D1578457

WHITAKER'S ALMANACK
2011

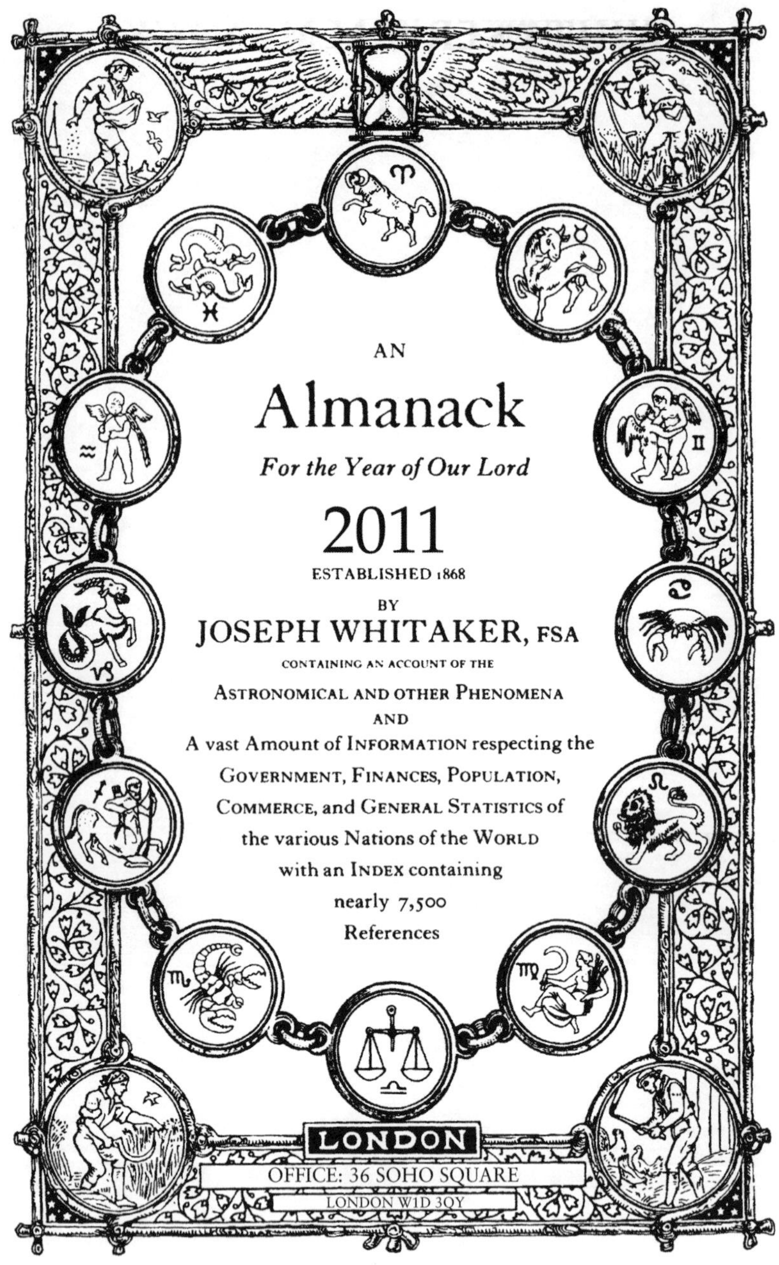

The traditional design of the title page for Whitaker's Almanack which has appeared in each edition since 1868

WHITAKER'S ALMANACK

2011

A & C BLACK

LONDON

A & C Black Publishers Ltd
36 Soho Square, London W1D 3QY

Whitaker's Almanack published annually since 1868

Published in the USA by Bloomsbury Academic & Professional

STANDARD EDITION
Cloth covers
978–1-4081–2848–0

CONCISE EDITION
Paperback
978–1-4081–2851–0

JACKET PHOTOGRAPHS
Main image: Prime Minister David Cameron welcomes Deputy Prime Minister Nick Clegg to Downing Street for their first day of coalition government. © Matt Cardy/Getty Images
Spine: Smoke and ash billow from the Eyjafjallajökull volcano in Iceland on 21 April 2010. © Emmanuel Dunand/AFP/Getty Images
Top, from left to right:
1. England coach Fabio Capello speaks during a press conference, a day after losing to Germany in the 2010 World Cup. © Paul Ellis/AFP/Getty Images
2. A protester raises his fist in front of the Greek parliament in the centre of Athens on 6 May 2010 as lawmakers vote on a drastic austerity package. © Aris Messinis/AFP/Getty Images
3. Jessica Ennis of Great Britain receives the gold medal in the women's heptathlon during day six of the 20th European Athletics Championships in Barcelona, Spain. © Jasper Juinen/Getty Images
4. Fire boats battle a blaze at the offshore oil rig Deepwater Horizon in the Gulf of Mexico. © US Coast Guard via Getty Images
5. US singer Lady Gaga looks on during the German TV show *Wetten dass . . . ? (Bet it . . . ?)* © AP Photo/Axel Heimken

Typeset in the UK by RefineCatch Ltd, Bungay, Suffolk NR35 1EF

Printed in the UK by CPI William Clowes, Beccles, Suffolk NR34 7TL

Whitaker's Almanack was compiled with the assistance of: Amnesty International; Christian Research; Euromonitor International; Keesing's Worldwide; Oxford Cartographers; Press Association; Transparency International: the global coalition against corruption; UK Hydrographic Office; the UNESCO Institute for Statistics (UIS); WM/Reuters; and the World Gazetteer/Stefan Helders (W www.world-gazetteer.com).

Material was reproduced from (in addition to that indicated): *CIA World Factbook 2010; The Diplomatic List January 2010* © Crown Copyright; *Human Development Indicators 2009* published by the UN Development Programme; *International Financial Statistics Year Book 2009* and *World Economic Outlook Database* © International Monetary Fund; *The Military Balance 2010* published by Routledge for the International Institute for Strategic Studies (IISS); Ordnance Survey of Northern Ireland, permit number 100036 © Crown Copyright; *People in Power* © Cambridge International Reference on Current Affairs (CIRCA); 2010 *World Development Indicators* published by The World Bank; the *World Health Organisation Statistical Information System,* and *World Urbanisation Prospects: The 2009 Revision* published by the UN Population Division. Crown copyright material is reproduced with the permission of the Controller of Her Majesty's Stationery Office.

This book is produced using paper that is made from wood grown in managed, sustainable forests. It is natural, renewable and recyclable. The logging and manufacturing processes conform to the environmental regulations of the country of origin.

A CIP catalogue record for this book is available from the British Library.

EDITORIAL STAFF
Publisher (Yearbooks) and Editor-in-Chief: Claire Fogg
Acting Deputy Editor: Clare Bryant
Project Editors: Ruth Craven (UK); Ross Fulton (International)
Editorial Assistant: Matt Munday

Thanks to Omer Ali, Sophie Hughes and Ruth Northey

CONTRIBUTORS (where not listed)
Gordon Taylor (Astronomy); Hilary Marsden (Countries of the World); Jill Papworth (Education and Taxation); Karen Harries-Rees (Environment); Graham Bartram (Flags); V. P. Kanitkar (Hindu Calendar); Clive Longhurst (Insurance); Duncan Murray, Chris Priestley (Legal Notes); Stan Greenberg, Alex Hazle (Sport); Philip Eden (Weather) and Russell Ash (World in Figures)

CONTENTS

PREFACE

Undoubtedly it has been a momentous year for UK politics: the first televised leaders' debates in the UK, the first coalition government since the Second World War, the youngest prime minister since 1812 and the first Liberal Democrat to take prime minister's questions.

The electoral campaign was something that took on a life of its own. When the three main party leaders agreed to televised live debates, they – like the viewers at home – could not have anticipated the outcome. Commentators seemed to think that Gordon Brown, a prime minister perilously low in the popularity polls, agreed because he had nothing to lose, everything to gain. Could he come across as the serious man of letters, of detail, of experience, when pitched head-to-head with his rivals? David Cameron perhaps agreed because he too had plenty to gain, not to mention past form as a politician well versed in the art of public relations. The man, though, who simply had so much to gain that no one actually saw him coming was, of course, Nick Clegg. If this was a race, then he was the outsider; the one with less than a sporting chance to get to the finish. Or so it seemed.

Three TV debates later and the political arena had become a very different place. Mr Clegg had surprised us all with his ease in front of the camera and a readiness to engage with his audience – often on first-name terms. The Liberal Democrats no longer appeared such a fanciful choice. In the general election that finally arrived on 6 May 2010, no party won an outright majority, and so, after days of deliberation, the coalition was born. Such events command our attention, but the detail can so easily get overlooked, distorted or forgotten. That's why, in the shape of *Whitaker's Almanack,* we are committed to bringing you a reliable, comprehensive work of reference featuring a host of essential facts and figures. Within these pages you will find full general election results (for each and every constituency) plus lists galore including those MPs who were defeated at the general election, those who retired, and those who newly took office. We also detail the number of women MPs by party, the average age of MPs and the number of votes cast at the general elections of 2001, 2005 and 2010. Should you want to gauge how the coalition is faring – and which party is managing to get their policies across as pledged – you will find details of the key manifesto commitments from both the Conservatives and the Liberal Democrats.

Nor have we forgotten the saga of MPs' expenses which set the tone in 2009. Updated information regarding members pay and allowances (including details of staffing allowance and accommodation expenses) is in the Parliament section of this year's *Almanack.* Elsewhere you'll find all the eclectic content that continues to make *Whitaker's Almanack* so special more than 140 years after its first publication. Alongside in-depth information about the structure of UK society, there are entries on all the countries of the world; plus everything from astronomy to Zoroastrianism; military titles to internet domain names; protected wildlife and habitats to utilities and transport.

At around 1,100 words a page across nearly 1,400 pages, it's no small feat. This year, more than most, has proved an editorial rollercoaster of documenting the UK's changing infrastructures and institutions. And so I would like to thank the dedicated team of in-house editors and expert contributors whose meticulous efforts have managed to bring such an impressive spectrum of information together in one volume. On a final note, *Whitaker's* wouldn't be *Whitaker's* without its readers, their vital feedback and useful suggestions. We value all your correspondence and I'd like to take this opportunity to thank you for your ongoing support.

Dr Claire Fogg
Editor-in-Chief
September 2010

THE YEAR 2011

CHRONOLOGICAL CYCLES AND ERAS

Dominical Letter	B
Epact	25
Golden Number (Lunar Cycle)	XVII
Julian Period	6724
Roman Indiction	4
	Beginning
Muslim year AH 1432*	7 Dec 2010
Japanese year Heisei 23	1 Jan
Roman year 2764 AUC	14 Jan
Regnal year 60	6 Feb
Chinese year of the Rabbit	3 Feb
Sikh new year	14 Mar
Hindu new year (Chaitra)	4 Apr
Indian (Saka) year 1933	22 Mar
Jewish year AM 5772*	2 Sep

* Year begins at sunset on the previous day

RELIGIOUS CALENDARS

CHRISTIAN

Epiphany	6 Jan
Presentation of Christ in the Temple	2 Feb
Ash Wednesday	9 Mar
The Annunciation	25 Mar
Palm Sunday	17 Apr
Maundy Thursday	21 Apr
Good Friday	22 Apr
Easter Day (western churches)	24 Apr
Easter Day (Eastern Orthodox)	24 Apr
Rogation Sunday	29 May
Ascension Day	2 Jun
Corpus Christi	2 Jun
Pentecost (Whit Sunday)	12 Jun
Trinity Sunday	19 Jun
All Saints' Day	1 Nov
Advent Sunday	27 Nov
Christmas Day	25 Dec

HINDU

Makara Sankranti	14 Jan
Vasant Panchami (Sarasvati Puja)	8 Feb
Mahashivaratri	3 Mar
Holi	19 Mar
Chaitra (Spring new year)	4 Apr
Ramanavami	12 Apr
Raksha Bandhan	13 Aug
Janmashtami	21 Aug
Ganesh Chaturthi, first day	1 Sep
Navaratri festival (Durga Puja), first day	28 Sep
Dasara	6 Oct
Diwali (New Year festival of lights), first day	26 Oct

JEWISH

Purim	20 Mar
Pesach (Passover), first day	19 Apr
Shavuoth (Feast of Weeks), first day	8 Jun
Rosh Hashanah (Jewish new year)	29 Sep
Yom Kippur (Day of Atonement)	8 Oct
Succoth (Feast of Tabernacles), first day	13 Oct
Hanukkah, first day	21 Dec

MUSLIM

Al-Hijra (Muslim new year)	7 Dec 2010
Ashura	16 Dec 2010
Ramadan, first day	1 Aug
Eid-ul-Fitr	30 Aug
Hajj	4 Nov
Eid-ul-Adha	6 Nov

SIKH

Birthday of Guru Gobind Singh Ji	5 Jan
1 Chet (Sikh new year)	14 Mar
Baisakhi Mela	13 Apr
Birthday of Guru Nanak Dev Ji	14 Apr†
Martyrdom of Guru Arjan Dev Ji	16 Jun
Martyrdom of Guru Tegh Bahadur Ji	24 Nov

† This festival is also currently celebrated according to the lunar calendar

CIVIL CALENDAR

Countess of Wessex's birthday	20 Jan
Accession of the Queen	6 Feb
Duke of York's birthday	19 Feb
St David's Day	1 Mar
Commonwealth Day	14 Mar
Earl of Wessex's birthday	10 Mar
St Patrick's Day	17 Mar
Birthday of the Queen	21 Apr
St George's Day	23 Apr
Europe Day	9 May
Coronation Day	2 Jun
Duke of Edinburgh's birthday	10 Jun
The Queen's Official Birthday	11 Jun
Duchess of Cornwall's birthday	17 Jul
Princess Royal's birthday	15 Aug
Lord Mayor's Day	12 Nov
Prince of Wales' birthday	14 Nov
Remembrance Sunday	13 Nov
Wedding Day of the Queen	20 Nov
St Andrew's Day	30 Nov

LEGAL CALENDAR

LAW TERMS

Hilary Term	11 Jan to 20 April
Easter Term	3 May to 27 May
Trinity Term	7 Jun to 30 Jul
Michaelmas Term	1 Oct to 21 Dec

QUARTER DAYS	TERM DAYS
England, Wales and Northern Ireland	*Scotland*
Lady – 25 Mar	Candlemas – 28 Feb
Midsummer – 24 Jun	Whitsunday – 28 May
Michaelmas – 29 Sep	Lammas – 28 Aug
Christmas – 25 Dec	Martinmas – 28 Nov

2011

JANUARY						
Sunday		2	9	16	23	30
Monday		3	10	17	24	31
Tuesday		4	11	18	25	
Wednesday		5	12	19	26	
Thursday		6	13	20	27	
Friday		7	14	21	28	
Saturday	1	8	15	22	29	

FEBRUARY					
Sunday		6	13	20	27
Monday		7	14	21	28
Tuesday	1	8	15	22	
Wednesday	2	9	16	23	
Thursday	3	10	17	24	
Friday	4	11	18	25	
Saturday	5	12	19	26	

MARCH					
Sunday		6	13	20	27
Monday		7	14	21	28
Tuesday	1	8	15	22	29
Wednesday	2	9	16	23	30
Thursday	3	10	17	24	31
Friday	4	11	18	25	
Saturday	5	12	19	26	

APRIL					
Sunday		3	10	17	24
Monday		4	11	18	25
Tuesday		5	12	19	26
Wednesday		6	13	20	27
Thursday		7	14	21	28
Friday	1	8	15	22	29
Saturday	2	9	16	23	30

MAY					
Sunday	1	8	15	22	29
Monday	2	9	16	23	30
Tuesday	3	10	17	24	31
Wednesday	4	11	18	25	
Thursday	5	12	19	26	
Friday	6	13	20	27	
Saturday	7	14	21	28	

JUNE					
Sunday		5	12	19	26
Monday		6	13	20	27
Tuesday		7	14	21	28
Wednesday	1	8	15	22	29
Thursday	2	9	16	23	30
Friday	3	10	17	24	
Saturday	4	11	18	25	

JULY						
Sunday		3	10	17	24	31
Monday		4	11	18	25	
Tuesday		5	12	19	26	
Wednesday		6	13	20	27	
Thursday		7	14	21	28	
Friday	1	8	15	22	29	
Saturday	2	9	16	23	30	

AUGUST					
Sunday		7	14	21	28
Monday	1	8	15	22	29
Tuesday	2	9	16	23	30
Wednesday	3	10	17	24	31
Thursday	4	11	18	25	
Friday	5	12	19	26	
Saturday	6	13	20	27	

SEPTEMBER					
Sunday		4	11	18	25
Monday		5	12	19	26
Tuesday		6	13	20	27
Wednesday		7	14	21	28
Thursday	1	8	15	22	29
Friday	2	9	16	23	30
Saturday	3	10	17	24	

OCTOBER						
Sunday		2	9	16	23	30
Monday		3	10	17	24	31
Tuesday		4	11	18	25	
Wednesday		5	12	19	26	
Thursday		6	13	20	27	
Friday		7	14	21	28	
Saturday	1	8	15	22	29	

NOVEMBER					
Sunday		6	13	20	27
Monday		7	14	21	28
Tuesday	1	8	15	22	29
Wednesday	2	9	16	23	30
Thursday	3	10	17	24	
Friday	4	11	18	25	
Saturday	5	12	19	26	

DECEMBER					
Sunday		4	11	18	25
Monday		5	12	19	26
Tuesday		6	13	20	27
Wednesday		7	14	21	28
Thursday	1	8	15	22	29
Friday	2	9	16	23	30
Saturday	3	10	17	24	31

PUBLIC HOLIDAYS	*England and Wales*	*Scotland*	*Northern Ireland*
New Year	3 January†	3, 4† January	3 January†
St Patrick's Day	—	—	17 March
*Good Friday	22 April	22 April	22 April
Easter Monday	25 April	—	25 April
Early May	2 May†	2 May	2 May†
Spring	30 May	30 May†	30 May
Battle of the Boyne	—	—	12 July‡
Summer	29 August	1 August	29 August
St Andrew's Day	—	30 Nov§	—
*Christmas	26, 27 December	26†, 27 December	26, 27 December

* In England, Wales and Northern Ireland, Christmas Day and Good Friday are common law holidays

† Subject to royal proclamation

‡ Subject to proclamation by the Secretary of State for Northern Ireland

§ The St Andrew's Day Holiday (Scotland) Bill was approved by parliament on 29 November 2006; it does not oblige employers to change their existing pattern of holidays but provides the legal framework in which the St Andrew's Day bank holiday could be substituted for an existing local holiday from another date in the year

Note: In the Channel Islands, Liberation Day is a bank and public holiday

2012

JANUARY					
Sunday	1	8	15	22	29
Monday	2	9	16	23	30
Tuesday	3	10	17	24	31
Wednesday	4	11	18	25	
Thursday	5	12	19	26	
Friday	6	13	20	27	
Saturday	7	14	21	28	

FEBRUARY					
Sunday		5	12	19	26
Monday		6	13	20	27
Tuesday		7	14	21	28
Wednesday	1	8	15	22	29
Thursday	2	9	16	23	
Friday	3	10	17	24	
Saturday	4	11	18	25	

MARCH					
Sunday		4	11	18	25
Monday		5	12	19	26
Tuesday		6	13	20	27
Wednesday		7	14	21	28
Thursday	1	8	15	22	29
Friday	2	9	16	23	30
Saturday	3	10	17	24	31

APRIL					
Sunday	1	8	15	22	29
Monday	2	9	16	23	30
Tuesday	3	10	17	24	
Wednesday	4	11	18	25	
Thursday	5	12	19	26	
Friday	6	13	20	27	
Saturday	7	14	21	28	

MAY					
Sunday		6	13	20	27
Monday		7	14	21	28
Tuesday	1	8	15	22	29
Wednesday	2	9	16	23	30
Thursday	3	10	17	24	31
Friday	4	11	18	25	
Saturday	5	12	19	26	

JUNE					
Sunday		3	10	17	24
Monday		4	11	18	25
Tuesday		5	12	19	26
Wednesday		6	13	20	27
Thursday		7	14	21	28
Friday	1	8	15	22	29
Saturday	2	9	16	23	30

JULY					
Sunday	1	8	15	22	29
Monday	2	9	16	23	30
Tuesday	3	10	17	24	31
Wednesday	4	11	18	25	
Thursday	5	12	19	26	
Friday	6	13	20	27	
Saturday	7	14	21	28	

AUGUST					
Sunday		5	12	19	26
Monday		6	13	20	27
Tuesday		7	14	21	28
Wednesday	1	8	15	22	29
Thursday	2	9	16	23	30
Friday	3	10	17	24	31
Saturday	4	11	18	25	

SEPTEMBER						
Sunday		2	9	16	23	30
Monday		3	10	17	24	
Tuesday		4	11	18	25	
Wednesday		5	12	19	26	
Thursday		6	13	20	27	
Friday		7	14	21	28	
Saturday	1	8	15	22	29	

OCTOBER					
Sunday		7	14	21	28
Monday	1	8	15	22	29
Tuesday	2	9	16	23	30
Wednesday	3	10	17	24	31
Thursday	4	11	18	25	
Friday	5	12	19	26	
Saturday	6	13	20	27	

NOVEMBER					
Sunday		4	11	18	25
Monday		5	12	19	26
Tuesday		6	13	20	27
Wednesday		7	14	21	28
Thursday	1	8	15	22	29
Friday	2	9	16	23	30
Saturday	3	10	17	24	

DECEMBER						
Sunday		2	9	16	23	30
Monday		3	10	17	24	31
Tuesday		4	11	18	25	
Wednesday		5	12	19	26	
Thursday		6	13	20	27	
Friday		7	14	21	28	
Saturday	1	8	15	22	29	

PUBLIC HOLIDAYS	*England and Wales*	*Scotland*	*Northern Ireland*
New Year	2 January†	2, 3† January	2 January†
St Patrick's Day	—	—	17 March
*Good Friday	6 April	6 April	6 April
Easter Monday	9 April	—	9 April
Early May	7 May†	7 May	7 May†
Spring	4 June	28 May†	4 June
Queen's Diamond Jubilee	5 June	5 June	5 June
Battle of the Boyne	—	—	12 July‡
Summer	27 August	6 August	27 August
St Andrew's Day	—	30 Nov§	—
*Christmas	25, 26 December	25†, 26 December	25, 26 December

* In England, Wales and Northern Ireland, Christmas Day and Good Friday are common law holidays

† Subject to royal proclamation

‡ Subject to proclamation by the Secretary of State for Northern Ireland

§ The St Andrew's Day Holiday (Scotland) Bill was approved by parliament on 29 November 2006; it does not oblige employers to change their existing pattern of holidays but provides the legal framework in which the St Andrew's Day bank holiday could be substituted for an existing local holiday from another date in the year

Note: In the Channel Islands, Liberation Day is a bank and public holiday

FORTHCOMING EVENTS

* Provisional dates
† Venue not confirmed

JANUARY 2011

7–16	London Boat Show, Excel, London Docklands
13–30	Celtic Connections Music Festival, Glasgow
15–30	London International Mime Festival
18–20	UK Open Dance Championships, Bournemouth International Centre
19–23	London Art Fair, Business Design Centre
29–30	RSPB Big Garden Birdwatch

FEBRUARY

3–6	London Motorcycle Show, Excel, London Docklands
4–20	Leicester Comedy Festival
13	British Academy Film Awards, Royal Opera House, London
13–21	Jorvik Viking Festival, Jorvik Viking Centre, York
25–27	Ceramic Art London, Royal College of Art
26–6 Mar	Bath Literature Festival

MARCH

3	World Book Day
8	International Women's Day
10–13	Affordable Art Fair, Battersea Park, London
10–13	Crufts Dog Show, NEC, Birmingham
11–20	National Science and Engineering Week
11–27	Ideal Home Show, Earls Court, London
20–28	Oxford Literary Festival
23–29	BADA Antiques and Fine Art Fair, Duke of York's Square, London

APRIL

11–13	London Book Fair, Earls Court, London
22	Earth Day

MAY

21 May–28 Aug	Glyndebourne Festival
24–28	RHS Chelsea Flower Show, Royal Hospital, Chelsea
26–5 Jun	Hay Festival, Hay-on-Wye, Hereford

JUNE

10–26	Aldeburgh Festival of Music and the Arts, Snape, Suffolk
*11	Trooping the Colour, Horse Guards Parade, London
7–15 Aug	Royal Academy of Arts Summer Exhibition, Burlington House, London
22–26	Glastonbury Festival of Contemporary Performing Arts, Somerset
30–10 Jul	New Designers Exhibition, Business Design Centre, London

JULY

1–16	Cheltenham Music Festival
2	Pride Parade, London
*5–10	RHS Hampton Court Palace Flower Show, Surrey
8–16	York Early Music Festival
9–27	Buxton Festival, Derbyshire
Mid-Jul–Mid-Sep	BBC Promenade Concerts, Royal Albert Hall, London
*20–24	RHS Flower Show, Tatton Park, Cheshire
*21–30	The Welsh Proms, St David's Hall, Cardiff
28–31	Cambridge Folk Festival
29–31	WOMAD Festival, Charlton Park, Wiltshire
29–7 Aug	Edinburgh Jazz and Blues Festival
30–6 Aug	National Eisteddfod of Wales, Wrexham

AUGUST

5–27	Edinburgh Military Tattoo, Edinburgh Castle
6–13	Three Choirs Festival, Worcester
*12–4 Sep	Edinburgh International Festival
*28–29	Notting Hill Carnival, London

SEPTEMBER

2–6 Nov	Blackpool Illuminations, Blackpool Promenade
3	Braemar Royal Highland Gathering, Aberdeenshire
*6	Mercury Music Prize
8	International Literacy Day
*8–11	Heritage Open Days, England (nationwide)
*9–11	RHS Wisley Flower Show, RHS Garden, Wisley
12–15	TUC Annual Congress, Manchester
17–21	Liberal Democrat Party Conference, Birmingham
25–29	Labour Party Conference, Liverpool

OCTOBER

*2–5	Conservative Party Conference, Manchester
6	National Poetry Day
13–16	Frieze Art Fair, Regent's Park, London
Mid-Oct	Booker Prize
Mid-Oct	London Film Festival
Mid-Oct–Jan	Turner Prize Exhibition, Tate Britain, London

NOVEMBER

6	London to Brighton Veteran Car Run
*11–13	Classic Motor Show, NEC, Birmingham
*12	Lord Mayor's Procession and Show, City of London
Mid-Nov	CBI Annual Conference

SPORTS EVENTS

JANUARY 2011

3–7	Cricket: Ashes Fifth Test, Sydney, Australia
9–16	Snooker: Masters, Wembley Arena, London

FEBRUARY

4–6	Badminton: English National Championships, Manchester
4–19 Mar	Rugby Union: Six Nations Championship
8–13	Squash: British National Championships, Manchester
12–13	Rugby League: Super League, Millennium Stadium, Cardiff
19–2 Apr	Cricket: World Cup, Bangladesh, India and Sri Lanka
27	Football: League Cup Final, Wembley Stadium, London

MARCH

26	Rowing: Oxford and Cambridge Boat Race, Putney to Mortlake, London

APRIL

9	Horse racing: Grand National, Aintree, Liverpool
16–2 May	Snooker: World Championship, Crucible Theatre, Sheffield
17	Athletics: London Marathon
21–25	Equestrian: Badminton Horse Trials, Badminton

MAY

7–8	Horse racing: Guineas Festival, Newmarket
11–15	Royal Windsor Horse Show, Home Park, Windsor
14	Football: FA Cup Final, Wembley Stadium, London
†21	Football: FA Women's Cup Final
21	Football: Scottish FA Cup Final, Hampden Park, Glasgow
22	Rugby Union: Heineken Cup Final, Millennium Stadium, Cardiff
28	Football: UEFA Champions League Final, Wembley Stadium, London
28–10 Jun	Motorcycling: TT Races, Isle of Man

JUNE

4	Horse racing: The Derby, Epsom Downs
13–18	Golf: British Amateur Golf Championship, Hillside & Hesketh, Lancashire
14–18	Horse racing: Royal Ascot
20–3 Jul	Tennis: Wimbledon Championship, All England Lawn Tennis Club, London
26–17 Jul	Football: Women's World Cup, Germany
29–3 Jul	Rowing: Henley Royal Regatta, Henley-on-Thames

JULY

2–24	Cycling: Tour de France
9–23	Shooting: NRA Imperial Meeting, Bisley Camp, Surrey
14–17	Golf: Open Championship, Royal St George, Kent
16–31	Swimming: World Championships, Shanghai
*23	Horse racing: King George VI and Queen Elizabeth Diamond Stakes, Ascot
28–31	Golf: Women's British Open, Carnoustie and St Andrews, Scotland

AUGUST

6–13	Sailing: Cowes Week, Isle of Wight
8–14	Badminton World Championships, Wembley Arena, London
*27	Rugby League: Challenge Cup Final, Wembley Stadium, London
27–4 Sep	Athletics: World Championships, Daegu, Republic of Korea

SEPTEMBER

1–4	Equestrian: Burghley Horse Trials, Stamford, Lincolnshire
7–10	Horse racing: St Leger, Doncaster
7–13	Commonwealth Youth Games, Isle of Man
*29–1 Oct	Horse racing: Cambridgeshire Meeting, Newmarket
Late Sep–Early Oct	Athletics: Great North Run, Newcastle

OCTOBER

5–9	Equestrian: Horse of the Year Show, NEC, Birmingham
*14–17	Horse racing: Champions Meeting, Newmarket
Early–Mid-Oct	Rugby League: Super League Final, Old Trafford, Manchester

CENTENARIES

2011

1511
30 Jul Giorgio Vasari, Italian painter, architect and writer, born

1711
7 May David Hume, philosopher, born
31 Oct Laura Bassi, Italian physicist, born

1811
31 Mar Robert Bunsen, German chemist, born
11 May Chang and Eng Bunker, conjoined twins from Siam (now Thailand), born
14 Jun Harriet Beecher Stowe, American writer, born
13 Jul Sir George Gilbert Scott, architect, born
18 Jul William Makepeace Thackeray, novelist, born
22 Oct Franz Liszt, Hungarian composer and pianist, born
27 Oct Isaac Singer, American inventor, born
16 Nov John Bright, co-founder of the Anti-Corn Law League, born
21 Nov Heinrich von Kleist, German writer, died
21 Dec Archibald Campbell Tait, Archbishop of Canterbury, born

1911
30 Jan Roy Eldridge, American jazz musician, born
6 Mar Sir Charles Frank, theoretical physicist, born
26 Mar Tennessee Williams, American playwright, born
17 May Maureen O'Sullivan, Irish actor, born
18 May Gustav Mahler, Austrian composer, died
29 May Sir William S. Gilbert, playwright and librettist, died
15 Jun Revd W. V. Awdry, children's writer, born
24 Jun Juan Manuel Fangio, Argentine Formula One racing driver, born
30 Jun Ruskin Spear, painter, born
16 Jul Ginger Rogers, American actor, born
19 Sep Sir William Golding, novelist and Nobel prize winner (1983), born
29 Sep Prof. R. V. Jones, military intelligence scientist, born
29 Oct Joseph Pulitzer, Hungarian-American publisher and journalist, died
12 Nov Revd Dr Chad Varah, founder of the Samaritans, born
5 Dec Wladyslaw Szpilman, Polish pianist and composer, born
30 Dec Jeanette Nolan, American actor, born

2012

1512
5 Mar Gerardus Mercator, Flemish-German cartographer, born
10 Apr King James V of Scotland, born

1612
17 Jan Sir Thomas Fairfax, commander of the New Model Army, born

1712
28 Jun Jean-Jacques Rousseau, French philosopher, born
12 Jul Richard Cromwell, Lord Protector 1658–9, died
14 Oct William Grenville, First Lord of the Treasury 1763–5, born

1812
7 Feb Charles Dickens, novelist and essayist, born
1 Mar Augustus Pugin, architect, born
6 Apr Alexander Herzen, Russian political theorist and writer, born
7 May Robert Browning, poet, born
11 May Spencer Perceval, Prime Minister 1809–12, died
12 May Edward Lear, poet and illustrator, born
19 Sep Mayer Amschel Rothschild, German banker, died
16 Nov John Walter, founder of *The Times,* died

1912
28 Jan Jackson Pollock, painter, born
10 Feb Sir Joseph Lister, surgeon, died
27 Feb Lawrence Durrell, novelist and poet, born
14 Mar Cliff Bastin, football player, born
27 Mar James Callaghan, Prime Minister 1976–9, born
20 Apr Bram Stoker, Irish novelist, died
28 May Patrick White, Australian novelist, born
30 May Wilbur Wright, American aviation pioneer, died
13 Jun Sir Georg Solti, conductor, born
14 Jul Woody Guthrie, American musician, born
17 Jul Jules Henri Poincaré, French mathematican, died
13 Aug Ben Hogan, American golfer, born
20 Aug Gen. William Booth, founder of the Salvation Army, died
23 Aug Gene Kelly, actor and choreographer, born

THE UNITED KINGDOM

THE UK IN FIGURES

The United Kingdom comprises Great Britain (England, Wales and Scotland) and Northern Ireland. The Isle of Man and the Channel Islands are Crown dependencies with their own legislative systems and are not part of the UK.

ABBREVIATIONS

AAS	*Annual Abstract of Statistics*
ST	*Social Trends*

All data is for the UK unless otherwise stated.

AREA OF THE UNITED KINGDOM

	Sq. km	*Sq. miles*
United Kingdom	243,122	93,870
England	130,280	50,301
Wales	20,733	8,005
Scotland	77,958	30,100
Northern Ireland	14,150	5,463

Source: ONS – *AAS 2010* (Crown copyright)

POPULATION

The first official census of population in England, Wales and Scotland was taken in 1801 and a census has been taken every ten years since, except in 1941 when there was no census because of the Second World War. The last official census in the UK was taken on 29 April 2001 and the next is due in April 2011.

The first official census of population in Ireland was taken in 1841. However, all figures given below refer only to the area which is now Northern Ireland. Figures for Northern Ireland in 1921 and 1931 are estimates based on the censuses taken in 1926 and 1937 respectively.

Estimates of the population of England before 1801, calculated from the number of baptisms, burials and marriages, are:

1570	4,160,221	1670	5,773,646
1600	4,811,718	1700	6,045,008
1630	5,600,517	1750	6,517,035

Further details are available on the Office for National Statistics (ONS) website (W www.statistics.gov.uk).

CENSUS RESULTS *Thousands*

	United Kingdom			England and Wales			Scotland			Northern Ireland		
	Total	*Male*	*Female*	*Total*	*Male*	*Female*	*Total*	*Male*	*Female*	*Total*	*Male*	*Female*
1801	—	—	—	8,893	4,255	4,638	1,608	739	869	—	—	—
1811	13,368	6,368	7,000	10,165	4,874	5,291	1,806	826	980	—	—	—
1821	15,472	7,498	7,974	12,000	5,850	6,150	2,092	983	1,109	—	—	—
1831	17,835	8,647	9,188	13,897	6,771	7,126	2,364	1,114	1,250	—	—	—
1841	20,183	9,819	10,364	15,914	7,778	8,137	2,620	1,242	1,378	1,649	800	849
1851	22,259	10,855	11,404	17,928	8,781	9,146	2,889	1,376	1,513	1,443	698	745
1861	24,525	11,894	12,631	20,066	9,776	10,290	3,062	1,450	1,612	1,396	668	728
1871	27,431	13,309	14,122	22,712	11,059	11,653	3,360	1,603	1,757	1,359	647	712
1881	31,015	15,060	15,955	25,974	12,640	13,335	3,736	1,799	1,936	1,305	621	684
1891	34,264	16,593	17,671	29,003	14,060	14,942	4,026	1,943	2,083	1,236	590	646
1901	38,237	18,492	19,745	32,528	15,729	16,799	4,472	2,174	2,298	1,237	590	647
1911	42,082	20,357	21,725	36,070	17,446	18,625	4,761	2,309	2,452	1,251	603	648
1921	44,027	21,033	22,994	37,887	18,075	19,811	4,882	2,348	2,535	1,258	610	648
1931	46,038	22,060	23,978	39,952	19,133	20,819	4,843	2,326	2,517	1,243	601	642
1951	50,225	24,118	26,107	43,758	21,016	22,742	5,096	2,434	2,662	1,371	668	703
1961	52,709	25,481	27,228	46,105	22,304	23,801	5,179	2,483	2,697	1,425	694	731
1971	55,515	26,952	28,562	48,750	23,683	25,067	5,229	2,515	2,714	1,536	755	781
1981	55,848	27,104	28,742	49,155	23,873	25,281	5,131	2,466	2,664	1,533*	750	783
1991	56,467	27,344	29,123	49,890	24,182	25,707	4,999	2,392	2,607	1,578	769	809
2001	58,789	28,581	30,208	52,042	25,327	26,715	5,062	2,432	2,630	1,685	821	864

* Figure includes 44,500 non-enumerated persons

ISLANDS

	Isle of Man			Jersey			Guernsey†		
	Total	*Male*	*Female*	*Total*	*Male*	*Female*	*Total*	*Male*	*Female*
1901	54,752	25,496	29,256	52,576	23,940	28,636	40,446	19,652	20,794
1921	60,284	27,329	32,955	49,701	22,438	27,263	38,315	18,246	20,069
1951	55,123	25,749	29,464	57,296	27,282	30,014	43,652	21,221	22,431
1971	56,289	26,461	29,828	72,532	35,423	37,109	51,458	24,792	26,666
1991	69,788	33,693	36,095	84,082	40,862	43,220	58,867	28,297	30,570
2001	76,315	37,372	38,943	87,186	42,485	44,701	59,807	29,138	30,669
2006	80,058	39,523	40,535						

† Includes Herm, Jethou and Lithou

Source: ONS – Census Reports (Crown copyright)

RESIDENT POPULATION

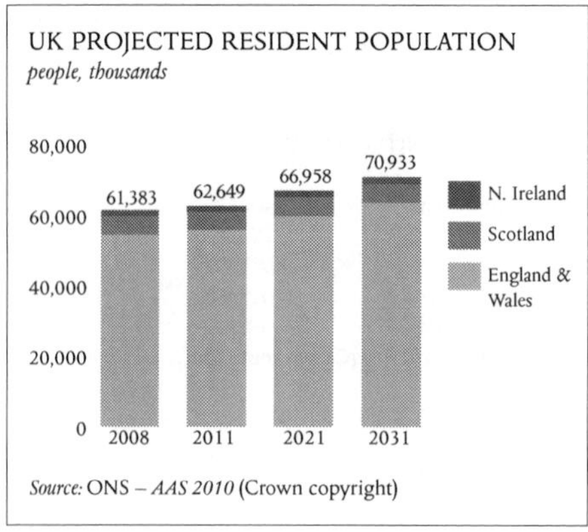

Source: ONS – AAS 2010 (Crown copyright)

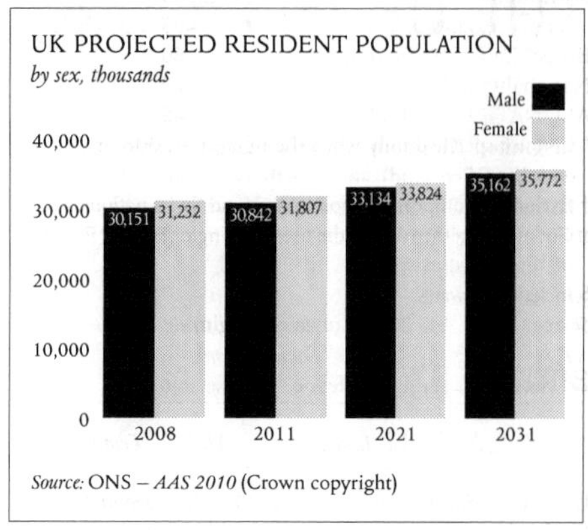

Source: ONS – AAS 2010 (Crown copyright)

BY AGE AND SEX

	Thousands	
	Male	*Female*
Under 1	404	385
1–4	1,492	1,420
5–9	1,737	1,658
10–14	1,873	1,785
15–19	2,049	1,939
20–29	4,235	4,067
30–44	6,449	6,529
45–59	5,815	5,978
60–64	1,778	1,861
65–74	2,447	2,708
75–84	1,452	1,988
85+	422	914

Source: ONS – *AAS 2010* (Crown copyright)

BY ETHNIC GROUP

	Thousands
White	
British	49,139
Other	3,188
Mixed	
White and black Caribbean	241
White and black African	98
White and Asian	187
Other mixed	151
Asian	
Indian	1,245
Pakistani	995
Bangladeshi	364
Other Asian	501
Black	
Black Caribbean	618
Black African	829
Black other	83
Chinese	255
Other	903
ALL*	60,554

* Includes those who did not state their ethnic origin and those in Northern Ireland who stated their ethnicity as white

Source: ONS – *AAS 2010* (Crown copyright)

IMMIGRATION

ACCEPTANCES FOR SETTLEMENT IN THE UK

*Region**	*Number of persons*	
	2006	*2008*
Europe: total†	15,580	9,955
Accession States: total	5,860	–
Bulgaria	4,250	–
Romania	1,610	–
Remainder of Europe: total	9,715	9,955
Albania	1,185	1,250
Russia	1,375	1,255
Serbia and Montenegro‡	2,070	1,520
Turkey	3,040	3,670
Americas: total	12,085	11,585
Canada	1,125	1,190
Jamaica	2,900	2,750
USA	3,845	3,335
Africa: total	32,240	40,395
Dem. Rep. of the Congo	1,345	1,845
Ghana	2,870	3,885
Kenya	1,670	1,890
Mauritius	675	1,035
Nigeria	4,440	5,145
Sierra Leone	1,145	905
Somalia	2,125	2,425
South Africa	5,665	6,955
Zambia	460	1,000
Zimbabwe	3,415	6,330
Asia: total	70,045	82,605
Indian subcontinent: total	25,005	39,800
Bangladesh	2,850	4,325
India	11,190	22,880
Pakistan	10,960	12,595
Middle East: total	9,795	7,700
Iran	1,035	1,470
Iraq	7,285	4,170
Remainder of Asia: total	35,245	35,100
Afghanistan	7,395	2,915
China§	3,320	6,890
Japan	1,255	915
Malaysia	1,785	2,190
Nepal	6,940	2,920
Philippines	6,315	11,290
Sri Lanka	3,080	3,315
Thailand	2,425	1,740

Oceania: total	4,215	4,040
Australia	2,645	2,620
New Zealand	1,405	1,335
British Overseas Citizens	60	25
Nationality unknown	220	135
ALL NATIONALITIES	134,445	148,740

* Country specified only when the figure for 2006 or 2008 is over 1,000

† Excluding European Economic Area and Swiss nationals

‡ Counted together due to the use of a single (Federal Republic of Yugoslavia) passport

§ Includes Taiwan

Source: ONS – *AAS 2010* (Crown copyright)

BIRTHS

	Live births	*Male*	*Female*	*Birth rate**
United Kingdom	794,400	407,000	388,000	12.9
England and Wales	708,700	363,000	346,000	13.0
Scotland	60,000	31,000	29,000	11.6
Northern Ireland	25,600	13,000	12,000	12.4

* Live births per 1,000 population

Source: ONS – *AAS 2010* (Crown copyright)

FERTILITY RATES

Total fertility rate is the average number of children which would be born to a woman if she experienced the age-specific fertility rates of the period in question throughout her child-bearing life span. The figures for the years 1960–2 are estimates.

	1960–2	*1998*	*2008*
United Kingdom	2.80	1.71	1.96
England and Wales	2.77	1.72	1.97
Scotland	2.98	1.55	1.80
Northern Ireland	3.47	1.90	2.11

Source: ONS – *AAS 2010* (Crown copyright)

TOP TEN BABY NAMES

	1934		*2008*	
	Girls	*Boys*	*Girls*	*Boys*
1	Margaret	John	Olivia	Jack
2	Jean	Peter	Ruby	Oliver
3	Mary	William	Emily	Thomas
4	Joan	Brian	Grace	Harry
5	Patricia	David	Jessica	Joshua
6	Sheila	James	Chloe	Alfie
7	Barbara	Michael	Sophie	Charlie
8	Doreen	Ronald	Lily	Daniel
9	June	Kenneth	Amelia	James
10	Shirley	George	Evie	William

Source: ONS – *AAS 2010* (Crown copyright)

LEGAL ABORTIONS

	1998	*2008*
England and Wales	177,871	195,296
Scotland	12,458	13,762

Source: ONS – *AAS 2010* (Crown copyright)

DEATHS

Men	*Deaths*	*Death rate**
United Kingdom	276,745	9.2
England and Wales	243,014	
Scotland	26,504	
Northern Ireland	7,227	
Women		
United Kingdom	302,952	9.7
England and Wales	266,076	
Scotland	29,196	
Northern Ireland	7,680	

* Per 1,000 population

Source: ONS – *AAS 2010* (Crown copyright)

INFANT MORTALITY RATE*

United Kingdom	4.7
England and Wales	4.8
Scotland	4.2
Northern Ireland	4.7

* Deaths of infants under one year of age per 1,000 live births

Source: ONS – *AAS 2010* (Crown copyright)

MARRIAGE AND DIVORCE

	Marriages	*Divorces*
United Kingdom	273,920	144,220
England and Wales	235,367	128,534
Scotland	29,866	12,773
Northern Ireland	8,687	2,913

Figures are for 2007

Source: ONS – *AAS 2010* (Crown copyright)

HOUSEHOLDS

BY TYPE (GREAT BRITAIN)

Percentages

	1971	*1991*	*2009*
One person			
Under state pension age	6	11	14
Over state pension age	12	16	14
One family households			
Couple			
No children	27	28	29
1–2 dependent children	26	20	18
3 or more dependent children	9	5	3
Non-dependent children only	8	8	6
Lone parent			
Dependent children	3	6	7
Non-dependent children only	4	4	3
Two or more unrelated adults	4	3	3
Multi-family households	1	1	1
All households (=100%) *(millions)*	18.6	22.4	25.2

Source: ONS – *ST 2010* (Crown copyright)

BY SIZE (GREAT BRITAIN)

Percentages

	1971	*1991*	*2009*
One person	18	27	29
Two people	32	34	35
Three people	19	16	16
Four people	17	16	14
Five people	8	5	4
Six or more people	6	2	2
All households (=100%) *(millions)*	18.6	22.4	25.2
Average household size *(people)*	2.9	2.5	2.4

Source: ONS – *ST 2010* (Crown copyright)

DEPENDENT CHILDREN LIVING IN DIFFERENT FAMILY TYPES

Millions

	1997	*2005*	*2009*
Married couple	9.6	8.6	8.3
Cohabiting couple	1.0	1.5	1.7
Female lone parent	2.5	2.8	2.9
Male lone parent	0.2	0.3	0.3

Source: ONS – *ST 2010* (Crown copyright)

MORTGAGES

	1999	*2005*	*2009*
Mortgages* *(thousands)*	10,987	11,608	11,401
Loans in arrears at end-period* *(thousands)*			
By 6–12 months	57	39	92
By 12+ months	30	15	68
Properties repossessed in period	30	15	48

* Estimates cover only members of the Council of Mortgage Lenders, which account for 98 per cent of all outstanding mortgages

Source: ONS – *AAS 2010* (Crown copyright)

TYPE OF ACCOMMODATION (GREAT BRITAIN)

Percentages by tenure 2008

	House or bungalow			*Flat or maisonette*	
	Detached	*Semi-detached*	*Terraced*	*Purpose-built*	*Other*
Owner-occupied	32	34	25	6	2
Owned outright	39	35	19	6	2
Owned with mortgage	27	34	30	6	2
Rented from social sector	1	24	30	41	3
Council	1	24	31	42	2
Housing association	1	25	30	40	4
Rented privately	12	20	35	20	13
Furnished	6	14	35	30	14
Unfurnished	13	21	34	18	13
All tenures	24	31	27	14	3

Source: ONS – *AAS 2010* (Crown copyright)

HEALTH

DEATHS BY CAUSE, 2008

	England and Wales	*Scotland*	*N. Ireland*
Total deaths	509,090	55,700	14,907
Deaths from natural causes	488,743	53,439	14,053
Certain infectious and parasitic diseases	6,499	936	183
Intestinal infectious diseases	2,690	183	69
Respiratory and other tuberculosis	384	46	6
Meningococcal infection	77	4	2
Viral hepatitis	218	24	2
AIDS (HIV – disease)	249	18	–
Neoplasms	141,143	15,525	4,086
Malignant neoplasms	137,831	15,269	3,971
Malignant neoplasm of trachea, bronchus and lung	30,326	4,080	927
Malignant neoplasm of skin	1,847	171	57
Malignant neoplasm of breast	10,779	1,050	312
Malignant neoplasm of cervix uteri	830	102	28
Malignant neoplasm of prostate	9,157	792	226
Leukaemia	3,924	366	102
Diseases of the blood and blood-forming organs and certain disorders involving the immune mechanism	952	85	36
Endocrine, nutritional and metabolic diseases	7,426	991	254
Diabetes mellitus	5,541	733	181
Mental and behavioural disorders	18,348	3,362	575
Vascular and unspecified dementia	16,610	2,590	520
Alcohol abuse	685	342	46
Drug dependence and non-dependent abuse of drugs	844	395	2
Diseases of the nervous system and sense organs	17,554	1,619	600
Meningitis (excluding meningococcal)	159	20	3
Alzheimer's disease	6,231	624	293
Diseases of the circulatory system	168,238	17,849	4,752
Ischaemic heart diseases	76,985	8,841	2,410
Cerebrovascular diseases	46,446	5,367	1,329
Diseases of the respiratory system	71,751	7,443	2,096
Influenza	39	10	2
Pneumonia	28,929	2,453	900
Bronchitis, emphysema and other chronic obstructive pulmonary diseases	24,816	2,848	680
Asthma	1,071	103	31
Diseases of the digestive system	25,997	3,119	682
Gastric and duodenal ulcer	2,912	220	52
Chronic liver disease	6,470	1,059	204
Diseases of the skin and subcutaneous tissue	1,895	159	24
Diseases of the musculo-skeletal system and connective tissue	4,398	351	85
Osteoporosis	1,420	107	15
Diseases of the genito-urinary system	11,886	1,279	400
Complications of pregnancy, childbirth and the puerperium	44	5	–
Certain conditions originating in the perinatal period*	234	134	67
Congenital malformations, deformations and chromosomal abnormalities*	1,139	144	74
Symptoms, signs and abnormal findings not classified elsewhere	11,149	438	139
Senility without mention of psychosis (old age)	9,320	235	107
Sudden infant death syndrome	176	22	3
Deaths from external causes	17,628	2,261	854
All accidents	12,306	1,261	525
Suicide and intentional self-harm	3,438	569	252
Homicide and assault	340†	88	40

* Excludes neonatal deaths (those at age under 28 days): for England and Wales neonatal deaths are included in the total number of deaths but excluded from the cause figures

† This will not be a true figure as registration of homicide and assault deaths in England and Wales is often delayed by adjourned inquests

Source: ONS – *AAS 2010* (Crown copyright)

ALCOHOL CONSUMPTION* BY AGE (GREAT BRITAIN)
Percentages

	16–24	*25–44*	*45–64*	*65+*	*All 16+*
Men					
No units	37	28	26	34	30
Up to 4 units	21	30	33	44	33
4–8 units	12	15	20	14	16
8+ units	30	27	21	7	21
Women					
No units	48	41	40	57	45
Up to 3 units	16	22	28	33	26
3–6 units	12	16	19	8	15
6+ units	24	20	13	2	14

* Maximum consumed on any one day in the previous week. Department of Health guidelines recommend that men should not regularly drink more than three to four units of alcohol per day and women should not regularly drink more than two to three units per day. A unit of alcohol is 8 grams by weight or 10ml by volume of pure alcohol, ie the amount contained in half a pint of ordinary-strength beer or lager, a single pub measure of spirits or a small glass of ordinary-strength wine

Source: ONS – *ST 2010* (Crown copyright)

NOTIFICATIONS OF INFECTIOUS DISEASES

	2000	*2008*
Measles	2,865	5,331
Mumps	3,367	8,682
Rubella	2,064	1,230
Whooping cough	866	1,676
Scarlet fever	2,544	3,983
Dysentery	1,613	1,289
Food poisoning	98,076	77,854
Typhoid and paratyphoid fevers	205	418
Hepatitis	4,530	6,515
Tuberculosis	7,100	7,878
Malaria	1,166	403

Source: ONS – *AAS 2010* (Crown copyright)

BODY MASS INDEX (BMI)* BY WEIGHT CLASSIFICATION (ENGLAND)
Percentages

	2000	*2008*
Underweight (BMI less than 18.5)	1.5	1.8
Normal (18.5 to less than 25)	38.6	36.8
Overweight (25 to less than 30)	38.8	36.9
Obese† (30 and over)	21.2	24.5
Morbidly obese (40 and over)	1.5	2.0

* BMI is the most widely used measure of obesity among adults aged 16 and over. BMI standardises weight for height and is calculated as weight (kg)/height $(m)^2$

† Includes morbidly obese

Source: ONS – *ST 2010* (Crown copyright)

CIGARETTE SMOKING HABITS
Percentages

	2000	*2008*
Men		
Current cigarette smoker	29	22
Light to moderate (fewer than 20 cigarettes a day)	18	15
Heavy (20 or more a day)	10	7
Ex-regular smoker	27	30
Never or only occasionally smoked	44	49
Women		
Current cigarette smoker	25	21
Light to moderate (fewer than 20 cigarettes a day)	19	15
Heavy (20 or more a day)	6	5
Ex-regular smoker	20	22
Never or only occasionally smoked	54	58

Source: ONS – *ST 2010* (Crown copyright)

THE NATIONAL FLAG

The national flag of the United Kingdom is the Union Flag, generally known as the Union Jack.

The Union Flag is a combination of the cross of St George, patron saint of England, the cross of St Andrew, patron saint of Scotland and the cross of St Patrick, patron saint of Ireland.

Cross of St George: cross Gules in a field Argent (red cross on a white ground)

Cross of St Andrew: saltire Argent in a field Azure (white diagonal cross on a blue ground)

Cross of St Patrick: saltire Gules in a field Argent (red diagonal cross on a white ground)

The Union Flag was first introduced in 1606 after the union of the kingdoms of England and Scotland under one sovereign. The cross of St Patrick was added in 1801 after the union of Great Britain and Ireland.

See also Flags of the World colour plates.

FLYING THE UNION FLAG

The correct orientation of the Union Flag when flying is with the broader diagonal band of white uppermost in the hoist (ie near the pole) and the narrower diagonal band of white uppermost in the fly (ie furthest from the pole).

The flying of the Union Flag on government buildings is decided by the Department for Culture, Media and Sport at the Queen's command. There is no formal definition of a government building but it is generally accepted to mean a building owned or used by the Crown and predominantly occupied or used by civil servants or the Armed Forces. It is now customary for the Union Flag to be flown at Buckingham Palace, Windsor Castle and Sandringham when the Queen is not in residence. Individuals, local authorities and other organisations may fly the Union Flag whenever they wish, subject to compliance with any local planning requirement.

FLAGS AT HALF-MAST

Flags are flown at half-mast (ie two-thirds up between the top and bottom of the flagstaff) on the following occasions:

- from the announcement of the death up to the funeral of the sovereign, except on Proclamation Day, when flags are hoisted right up from 11am to sunset
- the death or funeral of a member of the royal family*
- the funerals of foreign rulers*
- the funerals of prime ministers and ex-prime ministers of the UK*
- other occasions by special command of the Queen

On occasions when days for flying flags coincide with days for flying flags at half-mast, the following rules are observed. Flags are flown at full mast:

- although a member of the royal family, or a near relative of the royal family, may be lying dead, unless special commands are received from the Queen to the contrary
- although it may be the day of the funeral of a foreign ruler

If the body of a very distinguished subject is lying at a government office, the flag may fly at half-mast on that office until the body has left (provided it is a day on which the flag would fly) and then the flag is to be hoisted right up. On all other government buildings the flag will fly as usual.

DAYS FOR FLYING FLAGS

On 25 March 2008 the DCMS announced that UK government buildings in England, Scotland and Wales have the freedom to fly the Union Flag at all times, if they wish to do so, and not just on the established days listed below. In addition, on the patron saints' days of Scotland and Wales, the appropriate national flag may be flown alongside the Union Flag on Whitehall government buildings. Flags are hoisted from 8am to sunset.

Countess of Wessex's birthday	20 Jan
Accession of the Queen	6 Feb
Duke of York's birthday	19 Feb
St David's Day (in Wales only)†	1 Mar
Earl of Wessex's birthday	10 Mar
Commonwealth Day (2011)	14 Mar
St Patrick's Day (in Northern Ireland only)‡	17 Mar
The Queen's birthday	21 Apr
St George's Day (in England only)†	23 Apr
Europe Day†	9 May
Coronation Day	2 Jun
Duke of Edinburgh's birthday	10 Jun
The Queen's official birthday (2011)	11 Jun
Duchess of Cornwall's birthday	17 Jul
Princess Royal's birthday	15 Aug
Remembrance Day (2011)	13 Nov
Prince of Wales' birthday	14 Nov
Wedding Day of the Queen	20 Nov
St Andrew's Day (in Scotland only)†	30 Nov
Opening of parliament by the Queen§	
Prorogation of parliament by the Queen§	

THE ROYAL STANDARD

The Royal Standard comprises four quarterings – two for England (three lions passant), one for Scotland¶ (a lion rampant) and one for Ireland (a harp).

The Royal Standard is flown when the Queen is in residence at a royal palace, on transport being used by the Queen for official journeys and from Victoria Tower when the Queen attends parliament. It may also be flown on any building (excluding ecclesiastical buildings) during a visit by the Queen. If the Queen is to be present in a building advice on flag flying can be obtained from the DCMS.

The Royal Standard is never flown at half-mast, even after the death of the sovereign, as the new monarch immediately succeeds to the throne.

* Subject to special commands from the Queen in each case

† The appropriate national flag, or the European flag, may be flown in addition to the Union Flag (where there are two or more flagpoles), but not in a superior position

‡ Only the Union Flag should be flown

§ Only in the Greater London area, whether or not the Queen performs the ceremony in person

¶ In Scotland a version with two Scottish quarterings is used

THE ROYAL FAMILY

THE SOVEREIGN

ELIZABETH II, by the Grace of God, of the United Kingdom of Great Britain and Northern Ireland and of her other Realms and Territories Queen, Head of the Commonwealth, Defender of the Faith
Her Majesty Elizabeth Alexandra Mary of Windsor, elder daughter of King George VI and of HM Queen Elizabeth the Queen Mother
Born 21 April 1926, at 17 Bruton Street, London W1
Ascended the throne 6 February 1952
Crowned 2 June 1953, at Westminster Abbey
Married 20 November 1947, in Westminster Abbey, HRH the Prince Philip, Duke of Edinburgh
Official residences Buckingham Palace, London SW1A 1AA; Windsor Castle, Berks; Palace of Holyroodhouse, Edinburgh
Private residences Sandringham, Norfolk; Balmoral Castle, Aberdeenshire

HUSBAND OF THE QUEEN

HRH THE PRINCE PHILIP, DUKE OF EDINBURGH, KG, KT, OM, GBE, Royal Victorian Chain, AC, QSO, PC, Ranger of Windsor Park
Born 10 June 1921, son of Prince and Princess Andrew of Greece and Denmark, naturalised a British subject 1947, created Duke of Edinburgh, Earl of Merioneth and Baron Greenwich 1947

CHILDREN OF THE QUEEN

HRH THE PRINCE OF WALES (Prince Charles Philip Arthur George), KG, KT, GCB, OM and Great Master of the Order of the Bath, AK, QSO, PC, ADC(P)
Born 14 November 1948, created Prince of Wales and Earl of Chester 1958, succeeded as Duke of Cornwall, Duke of Rothesay, Earl of Carrick and Baron Renfrew, Lord of the Isles and Great Steward of Scotland 1952
Married (1) 29 July 1981 Lady Diana Frances Spencer (Diana, Princess of Wales (1961–97), youngest daughter of the 8th Earl Spencer and the Hon. Mrs Shand Kydd), marriage dissolved 1996; (2) 9 April 2005 Mrs Camilla Rosemary Parker Bowles, now HRH the Duchess of Cornwall (*born* 17 July 1947, daughter of Major Bruce Shand and the Hon. Mrs Rosalind Shand)
Residences Clarence House, London SW1A 1BA; Highgrove, Doughton, Tetbury, Glos GL8 8TN; Birkhall, Ballater, Aberdeenshire
Issue
1. HRH Prince William of Wales (Prince William Arthur Philip Louis), KG, *born* 21 June 1982
2. HRH Prince Henry of Wales (Prince Henry Charles Albert David), *born* 15 September 1984

HRH THE PRINCESS ROYAL (Princess Anne Elizabeth Alice Louise), KG, KT, GCVO
Born 15 August 1950, declared the Princess Royal 1987
Married (1) 14 November 1973 Captain Mark Anthony Peter Phillips, CVO (*born* 22 September 1948); marriage dissolved 1992; (2) 12 December 1992 Captain Timothy James Hamilton Laurence, MVO, RN (*born* 1 March 1955)
Residence Gatcombe Park, Minchinhampton, Glos GL6 9AT
Issue
1. Peter Mark Andrew Phillips, *born* 15 November 1977, *married* 17 May 2008 Autumn Patricia Kelly
2. Zara Anne Elizabeth Phillips, MBE, *born* 15 May 1981

HRH THE DUKE OF YORK (Prince Andrew Albert Christian Edward), KG, KCVO, ADC(P)
Born 19 February 1960, created Duke of York, Earl of Inverness and Baron Killyleagh 1986
Married 23 July 1986 Sarah Margaret Ferguson, now Sarah, Duchess of York (*born* 15 October 1959, younger daughter of Major Ronald Ferguson and Mrs Hector Barrantes), marriage dissolved 1996
Residence Royal Lodge, Windsor Great Park, Berks
Issue
1. HRH Princess Beatrice of York (Princess Beatrice Elizabeth Mary), *born* 8 August 1988
2. HRH Princess Eugenie of York (Princess Eugenie Victoria Helena), *born* 23 March 1990

HRH THE EARL OF WESSEX (Prince Edward Antony Richard Louis), KG, KCVO
Born 10 March 1964, created Earl of Wessex, Viscount Severn 1999
Married 19 June 1999 Sophie Helen Rhys-Jones, now HRH the Countess of Wessex, GCVO (*born* 20 January 1965, daughter of Mr and Mrs Christopher Rhys-Jones)
Residence Bagshot Park, Bagshot, Surrey GU19 5HS
Issue
1. Lady Louise Windsor (Louise Alice Elizabeth Mary Mountbatten-Windsor), *born* 8 November 2003
2. Viscount Severn (James Alexander Philip Theo Mountbatten-Windsor), *born* 17 December 2007

NEPHEW AND NIECE OF THE QUEEN

Children of HRH the Princess Margaret, Countess of Snowdon and the Earl of Snowdon (*see* House of Windsor):

DAVID ALBERT CHARLES ARMSTRONG-JONES, VISCOUNT LINLEY, *born* 3 November 1961, *married* 8 October 1993 the Hon. Serena Stanhope, and has issue, Hon. Charles Patrick Inigo Armstrong-Jones, *born* 1 July 1999; Hon. Margarita Elizabeth Alleyne Armstrong-Jones, *born* 14 May 2002

LADY SARAH CHATTO (Sarah Frances Elizabeth), *born* 1 May 1964, *married* 14 July 1994 Daniel Chatto, and has issue, Samuel David Benedict Chatto, *born* 28 July 1996; Arthur Robert Nathaniel Chatto, *born* 5 February 1999

COUSINS OF THE QUEEN

Child of HRH the Duke of Gloucester and HRH Princess Alice, Duchess of Gloucester (*see* House of Windsor):

HRH THE DUKE OF GLOUCESTER (Prince Richard Alexander Walter George), KG, GCVO, Grand Prior of the Order of St John of Jerusalem

Born 26 August 1944
Married 8 July 1972 Birgitte Eva van Deurs, now HRH the Duchess of Gloucester, GCVO (*born* 20 June 1946, daughter of Asger Henriksen and Vivian van Deurs)
Residence Kensington Palace, London W8 4PU
Issue
1. Earl of Ulster (Alexander Patrick Gregers Richard), *born* 24 October 1974 *married* 22 June 2002 Dr Claire Booth, and has issue, Lord Culloden (Xan Richard Anders), *born* 12 March 2007; Lady Cosima Windsor (Cosima Rose Alexandra), *born* 20 May 2010
2. Lady Davina Lewis (Davina Elizabeth Alice Benedikte), *born* 19 November 1977 *married* 31 July 2004 Gary Lewis
3. Lady Rose Gilman (Rose Victoria Birgitte Louise), *born* 1 March 1980 *married* 19 July 2008 George Gilman

Children of HRH the Duke of Kent and Princess Marina, Duchess of Kent (*see* House of Windsor):

HRH THE DUKE OF KENT (Prince Edward George Nicholas Paul Patrick), KG, GCMG, GCVO, ADC(P)
Born 9 October 1935
Married 8 June 1961 Katharine Lucy Mary Worsley, now HRH the Duchess of Kent, GCVO (*born* 22 February 1933, daughter of Sir William Worsley, Bt.)
Residence Wren House, Palace Green, London W8 4PY
Issue
1. Earl of St Andrews (George Philip Nicholas), *born* 26 June 1962, *married* 9 January 1988 Sylvana Tomaselli, and has issue, Baron Downpatrick (Edward Edmund Maximilian George), *born* 2 December 1988; Lady Marina-Charlotte Windsor (Marina-Charlotte Alexandra Katharine Helen), *born* 30 September 1992; Lady Amelia Windsor (Amelia Sophia Theodora Mary Margaret), *born* 24 August 1995
2. Lady Helen Taylor (Helen Marina Lucy), *born* 28 April 1964, *married* 18 July 1992 Timothy Taylor, and has issue, Columbus George Donald Taylor, *born* 6 August 1994; Cassius Edward Taylor, *born* 26 December 1996; Eloise Olivia Katharine Taylor, *born* 3 March 2003; Estella Olga Elizabeth Taylor, *born* 21 December 2004
3. Lord Nicholas Windsor (Nicholas Charles Edward Jonathan), *born* 25 July 1970, *married* 4 November 2006 Paola Doimi de Frankopan, and has issue, Albert Louis Philip Edward Windsor, *born* 22 September 2007; Leopold Ernest Augustus Guelph Windsor, *born* 8 September 2009

HRH PRINCESS ALEXANDRA, THE HON. LADY OGILVY (Princess Alexandra Helen Elizabeth Olga Christabel), KG, GCVO
Born 25 December 1936
Married 24 April 1963 the Rt. Hon. Sir Angus Ogilvy, KCVO (1928–2004), second son of 12th Earl of Airlie
Residence Thatched House Lodge, Richmond Park, Surrey TW10 5HP
Issue
1. James Robert Bruce Ogilvy, *born* 29 February 1964, *married* 30 July 1988 Julia Rawlinson, and has issue, Flora Alexandra Ogilvy, *born* 15 December 1994; Alexander Charles Ogilvy, *born* 12 November 1996
2. Marina Victoria Alexandra Ogilvy, *born* 31 July 1966, *married* 2 February 1990 Paul Mowatt (marriage dissolved 1997), and has issue, Zenouska May Mowatt, *born* 26 May 1990; Christian Alexander Mowatt, *born* 4 June 1993

HRH PRINCE MICHAEL OF KENT (Prince Michael George Charles Franklin), GCVO
Born 4 July 1942
Married 30 June 1978 Baroness Marie-Christine Agnes Hedwig Ida von Reibnitz, now HRH Princess Michael of Kent (*born* 15 January 1945, daughter of Baron Gunther von Reibnitz)
Residence Kensington Palace, London W8 4PU
Issue
1. Lord Frederick Windsor (Frederick Michael George David Louis), *born* 6 April 1979, *married* 12 September 2009 Sophie Winkleman
2. Lady Gabriella Windsor (Gabriella Marina Alexandra Ophelia), *born* 23 April 1981

ORDER OF SUCCESSION

1	HRH the Prince of Wales
2	HRH Prince William of Wales
3	HRH Prince Henry of Wales
4	HRH the Duke of York
5	HRH Princess Beatrice of York
6	HRH Princess Eugenie of York
7	HRH the Earl of Wessex
8	Viscount Severn
9	Lady Louise Windsor
10	HRH the Princess Royal
11	Peter Phillips
12	Zara Phillips
13	Viscount Linley
14	Hon. Charles Armstrong-Jones
15	Hon. Margarita Armstrong-Jones
16	Lady Sarah Chatto
17	Samuel Chatto
18	Arthur Chatto
19	HRH the Duke of Gloucester
20	Earl of Ulster
21	Lord Culloden
22	Lady Cosima Windsor
23	Lady Davina Lewis
24	Lady Rose Gilman
25	HRH the Duke of Kent
26	Lady Amelia Windsor
27	Lady Helen Taylor
28	Columbus Taylor
29	Cassius Taylor
30	Eloise Taylor
31	Estella Taylor
32	Lord Frederick Windsor
33	Lady Gabriella Windsor
34	HRH Princess Alexandra, the Hon. Lady Ogilvy
35	James Ogilvy
36	Alexander Ogilvy
37	Flora Ogilvy
38	Marina Ogilvy
39	Christian Mowatt

HRH Prince Michael of Kent, and the Earl of St Andrews both lost the right of succession to the throne through marriage to a Roman Catholic. Lord Nicholas Windsor, Baron Downpatrick and Lady Marina-Charlotte Windsor renounced their rights to the throne on converting to Roman Catholicism in 2001, 2003 and 2008 respectively. Their children remain in succession provided that they are in communion with the Church of England.

PRIVATE SECRETARIES TO THE ROYAL FAMILY

THE QUEEN
Office: Buckingham Palace, London SW1A 1AA
T 020-7930 4832 W www.royal.gov.uk
Private Secretary to the Queen, Christopher Geidt, CVO, OBE

PRINCE PHILIP, THE DUKE OF EDINBURGH
Office: Buckingham Palace, London SW1A 1AA
T 020-7930 4832
Private Secretary, Brig. Sir Miles Hunt-Davis, KCVO, CBE

THE PRINCE OF WALES AND THE DUCHESS OF CORNWALL
Office: Clarence House, London SW1A 1BA
T 020-7930 4832
Principal Private Secretary, Sir Michael Peat, KCVO

PRINCES WILLIAM AND HENRY OF WALES
Office: Clarence House, London SW1A 1BA
T 020-7930 4832
Private Secretary, James Lowther-Pinkerton, MVO, MBE

THE DUKE OF YORK
Office: Buckingham Palace, London SW1A 1AA
T 020-7930 4832
Private Secretary, Alastair Watson

THE EARL AND COUNTESS OF WESSEX
Office: Bagshot Park, Surrey GU19 5PL
T 01276-707040
Private Secretary, Brig. J. Smedley, LVO

THE PRINCESS ROYAL
Office: Buckingham Palace, London SW1A 1AA
T 020-7024 4199
Private Secretary, Capt. N. P. Wright, LVO, RN

THE DUKE AND DUCHESS OF GLOUCESTER
Office: Kensington Palace, London W8 4PU
T 020-7368 1000
Private Secretary, Alistair Wood, MBE

THE DUKE OF KENT
Office: St James's Palace, London SW1A 1BQ
T 020-7930 4872
Private Secretary, N. Adamson, CVO, OBE

THE DUCHESS OF KENT
Office: Wren House, Palace Green, London W8 4PY
T 020-7937 2730
Personal Secretary, Chloe Hill

PRINCE AND PRINCESS MICHAEL OF KENT
Office: Kensington Palace, London W8 4PU
T 020-7938 3519
W www.princemichael.org.uk
Private Secretary, Nicholas Chance, LVO

PRINCESS ALEXANDRA, THE HON. LADY OGILVY
Office: Buckingham Palace, London SW1A 1AA
T 020-7024 4270
Private Secretary, Diane Duke

ROYAL HOUSEHOLD

The PRIVATE SECRETARY is responsible for:

- informing and advising the Queen on constitutional, governmental and political matters in the UK, her other Realms and the wider Commonwealth, including communications with the prime minister and government departments
- organising the Queen's domestic and overseas official programme
- the Queen's speeches, messages, patronage, photographs, portraits and official presents
- communications in connection with the role of the royal family
- dealing with correspondence to the Queen from members of the public
- organising and coordinating royal travel
- coordinating and initiating research to support engagements by members of the royal family

The COMMUNICATIONS AND PRESS SECRETARY is in charge of Buckingham Palace's press office and reports to the private secretary. The press secretary is responsible for:

- developing communications strategies to enhance the public understanding of the role of the monarchy
- briefing the British and international media on the role and duties of the Queen and issues relating to the royal family
- responding to media enquiries
- arranging media facilities in the UK and overseas to support royal functions and engagements
- the management of the royal website

The private secretary is keeper of the royal archives and is responsible for the care of the records of the sovereign and the royal household from previous reigns, preserved in the royal archives at Windsor. As keeper, it is the private secretary's responsibility to ensure the proper management of the records of the present reign with a view to their transfer to the archives as and when appropriate. The private secretary is an *ex officio* trustee of the Royal Collection Trust.

The KEEPER OF THE PRIVY PURSE AND TREASURER to the Queen is responsible for:

- the Queen's Civil List, which is the money paid from the government's Consolidated Fund to meet official expenditure relating to the Queen's duties as head of state and head of the Commonwealth
- through the director of personnel, the planning and management of personnel policy across the royal household, the administration of all its pension schemes and private estates employees, and the allocation of employee and pensioner housing
- information technology systems
- internal audit services
- health and safety; insurance matters
- the privy purse, which is mainly financed by the net income of the Duchy of Lancaster, and meets both official and private expenditure incurred by the Queen
- liaison with other members of the royal family and their households on financial matters
- the Queen's private estates at Sandringham and Balmoral, the Queen's Racing Establishment and the Royal Studs and liaison with the Ascot Authority

- the Home Park at Windsor and liaison with the Crown Estate Commissioners concerning the Home Park and the Great Park at Windsor
- the Royal Philatelic Collection
- administrative aspects of the Military Knights of Windsor
- administration of the Royal Victorian Order, of which the keeper of the privy purse is secretary, Long and Faithful Service Medals, and the Queen's cups, medals and prizes, and policy on commemorative medals

The keeper of the privy purse is one of three royal trustees (in respect of his responsibilities for the Civil List) and is receiver-general of the Duchy of Lancaster and a member of the Duchy's Council.

The keeper of the privy purse is responsible for property services at occupied royal palaces in England, comprising Buckingham Palace, St James's Palace, Clarence House, Marlborough House Mews, the residential and office areas of Kensington Palace, Windsor Castle and buildings in the Home and Great Parks of Windsor and Hampton Court Mews and Paddocks. The costs of property services for occupied royal palaces are met from a grant-in-aid from the Department for Culture, Media and Sport (DCMS).

The keeper of the privy purse also oversees royal communications and information expenditure, which is met from the property services grant-in-aid, and the financial aspects of royal travel, met from a grant-in-aid provided by the Department for Transport.

The keeper of the privy purse is an *ex officio* trustee of the Historic Royal Palaces Trust and the Royal Collection Trust.

The Queen's Civil List and the grants-in-aid for property services and royal travel are provided by the government in return for the net surplus from the Crown Estate and other hereditary revenues.

The DIRECTOR OF THE PROPERTY SECTION has day-to-day responsibility for the royal household's property section:

- fire and health and safety
- repairs and refurbishment of buildings and new building work
- utilities and telecommunications
- putting up stages, tents and other work in connection with ceremonial occasions, garden parties and other official functions

The property section is also responsible, on a sub-contract basis from the DCMS, for the maintenance of Marlborough House (which is occupied by the Commonwealth Secretariat).

The MASTER OF THE HOUSEHOLD is responsible for:

- delivering the majority of the official and private entertaining in the Queen's annual programme at residences in the UK, and on occasion overseas
- periodic support for entertaining by other members of the royal family
- furnishings and internal decorative refurbishment in conjunction with the director of the Royal Collection and Property Services
- travel arrangements for employees and baggage movements between residences
- housekeeping, catering and service provision for the royal household

The COMPTROLLER, LORD CHAMBERLAIN'S OFFICE is responsible for:

- the organisation of all ceremonial engagements, including state visits to the Queen in the UK, royal weddings and funerals, the state opening of parliament, Guards of Honour at Buckingham Palace, investitures, and the Garter and Thistle ceremonies
- garden parties at Buckingham Palace and the Palace of Holyroodhouse (except for catering and tents)
- the Crown Jewels, which are part of the Royal Collection, when they are in use on state occasions
- coordination of the arrangements for the Queen to be represented at funerals and memorial services and at the arrival and departure of visiting heads of state
- advising on matters of precedence, style and titles, dress, flying of flags, gun salutes, mourning and other ceremonial issues
- supervising the applications from tradesmen for Royal Warrants of Appointment
- advising on the commercial use of royal emblems and contemporary royal photographs
- the ecclesiastical household, the medical household, the body guards and certain ceremonial appointments such as Gentlemen Ushers and Pages of Honour
- the lords in waiting, who represent the Queen on various occasions and escort visiting heads of state during incoming state visits
- the Queen's bargemaster and watermen and the Queen's swans
- the Royal Almonry

The comptroller is also responsible for the Royal Mews, assisted by the CROWN EQUERRY, who has day-to-day responsibility for:

- the provision of carriage processions for the state opening of parliament, state visits, Trooping of the Colour, Royal Ascot, the Garter Ceremony, the Thistle Service, the presentation of credentials to the Queen by incoming foreign ambassadors and high commissioners, and other state and ceremonial occasions
- the provision of chauffeur-driven cars
- coordinating travel arrangements by road in respect of the Queen's official engagements
- supervision and administration of the Royal Mews at Buckingham Palace, Windsor Castle, Hampton Court and the Palace of Holyroodhouse

The comptroller also has overall responsibility for the MARSHAL OF THE DIPLOMATIC CORPS, who is responsible for the relationship between the royal household and the Diplomatic Heads of Mission in London; and the SECRETARY OF THE CENTRAL CHANCERY OF THE ORDERS OF KNIGHTHOOD, who administers the Orders of Chivalry, makes arrangements for investitures and the distribution of insignia, and ensures the proper public notification of awards through the *London Gazette*.

The DIRECTOR OF THE ROYAL COLLECTION is responsible for:

- the administration and custodial control of the Royal Collection in all royal residences

- the care, display, conservation and restoration of items in the collection
- initiating and assisting research into the collection and publishing catalogues and books on the collection
- making the collection accessible to the public and educating and informing the public about the collection

The Royal Collection, which contains a large number of works of art, is held by the Queen as sovereign in trust for her successors and the nation and is not owned by her as an individual. The administration, conservation and presentation of the Royal Collection are funded by the Royal Collection Trust solely from income from visitors to Windsor Castle, Buckingham Palace and the Palace of Holyroodhouse. The Royal Collection Trust is chaired by the Prince of Wales. The Lord Chamberlain, the private secretary and the keeper of the privy purse are *ex officio* trustees and there are three external trustees appointed by the Queen.

The director of the Royal Collection is also at present the SURVEYOR OF THE QUEEN'S WORKS OF ART. The ROYAL LIBRARIAN is responsible for all books, manuscripts, coins and medals, insignia and works of art on paper including the watercolours, prints and drawings in the Print Room at Windsor Castle, and the SURVEYOR OF THE QUEEN'S PICTURES is responsible for pictures and miniatures.

Royal Collection Enterprises Limited is the trading subsidiary of the Royal Collection Trust. The company, whose chair is the Keeper of the Privy Purse, is responsible for:

- managing access by the public to Windsor Castle (including Frogmore House), Buckingham Palace (including the Royal Mews and the Queen's Gallery) and the Palace of Holyroodhouse (including the Queen's Gallery)
- running shops at each location
- managing the images and intellectual property rights of the Royal Collection

The director of the Royal Collection is also an *ex officio* trustee of the Historic Royal Palaces Trust.

SENIOR MANAGEMENT OF THE ROYAL HOUSEHOLD

Lord Chamberlain, Earl Peel, GCVO, PC

HEADS OF DEPARTMENT

Private Secretary to The Queen, Rt. Hon. Christopher Geidt, CVO, OBE
Keeper of the Privy Purse, Sir Alan Reid, KCVO
Master of the Household, Air Vice-Marshal David Walker, OBE, MVO
Comptroller, Lord Chamberlain's Office, Lt.-Col. Andrew Ford
Director of the Royal Collection, Jonathan Marsden, LVO

NON-EXECUTIVE MEMBERS

Private Secretary to the Duke of Edinburgh, Brig. Sir Miles Hunt-Davis, KCVO, CBE
Private Secretary to the Prince of Wales and the Duchess of Cornwall, Sir Michael Peat, KCVO

THE POET LAUREATE

The post of Poet Laureate was officially established when John Dryden was appointed by royal warrant as Poet Laureate and Historiographer Royal in 1668. The post is attached to the royal household and was originally conferred on the holder for life; in 1999 the length of appointment was changed to a ten-year term. It is customary for the Poet Laureate to write verse to mark events of national importance. The postholder currently receives an honorarium of £5,750 a year.
The Poet Laureate, Carol Ann Duffy, *apptd* 2009

ROYAL SALUTES

ENGLAND

The basic royal salute is 21 rounds with an extra 20 rounds fired at Hyde Park because it is a royal park. At the Tower of London 62 rounds are fired on royal anniversaries (21 plus a further 20 because the Tower is a royal palace and a further 21 'for the City of London') and 41 on other occasions. When the Queen's official birthday coincides with the Duke of Edinburgh's birthday, 124 rounds are fired from the Tower (62 rounds for each birthday). Gun salutes occur on the following royal anniversaries:

- Accession Day
- The Queen's birthday
- Coronation Day
- Duke of Edinburgh's birthday
- The Queen's Official Birthday
- The Prince of Wales' birthday
- State opening of parliament

Gun salutes also occur when parliament is prorogued by the sovereign, on royal births and when a visiting head of state meets the sovereign in London, Windsor or Edinburgh.

In London, salutes are fired at Hyde Park and the Tower of London although on some occasions (state visits, state opening of parliament and the Queen's birthday parade) Green Park is used instead of Hyde Park. Other military saluting stations in England are at Colchester, Dover, Plymouth, Woolwich and York.

Constable of the Royal Palace and Fortress of London, Gen. Sir Richard Dannatt, GCB, CBE, MC
Lieutenant of the Tower of London, Lt.-Gen. Sir Cedric Delves, KBE, DSO
Resident Governor and Keeper of the Jewel House, Maj.-Gen. Keith Cima, CB
Master Gunner of St James's Park, Gen. Sir Alex Harley, KBE, CB
Master Gunner within the Tower, HRH Prince Michael of Kent, GCVO

SCOTLAND

Royal salutes are authorised at Edinburgh Castle and Stirling Castle. A salute of 21 guns is fired on the following occasions:

- the anniversaries of the birth, accession and coronation of the sovereign

• the anniversary of the birth of the Duke of Edinburgh

A salute of 21 guns is fired in Edinburgh on the occasion of the opening of the general assembly of the Church of Scotland. A salute of 21 guns may also be fired in Edinburgh on the arrival of HM The Queen or a member of the royal family who is a Royal Highness on an official visit.

Military saluting stations are also situated at Cardiff Castle in Wales, Hillsborough Castle in Northern Ireland and in Gibraltar.

ROYAL FINANCES

FUNDING

CIVIL LIST

The Civil List dates back to the late 17th century. It was originally used by the sovereign to supplement hereditary revenues for paying the salaries of judges, ambassadors and other government officers as well as the expenses of the royal household. In 1760, on the accession of George III, it was decided that the Civil List would be provided by parliament to cover all relevant expenditure in return for the king surrendering the hereditary revenues of the Crown (principally the net surplus of the Crown Estate). At that time parliament undertook to pay the salaries of judges, ambassadors etc. In 1831 parliament agreed also to meet the costs of the royal palaces in return for a reduction in the Civil List. Each sovereign has agreed to continue this arrangement. The Civil List now meets the central staff costs and running expenses of the Queen's official household.

Until 1972, the amount of money allocated annually under the Civil List was set for the duration of a reign. The system was then altered to a fixed annual payment for ten years but from 1975 high inflation made an annual review necessary. The system of payments reverted to the practice of a fixed annual payment of £7.9m for a ten-year period to 31 December 2000; during this period annual Civil List expenditure reached £6.5m, and a reserve of £35m was established. In order to draw down the reserve, the annual Civil List payment was left at £7.9m for a further ten years to 31 December 2010.

The legislative requirement is for Civil List accounts to be submitted to parliament, in the form of Royal Trustees Reports, at ten-yearly intervals, but from June 2002 accounts have been published annually. The ninth annual accounts for the year ending 31 December 2009 were published in June 2010:

	2008	*2009*
Civil List payment	£7,900,000	£7,900,000
Draw-down from the Civil List reserve	£6,400,000	£6,500,000
Net Receipts	£14,300,000	£14,400,000
Net Civil List Expenditure	(£13,900,000)	(£14,200,000)

PARLIAMENTARY ANNUITIES

The Civil List Acts provide for other members of the royal family to receive parliamentary annuities from government funds to meet the expenses of carrying out their official duties. Since 1993 the Queen has reimbursed all the annuities except those paid to the late Queen Elizabeth the Queen Mother and the Duke of Edinburgh.

The Prince of Wales does not receive a parliamentary annuity. He derives his income from the revenues of the Duchy of Cornwall and these monies meet the official and private expenses of the Prince of Wales and his family (*see* Prince of Wales' Funding).

In 2000 the annual amounts payable to members of the royal family, excluding the Earl of Wessex, were reset at their 1990 levels for the next ten years. The Earl of Wessex had his annuity increased by £45,000 to £141,000 on the occasion of his marriage in 1999.

The annual payments remain as follows until December 2011:

The Duke of Edinburgh	£359,000
The Duke of York	£249,000
The Earl of Wessex	£141,000
The Princess Royal	£228,000
The Duke and Duchess of Gloucester	£175,000
The Duke and Duchess of Kent	£236,000
Princess Alexandra	£225,000
Subtotal	£1,613,000
Refunded to the Treasury by the Queen	(£1,254,000)
TOTAL	£359,000

GRANTS-IN-AID

Grants-in-aid are provided to the royal household annually by the Department for Culture, Media and Sport for property services and communications and information, and by the Department for Transport for royal travel. Property services meets the cost of property maintenance, utilities, telephones and related services at the occupied royal palaces in England (*see* Royal Household section for a list of occupied palaces). Communications and Information meets the cost of these services in connection with official royal functions and engagements in England and Scotland. Royal travel meets the cost of official royal travel by air and rail.

GRANTS-IN-AID 2009–10:

	Grant-in-aid voted by parliament	*Total net expenditure*
Property Services	£15,000,000	£15,400,000
Marlborough House Maintenance	£600,000	£500,000
Communications and Information	£500,000	£400,000
Royal Travel	£7,300,000	£3,900,000

THE PRIVY PURSE AND THE DUCHY OF LANCASTER

The funds received by the privy purse pay for official expenses incurred by the Queen as head of state and for some of the Queen's private expenditure. The revenues of the Duchy of Lancaster are the principal source of income for the privy purse. The revenues of the Duchy were retained by George III in 1760 when the hereditary revenues were surrendered in exchange for the Civil List. The Duchy's affairs are the responsibility of the Duchy Council which reports to the Chancellor of the Duchy of Lancaster, who in turn is accountable directly to the sovereign rather than to parliament. However the chancellor does answer parliamentary questions on matters relating to the Duchy of Lancaster's responsibilities.

THE DUCHY OF LANCASTER, 1 Lancaster Place, London WC2E 7ED
E info@duchyoflancaster.co.uk
W www.duchyoflancaster.co.uk
Chancellor of the Duchy of Lancaster, Rt. Hon. Baroness Royall of Blaisdon, *apptd* 2009
Chair of the Council, Lord Shuttleworth
Clerk and Chief Executive, Paul Clarke, CVO, FRICS
Receiver-General, Sir Alan Reid, KCVO
Attorney-General, Robert Hildyard, QC

PERSONAL INCOME
The Queen's personal income derives mostly from investments, and is used to meet private expenditure.

EXPENDITURE MET BY GOVERNMENT DEPARTMENTS AND THE CROWN ESTATE 2009–10:

Administration of honours	£600,000
Equerries, orderlies and other personnel	£1,000,000
Maintenance of Holyroodhouse	£1,100,000
State visits to and by the Queen and liaison with the Diplomatic Corps	£200,000
Ceremonial occasions	£300,000
Maintenance of Home Park, Windsor Castle	£600,000
Other	£100,000
Total	£3,900,000

PRINCE OF WALES' FUNDING

The Duchy Estate was created in 1337 by Edward III for his son and heir Prince Edward (the Black Prince) who became the Duke of Cornwall. The Duchy's primary function is to provide an income from its assets for the Prince of Wales. Under a 1337 charter, confirmed by subsequent legislation, the Prince of Wales is not entitled to the proceeds or profit on the sale of Duchy assets but only to the annual income which is generated from these assets. The Duchy is responsible for the sustainable and commercial management of its properties, investment portfolio and approximately 54,521 hectares of land, based mostly in the south-west of England. The Prince of Wales has chosen to use a proportion of his income to meet the cost of his public and charitable work in addition to providing a private source of income. The Duchy also funds the public, charitable and private activities of the Duchess of Cornwall and princes William and Harry. Proceeds from the Duchy are voluntarily subject to income tax.

THE DUCHY OF CORNWALL, 10 Buckingham Gate, London SW1E 6LA
T 020-7834 7346 E London@duchyofcornwall.org
W www.duchyofcornwall.org
Lord Warden of the Stannaries, Sir Nicholas Bacon, Bt.
Receiver-General, James Leigh-Pemberton
Attorney-General, Jonathan Crow, QC
Secretary and Keeper of the Records, Bertie Ross

TAXATION

The sovereign is not legally liable to pay income tax or capital gains tax. After income tax was reintroduced in 1842, some income tax was paid voluntarily by the sovereign but over a long period these payments were phased out. In 1992 the Queen offered to pay income and capital gains tax on a voluntary basis from 6 April 1993, and the Prince of Wales offered to pay tax on a voluntary basis on his income from the Duchy of Cornwall (he was already taxed in all other respects).

The main provisions for the Queen and the Prince of Wales to pay tax, set out in a Memorandum of Understanding on Royal Taxation presented to parliament on 11 February 1993, are that the Queen will pay income tax and capital gains tax in respect of her private income and assets, and on the proportion of the income and capital gains of the Privy Purse used for private purposes. Inheritance tax will be paid on the Queen's assets, except for those which pass to the next sovereign, whether automatically or by gift or bequest. The Prince of Wales will pay income tax on income from the Duchy of Cornwall used for private purposes.

The Prince of Wales has confirmed that he intends to pay tax on the same basis following his accession to the throne. Other members of the royal family are subject to tax as for any taxpayer.

MILITARY RANKS AND TITLES

THE QUEEN

ROYAL NAVY
Lord High Admiral of the United Kingdom

ARMY
Colonel-in-Chief
The Life Guards; The Blues and Royals (Royal Horse Guards and 1st Dragoons); The Royal Scots Dragoon Guards (Carabiniers and Greys); The Queen's Royal Lancers; Royal Tank Regiment; Corps of Royal Engineers; Grenadier Guards; Coldstream Guards; Scots Guards; Irish Guards; Welsh Guards; The Royal Regiment of Scotland; The Duke of Lancaster's Regiment (King's, Lancashire and Border); The Royal Welsh; Adjutant General's Corps; The Royal Mercian and Lancastrian Yeomanry; The Governor General's Horse Guards (of Canada); The King's Own Calgary Regiment (Royal Canadian Armoured Corps); Canadian Military Engineers Branch; Royal 22e Regiment (of Canada); Governor General's Foot Guards (of Canada); The Canadian Grenadier Guards; Le Régiment de la Chaudière (of Canada); 2nd Battalion Royal New Brunswick Regiment (North Shore); 48th Highlanders of Canada; The Argyll and Sutherland Highlanders of Canada (Princess Louise's); The Calgary Highlanders; Royal Australian Engineers; Royal Australian Infantry Corps; Royal Australian Army Ordnance Corps; Royal Australian Army Nursing Corps; The Corps of Royal New Zealand Engineers; Royal New Zealand Infantry Regiment; The Malawi Rifles; The Royal Malta Artillery

Affiliated Colonel-in-Chief
The Queen's Gurkha Engineers

Captain-General
Royal Regiment of Artillery; The Honourable Artillery Company; Combined Cadet Force; Royal Regiment of Canadian Artillery; Royal Regiment of Australian Artillery; Royal Regiment of New Zealand Artillery; Royal New Zealand Armoured Corps

Royal Colonel
The Argyll and Sutherland Highlanders, 5th Battalion The Royal Regiment of Scotland

Patron
Royal Army Chaplains' Department

ROYAL AIR FORCE
Air Commodore-in-Chief
Royal Auxiliary Air Force; Royal Air Force Regiment; Air Reserve of Canada; Royal Australian Air Force Reserve; Territorial Air Force (of New Zealand)

Commandant-in-Chief
RAF College, Cranwell

Royal Honorary Air Commodore
RAF Marham; 603 (City of Edinburgh) Squadron Royal Auxiliary Air Force

PRINCE PHILIP, DUKE OF EDINBURGH

ROYAL NAVY
Admiral of the Fleet
Admiral of the Fleet, Royal Australian Navy
Admiral of the Fleet, Royal New Zealand Navy
Admiral of the Royal Canadian Sea Cadets

ROYAL MARINES
Captain-General

ARMY
Field Marshal
Field Marshal, Australian Military Forces
Field Marshal, New Zealand Army
Colonel-in-Chief
The Queen's Royal Hussars (Queen's Own and Royal Irish); The Rifles; Corps of Royal Electrical and Mechanical Engineers; Intelligence Corps; Army Cadet Force Association; The Royal Canadian Regiment; The Royal Hamilton Light Infantry (Wentworth Regiment of Canada); The Cameron Highlanders of Ottawa; The Queen's Own Cameron Highlanders of Canada; The Seaforth Highlanders of Canada; The Royal Canadian Army Cadets; The Royal Australian Corps of Electrical and Mechanical Engineers; The Australian Army Cadet Corps

Colonel
Grenadier Guards

Royal Colonel
The Highlanders, 4th Battalion The Royal Regiment of Scotland

Honorary Colonel
City of Edinburgh University Officers' Training Corps; The Trinidad and Tobago Regiment

Member
Honourable Artillery Company

ROYAL AIR FORCE
Marshal of the Royal Air Force
Marshal of the Royal Australian Air Force
Marshal of the Royal New Zealand Air Force
Air Commodore-in-Chief
Air Training Corps; Royal Canadian Air Cadets

Honorary Air Commodore
RAF Kinloss

THE PRINCE OF WALES

ROYAL NAVY
Admiral
Commodore-in-Chief
Royal Naval Command Plymouth

ARMY
General
Colonel-in-Chief
The Royal Dragoon Guards; The Parachute Regiment; The Royal Gurkha Rifles; Army Air Corps; The Royal Canadian Dragoons; Lord Strathcona's Horse (Royal Canadians); The Royal Regiment of Canada; Royal Winnipeg Rifles; Royal Australian Armoured Corps; The Royal Pacific Islands Regiment; 1st The Queen's Dragoon Guards; The Black Watch (Royal Highland Regiment) of Canada; The Toronto Scottish Regiment (Queen Elizabeth The Queen Mother's Own); The Mercian Regiment

Royal Colonel
The Black Watch, 3rd Battalion The Royal Regiment of Scotland; 51st Highland, 7th Battalion The Royal Regiment of Scotland (Territorial Army)

Colonel
The Welsh Guards

Royal Honorary Colonel
The Queen's Own Yeomanry

ROYAL AIR FORCE
Air Chief Marshal
Honorary Air Commodore
RAF Valley

Air Commodore-in-Chief
Royal New Zealand Air Force

Colonel-in-Chief
Air Reserve Canada

THE DUCHESS OF CORNWALL

ROYAL NAVY
Commodore-in-Chief
Naval Medical Services; Royal Naval Chaplaincy Services

ARMY
Royal Colonel
4th Battalion The Rifles

ROYAL AIR FORCE
Honorary AIr Commodore
RAF Halton; RAF Leeming

PRINCE WILLIAM OF WALES

ROYAL NAVY
Lieutenant
Commodore-in-Chief
Scotland Command; Submarines Command

ARMY
Lieutenant
The Blues and Royals (Royal Horse Guards and 1st Dragoons)

ROYAL AIR FORCE
Flight Lieutenant
Honorary Air Commandant
RAF Coningsby

PRINCE HENRY OF WALES

ROYAL NAVY
Commodore-in-Chief
Small Ships and Diving Command

ARMY
Lieutenant
The Blues and Royals (Royal Horse Guards and 1st Dragoons)

ROYAL AIR FORCE
Honorary Air Commandant
RAF Honington

THE DUKE OF YORK

ROYAL NAVY
Commander
Admiral of the Marine Society and Sea Cadets
Rear Admiral

ARMY
Colonel-in-Chief
The Royal Irish Regiment (27th (Inniskilling), 83rd, 87th and The Ulster Defence Regiment); 9th/12th Royal Lancers (The Prince of Wales's); The Royal Highland Fusiliers, 2nd Battalion The Royal Regiment of Scotland; The Yorkshire Regiment; Small Arms School Corps; The Queen's York Rangers (First Americans); Royal New Zealand Army Logistics Regiment; The Royal Highland Fusiliers of Canada; The Princess Louise Fusiliers (Canada)

ROYAL AIR FORCE
Honorary Air Commodore
RAF Lossiemouth

THE EARL OF WESSEX

ROYAL NAVY
Commodore-in-Chief
Royal Fleet Auxiliary

Patron
Royal Fleet Auxiliary Association

ARMY
Colonel-in-Chief
Hastings and Prince Edward Regiment; Saskatchewan Dragoons

Royal Colonel
2nd Battalion, The Rifles

Royal Honorary Colonel
Royal Wessex Yeomanry

ROYAL AIR FORCE
Honorary Air Commodore
RAF Waddington

THE COUNTESS OF WESSEX

ARMY
Colonel-in-Chief
Queen Alexandra's Royal Army Nursing Corps; The Lincoln and Welland Regiment; South Alberta Light Horse Regiment

Royal Colonel
5th Battalion, The Rifles

ROYAL AIR FORCE
Honorary Air Commodore
RAF Wittering

THE PRINCESS ROYAL

ROYAL NAVY
Vice-Admiral (Chief Commandant for Women in the Royal Navy)
Commodore-in-Chief
HM Naval Base Portsmouth

ARMY
Colonel-in-Chief
The King's Royal Hussars; Royal Corps of Signals; Royal Logistic Corps; The Royal Army Veterinary Corps; 8th Canadian Hussars (Princess Louise's); Royal Newfoundland Regiment; Canadian Forces Communications and Electronics Branch; The Grey and Simcoe Foresters (Royal Canadian Armoured Corps); The Royal Regina Rifle Regiment; Canadian Forces Medical Branch; Royal Australian Corps of Signals; Royal New Zealand Corps of Signals; Royal New Zealand Nursing Corps

Affiliated Colonel-in-Chief
The Queen's Gurkha Signals; The Queen's Own Gurkha Transport Regiment

Royal Colonel
1st Battalion The Royal Regiment of Scotland; 52nd Lowland, 6th Battalion The Royal Regiment of Scotland

Colonel
The Blues and Royals (Royal Horse Guards and 1st Dragoons)

Honorary Colonel
University of London Officers' Training Corps

Commandant-in-Chief
First Aid Nursing Yeomanry (Princess Royal's Volunteer Corps)

ROYAL AIR FORCE
Honorary Air Commodore
RAF Lyneham; University of London Air Squadron

THE DUKE OF GLOUCESTER

ARMY
Colonel-in-Chief
The Royal Anglian Regiment; Royal Army Medical Corps; Royal New Zealand Army Medical Corps

Deputy Colonel-in-Chief
The Royal Logistic Corps

Royal Colonel
6th Battalion, The Rifles

Honorary Colonel
Royal Monmouthshire Royal Engineers (Militia)

ROYAL AIR FORCE
Honorary Air Marshal
Honorary Air Commodore
RAF Odiham; No. 501 (County of Gloucester) Squadron Royal Auxiliary Air Force

THE DUCHESS OF GLOUCESTER

ARMY
Colonel-in-Chief
Royal Army Dental Corps; Royal Australian Army Educational Corps; Royal New Zealand Army Educational Corps; Canadian Forces Dental Services

Deputy Colonel-in-Chief
Adjutant-General's Corps

Royal Colonel
7th Battalion, The Rifles

Vice-Patron
Adjutant General's Corps Regimental Association

Patron
Royal Army Educational Corps Association; Army Families Federation

THE DUKE OF KENT

ARMY
Field Marshal
Colonel-in-Chief
The Royal Regiment of Fusiliers; Lorne Scots (Peel, Dufferin and Hamilton Regiment)

Deputy Colonel-in-Chief
The Royal Scots Dragoon Guards (Carabiniers and Greys)

Royal Colonel
1st Battalion The Rifles

Colonel
Scots Guards

ROYAL AIR FORCE
Honorary Air Chief Marshal
Honorary Air Commodore
RAF Leuchars

THE DUCHESS OF KENT

ARMY
Deputy Colonel-in-Chief
The Royal Dragoon Guards; Adjutant-General's Corps; The Royal Logistic Corps

PRINCE MICHAEL OF KENT

ROYAL NAVY
Honorary Rear Admiral Royal Naval Reserve

ARMY
Colonel-in-Chief
Essex and Kent Scottish Regiment (Ontario)

Regimental Colonel
Honourable Artillery Company

Major (retired)
King's Royal Hussars

ROYAL AIR FORCE
Honorary Air Commodore
RAF Benson

PRINCESS ALEXANDRA, THE HON. LADY OGILVY

ROYAL NAVY
Patron
Queen Alexandra's Royal Naval Nursing Service

ARMY
Colonel-in-Chief
The Queen's Own Rifles of Canada; The Canadian Scottish Regiment (Princess Mary's)

Deputy Colonel-in-Chief
The Queen's Royal Lancers

Royal Colonel
3rd Battalion The Rifles

Royal Honorary Colonel
The Royal Yeomanry

ROYAL AIR FORCE
Patron and Air Chief Commandant
Princess Mary's RAF Nursing Service

Honorary Air Commodore
RAF Cottesmore

KINGS AND QUEENS

ENGLISH KINGS AND QUEENS 927 TO 1603

HOUSES OF CERDIC AND DENMARK

Reign

927–939 ÆTHELSTAN
Son of Edward the Elder, by Ecgwynn, and grandson of Alfred
Acceded to Wessex and Mercia *c.*924, established direct rule over Northumbria 927, effectively creating the Kingdom of England
Reigned 15 years

939–946 EDMUND I
Born 921, son of Edward the Elder, by Eadgifu
Married (1) Ælfgifu (2) Æthelflæd
Killed aged 25, *reigned* 6 years

946–955 EADRED
Son of Edward the Elder, by Eadgifu
Reigned 9 years

955–959 EADWIG
Born before 943, son of Edmund and Ælfgifu
Married Ælfgifu
Reigned 3 years

959–975 EDGAR I
Born 943, son of Edmund and Ælfgifu
Married (1) Æthelflæd (2) Wulfthryth (3) Ælfthryth
Died aged 32, *reigned* 15 years

975–978 EDWARD I (the Martyr)
*Born c.*962, son of Edgar and Æthelflæd
Assassinated aged *c.*16, *reigned* 2 years

978–1016 ÆTHELRED (the Unready)
Born 968/969, son of Edgar and Ælfthryth
Married (1) Ælfgifu (2) Emma, daughter of Richard I, Count of Normandy
1013–14 dispossessed of kingdom by Swegn Forkbeard (King of Denmark 987–1014)
Died aged *c.*47, *reigned* 38 years

1016 (Apr–Nov) EDMUND II (Ironside)
Born before 993, son of Æthelred and Ælfgifu
Married Ealdgyth
Died aged over 23, *reigned* 7 months

1016–1035 CNUT (Canute)
*Born c.*995, son of Swegn Forkbeard, King of Denmark, and Gunhild
Married (1) Ælfgifu (2) Emma, widow of Æthelred the Unready
Gained submission of West Saxons 1015, Northumbrians 1016, Mercia 1016, King of all England after Edmund's death, King of Denmark 1019–35, King of Norway 1028–35
Died aged *c.*40, *reigned* 19 years

1035–1040 HAROLD I (Harefoot)
Born 1016/17, son of Cnut and Ælfgifu
Married Ælfgifu
1035 recognised as regent for himself and his brother Harthacnut; 1037 recognised as king
Died aged *c.*23, *reigned* 4 years

1040–1042 HARTHACNUT (Harthacanute)
*Born c.*1018, son of Cnut and Emma
Titular king of Denmark from 1028
Acknowledged King of England 1035–7 with Harold I as regent; effective king after Harold's death
Died aged *c.*24, *reigned* 2 years

1042–1066 EDWARD II (the Confessor)
Born between1002 and 1005, son of Æthelred the Unready and Emma
Married Eadgyth, daughter of Godwine, Earl of Wessex
Died aged over 60, *reigned* 23 years

1066 (Jan–Oct) HAROLD II (Godwinesson)
*Born c.*1020, son of Godwine, Earl of Wessex, and Gytha
Married (1) Eadgyth (2) Ealdgyth
Killed in battle aged *c.*46, *reigned* 10 months

THE HOUSE OF NORMANDY

1066–1087 WILLIAM I (the Conqueror)
Born 1027/8, son of Robert I, Duke of Normandy; obtained the Crown by conquest
Married Matilda, daughter of Baldwin, Count of Flanders
Died aged *c.*60, *reigned* 20 years

1087–1100 WILLIAM II (Rufus)
Born between 1056 and 1060, third son of William I; succeeded his father in England only
Killed aged *c.*40, *reigned* 12 years

1100–1135 HENRY I (Beauclerk)
Born 1068, fourth son of William I
Married (1) Edith or Matilda, daughter of Malcolm III of Scotland (2) Adela, daughter of Godfrey, Count of Louvain
Died aged 67, *reigned* 35 years

1135–1154 STEPHEN
Born not later than 1100, third son of Adela, daughter of William I, and Stephen, Count of Blois
Married Matilda, daughter of Eustace, Count of Boulogne
1141 (Feb–Nov) held captive by adherents of Matilda, daughter of Henry I, who contested the crown until 1153
Died aged over 53, *reigned* 18 years

THE HOUSE OF ANJOU (PLANTAGENETS)

1154–1189 HENRY II (Curtmantle)
Born 1133, son of Matilda, daughter of Henry I, and Geoffrey, Count of Anjou
Married Eleanor, daughter of William, Duke of Aquitaine, and divorced queen of Louis VII of France
Died aged 56, *reigned* 34 years

1189–1199 RICHARD I (Coeur de Lion)
Born 1157, third son of Henry II
Married Berengaria, daughter of Sancho VI, King of Navarre
Died aged 42, *reigned* 9 years

1199–1216 JOHN (Lackland)
Born 1167, fifth son of Henry II
Married (1) Isabella or Avisa, daughter of William, Earl of Gloucester (divorced) (2) Isabella, daughter of Aymer, Count of Angoulême
Died aged 48, *reigned* 17 years

1216–1272 HENRY III
Born 1207, son of John and Isabella of Angoulême
Married Eleanor, daughter of Raymond, Count of Provence
Died aged 65, *reigned* 56 years

1272–1307 EDWARD I (Longshanks)
Born 1239, eldest son of Henry III
Married (1) Eleanor, daughter of Ferdinand III, King of Castile (2) Margaret, daughter of Philip III of France
Died aged 68, *reigned* 34 years

1307–1327 EDWARD II
Born 1284, eldest surviving son of Edward I and Eleanor
Married Isabella, daughter of Philip IV of France
Deposed Jan 1327, *killed* Sep 1327 aged 43, *reigned* 19 years

1327–1377 EDWARD III
Born 1312, eldest son of Edward II
Married Philippa, daughter of William, Count of Hainault
Died aged 64, *reigned* 50 years

1377–1399 RICHARD II
Born 1367, son of Edward (the Black Prince), eldest son of Edward III
Married (1) Anne, daughter of Emperor Charles IV (2) Isabelle, daughter of Charles VI of France
Deposed Sep 1399, *killed* Feb 1400 aged 33, *reigned* 22 years

THE HOUSE OF LANCASTER

1399–1413 HENRY IV
Born 1366, son of John of Gaunt, fourth son of Edward III, and Blanche, daughter of Henry, Duke of Lancaster
Married (1) Mary, daughter of Humphrey, Earl of Hereford (2) Joan, daughter of Charles, King of Navarre, and widow of John, Duke of Brittany
Died aged *c.*47, *reigned* 13 years

1413–1422 HENRY V
Born 1387, eldest surviving son of Henry IV and Mary
Married Catherine, daughter of Charles VI of France
Died aged 34, *reigned* 9 years

1422–1471 HENRY VI
Born 1421, son of Henry V
Married Margaret, daughter of René, Duke of Anjou and Count of Provence
Deposed Mar 1461, *restored* Oct 1470
Deposed Apr 1471, *killed* May 1471 aged 49, *reigned* 39 years

THE HOUSE OF YORK

1461–1483 EDWARD IV
Born 1442, eldest son of Richard of York (grandson of Edmund, fifth son of Edward III; and son of Anne, great-granddaughter of Lionel, third son of Edward III)
Married Elizabeth Woodville, daughter of Richard, Lord Rivers, and widow of Sir John Grey
Acceded Mar 1461, *deposed* Oct 1470, *restored* Apr 1471
Died aged 40, *reigned* 21 years

1483 (Apr–Jun) EDWARD V
Born 1470, eldest son of Edward IV
Deposed Jun 1483, *died* probably Jul–Sep 1483, aged 12, *reigned* 2 months

1483–1485 RICHARD III
Born 1452, fourth son of Richard of York
Married Anne Neville, daughter of Richard, Earl of Warwick, and widow of Edward, Prince of Wales, son of Henry VI
Killed in battle aged 32, *reigned* 2 years

THE HOUSE OF TUDOR

1485–1509 HENRY VII
Born 1457, son of Margaret Beaufort (great-granddaughter of John of Gaunt, fourth son of Edward III) and Edmund Tudor, Earl of Richmond
Married Elizabeth, daughter of Edward IV
Died aged 52, *reigned* 23 years

1509–1547 HENRY VIII
Born 1491, second son of Henry VII
Married (1) Catherine, daughter of Ferdinand II, King of Aragon, and widow of his elder brother Arthur (divorced) (2) Anne, daughter of Sir Thomas Boleyn (executed) (3) Jane, daughter of Sir John Seymour (died in childbirth) (4) Anne, daughter of John, Duke of Cleves (divorced) (5) Catherine Howard, niece of the Duke of Norfolk (executed) (6) Catherine, daughter of Sir Thomas Parr and widow of Lord Latimer
Died aged 55, *reigned* 37 years

1547–1553 EDWARD VI
Born 1537, son of Henry VIII and Jane Seymour
Died aged 15, *reigned* 6 years

1553 *(6/10–19 Jul) JANE
Born 1537, daughter of Frances (daughter of Mary Tudor, the younger daughter of Henry VII) and Henry Grey, Duke of Suffolk
Married Lord Guildford Dudley, son of the Duke of Northumberland
Deposed Jul 1553, *executed* Feb 1554 aged 16, *reigned* 13/9 days

1553–1558 MARY I
Born 1516, daughter of Henry VIII and Catherine of Aragon
Married Philip II of Spain
Died aged 42, *reigned* 5 years

1558–1603 ELIZABETH I
Born 1533, daughter of Henry VIII and Anne Boleyn
Died aged 69, *reigned* 44 years

* Depending on whether the date of her predecessor's death (6 July) or that of her official proclamation as Queen (10 July) is taken as the beginning of her reign.

BRITISH KINGS AND QUEENS SINCE 1603

THE HOUSE OF STUART

Reign

1603–1625 JAMES I (VI OF SCOTLAND)
Born 1566, son of Mary, Queen of Scots (granddaughter of Margaret Tudor, elder daughter of Henry VII), and Henry Stewart, Lord Darnley
Married Anne, daughter of Frederick II of Denmark
Died aged 58, *reigned* 22 years

1625–1649 CHARLES I
Born 1600, second son of James I
Married Henrietta Maria, daughter of Henry IV of France
Executed 1649 aged 48, *reigned* 23 years

INTERREGNUM 1649–1660

1649–1653 Government by a council of state
1653–1658 Oliver Cromwell, Lord Protector
1658–1659 Richard Cromwell, Lord Protector

Reign

1660–1685 CHARLES II
Born 1630, eldest son of Charles I
Married Catherine, daughter of John IV of Portugal
Died aged 54, *reigned* 24 years

1685–1688 JAMES II (VII OF SCOTLAND)
Born 1633, second son of Charles I
Married (1) Lady Anne Hyde, daughter of Edward, Earl of Clarendon (2) Mary, daughter of Alphonso, Duke of Modena
Reign ended with flight from kingdom Dec 1688
Died 1701 aged 67, *reigned* 3 years

INTERREGNUM

11 Dec 1688 to 12 Feb 1689

Reign

1689–1702 WILLIAM III
Born 1650, son of William II, Prince of Orange, and Mary Stuart, daughter of Charles I
Married Mary, elder daughter of James II
Died aged 51, *reigned* 13 years

and

1689–1694 MARY II
Born 1662, elder daughter of James II and Anne
Died aged 32, *reigned* 5 years

1702–1714 ANNE
Born 1665, younger daughter of James II and Anne
Married Prince George of Denmark, son of Frederick III of Denmark
Died aged 49, *reigned* 12 years

THE HOUSE OF HANOVER

1714–1727 GEORGE I (Elector of Hanover)
Born 1660, son of Sophia (daughter of Frederick, Elector Palatine, and Elizabeth Stuart, daughter of James I) and Ernest Augustus, Elector of Hanover
Married Sophia Dorothea, daughter of George William, Duke of Lüneburg-Celle
Died aged 67, *reigned* 12 years

1727–1760 GEORGE II
Born 1683, son of George I
Married Caroline, daughter of John Frederick, Margrave of Brandenburg-Anspach
Died aged 76, *reigned* 33 years

1760–1820 GEORGE III
Born 1738, son of Frederick, eldest son of George II
Married Charlotte, daughter of Charles Louis, Duke of Mecklenburg-Strelitz
Died aged 81, *reigned* 59 years

REGENCY 1811–1820

Prince of Wales regent owing to the insanity of George III

Reign

1820–1830 GEORGE IV
Born 1762, eldest son of George III
Married Caroline, daughter of Charles, Duke of Brunswick-Wolfenbüttel
Died aged 67, *reigned* 10 years

1830–1837 WILLIAM IV
Born 1765, third son of George III
Married Adelaide, daughter of George, Duke of Saxe-Meiningen
Died aged 71, *reigned* 7 years

1837–1901 VICTORIA
Born 1819, daughter of Edward, fourth son of George III
Married Prince Albert of Saxe-Coburg and Gotha
Died aged 81, *reigned* 63 years

THE HOUSE OF SAXE-COBURG AND GOTHA

1901–1910 EDWARD VII
Born 1841, eldest son of Victoria and Albert
Married Alexandra, daughter of Christian IX of Denmark
Died aged 68, *reigned* 9 years

THE HOUSE OF WINDSOR

1910–1936 GEORGE V
Born 1865, second son of Edward VII
Married Victoria Mary, daughter of Francis, Duke of Teck
Died aged 70, *reigned* 25 years

1936 (20 Jan–11 Dec) EDWARD VIII
Born 1894, eldest son of George V
Married (1937) Mrs Wallis Simpson
Abdicated 1936, *died* 1972 aged 77, *reigned* 10 months

1936–1952 GEORGE VI
Born 1895, second son of George V
Married Lady Elizabeth Bowes-Lyon, daughter of 14th Earl of Strathmore and Kinghorne
Died aged 56, *reigned* 15 years

1952– ELIZABETH II
Born 1926, elder daughter of George VI
Married Philip, son of Prince Andrew of Greece

KINGS AND QUEENS OF SCOTS 1016 TO 1603

Reign

1016–1034 MALCOLM II
*Born c.*954, son of Kenneth II
Acceded to Alba 1005, secured Lothian *c.*1016, obtained Strathclyde for his grandson Duncan *c.*1016, thus reigning over an area approximately the same as that governed by later rulers of Scotland
Died aged *c.*80, *reigned* 18 years

THE HOUSE OF ATHOLL

1034–1040 DUNCAN I
Son of Bethoc, daughter of Malcolm II, and Crinan, Mormaer of Atholl
Married a cousin of Siward, Earl of Northumbria
Reigned 5 years

1040–1057 MACBETH
*Born c.*1005, son of a daughter of Malcolm II and Finlaec, Mormaer of Moray
Married Gruoch, granddaughter of Kenneth III
Killed aged *c.*52, *reigned* 17 years

1057–1058 (Aug–Mar) LULACH
*Born c.*1032, son of Gillacomgan, Mormaer of Moray, and Gruoch (and stepson of Macbeth)
Died aged *c.*26, *reigned* 7 months

1058–1093 MALCOLM III (Canmore)
*Born c.*1031, elder son of Duncan I
Married (1) Ingibiorg (2) Margaret (St Margaret), granddaughter of Edmund II of England
Killed in battle aged *c.*62, *reigned* 35 years

1093–1097 DONALD III BÁN
*Born c.*1033, second son of Duncan I
Deposed May 1094, *restored* Nov 1094, *deposed* Oct 1097, *reigned* 3 years

1094 (May–Nov) DUNCAN II
*Born c.*1060, elder son of Malcolm III and Ingibiorg
Married Octreda of Dunbar
Killed aged *c.*34, *reigned* 6 months

1097–1107 EDGAR
*Born c.*1074, second son of Malcolm III and Margaret
Died aged *c.*32, *reigned* 9 years

1107–1124 ALEXANDER I (the Fierce)
*Born c.*1077, fifth son of Malcolm III and Margaret
Married Sybilla, illegitimate daughter of Henry I of England
Died aged *c.*47, *reigned* 17 years

1124–1153 DAVID I (the Saint)
*Born c.*1085, sixth son of Malcolm III and Margaret
Married Matilda, daughter of Waltheof, Earl of Huntingdon
Died aged *c.*68, *reigned* 29 years

1153–1165 MALCOLM IV (the Maiden)
*Born c.*1141, son of Henry, Earl of Huntingdon, second son of David I
Died aged *c.*24, *reigned* 12 years

1165–1214 WILLIAM I (the Lion)
*Born c.*1142, brother of Malcolm IV
Married Ermengarde, daughter of Richard, Viscount of Beaumont
Died aged *c.*72, *reigned* 49 years

1214–1249 ALEXANDER II
Born 1198, son of William I
Married (1) Joan, daughter of John, King of England (2) Marie, daughter of Ingelram de Coucy
Died aged 50, *reigned* 34 years

1249–1286 ALEXANDER III
Born 1241, son of Alexander II and Marie
Married (1) Margaret, daughter of Henry III of England (2) Yolande, daughter of the Count of Dreux
Killed accidentally aged 44, *reigned* 36 years

1286–1290 MARGARET (the Maid of Norway)
Born 1283, daughter of Margaret (daughter of Alexander III) and Eric II of Norway
Died aged 7, *reigned* 4 years

FIRST INTERREGNUM 1290–1292

Throne disputed by 13 competitors. Crown awarded to John Balliol by adjudication of Edward I of England

THE HOUSE OF BALLIOL

Reign

1292–1296 JOHN (Balliol)
*Born c.*1250, son of Dervorguilla, great-great-granddaughter of David I, and John de Balliol
Married Isabella, daughter of John, Earl of Surrey
Abdicated 1296, *died* 1313 aged *c.*63, *reigned* 3 years

SECOND INTERREGNUM 1296–1306

Edward I of England declared John Balliol to have forfeited the throne for contumacy in 1296 and took the government of Scotland into his own hands

THE HOUSE OF BRUCE

Reign

1306–1329 ROBERT I (Bruce)
Born 1274, son of Robert Bruce and Marjorie, countess of Carrick, and great-grandson of the second daughter of David, Earl of Huntingdon, brother of William I
Married (1) Isabella, daughter of Donald, Earl of Mar (2) Elizabeth, daughter of Richard, Earl of Ulster
Died aged 54, *reigned* 23 years

1329–1371 DAVID II
Born 1324, son of Robert I and Elizabeth
Married (1) Joanna, daughter of Edward II of England (2) Margaret Drummond, widow of Sir John Logie (divorced)
Died aged 46, *reigned* 41 years

1332 (Sep–Dec) Edward Balliol, son of John Balliol

1333–1336 Edward Balliol

THE HOUSE OF STEWART

1371–1390 ROBERT II (Stewart)
Born 1316, son of Marjorie (daughter of Robert I) and Walter, High Steward of Scotland
Married (1) Elizabeth, daughter of Sir Robert Mure of Rowallan (2) Euphemia, daughter of Hugh, Earl of Ross
Died aged 74, *reigned* 19 years

1390–1406 ROBERT III
*Born c.*1337, son of Robert II and Elizabeth

	Married Annabella, daughter of Sir John Drummond of Stobhall *Died* aged *c.*69, *reigned* 16 years
1406–1437	JAMES I *Born* 1394, son of Robert III *Married* Joan Beaufort, daughter of John, Earl of Somerset *Assassinated* aged 42, *reigned* 30 years
1437–1460	JAMES II *Born* 1430, son of James I *Married* Mary, daughter of Arnold, Duke of Gueldres *Killed* accidentally aged 29, *reigned* 23 years
1460–1488	JAMES III *Born* 1452, son of James II *Married* Margaret, daughter of Christian I of Denmark *Assassinated* aged 36, *reigned* 27 years
1488–1513	JAMES IV *Born* 1473, son of James III *Married* Margaret Tudor, daughter of Henry VII of England *Killed* in battle aged 40, *reigned* 25 years
1513–1542	JAMES V *Born* 1512, son of James IV *Married* (1) Madeleine, daughter of Francis I of France (2) Mary of Lorraine, daughter of the Duc de Guise *Died* aged 30, *reigned* 29 years
1542–1567	MARY *Born* 1542, daughter of James V and Mary *Married* (1) the Dauphin, afterwards Francis II of France (2) Henry Stewart, Lord Darnley (3) James Hepburn, Earl of Bothwell *Abdicated* 1567, prisoner in England from 1568, *executed* 1587, *reigned* 24 years
1567–1625	JAMES VI (and I of England) *Born* 1566, son of Mary, Queen of Scots, and Henry, Lord Darnley Acceded 1567 to the Scottish throne, *reigned* 58 years Succeeded 1603 to the English throne, so joining the English and Scottish crowns in one person. The two kingdoms remained distinct until 1707 when the parliaments of the kingdoms became conjoined

WELSH SOVEREIGNS AND PRINCES

Wales was ruled by sovereign princes from the earliest times until the death of Llywelyn in 1282. The first English Prince of Wales was the son of Edward I, who was born in Caernarvon town on 25 April 1284. According to a discredited legend, he was presented to the Welsh chieftains as their prince, in fulfilment of a promise that they should have a prince who 'could not speak a word of English' and should be native born. This son, who afterwards became Edward II, was created 'Prince of Wales and Earl of Chester' at the Lincoln Parliament on 7 February 1301.

The title Prince of Wales is borne after individual conferment and is not inherited at birth, though some Princes have been declared and styled Prince of Wales but never formally so created (*s.*). The title was conferred on Prince Charles by the Queen on 26 July 1958. He was invested at Caernarvon on 1 July 1969.

INDEPENDENT PRINCES AD 844 TO 1282

844–878	Rhodri the Great
878–916	Anarawd, son of Rhodri
916–950	Hywel Dda, the Good
950–979	Iago ab Idwal (or Ieuaf)
979–985	Hywel ab Ieuaf, the Bad
985–986	Cadwallon, his brother
986–999	Maredudd ab Owain ap Hywel Dda
999–1008	Cynan ap Hywel ab Ieuaf
1018–1023	Llywelyn ap Seisyll
1023–1039	Iago ab Idwal ap Meurig
1039–1063	Gruffydd ap Llywelyn ap Seisyll
1063–1075	Bleddyn ap Cynfyn
1075–1081	Trahaern ap Caradog
1081–1137	Gruffydd ap Cynan ab Iago
1137–1170	Owain Gwynedd
1170–1194	Dafydd ab Owain Gwynedd
1194–1240	Llywelyn Fawr, the Great
1240–1246	Dafydd ap Llywelyn
1246–1282	Llywelyn ap Gruffydd ap Llywelyn

ENGLISH PRINCES SINCE 1301

1301	Edward (Edward II)
1343	Edward the Black Prince, son of Edward III
1376	Richard (Richard II), son of the Black Prince
1399	Henry of Monmouth (Henry V)
1454	Edward of Westminster, son of Henry VI
1471	Edward of Westminster (Edward V)
1483	Edward, son of Richard III (*d.* 1484)
1489	Arthur Tudor, son of Henry VII
1504	Henry Tudor (Henry VIII)
1610	Henry Stuart, son of James I (*d.* 1612)
1616	Charles Stuart (Charles I)
*c.*1638 (*s.*)	Charles Stuart (Charles II)
1688 (*s.*)	James Francis Edward Stuart (The Old Pretender), son of James II (*d.* 1766)
1714	George Augustus (George II)
1729	Frederick Lewis, son of George II (*d.* 1751)
1751	George William Frederick (George III)
1762	George Augustus Frederick (George IV)
1841	Albert Edward (Edward VII)
1901	George (George V)
1910	Edward (Edward VIII)
1958	Charles, son of Elizabeth II

PRINCESSES ROYAL

The style Princess Royal is conferred at the sovereign's discretion on his or her eldest daughter. It is an honorary title, held for life, and cannot be inherited or passed on. It was first conferred on Princess Mary, daughter of Charles I, in approximately 1642.

*c.*1642	Princess Mary (1631–60), daughter of Charles I
1727	Princess Anne (1709–59), daughter of George II
1766	Princess Charlotte (1766–1828), daughter of George III
1840	Princess Victoria (1840–1901), daughter of Victoria
1905	Princess Louise (1867–1931), daughter of Edward VII
1932	Princess Mary (1897–1965), daughter of George V
1987	Princess Anne (*b.* 1950), daughter of Elizabeth II

THE HOUSE OF WINDSOR

King George V assumed by royal proclamation (17 July 1917) for his House and family, as well as for all descendants in the male line of Queen Victoria who are subjects of these realms, the name of Windsor.

KING GEORGE V
(George Frederick Ernest Albert), second son of King Edward VII *born* 3 June 1865 *married* 6 July 1893 HSH Princess Victoria Mary Augusta Louise Olga Pauline Claudine Agnes of Teck (Queen Mary *born* 26 May 1867 *died* 24 March 1953) *succeeded* to the throne 6 May 1910 *died* 20 January 1936. *Issue*

1. HRH PRINCE EDWARD Albert Christian George Andrew Patrick David *born* 23 June 1894 *succeeded* to the throne as King Edward VIII, 20 January 1936 *abdicated* 11 December 1936 *created* Duke of Windsor 1937 *married* 3 June 1937 Mrs Wallis Simpson (Her Grace The Duchess of Windsor *born* 19 June 1896 *died* 24 April 1986) *died* 28 May 1972

2. HRH PRINCE ALBERT Frederick Arthur George *born* 14 December 1895 *created* Duke of York 1920 *married* 26 April 1923 Lady Elizabeth Bowes-Lyon, youngest daughter of the 14th Earl of Strathmore and Kinghorne (HM Queen Elizabeth the Queen Mother *born* 4 August 1900 *died* 30 March 2002) *succeeded* to the throne as King George VI, 11 December 1936 *died* 6 February 1952. *Issue*
   (1) HRH Princess Elizabeth Alexandra Mary *succeeded* to the throne as Queen Elizabeth II, 6 February 1952 (*see* Royal Family)
   (2) HRH Princess Margaret Rose (later HRH The Princess Margaret, Countess of Snowdon) *born* 21 August 1930 *married* 6 May 1960 Anthony Charles Robert Armstrong-Jones, GCVO *created* Earl of Snowdon 1961 (marriage dissolved 1978) *died* 9 February 2002, having had issue (*see* Royal Family)

3. HRH PRINCESS (Victoria Alexandra Alice) MARY *born* 25 April 1897 *created* Princess Royal 1932 *married* 28 February 1922 Viscount Lascelles, later the 6th Earl of Harewood (1882–1947) *died* 28 March 1965. *Issue*
   (1) George Henry Hubert Lascelles, 7th Earl of Harewood, KBE *born* 7 February 1923 *married* (1) 1949 Maria (Marion) Stein (marriage dissolved 1967) *issue (a)* David Henry George, Viscount Lascelles *born* 1950 *(b)* James Edward *born* 1953 *(c)* (Robert) Jeremy Hugh *born* 1955 (2) 1967 Patricia Tuckwell *issue (d)* Mark Hubert *born* 1964
   (2) Gerald David Lascelles (1924–98) *married* (1) 1952 Angela Dowding (marriage dissolved 1978) *issue (a)* Henry Ulick *born* 1953 (2) 1978 Elizabeth Collingwood (Elizabeth Colvin) *issue (b)* Martin David *born* 1962

4. HRH PRINCE HENRY William Frederick Albert *born* 31 March 1900 *created* Duke of Gloucester, Earl of Ulster and Baron Culloden 1928 *married* 6 November 1935 Lady Alice Christabel Montagu-Douglas-Scott, daughter of the 7th Duke of Buccleuch and Queensberry (HRH Princess Alice, Duchess of Gloucester *born* 25 December 1901 *died* 29 October 2004) *died* 10 June 1974. *Issue*
   (1) HRH Prince William Henry Andrew Frederick *born* 18 December 1941 accidentally *killed* 28 August 1972
   (2) HRH Prince Richard Alexander Walter George (HRH The Duke of Gloucester, *see* Royal Family)

5. HRH PRINCE GEORGE Edward Alexander Edmund *born* 20 December 1902 *created* Duke of Kent, Earl of St Andrews and Baron Downpatrick 1934 *married* 29 November 1934 HRH Princess Marina of Greece and Denmark (*born* 30 November 1906 *died* 27 August 1968) *killed* on active service 25 August 1942. *Issue*
   (1) HRH Prince Edward George Nicholas Paul Patrick (HRH The Duke of Kent, *see* Royal Family)
   (2) HRH Princess Alexandra Helen Elizabeth Olga Christabel (HRH Princess Alexandra, the Hon. Lady Ogilvy, *see* Royal Family)
   (3) HRH Prince Michael George Charles Franklin (HRH Prince Michael of Kent, *see* Royal Family)

6. HRH PRINCE JOHN Charles Francis *born* 12 July 1905 *died* 18 January 1919

DESCENDANTS OF QUEEN VICTORIA

I. HRH Princess Victoria Adelaide Mary Louisa, Princess Royal (1840–1901) *m* Friedrich III (1831–88), later German Emperor

1. HIM Wilhelm II (1859–1941), later German Emperor *m* (1) Princess Augusta Victoria of Schleswig-Holstein-Sonderburg-Augustenburg (1858–1921) (2) Princess Hermine of Reuss (1887–1947). *Issue* Wilhelm (1882–1951); Eitel-Friedrich (1883–1942); Adalbert (1884–1948); August Wilhelm (1887–1949); Oskar (1888–1958); Joachim (1890–1920); Viktoria Luise (1892–1980)

2. Charlotte (1860–1919) *m* Bernhard, Duke of Saxe-Meiningen (1851–1928). *Issue* Feodora (1879–1945)

3. Heinrich (1862–1929) *m* Princess Irene of Hesse (*see* III.3). *Issue* Waldemar (1889–1945); Sigismund (1896–1978); Heinrich (1900–4)

4. Sigismund (1864–6)

5. Victoria (1866–1929) *m* (1) Prince Adolf of Schaumburg-Lippe (1859–1916) (2) Alexander Zubkov (1900–36)

6. Waldemar (1868–79)

7. Sophie (1870–1932) *m* Constantine I (1868–1923), later King of the Hellenes. *Issue* George II (1890–1947); Alexander I (1893–1920); Helena (1896–1982); Paul I (1901–64); Irene (1904–74); Katherine (1913–2007)

8. Margarethe (1872–1954) *m* Prince Friedrich Karl of Hesse (1868–1940). *Issue* Friedrich Wilhelm (1893–1916); Maximilian (1894–1914); Philipp (1896–1980); Wolfgang (1896–1989); Richard (1901–69); Christoph (1901–43)

II. HRH Prince Albert Edward (HM KING EDWARD VII) (1841–1910) *succeeded* 22 Jan 1901 *m* HRH Princess Alexandra of Denmark (1844–1925)

1. Albert Victor, Duke of Clarence and Avondale (1864–92)

2. George (HM KING GEORGE V) (1865–1936) (*see* House of Windsor)

3. Louise (1867–1931), later Princess Royal *m* 1st Duke of Fife (1849–1912). *Issue* Alexandra (1891–1959); Maud (1893–1945)

4. Victoria (1868–1935)

5. Maud (1869–1938) *m* Prince Carl of Denmark (1872–1957), later King Haakon VII of Norway. *Issue* Olav V (1903–91)

6. Alexander (6–7 Apr 1871)

III. HRH Princess Alice Maud Mary (1843–78) *m* Prince Ludwig (1837–92), later Grand Duke of Hesse

1. Victoria (1863–1950) *m* Prince Louis of Battenberg (1854–1921), later 1st Marquess of Milford Haven. *Issue* Alice (1885–1969); Louise (1889–1965); George (1892–1938); Louis (1900–79)

2. Elizabeth (1864–1918) *m* Grand Duke Sergius of Russia (1857–1905)

3. Irene (1866–1953) *m* Prince Heinrich of Prussia (*see* I.3)

4. Ernst Ludwig (1868–1937), Grand Duke of Hesse, *m* (1) Princess Victoria Melita of Saxe-Coburg (see IV.3) (2) Princess Eleonore of Solms-Hohensolms-Lich (1871–1937). *Issue* Elizabeth (1895–1903); George (1906–37); Ludwig (1908–68)

5. Frederick William (1870–3)

6. Alix (Tsaritsa of Russia) (1872–1918) *m* Nicholas II, Tsar of All the Russias (1868–1918). *Issue* Olga (1895–1918); Tatiana (1897–1918); Marie (1899–1918); Anastasia (1901–18); Alexis (1904–18)

7. Marie (1874–8)

IV. HRH Prince Alfred Ernest Albert, Duke of Edinburgh (1844–1900) *succeeded* as Duke of Saxe-Coburg and Gotha 1893 *m* Grand Duchess Marie Alexandrovna of Russia (1853–1920)

QUEEN VICTORIA (Alexandrina Victoria) (1819–1901) *succeeded* 20 Jun 1837 *m* (Francis) Albert Augustus Charles Emmanuel, Duke of Saxony, Prince of Saxe-Coburg and Gotha (HRH Albert, Prince Consort) (1819–61)

1. Alfred, Prince of Saxe-Coburg (1874–99)

2. Marie (1875–1938) *m* Ferdinand (1865–1927), later King of Roumania. *Issue* Carol II (1893–1953); Elisabeth (1894–1956); Marie (1900–61); Nicolas (1903–78); Ileana (1909–91); Mircea (1913–16)

3. Victoria Melita (1876–1936) *m* (1) Grand Duke Ernst Ludwig of Hesse (*see* III.4) (2) Grand Duke Kirill of Russia (1876–1938). *Issue* Marie (1907–51); Kira (1909–67); Vladimir (1917–92)

4. Alexandra (1878–1942) *m* Ernst, Prince of Hohenlohe Langenburg (1863–1950). *Issue* Gottfried (1897–1960); Maria (1899–1967); Alexandra (1901–63); Irma (1902–86)

5. Beatrice (1884–1966) *m* Alfonso of Orleans, Infante of Spain (1886–1975). *Issue* Alvaro (1910–97); Alonso (1912–36); Ataulfo (1913–74)

V. HRH Princess Helena Augusta Victoria (1846–1923) *m* Prince Christian of Schleswig-Holstein-Sonderburg-Augustenburg (1831–1917)

1. Christian Victor (1867–1900)

2. Albert (1869–1931), later Duke of Schleswig-Holstein

3. Helena (1870–1948)

4. Marie Louise (1872–1956), *m* Prince Aribert of Anhalt (1864–1933)

5. Harold (12–20 May 1876)

VI. HRH Princess Louise Caroline Alberta (1848–1939) *m* Marquess of Lorne (1845–1914), later 9th Duke of Argyll

VII. HRH Prince Arthur William Patrick Albert, Duke of Connaught (1850–1942) *m* Princess Louisa of Prussia (1860–1917)

1. Margaret (1882–1920) *m* Crown Prince Gustaf Adolf (1882–1973), later King of Sweden. *Issue* Gustaf Adolf (1906–47); Sigvard (1907–2002); Ingrid (1910–2000); Bertil (1912–97); Count Carl Bernadotte (*b* 1916)

2. Arthur (1883–1938) *m* HH Duchess of Fife (1891–1959). *Issue* Alastair Arthur (1914–43)

3. (Victoria) Patricia (1886–1974) *m* Adm. Hon. Sir Alexander Ramsay (1881–1972). *Issue* Alexander (1919–2000)

VIII. HRH Prince Leopold George Duncan Albert, Duke of Albany (1853–84) *m* Princess Helena of Waldeck (1861–1922)

1. Alice (1883–1981) *m* Prince Alexander of Teck (1874–1957), later 1st Earl of Athlone. *Issue* May (1906–94); Rupert (1907–28); Maurice (Mar–Sep 1910)

2. Charles Edward (1884–1954), Duke of Albany until title suspended 1917, Duke of Saxe-Coburg-Gotha, *m* Princess Victoria Adelheid of Schleswig-Holstein-Sonderburg-Glücksburg (1885–1970). *Issue* Johann Leopold (1906–72); Sibylla (1908–72); Dietmar Hubertus (1909–43); Caroline (1912–83); Friedrich Josias (1918–98)

IX. HRH Princess Beatrice Mary Victoria Feodore (1857–1944) *m* Prince Henry of Battenberg (1858–96)

1. Alexander, 1st Marquess of Carisbrooke (1886–1960) *m* Lady Irene Denison (1890–1956). *Issue* Iris (1920–82)

2. Victoria Eugénie (1887–1969) *m* Alfonso XIII, King of Spain (1886–1941). *Issue* Alfonso (1907–38); Jaime (1908–75); Beatriz (1909–2002); Maria (1911–96); Juan (1913–93); Gonzalo (1914–34)

3. Maj. Lord Leopold Mountbatten (1889–1922)

4. Maurice (1891–1914)

PRECEDENCE

ENGLAND AND WALES

The Sovereign
The Prince Philip, Duke of Edinburgh
The Prince of Wales
The Sovereign's younger sons
The Sovereign's grandsons
The Sovereign's cousins
Archbishop of Canterbury
Lord High Chancellor
Archbishop of York
The Prime Minister
Lord President of the Council
Speaker of the House of Commons
Speaker of the House of Lords
President of the Supreme Court
Lord Chief Justice of England and Wales
Lord Privy Seal
Ambassadors and High Commissioners
Lord Great Chamberlain
Earl Marshal
Lord Steward of the Household
Lord Chamberlain of the Household
Master of the Horse
Dukes, according to their patent of creation:
1. of England
2. of Scotland
3. of Great Britain
4. of Ireland
5. those created since the Union
Eldest sons of Dukes of the Blood Royal
Ministers, Envoys, and other important overseas visitors
Marquesses, according to their patent of creation:
1. of England
2. of Scotland
3. of Great Britain
4. of Ireland
5. those created since the Union
Dukes' eldest sons
Earls, according to their patent of creation:
1. of England
2. of Scotland
3. of Great Britain
4. of Ireland
5. those created since the Union
Younger sons of Dukes of Blood Royal
Marquesses' eldest sons
Dukes' younger sons
Viscounts, according to their patent of creation:
1. of England
2. of Scotland
3. of Great Britain
4. of Ireland
5. those created since the Union
Earls' eldest sons
Marquesses' younger sons
Bishop of London
Bishop of Durham
Bishop of Winchester
Other English Diocesan Bishops according to seniority of consecration
Retired Church of England Diocesan Bishops, according to seniority of consecration
Suffragan Bishops, according to seniority of consecration
Secretaries of State, if of the degree of a Baron
Barons, according to their patent of creation:
1. of England
2. of Scotland (Lords of Parliament)
3. of Great Britain
4. of Ireland
5. those created since the Union, including Life Barons
Master of the Rolls
Deputy President of the Supreme Court
Justices of the Supreme Court, according to seniority of appointment
Treasurer of the Household
Comptroller of the Household
Vice-Chamberlain of the Household
Secretaries of State under the degree of Baron
Viscounts' eldest sons
Earls' younger sons
Barons' eldest sons
Knights of the Garter
Privy Counsellors
Chancellor of the Order of the Garter
Chancellor of the Exchequer
Chancellor of the Duchy of Lancaster
President of the Queen's Bench Division
President of the Family Division
Chancellor of the High Court
Lord Justices of Appeal, according to seniority of appointment
Judges of the High Court, according to seniority of appointment
Viscounts' younger sons
Barons' younger sons
Sons of Life Peers
Baronets, according to date of patent
Knights of the Thistle
Knights Grand Cross of the Bath
Knights Grand Commanders of the Star of India
Knights Grand Cross of St Michael and St George
Knights Grand Commanders of the Indian Empire
Knights Grand Cross of the Royal Victorian Order
Knights Grand Cross of the British Empire
Knights Commanders of the Bath
Knights Commanders of the Star of India
Knights Commanders of St Michael and St George
Knights Commanders of the Indian Empire
Knights Commanders of the Royal Victorian Order
Knights Commanders of the British Empire
Knights Bachelor
Circuit Judges, according to priority and order of their respective appointments
Master of the Court of Protection
Companions of the Bath
Companions of the Star of India
Companions of St Michael and St George
Companions of the Indian Empire
Commanders of the Royal Victorian Order
Commanders of the British Empire
Companions of the Distinguished Service Order
Lieutenants of the Royal Victorian Order
Officers of the British Empire
Companions of the Imperial Service Order
Eldest sons of younger sons of peers
Baronets' eldest sons
Eldest sons of knights, in the same order as their fathers
Members of the Royal Victorian Order
Members of the British Empire
Younger sons of baronets
Younger sons of knights, in the same order as their fathers
Esquires
Gentlemen

WOMEN

Women take the same rank as their husbands or as their brothers; but the daughter of a peer marrying a commoner retains her title as Lady or Honourable. Daughters of peers rank next immediately after the wives of their elder brothers, and before their younger brothers' wives. Daughters of peers marrying peers of a lower degree take the same order of precedence as that of their husbands; thus the daughter of a Duke marrying a Baron becomes of the rank of Baroness only, while her sisters married to commoners retain their rank and take precedence over the Baroness. Merely official rank on the husband's part does not give any similar precedence to the wife.

Peeresses in their own right take the same precedence as peers of the same rank, ie from their date of creation.

SCOTLAND

The Sovereign
The Prince Philip, Duke of Edinburgh
The Lord High Commissioner to the General Assembly of the Church of Scotland (while that assembly is sitting)
The Duke of Rothesay (eldest son of the Sovereign)
The Sovereign's younger sons
Grandsons of the Sovereign
The Sovereign's cousins
Lord-Lieutenants
Lord Provosts of cities being *ex-officio* Lord-Lieutenants of those cities during their term of office*
Sheriffs Principal, successively, within their own localities and during holding of office
Lord Chancellor of Great Britain
Moderator of the General Assembly of the Church of Scotland
Keeper of the Great Seal of Scotland (the First Minister)
The Presiding Officer
The Secretary of State for Scotland
Hereditary High Constable of Scotland
Hereditary Master of the Household in Scotland
Dukes, in the same order as in England
Eldest sons of Dukes of the Blood Royal
Marquesses, as in England
Eldest sons of Dukes
Earls, as in England
Younger sons of Dukes of Blood Royal
Eldest sons of Marquesses
Dukes' younger sons
Lord Justice General
Lord Clerk Register
Lord Advocate
The Advocate-General
Lord Justice Clerk
Viscounts, as in England
Eldest sons of Earls
Marquesses' younger sons
Lords of Parliament or Barons, as in England
Eldest sons of Viscounts
Earls' younger sons
Eldest sons of Lords of Parliament or Barons
Knights of the Garter
Knights of the Thistle
Privy Counsellors
Senators of the College of Justice (Lords of Session)
Viscounts' younger sons
Younger sons of Lords of Parliament or Barons
Baronets
Knights Grand Cross and Knights Grand Commanders of orders, as in England
Knights Commanders of orders, as in England
Solicitor-General for Scotland
Lord Lyon King of Arms
Sheriffs Principal, when not within own county
Knights Bachelor
Sheriffs
Companions of Orders, as in England
Commanders of the Royal Victorian Order
Commanders of the British Empire
Companions of the Distinguished Service Order
Lieutenants of the Royal Victorian Order
Officers of the British Empire
Companions of the Imperial Service Order
Eldest sons of younger sons of peers
Eldest sons of baronets
Eldest sons of knights, as in England
Members of the Royal Victorian Order
Members of the British Empire
Baronets' younger sons
Knights' younger sons
Esquires
Gentlemen

* The Lord Provosts of the city districts of Aberdeen, Dundee, Edinburgh and Glasgow are Lord-Lieutenants for those districts *ex officio* and take precedence as such

THE PEERAGE

ABBREVIATIONS AND SYMBOLS

S.	Scottish title	*c.p.*	civil partnership
I.	Irish title	*w.*	widower or widow
**	hereditary peer remaining in the House of Lords	M.	minor
°	there is no 'of' in the title	†	heir not ascertained at time of going to press
b.	born	F_	represents forename
s.	succeeded	S_	represents surname
m.	married	cr.	created

The rules which govern the creation and succession of peerages are extremely complicated. There are, technically, five separate peerages, the Peerage of England, of Scotland, of Ireland, of Great Britain, and of the United Kingdom. The Peerage of Great Britain dates from 1707 when an Act of Union combined the two kingdoms of England and Scotland and separate peerages were discontinued. The Peerage of the United Kingdom dates from 1801 when Great Britain and Ireland were combined under an Act of Union. Some Scottish peers have received additional peerages of Great Britain or of the United Kingdom since 1707, and some Irish peers additional peerages of the United Kingdom since 1801.

The Peerage of Ireland was not entirely discontinued from 1801 but holders of Irish peerages, whether predating or created subsequent to the Union of 1801, were not entitled to sit in the House of Lords if they had no additional English, Scottish, Great Britain or United Kingdom peerage. However, they are eligible for election to the House of Commons and to vote in parliamentary elections. An Irish peer holding a peerage of a lower grade which enabled him to sit in the House of Lords was introduced there by the title which enabled him to sit, though for all other purposes he was known by his higher title.

In the Peerage of Scotland there is no rank of Baron; the equivalent rank is Lord of Parliament, abbreviated to 'Lord' (the female equivalent is 'Lady').

All peers of England, Scotland, Great Britain or the United Kingdom who are 21 years or over, and of British, Irish or Commonwealth nationality were entitled to sit in the House of Lords until the House of Lords Act 1999, when hereditary peers lost the right to sit. However, section two of the act provided an exception for 90 hereditary peers plus the holders of the office of Earl Marshal and Lord Great Chamberlain to remain as members of the House of Lords for their lifetime or pending further reform. Of the 90 hereditary peers, 75 were elected by the hereditary peers in their political party, or Crossbench grouping, and the remaining 15 by the whole house. Until 7 November 2002 any vacancy arising due to the death of one of the 90 excepted hereditary peers was filled by the runner-up to the original election. From 7 November 2002 any vacancy due to a death has been filled by holding a by-election. By-elections are conducted in accordance with arrangements made by the Clerk of the Parliaments and have to take place within three months of a vacancy occurring. If the vacancy is among the 75, only the excepted hereditary peers in the relevant party or Crossbench grouping are entitled to vote. If the vacancy is among the other 15, the whole house is entitled to vote.

In the list below, peers currently holding one of the 92 hereditary places in the House of Lords are indicated by ** .

In July 2008 proposed further reforms to the House of Lords were presented to parliament in a white paper *An Elected Second Chamber: Further Reform of the House of Lords.*

HEREDITARY WOMEN PEERS

Most hereditary peerages pass on death to the nearest male heir, but there are exceptions, and several are held by women.

A woman peer in her own right retains her title after marriage, and if her husband's rank is the superior she is designated by the two titles jointly, the inferior one second. Her hereditary claim still holds good in spite of any marriage whether higher or lower. No rank held by a woman can confer any title or even precedence upon her husband but the rank of a hereditary woman peer in her own right is inherited by her eldest son (or in some cases daughter).

After the Peerage Act 1963, hereditary women peers in their own right were entitled to sit in the House of Lords, subject to the same qualifications as men, until the House of Lords Act 1999.

LIFE PEERS

Since 1876 non-hereditary or life peerages have been conferred on certain eminent judges to enable the judicial functions of the House of Lords to be carried out. These lords were known as Lords of Appeal in Ordinary or law lords. The judicial role of the House of Lords as the highest appeal court in the UK ended on 30 July 2009 and since 1 October 2009 the UK Supreme Court has assumed jurisdiction on points of law for all civil cases in the UK and all criminal cases in England, Wales and Northern Ireland. Life peers who transferred to the supreme court as Justices of the Supreme Court are disqualified from sitting or voting in the House of Lords until retirement from the supreme court. On retirement they are able to return to the House of Lords as full members. Newly-appointed Justices of the Supreme Court will no longer automatically be given seats in the House of Lords. (*See also* Law Courts and Offices.)

Justices of the Supreme Court currently disqualified from sitting or voting in the House of Lords until retirement are marked with a '§' in the list of life peerages which follows.

Since 1958 life peerages have been conferred upon distinguished men and women from all walks of life, giving them seats in the House of Lords in the degree of Baron or Baroness. They are addressed in the same way as hereditary lords and barons, and their children have similar courtesy titles.

PEERAGES EXTINCT SINCE THE LAST EDITION

BARONY: Sysonby (cr. 1935)
LIFE PEERAGES: Bernstein of Craigweil (cr. 2000); Chapman (cr. 2004); David (cr. 1978); Delacourt-Smith of Alteryn (cr. 1974); Elles (cr. 1972); Flowers (cr. 1979); Laing of Dunphail (cr. 1991); Lyell of Markyate (cr. 2005); Park of Monmouth (cr. 1990); McIntosh of Haringey (cr. 1982); Plummer of St Marylebone (cr. 1981); Quinton (cr. 1982); Richardson of Duntisbourne (cr. 1983); Steinberg (cr. 2004); Walker of Worcester (cr. 1992); Wolfson (cr. 1985)

DISCLAIMER OF PEERAGES

The Peerage Act 1963 enables peers to disclaim their peerages for life. Peers alive in 1963 could disclaim within twelve months after the passing of the act (31 July 1963); a person subsequently succeeding to a peerage may disclaim within 12 months (one month if an MP) after the date of succession, or of reaching 21, if later. The disclaimer is irrevocable but does not affect the descent of the peerage after the disclaimant's death, and children of a disclaimed peer may, if they wish, retain their precedence and any courtesy titles and styles borne as children of a peer. The disclaimer permitted the disclaimant to sit in the House of Commons if elected as an MP. As the House of Lords Act 1999 removed hereditary peers from the House of Lords, they are now entitled to sit in the House of Commons without having to disclaim their titles.

The following peerages are currently disclaimed:

EARLDOM: Selkirk (1994)
VISCOUNTCY: Stansgate (1963)
BARONIES: Merthyr (1977); Reith (1972); Sanderson of Ayot (1971); Silkin (2002)
PEERS WHO ARE MINORS (ie under 21 years of age)
VISCOUNT: Selby (*b.* 1993)
BARONS: Glenconner (*b.* 1994); Hawke (*b.* 1995)

FORMS OF ADDRESS

Forms of address are given under the style for each individual rank of the peerage. Both formal and social forms of address are given where usage differs; nowadays, the social form is generally preferred to the formal, which increasingly is used only for official documents and on very formal occasions.

ROLL OF THE PEERAGE

Crown Office, House of Lords, London SW1A 0PW

The Roll of the Peerage is kept at the Crown Office and maintained by the Registrar of the Peerage in accordance with the terms of a 2004 royal warrant. The roll records the names of all living life peers and hereditary peers who have proved their succession to the satisfaction of the Lord Chancellor. The Roll of the Peerage is maintained in addition to the Clerk of the Parliaments' register of hereditary peers eligible to stand for election in House of Lords' by-elections.

A person whose name is not entered on the Roll of Peerage can not be addressed or mentioned by the title of a peer in any official document.

Registrar, Ian Denyer, MVO
Assistant Registrar, Grant Bavister

HEREDITARY PEERS

as at 31 August 2010

PEERS OF THE BLOOD ROYAL

Style, His Royal Highness the Duke of _/His Royal Highness the Earl of_
Style of address (formal) May it please your Royal Highness; *(informal)* Sir

Created	*Title, order of succession, name, etc*	*Heir*
	Dukes	
1947	*Edinburgh (1st),* HRH the Prince Philip, Duke of Edinburgh	The Prince of Wales *
1337	*Cornwall,* HRH the Prince of Wales, *s.* 1952	‡
1398 S.	*Rothesay,* HRH the Prince of Wales, *s.* 1952	‡
1986	*York (1st),* Prince Andrew, HRH the Duke of York	None
1928	*Gloucester (2nd),* Prince Richard, HRH the Duke of Gloucester, *s.* 1974	Earl of Ulster
1934	*Kent (2nd),* Prince Edward, HRH the Duke of Kent, *s.* 1942	Earl of St Andrews
	Earl	
1999	*Wessex (1st),* Prince Edward, HRH the Earl of Wessex	Viscount Severn

* In June 1999 Buckingham Palace announced that the current Earl of Wessex will be granted the Dukedom of Edinburgh when the title reverts to the Crown. The title will only revert to the Crown on both the death of the current Duke of Edinburgh and the Prince of Wales' succession as king

‡ The title is held by the sovereign's eldest son from the moment of his birth or the sovereign's accession

DUKES

Coronet, Eight strawberry leaves

Style, His Grace the Duke of _
Envelope (formal), His Grace the Duke of _; *(social),* The Duke of _. *Letter (formal),* My Lord Duke; *(social),* Dear Duke. *Spoken (formal),* Your Grace; *(social),* Duke
Wife's style, Her Grace the Duchess of _
Envelope (formal), Her Grace the Duchess of _; *(social),* The Duchess of _. *Letter (formal),* Dear Madam; *(social),* Dear Duchess. *Spoken,* Duchess
Eldest son's style, Takes his father's second title as a courtesy title (*see* Courtesy Titles)
Younger sons' style, 'Lord' before forename (F_) and surname (S_)
Envelope, Lord F_ S_. *Letter (formal),* My Lord; *(social),* Dear Lord F_. *Spoken (formal),* My Lord; *(social),* Lord F_
Daughters' style, 'Lady' before forename (F_) and surname (S_)
Envelope, Lady F_ S_. *Letter (formal),* Dear Madam; *(social),* Dear Lady F_. *Spoken,* Lady F_

Created	*Title, order of succession, name, etc*	*Heir*
1868 I.	*Abercorn (5th),* James Hamilton, KG, *b.* 1934, *s.* 1979, *m.*	Marquess of Hamilton, *b.* 1969
1701 S.	*Argyll (13th),* Torquhil Ian Campbell, *b.* 1968, *s.* 2001	Marquess of Lorne, *b.* 2004
1703 S.	*Atholl (11th),* John Murray, *b.* 1929, *s.* 1996, *m.*	Marquis of Tullibardine, *b.* 1960
1682	*Beaufort (11th),* David Robert Somerset, *b.* 1928, *s.* 1984, *m.*	Marquess of Worcester, *b.* 1952
1694	*Bedford (15th),* Andrew Ian Henry Russell, *b.* 1962, *s.* 2003, *m.*	Marquess of Tavistock, *b.* 2005
1663 S.	*Buccleuch (10th) and Queensberry (12th) (S. 1684),* Richard Walter John Montagu Douglas Scott, KBE, *b.* 1954, *s.* 2007, *m.*	Earl of Dalkeith, *b.* 1984
1694	*Devonshire (12th),* Peregrine Andrew Morny Cavendish, KCVO, CBE, *b.* 1944, *s.* 2004, *m.*	Marquess of Hartington, *b.* 1969
1900	*Fife (3rd),* James George Alexander Bannerman Carnegie, *b.* 1929, *s.* 1959	Earl of Southesk, *b.* 1961
1675	*Grafton (11th),* Hugh Denis Charles FitzRoy, KG, *b.* 1919, *s.* 1970, *m.*	Earl of Euston, *b.* 1978
1643 S.	*Hamilton (16th) and Brandon (13th) (1711),* Alexander Douglas Douglas-Hamilton, *b.* 1978, *s.* 2010 *Premier Peer of Scotland*	Lord John W., *b.* 1979
1766 I.	*Leinster (9th),* Maurice FitzGerald, *b.* 1948, *s.* 2004, *m. Premier Duke, Marquess and Earl of Ireland*	Lord John F., *b.* 1952

1719	*Manchester (13th),* Alexander Charles David Drogo Montagu, *b.* 1962, *s.* 2002, *m.*	Lord Kimble W. D. M., *b.* 1964
1702	*Marlborough (11th),* John George Vanderbilt Henry Spencer-Churchill, *b.* 1926, *s.* 1972, *m.*	Marquess of Blandford, *b.* 1955
1707 S.	** *Montrose (8th),* James Graham, *b.* 1935, *s.* 1992, *m.*	Marquis of Graham, *b.* 1973
1483	** *Norfolk (18th),* Edward Wiliam Fitzalan-Howard, *b.* 1956, *s.* 2002, *m.* *Premier Duke and Earl Marshal*	Earl of Arundel and Surrey, *b.* 1987
1766	*Northumberland (12th),* Ralph George Algernon Percy, *b.* 1956, *s.* 1995, *m.*	Earl Percy, *b.* 1984
1675	*Richmond (10th) and Gordon (5th) (1876),* Charles Henry Gordon Lennox, *b.* 1929, *s.* 1989, *m.*	Earl of March and Kinrara, *b.* 1955
1707 S.	*Roxburghe (10th),* Guy David Innes-Ker, *b.* 1954, *s.* 1974, *m. Premier Baronet of Scotland*	Marquis of Bowmont and Cessford, *b.* 1981
1703	*Rutland (11th),* David Charles Robert Manners, *b.* 1959, *s.* 1999, *m.*	Marquess of Granby, *b.*1999
1684	*St Albans (14th),* Murray de Vere Beauclerk, *b.* 1939, *s.* 1988, *m.*	Earl of Burford, *b.* 1965
1547	*Somerset (19th),* John Michael Edward Seymour, *b.* 1952, *s.* 1984, *m.*	Lord Seymour, *b.* 1982
1833	*Sutherland (7th),* Francis Ronald Egerton, *b.* 1940, *s.* 2000, *m.*	Marquess of Stafford, *b.* 1975
1814	*Wellington (8th),* Arthur Valerian Wellesley, KG, LVO, OBE, MC, *b.* 1915, *s.* 1972, *m.*	Marquess of Douro, *b.* 1945
1874	*Westminster (6th),* Gerald Cavendish Grosvenor, KG, CB, OBE, *b.* 1951, *s.* 1979, *m.*	Earl Grosvenor, *b.* 1991

MARQUESSES

Coronet, Four strawberry leaves alternating with four silver balls

Style, The Most Hon. the Marquess (of) _ . In Scotland the spelling 'Marquis' is preferred for pre-Union creations
Envelope (formal), The Most Hon. the Marquess of _; *(social),* The Marquess of _. *Letter (formal),* My Lord; *(social),* Dear Lord _. *Spoken (formal),* My Lord; *(social),* Lord _
Wife's style, The Most Hon. the Marchioness (of) _
Envelope (formal), The Most Hon. the Marchioness of _; *(social),* The Marchioness of _. *Letter (formal),* Madam; *(social),* Dear Lady _. *Spoken,* Lady _
Eldest son's style, Takes his father's second title as a courtesy title (*see* Courtesy Titles)
Younger sons' style, 'Lord' before forename and surname, as for Duke's younger sons
Daughters' style, 'Lady' before forename and surname, as for Duke's daughter

Created	*Title, order of succession, name, etc*	*Heir*
1916	*Aberdeen and Temair (7th),* Alexander George Gordon, *b.* 1955, *s.* 2002, *m.*	Earl of Haddo, *b.* 1983
1876	*Abergavenny (6th) and 10th Earl, Abergavenny, 1784,* Christopher George Charles Nevill, *b.* 1955, *s.* 2000, *m.*	To Earldom only, David M. R. N., *b.* 1941
1821	*Ailesbury (8th),* Michael Sidney Cedric Brudenell-Bruce, *b.* 1926, *s.* 1974	Earl of Cardigan, *b.* 1952
1831	*Ailsa (8th),* Archibald Angus Charles Kennedy, *b.* 1956, *s.* 1994	Lord David T. K., *b.* 1958
1815	*Anglesey (7th),* George Charles Henry Victor Paget, *b.* 1922, *s.* 1947, *m.*	Earl of Uxbridge, *b.* 1950
1789	*Bath (7th),* Alexander George Thynn, *b.* 1932, *s.* 1992, *m.*	Viscount Weymouth, *b.* 1974
1826	*Bristol (8th),* Frederick William Augustus Hervey, *b.* 1979, *s.* 1999	Timothy H. H., *b.* 1960
1796	*Bute (7th),* John Colum Crichton-Stuart, *b.* 1958, *s.* 1993, *m.*	Earl of Dumfries, *b.* 1989
1812	° *Camden (6th),* David George Edward Henry Pratt, *b.* 1930, *s.* 1983	Earl of Brecknock, *b.* 1965
1815	** *Cholmondeley (7th),* David George Philip Cholmondeley, KCVO, *b.* 1960, *s.* 1990, *m. Lord Great Chamberlain*	Earl of Rocksavage, *b.* 2010
1816 I.	° *Conyngham (8th),* Henry Vivian Pierpoint Conyngham, *b.* 1951, *s.* 2009, *m.*	Earl of Mount Charles, *b.* 1975
1791 I.	*Donegall (8th),* Arthur Patrick Chichester, *b.* 1952, *s.* 2007, *m.*	Earl of Belfast, *b.* 1990
1789 I.	*Downshire (9th),* (Arthur Francis) Nicholas Wills Hill, *b.* 1959, *s.* 2003, *m.*	Earl of Hillsborough, *b.* 1996
1801 I.	*Ely (9th),* Charles John Tottenham, *b.* 1943, *s.* 2006, *m.*	Lord Timothy C. T., *b.* 1948
1801	*Exeter (8th),* (William) Michael Anthony Cecil, *b.* 1935, *s.* 1988, *m.*	Lord Burghley, *b.* 1970

1800 I.	*Headfort (7th),* Thomas Michael Ronald Christopher Taylour, *b.* 1959, *s.* 2005, *m.*	Earl of Bective, *b.* 1989
1793	*Hertford (9th),* Henry Jocelyn Seymour, *b.* 1958, *s.* 1997, *m.*	Earl of Yarmouth, *b.* 1993
1599 S.	*Huntly (13th),* Granville Charles Gomer Gordon, *b.* 1944, *s.* 1987, *m.* *Premier Marquess of Scotland*	Earl of Aboyne, *b.* 1973
1784	*Lansdowne (9th),* Charles Maurice Mercer Nairne Petty-Fitzmaurice, LVO *b.* 1941, *s.* 1999, *m.*	Earl of Kerry, *b.* 1970
1902	*Linlithgow (4th),* Adrian John Charles Hope, *b.* 1946, *s.* 1987, *m.*	Earl of Hopetoun, *b.* 1969
1816 I.	*Londonderry (9th),* Alexander Charles Robert Vane-Tempest-Stewart, *b.* 1937, *s.* 1955, *m.*	Viscount Castlereagh, *b.* 1972
1701 S.	*Lothian (13th),* Michael Andrew Foster Jude Kerr (Michael Ancram), PC, *b.* 1945, *s.* 2004, *m.*	Lord Ralph W. F. J. K., *b.* 1957
1917	*Milford Haven (4th),* George Ivar Louis Mountbatten, *b.* 1961, *s.* 1970, *m.*	Earl of Medina, *b.* 1991
1838	*Normanby (5th),* Constantine Edmund Walter Phipps, *b.* 1954, *s.* 1994, *m.*	Earl of Mulgrave, *b.* 1994
1812	*Northampton (7th),* Spencer Douglas David Compton, *b.* 1946, *s.* 1978, *m.*	Earl Compton, *b.* 1973
1682 S.	*Queensberry (12th),* David Harrington Angus Douglas, *b.* 1929, *s.* 1954	Viscount Drumlanrig, *b.* 1967
1926	*Reading (4th),* Simon Charles Henry Rufus Isaacs, *b.* 1942, *s.* 1980, *m.*	Viscount Erleigh, *b.* 1986
1789	*Salisbury (7th) and Baron Gascoyne-Cecil (life peerage, 1999),* Robert Michael James Gascoyne-Cecil, PC, *b.* 1946, *s.* 2003, *m.*	Viscount Cranborne, *b.* 1970
1800 I.	*Sligo (11th),* Jeremy Ulick Browne, *b.* 1939, *s.* 1991, *m.*	Sebastian U. B., *b.* 1964
1787	° *Townshend (8th),* Charles George Townshend, *b.* 1945, *s.* 2010, *m.*	Viscount Raynham, *b.* 1977
1694 S.	*Tweeddale (14th),* Charles David Montagu Hay, *b.* 1947, *s.* 2005	(Lord) Alistair J. M. H., *b.* 1955
1789 I.	*Waterford (8th),* John Hubert de la Poer Beresford, *b.* 1933, *s.* 1934, *m.*	Earl of Tyrone, *b.* 1958
1551	*Winchester (18th),* Nigel George Paulet, *b.* 1941, *s.* 1968, *m.* *Premier Marquess of England*	Earl of Wiltshire, *b.* 1969
1892	*Zetland (4th),* Lawrence Mark Dundas, *b.* 1937, *s.* 1989, *m.*	Earl of Ronaldshay, *b.* 1965

EARLS

Coronet, Eight silver balls on stalks alternating with eight gold strawberry leaves

Style, The Rt. Hon. the Earl (of) _

Envelope (formal), The Rt. Hon. the Earl (of) _; *(social),* The Earl (of) _. *Letter (formal),* My Lord; *(social),* Dear Lord _. *Spoken (formal),* My Lord; *(social),* Lord _.

Wife's style, The Rt. Hon. the Countess (of) _

Envelope (formal), The Rt. Hon. the Countess (of) _; *(social),* The Countess (of) _. *Letter (formal),* Madam; *(social),* Lady _. *Spoken (formal),* Madam; *(social),* Lady _.

Eldest son's style, Takes his father's second title as a courtesy title (*see* Courtesy Titles)

Younger sons' style, 'The Hon.' before forename and surname, as for Baron's children

Daughters' style, 'Lady' before forename and surname, as for Duke's daughter

Created	*Title, order of succession, name, etc*	*Heir*
1639 S.	*Airlie (13th),* David George Coke Patrick Ogilvy, KT, GCVO, PC, Royal Victorian Chain, *b.* 1926, *s.* 1968, *m.*	Lord Ogilvy, *b.* 1958
1696	*Albemarle (10th),* Rufus Arnold Alexis Keppel, *b.* 1965, *s.* 1979, *m.*	Viscount Bury, *b.* 2003
1952	° *Alexander of Tunis (2nd),* Shane William Desmond Alexander, *b.* 1935, *s.* 1969, *m.*	Hon. Brian J. A., *b.* 1939
1662 S.	*Annandale and Hartfell (11th),* Patrick Andrew Wentworth Hope Johnstone, *b.* 1941, *s.* 1983, *m.* claim established 1985	Lord Johnstone, *b.* 1971
1789 I.	° *Annesley (11th),* Philip Harrison Annesley, *b.* 1927, *s.* 2001, *m.*	Hon. Michael R. A., *b.* 1933
1785 I.	*Antrim (9th),* Alexander Randal Mark McDonnell, *b.* 1935, *s.* 1977, *m.*	Viscount Dunluce, *b.* 1967
1762 I.	** *Arran (9th),* Arthur Desmond Colquhoun Gore, *b.* 1938, *s.* 1983, *m.*	Paul A. G., CMG, CVO, *b.* 1921
1955	° ** *Attlee (3rd),* John Richard Attlee, *b.* 1956, *s.* 1991, *m.*	None
1714	*Aylesford (12th),* Charles Heneage Finch-Knightley, *b.* 1947, *s.* 2008, *m.*	Lord Guernsey, *b.* 1985

1937	** *Baldwin of Bewdley (4th),* Edward Alfred Alexander Baldwin, *b.* 1938, *s.* 1976, *w.*	Viscount Corvedale, *b.* 1973
1922	*Balfour (5th),* Roderick Francis Arthur Balfour, *b.* 1948, *s.* 2003, *m.*	Charles G. Y. B., *b.* 1951
1772	° *Bathurst (8th),* Henry Allen John Bathurst, *b.* 1927, *s.* 1943, *m.*	Lord Apsley, *b.* 1961
1919	° *Beatty (3rd),* David Beatty, *b.* 1946, *s.* 1972, *m.*	Viscount Borodale, *b.* 1973
1797 I.	° *Belmore (8th),* John Armar Lowry-Corry, *b.* 1951, *s.* 1960, *m.*	Viscount Corry, *b.* 1985
1739 I.	*Bessborough (12th),* Myles Fitzhugh Longfield Ponsonby, *b.* 1941, *s.* 2002, *m.*	Viscount Duncannon, *b.* 1974
1815	*Bradford (7th),* Richard Thomas Orlando Bridgeman, *b.* 1947, *s.* 1981, *m.*	Viscount Newport, *b.* 1980
1469 S.	*Buchan (17th),* Malcolm Harry Erskine, *b.* 1930, *s.* 1984, *m.*	Lord Cardross, *b.* 1960
1746	*Buckinghamshire (10th),* (George) Miles Hobart-Hampden, *b.* 1944, *s.* 1983, *m.*	Sir John Hobart, Bt., *b.* 1945
1800	° *Cadogan (8th),* Charles Gerald John Cadogan, *b.* 1937, *s.* 1997, *m.*	Viscount Chelsea, *b.* 1966
1878	° *Cairns (6th),* Simon Dallas Cairns, CVO, CBE, *b.* 1939, *s.* 1989, *m.*	Viscount Garmoyle, *b.* 1965
1455 S.	** *Caithness (20th),* Malcolm Ian Sinclair, PC, *b.* 1948, *s.* 1965, *w.*	Lord Berriedale, *b.* 1981
1800 I.	*Caledon (7th),* Nicholas James Alexander, *b.* 1955, *s.* 1980, *m.*	Viscount Alexander, *b.* 1990
1661	*Carlisle (13th),* George William Beaumont Howard, *b.* 1949, *s.* 1994	Hon. Philip C. W. H., *b.* 1963
1793	*Carnarvon (8th),* George Reginald Oliver Molyneux Herbert, *b.* 1956, *s.* 2001, *m.*	Lord Porchester, *b.* 1992
1748 I.	*Carrick (10th),* David James Theobald Somerset Butler, *b.* 1953, *s.* 1992, *m.*	Viscount Ikerrin, *b.* 1975
1800 I.	° *Castle Stewart (8th),* Arthur Patrick Avondale Stuart, *b.* 1928, *s.* 1961, *m.*	Viscount Stuart, *b.* 1953
1814	°** *Cathcart (7th),* Charles Alan Andrew Cathcart, *b.* 1952, *s.* 1999, *m.*	Lord Greenock, *b.* 1986
1647 I.	*Cavan,* The 12th Earl died in 1988.	†Roger C. Lambart, *b.* 1944
1827	° *Cawdor (7th),* Colin Robert Vaughan Campbell, *b.* 1962, *s.* 1993, *m.*	Viscount Emlyn, *b.* 1998
1801	*Chichester (9th),* John Nicholas Pelham, *b.* 1944, *s.* 1944, *m.*	Richard A. H. P., *b.* 1952
1803 I.	** *Clancarty (9th),* Nicholas Power Richard Le Poer Trench, *b.* 1952, *s.* 1995, *m.*	None
1776 I.	*Clanwilliam (8th),* Patrick James Meade, *b.* 1960, *s.* 2009, *m.*	Lord Gillford, *b.* 1998
1776	*Clarendon (8th),* George Edward Laurence Villiers, *b.* 1976, *s.* 2009, *m.*	Lord Hyde, *b.* 2008
1620 I.	*Cork and Orrery (15th),* John Richard Boyle, *b.* 1945, *s.* 2003, *m.*	Viscount Dungarvan, *b.* 1978
1850	*Cottenham (9th),* Mark John Henry Pepys, *b.* 1983, *s.* 2000	Hon. Sam R. P., *b.* 1986
1762 I.	** *Courtown (9th),* James Patrick Montagu Burgoyne Winthrop Stopford, *b.* 1954, *s.* 1975, *m.*	Viscount Stopford, *b.* 1988
1697	*Coventry (13th),* George William Coventry, *b.* 1939, *s.* 2004, *m.*	David D. S. C., *b.* 1973
1857	° *Cowley (7th),* Garret Graham Wellesley, *b.* 1934, *s.* 1975, *w.*	Viscount Dangan, *b.* 1965
1892	*Cranbrook (5th),* Gathorne Gathorne-Hardy, *b.* 1933, *s.* 1978, *m.*	Lord Medway, *b.* 1968
1801 M.	*Craven (9th),* Benjamin Robert Joseph Craven, *b.* 1989, *s.* 1990	Rupert J. E. C., *b.* 1926
1398 S.	*Crawford (29th) and Balcarres (12th) (S. 1651) and Baron Balniel (life peerage, 1974),* Robert Alexander Lindsay, KT, GCVO, PC, *b.* 1927, *s.* 1975, *m. Premier Earl on Union Roll*	Lord Balniel, *b.* 1958
1861	*Cromartie (5th),* John Ruaridh Blunt Grant Mackenzie, *b.* 1948, *s.* 1989, *m.*	Viscount Tarbat, *b.* 1987
1901	*Cromer (4th),* Evelyn Rowland Esmond Baring, *b.* 1946, *s.* 1991, *m.*	Viscount Errington, *b.* 1994
1633 S.	*Dalhousie (17th),* James Hubert Ramsay, *b.* 1948, *s.* 1999, *m., Lord Steward*	Lord Ramsay, *b.* 1981
1725 I.	*Darnley (11th),* Adam Ivo Stuart Bligh, *b.* 1941, *s.* 1980, *m.*	Lord Clifton, *b.* 1968
1711	*Dartmouth (10th),* William Legge, *b.* 1949, *s.* 1997, *m.*	Hon. Rupert L., *b.* 1951
1761	° *De La Warr (11th),* William Herbrand Sackville, *b.* 1948, *s.* 1988, *m.*	Lord Buckhurst, *b.* 1979
1622	*Denbigh (12th) and Desmond (11th) (I. 1622),* Alexander Stephen Rudolph Feilding, *b.* 1970, *s.* 1995, *m.*	Viscount Feilding, *b.* 2005
1485	*Derby (19th),* Edward Richard William Stanley, *b.* 1962, *s.* 1994, *m.*	Lord Stanley, *b.* 1998
1553	*Devon (18th),* Hugh Rupert Courtenay, *b.* 1942, *s.* 1998, *m.*	Lord Courtenay, *b.* 1975
1800 I.	*Donoughmore (8th),* Richard Michael John Hely-Hutchinson, *b.* 1927, *s.* 1981, *w.*	Viscount Suirdale, *b.* 1952
1661 I.	*Drogheda (12th),* Henry Dermot Ponsonby Moore, *b.* 1937, *s.* 1989, *m.*	Viscount Moore, *b.* 1983
1837	*Ducie (7th),* David Leslie Moreton, *b.* 1951, *s.* 1991, *m.*	Lord Moreton, *b.* 1981
1860	*Dudley (4th),* William Humble David Ward, *b.* 1920, *s.* 1969, *m.*	Viscount Ednam, *b.* 1947
1660 S.	** *Dundee (12th),* Alexander Henry Scrymgeour, *b.* 1949, *s.* 1983, *m.*	Lord Scrymgeour, *b.* 1982
1669 S.	*Dundonald (15th),* Iain Alexander Douglas Blair Cochrane, *b.* 1961, *s.* 1986, *m.*	Lord Cochrane, *b.* 1991
1686 S.	*Dunmore (12th),* Malcolm Kenneth Murray, *b.* 1946, *s.* 1995, *m.*	Hon. Geoffrey C. M., *b.*1949
1822 I.	*Dunraven and Mount-Earl (7th),* Thady Windham Thomas Wyndham-Quin, *b.* 1939, *s.* 1965, *m.*	None

1833		*Durham (7th),* Edward Richard Lambton, *b.* 1961, *s.* 2006, *m.*	Viscount Lambton, *b.* 1985
1837		*Effingham (7th),* David Mowbray Algernon Howard, *b.* 1939, *s.* 1996, *m.*	Lord Howard of Effingham, *b.* 1971
1507 S.		*Eglinton (18th) and Winton (9th) (S. 1600),* Archibald George Montgomerie, *b.* 1939, *s.* 1966, *m.*	Lord Montgomerie, *b.* 1966
1733 I.		*Egmont (12th),* Thomas Frederick Gerald Perceval, *b.* 1934, *s.* 2001, *m.*	Hon. Donald W. P., *b.* 1954
1821		*Eldon (5th),* John Joseph Nicholas Scott, *b.* 1937, *s.* 1976, *m.*	Viscount Encombe, *b.* 1962
1633 S.		*Elgin (11th) and Kincardine (15th) (S. 1647),* Andrew Douglas Alexander Thomas Bruce, KT, *b.* 1924, *s.* 1968, *m.*	Lord Bruce, *b.* 1961
1789 I.		*Enniskillen (7th),* Andrew John Galbraith Cole, *b.* 1942, *s.* 1989, *m.*	Arthur G. C., *b.* 1920
1789 I.		*Erne (6th),* Henry George Victor John Crichton, *b.* 1937, *s.* 1940, *m.*	Viscount Crichton, *b.* 1971
1452 S.	**	*Erroll (24th),* Merlin Sereld Victor Gilbert Hay, *b.* 1948, *s.* 1978, *m.* *Hereditary Lord High Constable and Knight Marischal of Scotland*	Lord Hay, *b.* 1984
1661		*Essex (11th),* Frederick Paul de Vere Capell, *b.* 1944, *s.* 2005	William J. C., *b.* 1952
1711	° **	*Ferrers (13th),* Robert Washington Shirley, PC, *b.* 1929, *s.* 1954, *m.*	Viscount Tamworth, *b.* 1952
1789	°	*Fortescue (8th),* Charles Hugh Richard Fortescue, *b.* 1951, *s.* 1993, *m.*	John A. F. F., *b.* 1955
1841		*Gainsborough (6th),* Anthony Baptist Noel, *b.* 1950, *s.* 2009, *m.*	Viscount Campden, *b.* 1977
1623 S.		*Galloway (13th),* Randolph Keith Reginald Stewart, *b.* 1928, *s.* 1978, *w.*	Andrew C. S., *b.* 1949
1703 S.	**	*Glasgow (10th),* Patrick Robin Archibald Boyle, *b.* 1939, *s.* 1984, *m.*	Viscount of Kelburn, *b.* 1978
1806 I.		*Gosford (7th),* Charles David Nicholas Alexander John Sparrow Acheson, *b.* 1942, *s.* 1966, *m.*	Hon. Patrick B. V. M. A., *b.* 1915
1945		*Gowrie (2nd),* Alexander Patrick Greysteil Hore-Ruthven, PC, *b.* 1939, *s.* 1955, *m.*	Viscount Ruthven of Canberra, *b.* 1964
1684 I.		*Granard (10th),* Peter Arthur Edward Hastings Forbes, *b.* 1957, *s.* 1992, *m.*	Viscount Forbes, *b.* 1981
1833	°	*Granville (6th),* Granville George Fergus Leveson-Gower, *b.* 1959, *s.* 1996, *m.*	Lord Leveson, *b.* 1999
1806	°	*Grey (6th),* Richard Fleming George Charles Grey, *b.* 1939, *s.* 1963, *m.*	Philip K. G., *b.* 1940
1752		*Guilford (10th),* Piers Edward Brownlow North, *b.* 1971, *s.* 1999, *m.*	Lord North, *b.* 2002
1619 S.		*Haddington (13th),* John George Baillie-Hamilton, *b.* 1941, *s.* 1986, *m.*	Lord Binning, *b.* 1985
1919	°	*Haig (3rd),* Alexander Douglas Derrick Haig, *b.* 1961, *s.* 2009, *m.*	None
1944		*Halifax (3rd),* Charles Edward Peter Neil Wood, *b.* 1944, *s.* 1980, *m.*	Lord Irwin, *b.* 1977
1898		*Halsbury (4th),* Adam Edward Giffard, *b.* 1934, *s.* 2000, *m.*	None
1754		*Hardwicke (10th),* Joseph Philip Sebastian Yorke, *b.* 1971, *s.* 1974, *m.*	Viscount Royston, *b.* 2009
1812		*Harewood (7th),* George Henry Hubert Lascelles, KBE, *b.* 1923, *s.* 1947, *m.*	Viscount Lascelles, *b.* 1950
1742		*Harrington (12th),* Charles Henry Leicester Stanhope, *b.* 1945, *s.* 2009, *m.*	Viscount Petersham, *b.* 1967
1809		*Harrowby (8th),* Dudley Adrian Conroy Ryder, *b.* 1951, *s.* 2007, *m.*	Viscount Sandon, *b.* 1981
1605 S.	**	*Home (15th),* David Alexander Cospatrick Douglas-Home, CVO, CBE, *b.* 1943, *s.* 1995, *m.*	Lord Dunglass, *b.* 1987
1821	° **	*Howe (7th),* Frederick Richard Penn Curzon, *b.* 1951, *s.* 1984, *m.*	Viscount Curzon, *b.* 1994
1529		*Huntingdon (16th),* William Edward Robin Hood Hastings Bass, LVO, *b.* 1948, *s.* 1990, *m.*	Hon. Simon A. R. H. H. B., *b.* 1950
1885		*Iddesleigh (5th),* John Stafford Northcote, *b.* 1957, *s.* 2004, *m.*	Viscount St Cyres, *b.* 1985
1756		*Ilchester (10th),* Robin Maurice Fox-Strangways, *b.* 1942, *s.* 2006, *m.*	Lord Stavordale, *b.* 1972
1929		*Inchcape (4th),* (Kenneth) Peter (Lyle) Mackay, *b.* 1943, *s.* 1994, *m.*	Viscount Glenapp, *b.* 1979
1919		*Iveagh (4th),* Arthur Edward Rory Guinness, *b.* 1969, *s.* 1992	Viscount Elveden, *b.* 2003
1925	°	*Jellicoe (3rd),* Patrick John Bernard Jellicoe, *b.* 1950, *s.* 2007	Viscount Brocas, *b.* 1970
1697		*Jersey (10th),* George Francis William Child Villiers, *b.* 1976, *s.* 1998 *m.*	Hon. Jamie C. C. V., *b.* 1994
1822 I.		*Kilmorey (6th),* Sir Richard Francis Needham, PC, *b.* 1942, *s.* 1977, *m.*, (does not use title)	Viscount Newry and Mourne, *b.* 1966
1866		*Kimberley (5th),* John Armine Wodehouse, *b.* 1951, *s.* 2002, *m.*	Lord Wodehouse, *b.* 1978
1768 I.		*Kingston (12th),* Robert Charles Henry King-Tenison, *b.* 1969, *s.* 2002, *m.*	Viscount Kingsborough, *b.* 2000
1633 S.		*Kinnoull (15th),* Arthur William George Patrick Hay, *b.* 1935, *s.* 1938, *m.*	Viscount Dupplin, *b.* 1962
1677 S.		*Kintore (14th),* James William Falconer Keith, *b.* 1976, *s.* 2004	Lady Iona D. M. G. K., *b.* 1978
1914	°	*Kitchener of Khartoum (3rd),* Henry Herbert Kitchener, TD, *b.* 1919, *s.* 1937	None
1624 S.		*Lauderdale (18th),* Ian Maitland, *b.* 1937, *s.* 2008, *m.*	Viscount Maitland, *b.* 1965
1837		*Leicester (7th),* Edward Douglas Coke, *b.* 1936, *s.* 1994, *m.*	Viscount Coke, *b.* 1965
1641 S.		*Leven (14th) and Melville (13th) (S. 1690),* Alexander Robert Leslie Melville, *b.* 1924, *s.* 1947, *m.*	Lord Balgonie, *b.* 1984

1831	*Lichfield (6th)*, Thomas William Robert Hugh Anson, *b.* 1978, *s.* 2005, *m.*	George R. A., *b.* 1960
1803 I.	*Limerick (7th)*, Edmund Christopher Pery, *b.* 1963, *s.* 2003, *m.*	Viscount Glentworth, *b.* 1991
1572	*Lincoln (19th)*, Robert Edward Fiennes-Clinton, *b.* 1972, *s.* 2001	Hon. William R. F.-C., *b.* 1980
1633 S.	** *Lindsay (16th)*, James Randolph Lindesay-Bethune, *b.* 1955, *s.* 1989, *m.*	Viscount Garnock, *b.* 1990
1626	*Lindsey (14th) and Abingdon (9th) (1682)*, Richard Henry Rupert Bertie, *b.* 1931, *s.* 1963, *m.*	Lord Norreys, *b.* 1958
1776 I.	*Lisburne (8th)*, John David Malet Vaughan, *b.* 1918, *s.* 1965, *m.*	Viscount Vaughan, *b.* 1945
1822 I.	** *Listowel (6th)*, Francis Michael Hare, *b.* 1964, *s.* 1997, *m.*	Hon. Timothy P. H., *b.* 1966
1905	** *Liverpool (5th)*, Edward Peter Bertram Savile Foljambe, *b.* 1944, *s.* 1969, *m.*	Viscount Hawkesbury, *b.* 1972
1945	° *Lloyd George of Dwyfor (4th)*, David Richard Owen Lloyd George, *b.* 1951, *s.* 2010, *m.*	Viscount Gwynedd, *b.* 1986
1785 I.	*Longford (8th)*, Thomas Frank Dermot Pakenham, *b.* 1933, *s.* 2001, *m.*, (does not use title)	Hon. Edward M. P., *b.* 1970
1807	*Lonsdale (8th)*, Hugh Clayton Lowther, *b.* 1949, *s.* 2006, *m.*	Hon. William J. L., *b.* 1957
1633 S.	*Loudoun (14th)*, Michael Edward Abney-Hastings, *b.* 1942, *s.* 2002, *m.*	Lord Mauchline, *b.* 1974
1838	*Lovelace (5th)*, Peter Axel William Locke King, *b.* 1951, *s.* 1964, *m.*	None
1795 I.	*Lucan (7th)*, Richard John Bingham, *b.* 1934, *s.* 1964, *m.* (missing since 8 November 1974)	Lord Bingham, *b.* 1967
1880	*Lytton (5th)*, John Peter Michael Scawen Lytton, *b.* 1950, *s.* 1985, *m.*	Viscount Knebworth, *b.* 1989
1721	*Macclesfield (9th)*, Richard Timothy George Mansfield Parker, *b.* 1943, *s.* 1992, *m.*	Hon. J. David G. P., *b.* 1945
1800	*Malmesbury (7th)*, James Carleton Harris, *b.* 1946, *s.* 2000, *m.*	Viscount FitzHarris, *b.* 1970
1776	*Mansfield and Mansfield (8th) (1792)*, William David Mungo James Murray, *b.* 1930, *s.* 1971, *m.*	Viscount Stormont, *b.* 1956
1565 S.	*Mar (14th) and Kellie (16th) (S. 1616) and Baron Erskine of Alloa Tower (life peerage, 2000)*, James Thorne Erskine, *b.* 1949, *s.* 1994, *m.*	Hon. Alexander D. E., *b.* 1952
1785 I.	*Mayo (11th)*, Charles Diarmuidh John Bourke, *b.* 1953, *s.* 2006, *m.*	Lord Naas, *b.* 1985
1627 I.	*Meath (15th)*, John Anthony Brabazon, *b.* 1941, *s.* 1998, *m.*	Lord Ardee, *b.* 1977
1766 I.	*Mexborough (8th)*, John Christopher George Savile, *b.* 1931, *s.* 1980, *m.*	Viscount Pollington, *b.* 1959
1813	*Minto (7th)*, Gilbert Timothy George Lariston Elliot-Murray-Kynynmound, *b.* 1953, *s.* 2005, *m.*	Viscount Melgund, *b.* 1984
1562 S.	*Moray (20th)*, Douglas John Moray Stuart, *b.* 1928, *s.* 1974, *m.*	Lord Doune, *b.* 1966
1815	*Morley (6th)*, John St Aubyn Parker, KCVO, *b.* 1923, *s.* 1962, *m.*	Viscount Boringdon, *b.* 1956
1458 S.	*Morton (22nd)*, John Charles Sholto Douglas, *b.* 1927, *s.* 1976, *m.*	Lord Aberdour, *b.* 1952
1789	*Mount Edgcumbe (8th)*, Robert Charles Edgcumbe, *b.* 1939, *s.* 1982	Piers V. E., *b.* 1946
1805	° *Nelson (10th)*, Simon John Horatio Nelson, *b.* 1971, *s.* 2009, *m.*	Viscount Merton, *b.* 1994
1660 S.	*Newburgh (12th)*, Don Filippo Giambattista Camillo Francesco Aldo Maria Rospigliosi, *b.* 1942, *s.* 1986, *m.*	Princess Donna Benedetta F. M. R., *b.* 1974
1827 I.	*Norbury (7th)*, Richard James Graham-Toler, *b.* 1967, *s.* 2000	None
1806 I.	*Normanton (6th)*, Shaun James Christian Welbore Ellis Agar, *b.* 1945, *s.* 1967, *m.*	Viscount Somerton, *b.* 1982
1647 S.	*Northesk (15th)*, Patrick Charles Carnegy, *b.* 1940, *s.* 2010	Colin D. C., *b.* 1942
1801	** *Onslow (7th)*, Michael William Coplestone Dillon Onslow, *b.* 1938, *s.* 1971, *m.*	Viscount Cranley, *b.* 1967
1696 S.	*Orkney (9th)*, (Oliver) Peter St John, *b.* 1938, *s.* 1998, *m.*	Viscount Kirkwall, *b.* 1969
1328 I.	*Ormonde and Ossory (I. 1527)*, The 25th/18th Earl (7th Marquess) died in 1988	†Viscount Mountgarret *b.* 1961 (*see* that title)
1925	*Oxford and Asquith (2nd)*, Julian Edward George Asquith, KCMG, *b.* 1916, *s.* 1928, *w.*	Viscount Asquith, OBE, *b.* 1952
1929	° ** *Peel (3rd)*, William James Robert Peel, GCVO, PC, *b.* 1947, *s.* 1969, *m.* *Lord Chamberlain*	Viscount Clanfield, *b.* 1976
1551	*Pembroke (18th) and Montgomery (15th) (1605)*, William Alexander Sidney Herbert, *b.* 1978, *s.* 2003, *m.*	Earl of Carnarvon *b.* 1956 (*see* that title)
1605 S.	*Perth (18th)*, John Eric Drummond, *b.* 1935, *s.* 2002, *m.*	Viscount Strathallan, *b.* 1965
1905	*Plymouth (3rd)*, Other Robert Ivor Windsor-Clive, *b.* 1923, *s.* 1943, *m.*	Viscount Windsor, *b.* 1951
1785	*Portarlington (7th)*, George Lionel Yuill Seymour Dawson-Damer, *b.* 1938, *s.* 1959, *m.*	Viscount Carlow, *b.* 1965
1689	*Portland (12th)*, Count Timothy Charles Robert Noel Bentinck, *b.* 1953, *s.* 1997, *m.*	Viscount Woodstock, *b.* 1984
1743	*Portsmouth (10th)*, Quentin Gerard Carew Wallop, *b.* 1954, *s.* 1984, *m.*	Viscount Lymington, *b.* 1981
1804	*Powis (8th)*, John George Herbert, *b.* 1952, *s.* 1993, *m.*	Viscount Clive, *b.* 1979
1765	*Radnor (9th)*, William Pleydell-Bouverie, *b.* 1955, *s.* 2008, *m.*	Viscount Folkestone, *b.* 1999
1831 I.	*Ranfurly (7th)*, Gerald Françoys Needham Knox, *b.* 1929, *s.* 1988, *m.*	Viscount Northland, *b.* 1957
1771 I.	*Roden (10th)*, Robert John Jocelyn, *b.* 1938, *s.* 1993, *m.*	Viscount Jocelyn, *b.* 1989

1801	*Romney (8th),* Julian Charles Marsham, *b.* 1948, *s.* 2004, *m.*	Viscount Marsham, *b.* 1977
1703 S.	*Rosebery (7th),* Neil Archibald Primrose, *b.* 1929, *s.* 1974, *m.*	Lord Dalmeny, *b.* 1967
1806 I.	*Rosse (7th),* William Brendan Parsons, *b.* 1936, *s.* 1979, *m.*	Lord Oxmantown, *b.* 1969.
1801	** *Rosslyn (7th),* Peter St Clair-Erskine, *b.* 1958, *s.* 1977, *m.*	Lord Loughborough, *b.* 1986
1457 S.	*Rothes (22nd),* James Malcolm David Leslie, *b.* 1958, *s.* 2005, *m.*	Hon. Alexander J. L., *b.* 1962
1861	° *Russell (6th),* Nicholas Lyulph Russell, *b.* 1968, *s.* 2004	Hon. John F. R., *b.* 1971
1915	° *St Aldwyn (3rd),* Michael Henry Hicks Beach, *b.* 1950, *s.* 1992, *m.*	Hon. David S. H. B., *b.* 1955
1815	*St Germans (10th),* Peregrine Nicholas Eliot, *b.* 1941, *s.* 1988	Lord Eliot, *b.* 2004
1660	** *Sandwich (11th),* John Edward Hollister Montagu, *b.* 1943, *s.* 1995, *m.*	Viscount Hinchingbrooke, *b.* 1969
1690	*Scarbrough (13th),* Richard Osbert Lumley, *b.* 1973, *s.* 2004	Hon. Thomas H. L., *b.* 1980
1701 S.	*Seafield (13th),* Ian Derek Francis Ogilvie-Grant, *b.* 1939, *s.* 1969, *m.*	Viscount Reidhaven, *b.* 1963
1882	** *Selborne (4th),* John Roundell Palmer, KBE, *b.* 1940, *s.* 1971, *m.*	Viscount Wolmer, *b.* 1971
1646 S.	*Selkirk,* Disclaimed for life 1994. (*see* Lord Selkirk of Douglas, Life Peers)	Master of Selkirk, *b.* 1978
1672	*Shaftesbury (12th),* Nicholas Edmund Anthony Ashley-Cooper, *b.* 1979, *s.* 2005	None
1756 I.	*Shannon (9th),* Richard Bentinck Boyle, *b.* 1924, *s.* 1963	Viscount Boyle, *b.* 1960
1442	** *Shrewsbury and Waterford (22nd) (I. 1446),* Charles Henry John Benedict Crofton Chetwynd Chetwynd-Talbot, *b.* 1952, *s.* 1980, *m. Premier Earl of England and Ireland*	Viscount Ingestre, *b.* 1978
1961	*Snowdon (1st) and Baron Armstrong-Jones (life peerage, 1999),* Antony Charles Robert Armstrong-Jones, GCVO, *b.* 1930, *m.*	Viscount Linley, *b.* 1961
1765	° *Spencer (9th),* Charles Edward Maurice Spencer, *b.* 1964, *s.* 1992, *m.*	Viscount Althorp, *b.* 1994
1703 S.	** *Stair (14th),* John David James Dalrymple, *b.* 1961, *s.* 1996, *m.*	Hon. David H. D., *b.* 1963
1984	*Stockton (2nd),* Alexander Daniel Alan Macmillan, MEP, *b.* 1943, *s.* 1986, *m.*	Viscount Macmillan of Ovenden, *b.* 1974
1821	*Stradbroke (6th),* Robert Keith Rous, *b.* 1937, *s.* 1983, *m.*	Viscount Dunwich, *b.* 1961
1847	*Strafford (8th),* Thomas Edmund Byng, *b.* 1936, *s.* 1984, *m.*	Viscount Enfield, *b.* 1964
1606 S.	*Strathmore and Kinghorne (18th) (S. 1677),* Michael Fergus Bowes Lyon, *b.* 1957, *s.* 1987, *m.*	Lord Glamis, *b.* 1986
1603	*Suffolk (21st) and Berkshire (14th) (1626),* Michael John James George Robert Howard, *b.* 1935, *s.* 1941, *m.*	Viscount Andover, *b.* 1974
1955	*Swinton (3rd),* Nicholas John Cunliffe-Lister, *b.* 1939, *s.* 2006, *m.*	Lord Masham *b.* 1970
1714	*Tankerville (10th),* Peter Grey Bennet, *b.* 1956, *s.* 1980	Adrian G. B., *b.* 1958
1822	° *Temple of Stowe (8th),* (Walter) Grenville Algernon Temple-Gore-Langton, *b.* 1924, *s.* 1988, *m.*	Lord Langton, *b.* 1955
1815	*Verulam (7th),* John Duncan Grimston, *b.* 1951, *s.* 1973, *m.*	Viscount Grimston, *b.* 1978
1729	° *Waldegrave (13th),* James Sherbrooke Waldegrave, *b.* 1940, *s.* 1995, *m.*	Viscount Chewton, *b.* 1986
1759	*Warwick (9th) and Brooke (9th) (1746),* Guy David Greville, *b.* 1957, *s.* 1996, *m.*	Lord Brooke, *b.* 1982
1633 S.	*Wemyss (13th) and March (9th) (S. 1697),* James Donald Charteris, *b.* 1948, *s.* 2008, *m.*	Lord Elcho, *b.* 1984
1621 I.	*Westmeath (13th),* William Anthony Nugent, *b.* 1928, *s.* 1971, *m.*	Hon. Sean C. W. N., *b.* 1965
1624	*Westmorland (16th),* Anthony David Francis Henry Fane, *b.* 1951, *s.* 1993, *m.*	Hon. Harry St C. F., *b.* 1953
1876	*Wharncliffe (5th),* Richard Alan Montagu Stuart Wortley, *b.* 1953, *s.* 1987, *m.*	Viscount Carlton, *b.* 1980
1801	*Wilton (8th),* Francis Egerton Grosvenor, *b.* 1934, *s.* 1999, *m.*	Viscount Grey de Wilton, *b.*1959
1628	*Winchilsea (17th) and Nottingham (12th) (1681),* Daniel James Hatfield Finch Hatton, *b.* 1967, *s.* 1999, *m.*	Viscount Maidstone, *b.* 1998
1766	° *Winterton (8th),* (Donald) David Turnour, *b.* 1943, *s.* 1991, *m.*	Robert C. T., *b.* 1950
1956	*Woolton (3rd),* Simon Frederick Marquis, *b.* 1958, *s.* 1969, *m.*	None
1837	*Yarborough (8th),* Charles John Pelham, *b.* 1963, *s.* 1991, *m.*	Lord Worsley, *b.* 1990

COUNTESSES IN THEIR OWN RIGHT

Style, The Rt. Hon. the Countess (of) _
Envelope (formal), The Rt. Hon. the Countess (of) _; *(social),* The Countess (of) _. *Letter (formal),* Madam; *(social),* Lady _. *Spoken (formal),* Madam; *(social),* Lady _.
Husband, Untitled
Children's style, As for children of an Earl

Created	*Title, order of succession, name, etc*	*Heir*
1643 S.	*Dysart (12th in line),* Katherine Grant of Rothiemurchus, *b.* 1918, *s.* 2003 *w.*	Lord Huntingtower, *b.* 1946
c.1115 S.	** *Mar (31st in line),* Margaret of Mar, *b.* 1940, *s.* 1975, *m.* Premier Earldom of Scotland	Mistress of Mar, *b.* 1963
1947	° *Mountbatten of Burma (2nd in line),* Patricia Edwina Victoria Knatchbull, CBE, *b.* 1924, *s.* 1979, *w.*	Lord Romsey, (*also* Lord Brabourne (8th) *see* that title)
c.1235 S.	*Sutherland* (24th in line),* Elizabeth Millicent Sutherland, *b.* 1921, *s.* 1963, *w.*	Lord Strathnaver, *b.* 1947

VISCOUNTS

Coronet, Sixteen silver balls

Style, The Rt. Hon. the Viscount _
Envelope (formal), The Rt. Hon. the Viscount _; *(social),* The Viscount _. *Letter (formal),* My Lord; *(social),* Dear Lord _. *Spoken,* Lord _.
Wife's style, The Rt. Hon. the Viscountess _
Envelope (formal), The Rt. Hon. the Viscountess _; *(social),* The Viscountess _. *Letter (formal),* Madam; *(social),* Dear Lady _. *Spoken,* Lady _.
Children's style, 'The Hon.' before forename and surname, as for Baron's children
In Scotland, the heir apparent to a Viscount may be styled 'The Master of _ (title of peer)'

Created	*Title, order of succession, name, etc*	*Heir*
1945	*Addison (4th),* William Matthew Wand Addison, *b.* 1945, *s.* 1992, *m.*	Hon. Paul W. A., *b.* 1973
1946	*Alanbrooke (3rd),* Alan Victor Harold Brooke, *b.* 1932, *s.* 1972	None
1919	** *Allenby (3rd),* Lt.-Col. Michael Jaffray Hynman Allenby, *b.* 1931, *s.* 1984, *m.*	Hon. Henry J. H. A., *b.* 1968
1911	*Allendale (4th),* Wentworth Peter Ismay Beaumont, *b.* 1948, *s.* 2002, *m.*	Hon. Wentworth A. I. B., *b.* 1979
1642 S.	*of Arbuthnott (16th),* John Campbell Arbuthnott, KT, CBE, DSC, *b.* 1924, *s.* 1966, *m.*	Master of Arbuthnott, *b.* 1950
1751 I.	*Ashbrook (11th),* Michael Llowarch Warburton Flower, *b.* 1935, *s.* 1995, *m.*	Hon. Rowland F. W. F., *b.* 1975
1917	** *Astor (4th),* William Waldorf Astor, *b.* 1951, *s.* 1966, *m.*	Hon. William W. A., *b.* 1979
1781 I.	*Bangor (8th),* William Maxwell David Ward, *b.* 1948, *s.* 1993, *m.*	Hon. E. Nicholas W., *b.* 1953
1925	*Bearsted (5th),* Nicholas Alan Samuel, *b.* 1950, *s.* 1996, *m.*	Hon. Harry R. S., *b.* 1988
1963	*Blakenham (2nd),* Michael John Hare, *b.* 1938, *s.* 1982, *m.*	Hon. Caspar J. H., *b.* 1972
1935	*Bledisloe (4th),* Rupert Edward Ludlow Bathurst, *b.* 1964, *s.* 2009, *m.*	Hon. Benjamin B., *b.* 2004
1712	*Bolingbroke (7th) and St John (8th) (1716),* Kenneth Oliver Musgrave St John, *b.* 1927, *s.* 1974	Hon. Henry F. St J., *b.* 1957
1960	*Boyd of Merton (2nd),* Simon Donald Rupert Neville Lennox-Boyd, *b.* 1939, *s.* 1983, *m.*	Hon. Benjamin A. L.-B., *b.* 1964
1717 I.	*Boyne (11th),* Gustavus Michael Stucley Hamilton-Russell, *b.* 1965, *s.* 1995, *m.*	Hon. Gustavus A. E. H.-R., *b.* 1999
1929	*Brentford (4th),* Crispin William Joynson-Hicks, *b.* 1933, *s.* 1983, *m.*	Hon. Paul W. J.-H., *b.* 1971
1929	** *Bridgeman (3rd),* Robin John Orlando Bridgeman, *b.* 1930, *s.* 1982, *m.*	Hon. Luke R. O. B., *b.* 1971

1868		*Bridport (4th) and 7th Duke, Bronte in Sicily, 1799,* Alexander Nelson Hood, *b.* 1948, *s.* 1969, *m.*	Hon. Peregrine A. N. H., *b.* 1974
1952	**	*Brookeborough (3rd),* Alan Henry Brooke, *b.* 1952, *s.* 1987, *m.*	Hon. Christopher A. B., *b.* 1954
1933		*Buckmaster (4th),* Adrian Charles Buckmaster, *b.* 1949, *s.* 2007, *m.*	Hon. Andrew N. B., *b.* 1980
1939		*Caldecote (3rd),* Piers James Hampden Inskip, *b.* 1947, *s.* 1999, *m.*	Hon. Thomas J. H. I., *b.* 1985
1941		*Camrose (4th),* Adrian Michael Berry, *b.* 1937, *s.* 2001, *m.*	Hon. Jonathan W. B., *b.* 1970
1954		*Chandos (3rd) and Baron Lyttelton of Aldershot (life peerage, 2000),* Thomas Orlando Lyttelton, *b.* 1953, *s.* 1980, *m.*	Hon. Oliver A. L., *b.* 1986
1665 I.		*Charlemont (15th),* John Dodd Caulfeild, *b.* 1966, *s.* 2001, *m.*	Hon. Shane A. C., *b.* 1996
1921		*Chelmsford (4th)* Frederic Corin Piers Thesiger, *b.* 1962, *s.* 1999, *m.*	Hon. Frederic T. *b.* 2006
1717 I.		*Chetwynd (10th),* Adam Richard John Casson Chetwynd, *b.* 1935, *s.* 1965, *m.*	Hon. Adam D. C., *b.* 1969
1911		*Chilston (4th),* Alastair George Akers-Douglas, *b.* 1946, *s.* 1982, *m.*	Hon. Oliver I. A.-D., *b.* 1973
1902		*Churchill (3rd) and 5th UK Baron Churchill (1815),* Victor George Spencer, *b.* 1934, *s.* 1973	To Barony only, Richard H. R. S., *b.* 1926
1718		*Cobham (12th),* Christopher Charles Lyttelton, *b.* 1947, *s.* 2006, *m.*	Hon. Oliver C. L., *b.* 1976
1902		*Colville of Culross (5th),* Charles Mark Townshend Colville, *b.* 1959, *s.* 2010	Hon. Richmond J. I. C., *b.* 1961
1826		*Combermere (6th),* Thomas Robert Wellington Stapleton-Cotton, *b.* 1969, *s.* 2000	Hon. David P. D. S.-C., *b.* 1932
1917		*Cowdray (4th),* Michael Orlando Weetman Pearson, *b.* 1944, *s.* 1995, *m.*	Hon. Peregrine J. D. P., *b.* 1994
1927	**	*Craigavon (3rd),* Janric Fraser Craig, *b.* 1944, *s.* 1974	None
1943		*Daventry (4th),* James Edward FitzRoy Newdegate, *b.* 1960, *s.* 2000, *m.*	Hon. Humphrey J. F. N., *b.* 1995
1937		*Davidson (2nd),* John Andrew Davidson, *b.* 1928, *s.* 1970, *m.*	Hon. Malcolm W. M. D., *b.* 1934
1956		*De L'Isle (2nd),* Philip John Algernon Sidney, MBE, *b.* 1945, *s.* 1991, *m.*	Hon. Philip W. E. S., *b.* 1985
1776 I.		*De Vesci (7th),* Thomas Eustace Vesey, *b.* 1955, *s.* 1983, *m.*	Hon. Oliver I. V., *b.* 1991
1917		*Devonport (3rd),* Terence Kearley, *b.* 1944, *s.* 1973	Chester D. H. K., *b.* 1932
1964		*Dilhorne (2nd),* John Mervyn Manningham-Buller, *b.* 1932, *s.* 1980, *m.*	Hon. James E. M.-B., *b.* 1956
1622 I.		*Dillon (22nd),* Henry Benedict Charles Dillon, *b.* 1973, *s.* 1982	Hon. Richard A. L. D., *b.* 1948
1785 I.		*Doneraile (10th),* Richard Allen St Leger, *b.* 1946, *s.* 1983, *m.*	Hon. Nathaniel W. R. St J. St L., *b.* 1971
1680 I.		*Downe (12th),* Richard Henry Dawnay, *b.* 1967, *s.* 2002	Thomas P. D., *b.* 1978
1959		*Dunrossil (3rd),* Andrew William Reginald Morrison, *b.* 1953, *s.* 2000, *m.*	Hon. Callum A. B. M., *b.* 1994
1964	**	*Eccles (2nd),* John Dawson Eccles, CBE, *b.* 1931, *s.* 1999, *m.*	Hon. William D. E., *b.* 1960
1897		*Esher (5th),* Christopher Lionel Baliol Brett, *b.* 1936, *s.* 2004, *m.*	Hon. Matthew C. A. B., *b.* 1963
1816		*Exmouth (10th),* Paul Edward Pellew, *b.* 1940, *s.* 1970, *m.*	Hon. Edward F. P., *b.* 1978
1620 S.	**	*of Falkland (15th),* Lucius Edward William Plantagenet Cary, *b.* 1935, *s.* 1984, *m. Premier Scottish Viscount on the Roll*	Master of Falkland, *b.* 1963
1720		*Falmouth (9th),* George Hugh Boscawen, *b.* 1919, *s.* 1962, *w.*	Hon. Evelyn A. H. B., *b.* 1955
1720 I.		*Gage (8th),* (Henry) Nicolas Gage, *b.* 1934, *s.* 1993, *m.*	Hon. Henry W. G., *b.* 1975
1727 I.		*Galway (12th),* George Rupert Monckton-Arundell, *b.* 1922, *s.* 1980, *m.*	Hon. J. Philip M., *b.* 1952
1478 I.		*Gormanston (17th),* Jenico Nicholas Dudley Preston, *b.* 1939, *s.* 1940, *m. Premier Viscount of Ireland*	Hon. Jenico F. T. P., *b.* 1974
1816 I.		*Gort (9th),* Foley Robert Standish Prendergast Vereker, *b.* 1951, *s.* 1995, *m.*	Hon. Robert F. P. V., *b.* 1993
1900	**	*Goschen (4th),* Giles John Harry Goschen, *b.* 1965, *s.* 1977, *m.*	Hon. Alexander J. E. G., *b.* 2001
1849		*Gough (5th),* Shane Hugh Maryon Gough, *b.* 1941, *s.* 1951	None
1929		*Hailsham (3rd),* Douglas Martin Hogg, PC, QC, MP, *b.* 1945, *s.* 2001, *m.*	Hon. Quintin J. N. M. H., *b.* 1973
1891		*Hambleden (4th),* William Herbert Smith, *b.* 1930, *s.* 1948, *m.*	Hon. William H. B. S., *b.* 1955
1884		*Hampden (7th),* Francis Anthony Brand, *b.* 1970, *s.* 2008, *m.*	Hon. Lucian A. B., *b.* 2005
1936		*Hanworth (3rd),* David Stephen Geoffrey Pollock, *b.* 1946, *s.* 1996, *m.*	Harold W. C. P., *b.* 1988
1791 I.		*Harberton (11th),* Henry Robert Pomeroy, *b.* 1958, *s.* 2004, *m.*	Hon. Patrick C. P., b. 1995
1846		*Hardinge (7th),* Andrew Hartland Hardinge, *b.* 1960, *s.* 2004, *m.*	Hon. Thomas H. de M. H., *b.* 1993
1791 I.		*Hawarden (9th),* (Robert) Connan Wyndham Leslie Maude, *b.* 1961, *s.* 1991, *m.*	Hon. Varian J. C. E. M., *b.* 1997
1960		*Head (2nd),* Richard Antony Head, *b.* 1937, *s.* 1983, *m.*	Hon. Henry J. H., *b.* 1980
1550		*Hereford (19th),* Charles Robin De Bohun Devereux, *b.* 1975, *s.* 2004, *Premier Viscount of England*	Hon. Edward M. de B. D., *b.* 1977
1842		*Hill (9th),* Peter David Raymond Charles Clegg-Hill, *b.* 1945, *s.* 2003	Hon. Michael C. D. C.-H., *b.* 1988

1796	*Hood (8th),* Henry Lyttleton Alexander Hood, *b.* 1958, *s.* 1999, *m.*	Hon. Archibald L. S. H., *b.* 1993
1945	*Kemsley (3rd),* Richard Gomer Berry, *b.* 1951, *s.* 1999, *m.*	Hon. Luke G. B., *b.* 1998
1911	*Knollys (3rd),* David Francis Dudley Knollys, *b.* 1931, *s.* 1966, *m.*	Hon. Patrick N. M. K., *b.* 1962
1895	*Knutsford (6th),* Michael Holland-Hibbert, *b.* 1926, *s.* 1986, *m.*	Hon. Henry T. H.-H., *b.* 1959
1954	*Leathers (3rd),* Christopher Graeme Leathers, *b.* 1941, *s.* 1996, *m.*	Hon. James F. L., *b.* 1969
1781 I.	*Lifford (9th),* (Edward) James Wingfield Hewitt, *b.* 1949, *s.* 1987, *m.*	Hon. James T. W. H., *b.* 1979
1921	*Long (4th),* Richard Gerard Long, CBE, *b.* 1929, *s.* 1967, *m.*	Hon. James R. L., *b.* 1960
1957	*Mackintosh of Halifax (3rd),* (John) Clive Mackintosh, *b.* 1958, *s.* 1980, *m.*	Hon. Thomas H. G. M., *b.* 1985
1955	*Malvern (3rd),* Ashley Kevin Godfrey Huggins, *b.* 1949, *s.* 1978	Hon. M. James H., *b.* 1928
1945	*Marchwood (3rd),* David George Staveley Penny, *b.* 1936, *s.* 1979, *w.*	Hon. Peter G. W. P., *b.* 1965
1942	*Margesson (2nd),* Francis Vere Hampden Margesson, *b.* 1922, *s.* 1965, *m.*	Capt. Hon. Richard F. D. M., *b.* 1960
1660 I.	*Massereene (14th) and Ferrard (7th) (I. 1797),* John David Clotworthy Whyte-Melville Foster Skeffington, *b.* 1940, *s.* 1992, *m.*	Hon. Charles J. C. W.-M. F. S., *b.* 1973
1802	*Melville (9th),* Robert David Ross Dundas, *b.* 1937, *s.* 1971, *m.*	Hon. Robert H. K. D., *b.* 1984
1916	*Mersey (5th),* Edward John Hallam Bigham, *b.* 1966, *s.* 2006, *m.*	Hon. David E. H. B., *b.* 1938
1717 I.	*Midleton (12th),* Alan Henry Brodrick, *b.* 1949, *s.* 1988, *m.*	Hon. Ashley R. B., *b.* 1980
1962	*Mills (3rd),* Christopher Philip Roger Mills, *b.* 1956, *s.* 1988, *m.*	None
1716 I.	*Molesworth (12th),* Robert Bysse Kelham Molesworth, *b.* 1959, *s.* 1997	Hon. William J. C. M., *b.* 1960
1801 I.	*Monck (7th),* Charles Stanley Monck, *b.* 1953, *s.* 1982 (Does not use title)	Hon. George S. M., *b.* 1957
1957	*Monckton of Brenchley (3rd),* Christopher Walter Monckton, *b.* 1952, *s.* 2006, *m.*	Hon. Timothy D. R. M., *b.* 1955
1946	** *Montgomery of Alamein (2nd),* David Bernard Montgomery, CBE, *b.* 1928, *s.* 1976, *m.*	Hon. Henry D. M., *b.* 1954
1550 I.	*Mountgarret (18th),* Piers James Richard Butler, *b.* 1961, *s.* 2004	Hon. Edmund H. R. B., *b.* 1962
1952	*Norwich (2nd),* John Julius Cooper, CVO, *b.* 1929, *s.* 1954, *m.*	Hon. Jason C. D. B. C., *b.* 1959
1651 S.	*of Oxfuird (14th),* Ian Arthur Alexander Makgill, *b.* 1969, *s.* 2003	Hon. Robert E. G. M., *b.* 1969
1873	*Portman (10th),* Christopher Edward Berkeley Portman, *b.* 1958, *s.* 1999, *m.*	Hon. Luke O. B. P., *b.* 1984
1743 I.	*Powerscourt (10th),* Mervyn Niall Wingfield, *b.* 1935, *s.* 1973, *m.*	Hon. Mervyn A. W., *b.* 1963
1900	*Ridley (4th),* Matthew White Ridley, KG, GCVO, TD, *b.* 1925, *s.* 1964, *w.*	Hon. Matthew W. R., *b.* 1958
1960	*Rochdale (2nd),* St John Durival Kemp, *b.* 1938, *s.* 1993, *m.*	Hon. Jonathan H. D. K., *b.* 1961
1919	*Rothermere (4th),* (Harold) Jonathan Esmond Vere Harmsworth, *b.* 1967, *s.* 1998, *m.*	Hon. Vere R. J. H. H., *b.* 1994
1937	*Runciman of Doxford (3rd),* Walter Garrison Runciman (Garry), CBE, *b.* 1934, *s.* 1989, *m.*	Hon. David W. R., *b.* 1967
1918	*St Davids (4th),* Rhodri Colwyn Philipps, *b.* 1966, *s.* 2009, *m.*	Hon. Roland A. J. E. P., *b.* 1970
1801	*St Vincent (8th),* Edward Robert James Jervis, *b.* 1951, *s.* 2006, *m.*	Hon. James R. A. J., *b.* 1982
1937	*Samuel (3rd),* David Herbert Samuel, OBE, PHD, *b.* 1922, *s.* 1978, *m.*	Hon. Dan J. S., *b.* 1925
1911	*Scarsdale (4th),* Peter Ghislain Nathaniel Curzon, *b.* 1949, *s.* 2000, *m.*	Hon. David J. N. C., *b.* 1958
1905 M.	*Selby (6th),* Christopher Rolf Thomas Gully, *b.* 1993, *s.* 2001	Hon. (James) Edward H. G. G., *b.* 1945
1805	*Sidmouth (8th),* Jeremy Francis Addington, *b.* 1947, *s.* 2005, *w.*	Hon. Steffan A., *b.* 1966
1940	** *Simon (3rd),* Jan David Simon, *b.* 1940, *s.* 1993, *m.*	None
1960	** *Slim (2nd),* John Douglas Slim, OBE, *b.* 1927, *s.* 1970, *m.*	Hon. Mark W. R. S., *b.* 1960
1954	*Soulbury (4th),* Oliver Peter Ramsbotham, *b.* 1943, *s.* 2010, *m.*	Hon. Edward H. R., *b.* 1966
1776 I.	*Southwell (7th),* Pyers Anthony Joseph Southwell, *b.* 1930, *s.* 1960, *m.*	Hon. Richard A. P. S., *b.* 1956
1942	*Stansgate,* Anthony Neil Wedgwood Benn, *b.* 1925, *s.* 1960, *w.* Disclaimed for life 1963.	Stephen M. W. B., *b.* 1951
1959	*Stuart of Findhorn (3rd),* James Dominic Stuart, *b.* 1948, *s.* 1999, *m.*	Hon. Andrew M. S., *b.* 1957
1957	** *Tenby (3rd),* William Lloyd George, *b.* 1927, *s.* 1983, *m.*	Hon. Timothy H. G. L. G., *b.* 1962
1952	*Thurso (3rd),* John Archibald Sinclair, MP, *b.* 1953, *s.* 1995, *m.*	Hon. James A. R. S., *b.* 1984
1721	*Torrington (11th),* Timothy Howard St George Byng, *b.* 1943, *s.* 1961, *m.*	Colin H. C.-B., *b.* 1960
1936	** *Trenchard (3rd),* Hugh Trenchard, *b.* 1951, *s.* 1987, *m.*	Hon. Alexander T. T., *b.* 1978
1921	** *Ullswater (2nd),* Nicholas James Christopher Lowther, PC, LVO, *b.* 1942, *s.* 1949, *m.*	Hon. Benjamin J. L., *b.* 1975
1622 I.	*Valentia (16th),* Frances William Dighton Annesley, *b.* 1959, *s.* 2005, *m.*	Hon. Peter J. A., *b.* 1967
1952	** *Waverley (3rd),* John Desmond Forbes Anderson, *b.* 1949, *s.* 1990	Hon. Forbes A. R. A., *b.* 1996

1938	*Weir (3rd),* William Kenneth James Weir, *b.* 1933, *s.* 1975, *m.*	Hon. James W. H. W., *b.* 1965
1918	*Wimborne (4th),* Ivor Mervyn Vigors Guest, *b.* 1968, *s.* 1993	Hon. Julien J. G., *b.* 1945
1923	** *Younger of Leckie (5th),* James Edward George Younger, *b.* 1955, *s.* 2003, *m.*	Hon. Alexander W. G. Y., *b.* 1993

BARONS/LORDS

Coronet, Six silver balls

Style, The Rt. Hon. the Lord _
Envelope (formal), The Rt. Hon. Lord _; *(social),* The Lord _. *Letter (formal),* My Lord; *(social),* Dear Lord _. *Spoken,* Lord _.
In the Peerage of Scotland there is no rank of Baron; the equivalent rank is Lord of Parliament and Scottish peers should always be styled 'Lord', never 'Baron'.
Wife's style, The Rt. Hon. the Lady _
Envelope (formal), The Rt. Hon. Lady _; *(social),* The Lady _. *Letter (formal),* My Lady; *(social),* Dear Lady _. *Spoken,* Lady _
Children's style, 'The Hon.' before forename (F_) and surname (S_)
Envelope, The Hon. F_ S_. *Letter,* Dear Mr/Miss/Mrs S_. *Spoken,* Mr/Miss/Mrs S_
In Scotland, the heir apparent to a Lord may be styled 'The Master of _ (title of peer)'

Created	*Title, order of succession, name, etc*	*Heir*
1911	*Aberconway (4th),* (Henry) Charles McLaren, *b.* 1948, *s.* 2003, *m.*	Hon. Charles S. M., *b.* 1984
1873	** *Aberdare (5th),* Alastair John Lyndhurst Bruce, *b.* 1947, *s.* 2005, *m.*	Hon. Hector M. N. B., *b.* 1974
1835	*Abinger (9th),* James Harry Scarlett, *b.* 1959, *s.* 2002, *m.*	Hon. Peter R. S., *b.* 1961
1869	*Acton (4th) and Acton of Bridgnorth (life peerage, 2000),* Richard Gerald Lyon-Dalberg-Acton, *b.* 1941, *s.* 1989, *m.*	Hon. John C. F. H. L.-D.-A., *b.* 1966
1887	** *Addington (6th),* Dominic Bryce Hubbard, *b.* 1963, *s.* 1982	Hon. Michael W. L. H., *b.* 1965
1896	*Aldenham (6th) and Hunsdon of Hunsdon (4th) (1923),* Vicary Tyser Gibbs, *b.* 1948, *s.* 1986, *m.*	Hon. Humphrey W. F. G., *b.* 1989
1962	*Aldington (2nd),* Charles Harold Stuart Low, *b.* 1948, *s.* 2000, *m.*	Hon. Philip T. A. L., *b.* 1990
1945	*Altrincham (3rd),* Anthony Ulick David Dundas Grigg, *b.* 1934, *s.* 2001, *m.*	Hon. (Edward) Sebastian G., *b.* 1965
1929	*Alvingham (2nd),* Maj.-Gen. Robert Guy Eardley Yerburgh, CBE, *b.* 1926, *s.* 1955, *m.*	Capt. Hon. Robert R. G. Y., *b.* 1956
1892	*Amherst of Hackney (5th),* Hugh William Amherst Cecil, *b.* 1968, *s.* 2009, *m.*	Hon. Jack W. A. C., *b.* 2001
1881	** *Ampthill (4th),* Geoffrey Denis Erskine Russell, CBE, PC *b.* 1921, *s.* 1973	Hon. David W. E. R., *b.* 1947
1947	*Amwell (3rd),* Keith Norman Montague, *b.* 1943, *s.* 1990, *m.*	Hon. Ian K. M., *b.* 1973
1863	*Annaly (6th),* Luke Richard White, *b.* 1954, *s.* 1990, *m.*	Hon. Luke H. W., *b.* 1990
1885	*Ashbourne (4th),* Edward Barry Greynville Gibson, *b.* 1933, *s.* 1983, *m.*	Hon. Edward C. d'O. G., *b.* 1967
1835	*Ashburton (7th),* John Francis Harcourt Baring, KG, KCVO, *b.* 1928, *s.* 1991, *m.*	Hon. Mark F. R. B., *b.* 1958
1892	*Ashcombe (4th),* Henry Edward Cubitt, *b.* 1924, *s.* 1962, *m.*	Mark E. C., *b.* 1964
1911	*Ashton of Hyde (4th),* Thomas Henry Ashton, *b.* 1958, *s.* 2008, *m.*	Hon. John E. A., *b.* 1966
1800 I.	*Ashtown (8th),* Roderick Nigel Godolphin Trench, *b.* 1944, *s.* 2010, *m.*	Hon. Timothy R. H. T., *b.* 1968
1956	** *Astor of Hever (3rd),* John Jacob Astor, *b.* 1946, *s.* 1984, *m.*	Hon. Charles G. J. A., *b.* 1990
1789 I.	*Auckland (10th) and Auckland (10th) (1793),* Robert Ian Burnard Eden, *b.* 1962, *s.* 1997, *m.*	Henry V. E., *b.* 1958
1313	*Audley,* Barony in abeyance between three co-heiresses since 1997	
1900	** *Avebury (4th),* Eric Reginald Lubbock, *b.* 1928, *s.* 1971, *m.*	Hon. Lyulph A. J. L., *b.* 1954
1718 I.	*Aylmer (14th),* (Anthony) Julian Aylmer, *b.* 1951, *s.* 2006, *m.*	Hon. Michael H. A., *b.* 1991
1929	*Baden-Powell (3rd),* Robert Crause Baden-Powell, *b.* 1936, *s.* 1962, *m.*	Hon. David M. B.-P., *b.* 1940
1780	*Bagot (10th),* (Charles Hugh) Shaun Bagot, *b.* 1944, *s.* 2001, *m.*	Richard C. V. B., *b.* 1941
1953	*Baillieu (3rd),* James William Latham Baillieu, *b.* 1950, *s.* 1973, *m.*	Hon. Robert L. B., *b.* 1979
1607 S.	*Balfour of Burleigh (8th),* Robert Bruce, *b.* 1927, *s.* 1967, *m.*	Hon. Victoria B., *b.* 1973
1945	*Balfour of Inchrye (2nd),* Ian Balfour, *b.* 1924, *s.* 1988, *w.*	None
1924	*Banbury of Southam (3rd),* Charles William Banbury, *b.* 1953, *s.* 1981, *m.*	None
1698	*Barnard (11th),* Harry John Neville Vane, TD, *b.* 1923, *s.* 1964	Hon. Henry F. C. V., *b.* 1959

1887	*Basing (6th),* Stuart Anthony Whitfield Sclater-Booth, *b.* 1969, *s.* 2007, *m.*	Hon. Luke W. S.-B., *b.* 2000
1917	*Beaverbrook (3rd),* Maxwell William Humphrey Aitken, *b.* 1951, *s.* 1985, *m.*	Hon. Maxwell F. A., *b.* 1977
1647 S.	*Belhaven and Stenton (13th),* Robert Anthony Carmichael Hamilton, *b.* 1927, *s.* 1961, *m.*	Master of Belhaven, *b.* 1953
1848 I.	*Bellew (8th),* Bryan Edward Bellew, *b.* 1943, *s.* 2010, *m.*	Hon. Anthony R. B. B., *b.* 1972
1856	*Belper (5th),* Richard Henry Strutt, *b.* 1941, *s.* 1999, *m.*	Hon. Michael H. S., *b.* 1969
1421	*Berkeley (18th) and Gueterbock (life peerage, 2000),* Anthony Fitzhardinge Gueterbock, OBE, *b.* 1939, *s.* 1992, *m.*	Hon. Thomas F. G., *b.* 1969
1922	*Bethell (5th),* James Nicholas Bethell, *b.* 1967, *s.* 2007, *m.*	Hon. Jacob N. D. B., *b.* 200–
1938	*Bicester (3rd),* Angus Edward Vivian Smith, *b.* 1932, *s.* 1968	Hugh C. V. S., *b.* 1934
1903	*Biddulph (5th),* (Anthony) Nicholas Colin Maitland Biddulph, *b.* 1959, *s.* 1988, *m.*	Hon. Robert J. M. B., *b.* 1994
1938	*Birdwood (3rd),* Mark William Ogilvie Birdwood, *b.* 1938, *s.* 1962, *m.*	None
1958	*Birkett (2nd),* Michael Birkett, *b.* 1929, *s.* 1962, *w.*	Hon. Thomas B., *b.* 1982
1907	*Blyth (5th),* James Audley Ian Blyth, *b.* 1970, *s.* 2009, *m.*	Hon. Hugo A. J. B., *b.* 2006
1797	*Bolton (8th),* Harry Algar Nigel Orde-Powlett, *b.* 1954, *s.* 2001, *m.*	Hon. Thomas O.-P., *b.* 1979
1452 S.	*Borthwick (24th),* John Hugh Borthwick, *b.* 1940, *s.* 1996, *m.*	Hon. James H. A. B. of Glengelt, *b.* 1940
1922	*Borwick (5th),* (Geoffrey Robert) James Borwick, *b.* 1955, *s.* 2007, *m.*	Hon. Edwin D. W. B., *b.* 1984
1761	*Boston (11th),* George William Eustace Boteler Irby, *b.* 1971, *s.* 2007, *m.*	Hon. Thomas W. G. B. I., *b.* 1999
1942	** *Brabazon of Tara (3rd),* Ivon Anthony Moore-Brabazon, *b.* 1946, *s.* 1974, *m.*	Hon. Benjamin R. M.-B., *b.* 1983
1880	*Brabourne (8th),* Norton Louis Philip Knatchbull, *b.* 1947, *s.* 2005, *m.* (*also* Lord Romsey heir to Countess Mountbatten of Burma, *see* that title)	Hon. Nicholas L. C. N. K., *b.* 1981
1925	*Bradbury (3rd),* John Bradbury, *b.* 1940, *s.* 1994, *m.*	Hon. John B., *b.* 1973
1962	*Brain (2nd),* Christopher Langdon Brain, *b.* 1926, *s.* 1966, *m.*	Hon. Michael C. B., *b.* 1928
1938	*Brassey of Apethorpe (3rd),* David Henry Brassey, OBE, *b.* 1932, *s.* 1967, *m.*	Hon. Edward B., *b.* 1964
1788	*Braybrooke (10th),* Robin Henry Charles Neville, *b.* 1932, *s.* 1990, *m.*	Richard R. N., *b.* 1977
1957	** *Bridges (2nd),* Thomas Edward Bridges, GCMG, *b.* 1927, *s.* 1969, *m.*	Hon. Mark T. B., *b.* 1954
1945	*Broadbridge (4th),* Martin Hugh Broadbridge, *b.* 1929, *s.* 2000, *w.*	Hon. Richard J. M. B., *b.* 1959
1933	*Brocket (3rd),* Charles Ronald George Nall-Cain, *b.* 1952, *s.* 1967, *w.*	Hon. Alexander C. C. N.-C., *b.* 1984
1860	** *Brougham and Vaux (5th),* Michael John Brougham, CBE, *b.* 1938, *s.* 1967	Hon. Charles W. B., *b.* 1971
1776	*Brownlow (7th),* Edward John Peregrine Cust, *b.* 1936, *s.* 1978, *m.*	Hon. Peregrine E. Q. C., *b.* 1974
1942	*Bruntisfield (3rd),* Michael John Victor Warrender, *b.* 1949, *s.* 2007, *m.*	Hon. John M. P. C. W., *b.* 1996
1950	*Burden (4th),* Fraser William Elsworth Burden, *b.* 1964, *s.* 2000, *m.*	Hon. Ian S. B., *b.* 1967
1529	*Burgh (8th),* (Alexander) Gregory Disney Leith, *b.* 1958, *s.* 2001, *m.*	Hon. Alexander J. S. L., *b.* 1986
1903	*Burnham (7th),* Harry Frederick Alan Lawson, *b.* 1968, *s.* 2005	None
1897	*Burton (3rd),* Michael Evan Victor Baillie, *b.* 1924, *s.* 1962, *m.*	Hon. Evan M. R. B., *b.* 1949
1643	*Byron (13th),* Robert James Byron, *b.* 1950, *s.* 1989, *m.*	Hon. Charles R. G. B., *b.* 1990
1937	*Cadman (3rd),* John Anthony Cadman, *b.* 1938, *s.* 1966, *m.*	Hon. Nicholas A. J. C., *b.* 1977
1945	*Calverley (3rd),* Charles Rodney Muff, *b.* 1946, *s.* 1971, *m.*	Hon. Jonathan E. M., *b.* 1975
1383	*Camoys (7th),* (Ralph) Thomas Campion George Sherman Stonor, GCVO, PC, *b.* 1940, *s.* 1976, *m.*	Hon. R. William R. T. S., *b.* 1974
1715 I.	*Carbery (11th),* Peter Ralfe Harrington Evans-Freke, *b.* 1920, *s.* 1970, *w.*	Hon. Michael P. E.-F., *b.* 1942
1834 I.	*Carew (7th) and Carew (7th) (1838),* Patrick Thomas Conolly-Carew, *b.* 1938, *s.* 1994, *m.*	Hon. William P. C.-C., *b.* 1973
1916	*Carnock (5th),* Adam Nicolson, *b.* 1957, *s.* 2008, *m.*	Hon. Thomas N., *b.* 1984
1796 I.	*Carrington (6th) and Carrington (6th) (1797) and Carington of Upton (life peerage, 1999),* Peter Alexander Rupert Carington, KG, GCMG, CH, MC, PC, *b.* 1919, *s.* 1938, *w.*	Hon. Rupert F. J. C., *b.* 1948
1812 I.	*Castlemaine (8th),* Roland Thomas John Handcock, MBE, *b.* 1943, *s.* 1973, *m.*	Hon. Ronan M. E. H., *b.* 1989
1936	*Catto (3rd),* Innes Gordon Catto, *b.* 1950, *s.* 2001, *m.*	Hon. Alexander G. C., *b.* 1952
1918	*Cawley (4th),* John Francis Cawley, *b.* 1946, *s.* 2001, *m.*	Hon. William R. H. C., *b.* 1981
1858	*Chesham (7th),* Charles Gray Compton Cavendish, *b.* 1974, *s.* 2009, *m.*	Hon. Oliver N.B.C., *b.* 2007
1945	*Chetwode (2nd),* Philip Chetwode, *b.* 1937, *s.* 1950, *m.*	Hon. Roger C., *b.* 1968
1945	** *Chorley (2nd),* Roger Richard Edward Chorley, *b.* 1930, *s.* 1978, *m.*	Hon. Nicholas R. D. C., *b.* 1966
1858	*Churston (5th),* John Francis Yarde-Buller, *b.* 1934, *s.* 1991, *m.*	Hon. Benjamin F. A. Y.-B., *b.* 1974

1800 I.		*Clanmorris (8th),* Simon John Ward Bingham, *b.* 1937, *s.* 1988, *m.*	Robert D. de B. B., *b.* 1942
1672		*Clifford of Chudleigh (14th),* Thomas Hugh Clifford, *b.* 1948, *s.* 1988, *m.*	Hon. Alexander T. H. C., *b.* 1985
1299		*Clinton (22nd),* Gerard Nevile Mark Fane Trefusis, *b.* 1934, *s.* 1965, *m.*	Hon. Charles P. R. F. T., *b.* 1962
1955		*Clitheroe (2nd),* Ralph John Assheton, *b.* 1929, *s.* 1984, *m.*	Hon. Ralph C. A., *b.* 1962
1919		*Clwyd (4th),* (John) Murray Roberts, *b.* 1971, *s.* 2006	Hon. Jeremy T. R., *b.* 1973
1948		*Clydesmuir (3rd),* David Ronald Colville, *b.* 1949, *s.* 1996, *m.*	Hon. Richard C., *b.* 1980
1960	**	*Cobbold (2nd),* David Antony Fromanteel Lytton Cobbold, *b.* 1937, *s.* 1987, *m.*	Hon. Henry F. L. C., *b.* 1962
1919		*Cochrane of Cults (4th),* (Ralph Henry) Vere Cochrane, *b.* 1926, *s.* 1990, *m.*	Hon. Thomas H. V. C., *b.* 1957
1954		*Coleraine (2nd),* (James) Martin (Bonar) Law, *b.* 1931, *s.* 1980, *m.*	Hon. James P. B. L., *b.* 1975
1873		*Coleridge (5th),* William Duke Coleridge, *b.* 1937, *s.* 1984, *m.*	Hon. James D. C., *b.* 1967
1946		*Colgrain (4th),* Alastair Colin Leckie Campbell, *b.* 1951, *s.* 2008, *m.*	Hon. Thomas C. D. C., *b.* 1984
1917	**	*Colwyn (3rd),* (Ian) Anthony Hamilton-Smith, CBE, *b.* 1942, *s.* 1966, *m.*	Hon. Craig P. H.-S., *b.* 1968
1956		*Colyton (2nd),* Alisdair John Munro Hopkinson, *b.* 1958, *s.* 1996, *m.*	Hon. James P. M. H., *b.* 1983
1841		*Congleton (8th),* Christopher Patrick Parnell, *b.* 1930, *s.* 1967, *m.*	Hon. John P. C. P., *b.* 1959
1927		*Cornwallis (4th),* Fiennes Wykeham Jeremy Cornwallis, *b.* 1946, *s.* 2010, *m.*	Hon. Fiennes A. W. M. C., *b.* 1987
1874		*Cottesloe (5th),*John Tapling Fremantle, *b.* 1927, *s.* 1994, *m.*	Hon. Thomas F. H. F., *b.* 1966
1929		*Craigmyle (4th),* Thomas Columba Shaw, *b.* 1960, *s.* 1998, *m.*	Hon. Alexander F. S., *b.* 1988
1899		*Cranworth (3rd),* Philip Bertram Gurdon, *b.* 1940, *s.* 1964, *m.*	Hon. Sacha W. R. G., *b.* 1970
1959	**	*Crathorne (2nd),* Charles James Dugdale, *b.* 1939, *s.* 1977, *w.*	Hon. Thomas A. J. D., *b.* 1977
1892		*Crawshaw (5th),* David Gerald Brooks, *b.* 1934, *s.* 1997, *m.*	Hon. John P. B., *b.* 1938
1940		*Croft (3rd),* Bernard William Henry Page Croft, *b.* 1949, *s.* 1997, *m.*	None
1797 I.		*Crofton (8th),* Edward Harry Piers Crofton, *b.* 1988, *s.* 2007	Hon. Charles M. G. C., *b.* 1988
1375		*Cromwell (7th),* Godfrey John Bewicke-Copley, *b.* 1960, *s.* 1982, *m.*	Hon. David G. B.-C., *b.* 1997
1947		*Crook (3rd),* Robert Douglas Edwin Crook, *b.* 1955, *s.* 2001, *m.*	Hon. Matthew R. C., *b.* 1990
1920		*Cullen of Ashbourne (3rd),* Edmund Willoughby Marsham Cokayne, *b.* 1916, *s.* 2000, *w.*	(Hon.) John O'B. M. C., *b.*1920
1914		*Cunliffe (3rd),* Roger Cunliffe, *b.* 1932, *s.* 1963, *m.*	Hon. Henry C., *b.* 1962
1332		*Darcy de Knayth (19th),* Caspar David Ingrams, *b.* 1962, *s.* 2008, *m.*	Hon. Thomas R. I., *b.* 1999
1927		*Daresbury (4th),* Peter Gilbert Greenall, *b.* 1953, *s.* 1996, *m.*	Hon. Thomas E. G., *b.* 1984
1924		*Darling (3rd),* (Robert) Julian Henry Darling, *b.* 1944, *s.* 2003, *m.*	Hon. Robert J. C. D., *b.* 1972
1946		*Darwen (3rd),* Roger Michael Davies, *b.* 1938, *s.* 1988, *m.*	Hon. Paul D., *b.* 1962
1932		*Davies (3rd),* David Davies, *b.* 1940, *s.* 1944, *m.*	Hon. David D. D., *b.* 1975
1812 I.		*Decies (7th),* Marcus Hugh Tristram de la Poer Beresford, *b.* 1948, *s.* 1992, *m.*	Hon. Robert M. D. de la P. B., *b.* 1988
1299		*de Clifford (27th),* John Edward Southwell Russell, *b.* 1928, *s.* 1982, *m.*	Hon. William S. R., *b.* 1930
1851		*De Freyne (8th),* Fulke Charles Arthur John French, *b.* 1957, *s.* 2009	Hon. Alexander J. C. F., *b.* 1988
1821		*Delamere (5th),* Hugh George Cholmondeley, *b.* 1934, *s.* 1979, *m.*	Hon. Thomas P. G. C., *b.* 1968
1838	**	*de Mauley (7th),* Rupert Charles Ponsonby, *b.* 1957, *s.* 2002, *m.*	Ashley G. P., *b.* 1959
1937	**	*Denham (2nd),* Bertram Stanley Mitford Bowyer, KBE, PC, *b.* 1927, *s.* 1948, *m.*	Hon. Richard G. G. B., *b.* 1959
1834		*Denman (5th),* Charles Spencer Denman, CBE, MC, TD, *b.* 1916, *s.* 1971, *w.*	Hon. Richard T. S. D., *b.* 1946
1887		*De Ramsey (4th),* John Ailwyn Fellowes, *b.* 1942, *s.* 1993, *m.*	Hon. Freddie J. F., *b.* 1978
1264		*de Ros (28th),* Peter Trevor Maxwell, *b.* 1958, *s.* 1983, *m. Premier Baron of England*	Hon. Finbar J. M., *b.* 1988
1881		*Derwent (5th),* Robin Evelyn Leo Vanden-Bempde-Johnstone, LVO, *b.* 1930, *s.* 1986, *m.*	Hon. Francis P. H. V.-B.-J., *b.* 1965
1831		*de Saumarez (7th),* Eric Douglas Saumarez, *b.* 1956, *s.* 1991, *m.*	Hon. Victor T. S., *b.* 1956
1910		*de Villiers (4th),* Alexander Charles de Villiers, *b.* 1940, *s.* 2001, *m.*	None
1930		*Dickinson (2nd),* Richard Clavering Hyett Dickinson, *b.* 1926, *s.* 1943, *m.*	Hon. Martin H. D., *b.* 1961
1620 I.		*Digby (12th) and Digby (5th) (1765),* Edward Henry Kenelm Digby, KCVO, *b.* 1924, *s.* 1964, *m.*	Hon. Henry N. K. D., *b.* 1954
1615		*Dormer (17th),* Geoffrey Henry Dormer, *b.* 1920, *s.* 1995, *m.*	Hon. William R. D., *b.* 1960
1943		*Dowding (3rd),* Piers Hugh Tremenheere Dowding, *b.* 1948, *s.* 1992	Hon. Mark D. J. D., *b.* 1949
1439		*Dudley (15th),* Jim Anthony Hill Wallace, *b.* 1930, *s.* 2002, *m.*	Hon. Jeremy W. G. W., *b.* 1964
1800 I.		*Dufferin and Clandeboye (11th),* John Francis Blackwood, *b.* 1944, *s.* 1991 (claim to the peerage not yet established), *m.*	Hon. Francis S. B., *b.* 1979
1929		*Dulverton (3rd),* (Gilbert) Michael Hamilton Wills, *b.* 1944, *s.* 1992, *m.*	Hon. Robert A. H. W., *b.* 1983
1800 I.		*Dunalley (7th),* Henry Francis Cornelius Prittie, *b.* 1948, *s.* 1992, *m.*	Hon. Joel H. P., *b.* 1981
1324 I.		*Dunboyne (29th),* John Fitzwalter Butler, *b.* 1951, *s.* 2004, *m.*	Hon. Richard P. T. B., *b.* 1983
1892		*Dunleath (6th),* Brian Henry Mulholland, *b.* 1950, *s.* 1997, *m.*	Hon. Andrew H. M., *b.* 1981
1439 I.		*Dunsany (20th),* Edward John Carlos Plunkett, *b.* 1939, *s.* 1999, *m.*	Hon. Randal P., *b.* 1983

1780	*Dynevor (10th),* Hugo Griffith Uryan Rhys, *b.* 1966, *s.* 2008	Robert D. A. R., *b.* 1963
1963	*Egremont (2nd) and Leconfield (7th) (1859),* John Max Henry Scawen Wyndham, *b.* 1948, *s.* 1972, *m.*	Hon. George R. V. W., *b.* 1983
1643	*Elibank (14th),* Alan D'Ardis Erskine-Murray, *b.* 1923, *s.* 1973, *w.*	Master of Elibank, *b.* 1964
1802	*Ellenborough (8th),* Richard Edward Cecil Law, *b.* 1926, *s.* 1945, *m.*	Maj. Hon. Rupert E. H. L., *b.* 1955
1509 S.	*Elphinstone (19th) and Elphinstone (5th) (1885),* Alexander Mountstuart Elphinstone, *b.* 1980, *s.* 1994, *m.*	Hon. Angus J. E., *b.* 1982
1934	** *Elton (2nd),* Rodney Elton, TD, *b.* 1930, *s.* 1973, *m.*	Hon. Edward P. E., *b.* 1966
1627 S.	*Fairfax of Cameron (14th),* Nicholas John Albert Fairfax, *b.* 1956, *s.* 1964, *m.*	Hon. Edward N. T. F., *b.* 1984
1961	*Fairhaven (3rd),* Ailwyn Henry George Broughton, *b.* 1936, *s.* 1973, *m.*	Maj. Hon. James H. A. B., *b.* 1963
1916	*Faringdon (3rd),* Charles Michael Henderson, KCVO, *b.* 1937, *s.* 1977, *m.*	Hon. James H. H., *b.* 1961
1756 I.	*Farnham (13th),* Simon Kenlis Maxwell, *b.* 1933, *s.* 2001, *m.*	Hon. Robin S. M., *b.* 1965
1856 I.	*Fermoy (6th),* Patrick Maurice Burke Roche, *b.* 1967, *s.* 1984, *m.*	Hon. E. Hugh B. R., *b.* 1972
1826	*Feversham (7th),* Jasper Orlando Slingsby Duncombe, *b.* 1968, *s.* 2009	Hon. Jake B. D., *b.* 1972
1798 I.	*ffrench (8th),* Robuck John Peter Charles Mario ffrench, *b.* 1956, *s.* 1986, *m.*	Hon. John C. M. J. F. ff., *b.* 1928
1909	*Fisher (3rd),* John Vavasseur Fisher, DSC, *b.* 1921, *s.* 1955, *m.*	Hon. Patrick V. F., *b.* 1953
1295	*Fitzwalter (22nd),* Julian Brook Plumptre, *b.* 1952, *s.* 2004, *m.*	Hon. Edward B. P., *b.* 1989
1776	*Foley (8th),* Adrian Gerald Foley, *b.* 1923, *s.* 1927, *m.*	Hon. Thomas H. F., *b.* 1961
1445	*Forbes (22nd),* Nigel Ivan Forbes, KBE, *b.* 1918, *s.* 1953, *m. Premier Lord of Scotland*	Master of Forbes, *b.* 1946
1821	*Forester (9th),* Charles Richard George Weld-Forester, *b.* 1975, *s.* 2004,	Wolstan W. W.-F., *b.* 1941
1922	*Forres (4th),* Alastair Stephen Grant Williamson, *b.* 1946, *s.* 1978, *m.*	Hon. George A. M. W., *b.* 1972
1917	*Forteviot (4th),* John James Evelyn Dewar, *b.* 1938, *s.* 1993, *w.*	Hon. Alexander J. E. D., *b.* 1971
1951	** *Freyberg (3rd),* Valerian Bernard Freyberg, *b.* 1970, *s.* 1993	Hon. Joseph J. F., *b.* 2007
1917	*Gainford (3rd),* Joseph Edward Pease, *b.* 1921, *s.* 1971, *m.*	Hon. George P., *b.* 1926
1818 I.	*Garvagh (5th),* (Alexander Leopold Ivor) George Canning, *b.* 1920, *s.* 1956, *m.*	Hon. Spencer G. S. de R. C., *b.* 1953
1942	** *Geddes (3rd),* Euan Michael Ross Geddes, *b.* 1937, *s.* 1975, *m.*	Hon. James G. N. G., *b.* 1969
1876	*Gerard (5th),* Anthony Robert Hugo Gerard, *b.* 1949, *s.* 1992, *m.*	Hon. Rupert B. C. G., *b.* 1981
1824	*Gifford (6th),* Anthony Maurice Gifford, *b.* 1940, *s.* 1961, *m.*	Hon. Thomas A. G., *b.* 1967
1917	*Gisborough (3rd),* Thomas Richard John Long Chaloner, *b.* 1927, *s.* 1951, *m.*	Hon. T. Peregrine L. C., *b.* 1961
1960	*Gladwyn (2nd),* Miles Alvery Gladwyn Jebb, *b.* 1930, *s.* 1996	None
1899	*Glanusk (5th),* Christopher Russell Bailey, *b.* 1942, *s.* 1997, *m.*	Hon. Charles H. B., *b.* 1976
1918	** *Glenarthur (4th),* Simon Mark Arthur, *b.* 1944, *s.* 1976, *m.*	Hon. Edward A. A., *b.* 1973
1911	*Glenconner (4th),* Cody Charles Edward Tennant, *b.* 1994, *s.* 2010	None
1964	*Glendevon (3rd),* Jonathan Charles Hope, *b.* 1952, *s.* 2009	None
1922	*Glendyne (4th),* John Nivison, *b.* 1960, *s.* 2008	None
1939	** *Glentoran (3rd),* (Thomas) Robin (Valerian) Dixon, CBE, *b.* 1935, *s.* 1995, *m.*	Hon. Daniel G. D., *b.* 1959
1909	*Gorell (5th),* John Picton Gorell Barnes, *b.* 1959, *s.* 2007, *m.*	Hon. Oliver G. B., *b.* 1993
1953	** *Grantchester (3rd),* Christopher John Suenson-Taylor, *b.* 1951, *s.* 1995, *m.*	Hon. Jesse D. S.-T., *b.* 1977
1782	*Grantley (8th),* Richard William Brinsley Norton, *b.* 1956, *s.* 1995	Hon. Francis J. H. N., *b.* 1960
1794 I.	*Graves (10th),* Timothy Evelyn Graves, *b.* 1960, *s.* 2002	None
1445 S.	*Gray (23rd),* Andrew Godfrey Diarmid Stuart Campbell-Gray, *b.* 1964, *s.* 2003, *m.*	Master of Gray, *b.* 1996
1950	*Greenhill (3rd),* Malcolm Greenhill, *b.* 1924, *s.* 1989	None
1927	** *Greenway (4th),* Ambrose Charles Drexel Greenway, *b.* 1941, *s.* 1975, *m.*	Hon. Nigel. P. G., *b.* 1944
1902	*Grenfell (3rd) and Grenfell of Kilvey (life peerage, 2000),* Julian Pascoe Francis St Leger Grenfell, *b.* 1935, *s.* 1976, *m.*	Francis P. J. G., *b.* 1938
1944	*Gretton (4th),* John Lysander Gretton, *b.* 1975, *s.* 1989	Hon. John F. B. G., *b.* 2008
1397	*Grey of Codnor (6th),* Richard Henry Cornwall-Legh, *b.* 1936, *s.* 1996, *m.*	Hon. Richard S. C. C.-L., *b.* 1976
1955	*Gridley (3rd),* Richard David Arnold Gridley, *b.* 1956, *s.* 1996, *m.*	Peter A. C. G., *b.* 1940
1964	*Grimston of Westbury (3rd),* Robert John Sylvester Grimston, *b.* 1951, *s.* 2003, *m.*	Hon. Gerald C. W. G., *b.* 1953
1886	*Grimthorpe (5th),* Edward John Beckett, *b.* 1954, *s.* 2003, *m.*	Hon. Harry M. B., *b.* 1993
1945	*Hacking (3rd),* Douglas David Hacking, *b.* 1938, *s.* 1971, *m.*	Hon. Douglas F. H., *b.* 1968
1950	*Haden-Guest (5th),* Christopher Haden-Guest, *b.* 1948, *s.* 1996, *m.*	Hon. Nicholas H.-G., *b.* 1951

1886	*Hamilton of Dalzell (5th)*, Gavin Goulburn Hamilton, *b.* 1968, *s.* 2006, *m.*	Hon. Robert P. H., *b.* 1971
1874	*Hampton (7th)*, John Humphrey Arnott Pakington, *b.* 1964, *s.* 2003, *m.*	Hon. Charles R. C. P., *b.* 2005
1939	*Hankey (3rd)*, Donald Robin Alers Hankey, *b.* 1938, *s.* 1996, *m.*	Hon. Alexander M. A. H., *b.* 1947
1958	*Harding of Petherton (2nd)*, John Charles Harding, *b.* 1928, *s.* 1989, *m.*	Hon. William A. J. H., *b.* 1969
1910	*Hardinge of Penshurst (4th)*, Julian Alexander Hardinge, *b.* 1945, *s.* 1997	Hon. Hugh F. H., *b.* 1948
1876	*Harlech (6th)*, Francis David Ormsby-Gore, *b.* 1954, *s.* 1985, *m.*	Hon. Jasset D. C. O.-G., *b.* 1986
1939	*Harmsworth (3rd)*, Thomas Harold Raymond Harmsworth, *b.* 1939, *s.* 1990, *m.*	Hon. Dominic M. E. H., *b.* 1973
1815	*Harris (8th)*, Anthony Harris, *b.* 1942, *s.* 1996, *m.*	Rear-Adm. Michael G. T. H., *b.* 1941
1954	*Harvey of Tasburgh (3rd)*, Charles John Giuseppe Harvey, *b.* 1951, *s.* 2010, *m.*	Hon. John H., *b.* 1993
1295	*Hastings (23rd)*, Delaval Thomas Harold Astley, *b.* 1960, *s.* 2007, *m.*	Hon. Jacob A. A., *b.* 1991
1835	*Hatherton (8th)*, Edward Charles Littleton, *b.* 1950, *s.* 1985, *m.*	Hon. Thomas E. L., *b.* 1977
1776	*Hawke (12th)*, William Martin Theodore Hawke, *b.* 1995, *s.* 2010	None
1927	*Hayter (4th)*, George William Michael Chubb, *b.* 1943, *s.* 2003, *m.*	Hon. Thomas F. F. C., *b.*1986
1945	*Hazlerigg (3rd)*, Arthur Grey Hazlerigg, *b.* 1951, *s.* 2002, *m.*	Hon. Arthur W. G. H. *b.* 1987
1943	*Hemingford (3rd)*, (Dennis) Nicholas Herbert, *b.* 1934, *s.* 1982, *m.*	Hon. Christopher D. C. H., *b.* 1973
1906	*Hemphill (5th)*, Peter Patrick Fitzroy Martyn Martyn-Hemphill, *b.* 1928, *s.* 1957, *m.*	Hon. Charles A. M. M.-H., *b.* 1954
1799 I.	** *Henley (8th) and Northington (6th) (1885)*, Oliver Michael Robert Eden, *b.* 1953, *s.* 1977, *m.*	Hon. John W. O. E., *b.* 1988
1800 I.	*Henniker (9th) and Hartismere (6th) (1866)*, Mark Ian Philip Chandos Henniker-Major, *b.* 1947, *s.* 2004, *m.*	Hon. Edward G. M. H.-M., *b.* 1985
1461	*Herbert (19th)*, David John Seyfried Herbert, *b.* 1952, *s.* 2002, *m.*	Hon. Oliver R. S. H., *b.* 1976
1935	*Hesketh (3rd)*, Thomas Alexander Fermor-Hesketh, KBE, PC, *b.* 1950, *s.* 1955, *m.*	Hon. Frederick H. F.-H., *b.* 1988
1828	*Heytesbury (7th)*, James William Holmes à Court, *b.* 1967, *s.* 2004, *m.*	Peter M. H.. H. à. C., *b.* 1968
1886	*Hindlip (6th)*, Charles Henry Allsopp, *b.* 1940, *s.* 1993, *m.*	Hon. Henry W. A., *b.* 1973
1950	*Hives (3rd)*, Matthew Peter Hives, *b.* 1971, *s.* 1997	Hon. Michael B. H., *b.* 1926
1912	*Hollenden (4th)*, Ian Hampden Hope-Morley, *b.* 1946, *s.* 1999, *m.*	Hon. Edward H.-M., *b.* 1981
1897	*Holm Patrick (4th)*, Hans James David Hamilton, *b.* 1955, *s.* 1991, *m.*	Hon. Ion H. J. H., *b.* 1956
1797 I.	*Hotham (8th)*, Henry Durand Hotham, *b.* 1940, *s.* 1967, *m.*	Hon. William B. H., *b.* 1972
1881	*Hothfield (6th)*, Anthony Charles Sackville Tufton, *b.* 1939, *s.* 1991, *m.*	Hon. William S. T., *b.* 1977
1930	*Howard of Penrith (3rd)*, Philip Esme Howard, *b.* 1945, *s.* 1999, *m.*	Hon. Thomas Philip H., *b.* 1974
1960	*Howick of Glendale (2nd)*, Charles Evelyn Baring, *b.* 1937, *s.* 1973, *m.*	Hon. David E. C. B., *b.* 1975
1796 I.	*Huntingfield (7th)*, Joshua Charles Vanneck, *b.* 1954, *s.* 1994, *m.*	Hon. Gerard C. A. V., *b.* 1985
1866	** *Hylton (5th)*, Raymond Hervey Jolliffe, *b.* 1932, *s.* 1967, *m.*	Hon. William H. M. J., *b.* 1967
1933	*Iliffe (3rd)*, Robert Peter Richard Iliffe, *b.* 1944, *s.* 1996, *m.*	Hon. Edward R. I., *b.* 1968
1543 I.	*Inchiquin (18th)*, Conor Myles John O'Brien, *b.* 1943, *s.* 1982, *m.*	Conor J. A. O'B., *b.* 1952
1962	*Inchyra (2nd)*, Robert Charles Reneke Hoyer Millar, *b.* 1935, *s.* 1989, *m.*	Hon. C. James C. H. M., *b.* 1962
1964	** *Inglewood (2nd)*, (William) Richard Fletcher-Vane, *b.* 1951, *s.* 1989, *m.*	Hon. Henry W. F. F.-V., *b.* 1990
1919	*Inverforth (4th)*, Andrew Peter Weir, *b.* 1966, *s.* 1982	Hon. Benjamin A. W., *b.* 1997
1941	*Ironside (2nd)*, Edmund Oslac Ironside, *b.* 1924, *s.* 1959, *m.*	Hon. Charles E. G. I., *b.* 1956
1952	*Jeffreys (3rd)*, Christopher Henry Mark Jeffreys, *b.* 1957, *s.* 1986, *m.*	Hon. Arthur M. H. J., *b.* 1989
1906	*Joicey (5th)*, James Michael Joicey, *b.* 1953, *s.* 1993, *m.*	Hon. William J. J., *b.* 1990
1937	*Kenilworth (4th)*, (John) Randle Siddeley, *b.* 1954, *s.* 1981, *m.*	Hon. William R. J. S., *b.* 1992
1935	*Kennet (3rd)*, William Aldus Thoby Young, *b.* 1957, *s.* 2009, *m.*	Hon. Archibald W. K. Y., *b.* 1992
1776 I.	*Kensington (8th) and Kensington (5th) (1886)*, Hugh Ivor Edwardes, *b.* 1933, *s.* 1981, *m.*	Hon. W. Owen A. E., *b.* 1964
1951	*Kenswood (2nd)*, John Michael Howard Whitfield, *b.* 1930, *s.* 1963, *m.*	Hon. Michael C. W., *b.* 1955
1788	*Kenyon (6th)*, Lloyd Tyrell-Kenyon, *b.* 1947, *s.* 1993, *m.*	Hon. Lloyd N. T.-K., *b.* 1972
1947	*Kershaw (4th)*, Edward John Kershaw, *b.* 1936, *s.* 1962, *m.*	Hon. John C. E. K., *b.* 1971
1943	*Keyes (3rd)*, Charles William Packe Keyes, *b.* 1951, *s.* 2005, *m.*	Hon. (Leopold R.) J. K., *b.* 1956
1909	*Kilbracken (4th)*, Christopher John Godley, *b.* 1945, *s.* 2006, *m.*	Hon. James J. G., *b.* 1972
1900	*Killanin (4th)*, (George) Redmond Fitzpatrick Morris, *b.* 1947, *s.* 1999, *m.*	Hon. Luke M. G. M., *b.* 1975
1943	*Killearn (3rd)*, Victor Miles George Aldous Lampson, *b.* 1941, *s.* 1996, *m.*	Hon. Miles H. M. L., *b.* 1977
1789 I.	*Kilmaine (7th)*, John David Henry Browne, *b.* 1948, *s.* 1978, *m.*	Hon. John F. S. B., *b.* 1983

1831	*Kilmarnock (8th),* Dr Robin Jordan Boyd, *b.* 1941, *s.* 2009, *m.*	Hon. Simon J. B., *b.* 1978
1941	*Kindersley (3rd),* Robert Hugh Molesworth Kindersley, *b.* 1929, *s.* 1976, *m.*	Hon. Rupert J. M. K., *b.* 1955
1223 I.	*Kingsale (36th),* Nevinson Mark de Courcy, *b.* 1958, *s.* 2005, *m., Premier Baron of Ireland*	Joseph K. C. de C., *b.* 1955
1902	*Kinross (5th),* Christopher Patrick Balfour, *b.* 1949, *s.* 1985, *m.*	Hon. Alan I. B., *b.* 1978
1951	*Kirkwood (3rd),* David Harvie Kirkwood, PHD, *b.* 1931, *s.* 1970, *m.*	Hon. James S. K., *b.* 1937
1800 I.	*Langford (9th),* Col. Geoffrey Alexander Rowley-Conwy, OBE, *b.* 1912, *s.* 1953, *m.*	Hon. Owain G. R.-C., *b.* 1958
1942	*Latham (2nd),* Dominic Charles Latham, *b.* 1954, *s.* 1970	Anthony M. L., *b.* 1954
1431	*Latymer (9th),* Crispin James Alan Nevill Money-Coutts, *b.* 1955, *s.* 2003, *m.*	Hon. Drummond W. T. M.-C., *b.* 1986
1869	*Lawrence (5th),* David John Downer Lawrence, *b.* 1937, *s.* 1968	None
1947	*Layton (3rd),* Geoffrey Michael Layton, *b.* 1947, *s.* 1989, *m.*	Jonathan F., *b.* 1942
1839	*Leigh (6th),* Christopher Dudley Piers Leigh, *b.* 1960, *s.* 2003, *m.*	Hon. Rupert D. L., *b.* 1994
1962	*Leighton of St Mellons (3rd),* Robert William Henry Leighton Seager, *b.* 1955, *s.* 1998	Hon. Simon J. L. S., *b.* 1957
1797	*Lilford (8th),* Mark Vernon Powys, *b.* 1975, *s.* 2005	Robert C. L. P., *b.* 1930
1945	*Lindsay of Birker (3rd),* James Francis Lindsay, *b.* 1945, *s.* 1994, *m.*	Alexander S. L., *b.* 1940
1758 I.	*Lisle (9th),* (John) Nicholas Geoffrey Lysaght, *b.* 1960, *s.* 2003	Hon. David J. L., *b.* 1963
1850	*Londesborough (9th),* Richard John Denison, *b.* 1959, *s.* 1968, *m.*	Hon. James F. D., *b.* 1990
1541 I.	*Louth (16th),* Otway Michael James Oliver Plunkett, *b.* 1929, *s.* 1950, *m.*	Hon. Jonathan O. P., *b.* 1952
1458 S.	*Lovat (16th) and Lovat (5th) (1837),* Simon Fraser, *b.* 1977, *s.* 1995	Hon. Jack F., *b.* 1984
1946	*Lucas of Chilworth (3rd),* Simon William Lucas, *b.* 1957, *s.* 2001, *m.*	Hon. John R. M. L., *b.* 1995
1663	** *Lucas (11th) and Dingwall (14th) (S. 1609),* Ralph Matthew Palmer, *b.* 1951, *s.* 1991	Hon. Lewis E. P., *b.* 1987
1929	** *Luke (3rd),* Arthur Charles St John Lawson-Johnston, *b.* 1933, *s.* 1996, *m.*	Hon. Ian J. St J. L.-J., *b.* 1963
1914	** *Lyell (3rd),* Charles Lyell, *b.* 1939, *s.* 1943	None
1859	*Lyveden (7th),* Jack Leslie Vernon, *b.* 1938, *s.* 1999, *m.*	Hon. Colin R. V., *b.* 1967
1959	*MacAndrew (3rd),* Christopher Anthony Colin MacAndrew, *b.* 1945, *s.* 1989, *m.*	Hon. Oliver C. J. M., *b.* 1983
1776 I.	*Macdonald (8th),* Godfrey James Macdonald of Macdonald, *b.* 1947, *s.* 1970, *m.*	Hon. Godfrey E. H. T. M., *b.* 1982
1937	*McGowan (4th),* Harry John Charles McGowan, *b.* 1971, *s.* 2003, *m.*	Hon. Dominic J. W. McG., *b.* 1951
1922	*Maclay (3rd),* Joseph Paton Maclay, *b.* 1942, *s.* 1969, *m.*	Hon. Joseph P. M., *b.* 1977
1955	*McNair (3rd),* Duncan James McNair, *b.* 1947, *s.* 1989, *m.*	Hon. William S. A. M., *b.* 1958
1951	*Macpherson of Drumochter (3rd),* James Anthony Macpherson, *b.* 1978, *s.* 2008	None
1937	** *Mancroft (3rd),* Benjamin Lloyd Stormont Mancroft, *b.* 1957, *s.* 1987, *m.*	Hon. Arthur L. S. M., *b.* 1995
1807	*Manners (6th),* John Hugh Robert Manners, *b.* 1956, *s.* 2008	Hon. Richard N. M., *b.* 1924
1922	*Manton (4th),* Miles Ronald Marcus Watson, *b.* 1958, *s.* 2003, *m.*	Hon. Thomas N. C. D. W., *b.* 1985
1908	*Marchamley (4th),* William Francis Whiteley, *b.* 1968, *s.* 1994	None
1964	*Margadale (3rd),* Alastair John Morrison, *b.* 1958, *s.* 2003, *m.*	Hon. Declan J. M., *b.* 1993
1961	*Marks of Broughton (3rd),* Simon Richard Marks, *b.* 1950, *s.* 1998, *m.*	Hon. Michael M., *b.* 1989
1964	*Martonmere (2nd),* John Stephen Robinson, *b.* 1963, *s.* 1989	Hon. James I. R., *b.* 2003
1776 I.	*Massy (10th),* David Hamon Somerset Massy, *b.* 1947, *s.* 1995	Hon. John H. M., *b.* 1950
1935	*May (4th),* Jasper Bertram St John May, *b.* 1965, *s.* 2006	None
1928	*Melchett (4th),* Peter Robert Henry Mond, *b.* 1948, *s.* 1973	None
1925	*Merrivale (4th),* Derek John Philip Duke, *b.* 1948, *s.* 2007, *m.*	Hon. Thomas D., *b.* 1980
1911	*Merthyr,* Trevor Oswin Lewis, CBE, *b.* 1935, *s.* 1977, *m.* Disclaimed for life 1977	David T. L., *b.* 1977
1919	*Meston (3rd),* James Meston, *b.* 1950, *s.* 1984, *m.*	Hon. Thomas J. D. M., *b.* 1977
1838	** *Methuen (7th),* Robert Alexander Holt Methuen, *b.* 1931, *s.* 1994, *m.*	James P. A. M.-C., *b.* 1952
1711	*Middleton (12th),* (Digby) Michael Godfrey John Willoughby, MC, *b.* 1921, *s.* 1970	Hon. Michael C. J. W., *b.* 1948
1939	*Milford (4th),* Guy Wogan Philipps, *b.* 1961, *s.* 1999, *m.*	Hon. Archie S. P., *b.* 1997
1933	*Milne (3rd),* George Alexander Milne, *b.* 1941, *s.* 2005	Hon. Iain C. L. M., *b.* 1949
1951	*Milner of Leeds (3rd),* Richard James Milner, *b.* 1959, *s.* 2003, *m.*	None
1947	*Milverton (2nd), Revd* Fraser Arthur Richard Richards, *b.* 1930, *s.* 1978, *m.*	Hon. Michael H. R., *b.* 1936
1873	*Moncreiff (6th),* Rhoderick Harry Wellwood Moncreiff, *b.* 1954, *s.* 2002, *m.*	Hon. Harry J. W. M., *b.* 1986

1884	*Monk Bretton (3rd),* John Charles Dodson, *b.* 1924, *s.* 1933, *m.*	Hon. Christopher M. D., *b.* 1958
1885	*Monkswell (5th),* Gerard Collier, *b.* 1947, *s.* 1984, *m.*	Hon. James A. C., *b.* 1977
1728	** *Monson (11th),* John Monson, *b.* 1932, *s.* 1958, *m.*	Hon. Nicholas J. M., *b.* 1955
1885	** *Montagu of Beaulieu (3rd),* Edward John Barrington Douglas-Scott-Montagu, *b.* 1926, *s.* 1929, *m.*	Hon. Ralph D.-S.-M., *b.* 1961
1839	*Monteagle of Brandon (6th),* Gerald Spring Rice, *b.* 1926, *s.* 1946, *m.*	Hon. Charles J. S. R., *b.* 1953
1943	** *Moran (2nd),* (Richard) John (McMoran) Wilson, KCMG, *b.* 1924, *s.* 1977, *m.*	Hon. James M. W., *b.* 1952
1918	*Morris (3rd),* Michael David Morris, *b.* 1937, *s.* 1975, *m.*	Hon. Thomas A. S. M., *b.* 1982
1950	*Morris of Kenwood (3rd),* Jonathan David Morris, *b.* 1968, *s.* 2004, *m.*	Hon. Benjamin J. M., *b.* 1998
1831	*Mostyn (6th),* Llewellyn Roger Lloyd-Mostyn, *b.* 1948, *s.* 2000, *m.*	Hon. Gregory P. R. L.-M., *b.* 1984
1933	*Mottistone (4th),* David Peter Seely, CBE, *b.* 1920, *s.* 1966, *m.*	Hon. Peter J. P. S., *b.* 1949
1945	*Mountevans (3rd),* Edward Patrick Broke Evans, *b.* 1943, *s.* 1974, *m.*	Hon. Jeffrey de C. R. E., *b.* 1948
1283	*Mowbray (27th), Segrave (28th) (1295) and Stourton (24th) (1448),* Edward William Stephen Stourton, *b.* 1953, *s.* 2006, *m.*	Hon. James C. P. S., *b.* 1991
1932	*Moyne (3rd),* Jonathan Bryan Guinness, *b.* 1930, *s.* 1992, *m.*	Hon. Jasper J. R. G., *b.* 1954
1929	** *Moynihan (4th),* Colin Berkeley Moynihan, *b.* 1955, *s.* 1997, *m.*	Hon. Nicholas E. B. M., *b.* 1994
1781 I.	*Muskerry (9th),* Robert Fitzmaurice Deane, *b.* 1948, *s.* 1988, *m.*	Hon. Jonathan F. D., *b.* 1986
1627 S.	*Napier (14th) and Ettrick (5th) (1872),* Francis Nigel Napier, KCVO, *b.* 1930, *s.* 1954, *m.*	Master of Napier, *b.* 1962
1868	*Napier of Magdala (6th),* Robert Alan Napier, *b.* 1940, *s.* 1987, *m.*	Hon. James R. N., *b.* 1966
1940	*Nathan (3rd),* Rupert Harry Bernard Nathan, *b.* 1957, *s.* 2007, *m.*	None
1960	*Nelson of Stafford (4th),* Alistair William Henry Nelson, *b.* 1973, *s.* 2006	Hon. James J. N., *b.* 1947
1959	*Netherthorpe (3rd),* James Frederick Turner, *b.* 1964, *s.* 1982, *m.*	Hon. Andrew J. E. T., *b.* 1993
1946	*Newall (2nd),* Francis Storer Eaton Newall, *b.* 1930, *s.* 1963, *m.*	Hon. Richard H. E. N., *b.* 1961
1776 I.	*Newborough (8th),* Robert Vaughan Wynn, *b.* 1949, *s.* 1998, *m.*	Hon. Charles H. R. W., *b.* 1923
1892	*Newton (5th),* Richard Thomas Legh, *b.* 1950, *s.* 1992, *m.*	Hon. Piers R. L., *b.* 1979
1930	*Noel-Buxton (3rd),* Martin Connal Noel-Buxton, *b.* 1940, *s.* 1980, *m.*	Hon. Charles C. N.-B., *b.* 1975
1957	*Norrie (2nd),* (George) Willoughby Moke Norrie, *b.* 1936, *s.* 1977, *m.*	Hon. Mark W. J. N., *b.* 1972
1884	** *Northbourne (5th),* Christopher George Walter James, *b.* 1926, *s.* 1982, *m.*	Hon. Charles W. H. J., *b.* 1960
1866	** *Northbrook (6th),* Francis Thomas Baring, *b.* 1954, *s.* 1990, *m.*	To the Baronetcy, Peter B. *b.* 1939
1878	*Norton (8th),* James Nigel Arden Adderley, *b.* 1947, *s.* 1993, *m.*	Hon. Edward J. A. A., *b.* 1982
1906	*Nunburnholme (6th),* Stephen Charles Wilson, *b.* 1973, *s.* 2000	Hon. David M. W., *b.* 1954
1950	*Ogmore (3rd),* Morgan Rees-Williams, *b.* 1937, *s.* 2004, *m.*	Hon. Tudor D. R.-W., *b.* 1991
1870	*O'Hagan (4th),* Charles Towneley Strachey, *b.* 1945, *s.* 1961	Hon. Richard T. S., *b.* 1950
1868	*O'Neill (4th),* Raymond Arthur Clanaboy O'Neill, KCVO, TD, *b.* 1933, *s.* 1944, *m.*	Hon. Shane S. C. O'N., *b.* 1965
1836 I.	*Oranmore and Browne (5th) and Mereworth (3rd) (1926),* Dominick Geoffrey Thomas Browne, *b.* 1929, *s.* 2002	Hon. Martin M. D. B., *b.* 1931
1933	** *Palmer (4th),* Adrian Bailie Nottage Palmer, *b.* 1951, *s.* 1990, *m.*	Hon. Hugo B. R. P., *b.* 1980
1914	*Parmoor (5th),* Michael Leonard Seddon Cripps, *b.* 1942, *s.* 2008, *m.*	Hon. Henry W. A. C., *b.* 1976
1937	*Pender (3rd),* John Willoughby Denison-Pender, *b.* 1933, *s.* 1965, *m.*	Hon. Henry J. R. D.-P., *b.* 1968
1866	*Penrhyn (7th),* Simon Douglas-Pennant, *b.* 1938, *s.* 2003, *m.*	Hon. Edward S. D.-P., *b.* 1966
1603	*Petre (18th),* John Patrick Lionel Petre, *b.* 1942, *s.* 1989, *m.*	Hon. Dominic W. P., *b.* 1966
1918	*Phillimore (5th),* Francis Stephen Phillimore, *b.* 1944, *s.* 1994, *m.*	Hon. Tristan A. S. P., *b.* 1977
1945	*Piercy (3rd),* James William Piercy, *b.* 1946, *s.* 1981	Hon. Mark E. P. P., *b.* 1953
1827	*Plunket (8th),* Robin Rathmore Plunket, *b.* 1925, *s.* 1975, *m.*	Hon. Shaun A. F. S. P., *b.* 1931
1831	*Poltimore (7th),* Mark Coplestone Bampfylde, *b.* 1957, *s.* 1978, *m.*	Hon. Henry A. W. B., *b.* 1985
1690 S.	*Polwarth (11th),* Andrew Walter Hepburne-Scott, *b.* 1947, *s.* 2005, *m.*	Master of Polwarth, *b.* 1973
1930	*Ponsonby of Shulbrede (4th) and Ponsonby of Roehampton (life peerage, 2000),* Frederick Matthew Thomas Ponsonby, *b.* 1958, *s.* 1990	None
1958	*Poole (2nd),* David Charles Poole, *b.* 1945, *s.* 1993, *m.*	Hon. Oliver J. P., *b.* 1972
1852	*Raglan (6th),* Geoffrey Somerset, *b.* 1932, *s.* 2010, *m.*	Hon. Arthur G. S., *b.* 1960
1932	*Rankeillour (5th),* Michael Richard Hope, *b.* 1940, *s.* 2005, *m.*	James F. H., *b.* 1968
1953	*Rathcavan (3rd),* Hugh Detmar Torrens O'Neill, *b.* 1939, *s.* 1994, *m.*	Hon. François H. N. O'N., *b.* 1984
1916	*Rathcreedan (3rd),* Christopher John Norton, *b.* 1949, *s.* 1990, *m.*	Hon. Adam G. N., *b.* 1952
1868 I.	*Rathdonnell (5th),* Thomas Benjamin McClintock-Bunbury, *b.* 1938, *s.* 1959, *m.*	Hon. William L. M.-B., *b.* 1966
1911	*Ravensdale (3rd),* Nicholas Mosley, MC, *b.* 1923, *s.* 1966, *m.*	Hon. Daniel N. M., *b.* 1982

1821	*Ravensworth (9th),* Thomas Arthur Hamish Liddell, *b.* 1954, *s.* 2004, *m.*	Hon. Henry A. T. L., *b.* 1987
1821	*Rayleigh (6th),* John Gerald Strutt, *b.* 1960, *s.* 1988, *m.*	Hon. John F. S., *b.* 1993
1937	** *Rea (3rd),* John Nicolas Rea, MD, *b.* 1928, *s.* 1981, *m.*	Hon. Matthew J. R., *b.* 1956
1628 S.	** *Reay (14th),* Hugh William Mackay, *b.* 1937, *s.* 1963, *m.*	Master of Reay, *b.* 1965
1902	*Redesdale (6th) and Mitford (life peerage 2000),* Rupert Bertram Mitford, *b.* 1967, *s.* 1991, *m.*	Hon. Bertram D. M., *b.* 2000
1940	*Reith,* Christopher John Reith, *b.* 1928, *s.* 1971, *m.* Disclaimed for life 1972.	Hon. James H. J. R., *b.* 1971
1928	*Remnant (3rd),* James Wogan Remnant, CVO, *b.* 1930, *s.* 1967, *m.*	Hon. Philip J. R., *b.* 1954
1806 I.	*Rendlesham (9th),* Charles William Brooke Thellusson, *b.* 1954, *s.* 1999, *m.*	Hon. Peter R. T., *b.* 1920
1933	*Rennell (4th),* James Roderick David Tremayne Rodd, *b.* 1978, *s.* 2006	None
1964	*Renwick (2nd),* Harry Andrew Renwick, *b.* 1935, *s.* 1973, *m.*	Hon. Robert J. R., *b.* 1966
1885	*Revelstoke (6th),* James Cecil Baring, *b.* 1938, *s.* 2003, *m.*	Hon. Alexander R. B., *b.* 1970
1905	*Ritchie of Dundee (6th),* Charles Rupert Rendall Ritchie, *b.* 1958, *s.* 2008, *m.*	Hon. Sebastian R., *b.* 2004
1935	*Riverdale (3rd),* Anthony Robert Balfour, *b.* 1960, *s.* 1998	Arthur M. B., *b.* 1938
1961	*Robertson of Oakridge (3rd),* William Brian Elworthy Robertson, *b.* 1975, *s.* 2009, *m.*	None
1938	*Roborough (3rd),* Henry Massey Lopes, *b.* 1940, *s.* 1992, *m.*	Hon. Massey J. H. L., *b.* 1969
1931	*Rochester (2nd),* Foster Charles Lowry Lamb, *b.* 1916, *s.* 1955, *w.*	Hon. David C. L., *b.* 1944
1934	*Rockley (3rd),* James Hugh Cecil, *b.* 1934, *s.* 1976, *m.*	Hon. Anthony R. C., *b.* 1961
1782	*Rodney (10th),* George Brydges Rodney, *b.* 1953, *s.* 1992, *m.*	Hon. John G. B. R., *b.* 1999
1651 S.	*Rollo (14th) and Dunning (5th) (1869),* David Eric Howard Rollo, *b.* 1943, *s.* 1997, *m.*	Master of Rollo, *b.* 1972
1959	*Rootes (3rd),* Nicholas Geoffrey Rootes, *b.* 1951, *s.* 1992, *m.*	William B. R., *b.* 1944
1796 I.	*Rossmore (7th) and Rossmore (6th) (1838),* William Warner Westenra, *b.* 1931, *s.* 1958, *m.*	Hon. Benedict W. W., *b.* 1983
1939	** *Rotherwick (3rd),* (Herbert) Robin Cayzer, *b.* 1954, *s.* 1996, *m.*	Hon. H. Robin C., *b.* 1989
1885	*Rothschild (4th),* (Nathaniel Charles) Jacob Rothschild, OM, GBE, *b.* 1936, *s.* 1990, *m.*	Hon. Nathaniel P. V. J. R., *b.* 1971
1911	*Rowallan (4th),* John Polson Cameron Corbett, *b.* 1947, *s.* 1993	Hon. Jason W. P. C. C., *b.* 1972
1947	*Rugby (3rd),* Robert Charles Maffey, *b.* 1951, *s.* 1990, *m.*	Hon. Timothy J. H. M., *b.* 1975
1919	*Russell of Liverpool (3rd),* Simon Gordon Jared Russell, *b.* 1952, *s.* 1981, *m.*	Hon. Edward C. S. R., *b.* 1985
1876	*Sackville (7th),* Robert Bertrand Sackville-West, *b.* 1958, *s.* 2004, *m.*	Hon. Arthur S-W., *b.* 2000
1964	*St Helens (2nd),* Richard Francis Hughes-Young, *b.* 1945, *s.* 1980, *m.*	Hon. Henry T. H.-Y., *b.* 1986
1559	** *St John of Bletso (21st),* Anthony Tudor St John, *b.* 1957, *s.* 1978, *m.*	Hon. Oliver B. St J., *b.* 1995
1887	*St Levan (4th),* John Francis Arthur St Aubyn, DSC, *b.* 1919, *s.* 1978, *w.*	James P. S. St. A., *b.* 1950
1885	*St Oswald (6th),* Charles Rowland Andrew Winn, *b.* 1959, *s.* 1999, *m.*	Hon. Rowland C. S. H. W., *b.* 1986
1960	*Sanderson of Ayot (2nd),* Alan Lindsay Sanderson, *b.* 1931, *s.* 1971, *m.* Disclaimed for life 1971.	Hon. Michael S., *b.* 1959
1945	*Sandford (3rd),* James John Mowbray Edmondson, *b.* 1949, *s.* 2009, *m.*	Hon. Devon J. E., *b.* 1986
1871	*Sandhurst (6th),* Guy Rees John Mansfield, *b.* 1949, *s.* 2002, *m.*	Hon. Edward J. M., *b.* 1982
1802	*Sandys (7th),* Richard Michael Oliver Hill, *b.* 1931, *s.* 1961, *m.*	The Marquess of Downshire
1888	*Savile (4th),* John Anthony Thornhill Lumley-Savile, *b.* 1947, *s.* 2008, *m.*	Hon. James G. A. L-S., *b.* 1975
1447	*Saye and Sele (21st),* Nathaniel Thomas Allen Fiennes, *b.* 1920, *s.* 1968, *m.*	Hon. Martin G. F., *b.* 1961
1826	*Seaford (6th),* Colin Humphrey Felton Ellis, *b.* 1946, *s.* 1999, *m.*	Hon. Benjamin F. T. E., *b.* 1976
1932	** *Selsdon (3rd),* Malcolm McEacharn Mitchell-Thomson, *b.* 1937, *s.* 1963, *m.*	Hon. Callum M. M. M.-T., *b.* 1969
1489 S.	*Sempill (21st),* James William Stuart Whitemore Sempill, *b.* 1949, *s.* 1995, *m.*	Master of Sempill, *b.* 1979
1916	*Shaughnessy (5th),* Charles George Patrick Shaughnessy, *b.* 1955, *s.* 2007, *m.*	David J. S., *b.* 1957
1946	*Shepherd (3rd),* Graham George Shepherd, *b.* 1949, *s.* 2001, *m.*	Hon. Patrick M. S., *b.* 19–
1964	*Sherfield (3rd),* Dwight William Makins, *b.* 1951, *s.* 2006, *m.*	None
1902	*Shuttleworth (5th),* Charles Geoffrey Nicholas Kay-Shuttleworth, *b.* 1948, *s.* 1975, *m.*	Hon. Thomas E. K.-S., *b.* 1976
1950	*Silkin (3rd),* Christopher Lewis Silkin, *b.* 1947, *s.* 2001. Disclaimed for life 2002.	Rory L. S., *b.* 1954
1963	*Silsoe (3rd),* Simon Rupert Trustram Eve *b.* 1966, *s.* 2005	Hon. Peter N. T. E., *b.* 1930
1947	*Simon of Wythenshawe (3rd),* Matthew Simon, *b.* 1955, *s.* 2002	Martin S., *b.* 1944
1449 S.	*Sinclair (18th),* Matthew Murray Kennedy St Clair *b.* 1968, *s.* 2004, *m.*	Hugh A. C. St C., *b.* 1957

1957	*Sinclair of Cleeve (3rd),* John Lawrence Robert Sinclair, *b.* 1953, *s.* 1985	None
1919	*Sinha (6th),* Arup Kumar Sinha, *b.* 1966, *s.* 1999	Hon. Dilip K. S., *b.* 1967
1828	** *Skelmersdale (7th),* Roger Bootle-Wilbraham, *b.* 1945, *s.* 1973, *m.*	Hon. Andrew B.-W., *b.* 1977
1916	*Somerleyton (3rd),* Savile William Francis Crossley, GCVO, *b.* 1928, *s.* 1959, *m.*	Hon. Hugh F. S. C., *b.* 1971
1784	*Somers (9th),* Philip Sebastian Somers Cocks, *b.* 1948, *s.* 1995	Alan B. C., *b.* 1930
1780	*Southampton (6th),* Charles James FitzRoy, *b.* 1928, *s.* 1989, *m.*	Hon. Edward C. F., *b.* 1955
1959	*Spens (4th),* Patrick Nathaniel George Spens, *b.* 1968, *s.* 2001, *m.*	Hon. Peter L. S., *b.* 2000
1640	*Stafford (15th),* Francis Melfort William Fitzherbert, *b.* 1954, *s.* 1986, *m.*	Hon. Benjamin J. B. F., *b.* 1983
1938	*Stamp (4th),* Trevor Charles Bosworth Stamp, MD, *b.* 1935, *s.* 1987, *m.*	Hon. Nicholas C. T. S., *b.* 1978
1839	*Stanley of Alderley (8th), Sheffield (8th) (I. 1738) and Eddisbury (7th) (1848),* Thomas Henry Oliver Stanley, *b.* 1927, *s.* 1971, *m.*	Hon. Richard O. S., *b.* 1956
1318	** *Strabolgi (11th),* David Montague de Burgh Kenworthy, *b.* 1914, *s.* 1953, *m.*	Andrew D. W. K., *b.* 1967
1954	*Strang (2nd),* Colin Strang, *b.* 1922, *s.* 1978, *m.*	None
1628	*Strange (17th),* Adam Humphrey Drummond of Megginch, *b.* 1953, *s.* 2005 *m.*	Hon. John A. H. D. of M. *b.* 1992
1955	*Strathalmond (3rd),* William Roberton Fraser, *b.* 1947, *s.* 1976, *m.*	Hon. William G. F., *b.* 1976
1936	*Strathcarron (3rd),* Ian David Patrick Macpherson, *b.* 1949, *s.* 2006, *m.*	Hon. Rory D. A. M., *b.* 1982
1955	** *Strathclyde (2nd),* Thomas Galloway Dunlop du Roy de Blicquy Galbraith, PC, *b.* 1960, *s.* 1985, *m.*	Hon. Charles W. du R. de B. G., *b.* 1962
1900	*Strathcona and Mount Royal (4th),* Donald Euan Palmer Howard, *b.* 1923, *s.* 1959, *m.*	Hon. D. Alexander S. H., *b.* 1961
1836	*Stratheden (6th) and Campbell (6th) (1841),* Donald Campbell, *b.* 1934, *s.* 1987, *m.*	Hon. David A. C., *b.* 1963
1884	*Strathspey (6th),* James Patrick Trevor Grant of Grant, *b.* 1943, *s.* 1992, *m.*	Hon. Michael P. F. G., *b.* 1953
1838	*Sudeley (7th),* Merlin Charles Sainthill Hanbury-Tracy, *b.* 1939, *s.* 1941	D. Andrew J. H.-T., *b.* 1928
1786	*Suffield (11th),* Anthony Philip Harbord-Hamond, MC, *b.* 1922, *s.* 1951, *w.*	Hon. Charles A. A. H.-H., *b.* 1953
1893	*Swansea (5th),* Richard Anthony Hussey Vivian, *b.* 1957, *s.* 2005, *m.*	Hon. James H. H. V., *b.* 1999
1907	*Swaythling (5th),* Charles Edgar Samuel Montagu, *b.* 1954, *s.* 1998, *m.*	Hon. Anthony T. S. M., *b.* 1931
1919	** *Swinfen (3rd),* Roger Mynors Swinfen Eady, *b.* 1938, *s.* 1977, *m.*	Hon. Charles R. P. S. E., *b.* 1971
1831 I.	*Talbot of Malahide (10th),* Reginald John Richard Arundell, *b.* 1931, *s.* 1987, *m.*	Hon. Richard J. T. A., *b.* 1957
1946	*Tedder (3rd),* Robin John Tedder, *b.* 1955, *s.* 1994, *m.*	Hon. Benjamin J. T., *b.* 1985
1884	*Tennyson (6th),* David Harold Alexander Tennyson, *b.* 1960, *s.* 2006	Alan J. D. T., *b.* 1965
1918	*Terrington (6th),* Christopher Richard James Woodhouse, MB, *b.* 1946, *s.* 2001, *m.*	Hon. Jack H. L. W., *b.* 1978
1940	*Teviot (2nd),* Charles John Kerr, *b.* 1934, *s.* 1968, *m.*	Hon. Charles R. K., *b.* 1971
1616	*Teynham (20th),* John Christopher Ingham Roper-Curzon, *b.* 1928, *s.* 1972, *m.*	Hon. David J. H. I. R.-C., *b.* 1965
1964	*Thomson of Fleet (3rd),* David Kenneth Roy Thomson, *b.* 1957, *s.* 2006, *m.*	Hon. Benjamin T., *b.* 2006
1792	*Thurlow (8th),* Francis Edward Hovell-Thurlow-Cumming-Bruce, KCMG, *b.* 1912, *s.* 1971, *w.*	Hon. Roualeyn R. H.-T.-C.-B., *b.* 1952
1876	*Tollemache (5th),* Timothy John Edward Tollemache, *b.* 1939, *s.* 1975, *m.*	Hon. Edward J. H. T., *b.* 1976
1564 S.	*Torphichen (15th),* James Andrew Douglas Sandilands, *b.* 1946, *s.* 1975, *m.*	Robert P. S., *b.* 1950
1947	** *Trefgarne (2nd),* David Garro Trefgarne, PC, *b.* 1941, *s.* 1960, *m.*	Hon. George G. T., *b.* 1970
1921	*Trevethin (4th) and Oaksey (2nd) (1947),* John Geoffrey Tristram Lawrence, OBE, *b.* 1929, *s.* 1971, *m.*	Hon. Patrick J. T. L., *b.* 1960
1880	*Trevor (5th),* Marke Charles Hill-Trevor, *b.* 1970, *s.* 1997, *m.*	Hon. Iain R. H.-T., *b.* 1971
1461 I.	*Trimlestown (21st),* Raymond Charles Barnewall, *b.* 1930, *s.* 1997	None
1940	*Tryon (3rd),* Anthony George Merrik Tryon, *b.* 1940, *s.* 1976	Hon. Charles G. B. T., *b.* 1976
1935	*Tweedsmuir (4th),* John William de l'Aigle (Toby) Buchan, *b.* 1950, *s.* 2008, *m.*	Hon. John A. G. B., *b.* 1986
1523	*Vaux of Harrowden (11th),* Anthony William Gilbey, *b.* 1940, *s.* 2002, *m.*	Hon. Richard H. G. G., *b.*1965
1800 I.	*Ventry (8th),* Andrew Wesley Daubeny de Moleyns, *b.* 1943, *s.* 1987, *m.*	Hon. Francis W. D. de M., *b.* 1965
1762	*Vernon (11th),* Anthony William Vernon-Harcourt, *b.* 1939, *s.* 2000, *m.*	Hon. Simon A. V-H., *b.* 1969
1922	*Vestey (3rd),* Samuel George Armstrong Vestey, KCVO, *b.* 1941, *s.* 1954, *m.*	Hon. William G. V., *b.* 1983

1841	*Vivian (7th),* Charles Crespigny Hussey Vivian, *b.* 1966, *s.* 2004	Hon. Victor A. R. B. V., *b.* 1940
1934	*Wakehurst (3rd),* (John) Christopher Loder, *b.* 1925, *s.* 1970, *m.*	Hon. Timothy W. L., *b.* 1958
1723	** *Walpole (10th) and Walpole of Wolterton (8th) (1756),* Robert Horatio Walpole, *b.* 1938, *s.* 1989, *m.*	Hon. Jonathan R. H. W., *b.* 1967
1780	*Walsingham (9th),* John de Grey, MC, *b.* 1925, *s.* 1965, *m.*	Hon. Robert de. G., *b.* 1969
1936	*Wardington (3rd),* William Simon Pease, *b.* 1925, *s.* 2005, *m.*	None
1792 I.	*Waterpark (7th),* Frederick Caryll Philip Cavendish, *b.* 1926, *s.* 1948, *m.*	Hon. Roderick A. C., *b.* 1959
1942	*Wedgwood (4th),* Piers Anthony Weymouth Wedgwood, *b.* 1954, *s.* 1970, *m.*	Antony J. W., *b.* 1944
1861	*Westbury (6th),* Richard Nicholas Bethell, MBE, *b.* 1950, *s.* 2001, *m.*	Hon. Alexander B., *b.* 1986
1944	*Westwood (3rd),* (William) Gavin Westwood, *b.* 1944, *s.* 1991, *m.*	Hon. W. Fergus W., *b.* 1972
1544/5	*Wharton (12th),* Myles Christopher David Robertson, *b.* 1964, *s.* 2000, *m.*	Hon. Christopher J. R., *b.* 1969
1935	*Wigram (2nd),* (George) Neville (Clive) Wigram, MC, *b.* 1915, *s.* 1960, *w.*	Maj. Hon. Andrew F. C. W., *b.* 1949
1491	** *Willoughby de Broke (21st),* Leopold David Verney, *b.* 1938, *s.* 1986, *m.*	Hon. Rupert G. V., *b.* 1966
1937	*Windlesham (3rd) and Hennessy (life peerage, 1999),* David James George Hennessy, CVO, PC, *b.* 1932, *s.* 1962, *w.*	Hon. James R. H., *b.* 1968
1951	*Wise (2nd),* John Clayton Wise, *b.* 1923, *s.* 1968, *m.*	Hon. Christopher J. C. W., *b.* 1949
1869	*Wolverton (7th),* Christopher Richard Glyn, *b.* 1938, *s.* 1988	Miles J. G., *b.* 1966
1928	*Wraxall (3rd),* Eustace Hubert Beilby Gibbs, KCVO, CMG, *b.* 1929, *s.* 2001, *m.*	Hon. Anthony H. G., *b.* 1958
1915	*Wrenbury (3rd),* Revd John Burton Buckley, *b.* 1927, *s.* 1940, *m.*	Hon. William E. B., *b.* 1966
1838	*Wrottesley (6th),* Clifton Hugh Lancelot de Verdon Wrottesley, *b.* 1968, *s.* 1977, *m.*	Hon. Victor E. F. de V. W., *b.* 2004
1829	*Wynford (9th),* John Philip Robert Best, *b.* 1950, *s.* 2002, *m.*	Hon. Harry R. F. B., *b.* 1987
1308	*Zouche (18th),* James Assheton Frankland, *b.* 1943, *s.* 1965, *m.*	Hon. William T. A. F., *b.* 1984

BARONESSES/LADIES IN THEIR OWN RIGHT

Style, The Rt. Hon. the Lady _ , *or* The Rt. Hon. the Baroness _ , according to her preference. Either style may be used, except in the case of Scottish titles (indicated by S.), which are not baronies (*see* page 44) and whose holders are always addressed as Lady.

Envelope, may be addressed in same way as a Baron's wife or, if she prefers *(formal),* The Rt. Hon. the Baroness _; *(social),* The Baroness _. Otherwise as for a Baron's wife

Husband, Untitled

Children's style, As for children of a Baron

Created	*Title, order of succession, name, etc*	*Heir*
1664	*Arlington,* Jennifer Jane Forwood, *b.* 1939, *s.* 1999, *w.* Title called out of abeyance 1999	Hon. Patrick J. D. F., *b.* 1967
1455	*Berners (16th),* Pamela Vivien Kirkham, *b.* 1929, *s.* 1995, *m.*	Hon. Rupert W. T. K., *b.* 1953
1529	*Braye (8th),* Mary Penelope Aubrey-Fletcher, *b.* 1941, *s.* 1985, *m.*	Two co-heirs
1321	*Dacre (27th),* Rachel Leila Douglas-Home, *b.* 1929, *s.* 1970, *w.*	Hon. James T. A. D.-H., *b.* 1952
1490 S.	*Herries of Terregles (14th),* Anne Elizabeth Fitzalan-Howard, *b.* 1938, *s.* 1975, *w.*	Lady Mary Mumford, *b.* 1940
1597	*Howard de Walden (10th),* Mary Hazel Caridwen Czernin, *b.* 1935, *s.* 2004, *m.* Title called out of abeyance 2004	Hon. Peter J. J. C. *b.* 1966
1602 S.	*Kinloss (12th),* Beatrice Mary Grenville Freeman-Grenville, *b.* 1922, *s.* 1944, *w.*	Master of Kinloss, *b.* 1953
1445 S.	** *Saltoun (20th),* Flora Marjory Fraser, *b.* 1930, *s.* 1979, *w.*	Hon. Katharine I. M. I. F., *b.* 1957
1313	*Willoughby de Eresby (27th),* (Nancy) Jane Marie Heathcote-Drummond-Willoughby, *b.* 1934, *s.* 1983	Two co-heirs

LIFE PEERS

Style, The Rt. Hon. the Lord _ /The Rt. Hon. the Lady _, *or* The Rt. Hon. the Baroness _, according to her preference

Envelope (formal), The Rt. Hon. Lord _/Lady_/ Baroness_; *(social)*, The Lord _/Lady_/Baroness_ *Letter (formal)*, My Lord/Lady; *(social)*, Dear Lord/ Lady _. *Spoken*, Lord/Lady _

Wife's style, The Rt. Hon. the Lady _

Husband, Untitled

Children's style, 'The Hon.' before forename (F_) and surname (S_)

Envelope, The Hon. F_ S_. *Letter*, Dear Mr/Miss/Mrs S_. *Spoken*, Mr/Miss/Mrs S_

NEW LIFE PEERAGES

1 September 2009 to 31 August 2010:
Richard Beecroft Allan; Hilary Jane Armstrong, PC; Sir Jeremy Hugh Beecham; Floella Karen Yunies Benjamin, OBE; Sir Michael George Bichard, KCB; Guy Vaughan Black; Sir Ian Warwick Blair, QPM; Paul Yaw Boateng, PC; Timothy Eric Boswell; Desmond Henry Browne, PC; Angela Frances Browning; John Quentin Davies; Rita Margaret Donaghy, CBE; Jean Lesley Patricia Drake, CBE; Dame Ellen Margaret Eaton, DBE; Meral Hussein Ece, OBE; Edward Peter Lawless Faulks, QC; John Gardiner; Michael James German, OBE; Dame Tanni Carys Davina Grey-Thompson, DBE; John Selwyn Gummer, PC; Anthony William Hall, CBE; Dr Dianne Hayter; Anna Healy; Jonathan Hopkin Hill, CBE; Michael Howard, PC, QC; Beverley Hughes, PC; John Matthew Patrick Hutton, PC; Prof. Ajay Kumar Kakkar; Roy Francis Kennedy; James Philip Knight, PC; Helen Lawrie Liddell, PC; Roger John Liddle; Thomas McLaughlin McAvoy, PC; Dr Jack Wilson McConnell, PC; Sir Kenneth Donald John MacDonald, QC; John Francis McFall, PC; John Craddock Maples; John Stephen Monks; Helen Margaret Newlove; Susan Nye; Revd Ian Richard Kyle Paisley, PC; Kathryn Jane Parminter; Dolar Amarshi Popat; John Leslie Prescott, PC; Dr John Reid, PC; Shireen Olive Ritchie; Sir James Meyer Sassoon; Maeve Christina Mary Sherlock, OBE; John Warren Shipley, OBE; Angela Evans Smith, PC; Sir William Michael Hardy Spicer; Deborah Stedman-Scott, OBE; Robert Wilfrid Stevenson; Matthew Owen John Taylor; James Donnelly Touhig, PC; Nathanael Ming-Yan Wei; Margaret Eileen Joyce Wheeler, MBE; Michael Charles Williams; George Philip Willis; Michael David Wills, PC; Hon. Simon Adam Wolfson

SYMBOLS

* Hereditary peer who has been granted a life peerage. For further details, please refer to the Hereditary Peers section. For example, life peer *Balniel* can be found under his hereditary title *Earl of Crawford and Balcarres*

§ Justices of the Supreme Court currently disqualified from sitting or voting in the House of Lords until they retire from the supreme court. For further information *see* Law Courts and Offices

‡ Title not confirmed at time of going to press

CREATED UNDER THE APPELLATE JURISDICTION ACT 1876 (AS AMENDED)

BARONS

Created

2004 §*Brown of Eaton-under-Heywood*, Simon Denis Brown, PC, *b.* 1937, *m.*
1991 *Browne-Wilkinson*, Nicolas Christopher Henry Browne-Wilkinson, PC, *b.* 1930, *m.*
2004 *Carswell*, Robert Douglas Carswell, PC, *b.* 1934, *m.*
2009 §*Collins of Mapesbury*, Lawrence Antony Collins, PC, *b.* 1941
1986 *Goff of Chieveley*, Robert Lionel Archibald Goff, PC, *b.* 1926, *m.*
1985 *Griffiths*, (William) Hugh Griffiths, MC, PC, *b.* 1923, *m.*
1995 *Hoffmann*, Leonard Hubert Hoffmann, PC, *b.* 1934, *m.*
1997 *Hutton*, (James) Brian (Edward) Hutton, PC, *b.* 1931, *m.*
2009 §*Kerr of Tonaghmore*, Brian Francis Kerr, PC, *b.* 1948, *m.*
1993 *Lloyd of Berwick*, Anthony John Leslie Lloyd, PC, *b.* 1929, *m.*
2005 §*Mance*, Jonathan Hugh Mance, PC, *b.* 1943, *m.*
1998 *Millett*, Peter Julian Millett, PC, *b.* 1932, *m.*
1992 *Mustill*, Michael John Mustill, PC, *b.* 1931, *m.*
2007 *Neuberger of Abbotsbury*, David Edmond Neuberger, PC, *b.* 1948, *m.*, *Master of the Rolls*
1994 *Nicholls of Birkenhead*, Donald James Nicholls, PC, *b.* 1933, *m.*
1999 §*Phillips of Worth Matravers*, Nicholas Addison Phillips, b. 1938, *m.*
1997 §*Saville of Newdigate*, Mark Oliver Saville, PC, *b.* 1936, *m.*
2000 *Scott of Foscote*, Richard Rashleigh Folliott Scott, PC, *b.* 1934, *m.*
1995 *Steyn*, Johan van Zyl Steyn, PC, *b.* 1932, *m.*
1982 *Templeman*, Sydney William Templeman, MBE, PC, *b.* 1920, *w.*
2003 §*Walker of Gestingthorpe*, Robert Walker, PC, *b.* 1938, *m.*
1992 *Woolf*, Harry Kenneth Woolf, PC, *b.* 1933, *m.*

BARONESSES

2004 §*Hale of Richmond*, Brenda Marjorie Hale, DBE, PC, *b.* 1945, *m.*

CREATED UNDER THE LIFE PEERAGES ACT 1958

BARONS

Created

2000 **Acton of Bridgnorth*, Lord Acton, *b.* 1941, *m.* (*see* Hereditary Peers)
2001 *Adebowale*, Victor Olufemi Adebowale, CBE, *b.* 1962
2005 *Adonis*, Andrew Adonis, PC, *b.* 1963, *m.*

1998 *Ahmed,* Nazir Ahmed, *b.* 1957, *m.*
1996 *Alderdice,* John Thomas Alderdice, *b.* 1955, *m.*
2010 *Allan of Hallam,* Richard Beecroft Allan, *b.* 1966
1998 *Alli,* Waheed Alli, *b.* 1964
2004 *Alliance,* David Alliance, CBE, *b.* 1932
1997 *Alton of Liverpool,* David Patrick Paul Alton, *b.* 1951, *m.*
2005 *Anderson of Swansea,* Donald Anderson, PC, *b.* 1939, *m.*
1992 *Archer of Sandwell,* Peter Kingsley Archer, PC, QC, *b.* 1926, *m.*
1992 *Archer of Weston-super-Mare,* Jeffrey Howard Archer, *b.* 1940, *m.*
1988 *Armstrong of Ilminster,* Robert Temple Armstrong, GCB, CVO, *b.* 1927, *m.*
1999 **Armstrong-Jones,* Earl of Snowdon, GCVO, *b.* 1930, *m.* (*see* Hereditary Peers)
2000 *Ashcroft,* Michael Anthony Ashcroft, KCMG,
2001 *Ashdown of Norton-sub-Hamdon,* Jeremy John Durham (Paddy) Ashdown, GCMG, KBE, PC, *b.* 1941, *m.*
1992 *Ashley of Stoke,* Jack Ashley, CH, PC, *b.* 1922, *w.*
1993 *Attenborough,* Richard Samuel Attenborough, CBE, *b.* 1923, *m.*
1998 *Bach,* William Stephen Goulden Bach, *b.* 1946, *m.*
1997 *Bagri,* Raj Kumar Bagri, CBE, *b.* 1930, *m.*
1997 *Baker of Dorking,* Kenneth Wilfred Baker, CH, PC, *b.* 1934, *m.*
2004 *Ballyedmond,* Dr Edward Haughey, OBE, *b.* 1944, *m.*
1974 **Balniel,* The Earl of Crawford and Balcarres, *b.* 1927, *m.* (*see* Hereditary Peers)
2010 *Bannside,* Revd Ian Richard Kyle Paisley, PC, *b.* 1926, *m.*
1992 *Barber of Tewkesbury,* Derek Coates Barber, *b.* 1918, *m.*
1983 *Barnett,* Joel Barnett, PC, *b.* 1923, *m.*
1997 *Bassam of Brighton,* (John) Steven Bassam, PC, *b.* 1953
2008 *Bates,* Michael Walton Bates, *b.* 1961
2010 *Beecham,* Jeremy Hugh Beecham, *b.* 1944, *m.*
1998 *Bell,* Timothy John Leigh Bell, *b.* 1941, *m.*
2001 *Best,* Richard Stuart Best, OBE, *b.* 1945, *m.*
2007 *Bew,* Prof. Paul Anthony Elliott Bew, *b.* 1950, *m.*
2001 *Bhatia,* Amirali Alibhai Bhatia, OBE, *b.* 1932, *m.*
2004 *Bhattacharyya,* Prof. (Sushantha) Kumar Bhattacharyya, CBE *b.* 1932, *m.*
2010 *Bichard,* Michael George Bichard, KCB, *b.* 1947
2006 *Bilimoria,* Karan Faridoon Bilimoria, CBE, *b.* 1961, *m.*
2005 *Bilston,* Dennis Turner, *b.* 1942, *m.*
1996 *Bingham of Cornhill,* Thomas Henry Bingham, KG, PC, *b.* 1933, *m.*
2000 *Birt,* John Francis Hodgess Birt, *b.* 1944, *m.*
2010 *Black of Brentwood,* Guy Vaughan Black, *b.* 1964, *c. p.*
2001 *Black of Crossharbour,* Conrad Moffat Black, OC, PC, *b.* 1944, *m.*
1997 *Blackwell,* Norman Roy Blackwell, *b.* 1952, *m.*
2010 *Blair of Boughton,* Ian Warwick Blair, QPM *b.* 1953, *m.*
1995 *Blyth of Rowington,* James Blyth, *b.* 1940, *m.*
2010 *Boateng,* Paul Yaw Boateng, PC, *b.* 1951, *m.*
1996 *Borrie,* Gordon Johnson Borrie, QC, *b.* 1931, *m.*
1976 *Boston of Faversham,* Terence George Boston, QC, *b.* 1930, *m.*
2010 *Boswell of Aynho,* Timothy Eric Boswell, *b.* 1942, *m.*
1996 *Bowness,* Peter Spencer Bowness, CBE, *b.* 1943, *m.*
2003 *Boyce,* Michael Boyce, GCB, OBE, *b.* 1943
2006 *Boyd of Duncansby,* Colin David Boyd, PC, *b.* 1953, *m.*
2006 *Bradley,* Keith John Charles Bradley, PC, *b.* 1950, *m.*
1999 *Bradshaw,* William Peter Bradshaw, *b.* 1936, *m.*
1998 *Bragg,* Melvyn Bragg, *b.* 1939, *m.*
1987 *Bramall,* Edwin Noel Westby Bramall, KG, GCB, OBE, MC, *b.* 1923, *m.*
2000 *Brennan,* Daniel Joseph Brennan, QC, *b.* 1942, *m.*
1999 *Brett,* William Henry Brett, *b.* 1942, *m.*
1976 *Briggs,* Asa Briggs, FBA, *b.* 1921, *m.*
2000 *Brittan of Spennithorne,* Leon Brittan, PC, QC, *b.* 1939, *m.*
2004 *Broers,* Prof. Alec (Nigel) Broers, *b.* 1938, *m.*
1997 *Brooke of Alverthorpe,* Clive Brooke, *b.* 1942, *m.*
2001 *Brooke of Sutton Mandeville,* Peter Leonard Brooke, CH, PC, *b.* 1934, *m.*
1998 *Brookman,* David Keith Brookman, *b.* 1937, *m.*
1979 *Brooks of Tremorfa,* John Edward Brooks, *b.* 1927, *m.*
2006 *Browne of Belmont,* Wallace Hamilton Browne, *b.* 1947
2010 *Browne of Ladyton,* Desmond Henry Browne, PC, *b.* 1952
2001 *Browne of Madingley,* Edmund John Phillip Browne, *b.* 1948
2006 *Burnett,* John Patrick Aubone Burnett, *b.* 1945, *m.*
1998 *Burns,* Terence Burns, GCB, *b.* 1944, *m.*
1998 *Butler of Brockwell,* (Frederick Edward) Robin Butler, KG, GCB, CVO, PC, *b.* 1938, *m.*
2004 *Cameron of Dillington,* Ewen (James Hanning) Cameron, *b.* 1949, *m.*
1984 *Cameron of Lochbroom,* Kenneth John Cameron, PC, *b.* 1931, *m.*
1981 *Campbell of Alloway,* Alan Robertson Campbell, QC, *b.* 1917, *m.*
2001 *Campbell-Savours,* Dale Norman Campbell-Savours, *b.* 1943, *m.*
2002 *Carey of Clifton,* Rt. Revd George Leonard Carey, PC, *b.* 1935, *m.*
1999 **Carington of Upton,* Lord Carrington, GCMG, *b.* 1919, *m.* (*see* Hereditary Peers)
1999 *Carlile of Berriew,* Alexander Charles Carlile, QC, *b.* 1948, *m.*
1975 *Carr of Hadley,* (Leonard) Robert Carr, PC, *b.* 1916, *m.*
2008 *Carter of Barnes,* Stephen Andrew Carter, CBE, *b.* 1964, *m.*
2004 *Carter of Coles,* Patrick Robert Carter, *b.* 1946, *m.*
1990 *Cavendish of Furness,* (Richard) Hugh Cavendish, *b.* 1941, *m.*
1996 *Chadlington,* Peter Selwyn Gummer, *b.* 1942, *m.*
1964 *Chalfont,* (Alun) Arthur Gwynne Jones, OBE, MC, PC, *b.* 1919, *w.*
2005 *Chidgey,* David William George Chidgey, *b.* 1942, *m.*
1987 *Chilver,* (Amos) Henry Chilver, FRS, FRENG, *b.* 1926, *m.*
1977 *Chitnis,* Pratap Chidamber Chitnis, *b.* 1936, *m.*
1998 *Christopher,* Anthony Martin Grosvenor Christopher, CBE, *b.* 1925, *m.*
2001 *Clark of Windermere,* David George Clark, PC, PHD, *b.* 1939, *m.*

1998 *Clarke of Hampstead,* Anthony James Clarke, CBE, *b.* 1932, *m.*
2009 §*Clarke of Stone-Cum-Ebony,* Anthony Peter Clarke, PC, *b.* 1943, *m.*
1998 *Clement-Jones,* Timothy Francis Clement-Jones, CBE, *b.* 1949, *m.*
1990 *Clinton-Davis,* Stanley Clinton Clinton-Davis, PC, *b.* 1928, *m.*
2000 *Coe,* Sebastian Newbold Coe, KBE, *b.* 1956, *m.*
2001 *Condon,* Paul Leslie Condon, QPM, *b.* 1947, *m.*
1997 *Cope of Berkeley,* John Ambrose Cope, PC, *b.* 1937, *m.*
2001 *Corbett of Castle Vale,* Robin Corbett, *b.* 1933, *m.*
2006 *Cotter,* Brian Joseph Michael Cotter, *b.* 1938, *m.*
1991 *Craig of Radley,* David Brownrigg Craig, GCB, OBE, *b.* 1929, *m.*
1987 *Crickhowell,* (Roger) Nicholas Edwards, PC, *b.* 1934, *m.*
2006 *Crisp,* (Edmund) Nigel (Ramsay) Crisp, KCB, *b.* 1952, *m.*
1978 *Croham,* Douglas Albert Vivian Allen, GCB, *b.* 1917, *w.*
2003 *Cullen of Whitekirk,* William Douglas Cullen, KT, PC, *b.* 1935, *m.*
2005 *Cunningham of Felling,* John Anderson Cunningham, PC, *b.* 1939, *m.*
1996 *Currie of Marylebone,* David Anthony Currie, *b.* 1946, *m.*
2007 *Darzi of Denham,* Ara Warkes Darzi, KBE, *b.* 1960, *m.*
2006 *Davidson of Glen Clova,* Neil Forbes Davidson, QC, *b.* 1950, *m.*
2009 *Davies of Abersoch,* Evan Mervyn Davies, CBE, *b.* 1952, *m.*
1997 *Davies of Coity,* (David) Garfield Davies, CBE, *b.* 1935, *m.*
1997 *Davies of Oldham,* Bryan Davies, PC, *b.* 1939, *m.*
2010 *Davies of Stamford,* John Quentin Davies, *b.* 1944, *m.*
2006 *Dear,* Geoffrey (James) Dear, QPM, *b.* 1937, *m.*
2010 *Deben,* John Selwyn Gummer, PC, *b.* 1939, *m.*
1991 *Desai,* Prof. Meghnad Jagdishchandra Desai, PHD, *b.* 1940, *m.*
1997 *Dholakia,* Navnit Dholakia, OBE, *b.* 1937, *m.*
1997 *Dixon,* Donald Dixon, PC, *b.* 1929, *m.*
1993 *Dixon-Smith,* Robert William Dixon-Smith, *b.* 1934, *m.*
1985 *Donoughue,* Bernard Donoughue, DPHIL, *b.* 1934
2004 *Drayson,* Paul Rudd Drayson, PC, *b.* 1960, *m.*
1994 *Dubs,* Alfred Dubs, *b.* 1932, *m.*
2004 *Dykes,* Hugh John Maxwell Dykes, *b.* 1939, *m.*
1995 *Eames,* Robert Henry Alexander Eames, OM, PHD, *b.* 1937, *m.*
1992 *Eatwell,* John Leonard Eatwell, PHD, *b.* 1945
1983 *Eden of Winton,* John Benedict Eden, PC, *b.* 1925, *m.*
1999 *Elder,* Thomas Murray Elder, *b.* 1950
1992 *Elis-Thomas,* Dafydd Elis Elis-Thomas, PC, *b.* 1946, *m.*
1985 *Elliott of Morpeth,* Robert William Elliott, *b.* 1920, *m.*
1981 *Elystan-Morgan,* Dafydd Elystan Elystan-Morgan, *b.* 1932, *w.*
2000 **Erskine of Alloa Tower,* Earl of Mar and Kellie, *b.* 1949, *m.* (*see* Hereditary Peers)
1997 *Evans of Parkside,* John Evans, *b.* 1930, *m.*
2000 *Evans of Temple Guiting,* Matthew Evans, CBE, *b.* 1941, *m.*
1998 *Evans of Watford,* David Charles Evans, *b.* 1942, *m.*
1983 *Ezra,* Derek Ezra, MBE, *b.* 1919, *m.*
1997 *Falconer of Thoroton,* Charles Leslie Falconer, QC, *b.* 1951, *m.*
1999 *Faulkner of Worcester,* Richard Oliver Faulkner, *b.* 1946, *m.*
2010 *Faulks,* Edward Peter Lawless Faulks, QC, *b.* 1950, *m.*
2001 *Fearn, Ronald Cyril Fearn,* OBE, *b.* 1931, *m.*
1996 *Feldman,* Basil Feldman, *b.* 1926, *m.*
1999 *Fellowes,* Robert Fellowes, GCB, GCVO, PC, *b.* 1941, *m.*
1999 *Filkin,* David Geoffrey Nigel Filkin, CBE, *b.* 1944
1999 *Forsyth of Drumlean,* Michael Bruce Forsyth, *b.* 1954, *m.*
2005 *Foster of Bishop Auckland,* Derek Foster, PC, *b.* 1937, *m.*
1999 *Foster of Thames Bank,* Norman Robert Foster, OM, *b.* 1935, *m.*
2005 *Foulkes of Cumnock,* George Foulkes, PC, *b.* 1942, *m.*
2001 *Fowler,* (Peter) Norman Fowler, PC, *b.* 1938, *m.*
1989 *Fraser of Carmyllie,* Peter Lovat Fraser, PC, QC, *b.* 1945, *m.*
1997 *Freeman,* Roger Norman Freeman, PC, *b.* 1942, *m.*
2009 *Freud,* David Anthony Freud, *b.* 1950 *m.*
2000 *Fyfe of Fairfield,* George Lennox Fyfe, *b.* 1941, *m.*
2010 *Gardiner of Kimble,* John Gardiner, *b.* 1956, *m.*
1997 *Garel-Jones,* (William Armand) Thomas Tristan Garel-Jones, PC, *b.* 1941, *m.*
1999* *Gascoyne-Cecil,* The Marquess of Salisbury, PC, *b.* 1946, *m.* (*see* Hereditary Peers)
1999 *Gavron,* Robert Gavron, CBE, *b.* 1930, *m.*
2010 *German,* Michael James German, OBE, *b.* 1945, *m.*
2004 *Giddens,* Prof. Anthony Giddens, *b.* 1938, *m.*
1997 *Gilbert,* John William Gilbert, PC, PHD, *b.* 1927, *m.*
1977 *Glenamara,* Edward Watson Short, CH, PC, *b.* 1912, *m.*
1999 *Goldsmith,* Peter Henry Goldsmith, QC, *b.* 1950, *m.*
1997 *Goodhart,* William Howard Goodhart, QC, *b.* 1933, *m.*
2005 *Goodlad,* Alastair Robertson Goodlad, KCMG, *b.* 1943, *m.*
1997 *Gordon of Strathblane,* James Stuart Gordon, CBE, *b.* 1936, *m.*
2004 *Gould of Brookwood,* Philip Gould *b.* 1950 *m.*
1999 *Grabiner,* Anthony Stephen Grabiner, QC, *b.* 1945, *m.*
1983 *Graham of Edmonton,* (Thomas) Edward Graham, *b.* 1925, *m.*
2000 *Greaves,* Anthony Robert Greaves, *b.* 1942, *m.*
2000 **Grenfell of Kilvey,* Lord Grenfell, *b.* 1935, *m.* (*see* Hereditary Peers)
2004 *Griffiths of Burry Port,* Revd Dr Leslie John Griffiths, *b.* 1942, *m.*
1991 *Griffiths of Fforestfach,* Brian Griffiths, *b.* 1941, *m.*
2001 *Grocott,* Bruce Joseph Grocott, PC, *b.* 1940, *m.*

2000 **Guelerbock*, Lord Berkley, OBE, *b.* 1939, *m.* (*see* Hereditary Peers)
2000 *Guthrie of Craigiebank,* Charles Ronald Llewelyn Guthrie, GCB, LVO, OBE *b.* 1938, *m.*
1995 *Habgood,* Rt. Revd John Stapylton Habgood, PC, PHD, *b.* 1927, *m.*
2010 *Hall of Birkenhead,* Anthony William Hall, CBE, *b.* 1951, *m.*
2007 *Hameed,* Dr Khalid Hameed, *b.* 1941, *m.*
2005 *Hamilton of Epsom,* Archibald Gavin Hamilton, PC, *b.* 1941, *m.*
2001 *Hannay of Chiswick,* David Hugh Alexander Hannay, GCMG, CH, *b.* 1935, *m.*
1998 *Hanningfield,* Paul Edward Winston White, *b.* 1940
1997 *Hardie,* Andrew Rutherford Hardie, QC, PC, *b.* 1946, *m.*
2006 *Harries of Pentregarth,* Rt. Revd Richard Douglas Harries, *b.* 1936, *m.*
1998 *Harris of Haringey,* (Jonathan) Toby Harris, *b.* 1953, *m.*
1996 *Harris of Peckham,* Philip Charles Harris, *b.* 1942, *m.*
1999 *Harrison,* Lyndon Henry Arthur Harrison, *b.* 1947, *m.*
2004 *Hart of Chilton,* Garry Richard Rushby Hart, *b.* 1940, *m.*
1993 *Haskel,* Simon Haskel, *b.* 1934, *m.*
1998 *Haskins,* Christopher Robin Haskins, *b.* 1937, *m.*
2005 *Hastings of Scarisbrick,* Michael John Hastings, CBE, *b.* 1958, *m.*
1997 *Hattersley,* Roy Sidney George Hattersley, PC, *b.* 1932, *m.*
2004 *Haworth,* Alan Robert Haworth, *b.* 1948, *m.*
1992 *Hayhoe,* Bernard John (Barney) Hayhoe, PC, *b.* 1925, *m.*
1992 *Healey,* Denis Winston Healey, CH, MBE, PC, *b.* 1917, *w.*
1999 **Hennessey*, Lord Windlesham, CVO, *b.* 1932, *m.* (*see* Hereditary Peers)
2001 *Heseltine,* Michael Ray Dibdin Heseltine, CH, PC, *b.* 1933, *m.*
1997 *Higgins,* Terence Langley Higgins, KBE, PC, *b.* 1928, *m.*
2010 *Hill of Oareford,* Jonathan Hopkin Hill, CBE, *b.* 1960, *m.*
2000 *Hodgson of Astley Abbotts,* Robin Granville Hodgson, CBE, *b.* 1942, *m.*
1991 *Hollick,* Clive Richard Hollick, *b.* 1945, *m.*
1979 *Hooson,* (Hugh) Emlyn Hooson, QC, *b.* 1925, *m.*
2005 *Hope of Thornes,* Rt. Revd David Michael Hope, KCVO, PC, *b.* 1940
1995 §*Hope of Craighead,* (James Arthur) David Hope, KT, PC, *b.* 1938, *m.*
2010 *Howard of Lympne,* Michael Howard, PC, QC, *b.* 1941, *m.*
2004 *Howard of Rising,* Greville Patrick Charles Howard, *b.* 1941, *m.*
2005 *Howarth of Newport,* Alan Thomas Howarth, CBE, PC, *b.* 1944
1992 *Howe of Aberavon,* (Richard Edward) Geoffrey Howe, CH, PC, QC, *b.* 1926, *m.*
1997 *Howell of Guildford,* David Arthur Russell Howell, PC, *b.* 1936, *m.*
1978 *Howie of Troon,* William Howie, *b.* 1924, *w.*
1997 *Hoyle,* (Eric) Douglas Harvey Hoyle, *b.* 1930, *w.*
1997 *Hughes of Woodside,* Robert Hughes, *b.* 1932, *m.*
2000 *Hunt of Chesterton,* Julian Charles Roland Hunt, CBE, *b.* 1941, *m.*
1997 *Hunt of Kings Heath,* Philip Alexander Hunt, OBE, PC, *b.* 1949, *m.*
1997 *Hunt of Wirral,* David James Fletcher Hunt, MBE, PC, *b.* 1942, *m.*
1997 *Hurd of Westwell,* Douglas Richard Hurd, CH, CBE, PC, *b.* 1930, *w.*
1978 *Hutchinson of Lullington,* Jeremy Nicolas Hutchinson, QC, *b.* 1915, *w.*
2010 *Hutton of Furness,* John Matthew Patrick Hutton, PC, *b.* 1955, *m.*
1999 *Imbert,* Peter Michael Imbert, CVO, QPM, *b.* 1933, *m.*
1997 *Inge,* Peter Anthony Inge, KG, GCB, PC, *b.* 1935, *m.*
1987 *Irvine of Lairg,* Alexander Andrew Mackay Irvine, PC, QC, *b.* 1940, *m.*
1997 *Jacobs,* (David) Anthony Jacobs, *b.* 1931, *m.*
2006 *James of Blackheath,* David Noel James, CBE, *b.* 1937, *m.*
1997 *Janner of Braunstone,* Greville Ewan Janner, QC, *b.* 1928, *w.*
2007 *Janvrin,* Robin Berry Janvrin, GCB, GCVO, PC, *b.* 1946, *m.*
2006 *Jay of Ewelme,* Michael (Hastings) Jay, GCMG, *b.* 1946, *m.*
1987 *Jenkin of Roding,* (Charles) Patrick (Fleeming) Jenkin, PC, *b.* 1926, *m.*
2000 *Joffe,* Joel Goodman Joffe, CBE, *b.* 1932, *m.*
2001 *Jones,* (Stephen) Barry Jones, *b.* 1937, *m.*
2007 *Jones of Birmingham,* Digby Marritt Jones, *b.* 1955, *m.*
2005, *Jones of Cheltenham,* Nigel David Jones, *b.* 1948, *m.*
1997 *Jopling,* (Thomas) Michael Jopling, PC, *b.* 1930, *m.*
2000 *Jordan,* William Brian Jordan, CBE, *b.* 1936, *m.*
1991 *Judd,* Frank Ashcroft Judd, *b.* 1935, *m.*
2008 *Judge,* Igor Judge, PC, *b.* 1941, *m., Lord Chief Justice of England and Wales*
2010 *Kakkar,* Prof. Ajay Kumar Kakkar, *b.* 1964
2004 *Kalms,* Harold Stanley Kalms, *b.* 1931, *m.*
2010 *Kennedy of Southwark,* Roy Francis Kennedy, *b.* 1962
2004 *Kerr of Kinlochard,* John (Olav) Kerr, GCMG, *b.* 1942, *m.*
2001 *Kilclooney,* John David Taylor, PC (NI), *b.* 1937, *m.*
1996 *Kilpatrick of Kincraig,* Robert Kilpatrick, CBE, *b.* 1926, *m.*
1985 *Kimball,* Marcus Richard Kimball, *b.* 1928, *m.*
2001 *King of Bridgwater,* Thomas Jeremy King, CH, PC, *b.* 1933, *m.*
1999 *King of West Bromwich,* Tarsem King, *b.* 1937
1993 *Kingsdown,* Robert (Robin) Leigh-Pemberton, KG, PC, *b.* 1927, *m.*
2005 *Kinnock,* Neil Gordon Kinnock, PC, *b.* 1942, *m.*
1999 *Kirkham,* Graham Kirkham, *b.* 1944, *m.*
1975 *Kirkhill,* John Farquharson Smith, *b.* 1930, *m.*
2005 *Kirkwood of Kirkhope,* Archibald Johnstone Kirkwood, *b.* 1946, *m.*
2007 *Krebs,* Prof. John (Richard) Krebs, FRS, *b.* 1945, *m.*
2010 *Knight of Weymouth,* James Philip Knight, PC, *b.* 1965, *m.*

1987 *Knights,* Philip Douglas Knights, CBE, QPM, *b.* 1920, *m.*
2004 *Laidlaw,* Irvine Alan Stewart Laidlaw, *b.* 1942, *m.*
1999 *Laird,* John Dunn Laird, *b.* 1944, *m.*
1998 *Laming,* (William) Herbert Laming, CBE, *b.* 1936, *m.*
1998 *Lamont of Lerwick,* Norman Stewart Hughson Lamont, PC, *b.* 1942, *m.*
1997 *Lang of Monkton,* Ian Bruce Lang, PC, *b.* 1940, *m.*
1992 *Lawson of Blaby,* Nigel Lawson, PC, *b.* 1932, *m.*
2000 *Layard,* Peter Richard Grenville Layard, *b.* 1934, *m.*
1999 *Lea of Crondall,* David Edward Lea, OBE, *b.* 1937
2006 *Leach of Fairford,* Charles Guy Rodney Leach, *b.* 1934, *m.*
2006 *Lee of Trafford,* John Robert Louis Lee, *b.* 1942, *m.*
2004 *Leitch,* Alexander Park Leitch, *b.* 1947, *m.*
1993 *Lester of Herne Hill,* Anthony Paul Lester, QC, *b.* 1936, *m.*
1997 *Levene of Portsoken,* Peter Keith Levene, KBE, *b.* 1941, *m.*
1997 *Levy,* Michael Abraham Levy, *b.* 1944, *m.*
1989 *Lewis of Newnham,* Jack Lewis, FRS, *b.* 1928, *m.*
2010 *Liddle,* Roger John Liddle, *b.* 1947, *m.*
1999 *Lipsey,* David Lawrence Lipsey, *b.* 1948, *m.*
2001 *Livsey of Talgarth,* Richard Arthur Lloyd Livsey, CBE, *b.* 1935, *m.*
1997 *Lloyd-Webber,* Andrew Lloyd Webber, *b.* 1948, *m.*
1997 *Lofthouse of Pontefract,* Geoffrey Lofthouse, *b.* 1925, *w.*
2006 *Low of Dalston,* Prof. Colin Mackenzie Low, CBE, *b.* 1942, *m.*
2000 *Luce,* Richard Napier Luce, KG, GCVO, PC, *b.* 1936, *m.*
2000 **Lyttleton of Aldershot,* The Viscount Chandos, *b.* 1953, *m.* (*see* Hereditary Peers)
1984 *McAlpine of West Green,* (Robert) Alistair McAlpine, *b.* 1942, *m.*
2010 *McAvoy,* Thomas McLaughlin McAvoy, PC, *b.* 1943, *m.*
1988 *Macaulay of Bragar,* Donald Macaulay, QC, *b.* 1933, *m.*
1975 *McCarthy,* William Edward John McCarthy, DPHIL, *b.* 1925, *m.*
1976 *McCluskey,* John Herbert McCluskey, *b.* 1929, *m.*
1989 *McColl of Dulwich,* Ian McColl, CBE, FRCS, FRCSE, *b.* 1933, *m.*
2010 *McConnell of Glenscorrodale,* Dr Jack Wilson McConnell, PC, *b.* 1960, *m.*
2010 *MacDonald of River Glaven,* Kenneth Donald John MacDonald, QC, *b.* 1953, *m.*
1998 *Macdonald of Tradeston,* Angus John Macdonald, CBE, *b.* 1940, *m.*
2010 *McFall of Alcluith,* John Francis McFall, PC, *b.* 1944, *m.*
1991 *Macfarlane of Bearsden,* Norman Somerville Macfarlane, KT, FRSE, *b.* 1926, *m.*
2001 *MacGregor of Pulham Market,* John Roddick Russell MacGregor, CBE, PC, *b.* 1937, *m.*
1979 *Mackay of Clashfern,* James Peter Hymers Mackay, KT, PC, FRSE, *b.* 1927, *m.*
1995 *Mackay of Drumadoon,* Donald Sage Mackay, PC, *b.* 1946, *m.*
2004 *McKenzie of Luton,* William David McKenzie, *b.* 1946, *m.*
1999 *Mackenzie of Culkein,* Hector Uisdean MacKenzie, *b.* 1940
1998 *Mackenzie of Framwellgate,* Brian Mackenzie, OBE, *b.* 1943, *m.*
1974 *Mackie of Benshie,* George Yull Mackie, CBE, DSO, DFC, *b.* 1919, *m.*
1996 *MacLaurin of Knebworth,* Ian Charter MacLaurin, *b.* 1937, *m.*
2001 *Maclennon of Rogart,* Robert Adam Ross Maclennan, PC, *b.* 1936, *m.*
1995 *McNally,* Tom McNally, PC, *b.* 1943, *m.*
2001 *Maginnis of Drumglass,* Kenneth Wiggins Maginnis, *b.* 1938, *m.*
2007 *Malloch-Brown,* George Mark Malloch Brown, KCMG, PC, *b.* 1953, *m.*
2008 *Mandelson,* Peter Benjamin Mandelson, PC, *b.* 1953
2010 *Maples,* John Craddock Maples, *b.* 1943, *m.*
2006 *Marland,* Jonathan Peter Marland, *b.* 1956, *m.*
1991 *Marlesford,* Mark Shuldham Schreiber, *b.* 1931, *m.*
1981 *Marsh,* Richard William Marsh, PC, *b.* 1928, *m.*
1998 *Marshall of Knightsbridge,* Colin Marsh Marshall, *b.* 1933, *m.*
2009 *Martin of Springburn,* Michael Martin, PC, *b.* 1945, *m.*
1987 *Mason of Barnsley,* Roy Mason, PC, *b.* 1924, *m.*
2005 *Mawhinney,* Brian Stanley Mawhinney, PC, *b.* 1940, *m.*
2007 *Mawson,* Revd Andrew Mawson, OBE, *b.* 1954, *m.*
2004 *Maxton,* John Alston Maxton, *b.* 1936, *m.*
2001 *May of Oxford,* Robert McCredie May, OM, *b.* 1936, *m.*
1997 *Mayhew of Twysden,* Patrick Barnabas Burke Mayhew, QC, PC, *b.* 1929, *m.*
2000 *Mitchell,* Parry Andrew Mitchell, *b.* 1943, *m.*
2000 **Mitford,* Lord Redesdale, *b.* 1967, *m.* (*see* Hereditary Peers)
2008 *Mogg,* John (Frederick) Mogg, KCMG, *b.* 1943 *m.*
1997 *Molyneaux of Killead,* James Henry Molyneaux, KBE, PC, *b.* 1920
2010 *Monks,* John Stephen Monks, *b.* 1945, *m.*
2005 *Moonie,* Dr. Lewis George Moonie, *b.* 1947, *m.*
1992 *Moore of Lower Marsh,* John Edward Michael Moore, PC, *b.* 1937, *w.*
2000 *Morgan,* Kenneth Owen Morgan, *b.* 1934, *m.*
2001 *Morris of Aberavon,* John Morris, KG, QC, *b.* 1931, *m.*
2006 *Morris of Handsworth,* William Manuel Morris, *b.* 1938, *m.*
1997 *Morris of Manchester,* Alfred Morris, PC, *b.* 1928, *m.*
2006 *Morrow,* Maurice George Morrow, *m.*
2001 *Moser,* Claus Adolf Moser, KCB, CBE, *b.* 1922, *m.*
2008 *Myners,* Paul Myners, CBE, *b.* 1948, *m.*
1997 *Naseby,* Michael Wolfgang Laurence Morris, PC, *b.* 1936, *m.*
1997 *Neill of Bladen,* (Francis) Patrick Neill, QC, *b.* 1926, *m.*
1997 *Newby,* Richard Mark Newby, OBE, *b.* 1953, *m.*

1997 *Newton of Braintree,* Antony Harold Newton, OBE, PC, *b.* 1937, *m.*
1994 *Nickson,* David Wigley Nickson, KBE, FRSE, *b.* 1929, *m.*
1975 *Northfield,* (William) Donald Chapman, *b.* 1923
1998 *Norton of Louth,* Philip Norton, *b.* 1951
2000 *Oakeshott of Seagrove Bay,* Matthew Alan Oakeshott, *b.* 1947, *m.*
2005 *O'Neill of Clackmannan,* Martin John O'Neill, *b.* 1945, *m.*
2001 *Ouseley,* Herman George Ouseley, *b.* 1945, *m.*
1992 *Owen,* David Anthony Llewellyn Owen, CH, PC, *b.* 1938, *m.*
1999 *Oxburgh,* Ernest Ronald Oxburgh, KBE, FRS, PHD, *b.* 1934, *m.*
1991 *Palumbo,* Peter Garth Palumbo, *b.* 1935, *m.*
2008 *Pannick,* David Philip Pannick, QC, *b.* 1956, *m.*
2000 *Parekh,* Bhikhu Chhotalal Parekh, *b.* 1935, *m.*
1992 *Parkinson,* Cecil Edward Parkinson, PC, *b.* 1931, *m.*
1999 *Patel,* Narendra Babubhai Patel, *b.* 1938
2000 *Patel of Blackburn,* Adam Hafejee Patel, *b.* 1940
2006 *Patel of Bradford,* Prof. Kamlesh Kumar Patel, OBE, *b.* 1960 *m.*
2005 *Patten of Barnes,* Christopher Francis Patten, CH, PC, *b.* 1944, *m.*
1997 *Patten,* John Haggitt Charles Patten, PC, *b.* 1945, *m.*
1996 *Paul,* Swraj Paul, PC, *b.* 1931, *m.*
1990 *Pearson of Rannoch,* Malcolm Everard MacLaren Pearson, *b.* 1942, *m.*
2001 *Pendry,* Thomas Pendry, *b.* 1934, *m.*
1987 *Peston,* Maurice Harry Peston, *b.* 1931, *m.*
1998 *Phillips of Sudbury,* Andrew Wyndham Phillips, OBE, *b.* 1939, *m.*
1996 *Pilkington of Oxenford,* Revd Canon Peter Pilkington, *b.* 1933, *w.*
1992 *Plant of Highfield,* Prof. Raymond Plant, PHD, *b.* 1945, *m.*
1987 *Plumb,* (Charles) Henry Plumb, *b.* 1925, *m.*
2000 **Ponsonby of Roehampton,* Lord Ponsonby of Shulbrede, *b.* 1958 (*see* Hereditary Peers)
2010 *Popat,* Dolar Amarshi Popat, *b.* 1953, *m.*
2000 *Powell of Bayswater,* Charles David Powell, KCMG, *b.* 1941
2010 *Prescott,* John Leslie Prescott, PC, *b.* 1938, *m.*
1987 *Prior,* James Michael Leathes Prior, PC, *b.* 1927, *m.*
1982 *Prys-Davies,* Gwilym Prys Prys-Davies, *b.* 1923, *m.*
1997 *Puttnam,* David Terence Puttnam, CBE, *b.* 1941, *m.*
1994 *Quirk,* Prof. (Charles) Randolph Quirk, CBE, FBA, *b.* 1920, *m.*
2001 *Radice,* Giles Heneage Radice, PC, *b.* 1936
2005 *Ramsbotham,* Gen. David John Ramsbotham, GCB, CBE, *b.* 1934, *m.*
2004 *Rana,* Dr Diljit Singh Rana, MBE, *b.* 1938, *m.*
1997 *Randall of St Budeaux,* Stuart Jeffrey Randall, *b.* 1938, *m.*
1997 *Razzall,* (Edward) Timothy Razzall, CBE, *b.* 1943, *m.*
2005 *Rees of Ludlow,* Prof. Martin John Rees, OM, *b.* 1942, *m.*
1988 *Rees-Mogg,* William Rees-Mogg, *b.* 1928, *m.*
2010 *Reid of Cardowan,* Dr John Reid, PC, *b.* 1947, *m.*
1991 *Renfrew of Kaimsthorn,* (Andrew) Colin Renfrew, FBA, *b.* 1937, *m.*
1999 *Rennard,* Christopher John Rennard, MBE, *b.* 1960
1997 *Renton of Mount Harry,* (Ronald) Timothy Renton, PC, *b.* 1932, *m.*
1997 *Renwick of Clifton,* Robin William Renwick, KCMG, *b.* 1937, *m.*
1990 *Richard,* Ivor Seward Richard, PC, QC, *b.* 1932, *m.*
1992 *Rix,* Brian Norman Roger Rix, CBE, *b.* 1924, *m.*
2004 *Roberts of Llandudno,* Revd John Roger Roberts, *b.* 1935, *m.*
1997 *Roberts of Conwy,* (Ieuan) Wyn (Pritchard) Roberts, PC, *b.* 1930, *m.*
1999 *Robertson of Port Ellen,* George Islay MacNeill Robertson, KT, GCMG, PC, *b.* 1946, *m.*
1992 §*Rodger of Earlsferry,* Alan Ferguson Rodger, PC, QC, FBA, *b.* 1944
1992 *Rodgers of Quarry Bank,* William Thomas Rodgers, PC, *b.* 1928, *w.*
1999 *Rogan,* Dennis Robert David Rogan, *b.* 1942, *m.*
1996 *Rogers of Riverside,* Richard George Rogers, CH, RA, RIBA, *b.* 1933, *m.*
2001 *Rooker,* Jeffrey William Rooker, PC, *b.* 1941, *m.*
2000 *Roper,* John Francis Hodgess Roper, PC, *b.* 1935, *m.*
2004 *Rosser,* Richard Andrew Rosser, *b.* 1944, *m.*
2006 *Rowe-Beddoe,* David (Sydney) Rowe-Beddoe, *b.* 1937, *m.*
2004 *Rowlands,* Edward Rowlands, CBE, *b.* 1940, *m.*
1997 *Ryder of Wensum,* Richard Andrew Ryder, OBE, PC, *b.* 1949, *m.*
1996 *Saatchi,* Maurice Saatchi, *b.* 1946, *m.*
2009 ‡*Sacks,* Chief Rabbi Dr Jonathan Henry Sacks, *b.* 1948, *m.*
1989 *Sainsbury of Preston Candover,* John Davan Sainsbury, KG, *b.* 1927, *m.*
1997 *Sainsbury of Turville,* David John Sainsbury, *b.* 1940, *m.*
1987 *St John of Fawsley,* Norman Antony Francis St John-Stevas, PC, *b.* 1929
1997 *Sandberg,* Michael Graham Ruddock Sandberg, CBE, *b.* 1927, *m.*
1985 *Sanderson of Bowden,* Charles Russell Sanderson, *b.* 1933, *m.*
2010 *Sassoon,* James Meyer Sassoon, *b.* 1955, *m.*
1998 *Sawyer,* Lawrence (Tom) Sawyer, *b.* 1943
1997 *Selkirk of Douglas,* James Alexander Douglas-Hamilton, MSP, PC, QC, *b.* 1942, *m.*
1996 *Sewel,* John Buttifant Sewel, CBE, *b.* 1946
1999 *Sharman,* Colin Morven Sharman, OBE, *b.* 1943, *m.*
1994 *Shaw of Northstead,* Michael Norman Shaw, *b.* 1920, *m.*
2006 *Sheikh,* Mohamed Iltaf Sheikh, *b.* 1941, *m.*
2001 *Sheldon,* Robert Edward Sheldon, PC, *b.* 1923, *m.*
1994 *Sheppard of Didgemere,* Allan John George Sheppard, KCVO, *b.* 1932, *m.*
2010 *Shipley,* John Warren Shipley, OBE, *b.* 1946
2000 *Shutt of Greetland,* David Trevor Shutt, OBE, PC, *b.* 1942
1997 *Simon of Highbury,* David Alec Gwyn Simon, CBE, *b.* 1939, *m.*
1997 *Simpson of Dunkeld,* George Simpson, *b.* 1942, *m.*
1991 *Skidelsky,* Robert Jacob Alexander Skidelsky, DPHIL, *b.* 1939, *m.*

1997 *Smith of Clifton,* Trevor Arthur Smith, *b.* 1937, *m.*
2005 *Smith of Finsbury,* Christopher Robert Smith, PC, *b.* 1951
2008 *Smith of Kelvin,* Robert (Haldane) Smith, *b.* 1944, *m.*
1999 *Smith of Leigh,* Peter Richard Charles Smith, *b.* 1945, *m.*
2004 *Snape,* Peter Charles Snape, *b.* 1942
2005 *Soley,* Clive Stafford Soley, *b.* 1939
1990 *Soulsby of Swaffham Prior,* Ernest Jackson Lawson Soulsby, PHD, *b.* 1926, *m.*
2010 *Spicer,* (William) Michael Hardy Spicer, *b.* 1943, *m.*
1997 *Steel of Aikwood,* David Martin Scott Steel, KT, KBE, PC, *b.* 1938, *m.*
1991 *Sterling of Plaistow,* Jeffrey Maurice Sterling, GCVO, CBE, *b.* 1934, *m.*
2007 *Stern of Brentford,* Nicholas Herbert Stern, *b.* 1946, *m.*
2005 *Stevens of Kirkwhelpington,* John Arthur Stevens, *b.* 1942, *m.*
1987 *Stevens of Ludgate,* David Robert Stevens, *b.* 1936, *m.*
2010 *Stevenson of Balmacara,* Robert Wilfrid Stevenson, *b.* 1947, *m.*
1999 *Stevenson of Coddenham,* Henry Dennistoun Stevenson, CBE, *b.* 1945, *m.*
1992 *Stewartby,* (Bernard Harold) Ian (Halley) Stewart, RD, PC, FBA, FRSE, *b.* 1935, *m.*
1983 *Stoddart of Swindon,* David Leonard Stoddart, *b.* 1926, *m.*
1997 *Stone of Blackheath,* Andrew Zelig Stone, *b.* 1942, *m.*
2009 *Sugar,* Alan Michael Sugar, *b.* 1947, *m.*
2001 *Sutherland of Houndwood,* Stewart Ross Sutherland, KT, *b.* 1941, *m.*
1971 *Tanlaw,* Simon Brooke Mackay, *b.* 1934, *m.*
1996 *Taverne,* Dick Taverne, QC, *b.* 1928, *m.*
2010 *Taylor of Goss Moor,* Matthew Owen John Taylor, *b.* 1963, *m.*
1978 *Taylor of Blackburn,* Thomas Taylor, CBE, *b.* 1929, *m.*
2006 *Taylor of Holbeach,* John Derek Taylor, CBE, *b.* 1943, *m.*
1996 *Taylor of Warwick,* John David Beckett Taylor, *b.* 1952, *m.*
1992 *Tebbit,* Norman Beresford Tebbit, CH, PC, *b.* 1931, *m.*
2001 *Temple-Morris,* Peter Temple-Morris, *b.* 1938, *m.*
2006 *Teverson,* Robin Teverson, *b.* 1952, *m.*
1996 *Thomas of Gresford,* Donald Martin Thomas, OBE, QC, *b.* 1937, *m.*
1997 *Thomas of Macclesfield,* Terence James Thomas, CBE, *b.* 1937, *m.*
1981 *Thomas of Swynnerton,* Hugh Swynnerton Thomas, *b.* 1931, *m.*
1990 *Tombs,* Francis Leonard Tombs, FENG, *b.* 1924, *w.*
1998 *Tomlinson,* John Edward Tomlinson, *b.* 1939
1994 *Tope,* Graham Norman Tope, CBE, *b.* 1943, *m.*
1981 *Tordoff,* Geoffrey Johnson Tordoff, *b.* 1928, *m.*
2010 *Touhig,* James Donnelly Touhig, PC, *b.* 1947, *m.*
2004 *Triesman,* David Maxim Triesman, *b.* 1943
2006 *Trimble,* William David Trimble, PC, *b.* 1944, *m.*
2004 *Truscott,* Dr Peter Derek Truscott, *b.* 1959, *m.*
1993 *Tugendhat,* Christopher Samuel Tugendhat, *b.* 1937, *m.*
2004 *Tunnicliffe,* Denis Tunnicliffe, CBE, *b.* 1943, *m.*
2000 *Turnberg,* Leslie Arnold Turnberg, MD, *b.* 1934, *m.*
2005 *Turnbull,* Andrew Turnbull, KCB, CVO, *b.* 1945, *m.*
2005 *Turner of Ecchinswell,* (Jonathan) Adair Turner, *b.* 1955, *m.*
2005 *Tyler,* Paul Archer Tyler, CBE, *b.* 1941, *m.*
2004 *Vallance of Tummel,* Iain (David Thomas) Vallance, *b.* 1943, *m.*
1996 *Vincent of Coleshill,* Richard Frederick Vincent, GBE, KCB, DSO, *b.* 1931, *m.*
1985 *Vinson,* Nigel Vinson, LVO, *b.* 1931, *m.*
1990 *Waddington,* David Charles Waddington, GCVO, PC, QC, *b.* 1929, *m.*
1990 *Wade of Chorlton,* (William) Oulton Wade, *b.* 1932, *m.*
1992 *Wakeham,* John Wakeham, PC, *b.* 1932, *m.*
1999 *Waldegrave of North Hill,* William Arthur Waldegrave, PC, *b.* 1946, *m.*
2007 *Walker of Aldringham,* Michael John Dawson Walker, GCB, CMG, CBE, *b.* 1944, *m.*
1995 *Wallace of Saltaire,* William John Lawrence Wallace, PHD, *b.* 1941, *m.*
2007 *Wallace of Tankerness,* James Robert Wallace, PC, QC, *b.* 1954, *m.*
1989 *Walton of Detchant,* John Nicholas Walton, TD, FRCP, *b.* 1922, *w.*
1998 *Warner,* Norman Reginald Warner, PC, *b.* 1940, *m.*
1997 *Watson of Invergowrie,* Michael Goodall Watson, *b.* 1949, *m.*
1999 *Watson of Richmond,* Alan John Watson, CBE, *b.* 1941, *m.*
1977 *Wedderburn of Charlton,* (Kenneth) William Wedderburn, FBA, QC, *b.* 1927, *m.*
2010 *Wei,* Nathanael Ming-Yan Wei, *b.* 1977, *m.*
1976 *Weidenfeld,* (Arthur) George Weidenfeld, *b.* 1919, *m.*
2007 *West of Spithead,* Adm. Alan William John West, GCB, DSC, PC, *b.* 1948, *m.*
1996 *Whitty,* John Lawrence (Larry) Whitty, *b.* 1943, *m.*
2010 *Williams of Baglan,* Michael Charles Williams, *b.* 1949
1985 *Williams of Elvel,* Charles Cuthbert Powell Williams, CBE, *b.* 1933, *m.*
1999 *Williamson of Horton,* David (Francis) Williamson, GCMG, CB, PC, *b.* 1934, *m.*
2010 *Willis of Knaresborough,* George Philip Willis, *b.* 1941, *m.*
2010 *Wills,* Michael David Wills, PC, *b.* 1952, *m.*
2002 *Wilson of Dinton,* Richard Thomas James Wilson, GCB, *b.* 1942, *m.*
1992 *Wilson of Tillyorn,* David Clive Wilson, KT, GCMG, PHD, *b.* 1935, *m.*
1995 *Winston,* Robert Maurice Lipson Winston, FRCOG, *b.* 1940, *m.*
2010 *Wolfson of Aspley Guise,* Simon David Wolfson, *b.* 1967
1991 *Wolfson of Sunningdale,* David Wolfson, *b.* 1935, *m.*
1999 *Woolmer of Leeds,* Kenneth John Woolmer, *b.* 1940, *m.*
1994 *Wright of Richmond,* Patrick Richard Henry Wright, GCMG, *b.* 1931, *m.*
2004 *Young of Norwood Green,* Anthony (Ian) Young, *b.* 1942, *m.*

1984 *Young of Graffham,* David Ivor Young, PC, *b.* 1932, *m.*

BARONESSES

Created

2005 *Adams of Craigielea,* Katherine Patricia Irene Adams, *b.* 1947, *w.*

1997 *Amos,* Valerie Ann Amos, *b.* 1954

2007 *Afshar,* Prof. Haleh Afshar, OBE, , *b.* 1944, *m.*

2000 *Andrews,* Elizabeth Kay Andrews, OBE, *b.* 1943, *m.*

1996 *Anelay of St Johns,* Joyce Anne Anelay, DBE, PC, *b.* 1947, *m.*

2010 *Armstrong of Hill Top,* Hilary Jane Armstrong, PC, *b.* 1945, *m.*

1999 *Ashton of Upholland,* Catherine Margaret Ashton, PC, *b.* 1956, *m.*

1999 *Barker,* Elizabeth Jean Barker, *b.* 1961

2010 *Benjamin,* Floella Karen Yunies Benjamin, OBE, *b.* 1949, *m.*

2000 *Billingham,* Angela Theodora Billingham, DPHIL, *b.* 1939, *w.*

1987 *Blackstone,* Tessa Ann Vosper Blackstone, PHD, *b.* 1942

1999 *Blood,* May Blood, MBE, *b.* 1938

2000 *Boothroyd,* Betty Boothroyd, OM, PC, *b.* 1929

2004 *Bonham-Carter of Yarnbury,* Jane Bonham Carter, *b.* 1957, *w.*

2005 *Bottomley of Nettlestone,* Virginia Hilda Brunette Maxwell Bottomley, PC, *b.* 1948, *m.*

2010 *Browning,* Angela Frances Browning, *b.* 1946, *m.*

1998 *Buscombe,* Peta Jane Buscombe, *b.* 1954, *m.*

2006 *Butler-Sloss,* (Ann) Elizabeth (Oldfield) Butler-Sloss, GBE, PC *b.* 1933, *m.*

1996 *Byford,* Hazel Byford, DBE, *b.* 1941, *m.*

2008 *Campbell of Loughborough,* Susan Catherine Campbell, CBE, *b.* 1948

2007 *Campbell of Surbiton,* Jane Susan Campbell, DBE, *b.* 1959, *m.*

1982 *Carnegy of Lour,* Elizabeth Patricia Carnegy of Lour, *b.* 1925

1992 *Chalker of Wallasey,* Lynda Chalker, PC, *b.* 1942, *m.*

2005 *Clark of Calton,* Dr Lynda Margaret Clark, QC, *b.* 1949

2000 *Cohen of Pimlico,* Janet Cohen, *b.* 1940, *m.*

2005 *Corston,* Jean Ann Corston, PC, *b.* 1942, *w.*

2007 *Coussins,* Jean Coussins, *b.* 1950

1982 *Cox,* Caroline Anne Cox, *b.* 1937, *m.*

1998 *Crawley,* Christine Mary Crawley, *b.* 1950, *m.*

1990 *Cumberlege,* Julia Frances Cumberlege, CBE, *b.* 1943, *m.*

1993 *Dean of Thornton-le-Fylde,* Brenda Dean, PC, *b.* 1943, *m.*

2005 *Deech,* Ruth Lynn Deech, DBE, *b.* 1943, *m.*

2010 *Donaghy,* Rita Margaret Donaghy, CBE, *b.* 1944, *m.*

2010 *Drake,* Jean Lesley Patricia Drake, CBE, *b.* 1948

2004 *D'Souza,* Dr Frances Gertrude Claire D'Souza, CMG, PC, *b.* 1944, *m.*

1990 *Dunn,* Lydia Selina Dunn, DBE, *b.* 1940, *m.*

2010 *Eaton,* Ellen Margaret Eaton, DBE

1990 *Eccles of Moulton,* Diana Catherine Eccles, *b.* 1933, *m.*

1997 *Emerton,* Audrey Caroline Emerton, DBE, *b.* 1935

1974 *Falkender,* Marcia Matilda Falkender, CBE, *b.* 1932

2004 *Falkner of Margravine,* Kishwer Falkner, *b.* 1955, *m.*

1994 *Farrington of Ribbleton,* Josephine Farrington, *b.* 1940, *m.*

2001 *Finlay of Llandaff,* Ilora Gillian Finlay, *b.* 1949, *m.*

1990 *Flather,* Shreela Flather, *m.*

1997 *Fookes,* Janet Evelyn Fookes, DBE, *b.* 1936

2006 *Ford,* Margaret Anne Ford, *b.* 1957, *m.*

2005 *Fritchie,* Irene Tordoff Fritchie, DBE, *b.* 1942, *m.*

1999 *Gale,* Anita Gale, *b.* 1940

2007 *Garden of Frognal,* Susan Elizabeth Garden, *b.* 1944, *m.*

1981 *Gardner of Parkes,* (Rachel) Trixie (Anne) Gardner, *b.* 1927, *w.*

2000 *Gibson of Market Rasen,* Anne Gibson, OBE, *b.* 1940, *m.*

2001 *Golding,* Llinos Golding, *b.* 1933, *m.*

1998 *Goudie,* Mary Teresa Goudie, *b.* 1946, *m.*

1993 *Gould of Potternewton,* Joyce Brenda Gould, *b.* 1932, *m.*

2001 *Greenfield,* Susan Adele Greenfield, CBE, *b.* 1950, *m.*

2000 *Greengross,* Sally Ralea Greengross, OBE, *b.* 1935, *m.*

2010 *Grey-Thompson,* Tanni Carys Davina Grey-Thompson, DBE, *b.* 1969, *m.*

1991 *Hamwee,* Sally Rachel Hamwee, *b.* 1947

1999 *Hanham,* Joan Brownlow Hanham, CBE, *b.* 1939, *m.*

1999 *Harris of Richmond,* Angela Felicity Harris, *b.* 1944

1996 *Hayman,* Helene Valerie Hayman, PC, *b.* 1949, *m.*

2010 *Hayter of Kentish Town,* Dr Dianne Hayter, *b.* 1949, *m.*

2010 *Healy of Primrose Hill,* Anna Healy, *b.* 1955, *m.*

2004 *Henig,* Ruth Beatrice Henig, CBE, *b.* 1943, *m.*

1991 *Hilton of Eggardon,* Jennifer Hilton, QPM, *b.* 1936

1995 *Hogg,* Sarah Elizabeth Mary Hogg, *b.* 1946, *m.*

1990 *Hollis of Heigham,* Patricia Lesley Hollis, DPHIL, *b.* 1941, *m.*

1985 *Hooper,* Gloria Dorothy Hooper, CMG, *b.* 1939

2001 *Howarth of Breckland,* Valerie Georgina Howarth, OBE, *b.* 1940

2001 *Howe of Idlicote,* Elspeth Rosamond Morton Howe, CBE, *b.* 1932, *m.*

1999 *Howells of St Davids,* Rosalind Patricia-Anne Howells, *b.* 1931, *m.*

2010 *Hughes of Stretford,* Beverley Hughes, PC, *b.* 1950, *m.*

2010 *Hussein-Ece,* Meral Hussein Ece, OBE, *b.* 1953

1991 *James of Holland Park,* Phyllis Dorothy White (P. D. James), OBE, *b.* 1920, *w.*

1992 *Jay of Paddington,* Margaret Ann Jay, PC, *b.* 1939, *m.*

2006 *Jones of Whitchurch,* Margaret Beryl Jones, *b.* 1955

1997 *Kennedy of the Shaws,* Helena Ann Kennedy, QC, *b.* 1950, *m.*

2006 *Kingsmill,* Denise Patricia Byrne Kingsmill, CBE, *b.* 1947, *m.*

2009 *Kinnock of Holyhead,* Glenys Elizabeth Kinnock, *b.* 1944, *m.*

1997 *Knight of Collingtree,* (Joan Christabel) Jill Knight, DBE, *b.* 1927, *w.*

2010 *Liddell of Coatdyke,* Helen Lawrie Liddell, PC, *b.* 1950, *m.*
1997 *Linklater of Butterstone,* Veronica Linklater, *b.* 1943, *m.*
1978 *Lockwood,* Betty Lockwood, *b.* 1924, *w.*
1997 *Ludford,* Sarah Ann Ludford, *b.* 1951
2004 *McDonagh,* Margaret Josephine McDonagh
1979 *McFarlane of Llandaff,* Jean Kennedy McFarlane, *b.* 1926
1999 *McIntosh of Hudnall,* Genista Mary McIntosh, *b.* 1946
1997 *Maddock,* Diana Margaret Maddock, *b.* 1945, *m.*
2008 *Manningham-Buller,* Elizabeth (Lydia) Manningham-Buller, DCB, *b.* 1948, *m.*
1991 *Mallalieu,* Ann Mallalieu, QC, *b.* 1945, *m.*
1970 *Masham of Ilton,* Susan Lilian Primrose Cunliffe-Lister, *b.* 1935, *w.*
1999 *Massey of Darwen,* Doreen Elizabeth Massey, *b.* 1938, *m.*
2006 *Meacher,* Molly Christine Meacher, *b.* 1940, *m.*
1998 *Miller of Chilthorne Domer,* Susan Elizabeth Miller, *b.* 1954
1993 *Miller of Hendon,* Doreen Miller, MBE, *b.* 1933, *m.*
2004 *Morgan of Drefelin,* Delyth Jane Morgan, *b.* 1961, *m.*
2001 *Morgan of Huyton,* Sally Morgan, *b.* 1959, *m.*
2004 *Morris of Bolton,* Patricia Morris, OBE, *b.* 1953
2005 *Morris of Yardley,* Estelle Morris, PC, *b.* 1952
2004 *Murphy,* Elaine Murphy, *b.* 1947, *m.*
2004 *Neuberger,* Rabbi Julia (Babette Sarah) Neuberger, DBE, *b.* 1950, *m.*
2007 *Neville-Jones,* (Lilian) Pauline Neville-Jones, DCMG, PC, *b.* 1939
2010 *Newlove,* Helen Margaret Newlove, *w.*
1997 *Nicholson of Winterbourne,* Emma Harriet Nicholson, MEP, *b.* 1941, *m.*
1982 *Nicol,* Olive Mary Wendy Nicol, *b.* 1923, *m.*
2000 *Noakes,* Shiela Valerie Masters, DBE, *b.* 1949, *m.*
2000 *Northover,* Lindsay Patricia Granshaw, *b.* 1954
2010 *Nye,* Susan Nye, *b.* 1955, *m.*
1991 *O'Cathain,* Detta O'Cathain, OBE, *b.* 1938, *m.*
2009 *O'Loan,* Nuala Patricia, DBE, *b.* 1951, *m.*
1999 *O'Neill of Bengarve,* Onora Sylvia O'Neill, CBE, PHD, *b.* 1941
1989 *Oppenheim-Barnes,* Sally Oppenheim-Barnes, PC, *b.* 1930, *m.*
2006 *Paisley of St George's,* Eileen Emily Paisley, *m.*
2010 *Parminter,* Kathryn Jane Parminter, *b.* 1964, *m.*
1991 *Perry of Southwark,* Pauline Perry, *b.* 1931, *m.*
1997 *Pitkeathley,* Jill Elizabeth Pitkeathley, OBE, *b.* 1940
1981 *Platt of Writtle,* Beryl Catherine Platt, CBE, FENG, *b.* 1923, *m.*
1999 *Prashar,* Usha Kumari Prashar, CBE, PC, *b.* 1948, *m.*
2004 *Prosser,* Margaret Theresa Prosser, OBE, *b.* 1937
2006 *Quin,* Joyce Gwendoline Quin, PC *b.* 1944
1996 *Ramsay of Cartvale,* Margaret Mildred (Meta) Ramsay, *b.* 1936
1994 *Rawlings,* Patricia Elizabeth Rawlings, *b.* 1939
1997 *Rendell of Babergh,* Ruth Barbara Rendell, CBE, *b.* 1930, *m.*
1998 *Richardson of Calow,* Kathleen Margaret Richardson, OBE, *b.* 1938, *m.*
2010 *Ritchie of Brompton,* Shireen Olive Ritchie, *b.* 1945
2004 *Royall of Blaisdon,* Janet Anne Royall, PC, *b.* 1955, *m.*
1997 *Scotland of Asthal,* Patricia Janet Scotland, QC, *b.* 1955, *m.*
2000 *Scott of Needham Market,* Rosalind Carol Scott, *b.* 1957
1991 *Seccombe,* Joan Anna Dalziel Seccombe, DBE, *b.* 1930, *m.*
1998 *Sharp of Guildford,* Margaret Lucy Sharp, *b.* 1938, *m.*
1973 *Sharples,* Pamela Sharples, *b.* 1923, *m.*
2005 *Shephard of Northwold,* Gillian Patricia Shephard, PC, *b.* 1940, *m.*
2010 *Sherlock,* Maeve Christina Mary Sherlock, OBE, *b.* 1960
2010 *Smith of Basildon,* Angela Evans Smith, PC, *b.* 1959, *m.*
1995 *Smith of Gilmorehill,* Elizabeth Margaret Smith, *b.* 1940, *w.*
2010 *Stedman-Scott,* Deborah Stedman-Scott, OBE, *b.* 1955
1999 *Stern,* Vivien Helen Stern, CBE, *b.* 1941
1996 *Symons of Vernham Dean,* Elizabeth Conway Symons, *b.* 1951
2005 *Taylor of Bolton,* Winifred Ann Taylor, PC *b.* 1947, *m.*
1992 *Thatcher,* Margaret Hilda Thatcher, KG, OM, PC, FRS, *b.* 1925, *w.*
1994 *Thomas of Walliswood,* Susan Petronella Thomas, OBE, *b.* 1935, *m.*
2006 *Thomas of Winchester,* Celia Marjorie Thomas, MBE, *b.* 1945
1998 *Thornton,* (Dorothea) Glenys Thornton, *b.* 1952, *m.*
2005 *Tonge,* Dr. Jennifer Louise Tonge, *b.* 1941, *m.*
1980 *Trumpington,* Jean Alys Barker, DCVO, PC, *b.* 1922, *w.*
1985 *Turner of Camden,* Muriel Winifred Turner, *b.* 1927, *m.*
1998 *Uddin,* Manzila Pola Uddin, *b.* 1959, *m.*
2007 *Vadera,* Shriti Vadera, PC
2005 *Valentine,* Josephine Clare Valentine
2006 *Verma,* Sandip Verma, *b.* 1959, *m.*
2004 *Wall of New Barnet,* Margaret Mary Wall, *b.* 1941, *m.*
2000 *Walmsley,* Joan Margaret Walmsley, *b.* 1943
1985 *Warnock,* Helen Mary Warnock, DBE, *b.* 1924, *w.*
2007 *Warsi,* Sayeeda Hussain Warsi, PC, *b.* 1971
1999 *Warwick of Undercliffe,* Diana Mary Warwick, *b.* 1945, *m.*
2010 *Wheeler,* Margaret Eileen Joyce Wheeler, MBE, *b.* 1949
1999 *Whitaker,* Janet Alison Whitaker, *b.* 1936
1996 *Wilcox,* Judith Ann Wilcox, *b.* 1940, *w.*
1999 *Wilkins,* Rosalie Catherine Wilkins, *b.* 1946
1993 *Williams of Crosby,* Shirley Vivien Teresa Brittain Williams, PC, *b.* 1930, *w.*
2004 *Young of Hornsey,* Prof. Margaret Omolola Young, OBE, *b.* 1951, *m.*
1997 *Young of Old Scone,* Barbara Scott Young, *b.* 1948

LORDS SPIRITUAL

The Lords Spiritual are the Archbishops of Canterbury and York and 24 diocesan bishops of the Church of England. The Bishops of London, Durham and Winchester always have seats in the House of Lords; the other 21 seats are filled by the remaining diocesan bishops in order of seniority. The Bishop of Sodor and Man and the Bishop of Gibraltar are not eligible to sit in the House of Lords.

ARCHBISHOPS

Style, The Most Revd and Rt. Hon. the Lord Archbishop of_
Addressed as Archbishop *or* Your Grace

INTRODUCED TO HOUSE OF LORDS

2003 *Canterbury* (104th), Rowan Douglas Williams, PC, DPHIL, *b.* 1950, *m., cons.* 1992, *elected* 2002
2005 *York* (97th), John Mugabi Tucker Sentamu, PC, PHD, *b.* 1949, *m., cons.* 1996, *elected* 2005, *trans.* 2005

BISHOPS

Style, The Rt. Revd the Lord Bishop of _
Addressed as My Lord
elected date of confirmation as diocesan bishop

INTRODUCED TO HOUSE OF LORDS
(as at 31 August 2010)

1996 *London* (132nd), Richard John Carew Chartres, KCVO, PC, *b.* 1947, *m., cons.* 1992, *elected* 1995
2003 *Durham* (72nd), *vacant*
1996 *Winchester* (96th), Michael Charles Scott-Joynt, *b.* 1943, *m., cons.* 1987, *elected* 1995
1997 *Manchester* (11th), Nigel Simeon McCulloch, *b.* 1942, *m., cons.* 1986, *elected* 1992, *trans.* 2002
1998 *Salisbury* (77th), David Staffurth Stancliffe, *b.* 1942, *m., cons.* 1993, *elected* 1993
2001 *Chester* (40th), Peter Robert Forster, PHD, *m., b.* 1950, *cons.* 1996, *elected* 1996
2003 *Newcastle* (11th), (John) Martin Wharton, *b.* 1944, *m., cons.* 1992, *elected* 1997
2003 *Liverpool* (7th), James Stuart Jones, *b.* 1948, *m., cons.* 1994, *elected* 1998
2003 *Leicester* (6th), Timothy John Stevens, *b.* 1946, *m., cons.* 1995, *elected* 1999
2004 *Norwich* (71st), Graham Richard James, *b.* 1951, *m., cons.* 1993, *elected* 1999
2005 *Exeter* (70th), Michael Lawrence Langrish, *b.* 1946, *m., cons.* 1993, *elected* 2000
2006 *Ripon and Leeds* (12th), John Richard Packer, *b.* 1946, *m., cons.* 1996, *elected* 2000
2008 *Chichester* (102nd), John William Hind, *b.* 1945, *m., cons.* 1991, *elected* 2001
2008 *Lincoln* (71st), Dr John Charles Saxbee, *b.* 1946, *m., cons.* 1994, *elected* 2001
2008 *Bath and Wells* (77th), Peter Bryan Price, *b.* 1944, *m., cons.* 1997, *elected* 2002
2009 *Wakefield* (12th), Stephen George Platten, *b.* 1947, *m., cons.* 2003, *elected* 2003
2009 *Bristol* (55th), Michael Arthur Hill, *b.* 1947, *m., cons.* 1998, *elected* 2003
2009 *Lichfield* (98th), Jonathan Michael Gledhill, *b.* 1949, *m., cons.* 1996, *elected* 2003
2009 *Blackburn* (8th), Nicholas Stewart Reade, *b.* 1946, *cons.* 2004, *elected* 2004
2009 *Hereford* (104th), Anthony Martin Priddis, *b.* 1948, *cons.* 1996, *elected* 2004
2009 *Gloucester* (40th), Michael Francis Perham, *b.* 1947, *m., cons.* 2004, *elected* 2004
2010 *Guildford* (9th), Christopher John Hill, *b.* 1945, *m., cons.* 1996, *elected* 2004
2010 *Derby* (7th), Alastair Llewellyn John Redfern, *b.* 1948, *m., cons.* 1997, *elected* 2005
2010 *Birmingham* (9th), David Andrew Urquhart, *b.* 1952, *cons.* 2000, *elected* 2006

BISHOPS AWAITING SEATS, in order of seniority
(as at 31 August 2010)

Oxford (42nd), John Lawrence Pritchard, *b.* 1948, *m., cons.* 2002, *elected* 2007
St Edmundsbury and Ipswich (10th), (William) Nigel Stock, *b.* 1950, *m., cons.* 2000, *elected* 2007
Worcester (113th), John Geoffrey Inge, PHD, *b.* 1955, *m., cons.* 2003, *elected* 2007
Coventry (9th), Christopher John Cocksworth, PHD, *b.* 1959, *m., cons.* 2008, *elected* 2008
Truro (15th), Timothy Martin Thornton, *b.* 1957, *m., cons.* 2001, *elected* 2008
Sheffield (7th), Stephen John Lindsey Croft, *b.* 1957, *m., cons.* 2009, *elected* 2009
St Albans (10th), Alan Gregory Clayton Smith, *b.* 1957, *cons.* 2001, *elected* 2009
Carlisle (66th), James Newcome, *b.* 1953, *m., cons.* 2002, *elected* 2009
Southwell and Nottingham (11th), Paul Butler, *b.* 1955, *m., cons.* 2004, *elected* 2009
Peterborough (38th), Donald Spargo Allister, *b.* 1952, *m., cons.* 2010, *elected* 2010
Portsmouth (9th), Christopher Richard James Foster, *b.* 1953, *m., cons.* 2001, *elected* 2010
Chelmsford (10th), Stephen Cottrell, *b.* 1958, *m., cons.* 2004, *elected* 2010
Rochester (107th), James Langstaff, *b.* 1956, *m., cons.* 2004, *elected* 2010
Ely (69th), vacant
Southwark (10th), vacant
Bradford (10th), vacant

COURTESY TITLES AND PEERS' SURNAMES

COURTESY TITLES

The heir apparent to a Duke, Marquess or Earl uses the highest of his father's other titles as a courtesy title. For example, the Marquess of Blandford is heir to the Dukedom of Marlborough, and Viscount Amberley to the Earldom of Russell. Titles of second heirs (when in use) are also given, and the courtesy title of the father of a second heir is indicated by * eg Earl of Mornington, eldest son of *Marquess of Douro.

The holder of a courtesy title is not styled 'the Most Hon.' or 'the Rt. Hon.', and in correspondence 'the' is omitted before the title. The heir apparent to a Scottish title may use the title 'Master'.

MARQUESSES
*Blandford – *Marlborough, D.*
Bowmont and Cessford – *Roxburghe, D.*
*Douro – *Wellington, D.*
Graham – *Montrose, D.*
*Hamilton – *Abercorn, D.*
Hartington – *Devonshire, D.*
Lorne – *Argyll, D.*
Stafford – *Sutherland, D.*
Tavistock – *Bedford, D.*
Tullibardine – *Atholl, D.*
*Worcester – *Beaufort, D.*

EARLS
Aboyne – *Huntly, M.*
Arundel and Surrey – *Norfolk, D.*
Bective – *Headfort, M.*
Belfast – *Donegall, M.*
Brecknock – *Camden, M.*
Burford – *St Albans, D.*
*Cardigan – *Ailesbury, M.*
Compton – *Northampton, M.*
*Dalkeith – *Buccleuch, D.*
Dumfries – *Bute, M.*
*Euston – *Grafton, D.*
Glamorgan – **Worcester, M.*
Grosvenor – *Westminster, D.*
Haddo – *Aberdeen and Temair, M.*
Hillsborough – *Downshire, M.*
Hopetoun – *Linlithgow, M.*
Kerry – *Lansdowne, M.*
March and Kinrara – *Richmond, D.*
Medina – *Milford Haven, M.*
*Mount Charles – *Conyngham, M.*
Mornington – **Douro, M.*
Mulgrave – *Normanby, M.*
Percy – *Northumberland, D.*
Rocksavage – *Cholmondley, M.*
Ronaldshay – *Zetland, M.*
*St Andrews – *Kent, D.*
*Southesk – *Fife, D.*
Sunderland – **Blandford, M.*
*Tyrone – *Waterford, M.*
Ulster – *Gloucester, D.*
*Uxbridge – *Anglesey, M.*
Wiltshire – *Winchester, M.*
Yarmouth – *Hertford, M.*

VISCOUNTS
Alexander – *Caledon, E.*
Althorp – *Spencer, E.*
Andover – *Suffolk and Berkshire, E.*
Asquith – *Oxford and Asquith, E.*
Boringdon – *Morley, E.*
Borodale – *Beatty, E.*
Boyle – *Shannon, E.*
Brocas – *Jellicoe, E.*
Bury – *Albermarle, E.*
Campden – *Gainsborough, E.*
Carlow – *Portarlington, E.*
Carlton – *Wharncliffe, E.*
Castlereagh – *Londonderry, M.*
Chelsea – *Cadogan, E.*
Chewton – *Waldegrave, E.*
Clanfield – *Peel, E.*
Clive – *Powis, E.*
Coke – *Leicester, E.*
Corry – *Belmore, E.*
Corvedale – *Baldwin of Bewdley, E.*
Cranborne – *Salisbury, M.*
Cranley – *Onslow, E.*
Crichton – *Erne, E.*
Curzon – *Howe, E.*
Dangan – *Cowley, E.*
Drumlanrig – *Queensberry, M.*
Duncannon – *Bessborough, E.*
Dungarvan – *Cork and Orrery, E.*
Dunluce – *Antrim, E.*
Dunwich – *Stradbroke, E.*
Dupplin – *Kinnoull, E.*
Ednam – *Dudley, E.*
Elveden – *Iveagh, E.*
Emlyn – *Cawdor, E*
Encombe – *Eldon, E.*
Enfield – *Strafford, E.*
Erleigh – *Reading, M.*
Errington – *Cromer, E.*
Feilding – *Denbigh and Desmond, E.*
FitzHarris – *Malmesbury, E.*
Folkestone – *Radnor, E.*
Forbes – *Granard, E.*
Garmoyle – *Cairns, E.*
Garnock – *Lindsay, E.*
Glenapp – *Inchcape, E.*
Glentworth – *Limerick, E.*
Grey de Wilton – *Wilton, E.*
Grimstone – *Verulam, E.*
Gwynedd – *Lloyd George of Dwyfor, E.*
Hawkesbury – *Liverpool, E.*
Hinchingbrooke – *Sandwich, E.*
Ikerrin – *Carrick, E.*
Ingestre – *Shrewsbury, E.*
Jocelyn – *Roden, E.*
Kelburn – *Glasgow, E.*
Kingsborough – *Kingston, E.*
Kirkwall – *Orkney, E.*
Knebworth – *Lytton, E.*
Lambton – *Durham, E.*
Lascelles – *Harewood, E.*
Linley – *Snowdon, E.*
Lymington – *Portsmouth, E.*
Macmillan of Ovenden – *Stockton, E.*
Maidstone – *Winchilsea, E*
Maitland – *Lauderdale, E.*
Mandeville – *Manchester, D.*
Marsham – *Romney, E.*
Melgund – *Minto, E.*
Merton – *Nelson, E.*
Moore – *Drogheda, E.*
Newport – *Bradford, E.*
Northland – *Ranfurly, E*
Newry and Mourne – *Kilmorey, E.*
Petersham – *Harrington, E.*
Pollington – *Mexborough, E*
Raynham – *Townshend, M.*
Reidhaven – *Seafield, E.*
Royston – *Hardwicke, E.*
Ruthven of Canberra – *Gowrie, E.*
St Cyres – *Iddesleigh, E.*
Sandon – *Harrowby, E.*
Savernake – **Cardigan, E.*
Severn – *Wessex, E.*
Somerton – *Normanton, E.*
Stopford – *Courtown, E.*
Stormont – *Mansfield, E.*
Strabane – **Hamilton, M.*
Strathallan – *Perth, E.*
Stuart – *Castle Stewart, E.*
Suirdale – *Donoughmore, E.*
Tamworth – *Ferrers, E.*
Tarbat – *Cromartie, E.*
Vaughan – *Lisburne, E.*
Weymouth – *Bath, M.*
Windsor – *Plymouth, E.*
Wolmer – *Selborne, E.*
Woodstock – *Portland, E.*

BARONS (LORDS)
Aberdour – *Morton, E.*
Apsley – *Bathurst, E.*
Ardee – *Meath, E.*
Balgonie – *Leven and Melville, E.*
Balniel – *Crawford and Balcarres, E.*
Berriedale – *Caithness, E.*
Bingham – *Lucan, E.*
Binning – *Haddington, E.*
Brooke – *Warwick, E.*
Bruce – *Elgin, E.*
Burghley – *Exeter, M.*
Cardross – *Buchan, E.*
Carnegie – **Southesk, E.*
Clifton – *Darnley, E.*
Cochrane – *Dundonald, E.*
Courtenay – *Devon, E.*
Dalmeny – *Rosebery, E.*
Doune – *Moray, E.*
Downpatrick – **St Andrews, E.*
Dunglass – *Home, E.*
Elcho – *Wemyss and March, E.*
Eliot – *St Germans, E.*
Formartine – **Haddo, E.*
Gillford – *Clanwilliam, E.*
Glamis – *Strathmore, E.*
Greenock – *Cathcart, E.*
Guernsey – *Aylesford, E.*
Hay – *Erroll, E.*
Howard of Effingham – *Effingham, E.*
Huntingtower – *Dysart, C.*

Irwin – *Halifax, E.*
Johnstone – *Annandale and Hartfell, E.*
Langton – *Temple of Stowe, E.*
La Poer – **Tyrone, E.*
Leveson – *Granville, E*
Loughborough – *Rosslyn, E.*
Masham – *Swinton, E.*
Mauchline – *Loudoun, C.*
Medway – *Cranbrook, E.*
Montgomerie – *Eglinton and Winton, E.*
Moreton – *Ducie, E.*
Naas – *Mayo, E.*
Norreys – *Lindsey and Abingdon, E.*
North – *Guilford, E.*
Ogilvy – *Airlie, E.*
Oxmantown – *Rosse, E.*
Paget de Beaudesert – **Uxbridge, E.*
Porchester – *Carnarvon, E.*
Ramsay – *Dalhousie, E.*
Romsey – *Mountbatten of Burma, C.*
Scrymgeour – *Dundee, E.*
Seymour – *Somerset, D.*
Stanley – *Derby, E.*
Stavordale – *Ilchester, E.*
Strathnaver – *Sutherland, C.*
Wodehouse – *Kimberley, E.*
Worsley – *Yarborough, E.*

PEERS' SURNAMES

The following symbols indicate the rank of the peer holding each title:

C.	Countess
D.	Duke
E.	Earl
M.	Marquess
V.	Viscount
*	Life Peer

Where no designation is given, the title is that of a hereditary Baron or Baroness.

Abney-Hastings – *Loudoun, C.*
Acheson – *Gosford, E.*
Adams – *A. of Craigielea**
Adderley – *Norton*
Addington – *Sidmouth, V.*
Adebowale – *A. of Thornes**
Agar – *Normanton, E.*
Aitken – *Beaverbrook*
Akers-Douglas – *Chilston, V.*
Alexander – *A. of Tunis, E.*
Alexander – *Caledon, E.*
Allan – *A. of Hallam**
Allen – *Croham**
Allsopp – *Hindlip*
Alton – *A. of Liverpool**
Anderson – *A. of Swansea**
Anderson – *Waverley, V.*
Anelay – *A. of St Johns**
Annesley – *Valentia, V.*
Anson – *Lichfield, E.*
Archer – *A. of Sandwell**
Archer – *A. of Weston-super-Mare**
Armstrong – *A. of Hill Top**
Armstrong – *A. of Ilminster**
Armstrong-Jones – *Snowdon, E.*
Arthur – *Glenarthur*
Arundell – *Talbot of Malahide*
Ashdown – *A. of Norton-sub-Hamdon**
Ashley – *A. of Stoke**
Ashley-Cooper – *Shaftesbury, E.*
Ashton – *A. of Hyde*
Ashton – *A. of Upholland**
Asquith – *Oxford and Asquith, E.*
Assheton – *Clitheroe*
Astley – *Hastings*
Astor – *A. of Hever*
Aubrey-Fletcher – *Braye*
Bailey – *Glanusk*
Baillie – *Burton*
Baillie Hamilton – *Haddington, E.*
Baker – *B. of Dorking**
Baldwin – *B. of Bewdley, E.*
Balfour – *B. of Inchrye*
Balfour – *Kinross*
Balfour – *Riverdale*
Bampfylde – *Poltimore*
Banbury – *B. of Southam*
Barber – *B. of Tewkesbury**
Baring – *Ashburton*
Baring – *Cromer, E.*
Baring – *Howick of Glendale*
Baring – *Northbrook*
Baring – *Revelstoke*
Barker – *Trumpington**
Barnes – *Gorell*
Barnewall – *Trimlestown*
Bassam – *B. of Brighton**
Bathurst – *Bledisloe, V.*
Beauclerk – *St Albans, D.*
Beaumont – *Allendale, V.*
Beckett – *Grimthorpe*
Benn – *Stansgate, V.*
Bennet – *Tankerville, E.*
Bentinck – *Portland, E.*
Beresford – *Decies*
Beresford – *Waterford, M.*
Berry – *Camrose, V.*
Berry – *Kemsley, V.*
Bertie – *Lindsey, E.*
Best – *Wynford*
Bethell – *Westbury*
Bewicke-Copley – *Cromwell*
Bigham – *Mersey, V.*
Bingham – *B. of Cornhill**
Bingham – *Clanmorris*
Bingham – *Lucan, E.*
Black – *B. of Brentwood**
Black – *B. of Crossharbour**
Blair – *B. of Boughton**
Bligh – *Darnley, E.*
Blyth – *B. of Rowington**
Bonham Carter – *B.-C. of Yarnbury**
Bootle-Wilbraham – *Skelmersdale*
Boscawen – *Falmouth, V.*
Boston – *B. of Faversham**
Boswell – *B. of Aynho**
Bottomley – *B. of Nettlestone**
Bourke – *Mayo, E.*
Bowes Lyon – *Strathmore, E.*
Bowyer – *Denham*
Boyd – *Kilmarnock*
Boyd – *B. of Duncansby**
Boyle – *Cork and Orrery, E.*
Boyle – *Glasgow, E.*
Boyle – *Shannon, E.*
Brabazon – *Meath, E.*
Brand – *Hampden, V.*
Brassey – *B. of Apethorpe*
Brett – *Esher, V.*
Bridgeman – *Bradford, E.*
Brittan – *B. of Spennithorne**
Brodrick – *Midleton, V.*
Brooke – *Alanbrooke, V.*
Brooke – *B. of Alverthorpe**
Brooke – *Brookeborough, V.*
Brooke – *B. of Sutton Mandeville**
Brooks – *B. of Tremorfa**
Brooks – *Crawshaw*
Brougham – *Brougham and Vaux*
Broughton – *Fairhaven*
Brown – *B. of Eaton-under-Heywood**
Browne – *B. of Belmont**
Browne – *B. of Ladyton**
Browne – *B. of Madingley**
Browne – *Kilmaine*
Browne – *Oranmore and Browne*
Browne – *Sligo, M.*
Bruce – *Aberdare*
Bruce – *Balfour of Burleigh*
Bruce – *Elgin and Kincardine, E.*
Brudenell-Bruce – *Ailesbury, M.*
Buchan – *Tweedsmuir*
Buckley – *Wrenbury*
Butler – *B. of Brockwell**
Butler – *Carrick, E.*
Butler – *Dunboyne*
Butler – *Mountgarret, V.*
Byng – *Strafford, E.*
Byng – *Torrington, V.*
Cambell-Savours – *C.-S. of Allerdale**
Cameron – *C. of Dillington**
Cameron – *C. of Lochbroom**
Campbell – *Argyll, D.*
Campbell – *C. of Alloway**
Campbell – *C. of Loughborough**
Campbell – *C. of Surbiton**
Campbell – *Cawdor, E.*
Campbell – *Colgrain*
Campbell – *Stratheden and Campbell*
Campbell-Gray – *Gray*
Canning – *Garvagh*
Capell – *Essex, E.*
Carey – *C. of Clifton**
Carington – *Carrington*
Carlisle – *C. of Berriew**
Carnegie – *Fife, D.*
Carnegy – *Northesk, E.*
Carr – *C. of Hadley**
Carter – *C. of Barnes**
Carter – *C. of Coles**
Cary – *Falkland, V.*
Caulfeild – *Charlemont, V.*
Cavendish – *C. of Furness**
Cavendish – *Chesham*
Cavendish – *Devonshire, D.*
Cavendish – *Waterpark*
Cayzer – *Rotherwick*
Cecil – *Amherst of Hackney*
Cecil – *Exeter, M.*
Cecil – *Rockley*
Chalker – *C. of Wallasey**
Chaloner – *Gisborough*
Chapman – *C. of Leeds**
Chapman – *Northfield**
Charteris – *Wemyss and March, E.*
Chetwynd-Talbot – *Shrewsbury, E.*
Chichester – *Donegall, M.*
Child Villiers – *Jersey, E.*
Cholmondeley – *Delamere*
Chubb – *Hayter*

Clark – *C. of Calton**
Clarke – *C. of Hampstead**
Clarke – *C. of Stone-Cum-Ebony**
Clegg-Hill – *Hill, V.*
Clifford – *C. of Chudleigh*
Cochrane – *C. of Cults*
Cochrane – *Dundonald, E.*
Cocks – *Somers*
Cohen – *C. of Pimlico**
Cokayne – *Cullen of Ashbourne*
Coke – *Leicester, E.*
Cole – *Enniskillen, E.*
Collier – *Monkswell*
Collins – *C. of Mapesbury**
Colville – *Clydesmuir*
Colville – *C. of Culross, V.*
Compton – *Northampton, M.*
Conolly-Carew – *Carew*
Cooper – *Norwich, V*
Cope – *C. of Berkeley**
Corbett – *C. of Castle Vale**.
Corbett – *Rowallan*
Cornwall-Leigh – *Grey of Condor*
Courtenay – *Devon, E.*
Craig – *C. of Radley**
Craig – *Craigavon, V.*
Crichton – *Erne, E.*
Crichton-Stuart – *Bute, M.*
Cripps – *Parmoor*
Crossley – *Somerleyton*
Cubitt – *Ashcombe*
Cunliffe-Lister – *Masham of Ilton**
Cunliffe-Lister – *Swinton, E.*
Cunningham – *C. of Felling**
Currie – *C. of Marylebone**
Curzon – *Howe, E.*
Curzon – *Scarsdale, V.*
Cust – *Brownlow*
Czernin – *Howard de Walden*
Dalrymple – *Stair, E.*
Darzi – *D. of Denham**
Daubeny de Moleyns – *Ventry*
Davidson – *D. of Glen Clova**
Davies – *D. of Abersoch**
Davies – *D. of Coity**
Davies – *Darwen*
Davies – *D. of Oldham**
Davies – *D. of Stamford**
Dawnay – *Downe, V.*
Dawson-Damer – *Portarlington, E.*
Dean – *D. of Thornton-le-Fylde**
Deane – *Muskerry*
de Courcy – *Kingsale*
de Grey – *Walsingham*
Denison – *Londesborough*
Denison-Pender – *Pender*
Devereux – *Hereford, V.*
Dewar – *Forteviot*
Dixon – *Glentoran*
Dodson – *Monk Bretton*
Douglas – *Morton, E.*
Douglas – *Queensberry, M.*
Douglas-Hamilton – *Hamilton, D.*
Douglas-Hamilton – *Selkirk, E.*
Douglas-Hamilton – *Selkirk of Douglas**
Douglas-Home – *Dacre*
Douglas-Home – *Home, E.*
Douglas-Pennant – *Penrhyn*
Douglas-Scott-Montagu – *Montagu of Beaulieu*
Drummond – *Perth, E.*
Drummond of Megginch – *Strange*
Dugdale – *Crathorne*
Duke – *Merrivale*
Duncombe – *Feversham*
Dundas – *Melville, V.*
Dundas – *Zetland, M.*
Eady – *Swinfen*
Eccles – *E. of Moulton**
Ece – *Hussein-Ece**
Eden – *Auckland*
Eden – *E. of Winton**
Eden – *Henley*
Edgcumbe – *Mount Edgcumbe, E.*
Edmondson – *Sandford*
Edwardes – *Kensington*
Edwards – *Crickhowell**
Egerton – *Sutherland, D.*
Eliot – *St Germans, E.*
Elliott – *E. of Morpeth**
Elliot-Murray-Kynynmound – *Minto, E.*
Ellis – *Seaford*
Erskine – *Buchan, E.*
Erskine – *Mar and Kellie, E.*
Erskine-Murray – *Elibank*
Evans – *E. of Parkside**
Evans – *E. of Temple Guiting**
Evans – *E. of Watford**
Evans – *Mountevans*
Evans-Freke – *Carbery*
Eve – *Silsoe*
Fairfax – *F. of Cameron*
Falconer – *F. of Thoroton**
Falkner – *F. of Margravine**
Fane – *Westmorland, E.*
Farrington – *F. of Ribbleton**
Faulkner – *F. of Worcester**
Fearn – *F. of Southport**
Feilding – *Denbigh and Desmond, E.*
Felton – *Seaford*
Fellowes – *De Ramsey*
Fermor-Hesketh – *Hesketh*
Fiennes – *Saye and Sele*
Fiennes-Clinton – *Lincoln, E.*
Finch Hatton – *Winchilsea, E.*
Finch-Knightley – *Aylesford, E.*
Finlay – *F. of Llandaff**
Fitzalan-Howard – *Herries of Terregles*
Fitzalan-Howard – *Norfolk, D.*
FitzGerald – *Leinster, D.*
Fitzherbert – *Stafford*
FitzRoy – *Grafton, D.*
FitzRoy – *Southampton*
FitzRoy Newdegate – *Daventry, V.*
Fletcher-Vane – *Inglewood*
Flower – *Ashbrook, V.*
Foljambe – *Liverpool, E.*
Forbes – *Granard, E*
Forsyth – *F. of Drumlean**
Forwood – *Arlington*
Foster – *F. of Thames Bank**
Foulkes – *F. of Cumnock**
Fowler – *F. of Sutton Caulfield**
Fox-Strangways – *Ilchester, E.*
Frankland – *Zouche*
Fraser – *F. of Carmyllie**
Fraser – *F. of Kilmorack**
Fraser – *Lovat*
Fraser – *Saltoun*
Fraser – *Strathalmond*
Freeman-Grenville – *Kinloss*
Fremantle – *Cottesloe*
French – *De Freyne*
Fyfe – *F. of Fairfield**
Galbraith – *Strathclyde*
Garden – *G. of Frognal**
Gardiner – *G. of Kimble**
Gardner – *G. of Parkes**
Gascoyne-Cecil – *M. of Salisbury**
Gathorne-Hardy – *Cranbrook, E.*
Gibbs – *Aldenham*
Gibbs – *Wraxall*
Gibson – *Ashbourne*
Gibson – *G. of Market Rasen**
Giffard – *Halsbury, E.*
Gilbey – *Vaux of Harrowden*
Glyn – *Wolverton*
Godley – *Kilbracken*
Goff – *G. of Chieveley**
Golding – *G. of Newcastle-under-Lyme**
Gordon – *Aberdeen, M.*
Gordon – *G. of Strathblane**
Gordon – *Huntly, M.*
Gordon Lennox – *Richmond, D.*
Gore – *Arran, E.*
Gould – *G. of Brookwood**
Gould – *G. of Potternewton**
Graham – *G. of Edmonton**
Graham – *Montrose, D.*
Graham-Toler – *Norbury, E.*
Granshaw – *Northover**
Grant of Grant – *Strathspey*
Grant of Rothiemurchus – *Dysart, C.*
Granville – *G. of Eye**
Greenall – *Daresbury*
Greville – *Warwick, E.*
Griffiths – *G. of Burry Port**
Griffiths – *G. of Fforestfach**
Grigg – *Altrincham*
Grimston – *G. of Westbury*
Grimston – *Verulam, E.*
Grosvenor – *Westminster, D.*
Grosvenor – *Wilton and Ebury, E*
Guest – *Wimborne, V*
Gueterbock – *Berkeley*
Guinness – *Iveagh, E.*
Guinness – *Moyne*
Gully – *Selby, V.*
Gummer – *Chadlington**
Gummer – *Deben**
Gurdon – *Cranworth*
Guthrie – *G. of Craigiebank**
Gwynne Jones – *Chalfont**
Hale – *H. of Richmond**
Hall – *H. of Birkenhead**
Hamilton – *Abercorn, D.*
Hamilton – *Belhaven and Stenton*
Hamilton – *H. of Dalzell*
Hamilton – *H. of Epsom**
Hamilton – *Holm Patrick*
Hamilton-Russell – *Boyne, V.*
Hamilton-Smith – *Colwyn*
Hanbury-Tracy – *Sudeley*
Handcock – *Castlemaine*
Hannay – *H. of Chiswick**
Harbord-Hamond – *Suffield*
Harding – *H. of Petherton*
Hardinge – *H. of Penshurst*
Hare – *Blakenham, V.*
Hare – *Listowel, E.*
Harmsworth – *Rothermere, V.*
Harries – *H. of Pentregarth**
Harris – *H. of Haringey**

Harris – *H. of Peckham**
Harris – *H. of Richmond**
Harris – *Malmesbury, E.*
Hart – *H. of Chilton**
Harvey – *H. of Tasburgh*
Hastings – *H. of Scarisbrick**
Hastings Bass – *Huntingdon, E.*
Haughey – *Ballyedmond**
Hay – *Erroll, E.*
Hay – *Kinnoull, E.*
Hay – *Tweeddale, M.*
Hayter – *H. of Kentish Town**
Healy – *H. of Primrose Hill**
Heathcote-Drummond-Willoughby – *Willoughby de Eresby*
Hely-Hutchinson – *Donoughmore, E.*
Henderson – *Faringdon*
Hennessy – *Windlesham*
Henniker-Major – *Henniker*
Hepburne-Scott – *Polwarth*
Herbert – *Carnarvon, E.*
Herbert – *Hemingford*
Herbert – *Pembroke, E.*
Herbert – *Powis, E.*
Hervey – *Bristol, M.*
Heseltine – *H. of Thenford**
Hewitt – *Lifford, V.*
Hicks Beach – *St Aldwyn, E.*
Hill – *Downshire, M.*
Hill – *H. of Oareford**
Hill – *Sandys*
Hill-Trevor – *Trevor*
Hilton – *H. of Eggardon**
Hobart-Hampden – *Buckinghamshire, E.*
Hodgson – *H. of Astley Abbotts**
Hogg – *Hailsham, V.*
Holland-Hibbert – *Knutsford, V.*
Hollis – *H. of Heigham**
Holmes à Court – *Heytesbury*
Hood – *Bridport, V.*
Hope – *Glendevon*
Hope – *H. of Craighead**
Hope – *H. of Thornes**
Hope – *Linlithgow, M.*
Hope – *Rankeillour*
Hope Johnstone – *Annandale and Hartfell, E.*
Hope-Morley – *Hollenden*
Hopkinson – *Colyton*
Hore Ruthven – *Gowrie, E.*
Hovell-Thurlow-Cumming-Bruce – *Thurlow*
Howard – *Carlisle, E.*
Howard – *Effingham, E.*
Howard – *H. of Lympne**
Howard – *H. of Penrith*
Howard – *H. of Rising**
Howard – *Strathcona*
Howard – *Suffolk and Berkshire, E.*
Howarth – *H. of Breckland**
Howarth – *H. of Newport**
Howe – *H. of Aberavon**
Howe – *H. of Idlicote**
Howell – *H. of Guildford**
Howells – *H. of St. Davids**
Howie – *H. of Troon**
Hubbard – *Addington*
Huggins – *Malvern, V.*
Hughes – *H. of Stretford**
Hughes – *H. of Woodside**
Hughes-Young – *St Helens*
Hunt – *H. of Chesterton**
Hunt – *H. of Kings Heath**
Hunt – *H. of Wirral**
Hurd – *H. of Westwell**
Hutchinson – *H. of Lullington**
Hutton – *H. of Furness**
Ingrams – *Darcy de Knayth*
Innes-Ker – *Roxburghe, D.*
Inskip – *Caldecote, V.*
Irby – *Boston*
Irvine – *I. of Lairg**
Isaacs – *Reading, M.*
James – *J. of Blackheath**
James – *J. of Holland Park**
James – *Northbourne*
Janner – *J. of Braunstone**
Jay – *J. of Ewelme**
Jay – *J. of Paddington**
Jebb – *Gladwyn*
Jenkin – *J. of Roding**
Jervis – *St Vincent, V.*
Jocelyn – *Roden, E.*
Jolliffe – *Hylton*
Jones – *J. of Birmingham**
Jones – *J. of Cheltenham**
Jones – *J. of Deeside**
Jones – *J. of Whitchurch**
Joynson-Hicks – *Brentford, V.*
Kay-Shuttleworth – *Shuttleworth*
Kearley – *Devonport, V.*
Keith – *Kintore, E.*
Kemp – *Rochdale, V.*
Kennedy – *Ailsa, M*
Kennedy – *K. of the Shaws**
Kennedy – *K. of Southwark**
Kenworthy – *Strabolgi*
Keppel – *Albemarle, E.*
Kerr – *K. of Kinlochard**
Kerr – *K. of Tonaghmore**
Kerr – *Lothian, M.*
Kerr – *Teviot*
Kilpatrick – *K. of Kincraig**
King – *Lovelace, E.*
King – *K. of West Bromwich**
King-Tenison – *Kingston, E.*
Kinnock – *K. of Holyhead**
Kirkham – *Berners*
Kirkwood – *K. of Kirkhope**
Kitchener – *K. of Khartoum, E.*
Knatchbull – *Brabourne*
Knatchbull – *Mountbatten of Burma, C.*
Knight – *K. of Collingtree**
Knight – *K. of Weymouth**
Knox – *Ranfurly, E.*
Lamb – *Rochester*
Lambton – *Durham, E.*
Lamont – *L. of Lerwick**
Lampson – *Killearn*
Lang – *L. of Monkton**
Lascelles – *Harewood, E.*
Law – *Coleraine*
Law – *Ellenborough*
Lawrence – *Trevethin and Oaksey*
Lawson – *Burnham*
Lawson – *L. of Blaby**
Lawson-Johnston – *Luke*
Lea – *L. of Crondall**
Leach – *L. of Fairford**
Lee – *L. of Trafford**
Legge – *Dartmouth, E.*
Legh – *Grey of Codnor*
Legh – *Newton*
Leigh-Pemberton – *Kingsdown**
Leith – *Burgh*
Lennox-Boyd – *Boyd of Merton, V.*
Le Poer Trench – *Clancarty, E.*
Leslie – *Rothes, E.*
Leslie Melville – *Leven and Melville, E.*
Lester – *L. of Herne Hill**
Levene – *L. of Portsoken**
Leveson-Gower – *Granville, E.*
Lewis – *L. of Newnham**
Lewis – *Merthyr*
Liddell – *L. of Coatdyke**
Liddell – *Ravensworth*
Lindesay-Bethune – *Lindsay, E.*
Lindsay – *Crawford, E.*
Lindsay – *L. of Birker*
Linklater – *L. of Butterstone**
Littleton – *Hatherton*
Lloyd – *L. of Berwick**
Lloyd George – *Lloyd George of Dwyfor, E.*
Lloyd George – *Tenby, V.*
Lloyd-Mostyn – *Mostyn*
Loder – *Wakehurst*
Lofthouse – *L. of Pontefract**
Lopes – *Roborough*
Lour – *Carnegy of Lour**
Low – *Aldington*
Low – *L. of Dalston**
Lowry-Corry – *Belmore, E.*
Lowther – *Lonsdale, E.*
Lowther – *Ullswater, V.*
Lubbock – *Avebury*
Lucas – *L. of Chilworth*
Lumley – *Scarbrough, E.*
Lumley-Savile – *Savile*
Lyon-Dalberg-Acton – *Acton*
Lysaght – *Lisle*
Lyttelton – *Chandos, V.*
Lyttelton – *Cobham, V.*
Lytton Cobbold – *Cobbold*
McAlpine – *M. of West Green**
Macaulay – *M. of Bragar**
McClintock-Bunbury – *Rathdonnell*
McColl – *M. of Dulwich**
McConnell – *M. of Glenscorrodale**
MacDonald – *M. of River Glaven**
Macdonald – *M. of Tradeston**
McDonnell – *Antrim, E.*
McFall – *M. of Alcluith**
Macfarlane – *M. of Bearsden**
McFarlane – *M. of Llandaff**
MacGregor – *M. of Pulham Market**
McIntosh – *M. of Hudnall**
McKenzie – *M. of Luton**
Mackay – *Inchcape, E.*
Mackay – *M. of Clashfern**
Mackay – *M. of Drumadoon**
Mackay – *Reay*
Mackay – *Tanlaw**
MacKenzie – *M. of Culkein**
MacKenzie – *M. of Framwellgate**
Mackenzie – *Cromartie, E.*
Mackie – *M. of Benshie**
Mackintosh – *M. of Halifax, V.*
McLaren – *Aberconway*
*MacLaurin – M. of Knebworth**
MacLennan – *M. of Rogart**
Macmillan – *Stockton, E.*
Macpherson – *M. of Drumochter*

Macpherson – *Strathcarron*
Maffey – *Rugby*
Maginnis – *M. of Drumglass**
Maitland – *Lauderdale, E.*
Makgill – *Oxfuird, V.*
Makins – *Sherfield*
Manners – *Rutland, D.*
Manningham-Buller – *Dilhorne, V.*
Mansfield – *Sandhurst*
Marks – *M. of Broughton*
Marquis – *Woolton, E.*
Marshall – *M. of Knightsbridge**
Marsham – *Romney, E.*
Martin – *M. of Springburn**
Martyn-Hemphill – *Hemphill*
Mason – *M. of Barnsley**
Massey – *M. of Darwen**
Masters – *Noakes**
Maude – *Hawarden, V.*
Maxwell – *de Ros*
Maxwell – *Farnham*
May – *M. of Oxford**
Mayhew – *M. of Twysden**
Meade – *Clanwilliam, E.*
Mercer Nairne Petty-Fitzmaurice – *Lansdowne, M.*
Millar – *Inchyra*
Miller – *M. of Chiltorne Domer**
Miller – *M. of Hendon**
Milner – *M. of Leeds*
Mitchell-Thomson – *Selsdon*
Mitford – *Redesdale*
Molyneaux – *M. of Killead**
Monckton – *M. of Brenchley, V.*
Monckton-Arundell – *Galway, V.*
Mond – *Melchett*
Money-Coutts – *Latymer*
Montagu – *Manchester, D.*
Montagu – *Sandwich, E.*
Montagu – *Swaythling*
Montagu Douglas Scott – *Buccleuch, D.*
Montagu Stuart Wortley – *Wharncliffe, E.*
Montague – *Amwell*
Montgomerie – *Eglinton, E.*
Montgomery – *M. of Alamein, V.*
Moore – *Drogheda, E.*
Moore – *M. of Lower Marsh**
Moore-Brabazon – *Brabazon of Tara*
Moreton – *Ducie, E*
Morgan – *M. of Drefelin**
Morgan – *M. of Huyton**
Morris – *Killanin*
Morris – *M. of Aberavon**
Morris – *M. of Bolton**
Morris – *M. of Handsworth**
Morris – *M. of Manchester**
Morris – *M. of Kenwood*
Morris – *M. of Yardley**
Morris – *Naseby**
Morrison – *Dunrossil, V.*
Morrison – *Margadale*
Moser – *M. of Regents Park**
Mosley – *Ravensdale*
Mountbatten – *Milford Haven, M.*
Muff – *Calverley*
Mulholland – *Dunleath*
Murray – *Atholl, D.*
Murray – *Dunmore, E.*
Murray – *Mansfield and Mansfield, E.*
Nall-Cain – *Brocket*
Napier – *Napier and Ettrick*
Napier – *N. of Magdala*
Needham – *Kilmorey, E.*
Neill – *N. of Bladen**
Nelson – *N. of Stafford*
Neuberger – *N. of Abbotsbury**
Nevill – *Abergavenny, M.*
Neville – *Braybrooke*
Newton – *N. of Braintree**
Nicholls – *N. of Birkenhead**
Nicolson – *Carnock*
Nicholson – *N. of Winterboune**
Nivison – *Glendyne*
Noel – *Gainsborough, E.*
North – *Guilford, E.*
Northcote – *Iddesleigh, E.*
Norton – *Grantley*
Norton – *N. of Louth**
Norton – *Rathcreedan*
Nugent – *Westmeath, E.*
Oakeshott – *O. of Seagrove Bay**
O'Brien – *Inchiquin*
Ogilvie-Grant – *Seafield, E.*
Ogilvy – *Airlie, E.*
O'Neill – *O'N. of Bengarve**
O'Neill – *O'N. of Clackmannan**
O'Neill – *Rathcavan*
Orde-Powlett – *Bolton*
Ormsby-Gore – *Harlech*
Ouseley – *O. of Peckham Rye**
Paget – *Anglesey, M.*
Paisley – *Bannside**
Paisley – *P. of St George's**
Pakenham – *Longford, E.*
Pakington – *Hampton*
Palmer – *Lucas and Dingwall*
Palmer – *Selborne, E.*
Parker – *Macclesfield, E.*
Parker – *Morley, E.*
Parnell – *Congleton*
Parsons – *Rosse, E.*
Patel – *P. of Blackburn**
Patel – *P. of Bradford**
Patten – *P. of Barnes**
Paulet – *Winchester, M.*
Pearson – *Cowdray, V.*
Pearson – *P. of Rannoch**
Pease – *Gainford*
Pease – *Wardington*
Pelham – *Chichester, E.*
Pelham – *Yarborough, E.*
Pellew – *Exmouth, V*
Pendry – *P. of Stalybridge**.
Penny – *Marchwood, V.*
Pepys – *Cottenham, E.*
Perceval – *Egmont, E.*
Percy – *Northumberland, D.*
Perry – *P. of Southwark**
Pery – *Limerick, E.*
Philipps – *Milford*
Philipps – *St Davids, V.*
Phillips – *P. of Sudbury**
Phillips – *P. of Worth Matravers**
Phipps – *Normanby, M.*
Pilkington – *P. of Oxenford**
Plant – *P. of Highfield**
Platt – *P. of Writtle**
Pleydell-Bouverie – *Radnor, E.*
Plumptre – *Fitzwalter*
Plunkett – *Dunsany*
Plunkett – *Louth*
Pollock – *Hanworth, V.*
Pomeroy – *Harberton, V.*
Ponsonby – *Bessborough, E.*
Ponsonby – *de Mauley*
Ponsonby – *P. of Shulbrede*
Powell – *P. of Bayswater**
Powys – *Lilford*
Pratt – *Camden, M.*
Preston – *Gormanston, V.*
Primrose – *Rosebery, E.*
Prittie – *Dunalley*
Ramsay – *Dalhousie, E.*
Ramsay – *R. of Cartvale**
Ramsbotham – *Soulbury, V.*
Randall – *R. of St. Budeaux**
Rees – *R. of Ludlow**
Rees-Williams – *Ogmore*
Reid – *R. of Cardowan**
Rendell – *R. of Babergh**
Renfrew – *R. of Kaimsthorn**
Renton – *R. of Mount Harry**
Renwick – *R. of Clifton**
Rhys – *Dynevor*
Richards – *Milverton*
Richardson – *R. of Calow**
Ritchie – *R. of Brompton**
Ritchie – *R. of Dundee*
Roberts – *Clwyd*
Roberts – *R. of Conway**
Roberts – *R. of Llandudno**
Robertson – *R. of Oakridge*
Robertson – *R. of Port Ellen**
Robertson – *Wharton*
Robinson – *Martonmere*
Roche – *Fermoy*
Rodd – *Rennell*
Rodger – *R. of Earlsferry**
Rodgers – *R. of Quarry Bank**
Rogers – *R. of Riverside**
Roper-Curzon – *Teynham*
Rospigliosi – *Newburgh, E.*
Rous – *Stradbroke, E.*
Rowley-Conwy – *Langford*
Royall – *R. of Blaisdon**
Runciman – *R. of Doxford, V.*
Russell – *Ampthill*
Russell – *Bedford, D.*
Russell – *de Clifford*
Russell – *R. of Liverpool*
Ryder – *Harrowby, E.*
Ryder – *R. of Wensum**
Sackville – *De La Warr, E.*
Sackville-West – *Sackville*
Sainsbury – *S. of Preston Candover**
Sainsbury – *S. of Turville**
St Aubyn – *St Levan*
St Clair – *Sinclair*
St Clair-Erskine – *Rosslyn, E.*
St John – *Bolingbroke and St John, V.*
St John – *St John of Blesto*
St John-Stevas – *St John of Fawsley**
St Leger – *Doneraile, V.*
Samuel – *Bearsted, V.*
Sanderson – *S. of Ayot*
Sanderson – *S. of Bowden**
Sandilands – *Torphichen*
Saumarez – *De Saumarez*
Savile – *Mexborough, E.*
Saville – *S. of Newdigate**
Scarlett – *Abinger*
Schreiber – *Marlesford**
Sclater-Booth – *Basing*
Scotland – *S. of Asthal**
Scott – *Eldon, E*
Scott – *S. of Foscotte**
Scott – *S. of Needham Market**.
Scrymgeour – *Dundee, E.*
Seager – *Leighton of St Mellons*

Seely – *Mottistone*
Seymour – *Hertford, M.*
Seymour – *Somerset, D.*
Sharp – *S. of Guildford**
Shaw – *Craigmyle*
Shaw – *S. of Northstead**
Shephard – *S. of Northwood**
Sheppard – *S. of Didgemere**
Shirley – *Ferrers, E.*
Short – *Glenamara**
Shutt – *S. of Greetland**
Siddeley – *Kenilworth*
Sidney – *De L'Isle, V.*
Simon – *S. of Highbury**
Simon – *S. of Wythenshawe*
Simpson – *S. of Dunkeld**
Sinclair – *Caithness, E.*
Sinclair – *S. of Cleeve*
Sinclair – *Thurso, V.*
Skeffington – *Massereene, V.*
Smith – *Bicester*
Smith – *Hambleden, V.*
Smith – *Kirkhill**
Smith – *S. of Basildon**
Smith – *S. of Clifton**
Smith – *Smith of Finsbury**
Smith – *S. of Gilmorehill**
Smith – *S. of Kelvin**
Smith – *S. of Leigh**
Somerset – *Beaufort, D.*
Somerset – *Raglan*
Soulsby – *S. of Swaffham Prior**
Spencer – *Churchill, V.*
Spencer-Churchill – *Marlborough, D.*
Spring Rice – *Monteagle of Brandon*
Stanhope – *Harrington, E.*
Stanley – *Derby, E.*
Stanley – *of Alderley and Sheffield*
Stapleton-Cotton – *Combermere, V.*
Steel – *S. of Aikwood**
Sterling – *S. of Plaistow**
Stern – *S. of Brentford**
Stevens – *S. of Kirkwhelpington**
Stevens – *S. of Ludgate**
Stevenson – *S. of Balmacara**
Stevenson – *S. of Coddenham**
Stewart – *Galloway, E.*
Stewart – *Stewartby**
Stoddart – *S. of Swindon**
Stone – *S. of Blackheath**
Stonor – *Camoys*
Stopford – *Courtown, E.*
Stourton – *Mowbray*
Strachey – *O'Hagan*
Strutt – *Belper*
Strutt – *Rayleigh*
Stuart – *Castle Stewart, E.*
Stuart – *Moray, E.*
Stuart – *S. of Findhorn, V.*
Suenson-Taylor – *Grantchester*
Sutherland – *S. of Houndwood**
Symons – *S. of Vernham Dean**
Taylor – *Kilclooney**
Taylor – *T. of Blackburn**
Taylor – *T. of Bolton**
Taylor – *T. of Goss Moor**
Taylor – *T. of Holbeach**
Taylor – *T. of Warwick**
Taylour – *Headfort, M.*
Temple-Gore-Langton – *Temple of Stowe, E*
Temple-Morris – *Temple-Morris of Llandaff**
Tennant – *Glenconner*
Thellusson – *Rendlesham*
Thesiger – *Chelmsford, V.*
Thomas – *T. of Gresford**
Thomas – *T. of Macclesfield**
Thomas – *T. of Swynnerton**
Thomas – *T. of Walliswood**
Thomas – *T. of Winchester**
Thomson – *T. of Fleet*
Thynn – *Bath, M.*
Tottenham – *Ely, M.*
Trefusis – *Clinton*
Trench – *Ashtown*
Tufton – *Hothfield*
Turner – *Bilston**
Turner – *Netherthorpe*
Turner – *T. of Camden**
Turner – *T. of Ecchinswell**
Turnour – *Winterton, E.*
Tyrell-Kenyon – *Kenyon*
Vanden-Bempde-Johnstone – *Derwent*
Vane – *Barnard*
Vane-Tempest-Stewart – *Londonderry, M.*
Vanneck – *Huntingfield*
Vaughan – *Lisburne, E.*
Vereker – *Gort, V.*
Verney – *Willoughby de Broke*
Vernon – *Lyveden*
Vesey – *De Vesci, V.*
Villiers – *Clarendon, E.*
Vincent – *V. of Coleshill**
Vivian – *Swansea*
Wade – *W. of Chorlton**
Waldegrave – *W. of North Hill**
Walker – *W. of Aldringham**
Walker – *W. of Gestingthorpe**
Wall – *W. of New Barnett**
Wallace – *Dudley*
Wallace – *W. of Saltaire**
Wallace – *W. of Tankerness**
Wallace – *W. of Tummel**
Wallop – *Portsmouth, E.*
Walton – *W. of Detchant**
Ward – *Bangor, V.*
Ward – *Dudley, E.*
Warrender – *Bruntisfield*
Warwick – *W. of Undercliffe**
Watson – *W. of Invergowrie**
Watson – *Manton*
Watson – *W. of Richmond**
Webber – *Lloyd-Webber**
Wedderburn – *W. of Charlton**
Weir – *Inverforth*
Weld-Forester – *Forester*
Wellesley – *Cowley, E.*
Wellesley – *Wellington, D.*
West – *W. of Spithead**
Westenra – *Rossmore*
White – *Annaly*
White – *Hanningfield**
Whiteley – *Marchamley*
Whitfield – *Kenswood*
Williams – *W. of Baglan**
Williams – *W. of Crosby**
Williams – *W. of Elve**
Williamson – *Forres*
Williamson – *W. of Horton**
Willis – *W. of Knaresborough**
Willoughby – *Middleton*
Wills – *Dulverton*
Wilson – *Moran*
Wilson – *Nunburnholme*
Wilson – *W. of Dinton**
Wilson – *W. of Tillyorn**
Windsor – *Gloucester, D.*
Windsor – *Kent, D.*
Windsor-Clive – *Plymouth, E.*
Wingfield – *Powerscourt, V.*
Winn – *St Oswald*
Wodehouse – *Kimberley, E.*
Wolfson – *W. of Aspley Guise**
Wolfson – *W. of Sunningdale**
Wood – *Halifax, E.*
Woodhouse – *Terrington*
Woolmer – *W. of Leeds**
Wright – *W. of Richmond**
Wyndham – *Egremont and Leconfield*
Wyndham-Quin – *Dunraven, E.*
Wynn – *Newborough*
Yarde-Buller – *Churston*
Yerburgh – *Alvingham*
Yorke – *Hardwicke, E.*
Young – *Kennet*
Young – *Y. of Graffham**
Young – *Y. of Hornsey**
Young – *Y. of Norwood Green**
Young – *Y. of Old Scone**
Younger – *Y. of Leckie, V.*

ORDERS OF CHIVALRY

THE MOST NOBLE ORDER OF THE GARTER (1348)

KG
Ribbon, Blue
Motto, Honi soit qui mal y pense
(Shame on him who thinks evil of it)

The number of Knights and Lady Companions is limited to 24

SOVEREIGN OF THE ORDER
The Queen

LADIES OF THE ORDER
HRH The Princess Royal, 1994
HRH Princess Alexandra, The Hon. Lady Ogilvy, 2003

ROYAL KNIGHTS
HRH The Prince Philip, Duke of Edinburgh, 1947
HRH The Prince of Wales, 1958
HRH The Duke of Kent, 1985
HRH The Duke of Gloucester, 1997
HRH The Duke of York, 2006
HRH The Earl of Wessex, 2006
HRH Prince William of Wales, 2008

EXTRA KNIGHT COMPANIONS AND LADIES
Grand Duke Jean of Luxembourg, 1972
HM The Queen of Denmark, 1979
HM The King of Sweden, 1983
HM The King of Spain, 1988
HM The Queen of the Netherlands, 1989
HIM The Emperor of Japan, 1998
HM The King of Norway, 2001

KNIGHTS AND LADY COMPANIONS
Duke of Grafton, 1976
Lord Carrington, 1985
Duke of Wellington, 1990
Lord Bramall, 1990
Viscount Ridley, 1992
Lord Sainsbury of Preston Candover, 1992
Lord Ashburton, 1994
Lord Kingsdown, 1994
Sir Ninian Stephen, 1994
Baroness Thatcher, 1995
Sir Timothy Colman, 1996
Duke of Abercorn, 1999
Sir William Gladstone, 1999
Lord Inge, 2001
Sir Anthony Acland, 2001
Duke of Westminster, 2003
Lord Butler of Brockwell, 2003
Lord Morris of Aberavon, 2003
Lady Soames, 2005
Lord Bingham of Cornhill, 2005
Sir John Major, 2005
Lord Luce, 2008
Sir Thomas Dunne, 2008

Prelate, Bishop of Winchester
Chancellor, Lord Carrington, KG, GCMG, CH, MC
Register, Dean of Windsor
Garter King of Arms, Thomas Woodcock, LVO
Gentleman Usher of the Black Rod, Lt.-Gen. Sir Frederick Viggers, KCB, CMG, MBE
Secretary, Patric Dickinson, LVO

THE MOST ANCIENT AND MOST NOBLE ORDER OF THE THISTLE (REVIVED 1687)

KT
Ribbon, Green
Motto, Nemo me impune lacessit
(No one provokes me with impunity)

The number of Knights and Ladies of the Thistle is limited to 16

SOVEREIGN OF THE ORDER
The Queen

ROYAL LADY OF THE ORDER
HRH The Princess Royal, 2000

ROYAL KNIGHTS
HRH The Prince Philip, Duke of Edinburgh, 1952
HRH The Prince of Wales, Duke of Rothesay, 1977

KNIGHTS AND LADIES
Earl of Elgin and Kincardine, 1981
Earl of Airlie, 1985
Viscount of Arbuthnott, 1996
Earl of Crawford and Balcarres, 1996
Lady Marion Fraser, 1996
Lord Macfarlane of Bearsden, 1996
Lord Mackay of Clashfern, 1997
Lord Wilson of Tillyorn, 2000
Lord Sutherland of Houndwood, 2002
Sir Eric Anderson, 2002
Lord Steel of Aikwood, 2004
Lord Robertson of Port Ellen, 2004
Lord Cullen of Whitekirk, 2007
Sir Garth Morrison, 2007
Lord Hope of Craighead, 2009
Lord Patel, 2009

Chancellor, Earl of Airlie, KT, GCVO, PC
Dean, Very Revd Gilleasbuig Macmillan, CVO
Secretary and Lord Lyon King of Arms, David Sellar
Gentleman Usher of the Green Rod, Rear-Adm. Christopher Layman, CB, DSO, LVO

THE MOST HONOURABLE ORDER OF THE BATH (1725)

GCB *Military* GCB *Civil*

GCB	Knight (or Dame) Grand Cross
KCB	Knight Commander
DCB	Dame Commander
CB	Companion

Ribbon, Crimson
Motto, Tria juncta in uno
(Three joined in one)

Remodelled 1815, and enlarged many times since. The order is divided into civil and military divisions. Women became eligible for the order from 1 January 1971.

THE SOVEREIGN

GREAT MASTER AND FIRST OR PRINCIPAL KNIGHT GRAND CROSS
HRH The Prince of Wales, KG, KT, GCB, OM

Dean of the Order, Dean of Westminster
Bath King of Arms, Adm. Lord Boyce, GCB, OBE
Registrar and Secretary, Rear-Adm. Iain Henderson, CB, CBE
Genealogist, Thomas Woodcock, LVO
Gentleman Usher of the Scarlet Rod, Maj.-Gen. Charles Vyvyan, CB, CBE
Deputy Secretary, Secretary of the Central Chancery of the Orders of Knighthood
Chancery, Central Chancery of the Orders of Knighthood, St James's Palace, London SW1A 1BH

THE ORDER OF MERIT (1902)

OM *Military* OM *Civil*

OM
Ribbon, Blue and crimson

This order is designed as a special distinction for eminent men and women without conferring a knighthood upon them. The order is limited in numbers to 24, with the addition of foreign honorary members.

THE SOVEREIGN

HRH The Prince Philip, Duke of Edinburgh, 1968
Revd Prof. Owen Chadwick, KBE, 1983
Sir Andrew Huxley, 1983
Dr Frederick Sanger, 1986
Baroness Thatcher, 1990
Dame Joan Sutherland, 1991
Sir Michael Atiyah, 1992
Lucian Freud, 1993
Sir Aaron Klug, 1995
Lord Foster of Thames Bank, 1997
Sir Anthony Caro, 2000
Prof. Sir Roger Penrose, 2000
Sir Tom Stoppard, 2000
HRH The Prince of Wales, 2002
Lord May of Oxford, 2002
Lord Rothschild, 2002
Sir David Attenborough, 2005
Baroness Boothroyd, 2005
Sir Michael Howard, 2005
Sir Timothy Berners-Lee, KBE, 2007
Lord Eames, 2007
Lord Rees of Ludlow, 2007
Rt. Hon. Jean Chrétien, QC, 2009

Honorary Member, Nelson Mandela, 1995

Secretary and Registrar, Lord Fellowes, GCB, GCVO, PC, QSO
Chancery, Central Chancery of the Orders of Knighthood, St James's Palace, London SW1A 1BH

THE MOST DISTINGUISHED ORDER OF ST MICHAEL AND ST GEORGE (1818)

GCMG KCMG

GCMG Knight (or Dame) Grand Cross
KCMG Knight Commander
DCMG Dame Commander
CMG Companion

Ribbon, Saxon blue, with scarlet centre
Motto, Auspicium melioris aevi *(Token of a better age)*

THE SOVEREIGN

GRAND MASTER
HRH The Duke of Kent, KG, GCMG, GCVO, ADC

Prelate, Rt. Revd David Urquhart
Chancellor, Sir Christopher Mallaby, GCMG, GCVO
Secretary, Permanent Under-Secretary of State at the Foreign and Commonwealth Office and Head of the Diplomatic Service
Registrar, Sir David Manning, GCMG, CVO
King of Arms, Sir Jeremy Greenstock, GCMG
Gentleman Usher of the Blue Rod, Sir Anthony Figgis, KCVO, CMG
Dean, Dean of St Paul's
Deputy Secretary, Secretary of the Central Chancery of the Orders of Knighthood
Hon. Geneaologist, Timothy Duke
Chancery, Central Chancery of the Orders of Knighthood, St James's Palace, London SW1A 1BH

GCIE Knight Grand Commander
KCIE Knight Commander
CIE Companion

THE IMPERIAL ORDER OF THE CROWN OF INDIA (1877) FOR LADIES

CI

Badge, the royal cipher of Queen Victoria in jewels within an oval, surmounted by an heraldic crown and attached to a bow of light blue watered ribbon, edged white

The honour does not confer any rank or title upon the recipient

No conferments have been made since 1947

HM The Queen, 1947

THE ROYAL VICTORIAN ORDER (1896)

GCVO KCVO

GCVO Knight or Dame Grand Cross
KCVO Knight Commander
DCVO Dame Commander
CVO Commander
LVO Lieutenant
MVO Member

Ribbon, Blue, with red and white edges
Motto, Victoria

THE SOVEREIGN
GRAND MASTER
HRH The Princess Royal

Chancellor, Lord Chamberlain
Secretary, Keeper of the Privy Purse
Registrar, Secretary of the Central Chancery of the Orders of Knighthood
Chaplain, Chaplain of the Queen's Chapel of the Savoy
Hon. Genealogist, David White

THE MOST EXCELLENT ORDER OF THE BRITISH EMPIRE (1917)

GBE KBE

The order was divided into military and civil divisions in December 1918

GBE	Knight or Dame Grand Cross
KBE	Knight Commander
DBE	Dame Commander
CBE	Commander
OBE	Officer
MBE	Member

Ribbon, Rose pink edged with pearl grey with vertical pearl stripe in centre (military division); without vertical pearl stripe (civil division)
Motto, For God and the Empire

THE SOVEREIGN

GRAND MASTER
HRH The Prince Philip, Duke of Edinburgh, KG, KT, OM, GBE, PC

Prelate, Bishop of London
King of Arms, Air Chief Marshal Sir Patrick Hine, GCB, GBE
Registrar, Secretary of the Central Chancery of the Orders of Knighthood
Secretary, Secretary of the Cabinet and Head of the Home Civil Service
Dean, Dean of St Paul's
Gentleman Usher of the Purple Rod, Sir Alexander Michael Graham, GBE, DCL
Chancery, Central Chancery of the Orders of Knighthood, St James's Palace, London SW1A 1BH

ORDER OF THE COMPANIONS OF HONOUR (1917)

CH

Ribbon, Carmine, with gold edges
This order consists of one class only and carries with it no title. The number of awards is limited to 65 (excluding honorary members).

Anthony, Rt. Hon. John, 1981
Ashley of Stoke, Lord, 1975
Attenborough, Sir David, 1995
Baker, Dame Janet, 1993
Baker of Dorking, Lord, 1992
Birtwistle, Sir Harrison, 2000
Brenner, Sydney, 1986
Brook, Peter, 1998
Brooke of Sutton Mandeville, Lord, 1992
Carrington, Lord, 1983
Christie, Sir George, 2001
Davis, Sir Colin, 2001
De Chastelain, Gen. John, 1999
Dench, Dame Judi, 2005
Fraser, Rt. Hon. Malcolm, 1977
Freud, Lucian, 1983
Glenamara, Lord, 1976
Hamilton, Richard, 1999
Hannay of Chiswick, Lord, 2003
Hawking, Prof. Stephen, 1989
Healey, Lord, 1979
Heseltine, Lord, 1997
Hobsbawm, Prof. Eric, 1998
Hockney, David, 1997
Hodgkin, Sir Howard, 2002
Howard, Sir Michael, 2002
Howe of Aberavon, Lord, 1996
Hurd of Westwell, Lord, 1995
King of Bridgewater, Lord, 1992
Lessing, Doris, 1999
Lovelock, Prof. James, 2002
McKellen, Sir Ian Murray, 2008
McKenzie, Prof. Dan Peter, 2003
Mahon, Sir Denis, 2002
Major, Rt. Hon. Sir John, 1998
Owen, Lord, 1994
Patten of Barnes, Rt. Hon. Lord, 1997
Pawson, Prof. Anthony James, 2006
Riley, Bridget, 1998
Rogers of Riverside, Lord, 2008
Sanger, Dr. Frederick, 1981
Somare, Rt. Hon. Sir Michael, 1978
Talboys, Rt. Hon. Sir Brian, 1981
Tebbit, Lord, 1987

Honorary Members, Lee Kuan Yew, 1970; Prof. Amartya Sen, 2000; Bernard Haitink, 2002
Secretary and Registrar, Secretary of the Central Chancery of the Orders of Knighthood

THE DISTINGUISHED SERVICE ORDER (1886)

DSO

Ribbon, Red, with blue edges

Bestowed in recognition of especial services in action of commissioned officers in the Navy, Army and Royal Air Force and (since 1942) Mercantile Marine. The members are Companions only. A bar may be awarded for any additional act of service.

THE IMPERIAL SERVICE ORDER (1902)

ISO

Ribbon, Crimson, with blue centre

Appointment as companion of this order is open to members of the civil services whose eligibility is determined by the grade they hold. The order consists of the sovereign and companions to a number not exceeding 1,900, of whom 1,300 may belong to the home civil services and 600 to overseas civil services. The then prime minister announced in March 1993 that he would make no further recommendations for appointments to the order.

Secretary, Secretary of the Cabinet and Head of the Home Civil Service
Registrar, Secretary of the Central Chancery of the Orders of Knighthood

THE ROYAL VICTORIAN CHAIN (1902)

It confers no precedence on its holders

HM THE QUEEN

HM The King of Thailand, 1960
HM The Queen of Denmark, 1974
HM The King of Sweden, 1975
HM The Queen of the Netherlands, 1982
Gen. Antonio Eanes, 1985
HM The King of Spain, 1986
Dr Richard von Weizsäcker, 1992
HM The King of Norway, 1994
Earl of Airlie, 1997
Rt. Revd and Rt. Hon. Lord Carey of Clifton, 2002
HRH Prince Philip, Duke of Edinburgh, 2007
HM The King of Saudi Arabia, 2007

BARONETAGE AND KNIGHTAGE

BARONETS

Style, 'Sir' before forename and surname, followed by 'Bt'.
Envelope, Sir F_ S_, Bt. *Letter (formal)*, Dear Sir; *(social)*, Dear Sir F_. *Spoken*, Sir F_
Wife's style, 'Lady' followed by surname
Envelope, Lady S_. *Letter (formal)*, Dear Madam; *(social)*, Dear Lady S_. *Spoken*, Lady S_
Style of Baronetess, 'Dame' before forename and surname, followed by 'Btss.' (*see also* Dames)

There are five different creations of baronetcies: Baronets of England (creations dating from 1611); Baronets of Ireland (creations dating from 1619); Baronets of Scotland or Nova Scotia (creations dating from 1625); Baronets of Great Britain (creations after the Act of Union 1707 which combined the kingdoms of England and Scotland); and Baronets of the United Kingdom (creations after the union of Great Britain and Ireland in 1801).

Badge of Baronets of the United Kingdom

Badge of Baronets of Nova Scotia

Badge of Ulster

The patent of creation limits the destination of a baronetcy, usually to male descendants of the first baronet, although special remainders allow the baronetcy to pass, if the male issue of sons fail, to the male issue of daughters of the first baronet. In the case of baronetcies of Scotland or Nova Scotia, a special remainder of 'heirs male and of tailzie' allows the baronetcy to descend to heirs general, including women. There are four existing Scottish baronets with such a remainder.

The Official Roll of the Baronetage is kept at the Crown Office and maintained by the Registrar and Assistant Registrar of the Baronetage. Anyone who considers that he or she is entitled to be entered on the roll may apply through the Crown Office to prove their succession. Every person succeeding to a baronetcy must exhibit proofs of succession to the Lord Chancellor. A person whose name is not entered on the official roll will not be addressed or mentioned by the title of baronet or baronetess in any official document, nor will he or she be accorded precedence as a baronet of baronetess.

BARONETCIES EXTINCT SINCE THE LAST EDITION

Hamilton (cr. 1776 and 1819)

OFFICIAL ROLL OF THE BARONETAGE, Crown Office, House of Lords, London SW1A 0PW T 020-7219 2632
Registrar, Ian Denyer, MVO
Assistant Registrar, Grant Bavister

KNIGHTS

Style, 'Sir' before forename and surname, followed by appropriate post-nominal initials if a Knight Grand Cross, Knight Grand Commander or Knight Commander
Envelope, Sir F_ S_. *Letter (formal)*, Dear Sir; *(social)*, Dear Sir F_. *Spoken*, Sir F_
Wife's style, 'Lady' followed by surname
'*Envelope*, Lady S_. *Letter (formal)*, Dear Madam; *(social)*, Dear Lady S_. *Spoken*, Lady S_

The prefix 'Sir' is not used by knights who are clerics of the Church of England, who do not receive the accolade. Their wives are entitled to precedence as the wife of a knight but not to the style of 'Lady'.

ORDERS OF KNIGHTHOOD

Knight Grand Cross, Knight Grand Commander, and Knight Commander are the higher classes of the Orders of Chivalry (*see* Orders of Chivalry). Honorary knighthoods of these orders may be conferred on men who are citizens of countries of which the Queen is not head of state. As a rule, the prefix 'Sir' is not used by honorary knights.

KNIGHTS BACHELOR

The Knights Bachelor do not constitute a royal order, but comprise the surviving representation of the ancient state orders of knighthood. The Register of Knights Bachelor, instituted by James I in the 17th century, lapsed, and in 1908 a voluntary association under the title of the Society of Knights (now the Imperial Society of Knights Bachelor) was formed with the primary objectives of continuing the various registers dating from 1257 and obtaining the uniform registration of every created Knight Bachelor. In 1926 a design for a badge to be worn by Knights Bachelor was approved and adopted; in 1974 a neck badge and miniature were added.

THE IMPERIAL SOCIETY OF KNIGHTS BACHELOR, 1 Throgmorton Avenue, London EC2N 2BY
Knight Principal, Sir Robert Balchin
Prelate, Rt. Revd and Rt. Hon. Bishop of London
Registrar, Sir Paul Judge
Hon. Treasurer, Sir Colin Berry
Clerk to the Council, Col. Simon Doughty

LIST OF BARONETS AND KNIGHTS *as at 31 August 2010*

†	Not registered on the Official Roll of the Baronetage at the time of going to press
()	The date of creation of the baronetcy is given in parentheses
I	Baronet of Ireland
NS	Baronet of Nova Scotia
S	Baronet of Scotland

A full entry in italic type indicates that the recipient of a knighthood died during the year in which the honour was conferred. The name is included for purposes of record. Peers are not included in this list.

Aaronson, Sir Michael John, Kt., CBE
Abbott, *Adm.* Sir Peter Charles, GBE, KCB
Abdy, Sir Valentine Robert Duff, Bt. (1850)
Abed, *Dr* Sir Fazle Hasan, KCMG
Ackers-Jones, Sir David, KBE, CMG
Ackroyd, Sir Timothy Robert Whyte, Bt. (1956)
Acland, Sir Antony Arthur, KG, GCMG, GCVO
Acland, *Lt.-Col.* Sir (Christopher) Guy (Dyke), Bt. (1890), MVO
†Acland, Sir Dominic Dyke, Bt. (1644)
Adam, Sir Kenneth Hugo, Kt., OBE
Adams, Sir Geoffrey Doyne, KCMG
Adams, Sir William James, KCMG
Adsetts, Sir William Norman, Kt., OBE
Adye, Sir John Anthony, KCMG
Aga Khan IV, HH Prince Karim, KBE
Agnew, Sir Crispin Hamlyn, Bt. (S. 1629)
Agnew, Sir John Keith, Bt. (1895)
Agnew, Sir Rudolph Ion Joseph, Kt.
Agnew-Somerville, Sir Quentin Charles Somerville, Bt. (1957)
Ah Koy, Sir James Michael, KBE
Aikens, *Rt. Hon.* Sir Richard John Pearson, Kt.
†Ainsworth, Sir Anthony Thomas Hugh, Bt. (1916)
Aird, Sir (George) John, Bt. (1901)
Airy, *Maj.-Gen.* Sir Christopher John, KCVO, CBE
Aitchison, Sir Charles Walter de Lancey, Bt. (1938)
Ajegbo, Sir Keith Onyema, Kt., OBE
Akenhead, *Hon.* Sir Robert, Kt.
Alberti, *Prof.* Sir Kurt George Matthew Mayer, Kt.
Albu, Sir George, Bt. (1912)
Alcock, *Air Chief Marshal* Sir (Robert James) Michael, GCB, KBE
Aldous, *Rt. Hon.* Sir William, Kt.
†Alexander, Sir Richard, Bt. (1945)
Alexander, Sir Douglas, Bt. (1921)
Allen, *Prof.* Sir Geoffrey, Kt., PHD, FRS
Allen, Sir John Derek, Kt., CBE
Allen, Sir Mark John Spurgeon, Kt., CMG
Allen, *Hon.* Sir Peter Austin Philip Jermyn, Kt.
Allen, Sir Thomas Boaz, Kt., CBE
Allen, *Hon.* Sir William Clifford, KCMG
Allen, Sir William Guilford, Kt.
Alleyne, Sir George Allanmoore Ogarren, Kt.
Alleyne, *Revd* John Olpherts Campbell, Bt. (1769)
Allinson, Sir (Walter) Leonard, KCVO, CMG
Alliott, *Hon.* Sir John Downes, Kt.
Allison, *Air Chief Marshal* Sir John Shakespeare, KCB, CBE
Amet, *Hon.* Sir Arnold Karibone, Kt.
Amory, Sir Ian Heathcoat, Bt. (1874)
Anderson, *Dr* Sir James Iain Walker, Kt., CBE
Anderson, Sir John Anthony, KBE
Anderson, Sir Leith Reinsford Steven, Kt., CBE
Anderson, *Prof.* Sir Roy Malcolm, Kt.
Anderson, Sir (William) Eric Kinloch, KT.
Anderson, *Prof.* Sir (William) Ferguson, Kt., OBE
Anderton, Sir (Cyril) James, Kt., CBE, QPM
Andrew, Sir Robert John, KCB
Andrews, Sir Derek Henry, KCB, CBE
Andrews, Sir Ian Charles Franklin, Kt., CBE, TD
Annesley, Sir Hugh Norman, Kt., QPM
Anson, *Vice-Adm.* Sir Edward Rosebery, KCB
Anson, Sir John, KCB
Anson, *Rear-Adm.* Sir Peter, Bt. CB (1831)
Anstruther, Sir Sebastian Paten Campbell, Bt. (S. 1694)
†Anstruther, Sir Tobias Alexander Campbell, Bt. (1798)
Anstruther-Gough-Calthorpe, Sir Euan Hamilton, Bt. (1929)
Antrobus, Sir Edward Philip, Bt. (1815)
Appleyard, Sir Leonard Vincent, KCMG
Appleyard, Sir Raymond Kenelm, KBE
Arbib, Sir Martyn, Kt.
Arbuthnot, Sir Keith Robert Charles, Bt. (1823)
Arbuthnot, Sir William Reierson, Bt. (1964)
Arbuthnott, *Prof.* Sir John Peebles, Kt., PHD, FRSE
†Archdale, Sir Nicholas Edward, Bt. (1928)
Arculus, Sir Ronald, KCMG, KCVO
Arculus, Sir Thomas David Guy, Kt.
Armitage, *Air Chief Marshal* Sir Michael John, KCB, CBE
Armour, *Prof.* Sir James, Kt., CBE
Armstrong, Sir Christopher John Edmund Stuart, Bt. (1841), MBE
Armstrong, Sir Patrick John, Kt., CBE
Armstrong, Sir Richard, Kt., CBE
Armytage, Sir John Martin, Bt. (1738)
Arnold, *Hon.* Sir Richard David, Kt.
Arnold, Sir Thomas Richard, Kt.
Arnott, Sir Alexander John Maxwell, Bt. (1896)
Arrindell, Sir Clement Athelston, GCMG, GCVO, QC
Arthur, Sir Gavyn Farr, Kt.
Arthur, *Lt.-Gen.* Sir (John) Norman Stewart, KCB, CVO
Arthur, Sir Michael Anthony, KCMG
Arthur, Sir Stephen John, Bt. (1841)
Arulkumaran, *Prof.* Sir Sabaratnam, Kt.
Asbridge, Sir Jonathan Elliott, Kt.
Ash, *Prof.* Sir Eric Albert, Kt., CBE, FRS, FRENG
Ashburnham, Sir James Fleetwood, Bt. (1661)
Ashmore, *Admiral of the Fleet* Sir Edward Beckwith, GCB, DSC
Ashworth, *Dr* Sir John Michael, Kt.
Aske, Sir Robert John Bingham, Bt. (1922)
Askew, Sir Bryan, Kt.
Asscher, Prof. Sir (Adolf) William, Kt., MD, FRCP
Astill, *Hon.* Sir Michael John, Kt.
Astley-Cooper, Sir Alexander Paston, Bt. (1821)
Astwood, *Hon.* Sir James Rufus, KBE
Atcherley, Sir Harold Winter, Kt.
Atiyah, Sir Michael Francis, Kt., OM, PHD, FRS
Atkins, *Rt. Hon.* Sir Robert James, Kt.
Atkinson, *Prof.* Sir Anthony Barnes, Kt.
Atkinson, *Air Marshal* Sir David William, KBE
Atkinson, Sir Frederick John, KCB
Atkinson, Sir John Alexander, KCB, DFC
Atkinson, Sir Robert, Kt., DSC, FRENG
Atkinson, Sir William Samuel, Kt.
Atopare, Sir Sailas, GCMG
Attenborough, Sir David Frederick, Kt., OM, CH, CVO, CBE, FRS
Aubrey-Fletcher, Sir Henry Egerton, Bt. (1782)

Audland, Sir Christopher John, KCMG
Augier, *Prof.* Sir Fitz-Roy Richard, Kt.
Auld, *Rt. Hon.* Sir Robin Ernest, Kt.
Austin, Sir Anthony Leonard, Bt. (1894)
Austin, *Air Marshal* Sir Roger Mark, KCB, AFC
Austen-Smith, *Air Marshal* Sir Roy David, KBE, CB, CVO, DFC
Avei, Sir Moi, KBE
Axford, Sir William Ian, Kt.
Ayckbourn, Sir Alan, Kt., CBE
Aykroyd, Sir James Alexander Frederic, Bt. (1929)
†Aykroyd, Sir Henry Robert George, Bt. (1920)
Aylmer, Sir Richard John, Bt. (I. 1622)
Aylward, *Prof.* Sir Mansel, Kt., CB
Aynsley-Green, *Prof.* Sir Albert, Kt.

Bacha, Sir Bhinod, Kt., CMG
Backhouse, Sir Alfred James Stott, Bt. (1901)
Bacon, Sir Nicholas Hickman Ponsonby, Bt., OBE (1611 and 1627), *Premier Baronet of England*
Bacon, Sir Sidney Charles, Kt., CB, FRENG.
Baddeley, Sir John Wolsey Beresford, Bt. (1922)
Badge, Sir Peter Gilmour Noto, Kt.
Baer, Sir Jack Mervyn Frank, Kt.
Bagge, Sir (John) Jeremy Picton, Bt. (1867)
Bagnall, *Air Chief Marshal* Sir Anthony, GBE, KCB
Bailey, Sir Alan Marshall, KCB
Bailey, Sir Brian Harry, Kt., OBE
Bailey, Sir John Bilsland, KCB
†Bailey, Sir John Richard, Bt. (1919)
Bailey, Sir Richard John, Kt., CBE
Bailhache, Sir Philip Martin, Kt.
Baillie, Sir Adrian Louis, Bt. (1823)
Bain, *Prof.* Sir George Sayers, Kt.
Baird, Sir Charles William Stuart, Bt. (1809)
†Baird, Sir James Andrew Gardiner, Bt. (S. 1695)
Baird, *Air Marshal* Sir John Alexander, KBE
Baird, *Vice-Adm.* Sir Thomas Henry Eustace, KCB
Bairsto, *Air Marshal* Sir Peter Edward, KBE, CB
Baker, Sir Bryan William, Kt.
Baker, *Prof.* Sir John Hamilton, Kt., QC
Baker, Sir John William, Kt., CBE
Baker, *Hon.* Sir Jonathan Leslie, Kt.
Baker, *Rt. Hon.* Sir (Thomas) Scott (Gillespie), Kt.
Balchin, Sir Robert George Alexander, Kt.
Balderstone, Sir James Schofield, Kt.
Baldwin, *Prof.* Sir Jack Edward, Kt., FRS
Ball, *Air Marshal* Sir Alfred Henry Wynne, KCB, DSO, DFC
Ball, Sir Christopher John Elinger, Kt.
Ball, *Prof.* Sir John Macleod, Kt.
Ball, Sir Richard Bentley, Bt. (1911)
Ball, *Prof.* Sir Robert James, Kt., PHD
Ballantyne, *Dr* Sir Frederick Nathaniel, GCMG
Bamford, Sir Anthony Paul, Kt.
Band, *Adm.* Sir Jonathon, GCB
Banham, Sir John Michael Middlecott, Kt.
Bannerman, Sir David Gordon, Bt., OBE (S. 1682)
Bannister, Sir Roger Gilbert, Kt., CBE, DM, FRCP
Barber, Sir Michael Bayldon, Kt.
Barber, Sir (Thomas) David, Bt. (1960)
Barbour, *Very Revd* Robert Alexander Stewart, KCVO, MC
Barclay, Sir Colville Herbert Sanford, Bt. (S. 1668)
Barclay, Sir David Rowat, Kt.
Barclay, Sir Frederick Hugh, Kt.
Barclay, Sir Peter Maurice, Kt., CBE
Barder, Sir Brian Leon, KCMG
Baring, Sir John Francis, Bt. (1911)
Barker, Sir Colin, Kt.
Barker, *Hon.* Sir (Richard) Ian, Kt.
Barling, *Hon.* Sir Gerald Edward, Kt.
Barlow, Sir Christopher Hilaro, Bt. (1803)
Barlow, Sir Frank, Kt., CBE
Barlow, Sir (George) William, Kt., FRENG
Barlow, Sir James Alan, Bt. (1902)
Barlow, Sir John Kemp, Bt. (1907)
Barnes, *The Most Revd* Brian James, KBE
Barnes, Sir (James) David (Francis), Kt., CBE
Barnes, Sir Kenneth, KCB
Barnett, *Hon.* Sir Michael Lancelot Patrick, Kt.
Barnewall, Sir Reginald Robert, Bt. (I. 1623)
Baron, Sir Thomas, Kt., CBE
†Barran, Sir John Ruthven, Bt. (1895)
Barratt, Sir Lawrence Arthur, Kt.
Barratt, Sir Richard Stanley, Kt., CBE, QPM
Barrett, Sir Stephen Jeremy, KCMG
Barrett-Lennard, Sir Peter John, Bt. (1801)
Barrington, Sir Benjamin, Bt. (1831)
Barrington, Sir Nicholas John, KCMG, CVO
Barrington-Ward, *Rt. Revd* Simon, KCMG
Barron, Sir Donald James, Kt.
Barrow, Sir Anthony John Grenfell, Bt. (1835)
Barry, Sir (Lawrence) Edward (Anthony Tress), Bt. (1899)
Barter, Sir Peter Leslie Charles, Kt., OBE
†Bartlett, Sir Andrew Alan, Bt. (1913)
Barttelot, *Col.* Sir Brian Walter de Stopham, Bt. (1875), OBE
Bate, Sir David Lindsay, KBE
Bates, Sir James Geoffrey, Bt. (1880)
Bates, Sir Richard Dawson Hoult, Bt. (1937)
Bateson, *Prof.* Sir Patrick, Kt.
Bather, Sir John Knollys, KCVO
Batho, Sir Peter Ghislain, Bt. (1928)
Bathurst, *Admiral of the Fleet* Sir (David) Benjamin, GCB
Batten, Sir John Charles, KCVO
Battersby, *Prof.* Sir Alan Rushton, Kt., FRS
Battishill, Sir Anthony Michael William, GCB
Baulcombe, *Prof.* Sir David Charles, Kt., FRS
Baxendell, Sir Peter Brian, Kt., CBE, FRENG
Bayly, *Prof.* Sir Christopher Alan, Kt.
Bayne, Sir Nicholas Peter, KCMG
Baynes, Sir Christopher Rory, Bt. (1801)
Bazley, Sir Thomas John Sebastian, Bt. (1869)
Beach, *Gen.* Sir (William Gerald) Hugh, GBE, KCB, MC
Beache, *Hon.* Sir Vincent Ian, KCMG
Beale, *Lt.-Gen.* Sir Peter John, KBE, FRCP
Beamish, Sir Adrian John, KCMG
Bean, *Hon.* Sir David Michael, Kt
Beaumont, *Capt.* Hon. Sir (Edward) Nicholas (Canning), KCVO
Beaumont, Sir George (Howland Francis), Bt. (1661)
Beatson, *Hon.* Sir Jack, Kt.
Beavis, *Air Chief Marshal* Sir Michael Gordon, KCB, CBE, AFC
Beck, Sir Edgar Philip, Kt.
Beckett, Sir Richard Gervase, Bt. (1921), QC
Beckett, Sir Terence Norman, KBE, FRENG
Beckwith, Sir John Lionel, Kt., CBE
Beddington, *Prof.* Sir John Rex, Kt., CMG
Beecham, Sir John Stratford Roland, Bt. (1914)
Beetham, *Marshal of the Royal Air Force* Sir Michael James, GCB, CBE, DFC, AFC
Beevor, Sir Thomas Agnew, Bt. (1784)
Beith, *Rt. Hon.* Sir Alan James, Kt.
Beldam, *Rt. Hon.* Sir (Alexander) Roy (Asplan), Kt.
Belich, Sir James, Kt.
Bell, Sir David Charles Maurice, Kt.
Bell, *Prof.* Sir John Irving, Kt.
Bell, Sir John Lowthian, Bt. (1885)
Bell, *Prof.* Sir Peter Robert Frank, Kt.
Bell, *Hon.* Sir Rodger, Kt.
Bell, Sir Stuart, Kt.
Bellamy, *Hon.* Sir Christopher William, Kt.
Bellingham, Sir Anthony Edward Norman, Bt. (1796)
Bender, Sir Brian Geoffrey, KCB
Benn, Sir (James) Jonathan, Bt. (1914)
Bennett, *Air Vice-Marshal* Sir Erik Peter, KBE, CB

Bennett, *Hon.* Sir Hugh Peter Derwyn, Kt.
Bennett, *Gen.* Sir Phillip Harvey, KBE, DSO
Bennett, Sir Richard Rodney, Kt., CBE
Bennett, Sir Ronald Wilfrid Murdoch, Bt. (1929)
Benson, Sir Christopher John, Kt.
Benyon, Sir William Richard, Kt.
Beresford, Sir (Alexander) Paul, Kt.
Beresford-Peirse, Sir Henry Grant de la Poer, Bt. (1814)
Berghuser, *Hon.* Sir Eric, Kt., MBE
Beringer, *Prof.* Sir John Evelyn, Kt., CBE
Berman, Sir Franklin Delow, KCMG
Berners-Lee, Sir Timothy John, OM, KBE, FRS
Bernard, Sir Dallas Edmund, Bt. (1954)
Bernstein, Sir Howard, Kt.
Berney, Sir Julian Reedham Stuart, Bt. (1620)
Berridge, *Prof.* Sir Michael John, Kt., FRS
Berriman, Sir David, Kt.
Berry, *Prof.* Sir Colin Leonard, Kt., FRCPATH
Berry, *Prof.* Sir Michael Victor, Kt., FRS
Berthoud, Sir Martin Seymour, KCVO, CMG
Best, Sir Richard Radford, KCVO, CBE
Best-Shaw, Sir John Michael Robert, Bt. (1665)
Bethel, Sir Baltron Benjamin, KCMG
Bethlehem, Sir Daniel, KCMG
Bett, Sir Michael, Kt., CBE
Bettison, Sir Norman George, Kt., QPM
Bevan, Sir Martyn Evan Evans, Bt. (1958)
Bevan, Sir Nicolas, Kt., CB
Bevan, Sir Timothy Hugh, Kt.
Beverley, *Lt.-Gen.* Sir Henry York La Roche, KCB, OBE, RM
Bibby, Sir Michael James, Bt. (1959)
Bickersteth, *Rt. Revd* John Monier, KCVO
Biddulph, Sir Ian D'Olier, Bt. (1664)
Bidwell, Sir Hugh Charles Philip, GBE
Biggam, Sir Robin Adair, Kt.
Biggs, Sir Norman Paris, Kt.
Bilas, Sir Angmai Simon, Kt., OBE
Billière, *Gen.* Sir Peter Edgar de la Cour de la, KCB, KBE, DSO, MC
Bindman, Sir Geoffrey Lionel, Kt.
Bingham, *Hon.* Sir Eardley Max, Kt.
Birch, Sir John Allan, KCVO, CMG
Birch, Sir Roger, Kt., CBE, QPM
Bird, Sir Richard Geoffrey Chapman, Bt. (1922)
Birkin, Sir John Christian William, Bt. (1905)
Birkin, Sir (John) Derek, Kt., TD
Birkmyre, Sir James, Bt. (1921)
Birrell, Sir James Drake, Kt.
Birtwistle, Sir Harrison, Kt., CH
Bischoff, Sir Winfried Franz Wilhelm, Kt.
Bishop, Sir Michael David, Kt., CBE
Bisson, *Rt. Hon.* Sir Gordon Ellis, Kt.
Black, *Adm.* Sir (John) Jeremy, GBE, KCB, DSO
Black, Sir Robert David, Bt. (1922)
Blackburn, *Vice-Adm.* Sir David Anthony James, KCVO, CB
Blackburne, *Hon.* Sir William Anthony, Kt.
Blackett, Sir Hugh Francis, Bt. (1673)
Blackham, *Vice-Adm.* Sir Jeremy Joe, KCB
Blackman, Sir Frank Milton, KCVO, OBE
Blair, *Lt.-Gen.* Sir Chandos, KCVO, OBE, MC
†Blair, Sir Patrick David Hunter, Bt. (1786)
Blair, *Hon.* Sir William James Lynton, Kt.
Blake, Sir Alfred Lapthorn, KCVO, MC
Blake, Sir Francis Michael, Bt. (1907)
Blake, *Hon.* Sir Nicholas John Gorrod, Kt.
Blake, Sir Peter Thomas, Kt., CBE
Blake, Sir Anthony Teilo Bruce, Bt. (I. 1622)
Blaker, Sir John, Bt. (1919)
Blakiston, Sir Ferguson Arthur James, Bt. (1763)
Blanch, Sir Malcolm, KCVO
Bland, Sir (Francis) Christopher (Buchan), Kt.
Bland, *Lt.-Col.* Sir Simon Claud Michael, KCVO
Blank, Sir Maurice Victor, Kt.
Blatherwick, Sir David Elliott Spiby, KCMG, OBE
Blelloch, Sir John Nial Henderson, KCB
Blennerhassett, Sir (Marmaduke) Adrian Francis William, Bt. (1809)
Blewitt, *Maj.* Sir Shane Gabriel Basil, GCVO
Blofeld, *Hon.* Sir John Christopher Calthorpe, Kt.
Blois, Sir Charles Nicholas Gervase, Bt. (1686)
Blom-Cooper, Sir Louis Jacques, Kt., QC
Blomefield, Sir Thomas Charles Peregrine, Bt. (1807)
Bloomfield, Sir Kenneth Percy, KCB
Blundell, Sir Thomas Leon, Kt., FRS
Blunden, Sir George, Kt.
†Blunden, Sir Hubert Chisholm, Bt. (I. 1766)
Blunt, Sir David Richard Reginald Harvey, Bt. (1720)
Blyth, Sir Charles (Chay), Kt., CBE, BEM
Boardman, *Prof.* Sir John, Kt., FSA, FBA
Bodey, *Hon.* Sir David Roderick Lessiter, Kt.
Bodmer, Sir Walter Fred, Kt., PHD, FRS
Body, Sir Richard Bernard Frank Stewart, Kt.
Bogan, Sir Nagora, KBE
Boileau, Sir Guy (Francis), Bt. (1838)
Boles, Sir Jeremy John Fortescue, Bt. (1922)
Boles, Sir John Dennis, Kt., MBE
Bolt, *Air Marshal* Sir Richard Bruce, KBE, CB, DFC, AFC
Bona, Sir Kina, KBE
Bonallack, Sir Michael Francis, Kt., OBE
Bond, Sir John Reginald Hartnell, Kt.
Bond, *Prof.* Sir Michael Richard, Kt., FRCPSYCH, FRCPGLAS, FRCSE
Bone, *Prof.* Sir James Drummond, Kt., FRSE
Bone, Sir Roger Bridgland, KCMG
Bonfield, Sir Peter Leahy, Kt., CBE, FRENG
†Bonham, Sir George Martin Antony, Bt. (1852)
Bonington, Sir Christian John Storey, Kt., CBE
Bonsall, Sir Arthur Wilfred, KCMG, CBE
Bonsor, Sir Nicholas Cosmo, Bt. (1925)
Boord, Sir Nicolas John Charles, Bt. (1896)
Boorman, *Lt.-Gen.* Sir Derek, KCB
Booth, Sir Christopher Charles, Kt., MD, FRCP
Booth, Sir Clive, Kt.
Booth, Sir Douglas Allen, Bt. (1916)
Booth, Sir Gordon, KCMG, CVO
Boothby, Sir Brooke Charles, Bt. (1660)
Bore, Sir Albert, Kt.
Boreel, Sir Stephan Gerard, Bt. (1645)
Borthwick, Sir Anthony Thomas, Bt. (1908)
Borysiewicz, *Prof.* Sir Leszek Krzysztof, Kt.
Bossom, *Hon.* Sir Clive, Bt. (1953)
Boswell, *Lt.-Gen.* Sir Alexander Crawford Simpson, KCB, CBE
Bosworth, Sir Neville Bruce Alfred, Kt., CBE
Botham, Sir Ian Terence, Kt., OBE
Bottoms, *Prof.* Sir Anthony Edward, Kt.
Bottomley, Sir James Reginald Alfred, KCMG
Boughey, Sir John George Fletcher, Bt. (1798)
Boulton, Sir Clifford John, GCB
†Boulton, Sir John Gibson, Bt. (1944)
Bouraga, Sir Phillip, KBE
Bourn, Sir John Bryant, KCB
Bowater, Sir Euan David Vansittart, Bt. (1939)
†Bowater, Sir Michael Patrick, Bt. (1914)
Bowden, Sir Andrew, Kt., MBE
Bowden, Sir Nicholas Richard, Bt. (1915)
Bowen, Sir Barry Manfield, KCMG
Bowen, Sir Geoffrey Fraser, Kt.

Bowen, Sir Mark Edward Mortimer, Bt. (1921)
Bowes Lyon, Sir Simon Alexander, KCVO
†Bowlby, Sir Richard Peregrine Longstaff, Bt. (1923)
Bowman, Sir Edwin Geoffrey, KCB
Bowman, Sir Jeffery Haverstock, Kt.
Bowman-Shaw, Sir (George) Neville, Kt.
Bowness, Sir Alan, Kt., CBE
Bowyer-Smyth, Sir Thomas Weyland, Bt. (1661)
Boyce, Sir Graham Hugh, KCMG
Boyce, Sir Robert Charles Leslie, Bt. (1952)
Boyd, Sir Alexander Walter, Bt. (1916)
Boyd, Sir John Dixon Iklé, KCMG
Boyd, *Prof.* Sir Robert David Hugh, Kt.
Boyd-Carpenter, Sir (Marsom) Henry, KCVO
Boyd-Carpenter, *Lt.-Gen. Hon.* Sir Thomas Patrick John, KBE
Boyle, Sir Stephen Gurney, Bt. (1904)
Boyson, *Rt. Hon.* Sir Rhodes, Kt.
Brabham, Sir John Arthur, Kt., OBE
Bracewell-Smith, Sir Charles, Bt. (1947)
Bradbeer, Sir John Derek Richardson, Kt., OBE, TD
Bradfield, *Dr* Sir John Richard Grenfell, Kt., CBE
Bradford, Sir Edward Alexander Slade, Bt. (1902)
Brady, *Prof.* Sir John Michael, Kt., FRS
Braithwaite, *Rt. Hon.* Sir Nicholas Alexander, Kt., OBE
Braithwaite, Sir Rodric Quentin, GCMG
Bramley, *Prof.* Sir Paul Anthony, Kt.
Branson, Sir Richard Charles Nicholas, Kt.
Bratza, *Hon.* Sir Nicolas Dušan, Kt.
Breckenridge, *Prof.* Sir Alasdair Muir, Kt., CBE
Brennan, *Hon.* Sir (Francis) Gerard, KBE
Brenton, Sir Anthony Russell, KCMG
Brewer, Sir David William, Kt., CMG
Brierley, Sir Ronald Alfred, Kt.
Briggs, *Hon.* Sir Michael Townley Featherstone, Kt.
Brighouse, *Prof.* Sir Timothy Robert Peter, Kt.
Bright, Sir Graham Frank James, Kt.
Bright, Sir Keith, Kt.
Brigstocke, *Adm.* Sir John Richard, KCB
Brinckman, Sir Theodore George Roderick, Bt. (1831)
†Brisco, Sir Campbell Howard, Bt. (1782)
Briscoe, Sir Brian Anthony, Kt.
Briscoe, Sir John Geoffrey James, Bt. (1910)
Brittan, Sir Samuel, Kt.
Britton, Sir Paul John James, Kt., CB
†Broadbent, Sir Andrew George, Bt. (1893)
Broadbent, Sir Richard John, KCB
Brocklebank, Sir Aubrey Thomas, Bt. (1885)
Brodie, Sir Benjamin David Ross, Bt. (1834)
Brooke, Sir Rodney George, Kt., CBE
Brooking, Sir Trevor, Kt., CBE
Bromhead, Sir John Desmond Gonville, Bt. (1806)
Bromley, Sir Michael Roger, KBE
Bromley, Sir Rupert Charles, Bt. (1757)
Bromley-Davenport, Sir William Arthur, KCVO
Brook, *Prof.* Sir Richard John, Kt. OBE
†Brooke, Sir Alistair Weston, Bt. (1919)
Brooke, Sir Francis George Windham, Bt. (1903)
Brooke, *Rt. Hon.* Sir Henry, Kt.
Brooke, Sir (Richard) David Christopher, Bt. (1662)
Brooking, Sir Trevor David, Kt., CBE
Brooks, Sir Timothy Gerald Martin, KCVO
Brooksbank, Sir (Edward) Nicholas, Bt. (1919)
Broomfield, Sir Nigel Hugh Robert Allen, KCMG
†Broughton, Sir David Delves, Bt. (1661)
Broun, Sir Wayne Hercules, Bt. (S. 1686)
Brown, Sir (Austen) Patrick, KCB
Brown, *Adm.* Sir Brian Thomas, KCB, CBE
Brown, Sir David, Kt.
Brown, *Hon.* Sir Douglas Dunlop, Kt.
Brown, Sir George Francis Richmond, Bt. (1863)
Brown, Sir Mervyn, KCMG, OBE
Brown, Sir Peter Randolph, Kt.
Brown, *Rt. Hon.* Sir Stephen, GBE
Brown, Sir Stephen David Reid, KCVO
Browne, Sir Nicholas Walker, KBE, CMG
Brownrigg, Sir Nicholas (Gawen), Bt. (1816)
Browse, *Prof.* Sir Norman Leslie, Kt., MD, FRCS
Bruce, Sir (Francis) Michael Ian, Bt. (S. 1628)
†Bruce-Clifton, Sir Hervey Hamish Peter, Bt. (1804)
Bruce-Gardner, Sir Robert Henry, Bt. (1945)
Brunner, Sir Hugo Laurence Joseph, KCVO
Brunner, Sir John Henry Kilian, Bt. (1895)
Brunton, Sir Gordon Charles, Kt.
†Brunton, Sir James Lauder, Bt. (1908)
Bryan, Sir Arthur, Kt.
Buchan-Hepburn, Sir John Alastair Trant Kidd, Bt. (1815)
Buchanan, Sir Andrew George, Bt. (1878)
Buchanan, *Vice-Adm.* Sir Peter William, KBE
Buchanan, Sir Robert Wilson (Robin), Kt.
†Buchanan-Jardine, Sir John Christopher Rupert, Bt. (1885)
Buckland, Sir Ross, Kt.
Buckley, Sir Michael Sidney, Kt.
Buckley, *Lt.-Cdr.* Sir (Peter) Richard, KCVO
Buckley, *Hon.* Sir Roger John, Kt.
Buckworth-Herne-Soame, Sir Charles John, Bt. (1697)
Budd, Sir Alan Peter, Kt.
Budd, Sir Colin Richard, KCMG
Bull, Sir George Jeffrey, Kt.
Bull, Sir Simeon George, Bt. (1922)
Bullock, Sir Stephen Michael, Kt.
Bultin, Sir Bato, Kt., MBE
Bunbury, Sir Michael William, Bt. (1681), KCVO
Bunyard, Sir Robert Sidney, Kt., CBE, QPM
Burbidge, Sir Peter Dudley, Bt. (1916)
Burden, Sir Anthony Thomas, Kt., QPM
Burdett, Sir Savile Aylmer, Bt. (1665)
Burgen, Sir Arnold Stanley Vincent, Kt., FRS
Burgess, *Gen.* Sir Edward Arthur, KCB, OBE
Burgess, Sir (Joseph) Stuart, Kt., CBE, PHD, FRSC
Burgess, *Prof.* Sir Robert George, Kt.
Burgh, Sir John Charles, KCMG, CB
Burke, Sir James Stanley Gilbert, Bt. (I. 1797)
Burke, Sir (Thomas) Kerry, Kt.
Burn, *Prof.* Sir John, Kt.
Burnell-Nugent, *Vice-Adm.* Sir James Michael, KCB, CBE, ADC
Burnet, Sir James William Alexander (Sir Alastair Burnet), Kt.
Burnett, *Air Chief Marshal* Sir Brian Kenyon, GCB, DFC, AFC
Burnett, Sir Charles David, Bt., (1913)
Burnett, *Hon.* Sir Ian Duncan, Kt.
Burnett, Sir Walter John, Kt.
Burney, Sir Nigel Dennistoun, Bt. (1921)
Burns, Sir (Robert) Andrew, KCMG
Burnton, *Rt. Hon.* Sir Stanley Jeffrey, Kt.
Burrell, Sir Charles Raymond, Bt. (1774)
Burridge, *Air Chief Marshal* Sir Brian Kevin, KCB, CBE, ADC
Burston, Sir Samuel Gerald Wood, Kt., OBE
Burt, Sir Peter Alexander, Kt.
Burton, Sir Carlisle Archibald, Kt., OBE
Burton, *Lt.-Gen.* Sir Edmund Fortescue Gerard, KBE
Burton, Sir Graham Stuart, KCMG
Burton, *Hon.* Sir Michael John, Kt.
Burton, Sir Michael St Edmund, KCVO, CMG

Bush, *Adm.* Sir John Fitzroy Duyland, GCB, DSC
Butler, *Hon.* Sir Arlington Griffith, KCMG
Butler, Sir Michael Dacres, GCMG
Butler, Sir (Reginald) Michael (Thomas), Bt. (1922)
Butler, Sir Percy James, Kt., CBE
Butler, *Hon.* Sir Richard Clive, Kt.
Butler, Sir Richard Pierce, Bt. (1628)
Butterfield, *Hon.* Sir Alexander Neil Logie, Kt.
Butterfill, Sir John Valentine, Kt.
Buxton, Sir Jocelyn Charles Roden, Bt. (1840)
Buxton, *Rt. Hon.* Sir Richard Joseph, Kt.
Buzzard, Sir Anthony Farquhar, Bt. (1929)
Byatt, Sir Hugh Campbell, KCVO, CMG
Byatt, Sir Ian Charles Rayner, Kt.
Byford, Sir Lawrence, Kt., CBE, QPM
Byron, *Rt. Hon.* Sir Charles Michael Dennis, Kt.

†Cable-Alexander, Sir Patrick Desmond William, Bt. (1809)
Cadbury, Sir (George) Adrian (Hayhurst), Kt.
Cadbury, Sir (Nicholas) Dominic, Kt.
Cadogan, *Prof.* Sir John Ivan George, Kt., CBE, FRS, FRSE
Cahn, Sir Albert Jonas, Bt. (1934)
Cahn, Sir Andrew Thomas, KCMG
Caine, Sir Michael (Maurice Micklewhite), Kt., CBE
Caines, Sir John, KCB
Caldwell, Sir Edward George, KCB
Callaghan, Sir William Henry, Kt.
Callan, Sir Ivan Roy, KCVO, CMG
Calman, *Prof.* Sir Kenneth Charles, KCB, MD, FRCP, FRCS, FRSE
Calne, *Prof.* Sir Roy Yorke, Kt., FRS
Calvert-Smith, Sir David, Kt., QC
Cameron, Sir Hugh Roy Graham, Kt., QPM
Campbell, *Prof.* Sir Colin Murray, Kt.
Campbell, Sir Ian Tofts, Kt., CBE, VRD
Campbell, Sir Ilay Mark, Bt. (1808)
Campbell, Sir James Alexander Moffat Bain, Bt. (S. 1668)
Campbell, Sir Lachlan Philip Kemeys, Bt. (1815)
Campbell, Sir Roderick Duncan Hamilton, Bt. (1831)
Campbell, Sir Robin Auchinbreck, Bt. (S. 1628)
Campbell, *Rt. Hon.* Sir Walter Menzies, Kt., CBE, QC
Campbell, *Rt. Hon.* Sir William Anthony, Kt.
Campbell-Orde, Sir John Alexander, Bt. (1790)
Cannadine, *Prof.* Sir David Nicholas, Kt.
†Carden, Sir Christopher Robert, Bt. (1887)
†Carden, Sir John Craven, Bt. (I. 1787)
Carew, Sir Rivers Verain, Bt. (1661)
Carey, Sir de Vic Graham, Kt.
Carey, Sir Peter Willoughby, GCB
Carleton-Smith, *Maj.-Gen.* Sir Michael Edward, Kt., CBE
Carlisle, Sir James Beethoven, GCMG
Carlisle, Sir John Michael, Kt.
Carlisle, Sir Kenneth Melville, Kt.
Carnegie, *Lt.-Gen.* Sir Robin Macdonald, KCB, OBE
Carnegie, Sir Roderick Howard, Kt.
Carnwath, *Rt. Hon.* Sir Robert John Anderson, Kt., CVO
Caro, Sir Anthony Alfred, Kt., OM, CBE
Carr, Sir (Albert) Raymond (Maillard), Kt.
Carr, Sir Peter Derek, Kt., CBE
Carr, *Very Revd Dr* Arthur Wesley, KCVO
Carr-Ellison, *Col.* Sir Ralph Harry, KCVO, TD
Carrick, *Hon.* Sir John Leslie, KCMG
Carrick, Sir Roger John, KCMG, LVO
Carruthers, Sir Ian James, Kt., OBE
Carsberg, *Prof.* Sir Bryan Victor, Kt.
Carter, *Prof.* Sir David Craig, Kt., FRCSE, FRCSGLAS, FRCPE
Carter, Sir John Alexander, Kt.
Carter, Sir John Gordon Thomas, Kt.
Carter, Sir Philip David, Kt., CBE
Carter, Sir Richard Henry Alwyn, Kt.
Cartledge, Sir Bryan George, KCMG
Cary, Sir Roger Hugh, Bt. (1955)
Casey, *Rt. Hon.* Sir Maurice Eugene, Kt.
Cash, Sir Andrew John, Kt., OBE
Cass, Sir Geoffrey Arthur, Kt.
Cassel, Sir Timothy Felix Harold, Bt. (1920)
Cassels, Sir John Seton, Kt., CB
Cassels, *Adm.* Sir Simon Alastair Cassillis, KCB, CBE
Cassidi, *Adm.* Sir (Arthur) Desmond, GCB
Castell, Sir William Martin, Kt.
Castledine, *Prof.* Sir George, Kt.
Catherwood, Sir (Henry) Frederick (Ross), Kt.
Catto, *Prof.* Sir Graeme Robertson Dawson, Kt.
Cave, Sir John Charles, Bt. (1896)
Cave-Browne-Cave, Sir Robert, Bt. (1641)
Cayley, Sir Digby William David, Bt. (1661)
Cayzer, Sir James Arthur, Bt. (1904)
Cazalet, *Hon.* Sir Edward Stephen, Kt.
Cazalet, Sir Peter Grenville, Kt.
Cecil, *Rear-Adm.* Sir (Oswald) Nigel Amherst, KBE, CB
Chadwick, *Rt. Hon.* Sir John Murray, Kt.
Chadwick, Sir Joshua Kenneth Burton, Bt. (1935)
Chadwick, *Revd Prof.* (William) Owen, OM, KBE, FBA
Chadwyck-Healey, Sir Charles Edward, Bt. (1919)
Chakrabarti, Sir Sumantra, KCB
Chalmers, Sir Iain Geoffrey, Kt.
Chalmers, Sir Neil Robert, Kt.
Chalstrey, Sir (Leonard) John, Kt., MD, FRCS
Chan, *Rt. Hon.* Sir Julius, GCMG, KBE
Chan, Sir Thomas Kok, Kt., OBE
Chance, Sir (George) Jeremy ffolliott, Bt. (1900)
Chandler, Sir Colin Michael, Kt.
Chandler, Sir Geoffrey, Kt., CBE
Chantler, *Prof.* Sir Cyril, Kt., MD, FRCP
Chaplin, Sir Malcolm Hilbery, Kt., CBE
Chapman, Sir David Robert Macgowan, Bt. (1958)
Chapman, Sir George Alan, Kt.
Chapman, Sir Sidney Brookes, Kt., MP
Chapple, *Field Marshal* Sir John Lyon, GCB, CBE
Charles, *Hon.* Sir Arthur William Hessin, Kt.
Charlton, Sir Robert (Bobby), Kt., CBE
Charnley, Sir (William) John, Kt., CB, FRENG
Chartres, *Rt. Revd and Rt. Hon.* Richard John Carew, KCVO
Chataway, *Rt. Hon.* Sir Christopher, Kt.
Chatfield, Sir John Freeman, Kt., CBE
†Chaytor, Sir Bruce Gordon, Bt. (1831)
Checketts, *Sqn. Ldr.* Sir David John, KCVO
Checkland, Sir Michael, Kt.
Cheshire, *Air Chief Marshal* Sir John Anthony, KBE, CB
Chessells, Sir Arthur David (Tim), Kt.
†Chetwynd, Sir Robin John Talbot, Bt. (1795)
Cheyne, Sir Patrick John Lister, Bt. (1908)
Chichester, Sir James Henry Edward, Bt. (1641)
Chichester-Clark, Sir Robin, Kt.
Chilcot, *Rt. Hon.* Sir John Anthony, GCB
Child, Sir (Coles John) Jeremy, Bt. (1919)
Chilwell, *Hon.* Sir Muir Fitzherbert, Kt.
Chinn, Sir Trevor Edwin, Kt., CVO
Chipperfield, *Prof.* Sir David Alan, Kt., CBE
Chipperfield, Sir Geoffrey Howes, KCB
Chisholm, Sir John Alexander Raymond, Kt., FRENG
Chitty, Sir Thomas Willes, Bt. (1924)
Cholmeley, Sir Hugh John Frederick Sebastian, Bt. (1806)
Chow, Sir Chung Kong, Kt.
Chow, Sir Henry Francis, Kt., OBE

Christie, Sir George William Langham, Kt., CH
Christopher, Sir Duncan Robin Carmichael, KBE, CMG
Chung, Sir Sze-yuen, GBE, FRENG
Clark, Sir Francis Drake, Bt. (1886)
Clark, Sir John Arnold, Kt.
Clark, Sir Jonathan George, Bt. (1917)
Clark, Sir Robert Anthony, Kt., DSC
Clark, Sir Terence Joseph, KBE, CMG, CVO
Clarke, Sir (Charles Mansfield) Tobias, Bt. (1831)
Clarke, *Hon.* Sir Christopher Simon Courtenay Stephenson, Kt.
Clarke, Sir Christopher James, Kt., OBE
Clarke, *Hon.* Sir David Clive, Kt.
Clarke, Sir Ellis Emmanuel Innocent, GCMG
Clarke, Sir Jonathan Dennis, Kt.
Clarke, Sir Robert Cyril, Kt.
†Clarke, Sir Rupert Grant Alexander, Bt. (1882)
Clay, Sir Edward, KCMG
Clay, Sir Richard Henry, Bt. (1841)
Clayton, Sir David Robert, Bt. (1732)
Cleaver, Sir Anthony Brian, Kt.
Clementi, Sir David Cecil, Kt.
Cleminson, Sir James Arnold Stacey, KBE, MC
Clerk, Sir Robert Maxwell, Bt. (1679), OBE
Clerke, Sir John Edward Longueville, Bt. (1660)
Clifford, Sir Roger Joseph, Bt. (1887)
Clifford, Sir Timothy Peter Plint, Kt.
Clucas, Sir Kenneth Henry, KCB
Coates, Sir Anthony Robert Milnes, Bt. (1911)
Coates, Sir David Frederick Charlton, Bt. (1921)
Coats, Sir Alastair Francis Stuart, Bt. (1905)
Cochrane, Sir (Henry) Marc (Sursock), Bt. (1903)
Cockburn, Sir John Elliot, Bt. (S. 1671)
Cockburn-Campbell, Sir Alexander Thomas, Bt. (1821)
Cockell, Sir Merrick, Kt.
Cockshaw, Sir Alan, Kt., FRENG
†Codrington, Sir Christopher George Wayne, Bt. (1876)
†Codrington, Sir Giles Peter, Bt. (1721)
Coghill, Sir Patrick Kendal Farley, Bt. (1778)
Coghlin, *Rt. Hon.* Sir Patrick, Kt.
Cohen, Sir Edward, Kt.
Cohen, Sir Ivor Harold, Kt., CBE, TD
Cohen, *Prof.* Sir Philip, Kt., PHD, FRS
Cohen, Sir Ronald, Kt.
Cole, Sir (Robert) William, Kt.
Coleman, Sir Robert John, KCMG
Coleridge, *Hon.* Sir Paul James Duke, Kt.
Coles, Sir (Arthur) John, GCMG
Colfox, Sir (William) John, Bt. (1939)
Collett, Sir Christopher, GBE
Collett, Sir Ian Seymour, Bt. (1934)
Collins, Sir Alan Stanley, KCVO, CMG
Collins, *Hon.* Sir Andrew David, Kt.
Collins, Sir Bryan Thomas Alfred, Kt., OBE, QFSM
Collins, Sir John Alexander, Kt
Collins, Sir Kenneth Darlingston, Kt.
Collyear, Sir John Gowen, Kt.
Colman, *Hon.* Sir Anthony David, Kt.
Colman, Sir Michael Jeremiah, Bt. (1907)
Colman, Sir Timothy, KG
†Colquhoun of Luss, Sir Malcolm Rory, Bt. (1786)
Colt, Sir Edward William Dutton, Bt. (1694)
Colthurst, Sir Charles St John, Bt. (1744)
Conant, Sir John Ernest Michael, Bt. (1954)
Connell, *Hon.* Sir Michael Bryan, Kt.
Conner, *Rt. Revd* Sir David John, KCVO
Connery, Sir Sean, Kt.
Connor, Sir William Joseph, Kt.
Conran, Sir Terence Orby, Kt.
Cons, *Hon.* Sir Derek, Kt.
Conway, *Prof.* Sir Gordon Richard, KCMG, FRS
Cook, Sir Christopher Wymondham Rayner Herbert, Bt. (1886)
Cook, *Prof.* Sir Peter Frederic Chester, Kt.
Cooke, *Col.* Sir David William Perceval, Bt. (1661)
Cooke, Sir Howard Felix Hanlan, GCMG, GCVO
Cooke, *Hon.* Sir Jeremy Lionel, Kt.
Cooke, *Prof.* Sir Ronald Urwick, Kt.
Cooksey, Sir David James Scott, GBE
Cooper, *Gen.* Sir George Leslie Conroy, GCB, MC
Cooper, Sir Henry, Kt.
Cooper, Sir Richard Adrian, Bt. (1905)
Cooper, *Maj.-Gen.* Sir Simon Christie, GCVO
Cooper, Sir William Daniel Charles, Bt. (1863)
Coote, Sir Christopher John, Bt. (I. 1621), *Premier Baronet of Ireland*
Copas, *Most Revd* Virgil, KBE
Copisarow, Sir Alcon Charles, Kt.
Corbett, *Maj.-Gen.* Sir Robert John Swan, KCVO, CB
Cordy-Simpson, *Lt.-Gen.* Sir Roderick Alexander, KBE, CB
Corfield, Sir Kenneth George, Kt., FRENG
Cormack, Sir Patrick Thomas, Kt.
Corness, Sir Colin Ross, Kt.
Cornforth, Sir John Warcup, Kt., CBE, DPHIL, FRS
Corry, Sir James Michael, Bt. (1885)
Cortazzi, Sir (Henry Arthur) Hugh, GCMG
Cory, Sir (Clinton Charles) Donald, Bt. (1919)
Cory-Wright, Sir Richard Michael, Bt. (1903)
Cossons, Sir Neil, Kt., OBE
Cotter, Sir Patrick Laurence Delaval, Bt. (I. 1763)
Cotterell, Sir John Henry Geers, Bt. (1805)
Cottrell, Sir Alan Howard, Kt., PHD, FRS, FRENG
†Cotts, Sir Richard Crichton Mitchell, Bt. (1921)
Coulson, *Hon.* Sir Peter David William, Kt.
Couper, Sir James George, Bt. (1841)
Courtenay, Sir Thomas Daniel, Kt.
Cousins, *Air Chief Marshal* Sir David, KCB, AFC
Coville, *Air Marshal* Sir Christopher Charles Cotton, KCB
Cowan, *Gen.* Sir Samuel, KCB, CBE
Coward, *Vice-Adm.* Sir John Francis, KCB, DSO
Cowen, *Rt. Hon. Prof.* Sir Zelman, GCMG, GCVO
Cowie, Sir Thomas (Tom), Kt., OBE
Cowper-Coles, Sir Sherard Louis, KCMG, LVO
Cox, Sir Alan George, Kt., CBE
Cox, *Prof.* Sir David Roxbee, Kt.
Cox, Sir George Edwin, Kt.
Craft, *Prof.* Sir Alan William, Kt.
Craig, Sir (Albert) James (Macqueen), GCMG
Craig-Cooper, Sir (Frederick Howard) Michael, Kt., CBE, TD
Crane, *Hon.* Sir Peter Francis, Kt.
Crane, *Prof.* Sir Peter Robert, Kt.
Cranston, *Hon.* Sir Ross Frederick, Kt.
Craufurd, Sir Robert James, Bt. (1781)
Craven, Sir John Anthony, Kt.
Craven, Sir Philip Lee, Kt., MBE
Crawford, *Prof.* Sir Frederick William, Kt., FRENG
Crawford, Sir Robert William Kenneth, Kt. CBE
Crawley-Boevey, Sir Thomas Michael Blake, Bt. (1784)
Crew, Sir (Michael) Edward, Kt., QPM
Crewe, *Prof.* Sir Ivor Martin, Kt.
Cresswell, *Hon.* Sir Peter John, Kt.
Crichton-Brown, Sir Robert, KCMG, CBE, TD
Crisp, Sir John Charles, Bt. (1913)
Critchett, Sir Charles George Montague, Bt. (1908)
Crockett, Sir Andrew Duncan, Kt.
Croft, Sir Owen Glendower, Bt. (1671)
Croft, Sir Thomas Stephen Hutton, Bt. (1818)
†Crofton, Sir Hugh Denis, Bt. (1801)
†Crofton, Sir Julian Malby, Bt. (1838)
Crombie, Sir Alexander, Kt.
Crompton, Sir Dan, Kt., CBE, QPM
Crosby, Sir James Robert, Kt.

Crossland, *Prof.* Sir Bernard, Kt., CBE, FRENG
Crossley, Sir Sloan Nicholas, Bt. (1909)
Crowe, Sir Brian Lee, KCMG
Cruickshank, Sir Donald Gordon, Kt.
Cruthers, Sir James Winter, Kt.
Cubbon, Sir Brian Crossland, GCB
Cubie, *Dr* Sir Andrew, Kt., CBE
Cubitt, Sir Hugh Guy, Kt., CBE
Cullen, Sir (Edward) John, Kt., FRENG
Culme-Seymour, Sir Michael Patrick, Bt. (1809)
Culpin, Sir Robert Paul, Kt.
Cummins, Sir Michael John Austin, Kt.
Cunliffe, *Prof.* Sir Barrington, Kt., CBE
Cunliffe, Sir David Ellis, Bt. (1759)
Cunliffe, Sir Jonathan Stephen, Kt., CB
Cunliffe-Owen, Sir Hugo Dudley, Bt. (1920)
Cunningham, *Lt.-Gen.* Sir Hugh Patrick, KBE
Cunningham, Sir Roger Keith, Kt., CBE
Cunynghame, Sir Andrew David Francis, Bt. (S. 1702)
†Currie, Sir Donald Scott, Bt. (1847)
Curry, Sir Donald Thomas Younger, Kt., CBE
Curtain, Sir Michael, KBE
Curtis, Sir Barry John, Kt.
Curtis, *Hon.* Sir Richard Herbert, Kt.
Curtis, Sir William Peter, Bt. (1802)
Curtiss, *Air Marshal* Sir John Bagot, KCB, KBE
Curwen, Sir Christopher Keith, KCMG
Cuschieri, *Prof.* Sir Alfred, Kt.

Dain, Sir David John Michael, KCVO
Dales, Sir Richard Nigel, KCVO
Dalrymple-Hay, Sir Malcolm John Robert, Bt. (1798)
†Dalrymple-White, Sir Jan Hew, Bt. (1926)
Dalton, *Vice-Adm.* Sir Geoffrey Thomas James Oliver, KCB
Dalton, Sir Richard John, KCMG
Dalton, *Air Chief Marshal* Sir Stephen Gary George, KCB
Dalyell, Sir Tam (Thomas), Bt. (NS 1685)
Daniel, Sir John Sagar, Kt., DSC
Dannatt, *Gen.* Sir (Francis) Richard, GCB, CBE, MC
Darell, Sir Jeffrey Lionel, Bt. (1795), MC
Darling, Sir Clifford, GCVO
Darrington, Sir Michael John, Kt.
Darroch, Sir Nigel Kim, KCMG
Dasgupta, *Prof.* Sir Partha Sarathi, Kt.
†Dashwood, Sir Edward John Francis, Bt. (1707), *Premier Baronet of Great Britain*
Dashwood, Sir Richard James, Bt. (1684)
Daunt, Sir Timothy Lewis Achilles, KCMG
Davenport-Handley, Sir David John, Kt., OBE
David, Sir Jean Marc, Kt., CBE, QC
David, *His Hon.* Sir Robin (Robert) Daniel George, Kt.
Davies, Sir Alan Seymour, Kt.
Davies, Sir (Charles) Noel, Kt.
Davies, *Prof.* Sir David Evan Naughton, Kt., CBE, FRS, FRENG
Davies, *Hon.* Sir (David Herbert) Mervyn, Kt., MC, TD
Davies, Sir David John, Kt.
Davies, Sir Frank John, Kt., CBE
Davies, *Prof.* Sir Graeme John, Kt., FRENG
Davies, Sir John Howard, Kt.
Davies, Sir John Michael, KCB
Davies, Sir Peter Maxwell, Kt., CBE
Davies, Sir Rhys Everson, Kt., QC
Davis, Sir Andrew Frank, Kt., CBE
Davis, Sir Colin Rex, Kt., CH, CBE
Davis, Sir Crispin Henry Lamert, Kt.
Davis, Sir John Gilbert, Bt. (1946)
Davis, *Hon.* Sir Nigel Anthony Lambert, Kt.
Davis, Sir Peter John, Kt.
Davis-Goff, Sir Robert (William), Bt. (1905)
Davison, *Rt. Hon.* Sir Ronald Keith, GBE, CMG
†Davson, Sir George Trenchard Simon, Bt. (1927)
Dawanincura, Sir John Norbert, Kt., OBE
Dawbarn, Sir Simon Yelverton, KCVO, CMG
Dawson, *Hon.* Sir Daryl Michael, KBE, CB
Dawson, Sir Nicholas Antony Trevor, Bt. (1920)
Dawtry, Sir Alan (Graham), Kt., CBE, TD
Day, Sir Derek Malcolm, KCMG
Day, *Air Chief Marshal* Sir John Romney, KCB, OBE, ADC
Day, Sir (Judson) Graham, Kt.
Day, Sir Michael John, Kt., OBE
Day, Sir Simon James, Kt.
Deane, *Hon.* Sir William Patrick, KBE
Dearlove, Sir Richard Billing, KCMG, OBE
de Bellaigue, Sir Geoffrey, GCVO
†Debenham, Sir Thomas Adam, Bt. (1931)
de Deney, Sir Geoffrey Ivor, KCVO
Deeny, *Hon.* Sir Donnell Justin Patrick, Kt.
De Halpert, *Rear-Adm.* Sir Jeremy Michael, KCVO, CB
de Hoghton, Sir (Richard) Bernard (Cuthbert), Bt. (1611)
De la Bère, Sir Cameron, Bt. (1953)
de la Rue, Sir Andrew George Ilay, Bt. (1898)
De Silva, Sir George Desmond Lorenz, Kt., QC
Dellow, Sir John Albert, Kt., CBE
Delves, *Lt.-Gen.* Sir Cedric Norman George, KBE
Denholm, Sir John Ferguson (Ian), Kt., CBE
Denison-Smith, *Lt.-Gen.* Sir Anthony Arthur, KBE
Denny, Sir Anthony Coningham de Waltham, Bt. (I. 1782)
Denny, Sir Charles Alistair Maurice, Bt. (1913)
Derbyshire, Sir Andrew George, Kt.
Derham, Sir Peter John, Kt.
†de Trafford, Sir John Humphrey, Bt. (1841)
Deverell, *Gen.* Sir John Freegard, KCB, OBE
Devesi, Sir Baddeley, GCMG, GCVO
De Ville, Sir Harold Godfrey Oscar, Kt., CBE
Devitt, Sir James Hugh Thomas, Bt. (1916)
de Waal, Sir (Constant Henrik) Henry, KCB, QC
Dewey, Sir Anthony Hugh, Bt. (1917)
De Witt, Sir Ronald Wayne, Kt.
Dhenin, *Air Marshal* Sir Geoffrey Howard, KBE, AFC, GM, MD
Dick-Lauder, Sir Piers Robert, Bt. (S. 1690)
Dilke, Sir Charles John Wentworth, Bt. (1862)
Dillon, Sir Andrew Patrick, Kt., CBE
Dillwyn-Venables-Llewelyn, Sir John Michael, Bt. (1890)
Dixon, Sir Jeremy, Kt.
Dixon, Sir Jonathan Mark, Bt. (1919)
Dixon, Sir Peter John Bellett, Kt.
Djanogly, Sir Harry Ari Simon, Kt., CBE
Dobson, *Vice-Adm.* Sir David Stuart, KBE
Dodds, Sir Ralph Jordan, Bt. (1964)
Dollery, Sir Colin Terence, Kt.
Don-Wauchope, Sir Roger (Hamilton), Bt. (S. 1667)
Donald, Sir Alan Ewen, KCMG
Donald, *Air Marshal* Sir John George, KBE
Donaldson, *Prof.* Sir Liam Joseph, Kt.
Donne, *Hon.* Sir Gaven John, KBE
Donne, Sir John Christopher, Kt.
Donnelly, Sir Joseph Brian, KBE, CMG
Dorey, Sir Graham Martyn, Kt.
Dorman, Sir Philip Henry Keppel, Bt. (1923)
Doughty, Sir William Roland, Kt.
Douglas, *Prof.* Sir Neil James, Kt.
Douglas, *Hon.* Sir Roger Owen, Kt.
Dowell, Sir Anthony James, Kt., CBE
Dowling, Sir Robert, Kt.
Downey, Sir Gordon Stanley, KCB
Downs, Sir Diarmuid, Kt., CBE, FRENG
Downward, *Maj.-Gen.* Sir Peter Aldcroft, KCVO, CB, DSO, DFC

Dowson, Sir Philip Manning, Kt., CBE, PRA
Doyle, Sir Reginald Derek Henry, Kt., CBE
D'Oyly, Sir Hadley Gregory Bt. (1663)
Drake, *Hon.* Sir (Frederick) Maurice, Kt., DFC
Drewry, *Lt.-Gen.* Sir Christopher Francis, KCB, CBE
Drinkwater, Sir John Muir, Kt., QC
Drury, Sir (Victor William) Michael, Kt., OBE
Dryden, Sir John Stephen Gyles, Bt. (1733 and 1795)
du Cann, *Rt. Hon.* Sir Edward Dillon Lott, KBE
†Duckworth, Sir James Edward Dyce, Bt. (1909)
du Cros, Sir Claude Philip Arthur Mallet, Bt. (1916)
Dudley-Williams, Sir Alastair Edgcumbe James, Bt. (1964)
Duff, *Prof.* Sir Gordon William, Kt.
Duff-Gordon, Sir Andrew Cosmo Lewis, Bt. (1813)
Duffell, *Lt.-Gen.* Sir Peter Royson, KCB, CBE, MC
Duffy, Sir (Albert) (Edward) Patrick, Kt., PHD
Dugdale, Sir William Stratford, Bt. (1936), MC
Duggin, Sir Thomas Joseph, Kt.
Dummett, *Prof.* Sir Michael Anthony Eardley, Kt., FBA
Dunbar, Sir Archibald Ranulph, Bt. (S. 1700)
Dunbar, Sir Robert Drummond Cospatrick, Bt. (S. 1698)
Dunbar, Sir James Michael, Bt. (S. 1694)
Dunbar of Hempriggs, Sir Richard Francis, Bt. (S. 1706)
Dunbar-Nasmith, *Prof.* Sir James Duncan, Kt., CBE
Duncan, Sir James Blair, Kt.
Dunlop, Sir Thomas, Bt. (1916)
Dunn, *Rt. Hon.* Sir Robin Horace Walford, Kt., MC
Dunne, Sir Thomas Raymond, KG, KCVO
Dunning, Sir Simon William Patrick, Bt. (1930)
Dunnington-Jefferson, Sir Mervyn Stewart, Bt. (1958)
Dunstan, *Lt.-Gen.* Sir Donald Beaumont, KBE, CB
Dunt, *Vice-Adm.* Sir John Hugh, KCB
Duntze, Sir Daniel Evans Bt. (1774)
Dupre, Sir Tumun, Kt., MBE
Dupree, Sir (Thomas William James) David, Bt. (1921)
Durand, Sir Edward Alan Christopher David Percy, Bt. (1892)
Durant, Sir (Robert) Anthony (Bevis), Kt.
Durie, Sir David Robert Campbell, KCMG
Durrant, Sir William Alexander Estridge, Bt. (1784)
Duthie, *Prof.* Sir Herbert Livingston, Kt.
Duthie, Sir Robert Grieve (Robin), Kt., CBE
Dutton, *Lt-Gen.* Sir James Benjamin, KCB, CBE
Dwyer, Sir Joseph Anthony, Kt.
Dyke, Sir David William Hart, Bt. (1677)
Dymock, *Vice-Adm.* Sir Anthony Knox, KBE, CB
Dyson, Sir James, Kt., CBE
Dyson, *Rt. Hon.* Sir John Anthony, Kt.

Eady, *Hon.* Sir David, Kt.
Eardley-Wilmot, Sir Michael John Assheton, Bt. (1821)
Earle, Sir (Hardman) George (Algernon), Bt. (1869)
Eaton, *Adm.* Sir Kenneth John, GBE, KCB
Eberle, *Adm.* Sir James Henry Fuller, GCB
Ebrahim, Sir (Mahomed) Currimbhoy, Bt. (1910)
Eckersley, Sir Donald Payze, Kt., OBE
Eddington, Sir Roderick Ian, Kt.
Edge, *Capt.* Sir (Philip) Malcolm, KCVO
†Edge, Sir William, Bt. (1937)
Edmonstone, Sir Archibald Bruce Charles, Bt. (1774)
Edward, *Rt. Hon.* Sir David Alexander Ogilvy, KCMG
Edwardes, Sir Michael Owen, Kt.
Edwards, Sir Christopher John Churchill, Bt. (1866)
Edwards, *Prof.* Sir Christopher Richard Watkin, Kt.
Edwards, Sir Llewellyn Roy, Kt.
Edwards, Sir Robert Paul, Kt.
Edwards, *Prof.* Sir Samuel Frederick, Kt., FRS
†Edwards-Moss, Sir David John, Bt. (1868)
Edwards-Stuart, *Hon.* Sir Antony James Cobham, Kt.
Egan, Sir John Leopold, Kt.
Ehrman, Sir William Geoffrey, KCMG
Eichelbaum, *Rt. Hon.* Sir Thomas, GBE
Elder, Sir Mark Philip, Kt., CBE
Eldon, Sir Stewart Graham, KCMG, OBE
Elias, *Rt. Hon.* Sir Patrick, Kt.
Eliott of Stobs, Sir Charles Joseph Alexander, Bt. (S. 1666)
Elliot, Sir Gerald Henry, Kt.
Elliott, Sir Clive Christopher Hugh, Bt. (1917)
Elliott, Sir David Murray, KCMG, CB
Elliott, *Prof.* Sir John Huxtable, Kt., FBA
Elliott, *Prof.* Sir Roger James, Kt., FRS
Elphinstone, Sir John, Bt. (S. 1701)
Elphinstone, Sir John Howard Main, Bt. (1816)
Elton, Sir Arnold, Kt., CBE
Elton, Sir Charles Abraham Grierson, Bt. (1717)
Elton, Sir Leslie, Kt.
Elvidge, Sir John, KCB
Elwes, *Dr* Sir Henry William, KCVO
Elwes, Sir Jeremy Vernon, Kt., CBE
Elwood, Sir Brian George Conway, Kt., CBE
Elworthy, *Air Cdre. Hon.* Sir Timothy Charles, KCVO, CBE
Empey, Sir Reginald Norman Morgan, Kt., OBE
Enderby, *Prof.* Sir John Edwin, Kt. CBE, FRS
Engle, Sir George Lawrence Jose, KCB, QC
English, Sir Terence Alexander Hawthorne, KBE, FRCS
Ennals, Sir Paul Martin, Kt., CBE
Epstein, *Prof.* Sir (Michael) Anthony, Kt., CBE, FRS
Errington, *Col.* Sir Geoffrey Frederick, Bt. (1963), OBE
Errington, Sir Lancelot, KCB
Erskine, Sir (Thomas) Peter Neil, Bt. (1821)
Erskine-Hill, Sir Alexander Rodger, Bt. (1945)
Esmonde, Sir Thomas Francis Grattan, Bt. (I. 1629)
Esplen, Sir John Graham, Bt. (1921)
Esquivel, *Rt. Hon.* Sir Manuel, KCMG
Essenhigh, *Adm.* Sir Nigel Richard, GCB
Etherington, Sir Stuart James, Kt.
Etherton, *Rt. Hon.* Sir Terence Michael Elkan Barnet, Kt.
Evans, Sir Anthony Adney, Bt. (1920)
Evans, *Rt. Hon.* Sir Anthony Howell Meurig, Kt., RD
Evans, *Prof.* Sir Christopher Thomas, Kt., OBE
Evans, *Air Chief Marshal* Sir David George, GCB, CBE
Evans, *Hon.* Sir David Roderick, Kt.
Evans, Sir Harold Matthew, Kt.
Evans, *Hon.* Sir Haydn Tudor, Kt.
Evans, *Prof.* Sir John Grimley, Kt., FRCP
Evans, Sir John Stanley, Kt., QPM
Evans, *Prof.* Sir Martin John, Kt., FRS
Evans, Sir Richard Harry, Kt., CBE
Evans, Sir Richard Mark, KCMG, KCVO
Evans, Sir Robert, Kt., CBE, FRENG
Evans-Lombe, *Hon.* Sir Edward Christopher, Kt.
†Evans-Tipping, Sir David Gwynne, Bt. (1913)
Eveleigh, *Rt. Hon.* Sir Edward Walter, Kt., ERD
Everard, Sir Robin Charles, Bt. (1911)
Every, Sir Henry John Michael, Bt. (1641)
Ewans, Sir Martin Kenneth, KCMG
Ewart, Sir William Michael, Bt. (1887)

Ewbank, *Hon.* Sir Anthony Bruce, Kt.
Eyre, Sir Reginald Edwin, Kt.
Eyre, Sir Richard Charles Hastings, Kt., CBE

Fagge, Sir John Christopher Frederick, Bt. (1660)
Fairbairn, Sir (James) Brooke, Bt. (1869)
Fairlie-Cuninghame, Sir Robert Henry, Bt. (S. 1630)
Fairweather, Sir Patrick Stanislaus, KCMG
Faldo, Sir Nicholas Alexander, Kt., MBE
†Falkiner, Sir Benjamin Simon Patrick, Bt. (I. 1778)
Fall, Sir Brian James Proetel, GCVO, KCMG
Falle, Sir Samuel, KCMG, KCVO, DSC
Fang, *Prof.* Sir Harry, Kt., CBE
Fareed, Sir Djamil Sheik, Kt.
Farmer, Sir Thomas, Kt., CVO, CBE
Farquhar, Sir Michael Fitzroy Henry, Bt. (1796)
Farquharson, Sir Angus Durie Miller, KCVO, OBE
Farquharson, *Rt. Hon.* Sir Donald Henry, Kt.
Farrell, Sir Terence, Kt., CBE
Farrer, Sir (Charles) Matthew, GCVO
Farrington, Sir Henry William, Bt. (1818)
Fat, Sir (Maxime) Edouard (Lim Man) Lim, Kt.
Faulkner, Sir (James) Dennis (Compton), Kt., CBE, VRD
Fay, Sir (Humphrey) Michael Gerard, Kt.
Fayrer, Sir John Lang Macpherson, Bt. (1896)
Feachem, *Prof.* Sir Richard George Andrew, KBE
Fean, Sir Thomas Vincent, KCVO
Feilden, Sir Henry Wemyss, Bt. (1846)
Feldmann, *Prof.* Sir Marc, Kt.
Fell, Sir David, KCB
Fender, Sir Brian Edward Frederick, Kt., CMG, PHD
Fenn, Sir Nicholas Maxted, GCMG
Fennell, *Hon.* Sir (John) Desmond Augustine, Kt., OBE
Fenwick, Sir Leonard Raymond, Kt., CBE
Fergus, Sir Howard Archibald, KBE
Ferguson, Sir Alexander Chapman, Kt., CBE
Ferguson-Davie, Sir Michael, Bt. (1847)
Fergusson of Kilkerran, Sir Charles, Bt. (S. 1703)
Fergusson, Sir Ewan Alastair John, GCMG, GCVO
Fermor, Sir Patrick Michael Leigh, Kt., DSO, OBE
Fersht, *Prof.* Sir Alan Roy, Kt., FRS
Ferris, *Hon.* Sir Francis Mursell, Kt., TD
ffolkes, Sir Robert Francis Alexander, Bt. (1774), OBE
Field, Sir Malcolm David, Kt.
Field, *Hon.* Sir Richard Alan, Kt.
Fielding, Sir Colin Cunningham, Kt., CB
Fielding, Sir Leslie, KCMG
Fields, Sir Allan Clifford, KCMG
Fieldsend, *Hon.* Sir John Charles Rowell, KBE
Fiennes, Sir Ranulph Twisleton-Wykeham, Bt. (1916), OBE
Figg, Sir Leonard Clifford William, KCMG
Figgis, Sir Anthony St John Howard, KCVO, CMG
Finch, Sir Robert Gerard, Kt.
Finlay, Sir David Ronald James Bell, Bt. (1964)
Finlayson, Sir Garet Orlando, KCMG, OBE
Finney, Sir Thomas, Kt., OBE
†Fison, Sir Charles William, Bt. (1905)
†Fitzgerald, *Revd* Daniel Patrick, Bt. (1903)
FitzGerald, Sir Adrian James Andrew, Bt. (1880)
FitzHerbert, Sir Richard Ranulph, Bt. (1784)
Fitzpatrick, *Air Marshal* Sir John Bernard, KBE, CB
Flanagan, Sir Ronald, GBE
Flanagan, Sir Maurice, KBE
Flaux, *Hon.* Sir Julian Martin, Kt.
Floissac, *Hon.* Sir Vincent Frederick, Kt., CMG, OBE
Floud, *Prof.* Sir Roderick Castle, Kt.
Floyd, *Hon.* Sir Christopher David, Kt.
Floyd, Sir Giles Henry Charles, Bt. (1816)
Foley, *Lt.-Gen.* Sir John Paul, KCB, OBE, MC
Follett, *Prof.* Sir Brian Keith, Kt., FRS
Foot, Sir Geoffrey James, Kt.
Foots, Sir James William, Kt.
Forbes, Sir James Thomas Stewart, Bt. (1823)
Forbes, *Adm.* Sir Ian Andrew, KCB, CBE
Forbes, *Vice-Adm.* Sir John Morrison, KCB
Forbes, *Hon.* Sir Thayne John, Kt.
†Forbes Adam, Revd Stephen Timothy Beilby, Bt. (1917)
Forbes-Leith, Sir George Ian David, Bt. (1923)
Forbes of Craigievar, Sir Andrew Iain Ochoncar, Bt. (S. 1630)
Ford, Sir Andrew Russell, Bt. (1929)
Ford, Sir David Robert, KBE, LVO
Ford, Sir John Archibald, KCMG, MC
Ford, *Gen.* Sir Robert Cyril, GCB, CBE
Foreman, Sir Philip Frank, Kt., CBE, FRENG
Forestier-Walker, Sir Michael Leolin, Bt. (1835)
Forman, Sir John Denis, Kt., OBE
Forrest, *Prof.* Sir (Andrew) Patrick (McEwen), Kt.
Forte, Hon. Sir Rocco John Vincent, Kt.
Forwood, Sir Peter Noel, Bt. (1895)
Foskett, *Hon.* Sir David Robert, Kt.
Foster, Sir Andrew William, Kt.
Foster, *Prof.* Sir Christopher David, Kt.
†Foster, Sir Saxby Gregory, Bt. (1930)
Foulkes, Sir Arthur Alexander, GCMG
Foulkes, Sir Nigel Gordon, Kt.
Fountain, *Hon.* Sir Cyril Stanley Smith, Kt.
Fowke, Sir David Frederick Gustavus, Bt. (1814)
Fowler, Sir (Edward) Michael Coulson, Kt.
Fox, Sir Christopher, Kt., QPM
Fox, Sir Paul Leonard, Kt., CBE
France, Sir Christopher Walter, GCB
Francis, Sir Horace William Alexander, Kt., CBE, FRENG
Frank, Sir Robert Andrew, Bt. (1920)
Franklin, Sir Michael David Milroy, KCB, CMG
Fraser, Sir Alasdair MacLeod, Kt.
Fraser, Sir Charles Annand, KCVO
Fraser, *Gen.* Sir David William, GCB, OBE
Fraser, Sir Iain Michael Duncan, Bt. (1943)
Fraser, Sir James Murdo, KBE
Fraser, Sir William Kerr, GCB
Frayling, *Prof.* Sir Christopher John, Kt.
Frederick, Sir Christopher St John, Bt. (1723)
Freedman, *Rt. Hon. Prof.* Sir Lawrence David, KCMG, CBE
Freeland, Sir John Redvers, KCMG
Freeman, Sir James Robin, Bt. (1945)
Freer, *Air Chief Marshal* Sir Robert William George, GBE, KCB
French, *Air Marshal* Sir Joseph Charles, KCB, CBE
Frere, *Vice-Adm.* Sir Richard Tobias, KCB
Fretwell, Sir (Major) John (Emsley), GCMG
Friend *Prof.* Sir Richard Henry, Kt.
Froggatt, Sir Leslie Trevor, Kt.
Froggatt, Sir Peter, Kt.
Frossard, Sir Charles Keith, KBE
Frost, Sir David Paradine, Kt., OBE
Fry, Sir Graham Holbrook, KCMG
Fry, Sir Peter Derek, Kt.
Fry, *Lt.-Gen.* Sir Robert Allan, KCB, CBE
Fulford, *Hon.* Sir Adrian Bruce, Kt.
Fuller, Sir James Henry Fleetwood, Bt. (1910)
Fuller, *Hon.* Sir John Bryan Munro, Kt.
Fulton, *Lt.-Gen.* Sir Robert Henry Gervase, KBE
Furness, Sir Stephen Roberts, Bt. (1913)

Gage, *Rt. Hon.* Sir William Marcus, Kt., QC
Gains, Sir John Christopher, Kt.
Gainsford, Sir Ian Derek, Kt.
Galsworthy, Sir Anthony Charles, KCMG
Galway, Sir James, Kt., OBE
Gamble, Sir David Hugh Norman, Bt. (1897)
Gambon, Sir Michael John, Kt., CBE
Gammell, Sir William Benjamin Bowring, Kt.
Gardiner, Sir John Eliot, Kt., CBE
Gardner, *Prof.* Sir Richard Lavenham, Kt.
Gardner, Sir Roy Alan, Kt.
Garland, *Hon.* Sir Patrick Neville, Kt.
Garland, *Hon.* Sir Ransley Victor, KBE
Garland, *Dr* Sir Trevor, KBE
Garner, Sir Anthony Stuart, Kt.
Garnett, *Adm.* Sir Ian David Graham, KCB
Garnier, *Rear-Adm.* Sir John, KCVO, CBE
Garrard, Sir David Eardley, Kt.
Garrett, Sir Anthony Peter, Kt., CBE
Garrick, Sir Ronald, Kt., CBE, FRENG
Garthwaite, Sir (William) Mark (Charles), Bt. (1919)
Gaskell, Sir Richard Kennedy Harvey, Kt.
Geno, Sir Makena Viora, KBE
Gent, Sir Christopher Charles, Kt.
George, Sir Arthur Thomas, Kt.
George, *Prof.* Sir Charles Frederick, MD, FRCP
George, Sir Richard William, Kt., CVO
Gerken, *Vice-Adm.* Sir Robert William Frank, KCB, CBE
Gershon, Sir Peter Oliver, Kt., CBE
Gethin, Sir Richard Joseph St Lawrence, Bt. (I. 1665)
Gibb, Sir Francis Ross (Frank), Kt., CBE, FRENG
Gibbings, Sir Peter Walter, Kt.
Gibbons, Sir (John) David, KBE
Gibbons, Sir William Edward Doran, Bt. (1752)
Gibbs, *Hon.* Sir Richard John Hedley, Kt.
Gibbs, Sir Roger Geoffrey, Kt.
†Gibson, *Revd* Christopher Herbert, Bt. (1931)
Gibson, Sir Ian, Kt., CBE
Gibson, *Rt. Hon.* Sir Peter Leslie, Kt.
Gibson-Craig-Carmichael, Sir David Peter William, Bt. (S. 1702 and 1831)
Gieve, Sir Edward John Watson, KCB
Giffard, Sir (Charles) Sydney (Rycroft), KCMG
Gilbart-Denham, *Lt.-Col.* Sir Seymour Vivian, KCVO
Gilbert, *Air Chief Marshal* Sir Joseph Alfred, KCB, CBE
Gilbert, *Rt. Hon.* Sir Martin John, Kt., CBE
†Gilbey, Sir Walter Gavin, Bt. (1893)
Gill, Sir Anthony Keith, Kt.
Gill, Sir Arthur Benjamin Norman, Kt., CBE
Gill, Sir Robin Denys, KCVO
Gillam, Sir Patrick John, Kt.
Gillen, *Hon.* Sir John de Winter, Kt.
Gillett, Sir Nicholas Danvers Penrose, Bt. (1959)
Gillinson, Sir Clive Daniel, Kt., CBE
Gilmore, *Prof.* Sir Ian Thomas, Kt.
Gilmour, Sir John, Bt. (1897)
Gina, Sir Lloyd Maepeza, KBE
Giordano, Sir Richard Vincent, KBE
Girolami, Sir Paul, Kt.
Girvan, *Rt. Hon.* Sir (Frederick) Paul, Kt.
Gladstone, Sir (Erskine) William, Bt. (1846), KG
Glean, Sir Carlyle Arnold, GCMG
Glenn, Sir (Joseph Robert) Archibald, Kt., OBE
Glidewell, *Rt. Hon.* Sir Iain Derek Laing, Kt.
Glover, Sir Victor Joseph Patrick, Kt.
Glyn, Sir Richard Lindsay, Bt. (1759 and 1800)
Gobbo, Sir James Augustine, Kt., AC
Goldberg, *Prof.* Sir David Paul Brandes, Kt.
Goldring, *Rt. Hon.* Sir John Bernard, Kt.
Gomersall, Sir Stephen John, KCMG
Gonsalves-Sabola, *Hon.* Sir Joaquim Claudino, Kt
Gooch, Sir Miles Peter, Bt. (1866)
Gooch, Sir Arthur Brian Sherlock Heywood, Bt. (1746)
Good, Sir John James Griffen, Kt. CBE
Goodall, Sir (Arthur) David Saunders, GCMG
Goodall, *Air Marshal* Sir Roderick Harvey, KBE, CB, AFC
Goode, Prof. Sir Royston Miles, Kt., CBE, QC
Goodenough, Sir Anthony Michael, KCMG
Goodenough, Sir William McLernon, Bt. (1943)
Goodhart, Sir Philip Carter, Kt.
Goodhart, Sir Robert Anthony Gordon, Bt. (1911)
Goodison, Sir Nicholas Proctor, Kt.
Goodman, Sir Patrick Ledger, Kt., CBE
Goodson, Sir Mark Weston Lassam, Bt. (1922)
Goodwin, Sir Frederick, KBE
Goodwin, Sir Frederick Anderson, Kt.
Goodwin, Sir Matthew Dean, Kt., CBE
Goody, *Prof.* Sir John Rankine, Kt.
†Goold, Sir George William, Bt. (1801)
Gordon, Sir Donald, Kt.
Gordon, Sir Gerald Henry, Kt., CBE, QC
Gordon, Sir Robert James, Bt. (S. 1706)
Gordon-Cumming, Sir Alexander Penrose, Bt. (1804)
Gore, Sir Hugh Frederick Corbet, Bt. (I. 1622)
Gore-Booth, Sir Josslyn Henry Robert, Bt. (I. 1760)
Goring, Sir William Burton Nigel, Bt. (1627)
Gorman, Sir John Reginald, Kt., CVO, CBE, MC
Goschen, Sir (Edward) Alexander, Bt. (1916)
Gosling, Sir (Frederick) Donald, KCVO
Goswell, Sir Brian Lawrence, Kt.
Gough, Sir Charles Brandon, Kt.
Goulden, Sir (Peter) John, GCMG
Goulding, Sir (William) Lingard Walter, Bt. (1904)
Gourlay, *Gen.* Sir (Basil) Ian (Spencer), KCB, OBE, MC, RM
Gourlay, Sir Simon Alexander, Kt.
Gow, *Gen.* Sir (James) Michael, GCB
Gowans, Sir James Learmonth, Kt., CBE, FRCP, FRS
Gozney, Sir Richard Hugh Turton, KCMG
†Graaff, Sir David de Villiers, Bt. (1911)
Grabham, Sir Anthony Henry, Kt.
Graham, *Dr* Sir Albert Cecil, Kt.
Graham, Sir Alexander Michael, GBE
Graham, Sir James Bellingham, Bt. (1662)
Graham, Sir James Fergus Surtees, Bt. (1783)
Graham, Sir James Thompson, Kt., CMG
Graham, Sir John Alexander Noble, Bt. (1906), GCMG
Graham, Sir John Alistair, Kt.
Graham, Sir John Moodie, Bt. (1964)
Graham, Sir Norman William, Kt., CB
Graham, Sir Peter, KCB, QC
Graham, *Lt.-Gen.* Sir Peter Walter, KCB, CBE
†Graham, Sir Ralph Stuart, Bt. (1629)
Graham-Moon, Sir Peter Wilfred Giles, Bt. (1855)
Graham-Smith, *Prof.* Sir Francis, Kt.
Grant, Sir Archibald, Bt. (S. 1705)
Grant, Sir Clifford, Kt.
Grant, Sir Ian David, Kt., CBE
Grant, Sir (John) Anthony, Kt.
Grant, Sir John Douglas Kelso, KCMG
Grant, Sir Patrick Alexander Benedict, Bt. (S. 1688)
Grant, Sir Paul Joseph Patrick, Kt.
Grant, *Lt.-Gen.* Sir Scott Carnegie, KCB
Grant-Suttie, Sir James Edward, Bt. (S. 1702)
Granville-Chapman, *Lt.-Gen.* Sir Timothy John, GBE, KCB, ADC
Gratton-Bellew, Sir Henry Charles, Bt. (1838)
Gray, *Hon.* Sir Charles Anthony St John, Kt.

Gray, Sir Charles Ireland, Kt., CBE
Gray, *Prof.* Sir Denis John Pereira, Kt., OBE, FRCGP
Gray, Sir John Archibald Browne, Kt., SCD, FRS
Gray, *Dr.* Sir John Armstrong Muir, Kt., CBE
Gray, *Lt.-Gen.* Sir Michael Stuart, KCB, OBE
Gray, Sir Robert McDowall (Robin), Kt.
Gray, Sir William Hume, Bt. (1917)
Graydon, *Air Chief Marshal* Sir Michael James, GCB, CBE
Grayson, Sir Jeremy Brian Vincent Harrington, Bt. (1922)
Green, Sir Allan David, KCB, QC
Green, Sir Andrew Fleming, KCMG
Green, Sir Edward Patrick Lycett, Bt. (1886)
Green, Sir Gregory David, KCMG
Green, *Hon.* Sir Guy Stephen Montague, KBE
Green, Sir Kenneth, Kt.
Green, *Prof.* Sir Malcolm, Kt.
Green, Sir Owen Whitley, Kt.
Green, Sir Philip Green, Kt.
Green-Price, Sir Robert John, Bt. (1874)
Greenaway, Sir John Michael Burdick, Bt. (1933)
Greenbury, Sir Richard, Kt.
Greener, Sir Anthony Armitage, Kt.
Greengross, Sir Alan David, Kt.
Greenstock, Sir Jeremy Quentin, GCMG
Greenwell, Sir Edward Bernard, Bt. (1906)
Greenwood, *Prof.* Sir Christopher John, Kt., CMG
Gregson, Sir Peter Lewis, GCB
Greig, Sir (Henry Louis) Carron, KCVO, CBE
Grey, Sir Anthony Dysart, Bt. (1814)
†Grey-Egerton, Sir David Boswell, Bt. (1617), CB, OBE, MC
Grierson, Sir Ronald Hugh, Kt.
Griffiths, Sir Eldon Wylie, Kt.
Grigson, *Hon.* Sir Geoffrey Douglas, Kt.
Grimshaw, Sir Nicholas Thomas, Kt., CBE
Grimwade, Sir Andrew Sheppard, Kt., CBE
Grose, *Vice-Adm.* Sir Alan, KBE
Gross, *Hon.* Sir Peter Henry, Kt.
Grossart, Sir Angus McFarlane McLeod, Kt., CBE
Grotrian, Sir Philip Christian Brent, Bt. (1934)
Grove, Sir Charles Gerald, Bt. (1874)
Grundy, Sir Mark, Kt.
Guinness, Sir Howard Christian Sheldon, Kt., VRD
Guinness, Sir John Ralph Sidney, Kt., CB
Guinness, Sir Kenelm Ernest Lee, Bt. (1867)
†Guise, Sir Christopher James, Bt. (1783)
Gull, Sir Rupert William Cameron, Bt. (1872)
Gumbs, Sir Emile Rudolph, Kt.
Gunn, Sir Robert Norman, Kt.
†Gunning, Sir Charles Theodore, Bt. (1778)
Gunston, Sir John Wellesley, Bt. (1938)
Gurdon, *Prof.* Sir John Bertrand, Kt., DPHIL, FRS
Guthrie, Sir Malcolm Connop, Bt. (1936)
Gwynn-Jones, Sir Peter Llewellyn, KCVO

Haddacks, *Vice-Adm.* Sir Paul Kenneth, KCB
Hadfield, Sir Ronald, Kt., QPM
Hadlee, Sir Richard John, Kt., MBE
Hagart-Alexander, Sir Claud, Bt. (1886)
Hague, *Prof.* Sir Douglas Chalmers, Kt., CBE
Haines, *Prof.* Sir Andrew Paul, Kt.
Haji-Ioannou, Sir Stelios, Kt.
Halberg, Sir Murray Gordon, Kt., MBE
Hall, Sir Basil Brodribb, KCB, MC, TD
Hall, *Prof.* Sir David Michael Baldock, Kt.
Hall, Sir Ernest, Kt., OBE
Hall, Sir Graham Joseph, Kt.
Hall, Sir Iain Robert, Kt.
Hall, Sir (Frederick) John (Frank), Bt. (1923)
Hall, Sir John, Kt.
Hall, Sir John Bernard, Bt. (1919)
Hall, Sir John Douglas Hoste, Bt. (S. 1687)
Hall, HE *Prof.* Sir Kenneth Octavius, GCMG
Hall, Sir Peter Edward, KBE, CMG
Hall, *Prof.* Sir Peter Geoffrey, Kt., FBA
Hall, Sir Peter Reginald Frederick, Kt., CBE
Hall, Sir William Joseph, KCVO
Halpern, Sir Ralph Mark, Kt.
Halsey, *Revd* John Walter Brooke, Bt. (1920)
Halstead, Sir Ronald, Kt., CBE
Hamblen, *Hon.* Sir Nicholas Archibald, Kt.
†Hambling, Sir Herbert Peter Hugh, Bt. (1924)
Hamilton, Sir Andrew Caradoc, Bt. (S. 1646)
Hamilton, Sir James Arnot, KCB, MBE, FRENG
Hamilton, Sir Nigel, KCB
Hamilton-Dalrymple, *Maj.* Sir Hew Fleetwood, Bt. (S. 1697), GCVO
Hamilton-Spencer-Smith, Sir John, Bt. (1804)
Hammick, Sir Stephen George, Bt. (1834)
Hammond, Sir Anthony Hilgrove, KCB, QC
Hampel, Sir Ronald Claus, Kt.
Hampson, Sir Stuart, Kt.
Hampton, Sir (Leslie) Geoffrey, Kt.
Hampton, Sir Philip Roy, Kt.
Hanbury-Tenison, Sir Richard, KCVO
Hancock, Sir David John Stowell, KCB
†Hanham, Sir William John Edward, Bt. (1667)
Hankes-Drielsma, Sir Claude Dunbar, KCVO
Hanley, *Rt. Hon.* Sir Jeremy James, KCMG
Hanmer, Sir Wyndham Richard Guy, Bt. (1774)
Hannam, Sir John Gordon, Kt.
Hanson, Sir (Charles) Rupert (Patrick), Bt. (1918)
Hanson, Sir John Gilbert, KCMG, CBE
Harcourt-Smith, *Air Chief Marshal* Sir David, GBE, KCB, DFC
Hardie Boys, *Rt. Hon.* Sir Michael, GCMG
Harding, Sir George William, KCMG, CVO
Harding, *Marshal of the Royal Air Force* Sir Peter Robin, GCB
Harding, Sir Roy Pollard, Kt., CBE
Hardy, Sir David William, Kt.
Hardy, Sir James Gilbert, Kt., OBE
Hardy, Sir Richard Charles Chandos, Bt. (1876)
Hare, Sir David, Kt., FRSL
Hare, Sir Nicholas Patrick, Bt. (1818)
Haren, *Dr* Sir Patrick Hugh, Kt.
†Harford, Sir Mark John, Bt. (1934)
Harington, Sir Nicholas John, Bt. (1611)
Harkness, *Very Revd* James, KCVO, CB, OBE
Harland, *Air Marshal* Sir Reginald Edward Wynyard, KBE, CB
Harley, *Gen.* Sir Alexander George Hamilton, KBE, CB
Harman, *Hon.* Sir Jeremiah LeRoy, Kt.
Harman, Sir John Andrew, Kt.
Harmsworth, Sir Hildebrand Harold, Bt. (1922)
Harper, Sir Ewan William, Kt. CBE
Harper, *Prof.* Sir Peter Stanley, Kt., CBE
Harris, *Prof.* Sir Henry, Kt., FRCP, FRCPATH, FRS
Harris, Sir Jack Wolfred Ashford, Bt. (1932)
Harris, *Air Marshal* Sir John Hulme, KCB, CBE
Harris, *Prof.* Sir Martin Best, Kt., CBE
Harris, Sir Michael Frank, Kt.
Harris, Sir (Theodore) Wilson, Kt.
Harris, Sir Thomas George, KBE, CMG,
Harrison, *Prof.* Sir Brian Howard, Kt.
Harrison, Sir David, Kt., CBE, FRENG
Harrison, *Hon.* Sir Michael Guy Vicat, Kt.

Harrison, Sir Michael James Harwood, Bt. (1961)
Harrison, Sir (Robert) Colin, Bt. (1922)
Harrison, Sir Terence, Kt., FRENG
Harrop, Sir Peter John, KCB
Hart, *Hon.* Sir Anthony Ronald, Kt.
Hart, Sir David Michael, Kt., OBE
Hart, Sir Graham Allan, KCB
Hartwell, Sir (Francis) Anthony Charles Peter, Bt. (1805)
Harvey, Sir Charles Richard Musgrave, Bt. (1933)
Harvie, Sir John Smith, Kt., CBE
Harvie-Watt, Sir James, Bt. (1945)
Harwood, Sir Ronald, Kt., CBE
Haselhurst, *Rt. Hon.* Sir Alan Gordon Barraclough, Kt.
Haskard, Sir Cosmo Dugal Patrick Thomas, KCMG, MBE
Hastie, *Cdre* Sir Robert Cameron, KCVO, CBE, RD
Hastings, Sir Max Macdonald, Kt.
Hastings, *Dr* Sir William George, Kt., CBE
Hatter, Sir Maurice, Kt.
Havelock-Allan, Sir (Anthony) Mark David, Bt. (1858)
Hawkes, Sir John Garry, Kt., CBE
Hawkins, Sir Richard Caesar, Bt. (1778)
†Hawley, Sir Henry Nicholas, Bt. (1795)
Hawley, Sir James Appleton, KCVO, TD
Haworth, Sir Philip, Bt. (1911)
Hawthorne, *Prof.* Sir William Rede, Kt., CBE, SCD, FRS, FRENG
Hay, Sir David Russell, Kt., CBE, FRCP, MD
Hay, Sir John Erroll Audley, Bt. (S. 1663)
†Hay, Sir Ronald Frederick Hamilton, Bt. (S. 1703)
Hayes, Sir Brian, Kt., CBE, QPM
Hayes, Sir Brian David, GCB
Hayman-Joyce, *Lt.-Gen.* Sir Robert John, KCB, CBE
Hayter, Sir Paul David Grenville, KCB, LVO
Hayward, Sir Anthony William Byrd, Kt.
Hayward, Sir Jack Arnold, Kt., OBE
Head, Sir Richard Douglas Somerville, Bt. (1838)
Heap, Sir Peter William, KCMG
Heap, *Prof.* Sir Robert Brian, Kt., CBE, FRS
Hearne, Sir Graham James, Kt., CBE
Heathcote, *Brig.* Sir Gilbert Simon, Bt. (1733), CBE
†Heathcote, Sir Timothy Gilbert, Bt. (1733)
Heatley, Sir Peter, Kt., CBE
Hedley, *Hon.* Sir Mark, Kt.
Hegarty, Sir John Kevin, Kt.
Heiser, Sir Terence Michael, GCB
Henderson, Sir Denys Hartley, Kt.
Henderson, *Hon.* Sir Launcelot Dinadan James, Kt.
Henderson, *Maj.* Sir Richard Yates, KCVO
Hendry, *Prof.* Sir David Forbes, Kt.
Hennessy, Sir James Patrick Ivan, KBE, CMG
†Henniker, Sir Adrian Chandos, Bt. (1813)
Henniker-Heaton, Sir Yvo Robert, Bt. (1912)
Henriques, *Hon.* Sir Richard Henry Quixano, Kt.
Henry, *Hon.* Sir Geoffrey Arama, KBE
†Henry, Sir Patrick Denis, Bt. (1923)
Henshaw, Sir David George, Kt.
Hepple, *Prof.* Sir Bob Alexander, Kt.
Herbecq, Sir John Edward, KCB
Herbert, *Adm.* Sir Peter Geoffrey Marshall, KCB, OBE
Heron, Sir Conrad Frederick, KCB, OBE
Heron, Sir Michael Gilbert, Kt.
Heron-Maxwell, Sir Nigel Mellor, Bt. (S. 1683)
Hervey, Sir Roger Blaise Ramsay, KCVO, CMG
Hervey-Bathurst, Sir Frederick John Charles Gordon, Bt. (1818)
Heseltine, *Rt. Hon.* Sir William Frederick Payne, GCB, GCVO
Hewetson, Sir Christopher Raynor, Kt., TD
Hewett, Sir Richard Mark John, Bt. (1813)
Hewitt, Sir (Cyrus) Lenox (Simson), Kt., OBE
Hewitt, Sir Nicholas Charles Joseph, Bt. (1921)
Heygate, Sir Richard John Gage, Bt. (1831)
Heywood, Sir Peter, Bt. (1838)
Hickinbottom, *Hon.* Sir Gary Robert, Kt.
Hickman, Sir (Richard) Glenn, Bt. (1903)
Hicks, Sir Robert, Kt.
Hidden, *Hon.* Sir Anthony Brian, Kt.
Hielscher, Sir Leo Arthur, Kt.
Higgins, *Rt. Hon.* Sir Malachy Joseph, Kt.
Higginson, Sir Gordon Robert, Kt., PHD, FRENG
Hill, Sir Arthur Alfred, Kt., CBE
Hill, Sir Brian John, Kt.
Hill, Sir James Frederick, Bt. (1917)
Hill, Sir John Alfred Rowley, Bt. (I. 1779)
Hill, *Vice-Adm.* Sir Robert Charles Finch, KBE, FRENG
Hill-Norton, *Vice-Adm. Hon.* Sir Nicholas John, KCB
Hill-Wood, Sir Samuel Thomas, Bt. (1921)
Hillhouse, Sir (Robert) Russell, KCB
Hills, Sir Graham John, Kt.
Hine, *Air Chief Marshal* Sir Patrick Bardon, GCB, GBE
Hirsch, *Prof.* Sir Peter Bernhard, Kt., PHD., FRS
Hirst, *Rt. Hon.* Sir David Cozens-Hardy, Kt.
Hirst, Sir Michael William, Kt.
Hoare, *Prof.* Sir Charles Anthony Richard, Kt., FRS
Hoare, Sir David John, Bt. (1786)
Hoare, Sir Charles James, Bt. (I. 1784)
Hobart, Sir John Vere, Bt. (1914)
Hobbs, *Maj.-Gen.* Sir Michael Frederick, KCVO, CBE
Hobday, Sir Gordon Ivan, Kt.
Hobhouse, Sir Charles John Spinney, Bt. (1812)
Hobson, Sir Ronald, KCVO
†Hodge, Sir Andrew Rowland, Bt. (1921)
Hodge, Sir James William, KCVO, CMG
Hodgkin, Sir (Gordon) Howard (Eliot), Kt., CH, CBE
Hodgkinson, Sir Michael Stewart, Kt.
Hodgson, Sir Maurice Arthur Eric, Kt., FRENG
Hodson, Sir Michael Robin Adderley, Bt. (I. 1789)
Hogg, Sir Christopher Anthony, Kt.
†Hogg, Sir Piers Michael James, Bt. (1846)
Holcroft, Sir Peter George Culcheth, Bt. (1921)
Holderness, Sir Martin William, Bt. (1920)
Holden, Sir Paul, Bt. (1893)
Holden, Sir John David, Bt. (1919)
Holden-Brown, Sir Derrick, Kt.
Holder, Sir John Henry, Bt. (1898)
Holdgate, Sir Martin Wyatt, Kt., CB, PHD
Holdsworth, Sir (George) Trevor, Kt., CVO
Holland, *Hon.* Sir Alan Douglas, Kt.
Holland, *Hon.* Sir Christopher John, Kt.
Holland, Sir Clifton Vaughan, Kt.
Holland, Sir Geoffrey, KCB
Holland, Sir John Anthony, Kt.
Holland, Sir Philip Welsby, Kt.
Holliday, *Prof.* Sir Frederick George Thomas, Kt., CBE, FRSE
Hollom, Sir Jasper Quintus, KBE
Holloway, *Hon.* Sir Barry Blyth, KBE
Holm, Sir Ian (Holm Cuthbert), Kt., CBE
Holman, *Hon.* Sir (Edward) James, Kt.
Holman, *Prof.* Sir John Stranger, Kt.
Holmes, *Prof.* Sir Frank Wakefield, Kt.
Holmes, Sir John Eaton, GCVO, KBE, CMG
Holmes-Sellors, Sir Patrick John, KCVO
Holroyd, *Air Marshal* Sir Frank Martyn, KBE, CB
Holroyd, Sir Michael De Courcy Fraser, Kt., CBE
Holroyde, *Hon.* Sir Timothy Victor, Kt.
Holt, *Prof.* Sir James Clarke, Kt.
Holt, Sir Michael, Kt., CBE
Home, Sir William Dundas, Bt. (S. 1671)
Honywood, Sir Filmer Courtenay William, Bt. (1660)

†Hood, Sir John Joseph Harold, Bt. (1922)
Hookway, Sir Harry Thurston, Kt.
Hooper, *Rt. Hon.* Sir Anthony, Kt.
Hope, Sir Colin Frederick Newton, Kt.
Hope, Sir Alexander Archibald Douglas, Bt. (S. 1628)
Hope-Dunbar, Sir David, Bt. (S. 1664)
Hopkin, *Prof.* Sir Deian Rhys, Kt.
Hopkin, Sir Royston Oliver, KCMG
Hopkins, Sir Anthony Philip, Kt., CBE
Hopkins, Sir Michael John, Kt., CBE, RA, RIBA
Hopwood, *Prof.* Sir David Alan, Kt., FRS
Hordern, *Rt. Hon.* Sir Peter Maudslay, Kt.
Horlick, *Vice-Adm.* Sir Edwin John, KBE, FRENG
Horlick, Sir James Cunliffe William, Bt. (1914)
Horlock, *Prof.* Sir John Harold, Kt., FRS, FRENG
Horn, *Prof.* Sir Gabriel, Kt., FRS
Horn-Smith, Sir Julian Michael, Kt.
Hornby, Sir Derek Peter, Kt.
Horne, Sir Alan Gray Antony, Bt. (1929)
Horne, *Dr* Sir Alistair Allan, Kt. CBE
Horsbrugh-Porter, Sir John Simon, Bt. (1902)
Horsfall, Sir Edward John Wright, Bt. (1909)
Hort, Sir Andrew Edwin Fenton, Bt. (1767)
Horton, Sir Robert Baynes, Kt.
Hosker, Sir Gerald Albery, KCB, QC
Hoskins, *Prof.* Sir Brian John, Kt. CBE, FRS
†Hoskyns, Sir Edwyn Wren, Bt. (1676)
Hoskyns, Sir John Austin Hungerford Leigh, Kt.
Hotung, Sir Joseph Edward, Kt.
Houghton, *Lt.-Gen.* Sir John Nicholas Reynolds, KCB, CBE
Houghton, Sir John Theodore, Kt., CBE, FRS
Houldsworth, Sir Richard Thomas Reginald, Bt. (1887)
Hourston, Sir Gordon Minto, Kt.
Housden, Sir Peter James, KCB
House, *Lt.-Gen.* Sir David George, GCB, KCVO, CBE, MC
Houssemayne du Boulay, Sir Roger William, KCVO, CMG
Houstoun-Boswall, Sir (Thomas) Alford, Bt. (1836)
Howard, Sir David Howarth Seymour, Bt. (1955)
Howard, *Prof.* Sir Michael Eliot, Kt., OM, CH, CBE, MC
Howard-Lawson, Sir John Philip, Bt. (1841)
Howells, Sir Eric Waldo Benjamin, Kt., CBE
Howes, Sir Christopher Kingston, KCVO, CB
Howlett, *Gen.* Sir Geoffrey Hugh Whitby, KBE, MC
Hoy, Sir Christopher Andrew, Kt., MBE
Hugh-Jones, Sir Wynn Normington, Kt., LVO
Hugh-Smith, Sir Andrew Colin, Kt.
Hughes, *Rt. Hon.* Sir Anthony Philip Gilson, Kt.
Hughes, Sir Thomas Collingwood, Bt. (1773)
Hughes, Sir Trevor Poulton, KCB
†Hughes-Morgan, Sir (Ian) Parry David, Bt. (1925)
Hull, *Prof.* Sir David, Kt.
Hulse, Sir Edward Jeremy Westrow, Bt. (1739)
Hum, Sir Christopher Owen, KCMG
Humphreys, *Prof.* Sir Colin John, Kt., CBE
Hunt, Sir John Leonard, Kt.
Hunt, *Adm.* Sir Nicholas John Streynsham, GCB, LVO
Hunt, Sir Rex Masterman, Kt., CMG
Hunt, *Dr* Sir Richard Timothy, Kt.
Hunt-Davis, *Brig.* Sir Miles Garth, KCVO, CBE
Hunter, Sir Alistair John, KCMG
Hunter, *Prof.* Sir Laurence Colvin, Kt., CBE, FRSE
Hunter, *Dr* Sir Philip John, Kt., CBE
Hunter, Sir Thomas Blane, Kt.
Huntington-Whiteley, Sir Hugo Baldwin, Bt. (1918)
Hurn, Sir (Francis) Roger, Kt.
Hurst, Sir Geoffrey Charles, Kt., MBE
Husbands, Sir Clifford Straugh, GCMG
Hutchison, Sir James Colville, Bt. (1956)
Hutchison, *Rt. Hon.* Sir Michael, Kt.
Hutchison, Sir Robert, Bt. (1939)
Hutt, Sir Dexter Walter, Kt.
Huxley, *Prof.* Sir Andrew Fielding, Kt., OM, FRS
Huxtable, *Gen.* Sir Charles Richard, KCB, CBE
Hytner, Sir Nicholas, Kt.

Ibbs, Sir (John) Robin, KBE
Imbert-Terry, Sir Michael Edward Stanley, Bt. (1917)
Imray, Sir Colin Henry, KBE, CMG
Ingham, Sir Bernard, Kt.
Ingilby, Sir Thomas Colvin William, Bt. (1866)
Inglis, Sir Brian Scott, Kt.
Inglis of Glencorse, Sir Roderick John, Bt. (S. 1703)
Ingram, Sir James Herbert Charles, Bt. (1893)
Ingram, Sir John Henderson, Kt., CBE
Inkin, Sir Geoffrey David, Kt., OBE
†Innes, Sir Alastair Charles Deverell, Bt. (NS 1686)
Innes of Edingight, Sir Malcolm Rognvald, KCVO
Innes, Sir Peter Alexander Berowald, Bt. (S. 1628)
Insall, Sir Donald William, Kt., CBE
Irvine, Sir Donald Hamilton, Kt., CBE, MD, FRCGP
Irving, *Prof.* Sir Miles Horsfall, Kt., MD, FRCS, FRCSE
Irwin, *Lt.-Gen.* Sir Alistair Stuart Hastings, KCB, CBE
Irwin, *Hon.* Sir Stephen John, Kt.
Isaacs, Sir Jeremy Israel, Kt.
†Isham, Sir Norman Murray Crawford, Bt., OBE (1627)
Ivory, Sir Brian Gammell, Kt., CBE

Jack, *Hon.* Sir Alieu Sulayman, Kt.
Jack, Sir David, Kt., CBE, FRS, FRSE
Jack, *Hon.* Sir Raymond Evan, Kt.
Jackling, Sir Roger Tustin, KCB, CBE
Jackson, Sir Barry Trevor, Kt.
Jackson, Sir Kenneth Joseph, Kt.
Jackson, *Gen.* Sir Michael David, GCB, CBE
Jackson, Sir Michael Roland, Bt. (1902)
Jackson, Sir Nicholas Fane St George, Bt. (1913)
Jackson, Sir Keith Arnold, Bt. (1815)
Jackson, *Rt. Hon.* Sir Rupert Matthew, Kt.
Jackson, Sir (William) Roland Cedric, Bt. (1869)
Jacob, *Rt. Hon.* Sir Robert Raphael Hayim (Robin), Kt.
Jacobi, Sir Derek George, Kt., CBE
Jacobi, *Dr* Sir James Edward, Kt., OBE
Jacobs, Sir Cecil Albert, Kt., CBE
Jacobs, *Rt. Hon.* Sir Francis Geoffrey, KCMG, QC
Jacobs, *Hon.* Sir Kenneth Sydney, KBE
Jacomb, Sir Martin Wakefield, Kt.
Jaffray, Sir William Otho, Bt. (1892)
Jagger, Sir Michael Philip, Kt.
James, Sir Cynlais Morgan, KCMG
James, Sir Jeffrey Russell, KBE
James, Sir John Nigel Courtenay, KCVO, CBE
James, Sir Stanislaus Anthony, GCMG, OBE
Jamieson, *Air Marshal* Sir David Ewan, KBE, CB
Jansen, Sir Ross Malcolm, KBE
Jardine of Applegirth, Sir William Murray, Bt. (S. 1672)
Jardine, Sir Andrew Colin Douglas, Bt. (1916)
Jarman, *Prof.* Sir Brian, Kt., OBE
Jarratt, Sir Alexander Anthony, Kt., CB
Jarvis, Sir Gordon Ronald, Kt.
Jawara, *Hon.* Sir Dawda Kairaba, Kt.
Jay, Sir Antony Rupert, Kt., CVO
Jeewoolall, Sir Ramesh, Kt.
Jefferson, Sir George Rowland, Kt., CBE, FRENG
Jeffrey, Sir William Alexander, KCB
Jeffreys, *Prof.* Sir Alec John, Kt., FRS
Jeffries, *Hon.* Sir John Francis, Kt.
Jehangir, Sir Cowasji, Bt. (1908)
†Jejeebhoy, Sir Jehangir, Bt. (1857)

Jenkins, Sir Brian Garton, GBE
Jenkins, Sir Elgar Spencer, Kt., OBE
Jenkins, Sir James Christopher, KCB, QC
Jenkins, Sir Michael Nicholas Howard, Kt., OBE
Jenkins, Sir Michael Romilly Heald, KCMG
Jenkins, Sir Simon, Kt.
Jenkinson, Sir John Banks, Bt. (1661)
Jenks, Sir (Richard) Peter, Bt. (1932)
Jenner, *Air Marshal* Sir Timothy Ivo, KCB
Jennings, Sir John Southwood, Kt., CBE, FRSE
Jennings, Sir Peter Neville Wake, Kt., CVO
Jephcott, Sir Neil Welbourn, Bt. (1962)
Jessel, Sir Charles John, Bt. (1883)
Jewkes, Sir Gordon Wesley, KCMG
Job, Sir Peter James Denton, Kt.
John, Sir David Glyndwr, KCMG
John, Sir Elton Hercules (Reginald Kenneth Dwight), Kt., CBE
Johns, *Vice-Adm.* Sir Adrian James, KCB, CBE, ADC
Johns, *Air Chief Marshal* Sir Richard Edward, GCB, KCVO, CBE
Johnson, Sir Colpoys Guy, Bt. (1755)
Johnson, *Gen.* Sir Garry Dene, KCB, OBE, MC
Johnson, Sir John Rodney, KCMG
†Johnson, Sir Patrick Eliot, Bt. (1818)
Johnson, *Hon.* Sir Robert Lionel, Kt.
Johnson-Ferguson, Sir Ian Edward, Bt. (1906)
Johnston, *Lt.-Gen.* Sir Maurice Robert, KCB, CVO, OBE
Johnston, Sir Thomas Alexander, Bt. (S. 1626)
Johnston, Sir William Ian Ridley, Kt., CBE, QPM
Johnstone, Sir Geoffrey Adams Dinwiddie, KCMG
Johnstone, Sir (George) Richard Douglas, Bt. (S. 1700)
Johnstone, Sir (John) Raymond, Kt., CBE
Jolliffe, Sir Anthony Stuart, GBE
Jolly, Sir Arthur Richard, KCMG
Jonas, Sir John Peter, Kt., CBE
Jones, Sir Alan Jeffrey, Kt.
Jones, Sir David Charles, Kt., CBE
Jones, Sir Harry George, Kt., CBE
Jones, Sir John Francis, Kt.
Jones, Sir Keith Stephen, Kt.
Jones, Sir Kenneth Lloyd, Kt., QPM
Jones, Sir Lyndon, Kt.
Jones, Sir Mark Ellis Powell, Kt.
Jones, Sir (Owen) Trevor, Kt.
Jones, Sir Richard Anthony Lloyd, KCB
Jones, Sir Robert Edward, Kt.
Jones, Sir Roger Spencer, Kt., OBE
Jones, Sir Simon Warley Frederick Benton, Bt. (1919)
†Joseph, *Hon.* Sir James Samuel, Bt. (1943)
Jowell, *Prof.* Sir Roger Mark, Kt. CBE
Jowitt, *Hon.* Sir Edwin Frank, Kt.
Judge, Sir Paul Rupert, Kt.
Jugnauth, *Rt. Hon.* Sir Anerood, KCMG
Jungius, *Vice-Adm.* Sir James George, KBE

Kaberry, *Hon.* Sir Christopher Donald, Bt. (1960)
Kabui, Sir Frank Utu Ofagioro, GCMG, OBE
Kadoorie, *Hon.* Sir Michael David, Kt.
Kakaraya, Sir Pato, KBE
Kamit, Sir Leonard Wilson, Kt., CBE
Kan Yuet-Keung, Sir, GBE
Kao, *Prof.* Sir Charles Kuen, KBE
Kaputin, Sir John Rumet, KBE, CMG
Kaufman, *Rt. Hon.* Sir Gerald Bernard, Kt.
Kavali, Sir Thomas, Kt., OBE
Kay, *Prof.* Sir Andrew Watt, Kt.
Kay, *Rt. Hon.* Sir Maurice Ralph, Kt.
Kaye, Sir Paul Henry Gordon, Bt. (1923)
Keane, Sir Richard Michael, Bt. (1801)
Kearney, *Hon.* Sir William John Francis, Kt., CBE
Keegan, Sir John Desmond Patrick, Kt., OBE
Keene, *Rt. Hon.* Sir David Wolfe, Kt.
Keith, *Hon.* Sir Brian Richard, Kt.
Keith, *Prof.* Sir James, KBE
†Kellett, Sir Stanley Charles, Bt. (1801)
Kelly, Sir Christopher William, KCB
Kelly, Sir David Robert Corbett, Kt., CBE
Kemakeza, Sir Allan, Kt.
Kemball, *Air Marshal* Sir (Richard) John, KCB, CBE
Kemp-Welch, Sir John, Kt.
Kenilorea, *Rt. Hon.* Sir Peter, KBE
Kennaway, Sir John Lawrence, Bt. (1791)
Kennedy, Sir Francis, KCMG, CBE
Kennedy, *Hon.* Sir Ian Alexander, Kt.
Kennedy, *Prof.* Sir Ian McColl, Kt.
†Kennedy, Sir Michael Edward, Bt. (1836)
Kennedy, *Rt. Hon.* Sir Paul Joseph Morrow, Kt.
Kennedy, *Air Chief Marshal* Sir Thomas Lawrie, GCB, AFC
Kenny, Sir Anthony John Patrick, Kt., DPHIL, DLITT, FBA
Kenny, *Gen.* Sir Brian Leslie Graham, GCB, CBE
Kentridge, Sir Sydney Woolf, KCMG, QC
Kenyon, Sir Nicholas Roger, Kt., CBE
Keogh, *Prof.* Sir Bruce Edward, KBE
Kerr, *Adm.* Sir John Beverley, GCB
Kerry, Sir Michael James, KCB, QC
Kershaw, *Prof.* Sir Ian, Kt.
Kerslake, Sir Robert Walker, Kt.
Keswick, Sir Henry Neville Lindley, Kt.
Keswick, Sir John Chippendale Lindley, Kt.
Kevau, *Prof.* Sir Isi Henao, Kt., CBE
Kikau, *Ratu* Sir Jone Latianara, KBE
Kimber, Sir Timothy Roy Henry, Bt. (1904)
King, *Prof.* Sir David Anthony, Kt., FRS
King, Sir John Christopher, Bt. (1888)
King, *Vice-Adm.* Sir Norman Ross Dutton, KBE
King, *Hon.* Sir Timothy Roger Alan, Kt.
King, Sir Wayne Alexander, Bt. (1815)
Kingman, *Prof.* Sir John Frank Charles, Kt., FRS
Kingsland, Sir Richard, Kt., CBE, DFC
Kingsley, Sir Ben, Kt.
Kinloch, Sir David, Bt. (S. 1686)
Kinloch, Sir David Oliphant, Bt. (1873)
Kipalan, Sir Albert, Kt.
Kirkpatrick, Sir Ivone Elliott, Bt. (S. 1685)
Kirkwood, *Hon.* Sir Andrew Tristram Hammett, Kt.
Kiszely, *Lt.-Gen.* Sir John Panton, KCB, MC
Kitchin, *Hon.* Sir David James Tyson, Kt.
Kitson, *Gen.* Sir Frank Edward, GBE, KCB, MC
Kitson, Sir Timothy Peter Geoffrey, Kt.
Kleinwort, Sir Richard Drake, Bt. (1909)
Klug, Sir Aaron, Kt., OM
Knight, Sir Harold Murray, KBE, DSC
Knight, Sir Kenneth John, Kt., CBE, QFSM
Knight, *Air Chief Marshal* Sir Michael William Patrick, KCB, AFC
Knight, *Prof.* Sir Peter, Kt.
Knill, Sir Thomas John Pugin Bartholomew, Bt. (1893)
Knowles, Sir Charles Francis, Bt. (1765)
Knowles, Sir Durward Randolph, Kt., OBE
Knowles, Sir Nigel Graham, Kt.
Knox, Sir David Laidlaw, Kt.
Knox, *Hon.* Sir John Leonard, Kt.
Knox-Johnston, Sir William Robert Patrick (Sir Robin), Kt., CBE, RD
Kohn, *Dr* Sir Ralph, Kt., FRS
Koraea, Sir Thomas, Kt.
Kornberg, *Prof.* Sir Hans Leo, Kt., DSC, SCD, PHD, FRS
Korowi, Sir Wiwa, GCMG
Kroto, *Prof.* Sir Harold Walter, Kt., FRS
Kulukundis, Sir Elias George (Eddie), Kt., OBE
Kurongku, *Most Revd* Peter, KBE
Kwok-Po Li, *Dr* Sir David, Kt., OBE

Lachmann, *Prof.* Sir Peter Julius, Kt.
Lacon, Sir Edmund Vere, Bt. (1818)
Lacy, Sir Patrick Brian Finucane, Bt. (1921)
Laidlaw, Sir Christopher Charles Fraser, Kt.
Laing, Sir (John) Martin (Kirby), Kt., CBE
Laird, Sir Gavin Harry, Kt., CBE
Lake, Sir (Atwell) Graham, Bt. (1711)
Lakin, Sir Michael, Bt. (1909)
Lamb, Sir Albert Thomas, KBE, CMG, DFC
Lamb, *Lt.-Gen.* Sir Graeme Cameron Maxwell, KBE, CMG, DSO
Lambert, Sir John Henry, KCVO, CMG
†Lambert, Sir Peter John Biddulph, Bt. (1711)
Lampl, Sir Frank William, Kt.
Lampl, Sir Peter, Kt., OBE
Lamport, Sir Stephen Mark Jeffrey, KCVO
Landale, Sir David William Neil, KCVO
Landau, Sir Dennis Marcus, Kt.
Lander, Sir Stephen James, KCB
Lane, Prof. Sir David Philip, Kt.
Langham, Sir John Stephen, Bt. (1660)
Langlands, Sir Robert Alan, Kt.
Langley, *Hon.* Sir Gordon Julian Hugh, Kt.
Langrishe, Sir James Hercules, Bt. (I. 1777)
Langstaff, *Hon.* Sir Brian Frederick James, Kt.
Lankester, Sir Timothy Patrick, KCB
Lapli, Sir John Ini, GCMG
Lapthorne, Sir Richard Douglas, Kt., CBE
Large, Sir Andrew McLeod Brooks, Kt.
Latasi, *Rt. Hon.* Sir Kamuta, KCMG, OBE
Latham, *Rt. Hon.* Sir David Nicholas Ramsey, Kt.
Latham, Sir Michael Anthony, Kt.
Latham, Sir Richard Thomas Paul, Bt. (1919)
Latimer, Sir (Courtenay) Robert, Kt., CBE
Latimer, Sir Graham Stanley, KBE
Latour-Adrien, *Hon.* Sir Maurice, Kt.
Laughton, Sir Anthony Seymour, Kt.
Laurie, Sir Robert Bayley Emilius, Bt. (1834)
Lauterpacht, Sir Elihu, Kt., CBE, QC
Lauti, *Rt. Hon.* Sir Toaripi, GCMG
Lawes, Sir (John) Michael Bennet, Bt. (1882)
Lawler, Sir Peter James, Kt., OBE
Lawrence, Sir Clive Wyndham, Bt. (1906)
Lawrence, Sir Edmund Wickham, KCMG, OBE
Lawrence, Sir Henry Peter, Bt. (1858)
Lawrence, Sir Ivan John, Kt., QC
Lawrence, Sir John Patrick Grosvenor, Kt., CBE
Lawrence, Sir William Fettiplace, Bt. (1867)
Lawrence-Jones, Sir Christopher, Bt. (1831)
Laws, *Rt. Hon.* Sir John Grant McKenzie, Kt.
Lawson, Sir Charles John Patrick, Bt. (1900)
Lawson, *Gen.* Sir Richard George, KCB, DSO, OBE
†Lawson-Tancred, Sir Andrew Peter, Bt. (1662)
Lawton, *Prof.* Sir John Hartley, Kt., CBE, FRS
Layard, *Adm.* Sir Michael Henry Gordon, KCB, CBE
Lea, *Vice-Adm.* Sir John Stuart Crosbie, KBE
Lea, Sir Thomas William, Bt. (1892)
Leach, *Admiral of the Fleet* Sir Henry Conyers, GCB
Leahy, Sir Daniel Joseph, Kt.
Leahy, Sir John Henry Gladstone, KCMG
Leahy, Sir Terence Patrick, Kt.
Learmont, *Gen.* Sir John Hartley, KCB, CBE
Leaver, Sir Christopher, GBE
Le Bailly, *Vice-Adm.* Sir Louis Edward Stewart Holland, KBE, CB
Le Cheminant, *Air Chief Marshal* Sir Peter de Lacey, GBE, KCB, DFC
†Lechmere, Sir Nicholas Anthony Hungerford, Bt. (1818)
Ledger, Sir Philip Stevens, Kt., CBE, FRSE
Lee, Sir Christopher Frank Carandini, Kt., CBE
Lee, Sir Quo-wei, Kt., CBE
Leeds, Sir Christopher Anthony, Bt. (1812)
Lees, Sir David Bryan, Kt.
Lees, Sir Thomas Edward, Bt. (1897)
Lees, Sir Thomas Harcourt Ivor, Bt. (1804)
Lees, Sir (William) Antony Clare, Bt. (1937)
Leese, Sir Richard Charles, Kt., CBE
le Fleming, Sir David Kelland, Bt. (1705)
Legard, Sir Charles Thomas, Bt. (1660)
Legg, Sir Thomas Stuart, KCB, QC
Leggatt, *Rt. Hon.* Sir Andrew Peter, Kt.
Leggatt, Sir Hugh Frank John, Kt.
Leggett, *Prof.* Sir Anthony James, KBE
Leigh, Sir Geoffrey Norman, Kt.
Leigh, Sir Richard Henry, Bt. (1918)
Leighton, Sir Michael John Bryan, Bt. (1693)
Leith-Buchanan, Sir Gordon Kelly McNicol, Bt. (1775)
Le Marchant, Sir Francis Arthur, Bt. (1841)
Lennox-Boyd, The Hon. Sir Mark Alexander, Kt.
Leon, Sir John Ronald, Bt. (1911)
Lepping, Sir George Geria Dennis, GCMG, MBE
Le Quesne, Sir (John) Godfray, Kt., QC
Lee-Steere, Sir Ernest Henry, KBE
Leslie, Sir John Norman Ide, Bt. (1876)
Lester, Sir James Theodore, Kt.
Lethbridge, Sir Thomas Periam Hector Noel, Bt. (1804)
Lever, Sir Jeremy Frederick, KCMG, QC
Lever, Sir Paul, KCMG
Lever, Sir (Tresham) Christopher Arthur Lindsay, Bt. (1911)
Leveson, *Rt. Hon.* Sir Brian Henry, Kt.
Levine, Sir Montague Bernard, Kt.
Levinge, Sir Richard George Robin, Bt. (I. 1704)
Lewinton, Sir Christopher, Kt.
Lewis, Sir David Thomas Rowell, Kt.
Lewis, Sir John Anthony, Kt., OBE
Lewis, Sir Lawrence Vernon Harcourt, KCMG, GCM
Lewis, Sir Leigh Warren, KCB
Lewis, Sir Terence Murray, Kt., OBE, GM, QPM
Lewison, *Hon.* Sir Kim Martin Jordan, Kt.
Ley, Sir Ian Francis, Bt. (1905)
Li, Sir Ka-Shing, KBE
Lickiss, Sir Michael Gillam, Kt.
Liddington, Sir Bruce, Kt.
Liggins, *Prof.* Sir Graham Collingwood, Kt., CBE, FRS
Lightman, *Hon.* Sir Gavin Anthony, Kt.
Lighton, Sir Thomas Hamilton, Bt. (I. 1791)
Likierman, *Prof.* Sir John Andrew, Kt.
Lilleyman, *Prof.* Sir John Stuart, Kt.
Limon, Sir Donald William, KCB
Linacre, Sir (John) Gordon (Seymour), Kt., CBE, AFC, DFM
Lindop, Sir Norman, Kt.
Lindsay, *Hon.* Sir John Edmund Frederic, Kt.
†Lindsay, Sir James Martin Evelyn, Bt. (1962)
†Lindsay-Hogg, Sir Michael Edward, Bt. (1905)
Lipton, Sir Stuart Anthony, Kt.
Lipworth, Sir (Maurice) Sydney, Kt.
Lister-Kaye, Sir John Phillip Lister, Bt. (1812)
Lithgow, Sir William James, Bt. (1925)
Little, *Most Revd* Thomas Francis, KBE
Llewellyn, Sir Roderic Victor, Bt. (1922)
Llewellyn-Smith, *Prof.* Sir Christopher Hubert, Kt.
Lloyd, *Prof.* Sir Geoffrey Ernest Richard, Kt., FBA
Lloyd, Sir Nicholas Markley, Kt.
Lloyd, *Rt. Hon.* Sir Peter Robert Cable, Kt.
Lloyd, Sir Richard Ernest Butler, Bt. (1960)

Lloyd, *Hon.* Sir Timothy Andrew Wigram, Kt.
Lloyd-Edwards, *Capt.* Sir Norman, KCVO, RD
Lloyd Jones, Sir David, Kt.
Loader, Air Marshal Sir Clive Robert, KCB, OBE
Lobo, Sir Rogerio Hyndman, Kt., CBE
Lockhead, Sir Moir, Kt., OBE
†Loder, Sir Edmund Jeune, Bt. (1887)
Logan, Sir David Brian Carleton, KCMG
Lokoloko, Sir Tore, GCMG, GCVO, OBE
Longmore, *Rt. Hon.* Sir Andrew Centlivres, Kt.
Loram, *Vice-Adm.* Sir David Anning, KCB, CVO
Lord, Sir Michael Nicholson, Kt.
Lorimer, Sir (Thomas) Desmond, Kt.
Los, *Hon.* Sir Kubulan, Kt., CBE
Loughran, Sir Gerald Finbar, KCB
Louisy, *Rt. Hon.* Sir Allan Fitzgerald Laurent, KCMG
Lovell, Sir (Alfred Charles) Bernard, Kt., OBE, FRS
Lovelock, Sir Douglas Arthur, KCB
Lovill, Sir John Roger, Kt., CBE
Lowa, *Rt. Revd* Sir Samson, KBE
Lowe, *Air Chief Marshal* Sir Douglas Charles, GCB, DFC, AFC
Lowe, Sir Frank Budge, Kt.
Lowe, Sir Thomas William Gordon, Bt. (1918)
Lowson, Sir Ian Patrick, Bt. (1951)
Lowther, *Col.* Sir Charles Douglas, Bt. (1824)
Lowther, Sir John Luke, KCVO, CBE
Loyd, Sir Julian St John, KCVO
Lu, Sir Tseng Chi, Kt.
Lucas, *Prof.* Sir Colin Renshaw, Kt.
Lucas, Sir Thomas Edward, Bt. (1887)
Lucas-Tooth, Sir (Hugh) John, Bt. (1920)
Lumsden, Sir David James, Kt.
Lushington, Sir John Richard Castleman, Bt. (1791)
Lyall Grant, Sir Mark Justin, KCMG
Lygo, *Adm.* Sir Raymond Derek, KCB
Lyle, Sir Gavin Archibald, Bt. (1929)
Lynch-Blosse, *Capt.* Sir Richard Hely, Bt. (1622)
Lynch-Robinson, Sir Dominick Christopher, Bt. (1920)
Lyne, *Rt. Hon.* Sir Roderic Michael John, KBE, CMG
Lyons, Sir John, Kt.
Lyons, Sir Michael Thomas, Kt.

McAllister, Sir Ian Gerald, Kt., CBE
McAlpine, Sir William Hepburn, Bt. (1918)
Macara, Sir Alexander Wiseman, Kt., FRCP, FRCGP
McCaffrey, Sir Thomas Daniel, Kt.
McCallum, Sir Donald Murdo, Kt., CBE, FRENG
McCamley, Sir Graham Edward, KBE
McCarthy, Sir Callum, Kt.
McCartney, *Rt. Hon.* Sir Ian, Kt.
McCartney, Sir (James) Paul, Kt., MBE
Macartney, Sir John Ralph, Bt. (I. 1799)
McClement, *Vice-Admiral* Sir Timothy Pentreath, KCB, OBE
McClintock, Sir Eric Paul, Kt.
McCloskey, *Hon.* Sir John Bernard, Kt.
McColl, Sir Colin Hugh Verel, KCMG
McColl, *Gen.* Sir John Chalmers, KCB, CBE, DSO
McCollum, *Rt. Hon.* Sir William, Kt.
McCombe, *Hon.* Sir Richard George Bramwell, Kt.
McConnell, Sir Robert Shean, Bt. (1900)
MacCormac, Sir Richard Cornelius, Kt., CBE
†McCowan, Sir David William, Bt. (1934)
McCullough, *Hon.* Sir (Iain) Charles (Robert), Kt.
MacDermott, *Rt. Hon.* Sir John Clarke, Kt.
Macdonald, Sir Alasdair Uist, Kt., CBE
Macdonald, Sir Kenneth Carmichael, KCB
McDonald, Sir Trevor, Kt., OBE
Macdonald of Sleat, Sir Ian Godfrey Bosville, Bt. (S. 1625)
McDowell, Sir Eric Wallace, Kt., CBE
MacDuff, *Hon.* Sir Alistair Geoffrey, Kt.
Mace, *Lt.-Gen.* Sir John Airth, KBE, CB
McEwen, Sir John Roderick Hugh, Bt. (1953)
McFarland, Sir John Talbot, Bt. (1914)
MacFarlane, *Prof.* Sir Alistair George James, Kt., CBE, FRS
McFarlane, Sir Andrew Ewart, Kt.
Macfarlane, Sir (David) Neil, Kt.
McGeechan, Sir Ian Robert, Kt., OBE
McGrath, Sir Brian Henry, GCVO
Macgregor, Sir Ian Grant, Bt. (1828)
McGregor, Sir James David, Kt., OBE
MacGregor of MacGregor, Sir Malcolm Gregor Charles, Bt. (1795)
McGrigor, Sir James Angus Rhoderick Neil, Bt. (1831)
McIntosh, Sir Neil William David, Kt., CBE
McIntosh, Sir Ronald Robert Duncan, KCB
McIntyre, Sir Donald Conroy, Kt., CBE
McIntyre, Sir Meredith Alister, Kt.
Mackay, *Hon.* Sir Colin Crichton, Kt.
MacKay, *Prof.* Sir Donald Iain, Kt.
MacKay, Sir Francis Henry, Kt.
McKay, Sir Neil Stuart, Kt., CB
McKay, Sir William Robert, KCB
Mackay-Dick, *Maj.-Gen.* Sir Iain Charles, KCVO, MBE
Mackechnie, Sir Alistair John, Kt.
McKellen, Sir Ian Murray, Kt., CH, CBE
Mackenzie, Sir (James William) Guy, Bt. (1890)
Mackenzie, *Gen.* Sir Jeremy John George, GCB, OBE
†Mackenzie, Sir Peter Douglas, Bt. (S. 1673)
†Mackenzie, Sir Roderick McQuhae, Bt. (S. 1703)
Mackeson, Sir Rupert Henry, Bt. (1954)
McKillop, Sir Thomas Fulton Wilson, Kt.
McKinnon, *Rt. Hon.* Sir Donald Charles, GCVO
McKinnon, Sir James, Kt.
McKinnon, *Hon.* Sir Stuart Neil, Kt.
Mackintosh, Sir Cameron Anthony, Kt.
Mackworth, Sir Digby (John), Bt. (1776)
McLaughlin, Sir Richard, Kt.
Maclean of Dunconnell, Sir Charles Edward, Bt. (1957)
Maclean, Sir Lachlan Hector Charles, Bt. (NS 1631)
Maclean, Sir Murdo, Kt.
McLeod, Sir Charles Henry, Bt. (1925)
MacLeod, Sir (John) Maxwell Norman, Bt. (1924)
Macleod, Sir (Nathaniel William) Hamish, KBE
McLintock, Sir Michael William, Bt. (1934)
Maclure, Sir John Robert Spencer, Bt. (1898)
McMahon, Sir Brian Patrick, Bt. (1817)
McMahon, Sir Christopher William, Kt.
McMaster, Sir Brian John, Kt., CBE
McMichael, *Prof.* Sir Andrew James, Kt., FRS
Macmillan, Sir (Alexander McGregor) Graham, Kt.
MacMillan, *Lt.-Gen.* Sir John Richard Alexander, KCB, CBE
McMullin, *Rt. Hon.* Sir Duncan Wallace, Kt.
McMurtry, Sir David, Kt., CBE
Macnaghten, Sir Malcolm Francis, Bt. (1836)
McNair-Wilson, Sir Patrick Michael Ernest David, Kt.
McNamara, *Air Chief Marshal* Sir Neville Patrick, KBE
Macnaughton, *Prof.* Sir Malcolm Campbell, Kt.
McNee, Sir David Blackstock, Kt., QPM
McNulty, Sir (Robert William) Roy, Kt., CBE
MacPhail, Sir Bruce Dugald, Kt.
MacPherson, Sir Nicholas, KCB
Macpherson, Sir Ronald Thomas Steward (Tommy), CBE, MC, TD

Macpherson of Cluny, *Hon.* Sir William Alan, Kt., TD
McQuarrie, Sir Albert, Kt.
MacRae, Sir (Alastair) Christopher (Donald Summerhayes), KCMG
Macready, Sir Nevil John Wilfrid, Bt. (1923)
MacSween, *Prof.* Sir Roderick Norman McIver, Kt.
Mactaggart, Sir John Auld, Bt. (1938)
McWilliam, Sir Michael Douglas, KCMG
McWilliams, Sir Francis, GBE
Madden, Sir David Christopher Andrew, KCMG
†Madden, Sir Charles Jonathan, Bt. (1919)
Maddison, *Hon.* Sir David George, Kt.
Madejski, Sir John Robert, Kt., OBE
Madel, Sir (William) David, Kt.
Magee, Sir Ian Bernard Vaughan, Kt., CB
Magnus, Sir Laurence Henry Philip, Bt. (1917)
Mahon, Sir (John) Denis, Kt., CH, CBE
Mahon, Sir William Walter, Bt. (1819)
Maiden, Sir Colin James, Kt., DPHIL
Maini, *Prof.* Sir Ravinder Nath, Kt.
Maino, Sir Charles, KBE
†Maitland, Sir Charles Alexander, Bt. (1818)
Major, *Rt. Hon.* Sir John, KG, CH
Malbon, *Vice-Adm.* Sir Fabian Michael, KBE
Malcolm, Sir James William Thomas Alexander, Bt. (S. 1665)
Malet, Sir Harry Douglas St Lo, Bt. (1791)
Mallaby, Sir Christopher Leslie George, GCMG, GCVO
Mallet, Sir William George, GCMG, CBE
Mallick, *Prof.* Sir Netar Prakash, Kt.
Mallinson, Sir William James, Bt. (1935)
Malpas, Sir Robert, Kt., CBE
Mancham, Sir James Richard Marie, KBE
†Mander, Sir (Charles) Nicholas, Bt. (1911)
Manduell, Sir John, Kt., CBE
Mann, *Hon.* Sir George Anthony, Kt.
Mann, *Rt. Revd* Michael Ashley, KCVO
Mann, Sir Rupert Edward, Bt. (1905)
Manning, Sir David Geoffrey, GCMG, CVO
Mano, Sir Koitaga, Kt., MBE
Mansel, Sir Philip, Bt. (1622)
Mansfield, *Prof.* Sir Peter, Kt.
Manuella, Sir Tulaga, GCMG, MBE
Manzie, Sir (Andrew) Gordon, KCB
Margetson, Sir John William Denys, KCMG
Margetts, Sir Robert John, Kt., CBE
Mark, Sir Robert, GBE
Markesinis, *Prof.* Sir Basil Spyridonos, Kt. QC
Markham, *Prof.* Sir Alexander Fred, Kt.
Markham, Sir (Arthur) David, Bt. (1911)
Marling, Sir Charles William Somerset, Bt. (1882)
Marmot, Prof. Sir Michael Gideon, Kt.
Marr, Sir Leslie Lynn, Bt. (1919)
Marriner, Sir Neville, Kt., CBE
†Marsden, Sir Simon Neville Llewelyn, Bt. (1924)
Marsh, *Prof.* Sir John Stanley, Kt., CBE
Marshall, Sir Michael John, Kt., CBE
Marshall, *Prof.* Sir (Oshley) Roy, Kt., CBE
Marshall, Sir Peter Harold Reginald, KCMG
Martin, Sir Clive Haydon, Kt., OBE
Martin, Sir George Henry, Kt., CBE
Martin, *Vice-Adm.* Sir John Edward Ludgate, KCB, DSC
Martin, *Prof.* Sir Laurence Woodward, Kt.
Martin, Sir (Robert) Bruce, Kt., QC
Marychurch, Sir Peter Harvey, KCMG
Masefield, Sir Charles Beech Gordon, Kt.
Mason, *Hon.* Sir Anthony Frank, KBE
Mason, Sir (Basil) John, Kt., CB, DSC, FRS
Mason, *Prof.* Sir David Kean, Kt., CBE
Mason, Sir Gordon Charles, Kt., OBE
Mason, Sir John Peter, Kt., CBE
Mason, Sir Peter James, KBE
Mason, *Prof.* Sir Ronald, KCB, FRS
Massey, *Vice-Adm.* Sir Alan, KCB, CBE, ADC
Massie, Sir Herbert William, Kt., CBE
Matane, HE Sir Paulias Nguna, GCMG, OBE
Mathers, Sir Robert William, Kt.
Matheson of Matheson, Sir Fergus John, Bt. (1882)
Mathewson, Sir George Ross, Kt., CBE, PHD, FRSE
Matthews, Sir Terence Hedley, Kt., OBE
Maud, *Hon.* Sir Humphrey John Hamilton, KCMG
Maughan, Sir Deryck, Kt.
Mawer, Sir Philip John Courtney, Kt.
Maxwell, Sir Michael Eustace George, Bt. (S. 1681)
Maxwell-Scott, Sir Dominic James, Bt. (1642)
May, *Rt. Hon.* Sir Anthony Tristram Kenneth, Kt.
Mayhew-Sanders, Sir John Reynolds, Kt.
Maynard, *Hon.* Sir Clement Travelyan, Kt.
Meadow, *Prof.* Sir (Samuel) Roy, Kt., FRCP, FRCPE
Medlycott, Sir Mervyn Tregonwell, Bt. (1808)
Meeran, *His Hon.* Sir Goolam Hoosen Kader, Kt.
Meldrum, Sir Graham, Kt., CBE, QFSM
Melhuish, Sir Michael Ramsay, KBE, CMG
Mellars, *Prof.* Sir Paul Anthony, Kt., FBA
Mellon, Sir James, KCMG
Melmoth, Sir Graham John, Kt.
Melville, *Prof.* Sir David, Kt., CBE
Merifield, Sir Anthony James, KCVO, CB
†Meyer, Sir (Anthony) Ashley Frank, Bt. (1910)
Meyer, Sir Christopher John Rome, KCMG
Meyjes, Sir Richard Anthony, Kt.
†Meyrick, Sir Timothy Thomas Charlton, Bt. (1880)
Miakwe, *Hon.* Sir Akepa, KBE
Michael, Sir Duncan, Kt.
Michael, *Dr* Sir Jonathan, Kt.
Michael, Sir Peter Colin, Kt., CBE
Michels, Sir David Michael Charles, Kt.
Middleton, Sir John Maxwell, Kt.
Middleton, Sir Peter Edward, GCB
Miers, Sir (Henry) David Alastair Capel, KBE, CMG
Milbank, Sir Anthony Frederick, Bt. (1882)
Milborne-Swinnerton-Pilkington, Sir Thomas Henry, Bt. (S. 1635)
Milburn, Sir Anthony Rupert, Bt. (1905)
Miles, Sir Peter Tremayne, KCVO
Miles, Sir William Napier Maurice, Bt. (1859)
Millais, Sir Geoffrey Richard Everett, Bt. (1885)
Millar, *Prof.* Sir Fergus Graham Burtholme, Kt.
Millard, Sir Guy Elwin, KCMG, CVO
Miller, Sir Albert Joel, KCMG, MVO, MBE, QPM, CPM
Miller, Sir Donald John, Kt., FRSE, FRENG
Miller, *Air Marshal* Sir Graham Anthony, KBE
†Miller, Sir Anthony Thomas, Bt. (1705)
Miller, Sir Hilary Duppa (Hal), Kt.
Miller, Sir Jonathan Wolfe, Kt., CBE
Miller, Sir Peter North, Kt.
Miller, Sir Robin Robert William, Kt.
Miller, Sir Ronald Andrew Baird, Kt., CBE
Miller of Glenlee, Sir Stephen William Macdonald, Bt. (1788)
Mills, Sir Ian, Kt.
Mills, Sir Keith, Kt.
Mills, Sir Peter Frederick Leighton, Bt. (1921)
Milman, Sir David Patrick, Bt. (1800)
Milne, Sir John Drummond, Kt.

Milne-Watson, Sir Andrew Michael, Bt. (1937)
Milner, Sir Timothy William Lycett, Bt. (1717)
Milton, Sir Simon, Kt.
Milton-Thompson, *Surgeon Vice-Adm.* Sir Godfrey James, KBE
Mirrlees, *Prof.* Sir James Alexander, Kt., FBA
Mitchell, Sir David Bower, Kt.
Mitchell, *Rt. Hon.* Sir James FitzAllen, KCMG
Mitchell, *Very Revd* Patrick Reynolds, KCVO
Mitchell, *Hon.* Sir Stephen George, Kt.
Mitting, *Hon.* Sir John Edward, Kt.
Moate, Sir Roger Denis, Kt.
Moberly, Sir Patrick Hamilton, KCMG
Moffat, Sir Brian Scott, Kt., OBE
Moffat, *Lt.-Gen.* Sir (William) Cameron, KBE
Moir, Sir Christopher Ernest, Bt. (1916)
†Molesworth-St Aubyn, Sir William, Bt. (1689)
†Molony, Sir Thomas Desmond, Bt. (1925)
Moncada, *Prof.* Sir Salvador, Kt.
Monck, Sir Nicholas Jeremy, KCB
Money-Coutts, Sir David Burdett, KCVO
Montagu, Sir Nicholas Lionel John, KCB
Montagu-Pollock, Sir Giles Hampden, Bt. (1872)
Montague, Sir Adrian Alastair, Kt., CBE
Montague-Browne, Sir Anthony Arthur Duncan, KCMG, CBE, DFC
Montgomery, Sir (Basil Henry) David, Bt. (1801), CVO
Montgomery, Sir (William) Fergus, Kt.
Montgomery-Cuninghame, Sir John Christopher Foggo, Bt. (NS 1672)
Moody-Stuart, Sir Mark, KCMG
Moollan, Sir Abdool Hamid Adam, Kt.
Moollan, *Hon.* Sir Cassam (Ismael), Kt.
†Moon, Sir Roger, Bt. (1887)
Moorcroft, Sir William, Kt.
Moore, *Most Revd* Desmond Charles, KBE
Moore, Sir Francis Thomas, Kt.
Moore, Sir John Michael, KCVO, CB, DSC
Moore, *Vice Adm.* Sir Michael Antony Claës, KBE, LVO
Moore, *Prof.* Sir Norman Winfrid, Bt. (1919)
Moore, Sir Patrick Alfred Caldwell, Kt., CBE
Moore, Sir Patrick William Eisdell, Kt., OBE
Moore, Sir Roger George, KBE
Moore, Sir William Roger Clotworthy, Bt. (1932), TD
Moore-Bick, *Rt. Hon.* Sir Martin James, Kt.
Moores, Sir Peter, Kt., CBE
Morauta, Sir Mekere, KCMG
Mordaunt, Sir Richard Nigel Charles, Bt. (1611)
Moreton, Sir John Oscar, KCMG, KCVO, MC
Morgan, *Vice-Adm.* Sir Charles Christopher, KBE
Morgan, *Rt. Hon.* Sir (Charles) Declan, Kt.
Morgan, Sir Graham, Kt.
Morgan, Sir John Albert Leigh, KCMG
Morgan, *Hon.* Sir Paul Hyacinth, Kt.
Morgan-Giles, *Rear-Adm.* Sir Morgan Charles, Kt., DSO, OBE, GM
Morison, *Hon.* Sir Thomas Richard Atkin, Kt.
Morland, *Hon.* Sir Michael, Kt.
Morland, Sir Robert Kenelm, Kt.
Morpeth, Sir Douglas Spottiswoode, Kt., TD
†Morris, Sir Allan Lindsay, Bt. (1806)
Morris, *Air Marshal* Sir Arnold Alec, KBE, CB
Morris, Sir Derek James, Kt.
Morris, Sir Keith Elliot Hedley, KBE, CMG
Morris, *Prof.* Sir Peter John, Kt.
Morris, Sir Trefor Alfred, Kt., CBE, QPM
Morris, *Very Revd* William James, KCVO
Morrison, Sir (Alexander) Fraser, Kt., CBE
Morrison, Sir Kenneth Duncan, Kt., CBE
Morrison, Sir (William) Garth, KT, CBE
Morrison-Bell, Sir William Hollin Dayrell, Bt. (1905)
Morrison-Low, Sir James Richard, Bt. (1908)
Morritt, *Rt. Hon.* Sir (Robert) Andrew, Kt., CVO
Morse, Sir Christopher Jeremy, KCMG
Moseley, Sir George Walker, KCB
Moses, *Rt. Hon.* Sir Alan George, Kt.
Moses, *Very Revd* Dr John Henry, KCVO
Moss, Sir David Joseph, KCVO, CMG
Moss, Sir Stephen Alan, Kt.
Moss, Sir Stirling Craufurd, Kt., OBE
Mostyn, Sir William Basil John, Bt. (1670)
Motion, Sir Andrew, Kt.
Mott, Sir John Harmer, Bt. (1930)
Mottram, Sir Richard Clive, GCB
†Mount, Sir (William Robert) Ferdinand, Bt. (1921)
†Mountain, Sir Edward Brian Stanford, Bt. (1922)
Mountfield, Sir Robin, KCB
Mowbray, Sir John Robert, Bt. (1880)
Moylan, *Hon.* Sir Andrew John Gregory, Kt.
†Muir, Sir Richard James Kay, Bt. (1892)
Muir-Mackenzie, Sir Alexander Alwyne Henry Charles Brinton, Bt. (1805)
Mulcahy, Sir Geoffrey John, Kt.
Mummery, *Rt. Hon.* Sir John Frank, Kt.
Munby, *Rt. Hon.* Sir James Lawrence, Kt.
Munn, Sir James, Kt., OBE
Munro, Sir Alan Gordon, KCMG
†Munro, Sir Ian Kenneth, Bt. (S. 1634)
Munro, Sir Alasdair Thomas Ian, Bt. (1825)
Muria, *Hon.* Sir Gilbert John Baptist, Kt.
Murray, Sir David Edward, Kt.
Murray, *Rt. Hon.* Sir Donald Bruce, Kt.
Murray, *Prof.* Sir Kenneth, Kt.
Murray, Sir Nigel Andrew Digby, Bt. (S. 1628)
Murray, Sir Patrick Ian Keith, Bt. (S. 1673)
Murray, Sir Robert Sydney, Kt., CBE
†Murray, Sir Rowland William, Bt. (S. 1630)
Musgrave, Sir Christopher John Shane, Bt. (1782)
Musgrave, Sir Christopher Patrick Charles, Bt. (1611)
Myers, Sir Philip Alan, Kt., OBE, QPM
Myers, *Prof.* Sir Rupert Horace, KBE
Mynors, Sir Richard Baskerville, Bt. (1964)

Naipaul, Sir Vidiadhar Surajprasad, Kt.
Nairn, Sir Michael, Bt. (1904)
Nairne, *Rt. Hon.* Sir Patrick Dalmahoy, GCB, MC
Naish, Sir (Charles) David, Kt.
Nalau, Sir Jerry Kasip, KBE
Nall, Sir Edward William Joseph Bt. (1954)
Namaliu, *Rt. Hon.* Sir Rabbie Langanai, KCMG
†Napier, Sir Charles Joseph, Bt. (1867)
Napier, Sir John Archibald Lennox, Bt. (S. 1627)
Napier, Sir Oliver John, Kt.
Naylor, Sir Robert, Kt.
Naylor-Leyland, Sir Philip Vyvyan, Bt. (1895)
Neal, Sir Eric James, Kt., CVO
Neale, Sir Gerrard Anthony, Kt.
Neave, Sir Paul Arundell, Bt. (1795)
Neill, *Rt. Hon.* Sir Brian Thomas, Kt.
Neill, Sir (James) Hugh, KCVO, CBE, TD
†Nelson, Sir Jamie Charles Vernon Hope, Bt. (1912)
Nelson, *Hon.* Sir Robert Franklyn, Kt.
Neubert, Sir Michael John, Kt.
New, *Maj.-Gen.* Sir Laurence Anthony Wallis, Kt., CB, CBE
Newall, Sir Paul Henry, Kt., TD

Newby, *Prof.* Sir Howard Joseph, Kt., CBE
Newey, *Hon.* Sir Guy Richard, Kt.
Newington, Sir Michael John, KCMG
Newman, Sir Francis Hugh Cecil, Bt. (1912)
Newman, Sir Geoffrey Robert, Bt. (1836)
Newman, *Hon.* Sir George Michael, Kt.
Newman, Sir Kenneth Leslie, GBE, QPM
Newman, *Vice-Adm.* Sir Roy Thomas, KCB
Newman Taylor, *Prof.* Sir Anthony John, Kt., CBE
Newsam, Sir Peter Anthony, Kt.
†Newson-Smith, Sir Peter Frank Graham, Bt. (1944)
Newton, Sir (Charles) Wilfred, Kt., CBE
†Newton, *Revd* George Peter Howgill, Bt. (1900)
Newton, Sir John Garnar, Bt. (1924)
Ngata, Sir Henare Kohere, KBE
Nice, Sir Geoffrey, Kt., QC
Nicol, *Hon.* Sir Andrew George Lindsay, Kt.
Nichol, Sir Duncan Kirkbride, Kt., CBE
Nicholas, Sir David, Kt., CBE
Nicholas, Sir John William, KCVO, CMG
Nicholls, Sir Nigel Hamilton, KCVO, CBE
Nichols, Sir Richard Everard, Kt.
Nicholson, Sir Bryan Hubert, GBE, Kt.
†Nicholson, Sir Charles Christian, Bt. (1912)
Nicholson, Sir David, KCB, CBE
Nicholson, *Rt. Hon.* Sir Michael, Kt.
Nicholson, Sir Paul Douglas, Kt.
Nicholson, Sir Robin Buchanan, Kt., PHD, FRS, FRENG
Nicoll, Sir William, KCMG
Nightingale, Sir Charles Manners Gamaliel, Bt. (1628)
Nixon, Sir Simon Michael Christopher, Bt. (1906)
Noble, Sir David Brunel, Bt. (1902)
Noble, Sir Iain Andrew, Bt., OBE (1923)
Nombri, Sir Joseph Karl, Kt., ISO, BEM
Noon, Sir Gulam Kaderbhoy, Kt., MBE
Norman, Sir Arthur Gordon, KBE, DFC
Norman, Sir Mark Annesley, Bt. (1915)
Norman, Sir Ronald, Kt., OBE
Norman, Sir Torquil Patrick Alexander, Kt., CBE
Normington, Sir David John, KCB
Norrington, Sir Roger Arthur Carver, Kt., CBE
Norris, *Hon.* Sir Alastair Hubert, Kt.
Norriss, Air Marshal Sir Peter Coulson, KBE, CB, AFC
North, Sir Peter Machin, Kt., CBE, QC, DCL, FBA
North, Sir Thomas Lindsay, Kt.
North, Sir (William) Jonathan (Frederick), Bt. (1920)
Norton-Griffiths, Sir John, Bt. (1922)
Nossal, Sir Gustav Joseph Victor, Kt., CBE
Nott, *Rt. Hon.* Sir John William Frederic, KCB
Nourse, *Rt. Hon.* Sir Martin Charles, Kt.
Nugent, Sir John Edwin Lavallin, Bt. (I. 1795)
†Nugent, Sir Christopher George Ridley, Bt. (1806)
†Nugent, Sir (Walter) Richard Middleton, Bt. (1831)
Nunn, Sir Trevor Robert, Kt., CBE
Nunneley, Sir Charles Kenneth Roylance, Kt.
Nursaw, Sir James, KCB, QC
Nurse, Sir Paul Maxime, Kt.
†Nuttall, Sir Harry, Bt. (1922)
Nutting, Sir John Grenfell, Bt. (1903), QC

Oakeley, Sir John Digby Atholl, Bt. (1790)
Oakes, Sir Christopher, Bt. (1939)
†Oakshott, Hon. Sir Michael Arthur John, Bt. (1959)
Oates, Sir Thomas, Kt., CMG, OBE
O'Brien, Sir Frederick William Fitzgerald, Kt.
O'Brien, Sir Timothy John, Bt. (1849)
O'Brien, Sir William, Kt.
O'Brien, *Adm.* Sir William Donough, KCB, DSC
O'Connell, Sir Bernard, Kt.
O'Connell, Sir Maurice James Donagh MacCarthy, Bt. (1869)
O'Connor, Sir Denis Francis, Kt., CBE, QPM
O'Dea, Sir Patrick Jerad, KCVO
Odell, Sir Stanley John, Kt.
Odgers, Sir Graeme David William, Kt.
O'Donnell, Sir Augustine Thomas, KCB
O'Donnell, Sir Christopher John, Kt.
O'Donoghue, *Lt.-Gen.* Sir Kevin, KCB, CBE
O'Dowd, Sir David Joseph, Kt., CBE, QPM
Ogden, *Dr* Sir Peter James, Kt.
Ogden, Sir Robert, Kt., CBE
Ogilvy, Sir Francis Gilbert Arthur, Bt. (S. 1626)
Ogilvy-Wedderburn, Sir Andrew John Alexander, Bt. (1803)
Ognall, *Hon.* Sir Harry Henry, Kt.
Ohlson, Sir Brian Eric Christopher, Bt. (1920)
Oldham, *Dr* Sir John, Kt., OBE
Oliver, Sir James Michael Yorrick, Kt.
Oliver, Sir Stephen John Lindsay, Kt., QC
O'Loghlen, Sir Colman Michael, Bt. (1838)
Olver, Sir Stephen John Linley, KBE, CMG
Omand, Sir David Bruce, GCB
O'Nions, Prof. Sir Robert Keith, Kt., FRS, PHD
Ondaatje, Sir Christopher, Kt., CBE
Onslow, Sir John Roger Wilmot, Bt. (1797)
Oppenheimer, Sir Michael Bernard Grenville, Bt. (1921)
Oppenshaw, Sir Charles Peter Lawford, Kt., QC
Orde, Sir Hugh Stephen Roden, Kt., OBE, QPM
O'Regan, *Dr* Sir Stephen Gerard (Tipene), Kt.
O'Reilly, Sir Anthony John Francis, Kt.
O'Reilly, *Prof.* Sir John James, Kt.
Orr, Sir John, Kt., OBE
Orr-Ewing, Sir (Alistair) Simon, Bt. (1963)
Orr-Ewing, Sir Archibald Donald, Bt. (1886)
Osborn, Sir John Holbrook, Kt.
Osborn, Sir Richard Henry Danvers, Bt. (1662)
Osborne, Sir Peter George, Bt. (I. 1629)
O'Shea, *Prof.* Sir Timothy Michael Martin, Kt.
Osmotherly, Sir Edward Benjamin Crofton, Kt., CB
O'Sullevan, Sir Peter John, Kt., CBE
Oswald, *Admiral of the Fleet* Sir (John) Julian Robertson, GCB
Oswald, Sir (William Richard) Michael, KCVO
Otton, Sir Geoffrey John, KCB
Otton, *Rt. Hon.* Sir Philip Howard, Kt.
Oulton, Sir Antony Derek Maxwell, GCB, QC
Ouseley, *Hon.* Sir Brian Walter, Kt.
Outram, Sir Alan James, Bt. (1858)
Owen, Sir Geoffrey, Kt.
Owen, *Hon.* Sir John Arthur Dalziel, Kt.
Owen, *Hon.* Sir Robert Michael, Kt.
Owen-Jones, Sir Lindsay Harwood, KBE

Packer, Sir Richard John, KCB
Paget, Sir Julian Tolver, Bt. (1871), CVO
Paget, Sir Richard Herbert, Bt. (1886)
Paine, Sir Christopher Hammon, Kt., FRCP, FRCR
Pakenham, *Hon.* Sir Michael Aiden, KBE, CMG
Palin, *Air Chief Marshal* Sir Roger Hewlett, KCB, OBE
Palliser, *Rt. Hon.* Sir (Arthur) Michael, GCMG
Palmer, Sir Albert Rocky, Kt.
Palmer, Sir (Charles) Mark, Bt. (1886)

Palmer, Sir Geoffrey Christopher John, Bt. (1660)
Palmer, *Rt. Hon.* Sir Geoffrey Winston Russell, KCMG
Palmer, Sir John Edward Somerset, Bt. (1791)
Palmer, *Maj.-Gen.* Sir (Joseph) Michael, KCVO
Palmer, Sir Reginald Oswald, GCMG, MBE
Parbo, Sir Arvi Hillar, Kt.
Park, *Hon.* Sir Andrew Edward Wilson, Kt.
Parker, Sir Alan William, Kt., CBE
Parker, Sir Eric Wilson, Kt.
Parker, *Rt. Hon.* Sir Jonathan Frederic, Kt.
Parker, *Hon.* Sir Kenneth Blades, Kt.
Parker, *Maj.* Sir Michael John, KCVO, CBE
Parker, *Lt.-Gen.* Sir Nicholas Ralph, KCB, CBE
Parker, Sir Richard (William) Hyde, Bt. (1681)
Parker, *Rt. Hon.* Sir Roger Jocelyn, Kt.
Parker, Sir (Thomas) John, Kt.
Parker, Sir William Peter Brian, Bt. (1844)
Parkes, Sir Edward Walter, Kt., FRENG
Parkinson, Sir Michael, Kt., CBE
Parry, Sir Emyr Jones, GCMG
Parry-Evans, *Air Chief Marshal* Sir David, GCB, CBE
Parsons, Sir John Christopher, KCVO
Parsons, Sir Richard Edmund (Clement Fownes), KCMG
Partridge, Sir Michael John Anthony, KCB
Partridge, Sir Nicholas Wyndham, Kt., OBE
Pascoe, *Gen.* Sir Robert Alan, KCB, MBE
Pasley, Sir Robert Killigrew Sabine, Bt. (1794)
Paston-Bedingfeld, *Capt.* Sir Edmund George Felix, Bt. (1661)
Paterson, Sir Dennis Craig, Kt.
Patey, Sir William Charters, KCMG
Patnick, Sir (Cyril) Irvine, Kt., OBE
Patten, *Rt. Hon.* Sir Nicholas John, Kt.
Pattie, *Rt. Hon.* Sir Geoffrey Edwin, Kt.
Pattison, *Prof.* Sir John Ridley, Kt., DM, FRCPATH
Pattullo, Sir (David) Bruce, Kt., CBE
Pauncefort-Duncombe, Sir Philip Digby, Bt. (1859)
Peach, Sir Leonard Harry, Kt.
Peach, *Air Marshal* Sir Stuart William, KCB, CBE
Peacock, *Prof.* Sir Alan Turner, Kt., DSC
Pearce, Sir (Daniel Norton) Idris, Kt., CBE, TD
Pearse, Sir Brian Gerald, Kt.
Pearson, Sir Francis Nicholas Fraser, Bt. (1964)
Pearson, Sir Keith, Kt.
Pearson, *Gen.* Sir Thomas Cecil Hook, KCB, CBE, DSO
Peart, *Prof.* Sir William Stanley, Kt., MD, FRS
Pease, Sir Joseph Gurney, Bt. (1882)
Pease, Sir Richard Thorn, Bt. (1920)
Peat, Sir Gerrard Charles, KCVO
Peat, Sir Michael Charles Gerrard, KCVO
Peckham, *Prof.* Sir Michael John, Kt.,
Peek, *Vice-Adm.* Sir Richard Innes, KBE, CB, DSC
Peek, Sir Richard Grenville, Bt. (1874)
Peirse, *Air Vice-Marshal* Sir Richard Charles Fairfax, KCVO, CB
Pelgen, Sir Harry Friedrich, Kt., MBE
Peliza, Sir Robert John, KBE, ED
Pelly, Sir Richard John, Bt. (1840)
Pemberton, Sir Francis Wingate William, Kt., CBE
Pendry, *Prof.* Sir John Brian, Kt., FRS
Penrose, *Prof.* Sir Roger, Kt., OM, FRS
Penry-Davey, *Hon.* Sir David Herbert, Kt.
Pepper, *Dr.* Sir David Edwin, KCMG
Pepper, *Prof.* Sir Michael, Kt.
Perowne, *Vice-Adm.* Sir James Francis, KBE
Perring, Sir John Raymond, Bt. (1963)
Perris, Sir David (Arthur), Kt., MBE
Perry, Sir David Howard, KCB
Perry, Sir Michael Sydney, GBE
Pervez, Sir Mohammed Anwar, Kt., OBE
Peters, *Prof.* Sir David Keith, Kt., FRCP
Peterson, Sir Christopher Matthew, Kt., CBE, TD
†Petit, Sir Jehangir, Bt. (1890)
Peto, Sir Henry George Morton, Bt. (1855)
Peto, Sir Henry Christopher Morton Bampfylde, Bt. (1927)
Peto, *Prof.* Sir Richard, Kt., FRS
Petrie, Sir Peter Charles, Bt. (1918), CMG
Pettigrew, Sir Russell Hilton, Kt.
Pettitt, Sir Dennis, Kt.
†Philipson-Stow, Sir (Robert) Matthew, Bt. (1907)
Phillips, Sir Fred Albert, Kt., CVO
Phillips, Sir (Gerald) Hayden, GCB
Phillips, Sir John David, Kt., QPM
Phillips, Sir Jonathan, KCB
Phillips, Sir Peter John, Kt., OBE
Phillips, Sir Robin Francis, Bt. (1912)
Phillips, Sir Tom Richard Vaughan, KCMG
Pickard, Sir (John) Michael, Kt.
Pickthorn, Sir James Francis Mann, Bt. (1959)
Pidgeon, Sir John Allan Stewart, Kt.
†Piers, Sir James Desmond, Bt. (I. 1661)
Piggott-Brown, Sir William Brian, Bt. (1903)
Pigot, Sir George Hugh, Bt. (1764)
Pigott, *Lt.-Gen.* Sir Anthony David, KCB, CBE
Pigott, Sir Berkeley Henry Sebastian, Bt. (1808)
Pike, *Lt.-Gen.* Sir Hew William Royston, KCB, DSO, MBE
Pike, Sir Michael Edmund, KCVO, CMG
Pike, Sir Philip Ernest Housden, Kt., QC
Pilditch, Sir Richard Edward, Bt. (1929)
Pile, Sir Frederick Devereux, Bt. (1900), MC
Pill, *Rt. Hon.* Sir Malcolm Thomas, Kt.
Pilling, Sir Joseph Grant, KCB
Pinsent, Sir Christopher Roy, Bt. (1938)
Pinsent, Sir Matthew Clive, Kt., CBE
Pitakaka, Sir Moses Puibangara, GCMG
Pitcher, Sir Desmond Henry, Kt.
Pitchers, *Hon.* Sir Christopher (John), Kt.
Pitchford, *Rt. Hon.* Sir Christopher John, Kt.
Pitoi, Sir Sere, Kt., CBE
Pitt, Sir Michael Edward, Kt.
Plastow, Sir David Arnold Stuart, Kt.
Platt, Sir Harold Grant, Kt.
Platt, Sir Martin Philip, Bt. (1959)
Pledger, *Air Chief Marshal* Sir Malcolm David, KCB, OBE, AFC
Plender, *Hon.* Sir Richard Owen, Kt.
Plumbly, Sir Derek John, KCMG
Pogo, *Most Revd* Ellison Leslie, KBE
Pohai, Sir Timothy, Kt., MBE
Pole, Sir (John) Richard (Walter Reginald) Carew, Bt. (1628)
Pole, Sir Peter Van Notten, Bt. (1791)
Polkinghorne, *Revd Canon* John Charlton, KBE, FRS
Pollard, Sir Charles, Kt.
†Pollen, Sir Richard John Hungerford, Bt. (1795)
Pollock, Sir George Frederick, Bt. (1866)
Ponder, *Prof.* Sir Bruce Anthony John, Kt.
†Ponsonby, Sir Charles Ashley, Bt. (1956)
Poore, Sir Roger Ricardo, Bt. (1795)
Pope, Sir Joseph Albert, Kt., DSC, PHD
Popplewell, *Hon.* Sir Oliver Bury, Kt.
†Porritt, Sir Jonathon Espie, Bt. (1963)
Portal, Sir Jonathan Francis, Bt. (1901)
Porter, *Rt. Hon.* Sir Robert Wilson, Kt., PC (NI)
Potter, *Rt. Hon.* Sir Mark Howard, Kt.
Potts, *Hon.* Sir Francis Humphrey, Kt.
Pound, Sir John David, Bt. (1905)
Povey, Sir Keith, Kt., QPM
Powell, Sir John Christopher, Kt.
Powell, Sir Nicholas Folliott Douglas, Bt. (1897)
Power, Sir Alastair John Cecil, Bt. (1924)

Power, *Hon.* Sir Noel Plunkett, Kt.
Prance, *Prof.* Sir Ghillean Tolmie, Kt., FRS
Pratchett, Sir Terence David John, Kt., OBE
Prendergast, Sir (Walter) Kieran, KCVO, CMG
Prescott, Sir Mark, Bt. (1938)
†Preston, Sir Philip Charles Henry Hulton, Bt. (1815)
Prevost, Sir Christopher Gerald, Bt. (1805)
Price, Sir David Ernest Campbell, Kt.
Price, Sir Francis Caradoc Rose, Bt. (1815)
Price, Sir Frank Leslie, Kt.
Prideaux, Sir Humphrey Povah Treverbian, Kt., OBE
Priestly, Sir Julian Gordon, KCMG
†Primrose, Sir John Ure, Bt. (1903)
Pringle, *Air Marshal* Sir Charles Norman Seton, KBE, FRENG
Pringle, *Hon.* Sir John Kenneth, Kt.
Pringle, *Lt.-Gen.* Sir Steuart (Robert), Bt. (S. 1683), KCB
Pritchard, Sir Neil, KCMG
†Prichard-Jones, Sir David John Walter, Bt. (1910)
Proby, Sir William Henry, Bt. (1952)
Proctor-Beauchamp, Sir Christopher Radstock, Bt. (1745)
Prosser, Sir David John, Kt.
Prosser, Sir Ian Maurice Gray, Kt.
Pryke, Sir Christopher Dudley, Bt. (1926)
Puapua, *Rt. Hon.* Sir Tomasi, GCMG, KBE
Purves, Sir William, Kt., CBE, DSO
Purvis, *Vice-Adm.* Sir Neville, KCB

Quan, Sir Henry (Francis), KBE
Quigley, Sir (William) George (Henry), Kt., CB, PHD
Quilter, Sir Anthony Raymond Leopold Cuthbert, Bt. (1897)
Quinton, Sir James Grand, Kt.

Radcliffe, Sir Sebastian Everard, Bt. (1813)
Radda, *Prof.* Sir George Karoly, Kt., CBE, FRS
Rae, Sir William, Kt., QPM
Raeburn, Sir Michael Edward Norman, Bt. (1923)
Raikes, *Vice-Adm.* Sir Iwan Geoffrey, KCB, CBE, DSC
Raison, *Rt. Hon.* Sir Timothy Hugh Francis, Kt.
Rake, Sir Michael Derek Vaughan, Kt.
†Ralli, Sir David Charles, Bt. (1912)
Ramdanee, Sir Mookteswar Baboolall Kailash, Kt.
Ramphal, Sir Shridath Surendranath, GCMG
Ramphul, Sir Baalkhristna, Kt.
Ramphul, Sir Indurduth, Kt.
Ramsay, Sir Alexander William Burnett, Bt. (1806)
Ramsay, Sir Allan John (Hepple), KBE, CMG
Ramsay-Fairfax-Lucy, Sir Edmund John William Hugh, Bt. (1836)
Ramsden, Sir John Charles Josslyn, Bt. (1689)
Ramsey, *Dr* Sir Frank Cuthbert, KCMG
Ramsey, *Hon.* Sir Vivian Arthur, Kt.
Rankin, Sir Ian Niall, Bt. (1898)
Rasch, Sir Simon Anthony Carne, Bt. (1903)
Rashleigh, Sir Richard Harry, Bt. (1831)
Ratford, Sir David John Edward, KCMG, CVO
Rattee, *Hon.* Sir Donald Keith, Kt.
Rattle, Sir Simon Dennis, Kt., CBE
Rawlins, *Surgeon Vice-Adm.* Sir John Stuart Pepys, KBE
Rawlins, *Prof.* Sir Michael David, Kt., FRCP, FRCPED
Rawlinson, Sir Anthony Henry John, Bt. (1891)
Rea, *Prof.* Sir Desmond, Kt., OBE
Read, *Air Marshal* Sir Charles Frederick, KBE, CB, DFC, AFC
Read, *Prof.* Sir David John, Kt.
Read, Sir John Emms, Kt.
†Reade, Sir Kenneth Ray, Bt. (1661)
Reardon-Smith, Sir (William) Antony (John), Bt. (1920)
Reay, *Lt.-Gen.* Sir (Hubert) Alan John, KBE
Redgrave, *Maj.-Gen.* Sir Roy Michael Frederick, KBE, MC
Redgrave, Sir Steven Geoffrey, Kt., CBE
Redmayne, Sir Giles Martin, Bt. (1964)
Redwood, Sir Peter Boverton, Bt. (1911)
Reece, Sir Charles Hugh, Kt.
Reedie, Sir Craig Collins, Kt., CBE
Rees, Sir David Allan, Kt., PHD, DSC, FRS
Rees, Sir Richard Ellis Meuric, Kt., CBE
Reeve, Sir Anthony, KCMG, KCVO
Reeves, *Most Revd* Paul Alfred, GCMG, GCVO
Reffell, *Adm.* Sir Derek Roy, KCB
Refshauge, *Maj.-Gen.* Sir William Dudley, Kt., CBE
Reich, Sir Erich Arieh, Kt.
Reid, Sir Alexander James, Bt. (1897)
Reid, Sir Hugh, Bt. (1922)
Reid, Sir (Philip) Alan, KCVO
Reid, Sir Robert Paul, Kt.
Reid, Sir William Kennedy, KCB
Reiher, Sir Frederick Bernard Carl, KCMG, KBE
Reilly, *Lt.-Gen.* Sir Jeremy Calcott, KCB, DSO
Renals, Sir Stanley, Bt. (1895)
Renouf, Sir Clement William Bailey, Kt.
Renshaw, Sir John David Bine, Bt. (1903)
Renwick, Sir Richard Eustace, Bt. (1921)
Reporter, Sir Shapoor Ardeshirji, KBE
Reynolds, Sir David James, Bt. (1923)
Reynolds, Sir Peter William John, Kt., CBE
Rhodes, Sir John Christopher Douglas, Bt. (1919)
Ribeiro, Bernard Francisco, Kt., CBE
Rice, *Prof.* Sir Charles Duncan, Kt.
Rice, *Maj.-Gen.* Sir Desmond Hind Garrett, KCVO, CBE
Rice, Sir Timothy Miles Bindon, Kt.
Richard, Sir Cliff, Kt., OBE
Richards, Sir Brian Mansel, Kt., CBE, PHD
Richards, *Hon.* Sir David Anthony Stewart, Kt.
Richards, Sir David Gerald, Kt.
Richards, *Lt.-Gen.* Sir David, Julian, KCB, CBE, DSO
Richards, Sir Francis Neville, KCMG, CVO
Richards, *Prof.* Sir Michael Adrian, Kt., CBE
Richards, Sir Rex Edward, Kt., DSC, FRS
Richards, *Rt. Hon.* Sir Stephen Price, Kt.
Richardson, Sir Anthony Lewis, Bt. (1924)
Richardson, *Rt. Hon.* Sir Ivor Lloyd Morgan, Kt.
Richardson, *Lt.-Gen.* Sir Robert Francis, KCB, CVO, CBE
Richardson, Sir Thomas Legh, KCMG
Richardson-Bunbury, Sir (Richard David) Michael, Bt. (I. 1787)
Richmond, Sir David Frank, KBE, CMG
Richmond, *Prof.* Sir Mark Henry, Kt., FRS
Ricketts, Sir Stephen Tristram, Bt. (1828)
Ricks, *Prof.* Sir Christopher Bruce, Kt.
†Riddell, Sir Walter John, Bt. (S. 1628)
Ridley, Sir Adam (Nicholas), Kt.
Ridley, Sir Michael Kershaw, KCVO
Rifkind, *Rt. Hon.* Sir Malcolm Leslie, KCMG
Rigby, Sir Anthony John, Bt. (1929)
Rigby, Sir Peter, Kt.
Rimer, *Hon.* Sir Colin Percy Farquharson, Kt.
Ripley, Sir William Hugh, Bt. (1880)
Risk, Sir Thomas Neilson, Kt.
Ritako, Sir Thomas Baha, Kt., MBE
Ritblat, Sir John Henry, Kt.
†Rivett-Carnac, Sir Jonathan James, Bt. (1836)
Rix, *Rt. Hon.* Sir Bernard Anthony, Kt.
Robati, Sir Pupuke, KBE
Robb, Sir John Weddell, Kt.
Roberts, *Hon.* Sir Denys Tudor Emil, KBE,
Roberts, Sir Derek Harry, Kt., CBE, FRS, FRENG

Roberts, *Prof.* Sir Edward Adam, KCMG
Roberts, Sir Gilbert Howland Rookehurst, Bt. (1809)
Roberts, Sir Hugh Ashley, GCVO
Roberts, Sir Ivor Anthony, KCMG
Roberts, *Dr* Sir Richard John, Kt.
Roberts, *Maj.-Gen.* Sir Sebastian John Lechmere, KCVO, OBE
Roberts, Sir Samuel, Bt. (1919)
Roberts, Sir William James Denby, Bt. (1909)
Robertson, Sir Simon Manwaring, Kt.
Robins, Sir Ralph Harry, Kt., FRENG
Robinson, Sir Christopher Philipse, Bt. (1854)
Robinson, Sir Gerrard Jude, Kt.
Robinson, Sir Ian, Kt.
Robinson, Sir John James Michael Laud, Bt. (1660)
Robinson, *Dr* Sir Kenneth, Kt.
Robinson, Sir Wilfred Henry Frederick, Bt. (1908)
Robson, Sir John Adam, KCMG
Robson, Sir Stephen Arthur, Kt., CB
Roch, *Rt. Hon.* Sir John Ormond, Kt.
Roche, Sir David O'Grady, Bt. (1838)
Roche, Sir Henry John, Kt.
Rodgers, Sir (Andrew) Piers (Wingate Aikin-Sneath), Bt. (1964)
Rodley, *Prof.* Sir Nigel, KBE
Rogers, *Air Chief Marshal* Sir John Robson, KCB, CBE
Rogers, Sir Peter, Kt.
Rollo, *Lt.-Gen.* Sir William Raoul, KCB, CBE
Ropner, Sir John Bruce Woollacott, Bt. (1952)
Ropner, Sir Robert Clinton, Bt. (1904)
Rose, Sir Arthur James, Kt., CBE
Rose, *Rt. Hon.* Sir Christopher Dudley Roger, Kt.
Rose, Sir Clive Martin, GCMG
Rose, Sir David Lancaster, Bt. (1874)
Rose, *Gen.* Sir (Hugh) Michael, KCB, CBE, DSO, QGM
Rose, Sir John Edward Victor, Kt.
Rose, Sir Julian Day, Bt. (1872 and 1909)
Rose, Sir Stuart Alan Ransom, Kt.
Rosenthal, Sir Norman Leon, Kt.
Ross, *Maj.* Sir Andrew Charles Paterson, Bt. (1960)
Ross, *Lt.-Gen.* Sir Robert Jeremy, KCB, OBE
Ross, *Lt.-Col.* Sir Walter Hugh Malcolm, GCVO, OBE
Rossi, Sir Hugh Alexis Louis, Kt.
Roth, *Hon.* Sir Peter Marcel, Kt.
Rothschild, Sir Evelyn Robert Adrian de, Kt.
Rove, *Revd* Ikan, KBE
Rowe, *Rear-Adm.* Sir Patrick Barton, KCVO, CBE
Rowe-Ham, Sir David Kenneth, GBE
Rowland, Sir (John) David, Kt.
Rowland, Sir Geoffrey Robert, Kt.
Rowlands, Sir David, KCB
Rowley, Sir Richard Charles, Bt. (1836)
Rowling, Sir John Reginald, Kt.
Rowlinson, *Prof.* Sir John Shipley, Kt., FRS
Royce, *Hon.* Sir Roger John, Kt.
Royden, Sir Christopher John, Bt. (1905)
Rubin *Prof.* Sir Peter Charles, Kt.
Rudd, Sir (Anthony) Nigel (Russell), Kt.
Rudge, Sir Alan Walter, Kt., CBE, FRS
Rugge-Price, Sir James Keith Peter, Bt. (1804)
Ruggles-Brise, Sir Timothy Edward, Bt. (1935)
Rumbold, Sir Henry John Sebastian, Bt. (1779)
Runchorelal, Sir (Udayan) Chinubhai Madhowlal, Bt. (1913)
Rusby, *Vice-Adm.* Sir Cameron, KCB, LVO
Rushdie, Sir (Ahmed) Salman, Kt.
†Russell, Sir (Arthur) Mervyn, Bt. (1812)
Russell, Sir Charles Dominic, Bt. (1916)
Russell, Sir George, Kt., CBE
Russell, Sir Muir, KCB
Rutter, *Prof.* Sir Michael Llewellyn, Kt., CBE, MD, FRS
Ryan, Sir Derek Gerald, Bt. (1919)
Rycroft, Sir Richard John, Bt. (1784)
Ryder, *Hon.* Sir Ernest Nigel Ryder, Kt., TD
Ryrie, Sir William Sinclair, KCB

Sacranie, Sir Iqbal Abdul Karim Mussa, Kt., OBE
Sainsbury, *Rt. Hon.* Sir Timothy Alan Davan, Kt.
†St Clair-Ford, Sir Colin Anson, Bt. (1793)
St George, Sir John Avenel Bligh, Bt. (I. 1766)
St John-Mildmay, Sir Walter John Hugh, Bt. (1772)
St Omer, *Hon. Dr* Sir Dunstan Gerbert Raphael, KCMG
Sainty, Sir John Christopher, KCB
Sales, *Hon.* Sir Philip James, Kt.
Salisbury, Sir Robert William, Kt.
Salt, Sir Patrick MacDonnell, Bt. (1869)
Salt, Sir (Thomas) Michael John, Bt. (1899)
†Salusbury-Trelawny, Sir John William Richard, Bt. (1628)
Sampson, Sir Colin, Kt., CBE, QPM
Samuel, Sir John Michael Glen, Bt. (1898)
Samuelson, Sir James Francis, Bt. (1884)
Samuelson, Sir Sydney Wylie, Kt., CBE
Samworth, Sir David Chetwode, Kt., CBE
Sanders, Sir Robert Tait, KBE, CMG
Sanders, Sir Ronald Michael, KCMG
Sanderson, Sir Frank Linton, Bt. (1920)
Sands, Sir Roger Blakemore, KCB
Sarei, Sir Alexis Holyweek, Kt., CBE
Sargent, Sir William Desmond, Kt., CBE
Satchwell, Sir Kevin Joseph, Kt.
Saunders, *Hon.* Sir John Henry Boulton, Kt.
Savile, Sir James Wilson Vincent, Kt., OBE
Savill, *Prof.* Sir John Stewart, Kt.
Savory, Sir Michael Berry, Kt.
Sawers, Sir Robert John, KCMG
Saxby, *Prof.* Sir Robin Keith, Kt.
Scarlett, Sir John McLeod, KCMG, OBE
Scheele, Sir Nicholas Vernon, KCMG
Schiemann, *Rt. Hon.* Sir Konrad Hermann Theodor, Kt.
Scholar, Sir Michael Charles, KCB
Scholey, Sir David Gerald, Kt., CBE
Scholey, Sir Robert, Kt., CBE, FRENG
Scholtens, Sir James Henry, KCVO
Schreier, Sir Bernard, Kt.
Schubert, Sir Sydney, Kt.
Scipio, Sir Hudson Rupert, Kt.
Scoon, Sir Paul, GCMG, GCVO, OBE
Scott, Sir Anthony Percy, Bt. (1913)
Scott, Sir David Aubrey, GCMG
Scott, *Prof.* Sir George Peter, Kt.
Scott, Sir James Jervoise, Bt. (1962)
Scott, Sir Kenneth Bertram Adam, KCVO, CMG
Scott, Sir Oliver Christopher Anderson, Bt. (1909)
Scott, *Prof.* Sir Philip John, KBE
Scott, Sir Ridley, Kt.
Scott, Sir Robert David Hillyer, Kt.
Scott, Sir Walter John, Bt. (1907)
Scott-Lee, Sir Paul Joseph, Kt., QPM
Seale, Sir Clarence David, Kt.
Seale, Sir John Henry, Bt. (1838)
Seaman, Sir Keith Douglas, KCVO, OBE
Sebastian, Sir Cuthbert Montraville, GCMG, OBE
†Sebright, Sir Rufus Hugo Giles, Bt. (1626)
Seccombe, Sir (William) Vernon Stephen, Kt.
Seconde, Sir Reginald Louis, KCMG, CVO
Sedley, *Rt. Hon.* Sir Stephen John, Kt.
Seely, Sir Nigel Edward, Bt. (1896)
Seeto, Sir Ling James, Kt., MBE
Seeyave, Sir Rene Sow Choung, Kt., CBE
Seligman, Sir Peter Wendel, Kt., CBE
Semple, Sir John Laughlin, KCB
Sergeant, Sir Patrick, Kt.
Serota, Sir Nicholas Andrew, Kt.
†Seton, Sir Charles Wallace, Bt. (S. 1683)
Seton, Sir Iain Bruce, Bt. (S. 1663)
Severne, *Air Vice-Marshal* Sir John de Milt, KCVO, OBE, AFC
Shaffer, Sir Peter Levin, Kt., CBE
Shakerley, Sir Geoffrey Adam, Bt. (1838)

Shakespeare, Sir Thomas William, Bt. (1942)
Sharp, Sir Adrian, Bt. (1922)
Sharp, Sir Leslie, Kt., QPM
Sharp, Sir Sheridan Christopher Robin, Bt. (1920)
Sharples, Sir James, Kt., QPM
Shaw, Sir Brian Piers, Kt.
Shaw, Sir (Charles) Barry, Kt., CB, QC
Shaw, Sir Charles De Vere, Bt. (1821)
Shaw, *Prof.* Sir John Calman, Kt., CBE
Shaw, Sir Neil McGowan, Kt.
Shaw, Sir Roy, Kt.
Shaw, Sir Run Run, Kt., CBE
Shaw-Stewart, Sir Ludovic Houston, Bt. (S. 1667)
Shearing, Sir George Albert, Kt. OBE
Shebbeare, Sir Thomas Andrew, KCVO
Sheehy, Sir Patrick, Kt.
Sheffield, Sir Reginald Adrian Berkeley, Bt. (1755)
Shehadie, Sir Nicholas Michael, Kt., OBE
Sheil, *Rt. Hon.* Sir John, Kt.
Sheinwald, Sir Nigel Elton, KCMG
Shelley, Sir John Richard, Bt. (1611)
Shepherd, Sir Colin Ryley, Kt.
Shepherd, Sir John Alan, KCVO, CMG
Sher, Sir Antony, KBE
Sherbourne, Sir Stephen Ashley, Kt., CBE
Sherston-Baker, Sir Robert George Humphrey, Bt. (1796)
Shiffner, Sir Henry David, Bt. (1818)
Silber, *Hon.* Sir Stephen Robert, Kt.
Shinwell, Sir (Maurice) Adrian, Kt.
Shirreff, *Lt.-Gen.* Sir Alexander Richard David, KBE, CBE
Shock, Sir Maurice, Kt.
Short, Sir Apenera Pera, KBE
Shortridge, Sir Jon Deacon, KCB
Shuckburgh, Sir Rupert Charles Gerald, Bt. (1660)
Sieff, *Hon.* Sir David, Kt.
Silber, *Rt. Hon.* Sir Stephen Robert, Kt.
Simeon, Sir Richard Edmund Barrington, Bt. (1815)
Simmonds, *Rt. Hon. Dr* Sir Kennedy Alphonse, KCMG
Simmons, *Air Marshal* Sir Michael George, KCB, AFC
Simmons, Sir Stanley Clifford, Kt.
Simms, Sir Neville Ian, Kt., FRENG
Simon, *Hon.* Sir Peregrine Charles Hugh, Kt.
Simonet, Sir Louis Marcel Pierre, Kt., CBE
Simpson, *Dr* Sir Peter Jeffery, Kt.
Sims, Sir Roger Edward, Kt.
Sinclair, Sir Clive Marles, Kt.
Sinclair, Sir Ian McTaggart, KCMG, QC
Sinclair, Sir Patrick Robert Richard, Bt. (S. 1704)
Sinclair, Sir Robert John, Kt.
Sinclair-Lockhart, Sir Simon John Edward Francis, Bt. (S. 1636)
Sinden, Sir Donald Alfred, Kt., CBE
Singer, *Hon.* Sir Jan Peter, Kt.
Singh, *His Hon.* Sir Mota, Kt., QC
Singh, Sir Pritpal, Kt.
Singleton, Sir Roger, Kt., CBE
Sione, Sir Tomu Malaefone, GCMG, OBE
†Sitwell, Sir George Reresby Sacheverell, Bt. (1808)
Skeggs, Sir Clifford George, Kt.
Skehel, Sir John James, Kt., FRS
Skingsley, *Air Chief Marshal* Sir Anthony Gerald, GBE, KCB
Skinner, Sir (Thomas) Keith (Hewitt), Bt. (1912)
Skipwith, Sir Patrick Alexander d'Estoteville, Bt. (1622)
Slack, Sir William Willatt, KCVO, FRCS
Slade, Sir Benjamin Julian Alfred, Bt. (1831)
Slade, *Rt. Hon.* Sir Christopher John, Kt.
Slaney, *Prof.* Sir Geoffrey, KBE
Slater, *Adm.* Sir John (Jock) Cunningham Kirkwood, GCB, LVO
Sleight, Sir Richard, Bt. (1920)
Sloman, Sir Albert Edward, Kt., CBE
Smart, Sir Jack, Kt., CBE
Smiley, *Lt.-Col.* Sir John Philip, Bt. (1903)
Smith, Sir Alan, Kt., CBE, DFC
Smith, *Hon.* Sir Andrew Charles, Kt.
Smith, Sir Andrew Thomas, Bt. (1897)
†Smith, Sir Robert Christopher Sydney Winwood, Bt. (1809)
Smith, *Prof.* Sir Colin Stansfield, Kt., CBE
Smith, Sir Cyril, Kt., MBE
Smith, *Prof.* Sir David Cecil, Kt., FRS
Smith, Sir David Iser, KCVO
Smith, Sir Dudley (Gordon), Kt.
Smith, *Prof.* Sir Eric Brian, Kt., PHD
Smith, Sir John Alfred, Kt., QPM
Smith, Sir Joseph William Grenville, Kt.
Smith, Sir Kevin, Kt., CBE
Smith, Sir Michael John Llewellyn, KCVO, CMG
Smith, Sir (Norman) Brian, Kt., CBE, PHD
Smith, Sir Paul Brierley, Kt., CBE
Smith, *Hon.* Sir Peter (Winston), Kt.
Smith, Sir Robert Courtney, Kt., CBE
Smith, Sir Robert Hill, Bt. (1945)
Smith, *Gen.* Sir Rupert Anthony, KCB, DSO, OBE, QGM
Smith-Dodsworth, Sir John Christopher, Bt. (1784)
Smith-Gordon, Sir (Lionel) Eldred (Peter), Bt. (1838)
Smith-Marriott, Sir Hugh Cavendish, Bt. (1774)
Smurfit, *Dr.* Sir Michael William Joseph, KBE
Smyth, Sir Timothy John, Bt. (1955)
Snyder, Sir Michael John, Kt.
Soar, *Vice-Adm.* Sir Trevor Alan, KCB, OBE
Sobers, Sir Garfield St Auburn, Kt.
Solomon, Sir Harry, Kt.
Somare, *Rt. Hon.* Sir Michael Thomas, GCMG, CH
Somerville, *Brig.* Sir John Nicholas, Kt., CBE
Songo, Sir Bernard Paul, Kt., CMG, OBE
Sorrell, Sir John William, Kt., CBE
Sorrell, Sir Martin Stuart, Kt.
Soulsby, Sir Peter Alfred, Kt.
Soutar, *Air Marshal* Sir Charles John Williamson, KBE
Southby, Sir John Richard Bilbe, Bt. (1937)
Southern, *Prof.* Sir Edwin Mellor, Kt
Southgate, Sir Colin Grieve, Kt.
Southgate, Sir William David, Kt.
Southward, *Dr* Sir Nigel Ralph, KCVO
Sowrey, *Air Marshal* Sir Frederick Beresford, KCB, CBE, AFC
Sparrow, Sir John, Kt.
Spearman, Sir Alexander Young Richard Mainwaring, Bt. (1840)
Spedding, *Prof.* Sir Colin Raymond William, Kt., CBE
Speed, Sir (Herbert) Keith, Kt., RD
Speelman, Sir Cornelis Jacob, Bt. (1686)
Spencer, Sir Derek Harold, Kt., QC
Spencer, *Vice-Adm.* Sir Peter, KCB
Spencer-Nairn, Sir Robert Arnold, Bt. (1933)
Spicer, Sir James Wilton, Kt.
Spicer, Sir Nicholas Adrian Albert, Bt. (1906)
Spiers, Sir Donald Maurice, Kt., CB, TD
Spooner, Sir James Douglas, Kt.
Spratt, *Col.* Sir Greville Douglas, GBE, TD
Spring, Sir Dryden Thomas, Kt.
Squire, *Air Chief Marshal* Sir Peter Ted, GCB, DFC, AFC, ADC
Stadlen, *Hon.* Sir Nicholas Felix, Kt.
Stagg, Sir Charles Richard Vernon, KCMG
Stainton, Sir (John) Ross, Kt., CBE
Staite, Sir Richard John, Kt., OBE
Stamer, Sir (Lovelace) Anthony, Bt. (1809)
Stanhope, *Adm.* Sir Mark, GCB, OBE, ADC
Stanier, Sir Beville Douglas, Bt. (1917)
Stanley, *Rt. Hon.* Sir John Paul, Kt., MP
Staples, Sir Richard Molesworth, Bt. (I. 1628)
Starkey, Sir John Philip, Bt. (1935)
Staughton, *Rt. Hon.* Sir Christopher Stephen Thomas Jonathan Thayer, Kt.
Stear, *Air Chief Marshal* Sir Michael James Douglas, KCB, CBE
Steel, *Hon.* Sir David William, Kt.
Steer, Sir Alan William, Kt.

Stephen, *Rt. Hon.* Sir Ninian Martin, KG, GCMG, GCVO, KBE
Stephens, Sir (Edwin) Barrie, Kt.
Stephens, Sir William Benjamin Synge, Kt.
Stephenson, Sir Henry Upton, Bt. (1936)
Stephenson, Sir Paul Robert, Kt., QPM
Sternberg, Sir Sigmund, Kt.
Stevens, Sir Jocelyn Edward Greville, Kt., CVO
Stevenson, Sir Hugh Alexander, Kt.
Stevenson, Sir Simpson, Kt.
Stewart, Sir Alan d'Arcy, Bt. (I. 1623)
Stewart, Sir Brian John, Kt., CBE
Stewart, Sir David James Henderson, Bt. (1957)
Stewart, Sir David John Christopher, Bt. (1803)
Stewart, Sir James Douglas, Kt.
Stewart, Sir James Moray, KCB
Stewart, Sir (John) Simon (Watson), Bt. (1920)
Stewart, Sir John Young, Kt., OBE
Stewart, Sir Patrick, Kt., OBE
Stewart, *Lt.-Col.* Sir Robert Christie, KCVO, CBE, TD
Stewart, Sir Robin Alastair, Bt. (1960)
Stewart, *Prof.* Sir William Duncan Paterson, Kt., FRS, FRSE
Stewart-Clark, Sir John, Bt. (1918)
Stewart-Richardson, Sir Simon Alaisdair, Bt. (S. 1630)
Stewart-Wilson, *Lt.-Col.* Sir Blair Aubyn, KCVO
Stibbon, *Gen.* Sir John James, KCB, OBE
Stirling, Sir Alexander John Dickson, KBE, CMG
Stirling, Sir Angus Duncan Aeneas, Kt.
Stirling-Hamilton, Sir Malcolm William Bruce, Bt. (S. 1673)
Stirling of Garden, *Col.* Sir James, KCVO, CBE, TD
Stirrup, *Air Chief Marshal* Sir Graham Eric (Jock), GCB, AFC, ADC
Stockdale, Sir Thomas Minshull, Bt. (1960)
Stoddart, *Prof.* Sir James Fraser, Kt.
Stoker, *Prof.* Sir Michael George Parke, Kt., CBE, FRCP, FRS, FRSE
Stonhouse, *Revd* Michael Philip, Bt. (1628 and 1670)
Stonor, *Air Marshal* Sir Thomas Henry, KCB
Stoppard, Sir Thomas, Kt., OM, CBE
Storey, *Hon.* Sir Richard, Bt., CBE (1960)
Stothard, Sir Peter Michael, Kt.
Stott, Sir Adrian George Ellingham, Bt. (1920)
Stoute, Sir Michael Ronald, Kt.
Stowe, Sir Kenneth Ronald, GCB, CVO
Stracey, Sir John Simon, Bt. (1818)
Strachan, Sir Curtis Victor, Kt., CVO
Strachey, Sir Charles, Bt. (1801)
Straker, Sir Louis Hilton, KCMG
Strang Steel, Sir (Fiennes) Michael, Bt. (1938)
Street, *Hon.* Sir Laurence Whistler, KCMG
Streeton, Sir Terence George, KBE, CMG
Strickland-Constable, Sir Frederic, Bt. (1641)
Stringer, Sir Donald Edgar, Kt., CBE
Stringer, Sir Howard, Kt.
Strong, Sir Roy Colin, Kt., PHD, FSA
Stronge, Sir James Anselan Maxwell, Bt. (1803)
Stuart, Sir James Keith, Kt.
Stuart, Sir Kenneth Lamonte, Kt.
†Stuart, Sir Phillip Luttrell, Bt. (1660)
†Stuart-Forbes, Sir William Daniel, Bt. (S. 1626)
Stuart-Menteth, Sir Charles Greaves, Bt. (1838)
Stuart-Paul, *Air Marshal* Sir Ronald Ian, KBE
Stuart-Smith, *Rt. Hon.* Sir Murray, Kt.
Stubbs, Sir William Hamilton, Kt., PHD
Stucley, *Lt.* Sir Hugh George Coplestone Bampfylde, Bt. (1859)
Studd, Sir Edward Fairfax, Bt. (1929)
Studholme, Sir Henry William, Bt. (1956)
Sturridge, Sir Nicholas Anthony, KCVO
Stuttard, Sir John Boothman, Kt.
†Style, Sir William Frederick, Bt. (1627)
Sullivan, *Rt. Hon.* Sir Jeremy Mirth, Kt.
Sullivan, Sir Richard Arthur, Bt. (1804)
Sulston, Sir John Edward, Kt.
Sumner, *Hon.* Sir Christopher John, Kt.
Sunderland, Sir John Michael, Kt.
Sutherland, Sir John Brewer, Bt. (1921)
Sutherland, Sir William George MacKenzie, Kt.
Sutton, *Air Marshal* Sir John Matthias Dobson, KCB
Sutton, Sir Richard Lexington, Bt. (1772)
Swaffield, Sir James Chesebrough, Kt., CBE, RD
Swaine, Sir John Joseph, Kt., CBE
Swan, Sir Conrad Marshall John Fisher, KCVO, PHD
Swan, Sir John William David, KBE
Swann, Sir Michael Christopher, Bt. (1906), TD
Sweeney, Sir George, Kt.
Sweeney, *Hon.* Sir Nigel Hamilton, Kt.
Sweeting, *Prof.* Sir Martin Nicholas, Kt., OBE, FRS
Sweetnam, Sir (David) Rodney, KCVO, CBE, FRCS
Swinburn, *Lt.-Gen.* Sir Richard Hull, KCB
Swinnerton-Dyer, *Prof.* Sir (Henry) Peter (Francis), Bt. (1678), KBE, FRS
Swinton, *Maj.-Gen.* Sir John, KCVO, OBE
Swire, Sir Adrian Christopher, Kt.
Swire, Sir John Anthony, Kt., CBE
Sykes, Sir David Michael, Bt. (1921)
Sykes, Sir Francis John Badcock, Bt. (1781)
Sykes, Sir Hugh Ridley, Kt.
Sykes, *Prof.* Sir (Malcolm) Keith, Kt.
Sykes, Sir Richard, Kt.
Sykes, Sir Tatton Christopher Mark, Bt. (1783)
Symons, *Vice-Adm.* Sir Patrick Jeremy, KBE
Synge, Sir Robert Carson, Bt. (1801)
Synnott, Sir Hilary Nicholas Hugh, KCMG

Talboys, *Rt. Hon.* Sir Brian Edward, CH, KCB
Tang, Sir David Wing-cheung, KBE
Tapps-Gervis-Meyrick, Sir George Christopher Cadafael, Bt. (1791)
Tapsell, Sir Peter Hannay Bailey, Kt., MP
Tate, Sir (Henry) Saxon, Bt. (1898)
Taureka, *Dr* Sir Reubeh, KBE
Tauvasa, Sir Joseph James, KBE
Tavare, Sir John, Kt., CBE
Tavener, *Prof.* Sir John Kenneth, Kt.
Taylor, Sir (Arthur) Godfrey, Kt.
Taylor, Sir Cyril Julian Hebden, GBE
Taylor, Sir Edward Macmillan (Teddy), Kt.
Taylor, Sir Hugh Henderson, KCB
Taylor, *Rt. Revd* John Bernard, KCVO
Taylor, *Dr* Sir John Michael, Kt., OBE
Taylor, *Prof.* Sir Martin John, Kt., FRS
Taylor, Sir Nicholas Richard Stuart, Bt. (1917)
Taylor, *Prof.* Sir William, Kt., CBE
Taylor, Sir William George, Kt.
Teagle, *Vice-Adm.* Sir Somerford Francis, KBE
Teare, *Hon.* Sir Nigel John Martin, Kt.
Teasdale, *Prof.* Sir Graham Michael, Kt.
Tebbit, Sir Donald Claude, GCMG
Tebbit, Sir Kevin Reginald, KCB, CMG
Telito, *HE Revd* Filoimea, GCMG, MBE
Temple, *Prof.* Sir John Graham, Kt.
Temple, Sir Richard, Bt. (1876), Chartier
Temu, *Hon. Dr* Sir Puka, KBE, CMG
Tennant, Sir Anthony John, Kt.
Tennyson-D'Eyncourt, Sir Mark Gervais, Bt. (1930)
Terry, *Air Marshal* Sir Colin George, KBE, CB
Terry, *Air Chief Marshal* Sir Peter David George, GCB, AFC
Thatcher, Sir Mark, Bt. (1990)
Thomas, Sir David John Godfrey, Bt. (1694)

Thomas, Sir Derek Morison David, KCMG
Thomas, Sir Gilbert Stanley, Kt., OBE
Thomas, Sir Jeremy Cashel, KCMG
Thomas, Sir (John) Alan, Kt.
Thomas, *Prof.* Sir John Meurig, Kt., FRS
Thomas, Sir Keith Vivian, Kt.
Thomas, *Dr* Sir Leton Felix, KCMG, CBE
Thomas, Sir Philip Lloyd, KCVO, CMG
Thomas, Sir Quentin Jeremy, Kt., CB
Thomas, *Rt. Hon.* Sir Roger John Laugharne, Kt.
Thomas, *Hon.* Sir Swinton Barclay, Kt.
Thomas, Sir William Michael, Bt. (1919)
Thomas, Sir (William) Michael (Marsh), Bt. (1918)
Thompson, Sir Christopher Peile, Bt. (1890)
Thompson, Sir Clive Malcolm, Kt.
Thompson, Sir David Albert, KCMG
Thompson, Sir Gilbert Williamson, Kt., OBE
Thompson, *Prof.* Sir Michael Warwick, Kt., DSC
Thompson, Sir Nicholas Annesley, Bt. (1963)
Thompson, Sir Nigel Cooper, KCMG, CBE
Thompson, Sir Paul Anthony, Bt. (1963)
Thompson, Sir Peter Anthony, Kt.
Thompson, *Dr* Sir Richard Paul Hepworth, KCVO
Thompson, Sir Thomas d'Eyncourt John, Bt. (1806)
Thomson, Sir (Frederick Douglas) David, Bt. (1929)
Thomson, Sir John Adam, GCMG
Thomson, Sir Mark Wilfrid Home, Bt. (1925)
Thomson, Sir Thomas James, Kt., CBE, FRCP
Thorn, Sir John Samuel, Kt., OBE
Thorne, Sir Neil Gordon, Kt., OBE, TD
Thornton, *Air Marshal* Sir Barry Michael, KCB
Thornton, Sir (George) Malcolm, Kt.
Thornton, Sir Peter Eustace, KCB
Thornton, Sir Richard Eustace, KCVO, OBE
†Thorold, Sir (Anthony) Oliver, Bt. (1642)
Thorpe, *Rt. Hon.* Sir Mathew Alexander, Kt.
Thurecht, Sir Ramon Richard, Kt., OBE
Thwaites, Sir Bryan, Kt., PHD
Tickell, Sir Crispin Charles Cervantes, GCMG, KCVO
Tidmarsh, Sir James Napier, KCVO, MBE
Tikaram, Sir Moti, KBE
Tilt, Sir Robin Richard, Kt.
Tiltman, Sir John Hessell, KCVO
Timmins, *Col.* Sir John Bradford, KCVO, OBE, TD
Tims, Sir Michael David, KCVO
Tindle, Sir Ray Stanley, Kt., CBE
Tirvengadum, Sir Harry Krishnan, Kt.
Tjoeng, Sir James Neng, KBE
Tod, *Vice-Adm.* Sir Jonathan James Richard, KCB, CBE
Todd, *Prof.* Sir David, Kt., CBE
Todd, Sir Ian Pelham, KBE, FRCS
Toka, Sir Mahuru Dadi, Kt., MBE
Tollemache, Sir Lyonel Humphry John, Bt. (1793)
Tomkys, Sir (William) Roger, KCMG
Tomlinson, *Prof.* Sir Bernard Evans, Kt., CBE
Tomlinson, Sir John Rowland, Kt., CBE
Tomlinson, Sir Michael John, Kt., CBE
Tomlinson, *Hon.* Sir Stephen Miles, Kt.
Tooke, *Prof.* Sir John Edward, Kt.
Tooley, Sir John, Kt.
ToRobert, Sir Henry Thomas, KBE
Torpy, *Air Marshal* Sir Glenn Lester, GCB, CBE, DSO
Torry, Sir Peter James, GCVO, KCMG
Tory, Sir Geofroy William, KCMG
Touche, Sir Anthony George, Bt. (1920)
Touche, Sir Rodney Gordon, Bt. (1962)
Toulson, *Rt. Hon.* Sir Roger Grenfell, Kt.
Tovadek, Sir Martin, Kt. CMG
Tovey, Sir Brian John Maynard, KCMG
ToVue, Sir Ronald, Kt., OBE
Towneley, Sir Simon Peter Edmund Cosmo William, KCVO
Townsend, Sir Cyril David, Kt.
Traill, Sir Alan Towers, GBE
Treacher, *Adm.* Sir John Devereux, KCB
Treacy, *Hon.* Sir Colman Maurice, Kt.
Treacy, *Hon.* Sir (James Mary) Seamus, Kt.
Treitel, *Prof.* Sir Guenter Heinz, Kt., FBA, QC
Trescowthick, Sir Donald Henry, KBE
Trevelyan, Sir Geoffrey Washington, Bt. (1662 and 1874)
Trezise, Sir Kenneth Bruce, Kt., OBE
Trippier, Sir David Austin, Kt., RD
Tritton, Sir Anthony John Ernest, Bt. (1905)
Trollope, Sir Anthony Simon, Bt. (1642)
Trotman-Dickenson, Sir Aubrey Fiennes, Kt.
Trotter, Sir Neville Guthrie, Kt.
Trotter, Sir Ronald Ramsay, Kt.
Troubridge, Sir Thomas Richard, Bt. (1799)
Trousdell, *Lt.-Gen.* Sir Philip Charles Cornwallis, KBE, CB
Truscott, Sir Ralph Eric Nicholson, Bt. (1909)
Tsang, Sir Donald Yam-keun, KBE
Tuamure-Maoate, *Dr* Sir Terepai, KBE
Tuck, Sir Bruce Adolph Reginald, Bt. (1910)
Tucker, *Hon.* Sir Richard Howard, Kt.
Tuckey, *Rt. Hon.* Sir Simon Lane, Kt.
Tugendhat, *Hon.* Sir Michael George, Kt.
Tuita, Sir Mariano Kelesimalefo, KBE
Tuite, Sir Christopher Hugh, Bt. (1622), PHD
Tuivaga, Sir Timoci Uluiburotu, Kt.
Tully, Sir William Mark, KBE
†Tupper, Sir Charles Hibbert, Bt. (1888)
Turbott, Sir Ian Graham, Kt., CMG, CVO
Turing, Sir John Dermot, Bt. (S. 1638)
Turner, Sir Colin William Carstairs, Kt., CBE, DFC
Turner, *Hon.* Sir Michael John, Kt.
Turnquest, Sir Orville Alton, GCMG, QC
Tusa, Sir John, Kt.
Tweedie, *Prof.* Sir David Philip, Kt.
Tyree, Sir (Alfred) William, Kt., OBE
Tyrwhitt, Sir Reginald Thomas Newman, Bt. (1919)

Underhill, *Hon.* Sir Nicholas Edward, Kt.
Underwood, *Prof.* Sir James Cressee Elphinstone, Kt.
Unwin, Sir (James) Brian, KCB
Ure, Sir John Burns, KCMG, LVO
Urquhart, Sir Brian Edward, KCMG, MBE
Urwick, Sir Alan Bedford, KCVO, CMG
Usher, Sir Andrew John, Bt. (1899)
Utting, Sir William Benjamin, Kt., CB

Vardy, Sir Peter, Kt.
Varney, Sir David Robert, Kt.
Vasquez, Sir Alfred Joseph, Kt., CBE, QC
Vassar-Smith, Sir John Rathbone, Bt. (1917)
Vavasour, Sir Eric Michael Joseph Marmaduke, Bt. (1828)
Veness, Sir David, Kt., CBE, QPM
Venner, Sir Kenneth Dwight Vincent, KBE
Vereker, Sir John Michael Medlicott, KCB
†Verney, Sir John Sebastian, Bt. (1946)
Verney, *Hon.* Sir Lawrence John, Kt., TD
†Verney, Sir Edmund Ralph, Bt. (1818)
Vernon, Sir James William, Bt. (1914)
Vernon, Sir (William) Michael, Kt.
Vestey, Sir Paul Edmund, Bt. (1921)
Vickers, *Prof.* Sir Brian William, Kt.
Vickers, Sir John Stuart, Kt.

Vickers, *Lt.-Gen.* Sir Richard Maurice Hilton, KCB, CVO, OBE
Vickers, Sir Roger Henry, KCVO
Viggers, *Lt-Gen.* Sir Frederick Richard, KCB, CMG, MBE
Viggers, Sir Peter John, Kt.
Vincent, Sir William Percy Maxwell, Bt. (1936)
Vineall, Sir Anthony John Patrick, Kt.
Vines, Sir William Joshua, Kt., CMG
von Schramek, Sir Eric Emil, Kt.
Vos, *Hon.* Sir Geoffrey Michael, Kt.
†Vyvyan, Sir Ralph Ferrers Alexander, Bt. (1645)

Wade-Gery, Sir Robert Lucian, KCMG, KCVO
Waena, Sir Nathaniel Rahumaea, GCMG
Waine, *Rt. Revd* John, KCVO
Waite, *Rt. Hon.* Sir John Douglas, Kt.
Waka, Sir Lucas Joseph, Kt., OBE
Wake, Sir Hereward, Bt. (1621), MC
Wakefield, Sir (Edward) Humphry (Tyrell), Bt. (1962)
Wakefield, Sir Norman Edward, Kt.
Wakefield, Sir Peter George Arthur, KBE, CMG
Wakeford, Sir Geoffrey Michael Montgomery, Kt., OBE
Wakeham, *Prof.* Sir William Arnot, Kt.
Wakeley, Sir John Cecil Nicholson, Bt. (1952), FRCS
Wald, *Prof.* Sir Nicholas John, Kt.
Wales, Sir Robert Andrew, Kt.
Waley-Cohen, Sir Stephen Harry, Bt. (1961)
Walford, Sir Christopher Rupert, Kt.
Walker, *Gen.* Sir Antony Kenneth Frederick, KCB
†Walker, Sir Christopher Robert Baldwin, Bt. (1856)
Walker, Sir David Alan, Kt.
Walker, Sir Harold Berners, KCMG
Walker, Sir John Ernest, Kt., DPHIL, FRS
Walker, *Air Marshal* Sir John Robert, KCB, CBE, AFC
Walker, Sir Miles Rawstron, Kt., CBE
Walker, Sir Patrick Jeremy, KCB
Walker, *Hon.* Sir Paul James, Kt.
Walker, Sir Rodney Myerscough, Kt.
Walker, Sir Roy Edward, Bt. (1906)
Walker, *Hon.* Sir Timothy Edward, Kt.
Walker, Sir Victor Stewart Heron, Bt. (1868)
Walker-Okeover, Sir Andrew Peter Monro, Bt. (1886)
Walker-Smith, Sir John Jonah, Bt. (1960)
Wall, Sir (John) Stephen, GCMG, LVO
Wall, *Rt. Hon.* Sir Nicholas Peter Rathbone, Kt.
Wall, *Gen.* Sir Peter Anthony, KCB, CBE
Wallace, *Lt.-Gen.* Sir Christopher Brooke Quentin, KBE
Wallace, *Prof.* David James, Kt., CBE, FRS
Waller, *Rt. Hon.* Sir (George) Mark, Kt.
Waller, Sir John Michael, Bt. (I. 1780)
Wallis, Sir Peter Gordon, KCVO
Wallis, Sir Timothy William, Kt.
Walmsley, *Vice-Adm.* Sir Robert, KCB
Walport, *Dr* Sir Mark Jeremy, Kt.
†Walsham, Sir Timothy John, Bt. (1831)
Walters, Sir Dennis Murray, Kt., MBE
Walters, Sir Frederick Donald, Kt.
Walters, Sir Peter Ingram, Kt.
Walters, Sir Roger Talbot, KBE, FRIBA
Wamiri, Sir Akapite, KBE
Wan, Sir Wamp, Kt., MBE
Wanless, Sir Derek, Kt.
Ward, *Rt. Hon.* Sir Alan Hylton, Kt.
Ward, Sir Austin, Kt., QC
Ward, *Prof.* Sir John MacQueen, Kt., CBE
Ward, Sir Joseph James Laffey, Bt. (1911)
Ward, Sir Timothy James, Kt.
Wardale, Sir Geoffrey Charles, KCB
Wardlaw, Sir Henry Justin, Bt. (NS. 1631)
Waring, Sir (Alfred) Holburt, Bt. (1935)
Warmington, Sir Rupert Marshall, Bt. (1908)
Warner, Sir (Edward Courtenay) Henry, Bt. (1910)
Warner, Sir Gerald Chierici, KCMG
Warren, Sir (Frederick) Miles, KBE
Warren, Sir Kenneth Robin, Kt.
Warren, Sir Nicholas Roger, Kt.
Wass, Sir Douglas William Gretton, GCB
Waterhouse, *Hon.* Sir Ronald Gough, GBE
Waterlow, Sir Christopher Rupert, Bt. (1873)
Waterlow, Sir (James) Gerard, Bt. (1930)
Waters, *Gen.* Sir (Charles) John, GCB, CBE
Waters, Sir (Thomas) Neil (Morris), Kt.
Waterworth, Sir Alan William, KCVO
Wates, Sir Christopher Stephen, Kt.
Watson, Sir Bruce Dunstan, Kt.
Watson, *Prof.* Sir David John, Kt., PHD
Watson, Sir (James) Andrew, Bt. (1866)
Watson, Sir Ronald Matthew, Kt., CBE
Watson, Sir Simon Conran Hamilton, Bt. (1895)
Watt, *Gen.* Sir Charles Redmond, KCB, KCVO, CBE, ADC
Watts, Sir John Augustus Fitzroy, KCMG, CBE
Watts, Sir Philip Beverley, KCMG
Weatherall, *Prof.* Sir David John, Kt., FRS
Weatherall, *Vice-Adm.* Sir James Lamb, KCVO, KBE
Weatherup, *Hon.* Sir Ronald Eccles, Kt.
Webb, *Prof.* Sir Adrian Leonard, Kt.
Webb-Carter, *Gen.* Sir Evelyn John, KCVO, OBE
Webster, *Vice-Adm.* Sir John Morrison, KCB
Wedgwood, Sir (Hugo) Martin, Bt. (1942)
Weekes, Sir Everton DeCourcey, KCMG, OBE
Weinberg, Sir Mark Aubrey, Kt.
Weir, *Hon.* Sir Reginald George, Kt.
Weir, Sir Roderick Bignell, Kt.
Welby, Sir (Richard) Bruno Gregory, Bt. (1801)
Welch, Sir John Reader, Bt. (1957)
Weldon, Sir Anthony William, Bt. (I. 1723)
Weller, Sir Arthur Burton, Kt., CBE
†Wells, Sir Christopher Charles, Bt. (1944)
Wells, Sir John Julius, Kt.
Wells, Sir William Henry Weston, Kt., FRICS
Wesker, Sir Arnold, Kt.
Westbrook, Sir Neil Gowanloch, Kt., CBE
Westmacott, Sir Peter John, KCMG
Weston, Sir Michael Charles Swift, KCMG, CVO
Weston, Sir (Philip) John, KCMG
Whalen, Sir Geoffrey Henry, Kt., CBE
Wheeler, Sir Harry Anthony, Kt., OBE
Wheeler, *Rt. Hon.* Sir John Daniel, Kt.
Wheeler, Sir John Frederick, Bt. (1920)
Wheeler, *Gen.* Sir Roger Neil, GCB, CBE
Wheeler-Booth, Sir Michael Addison John, KCB
Wheler, Sir Trevor Woodford, Bt. (1660)
Whitaker, Sir John James Ingham (Jack), Bt. (1936)
Whitbread, Sir Samuel Charles, KCVO
Whitchurch, Sir Graeme Ian, Kt., OBE
White, *Prof.* Sir Christopher John, Kt., CVO
White, Sir Christopher Robert Meadows, Bt. (1937)
White, Sir David (David Jason), Kt., OBE
White, Sir David Harry, Kt.
White, *Hon.* Sir Frank John, Kt.
White, Sir George Stanley James, Bt. (1904)
White, *Adm.* Sir Hugo Moresby, GCB, CBE
White, Sir John Woolmer, Bt. (1922)
White, Sir Nicholas Peter Archibald, Bt. (1802)
White, Sir Willard Wentworth, Kt., CBE

Whitehead, Sir John Stainton, GCMG, CVO
Whitehead, Sir Philip Henry Rathbone, Bt. (1889)
Whiteley, *Gen.* Sir Peter John Frederick, GCB, OBE, RM
Whitfield, Sir William, Kt., CBE
Whitmore, Sir Clive Anthony, GCB, CVO
Whitmore, Sir John Henry Douglas, Bt. (1954)
Whitney, Sir Raymond William, Kt., OBE
Whitson, Sir Keith Roderick, Kt.
Wickerson, Sir John Michael, Kt.
Wicks, Sir Nigel Leonard, GCB, CVO, CBE
†Wigan, Sir Michael Iain, Bt. (1898)
Wiggin, Sir Alfred William (Jerry), Kt., TD
†Wiggin, Sir Charles Rupert John, Bt. (1892)
†Wigram, Sir John Woolmore, Bt. (1805)
Wilbraham, Sir Richard Baker, Bt. (1776)
Wiles, *Prof.* Sir Andrew John, KBE
Wilkes, *Prof.* Sir Maurice Vincent, Kt.
Wilkes, *Gen.* Sir Michael John, KCB, CBE
Wilkie, *Hon.* Sir Alan Fraser, Kt.
Wilkinson, Sir (David) Graham (Brook) Bt. (1941)
Wilkinson, *Prof.* Sir Denys Haigh, Kt., FRS
Willcocks, Sir David Valentine, Kt., CBE, MC
Willcocks, *Lt.-Gen.* Sir Michael Alan, KCB, CVO
Williams, Sir (Arthur) Gareth Ludovic Emrys Rhys, Bt. (1918)
Williams, *Prof.* Sir Bruce Rodda, KBE
Williams, Sir Charles Othniel, Kt.
Williams, Sir Daniel Charles, GCMG, QC
Williams, *Adm.* Sir David, GCB
Williams, Sir David Innes, Kt.
Williams, Sir David Reeve, Kt., CBE
Williams, *Hon.* Sir Denys Ambrose, KCMG
Williams, Sir Donald Mark, Bt. (1866)
Williams, *Prof.* Sir (Edward) Dillwyn, Kt., FRCP
Williams, Sir Francis Owen Garbett, Kt., CBE
Williams, *Hon.* Sir (John) Griffith, Kt.
Williams, Sir (Lawrence) Hugh, Bt. (1798)
Williams, Sir Osmond, Bt. (1909), MC
Williams, Sir Peter Michael, Kt.
Williams, Sir (Robert) Philip Nathaniel, Bt. (1915)
Williams, Sir Robin Philip, Bt. (1953)
Williams, *Prof.* Sir Roger, Kt.
Williams, Sir (William) Maxwell (Harries), Kt.
Williams, *Hon.* Sir Wyn Lewis
Williams-Bulkeley, Sir Richard Thomas, Bt. (1661)
Williams-Wynn, Sir David Watkin, Bt. (1688)
Williamson, Sir George Malcolm, Kt.
Williamson, *Marshal of the Royal Air Force* Sir Keith Alec, GCB, AFC
Williamson, Sir Robert Brian, Kt., CBE
Willink, Sir Edward Daniel, Bt. (1957)
Wills, Sir David James Vernon, Bt. (1923)
Wills, Sir David Seton, Bt. (1904)
Wilmot, Sir David, Kt., QPM
Wilmot, Sir Henry Robert, Bt. (1759)
Wilmut, *Prof.* Sir Ian, Kt., OBE
Wilsey, *Gen.* Sir John Finlay Willasey, GCB, CBE
Wilshaw, Sir Michael, Kt.
Wilson, *Prof.* Sir Alan Geoffrey, Kt.
Wilson, Sir Anthony, Kt.
Wilson, *Vice-Adm.* Sir Barry Nigel, KCB
Wilson, Sir David, Bt. (1920)
Wilson, Sir David Mackenzie, Kt.
Wilson, Sir James William Douglas, Bt. (1906)
Wilson, *Brig.* Sir Mathew John Anthony, Bt. (1874), OBE, MC
Wilson, *Rt. Hon.* Sir Nicholas Allan Roy, Kt.
Wilson, Sir Robert Peter, KCMG
Wilson, *Air Chief Marshal* Sir (Ronald) Andrew (Fellowes), KCB, AFC
Wilton, Sir (Arthur) John, KCMG, KCVO, MC
Wingate, *Capt.* Sir Miles Buckley, KCVO
Winkley, Sir David Ross, Kt.
Winnington, Sir Anthony Edward, Bt. (1755)
Winship, Sir Peter James Joseph, Kt., CBE
Winter, *Dr* Sir Gregory Winter, Kt., CBE
Winterton, Sir Nicholas Raymond, Kt.
Wisdom, Sir Norman, Kt., OBE
Wiseman, Sir John William, Bt. (1628)
Wolfendale, *Prof.* Sir Arnold Whittaker, Kt., FRS
Wolseley, Sir Charles Garnet Richard Mark, Bt. (1628)
†Wolseley, Sir James Douglas, Bt. (I. 1745)
†Wombell, Sir George Philip Frederick, Bt. (1778)
Womersley, Sir Peter John Walter, Bt. (1945)
Woo, Sir Leo Joseph, Kt.
Woo, Sir Po-Shing, Kt.
Wood, Sir Andrew Marley, GCMG
Wood, Sir Anthony John Page, Bt. (1837)
Wood, Sir Ian Clark, Kt., CBE
Wood, *Hon.* Sir John Kember, Kt., MC
Wood, Sir Martin Francis, Kt., OBE
Wood, Sir Michael Charles, KCMG
Wood, *Hon.* Sir Roderic Lionel James, Kt.
Woodard, *Rear Adm.* Sir Robert Nathaniel, KCVO
Woodcock, Sir John, Kt., CBE, QPM
Woodhead, *Vice-Adm.* Sir (Anthony) Peter, KCB
Woodhouse, *Rt. Hon.* Sir (Arthur) Owen, KBE, DSC
Woodroffe, *Most Revd* George Cuthbert Manning, KBE
Woods, Sir Robert Kynnersley, Kt., CBE
Woodward, Sir Clive Ronald, Kt., OBE
Woodward, *Adm.* Sir John Forster, GBE, KCB
Woodward, Sir Thomas Jones (Tom Jones), Kt., OBE
Worsley, *Gen.* Sir Richard Edward, GCB, OBE
Worsley, Sir (William) Marcus (John), Bt. (1838)
Worsthorne, Sir Peregrine Gerard, Kt.
Wratten, *Air Chief Marshal* Sir William John, GBE, CB, AFC
Wraxall, Sir Charles Frederick Lascelles, Bt. (1813)
Wrey, Sir George Richard Bourchier, Bt. (1628)
Wrigglesworth, Sir Ian William, Kt.
Wright, Sir Allan Frederick, KBE
Wright, Sir David John, GCMG, LVO
Wright, *Hon.* Sir (John) Michael, Kt.
Wright, *Prof.* Sir Nicholas Alcwyn, Kt.
Wright, Sir Peter Robert, Kt., CBE
Wright, *Air Marshal* Sir Robert Alfred, KBE, AFC
Wright, Sir Stephen John Leadbetter, KCMG
Wrightson, Sir Charles Mark Garmondsway, Bt. (1900)
Wrigley, *Prof.* Sir Edward Anthony (Sir Tony), Kt., PHD, PBA
Wrixon-Becher, Sir John William Michael, Bt. (1831)
Wroughton, Sir Philip Lavallin, KCVO
Wu, Sir Gordon Ying Sheung, KCMG
Wynne, Sir Graham Robert, Kt., CBE

Yacoub, *Prof.* Sir Magdi Habib, Kt., FRCS
Yaki, Sir Roy, KBE
Yang, *Hon.* Sir Ti Liang, Kt.
Yapp, Sir Stanley Graham, Kt.
Yardley, Sir David Charles Miller, Kt., LLD
Yarrow, Sir Eric Grant, Bt. (1916), MBE
Yocklunn, Sir John (Soong Chung), KCVO
Yoo Foo, Sir (François) Henri, Kt.
Young, Sir Brian Walter Mark, Kt.
Young, Sir Colville Norbert, GCMG, MBE
Young, Sir Dennis Charles, KCMG

Young, *Rt. Hon.* Sir George Samuel Knatchbull, Bt. (1813)
Young, Sir Jimmy Leslie Ronald, Kt., CBE
Young, Sir John Kenyon Roe, Bt. (1821)
Young, Sir John Robertson, GCMG
Young, Sir Leslie Clarence, Kt., CBE
Young, Sir Nicholas Charles, Kt.
Young, Sir Robin Urquhart, KCB
Young, Sir Roger William, Kt.
Young, Sir Stephen Stewart Templeton, Bt. (1945)
Young, Sir William Neil, Bt. (1769)
Younger, Sir Julian William Richard, Bt. (1911)
Yuwi, Sir Matiabe, KBE

Zeeman, *Prof.* Sir (Erik) Christopher, Kt., FRS
Zissman, Sir Bernard Philip, Kt.
Zochonis, Sir John Basil, Kt.
Zunz, Sir Gerhard Jacob (Jack), Kt., FRENG
Zurenuoc, Sir Zibang, KBE

BARONETESS

Maxwell Macdonald (formerly Stirling-Maxwell), Dame Ann, Btss. (NS 1682)

THE ORDER OF ST JOHN

THE MOST VENERABLE ORDER OF THE HOSPITAL OF ST JOHN OF JERUSALEM (1888)

GCStJ	Bailiff/Dame Grand Cross
KStJ	Knight of Justice/Grace
DStJ	Dame of Justice/Grace
CStJ	Commander
OstJ	Officer
SBStJ	Serving Brother
SSStJ	Serving Sister

Motto, Pro Fide, Pro Utilitate Hominum

The Order of St John, founded in the early 12th century in Jerusalem, was a religious order with a particular duty to care for the sick. In Britain the order was dissolved by Henry VIII in 1540 but the British branch was revived in the early 19th century. The branch was not accepted by the Grand Magistracy of the Order in Rome but its search for a role in the tradition of the hospitallers led to the founding of the St John Ambulance Association in 1877 and later the St John Ambulance Brigade; in 1882 the St John Ophthalmic Hospital was founded in Jerusalem. A royal charter was granted in 1888 establishing the Order of St John as a British Order of Chivalry with the sovereign as its head.

Since October 1999 the whole order worldwide has been governed by a Grand Council which includes a representative from each of the eight priories (England, Scotland, Wales, South Africa, New Zealand, Canada, Australia and the USA). In addition there are also two commanderies in Northern Ireland and Western Australia. There are also branches in about 30 other Commonwealth countries. Apart from the St John Ambulance Foundation, the Order is also responsible for the Jerusalem Eye Hospital. Admission to the order is usually conferred in recognition of service to either one of these institutions. Membership does not confer any rank, style, title or precedence on a recipient.

SOVEREIGN HEAD OF THE ORDER
HM The Queen

GRAND PRIOR
HRH The Duke of Gloucester, KG, GCVO

Lord Prior, Prof. Anthony Mellows, OBE, TD
Prelate, Rt. Revd John Nicholls
Deputy Lord Prior, Capt. Sir Norman Lloyd-Edwards, KCVO, RD, RNR
Sub Prior, Prof. Villis Marshall, AC
Secretary General, Rear-Adm. Andrew Gough, CB
Headquarters, 3 Charterhouse Mews, London EC1M 6BB
T 020-7251 3292

DAMES

DAMES GRAND CROSS AND DAMES COMMANDERS

Style, 'Dame' before forename and surname, followed by appropriate post-nominal initials. Where such an award is made to a lady already in possession of a higher title, the appropriate initials follow her name
Envelope, Dame F_ S_, followed by appropriate post-nominal letters. *Letter (formal),* Dear Madam; *(social),* Dear Dame F_. *Spoken,* Dame F_
Husband, Untitled

Dame Grand Cross and Dame Commander are the higher classes for women of the Order of the Bath, the Order of St Michael and St George, the Royal Victorian Order, and the Order of the British Empire. Dames Grand Cross rank after the wives of Baronets and before the wives of Knights Grand Cross. Dames Commanders rank after the wives of Knights Grand Cross and before the wives of Knights Commanders.

Honorary Dames Commanders may be conferred on women who are citizens of countries of which the Queen is not head of state.

LIST OF DAMES
As at 31 August 2010

Women peers in their own right and life peers are not included in this list. Female members of the royal family are not included in this list; details of the orders they hold can be found within the Royal Family section.

If a dame has a double barrelled or hyphenated surname, she is listed under the first element of the name. *A full entry in italic type* indicates that the recipient of an honour died during the year in which the honour was conferred. The name is included for the purposes of record.

Abaijah, Dame Josephine, DBE
Abramsky, Dame Jennifer Gita, DBE
Airlie, The Countess of, DCVO
Albemarle, The Countess of, DBE
Allen, *Prof.* Dame Ingrid Victoria, DBE
Andrews, Dame Julie, DBE
Anglesey, The Marchioness of, DBE
Anson, Lady (Elizabeth Audrey), DBE
Anstee, Dame Margaret Joan, DCMG
Arden, *Rt. Hon.* Dame Mary Howarth (Mrs Mance), DBE
Atkins, Dame Eileen, DBE
Baker, Dame Janet Abbott (Mrs Shelley), CH, DBE
Bakewell, Dame Joan Dawson, DBE
Barbour, Dame Margaret (Mrs Ash), DBE
Baron, *Hon.* Dame Florence Jacqueline, DBE
Barrow, Dame Jocelyn Anita (Mrs Downer), DBE
Barstow, Dame Josephine Clare (Mrs Anderson), DBE
Bassey, Dame Shirley, DBE
Beasley, *Prof.* Dame Christine Joan, DBE
Beaurepaire, Dame Beryl Edith, DBE
Beer, *Prof.* Dame Gillian Patricia Kempster, DBE, FBA
Beral, *Prof.* Dame Valerie, DBE
Bergquist, *Prof.* Dame Patricia Rose, DBE
Bertschinger, *Dr* Dame Claire, DBE
Bevan, Dame Yasmin, DBE
Bewley, Dame Beulah Rosemary, DBE
Bibby, Dame Enid, DBE
Black, *Prof.* Dame Carol Mary, DBE
Black, *Hon.* Dame Jill Margaret, DBE
Blackadder, Dame Elizabeth Violet, DBE
Blaize, Dame Venetia Ursula, DBE
Blaxland, Dame Helen Frances, DBE
Blume, Dame Hilary Sharon Braverman, DBE
Booth, *Hon.* Dame Margaret Myfanwy Wood, DBE
Bowtell, Dame Ann Elizabeth, DCB
Boyd, Dame Vivienne Myra, DBE
Brain, Dame Margaret Anne (Mrs Wheeler), DBE
Brennan, Dame Maureen, DBE
Bridges, Dame Mary Patricia, DBE
Brindley, Dame Lynne Janie, DBE
Brittan, Dame Diana (Lady Brittan of Spennithorne), DBE
Browne, Lady Moyra Blanche Madeleine, DBE
Buckland, Dame Yvonne Helen Elaine, DBE
Burnell, *Prof.* Dame Susan Jocelyn Bell, DBE
Burslem, Dame Alexandra Vivien, DBE
Byatt, Dame Antonia Susan, DBE, FRSL
Bynoe, Dame Hilda Louisa, DBE
Caldicott, Dame Fiona, DBE, FRCP, FRCPSYCH
Cameron, *Prof.* Dame Averil Millicent, DBE
Campbell-Preston, Dame Frances Olivia, DCVO
Cartwright, Dame Silvia Rose, DBE
Clark, *Prof.* Dame Jill MacLeod, DBE
Clark, *Prof.* Dame (Margaret) June, DBE, PHD
Clayton, Dame Barbara Evelyn (Mrs Klyne), DBE
Cleverdon, Dame Julia Charity, DCVO, CBE
Collarbone, Dame Patricia, DBE
Contreras, *Prof.* Dame Marcela, DBE
Corsar, *Hon.* Dame Mary Drummond, DBE
Coward, Dame Pamela Sarah, DBE
Cox, *Hon.* Dame Laura Mary, DBE
Dacon, Dame Monica Jessie, DBE, CMG
Davies, *Prof.* Dame Kay Elizabeth, DBE
Davies, *Hon.* Dame Nicola Velfor, DBE
Davies, *Prof.* Dame Sally Claire, DBE
Davies, Dame Wendy Patricia, DBE
Davis, Dame Karlene Cecile, DBE
Dawson, *Prof.* Dame Sandra Jane Noble, DBE
Dell, Dame Miriam Patricia, DBE
Dench, Dame Judith Olivia (Mrs Williams), CH, DBE
Descartes, Dame Marie Selipha Sesenne, DBE, BEM
Devonshire, The Duchess of, DCVO
Digby, Lady, DBE
Dobbs, *Hon.* Dame Linda Penelope, DBE
Docherty, Dame Jacqueline, DBE
Donald, *Prof.* Dame Athene Margaret, DBE, FRS
Dowling, *Prof.* Dame Ann Patricia, DBE
Duffield, Dame Vivien Louise, DBE
Dumont, Dame Ivy Leona, DCMG
Dunnell, Dame Karen, DCB
Dyche, Dame Rachael Mary, DBE
Elcoat, Dame Catherine Elizabeth, DBE
Ellison, Dame Jill, DBE
Else, Dame Jean, DBE

Elton, Dame Susan Richenda (Lady Elton), DCVO
Engel, Dame Pauline Frances (Sister Pauline Engel), DBE
Esteve-Coll, Dame Elizabeth Anne Loosemore, DBE
Evans, Dame Anne Elizabeth Jane, DBE
Evans, Dame Madeline Glynne Dervel, DBE, CMG
Farnham, Dame Marion (Lady Farnham), DCVO
Fawcett, Dame Amelia Chilcott, DBE
Fenner, Dame Peggy Edith, DBE
Fielding, Dame Pauline, DBE
Finch, *Prof.* Dame Janet Valerie, DBE
Fisher, Dame Jacqueline, DBE
Forgan, Dame Elizabeth Anne Lucy, DBE
Furse, Dame Clara Hedwig Frances, DBE
Fradd, Dame Elizabeth, DBE
Fraser, Dame Dorothy Rita, DBE
Friend, Dame Phyllis Muriel, DBE
Fry, Dame Margaret Louise, DBE
Gallagher, Dame Monica Josephine, DBE
Gaymer, Dame Janet Marion, DBE, QC
Ghosh, Dame Helen Frances, DCB
Glen-Haig, Dame Mary Alison, DBE
Glenn, *Prof.* Dame Hazel Gillian, DBE
Glennie, *Dr* Dame Evelyn Elizabeth Ann, DBE
Gloster, *Hon.* Dame Elisabeth (Lady Popplewell), DBE
Glover, Dame Audrey Frances, DBE, CMG
Goodall, *Dr* Dame (Valerie) Jane, DBE
Goodfellow, *Prof.* Dame Julia Mary, DBE
Goodman, Dame Barbara, DBE
Gordon, Dame Minita Elmira, GCMG, GCVO
Gordon, *Hon.* Dame Pamela Felicity, DBE
Gow, Dame Jane Elizabeth (Mrs Whiteley), DBE
Grafton, The Duchess of, GCVO
Grant, Dame Mavis, DBE
Green, Dame Pauline, DBE
Grey, Dame Beryl Elizabeth (Mrs Svenson), DBE
Griffiths, Dame Anne, DCVO
Grimthorpe, The Lady, DCVO
Guilfoyle, Dame Margaret Georgina Constance, DBE
Guthardt, *Revd Dr* Dame Phyllis Myra, DBE
Hakin, *Dr* Dame Barbara Ann, DBE
Hall, *Prof.* Dame Wendy, DBE
Hallett, *Rt. Hon.* Dame Heather Carol, DBE
Harbison, Dame Joan Irene, DBE
Harper, Dame Elizabeth Margaret Way, DBE
Harris, Lady Pauline, DBE
Hassan, Dame Anna Patricia Lucy, DBE
Hay, Dame Barbara Logan, DCMG, MBE
Henderson, Dame Fiona Douglas, DCVO
Hercus, *Hon.* Dame (Margaret) Ann, DCMG
Higgins, *Prof.* Dame Joan Margaret, DBE
Higgins, *Prof.* Dame Julia Stretton, DBE, FRS
Higgins, *Prof.* Dame Rosalyn, DBE, QC
Hill, *Air Cdre* Dame Felicity Barbara, DBE
Hine, Dame Deirdre Joan, DBE, FRCP
Hodgson, Dame Patricia Anne, DBE
Hogg, *Hon.* Dame Mary Claire (Mrs Koops), DBE
Holborow, Lady Mary Christina, DCVO
Hollows, Dame Sharon, DBE
Holmes, Dame Kelly, DBE
Holroyd, Lady Margaret, DBE
Holt, Dame Denise Mary, DCMG
Hoodless, Dame Elisabeth Anne, DBE
Hufton, *Prof.* Dame Olwen, DBE
Husband, *Prof.* Dame Janet Elizabeth Siarey, DBE
Hussey, Dame Susan Katharine (Lady Hussey of North Bradley), DCVO
Hutton, Dame Deirdre Mary, DBE
Imison, Dame Tamsyn, DBE
Ion, *Dr* Dame Susan Elizabeth, DBE
Isaacs, Dame Albertha Madeline, DBE
James, Dame Naomi Christine (Mrs Haythorne), DBE
Jenkins, Dame (Mary) Jennifer (Lady Jenkins of Hillhead), DBE
Johnson, *Prof.* Dame Louise Napier, DBE, FRS
Jonas, Dame Judith Mayhew
Jones, Dame Gwyneth (Mrs Haberfeld-Jones), DBE
Jordan, *Prof.* Dame Carole, DBE
Keegan, Dame Elizabeth Mary, DBE
Keegan, Dame Geraldine Mary Marcella, DBE
Kekedo, Dame Rosalina Violet, DBE
Kelleher, Dame Joan, DBE
Kellett-Bowman, Dame (Mary) Elaine, DBE
Kelly, Dame Barbara Mary, DBE
Kelly, Dame Lorna May Boreland, DBE
Kershaw, Dame Janet Elizabeth Murray (Dame Betty), DBE
Kettlewell, *Comdt.* Dame Marion Mildred, DBE
Kidu, Lady, DBE
King, *Hon.* Dame Eleanor Warwick, DBE
Kinnair, Dame Donna, DBE
Kirby, Dame Carolyn Emma, DBE
Kirby, Dame Georgina Kamiria, DBE
Kramer, *Prof.* Dame Leonie Judith, DBE
Laine, Dame Cleo (Clementine) Dinah (Lady Dankworth), DBE
Lake-Tack, *HE* Dame Louise Agnetha, GCMG
Lamb, Dame Dawn Ruth, DBE
Leather, Dame Susan Catherine, DBE
Leslie, Dame Ann Elizabeth Mary, DBE
Lewis, Dame Edna Leofrida (Lady Lewis), DBE
Lott, Dame Felicity Ann Emwhyla (Mrs Woolf), DBE
Louisy, Dame (Calliopa) Pearlette, GCMG
Lynn, Dame Vera (Mrs Lewis), DBE
MacArthur, Dame Ellen Patricia, DBE
Macdonald, Dame Mary Beaton, DBE
McDonald, Dame Mavis, DCB
Macmillan of Ovenden, Katharine, Viscountess, DBE
Macur, *Hon.* Dame Julia Wendy, DBE
Mayhew, Dame Judith, DBE
Major, Dame Malvina Lorraine (Mrs Fleming), DBE
Major, Dame Norma Christina Elizabeth, DBE
Marsden, *Dr* Dame Rosalind Mary, DCMG
Marsh, Dame Mary Elizabeth, DBE
Mason, Dame Monica Margaret, DBE
Mellor, Dame Julie Thérèse Mellor, DBE
Metge, *Dr* Dame (Alice) Joan, DBE
Middleton, Dame Elaine Madoline, DCMG, MBE
Mills, Dame Barbara Jean Lyon, DBE, QC
Mirren, Dame Helen, DBE
Monroe, *Prof.* Dame Barbara, DBE
Moores, Dame Yvonne, DBE
Morgan, *Dr* Dame Gillian Margaret, DBE
Morrison, *Hon.* Dame Mary Anne, DCVO
Muirhead, Dame Lorna Elizabeth Fox, DBE
Muldoon, Lady Thea Dale, DBE, QSO
Mullally, *Revd* Dame Sarah Elisabeth, DBE
Mumford, Lady Mary Katharine, DCVO
Murdoch, Dame Elisabeth Joy, DBE
Nelson, *Prof.* Dame Janet Laughland, DBE
Neville, Dame Elizabeth, DBE, QPM
Ogilvie, Dame Bridget Margaret, DBE, PHD, DSC
Oliver, Dame Gillian Frances, DBE
Ollerenshaw, Dame Kathleen Mary, DBE, DPHIL
Owers, Dame Anne Elizabeth (Mrs Cook), DBE
Oxenbury, Dame Shirley Anne, DBE
Paraskeva, *Rt. Hon.* Dame Janet, DBE

Park, Dame Merle Florence (Mrs Bloch), DBE
Parker, *Hon.* Dame Judith Mary Frances, DBE
Partridge, *Prof.* Dame Linda, DBE
Pauffley, *Hon.* Dame Anna Evelyn Hamilton, DBE
Penhaligon, Dame Annette (Mrs Egerton), DBE
Perkins, Dame Mary Lesley, DBE
Peters, Dame Mary Elizabeth, DBE
Pindling, Lady (Marguerite M.), DCMG
Platt, Dame Denise, DBE
Plowright, Dame Joan Ann, DBE
Polak, *Prof.* Dame Julia Margaret, DBE
Poole, Dame Avril Anne Barker, DBE
Porter, Dame Shirley (Lady Porter), DBE
Powell, Dame Sally Ann Vickers, DBE
Prendergast, Dame Simone Ruth, DBE
Price, Dame Margaret Berenice, DBE
Pringle, Dame Anne Fyfe, DCMG
Proudman, *Hon.* Dame Sonia Rosemary Susan, DBE
Pugh, *Dr* Dame Gillian Mary, DBE
Quinn, Dame Sheila Margaret Imelda, DBE
Rafferty, *Hon.* Dame Anne Judith, DBE
Rawson, *Prof.* Dame Jessica Mary, DBE
Rebuck, Dame Gail Ruth, DBE
Rees, *Prof.* Dame Lesley Howard, DBE
Reeves, Dame Helen May, DBE
Rego, Dame Paula Figueiroa, DBE
Reynolds, Dame Fiona Claire, DBE
Richardson, Dame Mary, DBE
Rigg, Dame Diana, DBE
Rimington, Dame Stella, DCB
Ritterman, Dame Janet, DBE
Roberts, Dame Jane Elisabeth, DBE
Robins, Dame Ruth Laura, DBE
Robottom, Dame Marlene, DBE
Roe, Dame Marion Audrey, DBE
Roe, Dame Raigh Edith, DBE
Ronson, Dame Gail, DBE
Rothwell, *Prof.* Dame Nancy Jane, DBE
Runciman of Doxford, The Viscountess, DBE
Russell, *Dr* Dame Philippa Margaret, DBE
Salas, Dame Margaret Laurence, DBE
Salmond, *Prof.* Dame Mary Anne, DBE
Savill, Dame Rosalind Joy, DBE
Sawyer, *Rt. Hon.* Dame Joan Augusta, DBE
Scardino, Dame Marjorie, DBE
Scott, Dame Catherine Margaret (Mrs Denton), DBE
Seward, Dame Margaret Helen Elizabeth, DBE
Sharp, *Hon.* Dame Victoria Madeleine, DBE
Shedrick, *Dr* Dame Daphne Marjorie, DBE
Shirley, Dame Stephanie, DBE
Shovelton, Dame Helena, DBE
Sibley, Dame Antoinette (Mrs Corbett), DBE
Silver, *Dr* Dame Ruth Muldoon, DBE
Slade, *Hon.* Dame Elizabeth Ann, DBE
Smith, Dame Dela, DBE
Smith, *Rt. Hon.* Dame Janet Hilary (Mrs Mathieson), DBE
Smith, *Hon.* Dame Jennifer Meredith, DBE
Smith, Dame Margaret Natalie (Maggie) (Mrs Cross), DBE
Soames, Lady Mary, KG, DBE
Southgate, *Prof.* Dame Lesley Jill, DBE
Spencer, Dame Rosemary Jane, DCMG
Steel, *Hon.* Dame (Anne) Heather (Mrs Beattie), DBE
Stocking, Dame Barbara Mary, DBE
Strachan, Dame Valerie Patricia Marie, DCB
Strathern, *Prof.* Dame Anne Marilyn, DBE
Strathie, Dame Lesley Ann, DCB
Street, Dame Susan Ruth, DCB
Stringer, *Prof.* Dame Joan Kathleen, DBE
Sutherland, Dame Joan (Mrs Bonynge), OM, DBE
Sutherland, Dame Veronica Evelyn, DBE, CMG
Swift, *Hon.* Dame Caroline Jane (Mrs Openshaw), DBE, QC
Symmonds, Dame Olga Patricia, DBE
Tanner, *Dr* Dame Mary Elizabeth, DBE
Taylor, Dame Elizabeth, DBE
Taylor, Dame Meg, DBE
Te Kanawa, Dame Kiri Janette, DBE
Thomas, *Prof.* Dame Jean Olwen, DBE
Thomas, Dame Maureen Elizabeth (Lady Thomas), DBE
Tickell, Dame Clare Oriana, DBE
Tinson, Dame Sue, DBE
Tizard, Dame Catherine Anne, GCMG, GCVO, DBE
Tokiel, Dame Rosa, DBE
Trotter, Dame Janet Olive, DBE
Turner-Warwick, Dame Margaret Elizabeth Harvey, DBE, FRCP, FRCPED
Twelftree, Dame Marcia, DBE
Uchida, Dame Mitsuko, DBE
Uprichard, Dame Mary Elizabeth, DBE
Varley, Dame Joan Fleetwood, DBE
Wagner, Dame Gillian Mary Millicent (Lady Wagner), DBE
Wall, Dame (Alice) Anne, (Mrs Michael Wall), DCVO
Wallis, Dame Sheila Ann, DBE
Warburton, Dame Anne Marion, DCVO, CMG
Waterhouse, Dr Dame Rachel Elizabeth, DBE
Waterman, *Dr* Dame Fanny, DBE
Webb, *Prof.* Dame Patricia, DBE
Weir, Dame Gillian Constance (Mrs Phelps), DBE
Weller, Dame Rita, DBE
Weston, Dame Margaret Kate, DBE
Westwood, Dame Vivienne Isabel, DBE
Wheldon, Dame Juliet Louise, DCB, QC
Williams, Dame Josephine, DBE
Wilson, Dame Jacqueline, DBE
Wilson-Barnett, *Prof.* Dame Jenifer, DBE
Winstone, Dame Dorothy Gertrude, DBE, CMG
Wong Yick-ming, Dame Rosanna, DBE
Zaffar, Dame Naila, DBE

DECORATIONS AND MEDALS

PRINCIPAL DECORATIONS AND MEDALS

IN ORDER OF WEAR

VICTORIA CROSS (VC), 1856 (*see* below)
GEORGE CROSS (GC), 1940 (*see* below)

BRITISH ORDERS OF KNIGHTHOOD (*see also* Orders of Chivalry)
Order of the Garter
Order of the Thistle
Order of St Patrick
Order of the Bath
Order of Merit
Order of the Star of India
Order of St Michael and George
Order of the Indian Empire
Order of the Crown of India
Royal Victorian Order (Classes I, II and III)
Order of the British Empire (Classes I, II and III)
Order of the Companions of Honour
Distinguished Service Order
Royal Victorian Order (Class IV)
Order of the British Empire (Class IV)
Imperial Service Order
Royal Victorian Order (Class V)
Order of the British Empire (Class V)

BARONET'S BADGE

KNIGHT BACHELOR'S BADGE

INDIAN ORDER OF MERIT (MILITARY)

DECORATIONS
Conspicuous Gallantry Cross (CGC), 1995
Royal Red Cross Class I (RRC), 1883
Distinguished Service Cross (DSC), 1914
Military Cross (MC), December 1914
Distinguished Flying Cross (DFC), 1918
Air Force Cross (AFC), 1918
Royal Red Cross Class II (ARRC)
Order of British India
Kaisar-i-Hind Medal
Order of St John

MEDALS FOR GALLANTRY AND DISTINGUISHED CONDUCT
Union of South Africa Queen's Medal for Bravery, in Gold
Distinguished Conduct Medal (DCM), 1854
Conspicuous Gallantry Medal (CGM), 1874
Conspicuous Gallantry Medal (Flying)
George Medal (GM), 1940
Queen's Police Medal for Gallantry
Queen's Fire Service Medal for Gallantry
Royal West African Frontier Force Distinguished Conduct Medal
King's African Rifles Distinguished Conduct Medal
Indian Distinguished Service Medal
Union of South Africa Queen's Medal for Bravery, in Silver
Distinguished Service Medal (DSM), 1914
Military Medal (MM), 1916
Distinguished Flying Medal (DFM), 1918
Air Force Medal (AFM)
Constabulary Medal (Ireland)
Medal for Saving Life at Sea (Sea Gallantry Medal)
Indian Order of Merit (Civil)
Indian Police Medal for Gallantry
Ceylon Police Medal for Gallantry
Sierra Leone Police Medal for Gallantry
Sierra Leone Fire Brigades Medal for Gallantry
Colonial Police Medal for Gallantry (CPM)
Queen's Gallantry Medal (QGM), 1974
Royal Victorian Medal (RVM), Gold, Silver and Bronze
British Empire Medal (BEM)
Canada Medal
Queen's Police Medal for Distinguished Service (QPM)
Queen's Fire Service Medal for Distinguished Service (QFSM)
Queen's Volunteer Reserves Medal
Queen's Medal for Chiefs

CAMPAIGN MEDALS AND STARS
Including authorised United Nations, European Community/Union and North Atlantic Treaty Organisation medals (in order of date of campaign for which awarded)

POLAR MEDALS (in order of date)

IMPERIAL SERVICE MEDAL

POLICE MEDALS FOR VALUABLE SERVICE
Indian Police Medal for Meritorious Service
Ceylon Police Medal for Merit
Sierra Leone Police Medal for Meritorious Service
Sierra Leone Fire Brigades Medal for Meritorious Service
Colonial Police Medal for Meritorious Service

BADGE OF HONOUR

JUBILEE, CORONATION AND DURBAR MEDALS
Queen Victoria, King Edward VII, King George V, King George VI, Queen Elizabeth II, Visit Commemoration and Long and Faithful Service Medals

EFFICIENCY AND LONG SERVICE DECORATIONS AND MEDALS
Medal for Meritorious Service
Accumulated Campaign Service Medal
Medal for Long Service and Good Conduct (Military)
Naval Long Service and Good Conduct Medal
Medal for Meritorious Service (Royal Navy 1918–28)
Indian Long Service and Good Conduct Medal
Indian Meritorious Service Medal
Royal Marines Meritorious Service Medal (1849–1947)
Royal Air Force Meritorious Service Medal (1918–1928)
Royal Air Force Long Service and Good Conduct Medal
Medal for Long Service and Good Conduct (Ulster Defence Regiment)
Indian Long Service and Good Conduct Medal
Royal West African Frontier Force Long Service and Good Conduct Medal

oyal Sierra Leone Military Forces Long Service and Good Conduct Medal
ing's African Rifles Long Service and Good Conduct Medal
ndian Meritorious Service Medal
olice Long Service and Good Conduct Medal
ire Brigade Long Service and Good Conduct Medal
frican Police Medal for Meritorious Service
oyal Canadian Mounted Police Long Service Medal
eylon Police Long Service Medal
eylon Fire Services Long Service Medal
ierra Leone Police Long Service Medal
olonial Police Long Service Medal
ierra Leone Fire Brigades Long Service Medal
lauritius Police Long Service and Good Conduct Medal
lauritius Fire Services Long Service and Good Conduct Medal
lauritius Prisons Service Long Service and Good Conduct Medal
olonial Fire Brigades Long Service Medal
olonial Prison Service Medal
Iong Kong Disciplined Services Medal
rmy Emergency Reserve Decoration (ERD)
olunteer Officers' Decoration (VD)
olunteer Long Service Medal
olunteer Officers' Decoration (for India and the Colonies)
olunteer Long Service Medal (for India and the Colonies)
olonial Auxiliary Forces Officers' Decoration
olonial Auxiliary Forces Long Service Medal
ledal for Good Shooting (Naval)
lilitia Long Service Medal
mperial Yeomanry Long Service Medal
erritorial Decoration (TD), 1908
eylon Armed Services Long Service Medal
fficiency Decoration (ED)
erritorial Efficiency Medal
fficiency Medal
pecial Reserve Long Service and Good Conduct Medal
ecoration for Officers of the Royal Navy Reserve (RD), 1910
ecoration for Officers of the Royal Naval Volunteer Reserve (VRD)
oyal Naval Reserve Long Service and Good Conduct Medal
oyal Naval Volunteer Reserve Long Service and Good Conduct Medal
oyal Naval Auxiliary Sick Berth Reserve Long Service and Good Conduct Medal
oyal Fleet Reserve Long Service and Good Conduct Medal
oyal Naval Wireless Auxiliary Reserve Long Service and Good Conduct Medal
oyal Naval Auxiliary Service Medal
ir Efficiency Award (AE), 1942
olunteer Reserves Service Medal
lster Defence Regiment Medal
orthern Ireland Home Service Medal
ueen's Medal (for Champion Shots of the RN and RM)
ueen's Medal (for Champion Shots of the New Zealand Naval Forces)
ueen's Medal (for Champion Shots in the Military Forces)
ueen's Medal (for Champion Shots of the Air Forces)
adet Forces Medal, 1950
oastguard Auxiliary Service Long Service Medal
pecial Constabulary Long Service Medal
anadian Forces Decoration
oyal Observer Corps Medal
ivil Defence Long Service Medal
Ambulance Service (Emergency Duties) Long Service and Good Conduct Medal
Royal Fleet Auxiliary Service Medal Rhodesia Medal
Royal Ulster Constabulary Service Medal
Northern Ireland Prison Service Medal
Union of South Africa Commemoration Medal
Indian Independence Medal
Pakistan Medal
Ceylon Armed Services Inauguration Medal
Ceylon Police Independence Medal (1948)
Sierra Leone Independence Medal
Jamaica Independence Medal
Uganda Independence Medal
Malawi Independence Medal
Fiji Independence Medal
Papua New Guinea Independence Medal
Solomon Islands Independence Medal
Service Medal of the Order of St John
Badge of the Order of the League of Mercy
Voluntary Medical Service Medal (1932)
Women's Royal Voluntary Service Medal
South African Medal for War Services
Colonial Special Constabulary Medal

HONORARY MEMBERSHIP OF COMMONWEALTH ORDERS

OTHER COMMONWEALTH MEMBERS' ORDERS, DECORATIONS AND MEDALS

FOREIGN ORDERS

FOREIGN DECORATIONS

FOREIGN MEDALS

THE VICTORIA CROSS (1856)

FOR CONSPICUOUS BRAVERY

VC

Ribbon, Crimson, for all Services (until 1918 it was blue for the Royal Navy)

Instituted on 29 January 1856, the Victoria Cross was awarded retrospectively to 1854, the first being held by Lt. C. D. Lucas, RN, for bravery in the Baltic Sea on 21 June 1854 (gazetted 24 February 1857). The first 62 crosses were presented by Queen Victoria in Hyde Park, London, on 26 June 1857.

The Victoria Cross is worn before all other decorations, on the left breast, and consists of a cross-pattée of bronze, 3.8cm in diameter, with the royal crown surmounted by a lion in the centre, and beneath there is the inscription *For Valour.* Holders of the VC currently receive a tax-free annuity of £1,500, irrespective of need or other conditions. In 1911, the right to receive the cross was extended to Indian soldiers, and in 1920 to matrons, sisters and nurses, the staff of the nursing services and other services pertaining to hospitals and nursing, and to civilians of either sex regularly or temporarily under the orders, direction or supervision of the naval, military, or air forces of the crown.

SURVIVING RECIPIENTS OF THE VICTORIA CROSS
as at 31 August 2010

Apiata, *Cpl.* B. H. (New Zealand Special Air Service)
2004 *Afghanistan*
Beharry, *Pte.* J. G. (Princess of Wales's Royal Regiment)
2005 *Iraq*
Cruickshank, *Flt. Lt.* J. A. (RAFVR)
1944 *World War*
Donaldson, *Trooper* M. G. S. (Australian Special Air Service)
2008 *Afghanistan*
Lachhiman Gurung, *Havildar* (8th Gurkha Rifles)
1945 *World War*
Payne, *WO* K., DSC (USA) (Australian Army Training Team)
1969 *Vietnam*
Rambahadur Limbu, *Capt.*, MVO (10th Princess Mary's Gurkha Rifles)
1965 *Sarawak*
Speakman-Pitts, *Sgt.* W. (Black Watch, attached KOSB)
1951 *Korea*
Tulbahadur Pun, *Lt.* (6th Gurkha Rifles)
1944 *World War*

THE GEORGE CROSS (1940)

FOR GALLANTRY

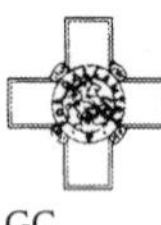

GC

Ribbon, Dark blue, threaded through a bar adorned with laurel leaves
Instituted 24 September 1940 (with amendments, 3 November 1942)

The George Cross is worn before all other decorations (except the VC) on the left breast (when worn by a woman it may be worn on the left shoulder from a ribbon of the same width and colour fashioned into a bow). It consists of a plain silver cross with four equal limbs, the cross having in the centre a circular medallion bearing a design showing St George and the Dragon. The inscription *For Gallantry* appears round the medallion and in the angle of each limb of the cross is the royal cypher 'G VI' forming a circle concentric with the medallion. The reverse is plain and bears the name of the recipient and the date of the award. The cross is suspended by a ring from a bar adorned with laurel leaves on dark blue ribbon 3.8cm wide.

The cross is intended primarily for civilians; awards to the fighting services are confined to actions for which purely military honours are not normally granted. It is awarded only for acts of the greatest heroism or of the most conspicuous courage in circumstances of extreme danger. From 1 April 1965, holders of the cross have received a tax-free annuity, which is currently £1,500. The cross has twice been awarded collectively rather than to an individual: to Malta (1942) and the Royal Ulster Constabulary (1999).

In October 1971 all surviving holders of the Albert Medal and the Edward Medal exchanged those decorations for the George Cross.

SURVIVING RECIPIENTS OF THE GEORGE CROSS
as at 31 August 2010

If the recipient originally received the Albert Medal (AM) or the Edward Medal (EM), this is indicated by the initial in parentheses.

Archer, *Col.* B. S. T., GC, OBE, ERD, 1941
Bamford, J., GC, 1952
Beaton, J., GC, CVO, 1974
Butson, *Lt.-Col.* A. R. C., GC, CD, MD (AM), 1948
Croucher, *Lance Cpl.* M., GC, 2008
Finney, *Trooper* C., GC, 2003
Flintoff, H. H., GC (EM), 1944
Gledhill, A. J., GC, 1967
Gregson, J. S., GC (AM), 1943
Hughes, *Staff Sgt.* K. S., GC, 2010
Johnson, *WO1 (SSM)* B., GC, 1990
Kinne, D. G., GC, 1954
Lowe, A. R., GC (AM), 1949
Norton, *Maj.* P. A., GC, 2006
Pratt, M. K., GC, 1978
Purves, Mrs M., GC (AM), 1949
Raweng, Awang anak, GC, 1951
Stevens, H. W., GC, 1958
Walker, C., GC, 1972
Walker, C. H., GC (AM), 1942
Wooding, E. A., GC (AM), 1945

AWARDED POSTHUMOUSLY IN 2009–10
Schmid, *Staff Sgt.* O. S. G., GC, 2010

THE ELIZABETH CROSS (2009)

EC

Instituted 1 July 2009

The Elizabeth Cross consists of a silver cross with a laurel wreath passing between the arms, which bear the floral symbols of England (rose), Scotland (thistle), Ireland (shamrock) and Wales (daffodil). The centre of the cross bears the royal cypher and the reverse is inscribed with the name of the person for whom it is in honour. The cross is accompanied by a memorial scroll and a miniature.

The cross was created to commemorate UK armed forces personnel who have died on operations or as a result of an act of terrorism. It may be granted to and worn by the next of kin of any eligible personnel who died from 1 January 1948 to date. It offers the wearer no precedence. Those that are eligible include the next of kin of personnel who died while serving on a medal earning operation, as a result of an act of terrorism, or on a non-medal earning operation where death was caused by the inherent high risk of the task.

The Elizabeth Cross is not intended as a posthumous medal for the fallen but as an emblem of national recognition of the loss and sacrifice made by the personnel and their families.

CHIEFS OF CLANS IN SCOTLAND

Only chiefs of whole Names or Clans are included, except certain special instances (marked *) who, though not chiefs of a whole Name, were or are for some reason (eg the Macdonald forfeiture) independent. Under decision (*Campbell-Gray,* 1950) that a bearer of a 'double or triple-barrelled' surname cannot be held chief of a part of such, several others cannot be included in the list at present.

THE ROYAL HOUSE: HM The Queen

AGNEW: Sir Crispin Agnew of Lochnaw, Bt., QC
ANSTRUTHER: Tobias Anstruther of Anstruther and Balcaskie
ARBUTHNOTT: Viscount of Arbuthnott, KT, CBE, DSC
BANNERMAN: Sir David Bannerman of Elsick, Bt.
BARCLAY: Peter C. Barclay of Towie Barclay and of that Ilk
BORTHWICK: Lord Borthwick
BOYLE: Earl of Glasgow
BRODIE: Alexander Brodie of Brodie
BROUN OF COLSTOUN: Sir Wayne Broun of Colstoun, Bt.
BRUCE: Earl of Elgin and Kincardine, KT
BUCHAN: David Buchan of Auchmacoy
BURNETT: J. C. A. Burnett of Leys
CAMERON: Donald Cameron of Lochiel
CAMPBELL: Duke of Argyll
CARMICHAEL: Richard Carmichael of Carmichael
CARNEGIE: Duke of Fife
CATHCART: Earl Cathcart
CHARTERIS: Earl of Wemyss and March
CLAN CHATTAN: K. Mackintosh of Clan Chattan
CHISHOLM: Hamish Chisholm of Chisholm *(The Chisholm)*
COCHRANE: Earl of Dundonald
COLQUHOUN: Sir Malcolm Rory Colquhoun of Luss, Bt.
CRANSTOUN: David Cranstoun of that Ilk
CUMMING: Sir Alastair Cumming of Altyre, Bt.
DARROCH: Capt. Duncan Darroch of Gourock
DAVIDSON: Alister Davidson of Davidston
DEWAR: Michael Dewar of that Ilk and Vogrie
DRUMMOND: Earl of Perth
DUNBAR: Sir James Dunbar of Mochrum, Bt.
DUNDAS: David Dundas of Dundas
DURIE: Andrew Durie of Durie, CBE
ELIOTT: Mrs Margaret Eliott of Redheugh
ERSKINE: Earl of Mar and Kellie
FARQUHARSON: Capt. A. Farquharson of Invercauld, MC
FERGUSSON: Sir Charles Fergusson of Kilkerran, Bt.
FORBES: Lord Forbes, KBE
FORSYTH: Alistair Forsyth of that Ilk
FRASER: Lady Saltoun
*FRASER (OF LOVAT): Lord Lovat
GAYRE: R. Gayre of Gayre and Nigg
GORDON: Marquess of Huntly
GRAHAM: Duke of Montrose
GRANT: Lord Strathspey
GUTHRIE: Alexander Guthrie of Guthrie
HAIG: Earl Haig, OBE
HALDANE: Martin Haldane of Gleneagles
HANNAY: David Hannay of Kirkdale and of that Ilk
HAY: Earl of Erroll
HENDERSON: Alistair Henderson of Fordell
HUNTER: Pauline Hunter of Hunterston
IRVINE OF DRUM: David Irvine of Drum
JARDINE: Sir William Jardine of Applegirth, Bt.
JOHNSTONE: Earl of Annandale and Hartfell
KEITH: Earl of Kintore
KENNEDY: Marquess of Ailsa
KERR: Marquess of Lothian, PC
KINCAID: Madam Arabella Kincaid of Kincaid
LAMONT: Revd Peter Lamont of that Ilk
LEASK: Jonathan Leask of that Ilk
LENNOX: Edward Lennox of that Ilk
LESLIE: Earl of Rothes
LINDSAY: Earl of Crawford and Balcarres, KT, GCVO, PC
LIVINGSTONE (or MACLEA): Niall Livingstone of the Bachuil
LOCKHART: Angus Lockhart of the Lee
LUMSDEN: Gillem Lumsden of that Ilk and Blanerne
MACALESTER: William St J. McAlester of Loup and Kennox
MACARTHUR; John MacArthur of that Ilk
MCBAIN: J. H. McBain of McBain
MACDONALD: Lord Macdonald *(The Macdonald of Macdonald)*
*MACDONALD OF CLANRANALD: Ranald Macdonald of Clanranald
*MACDONALD OF KEPPOCH: Ranald MacDonald of Keppoch
*MACDONALD OF SLEAT (CLAN HUSTEAIN): Sir Ian Macdonald of Sleat, Bt.
*MACDONELL OF GLENGARRY: Ranald MacDonell of Glengarry
MACDOUGALL: Morag MacDougall of MacDougall
MACDOWALL: Fergus Macdowall of Garthland
MACGREGOR: Sir Malcolm MacGregor of MacGregor, Bt.
MACINTYRE: Donald MacIntyre of Glenoe
MACKAY: Lord Reay
MACKENZIE: Earl of Cromartie
MACKINNON: Anne Mackinnon of Mackinnon
MACKINTOSH: John Mackintosh of Mackintosh *(The Mackintosh of Mackintosh)*
MACLACHLAN: Euan MacLachlan of MacLachlan
MACLAREN: Donald MacLaren of MacLaren and Achleskine
MACLEAN: Hon. Sir Lachlan Maclean of Duart, Bt., CVO
MACLENNAN: Ruaraidh MacLennan of MacLennan
MACLEOD: Hugh MacLeod of MacLeod
MACMILLAN: George MacMillan of MacMillan
MACNAB: J. C. Macnab of Macnab *(The Macnab)*
MACNAGHTEN: Sir Malcolm Macnaghten of Macnaghten and Dundarave, Bt.
MACNEACAIL: John Macneacail of Macneacail and Scorrybreac
MACNEIL OF BARRA: Rory Macneil of Barra *(The Macneil of Barra)*

MACPHERSON: Hon. Sir William Macpherson of Cluny, TD
MACTAVISH: Steven MacTavish of Dunardry
MACTHOMAS: Andrew MacThomas of Finegand
MAITLAND: Earl of Lauderdale
MAKGILL: Viscount of Oxfuird
MALCOLM (MACCALLUM): Robin N. L. Malcolm of Poltalloch
MAR: Countess of Mar
MARJORIBANKS: Andrew Marjoribanks of that Ilk
MATHESON: Maj. Sir Fergus Matheson of Matheson, Bt.
MENZIES: David Menzies of Menzies
MOFFAT: Madam Moffat of that Ilk
MONCREIFFE: Hon. Peregrine Moncreiffe of that Ilk
MONTGOMERIE: Earl of Eglinton and Winton
MORRISON: Dr Iain Morrison of Ruchdi
MUNRO: Hector Munro of Foulis
MURRAY: Duke of Atholl
NESBITT (or NISBET): Mark Nesbitt of that Ilk
OGILVY: Earl of Airlie, KT, GCVO, PC
OLIPHANT: Richard Oliphant of that Ilk
RAMSAY: Earl of Dalhousie
RIDDELL: Sir John Riddell of Riddell, Bt., KCVO
ROBERTSON: Alexander Robertson of Struan *(Struan-Robertson)*
ROLLO: Lord Rollo
ROSE: Miss Elizabeth Rose of Kilravock
ROSS: David Ross of that Ilk and Balnagowan
RUTHVEN: Earl of Gowrie, PC
SCOTT: Duke of Buccleuch and Queensberry, KBE
SCRYMGEOUR: Earl of Dundee
SEMPILL: Lord Sempill
SHAW: John Shaw of Tordarroch
SINCLAIR: Earl of Caithness
SKENE: Danus Skene of Skene
STIRLING: Fraser Stirling of Cader
STRANGE: Maj. Timothy Strange of Balcaskie
SUTHERLAND: Countess of Sutherland
SWINTON: John Swinton of that Ilk
TROTTER: Alexander Trotter of Mortonhall
URQUHART: Kenneth Urquhart of Urquhart
WALLACE: Ian Wallace of that Ilk
WEDDERBURN: Master of Dundee
WEMYSS: Michael Wemyss of that Ilk

THE PRIVY COUNCIL

The sovereign in council, or Privy Council, was the chief source of executive power until the system of cabinet government developed in the 18th century. Now the Privy Council's main functions are to advise the sovereign and to exercise its own statutory responsibilities independent of the sovereign in council.

Membership of the Privy Council is automatic upon appointment to certain government and judicial positions in the UK, eg cabinet ministers must be Privy Counsellors and are sworn in on first assuming office. Membership is also accorded by the Queen to eminent people in the UK and independent countries of the Commonwealth of which she is Queen, on the recommendation of the prime minister. Membership of the council is retained for life, except for very occasional removals.

The administrative functions of the Privy Council are carried out by the Privy Council Office under the direction of the president of the council, who is always a member of the cabinet. (*See also* Parliament)

President of the Council, Rt. Hon. Nick Clegg
Clerk of the Council, Judith Simpson

Style The Right (or Rt.) Hon._
*Envelope, The Right (or Rt.) Hon. F_ S_*
*Letter, Dear Mr/Miss/Mrs S_*
*Spoken, Mr/Miss/Mrs S_*

It is incorrect to use the letters PC after the name in conjunction with the prefix The Rt. Hon., unless the Privy Counsellor is a peer below the rank of Marquess and so is styled The Rt. Hon. because of his/her rank.

MEMBERS *as at August 2010*

HRH The Duke of Edinburgh, 1951
HRH The Prince of Wales, 1977

Abernethy, *Hon.* Lord (Alastair Cameron), 2005
Adonis, Lord, 2009
Aikens, Sir Richard, 2008
Ainsworth, Robert, 2005
Airlie, Earl of, 1984
Aldous, Sir William, 1995
Alebua, Ezekiel, 1988
Alexander, Douglas, 2005
Alexander, Danny, 2010
Amos, Baroness, 2003
Ampthill, Lord, 1995
Ancram, Michael, 1996
Anderson of Swansea, Lord, 2000
Anelay of St Johns, Baroness, 2009
Angiolini, Elish, 2006
Anthony, Douglas, 1971
Arbuthnot, James, 1998
Archer of Sandwell, Lord, 1977
Arden, Dame Mary, 2000
Armstrong of Hill Top, Baroness, 1999
Arthur, *Hon.* Owen, 1995
Ashdown of Norton-sub-Hamdon, Lord, 1989
Ashley of Stoke, Lord, 1979
Ashton of Upholland, Baroness, 2006
Atkins, Sir Robert, 1995
Auld, Sir Robin, 1995
Baker, Sir Thomas, 2002
Baker of Dorking, Lord, 1984
Balls, Ed, 2007
Bannside, Lord, 2005
Barnett, Lord, 1975
Barron, Kevin, 2001
Bassam of Brighton, Lord, 2009
Battle, John, 2002
Beckett, Margaret, 1993
Beith, Sir Alan, 1992
Beldam, Sir Roy, 1989
Benn, Anthony, 1964
Benn, Hilary, 2003
Bercow, John, 2009
Bingham of Cornhill, Lord, 1986
Birch, William, 1992
Bisson, Sir Gordon, 1987
Blackstone, Baroness, 2001
Blair, Anthony, 1994
Blanchard, Peter, 1998
Blears, Hazel, 2005
Blunkett, David, 1997
Boateng, Lord, 1999
Bolger, James, 1991
Boothroyd, Baroness, 1992
Boscawen, *Hon.* Robert, 1992
Bottomley of Nettlestone, Baroness, 1992
Boyd of Duncansby, Lord, 2000
Boyson, Sir Rhodes, 1987
Bradley, Lord, 2001
Bradshaw, Ben, 2009
Brathwaite, Sir Nicholas, 1991
Brittan of Spennithorne, Lord, 1981
Brooke, Sir Henry, 1996
Brooke of Sutton Mandeville, Lord, 1988
Brown, Gordon, 1996
Brown, Nicholas, 1997
Brown, Sir Stephen, 1983
Brown of Eaton-under-Heywood, Lord, 1992
Browne of Ladyton, Lord, 2005
Browne-Wilkinson, Lord, 1983
Bruce, Malcolm, 2006
Burnham, Andy, 2007
Burnton, Sir Stanley, 2008
Butler of Brockwell, Lord, 2004
Butler-Sloss, Baroness, 1988
Buxton, Sir Richard, 1997
Byers, Stephen, 1998
Byrne, Liam, 2008
Byron, Sir Dennis, 2004
Cable, Vincent, 2010
Caborn, Richard, 1999
Caithness, Earl of, 1990
Cameron, David, 2005
Cameron of Lochbroom, Lord, 1984
Camoys, Lord, 1997
Campbell, Sir Walter Menzies, 1999
Campbell, Sir William, 1999
Canterbury, Archbishop of, 2002
Carey of Clifton, Lord, 1991
Carloway, *Hon.* Lord (Colin Sutherland), 2008
Carnwath, Sir Robert, 2002
Carr of Hadley, Lord, 1963
Carrington, Lord, 1959
Carswell, Lord, 1993
Casey, Sir Maurice, 1986
Chadwick, Sir John, 1997
Chalfont, Lord, 1964
Chalker of Wallasey, Baroness, 1987
Chan, Sir Julius, 1981
Chataway, Sir Christopher, 1970
Chilcot, Sir John, 2004
Christie, Perry, 2004
Clark, Greg, 2010
Clark, Helen, 1990
Clark of Windermere, Lord, 1997
Clarke, Charles, 2001
Clarke, Kenneth, 1984
Clarke, *Hon.* Lord (Matthew Clarke), 2008
Clarke, Thomas, 1997
Clarke of Stone-Cum-Ebony, Lord, 1998
Clegg, Nicholas, 2008
Clinton-Davis, Lord, 1998
Clwyd, Ann, 2004
Coghlin, Sir Patrick, 2009
Collins of Mapesbury, Lord, 2007
Cooper, Yvette, 2007
Cope of Berkeley, Lord, 1988
Corston, Baroness, 2003
Cosgrove, *Hon.* Lady (Hazel Cosgrove), 2003
Coulsfield, *Hon.* Lord (John Coulsfield), 2000
Cowen, Sir Zelman, 1981
Crawford and Balcarres, Earl of, 1972
Creech, *Hon.* Wyatt, 1999

Crickhowell, Lord, 1979
Cullen of Whitekirk, Lord, 1997
Cunningham of Felling, Lord, 1993
Curry, David, 1996
Darling, Alistair, 1997
Darzi of Denham, Lord, 2009
Davies, Denzil, 1978
Davies, Ronald, 1997
Davies of Oldham, Lord, 2006
Davis, David, 1997
Davis, Terence, 1999
Davison, Sir Ronald, 1978
de la Bastide, Michael, 2004
Dean of Thornton-le-Fylde, Baroness, 1998
Deben, Lord, 1985
Denham, John, 2000
Denham, Lord, 1981
Dixon, Lord, 1996
Dobson, Frank, 1997
Dodds, Nigel, 2010
Donaldson, Jeffrey, 2007
Dorrell, Stephen, 1994
Drayson, Lord, 2008
D'Souza, Baroness, 2009
du Cann, Sir Edward, 1964
Duncan, Alan, 2010
Duncan Smith, Iain, 2001
Dunn, Sir Robin, 1980
Dyson, Sir John, 2001
Eassie, *Hon.* Lord (Ronald Mackay), 2006
East, Paul, 1998
Eden of Winton, Lord, 1972
Edward, Sir David, 2005
Eggar, Timothy, 1995
Eichelbaum, Sir Thomas, 1989
Elias, Sir Patrick, 2009
Elias, *Hon.* Dame, Sian, 1999
Elis-Thomas, Lord, 2004
Esquivel, Manuel, 1986
Etherton, Sir Terence, 2008
Evans, Sir Anthony, 1992
Eveleigh, Sir Edward, 1977
Falconer of Thoroton, Lord, 2003
Farquharson, Sir Donald, 1989
Fellowes, Lord, 1990
Fergusson, Alexander, 2010
Ferrers, Earl, 1982
Field, Frank, 1997
Flint, Caroline, 2008
Floissac, Sir Vincent, 1992
Forsyth of Drumlean, Lord, 1995
Foster of Bishop Auckland, Lord, 1993
Foulkes of Cumnock, Lord, 2002
Fowler, Lord, 1979
Fox, Liam, 2010
Francois, Mark, 2010
Fraser, Malcolm, 1976
Fraser of Carmyllie, Lord, 1989
Freedman, Sir Lawrence, 2009
Freeman, John, 1966
Freeman, Lord, 1993
Gage, Sir William, 2004
Garel-Jones, Lord, 1992
Gault, Thomas, 1992
Geidt, Christopher, 2007
George, Bruce, 2000
Gibson, Sir Peter, 1993
Gilbert, Lord, 1978
Gilbert, Sir Martin, 2009
Gill, *Hon.* Lord (Brian Gill), 2002
Gillan, Cheryl, 2010
Girvan, Sir (Frederick) Paul, 2007
Glenamara, Lord, 1964
Glidewell, Sir Iain, 1985
Goff of Chieveley, Lord, 1982
Goggins, Paul, 2009
Goldring, Sir John, 2008
Goldsmith, Lord, 2002
Goodlad, Lord, 1992
Gove, Michael, 2010
Gowrie, Earl of, 1984
Graham, Sir Douglas, 1998
Graham of Edmonton, Lord, 1998
Grayling, Chris, 2010
Grieve, Dominic, 2010
Griffiths, Lord, 1980
Grocott, Lord, 2002
Habgood, Rt. Revd Lord, 1983
Hague, William, 1995
Hain, Peter, 2001
Hale of Richmond, Baroness, 1999
Hallett, Dame Heather, 2005
Hamilton, *Hon.* Lord (Arthur Hamilton), 2002
Hamilton of Epsom, Lord, 1991
Hammond, Philip, 2010
Hanley, Sir Jeremy, 1994
Hanson, David, 2007
Hardie, Lord, 1997
Hardie Boys, Sir Michael, 1989
Harman, Harriet, 1997
Harrison, Walter, 1977
Haselhurst, Sir Alan, 1999
Hattersley, Lord, 1975
Hayhoe, Lord, 1985
Hayman, Baroness, 2000
Healey, John, 2008
Healey, Lord, 1964
Heathcoat-Amory, David, 1996
Henry, John, 1996
Herbert, Nick, 2010
Heseltine, Lord, 1979
Heseltine, Sir William, 1986
Hesketh, Lord, 1991
Hewitt, Patricia, 2001
Higgins, Lord, 1979
Higgins, Sir Malachy, 2007
Hill, Keith, 2003
Hirst, Sir David, 1992
Hodge, Margaret, 2003
Hoffmann, Lord, 1992
Hogg, *Hon.* Douglas, 1992
Hollis of Heigham, Baroness, 1999
Hoon, Geoffrey, 1999
Hooper, Sir Anthony, 2004
Hope of Craighead, Lord, 1989
Hope of Thornes, Lord, 1991
Hordern, Sir Peter, 1993
Howard of Lympne, Lord, 1990
Howarth, George, 2005
Howarth of Newport, Lord, 2000
Howe of Aberavon, Lord, 1972
Howell of Guildford, Lord, 1979
Howells, Kim, 2009
Hughes, Sir Anthony, 2006
Hughes of Stretford, Baroness, 2004
Huhne, Chris, 2010
Hunt, Jeremy, 2010
Hunt, Jonathon, 1989
Hunt of Kings Heath, Lord, 2009
Hunt of Wirral, Lord, 1990
Hurd of Westwell, Lord, 1982
Hutchison, Sir Michael, 1995
Hutton, Lord, 1988
Hutton of Furness, Lord, 2001
Inge, Lord, 2004
Ingraham, Hubert, 1993
Ingram, Adam, 1999
Irvine of Lairg, Lord, 1997
Jack, Michael, 1997
Jackson, Sir Rupert, 2008
Jacob, Sir Robert, 2004
Jacobs, Francis, 2005
Janvrin, Lord, 1998
Jay of Paddington, Baroness, 1998
Jenkin of Roding, Lord, 1973
Johnson, Alan, 2003
Jones, Lord, 1999
Jopling, Lord, 1979
Jowell, Tessa, 1998
Judge, Lord, 1996
Jugnauth, Sir Anerood, 1987
Kaufman, Sir Gerald, 1978
Kay, Sir Maurice, 2004
Keene, Sir David, 2000
Keith, Sir Kenneth, 1998
Kelly, Ruth, 2004
Kenilorea, Sir Peter, 1979
Kennedy, Charles, 1999
Kennedy, Jane, 2003
Kennedy, Sir Paul, 1992
Kerr of Tonaghmore, Lord, 2004
Khan, Sadiq, 2009
King of Bridgwater, Lord, 1979
Kingarth, *Hon.* Lord (Derek Emslie), 2006
Kingsdown, Lord, 1987
Kinnock, Lord, 1983
Kirkwood, *Hon.* Lord (Ian Kirkwood), 2000
Knight, Gregory, 1995
Knight of Weymouth, Lord, 2008
Lammy, David, 2008
Lamont of Lerwick, Lord, 1986
Lang of Monkton, Lord, 1990
Lansley, Andrew, 2010
Latasi, Sir Kamuta, 1996
Latham, Sir David, 2000
Lauti, Sir Toaripi, 1979
Laws, Sir John, 1999
Lawson of Blaby, Lord, 1981
Leggatt, Sir Andrew, 1990
Letwin, Oliver, 2002
Leveson, Sir Brian, 2006
Liddell of Coatdyke, Baroness, 1998
Lilley, Peter, 1990
Lloyd of Berwick, Lord, 1984
Lloyd, Sir Peter, 1994
Lloyd, Sir Timothy, 2005
London, Bishop of, 1995
Longmore, Sir Andrew, 2001

Louisy, Sir Allan, 1981
Luce, Lord, 1986
Lyne, Sir Roderic, 2009
McAvoy, Lord, 2003
McCartney, Sir Ian, 1999
McCollum, Sir Liam, 1997
McConnell of Glenscorrodale, Lord, 2001
MacDermott, Sir John, 1987
Macdonald of Tradeston, Lord, 1999
McFadden, Patrick, 2008
McFall of Alcluith, Lord, 2004
MacGregor of Pulham Market, Lord, 1985
McGuire, Anne, 2008
Mackay, Andrew, 1998
McKay, Sir Ian, 1992
Mackay of Clashfern, Lord, 1979
Mackay of Drumadoon, Lord, 1996
McKinnon, Sir Donald, 1992
Maclean, David, 1995
Maclean, *Hon.* Lord (Ranald MacLean), 2001
McLeish, Henry, 2000
Maclennan of Rogart, Lord, 1997
McLoughlin, Patrick, 2005
McMullin, Sir Duncan, 1980
McNally, Lord, 2005
McNulty, Anthony, 2007
MacShane, Denis, 2005
Major, Sir John, 1987
Malloch-Brown, Lord, 2007
Mance, Lord, 1999
Mandelson, Lord, 1998
Marnoch, *Hon.* Lord (Michael Marnoch), 2001
Marsh, Lord, 1966
Martin of Springburn, Lord, 2000
Mason of Barnsley, Lord, 1968
Mates, Michael, 2004
Maude, *Hon.* Francis, 1992
Mawhinney, Lord, 1994
May, Sir Anthony, 1998
May, Theresa, 2003
Mayhew of Twysden, Lord, 1986
Meacher, Michael, 1997
Mellor, David, 1990
Michael, Alun, 1998
Milburn, Alan, 1998
Miliband, David, 2005
Miliband, Ed, 2007
Millan, Bruce, 1975
Millett, Lord, 1994
Mitchell, Andrew, 2010
Mitchell, Sir James, 1985
Mitchell, Dr Keith, 2004
Molyneaux of Killead, Lord, 1983
Moore, Michael, 1990
Moore, Michael, 2010
Moore of Lower Marsh, Lord, 1986
Moore-Bick, Sir Martin, 2005
Morgan, Sir Declan, 2009
Morgan, Rhodri, 2000
Morley, Elliot, 2007
Morris, Charles, 1978
Morris of Aberavon, Lord, 1970
Morris of Manchester, Lord, 1979
Morris of Yardley, Baroness, 1999
Morritt, Sir Robert, 1994
Moses, Sir Alan, 2005
Moyle, Roland, 1978
Mummery, Sir John, 1996
Munby, Sir James, 2009
Mundell, David, 2010
Murphy, James, 2008
Murphy, Paul, 1999
Murray, *Hon.* Lord (Ronald Murray), 1974
Murray, Sir Donald, 1989
Musa, Wilbert, 2005
Mustill, Lord, 1985
Nairne, Sir Patrick, 1982
Namaliu, Sir Rabbie, 1989
Naseby, Lord, 1994
Needham, Sir Richard, 1994
Neill, Sir Brian, 1985
Neuberger of Abbotsbury, Lord, 2004
Neville-Jones, Baroness, 2010
Newton of Braintree, Lord, 1988
Nicholls of Birkenhead, Lord, 1995
Nicholson, Sir Michael, 1995
Nimmo Smith, *Hon.* Lord (William Nimmo Smith), 2005
Nott, Sir John, 1979
Nourse, Sir Martin, 1985
O'Brien, Mike, 2009
O'Donnell, Turlough, 1979
Oppenheim-Barnes, Baroness, 1979
Osborne, *Hon.* Lord (Kenneth Osborne), 2001
Otton, Sir Philip, 1995
Owen, Lord, 1976
Paeniu, Bikenibeu, 1991
Palliser, Sir Michael, 1983
Palmer, Sir Geoffrey, 1986
Paraskeva, Dame Janet, 2010
Parker, Sir Jonathan, 2000
Parker, Sir Roger, 1983
Parkinson, Lord, 1981
Paterson, Owen, 2010
Paton, *Hon.* Lady (Ann Paton), 2007
Patten, Lord, 1990
Patten, Sir Nicholas, 2009
Patten of Barnes, Lord, 1989
Patterson, Percival, 1993
Pattie, Sir Geoffrey, 1987
Paul, Lord, 2009
Peel, Earl, 2006
Pendry, Lord, 2000
Penrose, *Hon.* Lord (George Penrose), 2000
Peters, Winston, 1998
Philip, *Hon.* Lord (Alexander Philip), 2005
Phillips of Worth Matravers, Lord, 1995
Pickles, Eric, 2010
Pill, Sir Malcolm, 1995
Pitchford, Sir Christopher, 2010
Portillo, Michael, 1992
Potter, Sir Mark, 1996
Prashar, Baroness, 2009
Prescott, Lord, 1994
Price, George, 1982
Primarolo, Dawn, 2002
Prior, Lord, 1970
Prosser, *Hon.* Lord (William Prosser), 2000
Puapua, Sir Tomasi, 1982
Purnell, James, 2007
Quin, Baroness, 1998
Radice, Lord, 1999
Raison, Sir Timothy, 1982
Ramsden, James, 1963
Randall, John, 2010
Raynsford, Nick, 2001
Redwood, John, 1993
Reed, Lord, 2008
Reid, George, 2004
Reid of Cardowan, Lord, 1998
Renton of Mount Harry, Lord, 1989
Richard, Lord, 1993
Richards, Sir Stephen, 2005
Richardson, Sir Ivor, 1978
Riddell, Peter, 2010
Rifkind, Sir Malcolm, 1986
Rimer, Sir Colin, 2007
Rix, Sir Bernard, 2000
Roberts of Conwy, Lord, 1991
Robertson of Port Ellen, Lord, 1997
Robinson, Peter, 2007
Roch, Sir John, 1993
Rodger of Earlsferry, Lord, 1992
Rodgers of Quarry Bank, Lord, 1975
Rooker, Lord, 1999
Roper, Lord, 2005
Rose, Sir Christopher, 1992
Ross, *Hon.* Lord (Donald MacArthur), 1985
Royall of Blaisdon, Baroness, 2008
Ruddock, Joan, 2010
Ryan, Joan, 2007
Ryder of Wensum, Lord, 1990
Sainsbury, Sir Timothy, 1992
St John of Fawsley, Lord, 1979
Salisbury, Marquess of, 1994
Salmond, Alex, 2007
Sandiford, Erskine, 1989
Saville of Newdigate, Lord, 1994
Sawyer, Dame Joan, 2004
Schiemann, Sir Konrad, 1995
Scotland of Asthal, Baroness, 2001
Scott of Foscote, Lord, 1991
Seaga, Edward, 1981
Sedley, Sir Stephen, 1999
Selkirk of Douglas, Lord, 1996
Shapps, Grant, 2010
Sheldon, Lord, 1977
Shephard of Northwold, Baroness, 1992
Sheil, Sir John, 2005
Shipley, Jennifer, 1998
Short, Clare, 1997
Shutt of Greetland, Lord, 2009
Simmonds, Kennedy Sir, 1984
Sinclair, Ian, 1977
Slade, Sir Christopher, 1982
Smith, Andrew, 1997
Smith, Dame Janet, 2002
Smith, Jacqueline, 2003
Smith of Basildon, Baroness, 2009

Smith of Finsbury, Lord, 1997
Somare, Sir Michael, 1977
Spellar, John, 2001
Spelman, Caroline, 2010
Stanley, Sir John, 1984
Staughton, Sir Christopher, 1988
Steel of Aikwood, Lord, 1977
Stephen, Sir Ninian, 1979
Stewartby, Lord, 1989
Steyn, Lord, 1992
Strang, Gavin, 1997
Strathclyde, Lord, 1995
Straw, Jack, 1997
Stuart-Smith, Sir Murray, 1988
Sullivan, Sir Jeremy, 2009
Sutherland, *Hon.* Lord (Ranald Sutherland), 2000
Symons of Vernham Dean, Baroness, 2001
Talboys, Sir Brian, 1977
Taylor of Bolton, Baroness, 1997
Tebbit, Lord, 1981
Templeman, Lord, 1978
Thatcher, Baroness, 1970
Thomas, Edmund, 1996
Thomas, Sir Roger, 2003
Thomas, Sir Swinton, 1994
Thorpe, Jeremy, 1967
Thorpe, Sir Matthew, 1995
Timms, Stephen, 2006
Tipping, Andrew, 1998
Tizard, Robert, 1986
Touhig, Lord, 2006
Toulson, Sir Roger, 2007
Trefgarne, Lord, 1989
Trimble, Lord, 1997
Trumpington, Baroness, 1992
Tuckey, Sir Simon, 1998
Ullswater, Viscount, 1994
Upton, Simon, 1999
Vadera, Baroness, 2009
Vaz, Keith, 2006
Villiers, Theresa, 2010
Waddington, Lord, 1987
Waite, Sir John, 1993
Wakeham, Lord, 1983
Waldegrave of North Hill, Lord, 1990
Walker of Gestingthorpe, Lord, 1997
Wall, Sir Nicholas, 2004
Wallace of Tankerness, Lord, 2000
Waller, Sir Mark, 1996
Ward, Sir Alan, 1995
Warner, Lord, 2006
Warsi, Baroness, 2010
West of Spithead, Lord, 2010
Wheatley, *Hon.* Lord (John Wheatley), 2007
Wheeler, Sir John, 1993
Whitty, Lord, 2005
Wicks, Malcolm, 2008
Widdecombe, Ann, 1997
Wigley, Dafydd, 1997
Willetts, David, 2010
Williams, Alan, 1977
Williams of Crosby, Baroness, 1974
Williamson of Horton, Lord, 2007
Wills, Lord, 2008
Wilson, Brian, 2003
Wilson, Sir Nicholas, 2005
Windlesham, Lord, 1973
Winterton, Rosie, 2006
Wingti, Paias, 1987
Withers, Reginald, 1977
Woodhouse, Sir Owen, 1974
Woodward, Shaun, 2007
Woolf, Lord, 1986
York, Archbishop of, 2005
Young, Sir George, 1993
Young of Graffham, Lord, 1984
Zacca, Edward, 1992

PRIVY COUNCIL OF NORTHERN IRELAND

The Privy Council of Northern Ireland had responsibilities in Northern Ireland similar to those of the Privy Council in Great Britain until the Northern Ireland Act 1974. Membership of the Privy Council of Northern Ireland is retained for life. Since the Northern Ireland Constitution Act 1973 no further appointments have been made. The postnominal initials PC (NI) are used to differentiate its members from those of the Privy Council.

MEMBERS *as at August 2010*
Bailie, Robin, 1971
Bleakley, David, 1971
Craig, William, 1963
Dobson, John, 1969
Kilclooney, Lord, 1970
Kirk, Herbert, 1962
Porter, Sir Robert, 1969

PARLIAMENT

The United Kingdom constitution is not contained in any single document but has evolved over time, formed partly by statute, partly by common law and partly by convention. A constitutional monarchy, the United Kingdom is governed by ministers of the crown in the name of the sovereign, who is head both of the state and of the government.

The organs of government are the legislature (parliament), the executive and the judiciary. The executive consists of HM government (the cabinet and other ministers), government departments and local authorities (*see* Government Departments, Public Bodies and Local Government sections). The judiciary (*see* Law Courts and Offices section) pronounces on the law, both written and unwritten, interprets statutes and is responsible for the enforcement of the law; the judiciary is independent of both the legislature and the executive.

THE MONARCHY

The sovereign personifies the state and is, in law, an integral part of the legislature, head of the executive, head of the judiciary, commander-in-chief of all armed forces of the crown and supreme governor of the Church of England. The seat of the monarchy is in the United Kingdom. In the Channel Islands and the Isle of Man, which are crown dependencies, the sovereign is represented by a lieutenant-governor. In the member states of the Commonwealth of which the sovereign is head of state, her representative is a governor-general; in UK overseas territories the sovereign is usually represented by a governor, who is responsible to the British government.

Although in practice the powers of the monarchy are now very limited, and restricted mainly to the advisory and ceremonial, there are important acts of government which require the participation of the sovereign. These include summoning, proroguing and dissolving parliament, giving royal assent to bills passed by parliament, appointing important office-holders, eg government ministers, judges, bishops and governors, conferring peerages, knighthoods and other honours, and granting pardon to a person wrongly convicted of a crime. The sovereign appoints the prime minister; by convention this office is held by the leader of the political party which enjoys, or can secure, a majority of votes in the House of Commons. In international affairs the sovereign as head of state has the power to declare war and make peace, to recognise foreign states and governments, to conclude treaties and to annex or cede territory. However, as the sovereign entrusts executive power to ministers of the crown and acts on the advice of her ministers, which she cannot ignore, royal prerogative powers are in practice exercised by ministers, who are responsible to parliament.

Ministerial responsibility does not diminish the sovereign's importance to the smooth working of government. She holds meetings of the Privy Council (*see* below), gives audiences to her ministers and other officials at home and overseas, receives accounts of cabinet decisions, reads dispatches and signs state papers; she must be informed and consulted on every aspect of national life; and she must show complete impartiality.

COUNSELLORS OF STATE

In the event of the sovereign's absence abroad, it is necessary to appoint counsellors of state under letters patent to carry out the chief functions of the monarch, including the holding of Privy Councils and giving royal assent to acts passed by parliament. The normal procedure is to appoint as counsellors three or four members of the royal family among those remaining in the UK.

In the event of the sovereign on accession being under the age of 18 years, or at any time unavailable or incapacitated by infirmity of mind or body for the performance of the royal functions, provision is made for a regency.

THE PRIVY COUNCIL

The sovereign in council, or Privy Council, was the chief source of executive power until the system of cabinet government developed. Its main function today is to advise the sovereign on the approval of various statutory functions and acts of the royal prerogative. These powers are exercised through orders in council and royal proclamations, approved by the Queen at meetings of the Privy Council. The council is also able to exercise a number of statutory duties without approval from the sovereign, including powers of supervision over the registering bodies for the medical and allied professions. These duties are exercised through orders in council.

Although appointment as a privy counsellor is for life, only those who are currently government ministers are involved in the day-to-day business of the council. A full council is summoned only on the death of the sovereign or when the sovereign announces his or her intention to marry. (For a full list of privy counsellors, *see* the Privy Council section.)

There are a number of advisory Privy Council committees whose meetings the sovereign does not attend. Some are prerogative committees, such as those dealing with legislative matters submitted by the legislatures of the Channel Islands and the Isle of Man or with applications for charters of incorporation; and some are provided for by statute, eg those for the universities of Oxford and Cambridge and the Scottish universities.

Administrative work is carried out by the Privy Council Office under the direction of the Lord President of the Council, a cabinet minister.

JUDICIAL COMMITTEE OF THE PRIVY COUNCIL

Supreme Court Building, Parliament Square, London SW1P 3BD
T 020-7960 1500 **E** jcpcregistry@jcpc.gsi.gov.uk

The Judicial Committee of the Privy Council is the court of final appeal from courts of the UK dependencies, courts of independent Commonwealth countries which have retained the right of appeal and courts of the Channel Islands and the Isle of Man.

It also has certain jurisdiction within the United Kingdom, the most important of which is that it is the court of final appeal for 'devolution issues', ie issues as to the legal competences and functions of the legislative and executive authorities established in Scotland, Wales and Northern Ireland by the devolution legislation of 1998.

The committee is composed of privy counsellors who hold, or have held, high judicial office. Only three or five judges hear each case, and these are usually justices of the Supreme Court.

PARLIAMENT

Parliament is the supreme law-making authority and can legislate for the UK as a whole or for any parts of it separately (the Channel Islands and the Isle of Man are crown dependencies and not part of the UK). The main functions of parliament are to pass laws, to provide (by voting taxation) the means of carrying on the work of government and to scrutinise government policy and administration, particularly proposals for expenditure. International treaties and agreements are by custom presented to parliament before ratification.

Parliament emerged during the late 13th and early 14th centuries. The officers of the king's household and the king's judges were the nucleus of early parliaments, joined by such ecclesiastical and lay magnates as the king might summon to form a prototype 'House of Lords', and occasionally by the knights of the shires, burgesses and proctors of the lower clergy. By the end of Edward III's reign a 'House of Commons' was beginning to appear; the first known Speaker was elected in 1377.

Parliamentary procedure is based on custom and precedent, partly formulated in the standing orders of both houses of parliament, and each house has the right to control its own internal proceedings and to commit for contempt. The system of debate in the two houses is similar; when a motion has been moved, the Speaker proposes the question as the subject of a debate. Members speak from wherever they have been sitting. Questions are decided by a vote on a simple majority. Draft legislation is introduced, in either house, as a bill. Bills can be introduced by a government minister or a private member, but in practice the majority of bills which become law are introduced by the government. To become law, a bill must be passed by each house (for parliamentary stages, *see* Parliamentary Information) and then sent to the sovereign for the royal assent, after which it becomes an act of parliament.

Proceedings of both houses are public, except on extremely rare occasions. The minutes (called *Votes and Proceedings in the Commons,* and *Minutes of Proceedings in the Lords)* and the speeches *(The Official Report of Parliamentary Debates,* Hansard) are published daily. Proceedings are also recorded for transmission on radio and television and stored in the Parliamentary Recording Unit before transfer to the National Sound Archive. Television cameras have been allowed into the House of Lords since 1985 and into the House of Commons since 1989; committee meetings may also be televised.

By the Parliament Act of 1911, the maximum duration of a parliament is five years (if not previously dissolved), the term being reckoned from the date given on the writs for the new parliament. The maximum life has been prolonged by legislation in such rare circumstances as the two world wars (31 January 1911 to 25 November 1918; 26 November 1935 to 15 June 1945). Dissolution and writs for a general election are ordered by the sovereign on the advice of the prime minister. The life of a parliament is divided into sessions, usually of one year in length, beginning and ending most often in October or November.

DEVOLUTION

The Scottish parliament and the National Assembly for Wales have legislative power over all devolved matters, ie matters not reserved to Westminster or otherwise outside its powers. The Northern Ireland Assembly has legislative authority in the fields previously administered by the Northern Ireland departments. The assembly was suspended in October 2002 and dissolved in April 2003, before being reinstated on 8 May 2007. For further information, *see* the Regional Government section.

THE HOUSE OF LORDS

London SW1A 0PW
T 020-7219 3000 Information Office 020-7219 3107
E hlinfo@parliament.uk **W** www.parliament.uk

The House of Lords is the second chamber, or 'Upper House', of the UK's bicameral parliament. Until the beginning of the 20th century, the House of Lords had considerable power, being able to veto any bill submitted to it by the House of Commons. Today the main functions of the House of Lords are to contribute to the legislative process, to act as a check on the government, and to provide a forum of independent expertise. Its judicial role as final court of appeal ended in 2009 as a result of the establishment of a new UK supreme court (*see* Law Courts and Offices section).

The House of Lords has a number of select committees. Some relate to the internal affairs of the house – such as its management and administration – while others carry out important investigative work on matters of public interest. The main areas of work are: Europe, science, the economy, the constitution and communications. House of Lords investigative committees look at broader issues and do not mirror government departments as the select committees in the House of Commons do.

On 12 June 2003 the government announced reforms of the judicial function and the role of the Lord Chancellor as a judge and Speaker of the House of Lords. In 2006 the position of Lord Chancellor was significantly altered by the Constitutional Reform Act 2005. The office holder is no longer speaker of the House of Lords nor head of the judiciary in England and Wales, but remains a cabinet minister (the Lord Chancellor and Secretary of State for Justice), currently in the House of Commons. The function of speaker of the House of Lords was devolved to the newly created post of Lord Speaker. The Rt. Hon. Baroness Hayman was elected as the first Lord Speaker by the house on 4 July 2006.

Members of the House of Lords comprise life peers created under the Life Peerages Act 1958, 92 hereditary peers under the House of Lords Act 1999 and Lords of Appeal in Ordinary, ie law lords, under the Appellate Jurisdiction Act 1876*. The Archbishops of Canterbury and York, the Bishops of London, Durham and Winchester, and the 21 senior diocesan bishops of the Church of England are also members.

The House of Lords Act provides for 90 elected hereditary peers to remain in the House of Lords until longer-term reform of the House has been carried out; 42 Conservative, 28 crossbench, three Liberal Democrat and two Labour. Elections for each of the party groups and the crossbenches were held in October and November 1999. Fifteen office holders were elected by the whole house. Two hereditary peers with royal duties, the Earl Marshal and the Lord Great Chamberlain, are also members.

Peers are disqualified from sitting in the house if they are:

- aliens, ie any peer who is not a British citizen, a Commonwealth citizen (under the British Nationality Act 1981) or a citizen of the Republic of Ireland
- under the age of 21
- undischarged bankrupts or, in Scotland, those whose estate is sequestered
- a non-domiciled resident in the UK for tax purposes
- convicted of treason

Bishops retire at the age of 70 and cease to be members of the house at that time.

Members who do not wish to attend sittings of the House of Lords may apply for leave of absence for the duration of a parliament.

Members of the House of Lords are unpaid but are entitled to allowances for attendance at sittings of the house. The daily maxima, between 1 August 2009 and 31 July 2010, were £174 for overnight subsistence, £86.50 for day subsistence and incidental travel, and £75 for office costs.

* Although the office of Lord of Appeal in Ordinary no longer exists, retired law lords remain in the House of Lords as life peers. Law lords who became justices of the UK supreme court are not permitted to sit or vote in the House of Lords until they retire.

COMPOSITION *as at 4 August 2010*

Archbishops and bishops	26
Life peers under the Appellate Jurisdiction Act 1876	23
Life peers under the Life Peerages Act 1958	614
Peers under the House of Lords Act 1999	92
Total	755

STATE OF THE PARTIES *as at 4 August 2010†*

Conservative	188
Labour	225
Liberal Democrat	75
Crossbench	182
Archbishops and bishops	26
Other	26
Total	722

† Excluding 16 peers on leave of absence, 16 disqualified as senior members of the judiciary and one disqualified as an MEP

HOUSE OF LORDS PAY BANDS

Staff are placed in the following pay bands according to their level of responsibility and taking account of other factors such as experience and marketability.

Judicial group 4	£172,000
Senior band 3	£101,500–£145,000
Senior band 2	£82,900–£135,000
Senior band 1A	£67,600–£113,000
Senior band 1	£58,200–£100,000
Band A1	£56,723–£72,788
Band A2	£47,164–£60,221

OFFICERS AND OFFICIALS

The house is presided over by the Lord Speaker, whose powers differ from those of the Speaker of the House of Commons. The Lord Speaker has no power to maintain order because the House of Lords is self-regulating.

A panel of deputy speakers is appointed by Royal Commission. The first deputy speaker is the Chair of Committees, appointed at the beginning of each session, who is a salaried officer of the house. He or she takes the chair when the whole house is in committee and in some select committees. He or she is assisted by a panel of deputy chairs, headed by the salaried Principal Deputy Chair of Committees, who is also chair of the European Union Committee of the house.

The Clerk of the Parliaments is the accounting officer and the chief permanent official responsible for the administration of the house. The Gentleman Usher of the Black Rod is responsible for security and other services and also has royal duties as secretary to the Lord Great Chamberlain.

Lord Speaker (£104,386), Rt. Hon. Baroness Hayman
Chair of Committees (£84,524), Lord Brabazon of Tara
Principal Deputy Chair of Committees (£79,076), Lord Roper
Clerk of the Parliaments (Judicial Group 4), M. G. Pownall
Clerk Assistant (Senior Band 3), D. R. Beamish, LLM
Reading Clerk and Clerk of the Overseas Office (Senior Band 2), Dr R. H. Walters, DPHIL
Clerk of the Committees (Senior Band 2), E. C. Ollard
Director of Facilities (Senior Band 2), C. V. Woodall
Finance Director (Senior Band 1A), Dr F. P. Tudor
Head of Human Resources (Senior Band 1A), S. P. Burton
Clerk of the Judicial Office and Registrar of Members' Interests (Senior Band 1A), B. P. Keith
Director of Information Services and Librarian (Senior Band 2), Dr E. Hallam Smith
Clerk of Public and Private Bill Office and Examiner of Petitions for Private Bills in the House of Lords (Senior Band 1A), T. V. Mohan
Editor of the Official Report (Senior Band 1), A. S. Nicholls
Clerk of the Records (Senior Band 1), Dr C. Shenton
Deputy Finance Director and Head of Finance (Senior Band 1), J. P. Smith
Director of Public Information (Band A1), B. Hiscock
Counsel to the Chairman of Committees (Senior Band 2), M. Thomas
Second Counsel to the Chairman of Committees (Senior Band 2), A. Roberts
Legal Adviser to the Human Rights Committee (Senior Band 2), M. Hunt
Change Manager (Senior Band 1), Mrs M. E. Ollard
Clerk of the Journals (Senior Band 1), C. Johnson
Clerk of the European Union Committee (Senior Band 1A), A. Makower
Clerks of Select Committees (Senior Band 1), Ms C. Salmon Percival; Ms C. K. Mawson
Gentleman Usher of the Black Rod and Serjeant-at-Arms (Senior Band 2), Lt.-Gen. Sir Frederick Viggers, KCB, CMG, MBE
Yeoman Usher of the Black Rod and Deputy Serjeant-at-Arms (Band A2), T. Lloyd-Jukes

LORD GREAT CHAMBERLAIN'S OFFICE

Lord Great Chamberlain, Marquess of Cholmondeley
Secretary to the Lord Great Chamberlain, Lt.-Gen. Sir Frederick Viggers, KCB, CMG, MBE

SELECT COMMITTEES

The main House of Lords select committees, as at August 2010, are as follows:

Administration and Works Committee – Chair, vacant; *Clerk,* Tom Wilson
Communications Committee – Chair, Earl of Onslow; *Clerk,* Ralph Publicover
Constitution Committee – Chair, Baroness Jay of Paddington; *Clerk,* Anna Murphy
Delegated Powers and Regulatory Reform – Chair, Baroness Thomas of Winchester; *Clerk,* vacant
Economic Affairs – Chair, Lord MacGregor of Pulham Market; *Clerk,* Bill Sinton
European Union – Chair, Lord Roper; *Clerks,* Andrew Makower; James Whittle
European Union – Sub-committees:
A (Economic and Financial Affairs and International Trade) – Chair, Lord Harrison; *Clerk,* Antony Willott
B (Internal Market, Energy and Transport) – Chair, Baroness O'Cathain; *Clerk,* John Turner
C (Foreign Affairs, Defence and Development Policy) – Chair, Lord Teverson; *Clerk,* Kathryn Colvin
D (Agriculture, Fisheries and Environment) – Chair, Lord Carter of Coles; *Clerk,* Paul Bristow
E (Justice and Institutions) – Chair, Lord Bowness; *Clerk,* Talitha Rowland
F (Home Affairs) – Chair, Lord Hannay of Chiswick; *Clerk,* Michael Collon
G (Social Policies and Consumer Protection) – Chair, Baroness Young of Hornsey; *Clerk,* Talitha Rowland
House Committee – Chair, Baroness Hayman; *Clerk,* Chis Clarke
Liaison Committee – Chair, Lord Brabazon of Tara; *Clerk,* Edward Ollard
Privileges and Conduct – Chair, Lord Brabazon of Tara; *Clerk,* vacant
Lords' Conduct Sub-committee – Chair, Baroness Manningham-Buller; *Clerk,* vacant
Merits of Statutory Instruments – Chair, Rt. Hon. Lord Goodlad; *Clerk,* vacant
Refreshment Committee – Chair, Lord Brabazon of Tara; *Clerk,* vacant
Science and Technology – Chair, Lord Krebs; *Clerk,* Christine Salmon Percival
Selection Committee – Chair, Lord Brabazon of Tara; *Clerk,* vacant
Human Rights Joint Committee – Chair, vacant; *Clerk,* vacant
Security Joint Committee – Chair, John Randall, MP; *Clerks,* Mr Wilson (Commons); Mr Clarke (Lords)
Statutory Instruments Joint Committee – Chair, George Mudie, MP; *Clerk,* John Whatley

THE HOUSE OF COMMONS

London SW1A 0AA
T 020-7219 3000 **W** www.parliament.uk

HOUSE OF COMMONS INFORMATION OFFICE
Norman Shaw Building (North), London SW1A 2TT
T 020-7219 4272 **E** hcinfo@parliament.uk

The members of the House of Commons are elected by universal adult suffrage. For electoral purposes, the United Kingdom is divided into constituencies, each of which returns one member to the House of Commons, the member being the candidate who obtains the largest number of votes cast in the constituency. To ensure equitable representation, the four Boundary Commissions keep constituency boundaries under review and recommend any redistribution of seats which may seem necessary because of population movements etc. At the 2010 general election the number of seats increased from 646 to 650. Of the present 650 seats, there are 533 for England, 40 for Wales, 59 for Scotland and 18 for Northern Ireland.

NUMBER OF SEATS IN THE HOUSE OF COMMONS

Year	*Seats*	*Year*	*Seats*
1945	640	1992	651
1948	625	1997	659
1955	630	2005	646
1970	635	2010	650
1983	650		

ELECTIONS

Elections are by secret ballot, each elector casting one vote; voting is not compulsory. For entitlement to vote in parliamentary elections, *see* Legal Notes. When a seat becomes vacant between general elections, a by-election is held.

British subjects and citizens of the Irish Republic can stand for election as MPs provided they are 18 or over and not subject to disqualification. Those disqualified from sitting in the house include:

- undischarged bankrupts
- people sentenced to more than one year's imprisonment
- members of the House of Lords (but hereditary peers not sitting in the Lords are eligible)
- holders of certain offices listed in the House of Commons Disqualification Act 1975, eg members of the judiciary, civil service, regular armed forces, police forces, some local government officers and some members of public corporations and government commissions

A candidate does not require any party backing but his or her nomination for election must be supported by the signatures of ten people registered in the constituency. A candidate must also deposit £500 with the returning officer, which is forfeit if the candidate does not receive more than 5 per cent of the votes cast. All election expenses at a general election, except the candidate's personal expenses, are subject to a statutory limit of £7,150, plus five pence for each elector in a borough constituency or seven pence for each elector in a county constituency.

See pages 138–183 for an alphabetical list of MPs and results of the general election in 2010.

STATE OF THE PARTIES *AS AT AUGUST 2010**

Party	*Seats*
Conservative	305
Labour	256
Liberal Democrats	57
Democratic Unionist Party	8
Scottish National Party	6
Sinn Fein (have not taken their seats)	5
Plaid Cymru	3
Social Democratic & Labour Party	3
Alliance	1
Green	1
Independent	1
The Speaker and three Deputy Speakers	4
Total	650

* Working majority of 83; 305 Conservative and 57 Liberal Democrat MPs less 279 of all other parties (excluding the speaker, deputy speakers and Sinn Fein)

BUSINESS
The week's business of the house is outlined each Thursday by the leader of the house, after consultation between the chief government whip and the chief opposition whip. A quarter to a third of the time will be taken up by the government's legislative programme and the rest by other business. As a rule, bills likely to raise political controversy are introduced in the Commons before going on to the Lords, and the Commons claims exclusive control in respect of national taxation and expenditure. Bills such as the finance bill, which imposes taxation, and the consolidated fund bills, which authorise expenditure, must begin in the Commons. A bill of which the financial provisions are subsidiary may begin in the Lords, and the Commons may waive its rights in regard to Lords' amendments affecting finance.

The Commons has a public register of MPs' financial and certain other interests; this is published annually as a House of Commons paper. Members must also disclose any relevant financial interest or benefit in a matter before the house when taking part in a debate, in certain other proceedings of the house, or in consultations with other MPs, with ministers or with civil servants.

MEMBERS' PAY AND ALLOWANCES
Since 1911 members of the House of Commons have received salary payments; facilities for free travel were introduced in 1924. Salary rates for the last 30 years are as follows:

1979 Jun	£9,450	1996 Jan	£34,085
1980 Jun	11,750	1996 Jul	43,000
1981 Jun	13,950	1997 Apr	43,860
1982 Jun	14,910	1998 Apr	45,066
1983 Jun	15,308	1999 Apr	47,008
1984 Jan	16,106	2000 Apr	48,371
1985 Jan	16,904	2001 Apr	49,822
1986 Jan	17,702	2002 Apr	55,118
1987 Jan	18,500	2003 Apr	56,358
1988 Jan	22,548	2004 Apr	57,485
1989 Jan	24,107	2005 Apr	59,095
1990 Jan	26,701	2006 Apr	59,686
1991 Jan	28,970	2007 Apr	61,181
1992 Jan	30,854	2008 Apr	63,291
1993 Jan	30,854	2009 Apr	64,766
1994 Jan	31,687	2010 Apr	65,738
1995 Jan	33,189		

During 2010–11, MPs received administrative expenditure (£10,394), office rental expenditure (£10,663–£12,761) and a staffing allowance (up to £109,548).

Since 1972 MPs have been able to claim reimbursement for the additional cost of staying overnight away from their main residence while on parliamentary business. During 2010–11 MPs could claim a maximum of £105 per night. Rental accommodation expenses (£19,900 per year), and mortgage interest expenses (£17,500), are only payable to non-London area MPs.

With effect from the May 2010 general election, responsibility for MPs' expenses has passed to the new Independent Parliamentary Standards Authority.

Members of staff who are paid out of the allowances can benefit from a sum not exceeding 10 per cent of their gross salary which is paid into the Portcullis Pension Plan.

MEMBERS' PENSIONS
Pension arrangements for MPs were first introduced in 1964. Under the Parliamentary Contributory Pension Fund (PCPF), MPs receive a pension on retirement based upon their salary in their final year, and upon their number of years' service as an MP. Members may pay a contribution rate of 5.9, 7.9 or 11.9 per cent and build up a pension of 1.6, 2 or 2.5 per cent of salary for each year of service. Pensions are normally payable at age 65; upon retirement at 65, the pension payable is subject to a maximum of 66.6 per cent of salary, inclusive of pensions from employment or self-employment prior to becoming an MP. There are provisions in place for: early retirement for those MPs who cease to serve between the ages of 55 and 65; MPs of any age who retire due to ill health; and pensions for widows/widowers of MPs. All pensions are index-linked. There is also an Exchequer contribution; currently 28.7 per cent of an MP's salary.

The House of Commons Members' Fund provides for annual or lump sum grants to ex-MPs, their widows or widowers, and children of those who either ceased to serve as an MP prior to the PCPF being established or who are experiencing hardship. Members contribute £24 a year and the Exchequer £215,000 a year to the fund.

HOUSE OF COMMONS PAY BANDS
Staff are placed in the following Senior Civil Service pay bands. These pay bands apply to the most senior staff in departments and agencies.

Pay Band 1	£58,200–£93,380
Pay Band 1A	£67,600–£105,560
Pay Band 2	£82,900–£124,845
Pay Band 3	£101,500–£139,829

OFFICERS AND OFFICIALS
The House of Commons is presided over by the Speaker, who has considerable powers to maintain order. A deputy speaker, called the chairman of ways and means, and two deputy chairs may preside over sittings of the House of Commons; they are elected by the house, and, like the Speaker, neither speak nor vote other than in their official capacity.

The staff of the house are employed by a commission chaired by the Speaker. The heads of the six House of Commons departments are permanent officers of the house, not MPs. The Clerk of the House is the principal adviser to the Speaker on the privileges and procedures of the house, the conduct of the business of the house, and committees. The Serjeant-at-Arms is responsible for security and ceremonial functions of the house.

Speaker (£145,492)*, Rt. Hon. John Bercow, MP (Buckingham)

Chairman of Ways and Means (£107,108), Lindsay Hoyle, MP

First Deputy Chairman of Ways and Means (£102,098), Nigel Evans, MP

Second Deputy Chairman of Ways and Means (£102,098), Dawn Primarolo, MP

Parliamentary Commissioner for Standards in Public Life, John Lyon, CB

* Salaries in brackets are the maximum available. Ministers have opted not to take a pay rise for 2010–11

OFFICES OF THE SPEAKER AND CHAIRMAN OF WAYS AND MEANS

Speaker's Secretary, A. Sinclair

Chaplain to the Speaker, Revd Canon R. Wright

Secretary to the Chairman of Ways and Means, M. Clark
Clerk of the House of Commons and Chief Executive, Dr M. R. Jack

OFFICE OF THE CHIEF EXECUTIVE
Head of Office, Ms P. Helme
Director of Internal Audit, P. Dillon-Robinson

DEPARTMENT OF CHAMBER AND COMMITTEE SERVICES

Director-General and Clerk Assistant, R. J. Rogers
Principal Clerks
Table Office, A. R. Kennon
Journals, L. Laurence Smyth
Overseas Office, M. Hutton
Director of Departmental Services, Colin Lee

VOTE OFFICE
Deliverer of the Vote, Ms C. Fogarty
Deputy Deliverers of the Vote, O. B. T. Sweeney *(Parliamentary)*; Ms J. Pitt *(Production)*

COMMITTEE DIRECTORATE
Clerk of Committees, Ms J. Sharpe
Principal Clerk and Deputy Head of Committee Office, R. W. G. Wilson
Clerk of Domestic Committees/Secretary to the Commission, D. J. Gerhold
Select Committees, P. A. Evans; C. J. Poyser
Head of Scrutiny Unit, C. Shaw
Director of Broadcasting, T. Jeffes

LEGISLATION DIRECTORATE
Clerk of Legislation, D. Natzler

Principal Clerks
Delegated Legislation, J. Benger
Bills, S. J. Patrick
National Parliament Office (Brussels), Ms L. Kurien
Ways and Means Office, M. Clark

OFFICIAL REPORT DIRECTORATE
Editor, Miss L. Sutherland
Deputy Editors, Ms V. Widgery; A. Newton

SERJEANT-AT-ARMS DIRECTORATE
Serjeant-at-Arms, Mrs J. Pay
Deputy Serjeant-at-Arms, M. Naworynsky
Assistant Serjeant-at-Arms, L. Ward

LEGAL SERVICES OFFICE
Speaker's Counsel and Head of Legal Services Office, M. Carpenter
Counsel for European Legislation, P. Hardy
Counsel for Legislation, Peter Davis
Deputy Counsel, P. Brooksbank; Ms C. Cogger
Senior Assistant Counsel, Ms V. Daly
Assistant Counsel, G. Beck; Ms H. Emes

DEPARTMENT OF INFORMATION SERVICES

Director-General and Librarian, J. Pullinger
Directors, R. Clements *(Service Delivery);* Prof. D. Cope *(Parliamentary Office of Science and Technology);* B. Morgan *(Research);* R. Twigger *(Information Services);* Ms A. Walker *(Public Information);* S. Wise *(Information Management);* Ms H. Wood *(SPIRE Programme)*
Heads of Sections, C. Barclay; Mrs D. Clark; R. Cracknell; T. Edmonds; Ms O. Gay; Mrs C. Gillie; M. Hay; V. Launert; S. McGinness; Mrs K. Marke; Ms C. Meredith; Ms V. Miller; T. O'Leary; Ms P. J. Strickland
Media and Communications Adviser, Ms E. Parratt
Parliamentary Outreach Officer, Ms C. Cowan
Visitor and Information Manager, C. Weeds

DEPARTMENT OF RESOURCES

Director-General of Resources, A. J. Walker
Director of Business Management and Development, Ms J. Rissen
Director of Human Resource Management, Mrs H. Bryson
Director of Finance Policy, C. Ridley
Director of Commercial Services, Ms B. Mohan
Head of Occupational Health, Safety and Welfare Service, Dr M. McDougall

DEPARTMENT OF FACILITIES

Director-General, J. Borley
Director of Business Management, J. Greenaway
Parliamentary Director of Estates, M. Barlex
Director of Accommodation Services, J. Robertson
Director of Facilities Finance, P. Collins
Executive Officer, M. Trott
Head of Human Resources and Development, vacant

CATERING AND RETAIL SERVICES DIRECTORATE
Director of Catering Services, Mrs S. Harrison
Catering Operations Manager (Outbuildings), Ms D. Herd
Food and Beverage Operations Manager, Palace of Westminster, R. Gibbs
Executive Chef, M. Hill
Retail Manager, Mrs M. DeSouza

PARLIAMENTARY INFORMATION AND COMMUNICATION TECHNOLOGY (ICT)

Director of Parliamentary ICT, Ms J. Miller
Director of Technology Directorate, I. Montgomery
Director of Operations and Members Services, M. Taylor
Director of Resources, F. Reid
Director of Programmes and Project Development, R. Ware

NATIONAL AUDIT OFFICE

157–197 Buckingham Palace Road, London SW1W 9SP
T 020-7798 7000
E enquiries@nao.gsi.gov.uk W www.nao.org.uk

The National Audit Office came into existence under the National Audit Act 1983 to replace and continue the work of the former Exchequer and Audit Department. The act reinforced the office's total financial and operational independence from the government and brought its head, the Comptroller and Auditor-General, into a closer relationship with parliament as an officer of the House of Commons.

The National Audit Office provides independent information, advice and assurance to parliament and the public about all aspects of the financial operations of government departments and many other bodies receiving public funds. It does this by examining and certifying the accounts of these organisations. It also regularly publishes reports to parliament on the results of its value for money investigations of the economy (the efficiency and effectiveness with which public resources have been used). The National Audit Office is also the auditor by agreement of the accounts of certain international and other organisations. In addition, the office authorises the issue of public funds to government departments.

Comptroller and Auditor-General, Amyas Morse
Private Secretary, Laura Brackwell
Chief Operating Officer, Michael Whitehouse
Leadership Team, Gabrielle Cohen; Ed Humpherson; Wendy Kenway-Smith; Martin Sinclair

SELECT COMMITTEES
The more significant committees, as at June 2010, are:

DEPARTMENTAL COMMITTEES
Business, Innovation and Skills – Chair, Adrian Bailey, MP; *Clerk,* James Davies
Children, Schools and Families – Chair, Graham Stuart, MP, *Clerk,* Kenneth Fox
Communities and Local Government – Chair, Clive Betts, MP; *Clerk,* Huw Yardley
Culture, Media and Sport – Chair, John Whittingdale, MP; *Clerk,* Tracey Garratty
Defence – Chair, Rt. Hon. James Arbuthnot, MP; *Clerk,* Mike Hennessy
Energy and Climate Change – Chair, Tim Yeo, MP; *Clerk,* Tom Goldsmith
Environment, Food and Rural Affairs – Chair, Ann McIntosh, MP; *Clerk,* Richard Cooke
Foreign Affairs – Chair, Richard Ottaway, MP; *Clerk,* Dr Robin James
Health – Chair, Stephen Dorell, MP; *Clerk,* David Lloyd
Home Affairs – Chair, Rt. Hon. Keith Vaz, MP; *Clerk,* Elizabeth Flood
International Development – Chair, Rt. Hon. Malcolm Bruce, MP; *Clerk,* David Harrison
Justice – Chair, Rt. Hon. Sir Alan Beith, MP; *Clerk,* vacant
Northern Ireland Affairs – Chair, Laurence Robertson, MP; *Clerk,* Alison Groves
Scottish Affairs – Chair, Ian Davidson, MP; *Clerk,* Nerys Welfoot
Transport – Chair, Louise Ellman, MP; *Clerk,* Adrian Jenner
Treasury – Chair, Andrew Tyrie, MP; *Clerk,* Eve Samson
Welsh Affairs – Chair, David T. C. Davies, MP; *Clerk,* Alison Groves
Work and Pensions – Chair, Anne Begg, MP; *Clerk,* Carol Oxborough

NON-DEPARTMENTAL COMMITTEES
Environmental Audit – Chair, Joan Walley, MP; *Clerk,* Gordon Clarke
Political and Constitutional Reform – Chair, Graham Allen, MP; *Clerk,* vacant
Procedure – Chair, Rt. Hon. Greg Knight, MP; *Clerk,* Dr Lynn Gardner
Public Accounts – Chair, Margaret Hodge, MP; *Clerk,* Mark Etherton
Public Administration – Chair, Bernard Jenkin, MP; *Clerk,* Steven Mark
Science and Technology – Chair, Andrew Miller; *Clerk,* Glenn McKee

PARLIAMENTARY INFORMATION

The following is a short glossary of aspects of the work of parliament. Unless otherwise stated, references are to House of Commons procedures.

BILL – Proposed legislation is termed a bill. The stages of a public bill (for private bills, *see* below) in the House of Commons are as follows:

First reading: This stage introduces the legislation to the house and, for government Bills, merely constitutes an order to have the bill printed.

Second reading: The debate on the principles of the bill.

Committee stage: The detailed examination of a bill, clause by clause. In most cases this takes place in a public bill committee, or the whole house may act as a committee. Public bill committees may take evidence before embarking on detailed scrutiny of the bill. Very rarely, a bill may be examined by a select committee.

Report stage: Detailed review of a bill as amended in committee, on the floor of the house, and an opportunity to make further changes.

Third reading: Final debate on the full bill in the Commons.

Public bills go through the same stages in the House of Lords, but with important differences: the committee stage is taken in committee of the whole house or in a grand committee, in which any peer may participate. There are no time limits, all amendments are debated, and further amendments can be made at third reading.

A bill may start in either house, and has to pass through both houses to become law. Both houses have to agree the final text of a bill, so that amendments made by the second house are then considered in the originating house, and if not agreed, sent back or themselves amended, until agreement is reached.

CHILTERN HUNDREDS – A nominal office of profit under the crown, the acceptance of which requires an MP to vacate his/her seat. The Manor of Northstead is similar. These are the only means by which an MP may resign.

CONSOLIDATED FUND BILL – A bill to authorise issue of money to maintain government services. The bill is dealt with without debate.

EARLY DAY MOTION – A motion put on the notice paper by an MP without, in general, the real prospect of its being debated. Such motions are expressions of back-bench opinion.

FATHER OF THE HOUSE – The MP whose continuous service in the House of Commons is the longest. The present Father of the House is Sir Peter Tapsell, MP.

GRAND COMMITTEES – There are three grand committees in the House of Commons, one each for Northern Ireland, Scotland and Wales; they consider matters relating specifically to that country. In the House of Lords, bills may be sent to a grand committee instead of a committee of the whole house (*see also* Bill).

HOURS OF MEETING – The House of Commons normally meets on Mondays and Tuesdays at 2.30pm, Wednesdays at 11.30am, Thursdays at 10.30am and some Fridays at 9.30am. (*See also* Westminster Hall Sittings, below.) The House of Lords normally meets at 2.30pm Mondays and Tuesdays, 3pm on Wednesdays and at 11am on Thursdays. The House of Lords occasionally sits on Fridays at 10am.

LEADER OF THE OPPOSITION – In 1937 the office of leader of the opposition was recognised and a salary was assigned to the post. In 2010–11 this was £139,355 (including a parliamentary salary of £65,738). The present acting leader of the opposition is the Rt. Hon. Harriet Harman, QC, MP.

THE LORD CHANCELLOR – The office of Lord High Chancellor of Great Britain was significantly altered by the Constitutional Reform Act 2005. Previously, the Lord Chancellor was (*ex officio*) the Speaker of the House of Lords, and took part in debates and voted in divisions in the House of Lords. The Department for Constitutional Affairs was created in 2003, which became the Ministry of Justice in 2007, incorporating most of the responsibilities of the Lord Chancellor's department. The role of Speaker has been transferred to the post of Lord Speaker. The Constitutional Reform Act 2005 also brought to an end the Lord Chancellor's role as head of the judiciary. A Judicial Appointments Commission was created in April 2006, and a supreme court (separate from the House of Lords) was established in 2009.

THE LORD SPEAKER – The first Lord Speaker of the House of Lords, the Rt. Hon. Baroness Hayman, took up office on 4 July 2006. Unlike in the case of the Lord Chancellor, the Lord Speaker is independent of the government and elected by members of the House of Lords rather than appointed by the prime minister. Although the Lord Speaker's primary role is to preside over proceedings in the House of Lords, she does not have the same powers as the speaker of the House of Commons. For example, the Lord Speaker is not responsible for maintaining order during debates, as this is the responsibility of the house as a whole. The Lord Speaker sits in the Lords on one of the woolsacks, which are couches covered in red cloth and stuffed with wool.

THE LORD GREAT CHAMBERLAIN – The Lord Great Chamberlain is a Great Officer of State, the office being hereditary since the grant of Henry I to the family of De Vere, Earls of Oxford. It is now a joint hereditary office rotating on the death of the sovereign between the Cholmondeley, Carington and Ancaster families.

The Lord Great Chamberlain, currently the Marquess of Cholmondeley, is responsible for the royal apartments in the Palace of Westminster, the Royal Gallery, the administration of the Chapel of St Mary Undercroft and, in conjunction with the Lord Speaker and the Speaker of the House of Commons, Westminster Hall. The Lord Great Chamberlain has the right to perform specific services at a coronation, he carries out ceremonial duties in the Palace of Westminster when the sovereign visits the palace and has particular responsibility for the internal administrative arrangements within the House of Lords for state openings of parliament.

OPPOSITION DAY – A day on which the topic for debate is chosen by the opposition. There are 20 such days in a normal session. On 17 days, subjects are chosen by the leader of the opposition; on the remaining three days by the leader of the next largest opposition party.

PARLIAMENT ACTS 1911 AND 1949 – Under these acts, bills may become law without the consent of the Lords, though the House of Lords has the power to delay a public bill for a parliamentary session.

PRIME MINISTER'S QUESTIONS – The prime minister answers questions from 12 to 12.30pm on Wednesdays.

PRIVATE BILL – A bill promoted by a body or an individual to give powers additional to, or in conflict with, the general law, and to which a special procedure applies to enable people affected to object.

PRIVATE MEMBER'S BILL – A public bill promoted by an MP or peer who is not a member of the government.

PRIVATE NOTICE QUESTION – A question adjudged of urgent importance on submission to the Speaker (in the Lords, the Lord Speaker), answered at the end of oral questions.

PRIVILEGE – The House of Commons has rights and immunities to protect it from obstruction in carrying out its duties. These are known as parliamentary privilege and enable Members of Parliament to debate freely. The most important privilege is that of freedom of speech. MPs cannot be prosecuted for sedition or sued for libel or slander over anything said during proceedings in the house. This enables them to raise in the house questions affecting the public good which might be difficult to raise outside owing to the possibility of being sued. The House of Lords has similar privileges.

QUESTION TIME – Oral questions are answered by ministers in the Commons from 2.30 to 3.30pm on Mondays and Tuesdays, 11.30am to 12.30pm on Wednesdays, and 10.30 to 11.30am on Thursdays. Questions are also taken at the start of the Lords sittings, with a daily limit of four oral questions.

ROYAL ASSENT – The royal assent is signified by letters patent to such bills and measures as have passed both Houses of Parliament (or bills which have been passed under the Parliament Acts 1911 and 1949). The sovereign has not given royal assent in person since 1854. On occasion, for instance in the prorogation of parliament, royal assent may be pronounced to the two houses by Lords Commissioners. More usually royal assent is notified to each house sitting separately in accordance with the Royal Assent Act 1967. The old French formulae for royal assent are then endorsed on the acts by the Clerk of the Parliaments.

The power to withhold assent resides with the sovereign but has not been exercised in the UK since 1707.

SELECT COMMITTEES – Consisting usually of 10 to 15 members of all parties, select committees are a means used by both houses in order to investigate certain matters.

Most select committees in the House of Commons are tied to departments: each committee investigates subjects within a government department's remit. There are other select committees dealing with matters such as public accounts (ie the spending by the government of money voted by parliament) and European legislation, and also committees advising on procedures and domestic administration of the house. Major select committees usually take evidence in public; their evidence and reports are published on the parliament website and in hard copy by TSO (The Stationery Office). House of Commons select committees are reconstituted after a general election.

In the House of Lords, select committees do not mirror government departments but cover broader issues. There is a select committee on the European Union (EU), which has seven sub-committees dealing with specific areas of EU policy, a select committee on science and technology, a select committee on economic affairs and also one on the constitution. There is also a select committee on delegated powers and regulatory reform and one on privileges and conduct. In addition, *ad hoc* select committees have been set up from time to time to investigate specific subjects. There are also joint committees of the two houses, eg the committees on statutory instruments and on human rights.

THE SPEAKER – The Speaker of the House of Commons is the spokesperson and chair of the Chamber. He or she is elected by the house at the beginning of each parliament or when the previous Speaker retires or dies. The Speaker neither speaks in debates nor votes in divisions except when the voting is equal.

VACANT SEATS – When a vacancy occurs in the House of Commons during a session of parliament, the writ for the by-election is moved by a whip of the party to which the member whose seat has been vacated belonged. If the house is in recess, the Speaker can issue a warrant for a writ, should two members certify to him that a seat is vacant.

WESTMINSTER HALL SITTINGS – Following a report by the Modernisation of the House of Commons Select Committee, the Commons decided in May 1999 to set up a second debating forum. It is known as 'Westminster Hall' and sittings are in the Grand Committee Room on Tuesdays from 9.30 to 11.30am, Wednesdays from 9.30 to 11.30am and from 2 to 5pm, and Thursdays from 2.30 to 5.30pm. Sittings will be open to the public at the times indicated.

WHIPS – In order to secure the attendance of members of a particular party in parliament, particularly on the occasion of an important vote, whips (originally known as 'whippers-in') are appointed. The written appeal or circular letter issued by them is also known as a 'whip', its urgency being denoted by the number of times it is underlined. Failure to respond to a three-line whip is tantamount in the Commons to secession (at any rate temporarily) from the party. Whips are provided with office accommodation in both houses, and government and some opposition whips receive salaries from public funds.

PARLIAMENTARY ARCHIVES
Houses of Parliament, London SW1A 0PW
T 020-7219 3074
E archives@parliament.uk W www.parliament.uk/archives

Since 1497, the records of parliament have been kept within the Palace of Westminster. They are in the custody of the Clerk of the Parliaments. In 1946 the House of Lords Record Office, which became the Parliamentary Archives in 2006, was established to supervise their preservation and their availability to the public. Some three million documents are preserved, including acts of parliament from 1497, journals of the House of Lords from 1510, minutes and committee proceedings from 1610, and papers laid before parliament from 1531. Among the records are the Petition of Right, the death warrant of Charles I, the Declaration of Breda, and the Bill of Rights. Records are made available through a public search room.
Clerk of the Records, Dr Caroline Shenton

GOVERNMENT OFFICE

The government is the body of ministers responsible for the administration of national affairs, determining policy and introducing into parliament any legislation necessary to give effect to government policy. The majority of ministers are members of the House of Commons but members of the House of Lords, or of neither house, may also hold ministerial responsibility. The prime minister is, by current convention, always a member of the House of Commons.

THE PRIME MINISTER

The office of prime minister, which had been in existence for nearly 200 years, was officially recognised in 1905 and its holder was granted a place in the table of precedence. The prime minister, by tradition also First Lord of the Treasury and Minister for the Civil Service, is appointed by the sovereign and is usually the leader of the party which enjoys, or can secure, a majority in the House of Commons. Other ministers are appointed by the sovereign on the recommendation of the prime minister, who also allocates functions among ministers and has the power to obtain their resignation or dismissal individually.

The prime minister informs the sovereign on state and political matters, advises on the dissolution of parliament, and makes recommendations for important crown appointments, ie the award of honours, etc.

As the chair of cabinet meetings and leader of a political party, the prime minister is responsible for translating party policy into government activity. As leader of the government, the prime minister is responsible to parliament and to the electorate for the policies and their implementation.

The prime minister also represents the nation in international affairs, eg summit conferences.

THE CABINET

The cabinet developed during the 18th century as an inner committee of the Privy Council, which was the chief source of executive power until that time. The cabinet is composed of about 20 ministers chosen by the prime minister, usually the heads of government departments (generally known as secretaries of state unless they have a special title, eg Chancellor of the Exchequer), the leaders of the two houses of parliament, and the holders of various traditional offices.

The cabinet's functions are the final determination of policy, control of government and coordination of government departments. The exercise of its functions is dependent upon enjoying majority support in the House of Commons. Cabinet meetings are held in private, taking place once or twice a week during parliamentary sittings and less often during a recess. Proceedings are confidential, the members being bound by their oath as privy counsellors not to disclose information about the proceedings.

The convention of collective responsibility means that the cabinet acts unanimously even when cabinet ministers do not all agree on a subject. The policies of departmental ministers must be consistent with the policies of the government as a whole, and once the government's policy has been decided, each minister is expected to support it or resign.

The convention of ministerial responsibility holds a minister, as the political head of his or her department, accountable to parliament for the department's work. Departmental ministers usually decide all matters within their responsibility, although on matters of political importance they normally consult their colleagues collectively. A decision by a departmental minister is binding on the government as a whole.

POLITICAL PARTIES

Before the reign of William and Mary the principal officers of state were chosen by and were responsible to the sovereign alone, and not to parliament or the nation at large. Such officers acted sometimes in concert with one another but more often independently, and the fall of one did not, of necessity, involve that of others, although all were liable to be dismissed at any moment.

In 1693 the Earl of Sunderland recommended to William III the advisability of selecting a ministry from the political party which enjoyed a majority in the House of Commons, and the first united ministry was drawn in 1696 from the Whigs, to which party the king owed his throne. This group became known as the 'Junto' and was regarded with suspicion as a novelty in the political life of the nation, being a small section meeting in secret apart from the main body of ministers. It may be regarded as the forerunner of the cabinet and in the course of time it led to the establishment of the principle of joint responsibility of ministers, so that internal disagreement caused a change of personnel or resignation of the whole body of ministers.

The accession of George I, who was unfamiliar with the English language, led to a disinclination on the part of the sovereign to preside at meetings of his ministers and caused the emergence of a prime minister, a position first acquired by Robert Walpole in 1721 and retained by him without interruption for 20 years and 326 days.

DEVELOPMENT OF PARTIES

In 1828 the Whigs became known as Liberals, a name originally given by opponents to imply laxity of principles, but gradually accepted by the party to indicate its claim to be pioneers and champions of political reform and progressive legislation. In 1861 a Liberal Registration Association was founded and Liberal Associations became widespread. In 1877 a National Liberal Federation was formed, with its headquarters in London. The Liberal Party was in power for long periods during the second half of the 19th century and for several years during the first quarter of the 20th century, but after a split in the party in 1931, the numbers elected remained small. In 1988, a majority of the Liberals agreed on a merger with the Social Democratic Party under the title Social and Liberal Democrats; since 1989 they have been known as the Liberal Democrats. A minority continue separately as the Liberal Party.

Soon after the change from Whig to Liberal, the Tory Party became known as Conservative, a name believed to have been invented by John Wilson Croker in 1830 and to have been generally adopted around the time of the passing of the Reform Act of 1832 – to indicate that the preservation of national institutions was the leading principle of the party. After the Home Rule crisis of 1886 the dissentient Liberals entered into a compact with the Conservatives, under which the latter undertook not to contest their seats, but a separate Liberal Unionist organisation was maintained until 1912, when it was united with the Conservatives.

Labour candidates for parliament made their first appearance at the general election of 1892, when there were 27 standing as Labour or Liberal-Labour. In 1900 the Labour Representation Committee (LRC) was set up in order to establish a distinct Labour group in parliament, with its own whips, its own policy, and a readiness to cooperate with any party which might be engaged in promoting legislation in the direct interests of labour. In 1906 the LRC became known as the Labour Party.

The Green Party was founded in 1973 and campaigns for social and environmental justice. The party began as 'People', was renamed the Ecology Party, and became the Green Party in 1985.

Plaid Cymru was founded in 1926 to provide an independent political voice for Wales and to campaign for self-government in Wales.

The Scottish National Party was founded in 1934 to campaign for independence for Scotland.

The Social Democratic and Labour Party was founded in 1970, emerging from the civil rights movement of the 1960s, with the aim of promoting reform, reconciliation and partnership across the sectarian divide in Northern Ireland, and of opposing violence from any quarter.

The Democratic Unionist Party was founded in 1971 to resist moves by the Ulster Unionist Party which were considered a threat to the Union. Its aim is to maintain Northern Ireland as an integral part of the UK.

The Alliance Party of Northern Ireland was formed in 1970 as a non-sectarian unionist party.

Sinn Fein first emerged in the 1900s as a federation of nationalist clubs. It is a left-wing republican and labour party that seeks to end British governance in Ireland and achieve a 32-county republic.

GOVERNMENT AND OPPOSITION

The government is formed by the party which wins the largest number of seats in the House of Commons at a general election, or which has the support of a majority of members in the House of Commons. By tradition, the leader of the majority party is asked by the sovereign to form a government, while the largest minority party becomes the official opposition with its own leader and a shadow cabinet. Leaders of the government and opposition sit on the front benches of the Commons with their supporters (the back-benchers) sitting behind them.

FINANCIAL SUPPORT

Financial support for opposition parties in the House of Commons was introduced in 1975 and is commonly known as Short Money, after Edward Short, the leader of the house at that time, who introduced the scheme. Short Money allocation for 2010–11* is:

Democratic Unionists	£129,249
Green Party	£51,326
Labour	£4,592,546
Plaid Cymru	£51,326
SDLP	£54,832
SNP	£145,610

*Pro-rata amounts from 6 May 2010

A specific allocation for the leader of the opposition's office was introduced in April 1999 and has been set at £604,493 for the years 2010–11.

Financial support for opposition parties in the House of Lords was introduced in 1996 and is commonly known as Cranborne Money.

The parties included here are those with MPs sitting in the House of Commons in the present parliament.

ALLIANCE PARTY OF NORTHERN IRELAND

88 University Street, Belfast BT7 1HE
T 028-9032 4274 E alliance@allianceparty.org
W www.allianceparty.org

Party Leader, David Ford
Deputy Party Leader, Naomi Long, MP
President, Colm Cavanagh
Chair, Michael Long
Hon. Treasurers, Stewart Dickson; Dan McGuinness

CONSERVATIVE PARTY

Conservative Campaign Headquarters, 30 Millbank, London SW1P 4DP
T 020-7222 9000
W www.conservatives.com

Parliamentary Party Leader, Rt. Hon. David Cameron, MP
Leader in the Lords and Chancellor of the Duchy of Lancaster, Rt. Hon. Lord Strathclyde
Leader in the Commons and Lord Privy Seal, Rt. Hon. Sir George Young, Bt., MP
Chairs, Andrew Feldman; Baroness Warsi
Party Treasurer, Michael Spencer

GREEN PARTY

1A Waterlow Road, London N19 5NJ
T 020-7272 4474
E office@greenparty.org.uk W www.greenparty.org.uk
Party Leader, Dr Caroline Lucas, MP
Deputy Leader, Adrian Ramsay
Chair of Party Executive, Jayne Forbes
Finance Coordinator, Dean Walton

LABOUR PARTY

39 Victoria Street, London SW1H 0HA
T 0870-590 0200 W www.labour.org.uk
General Secretary, Ray Collins
General Secretary, Welsh Labour, Chris Roberts
General Secretary, Scottish Labour Party, Colin Smyth

SHADOW CABINET AS AT AUGUST 2010
Leader of the Opposition (acting), Rt. Hon. Harriet Harman, QC, MP
Deputy Prime Minister, Secretary of State for Justice and Lord Chancellor, Rt. Hon. Jack Straw, MP
Secretary of State for Foreign and Commonwealth Affairs, Rt. Hon. David Miliband, MP
Chancellor of the Exchequer, Rt. Hon. Alistair Darling, MP
Secretary of State for Business, Innovation and Skills, Rt. Hon. Pat McFadden, MP
Secretary of State for the Cabinet Office and Chancellor of the Duchy of Lancaster, Rt. Hon. Tessa Jowell, MP
Secretary of State for Communities and Local Government, Rt. Hon. John Denham, MP
Secretary of State for Culture, Olympics, Media and Sport, Rt. Hon. Ben Bradshaw, MP
Secretary of State for Defence, Rt. Hon. Bob Ainsworth, MP
Secretary of State for Education, Rt. Hon. Ed Balls, MP
Secretary of State for Energy and Climate Change, Rt. Hon. Ed Miliband, MP
Secretary of State for Environment, Food and Rural Affairs, Rt. Hon. Hilary Benn, MP
Secretary of State for Health, Rt. Hon. Andy Burnham, MP
Secretary of State for Home Affairs, Rt. Hon. Alan Johnson, MP
**Minister for Housing,* Rt. Hon. John Healey, MP
Secretary of State for International Development, Rt. Hon. Douglas Alexander, MP
Secretary of State for Northern Ireland, Rt. Hon. Shaun Woodward
Secretary of State for Scotland, Rt. Hon. Jim Murphy, MP
**Secretary of State for Transport,* Rt. Hon. Sadiq Khan, MP
Chief Secretary to the Treasury, Rt. Hon. Liam Byrne, MP
Secretary of State for Wales, Rt. Hon. Peter Hain, MP
Secretary of State for Work and Pensions and Minister for Women and Equalities, Rt. Hon. Yvette Cooper, MP
Leader in the House of Commons and Lord Privy Seal, Rt. Hon. Rosie Winterton, MP
Leader in the House of Lords, Rt. Hon. Baroness Royall of Blaisdon
Spokesman for the Deputy Prime Minister in the House of Lords, Rt. Hon. Lord Hunt of Kings Heath
**Attorney-General,* Baroness Scotland of Asthal, QC
Parliamentary Party Chair, Tony Lloyd, MP

LABOUR WHIPS
House of Lords, Lord Bassam of Brighton
House of Commons, Nick Brown, MP
* Attends Cabinet meetings but is not a Cabinet member

LIBERAL DEMOCRATS

4 Cowley Street, London SW1P 3NB
T 020-7222 7999
E info@libdems.org.uk W www.libdems.org.uk
Parliamentary Party Leader, Rt. Hon. Nick Clegg, MP
Deputy Party Leader, Simon Hughes, MP
Leader in the Lords, Rt. Hon. Lord McNally
Leader in the Commons, David Heath, MP
President, Baroness Ros Scott
Chief Executive (interim), Chris Fox
Hon. Treasurer, Lord Razzall

NORTHERN IRELAND DEMOCRATIC UNIONIST PARTY

91 Dundela Avenue, Belfast BT4 3BU
T 028-9047 1155
E info@dup.org.uk W www.dup.org.uk
Parliamentary Party Leader, Peter Robinson, MLA
Deputy Leader, Nigel Dodds, MP, MLA
Chair, Lord Morrow, MLA
Hon Treasurer, Gregory Campbell, MP, MLA
Party Secretary, Michelle McIlveen, MLA

PLAID CYMRU – THE PARTY OF WALES

Ty Gwynfor, Marine Chambers, Anson Court, Atlantic Wharf, Caerdydd CF10 4AL
T 029-2047 2272
E post@plaidcymru.org W www.plaidcymru.org
Party Leader, Ieuan Wyn Jones, AM
Party President, Jill Evans, MEP
Parliamentary Group Leader, Elfyn Llwyd, MP
Chief Executive, Dr Gwenllian Lansdown

SCOTTISH NATIONAL PARTY

3 Jackson's Entry, Edinburgh EH8 8PJ
T 0131-525 8900
E snp.hq@snp.org W www.snp.org
Westminster Parliamentary Party Leader, Angus Robertson, MP
Westminster Parliamentary Party Chief Whip, Stewart Hosie, MP
Scottish Parliamentary Party Leader, Alex Salmond, MSP
Scottish Parliamentary Party Chief Whip, Brian Adam, MSP
National Treasurer, Cllr Colin Beattie
National Secretary, William Henderson
Chief Executive, Peter Murrell

SINN FEIN

53 Falls Road, Belfast BT12 4PD
T 028-9022 3000
E sfadmin@eircom.net W www.ardfheis.com
Party President, Gerry Adams, MP, MLA
Vice-President, Mary Lou McDonald, MEP
Chair, Declan Kearney
Treasurers, Rita O'Hare; Maurice Quinlivan
General Secretary, Dawn Doyle

SOCIAL DEMOCRATIC AND LABOUR PARTY

121 Ormeau Road, Belfast BT7 1SH
T 028-9024 7700 E info@sdlp.ie W www.sdlp.ie
Parliamentary Party Leader, Margaret Ritchie, MP, MLA
Deputy Leader, Patsy McGlone, MLA
Party Whip, Pat Ramsey, MLA
Chair, Joe Byrne
Treasurer, Peter McEvoy
General Secretary, Gerry Cosgrove

MEMBERS OF PARLIAMENT as at 1 September 2010

* New MP
† Previously MP in another seat
‡ Previously MP for another party

Abbott, Diane (*b.* 1953) *Lab., Hackney North & Stoke Newington,* Maj. 14,461
Adams, Gerry (*b.* 1948) *SF, Belfast West,* Maj. 17,579
***Adams**, Nigel (*b.* 1966) *C., Selby and Ainsty,* Maj. 12,265
Afriyie, Adam (*b.* 1965) *C., Windsor,* Maj. 19,054
Ainsworth, Rt. Hon. Robert (*b.* 1952) *Lab., Coventry North East,* Maj. 11,775
***Aldous**, Peter (*b.* 1961) *C., Waveney,* Maj. 769
Alexander, Danny (*b.* 1972) *LD, Inverness, Nairn, Badenoch & Strathspey,* Maj. 8,765
Alexander, Rt. Hon. Douglas (*b.* 1967) *Lab., Paisley & Renfrewshire South,* Maj. 16,614
***Alexander,** Heidi (*b.* 1975) *Lab., Lewisham East,* Maj. 6,216
***Ali**, Rushanara, *Lab., Bethnal Green and Bow,* Maj. 11,574
Allen, Graham (*b.* 1953) *Lab., Nottingham North,* Maj. 8,138
Amess, David (*b.* 1952) *C., Southend West,* Maj. 7,270
Anderson, David (*b.* 1953) *Lab., Blaydon,* Maj. 9,117
***Andrew**, Stuart (*b.* 1971) *C., Pudsey,* Maj. 1,659
Arbuthnot, Rt. Hon. James (*b.* 1952) *C., Hampshire North East,* Maj. 18,597
Austin, Ian (*b.* 1965) *Lab., Dudley North,* Maj. 649
Bacon, Richard (*b.* 1962) *C., Norfolk South,* Maj. 10,940
***Bagshawe**, Louise (*b.* 1971) *C., Corby,* Maj. 1,951
Bailey, Adrian (*b.* 1945) *Lab. (Co-op), West Bromwich West,* Maj. 5,651
Bain, William (*b.* 1972) *Lab., Glasgow North East,* Maj. 15,942
Baker, Norman (*b.* 1957) *LD, Lewes,* Maj. 7,647
***Baker**, Steven (*b.* 1971) *C., Wycombe,* Maj. 9,560
Baldry, Tony (*b.* 1950) *C., Banbury,* Maj. 18,227
***Baldwin**, Harriett (*b.* 1960) *C., West Worcestershire,* Maj. 6,804
Balls, Rt. Hon. Ed (*b.* 1967) *Lab. (Co-op), Morley and Outwood,* Maj. 1,101
Banks, Gordon (*b.* 1955) *Lab., Ochil & Perthshire South,* Maj. 5,187
***Barclay**, Stephen (*b.* 1972) *C., Cambridgeshire North East,* Maj. 16,425
Barker, Gregory (*b.* 1966) *C., Bexhill & Battle,* Maj. 12,880
Baron, John (*b.* 1959) *C., Basildon and Billericay,* Maj. 12,398
Barron, Rt. Hon. Kevin (*b.* 1946) *Lab., Rother Valley,* Maj. 5,866
***Barwell**, Gavin (*b.* 1972) *C., Croydon Central,* Maj. 2,969
Bayley, Hugh (*b.* 1952) *Lab., York Central,* Maj. 6,451
***Bebb**, Guto (*b.* 1968) *C., Aberconwy,* Maj. 3,398
Beckett, Rt. Hon. Margaret (*b.* 1943) *Lab., Derby South,* Maj. 6,122
Begg, Anne (*b.* 1955) *Lab., Aberdeen South,* Maj. 3,506
Beith, Rt. Hon. Sir Alan (*b.* 1943) *LD, Berwick-upon-Tweed,* Maj. 2,690
Bell, Sir Stuart (*b.* 1938) *Lab., Middlesbrough,* Maj. 8,689
Bellingham, Henry (*b.* 1955) *C., Norfolk North West,* Maj. 14,810
Benn, Rt. Hon. Hilary (*b.* 1953) *Lab., Leeds Central,* Maj. 10,645
Benton, Joe (*b.* 1933) *Lab., Bootle,* Maj. 21,181
Benyon, Richard (*b.* 1960) *C., Newbury,* Maj. 12,248
Bercow, John (*b.* 1963) *The Speaker, Buckingham,* Maj. 12,529
Beresford, Sir Paul (*b.* 1946) *C., Mole Valley,* Maj. 15,653
***Berger**, Luciana (*b.* 1981) *Lab. (Co-op), Liverpool, Wavertree,* Maj. 7,167
***Berry**, Jake (*b.* 1978) *C., Rossendale and Darwen,* Maj. 4,493
Betts, Clive (*b.* 1950) *Lab., Sheffield South East,* Maj. 10,505
***Bingham**, Andrew (*b.* 1962) *C., High Peak,* Maj. 4,677
Binley, Brian (*b.* 1942) *C., Northampton South,* Maj. 6,004
***Birtwistle**, Gordon (*b.* 1943) *LD, Burnley,* Maj. 1,818
***Blackman**, Bob (*b.* 1956) *C., Harrow East,* Maj. 3,403
Blackman-Woods, Dr Roberta (*b.* 1957) *Lab., Durham, City of,* Maj. 3,067
***Blackwood**, Nicola (*b.* 1979) *C., Oxford West and Abingdon,* Maj. 176
Blears, Rt. Hon. Hazel (*b.* 1956) *Lab., Salford and Eccles,* Maj. 5,725
***Blenkinsop**, Tom (*b.* 1980) *Lab., Middlesbrough South and East Cleveland,* Maj. 1,677
***Blomfield**, Paul (*b.* 1953) *Lab., Sheffield Central,* Maj. 165
Blunkett, Rt. Hon. David (*b.* 1947) *Lab., Sheffield, Brightside and Hillsborough,* Maj. 13,632
Blunt, Crispin (*b.* 1960) *C., Reigate,* Maj. 13,591
***Boles**, Nick (*b.* 1965) *C., Grantham and Stamford,* Maj. 14,826
Bone, Peter (*b.* 1952) *C., Wellingborough,* Maj. 11,787
Bottomley, Peter (*b.* 1944) *C., Worthing West,* Maj. 11,729
***Bradley**, Karen (*b.* 1970) *C., Staffordshire Moorlands,* Maj. 6,689
Bradshaw, Ben (*b.* 1960) *Lab., Exeter,* Maj. 2,721
Brady, Graham (*b.* 1967) *C., Altrincham & Sale West,* Maj. 11,595
Brake, Tom (*b.* 1962) *LD, Carshalton & Wallington,* Maj. 5,260
***Bray**, Angie (*b.* 1953) *C., Ealing Central and Acton,* Maj. 3,716
Brazier, Julian (*b.* 1953) *C., Canterbury,* Maj. 6,048
Brennan, Kevin (*b.* 1959) *Lab., Cardiff West,* Maj. 4,750
***Bridgen**, Andrew (*b.* 1964) *C., Leicestershire North West,* Maj. 7,511
***Brine**, Steve (*b.* 1974) *C., Winchester,* Maj. 24,107
†**Brokenshire**, James (*b.* 1968) *C., Old Bexley and Sidcup,* Maj. 15,857
Brooke, Annette (*b.* 1947) *LD, Dorset Mid & Poole North,* Maj. 269
Brown, Rt. Hon. Gordon (*b.* 1951) *Lab., Kirkcaldy & Cowdenbeath,* Maj. 23,009
Brown, Lyn (*b.* 1960) *Lab., West Ham,* Maj. 22,534
Brown, Rt. Hon. Nicholas (*b.* 1950) *Lab., Newcastle upon Tyne East,* Maj. 4,453
Brown, Russell (*b.* 1951) *Lab., Dumfries & Galloway,* Maj. 7,449
Browne, Jeremy (*b.* 1970) *LD, Taunton Deane,* Maj. 3,993
***Bruce**, Fiona (*b.* 1957) *C., Congleton,* Maj. 7,063
Bruce, Rt. Hon. Malcolm (*b.* 1944) *LD, Gordon,* Maj. 6,748

Bryant, Chris (*b.* 1962) *Lab., Rhondda,* Maj. 11,553
Buck, Karen (*b.* 1958) *Lab., Westminster North,* Maj. 2,126
***Buckland**, Robert (*b.* 1968) *C., Swindon South,* Maj. 3,544
Burden, Richard (*b.* 1954) *Lab., Birmingham Northfield,* Maj. 2,782
***Burley**, Aidan (*b.* 1979) *C., Cannock Chase,* Maj. 3,195
Burnham, Rt. Hon. Andy (*b.* 1970) *Lab., Leigh,* Maj. 15,011
***Burns**, Conor (*b.* 1972) *C., Bournemouth West,* Maj. 5,583
Burns, Simon (*b.* 1952) *C., Chelmsford,* Maj. 5,110
Burrowes, David (*b.* 1969) *C., Enfield Southgate,* Maj. 7,626
Burstow, Paul (*b.* 1962) *LD, Sutton & Cheam,* Maj. 1,608
Burt, Alistair (*b.* 1955) *C., Bedfordshire North East,* Maj. 18,942
Burt, Lorely (*b.* 1957) *LD, Solihull,* Maj. 175
***Byles**, Daniel (*b.* 1974) *C., Warwickshire North,* Maj. 54
Byrne, Liam (*b.* 1970) *Lab., Birmingham Hodge Hill,* Maj. 10,302
Cable, Dr Vincent (*b.* 1943) *LD, Twickenham,* Maj. 12,140
***Cairns**, Alun (*b.* 1970) C., Vale of Glamorgan, Maj. 4,307
Cairns, David (*b.* 1966) *Lab., Inverclyde,* Maj. 14,416
Cameron, Rt. Hon. David (*b.* 1966) *C., Witney,* Maj. 22,740
Campbell, Alan (*b.* 1957) *Lab., Tynemouth,* Maj. 5,739
Campbell, Gregory (*b.* 1953) *DUP, Londonderry East,* Maj. 5,355
Campbell, Rt. Hon. Sir Menzies (*b.* 1941) *LD, Fife North East,* Maj. 9,048
Campbell, Ronnie (*b.* 1943) *Lab., Blyth Valley,* Maj. 6,668
Carmichael, Alistair (*b.* 1965) *LD, Orkney & Shetland,* Maj. 9,928
***Carmichael**, Neil (*b.* 1961) *C., Stroud,* Maj. 1,299
Carswell, Douglas (*b.* 1971) *C., Clacton,* Maj. 12,068
Cash, Bill (*b.* 1940) *C., Stone,* Maj. 13,292
Caton, Martin (*b.* 1951) *Lab., Gower,* Maj. 2,683
***Chapman**, Jenny (*b.* 1973) *Lab., Darlington,* Maj. 3,388
***Chishti**, Rehman (*b.* 1978) *C., Gillingham & Rainham,* Maj. 8,680
Chope, Christopher (*b.* 1947) *C., Christchurch,* Maj. 15,410
Clappison, James (*b.* 1956) *C., Hertsmere,* Maj. 17,605
Clark, Greg (*b.* 1967) *C., Tunbridge Wells,* Maj. 15,576
Clark, Katy (*b.* 1967) *Lab., Ayrshire North & Arran,* Maj. 9,895
Clarke, Rt. Hon. Kenneth (*b.* 1940) *C., Rushcliffe,* Maj. 15,811
Clarke, Rt. Hon. Thomas (*b.* 1941) *Lab., Coatbridge, Chryston & Bellshill,* Maj. 20,714
Clegg, Rt. Hon. Nick (*b.* 1967) *LD, Sheffield Hallam,* Maj. 15,284
Clifton-Brown, Geoffrey (*b.* 1953) *C., Cotswold,* Maj. 12,864
Clwyd, Rt. Hon. Ann (*b.* 1937) *Lab., Cynon Valley,* Maj. 9,617
Coaker, Vernon (*b.* 1953) *Lab., Gedling,* Maj. 1,859
Coffey, Ann (*b.* 1946) *Lab., Stockport,* Maj. 6,784
***Coffey**, Therese (*b.* 1971) *C., Suffolk Coastal,* Maj. 9,128
***Collins**, Damian (*b.* 1974) *C., Folkestone and Hythe,* Maj. 10,122
***Colvile**, Oliver (*b.* 1959) *C., Plymouth, Sutton & Devonport,* Maj. 1,149
Connarty, Michael (*b.* 1947) *Lab., Linlithgow & Falkirk East,* Maj. 12,553
Cooper, Rosie (*b.* 1950) *Lab., Lancashire West,* Maj. 4,343
Cooper, Rt. Hon. Yvette (*b.* 1969) *Lab., Pontefract & Castleford,* Maj. 10,979
Corbyn, Jeremy (*b.* 1949) *Lab., Islington North,* Maj. 12,401
Cox, Geoffrey (*b.* 1960) *C., Devon West & Torridge,* Maj. 2,957
Crabb, Stephen (*b.* 1973) *C., Preseli Pembrokeshire,* Maj. 4,605
Crausby, David (*b.* 1946) *Lab., Bolton North East,* Maj. 4,084
Creagh, Mary (*b.* 1967) *Lab., Wakefield,* Maj. 1,613
***Creasy**, Stella (*b.* 1977) *Lab. (Co-op), Walthamstow,* Maj. 9,478
***Crockart**, Mike (*b.* 1966) *LD, Edinburgh West,* Maj. 3,803
***Crouch**, Tracey (*b.* 1975) *C., Chatham & Aylesford,* Maj. 6,069
Cruddas, Jonathan (*b.* 1965) *Lab., Dagenham & Rainham,* Maj. 2,630
***Cryer**, John (*b.* 1964) *Lab., Leyton & Wanstead,* Maj. 6,416
***Cunningham**, Alex (*b.* 1955) *Lab., Stockton North,* Maj. 6,676
Cunningham, Jim (*b.* 1941) *Lab., Coventry South,* Maj. 3,845
Cunningham, Tony (*b.* 1952) *Lab., Workington,* Maj. 4,575
***Curran**, Margaret (*b.* 1958) *Lab., Glasgow East,* Maj. 11,840
***Dakin**, Nick (*b.* 1955) *Lab., Scunthorpe,* Maj. 2,549
***Danczuk**, Simon (*b.* 1966) *Lab., Rochdale,* Maj. 889
Darling, Rt. Hon. Alistair (*b.* 1953) *Lab., Edinburgh South West,* Maj. 8,447
Davey, Edward (*b.* 1965) *LD, Kingston & Surbiton,* Maj. 7,560
David, Wayne (*b.* 1957) *Lab., Caerphilly,* Maj. 10,775
Davidson, Ian (*b.* 1950) *Lab. (Co-op), Glasgow South West,* Maj. 14,671
Davies, David (*b.* 1970) *C., Monmouth,* Maj. 10,425
***Davies**, Geraint (*b.* 1960) *Lab. (Co-op), Swansea West,* Maj. 504
***Davies**, Glyn (*b.* 1944) *C., Montgomeryshire,* Maj. 1,184
Davies, Philip (*b.* 1972) *C., Shipley,* Maj. 9,944
Davis, Rt. Hon. David (*b.* 1948) *C., Haltemprice & Howden,* Maj. 11,602
***de Bois**, Nick (*b.* 1959) *C., Enfield North,* Maj. 1,692
***De Piero**, Gloria (*b.* 1972) *Lab., Ashfield,* Maj. 192
Denham, Rt. Hon. John (*b.* 1953) *Lab., Southampton Itchen,* Maj. 192
***Dinenage**, Caroline (*b.* 1971) *C., Gosport,* Maj. 14,413
Djanogly, Jonathan (*b.* 1965) *C., Huntingdon,* Maj. 10,819
Dobbin, Jim (*b.* 1941) *Lab. (Co-op), Heywood & Middleton,* Maj. 5,971
Dobson, Rt. Hon. Frank (*b.* 1940) *Lab., Holborn & St Pancras,* Maj. 9,942
***Docherty**, Thomas, *Lab., Dunfermline & Fife West,* Maj. 5,470
Dodds, Nigel (*b.* 1958) *DUP, Belfast North,* Maj. 2,224
Doherty, Pat (*b.* 1945) *SF, Tyrone West,* Maj. 10,685
‡**Donaldson**, Rt. Hon. Jeffrey (*b.* 1962) *DUP, Lagan Valley,* Maj. 10,486
Donohoe, Brian (*b.* 1948) *Lab., Ayrshire Central,* Maj. 12,007

Doran, Frank (*b.* 1949) *Lab., Aberdeen North,* Maj. 8,361
Dorrell, Rt. Hon. Stephen (*b.* 1952) *C., Charnwood,* Maj. 15,029
Dorries, Nadine (*b.* 1958) *C., Bedfordshire Mid,* Maj. 15,152
Dowd, Jim (*b.* 1951) *Lab., Lewisham West & Penge,* Maj. 5,828
***Doyle**, Gemma, *Lab. (Co-op), Dunbartonshire West,* Maj. 17,408
***Doyle-Price**, Jackie (*b.* 1969) *C., Thurrock,* Maj. 92
***Drax**, Richard (*b.* 1958) *C., Dorset South,* Maj. 7,443
***Dromey**, Jack (*b.* 1948) *Lab., Birmingham Erdington,* Maj. 3,277
Duddridge, James (*b.* 1971) *C., Rochford & Southend East,* Maj. 11,050
***Dugher**, Michael (*b.* 1975) *Lab., Barnsley East,* Maj. 11,090
Duncan, Alan (*b.* 1957) *C., Rutland & Melton,* Maj. 14,000
Duncan Smith, Rt. Hon. Iain (*b.* 1954) *C., Chingford & Woodford Green,* Maj. 12,963
Dunne, Philip (*b.* 1958) *C., Ludlow,* Maj. 9,749
Durkan, Mark (*b.* 1960) *SDLP, Foyle,* Maj. 4,824
Eagle, Angela (*b.* 1961) *Lab., Wallasey,* Maj. 8,507
Eagle, Maria (*b.* 1961) *Lab., Garston & Halewood,* Maj. 16,877
***Edwards**, Jonathan (*b.* 1976) *PC, Carmarthen East and Dinefwr,* Maj. 3,481
Efford, Clive (*b.* 1958) *Lab., Eltham,* Maj. 1,663
***Elliott**, Julie (*b.* 1963) *Lab., Sunderland Central,* Maj. 6,725
***Ellis**, Michael (*b.* 1967) *C., Northampton North,* Maj. 1,936
***Ellison**, Jane (*b.*1964) *C., Battersea,* Maj. 5,977
Ellman, Louise (*b.* 1945) *Lab. (Co-op), Liverpool Riverside,* Maj. 14,173
Ellwood, Tobias (*b.* 1966) *C., Bournemouth East,* Maj. 7,728
***Elphicke**, Charlie (*b.* 1971) *C., Dover,* Maj. 5,274
Engel, Natascha (*b.* 1967) *Lab., Derbyshire North East,* Maj. 2,445
***Esterson**, Bill (*b.* 1966) *Lab., Sefton Central,* Maj. 3,862
***Eustice**, George (*b.* 1971) *C., Camborne & Redruth,* Maj. 66
***Evans**, Chris (*b.* 1976) *Lab. (Co-op), Islwyn,* Maj. 12,215
***Evans**, Graham (*b.* 1963) *C., Weaver Vale,* Maj. 991
***Evans**, Jonathan (*b.* 1950) *C., Cardiff North,* Maj. 194
Evans, Nigel (*b.* 1957) *C., Ribble Valley,* Maj. 14,769
Evennett, David (*b.* 1949) *C., Bexleyheath & Crayford,* Maj. 10,344
Fabricant, Michael (*b.* 1950) *C., Lichfield,* Maj. 17,683
Fallon, Michael (*b.* 1952) *C., Sevenoaks,* Maj. 17,515
Farrelly, Paul (*b.* 1962) *Lab., Newcastle-under-Lyme,* Maj. 1,552
Farron, Tim (*b.* 1970) *LD, Westmorland & Lonsdale,* Maj. 12,264
Featherstone, Lynne (*b.* 1951) *LD, Hornsey & Wood Green,* Maj. 6,875
Field, Rt. Hon. Frank (*b.* 1942) *Lab., Birkenhead,* Maj. 15,195
Field, Mark (*b.* 1934) *C., Cities of London & Westminster,* Maj. 11,076
Fitzpatrick, Jim (*b.* 1952) *Lab., Poplar & Limehouse,* Maj. 6,030
Flello, Robert (*b.* 1966) *Lab., Stoke-on-Trent South,* Maj. 4,130
Flint, Rt. Hon. Caroline (*b.* 1961) *Lab., Don Valley,* Maj. 3,595
Flynn, Paul (*b.* 1935) *Lab., Newport West,* Maj. 3,544
Foster, Don (*b.* 1947) *LD, Bath,* Maj. 11,883
***Fovargue**, Yvonne (*b.* 1956) *Lab., Makerfield,* Maj. 12,490
Fox, Dr Liam (*b.* 1961) *C., North Somerset,* Maj. 7,862
Francis, Dr Hywel (*b.* 1946) *Lab., Aberavon,* Maj. 11,039
Francois, Mark (*b.* 1965) *C., Rayleigh & Wickford,* Maj. 22,338
***Freeman**, George (*b.* 1967) *C., Norfolk Mid,* Maj. 13,856
***Freer**, Mike (*b.* 1960) *C., Finchley & Golders Green,* Maj. 5,809
***Fullbrook**, Lorraine (*b.* 1959) *C., Ribble South,* Maj. 5,554
***Fuller**, Richard (*b.* 1962) *C., Bedford,* Maj. 1,353
Gale, Roger (*b.* 1943) *C., Thanet North,* Maj. 13,528
Gapes, Mike (*b.* 1952) *Lab. (Co-op), Ilford South,* Maj. 11,297
Gardiner, Barry (*b.* 1957) *Lab., Brent North,* Maj. 8,028
Garnier, Edward (*b.* 1952) *C., Harborough,* Maj. 9,877
***Garnier**, Mark (*b.* 1963) *C. Wyre Forest,* Maj. 2,643
Gauke, David (*b.* 1971) *C., Hertfordshire South West,* Maj. 14,920
George, Andrew (*b.* 1958) *LD, St Ives,* Maj. 1,719
Gibb, Nick (*b.* 1960) *C., Bognor Regis & Littlehampton,* Maj. 13,063
***Gilbert**, Stephen (*b.* 1976) *LD, St Austell & Newquay,* Maj. 1,312
Gildernew, Michelle (*b.* 1970) *SF, Fermanagh & South Tyrone,* Maj. 4
Gillan, Cheryl (*b.* 1952) *C., Chesham & Amersham,* Maj. 16,710
***Gilmore**, Sheila (*b.* 1950) *Lab., Edinburgh East,* Maj. 9,181
***Glass**, Pat (*b.* 1956) *Lab., Durham North West,* Maj. 7,612
***Glen**, John (*b.* 1974) *C., Salisbury,* Maj. 5,966
***Glindon**, Mary (*b.* 1957) *Lab., Tyneside North,* Maj. 12,884
Godsiff, Roger (*b.* 1946) *Lab., Birmingham Hall Green,* Maj. 3,799
Goggins, Paul (*b.* 1953) *Lab., Wythenshawe & Sale East,* Maj. 7,575
***Goldsmith**, Zac (*b.* 1975) *C., Richmond Park,* Maj. 4,091
Goodman, Helen (*b.* 1958) *Lab., Bishop Auckland,* Maj. 5,218
Goodwill, Robert (*b.* 1956) *C., Scarborough & Whitby,* Maj. 8,130
Gove, Michael (*b.* 1967) *C., Surrey Heath,* Maj. 17,289
***Graham**, Richard (*b.* 1958) *C., Gloucester,* Maj. 2,420
***Grant**, Helen (*b.* 1961) *C., Maidstone & the Weald,* Maj. 5,889
Gray, James (*b.* 1954) *C., Wiltshire North,* Maj. 7,483
Grayling, Chris (*b.* 1962) *C., Epsom & Ewell,* Maj. 16,134
***Greatrex**, Tom (*b.* 1974) *Lab. (Co-op), Rutherglen & Hamilton West,* Maj. 21,002
Green, Damian (*b.* 1956) *C., Ashford,* Maj. 17,297
***Green**, Kate (*b.* 1960) *Lab., Stretford and Urmston,* Maj. 8,935
Greening, Justine (*b.* 1969) *C., Putney,* Maj. 10,053
***Greenwood**, Lilian (*b.* 1966) *Lab., Nottingham South,* Maj. 1,772
Grieve, Dominic (*b.* 1956) *C., Beaconsfield,* Maj. 21,782
Griffith, Nia (*b.* 1956) *Lab., Llanelli,* Maj. 4,701

***Griffiths**, Andrew (*b.* 1970) *C., Burton,* Maj. 6,304
***Gummer**, Benedict (*b.* 1978) *C., Ipswich,* Maj. 2,079
Gwynne, Andrew (*b.* 1974) *Lab., Denton & Reddish,* Maj. 9,831
***Gyimah**, Sam (*b.* 1976) *C., Surrey East,* Maj. 16,874
Hague, Rt. Hon. William (*b.* 1961) *C., Richmond (Yorks),* Maj. 23,336
Hain, Rt. Hon. Peter (*b.* 1950) *Lab., Neath,* Maj. 9,775
***Halfon**, Robert (*b.* 1969) *C., Harlow,* Maj. 4,925
***Hames**, Duncan (*b.* 1977) *LD, Chippenham,* Maj. 2,470
Hamilton, David (*b.* 1950) *Lab., Midlothian,* Maj. 4,545
Hamilton, Fabian (*b.* 1955) *Lab., Leeds North East,* Maj. 10,349
Hammond, Philip (*b.* 1955) *C., Runnymede & Weybridge,* Maj. 16,509
Hammond, Stephen (*b.* 1962) *C., Wimbledon,* Maj. 11,408
***Hancock**, Matthew (*b.* 1978) *C., Suffolk West,* Maj. 13,050
Hancock, Mike (*b.* 1946) *LD, Portsmouth South,* Maj. 5,200
Hands, Greg (*b.* 1965) *C., Chelsea & Fulham,* Maj. 16,722
Hanson, Rt. Hon. David (*b.* 1957) *Lab., Delyn,* Maj. 2,272
Harman, Rt. Hon. Harriet (*b.* 1950) *Lab., Camberwell & Peckham,* Maj. 17,187
Harper, Mark (*b.* 1970) *C., Forest of Dean,* Maj. 11,064
***Harrington**, Richard (b. 1957) *C., Watford,* Maj. 1,425
***Harris**, Rebecca (*b.* 1967) *C., Castle Point,* Maj. 7,632
Harris, Tom (*b.* 1964) *Lab., Glasgow South,* Maj. 12,658
***Hart**, Simon (*b.* 1963) *C., Carmarthen West & Pembrokeshire South,* Maj. 3,423
Harvey, Nick (*b.* 1961) *LD, Devon North,* Maj. 5,821
Haselhurst, Rt. Hon. Sir Alan (*b.* 1937) *C., Deputy Speaker, Saffron Walden,* Maj. 15,242
Havard, Dai (*b.* 1949) *Lab., Merthyr Tydfil & Rhymney,* Maj. 4,056
Hayes, John (*b.* 1958) *C., South Holland & The Deepings,* Maj. 21,880
Heald, Oliver (*b.* 1954) *C., Hertfordshire North East,* Maj. 15,194
Healey, Rt. Hon. John (*b.* 1960) *Lab., Wentworth and Dearne,* Maj. 13,920
Heath, David (*b.* 1954) *LD, Somerton & Frome,* Maj. 1,817
***Heaton-Harris**, Chris (*b.* 1967) *C., Daventry,* Maj. 19,188
Hemming, John (*b.* 1960) *LD, Birmingham Yardley,* Maj. 3,002
***Henderson**, Gordon (*b.* 1948) *C., Sittingbourne & Sheppey,* Maj. 12,383
Hendrick, Mark (*b.* 1958) *Lab. (Co-op), Preston,* Maj. 7,733
Hendry, Charles (*b.* 1959) *C., Wealden,* Maj. 17,179
Hepburn, Stephen (*b.* 1959) *Lab., Jarrow,* Maj. 12,908
Herbert, Nick (*b.* 1963) *C., Arundel & South Downs,* Maj. 16,691
‡Hermon, Lady Sylvia (*b.* 1956) *Ind., Down North,* Maj. 14,364
Heyes, David (*b.* 1946) *Lab., Ashton-under-Lyne,* Maj. 9,094
Hillier, Meg (*b.* 1969) *Lab. (Co-op), Hackney South & Shoreditch,* Maj. 14,288
***Hilling**, Julie, *Lab., Bolton West,* Maj. 92
***Hinds**, Damian (*b.* 1969) *C., Hampshire East,* Maj. 13,497
Hoban, Mark (*b.* 1964) *C., Fareham,* Maj. 17,092
Hodge, Rt. Hon. Margaret (*b.* 1944) *Lab., Barking,* Maj. 16,555
Hodgson, Sharon (*b.* 1966) *Lab., Washington and Sunderland West,* Maj. 11,458
Hoey, Kate (*b.* 1946) *Lab., Vauxhall,* Maj. 10,651
***Hollingbery**, George (*b.* 1963) *C., Meon Valley,* Maj. 12,125
Hollobone, Philip (*b.* 1964) *C., Kettering,* Maj. 9,094
Holloway, Adam (*b.* 1965) *C., Gravesham,* Maj. 9,312
Hood, Jim (*b.* 1948) *Lab., Lanark & Hamilton East,* Maj. 13,478
Hopkins, Kelvin (*b.* 1941) *Lab., Luton North,* Maj. 7,520
***Hopkins**, Kris (*b.* 1963) *C., Keighley,* Maj. 2,940
Horwood, Martin (*b.* 1962) *LD, Cheltenham,* Maj. 4,920
Hosie, Stewart (*b.* 1963) *SNP, Dundee East,* Maj. 1,821
Howarth, Rt. Hon. George (*b.* 1949) *Lab., Knowsley,* Maj. 25,690
Howarth, Gerald (*b.* 1947) *C., Aldershot,* Maj. 5,586
Howell, John (*b.* 1955) *C., Henley,* Maj. 16,588
Hoyle, Lindsay (*b.* 1957) *Lab., Chorley,* Maj. 2,593
Hughes, Simon (*b.* 1951) *LD, Bermondsey & Old Southwark,* Maj. 8,530
Huhne, Chris (*b.* 1954) *LD, Eastleigh,* Maj. 3,864
Hunt, Jeremy (*b.* 1966) *C., Surrey South West,* Maj. 16,318
***Hunt**, Tristram (*b.* 1974) *Lab., Stoke-on-Trent Central,* Maj. 5,566
Hunter, Mark (*b.* 1957) *LD, Cheadle,* Maj. 3,272
***Huppert**, Julian (*b.* 1978) *LD, Cambridge,* Maj. 6,792
Hurd, Nick (*b.* 1962) *C., Ruislip, Northwood & Pinner,* Maj. 19,060
Illsley, Eric (*b.* 1955) *Lab., Barnsley Central,* Maj. 11,093
Irranca-Davies, Huw (*b.* 1963) *Lab., Ogmore,* Maj. 13,246
Jackson, Glenda (*b.* 1936) *Lab., Hampstead & Kilburn,* Maj. 42
Jackson, Stewart (*b.* 1965) *C., Peterborough,* Maj. 4,861
***James**, Margot (*b.* 1957) *C., Stourbridge,* Maj. 5,164
James, Sian (*b.* 1959) *Lab., Swansea East,* Maj. 10,838
***Jamieson**, Cathy (b. 1956) *Lab. (Co-op), Kilmarnock & Loudoun,* Maj. 12,378
***Javid**, Sajid (*b.* 1969) *C., Bromsgrove,* Maj. 11,308
Jenkin, Bernard (*b.* 1959) *C., Harwich & Essex North,* Maj. 11,447
Johnson, Rt. Hon. Alan (*b.* 1950) *Lab., Hull West & Hessle,* Maj. 5,740
Johnson, Diana (*b.* 1966) *Lab., Kingston upon Hull North,* Maj. 641
***Johnson**, Gareth (*b.* 1969) *C., Dartford,* Maj. 24,428
***Johnson**, Jo (*b.* 1971) *C., Orpington,* Maj. 17,200
***Jones**, Andrew (*b.* 1963) *C., Harrogate & Knaresborough,* Maj. 1,039
Jones, David (*b.* 1952) *C., Clwyd West,* Maj. 6,419
***Jones**, Graham, *Lab., Hyndburn,* Maj. 3,090
Jones, Helen (*b.* 1954) *Lab., Warrington North,* Maj. 6,771
Jones, Kevan (*b.* 1964) *Lab., Durham North,* Maj. 12,076
***Jones**, Marcus (*b.* 1974) *C., Nuneaton,* Maj. 2,069
***Jones**, Susan (*b.* 1968) *Lab., Clwyd South,* Maj. 2,834
Jowell, Rt. Hon. Tessa (*b.* 1947) *Lab., Dulwich & West Norwood,* Maj. 9,365
Joyce, Eric (*b.* 1960) *Lab., Falkirk,* Maj. 7,843
Kaufman, Rt. Hon. Sir Gerald (*b.* 1930) *Lab., Manchester Gorton,* Maj. 6,703
Kawczynski, Daniel (*b.* 1972) *C., Shrewsbury & Atcham,* Maj. 7,944
Keeley, Barbara (*b.* 1952) *Lab., Worsley & Eccles South,* Maj. 4,337

Keen, Alan (*b.* 1937) *Lab. (Co-op), Feltham & Heston,* Maj. 4,658
*__Kelly__, Chris (b. 1978) *C., Dudley South,* Maj. 3,856
*__Kendall__, Elizabeth (*b.* 1971) *Lab., Leicester West,* Maj. 4,017
Kennedy, Rt. Hon. Charles (*b.* 1959) *LD, Ross, Skye & Lochaber,* Maj. 13,070
Khan, Rt. Hon. Sadiq (*b.* 1970) *Lab., Tooting,* Maj. 2,524
*__Kirby__, Simon (*b.* 1964) *C., Brighton Kemptown,* Maj. 1,328
Knight, Rt. Hon. Greg (*b.* 1949) *C., Yorkshire East,* Maj. 13,486
*__Kwarteng__, Kwasi (*b.* 1975) *C., Spelthorne,* Maj. 10,019
Laing, Eleanor (*b.* 1958) *C., Epping Forest,* Maj. 15,131
Lamb, Norman (*b.* 1957) *LD, Norfolk North,* Maj. 11,626
Lammy, Rt. Hon. David (*b.* 1972) *Lab., Tottenham,* Maj. 16,931
Lancaster, Mark (*b.* 1970) *C., Milton Keynes North,* Maj. 8,961
Lansley, Andrew (*b.* 1956) *C., Cambridgeshire South,* Maj. 7,838
*__Latham__, Pauline (*b.* 1948) *C., Derbyshire Mid,* Maj. 11,292
*__Lavery__, Ian, *Lab., Wansbeck,* Maj. 7,031
Laws, David (*b.* 1965) *LD, Yeovil,* Maj. 13,036
Lazarowicz, Mark (*b.* 1953) *Lab. (Co-op), Edinburgh North & Leith,* Maj. 1,724
*__Leadsom__, Andrea (*b.* 1963) *C., Northamptonshire South,* Maj. 20,478
*__Lee__, Jessica (*b.* 1976) *C., Erewash,* Maj. 2,501
*__Lee__, Philip (*b.* 1970) *C., Bracknell,* Maj. 15,074
Leech, John (*b.* 1971) *LD, Manchester Withington,* Maj. 1,850
*__Lefroy__, Jeremy (*b.* 1959) *C., Stafford,* Maj. 5,460
Leigh, Edward (*b.* 1950) *C., Gainsborough,* Maj. 10,559
*__Leslie__, Charlotte (*b.* 1978) *C., Bristol North West,* Maj. 3,274
*__Leslie__, Christopher (*b.* 1972) *Lab. (Co-op), Nottingham East,* Maj. 6,969
Letwin, Rt. Hon. Oliver (*b.* 1956) *C., Dorset West,* Maj. 3,923
*__Lewis__, Brandon (b. 1971) C., *Great Yarmouth,* Maj. 4,276
Lewis, Ivan (*b.* 1967) *Lab., Bury South,* Maj. 3,292
Lewis, Dr Julian (*b.* 1951) *C., New Forest East,* Maj. 11,307
Liddell-Grainger, Ian (*b.* 1959) *C., Bridgwater & Somerset West,* Maj. 9,249
Lidington, David (*b.* 1956) *C., Aylesbury,* Maj. 12,618
Lilley, Rt. Hon. Peter (*b.* 1943) *C., Hitchin & Harpenden,* Maj. 15,271
*__Lloyd__, Stephen (*b.* 1957) *LD, Eastbourne,* Maj. 3,435
Lloyd, Tony (*b.* 1950) *Lab., Manchester Central,* Maj. 10,439
Llwyd, Elfyn (*b.* 1951) *PC, Dwyfor Meirionnydd,* Maj. 6,367
*__Long__, Naomi (*b.* 1971) *All. Belfast East,* Maj. 1,533
*__Lopresti,__ Jack (*b.* 1969) *C., Filton & Bradley Stoke,* Maj. 6,914
*__Lord__, Jonathan (*b.* 1962) *C., Woking,* Maj. 6,807
Loughton, Tim (*b.* 1962) *C., Worthing East & Shoreham,* Maj. 11,105
Love, Andy (*b.* 1949) *Lab. (Co-op), Edmonton,* Maj. 9,613
*__Lucas__, Caroline (*b.* 1960) *Green, Brighton Pavilion,* Maj. 1,252
Lucas, Ian (*b.* 1960) *Lab., Wrexham,* Maj. 3,658
Luff, Peter (*b.* 1955) *C., Worcestershire Mid,* Maj. 15,864
*__Lumley__, Karen (*b.* 1964) *C., Redditch,* Maj. 5,821
McCabe, Stephen (*b.* 1955) *Lab., Birmingham Selly Oak,* Maj. 3,482
*__McCann__, Michael (*b.* 1964) *Lab., East Kilbride, Strathaven & Lesmahagow,* Maj. 14,503
McCarthy, Kerry (*b.* 1965) *Lab., Bristol East,* Maj. 3,722
*__McCartney__, Jason (*b.* 1968) *C., Colne Valley,* Maj. 4,837
*__McCartney__, Karl (*b.* 1968) *C., Lincoln,* Maj. 1,058
*__McClymont__, Gregg (*b.* 1976) *Lab., Cumbernauld, Kilsyth & Kirkintilloch East,* Maj. 13,755
McCrea, Revd Dr William (*b.* 1948) *DUP, Antrim South,* Maj. 1,183
McDonagh, Siobhain (*b.* 1960) *Lab., Mitcham & Morden,* Maj. 13,666
McDonnell, Dr Alasdair (*b.* 1949) *SDLP, Belfast South,* Maj. 5,926
McDonnell, John (*b.* 1951) *Lab., Hayes & Harlington,* Maj. 10,824
McFadden, Rt. Hon. Pat (*b.* 1965) *Lab., Wolverhampton South East,* Maj. 6,593
*__McGovern__, Alison (*b.* 1980) *Lab., Wirral South,* Maj. 531
McGovern, James (*b.* 1956) *Lab., Dundee West,* Maj. 7,278
McGuinness, Martin (*b.* 1950) *SF, Ulster Mid,* Maj. 15,363
McGuire, Rt. Hon. Anne (*b.* 1949) *Lab., Stirling,* Maj. 8,354
McKechin, Ann (*b.* 1961) *Lab., Glasgow North,* Maj. 3,898
*__McKinnell__, Catherine (*b.* 1976) *Lab., Newcastle upon Tyne North,* Maj. 3,414
*__MacLeod__, Mary (*b.* 1969) *C., Brentford & Isleworth,* Maj. 1,958
McLoughlin, Rt. Hon. Patrick (*b.* 1957) *C., Derbyshire Dales,* Maj. 13,866
MacNeil, Angus (*b.* 1970) *SNP, Na h-Eileanan an Iar,* Maj. 1,885
*__McPartland__, Stephen (*b.* 1976) *C., Stevenage,* Maj. 3,578
MacShane, Rt. Hon. Denis (*b.* 1948) *Lab., Rotherham,* Maj. 10,462
Mactaggart, Fiona (*b.* 1953) *Lab., Slough,* Maj. 5,523
*__McVey__, Esther (*b.* 1967) *C., Wirral West,* Maj. 2,436
Mahmood, Khalid (*b.* 1961) *Lab., Birmingham Perry Barr,* Maj. 11,908
*__Mahmood__, Shabana (*b.* 1980) *Lab., Birmingham Ladywood,* Maj. 10,105
Main, Anne (*b.* 1957) *C., St Albans,* Maj. 2,305
Mann, John (*b.* 1960) *Lab., Bassetlaw,* Maj. 8,215
Marsden, Gordon (*b.* 1953) *Lab., Blackpool South,* Maj. 1,852
Maude, Rt. Hon. Francis (*b.* 1953) *C., Horsham,* Maj. 11,460
May, Rt. Hon. Theresa (*b.* 1956) *C., Maidenhead,* Maj. 16,769
*__Maynard__, Paul (*b.* 1975) *C., Blackpool North & Cleveleys,* Maj. 2,150
Meacher, Rt. Hon. Michael (*b.* 1939) *Lab., Oldham West & Royton,* Maj. 9,352
Meale, Alan (*b.* 1949) *Lab., Mansfield,* Maj. 6,012
*__Mearns__, Ian (*b.* 1957) *Lab., Gateshead,* Maj. 12,549
*__Menzies__, Mark (*b.* 1971) *C., Fylde,* Maj. 13,185
Mercer, Patrick (*b.* 1956) *C., Newark,* Maj. 16,152
*__Metcalfe__, Stephen (*b.* 1966) *C., Basildon South & Thurrock East,* Maj. 5,772
Michael, Rt. Hon. Alun (*b.* 1943) *Lab. (Co-op), Cardiff South & Penarth,* Maj. 4,709

Miliband, Rt. Hon. David (*b.* 1966) *Lab., South Shields,* Maj. 11,109
Miliband, Rt. Hon. Edward (*b.* 1969) *Lab., Doncaster North,* Maj. 10,909
Miller, Andrew (*b.* 1949) *Lab., Ellesmere Port & Neston,* Maj. 4,331
Miller, Maria (*b.* 1964) *C., Basingstoke,* Maj. 13,176
*__Mills__, Nigel (*b.* 1974) *C., Amber Valley,* Maj. 536
Milton, Anne (*b.* 1955) *C., Guildford,* Maj. 7,782
Mitchell, Andrew (*b.* 1956) *C., Sutton Coldfield,* Maj. 17,005
Mitchell, Austin (*b.* 1934) *Lab., Great Grimsby,* Maj. 714
Moon, Madeleine (*b.* 1950) *Lab., Bridgend,* Maj. 2,263
Moore, Michael (*b.* 1965) *LD, Berwickshire, Roxburgh & Selkirk,* Maj. 5,675
*__Mordaunt__, Penny (*b.* 1973) *C., Portsmouth North,* Maj. 7,289
Morden, Jessica (*b.* 1968) *Lab., Newport East,* Maj. 1,650
*__Morgan__, Nicky (*b.* 1972) *C., Loughborough,* Maj. 3,744
*__Morrice__, Graeme (*b.* 1959) *Lab., Livingston,* Maj. 10,791
*__Morris__, Anne Marie (*b.* 1957) *C., Newton Abbot,* Maj. 523
*__Morris__, David (*b.* 1966) *C., Morecambe & Lunesdale,* Maj. 866
*__Morris__, Grahame (*b.* 1961) *Lab., Easington,* Maj. 14,982
*__Morris__, James (*b.* 1967) *C., Halesowen & Rowley Regis,* Maj. 2,023
*__Mosley__, Stephen (*b.* 1972) *C., Chester, City of,* Maj. 2,583
*__Mowat__, David (*b.* 1957) *C., Warrington South,* Maj. 1,553
Mudie, George (*b.* 1945) *Lab., Leeds East,* Maj. 10,293
Mulholland, Greg (*b.* 1970) *LD, Leeds North West,* Maj. 9,103
Mundell, David (*b.* 1962) *C., Dumfriesshire, Clydesdale & Tweeddale,* Maj. 4,194
Munn, Meg (*b.* 1959) *Lab. (Co-op), Sheffield Heeley,* Maj. 5,807
*__Munt__, Tessa (*b.* 1959) *LD, Wells,* Maj. 800
Murphy, Conor (*b.* 1963) *SF, Newry & Armagh,* Maj. 8,331
Murphy, Rt. Hon. Jim (*b.* 1967) *Lab., Renfrewshire East,* Maj. 10,420
Murphy, Rt. Hon. Paul (*b.* 1948) *Lab., Torfaen,* Maj. 9,306
*__Murray__, Ian (*b.* 1976) *Lab., Edinburgh South,* Maj. 316
*__Murray__, Sheryll (*b.* 1956) *C., Cornwall South East,* Maj. 3,220
Murrison, Dr Andrew (*b.* 1961) *C., Wiltshire South West,* Maj. 10,367
*__Nandy__, Lisa (*b.* 1979) *Lab., Wigan,* Maj. 10,487
*__Nash__, Pamela (*b.* 1984) *Lab., Airdrie & Shotts,* Maj. 12,408
Neill, Bob (*b.* 1952) *C., Bromley & Chislehurst,* Maj. 13,900
Newmark, Brooks (*b.* 1958) *C., Braintree,* Maj. 16,121
*__Newton__, Sarah (*b.* 1962) *C., Truro & Falmouth,* Maj. 435
*__Nokes__, Caroline (*b.* 1972) *C., Romsey & Southampton North,* Maj. 4,156
*__Norman__, Jesse (*b.* 1962) *C., Hereford & Herefordshire South,* Maj. 2,481
*__Nuttall__, David (*b.* 1962) *C., Bury North,* Maj. 2,243
O'Brien, Stephen (*b.* 1957) *C., Eddisbury,* Maj. 13,255
*__O'Donnell__, Fiona (*b.* 1960) *Lab., East Lothian,* Maj. 12,258
*__Offord__, Matthew (*b.* 1969) *C., Hendon,* Maj. 106
*__Ollerenshaw__, Eric (*b.* 1950) *C., Lancaster & Fleetwood,* Maj. 333
*__Onwurah__, Chinyelu (*b.* 1965) *Lab., Newcastle upon Tyne Central,* Maj. 7,464
*__Opperman__, Guy (*b.* 1965) *C., Hexham,* Maj. 5,788
Osborne, George (*b.* 1971) *C., Tatton,* Maj. 14,487
Osborne, Sandra (*b.* 1956) *Lab., Ayr, Carrick & Cumnock,* Maj. 9,911
Ottaway, Richard (*b.* 1945) *C., Croydon South,* Maj. 15,818
Owen, Albert (*b.* 1960) *Lab., Ynys Mon,* Maj. 2,461
Paice, James (*b.* 1949) *C., Cambridgeshire South East,* Maj. 5,946
*__Paisley Junior__, Ian (*b.* 1966) *DUP, Antrim North,* Maj. 12,558
*__Parish__, Neil (*b.* 1956) *C., Tiverton & Honiton,* Maj. 9,320
*__Patel__, Priti (*b.* 1972) *C., Witham,* Maj. 15,196
Paterson, Owen (*b.* 1956) *C., Shropshire North,* Maj. 15,828
*__Pawsey__, Mark (*b.* 1957) *C., Rugby,* Maj. 6,000
*__Pearce__, Teresa (*b.* 1955) *Lab., Erith & Thamesmead,* Maj. 5,703
Penning, Michael (*b.* 1957) *C., Hemel Hempstead,* Maj. 13,406
Penrose, John (*b.* 1964) *C., Weston-Super-Mare,* Maj. 2,691
*__Percy__, Andrew, *C., Brigg & Goole,* Maj. 5,147
*__Perkins__, Toby (*b.* 1970) *Lab., Chesterfield,* Maj. 549
*__Perry__, Claire (*b.* 1964) *C., Devizes,* Maj. 13,005
*__Phillips__, Stephen (*b.* 1970) *C., Sleaford & Hykeham North,* Maj. 19,905
*__Phillipson__, Bridget (*b.* 1983) *Lab., Houghton & Sunderland South,* Maj. 10,990
Pickles, Eric (*b.* 1952) *C., Brentwood & Ongar,* Maj. 16,920
*__Pincher__, Chris (*b.* 1969) *C., Tamworth,* Maj. 6,090
*__Poulter__, Daniel (*b.* 1978) *C., Suffolk Central & Ipswich North,* Maj. 13,786
Pound, Stephen (*b.* 1948) *Lab., Ealing North,* Maj. 9,301
Primarolo, Rt. Hon. Dawn (*b.* 1954) *Lab., Bristol South,* Maj. 4,734
Prisk, Mark (*b.* 1962) *C., Hertford & Stortford,* Maj. 15,437
Pritchard, Mark (*b.* 1966) *C., The Wrekin,* Maj. 9,450
Pugh, Dr John (*b.* 1948) *LD, Southport,* Maj. 6,024
*__Qureshi__, Yasmin (*b.* 1963) *Lab., Bolton South East,* Maj. 8,634
*__Raab__, Dominic (*b.* 1974) *C., Esher & Walton,* Maj. 18,593
Randall, John (*b.* 1955) *C., Uxbridge & Ruislip South,* Maj. 11,216
Raynsford, Rt. Hon. Nick (*b.* 1945) *Lab., Greenwich & Woolwich,* Maj. 10,153
*__Reckless__, Mark (*b.* 1970) *C., Rochester & Strood,* Maj. 9,953
Redwood, Rt. Hon. John (*b.* 1951) *C., Wokingham,* Maj. 13,492
Reed, Jamie (*b.* 1973) *Lab., Copeland,* Maj. 3,833
*__Rees-Mogg__, Jacob (*b.* 1969) *C., Somerset North East,* Maj. 4,914
*__Reevell__, Simon (*b.* 1966) *C., Dewsbury,* Maj. 1,526
*__Reeves__, Rachel (*b.* 1979) *Lab., Leeds West,* Maj. 7,016
Reid, Alan (*b.* 1954) *LD, Argyll & Bute,* Maj. 3,431
*__Reynolds__, Emma (*b.* 1977) *Lab., Wolverhampton North East,* Maj. 2,484
*__Reynolds__, Jonathan (*b.* 1980) *Lab. (Co-op), Stalybridge & Hyde,* Maj. 2,744

Rifkind, Rt. Hon. Sir Malcolm (*b.* 1946) *C., Kensington,* Maj. 8,616
Riordan, Linda (*b.* 1953) *Lab. (Co-op), Halifax,* Maj. 1,472
***Ritchie**, Margaret (*b.* 1958) *SDLP, South Down,* Maj. 8,412
Robathan, Andrew (*b.* 1951) *C., Leicestershire South,* Maj. 15,524
Robertson, Angus (*b.* 1969) *SNP, Moray,* Maj. 5,590
Robertson, Hugh (*b.* 1962) *C., Faversham & Kent Mid,* Maj. 17,088
Robertson, John (*b.* 1952) *Lab., Glasgow North West,* Maj. 13,611
Robertson, Laurence (*b.* 1958) *C., Tewkesbury,* Maj. 6,310
Robinson, Geoffrey (*b.* 1938) *Lab., Coventry North West,* Maj. 6,288
Rogerson, Dan (*b.* 1975) *LD, Cornwall North,* Maj. 2,981
Rosindell, Andrew (*b.* 1966) *C., Romford,* Maj. 16,954
***Rotheram**, Steve (*b.* 1961) *Lab., Liverpool Walton,* Maj. 19,818
Roy, Frank (*b.* 1958) *Lab., Motherwell & Wishaw,* Maj. 16,806
Roy, Lindsay (*b.* 1949) *Lab., Glenrothes,* Maj. 16,455
Ruane, Christopher (*b.* 1958) *Lab., Vale of Clwyd,* Maj. 2,509
***Rudd**, Amber (*b.* 1963) *C., Hastings & Rye,* Maj. 1,993
Ruddock, Joan (*b.* 1943) *Lab., Lewisham Deptford,* Maj. 12,499
Ruffley, David (*b.* 1962) *C., Bury St Edmunds,* Maj. 12,380
Russell, Bob (*b.* 1946) *LD, Colchester,* Maj. 6,982
***Rutley**, David (*b.* 1961) *C., Macclesfield,* Maj. 11,959
Sanders, Adrian (*b.* 1959) *LD, Torbay,* Maj. 4,078
***Sandys**, Laura (*b.* 1964) *C., Thanet South,* Maj. 7,617
***Sarwar**, Anas (*b.* 1983) *Lab., Glasgow Central,* Maj. 10,551
Scott, Lee (*b.* 1956) *C., Ilford North,* Maj. 5,404
Seabeck, Alison (*b.* 1954) *Lab., Plymouth Moor View,* Maj. 1,588
Selous, Andrew (*b.* 1962) *C., Bedfordshire South West,* Maj. 16,649
***Shannon**, Jim (*b.* 1955) *DUP, Strangford,* Maj. 5,876
Shapps, Grant (*b.* 1968) *C., Welwyn Hatfield,* Maj. 7,423
***Sharma**, Alok (*b.* 1967) *C., Reading West,* Maj. 6,004
Sharma, Virendra (*b.* 1947) *Lab., Ealing Southall,* Maj. 9,291
Sheerman, Barry (*b.* 1940) *Lab. (Co-op), Huddersfield,* Maj. 4,472
***Shelbrooke**, Alec (*b.* 1976) *C., Elmet & Rothwell,* Maj. 4,521
Shepherd, Richard (*b.* 1942) *C., Aldridge-Brownhills,* Maj. 15,256
Sheridan, James (*b.* 1952) *Lab., Paisley & Renfrewshire North,* Maj. 15,280
***Shuker**, Gavin (*b.* 1981) *Lab. (Co-op), Luton South,* Maj. 2,329
Simmonds, Mark (*b.* 1964) *C., Boston & Skegness,* Maj. 12,426
Simpson, David (*b.* 1959) *DUP, Upper Bann,* Maj. 3,361
†**Simpson**, Keith (*b.* 1949) *C., Broadland,* Maj. 7,292
Singh, Marsha (*b.* 1954) *Lab., Bradford West,* Maj. 5,763
***Skidmore**, Chris (*b.* 1981) *C., Kingswood,* Maj. 2,445
Skinner, Dennis (*b.* 1932) *Lab., Bolsover,* Maj. 11,182
†**Slaughter**, Andrew (*b.* 1960) *Lab., Hammersmith,* Maj. 3,549
Smith, Rt. Hon. Andrew (*b.* 1951) *Lab., Oxford East,* Maj. 4,581
Smith, Angela C. (*b.* 1961) *Lab., Penistone & Stocksbridge,* Maj. 3,049
Smith, Chloe (*b.* 1982) *C., Norwich North,* Maj. 3,901
***Smith**, Henry (*b.* 1969) *C., Crawley,* Maj. 5,928
***Smith**, Julian (*b.* 1971) *C., Skipton & Ripon,* Maj. 9,950
***Smith**, Nick, (*b.* 1960) *Lab., Blaenau Gwent,* Maj. 10,516
***Smith**, Owen (*b.* 1970) *Lab., Pontypridd,* Maj. 2,785
Smith, Sir Robert (*b.* 1958) *LD, Aberdeenshire West & Kincardine,* Maj. 6,684
Soames, Hon. Nicholas (*b.* 1948) *C., Sussex Mid,* Maj. 7,402
***Soubry**, Anna (*b.* 1956) *C., Broxtowe,* Maj. 389
Soulsby, Sir Peter (*b.* 1948) *Lab., Leicester South,* Maj. 8,808
Spellar, Rt. Hon. John (*b.* 1947) *Lab., Warley,* Maj. 10,756
Spelman, Caroline (*b.* 1958) *C., Meriden,* Maj. 16,253
***Spencer**, Mark (*b.* 1970) *C., Sherwood,* Maj. 214
Stanley, Rt. Hon. Sir John (*b.* 1942) *C., Tonbridge & Malling,* Maj. 18,178
***Stephenson**, Andrew (*b.* 1981) *C., Pendle,* Maj. 3,585
***Stevenson**, John (*b.* 1963) *C., Carlisle,* Maj. 853
***Stewart**, Bob (*b.* 1949) *C., Beckenham,* Maj. 17,784
***Stewart**, Iain (*b.* 1972) *C., Milton Keynes South,* Maj. 5,201
***Stewart**, Rory (*b.* 1973) *C., Penrith & The Border,* Maj. 11,241
Straw, Rt. Hon. Jack (*b.* 1946) *Lab., Blackburn,* Maj. 9,856
Streeter, Gary (*b.* 1955) *C., Devon South West,* Maj. 15,874
***Stride**, Mel (*b.* 1961) *C., Devon Central,* Maj. 9,230
Stringer, Graham (*b.* 1950) *Lab., Blackley & Broughton,* Maj. 12,303
Stuart, Gisela (*b.* 1955) *Lab., Birmingham Edgbaston,* Maj. 1,274
Stuart, Graham (*b.* 1962) *C., Beverley & Holderness,* Maj. 12,987
Stunell, Andrew (*b.* 1942) *LD, Hazel Grove,* Maj. 6,371
***Sturdy**, Julian (*b.* 1971) *C., York Outer,* Maj. 3,688
Sutcliffe, Gerry (*b.* 1953) *Lab., Bradford South,* Maj. 4,622
***Swales**, Ian (*b.* 1953) *LD, Redcar,* Maj. 5,214
Swayne, Desmond (*b.* 1956) *C., New Forest West,* Maj. 16,896
Swinson, Jo (*b.* 1980) *LD, Dunbartonshire East,* Maj. 2,184
Swire, Hugo (*b.* 1959) *C., Devon East,* Maj. 9,114
Syms, Robert (*b.* 1956) *C., Poole,* Maj. 7,541
Tami, Mark (*b.* 1963) *Lab., Alyn & Deeside,* Maj. 2,919
Tapsell, Sir Peter (*b.* 1930) *C., Louth & Horncastle,* Maj. 13,871
Teather, Sarah (*b.* 1974) *LD, Brent Central,* Maj. 1,345
Thomas, Gareth (*b.* 1967) *Lab. (Co-op), Harrow West,* Maj. 3,143
Thornberry, Emily (*b.* 1960) *Lab., Islington South & Finsbury,* Maj. 3,569
Thurso, John (*b.* 1953) *LD, Caithness, Sutherland & Easter Ross,* Maj. 4,826
Timms, Rt. Hon. Stephen (*b.* 1955) *Lab., East Ham,* Maj. 27,826
Timpson, Edward (*b.* 1973) *C., Crewe & Nantwich,* Maj. 6,046
***Tomlinson**, Justin (*b.* 1976) *C., Swindon North,* Maj. 7,060

Tredinnick, David (*b.* 1950) *C., Bosworth,* Maj. 5,032
Trickett, Jon (*b.* 1950) *Lab., Hemsworth,* Maj. 9,844
***Truss**, Elizabeth (*b.* 1975) *C., Norfolk South West,* Maj. 13,140
Turner, Andrew (*b.* 1953) *C., Isle of Wight,* Maj. 10,527
***Turner**, Karl (*b.* 1971) *Lab., Kingston upon Hull East,* Maj. 8,597
Twigg, Derek (*b.* 1959) *Lab., Halton,* Maj. 15,504
***Twigg**, Stephen (*b.* 1966) *Lab. (Co-op), Liverpool Derby West,* Maj. 18,467
Tyrie, Andrew (*b.* 1957) *C., Chichester,* Maj. 15,877
***Umunna**, Chuka (*b.* 1978) *Lab., Streatham,* Maj. 3,259
***Uppal**, Paul (*b.* 1967) *C., Wolverhampton South West,* Maj. 691
Vaizey, Ed (*b.* 1969) *C., Wantage,* Maj. 13,547
Vara, Shailesh (*b.* 1960) *C., Cambridgeshire North West,* Maj. 16,677
Vaz, Rt. Hon. Keith (*b.* 1956) *Lab., Leicester East,* Maj. 14,082
***Vaz**, Valerie (*b.* 1954) *Lab., Walsall South,* Maj. 1,755
***Vickers**, Martin (*b.* 1950) *C., Cleethorpes,* Maj. 4,298
Villiers, Theresa (*b.* 1968) *C., Chipping Barnet,* Maj. 11,927
Walker, Charles (*b.* 1967) *C., Broxbourne,* Maj. 18,804
***Walker**, Robin (*b.* 1978) *C., Worcester,* Maj. 2,982
Wallace, Ben (*b.* 1970) *C., Wyre & Preston North,* Maj. 15,844
Walley, Joan (*b.* 1949) *Lab., Stoke-on-Trent North,* Maj. 8,235
Walter, Robert (*b.* 1948) *C., Dorset North,* Maj. 7,625
***Ward**, David, (*b.* 1953) *LD, Bradford East,* Maj. 365
Watkinson, Angela (*b.* 1941) *C., Hornchurch & Upminster,* Maj. 16,371
Watson, Tom (*b.* 1967) *Lab., West Bromwich East,* Maj. 6,696
Watts, Dave (*b.* 1951) *Lab., St Helens North,* Maj. 13,101
***Weatherley**, Mike (*b.* 1957) *C., Hove,* Maj. 1,868
Webb, Prof. Steve (*b.* 1965) *LD, Thornbury & Yate,* Maj. 7,116
Weir, Michael (*b.* 1957) *SNP, Angus,* Maj. 3,282
***Wharton**, James (*b.* 1984) *C., Stockton South,* Maj. 332
***Wheeler**, Heather (*b.* 1959) *C., Derbyshire South,* Maj. 7,128
***White**, Chris (*b.* 1967) *C., Warwick & Leamington,* Maj. 3,513
***Whiteford**, Eilidh (*b.* 1969) *SNP, Banff & Buchan,* Maj. 4,027
Whitehead, Dr Alan (*b.* 1950) *Lab., Southampton Test,* Maj. 2,413
***Whittaker**, Craig (*b.* 1962) *C., Calder Valley,* Maj. 6,431
Whittingdale, John (*b.* 1959) *C., Maldon,* Maj. 19,407
Wicks, Malcolm (*b.* 1947) *Lab., Croydon North,* Maj. 16,483
Wiggin, Bill (*b.* 1966) *C., Herefordshire North,* Maj. 9,887
Willetts, David (*b.* 1956) *C., Havant,* Maj. 12,160
Williams, Hywel (*b.* 1953) *PC, Arfon,* Maj. 1,455
Williams, Mark (*b.* 1966) *LD, Ceredigion,* Maj. 8,324
Williams, Roger (*b.* 1948) *LD, Brecon & Radnorshire,* Maj. 3,747
Williams, Stephen (*b.* 1966) *LD, Bristol West,* Maj. 11,366
***Williamson**, Chris (*b.* 1956) *Lab., Derby North,* Maj. 613
***Williamson**, Gavin (*b.* 1976) *C., Staffordshire South,* Maj. 16,590
Willott, Jenny (*b.* 1974) *LD, Cardiff Central,* Maj. 4,576
Wilson, Phil (*b.* 1959) *Lab., Sedgefield,* Maj. 8,696
Wilson, Rob (*b.* 1965) *C., Reading East,* Maj. 7,605
Wilson, Sammy (*b.* 1953) *DUP, Antrim East,* Maj. 6,770
Winnick, David (*b.* 1933) *Lab., Walsall North,* Maj. 990
Winterton, Rt. Hon. Rosie (*b.* 1958) *Lab., Doncaster Central,* Maj. 6,229
Wishart, Peter (*b.* 1962) *SNP, Perth & Perthshire North,* Maj. 4,379
***Wollaston**, Sarah (*b.* 1962) *C., Totnes,* Maj. 4,927
Wood, Mike (*b.* 1946) *Lab., Batley & Spen,* Maj. 4,406
***Woodcock**, John (*b.* 1978) *Lab. (Co-op), Barrow & Furness,* Maj. 5,208
Woodward, Rt. Hon. Shaun (*b.* 1958) *Lab., St Helens South & Whiston,* Maj. 14,122
Woolas, Phil (*b.* 1959) *Lab., Oldham East & Saddleworth,* Maj. 103
Wright, David (*b.* 1967) *Lab., Telford,* Maj. 981
Wright, Iain (*b.* 1972) *Lab., Hartlepool,* Maj. 5,509
Wright, Jeremy (*b.* 1972) *C., Kenilworth & Southam,* Maj. 12,552
***Wright**, Simon (*b.* 1979) *LD, Norwich South,* Maj. 310
Yeo, Tim (*b.* 1945) *C., Suffolk South,* Maj. 8,689
Young, Rt. Hon. Sir George (*b.* 1941) *C., Hampshire North West,* Maj. 18,583
***Zahawi**, Nadhim (*b.* 1967) *C., Stratford-on-Avon,* Maj. 11,346

GENERAL ELECTION RESULTS

The results of voting in each parliamentary division at the general election of 6 May 2010 are given below.

BOUNDARY CHANGES

The constituency boundaries were redrawn for the 2010 election in England, Wales and Northern Ireland. As a result of the review the number of constituencies increased from 646 to 650, with four new seats in England. Only 138 constituencies had no boundary changes, 59 of them in Scotland.

For the majority of constituencies where a boundary change has taken place, it is not appropriate to make a direct comparison between the results of 2005 and 2010. The seat of Hammersmith, for example, comprises 60 per cent of the old Hammersmith and Fulham constituency and 40 per cent of the old Ealing and Shepherds Bush constituency; it cannot therefore be described as a simple hold for the Labour party. The term 'notional' used here refers to a theoretical set of results, published by Professors Rallings and Thrasher of Plymouth University, which estimates the way each new constituency might have voted in the 2005 general election.

KEY

* New MP

† Previously MP in another seat

‡ Previously MP for another party

§ Notional result; *see* explanation of boundary changes

E. Electorate

T. Turnout

Abbreviations

AD	Apolitical Democrats
Alliance	Alliance
Animals	Animals Count
Anti-War	Fight for an Anti-War Government
APP	Animal Protection Party
Battersea	Putting the People of Battersea First
BB	A Better Britain for All
BCP	Basingstoke Common Man
Bean	New Millennium Bean
Beer	Reduce Tax on Beer Party
Best	The Best of a Bad Bunch
BIB	Bushra Irfan of Blackburn
BIC	Bromsgrove Independent Conservative
Blaenau Voice	Blaenau Gwent People's Voice
Blue	Blue Environment Party
BNP	British National Party
BP Elvis	Bus-Pass Elvis Party
C.	Conservative
Ch. M.	Christian Movement for Great Britain
Ch. P.	Christian Party
Christian	Christian
CIP	Campaign for Independent Politicians
City Ind.	City Independent
Clause 28	Clause 28, Children's Protection Christian Democrats
CNBPG	Community Need Before Private Greed
Comm.	Communist Party
Comm. Brit.	Communist Party of Britain
Comm. Lge	Communist League
Cornish D.	Cornish Democrats
CPA	Christian People's Alliance
CSP	Common Sense Party
Currency	Virtue Currency Cognitive Appraisal Party
D. Nat.	Democratic Nationalist
DDP	Direct Democracy Party
Deficit	Cut the Deficit Party
Dem. Lab.	Democratic Labour Party
DUP	Democratic Unionist Party
Eng. Dem.	English Democrats
Eng. Ind.	English Independence Party
F and R	For Freedom and Responsibility
FDP	Fancy Dress Party
Good	The Common Good
Green	Green
Green Belt	Independent Save Our Green Belt
Green Soc.	Alliance for Green Socialism
Humanity	Humanity
Impact	Impact Party
Ind.	Independent
Ind. CCF	New Independent Conservative Chelsea and Fulham
Ind. CHC	Independent Community and Health Concern
Ind. EACPS	Independent Ealing Action Communities Public Services
Ind. Fed.	Independents Federation UK
Ind. People	Independent People Together
Ind. Rantzen	Independent Rantzen
Ind. Voice	Independent Voice for Halifax
Integrity	Integrity UK
IZB	Islam Zinda Baad Platform
J & AC	Justice & Anti-Corruption Party
Jacobite	Scottish Jacobite Party
Joy	The Joy of Talk
JP	Justice Party
King George	Save King George Hospital
Lab.	Labour
Lab. (Co-op)	Labour and Co-operative
Land	Land is Power
LD	Liberal Democrat
Leave EU	Independent Leave the EU Alliance
Lib.	Liberal
Libertarian	Libertarian Party
Lincs. Ind.	Lincolnshire Independents
LLPBPP	Local Liberals People Before Politics Party
Loony	Monster Raving Loony Party
LTT	Lawfulness Trustworthiness and Transparency
Macc. Ind.	The Macclesfield Independent
Magna Carta	The Magna Carta Party
Mansfield Ind.	Mansfield Independent Forum
Meb. Ker.	Mebyon Kernow
Med. Ind.	Medway Independent
Mid. England	Middle England Party
MP Expense	A Vote Against MP Expense Abuse
MRP	Money Reform Party
Nat. Dem.	National Democrat
ND	No Description
New Party	The New Party
NF	National Front
NFP	Nationwide Reform Party
No Vote	No Candidate Deserves My Vote
Nobody	Nobody Party
NSPS	Northampton – Save Our Public Services
Parenting	Equal Parenting Alliance
PBP	People Before Profit
PC	Plaid Cymru
Pirate	Pirate Party UK
PNDP	People's National Democratic Party
Poetry	The True English (Poetry) Party
PP Essex	Peoples Party Essex
PPN-V	Peace Party Non-Violence Justice Environment
R and E	Citizens for Undead Rights and Equality
RA	Solihull and Meridien Residents' Association
Reform	Reform 2000
Respect	Respect the Unity Coalition
RP	The Restoration Party
RRG	Radical Reform Group

SACL	Scotland Against Crooked Lawyers	South	All the South Party	UKIP	UK Independence Party
Save QM	Independents to Save Queen Mary's Hospital	Speaker	The Speaker	UPS	Unity for Peace and Socialism
Science	The Science Party	SSP	Scottish Socialist Party	Voice	United Voice
SDLP	Social Democratic and Labour Party	Staffs Ind.	Staffordshire Independent Group	Wessex Reg.	Wessex Regionalist
SEP	Socialist Equality Party	Tendring	Tendring First	Workers Lib.	Alliance for Workers Liberty
SF	Sinn Fein	TOC	Tamsin Omond to the Commons	WP	Workers' Party
SMA	Scrap Members Allowances	Trust	Trust	WRP	Workers' Revolutionary Party
Snouts	Get Snouts Out The Trough	TUSC	Trade Unionist and Socialist Coalition	You	You Party
SNP	Scottish National Party	TUV	Traditional Unionist Voice	Youth	Youth Party
Soc.	Socialist Party	UCUNF	Ulster Conservatives and Unionists – New Force	YP	Go Mad and Vote For Yourself Party
Soc. Alt.	Socialist Alternative Party	UK Integrity	Independents Federation UK – Honest Integrity Democracy	YRDPL	Your Right to Democracy Party Limited
Soc. Dem.	Social Democratic Party				
Soc. Lab.	Socialist Labour Party				

PARLIAMENTARY CONSTITUENCIES AS AT 6 MAY 2010 GENERAL ELECTION

UK Turnout
E. 45,533,536 T. 29,643,522 (65.1%)

ENGLAND

§ALDERSHOT
E. 71,469 T. 45,384 (63.50%) C. hold
Gerald Howarth, C. 21,203
Adrian Collett, LD 15,617
Jonathan Slater, Lab. 5,489
Robert Snare, UKIP 2,041
Gary Crowd, Eng. Ind. 803
Juliana Brimicombe, Ch. P. 231
C. majority 5,586 (12.31%)
Notional 1.41% swing C. to LD
(2005: C. majority 6,345 (15.12%))

§ALDRIDGE-BROWNHILLS
E. 59,355 T. 38,634 (65.09%) C. hold
Richard Shepherd, C. 22,913
Ashiq Hussain, Lab. 7,647
Ian Jenkins, LD 6,833
Karl Macnaughton, Green 847
Sue Gray, Ch. P. 394
C. majority 15,266 (39.51%)
Notional 12.01% swing Lab. to C.
(2005: C. majority 5,732 (15.49%))

§ALTRINCHAM & SALE WEST
E. 71,254 T. 49,393 (69.32%) C. hold
Graham Brady, C. 24,176
Jane Brophy, LD 12,581
Tom Ross, Lab. 11,073
Kenneth Bullman, UKIP 1,563
C. majority 11,595 (23.47%)
Notional 0.83% swing C. to LD
(2005: C. majority 7,618 (17.57%))

§AMBER VALLEY
E. 70,171 T. 45,958 (65.49%) C. gain
*Nigel Mills, C. 17,746
Judy Mallaber, Lab. 17,210
Tom Snowdon, LD 6,636
Michael Clarke, BNP 3,195
Sue Ransome, UKIP 906
Sam Thing, Loony 265
C. majority 536 (1.17%)
Notional 6.85% swing Lab. to C.
(2005: Lab. majority 5,512 (12.53%))

§ARUNDEL & SOUTH DOWNS
E. 77,564 T. 55,982 (72.18%) C. hold
Nick Herbert, C. 32,333
Derek Deedman, LD 15,642
Tim Lunnon, Lab. 4,835
Stuart Bower, UKIP 3,172
C. majority 16,691 (29.81%)
Notional 3.00% swing LD to C.
(2005: C. majority 12,291 (23.81%))

§ASHFIELD
E. 77,379 T. 48,196 (62.29%) Lab. hold
*Gloria De Piero, Lab. 16,239
Jason Zadrozny, LD 16,047
Garry Hickton, C. 10,698
Edward Holmes, BNP 2,781
Tony Ellis, Eng. Dem. 1,102
Terry Coleman, UKIP 933
Eddie Smith, Ind. 396
Lab. majority 192 (0.40%)
Notional 17.23% swing Lab. to LD
(2005: Lab. majority 10,370 (24.28%))

§ASHFORD
E. 81,269 T. 55,185 (67.90%) C. hold
Damian Green, C. 29,878
Chris Took, LD 12,581
Chris Clark, Lab. 9,204
Jeffrey Elenor, UKIP 2,508
Steve Campkin, Green 1,014
C. majority 17,297 (31.34%)
Notional 2.25% swing C. to LD
(2005: C. majority 12,268 (25.02%))

§ASHTON UNDER LYNE
E. 67,564 T. 38,432 (56.88%) Lab. hold
David Heyes, Lab. 18,604
Seema Kennedy, C. 9,510
Paul Larkin, LD 5,703
David Lomas, BNP 2,929
Angela McManus, UKIP 1,686
Lab. majority 9,094 (23.66%)
Notional 7.34% swing Lab. to C.
(2005: Lab. majority 13,199 (38.33%))

§AYLESBURY
E. 77,934 T. 53,162 (68.21%) C. hold
David Lidington, C. 27,736
Steven Lambert, LD 15,118
Kathryn White, Lab. 6,695
Chris Adams, UKIP 3,613
C. majority 12,618 (23.73%)
Notional 2.12% swing LD to C.
(2005: C. majority 9,314 (19.49%))

§BANBURY
E. 86,986 T. 56,241 (64.66%) C. hold
Tony Baldry, C. 29,703
David Rundle, LD 11,476
Les Sibley, Lab. 10,773
Dr David Fairweather, UKIP 2,806
Alastair White, Green 959
Roseanne Edwards, Ind. 524
C. majority 18,227 (32.41%)
Notional 1.51% swing LD to C.
(2005: C. majority 10,090 (18.79%))

§BARKING
E. 73,864 T. 45,343 (61.39%) Lab. hold
Margaret Hodge, Lab. 24,628
Simon Marcus, C. 8,073
Nick Griffin, BNP 6,620
Dominic Carman, LD 3,719
Frank Maloney, UKIP 1,300
George Hargreaves, Ch. P. 482
Jayne Forbes, Green 317
Crucial Chris Dowling, Loony 82
Thomas Darwood, Ind. 77
Dapo Sijuwola, RP 45
Lab. majority 16,555 (36.51%)
Notional 1.73% swing C. to Lab.
(2005: Lab. majority 12,183 (33.04%))

§BARNSLEY CENTRAL
E. 65,543 T. 37,001 (56.45%) Lab. hold
Eric Illsley, Lab. 17,487
Christopher Wiggin, LD 6,394
Piers Tempest, C. 6,388
Ian Sutton, BNP 3,307
David Silver, UKIP 1,727
Donald Wood, Ind. 732
Tony Devoy, Ind. 610
Terry Robinson, Soc. Lab. 356
Lab. majority 11,093 (29.98%)
Notional 4.17% swing Lab. to LD
(2005: Lab. majority 11,839 (38.32%))

§BARNSLEY EAST
E. 68,435 T. 38,386 (56.09%) Lab. hold
*Michael Dugher, Lab. 18,059
John Brown, LD 6,969
James Hockney, C. 6,329
Colin Porter, BNP 3,301
Tony Watson, UKIP 1,731
Kevin Hogan, Ind. 712
Eddie Devoy, Ind. 684
Ken Capstick, Soc. Lab. 601
Lab. majority 11,090 (28.89%)
Notional 14.02% swing Lab. to LD
(2005: Lab. majority 18,298 (56.94%))

§BARROW & FURNESS
E. 68,758 T. 44,124 (64.17%)
Lab. Co-op hold
*John Woodcock, Lab. Co-op 21,226
John Gough, C. 16,018
Barry Rabone, LD 4,424
John Smith, UKIP 841
Mike Ashburner, BNP 840
Christopher Loynes, Green 530
Brian Greaves, Ind. 245
Lab. Co-op majority 5,208 (11.80%)
Notional 0.37% swing Lab. to C.
(2005: Lab. majority 4,843 (12.54%))

§BASILDON & BILLERICAY
E. 65,482 T. 41,569 (63.48%) C. hold
John Baron, C. 21,922
Allan Davies, Lab. 9,584
Mike Hibbs, LD 6,538
Irene Bateman, BNP 1,934
Alan Broad, UKIP 1,591
C. majority 12,338 (29.68%)
Notional 9.23% swing Lab. to C.
(2005: C. majority 4,559 (11.22%))

§BASILDON SOUTH & THURROCK EAST
E. 71,815 T. 44,735 (62.29%) C. gain
*Stephen Metcalfe, C. 19,624
Angela Smith, Lab. Co-op 13,852
Geoff Williams, LD 5,977
Kerry Smith, UKIP 2,639
Chris Roberts, BNP 2,518
None Of The Above X, ND 125
C. majority 5,772 (12.90%)
Notional 7.52% swing Lab. to C.
(2005: Lab. majority 905 (2.14%))

§BASINGSTOKE
E. 75,470 T. 50,654 (67.12%) C. hold
Maria Miller, C. 25,590
John Shaw, LD 12,414
Funda Pepperell, Lab. 10,327
Stella Howell, UKIP 2,076
Steve Saul, BCP 247
C. majority 13,176 (26.01%)
Notional 4.55% swing LD to C.
(2005: C. majority 2,651 (6.27%))

§BASSETLAW
E. 76,542 T. 49,577 (64.77%) Lab. hold
John Mann, Lab. 25,018
Keith Girling, C. 16,803
David Dobbie, LD 5,570
Andrea Hamilton, UKIP 1,779
Grahame Whithurst, Ind. 407
Lab. majority 8,215 (16.57%)
Notional 0.67% swing Lab. to C.
(2005: Lab. majority 8,256 (17.92%))

§BATH
E. 65,603 T. 47,086 (71.77%) LD hold
Don Foster, LD 26,651
Fabian Richter, C. 14,768
Hattie Ajderian, Lab. 3,251
Eric Lucas, Green 1,120
Ernie Warrender, UKIP 890
Steve Hewett, Ch. P. 250
ANON, ND 69
Sean Geddis, Ind. 56
Robert Craig, South 31
LD majority 11,883 (25.24%)
Notional 5.84% swing C. to LD
(2005: LD majority 5,624 (13.56%))

§BATLEY & SPEN
E. 76,732 T. 51,109 (66.61%) Lab. hold
Mike Wood, Lab. 21,565
Janice Small, C. 17,159
Neil Bentley, LD 8,095
David Exley, BNP 3,685
Matt Blakeley, Green 605
Lab. majority 4,406 (8.62%)
Notional 2.46% swing Lab. to C.
(2005: Lab. majority 6,060 (13.54%))

§BATTERSEA
E. 74,300 T. 48,792 (65.67%) C. gain
*Jane Ellison, C. 23,103
Martin Linton, Lab. 17,126
Layla Moran, LD 7,176
Guy Evans, Green 559
Christopher MacDonald, UKIP 505
Hugh Salmon, Battersea 168
Tom Fox, Ind. 155
C. majority 5,977 (12.25%)
Notional 6.53% swing Lab. to C.
(2005: Lab. majority 332 (0.81%))

§BEACONSFIELD
E. 74,982 T. 52,490 (70.00%) C. hold
Dominic Grieve, C. 32,053
John Edwards, LD 10,271
Jeremy Miles, Lab. 6,135
Delphine Gray-Fisk, UKIP 2,597
Jem Bailey, Green 768
Andrew Cowen, MP Expense 475
Quentin Baron, Ind. 191
C. majority 21,782 (41.50%)
Notional 4.70% swing LD to C.
(2005: C. majority 14,794 (32.09%))

§BECKENHAM
E. 66,219 T. 47,686 (72.01%) C. hold
*Bob Stewart, C. 27,597
Steve Jenkins, LD 9,813
Damien Egan, Lab. 6,893
Owen Brolly, UKIP 1,551
Roger Tonks, BNP 1,001
Ann Garrett, Green 608
Dan Eastgate, Eng. Dem. 223
C. majority 17,784 (37.29%)
Notional 3.15% swing C. to LD
(2005: C. majority 16,913 (40.40%))

§BEDFORD
E. 68,491 T. 45,102 (65.85%) C. gain
*Richard Fuller, C. 17,546
Patrick Hall, Lab. 16,193
Henry Vann, LD 8,957
Mark Adkin, UKIP 1,136
William Dewick, BNP 757
Ben Foley, Green 393
Samrat Bhandari, Ind. 120
C. majority 1,353 (3.00%)
Notional 5.52% swing Lab. to C.
(2005: Lab. majority 3,413 (8.04%))

§BEDFORDSHIRE MID
E. 76,023 T. 54,897 (72.21%) C. hold
Nadine Dorries, C. 28,815
Linda Jack, LD 13,663
David Reeves, Lab. 8,108
Bill Hall, UKIP 2,826
Malcolm Bailey, Green 773
John Cooper, Eng. Dem. 712
C. majority 15,152 (27.60%)
Notional 2.26% swing LD to C.
(2005: C. majority 11,593 (23.08%))

§BEDFORDSHIRE NORTH EAST
E. 78,060 T. 55,552 (71.17%) C. hold
Alistair Burt, C. 30,989
Mike Pitt, LD 12,047
Edward Brown,Lab. 8,957
Brian Capell, UKIP 2,294
Ian Seeby, BNP 1,265
C. majority 18,942 (34.10%)
Notional 2.55% swing LD to C.
(2005: C. majority 12,128 (24.59%))

BEDFORDSHIRE SOUTH WEST
E. 76,559 T. 50,774 (66.32%) C. hold
Andrew Selous, C. 26,815
Rod Cantrill, LD 10,166
Jennifer Bone, Lab. 9,948
Martin Newman, UKIP 2,142
Mark Tolman, BNP 1,703
C. majority 16,649 (32.79%)
0.69% swing LD to C.
(2005: C. majority 8,277 (18.07%))

§BERMONDSEY & OLD SOUTHWARK
E. 77,623 T. 44,651 (57.52%) LD hold
Simon Hughes, LD 21,590
Val Shawcross, Lab. 13,060
Loanna Morrison, C. 7,638
Stephen Tyler, BNP 1,370
Tom Chance, Green 718
Alan Kirkby, Ind. 155
Steve Freeman, ND 120
LD majority 8,530 (19.10%)
Notional 1.55% swing Lab. to LD
(2005: LD majority 5,769 (16.00%))

§BERWICK-UPON-TWEED
E. 57,403 T. 38,439 (66.96%) LD hold
Sir Alan Beith, LD 16,806
Anne-Marie Trevelyan, C. 14,116
Alan Strickland, Lab. 5,061
Michael Weatheritt, UKIP 1,243
Peter Mailer, BNP 1,213
LD majority 2,690 (7.00%)
Notional 8.29% swing LD to C.
(2005: LD majority 8,585 (23.58%))

§BETHNAL GREEN & BOW
E. 81,243 T. 50,728 (62.44%) Lab. gain
*Rushanara Ali, Lab. 21,784
Ajmal Masroor, LD 10,210
Abjol Miah, Respect 8,532
Zakir Khan, C. 7,071
Jeffrey Marshall, BNP 1,405
Farid Bakht, Green 856
Patrick Brooks, Ind. 277
Alexander Van Terheyden, Pirate 213
Hasib Hikmat, Voice 209
Haji Choudhury, Ind. 100
Ahmed Malik, Ind. 71
Lab. majority 11,574 (22.82%)
Notional 14.11% swing Respect to Lab.
(2005: Respect majority 804 (2.10%))

§BEVERLEY & HOLDERNESS
E. 79,611 T. 53,199 (66.82%) C. hold
Graham Stuart, C. 25,063
Craig Dobson, LD 12,076
Ian Saunders, Lab. 11,224
Neil Whitelam, BNP 2,080
Andrew Horsfield, UKIP 1,845
Bill Rigby, Green 686
Ron Hughes, Ind. 225
C. majority 12,987 (24.41%)
Notional 1.58% swing LD to C.
(2005: C. majority 3,097 (6.23%))

§BEXHILL & BATTLE
E. 79,208 T. 54,587 (68.92%) C. hold
Greg Barker, C. 28,147
Mary Varrall, LD 15,267
James Royston, Lab. 6,524
Stuart Wheeler, Trust 2,699
Neil Jackson, BNP 1,950
C. majority 12,880 (23.60%)
Notional 3.96% swing C. to LD
(2005: C. majority 15,893 (31.52%))

§BEXLEYHEATH & CRAYFORD
E. 64,985 T. 43,182 (66.45%) C. hold
David Evennett, C. 21,794
Howard Dawber, Lab. 11,450
Karelia Scott, LD 5,502
Stephen James, BNP 2,042
John Dunford, UKIP 1,557
John Griffiths, Eng. Dem. 466
Adrian Ross, Green 371
C. majority 10,344 (23.95%)
Notional 5.81% swing Lab. to C.
(2005: C. majority 5,167 (12.33%))

§BIRKENHEAD
E. 62,773 T. 35,323 (56.27%) Lab. hold
Frank Field, Lab. 22,082
Andrew Gilbert, C. 6,687
Stuart Kelly, LD 6,554
Lab. majority 15,395 (43.58%)
Notional 2.34% swing Lab. to C.
(2005: Lab. majority 14,638 (46.21%))

§BIRMINGHAM EDGBASTON
E. 68,573 T. 41,571 (60.62%) Lab. hold
Gisela Stuart, Lab. 16,894
Deirdre Alden, C. 15,620
Roger Harmer, LD 6,387
Trevor Lloyd, BNP 1,196
Greville Warwick, UKIP 732
Phil Simpson, Green 469
Harry Takhar, Impact 146
Charith Fernando, Ch. P. 127
Lab. majority 1,274 (3.06%)
Notional 0.47% swing Lab. to C.
(2005: Lab. majority 1,555 (4.01%))

§BIRMINGHAM ERDINGTON
E. 66,405 T. 35,546 (53.53%) Lab. hold
*Jack Dromey, Lab. 14,869
Robert Alden, C. 11,592
Ann Holtom, LD 5,742
Kevin McHugh, BNP 1,815
Maria Foy, UKIP 842
Tony Tomkins, Ind. 240
Terry Williams, NF 229
Timothy Gray, Ch. P. 217
Lab. majority 3,277 (9.22%)
Notional 10.43% swing Lab. to C.
(2005: Lab. majority 9,677 (30.07%))

§BIRMINGHAM HALL GREEN
E. 76,580 T. 48,727 (63.63%) Lab. hold
Roger Godsiff, Lab. 16,039
Salma Yaqoob, Respect 12,240
Jerry Evans, LD 11,988
Jo Barker, C. 7,320
Alan Blumenthal, UKIP 950
Andrew Gardner, Ind. 190
Lab. majority 3,799 (7.80%)
Notional 11.07% swing Lab. to Respect
(2005: Lab. majority 6,649 (15.90%))

§BIRMINGHAM HODGE HILL
E. 75,040 T. 42,472 (56.60%) Lab. hold
Liam Byrne, Lab. 22,077
Tariq Khan, LD 11,775
Shailesh Parekh, C. 4,936
Richard Lumby, BNP 2,333
Waheed Rafiq, UKIP 714
Peter Johnson, Soc. Dem. 637
Lab. majority 10,302 (24.26%)
Notional 3.61% swing LD to Lab.
(2005: Lab. majority 7,063 (17.05%))

§BIRMINGHAM LADYWOOD
E. 73,646 T. 35,833 (48.66%) Lab. hold
*Shabana Mahmood, Lab. 19,950
Ayoub Khan, LD 9,845
Nusrat Ghani, C. 4,277
Christopher Booth, UKIP 902
Peter Beck, Green 859
Lab. majority 10,105 (28.20%)
Notional 2.49% swing LD to Lab.
(2005: Lab. majority 6,804 (23.23%))

§BIRMINGHAM NORTHFIELD
E. 71,338 T. 41,814 (58.61%) Lab. hold
Richard Burden, Lab. 16,841
Keely Huxtable, C. 14,059
Mike Dixon, LD 6,550
Les Orton, BNP 2,290
John Borthwick, UKIP 1,363
Susan Pearce, Green 406
Dick Rodgers, Good 305
Lab. majority 2,782 (6.65%)
Notional 6.64% swing Lab. to C.
(2005: Lab. majority 7,879 (19.93%))

§BIRMINGHAM PERRY BARR
E. 71,304 T. 42,045 (58.97%) Lab. hold
Khalid Mahmood, Lab. 21,142
Karen Hamilton, LD 9,234
William Norton, C. 8,960
Melvin Ward, UKIP 1,675
John Tyrrell, Soc. Lab. 527
Deborah Hey-Smith, Ch. P. 507
Lab. majority 11,908 (28.32%)
Notional 4.05% swing LD to Lab.
(2005: Lab. majority 7,825 (20.22%))

§BIRMINGHAM SELLY OAK
E. 74,805 T. 46,563 (62.25%) Lab. hold
Steve McCabe, Lab. 17,950
Nigel Dawkins, C. 14,468
David Radcliffe, LD 10,371
Lynette Orton, BNP 1,820
Jeffery Burgess, UKIP 1,131
James Burn, Green 664
Samuel Leeds, Ch. P. 159
Lab. majority 3,482 (7.48%)
Notional 4.83% swing Lab. to C.
(2005: Lab. majority 7,564 (17.14%))

§BIRMINGHAM YARDLEY
E. 72,321 T. 40,850 (56.48%) LD hold
John Hemming, LD 16,162
Lynnette Kelly, Lab. 13,160
Meirion Jenkins, C. 7,836
Tanya Lumby, BNP 2,153
Graham Duffen, UKIP 1,190
Paul Morris, NF 349
LD majority 3,002 (7.35%)
Notional 0.02% swing Lab. to LD
(2005: LD majority 2,864 (7.30%))

§BISHOP AUCKLAND
E. 68,370 T. 41,136 (60.17%) Lab. hold
Helen Goodman, Lab. 16,023
Barbara Harrison, C. 10,805
Mark Wilkes, LD 9,189
Adam Walker, BNP 2,036
Sam Zair, LLPBPP 1,964
Dave Brothers, UKIP 1,119
Lab. majority 5,218 (12.68%)
Notional 7.20% swing Lab. to C.
(2005: Lab. majority 10,047 (26.35%))

§BLACKBURN
E. 72,331 T. 45,499 (62.90%) Lab. hold
Jack Straw, Lab. 21,751
Michael Law-Riding, C. 11,895
Paul English, LD 6,918
Robin Evans, BNP 2,158
Bushra Irfanullah, BIB 1,424
Bobby Anwar, UKIP 942
Grace Astley, Ind. 238
Janis Sharp, Ind. 173
Lab. majority 9,856 (21.66%)
Notional 1.11% swing C. to Lab.
(2005: Lab. majority 8,048 (19.45%))

§BLACKLEY & BROUGHTON
E. 69,489 T. 34,204 (49.22%) Lab. hold
Graham Stringer, Lab. 18,563
James Edsberg, C. 6,260
William Hobhouse, LD 4,861
Derek Adams, BNP 2,469
Kay Phillips, Respect 996
Bob Willescroft, UKIP 894
Shafiq-Uz Zaman, Ch. P. 161
Lab. majority 12,303 (35.97%)
Notional 6.74% swing Lab. to C.
(2005: Lab. majority 13,060 (43.35%))

§BLACKPOOL NORTH & CLEVELEYS
E. 65,888 T. 40,591 (61.61%) C. gain
*Paul Maynard, C. 16,964
Penny Martin, Lab. 14,814
Bill Greene, LD 5,400
Roy Hopwood, UKIP 1,659
James Clayton, BNP 1,556
Tony Davies, Loony 198
C. majority 2,150 (5.30%)
Notional 6.89% swing Lab. to C.
(2005: Lab. majority 3,241 (8.48%))

§BLACKPOOL SOUTH
E. 63,025 T. 35,191 (55.84%) Lab. hold
Gordon Marsden, Lab. 14,448
Ron Bell, C. 12,597
Doreen Holt, LD 5,082
Roy Goodwin, BNP 1,482
Hamish Howitt, UKIP 1,352
Si Thu Tun, Integrity 230
Lab. majority 1,851 (5.26%)
Notional 6.21% swing Lab. to C.
(2005: Lab. majority 5,911 (17.67%))

§BLAYDON
E. 67,808 T. 44,913 (66.24%) Lab. hold
Dave Anderson, Lab. 22,297
Neil Bradbury, LD 13,180
Glenn Hall, C. 7,159
Keith McFarlane, BNP 2,277
Lab. majority 9,117 (20.30%)
Notional 3.28% swing LD to Lab.
(2005: Lab. majority 5,748 (13.75%))

BLYTH VALLEY
E. 64,263 T. 38,566 (60.01%) Lab. hold
Ronnie Campbell, Lab. 17,156
Jeffrey Reid, LD 10,488
Barry Flux, C. 6,412
Steve Fairbairn, BNP 1,699
James Condon, UKIP 1,665
Barry Elliott, Ind. 819
Allan White, Eng. Dem. 327
Lab. majority 6,668 (17.29%)
3.27% swing Lab. to LD
(2005: Lab. majority 8,527 (23.84%))

§BOGNOR REGIS & LITTLEHAMPTON
E. 70,812 T. 46,852 (66.16%) C. hold
Nick Gibb, C. 24,087
Simon McDougall, LD 11,024
Michael Jones, Lab. 6,580
Douglas Denny, UKIP 3,036
Andrew Moffat, BNP 1,890
Melissa Briggs, Ind. 235
C. majority 13,063 (27.88%)
Notional 2.31% swing LD to C.
(2005: C. majority 8,617 (20.15%))

§BOLSOVER
E. 72,766 T. 43,988 (60.45%) Lab. hold
Dennis Skinner, Lab. 21,994
Lee Rowley, C. 10,812
Denise Hawksworth, LD 6,821
Martin Radford, BNP 2,640
Ray Calladine, UKIP 1,721
Lab. majority 11,182 (25.42%)
Notional 11.23% swing Lab. to C.
(2005: Lab. majority 19,260 (47.68%))

§BOLTON NORTH EAST
E. 67,281 T. 43,277 (64.32%) Lab. hold
David Crausby, Lab. 19,870
Deborah Dunleavy, C. 15,786
Paul Ankers, LD 5,624
Neil Johnson, UKIP 1,815
Norma Armston, You 182
Lab. majority 4,084 (9.44%)
Notional 1.27% swing Lab. to C.
(2005: Lab. majority 4,527 (11.99%))

§BOLTON SOUTH EAST
E. 69,928 T. 39,604 (56.64%) Lab. hold
*Yasmin Qureshi, Lab. 18,782
Andy Morgan, C. 10,148
Donal O'Hanlon, LD 6,289
Sheila Spink, BNP 2,012
Ian Sidaway, UKIP 1,564
Alan Johnson, Green 614
Navaid Syed, CPA 195
Lab. majority 8,634 (21.80%)
Notional 5.61% swing Lab. to C.
(2005: Lab. majority 11,483 (33.03%))

§BOLTON WEST
E. 71,250 T. 47,576 (66.77%) Lab. hold
*Julie Hilling, Lab. 18,327
Susan Williams, C. 18,235
Jackie Pearcey, LD 8,177
Harry Lamb, UKIP 1,901
Rachel Mann, Green 545
Jimmy Jones, Ind. 254
Doug Bagnall, You 137
Lab. majority 92 (0.19%)
Notional 5.88% swing Lab. to C.
(2005: Lab. majority 5,041 (11.95%))

§BOOTLE
E. 71,426 T. 41,277 (57.79%) Lab. hold
Joe Benton, Lab. 27,426
James Murray, LD 6,245
Sohail Qureshi, C. 3,678
Paul Nuttall, UKIP 2,514
Charles Stewart, BNP 942
Pete Glover, TUSC 472
Lab. majority 21,181 (51.31%)
Notional 1.59% swing Lab. to LD
(2005: Lab. majority 20,125 (54.48%))

§BOSTON & SKEGNESS
E. 70,529 T. 43,125 (61.15%) C. hold
Mark Simmonds, C. 21,325
Paul Kenny, Lab. 8,899
Philip Smith, LD 6,371
Christopher Pain, UKIP 4,081
David Owens, BNP 2,278
Peter Wilson, Ind. 171
C. majority 12,426 (28.81%)
Notional 7.00% swing Lab. to C.
(2005: C. majority 6,391 (14.81%))

§BOSWORTH
E. 77,296 T. 54,274 (70.22%) C. hold
David Tredinnick, C. 23,132
Michael Mullaney, LD 18,100
Rory Palmer, Lab. 8,674
John Ryde, BNP 2,458
Dutch Veldhuizen, UKIP 1,098
James Lampitt, Eng. Dem. 615
Michael Brooks, Science 197
C. majority 5,032 (9.27%)
Notional 5.87% swing C. to LD
(2005: C. majority 5,335 (10.72%))

§BOURNEMOUTH EAST
E. 71,125 T. 44,024 (61.90%) C. hold
Tobias Ellwood, C. 21,320
Lisa Northover, LD 13,592
David Stokes, Lab. 5,836
David Hughes, UKIP 3,027
Steven Humphrey, Ind. 249
C. majority 7,728 (17.55%)
Notional 1.76% swing LD to C.
(2005: C. majority 5,874 (14.04%))

§BOURNEMOUTH WEST
E. 71,753 T. 41,659 (58.06%) C. hold
*Conor Burns, C. 18,808
Alasdair Murray, LD 13,225
Sharon Carr-Brown, Lab. 6,171
Philip Glover, UKIP 2,999
Harvey Taylor, Ind. 456
C. majority 5,583 (13.40%)
Notional 2.92% swing LD to C.
(2005: C. majority 2,766 (7.55%))

§BRACKNELL
E. 76,885 T. 52,140 (67.82%) C. hold
*Phillip Lee, C. 27,327
Ray Earwicker, LD 11,623
John Piasecki, Lab. 8,755
Murray Barter, UKIP 2,297
Mark Burke, BNP 1,253
David Young, Green 825
Dan Haycocks, SMA 60
C. majority 15,704 (30.12%)
Notional 0.97% swing C. to LD
(2005: C. majority 10,037 (21.96%))

§BRADFORD EAST
E. 65,116 T. 40,457 (62.13%) LD gain
*David Ward, LD 13,637
Terry Rooney, Lab. 13,272
Mohammed Riaz, C. 10,860
Neville Poynton, BNP 1,854
Raja Hussain, Ind. 375
Peter Shields, Ind. 237
Gerry Robinson, NF 222
LD majority 365 (0.90%)
Notional 7.57% swing Lab. to LD
(2005: Lab. majority 5,227 (14.24%))

§BRADFORD SOUTH
E. 63,580 T. 37,995 (59.76%) Lab. hold
Gerry Sutcliffe, Lab. 15,682
Matt Palmer, C. 11,060
Alun Griffiths, LD 6,948
Sharon Sutton, BNP 2,651
Jamie Illingworth, UKIP 1,339
James Lewthwaite, D Nat 315
Lab. majority 4,622 (12.16%)
Notional 5.91% swing Lab. to C.
(2005: Lab. majority 8,444 (23.99%))

§BRADFORD WEST
E. 62,519 T. 40,576 (64.90%) Lab. hold
Marsha Singh, Lab. 18,401
Zahid Iqbal, C. 12,638
David Hall-Matthews, LD 4,732
Jenny Sampson, BNP 1,370
Arshad Ali, Respect 1,245
David Ford, Green 940
Jason Smith, UKIP 812
Neil Craig, D. Nat. 438
Lab. majority 5,763 (14.20%)
Notional 2.93% swing C. to Lab.
(2005: Lab. majority 3,050 (8.34%))

§BRAINTREE
E. 71,162 T. 49,203 (69.14%) C. hold
Brooks Newmark, C. 25,901
Bill Edwards, Lab. 9,780
Steve Jarvis, LD 9,247
Michael Ford, UKIP 2,477
Paul Hooks, BNP 1,080
Daisy Blench, Green 718
C. majority 16,121 (32.76%)
Notional 6.74% swing Lab. to C.
(2005: C. majority 8,658 (19.28%))

§BRENT CENTRAL
E. 74,076 T. 45,324 (61.19%) LD gain
Sarah Teather, LD 20,026
Dawn Butler, Lab. 18,681
Sachin Rajput, C. 5,068
Shahar Ali, Green 668
Errol Williams, Ch. P. 488
Abdi Duale, Respect 230
Dean McCastree, Ind. 163
LD majority 1,345 (2.97%)
Notional 10.99% swing Lab. to LD
(2005: Lab. majority 7,469 (19.02%))

§BRENT NORTH
E. 83,896 T. 52,298 (62.34%) Lab. hold
Barry Gardiner, Lab. 24,514
Harshadbhai Patel, C. 16,486
James Allie, LD 8,879
Atiq Malik, Ind. 734
Martin Francis, Green 725
Sunita Webb, UKIP 380
Jannen Vamadeva, Ind. 333
Arvind Tailor, Eng. Dem. 247
Lab. majority 8,028 (15.35%)
Notional 2.35% swing Lab. to C.
(2005: Lab. majority 8,830 (20.04%))

§BRENTFORD & ISLEWORTH
E. 83,546 T. 53,765 (64.35%) C. gain
*Mary Macleod, C. 20,022
Ann Keen, Lab. 18,064
Andrew Dakers, LD 12,718
Jason Hargreaves, UKIP 863
John Hunt, Green 787
Paul Winnet, BNP 704
David Cunningham, Eng. Dem. 230
Aamir Bhatti, Ch. P. 210
Evangeline Pillai, CPA 99
Teresa Vanneck-Surplice, Ind. 68
C. majority 1,958 (3.64%)
Notional 5.96% swing Lab. to C.
(2005: Lab. majority 3,633 (8.29%))

§BRENTWOOD & ONGAR
E. 73,224 T. 50,592 (69.09%) C. hold
Eric Pickles, C. 28,793
David Kendall, LD 11,872
Heidi Benzing, Lab. 4,992
Michael McGough, UKIP 2,037
Paul Morris, BNP 1,447
Jess Barnecutt, Green 584
Robin Tilbrook, Eng. Dem. 491
James Sapwell, Ind. 263
Danny Attfield, ND 113
C. majority 16,921 (33.45%)
Notional 3.12% swing LD to C.
(2005: C. majority 12,522 (27.21%))

§BRIDGWATER & SOMERSET WEST
E. 76,560 T. 54,493 (71.18%) C. hold
Ian Liddell-Grainger, C. 24,675
Theo Butt Philip, LD 15,426
Kathryn Pearce, Lab. 9,332
Peter Hollings, UKIP 2,604
Donna Treanor, BNP 1,282
Charles Graham, Green 859
Bob Cudlipp, Ind. 315
C. majority 9,249 (16.97%)
Notional 2.88% swing C. to LD
(2005: C. majority 10,081 (19.77%))

§BRIGG & GOOLE
E. 67,345 T. 43,874 (65.15%) C. gain
*Andrew Percy, C. 19,680
Ian Cawsey, Lab. 14,533
Richard Nixon, LD 6,414
Nigel Wright, UKIP 1,749
Stephen Ward, BNP 1,498
C. majority 5,147 (11.73%)
Notional 9.79% swing Lab. to C.
(2005: Lab. majority 3,217 (7.84%))

§BRIGHTON KEMPTOWN
E. 66,017 T. 42,705 (64.69%) C. gain
*Simon Kirby, C. 16,217
Simon Burgess, Lab. Co-op 14,889
Juliet Williams, LD 7,691
Ben Duncan, Green 2,330
James Chamberlain-Webber, UKIP 1,384
Dave Hill, TUSC 194
C. majority 1,328 (3.11%)
Notional 3.97% swing Lab. to C.
(2005: Lab. majority 1,853 (4.83%))

§BRIGHTON PAVILION
E. 74,004 T. 51,834 (70.04%) Green gain
*Dr Caroline Lucas, Green 16,238
Nancy Platts, Lab. 14,986
Charlotte Vere, C. 12,275
Bernadette Millam, LD 7,159
Nigel Carter, UKIP 948
Ian Fyvie, Soc. Lab. 148
Soraya Kara, R and E 61
Leo Atreides, ND 19
Green majority 1,252 (2.42%)
Notional 8.45% swing Lab. to Green
(2005: Lab. majority 5,867 (13.11%))

§BRISTOL EAST
E. 69,448 T. 45,017 (64.82%) Lab. hold
Kerry McCarthy, Lab. 16,471
Adeela Shafi, C. 12,749
Mike Popham, LD 10,993
Brian Jenkins, BNP 1,960
Philip Collins, UKIP 1,510
Glenn Vowles, Green 803
Stephen Wright, Eng. Dem. 347
Rae Lynch, TUSC 184
Lab. majority 3,722 (8.27%)
Notional 4.54% swing Lab. to C.
(2005: Lab. majority 7,335 (17.35%))

§BRISTOL NORTH WEST
E. 73,469 T. 50,336 (68.51%) C. gain
*Charlotte Leslie, C. 19,115
Paul Harrod, LD 15,841
Sam Townend, Lab. 13,059
Robert Upton, UKIP 1,175
Ray Carr, Eng. Dem. 635
Alex Dunn, Green 511
C. majority 3,274 (6.50%)
Notional 8.86% swing Lab. to C.
(2005: Lab. majority 2,781 (5.69%))

§BRISTOL SOUTH
E. 78,579 T. 48,377 (61.56%) Lab. hold
Dawn Primarolo, Lab. 18,600
Mark Wright, LD 13,866
Mark Lloyd Davies, C. 11,086
Colin Chidsey, BNP 1,739
Colin McNamee, UKIP 1,264
Charlie Bolton, Green 1,216
Craig Clarke, Eng. Dem. 400
Tom Baldwin, TUSC 206
Lab. majority 4,734 (9.79%)
Notional 7.53% swing Lab. to LD
(2005: Lab. majority 10,928 (24.86%))

§BRISTOL WEST
E. 82,728 T. 55,347 (66.90%) LD hold
Stephen Williams, LD 26,593
Paul Smith, Lab. 15,227
Nick Yarker, C. 10,169
Ricky Knight, Green 2,090
Chris Lees, UKIP 655
Danny Kushlick, Ind. 343
Jon Baker, Eng. Dem. 270
LD majority 11,366 (20.54%)
Notional 9.00% swing Lab. to LD
(2005: LD majority 1,147 (2.55%))

§BROADLAND
E. 73,168 T. 52,676 (71.99%) C. hold
Keith Simpson, C. 24,338
Daniel Roper, LD 17,046
Allyson Barron, Lab. 7,287
Stuart Agnew, UKIP 2,382
Edith Crowther, BNP 871
Susan Curran, Green 752
C. majority 7,292 (13.84%)
Notional 0.06% swing C. to LD
(2005: C. majority 6,573 (13.97%))

§BROMLEY & CHISLEHURST
E. 65,427 T. 44,037 (67.31%) C. hold
Bob Neill, C. 23,569
Sam Webber, LD 9,669
Chris Kirby, Lab. 7,295
Emmett Jenner, UKIP 1,451
Rowena Savage, BNP 1,070
Roisin Robertson, Green 607
Jon Cheeseman, Eng. Dem. 376
C. majority 13,900 (31.56%)
Notional 5.13% swing LD to C.
(2005: C. majority 8,236 (20.57%))

BROMSGROVE
E. 73,086 T. 51,630 (70.64%) C. hold
*Sajid Javid, C. 22,558
Sam Burden, Lab. 11,250
Philip Ling, LD 10,124
Steven Morson, UKIP 2,950
Adrian Kriss, BIC 2,182
Elizabeth Wainwright, BNP 1,923
Mark France, Ind. 336
Ken Wheatley, Ind. 307
C. majority 11,308 (21.90%)
0.41% swing Lab. to C.
(2005: C. majority 10,080 (21.08%))

BROXBOURNE
E. 71,391 T. 45,658 (63.95%) C. hold
Charles Walker, C. 26,844
Michael Watson, Lab. 8,040
Allan Witherick, LD 6,107
Steve McCole, BNP 2,159
Martin Harvey, UKIP 1,890
Debbie LeMay, Eng. Dem. 618
C. majority 18,804 (41.18%)
6.43% swing Lab. to C.
(2005: C. majority 11,509 (28.33%))

§BROXTOWE
E. 72,042 T. 52,727 (73.19%) C. gain
*Anna Soubry, C. 20,585
Nick Palmer, Lab. 20,196
David Watts, LD 8,907
Mike Shore, BNP 1,422
Chris Cobb, UKIP 1,194
David Mitchell, Green 423
C. majority 389 (0.74%)
Notional 2.59% swing Lab. to C.
(2005: Lab. majority 2,139 (4.44%))

§BUCKINGHAM
E. 74,996 T. 48,335 (64.45%)
Speaker hold
‡John Bercow, Speaker 22,860
John Stevens, Ind. 10,331
Nigel Farage, UKIP 8,401
Patrick Phillips, Ind. 2,394
Debbie Martin, Ind. 1,270
Lynne Mozar, BNP 980
Colin Dale, Loony 856
Geoff Howard, Ind. 435
David Hews, Ch. P. 369
Anthony Watts, Ind. 332
Simon Strutt, Deficit 107
Speaker majority 12,529 (25.92%)
(2005: C. majority 18,716 (37.83%))

BURNLEY
E. 66,616 T. 41,845 (62.82%) LD gain
*Gordon Birtwistle, LD 14,932
Julie Cooper, Lab. 13,114
Richard Ali, C. 6,950
Sharon Wilkinson, BNP 3,747
Andrew Brown, Ind. 1,876
John Wignall, UKIP 929
Andrew Hennessey, Ind. 297
LD majority 1,818 (4.34%)
9.58% swing Lab. to LD
(2005: Lab. majority 5,778 (14.82%))

§BURTON
E. 74,874 T. 49,823 (66.54%) C. gain
*Andrew Griffiths, C. 22,188
Ruth Smeeth, Lab. 15,884
Michael Rodgers, LD 7,891
Alan Hewitt, BNP 2,409
Philip Lancaster, UKIP 1,451
C. majority 6,304 (12.65%)
Notional 8.73% swing Lab. to C.
(2005: Lab. majority 2,132 (4.81%))

§BURY NORTH
E. 66,759 T. 44,961 (67.35%) C. gain
*David Nuttall, C. 18,070
Maryam Khan, Lab. 15,827
Richard Baum, LD 7,645
John Maude, BNP 1,825
Stephen Evans, UKIP 1,282
Bill Brison, Ind. 181
Graeme Lambert, Pirate 131
C. majority 2,243 (4.99%)
Notional 5.02% swing Lab. to C.
(2005: Lab. majority 2,059 (5.05%))

§BURY SOUTH
E. 73,544 T. 48,267 (65.63%) Lab. hold
Ivan Lewis, Lab. 19,508
Michelle Wiseman, C. 16,216
Vic D'Albert, LD 8,796
Jean Purdy, BNP 1,743
Paul Chadwick, UKIP 1,017
Valerie Morris, Eng. Dem. 494
George Heron, Green 493
Lab. majority 3,292 (6.82%)
Notional 8.01% swing Lab. to C.
(2005: Lab. majority 9,779 (22.84%))

§BURY ST EDMUNDS
E. 84,727 T. 58,718 (69.30%) C. hold
David Ruffley, C. 27,899
David Chappell, LD 15,519
Kevin Hind, Lab. 9,776
John Howlett, UKIP 3,003
Mark Ereira-Guyer, Green 2,521
C. majority 12,380 (21.08%)
Notional 2.76% swing C. to LD
(2005: C. majority 10,080 (19.03%))

§CALDER VALLEY
E. 76,903 T. 51,780 (67.33%) C. gain
*Craig Whittaker, C. 20,397
Steph Booth, Lab. 13,966
Hilary Myers, LD 13,037
John Gregory, BNP 1,823
Greg Burrows, UKIP 1,173
Kate Sweeny, Green 858
Tim Cole, Ind. 194
Barry Greenwood, Ind. 175
Paul Rogan, Eng. Dem. 157
C. majority 6,431 (12.42%)
Notional 7.58% swing Lab. to C.
(2005: Lab. majority 1,303 (2.73%))

§CAMBERWELL & PECKHAM
E. 78,618 T. 46,659 (59.35%) Lab. hold
Harriet Harman, Lab. 27,619
Columba Blango, LD 10,432
Andy Stranack, C. 6,080
Jenny Jones, Green 1,361
Yohara Robby Munilla, Eng. Dem. 435
Joshua Ogunleye, WRP 211
Margaret Sharkey, Soc. Lab. 184
Decima Francis, Ind. 93
Steven Robbins, Ind. 87
Patricia Knox, ND 82
Jill Mountford, Workers Lib 75
Lab. majority 17,187 (36.84%)
Notional 3.00% swing Lab. to LD
(2005: Lab. majority 16,608 (42.83%))

§CAMBORNE & REDRUTH
E. 63,968 T. 42,493 (66.43%) C. gain
*George Eustice, C. 15,969
Julia Goldsworthy, LD 15,903
Jude Robinson, Lab. 6,945
Derek Elliott, UKIP 2,152
Loveday Jenkin, Meb. Ker. 775
Euan McPhee, Green 581
Robert Hawkins, Soc. Lab. 168
C. majority 66 (0.16%)
Notional 5.21% swing LD to C.
(2005: LD majority 2,733 (7.08%))

§CAMBRIDGE
E. 77,081 T. 50,130 (65.04%) LD hold
*Julian Huppert, LD 19,621
Nick Hillman, C. 12,829
Daniel Zeichner, Lab. 12,174
Tony Juniper, Green 3,804
Peter Burkinshaw, UKIP 1,195
Martin Booth, TUSC 362
Holborn Old, Ind. 145
LD majority 6,792 (13.55%)
Notional 6.98% swing LD to C.
(2005: LD majority 5,834 (12.27%))

§CAMBRIDGESHIRE NORTH EAST
E. 73,224 T. 52,264 (71.38%) C. hold
*Stephen Barclay, C. 26,862
Lorna Spenceley, LD 10,437
Peter Roberts, Lab. 9,274
Robin Talbot, UKIP 2,991
Susan Clapp, BNP 1,747
Debra Jordan, Ind. 566
Graham Murphy, Eng. Dem. 387
C. majority 16,425 (31.43%)
Notional 0.79% swing LD to C.
(2005: C. majority 7,726 (16.30%))

§CAMBRIDGESHIRE NORTH WEST
E. 88,857 T. 58,283 (65.59%) C. hold
Shailesh Vara, C. 29,425
Kevin Wilkins, LD 12,748
Chris York, Lab. 9,877
Robert Brown, UKIP 4,826
Stephen Goldspink, Eng. Dem. 1,407
C. majority 16,677 (28.61%)
Notional 2.64% swing LD to C.
(2005: C. majority 10,925 (20.62%))

§CAMBRIDGESHIRE SOUTH
E. 78,995 T. 59,056 (74.76%) C. hold
Andrew Lansley, C. 27,995
Sebastian Kindersley, LD 20,157
Tariq Sadiq, Lab. 6,024
Robin Page, Ind. 1,968
Helene Davies-Green, UKIP 1,873
Simon Saggers, Green 1,039
C. majority 7,838 (13.27%)
Notional 2.46% swing C. to LD
(2005: C. majority 9,634 (18.20%))

§CAMBRIDGESHIRE SOUTH EAST
E. 83,068 T. 57,602 (69.34%) C. hold
Jim Paice, C. 27,629
Jonathan Chatfield, LD 21,683
John Cowan, Lab. 4,380
Andy Monk, UKIP 2,138
Simon Sedgwick-Jell, Green 766
Geoffrey Woollard, Ind. 517
Daniel Bell, CPA 489
C. majority 5,946 (10.32%)
Notional 2.67% swing C. to LD
(2005: C. majority 8,110 (15.66%))

§CANNOCK CHASE
E. 74,509 T. 45,559 (61.15%) C. gain
*Aidan Burley, C. 18,271
Susan Woodward, Lab. 15,076
Jon Hunt, LD 7,732
Terence Majorowicz, BNP 2,168
Malcolm McKenzie, UKIP 1,580
Ron Turville, Ind. 380
Royston Jenkins, Snouts 259
Mike Walters, Ind. 93
C. majority 3,195 (7.01%)
Notional 14.01% swing Lab. to C.
(2005: Lab. majority 8,726 (21.00%))

§CANTERBURY
E. 76,808 T. 49,209 (64.07%) C. hold
Julian Brazier, C. 22,050
Guy Voizey, LD 16,002
Jean Samuel, Lab. 7,940
Howard Farmer, UKIP 1,907
Geoff Meaden, Green 1,137
Anne Belsey, MRP 173
C. majority 6,048 (12.29%)
Notional 5.36% swing C. to LD
(2005: C. majority 7,579 (16.37%))

§CARLISLE
E. 65,263 T. 42,200 (64.66%) C. gain
*John Stevenson, C. 16,589
Michael Boaden, Lab. 15,736
Neil Hughes, LD 6,567
Paul Stafford, BNP 1,086
Michael Owen, UKIP 969
John Reardon, Green 614
John Metcalfe, TUSC 376
Peter Howe, ND 263
C. majority 853 (2.02%)
Notional 7.74% swing Lab. to C.
(2005: Lab. majority 5,085 (13.46%))

§CARSHALTON & WALLINGTON
E. 66,520 T. 45,918 (69.03%) LD hold
Tom Brake, LD 22,180
Dr Ken Andrew, C. 16,920
Shafi Khan, Lab. 4,015
Frank Day, UKIP 1,348
Charlotte Lewis, BNP 1,100
George Dow, Green 355
LD majority 5,260 (11.46%)
Notional 4.26% swing C. to LD
(2005: LD majority 1,225 (2.93%))

CASTLE POINT
E. 67,284 T. 45,026 (66.92%) C. gain
*Rebecca Harris, C. 19,806
Bob Spink, Green Belt 12,174
Julian Ware-Lane, Lab. 6,609
Brendan D'Cruz, LD 4,232
Philip Howell, BNP 2,205
C. majority 7,632 (16.95%)
(2005: C. majority 8,201 (17.91%))

§CHARNWOOD
E. 74,473 T. 53,542 (71.89%) C. hold
Stephen Dorrell, C. 26,560
Robin Webber-Jones, LD 11,531
Eric Goodyer, Lab. 10,536
Cathy Duffy, BNP 3,116
Miles Storier, UKIP 1,799
C. majority 15,029 (28.07%)
Notional 0.10% swing C. to LD
(2005: C. majority 8,613 (18.05%))

§CHATHAM & AYLESFORD
E. 71,122 T. 43,807 (61.59%) C. gain
*Tracey Crouch, C. 20,230
Jonathan Shaw, Lab. 14,161
John McClintock, LD 5,832
Colin McCarthy-Stewart, BNP 1,365
Steve Newton, UKIP 1,314
Sean Varnham, Eng. Dem. 400
Dave Arthur, Green 396
Maureen Smith, Ch. P. 109
C. majority 6,069 (13.85%)
Notional 11.05% swing Lab. to C.
(2005: Lab. majority 3,289 (8.25%))

§CHEADLE
E. 72,458 T. 52,512 (72.47%) LD hold
Mark Hunter, LD 24,717
Ben Jeffreys, C. 21,445
Martin Miller, Lab. 4,920
Tony Moore, UKIP 1,430
LD majority 3,272 (6.23%)
Notional 0.59% swing LD to C.
(2005: LD majority 3,672 (7.41%))

§CHELMSFORD
E. 77,529 T. 54,593 (70.42%) C. hold
Simon Burns, C. 25,207
Stephen Robinson, LD 20,097
Peter Dixon, Lab. 5,980
Ken Wedon, UKIP 1,527
Mike Bateman, BNP 899
Angela Thomson, Green 476
Claire Breed, Eng. Dem. 254
Ben Sherman, Beer 153
C. majority 5,110 (9.36%)
Notional 0.08% swing LD to C.
(2005: C. majority 4,358 (9.20%))

§CHELSEA & FULHAM
E. 66,295 T. 39,856 (60.12%) C. hold
Greg Hands, C. 24,093
Alexander Hilton, Lab. 7,371
Dirk Hazell, LD 6,473
Julia Stephenson, Green 671
Timothy Gittos, UKIP 478
Brian McDonald, BNP 388
Roland Courtenay, Ind. CCF 196
George Roseman, Eng. Dem. 169
Godfrey Spickernell, Blue 17
C. majority 16,722 (41.96%)
Notional 6.08% swing Lab. to C.
(2005: C. majority 10,253 (29.79%))

§CHELTENHAM
E. 78,998 T. 52,786 (66.82%) LD hold
Martin Horwood, LD 26,659
Mark Coote, C. 21,739
James Green, Lab. 2,703
Peter Bowman, UKIP 1,192
Dancing Ken Hanks, Loony 493
LD majority 4,920 (9.32%)
Notional 4.33% swing C. to LD
(2005: LD majority 316 (0.66%))

§CHESHAM & AMERSHAM
E. 70,333 T. 52,444 (74.57%) C. hold
Cheryl Gillan, C. 31,658
Tim Starkey, LD 14,948
Anthony Gajadharsingh, Lab. 2,942
Alan Stevens, UKIP 2,129
Nick Wilkins, Green 767
C. majority 16,710 (31.86%)
Notional 2.28% swing LD to C.
(2005: C. majority 12,974 (27.31%))

§CHESTER, CITY OF
E. 68,874 T. 46,790 (67.94%) C. gain
*Stephen Mosley, C. 18,995
Christine Russell, Lab. 16,412
Elizabeth Jewkes, LD 8,930
Allan Weddell, UKIP 1,225
Ed Abrams, Eng. Dem. 594
Tom Barker, Green 535
John Whittingham, Ind. 99
C. majority 2,583 (5.52%)
Notional 3.86% swing Lab. to C.
(2005: Lab. majority 973 (2.20%))

§CHESTERFIELD
E. 71,878 T. 45,839 (63.77%) Lab. gain
*Toby Perkins, Lab. 17,891
Paul Holmes, LD 17,342
Carolyn Abbott, C. 7,214
David Phillips, UKIP 1,432
Ian Jerram, Eng. Dem. 1,213
Duncan Kerr, Green 600
John Noneoftheabove Daramy, Ind. 147
Lab. majority 549 (1.20%)
Notional 3.78% swing LD to Lab.
(2005: LD majority 2,733 (6.36%))

§CHICHESTER
E. 81,462 T. 56,787 (69.71%) C. hold
Andrew Tyrie, C. 31,427
Martin Lury, LD 15,550
Simon Holland, Lab. 5,937
Andrew Moncrieff, UKIP 3,873
C. majority 15,877 (27.96%)
Notional 3.82% swing LD to C.
(2005: C. majority 10,457 (20.32%))

CHINGFORD & WOODFORD GREEN
E. 64,831 T. 43,106 (66.49%) C. hold
Iain Duncan Smith, C. 22,743
Cath Arakelian, Lab. 9,780
Geoffrey Seeff, LD 7,242
Julian Leppert, BNP 1,288
Nick Jones, UKIP 1,133
Lucy Craig, Green 650
None of The Above, Ind. 202
Barry White, Ind. 68
C. majority 12,963 (30.07%)
1.27% swing Lab. to C.
(2005: C. majority 10,641 (27.53%))

§CHIPPENHAM
E. 72,105 T. 52,385 (72.65%) LD hold
*Duncan Hames, LD 23,970
Wilfred Emmanuel-Jones, C. 21,500
Greg Lovell, Lab. 3,620
Julia Reid, UKIP 1,783
Michael Simpkins, BNP 641
Samantha Fletcher, Green 446
John Maguire, Eng. Dem. 307
Richard Sexton, Ch. P. 118
LD majority 2,470 (4.72%)
Notional 0.01% swing C. to LD
(2005: LD majority 2,183 (4.70%))

§CHIPPING BARNET
E. 77,798 T. 50,608 (65.05%) C. hold
Theresa Villiers, C. 24,700
Damien Welfare, Lab. 12,773
Stephen Barber, LD 10,202
James Fluss, UKIP 1,442
Kate Tansley, Green 1,021
Philip Clayton, Ind. 470
C. majority 11,927 (23.57%)
Notional 5.77% swing Lab. to C.
(2005: C. majority 5,457 (12.02%))

§CHORLEY
E. 70,950 T. 49,774 (70.15%) Lab. hold
Lindsay Hoyle, Lab. 21,515
Alan Cullens, C. 18,922
Stephen Fenn, LD 6,957
Nick Hogan, UKIP 2,021
Chris Curtis, Ind. 359
Lab. majority 2,593 (5.21%)
Notional 5.60% swing Lab. to C.
(2005: Lab. majority 7,285 (16.41%))

§CHRISTCHURCH
E. 68,861 T. 49,416 (71.76%) C. hold
Christopher Chope, C. 27,888
Martyn Hurll, LD 12,478
Robert Deeks, Lab. 4,849
David Williams, UKIP 4,201
C. majority 15,410 (31.18%)
Notional 0.05% swing C. to LD
(2005: C. majority 14,640 (31.28%))

§CITIES OF LONDON & WESTMINSTER
E. 66,489 T. 36,931 (55.54%) C. hold
Mark Field, C. 19,264
David Rowntree, Lab. 8,188
Naomi Smith, LD 7,574
Dr Derek Chase, Green 778
Paul Weston, UKIP 664
Frank Roseman, Eng. Dem. 191
Dennis Delderfield, Ind. 98
Jack Nunn, Pirate 90
Mad Cap'n Tom, Ind. 84
C. majority 11,076 (29.99%)
Notional 3.51% swing Lab. to C.
(2005: C. majority 7,352 (22.96%))

§CLACTON
E. 67,194 T. 43,123 (64.18%) C. hold
Douglas Carswell, C. 22,867
Ivan Henderson, Lab. 10,799
Michael Green, LD 5,577
Jim Taylor, BNP 1,975
Terry Allen, Tendring 1,078
Chris Southall, Green 535
Christopher Humphrey, Ind. 292
C. majority 12,068 (27.99%)
Notional 9.74% swing Lab. to C.
(2005: C. majority 3,629 (8.50%))

CLEETHORPES
E. 70,214 T. 44,966 (64.04%) C. gain
*Martin Vickers, C. 18,939
Shona McIsaac, Lab. 14,641
Malcolm Morland, LD 8,192
Stephen Harness, UKIP 3,194
C. majority 4,298 (9.56%)
7.81% swing Lab. to C.
(2005: Lab. majority 2,642 (6.06%))

§COLCHESTER
E. 74,062 T. 46,139 (62.30%) LD hold
Bob Russell, LD 22,151
Will Quince, C. 15,169
Jordan Newell, Lab. 5,680
John Pitts, UKIP 1,350
Sidney Chaney, BNP 705
Peter Lynn, Green 694
Eddie Bone, Eng. Dem. 335
Garryck Noble, PP Essex 35
Paul Shaw, ND 20
LD majority 6,982 (15.13%)
Notional 0.24% swing LD to C.
(2005: LD majority 6,388 (15.60%))

§COLNE VALLEY
E. 80,062 T. 55,296 (69.07%) C. gain
*Jason McCartney, C. 20,440
Nicola Turner, LD 15,603
Debbie Abrahams, Lab. 14,589
Barry Fowler, BNP 1,893
Melanie Roberts, UKIP 1,163
Chas Ball, Green 867
Dr Jackie Grunsell, TUSC 741
C. majority 4,837 (8.75%)
Notional 6.55% swing Lab. to C.
(2005: Lab. majority 1,267 (2.51%))

CONGLETON
E. 73,692 T. 50,780 (68.91%) C. hold
*Fiona Bruce, C. 23,250
Peter Hirst, LD 16,187
David Bryant, Lab. 8,747
Lee Slaughter, UKIP 2,147
Paul Edwards, Ind. 276
Paul Rothwell, ND 94
Adam Parton, Ind. 79
C. majority 7,063 (13.91%)
2.30% swing C. to LD
(2005: C. majority 8,246 (17.66%))

§COPELAND
E. 63,291 T. 42,787 (67.60%) Lab. hold
Jamie Reed, Lab. 19,699
Christopher Whiteside, C. 15,866
Frank Hollowell, LD 4,365
Clive Jefferson, BNP 1,474
Ted Caley-Knowles, UKIP 994
Jill Perry, Green 389
Lab. majority 3,833 (8.96%)
Notional 2.14% swing Lab. to C.
(2005: Lab. majority 5,157 (13.24%))

CORBY
E. 78,305 T. 54,236 (69.26%) C. gain
*Louise Bagshawe, C. 22,886
Phil Hope, Lab. 20,991
Portia Wilson, LD 7,834
Roy Davies, BNP 2,525
C. majority 1,895 (3.49%)
3.31% swing Lab. to C.
(2005: Lab. (Co-op) majority 1,517 (3.13%))

§CORNWALL NORTH
E. 68,662 T. 46,844 (68.22%) LD hold
Dan Rogerson, LD 22,512
Sian Flynn, C. 19,531
Miriel O'Connor, UKIP 2,300
Janet Hulme, Lab. 1,971
Joanie Willett, Meb. Ker. 530
LD majority 2,981 (6.36%)
Notional 0.25% swing LD to C.
(2005: LD majority 2,892 (6.87%))

§CORNWALL SOUTH EAST
E. 72,237 T. 49,617 (68.69%) C. gain
*Sheryll Murray, C. 22,390
Karen Gillard, LD 19,170
Michael Sparling, Lab. 3,507
Stephanie McWilliam, UKIP 3,083
Roger Creagh-Osborne, Green 826
Roger Holmes, Meb. Ker. 641
C. majority 3,220 (6.49%)
Notional 9.13% swing LD to C.
(2005: LD majority 5,485 (11.77%))

§COTSWOLDS, THE
E. 76,728 T. 54,832 (71.46%) C. hold
Geoffrey Clifton-Brown, C. 29,075
Mike Collins, LD 16,211
Mark Dempsey, Lab. 5,886
Adrian Blake, UKIP 2,292
Kevin Lister, Green 940
Alex Steel, Ind. 428
C. majority 12,864 (23.46%)
Notional 1.08% swing LD to C.
(2005: C. majority 10,742 (21.29%))

§COVENTRY NORTH EAST
E. 73,035 T. 43,383 (59.40%) Lab. hold
Bob Ainsworth, Lab. 21,384
Hazel Noonan, C. 9,609
Russell Field, LD 7,210
Tom Gower, BNP 1,863
Dave Nellist, Soc. Alt. 1,592
Chris Forbes, UKIP 1,291
Ron Lebar, Ch. M. 434
Lab. majority 11,775 (27.14%)
Notional 5.47% swing Lab. to C.
(2005: Lab. majority 14,621 (38.08%))

§COVENTRY NORTH WEST
E. 72,871 T. 46,560 (63.89%) Lab. hold
Geoffrey Robinson, Lab. 19,936
Gary Ridley, C. 13,648
Vincent McKee, LD 8,344
Edward Sheppard, BNP 1,666
Mark Nattrass, UKIP 1,295
John Clarke, Ind. 640
Justin Wood, Green 497
Nikki Downes, Soc. Alt. 370
William Sidhu, Ch. M. 164
Lab. majority 6,288 (13.51%)
Notional 3.92% swing Lab. to C.
(2005: Lab. majority 8,934 (21.35%))

§COVENTRY SOUTH
E. 73,652 T. 45,924 (62.35%) Lab. hold
Jim Cunningham, Lab. 19,197
Kevin Foster, C. 15,352
Brian Patton, LD 8,278
Mark Taylor, UKIP 1,767
Judy Griffiths, Soc. Alt. 691
Stephen Gray, Green 639
Lab. majority 3,845 (8.37%)
Notional 3.41% swing Lab. to C.
(2005: Lab. majority 6,237 (15.18%))

CRAWLEY
E. 72,781 T. 47,504 (65.27%) C. gain
*Henry Smith, C. 21,264
Chris Oxlade, Lab. 15,336
John Vincent, LD 6,844
Richard Trower, BNP 1,672
Chris French, UKIP 1,382
Phil Smith, Green 598
Arshad Khan, JP 265
Andrew Hubner, Ind. 143
C. majority 5,928 (12.48%)
6.28% swing Lab. to C.
(2005: Lab. majority 37 (0.09%))

§CREWE & NANTWICH
E. 77,460 T. 51,084 (65.95%) C. hold
Edward Timpson, C. 23,420
David Williams, Lab. 17,374
Roy Wood, LD 7,656
James Clutton, UKIP 1,414
Phil Williams, BNP 1,043
Mike Parsons, Ind. 177
C. majority 6,046 (11.84%)
Notional 13.67% swing Lab. to C.
(2005: Lab. majority 6,999 (15.50%))

§CROYDON CENTRAL
E. 78,880 T. 49,757 (63.08%) C. gain
*Gavin Barwell, C. 19,657
Gerry Ryan, Lab. (Co-op) 16,688
Peter Lambell, LD 6,553
Andrew Pelling, Ind. 3,239
Cliff Le May, BNP 1,448
Ralph Atkinson, UKIP 997
Bernice Golberg, Green 581
James Gitau, Ch. P. 264
John Cartwright, Loony 192
Michael Castle, Ind. 138
C. majority 2,969 (5.97%)
Notional 3.34% swing Lab. to C.
(2005: Lab. majority 328 (0.72%))

§CROYDON NORTH
E. 85,212 T. 51,678 (60.65%) Lab. hold
Malcolm Wicks, Lab. 28,949
Jason Hadden, C. 12,466
Gerry Jerome, LD 7,226
Shasha Khan, Green 1,017
Jonathan Serter, UKIP 891
Novlette Williams, Ch. P. 586
Mohommad Shaikh, Respect 272
Ben Stevenson, Comm. 160
Mohamed Seyed, Ind. 111
Lab. majority 16,483 (31.90%)
Notional 0.27% swing C. to Lab.
(2005: Lab. majority 14,185 (31.37%))

§CROYDON SOUTH
E. 81,301 T. 56,322 (69.28%) C. hold
Richard Ottaway, C. 28,684
Simon Rix, LD 12,866
Jane Avis, Lab. 11,287
Jeffrey Bolter, UKIP 2,504
Gordon Ross, Green 981
C. majority 15,818 (28.08%)
Notional 1.75% swing C. to LD
(2005: C. majority 14,228 (27.95%))

§DAGENHAM & RAINHAM
E. 69,764 T. 44,232 (63.40%) Lab. hold
Jon Cruddas, Lab. 17,813
Simon Jones, C. 15,183
Michael Barnbrook, BNP 4,952
Joseph Bourke, LD 3,806
Craig Litwin, UKIP 1,569
Gordon Kennedy, Ind. 308
Paula Watson, Ch. P. 305
Debbie Rosaman, Green 296
Lab. majority 2,630 (5.95%)
Notional 4.87% swing Lab. to C.
(2005: Lab. majority 6,372 (15.69%))

§DARLINGTON
E. 69,352 T. 42,896 (61.85%) Lab. hold
*Jenny Chapman, Lab. 16,891
Edward Legard, C. 13,503
Mike Barker, LD 10,046
Amanda Foster, BNP 1,262
Charlotte Bull, UKIP 1,194
Lab. majority 3,388 (7.90%)
Notional 9.14% swing Lab. to C.
(2005: Lab. majority 10,417 (26.18%))

§DARTFORD
E. 76,271 T. 50,080 (65.66%) C. gain
*Gareth Johnson, C. 24,428
John Adams, Lab. 13,800
James Willis, LD 7,361
Gary Rogers, Eng. Dem. 2,178
Richard Palmer, UKIP 1,842
Stephane Tindame, Ind. 264
John Crockford, FDP 207
C. majority 10,628 (21.22%)
Notional 11.56% swing Lab. to C.
(2005: Lab. majority 860 (1.90%))

§DAVENTRY
E. 71,451 T. 51,774 (72.46%) C. hold
*Chris Heaton-Harris, C. 29,252
Christopher McGlynn, LD 10,064
Paul Corazzo, Lab. 8,168
Jim Broomfield, UKIP 2,333
Alan Bennett-Spencer, Eng. Dem. 1,187
Steve Whiffen, Green 770
C. majority 19,188 (37.06%)
Notional 0.71% swing C. to LD
(2005: C. majority 11,776 (25.15%))

§DENTON & REDDISH
E. 64,765 T. 37,635 (58.11%) Lab. hold
Andrew Gwynne, Lab. 19,191
Julie Searle, C. 9,360
Stephen Broadhurst, LD 6,727
William Robinson, UKIP 2,060
Jeff Dennis, Ind. 297
Lab. majority 9,831 (26.12%)
Notional 6.25% swing Lab. to C.
(2005: Lab. majority 13,128 (38.62%))

§DERBY NORTH
E. 71,484 T. 45,080 (63.06%) Lab. hold
*Chris Williamson, Lab. 14,896
Stephen Mold, C. 14,283
Lucy Care, LD 12,638
Peter Cheeseman, BNP 2,000
Elizabeth Ransome, UKIP 829
David Gale, Ind. 264
David Geraghty, Pirate 170
Lab. majority 613 (1.36%)
Notional 7.39% swing Lab. to C.
(2005: Lab. majority 5,691 (14.58%))

§DERBY SOUTH
E. 71,012 T. 41,188 (58.00%) Lab. hold
Margaret Beckett, Lab. 17,851
Jack Perschke, C. 11,729
David Batey, LD 8,430
Stephen Fowke, UKIP 1,821
Alan Graves, Ind. 1,357
Lab. majority 6,122 (14.86%)
Notional 9.26% swing Lab. to C.
(2005: Lab. majority 11,655 (28.99%))

§DERBYSHIRE DALES
E. 63,367 T. 46,780 (73.82%) C. hold
Patrick McLoughlin, C. 24,378
Joe Naitta, LD 10,512
Colin Swindell, Lab. 9,061
Ian Guiver, UKIP 1,779
Josh Stockell, Green 772
Nick The Flying Brick Delves, Loony 228
Amila Y'mech, Humanity 50
C. majority 13,866 (29.64%)
Notional 3.74% swing LD to C.
(2005: C. majority 8,810 (20.82%))

§DERBYSHIRE MID
E. 66,297 T. 47,342 (71.41%) C. hold
*Pauline Latham, C. 22,877
Hardyal Dhindsa, Lab. 11,585
Sally McIntosh, LD 9,711
Lewis Allsebrook, BNP 1,698
Anthony Kay, UKIP 1,252
RU Seerius, Loony 219
C. majority 11,292 (23.85%)
Notional 5.66% swing Lab. to C.
(2005: C. majority 5,329 (12.54%))

§DERBYSHIRE NORTH EAST
E. 71,422 T. 47,034 (65.85%) Lab. hold
Natascha Engel, Lab. 17,948
Huw Merriman, C. 15,503
Richard Bull, LD 10,947
James Bush, UKIP 2,636
Lab. majority 2,445 (5.20%)
Notional 8.56% swing Lab. to C.
(2005: Lab. majority 9,564 (22.31%))

§DERBYSHIRE SOUTH
E. 70,610 T. 50,419 (71.40%) C. gain
*Heather Wheeler, C. 22,935
Michael Edwards, Lab. 15,807
Alexis Diouf, LD 8,012
Peter Jarvis, BNP 2,193
Charles Swabey, UKIP 1,206
Paul Liversuch, Soc. Lab. 266
C. majority 7,128 (14.14%)
Notional 9.80% swing Lab. to C.
(2005: Lab. majority 2,436 (5.45%))

§DEVIZES
E. 67,374 T. 46,340 (68.78%) C. hold
*Claire Perry, C. 25,519
Fiona Hornby, LD 12,514
Jurab Ali, Lab. 4,711
Patricia Bryant, UKIP 2,076
Mark Fletcher, Green 813
Martin Houlden, Ind. 566
Nic Coombe, Libertarian 141
C. majority 13,005 (28.06%)
Notional 0.33% swing C. to LD
(2005: C. majority 12,259 (28.63%))

§DEVON CENTRAL
E. 71,204 T. 53,873 (75.66%) C. hold
*Mel Stride, C. 27,737
Philip Hutty, LD 18,507
Moira Macdonald, Lab. 3,715
Bob Edwards, UKIP 2,870
Colin Mathews, Green 1,044
C. majority 9,230 (17.13%)
Notional 6.07% swing LD to C.
(2005: C. majority 2,338 (4.99%))

§DEVON EAST
E. 73,109 T. 53,092 (72.62%) C. hold
Hugo Swire, C. 25,662
Paull Robathan, LD 16,548
Gareth Manson, Lab. 5,721
Mike Amor, UKIP 4,346
Sharon Pavey, Green 815
C. majority 9,114 (17.17%)
Notional 1.03% swing C. to LD
(2005: C. majority 9,168 (19.23%))

§DEVON NORTH
E. 74,508 T. 51,321 (68.88%) LD hold
Nick Harvey, LD 24,305
Philip Milton, C. 18,484
Stephen Crowther, UKIP 3,720
Mark Cann, Lab. 2,671
L'Anne Knight, Green 697
Gary Marshall, BNP 614
Rodney Cann, Ind. 588
Nigel Vidler, Eng. Dem. 146
Gerrard Sables, Comm. Brit. 96
LD majority 5,821 (11.34%)
Notional 0.32% swing C. to LD
(2005: LD majority 5,276 (10.71%))

§DEVON SOUTH WEST
E. 70,059 T. 49,860 (71.17%) C. hold
Gary Streeter, C. 27,908
Anna Pascoe, LD 12,034
Luke Pollard, Lab. 6,193
Hugh Williams, UKIP 3,084
Vaughan Brean, Green 641
C. majority 15,874 (31.84%)
Notional 5.64% swing LD to C.
(2005: C. majority 9,442 (20.12%))

§DEVON WEST & TORRIDGE
E. 76,574 T. 55,257 (72.16%) C. hold
Geoffrey Cox, C. 25,230
Adam Symons, LD 22,273
Robin Julian, UKIP 3,021
Darren Jones, Lab. 2,917
Cathrine Simmons, Green 1,050
Nick Baker, BNP 766
C. majority 2,957 (5.35%)
Notional 0.01% swing C. to LD
(2005: C. majority 2,732 (5.37%))

§DEWSBURY
E. 78,901 T. 54,008 (68.45%) C. gain
*Simon Reevell, C. 18,898
Shahid Malik, Lab. 17,372
Andrew Hutchinson, LD 9,150
Khizar Iqbal, Ind. 3,813
Roger Roberts, BNP 3,265
Adrian Cruden, Green 849
Michael Felse, Eng. Dem. 661
C. majority 1,526 (2.83%)
Notional 5.85% swing Lab. to C.
(2005: Lab. majority 3,999 (8.88%))

§DON VALLEY
E. 73,214 T. 43,430 (59.32%) Lab. hold
Caroline Flint, Lab. 16,472
Matthew Stephens, C. 12,877
Edward Simpson, LD 7,422
Erwin Toseland, BNP 2,112
William Shaw, UKIP 1,904
Bernie Aston, Eng. Dem. 1,756
Martin Williams, Ind. 887
Lab. majority 3,595 (8.28%)
Notional 10.64% swing Lab. to C.
(2005: Lab. majority 11,333 (29.56%))

§DONCASTER CENTRAL
E. 75,207 T. 41,745 (55.51%) Lab. hold
Rosie Winterton, Lab. 16,569
Gareth Davies, C. 10,340
Patrick Wilson, LD 8,795
Lawrence Parramore, Eng. Dem. 1,816
John Bettney, BNP 1,762
Michael Andrews, UKIP 1,421
Scott Pickles, Ind. 970
Derek Williams, R and E 72
Lab. majority 6,229 (14.92%)
Notional 8.72% swing Lab. to C.
(2005: Lab. majority 10,325 (27.33%))

§DONCASTER NORTH
E. 72,381 T. 41,483 (57.31%) Lab. hold
Ed Miliband, Lab. 19,637
Sophie Brodie, C. 8,728
Edward Sanderson, LD 6,174
Pamela Chambers, BNP 2,818
Wayne Crawshaw, Eng. Dem. 2,148
Liz Andrews, UKIP 1,797
Bill Rawcliffe, TUSC
Lab. majority 10,909 (26.30%)
Notional 2.77% swing Lab. to C.
(2005: Lab. majority 12,027 (31.85%))

§DORSET MID & POOLE NORTH
E. 72,647 T. 46,788 (64.40%) LD hold
Annette Brooke, LD 21,100
Nick King, C. 20,831
Darren Brown, Lab. 2,748
Dave Evans, UKIP 2,109
LD majority 269 (0.57%)
Notional 6.27% swing LD to C.
(2005: LD majority 5,931 (13.12%))

§DORSET NORTH
E. 73,698 T. 54,141 (73.46%) C. hold
Bob Walter, C. 27,640
Emily Gasson, LD 20,015
Mike Bunney, Lab. 2,910
Jeremy Nieboer, UKIP 2,812
Anna Hayball, Green 546
Roger Monksummers, Loony 218
C. majority 7,625 (14.08%)
Notional 2.75% swing LD to C.
(2005: C. majority 4,200 (8.58%))

DORSET SOUTH
E. 73,838 T. 50,310 (68.14%) C. gain
*Richard Drax, C. 22,667
Jim Knight, Lab. 15,224
Ros Kayes, LD 9,557
Mike Hobson, UKIP 2,034
Brian Heatley, Green 595
Andy Kirkwood, YP 233
C. majority 7,443 (14.79%)
9.26% swing Lab. to C.
(2005: Lab. majority 1,812 (3.73%))

DORSET WEST
E. 76,869 T. 57,337 (74.59%) C. hold
Oliver Letwin, C. 27,287
Sue Farrant, LD 23,364
Dr Steve Bick, Lab. 3,815
Oliver Chisholm, UKIP 2,196
Susan Greene, Green 675
C. majority 3,923 (6.84%)
1.11% swing LD to C.
(2005: C. majority 2,461 (4.62%))

§DOVER
E. 71,832 T. 50,385 (70.14%) C. gain
*Charlie Elphicke, C. 22,174
Gwyn Prosser, Lab. 16,900
John Brigden, LD 7,962
Victor Matcham, UKIP 1,747
Dennis Whiting, BNP 1,104
Michael Walters, Eng. Dem. 216
David Clark, CPA 200
George Lee-Delisle, Ind. 82
C. majority 5,274 (10.47%)
Notional 10.43% swing Lab. to C.
(2005: Lab. majority 5,005 (10.40%))

§DUDLEY NORTH
E. 60,838 T. 38,602 (63.45%) Lab. hold
Ian Austin, Lab. 14,923
Graeme Brown, C. 14,274
Mike Beckett, LD 4,066
Malcolm Davis, UKIP 3,267
Ken Griffiths, BNP 1,899
Kevin Inman, NF 173
Lab. majority 649 (1.68%)
Notional 4.73% swing Lab. to C.
(2005: Lab. majority 4,106 (11.14%))

§DUDLEY SOUTH
E. 60,572 T. 38,165 (63.01%) C. gain
*Chris Kelly, C. 16,450
Rachel Harris, Lab. 12,594
Jonathan Bramall, LD 5,989
Philip Rowe, UKIP 3,132
C. majority 3,856 (10.10%)
Notional 9.51% swing Lab. to C.
(2005: Lab. majority 3,222 (8.91%))

§DULWICH & WEST NORWOOD
E. 72,817 T. 48,214 (66.21%) Lab. hold
Tessa Jowell, Lab. 22,461
Jonathan Mitchell, LD 13,096
Kemi Adegoke, C. 10,684
Shane Collins, Green 1,266
Elizabeth Jones, UKIP 707
Lab. majority 9,365 (19.42%)
Notional 0.84% swing Lab. to LD
(2005: Lab. majority 7,853 (19.75%))

DURHAM, CITY OF
E. 68,832 T. 46,252 (67.20%) Lab. hold
Roberta Blackman-Woods, Lab. 20,496
Carol Woods, LD 17,429
Nick Varley, C. 6,146
Ralph Musgrave, BNP 1,153
Nigel Coghill-Marshall, UKIP 856
Jonathan Collings, Ind. 172
Lab. majority 3,067 (6.63%)
0.37% swing Lab. to LD
(2005: Lab. majority 3,274 (7.38%))

§DURHAM NORTH
E. 67,548 T. 40,967 (60.65%) Lab. hold
Kevan Jones, Lab. 20,698
David Skelton, C. 8,622
Ian Lindley, LD 8,617
Pete Molloy, BNP 1,686
Bruce Reid, UKIP 1,344
Lab. majority 12,076 (29.48%)
Notional 8.93% swing Lab. to C.
(2005: Lab. majority 16,781 (44.94%))

§DURHAM NORTH WEST
E. 70,618 T. 43,815 (62.05%) Lab. hold
*Pat Glass, Lab. 18,539
Owen Temple, LD 10,927
Michelle Tempest, C. 8,766
Watts Stelling, Ind. 2,472
Michael Stewart, BNP 1,852
Andrew McDonald, UKIP 1,259
Lab. majority 7,612 (17.37%)
Notional 8.33% swing Lab. to LD
(2005: Lab. majority 13,443 (34.03%))

§EALING CENTRAL & ACTON
E. 63,489 T. 47,200 (74.34%) C. gain
*Angie Bray, C. 17,944
Bassam Mahfouz, Lab. 14,228
Jon Ball, LD 13,041
Julie Carter, UKIP 765
Sarah Edwards, Green 737
Suzanne Fernandes, Ch. P. 295
Sam Akaki, Ind. EACPS 190
C. majority 3,716 (7.87%)
Notional 5.02% swing Lab. to C.
(2005: Lab. majority 839 (2.16%))

§EALING NORTH
E. 67,902 T. 47,678 (70.22%) Lab. hold
Stephen Pound, Lab. 24,023
Ian Gibb, C. 14,722
Chris Lucas, LD 6,283
Dave Furness, BNP 1,045
Ian De Wulverton, UKIP 685
Christopher Warleigh-Lack, Green 505
Petar Ljubisic, Ch. P. 415
Lab. majority 9,301 (19.51%)
Notional 0.45% swing C. to Lab.
(2005: Lab. majority 8,126 (18.61%))

§EALING SOUTHALL
E. 60,379 T. 42,756 (70.81%) Lab. hold
Virendra Sharma, Lab. 22,024
Gurcharan Singh, C. 12,733
Nigel Bakhai, LD 6,383
Suneil Basu, Green 705
Mehboob Anil, Ch. P. 503
Sati Chaggar, Eng. Dem. 408
Lab. majority 9,291 (21.73%)
Notional 8.30% swing Lab. to C.
(2005: Lab. majority 13,140 (38.33%))

§EASINGTON
E. 63,873 T. 34,914 (54.66%) Lab. hold
*Grahame Morris, Lab. 20,579
Tara Saville, LD 5,597
Richard Harrison, C. 4,790
Cheryl Dunn, BNP 2,317
Martyn Aiken, UKIP 1,631
Lab. majority 14,982 (42.91%)
Notional 7.74% swing Lab. to LD
(2005: Lab. majority 18,874 (58.39%))

§EAST HAM
E. 90,675 T. 50,373 (55.55%) Lab. hold
Stephen Timms, Lab. 35,471
Paul Shea, C. 7,645
Chris Brice, LD 5,849
Barry O'Connor, Eng. Dem. 822
Judy Maciejowska, Green 586
Lab. majority 27,826 (55.24%)
Notional 7.71% swing C. to Lab.
(2005: Lab. majority 13,649 (33.08%))

§EASTBOURNE
E. 77,840 T. 52,124 (66.96%) LD gain
*Stephen Lloyd, LD 24,658
Nigel Waterson, C. 21,223
Dave Brinson, Lab. 2,497
Stephen Shing, Ind. 1,327
Roger Needham, UKIP 1,305
Colin Poulter, BNP 939
Michael Baldry, Ind. 101
Keith Gell, Ind. 74
LD majority 3,435 (6.59%)
Notional 4.00% swing C. to LD
(2005: C. majority 672 (1.41%))

§EASTLEIGH
E. 77,435 T. 53,650 (69.28%) LD hold

Chris Huhne, LD	24,966
Maria Hutchings, C.	21,102
Leo Barraclough, Lab.	5,153
Ray Finch, UKIP	1,933
Tony Stephen Pewsey, Eng. Dem.	249
Dave Stone, Ind.	154
Keith Low, Nat. Dem.	93

LD majority 3,864 (7.20%)
Notional 3.04% swing C. to LD
(2005: LD majority 534 (1.12%))

§EDDISBURY
E. 65,306 T. 45,414 (69.54%) C. hold

Stephen O'Brien, C.	23,472
Robert Thompson, LD	10,217
Pat Merrick, Lab.	9,794
Charles Dodman, UKIP	1,931

C. majority 13,255 (29.19%)
Notional 0.13% swing LD to C.
(2005: C. majority 6,408 (14.83%))

§EDMONTON
E. 63,902 T. 40,377 (63.19%)
Lab. (Co-op) hold

Andy Love, Lab. (Co-op)	21,665
Andrew Charalambous, C.	12,052
Iarla Kilbane-Dawe, LD	4,252
Roy Freshwater, UKIP	1,036
Jack Johnson, Green	516
Erol Basarik, Reform	379
Clive Morrison, Ch. P.	350
David Mclean, Ind.	127

Lab. (Co-op) majority 9,613 (23.81%)
Notional 2.26% swing Lab. (Co-op) to C.
(2005: Lab. (Co-op) majority 10,312 (28.33%))

§ELLESMERE PORT & NESTON
E. 63,097 T. 44,233 (70.10%) Lab. hold

Andrew Miller, Lab.	19,750
Stuart Penketh, C.	15,419
Denise Aspinall, LD	6,663
Henry Crocker, UKIP	1,619
Jonathan Starkey, Ind.	782

Lab. majority 4,331 (9.79%)
Notional 3.10% swing Lab. to C.
(2005: Lab. majority 6,713 (15.99%))

§ELMET & ROTHWELL
E. 77,724 T. 55,789 (71.78%) C. gain

*Alec Shelbrooke, C.	23,778
James Lewis, Lab.	19,257
Stewart Golton, LD	9,109
Sam Clayton, BNP	1,802
Darren Oddy, UKIP	1,593
Christopher Nolan, Ind.	250

C. majority 4,521 (8.10%)
Notional 9.77% swing Lab. to C.
(2005: Lab. majority 6,078 (11.43%))

§ELTHAM
E. 62,590 T. 41,964 (67.05%) Lab. hold

Clive Efford, Lab.	17,416
David Gold, C.	15,753
Steven Toole, LD	5,299
Roberta Woods, BNP	1,745
Ray Adams, UKIP	1,011
Arthur Hayles, Green	419
Mike Tibby, Eng. Dem.	217
Andrew Graham, Ind.	104

Lab. majority 1,663 (3.96%)
Notional 1.82% swing Lab. to C.
(2005: Lab. majority 2,904 (7.60%))

§ENFIELD NORTH
E. 66,258 T. 44,453 (67.09%) C. hold

*Nick de Bois, C.	18,804
Joan Ryan, Lab.	17,112
Paul Smith, LD	5,403
Tony Avery, BNP	1,228
Madge Jones, UKIP	938
Bill Linton, Green	489
Anthony Williams, Ch. P.	161
Raquel Weald, Eng. Dem.	131
Anna Athow, WRP	96
Gonul Daniels, Ind.	91

C. majority 1,692 (3.81%)
Notional 0.73% swing Lab. to C.
(2005: C. majority 937 (2.35%))

§ENFIELD SOUTHGATE
E. 64,138 T. 44,352 (69.15%) C. hold

David Burrowes, C.	21,928
Bambos Charalambous, Lab.	14,302
Johar Khan, LD	6,124
Peter Krakowiak, Green	632
Bob Brock, UKIP	505
Dr Asit Mukhopadhyay, Ind.	391
Samad Billoo, Respect	174
Ben Weald, Eng. Dem.	173
Mal Malakounides, ND	88
Jeremy Sturgess, BB	35

C. majority 7,626 (17.19%)
Notional 7.24% swing Lab. to C.
(2005: C. majority 1,127 (2.72%))

§EPPING FOREST
E. 72,198 T. 46,584 (64.52%) C. hold

Eleanor Laing, C.	25,148
Ann Haigh, LD	10,017
Katie Curtis, Lab.	6,641
Pat Richardson, BNP	1,982
Andrew Smith, UKIP	1,852
Simon Pepper, Green	659
Kim Sawyer, Eng. Dem.	285

C. majority 15,131 (32.48%)
Notional 1.08% swing C. to LD
(2005: C. majority 13,473 (31.33%))

§EPSOM & EWELL
E. 78,104 T. 54,955 (70.36%) C. hold

Chris Grayling, C.	30,868
Jonathan Lees, LD	14,734
Craig Montgomery, Lab.	6,538
Elizabeth Wallace, UKIP	2,549
Peter Ticher, RRG	266

C. majority 16,134 (29.36%)
Notional 2.05% swing C. to LD
(2005: C. majority 16,342 (33.47%))

§EREWASH
E. 69,654 T. 47,642 (68.40%) C. gain

*Jessica Lee, C.	18,805
Cheryl Pidgeon, Lab.	16,304
Martin Garnett, LD	8,343
Mark Bailey, BNP	2,337
Jodie Sutton, UKIP	855
Lee Fletcher, Green	534
Luke Wilkins, Ind.	464

C. majority 2,501 (5.25%)
Notional 10.45% swing Lab. to C.
(2005: Lab. majority 6,782 (15.66%))

§ERITH & THAMESMEAD
E. 69,918 T. 42,476 (60.75%) Lab. hold

*Teresa Pearce, Lab.	19,068
Colin Bloom, C.	13,365
Alexander Cunliffe, LD	5,116
Kevin Saunders, BNP	2,184
Pamela Perrin, UKIP	1,139
Laurence Williams, Eng. Dem.	465
Abbey Akinoshun, ND	438
Sid Cordle, CPA	379
Marek Powley, Green	322

Lab. majority 5,703 (13.43%)
Notional 6.34% swing Lab. to C.
(2005: Lab. majority 9,870 (26.11%))

ESHER & WALTON
E. 75,338 T. 54,543 (72.40%) C. hold

*Dominic Raab, C.	32,134
Lionel Blackman, LD	13,541
Francis Eldergill, Lab.	5,829
Bernard Collignon, UKIP	1,783
Tony Popham, Ind.	378
Chinners Chinnery, Loony	341
Mike Kearsley, Eng. Dem.	307
Andy Lear, Best	230

C. majority 18,593 (34.09%)
8.97% swing LD to C.
(2005: C. majority 7,727 (16.14%))

§EXETER
E. 77,157 T. 52,247 (67.72%) Lab. hold

Ben Bradshaw, Lab.	19,942
Hannah Foster, C.	17,221
Graham Oakes, LD	10,581
Keith Crawford, UKIP	1,930
Chris Gale, Lib.	1,108
Paula Black, Green	792
Robert Farmer, BNP	673

Lab. majority 2,721 (5.21%)
Notional 6.03% swing Lab. to C.
(2005: Lab. majority 8,559 (17.27%))

FAREHAM
E. 75,878 T. 54,345 (71.62%) C. hold

Mark Hoban, C.	30,037
Alex Bentley, LD	12,945
James Carr, Lab.	7,719
Steve Richards, UKIP	2,235
Peter Doggett, Green	791
Joe Jenkins, Eng. Dem.	618

C. majority 17,092 (31.45%)
1.73% swing LD to C.
(2005: C. majority 11,702 (24.09%))

§FAVERSHAM & KENT MID
E. 68,858 T. 46,712 (67.84%) C. hold

Hugh Robertson, C.	26,250
David Naghi, LD	9,162
Ash Rehal, Lab.	7,748
Sarah Larkins, UKIP	1,722
Tim Valentine, Green	890
Graham Kemp, NF	542
Hairy Knorm Davidson, Loony	398

C. majority 17,088 (36.58%)
Notional 1.62% swing LD to C.
(2005: C. majority 8,927 (21.00%))

§FELTHAM & HESTON
E. 81,058 T. 48,526 (59.87%)
Lab. (Co-op) hold
Alan Keen, Lab. (Co-op) 21,174
Mark Bowen, C. 16,516
Munira Wilson, LD 6,669
John Donnelly, BNP 1,714
Jerry Shadbolt, UKIP 992
Elizabeth Anstis, Green 530
Dharmendra Tripathi, Ind. 505
Asa Khaira, Ind. 180
Roger Williams, Ind. 168
Matthew Linley, WRP 78
Lab. (Co-op) majority 4,658 (9.60%)
Notional 4.83% swing Lab. (Co-op) to C.
(2005: Lab. (Co-op) majority 7,598 (19.25%))

§FILTON & BRADLEY STOKE
E. 69,003 T. 48,301 (70.00%) C. hold
*Jack Lopresti, C. 19,686
Ian Boulton, Lab. 12,772
Peter Tyzack, LD 12,197
John Knight, UKIP 1,506
David Scott, BNP 1,328
Jon Lucas, Green 441
Ruth Johnson, Ch. P. 199
Vote Zero None of the Above, ND 172
C. majority 6,914 (14.31%)
Notional 6.37% swing Lab. to C.
(2005: C. majority 653 (1.58%))

§FINCHLEY & GOLDERS GREEN
E. 77,198 T. 47,157 (61.09%) C. hold
*Mike Freer, C. 21,688
Alison Moore, Lab. 15,879
Laura Edge, LD 8,036
Susan Cummins, UKIP 817
Donald Lyven, Green 737
C. majority 5,809 (12.32%)
Notional 5.81% swing Lab. to C.
(2005: C. majority 294 (0.70%))

§FOLKESTONE & HYTHE
E. 78,003 T. 52,800 (67.69%) C. hold
*Damian Collins, C. 26,109
Lynne Beaumont, LD 15,987
Donald Worsley, Lab. 5,719
Frank McKenna, UKIP 2,439
Harry Williams, BNP 1,662
Penny Kemp, Green 637
David Plumstead, Ind. 247
C. majority 10,122 (19.17%)
Notional 2.58% swing C. to LD
(2005: C. majority 12,446 (24.33%))

FOREST OF DEAN
E. 68,419 T. 48,763 (71.27%) C. hold
Mark Harper, C. 22,853
Bruce Hogan, Lab. 11,789
Chris Coleman, LD 10,676
Tim Congdon, UKIP 2,522
James Greenwood, Green 923
C. majority 11,064 (22.69%)
9.19% swing Lab. to C.
(2005: C. majority 2,049 (4.30%))

§FYLDE
E. 65,917 T. 43,690 (66.28%) C. hold
*Mark Menzies, C. 22,826
Bill Winlow, LD 9,641
Liam Robinson, Lab. 8,624
Martin Bleeker, UKIP 1,945
Philip Mitchell, Green 654
C. majority 13,185 (30.18%)
Notional 4.15% swing C. to LD
(2005: C. majority 11,117 (28.67%))

§GAINSBOROUGH
E. 72,144 T. 49,251 (68.27%) C. hold
Edward Leigh, C. 24,266
Pat O'Connor, LD 13,707
Jamie McMahon, Lab. 7,701
Steve Pearson, UKIP 2,065
Malcolm Porter, BNP 1,512
C. majority 10,559 (21.44%)
Notional 1.80% swing LD to C.
(2005: C. majority 7,895 (17.73%))

§GARSTON & HALEWOOD
E. 71,312 T. 42,825 (60.05%) Lab. hold
Maria Eagle, Lab. 25,493
Paula Keaveney, LD 8,616
Richard Downey, C. 6,908
Tony Hammond, UKIP 1,540
Diana Raby, Respect 268
Lab. majority 16,877 (39.41%)
Notional 5.74% swing LD to Lab.
(2005: Lab. majority 10,814 (27.92%))

§GATESHEAD
E. 66,492 T. 38,257 (57.54%) Lab. hold
*Ian Mearns, Lab. 20,712
Frank Hindle, LD 8,163
Hazel Anderson, C. 5,716
Kevin Scott, BNP 1,787
John Tennant, UKIP 1,103
Andy Redfern, Green 379
Elaine Brunskill, TUSC 266
David Walton, Ch. P. 131
Lab. majority 12,549 (32.80%)
Notional 3.94% swing Lab. to LD
(2005: Lab. majority 14,245 (40.68%))

§GEDLING
E. 70,590 T. 48,190 (68.27%) Lab. hold
Vernon Coaker, Lab. 19,821
Bruce Laughton, C. 17,962
Julia Bateman, LD 7,350
Stephen Adcock, BNP 1,598
Dave Marshall, UKIP 1,459
Lab. majority 1,859 (3.86%)
Notional 2.89% swing Lab. to C.
(2005: Lab. majority 4,335 (9.63%))

§GILLINGHAM & RAINHAM
E. 70,865 T. 46,786 (66.02%) C. gain
*Rehman Chishti, C. 21,624
Paul Clark, Lab. 12,944
Andrew Stamp, LD 8,484
Robert Oakley, UKIP 1,515
Brian Ravenscroft, BNP 1,149
Dean Lacey, Eng. Dem. 464
Trish Marchant, Green 356
Gordon Bryan, ND 141
George Meegan, Med. Ind. 109
C. majority 8,680 (18.55%)
Notional 9.29% swing Lab. to C.
(2005: Lab. majority 15 (0.03%))

§GLOUCESTER
E. 79,322 T. 50,764 (64.00%) C. gain
*Richard Graham, C. 20,267
Parmjit Dhanda, Lab. 17,847
Jeremy Hilton, LD 9,767
Mike Smith, UKIP 1,808
Alan Platt, Eng. Dem. 564
Bryan Meloy, Green 511
C. majority 2,420 (4.77%)
Notional 8.86% swing Lab. to C.
(2005: Lab. majority 6,063 (12.95%))

GOSPORT
E. 72,720 T. 46,939 (64.55%) C. hold
*Caroline Dinenage, C. 24,300
Rob Hylands, LD 9,887
Graham Giles, Lab. 7,944
Andrew Rice, UKIP 1,496
Barry Bennett, BNP 1,004
Bob Shaw, Eng. Dem. 622
Andrea Smith, Green 573
David Smith, Ind. 493
Charles Read, Ind. 331
Brian Hart, Ind. 289
C. majority 14,413 (30.71%)
1.27% swing LD to C.
(2005: C. majority 5,730 (13.32%))

§GRANTHAM & STAMFORD
E. 78,000 T. 52,799 (67.69%) C. hold
*Nicholas Boles, C. 26,552
Harrish Bisnauthsing, LD 11,726
Mark Bartlett, Lab. 9,503
Christopher Robinson, BNP 2,485
Tony Wells, UKIP 1,604
Mark Horn, Lincs Ind. 929
C. majority 14,826 (28.08%)
Notional 1.18% swing C. to LD
(2005: C. majority 7,308 (15.77%))

GRAVESHAM
E. 70,195 T. 47,303 (67.39%) C. hold
Adam Holloway, C. 22,956
Kathryn Smith, Lab. (Co-op) 13,644
Anna Arrowsmith, LD 6,293
Geoffrey Clark, UKIP 2,265
Steven Uncles, Eng. Dem. 1,005
Richard Crawford, Green 675
Alice Dartnell, Ind. 465
C. majority 9,312 (19.69%)
9.12% swing Lab. (Co-op) to C.
(2005: C. majority 654 (1.45%))

GREAT GRIMSBY
E. 61,229 T. 32,954 (53.82%) Lab. hold
Austin Mitchell, Lab. 10,777
Victoria Ayling, C. 10,063
Andrew de Freitas, LD 7,388
Henry Hudson, UKIP 2,043
Steve Fyfe, BNP 1,517
Ernie Brown, Ind. 835
Adrian Howe, PNDP 331
Lab. majority 714 (2.17%)
10.53% swing Lab. to C.
(2005: Lab. majority 7,654 (23.22%))

GREAT YARMOUTH
E. 70,315 T. 43,057 (61.23%) C. gain
*Brandon Lewis, C. 18,571
Tony Wright, Lab. 14,295
Simon Partridge, LD 6,188
Alan Baugh, UKIP 2,066
Bosco Tann, BNP 1,421
Laura Biggart, Green 416
Margaret McMahon-Morris, LTT 100
C. majority 4,276 (9.93%)
8.66% swing Lab. to C.
(2005: Lab. majority 3,055 (7.38%))

§GREENWICH & WOOLWICH
E. 65,489 T. 41,188 (62.89%) Lab. hold
Nick Raynsford, Lab. 20,262
Spencer Drury, C. 10,109
Joseph Lee, LD 7,498
Lawrence Rustem, BNP 1,151
Andy Hewett, Green 1,054
Edward Adeleye, Ch. P. 443
Topo Wresniwiro, Eng. Dem. 339
Onay Kasab, TUSC 267
Dr Tammy Alingham, Ind. 65
Lab. majority 10,153 (24.65%)
Notional 5.12% swing Lab. to C.
(2005: Lab. majority 11,638 (32.77%))

§GUILDFORD
E. 77,082 T. 55,567 (72.09%) C. hold
Anne Milton, C. 29,618
Sue Doughty, LD 21,836
Tim Shand, Lab. 2,812
Mazhar Manzoor, UKIP 1,021
John Morris, PPN-V 280
C. majority 7,782 (14.00%)
Notional 6.91% swing LD to C.
(2005: C. majority 89 (0.17%))

§HACKNEY NORTH & STOKE NEWINGTON
E. 73,874 T. 46,488 (62.93%) Lab. hold
Diane Abbott, Lab. 25,553
Keith Angus, LD 11,092
Darren Caplan, C. 6,759
Matt Sellwood, Green 2,133
Maxine Hargreaves, Ch. P. 299
Suzanne Moore, ND 285
Knigel Knapp, Loony 182
Paul Shaer, Ind. 96
Alessandra Williams, Ind. 61
Dr Jack Pope-De-Locksley, Magna Carta 28
Lab. majority 14,461 (31.11%)
Notional 2.61% swing LD to Lab.
(2005: Lab. majority 8,002 (25.88%))

§HACKNEY SOUTH & SHOREDITCH
E. 72,816 T. 42,858 (58.86%) Lab. hold
Meg Hillier, Lab. 23,888
Dave Raval, LD 9,600
Simon Nayyar, C. 5,800
Polly Lane, Green 1,493
Michael King, UKIP 651
Ben Rae, Lib. 539
John Williams, Ch. P. 434
Nusret Sen, DDP 202
Paul Davies, Comm. Lge 110
Denny De La Haye, Ind. 95
Jane Tuckett, Ind. 26
Michael Spinks, Ind. 20
Lab. majority 14,288 (33.34%)
Notional 0.99% swing LD to Lab.
(2005: Lab. majority 9,629 (31.37%))

§HALESOWEN & ROWLEY REGIS
E. 63,693 T. 43,979 (69.05%) C. gain
*James Morris, C. 18,115
Sue Hayman, Lab. 16,092
Philip Tibbets, LD 6,515
Derek Baddeley, UKIP 2,824
Derek Thompson, Ind. 433
C. majority 2,023 (4.60%)
Notional 7.13% swing Lab. to C.
(2005: Lab. majority 4,010 (9.66%))

§HALIFAX
E. 70,380 T. 43,555 (61.89%) Lab. hold
Linda Riordan, Lab. 16,278
Philip Allott, C. 14,806
Elisabeth Wilson, LD 8,335
Tom Bates, BNP 2,760
Diane Park, Ind. Voice 722
Jay Sangha, UKIP 654
Lab. majority 1,472 (3.38%)
Notional 2.69% swing Lab. to C.
(2005: Lab. majority 3,481 (8.75%))

§HALTEMPRICE & HOWDEN
E. 70,403 T. 48,737 (69.23%) C. hold
David Davis, C. 24,486
Jon Neal, LD 12,884
Danny Marten, Lab. 7,630
James Cornell, BNP 1,583
Joanne Robinson, Eng. Dem. 1,485
Shan Oakes, Green 669
C. majority 11,602 (23.81%)
Notional 6.64% swing LD to C.
(2005: C. majority 5,080 (10.52%))

§HALTON
E. 68,884 T. 41,338 (60.01%) Lab. hold
Derek Twigg, Lab. 23,843
Ben Jones, C. 8,339
Frank Harasiwka, LD 5,718
Andrew Taylor, BNP 1,563
John Moore, UKIP 1,228
Jim Craig, Green 647
Lab. majority 15,504 (37.51%)
Notional 2.87% swing Lab. to C.
(2005: Lab. majority 16,060 (43.25%))

§HAMMERSMITH
E. 72,348 T. 47,452 (65.59%) Lab. hold
Andy Slaughter, Lab. 20,810
Shaun Bailey, C. 17,261
Merlene Emerson, LD 7,567
Rollo Miles, Green 696
Vanessa Crichton, UKIP 551
Lawrence Searle, BNP 432
Stephen Brennan, Ind. 135
Lab. majority 3,549 (7.48%)
Notional 0.48% swing Lab. to C.
(2005: Lab. majority 3,673 (8.44%))

§HAMPSHIRE EAST
E. 72,250 T. 51,317 (71.03%) C. hold
*Damian Hinds, C. 29,137
Adam Carew, LD 15,640
Jane Edbrooke, Lab. 4,043
Hugh McGuinness, UKIP 1,477
Matt Williams, Eng. Dem. 710
Don Jerrard, J & AC 310
C. majority 13,497 (26.30%)
Notional 6.61% swing LD to C.
(2005: C. majority 5,968 (13.09%))

§HAMPSHIRE NORTH EAST
E. 72,196 T. 52,939 (73.33%) C. hold
James Arbuthnot, C. 32,075
Denzil Coulson, LD 13,478
Barry Jones, Lab. 5,173
Ruth Duffin, UKIP 2,213
C. majority 18,597 (35.13%)
Notional 4.52% swing LD to C.
(2005: C. majority 11,189 (26.09%))

§HAMPSHIRE NORTH WEST
E. 76,040 T. 53,292 (70.08%) C. hold
Sir George Young, C. 31,072
Thomas McCann, LD 12,489
Sarah Evans, Lab. 6,980
Stan Oram, UKIP 2,751
C. majority 18,583 (34.87%)
Notional 4.67% swing LD to C.
(2005: C. majority 12,683 (25.53%))

§HAMPSTEAD & KILBURN
E. 79,713 T. 52,822 (66.27%) Lab. hold
Glenda Jackson, Lab. 17,332
Chris Philp, C. 17,290
Edward Fordham, LD 16,491
Bea Campbell, Green 759
Magnus Nielsen, UKIP 408
Victoria Moore, BNP 328
Tamsin Omond, TOC 123
Gene Alcantara, Ind. 91
Lab. majority 42 (0.08%)
Notional 6.65% swing Lab. to C.
(2005: Lab. majority 474 (1.14%))

§HARBOROUGH
E. 77,917 T. 54,945 (70.52%) C. hold
Edward Garnier, C. 26,894
Zuffar Haq, LD 17,097
Kevin McKeever, Lab. 6,981
Geoff Dickens, BNP 1,715
Marrietta King, UKIP 1,462
David Ball, Eng. Dem. 568
Jeff Stephenson, Ind. 228
C. majority 9,797 (17.83%)
Notional 4.73% swing LD to C.
(2005: C. majority 4,047 (8.38%))

§HARLOW
E. 67,439 T. 43,878 (65.06%) C. gain
*Robert Halfon, C. 19,691
Bill Rammell, Lab. 14,766
David White, LD 5,990
Eddy Butler, BNP 1,739
John Croft, UKIP 1,591
Oluyemi Adeeko, Ch. P. 101
C. majority 4,925 (11.22%)
Notional 5.90% swing Lab. to C.
(2005: Lab. majority 230 (0.58%))

§HARROGATE & KNARESBOROUGH
E. 75,269 T. 53,134 (70.59%) C. gain
*Andrew Jones, C. 24,305
Claire Kelley, LD 23,266
Kevin McNerney, Lab. 3,413
Steven Gill, BNP 1,094
John Upex, UKIP 1,056
C. majority 1,039 (1.96%)
Notional 9.09% swing LD to C.
(2005: LD majority 7,980 (16.22%))

§HARROW EAST
E. 68,554 T. 48,006 (70.03%) C. gain
*Bob Blackman, C. 21,435
Tony McNulty, Lab. 18,032
Nahid Boethe, LD 6,850
Abhijit Pandya, UKIP 896
Madeleine Atkins, Green 793
C. majority 3,403 (7.09%)
Notional 6.99% swing Lab. to C.
(2005: Lab. majority 2,934 (6.89%))

§HARROW WEST
E. 71,510 T. 46,116 (64.49%) Lab. (Co-op) hold
Gareth Thomas, Lab. (Co-op) 20,111
Dr Rachel Joyce, C. 16,968
Christopher Noyce, LD 7,458
Herbert Crossman, UKIP 954
Rowan Langley, Green 625
Lab. (Co-op) majority 3,143 (6.82%)
Notional 5.72% swing Lab. (Co-op) to C.
(2005: Lab. (Co-op) majority 7,742 (18.26%))

HARTLEPOOL
E. 68,923 T. 38,242 (55.49%) Lab. hold
Iain Wright, Lab. 16,267
Alan Wright, C. 10,758
Reg Clark, LD 6,533
Stephen Allison, UKIP 2,682
Ronnie Bage, BNP 2,002
Lab. majority 5,509 (14.41%)
12.82% swing Lab. to C.
(2005: Lab. majority 7,478 (21.10%))

§HARWICH & ESSEX NORTH
E. 70,743 T. 49,000 (69.26%) C. hold
Bernard Jenkin, C. 23,001
James Raven, LD 11,554
Darren Barrenger, Lab. 9,774
Simon Anselmi, UKIP 2,527
Stephen Robey, BNP 1,065
Chris Fox, Green 909
Peter Thompson Bates, Ind. 170
C. majority 11,447 (23.36%)
Notional 0.00% swing C. to LD
(2005: C. majority 5,583 (11.73%))

§HASTINGS & RYE
E. 78,000 T. 49,814 (63.86%) C. gain
*Amber Rudd, C. 20,468
Michael Foster, Lab. 18,475
Nicholas Perry, LD 7,825
Anthony Smith, UKIP 1,397
Nicholas Prince, BNP 1,310
Rodney Bridger, Eng. Dem. 339
C. majority 1,993 (4.00%)
Notional 3.27% swing Lab. to C.
(2005: Lab. majority 1,156 (2.54%))

§HAVANT
E. 69,712 T. 43,903 (62.98%) C. hold
David Willetts, C. 22,433
Alex Payton, LD 10,273
Robert Smith, Lab. 7,777
Gary Kerrin, UKIP 2,611
Fungus Addams, Eng. Dem. 809
C. majority 12,160 (27.70%)
Notional 1.79% swing LD to C.
(2005: C. majority 6,395 (15.58%))

§HAYES & HARLINGTON
E. 70,233 T. 42,637 (60.71%) Lab. hold
John McDonnell, Lab. 23,377
Scott Seaman-Digby, C. 12,553
Satnam Kaur Khalsa, LD 3,726
Chris Forster, BNP 1,520
Andrew Cripps, NF 566
Cliff Dixon, Eng. Dem. 464
Jessica Lee, Green 348
Aneel Shahzad, Ch. P. 83
Lab. majority 10,824 (25.39%)
Notional 1.65% swing Lab. to C.
(2005: Lab. majority 10,594 (28.68%))

§HAZEL GROVE
E. 63,074 T. 41,981 (66.56%) LD hold
Andrew Stunell, LD 20,485
Annesley Abercorn, C. 14,114
Richard Scorer, Lab. 5,234
John Whittaker, UKIP 2,148
LD majority 6,371 (15.18%)
Notional 2.37% swing LD to C.
(2005: LD majority 7,694 (19.92%))

§HEMEL HEMPSTEAD
E. 72,754 T. 49,471 (68.00%) C. hold
Mike Penning, C. 24,721
Dr Richard Grayson, LD 11,315
Ayfer Orhan, Lab. 10,295
Janet Price, BNP 1,615
David Alexander, UKIP 1,254
Mick Young, Ind. 271
C. majority 13,406 (27.10%)
Notional 1.94% swing LD to C.
(2005: C. majority 168 (0.36%))

§HEMSWORTH
E. 72,552 T. 43,840 (60.43%) Lab. hold
Jon Trickett, Lab. 20,506
Ann Myatt, C. 10,662
Alan Belmore, LD 5,667
Ian Womersley, Ind. 3,946
Ian Kitchen, BNP 3,059
Lab. majority 9,844 (22.45%)
Notional 7.03% swing Lab. to C.
(2005: Lab. majority 14,026 (36.51%))

§HENDON
E. 78,923 T. 46,374 (58.76%) C. gain
*Matthew Offord, C. 19,635
Andrew Dismore, Lab. 19,529
Matthew Harris, LD 5,734
Robin Lambert, UKIP 958
Andrew Newby, Green 518
C. majority 106 (0.23%)
Notional 4.14% swing Lab. to C.
(2005: Lab. majority 3,231 (8.06%))

§HENLEY
E. 75,005 T. 53,520 (71.36%) C. hold
John Howell, C. 30,054
Andrew Crick, LD 13,466
Richard McKenzie, Lab. 5,835
Laurence Hughes, UKIP 1,817
Mark Stevenson, Green 1,328
John Bews, BNP 1,020
C. majority 16,588 (30.99%)
Notional 1.93% swing LD to C.
(2005: C. majority 13,366 (27.13%))

§HEREFORD & HEREFORDSHIRE SOUTH
E. 71,435 T. 48,381 (67.73%) C. gain
*Jesse Norman, C. 22,366
Sarah Carr, LD 19,885
Philippa Roberts, Lab. 3,506
Valentine Smith, UKIP 1,638
John Oliver, BNP 986
C. majority 2,481 (5.13%)
Notional 3.76% swing LD to C.
(2005: LD majority 1,089 (2.39%))

§HEREFORDSHIRE NORTH
E. 66,525 T. 47,568 (71.50%) C. hold
Bill Wiggin, C. 24,631
Lucy Hurds, LD 14,744
Neil Sabharwal, Lab. 3,373
Jonathan Oakton, UKIP 2,701
Felicity Norman, Green 1,533
John King, Ind. 586
C. majority 9,887 (20.78%)
Notional 3.82% swing C. to LD
(2005: C. majority 12,688 (28.43%))

§HERTFORD & STORTFORD
E. 78,459 T. 55,377 (70.58%) C. hold
Mark Prisk, C. 29,810
Andrew Lewin, LD 14,373
Steve Terry, Lab. 7,620
David Sodey, UKIP 1,716
Roy Harris, BNP 1,297
Loucas Xenophontos, Ind. 325
Martin Adams, Ind. 236
C. majority 15,437 (27.88%)
Notional 1.95% swing C. to LD
(2005: C. majority 12,756 (25.95%))

§HERTFORDSHIRE NORTH EAST
E. 72,200 T. 50,425 (69.84%) C. hold
Oliver Heald, C. 26,995
Hugh Annand, LD 11,801
David Kirkman, Lab. 8,291
Adrianne Smyth, UKIP 2,075
Rosemary Bland, Green 875
Richard Campbell, Ind. 209
David Ralph, YRDPL 143
Philip Reichardt, Ind. 36
C. majority 15,194 (30.13%)
Notional 1.19% swing LD to C.
(2005: C. majority 9,510 (19.75%))

§HERTFORDSHIRE SOUTH WEST
E. 78,248 T. 56,750 (72.53%) C. hold
David Gauke, C. 30,773
Christopher Townsend, LD 15,853
Harry Mann, Lab. 6,526
Mark Benson, UKIP 1,450
Deirdre Gates, BNP 1,302
James Hannaway, Ind. 846
C. majority 14,920 (26.29%)
Notional 4.66% swing LD to C.
(2005: C. majority 8,640 (16.97%))

HERTSMERE
E. 73,062 T. 47,270 (64.70%) C. hold
James Clappison, C. 26,476
Sam Russell, Lab. 8,871
Anthony Rowlands, LD 8,210
David Rutter, UKIP 1,712
Daniel Seabrook, BNP 1,397
Arjuna Krishna-Das, Green 604
C. majority 17,605 (37.24%)
5.59% swing Lab. to C.
(2005: C. majority 11,093 (26.06%))

§HEXHAM
E. 61,375 T. 43,483 (70.85%) C. hold
*Guy Opperman, C. 18,795
Andrew Duffield, LD 13,007
Antoine Tinnion, Lab. 8,253
Steve Ford, Ind. 1,974
Quentin Hawkins, BNP 1,205
Colin Moss, Ind. 249
C. majority 5,788 (13.31%)
Notional 1.70% swing C. to LD
(2005: C. majority 4,957 (12.03%))

§HEYWOOD & MIDDLETON
E. 80,171 T. 46,125 (57.53%) Lab. hold
Jim Dobbin, Lab. 18,499
Michael Holly, C. 12,528
Wera Hobhouse, LD 10,474
Peter Greenwood, BNP 3,239
Victoria Cecil, UKIP 1,215
Chrissy Lee, Ind. 170
Lab. majority 5,971 (12.95%)
Notional 6.82% swing Lab. to C.
(2005: Lab. majority 11,034 (26.58%))

§HIGH PEAK
E. 71,973 T. 50,337 (69.94%) C. gain
*Andrew Bingham, C. 20,587
Caitlin Bisknell, Lab. 15,910
Alistair Stevens, LD 10,993
Sylvia Hall, UKIP 1,690
Peter Allen, Green 922
Lance Dowson, Ind. 161
Tony Alves, ND 74
C. majority 4,677 (9.29%)
Notional 6.54% swing Lab. to C.
(2005: Lab. majority 1,750 (3.80%))

§HITCHIN & HARPENDEN
E. 73,851 T. 54,707 (74.08%) C. hold
Peter Lilley, C. 29,869
Nigel Quinton, LD 14,598
Oliver de Botton, Lab. 7,413
Graham Wilkinson, UKIP 1,663
Richard Wise, Green 807
Margaret Henderson, Ind. 109
Simon Byron, R and E 108
Eric Hannah, YRDPL 90
Peter Rigby, Ind. 50
C. majority 15,271 (27.91%)
Notional 2.50% swing LD to C.
(2005: C. majority 11,064 (22.90%))

§HOLBORN & ST PANCRAS
E. 86,863 T. 54,649 (62.91%) Lab. hold
Frank Dobson, Lab. 25,198
Jo Shaw, LD 15,256
George Lee, C. 11,134
Natalie Bennett, Green 1,480
Robert Carlyle, BNP 779
Max Spencer, UKIP 587
John Chapman, Ind. 96
Mikel Susperregi, Eng. Dem. 75
Iain Meek, Ind. 44
Lab. majority 9,942 (18.19%)
Notional 0.38% swing Lab. to LD
(2005: Lab. majority 8,348 (18.95%))

§HORNCHURCH & UPMINSTER
E. 78,487 T. 53,390 (68.02%) C. hold
Angela Watkinson, C. 27,469
Kath McGuirk, Lab. 11,098
Karen Chilvers, LD 7,426
William Whelpley, BNP 3,421
Lawrence Webb, UKIP 2,848
Melanie Collins, Green 542
David Durant, Ind. 305
Johnson Olukotun, Ch. P. 281
C. majority 16,371 (30.66%)
Notional 7.14% swing Lab. to C.
(2005: C. majority 8,058 (16.38%))

HORNSEY & WOOD GREEN
E. 79,916 T. 55,042 (68.87%) LD hold
Lynne Featherstone, LD 25,595
Karen Jennings, Lab. 18,720
Richard Merrin, C. 9,174
Pete McAskie, Green 1,261
Stephane De Roche, Ind. 201
Rohen Kapur, Ind. 91
LD majority 6,875 (12.49%)
3.72% swing Lab. to LD
(2005: LD majority 2,395 (5.06%))

§HORSHAM
E. 76,835 T. 55,841 (72.68%) C. hold
Francis Maude, C. 29,447
Godfrey Newman, LD 17,987
Andrew Skudder, Lab. 4,189
Harry Aldridge, UKIP 2,839
Nick Fitter, Green 570
Steve Lyon, Ch. P. 469
Jim Duggan, PPN-V 253
Derek Kissach, Ind. 87
C. majority 11,460 (20.52%)
Notional 0.57% swing C. to LD
(2005: C. majority 10,780 (21.66%))

§HOUGHTON & SUNDERLAND SOUTH
E. 68,729 T. 38,021 (55.32%) Lab. hold
*Bridget Phillipson, Lab. 19,137
Robert Oliver, C. 8,147
Chris Boyle, LD 5,292
Colin Wakefield, Ind. 2,462
Karen Allen, BNP 1,961
Richard Elvin, UKIP 1,022
Lab. majority 10,990 (28.91%)
Notional 8.44% swing Lab. to C.
(2005: Lab. majority 16,986 (45.78%))

§HOVE
E. 71,708 T. 49,819 (69.47%) C. gain
*Mike Weatherley, C. 18,294
Celia Barlow, Lab. 16,426
Paul Elgood, LD 11,240
Ian Davey, Green 2,568
Paul Perrin, UKIP 1,206
Brian Ralfe, Ind. 85
C. majority 1,868 (3.75%)
Notional 2.37% swing Lab. to C.
(2005: Lab. majority 448 (1.00%))

§HUDDERSFIELD
E. 66,316 T. 40,524 (61.11%) Lab. hold
Barry Sheerman, Lab. 15,725
Karen Tweed, C. 11,253
James Blanchard, LD 10,023
Andrew Cooper, Green 1,641
Rachel Firth, BNP 1,563
Paul Cooney, TUSC 319
Lab. majority 4,472 (11.04%)
Notional 7.14% swing Lab. to C.
(2005: Lab. majority 7,883 (22.29%))

§HULL EAST
E. 67,530 T. 34,184 (50.62%) Lab. hold
*Karl Turner, Lab. 16,387
Jeremy Wilcock, LD 7,790
Christine Mackay, C. 5,667
Mike Hookem, UKIP 2,745
Joe Uttley, NF 880
Mike Burton, Eng. Dem. 715
Lab. majority 8,597 (25.15%)
Notional 5.35% swing Lab. to LD
(2005: Lab. majority 11,740 (35.84%))

§HULL NORTH
E. 64,082 T. 33,291 (51.95%) Lab. hold
Diana Johnson, Lab. 13,044
Denis Healy, LD 12,403
Victoria Aitken, C. 4,365
John Mainprize, BNP 1,443
Paul Barlow, UKIP 1,358
Martin Deane, Green 478
Michael Cassidy, Eng. Dem. 200
Lab. majority 641 (1.93%)
Notional 12.18% swing Lab. to LD
(2005: Lab. majority 7,384 (26.29%))

§HULL WEST & HESSLE
E. 69,017 T. 31,505 (45.65%) Lab. hold
Alan Johnson, Lab. 13,378
Mike Ross, LD 7,636
Gary Shores, C. 6,361
Ken Hordon, UKIP 1,688
Edward Scott, BNP 1,416
Peter Mawer, Eng. Dem. 876
Keith Gibson, TUSC 150
Lab. majority 5,742 (18.23%)
Notional 7.92% swing Lab. to LD
(2005: Lab. majority 9,430 (34.06%))

§HUNTINGDON
E. 83,557 T. 54,266 (64.94%) C. hold
Jonathan Djanogly, C. 26,516
Martin Land, LD 15,697
Anthea Cox, Lab. 5,982
Ian Curtis, UKIP 3,258
Jonathan Salt, Ind. 1,432
John Clare, Green 652
Lord Toby Jug, Loony 548
Carrie Holliman, APP 181
C. majority 10,819 (19.94%)
Notional 2.08% swing C. to LD
(2005: C. majority 11,652 (24.10%))

§HYNDBURN
E. 67,221 T. 42,672 (63.48%) Lab. hold
*Graham Jones, Lab. 17,531
Karen Buckley, C. 14,441
Andrew Rankine, LD 5,033
David Shapcott, BNP 2,137
Granville Barker, UKIP 1,481
The Revd Kevin Logan, CPA 795
Kerry Gormley, Green 463
Christopher Reid, Eng. Dem. 413
Craig Hall, Ind. 378
Lab. majority 3,090 (7.24%)
Notional 3.28% swing Lab. to C.
(2005: Lab. majority 5,528 (13.80%))

§ILFORD NORTH
E. 71,995 T. 47,018 (65.31%) C. hold
Lee Scott, C. 21,506
Sonia Klein, Lab. 16,102
Alex Berhanu, LD 5,966
Danny Warville, BNP 1,545
Henri van der Stighelen, UKIP 871
Caroline Allen, Green 572
The Revd Robert Hampson, CPA 456
C. majority 5,404 (11.49%)
Notional 3.68% swing Lab. to C.
(2005: C. majority 1,735 (4.14%))

ILFORD SOUTH
E. 75,246 T. 51,191 (68.03%)
Lab. (Co-op) hold
Mike Gapes, Lab. (Co-op) 25,301
Toby Boutle, C. 14,014
Anood Al-Samerai, LD 8,679
Wilson Chowdhry, Green 1,319
Terry Murray, UKIP 1,132
John Jestico, King George 746
Lab. (Co-op) majority 11,287 (22.05%)
0.22% swing C. to Lab. (Co-op)
(2005: Lab. (Co-op) majority 9,228 (21.61%))

§IPSWICH
E. 78,371 T. 46,941 (59.90%) C. gain
*Benedict Gummer, C. 18,371
Chris Mole, Lab. 16,292
Mark Dyson, LD 8,556
Chris Streatfield, UKIP 1,365
Dennis Boater, BNP 1,270
Tim Glover, Green 775
Kim Christofi, Ch. P. 149
Peter Turtill, Ind. 93
Sally Wainman, Ind. 70
C. majority 2,079 (4.43%)
Notional 8.12% swing Lab. to C.
(2005: Lab. majority 5,235 (11.81%))

ISLE OF WIGHT
E. 109,966 T. 70,264 (63.90%) C. hold
Andrew Turner, C. 32,810
Jill Wareham, LD 22,283
Mark Chiverton, Lab. 8,169
Mike Tarrant, UKIP 2,435
Geoff Clynch, BNP 1,457
Ian Dunsire, Eng. Dem. 1,233
Bob Keats, Green 931
Paul Martin, Mid. England 616
Pete Harris, Ind. 175
Paul Randle-Jolliffe, Ind. 89
Edward Corby, Ind. 66
C. majority 10,527 (14.98%)
2.22% swing C. to LD
(2005: C. majority 12,978 (19.42%))

ISLINGTON NORTH
E. 68,120 T. 44,554 (65.41%) Lab. hold
Jeremy Corbyn, Lab. 24,276
Rhodri Jamieson-Ball, LD 11,875
Adrian Berrill-Cox, C. 6,339
Emma Dixon, Green 1,348
Dominic Lennon, UKIP 716
Lab. majority 12,401 (27.83%)
3.25% swing LD to Lab.
(2005: Lab. majority 6,716 (21.32%))

ISLINGTON SOUTH & FINSBURY
E. 67,649 T. 43,555 (64.38%) Lab. hold
Emily Thornberry, Lab. 18,407
Bridget Fox, LD 14,838
Antonia Cox, C. 8,449
James Humphreys, Green 710
Rose-Marie McDonald, UKIP 701
John Dodds, Eng. Dem. 301
Richard Deboo, Animals 149
Lab. majority 3,569 (8.19%)
3.32% swing LD to Lab.
(2005: Lab. majority 484 (1.56%))

§JARROW
E. 64,350 T. 38,784 (60.27%) Lab. hold
Stephen Hepburn, Lab. 20,910
Jeffrey Milburn, C. 8,002
Tom Appleby, LD 7,163
Andy Swaddle, BNP 2,709
Lab. majority 12,908 (33.28%)
Notional 6.38% swing Lab. to C.
(2005: Lab. majority 12,749 (36.35%))

KEIGHLEY
E. 65,893 T. 47,692 (72.38%) C. gain
*Kris Hopkins, C. 20,003
Jane Thomas, Lab. 17,063
Nader Fekri, LD 7,059
Andrew Brons, BNP 1,962
Paul Latham, UKIP 1,470
Steven Smith, NF 135
C. majority 2,940 (6.16%)
8.32% swing Lab. to C.
(2005: Lab. majority 4,852 (10.48%))

§KENILWORTH & SOUTHAM
E. 59,630 T. 48,431 (81.22%) C. hold
Jeremy Wright, C. 25,945
Nigel Rock, LD 13,393
Nicholas Milton, Lab. 6,949
John Moore, UKIP 1,214
James Harrison, Green 568
Joe Rukin, Ind. 362
C. majority 12,552 (25.92%)
Notional 1.20% swing C. to LD
(2005: C. majority 10,956 (24.80%))

§KENSINGTON
E. 65,961 T. 35,150 (53.29%) C. hold
Sir Malcolm Rifkind, C. 17,595
Sam Gurney, Lab. 8,979
Robin Meltzer, LD 6,872
Lady Caroline Pearson, UKIP 754
Zahra-Melan Ebrahimi-Fardouee, Green 753
Eddie Adams, Green Soc. 197
C. majority 8,616 (24.51%)
Notional 5.19% swing Lab. to C.
(2005: C. majority 4,540 (14.13%))

§KETTERING
E. 68,837 T. 47,328 (68.75%) C. hold
Philip Hollobone, C. 23,247
Phil Sawford, Lab. 14,153
Chris Nelson, LD 7,498
Clive Skinner, BNP 1,366
Derek Hilling, Eng. Dem. 952
Dave Bishop, BP Elvis 112
C. majority 9,094 (19.21%)
Notional 9.41% swing Lab. to C.
(2005: C. majority 176 (0.39%))

§KINGSTON & SURBITON
E. 81,116 T. 57,111 (70.41%) LD hold
Edward Davey, LD 28,428
Helen Whately, C. 20,868
Max Freedman, Lab. 5,337
Jonathan Greensted, UKIP 1,450
Chris Walker, Green 555
Monkey the Drummer, Loony 247
Anthony May, CPA 226
LD majority 7,560 (13.24%)
Notional 2.43% swing LD to C.
(2005: LD majority 9,084 (18.11%))

§KINGSWOOD
E. 66,361 T. 47,906 (72.19%) C. gain.
*Chris Skidmore, C. 19,362
Roger Berry, Lab. 16,917
Sally Fitzharris, LD 8,072
Neil Dowdney, UKIP 1,528
Michael Carey, BNP 1,311
Nick Foster, Green 383
Michael Blundell, Eng. Dem. 333
C. majority 2,445 (5.10%)
Notional 9.43% swing Lab. to C.
(2005: Lab. majority 6,145 (13.76%))

§KNOWSLEY
E. 79,561 T. 44,658 (56.13%) Lab. hold
George Howarth, Lab. 31,650
Flo Clucas, LD 5,964
David Dunne, C. 4,004
Steven Greenhalgh, BNP 1,895
Anthony Rundle, UKIP 1,145
Lab. majority 25,686 (57.52%)
Notional 0.25% swing Lab. to LD
(2005: Lab. majority 24,333 (58.02%))

LANCASHIRE WEST
E. 75,975 T. 48,473 (63.80%) Lab. hold
Rosie Cooper, Lab. 21,883
Adrian Owens, C. 17,540
John Gibson, LD 6,573
Damon Noone, UKIP 1,775
Peter Cranie, Green 485
David Braid, Clause 28 217
Lab. majority 4,343 (8.96%)
2.57% swing Lab. to C.
(2005: Lab. majority 6,084 (14.10%))

§LANCASTER & FLEETWOOD
E. 69,908 T. 42,701 (61.08%) C. gain
*Eric Ollerenshaw, C. 15,404
Clive Grunshaw, Lab. 15,071
Stuart Langhorn, LD 8,167
Gina Dowding, Green 1,888
Fred McGlade, UKIP 1,020
Debra Kent, BNP 938
Keith Riley, Ind. 213
C. majority 333 (0.78%)
Notional 4.80% swing Lab. to C.
(2005: Lab. majority 3,428 (8.82%))

§LEEDS CENTRAL
E. 64,698 T. 37,394 (57.80%) Lab. hold
Hilary Benn, Lab. 18,434
Michael Taylor, LD 7,789
Alan Lamb, C. 7,541
Kevin Meeson, BNP 3,066
Dave Procter, Ind. 409
We Beat The Scum One-Nil, ND 155
Lab. majority 10,645 (28.47%)
Notional 4.76% swing Lab. to LD
(2005: Lab. majority 12,916 (37.98%))

§LEEDS EAST
E. 65,067 T. 37,813 (58.11%) Lab. hold
George Mudie, Lab. 19,056
Barry Anderson, C. 8,763
Andrew Tear, LD 6,618
Trevor Brown, BNP 2,947
Michael Davies, Green Soc. 429
Lab. majority 10,293 (27.22%)
Notional 5.49% swing Lab. to C.
(2005: Lab. majority 13,689 (38.21%))

§LEEDS NORTH EAST
E. 67,899 T. 47,535 (70.01%) Lab. hold
Fabian Hamilton, Lab. 20,287
Matthew Lobley, C. 15,742
Aqila Choudhry, LD 9,310
Warren Hendon, UKIP 842
Tom Redmond, BNP 758
Celia Foote, Green Soc. 596
Lab. majority 4,545 (9.56%)
Notional 2.97% swing Lab. to C.
(2005: Lab. majority 6,762 (15.51%))

§LEEDS NORTH WEST
E. 65,399 T. 43,483 (66.49%) LD hold
Greg Mulholland, LD 20,653
Julia Mulligan, C. 11,550
Judith Blake, Lab. 9,132
Geoffrey Bulmer, BNP 766
Mark Thackray, UKIP 600
Martin Hemingway, Green 508
Alan Procter, Eng. Dem. 153
Trevor Bavage, Green Soc. 121
LD majority 9,103 (20.93%)
Notional 5.44% swing C. to LD
(2005: LD majority 2,064 (4.96%))

§LEEDS WEST
E. 67,453 T. 38,752 (57.45%) Lab. hold
*Rachel Reeves, Lab. 16,389
Ruth Coleman, LD 9,373
Joe Marjoram, C. 7,641
Joanna Beverley, BNP 2,377
David Blackburn, Green 1,832
Jeff Miles, UKIP 1,140
Lab. majority 7,016 (18.10%)
Notional 10.36% swing Lab. to LD
(2005: Lab. majority 13,699 (38.83%))

§LEICESTER EAST
E. 72,986 T. 47,995 (65.76%) Lab. hold
Keith Vaz, Lab. 25,804
Jane Hunt, C. 11,722
Ali Asghar, LD 6,817
Colin Gilmore, BNP 1,700
Mo Taylor, Green 733
Felicity Ransome, UKIP 725
Avtar Sadiq, UPS 494
Lab. majority 14,082 (29.34%)
Notional 4.77% swing Lab. to C.
(2005: Lab. majority 16,400 (38.89%))

§LEICESTER SOUTH
E. 77,175 T. 47,124 (61.06%) Lab. hold
Sir Peter Soulsby, Lab. 21,479
Parmjit Singh Gill, LD 12,671
Ross Grant, C. 10,066
Adrian Waudby, BNP 1,418
Dave Dixey, Green 770
Christopher Lucas, UKIP 720
Lab. majority 8,808 (18.69%)
Notional 4.96% swing LD to Lab.
(2005: Lab. majority 3,727 (8.78%))

§LEICESTER WEST
E. 64,900 T. 35,819 (55.19%) Lab. hold
*Elizabeth Kendall, Lab. 13,745
Celia Harvey, C. 9,728
Peter Coley, LD 8,107
Gary Reynolds, BNP 2,158
Stephen Ingall, UKIP 883
Geoff Forse, Green 639
Steven Huggins, Ind. 181
Steve Score, TUSC 157
Shaun Dyer, Pirate 113
David Bowley, Ind. 108
Lab. majority 4,017 (11.21%)
Notional 7.60% swing Lab. to C.
(2005: Lab. majority 8,539 (26.42%))

LEICESTERSHIRE NORTH WEST
E. 71,219 T. 51,952 (72.95%) C. gain
*Andrew Bridgen, C. 23,147
Ross Willmott, Lab. (Co-op) 15,636
Paul Reynolds, LD 8,639
Ian Meller, BNP 3,396
Martin Green, UKIP 1,134
C. majority 7,511 (14.46%)
11.98% swing Lab. (Co-op) to C.
(2005: Lab. (Co-op) majority 4,477 (9.50%))

§LEICESTERSHIRE SOUTH
E. 76,639 T. 54,577 (71.21%) C. hold
Andrew Robathan, C. 27,000
Aladdin Ayesh, LD 11,476
Sally Gimson, Lab. 11,392
Paul Preston, BNP 2,721
John Williams, UKIP 1,988
C. majority 15,524 (28.44%)
Notional 1.03% swing LD to C.
(2005: C. majority 7,704 (15.77%))

§LEIGH
E. 76,350 T. 44,332 (58.06%) Lab. hold
Andy Burnham, Lab. 21,295
Shazia Awan, C. 9,284
Chris Blackburn, LD 8,049
Gary Chadwick, BNP 2,724
Mary Lavelle, UKIP 1,535
Norman Bradbury, Ind. 988
Terry Dainty, Ind. 320
Ryan Hessell, Ch. P. 137
Lab. majority 12,011 (27.09%)
Notional 7.17% swing Lab. to C.
(2005: Lab. majority 15,098 (38.73%))

§LEWES
E. 68,708 T. 50,088 (72.90%) LD hold
Norman Baker, LD 26,048
Jason Sugarman, C. 18,401
Hratche Koundarjian, Lab. 2,508
Peter Charlton, UKIP 1,728
Susan Murray, Green 729
David Lloyd, BNP 594
Ondrej Soucek, Ind. 80
LD majority 7,647 (15.27%)
Notional 0.81% swing LD to C.
(2005: LD majority 7,889 (16.89%))

§LEWISHAM DEPTFORD
E. 67,058 T. 41,220 (61.47%) Lab. hold
Joan Ruddock, Lab. 22,132
Tam Langley, LD 9,633
Gemma Townsend, C. 5,551
Darren Johnson, Green 2,772
Ian Page, Soc. Alt. 645
Malcolm Martin, CPA 487
Lab. majority 12,499 (30.32%)
Notional 3.56% swing Lab. to LD
(2005: Lab. majority 13,012 (37.43%))

§LEWISHAM EAST
E. 65,926 T. 41,719 (63.28%) Lab. hold
*Heidi Alexander, Lab. 17,966
Pete Pattisson, LD 11,750
Jonathan Clamp, C. 9,850
Roderick Reed, UKIP 771
Priscilla Cotterell, Green 624
James Rose, Eng. Dem. 426
George Hallam, CNBPG 332
Lab. majority 6,216 (14.90%)
Notional 6.41% swing Lab. to LD
(2005: Lab. majority 8,758 (23.31%))

§LEWISHAM WEST & PENGE
E. 69,022 T. 45,028 (65.24%) Lab. hold
Jim Dowd, Lab. 18,501
Alex Feakes, LD 12,673
Chris Phillips, C. 11,489
Peter Staveley, UKIP 1,117
Romayne Phoenix, Green 931
Stephen Hammond, CPA 317
Lab. majority 5,828 (12.94%)
Notional 3.10% swing Lab. to LD
(2005: Lab. majority 7,779 (19.15%))

§LEYTON & WANSTEAD
E. 63,541 T. 40,159 (63.20%) Lab. hold
*John Cryer, Lab. 17,511
Farooq Qureshi, LD 11,095
Ed Northover, C. 8,928
Graham Wood, UKIP 1,080
Ashley Gunstock, Green 562
Jim Clift, BNP 561
Sonika Bhatti, Ch. P. 342
Martin Levin, Ind. Fed. 80
Lab. majority 6,416 (15.98%)
Notional 2.57% swing Lab. to LD
(2005: Lab. majority 7,253 (21.11%))

§LICHFIELD
E. 72,586 T. 51,563 (71.04%) C. hold
Michael Fabricant, C. 28,048
Ian Jackson, LD 10,365
Steve Hyden, Lab. 10,230
Karen Maunder, UKIP 2,920
C. majority 17,683 (34.29%)
Notional 0.74% swing LD to C.
(2005: C. majority 7,791 (16.49%))

§LINCOLN
E. 73,540 T. 45,721 (62.17%) C. gain
*Karl McCartney, C. 17,163
Gillian Merron, Lab. 16,105
Reg Shore, LD 9,256
Robert West, BNP 1,367
Nick Smith, UKIP 1,004
Ernest Coleman, Eng. Dem. 604
Gary Walker, Ind. 222
C. majority 1,058 (2.31%)
Notional 5.89% swing Lab. to C.
(2005: Lab. majority 3,806 (9.47%))

§LIVERPOOL RIVERSIDE
E. 74,539 T. 38,801 (52.05%) Lab. hold
Louise Ellman, Lab. 22,998
Richard Marbrow, LD 8,825
Kegang Wu, C. 4,243
Tom Crone, Green 1,355
Peter Stafford, BNP 706
Pat Gaskell, UKIP 674
Lab. majority 14,173 (36.53%)
Notional 0.30% swing LD to Lab.
(2005: Lab. majority 11,731 (35.93%))

§LIVERPOOL WALTON
E. 62,612 T. 34,335 (54.84%) Lab. hold
*Steve Rotheram, Lab. 24,709
Patrick Moloney, LD 4,891
Adam Marsden, C. 2,241
Peter Stafford, BNP 1,104
Joe Nugent, UKIP 898
John Manwell, CPA 297
Daren Ireland, TUSC 195
Lab. majority 19,818 (57.72%)
Notional 1.47% swing LD to Lab.
(2005: Lab. majority 17,611 (54.77%))

§LIVERPOOL WAVERTREE
E. 62,518 T. 37,914 (60.64%)
Lab. (Co-op) hold
*Luciana Berger, Lab. (Co-op) 20,132
Colin Eldridge, LD 12,965
Andrew Garnett, C. 2,830
Neil Miney, UKIP 890
Rebecca Lawson, Green 598
Kim Singleton, Soc. Lab. 200
Steven McEllenborough, BNP 150
Frank Dunne, Ind. 149
Lab. (Co-op) majority 7,167 (18.90%)
Notional 5.00% swing LD to Lab. (Co-op)
(2005: Lab. (Co-op) majority 2,911 (8.91%))

§LIVERPOOL WEST DERBY
E. 63,082 T. 35,784 (56.73%)
Lab. (Co-op) hold
*Stephen Twigg, Lab. (Co-op) 22,953
Paul Twigger, LD 4,486
Stephen Radford, Lib 3,327
Pamela Hall, C. 3,311
Hilary Jones, UKIP 1,093
Kai Andersen, Soc. Lab. 614
Lab. (Co-op) majority 18,467 (51.61%)
Notional 3.16% swing LD to Lab. (Co-op)
(2005: Lab. (Co-op) majority 13,874 (45.29%))

§LOUGHBOROUGH
E. 77,502 T. 52,838 (68.18%) C. gain
*Nicky Morgan, C. 21,971
Andy Reed, Lab. (Co-op) 18,227
Mike Willis, LD 9,675
Kevan Stafford, BNP 2,040
John Foden, UKIP 925
C. majority 3,744 (7.09%)
Notional 5.48% swing Lab. (Co-op) to C.
(2005: Lab. (Co-op) majority 1,816 (3.88%))

§LOUTH & HORNCASTLE
E. 77,650 T. 50,494 (65.03%) C. hold
Sir Peter Tapsell, C. 25,065
Fiona Martin, LD 11,194
Patrick Mountain, Lab. 8,760
Julia Green, BNP 2,199
Pat Nurse, UKIP 2,183
Daniel Simpson, Lincs Ind. 576
Colin Mair, Eng. Dem. 517
C. majority 13,871 (27.47%)
Notional 0.80% swing LD to C.
(2005: C. majority 9,813 (21.08%))

LUDLOW
E. 66,631 T. 48,732 (73.14%) C. hold
Philip Dunne, C. 25,720
Heather Kidd, LD 15,971
Anthony Hunt, Lab. 3,272
Christopher Gill, UKIP 2,127
Christina Evans, BNP 1,016
Jacqui Morrish, Green 447
Alan Powell, Loony 179
C. majority 9,749 (20.01%)
7.82% swing LD to C.
(2005: C. majority 2,027 (4.36%))

§LUTON NORTH
E. 65,062 T. 43,018 (66.12%) Lab. hold
Kelvin Hopkins, Lab. 21,192
Jeremy Brier, C. 13,672
Rabi Martins, LD 4,784
Colin Brown, UKIP 1,564
Shelley Rose, BNP 1,316
Simon Hall, Green 490
Lab. majority 7,520 (17.48%)
Notional 0.55% swing C. to Lab.
(2005: Lab. majority 6,439 (16.39%))

§LUTON SOUTH
E. 59,962 T. 42,216 (70.40%)
Lab. (Co-op) hold
*Gavin Shuker, Lab. (Co-op) 14,725
Nigel Huddleston, C. 12,396
Qurban Hussain, LD 9,567
Esther Rantzen, Ind. Rantzen 1,872
Tony Blakey, BNP 1,299
Charles Lawman, UKIP 975
Stephen Rhodes, Ind. 463
Marc Scheimann, Green 366
Joe Hall, Ind. 264
Faruk Choudhury, Ind. 130
Stephen Lathwell, Ind. 84
Frank Sweeney, WRP 75
Lab. (Co-op) majority 2,329 (5.52%)
Notional 4.59% swing Lab. (Co-op) to C.
(2005: Lab. (Co-op) majority 5,698 (14.71%))

§MACCLESFIELD
E. 73,417 T. 50,059 (68.18%) C. hold
*David Rutley, C. 23,503
Roger Barlow, LD 11,544
Adrian Heald, Lab. 10,164
Brendan Murphy, Macc. Ind. 2,590
Jacqueline Smith, UKIP 1,418
John Knight, Green 840
C. majority 11,959 (23.89%)
Notional 3.11% swing C. to LD
(2005: C. majority 9,464 (20.66%))

§MAIDENHEAD
E. 72,844 T. 53,720 (73.75%) C. hold
Theresa May, C. 31,937
Tony Hill, LD 15,168
Pat McDonald, Lab. 3,795
Kenneth Wight, UKIP 1,243
Tim Rait, BNP 825
Peter Forbes, Green 482
Peter Prior, F and R 270
C. majority 16,769 (31.22%)
Notional 7.82% swing LD to C.
(2005: C. majority 7,650 (15.58%))

§MAIDSTONE & THE WEALD
E. 71,041 T. 48,928 (68.87%) C. hold
*Helen Grant, C. 23,491
Peter Carroll, LD 17,602
Rav Seeruthun, Lab. 4,769
Gareth Kendall, UKIP 1,637
Stuart Jeffery, Green 655
Gary Butler, NF 643
Heidi Simmonds, Ch. P. 131
C. majority 5,889 (12.04%)
Notional 8.48% swing C. to LD
(2005: C. majority 12,922 (28.99%))

§MAKERFIELD
E. 73,641 T. 43,771 (59.44%) Lab. hold
*Yvonne Fovargue, Lab. 20,700
Itrat Ali, C. 8,210
David Crowther, LD 7,082
Bob Brierley, Ind. 3,424
Ken Haslam, BNP 3,229
John Mather, Ind. 1,126
Lab. majority 12,490 (28.53%)
Notional 9.98% swing Lab. to C.
(2005: Lab. majority 17,903 (48.49%))

§MALDON
E. 68,861 T. 47,895 (69.55%) C. hold
John Whittingdale, C. 28,661
Elfreda Tealby-Watson, LD 9,254
Swatantra Nandanwar, Lab. 6,070
Jesse Pryke, UKIP 2,446
Len Blaine, BNP 1,464
C. majority 19,407 (40.52%)
Notional 0.40% swing C. to LD
(2005: C. majority 13,631 (32.13%))

§MANCHESTER CENTRAL
E. 90,110 T. 39,927 (44.31%) Lab. hold
Tony Lloyd, Lab. 21,059
Marc Ramsbottom, LD 10,620
Suhail Rahuja, C. 4,704
Tony Trebilcock, BNP 1,636
Gayle O'Donovan, Green 915
Nicola Weatherill, UKIP 607
Ron Sinclair, Soc. Lab. 153
John Cartwright, Ind. 120
Jonty Leff, WRP 59
Robert Skelton, SEP 54
Lab. majority 10,439 (26.15%)
Notional 6.11% swing Lab. to LD
(2005: Lab. majority 11,636 (38.36%))

§MANCHESTER GORTON
E. 75,933 T. 38,325 (50.47%) Lab. hold
Gerald Kaufman, Lab. 19,211
Qassim Afzal, LD 12,508
Caroline Healy, C. 4,224
Justine Hall, Green 1,048
Karen Reissman, TUSC 507
Mohammed Zulfikar, Respect 337
Peter Harrison, Ch. P. 254
Tim Dobson, Pirate 236
Lab. majority 6,703 (17.49%)
Notional 1.06% swing Lab. to LD
(2005: Lab. majority 6,355 (19.61%))

§MANCHESTER WITHINGTON
E. 74,371 T. 45,031 (60.55%) LD hold
John Leech, LD 20,110
Lucy Powell, Lab. 18,216
Christopher Green, C. 5,005
Brian Candeland, Green 798
Bob Gutfreund-Walmsley, UKIP 698
Yasmin Zalzala, Ind. 147
Marcus Farmer, Ind. 57
LD majority 1,894 (4.21%)
Notional 1.41% swing Lab. to LD
(2005: LD majority 531 (1.39%))

§MANSFIELD
E. 80,069 T. 48,395 (60.44%) Lab. hold
Joseph Meale, Lab. 18,753
Tracy Critchlow, C. 12,741
Michael Wyatt, LD 7,469
Andre Camilleri, Mansfield Ind. 4,339
David Hamilton, UKIP 2,985
Rachel Hill, BNP 2,108
Lab. majority 6,012 (12.42%)
Notional 9.49% swing Lab. to C.
(2005: Lab. majority 13,776 (31.39%))

§MEON VALLEY
E. 70,488 T. 51,238 (72.69%) C. hold
*George Hollingbery, C. 28,818
Liz Leffman, LD 16,693
Howard Linsley, Lab. 3,266
Steve Harris, UKIP 1,490
Pat Harris, Eng. Dem. 582
Sarah Coats, APP 255
Graeme Quar, Ind. 134
C. majority 12,125 (23.66%)
Notional 9.38% swing LD to C.
(2005: C. majority 2,378 (4.91%))

§MERIDEN
E. 83,826 T. 52,162 (62.23%) C. hold
Caroline Spelman, C. 26,956
Ed Williams, Lab. 10,703
Simon Slater, LD 9,278
Frank O'Brien, BNP 2,511
Barry Allcock, UKIP 1,378
Elly Stanton, Green 678
Nikki Sinclaire, RA 658
C. majority 16,253 (31.16%)
Notional 7.90% swing Lab. to C.
(2005: C. majority 7,412 (15.37%))

§MIDDLESBROUGH
E. 65,148 T. 33,455 (51.35%) Lab. hold
Sir Stuart Bell, Lab. 15,351
Chris Foote-Wood, LD 6,662
John Walsh, C. 6,283
Joan McTigue, Ind. 1,969
Michael Ferguson, BNP 1,954
Robert Parker, UKIP 1,236
Lab. majority 8,689 (25.97%)
Notional 6.45% swing Lab. to LD
(2005: Lab. majority 12,476 (38.87%))

§MIDDLESBROUGH SOUTH & CLEVELAND EAST
E. 72,664 T. 46,214 (63.60%) Lab. hold
*Tom Blenkinsop, Lab. 18,138
Paul Bristow, C. 16,461
Nick Emmerson, LD 7,340
Stuart Lightwing, UKIP 1,881
Shaun Gatley, BNP 1,576
Mike Allen, Ind. 818
Lab. majority 1,677 (3.63%)
Notional 7.44% swing Lab. to C.
(2005: Lab. majority 8,096 (18.51%))

§MILTON KEYNES NORTH
E. 85,841 T. 53,888 (62.78%) C. gain
Mark Lancaster, C. 23,419
Andrew Pakes, Lab. 14,458
Jill Hope, LD 11,894
Michael Phillips, UKIP 1,772
Richard Hamilton, BNP 1,154
Alan Francis, Green 733
Revd John Lennon, CPA 206
Matt Bananamatt Fensome, Loony 157
Anant Vyas, Ind. 95
C. majority 8,961 (16.63%)
Notional 9.17% swing Lab. to C.
(2005: Lab. majority 848 (1.71%))

§MILTON KEYNES SOUTH
E. 90,487 T. 55,333 (61.15%) C. gain
*Iain Stewart, C. 23,034
Phyllis Starkey, Lab. 17,833
Peter Jones, LD 9,787
Philip Pinto, UKIP 2,074
Matthew Tait, BNP 1,502
Katrina Deacon, Green 774
Suzanne Nti, CPA 245
Jonathan Worth, NFP 84
C. majority 5,201 (9.40%)
Notional 6.22% swing Lab. to C.
(2005: Lab. majority 1,497 (3.04%))

§MITCHAM & MORDEN
E. 65,939 T. 43,797 (66.42%) Lab. hold
Siobhain McDonagh, Lab. 24,722
Melanie Hampton, C. 11,056
Diana Coman, LD 5,202
Tony Martin, BNP 1,386
Andrew Mills, UKIP 857
Smarajit Roy, Green 381
Rathy Alagaratnam, Ind. 155
Ernest Redgrave, Ind. 38
Lab. majority 13,666 (31.20%)
Notional 0.44% swing Lab. to C.
(2005: Lab. majority 12,739 (32.08%))

MOLE VALLEY
E. 72,612 T. 54,324 (74.81%) C. hold
Sir Paul Beresford, C. 31,263
Alice Humphreys, LD 15,610
James Dove, Lab. 3,804
Leigh Jones, UKIP 2,752
Rob Sedgwick, Green 895
C. majority 15,653 (28.81%)
2.27% swing LD to C.
(2005: C. majority 11,997 (24.28%))

§MORECAMBE & LUNESDALE
E. 69,965 T. 43,616 (62.34%) C. gain
*David Morris, C. 18,035
Geraldine Smith, Lab. 17,169
Leslie Jones, LD 5,971
Mark Knight, UKIP 1,843
Chris Coates, Green 598
C. majority 866 (1.99%)
Notional 6.86% swing Lab. to C.
(2005: Lab. majority 4,849 (11.74%))

§MORLEY & OUTWOOD
E. 74,200 T. 48,856 (65.84%)
Lab. (Co-op) hold
Ed Balls, Lab. (Co-op) 18,365
Antony Calvert, C. 17,264
James Monaghan, LD 8,186
Chris Beverley, BNP 3,535
David Daniel, UKIP 1,506
Lab. (Co-op) majority 1,101 (2.25%)
Notional 9.35% swing Lab. (Co-op) to C.
(2005: Lab. (Co-op) majority 8,669 (20.95%))

§NEW FOREST EAST
E. 72,858 T. 50,036 (68.68%) C. hold
Julian Lewis, C. 26,443
Terry Scriven, LD 15,136
Peter Sopowski, Lab. 4,915
Peter Day, UKIP 2,518
Beverley Golden, Green 1,024
C. majority 11,307 (22.60%)
Notional 3.20% swing LD to C.
(2005: C. majority 7,653 (16.21%))

§NEW FOREST WEST
E. 68,332 T. 47,572 (69.62%) C. hold
Desmond Swayne, C. 27,980
Mike Plummer, LD 11,084
Janice Hurne, Lab. 4,666
Martin Lyon, UKIP 2,783
Janet Richards, Green 1,059
C. majority 16,896 (35.52%)
Notional 0.60% swing C. to LD
(2005: C. majority 16,183 (36.71%))

§NEWARK
E. 71,785 T. 51,228 (71.36%) C. hold
Patrick Mercer, C. 27,590
Dr Ian Campbell, Lab. 11,438
Pauline Jenkins, LD 10,246
Tom Irvine, UKIP 1,954
C. majority 16,152 (31.53%)
Notional 4.68% swing Lab. to C.
(2005: C. majority 10,077 (22.17%))

§NEWBURY
E. 83,411 T. 58,589 (70.24%) C. hold
Richard Benyon, C. 33,057
David Rendel, LD 20,809
Hannah Cooper, Lab. 2,505
David Black, UKIP 1,475
Adrian Hollister, Green 490
Brian Burgess, Ind. 158
David Yates, AD 95
C. majority 12,248 (20.90%)
Notional 7.24% swing LD to C.
(2005: C. majority 3,452 (6.42%))

NEWCASTLE-UNDER-LYME
E. 69,433 T. 43,191 (62.21%) Lab. hold
Paul Farrelly, Lab. 16,393
Robert Jenrick, C. 14,841
Nigel Jones, LD 8,466
David Nixon, UKIP 3,491
Lab. majority 1,552 (3.59%)
8.39% swing Lab. to C.
(2005: Lab. majority 8,108 (20.38%))

§NEWCASTLE UPON TYNE CENTRAL
E. 60,507 T. 34,157 (56.45%) Lab. hold
*Chinyelu Onwurah, Lab. 15,694
Gareth Kane, LD 8,228
Nick Holder, C. 6,611
Ken Booth, BNP 2,302
Martin Davies, UKIP 754
John Pearson, Green 568
Lab. majority 7,466 (21.86%)
Notional 0.60% swing Lab. to LD
(2005: Lab. majority 7,509 (23.07%))

§NEWCASTLE UPON TYNE EAST
E. 64,487 T. 37,840 (58.68%) Lab. hold
Nicholas Brown, Lab. 17,043
Wendy Taylor, LD 12,590
Dominic Llewellyn, C. 6,068
Alan Spence, BNP 1,342
Andrew Gray, Green 620
Martin Levy, Comm. 177
Lab. majority 4,453 (11.77%)
Notional 4.60% swing Lab. to LD
(2005: Lab. majority 6,987 (20.97%))

§NEWCASTLE UPON TYNE NORTH
E. 67,110 T. 43,946 (65.48%) Lab. hold
*Catherine McKinnell, Lab. 17,950
Ronald Beadle, LD 14,536
Stephen Parkinson, C. 7,966
Terry Gibson, BNP 1,890
Ian Proud, UKIP 1,285
Anna Heyman, Green 319
Lab. majority 3,414 (7.77%)
Notional 4.54% swing Lab. to LD
(2005: Lab. majority 6,878 (16.84%))

§NEWTON ABBOT
E. 69,343 T. 48,283 (69.63%) C. gain
*Anne-Marie Morris, C. 20,774
Richard Younger-Ross, LD 20,251
Patrick Canavan, Lab. 3,387
Jackie Hooper, UKIP 3,088
Corinne Lindsey, Green 701
Keith Sharp, Ind. 82
C. majority 523 (1.08%)
Notional 5.79% swing LD to C.
(2005: LD majority 4,830 (10.50%))

§NORFOLK MID
E. 74,260 T. 50,765 (68.36%) C. hold
*George Freeman, C. 25,123
David Newman, LD 11,267
Elizabeth Hughes, Lab. 8,857
Toby Coke, UKIP 2,800
Tim Birt, Green 1,457
Christine Kelly, BNP 1,261
C. majority 13,856 (27.29%)
Notional 0.02% swing C. to LD
(2005: C. majority 7,793 (16.29%))

§NORFOLK NORTH
E. 67,841 T. 49,661 (73.20%) LD hold
Norman Lamb, LD 27,554
Trevor Ivory, C. 15,928
Phil Harris, Lab. 2,896
Michael Baker, UKIP 2,680
Andrew Boswell, Green 508
Simon Mann, Ind. 95
LD majority 11,626 (23.41%)
Notional 3.06% swing C. to LD
(2005: LD majority 8,575 (17.28%))

§NORFOLK NORTH WEST
E. 73,207 T. 47,800 (65.29%) C. hold
Henry Bellingham, C. 25,916
William Summers, LD 11,106
Manish Sood, Lab. 6,353
John Gray, UKIP 1,841
David Fleming, BNP 1,839
Michael de Whalley, Green 745
C. majority 14,810 (30.98%)
Notional 2.09% swing C. to LD
(2005: C. majority 8,417 (18.34%))

§NORFOLK SOUTH
E. 76,165 T. 54,993 (72.20%) C. hold
Richard Bacon, C. 27,133
Jacky Howe, LD 16,193
Mick Castle, Lab. 7,252
Evan Heasley, UKIP 2,329
Helen Mitchell, BNP 1,086
Jo Willcott, Green 1,000
C. majority 10,940 (19.89%)
Notional 3.25% swing LD to C.
(2005: C. majority 6,719 (13.39%))

§NORFOLK SOUTH WEST
E. 74,298 T. 49,150 (66.15%) C. hold
*Elizabeth Truss, C. 23,753
Stephen Gordon, LD 10,613
Peter Smith, Lab. 9,119
Kay Hipsey, UKIP 3,061
Dennis Pearce, BNP 1,774
Lori Allen, Green 830
C. majority 13,140 (26.73%)
Notional 0.48% swing LD to C.
(2005: C. majority 6,817 (15.00%))

§NORMANTON, PONTEFRACT & CASTLEFORD
E. 82,239 T. 46,239 (56.23%) Lab. hold
Yvette Cooper, Lab. 22,293
Nick Pickles, C. 11,314
Chris Rush, LD 7,585
Graham Thewlis-Hardy, BNP 3,864
Gareth Allen, Ind. 1,183
Lab. majority 10,979 (23.74%)
Notional 12.49% swing Lab. to C.
(2005: Lab. majority 20,608 (48.73%))

§NORTHAMPTON NORTH
E. 64,230 T. 40,271 (62.70%) C. gain
*Michael Ellis, C. 13,735
Sally Keeble, Lab. 11,799
Andrew Simpson, LD 11,250
Ray Beasley, BNP 1,316
Jim Macarthur, UKIP 1,238
Tony Lochmuller, Green 443
Eamonn Fitzpatrick, Ind. 334
Timothy Webb, Ch. P. 98
Malcolm Mildren, Ind. 58
C. majority 1,936 (4.81%)
Notional 6.90% swing Lab. to C.
(2005: Lab. majority 3,340 (9.00%))

§NORTHAMPTON SOUTH
E. 66,923 T. 38,978 (58.24%) C. gain
*Brian Binley, C. 15,917
Clyde Loakes, Lab. 9,913
Paul Varnsverry, LD 7,579
Tony Clarke, Ind. 2,242
Derek Clark, UKIP 1,897
Kevin Sills, Eng. Dem. 618
Julie Hawkins, Green 363
Dave Green, NSPS 325
Kevin Willsher, Ind. 65
Liam Costello, SMA 59
C. majority 6,004 (15.40%)
Notional 9.59% swing Lab. to C.
(2005: Lab. majority 1,445 (3.78%))

§NORTHAMPTONSHIRE SOUTH
E. 82,032 T. 59,890 (73.01%) C. hold
*Andrea Leadsom, C. 33,081
Scott Collins, LD 12,603
Matthew May, Lab. 10,380
Barry Mahoney, UKIP 2,406
Tony Tappy, Eng. Dem. 735
Marcus Rock, Green 685
C. majority 20,478 (34.19%)
Notional 0.12% swing C. to LD
(2005: C. majority 11,356 (22.85%))

§NORWICH NORTH
E. 65,258 T. 42,573 (65.24%) C. gain
Chloe Smith, C. 17,280
John Cook, Lab. 13,379
John Stephen, LD 7,783
Glenn Tingle, UKIP 1,878
Jessica Goldfinch, Green 1,245
Thomas Richardson, BNP 747
Bill Holden, Ind. 143
Andrew Holland, Ch. P. 118
C. majority 3,901 (9.16%)
Notional 12.88% swing Lab. to C.
(2005: Lab. majority 6,769 (16.60%))

§NORWICH SOUTH
E. 73,649 T. 47,551 (64.56%) LD gain
*Simon Wright, LD 13,960
Charles Clarke, Lab. 13,650
Antony Little, C. 10,902
Adrian Ramsay, Green 7,095
Steve Emmens, UKIP 1,145
Leonard Heather, BNP 697
Gabriel Polley, WRP 102
LD majority 310 (0.65%)
Notional 4.03% swing Lab. to LD
(2005: Lab. majority 3,023 (7.40%))

§NOTTINGHAM EAST
E. 58,707 T. 33,112 (56.40%) Lab. (Co-op) hold
*Christopher Leslie, Lab. (Co-op) 15,022
Sam Boote, LD 8,053
Ewan Lamont, C. 7,846
Pat Wolfe, UKIP 1,138
Benjamin Hoare, Green 928
Parvaiz Sardar, Ch. P. 125
Lab. (Co-op) majority 6,969 (21.05%)
Notional 1.89% swing Lab. (Co-op) to LD
(2005: Lab. (Co-op) majority 7,083 (24.22%))

§NOTTINGHAM NORTH
E. 63,240 T. 34,285 (54.21%) Lab. hold
Graham Allen, Lab. 16,646
Martin Curtis, C. 8,508
Tim Ball, LD 5,849
Bob Brindley, BNP 1,944
Irenea Marriott, UKIP 1,338
Lab. majority 8,138 (23.74%)
Notional 8.65% swing Lab. to C.
(2005: Lab. majority 12,870 (41.04%))

§NOTTINGHAM SOUTH
E. 67,441 T. 40,789 (60.48%) Lab. hold
*Lilian Greenwood, Lab. 15,209
Rowena Holland, C. 13,437
Tony Sutton, LD 9,406
Tony Woodward, BNP 1,140
Ken Browne, UKIP 967
Matthew Butcher, Green 630
Lab. majority 1,772 (4.34%)
Notional 7.43% swing Lab. to C.
(2005: Lab. majority 6,665 (19.20%))

§NUNEATON
E. 67,837 T. 44,646 (65.81%) C. gain
*Marcus Jones, C. 18,536
Jayne Innes, Lab. 16,467
Christina Jebb, LD 6,846
Martyn Findley, BNP 2,797
C. majority 2,069 (4.63%)
Notional 7.19% swing Lab. to C.
(2005: Lab. majority 3,894 (9.74%))

§OLD BEXLEY & SIDCUP
E. 65,665 T. 45,492 (69.28%) C. hold
James Brokenshire, C. 24,625
Rick Everitt, Lab. 8,768
Duncan Borrowman, LD 6,996
John Brooks, BNP 2,132
David Coburn, UKIP 1,532
Elaine Cheeseman, Eng. Dem. 520
John Hemming-Clark, Save QM 393
Jonathan Rooks, Green 371
Napoleon Dynamite, Loony 155
C. majority 15,857 (34.86%)
Notional 6.43% swing Lab. to C.
(2005: C. majority 9,309 (22.00%))

§OLDHAM EAST & SADDLEWORTH
E. 72,765 T. 44,520 (61.18%) Lab. hold
Phil Woolas, Lab. 14,186
Elwyn Watkins, LD 14,083
Kashif Ali, C. 11,773
Alwyn Stott, BNP 2,546
David Bentley, UKIP 1,720
Gulzar Nazir, Ch. P. 212
Lab. majority 103 (0.23%)
Notional 5.08% swing Lab. to LD
(2005: Lab. majority 4,245 (10.39%))

§OLDHAM WEST & ROYTON
E. 72,651 T. 42,910 (59.06%) Lab. hold
Michael Meacher, Lab. 19,503
Kamran Ghafoor, C. 10,151
Mark Alcock, LD 8,193
David Joines, BNP 3,049
Helen Roberts, UKIP 1,387
Shahid Miah, Respect 627
Lab. majority 9,352 (21.79%)
Notional 2.74% swing Lab. to C.
(2005: Lab. majority 10,454 (27.13%))

§ORPINGTON
E. 67,732 T. 48,911 (72.21%) C. hold
*Joseph Johnson, C. 29,200
David McBride, LD 12,000
Stephen Morgan, Lab. 4,400
Mick Greenhough, UKIP 1,360
Tess Culnane, BNP 1,241
Tamara Galloway, Green 511
Chriss Snape, Eng. Dem. 199
C. majority 17,200 (35.17%)
Notional 12.19% swing LD to C.
(2005: C. majority 5,221 (10.79%))

§OXFORD EAST
E. 81,886 T. 51,651 (63.08%) Lab. hold
Andrew Smith, Lab. 21,938
Steve Goddard, LD 17,357
Edward Argar, C. 9,727
Sushila Dhall, Green 1,238
Julia Gasper, UKIP 1,202
David O'Sullivan, SEP 116
Roger Crawford, Parenting 73
Lab. majority 4,581 (8.87%)
Notional 4.07% swing LD to Lab.
(2005: Lab. majority 332 (0.73%))

§OXFORD WEST & ABINGDON
E. 86,458 T. 56,480 (65.33%) C. gain
*Nicola Blackwood, C. 23,906
Evan Harris, LD 23,730
Richard Stevens, Lab. 5,999
Paul Williams, UKIP 1,518
Chris Goodall, Green 1,184
Keith Mann, APP 143
C. majority 176 (0.31%)
Notional 6.87% swing LD to C.
(2005: LD majority 6,816 (13.43%))

PENDLE
E. 66,417 T. 45,045 (67.82%) C. gain
*Andrew Stephenson, C. 17,512
Gordon Prentice, Lab. 13,927
Afzal Anwar, LD 9,095
James Jackman, BNP 2,894
Graham Cannon, UKIP 1,476
Richard Masih, Ch. P. 141
C. majority 3,585 (7.96%)
6.63% swing Lab. to C.
(2005: Lab. majority 2,180 (5.30%))

§PENISTONE & STOCKSBRIDGE
E. 68,501 T. 46,516 (67.91%) Lab. hold
Angela Smith, Lab. 17,565
Spencer Pitfield, C. 14,516
Ian Cuthbertson, LD 9,800
Paul James, BNP 2,207
Grant French, UKIP 1,936
Paul McEnhill, Eng. Dem. 492
Lab. majority 3,049 (6.55%)
Notional 7.45% swing Lab. to C.
(2005: Lab. majority 8,617 (20.43%))

§PENRITH & THE BORDER
E. 64,548 T. 45,087 (69.85%) C. hold
*Rory Stewart, C. 24,071
Peter Thornton, LD 12,830
Barbara Cannon, Lab. 5,834
John Stanyer, UKIP 1,259
Chris Davidson, BNP 1,093
C. majority 11,241 (24.93%)
Notional 0.32% swing C. to LD
(2005: C. majority 10,795 (25.58%))

§PETERBOROUGH
E. 70,316 T. 44,927 (63.89%) C. hold
Stewart Jackson, C. 18,133
Ed Murphy, Lab. 13,272
Nick Sandford, LD 8,816
Frances Fox, UKIP 3,007
Rob King, Eng. Dem. 770
Fiona Radic, Green 523
John Swallow, Ind. 406
C. majority 4,861 (10.82%)
Notional 0.94% swing Lab. to C.
(2005: C. majority 4,005 (8.93%))

§PLYMOUTH MOOR VIEW
E. 67,261 T. 41,526 (61.74%) Lab. hold
Alison Seabeck, Lab. 15,433
Matthew Groves, C. 13,845
Stuart Bonar, LD 7,016
Bill Wakeham, UKIP 3,188
Roy Cook, BNP 1,438
Wendy Miller, Green 398
David Marchesi, Soc. Lab. 208
Lab. majority 1,588 (3.82%)
Notional 7.77% swing Lab. to C.
(2005: Lab. majority 7,740 (19.37%))

§PLYMOUTH SUTTON & DEVONPORT
E. 71,035 T. 43,894 (61.79%) C. gain
*Oliver Colville, C. 15,050
Linda Gilroy, Lab. (Co-op) 13,901
Judy Evans, LD 10,829
Andrew Leigh, UKIP 2,854
Tony Brown, Green 904
Brian Gerrish, Ind. 233
Robert Hawkins, Soc. Lab. 123
C. majority 1,149 (2.62%)
Notional 6.86% swing Lab. (Co-op) to C.
(2005: Lab. (Co-op) majority 4,472 (11.11%))

§POOLE
E. 64,661 T. 47,436 (73.36%) C. hold
Robert Syms, C. 22,532
Philip Eades, LD 14,991
Jason Sanderson, Lab. 6,041
Nick Wellstead, UKIP 2,507
David Holmes, BNP 1,188
Ian Northover, Ind. 177
C. majority 7,541 (15.90%)
Notional 0.79% swing LD to C.
(2005: C. majority 6,035 (14.32%))

§POPLAR & LIMEHOUSE
E. 74,956 T. 46,700 (62.30%) Lab. hold
Jim Fitzpatrick, Lab. 18,679
Tim Archer, C. 12,649
George Galloway, Respect 8,160
Jonathan Fryer, LD 5,209
Wayne Lochner, UKIP 565
Andrew Osborne, Eng. Dem. 470
Chris Smith, Green 449
Kabir Mahmud, Ind. 293
Mohammed Hoque, Ind. 167
Jim Thornton, Ind. 59
Lab. majority 6,030 (12.91%)
Notional 1.04% swing C. to Lab.
(2005: Lab. majority 3,823 (10.84%))

§PORTSMOUTH NORTH
E. 70,329 T. 44,118 (62.73%) C. gain
*Penny Mordaunt, C. 19,533
Sarah McCarthy-Fry, Lab. (Co-op) 12,244
Darren Sanders, LD 8,874
Mike Fitzgerald, UKIP 1,812
David Knight, Eng. Dem. 1,040
Iain Maclennan, Green 461
Mick Tosh, TUSC 154
C. majority 7,289 (16.52%)
Notional 8.64% swing Lab. (Co-op) to C.
(2005: Lab. (Co-op) majority 315 (0.77%))

§PORTSMOUTH SOUTH
E. 70,242 T. 41,264 (58.75%) LD hold
Mike Hancock, LD 18,921
Flick Drummond, C. 13,721
John Ferrett, Lab. 5,640
Christopher Martin, UKIP 876
Geoff Crompton, BNP 873
Tim Dawes, Green 716
Ian DuCane, Eng. Dem. 400
Les Cummings, J & AC 117
LD majority 5,200 (12.60%)
Notional 2.30% swing C. to LD
(2005: LD majority 2,955 (8.00%))

§PRESTON
E. 62,460 T. 32,505 (52.04%) Lab. (Co-op) hold
Mark Hendrick, Lab. (Co-op) 15,668
Mark Jewell, LD 7,935
Nerissa Warner-O'Neill, C. 7,060
Richard Muirhead, UKIP 1,462
George Ambroze, Ch. P. 272
Krishna Tayya, Ind. 108
Lab. (Co-op) majority 7,733 (23.79%)
Notional 2.50% swing Lab. (Co-op) to LD
(2005: Lab. (Co-op) majority 8,338 (27.67%))

§PUDSEY
E. 69,257 T. 49,083 (70.87%) C. gain
*Stuart Andrew, C. 18,874
Jamie Hanley, Lab. 17,215
Jamie Matthews, LD 10,224
Ian Gibson, BNP 1,549
David Dews, UKIP 1,221
C. majority 1,659 (3.38%)
Notional 7.56% swing Lab. to C.
(2005: Lab. majority 5,204 (11.74%))

§PUTNEY
E. 63,370 T. 40,785 (64.36%) C. hold
Justine Greening, C. 21,223
Stuart King, Lab. 11,170
James Sandbach, LD 6,907
Bruce Mackenzie, Green 591
Peter Darby, BNP 459
Hugo Wareham, UKIP 435
C. majority 10,053 (24.65%)
Notional 9.92% swing Lab. to C.
(2005: C. majority 1,723 (4.80%))

§RAYLEIGH & WICKFORD
E. 75,905 T. 52,343 (68.96%) C. hold
Mark Francois, C. 30,257
Susan Gaszczak, LD 7,919
Michael Le-Surf, Lab. 7,577
John Hayter, Eng. Dem. 2,219
Tino Callaghan, UKIP 2,211
Anthony Evennett, BNP 2,160
C. majority 22,338 (42.68%)
Notional 2.13% swing LD to C.
(2005: C. majority 12,983 (27.37%))

§READING EAST
E. 74,922 T. 49,985 (66.72%) C. hold
Rob Wilson, C. 21,269
Gareth Epps, LD 13,664
Anneliese Dodds, Lab. 12,729
Adrian Pitfield, UKIP 1,086
Rob White, Green 1,069
Joan Lloyd, Ind. 111
Michael Turberville, Ind. 57
C. majority 7,605 (15.21%)
Notional 1.97% swing LD to C.
(2005: C. majority 739 (1.71%))

§READING WEST
E. 72,118 T. 47,530 (65.91%) C. gain
*Alok Sharma, C. 20,523
Naz Sarkar, Lab. 14,519
Daisy Benson, LD 9,546
Bruce Hay, UKIP 1,508
Howard Thomas, CSP 852
Adrian Windisch, Green 582
C. majority 6,004 (12.63%)
Notional 12.05% swing Lab. to C.
(2005: Lab. majority 4,931 (11.47%))

REDCAR
E. 67,125 T. 41,963 (62.51%) LD gain
*Ian Swales, LD 18,955
Vera Baird, Lab. 13,741
Steve Mastin, C. 5,790
Martin Bulmer, UKIP 1,875
Kevin Broughton, BNP 1,475
Hannah Walter, TUSC 127
LD majority 5,214 (12.43%)
21.80% swing Lab. to LD
(2005: Lab. majority 12,116 (31.18%))

§REDDITCH
E. 68,550 T. 44,018 (64.21%) C. gain
*Karen Lumley, C. 19,138
Jacqui Smith, Lab. 13,317
Nicholas Lane, LD 7,750
Anne Davis, UKIP 1,497
Andy Ingram, BNP 1,394
Kevin White, Green 393
Vincent Schittone, Eng. Dem. 255
Scott Beverley, Ch. P. 101
Paul Swansborough, Ind. 100
Derek Fletcher, Nobody 73
C. majority 5,821 (13.22%)
Notional 9.21% swing Lab. to C.
(2005: Lab. majority 2,163 (5.20%))

§REIGATE
E. 71,604 T. 49,978 (69.80%) C. hold
Crispin Blunt, C. 26,688
Jane Kulka, LD 13,097
Robert Hull, Lab. 5,672
Joe Fox, UKIP 2,089
Keith Brown, BNP 1,345
Jonathan Essex, Green 1,087
C. majority 13,591 (27.19%)
Notional 0.89% swing LD to C.
(2005: C. majority 11,093 (25.41%))

§RIBBLE VALLEY
E. 78,068 T. 52,287 (66.98%) C. hold
Nigel Evans, C. 26,298
Paul Foster, Lab. 11,529
Allan Knox, LD 10,732
Stephen Rush, UKIP 3,496
Tony Johnson, ND 232
C. majority 14,769 (28.25%)
Notional 6.58% swing Lab. to C.
(2005: C. majority 6,953 (15.09%))

§RICHMOND (YORKS)
E. 79,478 T. 53,412 (67.20%) C. hold
William Hague, C. 33,541
Lawrence Meredith, LD 10,205
Eileen Driver, Lab. 8,150
Leslie Rowe, Green 1,516
C. majority 23,336 (43.69%)
Notional 0.64% swing LD to C.
(2005: C. majority 19,450 (38.73%))

§RICHMOND PARK
E. 77,060 T. 59,268 (76.91%) C. gain
*Zac Goldsmith, C. 29,461
Susan Kramer, LD 25,370
Eleanor Tunnicliffe, Lab. 2,979
Peter Dul, UKIP 669
James Page, Green 572
Susan May, CPA 133
Charles Hill, Ind. 84
C. majority 4,091 (6.90%)
Notional 7.00% swing LD to C.
(2005: LD majority 3,613 (7.09%))

§ROCHDALE
E. 78,952 T. 45,907 (58.15%) Lab. hold
*Simon Danczuk, Lab. 16,699
Paul Rowen, LD 15,810
Mudasir Dean, C. 8,305
Chris Jackson, NF 2,236
Colin Denby, UKIP 1,999
Mohammed Salim, IZB 545
John Whitehead, Ind. 313
Lab. majority 889 (1.94%)
Notional 0.79% swing LD to Lab.
(2005: Lab. majority 149 (0.35%))

§ROCHESTER & STROOD
E. 73,882 T. 47,971 (64.93%) C. hold
*Mark Reckless, C. 23,604
Teresa Murray, Lab. 13,651
Geoffrey Juby, LD 7,800
Ron Sands, Eng. Dem. 2,182
Simon Marchant, Green 734
C. majority 9,953 (20.75%)
Notional 9.81% swing Lab. to C.
(2005: C. majority 503 (1.14%))

§ROCHFORD & SOUTHEND EAST
E. 71,080 T. 41,631 (58.57%) C. hold
James Duddridge, C. 19,509
Kevin Bonavia, Lab. 8,459
Graham Longley, LD 8,084
James Moyies, UKIP 2,405
Geoff Strobridge, BNP 1,856
Andrew Vaughan, Green 707
Anthony Chytry, Ind. 611
C. majority 11,050 (26.54%)
Notional 6.37% swing Lab. to C.
(2005: C. majority 5,307 (13.80%))

§ROMFORD
E. 71,193 T. 46,481 (65.29%) C. hold
Andrew Rosindell, C. 26,031
Rachel Voller, Lab. 9,077
Helen Duffett, LD 5,572
Robert Bailey, BNP 2,438
Gerard Batten, UKIP 2,050
Dr Peter Thorogood, Eng. Dem. 603
Gary Haines, Green 447
Philip Hyde, Ind. 151
David Sturman, Ind. 112
C. majority 16,954 (36.48%)
Notional 3.94% swing Lab. to C.
(2005: C. majority 12,120 (28.59%))

§ROMSEY & SOUTHAMPTON NORTH
E. 66,901 T. 48,939 (73.15%) C. gain
*Caroline Nokes, C. 24,345
Sandra Gidley, LD 20,189
Aktar Beg, Lab. 3,116
John Meropoulos, UKIP 1,289
C. majority 4,156 (8.49%)
Notional 4.48% swing LD to C.
(2005: LD majority 204 (0.46%))

§ROSSENDALE & DARWEN
E. 73,003 T. 47,128 (64.56%) C. gain
*Jake Berry, C. 19,691
Janet Anderson, Lab. 15,198
Robert Sheffield, LD 8,541
David Duthie, UKIP 1,617
Kevin Bryan, NF 1,062
Michael Johnson, Eng. Dem. 663
Tony Melia, Impact 243
Mike Sivieri, Ind. 113
C. majority 4,493 (9.53%)
Notional 8.94% swing Lab. to C.
(2005: Lab. majority 3,696 (8.35%))

§ROTHER VALLEY
E. 72,841 T. 46,758 (64.19%) Lab. hold
Kevin Barron, Lab. 19,147
Lynda Donaldson, C. 13,281
Wesley Paxton, LD 8,111
Will Blair, BNP 3,606
Tina Dowdall, UKIP 2,613
Lab. majority 5,866 (12.55%)
Notional 7.96% swing Lab. to C.
(2005: Lab. majority 11,558 (28.47%))

§ROTHERHAM
E. 63,565 T. 37,506 (59.00%) Lab. hold
Denis MacShane, Lab. 16,741
Jackie Whiteley, C. 6,279
Rebecca Taylor, LD 5,994
Marlene Guest, BNP 3,906
Peter Thirlwall, Ind. 2,366
Caven Vines, UKIP 2,220
Lab. majority 10,462 (27.89%)
Notional 8.27% swing Lab. to C.
(2005: Lab. majority 13,865 (41.33%))

§RUGBY
E. 68,914 T. 47,468 (68.88%) C. gain
*Mark Pawsey, C. 20,901
Andy King, Lab. 14,901
Jerry Roodhouse, LD 9,434
Mark Badrick, BNP 1,375
Roy Sandison, Green 451
Barry Milford, UKIP 406
C. majority 6,000 (12.64%)
Notional 8.92% swing Lab. to C.
(2005: Lab. majority 2,397 (5.20%))

§RUISLIP, NORTHWOOD & PINNER
E. 70,873 T. 50,205 (70.84%) C. hold
Nick Hurd, C. 28,866
Anita McDonald, Lab. 9,806
Thomas Papworth, LD 8,345
Jason Pontey, UKIP 1,351
Ian Edward, NF 899
Graham Lee, Green 740
Ruby Akhtar, Ch. P. 198
C. majority 19,060 (37.96%)
Notional 3.63% swing Lab. to C.
(2005: C. majority 13,274 (30.71%))

RUNNYMEDE & WEYBRIDGE
E. 72,566 T. 48,150 (66.35%) C. hold
Philip Hammond, C. 26,915
Andrew Falconer, LD 10,406
Paul Greenwood, Lab. 6,446
Toby Micklethwait, UKIP 3,146
Jenny Gould, Green 696
David Sammons, Ind. 541
C. majority 16,509 (34.29%)
0.38% swing LD to C.
(2005: C. majority 12,349 (28.37%))

§RUSHCLIFFE
E. 72,955 T. 53,687 (73.59%) C. hold
Kenneth Clarke, C. 27,470
Karrar Khan, LD 11,659
Andrew Clayworth, Lab. 11,128
Matthew Faithfull, UKIP 2,179
Richard Mallender, Green 1,251
C. majority 15,811 (29.45%)
Notional 0.63% swing C. to LD
(2005: C. majority 9,932 (20.60%))

§RUTLAND & MELTON
E. 77,185 T. 55,220 (71.54%) C. hold
Alan Duncan, C. 28,228
Grahame Hudson, LD 14,228
John Morgan, Lab. 7,893
Peter Baker, UKIP 2,526
Keith Addison, BNP 1,757
Leigh Higgins, Ind. 588
C. majority 14,000 (25.35%)
Notional 3.65% swing C. to LD
(2005: C. majority 12,998 (26.29%))

§SAFFRON WALDEN
E. 76,035 T. 54,369 (71.51%) C. hold
Sir Alan Haselhurst, C. 30,155
Peter Wilcock, LD 14,913
Barbara Light, Lab. 5,288
Roger Lord, UKIP 2,228
Christine Mitchell, BNP 1,050
Reza Hossain, Green 735
C. majority 15,242 (28.03%)
Notional 3.39% swing LD to C.
(2005: C. majority 10,483 (21.25%))

§ST ALBANS
E. 70,058 T. 52,835 (75.42%) C. hold
Anne Main, C. 21,533
Sandy Walkington, LD 19,228
Roma Mills, Lab. 9,288
John Stocker, UKIP 2,028
Jack Easton, Green 758
C. majority 2,305 (4.36%)
Notional 3.74% swing C. to LD
(2005: C. majority 1,334 (2.94%))

§ST AUSTELL & NEWQUAY
E. 76,346 T. 47,238 (61.87%) LD hold
*Stephen Gilbert, LD 20,189
Caroline Righton, C. 18,877
Lee Jameson, Lab. 3,386
Dick Cole, Meb. Ker. 2,007
Clive Medway, UKIP 1,757
James Fitton, BNP 1,022
LD majority 1,312 (2.78%)
Notional 4.83% swing LD to C.
(2005: LD majority 5,723 (12.44%))

§ST HELENS NORTH
E. 74,985 T. 44,556 (59.42%) Lab. hold
Dave Watts, Lab. 23,041
Paul Greenall, C. 9,940
John Beirne, LD 8,992
Gary Robinson, UKIP 2,100
Stephen Whatham, Soc. Lab. 483
Lab. majority 13,101 (29.40%)
Notional 4.55% swing Lab. to C.
(2005: Lab. majority 15,265 (36.49%))

§ST HELENS SOUTH & WHISTON
E. 77,975 T. 46,081 (59.10%) Lab. hold
Shaun Woodward, Lab. 24,364
Brian Spencer, LD 10,242
Val Allen, C. 8,209
James Winstanley, BNP 2,040
John Sumner, UKIP 1,226
Lab. majority 14,122 (30.65%)
Notional 1.94% swing LD to Lab.
(2005: Lab. majority 10,987 (26.76%))

§ST IVES
E. 66,930 T. 45,921 (68.61%) LD hold
Andrew George, LD 19,619
Derek Thomas, C. 17,900
Philippa Latimer, Lab. 3,751
Mick Faulkner, UKIP 2,560
Tim Andrewes, Green 1,308
Jonathan Rogers, Cornish D. 396
Simon Reed, Meb. Ker. 387
LD majority 1,719 (3.74%)
Notional 10.39% swing LD to C.
(2005: LD majority 10,711 (24.52%))

§SALFORD & ECCLES
E. 75,482 T. 41,533 (55.02%) Lab. hold
Hazel Blears, Lab. 16,655
Norman Owen, LD 10,930
Matthew Sephton, C. 8,497
Tina Wingfield, BNP 2,632
Duran O'Dwyer, UKIP 1,084
David Henry, TUSC 730
Stephen Morris, Eng. Dem. 621
Richard Carvath, Ind. 384
Lab. majority 5,725 (13.78%)
Notional 9.43% swing Lab. to LD
(2005: Lab. majority 10,707 (32.64%))

§SALISBURY
E. 67,429 T. 48,481 (71.90%) C. hold
*John Glen, C. 23,859
Nick Radford, LD 17,893
Tom Gann, Lab. 3,690
Frances Howard, UKIP 1,392
Sean Witheridge, BNP 765
Nick Startin, Green 506
King Arthur, Ind. 257
John Holme, Ind. 119
C. majority 5,966 (12.31%)
Notional 3.60% swing C. to LD
(2005: C. majority 8,860 (19.50%))

SCARBOROUGH & WHITBY
E. 75,443 T. 49,282 (65.32%) C. hold
Robert Goodwill, C. 21,108
Annajoy David, Lab. 12,978
Tania Exley-Moore, LD 11,093
Michael James, UKIP 1,484
Trisha Scott, BNP 1,445
Dilys Cluer, Green 734
Peter Popple, Ind. 329
Juliet Boddington, Green Soc. 111
C. majority 8,130 (16.50%)
6.92% swing Lab. to C.
(2005: C. majority 1,245 (2.65%))

§SCUNTHORPE
E. 63,089 T. 37,034 (58.70%) Lab. hold
*Nic Dakin, Lab. 14,640
Caroline Johnson, C. 12,091
Neil Poole, LD 6,774
Jane Collins, UKIP 1,686
Douglas Ward, BNP 1,447
Natalie Hurst, Green 396
Lab. majority 2,549 (6.88%)
Notional 9.18% swing Lab. to C.
(2005: Lab. majority 8,638 (25.24%))

§SEDGEFIELD
E. 64,727 T. 40,222 (62.14%) Lab. hold
Phil Wilson, Lab. 18,141
Neil Mahapatra, C. 9,445
Alan Thompson, LD 8,033
Mark Walker, BNP 2,075
Brian Gregory, UKIP 1,479
Paul Gittins, Ind. 1,049
Lab. majority 8,696 (21.62%)
Notional 11.60% swing Lab. to C.
(2005: Lab. majority 18,198 (44.82%))

§SEFTON CENTRAL
E. 67,512 T. 48,463 (71.78%) Lab. hold
*Bill Esterson, Lab. 20,307
Debi Jones, C. 16,445
Richard Clein, LD 9,656
Peter Harper, UKIP 2,055
Lab. majority 3,862 (7.97%)
Notional 2.03% swing Lab. to C.
(2005: Lab. majority 4,950 (12.02%))

§SELBY & AINSTY
E. 72,789 T. 51,728 (71.07%) C. hold
*Nigel Adams, C. 25,562
Jan Marshall, Lab. 13,297
Tom Holvey, LD 9,180
Darren Haley, UKIP 1,635
Duncan Lorriman, BNP 1,377
Graham Michael, Eng. Dem. 677
C. majority 12,265 (23.71%)
Notional 9.70% swing Lab. to C.
(2005: C. majority 2,060 (4.31%))

§SEVENOAKS
E. 69,591 T. 49,408 (71.00%) C. hold
Michael Fallon, C. 28,076
Alan Bullion, LD 10,561
Gareth Siddorn, Lab. 6,541
Chris Heath, UKIP 1,782
Paul Golding, BNP 1,384
Louise Uncles, Eng. Dem. 806
Mark Ellis, Ind. 258
C. majority 17,515 (35.45%)
Notional 3.13% swing LD to C.
(2005: C. majority 13,060 (29.19%))

§SHEFFIELD BRIGHTSIDE & HILLSBOROUGH
E. 68,186 T. 38,914 (57.07%) Lab. hold
David Blunkett, Lab. 21,400
Jonathan Harston, LD 7,768
John Sharp, C. 4,468
John Sheldon, BNP 3,026
Pat Sullivan, UKIP 1,596
Maxine Bowler, TUSC 656
Lab. majority 13,632 (35.03%)
Notional 10.77% swing Lab. to LD
(2005: Lab. majority 18,801 (56.58%))

§SHEFFIELD CENTRAL
E. 69,519 T. 41,468 (59.65%) Lab. hold
*Paul Blomfield, Lab. 17,138
Paul Scriven, LD 16,973
Andrew Lee, C. 4,206
Jillian Creasy, Green 1,556
Tracey Smith, BNP 903
Jeffrey Shaw, UKIP 652
Rod Rodgers, Ind. 40
Lab. majority 165 (0.40%)
Notional 7.36% swing Lab. to LD
(2005: Lab. majority 5,025 (15.12%))

§SHEFFIELD HALLAM
E. 69,378 T. 51,135 (73.70%) LD hold
Nick Clegg, LD 27,324
Nicola Bates, C. 12,040
Jack Scott, Lab. 8,228
Nigel James, UKIP 1,195
Steve Barnard, Green 919
David Wildgoose, Eng. Dem. 586
Martin Fitzpatrick, Ind. 429
Ray Green, Ch. P. 250
Mark Adshead, Loony 164
LD majority 15,284 (29.89%)
Notional 6.86% swing C. to LD
(2005: LD majority 7,416 (16.17%))

§SHEFFIELD HEELEY
E. 65,869 T. 40,871 (62.05%) Lab. hold
Meg Munn, Lab. 17,409
Simon Clement-Jones, LD 11,602
Anne Crampton, C. 7,081
John Beatson, BNP 2,260
Charlotte Arnott, UKIP 1,530
Gareth Roberts, Green 989
Lab. majority 5,807 (14.21%)
Notional 9.23% swing Lab. to LD
(2005: Lab. majority 12,340 (32.67%))

§SHEFFIELD SOUTH EAST
E. 67,284 T. 41,408 (61.54%) Lab. hold
Clive Betts, Lab. 20,169
Gail Smith, LD 9,664
Nigel Bonson, C. 7,202
Christopher Hartigan, BNP 2,345
Jonathan Arnott, UKIP 1,889
Steven Andrew, Comm. Brit. 139
Lab. majority 10,505 (25.37%)
Notional 9.00% swing Lab. to LD
(2005: Lab. majority 15,843 (43.36%))

§SHERWOOD
E. 71,043 T. 48,954 (68.91%) C. gain
*Mark Spencer, C. 19,211
Emilie Oldknow, Lab. 18,997
Kevin Moore, LD 7,283
James North, BNP 1,754
Margot Parker, UKIP 1,490
Russ Swan, Ind. 219
C. majority 214 (0.44%)
Notional 8.17% swing Lab. to C.
(2005: Lab. majority 6,869 (15.90%))

§SHIPLEY
E. 67,689 T. 49,427 (73.02%) C. hold
Philip Davies, C. 24,002
Susan Hinchcliffe, Lab. 14,058
John Harris, LD 9,890
Kevin Warnes, Green 1,477
C. majority 9,944 (20.12%)
Notional 9.58% swing Lab. to C.
(2005: C. majority 450 (0.97%))

SHREWSBURY & ATCHAM
E. 75,438 T. 53,045 (70.32%) C. hold
Daniel Kawczynski, C. 23,313
Charles West, LD 15,369
Jon Tandy, Lab. 10,915
Peter Lewis, UKIP 1,627
James Whittall, BNP 1,168
Alan Whittaker, Green 565
James Gollings, Impact 88
C. majority 7,944 (14.98%)
0.06% swing LD to C.
(2005: C. majority 1,808 (3.59%))

SHROPSHIRE NORTH
E. 78,926 T. 51,869 (65.72%) C. hold
Owen Paterson, C. 26,692
Ian Croll, LD 10,864
Ian McLaughlan, Lab. 9,406
Sandra List, UKIP 2,432
Phil Reddall, BNP 1,667
Steve Boulding, Green 808
C. majority 15,828 (30.52%)
0.33% swing LD to C.
(2005: C. majority 11,020 (23.69%))

§SITTINGBOURNE & SHEPPEY
E. 75,354 T. 48,578 (64.47%) C. hold
*Gordon Henderson, C. 24,313
Angela Harrison, Lab. 11,930
Keith Nevols, LD 7,943
Ian Davison, UKIP 2,610
Lawrence Tames, BNP 1,305
Mad Mike Young, Loony 319
David Cassidy, Ind. 158
C. majority 12,383 (25.49%)
Notional 12.72% swing Lab. to C.
(2005: C. majority 22 (0.05%))

§SKIPTON & RIPON
E. 77,381 T. 54,724 (70.72%) C. hold
*Julian Smith, C. 27,685
Helen Flynn, LD 17,735
Claire Hazelgrove, Lab. 5,498
Rodney Mills, UKIP 1,909
Bernard Allen, BNP 1,403
Roger Bell, Ind. 315
Dylan Gilligan, Youth 95
Robert Leakey, Currency 84
C. majority 9,950 (18.18%)
Notional 2.63% swing C. to LD
(2005: C. majority 11,596 (23.43%))

§SLEAFORD & NORTH HYKEHAM
E. 85,550 T. 59,530 (69.59%) C. hold
*Stephen Phillips, C. 30,719
David Harding-Price, LD 10,814
James Normington, Lab. 10,051
Marianne Overton, Lincs Ind. 3,806
Rodger Doughty, UKIP 2,163
Mike Clayton, BNP 1,977
C. majority 19,905 (33.44%)
Notional 0.46% swing LD to C.
(2005: C. majority 12,687 (24.15%))

§SLOUGH
E. 77,068 T. 47,742 (61.95%) Lab. hold
Fiona Mactaggart, Lab. 21,884
Diana Coad, C. 16,361
Chris Tucker, LD 6,943
Peter Mason-Apps, UKIP 1,517
Miriam Kennet, Green 542
Sunil Chaudhary, Ch. P. 495
Lab. majority 5,523 (11.57%)
Notional 4.14% swing Lab. to C.
(2005: Lab. majority 7,924 (19.86%))

§SOLIHULL
E. 77,863 T. 55,129 (70.80%) LD gain
Lorely Burt, LD 23,635
Maggie Throup, C. 23,460
Sarah-Jayne Merrill, Lab. 4,891
Andrew Terry, BNP 1,624
John Ison, UKIP 1,200
Neill Watts, RA 319
LD majority 175 (0.32%)
Notional 0.28% swing C. to LD
(2005: C. majority 124 (0.25%))

§SOMERSET NORTH
E. 77,304 T. 57,941 (74.95%) C. hold
Dr Liam Fox, C. 28,549
Brian Mathew, LD 20,687
Steven Parry-Hearn, Lab. 6,448
Susan Taylor, UKIP 2,257
C. majority 7,862 (13.57%)
Notional 0.98% swing LD to C.
(2005: C. majority 6,007 (11.61%))

§SOMERSET NORTH EAST
E. 67,412 T. 51,203 (75.96%) C. hold
*Jacob Rees-Mogg, C. 21,130
Dan Norris, Lab. 16,216
Gail Coleshill, LD 11,433
Peter Sandell, UKIP 1,754
Michael Jay, Green 670
C. majority 4,914 (9.60%)
Notional 4.57% swing Lab. to C.
(2005: C. majority 212 (0.46%))

§SOMERTON & FROME
E. 81,548 T. 60,612 (74.33%) LD hold
David Heath, LD 28,793
Annunziata Rees-Mogg, C. 26,976
David Oakensen, Lab. 2,675
Barry Harding, UKIP 1,932
Niall Warry, Leave EU 236
LD majority 1,817 (3.00%)
Notional 0.94% swing C. to LD
(2005: LD majority 595 (1.12%))

§SOUTH HOLLAND & THE DEEPINGS
E. 76,243 T. 50,188 (65.83%) C. hold
John Hayes, C. 29,639
Jennifer Conroy, LD 7,759
Gareth Gould, Lab. 7,024
Richard Fairman, UKIP 3,246
Roy Harban, BNP 1,796
Ashley Baxter, Green 724
C. majority 21,880 (43.60%)
Notional 0.27% swing C. to LD
(2005: C. majority 15,127 (32.48%))

§SOUTH RIBBLE
E. 75,822 T. 51,458 (67.87%) C. gain
*Lorraine Fullbrook, C. 23,396
David Borrow, Lab. 17,842
Peter Fisher, LD 7,271
David Duxbury, UKIP 1,895
Rosalind Gauci, BNP 1,054
C. majority 5,554 (10.79%)
Notional 8.11% swing Lab. to C.
(2005: Lab. majority 2,528 (5.42%))

§SOUTH SHIELDS
E. 63,294 T. 36,518 (57.70%) Lab. hold
David Miliband, Lab. 18,995
Karen Allen, C. 7,886
Stephen Psallidas, LD 5,189
Donna Watson, BNP 2,382
Shirley Ford, Green 762
Siamak Kaikavoosi, Ind. 729
Victor Thompson, Ind. 316
Sam Navabi, Ind. 168
Roger Nettleship, Anti-War 91
Lab. majority 11,109 (30.42%)
Notional 6.36% swing Lab. to C.
(2005: Lab. majority 13,368 (41.61%))

§SOUTHAMPTON ITCHEN
E. 74,532 T. 44,412 (59.59%) Lab. hold
John Denham, Lab. 16,326
Royston Smith, C. 16,134
David Goodall, LD 9,256
Alan Kebbell, UKIP 1,928
John Spottiswoode, Green 600
Tim Cutter, TUSC 168
Lab. majority 192 (0.43%)
Notional 10.28% swing Lab. to C.
(2005: Lab. majority 8,479 (21.00%))

§SOUTHAMPTON TEST
E. 71,931 T. 44,187 (61.43%) Lab. hold
Alan Whitehead, Lab. 17,001
Jeremy Moulton, C. 14,588
David Callaghan, LD 9,865
Pearline Hingston, UKIP 1,726
Chris Bluemel, Green 881
Charles Sanderson, Ind. 126
Lab. majority 2,413 (5.46%)
Notional 6.86% swing Lab. to C.
(2005: Lab. majority 7,817 (19.17%))

§SOUTHEND WEST
E. 66,527 T. 43,606 (65.55%) C. hold
David Amess, C. 20,086
Peter Welch, LD 12,816
Thomas Flynn, Lab. 5,850
Garry Cockrill, UKIP 1,714
Tony Gladwin, BNP 1,333
Barry Bolton, Green 644
Dr Vel, Ind. 617
Terry Phillips, Eng. Dem. 546
C. majority 7,270 (16.67%)
Notional 2.77% swing C. to LD
(2005: C. majority 9,008 (22.20%))

SOUTHPORT
E. 67,202 T. 43,757 (65.11%) LD hold
John Pugh, LD 21,707
Brenda Porter, C. 15,683
Jim Conalty, Lab. 4,116
Terry Durrance, UKIP 2,251
LD majority 6,024 (13.77%)
2.23% swing C. to LD
(2005: LD majority 3,838 (9.32%))

SPELTHORNE
E. 70,479 T. 47,304 (67.12%) C. hold
Kwasi Kwarteng, C. 22,261
Mark Chapman, LD 12,242
Adam Tyler-Moore, Lab. 7,789
Christopher Browne, UKIP 4,009
Ian Swinglehurst, Ind. 314
Rod Littlewood, Best 244
Paul Couchman, TUSC 176
John Gore, CIP 167
Grahame Leon-Smith, Ind. Fed. 102
C. majority 10,019 (21.18%)
0.11% swing C. to LD
(2005: C. majority 9,936 (23.20%))

§STAFFORD
E. 70,587 T. 50,239 (71.17%) C. gain
Jeremy Lefroy, C. 22,047
David Kidney, Lab. 16,587
Barry Stamp, LD 8,211
Roy Goode, UKIP 1,727
Roland Hynd, BNP 1,103
Mike Shone, Green 564
C. majority 5,460 (10.87%)
Notional 7.44% swing Lab. to C.
(2005: Lab. majority 1,852 (4.01%))

§STAFFORDSHIRE MOORLANDS
E. 62,071 T. 43,815 (70.59%) C. hold
*Karen Bradley, C. 19,793
Charlotte Atkins, Lab. 13,104
Henry Jebb, LD 7,338
Steve Povey, UKIP 3,580
C. majority 6,689 (15.27%)
Notional 5.71% swing Lab. to C.
(2005: C. majority 1,618 (3.86%))

§STAFFORDSHIRE SOUTH
E. 73,390 T. 50,440 (68.73%) C. hold
*Gavin Williamson, C. 26,834
Kevin McElduff, Lab. 10,244
Sarah Fellows, LD 8,427
Mike Nattrass, UKIP 2,753
David Bradnock, BNP 1,928
Andrew Morris, Ind. 254
C. majority 16,590 (32.89%)
Notional 1.12% swing Lab. to C.
(2005: C. majority 8,346 (30.65%))

§STALYBRIDGE & HYDE
E. 69,037 T. 40,879 (59.21%) Lab. hold
*Jonathan Reynolds, Lab. 16,189
Rob Adlard, C. 13,445
John Potter, LD 6,965
Anthony Jones, BNP 2,259
John Cooke, UKIP 1,342
Ruth Bergan, Green 679
Lab. majority 2,744 (6.71%)
Notional 8.47% swing Lab. to C.
(2005: Lab. majority 8,455 (23.64%))

§STEVENAGE
E. 68,937 T. 44,651 (64.77%) C. gain
*Stephen McPartland, C. 18,491
Sharon Taylor, Lab. (Co-op) 14,913
Julia Davies, LD 7,432
Marion Mason, UKIP 2,004
Andrew Green, BNP 1,007
Charles Vickers, Eng. Dem. 366
Stephen Phillips, No Vote 327
David Cox, Ind. 80
Andrew Ralph, YRDPL 31
C. majority 3,578 (8.01%)
Notional 8.03% swing Lab. (Co-op) to C.
(2005: Lab. (Co-op) majority 3,288 (8.05%))

§STOCKPORT
E. 63,525 T. 39,128 (61.59%) Lab. hold
Ann Coffey, Lab. 16,697
Stephen Holland, C. 9,913
Stuart Bodsworth, LD 9,778
Duncan Warner, BNP 1,201
Mike Kelly, UKIP 862
Peter Barber, Green 677
Lab. majority 6,784 (17.34%)
Notional 5.74% swing Lab. to C.
(2005: Lab. majority 9,982 (28.82%))

§STOCKTON NORTH
E. 67,363 T. 39,498 (58.63%) Lab. hold
*Alex Cunningham, Lab. 16,923
Ian Galletley, C. 10,247
Philip Latham, LD 6,342
James Macpherson, BNP 1,724
Frank Cook, Ind. 1,577
Gordon Parkin, UKIP 1,556
Ian Saul, Eng. Dem. 1,129
Lab. majority 6,676 (16.90%)
Notional 8.35% swing Lab. to C.
(2005: Lab. majority 12,742 (33.60%))

§STOCKTON SOUTH
E. 74,552 T. 50,284 (67.45%) C. gain
*James Wharton, C. 19,577
Dari Taylor, Lab. 19,245
Jacquie Bell, LD 7,600
Neil Sinclair, BNP 1,553
Peter Braney, UKIP 1,471
Yvonne Hossack, Ind. 536
Ted Strike, Ch. P. 302
C. majority 332 (0.66%)
Notional 7.05% swing Lab. to C.
(2005: Lab. majority 5,834 (13.44%))

§STOKE-ON-TRENT CENTRAL
E. 60,995 T. 32,470 (53.23%) Lab. hold
*Tristram Hunt, Lab. 12,605
John Redfern, LD 7,039
Norsheen Bhatti, C. 6,833
Simon Darby, BNP 2,502
Carol Lovatt, UKIP 1,402
Paul Breeze, Ind. 959
Gary Elsby, Ind. 399
Brian Ward, City Ind. 303
Alby Walker, Ind. 295
Matthew Wright, TUSC 133
Lab. majority 5,566 (17.14%)
Notional 8.33% swing Lab. to LD
(2005: Lab. majority 9,717 (33.80%))

§STOKE-ON-TRENT NORTH
E. 72,052 T. 40,196 (55.79%) Lab. hold
Joan Walley, Lab. 17,815
Andy Large, C. 9,580
John Fisher, LD 7,120
Melanie Baddeley, BNP 3,196
Geoffrey Locke, UKIP 2,485
Lab. majority 8,235 (20.49%)
Notional 8.77% swing Lab. to C.
(2005: Lab. majority 13,666 (38.03%))

§STOKE-ON-TRENT SOUTH
E. 68,031 T. 39,852 (58.58%) Lab. hold
Rob Flello, Lab. 15,446
James Rushton, C. 11,316
Zulfiqar Ali, LD 6,323
Michael Coleman, BNP 3,762
Mark Barlow, UKIP 1,363
Terry Follows, Staffs Ind. 1,208
Mark Breeze, Ind. 434
Lab. majority 4,130 (10.36%)
Notional 6.15% swing Lab. to C.
(2005: Lab. majority 8,324 (22.67%))

§STONE
E. 66,979 T. 47,229 (70.51%) C. hold
Bill Cash, C. 23,890
Christine Tinker, LD 10,598
Jo Lewis, Lab. 9,770
Andrew Illsley, UKIP 2,481
Damon Hoppe, Green 490
C. majority 13,292 (28.14%)
Notional 0.81% swing C. to LD
(2005: C. majority 8,191 (18.72%))

§STOURBRIDGE
E. 69,637 T. 47,234 (67.83%) C. gain
*Margot James, C. 20,153
Lynda Waltho, Lab. 14,989
Christopher Bramall, LD 7,733
Maddy Westrop, UKIP 2,103
Robert Weale, BNP 1,696
Will Duckworth, Green 394
Alun Nicholas, Ind. 166
C. majority 5,164 (10.93%)
Notional 6.93% swing Lab. to C.
(2005: Lab. majority 1,280 (2.92%))

§STRATFORD-ON-AVON
E. 69,516 T. 50,542 (72.71%) C. hold
*Nadhim Zahawi, C. 26,052
Martin Turner, LD 14,706
Robert Johnston, Lab. 4,809
Brett Parsons, UKIP 1,846
George Jones, BNP 1,097
Neil Basnett, Ind. 1,032
Karen Varga, Green 527
Fred Bishop, Eng. Dem. 473
C. majority 11,346 (22.45%)
Notional 0.72% swing C. to LD
(2005: C. majority 10,928 (23.90%))

§STREATHAM
E. 74,531 T. 46,837 (62.84%) Lab. hold
*Chuka Umunna, Lab. 20,037
Chris Nicholson, LD 16,778
Rahoul Bhansali, C. 8,578
Rebecca Findlay, Green 861
Geoffrey Macharia, Ch. P. 237
Janus Polenceus, Eng. Dem. 229
Paul Lepper, WRP 117
Lab. majority 3,259 (6.96%)
Notional 5.25% swing Lab. to LD
(2005: Lab. majority 6,584 (17.47%))

§STRETFORD & URMSTON
E. 70,091 T. 44,910 (64.07%) Lab. hold
*Kate Green, Lab. 21,821
Alex Williams, C. 12,886
Steve Cooke, LD 7,601
David Owen, UKIP 1,508
Margaret Westbrook, Green 916
Samuel Jacob, Ch. P. 178
Lab. majority 8,935 (19.90%)
Notional 0.69% swing Lab. to C.
(2005: Lab. majority 8,310 (21.28%))

§STROUD
E. 78,305 T. 57,973 (74.03%) C. gain
*Neil Carmichael, C. 23,679
David Drew, Lab. (Co-op) 22,380
Dennis Andrewartha, LD 8,955
Martin Whiteside, Green 1,542
Steve Parker, UKIP 1,301
Alan Lomas, Ind. 116
C. majority 1,299 (2.24%)
Notional 2.05% swing Lab. (Co-op) to C.
(2005: Lab. (Co-op) majority 996 (1.85%))

§SUFFOLK CENTRAL & IPSWICH NORTH
E. 75,848 T. 53,420 (70.43%) C. hold
*Daniel Poulter, C. 27,125
Andrew Aalders-Dunthorne, LD 13,339
Bhavna Joshi, Lab. 8,636
Roy Philpot, UKIP 2,361
Andrew Stringer, Green 1,452
Mark Trevitt, Ind. 389
Richard Vass, New Party 118
C. majority 13,786 (25.81%)
Notional 0.76% swing LD to C.
(2005: C. majority 7,786 (16.07%))

§SUFFOLK COASTAL
E. 76,687 T. 54,893 (71.58%) C. hold
*Therese Coffey, C. 25,475
Daisy Cooper, LD 16,347
Adam Leeder, Lab. 8,812
Prof. Stephen Bush, UKIP 3,156
Rachel Fulcher, Green 1,103
C. majority 9,128 (16.63%)
Notional 2.91% swing C. to LD
(2005: C. majority 9,674 (18.43%))

§SUFFOLK SOUTH
E. 72,498 T. 51,416 (70.92%) C. hold
Tim Yeo, C. 24,550
Nigel Bennett, LD 15,861
Emma Bishton, Lab. 7,368
David Campbell Bannerman, UKIP 3,637
C. majority 8,689 (16.90%)
Notional 1.63% swing LD to C.
(2005: C. majority 6,664 (13.64%))

§SUFFOLK WEST
E. 74,413 T. 48,089 (64.62%) C. hold
*Matthew Hancock, C. 24,312
Belinda Brooks-Gordon, LD 11,262
Ohid Ahmed, Lab. 7,089
Ian Smith, UKIP 3,085
Ramon Johns, BNP 1,428
Andrew Appleby, Ind. 540
Colin Young, CPA 373
C. majority 13,050 (27.14%)
Notional 2.28% swing C. to LD
(2005: C. majority 8,735 (19.92%))

§SUNDERLAND CENTRAL
E. 74,485 T. 42,463 (57.01%) Lab. hold
*Julie Elliott, Lab. 19,495
Lee Martin, C. 12,770
Paul Dixon, LD 7,191
John McCaffrey, BNP 1,913
Pauline Featonby-Warren, UKIP 1,094
Lab. majority 6,725 (15.84%)
Notional 4.85% swing Lab. to C.
(2005: Lab. majority 9,464 (25.53%))

SURREY EAST
E. 76,855 T. 54,640 (71.09%) C. hold
*Sam Gyimah, C. 31,007
David Lee, LD 14,133
Mathew Rodda, Lab. 4,925
Helena Windsor, UKIP 3,770
Martin Hogbin, Loony 422
Sandy Pratt, Ind. 383
C. majority 16,874 (30.88%)
0.72% swing C. to LD
(2005: C. majority 15,921 (32.32%))

SURREY HEATH
E. 77,690 T. 54,347 (69.95%) C. hold
Michael Gove, C. 31,326
Alan Hilliar, LD 14,037
Matthew Willey, Lab. 5,552
Mark Stroud, UKIP 3,432
C. majority 17,289 (31.81%)
4.58% swing LD to C.
(2005: C. majority 10,845 (22.66%))

§SURREY SOUTH WEST
E. 77,980 T. 57,259 (73.43%) C. hold
Jeremy Hunt, C. 33,605
Mike Simpson, LD 17,287
Richard Mollet, Lab. 3,419
Roger Meekins, UKIP 1,486
Cherry Allan, Green 690
Helen Hamilton, BNP 644
Luke Leighton, Pirate 94
Arthur Price, Ind. 34
C. majority 16,318 (28.50%)
Notional 8.63% swing LD to C.
(2005: C. majority 5,969 (11.23%))

§SUSSEX MID
E. 77,182 T. 55,855 (72.37%) C. hold
Nicholas Soames, C. 28,329
Serena Tierney, LD 20,927
David Boot, Lab. 3,689
Marc Montgomery, UKIP 1,423
Paul Brown, Green 645
Stuart Minihane, BNP 583
Baron Von Thunderclap, Loony 259
C. majority 7,402 (13.25%)
Notional 0.32% swing LD to C.
(2005: C. majority 6,462 (12.62%))

§SUTTON & CHEAM
E. 66,658 T. 48,508 (72.77%) LD hold
Paul Burstow, LD 22,156
Philippa Stroud, C. 20,548
Kathy Allen, Lab. 3,376
John Clarke, BNP 1,014
David Pickles, UKIP 950
Peter Hickson, Green 246
John Dodds, Eng. Dem. 106
Matthew Connolly, CPA 52
Martin Cullip, Libertarian 41
Dr Brian Hammond, UK Integrity 19
LD majority 1,608 (3.31%)
Notional 1.45% swing LD to C.
(2005: LD majority 2,689 (6.22%))

§SUTTON COLDFIELD
E. 74,489 T. 50,589 (67.91%) C. hold
Andrew Mitchell, C. 27,303
Robert Pocock, Lab. 10,298
Richard Brighton, LD 9,117
Robert Grierson, BNP 1,749
Edward Siddall-Jones, UKIP 1,587
Joe Rooney, Green 535
C. majority 17,005 (33.61%)
Notional 3.44% swing Lab. to C.
(2005: C. majority 12,318 (26.72%))

§SWINDON NORTH
E. 78,391 T. 50,295 (64.16%) C. gain
*Justin Tomlinson, C. 22,408
Victor Agarwal, Lab. 15,348
Jane Lock, LD 8,668
Stephen Halden, UKIP 1,842
Reginald Bates, BNP 1,542
Bill Hughes, Green 487
C. majority 7,060 (14.04%)
Notional 10.14% swing Lab. to C.
(2005: Lab. majority 2,675 (6.25%))

§SWINDON SOUTH
E. 72,622 T. 47,119 (64.88%) C. gai
*Robert Buckland, C. 19,68
Anne Snelgrove, Lab. 16,14
Damon Hooton, LD 8,30
Robin Tingey, UKIP 2,02
Jenni Miles, Green 61
Alastair Kirk, Ch. P. 17
Karsten Evans, Ind. 16
C. majority 3,544 (7.52%)
Notional 5.51% swing Lab. to C.
(2005: Lab. majority 1,493 (3.50%))

TAMWORTH
E. 72,693 T. 46,390 (63.82%) C. gain
*Christopher Pincher, C. 21,238
Brian Jenkins, Lab. 15,148
Jenny Pinkett, LD 7,516
Paul Smith, UKIP 2,253
Charlene Detheridge, Ch. P. 235
C. majority 6,090 (13.13%)
9.50% swing Lab. to C.
(2005: Lab. majority 2,569 (5.87%))

§TATTON
E. 65,689 T. 45,231 (68.86%) C. hold
George Osborne, C. 24,687
David Lomax, LD 10,200
Richard Jackson, Lab. 7,803
Sarah Flannery, Ind. 2,243
Michael Gibson, Poetry 298
C. majority 14,487 (32.03%)
Notional 1.17% swing LD to C.
(2005: C. majority 11,537 (27.73%))

§TAUNTON DEANE
E. 82,537 T. 58,150 (70.45%) LD hold
Jeremy Browne, LD 28,531
Mark Formosa, C. 24,538
Martin Jevon, Lab. 2,967
Tony McIntyre, UKIP 2,114
LD majority 3,993 (6.87%)
Notional 1.78% swing C. to LD
(2005: LD majority 1,868 (3.30%))

§TELFORD
E. 65,061 T. 41,310 (63.49%) Lab. hold
David Wright, Lab. 15,974
Tom Biggins, C. 14,996
Phil Bennion, LD 6,399
Denis Allen, UKIP 2,428
Phil Spencer, BNP 1,513
Lab. majority 978 (2.37%)
Notional 6.32% swing Lab. to C.
(2005: Lab. majority 5,651 (15.01%))

§TEWKESBURY
E. 76,655 T. 53,961 (70.39%) C. hold
Laurence Robertson, C. 25,472
Alistair Cameron, LD 19,162
Stuart Emmerson, Lab. 6,253
Brian Jones, UKIP 2,230
Matthew Sidford, Green 525
George Ridgeon, Loony 319
C. majority 6,310 (11.69%)
Notional 4.04% swing C. to LD
(2005: C. majority 9,130 (19.78%))

§THANET NORTH
E. 69,432 T. 43,343 (62.43%) C. hold
Roger Gale, C. 22,826
Michael Britton, Lab. 9,298
Laura Murphy, LD 8,400
Rosamund Parker, UKIP 2,819
C. majority 13,528 (31.21%)
Notional 7.94% swing Lab. to C.
(2005: C. majority 6,118 (15.33%))

§THANET SOUTH
E. 71,596 T. 45,933 (64.16%) C. hold
*Laura Sandys, C. 22,043
Dr Stephen Ladyman, Lab. 14,426
Peter Bucklitsch, LD 6,935
Trevor Shonk, UKIP 2,529
C. majority 7,617 (16.58%)
Notional 7.41% swing Lab. to C.
(2005: C. majority 810 (1.76%))

§THIRSK & MALTON
E. 76,231 T. 38,142 (50.03%) C. hold
Anne McIntosh, C. 20,167
Howard Keal, LD 8,886
Jonathan Roberts, Lab. 5,169
Toby Horton, UKIP 2,502
John Clark, Lib. 1,418
C. majority 11,281 (29.58%)
Notional 1.75% swing C. to LD
(2005: C. majority 14,117 (28.50%))

§THORNBURY & YATE
E. 64,092 T. 48,226 (75.24%) LD hold
Steve Webb, LD 25,032
Matthew Riddle, C. 17,916
Roxanne Egan, Lab. 3,385
Jenny Knight, UKIP 1,709
Thomas Beacham, Ind. Fed. 126
Anthony Clements, ND 58
LD majority 7,116 (14.76%)
Notional 4.35% swing LD to C.
(2005: LD majority 11,060 (23.45%))

§THURROCK
E. 92,390 T. 45,821 (49.60%) C. gain
*Jackie Doyle-Price, C. 16,869
Carl Morris, Lab. 16,777
Carys Davis, LD 4,901
Emma Colgate, BNP 3,618
Clive Broad, UKIP 3,390
Arinola Araba, Ch. P. 266
C. majority 92 (0.20%)
Notional 6.61% swing Lab. to C.
(2005: Lab. majority 5,358 (13.02%))

§TIVERTON & HONITON
E. 76,810 T. 54,894 (71.47%) C. hold
*Neil Parish, C. 27,614
Jon Underwood, LD 18,294
Vernon Whitlock, Lab. 4,907
Daryl Stanbury, UKIP 3,277
Cathy Connor, Green 802
C. majority 9,320 (16.98%)
Notional 0.28% swing C. to LD
(2005: C. majority 9,007 (17.55%))

TONBRIDGE & MALLING
E. 71,790 T. 51,314 (71.48%) C. hold
Sir John Stanley, C. 29,723
Elizabeth Simpson, LD 11,545
Daniel Griffiths, Lab. 6,476
David Waller, UKIP 1,911
Steve Dawe, Green 764
Mike Easter, NF 505
Lisa Rogers, Eng. Dem. 390
C. majority 18,178 (35.43%)
1.02% swing LD to C.
(2005: C. majority 13,352 (28.99%))

§TOOTING
E. 73,836 T. 50,655 (68.60%) Lab. hold
Sadiq Khan, Lab. 22,038
Mark Clarke, C. 19,514
Nasser Butt, LD 7,509
Strachan McDonald, UKIP 624
Roy Vickery, Green 609
Susan John-Richards, Ind. 190
Shereen Paul, Ch. P. 171
Lab. majority 2,524 (4.98%)
Notional 3.60% swing Lab. to C.
(2005: Lab. majority 5,169 (12.17%))

§TORBAY
E. 76,151 T. 49,210 (64.62%) LD hold
Adrian Sanders, LD 23,126
Marcus Wood, C. 19,048
David Pedrick-Friend, Lab. 3,231
Julien Parrott, UKIP 2,628
Ann Conway, BNP 709
Sam Moss, Green 468
LD majority 4,078 (8.29%)
Notional 1.14% swing C. to LD
(2005: LD majority 2,727 (6.01%))

§TOTNES
E. 67,937 T. 47,843 (70.42%) C. hold
*Dr Sarah Wollaston, C. 21,940
Julian Brazil, LD 17,013
Carole Whitty, Lab. 3,538
Jeff Beer, UKIP 2,890
Lydia Somerville, Green 1,181
Mike Turner, BNP 624
Simon Drew, Ind. 390
Dr Stephen Hopwood, Ind. 267
C. majority 4,927 (10.30%)
Notional 2.27% swing LD to C.
(2005: C. majority 2,693 (5.76%))

TOTTENHAM
E. 69,933 T. 40,687 (58.18%) Lab. hold
David Lammy, Lab. 24,128
David Schmitz, LD 7,197
Sean Sullivan, C. 6,064
Jenny Sutton, TUSC 1,057
Anne Gray, Green 980
Winston McKenzie, UKIP 466
Neville Watson, Ind. People 265
Abimbola Kadara, Ch. P. 262
Sheik Thompson, Ind. 143
Errol Carr, Ind. 125
Lab. majority 16,931 (41.61%)
0.22% swing LD to Lab.
(2005: Lab. majority 13,034 (41.16%))

§TRURO & FALMOUTH
E. 70,598 T. 48,768 (69.08%) C. gain
*Sarah Newton, C. 20,349
Terrye Teverson, LD 19,914
Charlotte Mackenzie, Lab. 4,697
Harry Blakeley, UKIP 1,911
Loic Rich, Meb. Ker. 1,039
Ian Wright, Green 858
C. majority 435 (0.89%)
Notional 5.07% swing LD to C.
(2005: LD majority 3,931 (9.25%))

§TUNBRIDGE WELLS
E. 72,042 T. 50,320 (69.85%) C. hold
Greg Clark, C. 28,302
David Hallas, LD 12,726
Gary Heather, Lab. 5,448
Victor Webb, UKIP 2,054
Hazel Dawe, Green 914
Andrew McBride, BNP 704
Farel Bradbury, Ind. 172
C. majority 15,576 (30.95%)
Notional 2.79% swing LD to C.
(2005: C. majority 11,572 (25.38%))

TWICKENHAM
E. 79,861 T. 59,721 (74.78%) LD hold
Vince Cable, LD 32,483
Deborah Thomas, C. 20,343
Brian Tomlinson, Lab. 4,583
Brian Gilbert, UKIP 868
Steve Roest, Green 674
Chris Hurst, BNP 654
Harry Cole, R and E 76
Paul Armstrong, Magna Carta 40
LD majority 12,140 (20.33%)
0.52% swing C. to LD
(2005: LD majority 9,965 (19.28%))

§TYNEMOUTH
E. 75,680 T. 52,668 (69.59%) Lab. hold
Alan Campbell, Lab. 23,860
Wendy Morton, C. 18,121
John Appleby, LD 7,845
Dorothy Brooke, BNP 1,404
Natasha Payne, UKIP 900
Julia Erskine, Green 538
Lab. majority 5,739 (10.90%)
Notional 0.38% swing Lab. to C.
(2005: Lab. majority 5,490 (11.65%))

§TYNESIDE NORTH
E. 77,690 T. 46,405 (59.73%) Lab. hold
*Mary Glindon, Lab. 23,505
David Ord, LD 10,621
Gagan Mohindra, C. 8,514
John Burrows, BNP 1,860
Claudia Blake, UKIP 1,306
Bob Batten, NF 599
Lab. majority 12,884 (27.76%)
Notional 4.81% swing Lab. to LD
(2005: Lab. majority 14,929 (37.38%))

§UXBRIDGE & RUISLIP SOUTH
E. 71,168 T. 45,076 (63.34%) C. hold
John Randall, C. 21,758
Sidharath Garg, Lab. 10,542
Michael Cox, LD 8,995
Dianne Neal, BNP 1,396
Mark Wadsworth, UKIP 1,234
Mike Harling, Green 477
Roger Cooper, Eng. Dem. 403
Francis Mcallister, NF 271
C. majority 11,216 (24.88%)
Notional 3.44% swing Lab. to C.
(2005: C. majority 7,178 (18.01%))

§VAUXHALL
E. 74,811 T. 43,191 (57.73%) Lab. hold
Kate Hoey, Lab. 21,498
Caroline Pidgeon, LD 10,847
Glyn Chambers, C. 9,301
Joseph Healy, Green 708
Jose Navarro, Eng. Dem. 289
Lana Martin, Ch. P. 200
Daniel Lambert, Soc. 143
Jeremy Drinkall, WP 109
James Kapetanos, APP 96
Lab. majority 10,651 (24.66%)
Notional 0.06% swing LD to Lab.
(2005: Lab. majority 8,503 (24.54%))

§WAKEFIELD
E. 70,834 T. 44,444 (62.74%) Lab. hold
Mary Creagh, Lab. 17,454
Alex Story, C. 15,841
David Smith, LD 7,256
Ian Senior, BNP 2,581
Miriam Hawkins, Green 873
Mark Harrop, Ind. 439
Lab. majority 1,613 (3.63%)
Notional 6.94% swing Lab. to C.
(2005: Lab. majority 7,349 (17.50%))

§WALLASEY
E. 65,915 T. 41,654 (63.19%) Lab. hold
Angela Eagle, Lab. 21,578
Leah Fraser, C. 13,071
Steve Pitt, LD 5,693
Derek Snowden, UKIP 1,205
Emmanuel Mwaba, Ind. 107
Lab. majority 8,507 (20.42%)
Notional 1.78% swing Lab. to C.
(2005: Lab. majority 9,130 (23.98%))

§WALSALL NORTH
E. 65,183 T. 36,187 (55.52%) Lab. hold
David Winnick, Lab. 13,385
Helyn Clack, C. 12,395
Nadia Fazal, LD 4,754
Christopher Woodall, BNP 2,930
Elizabeth Hazell, UKIP 1,737
Peter Smith, Dem. Lab. 842
Babar Shakir, Ch. P. 144
Lab. majority 990 (2.74%)
Notional 9.03% swing Lab. to C.
(2005: Lab. majority 6,901 (20.79%))

§WALSALL SOUTH
E. 64,830 T. 40,882 (63.06%) Lab. hold
*Valerie Vaz, Lab. 16,211
Richard Hunt, C. 14,456
Dr Murli Sinha, LD 5,880
Derek Bennett, UKIP 3,449
Gulzaman Khan, Ch. P. 482
Mohammed Mulia, ND 404
Lab. majority 1,755 (4.29%)
Notional 8.24% swing Lab. to C.
(2005: Lab. majority 7,910 (20.77%))

WALTHAMSTOW
E. 64,625 T. 40,994 (63.43%) Lab. hold
*Stella Creasy, Lab. 21,252
Farid Ahmed, LD 11,774
Andy Hemsted, C. 5,734
Judith Chisholm-Benli, UKIP 823
Daniel Perrett, Green 767
Nancy Taaffe, TUSC 279
Ashar Mall, Ch. P. 248
Paul Warburton, Ind. 117
Lab. majority 9,478 (23.12%)
0.04% swing Lab. to LD
(2005: Lab. majority 7,993 (23.21%))

WANSBECK
E. 63,045 T. 38,273 (60.71%) Lab. hold
*Ian Lavery, Lab. 17,548
Simon Reed, LD 10,517
Campbell Storey, C. 6,714
Stephen Finlay, BNP 1,418
Linda Lee-Stokoe, UKIP 974
Nic Best, Green 601
Malcolm Reid, Ind. 359
Michael Flynn, Ch. P. 142
Lab. majority 7,031 (18.37%)
5.19% swing Lab. to LD
(2005: Lab. majority 10,581 (28.75%))

§WANTAGE
E. 80,456 T. 56,341 (70.03%) C. hold
Ed Vaizey, C. 29,284
Alan Armitage, LD 15,737
Steven Mitchell, Lab. 7,855
Jacqueline Jones, UKIP 2,421
Adam Twine, Green 1,044
C. majority 13,547 (24.04%)
Notional 4.30% swing LD to C.
(2005: C. majority 8,039 (15.44%))

§WARLEY
E. 63,106 T. 38,270 (60.64%) Lab. hold
John Spellar, Lab. 20,240
Jasbir Parmar, C. 9,484
Edward Keating, LD 5,929
Nigel Harvey, UKIP 2,617
Lab. majority 10,756 (28.11%)
Notional 1.94% swing Lab. to C.
(2005: Lab. majority 11,206 (31.99%))

§WARRINGTON NORTH
E. 71,601 T. 44,211 (61.75%) Lab. hold
Helen Jones, Lab. 20,135
Paul Campbell, C. 13,364
David Eccles, LD 9,196
Albert Scott, Ind. 1,516
Lab. majority 6,771 (15.32%)
Notional 6.61% swing Lab. to C.
(2005: Lab. majority 11,382 (28.53%))

§WARRINGTON SOUTH
E. 80,506 T. 54,874 (68.16%) C. gain
*David Mowat, C. 19,641
Nick Bent, Lab. 18,088
Jo Crotty, LD 15,094
James Ashington, UKIP 1,624
Steph Davies, Green 427
C. majority 1,553 (2.83%)
Notional 6.00% swing Lab. to C.
(2005: Lab. majority 4,337 (9.17%))

§WARWICK & LEAMINGTON
E. 58,030 T. 49,032 (84.49%) C. gain
*Chris White, C. 20,876
James Plaskitt, Lab. 17,363
Alan Beddow, LD 8,977
Christopher Lenton, UKIP 926
Ian Davison, Green 693
Jim Cullinane, Ind. 197
C. majority 3,513 (7.16%)
Notional 8.76% swing Lab. to C.
(2005: Lab. majority 4,393 (10.35%))

§WARWICKSHIRE NORTH
E. 70,143 T. 47,265 (67.38%) C. gain
*Dan Byles, C. 18,993
Mike O'Brien, Lab. 18,939
Stephen Martin, LD 5,481
Jason Holmes, BNP 2,106
Steven Fowler, UKIP 1,335
David Lane, Eng. Dem. 411
C. majority 54 (0.11%)
Notional 7.69% swing Lab. to C.
(2005: Lab. majority 6,684 (15.27%))

§WASHINGTON & SUNDERLAND WEST
E. 68,910 T. 37,334 (54.18%) Lab. hold
Sharon Hodgson, Lab. 19,615
Ian Cuthbert, C. 8,157
Peter Andras, LD 6,382
Ian McDonald, BNP 1,913
Linda Hudson, UKIP 1,267
Lab. majority 11,458 (30.69%)
Notional 11.56% swing Lab. to C.
(2005: Lab. majority 17,060 (52.56%))

§WATFORD
E. 80,798 T. 55,208 (68.33%) C. gain
*Richard Harrington, C. 19,291
Sal Brinton, LD 17,866
Claire Ward, Lab. 14,750
Andrew Emerson, BNP 1,217
Graham Eardley, UKIP 1,199
Ian Brandon, Green 885
C. majority 1,425 (2.58%)
Notional 6.08% swing Lab. to C.
(2005: Lab. majority 1,151 (2.33%))

§WAVENEY
E. 78,532 T. 51,141 (65.12%) C. gain
*Peter Aldous, C. 20,571
Bob Blizzard, Lab. 19,802
Alan Dean, LD 6,811
Jack Tyler, UKIP 2,684
Graham Elliott, Green 1,167
Louis Barfe, Ind. 106
C. majority 769 (1.50%)
Notional 6.75% swing Lab. to C.
(2005: Lab. majority 5,950 (12.00%))

§WEALDEN
E. 76,537 T. 54,969 (71.82%) C. hold
Charles Hendry, C. 31,090
Chris Bowers, LD 13,911
Lorna Blackmore, Lab. 5,266
Dan Docker, UKIP 3,319
David Jonas, Green 1,383
C. majority 17,179 (31.25%)
Notional 2.79% swing LD to C.
(2005: C. majority 12,812 (25.66%))

§WEAVER VALE
E. 66,538 T. 43,990 (66.11%) C. gain
*Graham Evans, C. 16,953
John Stockton, Lab. 15,962
Peter Hampson, LD 8,196
Colin Marsh, BNP 1,063
Paul Remfry, UKIP 1,018
Howard Thorp, Green 338
Mike Cooksley, Ind. 270
Tom Reynolds, Ind. 133
Will Charlton, Ind. 57
C. majority 991 (2.25%)
Notional 8.14% swing Lab. to C.
(2005: Lab. majority 5,277 (14.03%))

§WELLINGBOROUGH
E. 76,857 T. 51,661 (67.22%) C. hold
Peter Bone, C. 24,918
Jayne Buckland, Lab. 13,131
Kevin Barron, LD 8,848
Adrian Haynes, UKIP 1,636
Rob Walker, BNP 1,596
Terry Spencer, Eng. Dem. 530
Jonathan Hornett, Green 480
Paul Crofts, TUSC 249
Gary Donaldson, Ind. 240
Marcus Lavin, Ind. 33
C. majority 11,787 (22.82%)
Notional 10.78% swing Lab. to C.
(2005: C. majority 610 (1.25%))

WELLS
E. 79,432 T. 55,864 (70.33%) LD gain
*Tessa Munt, LD 24,560
David Heathcoat-Amory, C. 23,760
Andy Merryfield, Lab. 4,198
Jake Baynes, UKIP 1,711
Richard Boyce, BNP 1,004
Chris Briton, Green 631
LD majority 800 (1.43%)
3.59% swing C. to LD
(2005: C. majority 3,040 (5.74%))

WELWYN HATFIELD
E. 72,058 T. 48,972 (67.96%) C. hold
Grant Shapps, C. 27,894
Mike Hobday, Lab. 10,471
Paul Zukowskyj, LD 8,010
David Platt, UKIP 1,643
Jill Weston, Green 796
Nigel Parker, Ind. 158
C. majority 17,423 (35.58%)
11.14% swing Lab. to C.
(2005: C. majority 5,946 (13.30%))

§WENTWORTH & DEARNE
E. 72,586 T. 42,106 (58.01%) Lab. hold
John Healey, Lab. 21,316
Michelle Donelan, C. 7,396
Nick Love, LD 6,787
John Wilkinson, UKIP 3,418
George Baldwin, BNP 3,189
Lab. majority 13,920 (33.06%)
Notional 7.49% swing Lab. to C.
(2005: Lab. majority 17,551 (45.55%))

§WEST BROMWICH EAST
E. 62,824 T. 37,950 (60.41%) Lab. hold
Tom Watson, Lab. 17,657
Alistair Thompson, C. 10,961
Ian Garrett, LD 4,993
Terry Lewin, BNP 2,205
Mark Cowles, Eng. Dem. 1,150
Steve Grey, UKIP 984
Lab. majority 6,696 (17.64%)
Notional 7.68% swing Lab. to C.
(2005: Lab. majority 11,947 (33.00%))

§WEST BROMWICH WEST
E. 65,013 T. 36,171 (55.64%) Lab. hold
Adrian Bailey, Lab. 16,263
Andrew Hardie, C. 10,612
Sadie Smith, LD 4,336
Russ Green, BNP 3,394
Mac Ford, UKIP 1,566
Lab. majority 5,651 (15.62%)
Notional 7.64% swing Lab. to C.
(2005: Lab. majority 9,821 (30.90%))

§WEST HAM
E. 85,313 T. 46,951 (55.03%) Lab. hold
Lyn Brown, Lab. 29,422
Virginia Morris, C. 6,888
Martin Pierce, LD 5,392
Stan Gain, CPA 1,327
Kamran Malik, Ind. 1,245
Michael Davidson, NF 1,089
Kim Gandy, UKIP 766
Jane Lithgow, Green 645
Grace Agbogun-Toko, Ind. 177
Lab. majority 22,534 (47.99%)
Notional 4.16% swing C. to Lab.
(2005: Lab. majority 12,274 (31.76%))

§WESTMINSTER NORTH
E. 66,739 T. 39,598 (59.33%) Lab. hold
Karen Buck, Lab. 17,377
Joanne Cash, C. 15,251
Mark Blackburn, LD 5,513
Tristan Smith, Green 478
Stephen Curry, BNP 334
Jasna Badzak, UKIP 315
Dr Ali Bahaijoub, Ind. 101
Edward Roseman, Eng. Dem. 99
Gabriela Fajardo, Ch. P. 98
Abby Dharamsey, Ind. 32
Lab. majority 2,126 (5.37%)
Notional 0.61% swing Lab. to C.
(2005: Lab. majority 2,120 (6.59%))

§WESTMORLAND & LONSDALE
E. 67,881 T. 51,487 (75.85%) LD hold
Tim Farron, LD 30,896
Gareth McKeever, C. 18,632
Jonathan Todd, Lab. 1,158
John Mander, UKIP 801
LD majority 12,264 (23.82%)
Notional 11.06% swing C. to LD
(2005: LD majority 806 (1.70%))

§WESTON-SUPER-MARE
E. 78,487 T. 52,716 (67.17%) C. hold
John Penrose, C. 23,356
Mike Bell, LD 20,665
David Bradley, Lab. 5,772
Paul Spencer, UKIP 1,406
Peryn Parsons, BNP 1,098
John Peverelle, Eng. Dem. 275
Steve Satch, Ind. 144
C. majority 2,691 (5.10%)
Notional 0.42% swing LD to C.
(2005: C. majority 2,088 (4.26%))

§WIGAN
E. 75,564 T. 44,140 (58.41%) Lab. hold
*Lisa Nandy, Lab. 21,404
Michael Winstanley, C. 10,917
Mark Clayton, LD 6,797
Alan Freeman, UKIP 2,516
Charles Mather, BNP 2,506
Lab. majority 10,487 (23.76%)
Notional 7.69% swing Lab. to C.
(2005: Lab. majority 15,501 (39.15%))

§WILTSHIRE NORTH
E. 66,313 T. 48,699 (73.44%) C. hold
James Gray, C. 25,114
Mike Evemy, LD 17,631
Jason Hughes, Lab. 3,239
Charles Bennett, UKIP 1,908
Phil Chamberlain, Green 599
Philip Allnatt, Ind. 208
C. majority 7,483 (15.37%)
Notional 0.01% swing LD to C.
(2005: C. majority 6,888 (15.34%))

§WILTSHIRE SOUTH WEST
E. 71,645 T. 49,018 (68.42%) C. hold
Andrew Murrison, C. 25,321
Trevor Carbin, LD 14,954
Rebecca Rennison, Lab. 5,613
Michael Cuthbert-Murray, UKIP 2,684
Crispin Black, Ind. 446
C. majority 10,367 (21.15%)
Notional 1.15% swing LD to C.
(2005: C. majority 8,568 (18.85%))

§WIMBLEDON
E. 65,723 T. 47,395 (72.11%) C. hold
Stephen Hammond, C. 23,257
Shas Sheehan, LD 11,849
Andrew Judge, Lab. 10,550
Mark McAleer, UKIP 914
Rajeev Thacker, Green 590
David Martin, Ch. P. 235
C. majority 11,408 (24.07%)
Notional 0.42% swing LD to C.
(2005: C. majority 2,480 (5.69%))

§WINCHESTER
E. 73,806 T. 55,955 (75.81%) C. gain
*Steve Brine, C. 27,155
Martin Tod, LD 24,107
Patrick Davies, Lab. 3,051
Jocelyn Penn-Bull, UKIP 1,139
Mark Lancaster, Eng. Dem. 503
C. majority 3,048 (5.45%)
Notional 9.09% swing LD to C.
(2005: LD majority 6,524 (12.74%))

§WINDSOR
E. 69,511 T. 49,588 (71.34%) C. hold
Adam Afriyie, C. 30,172
Julian Tisi, LD 11,118
Amanjit Jhund, Lab. 4,910
John-Paul Rye, UKIP 1,612
Peter Phillips, BNP 950
Derek Wall, Green 628
Peter Hooper, Ind. 198
C. majority 19,054 (38.42%)
Notional 8.05% swing LD to C.
(2005: C. majority 9,605 (22.32%))

§WIRRAL SOUTH
E. 56,099 T. 39,906 (71.13%) Lab. hold
*Alison McGovern, Lab. 16,276
Jeff Clarke, C. 15,745
Jamie Saddler, LD 6,611
David Scott, UKIP 1,274
Lab. majority 531 (1.33%)
Notional 3.98% swing Lab. to C.
(2005: Lab. majority 3,538 (9.30%))

§WIRRAL WEST
E. 55,050 T. 39,372 (71.52%) C. hold
*Esther McVey, C. 16,726
Phillip Davies, Lab. 14,290
Peter Reisdorf, LD 6,630
Philip Griffiths, UKIP 899
David Kirwan, Ind. 506
David James, CSP 321
C. majority 2,436 (6.19%)
Notional 2.34% swing Lab. to C.
(2005: C. majority 569 (1.51%))

§WITHAM
E. 66,750 T. 46,835 (70.16%) C. hold
*Priti Patel, C. 24,448
Margaret Phelps, LD 9,252
John Spademan, Lab. 8,656
David Hodges, UKIP 3,060
James Abbott, Green 1,419
C. majority 15,196 (32.45%)
Notional 1.06% swing C. to LD
(2005: C. majority 7,241 (17.29%))

§WITNEY
E. 78,766 T. 57,769 (73.34%) C. hold
David Cameron, C. 33,973
Dawn Barnes, LD 11,233
Joe Goldberg, Lab. 7,511
Stuart Macdonald, Green 2,385
Nikolai Tolstoy, UKIP 2,001
Howling Hope, Loony 234
Paul Wesson, Ind. 166
Johnnie Cook, Ind. 151
Colin Bex, Wessex Reg. 62
Aaron Barschak, Ind. 53
C. majority 22,740 (39.36%)
Notional 6.29% swing LD to C.
(2005: C. majority 13,874 (26.78%))

WOKING
E. 73,838 T. 52,786 (71.49%) C. hold
*Jonathan Lord, C. 26,551
Rosie Sharpley, LD 19,744
Tom Miller, Lab. 4,246
Rob Burberry, UKIP 1,997
Julie Roxburgh, PPN-V 204
Ruth Temple, Magna Carta 44
C. majority 6,807 (12.90%)
0.73% swing C. to LD
(2005: C. majority 6,612 (14.36%))

§WOKINGHAM
E. 76,219 T. 54,528 (71.54%) C. hold
John Redwood, C. 28,754
Prue Bray, LD 15,262
George Davidson, Lab. 5,516
Mark Ashwell, Ind. 2,340
Ann Zebedee, UKIP 1,664
Marjory Bisset, Green 567
Top Cat Owen, Loony 329
Robin Smith, Ind. 96
C. majority 13,492 (24.74%)
Notional 4.65% swing LD to C.
(2005: C. majority 7,257 (15.44%))

§WOLVERHAMPTON NORTH EAST
E. 59,324 T. 34,894 (58.82%) Lab. hold
*Emma Reynolds, Lab. 14,448
Julie Rook, C. 11,964
Colin Ross, LD 4,711
Simon Patten, BNP 2,296
Paul Valdmanis, UKIP 1,138
Shangara Bhatoe, Soc. Lab. 337
Lab. majority 2,484 (7.12%)
Notional 9.00% swing Lab. to C.
(2005: Lab. majority 8,628 (25.12%))

§WOLVERHAMPTON SOUTH EAST
E. 60,450 T. 34,707 (57.41%) Lab. hold
Pat McFadden, Lab. 16,505
Ken Wood, C. 9,912
Richard Whitehouse, LD 5,277
Gordon Fanthom, UKIP 2,675
Sudhir Handa, Ind. 338
Lab. majority 6,593 (19.00%)
Notional 8.79% swing Lab. to C.
(2005: Lab. majority 12,309 (36.58%))

§WOLVERHAMPTON SOUTH WEST
E. 59,160 T. 40,160 (67.88%) C. gain
*Paul Uppal, C. 16,344
Rob Marris, Lab. 15,653
Robin Lawrence, LD 6,430
Amanda Mobberley, UKIP 1,487
Raymond Barry, Parenting 246
C. majority 691 (1.72%)
Notional 3.52% swing Lab. to C.
(2005: Lab. majority 2,114 (5.31%))

WORCESTER
E. 72,831 T. 48,974 (67.24%) C. gain
*Robin Walker, C. 19,358
Michael Foster, Lab. 16,376
Jackie Alderson, LD 9,525
Jack Bennett, UKIP 1,360
Spencer Lee Kirby, BNP 1,219
Louis Stephen, Green 735
Andrew Robinson, Pirate 173
Peter Nielsen, Ind. 129
Andrew Christian-Brookes, Ind. 99
C. majority 2,982 (6.09%)
6.43% swing Lab. to C.
(2005: Lab. majority 3,144 (6.78%))

§WORCESTERSHIRE MID
E. 72,171 T. 50,931 (70.57%) C. hold
Peter Luff, C. 27,770
Margaret Rowley, LD 11,906
Robin Lunn, Lab. 7,613
John White, UKIP 3,049
Gordon Matthews, Green 593
C. majority 15,864 (31.15%)
Notional 0.04% swing LD to C.
(2005: C. majority 12,906 (27.33%))

§WORCESTERSHIRE WEST
E. 73,270 T. 54,093 (73.83%) C. hold
*Harriett Baldwin, C. 27,213
Richard Burt, LD 20,459
Penelope Barber, Lab. 3,661
Caroline Bovey, UKIP 2,119
Malcolm Victory, Green 641
C. majority 6,754 (12.49%)
Notional 3.23% swing LD to C.
(2005: C. majority 3,053 (6.03%))

§WORKINGTON
E. 59,607 T. 39,259 (65.86%) Lab. hold
Tony Cunningham, Lab. 17,865
Judith Pattinson, C. 13,290
Stan Collins, LD 5,318
Martin Wingfield, BNP 1,496
Stephen Lee, UKIP 876
Rob Logan, Eng. Dem. 414
Lab. majority 4,575 (11.65%)
Notional 5.66% swing Lab. to C.
(2005: Lab. majority 8,226 (22.97%))

§WORSLEY & ECCLES SOUTH
E. 72,473 T. 41,701 (57.54%) Lab. hold
Barbara Keeley, Lab. 17,892
Iain Lindley, C. 13,555
Richard Gadsden, LD 6,883
Andrew Townsend, UKIP 2,037
Paul Whitelegg, Eng. Dem. 1,334
Lab. majority 4,337 (10.40%)
Notional 7.61% swing Lab. to C.
(2005: Lab. majority 10,001 (25.62%))

§WORTHING EAST & SHOREHAM
E. 74,001 T. 48,397 (65.40%) C. hold
Tim Loughton, C. 23,458
James Doyle, LD 12,353
Emily Benn, Lab. 8,087
Mike Glennon, UKIP 2,984
Susan Board, Green 1,126
Clive Maltby, Eng. Dem. 389
C. majority 11,105 (22.95%)
Notional 1.70% swing LD to C.
(2005: C. majority 8,180 (18.37%))

§WORTHING WEST
E. 75,945 T. 49,123 (64.68%) C. hold
Peter Bottomley, C. 25,416
Hazel Thorpe, LD 13,687
Ian Ross, Lab. 5,800
John Wallace, UKIP 2,924
David Aherne, Green 996
Stuart Dearsley, Christian 300
C. majority 11,729 (23.88%)
Notional 1.50% swing LD to C.
(2005: C. majority 9,383 (20.89%))

§WREKIN, THE
E. 65,544 T. 45,968 (70.13%) C. hold
Mark Pritchard, C. 21,922
Paul Kalinauckas, Lab. (Co-op) 12,472
Ali Cameron-Daw, LD 8,019
Malcolm Hurst, UKIP 2,050
Susan Harwood, BNP 1,505
C. majority 9,450 (20.56%)
Notional 8.85% swing Lab. (Co-op) to C.
(2005: C. majority 1,187 (2.85%))

§WYCOMBE
E. 74,502 T. 48,151 (64.63%) C. hold
*Steven Baker, C. 23,423
Steve Guy, LD 13,863
Andrew Lomas, Lab. 8,326
John Wiseman, UKIP 2,123
Madassar Khokar, Ind. 228
David Fitton, Ind. 188
C. majority 9,560 (19.85%)
Notional 4.83% swing C. to LD
(2005: C. majority 7,597 (17.29%))

§WYRE & PRESTON NORTH
E. 71,201 T. 51,308 (72.06%) C. hold
*Ben Wallace, C. 26,877
Danny Gallagher, LD 11,033
Cat Smith, Lab. 10,932
Nigel Cecil, UKIP 2,466
C. majority 15,844 (30.88%)
Notional 3.86% swing C. to LD
(2005: C. majority 12,082 (27.51%))

§WYRE FOREST
E. 76,711 T. 50,899 (66.35%) C. gain
*Mark Garnier, C. 18,793
Dr Richard Taylor, Ind. CHC 16,150
Nigel Knowles, Lab. 7,298
Neville Farmer, LD 6,040
Michael Wrench, UKIP 1,498
Gordon Howells, BNP 1,120
C. majority 2,643 (5.19%)
Notional 7.35% swing Ind. CHC to C.
(2005: Ind. CHC majority 4,613 (9.51%))

WYTHENSHAWE & SALE EAST
E. 79,923 T. 40,751 (50.99%) Lab. hold
Paul Goggins, Lab. 17,987
Janet Clowes, C. 10,412
Martin Eakins, LD 9,107
Bernard Todd, BNP 1,572
Chris Cassidy, UKIP 1,405
Lynn Worthington, TUSC 268
Lab. majority 7,575 (18.59%)
5.67% swing Lab. to C.
(2005: Lab. majority 10,827 (29.92%))

§YEOVIL
E. 82,314 T. 57,160 (69.44%) LD hold
David Laws, LD 31,843
Kevin Davis, C. 18,807
Lee Skevington, Lab. 2,991
Nigel Pearson, UKIP 2,357
Robert Baehr, BNP 1,162
LD majority 13,036 (22.81%)
Notional 2.74% swing C. to LD
(2005: LD majority 8,779 (17.33%))

§YORK CENTRAL
E. 74,908 T. 46,483 (62.05%) Lab. hold
Hugh Bayley, Lab. 18,573
Susan Wade Weeks, C. 12,122
Christian Vassie, LD 11,694
Andy Chase, Green 1,669
Jeff Kelly, BNP 1,171
Paul Abbott, UKIP 1,100
Eddie Vee, Loony 154
Lab. majority 6,451 (13.88%)
Notional 6.02% swing Lab. to C.
(2005: Lab. majority 10,344 (25.92%))

§YORK OUTER
E. 74,965 T. 53,300 (71.10%) C. gain
*Julian Sturdy, C. 22,912
Madeleine Kirk, LD 19,224
James Alexander, Lab. 9,108
Judith Morris, UKIP 1,100
Cathy Smurthwaite, BNP 956
C. majority 3,688 (6.92%)
Notional 3.68% swing LD to C.
(2005: LD majority 203 (0.44%))

§YORKSHIRE EAST
E. 80,342 T. 51,254 (63.79%) C. hold
Greg Knight, C. 24,328
Robert Adamson, LD 10,842
Paul Rounding, Lab. 10,401
Chris Daniels, UKIP 2,142
Gary Pudsey, BNP 1,865
Ray Allerston, Soc. Dem. 914
Michael Jackson, Green 762
C. majority 13,486 (26.31%)
Notional 0.06% swing C. to LD
(2005: C. majority 6,284 (13.31%))

WALES

ABERAVON
E. 50,789 T. 30,958 (60.95%) Lab. hold
Hywel Francis, Lab. 16,073
Keith Davies, LD 5,034
Caroline Jones, C. 4,411
Paul Nicholls-Jones, PC 2,198
Kevin Edwards, BNP 1,276
Andrew Tutton, Ind. 919
Captain Beany, Bean 558
Joe Callan, UKIP 489
Lab. majority 11,039 (35.66%)
5.32% swing Lab. to LD
(2005: Lab. majority 13,937 (46.30%))

§ABERCONWY
E. 44,593 T. 29,966 (67.20%) C. gain
*Guto Bebb, C. 10,734
Ronald Hughes, Lab. 7,336
Mike Priestley, LD 5,786
Phil Edwards, PC 5,341
Mike Wieteska, UKIP 632
Louise Wynne-Jones, Ch. P. 137
C. majority 3,398 (11.34%)
Notional 7.63% swing Lab. to C.
(2005: Lab. majority 1,070 (3.93%))

ALYN & DEESIDE
E. 60,931 T. 39,923 (65.52%) Lab. hold
Mark Tami, Lab. 15,804
Will Gallagher, C. 12,885
Paul Brighton, LD 7,308
Maurice Jones, PC 1,549
John Walker, BNP 1,368
James Howson, UKIP 1,009
Lab. majority 2,919 (7.31%)
8.15% swing Lab. to C.
(2005: Lab. majority 8,378 (23.60%))

§ARFON
E. 41,198 T. 26,078 (63.30%) PC gain
Hywel Williams, PC 9,383
Alan Pugh, Lab. 7,928
Robin Millar, C. 4,416
Sarah Green, LD 3,666
Elwyn Williams, UKIP 685
PC majority 1,455 (5.58%)
Notional 3.70% swing Lab. to PC
(2005: Lab. majority 456 (1.82%))

BLAENAU GWENT
E. 52,438 T. 32,395 (61.78%) Lab. gain
*Nick Smith, Lab. 16,974
Dai Davies, Blaenau Voice 6,458
Matt Smith, LD 3,285
Liz Stevenson, C. 2,265
Rhodri Davies, PC 1,333
Anthony King, BNP 1,211
Mike Kocan, UKIP 488
Alyson O'Connell, Soc. Lab. 381
Lab. majority 10,516 (32.46%)
(2005: Ind. Law majority 9,121 (25.87%))(2006: Ind. Davies majority 2,484 (9.14%))

BRECON & RADNORSHIRE
E. 53,589 T. 38,845 (72.49%) LD hold
Roger Williams, LD 17,929
Suzy Davies, C. 14,182
Christopher Lloyd, Lab. 4,096
Janet Davies, PC 989
Clive Easton, UKIP 876
Dorienne Robinson, Green 341
Jeffrey Green, Ch. P. 222
Lord Offa, Loony 210
LD majority 3,747 (9.65%)
0.27% swing LD to C.
(2005: LD majority 3,905 (10.18%))

§BRIDGEND
E. 58,700 T. 38,347 (65.33%) Lab. hold
Madeleine Moon, Lab. 13,931
Helen Baker, C. 11,668
Wayne Morgan, LD 8,658
Nick Thomas, PC 2,269
Brian Urch, BNP 1,020
David Fulton, UKIP 801
Lab. majority 2,263 (5.90%)
Notional 5.98% swing Lab. to C.
(2005: Lab. majority 6,089 (17.87%))

§CAERPHILLY
E. 62,134 T. 38,992 (62.75%) Lab. hold
Wayne David, Lab. 17,377
Maria Caulfield, C. 6,622
Lindsay Whittle, PC 6,460
Kay David, LD 5,988
Laurence Reid, BNP 1,635
Tony Jenkins, UKIP 910
Lab. majority 10,755 (27.58%)
Notional 6.57% swing Lab. to C.
(2005: Lab. majority 13,517 (37.32%))

CARDIFF CENTRAL
E. 61,162 T. 36,151 (59.11%) LD hold
Jenny Willott, LD 14,976
Jenny Rathbone, Lab. 10,400
Karen Robson, C. 7,799
Chris Williams, PC 1,246
Susan Davies, UKIP 765
Sam Coates, Green 575
Ross Saunders, TUSC 162
Mark Beech, Loony 142
Alun Mathias, Ind. 86
LD majority 4,576 (12.66%)
1.41% swing LD to Lab.
(2005: LD majority 5,593 (15.48%))

CARDIFF NORTH
E. 65,553 T. 47,630 (72.66%) C. gain
*Jonathan Evans, C. 17,860
Julie Morgan, Lab. 17,666
John Dixon, LD 8,724
Llywelyn Rhys, PC 1,588
Lawrence Gwynn, UKIP 1,130
Christopher von Ruhland, Green 362
Derek Thomson, Ch. P. 300
C. majority 194 (0.41%)
1.47% swing Lab. to C.
(2005: Lab. majority 1,146 (2.53%))

§CARDIFF SOUTH & PENARTH
E. 73,704 T. 44,370 (60.20%)
Lab. (Co-op) hold
Alun Michael, Lab. (Co-op) 17,263
Simon Hoare, C. 12,553
Dominic Hannigan, LD 9,875
Farida Aslam, PC 1,851
Simon Zeigler, UKIP 1,145
George Burke, Ind. 648
Matt Townsend, Green 554
Clive Bate, Ch. P. 285
Robert Griffiths, Comm 196
Lab. (Co-op) majority 4,710 (10.62%)
Notional 6.03% swing Lab. (Co-op) to C.
(2005: Lab. (Co-op) majority 8,955 (22.68%))

§CARDIFF WEST
E. 62,787 T. 40,957 (65.23%) Lab. hold
Kevin Brennan, Lab. 16,893
Angela Jones-Evans, C. 12,143
Rachael Hitchinson, LD 7,186
Mohammed Sarul Islam, PC 2,868
Mike Henessey, UKIP 1,117
Jake Griffiths, Green 750
Lab. majority 4,750 (11.60%)
Notional 5.33% swing Lab. to C.
(2005: Lab. majority 8,361 (22.25%))

§CARMARTHEN EAST & DINEFWR
E. 52,385 T. 38,011 (72.56%) PC hold
*Jonathan Edwards, PC 13,546
Christine Gwyther, Lab. 10,065
Andrew Morgan, C. 8,506
Bill Powell, LD 4,609
John Atkinson, UKIP 1,285
PC majority 3,481 (9.16%)
Notional 4.19% swing PC to Lab.
(2005: PC majority 6,551 (17.54%))

§CARMARTHEN WEST & PEMBROKESHIRE SOUTH
E. 57,519 T. 40,507 (70.42%) C. gain
*Simon Hart, C. 16,649
Nick Ainger, Lab. 13,226
John Gossage, LD 4,890
John Dixon, PC 4,232
Ray Clarke, UKIP 1,146
Henry Langen, Ind. 364
C. majority 3,423 (8.45%)
Notional 6.88% swing Lab. to C.
(2005: Lab. majority 2,043 (5.32%))

§CEREDIGION
E. 59,043 T. 38,258 (64.80%) LD hold
Mark Williams, LD 19,139
Penri James, PC 10,815
Luke Evetts, C. 4,421
Richard Boudier, Lab. 2,210
Elwyn Williams, UKIP 977
Leila Kiersch, Green 696
LD majority 8,324 (21.76%)
Notional 10.57% swing PC to LD
(2005: LD majority 218 (0.61%))

§CLWYD SOUTH
E. 53,748 T. 34,681 (64.53%) Lab. hold
*Susan Elan Jones, Lab. 13,311
John Bell, C. 10,477
Bruce Roberts, LD 5,965
Janet Ryder, PC 3,009
Sarah Hynes, BNP 1,100
Nick Powell, UKIP 819
Lab. majority 2,834 (8.17%)
Notional 5.83% swing Lab. to C.
(2005: Lab. majority 6,220 (19.84%))

§CLWYD WEST
E. 57,913 T. 38,111 (65.81%) C. hold
David Jones, C. 15,833
Donna Hutton, Lab. 9,414
Llyr Huws Gruffydd, PC 5,864
Michele Jones, LD 5,801
Warwick Nicholson, UKIP 864
Revd Dr David Griffiths, Ch. P. 239
Joe Blakesley, Ind. 96
C. majority 6,419 (16.84%)
Notional 8.35% swing Lab. to C.
(2005: C. majority 51 (0.14%))

§CYNON VALLEY
E. 50,656 T. 29,876 (58.98%) Lab. hold
Ann Clwyd, Lab. 15,681
Dafydd Trystan Davies, PC 6,064
Lee Thacker, LD 4,120
Juliette Ash, C. 3,010
Frank Hughes, UKIP 1,001
Lab. majority 9,617 (32.19%)
Notional 8.65% swing Lab. to PC
(2005: Lab. majority 14,390 (49.48%))

DELYN
E. 53,470 T. 36,984 (69.17%) Lab. hold
David Hanson, Lab. 15,083
Antoinette Sandbach, C. 12,811
Bill Brereton, LD 5,747
Peter Ryder, PC 1,844
Jennifer Matthys, BNP 844
Andrew Haigh, UKIP 655
Lab. majority 2,272 (6.14%)
6.70% swing Lab. to C.
(2005: Lab. majority 6,644 (19.54%))

§DWYFOR MEIRIONNYDD
E. 45,354 T. 28,906 (63.73%) PC hold
Elfyn Llwyd, PC 12,814
Simon Baynes, C. 6,447
Alwyn Humphreys, Lab. 4,021
Steve Churchman, LD 3,538
Louise Hughes, Ind. 1,310
Frank Wykes, UKIP 776
PC majority 6,367 (22.03%)
Notional 7.28% swing PC to C.
(2005: PC majority 8,706 (29.02%))

§GOWER
E. 61,696 T. 41,671 (67.54%) Lab. hold
Martin Caton, Lab. 16,016
Byron Davies, C. 13,333
Mike Day, LD 7,947
Darren Price, PC 2,760
Adrian Jones, BNP 963
Gordon Triggs, UKIP 652
Lab. majority 2,683 (6.44%)
Notional 5.26% swing Lab. to C.
(2005: Lab. majority 6,703 (16.95%))

§ISLWYN
E. 54,826 T. 34,690 (63.27%) Lab. (Co-op) hold
*Christopher Evans, Lab. (Co-op) 17,069
Daniel Thomas, C. 4,854
Steffan Lewis, PC 4,518
Asghar Ali, LD 3,597
Dave Rees, Ind. 1,495
John Voisey, BNP 1,320
Jason Crew, UKIP 936
Paul Taylor, Ind. 901
Lab. (Co-op) majority 12,215 (35.21%)
Notional 9.05% swing Lab. (Co-op) to C.
(2005: Lab. (Co-op) majority 17,582 (51.91%))

LLANELLI
E. 55,637 T. 37,461 (67.33%) Lab. hold
Nia Griffith, Lab. 15,916
Myfanwy Davies, PC 11,215
Christopher Salmon, C. 5,381
Myrddin Edwards, LD 3,902
Andrew Marshall, UKIP 1,047
Lab. majority 4,701 (12.55%)
3.96% swing Lab. to PC
(2005: Lab. majority 7,234 (20.47%))

MERTHYR TYDFIL & RHYMNEY
E. 54,715 T. 32,076 (58.62%) Lab. hold
Dai Havard, Lab. 14,007
Amy Kitcher, LD 9,951
Maria Hill, C. 2,412
Clive Tovey, Ind. 1,845
Glyndwr Cennydd Jones, PC 1,621
Richard Barnes, BNP 1,173
Adam Brown, UKIP 872
Alan Cowdell, Soc. Lab. 195
Lab. majority 4,056 (12.64%)
16.92% swing Lab. to LD
(2005: Lab. majority 13,934 (46.48%))

MONMOUTH
E. 62,768 T. 46,519 (74.11%) C. hold
David Davies, C. 22,466
Hamish Sandison, Lab. 12,041
Martin Blakebrough, LD 9,026
Jonathan Clark, PC 1,273
Derek Rowe, UKIP 1,126
Steve Millson, Green 587
C. majority 10,425 (22.41%)
6.25% swing Lab. to C.
(2005: C. majority 4,527 (9.92%))

§MONTGOMERYSHIRE
E. 48,730 T. 33,813 (69.39%) C. gain
*Glyn Davies, C. 13,976
Lembit Opik, LD 12,792
Heledd Fychan, PC 2,802
Nick Colbourne, Lab. 2,407
David Rowlands, UKIP 1,128
Milton Ellis, NF 384
Bruce Lawson, Ind. 324
C. majority 1,184 (3.50%)
Notional 13.15% swing LD to C.
(2005: LD majority 7,048 (22.80%))

§NEATH
E. 57,186 T. 37,122 (64.91%) Lab. hold
Peter Hain, Lab. 17,172
Alun Llewelyn, PC 7,397
Frank Little, LD 5,535
Emmeline Owens, C. 4,847
Michael Green, BNP 1,342
James Bevan, UKIP 829
Lab. majority 9,775 (26.33%)
Notional 4.58% swing Lab. to PC
(2005: Lab. majority 12,710 (35.49%))

NEWPORT EAST
E. 54,437 T. 34,448 (63.28%) Lab. hold
Jessica Morden, Lab. 12,744
Ed Townsend, LD 11,094
Dawn Parry, C. 7,918
Keith Jones, BNP 1,168
Fiona Cross, PC 724
David Rowlands, UKIP 677
Liz Screen, Soc. Lab. 123
Lab. majority 1,650 (4.79%)
8.35% swing Lab. to LD
(2005: Lab. majority 6,838 (21.49%))

NEWPORT WEST
E. 62,111 T. 39,720 (63.95%) Lab. hold
Paul Flynn, Lab. 16,389
Matthew Williams, C. 12,845
Veronica German, LD 6,587
Timothy Windsor, BNP 1,183
Hugh Moelwyn Hughes, UKIP 1,144
Jeff Rees, PC 1,122
Pippa Bartolotti, Green 450
Lab. majority 3,544 (8.92%)
3.18% swing Lab. to C.
(2005: Lab. majority 5,458 (15.27%))

§OGMORE
E. 55,527 T. 34,650 (62.40%) Lab. hold
Huw Irranca-Davies, Lab. 18,644
Emma Moore, C. 5,398
Jackie Radford, LD 5,260
Danny Clark, PC 3,326
Kay Thomas, BNP 1,242
Carolyn Passey, UKIP 780
Lab. majority 13,246 (38.23%)
Notional 4.28% swing Lab. to C.
(2005: Lab. majority 14,839 (46.29%))

§PONTYPRIDD
E. 58,219 T. 36,671 (62.99%) Lab. hold
*Owen Smith, Lab. 14,220
Michael Powell, LD 11,435
Lee Gonzalez, C. 5,932
Ioan Bellin, PC 2,673
David Bevan, UKIP 1,229
Simon Parsons, Soc. Lab. 456
Donald Watson, Ch. P. 365
John Matthews, Green 361
Lab. majority 2,785 (7.59%)
Notional 13.31% swing Lab. to LD
(2005: Lab. majority 11,694 (34.21%))

§PRESELI PEMBROKESHIRE
E. 57,419 T. 39,602 (68.97%) C. hold
Stephen Crabb, C. 16,944
Mari Rees, Lab. 12,339
Nick Tregoning, LD 5,759
Henry Jones-Davies, PC 3,654
Richard Lawson, UKIP 906
C. majority 4,605 (11.63%)
Notional 5.05% swing Lab. to C.
(2005: C. majority 601 (1.53%))

RHONDDA
E. 51,554 T. 31,072 (60.27%) Lab. hold
Chris Bryant, Lab. 17,183
Geraint Davies, PC 5,630
Paul Wasley, LD 3,309
Philip Howe, Ind. 2,599
Juliet Henderson, C. 1,993
Taffy John, UKIP 358
Lab. majority 11,553 (37.18%)
7.48% swing Lab. to PC
(2005: Lab. majority 16,242 (52.14%))

SWANSEA EAST
E. 59,823 T. 32,676 (54.62%) Lab. hold
Sian James, Lab. 16,819
Robert Speht, LD 5,981
Christian Holliday, C. 4,823
Dic Jones, PC 2,181
Clive Bennett, BNP 1,715
David Rogers, UKIP 839
Tony Young, Green 318
Lab. majority 10,838 (33.17%)
1.66% swing Lab. to LD
(2005: Lab. majority 11,249 (36.48%))

SWANSEA WEST
E. 61,334 T. 35,593 (58.03%) Lab. hold
*Geraint Davies, Lab. 12,335
Peter May, LD 11,831
Rene Kinzett, C. 7,407
Harri Roberts, PC 1,437
Alan Bateman, BNP 910
Tim Jenkins, UKIP 716
Keith Ross, Green 404
Ian McCloy, Ind. 374
Rob Williams, TUSC 179
Lab. majority 504 (1.42%)
5.74% swing Lab. to LD
(2005: Lab. majority 4,269 (12.90%))

TORFAEN
E. 61,178 T. 37,640 (61.53%) Lab. hold
Paul Murphy, Lab. 16,847
Jonathan Burns, C. 7,541
David Morgan, LD 6,264
Rhys ab Elis, PC 2,005
Jennifer Noble, BNP 1,657
Fred Wildgust, Ind. 1,419
Gareth Dunn, UKIP 862
Richard Turner-Thomas, Ind. 607
Owen Clarke, Green 438
Lab. majority 9,306 (24.72%)
8.19% swing Lab. to C.
(2005: Lab. majority 14,791 (41.11%))

§VALE OF CLWYD
E. 55,781 T. 35,534 (63.70%) Lab. hold
Chris Ruane, Lab. 15,017
Matt Wright, C. 12,508
Paul Penlington, LD 4,472
Caryl Wyn Jones, PC 2,068
Ian Si'Ree, BNP 827
Tom Turner, UKIP 515
Mike Butler, Green Soc. 127
Lab. majority 2,509 (7.06%)
Notional 3.56% swing Lab. to C.
(2005: Lab. majority 4,629 (14.18%))

§VALE OF GLAMORGAN
E. 70,262 T. 48,667 (69.27%) C. gain
*Alun Cairns, C. 20,341
Alana Davies, Lab. 16,034
Eluned Parrott, LD 7,403
Ian Johnson, PC 2,667
Kevin Mahoney, UKIP 1,529
Rhodri Thomas, Green 457
John Harrold, Ch. P. 236
C. majority 4,307 (8.85%)
Notional 6.11% swing Lab. to C.
(2005: Lab. majority 1,574 (3.37%))

WREXHAM
E. 50,872 T. 32,976 (64.82%) Lab. hold
Ian Lucas, Lab. 12,161
Tom Rippeth, LD 8,503
Gareth Hughes, C. 8,375
Arfon Jones, PC 2,029
Melvin Roberts, BNP 1,134
John Humberstone, UKIP 774
Lab. majority 3,658 (11.09%)
5.67% swing Lab. to LD
(2005: Lab. majority 6,819 (22.44%))

YNYS MON
E. 50,075 T. 34,444 (68.78%) Lab. hold
Albert Owen, Lab. 11,490
Dylan Rees, PC 9,029
Anthony Ridge-Newman, C. 7,744
Matt Wood, LD 2,592
Peter Rogers, Ind. 2,225
Elaine Gill, UKIP 1,201
The Rev David Owen, Ch. P. 163
Lab. majority 2,461 (7.14%)
1.82% swing PC to Lab.
(2005: Lab. majority 1,242 (3.50%))

SCOTLAND

ABERDEEN NORTH
E. 64,808 T. 37,701 (58.17%) Lab. hold
Frank Doran, Lab. 16,746
Joanna Strathdee, SNP 8,385
Kristian Chapman, LD 7,001
Stewart Whyte, C. 4,666
Roy Jones, BNP 635
Ewan Robertson, SSP 268
Lab. majority 8,361 (22.18%)
1.00% swing SNP to Lab.
(2005: Lab. majority 6,795 (18.55%))

ABERDEEN SOUTH
E. 64,031 T. 43,034 (67.21%) Lab. hold
Anne Begg, Lab. 15,722
John Sleigh, LD 12,216
Amanda Harvie, C. 8,914
Mark McDonald, SNP 5,102
Susan Ross, BNP 529
Rhonda Reekie, Green 413
Robert Green, SACL 138
Lab. majority 3,506 (8.15%)
2.45% swing LD to Lab.
(2005: Lab. majority 1,348 (3.24%))

ABERDEENSHIRE WEST & KINCARDINE
E. 66,110 T. 45,195 (68.36%) LD hold
Sir Robert Smith, LD 17,362
Alex Johnstone, C. 13,678
Dennis Robertson, SNP 7,086
Greg Williams, Lab. 6,159
Gary Raikes, BNP 513
Anthony Atkinson, UKIP 397
LD majority 3,684 (8.15%)
4.89% swing LD to C.
(2005: LD majority 7,471 (17.94%))

AIRDRIE & SHOTTS
E. 62,364 T. 35,849 (57.48%) Lab. hold
*Pamela Nash, Lab. 20,849
Sophia Coyle, SNP 8,441
Ruth Whitfield, C. 3,133
John Love, LD 2,898
John McGeechan, Ind. 528
Lab. majority 12,408 (34.61%)
3.93% swing Lab. to SNP
(2005: Lab. majority 14,084 (42.48%))

ANGUS
E. 62,863 T. 37,960 (60.39%) SNP hold
Mike Weir, SNP 15,020
Alberto Costa, C. 11,738
Kevin Hutchens, Lab. 6,535
Sanjay Samani, LD 4,090
Martin Gray, UKIP 577
SNP majority 3,282 (8.65%)
2.22% swing C. to SNP
(2005: SNP majority 1,601 (4.20%))

ARGYLL & BUTE
E. 67,165 T. 45,207 (67.31%) LD hold
Alan Reid, LD 14,292
Gary Mulvaney, C. 10,861
David Graham, Lab. 10,274
Michael MacKenzie, SNP 8,563
Elaine Morrison, Green 789
George Doyle, Ind. 272
John Black, Jacobite 156
LD majority 3,431 (7.59%)
2.72% swing LD to C.
(2005: LD majority 5,636 (13.04%))

AYR, CARRICK & CUMNOCK
E. 73,320 T. 45,893 (62.59%) Lab. hold
Sandra Osborne, Lab. 21,632
William Grant, C. 11,721
Charles Brodie, SNP 8,276
James Taylor, LD 4,264
Lab. majority 9,911 (21.60%)
0.30% swing Lab. to C.
(2005: Lab. majority 9,997 (22.19%))

AYRSHIRE CENTRAL
E. 68,352 T. 43,915 (64.25%) Lab. hold
Brian Donohoe, Lab. 20,950
Maurice Golden, C. 8,943
John Mullen, SNP 8,364
Andrew Chamberlain, LD 5,236
James McDaid, Soc. Lab. 422
Lab. majority 12,007 (27.34%)
1.51% swing C. to Lab.
(2005: Lab. majority 10,423 (24.31%))

AYRSHIRE NORTH & ARRAN
E. 74,953 T. 46,116 (61.53%) Lab. hold
Katy Clark, Lab. 21,860
Patricia Gibson, SNP 11,965
Philip Lardner, C. 7,212
Gillian Cole-Hamilton, LD 4,630
Louise McDaid, Soc. Lab. 449
Lab. majority 9,895 (21.46%)
2.26% swing Lab. to SNP
(2005: Lab. majority 11,296 (25.55%))

BANFF & BUCHAN
E. 64,300 T. 38,466 (59.82%) SNP hold
*Eilidh Whiteford, SNP 15,868
Jimmy Buchan, C. 11,841
Glen Reynolds, Lab. 5,382
Galen Milne, LD 4,365
Richard Payne, BNP 1,010
SNP majority 4,027 (10.47%)
10.67% swing SNP to C.
(2005: SNP majority 11,837 (31.81%))

BERWICKSHIRE, ROXBURGH & SELKIRK
E. 73,826 T. 49,014 (66.39%) LD hold
Michael Moore, LD 22,230
John Lamont, C. 16,555
Ian Miller, Lab. 5,003
Paul Wheelhouse, SNP 4,497
Sherry Fowler, UKIP 595
Chris Black, Jacobite 134
LD majority 5,675 (11.58%)
0.71% swing LD to C.
(2005: LD majority 5,901 (13.00%))

CAITHNESS, SUTHERLAND & EASTER ROSS
E. 47,257 T. 28,768 (60.88%) LD hold
John Thurso, LD 11,907
John Mackay, Lab. 7,081
Jean Urquhart, SNP 5,516
Alastair Graham, C. 3,744
Gordon Campbell, Ind. 520
LD majority 4,826 (16.78%)
6.38% swing LD to Lab.
(2005: LD majority 8,168 (29.53%))

COATBRIDGE, CHRYSTON & BELLSHILL
E. 70,067 T. 41,635 (59.42%) Lab. hold
Tom Clarke, Lab. 27,728
Frances McGlinchey, SNP 7,014
Kenneth Elder, LD 3,519
Fiona Houston, C. 3,374
Lab. majority 20,714 (49.75%)
0.58% swing Lab. to SNP
(2005: Lab. majority 19,519 (50.90%))

CUMBERNAULD, KILSYTH & KIRKINTILLOCH EAST
E. 64,037 T. 41,150 (64.26%) Lab. hold
*Gregg McClymont, Lab. 23,549
Julie Hepburn, SNP 9,794
Rod Ackland, LD 3,924
Stephanie Fraser, C. 3,407
William O'Neill, SSP 476
Lab. majority 13,755 (33.43%)
1.92% swing SNP to Lab.
(2005: Lab. majority 11,562 (29.58%))

DUMFRIES & GALLOWAY
E. 74,581 T. 52,173 (69.95%) Lab. hold
Russell Brown, Lab. 23,950
Peter Duncan, C. 16,501
Andrew Wood, SNP 6,419
Richard Brodie, LD 4,608
William Wright, UKIP 695
Lab. majority 7,449 (14.28%)
4.27% swing C. to Lab.
(2005: Lab. majority 2,922 (5.74%))

DUMFRIESSHIRE, CLYDESDALE & TWEEDDALE
E. 66,627 T. 45,892 (68.88%) C. hold
David Mundell, C. 17,457
Claudia Beamish, Lab. 13,263
Catriona Bhatia, LD 9,080
Aileen Orr, SNP 4,945
Steven McKeane, UKIP 637
Alis Ballance, Green 510
C. majority 4,194 (9.14%)
2.62% swing Lab. to C.
(2005: C. majority 1,738 (3.90%))

DUNBARTONSHIRE EAST
E. 63,795 T. 47,948 (75.16%) LD hold
Jo Swinson, LD 18,551
Mary Galbraith, Lab. 16,367
Mark Nolan, C. 7,431
Iain White, SNP 5,054
James Beeley, UKIP 545
LD majority 2,184 (4.55%)
2.07% swing LD to Lab.
(2005: LD majority 4,061 (8.69%))

DUNBARTONSHIRE WEST
E. 66,085 T. 42,266 (63.96%) Lab. (Co-op) hold
*Gemma Doyle, Lab. (Co-op) 25,905
Graeme McCormick, SNP 8,497
Helen Watt, LD 3,434
Martyn McIntyre, C. 3,242
Mitch Sorbie, UKIP 683
Katharine McGavigan, Soc. Lab. 505
Lab. (Co-op) majority 17,408 (41.19%)
5.50% swing SNP to Lab. (Co-op)
(2005: Lab. (Co-op) majority 12,553 (30.18%))

DUNDEE EAST
E. 65,471 T. 40,568 (61.96%) SNP hold
Stewart Hosie, SNP 15,350
Katrina Murray, Lab. 13,529
Chris Bustin, C. 6,177
Clive Sneddon, LD 4,285
Shiona Baird, Green 542
Mike Arthur, UKIP 431
Angela Gorrie, SSP 254
SNP majority 1,821 (4.49%)
1.76% swing Lab. to SNP
(2005: SNP majority 383 (0.97%))

DUNDEE WEST
E. 63,013 T. 37,126 (58.92%) Lab. hold
Jim McGovern, Lab. 17,994
Jim Barrie, SNP 10,716
John Barnett, LD 4,233
Colin Stewart, C. 3,461
Andy McBride, Ind. 365
Jim McFarlane, TUSC 357
Lab. majority 7,278 (19.60%)
2.52% swing SNP to Lab.
(2005: Lab. majority 5,379 (14.56%))

DUNFERMLINE & FIFE WEST
E. 73,769 T. 48,947 (66.35%) Lab. gain
*Thomas Docherty, Lab. 22,639
Willie Rennie, LD 17,169
Joe McCall, SNP 5,201
Belinda Hacking, C. 3,305
Otto Inglis, UKIP 633
Lab. majority 5,470 (11.18%)
8.05% swing Lab. to LD
(2005: Lab. majority 11,562 (27.27%))(2006: LD majority 1,800 (5.21%))

EAST KILBRIDE, STRATHAVEN & LESMAHAGOW
E. 76,534 T. 50,946 (66.57%) Lab. hold
*Michael McCann, Lab. 26,241
John McKenna, SNP 11,738
Graham Simpson, C. 6,613
John Loughton, LD 5,052
Kirsten Robb, Green 1,003
John Houston, Ind. 299
Lab. majority 14,503 (28.47%)
1.19% swing Lab. to SNP
(2005: Lab. majority 14,723 (30.84%))

EAST LOTHIAN
E. 73,438 T. 49,161 (66.94%) Lab. hold
*Fiona O'Donnell, Lab. 21,919
Michael Veitch, C. 9,661
Stuart Ritchie, LD 8,288
Andrew Sharp, SNP 7,883
James Mackenzie, Green 862
Jon Lloyd, UKIP 548
Lab. majority 12,258 (24.93%)
0.28% swing Lab. to C.
(2005: Lab. majority 7,620 (16.65%))

EDINBURGH EAST
E. 60,941 T. 39,865 (65.42%) Lab. hold
*Sheila Gilmore, Lab. 17,314
George Kerevan, SNP 8,133
Beverley Hope, LD 7,751
Martin Donald, C. 4,358
Robin Harper, Green 2,035
Gary Clark, TUSC 274
Lab. majority 9,181 (23.03%)
0.01% swing SNP to Lab.
(2005: Lab. majority 6,202 (15.62%))

EDINBURGH NORTH & LEITH
E. 69,204 T. 47,356 (68.43%) Lab. (Co-op) hold
Mark Lazarowicz, Lab. (Co-op) 17,740
Kevin Lang, LD 16,016
Iain McGill, C. 7,079
Calum Cashley, SNP 4,568
Kate Joester, Green 1,062
John Hein, Lib. 389
Willie Black, TUSC 233
David Jacobsen, Soc. Lab. 141
Cameron MacIntyre, Ind. 128
Lab. majority 1,724 (3.64%)
0.70% swing Lab. (Co-op) to LD
(2005: Lab. (Co-op) majority 2,153 (5.05%))

EDINBURGH SOUTH
E. 59,354 T. 43,801 (73.80%) Lab. hold
*Ian Murray, Lab. 15,215
Fred Mackintosh, LD 14,899
Neil Hudson, C. 9,452
Sandy Howat, SNP 3,354
Steve Burgess, Green 881
Lab. majority 316 (0.72%)
0.11% swing Lab. to LD
(2005: Lab. majority 405 (0.95%))

EDINBURGH SOUTH WEST
E. 66,359 T. 45,462 (68.51%) Lab. hold
Alistair Darling, Lab. 19,473
Jason Rust, C. 11,026
Tim McKay, LD 8,194
Kaukab Stewart, SNP 5,530
Clare Cooney, Green 872
Colin Fox, SSP 319
Caroline Bellamy, Comm. Lge 48
Lab. majority 8,447 (18.58%)
1.05% swing C. to Lab.
(2005: Lab. majority 7,242 (16.49%))

EDINBURGH WEST
E. 65,161 T. 46,447 (71.28%) LD hold
*Michael Crockart, LD 16,684
Cameron Day, Lab. 12,881
Stewart Geddes, C. 10,767
Sheena Cleland, SNP 6,115
LD majority 3,803 (8.19%)
11.35% swing LD to Lab.
(2005: LD majority 13,600 (30.05%))

FALKIRK
E. 81,869 T. 50,777 (62.02%) Lab. hold
Eric Joyce, Lab. 23,207
John McNally, SNP 15,364
Katie Mackie, C. 5,698
Kieran Leach, LD 5,225
Brian Goldie, UKIP 1,283
Lab. majority 7,843 (15.45%)
7.00% swing Lab. to SNP
(2005: Lab. majority 13,475 (29.45%))

FIFE NORTH EAST
E. 62,969 T. 40,064 (63.62%) LD hold
Sir Menzies Campbell, LD 17,763
Miles Briggs, C. 8,715
Mark Hood, Lab. 6,869
Rod Campbell, SNP 5,685
Mike Scott-Hayward, UKIP 1,032
LD majority 9,048 (22.58%)
5.01% swing LD to C.
(2005: LD majority 12,571 (32.60%))

GLASGOW CENTRAL
E. 60,062 T. 30,580 (50.91%) Lab. hold
*Anas Sarwar, Lab. 15,908
Osama Saeed, SNP 5,357
Chris Young, LD 5,010
John Bradley, C. 2,158
Alastair Whitelaw, Green 800
Ian Holt, BNP 616
James Nesbitt, SSP 357
Ramsay Urquhart, UKIP 246
Finlay Archibald, Pirate 128
Lab. majority 10,551 (34.50%)
0.54% swing SNP to Lab.
(2005: Lab. majority 8,531 (30.43%))

GLASGOW EAST
E. 61,516 T. 32,164 (52.29%) Lab. gain
*Margaret Curran, Lab. 19,797
John Mason, SNP 7,957
Kevin Ward, LD 1,617
Hamira Khan, C. 1,453
Joseph Finnie, BNP 677
Frances Curran, SSP 454
Arthur Thackeray, UKIP 209
Lab. majority 11,840 (36.81%)
3.42% swing Lab. to SNP
(2005: Lab. majority 13,507 (43.66%))(2008: SNP majority 365 (1.39%))

GLASGOW NORTH
E. 51,416 T. 29,613 (57.59%) Lab. hold
Ann McKechin, Lab. 13,181
Katy Gordon, LD 9,283
Patrick Grady, SNP 3,530
Erin Boyle, C. 2,089
Martin Bartos, Green 947
Thomas Main, BNP 296
Angela McCormick, TUSC 287
Lab. majority 3,898 (13.16%)
0.60% swing LD to Lab.
(2005: Lab. majority 3,338 (11.96%))

GLASGOW NORTH EAST
E. 59,859 T. 29,409 (49.13%) Lab. hold
Willie Bain, Lab. 20,100
Billy McAllister, SNP 4,158
Eileen Baxendale, LD 2,262
Ruth Davidson, C. 1,569
Walter Hamilton, BNP 798
Graham Campbell, TUSC 187
Kevin McVey, SSP 179
Jim Berrington, Soc. Lab. 156
Lab. majority 15,942 (54.21%)
(2005: Speaker majority 10,134 (35.66%))(2009: Lab. majority 8,111 (39.38%))

GLASGOW NORTH WEST
E. 60,968 T. 35,582 (58.36%) Lab. hold
John Robertson, Lab. 19,233
Natalie McKee, LD 5,622
Mags Park, SNP 5,430
Richard Sullivan, C. 3,537
Moira Crawford, Green 882
Scott Mclean, BNP 699
Marc Livingstone, Comm. 179
Lab. majority 13,611 (38.25%)
4.31% swing LD to Lab.
(2005: Lab. majority 10,093 (29.63%))

GLASGOW SOUTH
E. 65,029 T. 40,094 (61.66%) Lab. hold
Tom Harris, Lab. 20,736
Malcolm Fleming, SNP 8,078
Shabnum Mustapha, LD 4,739
Davena Rankin, C. 4,592
Marie Campbell, Green 961
Mike Coyle, BNP 637
Brian Smith, TUSC 351
Lab. majority 12,658 (31.57%)
1.51% swing Lab. to SNP
(2005: Lab. majority 10,832 (28.19%))

GLASGOW SOUTH WEST
E. 58,182 T. 31,781 (54.62%)
Lab. (Co-op) hold
Ian Davidson, Lab. (Co-op) 19,863
Chris Stephens, SNP 5,192
Isabel Nelson, LD 2,870
Maya Henderson Forrest, C. 2,084
Tommy Sheridan, TUSC 931
David Orr, BNP 841
Lab. (Co-op) majority 14,671 (46.16%)
0.65% swing SNP to Lab. (Co-op)
(2005: Lab. (Co-op) majority 13,896 (44.86%))

GLENROTHES
E. 67,893 T. 40,501 (59.65%) Lab. hold
Lindsay Roy, Lab. 25,247
David Alexander, SNP 8,799
Harry Wills, LD 3,108
Sheila Low, C. 2,922
Kris Seunarine, UKIP 425
Lab. majority 16,448 (40.61%)
6.04% swing SNP to Lab.
(2005: Lab. majority 10,664 (28.54%))(2008: Lab. majority 6,737 (18.61%))

GORDON
E. 73,420 T. 48,775 (66.43%) LD hold
Malcolm Bruce, LD 17,575
Richard Thomson, SNP 10,827
Barney Crockett, Lab. 9,811
Ross Thomson, C. 9,111
Sue Edwards, Green 752
Elise Jones, BNP 699
LD majority 6,748 (13.83%)
7.61% swing LD to SNP
(2005: LD majority 11,026 (24.81%))

INVERCLYDE
E. 59,209 T. 37,502 (63.34%) Lab. hold
David Cairns, Lab. 20,993
Innes Nelson, SNP 6,567
Simon Hutton, LD 5,007
David Wilson, C. 4,502
Peter Campbell, UKIP 433
Lab. majority 14,426 (38.47%)
3.64% swing SNP to Lab.
(2005: Lab. majority 11,259 (31.19%))

INVERNESS, NAIRN, BADENOCH & STRATHSPEY
E. 72,528 T. 47,086 (64.92%) LD hold
Danny Alexander, LD 19,172
Mike Robb, Lab. 10,407
John Finnie, SNP 8,803
Jim Ferguson, C. 6,278
Dr Donald Boyd, Ch. P. 835
Donnie MacLeod, Green 789
Ross Durance, UKIP 574
George MacDonald, TUSC 135
Kit Fraser, Joy 93
LD majority 8,765 (18.61%)
4.62% swing Lab. to LD
(2005: LD majority 4,148 (9.37%))

KILMARNOCK & LOUDOUN
E. 74,131 T. 46,553 (62.80%)
Lab. (Co-op) hold
*Cathy Jamieson, Lab. (Co-op) 24,460
George Leslie, SNP 12,082
Janette McAlpine, C. 6,592
Sebastian Tombs, LD 3,419
Lab. (Co-op) majority 12,378 (26.59%)
3.49% swing SNP to Lab. (Co-op)
(2005: Lab. (Co-op) majority 8,703 (19.61%))

KIRKCALDY & COWDENBEATH
E. 73,665 T. 45,802 (62.18%) Lab. hold
Gordon Brown, Lab. 29,559
Douglas Chapman, SNP 6,550
John Mainland, LD 4,269
Lindsay Paterson, C. 4,258
Peter Adams, UKIP 760
Susan Archibald, Ind. 184
Donald MacLaren of MacLaren, Ind. 165
Derek Jackson, Land 57
Lab. majority 23,009 (50.24%)
3.33% swing SNP to Lab.
(2005: Lab. majority 18,216 (43.58%))

LANARK & HAMILTON EAST
E. 74,773 T. 46,554 (62.26%) Lab. hold
Jim Hood, Lab. 23,258
Clare Adamson, SNP 9,780
Colin McGavigan, C. 6,981
Douglas Herbison, LD 5,249
Duncan McFarlane, Ind. 670
Rob Sale, UKIP 616
Lab. majority 13,478 (28.95%)
0.34% swing SNP to Lab.
(2005: Lab. majority 11,947 (27.41%))

LINLITHGOW & FALKIRK EAST
E. 80,907 T. 51,450 (63.59%) Lab. hold
Michael Connarty, Lab. 25,634
Tam Smith, SNP 13,081
Stephen Glenn, LD 6,589
Andrea Stephenson, C. 6,146
Lab. majority 12,553 (24.40%)
0.13% swing SNP to Lab.
(2005: Lab. majority 11,202 (24.15%))

LIVINGSTON
E. 75,924 T. 47,907 (63.10%) Lab. hold
*Graeme Morrice, Lab. 23,215
Lis Bardell, SNP 12,424
Charles Dundas, LD 5,316
Alison Adamson-Ross, C. 5,158
David Orr, BNP 960
Alistair Forrest, UKIP 443
Ally Hendry, SSP 242
Jim Slavin, Ind. 149
Lab. majority 10,791 (22.52%)
3.51% swing Lab. to SNP
(2005: Lab. majority 13,097 (29.54%))(2005: Lab. majority 2,680 (9.09%))

MIDLOTHIAN
E. 61,387 T. 39,242 (63.93%) Lab. hold
David Hamilton, Lab. 18,449
Colin Beattie, SNP 8,100
Ross Laird, LD 6,711
James Callander, C. 4,661
Ian Baxter, Green 595
Gordon Norrie, UKIP 364
George McCleery, Ind. 196
Willie Duncan, TUSC 166
Lab. majority 10,349 (26.37%)
1.07% swing Lab. to SNP
(2005: Lab. majority 7,265 (19.27%))

MORAY
E. 65,925 T. 41,004 (62.20%) SNP hold
Angus Robertson, SNP 16,273
Douglas Ross, C. 10,683
Kieron Green, Lab. 7,007
James Paterson, LD 5,956
Donald Gatt, UKIP 1,085
SNP majority 5,590 (13.63%)
0.50% swing SNP to C.
(2005: SNP majority 5,676 (14.63%))

MOTHERWELL & WISHAW
E. 66,918 T. 39,123 (58.46%) Lab. hold
Frank Roy, Lab. 23,910
Marion Fellows, SNP 7,104
Stuart Douglas, LD 3,840
Patsy Gilroy, C. 3,660
Ray Gunnion, TUSC 609
Lab. majority 16,806 (42.96%)
0.97% swing SNP to Lab.
(2005: Lab. majority 15,222 (41.02%))

NA H-EILEANAN AN IAR
E. 22,266 T. 14,717 (66.10%) SNP hold
Angus MacNeil, SNP 6,723
Donald John MacSween, Lab. 4,838
Murdo Murray, Ind. 1,412
Jean Davis, LD 1,097
Sheena Norquay, C. 647
SNP majority 1,885 (12.81%)
1.20% swing Lab. to SNP
(2005: SNP majority 1,441 (10.41%))

OCHIL & PERTHSHIRE SOUTH
E. 75,115 T. 50,469 (67.19%) Lab. hold
Gordon Banks, Lab. 19,131
Annabelle Ewing, SNP 13,944
Gerald Michaluk, C. 10,342
Graeme Littlejohn, LD 5,754
David Bushby, UKIP 689
Hilary Charles, Green 609
Lab. majority 5,187 (10.28%)
4.40% swing SNP to Lab.
(2005: Lab. majority 688 (1.47%))

ORKNEY & SHETLAND
E. 33,085 T. 19,346 (58.47%) LD hold
Alistair Carmichael, LD 11,989
Mark Cooper, Lab. 2,061
John Mowat, SNP 2,042
Frank Nairn, C. 2,032
Robert Smith, UKIP 1,222
LD majority 9,928 (51.32%)
6.98% swing Lab. to LD
(2005: LD majority 6,627 (37.35%))

PAISLEY & RENFREWSHIRE NORTH
E. 63,704 T. 43,707 (68.61%) Lab. hold
Jim Sheridan, Lab. 23,613
Mags MacLaren, SNP 8,333
Alistair Campbell, C. 6,381
Ruaraidh Dobson, LD 4,597
Gary Pearson, Ind. 550
Chris Rollo, SSP 233
Lab. majority 15,280 (34.96%)
4.03% swing SNP to Lab.
(2005: Lab. majority 11,001 (26.91%))

PAISLEY & RENFREWSHIRE SOUTH
E. 61,197 T. 39,998 (65.36%) Lab. hold
Douglas Alexander, Lab. 23,842
Andy Doig, SNP 7,228
Gordon McCaskill, C. 3,979
Ashay Ghai, LD 3,812
Paul Mack, Ind. 513
Jimmy Kerr, SSP 375
William Hendry, Ind. 249
Lab. majority 16,614 (41.54%)
3.27% swing SNP to Lab.
(2005: Lab. majority 13,232 (34.95%))

PERTH & PERTHSHIRE NORTH
E. 72,141 T. 48,268 (66.91%) SNP hold
Pete Wishart, SNP 19,118
Peter Lyburn, C. 14,739
Jamie Glackin, Lab. 7,923
Peter Barrett, LD 5,954
Douglas Taylor, Trust 534
SNP majority 4,379 (9.07%)
2.88% swing C. to SNP
(2005: SNP majority 1,521 (3.31%))

RENFREWSHIRE EAST
E. 66,249 T. 51,181 (77.26%) Lab. hold
Jim Murphy, Lab. 25,987
Richard Cook, C. 15,567
Gordon Macdonald, LD 4,720
Gordon Archer, SNP 4,535
Donald MacKay, UKIP 372
Lab. majority 10,420 (20.36%)
3.16% swing C. to Lab.
(2005: Lab. majority 6,657 (14.04%))

ROSS, SKYE & LOCHABER
E. 51,836 T. 34,838 (67.21%) LD hold
Charles Kennedy, LD 18,335
John McKendrick, Lab. 5,265
Alasdair Stephen, SNP 5,263
Donald Cameron, C. 4,260
Eleanor Scott, Green 777
Philip Anderson, UKIP 659
Ronnie Campbell, Ind. 279
LD majority 13,070 (37.52%)
3.14% swing LD to Lab.
(2005: LD majority 14,249 (43.79%))

RUTHERGLEN & HAMILTON WEST
E. 76,408 T. 46,981 (61.49%)
Lab. (Co-op) hold
*Tom Greatrex, Lab. (Co-op) 28,566
Graeme Horne, SNP 7,564
Ian Robertson, LD 5,636
Malcolm Macaskill, C. 4,540
Janice Murdoch, UKIP 675
Lab. (Co-op) majority 21,002 (44.70%)
1.51% swing SNP to Lab. (Co-op)
(2005: Lab. (Co-op) majority 16,112 (37.24%))

STIRLING
E. 66,080 T. 46,791 (70.81%) Lab. hold
Anne McGuire, Lab. 19,558
Bob Dalrymple, C. 11,204
Alison Lindsay, SNP 8,091
Graham Reed, LD 6,797
Mark Ruskell, Green 746
Paul Henke, UKIP 395
Lab. majority 8,354 (17.85%)
3.47% swing C. to Lab.
(2005: Lab. majority 4,767 (10.91%))

NORTHERN IRELAND

§ANTRIM EAST
E. 60,204 T. 30,502 (50.66%)
DUP hold
Sammy Wilson, DUP 13,993
Rodney McCune, UCUNF 7,223
Gerry Lynch, Alliance 3,377
Oliver McMullan, SF 2,064
Justin McCamphill, SDLP 2,019
Samuel Morrison, TUV 1,826
DUP majority 6,770 (22.20%)
Notional 0.2% swing UCUNF to DUP
(2005: DUP majority 6,996 (21.76%))

§ANTRIM NORTH
E. 73,338 T. 42,397 (57.81%)
DUP hold
*Ian Paisley Junior, DUP 19,672
Jim Allister, TUV 7,114
Daithi McKay, SF 5,265
Irwin Armstrong, UCUNF 4,634
Declan O'Loan, SDLP 3,738
Jayne Dunlop, Alliance 1,368
Lyle Cubitt, ND 606
DUP majority 12,558 (29.62%)
(2005: DUP majority 18,486 (41.80%))

§ANTRIM SOUTH
E. 63,054 T. 34,009 (53.94%)
DUP hold
Revd William McCrea, DUP 11,536
Sir Reg Empey, UCUNF 10,353
Mitchel McLaughlin, SF 4,729
Michelle Byrne, SDLP 2,955
Alan Lawther, Alliance 2,607
Melwyn Lucas, TUV 1,829
DUP majority 1,183 (3.48%)
Notional 3.6% swing DUP to UCUNF
(2005: DUP majority 3,778 (10.74%))

§BELFAST EAST
E. 59,007 T. 34,488 (58.45%)
Alliance gain
*Naomi Long, Alliance 12,839
Peter Robinson, DUP 11,306
Trevor Ringland, UCUNF 7,305
David Vance, TUV 1,856
Niall Donnelly, SF 817
Mary Muldoon, SDLP 365
Alliance majority 1,533 (4.45%)
Notional 22.87% swing DUP to Alliance
(2005: DUP majority 7,900 (22.87%))

§BELFAST NORTH
E. 65,504 T. 36,993 (56.47%)
DUP hold
Nigel Dodds, DUP 14,812
Gerry Kelly, SF 12,588
Alban Maginness, SDLP 4,544
Fred Cobain, UCUNF 2,837
William Webb, Alliance 1,809
Martin McAuley, Ind. 403
DUP majority 2,224 (6.01%)
Notional 5.00% swing DUP to SF
(2005: DUP majority 5,832 (16.02%))

§BELFAST SOUTH
E. 59,524 T. 34,186 (57.43%)
SDLP hold
Dr Alasdair McDonnell, SDLP 14,026
Jimmy Spratt, DUP 8,100
Paula Bradshaw, UCUNF 5,910
Anna Lo, Alliance 5,114
Adam McGibbon, Green 1,036
SDLP majority 5,926 (17.33%)
Notional 8.41% swing DUP to SDLP
(2005: SDLP majority 188 (0.52%))

§BELFAST WEST
E. 59,522 T. 32,133 (53.99%) SF hold
Gerry Adams, SF 22,840
Alex Attwood, SDLP 5,261
William Humphrey, DUP 2,436
Bill Manwaring, UCUNF 1,000
Maire Hendron, Alliance 596
SF majority 17,579 (54.71%)
Notional 1.07% swing SDLP to SF
(2005: SF majority 19,527 (52.57%))

DOWN NORTH
E. 60,698 T. 33,481 (55.16%)
Ind. hold
Lady Sylvia Hermon, Ind. 21,181
Ian Parsley, UCUNF 6,817
Stephen Farry, Alliance 1,876
Mary Kilpatrick, TUV 1,634
Steven Agnew, Green 1,043
Liam Logan, SDLP 680
Vincent Parker, SF 250
Ind. majority 14,364 (42.90%)
(2005: UUP majority 4,944 (15.31%))

§DOWN SOUTH
E. 70,784 T. 42,589 (60.17%)
SDLP hold
*Margaret Ritchie, SDLP 20,648
Caitriona Ruane, SF 12,236
Jim Wells, DUP 3,645
John McCallister, UCUNF 3,093
Ivor McConnell, TUV 1,506
Cadogan Enright, Green 901
David Griffin, Alliance 560
SDLP majority 8,412 (19.75%)
Notional 0.06% swing SDLP to SF
(2005: SDLP majority 8,801 (19.87%))

FERMANAGH & SOUTH TYRONE
E. 67,908 T. 46,803 (68.92%) SF hold
Michelle Gildernew, SF 21,304
Rodney Connor, Ind. 21,300
Fearghal McKinney, SDLP 3,574
Vasundhara Kamble, Alliance 437
John Stevenson, Ind. 188
SF majority 4 (0.01%)
(2005: SF majority 4,582 (9.39%))

§FOYLE
E. 65,843 T. 37,889 (57.54%)
SDLP hold
Mark Durkan, SDLP 16,922
Martina Anderson, SF 12,098
Maurice Devenney, DUP 4,489
Eammon McCann, PBP 2,936
David Harding, UCUNF 1,221
Keith McGrellis, Alliance 223
SDLP majority 4,824 (12.73%)
Notional 0.17% swing SDLP to SF
(2005: SDLP majority 5,570 (13.08%))

§LAGAN VALLEY
E. 65,257 T. 36,540 (55.99%)
DUP hold
Jeffrey Donaldson, DUP 18,199
Daphne Trimble, UCUNF 7,713
Trevor Lunn, Alliance 4,174
Keith Harbinson, TUV 3,154
Brian Heading, SDLP 1,835
Paul Butler, SF 1,465
DUP majority 10,486 (28.70%)
Notional 3.3% swing DUP to UCUNF
(2005: DUP majority 13,493 (35.33%))

§LONDONDERRY EAST
E. 63,220 T. 34,950 (55.28%)
DUP hold
Gregory Campbell, DUP 12,097
Cathal O hOisin, SF 6,742
Lesley Macaulay, UCUNF 6,218
Thomas Conway, SDLP 5,399
William Ross, TUV 2,572
Bernard Fitzpatrick, Alliance 1,922
DUP majority 5,355 (15.32%)
Notional 4.13% swing DUP to SF
(2005: DUP majority 8,192 (21.26%))

NEWRY & ARMAGH
E. 74,308 T. 44,906 (60.43%) SF hold
Conor Murphy, SF 18,857
Dominic Bradley, SDLP 10,526
Danny Kennedy, UCUNF 8,558
William Irwin, DUP 5,764
William Frazer, Ind. 656
Andrew Muir, Alliance 545
SF majority 8,331 (18.55%)
1.19% swing SDLP to SF
(2005: SF majority 8,195 (16.16%))

§STRANGFORD
E. 60,539 T. 32,505 (53.69%)
DUP hold
*Jim Shannon, DUP 14,926
Mike Nesbitt, UCUNF 9,050
Deborah Girvan, Alliance 2,828
Claire Hanna, SDLP 2,164
Terry Williams, TUV 1,814
Michael Coogan, SF 1,161
Barbara Haig, Green 562
DUP majority 5,876 (18.08%)
Notional 7.6% swing DUP to UCUNF
(2005: DUP majority 10,934 (33.32%))

TYRONE WEST
E. 61,148 T. 37,275 (60.96%) SF hold
Pat Doherty, SF 18,050
Thomas Buchanan, DUP 7,365
Ross Hussey, UCUNF 5,281
Joe Byrne, SDLP 5,212
Michael Bower, Alliance 859
Ciaran McClean, Ind. 508
SF majority 10,685 (28.67%)
3.79% swing DUP to SF
(2005: SF majority 5,005 (11.51%))

ULSTER MID
E. 64,594 T. 40,842 (63.23%) SF hold
Martin McGuinness, SF 21,239
Ian McCrea, DUP 5,876
Tony Quinn, SDLP 5,826
Sandra Overend, UCUNF 4,509
Walter Millar, TUV 2,995
Ian Butler, Alliance 397
SF majority 15,363 (37.62%)
6.73% swing DUP to SF
(2005: SF majority 10,976 (24.16%))

UPPER BANN
E. 74,732 T. 41,383 (55.38%)
DUP hold
David Simpson, DUP 14,000
Harry Hamilton, UCUNF 10,639
John O'Dowd, SF 10,237
Dolores Kelly, SDLP 5,276
Brendan Heading, Alliance 1,231
DUP majority 3,361 (8.12%)
Notional 1.9% swing DUP to UCUNF
(2005: DUP majority 5,298 (11.93%))

GENERAL ELECTION FACTS AND FIGURES

MPS DEFEATED AT THE 2010 GENERAL ELECTION

CONSERVATIVE
Heathcoat-Amory, David, *Wells*
Waterson, Nigel, *Eastbourne*

LABOUR
Ainger, Nick, *Carmarthen West & Pembrokeshire South*
Anderson, Janet, *Rossendale & Darwen*
Baird, Vera, *Redcar*
Barlow, Celia, *Hove*
Berry, Roger, *Kingswood*
Blizzard, Bob, *Waveney*
Borrow, David, *South Ribble*
Butler, Dawn, *Brent Central*
Cawsey, Ian, *Brigg & Goole*
Clark, Paul, *Gillingham & Rainham*
Clarke, Charles, *Norwich South*
Dhanda, Parmjit, *Gloucester*
Dismore, Andrew, *Hendon*
Drew, David, *Stroud*
Foster, Michael, *Worcester*
Foster, Michael Jabez, *Hastings & Rye*
Gilroy, Linda, *Plymouth Sutton & Devonport*
Hall, Patrick, *Bedford*
Hope, Phil, *Corby*
Jenkins, Brian, *Tamworth*
Keeble, Sally, *Northampton North*
Keen, Ann, *Brentford & Isleworth*
Kidney, David, *Stafford*
Knight, Jim, *Dorset South*
Linton, Martin, *Battersea*
McCarthy-Fry, Sarah, *Portsmouth North*
McIsaac, Shona, *Cleethorpes*
McNulty, Tony, *Harrow East*
Malik, Shahid, *Dewsbury*
Mallaber, Judy, *Amber Valler*
Marris, Rob, *Wolverhampton South West*
Merron, Gillian, *Lincoln*
Mole, Chris, *Ipswich*
Morgan, Julie, *Cardiff North*
O'Brien, Mike, *Warwickshire North*
Palmer, Nick, *Broxtowe*
Plaskitt, James, *Warwick & Leamington*
Prentice, Gordon, *Pendle*
Prosser, Gwyn, *Dover*
Rammell, Bill, *Harlow*
Reed, Andy, *Loughborough*
Rooney, Terry, *Bradford East*
Russell, Christine, *Chester, City of*
Shaw, Jonathan, *Chatham & Aylesford*
Smith, Angela E., *Basildon South & Thurrock East*
Smith, Geraldine, *Morecambe & Lunesdale*
Smith, Jacqui, *Redditch*
Snelgrove, Anne, *Swindon South*
Starkey, Phyllis, *Milton Keynes South*
Taylor, Dari, *Stockton South*
Waltho, Linda, *Stourbridge*
Ward, Claire, *Watford*
Wright, Anthony, *Great Yarmouth*

LIBERAL DEMOCRAT
Gidley, Sandra, *Romsey & Southampton North*
Goldsworthy, Julia, *Camborne & Redruth*
Harris, Evan, *Oxford West & Abingdon*
Holmes, Paul, *Chesterfield*
Kramer, Susan, *Richmond Park*
Opik, Lembit, *Montgomeryshire*
Rennie, Willie, *Dunfermline & Fife West*
Younger-Ross, Richard, *Newton Abbot*

OTHER
Davies, Dai (Blaenau Voice), *Blaenau Gwent*
Mason, John (SNP), *Glasgow East*
Robinson, Peter (DUP), *Belfast East*
Spink, Bob (Ind. Green Belt), *Castle Point*
Taylor, Richard (Ind. CHC), *Wyre Forest*

MPS WHO RETIRED AT THE 2010 GENERAL ELECTION

CONSERVATIVE
Ainsworth, Peter, *Surrey East*
Ancram, Michael, *Devizes*
Atkinson, Peter, *Hexham*
Boswell, Tim, *Daventry*
Browning, Angela, *Tiverton & Honiton*
Butterfill, Sir John, *Bournemouth West*
Cormack, Sir Patrick, *Staffordshire South*
Curry, David, *Skipton & Ripon*
Fraser, Christopher, *Norfolk South West*
Goodman, Paul, *Wycombe*
Greenway, John, *Ryedale*
Gummer, John, *Suffolk Coastal*
Hogg, Douglas, *Sleaford & North Hykeham*
Horam, John, *Orpington*
Howard, Michael, *Folkstone & Hythe*
Jack, Michael, *Fylde*
Key, Robert, *Salisbury*
Kirkbride, Julie, *Bromsgrove*
Lait, Jacqui, *Beckenham*
Lord, Sir Michael, *Suffolk Central & Ipswich North*
MacKay, Andrew, *Bracknell*
Maclean, David, *Penrith & The Border*
Malins, Humfrey, *Woking*
Maples, John, *Stratford on Avon*
Mates, Michael, *Hampshire East*
Moss, Malcolm, *Cambridgeshire North East*
Spicer, Michael, *Worcestershire West*
Spring, Richard, *Suffolk West*
Steen, Anthony, *Totnes*
Taylor, Ian, *Esher & Walton*
Viggers, Sir Peter, *Gosport*
Widdecombe, Ann, *Maidstone & The Weald*
Wilshire, David, *Spelthorne*
Winterton, Ann, *Congleton*
Winterton, Sir Nicholas, *Macclesfield*

LABOUR
Armstrong, Hilary, *Durham North West*
Austin, John, *Erith & Thamesmead*
Battle, John, *Leeds West*
Blackman, Liz, *Erewash*
Browne, Des, *Kilmarnock & Loudoun*
Burgon, Colin, *Elmet*
Byers, Stephen, *North Tyneside*
Caborn, Richard, *Sheffield Central*
Challen, Colin, *Morley & Rothwell*
Chapman, Ben, *Wirral South*
Chaytor, David, *Bury North*
Clapham, Michael, *Barnsley West & Penistone*

Clelland, David, *Tyne Bridge*
Cohen, Harry, *Leyton & Wanstead*
Cousins, Jim, *Newcastle Upon Tyne Central*
Cryer, Ann, *Keighley*
Cummings, John, *Easington*
Curtis-Thomas, Claire, *Crosby*
Davies, Quentin, *Grantham & Stamford*
Dean, Janet, *Burton*
Devine, Jim, *Livingston*
Ennis, Jeff, *Barnsley East & Mexborough*
Etherington, Bill, *Sunderland North*
Fisher, Mark, *Stoke on Trent Central*
Follett, Barbara, *Stevenage*
George, Bruce, *Walsall South*
Gerrard, Neil, *Walthamstow*
Griffiths, Nigel, *Edinburgh South*
Grogan, John, *Selby*
Hall, Mike, *Weaver Vale*
Heal, Sylvia, *Halesowen & Rowley Regis*
Henderson, Doug, *Newcastle Upon Tyne North*
Heppell, John, *Nottingham East*
Hesford, Stephen, *Wirral West*
Hewitt, Patricia, *Leicester West*
Hill, Keith, *Streatham*
Hoon, Geoff, *Ashfield*
Howells, Kim, *Pontypridd*
Hughes, Beverley, *Stretford & Urmston*
Humble, Joan, *Blackpool North & Fleetwood*
Hutton, John, *Barrow & Furness*
Iddon, Brian, *Bolton South East*
Ingram, Adam, *East Kilbride, Strathaven & Lesmahagow*
Jones, Lynne, *Birmingham Selly Oak*
Jones, Martyn, *Clwyd South*
Kelly, Ruth, *Bolton West*
Kemp, Fraser, *Houghton & Washington East*
Kennedy, Jane, *Liverpool Wavertree*
Kilfoyle, Peter, *Liverpool Walton*
Laxton, Bob, *Derby North*
Lepper, David, *Brighton Pavilion*
Levitt, Tom, *High Peak*
McAvoy, Tommy, *Rutherglen & Hamilton West*
McCafferty, Christine, *Calder Valley*
McCartney, Ian, *Makerfield*
McFall, John, *West Dunbartonshire*
McKenna, Rosemary, *Cumbernauld, Kislyth & Kirkintilloch East*
MacKinlay, Andrew, *Thurrock*
Marshall-Andrews, Bob, *Medway*
Martlew, Eric, *Carlisle*
Milburn, Alan, *Darlington*
Moffat, Ann, *East Lothian*
Moffat, Laura, *Crawley*
Moran, Margaret, *Luton South*
Morley, Elliot, *Scunthorpe*
Mountford, Kali, *Colne Valley*
Mullin, Chris, *Sunderland South*
Murphy, Denis, *Wansbeck*
Naysmith, Doug, *Bristol North West*
O'Hara, Eddie, *Knowsley South*
Olner, Bill, *Nuneaton*
Pearson, Ian, *Dudley South*
Pope, Greg, *Hyndburn*
Prentice, Bridget, *Lewisham East*
Prescott, John, *Hull East*
Purchase, Ken, *Wolverhampton North East*
Purnell, James, *Stalybridge & Hyde*
Reid, John, *Airdrie & Shotts*
Salter, Martin, *Reading West*
Sarwar, Mohammad, *Glasgow Central*
Simon, Sion, *Birmingham Erdington*
Simpson, Alan, *Nottingham South*
Smith, John, *Vale of Glamorgan*
Southworth, Helen, *Warrington South*
Stewart, Ian, *Eccles*
Stoate, Howard, *Dartford*
Strang, Gavin, *Edinburgh East*
Tipping, Paddy, *Sherwood*
Todd, Mark, *Derbyshire South*
Touhig, Dan, *Islwyn*
Truswell, Paul, *Pudsey*
Turner, Des, *Brighton Kemptown*
Turner, Neil, *Wigan*
Ussher, Kitty, *Burnley*
Vis, Rudi, *Finchley & Golders Green*
Williams, Alan, *Swansea West*
Williams, Betty, *Conwy*
Wills, Michael, *Swindon North*
Wright, Tony, *Cannock Chase*
Wyatt, Derek, *Sittingbourne & Sheppey*

LIBERAL DEMOCRAT
Barrett, John, *Edinburgh West*
Breed, Colin, *Cornwall South East*
Howarth, David, *Cambridge*
Keetch, Paul, *Hereford*
Oaten, Mark, *Winchester*
Taylor, Matthew, *Truro & St Austell*
Willis, Phil, *Harrogate & Knaresborough*

OTHER
Conway, Derek (Ind. C.), *Old Bexley & Sidcup*
McGrady, Eddie (SDLP), *Down South*
Paisley, Ian (DUP), *Antrim North*
Price, Adam (PC), *Carmarthen East & Dinefwr*
Salmond, Alex (SNP), *Banff & Buchan*
Short, Clare (Ind. Lab.), *Birmingham Ladywood*
Wareing, Robert (Ind.), *Liverpool West Derby*

NEW MPS

CONSERVATIVE
Adams, Nigel, *Selby & Ainsty*
Aldous, Peter, *Waveney*
Andrew, Stuart, *Pudsey*
Bagshawe, Louise, *Corby*
Baker, Steven, *Wycombe*
Baldwin, Harriett, *West Worcestershire*
Barclay, Stephen, *Cambridgeshire North East*
Barwell, Gavin, *Croydon Central*
Bebb, Guto, *Aberconwy*
Berry, Jake, *Rossendale & Darwen*
Bingham, Andrew, *High Peak*
Blackman, Bob, *Harrow East*
Blackwood, Nicola, *Oxford West & Abingdon*
Boles, Nick, *Grantham & Stamford*
Bradley, Karen, *Staffordshire Moorlands*
Bray, Angie, *Ealing Central & Acton*
Bridgen, Andrew, *Leicestershire North West*
Brine, Steve, *Winchester*
Bruce, Fiona, *Congleton*
Buckland, Robert, *Swindon South*
Burley, Aidan, *Cannock Chase*
Burns, Conor, *Bournemouth West*
Byles, Daniel, *Warwickshire North*
Cairns, Alun, *Vale of Glamorgan*
Carmichael, Neil, *Stroud*

Chishti, Rehman, *Gillingham & Rainham*
Coffey, Therese, *Suffolk Coastal*
Collins, Damian, *Folkestone & Hythe*
Colvile, Oliver, *Plymouth, Sutton & Devonport*
Crouch, Tracey, *Chatham & Aylesford*
Davies, Glyn, *Montgomeryshire*
de Bois, Nick, *Enfield North*
Dinenage, Caroline, *Gosport*
Doyle-Price, Jackie, *Thurrock*
Drax, Richard, *Dorset South*
Ellis, Michael, *Northampton North*
Ellison, Jane, *Battersea*
Elphicke, Charlie, *Dover*
Eustice, George, *Camborne & Redruth*
Evans, Graham, *Weaver Vale*
Evans, Jonathan, *Cardiff North*
Freeman, George, *Norfolk Mid*
Freer, Mike, *Finchley & Golders Green*
Fullbrook, Lorraine, *Ribble South*
Fuller, Richard, *Bedford*
Garnier, Mark, *Wyre Forest*
Glen, John, *Salisbury*
Goldsmith, Zac, *Richmond Park*
Graham, Richard, *Gloucester*
Grant, Helen, *Maidstone & the Weald*
Griffiths, Andrew, *Burton*
Gummer, Benedict, *Ipswich*
Gyimah, Sam, *Surrey East*
Halfon, Robert, *Harlow*
Hancock, Matthew, *Suffolk West*
Harrington, Richard, *Watford*
Harris, Rebecca, *Castle Point*
Hart, Simon, *Carmarthen West & Pembrokeshire South*
Heaton-Harris, Chris, *Daventry*
Henderson, Gordon, *Sittingbourne & Sheppey*
Hinds, Damian, *Hampshire East*
Hollingbery, George, *Meon Valley*
Hopkins, Kris, *Keighley*
James, Margot, *Stourbridge*
Javid, Sajid, *Bromsgrove*
Johnson, Gareth, *Dartford*
Johnson, Jo, *Orpington*
Jones, Andrew, *Harrogate & Knaresborough*
Jones, Marcus, *Nuneaton*
Kelly, Chris, *Dudley South*
Kirby, Simon, *Brighton Kemptown*
Kwarteng, Kwasi, *Spelthorne*
Latham, Pauline, *Derbyshire Mid*
Leadsom, Andrea, *Northamptonshire South*
Lee, Jessica, *Erewash*
Lee, Philip, *Bracknell*
Lefroy, Jeremy, *Stafford*
Leslie, Charlotte, *Bristol North West*
Lewis, Brandon, *Great Yarmouth*
Lopresti, Jack, *Filton & Bradley Stoke*
Lord, Jonathan, *Woking*
Lumley, Karen, *Redditch*
McCartney, Jason, *Colne Valley*
McCartney, Karl, *Lincoln*
MacLeod, Mary, *Brentford & Isleworth*
McPartland, Stephen, *Stevenage*
McVey, Esther, *Wirral West*
Maynard, Paul, *Blackpool North & Cleveleys*
Menzies, Mark, *Fylde*
Metcalfe, Stephen, *Basildon South & Thurrock East*
Mills, Nigel, *Amber Valley*
Mordaunt, Penny, *Portsmouth North*
Morgan, Nicky, *Loughborough*
Morris, Anne Marie, *Newton Abbot*
Morris, David, *Morecambe & Lunesdale*
Morris, James, *Halesowen & Rowley Regis*
Mosley, Stephen, *Chester, City of*
Mowat, David, *Warrington South*
Murray, Sheryll, *Cornwall South East*
Newton, Sarah, *Truro & Falmouth*
Nokes, Caroline, *Romsey & Southampton North*
Norman, Jesse, *Hereford & Herefordshire South*
Nuttall, David, *Bury North*
Offord, Matthew, *Hendon*
Ollerenshaw, Eric, *Lancaster & Fleetwood*
Opperman, Guy, *Hexham*
Parish, Neil, *Tiverton & Honiton*
Patel, Priti, *Witham*
Pawsey, Mark, *Rugby*
Percy, Andrew, *Brigg & Goole*
Perry, Claire, *Devizes*
Phillips, Stephen, *Sleaford & Hykeham North*
Pincher, Chris, *Tamworth*
Poulter, Daniel, *Suffolk Central & Ipswich North*
Raab, Dominic, *Esher & Walton*
Reckless, Mark, *Rochester & Strood*
Rees-Mogg, Jacob, *Somerset North East*
Reevell, Simon, *Dewsbury*
Rudd, Amber, *Hastings & Rye*
Rutley, David, *Macclesfield*
Sandys, Laura, *Thanet South*
Sharma, Alok, *Reading West*
Shelbrooke, Alec, *Elmet & Rothwell*
Skidmore, Chris, *Kingswood*
Smith, Henry, *Crawley*
Smith, Julian, *Skipton & Ripon*
Soubry, Anna, *Broxtowe*
Spencer, Mark, *Sherwood*
Stephenson, Andrew, *Pendle*
Stevenson, John, *Carlisle*
Stewart, Bob, *Beckenham*
Stewart, Iain, *Milton Keynes South*
Stewart, Rory, *Penrith & The Border*
Stride, Mel, *Devon Central*
Sturdy, Julian, *York Outer*
Tomlinson, Justin, *Swindon North*
Truss, Elizabeth, *Norfolk South West*
Uppal, Pau, *Wolverhampton South West*
Vickers, Martin, *Cleethorpes*
Walker, Robin, *Worcester*
Weatherley, Mike, *Hove*
Wharton, James, *Stockton South*
Wheeler, Heather, *Derbyshire South*
White, Chris, *Warwick & Leamington*
Whittaker, Craig, *Calder Valley*
Williamson, Gavin, *Staffordshire South*
Wollaston, Sarah, *Totnes*
Zahawi, Nadhim, *Stratford-on-Avon*

LABOUR
Alexander, Heidi, *Lewisham East*
Ali, Rushanara, *Bethnal Green & Bow*
Berger, Luciana, *Liverpool, Wavertree*
Blenkinsop, Tom, *Middlesbrough South & East Cleveland*
Blomfield, Paul, *Sheffield Central*
Chapman, Jenny, *Darlington*
Creasy, Stella, *Walthamstow*
Cryer, John, *Leyton & Wanstead*
Cunningham, Alex, *Stockton North*
Curran, Margaret, *Glasgow East*
Dakin, Nick, *Scunthorpe*

Danczuk, Simon, *Rochdale*
Davies, Geraint, *Swansea West*
De Piero, Gloria, *Ashfield*
Docherty, Thomas, *Dunfermline & Fife West*
Doyle, Gemma, *Dunbartonshire West*
Dromey, Jack, *Birmingham Erdington*
Dugher, Michael, *Barnsley East*
Elliott, Julie, *Sunderland Central*
Esterson, Bill, *Sefton Central*
Evans, Chris, *Islwyn*
Fovargue, Yvonne, *Makerfield*
Gilmore, Sheila, *Edinburgh East*
Glass, Pat, *Durham North West*
Glindon, Mary, *Tyneside North*
Greatrex, Tom, *Rutherglen & Hamilton West*
Green, Kate, *Stretford & Urmston*
Greenwood, Lilian, *Nottingham South*
Hilling, Julie, *Bolton West*
Hunt, Tristram, *Stoke-on-Trent Central*
Jamieson, Cathy, *Kilmarnock & Loudoun*
Jones, Graham, *Hyndburn*
Jones, Susan, *Clwyd South*
Kendall, Elizabeth, *Leicester West*
Lavery, Ian, *Wansbeck*
Leslie, Christopher, *Nottingham East*
McCann, Michael, *East Kilbride, Strathaven & Lesmahagow*
McClymont, Gregg, *Cumbernauld, Kilsyth & Kirkintilloch East*
McGovern, Alison, *Wirral South*
McKinnell, Catherine, *Newcastle upon Tyne North*
Mahmood, Shabana, *Birmingham Ladywood*
Mearns, Ian, *Gateshead*
Morrice, Graeme,*Livingston*
Morris, Grahame, *Easington*
Murray, Ian, *Edinburgh South*
Nandy, Lisa, *Wigan*
Nash, Pamela, *Airdrie & Shotts*
O'Donnell, Fiona, *East Lothian*
Onwurah, Chinyelu, *Newcastle upon Tyne Central*
Pearce, Teresa, *Erith & Thamesmead*
Perkins, Toby, *Chesterfield*
Phillipson, Bridget, *Houghton & Sunderland South*
Qureshi, Yasmin, *Bolton South East*
Reeves, Rachel, *Leeds West*
Reynolds, Emma, *Wolverhampton North East*
Reynolds, Jonathan, *Stalybridge & Hyde*
Rotheram, Steve, *Liverpool Walton*
Sarwar, Anas, *Glasgow Central*
Shuker, Gavin, *Luton South*
Smith, Nick, *Blaenau Gwent*
Smith, Owen, *Pontypridd*
Turner, Karl, *Kingston upon Hull East*
Twigg, Stephen, *Liverpool Derby West*
Umunna, Chuka, *Streatham*
Vaz, Valerie, *Walsall South*
Williamson, Chris, *Derby North*
Woodcock, John, *Barrow & Furness*

LIBERAL DEMOCRAT
Birtwhistle, Gordon, *Burnley*
Crockart, Michael, *Edinburgh West*
Gilbert, Stephen, *St Austell & Newquay*
Hames, Duncan, *Chippenham*
Huppert, Julian, *Cambridge*
Lloyd, Stephen, *Eastbourne*
Munt, Tessa, *Wells*
Swales, Ian, *Redcar*
Ward, David, *Bradford East*
Wright, Simon, *Norwich South*

OTHER
Edwards, Jonathan (PC), *Carmarthen East & Dinefwr*
Long, Naomi (Alliance), *Belfast East*
Lucas, Caroline (Green), *Brighton Pavilion*
Paisley Junior, Ian (DUP), *Antrim North*
Ritchie, Margaret (SDLP), *South Down*
Shannon, Jim (DUP), *Strangford*
Whiteford, Eilidh (SNP), *Banff & Buchan*

WOMEN MPS
by party

Labour	81 (31 per cent)
Conservative	48 (16 per cent)
Liberal Democrat	7 (12 per cent)
Alliance	1 (100 per cent)
Green	1 (100 per cent)
SDLP	1 (33 per cent)
Sinn Fein	1 (20 per cent)
SNP	1 (17 per cent)
Other	1 (50 per cent)
DUP	0
Plaid Cymru	0
SDLP	0
Total	142 (22 per cent)

AVERAGE AGE OF MPS
by party

Conservative	48
Liberal Democrat	50
Other	51
Labour	52
All Parties	50

Youngest MP: Pamela Nash (Lab.), *Airdrie & Shotts,* 25
Oldest MP: Sir Peter Tapsell (C.), *Louth & Horncastle,* 80

VOTES CAST 2001, 2005 AND 2010

	2001	*2005*	*2010*
Conservative	8,357,615	8,784,915	10,683,577
Labour	10,724,953	9,552,436	8,601,349
Liberal Democrat	4,814,321	5,985,454	6,827,312
UKIP	390,563	605,973	917,581
BNP	47,129	192,745	564,003
SNP	464,314	412,267	491,386
Green	166,477	283,414	284,823
Sinn Fein	175,933	174,530	171,942
DUP	181,999	241,856	168,216
Plaid Cymru	195,893	174,838	165,394
SDLP	169,865	125,626	110,970
UUP/ UCUNF*	216,839	127,414	102,361
Other	461,482	487,042	554,608
Total	26,367,383	27,148,510	29,643,522

* For the 2010 general election the Ulster Unionist Party formed an alliance with the Conservative Party in Northern Ireland and appeared on ballot papers as Ulster Conservatives and Unionists – New Force

SEATS CHANGING HANDS

CONSERVATIVE GAINS	
From Labour	87
From Liberal Democrats	12
From ICHC	1
Total	100
LABOUR GAINS	
From Independent	1
From Liberal Democrats	1
From Respect	1
From Speaker	1
Total	4
LIBERAL DEMOCRAT GAINS	
From Labour	5
From Conservative	3
Total	8
ALLIANCE GAIN	
From DUP	1
GREEN GAIN	
From Labour	1
INDEPENDENT GAIN	
From UUP	1
PLAID CYMRU GAIN	
From Labour	1
SPEAKER GAIN	
From Conservative	1

MAJORITIES

SMALLEST MAJORITIES

	Majority	*Majority (per cent)*
Fermanagh & South Tyrone, Michelle Gildernew, SF	4	0.0
Hampstead & Kilburn, Glenda Jackson, Lab.	42	0.1
Warwickshire North, Dan Byles, C.	54	0.1
Camborne & Redruth, George Eustice, C.	66	0.2
Bolton West, Julie Hilling, Lab.	92	0.2
Thurrock, Jackie Doyle-Price, C.	92	0.2
Hendon, Matthew Offord, Lab.	106	0.2
Oldham East & Saddleworth, Phil Woolas, Lab.	103	0.2
Oxford West & Abingdon, Nicola Blackwood, C.	176	0.3
Solihull, Lorely Burt, LD	175	0.3

LARGEST MAJORITIES

Liverpool Walton, Steve Rotherham, Lab.	19,818	57.7
Knowsley, George Howarth, Lab.	25,686	57.5
East Ham, Stephen Timms, Lab.	27,826	55.2
Belfast West, Gerry Adams, SF	17,579	54.7
Glasgow North East, Willie Bain, Lab.	15,942	54.2
Liverpool West Derby, Stephen Twigg, Lab.	18,467	51.6
Bootle, Joe Benton, Lab.	21,181	51.3
Orkney & Shetland, Alistair Carmichael, LD	9,928	51.3
Kirkcaldy & Cowdenbeath, Gordon Brown, Lab.	23,009	50.2
Coatbridge, Chryston & Bellshill, Tom Clarke, Lab.	20,714	49.8

TURNOUT

The UK parliamentary electorate on 6 May 2010 was 45,533,536. Overall turnout was 29,643,522, or 65.1 per cent. This excludes the 77,000 electors in the Thirsk & Malton constituency, where the election was held on 27 May 2010 owing to the death of a candidate.

HIGHEST TURNOUT	
East Renfrewshire	77.3%
Westmorland & Lonsdale	76.9%
Richmond Park	76.2%
Winchester	75.8%
Devon Central	75.7%
Charnwood	75.6%
Somerset North East	75.4%
St Albans	75.4%
Kenilworth & Southam	75.2%
Thornbury & Yate	75.2%

LOWEST TURNOUT	
Manchester Central	44.3%
Leeds Central	46.0%
Birmingham Ladywood	48.7%
Glasgow North East	49.1%
Blackley & Broughton	49.2%
Manchester Gorton	50.5%
Kingston upon Hull East	50.6%
Antrim East	50.7%
Glasgow Central	50.9%
Wythenshawe & Sale East	51.0%

VOTER TURNOUT 1945 – 2010

per cent

85 80 75 70 65 60 55

'45 '50 '51 '55 '59 '64 '66 '70 '74* '79 '83 '87 '92 '97 '01 '05 '10

* Average turnout – two elections were held in 1974

PARLIAMENTS SINCE 1970

Assembled	*Dissolved*	*yr*	*m.*	*d.*
29 June 1970	8 February 1974	3	7	10
6 March 1974	20 September 1974	0	6	14
22 October 1974	7 April 1979	4	5	16
9 May 1979	13 May 1983	4	0	4
15 June 1983	18 May 1987	3	11	3
17 June 1987	16 March 1992	4	8	28
27 April 1992	8 April 1997	4	11	12
7 May 1997	14 May 2001	4	0	7
13 June 2001	11 April 2005	3	9	29
11 May 2005	12 April 2010	4	11	1
11 May 2010				

MANIFESTO COMMITMENTS

Below are selected key manifesto commitments for the two political parties that formed a coalition government following the 2010 general election.

CONSERVATIVE, *INVITATION TO JOIN THE GOVERNMENT OF BRITAIN*

ECONOMY

- Cut £6bn of departmental spending in the financial year 2010–11
- Freeze public-sector pay for one year in 2011
- Review bringing forward the date when the pension age starts to rise
- Stop tax credits for families with incomes of over £50,000
- Cut most government contributions to child trust funds
- Raise the inheritance tax threshold to £1m
- Create a single work programme for all unemployed
- Introduce a levy on banks
- Put the Bank of England in charge of monitoring UK credit and debt

HEALTH

- Give patients a choice of NHS-level healthcare providers
- Put patients before targets
- Link GPs' pay to the quality of their results
- Voluntary one-off premiums to protect sale of homes to pay for residential care
- Weight health funding towards the poorest areas

EDUCATION

- Raise qualification for state-funded teacher training to at least a 2:2 degree
- Make Key Stage 2 tests and league tables more rigorous
- Reform the primary school curriculum
- Allow any good education provider to set up an academy school
- Give all existing schools the chance to gain academy status
- Allow communities to take over and run schools threatened by closure

CRIME

- Raise taxes on alcohol linked to antisocial drinking
- Anyone convicted of knife crime to face a jail sentence
- Reduce paperwork for the police
- Return charging discretion to the police for minor offences
- Increase prison capacity to stop the early release of prisoners
- Collect DNA of all existing prisoners; remove wrongly accused from the database

SOCIETY

- National Citizen Service programme for 16-year-olds
- Involve communities in the development of neighbourhoods
- Allow parents to share allocation of maternity and paternity leave
- Recognise marriage and civil partnerships in the tax system

IMMIGRATION

- Limit the number of non-EU economic migrants admitted into the UK
- Reduce net migration to tens of thousands a year
- Overseas students to pay a bond to study in the UK

POLITICAL REFORM

- Support the first-past-the-post system for Westminster elections
- Clean up the MPs' expenses system
- Cut ministers' pay and reduce the number of MPs
- All members of the Commons and Lords to be full UK taxpayers
- Make government data more transparent
- Abolish unnecessary non-departmental public bodies
- Allow electors to 'sack' MPs found guilty of serious wrongdoing
- Scrap ID cards and the National Identity Register

ENVIRONMENT

- Aim to reduce carbon emissions by 80 per cent by 2050
- Ten per cent cut in central government emissions in 12 months
- Clear the way for nuclear power stations
- Create renewable energy plants
- Give every home up to £6,500 of energy improvement measures

DEFENCE AND FOREIGN AFFAIRS

- Support the renewal of the Trident missile system
- Ensure that forces in Afghanistan have proper resources
- Ban any organisations that advocate hate or violence
- Strengthen alliances beyond Europe and North America
- Work towards greater stability in Afghanistan and Pakistan
- Ensure by law that Britain cannot concede powers to the EU or join the euro without a referendum
- Review which countries should get British aid

LIBERAL DEMOCRAT, *CHANGE THAT WORKS FOR YOU – BUILDING A FAIRER BRITAIN*

ECONOMY

- Postpone cuts in government spending until 2011–12
- Make the first £10,000 of earnings tax-free
- Introduce a mansion tax on properties worth over £2m
- Restrict tax credits; stop payments to child trust funds
- Introduce a levy on banks
- Break up the banks; separate low and high-risk banking
- Restore the link between basic state pension and earnings
- Set up a United Kingdom infrastructure bank
- Sell 49 per cent of Royal Mail

HEALTH

- Allow every patient to choose their GP
- Halve the size of the Department of Health
- NHS to pay for private treatment if deadlines are missed
- Establish local health boards to improve health services
- Overseas doctors to pass language and competence tests

EDUCATION
- Invest in a £2.5bn 'pupil premium' for disadvantaged pupils
- Scale back Key Stage 2 tests in favour of teacher assessment
- Replace the National Curriculum with a Minimum Curriculum Entitlement
- Replace academies with sponsor-managed schools commissioned by local authorities
- Scrap tuition fees for all students taking a first degree
- Scrap the target of 50 per cent of young people going to university

CRIME
- Review the tax system for alcohol
- Pay for 3,000 more police on the beat
- Reduce bureaucracy at police stations
- Reduce the number of short prison sentences
- Cancel the prison-building programme
- Remove profiles of innocent people from the DNA database

SOCIETY
- Allow parents to share allocation of maternity and paternity leave
- Share contact time between both parents in the event of family breakdown
- Right to request flexible working for all employees
- Scrap compulsory retirement ages

IMMIGRATION
- Introduce a regional points-based system for migrants
- Allow illegal immigrants living in the UK for ten years prior to 2010 to apply for citizenship
- Allow asylum seekers to work

POLITICAL REFORM
- Introduce the single-transferable-vote system for elections
- Introduce fixed-term parliaments
- Give the right to vote from age 16
- Replace the House of Lords with a fully elected second chamber
- Allow electors to 'sack' MPs found guilty of serious wrongdoing
- All members of the Commons and Lords to be full UK taxpayers
- Scrap ID cards and biometric passports

ENVIRONMENT
- Energy improvement package of up to £10,000 a household
- 100 per cent of electricity from non carbon-emitting sources by 2050
- Reduce carbon emissions by 30 per cent by 2020
- Aim to end the use of landfill
- Increase the general right of access to the countryside

DEFENCE AND FOREIGN AFFAIRS
- Oppose like-for-like replacement of the Trident missile system
- Cancel the Eurofighter Tranche 3B
- Be critical supporters of the Afghanistan mission
- Hold a full judicial inquiry into allegations of British complicity in torture
- Support cancellation of unpayable debts for the world's poorest countries
- Renew Franco-British and European defence cooperation
- Make the EU use its collective weight in foreign policy

THE GOVERNMENT

A coalition government formed of the Conservative Party and Liberal Democrat Party (since 12 May 2010)

as at 1 September 2010

* Liberal Democrats

THE CABINET

Prime Minister, First Lord of the Treasury and Minister for the Civil Service
Rt. Hon. David Cameron, MP
Deputy Prime Minister, Lord President of the Council (with special responsibility for political and constitutional reform)
*Rt. Hon. Nick Clegg, MP
First Secretary of State, Secretary of State for Foreign and Commonwealth Affairs
Rt. Hon. William Hague, MP
Chancellor of the Exchequer
Rt. Hon. George Osborne, MP
Secretary of State for Business, Innovation and Skills
*Rt. Hon. Dr Vincent Cable, MP
Secretary of State for Communities and Local Government
Rt. Hon. Eric Pickles, MP
Secretary of State for Culture, Olympics, Media and Sport
Rt. Hon. Jeremy Hunt, MP
Secretary of State for Defence
Rt. Hon. Dr Liam Fox, MP
Secretary of State for Education
Rt. Hon. Michael Gove, MP
Secretary of State for Energy and Climate Change
*Rt. Hon. Chris Huhne, MP
Secretary of State for Environment, Food and Rural Affairs
Rt. Hon. Caroline Spelman, MP
Secretary of State for Health
Rt. Hon. Andrew Lansley, CBE, MP
Secretary of State for the Home Department and Minister for Women and Equalities
Rt. Hon. Theresa May, MP
Secretary of State for International Development
Rt. Hon. Andrew Mitchell, MP
Secretary of State for Justice and Lord Chancellor
Rt. Hon. Kenneth Clarke, QC, MP
Secretary of State for Northern Ireland
Rt. Hon. Owen Paterson, MP
Secretary of State for Scotland
*Michael Moore, MP
Secretary of State for Transport
Rt. Hon. Philip Hammond, MP
Secretary of State for Wales
Rt. Hon. Cheryl Gillan, MP
Secretary of State for Work and Pensions
Rt. Hon. Iain Duncan Smith, MP
Chief Secretary to the Treasury
*Rt. Hon. Danny Alexander, MP (since 29 May 2010)
Leader of the House of Lords, Chancellor of the Duchy of Lancaster
Rt. Hon. Lord Strathclyde
Minister without Portfolio (Minister of State)
Rt. Hon. Baroness Warsi

ALSO ATTENDING CABINET MEETINGS
Attorney-General
†Rt. Hon. Dominic Grieve, QC, MP
Leader of the House of Commons and Lord Privy Seal
Rt. Hon. Sir George Young, Bt., MP
Minister for the Cabinet Office and Paymaster General
Rt. Hon. Francis Maude, MP
Minister for the Cabinet Office (providing policy advice to the prime minister)
Rt. Hon. Oliver Letwin, MP
Minister of State for Universities and Science
David Willetts, MP
Parliamentary Secretary to the Treasury and Chief Whip
Rt. Hon. Patrick McLoughlin, MP

† Only attends cabinet meetings when ministerial responsibilities are on the agenda

LAW OFFICERS

Attorney-General
Rt. Hon. Dominic Grieve, QC, MP
Solicitor-General
Edward Garnier, QC, MP
Advocate-General for Scotland
*Rt. Hon. Lord Wallace of Tankerness, QC

MINISTERS OF STATE

Business, Innovation and Skills
John Hayes, MP
Mark Prisk, MP
David Willetts, MP
Cabinet Office
Rt. Hon. Oliver Letwin, MP
Communities and Local Government
Greg Clark, MP
Grant Shapps, MP
Defence
*Nick Harvey, MP
Education
Nick Gibb, MP
John Hayes, MP
*Sarah Teather, MP
Energy and Climate Change
Gregory Barker, MP
Charles Hendry, MP
Environment, Food and Rural Affairs
Jim Paice, MP
Equalities Office
Rt. Hon. Theresa May, MP
Foreign and Commonwealth Office
*Jeremy Browne, MP
Rt. Hon. Lord Howell of Guildford
David Lidington, MP
Health
Simon Burns, MP
*Paul Burstow, MP
Home Office
Damian Green, MP
Nick Herbert, MP
Baroness Neville-Jones

International Development
Alan Duncan, MP
Justice
Nick Herbert, MP
*Rt. Hon. Lord McNally
Northern Ireland Office
Hugo Swire, MP
Transport
Theresa Villiers, MP
Work and Pensions
Chris Grayling, MP
*Steve Webb, MP

UNDER-SECRETARIES OF STATE

Business, Innovation and Skills
*Edward Davey, MP
Ed Vaizey, MP
Baroness Wilcox
Communities and Local Government
Baroness Hanham, CBE
Bob Neill, MP
*Andrew Stunell, OBE, MP
Culture, Media and Sport
John Penrose, MP
Hugh Robertson, MP
Ed Vaizey, MP
Defence
Lord Astor of Hever
Gerald Howarth, MP
Peter Luff, MP
Andrew Robathan, MP
Education
Lord Hill of Oareford, CBE
Tim Loughton, MP
Energy and Climate Change
Lord Marland
Environment, Food and Rural Affairs
Richard Benyon, MP
Lord Henley
Equalities Office
*Lynne Featherstone, MP
Foreign and Commonwealth Office
Henry Bellingham, MP
Alistair Burt, MP
Health
Earl Howe
Anne Milton, MP
Home Office
James Brokenshire, MP
*Lynne Featherstone, MP
International Development
Stephen O'Brien, MP
Justice
Crispin Blunt, MP
Jonathan Djanogly, MP
Scotland Office
David Mundell, MP
Transport
*Norman Baker, MP
Mike Penning, MP
Wales Office
David Jones, MP
Work and Pensions
Lord Freud
Maria Miller, MP

OTHER MINISTERS

Parliamentary Private Secretary to the Prime Minister
Desmond Swayne, MP
Cabinet Office
Mark Harper, MP *(Parliamentary Secretary)*
Nick Hurd, MP *(Parliamentary Secretary)*
Office of the Leader of the House of Commons
*David Heath, CBE, MP *(Parliamentary Secretary and Deputy Leader of the Commons)*
Treasury
Mark Hoban, MP *(Financial Secretary)*
Justine Greening, MP *(Economic Secretary)*
David Gauke, MP *(Exchequer Secretary)*
Lord Sassoon *(Commercial Secretary)*

GOVERNMENT WHIPS

HOUSE OF LORDS

Captain of the Honourable Corps of the Gentlemen-at-Arms (Chief Whip)
Rt. Hon. Baroness Anelay of St Johns, DBE
Captain of the Queen's Bodyguard of the Yeomen of the Guard (Deputy Chief Whip)
*Rt. Hon. Lord Shutt of Greetland, OBE
Lords-in-Waiting
Earl Attlee
Lord Astor of Hever
Lord De Mauley
Lord Taylor of Holbeach, CBE
*Lord Wallace of Saltaire
Baronesses-in-Waiting
*Baroness Northover
Baroness Rawlings
Baroness Verma

HOUSE OF COMMONS

Parliamentary Secretary to the Treasury (Chief Whip)
Rt. Hon. Patrick McLoughlin, MP
Treasurer of HM Household (Deputy Chief Whip)
John Randall, MP
Comptroller of HM Household (Deputy Chief Whip)
*Alistair Carmichael, MP
Vice-Chamberlain of HM Household
Mark Francois, MP
Lords Commissioners of HM Treasury
James Duddridge, MP; Michael Fabricant, MP; Brooks Newmark, MP; Angela Watkinson, MP; Jeremy Wright, MP
Assistant Whips
Stephen Crabb, MP; Philip Dunne, MP; Robert Goodwill, MP; *Mark Hunter, MP; *Norman Lamb, MP; Chloe Smith, MP; Shailesh Vara, MP; Bill Wiggin, MP

;OVERNMENT DEPARTMENTS

HE CIVIL SERVICE

nder the Next Steps programme, launched in 1988, any semi-autonomous executive agencies were stablished to carry out much of the work of the civil rvice. Executive agencies operate within a framework set y the responsible minister which specifies policies, bjectives and available resources. All executive agencies e set annual performance targets by their minister. Each gency has a chief executive, who is responsible for the ay-to-day operations of the agency and who is ccountable to the minister for the use of resources and r meeting the agency's targets. The minister accounts to arliament for the work of the agency. Nearly 75 per cent f civil servants now work in executive agencies. In the rst quarter of 2010 there were 493,000 permanent civil rvants, down from about 537,000 in June 2005.

The Senior Civil Service was created in 1996 and in lay 2010 comprised around 4,200 staff from permanent cretary to the former grade 5 level, including all agency hief executives. All government departments and xecutive agencies are now responsible for their own pay nd grading systems for civil servants outside the Senior ivil Service.

ALARIES 2010–11

IINISTERIAL SALARIES *from 1 April 2010*

linisters who are members of the House of Commons ceive a parliamentary salary of £65,738 in addition to eir ministerial salary.

Prime minister	£76,762
Cabinet minister (Commons)	£68,827
Cabinet minister (Lords)	£101,038
Minister of state (Commons)	£33,002
Minister of state (Lords)	£78,891
Parliamentary under-secretary (Commons)	£23,697
Parliamentary under-secretary (Lords)	£68,710

PECIAL ADVISERS' SALARIES *from 1 April 2010*

pecial advisers to government ministers are paid out of ublic funds; their salaries are negotiated individually, but re usually in the range of £40,352 to £106,864.

IVIL SERVICE SALARIES *from 1 April 2010*

Senior Civil Servants	
Permanent secretary	£141,800–£279,300
Band 3	£101,500–£208,100
Band 2	£82,900–£162,500
Band 1A	£67,600–£128,900
Band 1	£61,500–£117,800

taff are placed in pay bands according to their level of esponsibility and taking account of other factors such as xperience and marketability. Movement within and etween bands is based on performance. Following the elegation of responsibility for pay and grading to overnment departments and agencies from 1 April 1996, is no longer possible to show service-wide pay rates for taff outside the Senior Civil Service.

GOVERNMENT DEPARTMENTS

For more information on government departments, *see* W www.cabinetoffice.gov.uk/ministerial_responsibilities.aspx

ATTORNEY-GENERAL'S OFFICE

Attorney-General's Office, 20 Victoria Street, London SW1H 0NF
T 020-7271 2492
E correspondenceunit@attorneygeneral.gsi.gov.uk
W www.attorneygeneral.gov.uk
Attorney-General's Chambers, Royal Courts of Justice, Belfast BT1 3JY
T 028-9054 6082

The law officers of the crown for England and Wales are the Attorney-General and the Solicitor-General. The Attorney-General, assisted by the Solicitor-General, is the chief legal adviser to the government and is also ultimately responsible for all crown litigation. He has overall responsibility for the work of the Law Officers' Departments (the Treasury Solicitor's Department, the Crown Prosecution Service incorporating the Revenue and Customs Prosecutions Office, the Serious Fraud Office, the Army Prosecuting Authority, HM Crown Prosecution Service Inspectorate and the Attorney-General's Office). He has a specific statutory duty to superintend the discharge of their duties by the Director of Public Prosecutions (who heads the Crown Prosecution Service) and the Director of the Serious Fraud Office. The Director of Public Prosecutions for Northern Ireland and the Crown Solicitor for Northern Ireland are also responsible to the Attorney-General for the performance of their functions. The Attorney-General has specific responsibilities for the enforcement of the criminal law and also performs certain public interest functions, eg protecting charities and appealing unduly lenient sentences. He also deals with questions of law arising in bills and with issues of legal policy.

Attorney-General, Rt. Hon. Dominic Grieve, QC, MP
Private Secretary, D. Parish
Solicitor-General, Edward Garnier, QC, MP
Director-General, P. Fish
Director, Criminal Law, S. Patten

DEPARTMENT FOR BUSINESS, INNOVATION AND SKILLS

1 Victoria Street, London SW1H 0ET
T 020-7215 5000 W www.bis.gov.uk

The Department for Business, Innovation and Skills (BIS) was established in June 2009 by merging the Department for Business, Enterprise and Regulatory Reform and the Department for Innovation, Universities and Skills. It aims to build Britain's capabilities to compete in the global economy. The merger brought together expertise in enterprise, innovation, and world-class science and research. Among other roles, the department advocates the needs of business across government; promotes an enterprise environment; invests in the development of the higher education system; invests in the UK's science base; invests in skills through the further education system, aims to expand the number of apprenticeships; collaborates with regional development agencies to build

economic growth in England; and encourages innovation in the UK.
Secretary of State for Business, Innovation and Skills and President of the Board of Trade, Rt. Hon. Dr Vince Cable, MP
Principal Private Secretary, Joanna Crellin
Senior Private Secretary, Bryan Payne
Special Advisers, Katie Waring; Giles Wilkes
Minister of State, Rt. Hon. David Willetts, MP *(Universities and Science)*
Senior Private Secretary, Emma Payne
Special Adviser, Nick Hillman
Minister of State, John Hayes *(Further Education, Skills and Lifelong Learning)**
Private Secretary, Kellie Hurst
Minister of State, Mark Prisk, MP *(Business and Enterprise)*
Senior Private Secretary, Helen Mitchell
Parliamentary Under-Secretary of of State, Edward Davey, MP *(Employment Relations, Consumer and Postal Affairs)*
Private Secretary, Amy Jordan
Parliamentary Under-Secretary of State, Ed Vaizey, MP *(Culture, Communications and Creative Industries)*†
Private Secretary, Craig Westwood *(DCMS)*
Parliamentary Under-Secretary of State, Baroness Wilcox *(Business, Innovation and Skills)*
Private Secretary, Rachael Bishop
Permanent Secretary (acting), Philip Rutnam
Private Secretary, Karis Hewitt
Head of Parliamentary Unit, Ian Webster

* Jointly with the Department of Education
† Jointly with the Department for Culture, Media and Sport

MANAGEMENT BOARD
Chair, Philip Rutnam *(Acting Permanent Secretary of State)*
Members, Sir Andrew Cahn *(UK Trade and Investment);* Bernadette Kelly *(Fair Markets);* Stephen Lovegrove *(Shareholder Executive);* Stephen Marston *(Universities and Skills);* Howard Orme *(Finance and Commercial);* Vicky Pryce *(Economics and UK Government Economic Service);* Philip Rutnam *(Business);* Philip Rycroft *(Innovation and Enterprise, and Better Regulation Executive);* Rachel Sandby-Thomas *(The Solicitor and Legal, People and Communications);* Adrian Smith *(Science and Research)*
Non-Executive Members, Prof. Julia King; Dame Julie Mellor; Dr Brian Woods-Scawen

BETTER REGULATION EXECUTIVE
1 Victoria Street, London SW1 0ET
T 020-7215 5000 **E** breadmin@bis.gsi.gov.uk
W www.bis.gov.uk/betterregulation

The Better Regulation Executive is responsible for implementing the agenda for regulation; working across government to improve the way new laws and regulations are created; reducing unnecessary red tape; and providing the best environment for businesses to start up and grow.
Chair, Sir Don Curry
Chief Executive, Philip Rycroft

SHAREHOLDER EXECUTIVE
1 Victoria Street, London SW1H 0ET
T 020-7215 3909 **W** www.shareholderexecutive.gov.uk

The Shareholder Executive was set up in September 2003 to work with all departments in government to improve the government's capabilities and performance as a shareholder. Its goal is to create a climate of ownership that, while challenging, is genuinely supportive and provides the framework for its businesses to be successful. The executive's current remit covers over 30 businesses.
Chair, Philip Remnant
Chief Executive, Stephen Lovegrove

CABINET OFFICE

70 Whitehall, London SW1A 2AS
T 020-7276 1234; Switchboard 020-7276 3000
W www.cabinet-office.gov.uk

The Cabinet Office, alongside the Treasury, sits at the centre of the government. It has three core functions: to support the prime minister in defining and delivering the government's objectives; to support the cabinet in ensuring the coherence, quality and delivery of policy and operations across departments; and strengthening the Civil Service's capabilities in terms of organisation leadership and skills. The department is headed by the Minister for the Cabinet Office.
Prime Minister, First Lord of the Treasury and Minister for the Civil Service, Rt. Hon. David Cameron, MP
Principal Private Secretary to the Prime Minister, James Bowler
Deputy Prime Minister, Rt. Hon. Nick Clegg, MP
Minister for the Cabinet Office and Paymaster General, Rt. Hon. Francis Maude, MP
Parliamentary Private Secretary, Amber Batool, MP
Private Secretaries, Roger Cotes; Elizabeth McGarva
Minister of State, Rt. Hon. Oliver Letwin *(Government Policy),* MP
Assistant Private Secretaries, Nasira Ashraf; Kate Lalor
Parliamentary Secretary, Nick Hurd, MP *(Civil Society)*
Private Secretary, Kate Wilson
Parliamentary Secretary, Mark Harper, MP *(Political and Constitutional Reform)*
Private Secretary, Joanne Trimble-Bruce
Leader of the House of Lords and Chancellor of the Duchy of Lancaster, Rt. Hon. Lord Strathclyde
Private Secretaries, Phil Lloyd *(Head of Office);* Rebecca Russel-Ponte
Minister of State, Rt. Hon. Baroness Warsi *(without portfolio)*
Private Secretary, Cleo Blackman
Secretary of the Cabinet and Head of the Home Civil Service, Sir Gus O'Donnell, KCB
Principal Private Secretary, Paul Kissack
Private Secretary, Lynne Charles

MANAGEMENT BOARD
Chair, Sir Gus O'Donnell
Board Members, Alex Allan *(Permanent Secretary);* Ruth Carnall; Alexis Cleveland *(Corporate Services Group);* Sir Jon Cunliffe, CB *(Prime Minister's Adviser);* Jeremy Heywood *(Permanent Secretary, Prime Minister's Office);* Karen Jordan; Gill Rider *(Civil Service Capability Group);* Christina Scott *(Head, Civil Contingencies Secretariat);* Chris Wormald *(Domestic Policy Group)*

HONOURS AND APPOINTMENTS SECRETARIAT
Ground Floor, Admiralty Arch, The Mall, London SW1A 2WH
T 020-7276 2777
Permanent Secretary, Alex Allan
Prime Minister's Appointments Secretary, Sir Paul Britton, CB
Ceremonial Officer, Denis Brennan

DOMESTIC POLICY GROUP
Comprising Economic and Domestic Affairs, Economic Policy Coordination, the Strategy Unit, and European and Global Issues.
Director-General, Chris Wormald

ECONOMIC AND DOMESTIC AFFAIRS SECRETARIAT
Director, Robin Fellgett, CB
Deputy Directors, Scott McPherson *(MoJ, Home Office, Devolution);* Hannah Tooze *(Legislation, Home Affairs – Olympics);* Patrick White *(Health and Social Justice)*
Parliamentary Adviser, John Healey

ECONOMIC POLICY COORDINATION
Director of the National Economic Council Secretariat and Deputy Head, Economic and Domestic Affairs Secretariat, Jeremy Pocklington
Deputy Directors, Caleb Deeks *(Public Spending, Labour Market);* Debbie Gillat *(Business Banking and Reform)*

STRATEGY UNIT
Director, Gareth Davies
Deputy Directors, Miatta Fahnbulleh *(Localism);* Hugh Harris *(Welfare);* Axel Heitmueller *(Economy);* Halima Khan *(Value for Money);* Sophia Oliver *(Health and Social Care);* Harvey Redgrave *(Home Affairs);* Matt Robinson *(Strategic Challenges);* Chloe Ross *(Education and Family)*

EUROPEAN AND GLOBAL ISSUES SECRETARIAT
Director, Paul Rankin
Prime Minister's Adviser, Sir Jon Cunliffe, CB *(Europe and Global Issues)*
Senior Adviser, Jonathan Portes *(Economic Policy Issues)*
Deputy Directors, Harold Freeman *(International Economic Affairs);* Hermione Gough *(Economic Reform, Energy and Climate Change, Employment and Social Affairs);* Matthew Taylor *(EU Issues)*

NATIONAL SECURITY
Comprises the Joint Intelligence Organisation, National Security Secretariat, Foreign Policy and Intelligence, Security and Resilience

JOINT INTELLIGENCE ORGANISATION
Chair, Joint Intelligence Committee and Professional Head of Intelligence Analysis, Alex Allan
Chief of the Assessments Staff, Paul Rimmer
Deputy Professional Head of Intelligence Analysis, vacant

NATIONAL SECURITY SECRETARIAT
70 Whitehall, London SW1A 2AS
Prime Minister's National Security Adviser, Sir Peter Ricketts, KCMG
Deputy National Security Adviser, Simon McDonald, CMG *(Foreign Policy)*
Directors, Philip Barton, CMG, OBE *(Afghanistan and Pakistan);* Julian Miller, CB *(Foreign and Defence Policy)*

INTELLIGENCE, SECURITY AND RESILIENCE
Deputy National Security Adviser (Intelligence, Security and Resilience), vacant
Directors, Ciaran Martin *(Security and Intelligence);* Willam Nye *(Strategy and Counter-Terrorism);* Christina Scott *(Civil Contingencies Secretariat);* Neil Thompson *(Office of Cyber Security)*

EFFICIENCY AND REFORM GROUP
Chief Operating Officer, Ian Watmore
Director, Ben Jupp
Deputy Director, Paula McDonald, CBE *(Pay and Workforce Reform)*

OFFICE OF GOVERNMENT COMMERCE (OGC)
Rosebery Court, St Andrews Business Park, Norwich, Norfolk NR7 0HS
T 0845-000 4999 **E** servicedesk@ogc.gsi.gov.uk
W www.ogc.gov.uk

The Office of Government Commerce was set up in April 2000, and became part of the Efficiency and Reform Group in the Cabinet Office in June 2010. It is responsible for increasing the government's value for money by improving standards and capability in procurement, for example by commodities buying, delivering major capital projects, and maximising the effective use of government spending and a £30bn property estate.

BUYING SOLUTIONS
3rd Floor, Royal Liver Building, Pier Head, Liverpool L3 1PE
T 0345-410 2222 **E** info@buyingsolutions.gsi.gov.uk
W www.buyingsolutions.gov.uk

The agency provides a professional procurement service to public sector organisations delivering improved value for money. It was established in 2001 and is an executive agency of the Office of Government Commerce.
Chief Executive, Alison Littley

OFFICE OF THE CHIEF INFORMATION OFFICER
Cabinet Office Chief Information Officer, Lesley Hume
Deputy Director, Neill Goulder *(ICT Service Delivery)*

CIVIL SERVICE CAPABILITY GROUP
Admiralty Arch, The Mall, London SW1A 2WH

Comprises Civil Service Reform, Civil Service Workforce and Leadership and Talent Management
Head, Gill Rider

CIVIL SERVICE REFORM
Director, Brian Etheridge, CBE
Deputy Directors, Liz McKeown *(Analysis and Insight);* Adam Pemberton *(Strategy and Performance);* Ian Wood *(Capability Review)*

CIVIL SERVICE WORKFORCE
Director, Dusty Amroliwala
Deputy Directors, Jennifer Hutton *(Diversity, Health and Wellbeing Strategy);* John Whittaker, CBE *(Employment Policy);* Julia Wood *(Pay and Reward)*

LEADERSHIP AND TALENT MANAGEMENT
Director, Helen Dudley, CBE
Deputy Directors, Jacquie Heany *(HR Profession);* Joanne Peel *(Fast Stream);* Esther Wallington *(Senior Appointments and Talent Management)*

GOVERNMENT COMMUNICATION GROUP
Ripley House, 22/26 Whitehall, London SW1A 2WH
T 020-7276 2712
Permanent Secretary, Matt Tee *(Government Communication)*

Directors, Sue Jenkins *(Government Communication Group);* Andrew Stott *(Transparency and Digital Engagement);* Karen Wheeler, CBE *(Digital Delivery Programme)*
Deputy Director, Michael Warren *(Government Communication)*

COMMUNICATIONS
Director, Jenny Gray
Deputy Directors, Alison Potter-Drake *(Head of News);* Rishi Saha *(Digital Communication);* Emma Thwaites *(Strategic Communications);* John Toker *(Communications for Counter-Terrorism)*

OFFICE OF THE GOVERNMENT CHIEF INFORMATION OFFICER

Admiralty Arch, The Mall, London SW1A 2AH
HM Government Chief Information Officer, John Suffolk
Private Secretary and Secretary to the CIO Council, Sue Bateman
Special Projects, Andy Bloyce
Director, Martin Bellamy (IT Strategy and Policy)
Heads, Jo Clift *(Shared Services);* Owen Pengelly *(Central Sponsor for Information Assurance Unit)*

GOVERNMENT CLOUD PROGRAMME
Director, Chris Chant
Deputy Director, Andrew Tait *(Data Centre Strategy, G-Cloud and Apps Store)*

ICT STRATEGY AND POLICY
Deputy Government Chief Information Officer and Director, Bill McCluggage
Deputy Director, Rachel Gentry

SHARED ICT INFRASTRUCTURE
Director, Lesley Hume
Deputy Directors, Claire Baker *(Government IT Profession);* Kevin Docherty *(Cabinet Office ICT Strategy, Policy and Security);* Neill Goulder *(ICT Service Delivery);* John Stubley *(Public Service Network Programme);* Chris Thirkell *(Reliable Delivery)*

OFFICE FOR CIVIL SOCIETY

The Office for Civil Society replaced the Office for the Third Sector in May 2010 and takes a key role in delivering the government's Big Society agenda.
Director-General, Rolande Anderson
Deputy Directors, Sarah Benioff *(Participation);* Liz Liston-Jones *(Social Enterprise and Finance);* Juliet Mountford *(Strategy and Communications);* Pat Samuel, CBE *(Public Sector Partnerships);* Helen Stephenson *(OCS Support);* Jane Swift *(Social Exclusion Task Force);* Ann Watt *(Social Exclusion Task Force)*

CORPORATE SERVICES GROUP

Comprises Finance and Human Resources
Director-General, Alexis Cleveland, CB
Deputy Directors, Karen Cadman *(Head of Civil Service Pensions);* Roger Smethurst *(Knowledge and Information Management)*

FINANCE
Director, Bruce Mann, CB
Deputy Directors, Peter Lawrence *(Strategy, Planning and Performance);* Jerry Page *(Finance and Estates)*

HUMAN RESOURCES
Director, Janette Durbin
Deputy Director, Simon Fryer

PRIME MINISTER'S OFFICE

10 Downing Street, London SW1A 2AA
T 020-7930 4433 **W** www.number-10.gov.uk
Prime Minister, Rt. Hon David Cameron, MP
Parliamentary Private Secretary, Desmond Swayne, MP
Permanent Secretary, Jeremy Heywood, CB, CVO
Principal Private Secretary, James Bowler
Director of Communications, Andy Coulson
Prime Minister's Official Spokesman, Steve Field
Chief of Staff (Political), Ed Llewellyn
Deputy Chief of Staff (Political), Catherine Fall
Director of Policy, James O'Shaughnessy
Political Press Secretary to the Prime Minister, Gabby Bertin

DEPUTY PRIME MINISTER'S OFFICE AND CONSTITUTION REFORM

Principal Private Secretary to the Deputy Prime Minister, Calum Miller

CONSTITUTIONAL GROUP
Director General, Rowena Collins-Rice
Director, Vijay Rangarajan
Deputy Directors, Judith Simpson *(Constitutional Settlement and Clerk of the Privy Council);* Mark Sweeney *(Elections and Democracy)*

CROSS GOVERNMENT UNITS in the Cabinet Office comprises the Committee on Standards in Public Life (*see* Public Bodies), Independent Offices and the Office of the Parliamentary Counsel.

INDEPENDENT OFFICES

OFFICE OF THE COMMISSIONER FOR PUBLIC APPOINTMENTS (OCPA)
3rd Floor, 35 Great Smith Street, London SW1P 3BQ
T 020-7276 2625 **E** ocpa@gtnet.gov.uk
W www.publicappointmentscommissioner.org

The Commissioner for Public Appointments is responsible for monitoring, regulating and reporting on ministerial appointments to public bodies. The commissioner can investigate complaints about the way in which appointments were made or applicants treated.
Commissioner for Public Appointments, Dame Janet Gaymer, DBE, QC
Head of Office, Leila Brosnan

OFFICE OF THE CIVIL SERVICE COMMISSIONERS (OCSC)
35 Great Smith Street, London SW1P 3BQ
T 020-7276 2617 **W** www.civilservicecommissioners.org

The Civil Service Commissioners are regulators of the principle that selection for appointment to the Civil Service must be on merit on the basis of fair and open competition; they publish recruitment principles and audit departments and agencies' performance against these. They personally chair competitions for the most senior jobs in the civil service. In addition, they hear appeals from civil servants under the Civil Service Code.
First Commissioner, Dame Janet Paraskeva, DBE
Commissioners (part-time), Sir Michael Aaronson, CBE;

Mark Addison; Adele Biss; Peter Blausten; Dame Janet Gaymer, DBE, QC; Prof. Christine Hallett; Eliza Hermann; Bernard Knight; Sir Neil McIntosh; Anthea Millett, CBE; Ranjit Sondhi; Libby Watkins

OFFICE OF THE PARLIAMENTARY COUNSEL
36 Whitehall, London SW1A 2AY
T 020-7210 2588
W www.cabinetoffice.co.uk/parliamentarycounsel
First Parliamentary Counsel, Stephen Laws, CB
Chief Executive, Jim Barron, CBE

DEPARTMENT FOR COMMUNITIES AND LOCAL GOVERNMENT

Eland House, Bressenden Place, London SW1E 5DU
T 0303-444 0000 W www.communities.gov.uk

The Department for Communities and Local Government (CLG) was formed in May 2006 with a remit to promote community cohesion and prevent extremism, as well as responsibility for housing, urban regeneration and planning. It unites the communities and civil renewal functions previously undertaken by the Home Office, with responsibility for regeneration, neighbourhood renewal and local government (previously held by the Office of the Deputy Prime Minister, which was abolished following a cabinet reshuffle in May 2006).

The CLG also has responsibility for equality policy on race and faith (functions that were previously split between several government departments).

Secretary of State for Communities and Local Government, Rt. Hon. Eric Pickles, MP
Private Secretary, Nick Dexter
Parliamentary Private Secretary, Stephen Hammond, MP
Minister of State, Rt. Hon. Grant Shapps, MP *(Housing)*
Private Secretary, Mark Livesey
Minister of State, Rt. Hon. Greg Clark, MP *(Decentralisation)*
Private Secretary, Fakruz Zaman
Parliamentary Under-Secretary of State, Bob Neill, MP
Private Secretary, Lee Burge
Parliamentary Under-Secretary of State, Andrew Stunnell, MP
Private Secretary, Stella Michael
Parliamentary Under-Secretary of State, Baroness Hanham, CBE
Private Secretary, Katie Burton
Permanent Secretary (acting), Irene Lucas
Private Secretary, Jenan Hasan
Chief Scientific Adviser, Jeremy Watson

MANAGEMENT BOARD
Chair, Irene Lucas *(Acting Permanent Secretary of State)*
Members, Cindy Butts; Andrew Campbell; Stephen Hay; Richard McCarthy; Joe Montgomery; Stephen Park; Shirley Pointer; David Prout; David Rossington; Rob Vincent; Sarah Weir; Dame Jo Williams, DBE

DEPARTMENT FOR CULTURE, MEDIA AND SPORT

2–4 Cockspur Street, London SW1Y 5DH
T 020-7211 6200
E enquiries@culture.gov.uk W www.culture.gov.uk

The Department for Culture, Media and Sport (DCMS) was established in July 1997 and aims to improve the quality of life for all those in the UK through cultural and sporting activities while championing the tourism, creative and leisure industries. It is responsible for government policy relating to the arts, sport, the National Lottery, tourism, libraries, museums and galleries, broadcasting, creative industries – including film and the music industry – press freedom and regulation, licensing, gambling and the historic environment.

The department is also responsible for 55 public bodies that help deliver the department's strategic aims and objectives, the 2012 Olympic Games and Paralympic Games, the listing of historic buildings and scheduling of ancient monuments, the export licensing of cultural goods, and the management of the Government Art Collection and the Royal Parks (its sole executive agency). It has the responsibility for humanitarian assistance in the event of a disaster, as well as for the organisation of the annual Remembrance Day ceremony at the Cenotaph. In May 2005 the DCMS assumed responsibility for fashion design, advertising and the arts market from the then Department for Trade and Industry – now the Department for Business, Innovation and Skills – which it also works jointly with on design issues (including sponsorship of the Design Council) and on relations with the computer games and publishing industries.

Secretary of State for Culture, Olympics, Media and Sport, Rt. Hon. Jeremy Hunt, MP
Principal Private Secretary, Rita Patel
Special Advisers, Sue Beeby; Adam Smith
Parliamentary Private Secretary, Rob Wilson, MP
Parliamentary Under-Secretary of State, John Penrose, MP *(Tourism and Heritage)*
Private Secretary, Leonie Phillips
Parliamentary Under-Secretary of State, Hugh Robertson, MP *(Sport and the Olympics)*
Private Secretary, Graeme Brown
Parliamentary Under-Secretary of State, Ed Vaizey, MP *(Culture, Communications and Creative Industries)*
Private Secretary, Craig Westwood
Permanent Secretary, Jonathan Stephens
Private Secretary, Lizzie Glithero-West

MANAGEMENT BOARD
Chair, Jonathan Stephens *(Permanent Secretary of State)*
Members, Jeremy Beeton *(Government Olympic Executive);* Andrew Ramsay, CB *(Partnerships and Programmes)*

MINISTRY OF DEFENCE

see Defence section

DEPARTMENT FOR EDUCATION

Castle View House, East Lane, Runcorn, Cheshire WA7 2GJ
T 0870-001 2345 Public Enquiries 0870-000 2288
E inforequests@education.gsi.gov.uk W www.education.gov.uk

The Department for Education (DfE) was established in May 2010 in place of the Department for Children, Schools and Families (DCSF), in order to refocus the department on its core purpose of supporting teaching and learning. The department is responsible for education and children's services, but the Department for Business, Innovation and Skills is responsible for higher education.

The department's objectives include the expansion of the academies programme, to allow schools to apply to become independent of their local authority, and the introduction of the free schools programme, to allow any suitable proposers, such as parents, businesses or charities, to set up their own school.

Secretary of State for Education, Rt. Hon. Michael Gove, MP
Principal Private Secretary, Sinead O'Sullivan
Deputy Principal Private Secretary, Emma Cottrell

Private Secretaries, Sophie Taylor; Peter Walsh
Special Advisers, Henry de Zoete; Elena Narozanski
Parliamentary Private Secretary, David Evennett, MP
Minister of State, Sarah Teather, MP *(Children and Families)*
Private Secretary, Jo Israel
Parliamentary Private Secretary, Duncan Hames, MP
Minister of State, Nick Gibb, MP *(Schools)*
Private Secretary, Jessica Attree
Parliamentary Private Secretary, vacant
Minister of State, John Hayes, MP *(Further Education, Skills and Lifelong Learning)**
Private Secretary, Kellie Hurst
Parliamentary Under-Secretary of State, Lord Hill of Oareford, CBE *(Schools)*
Private Secretary, Jamie Weatherhead
Parliamentary Under-Secretary of State, Tim Loughton, MP *(Children and Families)*
Private Secretary, David Curtis
Parliamentary Clerk, Helen Heyden
Spokesperson in the House of Lords, Lord Hill of Oareford, CBE
Permanent Secretary, David Bell
Private Secretary, Bernie Serieux

MANAGEMENT BOARD
Chair, David Bell *(Permanent Secretary of State)*
Members, Philip Augar; Jon Coles; Sue Higgins; Tom Jeffery; Lesley Longstone

*Also works in the Department for Business, Innovation and Skills

DEPARTMENT OF ENERGY AND CLIMATE CHANGE

3 Whitehall Place, London SW1A 2HD
T 0300-060 4000 E correspondence@decc.gsi.gov.uk
W www.decc.gsi.gov.uk

The Department of Energy and Climate Change (DECC) was formed in 2008 to bring together energy policy, previously the responsibility of BERR (now the Department for Business, Innovation and Skills), and climate change mitigation policy, previously the responsibility of the Department for Environment, Food and Rural Affairs. DECC is responsible for tackling the threat of climate change by securing safe, clean and affordable energy in the UK, and by changing how we resource, manage and use our energy to create a low carbon and resource-efficient world.

Secretary of State for the Department for Energy and Climate Change, Rt. Hon. Chris Huhne, MP
Private Secretary, Ashley Ibbett
Parliamentary Private Secretary, Jenny Willott, MP
Minister of State, Charles Hendry, MP
Private Secretary, Emily Veitch
Parliamentary Private Secretary, vacant
Minister of State, Gregory Barker, MP
Private Secretary, David Watson
Parliamentary Private Secretary, vacant
Parliamentary Under-Secretary of State, Lord Marland
Private Secretary, Patrick Whitehead

MANAGEMENT BOARD
Permanent Secretary, Moira Wallace
Members, Will Cavendish *(International Energy and Climate Change)*; Edmund Hosker *(Corporate Support and Professional Services)*; Phil Wynn Owen *(National Climate Change and Consumer Support)*; Simon Virley *(Energy Markets and Infrastructure)*

DEPARTMENT FOR ENVIRONMENT, FOOD AND RURAL AFFAIRS

Nobel House, 17 Smith Square, London SW1P 3JR
T 020-7238 3000 **Helpline** 0845-933 5577
E helpline@defra.gsi.gov.uk W www.defra.gov.uk

The Department for Environment, Food and Rural Affairs (DEFRA) is responsible for government policy on the environment, rural matters and farming and food production. In association with the agriculture departments of the Scottish government, the National Assembly for Wales and the Northern Ireland Office, and with the Intervention Board, the department is responsible for negotiations in the EU on the common agricultural and fisheries policies, and for single European market questions relating to its responsibilities. Its remit includes international agricultural and food trade policy.

The department's five strategic priorities are climate change, adaptation and mitigation; sustainable consumption and production; the protection of natural resources and the countryside; sustainable rural communities; and sustainable farming and food, including animal health and welfare. DEFRA is also the lead government department for emergencies in animal and plant diseases, flooding, food and water supply, dealing with the consequences of a chemical, biological, radiological or nuclear incident, and other threats to the environment.

Secretary of State for Environment, Food and Rural Affairs, Rt. Hon. Caroline Spelman, MP
Principal Private Secretary, John Kittmer
Private Secretaries, Diane Duffy; Helen Emmett; Peter Featherstone; Dan Hamza-Goodacre; Rhys Jackson; Cathy Miller; Nathalie Simon; Alexandra Suzuki
Minister of State, Jim Paice, MP *(Agriculture and Food)*
Senior Private Secretary, Karen Morgan
Private Secretaries, Caroline Jack; Martin Jenkins; Dan Skerten; Samantha Suares
Parliamentary Private Secretary, Mark Simmons, MP
Parliamentary Under-Secretary of State, Richard Benyon, MP *(Natural Environment and Fisheries)*
Senior Private Secretary, Sarah Wardle
Private Secretaries, Zahra Ali; William Pryer; Nicole Roberts
Parliamentary Under-Secretary of State, Lord Henley
Senior Private Secretary, Mike Rowe
Private Secretaries, William Boohan; Helen Hazzledine; Frances Kirwan; Darryl Pearson; David Read; Lucillia Samuel
Permanent Secretary, Dame Helen Ghosh, DBE

MANAGEMENT BOARD
Chair, Dame Helen Ghosh, DBE *(Permanent Secretary of State)*
Members, Mike Anderson *(Strategy and Evidence)*; Alexis Cleveland; Bill Griffiths; Bill Stow *(Central Approvals Panel)*; Peter Unwin *(Environment and Rural)*; Prof. Robert Watson *(Chief Scientific Adviser)*; Katrina Williams *(Food and Farming)*

FOREIGN AND COMMONWEALTH OFFICE

King Charles Street, London SW1A 2AH
T 020-7008 1500 W www.fco.gov.uk

The Foreign and Commonwealth Office (FCO) provides, through its staff in the UK and through its diplomatic missions abroad, the means of communication between the British government and other governments – and international governmental organisations – on all matters falling within the field of international relations.

It is responsible for alerting the British government to the implications of developments overseas; promoting British interests overseas; protecting British citizens abroad; explaining British policies to, and cultivating relationships with, governments overseas; the discharge of British responsibilities to the overseas territories; entry clearance UK visas (with the Home Office); and promoting British business overseas (jointly with the Department for Business, Innovation and Skills through UK Trade and Investment).

Secretary of State for Foreign and Commonwealth Affairs, Rt. Hon. William Hague, MP
Principal Private Secretary, Lindsay Appleby
Special Advisers, Denzil Davidson; Arminka Helic
Parliamentary Private Secretary, Keith Simpson, MP
Minister of State, David Lidington, MP *(Europe)*
Private Secretary, Paul Heardman
Minister of State, Jeremy Browne, MP
Private Secretary, Hamish Cowell
Parliamentary Under-Secretary of State, Alistair Burt, MP
Private Secretary, Russ Dixon
Parliamentary Under-Secretary of State, Henry Bellingham
Private Secretary, Emily Maltman
Minister of State, Rt. Hon. Lord Howell of Guildford *(House of Lords; the Commonwealth and international energy policy)*
Private Secretary, Steve Mccready
Permanent Under-Secretary of State and Head of HM Diplomatic Service, Simon Fraser
Private Secretary, Aiden Liddle
Special Representatives, John Ashton *(Climate Change);* Sir Andrew Burns *(Post-Holocaust issues);* Michael Ryder *(Sudan)*

MANAGEMENT BOARD
Chief Executive (UKTI), Andrew Cahn
Members, Sir Geoffrey Adams *(Political);* Nick Baird *(Europe and Globalisation);* James Bevan *(Change and Delivery);* Robert Hannigan *(Defence and Intelligence);* Keith Luck *(Finance);* Alison Platt

GOVERNMENT EQUALITIES OFFICE

Eland House, Bressenden Place, London SW1E 5DU
T 0303-444 1204 E enquiries@geo.gsi.gov.uk
W www.equalities.gov.uk

The Government Equalities Office (GEO) was created in July 2007. The GEO is responsible for the government's overall strategy on equality. Its work includes leading the development of a more integrated approach on equality across government; sponsoring the Equality and Human Rights Commission and Women's National Commission; taking forward the Minister for Women's priorities; taking forward work on the equality bill and supporting the work of the National Equality Panel. The department is responsible for leading policy on gender equality and sexual orientation, and for integrating work on disability, age, race and religion or belief into the overall equality framework.

Minister for Women and Equality, Rt. Hon. Theresa May, MP
Private Secretary, Lucy Phipps
Solicitor-General, Edward Garnier MP
Parliamentary Under-Secretary of State, Lynne Featherstone, MP
Private Secretary, Mike Box

SENIOR MANAGEMENT TEAM
Director-General, Jonathan Rees
Deputy Head and Policy Director, Janice Shersby
Director, Corporate Services, Chris Bull
Chief Economist and Head of Evidence and Equality at Work, Helen Carrier
Gender Equality Policy and Inclusion, Helene Reardon-Bond, OBE
Strategy, Alison Pritchard
Non-Executive Directors, Peter Bungard; Judy McKnight; Janet Soo-Chung

DEPARTMENT OF HEALTH

Richmond House, 79 Whitehall, London SW1A 2NS
T 020-7210 3000 W www.dh.gov.uk

The Department of Health is responsible for the provision of the National Health Service (NHS) in England and for social care. The department's aims are to support, protect, promote and improve the nation's health; to secure the provision of comprehensive, high-quality care for all those who need it, regardless of their ability to pay, where they live or their age; and to provide responsive adult social care for those who lack the support they need.

The Department of Health is responsible for setting health and social care policy in England. The department's work sets standards and drives modernisation across all areas of the NHS, social care and public health.

Secretary of State for Health, Rt. Hon. Andrew Lansley, CBE, MP
Principal Private Secretary, Paul Macnaught
Parliamentary Private Secretary, Dr Andrew Murrison, MP
Minister of State, Simon Burns, MP *(Health)*
Private Secretary, Elizabeth Gunnion
Minister of State, Paul Burstow, MP *(Care Services)*
Private Secretary, Ian Ellis
Parliamentary Under-Secretary of State, Anne Milton, MP *(Public Health)*
Private Secretary, Giancarlo Laura
Parliamentary Under-Secretary of State, Earl Howe *(Quality)*
Parliamentary Clerk, Tim Elms

MANAGEMENT BOARD
Chair (acting), Richard Douglas
Members, David Behan, CBE *(Social Care, Local Government and Care Partnerships);* Richard Douglas, CB *(Finance and Operations);* Sir David Nicholson, KCB, CBE *(Chief Executive, NHS);* Mike Wheeler

NATIONAL CLINICAL DIRECTORS
Cancer, Prof. Mike Richards, CBE
Children, Young People and Community Services, Dr Sheila Shribman
Community Pharmacy, Jonathan Mason
Diabetes, Dr Rowan Hillson, MBE
Diagnostic Kidney Services, Dr Donal J. O'Donoghue
Emergency Access, Prof. Sir George Alberti
Equality and Human Rights, Surinder Sharma
Health and Work, Prof. Dame Carol Black
Heart Disease and Stroke, Prof. Roger Boyle, CBE
Hospital Pharmacy, Martin Stephens
Imaging, Dr Erika Denton
Learning Disabilities, Scott Watkin *(co-national director);* Anne Williams, CBE
Mental Health, Prof. Louis Appleby, CBE
Older People's Services, vacant

Pandemic Influenza Preparedness, Helen Shirley-Quirk
Patients and the Public, Joan Saddler, OBE
Primary Care, Dr David Colin-Thome
Service Reconfiguration, Prof. Sir George Alberti
Transplantation, Chris J. Rudge
Trauma Care, Prof. Keith Willett
Widening Participation in Learning, Prof. Bob Fryer, CBE

SOLICITOR'S OFFICE*
Solicitor, Gill Aitken
Director of DWP Legal Services, Isabel Letwin
Director of DH Legal Services, Frances Logan
* Also the solicitor's office for the Department for Work and Pensions

SPECIAL HEALTH AUTHORITIES
Care Quality Commission
W www.cqc.org.uk
Health Protection Agency
W www.hpa.org.uk
National Blood Service
W www.blood.co.uk
National Clinical Assessment Service
W www.ncas.npsa.nhs.uk
National Institute for Health and Clinical Excellence
W www.nice.org.uk
National Treatment Agency for Substance Misuse
W www.nta.nhs.uk
National Patient Safety Agency
W www.npsa.nhs.uk
NHS Appointments Commission
W www.appointments.org.uk
NHS Business Services Authority
W www.nhsbsa.nhs.uk
NHS Litigation Authority
W www.nhsla.com
UK Transplant
W www.uktransplant.org.uk

HOME OFFICE

2 Marsham Street, London SW1P 4DF
T 020-7035 4848 E public.enquiries@homeoffice.gsi.gov.uk
W www.homeoffice.gov.uk

The Home Office deals with those internal affairs in England and Wales which have not been assigned to other government departments. The Secretary of State for the Home Department is the link between the Queen and the public, and exercises certain powers on her behalf, including that of the royal pardon.

The Home Office aims to build a safe, just and tolerant society and to maintain and enhance public security and protection; to support and mobilise communities so that they are able to shape policy and improvement for their locality, overcome nuisance and anti-social behaviour, maintain and enhance social cohesion and enjoy their homes and public spaces peacefully; to deliver departmental policies and responsibilities fairly, effectively and efficiently; and to make the best use of resources. These objectives reflect the priorities of the government and the home secretary in areas of crime, citizenship and communities, namely to reduce crime and the fear of crime through visible, responsive and accountable policing; to reduce organised and international crime; to combat terrorism and other threats to national security; to ensure the effective delivery of justice; to reduce re-offending and protect the public; to reduce the availability and abuse of dangerous drugs; to regulate entry to, and settlement in, the UK in the interests of sustainable growth and social inclusion; and to support strong, active communities in which people of all races and backgrounds are valued and participate on equal terms.

The Home Office delivers these aims through the immigration services, its agencies and non-departmental public bodies, and by working with partners in private, public and voluntary sectors, individuals and communities. The home secretary is also the link between the UK government and the governments of the Channel Islands and the Isle of Man.

Secretary of State for the Home Department, Rt. Hon. Theresa May, MP
Principal Private Secretary, Gillian McGregor
Assistant Private Secretary, Natasha Chetty
Special Advisers, Fiona Cunningham; Nick Timothy
Minister of State, Rt. Hon. Baroness Neville-Jones, DCMG *(Security and Counter-Terrorism)*
Private Secretary, Tom Hartley
Minister of State, Damian Green, MP *(Immigration)*
Private Secretary, Emily Weighill
Minister of State, Nick Herbert, MP *(Security, Counter-Terrorism, Crime and Policing Reform)*
Private Secretary, Phil Lawley
Parliamentary Under-Secretary of State, James Brokenshire, MP *(Crime Prevention)*
Private Secretary, Dr Simon Pender
Parliamentary Under-Secretary of State, Lynne Featherstone, MP *(Equalities and Criminal Information)*
Private Secretary, Mike Box
Permanent Secretary of State, Sir David Normington, KCB
Private Secretary, Rachel Hopcroft

MANAGEMENT BOARD
Chair, Sir David Normington, KCB *(Permanent Secretary of State)*
Members, Derrick Anderson; Philip Augar; Yasmin Diamond *(Communications);* Charles Farr *(Office for Security and Counter Terrorism);* James Hall *(Identity and Passport Service);* John Heywood; Lin Homer, CB *(UK Border Agency);* Helen Kilpatrick *(Financial and Commercial);* Peter Makeham, CB *(Strategy and Reform);* Stephen Rimmer *(Crime and Policing Group);* Kevin White, CB *(Human Resources)*

DEPARTMENT FOR INTERNATIONAL DEVELOPMENT

1 Palace Street, London SW1 5HE
T 020-7023 0000
Abercrombie House, Eaglesham Road, East Kilbride, Glasgow G75 8EA
T 01355-844000 **Public Enquiries** 0845-300 4100
E enquiry@dfid.gov.uk W www.dfid.gov.uk

The Department for International Development (DFID) is responsible for promoting sustainable development and reducing poverty. The central focus of the government's policy, based on the 1997, 2000 and 2006 white papers on international development, is a commitment to the internationally agreed Millennium Development Goals, to be achieved by 2015. These seek to eradicate extreme poverty and hunger; achieve universal primary education; promote gender equality and empower women; reduce child mortality; improve maternal health; combat HIV/AIDS, malaria and other diseases; ensure environmental sustainability; and encourage a global partnership for development.

DFID's assistance is concentrated in the poorest countries of sub-Saharan Africa and Asia, but also contributes to poverty reduction and sustainable development in middle-income countries, including those in Latin America and Eastern Europe. It also responds to overseas emergencies. The department works in partnership with governments of developing countries, charities, non-government organisations and businesses. It also works with multilateral institutions, including the World Bank, United Nations agencies and the European Commission. The department has headquarters in London and East Kilbride, offices in many developing countries, and staff based in British embassies and high commissions around the world.

Secretary of State for International Development, Rt. Hon. Andrew Mitchell, MP
Principal Private Secretary, Melanie Speight
Private Secretary, Kate Joseph
Special Advisers, Philippa Buckley; Richard Parr
Parliamentary Clerk, Jo Smith
Minister of State, Alan Duncan, MP
Private Secretary, Alasdair Wardhaugh
Parliamentary Under-Secretary of State, Stephen O'Brien, MP
Private Secretary, Greg Hicks
House of Lords Spokesperson, Baroness Verma
Whips, Chloe Smith, MP *(Commons);* Earl Attlee *(Lords)*
Permanent Secretary, Minouche Shafik

MANAGEMENT BOARD
Chair, Minouche Shafik
Members, Michael Anderson *(Policy and Global Issues);* Richard Calvert *(Corporate Performance);* Doreen Langston; Mark Lowcock *(Country Programmes);* David MacLeod

CDC GROUP
Cardinal Place, 80 Victoria Street SW1E 5JL
T 020-7963 4700 **E** enquiries@cdcgroup.com
W www.cdcgroup.com

Founded in 1948, CDC is a government-owned Development Finance Institution that invests in the creation and growth of viable private businesses in poorer developing countries in order to contribute to economic growth and reduce poverty. The company is committed to investing over 75 per cent of its funds in low-income countries. CDC is a public limited company with the Department for International Development as its 100 per cent shareholder.

Chair, Richard Gillingwater, CBE
Chief Executive, Richard Laing

MINISTRY OF JUSTICE

102 Petty France, London SW1P 9AJ
T 020-3334 3555 **E** general.queries@justice.gsi.gov.uk
W www.justice.gov.uk

The Ministry of Justice (MoJ) was established in May 2007. MoJ is headed by the Lord Chancellor and Secretary of State for Justice who is responsible for improvements to the justice system so that it better serves the public. He is also responsible for some areas of constitutional policy (those not covered by the Deputy Prime Minister).

The MoJ's priorities are to reduce reoffending and protect the public; provide access to justice; increase confidence in the justice system; and uphold people's civil liberties. The Lord Chancellor is the government minister responsible to parliament for the judiciary, the court system and prisons and probation. The Lord Chief Justice has been the head of the judiciary since 2006.

MoJ incorporates the National Offender Management Service, which includes HM Prison Service and the National Probation Service, Her Majesty's Court Service and the Tribunals Service.

MoJ has several associated departments, non-departmental public bodies and executive agencies, including Her Majesty's Land Registry, the National Archives, the Legal Services Commission, and the Public Guardianship Office. The administrative functions of the Scotland Office and the Wales Office fall under MoJ but these offices report to the respective Secretaries of State for Scotland and Wales.

Lord Chancellor and Secretary of State for Justice, Rt. Hon. Kenneth Clarke, QC, MP
Principal Private Secretary, Darren Tierney
Special Advisers, David Hass; Kathryn Laing
Parliamentary Private Secretary, Ben Wallace, MP
Minister of State and Deputy Leader of the House of Lords, Rt. Hon. Lord McNally
Private Secretary, Emma Douglas
Minister of State, Nick Herbert*, MP
Private Secretary, Phil Lawley
Parliamentary Under-Secretary of State, Jonathan Djanogly, MP
Private Secretary, Sally Jones
Parliamentary Under-Secretary of State, Crispin Blunt, MP
Private Secretary, Jane Walker
Permanent Secretary, Sir Suma Chakrabarti
Private Secretary, Hannah Davenport
Parliamentary Clerk, Ann Nixon
* Also works in the Home Office

CORPORATE MANAGEMENT BOARD
Chair, Sir Suma Chakrabarti *(Permanent Secretary of State)*
Members, Anne Beasley *(Finance);* Anne Bulford; Helen Edwards *(Justice Policy);* Peter Handcock *(Access to Justice);* David MacLeod; Michael Spurr *(Chief Executive Officer, National Offender Management Service);* Jonathan Slater *(Transforming Justice);* Sharon White *(Law, Rights and International)*

NORTHERN IRELAND OFFICE

11 Millbank, London SW1P 4PN
T 020-7210 3000
Castle Buildings, Stormont, Belfast BT4 3SG
T 028-9052 0700 **W** www.nio.gov.uk

The Northern Ireland Office was established in 1972, when the Northern Ireland (Temporary Provisions) Act transferred the legislative and executive powers of the Northern Ireland parliament and government to the UK parliament and a secretary of state.

The Northern Ireland Office is responsible primarily for security issues, and for matters relating to the political and constitutional future of the province. It also deals with international issues as they affect Northern Ireland. In April 2010 the office transferred responsibility for policing and criminal justice to the Northern Ireland Assembly and Executive.

Under the terms of the 1998 Good Friday Agreement, power was devolved to the Northern Ireland Assembly in 1999. The assembly took on responsibility for the relevant areas of work previously undertaken by the departments of the Northern Ireland Office, covering agriculture and rural development, the environment, regional development, social development, education, higher education, training and employment, enterprise, trade and investment, culture, arts and leisure, health, social services, public safety and finance and personnel. In October 2002 the Northern Ireland Assembly was suspended and Northern Ireland returned to direct rule, but despite repeated setbacks, devolution was restored on 8 May 2007. For further details, *see* Regional Government section.

Secretary of State for Northern Ireland, Owen Paterson, MP
Minister of State, Hugo Swire, MP
Permanent Secretary and Head of the Northern Ireland Civil Service, Bruce Robinson

OFFICE OF THE ADVOCATE-GENERAL FOR SCOTLAND

Dover House, Whitehall, London SW1A 2AU
T 020-7270 6713
Office of the Solicitor to the Advocate-General, Victoria Quay, Leith, Edinburgh EH6 6QQ
T 0131-244 1635
E privateoffice@advocategeneral.gsi.gov.uk
W www.oag.gov.uk

The Advocate-General for Scotland is one of the three law officers of the crown, alongside the Attorney-General and the Solicitor-General for England and Wales. He is the legal adviser to the UK government on Scottish law and is supported by staff in the Office of the Advocate-General for Scotland. The office is divided into the Legal Secretariat, based mainly in London, and the Office of the Solicitor to the Advocate-General, based in Edinburgh.

The post was created as a consequence of the constitutional changes set out in the Scotland Act 1998, which created a devolved Scottish parliament. The Lord Advocate and the Solicitor-General for Scotland then became part of the Scottish government and the Advocate-General took over their previous role as legal adviser to the government on Scots law. *See also* Regional Government section and Ministry of Justice.

Advocate-General for Scotland, Lord Wallace of Tankerness, QC
Private Secretary, Alice Adamson

OFFICE OF THE LEADER OF THE HOUSE OF COMMONS

26 Whitehall, London SW1A 2WH
T 020-7276 1005
E leader@commonsleader.x.gsi.gov.uk
W www.commonsleader.gov.uk

The Office of the Leader of the House of Commons is responsible for the arrangement of government business in the House of Commons and for planning and supervising the government's legislative programme. The Leader of the House of Commons upholds the rights and privileges of the house and acts as a spokesperson for the government as a whole.

The leader reports regularly to the cabinet on parliamentary business and the legislative programme. In his capacity as leader of the house, he is a member of the Public Accounts Commission and of the House of Commons Commission. He also chairs the cabinet committee on the legislative programme. As Lord Privy Seal, he is chair of the board of trustees of the Chevening Estate.

The Deputy Leader of the House of Commons supports the leader in handling the government's business in the house. He is responsible for monitoring MPs' and peers' correspondence.

Leader of the House of Commons and Lord Privy Seal, Rt. Hon. Sir George Young, Bt., MP
Head of Office, Mike Winter
Private Secretary, Robert Foot
Deputy Leader of the House of Commons, David Heath, CBE, MP
Private Secretary, Ben Sneddon

PRIVY COUNCIL OFFICE

2 Carlton Gardens, London SW1Y 5AA
T 020-7747 5310 E pcosecretariat@pco.x.gsi.gov.uk
W www.privy-council.gov.uk

The primary function of the office is to act as the secretariat to the Privy Council. It is responsible for the arrangements leading to the making of all royal proclamations and orders in council; for certain formalities connected with ministerial changes; for considering applications for the granting (or amendment) of royal charters; for the scrutiny and approval of by-laws and statutes of chartered institutions and of the governing instruments of universities and colleges; for approving use of the word 'university' in a company name; and for the appointment of high sheriffs and many crown and Privy Council appointments to governing bodies. Under the relevant acts, the office is responsible for the approval of certain regulations and rules made by the governing bodies of the medical and certain allied professions.

The Lord President of the Council is the ministerial head of the office and presides at meetings of the Privy Council. The Clerk of the Council is the administrative head of the Privy Council office.

Lord President of the Council and Deputy Prime Minister, Rt. Hon. Nick Clegg, MP
Clerk of the Council, Judith Simpson
Head of Secretariat and Senior Clerk, Ceri King
Senior Clerks, Christopher Berry; Meriel McCullagh
Registrar of the Judicial Committee (acting), Louise di Mambro

SCOTLAND OFFICE

Dover House, Whitehall, London SW1A 2AU
T 020-7270 6754
1 Melville Crescent, Edinburgh EH3 7HW
T 0131-244 9010
E scottish.secretary@scotland.gsi.gov.uk
W www.scotlandoffice.gov.uk

The Scotland Office is the department of the Secretary of State for Scotland which represents Scottish interests within the UK government in matters reserved to the UK parliament. The Secretary of State for Scotland also exercises certain specific functions in relation to devolution, including those provided for in the Scotland Act 1998; maintains the stability of the devolution settlement for Scotland; and pays grants to the Scottish Consolidated Fund and manages other financial transactions.

Reserved matters include the constitution, foreign affairs, defence, international development, the civil service, financial and economic matters, national security, immigration and nationality, misuse of drugs, trade and industry, various aspects of energy regulation (eg coal, electricity, oil, gas and nuclear energy), various aspects of transport, social security, employment, abortion, genetics, surrogacy, medicines, broadcasting and equal opportunities. Devolved matters include health and social work, education and training, local government and housing, justice and police, agriculture, forestry, fisheries,

the environment, tourism, sports, heritage, economic development and internal transport. *See also* Regional Government section and Ministry of Justice.
Secretary of State for Scotland, Michael Moore, MP
Private Secretary, Kate Richards
Parliamentary Private Secretary, vacant
Parliamentary Under-Secretary of State, David Mundell, MP
Private Secretary, Barbara Reid
Spokesperson in the House of Lords, Lord Wallace of Tankerness, QC

DEPARTMENT FOR TRANSPORT

Great Minster House, 76 Marsham Street, London SW1P 4DR
T 020-7944 8300 **W** www.dft.gov.uk

The Department for Transport (DfT) is responsible for setting strategy and policy and establishing and managing relationships with the organisations that are responsible for delivery. Much of the department's work is delivered by seven executive agencies that employ around 90 per cent of the staff. The DfT's main responsibilities include aviation, crime and public transport, freight, regional and local transport, social inclusion, railways, roads and road safety, science and research, shipping and vehicles and sustainable travel.

The department's work focuses on the following objectives: supporting national economic competitiveness and growth by delivering reliable and efficient transport networks; reducing transport's emissions of carbon dioxide and other greenhouse gases; reducing the risk of death, injury or illness arising from transport and promoting travel modes that are beneficial to health; promoting equality of opportunity for all citizens; improving quality of life for transport users and non-transport users; and promoting a healthy natural environment.

Secretary of State for Transport, Rt. Hon. Philip Hammond, MP
Principal Private Secretary, Natasha Robinson
Minister of State, Theresa Villiers, MP
Private Secretary, Audy Utchanah
Parliamentary Under-Secretary of State, Norman Baker, MP
Private Secretary, James Conway
Parliamentary Under-Secretary of State, Mike Penning, MP
Private Secretary, Claire McAllister
Permanent Secretary, Robert Devereux
Private Secretary, Victoria Robb

MANAGEMENT BOARD
Chair, Robert Devereux *(Permanent Secretary of State)*
Members, Alan Cook; Sally Davis; Steve Gooding *(Motoring and Freight Services);* Richard Hatfield *(International Networks and Environment);* Bronwyn Hill *(City and Regional Networks);* Mike Mitchell *(National Networks);* Claire Moriarty *(Corporate Support Functions);* Ed Smith

HM TREASURY

1 Horse Guards Road, London SW1A 2HQ
T 020-7270 4558
E public.enquiries@hm-treasury.gsi.gov.uk
W www.hm-treasury.gov.uk

HM Treasury is the country's economics and finance ministry, and is responsible for formulating and implementing the government's financial and economic policy. It aims to raise the rate of sustainable growth, boost prosperity, and provide the conditions necessary for universal economic and employment opportunities. The Office of the Lord High Treasurer has been continuously in commission for over 200 years. The Lord High Commissioners of HM Treasury are the First Lord of the Treasury (who is also the prime minister), the Chancellor of the Exchequer and five junior lords. This board of commissioners is assisted at present by the chief secretary, the parliamentary secretary (who is also the government chief whip in the House of Commons), the financial secretary, the economic secretary, the exchequer secretary and the commercial secretary. The prime minister as first lord is not primarily concerned with the day-to-day aspects of Treasury business; neither are the parliamentary secretary and the junior lords as government whips. Treasury business is managed by the Chancellor of the Exchequer and the other Treasury ministers, assisted by the permanent secretary.

The chief secretary is responsible for public expenditure, including spending reviews and strategic planning; in-year control; public sector pay and pensions; Annually Managed Expenditure and welfare reform; efficiency in public services; procurement and capital investment. He also has responsibility for the Treasury's interest in devolution.

The financial secretary is the departmental minister for HM Revenue and Customs and the Valuation Office Agency and has responsibility for financial services policy including banking and financial services reform and regulation; financial stability; city competitiveness; wholesale and retail markets in the UK, Europe and internationally; and the Financial Services Authority. His other responsibilities include banking support; bank lending; UK Financial Investments; Equitable Life; and personal savings and pensions policy. He also provides support to the chancellor on EU and wider international finance issues.

The exchequer secretary is a title only used occasionally, normally when the post of paymaster-general is allocated to a minister outside of the Treasury (as it is at present; Francis Maude, MP was appointed paymaster-general and minister of the Cabinet Office in May 2010). The exchequer secretary's responsibilities include strategic oversight of the UK tax system; corporate and small business taxation, with input from the commercial secretary; departmental minister for HM Revenue and Customs and the Valuation Office Agency; lead minister on European and international tax issues; and has overall responsibility for the finance bill.

The economic secretary's responsibilities include environmental issues such as taxation of transport, international climate change and energy; North Sea oil taxation; tax credits and child poverty; assisting the chief secretary on welfare reform; charities and the voluntary sector; excise duties and gambling; stamp duty land tax; EU Budget; the Royal Mint; minister for HM Treasury Group; and working with the exchequer secretary on the finance bill.

The role of commercial secretary was created in 2010. Responsibilities include enterprise and productivity; corporate finance; assisting the financial secretary on financial services, banking policy promoting the government's financial services policies and the competitiveness of the UK; asset freezing and financial crime; foreign exchange reserves and debt management policy; National Savings and Investments; and the Debt Management Office. The commercial secretary is also the treasury spokesperson in the House of Lords.

Prime Minister and First Lord of the Treasury, Rt. Hon. David Cameron, MP
Chancellor of the Exchequer, Rt. Hon. George Osborne, MP

Principal Private Secretary, Dan Rosenfield
Private Secretary, Sophie Dean
Special Advisers, Catherine Macleod; Sam White
Council of Economic Advisers, Andrew Maugham; David Pinto-Duschinsky; Geoffrey Spence
Chief Secretary to the Treasury, Rt. Hon. Danny Alexander, MP
Private Secretary, Sophie Dean
Financial Secretary to the Treasury, Mark Hoban, MP
Private Secretary, Gemma Dawson
Exchequer Secretary to the Treasury, David Gauke, MP
Private Secretary, Mario Pisani
Economic Secretary to the Treasury, Justine Greening, MP
Private Secretary, Simon Whitfield
Commercial Secretary to the Treasury, Lord Sassoon
Permanent Secretary to the Treasury, Sir Nicholas Macpherson
Private Secretary and Speechwriter, Amber Batool
Parliamentary Secretary to the Treasury and Government Chief Whip, Rt. Hon. Patrick McLoughlin, MP
Parliamentary Private Secretary, vacant
Lords Commissioners of HM Treasury (Whips), James Duddridge, MP; Michael Fabricant, MP; Brooks Newmark, MP; Angela Watkinson, MP; Jeremy Wright, MP
Assistant Whips, Stephen Crabb, MP; Philip Dunne, MP; Robert Goodwill, MP; Mark Hunter, MP; Norman Lamb, MP*; Chloe Smith, MP; Shailesh Vera, MP; Bill Wiggin, MP

* Also Chief Parliamentary and Political Adviser to the Deputy Prime Minister

MANAGEMENT BOARD

Chair, Sir Nicholas Macpherson *(Permanent Secretary of State)*
Members, Andrew Hudson *(Public Services and Growth);* Edward Troup *(Budget, Tax and Welfare);* Louise Tulett *(Finance and Procurement);* Tom Scholar *(International and Finance);* Dave Ramsden *(Macroeconomic and Fiscal Policy);* Ray Shostak *(Director General, Performance Management)*

OFFICE OF GOVERNMENT COMMERCE (OGC)

Rosebery Court, St Andrews Business Park, Norwich, Norfolk NR7 0HS
T 0845-000 4999 E servicedesk@ogc.gsi.gov.uk
W www.ogc.gov.uk

The Office of Government Commerce was set up in April 2000, and became part of the Efficiency and Reform Group in the Cabinet Office in June 2010. It is responsible for increasing the government's value for money by improving standards and capability in procurement, for example by commodities buying, delivering major capital projects, and maximising the effective use of government spending and a £30bn property estate.

BUYING SOLUTIONS

3rd Floor, Royal Liver Building, Pier Head, Liverpool L3 1PE
T 0345-410 2222 E info@buyingsolutions.gsi.gov.uk
W www.buyingsolutions.gov.uk

The agency provides a professional procurement service to public sector organisations delivering improved value for money. It was established in 2001 and is an executive agency of the Office of Government Commerce.
Chief Executive, Alison Littley

THE PRIME MINISTER'S DELIVERY UNIT

1 Horse Guards Road, London SW1A 2HQ
T 020-7270 5867 E PMDU@hm-treasury.x.gsi.gov.uk
W www.hm-treasury.gov.uk

The Prime Minister's Delivery Unit was established in June 2001. Its role is to help the government to deliver improved and more efficient public services. The unit reports jointly to the prime minister and the chancellor, and works closely with Number 10, the Cabinet Office, HM Treasury and other departments on the critical priorities and actions needed to strengthen delivery across government.
Head of Unit, Ray Shostak, CBE

WALES OFFICE

Gwydyr House, Whitehall, London SW1A 2NP
T 020-7270 0534
E walesoffice@walesoffice.gsi.gov.uk
W www.walesoffice.gov.uk

The Wales Office was established in 1999 when most of the powers of the Welsh Office were handed over to the National Assembly for Wales. It is the department of the Secretary of State for Wales, who is the key government figure liaising with the devolved government in Wales and who represents Welsh interests in the cabinet and parliament. The secretary of state has the right to attend and speak at sessions of the National Assembly (and must consult the assembly on the government's legislative programme). *See also* Regional Government section and Ministry of Justice.
Secretary of State for Wales, Rt. Hon. Cheryl Gillan, MP
Principal Private Secretary, Stephen Hillcoat
Parliamentary Under-Secretary, David Jones, MP
Director of Office, Fiona Adams-Jones

DEPARTMENT FOR WORK AND PENSIONS

Caxton House, Tothill Street, London SW1H 9NA
T 020-7962 8000 E enquiries@dwp.gsi.gov.uk
W www.dwp.gov.uk

The Department for Work and Pensions was formed in June 2001 from parts of the former Department of Social Security, the Department for Education and Employment and the Employment Service. The department helps unemployed people of working age into work, helps employers to fill their vacancies and provides financial support to people unable to help themselves, through back-to-work programmes. The department also administers the child support system, social security benefits and the social fund. In addition, the department has reciprocal social security arrangements with other countries.
Secretary of State for Work and Pensions, Rt. Hon. Iain Duncan Smith, MP
Principal Private Secretary, John-Paul Marks
Private Secretaries, Melanie Hogger; Rachel Hunter; Mark Swindells; Phill Wells
Minister of State, Chris Grayling, MP *(Employment)*
Private Secretary, Sarah Ormerod
Parliamentary Private Secretary, vacant
Assistant Private Secretaries, Ann Lyle; Debbie McMahon; Cargill Sanderson
Minister of State, Steve Webb, MP *(Pensions)*
Private Secretary, Michael Dynan-Oakley
Assistant Private Secretaries, Biba Ahmed; Polly Fortune; Emily Holdup
Parliamentary Under-Secretary of State, Maria Miller, MP *(Disabled People)*

Private Secretary, Tash Shotton
Assistant Private Secretary, James Rogers
Parliamentary Under-Secretary of State, Lord Freud (*Welfare Reform)*
Private Secretary, Jessica Yuille
Assistant Private Secretaries, Lucy Fletcher; Manjula Pelpola

EXECUTIVE TEAM
Permanent Secretary and Head of Department, Leigh Lewis
Directors-General, Gill Aitken *(Legal Group);* Sue Garrard *(Communications and Customer Strategy);* Joe Harley *(IT and Chief Information Officer);* Richard Heaton *(Strategy, Information and Pensions);* Chris Last *(Human Resources);* Hunada Nouss *(Finance);* Sue Owen *(Welfare and Wellbeing);* Adam Sharples *(Employment)*

DEPARTMENTAL BOARD
Members, John Cross; Adrian Fawcett; Joe Harley; Leigh Lewis; Terry Moran; Richard Paul; Michael Sommers; Helen Stevenson

EXECUTIVE AGENCIES

Executive agencies are well-defined business units that carry out services with a clear focus on delivering specific outputs within a framework of accountability to ministers. They can be set up or disbanded without legislation, and they are organisationally independent from the department they are answerable to. In the following list the agencies are shown in the accounts of their sponsor departments. Legally they act on behalf of the relevant secretary of state. Their chief executives also perform the role of accounting officers, which means they are responsible for the money spent by their organisations. Staff employed by agencies are civil servants.

CABINET OFFICE

COI (CENTRAL OFFICE OF INFORMATION)
Hercules Road, London SE1 7DU
T 020-7928 2345 **W** www.coi.gov.uk
The COI was created to improve the effectiveness of and add value to government publicity programmes, through consultancy, procurement and project management services across all communication channels. Administrative responsibility for the COI rests with the minister for the Cabinet Office.
Chief Executive, M. Lund
Deputy Chief Executive, P. Buchanan

MANAGEMENT BOARD
Members, Ms A. Butler; M. Cross; I. Hamilton; G. Hooper; H. Lederer; Ms E. Lochhead; S. Marquis; N. Martinson; A. Wade; Mrs S. Whetton; C. Wood

ATTORNEY-GENERAL'S OFFICE

NATIONAL FRAUD AUTHORITY
PO Box 64170, London WC1A 9BP
T 020-3356 1000 **E** NFAcontact@attorneygeneral.gsi.gov.uk
W www.attorneygeneral.gov.uk/nfa
The National Fraud Authority (NFA) was established on 1 October 2008 to increase protection for the UK economy from the harm caused by fraud. It works with private, public and third sector organisations to initiate, coordinate and communicate counter-fraud activity across the economy. The authority's priorities are to tackle the key fraud threats to the UK, to act effectively to pursue fraudsters and hold them to account, and to improve the nation's long-term capability to prevent fraud. The NFA is also working to improve the support available to fraud victims and to build the UK's capability to share and act on knowledge about fraud, both nationally and internationally.
Chief Executive, Dr Bernard Herdan, CB

TREASURY SOLICITOR'S DEPARTMENT
1 Kemble Street, London WC2B 4TS
T 020-7210 3000
E thetreasurysolicitor@tsol.gsi.gov.uk
W www.tsol.gov.uk
The Treasury Solicitor's Department, which became an executive agency in 1996, provides legal services for many government departments and is answerable to the Attorney-General. Those departments without their own lawyers are provided with legal advice, and both they and other departments are provided with litigation services. The Treasury Solicitor is also the Queen's Proctor, and is responsible for collecting ownerless goods *(bona vacantia)* on behalf of the crown.
HM Procurator-General and Treasury Solicitor (Permanent Secretary), Paul Jenkins
Deputy Treasury Solicitor, Jonathan Jones

BONA VACANTIA DIVISION
Head of Division, Zane Denton

CENTRAL ADVISORY DIVISION
Head of Division, Iain Macleod

DEPARTMENT OF CULTURE, MEDIA AND SPORT ADVISORY DIVISION
Legal Adviser, Patrick Kilgarriff

DEPARTMENT FOR EDUCATION ADVISORY DIVISION
Legal Adviser, Claire Johnston

EUROPEAN DIVISION
Head of Division, Paul Berman

HM TREASURY ADVISORY DIVISION
Legal Adviser, Stephen Parker

LITIGATION AND EMPLOYMENT GROUP
Head of Division, Hugh Giles

DEPARTMENT FOR BUSINESS, INNOVATION AND SKILLS

COMPANIES HOUSE
Crown Way, Cardiff CF14 3UZ
T 0303-123 4500
E enquiries@companieshouse.gov.uk
W www.companieshouse.gov.uk
Companies House incorporates companies, registers company documents and provides company information.
Registrar of Companies for England and Wales, Gareth Jones
Registrar of Companies for Scotland, Dorothy Blair
Registrar of Companies for Northern Ireland, Helen Shilliday

THE INSOLVENCY SERVICE
21 Bloomsbury Street, London WC1B 3QW
Insolvency Enquiry Line 0845-602 9848
Redundancy Enquiry Line 0845-145 0004
W www.insolvency.gov.uk

The role of the service includes administration and investigation of the affairs of bankrupts, partners and companies in compulsory liquidation; dealing with the disqualification of directors in all corporate failures; authorising and regulating the insolvency profession; providing banking and investment services for bankruptcy and liquidation estate funds; assessing and paying statutory entitlement to redundancy payments when an employer cannot, or will not, pay its employees; and advising ministers on insolvency, redundancy and related issues.
Inspector-General and Chief Executive, Stephen Speed
Deputy Chief Executive, Graham Horne
Deputy Inspector-General, Les Cramp
Inspector of Companies and Head of Investigation and Enforcement Services, Robert Burns

INTELLECTUAL PROPERTY OFFICE
Concept House, Cardiff Road, Newport NP10 8QQ
T 0845-950 0505 E enquiries@ipo.gov.uk
W www.ipo.gov.uk
The Intellectual Property Office, formerly known as the Patent Office, was established in 1990 and became a trading fund in 1991. The office is responsible for intellectual property (IP) policy and operation in the UK, and aims to educate business, researchers and the public about the IP system; facilitate the appropriate protection and use of rights; provide services to assist business use of the IP system; and create a domestic and international legal and policy framework, which balances the interests of rights holders with the need for open competition and free markets.
Comptroller-General and Chief Executive, John Alty

NATIONAL MEASUREMENT OFFICE
Stanton Avenue, Teddington, Middx TW11 0JZ
T 020-8943 7272 E info@nmo.gov.uk
W www.nmo.bis.gov.uk
The National Measurement Office (NMO) was created in April 2009, merging the functions of the National Weights and Measures Laboratory and the National Measurement System. NMO is responsible for all aspects of the national measurement system and provides a legal metrology infrastructure necessary to facilitate fair competition, support innovation, promote international trade and protect consumers, health and the environment.
Chief Executive, Peter Mason

UK SPACE AGENCY
Polaris House, North Star Avenue, Swindon, Wiltshire SN2 1SZ
T 020-7215 5000
E ukspaceagencyinfo@ukspaceagency.bis.gsi.gov.uk
W www.ukspaceagency.bis.gov.uk
The UK Space Agency was established on 23 March 2010. It was created to provide a single voice for UK space ambitions, and is responsible for all strategic decisions on the UK civil space programme. Responsibilities of the UK Space Agency include coordinating UK civil space activity; supporting academic research; nurturing the UK space industry; raising the profile of UK space activities at home and abroad; working to increase understanding of space science and its practical benefits; and inspiring the next generation of UK scientists and engineers.
Chief Executive (acting), Dr David Williams

DEPARTMENT FOR COMMUNITIES AND LOCAL GOVERNMENT

FIRE SERVICE COLLEGE
Moreton-in-Marsh, Gloucestershire GL56 0RH
T 01608-650831 E enquiries@fireservicecollege.ac.uk
W www.fireservicecollege.ac.uk
The Fire Service College provides fire-related training, both practical and theoretical, consultancy, and library and information services to the UK fire and rescue service, other UK public sector organisations, the private sector, and the international market.
Chief Executive, Kim Robinson

ORDNANCE SURVEY
Romsey Road, Southampton SO16 4GU
T 0845-605 0505
E customerservices@ordnancesurvey.co.uk
W www.ordnancesurvey.co.uk
Ordnance Survey is the national mapping agency for Great Britain. It is a government department and executive agency operating as a trading fund since 1999.
Director-General and Chief Executive, Vanessa Lawrence, CB

PLANNING INSPECTORATE
Temple Quay House, 2 The Square, Temple Quay, Bristol BS1 6PN
T 0117-372 6372 E enquiries@planning-inspectorate.gsi.gov.uk
Crown Buildings, Cathays Park, Cardiff CF10 3NQ
T 029-2082 3866 E wales@planning-inspectorate.gsi.gov.uk
W www.planning-inspectorate.gov.uk
The main work of the inspectorate consists of the processing of planning and enforcement appeals, and holding examinations into development plan documents. It also deals with advertisement appeals; rights of way cases; cases arising from the Environmental Protection and Water acts, the Transport and Works Act 1992 and other highways legislation; and reporting on planning applications called in for decision by the Department for Communities and Local Government and the Welsh Assembly Government
Chief Executive, Katrine Sporle

THE QUEEN ELIZABETH II CONFERENCE CENTRE
Broad Sanctuary, London SW1P 3EE
T 020-7222 5000 F 020-7798 4200
E info@qeiicc.co.uk W www.qeiicc.co.uk
The centre provides secure conference facilities for national and international government and private sector use.
Chief Executive, Ernest Vincent

DEPARTMENT FOR CULTURE, MEDIA AND SPORT

THE ROYAL PARKS
The Old Police House, Hyde Park, London W2 2UH
T 020-7298 2000 E hq@royalparks.gsi.gov.uk
W www.royalparks.org.uk
Royal Parks is responsible for maintaining and developing over 2,000 hectares (5,000 acres) of urban parkland contained within the eight royal parks in London: Bushy Park (with the Longford river); Green Park; Greenwich Park; Hyde Park; Kensington Gardens; Regent's Park (with Primrose Hill); Richmond Park and St James's Park.
Chief Executive, Mark Camley

DEPARTMENT FOR ENVIRONMENT, FOOD AND RURAL AFFAIRS

ANIMAL HEALTH

Corporate Centre, Block C, Government Buildings, Whittington Road, Worcester WR5 2LQ
T 01905-763355
E corporate-office@animalhealth.gsi.gov.uk
W www.defra.gov.uk/animalhealth

Animal Health is an executive agency that also works on behalf of the Welsh Assembly Government, the Scottish government and the Food Standards Agency. It is the government's delivery agent for ensuring the health and welfare of farmed animals. It is also responsible for the prevention, detection and management of diseases in animals. Animal Health's main responsibilities include protecting the welfare of farmed animals; the eradication of endemic disease; import and export certification; animal by-product regulation; and preparedness for managing exotic animal diseases. Animal Health is also reponsible for licensing the trade in endangered species for conservation purposes; for ensuring that eggs are correctly labelled and there is compliance with marketing conditions; and for monitoring the standard of hygiene in relation to the nation's raw milk supply. Animal Health is scheduled to merge with the Veterinary Laboratories Agency in autumn 2010.

Chief Executive, Catherine Brown

CENTRE FOR ENVIRONMENT, FISHERIES AND AQUACULTURE SCIENCE (CEFAS)

Pakefield Road, Lowestoft, Suffolk NR33 0HT
T 01502-562244 W www.cefas.co.uk

Established in April 1997, the agency provides research and consultancy services in fisheries science and management, aquaculture, fish health and hygiene, environmental impact assessment, and environmental quality assessment.

Chief Executive, Richard Judge

FOOD AND ENVIRONMENT RESEARCH AGENCY

Sand Hutton, York YO41 1LZ
T 01904-462000
E info@fera.gsi.gov.uk W www.fera.defra.gov.uk

The Food and Environment Research Agency was formed on 1 April 2009 from the merger of the Central Science Laboratory, the Government Decontamination Service, and DEFRA's Plant Health division and Plant Varieties office. The agency's purpose is to support and develop a sustainable food chain, a healthy natural environment, and to protect the community from biological and chemical risks. It does this by providing evidence, analysis and professional advice to the government, international organisations and the private sector. The agency brings together expertise in policy issues, particularly relating to seed, plant and bee health; inspection services necessary to ensure protection for seeds, crops and horticulture; multi-disciplinary science to rapidly diagnose threats, evaluate risk and inform policy in food and environmental areas; and in responding to and recovering from unforeseen or emergency situations.

Chief Executive, Adrian Belton

RURAL PAYMENTS AGENCY

PO Box 1058, Newcastle Upon Tyne NE99 4YQ
T 0845-603 7777
E csc@rpa.gsi.gov.uk W www.rpa.gov.uk

The RPA was established in 2001. It is the single paying agency responsible for Common Agricultural Policy (CAP) schemes in England and for certain schemes throughout the UK; it is also responsible for operating cattle tracing services across Great Britain, conducting inspections of farms, processing plants and fresh produce markets in England, and managing the Rural Land Register.

Chief Executive, Tony Cooper
Chief Operating Officer (interim), Steve Pearce

VETERINARY LABORATORIES AGENCY

New Haw, Addlestone, Surrey KT15 3NB
T 01932-341111
E enquiries@vla.defra.gov.uk W www.vla.gov.uk

The Veterinary Laboratories Agency is a regional network of 16 veterinary laboratories and two surveillance centres, which provides all sectors of the animal health industry with animal disease surveillance, diagnostic services and veterinary scientific research. The Veterinary Laboratories Agency is scheduled to merge with Animal Health in autumn 2010.

Chief Executive, Prof. S. P. Borriello

VETERINARY MEDICINES DIRECTORATE

Woodham Lane, New Haw, Addlestone, Surrey KT15 3LS
T 01932-336911 E postmaster@vmd.defra.gsi.gov.uk
W www.vmd.gov.uk

The Veterinary Medicines Directorate is responsible for all aspects of the authorisation and control of veterinary medicines, including post-authorisation surveillance of residues in animals and animal products. It is also responsible for the development and enforcement of legislation concerning veterinary medicines and the provision of policy advice to ministers.

Chief Executive, Steve Dean

FOREIGN AND COMMONWEALTH OFFICE

FCO SERVICES

Hanslope Park, Milton Keynes MK19 7BH
T 01908-515789 E fco.services@fco.gov.uk
W www.fcoservices.gov.uk

FCO Services was established as an executive agency in April 2006 and became a trading fund in April 2008. It delivers a combination of secure IT, estates and logistical services to the FCO in the UK and at its missions overseas and to other UK government departments and public bodies. Its customers also include other governments and international institutions with whom the UK has close links.

Chief Executive, Chris Moxey

WILTON PARK CONFERENCE CENTRE

Wiston House, Steyning, W. Sussex BN44 3DZ
T 01903-815020 E admin@wiltonpark.org.uk
W www.wiltonpark.org.uk

Wilton Park organises international affairs conferences and is hired out to government departments and commercial users.

Chief Executive, Richard Burge

DEPARTMENT OF HEALTH

MEDICINES AND HEALTHCARE PRODUCTS REGULATORY AGENCY (MHRA)

Market Towers, 151 Buckingham Palace Road, London SW1W 9SS
E info@mhra.gsi.gov.uk W www.mhra.gov.uk

The MHRA is responsible for protecting and promoting public and patient safety by ensuring that medicines,

healthcare products and medical equipment meet appropriate standards of safety, quality, performance and effectiveness, and are used safely.
Chair, Prof. Sir Alasdair Breckenridge, CBE
Chief Executive, Prof. Kent Woods

HOME OFFICE

CRIMINAL RECORDS BUREAU
PO Box 110, Liverpool L69 3EF
T 0870-909 0811 **E** customerservices@crb.gov.uk
W www.crb.homeoffice.gov.uk
The Criminal Records Bureau was launched in March 2002 and provides access to criminal record information to enable organisations in the public, private and voluntary sectors to make safer recruitment decisions by identifying candidates who may be unsuitable for certain work – especially that which involves children or vulnerable adults.
Chief Executive, Steve Long

IDENTITY AND PASSPORT SERVICE
Globe House, 89 Eccleston Square, London SW1V 1PN
T Passport Advice Line 0300-222 0000, General Register Office 0845-603 7788
W www.ips.gov.uk, www.directgov.co.uk
The Identity and Passport Service was established in April 2006 and incorporates the UK Passport Service and the General Register Office. The UK Passport Service issues, renews and amends passports. The General Register Office is responsible for overseeing the system of civil registration in England and Wales, which involves administering the marriage laws; securing an effective system for the registration of births, adoptions, civil partnerships, marriages and deaths; maintaining an archive of births, civil partnerships, marriages and deaths; maintaining the adopted children's register, adoption contact register and other registers; and supplying certificates from the registers and the archives for research or family history purposes.
Chief Executive and Registrar-General, Sarah Rapson

UK BORDER AGENCY
2 Marsham Street, London SW1P 4DF
T 0870-606 7766 **E** ukbapublicenquiries@ukba.gsi.gov.uk
W www.ukba.homeoffice.gov.uk
The UK Border Agency was established in April 2008 and became an executive agency of the Home Office in April 2009. The agency brings together the work previously carried out by the Border and Immigration Agency, and, following Royal Assent to the Borders, Citizenship and Immigration Act in July 2009, customs detection work at the border from HM Revenue and Customs, and UK visa services from the Foreign and Commonwealth Office.
Chief Executive, Lin Homer
Board Members, Jonathan Sedgwick *(Deputy Chief Executive)*; Zila Bowell *(Chief Executive's Chief of Staff)*; Martin Baker; James Bevan; Kathryn Bishop; Brodie Clark; Matthew Coats; Melanie Dawes; Joe Dugdale; Mike Hawker; Justin Holliday; Martin Peach; Graham Sims; Mark Thomson; David Wood; Barbara Woodward; Rob Yeldham

MINISTRY OF JUSTICE

HER MAJESTY'S COURTS SERVICE
see Law Courts and Offices section

LAND REGISTRY
Lincoln's Inn Fields, London WC2A 3PH
T 0844-892 1111 **E** customersupport@landregistry.gsi.gov.uk
W www.landregistry.gov.uk
The registration of title to land was first introduced in England and Wales by the Land Registry Act 1862. Land Registry maintains and develops the Land Register for England and Wales, and is an executive agency and trading fund responsible to the Lord Chancellor and Secretary of State for Justice. The Land Register has been open to public inspection since 1990.
Chief Land Registrar and Chief Executive, Marco Pierleoni

NATIONAL ARCHIVES
Kew, Richmond, Surrey TW9 4DU
T 020-8876 3444
W www.nationalarchives.gov.uk
The National Archives is an executive agency of the Ministry of Justice, although it receives funding directly from HM Treasury and is answerable directly to legislature. It incorporates the Public Record Office, Historical Manuscripts Commission, Office of Public Sector Information and Her Majesty's Stationery Office. As the official archive of the UK government, it preserves, protects and makes accessible the historical collection of official records.

The National Archives also manages digital information including the UK government web archive which contains over one billion digital documents, and devises solutions for keeping government records readable now and in the future.

The organisation administers the UK's public records system under the Public Records Acts of 1958 and 1967. The records it holds span 1,000 years – from the Domesday Book to the latest government papers to be released – and fill more than 167km (104 miles) of shelving.
Chief Executive (acting), Oliver Morley

OFFICE OF PUBLIC SECTOR INFORMATION
102 Petty France, London SW1H 9AJ
T 020-3334 2780
W www.nationalarchives.gsi.gov.uk
The Office of Public Sector Information (OPSI) operates from within the National Archives as of October 2006, after previously being attached to the Cabinet Office. It is responsible for policy in relation to access and re-use of UK public sector information. The legal and statutory responsibilities of Her Majesty's Stationery Office (HMSO), in relation to statutory publishing and the management of crown copyright, operate from within the OPSI's wider remit.
Director/Controller, Carol Tullo

NATIONAL OFFENDER MANAGEMENT SERVICE
see Prison Service section

OFFICE OF THE PUBLIC GUARDIAN
PO Box 15118, Birmingham B16 6GX
T 0300-456 0300
E customerservices@publicguardian.gsi.gov.uk
W www.publicguardian.gov.uk
The Office of the Public Guardian supports and promotes decision making for those who lack capacity or would like to plan for their future, within the framework of the Mental Capacity Act 2005.
Chief Executive and Public Guardian, Martin John

TRIBUNALS SERVICE
see Tribunals section

DEPARTMENT FOR TRANSPORT

DRIVER AND VEHICLE LICENSING AGENCY (DVLA)
Longview Road, Swansea SA6 7JL
T 01792-782341 W www.dft.gov.uk/dvla
The agency was established as an executive agency in 1990 and became a trading fund in 2004. It is responsible for registering and licensing drivers and vehicles, and for collection and enforcement of vehicle excise duty (some £5.7bn annually). The DVLA also maintains records of all those who are entitled to drive various types of vehicle (currently around 44 million people), all vehicles entitled to travel on public roads (currently 34 million), and drivers' endorsements, disqualifications and medical conditions.
Chief Executive, Simon Tse

DRIVING STANDARDS AGENCY
The Axis Building, 112 Upper Parliament Street, Nottingham NG1 6LP
T 0115-936 6666 E customer.services@dsa.gsi.gov.uk
W www.dsa.gov.uk
The agency is responsible for carrying out theory and practical driving tests for car drivers, motorcyclists, bus and lorry drivers, and for maintaining the registers of approved driving instructors and large goods vehicle instructors. It also supervises Compulsory Basic Training (CBT) for learner motorcyclists. There are two area offices, which manage over 400 practical driving test centres across Britain.
Chief Executive, Rosemary Thew

GOVERNMENT CAR AND DESPATCH AGENCY
46 Ponton Road, London SW8 5AX
T 020-7217 3837 E info@gcda.gsi.gov.uk
W www.dft.gov.uk/gcda
The agency provides secure transport and mail distribution to government and the public sector.
Chief Executive (interim), Paul Markwick

HIGHWAYS AGENCY
123 Buckingham Palace Road, London SW1W 9HA
T 0845-955 6575 Information Line 0845-750 4030
E ha_info@highways.gsi.gov.uk W www.highways.gov.uk
The Highways agency is responsible for operating, maintaining and improving England's 7,050km (4,406 miles) of motorways and trunk roads – known as the strategic road network – on behalf of the Secretary of State for Transport.
Chief Executive, Graham Dalton

MARITIME AND COASTGUARD AGENCY
Spring Place, 105 Commercial Road, Southampton SO15 1EG
T 023-8032 9100 W www.mcga.gov.uk
The agency's aims are to prevent loss of life, continuously improve maritime safety and protect the marine environment.
Chief Executive, Sir Alan Massey
Chief Coastguard, Rod Johnson

VEHICLE CERTIFICATION AGENCY
1 Eastgate Office Centre, Eastgate Road, Bristol BS5 6XX
T 0117-952 4235 E enquiries@vca.gov.uk W www.vca.gov.uk
The agency is the UK authority responsible for ensuring that vehicles and vehicle parts have been designed and constructed to meet internationally agreed standards of safety and environmental protection.
Chief Executive, P. Markwick

VEHICLE AND OPERATOR SERVICES AGENCY
Berkeley House, Croydon Street, Bristol BS5 0DA
T 0300-123 9000
E enquiries@vosa.gov.uk W www.vosa.gov.uk
The Vehicle and Operator Services Agency was formed in April 2003 from the merger of the Vehicle Inspectorate and the Traffic Area Network. The agency works with the independent traffic commissioners to improve road safety and the environment; safeguard fair competition by promoting and enforcing compliance with commercial operator licensing requirements; process applications for licences to operate lorries and buses; register bus services; operate and administer testing schemes for all vehicles, including the supervision of the MOT testing scheme; enforce the law on vehicles to ensure that they comply with legal standards and regulations; enforce drivers' hours and licensing requirements; provide training and advice for commercial operators; and investigate vehicle accidents, defects and recalls.
Chief Executive, Alastair Peoples

HM TREASURY

NATIONAL SAVINGS AND INVESTMENTS
1 Drummond Gate, Pimlico, London SW1V 2QX
T 0500-007007 W www.nsandi.com
NS&I (National Savings and Investments) came into being in 1861 when the Palmerston government set up the Post Office Savings Bank, a savings scheme which aimed to encourage ordinary wage earners 'to provide for themselves against adversity and ill health'. NS&I was established as a government department in 1969. It became an executive agency of the Treasury in 1996 and is responsible for the design, marketing and administration of savings and investment products for personal savers and investors. It has almost 27 million customers with over £98bn invested. *See also* Banking and Finance.
Chief Executive, Jane Platt

ROYAL MINT
PO Box 500, Llantrisant, Pontyclun CF72 8YT
T 01443-222111 W www.royalmint.com
The Royal Mint has operated as a trading fund since 1975, and was established as an executive agency in 1990.

The prime responsibility of the Royal Mint is the provision of United Kingdom coinage, but it actively competes in world markets for a share of the available circulating coin business and about half of the coins and blanks it produces annually are exported. It also manufactures special proof and uncirculated quality coins in gold, silver and other metals; military and civil decorations and medals; commemorative and prize medals; and royal and official seals.
Master of the Mint, Chancellor of the Exchequer *(ex officio)*
Chief Executive, A. Stafford

UK DEBT MANAGEMENT OFFICE
Eastcheap Court, 11 Philpot Lane, London EC3M 8UD
T 0845-357 6500
W www.dmo.gov.uk

The UK Debt Management Office (DMO) was launched as an executive agency of HM Treasury in April 1998. The Chancellor of the Exchequer determines the policy and financial framework within which the DMO operates, but delegates operational decisions on debt and cash management and the day-to-day running of the office to the chief executive. The DMO's remit is to carry out the government's debt management policy of minimising financing costs over the long term, and to minimise the cost of offsetting the government's net cash flows over time, while operating at a level of risk approved by ministers in both cases. The DMO is also responsible for providing loans to local authorities through the Public Works Loan Board, for managing the assets of certain public sector bodies through the Commissioners for the Reduction of the National Debt, and for administering the operational delivery of the government's Credit Guarantee Scheme.
Chief Executive, Robert Stheeman

DEPARTMENT FOR WORK AND PENSIONS

JOBCENTRE PLUS

Quarry House, Quarry Hill, Leeds, West Yorkshire LS2 7UA
T 0845-606 0234 W www.dwp.gov.uk/jobcentreplus

Jobcentre Plus was formed in April 2002 following the merger of the Employment Service and some parts of the Benefits Agency. The agency administers claims for, and payment of, social security benefits to help people gain employment or improve their prospects for work, as well as helping employers to fill their vacancies.
Chief Executive, Darra Singh

THE PENSION, DISABILITY AND CARERS SERVICE

Room 204, Richmond House, 79 Whitehall, London SW1A 2NS
T DCS 0845-712 3456, Pension Service 0845-606 0265
W www.direct.gov.uk

The Pension, Disability and Carers Service was formed in 2008 from the Pension Service and the Disability and Carers Service (DCS). The agency serves over 15 million customers in Great Britain and abroad. The service administers benefits including disability living allowance, attendance allowance, carers allowance, state pension, pension credit and winter fuel payments.
Chief Executive, Terry Moran, CB

NON-MINISTERIAL GOVERNMENT DEPARTMENTS

Non-ministerial government departments are part of central government but are not headed by a minister and are not funded by a sponsor department. They are created to implement specific legislation, but do not have the ability to change it. Departments may have links to a minister, but the minister is not responsible for the department's overall performance. Staff employed by non-ministerial departments are civil servants.

CROWN ESTATE

16 New Burlington Place, London W1S 2HX
T 020-7851 5000 E enquiries@thecrownestate.co.uk
W www.thecrownestate.co.uk

The Crown Estate is valued at £6.6bn, and includes substantial blocks of urban property, primarily in London, almost 108,000 hectares (267,000 acres) of rural land, over half of the foreshore, and the sea bed out to the 12 nautical mile territorial limit throughout the UK. The Crown Estate is part of the hereditary possessions of the sovereign 'in right of the crown', managed under the provisions of the Crown Estate Act 1961. The Crown Estate has a duty to maintain and enhance the capital value of estate and the income obtained from it. Under the terms of the act, the Crown Estate pays its revenue surplus to the Treasury every year.
Chair, Sir Stuart Hampson
Chief Executive, Roger Bright

CROWN PROSECUTION SERVICE

Rose Court, 2 Southwark Bridge, London SE1 9HS
T 020-7796 8000 E enquiries@cps.gsi.gov.uk
W www.cps.gov.uk

The Crown Prosecution Service (CPS) is the independent body responsible for prosecuting people in England and Wales. The CPS was established as a result of the Prosecution of Offences Act 1985. It works closely with the police to advise on lines of inquiry and to decide on appropriate charges and other disposals in all but minor cases. *See also* Law Courts and Offices.

The Revenue and Customs Prosecutions Office, which prosecutes major drug trafficking and tax fraud cases in the UK, was incorporated into the CPS on 1 January 2010.
Director of Public Prosecutions, Keir Starmer, QC
Chief Executive, Peter Lewis

EXPORT CREDITS GUARANTEE DEPARTMENT (ECGD)

PO Box 2200, 2 Exchange Tower, Harbour Exchange Square, London E14 9GS
T 020-7512 7887 E help@ecgd.gsi.gov.uk
W www.ecgd.gov.uk

ECGD is the UK export credit agency and was established in 1919. A separate government department reporting to the Secretary of State for Business, Innovation and Skills, it has more than 90 years' experience of working closely with exporters, project sponsors, banks and buyers to help UK exporters of capital equipment and project-related goods and services. ECGD does this by providing help in arranging finance packages for buyers of UK goods by guaranteeing bank loans; insurance against non-payment to UK exporters; and overseas investment insurance – a facility that gives UK investors up to 15 years' insurance against political risks such as war, expropriation and restrictions on remittances.
Chief Executive and Accounting Officer, P. Crawford
Non-Executive Chair, G. Beringer, QC

FOOD STANDARDS AGENCY

Aviation House, 125 Kingsway, London WC2B 6NH
T 020-7276 8829
E helpline@foodstandards.gsi.gov.uk
W www.food.gov.uk, www.eatwell.gov.uk

The FSA was established in April 2000 to protect public health from risks arising in connection with the consumption of food, and otherwise to protect the interests of consumers in relation to food. The agency has the general function of developing policy in these areas and provides information and advice to the government, other public bodies and consumers. It also sets standards for and monitors food law enforcement by local authorities. The agency is a UK-wide non-ministerial government body, led by a board which has been appointed to act in the public interest. It has executive offices in Scotland, Wales and Northern Ireland. It is advised by advisory committees on food safety matters of special interest to each of these areas.

Chair, Lord Rooker
Deputy Chair, Dr Ian Reynolds
Chief Executive, Tim Smith

FOOD STANDARDS AGENCY NORTHERN IRELAND, 10C Clarendon Road, Belfast BT1 3BG
T 028-9041 7700 E infofsani@foodstandards.gsi.gov.uk
FOOD STANDARDS AGENCY SCOTLAND, St Magnus House, 6th Floor, 25 Guild Street, Aberdeen AB11 6NJ
T 01224-285100 E scotland@foodstandards.gsi.gov.uk
FOOD STANDARDS AGENCY WALES, 11th Floor, Southgate House, Wood Street, Cardiff CF10 1EW
T 029-2067 8999 E wales@foodstandards.gsi.gov.uk

FORESTRY COMMISSION

Silvan House, 231 Corstorphine Road, Edinburgh EH12 7AT
T 0131-334 0303 E enquiries@forestry.gsi.gov.uk
W www.forestry.gov.uk

The Forestry Commission is the government department responsible for forestry policy in Great Britain. It reports directly to forestry ministers (ie the Secretary of State for Environment, Food and Rural Affairs, the Scottish ministers and the National Assembly for Wales), to whom it is responsible for advice on forestry policy and for the implementation of that policy.

The commission's principal objectives are to protect Britain's forests and woodlands; expand Britain's forest area; enhance the economic value of forest resources; conserve and improve the biodiversity, landscape and cultural heritage of forests and woodlands; develop opportunities for woodland recreation; and increase public understanding of, and community participation in, forestry.

Chair, Pamela Warhurst
Director-General and Deputy Chair, T. Rollinson

FORESTRY COMMISSION ENGLAND, 620 Bristol Business Park, Coldharbour Lane, Bristol BS16 1EJ
T 0117-906 6000
FORESTRY COMMISSION SCOTLAND, Silvan House, 231 Corstorphine Road, Edinburgh EH12 7AT
T 0131-334 0303
FORESTRY COMMISSION WALES, Welsh Assembly Government, Rhodfa Padarn, Llanbadarn Fawr, Aberystwyth SY23 3UR T 0300-068 0300
NORTHERN RESEARCH STATION, Roslin, Midlothian EH25 9SY T 0131-445 2176

FOREST ENTERPRISE

Forest Enterprise England, 620 Bristol Business Park, Coldharbour Lane, Bristol BS16 1EJ
T 0117-906 6000
Forest Enterprise Scotland, 1 Highlander Way, Inverness Business and Retail Park, Inverness IV2 7GB
T 01463-232811

Forest Enterprise was established as an executive agency of the Forestry Commission in 1996 to manage the UK's forest estate; it ceased to exist as a single executive agency in March 2003, when three new agencies were created – one each for England, Wales and Scotland. Forest Enterprise Wales has since been wound up, with its responsibilities reabsorbed by the Forestry Commission.

The agencies in England and Scotland take their direction from their respective country governments but their basic remit is to provide environmental, social and economic benefits from the forests they manage.

Chief Executives, Simon Hodgson *(England)*; Dr Hugh Insley *(Scotland)*

FOREST RESEARCH

Alice Holt Lodge, Farnham, Surrey GU10 4LH
T 01420-22255
E research.info@forestry.gsi.gov.uk
W www.forestresearch.gov.uk

Forest Research is also an executive agency of the Forestry Commission. Its objectives are to inform and support forestry's contribution to the development and delivery of the policies of the government and devolved administrations; to provide research, development and monitoring services relevant to UK forestry interests; and to transfer knowledge actively and appropriately.

Chief Executive, Dr James Pendlebury
Research Director, Dr Peter Freer-Smith

GOVERNMENT ACTUARY'S DEPARTMENT

Finlaison House, 15–17 Furnival Street, London EC4A 1AB
T 020-7211 2601
Abbey Business Centre, The Beacon, 176 St Vincent Street, Glasgow G2 5SG
T 0141-249 6555
E enquiries@gad.gov.uk W www.gad.gov.uk

The Government Actuary's Department was established in 1919 and provides a consulting service to government departments, the public sector, and overseas governments. The actuaries advise on social security schemes and superannuation arrangements in the public sector at home and abroad, on population and other statistical studies, and on supervision of insurance companies and pension funds.

Government Actuary, T. J. Llanwarne
Deputy Government Actuary, G. Russell
Chief Actuaries (London), E. I. Battersby; S. Bell; I. A. Boonin; H. Duckers; A. Hale; D. J. Hughes; S. R. Humphrey; K. Kneller; M. Lunnon; S. Vivian
Chief Actuary (Glasgow), A. Murray

HM REVENUE AND CUSTOMS

Board of HM Revenue and Customs, 100 Parliament Street, London SW1A 2BQ
T 020-7147 0000 W www.hmrc.gov.uk

HMRC was formed following the integration of the Inland Revenue and HM Customs and Excise, which was made formal by parliament in April 2005. It administers, and advises the Chancellor of the Exchequer on, any matters connected with the following areas: income, corporation, capital gains, inheritance, insurance premium, stamp, land and petroleum revenue taxes; environmental taxes (climate change and aggregates levy, landfill tax); value added tax (VAT); customs duties and frontier protection; excise duties; National Insurance; tax credits, child benefit and the Child Trust Fund; enforcement of the minimum wage; and recovery of student loan repayments.

Chair, Mike Clasper

VALUATION OFFICE AGENCY

Wingate House, 93–107 Shaftesbury Avenue, London W1D 5BU
T 0300-056 1700 E customerservices@voa.gsi.gov.uk
W www.voa.gov.uk

Established in 1991, the Valuation Office is an executive agency of HM Revenue and Customs. It is responsible for compiling and maintaining the business rating and council tax valuation lists for England and Wales; valuing property throughout Great Britain for the purposes of taxes administered by the Inland Revenue; providing statutory and non-statutory property valuation services in

England, Wales and Scotland; and giving policy advice to ministers on property valuation matters. In April 2009 the VOA assumed responsibility for the functions of The Rent Service, which provided a rental valuation service to local authorities in England, and fair rent determinations for landlords and tenants.
Chief Executive, Penny Ciniewicz

NATIONAL SCHOOL OF GOVERNMENT

Sunningdale Park, Larch Avenue, Ascot, Berks SL5 0QE
T 01344-634000
E customer.services@nationalschool.gsi.gov.uk
W www.nationalschool.gov.uk

The National School of Government is the learning and development partner of the UK Civil Service. It became a separate non-ministerial department on 1 January 2007. It is run by public servants for public servants, and aims to improve services for citizens by using learning and development to raise the bar for public services.
Principal and Chief Executive, Rod Clark

OFFICE OF FAIR TRADING (OFT)

Fleetbank House, 2–6 Salisbury Square, London EC4Y 8JX
T 020-7211 8000
E enquiries@oft.gsi.gov.uk W www.oft.gov.uk

The OFT is a non-ministerial government department established by statute in 1973, and it is the UK's consumer and competition authority. It encourages businesses to comply with competition and consumer law and to improve their trading practices through self-regulation. It acts decisively to stop serious or flagrant offenders, studies markets and recommends action where required, and empowers consumers with the knowledge and skills to make informed choices.
Chair, Philip Collins
Chief Executive Officer, John Fingleton

CHARITY COMMISSION

PO Box 1227, Liverpool L69 3UG
T 0845-300 0218
W www.charity-commission.gov.uk

The Charity Commission is established by law as the independent regulator and registrar of charities in England and Wales. Its aim is to provide the best possible regulation of these charities in order to ensure their legal compliance and increase their efficiency, accountability and effectiveness, as well as to encourage public trust and confidence in them. The commission maintains a register of over 180,000 charities. It is accountable to parliament and both the charity tribunal and the high court for decisions made in exercising its legal powers. The commission has offices in London, Liverpool, Taunton and Newport.
Chair, Dame Suzi Leather
Chief Executive, Sam Younger, CBE

OFFICE OF GAS AND ELECTRICITY MARKETS (OFGEM)

9 Millbank, London SW1P 3GE
T 020-7901 7295 E consumeraffairs@ofgem.gov.uk
W www.ofgem.gov.uk

OFGEM is the regulator for Britain's gas and electricity industries. Its role is to protect and advance the interests of consumers by promoting competition where possible, and through regulation only where necessary. OFGEM operates under the direction and governance of the Gas and Electricity Markets Authority, which makes all major decisions and sets policy priorities for OFGEM. OFGEM's powers are provided for under the Gas Act 1986 and the Electricity Act 1989, as amended by the Utilities Act 2000. It also has enforcement powers under the Competition Act 1998 and the Enterprise Act 2002.
Chair, Lord Mogg, KCMG
Chief Executive, Alistair Buchanan

OFFICE OF RAIL REGULATION

1 Kemble Street, London WC2B 4AN
T 020-7282 2000 E contact.cct@orr.gsi.gov.uk
W www.rail-reg.gov.uk

The Office of the Rail Regulator was set up under the Railways Act 1993. It became the ORR in July 2004, under the provisions of the Railways and Transport Safety Act 2003. On 1 April 2006, in addition to its role as economic regulator, the ORR became the health and safety regulator for the rail industry. This transfer of responsibility from the Health and Safety Executive was given effect under the Railways Act 2005. The board and chair are appointed by the Secretary of State for Transport. The ORR's key roles are to ensure that Network Rail, the owner and operator of the national railway infrastructure (the track and signalling), manages the network efficiently and in a way that meets the needs of its users; to encourage continuous improvement in health and safety performance while securing compliance with relevant health and safety law, including taking enforcement action as necessary; and to develop policy and enhance relevant railway health and safety legislation. It is also responsible for licensing operators of railway assets, setting the terms for access by operators to the network and other railway facilities, and enforcing competition law in the rail sector.
Chair, Anna Walker
Chief Executive, Bill Emery

OFFICE FOR STANDARDS IN EDUCATION, CHILDREN'S SERVICES AND SKILLS (OFSTED)

Royal Exchange Buildings, St Ann's Square, Manchester M2 7LA
T 0300-123 1231 E enquiries@ofsted.gov.uk
W www.ofsted.gov.uk

Ofsted was established under the Education (Schools Act) 1992 and was relaunched on 1 April 2007 with a wider remit, bringing together four formerly separate inspectorates. It works to raise standards in services through the inspection and regulation of care for children and young people, and inspects education and training for children of all ages. *See also* The Education System.
HM Chief Inspector, Christine Gilbert, CBE
Chair, Zenna Atkins

POSTAL SERVICES COMMISSION (POSTCOMM)

Hercules House, 6 Hercules Road, London SE1 7DB
T 020-7593 2100 E info@psc.gov.uk W www.psc.gov.uk

Postcomm is an independent regulator set up by the Postal Services Act 2000 to protect the universal postal service, improve postal services by introducing competition to the UK postal market, licence postal operators dealing with mail costing less than £1 to deliver, and ensure that postal operators, including Royal Mail, meet the needs of their customers throughout the UK. Postcomm monitors and reports to the Department for Business, Innovation and Skills on the UK post office network.
Chair, Nigel Stapleton
Chief Executive, Tim Brown

SECURITY AND INTELLIGENCE SERVICES

GOVERNMENT COMMUNICATIONS HEADQUARTERS (GCHQ)

Hubble Road, Cheltenham GL51 0EX
T 01242-221491 E pressoffice@gchq.gsi.gov.uk
W www.gchq.gov.uk

GCHQ produces signals intelligence in support of national security and the UK's economic wellbeing, and in the prevention or detection of serious crime. Additionally, GCHQ's Information Assurance arm, CESG, is the national technical authority for information assurance, and provides advice and assistance to government departments, the armed forces and other national infrastructure bodies on the security of their communications and information systems. GCHQ was placed on a statutory footing by the Intelligence Services Act 1994 and is headed by a director who is directly accountable to the foreign secretary.
Director, Iain Lobban

SECRET INTELLIGENCE SERVICE (MI6)

PO Box 1300, London SE1 1BD
W www.mi6.gov.uk

The Secret Intelligence Service produces secret intelligence in support of the government's security, defence, foreign and economic policies. It was placed on a statutory footing by the Intelligence Services Act 1994 and is headed by a chief, known as 'C', who is directly accountable to the foreign secretary.
Chief, Sir John Sawers

SECURITY SERVICE (MI5)

PO Box 3255, London SW1P 1AE
T 020-7930 9000 W www.mi5.gov.uk

The Security Service is responsible for security intelligence work against covertly organised threats to the UK. These include terrorism, espionage and the proliferation of weapons of mass destruction. The Security Service also provides security advice to a wide range of organisations to help reduce vulnerability to threats from individuals, groups or countries hostile to UK interests. The home secretary has parliamentary accountability for the Security Service.
Director-General, Jonathan Evans

SERIOUS FRAUD OFFICE

Elm House, 10–16 Elm Street, London WC1X 0BJ
T 020-7239 7272
E public.enquiries@sfo.gsi.gov.uk W www.sfo.gov.uk

The Serious Fraud Office is an independent government department that investigates and prosecutes serious or complex fraud. It is part of the UK Criminal Justice System. The office is headed by a director who is appointed by and accountable to the Attorney-General, and has jurisdiction over England, Wales and Northern Ireland but not Scotland, the Isle of Man or the Channel Islands.
Director, Richard Alderman

UK STATISTICS AUTHORITY

Statistics House, Tredegar Park, Newport, Gwent NP10 8XG
T 0845-604 1857 E authority.enquiries@statistics.gov.uk
W www.statisticsauthority.gov.uk

The UK Statistics Authority was established on 1 April 2008 by the Statistics and Registration Service Act 2007 as an independent body operating at arm's length from government, reporting to the UK parliament and the devolved legislatures. Its overall objective is to promote and safeguard the production and publication of official statistics and ensure their quality and comprehensiveness. The authority's main functions are the oversight of the Office for National Statistics (ONS); monitoring and reporting on all UK official statistics; and independent assessment of official statistics.

BOARD
Chair, Sir Michael Scholar, KCB
Board Members, Lord Rowe-Beddoe *(Deputy Chair, ONS);* Richard Alldritt *(Head of Assessment);* Dr Colette Bowe; Partha Dasgupta; Jil Matheson *(National Statistician);* Moira Gibb, CBE; Prof. Sir Roger Jowell, CBE *(Deputy Chair, Statistical System);* Prof. Steve Nickell, FBA; Stephen Penneck *(Director-General, ONS);* Prof David Rhind, CBE, FRS, FBA; Sir John Shortridge, KCB

OFFICE FOR NATIONAL STATISTICS (ONS)

Cardiff Road, Newport NP10 8XG
T 0845-601 3034 E info@statistics.gov.uk
W www.statistics.gov.uk

The ONS was created in 1996 by the merger of the Central Statistical Office and the Office of Population Censuses and Surveys. On 1 April 2008 it became the executive office of the UK Statistics Authority. As part of these changes, the office's responsibility for the General Register Office transferred to the Identity and Passport Service of the Home Office.

The ONS is responsible for preparing, interpreting and publishing key statistics on the government, economy and society of the UK. Its key responsibilities include the provision of population estimates and projections and statistics on health and other demographic matters in England and Wales; the production of the UK National Accounts and other economic indicators; the organisation of population censuses in England and Wales and surveys for government departments and public bodies.
National Statistician, Jil Matheson
Director-General, Stephen Penneck

UK TRADE AND INVESTMENT

Europa Building, 450 Argyle Street, Glasgow G2 8LH
T 020-7215 8000 W www.ukti.gov.uk

UK Trade and Investment is a government organisation that helps UK-based companies succeed in international markets. It assists overseas companies to bring high quality investment to the UK economy.
Chief Executive, Sir Andrew Cahn

WATER SERVICES REGULATION AUTHORITY (OFWAT)

Centre City Tower, 7 Hill Street, Birmingham B5 4UA
T 0121-644 7500 E enquiries@ofwat.gsi.gov.uk
W www.ofwat.gov.uk

OFWAT is the independent economic regulator of the water and sewerage companies in England and Wales. It is responsible for ensuring that the water industry in England and Wales provides customers with a good quality service at a fair price. This is done by keeping bills for consumers as low as possible; monitoring and comparing the services that companies provide; scrutinising the companies' costs and investment; and encouraging competition where this benefits consumers.
Chair, Philip Fletcher
Chief Executive, Regina Finn

PUBLIC BODIES

The following section is a listing of public bodies and selected other civil service organisations.

Whereas executive agencies are either part of a government department or are one in their own right (*see* Government Departments section), public bodies carry out their functions to a greater or lesser extent at arm's length from central government. Ministers are ultimately responsible to parliament for the activities of the public bodies sponsored by their department and in almost all cases (except where there is separate statutory provision) ministers make the appointments to their boards. Departments are responsible for funding and ensuring good governance of their public bodies.

The term 'public body' is a general one which includes public corporations, such as the BBC; NHS bodies; and non-departmental public bodies (NDPBs). There were 766 NDPBs sponsored by UK government departments as at 31 March 2009. This figure is made up of 192 executive NDPBs, 405 advisory NDPBs, 19 tribunal NDPBs and 150 independent monitoring boards. The following is not a complete list of these organisations.

ADJUDICATOR'S OFFICE

8th Floor, Euston Tower, 286 Euston Road, London NW1 3US
T 0300-057 1111 W www.adjudicatorsoffice.gov.uk

The Adjudicator's Office investigates complaints about the way that HM Revenue and Customs, the Valuation Office Agency, the Office of the Public Guardian and the Insolvency Service have handled a person's affairs.
The Adjudicator, Judy Clements, OBE

ADMINISTRATIVE JUSTICE AND TRIBUNALS COUNCIL

81 Chancery Lane, London WC2A 1BQ
T 020-7855 5200 E enquiries@ajtc.gsi.gov.uk
W www.ajtc.gov.uk

The Administrative Justice and Tribunals Council (AJTC) is a permanent standing advisory body set up under the Tribunals, Courts and Enforcement Act. It consists of 15 members appointed by the Lord Chancellor, Scottish and Welsh ministers. It has Scottish and Welsh Committees which discharge its responsibilities in their respective territories. The Parliamentary Ombudsman is an *ex officio* member of the council and of its Scottish and Welsh Committees.

The principal functions of the AJTC are to keep the administrative justice system under review; keep under review and report on the constitution and working of listed tribunals; and keep under review and report on the constitution and working of statutory inquiries. It is consulted by and advises government departments on a wide range of subjects relating to adjudicative procedures.
Chair, Richard Thomas, CBE
Members, The Parliamentary Ombudsman *(ex officio),* Ann Abraham; Jodi Berg; Prof. Alice Brown, CBE; Prof. Andrew Coyle; Kate Dunlop; Richard Henderson; Sukhvinder Kaur-Stubbs; Penny Letts, OBE; Bronwyn McKenna; Bernard Quoroll; Prof. Mary Seneviratne; Dr Jonathan Spencer, CB; Dr Adrian Stokes, OBE; Brian Thompson; Prof. Sir Adrian Webb

WELSH COMMITTEE OF THE ADMINISTRATIVE JUSTICE AND TRIBUNALS COUNCIL
81 Chancery Lane, London WC2A 1BQ
T 020-7855 5200 E enquiries@ajtc.gsi.gov.uk
W www.ajtc.gov.uk
Chair, Prof. Sir Adrian Webb
Members, The Public Services Ombudsman for Wales *(ex officio)*; Bob Chapman; Gareth Lewis; Rhian Williams-Flew

SCOTTISH COMMITTEE OF THE ADMINISTRATIVE JUSTICE AND TRIBUNALS COUNCIL
George House, 126 George Street, Edinburgh EH2 4HH
T 0131-271 4300 W www.ajtc.gov.uk
Chair, Richard Henderson
Members, The Parliamentary Commissioner for Administration *(ex officio);* The Scottish Public Services Ombudsman *(ex officio);* Prof. Andrew Coyle; Annabell Fowles; Michael Menlowe; Michael Scanlan

ADVISORY, CONCILIATION AND ARBITRATION SERVICE (ACAS)

22nd Floor, Euston Tower, 286 Euston Road, London NW1 3JJ
T 020-7396 0022 **Helpline** 0845-747 4747
W www.acas.org.uk

The Advisory, Conciliation and Arbitration Service was set up under the Employment Protection Act 1975 (the provisions now being found in the Trade Union and Labour Relations (Consolidation) Act 1992).

ACAS is funded by the Department for Business, Innovation and Skills. A council sets its strategic direction, policies and priorities, and ensures that the agreed strategic objectives and targets are met. It consists of a chair and 11 employer, trade union and independent members, appointed by the Secretary of State for Business, Innovation and Skills. ACAS aims to improve organisations and working life through better employment relations, to provide up-to-date information, independent advice and high-quality training, and to work with employers and employees to solve problems and improve performance.

ACAS has 13 regional offices, in Birmingham, Bury St Edmunds, Bristol, Cardiff, Fleet, Glasgow, Leeds, Liverpool, London, Manchester, Newcastle upon Tyne, Nottingham and Paddock Wood.
Chair, Ed Sweeney
Chief Executive, John Taylor

ADVISORY COUNCIL ON NATIONAL RECORDS AND ARCHIVES

The National Archives, Kew, Surrey TW9 4DU
T 020-8392 5377
W www.nationalarchives.gov.uk/advisorycouncil

The Advisory Council on National Records and Archives advises the Lord Chancellor on all matters relating to the preservation, use of, and access to historical manuscripts, records and archives of all kinds. The council meets four times a year, and its main task is to consider requests for the extended closure of public records, or from departments that want to keep records. The council encompasses the statutory Advisory Council on Public Records and the Advisory Council on Historical Manuscripts.

Chair, Lord Neuberger of Abbotsbury, PC *(Master of the Rolls)*

AGRICULTURE AND HORTICULTURE DEVELOPMENT BOARD

Stoneleigh Park, Kenilworth, Warwickshire CV8 2TL
T 02476-692051 E info@ahdb.org.uk W www.ahdb.org.uk

The Agriculture and Horticulture Development Board (AHDB) is funded by the agriculture and horticulture industries through statutory levies, with the duty to improve efficiency and competitiveness within six sectors: pig meat in England; milk in Great Britain; beef and lamb in England; commercial horticulture in Great Britain; cereals and oilseeds in the UK; and potatoes in Great Britain. The AHDB represents about 75 per cent of total UK agricultural output. Levies raised from the six sectors are ring-fenced to ensure they can only be used to the benefit of the sectors from which they were raised. The AHDB board consists of ten members: the chairs for each of the six sector organisations, and four independent members.

Chairman, John Bridge
Independent members, Chris Bones; John Bridge; Lorraine Clinton; Clare Dodgson
Sector members, Tim Bennett (milk); Neil Bragg (horticulture); John Cross (beef and lamb); Stewart Houston (pig meat); Allan Stevenson (potatoes); Jonathan Tipples (cereals and oilseeds)
Chief Executive, Tom Taylor

ANCIENT MONUMENTS ADVISORY BOARD FOR WALES (CADW)

Plas Carew, Unit 5–7 Cefn Coed, Parc Nantgarw, Cardiff CF15 7QQ
T 01443-336000 E cadw@wales.gsi.gov.uk
W www.cadw.wales.gov.uk

The Ancient Monuments Advisory Board for Wales advises the Welsh Assembly Government on its statutory functions in respect of ancient monuments.

Chair, Richard Brewer
Members, Prof. Miranda Aldhouse-Green, FSA; Prof. Nancy Edwards; Prof. Ralph Griffiths, DLITT; John Hilling; Christopher Musson, MBE, FSA; Dr Emma Plunkett Dillon; Dr Anthony Ward; Prof. Alasdair Whittle, FBA, DPHIL

ARCHITECTURE AND DESIGN SCOTLAND

Bakehouse Close, 146 Canongate, Edinburgh EH8 8DD
T 0131-556 6699 E info@ads.org.uk
W www.ads.org.uk

Architecture and Design Scotland (A+DS) was established in 2005 by the Scottish government as the national champion for good architecture, urban design and planning in the built environment; it works with a wide range of organisations at national, regional and local levels. A+DS also assumed the independent design review and advisory role of the Royal Fine Art Commission for Scotland.

Chair, Karen Anderson
Chief Executive, Trevor Muir, OBE

ARMED FORCES' PAY REVIEW BODY

6th Floor, Kingsgate House, 66–74 Victoria Street, London SW1E 6SW
T 020-7215 8859 W www.ome.uk.com

The Armed Forces' Pay Review Body was appointed in 1971. It advises the prime minister and the Secretary of State for Defence on the pay and allowances of members of naval, military and air forces of the Crown.

Chair, Prof. Alasdair Smith
Members, Mary Carter; Very Revd. Dr Graham Forbes, CBE; Alison Gallico; Dr Peter Knight, CBE; Prof. Derek Leslie; Judy McKnight, CBE; John Steele; Air Vice-Marshall Ian Stewart (retd), CB

ARTS COUNCIL ENGLAND

14 Great Peter Street, London SW1P 3NQ
T 0845-300 6200
E enquiries@artscouncil.org.uk
W www.artscouncil.org.uk

Arts Council England is the national development agency for the arts in England. Using public money from government and the National Lottery, it supports a range of artistic activities, including theatre, music, literature, dance, photography, digital art, carnival and crafts. Between 2008 and 2011 Arts Council England will invest £1.3bn of public money from government and £300m from the National Lottery.

In 2002, the Arts Council of England and nine regional arts boards joined together to form a single development organisation for the arts. The governing council's members and chair are appointed by the Secretary of State for Culture, Olympics, Media and Sport usually for a term of four years, and meet approximately five times a year.

Chair, Dame Liz Forgan
Members, Diran Adebayo; Janet Barnes; Caroline Collier; Prof. Jon Cook; Ekow Eshun; Sheila Healy; Sir Nicholas Kenyon; Keith Khan; Francois Matarasso; Peter Phillips; Alice Rawsthorn; Anil Ruia, OBE; Alistair Spalding; Rosemary Squire, OBE
Chief Executive, Alan Davey

ARTS COUNCIL OF NORTHERN IRELAND

77 Malone Road, Belfast BT9 6AQ
T 028-9038 5200 E info@artscouncil-ni.org
W www.artscouncil-ni.org

The Arts Council of Northern Ireland is the prime distributor of government funds in support of the arts in Northern Ireland. It is funded by the Department of Culture, Arts and Leisure and from National Lottery funds.

Chair, Rosemary Kelly
Members, Eithne Benson; Kate Bond; Damien Coyle *(Vice-Chair);* Raymond Fullerton; David Irvine; Anthony Kennedy; Bill Montgomery; Ian Montgomery; Sharon O'Connor; Joseph Rice; Paul Seawright; Brian Sore; Peter Spratt; Janine Walker
Chief Executive, Roisin McDonough

ARTS COUNCIL OF WALES

Bute Place, Cardiff CF10 5AL
T 0845-873 4900 E feedback@artswales.org.uk
W www.artswales.org.uk

The Arts Council of Wales was established in 1994 by royal charter and is the development body for the arts in Wales. It funds arts organisations with funding from the National Assembly for Wales and is the distributor of National Lottery funds to the arts in Wales. The grant for 2009–10 was £27m from the National Assembly and £8.97m from the National Lottery.
Chair, Prof. Dai Smith
Members, Norah Campbell; Emma Evans; John Geraint; Maggie Hampton; Margaret Jervis, MBE; Robin Morrison; Osi Rhys Osmond; Richard Turner; Alan Watkin; Debbie Wilcox; Gerwyn Wiliams; John Carey Williams; Dr Kate Woodward
Chief Executive, Nick Capaldi

AUDIT COMMISSION

1st Floor, Millbank Tower, London SW1P 4HQ
T 0844-798 1212
E public-enquiries@audit-commission.gov.uk
W www.audit-commission.gov.uk

The Audit Commission was set up in 1983 and is an independent body responsible for ensuring that public money is spent economically, efficiently and effectively, to achieve high-quality local services for the public. Its remit covers around 11,000 bodies in England, which between them spend more than £200bn of public money each year. Its work covers local government, health, criminal justice organisations and public services.

The commission has a chair, a deputy chair and a board of up to 20 commissioners who are appointed by the Department for Communities and Local Government following consultation with key stakeholders.
Chair, Michael O'Higgins
Deputy Chair, Bahrat Shah
Commissioners, Lord Adebowale, CBE; Cllr Merrick Cockell; Jim Coulter; Dr Jennifer Dixon; Sheila Drew Smith, OBE; Cllr Stephen Houghton, CBE; Sir Thomas Legg, KCB, QC; Dame Denise Platt; Dr Raj Rajagopal; Jenny Watson; Cllr Chris White
Interim Chief Executive, Eugene Sullivan

AUDIT SCOTLAND

110 George Street, Edinburgh EH2 4LH
T 0845-146 1010 E info@auditscotland.gov.uk
W www.audit-scotland.gov.uk

Audit Scotland was set up in 2000 to provide services to the Accounts Commission and the Auditor General for Scotland. Together they help to ensure that public sector bodies in Scotland are held accountable for the proper, efficient and effective use of public funds.

Audit Scotland's work covers about 200 bodies including local authorities; police forces and fire rescue services; health boards; further education colleges; Scottish Water; the Scottish government; government agencies such as the Prison Service and non-departmental public bodies such as Scottish Enterprise.

Audit Scotland carries out financial and regularity audits to ensure that public sector bodies adhere to the highest standards of financial management and governance. It also performs audits to ensure that these bodies achieve the best value for money. All of Audit Scotland's work in connection with local authorities, fire and police boards is carried out for the Accounts Commission; its other work is undertaken for the Auditor-General.
Auditor-General, R. W. Black
Chair of the Accounts Commission, J. Baillie

BANK OF ENGLAND

Threadneedle Street, London EC2R 8AH
T 020-7601 4444 E enquiries@bankofengland.co.uk
W www.bankofengland.co.uk

The Bank of England was incorporated in 1694 under royal charter. It was nationalised in 1946 under the Bank of England Act of that year which gave HM Treasury statutory powers over the bank. It is the banker of the government and it manages the issue of banknotes. Since 1998 it has been operationally independent and its Monetary Policy Committee has been responsible for setting short-term interest rates to meet the government's inflation target. Its responsibility for banking supervision was transferred to the Financial Services Authority in the same year. As the central reserve bank of the country, the Bank of England keeps the accounts of British banks, and of most overseas central banks; the larger banks and building societies are required to maintain with it a proportion of their cash resources. The bank's core purposes are monetary stability and financial stability. The Banking Act 2009 increased the responsibilities of the bank, including giving the bank a new financial stability objective and creating a special resolution regime for dealing with failing banks.
Governor, Mervyn King
Deputy Governors, Charles Bean; Paul Tucker
Court of Directors, Brendan Barber; Roger Carr; Antonio Horta-Osorio; Sir David Lees; Susan Rice; John Stewart; Mark Tucker; Lord Adair Turner; Harrison Young
Monetary Policy Committee, The Governor; the Deputy Governors; Spencer Dale; Paul Fisher; David Miler; Adam Posen; Dr Andrew Sentance
Adviser to the Governor, Graham Nicholson
Chief Cashier and Executive Director, Banking Services, Andrew Bailey
The Auditor, Stephen Brown

BIG LOTTERY FUND

1 Plough Place, London EC4A 1DE
T 020-7211 1800 Advice Line 0845-410 2030
E general.enquiries@biglotteryfund.org.uk
W www.biglotteryfund.org.uk

The Big Lottery Fund was launched in 2004, merging the New Opportunities Fund and the Lottery Charities Board (Community Fund). The fund is responsible for giving out half of the money for good causes raised by the National Lottery. The money is distributed to charitable, benevolent and philanthropic organisations in the voluntary and community sectors, as well as health, education and environmental projects. The Big Lottery Fund also assumed the Millennium Commission's role of supporting large-scale regenerative projects.
Chair, Prof. Sir Clive Booth
Vice-Chair, Anna Southall
Regional Chairs, Sanjay Dighe *(England)*; Frank Hewitt *(Northern Ireland)*; Alison Magee *(Scotland)*; Huw Vaughan *(Wales)*
General Members, Judith Donovan, CBE; Roland Doven, MBE; John Gartside, OBE; Rajay Naik; Albert Tucker; Diana Whitworth
Chief Executive, Peter Wanless
Directors, Walter Rader *(Northern Ireland)*; Dharmendra Kanani *(Scotland)*; Ceri Doyle *(Wales)*

BOUNDARY COMMISSIONS

ENGLAND
2nd Floor, Steel House, 11 Tothill Street, London SW1H 9LJ
T 020-3334 0400 E information@justice.gsi.gov.uk
W www.boundarycommissionforengland.org.uk
Deputy Chair, Hon. Mr Justice Sales

WALES
1st Floor, Caradog House, 1–6 St Andrews Place, Cardiff CF10 3BE
T 029-2039 5031 E bcomm.wales@wales.gsi.gov.uk
W www.bcomm-wales.gov.uk
Deputy Chair, Hon. Justice Lloyd Jones

SCOTLAND
Thistle House, 91 Haymarket Terrace, Edinburgh EH12 5HD
T 0131-538 7510 F 0131-538 7511
E secretariat@scottishboundaries.gov.uk
W www.bcomm-scotland.gov.uk
Deputy Chair, Hon. Lord Woolman

NORTHERN IRELAND
Forestview, Purdy's Lane, Newtownbreda, Belfast BT8 7AR
T 028-9069 4800 E bcni@belfast.org.uk
W www.boundarycommission.org.uk
Deputy Chair, Hon. Mr Justice McLaughlin

The commissions, established in 1944, are constituted under the Parliamentary Constituencies Act 1986 (as amended). The Speaker of the House of Commons is *ex officio* chair of all four commissions in the UK. Each of the four commissions is required by law to keep the parliamentary constituencies in their part of the UK under review (in the case of the Scottish Commission this includes constituencies for the Scottish parliament). The latest Boundary Commission report for England was laid before parliament in February 2007, and the proposals took effect at the 2010 general election. The latest report from Northern Ireland was published in May 2006, from Wales in January 2005 and the most recent Scottish report on Westminster constituencies was completed in May 2010.

BRITISH BROADCASTING CORPORATION (BBC)

Television Centre, Wood Lane, London W12 7RJ
T 020-8743 8000; BBC Information Line 0870-010 0222
W www.bbc.co.uk

The BBC was incorporated under royal charter in 1926 as successor to the British Broadcasting Company Ltd. The BBC's current charter, which came into force on 1 January 2007 and extends to 31 December 2016, recognises the BBC's editorial independence and sets out its public purposes. The BBC Trust was formed under the new charter and replaces the Board of Governors; it sets the strategic direction of the BBC and has a duty to represent the interests of licence fee payers. The chair, vice-chair and other trustees are appointed by the Queen-in-Council. The BBC is financed by revenue from receiving licences for the home services and by grant-in-aid from parliament for the World Service (radio). *See also* Broadcasting.

BBC TRUST MEMBERS
Chair, Sir Michael Lyons
Vice-Chair, Chitra Bharucha
National Trustees, Alison Hastings *(England);* Rotha Johnston *(Northern Ireland);* Janet Lewis-Jones *(Wales);* Jeremy Peat *(Scotland)*
Trustees, Diane Coyle; Anthony Fry; Patricia Hodgson; David Liddiment; Mehmuda Mian; Richard Tait

EXECUTIVE BOARD
Director-General and Chair, Mark Thompson
Deputy Director-General, Mark Byford
Directors, Tim Davie *(Audio and Music);* Jana Bennett *(Vision);* Sharon Baylay *(Marketing, Communications and Audiences);* Erik Huggers *(Future Media and Technology);* Lucy Adams *(People);* Zarin Patel *(Chief Financial Officer)*
Chief Executive, BBC Worldwide, John Smith
Chief Operating Officer, Caroline Thomson
Senior Independent Director, Marcus Agius
Non-Executive Directors, Val Gooding, CBE; Dr Mike Lynch, OBE; David Robbie; Dr Samir Shah, OBE; Robert Webb, QC

STATION CONTROLLERS
BBC1, Jay Hunt
BBC2, Janice Hadlow
BBC3, Danny Cohen
BBC4, Richard Klein
BBC News Channel, Kevin Bakhurst
BBC Parliament, Peter Knowles
BBC Northern Ireland, Peter Johnston
BBC Scotland, Ken MacQuarrie
BBC Wales, Menna Richards
Radio 1, 1Xtra, Asian Network and Switch, Andy Parfitt
Radio 2 and 6 Music, Bob Shennan
Radio 3, Roger Wright
Radio 4, Gwyneth Williams
Radio 5 Live, Adrian Van Klaveren

BRITISH COUNCIL

Bridgewater House, 58 Whitworth Street, Manchester M1 6BB
T 0161-957 7000 E general.enquiries@britishcouncil.org
W www.britishcouncil.org

The British Council was established in 1934, incorporated by royal charter in 1940 and granted a supplemental charter in 1993. It is an independent, non-political organisation which promotes Britain abroad and is the UK's international organisation for educational and cultural relations. The British Council is represented in 216 towns and cities in 109 countries. Grant-in-aid received from the Foreign and Commonwealth Office in 2007–8 was £189m.
Chair, Vernon Ellis
Chief Executive, Martin Davidson, CMG

BRITISH FILM INSTITUTE (BFI)

21 Stephen Street, London W1T 1LN
T 020-7255 1444 W www.bfi.org.uk

The BFI, established in 1933, offers opportunities for people throughout the UK to experience, learn and discover more about the world of film and moving image culture. It incorporates the BFI National Archive, the BFI National Library, a range of DVD releases, publications and educational materials (including the monthly *Sight and Sound* magazine), BFI Southbank, BFI Distribution, the annual BFI London Film Festival as well as the BFI London Lesbian and Gay Film Festival, and the BFI IMAX cinema, and provides advice and support for regional cinemas and film festivals across the UK.

Chair, Greg Dyke
Director, Amanda Nevill

BRITISH LIBRARY

96 Euston Road, London NW1 2DB
T 0843-208 1144 E customer-services@bl.uk
W www.bl.uk

The British Library was established in 1973. It is the UK's national library and occupies a key position in the library and information network. It aims to serve scholarship, research, industry, commerce and all other major users of information. Its services are based on a collection of over 150 million separate items, including books, journals, manuscripts, maps, stamps, music, patents, newspapers and sound recordings in all written and spoken languages. The library is now based at three sites: London (St Pancras and Colindale) and Boston Spa, W. Yorks. The library's sponsoring department is the Department for Culture, Media and Sport.

Access to the reading rooms at St Pancras is limited to holders of a British Library reader's pass; information about eligibility is available from the reader admissions office. The exhibition galleries and public areas are open to all, free of charge.

BRITISH LIBRARY BOARD
Chair, Sir Colin Lucas
Chief Executive and Deputy Chair, Dame L. Brindley, DBE
Members, Ms D. Airey; R. S. Broadhurst, CBE; Prof. R. Burgess; Sir K. Calman; Lord Fellowes; Ms S. Forbes, CBE; Prof. W. Hall, CBE; Ms E. Mackay, CB; Prof. K. McLuskie; M. Semple, OBE

SCHOLARSHIP AND COLLECTIONS
Americas Collections, T 020-7412 7743
Asia, Pacific and Africa Collections, T 020-7412 7873
British and Irish Collections, T 020-7412 7538
British Library Newspapers, Colindale Avenue, London NW9 5HE T 020-7412 7353
British Library Sound Archive, T 020-7412 7676
Early Printed Collections, T 020-7412 7564
Map Library, T 020-7412 7702
Music Library, T 020-7412 7772
Philatelic Collections, T 020-7412 7635
Reader Information, T 020-7412 7676
West European Collections, T 020-7412 7572/7569

OPERATIONS AND SERVICES
Permission Clearance, T 020-7412 7755
Research Services, T 020-7412 7903

SCIENCE, TECHNOLOGY AND INNOVATION
Business, T 020-7412 7454
National Preservation Office, T 020-7412 7612
Patents, T 020-7412 7454
Science and Technology, T 020-7412 7494/7288
Social Science, Law and Official Publications, T 020-7412 7536

BRITISH LIBRARY, BOSTON SPA
Boston Spa, Wetherby, W. Yorks LS23 7BQ
T 01937-546060

BRITISH MUSEUM

Great Russell Street, London WC1B 3DG
T 020-7323 8000
E information@britishmuseum.org
W www.britishmuseum.org

The British Museum houses the national collection of antiquities, ethnography, coins and paper money, medals, prints and drawings. The British Museum may be said to date from 1753, when parliament approved the holding of a public lottery to raise funds for the purchase of the collections of Sir Hans Sloane and the Harleian manuscripts, and for their proper housing and maintenance. The building (Montagu House) was opened in 1759. The existing buildings were erected between 1823 and the present day, and the original collection has increased to its current dimensions by gifts and purchases. Total government grant-in-aid for 2010–11 was £47.3m.

BOARD OF TRUSTEES
Appointed by the Sovereign, Chief Emeka Anyaoku
Appointed by the Prime Minister, Karen Armstrong; Prof. Sir Christopher Bayly; Sir Ronald Cohen; Francis Finlay; Dame Liz Forgan, OBE; Val Gooding, CBE; Stephen Green; Bonnie Greer; Penny Hughes; George Iacobescu, CBE; Baroness Kennedy, QC; Richard Lambert; David Norgrove; Lord Stern of Brentford, FBA
Appointed by the Trustees of the British Museum, Lord Broers of Cambridge, FRS, FRENG; Niall Fitzgerald *(Chair);* Edmee P. Leventis; Lord Powell of Bayswater, KCMG
Appointed by the Royal Society, Dr Olga Kennard, OBE
Appointed by the Royal Academy, Antony Gormley, OBE

OFFICERS
Director, Neil MacGregor
Deputy Director, Dr Andrew Burnett
Director of Public Engagement, Joanna Mackle
Director of Administration, Chris Yates
Director of Visitor and Building Services, Stephen Gill
Director of Strategic Planning, Justin Morris
Heads of Departments, Carolyn Marsden-Smith *(Exhibitions);* Xerxes Mazda *(Learning and Audience);* Carol Hunt *(Membership)*

KEEPERS
Keeper of Africa, Oceania and the Americas, Jonathan King
Keeper of Ancient Egypt and Sudan, Vivian Davies
Keeper of Asia, Jan Stuart
Keeper of Coins and Medals, Philip Attwood
Keeper of Greece and Rome, J. Lesley Fitton
Keeper of the Middle East, John Curtis
Keeper of Prehistory and Europe, Jonathan Williams
Keeper of Prints and Drawings, Antony Griffiths
Conservation and Scientific Research, David Saunders

BRITISH PHARMACOPOEIA COMMISSION

151 Buckingham Palace Road, London SW1W 9SS
T 020-7084 2561 E bpcom@mhra.gsi.gov.uk
W www.pharmacopoeia.gov.uk

The British Pharmacopoeia Commission sets standards for medicinal products used in human and veterinary medicines and is responsible for publication of the *British Pharmacopoeia* (a publicly available statement of the standard that a product must meet throughout its shelf-life), the *British Pharmacopoeia (Veterinary)* and the *British Approved Names.* It has 15 members, including two lay members, who are appointed by the Appointments Commission (the body responsible for appointments to all of the Medicines Act advisory bodies).
Chair, Prof. A. D. Woolfson

Vice-Chair, V'lain Fenton-May
Secretary and Scientific Director, Dr M. G. Lee

BRITISH STANDARDS INSTITUTION

389 Chiswick High Road, London W4 4AL
T 020-8996 9001 E cservices@bsigroup.com
W www.bsigroup.com

British Standards – a part of the BSI Group – was the world's first national standards-making body, established in 1901, and is the recognised national standards body in the UK for the preparation, publication and marketing of national standards, both for products and for the service sector. About 90 per cent of its standards work is internationally linked. British Standards are issued for voluntary adoption, though in some cases compliance with a British Standard is required by legislation. Industrial and consumer products and services certified as complying with the relevant British Standard and operating an assessed quality management system are eligible to carry BSI's certification trade mark, known as the 'Kitemark'.
Chair, Sir David John, KCMG
Chief Executive, Howard Kerr

BRITISH WATERWAYS

64 Clarendon Road, Watford WD17 1DA
T 01923-201120
E enquiries.hq@britishwaterways.co.uk
W www.britishwaterways.co.uk

British Waterways conserves and manages the network of over 3,540km (2,200 miles) of canals and rivers in England, Scotland and Wales. Its sponsoring departments are the Department for Environment, Food and Rural Affairs in England and Wales, and the Scottish Government Transport Directive.

Its responsibilities include maintaining the waterways and structures on and around them; looking after wildlife and the waterway environment; and ensuring that canals and rivers are safe and enjoyable places to visit.
Chair, Tony Hales, CBE
Vice-Chair, John Bridgeman, CBE, TD
Chief Executive, Robin Evans, FRICS

CARE QUALITY COMMISSION

Finsbury Tower, 103–105 Bunhill Row, London EC1Y 8TG
T 0300-061 6161 E enquiries@cqc.org.uk
W www.cqc.org.uk

The Care Quality Commission (CQC) was established on 1 April 2009, bringing together the work of the Healthcare Commission, the Mental Health Act Commission and the Commission for Social Care Inspection. CQC is the independent regulator of health and adult social care in England, including those provided by the NHS, local authorities, private companies and voluntary organisations. Its main functions are to register health and social care providers; monitor and inspect all health and social care; enforce standards and to implement fines, public warnings or closures if these are not met; to review services regularly; and to report findings publicly.
Chair (acting), Jo Williams
Chief Executive, Cynthia Bower
Board, John Harwood; Prof. Deirdre Kelly; Martin Marshall; Olu Olasode; Kay Sheldon; Jo Williams

CENTRAL ARBITRATION COMMITTEE

22nd Floor, Euston Tower, 286 Euston Road, London NW1 3JJ
T 020-7904 2300 E enquiries@cac.gov.uk
W www.cac.gov.uk

The Central Arbitration Committee (CAC) is a permanent independent body with statutory powers whose main function is to adjudicate on applications relating to the statutory recognition and de-recognition of trade unions for collective bargaining purposes, where such recognition or de-recognition cannot be agreed voluntarily. In addition, the CAC has a statutory role in determining disputes between trade unions and employers over the disclosure of information for collective bargaining purposes, and in resolving applications and complaints under the information and consultation regulations, and performs a similar role in relation to the legislation on the European Works Council, European companies, European cooperative societies and cross-border mergers. The CAC also provides voluntary arbitration in industrial disputes.

The committee consists of a chair and 10 deputy chairs, 28 members experienced as representatives of employers and 25 members experienced as representatives of workers. Members of the committee are appointed by the Secretary of State for Business, Innovation and Skills after consulting ACAS.
Chair, Sir Michael Burton
Chief Executive, Graeme Charles

CERTIFICATION OFFICE FOR TRADE UNIONS AND EMPLOYERS' ASSOCIATIONS

Euston Tower, 286 Euston Road, London NW1 3JJ
T 020-7210 3734 E info@certoffice.org
W www.certoffice.org

The Certification Office is an independent statutory authority. The certification officer is appointed by the Secretary of State for Business, Innovation and Skills and is responsible for maintaining a list of trade unions and employers' associations; ensuring compliance with statutory requirements; keeping annual returns from trade unions and employers' associations available for public inspection; determining complaints concerning trade union elections, certain ballots and certain breaches of trade union rules; ensuring observance of statutory requirements governing mergers between trade unions and employers' associations; overseeing the political funds and finances of trade unions and employers' associations; and for certifying the independence of trade unions.
Certification Officer, David Cockburn

SCOTLAND
69A George Street, Edinburgh EH2 2JG
T 0131-220 7660
Assistant Certification Officer for Scotland, Christine Stuart

CHURCH COMMISSIONERS

Church House, Great Smith Street, London SW1P 3AZ
T 020-7898 1000 E commissioners.enquiry@c-of-e.org
W www.cofe.anglican.org/about/churchcommissioners

The Church Commissioners were established in 1948 by the amalgamation of Queen Anne's Bounty (established 1704) and the Ecclesiastical Commissioners (established 1836). They are responsible for the management of some of the Church of England's assets, the income from which is predominantly used to help pay for the stipend and pension of the clergy and to support the church's work throughout the country. The commissioners own UK and global company shares, over 43,000ha (106,000 acres) of agricultural land, a residential estate in central London, and commercial property across Great Britain, plus an interest in overseas property via managed funds. They also carry out administrative duties in connection with pastoral reorganisation and closed churches.

The commissioners are: the Archbishops of Canterbury and of York; four bishops, three clergy and four lay persons elected by the respective houses of the General Synod; two deans elected by all the deans; three persons nominated by the Queen; three persons nominated by the Archbishops of Canterbury and York; three persons nominated by the archbishops after consultation with others including the Lord Mayors of London and York and the vice-chancellors of the universities of Oxford and Cambridge; the First Lord of the Treasury; the Lord President of the Council; the home secretary; the Secretary of State for Culture, Olympics, Media and Sport; and the Speakers of the House of Commons and the House of Lords.

CHURCH ESTATES COMMISSIONERS
First, A. Whittam Smith
Second, Sir Stuart Bell, MP
Third, T. E. H. Walker

OFFICERS
Secretary, A. C. Brown
Director of Investments, T. Joy
Assistant Secretary, Pastoral and Redundant Churches, P. Lewis
Official Solicitor, S. Slack

COAL AUTHORITY

200 Lichfield Lane, Mansfield, Notts NG18 4RG
T 01623-637000 E thecoalauthority@coal.gov.uk
W www.coal.gov.uk

The Coal Authority was established under the Coal Industry Act 1994 to manage certain functions previously undertaken by British Coal, including ownership of unworked coal. It is responsible for licensing coal mining operations and for providing information on coal reserves and past and future coal mining. It settles subsidence damage claims which are not the responsibility of licensed coal mining operators. It deals with the management and disposal of property, and with surface hazards such as abandoned coal mine entries.
Chair, Dr Helen Mounsey
Chief Executive, Philip Lawrence

COMMISSION FOR ARCHITECTURE AND THE BUILT ENVIRONMENT (CABE)

1 Kemble Street, London WC2B 4AN
T 020-7070 6700 E info@cabe.org.uk
W www.cabe.org.uk

CABE was established in 1999 and is responsible for promoting the importance of high-quality architecture and urban design, and for encouraging the understanding of architecture through educational and regional initiatives. The commission offers free advice to local authorities, public sector clients and others embarking on building projects of any size or purpose. CABE has a board of 16 commissioners, appointed by the Secretary of State for Culture, Media and Sport for a maximum of two four-year terms.
Chair, Peter Finch, OBE
Chief Executive, Richard Simmons

COMMISSION FOR INTEGRATED TRANSPORT (CFIT)

2nd Floor, 55 Victoria Street, London SW1H 0EU
T 020-7944 8131 E cfit@dft.gsi.gov.uk
W www.independent.gov.uk/cfit

The CfIT was established in June 1999. Its role is to provide independent expert advice to the government in order to achieve a transport system that supports sustainable development. The CfIT also encourages best practice among local authorities and delivery agencies, and assesses both the impact of new technology on future policy options and transport policy initiatives from outside the UK. Members of the commission are appointed by the transport secretary.
Chair, Peter Hendy, CBE
Vice-Chair, David Leeder
Vice-Chair, Dr Lynn Sloman

COMMISSION FOR RURAL COMMUNITIES

John Dower House, Crescent Place, Cheltenham GL50 3RA
T 01242-521381 E info@ruralcommunities.gov.uk
W www.ruralcommunities.gov.uk

The Commission for Rural Communities was established in October 2006; it was formerly an operating division of the now-defunct Countryside Agency. It is a statutory body under the Natural Environment and Rural Communities Act 2006 and it aims to provide well-informed, independent advice to government and to ensure that policies reflect the needs of people living and working in rural England, with a particular focus on tackling disadvantage. Its three key roles are to be a rural advocate, an expert adviser and an independent watchdog. The commission is funded by an annual grant from the Department for Environment, Food and Rural Affairs and commissioners are appointed by the secretary of state.
Chair and Rural Advocate, Dr Stuart Burgess
Commissioners, Prof. Sheena Asthana; Richard Childs, QPM; Dr Jim Cox, OBE; Elinor Goodman; John Mills, CBE; Howard Petch, CBE; Sue Prince, OBE; Rachel Purchase; Prof. Mark Shucksmith, OBE; Prof. Michael Winter, OBE
Chief Executive, Sarah McAdam

COMMITTEE ON STANDARDS IN PUBLIC LIFE

35 Great Smith Street, London SW1P 3BQ
T 020-7276 2595 E public@standards.x.gsi.gov.uk
W www.public-standards.org.uk

The Committee on Standards in Public Life was set up in October 1994. It is a standing body whose chair and members are appointed by the prime minister; three members are nominated by the leaders of the three main political parties. The committee's remit is to examine concerns about standards of conduct of all holders of public office, including arrangements relating to financial and commercial activities, and to make recommendations as to any changes in present arrangements which might be

required to ensure the highest standards of propriety in public life. It is also charged with reviewing issues in relation to the funding of political parties. The committee does not investigate individual allegations of misconduct.
Chair, Sir Christopher Kelly, KCB
Members, Lloyd Clarke, QPM; Oliver Heald, MP; Rt. Hon. Alun Michael, MP; Sir Derek Morris; Dame Denise Platt, DBE; David Prince, CBE; Dr Elizabeth Vallance; Dr Brian Woods-Scawen, CBE

COMMONWEALTH WAR GRAVES COMMISSION

2 Marlow Road, Maidenhead, Berks SL6 7DX
T 01628-634221 E casualty.enq@cwgc.org
W www.cwgc.org

The Commonwealth War Graves Commission (formerly Imperial War Graves Commission) was founded by royal charter in 1917. It is responsible for the commemoration of around 1.7 million members of the forces of the Commonwealth who lost their lives in the two world wars. More than one million graves are maintained in 23,274 burial grounds throughout the world. Over three-quarters of a million men and women who have no known grave or who were cremated are commemorated by name on memorials built by the commission.

The funds of the commission are derived from the six participating governments, ie the UK, Canada, Australia, New Zealand, South Africa and India.
President, HRH The Duke of Kent, KG, GCMG, GCVO, ADC
Chair, Secretary of State for Defence (UK)
Vice-Chair, Adm. Sir Ian Garnett, KCB
Members, High Commissioners in London for Australia, Canada, South Africa, New Zealand and India; Air Chief Marshal Sir Joe French, KCB, CBE; Ian Henderson, CBE, FRICS; Lt.-Gen. Sir Alistair Irwin, KCB, CBE; Sara Jones, CBE; Alan Meale, MP; Keith Simpson, MP; Prof. Hew Strachan, FRSE; Sir Rob Young, GCMG
Director-General and Secretary to the Commission, Alan Pateman-Jones
Deputy Director-General, T. V. Reeves
Legal Adviser and Solicitor, G. C. Reddie

COMPETITION COMMISSION

Victoria House, Southampton Row, London WC1B 4AD
T 020-7271 0100 E info@cc.gsi.gov.uk
W www.competition-commission.org.uk

The commission was established in 1948 as the Monopolies and Restrictive Practices Commission (later the Monopolies and Mergers Commission); it became the Competition Commission in April 1999 under the Competition Act 1998. The commission conducts in-depth inquiries into mergers, markets, and the regulation of major industries. Every inquiry the commission undertakes is in response to a reference made to it by another authority, usually the Office of Fair Trading. The commission has no power to conduct inquiries on its own initiative. The Enterprise Act 2002 introduced a new regime for the assessment of mergers and markets in the UK – in most related investigations the commission is responsible for making decisions on the competition questions and for making and implementing decisions on appropriate remedies.

The commission has a full-time chair and three deputy chairs. There are usually around 40 part-time commission members, who usually carry out investigations in groups of four or five after appointment by the chair. All are appointed by the Secretary of State for Business, Innovation and Skills for eight-year terms.
Chair, Peter Freeman
Deputy Chairs, Laura Carstensen; Christopher Clarke; Dr Peter Davis; Diana Guy
Non-Executive Directors, Grey Denham; Dame Patricia Hodgson, DBE; Lesley Watkins
Chief Executive and Secretary, David Saunders

COMPETITION SERVICE

Victoria House, Bloomsbury Place, London WC1A 2EB
T 020-7979 7979 E info@catribunal.org.uk
W www.catribunal.org.uk

The Enterprise Act 2002 created the Competition Service, a corporate body and executive non-departmental public body whose purpose is to fund and provide support services to the Competition Appeal Tribunal (CAT). Support services include everything necessary to facilitate the carrying out by CAT of its statutory functions such as administrative staff, accommodation and office equipment.
Director, Operations, Jeremy Straker
President, Hon. Mr Justice Barling
Registrar, Charles Dhanowa, OBE

CONSUMER COUNCIL FOR WATER

Victoria Square House, Victoria Square, Birmingham B2 4AJ
T 0121-345 1000 E enquiries@ccwater.org.uk
W www.ccwater.org.uk

The Consumer Council for Water was established in 2005 under the Water Act 2003 to represent consumers' interests in respect of price, service and value for money from their water and sewerage services, and to investigate complaints from customers about their water company. There are four regional committees in England and one in Wales.
Chair, Dame Yve Buckland, DBE

CONSUMER FOCUS

4th Floor, Artillery House, Artillery Row, London SW1P 1RT
T 020-7799 7900 E contact@consumerfocus.org.uk
W www.consumerfocus.org.uk

Consumer Focus was formed from the merger of Energywatch, Postwatch and the National Consumer Council, and began operations in October 2008. The organisation works for the interests of consumers in private and public sectors throughout England, Scotland and Wales (and for postal services in Northern Ireland). Consumer Focus has legislative powers, including the right to investigate any complaint if it is of wider interest; the right to open up information from providers; and the ability to make an official 'super-complaint' about failing services. Consumer Focus is not a complaints-handling body or a statutory regulator; consumer complaints or requests for advice should be directed to Consumer Direct or Citizens Advice.
Chair, Larry Whitty
Chief Executive, Mike O'Connor

CORPORATION OF TRINITY HOUSE

Trinity House, Tower Hill, London EC3N 4DH
T 020-7481 6900 E enquiries@thls.org
W www.trinityhouse.co.uk

The Corporation of Trinity House is the General Lighthouse Authority for England, Wales and the Channel Islands, and was granted its first charter by Henry VIII in 1514. Its remit is to assist the safe passage of a variety of vessels through some of the busiest sea-lanes in the world; it does this by deploying and maintaining approximately 600 aids to navigation, ranging from lighthouses to a satellite navigation service. The corporation also has certain statutory jurisdiction over aids to navigation maintained by local harbour authorities and is responsible for marking or dispersing wrecks dangerous to navigation, except those occurring within port limits or wrecks of HM ships.

The statutory duties of Trinity House are funded by the General Lighthouse Fund, which is provided from light dues levied on ships calling at ports of the UK and the Republic of Ireland. The corporation is a deep-sea pilotage authority, authorised by the Secretary of State for Transport to license deep-sea pilots. In addition Trinity House is a charitable organisation that maintains a number of retirement homes for mariners and their dependants, funds a four-year training scheme for those seeking a career in the merchant navy, and also dispenses grants to a wide range of maritime charities. The charity work is wholly funded by its own activities.

The corporation is controlled by a board of Elder Brethren; a separate board controls the Lighthouse Service. The Elder Brethren also act as nautical assessors in marine cases in the Admiralty Division of the High Court.

ELDER BRETHREN

Master, HRH The Prince Philip, Duke of Edinburgh, KG, KT, PC

Deputy Master, Rear-Adm. Sir Jeremy de Halpert, KCVO, CB

Wardens, Capt. Duncan Glass, OBE *(Rental);* Capt. Nigel Pryke *(Nether)*

Elder Brethren, HRH The Prince of Wales, KG, KT, GCB; HRH The Duke of York, KG, KCVO, ADC; HRH The Princess Royal, KG, KT, GCVO; Capt. Roger Barker; Adm. Lord Boyce, GCB, OBE; Lord Browne of Madingley; Capt. John Burton-Hall, RD; Lord Carrington, KG, GCMG, CH, PC; Viscount Cobham; Capt. Sir Malcolm Edge, KCVO; Capt. Ian Gibb; Lord Greenway; Lord Mackay of Clashfern, KT, PC; Capt. Peter Mason, CBE; Cdre. Peter Melson, CVO, CBE, RN; Capt. David Orr; Sir John Parker; Douglas Potter; Capt. Derek Richards, RD, RNR; Lord Robertson of Port Ellen, KT, GCMG, PC; Rear-Adm. Sir Patrick Rowe, KCVO, CBE; Cdre. Jim Scorer; Sir Brian Shaw; Simon Sherrard; Adm. Sir Jock Slater, GCB, LVO; Capt. David Smith, OBE, RN; Cdre. David Squire, CBE, RFA; Cdre. Lord Sterling of Plaistow, CBE, GCVO, RNR; Capt. Colin Stewart, LVO; Sir Adrian Swire, AE; Capt. Sir Miles Wingate, KCVO; Capt. Thomas Woodfield, OBE; Capt. Richard Woodman

OFFICERS

Secretary, Cdr Graham Hockley

Director of Finance, Jerry Wedge

Director of Navigation, Capt. Roger Barker

Director of Operations, Cdre. Jim Scorer

COUNTRYSIDE COUNCIL FOR WALES/CYNGOR CEFN GWLAD CYMRU

Maes-y-Ffynnon, Penrhosgarnedd, Bangor, Gwynedd LL57 2DW
T 0845-130 6229 E enquiries@ccw.gov.uk
W www.ccw.gov.uk

The Countryside Council for Wales is the government's statutory adviser on sustaining natural beauty, wildlife and the opportunity for outdoor enjoyment in Wales and its inshore waters. It is funded by the National Assembly for Wales and accountable to the First Secretary, who appoints its members.

Chair, Morgan Parry

Chief Executive, Roger Thomas

COVENT GARDEN MARKET AUTHORITY

Covent House, New Covent Garden Market, London SW8 5NX
T 020-7720 2211 E info@cgma.co.uk
W www.newcoventgardenmarket.com

The Covent Garden Market Authority is constituted under the Covent Garden Market Acts 1961 to 1977, the board being appointed by the Department of Environment, Food and Rural Affairs. The authority owns and operates the 22.7ha (56 acre) New Covent Garden Markets (fruit, vegetables, flowers), which have been trading at the site since 1974.

Chair (part-time), Rt. Hon. Baroness Dean of Thornton-le-Fylde

Chief Executive, Jan Lloyd

CREATIVE SCOTLAND

12 Manor Place, Edinburgh EH3 7DD
T 0330-333 2000 E enquiries@creativescotland.com
W www.creativescotland.org.uk

Creative Scotland is the organisation tasked with leading the development of the arts, creative and screen industries across Scotland. It was created in 2010 as an amalgamation of the Scottish Arts Council and Scottish Screen, and it encourages and sustains the arts through investment in the form of grants, bursaries, loans and equity. It aims to provide informed advocacy for practising artists and producers while ensuring that as many people as possible can participate in creative activities. The intelligence it gathers from practitioners, partners and sector peers will be used to guide its future investments – the money for which is inherited from the grant-in-aid budgets of its two predecessor organisations. The draft budget for 2010–11 was £57.5m.

Chair, Sir Sandy Crombie

Board, Peter Cabrelli; Gwilym Gibbons; Steve Grimmond; Robin MacPherson; Gayle McPherson; Barclay Price; Gary West; Ruth Wishart

Chief Executive, Andrew Dixon

CRIMINAL CASES REVIEW COMMISSION

Alpha Tower, Suffolk Street Queensway, Birmingham B1 1TT
T 0121-633 1800 E info@ccrc.x.gsi.gov.uk
W www.ccrc.gov.uk

The Criminal Cases Review Commission is an independent body set up under the Criminal Appeal Act 1995. It is a non-departmental public body reporting to parliament via the Lord Chancellor and Secretary of State for Justice. It is responsible for investigating possible miscarriages of justice in England, Wales and Northern Ireland, and deciding whether or not to refer cases back to an appeal court. Membership of the commission is by royal appointment; the senior executive staff are appointed by the commission.

Chair, Richard Foster, CBE

Members, M. Allen; Ms P. Barrett; J. England;

Ms J. Goulding; A. MacGregor, QC; I. Nicholl; E. Smith; J. Weeden
Chief Executive, Claire Bassett

CRIMINAL INJURIES COMPENSATION AUTHORITY (CICA)

Tay House, 300 Bath Street, Glasgow G2 4LN
T 0800-358 3601 W www.cica.gov.uk

CICA is the government body responsible for administering the Criminal Injuries Compensation Scheme in England, Scotland and Wales (separate arrangements apply in Northern Ireland). CICA deals with every aspect of applications for compensation under the 1996, 2001 and 2008 Criminal Injuries Compensation Schemes. There is a separate avenue of appeal to the Tribunals Service – Criminal Injuries Compensation (*see* Tribunals section).
Chief Executive, Carole Oatway

CROFTERS COMMISSION

Great Glen House, Leachkin Road, Inverness IV3 8NW
T 01463-663450 E info@crofterscommission.org.uk
W www.crofterscommission.org.uk

The Crofters Commission, established in 1955 under the Crofters (Scotland) Act, is a government-funded organisation tasked with overseeing crofting legislation. It works with communities to regulate crofting and advises Scottish ministers on crofting matters. The commission administers the Croft House Grant Scheme and the Crofters' Cattle Improvement Scheme. It also provides a free enquiry service.
Convenor, Drew Ratter
Chief Executive, Nick Reiter

DESIGN COUNCIL

34 Bow Street, London WC2E 7DL
T 020-7420 5200 E info@designcouncil.org.uk
W www.design-council.org.uk

The Design Council is a campaigning organisation which works with partners in business, education and government to promote the effective use of good design; its aim is to make businesses more competitive and public services more effective. It is a registered charity with a royal charter and is co-sponsored by the Department for Business, Innovation and Skills and the Department for Culture, Media and Sport; the secretaries of state of these two departments appoint the chair and members of the council.
Chair, Lord Michael Bichard
Chief Executive, David Kester

ENGLISH HERITAGE (HISTORIC BUILDINGS AND MONUMENTS COMMISSION FOR ENGLAND)

1 Waterhouse Square, 138–142 Holborn, London EC1N 2ST
T 020-7973 3000 W www.english-heritage.org.uk

English Heritage was established under the National Heritage Act 1983. On 1 April 1999 it merged with the Royal Commission on the Historical Monuments of England to become the new lead body for England's historic environment. It is sponsored by the Department for Culture, Media and Sport and its duties are to carry out and sponsor archaeological, architectural and scientific surveys and research designed to increase the understanding of England's past and its changing condition; to identify buildings, monuments and landscapes for protection while also offering expert advice, skills and grants to conserve these sites; to encourage town planners to make imaginative re-use of historic buildings to aid regeneration of the centres of cities, towns and villages; to manage and curate selected sites; and to curate and make publicly accessible the National Monuments Record, whose records of over one million historic sites and buildings, and extensive collections of photographs, maps, drawings and reports, constitute the central database and archive of England's historic environment.
Chair, Baroness Andrews, OBE
Commissioners, Lynda Addison, OBE; Maria Adebowale; Joyce Bridges, CBE; Manish Chande; Prof. Sir Barry Cunliffe, CBE; David Fursdon; Prof. Ronald Hutton; Michael Jolly, CBE; Jane Kennedy; John Walker, CBE; Chris Wilkinson, OBE; Elizabeth Williamson, FSA
Chief Executive, Dr Simon Thurley

CUSTOMER SERVICES DEPARTMENT, PO Box 569, Swindon SN2 2YP T 0870-333 1181
E customers@english-heritage.org.uk
NATIONAL MONUMENTS RECORD CENTRE, Kemble Drive, Swindon SN2 2GZ T 01793-414600

ENVIRONMENT AGENCY

National Customer Contact Centre, PO Box 544, Rotherham S60 1BY
T 0870-850 6506 E enquiries@environment-agency.gov.uk
W www.environment-agency.gov.uk

The Environment Agency was established in 1996 under the Environment Act 1995 and is a non-departmental public body sponsored by the Department for Environment, Food and Rural Affairs and the National Assembly for Wales – around 60 per cent of the agency's funding is from the government, with the rest raised from various charging schemes. The agency is responsible for pollution prevention and control in England and Wales, and for the management and use of water resources, including flood defences, fisheries and navigation. It has head offices in London and Bristol, and eight regional offices.

THE BOARD
Chair, Lord Smith of Finsbury
Members, James Braithwaite, CBE; Andrew Brown; Prof. Ruth Hall; Julie Hill, MBE; Emma Howard Boyd; Robert Light; Dr Malcolm Smith; Cllr Kay Twitchen, OBE; John Varley; Jeremy Walker; Lady Warner, OBE; Lord Whitty
Chief Executive, Paul Leinster

EQUALITY AND HUMAN RIGHTS COMMISSION

Arndale House, The Arndale Centre, Manchester M4 3AQ
T 0161-829 8100 E info@equalityhumanrights.com
W www.equalityhumanrights.com

The Equality and Human Rights Commission (EHRC) is a statutory body, established under the Equality Act 2006 and launched in October 2007. It inherited the responsibilities of the Commission for Racial Equality, the Disability Rights Commission and the Equal Opportunities Commission. The EHRC's purpose is to

reduce inequality, eliminate discrimination, strengthen relations between people, and promote and protect human rights. It enforces equality legislation on age, disability and health, gender, race, religion and belief, sexual orientation or transgender status, and encourages compliance with the Human Rights Act 1998 throughout England, Wales and Scotland. For information on how to contact the helpline, visit the EHRC website.
Chair, Trevor Phillips
Deputy Chair, Baroness Prosser, OBE
Commissioners, Stephen Alambritis; Ann Beynon, OBE; Prof. Geraldine Van Bueren; Kay Carberry, CBE; Meral Hussein Ece, OBE; Baroness Greengross, OBE; Dr Jean Irvine, OBE; Kaliani Lyle; Angela Mason; Maeve Sherlock, OBE; Michael Smith; Simon Woolley

EQUALITY COMMISSION FOR NORTHERN IRELAND

Equality House, 7–9 Shaftesbury Square, Belfast BT2 7DP
T 028-9089 0890; Textphone 028-9050 0589
E information@equalityni.org W www.equalityni.org

The Equality Commission was set up in 1999 under the Northern Ireland Act 1998 and is responsible for promoting equality, keeping the relevant legislation under review, eliminating discrimination on the grounds of race, disability, sexual orientation, gender, age, religion and political opinion and for overseeing the statutory duty on public authorities to promote equality of opportunity.
Chief Commissioner, Bob Collins
Deputy Chief Commissioner, Jane Morrice
Chief Executive, Evelyn Collins, CBE

FOREIGN COMPENSATION COMMISSION (FCC)

Old Admiralty Building, London SW1A 2PA
T 020-7008 1321 E fcc@fco.gov.uk
W http://foi.fco.gov.uk/en/access-information/Ndpbs/fcc

The FCC was set up by the Foreign Compensation Act 1950 primarily to distribute, under orders in council, funds received from other governments in accordance with agreements to pay compensation for expropriated British property and other losses sustained by British nationals abroad. The FCC carries out both judicial and administrative functions, including the adjudication of claims by applicants and the investment and management of compensation funds. There are no active compensation programmes at present.
Chair, Dr John Barker

GAMBLING COMMISSION

Victoria Square House, Victoria Square, Birmingham B2 4BP
T 0121-230 6666 E info@gamblingcommission.gov.uk
W www.gamblingcommission.gov.uk

The Gambling Commission was established under the Gambling Act 2005, and took over the role previously occupied by the Gaming Board for Great Britain in regulating and licensing all commercial gambling – apart from spread betting and the National Lottery – ie casinos, bingo, betting, remote gambling, gaming machines and lotteries. It also advises local and central government on related issues, and is responsible for the protection of children and the vulnerable from being exploited or harmed by gambling. The commission is sponsored by the Department for Culture, Media and Sport, with its work funded mainly by licence fees paid by the gambling industry.
Chair, Brian Pomeroy
Chief Executive, Jenny Williams

GOVERNMENT OFFICES FOR THE ENGLISH REGIONS

The Government Office Network was set up in 1994 and consists of nine regional offices across England, and their corporate centre, the GO Network and central services. It aims to bring together the offices of individual central government departments in each region and so provide a more efficient and integrated service. The network now works for 13 central government departments implementing policies and programmes on the ground, monitoring and reporting on local priorities and responding to civil emergencies.

GOVERNMENT OFFICE NETWORK CENTRE AND SERVICES

4th Floor, Eland House, Bressenden Place, London SW1E 5DU
T 030-3444 0000 E goncsenquiries@goncs.gsi.gov.uk
W www.gonetwork.gos.gov.uk
Director-General, Joe Montgomery
Director, Brian Hackland

EAST MIDLANDS

The Belgrave Centre, Stanley Place, Talbot Street, Nottingham NG1 5GG
T 0115-971 9971 E enquiries@goem.gsi.gov.uk
Regional Director, Stephen Hillier

EAST OF ENGLAND

Eastbrook, Shaftesbury Road, Cambridge CB2 2DF
T 01223-372500 E enquiries.goeast@goeast.gsi.gov.uk
Regional Director, Paul Pugh

LONDON

Riverwalk House, 157–161 Millbank, London SW1P 4RR
T 020-7217 3111 E enquiries@gol.gsi.gov.uk
Regional Director, Chris Hayes

NORTH EAST

Citygate, Gallowgate, Newcastle upon Tyne NE1 4WH
T 0191-201 3300 E general.enquiries@gone.gsi.gov.uk
Regional Director, Jonathan Blackie

NORTH WEST

City Tower, Piccadilly Plaza, Manchester M1 4BE
T 0161-952 4000
Cunard Building, Pier Head, Liverpool L3 1QB
T 0151-224 6300
E gonwmailbox@gonw.gsi.gov.uk
Regional Director, Liz Meek

SOUTH EAST

Bridge House, 1 Walnut Tree Close, Guildford GU1 4GA
T 01483-882255 E info@gose.gsi.gov.uk
Regional Director, Colin Byrne

SOUTH WEST

2 Rivergate, Temple Quay, Bristol BS1 6EH
T 0117-900 1700
Mast House, Shepherds Wharf, 24 Sutton Road, Plymouth PL4 0HJ
T 01752-635000

Castle House, Pydar Street, Truro TR1 2UD
T 01872-264500
E swcontactus@gosw.gsi.gov.uk
Regional Director, Jon Bright

WEST MIDLANDS
5 St Philips Place, Colmore Row, Birmingham B3 2PW
T 0121-352 5050 E enquiries.team@gowm.gsi.gov.uk
Regional Director, Trudi Elliott

YORKSHIRE AND THE HUMBER
Lateral, 8 City Walk, Leeds LS11 9AT
T 0113-341 3000 E yhenquiries@goyh.gsi.gov.uk
Regional Director, Felicity Everiss

HEALTH AND SAFETY EXECUTIVE

Redgrave Court, Merton Road, Bootle, Merseyside L20 7HS
T 0845-345 0055 E hse.infoline@connaught.plc.uk
W www.hse.gov.uk

The Health and Safety Commission (HSC) and the Health and Safety Executive (HSE) merged on 1 April 2008 to form a single national regulatory body responsible for promoting the cause of better health and safety at work.

HSE regulates all industrial and commercial sectors except operations in the air and at sea. This includes agriculture, construction, manufacturing, services, transport, mines, offshore oil and gas, nuclear, quarries and major hazard sites in chemicals and petrochemicals.

HSE is responsible for developing and enforcing health and safety law, providing guidance and advice, commissioning research, inspection including accident and ill-health investigation, developing standards and licensing or approving some work activities such as nuclear power and asbestos removal. HSE is sponsored by the Department for Work and Pensions.

Chair, Judith Hackitt, CBE
Board Members, Sandy Blair; Danny Carrigan; Robin Dahlberg; Judith Donovan; David Gartside; Sayeed Khan; Hugh Robertson; Elizabeth Snape; John Spanswick
Chief Executive, Geoffrey Podger

HEALTH PROTECTION AGENCY (HPA)

7th Floor, Holborn Gate, 330 High Holborn, London WC1V 7PP
T 020-7759 2700 E hpa.enquiries@hpa.org.uk
W www.hpa.org.uk

The HPA was set up in 2003 and is responsible for providing an integrated approach to protecting public health through the provision of support and advice to the NHS, local authorities, emergency services, other non-departmental public bodies, the Department of Health and the devolved administrations.

The HPA works at local, regional, national and international levels to reduce the impact of infectious diseases and reduce exposure to chemicals, radiation and poisons, as well as ensure a rapid response when hazards occur. The HPA provides services in Northern Ireland and works closely with the devolved administrations, so that there is a coordinated response to incidents, trends and outbreaks on a national level. Research and development projects conducted by HPA scientists are primarily concerned with new methods of treating illness and assessing exposure to chemicals or radiation.

Chair, Dr David Heymann
Board Members, Dr Barbara Bannister, FRCP; Michael Beaumont; James T. Brown; Michael Carroll; Prof. Charles Easmon, CBE, FMEDSCI (Deputy Chair); Helen Froud; Prof. William Gelletly, OBE (adviser); Martin Hindle; Dr Rosemary Leonard, MBE; Prof. Alan Maryon Davis, FRCP (adviser); Dr Vanessa Mayatt; Deborah Oakley; Prof. Debby Reynolds
Chief Executive, Justin McCracken

HER MAJESTY'S OFFICERS OF ARMS

COLLEGE OF ARMS (HERALDS' COLLEGE)

Queen Victoria Street, London EC4V 4BT
T 020-7248 2762 E enquiries@college-of-arms.gov.uk
W www.college-of-arms.gov.uk

The Sovereign's Officers of Arms (Kings, Heralds and Pursuivants of Arms) were first incorporated by Richard III in 1484. The powers vested by the Crown in the Earl Marshal (the Duke of Norfolk) with regard to state ceremonial are largely exercised through the college. The college is also the official repository of the arms and pedigrees of English, Welsh, Northern Irish and Commonwealth (except Canadian) families and their descendants, and its records include official copies of the records of the Ulster King of Arms, the originals of which remain in Dublin. The 13 officers of the college specialise in genealogical and heraldic work for their respective clients.

Arms have long been, and still are, granted by letters patent from the Kings of Arms. A right to arms can only be established by the registration in the official records of the College of Arms of a pedigree showing direct male line descent from an ancestor already appearing therein as being entitled to arms, or by making application through the College of Arms for a grant of arms. Grants are made to corporations as well as to individuals.

Earl Marshal, Duke of Norfolk

KINGS OF ARMS
Garter, T. Woodcock, LVO, FSA
Clarenceux (and Earl Marshal's Secretary), P. L. Dickinson, LVO
Norroy and Ulster, vacant

HERALDS
York, H. E. Paston-Bedingfeld
Chester, T. H. S. Duke
Lancaster, R. J. B. Noel
Windsor (and Registrar), W. G. Hunt, TD
Somerset, D. V. White
Richmond, C. E. A. Cheesman

PURSUIVANT
Bluemantle, M. P. D. O'Donoghue

COURT OF THE LORD LYON

HM New Register House, Edinburgh EH1 3YT
T 0131-556 7255 W www.lyon-court.com

Her Majesty's Officers of Arms in Scotland perform ceremonial duties and in addition may be consulted by members of the public on heraldic and genealogical matters in a professional capacity.

KING OF ARMS
Lord Lyon King of Arms, David Sellar, FSA SCOT, FRHISTS

HERALDS
Albany, J. A. Spens, MVO, RD, WS
Rothesay, Sir Crispin Agnew of Lochnaw, Bt., QC
Ross, C. J. Burnett, FSA SCOT

PURSUIVANTS
Carrick, Mrs C. G. W. Roads, MVO, FSA SCOT
Unicorn, The Hon. Adam Bruce, WS
Ormond, Mark D. Dennis

EXTRAORDINARY OFFICERS
Orkney Herald Extraordinary, Sir Malcolm Innes of Edingight, KCVO, WS
Angus Herald Extraordinary, R. O. Blair, CVO, WS
Islay Herald Extraordinary, Alastair Campbell of Airds

HERALD PAINTER
Herald Painter, Mrs Y. Holton

HIGHLANDS AND ISLANDS ENTERPRISE

Cowan House, Inverness Retail and Business Park, Inverness IV2 7GF
T 01463-234171 E info@hient.co.uk
W www.hie.co.uk

Highlands and Islands Enterprise (HIE) was set up under the Enterprise and New Towns (Scotland) Act 1991. Its role is to deliver community and economic development in line with the Scottish government economic strategy. It focuses on helping high-growth businesses, improving regional competitiveness and strengthening communities. HIE's budget for 2010–11 is £83m.
Chair, W. Roe
Chief Executive (acting), Sandy Brady

HISTORIC ROYAL PALACES

Apartment 39, Hampton Court Palace, Surrey KT8 9AU
T 0844-482 7777 E operators@hrp.org.uk
W www.hrp.org.uk

Historic Royal Palaces was established in 1998 as a royal charter body with charitable status and is contracted by the Secretary of State for Culture, Olympics, Media and Sport to manage the palaces on his behalf. The palaces – the Tower of London, Hampton Court Palace, the Banqueting House, Kensington Palace and Kew Palace – are owned by the Queen on behalf of the nation.

The organisation is governed by a board comprising a chair and ten non-executive trustees. The chief executive is accountable to the board of trustees and ultimately to parliament. Historic Royal Palaces receives no funding from the government or the Crown.

TRUSTEES
Chair, Charles Mackay
Appointed by the Queen, Jonathan Marsden; Sir Trevor McDonald, OBE; Sir Adrian Montague, CBE; Sir Alan Reid, KCVO
Appointed by the Secretary of State, Sophie Andreae; Dawn Austwick, OBE; Sue Farr; John Hamer; Malcolm Reading
Ex officio, Gen. Sir Richard Dannatt, GCB, CBE, MC *(Constable of the Tower of London)*

OFFICERS
Chief Executive, Michael Day
Resident Governor, HM Tower of London, Maj.-Gen. Keith Cima, CB

HOMES AND COMMUNITIES AGENCY

110 Buckingham Palace Road, Victoria, London SW1W 9SA
T 0300-1234 500 E mail@homesandcommunities.co.uk
W www.homesandcommunities.co.uk

The Homes and Communities Agency (HCA) is the national housing regeneration agency for England. It is a non-departmental public body sponsored by the Department for Communities and Local Government. The HCA aims to create thriving communities and affordable homes by providing funding for affordable housing and bringing land back into productive use; it also strives to improve quality of life by raising standards for the physical and social environment. For 2008–11 the HCA has a budget of £18.6bn, of which £9.1bn will be invested in affordable homes for rent and sale through the National Affordable Housing Programme.
Chair, Robert Napier
Chief Executive, Bob Kerslake

HORSERACE TOTALISATOR BOARD

Westgate House, Tote Park, Chapel Lane, Wigan WN3 4HS
T 0800-666100 E customercare@totesport.com
W www.totesport.com

The Horserace Totalisator Board (the Tote) operates totalisators on approved racecourses in Great Britain, provides on- and off-course cash and credit offices, telephone betting and a website. It was established in 1928 (then the Racecourse Betting Control Board) and renamed following the Betting Levy Act 1961. With the Horserace Totalisator and Betting Levy Board Act 1972, the Tote was empowered to operate as a bookmaker, offering bets at fixed odds on any sporting event, and under the Horserace Totalisator Board Act 1997 to take bets on any event, except the National Lottery. It retains exclusivity over pools' betting on British horseracing. The chair and members of the board are appointed by the Secretary of State for Culture, Olympics, Media and Sport.
Chair, Mike Smith
Chief Executive, Trevor Beaumont

HUMAN FERTILISATION AND EMBRYOLOGY AUTHORITY (HFEA)

21 Bloomsbury Street, London WC1B 3HF
T 020-7291 8200 E admin@hfea.gov.uk
W www.hfea.gov.uk

The HFEA was established in 1991 under the Human Fertilisation and Embryology Act 1990. It is the UK's independent regulator tasked with overseeing safe and appropriate practice in fertility treatment and embryo research, including licensing and monitoring centres carrying out IVF, artificial insemination and human embryo research. The HFEA also provides a range of detailed information for patients, professionals and government, and maintains a formal register of information about donors, fertility treatments and children born as a result of those treatments.
Chair, Prof. Lisa Jardine, CBE
Chief Executive, Alan Doran

HUMAN GENETICS COMMISSION

Area 605, Wellington House, 133–155 Waterloo Road, London SE1 8UG
T 020-7972 4351 E hgc@dh.gsi.gov.uk
W www.hgc.gov.uk

The Human Genetics Commission was established in 1999, subsuming three previous advisory committees. Its remit is to give ministers strategic advice on how developments in human genetics will impact on people and healthcare, focusing in particular on the social and ethical implications.

Chair, Prof. Jonathan Montgomery
Members, Prof. Tim Aitman; Prof. Thomas Baldwin; Prof. Angus Clarke; Prof. Sarah Cunningham-Burley; Dr Paul Darragh; Dr Paul Debenham; Nicola Drury; Dr Frances Flinter; Ros Gardner; Prof. John Harris; Caroline Harrison; Alastair Kent; Dr Anneke Lucassen; Dr Duncan McHale; Dr Alice Maynard; Dr Lola Oni; Dr Rosalind Skinner; Dr Anita Thomas

HUMAN TISSUE AUTHORITY (HTA)

2nd Floor, Finlaison House, 15–17 Furnival Street, London EC4A 1AB
T 020-7211 3400 E enquiries@hta.gov.uk
W www.hta.gov.uk

The HTA was established on 1 April 2005 under the Human Tissue Act 2004, and is sponsored and part-funded by the Department of Health. Its role is to inform the public and Secretary of State for Health about issues within its remit, which include the import, export, storage and use of human bodies and tissue for scheduled purposes, and disposal of human tissue following its use in medical treatment or for scheduled purposes. The HTA is the competent authority under the EU tissues and cells directive for regulating human tissue banking for transplant services.

The HTA also supersedes and extends the role that was previously performed by the now-defunct Unrelated Live Transplant Regulatory Authority (ULTRA) in setting out the circumstances in which live 'transplantable material' (from both related and unrelated donors) will be allowed.

Chair, Baroness Diana Warwick
Chief Executive, Craig Muir

IMPERIAL WAR MUSEUM

Lambeth Road, London SE1 6HZ
T 020-7416 5000 E mail@iwm.org.uk
W www.iwm.org.uk

The museum, founded in 1917, illustrates and records all aspects of the two world wars and other military operations involving Britain and the Commonwealth since 1914. It was opened in its present home, formerly Bethlem Royal Hospital, in 1936. The museum is a multi-branch organisation that also includes the Churchill War Rooms in Whitehall; HMS *Belfast* in the Pool of London; Imperial War Museum Duxford in Cambridgeshire; and Imperial War Museum North in Trafford, Manchester.

The total projected grant-in-aid (including grants for special projects) for 2009–10 was £24.16m.

OFFICERS
Chair of Trustees, Air Chief Marshal Sir Peter Squire, GCB, DFC, AFC, DSc
Director-General, Diane Lees
Directors, Richard Ashton *(Imperial War Museum Duxford);* Jon Card *(Secretary, Finance);* Sue Coleman *(Development);* Jim Forrester *(Imperial War Museum North);* Phil Reed *(Churchill War Rooms and HMS Belfast);* Alan Stoneman *(Corporate Services);* Mark Whitmore *(Collections)*

INDEPENDENT REVIEW SERVICE FOR THE SOCIAL FUND

4th Floor, Centre City Podium, 5 Hill Street, Birmingham B5 4UB
T 0800-096 1926 E sfc@irs-review.org.uk
W www.irs-review.org.uk

The Social Fund Commissioner is appointed by the Secretary of State for Work and Pensions. The commissioner appoints Social Fund Inspectors, who provide an independent review for customers dissatisfied with decisions made in Jobcentre Plus offices throughout England, Scotland and Wales regarding the grants and loans available from the Discretionary Social Fund.

Social Fund Commissioner, Karamjit Singh, CBE

INDEPENDENT SAFEGUARDING AUTHORITY

PO Box 181, Darlington DL1 9FA
T 0300-123 1111 E info@vbs-info.org.uk
W www.isa-gov.org.uk

The Independent Safeguarding Authority (ISA) was created in 2008 to help prevent unsuitable people working with children and vulnerable adults in England, Wales and Northern Ireland. It assumed full responsibility for decisions to bar individuals from working with vulnerable people in January 2009. ISA works in partnership with the Criminal Records Bureau to assess each person who wants to work or volunteer with vulnerable people on a case-by-case basis. Once the scheme has been fully rolled out, employers who work with vulnerable people will only be allowed to recruit those who are ISA-registered. ISA is a non-departmental public body sponsored by the Home Office.

Chair, Sir Roger Singleton, CBE
Chief Executive, Adrian McAllister

INDUSTRIAL INJURIES ADVISORY COUNCIL

Second Floor, Caxton House, Tothill Street, London SW1H 9NA
T 020-7449 5618 E iiac@dwp.gsi.gov.uk
W www.iiac.org.uk

The Industrial Injuries Advisory Council was established under the National Insurance (Industrial Injuries) Act 1946, which came into effect on 5 July 1948. Statutory provisions governing its work are set out in section 171–173 of the Social Security Administration Act 1992 and corresponding Northern Ireland legislation. The council usually consists of 16 independent members appointed by the Secretary of State for Work and Pensions, and has three roles: to consider and advise on matters relating to industrial injuries benefit or its administration referred to it by the Secretary of State for Work and Pensions or the Department for Social Development in Northern Ireland; to consider and provide advice on any draft regulations that the secretary of state proposes to make on industrial injuries benefit or its administration; and to advise on any other matter relating to industrial injuries benefit or its administration.

Chair, Prof. Keith Palmer

INFORMATION COMMISSIONER'S OFFICE

Wycliffe House, Water Lane, Wilmslow, Cheshire SK9 5AF
T 0845-630 6060 E mail@ico.gsi.gov.uk
W www.ico.gov.uk

The Information Commissioner's Office (ICO) is sponsored by the Ministry of Justice and oversees and enforces the Freedom of Information Act 2000 and the Data Protection Act 1998, with the objective of promoting public access to official information and protecting personal information.

The Data Protection Act 1998 sets out rules for the processing of personal information and applies to records held on computers and some paper files. It works in two ways: it dictates that those who record and use personal information (data controllers) must be open about how the information is used and must follow the eight principles of 'good information handling', and it gives individuals certain rights to access their personal information.

The Freedom of Information Act 2000 is designed to help end the culture of unnecessary secrecy and open up the inner workings of the public sector to citizens and businesses. Under the Freedom of Information Act, public authorities must produce a publication scheme that sets out what information the public authority is obliged to publish by law.

The Information Commissioner's Office also enforces and oversees the environmental information regulations, and the privacy and electronic communications regulations.

The Information Commissioner reports annually to parliament on the performance of his functions under the acts and has obligations to assess breaches of the acts. As of April 2010, the ICO has been able to fine organisations up to £500,000 for serious breaches of the Data Protection Act.

Information Commissioner, Christopher Graham

JOINT NATURE CONSERVATION COMMITTEE

Monkstone House, City Road, Peterborough PE1 1JY
T 01733-562626 E communications@jncc.gov.uk
W www.jncc.gov.uk

The committee was established under the Environmental Protection Act 1990 and was reconstituted by the Natural Environment and Rural Communities Act 2006. It advises the government and devolved administrations on UK and international nature conservation issues. Its work contributes to maintaining and enriching biological diversity, conserving geological features and sustaining natural systems.

Chair, Dr Peter Bridgewater
Deputy Chair, Prof. Lynda Warren

LAW COMMISSION

Steel House, 11 Tothill Street, London SW1H 9LJ
T 020-3334 0200
E chief.executive@lawcommission.gsi.gov.uk
W www.lawcom.gov.uk

The Law Commission was set up under the Law Commissions Act 1965 to make proposals to the government for the examination of the law in England and Wales and for its revision where it is unsuited for modern requirements, obscure or otherwise unsatisfactory. It recommends to the lord chancellor programmes for the examination of different branches of the law and suggests whether the examination should be carried out by the commission itself or by some other body. The commission is also responsible for the preparation of Consolidation and Statute Law (Repeals) Bills.

Chair, Rt. Hon. Lord Justice Munby
Commissioners, E. J. Cooke; David Hertzell; Prof. David Ormerod; Frances Patterson, QC
Chief Executive, Mark Ormerod

LEGAL SERVICES COMMISSION

4 Abbey Orchard Street, London SW1P 2BS
T 020-7783 7000
W www.legalservices.gov.uk; www.communitylegaladvice.org.uk

The Legal Services Commission was created under the Access to Justice Act 1999 and replaced the Legal Aid Board in April 2000. It is a non-departmental public body which is sponsored by the Ministry of Justice.

The commission is responsible for two schemes. The Community Legal Service funds the delivery of civil legal and advice services, identifies priorities and unmet needs and develops suppliers and services to meet those needs. The Criminal Defence Service provides free legal advice and representation for people involved in criminal investigations or proceedings.

The commission produces free information leaflets which are available from solicitors' and advisory offices and from the commission's website.

Chief Executive, Carolyn Downs
Chair, Sir Bill Callaghan

MUSEUM OF LONDON

150 London Wall, London EC2Y 5HN
T 020-7001 9844
E info@museumoflondon.org.uk
W www.museumoflondon.org.uk

The Museum of London illustrates the history of London from prehistoric times to the present day. It opened in 1976 and is based on the amalgamation of the former Guildhall Museum and London Museum. The museum is controlled by a board of governors, appointed (ten each) by the prime minister and the City of London. The museum is currently funded by grants from the Greater London Authority and the City of London. In May 2010 the museum opened the Galleries of Modern London exhibit after a £20m refurbishment. The total grant-in-aid for 2008–9 was £16m.

Chair of Board of Governors, Michael Cassidy, CBE
Director, Prof. Jack Lohman

MUSEUMS, LIBRARIES AND ARCHIVES COUNCIL (MLA)

1st Floor, Grosvenor House, 14 Bennetts Hill, Birmingham B2 5RS
T 0121-345 7300 E info@mla.gov.uk
W www.mla.gov.uk

The MLA was launched in April 2000 and is the lead strategic agency for museums, libraries and archives. It is a non-departmental public body sponsored by the Department for Culture, Media and Sport. The MLA replaced the Museums and Galleries Commission (MGC) and the Library and Information Commission (LIC).

hair, Andrew Motion
oard Members, Geoffrey Bond, OBE; Patricia Cullen; Nick Dodd; Yinnon Ezra, MBE; Helen Forde; Glen Lawes; Karen Tyerman; Robert Wand
hief Executive, Roy Clare, CBE

IATIONAL ARMY MUSEUM

oyal Hospital Road, London SW3 4HT
020-7730 0717
info@national-army-museum.ac.uk
V www.national-army-museum.ac.uk

he National Army Museum was established by royal harter in 1960, and covers the history of five centuries of ne British Army from the Middle Ages to the present. It hronicles the campaigns and battles fought over this time s well as the social history and development of the Army, nd its impact on Britain, Europe and the world. The nuseum houses a wide array of artefacts, paintings, hotographs, uniforms and equipment.
hair, General Sir Jack Deverell, KCB, OBE
)irector, vacant

IATIONAL ENDOWMENT FOR SCIENCE, TECHNOLOGY AND THE ARTS (NESTA)

Plough Place, London EC4A 1DE
020-7438 2500 E nesta@nesta.org.uk
V www.nesta.org.uk

IESTA was established under the National Lottery Act 998 with a £200m endowment from the proceeds of the Iational Lottery. Its endowment is presently over £300m. IESTA invests in early-stage companies, informs and hapes policy, and delivers practical programmes to help olve the UK's biggest economic and social challenges.
hair, Sir John Chisholm
hief Executive, Jonathan Kestenbaum

IATIONAL GALLERIES OF SCOTLAND

he Dean Gallery, 73 Belford Road, Edinburgh EH4 3DS
0131-624 6200 E enquiries@nationalgalleries.org
V www.nationalgalleries.org

The National Galleries of Scotland comprise the National Gallery of Scotland, the Scottish National Portrait Gallery, the Scottish National Gallery of Modern Art, the Dean Gallery and the Royal Scottish Academy Building. There are also partner galleries at Paxton House, Berwickshire, and Duff House, Banffshire. Total government grant-in-aid for 2010–11 is £12.5m.

TRUSTEES
hair, Ben Thomson
Trustees, Ian Barr; Richard Burns; Herbert Coutts, MBE; James Dawney; Marc Ellington; James Knox; Ray Macfarlane; Alasdair Morton; Prof. Richard Thomson; Dr Ruth Wishart

OFFICERS
Director-General, John Leighton
Directors, M. Clarke *(National Gallery of Scotland);* Dr Simon Groom *(Scottish National Gallery of Modern Art and Dean Gallery);* J. Holloway *(Scottish National Portrait Gallery);* Catrin Tilley *(Director of Development and Communications)*

NATIONAL GALLERY

Trafalgar Square, London WC2N 5DN
T 020-7747 2885 E information@ng-london.org.uk
W www.nationalgallery.org.uk

The National Gallery, which houses a permanent collection of western European painting from the 13th to the 20th century, was founded in 1824, following a parliamentary grant of £60,000 for the purchase and exhibition of the Angerstein collection of pictures. The present site was first occupied in 1838; an extension to the north of the building with a public entrance in Orange Street was opened in 1975; the Sainsbury Wing was opened in 1991; and the Getty Entrance opened off Trafalgar Square at the east end of the main building in 2004. Total government grant-in-aid for 2010–11 is £28.19m.

BOARD OF TRUSTEES
Chair, M. Getty
Trustees, S. Burke; G. Dalal; Prof. D. Ekserdjian; Lady Heseltine; M. Hintze; Prof. A. Hurlbert; P. Lankester; J. Lessore; Lady Normanby; H. Rothschild; C. Thomson

OFFICERS
Director, Dr N. Penny
Director of Collections and Deputy Director, Dr S. Foister
Director of Conservation, Larry Keith
Director of Education, Information and Access, Jillian Barker
Director of Operations and Administration, Greg Perry
Director of Public Affairs and Development, S. Ward
Director of Scientific Research, Dr A. Roy
Senior Curator, D. Jaffé

NATIONAL HERITAGE MEMORIAL FUND

7 Holbein Place, London SW1W 8NR
T 020-7591 6000 E enquire@hlf.org.uk
W www.nhmf.org.uk

The National Heritage Memorial Fund was set up under the National Heritage Act 1980 in memory of people who have given their lives for the United Kingdom. The fund provides grants to organisations based in the UK, mainly so they can buy items of outstanding interest and of importance to the national heritage. These must either be at risk or have a memorial character. The fund is administered by a chair and 14 trustees who are appointed by the prime minister.

The National Heritage Memorial Fund receives an annual grant from the Department for Culture, Media and Sport. Under the the National Lottery etc Act 1993 the trustees of the fund became responsible for the distribution of funds for both the National Heritage Memorial Fund and the Heritage Lottery Fund.
Chair, Jenny Abramsky
Chief Executive, Carole Souter

NATIONAL LIBRARY OF SCOTLAND

George IV Bridge, Edinburgh EH1 1EW
T 0131-623 3700 E enquiries@nls.uk
W www.nls.uk

The library, which was founded as the Advocates' Library in 1682, became the National Library of Scotland (NLS) in 1925. It is funded by the Scottish government. It contains about 14 million books and pamphlets, two million maps, 25,000 newspaper and magazine titles and

100,000 manuscripts, including the John Murray Archive. It has an unrivalled Scottish collection as well as online catalogues and digital resources which can be accessed through the NLS website.

Material can be consulted in the reading rooms, which are open to anyone with a valid library card.

Chair of the Trustees, Prof. Michael Anderson, OBE, FBA, FRSE
National Librarian and Chief Executive, Martyn Wade
Directors, Cate Newton *(Collections and Research);* Duncan Campbell *(Corporate Services);* Alex Miller *(Customer Services);* Teri Wishart *(Development and External Relations)*

NATIONAL LIBRARY OF WALES/LLYFRGELL GENEDLAETHOL CYMRU

Aberystwyth SY23 3BU
T 01970-632800 E holi@llgc.org.uk
W www.llgc.org.uk

The National Library of Wales was founded by royal charter in 1907, and is funded by the National Assembly for Wales. It contains about five million printed books, 40,000 manuscripts, four million deeds and documents, numerous maps, prints and drawings, and a sound and moving image collection. It specialises in manuscripts and books relating to Wales and the Celtic peoples. It is the repository for pre-1858 Welsh probate records, manorial records and tithe documents, and certain legal records. Admission is by reader's ticket to the reading rooms but entry to the exhibition programme is free.

President, Rt. Hon. Dafydd Wigley
Heads of Departments, Avril Jones *(Collection Services);* David Michael *(Corporate Services);* R. Arwel Jones *(Public Services)*
Librarian, A. M. W. Green

NATIONAL LOTTERY COMMISSION

101 Wigmore Street, London W1U 1QU
T 020-7016 3400 E publicaffairs@natlotcomm.gov.uk
W www.natlotcomm.gov.uk

The National Lottery Commission replaced the Office of the National Lottery (OFLOT) in 1999 under the National Lottery Act 1998. The commission is responsible for the granting, varying and enforcing of licences to run the National Lottery. It also runs the competition to award the next licence. Its duties are to ensure that the National Lottery is run with all due propriety, that the interests of players are protected, and, subject to these two objectives, that returns to the good causes are maximised. The commission does not have a role in the distribution of funds to good causes: this is undertaken by 16 distributors; visit W www.lotteryfunding.org.uk for further information. Gaming and lotteries in the UK are officially regulated and may only be run by licensed operators or in licensed premises.

The Department for Culture, Media and Sport (DCMS) is responsible for gaming and lottery policy and laws. Empowered by the National Lottery Act 1993 (as amended), the DCMS directs the National Lottery Commission, who in turn regulates Camelot, the lottery operator. Camelot, a private company wholly owned by five shareholders, was granted a third licence to run the lottery from 1 February 2009 for ten years.

Chair, Dr Anne Wright, CBE
Chief Executive, Mark Harris

NATIONAL MARITIME MUSEUM

Greenwich, London SE10 9NF
T 020-8858 4422
W www.nmm.ac.uk

Established in 1934, the National Maritime Museum provides information on the maritime history of Great Britain and is the largest institution of its kind in the world, with over two million items in its collection related to seafaring, navigation and astronomy. The museum is in three groups of buildings in Greenwich Park: the main building, the Queen's House (built by Inigo Jones, 1616–35) and the Royal Observatory Greenwich (including Christopher Wren's Flamsteed House). In 2007 a £16m project opened a new astronomy centre and planetarium (now the only public planetarium in London) at the Royal Observatory.

Director, Kevin Fewster
Chair, Lord Sterling of Plaistow, GCVO, CBE

NATIONAL MUSEUM OF THE ROYAL NAVY

HM Naval Base (PP66), Portsmouth PO1 3NH
T 023-9272 7562 E info@nmrn.org.uk
W www.royalnavalmuseum.org

The National Museum of the Royal Navy and HMS *Victory* (formerly the Royal Naval Museum) is a subsidiary charity of the newly formed National Museum of the Royal Navy. It is located in Portsmouth Historic Dockyard alongside Nelson's flagship and is housed in three buildings offering exhibitions on the Navy from the 18th century onwards. The museum aims to provide an effective and accessible repository for the heritage of the Navy, and to raise public awareness of, and encourage scholarship and research into, the history and achievements of the Royal Navy.

Chair, Adm. Sir Peter Abbott, GBE, KCB

NATIONAL MUSEUMS AND GALLERIES NORTHERN IRELAND

Cultra, Holywood, Northern Ireland BT18 0EU
T 0845-608 0000 E info@nmni.com
W www.nmni.com

The organisation of National Museums and Galleries of Northern Ireland was established under the Museums and Galleries (Northern Ireland) Order in 1998 and includes the Ulster Museum, the Armagh County Museum, the Ulster Folk and Transport Museum, the Ulster American Folk Park and W5 at Odyssey (a wholly owned subsidiary).

Legislation requires National Museums and Galleries of Northern Ireland's board of trustees to care for, preserve and add to the collections; ensure that the collections are exhibited to the public; ensure that the significance of the collections is interpreted; and promote the awareness, appreciation and understanding of the public in relation to art, history and science, to the culture and way of life of the people and to the migration and settlement of people.

Chair, Dan Harvey, OBE
Trustees, Linda Beers; Lt-Col. (retd) Harvey Bicker, OBE; Neil Bodger; Pat Carvill, CB; Dame Geraldine Keegan; Joe Kelly; Dr Richard Browne McMinn; David Moore; Wendy Osborne, OBE; Anne Peoples; Tom Shaw, CBE; Dr Brian Scott; Dr Alastair Walker
Chief Executive, Tim Cooke

NATIONAL MUSEUMS LIVERPOOL

127 Dale Street, Liverpool L2 2JH
T 0151-207 0001
W www.liverpoolmuseums.org.uk

The board of trustees of the National Museums Liverpool (formerly National Museums and Galleries on Merseyside) is responsible for World Museum, the Merseyside Maritime Museum (also home to Seized! The Border and Customs Uncovered), the Lady Lever Art Gallery, the Walker Art Gallery, Sudley House, the National Conservation Centre, the International Slavery Museum and the Museum of Liverpool. Total government grant-in-aid for 2010–11 is £21.2m.

Chair of the Board of Trustees, Prof. P. Redmond, CBE
Director, Dr D. Fleming
Director of Art Galleries, R. King
Director, World Museum Liverpool, S. Judd
Director, Merseyside Maritime Museum, R. Mulhearn
Director of Urban History, Museum of Liverpool, J. Dugdale
Director of Collections Management, National Conservation Centre, S. A. Yates
Head of International Slavery Museum, Dr R. Benjamin

NATIONAL MUSEUMS SCOTLAND

Chambers Street, Edinburgh EH1 1JF
T 0131-225 7534 E info@nms.ac.uk W www.nms.ac.uk

National Museums Scotland (NMS) provides advice, expertise and support to the museums community across Scotland, and undertakes fieldwork that often involves collaboration at local, national and international levels. NMS comprises the National Museum of Scotland, the National War Museum, the National Museum of Rural Life, the National Museum of Flight, the National Museum of Costume and the National Museums Collection Centre. Its collections represent more than two centuries of collecting and include Scottish and classical archaeology, decorative and applied arts, world cultures and social history and science, technology and the natural world. Total grant-in-aid funding from the Scottish government for 2009–10 was £21.3m.

Up to 15 trustees can be appointed by the Minister for Culture and External Affairs for a term of four years, and may serve a second term.

Chair, Sir Angus Grossart, CBE, LLD, DLITT
Trustees, Dr Isabel F. Bruce, OBE; James Fiddes, OBE, FRICS; Dr Anna Gregor, CBE, FRCR, FRCP; Lesley Hart, MBE; Andrew Holmes; Michael Kirwan, FCA; Prof. Michael Lynch, FRSE, FSA SCOT; Prof. Malcolm McLeod, CBE, FRSE; Prof. Stuart Monro, OBE; Ian Ritchie, CBE, FRENG, FRSE; Sir John Ward, CBE, FRSE, FRSA; Iain Watt
Director, Dr Gordon Rintoul

NATIONAL MUSEUM WALES – AMGUEDDFA CYMRU

Cathays Park, Cardiff CF10 3NP
T 029-2039 7951 E post@museumwales.ac.uk
W www.museumwales.ac.uk

National Museum Wales – Amgueddfa Cymru aims to provide a complete illustration of the geology, mineralogy, zoology, botany, ethnography, archaeology, art, history and special industries of Wales. It is comprised of the National Museum Cardiff; St Fagans National History Museum; Big Pit – National Coal Museum, Blaenafon; the National Roman Legion Museum, Caerleon; the National Slate Museum, Llanberis; the National Wool Museum, Dre-fach Felindre; and the National Waterfront Museum, Swansea. Total funding from the Welsh Assembly government for 2009–10 was £25.8m.

President, Paul E. Loveluck, CBE
Vice-President, Elisabeth Elias
Director-General, vacant
Trustees, Prof. Anthony George Atkins; Carole-Anne Davies; Dr Haydn Edwards; Miriam Hazel Griffiths; Dr Iolo ap Gwynn; Emeritus Prof. Richard G. W. Jones; Prof. J. W. Last, CBE; Christina Macaulay; Peter W. Morgan; Prof. Jonathan Osmond; Victoria Mary Provis; Dr Keshav Singhal; David Beresford Vokes; Gareth Williams

NATIONAL PORTRAIT GALLERY

St Martin's Place, London WC2H 0HE
T 020-7312 2463
W www.npg.org.uk

The National Portrait Gallery was formed after a grant was made in 1856 to form a gallery of the portraits of the most eminent persons in British history. The present building was opened in 1896 and the Ondaatje Wing (including a new Balcony Gallery, Tudor Gallery, IT Gallery, lecture theatre and roof-top restaurant) opened in May 2000. There are three regional partnerships displaying portraits at Montacute House, Beningbrough Hall and Bodelwyddan Castle. Total government grant-in-aid for 2008–9 was £7.69m.

BOARD OF TRUSTEES
Chair, Prof. David Cannadine, FBA, FRSL
Trustees, Zeinab Badawi; Prof. Dame Carol Black, DBE; Sir Nicholas Blake, QC; Dr Rosalind P. Blakesley; Dr Augustus Casely-Hayford; Marchioness of Douro, OBE; Rt. Hon. Nick Clegg MP; Amelia Fawcett, CBE; Sir Nicholas Grimshaw, CBE, PRA; Rt. Hon. Lord Janvrin, GCB, GCVO, QSO; David Mach, RA; Sir William Proby Bt., CBE; David Ross; Marina Warner, CBE, FBA
Director, Sandy Nairne

NATURAL ENGLAND

1 East Parade, Sheffield S1 2ET
T 0845-600 3078 E enquiries@naturalengland.org.uk
W www.naturalengland.org.uk

Natural England was established on 1 October 2006 after the Natural Environment and Rural Communities Act received royal assent in March 2006. It is the government's advisor on the natural environment, providing practical advice, grounded in science, on how best to safeguard England's natural wealth. The organisation's remit is to ensure sustainable stewardship of the land and sea and to ensure England's environment can adapt and survive for future generations. Natural England works with farmers and land managers; business and industry; planners and developers; national, regional and local government; interest groups and local communities to help them improve their local environment.

Chief Executive, Dr Helen Phillips

NATURAL HISTORY MUSEUM

Cromwell Road, London SW7 5BD
T 020-7942 5000 W www.nhm.ac.uk

The Natural History Museum originates from the natural history departments of the British Museum, which grew extensively during the 19th century; in 1860 it was agreed that the natural history collections should be separated from the British Museum's collections of books, manuscripts and antiquities. Part of the site of the 1862 International Exhibition in South Kensington was acquired for the new museum, and the museum opened to the public in 1881. In 1963 the Natural History Museum became completely independent with its own board of trustees. The Natural History Museum at Tring, bequeathed by the second Lord Rothschild, has formed part of the museum since 1937. The Geological Museum merged with the Natural History Museum in 1985. In September 2009 the Natural History Museum opened the Darwin Centre, which contains public galleries, scientific research areas and space for 22 million zoological specimens, 17 million insect specimens and three million botanical specimens. Total government grant-in-aid for 2009–10 was £51.05m.

BOARD OF TRUSTEES
Chair, Oliver Stocken
Trustees, Daniel Alexander, QC; Prof. Sir Roy Anderson, FRS; Louise Charlton; Prof. David Drewry; Prof. Dianne Edwards, CBE, FRS; Prof. Alex Halliday, FRS; Ian J. Henderson, CBE, FRICS; Dr Derek Langslow, CBE; Prof. Jacquie McGlade; Prof. Georgina Mace, CBE, FRS; Sir David Omand, GCB, KCB

SENIOR STAFF
Director, Dr Michael Dixon
Director of Estates and Services, David Sanders
Director of Finance and Administration, Neil Greenwood
Director of Human Resources, Paul Brereton
Director, Natural History Museum at Tring, Teresa Wild
Director of Public Engagement Group, Sharon Ament
Director of Science, Richard Lane
Head of Audit and Review, David Thorpe
Head of Library and Information Services, Graham Higley
Keeper of Botany, Dr Johannes Vogel
Keeper of Entomology, Dr Malcolm Scoble
Keeper of Mineralogy, Dr Andy Fleet
Keeper of Palaeontology, Prof. Norman MacLeod
Keeper of Zoology, Prof. Phil Rainbow
Museum Manager, Ian Jenkinson

NHS PAY REVIEW BODY

6th Floor, Kingsgate House, 66–74 Victoria Street, London SW1E 6SW
T 020-7215 4453 W www.ome.uk.com

The NHS Pay Review Body (NHSPRB) makes recommendations to the prime minister, Secretary of State for Health and ministers in Scotland, Wales and Northern Ireland on the remuneration of all paid staff under agenda for change and employed in the NHS. The review body was established in 1983 for nurses and allied health professionals. Its remit has since expanded to cover over 1.8 million staff, ie almost all staff in the NHS, with the exception of dentists, doctors and very senior managers.
Chair, Prof. Gillian Morris
Members, Philip Ashmore; Prof. David Blackaby; Dame Denise Holt; Graham Jagger; Ian McKay; Prof. Alan Manning; Maureen Scott

NORTHERN IRELAND HUMAN RIGHTS COMMISSION

Temple Court, 39 North Street, Belfast BT1 1NA
T 028-9024 3987; Textphone 028-9024 9066
E information@nihrc.org W www.nihrc.org

The Northern Ireland Human Rights Commission was set up in March 1999. Its main functions are to keep under review the law and practice relating to human rights in Northern Ireland, to advise the government and to promote an awareness of human rights in Northern Ireland. It can also take cases to court. The members of the commission are appointed by the Secretary of State for Northern Ireland.
Chief Commissioner, Prof. Monica McWilliams
Commissioners, Thomas Duncan; Prof. Colin Harvey; Alan Henry; Ann Hope; Colin Larkin; Eamonn O'Neill; Geraldine Rice
Chief Executive, Peter O'Neill

NORTHERN LIGHTHOUSE BOARD

84 George Street, Edinburgh EH2 3DA
T 0131-473 3100 E enquiries@nlb.org.uk
W www.nlb.org.uk

The Northern Lighthouse Board is the general lighthouse authority for Scotland and the Isle of Man and owes its origin to an act of parliament passed in 1786. At present there are 19 commissioners who operate under the Merchant Shipping Act 1995.

The commissioners control 206 lighthouses, many lighted and unlighted buoys, a DGPS (differential global positioning system) station and an ELORAN (long-range navigation) system. *See also* Transport.
Chair, Sir Andrew Cubie, CBE, FRSE
Commissioners, Lord Advocate; Solicitor-General for Scotland; Lord Provosts of Edinburgh, Glasgow and Aberdeen; Convener of Highland Council; Convener of Argyll and Bute Council; Sheriffs-Principal of North Strathclyde, Tayside, Central and Fife, Grampian, Highlands and Islands, South Strathclyde, Dumfries and Galloway, Lothians and Borders and Glasgow and Strathkelvin; Capt. Mike Close; Alistair MacKenzie; Robert Quayle; John Ross, CBE; Alistair Whyte
Chief Executive, Roger Lockwood, CB

OFFICE FOR BUDGET RESPONSIBILITY

Correspondence and Enquiry Unit, 2/W1, 1 Horse Guards Road, London SW1A 2HQ
T 020-7270 4558 E enquiries@hm-treasury.gov.uk
W http://budgetresponsibility.independent.gov.uk

The Office for Budget Responsibility (OBR) was formed in May 2010 to make an independent assessment of the public finances and the economy for each Budget and Pre-Budget Report. It has direct control over the forecast and full access to the necessary data and analysis produced by the Treasury to make key judgements that drive the official projections.

The OBR presents a range of outcomes around its forecasts and uses these to confirm whether government policy is more than 50 per cent likely of achieving the fiscal mandate set by the Chancellor of the Exchequer. It also has a role in assessing the public sector balance sheet, including analysis of the costs of ageing, public service pensions and Private Finance Initiatives.
Committee, Sir Alan Budd; Geoffrey Dicks; Graham Parker

OFFICE OF COMMUNICATIONS (OFCOM)

Riverside House, 2A Southwark Bridge Road, London SE1 9HA
T 0300-123 3000 E contact@ofcom.org.uk
W www.ofcom.org.uk

OFCOM was established in 2003 under the Office of Communications Act 2002 as the independent regulator and competition authority for the UK communications industries with responsibility for television, radio, telecommunications and wireless communications services.
Chief Executive, Ed Richards
Chair, Colette Bowe
Deputy Chair, Philip Graf, CBE
Board Members, Millie Banerjee, CBE; Norman Blackwell; Tim Gardam; Stuart McIntosh; Mike McTighe; Peter Phillips

OFFICE OF MANPOWER ECONOMICS (OME)

6th Floor, Kingsgate House, 66–74 Victoria Street, London SW1E 6SW
T 020-7215 8253 **W** www.ome.uk.com

The OME was set up in 1971. It is an independent non-statutory organisation which is responsible for servicing independent review bodies that advise on the pay of various public sector groups, the School Staff Negotiating Body, the Police Negotiating Board and the Police Advisory Board for England and Wales. The OME is also responsible for servicing *ad hoc* bodies of inquiry and for undertaking research into pay and associated matters as requested by the government.
OME Director, Ian Jones
Director, Doctors' and Dentists' and NHS Pay Review Body Secretariats, Research and Analysis Group and OME Deputy Director, Margaret McEvoy
Director, Armed Forces' and Prison Service Secretariats, Jenny Eastabrook
Director, Doctors and Dentists and Senior Salaries Secretariats, Keith Masson
Director, School Teachers', School Support Staff Negotiating Body, Police Negotiating Board and Police Advisory Board for England and Wales Secretariats, Chris Dee

PARADES COMMISSION

Windsor House, 9–15 Bedford Street, Belfast BT2 7EL
T 028-9089 5900 **E** info@paradescommission.org
W www.paradescommission.org

The Parades Commission was set up under the Public Processions (Northern Ireland) Act 1998. Its function is to encourage and facilitate local accommodation of contentious parades; where this is not possible, the commission is empowered to make legal determinations about such parades, which may include imposing conditions on aspects of the notified parade (such as restrictions on routes/areas and exclusion of certain groups with a record of bad behaviour).

The chair and members are appointed by the Secretary of State for Northern Ireland; the membership must, as far as is practicable, be representative of the community in Northern Ireland.
Chair, Rena Shepherd
Members, Kelly Andrews; Michael Doherty; Edwin Graham; Dr Joe Hendron; Vilma Patterson, MBE; Alison Scott-McKinley

PAROLE BOARD FOR ENGLAND AND WALES

Grenadier House, 99–105 Horseferry Road, London SW1P 2DX
T 0845-251 2220 **E** info@paroleboard.gov.uk
W www.paroleboard.gov.uk

The Parole Board was established under the Criminal Justice Act 1967 and became an independent executive non-departmental public body under the Criminal Justice and Public Order Act 1994. It is the body that protects the public by making risk assessments about prisoners to decide who may safely be released into the community and who must remain in, or be returned to, custody. Board decisions are taken at two main types of panels of up to three members: 'paper panels' for the majority of cases, or oral hearings for decisions concerning prisoners serving life or indeterminate sentences for public protection.
Chair, Rt. Hon. Sir David Latham
Chief Executive, Linda Lennon, CBE

PAROLE BOARD FOR SCOTLAND

Saughton House, Broomhouse Drive, Edinburgh EH11 3XD
T 0131-244 8373
E paroleboardforscotlandexecutive@scotland.gsi.gov.uk
W www.scottishparoleboard.gov.uk

The board directs and advises the Scottish ministers on the release of prisoners on licence, and related matters.
Chair, Prof. A. Cameron
Vice-Chair, Ms K. McQuillan

PENSION PROTECTION FUND (PPF)

Knollys House, 17 Addiscombe Road, Croydon CR0 6SR
T 0845-600 2541 **E** information@ppf.gsi.gov.uk
W www.pensionprotectionfund.org.uk

The PPF became operational in 2005. It was established to pay compensation to members of eligible defined-benefit pension schemes where a qualifying insolvency event in relation to the employer occurs and where there is a lack of sufficient assets in the pension scheme. The PPF is also responsible for the Fraud Compensation Fund (which provides compensation to occupational pension schemes that suffer a loss that can be attributed to dishonesty). The chair and board of the PPF are appointed by, and accountable to, the Secretary of State for Work and Pensions, and are responsible for paying compensation, calculating annual levies (which help fund the PPF), and setting and overseeing investment strategy.
Chair, Lady Barbara Judge
Chief Executive, Alan Rubenstein

PENSIONS REGULATOR

Napier House, Trafalgar Place, Brighton BN1 4DW
T 0870-606 3636
E customersupport@thepensionsregulator.gov.uk
W www.thepensionsregulator.gov.uk

The Pensions Regulator was established in 2005 as the regulator of work-based pension schemes in the UK, replacing the Occupational Pensions Regulatory Authority (OPRA). It aims to protect the benefits of occupational and personal pension scheme members by working with trustees, employers, pension providers and advisors. The regulator's work focuses on encouraging better management and administration of schemes, ensuring that final salary schemes have a sensible funding plan, and encouraging money purchase schemes to provide members with the information they need to make informed choices about their pension fund. The Pensions Act gave the regulator a range of powers which can be used to protect scheme members, but a strong emphasis is placed on educating and enabling those responsible for

managing pension schemes, and powers are used as a last resort. The regulator offers two free online resources to help trustees and employers understand their role, duties and obligations.
Chair, David Norgrove
Chief Executive, Bill Galvin

POLICE ADVISORY BOARD FOR ENGLAND AND WALES

6th Floor, Kingsgate House, 66–74 Victoria Street, London SW1E 6SW
T 020-7215 8101 W www.ome.uk.com

The Police Advisory Board for England and Wales was established in 1965 and provides advice to the home secretary on general questions affecting the police in England and Wales. It also considers draft regulations which the secretary of state proposes to make with respect to matters other than hours of duty, leave, pay and allowances or the issue, use and return of police clothing, personal equipment and other effects.
Independent Chair, John Randall
Independent Deputy Chair, Prof. Gillian Morris

POLICE NEGOTIATING BOARD (PNB)

6th Floor, Kingsgate House, 66–74 Victoria Street, London SW1E 6SW
T 020-7215 8101 W www.ome.uk.com

The PNB was established in 1980 to negotiate pay; allowances; hours of duty; the issue, use and return of police clothing, personal equipment and accoutrements; leave; and pensions of United Kingdom police officers, and to make recommendations on these matters to the Secretary of State for Home Affairs, Northern Ireland secretary, and Scottish ministers.
Independent Chair, John Randall
Independent Deputy Chair, Prof. Gillian Morris

PRISON SERVICE PAY REVIEW BODY

6th Floor, Kingsgate House, 66–74 Victoria Street, London SW1E 6SW
T 020-7215 8369 W www.ome.uk.com

The Prison Service Pay Review Body was set up in 2001. It makes independent recommendations on the pay of prison governors, operational managers, prison officers and related grades for the Prison Service in England and Wales and for the Northern Ireland Prison Service.
Chair, Jerry Cope
Members, Prof. John Beath; Dr Henrietta Campbell; Richard Childs, QPM; Bronwen Mary Curtis, CBE; John Davies, OBE; David Lebrecht; Joseph Magee

REGIONAL DEVELOPMENT AGENCIES

5th Floor, Oceanic House, 1A Cockspur Street, London SW1Y 5BG
T 020-7968 0600 W www.englandsrdas.com

Regional Development Agencies (RDAs) were established to help the English regions improve their relative economic performance and reduce social and economic disparities within and between regions. Their five statutory objectives are to further economic development and regeneration; to promote business efficiency and competitiveness; to promote employment; to enhance the development and application of skills relevant to employment; and to contribute to sustainable development. There are nine RDAs in England, and they are financed through a single fund provided by contributing government departments (BIS, DCLG, DECC, DEFRA and DCMS). In 2009–10 the RDA's budget was £2.25bn; in 2010–11 it is £1.75bn.

RDA REGIONS

NORTH WEST: Renaissance House, Centre Park, Warrington WA1 1QN T 01925-400100 *Chair,* Robert Hough
YORKSHIRE: Victoria House, Victoria Place, Leeds LS11 5AE T 0113-394 9600 *Chair,* Terry Hodgkinson
NORTH EAST: Stella House, Goldcrest Way, Newburn Riverside, Newcastle upon Tyne NE15 8NY T 0191-229 6200 *Chair,* Margaret Fay, CBE
WEST MIDLANDS: 3 Priestley Wharf, Holt Street, Aston Science Park, Birmingham B7 4BN T 0121-380 3500 *Chair,* Sir Roy McNulty
EAST MIDLANDS: Apex Court, City Link, Nottingham NG2 4LA T 0115-988 8300 *Chair,* Dr Bryan Jackson, OBE
EAST OF ENGLAND: Victory House, Vision Park, Chivers Way, Histon, Cambridgeshire CB24 9ZR T 01223-713900 *Chair,* Will Pope
SOUTH WEST: Sterling House, Dix's Field, Exeter EX1 1QA T 01392-214747 *Chair,* Sir Harry Studholme
LONDON: Palestra, 197 Blackfriars Road, London SE1 8AA T 020-7593 8000 *Chair,* Harvey McGrath
SOUTH EAST: Cross Lanes, Guildford GU1 1YA T 01483-484200 *Chair,* Robert Douglas, CBE

REGISTRAR OF PUBLIC LENDING RIGHT

Richard House, Sorbonne Close, Stockton on Tees TS17 6DA
T 01642-604699 E authorservices@plr.uk.com
W www.plr.uk.com

Under the Public Lending Right (PLR) system, in operation since 1983, payment is made from public funds to authors whose books are lent out from public libraries. Payment is made once a year and the amount each author receives is proportionate to the number of times (established from a sample) that each registered book has been lent out during the previous year. The registrar of PLR, who is appointed by the Secretary of State for Culture, Olympics, Media and Sport, compiles the register of authors and books. Authors resident in all European Economic Area countries are eligible to apply. (The term 'author' covers writers, illustrators, translators and some editors/compilers.)

A payment of 6.29 pence was made in 2009–10 for each estimated loan of a registered book, up to a top limit of £6,600 for the books of any one registered author; the money for loans above this level is used to augment the remaining PLR payments. In 2010 the sum of £6.76m was paid out to 23,241 registered authors and assignees as the annual payment of PLR.
Registrar, Dr J. G. Parker

REVIEW BODY ON DOCTORS' AND DENTISTS' REMUNERATION

6th Floor, Kingsgate House, 66–74 Victoria Street, London SW1E 6SW
T 020-7215 8407 W www.ome.uk.com

The Review Body on Doctors' and Dentists' Remuneration was set up in 1971. It advises the prime minister, first ministers in Scotland, Wales and Northern Ireland, and the Ministers for Health, in England,

Scotland, Wales and Northern Ireland on the remuneration of doctors and dentists taking any part in the National Health Service.

Chair, Ron Amy, OBE

Members, Katrina Easterling; John Glennie; David Grafton; Sally Smedley; Prof. Steve Thompson; Prof. Ian Walker; David Williamson

ROYAL AIR FORCE MUSEUM

Grahame Park Way, London NW9 5LL

T 020-8205 2266 **E** london@rafmuseum.org

W www.rafmuseum.org

The museum has two sites, one at the former airfield at Hendon and the second at Cosford, in the West Midlands, both of which illustrate the development of aviation from before the Wright brothers to the present-day RAF. The museum's collection across both sites consists of over 170 aircraft, as well as artefacts, aviation memorabilia, fine art and photographs. Total government grant-in-aid for 2010–11, provided by the Ministry of Defence, is £7.36m.

Director-General, Air Vice-Marshal Peter Dye, OBE

ROYAL BOTANIC GARDEN EDINBURGH

20A Inverleith Row, Edinburgh EH3 5LR

T 0131-552 7171 **W** www.rbge.org.uk

The Royal Botanic Garden Edinburgh (RBGE) originated as the Physic Garden, established in 1670 beside the Palace of Holyroodhouse. The garden moved to its present 28-hectare site at Inverleith, Edinburgh, in 1821. There are also three regional gardens: Benmore Botanic Garden, near Dunoon, Argyll; Logan Botanic Garden, near Stranraer, Wigtownshire; and Dawyck Botanic Garden, near Stobo, Peeblesshire. Since 1986 RBGE has been administered by a board of trustees established under the National Heritage (Scotland) Act 1985. It receives an annual grant from the Scottish government's Rural and Environmental Research and Analysis Directorate.

The RBGE is an international centre for scientific research on plant diversity and for horticulture education and conservation. It has an extensive library, a herbarium with almost three million preserved plant specimens, and over 15,000 species in the living collections.

Chair of the Board of Trustees, Sir George Mathewson, CBE, LLD, FRSE

Regius Keeper, Prof. Stephen Blackmore, FRSE

ROYAL BOTANIC GARDENS KEW

Richmond, Surrey TW9 3AB

T 020-8332 5000

Wakehurst Place, Ardingly, W. Sussex RH17 6TN

T 01444-89000

E info@kew.org **W** www.kew.org

The Royal Botanic Gardens, Kew (RBG Kew) were originally laid out as a private garden for the now demolished White House for George III's mother, Princess Augusta, in 1759. The gardens were much enlarged in the 19th century, notably by the inclusion of the grounds of the former Richmond Lodge. In 1965 Kew acquired the gardens at Wakehurst Place on a long lease from the National Trust. Under the National Heritage Act 1983 a board of trustees was set up to administer the gardens, which in 1984 became an independent body supported by grant-in-aid from the Department of Environment, Food and Rural Affairs.

The functions of RBG Kew are to carry out research into plant sciences, to disseminate knowledge about plants and to provide the public with the opportunity to gain knowledge and enjoyment from the gardens' collections. There are extensive national reference collections of living and preserved plants and a comprehensive library and archive. The main emphasis is on plant conservation and biodiversity; Wakehurst Place houses the Millennium Seed Bank Partnership, which is the largest *ex situ* conservation project in the world – its aim is to save seed from 25 per cent of Earth's wild plant species by 2020.

BOARD OF TRUSTEES

Chair, Marcus Agius

Members, Prof. Jonathan Drori, CBE; Prof. Charles Godfray; Dr Sandy Harrison; Dr Geoffrey Hawtin; Mr Timothy Hornsby; Sir Henry Keswick; Mr George Loudon; Prof. Nicola Spence; Prof. Sir William Stewart; Ms Jennifer Ullman; Sir Ferrers Vyvyan

Director, Prof. Stephen Hopper

ROYAL COMMISSION ON ENVIRONMENTAL POLLUTION

Room 108, 55 Whitehall, London SW1A 2EY

T 0300-068 6474 **E** enquiries@rcep.org.uk

W www.rcep.org.uk

The commission was set up in 1970 to advise on national and international matters concerning the pollution of the environment. The commission's advice is mainly in the form of reports which are the outcome of studies, the most recent of which relates to the urban environment. Members are appointed by the Queen on the advice of the prime minister.

Chair, Prof. Sir John Lawton, CBE, FRS

Members, Prof. Jonathan Ayres; Prof. Michael H. Depledge; Prof. Maria Lee; Prof. Peter Liss; Prof. Gordon Mackerron; Prof. Peter Matthews; Prof. Judith Petts; Prof. Michael Roberts; Prof. Joanne Scott; Prof. Marian Scott; Prof. Lynda Warren

ROYAL COMMISSION ON THE ANCIENT AND HISTORICAL MONUMENTS OF SCOTLAND

John Sinclair House, 16 Bernard Terrace, Edinburgh EH8 9NX

T 0131-662 1456 **E** info@rcahms.gov.uk

W www.rcahms.gov.uk

The Royal Commission on the Ancient and Historical Monuments of Scotland (RCAHMS) was established by a royal warrant in 1908, which was revised in 1992, and is appointed to provide for the collecting, recording and interpretation of information on the architectural, industrial, archaeological and maritime heritage of Scotland, to give a picture of the human influence on Scotland's places from the earliest times to the present day. It is funded by the Scottish government. More than 15 million items, including photographs, maps, drawings and documents, are available through the search room, and online databases provide access to over 130,000 images and information on 280,000 buildings and sites. RCAHMS also holds Scotland's national collection of historical aerial photography as well as the Aerial Reconnaissance Archives (TARA) of international wartime photography.

Chair, Prof. John Hume, OBE, FSA SCOT

Commissioners, Kate Byrne; Tom Dawson, FSA SCOT; Mark Hopton, FSA SCOT; Dr Jeremy Huggett,

FSA SCOT; Prof. John Hunter, FSA, FSA SCOT; Paul Jardine; Gordon Masterton; Dr Stana Nenadic, FSA SCOT; Jude Quartson-Mochrie; Elspeth Reid
Chief Executive, Diana Murray, FSA, FSA SCOT

ROYAL COMMISSION ON THE ANCIENT AND HISTORICAL MONUMENTS OF WALES

Crown Building, Plas Crug, Aberystwyth SY23 1NJ
T 01970-621200 E nmr.wales@rcahmw.gov.uk
W www.rcahmw.gov.uk

The Royal Commission was established in 1908 and is currently empowered by a royal warrant of 2001 to survey, record, publish and maintain a database of ancient, historical and maritime sites and structures, and landscapes, in Wales. The commission is funded by the National Assembly for Wales and is also responsible for the National Monuments Record of Wales, which is open daily for public reference and has a public enquiry service. The commission is responsible for supplying archaeological information to Ordnance Survey, for the coordination of archaeological aerial photography in Wales, and for sponsorship of the regional Sites and Monuments Records.
Chair, Dr Eurwyn William, FSA
Vice-Chair, Dr Llinos Smith, FRHISTS
Commissioners, Prof. Antony D. Carr, FSA, FRHISTS; Mrs A. Eastham; Neil Harries; John W. Lloyd, CB; Jonathan Matthews Hudson; John Newman, FSA; Henry Owen-John; Mark Redknap; Prof. C. M. Williams, FRHISTS

ROYAL MAIL GROUP

100 Victoria Embankment, London EC4Y 0HQ
T 020-7250 2888 W www.royalmailgroup.com

Crown services for the carriage of government dispatches were set up in about 1516. The conveyance of public correspondence began in 1635 and the mail service was made a parliamentary responsibility with the setting up of a Post Office in 1657. Telegraphs came under Post Office control in 1870 and the Post Office Telephone Service began in 1880. The National Girobank service of the Post Office began in 1968. The Post Office ceased to be a government department in 1969 when responsibility for the running of the postal, telecommunications, giro and remittance services was transferred to a public authority of the same name.

The British Telecommunications Act 1981 separated the functions of the Post Office, making it solely responsible for postal services and Girobank. Girobank was privatised in 1990. The Postal Services Act 2000 turned the Post Office into a wholly owned public limited company establishing a regulatory regime under the Postal Service Commission. The Post Office Group changed its name to Consignia plc in March 2001 when its new corporate structure took effect; in November 2002 the name was changed to Royal Mail Group plc. As of 1 January 2006 the UK postal service market was fully liberalised, and any licensed operator is now able to deliver mail to businesses and residential customers.

Royal Mail processes and delivers around 71 million letters, packets and parcels to 28 million addresses every day; 20 million customers are served in the 11,900 Post Office branches each week. The Royal Mail Group directly employs around 168,000 people in the UK.

The chair, chief executive and members of the board are appointed by the Secretary of State for Business Innovation and Skills but responsibility for the running of Royal Mail Group as a whole rests with the board in its corporate capacity.

BOARD
Chair, Donald Brydon, CBE
Chief Executive (Royal Mail Group), Moya Greene
Managing Director, David Smith *(Post Office Ltd)*
Members, Ian Duncan *(Group Finance Director)*; Mark Higson *(Managing Director, Royal Mail Letters)*
Non-Executive Directors, Andrew Carr-Locke; Lord Currie; Richard Handover, CBE; Nick Horler; Cath Keers; Paul Murray; Orna Ni-Chionna; Les Owen; Baroness Prosser, OBE
Company Secretary, Jon Millidge

SCHOOL TEACHERS' REVIEW BODY

6th Floor, Kingsgate House, 66–74 Victoria Street, London SW1E 6SW
T 020-7215 8314 W www.ome.uk.com

The School Teachers' Review Body was set up under the School Teachers' Pay and Conditions Act 1991. It is required to examine and report on such matters relating to the statutory conditions of employment of school teachers in England and Wales as may be referred to it by the education secretary.
Chair, Dr Anne Wright, CBE
Members, Prof. Peter Dolton; Dewi Jones; Elizabeth Kidd; Esmond Lindop; Stella Pantelides; Jill Pullen; Anne Watts, CBE

SCIENCE MUSEUM

Exhibition Road, London SW7 2DD
T 0870-870 4868 E sciencem@sciencemuseum.org.uk
W www.sciencemuseum.org.uk

The Science Museum, part of the National Museum of Science & Industry (NMSI), houses the national collections of science, technology, industry and medicine. The museum began as the science collection of the South Kensington Museum and first opened in 1857. In 1883 it acquired the collections of the Patent Museum and in 1909 the science collections were transferred to the new Science Museum, leaving the art collections with the Victoria and Albert Museum. The Wellcome Wing was opened in July 2000.

Some of the museum's larger objects, ranging across aircraft, agricultural machinery, computing, mechanical engineering, and road and rail transport collections, are at Science Museum Swindon, Wilts. The NMSI also incorporates the National Railway Museum, York, the National Media Museum, Bradford, and Locomotion: the National Railway Museum at Shildon.

Total government grant-in-aid for 2008–9 was £39m.
Chair, Rt. Hon. Lord Waldegrave of North Hill
Trustees, Lady Chisholm; Sir Ron U. Cooke; Howard Covington; Prof. Dame Anne Dowling, FRENG; Lord Faulkner of Worcester; Dr Douglas Gurr; Lord Rees of Ludlow, FRS; Prof. Averil Macdonald; Sir Howard Newby, CBE; Dr Gill Samuels, CBE; Prof. Simon J. Schaffer; Dr Maggie Semple, OBE; Dr Tony Sewell; Martin G. Smith; Prof. Roderick A. Smith, FRENG; Janet Street-Porter; Christopher Swinson, OBE; Sir William Wells; Michael G. Wilson, OBE
Director of NMSI, Andrew Scott, CBE
Director of Science Museum, Prof. Chris Rapley, CBE

Director of National Media Museum, Colin Philpott
Director of National Railway Museum, Steve Davies, MBE

SCOTTISH CRIMINAL CASES REVIEW COMMISSION

5th Floor, Portland House, 17 Renfield Street, Glasgow G2 5AH
T 0141-270 7030 E info@sccrc.org.uk
W www.sccrc.org.uk

The commission is a non-departmental public body, funded by the Scottish Government Criminal Justice Directorate, and established in April 1999. It assumed the role previously performed by the Secretary of State for Scotland to consider alleged miscarriages of justice in Scotland and refer cases meeting the relevant criteria to the high court for determination. Members are appointed by the Queen on the recommendation of the First Minister; senior executive staff are appointed by the commission.

Chair, Jean Couper, CBE
Members, Gerrard Bann; Graham Bell, QC; Prof. Brian Caddy; Stewart Campbell; Prof. George Irving, CBE; Gerard McClay; Christopher Shead
Chief Executive, Gerard Sinclair

SCOTTISH ENTERPRISE

Atrium Court, 50 Waterloo Street, Glasgow G2 6HQ
T 0141-248 2700 E enquiries@scotent.co.uk
W www.scottish-enterprise.com

Scottish Enterprise was established in 1991 and its purpose is to stimulate the sustainable growth of Scotland's economy. It is mainly funded by the Scottish government and is responsible to the Scottish ministers. Working in partnership with the private and public sectors, Scottish Enterprise aims to further the development of Scotland's economy by helping ambitious and innovative businesses grow and become more successful. Scottish Enterprise is particularly interested in industries with competitive advantage in Scotland, including energy; life sciences; tourism; financial services; food and drink; and digital markets and enabling technologies.

Chair, Crawford Gillies
Chief Executive, Lena C. Wilson

SCOTTISH ENVIRONMENT PROTECTION AGENCY (SEPA)

Erskine Court, Castle Business Park, Stirling FK9 4TR
T 01786-457700; Hotline 0800-807060
E info@sepa.org.uk W www.sepa.org.uk

SEPA was established in 1996 and is the public body responsible for environmental protection in Scotland. It regulates potential pollution to land, air and water; the storage, transport and disposal of controlled waste; and the safekeeping and disposal of radioactive materials. It does this within a complex legislative framework of acts of parliament, EU directives and regulations, granting licences to operations of industrial processes and waste disposal. SEPA also operates Floodline (T 0845-988 1188), a public service providing information on the possible risk of flooding 24 hours a day, 365 days a year.

Chair, David Sigsworth
Chief Executive, Campbell Gemmell
Directors, John Ford *(Finance and Corporate Services);* Calum MacDonald *(Operations);* James Curran *(Science and Strategy)*

SCOTTISH LAW COMMISSION

140 Causewayside, Edinburgh EH9 1PR
T 0131-668 2131 E info@scotlawcom.gov.uk
W www.scotlawcom.gov.uk

The Scottish Law Commission, established in 1965, keeps the law in Scotland under review and makes proposals for its development and reform. It is responsible to the Scottish ministers through the Scottish Government Justice Department.

Chair (part-time), Hon. Lord Drummond Young
Chief Executive, M. McMillan
Commissioners, Ms L. Dunlop, QC; Prof. G. L. Gretton; P. Layden, QC, TDC; Prof. H. MacQueen

SCOTTISH LEGAL AID BOARD

44 Drumsheugh Gardens, Edinburgh EH3 7SW
T 0131-226 7061; Helpline 0845-122 8686
E general@slab.org.uk W www.slab.org.uk

The Scottish Legal Aid Board was set up under the Legal Aid (Scotland) Act 1986 to manage legal aid in Scotland. It reports to the Scottish government. Board members are appointed by Scottish ministers.

Chair, Iain A. Robertson, CBE
Members, Les Campbell; Joseph Hughes; Alastair Kinroy, QC; Denise Loney; Ray MacFarlane; Paul McBride, QC; Susan McPhee; Bill McQueen, CBE; Elaine Rosie; Sheriff Harry Small; Graham Watson
Chief Executive, Lindsay Montgomery, CBE

SCOTTISH NATURAL HERITAGE (SNH)

Great Glen House, Leachkin Road, Inverness IV3 8NW
T 01463-725000 E enquiries@snh.gov.uk
W www.snh.org.uk

SNH was established in 1992 under the Natural Heritage (Scotland) Act 1991. It is the government's adviser on all aspects of nature and landscape across Scotland and its role is to help the public understand, value and enjoy Scotland's nature.

Chair, Andrew Thin
Chief Executive, I. Jardine
Chief Scientific Adviser, S. Davies
Directors of Operations, G. Hogg *(North);* A. Bachell *(South);* J. Thomson *(Strategy and Communications)*
Director of Corporate Services, J. Moore

SCOTTISH PRISONS COMPLAINTS COMMISSION

Government Buildings, Broomhouse Drive,
Edinburgh EH11 3XD
T 0131-244 8423 E spcc@scotland.gsi.gov.uk

The commission was established in 1994. It is an independent body to which prisoners in Scottish prisons can make applications in relation to any matter where they have failed to obtain satisfaction from the Scottish Prison Service's internal grievance procedures. Clinical judgements made by medical officers, matters that are the subject of legal proceedings and matters relating to sentence, conviction, parole, and life licence decision-making are excluded from the commission's jurisdiction. The commissioner is appointed by the Scottish ministers.

Commissioner (interim), Richard Smith

SEAFISH INDUSTRY AUTHORITY

18 Logie Mill, Logie Green Road, Edinburgh EH7 4HS
T 0131-558 3331 E seafish@seafish.co.uk
W www.seafish.org

Established under the Fisheries Act 1981, the authority on seafood works with all sectors of the UK seafood industry to satisfy consumers, raise standards, improve efficiency and secure a sustainable and profitable future. Services range from research and development, economic consulting, market research and training and accreditation through to account management and legislative advice for the seafood industry. It is sponsored by the four UK fisheries departments, which appoint the board, and is funded by a levy on seafood.
Chair, Charles Howeson
Chief Executive, John Rutherford

SENIOR SALARIES REVIEW BODY

6th Floor, Kingsgate House, 66–74 Victoria Street, London SW1E 6SW
T 020-7215 8276 W www.ome.uk.com

The Senior Salaries Review Body (formerly the Top Salaries Review Body) was set up in 1971 to advise the prime minister on the remuneration of the judiciary, senior civil servants, senior officers of the armed forces and very senior managers in the NHS. In 1993 its remit was extended to cover the pay, pensions and allowances of MPs, ministers and others whose pay is determined by the Ministerial and Other Salaries Act 1975, and also the allowances of peers. If asked, it advises on the pay of officers and members of the devolved parliament and assemblies.
Chair, Bill Cockburn, CBE, TD
Members, Richard Disney; Martin Fish; Michael Langley; David Metcalf; Sir Peter North, CBE, QC; Alasdair Smith; Christopher Stephens; Bruce Warman; Paul Williams

SERIOUS ORGANISED CRIME AGENCY (SOCA)

PO Box 8000, London SE11 5EN
T 0370-496 7622 W www.soca.gov.uk

SOCA was established in April 2006. It took over the functions of the National Criminal Intelligence Service and the National Crime Squad, as well as the role of HM Revenue and Customs in investigating drug trafficking and related criminal finance, and some of the functions of the UK Immigration Service in dealing with organised immigration crime. Its remit is to prevent and detect serious organised crime and to gather, store, analyse and disseminate information on crime. SOCA is also tasked with providing support to law enforcement partners. SOCA officers can have the combined powers of police, customs and immigration officers, and the organisation works in partnership with agencies and officials from across the world.

The Secretary of State for Home Affairs appoints the chair and director-general, may set SOCA strategies and will judge the success of its efforts. Grant-in-aid is provided by the Home Office and for 2010–11 is estimated to be £432m.
Chair, Sir Ian Andrews
Director-General, vacant
Directors, Malcolm Cornberg *(Corporate Services);* Trevor Pearce *(Enforcement);* Paul Evans *(Intervention)*
Non-Executive Directors, Peter Clarke; Elizabeth France; Susan Garrard; Dame Janet Paraskeva, DBE; Francis Plowden

SKILLS FUNDING AGENCY

Cheylesmore House, Quinton Road, Coventry CV1 2WT
T 0845-377 5000 E info@skillsfundingagency.bis.gov.uk
W www.skillsfundingagency.bis.gov.uk

The Skills Funding Agency was established in April 2010 as one of two successor organisations of the Learning and Skills Council. As an agency of the Department of Business, Innovation and Skills, it funds and regulates adult further education and skills training in England and is part of a network of organisations which commission, manage and market training for adults. Its purpose is to ensure that people and businesses can access the skills training necessary for them to do their jobs, progress in their chosen fields and succeed in growing England's economy. Its annual budget is £4bn.
Chief Executive, Geoff Russell

STUDENT LOANS COMPANY LTD

100 Bothwell Street, Glasgow G2 7JD
T 0141-306 2000 W www.slc.co.uk

The Student Loans Company is wholly owned by the government. It processes and administers financial assistance for undergraduates who have secured a place at university or college, under the Student Loans Scheme (established in 1990) and the Income Contingent Loans Scheme (established in 1998). For 2009–10 support payments to students totalled £6.2bn, of which £2.7bn was in maintenance loans and £1.1bn was in maintenance grants and other non-repayable allowances. As at the end of the year the company had 3.2 million borrowers.
Chair, Sir Deian Hopkin
Chief Executive (interim), Ed Lester

TATE BRITAIN

Millbank, London SW1P 4RG
T 020-7887 8888 E visiting.britain@tate.org.uk
W www.tate.org.uk/britain

Tate Britain displays the national collection of British art from 1500 to the present day – with special attention and dedicated space given to Blake, Turner and Constable. The gallery opened in 1897, the cost of building (£80,000) being defrayed by Sir Henry Tate, who also contributed the nucleus of the present collection. The Turner wing was opened in 1910, and further galleries and a new sculpture hall followed in 1937. In 1979 a further extension was built, and the Clore Gallery was opened in 1987. The Centenary Development was opened in 2001.

There are four Tate galleries: Tate Britain and Tate Modern in London, Tate Liverpool and Tate St Ives; the entire Tate collection is available to view online.

BOARD OF TRUSTEES
Chair, Lord Browne of Madingley
Trustees, Helen Alexander; Tom Bloxham; Jeremy Deller; David Ekserdjian; Mala Gaonkar; Maja Hoffman; Patricia Lankester; Elisabeth Murdoch; Franck Petitgas; Monisha Shah; Bob Smith; Roberta Smith; Gareth Thomas; Wolfgang Tillmans

OFFICERS
Director, Sir Nicholas Serota
Director, Tate Britain, Dr Penelope Curtis
Director, Tate Liverpool, Dr Christoph Grunenberg
Director, Tate Modern, Chris Dercon
Artistic Director, Tate St Ives, Martin Clark
Executive Director, Tate St Ives, Mark Osterfield

TATE MODERN

Bankside, London SE1 9TG
T 020-7887 8888 E visiting.modern@tate.org.uk
W www.tate.org.uk/modern

Opened in May 2000, Tate Modern displays the Tate collection of international modern art dating from 1900 to the present day. It includes works by Dalí, Picasso, Matisse and Warhol as well as many contemporary works. It is housed in the former Bankside Power Station in London, which was redesigned by the Swiss architects Herzog and de Meuron.
Director, Chris Dercon

TENANT SERVICES AUTHORITY

Maple House, 149 Tottenham Court Road, London W1T 7BN
T 0845-230 7000 E enquiries@tsa.gsx.gov.uk
W www.tenantservicesauthority.org

The Tenant Services Authority (TSA) was established on 1 December 2008 as the regulator for affordable housing. It took over the regulatory powers of the Housing Corporation. The TSA's main aim is to raise the standards of services for tenants. In April 2010 the TSA became responsible for all affordable housing in England, whether it is provided by local authorities, housing associations or arm's-length management organisations.
Chair, Anthony Mayer
Chief Executive, Peter Marsh

TOURISM BODIES

Visit Britain, Visit Scotland, Visit Wales and the Northern Ireland Tourist Board are responsible for developing and marketing the tourist industry in their respective regions. Visit Wales is not listed here as it is part of the Welsh Assembly government, within the Department for Heritage, and not a public body.

VISIT BRITAIN
1 Palace Street, Victoria SW1E 5HE T 020-7578 1000
W www.visitbritain.com
Chair, Christopher Rodrigues, CBE
Chief Executive, Sandie Dawe, MBE

VISIT SCOTLAND
Ocean Point One, 94 Ocean Drive, Leith, Edinburgh EH6 6JH
T 0131-472 2222
E info@visitscotland.com W www.visitscotland.com
Chair, Dr Mike Cantlay
Chief Executive, Philip Riddle, OBE

NORTHERN IRELAND TOURIST BOARD
St Anne's Court, 59 North Street, Belfast BT1 1NB
T 028-9023 1221
E info@nitb.com W www.discovernorthernireland.com
Chair, Howard Hastings
Chief Executive, Alan Clarke

TRAINING AND DEVELOPMENT AGENCY FOR SCHOOLS

Piccadilly Gate, Store Street, Manchester M1 2WD
T 0870-496 0123 E corporatecomms@tda.gov.uk
W www.tda.gov.uk; www.teach.gov.uk

The Training and Development Agency for Schools (TDA) was launched in September 2005 and took on the role, and expanded the remit of, the Teacher Training Agency. The TDA aims to attract able and committed people to teaching, concentrating specifically on subjects where teachers are in short supply; provide schools and their staff with good information on training and development opportunities; and ensure that new teachers enter schools with appropriate skills and knowledge, through working closely with providers of initial teacher training.
Chief Executive, Graham Holley

TRANSPORT FOR LONDON (TFL)

Windsor House, 42–50 Victoria Street, London SW1H 0TL
T 020-7222 5600
E enquire@tfl.gov.uk W www.tfl.gov.uk

TfL was formed in July 2000 as a functional body of the Greater London Authority and is responsible for the capital's transport system. Its role is to implement the Mayor of London's transport strategy and manage the transport services across London for which the mayor has responsibility.

As a result, TfL is responsible for London's buses, London Underground, London Overground, the Docklands Light Railway (DLR) and the management of Croydon Tramlink, London River Services and Victoria Coach Station. It also runs the London Transport Museum; manages the Congestion Charging scheme and Low Emission Zone; regulates the city's taxis and private hire trade; maintains 580km of main roads and all of London's traffic lights; coordinates schemes for people with impaired mobility; runs Dial-a-Ride and the London boroughs taxi card scheme; and promotes walking and cycling initiatives.
Chair, Boris Johnson
Commissioner, Peter Hendy

UK ATOMIC ENERGY AUTHORITY

Culham Science Centre, Abingdon, Oxfordshire OX14 3DB
T 01235-528822
W www.uk-atomic-energy.org.uk

The UK Atomic Energy Authority was established by the Atomic Energy Authority Act 1954 and took over responsibility for the research and development of the civil nuclear power programme. The authority is responsible for managing UK fusion research, and reports to the Department for Business, Innovation and Skills. It also operates the Joint European Torus (JET) on behalf of the European Fusion Development Agency (EFDA) at Culham, Oxfordshire, as well as managing the records service for the Nuclear Decommissioning Authority (NDA) at Harwell. In October 2009, as part of the government's Operation Efficiency Programme (OEP), the authority sold its commercial arm, UKAEA Limited. This body continues to provide nuclear decommissioning, waste management and site environmental remediation services, as well as site management services at three NDA sites.
Chair, Lady Barbara Judge
Chief Executive, Prof. Steven Cowley

UK FILM COUNCIL

10 Little Portland Street, London W1W 7JG
T 020-7861 7861 E info@ukfilmcouncil.org.uk
W www.ukfilmcouncil.org.uk

The council was created in April 2000 by the Department for Culture, Media and Sport. The council's board comprises of 15 directors and was established as a private company limited by guarantee. It invests grant-in-aid and National Lottery funds in film development and production, training, international development and export promotion, distribution and exhibition, and education.

The Office of the British Film Commissioner (formerly UK Film Council International) is part of the same organisation, and was originally established in 1991. Its remit is to attract inward investment by promoting the UK as an international production centre to the film and television industries and encouraging the use of British locations, services, facilities and personnel.

Chair, Tim Bevan, CBE
Chief Executive, John Woodward
British Film Commissioner, Colin Brown

UNITED KINGDOM SPORTS COUNCIL (UK SPORT)

40 Bernard Street, London WC1N 1ST
T 020-7211 5100
E info@uksport.gov.uk W www.uksport.gov.uk

UK Sport was established by royal charter in 1996 and is accountable to parliament through the Department for Culture, Media and Sport. Its mission is to lead sport in the UK to world-class success. This means working with partner organisations to deliver medals at the Olympic and Paralympic Games and organising, bidding for and staging major sporting events in the UK; increasing the UK's sporting activity and influence overseas; and promoting sporting conduct, ethics and diversity in society. UK Sport is funded by a mix of grant-in-aid and National Lottery income, as well as private investment through Team 2012. Projected government grant-in-aid for 2010–11 is £62.9m and National Lottery funding is £49.8m.

Chair, Baroness Sue Campbell, CBE

VICTORIA AND ALBERT MUSEUM

Cromwell Road, London SW7 2RL
T 020-7942 2000 W www.vam.ac.uk

The Victoria and Albert Museum (V&A) is the national museum of fine and applied art and design. It descends directly from the Museum of Manufactures, which opened in Marlborough House in 1852 after the Great Exhibition of 1851. The museum was moved in 1857 to become part of the South Kensington Museum. It was renamed the Victoria and Albert Museum in 1899. It also houses the National Art Library and Print Room.

The museum administers the V&A Museum of Childhood at Bethnal Green, which was opened in 1872; the building is the most important surviving example of the type of glass and iron construction used by Paxton for the Great Exhibition. Total government grant-in-aid for 2010–11 is £44.3m.

Chair, Paul Ruddock
Trustees, D. Adjaye, OBE; E. Davies, OBE; T. Dixon, OBE; Ms B. Jackson, CBE; Prof. L. Jardine, CBE; S. McGuckin; Ms E. O' Connor; Ms M. Ogundehin; Rt. Hon. Sir T. Sainsbury; Dame M. Scardino, DBE; S. Shah, OBE; R. Stefanowski; Dr P. Thompson
Director of the V&A, Sir M. Jones

WALLACE COLLECTION

Hertford House, Manchester Square, London W1U 3BN
T 020-7563 9500 E collections@wallacecollection.org
W www.wallacecollection.org

The Wallace Collection was bequeathed to the nation by the widow of Sir Richard Wallace, in 1897, and Hertford House was subsequently acquired by the government. The collection contains works by Titian and Rembrandt, and includes porcelain, furniture and an array of arms and armour. Total government grant-in-aid for 2009–10 was estimated at £4.23m.

Director, Rosalind Savill

WOMEN'S NATIONAL COMMISSION

Eland House, Bressenden Place, London SW1E 5DU
T 0303-444 4009 E wnc@communities.gsi.gov.uk
W www.thewnc.org.uk

The Women's National Commission was established in 1969 as an independent advisory committee to the government. It is an umbrella organisation representing women and women's organisations in the UK. Its remit is to ensure that the informed opinions of women are given their due weight in the deliberations of the government and in public debate on matters of public interest, including those of special interest to women. The commission is an advisory NDPB sponsored by the Government Equalities Office.

Chair, Baroness Gould of Potternewton
Director, Barbara-Ann Collins
Deputy Director (Policy), Susan Green

YOUNG PEOPLE'S LEARNING AGENCY

Cheylesmore House, Quinton Road, Coventry CV1 2WT
T 0845-377 2000 E enquiries@ypla.gov.uk
W www.ypla.gov.uk

The Young People's Learning Agency (YPLA) was launched in April 2010 as one of two successor organisations of the Learning and Skills Council. It was established by the Apprenticeships, Skills, Children and Learning Act 2009 to support training and education for 16- to 19-year-olds in England. Its work falls into three areas: supporting local authorities to commission suitable education and training opportunities; funding academies for all their provision; and providing financial support to young learners, often in the form of Education Management Allowances.

The YPLA's board is made up of 12 members appointed by the Secretary of State for Education. Its budget for 2010 is £7bn.

Chair, Les Walton
Chief Executive, Peter Lauener

REGIONAL GOVERNMENT

LONDON

GREATER LONDON AUTHORITY (GLA)

City Hall, The Queen's Walk, London SE1 2AA
T 020-7983 4000 E mayor@london.gov.uk
W www.london.gov.uk

On 7 May 1998 London voted in favour of the formation of the Greater London Authority (GLA). The first elections to the GLA took place on 4 May 2000 and the new authority took over its responsibilities on 3 July 2000. In July 2002 the GLA moved to one of London's most spectacular buildings, newly built on a brownfield site on the south bank of the Thames, adjacent to Tower Bridge. The third and most recent election to the GLA took place on 1 May 2008.

The structure and objectives of the GLA stem from its main areas of responsibility: transport, policing, fire and emergency planning, economic development, planning, culture and health. There are four functional bodies that coordinate these functions and report to the GLA: the London Development Agency (LDA), the London Fire and Emergency Planning Authority (LFEPA), the Metropolitan Police Authority (MPA) and Transport for London (TfL).

The GLA consists of a directly elected mayor, the Mayor of London, and a separately elected assembly, the London Assembly. The mayor has the key role of decision making, with the assembly performing the tasks of regulating and scrutinising these decisions, and investigating issues of importance to Londoners. In addition, the GLA has around 600 permanent staff to support the activities of the mayor and the assembly, which are overseen by a head of paid service. The mayor may appoint two political advisers and not more than ten other members of staff, though he does not necessarily exercise this power, but he does not appoint the chief executive, the monitoring officer or the chief finance officer. These must be appointed jointly by the assembly and the mayor.

Every aspect of the assembly and its activities must be open to public scrutiny and therefore accountable. The assembly holds the mayor to account through scrutiny of his strategies, decisions and actions. This is carried out by direct questioning at assembly meetings and by conducting detailed investigations in committee.

People's Question Time and Mayor's Consultation Meetings give Londoners the chance to question the mayor and the London Assembly about plans, priorities and policies for London. Question time is held twice a year, and consultation meetings are held four times a year in different parts of London.

The role of the mayor can be broken down into a number of key areas:

- to represent and promote London at home and abroad and speak up for Londoners
- to devise strategies and plans to tackle London-wide issues, such as crime, transport, housing, planning, environment, accountability, business and skills, public services, society and culture, local government and the Olympic and Paralympic Games, sport and health; and to set budgets for TfL, the LDA, the MPA and the LFEPA
- the mayor is chair of TfL, and has the power to appoint the chair of the MPA and board members to TfL, the MPA and the LDA; he also makes appointments to the police and fire authorities
- with London's successful bid to host the 2012 Olympic and Paralympic Games, the previous mayor was the signatory to the contract with the International Olympic Committee undertaking that the games would be delivered

The role of the assembly can be broken down into a number of key areas:

- to check on and balance the mayor
- to scrutinise the mayor
- to have the power to amend the mayor's budget by a majority of two-thirds
- to have the power to summon the mayor, senior staff of the GLA and functional bodies
- to investigate issues of London-wide significance and make proposals to appropriate stakeholders
- to have representatives on the boards of the MPA, the LFEPA and the LDA

Mayor, Boris Johnson
Deputy Mayors, Richard Barnes (Statutory Deputy Mayor); Kit Malthouse (Policing); Sir Simon Milton (Policy and Planning, and Chief of Staff)
Chair of the London Assembly, Dee Doocey
Deputy Chair of the Assembly, Jennette Arnold

ELECTIONS AND VOTING SYSTEMS

The assembly is elected every four years at the same time as the mayor, and consists of 25 members. There is one member from each of the 14 GLA constituencies topped up with 11 London members who are representatives of political parties or individuals standing as independent candidates. The last election was on 1 May 2008.

Two distinct voting systems are used to appoint the existing mayor and the assembly. The mayor is elected using the supplementary vote system (SVS). With SVS, electors have two votes: one to give a first choice for mayor and one to give a second choice. Electors can only have one effective vote and so cannot vote twice for the same candidate. If one candidate gets more than half of all the first-choice votes, he or she becomes mayor. If no candidate gets more than half of the first-choice votes, the two candidates with the most first-choice votes remain in the election and all the other candidates drop out. The second-choice votes on the ballot papers of the candidates who drop out are then counted. Where these second-choice votes are for the two remaining candidates they are added to the first-choice votes these candidates already have. The candidate with the most first- and second-choice votes combined becomes the Mayor of London.

The assembly is appointed using the additional member system (AMS). Under AMS, electors have two votes. The first vote is for a constituency candidate. The second vote is for a party list or individual candidate contesting the London-wide assembly seats. The 14 constituency members are elected under the first-past-the-post system, the same system used in general and local elections. Electors vote for one candidate and the candidate with the most votes wins. The additional (London) members are drawn from party lists or are independent candidates who stand as London members; they are chosen using a form of proportional representation.

The Greater London Returning Officer (GLRO) is the independent official responsible for running the election in London. He is supported in this by returning officers in each of the 14 London constituencies.

GLRO, Leo Boland

TRANSPORT FOR LONDON (TFL)

TfL is the integrated body responsible for London's transport system. Its role is to implement the mayor's transport strategy for London and manage transport services across the capital for which the mayor has responsibility. TfL is directed by a management board whose members are chosen for their understanding of transport matters and are appointed by the mayor, who chairs the board. TfL's role is:

- to manage the London Underground, buses, Croydon Tramlink, London Overground and the Docklands Light Railway (DLR)
- to manage a network of main roads and all of London's traffic lights
- to regulate taxis and minicabs
- to run the London River Services, Victoria Coach Station and London Transport Museum
- to help to coordinate the Dial-a-Ride and Taxicard schemes for door-to-door services for transport users with mobility problems

The London Borough Councils maintain the role of highway and traffic authorities for 95 per cent of London's roads. A £5 congestion charge for motorists driving into central London between the hours of 7am and 6.30pm, Monday to Friday (excluding public holidays) was introduced on 17 February 2003, and was subsequently raised to £8 on 4 July 2005. On 19 February 2007, the charge zone roughly doubled in size after a westward expansion (although this is under consultation to be abolished), and the time zone changed to finish earlier at 6pm.

TfL introduced a low emission zone for London on 4 February 2008. It consisted of a £200 daily charge for polluting vehicles that entered the zone, which covered most of Greater London. Lorries over 12 tonnes that did not meet emissions standards were the first to be affected. Charges for vehicles exceeding three-and-a-half tonnes and buses and coaches exceeding five tonnes began on 7 July 2008; tougher emissions standards will be introduced in January 2012. Proposed additional charges, to apply to minibuses and vans from October 2010, have been suspended subject to public consultation.

Since May 2008, Londoners over pensionable age (or over 60 if born before 1950) and war veterans have received free travel on all transport services.

In the summer of 2010, the London cycle hire scheme launched with 6,000 new bicycles for hire from 400 docking stations across eight boroughs, the City and the Royal parks.

Transport Commissioner for London, Peter Hendy

LONDON DEVELOPMENT AGENCY (LDA)

The LDA promotes economic development and regeneration. It is one of the nine regional development agencies set up around the country to perform this task. It is run by a board of 12 members appointed by the mayor. The key aspects of the LDA's role are:

- to further the economic development and regeneration of London
- to promote business efficiency, investment and competitiveness
- to promote employment
- to invest in reducing London's carbon emissions
- to help London and its communities to benefit from the 2012 Olympic Games
- to promote London as a leading destination for business, education and tourism

The London boroughs retain powers to promote economic development in their local areas.

Chair, Harvey McGrath

THE ENVIRONMENT

The mayor is required to formulate strategies to tackle London's environmental issues including the quality of water, air and land; the use of energy and London's contribution to climate change targets; groundwater levels and traffic emissions; and municipal waste management.

METROPOLITAN POLICE AUTHORITY (MPA)

This body, which oversees the policing of London, consists of 23 members: 12 from the assembly and 11 independents. One of the independents is appointed directly by the home secretary. The role of the MPA is:

- to monitor and scrutinise the Metropolitan Police Service
- to maintain an efficient and effective police force
- to secure best value in the delivery of policing services
- to publish an annual policing plan
- to set police targets and monitor performance
- to be part of the appointment, discipline and removal of senior officers
- to be responsible for the police budget

The boundaries of the metropolitan police districts have been changed to be consistent with the 32 London boroughs. Areas beyond the GLA remit have been incorporated into the Surrey, Hertfordshire and Essex police areas. The City of London has its own police force.

Chair, Kit Malthouse

LONDON FIRE AND EMERGENCY PLANNING AUTHORITY (LFEPA)

In July 2000 the London Fire and Civil Defence Authority became the London Fire and Emergency Planning Authority. It consists of 17 members, eight drawn from the assembly, seven from the London boroughs and two mayoral appointees. The role of the LFEPA is:

- to set the strategy for the provision of fire services
- to ensure that the fire brigade can meet all the normal requirements efficiently
- to ensure that effective arrangements are made for the fire brigade to receive emergency calls and deal with them promptly
- to ensure members of the fire brigade are properly trained and equipped
- to ensure that information useful to the development of the fire brigades is gathered
- to ensure arrangements for advice and guidance on fire protection are made

Chair, Brian Coleman, FRSA

SALARIES *as at June 2010*	
Mayor	£143,911
Deputy Mayors	
Richard Barnes	£96,092
Kit Malthouse	£53,439
Sir Simon Milton	£127,784
Chair of the Assembly	£64,103
Assembly Members	£53,439

LONDON ASSEMBLY COMMITTEES

Chair, Audit Panel, Roger Evans
Chair, Budget and Performance Committee, John Biggs
Chair, Business Management and Administration Committee, Jennette Arnold
Chair, Confirmation Hearings Committee, various
Chair, Economic Development, Culture, Sport and Tourism Committee, Len Duvall
Chair, Environment Committee, Darren Johnson
Chair, Health and Public Services Committee, James Cleverly
Chair, Planning and Housing Committee, Nicky Gavron
Chair, Standards Committee, Claer Lloyd-Jones
Chair, Transport Committee, Valerie Shawcross

LONDON ASSEMBLY MEMBERS

as at 1 July 2010

Arbour, Tony, *C., South West,* Maj. 26,928
Arnold, Jennette, *Lab. North East,* Maj. 28,437
Bacon, Gareth, *C., London List*
Barnbrook, Richard, *BNP, London List*
Barnes, Richard, *C., Ealing and Hillingdon,* Maj. 28,638
Biggs, John, *Lab., City and East,* Maj. 31,553
Boff, Andrew, *C., London List*
Borwick, Victoria, *C., London List*
Cleverly, James, *C., Bexley and Bromley,* Maj. 75,237
Coleman, Brian, *C., Barnet and Camden,* Maj. 19,693
Doocey, Dee, *LD, London List*
Duvall, Len, *Lab., Greenwich and Lewisham,* Maj. 16,134
Evans, Roger, *C., Havering and Redbridge,* Maj. 43,025
Gavron, Nicky, *Lab., London List*
Johnson, Darren, *Green, London List*
Jones, Jenny, *Green, London List*
McCartney, Joanne, *Lab., Enfield and Haringey,* Maj. 1,402
Malthouse, Kit, *C., West Central,* Maj. 51,381
O'Connell, Stephen, *C., Croydon and Sutton,* Maj. 42,665
Pidgeon, Caroline, *LD, London List*
Qureshi, Murad, *Lab., London List*
Shah, Navin, *Lab., Brent and Harrow,* Maj. 1,649
Shawcross, Valerie, *Lab., Lambeth and Southwark,* Maj. 23,648
Tracey, Richard, *C., Merton and Wandsworth,* Maj. 26,293
Tuffrey, Michael, *LD, London List*

STATE OF THE PARTIES *as at 1 July 2010*

Party	*Seats*
Conservative (C.)	11
Labour (Lab.)	8
Liberal Democrats (LD)	3
Green	2
British National Party (BNP)	1

MAYORAL ELECTION RESULTS

as at 1 May 2008

E. 5,419,913 T. 45.33%

Change in turnout from 2004: + 8.38%
Good votes: 1st choice 2,415,952 (98.32%); 2nd choice 2,004,078 (82.94%)
Rejected votes: 1st choice 41,032 (1.67%); 2nd choice 412,054 (17.05%)

First	*Party*	*Votes*	*%*
Boris Johnson	C.	1,043,761	42.48
Ken Livingstone	Lab.	893,877	36.38
Brian Paddick	LD	236,685	9.63
Sian Berry	Green	77,374	3.15
Richard Barnbrook	BNP	69,710	2.84
Alan Craig	CPA	39,249	1.60
Gerard Batten	UKIP	24,222	0.91
Lindsey German	Left List	16,796	0.68
Matt O'Connor	Eng. Dem.	10,695	0.44
Winston McKenzie	Ind.	5,389	0.22

Second	*Party*	*Votes*	*%*
Brian Paddick	LD	641,412	26.11
Sian Berry	Green	331,727	13.50
Ken Livingstone	Lab.	303,198	12.34
Boris Johnson	C.	257,792	10.49
Richard Barnbrook	BNP	128,609	5.23
Gerard Batten	UKIP	113,651	4.63
Alan Craig	CPA	80,140	3.26
Matt O'Connor	Eng. Dem.	73,538	2.99
Winston McKenzie	Ind.	38,954	1.59
Lindsey German	Left List	35,057	1.43

LONDON ASSEMBLY ELECTION RESULTS

as at 1 May 2008

E. Electorate T. Turnout
See General Election Results for a list of party abbreviations

CONSTITUENCIES

E. 5,419,913 T. 45.28%

BARNET AND CAMDEN

E. 376,818 T. 47.77%

Brian Coleman, C.	72,659
Nicky Gavron, Lab.	52,966
Nick Russell, LD	22,213
Miranda Dunn, Green	16,782
Magnus Nielsen, UKIP	3,678
Clement Adebayo, CPA	3,536
David Stevens, Eng. Dem.	2,146
Dave Hoefling, Left List	2,074
Graham Dare, Veritas	510

C. majority 19,693

BEXLEY AND BROMLEY

E. 407,003 T. 49.85%

James Cleverly, C.	105,162
Alex Heslop, Lab.	29,925
Tom Papworth, LD,	21,244
Paul Winnett, NF	11,288
Ann Garrett, Green	9,261
Mick Greenhough, UKIP	8,021
John Hemming-Clark, Ind.	6,684
Miranda Suit, CPA	4,408
Steven Uncles, Eng. Dem.	2,907
David Davis, Left List	1,050

C. majority 75,237

BRENT AND HARROW
E. 367,337 T. 43.10%

Navin Shah, Lab.	57,716
Bob Blackman, C.	56,067
James Allie, LD	19,299
Shahrar Ali, Green	10,129
Zena Sherman, CPA	4,180
Sunita Webb, UKIP	3,021
Pat McManus, Left List	2,287
Arvind Tailor, Eng. Dem.	2,150

Lab. majority 1,649

CITY AND EAST
E. 470,863 T. 39.79%

John Biggs, Lab.	63,635
Philip Briscoe, C.	32,082
Hanif Abdulmuhit, Respect	26,760
Robert Bailey, BNP	18,020
Rajonuddin Jalal, LD	13,724
Heather Finlay, Green	11,478
Thomas Conquest, CPA	7,306
Michael McGough, UKIP	3,078
Graham Kemp, NF	2,350
Michael Gavan, Left List	2,274
John Griffiths, Eng. Dem.	2,048
Julie Crawford, Ind.	701

Lab. majority 31,553

CROYDON AND SUTTON
E. 360,221 T. 48.99%

Stephen O'Connell, C.	76,477
Shafi Khan, Lab.	33,812
Abigail Lock, LD	32,335
David Pickles, UKIP	9,440
Shasha Khan, Green	8,969
David Campanale, CPA	6,910
Richard Castle, Eng. Dem.	4,186
Zana Hussain, Left List	1,361

C. majority 42,665

EALING AND HILLINGDON
E. 401,671 T. 44.05%

Richard Barnes, C.	74,710
Ranjit Dheer, Lab.	46,072
Nigel Bakhai, LD	18,004
Sarah Edwards, Green	12,606
Ian Edward, NF	7,939
Mary Boyle, CPA	5,100
Lynnda Robson, UKIP	4,465
Salvinder Dhillon, Left List	2,390
Sati Chaggar, Eng. Dem.	1,853

C. majority 28,638

ENFIELD AND HARINGEY
E. 351,536 T. 46.04%

Joanne McCartney, Lab.	52,665
Matthew Laban, C.	51,263
Monica Whyte, LD	23,550
Pete McAskie, Green	12,473
Segun Johnson, CPA	5,779
Sait Akgul, Left List	5,639
Brian Hall, UKIP	4,682
Teresa Cannon, Eng. Dem.	2,282

Lab. majority 1,402

GREENWICH AND LEWISHAM
E. 347,252 T. 42.98%

Len Duvall, Lab.	53,174
Andy Jennings, C.	37,040
Brian Robson, LD	18,174
Susan Luxton, Green	15,607
Tess Culnane, NF	8,509
Stephen Hammond, CPA	5,079
Arnold Tarling, UKIP	3,910
Jennifer Jones, Left List	2,045
Johanna Munilla, Eng. Dem.	1,716
Chris Flood, Soc. Alt.	1,587

Lab. majority 16,134

HAVERING AND REDBRIDGE
E. 369,407 T. 45.46%

Roger Evans, C.	78,493
Balvinder Saund, Lab.	35,468
Farrukh Islam, LD	12,443
Lawrence Webb, UKIP	12,203
Ashley Gunstock, Green	9,126
Leo Brookes, Eng. Dem.	6,487
Paula Warren, CPA	5,533
Dr Peter Thorogood, Ind.	3,450
Carole Vincent, Left List	1,473

C. majority 43,025

LAMBETH AND SOUTHWARK
E. 395,202 T. 42.09%

Valerie Shawcross, Lab.	60,601
Caroline Pidgeon, LD	36,953
Shirley Houghton, C.	32,835
Shane Collins, Green	18,011
Geoffrey Macharia, CPA	4,432
Jens Winton, UKIP	3,012
Katt Young, Left List	1,956
Janus Polenceus, Eng. Dem.	1,867
Jasmijn De Boo, Animals Count	1,828
Daniel Lambert, Socialist	1,588

Lab. majority 23,648

MERTON AND WANDSWORTH
E. 362,542 T. 47.16%

Richard Tracey, C.	75,103
Leonie Cooper, Lab.	48,810
Shas Sheehan, LD	17,187
Roy Vickery, Green	14,124
Strachan McDonald, UKIP	4,286
Ellen Greco, CPA	4,053
Steve Scott, Eng. Dem.	2,160
Kris Stewart, Left List	1,714

C. majority 26,293

NORTH EAST
E. 451,787 T. 43.80%

Jennette Arnold, Lab.	73,551
Alexander Ellis, C.	45,114
Meral Ece, LD	28,973
Aled Fisher, Green	28,845
Unjum Mirza, Left List	6,019
Nicholas Jones, UKIP	5,349
Maxine Hargreaves, CPA	5,323
John Dodds, Eng. Dem.	3,637

Lab. majority 28,437

SOUTH WEST
E. 415,092 T. 46.15%

Tony Arbour, C.	76,913
Stephen Knight, LD	49,985
Ansuya Sodha, Lab.	30,190
John Hunt, Green	12,774
Andrew Cripps, NF	4,754
Peter Dul, UKIP	3,779
Sue May, CPA	3,718
Andrew Constantine, Free England Party	2,908
Roger Cooper, Eng. Dem.	1,874
Tansy Hoskins, Left List	1,526

C. majority 26,928

WEST CENTRAL
E. 343,182 T. 48.48%

Kit Malthouse, C.	86,651
Murad Qureshi, Lab.	35,270
Julia Stephenson, Green	16,874
Merlene Emerson, LD	15,934
Paul Wiffen, UKIP	3,060
Alex Vaughan, Eng. Dem.	1,858
Explo Nani-Kofi, Left List	1,630
Abby Dharamsey, Ind.	962

C. majority 51,381

TOP-UP MEMBERS

BRITISH NATIONAL PARTY
Richard Barnbrook

CONSERVATIVE
Andrew Boff
Victoria Borwick
Gareth Bacon

GREEN PARTY
Darren Johnson
Jenny Jones

LABOUR
Nicky Gavron
Murad Qureshi

LIBERAL DEMOCRAT
Dee Doocey
Caroline Pidgeon
Michael Tuffrey

WALES

WELSH ASSEMBLY GOVERNMENT

Cathays Park, Cardiff CF10 3NQ
T 0845-010 3300 W http://wales.gov.uk

The Welsh Assembly Government is comprised of the first minister, deputy first minister, Welsh ministers, the counsel general (the chief legal adviser), and the deputy Welsh ministers. The 60 assembly members delegate their executive powers, including the implementation of policies and legislation, to the first minister – who is elected by the whole assembly and is therefore usually the leader of the largest political party. In turn, the first minister delegates responsibility for delivering the executive functions to Welsh ministers, who together form the cabinet.

The Welsh Assembly Government has responsibility over the following devolved areas: agriculture, fisheries, forestry and rural development; ancient monuments and historic buildings; culture; economic development; education and training; environment; fire and rescue services; food; health and health services; highways and transport; housing; local government; the National Assembly for Wales; public administration; social welfare; sport and recreation; tourism; town and county planning; water and flood defence; and the Welsh language.

First Minister for Wales, Carwyn Jones, AM
Deputy First Minister for Wales, and Minister for the Economy and Transport, Ieuan Wyn Jones, AM
Minister for Business and Budget, Jane Hutt, AM
Minister for Children, Education and Lifelong Learning, Leighton Andrews, AM
Minister for Environment, Sustainability and Housing, Jane Davidson, AM
Minister for Health and Social Services, Edwina Hart, MBE, AM
Minister for Heritage, Alun Ffred Jones, AM
Minister for Rural Affairs, Elin Jones, AM
Minister for Social Justice and Local Government, Carl Sargeant, AM
Deputy Minister for Children, Huw Lewis, AM
Deputy Minister for Housing and Regeneration, Jocelyn Davies, AM
Deputy Minister for Science, Innovation and Skills, Lesley Griffiths, AM
Deputy Minister for Social Services, Gwenda Thomas, AM
Counsel General and Leader of the Legislative Programme, John Griffiths, AM
Clerk to the Assembly and Chief Executive of Assembly Commission, Claire Clancy

MANAGEMENT BOARD
Permanent Secretary, Dame Gillian Morgan
Director General, Children, Education, Lifelong Learning and Skills, David Hawker
Director General, Economy and Transport, Gareth Hall
Director General, Finance, Christine Daws
Director General, Health and Social Services, Paul Williams
Director General, People, Places and Corporate Services, Bernard Galton
Director General, Public Services and Local Government Delivery, Emyr Roberts
Director General, Sustainable Futures, Clive Bates
Non-Executive Directors, Kathryn Bishop; Elan Cross Stephens; James Turner

DEPARTMENTS
Central Service Departments
Children, Education, Lifelong Learning and Skills
Constitutional Affairs, Equality and Communication
Corporate Information and Services
Economy and Transport
Environment, Sustainability and Housing
Health and Social Services
Office of the Permanent Secretary
Public Health and Health Professions
Public Service Improvement
Rural Affairs and Heritage
Social Justice and Local Government

EXECUTIVE AGENCIES
CADW – Welsh Historic Monuments

ASSEMBLY COMMITTEES
Business
Children and Young People
Communities and Culture
Constitutional Affairs
Enterprise and Learning
Equality of Opportunity
European and External Affairs
Finance
Health, Wellbeing and Local Government
Legislation Committees
Petitions
Public Accounts
Scrutiny of First Minister
Standards of Conduct
Sustainability

ASSEMBLY COMMISSION
The Assembly Commission was created under the Government of Wales Act 2006. It is a corporate body which has responsibility for the provision of property, staff and services to support assembly members. The commission is made up of three directorates: the Assembly Business directorate, the Legal Services directorate and the directorate of the Chief Operating Officer. All three are supported by a corporate unit and are accountable to the chief executive. Membership of the Assembly Commission includes a presiding officer and four assembly members, with not more than one member (other than the presiding officer) from the same political group.

Presiding Officer, Lord Elis-Thomas, PC, AM
Members, Lorraine Barrett; Peter Black; Chris Franks; William Graham
Chief Executive, Clare Clancy

NATIONAL ASSEMBLY FOR WALES

Cardiff Bay, Cardiff CF99 1NA
T 0845-010 5500 W www.assemblywales.org

In July 1997 the government announced plans to establish a National Assembly for Wales. In a referendum in September 1997 about 50 per cent of the electorate voted, of whom 50.3 per cent voted in favour of the assembly. Elections are held every four years and the first elections took place on 6 May 1999, the second on 1 May 2003 and the third on 3 May 2007.

Welsh Assembly members are elected using the additional member system. Voters are given two votes: one for a constituency member and one for a regional member. The constituency members are elected under the first-past-the-post system, also used to elect constituency members to the London Assembly. Four regional members in each of the five constituencies are then chosen from party lists or independent candidates using a form of proportional representation.

Until 2007 the National Assembly for Wales had responsibility in Wales for ministerial functions relating to health and personal social services; education; the Welsh language, arts and culture; local government; housing; water and sewerage; environmental protection; sport; agriculture and fisheries; forestry; land use, including town and country planning and conservation; roads; tourism; and European Union matters.

The Government of Wales Act 2006 introduced a radical change to the functions and status of the National Assembly for Wales. With effect from 25 May 2007 the act formally separated the National Assembly for Wales (the legislature – made up of 60 elected assembly members) and the Welsh Assembly Government (the executive – comprising the first minister, Welsh ministers, deputy Welsh ministers and the counsel general). It also made changes to the electoral process: candidates are no longer permitted to stand for both a constituency and a regional list. The act enabled the National Assembly for Wales to formulate its own legislation (assembly measures) on devolved matters such as health, education, social services and local government; the assembly is given legislative competence (the legal authority to pass measures) on a case-by-case basis by the UK parliament.

The National Assembly for Wales also scrutinises and monitors the Welsh Assembly Government. It meets in the Senedd debating chamber. The 60 assembly members examine and approve assembly measures and approve certain items of subordinate legislation; approve budgets for the Welsh Assembly Government's programmes; hold Welsh ministers to account; and analyse and debate their decisions and policies.

Presiding Officer, Lord Dafydd Elis-Thomas, PC, AM

SALARIES *2009–10*	
First Minister*	£80,871
Minister/Presiding Officer*	£41,950
Deputy Minister/Deputy Presiding Officer*	£26,386
Assembly Members (AM)†	£53,852

* Also receives the assembly member salary

† Reduced by two-thirds if the member is already an MP or an MEP

MEMBERS OF THE NATIONAL ASSEMBLY FOR WALES

as at 29 June 2010

Andrews, Leighton, *Lab., Rhondda,* Maj. 6,215
Asghar, Mohammad, *C., South Wales East region*
Barrett, Lorraine Jayne, *Lab., Cardiff S. and Penarth,* Maj. 2,754
‡**Bates**, Michael, *Ind. LD, Montgomeryshire,* Maj. 1,979
Black, Peter, *LD, South Wales West region*
Bourne, Prof. Nicholas, *C., Mid and West Wales region*
Burnham, Eleanor, *LD, North Wales region*
Burns, Angela, *C., Carmarthen West and South Pembrokeshire,* Maj. 98
Butler, Rosemary Janet Mair, *Lab., Newport W.,* Maj. 1,401
Cairns, Alun, *C., South Wales West region*
Chapman, Christine, *Lab., Cynon Valley,* Maj. 5,623
Cuthbert, Jeffrey, *Lab., Caerphilly,* Maj. 2,287
Davidson, Jane Elizabeth, *Lab., Pontypridd,* Maj. 3,347
Davies, Alun, *Lab., Mid and West Wales region*
Davies, Andrew David, *Lab., Swansea West,* Maj. 1,511
Davies, Andrew Robert, *C., South Wales Central region*
Davies, Jocelyn, *PC, South Wales East region*
Davies, Paul, *C., Preseli Pembrokeshire,* Maj. 3,205
Elis-Thomas, Lord Dafydd, *PC, Dwyfor Meirionnydd,* Maj. 8,868
Evans, Nerys, *PC, Mid and West Wales region*
Franks, Christopher, *PC, South Wales Central region*
§**German**, Veronica, *LD, South Wales East region*
Gibbons, Brian, *Lab., Aberavon,* Maj. 6,571
Graham, William, *C., South Wales East region*
Gregory, Janice, *Lab., Ogmore,* Maj. 7,900
Griffiths, Albert John, *Lab., Newport East,* Maj. 875
Griffiths, Lesley, *Lab., Wrexham,* Maj. 1,250
Hart, Edwina, *Lab., Gower,* Maj. 1,192
Hutt, Jane, *Lab., Vale of Glamorgan,* Maj. 83
Isherwood, Mark, *C., North Wales region*
James, Irene, *Lab., Islwyn,* Maj. 2,218
Jenkins, Bethan, *PC, South Wales West region*
Jones, Alun Ffred, *PC, Arfon,* Maj. 5,018
Jones, Carwyn Howell, *Lab., Bridgend,* Maj. 2,556
Jones, Elin, *PC, Ceredigion,* Maj. 3,955
Jones, Gareth, *PC, Aberconwy,* Maj. 1,693
Jones, Helen Mary, *PC, Llanelli,* Maj. 3,884
Jones, Margaret Ann, *Lab., Vale of Clwyd,* Maj. 92
Law, Trish, *Ind., Blaenau Gwent,* Maj. 5,357
Lewis, Huw, *Lab., Merthyr Tydfil and Rhymney,* Maj. 4,581
Lloyd, Dr David, *PC, South Wales West region*
Lloyd, Val, *Lab., Swansea East,* Maj. 4,961
Melding, David, *C., South Wales Central region*
Mewies, Sandra Elaine, *Lab., Delyn,* Maj. 511
Millar, Darren, *C., Clwyd West,* Maj. 1,596
Morgan, Hywel Rhodri, *Lab., Cardiff West,* Maj. 3,698
Morgan, Jonathan, *C., Cardiff North,* Maj. 4,844
Neagle, Lynne, *Lab., Torfaen,* Maj. 5,396
Ramsay, Nicholas, *C., Monmouth,* Maj. 8,469
Randerson, Jennifer Elizabeth, *LD, Cardiff C.,* Maj. 6,565
Ryder, Janet, *PC, North Wales region*
Sargeant, Carl, *Lab., Alyn and Deeside,* Maj. 3,362
Sinclair, Karen, *Lab., Clwyd South,* Maj. 1,119
Thomas, Gwenda, *Lab., Neath,* Maj. 1,944
Thomas, Rhodri, *PC, Carmarthen East and Dinefwr,* Maj. 8,469
Watson, Joyce, *Lab., Mid and West Wales region*
Williams, Brynle, *C., North Wales region*
Williams, Kirsty, *LD, Brecon and Radnorshire,* Maj. 5,354
Wood, Leanne, *PC, South Wales Central region*
Wyn Jones, Ieuan, *PC, Ynys Mon,* Maj. 4,392

‡ Michael Bates was suspended from the Welsh Liberal Democrats on 16 April 2010 pending a court hearing relating to an incident that took place in January 2010

§ Michael German was made a working peer in the House of Lords in May 2010 and the vacancy was filled from the party's regional list

STATE OF THE PARTIES *as at 4 June 2009*

	Constituency AMs	*Regional AMs*	*AM total*
Labour (Lab.)	23*	2	25*
Conservative (C.)	5	8	13
Plaid Cymru (PC)	6*	7	13*
Liberal Democrats (LD)	2	3	5
Others	2	0	2
The Presiding Officer	1	0	1
The Deputy Presiding Officer	1	0	1
Total	40	20	60

* Excludes the presiding officer (PC) and deputy presiding officer (Lab.), who have no party allegiance while in post

NATIONAL ASSEMBLY ELECTION RESULTS

As at 3 May 2007

E. Electorate T. Turnout

See General Election Results for a list of party abbreviations

CONSTITUENCIES
E. 2,248,122 T. 43.5%

ABERAVON (S. WALES WEST)
E. 51,536 T. 20,528 (39.83%)
Lab. majority 6,571 (32.01%)
Brian Gibbons, Lab. 10,129
Linet Purcell, PC 3,558
Andrew Tutton, Neath Port Talbot Ratepayers Association 2,561
Daisy Meyland-Smith, C. 1,990
Claire Waller, LD 1,450
Captain Beany, Bean 840
4.82% swing Lab. to PC

ALYN AND DEESIDE (WALES N.)
E. 59,355 T. 21,095 (35.54%)
Carl Sargeant, Lab. 8,196
Will Gallagher, C. 4,834
Dennis Hutchinson, Ind. 3,241
Paul Brighton, LD 2,091
Dafydd Passe, PC 1,398
William Crawford, UKIP 1,335
Lab. majority 3,362 (15.94%)
3.66% swing Lab. to C.

BLAENAU GWENT (S. WALES EAST)
E. 52,816 T. 23,518 (44.53%)
Trish Law, Ind. 12,722
Keren Bender, Lab. 7,365
Gareth Lewis, LD 1,351
Natasha Asghar, PC 1,129
Bob Hayward, C. 951
Ind. majority 5,357 (22.78%)
46.5% swing Lab. to Ind.

BRECON AND RADNORSHIRE (WALES MID AND W.)
E. 55,428 T. 28,748 (51.87%)
Kirsty Williams, LD 15,006
Suzy Davies, C. 9,652
Neil Stone, Lab. 2,514
Arwel Lloyd, PC 1,576
LD majority 5,354 (18.62%)
0.58% swing LD to C.

BRIDGEND (S. WALES WEST)
E. 59,550 T. 24,552 (41.23%)
Carwyn Jones, Lab. 9,889
Emma Greenow, C. 7,333
Paul Warren, LD 3,730
Nicholas Thomas, PC 3,600
Lab. majority 2,556 (10.41%)
0.71% swing Lab. to C.

CAERNARFON (WALES N.)
E. 39,891 T. 19,573 (49.07%)
Alun Ffred Jones, PC 10,260
Martin Eaglestone, Lab. 5,242
Gerry Frobisher, C. 1,858
Mel ab Owain, LD 1,424
Elwyn Williams, UKIP 789
PC majority 5,018 (25.64%)
3.43% swing Lab. to PC

CAERPHILLY (S. WALES EAST)
E. 62,046 T. 26,922 (43.39%)
Jeff Cuthbert, Lab. 8,937
Lindsay Whittle, PC 7,000
Ron Davies, Ind. 6,071
Richard Foley, C. 3,227
Huw Price, LD 1,687
Lab. majority 1,937 (7.19%)
5.07% swing Lab. to PC

CARDIFF CENTRAL (S. WALES CENTRAL)
E. 62,202 T. 22,397 (36.01%)
Jenny Randerson, LD 11,462
Sue Lent, Lab. 4,897
Andrew Murphy, C. 3,137
Thomas Whitfield, PC 1,855
Frank Hughes, UKIP 1,046
LD majority 6,565 (29.31%)
2.71% swing LD to Lab.

CARDIFF NORTH (S. WALES CENTRAL)
E. 65,687 T. 33,702 (51.31%)
Jonathan Morgan, C. 15,253
Sophie Howe, Lab. 10,409
Ed Bridges, LD 4,287
Wyn Jones, PC 2,491
Dai Llewellyn, UKIP 1,262
C. majority 4,844 (14.37%)
8.16% swing Lab. to C.

CARDIFF SOUTH AND PENARTH (S. WALES CENTRAL)
E. 71,312 T. 26,728 (37.48%)
Lorraine Barrett, Lab. 10,106
Karen Robson, C. 7,352
Dominic Hannigan, LD 5,445
Jason Toby, PC 3,825
Lab. majority 2,754 (10.30%)
4.22% swing Lab. to C.

CARDIFF WEST (S. WALES CENTRAL)
E. 64,588 T. 26,889 (41.63%)
Rhodri Morgan, Lab. 10,390
Craig Williams, C. 6,692
Neil McEvoy, PC 5,719
Alison Goldsworthy, LD 4,088
Lab. majority 3,698 (13.75%)
8.77% swing Lab. to C.

CARMARTHEN EAST AND DINEFWR (WALES MID AND W.)
E. 52,528 T. 29,269 (55.72%)

Rhodri Glyn Thomas, PC	15,655
Kevin Madge, Lab.	7,186
Henrietta Hensher, C.	4,676
Ian Walton, LD	1,752

PC majority 8,469 (28.94%)
5.85% swing Lab. to PC

CARMARTHEN WEST AND SOUTH PEMBROKESHIRE (WALES MID AND W.)
E. 57,477 T. 28,568 (49.70%)

Angela Burns, C.	8,590
Christine Gwyther, Lab.	8,492
John Dixon, PC	8,340
John Gossage, LD	1,806
Malcolm Calver, Ind.	1,340

C. majority 98 (0.34%)
7.45% swing Lab. to C.

CEREDIGION (WALES MID AND W.)
E. 54,071 T. 30,108 (55.68%)

Elin Jones, PC	14,818
John Davies, LD	10,863
Trefor Jones, C.	2,369
Linda Grace, Lab.	1,530
Emyr Morgan, Ind.	528

PC majority 3,955 (13.14%)
2.20% swing PC to LD

CLWYD SOUTH (WALES N.)
E. 51,865 T. 19,498 (37.59%)

Karen Sinclair, Lab.	6,838
John Bell, C.	5,719
Nia Davies, PC	3,894
Frank Biggs, LD	1,838
David Rowlands, UKIP	1,209

Lab. majority 1,119 (5.74%)
6.04% swing Lab. to C.

CLWYD WEST (WALES N.)
E. 57,312 T. 26,205 (45.72%)

Darren Millar, C.	8,905
Alun Pugh, Lab.	7,309
Philip Edwards, PC	7,162
Simon Croft, LD	1,705
Warwick Nicholson, UKIP	1,124

C. majority 1,596 (6.09%)
4.13% swing Lab. to C.

CONWY (WALES N.)
E. 44,143 T. 20,699 (46.89%)

Gareth Jones, PC	7,983
Dylan Jones-Evans, C.	6,290
Denise Idris Jones, Lab.	4,508
Euron Hughes, LD	1,918

PC majority 1,693 (8.18%)
2.86% swing C. to PC

CYNON VALLEY (S. WALES CENTRAL)
E. 50,846 T. 19,517 (38.38%)

Christine Chapman, Lab.	11,058
Liz Walters, PC	5,435
Neill John, C.	2,024
Margaret Phelps, LD	1,000

Lab. majority 5,623 (28.81%)
7.16% swing Lab. to PC

DELYN (WALES N.)
E. 52,733 T. 21,668 (41.09%)

Sandy Mewies, Lab.	7,506
Antoinette Sandbach, C.	6,996
Meg Ellis, PC	3,179
Ian Matthews, LD	2,669
Derek Bigg, UKIP	1,318

Lab. majority 510 (2.35%)
3.63% swing Lab. to C.

GOWER (S. WALES WEST)
E. 61,520 T. 27,545 (44.77%)

Edwina Hart, Lab.	9,406
Byron Davis, C.	8,214
Darren Price, PC	5,106
Nick Tregoning, LD	2,924
Alex Lewis, UKIP	1,895

Lab. majority 1,192 (4.33%)
9.84% swing Lab. to C.

ISLWYN (S. WALES EAST)
E. 54,795 T. 23,564 (43.00%)

Irene James, Lab.	8,883
Kevin Etheridge, Ind.	6,665
Allan Pritchard, PC	5,084
Paul Williams, C.	1,797
Mark Maguire, LD	1,135

Lab. majority 2,218 (9.41%)
23.3% swing Lab. to Ind.

LLANELLI (WALES MID AND W.)
E. 56,154 T. 27,602 (49.15%)

Helen Mary Jones, PC	13,839
Catherine Thomas, Lab.	9,955
Andrew Morgan, C.	2,757
Jeremy Townsend, LD	1,051

PC majority 3,884 (14.07%)
7.08% swing Lab. to PC

MEIRIONNYDD NANT CONWY (WALES MID AND W.)
E. 46,718 T. 22,122 (47.35%)

Dafydd Elis-Thomas, PC	13,201
Mike Wood, C.	4,333
David Phillips, Lab.	2,749
Steve Churchman, LD	1,839

PC majority 8,868 (40.09%)
1.57% swing PC to C.

MERTHYR TYDFIL AND RHYMNEY (S. WALES EAST)
E. 54,025 T. 21,028 (38.92%)

Huw Lewis, Lab.	7,776
Amy Kitcher, LD	3,195
Clive Tovey, Ind.	2,622
Glyndwr Jones, PC	2,519
Jeff Edwards, Ind.	1,950
Giles Howard, C.	1,151
Jock Greer, Ind.	844
Vivienne Hadley, Ind.	809
Richard Williams, Ind.	162

Lab. majority 4,581 (21.79%)
15.77% swing Lab. to LD

MONMOUTH (S. WALES EAST)
E. 63,000 T. 29,565 (46.93%)

Nick Ramsay, C.	15,389
Richard Clark, Lab.	6,920
Jacqui Sullivan, LD	4,359
Jonathan Clark, PC	2,093
Ed Abrams, Eng. Dem.	804

C. majority 8,469 (28.65%)
0.99% swing C. to Lab.

MONTGOMERYSHIRE (WALES MID AND W.)
E. 48,377 T. 22,300 (46.10%)

Mick Bates, LD	8,704
Don Munford, C.	6,725
David Thomas, PC	3,076
Charles Lawson, UKIP	2,251
Rachel Maycock, Lab.	1,544

LD majority 1,979 (8.87%)
1.18% swing LD to C.

NEATH (S. WALES WEST)
E. 57,952 T. 25,200 (43.48%)

Gwenda Thomas, Lab.	10,934
Alun Llewelyn, PC	8,990
Andrew Sivertsen, C.	2,956
Sheila Waye, LD	2,320

Lab. majority 1,944 (7.71%)
7.29% swing Lab. to PC

NEWPORT EAST (S. WALES EAST)
E. 53,060 T. 19,906 (37.52%)

John Griffiths, Lab.	6,395
Ed Townsend, LD	5,520
Peter Fox, C.	4,512
Trefor Puw, PC	1,696
James Harris, Ind.	1,354
Mike Blundell, Eng. Dem.	429

Lab. majority 875 (4.40%)
12.00% swing Lab. to LD

NEWPORT WEST (S. WALES EAST)
E. 58,981 T. 23,659 (40.11%)

Rosemary Butler, Lab.	9,582
Matthew Evans, C.	8,181
Nigel Flanagan, LD	2,813
Brian Hancock, PC	2,449
Andrew Constantine, Eng. Dem.	634

Lab. majority 1,401 (5.92%)
5.79% swing Lab. to C.

OGMORE (S. WALES WEST)
E. 56,973 T. 22,766 (39.96%)

Janice Gregory, Lab.	11,761
Sian Caiach, PC	3,861
Norma Lloyd-Nesling, C.	2,663
Steve Smith, Ind.	2,337
Martin Plant, LD	2,144

Lab. majority 7,900 (34.70%)
2.65% swing Lab. to PC

PONTYPRIDD (S. WALES CENTRAL)
E. 57,512 T. 23,501 (40.86%)

Jane Davidson, Lab.	9,836
Michael Powell, LD	6,449
Richard Grigg, PC	4,181
Janice Charles, C.	3,035

Lab. majority 3,387 (14.41%)
11.08% swing Lab. to LD

PRESELI PEMBROKESHIRE (WALES MID AND W.)
E. 56,435 T. 28,720 (50.89%)

Paul Davies, C.	11,086
Tamsin Dunwoody, Lab.	7,881
John Osmond, PC	7,101
Hywel Davies, LD	2,652

C. majority 3,205 (11.16%)
8.52% swing Lab. to C.

RHONDDA (S. WALES CENTRAL)
E. 52,478 T. 22,107 (42.13%)

Leighton Andrews, Lab.	12,875
Jill Evans, PC	6,660
Karen Roberts, LD	1,441
Howard Parsons, C.	1,131

Lab. majority 6,215 (28.11%)
3.23% swing Lab. to PC

SWANSEA EAST (S. WALES WEST)
E. 59,186 T. 20,717 (35.00%)

Val Lloyd, Lab.	8,590
Helen Clarke, LD	3,629
Danny Bowles, PC	3,218
Bob Dowdle, C.	2,025
David Robinson, Ind.	1,618
Ray Welsby, Ind. Welsby	1,177
Gary Evans, Ind. Evans	460

Lab. majority 4,961 (23.95%)
0.49% swing LD to Lab.

SWANSEA WEST (S. WALES WEST)
E. 61,469 T. 22,879 (37.22%)

Andrew Davies, Lab.	7,393
Peter May, LD	5,882
Harri Davies, C.	4,379
Ian Titherington, PC	3,583
Richard Lewis, UKIP	1,642

Lab. majority 1,511 (6.60%)
5.75% swing Lab. to LD

TORFAEN (S. WALES EAST)
E. 62,592 T. 23,215 (37.09%)

Lynne Neagle, Lab.	9,921
Graham Smith, C.	4,525
Ian Williams, Ind.	3,348
Rhys ab Elis, PC	2,762
Patrick Legge, LD	2,659

Lab. majority 5,396 (23.24%)
6.18% swing Lab. to C.

VALE OF CLWYD (WALES N.)
E. 55,234 T. 22,275 (40.33%)

Ann Jones, Lab.	8,104
Matt Wright, C.	8,012
Mark Jones, PC	3,884
Mark Young, LD	2,275

Lab. majority 92 (0.41%)
7.40% swing Lab. to C.

VALE OF GLAMORGAN (S. WALES CENTRAL)
E. 68,856 T. 33,686 (48.92%)

Jane Hutt, Lab.	11,515
Gordon Kemp, C.	11,432
Barry Shaw, PC	4,671
Mark Hooper, LD	3,758
Kevin Mahoney, UKIP	2,310

Lab. majority 83 (0.25%)
4.02% swing Lab. to C.

WREXHAM (WALES N.)
E. 50,759 T. 19,567 (38.55%)

Lesley Griffiths, Lab.	5,633
John Marek, Ind.	4,383
Felicity Elphick, C.	3,372
Bruce Roberts, LD	3,268
Sion Aled Owen, PC	1,878
Peter Lewis, UKIP	1,033

Lab. majority 1,250 (6.39%)
6.0% swing Ind. to Lab.

YNYS MON (WALES N.)
E. 51,814 T. 26,820 (51.76%)

Ieuan Wyn Jones, PC	10,653
Peter Rogers, Ind.	6,261
Jonathan Austin, Lab.	4,681
James Roach, C.	3,480
Mandi Abrahams, LD	912
Francis Wykes, UKIP	833

PC majority 4,392 (16.38%)
10.5% swing PC to Ind.

REGIONS
E. 2,248,122 T. 43.4%

MID AND WEST WALES
E. 427,188 T. 216,957 (50.79%)

PC	67,258	(31.00%)
C.	49,606	(22.86%)
Lab.	39,979	(18.43%)
LD	28,790	(13.27%)
Green	8,768	(4.04%)
UKIP	8,191	(3.78%)
BNP	6,389	(2.94%)
Soc. Lab.	2,196	(1.01%)
Ind.	1,598	(0.74%)
Welsh Christian Party	1,493	(0.69%)
Ind. Evans	1,108	(0.51%)
Comm. Brit.	666	(0.31%)
Veritas	502	(0.23%)
CPA	413	(0.19%)

PC majority 17,652 (8.14%)
1.16% swing PC to C. (2003 PC majority 5,423)

ADDITIONAL MEMBERS
Nick Bourne, *C.*
Alun Davies, *Lab.*
Joyce Watson, *Lab.*
Nerys Evans, *PC*

NORTH WALES
E. 463,106 T. 196,442 (42.42%)

Lab.	51,831	(26.38%)
PC	50,558	(25.74%)
C.	50,266	(25.59%)
LD	15,275	(7.78%)
BNP	9,986	(5.08%)
UKIP	8,015	(4.08%)
Green	5,660	(2.88%)
Soc. Lab.	2,209	(1.12%)
Welsh Christian Party	1,300	(0.66%)
Comm. Brit.	700	(0.36%)
CPA	642	(0.33%)

Lab. majority 1,273 (0.65%)
4.72% swing Lab. to PC (2003 Lab. majority 13,610)

ADDITIONAL MEMBERS
Brynle Williams, *C.*
Mark Isherwood, *C.*
Eleanor Burnham, *LD*
Janet Ryder, *PC*

SOUTH WALES CENTRAL
E. 493,481 T. 208,294 (42.21%)

Lab.	70,799	(33.99%)
C.	45,147	(21.67%)
PC	32,207	(15.46%)
LD	29,262	(14.05%)
BNP	7,889	(3.79%)
Green	7,831	(3.76%)
UKIP	7,645	(3.67%)
Welsh Christian Party	1,987	(0.95%)
Soc. Lab.	1,744	(0.84%)
Respect	1,079	(0.52%)
Soc. Alt.	838	(0.40%)
Comm. Brit.	817	(0.39%)
CPA	757	(0.36%)
Socialist Equality Party	292	(0.14%)

Lab. majority 25,652 (12.32%)
5.16% swing Lab. to C. (2003 Lab. majority 40,965)

ADDITIONAL MEMBERS
David Melding, *C.*
Andrew Davies, *C.*
Leanne Wood, *PC.*
Chris Franks, *PC*

SOUTH WALES EAST
E. 461,315 T. 190,064 (41.20%)

Lab.	67,998	(35.78%)
C.	37,935	(19.96%)
PC	25,915	(13.63%)
LD	20,947	(11.02%)
BNP	8,940	(4.70%)
UKIP	8,725	(4.59%)
Green	5,414	(2.85%)
Ind.	4,876	(2.57%)
Soc. Lab.	3,693	(1.94%)
Welsh Christian Party	2,498	(1.31%)
Eng. Dem.	1,655	(0.87%)
Comm. Brit.	979	(0.52%)
CPA	489	(0.26%)

Lab. majority 30,063 (15.82%)
4.55% swing Lab. to C. (2003 Lab. majority 42,291)

ADDITIONAL MEMBERS
William Graham, *C.*
Michael German, *LD*
Jocelyn Davies, *PC*
Mohammed Asghar, *PC*

SOUTH WALES WEST
E. 408,186 T. 163,127 (39.96%)

Lab.	58,347	(35.77%)
PC	28,819	(17.67%)
C.	26,199	(16.06%)
LD	20,226	(12.40%)
BNP	8,993	(5.51%)
Green	6,130	(3.76%)
UKIP	5,914	(3.63%)
Soc. Lab.	2,367	(1.45%)
Welsh Christian Party	1,685	(1.03%)
Ind. James	1,186	(0.73%)
Soc. Alt.	1,027	(0.63%)
Respect	713	(0.44%)
Ind.	582	(0.36%)
Comm. Brit.	546	(0.33%)
CPA	393	(0.24%)

Lab. majority 29,528 (18.10%)
2.87% swing Lab. to PC (2003 Lab. majority 33,267)

ADDITIONAL MEMBERS
Alun Cairns, *C.*
Peter Black, *LD*
Bethan Jenkins, *PC*
Dai Lloyd, *PC*

SCOTLAND

SCOTTISH GOVERNMENT

St Andrew's House, Regent Road, Edinburgh EH1 3DG
T 0845-774 1741 **Enquiry Line** 0131-556 840
E ceu@scotland.gsi.gov.uk **W** www.scotland.gov.uk

The Scottish government is the devolved government for Scotland. It is responsible for most of the issues of day-to-day concern to the people of Scotland, including health, education, justice, rural affairs and transport, and manages an annual budget of over £30bn.

The government was known as the Scottish executive when it was established in 1999, following the first elections to the Scottish parliament. The current administration was formed after elections in May 2007.

The government is led by a first minister who is nominated by the parliament and in turn appoints the other Scottish ministers who make up the cabinet.

Civil servants in Scotland are accountable to Scottish ministers, who are themselves accountable to the Scottish parliament.

CABINET

First Minister, Rt. Hon. Alex Salmond, MSP
Minister for Culture and External Affairs, Fiona Hyslop, MSP
Minister for Parliamentary Business, Bruce Crawford, MSP
Deputy First Minister and Cabinet Secretary for Health and Wellbeing, Nicola Sturgeon, MSP
Minister for Housing and Communities, Alex Neil, MSP
Minister for Public Health and Sport, Shona Robison, MSP
Cabinet Secretary for Education and Lifelong Learning, Mike Russell, MSP
Minister for Children and Early Years, Adam Ingram, MSP
Minister for Skills and Lifelong Learning, Keith Brown, MSP
Cabinet Secretary for Finance and Sustainable Growth, John Swinney, MSP
Minister for Enterprise, Energy and Tourism, Jim Mather, MSP
Minister for Transport, Infrastructure and Climate Change, Stewart Stevenson, MSP
Cabinet Secretary for Justice, Kenny MacAskill, MSP
Minister for Community Safety, Fergus Ewing, MSP
Cabinet Secretary for Rural Affairs and the Environment, Richard Lochhead, MSP
Minister for Environment, Roseanna Cunningham, MSP

LAW OFFICERS

Lord Advocate, Elish Angiolini, QC
Solicitor-General for Scotland, Frank Mulholland, QC

STRATEGIC BOARD

Permanent Secretary, Sir John Elvidge, KCB
Director-General, Constitution and Corporate Change, Robert Gordon, CB
Director-General, Economy, and Chief Economic Adviser, Dr Andrew Goudie
Director-General, Education, Leslie Evans
Director-General, Environment, Paul Gray
Director-General, Finance, Alyson Stafford
Director-General, Justice and Communities, Stella Manzie, CBE
Director-General, and Chief Executive of NHS Scotland, Dr Kevin Woods
Non-Executive Directors, Prof. William Bound; David Fisher; Heather Logan

CHANGE AND CORPORATE SERVICES

Saughton House, Broomhouse Drive, Edinburgh EH11 3XD
Director of Constitution and Corporate Change, Robert Gordon, CB

ECONOMY DEPARTMENT

Victoria Quay, Edinburgh EH6 6QQ
Directorates: Built Environment; Culture, External Affairs and Tourism; DG Coordination – Economy, Business Management and Support; Energy; Inspectorate of Prosecution in Scotland; Office of the Chief Economic Adviser; Public Sector Simplification; Public Service Reform; Scottish Development International; Transport
Director-General and Chief Economic Adviser, Dr Andrew Goudie

EXECUTIVE AGENCIES

General Register Office of Scotland
Historic Scotland
National Archives of Scotland
Registers of Scotland
Transport Scotland

EDUCATION DEPARTMENT

Victoria Quay, Edinburgh EH6 6QQ
Directorates: Business; Children, Young People and Social Care; DG Coordination – Education; General Group; Learning; Lifelong Learning; Office of the Chief Scientific Adviser
Director-General, Leslie Evans

EXECUTIVE AGENCIES

HM Inspectorate of Education
Social Work Inspection Agency
Student Awards Agency for Scotland

RURAL AFFAIRS, ENVIRONMENT AND SERVICES DEPARTMENT

Victoria Quay, Edinburgh EH6 6QQ
Directorates: Planning and Environmental Appeals; Human Resources and Corporate Services; TUS; Marine Scotland; Office of the Scottish Parliamentary Counsel; Rural and Environment; Leader; Rural and Environment Research and Analysis Directorate; Rural Payments and Inspections Directorate; Scottish Government Legal Directorate; Legal Secretariat to the Lord Advocate; Scottish Procurement Directorate; SGLD Group 1: Healthier, Safer and Stronger; SGLD Group 2: Wealthier and Fairer, Smarter and Greener; SGLD Group B; Shaping Up Implementation Team; State Veterinary Service
Director-General, Paul Gray

HEALTH DEPARTMENT

St Andrew's House, Regent Road, Edinburgh EH1 3DG
Directorates: Chief Medical Officer and Public Health; Chief Nursing Officer; DG Coordination: Health; Health Delivery; Health Finance; Health Workforce; Healthcare Policy and Strategy; E Health; Equalities, Social Inclusion and Sport; Primary and Community Care; Scottish Academy for Health Policy and Management; Pandemic Flu
Director-General and Chief Executive of NHS Scotland, Dr Kevin Woods

JUSTICE AND COMMUNITIES DEPARTMENT

St Andrew's House, Regent Road, Edinburgh EH1 3DG
Directorates: Courts; Criminal Justice; DG Coordination – Justice and Communities; Housing and Regeneration; Judicial Appointments Board for Scotland; Justice;

Police and Community Safety; Scottish Prisons Complaints Commission
Director-General, Stella Manzie, CBE

EXECUTIVE AGENCIES
Accountant in Bankruptcy
Disclosure Scotland
HM Inspectorate of Constabulary
HMC Inspectorate of Fire Service
HMC Inspectorate of Prisons
Scottish Housing Regulator
Scottish Prison Service
Scottish Public Pensions Agency

CROWN OFFICE AND PROCURATOR FISCAL SERVICE
25 Chambers Street, Edinburgh EH1 1LA
T 0131-226 2626
Chief Executive and Crown Agent, Catherine Dyer

OFFICE OF THE PERMANENT SECRETARY
St Andrew's House, Regent Road, Edinburgh EH1 3DG
T 0131-556 8400
Permanent Secretary, Peter Housden

AUDIT SCOTLAND
110 George Street, Edinburgh EH2 4LH
T 0845-146 1010 E info@audit-scotland.gov.uk
W www.audit-scotland.gov.uk
Auditor-General, Robert W. Black
Accounts Commission Chair, Prof. John Baillie

SCOTTISH PARLIAMENT

Edinburgh EH99 1SP
T 0131-348 5000 **Textphone** 0800-092 7100
E sp.info@scottish.parliament.uk
W www.scottish.parliament.uk

In July 1997 the government announced plans to establish a Scottish parliament. In a referendum on 11 September 1997 about 60 per cent of the electorate voted. Of those who voted, 74.3 per cent voted in favour of the parliament and 63.5 per cent in favour of it having tax-raising powers. Elections are held every four years. The first elections were held on 6 May 1999, when around 59 per cent of the electorate voted. The first meeting was held on 12 May 1999 and the Scottish parliament was officially opened on 1 July 1999 at the Assembly Hall, Edinburgh. A new building to house parliament was opened, in the presence of the Queen, at Holyrood on 9 October 2004. On 3 May 2007 the third elections to the Scottish parliament took place.

The Scottish parliament has 129 members (including the presiding officer), comprising 73 constituency members and 56 additional regional members, mainly from party lists. It can introduce primary legislation and has the power to raise or lower the basic rate of income tax by up to three pence in the pound. Members of the Scottish parliament are elected using the additional member system, the same system used to elect London Assembly and Welsh Assembly members.

The areas for which the Scottish parliament is responsible include: education, health, law, environment, economic development, local government, housing, police, fire services, planning, financial assistance to industry, tourism, some transport, heritage and the arts, agriculture, social work, sports, public registers and records, forestry and food standards.

SALARIES *as at 1 April 2010*	
First Minister*	£83,826
Cabinet Secretaries*	£43,227
Lord Advocate*	£56,473
Solicitor-General for Scotland*	£40,837
Ministers*	£27,077
MSPs†	£57,521
Presiding Officer*	£43,227
Deputy Presiding Officer*	£27,077

* In addition to the MSP salary
† Reduced by two-thirds if the member is already an MP or an MEP

MEMBERS OF THE SCOTTISH PARLIAMENT

as at 29 June 2010

Adam, Brian, *SNP, Aberdeen North,* Maj. 3,749
Aitken, Bill, *C., Glasgow region*
Alexander, Wendy, *Lab., Paisley North,* Maj. 5,113
Allan, Alasdair, *SNP, Western Isles,* Maj. 687
Baillie, Jackie, *Lab., Dumbarton,* Maj. 1,611
Baker, Claire, *Lab., Mid Scotland and Fife region*
Baker, Richard, *Lab., North East Scotland region*
Boyack, Sarah, *Lab., Edinburgh Central,* Maj. 1,193
Brankin, Rhona, *Lab., Midlothian,* Maj. 1,702
Brocklebank, Ted, *C., Mid Scotland and Fife region*
Brown, Gavin, *C., Lothians region*
Brown, Keith, *SNP, Ochil,* Maj. 490
Brown, Robert E., *LD, Glasgow region*
Brownlee, Derek, *C., South of Scotland region*
Butler, Bill, *Lab., Glasgow Anniesland,* Maj. 4,306
Campbell, Aileen, *SNP, South of Scotland region*
Carlaw, Jackson, *C., West of Scotland region*
Chisholm, Malcolm, *Lab., Edinburgh North and Leith,* Maj. 2,444
Coffey, Willie, *SNP, Kilmarnock and Loudon,* Maj. 1,342
Constance, Angela, *SNP, Livingston,* Maj. 870
Craigie, Cathie, *Lab., Cumbernauld and Kilsyth,* Maj. 2,079
Crawford, Bruce, *SNP, Stirling,* Maj. 620
Cunningham, Roseanna, *SNP, Perth,* Maj. 2,495
Curran, Margaret, *Lab., Glasgow Baillieston,* Maj. 3,934
Don, Nigel, *SNP, North East Scotland region*
Doris, Bob, *SNP, Glasgow region*
Eadie, Helen, *Lab., Dunfermline East,* Maj. 3,993
Ewing, Fergus, *SNP, Inverness East, Nairn and Lochaber,* Maj. 5,471
Fabiani, Linda, *SNP, Central Scotland region*
Ferguson, Patricia, *Lab., Glasgow Maryhill,* Maj. 2,310
Fergusson, Alex, *C., Galloway and Upper Nithsdale,* Maj. 3,333
Finnie, Ross, *LD, West of Scotland region*
FitzPatrick, Joe, *SNP, Dundee West,* Maj. 1,946
Foulkes, George, *Lab., Lothians region*
Fraser, Murdo, *C., Mid Scotland and Fife region*
Gibson, Kenneth, *SNP, Cunninghame North,* Maj. 48
Gibson, Rob, *SNP, Highlands and Islands region*
Gillon, Karen, *Lab., Clydesdale,* Maj. 2,893
Glen, Marlyn, *Lab., North East Scotland region*
Godman, Trish, *Lab., Renfrewshire West,* Maj. 2,178
Goldie, Annabel, *C., West of Scotland region*
Gordon, Charlie, *Lab., Glasgow Cathcart,* Maj. 2,189
Grahame, Christine, *SNP, South of Scotland region*
Grant, Rhoda, *Lab., Highlands and Islands region*
Gray, Iain, *Lab., East Lothian,* Maj. 2,448
Harper, Robin, *Scot. Green, Lothians region*

Harvie, Christopher, *SNP, Mid Scotland and Fife region*
Harvie, Patrick, *Scot. Green, Glasgow region*
Henry, Hugh, *Lab., Paisley South,* Maj. 4,230
Hepburn, Jamie, *SNP, Central Scotland region*
Hume, Jim, *LD, South of Scotland region*
Hyslop, Fiona, *SNP, Lothians region*
Ingram, Adam, *SNP, South of Scotland region*
Jamieson, Cathy, *Lab., Carrick, Cumnock and Doon Valley,* Maj. 3,986
Johnstone, Alex, *C., North East Scotland region*
Kelly, James, *Lab., Glasgow Rutherglen,* Maj. 4,378
Kerr, Andy, *Lab., East Kilbride,* Maj. 1,972
Kidd, Bill, *SNP, Glasgow region*
Lamont, Johann, *Lab., Glasgow Pollok,* Maj. 4,393
Lamont, John, *C., Roxburgh and Berwickshire,* Maj. 1,985
Livingstone, Marilyn, *Lab., Kirkcaldy,* Maj. 2,622
Lochhead, Richard, *SNP, Moray,* Maj. 7,924
MacAskill, Kenny, *SNP, Edinburgh East and Musselburgh,* Maj. 1,382
Macdonald, Lewis, *Lab., Aberdeen Central,* Maj. 382
MacDonald, Margo, *Ind., Lothians region*
Macintosh, Kenneth, *Lab., Eastwood,* Maj. 913
McArthur, Liam, *LD, Orkney,* Maj. 2,476
McAveety, Frank, *Lab., Glasgow Shettleston,* Maj. 2,881
McCabe, Tom, *Lab., Hamilton South,* Maj. 3,652
McConnell, Jack, *Lab., Motherwell and Wishaw,* Maj. 5,938
McGrigor, Jamie, *C., Highlands and Islands region*
McInnes, Alison, *LD, North East Scotland region*
McKee, Ian, *SNP, Lothians region*
McKelvie, Christina, *SNP, Central Scotland region*
***McLaughlin**, Anne, *SNP, Glasgow*
McLetchie, David, *C., Edinburgh Pentlands,* Maj. 4,525
McMahon, Michael, *Lab., Hamilton North and Bellshill,* Maj. 4,865
McMillan, Stuart, *SNP, West of Scotland region*
McNeil, Duncan, *Lab., Greenock and Inverclyde,* Maj. 3,024
McNeill, Pauline, *Lab., Glasgow Kelvin,* Maj. 1,207
McNulty, Des, *Lab., Clydebank and Milngavie,* Maj. 3,179
Martin, Paul, *Lab., Glasgow Springburn,* Maj. 5,095
Marwick, Tricia, *SNP, Central Fife,* Maj. 1,166
Mather, Jim, *SNP, Argyll and Bute,* Maj. 815
Matheson, Michael, *SNP, Falkirk West,* Maj. 776
Maxwell, Stewart, *SNP, West of Scotland region*
Milne, Nanette, *C., North East Scotland region*
Mitchell, Margaret, *C., Central Scotland region*
Morgan, Alasdair, *SNP, South of Scotland region*
Mulligan, Mary, *Lab., Linlithgow,* Maj. 1,160
Munro, John F., *LD, Ross, Skye and Inverness West,* Maj. 3,486
Murray, Elaine, *Lab., Dumfries,* Maj. 2,839
Neil, Alex, *SNP, Central Scotland region*
O'Donnell, Hugh, *LD, Central Scotland region*
Oldfather, Irene, *Lab., Cunninghame South,* Maj. 2,168
Park, John, *Lab., Mid Scotland and Fife region*
Paterson, Gil, *SNP, West of Scotland region*
Peacock, Peter, *Lab., Highlands and Islands region*
Peattie, Cathy, *Lab., Falkirk East,* Maj. 1,872
Pringle, Michael, *LD, Edinburgh South,* Maj. 1,929
Purvis, Jeremy, *LD, Tweeddale, Ettrick and Lauderdale,* Maj. 598
Robison, Shona, *SNP, Dundee East,* Maj. 4,524
Rumbles, Mike, *LD, Aberdeenshire West and Kincardine,* Maj. 5,170
Russell, Michael, *SNP, South of Scotland region*
Salmond, Alex, *SNP, Gordon,* Maj. 2,062
Scanlon, Mary, *C., Highlands and Islands region*
Scott, John, *C., Ayr,* Maj. 3,906
Scott, Tavish, *LD, Shetland,* Maj. 4,909
Simpson, Richard, *Lab., Mid Scotland and Fife region*
Smith, Elaine, *Lab., Coatbridge and Chryston,* Maj. 4,510
Smith, Elizabeth, *C., Mid Scotland and Fife region*
Smith, Iain, *LD, Fife North East,* Maj. 5,016
Smith, Margaret, *LD, Edinburgh West,* Maj. 5,886
†Somerville, Shirley-Anne, *SNP, Lothians region*
Stephen, Nicol, *LD, Aberdeen South,* Maj. 2,732
Stevenson, Stewart, *SNP, Banff and Buchan,* Maj. 10,530
Stewart, David, *Lab., Highlands and Islands region*
Stone, Jamie, *LD, Caithness, Sutherland and Easter Ross,* Maj. 2,323
Sturgeon, Nicola, *SNP, Glasgow Govan,* Maj. 744
Swinney, John, *SNP, North Tayside,* Maj. 7,584
Thompson, Dave, *SNP, Highlands and Islands region*
Tolson, Jim, *LD, Dunfermline West,* Maj. 476
Watt, Maureen, *SNP, North East Scotland region*
Welsh, Andrew, *SNP, Angus,* Maj. 8,243
White, Sandra, *SNP, Glasgow region*
Whitefield, Karen, *Lab., Airdrie and Shotts,* Maj. 1,446
Whitton, David, *Lab., Strathkelvin and Bearsden,* Maj. 3,388
Wilson, Bill, *SNP, West of Scotland region*
Wilson, John, *SNP, Central Scotland region*

* Bashir Ahmad died on 6 February 2009 and was replaced by Anne McLaughlin on 9 February 2009
† Stefan Tymkewycz stepped down after his election to the Scottish parliament and was replaced by Shirley-Anne Somerville on 31 August 2007

STATE OF THE PARTIES *as at 29 June 2010*

	Constituency MSPs	*Regional MSPs*	*Total*
Scottish National Party (SNP)	21	26	47
Scottish Labour Party (Lab.)	37	9	46
Scottish Conservative and Unionist Party (C.)	3	13	16
Scottish Liberal Democrats (LD)	11	5	16
Scottish Green Party (Scot. Green)	0	2	2
Independent (Ind.)	0	1	1
Presiding Officer‡	1	0	1
Total	73	56	129

‡ The presiding officer was elected as a constituency member for the Conservatives but has no party allegiance while in post

The Presiding Officer, Alex Fergusson, MSP
Deputy Presiding Officers, Trish Godman, MSP *(Lab.);* Alasdair Morgan, MSP *(SNP)*

SCOTTISH PARLIAMENT ELECTION RESULTS

as at 3 May 2007

E. Electorate T. Turnout

See General Election Results for a list of party abbreviations

CONSTITUENCIES
E. 3,899,472 T. 51.7%

ABERDEEN CENTRAL
(Scotland North East Region)
E. 46,588 T. 21,120 (45.33%)

Lewis Macdonald, Lab.	7,232
Karen Shirron, SNP	6,850
John Stewart, LD	4,693
Andrew Jones, C.	2,345

Lab. majority 382 (1.81%)
2.06% swing Lab. to SNP

ABERDEEN NORTH
(Scotland North East Region)
E. 51,507 T. 24,891 (48.33%)

Brian Adam, SNP	11,406
Elaine Thomson, Lab.	7,657
Steve Delaney, LD	3,836
Carol Garvie, C.	1,992

SNP majority 3,749 (15.06%)
6.62% swing Lab. to SNP

ABERDEEN SOUTH
(Scotland North East Region)
E. 56,700 T. 29,885 (52.71%)

Nicol Stephen, LD	10,843
Maureen Watt, SNP	8,111
Rami Okasha, Lab.	5,499
David Davidson, C.	5,432

LD majority 2,732 (9.14%)
11.21% swing LD to SNP

ABERDEENSHIRE WEST AND KINCARDINE
(Scotland North East Region)
E. 65,233 T. 34,823 (53.38%)

Mike Rumbles, LD	14,314
Dennis Robertson, SNP	9,144
Stewart Whyte, C.	8,604
James Noble, Lab.	2,761

LD majority 5,170 (14.85%)
8.48% swing LD to SNP

AIRDRIE AND SHOTTS
(Scotland Central Region)
E. 57,660 T. 27,160 (47.10%)

Karen Whitefield, Lab.	11,907
Sophia Coyle, SNP	10,461
Iain McGill, C.	2,370
Robert Gorrie, LD	1,452
Mev Brown, Scottish Voice	970

Lab. majority 1,446 (5.32%)
15.23% swing Lab. to SNP

ANGUS
(Scotland North East Region)
E. 61,362 T. 31,960 (52.08%)

Andrew Welsh, SNP	15,686
Alex Johnstone, C.	7,443
Doug Bradley, Lab.	5,032
Scott Rennie, LD	3,799

SNP majority 8,243 (25.79%)
1.67% swing C. to SNP

ARGYLL AND BUTE
(Highlands and Islands Region)
E. 48,846 T. 28,792 (58.94%)

Jim Mather, SNP	9,944
George Lyon, LD	9,129
Jamie McGrigor, C.	5,571
Mary Galbraith, Lab.	4,148

SNP majority 815 (2.83%)
9.17% swing LD to SNP

AYR
(Scotland South Region)
E. 55,034 T. 31,025 (56.37%)

John Scott, C.	12,619
John Duncan, Lab.	8,713
Iain White, SNP	7,952
Stuart Ritchie, LD	1,741

C. majority 3,906 (12.59%)
3.30% swing Lab. to C.

BANFF AND BUCHAN
(Scotland North East Region)
E. 56,324 T. 27,285 (48.44%)

Stewart Stevenson, SNP	16,031
Geordie Burnett-Stuart, C.	5,501
Kay Barnett, Lab.	3,136
Alison McInnes, LD	2,617

SNP majority 10,530 (38.59%)
3.30% swing C. to SNP

CAITHNESS, SUTHERLAND AND EASTER ROSS
(Highlands and Islands Region)
E. 41,789 T. 22,334 (53.44%)

Jamie Stone, LD	8,981
Rob Gibson, SNP	6,658
John McKendrick, Lab.	3,152
Donald MacDonald, C.	2,586
Gordon Campbell, Ind.	957

LD majority 2,323 (10.40%)
4.38% swing LD to SNP

CARRICK, CUMNOCK AND DOON VALLEY
(Scotland South Region)
E. 65,166 T. 33,785 (51.84%)

Cathy Jamieson, Lab.	14,350
Adam Ingram, SNP	10,364
Tony Lewis, C.	6,729
Paul McGreal, LD	1,409
Hugh Hill, Ind.	809
Ray Barry, Equal Parenting Alliance	124

Lab. majority 3,986 (11.80%)
9.61% swing Lab. to SNP

CLYDEBANK AND MILNGAVIE
(Scotland West Region)
E. 48,700 T. 26,765 (54.96%)

Des McNulty, Lab.	11,617
Gil Paterson, SNP	8,438
Murray Roxburgh, C.	3,544
Ashay Ghai, LD	3,166

Lab. majority 3,179 (11.88%)
2.61% swing Lab. to SNP

CLYDESDALE
(Scotland South Region)
E. 66,011 T. 33,332 (50.49%)

Karen Gillon, Lab.	13,835
Aileen Campbell, SNP	10,942
Colin McGavigan, C.	5,604
Fraser Grieve, LD	2,951

Lab. majority 2,893 (8.68%)
5.94% swing Lab. to SNP

COATBRIDGE AND CHRYSTON
(Scotland Central Region)
E. 54,423 T. 25,725 (47.27%)

Elaine Smith, Lab.	11,860
Frances McGlinchey, SNP	7,350
Ross Thomson, C.	2,305
Julie McAnulty, Ind.	1,843
Doreen Nisbet, LD	1,519
Gaille McCann, Scottish Voice	848

Lab. majority 4,510 (17.53%)
9.19% swing Lab. to SNP

CUMBERNAULD AND KILSYTH
(Scotland Central Region)
E. 49,197 T. 26,382 (53.63%)

Cathie Craigie, Lab.	12,672
Jamie Hepburn, SNP	10,593
Hugh O'Donnell, LD	1,670
Anne Harding, C.	1,447

Lab. majority 2,079 (7.88%)
2.87% swing SNP to Lab.

CUNNINGHAME NORTH
(Scotland West Region)
E. 55,925 T. 30,241 (54.07%)

Kenneth Gibson, SNP	9,295
Allan Wilson, Lab.	9,247
Philip Lardner, C.	5,466
Campbell Martin, Ind.	4,423
Lewis Hutton, LD	1,810

SNP majority 48 (0.16%)
5.99% swing Lab. to SNP

CUNNINGHAME SOUTH
(Scotland South Region)
E. 49,969 T. 23,422 (46.87%)

Irene Oldfather, Lab.	10,270
Duncan Ross, SNP	8,102
Pat McPhee, C.	3,073
Iain Dale, LD	1,977

Lab. majority 2,168 (9.26%)
8.71% swing Lab. to SNP

DUMBARTON
(Scotland West Region)
E. 54,023 T. 30,054 (55.63%)

Jackie Baillie, Lab.	11,635
Graeme McCormick, SNP	10,024
Brian Pope, C.	4,701
Alex Mackie, LD	3,385
John Black, Scottish Jacobite Party	309

Lab. majority 1,611 (5.36%)
8.79% swing Lab. to SNP

DUMFRIES
(Scotland South Region)
E. 53,518 T. 33,419 (62.44%)

Elaine Murray, Lab.	13,707
Murray Tosh, C.	10,868
Michael Russell, SNP	6,306
Lynne Hume, LD	2,538

Lab. majority 2,839 (8.50%)
2.54% swing C. to Lab.

DUNDEE EAST
(Scotland North East Region)
E. 53,804 T. 26,869 (49.94%)

Shona Robison, SNP	13,314
Iain Luke, Lab.	8,790
Chris Bustin, C.	2,976
Clive Sneddon, LD	1,789

SNP majority 4,524 (16.84%)
8.25% swing Lab. to SNP

DUNDEE WEST
(Scotland North East Region)
E. 49,711 T. 24,268 (48.82%)

Joe Fitzpatrick, SNP	10,955
Jill Shimi, Lab.	9,009
Michael Charlton, LD	2,517
Belinda Don, C.	1,787

SNP majority 1,946 (8.02%)
6.14% swing Lab. to SNP

DUNFERMLINE EAST
(Scotland Mid and Fife Region)
E. 51,115 T. 24,568 (48.06%)

Helen Eadie, Lab.	10,995
Ewan Dow, SNP	7,002
Graeme Brown, C.	3,718
Karen Utting, LD	2,853

Lab. majority 3,993 (16.25%)
7.62% swing Lab. to SNP

DUNFERMLINE WEST
(Scotland Mid and Fife Region)
E. 56,953 T. 29,525 (51.84%)

Jim Tolson, LD	9,952
Scott Barrie, Lab.	9,476
Len Woods, SNP	7,296
Peter Lyburn, C.	2,363
Susan Archibald, Scottish Voice	438

LD majority 476 (1.61%)
10.77% swing Lab. to LD

EAST KILBRIDE
(Scotland Central Region)
E. 66,935 T. 35,902 (53.64%)

Andy Kerr, Lab.	15,334
Linda Fabiani, SNP	13,362
Graham Simpson, C.	4,114
David Clark, LD	3,092

Lab. majority 1,972 (5.49%)
5.00% swing Lab. to SNP

EAST LOTHIAN
(Scotland South Region)
E. 61,378 T. 34,471 (56.16%)

Iain Gray, Lab.	12,219
Andrew Sharp, SNP	9,771
Judy Hayman, LD	6,249
Bill Stevenson, C.	6,232

Lab. majority 2,448 (7.10%)
10.08% swing Lab. to SNP

EASTWOOD
(Scotland West Region)
E. 67,347 T. 42,187 (62.64%)

Ken Macintosh, Lab.	15,099
Jackson Carlaw, C.	14,186
Stewart Maxwell, SNP	7,972
Gordon MacDonald, LD	3,603
Frank McGhee, Ind.	1,327

Lab. majority 913 (2.16%)
3.68% swing Lab. to C.

EDINBURGH CENTRAL
(Lothians Region)
E. 55,953 T. 29,396 (52.54%)

Sarah Boyack, Lab.	9,155
Siobhan Mathers, LD	7,962
Shirley-Anne Somerville, SNP	7,496
Fiona Houston, C.	4,783

Lab. majority 1,193 (4.06%)
2.73% swing Lab. to LD

EDINBURGH EAST AND MUSSELBURGH
(Lothians Region)
E. 56,578 T. 29,967 (52.97%)

Kenny MacAskill, SNP	11,209
Norman Murray, Lab.	9,827
Gillian Cole-Hamilton, LD	5,473
Christine Wright, C.	3,458

SNP majority 1,382 (4.61%)
12.91% swing Lab. to SNP

EDINBURGH NORTH AND LEITH
(Lothians Region)
E. 60,340 T. 31,685 (52.51%)

Malcolm Chisholm, Lab.	11,020
Mike Crockart, LD	8,576
Davie Hutchison, SNP	8,044
Iain Whyte, C.	4,045

Lab. majority 2,444 (7.71%)
6.92% swing Lab. to LD

EDINBURGH PENTLANDS
(Lothians Region)
E. 57,891 T. 34,377 (59.38%)

David McLetchie, C.	12,927
Sheila Gilmore, Lab.	8,402
Ian McKee, SNP	8,234
Simon Clark, LD	4,814

C. majority 4,525 (13.16%)
3.42% swing Lab. to C.

EDINBURGH SOUTH
(Lothians Region)
E. 57,621 T. 32,573 (56.53%)

Mike Pringle, LD	11,398
Donald Anderson, Lab.	9,469
Robert Holland, SNP	6,117
Gavin Brown, C.	5,589

LD majority 1,929 (5.92%)
2.71% swing Lab. to LD

EDINBURGH WEST
(Lothians Region)
E. 59,814 T. 34,752 (58.10%)

Margaret Smith, LD	13,677
Sheena Cleland, SNP	7,791
Gordon Lindhurst, C.	7,361
Richard Meade, Lab.	5,343
John Wilson, Ind.	580

LD majority 5,886 (16.94%)
7.00% swing LD to SNP

FALKIRK EAST
(Scotland Central Region)
E. 57,663 T. 30,333 (52.60%)

Cathy Peattie, Lab.	13,184
Annabelle Ewing, SNP	11,312
Scott Campbell, C.	3,701
Natalie Maver, LD	2,136

Lab. majority 1,872 (6.17%)
9.00% swing Lab. to SNP

FALKIRK WEST
(Scotland Central Region)
E. 56,254 T. 28,785 (51.17%)

Michael Matheson, SNP	12,068
Dennis Goldie, Lab.	11,292
Stephen O'Rourke, C.	2,887
Callum Chomczuk, LD	2,538

SNP majority 776 (2.70%)
1.13% swing Lab. to SNP

FIFE CENTRAL
(Scotland Mid and Fife Region)
E. 58,215 T. 26,965 (46.32%)

Tricia Marwick, SNP	11,920
Christine May, Lab.	10,754
Elizabeth Riches, LD	2,288
Maurice Golden, C.	2,003

SNP majority 1,166 (4.32%)
7.56% swing Lab. to SNP

FIFE NORTH EAST
(Scotland Mid and Fife Region)
E. 61,078 T. 31,552 (51.66%)

Iain Smith, LD	13,307
Ted Brocklebank, C.	8,291
Roderick Campbell, SNP	6,735
Kenny Young, Lab.	2,557
Tony Campbell, Ind.	662

LD majority 5,016 (15.90%)
0.68% swing LD to C.

GALLOWAY AND UPPER NITHSDALE
(Scotland South Region)
E. 52,583 T. 30,318 (57.66%)

Alex Fergusson, C.	13,387
Alasdair Morgan, SNP	10,054
Stephen Hodgson, Lab.	4,935
Alastair Cooper, LD	1,631
Sandy Richardson, Ind.	311

C. majority 3,333 (10.99%)
5.33% swing SNP to C.

GLASGOW ANNIESLAND
(Glasgow Region)
E. 48,344 T. 22,139 (45.79%)

Bill Butler, Lab.	10,483
Bill Kidd, SNP	6,177
Bill Aitken, C.	3,154
Danica Gilland, LD	2,325

Lab. majority 4,306 (19.45%)
4.38% swing Lab. to SNP

GLASGOW BAILLIESTON
(Glasgow Region)
E. 44,367 T. 17,272 (38.93%)

Margaret Curran, Lab.	9,141
Lachie McNeill, SNP	5,207
Richard Sullivan, C.	1,276
David Jackson, LD	1,060
George Hargreaves, Scottish Christian Party	588

Lab. majority 3,934 (22.78%)
5.52% swing Lab. to SNP

GLASGOW CATHCART
(Glasgow Region)
E. 47,822 T. 21,657 (45.29%)

Charlie Gordon, Lab.	8,476
James Dornan, SNP	6,287
David Smith, Ind.	2,911
Davena Rankin, C.	2,324
Shabnum Mustapha, LD	1,659

Lab. majority 2,189 (10.11%)
6.40% swing Lab. to SNP

GLASGOW GOVAN
(Glasgow Region)
E. 47,405 T. 21,521 (45.40%)

Nicola Sturgeon, SNP	9,010
Gordon Jackson, Lab.	8,266
Chris Young, LD	1,891
Martyn McIntyre, C.	1,680
Asif Nasir, Ind.	423
Elinor McKenzie, Comm. Brit.	251

SNP majority 744 (3.46%)
4.65% swing Lab. to SNP

GLASGOW KELVIN
(Glasgow Region)
E. 55,096 T. 23,500 (42.65%)

Pauline McNeill, Lab.	7,875
Sandra White, SNP	6,668
Martin Bartos, Green	2,971
Katy Gordon, LD	2,843
Brian Cooklin, C.	1,943
Niall Walker, Ind.	744
Isobel Macleod, Scottish Christian Party	456

Lab. majority 1,207 (5.14%)
4.88% swing Lab. to SNP

GLASGOW MARYHILL
(Glasgow Region)
E. 46,060 T. 16,564 (35.96%)

Patricia Ferguson, Lab.	7,955
Bob Doris, SNP	5,645
Kenn Elder, LD	1,936
Heather MacLeod, C.	1,028

Lab. majority 2,310 (13.95%)
7.74% swing Lab. to SNP

GLASGOW POLLOK
(Glasgow Region)
E. 47,189 T. 19,416 (41.15%)

Johann Lamont, Lab.	10,456
Chris Stephens, SNP	6,063
Gerald Michaluk, C.	1,460
Christine Gilmore, LD	1,437

Lab. majority 4,393 (22.63%)
0.85% swing Lab. to SNP

GLASGOW RUTHERGLEN
(Glasgow Region)
E. 50,005 T. 24,252 (48.50%)

James Kelly, Lab.	10,237
Margaret Park, SNP	5,857
Robert Brown, LD	5,516
Christina Harcus, C.	2,094
Tom Greig, Scottish Christian Party	548

Lab. majority 4,380 (18.06%)
6.43% swing Lab. to SNP

GLASGOW SHETTLESTON
(Glasgow Region)
E. 44,278 T. 14,801 (33.43%)

Frank McAveety, Lab.	7,574
John McLaughlin, SNP	4,693
Ross Renton, LD	1,182
William MacNair, C.	946
Bob Graham, Scottish Christian Party	406

Lab. majority 2,881 (19.46%)
9.45% swing Lab. to SNP

GLASGOW SPRINGBURN
(Glasgow Region)
E. 47,021 T. 17,612 (37.46%)

Paul Martin, Lab.	10,024
Anne McLaughlin, SNP	4,929
Katy McCloskey, LD	1,108
Gordon Wilson, C.	1,067
David Johnston, Scottish Christian Party	484

Lab. majority 5,095 (28.93%)
7.09% swing Lab. to SNP

GORDON
(Scotland North East Region)
E. 65,431 T. 35,363 (54.05%)

Alex Salmond, SNP	14,650
Nora Radcliffe, LD	12,588
Nanette Milne, C.	5,348
Neil Cardwell, Lab.	2,276
Donald Marr, Ind.	199
Dave Mathers, Ind.	185
Bob Ingram, Scottish Enterprise Party	117

SNP majority 2,062 (5.83%)
10.66% swing LD to SNP

GREENOCK AND INVERCLYDE
(Scotland West Region)
E. 44,646 T. 23,105 (51.75%)

Duncan McNeil, Lab.	10,035
Stuart McMillan, SNP	7,011
Ross Finnie, LD	3,893
Charles Ferguson, C.	2,166

Lab. majority 3,024 (13.09%)
6.37% swing Lab. to SNP

HAMILTON NORTH AND BELLSHILL
(Scotland Central Region)
E. 53,854 T. 25,366 (47.10%)

Michael McMahon, Lab.	12,334
Alex Neil, SNP	7,469
James Callander, C.	2,835
Douglas Herbison, LD	1,726
Joe Gorman, Scottish Voice	571
Gordon Weir, Ind.	431

Lab. majority 4,865 (19.18%)
6.75% swing Lab. to SNP

HAMILTON SOUTH
(Scotland Central Region)
E. 48,838 T. 23,211 (47.53%)

Tom McCabe, Lab.	10,280
Christina McKelvie, SNP	6,628
Margaret Mitchell, C.	2,929
Michael McGlynn, Ind.	1,764
John Oswald, LD	1,610

Lab. majority 3,652 (15.73%)
3.89% swing Lab. to SNP

INVERNESS EAST, NAIRN AND LOCHABER
(Highlands and Islands Region)
E. 71,609 T. 39,609 (55.31%)

Fergus Ewing, SNP	16,443
Craig Harrow, LD	10,972
Linda Stewart, Lab.	7,559
Jamie Halcro-Johnston, C.	4,635

SNP majority 5,471 (13.81%)
0.48% swing SNP to LD

KILMARNOCK AND LOUDOUN
(Scotland Central Region)
E. 60,753 T. 33,435 (55.03%)

Willie Coffey, SNP	14,297
Margaret Jamieson, Lab.	12,955
Janette McAlpine, C.	4,127
Ron Aitken, LD	2,056

SNP majority 1,342 (4.01%)
3.93% swing Lab. to SNP

KIRKCALDY
(Scotland Mid and Fife Region)
E. 50,761 T. 24,195 (47.66%)

Marilyn Livingstone, Lab.	10,627
Chris Harvie, SNP	8,005
Alice Soper, LD	3,361
David Potts, C.	2,202

Lab. majority 2,622 (10.84%)
5.58% swing Lab. to SNP

LINLITHGOW
(Lothians Region)
E. 56,175 T. 29,637 (52.76%)

Mary Mulligan, Lab.	12,715
Fiona Hyslop, SNP	11,565
Donald Cameron, C.	3,125
Martin Oliver, LD	2,232

Lab. majority 1,150 (3.88%)
1.62% swing Lab. to SNP

LIVINGSTON
(Lothians Region)
E. 66,348 T. 33,224 (50.08%)

Angela Constance, SNP	13,159
Bristow Muldoon, Lab.	12,289
Ernie Walker, Action to Save St John's Hospital	2,814
David Brown, C.	2,804
Evan Bell, LD	2,158

SNP majority 870 (2.62%)
7.31% swing Lab. to SNP

MIDLOTHIAN
(Lothians Region)
E. 48,395 T. 25,111 (51.89%)

Rhona Brankin, Lab.	10,671
Colin Beattie, SNP	8,969
Ross Laird, LD	2,704
P. J. Lewis, C.	2,269
George McCleery, Had Enough Party	498

Lab. majority 1,702 (6.78%)
8.37% swing Lab. to SNP

MORAY
(Highlands and Islands Region)
E. 60,959 T. 30,274 (49.66%)

Richard Lochhead, SNP	15,045
Mary Scanlon, C.	7,121
Lee Butcher, Lab.	4,580
Dominique Rommel, LD	3,528

SNP majority 7,924 (26.17%)
3.24% swing C. to SNP

MOTHERWELL AND WISHAW
(Scotland Central Region)
E. 53,875 T. 26,150 (48.54%)

Jack McConnell, Lab.	12,574
Marion Fellows, SNP	6,636
Diane Huddleston, C.	1,990
John Swinburne, SSCUP	1,702
Stuart Douglas, LD	1,570
Tom Selfridge, Scottish Christian Party	1,491
Richard Leat, Anti-Trident Party	187

Lab. majority 5,938 (22.71%)
6.88% swing Lab. to SNP

OCHIL
(Scotland Mid and Fife Region)
E. 58,104 T. 31,553 (54.30%)

Keith Brown, SNP	12,147
Brian Fearon, Lab.	11,657
George Murray, C.	4,284
Lorraine Caddell, LD	3,465

SNP majority 490 (1.55%)
0.29% swing Lab. to SNP

ORKNEY
(Highlands and Islands Region)
E. 16,195 T. 8,653 (53.43%)

Liam McArthur, LD	4,113
John Mowat, SNP	1,637
Helen Gardiner, C.	1,632
Iain MacDonald, Lab.	1,134
Barrie Johnson, Ind.	137

LD majority 2,476 (28.61%)
1.95% swing LD to SNP

PAISLEY NORTH
(Scotland West Region)
E. 44,081 T. 23,206 (52.64%)

Wendy Alexander, Lab.	12,111
Andy Doig, SNP	6,998
Malcolm MacAskill, C.	1,721
Angela McGarrigle, LD	1,570
Iain Hogg, SSP	525
John Plott, Ind.	281

Lab. majority 5,113 (22.03%)
1.31% swing SNP to Lab.

PAISLEY SOUTH
(Scotland West Region)
E. 49,175 T. 25,527 (51.91%)

Hugh Henry, Lab.	12,123
Fiona McLeod, SNP	7,893
Eileen McCartin, LD	3,434
Tom Begg, C.	2,077

Lab. majority 4,230 (16.57%)
3.38% swing SNP to Lab.

PERTH
(Scotland and Mid Fife Region)
E. 62,220 T. 34,862 (56.03%)

Roseanna Cunningham, SNP	13,751
Liz Smith, C.	11,256
Peter Barrett, LD	4,767
Doug Maughan, Lab.	4,513
Jim Fairlie, Free Scot.	575

SNP majority 2,495 (7.16%)
2.43% swing C. to SNP

RENFREWSHIRE WEST
(Scotland West Region)
E. 50,787 T. 29,129 (57.36%)

Trish Godman, Lab.	10,467
Annabel Goldie, C.	8,289
Bill Wilson, SNP	8,167
Simon Hutton, LD	2,206

Lab. majority 2,178 (7.48%)
1.22% swing Lab. to C.

ROSS, SKYE AND INVERNESS WEST
(Highlands and Islands Region)
E. 59,237 T. 31,719 (53.55%)

John Farquhar Munro, LD	13,501
Dave Thompson, SNP	10,015
Maureen Macmillan, Lab.	4,789
John Hodgson, C.	3,122
Iain Brodie, Scottish Enterprise Party	292

LD majority 3,486 (10.99%)
6.32% swing LD to SNP

ROXBURGH AND BERWICKSHIRE
(Scotland South Region)
E. 47,862 T. 25,680 (53.65%)

John Lamont, C.	10,556
Euan Robson, LD	8,571
Aileen Orr, SNP	4,127
Mary Lockhart, Lab.	2,108
Jesse Rae, No Description	318

C. majority 1,985 (7.73%)
9.40% swing LD to C.

SHETLAND
(Highlands and Islands Region)
E. 17,108 T. 9,795 (57.25%)

Tavish Scott, LD	6,531
Val Simpson, SNP	1,622
Mark Jones, C.	972
Scott Burnett, Lab.	670

LD majority 4,909 (50.12%)
11.99% swing SNP to LD

STIRLING
(Scotland and Mid Fife Region)
E. 52,864 T. 32,625 (61.71%)

Bruce Crawford, SNP	10,447
Sylvia Jackson, Lab.	9,827
Bob Dalrymple, C.	8,081
Alex Cole-Hamilton, LD	3,693
Liz Law, Peace Party	577

SNP majority 620 (1.90%)
9.41% swing Lab. to SNP

STRATHKELVIN AND BEARSDEN
(Scotland West Region)
E. 60,389 T. 36,595 (60.60%)

David Whitton, Lab.	11,396
Robin Easton, SNP	8,008
Jean Turner, Ind.	6,742
Stephanie Fraser, C.	5,178
Cathy McInnes, LD	4,658
Bob Handyside, Scottish Christian Party	613

Lab. majority 3,388 (9.26%)
3.91% swing Lab. to SNP

TAYSIDE NORTH
(Scotland Mid and Fife Region)
E. 62,133 T. 35,396 (56.97%)

John Swinney, SNP	18,281
Murdo Fraser, C.	10,697
Michael Marna, Lab.	3,243
James Taylor, LD	3,175

SNP majority 7,584 (21.43%)
3.96% swing C. to SNP

TWEEDDALE, ETTRICK AND LAUDERDALE
(Scotland South Region)
E. 53,588 T. 30,327 (56.59%)

Jeremy Purvis, LD	10,656
Christine Grahame, SNP	10,058
Derek Brownlee, C.	5,594
Catherine Maxwell-Stuart, Lab.	4,019

LD majority 598 (1.97%)
0.02% swing LD to SNP

WESTERN ISLES
(Highlands and Islands Region)
E. 22,051 T. 13,625 (61.79%)

Alasdair Allan, SNP	6,354
Alasdair Morrison, Lab.	5,667
Ruaraidh Ferguson, LD	852
Dave Petrie, C.	752

SNP majority 687 (5.04%)
5.43% swing Lab. to SNP

REGIONS
E. 3,899,472 T. 52.4%

GLASGOW
E. 477,587 T. 206,618 (43.26%)

Lab.	78,838	(38.16%)
SNP	55,832	(27.02%)
LD	14,767	(7.15%)
C.	13,781	(6.67%)
Green	10,759	(5.21%)
Solidarity	8,525	(4.13%)
BNP	3,865	(1.87%)
SSCUP	3,703	(1.79%)
Scottish Christian Party	2,991	(1.45%)
Soc. Lab.	2,680	(1.30%)
CPA	2,626	(1.27%)
SSP	2,579	(1.25%)
Scottish Unionist Party	1,612	(0.78%)
Publican Party Smoking-Room in Pubs	952	(0.46%)
Ind. Shoaib	582	(0.28%)
Ind. Green	496	(0.24%)
UKIP	405	(0.20%)
Scottish Voice	389	(0.19%)
Ind. Nasir	317	(0.15%)
Scotland Against Crooked Lawyers	293	(0.14%)
Ind.	286	(0.14%)
Comm. Brit.	260	(0.13%)
Nine Per Cent Growth Party	80	(0.04%)

Lab. majority 23,006 (11.13%)
4.75% swing Lab. to SNP (2003 Lab. majority 42,146)

ADDITIONAL MEMBERS
Bill Aitken, *C.*
Robert Brown, *LD*
Bashir Ahmad, *SNP*
Sandra White, *SNP*
Bob Doris, *SNP*
Bill Kidd, *SNP*
Patrick Harvie, *Green*

HIGHLANDS AND ISLANDS
E. 337,794 T. 185,773 (55.00%)

SNP	63,979	(34.44%)
LD	37,001	(19.92%)
Lab.	32,952	(17.74%)
C.	23,334	(12.56%)
Green	8,602	(4.63%)
Scottish Christian Party	6,332	(3.41%)
SSCUP	3,841	(2.07%)
BNP	2,152	(1.16%)
Solidarity	1,833	(0.99%)
UKIP	1,287	(0.69%)
Soc. Lab.	1,027	(0.55%)
SSP	973	(0.52%)
Publican Party Smoking-Room in Pubs	914	(0.49%)
CPA	885	(0.48%)
Scottish Voice	450	(0.24%)
Scottish Enterprise Party	211	(0.11%)

SNP majority 26,978 (14.52%)
4.94% swing LD to SNP (2003 SNP majority 1,892)

ADDITIONAL MEMBERS
Mary Scanlon, *C.*
Jamie McGrigor, *C.*
Peter Peacock, *Lab.*
Rhoda Grant, *Lab.*
David Stewart, *Lab.*
Rob Gibson, *SNP*
Dave Thompson, *SNP*

LOTHIANS
E. 519,115 T. 287,039 (55.29%)

SNP	76,019	(26.48%)
Lab.	75,495	(26.30%)
C.	37,548	(13.08%)
LD	36,571	(12.74%)
Green	20,147	(7.02%)
Ind.	19,256	(6.71%)
SSCUP	4,176	(1.45%)
Solidarity	2,998	(1.04%)
BNP	2,637	(0.92%)
Soc. Lab.	2,190	(0.76%)
Scottish Christian Party	2,002	(0.70%)
SSP	1,994	(0.69%)
Publican Party Smoking-Room in Pubs	1,230	(0.43%)
Witchery Tour Party	867	(0.30%)
CPA	848	(0.30%)
UKIP	834	(0.29%)
Had Enough Party	670	(0.23%)
Scottish Voice	661	(0.23%)
Scotland Against Crooked Lawyers	322	(0.11%)
Ind. Scott	189	(0.07%)
Scottish Enterprise Party	183	(0.06%)
Ind. Wilson	129	(0.04%)
Ind. Thorp	73	(0.03%)

SNP majority 524 (0.18%)
4.22% swing Lab. to SNP (2003 Lab. majority 21,960)

ADDITIONAL MEMBERS
Gavin Brown, *C.*
George Foulkes, *Lab.*
Fiona Hyslop, *SNP*
Ian McKee, *SNP*
Stefan Tymkewycz, *SNP*
Robin Harper, *Green*
Margo MacDonald, *Ind.*

SCOTLAND CENTRAL
E. 559,452 T. 284,512 (50.86%)

Lab.	112,596	(39.58%)
SNP	89,210	(31.36%)
C.	24,253	(8.52%)
LD	14,648	(5.15%)
Green	7,204	(2.53%)
SSCUP	7,060	(2.48%)
Scottish Christian Party	5,575	(1.96%)
Solidarity	5,012	(1.76%)
CPA	4,617	(1.62%)
BNP	4,125	(1.45%)
Soc. Lab.	2,303	(0.81%)
SSP	2,188	(0.77%)
Scottish Voice	1,955	(0.69%)
Scottish Unionist Party	1,544	(0.54%)
Publican Party Smoking-Room in Pubs	1,500	(0.53%)
UKIP	722	(0.25%)

Lab. majority 23,386 (8.22%)
4.83% swing Lab. to SNP (2003 Lab. majority 47,044)

ADDITIONAL MEMBERS
Margaret Mitchell, *C.*
Hugh O'Donnell, *LD*
Alex Neil, *SNP*
Linda Fabiani, *SNP*
Jamie Hepburn, *SNP*
Christina McKelvie, *SNP*
John Wilson, *SNP*

SCOTLAND MID AND FIFE,
E. 513,443 T. 273,083 (53.19%)

SNP	90,090 (32.99%)
Lab.	71,922 (26.34%)
C.	44,341 (16.24%)
LD	36,195 (13.25%)
Green	10,318 (3.78%)
SSCUP	5,523 (2.02%)
BNP	2,620 (0.96%)
Solidarity	2,468 (0.90%)
Scottish Christian Party	1,698 (0.62%)
UKIP	1,587 (0.58%)
Soc. Lab.	1,523 (0.56%)
Publican Party Smoking-Room in Pubs	1,309 (0.48%)
SSP	1,116 (0.41%)
Scottish Voice	919 (0.34%)
CPA	790 (0.29%)
Free Scotland Party	664 (0.24%)

SNP majority 18,168 (6.65%)
4.45% swing Lab. to SNP (2003 Lab. majority 5,608)

ADDITIONAL MEMBERS
Murdo Fraser, *C.*
Liz Smith, *C.*
Ted Brocklebank, *C.*
John Park, *Lab.*
Claire Baker, *Lab.*
Richard Simpson, *Lab.*
Chris Harvie, *SNP*

SCOTLAND NORTH EAST
E. 506,660 T. 256,282 (50.58%)

SNP	105,265 (41.07%)
Lab.	52,125 (20.34%)
LD	40,934 (15.97%)
C.	37,666 (14.70%)
Green	8,148 (3.18%)
BNP	2,764 (1.08%)
Solidarity	2,004 (0.78%)
Scottish Christian Party	1,895 (0.74%)
CPA	1,173 (0.46%)
SSP	1,051 (0.41%)
UKIP	1,045 (0.41%)
SSCUP	930 (0.36%)
Scottish Voice	569 (0.22%)
Soc. Lab.	491 (0.19%)
Scottish Enterprise Party	222 (0.09%)

SNP majority 53,140 (20.73%)
6.82% swing Lab. to SNP (2003 SNP majority 17,274)

ADDITIONAL MEMBERS
Alex Johnstone, *C.*
Nanette Milne, *C.*
Richard Baker, *Lab.*
Marlyn Glen, *Lab.*
Alison McInnes, *LD*
Maureen Watt, *SNP*
Nigel Don, *SNP*

SCOTLAND SOUTH
E. 514,105 T. 276,910 (53.86%)
Lab. majority 2,709 (0.98%)

Lab.	79,762 (28.80%)
SNP	77,053 (27.83%)
C.	62,475 (22.56%)
LD	28,040 (10.13%)
Green	9,254 (3.34%)
SSCUP	5,335 (1.93%)
Solidarity	3,433 (1.24%)
BNP	3,212 (1.16%)
Scottish Christian Party	2,353 (0.85%)
Soc. Lab.	1,633 (0.59%)
UKIP	1,429 (0.52%)
SSP	1,114 (0.40%)
CPA	839 (0.30%)
Scottish Voice	490 (0.18%)
Ind.	488 (0.18%)

5.32% swing Lab. to SNP (2003 Lab. majority 15,128)

ADDITIONAL MEMBERS
Derek Brownlee, *C.*
Jim Hume, *LD*
Christine Grahame, *SNP*
Michael Russell, *SNP*
Adam Ingram, *SNP*
Alasdair Morgan, *SNP*
Aileen Campbell, *SNP*

SCOTLAND WEST
E. 475,073 T. 268,179 (56.45%)

Lab.	91,725 (34.20%)
SNP	75,953 (28.32%)
C.	40,637 (15.15%)
LD	22,515 (8.40%)
Green	8,152 (3.04%)
SSCUP	5,231 (1.95%)
Solidarity	4,774 (1.78%)
Scottish Christian Party	3,729 (1.39%)
BNP	3,241 (1.21%)
CPA	3,027 (1.13%)
Save Our NHS Group	2,682 (1.00%)
SSP	1,716 (0.64%)
Soc. Lab.	1,557 (0.58%)
Scottish Unionist Party	1,245 (0.46%)
UKIP	888 (0.33%)
Scottish Voice	522 (0.19%)
Scottish Jacobite Party	446 (0.17%)
Socialist Equality Party	139 (0.05%)

Lab. majority 15,772 (5.88%)
2.70% swing Lab. to SNP (2003 Lab. majority 12,351)

ADDITIONAL MEMBERS
Annabel Goldie, *C.*
Jackson Carlaw, *C.*
Ross Finnie, *LD*
Stewart Maxwell, *SNP*
Gil Paterson, *SNP*
Bill Wilson, *SNP*
Stuart McMillan, *SNP*

NORTHERN IRELAND

NORTHERN IRELAND EXECUTIVE

Stormont Castle, Stormont, Belfast BT4 3TT
T 028-9052 0700
W www.northernireland.gov.uk

The first minister and deputy first minister head the executive committee of ministers and, acting jointly, determine the total number of ministers in the executive. First and deputy first ministers are elected by Northern Ireland assembly members through a formula of parallel consent that requires a majority of designated unionists, a majority of designated nationalists and a majority of the whole assembly to vote in favour. The parties elected to the assembly select ministerial portfolios in proportion to party strengths using the d'Hondt nominating procedure.

The executive committee includes five DUP ministers, four SF ministers, two Ulster Unionist members, one Social Democratic and Labour Party minister and one Alliance minister alongside the first minister Peter Robinson, MLA of the DUP and the deputy first minister, Martin McGuinness, MLA, of SF.

EXECUTIVE COMMITTEE
First Minister, Rt. Hon. Peter Robinson, MLA
Deputy First Minister, Martin McGuinness, MP, MLA
Junior Ministers, Gerry Kelly, MLA; Robin Newton, MLA
Minister for Agriculture and Rural Development, Michelle Gildernew, MP, MLA
Minister for Culture, Arts and Leisure, Nelson McCousland, MLA
Minister for Education, Caitriona Ruane, MLA
Minister for Employment and Learning, Sir Reg Empey, MLA
Minister for Enterprise, Trade and Investment, Arlene Foster, MLA
Minister for Environment, Edwin Poots, MLA
Minister for Finance and Personnel, Sammy Wilson, MP, MLA
Minister for Health, Social Services and Public Safety, Michael McGimpsey, MLA
Minister for Justice, David Ford, MLA
Minister for Regional Development, Conor Murphy, MP, MLA
Minister for Social Development, Alex Attwood, MLA

OFFICE OF THE FIRST MINISTER AND DEPUTY FIRST MINISTER
Stormont Castle, Stormont, Belfast BT4 3TT
T 028-9052 8400 W www.ofmdfmni.gov.uk

DEPARTMENT OF AGRICULTURE AND RURAL DEVELOPMENT
Dundonald House, Upper Newtownards Road, Belfast BT4 3SB
T 028-9052 4420 W www.dardni.gov.uk

EXECUTIVE AGENCIES
Forest Service
Rivers Agency

DEPARTMENT OF CULTURE, ARTS AND LEISURE
Causeway Exchange, 1–7 Bedford Street, Belfast BT1 7FB
T 028-9025 8825 W www.dcalni.gov.uk

DEPARTMENT OF EDUCATION
Rathgael House, Balloo Road, Bangor, Co. Down BT19 7PR
T 028-9127 9279 W www.deni.gov.uk

DEPARTMENT FOR EMPLOYMENT AND LEARNING
Adelaide House, 39–49 Adelaide Street, Belfast BT2 8FD
T 028-9025 7777 W www.delni.gov.uk

DEPARTMENT OF ENTERPRISE, TRADE AND INVESTMENT
Netherleigh, Massey Avenue, Belfast BT4 2JP T 028-9052 9900
W www.detini.gov.uk

EXECUTIVE AGENCIES
General Consumer Council for Northern Ireland
Health and Safety Executive
Invest Northern Ireland
Northern Ireland Tourist Board

DEPARTMENT OF THE ENVIRONMENT
Clarence Court, 10–18 Adelaide Street, Belfast BT2 8GB
T 028-9054 0540 W www.doeni.gov.uk

EXECUTIVE AGENCIES
Driver and Vehicle Agency (Northern Ireland)
NI Environment Agency
Planning Service

DEPARTMENT OF FINANCE AND PERSONNEL
Rathgael House, Balloo Road, Bangor BT19 7PR
T 028-9185 8111 W www.dfpni.gov.uk

EXECUTIVE AGENCIES
Northern Ireland Statistics and Research Agency (Incorporates Land Registers of Northern Ireland and Ordnance Survey of Northern Ireland)
Land and Property Services

DEPARTMENT OF HEALTH, SOCIAL SERVICES AND PUBLIC SAFETY
Castle Buildings, Stormont, Belfast BT4 3SJ T 028-9052 0500
W www.dhsspsni.gov.uk

DEPARTMENT FOR REGIONAL DEVELOPMENT
Clarence Court, 10–18 Adelaide Street, Belfast BT2 8GB
T 028-9054 0540 W www.drdni.gov.uk

EXECUTIVE AGENCY
Roads Agency

DEPARTMENT FOR SOCIAL DEVELOPMENT
Lighthouse Building, 1 Cromac Place, Gasworks Business Park, Ormeau Road, Belfast BT7 2JB T 028-9082 9028
W www.dsdni.gov.uk

EXECUTIVE AGENCIES
Northern Ireland Housing Executive
Social Security Agency

DEPARTMENT OF JUSTICE
Block B, Castle Buildings, Stormont Estate, Belfast BT4 3SG
T 028-9076 3000 W www.dojni.gov.uk

EXECUTIVE AGENCIES
Northern Ireland Prison Service
Northern Ireland Courts and Tribunals Service
Compensation Agency
Forensic Science Agency
Youth Justice Agency

NORTHERN IRELAND AUDIT OFFICE
106 University Street, Belfast BT7 1EU
T 028-9025 1000 E info@niauditoffice.gov.uk
W www.niauditoffice.gov.uk
Comptroller and Auditor-General for Northern Ireland, J. M. Dowdall, CB

NORTHERN IRELAND AUTHORITY FOR UTILITY REGULATION
Queens House, 14 Queen Street, Belfast BT1 6ER
T 028-9031 1575 W www.niaur.gov.uk
Chair, Prof. Peter Matthews

NORTHERN IRELAND ASSEMBLY

Parliament Buildings, Stormont, Belfast BT4 3XX
T 028-9052 1333 W www.niassembly.gov.uk

The Northern Ireland Assembly was established as a result of the Belfast Agreement (also known as the Good Friday Agreement) in April 1998. The agreement was endorsed through a referendum held in May 1998 and subsequently given legal force through the Northern Ireland Act 1998.

The Northern Ireland Assembly has full legislative and executive authority for all matters that are the responsibility of the government's Northern Ireland departments – known as transferred matters. Excepted and reserved matters are defined in schedules 2 and 3 of the Northern Ireland Act 1998 and remain the responsibility of UK parliament.

The first assembly election occurred on 25 June 1998 and the 108 members elected met for the first time on 1 July 1998. Members of the Northern Ireland Assembly are elected by the single transferable vote system from 18 constituencies – six per constituency. Under the single transferable vote system every voter has a single vote that can be transferred from one candidate to another. Voters number their candidates in order of preference. Where candidates reach their quota of votes and are elected, surplus votes are transferred to other candidates according to the next preference on each voter's ballot slip. The candidate in each round with the fewest votes is eliminated and their surplus votes are redistributed according to the voter's next preference. The process is repeated until the required number of members are elected.

On 29 November 1999 the assembly appointed ten ministers as well as the chairs and deputy chairs for the ten statutory departmental committees. Devolution of powers to the Northern Ireland Assembly occurred on 2 December 1999, following several delays concerned with Sinn Fein's inclusion in the executive while Irish Republican Army (IRA) weapons were yet to be decommissioned.

Since the devolution of powers, the assembly has been suspended by the Secretary of State for Northern Ireland on four occasions. The first was between 11 February and 30 May 2000, with two 24-hour suspensions on 10 August and 22 September 2001 – all owing to a lack of progress in decommissioning. The final suspension took place on 14 October 2002 after unionists walked out of the executive following a police raid on Sinn Fein's office investigating alleged intelligence gathering.

The assembly was formally dissolved in April 2003 in anticipation of an election, which eventually took place on 26 November 2003. The results of the election changed the balance of power between the political parties, with an increase in the number of seats held by the Democratic Unionist Party (DUP) and Sinn Fein (SF), so that they became the largest parties. The assembly was restored to a state of suspension following the November election while political parties engaged in a review of the Belfast Agreement aimed at fully restoring the devolved institutions.

In July 2005 the leadership of the IRA formally ordered an end to its armed campaign; it authorised a representative to engage with the Independent International Commission on Decommissioning in order to verifiably put the arms beyond use. On 26 September 2005 General John de Chastelain, the chair of the commission, along with two independent church witnesses confirmed that the IRA's entire arsenal of weapons had been decommissioned.

Following the passing of the Northern Ireland Act 2006 the secretary of state created a non-legislative fixed-term assembly, whose membership consisted of the 108 members elected in the 2003 election. It first met on 15 May 2006 with the remit of making preparations for the restoration of devolved government; its discussions informed the next round of talks called by the British and Irish governments held at St Andrews. The St Andrews agreement of 13 October 2006 led to the establishment of the transitional assembly.

The Northern Ireland (St Andrews Agreement) Act 2006 set out a timetable to restore devolution, and also set the date for the third election to the assembly as 7 March 2007. The DUP and SF again had the largest number of Members of the Legislative Assembly (MLAs) elected, and although the initial restoration deadline of 26 March was missed, the leaders of the DUP and SF (Revd Dr Ian Paisley, MP, MLA and Gerry Adams, MLA, respectively) took part in a historic meeting and made a joint commitment to establish an executive committee in the assembly to which devolved powers were restored on 8 May 2007.

SALARIES *as at May 2010*	
Assembly Member	£43,101

NORTHERN IRELAND ASSEMBLY MEMBERS

as at May 2010

Adams, Gerry, *SF, West Belfast*
Anderson, Martina, *SF, Foyle*
Armstrong, Billy, *UUP, Mid Ulster*
Attwood, Alex, *SDLP, West Belfast*
Bannside, Lord (Revd Dr Ian Paisley), PC, *DUP, North Antrim*
Beggs, Roy, *UUP, East Antrim*
***Bell**, Jonathan, *DUP, Strangford*
Boylan, Cathal, *SF, Newry and Armagh*
Bradley, Dominic, *SDLP, Newry and Armagh*
Bradley, Mary, *SDLP, Foyle*
Bradley, P. J., *SDLP, South Down*
Brady, Mickey, *SF, Newry and Armagh*
Bresland, Allan, *DUP, West Tyrone*
Brolly, Francie, *SF, East Londonderry*
Browne of Belmont, Lord, *DUP, East Belfast*
Buchanan, Thomas, *DUP, West Tyrone*
Burns, Thomas, *SDLP, South Antrim*
Butler, Paul, *SF, Lagan Valley*
Campbell, Gregory, *DUP, East Londonderry*
Clarke, Trevor, *DUP, South Antrim*
Clarke, Willie, *SF, South Down*
Cobain, Fred, *UUP, North Belfast*

Coulter, Revd Dr Robert, *UUP, North Antrim*
Craig, Jonathan, *DUP, Lagan Valley*
Cree, Leslie, *UUP, North Down*
Dallat, John, *SDLP, East Londonderry*
Deeny, Dr Kieran, *Ind., West Tyrone*
Dodds, Nigel, *DUP, North Belfast*
Doherty, Pat, *SF, West Tyrone*
Donaldson, Jeffrey, *DUP, Lagan Valley*
Durkan, Mark, *SDLP, Foyle*
Easton, Alex, *DUP, North Down*
Elliot, Tom, *UUP, Fermanagh and South Tyrone*
Empey, Sir Reg, *UUP, East Belfast*
Farry, Stephen, *Alliance, North Down*
Ford, David, *Alliance, South Antrim*
Foster, Arlene, *DUP, Fermanagh and South Tyrone*
Gallagher, Tommy, *SDLP, Fermanagh and South Tyrone*
Gardiner, Samuel, *UUP, Upper Bann*
Gildernew, Michelle, *SF, Fermanagh and South Tyrone*
Hamilton, Simon, *DUP, Strangford*
Hay, William, *DUP, Foyle*
Hilditch, David, *DUP, East Antrim*
Irwin, William, *DUP, Newry and Armagh*
Kelly, Dolores, *SDLP, Upper Bann*
Kelly, Gerry, *SF, North Belfast*
Kennedy, Danny, *UUP, Newry and Armagh*
†Kinahan, Danny, *UUP, South Antrim*
‡Leonard, Billy, *SF, East Londonderry*
Lo, Anna, *Alliance, South Belfast*
Long, Naomi, *Alliance, East Belfast*
Lunn, Trevor, *Alliance, Lagan Valley*
Maginness, Alban, *SDLP, North Belfast*
Maskey, Alex, *SF, South Belfast*
Maskey, Paul, *SF, West Belfast*
McCallister, John, *UUP, South Down*
McCann, Fra, *SF, West Belfast*
McCann, Jennifer, *SF, West Belfast*
McCarthy, Kieran, *Alliance, Strangford*
McCartney, Raymond, *SF, Foyle*
McCausland, Nelson, *DUP, North Belfast*
McClarty, David, *UUP, East Londonderry*
McCrea, Basil, *UUP, Lagan Valley*
McCrea, Ian, *DUP, Mid Ulster*
McCrea, Dr William, *DUP, South Antrim*
§McDevitt, Conall, *SDLP, Belfast South*
McDonnell, Dr Alasdair, *SDLP, South Belfast*
McElduff, Barry, *SF, West Tyrone*
ℭMcFarland, Alan, *Ind., North Down*
McGill, Claire, *SF, West Tyrone*
McGimpsey, Michael, *UUP, South Belfast*
McGlone, Patsy, *SDLP, Mid Ulster*
McGuinness, Martin, *SF, Mid Ulster*
****McHugh**, Gerry, *Ind., Fermanagh and South Tyrone*
McIlveen, Michelle, *DUP, Strangford*
McKay, Daithi, *SF, North Antrim*
McLaughlin, Mitchel, *SF, South Antrim*
McNarry, David, *UUP, Strangford*
McQuillan, Adrian, *DUP, East Londonderry*
Molloy, Francie, *SF, Mid Ulster*
Morrow, Lord, *DUP, Fermanagh and South Tyrone*
Moutray, Stephen, *DUP, Upper Bann*
Murphy, Conor, *SF, Newry and Armagh*
Neeson, Sean, *Alliance, East Antrim*
Newton, Robin, *DUP, East Belfast*
Ni Chuilín, Caral, *SF, North Belfast*
O'Dowd, John, *SF, Upper Bann*
O'Loan, Declan, *SDLP, North Antrim*
O'Neill, Michelle, *SF, Mid Ulster*
Paisley, Ian Jr, *DUP, North Antrim*
Poots, Edwin, *DUP, Lagan Valley*
Purvis, Dawn, *PUP, East Belfast*
Ramsey, Pat, *SDLP, Foyle*
Ramsey, Sue, *SF, West Belfast*
Ritchie, Margaret, *SDLP, South Down*
Robinson, George, *DUP, East Londonderry*
Robinson, Ken, *UUP, East Antrim*
Robinson, Peter, *DUP, East Belfast*
††Ross, Alastair, *DUP, East Antrim*
Ruane, Caitriona, *SF, South Down*
Savage, George, *UUP, Upper Bann*
Shannon, Jim, *DUP, Strangford*
Simpson, David, *DUP, Upper Bann*
Spratt, Jimmy, *DUP, South Belfast*
Storey, Mervyn, *DUP, North Antrim*
Weir, Peter, *DUP, North Down*
Wells, Jim, *DUP, South Down*
Wilson, Brian, *Green, North Down*
Wilson, Sammy, *DUP, East Antrim*

* Iris Robinson resigned with effect from 12 January 2010 and was replaced by Jonathan Bell with effect from 25 January 2010

† David Burnside resigned with effect from 1 June 2009 and was replaced by Danny Kinahan with effect from 9 June 2009

‡ Francie Brolly resigned on 11 December 2009 and was replaced by Billy Leonard with effect from 7 January 2010

§ Carmel Hanna resigned with effect from 15 January 2010 and was replaced by Conall McDevitt with effect from 21 January 2010

ℭ Alan McFarland resigned from the UUP on 30 March 2010 and now sits as an independent member

** Gerry McHugh resigned from Sinn Fein on 29 November 2007 and now sits as an independent member

†† George Dawson died on 7 May 2007 and was replaced by Alastair Ross with effect from 14 May 2007

STATE OF THE PARTIES *as at May 2010*

Party	*Seats*
Democratic Unionist Party (DUP)	36
Sinn Fein (SF)	27
Ulster Unionist Party (UUP)	17
Social Democratic and Labour Party (SDLP)	16
Alliance Party (Alliance)	7
Independent (Ind.)	3
Progressive Unionist Party (PUP)	1
Green Party	1
Total	108

NORTHERN IRELAND ASSEMBLY ELECTION RESULTS

As at 7 March 2007
E. 1,107,904 T. 62.3%

E. Electorate T. Turnout
First = first-preference votes
Final = final total for that candidate, after all necessary transfers of lower-preference votes
R. = round
* = eliminated last
See General Election Results for a list of party abbreviations

ANTRIM EAST
E. 56,666 T. 30,293 (53.46%)

	First	*Final*	*Elected (R.)*
Sammy Wilson, DUP	6,755	6,755	First (1)
George Dawson, DUP	4,167	4,777	Second (2)
Sean Neeson, Alliance	3,114	5,191	Fourth (10)
Roy Beggs, UUP	3,076	5,115	Fifth (12)

David Hilditch, DUP	2,732	4,587	Third (3)
Ken Robinson, UUP	1,881	4,195	Sixth (13)
*Danny O'Connor, SDLP	1,769	3,298	
Stewart Dickson, Alliance	1,624		
Mark Dunn, UUP	1,617		
Oliver McMullan, SF	1,168		
Tom Robinson, UK Unionist Party	731		
Mark Bailey, Green	612		
John Anderson, Ind.	398		
Tim Lewis, C.	395		

ANTRIM NORTH
E. 72,814 T. 44,655 (61.33%)

	First	*Final*	*Elected (R.)*
Lord Bannside (Revd Ian Paisley), DUP	7,716	7,716	First (1)
Daithi McKay, SF	7,065	7,065	Second (1)
Ian Paisley Jr, DUP	6,106	7,264	Third (2)
Mervyn Storey, DUP	5,171	6,924	Fifth (8)
Revd Robert Coulter, UUP	5,047	6,579	Fourth (7)
Declan O'Loan, SDLP	3,281	6,498	Sixth (10)
*Deirdre Nelson, DUP	2,740	4,092	
Orla Black, SDLP	2,129		
Lyle Cubitt, UK Unionist Party	1,848		
Robert Swann, UUP	1,281		
Jayne Dunlop, Alliance	1,254		
Paul McGlinchey, Ind.	383		
James Gregg, Ind.	310		

ANTRIM SOUTH
E. 65,654 T. 38,481 (58.61%)

	First	*Final*	*Elected (R.)*
Mitchel McLaughlin, SF	6,313	6,313	First (1)
Revd William McCrea, DUP	6,023	6,023	Second (1)
David Ford, Alliance	5,007	5,495	Third (5)
David Burnside, UUP	4,507	6,926	Fourth (7)
Trevor Clarke, DUP	4,302	5,544	Fifth (8)
*Mel Lucas, DUP	2,840	4,429	
Thomas Burns, SDLP	2,721	5,396	Sixth (8)
Danny Kinahan, UUP	2,391		
Noreen McClelland, SDLP	1,526		
Stephen Nicholl, UUP	927		
Robert McCartney, UK Unionist Party	893		
Pete Whitcroft, Green	507		
Stephen O'Brien, C.	129		
Marcella Delaney, WP	89		

BELFAST EAST
E. 49,757 T. 29,873 (60.04%)

	First	*Final*	*Elected (R.)*
Peter Robinson, DUP	5,635	5,635	First (1)
Naomi Long, Alliance	5,585	5,585	Second (1)
Sir Reg Empey, UUP	4,139	4,620	Third (3)
Lord Wallace Browne, DUP	3,185	3,734	Fifth (10)
Dawn Purvis, Progressive Unionist Party	3,045	4,208	Fourth (10)
Robin Newton, DUP	2,335	3,517	Sixth (10)
*Michael Copeland, UUP	1,557	2,999	
Niall O'Donnghaile, SF	1,055		
Jim Rodgers, UUP	820		
Mary Muldoon, SDLP	816		
Steve Agnew, Green	653		
Glyn Chambers, C.	427		
Thomas Black, Socialist Party	225		
Joe Bell, WP	107		
Rainbow George, Make Politicians History	47		

BELFAST NORTH
E. 49,372 T. 30,067 (60.90%)

	First	*Final*	*Elected (R.)*
Nigel Dodds, DUP	6,973	6,973	First (1)
Gerry Kelly, SF	5,414	5,414	Second (1)
Caral Ni Chuilin, SF	3,680	4,587	Third (3)
Fred Cobain, UUP	2,498	3,967	Fifth (10)
Nelson McCausland, DUP	2,462	3,818	Sixth (10)
Alban Maginness, SDLP	2,212	4,830	Fourth (9)
Pat Convery, SDLP	1,868		
*William Humphrey, DUP	1,673	3,327	
Raymond McCord, Ind.	1,320		
Peter Emerson, Green	590		
Tommy McCullough, Alliance	486		
Robert McCartney, UK Unionist Party	360		
John Lavery, WP	139		
Rainbow George, Make Politicians History	40		

BELFAST SOUTH
E. 48,923 T. 30,533 (62.41%)

	First	*Final*	*Elected (R.)*
Jimmy Spratt, DUP	4,762	4,762	First (1)
Dr Alasdair McDonnell, SDLP	4,379	4,379	Second (1)
Alex Maskey, SF	3,996	4,167	Sixth (10)
Anna Lo, Alliance	3,829	4,415	Third (8)
Carmel Hanna, SDLP	3,748	4,262	Fifth (10)
Michael McGimpsey, UUP	2,647	4,927	Fourth (10)
*Christopher Stalford, DUP	2,035	3,275	
Dr Esmond Birnie, UUP	1,804		
Bob Stoker, UUP	1,122		
Brenda Cooke, Green	737		
Andrew Park, Progressive Unionist Party	410		
David Hoey, UK Unionist Party	298		
Jim Barbour, Socialist Party	248		
Paddy Lynn, WP	123		
Roger Lomas, C.	108		
Rainbow George, Make Politicians History	66		
Charles Smyth, Pro-Capitalism	22		
Geoffrey Wilson, Ind.	10		

BELFAST WEST
E. 50,792 T. 34,238 (67.41%)

	First	*Final*	*Elected (R.)*
Gerry Adams, SF	6,029	6,029	First (1)
Sue Ramsey, SF	4,715	5,267	Second (2)
Paul Maskey, SF	4,368	5,075	Third (6)
Jennifer McCann, SF	4,265	4,849	Fourth (6)
Fra McCann, SF	4,254	4,647	Sixth (6)
*Diane Dodds, DUP	3,661	4,166	
Alex Attwood, SDLP	3,036	4,779	Fifth (6)
Margaret Walsh, SDLP	1,074		
Sean Mitchell, People Before Profit	774		
Louis West, UUP	558		
John Lowry, WP	434		
Geraldine Taylor, Republican Sinn Fein	427		
Dan McGuinness, Alliance	127		
Rainbow George, Make Politicians History	68		

DOWN NORTH
E. 57,525 T. 30,930 (53.77%)

	First	*Final*	*Elected (R.)*
Alex Easton, DUP	4,946	4,946	First (1)
Peter Weir, DUP	3,376	4,380	Fifth (10)
Stephen Farry, Alliance	3,131	4,466	Second (8)
Leslie Cree, UUP	2,937	4,687	Third (10)
Brian Wilson, Green	2,839	4,572	Fourth (10)
Alan McFarland, UUP	2,245	3,986	Sixth (10)
*Alan Graham, DUP	2,147	3,255	
Marion Smith, UUP	2,098		
Robert McCartney, UK Unionist Party	1,806		
Brian Rowan, Ind.	1,194		
Alan Chambers, Ind.	1,129		
Liam Logan, SDLP	1,115		
James Leslie, C.	864		
Deaglan Page, SF	390		
Elaine Martin, Progressive Unionist Party	367		
Chris Carter, Ind.	123		

DOWN SOUTH
E. 71,704 T. 46,623 (65.02%)

	First	*Final*	*Elected (R.)*
Catriona Ruane, SF	6,334	6,676	First (7)
Margaret Ritchie, SDLP	5,838	6,945	Third (8)
P. J. Bradley, SDLP	5,652	6,650	Fourth (9)
Jim Wells, DUP	5,542	8,463	Fifth (10)
Willie Clarke, SF	5,138	7,382	Second (8)
John McCallister, UUP	4,447	7,721	Sixth (11)
*Michael Carr, SDLP	2,972	3,883	
Eamonn McConvey, SF	2,662		
William Burns, DUP	2,611		
Ciaran Mussen, Green	1,622		
Henry Reilly, UKIP	1,229		
David Griffin, Alliance	691		
Martin Cunningham, Ind.	434		
Nelson Wharton, UK Unionist Party	424		
Peter Bowles, C.	391		
Malachi Curran, Lab.	123		

FERMANAGH AND SOUTH TYRONE
E. 65,826 T. 46,845 (71.16%)

	First	*Final*	*Elected (R.)*
Arlene Foster, DUP	7,138	7,138	First (1)
Michelle Gildernew, SF	7,026	7,026	Second (1)
Tom Elliott, UUP	6,603	6,680	Third (2)
Gerry McHugh, SF	5,103	5,777	Sixth (8)
*Sean Lynch, SF	4,704	5,188	
Lord Morrow, DUP	4,700	7,014	Fifth (8)
Tommy Gallagher, SDLP	4,440	6,640	Fourth (7)
Kenny Donaldson, UUP	2,531		
Vincent Currie, SDLP	2,043		
Gerry McGeough, Ind.	814		
Allan Leonard, Alliance	521		
Michael McManus, Republican Sinn Fein	431		
Robert McCartney, UK Unionist Party	388		

FOYLE
E. 64,889 T. 41,455 (63.89%)

	First	*Final*	*Elected (R.)*
William Hay, DUP	6,960	6,960	First (1)
Mark Durkan, SDLP	6,401	6,401	Second (1)
Martina Anderson, SF	5,414	5,972	Third (6)
Raymond McCartney, SF	4,321	7,275	Fourth (8)
Pat Ramsey, SDLP	3,242	5,396	Fifth (10)
Lynn Fleming, SF	2,914		
Mary Bradley, SDLP	2,891	4,419	Sixth (10)
*Helen Quigley, SDLP	2,648	4,314	
Eamonn McCann, Socialist Environmental Alliance	2,045		
Peggy O'Hara, Ind.	1,789		
Peter Munce, UUP	1,755		
Adele Corry, Green	359		
Yvonne Boyle, Alliance	224		
Willie Frazer, Ind.	73		

LAGAN VALLEY
E. 70,101 T. 42,058 (60.00%)

	First	*Final*	*Elected (R.)*
Jeffrey Donaldson, DUP	9,793	9,793	First (1)
Paul Butler, SF	5,098	6,387	Second (6)
Basil McCrea, UUP	4,031	6,712	Third (7)
Trevor Lunn, Alliance	3,765	6,264	Fourth (7)
Jonathan Craig, DUP	3,471	6,147	Fifth (8)
Edwin Poots, DUP	3,457	5,386	Sixth (9)
*Paul Givan, DUP	3,377	4,728	
Marietta Farrell, SDLP	2,839		
Billy Bell, UUP	2,599		
Ronnie Crawford, UUP	1,147		
Michael Rogan, Green	922		
Robert McCartney, UK Unionist Party	853		
Neil Johnston, C.	387		
John Magee, WP	83		

LONDONDERRY EAST
E. 56,104 T. 34,180 (60.92%)

	First	*Final*	*Elected (R.)*
Gregory Campbell, DUP	6,845	6,845	First (1)
Francie Brolly, SF	4,476	5,003	Third (7)
George Robinson, DUP	3,991	4,869	Second (5)
David McClarty, UUP	2,875	4,409	Fifth (9)
Adrian McQuillan, DUP	2,650	4,074	Sixth (9)
John Dallat, SDLP	2,638	6,380	Fourth (8)
Billy Leonard, SF	2,321		
*Norman Hillis, UUP	2,054	3,195	
Orla Beattie, SDLP	1,797		
Barney Fitzpatrick, Alliance	1,401		
Edwin Stevenson, UUP	1,338		
Leslie Cubitt, UK Unionist Party	549		
Phillippe Moison, Green	521		
Michael McGonigle, Republican Sinn Fein	393		
Victor Christie, Ind.	73		

NEWRY AND ARMAGH
E. 70,823 T. 50,165 (70.83%)

	First	*Final*	*Elected (R.)*
Conor Murphy, SF	7,437	7,437	First (1)
Cathal Boylan, SF	7,105	7,105	Second (1)
Danny Kennedy, UUP	6,517	7,653	Fifth (5)
William Irwin, DUP	6,418	8,008	Fourth (5)
Mickey Brady, SF	6,337	7,514	Third (4)
Dominic Bradley, SDLP	5,318	6,311	Sixth (7)
*Sharon Haughey, SDLP	4,500	5,368	
Paul Berry, Ind.	2,317		
Davy Hyland, Ind.	2,188		
Willie Frazer, Ind.	605		
Arthur Morgan, Green	599		
Maire Hendron, Alliance	278		

STRANGFORD
E. 66,648 T. 36,340 (54.53%)

	First	*Final*	*Elected (R.)*
Iris Robinson, DUP	5,917	5,917	First (1)
Jim Shannon, DUP	4,788	5,178	Second (6)
Kieran McCarthy, Alliance	4,085	5,207	Third (9)
Simon Hamilton, DUP	3,889	4,998	Fifth (13)
David McNarry, UUP	3,709	6,036	Fourth (10)
Michelle McIlveen, DUP	3,468	4,579	Sixth (13)
*Joe Boyle, SDLP	3,068	4,548	
Angus Carson, UUP	2,128		
Dermot Kennedy, SF	1,089		
George Ennis, UK Unionist Party	872		
Stephanie Sim, Green	868		
Michael Henderson, UUP	675		
David Gregg, Ind.	650		
Bob Little, C.	508		
Cedric Wilson, Ind.	305		

TYRONE WEST
E. 58,367 T. 41,839 (71.68%)

	First	*Final*	*Elected (R.)*
Barry McElduff, SF	6,971	6,971	First (1)
Pat Doherty, SF	6,709	6,709	Second (1)
Clare McGill, SF	4,757	6,217	Third (3)
Tom Buchanan, DUP	4,625	6,208	Fourth (6)
Allan Bresland, DUP	4,244	5,543	Sixth (7)
Dr Kieran Deeny, Ind.	3,776	5,616	Fifth (7)
Derek Hussey, UUP	3,686		
*Josephine Deehan, SDLP	2,689	5,186	
Eugene McMenamin, SDLP	2,272		
Seamus Shiels, SDLP	1,057		
Joe O'Neill, Republican Sinn Fein	448		
Robert McCartney, UK Unionist Party	220		

ULSTER MID
E. 61,223 T. 44,728 (73.06%)

	First	*Final*	*Elected (R.)*
Martin McGuinness, SF	8,065	8,065	First (1)
Ian McCrea, DUP	7,608	7,608	Second (1)
Francie Molloy, SF	6,597	6,597	Third (1)
Michelle O'Neill, SF	6,432	6,432	Fourth (1)
Patsy McGlone, SDLP	4,976	6,430	Fifth (5)
Billy Armstrong, UUP	4,781	6,355	Sixth (7)
*Kate Lagan, SDLP	2,759	3,531	
Walter Millar, UK Unionist Party	1,210		
Ann Forde, DUP	1,021		
Brendan McLaughlin, Republican Sinn Fein	437		
Margaret Marshall, Alliance	221		
Harry Hutchinson, Ind.	170		

UPPER BANN
E. 70,716 T. 43,235 (61.14%)

	First	*Final*	*Elected (R.)*
John O'Dowd, SF	7,733	7,733	First (1)
David Simpson, DUP	6,828	6,828	Second (1)
Samuel Gardiner, UUP	5,135	7,265	Fourth (9)
Dolores Kelly, SDLP	4,689	6,191	Third (8)
Stephen Moutray, DUP	3,663	7,550	Fifth (11)
*Dessie Ward, SF	3,118	4,732	
Junior McCrum, DUP	2,975		
George Savage, UUP	2,167	5,998	Sixth (12)
Arnold Hatch, UUP	1,815		
David Calvert, No Description	1,332		
Helen Corry, Green	1,156		
Sheila McQuaid, Alliance	798		
Pat McAleenan, SDLP	761		
Barry Toman, Republican Sinn Fein	386		
David Fry, C.	248		
Suzanne Peeples, Ind.	78		

EUROPEAN PARLIAMENT

European parliament elections take place at five-yearly intervals; the first direct elections to the parliament were held in 1979. In mainland Britain, members of the European parliament (MEPs) were elected in all constituencies on a first-past-the-post basis until 1999, when a regional system of proportional representation was introduced; in Northern Ireland three MEPs have been elected by the single transferable vote system of proportional representation since 1979. From 1979 to 1994 the number of seats held by the UK in the European parliament was 81, which increased to 87 in the 1994 election, decreased to 78 following EU enlargement in 2004, and decreased to 72 for the 2009 election (England 59, Wales 4, Scotland 6, Northern Ireland 3) as a result of Bulgaria and Romania joining the EU in 2007. Under the Lisbon Treaty, which came into force in December 2009, the UK will gain an extra seat, but the UK authorities have yet to decide where that seat will be located.

At the 2009 European parliament elections all UK MEPs were elected under a 'closed-list' regional system of proportional representation, with England being divided into nine regions and Scotland, Wales and Northern Ireland each constituting a region. Since June 2004 residents of Gibraltar vote in the South West region. Parties submitted a list of candidates for each region in their own order of preference. Votes were cast for a party or an independent candidate, and the first seat in each region was allocated to the party or candidate with the highest number of votes. The rest of the seats in each region were then allocated broadly in proportion to each party's share of the vote. Each region returned the following number of members: East Midlands, 5; Eastern, 7; London, 8; North East, 3; North West, 8; South East, 10; South West, 6; West Midlands, 6; Yorkshire and the Humber, 6; Wales, 4; Northern Ireland, 3; Scotland, 6.

If a vacancy occurs due to the resignation or death of an MEP, it is filled by the next available person on that party's list. If an independent MEP resigns or dies, a by-election is held. Where an MEP leaves the party on whose list he/she was elected, there is no requirement to resign and he/she can remain in office until the next election.

British subjects and nationals of member states of the European Union are eligible for election to the European parliament provided they are 18 or over and not subject to disqualification. Since 1994, eligible citizens have had the right to vote in elections to the European parliament in the UK as long as they are entered on the electoral register.

In July 2009 an MEP statute introduced the same salary for all MEPs (€91,980/£76,389), fixed at a rate of 38.5 per cent of the basic salary of a European court of justice judge. Previously MEPs received a salary set at the level of the national parliamentary salary of their country.

The next elections to the European parliament will take place in 2014. For further information visit the UK's European parliament website (W www.europarl.org.uk).

UK MEMBERS *as at March 2010*

* Denotes membership of the last European parliament
† Previously sat as a member of the Conservative party
‡ Previously sat as a member of UUP

Agnew, John Stuart (*b.* 1949), *UKIP, Eastern*
Andreasen, Marta (*b.* 1954), *UKIP, South East*
***Ashworth**, Richard (*b.* 1947), *C., South East*
***Atkins**, Rt. Hon. Sir Robert (*b.* 1946), *C., North West*
***Batten**, Gerard (*b.* 1954), *UKIP, London*
Bearder, Catherine (*b.* 1949) *LD, South East*
***Bloom**, Godfrey (*b.* 1949), *UKIP, Yorkshire and the Humber*
***Bowles**, Sharon M. (*b.* 1953), *LD, South East*
***Bradbourn**, Philip, OBE (*b.* 1951), *C., West Midlands*
Brons, Andrew (*b.* 1947), *BNP, Yorkshire and the Humber*
Bufton, John (*b.* 1962), *UKIP, Wales*
***Callanan**, Martin (*b.* 1961), *C., North East*
Campbell Bannerman, David (*b.* 1960), *UKIP, Eastern*
***Cashman**, Michael (*b.* 1950), *Lab., West Midlands*
***Chichester**, Giles B. (*b.* 1946), *C., South West*
***Clark**, Derek (*b.* 1933), *UKIP, East Midlands*
Colman, Trevor (*b.* 1941), *UKIP, South West*
Dartmouth, Earl of (*b.* 1949), *UKIP, South West*
***Davies**, Christopher G. (*b.* 1954), *LD, North West*
***de Brún**, Bairbre (*b.* 1954), *SF, Northern Ireland*
***Deva**, Niranjan J. A. (Nirj), FRSA (*b.* 1948), *C., South East*
Dodds, Diane (*b.* 1958), *DUP, Northern Ireland*
***Duff**, Andrew N. (*b.* 1950), *LD, Eastern*
***Elles**, James E. M. (*b.* 1949), *C., South East*
***Evans**, Jill R. (*b.* 1959), *PC, Wales*
***Farage**, Nigel P. (*b.* 1964), *UKIP, South East*
Ford, Vicky (*b.* 1967), *C. Eastern*
Foster, Jacqueline (*b.* 1947), *C., North West*
Fox, Ashley (*b.* 1969), *C., South West*
Girling, Julie (*b.* 1956), *C., South West*
Griffin, Nick (*b.* 1959), *BNP, North West*
***Hall**, Fiona (*b.* 1955), *LD, North East*
***Hannan**, Daniel J. (*b.* 1971), *C., South East*
***Harbour**, Malcolm (*b.* 1947), *C., West Midlands*
***Helmer**, Roger (*b.* 1944), *C., East Midlands*
***Honeyball**, Mary (*b.* 1952), *Lab., London*
***Howitt**, Richard (*b.* 1961), *Lab., Eastern*
***Hudghton**, Ian (*b.* 1951), *SNP, Scotland*
***Hughes**, Stephen (*b.* 1952), *Lab., North East*
***Kamall**, Syed S. (*b.* 1967), *C., London*
***Karim**, Sajjad (*b.* 1970), *C., North West*
***Kirkhope**, Timothy J. R. (*b.* 1945), *C., Yorkshire and the Humber*
***Lambert**, Jean D. (*b.* 1950), *Green, London*
***Ludford**, Baroness Sarah (*b.* 1951), *LD, London*
***Lynne**, Elizabeth (*b.* 1948), *LD, West Midlands*
Lyon, George (*b.* 1956), *LD, Scotland*
***McAvan**, Linda (*b.* 1962), *Lab., Yorkshire and the Humber*
***McCarthy**, Arlene (*b.* 1960), *Lab., North West*
McClarkin, Emma (*b.* 1978), *C., East Midlands*
***†McMillan-Scott**, Edward H. C. (*b.* 1949), *LD, Yorkshire and the Humber*
***Martin**, David W. (*b.* 1954), *Lab., Scotland*
***Moraes**, Claude (*b.* 1965), *Lab., London*
***Nattrass**, Mike (*b.* 1945), *UKIP, West Midlands*
***Newton Dunn**, William F. (Bill) (*b.* 1941), *LD, East Midlands*
***‡Nicholson**, James (*b.* 1945), *UCUNF, Northern Ireland*
Nuttall, Paul (*b.* 1976), *UKIP, North West*
***Simpson**, Brian (*b.* 1953), *Lab., North West*
Sinclaire, Nikki (*b.* 1968), *UKIP, West Midlands*

***Skinner**, Peter W. (*b.* 1959), *Lab., South East*
***Smith**, Alyn (*b.* 1973), *SNP, Scotland*
***Stevenson**, Struan (*b.* 1948), *C., Scotland*
***Stihler**, Catherine D. (*b.* 1973), *Lab., Scotland*
***Sturdy**, Robert W. (*b.* 1944), *C., Eastern*
Swinburne, Kay (*b.* 1967), *C., Wales*
***Tannock**, Dr Charles (*b.* 1957), *C., London*
Taylor, Keith (*b.* 1953), *Green, South East*
***Van Orden**, Geoffrey (*b.* 1945), *C., Eastern*
Vaughan, Derek (*b.* 1961), *Lab., Wales*
***Wallis**, Diana (*b.* 1954), *LD, Yorkshire and the Humber*
***Watson**, Graham R. (*b.* 1956), *LD, South West*
***Willmott**, Glenis (*b.* 1951), *Lab., East Midlands*
Yannakoudakis, Marina (*b.* 1956), *C., London*

UK REGIONS *as at 4 June 2009 Election*

Abbreviations

AC	Animals Count
ChP	Christian Party
JT	Jury Team
Libertas	Libertas
No2EU	No2EU Yes to Democracy
Peace	Peace Party
Pensioners	Pensioners Party
Roman	Roman Party
SGB	Socialist Party of Great Britain
SLP	Socialist Labour Party
SSP	Scottish Socialist Party
TUV	Traditional Unionist Voice
UCUNF	Ulster Conservatives and Unionists – New Force
UKF	United Kingdom First
YD	Wai D (Your Decision)
Yes2EU	YES2EUROPE

For other abbreviations, *see* UK General Election Results. For detailed information on which areas of the country are covered by a particular region, please contact the Home Office.

E. 44,173,690 T. 34.48%

EASTERN

(Bedfordshire, Cambridgeshire, Essex, Hertfordshire, Luton, Norfolk, Peterborough, Southend-on-Sea, Suffolk, Thurrock)

E. 4,252,669	T. 38.0%
C.	500,331 (31.2%)
UKIP	313,921 (19.6%)
LD	221,235 (13.8%)
Lab.	167,833 (10.5%)
Green	141,016 (8.8%)
BNP	97,013 (6.1%)
UKF	38,185 (2.4%)
Eng. Dem.	32,211 (2.0%)
CPA	24,646 (1.5%)
No2EU	13,939 (0.9%)
SLP	13,599 (0.8%)
AC	13,201 (0.8%)
Libertas	9,940 (0.6%)
Ind.	9,916 (0.6%)
JT	6,354 (0.4%)
C. majority	186,410

(June 2004, C. maj. 169,366)

MEMBERS ELECTED
1. *G. Van Orden, *C.* 2. D. Campbell Bannerman, *UKIP* 3. *R. Sturdy, *C.* 4. *A. Duff, *LD* 5. *R. Howitt, *Lab.* 6. V. Ford, *C.* 7. J. Agnew, *UKIP*

EAST MIDLANDS

(Derby, Derbyshire, Leicester, Leicestershire, Lincolnshire, Northamptonshire, Nottingham, Nottinghamshire, Rutland)

E. 3,312,944	T. 37.51%
C.	370,275 (30.2%)
Lab.	206,945 (16.9%)
UKIP	201,984 (16.4%)
LD	151,428 (12.3%)
BNP	106,319 (8.7%)
Green	83,939 (6.8%)
Eng. Dem.	28,498 (2.3%)
UKF	20,561 (1.7%)
CPA	17,907 (1.5%)
SLP	13,590 (1.1%)
No2EU	11,375 (0.9%)
Libertas	7,882 (0.6%)
JT	7,362 (0.6%)
C. majority	204,243

(June 2004, C. maj. 4,864)

MEMBERS ELECTED
1. *R. Helmer, *C.* 2.*G. Willmott, *Lab.* 3. *D. Clark, *UKIP* 4. E. McClarkin, *C.* 5. *W. Newton Dunn, *LD*

LONDON

E. 5,257,624	T. 33.53%
C.	479,037 (27.4%)
Lab.	372,590 (21.3%)
LD	240,156 (13.7%)
Green	190,589 (10.9%)
UKIP	188,440 (10.8%)
BNP	86,420 (4.9%)
CPA	51,336 (2.9%)
Ind.	50,014 (2.9%)
Eng. Dem.	24,477 (1.4%)
No2EU	17,758 (1.0%)
SLP	15,306 (0.9%)
Libertas	8,444 (0.5%)
JT	7,284 (0.4%)
Ind, SC	4,918 (0.3%)
SGB	4,050 (0.2%)
Yes2EU	3,384 (0.2%)
Ind.	3,248 (0.2%)
Ind.	1,972 (0.1%)
Ind.	1,603 (0.1%)
C. majority	106,447

(June 2004, C. maj. 38,357)

MEMBERS ELECTED
1. *C. Tannock, *C.* 2. *C. Moraes, *Lab.* 3. *Baroness Ludford, *LD* 4. *S. Kamall, *C.* 5. *J. Lambert, *Green* 6. *G. Batten, *UKIP* 7. *M. Honeyball, *Lab.* 8. M. Yannakoudakis, *C.*

NORTH EAST

(Co. Durham, Darlington, Hartlepool, Middlesbrough, Northumberland, Redcar and Cleveland, Stockton-on-Tees, Tyne and Wear)

E. 1,939,709	T. 30.50%
Lab.	147,338 (25.0%)
C.	116,911 (19.8%)
LD	103,644 (17.6%)
UKIP	90,700 (15.4%)
BNP	52,700 (8.9%)
Green	34,081 (5.8%)
Eng. Dem.	13,007 (2.2%)
SLP	10,238 (1.7%)
No2EU	8,066 (1.4%)
CPA	7,263 (1.2%)
Libertas	3,010 (0.5%)
JT	2,904 (0.5%)
Lab. majority	30,427

(June 2004, Lab. maj. 121,088)

MEMBERS ELECTED
1. *S. Hughes, *Lab.* 2. *M. Callanan, *C.* 3. *Ms F. Hall, *LD*

NORTHERN IRELAND

(Northern Ireland forms a three-member seat with a single transferable vote system)

E. 1,141,979	T. 42.81%
	1st Pref. Votes
Bairbre de Brún, *SF*	126,184 (26.0%)
Diane Dodds, *DUP*	88,346 (18.2%)
Jim Nicholson, *UCUNF*	82,893 (17.1%)
Alban Maginness, *SDLP*	78,489 (16.2%)
Jim Allister, *TUV*	66,197 (13.7%)
Ian James Parsley, *Alliance*	26,699 (5.5%)
Steven Agnew, *Green*	15,764 (3.3%)

MEMBERS ELECTED
1. *B. de Brún, *SF* 2. *†J. Nicholson, *UCUNF* 3. D. Dodds, *DUP*

NORTH WEST

(Blackburn-with-Darwen, Blackpool, Cheshire, Cumbria, Greater Manchester, Halton, Lancashire, Merseyside, Warrington)

E. 1,651,825	T. 31.90%
C.	423,174 (25.6%)
Lab.	336,831 (20.4%)
UKIP	261,740 (15.8%)
LD	235,639 (14.3%)
BNP	132,094 (8.0%)
Green	127,133 (7.7%)
Eng. Dem.	40,027 (2.4%)
SLP	26,224 (1.6%)
CPA	25,999 (1.6%)
No2EU	23,580 (1.4%)
JT	8,783 (0.5%)
Libertas	6,980 (0.4%)
Ind.	3,621 (0.2%)
C. majority	86,343

(June 2004, Lab. maj. 66,942)

MEMBERS ELECTED
1. *Sir R. Atkins, *C.* 2. A. McCarthy, *Lab.* 3. P. Nuttall, *UKIP* 4. *C. Davies, *LD* 5. *S. Karim, *C.* 6. *B. Simpson, *Lab.* 7. J. Foster, *C.* 8. N. Griffin, *BNP*

SCOTLAND

E. 3,873,163	T. 28.60%
SNP	321,007 (29.1%)
Lab.	229,853 (20.8%)
C.	185,794 (16.8%)
LD	127,038 (11.5%)
Green	80,442 (7.3%)
UKIP	57,788 (5.2%)
BNP	27,174 (2.5%)
SLP	22,135 (2.0%)
CPA	16,738 (1.5%)
SSP	10,404 (0.9%)
Ind.	10,189 (0.9%)
No2EU	9,693 (0.9%)
JT	6,257 (0.6%)
SNP majority	91,154

(June 2004, Lab. maj. 79,360)

MEMBERS ELECTED
1. *I. Hudghton, *SNP* 2. *D. Martin, *Lab.* 3. *S. Stevenson, *C.* 4. *A. Smith, *SNP* 5. G. Lyon, *LD* 6. *C. Stihler, *Lab.*

SOUTH EAST

(Bracknell Forest, Brighton and Hove, Buckinghamshire, East Sussex, Hampshire, Isle of Wight, Kent, Medway, Milton Keynes, Newbury, Oxfordshire, Portsmouth, Reading, Slough, Southampton, Surrey, West Sussex, Windsor and Maidenhead, Wokingham)

E. 6,231,875	T. 38.19%
C.	812,288 (34.8%)
UKIP	440,002 (18.8%)
LD	330,340 (14.1%)
Green	271,506 (11.6%)
Lab.	192,592 (8.2%)
BNP	101,769 (4.4%)
Eng. Dem.	52,526 (2.2%)
CPA	35,712 (1.5%)
No2EU	21,455 (0.9%)
Libertas	16,767 (0.7%)
SLP	15,484 (0.7%)
UKF	15,261 (0.7%)
JT	14,172 (0.6%)
Peace Party	9,534 (0.4%)
Roman Party	5,450 (0.2%)
C. majority	372,286

(June 2004, C. maj. 345,259)

MEMBERS ELECTED
1. *D. Hannan, *C.* 2. *N. Farage, *UKIP* 3. *R. Ashworth, *C.* 4. *S. Bowles, *LD* 5. *Dr C. Lucas, *Green* 6. *N. Deva, *C.* 7. M. Andreasen, *UKIP* 8. *J. Elles, *C.* 9. *P. Skinner, *Lab.* 10. C. Bearder, *LD*

SOUTH WEST

(Bath and North East Somerset, Bournemouth, Bristol, Cornwall, Devon, Dorset, Gloucestershire, North Somerset, Plymouth, Poole, Somerset, South Gloucestershire, Swindon, Torbay, Wiltshire, Isles of Scilly, Gibraltar)

E. 3,998,479	T. 39.04%
C.	468,472 (30.2%)
UKIP	341,845 (22.1%)
LD	266,253 (17.2%)
Green	144,179 (9.3%)
Labour	118,716 (7.7%)
BNP	60,889 (3.9%)
Pensioners	37,785 (2.4%)
Eng. Dem.	25,313 (1.6%)
CPA	21,329 (1.4%)
Meb. Ker.	14,922 (1.0%)
SLP	10,033 (0.6%)
No2EU	9,741 (0.6%)
Ind.	8,971 (0.6%)
Libertas	7,292 (0.5%)
FPFT	7,151 (0.5%)
JT	5,758 (0.4%)
YD	789 (0.1%)
C. majority	126,627

(June 2004, C. maj. 130,587)

MEMBERS ELECTED
1. *G. Chichester, *C.* 2. T. Colman, *UKIP* 3. *G. Watson, *LD* 4. J. McCulloch Girling, *C.* 5. W. Dartmouth, *UKIP* 6. A. Fox, *C.*

WALES

E. 2,251,968	T. 30.50%
C.	145,193 (21.2%)
Lab.	138,852 (20.3%)
PC	126,702 (18.5%)
UKIP	87,585 (12.8%)
LD	73,082 (10.7%)
Green	38,160 (5.6%)
BNP	37,114 (5.4%)
ChP	13,037 (1.9%)
SLP	12,402 (1.8%)
No2EU	8,600 (1.3%)
JT	3,793 (0.6%)
C. majority	6,341

(June 2004, Lab. maj. 120,039)

MEMBERS ELECTED
1. K. Swinburne, *C.* 2. D. Vaughan. *Lab.* 3. *J. Evans, *PC* 4. J. Bufton, *UKIP*

WEST MIDLANDS

(Herefordshire, Shropshire, Staffordshire, Stoke-on-Trent, Telford and Wrekin, Warwickshire, West Midlands Metropolitan area, Worcestershire)

E. 4,056,370	T. 35.07%
C.	396,487 (28.1%)
UKIP	300,471 (21.3%)
Lab.	240,201 (17.0%)
LD	170,246 (12.0%)
BNP	121,967 (8.6%)
Green	88,244 (6.2%)
Eng. Dem.	32,455 (2.3%)
CPA	18,784 (1.3%)
SLP	14,724 (1.0%)
No2EU	13,415 (0.9%)
JT	8,721 (0.6%)
Libertas	6,961 (0.5%)
C. majority	96,016

(June 2004, C. maj. 56,324)

MEMBERS ELECTED
1. *P. Bradbourn, *C.* 2. *M. Nattrass, *UKIP* 3. *M. Cashman, *Lab.* 4. *M. Harbour, *C.* 5. *L. Lynne, *LD* 6. N. Sinclaire, *UKIP*

YORKSHIRE AND THE HUMBER

(East Riding of Yorkshire, Kingston-upon-Hull, North East Lincolnshire, North Lincolnshire, North Yorkshire, South Yorkshire, West Yorkshire, York)

E. 3,792,415	T. 32.51%
C.	299,802 (24.5%)
Lab.	230,009 (18.8%)
UKIP	213,750 (17.4%)
LD	161,552 (13.2%)
BNP	120,139 (9.8%)
Green	104,456 (8.5%)
Eng. Dem.	31,287 (2.6%)
SLP	19,380 (1.6%)
CPA	16,742 (1.4%)
No2EU	15,614 (1.3%)
JT	7,181 (0.6%)
Libertas	6,268 (0.5%)
C. majority	69,793

(June 1999, Lab. maj. 25,844)

MEMBERS ELECTED
1. *E. McMillan-Scott, *C.* 2. *L. McAvan, *Lab.* 3. *G. Bloom, *UKIP* 4. *D. Wallis, *LD* 5. *T. Kirkhope, *C.* 6. A. Brons, *BNP*

LOCAL GOVERNMENT

Major changes in local government were introduced in England and Wales in 1974 and in Scotland in 1975 by the Local Government Act 1972 and the Local Government (Scotland) Act 1973. Further significant alterations were made in England by the Local Government Acts of 1985, 1992 and 2000.

The structure in England was based on two tiers of local authorities (county councils and district councils) in the non-metropolitan areas; and a single tier of metropolitan councils in the six metropolitan areas of England and London borough councils in London.

Following reviews of the structure of local government in England by the Local Government Commission (now the Boundary Commission for England), 46 unitary (all-purpose) authorities were created between April 1995 and April 1998 to cover certain areas in the non-metropolitan counties. The remaining county areas continue to have two tiers of local authorities. The county and district councils in the Isle of Wight were replaced by a single unitary authority on 1 April 1995; the former counties of Avon, Cleveland, Humberside and Berkshire were replaced by unitary authorities; and Hereford and Worcester was replaced by a new county council for Worcestershire (with district councils) and a unitary authority for Herefordshire. On 1 April 2009 the county areas of Cornwall, Durham, Northumberland, Shropshire and Wiltshire were given unitary status and two new unitary authorities were created for Bedfordshire (Bedford and Central Bedfordshire) and Cheshire (Cheshire East and Cheshire West & Chester) replacing the two-tier county/district system in these areas.

The Local Government (Wales) Act 1994 and the Local Government etc (Scotland) Act 1994 abolished the two-tier structure in Wales and Scotland with effect from 1 April 1996, replacing it with a single tier of unitary authorities.

ELECTIONS

Local elections are normally held on the first Thursday in May. Generally, all British subjects, citizens of the Republic of Ireland, Commonwealth and other European Union citizens who are 18 years or over and resident on the qualifying date in the area for which the election is being held, are entitled to vote at local government elections. A register of electors is prepared and published annually by local electoral registration officers.

A returning officer has the overall responsibility for an election. Voting takes place at polling stations, arranged by the local authority and under the supervision of a presiding officer specially appointed for the purpose. Candidates, who are subject to various statutory qualifications and disqualifications designed to ensure that they are suitable to hold office, must be nominated by electors for the electoral area concerned.

In England, the Local Government Boundary Commission for England is responsible for carrying out periodic reviews of electoral arrangements, to consider whether the boundaries of wards or divisions within a local authority need to be altered to take account of changes in electorate; structural reviews, to consider whether a single, unitary authority should be established in an area instead of an existing two-tier system; and administrative boundary reviews of district or county authorities.

The Local Government Boundary Commission for Wales, the Local Government Boundary Commission for Scotland and the local government boundary commissioner for Northern Ireland (appointed when required by the Boundary Commission for Northern Ireland) are responsible for reviewing the electoral arrangements and boundaries of local authorities within their respective regions.

The Local Government Act 2000 provided for the secretary of state to change the frequency and phasing of elections in England and Wales.

LOCAL GOVERNMENT BOUNDARY COMMISSION FOR ENGLAND, Layden House, 76–86 Turnmill Street, London EC1M 5LG **T** 020-7296 6227 **E** reviews@lgbce.org.uk **W** www.lgbce.org.uk

LOCAL GOVERNMENT BOUNDARY COMMISSION FOR WALES, Caradog House, 1–6 St Andrew's Place, Cardiff CF10 3BE **T** 029-2039 5031 **E** lgbc.wales@wales.gsi.gov.uk **W** www.lgbc-wales.gov.uk

LOCAL GOVERNMENT BOUNDARY COMMISSION FOR SCOTLAND, Thistle House, 91 Haymarket Terrace, Edinburgh EH12 5HD **T** 0131-538 7510 **E** lgbcs@scottishboundaries.gov.uk **W** www.lgbc-scotland.gov.uk

BOUNDARY COMMISSION FOR NORTHERN IRELAND, Forestview, Purdy's Lane, Newtownbreda, Belfast BT8 7AR **T** 028-9069 4800 **E** bcni@belfast.org.uk **W** www.boundarycommission.org.uk

INTERNAL ORGANISATION

The council as a whole is the final decision-making body within any authority. Councils are free to a great extent to make their own internal organisational arrangements. The Local Government Act, given royal assent on 28 July 2000, allows councils to adopt one of three broad categories of a new constitution which include a separate executive.

These three categories are:

- A directly elected mayor with a cabinet selected by that mayor
- A cabinet, either elected by the council or appointed by its leader
- A directly elected mayor and council manager

Normally, questions of policy are settled by the full council, while the administration of the various services is the responsibility of committees of councillors. Day-to-day decisions are delegated to the council's officers, who act within the policies laid down by the councillors.

FINANCE

Local government in England, Wales and Scotland is financed from four sources: council tax, non-domestic rates, government grants and income from fees and charges for services.

COUNCIL TAX

Under the Local Government Finance Act 1992, from 1 April 1993 council tax replaced the community charge (which had been introduced in April 1989 in Scotland and April 1990 in England and Wales in place of domestic rates).

Council tax is a local tax levied by each local council. Liability for the council tax bill usually falls on the owner-occupier or tenant of a dwelling which is their sole or main residence. Council tax bills may be reduced because of the personal circumstances of people resident in a property, and there are discounts in the case of dwellings occupied by fewer than two adults.

In England, unitary and metropolitan authorities are responsible for collecting their own council tax from which the police authorities claim their share. In areas where there are two tiers of local authority, each county, district and police authority sets its own council tax rate; the district authorities collect the combined council tax and the county councils and police authorities claim their share from the district councils' collection funds. In Wales, each unitary authority and each police authority sets its own council tax rate. The unitary authorities collect the combined council tax and the police authorities claim their share from the funds. In Scotland, each local authority sets its own rate of council tax.

The tax relates to the value of the dwelling. In England and Scotland each dwelling is placed in one of eight valuation bands, ranging from A to H, based on the property's estimated market value as at 1 April 1991. In Wales there are nine bands, ranging from A to I, based on the estimated market value of property as at 1 April 2003.

The valuation bands and ranges of values in England, Wales and Scotland are:

England

A	Up to £40,000	E	£88,001–£120,000
B	£40,001–£52,000	F	£120,001–£160,000
C	£52,001–£68,000	G	£160,001–£320,000
D	£68,001–£88,000	H	Over £320,001

Wales

A	Up to £44,000	F	£162,001–£223,000
B	£44,001–£65,000	G	£223,001–£324,000
C	£65,001–£91,000	H	£324,001–£424,000
D	£91,001–£123,000	I	Over £424,001
E	£123,001–£162,000		

Scotland

A	Up to £27,000	E	£58,001–£80,000
B	£27,001–£35,000	F	£80,001–£106,000
C	£35,001–£45,000	G	£106,001–£212,000
D	£45,001–£58,000	H	Over £212,001

The council tax within a local area varies between the different bands according to proportions laid down by law. The charge attributable to each band as a proportion of the Band D charge set by the council is approximately:

A	67%	F	144%
B	78%	G	167%
C	89%	H	200%
D	100%	I	233%*
E	122%		

* Wales only

The average Band D council tax bill for each authority area is given in the tables on the following pages. There may be variations from the given figure within each district council area because of different parish or community precepts being levied.

NON-DOMESTIC RATES

Non-domestic (business) rates are collected by billing authorities; these are the district councils in those areas of England with two tiers of local government and are unitary authorities in other parts of England, in Wales and in Scotland. In respect of England and Wales, the Local Government Finance Act 1988 provides for liability for rates to be assessed on the basis of a poundage (multiplier) tax on the rateable value of property (hereditaments). Separate multipliers are set by the Department for Communities and Local Government (CLG) in England, the Welsh Assembly government and the Scottish government. Rates are collected by the billing authority for the area where a property is located. Rate income collected by billing authorities is paid into a national non-domestic rating (NNDR) pool and redistributed to individual authorities on the basis of the adult population figure as prescribed by CLG, the Welsh Assembly government or the Scottish government. The rates pools are maintained separately in England, Wales and Scotland. Actual payment of rates in certain cases is subject to transitional arrangements, to phase in the larger increases and reductions in rates resulting from the effects of the latest revaluation.

Rateable values for the 2010 rating lists came into effect on 1 April 2010. They are derived from the rental value of property as at 1 April 2003 and determined on certain statutory assumptions by the Valuation Office Agency in England and Wales, and by local area assessors in Scotland. New property which is added to the list, and significant changes to existing property, necessitate amendments to the rateable value on the same basis. Rating lists (valuation rolls in Scotland) remain in force until the next general revaluation. Such revaluations take place every five years, the next being in 2015.

Certain types of property are exempt from rates, eg agricultural land and buildings, certain businesses and some places of public religious worship. Charities and other non-profit-making organisations may receive full or partial relief. Empty commercial property in England and Wales is exempt from business rates for the first three months that the property is vacant (six months for an industrial property), after which full business rates are normally payable.* In Scotland an empty commercial property is exempt from business rates for the first three months and entitled to a 50 per cent discount thereafter, except for some types of premises, such as factories, which are entirely exempt.

* Empty property with a rateable value of less than £18,000 is exempt from business rates until 31 March 2011

GOVERNMENT GRANTS

In addition to specific grants in support of revenue expenditure on particular services, central government pays a revenue support grant to local authorities. This grant is paid to each local authority so that if each authority spends at the level of its standard spending assessment, all authorities in the same class can set broadly the same council tax.

COMPLAINTS

ENGLAND

In England the Local Government Ombudsman investigates complaints of injustice arising from maladministration by local authorities and certain other bodies. The Local Government Ombudsman will not usually consider a complaint unless the local authority concerned has had an opportunity to investigate and reply to a complainant.

The Local Government Act 2000 established a standards board, now called Standards for England, and an independent tribunal known as the Adjudication Panel for England. Standards for England's main task is to ensure that standards of ethical conduct are maintained and to investigate any allegations that councillors have breached the council's code of conduct. At the end of an investigation, a case may be referred to either the relevant local authority's standards committee or the Adjudication Panel, which has a number of sanctions at its disposal, up to and including the disqualification of a member from holding office for five years. In May 2010 the coalition government announced plans to abolish the standards board regime.

LOCAL GOVERNMENT STANDARDS IN ENGLAND, Tribunal Service, York House, 31–36 York Place, Leeds LS1 2ED **T** 0113-389 6013
E AP-enquiries@tribunals.gsi.gov.uk
W www.adjudicationpanel.tribunals.gov.uk

LOCAL GOVERNMENT OMBUDSMAN, PO Box 4771, Coventry CV4 0EH **T** 0300-061 0614 **E** advice@lgo.org.uk
W www.lgo.org.uk
Ombudsmen, Jane Martin, Tony Redmond, Anne Seex

STANDARDS FOR ENGLAND, 4th Floor, Griffin House, 40 Lever Street, Manchester M1 1BB **T** 0161-817 5300
E enquiries@standardsboard.gov.uk
W www.standardsforengland.gov.uk

WALES

The office of Public Services Ombudsman for Wales came into force on 1 April 2006, incorporating the functions of the Local Government Ombudsman for Wales.

PUBLIC SERVICES OMBUDSMAN FOR WALES, 1 Ffordd yr Hen Gae, Pencoed CF35 5LJ
T 0845-601 0987 **E** ask@ombudsman-wales.org.uk
W www.ombudsman-wales.org.uk
Ombudsman, Peter Tyndall

SCOTLAND

The Scottish Public Services Ombudsman is responsible for complaints regarding the maladministration of local government in Scotland.

SCOTTISH PUBLIC SERVICES OMBUDSMAN, 4 Melville Street, Edinburgh EH3 7NS **T** 0800-377 7330
E ask@spso.org.uk **W** www.spso.org.uk
Ombudsman, Jim Martin

NORTHERN IRELAND

The Northern Ireland Commissioner for Complaints fulfils a similar function in Northern Ireland, investigating complaints about local authorities and certain public bodies. Complaints are made to the relevant local authority in the first instance but may also be made directly to the commissioner.

NORTHERN IRELAND COMMISSIONER FOR COMPLAINTS, Freepost BEL 1478, Belfast BT1 6BR
T 0800-343424 **E** ombudsman@ni-ombudsman.org.uk
W www.ni-ombudsman.org.uk
Northern Ireland Commissioner for Complaints, Tom Frawley, CBE

THE QUEEN'S REPRESENTATIVES

The lord-lieutenant of a county is the permanent local representative of the Crown in that county. The appointment of lord-lieutenants is now regulated by the Lieutenancies Act 1997. They are appointed by the sovereign on the recommendation of the prime minister. The retirement age is 75. The office of lord-lieutenant dates from 1551, and its holder was originally responsible for maintaining order and for local defence in the county. The duties of the post include attending on royalty during official visits to the county, performing certain duties in connection with the armed forces (and in particular the reserve forces), and making presentations of honours and awards on behalf of the Crown. In England, Wales and Northern Ireland, the lord-lieutenant usually also holds the office of *Custos Rotulorum.* As such, he or she acts as head of the county's commission of the peace (which recommends the appointment of magistrates).

The office of sheriff (from the Old English *shire-reeve*) of a county was created in the tenth century. The sheriff was the special nominee of the sovereign, and the office reached the peak of its influence under the Norman kings. The Provisions of Oxford (1258) laid down a yearly tenure of office. Since the mid-16th century the office has been purely civil, with military duties taken over by the lord-lieutenant of the county. The sheriff (commonly known as 'high sheriff') attends on royalty during official visits to the county, acts as the returning officer during parliamentary elections in county constituencies, attends the opening ceremony when a high court judge goes on circuit, executes high court writs, and appoints under-sheriffs to act as deputies. The appointments and duties of the sheriffs in England and Wales are laid down by the Sheriffs Act 1887.

The serving high sheriff submits a list of names of possible future sheriffs to a tribunal, which chooses three names to put to the sovereign. The tribunal nominates the high sheriff annually on 12 November and the sovereign picks the name of the sheriff to succeed in the following year. The term of office runs from 25 March to the following 24 March (the civil and legal year before 1752). No person may be chosen twice in three years if there is any other suitable person in the county.

CIVIC DIGNITIES

District councils in England and local councils in Wales may petition for a royal charter granting borough or 'city' status to the council.

In England and Wales the chair of a borough or county borough council may be called a mayor, and the chair of a city council may be called a lord mayor (if lord mayoralty has been conferred on that city). Parish councils in England and community councils in Wales may call themselves 'town councils', in which case their chair is the town mayor.

In Scotland the chair of a local council may be known as a convenor; a provost is the mayoral equivalent. The chair of the councils for the cities of Aberdeen, Dundee, Edinburgh and Glasgow are lord provosts.

ENGLAND

In April 2009 five county councils were given unitary status, abolishing the two-tier district/county system within these areas, and a further four unitary authorities were created from the division of the county areas of Bedfordshire and Cheshire. Plans to create unitary authorities at Exeter, Norwich and Suffolk were revoked by the coalition government in May 2010. There are 27 counties, divided into 201 districts, 55 unitary authorities (plus the Isles of Scilly) and 36 metropolitan boroughs.

The populations of most of the unitary authorities are in the range of 100,000 to 300,000. The district councils have populations broadly in the range of 60,000 to 100,000; some, however, have larger populations, because of the need to avoid dividing large towns, and some in mainly rural areas have smaller populations.

The main conurbations outside Greater London – Tyne and Wear, West Midlands, Merseyside, Greater Manchester, West Yorkshire and South Yorkshire – are divided into 36 metropolitan boroughs, most of which have a population of over 200,000.

There are also about 8,700 town and parish councils with a population coverage of around 17 million.

ELECTIONS

For districts, counties and for about 8,000 parishes, there are elected councils, consisting of directly elected councillors. The councillors elect one of their number as chair annually.

In general, councils can have whole council elections, elections by thirds or elections by halves. However all metropolitan authorities must hold elections by thirds. The electoral cycle of any new unitary authority is specified in the appropriate statutory order under which it is established.

FUNCTIONS

In areas with a two-tier system of local governance, functions are divided between the district and county authorities, with those functions affecting the larger area or population generally being the responsibility of the county council. A few functions continue to be exercised over the larger area by joint bodies, made up of councillors from each authority within the area.

Generally the allocation of functions is as follows:

County councils: education; strategic planning; traffic, transport and highways; fire service; consumer protection; refuse disposal; smallholdings; social care; libraries

District councils: local planning; housing; highways (maintenance of certain urban roads and off-street car parks); building regulations; environmental health; refuse collection; cemeteries and crematoria; collection of council tax and non-domestic rates

Unitary and metropolitan councils: their functions are all those listed above, except that the fire service is exercised by a joint body

Concurrently by county and district councils: recreation (parks, playing fields, swimming pools); museums; encouragement of the arts, tourism and industry

PARISH COUNCILS

Parish or town councils are the most local tier of government in England. There are currently around 10,000 parishes in England, of which around 8,700 have councils served by approximately 70,000 councillors. Since 15 February 2008 local councils have been able to create new parish councils without seeking approval from the government. Around 80 per cent of parish councils represent populations of less than 2,500; parishes with no parish council can be grouped with neighbouring parishes under a common parish council. A parish council comprises at least five members, the number being fixed by the district council. Elections are held every four years, at the time of the election of the district councillor for the ward including the parish. Full parish councils must be formed for those parishes with more than 999 electors – below this number, parish meetings comprising the electors of the parish must be held at least twice a year.

Parish council functions include: allotments; encouragement of arts and crafts; community halls, recreational facilities (eg open spaces, swimming pools), cemeteries and crematoria; and many minor functions. They must also be given an opportunity to comment on planning applications. They may, like county and district councils, spend limited sums for the general benefit of the parish. They levy a precept on the district councils for their funds. Parish precepts for 2010–11 totalled £357m, an increase of 5 per cent on 2009–10.

REGIONAL DEVELOPMENT AGENCIES

Eight voluntary regional chambers were established for the East Midlands, the East of England, the North East, the North West, the South East, the South West, the West Midlands and Yorkshire and the Humber under the Regional Development Agencies Act 1998. The chambers operated within the same boundaries as the regional development agencies. The Regional Assemblies (Preparations) Act received royal assent on 8 May 2003, giving the chambers responsibility to act as regional planning bodies and to receive direct funding from central government for fulfilling this role.

After the *Sub-national Review of Economic Development and Regeneration* (July 2007), regional assemblies were abolished in 2010, with responsibility for regional planning being passed to the regional development agencies. Local authorities were given a new statutory duty to assess local economic conditions and have a stronger role in the area's economic development. In June 2010 the coalition government announced plans to abolish the regional development agencies, to be replaced with local economic partnerships (LEPs). Planning responsibilities are to pass back to local authorities.

FINANCE

The local government budget requirement (including parish precepts) for 2010–11 is £55.4bn; of this £26.3bn is to be raised through council tax, £21.5bn from redistributed business rates, £3.1bn from revenue support grant and £4.4bn from police grant.

In England, the average council tax per dwelling for 2010–11 is £1,195, up from £1,175 in 2009–10, an increase of 1.7 per cent. The average council tax bill for a Band D dwelling (occupied by two adults, including parish precepts) for 2010–11 is £1,439, an average increase of 1.8 per cent from 2009–10. The average Band D council tax is £1,484 in shire areas, £1,399 in metropolitan areas and £1,309 in London. Since 2006–7 the London figure has included a levy to fund the 2012 Olympic Games, which equates to a £20 a year increase on a Band D council tax.

The provisional amount estimated to be raised from national non-domestic rates from central and local lists is £19.5bn. The non-domestic rating multiplier for England for 2010–11 is 41.4p (40.7p for small businesses).

The City of London is able to set a different multiplier from the rest of England; for 2010–11 this is 41.8p (41.1p for small businesses).

Under the Local Government and Housing Act 1989, local authorities have four main ways of paying for capital expenditure: borrowing and other forms of extended credit; capital grants from central government towards some types of capital expenditure; 'usable' capital receipts from the sale of land, houses and other assets; and revenue.

The amount of capital expenditure which a local authority can finance by borrowing (or other forms of credit) is effectively limited by the credit approvals issued to it by central government. Most credit approvals can be used for any kind of local authority capital expenditure; these are known as basic credit approvals. Others (supplementary credit approvals) can be used only for the kind of expenditure specified in the approval, and so are often given to fund particular projects or services.

Local authorities can use all capital receipts from the sale of property or assets for capital spending, except in the case of sales of council houses. Generally, the 'usable' part of a local authority's capital receipts consists of 25 per cent of receipts from the sale of council houses and 50 per cent of other housing assets such as shops or vacant land. The balance has to be set aside as provision for repaying debt and meeting other credit liabilities.

EXPENDITURE

Local authority budgeted net expenditure for 2009–10 was:

Service	*£ million*
Education	42,991
Highways and transport	6,332
Social care	20,251
Housing (excluding HRA)	2,478
Cultural, environment and planning	10,533
Police	12,218
Fire and rescue	2,311
Courts	71
Central services	3,521
Mandatory rent allowances	10,126
Mandatory rent rebates	641
Rent rebates granted to HRA tenants	3,885
Other services	202
Net current expenditure	115,559
Capital financing	3,595
Capital expenditure charged to revenue account	1,750
Council tax benefit	3,623
Discretionary non-domestic rate relief	26
Bad debt provision	31
Flood defence payments to Environment Agency	31
Pensions interest cost and expected return on pensions assets	4,810
Less appropriations from pensions reserves	(4,896)
Less interest receipts	(720)
Less specific grants outside AEF	(21,011)
Gross revenue expenditure	102,823
Less specific grants inside AEF	(44,083)
Less area-based grant	(3,145)
Net revenue expenditure	55,640
Less appropriations from other revenue reserves	(1,635)
Less adjustments	(10)
BUDGET REQUIREMENT	54,016

HRA = Housing Revenue Account
AEF = aggregate external finance

LONDON

The Greater London Council was abolished in 1986 and London was divided into 32 borough councils, which have a status similar to the metropolitan borough councils in the rest of England, and the City of London Corporation.

In March 1998 the government announced proposals for a Greater London Authority (GLA) covering the area of the 32 London boroughs and the City of London, which would comprise a directly elected mayor and a 25-member assembly. A referendum was held in London on 7 May 1998; the turnout was approximately 34 per cent and 72 per cent of electors voted in favour of the GLA. A London mayor was elected on 4 May 2000 and the authority assumed its responsibilities on 3 July 2000 (*see also* Regional Government).

The GLA is responsible for transport, economic development, strategic planning, culture, health, the environment, the police and fire and emergency planning. The separately elected assembly scrutinises the mayor's activities and approves plans and budgets. There are 14 constituency assembly members, each representing a separate area of London (each constituency is made up of two or three complete London boroughs). Eleven additional members, making up the total assembly complement of 25 members, are elected on a London-wide basis, either as independents or from party political lists on the basis of proportional representation.

LONDON BOROUGH COUNCILS

The London boroughs have whole council elections every four years, in the year immediately following the county council election year. The most recent elections took place on 6 May 2010.

The borough councils have responsibility for the following functions: building regulations, cemeteries and crematoria, consumer protection, education, youth employment, environmental health, electoral registration, food, drugs, housing, leisure services, libraries, local planning, local roads, museums, parking, recreation (parks, playing fields, swimming pools), refuse collection and street cleaning, social services, town planning and traffic management.

CITY OF LONDON CORPORATION

The City of London Corporation is the local authority for the City of London. Its legal definition is the 'Mayor and Commonalty and Citizens of the City of London'. It is governed by the court of common council, which consists of the lord mayor, 25 other aldermen and 100 common councilmen. The lord mayor and two sheriffs are nominated annually by the City guilds (the livery companies) and elected by the court of aldermen. Aldermen and councilmen are elected from the 25 wards into which the City is divided; councilmen must stand for re-election annually. The council is a legislative assembly, and there are no political parties.

The corporation has the same functions as the London borough councils. In addition, it runs the City of London Police; is the health authority for the Port of London; has health control of animal imports throughout Greater London, including at Heathrow airport; owns and manages public open spaces throughout Greater London; runs the central criminal court; and runs Billingsgate, Smithfield and Spitalfields markets.

THE CITY GUILDS (LIVERY COMPANIES)

The livery companies of the City of London grew out of early medieval religious fraternities and began to emerge as trade and craft guilds, retaining their religious aspect, in the 12th century. From the early 14th century, only members of the trade and craft guilds could call themselves citizens of the City of London. The guilds began to be called livery companies, because of the distinctive livery worn by the most prosperous guild members on ceremonial occasions, in the late 15th century.

By the early 19th century the power of the companies within their trades had begun to wane, but those wearing the livery of a company continued to play an important role in the government of the City of London. Liverymen still have the right to nominate the lord mayor and sheriffs, and most members of the court of common council are liverymen.

WALES

The Local Government (Wales) Act 1994 abolished the two-tier structure of eight county and 37 district councils which had existed since 1974, and replaced it, from 1 April 1996, with 22 unitary authorities. The new authorities were elected in May 1995. Each unitary authority inherited all the functions of the previous county and district councils, except fire services (which are provided by three combined fire authorities, composed of representatives from the unitary authorities) and national parks (which are the responsibility of three independent national park authorities).

COMMUNITY COUNCILS

In Wales community councils are the equivalent of parishes in England. Unlike England, where many areas are not in any parish, communities have been established for the whole of Wales, approximately 865 communities in all. Community meetings may be convened as and when desired.

Community or town councils exist in 736 of the communities and further councils may be established at the request of a community meeting. Community councils have broadly the same range of powers as English parish councils. Community councillors are elected for a term of four years.

ELECTIONS

Elections take place every four years; the last elections took place in May 2008.

FINANCE

Total budgeted revenue expenditure for 2010–11 is £7.5bn, an increase of 3.3 per cent on 2009–10. Total budget requirement, which excludes expenditure financed by specific and special government grants and any use of reserves, is £5.8bn. This comprises revenue support grant of £3.3bn, support from the national non-domestic rate pool of £935m, police grant of £242m and £1.3bn to be raised through council tax. The non-domestic rating multiplier for Wales for 2010–11 is 40.9p. The average Band D council tax levied in Wales for 2010–11 is £1,127, comprising unitary authorities £927, police authorities £175 and community councils £25.

EXPENDITURE

Local authority budgeted net revenue expenditure for 2010–11 is:

Service	*£ million*
Education	2,574
Social services	1,431
Council fund housing, including housing benefit	923
Local environmental services	431
Roads and transport	324
Libraries, culture, heritage, sport and recreation	277
Planning, economic and community development	137
Council tax collection	30
Debt financing costs: counties	325
Central administrative and other revenue expenditure	248
Police	685
Fire	149
National parks	16
Gross revenue expenditure	7,549
Less specific and special government grants	(1,784)
Net revenue expenditure	5,765
Less appropriations from reserves	(13)
BUDGET REQUIREMENT	5,752

SCOTLAND

The Local Government etc (Scotland) Act 1994 abolished the two-tier structure of nine regional and 53 district councils which had existed since 1975 and replaced it, from 1 April 1996, with 29 unitary authorities on the mainland; the three islands councils remained. The new authorities were elected in April 1995.

In July 1999 the Scottish parliament assumed responsibility for legislation on local government. The government had established a commission on local government and the Scottish parliament (the McIntosh Commission) to make recommendations on the relationship between local authorities and the Scottish parliament and on increasing local authorities' accountability.

The local government in Scotland bill was introduced to the Scottish parliament in May 2002. The bill focused on three integrated core elements:

- A power for local authorities to promote and improve the well-being of their area and/or persons in it
- Statutory underpinning for community planning through the introduction of a duty on local authorities and key partners, including police, health boards and enterprise agencies
- A duty to secure best value

ELECTIONS

The unitary authorities consist of directly elected councillors. The Scottish Local Government (Elections) Act 2002 moved elections from a three-year to a four-year cycle; the last elections took place in May 2007.

FUNCTIONS

The functions of the councils and islands councils are: education; social work; strategic planning; the provision of infrastructure such as roads; consumer protection; flood prevention; coast protection; valuation and rating; the police and fire services; civil defence; electoral registration; public transport; registration of births, deaths and marriages; housing; leisure and recreation;

development and building control; environmental health; licensing; allotments; public conveniences; and the administration of district courts.

COMMUNITY COUNCILS

Scottish community councils differ from those in England and Wales. Their purpose as defined in statute is to ascertain and express the views of the communities they represent, and to take in the interests of their communities such action as appears to be expedient or practicable. Around 1,200 community councils have been established under schemes drawn up by local authorities in Scotland.

FINANCE

Budgeted total revenue support for 2010–11 is £11.1bn, comprising £8.1bn general revenue funding, non-domestic rate income of £2.1bn and ring-fenced grants of £533m. The non-domestic rate multiplier or poundage for 2010–11 is 40.7p. All non-domestic properties with a rateable value of £18,000 or less may be eligible for non-domestic rates relief of up to 100 per cent. The average Band D council tax for 2010–11 is £1,149.

EXPENDITURE

The 2010–11 net expenditure budget estimates for local authorities in Scotland were:

Service	*£ million*
Education	4,803
Cultural and related services	634
Social work services	2,844
Police	968
Roads and transport	494
Environmental services	695
Fire	276
Planning and development services	320
Other	1,902
TOTAL	12,937

NORTHERN IRELAND

For the purpose of local government, Northern Ireland has a system of 26 single-tier district councils.

ELECTIONS

Council members are elected for periods of four years at a time on the principle of proportional representation.

FUNCTIONS

The district councils have three main roles. These are:

Executive: responsibility for a wide range of local services including building regulations; community services; consumer protection; cultural facilities; environmental health; miscellaneous licensing and registration provisions, including dog control; litter prevention; recreational and social facilities; refuse collection and disposal; street cleaning; and tourist development

Representative: nominating representatives to sit as members of the various statutory bodies responsible for the administration of regional services such as drainage, education, fire, health and personal social services, housing, and libraries

Consultative: acting as the medium through which the views of local people are expressed on the operation in their area of other regional services – notably conservation (including water supply and sewerage services), planning and roads – provided by those departments of central government which have an obligation, statutory or otherwise, to consult the district councils about proposals affecting their areas

FINANCE

Local government in Northern Ireland is funded by a system of rates. The ratepayer receives a combined tax bill consisting of the regional rate and the district rate, which is set by each district council. The regional and district rates are both collected by the Land and Property Services Agency (formerly the Rate Collection Agency). The product of the district rates is paid over to each council while the product of the regional rate supports expenditure by the departments of the executive and assembly.

Since April 2007 domestic rates bills have been based on the capital value of a property, rather than the rental value. The capital value is defined as the price the property might reasonably be expected to realise had it been sold on the open market on 1 January 2005. Non-domestic rates bills are based on 2001 rental values.

Rate bills are calculated by multiplying the property's net annual rental value (in the case of non-domestic property), or capital value (in the case of domestic property), by the regional and district rate poundages respectively.

For 2010–11 the overall average domestic poundage is 0.67p compared to 0.66p in 2009–10. The overall average non-domestic rate poundage in 2010–11 is 54.33p compared to 52.35p in 2009–10.

POLITICAL COMPOSITION OF LOCAL COUNCILS

as at June 2010

Abbreviations

All.	Alliance
BNP	British National Party
C.	Conservative
DUP	Democratic Unionist Party
Green	Green
Ind.	Independent
Ind. Un.	Independent Unionist
Lab.	Labour
LD	Liberal Democrat
Lib.	Liberal
O.	Other
PC	Plaid Cymru
R	Residents Associations/Ratepayers
SD	Social Democrat
SDLP	Social Democratic and Labour Party
SF	Sinn Fein
SNP	Scottish National Party
Soc.	Socialist
UUP	Ulster Unionist Party
v.	Vacant

Total number of seats is given in parentheses after council name.

ENGLAND

COUNTY COUNCILS

Buckinghamshire (57)	C. 46; LD 11
Cambridgeshire (69)	C. 42; LD 23; Lab. 2; Green 1; O. 1
Cumbria (84)	C. 37; Lab. 24; LD 16; Ind. 5; O. 1; v. 1
Derbyshire (64)	C. 33; Lab. 22; LD 8; Ind. 1
Devon (62)	C. 41; LD 14; Lab. 4; Ind. 2; Green 1
Dorset (45)	C. 28; LD 16; Ind. 1
East Sussex (49)	C. 29; LD 13; Lab. 4; O. 2; Ind. 1
Essex (75)	C. 60; LD 12; Ind. 2; Lab. 1
Gloucestershire (63)	C. 41; LD 14; Lab. 4; O. 4; Green 1
Hampshire (78)	C. 51; LD 25; Lab. 1; O. 1
Hertfordshire (77)	C. 55; LD 16; Lab. 3; BNP 1; Green 1; v. 1
Kent (84)	C. 74; LD 7; Lab. 2; Ind. 1
Lancashire (84)	C. 51; Lab. 17; LD 9; Ind. 3; Green 2; BNP 1; O. 1
Leicestershire (55)	C. 36; LD 14; Lab. 4; BNP 1
Lincolnshire (77)	C. 61; Ind. 7; LD 5; Lab. 4
Norfolk (84)	C. 60; LD 13; Green 7; Lab. 3; O. 1
North Yorkshire (72)	C. 48; LD 11; Ind. 10; Lab. 1; Lib. 1; O. 1
Northamptonshire (73)	C. 56; LD 9; Lab. 6; Ind. 2
Nottinghamshire (67)	C. 36; Lab. 14; LD 9; O. 6; Ind. 2
Oxfordshire (74)	C. 52; LD 10; Lab. 9; Green 2; Ind. 1
Somerset (58)	C. 34; LD 22; Lab. 2
Staffordshire (62)	C. 49; O. 10; Lab. 3
Suffolk (75)	C. 55; LD 11; Lab. 4; Green 2; Ind. 2; O. 1
Surrey (80)	C. 55; LD. 13; Ind. 10; Lab. 1; v. 1
Warwickshire (62)	C. 38; LD 12; Lab. 11; Ind. 1
West Sussex (71)	C. 49; LD 20; Lab. 2
Worcestershire (57)	C. 41; LD 8; Lab. 3; O. 3; Lib. 1; Ind. 1

DISTRICT COUNCILS

Adur (29)	C. 25; Ind. 2; LD. 2
Allerdale (56)	O. 29; Lab. 22; Ind. 5
Amber Valley (45)	C. 29; Lab. 14; BNP 2
Arun (56)	C. 41; LD 9; Ind. 3; Lab. 3
Ashfield (33)	LD 13; Lab. 9; Ind. 8; O. 3
Ashford (43)	C. 28; LD 8; Ind. 2; O. 3; Lab. 2
Aylesbury Vale (59)	C. 37; LD 21; Ind. 1
Babergh (43)	C. 17; LD 16; Ind. 8; O. 1; v. 1
Barrow-in-Furness (36)	Lab. 16; C. 13; Ind. 4; Soc. 2; O. 1
Basildon (42)	C. 29; Lab. 10; LD 3
Basingstoke and Deane (60)	C. 34; LD 14; Lab. 9; Ind. 2; O. 1
Bassetlaw (48)	C. 25; Lab. 20; Ind. 3
Blaby (39)	C. 27; LD 7; Lab. 4; Ind. 1
Bolsover (37)	Lab. 28; Ind. 6; R 3
Boston (32)	O. 22; C. 7; Ind. 3
Braintree (60)	C. 42; Lab. 9; R 5; Green 2; Ind. 1; LD 1
Breckland (54)	C. 48; Ind. 3; Lab. 3
Brentwood (37)	C. 27; LD 8; Ind. 1; Lab. 1
Broadland (47)	C. 34; LD 12; Ind. 1
Bromsgrove (39)	C. 26; Lab. 6; Ind. 4; R 2; O. 1
Broxbourne (38)	C. 35; Lab. 3
Broxtowe (44)	C. 18; LD 13; Lab. 10; Ind. 2; v. 1
Burnley (45)	LD 23; Lab. 14; C. 5; BNP 2; Ind. 1
Cambridge (42)	LD 29; Lab. 9; Green 2; C. 1; Ind. 1
Cannock Chase (41)	LD 15; Lab. 13; C. 11; Ind.2
Canterbury (50)	C. 28; LD 18; Ind. 2; Lab. 2
Carlisle (52)	Lab. 23; C. 22; LD 5; Ind. 2
Castle Point (41)	C. 25; Ind. 16
Charnwood (52)	C. 32; Lab. 13; LD 5; BNP 1; Ind. 1
Chelmsford (57)	C. 31; LD 26
Cheltenham (40)	LD 25; C. 12; O. 3
Cherwell (50)	C. 44; LD 3; Lab. 2; v. 1
Chesterfield (48)	LD 37; Lab. 11
Chichester (48)	C. 33; LD 11; O. 2; Ind. 1; v. 1
Chiltern (40)	C. 29; LD 9; Ind. 2
Chorley (47)	C. 27; Lab. 15; LD 3; Ind. 2
Christchurch (24)	C. 17; LD 4; Ind. 3
Colchester (60)	LD 26; C. 24; Lab. 7; Ind. 3
Copeland (51)	Lab. 30; C. 18; Ind. 2; O.1
Corby (29)	Lab. 16; C. 8; LD 5
Cotswolds (44)	C. 37; LD 5; Ind. 2
Craven (30)	C. 18; Ind. 7; LD 4; O. 1
Crawley (37)	C. 26; Lab. 11
Dacorum (51)	C. 44; LD 5; Lab. 2
Dartford (44)	C. 26; Lab. 12; O. 6
Daventry (38)	C. 35; LD 2; Lab. 1
Derbyshire Dales (39)	C. 26; LD 8; Lab. 4; Ind. 1
Dover (45)	C. 28; Lab. 15; LD 2
East Cambridgeshire (39)	C. 24; LD 13; Ind. 2
East Devon (59)	C. 42; LD 10; Ind. 7

East Dorset (36)	C. 25; LD 10; v.1
East Hampshire (44)	C. 30; LD 14
East Hertfordshire (50)	C. 41; LD 5; Ind. 3; O. 1
East Lindsey (60)	C. 28; O. 21; Lab. 7; Ind. 2; LD 2
East Northamptonshire (40)	C. 38; Ind. 2
East Staffordshire (39)	C. 24; Lab. 12; LD 2; Ind. 1
Eastbourne (27)	LD 20; C. 7
Eastleigh (44)	LD 39; C. 4; Lab. 1
Eden (38)	O. 19; C. 12; LD 6; Ind. 1
Elmbridge (60)	C. 33; R 18; LD 7; O. 2
Epping Forest (58)	C. 37; R 10; LD 7; Ind. 2; BNP 1; Lab. 1
Epsom and Ewell (38)	R 22; LD 10; C. 4; Ind. 1; Lab. 1
Erewash (51)	C. 28; Lab. 19; Ind. 2; LD 2
Exeter (40)	v. 13; C. 8; Lab. 8; LD 8; Lib. 3
Fareham (31)	C. 23; LD 8
Fenland (40)	C. 38; Ind. 1; LD 1
Forest Heath (27)	C. 20; LD 3; Ind. 2; O. 2
Forest of Dean (48)	C. 25; Ind. 11; Lab. 8; LD 3; v. 1
Fylde (51)	C. 29; Ind. 16; O. 3; LD 2; v. 1
Gedling (50)	C. 28; Lab. 9; LD 8; Ind. 5
Gloucester (36)	C. 17; LD 11; Lab. 8
Gosport (34)	C. 22; LD 6; Lab. 3; Ind. 2; v. 1
Gravesham (44)	C. 27; Lab. 17
Great Yarmouth (39)	C. 24; Lab. 15
Guildford (48)	C. 26; LD 21; v. 1
Hambleton (44)	C. 39; Ind. 3; LD 2
Harborough (37)	C. 26; LD 11
Harlow (33)	C. 18; Lab. 10; LD 5
Harrogate (54)	C. 28; LD 22; Ind. 4
Hart (35)	C. 20; LD 10; O. 5
Hastings (32)	Lab 16; C. 14; LD 1; v. 1
Havant (38)	C. 34; LD 3; Lab 1
Hertsmere (39)	C. 34; Lab. 3; LD 2
High Peak (43)	C. 24; Lab. 9; LD 6; Ind. 2; O. 2
Hinckley and Bosworth (34)	LD 19; C. 12; Lab. 2; Ind. 1
Horsham (44)	C. 30; LD 12; Ind. 2
Huntingdonshire (52)	C. 37; LD 12; O. 2; Ind. 1
Hyndburn (35)	C. 17; Lab. 14; O. 3; Ind. 1
Ipswich (48)	Lab. 23; C. 18; LD 7
Kettering (36)	C. 28; Lab. 6; Ind. 2
King's Lynn and West Norfolk (62)	C. 53; Lab. 4; LD 4; Ind. 1
Lancaster (60)	O. 15; Lab. 13; Green 12; C. 11; LD 5; Ind. 4
Lewes (41)	LD 21; C. 18; Ind. 2
Lichfield (56)	C. 44; LD 6; Lab. 5; Ind. 1
Lincoln City (33)	C. 16; Lab. 16; LD 1
Maidstone (55)	C. 28; LD 23; Ind. 4
Maldon (31)	C. 27; Ind. 4
Malvern Hills (38)	C. 28; LD 6; Ind. 3; Green 1
Mansfield (46)	Ind. 26; Lab. 15; LD 4; C. 1
Melton (28)	C. 20; Ind. 3; Lab. 3; O. 2
Mendip (47)	C. 24; LD 21; Ind. 2
Mid Devon (42)	C. 18; Ind. 15; LD 9
Mid Suffolk (40)	C. 21; LD 10; Ind. 4; Green 3; O. 2
Mid Sussex (54)	C. 31; LD 22; Lab. 1
Mole Valley (41)	C. 18; LD 17; Ind. 5; O. 1
New Forest (60)	C. 46; LD 14
Newark and Sherwood (46)	C. 26; Ind. 7; Lab. 6; LD 4; O. 2; v. 1
Newcastle-under-Lyme (60)	C. 23; LD 18; Lab. 14; O. 5
North Devon (43)	C. 22; LD 17; Ind. 3; O. 1
North Dorset (33)	C. 17; LD 13; Ind. 3
North East Derbyshire (53)	Lab. 28; C. 10; Ind. 7; LD 7; v. 1
North Hertfordshire (49)	C. 33; LD 9; Lab. 7
North Kesteven (43)	C. 25; O. 12; Ind. 3; LD 3
North Norfolk (48)	LD 31; C. 16; O. 1
North Warwickshire (35)	C. 21; Lab. 14
North West Leicestershire (38)	C. 27; Lab. 5; LD 3; BNP 2; Ind. 1
Northampton (47)	LD 24; C. 15; Lab. 5; Ind. 3
Norwich (39)	v. 13; Green 9; Lab. 9; C. 4; LD 4
Nuneaton and Bedworth (34)	Lab. 17; C. 14; Ind. 2; BNP 1
Oadby and Wigston (26)	LD 21; C. 5
Oxford (48)	Lab. 25; LD 17; Green 5; O. 1
Pendle (49)	C. 17; LD 16; Lab. 12; BNP 2; Ind. 1; O. 1
Preston (57)	Lab. 24; C. 22; LD 8; Ind. 2; O. 1
Purbeck (24)	LD 12; C. 10; Ind. 2
Redditch (29)	C. 17; Lab. 9; LD 3
Reigate and Banstead (51)	C. 39; R 6; LD 3; Green 1; Ind. 1; Lab. 1
Ribble Valley (40)	C. 30; LD 9; Ind. 1
Richmondshire (34)	C. 17; O. 11; LD 6
Rochford (39)	C. 31; LD 5; Green 1; Ind. 1; v. 1
Rossendale (36)	C. 20; Lab. 12; LD 3; O. 1
Rother (38)	C. 28; LD 8; Ind. 2
Rugby (48)	C. 28; Lab. 11; LD 9
Runnymede (42)	C. 36; Ind. 6
Rushcliffe (50)	C. 34; LD 11; Green 2; Lab. 2; Ind. 1
Rushmoor (42)	C. 30; Lab. 6; LD 6
Ryedale (30)	C. 14; LD 8; Ind. 4; Lib. 3; O. 1
St Albans (58)	LD 30; C. 24; Lab. 3; Ind. 1
St Edmundsbury (45)	C. 36; O. 4; LD 3; Lab. 2
Scarborough (50)	C. 22; Ind. 15; LD 5; Green 3; O. 3; Lab. 2
Sedgemoor (50)	C. 36; Lab. 11; LD 3
Selby (41)	C. 30; Lab. 9; Ind. 2
Sevenoaks (54)	C. 41; LD 7; Lab. 4; Ind. 1; BNP 1
Shepway (46)	C. 38; LD 6; O. 2
South Bucks (40)	C. 36; Ind. 2; LD 2
South Cambridgeshire (57)	C. 29; LD 20; Ind. 6; Lab. 1; O. 1
South Derbyshire (36)	C. 21; Lab. 14; Ind. 1
South Hams (40)	C. 27; LD 10; Ind. 2; O. 1
South Holland (37)	C. 25; Ind. 11; O. 1
South Kesteven (58)	C. 34; Ind. 15; LD 6; Lab. 2; O. 1
South Lakeland (51)	LD 34; C. 16; Lab. 1
South Norfolk (46)	C. 39; LD 7
South Northamptonshire (42)	C. 35; Ind. 7
South Oxfordshire (48)	C. 37; LD 6; Ind. 2; Lab. 1; R 1; v. 1
South Ribble (55)	C. 42; Lab. 9; LD 2; O. 2
South Somerset (60)	LD 37; C. 17; Ind. 6
South Staffordshire (49)	C. 42; Ind. 5; Lab. 1; LD 1
Spelthorne (39)	C. 30; LD 9
Stafford (59)	C. 41; Lab. 12; LD 6
Staffordshire Moorlands (56)	C. 29; Ind. 10; LD 6; O. 6; Lab. 4; BNP 1

Stevenage (39)	Lab. 27; C. 9; LD 3
Stratford-on-Avon (53)	C. 31; LD 20; Ind. 2
Stroud (51)	C. 30; Lab. 7; LD 7; Green 6; Ind. 1
Suffolk Coastal (55)	C. 45; LD 9; Lab. 1
Surrey Heath (40)	C. 30; LD 7; Lab. 2; Ind. 1
Swale (47)	C. 33; Lab. 10; LD 3; Ind. 1
Tamworth (30)	C. 24; Lab. 5; Ind. 1
Tandridge (42)	C. 33; LD 8; Ind. 1
Taunton Deane (56)	C. 25; LD 25; Ind. 5; Lab. 1
Teignbridge (46)	LD 20; C. 19; Ind. 7
Tendring (60)	C. 28; O. 13; Lab. 7; Ind. 6; LD 6
Test Valley (48)	C. 33; LD 14; Ind. 1
Tewkesbury (38)	C. 19; LD 16; O. 2; Ind. 1
Thanet (56)	C. 32; Lab. 20; Ind. 4
Three Rivers (48)	LD 30; C. 14; Lab. 3; BNP 1
Tonbridge and Malling (53)	C. 46; LD 7
Torridge (36)	C. 17; Ind. 9; LD 5; O. 5
Tunbridge Wells (48)	C. 42; Lab. 6
Uttlesford (44)	C. 27; LD 14; Ind. 3
Vale of White Horse (51)	LD 34; C. 17
Warwick (46)	C. 24; Lab. 9; LD 9; Ind. 4
Watford (37)	LD 26; C. 4; Lab. 4; Green 3
Waveney (48)	C. 29; Lab. 15; LD 2; Green 1; Ind. 1
Waverley (57)	C. 50; Ind. 4; LD 3
Wealden (55)	C. 32; LD 13; O. 4; Ind. 3; Green 2; v. 1
Wellingborough (36)	C. 31; Lab. 4; Ind. 1
Welwyn and Hatfield (48)	C. 40; Lab. 5; LD 3
West Devon (31)	C. 12; Ind. 9; LD 8; O. 2
West Dorset (48)	C. 28; LD 14; Ind. 6
West Lancashire (54)	C. 31; Lab. 21; Ind. 1; v. 1
West Lindsey (37)	C. 22; LD 14; Ind. 1
West Oxfordshire (49)	C. 40; LD 7; Ind. 1; Lab. 1
West Somerset (31)	Ind. 15; C. 14; O. 2
Weymouth and Portland (36)	C. 18; LD 11; Lab. 5; Ind. 2
Winchester (57)	C. 29; LD 26; Ind. 2
Woking (36)	C. 18; LD 17; Ind. 1
Worcester (35)	C. 17; Lab. 13; LD 3; Ind. 2
Worthing (37)	C. 25; LD 12
Wychavon (45)	C. 34; LD 11
Wycombe (60)	C. 48; LD 8; Ind. 2; Lab. 2
Wyre (55)	C. 45; Lab. 7; LD. 1; Ind.1; v. 1
Wyre Forest (42)	C. 23; O. 8; Lib. 5; Lab. 3; LD 2; Ind. 1

LONDON BOROUGH COUNCILS

Barking and Dagenham (51)	Lab. 51
Barnet (63)	C. 39; Lab. 21; LD 3
Bexley (63)	C. 52; Lab. 11
Brent (63)	Lab. 40; LD 17; C. 6
Bromley (60)	C. 53; LD 4; Lab. 3
Camden (54)	Lab. 30; LD 13; C. 9; Green 1; v. 1
Croydon (70)	C. 37; Lab. 33
Ealing (69)	Lab. 40; C. 24; LD 5
Enfield (63)	Lab. 36; C. 27
Greenwich (51)	Lab. 40; C. 11
Hackney (57)	Lab. 50; C. 4; LD 3
Hammersmith and Fulham (46)	Lab. 31; C. 15
Haringey (57)	Lab. 34; LD 23
Harrow (63)	Lab. 34; C. 27; Ind. 1; LD 1
Havering (54)	C. 33; R 16; Lab. 5
Hillingdon (65)	C. 44; Lab. 21
Hounslow (60)	Lab. 35; C. 25
Islington (48)	Lab. 35; LD 13
Kensington and Chelsea (54)	C. 43; Lab. 9; LD 2
Kingston upon Thames (48)	LD 27; C. 21
Lambeth (63)	Lab. 44; LD 15; C. 4
Lewisham (55)	Lab. 40; LD 12; C. 2; Green 1
Merton (60)	Lab. 28; C. 27; R 3; LD 2
Newham (60)	Lab. 60
Redbridge (63)	C. 30; Lab. 26; LD 7
Richmond upon Thames (54)	C. 30; LD 24
Southwark (63)	Lab. 35; LD 25; C. 3
Sutton (54)	LD 43; C. 11
Tower Hamlets (51)	Lab. 41; C. 8; LD 1; O. 1
Waltham Forest (60)	Lab. 37; C. 18; LD 5
Wandsworth (60)	C. 47; Lab.13
Westminster (60)	C. 48; Lab. 12

METROPOLITAN BOROUGHS

Barnsley (63)	Lab. 37; Ind. 18; C. 6; LD 1; O. 1
Birmingham (120)	C. 45; Lab. 41; LD 31; O. 3
Bolton (60)	Lab. 30; C. 21; LD 8; Ind. 1
Bradford (90)	Lab. 39; C. 32; LD 14; Green 3; BNP 2
Bury (51)	C. 23; Lab. 20; LD 8
Calderdale (51)	C. 20; LD 17; Lab. 10; Ind. 3; BNP 1
Coventry (54)	Lab. 30; C. 22; LD 1; Soc. 1
Doncaster (64)	Lab. 34; LD 10; C. 9; O. 6; Ind. 5
Dudley (72)	C. 44; Lab. 26; LD 1; O. 1
Gateshead (66)	Lab. 45; LD 20; Lib. 1
Kirklees (69)	Lab. 24; LD 20; C. 19; Green 4; Ind. 2
Knowsley (63)	Lab. 54; LD 8; v. 1
Leeds (99)	Lab. 48; C. 22; LD 21; O. 6; Green 2
Liverpool (90)	Lab. 48; LD 37; Lib. 3; Green 2
Manchester (96)	Lab. 62; LD 33; C. 1
Newcastle-upon-Tyne (78)	LD 42; Lab. 34; Ind. 2
North Tyneside (60)	Lab. 29; C. 24; LD 7
Oldham (60)	Lab. 27; LD 27; C. 5; Ind. 1
Rochdale (60)	LD 26; Lab. 22; C. 11; Ind. 1
Rotherham (63)	Lab. 49; C. 9; Ind. 3; BNP 1; v. 1
St Helens (48)	Lab. 27; LD 15; C. 5; v. 1
Salford (60)	Lab. 39; C. 13; LD 5; O. 3
Sandwell (72)	Lab. 56; C. 11; LD 4; Ind. 1
Sefton (66)	LD 28; Lab. 23; C. 15
Sheffield (84)	LD 42; Lab. 38; Green 2; Ind. 1; v. 1
Solihull (51)	C. 23; LD 18; Lab. 7; O. 2; Ind. 1
South Tyneside (54)	Lab. 36; O. 12; C. 3; LD 2; Ind. 1
Stockport (63)	LD 37; Lab. 13; C. 9; Ind. 4
Sunderland (75)	Lab. 52; C. 18; Ind. 3; LD 1; v. 1
Tameside (57)	Lab. 46; C. 9; Ind. 2
Trafford (63)	C. 37; Lab. 21; LD 5
Wakefield (63)	Lab. 33; C. 24; Ind. 5; LD 1
Walsall (60)	C. 33; Lab. 17; LD 6; Ind. 2; O. 1; v. 1
Wigan (75)	Lab. 51; C. 8; Ind. 7; O. 6; LD 3
Wirral (66)	C. 27; Lab. 24; LD 15
Wolverhampton (60)	Lab. 30; C. 25; LD 5

UNITARY COUNCILS

Council	Composition
Bath and North East Somerset (65)	C. 31; LD 26; Lab. 5; Ind. 2; O. 1
Bedford (36)	LD 13; C. 8; Ind. 8; Lab. 7
Blackburn with Darwen (64)	Lab. 31; C. 19; LD 9; O. 5
Blackpool (42)	C. 27; Lab. 12; LD 3
Bournemouth (54)	C. 37; LD 9; Ind. 5; Lab. 3
Bracknell Forest (42)	C. 39; Lab. 3
Brighton and Hove (54)	C. 25; Green 13; Lab. 13; LD 2; Ind. 1
Bristol (70)	LD 38; Lab 17; C. 14; Green 1
Central Bedfordshire (66)	C. 54; LD 11; Ind. 1
Cheshire East (81)	C. 59; LD 12; Lab. 6; Ind. 4
Cheshire West and Chester (72)	C. 55; Lab. 13; LD 4
Cornwall (123)	C. 49; LD 39; Ind. 32; O. 3
Darlington (53)	Lab. 29; C. 18; LD 6
Derby (51)	Lab. 17; C. 16; LD 16; Ind. 2
Durham (126)	Lab. 67; LD 24; Ind. 21; C. 10; O. 3; v. 1
East Riding of Yorkshire (67)	C. 45; LD 13; Ind. 4; Lab. 3; SD 1; O. 1
Halton (56)	Lab. 37; LD 12; C. 6; Ind. 1
Hartlepool (48)	Lab. 24; Ind. 12; LD 5; C. 4; O. 3
Herefordshire (58)	C. 31; Ind. 11; LD 9; Lab. 2; Green 1; O. 5
Isles of Scilly (21)*	Ind. 21
Isle of Wight (40)	C. 24; Ind. 10; LD 4; Lab. 1; v. 1
Kingston-upon-Hull (59)	LD 33; Lab. 22; C. 2; O. 2
Leicester (54)	Lab. 38; C. 8; LD 6; Ind. 1; v. 1
Luton (48)	Lab. 26; LD 17; C. 5
Medway (55)	C. 33; Lab. 10; LD 8; Ind. 3; O. 1
Middlesbrough (49)	Lab. 28; O. 10; C. 6; Ind. 3; Green 1; LD 1
Milton Keynes (51)	LD 22; C. 17; Lab. 9; Ind. 3
North East Lincolnshire (42)	C. 15; LD 15; Lab. 10; Ind. 2
North Lincolnshire (43)	Lab. 22; C. 18; O. 2; Ind. 1
North Somerset (61)	C. 46; Ind. 6; LD 5; Lab. 3; Green 1
Northumberland (67)	LD 26; C. 19; Lab. 17; Ind. 5
Nottingham (55)	Lab. 42; C. 7; LD 6
Peterborough (57)	C. 40; Ind. 9; Lab. 3; LD 3; O. 2
Plymouth (57)	C. 36; Lab. 20; Ind. 1
Poole (42)	C. 23; LD 17; Ind. 2
Portsmouth (42)	LD 24; C. 16; Lab. 2
Reading (46)	Lab. 19; C. 17; LD 9; Ind. 1
Redcar and Cleveland (59)	Lab. 24; LD 16; C. 11; Ind. 5; O. 2; v. 1
Rutland (26)	C. 19; Ind. 5; LD 2
Shropshire (74)	C. 53; LD 12; Lab. 7; Ind. 2
Slough (41)	Lab. 23; C. 9; O. 9
South Gloucestershire (70)	C. 33; LD 28; Lab. 9
Southampton (48)	C. 28; Lab. 15; LD 5
Southend-on-Sea (51)	C. 28; LD 12; Ind. 7; Lab. 4
Stockton-on-Tees (56)	Lab. 22; O. 15; C. 13; LD 5; v. 1
Stoke-on-Trent (60)	Lab. 26; Ind. 9; C. 8; O. 8; BNP 5; LD 4
Swindon (59)	C. 41; Lab. 13; LD 4; Ind. 1
Telford and Wrekin (54)	C. 27; Lab. 17; O. 4; Ind. 3; LD 3
Thurrock (49)	C. 22; Lab. 22; O.3; Ind. 2
Torbay (37)	C. 24; LD 9; Ind. 4
Warrington (57)	Lab. 27; LD 24; C. 6
West Berkshire (52)	C. 36; LD 16
Wiltshire (98)	C. 61; LD 24; Ind. 8; O. 3; Lab. 2
Windsor and Maidenhead (57)	C. 36; LD 16; R 5
Wokingham (54)	C. 43; LD 11
York (47)	LD 20; Lab. 18; C. 7; Green 2

* Thirteen councillors are elected by the residents of the isle of St Mary's and two councillors each are elected by the residents of the four other islands (Bryher, St Agnes, St Martins and Tresco)

WALES

Council	Composition
Blaenau Gwent (42)	Lab. 17; Ind. 16; O. 7; LD 2
Bridgend (54)	Lab. 27; Ind. 14; C. 6; LD 6; PC 1
Caerphilly (73)	PC 32; Lab. 29; Ind. 11; v. 1
Cardiff (75)	LD 35; C. 17; Lab. 13; PC 7; Ind. 3
Carmarthenshire (74)	Ind. 30; PC 29; Lab. 11; O. 3; LD 1
Ceredigion (42)	PC 20; Ind. 12; LD 9; Lab. 1
Conwy (59)	C. 20; Ind. 14; PC 14; Lab. 6; LD 4; v. 1
Denbighshire (47)	C. 17; Ind. 10; PC 8; Lab. 5; O. 6; LD 1
Flintshire (70)	Ind. 25; Lab. 22; LD 12; C. 9; O. 1; PC 1
Gwynedd (75)	PC 35; Ind. 18; O. 12; LD 5; Lab. 4; O. 1
Merthyr Tydfil (33)	Ind. 13; Lab. 10; O. 6; LD 4
Monmouthshire (43)	C. 27; Lab. 6; LD 5; O. 5
Neath Port Talbot (64)	Lab. 38; PC 11; Ind. 6; LD 4; SD 3; O. 2
Newport (50)	Lab. 21; C. 17; LD 9; Ind. 2; PC 1
Pembrokeshire (60)	Ind. 39; O. 6; C. 5; Lab. 5; PC 5
Powys (73)	O. 45; LD 15; C. 9; Lab. 4
Rhondda Cynon Taff (75)	Lab. 45; PC 20; O. 5; Ind. 4; v. 1
Swansea (72)	Lab. 27; LD 24; O. 10; Ind. 6; C. 4; PC 1
Torfaen (44)	Lab. 18; Ind. 8; O. 8; C. 5; PC 3; LD 2
Vale of Glamorgan (47)	C. 25; Lab. 13; PC 6; Ind. 3
Wrexham (52)	Ind. 15; LD 12; Lab. 11; C. 5; O. 5; PC 4
Ynys Mon (Isle of Anglesey) (40)	O. 27; PC 8; Lab. 5

SCOTLAND

Aberdeen (43)	LD 14; SNP 13; Lab. 10; C. 4; Ind. 2
Aberdeenshire (68)	LD 21; SNP 20; C. 13; Ind. 9; O. 5
Angus (29)	SNP 13; Ind. 6; C. 5; LD 3; Lab. 2
Argyll and Bute (36)	Ind. 15; SNP 10; LD 6; C. 3; O. 2
Clackmannanshire (18)	Lab. 8; SNP 7; C. 1; Ind. 1; LD 1
Dumfries and Galloway (47)	C. 18; Lab. 14; SNP 10; LD 3; Ind. 2
Dundee (29)	SNP 14; Lab. 8; C. 3; Ind. 2; LD 2
East Ayrshire (32)	Lab. 15; SNP 14; C. 3
East Dunbartonshire (24)	SNP 8; Lab. 6; C. 4; LD 4; Ind. 2
East Lothian (23)	SNP 9; Lab. 7; LD 4; C. 2; Ind. 1
East Renfrewshire (20)	C. 7; Lab. 7; SNP 3; Ind. 2; LD 1
Edinburgh (58)	LD 17; Lab. 15; SNP 12; C. 11; Green 3
Eilean Siar (Western Isles) (31)	Ind. 25; SNP 4; Lab. 2
Falkirk (32)	Lab. 14; SNP 13; Ind. 3; C. 2
Fife (78)	Lab. 24; SNP 22; LD 21; Ind. 7; C. 4
Glasgow (79)	Lab. 47; SNP 19; LD 6; Green 5; C. 1; Ind. 1
Highland (80)	Ind. 25; LD 22; SNP 17; O. 9; Lab. 7
Inverclyde (20)	Lab. 8; SNP 5; LD 4; Ind. 2; C. 1
Midlothian (18)	Lab. 10; SNP 6; LD 2
Moray (26)	Ind. 11; SNP 10; C. 3; Lab. 2
North Ayrshire (30)	Lab. 12; SNP 8; Ind. 5; C. 3; LD 2
North Lanarkshire (70)	Lab. 41; SNP 22; Ind. 4; C. 1; LD 1; O. 1
Orkney Islands (21)	Ind. 21
Perth and Kinross (41)	SNP 18; C. 11; LD 7; Lab. 3; Ind. 2
Renfrewshire (40)	SNP 17; Lab. 16; LD 4; C. 2; Ind. 1
Scottish Borders (34)	C. 11; LD 10; SNP 6; Ind. 5; O. 2
Shetland Islands (22)	Ind. 11; O. 11
South Ayrshire (30)	C. 12; SNP 8; Lab. 6; Ind. 4
South Lanarkshire (67)	Lab. 32; SNP 23; C. 8; Ind. 2; LD 2
Stirling (22)	Lab. 8; SNP 7; C. 4; LD 3
West Dunbartonshire (22)	SNP 9; Lab. 8; Ind. 4; O. 1
West Lothian (32)	Lab. 14; SNP 13; O. 3; C. 1; Ind. 1

NORTHERN IRELAND

Antrim (19)	DUP 5; UUP 5; All. 3; SF 3; SDLP 2; O. 1
Ards (23)	DUP 11; UUP 6; All. 3; O. 2; SDLP 1
Armagh City (22)	SDLP 6; DUP 5; SF 5; UUP 5; Ind. Un. 1
Ballymena (24)	DUP 8; O. 6; UUP 4; Ind. 2; SDLP 2; C. 1; SF 1
Ballymoney (16)	DUP 7; SF 3; SDLP 2; UUP 2; Ind. 1; O. 1
Banbridge (17)	DUP 6; UUP 5; SDLP 3; All. 1; Ind. 1; O. 1
Belfast (51)	SF 14; DUP 13; UUP 9; SDLP 8; All. 4; O. 2; Ind. Un. 1
Carrickfergus (17)	DUP 8; UUP 4; All. 3; Ind. 2
Castlereagh (23)	DUP 12; All. 4; UUP 4; SDLP 2; O. 1
Coleraine (22)	DUP 8; UUP 8; SDLP 3; All. 1; Ind. Un. 1; SF 1
Cookstown (16)	SDLP 5; SF 5; DUP 3; UUP 3
Craigavon (26)	DUP 8; UUP 7; SF 6; SDLP 3; Ind. 2
Derry City (30)	SDLP 14; SF 10; DUP 5; UUP 1
Down (23)	SDLP 10; SF 5; DUP 3; UUP 3; C. 1; Green 1
Dungannon and South Tyrone (22)	SF 8; UUP 5; DUP 4; SDLP 4; Ind. 1
Fermanagh (23)	SF 7; SDLP 5; UUP 5; DUP 4; Ind. 2
Larne (15)	DUP 4; UUP 4; All. 2; Ind. 2; SDLP 2; O. 1
Limavady (15)	SF 6; SDLP 3; DUP 2; O. 2; UUP 2
Lisburn (30)	DUP 12; UUP 7; SF 4; All. 3; SDLP 3; O. 1
Magherafelt (16)	SF 6; DUP 4; Ind. Un. 2; SDLP 2; UUP 2
Moyle (15)	Ind. Un 4; DUP 3; SDLP 3; SF 3; UUP 2
Newry and Mourne (30)	SF 12; SDLP 9; DUP 2; Ind. 2; UUP 2; Green 1; O. 2
Newtownabbey (25)	DUP 12; UUP 6; All. 3; Ind. Un. 2; O. 1; SDLP 1
North Down (25)	DUP 8; UUP 8; All. 5; Ind. 2; C. 1; Green 1
Omagh (21)	SF 10; DUP 3; SDLP 3; UUP 3; Ind. 2
Strabane (16)	SF 7; DUP 3; Ind. 2; SDLP 2; UUP 2

ENGLAND

The region of England lies between 55° 46′ and 49° 57′ 30″ N. latitude (from a few miles north of the mouth of the Tweed to the Lizard), and between 1° 46′ E. and 5° 43′ W. longitude (from Lowestoft to Land's End). England is bounded on the north by the Cheviot Hills; on the south by the English Channel; on the east by the Straits of Dover (Pas de Calais) and the North Sea; and on the west by the Atlantic Ocean, Wales and the Irish Sea. It has a total area of 130,432 sq. km (50,360 sq. miles): land 130,279 sq. km (50,301 sq. miles); inland water 153 sq. km (59 sq. miles).

POPULATION

The population at the 2001 census was 49,138,831. The average density of the population in 2001 was 377 persons per sq. km (976 per sq. mile).

FLAG

The flag of England is the cross of St George, a red cross on a white field (cross gules in a field argent). The cross of St George, the patron saint of England, has been used since the 13th century.

RELIEF

There is a marked division between the upland and lowland areas of England. In the extreme north the Cheviot Hills (highest point, the Cheviot, 815m/2,674ft) form a natural boundary with Scotland. Running south from the Cheviots, though divided from them by the Tyne Gap, is the Pennine range (highest point, Cross Fell, 893m/2,930ft), the main orological feature of the country. The Pennines culminate in the Peak District of Derbyshire (Kinder Scout, 636m/2,088ft). West of the Pennines are the Cumbrian mountains, which include Scafell Pike (978m/3,210ft), the highest peak in England, and to the east are the Yorkshire Moors, their highest point being Urra Moor (454m/1,490ft).

In the west, the foothills of the Welsh mountains extend into the bordering English counties of Shropshire (the Wrekin, 407m/1,334ft; Long Mynd, 516m/1,694ft) and Hereford and Worcester (the Malvern Hills – Worcestershire Beacon, 425m/1,394ft). Extensive areas of highland and moorland are also to be found in the south-western peninsula formed by Somerset, Devon and Cornwall, principally Exmoor (Dunkery Beacon, 519m/1,704ft), Dartmoor (High Willhays, 621m/2,038ft) and Bodmin Moor (Brown Willy, 420m/1,377ft). Ranges of low, undulating hills run across the south of the country, including the Cotswolds in the Midlands and south-west, the Chilterns to the north of London, and the North (Kent) and South (Sussex) Downs of the south-east coastal areas.

The lowlands of England lie in the Vale of York, East Anglia and the area around the Wash. The lowest-lying are the Cambridgeshire Fens in the valleys of the Great Ouse and the river Nene, which are below sea-level in places. Since the 17th century extensive drainage has brought much of the Fens under cultivation. The North Sea coast between the Thames and the Humber, low-lying and formed of sand and shingle for the most part, is subject to erosion, and defences against further incursion have been built along many stretches.

HYDROGRAPHY

The Severn is the longest river in Great Britain, rising in the north-eastern slopes of Plynlimon (Wales) and entering England in Shropshire, with a total length of 354km (220 miles) from its source to its outflow into the Bristol Channel, where it receives the Bristol Avon on the east and the Wye on the west; its other tributaries are the Vyrnwy, Tern, Stour, Teme and Upper (or Warwickshire) Avon. The Severn is tidal below Gloucester, and a high bore or tidal wave sometimes reverses the flow as high as Tewkesbury (21.75km/13.5 miles above Gloucester). The scenery of the greater part of the river is very picturesque, and the Severn is a noted salmon river, with some of its tributaries being famous for trout. Navigation is assisted by the Gloucester and Berkeley Ship Canal (26km/16.25 miles), which admits vessels of 350 tons to Gloucester. The Severn Tunnel was begun in 1873 and completed in 1886 at a cost of £2m and after many difficulties caused by flooding. It is 7km (4 miles 628 yards) in length (of which 3.67km/2.25 miles are under the river). The Severn road bridge between Haysgate, Gwent, and Almondsbury, Glos, with a centre span of 988m (3,240ft), was opened in 1966.

The longest river wholly in England is the Thames, with a total length of 346km (215 miles) from its source in the Cotswold hills to the Nore, and is navigable by ocean-going ships to London Bridge. The Thames is tidal to Teddington (111km/69 miles from its mouth) and forms county boundaries almost throughout its course; on its banks are situated London, Windsor Castle, Eton College and Oxford University. Of the remaining English rivers, those flowing into the North Sea are the Tyne, Wear, Tees, Ouse and Trent from the Pennine Range, the Great Ouse (257km/160 miles), which rises in Northamptonshire, and the Orwell and Stour from the hills of East Anglia. Flowing into the English Channel are the Sussex Ouse from the Weald, the Itchen from the Hampshire Hills, and the Axe, Teign, Dart, Tamar and Exe from the Devonian hills. Flowing into the Irish Sea are the Mersey, Ribble and Eden from the western slopes of the Pennines and the Derwent from the Cumbrian mountains.

The English Lakes, notable for their picturesque scenery and poetic associations, lie in Cumbria's Lake District; the largest are Windermere (14.7 sq. km/5.7 sq. miles), Ullswater (8.8 sq. km/3.4 sq. miles) and Derwent Water (5.3 sq. km/2.0 sq. miles).

ISLANDS

The Isle of Wight is separated from Hampshire by the Solent. The capital, Newport, stands at the head of the estuary of the Medina, and Cowes (at the mouth) is the chief port. Other centres are Ryde, Sandown, Shanklin, Ventnor, Freshwater, Yarmouth, Totland Bay, Seaview and Bembridge.

Lundy (the name is derived from the Old Norse for 'puffin island'), 18km (11 miles) north-west of Hartland Point, Devon, is around 5km (3 miles) long and almost 1km (half a mile) wide on average, with a total area of around 452 hectares (1,116 acres), and a population of around 18. It became the property of the National Trust in 1969 and is now principally a bird sanctuary and the UK's first marine conservation zone.

The Isles of Scilly comprise around 140 islands and skerries (total area, 10 sq. km/6 sq. miles) situated 45 km (28 miles) south-west of Land's End in Cornwall. Only five are inhabited: St Mary's, St Agnes, Bryher, Tresco and St Martin's. The population at the 2001 census was 2,153. The entire group has been designated an Area of Outstanding Natural Beauty because of its unique flora and fauna. Tourism and the winter/spring flower trade for the home market form the basis of the economy of the islands. The island group is a recognised rural development area.

EARLY HISTORY

Archaeological evidence suggests that England has been inhabited since at least the Palaeolithic period, though the extent of the various Palaeolithic cultures was dependent upon the degree of glaciation. The succeeding Neolithic and Bronze Age cultures have left abundant remains throughout the country; the best-known of these are the henges and stone circles of Stonehenge (ten miles north of Salisbury, Wilts) and Avebury (Wilts), both of which are believed to have been of religious significance. In the latter part of the Bronze Age the Goidels, a people of the Celtic race, invaded the country and brought with them Celtic civilisation and dialects; as a result place names in England bear witness to the spread of the invasion across the whole region.

THE ROMAN CONQUEST

The Roman conquest of Gaul (57–50 BC) brought Britain into close contact with Roman civilisation, but although Julius Caesar raided the south of Britain in 55 and 54 BC, conquest was not undertaken until nearly 100 years later. In AD 43 the Emperor Claudius dispatched Aulus Plautius, with a well-equipped force of 40,000, and himself followed with reinforcements in the same year. Success was delayed by the resistance of Caratacus (Caractacus), the British leader from AD 48–51, who was finally captured and sent to Rome, and by a great revolt in AD 61 led by Boudicca (Boadicea), Queen of the Iceni, but the south of Britain was secured by AD 70, and Wales and the area north to the Tyne by about AD 80.

In AD 122, the Emperor Hadrian visited Britain and built a continuous rampart, since known as Hadrian's Wall, from Wallsend to Bowness (Tyne to Solway). The work was entrusted by the Emperor Hadrian to Aulus Platorius Nepos, legate of Britain from AD 122 to 126, and it was intended to form the northern frontier of the Roman Empire.

The Romans administered Britain as a province under a governor, with a well-defined system of local government, each Roman municipality ruling itself and its surrounding territory, while London was the centre of the road system and the seat of the financial officials of the Province of Britain. Colchester, Lincoln, York, Gloucester and St Albans stand on the sites of five Roman municipalities, and Wroxeter, Caerleon, Chester, Lincoln and York were at various times the sites of legionary fortresses. Well-preserved Roman towns have been uncovered at or near Silchester *(Calleva Atrebatum),* ten miles south of Reading, Wroxeter *(Viroconium Cornoviorum),* near Shrewsbury, and St Albans *(Verulamium)* in Hertfordshire.

Four main groups of roads radiated from London, and a fifth (the Fosse) ran obliquely from Lincoln through Leicester, Cirencester and Bath to Exeter. Of the four groups radiating from London, one ran south-east to Canterbury and the coast of Kent, a second to Silchester and thence to parts of western Britain and south Wales, a third (later known as Watling Street) ran through St Albans to Chester, with various branches, and the fourth reached Colchester, Lincoln, York and the eastern counties.

In the fourth century Britain was subjected to raids along the east coast by Saxon pirates, which led to the establishment of a system of coastal defences from the Wash to Southampton Water, with forts at Brancaster, Burgh Castle (Yarmouth), Walton (Felixstowe), Bradwell, Reculver, Richborough, Dover, Lympne, Pevensey and Porchester (Portsmouth). The Irish (Scoti) and Picts in the north were also becoming more aggressive and from around AD 350 incursions became more frequent and more formidable. As the Roman Empire came increasingly under attack towards the end of the fourth century, many troops were removed from Britain for service in other parts of the empire. The island was eventually cut off from Rome by the Teutonic conquest of Gaul, and with the withdrawal of the last Roman garrison early in the fifth century, the Romano-British were left to themselves.

SAXON SETTLEMENT

According to legend, the British King Vortigern called in the Saxons to defend his lands against the Picts. The Saxon chieftains Hengist and Horsa landed at Ebbsfleet, Kent, and established themselves in the Isle of Thanet, but the events during the one-and-a-half centuries between the final break with Rome and the re-establishment of Christianity are unclear. However, it would appear that over the course of this period the raids turned into large-scale settlement by invaders traditionally known as Angles (England north of the Wash and East Anglia), Saxons (Essex and southern England) and Jutes (Kent and the Weald), which pushed the Romano-British into the mountainous areas of the north and west. Celtic culture outside Wales and Cornwall survives only in topographical names. Various kingdoms established at this time attempted to claim overlordship of the whole country, hegemony finally being achieved by Wessex (with the capital at Winchester) in the ninth century. This century also saw the beginning of raids by the Vikings (Danes), which were resisted by Alfred the Great (871–899), who fixed a limit on the advance of Danish settlement by the Treaty of Wedmore (878), giving them the area north and east of Watling Street on the condition that they adopt Christianity.

In the tenth century the kings of Wessex recovered the whole of England from the Danes, but subsequent rulers were unable to resist a second wave of invaders. England paid tribute *(Danegeld)* for many years, and was invaded in 1013 by the Danes and ruled by Danish kings (including Cnut) from 1016 until 1042, when Edward the Confessor was recalled from exile in Normandy. On Edward's death in 1066 Harold Godwinson (brother-in-law of Edward and son of Earl Godwin of Wessex) was chosen to be King of England. After defeating (at Stamford Bridge, Yorkshire, 25 September 1066) an invading army under Harald Hadraada, King of Norway (aided by the outlawed Earl Tostig of Northumbria, Harold's brother), Harold was himself defeated at the Battle of Hastings on 14 October 1066, and the Norman conquest secured the throne of England for Duke William of Normandy, a cousin of Edward the Confessor.

CHRISTIANITY

Christianity reached the Roman province of Britain from Gaul in the third century (or possibly earlier). Alban, traditionally Britain's first martyr, was put to death as a Christian during the persecution of Diocletian (22 June 303) at his native town *Verulamium,* and the Bishops of *Londinium, Eboracum* (York), and *Lindum* (Lincoln) attended the Council of Arles in 314. However, the Anglo-Saxon invasions submerged the Christian religion in England until the sixth century: conversion was undertaken in the north from 563 by Celtic missionaries from Ireland led by St Columba, and in the south by a mission sent from Rome in 597 which was led by St Augustine, who became the first archbishop of Canterbury. England appears to have been converted again by the end of the seventh century and followed, after the Council of Whitby in 663, the practices of the Roman Church, which brought the kingdom into the mainstream of European thought and culture.

PRINCIPAL CITIES

There are 50 cities in England and space constraints prevent us from including profiles of them all. Below is a selection of England's principal cities with the date on which city status was conferred in parenthesis. Other cities are: Chichester (pre-1900), Derby (1977), Ely (pre-1900), Exeter (pre-1900), Gloucester (pre-1900), Hereford (pre-1900), Lancaster (1937), Lichfield (pre-1900), London (pre-1900), Peterborough (pre-1900), Plymouth (1928), Portsmouth (1926), Preston (2002), Ripon (pre-1900), Salford (1926), Sunderland (1992), Truro (pre-1900), Wakefield (pre-1900), Wells (pre-1900), Westminster (pre-1900), Wolverhampton (2000) and Worcester (pre-1900).

Certain cities have also been granted a lord mayoralty – this grant confers no additional powers or functions and is purely honorific. Cities with lord mayors are Birmingham, Bradford, Bristol, Canterbury, Chester, Coventry, Exeter, Kingston-upon-Hull, Leeds, Leicester, Liverpool, London, Manchester, Newcastle-upon-Tyne, Norwich, Nottingham, Oxford, Plymouth, Portsmouth, Sheffield, Stoke-on-Trent, Westminster and York.

BATH (PRE-1900)

Bath stands on the River Avon between the Cotswold Hills to the north and the Mendips to the south. In the early 18th century, Bath became England's premier spa town where the rich and celebrated members of fashionable society gathered to 'take the waters' and enjoy the town's theatres and concert rooms. During this period the architect John Wood laid the foundations for a new Georgian city to be built using the honey-coloured stone for which Bath is famous today.

Contemporary Bath is a thriving tourist destination and remains a leading cultural, religious and historical centre with many art galleries and historic sites including the Pump Room (1790); the Royal Crescent (1767); the Circus (1754); the 18th-century Assembly Rooms (housing the Museum of Costume); Pulteney Bridge (1771); the Guildhall and the Abbey, now over 500 years old, which is built on the site of a Saxon monastery. In 2006 the Bath Thermae Spa was completed and the hot springs re-opened to the public for the first time since 1978; combining five historic spa buildings with contemporary architecture, it is the only spa in the UK to utilise naturally occurring thermal waters.

BIRMINGHAM (PRE-1900)

Birmingham is Britain's second largest city, with a population of over one million. The generally accepted derivation of 'Birmingham' is the *ham* (dwelling-place) of the *ing* (family) of *Beorma,* presumed to have been Saxon. During the Industrial Revolution the town grew into a major manufacturing centre and in 1889 was granted city status.

Recent developments include Millennium Point, which houses Thinktank, the Birmingham science museum, and Brindleyplace, a development of shops, offices and leisure facilities on a former industrial site clustered around canals. In 2003 the Bullring shopping centre was officially opened as part of the city's urban regeneration programme.

The principal buildings are the Town Hall (1834–50), the Council House (1879), Victoria Law Courts (1891), the University of Birmingham (1906–9), the 13th-century Church of St Martin-in-the-Bull-Ring (rebuilt 1873), the cathedral (formerly St Philip's Church) (1711), the Roman Catholic cathedral of St Chad (1839–41), the Assay Office (1773), the Rotunda (1964) and the National Exhibition Centre (1976). There is also the Birmingham Museum and Art Gallery which was founded in 1885 and is home to a collection of Pre-Raphaelite paintings.

BRADFORD (PRE-1900)

During the Industrial Revolution of the 18th and 19th centuries Bradford expanded rapidly, largely as a result of the thriving wool industry.

Bradford city centre has a host of buildings with historical and cultural interest, including City Hall, with its 19th-century Lord Mayor's rooms and Victorian law court; Bradford Cathedral; the Priestley, a theatre and arts centre originally established as the Bradford Civic Playhouse by J. B. Priestley and friends; the National Media Museum which houses seven floors of interactive displays and three cinemas; Piece Hall Yard which incorporates the Bradford Club, a Victorian Gothic style building dating from 1837, and the Peace Museum.

BRIGHTON AND HOVE (2000)

Brighton and Hove is situated on the south coast of England, around 96 km (60 miles) south of London. Originally a fishing village called Brighthelmstone, it was transformed into a fashionable seaside resort in the 18th century when Dr Richard Russell popularised the benefits of his 'sea-water cure'; as one of the closest beaches to London, Brighton began to attract wealthy visitors. One of these was the Prince Regent (the future King George IV), who first visited in 1783 and became so fond of the city that in 1807 he bought the former farmhouse he had been renting, and gradually turned it into Brighton's most recognisable building, the Royal Pavilion. The Pavilion is renowned for its Indo-Saracenic exterior, featuring minarets and an enormous central dome designed by John Nash, combined with the lavish chinoiserie of Frederick Crace's and Robert Jones' interiors.

Brighton and Hove's Regency heritage can also be seen in the numerous elegant squares and crescents designed by Amon Wilds and Augustin Busby that dominate the seafront.

Brighton and Hove is once again a fashionable resort, known for its cafe culture, lively nightlife and thriving gay scene.

BRISTOL (PRE-1900)

Bristol was a royal borough before the Norman conquest. The earliest form of the name is *Bricgstow.*

The principal buildings include the 12th-century

Cathedral with Norman chapter house and gateway; the 14th-century Church of St Mary Redcliffe; Wesley's Chapel, Broadmead; the Merchant Venturers' Almshouses; the Council House (1956); the Guildhall; the Exchange (erected from the designs of John Wood in 1743); Cabot Tower; the University and Clifton College. The Roman Catholic cathedral at Clifton was opened in 1973.

The Clifton Suspension Bridge, with a span of 214m (702ft) over the Avon, was projected by Isambard Kingdom Brunel in 1836 but was not completed until 1864. Brunel's SS *Great Britain,* the first ocean-going propeller-driven ship, now forms a museum at the Western Dockyard, from where she was originally launched in 1843. The docks themselves have been extensively restored and redeveloped; the 19th-century two-storey former tea warehouse is now the Arnolfini centre for contemporary arts, and an 18th-century sail loft houses the Architecture Centre. Behind the baroque-domed facade of the former 'E' Shed are shops, cafes, restaurants and the Watershed Media Centre, and on Princes Wharf 1950s transit sheds, which formerly housed the Industrial Museum, are being renovated and converted into the new Museum of Bristol, due to open in 2011.

CAMBRIDGE (1951)

Cambridge, a settlement far older than its ancient university, lies on the River Cam (or Granta). The city is a county town and regional headquarters. Its industries include technology research and development, and biotechnology. Among its open spaces are Jesus Green, Sheep's Green, Coe Fen, Parker's Piece, Christ's Pieces, the University Botanic Garden, and the 'Backs' – lawns and gardens through which the Cam winds behind the principal line of college buildings. Historical sites east of the Cam include King's Parade, Great St Mary's Church, Gibbs' Senate House and King's College Chapel.

University and college buildings provide the outstanding features of Cambridge's architecture but several churches (especially St Benet's, the oldest building in the city, and Holy Sepulchre or the Round Church) are also notable. The Guildhall (1937) stands on a site, of which at least part has held municipal buildings since 1224.

CANTERBURY (PRE-1900)

Canterbury, seat of the Archbishop of Canterbury, the primate of the Church of England, dates back to prehistoric times. It was the Roman *Durovernum Cantiacorum* and the Saxon *Cant-wara-byrig* (stronghold of the men of Kent). It was here in 597 that St Augustine began the conversion of the English to Christianity, when Ethelbert, King of Kent, was baptised.

Of the Benedictine St Augustine's Abbey, burial place of the Jutish Kings of Kent, only ruins remain. St Martin's Church, on the eastern outskirts of the city, is stated by Bede to have been the place of worship of Queen Bertha, the Christian wife of King Ethelbert, before the advent of St Augustine.

In 1170 the rivalry of Church and State culminated in the murder in Canterbury Cathedral, by Henry II's knights, of Archbishop Thomas Becket. His shrine became a great centre of pilgrimage, as described in Chaucer's *Canterbury Tales.* After the Reformation pilgrimages ceased, but the prosperity of the city was strengthened by an influx of Huguenot refugees, who introduced weaving. The poet and playwright Christopher Marlowe was born and raised in Canterbury (the city is home to the 1,000-seat Marlowe Theatre) and there are also literary associations with Defoe, Dickens, Joseph Conrad and Somerset Maugham.

The cathedral, its architecture ranging from the 11th to the 15th centuries, is famous worldwide. Visitors are attracted particularly to the Martyrdom, the Black Prince's Tomb, the Warriors' Chapel and the many examples of medieval stained glass.

The medieval city walls are built on Roman foundations and the 14th-century West Gate is one of the finest buildings of its kind in the country.

The Canterbury Arts Festival takes place at a variety of venues throughout the city each autumn.

CARLISLE (PRE-1900)

Carlisle is situated at the confluence of the rivers Eden and Caldew, 497km (309 miles) north-west of London and around 16km (10 miles) from the Scottish border. It was granted a charter in 1158.

The city stands at the western end of Hadrian's Wall and dates from the original Roman settlement of *Luguvalium.* Granted to Scotland in the tenth century, Carlisle is not included in the Domesday Book. William Rufus reclaimed the area in 1092 and the castle and city walls were built to guard Carlisle and the western border; the citadel is a Tudor addition to protect the south of the city. Border disputes were common until the problem of the Debateable Lands was settled in 1552. During the Civil War the city remained Royalist; in 1745 Carlisle was besieged for the last time by the Young Pretender (Bonnie Prince Charlie).

The cathedral, originally a 12th-century Augustinian priory, was enlarged in the 13th and 14th centuries after the diocese was created in 1133. To the south is a restored tithe barn and nearby the 18th-century church of St Cuthbert, the third to stand on a site dating from the seventh century.

Carlisle is the major shopping, commercial and agricultural centre for the area, and industries include the manufacture of metal goods, biscuits and textiles. However, the largest employer is the services sector, most notably in central and local government, retailing and transport. The city occupies an important position at the centre of a network of major roads, as a stage on the main west coast rail services, and with its own airport at Crosby-on-Eden.

CHESTER (PRE-1900)

Chester is situated on the River Dee. Its recorded history dates from the first century when the Romans founded the fortress of *Deva.* The city's name is derived from the Latin *castra* (a camp or encampment). During the Middle Ages, Chester was the principal port of north-west England but declined with the silting of the Dee estuary and competition from Liverpool. The city was also an important military centre, notably during Edward I's Welsh campaigns and the Elizabethan Irish campaigns. During the Civil War, Chester supported the King and was besieged from 1643 to 1646. Chester's first charter was granted *c.*1175 and the city was incorporated in 1506. The office of sheriff is the earliest created in the country (1120s), and in 1992 the mayor was granted the title of Lord Mayor, who also enjoys the title 'Admiral of the Dee'.

The city's architectural features include the city walls (an almost complete two-mile circuit), the unique 13th-century Rows (covered galleries above the street-level shops), the Victorian Gothic Town Hall (1869), the castle (rebuilt 1788 and 1822) and numerous half-timbered buildings. The cathedral was a Benedictine abbey until the Dissolution of the Monasteries. Remaining monastic buildings include the chapter house, refectory and cloisters and there is a modern free-standing bell tower. The Norman church of St John the Baptist was a cathedral church in the early Middle Ages.

COVENTRY (PRE-1900)

Coventry is an important industrial centre, producing vehicles, machine tools, agricultural machinery, man-made fibres, aerospace components and telecommunications equipment. New investment has come from financial services, power transmission, professional services, leisure and education.

The city owes its beginning to Leofric, Earl of Mercia, and his wife Godiva who, in 1043, founded a Benedictine monastery. The guildhall of St Mary and three of the city's churches date from the 14th and 15th centuries, and 16th-century almshouses can still be seen. Coventry's first cathedral was destroyed during the Reformation, its second in the 1940 blitz (the walls and spire remain) and the new cathedral designed by Sir Basil Spence, consecrated in 1962, now draws numerous visitors.

Coventry is the home of the University of Warwick, Coventry University, Coventry Transport Museum, which specialises in British road transport, and the Skydome Arena.

DURHAM (PRE-1900)

The city of Durham is a major tourist attraction and its prominent Norman cathedral and castle are set high on a wooded peninsula overlooking the River Wear. The cathedral was founded as a shrine for the body of St Cuthbert in 995. The present building dates from 1093 and among its many treasures is the tomb of the Venerable Bede (673–735). Durham's prince bishops had unique powers up to 1836, being lay rulers as well as religious leaders. As a palatinate, Durham could have its own army, nobility, coinage and courts. The castle was the main seat of the prince bishops for nearly 800 years; it is now used as a college by the University of Durham. The university, founded in the early 19th century on the initiative of Bishop William Van Mildert, is England's third oldest.

Among other buildings of interest is the Guildhall in the Market Place which dates from the 14th century. Annual events include Durham's regatta in June (claimed to be the oldest rowing event in Britain) and the annual Gala (formerly Durham Miners' Gala) in July.

KINGSTON-UPON-HULL (PRE-1900)

Hull (officially Kingston-upon-Hull, so named by Edward I) lies at the junction of the River Hull with the Humber, 35km (22 miles) from the North Sea. It is one of the major seaports of the UK. The port provides a wide range of cargo services, including ro-ro and container traffic, and handles an estimated million passengers annually on daily sailings to Rotterdam and Zeebrugge. There is a variety of manufacturing and service industries. City status was accorded in 1897 and the office of mayor raised to the dignity of Lord Mayor in 1914.

The city, restored after heavy air raid damage during the Second World War, has good educational facilities with both the University of Hull and a campus of the University of Lincoln being within its boundaries. Hull is home to the world's only submarium, The Deep, which opened in 2002, and the state-of-the-art Truck Theatre, which opened in 2009 and won the RIBA building of the year award.

Tourism is a growing industry; the old town area has been renovated and includes museums, a marina and a shopping complex. Just west of the city is the Humber Bridge, a suspension bridge, opened in 1981, which crosses the Humber Estuary.

LEEDS (PRE-1900)

Leeds, situated in the lower Aire Valley, is a junction for road, rail, canal and air services and an important commercial centre. It was first incorporated by Charles I in 1626. The earliest forms of the name are *Loidis* or *Ledes,* the origins of which are obscure.

The principal buildings are the Civic Hall (1933), the Town Hall (1858), the Municipal Buildings and Art Gallery (1884) with the Henry Moore Gallery (1982), the Corn Exchange (1863) and the University. The parish church (St Peter's) was rebuilt in 1841; the 17th-century St John's Church has a fine interior with a famous English Renaissance screen; the last remaining 18th-century church in the city is Holy Trinity in Boar Lane (1727). Kirkstall Abbey (about three miles from the centre of the city), founded by Henry de Lacy in 1152, is one of the most complete examples of a Cistercian house now remaining. Temple Newsam, birthplace of Lord Darnley and largely rebuilt by Sir Arthur Ingram *c.*1620, was acquired by the council in 1922. Adel Church, about five miles from the centre of the city, is a fine Norman structure. The Royal Armouries Museum forms part of a group of museums that house the national collection of antique arms and armour.

LEICESTER (1919)

Leicester is situated in central England. The city was an important Roman settlement and also one of the five Viking boroughs of Danelaw. In 1485 Richard III was buried in Leicester following his death at the nearby Battle of Bosworth. In 1589 Queen Elizabeth I granted a charter to the city and the ancient title was confirmed by letters patent in 1919.

The textile industry was responsible for Leicester's early expansion and the city still maintains a strong manufacturing base. Cotton mills and factories are now undergoing extensive regeneration and are being converted into offices, apartments, bars and restaurants. The principal buildings include the two universities (the University of Leicester and De Montfort University), as well as the Town Hall, the 13th-century Guildhall, De Montfort Hall, Leicester Cathedral, the Jewry Wall (the UK's highest standing Roman wall), St Nicholas Church and St Mary de Castro church. The motte and Great Hall of Leicester can be seen from the castle gardens, situated next to the River Soar.

Leicester is now one of the UK's most ethnically diverse cities – home to the only Jain temple in the West and hosting the country's second-largest Caribbean carnival.

LINCOLN (PRE-1900)

Situated 64km (40 miles) inland on the River Witham, Lincoln derives its name from a contraction of *Lindum Colonia,* the settlement founded in AD 48 by the Romans to command the crossing of Ermine Street and Fosse Way. Sections of the third-century Roman city wall can be seen, including an extant gateway (Newport Arch), and excavations have discovered traces of a sewerage system unique in Britain. The Romans also drained the surrounding fenland and created a canal system, laying the foundations of Lincoln's agricultural prosperity and also the city's importance in the medieval wool trade as a port and staple town.

As one of the five boroughs of Danelaw, Lincoln was an important trading centre in the ninth and tenth centuries and prosperity from the wool trade lasted until the 14th century. This wealth enabled local merchants to build parish churches, of which three survive, and there are also remains of a 12th-century Jewish community (Jew's House and Court, Aaron's House). However, the removal of the staple to Boston in 1369 heralded a decline, from which the city only recovered fully in the 19th century, when improved fen drainage made Lincoln agriculturally important. Improved canal and rail links led to industrial development, mainly in the manufacture of machinery, components and engineering products.

The castle was built shortly after the Norman Conquest and is unusual in having two mounds; on one motte stands a keep (Lucy's Tower) added in the 12th century. It currently houses one of the four surviving copies of the Magna Carta. The cathedral was begun *c.*1073 when the first Norman bishop moved the see of Lindsey to Lincoln, but was mostly destroyed by fire and earthquake in the 12th century. Rebuilding was begun by St Hugh and completed over a century later. Other notable architectural features are the 12th-century High Bridge, the oldest in Britain still to carry buildings, and the Guildhall, situated above the 15th-century Stonebow gateway.

LIVERPOOL (PRE-1900)

Liverpool, on the north bank of the river Mersey, 5km (3 miles) from the Irish Sea, is the United Kingdom's foremost port for Atlantic trade. Tunnels link Liverpool with Birkenhead and Wallasey.

There are 2,100 acres of dockland on both sides of the river and the Gladstone and Royal Seaforth Docks can accommodate tanker-sized vessels. Liverpool Free Port was opened in 1984.

Liverpool was created a free borough in 1207 and a city in 1880. From the early 18th century it expanded rapidly with the growth of industrialisation and the transatlantic slave trade. Surviving buildings from this period include the Bluecoat Chambers (1717, formerly the Bluecoat School), the Town Hall (1754, rebuilt to the original design 1795), and buildings in Rodney Street, Canning Street and the suburbs. Notable from the 19th and 20th centuries are the Anglican cathedral, built from the designs of Sir Giles Gilbert Scott (the foundation stone was laid in 1904, but the building was only completed in 1980); the Catholic Metropolitan Cathedral (designed by Sir Frederick Gibberd, consecrated 1967) and St George's Hall (1842), regarded as one of the finest modern examples of classical architecture. The refurbished Albert Dock (designed by Jesse Hartley) contains the Merseyside Maritime Museum, the International Slavery Museum and the Tate Liverpool art gallery.

In 1852 an act was passed establishing a public library, museum and art gallery; as a result Liverpool had one of the first public libraries in the country. The Brown, Picton and Hornby libraries form one of the country's major collections. The Victoria Building of Liverpool University; the Royal Liver, Cunard and Mersey Docks & Harbour Company buildings at the Pier Head; the Municipal Buildings and the Philharmonic Hall are other examples of the city's fine architecture.

Six areas of Liverpool's maritime mercantile city were designated as UNESCO World Heritage Sites in 2004, and Liverpool was elected as the European Capital of Culture for 2008.

MANCHESTER (PRE-1900)

Manchester (the *Mamucium* of the Romans, who occupied it in AD 79) is a commercial and industrial centre engaged in the engineering, chemical, clothing, food processing and textile industries and in education. Banking, insurance and a growing leisure industry are among its prime commercial activities. The city is connected with the sea by the Manchester Ship Canal, opened in 1894, 57km (35.5 miles) long, and accommodating ships up to 15,000 tons.

The principal buildings are the Town Hall, erected in 1877 from the designs of Alfred Waterhouse, with a large extension of 1938; the Royal Exchange (1869, enlarged 1921); the Central Library (1934); Heaton Hall; the 17th-century Chetham Library; the Rylands Library (1900), which includes the Althorp collection; the university precinct; the 15th-century cathedral (formerly the parish church); the Manchester Central conference and exhibition centre and the Bridgewater Hall (1996) concert venue. Manchester is the home of the Hallé Orchestra, the Royal Northern College of Music, the Royal Exchange Theatre and numerous public art galleries.

To accommodate the Commonwealth Games held in the city in 2002, new sports facilities were built including a stadium, swimming pool complex and the National Cycling Centre.

The town received its first charter of incorporation in 1838 and was created a city in 1853.

NEWCASTLE UPON TYNE (PRE-1900)

Newcastle upon Tyne, on the north bank of the River Tyne, is 13km (8 miles) from the North Sea. A cathedral and university city, it is the administrative, commercial and cultural centre for north-east England and the principal port. It is an important manufacturing centre with a wide variety of industries.

The principal buildings include the Castle Keep (12th century), Black Gate (13th century), Blackfriars (13th century), West Walls (13th century), St Nicholas's Cathedral (15th century, fine lantern tower), St Andrew's Church (12th–14th century), St John's (14th–15th century), All Saints (1786 by Stephenson), St Mary's Roman Catholic Cathedral (1844), Trinity House (17th century), Sandhill (16th-century houses), Guildhall (Georgian), Grey Street (1834–9), Central Station (1846–50), Laing Art Gallery (1904), University of Newcastle Physics Building (1962) and Medical Building (1985), Civic Centre (1963) and the Central Library (1969). Open spaces include the Town Moor (927 acres) and Jesmond Dene. Numerous bridges span the Tyne at Newcastle, including the Tyne Bridge (1928) and the tilting Millennium Bridge (2001) – which links the city with Gateshead to the south.

The city's name is derived from the 'new castle' (1080) erected as a defence against the Scots. In 1400 it was made a county, and in 1882 a city.

NORWICH (PRE-1900)

Norwich grew from an early Anglo-Saxon settlement near the confluence of the rivers Yare and Wensum, and now serves as the provincial capital for the predominantly agricultural region of East Anglia. The name is thought to relate to the most northerly of a group of Anglo-Saxon villages or *wics*. The city's first known charter was granted in 1158 by Henry II.

Norwich serves its surrounding area as a market town and commercial centre, with banking and insurance prominent among the city's businesses. From the 14th century until the Industrial Revolution, Norwich was the regional centre of the woollen industry, but now the biggest single industry is financial services and principal trades are engineering, printing, shoemaking, the production of chemicals and clothing, food processing and technology. Norwich is accessible to seagoing vessels by means of the River Yare, entered at Great Yarmouth, 32km (20 miles) to the east.

Among many historic buildings are the cathedral (completed in the 12th century and surmounted by a 15th-century spire 96m (315ft) in height); the keep of the Norman castle (now a museum and art gallery); the 15th-century flint-walled Guildhall; some thirty medieval parish churches; St Andrew's and Blackfriars' Halls; the Tudor houses preserved in Elm Hill and the Georgian Assembly House. The University of East Anglia is on the city's western boundary.

NOTTINGHAM (PRE-1900)

Nottingham stands on the River Trent. *Snotingaham* or *Notingeham,* literally the homestead of the people of Snot, is the Anglo-Saxon name for the Celtic settlement of *Tigguocobauc,* or the house of caves. In 878, Nottingham became one of the five boroughs of Danelaw. William the Conqueror ordered the construction of Nottingham Castle, while the town itself developed rapidly under Norman rule. Its laws and rights were later formally recognised by Henry II's charter in 1155. The castle became a favoured residence of King John. In 1642 King Charles I raised his personal standard at Nottingham Castle at the start of the Civil War.

Nottingham is home to Notts County FC (the world's oldest football league side), Nottingham Forest FC, Nottingham Racecourse, Trent Bridge cricket ground and the National Watersports Centre. The principal industries include textiles, pharmaceuticals, food manufacturing, engineering and telecommunications. There are two universities within the city boundaries.

Architecturally, Nottingham has a wealth of notable buildings, particularly those designed in the Victorian era by T. C. Hine and Watson Fothergill. The city council owns the castle, of Norman origin but restored in 1878, Wollaton Hall (1580–8), Newstead Abbey (once home of Lord Byron), the Guildhall (1888) and Council House (1929). St Mary's, St Peter's and St Nicholas' churches are of interest, as is the Roman Catholic cathedral (Pugin, 1842–4). Nottingham was granted city status in 1897.

OXFORD (PRE-1900)

Oxford is a university city, an important industrial centre and a market town. Industry played a minor part in Oxford until the motor industry was established in 1912.

Oxford is known for its architecture, its oldest specimens being the reputedly Saxon tower of St Michael's Church, the remains of the Norman castle and city walls, and the Norman church at Iffley. It also has many Gothic buildings, such as the Divinity Schools, the Old Library at Merton College, William of Wykeham's New College, Magdalen and Christ Church colleges and many other college buildings. Later centuries are represented by the Laudian quadrangle at St John's College, the Renaissance Sheldonian Theatre by Wren, Trinity College Chapel, All Saints Church, Hawksmoor's mock-Gothic at All Souls College, and the 18th-century Queen's College. In addition to individual buildings, High Street and Radcliffe Square both form interesting architectural compositions. Most of the colleges have gardens, those of Magdalen, New College, St John's and Worcester being the largest.

The Oxford University Museum of Natural History, renowned for its spectacular neo-gothic architecture, houses the university's scientific collections of zoological, entomological and geological specimens and is attached to the neighbouring Pitt Rivers Museum which houses ethnographic and archaeological objects from around the world. The Ashmolean is the city's museum of art and archaeology and Modern Art Oxford hosts a programme of contemporary art exhibitions.

ST ALBANS (PRE-1900)

The origins of St Albans, situated on the River Ver, stem from the Roman town of *Verulamium.* Named after the first Christian martyr in Britain, who was executed there, St Albans has developed around the Norman abbey and cathedral church (consecrated 1115), built partly of materials from the old Roman city. The museums house Iron Age and Roman artefacts and the Roman theatre, unique in Britain, has a stage as opposed to an amphitheatre. Archaeological excavations in the city centre have revealed evidence of pre-Roman, Saxon and medieval occupation.

The town's significance grew to the extent that it was a signatory and venue for the drafting of the Magna Carta. It was also the scene of riots during the Peasants' Revolt, the French King John was imprisoned there after the Battle of Poitiers, and heavy fighting took place there during the Wars of the Roses.

Previously controlled by the Abbot, the town achieved a charter in 1553 and city status in 1877. The street market, first established in 1553, is still an important feature of the city, as are many hotels and inns, surviving from the days when St Albans was an important coach stop. Tourist attractions include historic churches and houses and a 15th-century clock tower.

The city is now home to a wide range of businesses, with special emphasis on information and legal services, and is home to the Royal National Rose Society.

SALISBURY (PRE-1900)

The history of Salisbury centres around the cathedral and cathedral close. The city evolved from an Iron Age camp a mile to the north of its current position which was strengthened by the Romans and called *Serviodunum.* The Normans built a castle and cathedral on the site and renamed it Sarum. In 1220 Bishop Richard Poore and the architect Elias de Derham decided to build a new Gothic style cathedral. The cathedral was completed 38 years later and a community known as New Sarum, now called Salisbury, grew around it. Originally the cathedral had a squat tower; the 123m (404ft) spire that makes the cathedral the tallest medieval structure in the world was added *c.*1315. A walled close with houses for the clergy was built around the cathedral; the Medieval Hall still stands today, alongside buildings dating from the 13th to the 20th century, including some designed by Sir Christopher Wren.

A prosperous wool and cloth trade allowed Salisbury to flourish until the 17th century. When the wool trade declined new crafts were established including cutlery, leather and basket work, saddlery, lacemaking, joinery and malting. By 1750 it had become an important road junction and coaching centre and in the Victorian era the railways enabled a new age of expansion and prosperity. Today Salisbury is a thriving tourist centre.

SHEFFIELD (PRE-1900)

Sheffield is situated at the junction of the Sheaf, Porter, Rivelin and Loxley valleys with the River Don and was created a city in 1893. Though its cutlery, silverware and plate have long been famous, Sheffield has other and now more important industries: special and alloy steels, engineering, tool-making, medical equipment and media-related industries (in its new cultural industries quarter). Sheffield has two universities and is an important research centre.

The parish church of St Peter and St Paul, founded in the 12th century, became the cathedral church of the Diocese of Sheffield in 1914. The Roman Catholic Cathedral Church of St Marie (founded 1847) was created a cathedral for the new diocese of Hallam in 1980. Parts of the present building date from *c.*1435. The principal buildings are the Town Hall (1897), the Cutlers' Hall (1832), City Hall (1932), Graves Art Gallery (1934), Mappin Art Gallery, the Crucible Theatre and the restored Lyceum theatre, which dates from 1897 and was reopened in 1990. Three major sporting and entertainment venues were opened between 1990 and 1991: Sheffield Arena, Don Valley Stadium and Pond's Forge. The Millennium Galleries opened in 2001.

SOUTHAMPTON (1964)

Southampton is a major seaport on the south coast of England, situated between the mouths of the Test and Itchen rivers. Southampton's natural deep-water harbour has made the area an important settlement since the Romans built the first port (known as *Clausentum*) in the first century, and Southampton's port has witnessed several important departures, including those of King Henry V in 1415 for the Battle of Agincourt, RMS *Titanic* in 1912, and the *Mayflower* in 1620.

The city's strategic importance, not only as a seaport but also as a centre for aircraft production, meant that it was heavily bombed during the Second World War; however, many historically significant structures remain, including the Wool House, dating from 1417 and now used as the Maritime Museum; parts of the Norman city walls which are among the most complete in the UK; the Bargate, which was originally the main gateway into the city; God's House Tower, now the Museum of Archaeology; St Michael's, the city's oldest church; and the Tudor Merchants Hall.

Home to the National Oceanography Centre, the international Southampton Boat Show and some of the country's principal watersports venues, Southampton's coastal setting and maritime history remain its main focus, but it also features extensive parks and a thriving entertainment scene.

STOKE-ON-TRENT (1925)

Stoke-on-Trent, standing on the River Trent and familiarly known as 'the potteries', is the main centre of employment for the population of north Staffordshire. The city is the largest clayware producer in the world (china, earthenware, sanitary goods, refractories, bricks and tiles) and also has a wide range of other manufacturing industries, including steel, chemicals, engineering and tyres. Extensive reconstruction has been carried out in recent years.

The city was formed by the federation of the separate municipal authorities of Tunstall, Burslem, Hanley, Stoke, Fenton, and Longton in 1910 and received its city status in 1925.

WINCHESTER (PRE-1900)

Winchester, the ancient capital of England, is situated on the River Itchen. The city is rich in architecture of all types, especially notable is the cathedral. Built in 1079–93 the cathedral exhibits examples of Norman, early English and Perpendicular styles and is the burial place of author Jane Austen. Winchester College, founded in 1382, is one of the country's most famous public schools, and the original building (1393) remains largely unaltered. St Cross Hospital, another great medieval foundation, lies one mile south of the city. The almshouses were founded in 1136 by Bishop Henry de Blois, and Cardinal Henry Beaufort added a new almshouse of 'Noble Poverty' in 1446. The chapel and dwellings are of great architectural interest, and visitors may still receive the 'Wayfarer's Dole' of bread and ale.

Excavations have done much to clarify the origins and development of Winchester. Part of the forum and several of the streets from the Roman town have been discovered. Excavations in the Cathedral Close have uncovered the entire site of the Anglo-Saxon cathedral (known as the Old Minster) and parts of the New Minster which was built by Alfred's son, Edward the Elder, and is the burial place of the Alfredian dynasty. The original burial place of St Swithun, before his remains were translated to a site in the present cathedral, was also uncovered.

Excavations in other parts of the city have thrown much light on Norman Winchester, notably on the site of the Royal Castle (adjacent to which the new Law Courts have been built) and in the grounds of Wolvesey Castle, where the great house built by Bishops Giffard and Henry de Blois in the 12th century has been uncovered. The Great Hall, built by Henry III between 1222 and 1236, survives and houses the Arthurian Round Table.

YORK (PRE-1900)

The city of York is an archiepiscopal seat. Its recorded history dates from AD 71, when the Roman Ninth Legion established a base under Petilius Cerealis that would later become the fortress of *Eburacum,* or *Eboracum.* In Anglo-Saxon times the city was the royal and ecclesiastical centre of Northumbria, and after capture by a Viking army in AD 866 it became the capital of the Viking kingdom of Jorvik. By the 14th century the city had become a great mercantile centre, mainly because of its control of the wool trade, and was used as the chief base against the Scots. Under the Tudors its fortunes declined, although Henry VIII made it the headquarters of the Council of the North. Excavations on many sites, including Coppergate, have greatly expanded knowledge of Roman, Viking and medieval urban life.

With its development as a railway centre in the 19th century the commercial life of York expanded, and today the city is home to the award-winning National Railway Museum. The principal industries are the manufacture of chocolate, scientific instruments and sugar.

The city is rich in examples of architecture of all periods. The earliest church was built in AD 627 and, from the 12th to 15th centuries, the present Minster was built in a succession of styles. Other examples within the city are the medieval city walls and gateways, churches and guildhalls. Domestic architecture includes the Georgian mansions of The Mount, Micklegate and Bootham.

LORD-LIEUTENANTS AND HIGH SHERIFFS

Area	*Lord-Lieutenant*	*High Sheriff (2010–11)*
Bedfordshire	Sir Samuel Whitbread, KCVO	Daniel Hanbury
Berkshire	Hon. Mary Bayliss	Catherine Stevenson
Bristol	Mary Prior, MBE	Lois Golding, OBE
Buckinghamshire	Sir Henry Aubrey-Fletcher	Countess Howe
Cambridgeshire	Hugh Duberly, CBE	Nigel Brown, OBE
Cheshire	David Briggs, MBE	Diana Barbour
Cornwall	Lady Mary Holborow, DCVO	Iain Mackie
Cumbria	J. Cropper	James Carr
Derbyshire	William Tucker	Fiona Cannon
Devon	Eric Dancer, CBE	Hon. Elizabeth d'Erlanger
Dorset	Valerie Pitt-Rivers	Hon. Timothy Palmer
Durham	Sir Paul Nicholson	Bernard Robinson, OBE
East Riding of Yorkshire	Hon. Susan Cunliffe-Lister	Adrian Horsley
East Sussex	Peter Field	Deborah Bedford
Essex	Lord Petre	Michael Hindmarch
Gloucestershire	Sir Henry Elwes, KCVO	Ceri Evans
Greater London	Sir David Brewer, CMG	Ranjit Mathrani
Greater Manchester	Warren Smith	Anil Ruia
Hampshire	Dame Mary Fagan, DCVO	Alan Lovell
Herefordshire	Countess of Darnley	Elizabeth Hunter
Hertfordshire	Countess of Verulam	Gerald Corbett
Isle of Wight	Maj.-Gen. Martin White, CB, CBE	Peter Kingston
Kent	Allan Willett, CMG	Peregrine Massey
Lancashire	Lord Shuttleworth	George Menderos
Leicestershire	Lady Gretton	Col. Robert Martin OBE
Lincolnshire	Anthony Worth	John Godfrey, CBE
Merseyside	Dame Lorna Fox Muirhead, DBE	Roy Morris
Norfolk	Richard Jewson	Charles Barratt
North Yorkshire	Lord Crathorne	Richard Compton
Northamptonshire	Lady Juliet Townsend, LVO	David Laing
Northumberland	Duchess of Northumberland	Hon. Katie Crosbie-Dawson
Nottinghamshire	Sir Andrew Buchanan, Bt.	Amanda Farr
Oxfordshire	Tim Stevenson, OBE	Marie-Jane Barnett
Rutland	Dr Laurence Howard, OBE	Sarah Forsyth
Shropshire	A. Heber-Percy	Hugh Trevor-Jones
Somerset	Lady Gass	Patricia Hunt
South Yorkshire	David Moody	Anthony Cooper
Staffordshire	Sir James Hawley, KCVO, TD	Ian Dudson, CBE
Suffolk	Lord Tollemache	Theresa Innes
Surrey	Mrs S. Goad	Robert Douglas, CBE
Tyne and Wear	N. Sherlock, OBE	Susan Winfield, OBE
Warwickshire	M. Dunne	Richard Hardy
West Midlands	Paul Sabapathy, CBE	Anita Bhalla
West Sussex	Susan Pyper	Elizabeth Bennett
West Yorkshire	Dr Ingrid Roscoe	Richard Clough
Wiltshire	John Bush, OBE	Dame Elizabeth Neville, DBE, QPM
Worcestershire	M. Brinton	Elizabeth Hunter

COUNTY COUNCILS

Council & Administrative Headquarters	*Telephone*	*Population**	*Council Tax†*	*Chief Executive*
Buckinghamshire, Aylesbury	01296-395000	493,300	£1,078	Chris Williams
Cambridgeshire, Cambridge	0345-045 5200	605,000	£1,048	Mark Lloyd
Cumbria, Carlisle	01228-606060	496, 600	£1,162	Jill Stannard *(acting)*
Derbyshire, Matlock	01629-580000	762,100	£1,077	Nick Hodgson
Devon, Exeter	0845-155 1015	754,700	£1,116	Phil Norrey
Dorset, Dorchester	01305-221000	407,800	£1,168	David Jenkins
East Sussex, Lewes	01273-481000	509,900	£1,158	Becky Shaw
Essex, Chelmsford	0845-743 0430	1,396,400	£1,087	Joanna Killian
Gloucestershire, Gloucester	01452-425000	582,600	£1,091	Peter Bungard
Hampshire, Winchester	01962-841841	1,285,900	£1,038	Andrew Smith
Hertfordshire, Hertford	01992-555644	1,078,400	£1,119	Caroline Tapster
Kent, Maidstone	01622-671411	1,406,600	£1,048	Peter Gilroy, OBE
Lancashire, Preston	0545-053 0000	1,169,000	£1,108	Ged Fitzgerald
Leicestershire, Leicester	0116-232 3232	645,800	£1,063	John Sinnott
Lincolnshire, Lincoln	01522-552222	698,000	£1,066	Tony McArdle
Norfolk, Norwich	0844-800 8020	850,800	£1,145	David White
North Yorkshire, Northallerton	01609-780780	599,200	£1,057	Richard Flinton
Northamptonshire, Northampton	01604-236236	685,000	£1,028	Paul Blankern *(acting)*
Nottinghamshire, Nottingham	0115-982 3823	776,500	£1,193	Mick Burrows
Oxfordshire, Oxford	01865-792422	639,800	£1,162	Joanna Simons
Somerset, Taunton	0845-345 9166	525,800	£1,027	Sheila Wheeler
Staffordshire, Stafford	01785-223121	828,900	£1,029	Nick Bell
Suffolk, Ipswich	0845-606 6067	715,700	£1,127	Andrea Hill
Surrey, Kingston upon Thames	0845-600 9009	1,109,700	£1,116	David McNulty
Warwickshire, Warwick	01926-410410	530,700	£1,155	Jim Graham
West Sussex, Chichester	01243-777100	781,500	£1,162	Mark Hammond
Worcestershire, Worcester	01905-763763	557,600	£1,039	Trish Haines

* *Source:* The Office of National Statistics – *Mid-2008 Population Estimates* (Crown copyright)

† Average 2010–11 Band D council tax in the county area exclusive of precepts for fire and police authorities. County councils claim their share of the combined council tax from the collection funds of the district authorities into whose area they fall. Average Band D council tax bills for the billing authority are given on the following pages

DISTRICT COUNCILS

District Council	*Telephone*	*Population**	*Council Tax†*	*Chief Executive*
Adur	01273-263000	60,700	£1,587	Ian Lowrie
Allerdale	01900-702702	94,500	£1,536	Harry Dyke *(acting)*
Amber Valley	01773-570222	121,100	£1,494	Peter Carney
Arun	01903-737500	146,600	£1,520	Ian Sumnall
Ashfield	01623-450000	116,500	£1,596	Philip Marshall *(acting)*
Ashford	01233-331111	113,500	£1,412	John Bunnett
Aylesbury Vale	01296-585858	176,000	£1,492	Andrew Grant
Babergh	01473-822801	87,000	£1,488	Patricia Rockall
Barrow-in-Furness	01229-876300	71,800	£1,562	Tom Campbell
Basildon	01268-533333	172,600	£1,544	Bala Mahendran
Basingstoke and Deane	01256-844844	161,700	£1,365	Tony Curtis
Bassetlaw	01909-533533	112,200	£1,598	David Hunter
Blaby	0116-275 0555	93,400	£1,495	Sandra Whiles
Bolsover	01246-240000	74,300	£1,565	Wesley Lumley
Boston	01205-314200	58,300	£1,427	Richard Harbord
Braintree	01376-552525	142,100	£1,480	Allan Reid
Breckland	01362-656870	131,800	£1,458	Sandra Dineen
Brentwood	01277-312500	73,200	£1,468	Joanna Killian
Broadland	01603-431133	123,300	£1,506	Colin Bland
Bromsgrove	01527-881288	92,800	£1,502	Kevin Dicks
Broxbourne	01992-785555	90,100	£1,380	Mike Walker
Broxtowe	0115-917 7777	112,000	£1,607	Ruth Hyde
Burnley	01282-425011	87,300	£1,577	Steve Rumbelow
CAMBRIDGE	01223-457000	122,800	£1,442	Antoinette Jackson
Cannock Chase	01543-462621	94,800	£1,490	Stephen Brown
CANTERBURY	01227-862000	149,700	£1,444	Colin Carmichael
CARLISLE	01228-817000	103,700	£1,561	Maggie Mooney
Castle Point	01268-882200	89,800	£1,523	David Marchant
Charnwood	01509-263151	167,100	£1,459	Geoffrey Parker *(acting)*
Chelmsford	01245-606606	167,100	£1,481	Steve Packham
Cheltenham	01242-262626	112,000	£1,481	Andrew North
Cherwell	01295-252535	138,200	£1,519	Mary Harpley
Chesterfield	01246-345345	100,800	£1,459	Huw Bowen
Chichester	01243-785166	110,500	£1,474	John Marsland
Chiltern	01494-729000	90,900	£1,506	Alan Goodrum
Chorley	01257-515151	104,800	£1,515	Donna Hall
Christchurch	01202-495000	45,800	£1,584	Michael Turvey
Colchester	01206-282222	181,000	£1,476	Adrian Pritchard
Copeland	0845-054 8600	70,300	£1,554	Paul Walker
Corby	01536-464000	55,800	£1,402	Chris Mallender
Cotswold	01285-623000	83,500	£1,486	David Neudegg
Craven	01756-700600	56,200	£1,523	Paul Shevlin
Crawley	01293-438000	101,300	£1,488	Lee Harris
Dacorum	01442-228000	139,600	£1,447	Daniel Zammit
Dartford	01322-343434	92,000	£1,442	Graham Harris
Daventry	01327-871100	79,700	£1,410	Simon Bovey
Derbyshire Dales	01629-761100	100,800	£1,537	David Wheatcroft
Dover	01304-821199	106,900	£1,459	Nadeem Aziz
East Cambridgeshire	01353-665555	82,300	£1,461	John Hill
East Devon	01395-516551	132,700	£1,499	Mark Williams
East Dorset	01202-886201	85,900	£1,638	David McIntosh
East Hampshire	01730-266551	111,700	£1,432	Sandy Hopkins
East Hertfordshire	01279-655261	135,500	£1,487	Anne Freimanis
East Lindsey	01507-601111	141,000	£1,388	Nigel Howells
East Northamptonshire	01832-742000	86,200	£1,409	David Oliver
East Staffordshire	01283-508000	109,100	£1,491	Andy O'Brien
Eastbourne	01323-410000	96,100	£1,603	Robert Cottrill
Eastleigh	023-8068 8000	121,000	£1,434	Bernie Topham
Eden	01768-817817	51,900	£1,550	Kevin Douglas
Elmbridge	01372-474474	132,400	£1,515	Robert Moran

District Council	*Telephone*	*Population**	*Council Tax†*	*Chief Executive*
Epping Forest	01992-564000	123,900	£1,490	Peter Haywood
Epsom and Ewell	01372-732000	72,400	£1,478	Frances Rutter *(acting)*
Erewash	0115-907 2244	111,300	£1,480	Jeremy Jaroszek
EXETER	01392-277888	123,500	£1,470	Philip Bostock
Fareham	01329-236100	110,300	£1,386	Peter Grimwood
Fenland	01354-654321	91,800	£1,540	Sandra Claxton
Forest Heath	01638-719000	64,700	£1,497	David Burnip
Forest of Dean	01594-810000	81,900	£1,501	Sue Pangbourne *(acting)*
Fylde	01253-658658	76,500	£1,522	Phillip Woodward
Gedling	0115-901 3901	112,100	£1,576	Peter Murdock
GLOUCESTER	01452-522232	115,300	£1,477	Julian Wain
Gosport	023-9258 4242	80,000	£1,448	Ian Lycett
Gravesham	01474-337000	98,000	£1,426	Glyn Thomson
Great Yarmouth	01493-856100	94,400	£1,492	Richard Packham
Guildford	01483-505050	135,700	£1,481	David Hill
Hambleton	0845-121 1555	87,100	£1,444	Peter Simpson
Harborough	01858-828282	82,800	£1,492	Sue Smith
Harlow	01279-446655	79,000	£1,537	Malcolm Morley
Harrogate	01423-500600	160,500	£1,553	Wallace Sampson
Hart	01252-622122	90,600	£1,456	Geoff Bonner
Hastings	01424 451066	86,400	£1,614	Roy Mawford
Havant	023-9247 4174	117,600	£1,438	Sandy Hopkins
Hertsmere	020-8207 2277	98,700	£1,447	Donald Graham
High Peak	0845-129 7777	93,200	£1,500	Simon Baker
Hinckley and Bosworth	01455-238141	105,200	£1,437	Steve Atkinson
Horsham	01403-215100	130,700	£1,479	Tom Crowley
Huntingdonshire	01480-388388	168,900	£1,471	David Monks
Hyndburn	01254-388111	81,600	£1,549	David Welsby
Ipswich	01473-432000	122,300	£1,600	Russell Williams *(acting)*
Kettering	01536-410333	90,700	£1,428	David Cook, MBE
King's Lynn and West Norfolk	01553-616200	144,800	£1,491	Ray Harding
LANCASTER	01524-582000	143,700	£1,523	Mark Cullinan
Lewes	01273-471600	95,200	£1,643	Jenny Rowlands
Lichfield	01543-308000	97,900	£1,453	Nina Dawes
LINCOLN	01522-881188	88,400	£1,481	Andrew Taylor
Maidstone	01622-602000	145,400	£1,493	Alison Broom
Maldon	01621-854477	63,100	£1,495	Fiona Marshall
Malvern Hills	01684-862151	74,800	£1,477	Chris Bocock
Mansfield	01623-463463	100,600	£1,610	Ruth Marlow
Melton	01664-502502	49,300	£1,487	Lynn Aisbett
Mendip	01749-648999	110,100	£1,464	Stuart Brown
Mid Devon	01884-255255	76,700	£1,559	Gerald Hirsch
Mid Suffolk	01449-720711	94,700	£1,491	Andrew Good
Mid Sussex	01444-458166	131,600	£1,505	vacant
Mole Valley	01306-885001	82,000	£1,470	Darren Mepham
New Forest	023-8028 5000	175,400	£1,466	David Yates
Newark and Sherwood	01636-650000	113,300	£1,651	Andrew Muter
Newcastle-under-Lyme	01782-717717	124,700	£1,460	Mark Barrow
North Devon	01271-327711	92,300	£1,553	M. Mansell *(acting)*
North Dorset	01258-454111	67,900	£1,586	Elizabeth Goodall
North East Derbyshire	01246-231111	98,200	£1,565	Mike Goodwin
North Hertfordshire	01462-474000	123,800	£1,480	John Campbell
North Kesteven	01529-414155	106,100	£1,444	Ian Fytche
North Norfolk	01263-513811	101,500	£1,510	Philip Burton
North Warwickshire	01827-715341	62,300	£1,581	Jeremy Hutchinson
North West Leicestershire	01530-454545	90,800	£1,506	Christine Fisher
Northampton	01604-837837	205,200	£1,445	David Kennedy
NORWICH	0344-980 3333	135,800	£1,562	Laura McGillivray
Nuneaton and Bedworth	02476-376376	122,000	£1,533	Christine Kerr
Oadby and Wigston	0116-288 8961	57,200	£1,489	Mark Hall
OXFORD	01865-249811	153,900	£1,583	Peter Sloman
Pendle	01282-661661	89,900	£1,572	Stephen Barnes
PRESTON	01772-906900	132,000	£1,580	Lorraine Norris
Purbeck	01929-556561	46,000	£1,626	Steve Mackenzie
Redditch	01527-64252	79,900	£1,501	Kevin Dicks *(acting)*
Reigate and Banstead	01737-276000	134,800	£1,514	John Jory
Ribble Valley	01200-425111	58,500	£1,476	Marshal Scott

District Council	*Telephone*	*Population**	*Council Tax†*	*Chief Executive*
Richmondshire	01748-829100	51,500	£1,538	Peter Simpson
Rochford	01702-546366	83,200	£1,519	Paul Warren
Rossendale	01706-217777	67,300	£1,574	Helen Lockwood
Rother	01424-787999	88,800	£1,588	Derek Stevens
Rugby	01788-533533	91,700	£1,517	Andrew Gabbitas *(acting)*
Runnymede	01932-838383	83,400	£1,452	Paul Turrell
Rushcliffe	0115-981 9911	109,800	£1,598	Allen Graham
Rushmoor	01252-398398	89,600	£1,430	Andrew Lloyd
Ryedale	01653-600666	53,500	£1,534	Janet Waggott
ST ALBANS	01727-866100	133,700	£1,473	Daniel Goodwin
St Edmundsbury	01284-763233	103,700	£1,501	Geoff Rivers
Scarborough	01723-232323	108,500	£1,552	Jim Dillon
Sedgemoor	0845-408 2540	112,800	£1,440	Mr Kerry Rickards
Selby	01757-705101	82,000	£1,529	Martin Connor
Sevenoaks	01732-227000	114,700	£1,501	Robin Hales
Shepway	01303-853000	100,100	£1,535	Alistair Stewart
South Bucks	01895-837200	64,800	£1,486	Chris Furness
South Cambridgeshire	0345-0450500	139,300	£1,452	Greg Harlock
South Derbyshire	01283-221000	92,700	£1,475	Frank McArdle
South Hams	01803-861234	83,500	£1,518	David Incoll
South Holland	01775-761161	83,400	£1,429	Terry Huggins
South Kesteven	01476-406080	132,00	£1,409	Beverly Agass *(acting)*
South Lakeland	01539-733333	104,400	£1,555	Peter Ridgway
South Norfolk	01508-533633	119,200	£1,528	Sandra Dinneen
South Northamptonshire	01327-322322	91,000	£1,448	Jean Morgan
South Oxfordshire	01491-823000	129,100	£1,507	David Buckle
South Ribble	01772-421491	107,200	£1,528	Jean Hunter
South Somerset	01935-462462	158,700	£1,478	Mark Williams
South Staffordshire	01902-696000	106,400	£1,418	Steve Winterflood
Spelthorne	01784-451499	91,200	£1,482	Roberto Tambini
Stafford	01785-619000	124,700	£1,440	Ian Thompson
Staffordshire Moorlands	01538-483483	95,500	£1,455	Simon Baker
Stevenage	01438-242242	80,000	£1,455	Nick Parry
Stratford-on-Avon	01789-267575	118,800	£1,510	Paul Lankester
Stroud	01453-766321	110,700	£1,532	David Hagg
Suffolk Coastal	01394-383789	125,600	£1,479	Stephen Baker
Surrey Heath	01276-707100	83,400	£1,518	Michael Willis
Swale	01795-417330	131,900	£1,431	Abdool Kara
Tamworth	01827-709709	75,800	£1,424	David Weatherley
Tandridge	01883-722000	83,500	£1,521	Stephen Weigel
Taunton Deane	01823-356356	108,700	£1,414	Penny James
Teignbridge	01626-361101	127,600	£1,539	Nicola Bulbeck
Tendring	01255-686868	147,600	£1,463	John Hawkins
Test Valley	01264-368000	115,400	£1,398	Roger Tetstall
Tewkesbury	01684-295010	79,100	£1,431	Michael Dawson
Thanet	01843-577000	129,900	£1,481	Richard Samuel
Three Rivers	01923-776611	87,700	£1,459	Dr Steven Halls
Tonbridge and Malling	01732-844522	117,100	£1,463	David Hughes
Torridge	01237-428700	65,600	£1,523	Nicola Bulbeck
Tunbridge Wells	01892-526121	107,400	£1,435	William Benson
Uttlesford	01799-510510	73,700	£1,495	John Mitchell
Vale of White Horse	01235-520202	116,900	£1,492	David Buckle
Warwick	01926-450000	135,700	£1,497	Chris Elliott
Watford	01923-226400	81,000	£1,516	Manny Lewis
Waveney	01502-562111	117,700	£1,446	Stephen Baker
Waverley	01483-523333	118,700	£1,519	Mary Orton
Wealden	01323-443322	143,300	£1,629	Charles Lant
Wellingborough	01933-229777	76,400	£1,370	Joe Hubbard
Welwyn & Hatfield	01707-357000	108,300	£1,498	Michel Saminaden
West Devon	01822-813600	52,900	£1,586	David Incoll
West Dorset	01305-251010	97,200	£1,598	David Clarke
West Lancashire	01695-577177	109,400	£1,515	William Taylor
West Lindsey	01427-676676	88,900	£1,481	Manjeet Gill
West Oxfordshire	01993-861000	101,600	£1,454	David Neudegg
West Somerset	01643-703704	35,500	£1,448	Adrian Dyer
Weymouth and Portland	01305-838000	65,000	£1,678	Tom Grainger
WINCHESTER	01962-840222	112,700	£1,434	Simon Eden

District Council	*Telephone*	*Population**	*Council Tax†*	*Chief Executive*
Woking	01483-755855	92,200	£1,520	Ray Morgan, OBE
WORCESTER	01905-723471	94,100	£1,457	Duncan Sharkey
Worthing	01903-239999	100,200	£1,516	Ian Lowrie
Wychavon	01386-565000	117,300	£1,441	Jack Hegarty
Wycombe	01494-461000	161,500	£1,457	Karen Satterford
Wyre	01253-891000	110,900	£1,507	Jim Corry
Wyre Forest	01562-732928	98,700	£1,502	Ian Miller

* *Source:* ONS – *Mid-2008 Population Estimates* (Crown copyright)
† Average Band D council tax bill for 2010–11
Councils in CAPITAL LETTERS have city status

METROPOLITAN BOROUGH COUNCILS

Metropolitan Borough Councils	*Telephone*	*Population**	*Council Tax†*	*Chief Executive*
Barnsley	01226-770770	225,900	£1,400	Philip Coppard
BIRMINGHAM	0121-303 9944	1,016,800	£1,261	Stephen Hughes
Bolton	01204-333333	262,800	£1,414	Sean Harriss
BRADFORD	01274-432001	501,700	£1,283	Tony Reeves
Bury	0161-253 5000	183,100	£1,457	Mark Sanders
Calderdale	01422-357257	201,800	£1,417	Owen Williams
COVENTRY	024-7683 3333	309,800	£1,471	Martin Reeves
Doncaster	01302-734444	291,600	£1,315	Robert Vincent
Dudley	0300-555 2345	306,500	£1,273	John Polychronakis
Gateshead	0191-433 3000	190,600	£1,600	Roger Kelly
Kirklees	01484-221000	403,900	£1,405	Rob Vincent
Knowsley	0151-489 6000	150,800	£1,484	Sheena Ramsey
LEEDS	0113-222 4444	770,800	£1,312	Tom Riordan
LIVERPOOL	0151-233 3000	434,900	£1,519	Colin Hilton
MANCHESTER	0161-234 5000	464,200	£1,327	Sir Howard Bernstein
NEWCASTLE UPON TYNE	0191-232 8520	273,600	£1,512	Barry Rowland *(acting)*
North Tyneside	0191-643 5991	197,300	£1,485	John Marsden
Oldham	0161-911 3000	219,700	£1,547	Charlie Parker
Rochdale	01706-647474	206,300	£1,482	Roger Ellis
Rotherham	01709-382121	253,900	£1,451	Martin Kimber
St Helens	01744-676789	177,500	£1,366	Carole Hudson
SALFORD	0161-794 4711	221,300	£1,523	Barbara Spicer
Sandwell	0121-569 2200	289,100	£1,323	Allison Fraser
Sefton	0151-922 4040	275,100	£1,488	Margaret Carney
SHEFFIELD	0114-272 6444	534,500	£1,478	John Mothersole
Solihull	0121-704 6000	205,500	£1,337	Mark Rogers
South Tyneside	0191-427 1717	151,600	£1,448	Martin Swales
Stockport	0161-480 4949	281,000	£1,561	Eamonn Boylan
SUNDERLAND	0191-520 5555	280,300	£1,343	Dave Smith
Tameside	0161-342 8355	215,500	£1,366	Steven Pleasant
Trafford	0161-912 2000	212,800	£1,303	Janet Callender
WAKEFIELD	0845-8506 506	322,300	£1,305	Joanne Roney, OBE
Walsall	01922-650000	255,400	£1,532	Paul Sheehan
Wigan	01942-244991	306,800	£1,370	Joyce Redfearn
Wirral	0151-606 2000	309,500	£1,464	Stephen Maddox
WOLVERHAMPTON	01902-556556	236,400	£1,464	Simon Warren

* *Source:* ONS – *Mid-2008 Population Estimates* (Crown copyright)
† Average Band D council tax bill for 2010–11
Councils in CAPITAL LETTERS have city status

UNITARY COUNCILS

Unitary Councils	*Telephone*	*Population**	*Council Tax†*	*Chief Executive*
Bath and North East Somerset	01225-477000	180,300	£1,461	John Everitt
Bedford	01234-267422	155,700	£1,564	Philip Simpkins
Blackburn with Darwen	01254-585585	140,700	£1,481	Graham Burgess
Blackpool	01253-477477	141,900	£1,516	Steve Weaver
Bournemouth	01202-451451	163,900	£1,499	Pam Donnellan
Bracknell Forest	01344-352000	114,700	£1,365	Timothy Wheadon
BRIGHTON AND HOVE	01273-290000	256,600	£1,483	John Barradell
BRISTOL	0117-922 2000	421,300	£1,567	Jan Ormondroyd
Central Bedfordshire	0300-300 8000	255,000	£1,641	Richard Carr
Cheshire East	0300-123 5500	361,500	£1,448	Erika Wenzel
Cheshire West and Chester	0300-123 8123	328,600	£1,486	Steve Robinson
Cornwall	0300-123 4100	532,200	£1,458	Kevin Lavery
Darlington	01325-380651	100,500	£1,394	Ada Burns
DERBY	01332-293111	239,200	£1,358	Adam Wilkinson
DURHAM	0300-123 7070	504,900	£1,602	George Garlick
East Riding of Yorkshire	01482-887700	335,000	£1,500	Nigel Pearson
Halton	0151-907 8300	119,800	£1,350	David Parr
Hartlepool	01429-266522	91,700	£1,671	Paul Walker
Herefordshire	01432-260000	179,300	£1,493	Chris Bull
Isle of Wight	01983-821000	140,200	£1,462	Joe Duckworth
Isles of Scilly‡	01720-422537	2,100	£1,187	Philip Hygate
KINGSTON-UPON-HULL	01482-609100	258,700	£1,341	Nicola Yates
LEICESTER	0116-254 9922	294,700	£1,409	Sheila Lock
Luton	01582-546000	191,800	£1,371	Trevor Holden
Medway	01634-333333	253,500	£1,329	Neil Davies
Middlesbrough	01642-245432	139,000	£1,514	Ian Parker
Milton Keynes	01908-691691	232,200	£1,389	David Hill
North East Lincolnshire	01472-313131	158,200	£1,503	Tony Hunter
North Lincolnshire	01724-296296	160,300	£1,555	Simon Driver
North Somerset	01934-888888	206,800	£1,423	Graham Turner
Northumberland	01670-533000	311,000	£1,490	Steve Stewart
NOTTINGHAM	0115-915 5555	292,400	£1,562	Jane Todd
PETERBOROUGH	01733-747474	164,000	£1,330	Gillian Beasley
PLYMOUTH	01752-668000	252,800	£1,473	Barry Keel
Poole	01202-633633	138,800	£1,450	John McBride
PORTSMOUTH	023-9282 2251	200,000	£1,357	David Williams
Reading	0118-9373737	145,700	£1,499	Michael Coughlin
Redcar and Cleveland	0164-277 4774	139,500	£1,556	Amanda Skelton
Rutland	01572-722577	39,200	£1,689	Helen Briggs
Shropshire	0345-678 9000	292,800	£1,491	Kim Ryley
Slough	01753-475111	121,200	£1,368	Ruth Bagley
South Gloucestershire	01454-868686	257,700	£1,528	Amanda Deeks
SOUTHAMPTON	023-8022 3855	234,600	£1,447	Brad Roynon
Southend-on-Sea	01702-215000	164,300	£1,320	Robert Tinlin
Stockton-on-Tees	01642-393939	191,900	£1,483	Neil Schneider
STOKE-ON-TRENT	01782-234567	240,100	£1,389	John van de Laarschot
Swindon	01793-445500	192,900	£1,394	Gavin Jones
Telford and Wrekin	01952-380000	162,100	£1,419	Victor Brownlees *(acting)*
Thurrock	01375-652652	151,600	£1,304	Graham Farrant
Torbay	01803-201201	134,000	£1,493	Elizabeth Raikes
Warrington	01925-444400	196,200	£1,369	Diana Terris
West Berkshire	01635-42400	152,800	£1,501	Nick Carter
Wiltshire	0300-456 0100	455,500	£1,512	Andrew Kerr
Windsor and Maidenhead	01628-683800	142,800	£1,223	Ian Trenholm
Wokingham	0118-974 6000	159,100	£1,462	Susan Law
YORK	01904-613161	195,400	£1,366	Kersten England

* *Source:* ONS – *Mid-2008 Population Estimates* (Crown copyright)
† Average Band D council tax bill for 2010–11
‡ Under the Isles of Scilly Clause the council has additional functions to other unitary authorities
Councils in CAPITAL LETTERS have city status

MAP OF COUNCILS IN ENGLAND

LONDON

THE CITY OF LONDON CORPORATION

The City of London is the historic centre at the heart of London known as 'the square mile' around which the vast metropolis has grown over the centuries. The City's residential population is roughly 8,000 and in addition, around a third of a million people work in the City. The civic government is carried on by the City of London Corporation through the court of Common Council.

The City is an international financial and business centre, generating about £30bn a year for the British economy. It includes the head offices of the principal banks, insurance companies and mercantile houses, in addition to buildings ranging from the historic Roman Wall and the 15th-century Guildhall, to the massive splendour of St Paul's Cathedral and the architectural beauty of Wren's spires.

The City of London was described by Tacitus in AD 62 as 'a busy emporium for trade and traders'. Under the Romans it became an important administration centre and hub of the road system. Little is known of London in Saxon times, when it formed part of the kingdom of the East Saxons. In 886 Alfred recovered London from the Danes and reconstituted it a burgh under his son-in-law. In 1066 the citizens submitted to William the Conqueror who in 1067 granted them a charter, which is still preserved, establishing them in the rights and privileges they had hitherto enjoyed.

THE MAYORALTY

The mayoralty was probably established about 1189, the first mayor being Henry Fitz Ailwyn who filled the office for 23 years and was succeeded by Fitz Alan (1212–14). A new charter was granted by King John in 1215, directing the mayor to be chosen annually, which has been done ever since, though in early times the same individual often held the office more than once. A familiar instance is that of 'Whittington, thrice Lord Mayor of London' (in reality four times: 1397, 1398, 1406 and 1419); and many modern cases have occurred. The earliest instance of the phrase 'lord mayor' in English is in 1414. It was used more generally in the latter part of the 15th century and became invariable from 1535 onwards. At Michaelmas the liverymen in Common Hall choose two aldermen who have served the office of sheriff for presentation to the Court of Aldermen, and one is chosen to be lord mayor for the following mayoral year.

LORD MAYOR'S DAY

The lord mayor of London was previously elected on the feast of St Simon and St Jude (28 October), and from the time of Edward I, at least, was presented to the King or to the Barons of the Exchequer on the following day, unless that day was a Sunday. The day of election was altered to 16 October in 1346, and after some further changes was fixed for Michaelmas Day in 1546, but the ceremonies of admittance and swearing-in of the lord mayor continued to take place on 28 and 29 October respectively until 1751. In 1752, at the reform of the calendar, the lord mayor was continued in office until 8 November, the 'new style' equivalent of 28 October. The lord mayor is now presented to the lord chief justice at the royal courts of justice on the second Saturday in November to make the final declaration of office, having been sworn in at Guildhall on the preceding day. The procession to the royal courts of justice is popularly known as the Lord Mayor's Show.

REPRESENTATIVES

Aldermen are mentioned in the 11th century and their office is of Saxon origin. They were elected annually between 1377 and 1394, when an act of parliament of Richard II directed them to be chosen for life.

The Common Council was, at an early date, substituted for a popular assembly called the *Folkmote*. At first only two representatives were sent from each ward, but now each of the City's 25 wards is represented by an alderman and at least two Common Councilmen (the number depending on the size of the ward).

OFFICERS

Sheriffs were Saxon officers; their predecessors were the *wic-reeves* and *portreeves* of London and Middlesex. At first they were officers of the Crown, and were named by the Barons of the Exchequer; but Henry I (in 1132) gave the citizens permission to choose their own sheriffs, and the annual election of sheriffs became fully operative under King John's charter of 1199. The citizens lost this privilege, as far as the election of the sheriff of Middlesex was concerned, by the Local Government Act 1888; but the liverymen continue to choose two sheriffs of the City of London, who are appointed on Midsummer Day and take office at Michaelmas.

The office of chamberlain is an ancient one, the first contemporary record of which is 1237. The town clerk (or common clerk) is first mentioned in 1274.

ACTIVITIES

The work of the City of London Corporation is assigned to a number of committees which present reports to the Court of Common Council. These committees are: Barbican Centre; Barbican Residential; Board of Governors of the City of London Freeman's School, the City of London School, the City of London School for Girls, the Guildhall School of Music and Drama and the Museum of London; City Bridge Trust; City Lands and Bridge House Estates; Community and Children's Services; Court of Aldermen; Court of Common Council; Education; Epping Forest and Commons; Establishment; Finance; Freedom Applications; Gresham (city side); Guildhall Improvement; Hampstead Heath Management; Joint Working Party of the Three Schools; Keats House Management; Libraries, Archives and Guildhall Art Gallery; Licensing; Livery; London Drug Policy Forum; Managers of West Ham Park; Markets; Open Spaces; Planning and Transportation; Police; Policy and Resources; Port Health and Environmental Services; Queen's Park and Highgate Wood Management and Standards Committees.

The City's estate, in the possession of which the City of London Corporation differs from other municipalities, is managed by the City Lands and Bridge House Estates Committee, the chairmanship of which carries with it the title of chief commoner.

The Honourable the Irish Society, which manages the City Corporation's estates in Ulster, consists of a governor and five other aldermen, the recorder, and 19 common councilmen, of whom one is elected deputy governor.

THE LORD MAYOR 2010–11
The Rt. Hon. the Lord Mayor, Michael Bear*
Private Secretary, William Chapman
* Provisional at time of going to press

THE SHERIFFS 2010–11
Richard Sermon; Alderman Fiona Woolf (Candlewick)

OFFICERS, ETC
Town Clerk, Chris Duffield
Chamberlain, Chris Bilsland
Chief Commoner (2010), Robin Sherlock
Clerk, The Honourable the Irish Society, C. Fisher

THE ALDERMEN
with office held and date of appointment to that office

Name and Ward	*CC*	*Ald.*	*Shff*	*Lord Mayor*
Lord Levene of Portsoken, KBE, *Aldgate*	1983	1984	1995	1998
Sir David Howard, Bt., *Cornhill*	1972	1986	1997	2000
Sir Robert Finch, *Coleman Street*	–	1992	1999	2003
Sir Michael Savory, *Bread Street*	1980	1996	2001	2004
Sir John Stuttard, *Lime Street*	–	2001	2005	2006
Sir David Lewis, *Broad Street*	–	2001	2006	2007
Ian Luder, *Castle Baynard*	1998	2005	2007	2008
Nicholas Anstee, Aldersgate	1987	1996	2003	2009

All the above have passed the Civic Chair

Simon Walsh, *Farringdon Wt.*	1989	2000	
Dr Andrew Parmley, *Vintry*	1992	2001	
Benjamin R. Hall, *Farringdon Wn.*	1995	2002	
Alison Gowman, *Dowgate*	1991	2002	
Gordon Haines, *Queenhithe*	–	2004	
Roger Gifford, *Cordwainer*	–	2004	2008
David Wootton, *Langbourn*	2002	2005	
Alan Yarrow, *Bridge & Bridge Without*	–	2007	
Jeffrey Evans, *Cheap*	–	2007	
Sir Paul Judge, *Tower*	–	2007	
Fiona Woolf, CBE, *Candlewick*	–	2007	
John White, TD, *Billingsgate*	–	2008	
David Graves, *Cripplegate*	–	2008	
John Garbutt, *Walbrook*	–	2009	
Neil Redcliffe, *Bishopsgate*	–	2009	
Philip Remnant, *Bassishaw*	–	2010	

THE COMMON COUNCIL
Deputy: each common councilman so described serves as deputy to the alderman of her/his ward.

Abrahams, G. C. (2000)	*Farringdon Wt.*
Absalom, J. D. (1994)	*Farringdon Wt.*
Ayers, *Deputy* K. E., MBE (1996)	*Bassishaw*
Bain-Stewart, A. (2005)	*Farringdon Wn.*
Barker, *Deputy* J. A., OBE (1981)	*Cripplegate Wn.*
Barrow, *Deputy* D. (2007)	*Aldgate*
Bennett, *Deputy* J. A. (2005)	*Broad Street*
Bird, J. L., OBE (1977)	*Tower*
Boleat, M. J. (2002)	*Cordwainer*
Bradshaw, D. J. (1991)	*Cripplegate Wn.*
Burleigh, I. B. (2005)	*Portsoken*
Cassidy, *Deputy* M. J., CBE (1989)	*Coleman Street*
Catt, R. M. (2004)	*Castle Baynard*
Cenci Di Bello, Mrs P. J. (2004)	*Farringdon Wn.*
Chadwick, R. A. H. (1994)	*Tower*
Challis, N. K. (2005)	*Castle Baynard*
Chapman, J. D. (2006)	*Langbourn*
Cohen, *Deputy* Mrs C. M., OBE (1986)	*Lime Street*
Cotgrove, D. (1991)	*Lime Street*
Cressey, N. (2009)	*Portsoken*
Currie, *Deputy* Miss S. E. M. (1985)	*Cripplegate Wt.*
Davies, P. S. (2009)	*Broad Street*
Day, M. J. (2005)	*Bishopsgate*
Dove, W. H., MBE (1993)	*Bishopsgate*
Duckworth, S. D. (2000)	*Bishopsgate*
Dudley, Revd Dr M. R. (2002)	*Aldersgate*
Duffield, R. W. (2004)	*Farringdon Wn.*
Dunphy, P. G. (2009)	*Cornhill*
Eskenzi, *Deputy* A. N., CBE (1970)	*Farringdon Wn.*
Eve, *Deputy* R. A. (1980)	*Cheap*
Everett, K. M. (1984)	*Candlewick*
Farr, M. C. (1998)	*Walbrook*
Farrow, M. W. W. (1996)	*Farringdon Wt.*
Fernandes, S. A. (2009)	*Coleman Street*
Fraser, S. J. (1993)	*Coleman Street*
Fraser, *Deputy* W. B., OBE (1981)	*Vintry*
Fredericks, M. B. (2008)	*Tower*
Galloway, A. D., OBE (1981)	*Bishopsgate*
Gillon, G. M. F. (1995)	*Cordwainer*
Ginsburg, *Deputy* S. (1990)	*Bishopsgate*
Graves, A. C. (1985)	*Bishopsgate*
Haines, *Deputy* Revd S. D. (2005)	*Cornhill*
Halliday, *Deputy* Mrs P. A., OBE (1992)	*Walbrook*
Hardwick, Dr P. B. (1987)	*Aldgate*
Harris, B. N. (2004)	*Bridge*
Henderson-Begg, M. (1977)	*Coleman Street*
Hoffman, T. D. D. (2002)	*Vintry*
Hudson, M. (2007)	*Castle Baynard*
Hughes-Penney, R. C. (2004)	*Farringdon Wn.*
Hunt, W. G., TD (2004)	*Castle Baynard*
James, Clare (2008)	*Farringdon Wn.*
Jones, *Deputy* H. L. M. (2004)	*Portsoken*
King, *Deputy* A. J. N. (1999)	*Queenhithe*
Knowles, *Deputy* S. K., MBE (1984)	*Candlewick*
Lawrence, *Deputy* G. A. (2002)	*Farringdon Wt.*
Leck, P. (1998)	*Aldersgate*
Littlechild, V. (2009)	*Cripplegate Wn.*
Llewelyn-Davies, A. (2009)	*Billingsgate*
Lodge, O. A. W., TD (2009)	*Bread Street*
Lord, C. E. (2009)	*Farringdon Wt.*
McGuinness, *Deputy* C. S. (1997)	*Castle Baynard*
Malins, *Deputy* J. H., QC (1981)	*Farringdon Wt.*
Martinelli, P. J. (2009)	*Farringdon Wt.*
Mayhew, J. P. (1996)	*Aldersgate*
Mead, Mrs W. (1997)	*Farringdon Wt.*
Merrett, R. A. (2009)	*Bassishaw*
Mooney, B. D. F. (1998)	*Queenhithe*
Moore, G. W. (2009)	*Cripplegate Wn.*
Morris, H. F. (2008)	*Aldgate*
Moys, Mrs S. D. (2001)	*Aldgate*
Nash, *Deputy* Mrs J. C., OBE (1983)	*Aldersgate*
Newman, Mrs B. P., CBE (1989)	*Aldersgate*
Owen, *Deputy* Mrs J., MBE (1975)	*Langbourn*

Owen-Ward, *Deputy* J. R., MBE (1983)	*Bridge*
Page, M. (2002)	*Farringdon Wn.*
Pembroke, Mrs A. M. F. (1978)	*Cheap*
Pollard, J. H. G. (2002)	*Dowgate*
Priest, H. J. S. (2009)	*Castle Baynard*
Pulman, *Deputy* G. A. G. (1983)	*Tower*
Punter, C. (1993)	*Cripplegate Wn.*
Quilter, S. D. (1998)	*Cripplegate Wt.*
Regan, *Deputy* R. D. (1998)	*Farringdon Wn.*
Regis, D. (2009)	*Portsoken*
Richardson, M. C. (2009)	*Coleman Street*
Robinson, Mrs D. C. (1989)	*Bishopsgate*
Rogula, E. (2008)	*Lime Street*
Scott, J. G. S. (1999)	*Broad Street*
Seaton, I. (2009)	*Bassishaw*
Sherlock, *Deputy* M. R. C. (1992)	*Dowgate*
Shilson, *Deputy*, G. R. E., DPHIL (2009)	*Bread Street*
Simons, J. L. (2004)	*Castle Baynard*
Snyder, *Deputy* Sir Michael (1986)	*Cordwainer*
Spanner, J. H., TD (2001)	*Farringdon Wt.*
Starling, Mrs A. J. (2006)	*Cripplegate Wt.*
Thompson, D. J. (2004)	*Aldgate*
Tomlinson, J. (2004)	*Cripplegate Wt.*
Tumbridge, J. R. (2009)	*Tower*
Twogood, M. (2004)	*Farringdon Wt.*
Welbank, *Deputy* M. (2005)	*Billingsgate*
Willoughby, *Deputy* P. J. (1985)	*Bishopsgate*

THE CITY GUILDS (LIVERY COMPANIES)

The constitution of the livery companies has been unchanged for centuries. There are three ranks of membership: freemen, liverymen and assistants. A person can become a freeman by patrimony (through a parent having been a freeman); by servitude (through having served an apprenticeship to a freeman); or by redemption (by purchase).

Election to the livery is the prerogative of the company, who can elect any of its freemen as liverymen. Assistants are usually elected from the livery and form a Court of Assistants which is the governing body of the company. The master (in some companies called the prime warden) is elected annually from the assistants.

The register for 2010–11 lists 24,947 liverymen of the guilds entitled to vote at elections at Common Hall.

The order of precedence, omitting extinct companies, is given in parentheses after the name of each company in the list below. In certain companies the election of master or prime warden for the year does not take place until the autumn. In such cases the master or prime warden for 2009–10, rather than 2010–11, is given.

THE TWELVE GREAT COMPANIES

In order of civic precedence

MERCERS *(1). Hall,* Mercers' Hall, Ironmonger Lane, London EC2V 8HE *Livery,* 230. *Clerk,* Menna McGregor *Master,* Sir David Clementi

GROCERS *(2). Hall,* Grocers' Hall, Princes Street, London EC2R 8AD *Livery,* 334. *Clerk,* Brig. Robert Pridham, OBE *Master,* Rory Macnamara

DRAPERS *(3). Hall,* Drapers' Hall, Throgmorton Avenue, London EC2N 2DQ *Livery,* 300. *Clerk,* Rear-Adm. A. B. Ross, CB, CBE *Master,* Maj. Gen. A. W. Lyons, CBE

FISHMONGERS *(4). Hall,* Fishmongers' Hall, London Bridge, London EC4R 9EL *Livery,* 353. *Clerk,* Nigel Cox *Prime Warden,* R. G. Holland-Martin

GOLDSMITHS *(5). Hall,* Goldsmiths' Hall, Foster Lane, London EC2V 6BN *Livery,* 285. *Clerk,* Richard Melly *Prime Warden,* A. M. J. Galsworthy, CVO, CBE

MERCHANT TAYLORS *(6/7). Hall,* Merchant Taylors' Hall, 30 Threadneedle Street, London EC2R 8JB *Livery,* 293. *Clerk,* Rear-Adm. Nicholas Harris, CB, MBE *Master,* Dr J. J. Oram

SKINNERS *(6/7). Hall,* Skinners' Hall, 8 Dowgate Hill, London EC4R 2SP *Livery,* 400. *Clerk,* Maj.-Gen. Brian Plummer, CBE *Master,* Hugh Carson

HABERDASHERS *(8). Hall,* Haberdashers' Hall, 18 West Smithfield, London EC1A 9HQ *Livery,* 309. *Clerk,* Rear-Adm. Richard Phillips, CB *Master,* B. L. H Powell, QC

SALTERS *(9). Hall,* Salters' Hall, 4 Fore Street, London EC2Y 5DE *Livery,* 163. *Clerk,* Capt. David Morris, RN *Master,* Dr Christopher Anderson

IRONMONGERS *(10). Hall,* Ironmongers' Hall, 1 Shaftesbury Place, London EC2Y 8AA *Livery,* 140. *Clerk,* Col. Hamon Massey *Master,* Maj.-Gen. P.A.J. Cordingley, DSO

VINTNERS *(11). Hall,* Vintners' Hall, Upper Thames Street, London EC4V 3BG *Livery,* 312. *Clerk,* Brig. Michael Smythe, OBE *Master,* Martin Mason

CLOTHWORKERS *(12). Hall,* Clothworkers' Hall, Dunster Court, Mincing Lane, London EC3R 7AH *Livery,* 200. *Clerk,* Andrew Blessley *Master,* Neil Foster

OTHER CITY GUILDS

In alphabetical order

ACTUARIES *(91).* 3rd Floor Cheapside House, 138 Cheapside, London EC2V 6BW *Livery,* 232. *Clerk,* David Johnson *Master,* Graham D. Clay

AIR PILOTS AND AIR NAVIGATORS *(81). Hall,* Cobham House, 9 Warwick Court, Gray's Inn, London WC1R 5DJ *Livery,* 600. *Clerk,* Paul Tacon *Grand Master,* HRH The Duke of York, KG, KCVO, ADC(P) *Master,* Dr M. A. Fopp

APOTHECARIES *(58). Hall,* Apothecaries' Hall, 14 Black Friars Lane, London EC4V 6EJ *Livery,* 1,271. *Clerk,* Ann Wallington-Smith *Master,* Dr R. Bethel

ARBITRATORS *(93).* 13 Hall Gardens, Colney Heath, St Albans, Herts AL4 0QF *Livery,* 175. *Clerk,* Gaye Duffy *Master,* Christopher Dancaster

ARMOURERS AND BRASIERS *(22). Hall,* Armourers' Hall, 81 Coleman Street, London EC2R 5BJ *Livery,* 128. *Clerk,* Cdre Christopher Waite *Master,* Prof. Sir Colin Humphreys

BAKERS *(19). Hall,* Bakers' Hall, 9 Harp Lane, London EC3R 6DP *Livery,* 350. *Clerk,* John Tompkins *Master,* David Goddard

BARBERS *(17). Hall,* Barber-Surgeons' Hall, Monkwell Square, Wood Street, London EC2Y 5BL *Livery,* 220. *Clerk,* Col. Peter Durrant, MBE *Master,* Dr J. S. Bolton, FRCPSYCH

BASKETMAKERS *(52).* Doric House, 108 Garstang Road West, Poulton le Fylde, Lancs FY6 7SN *Livery,* 300. *Clerk,* Roger de Pilkyngton *Prime Warden,* Peter Yarker

BLACKSMITHS *(40).* 48 Upwood Road, London SE12 8AN *Livery,* 235. *Clerk,* Christopher Jeal *Prime Warden,* Richard Chellew, CMG

BOWYERS *(38).* London, SW11, *Livery,* 86. *Clerk,* Richard Wilkinson *Master,* A. H. Mundy

BREWERS *(14). Hall,* Brewers' Hall, Aldermanbury Square, London EC2V 7HR *Livery,* 180. *Clerk,* Brig. D. J. Ross, CBE *Master,* N. J. Atkinson

BRODERERS *(48)*. Ember House, 35–37 Creek Road, East Molesey, Surrey KT8 9BE *Livery*, 125. *Clerk*, Peter J. C. Crouch *Master*, Dr Paul Woolley

BUILDERS MERCHANTS *(88)*. 4 College Hill, London EC4R 2RB *Livery*, 196. *Clerk*, T. Statham *Master*, Kenneth Pepperrell

BUTCHERS *(24)*. *Hall*, Butchers' Hall, 87 Bartholomew Close, London EC1A 7EB *Livery*, 630. *Clerk*, Cdre Anthony Morrow, CVO *Master*, Jeff Davies

CARMEN *(77)*. Five Kings House, 1 Queen Street Place, London EC4R 1QS *Livery*, 500. *Clerk*, Walter Gill *Master*, Robert Harold Russett

CARPENTERS *(26)*. *Hall*, Carpenters' Hall, 1 Throgmorton Avenue, London EC2N 2JJ *Livery*, 196. *Clerk*, Brig. Tim Gregson, MBE *Master*, Revd Dr W. Povey

CHARTERED ACCOUNTANTS *(86)*. Larksfield, Kent Hatch Road, Crockham Hill, Edenbridge, Kent TN8 6SX *Livery*, 292. *Clerk*, Peter Dickinson *Master*, Graham Ward, CBE

CHARTERED ARCHITECTS *(98)*. 82A Muswell Hill Road, London N10 3JR *Livery*, 150. *Clerk*, David Cole-Adams *Master*, Edward King

CHARTERED SECRETARIES AND ADMINISTRATORS *(87)*. 3rd Floor, Saddlers' House, 40 Gutter Lane, London EC2V 6BR *Livery*, 279. *Clerk*, Col. Michael Dudding, OBE, TD *Master*, Cdr. Rory F. Jackson

CHARTERED SURVEYORS *(85)*. 75 Meadway Drive, Horsell, Woking, Surrey GU21 4TF *Livery*, 345. *Clerk*, Amanda Jackson *Master*, Robert Bould

CLOCKMAKERS *(61)*. Salters' Hall, 4 Fore Street, London EC2Y 5DE *Livery*, 285. *Clerk*, Joe Buxton *Master*, Andrew C. Crisford, OBE

COACHMAKERS AND COACH-HARNESS MAKERS *(72)*. 49 Aldernay Street, London SW1V 4EX *Livery*, 400. *Clerk*, Lt.-Col. Peter Henderson, OBE *Master*, Vice-Adm. Timothy Laurence, CB, MVO

CONSTRUCTORS *(99)*. Forge Farmhouse, Glassenbury, Cranbrook, Kent TN17 2QE *Livery*, 160. *Clerk*, Tim Nicholson *Master*, Patricia Bessey-Newton

COOKS *(35)*. Coombe Ridge, Thursley Road, Churt, Farnham, Surrey GU10 2LQ *Livery*, 75. *Clerk*, Michael Thatcher, LLB *Master*, John Barrie Righton

COOPERS *(36)*. *Hall*, Coopers' Hall, 13 Devonshire Square, London EC2M 4TH *Livery*, 260. *Clerk*, Lt.-Col. Adrian Carroll *Master*, George Prescott

CORDWAINERS *(27)*. Clothworkers' Hall, Dunster Court, Mincing Lane, London EC3R 7AH *Livery*, 172. *Clerk*, John Miller *Master*, Oliver Chamberlain

CURRIERS *(29)*. Hedgerley, 10 The Leaze, Ashton Keynes, Wiltshire SN6 6PE *Livery*, 89. *Clerk*, Gp Capt. David Moss *Master*, Brian D. Price

CUTLERS *(18)*. *Hall*, Cutlers' Hall, Warwick Lane, London EC4M 7BR *Livery*, 100. *Clerk*, J. Allen *Master*, J. W. Prynne

DISTILLERS *(69)*. 1 The Sanctuary, Westminster, London SW1P 3JT *Livery*, 260. *Clerk*, Edward Macey-Dare *Master*, David Sills

DYERS *(13)*. *Hall*, Dyers' Hall, 10 Dowgate Hill, London EC4R 2ST *Livery*, 136. *Clerk*, J. R. Vaizey *Prime Warden*, A. Burdon-Cooper

ENGINEERS *(94)*. Wax Chandlers' Hall, 6 Gresham Street, London EC2V 7AD *Livery*, 320. *Clerk*, Wg Cdr A. G. Willenbruch, FRSE *Master*, J. H. Robinson, OBE, FRENG

ENVIRONMENTAL CLEANERS *(97)*. 121 Hacton Lane, Upminster, Essex RM14 2NL *Livery*, 280. *Clerk*, Neil Morley *Master*, Barrie P. Torbett

FAN MAKERS *(76)*. Skinners' Hall, 8 Dowgate Hill, London EC4R 2SP *Livery*, 202. *Clerk*, Martin J. Davies *Master*, John Hayes

FARMERS *(80)*. *Hall*, The Farmers' and Fletchers' Hall, 3 Cloth Street, London EC1A 7LD *Livery*, 300. *Clerk*, Col. David King, OBE *Master*, W. F. Balch

FARRIERS *(55)*. 19 Queen Street, Chipperfield, Kings Langley, Herts WD4 9BT *Livery*, 342. *Clerk*, Charlotte Clifford *Master*, Jeremy Fern

FELTMAKERS *(63)*. Post Cottage, Greywell, Hook, Hants RG29 1DA *Livery*, 173. *Clerk*, Maj. J. Coombs *Master*, Susan Wood

FIREFIGHTERS *(103)*. The Insurance Hall, 20 Aldermanbury, London EC2V 7HY *Livery*, 96. *Clerk*, Martin Bonham *Master*, Prof. David Bland, OBE

FLETCHERS *(39)*. *Hall*, The Farmers' and Fletchers' Hall, 3 Cloth Street, London EC1A 7LD *Livery*, 143. *Clerk*, Capt. Michael Johnson, RN *Master*, Robert Hall

FOUNDERS *(33)*. *Hall*, Founders' Hall, 1 Cloth Fair, London EC1A 7JQ *Livery*, 175. *Clerk*, A. Gillett *Master*, C. J. Allport

FRAMEWORK KNITTERS *(64)*. 86 Park Drive, Upminster, Essex RM14 3AS *Livery*, 200. *Clerk*, Alan Clark *Master*, George Turner

FRUITERERS *(45)*. Chapelstones, 84 High Street, Codford St Mary, Warminster BA12 0ND *Livery*, 283. *Clerk*, Lt.-Col. L. French *Master*, S. Bodger

FUELLERS *(95)*. 26 Merrick Square, London SE1 4JB *Livery*, 135. *Clerk*, Sir Anthony Reardon Smith, Bt. *Master*, Michael Byrne

FURNITURE MAKERS *(83)*. *Hall*, Furniture Makers' Hall, 12 Austin Friars, London EC2N 2HE *Livery*, 225. *Clerk*, Charles Kerrigan *Master*, Peter Head

GARDENERS *(66)*. 25 Luke Street, London EC2A 4AR *Livery*, 285. *Clerk*, Cdr Robert Woolgar, OBE *Master*, Dr Steven Dowbiggin, OBE

GIRDLERS *(23)*. *Hall*, Girdlers' Hall, Basinghall Avenue, London EC2V 5DD *Livery*, 80. *Clerk*, Brig. I. Rees *Master*, Lord Strathalmond

GLASS SELLERS *(71)*. 57 Witley Court, Coram Street, London WC1N 1HD *Livery*, 230. *Clerk*, Col. Audrey Smith *Master*, Richard Lawman

GLAZIERS AND PAINTERS OF GLASS *(53)*. *Hall*, Glaziers' Hall, 9 Montague Close, London SE1 9DD *Livery*, 292. *Clerk*, Alex Galloway, CVO *Master*, C. R. Freeman

GLOVERS *(62)*. London SW3 *Livery*, 250. *Clerk*, C. Blackshaw *Master*, O. Holmes

GOLD AND SILVER WYRE DRAWERS *(74)*. 9A Prince of Wales Mansions, Prince of Wales Drive, London SW11 4BG *Livery*, 300. *Clerk*, Cdr. R. House *Master*, J. C. Edgcumbe

GUNMAKERS *(73)*. The Proof House, 48–50 Commercial Road, London E1 1LP *Livery*, 350. *Clerk*, Col. William Chesshyre *Master*, Lord Sharman, OBE

HACKNEY CARRIAGE DRIVERS *(104)*. 25 The Grove, Parkfield, Latimer, Bucks HP5 1UE *Livery*, 98. *Clerk*, Mary Whitworth *Master*, James Rainbird

HORNERS *(54)*. St. Stephen's House, Hide Place, London SW1P 4NJ *Livery*, 225. *Clerk*, Raymond Layard *Master*, Colin Temple Richards

INFORMATION TECHNOLOGISTS *(100)*. *Hall*, Information Technologists' Hall, 39A Bartholomew Close, London EC1A 7JN *Livery*, 750. *Clerk*, Mike Jenkins *Master*, Charles Hughes

INNHOLDERS *(32)*. *Hall,* Innholders' Hall, 30 College Street, London EC4R 2RH *Livery,* 154. *Clerk,* Dougal Bulger *Master,* Peter Denley

INSURERS *(92)*. The Hall, 20 Aldermanbury, London EC2V 7HY *Livery,* 380. *Clerk,* L. Walters *Master,* Clive Haslock

INTERNATIONAL BANKERS *(106)*. 12 Austin Friars, London EC2N 2HE *Livery,* 152. *Clerk,* Wg Cdr Tim Woods, BEM *Master,* Robert Wigley

JOINERS AND CEILERS *(41)*. 75 Meadway Drive, Horsell, Woking, Surrey GU21 4TF *Livery,* 128. *Clerk,* Amanda Jackson *Master,* Paul Ridout

LAUNDERERS *(89)*. *Hall,* Launderers' Hall, 9 Montague Close, London Bridge, London SE1 9DD *Livery,* 215. *Clerk,* Mrs J. Polek *Master,* Martyn Lewis

LEATHERSELLERS *(15)*. *Hall,* Leathersellers' Hall, 15 St Helen's Place, London EC3A 6DQ *Livery,* 150. *Clerk,* David Santa-Olalla *Master,* Nigel Pullman

LIGHTMONGERS *(96)*. Crown Wharf, 11A Coldharbour, Blackwall Reach, London E14 9NS *Livery,* 185. *Clerk,* Derek Wheatly *Master,* Hugh Ogus

LORINERS *(57)*. Hampton House, High Street, East Grinstead, West Sussex RH19 3AW *Livery,* 435. *Clerk,* Peter Lusty *Master,* Elisabeth Hobday

MAKERS OF PLAYING CARDS *(75)*. 256 St David's Square, London E14 3WE *Livery,* 143. *Clerk,* David Barrett *Master,* Jonathan M. F. Crowther

MANAGEMENT CONSULTANTS *(105)*. Skinners' Hall, 8 Dowgate Hill, London EC4R 2SP *Livery,* 177. *Clerk,* Leslie Johnson *Master,* Vicky Pryce

MARKETORS *(90)*. 5a Nottingham Mansions, Nottingham Street, Marylebone, London W1U 5EN *Livery,* 267. *Clerk,* Mrs Adele Thorpe *Master,* James Surguy

MASONS *(30)*. 22 Cannon Hill, Southgate, London N14 6LG *Livery,* 150. *Clerk,* Heather Rowell *Master,* Richard Woodman-Bailey

MASTER MARINERS *(78)*. *Hall,* HQS Wellington, Temple Stairs, Victoria Embankment, London WC2R 2PN *Livery,* 197. *Clerk,* Cdre Angus Menzies *Master,* Capt. Graham M. Pepper, RFA

MUSICIANS *(50)*. 6th Floor, 2 London Wall Building, London EC2M 5PP *Livery,* 385. *Clerk,* Margaret Alford *Master,* Paul Campion

NEEDLEMAKERS *(65)*. PO Box 3682, Windsor, Berkshire SL4 3WR *Livery,* 200. *Clerk,* Philip Grant *Master,* Roger Staines

PAINTER-STAINERS *(28)*. *Hall,* Painters' Hall, 9 Little Trinity Lane, London EC4V 2AD *Livery,* 320. *Clerk,* Christopher Twyman *Master,* Peter Hamerson

PATTENMAKERS *(70)*. 3 The High Street, Sutton Valence, Kent ME17 3AG *Livery,* 200. *Clerk,* Col. R. Murfin, TD *Master,* Stuart Lamb

PAVIORS *(56)*. 3 Ridgemount Gardens, Enfield, Middx EN2 8QL *Livery,* 283. *Clerk,* John White *Master,* Thomas Barton

PEWTERERS *(16)*. *Hall,* Pewterers' Hall, Oat Lane, London EC2V 7DE *Livery,* 80. *Clerk,* Capt. Paddy Watson, RN *Master,* Prof. John Donaldson

PLAISTERERS *(46)*. *Hall,* Plaisterers' Hall, 1 London Wall, London EC2Y 5JU *Livery,* 236. *Clerk,* Nigel Bamping *Master,* Prof. Hubert Lacey

PLUMBERS *(31)*. Wax Chandlers' Hall, 6 Gresham Street, London EC2V 7AD *Livery,* 360. *Clerk,* Air Cdre Paul Nash, OBE *Master,* David Hamilton

POULTERS *(34)*. The Old Butchers, Station Road, Groombridge, Kent TN3 9QX *Livery,* 204. *Clerk,* Vernon Ashford *Master,* Brian Coombe

SADDLERS *(25)*. *Hall,* Saddlers' Hall, 40 Gutter Lane, London EC2V 6BR *Livery,* 75. *Clerk,* Col. N. Lithgow, CBE *Master,* P. L. H. Lewis

SCIENTIFIC INSTRUMENT MAKERS *(84)*. 9 Montague Close, London SE1 9DD *Livery,* 185. *Clerk,* Neville Watson *Master,* B. D. Fishwick

SCRIVENERS *(44)*. HQS Wellington, Temple Stairs, Victoria Embankment, London WC2R 2PN *Livery,* 193. *Clerk,* Paul Elliott *Master,* Ruth M. Campbell

SECURITY PROFESSIONALS *(108)*. 8 Palace Mews, London, SW6 7TQ *Livery,* 150. *Clerk,* Judith Pleasance *Master,* Don Randall, MBE

SHIPWRIGHTS *(59)*. Ironmongers Hall, Shaftesbury Place, London EC2Y 8AA *Livery,* 450. *Clerk,* Lt.-Col. Andy Milne, RN *Permanent Master,* HRH The Duke of Edinburgh, KG, KT, OM *Prime Warden,* Simon Sherrard

SOLICITORS *(79)*. 4 College Hill, London EC4R 2RB *Livery,* 350. *Clerk,* Neil Cameron *Master,* Alderman David Wootton

SPECTACLE MAKERS *(60)*. Apothecaries' Hall, Black Friars Lane, London EC4V 6EL *Livery,* 390. *Clerk,* Lt.-Col. John Salmon, OBE *Master,* W. M. Barton, FRCS

STATIONERS AND NEWSPAPER MAKERS *(47)*. *Hall,* Stationers' Hall, Ave Maria Lane, London EC4M 7DD *Livery,* 476. *Clerk,* William Alden, MBE *Master,* Christopher McKane

TALLOW CHANDLERS *(21)*. *Hall,* Tallow Chandlers' Hall, 4 Dowgate Hill, London EC4R 2SH *Livery,* 180. *Clerk,* Brig. R. Wilde, CBE *Master,* Robert Pick

TAX ADVISERS *(107)*. 191 West End Road, Ruislip, Middx HA4 6LD *Freemen,* 142. *Clerk,* Paul Herbage *Master,* Barbara Abraham

TIN PLATE WORKERS (ALIAS WIRE WORKERS) *(67)*. Highbanks, Ferry Road, Surlingham, Norwich, Norfolk NR14 7AR *Livery,* 220. *Clerk,* Michael Henderson-Begg *Master,* Maurice Frank Avent

TOBACCO PIPE MAKERS AND TOBACCO BLENDERS *(82)*. Green Meadow,Steep, Hants GU32 1AE *Livery,* 150. *Clerk,* Barbara Hines *Master,* Julian Keevil

TURNERS *(51)*. Skinner's Hall, 8 Dowgate Hill, London EC4R 2SP *Livery,* 186. *Clerk,* Edward Windsor Clive *Master,* P. Ellis

TYLERS AND BRICKLAYERS *(37)*. 30 Shelley Avenue, Tiptree CO5 OSF *Livery,* 155. *Clerk,* Barry Blumson *Master,* Michael Christopher

UPHOLDERS *(49)*. Hall in the Wood, 46 Quail Gardens, Selsdon Vale, Croydon CR2 8TF *Livery,* 209. *Clerk,* Jean Cody *Master,* Julian Squire

WATER CONSERVATORS *(102)*. The Lark, 2 Bell Lane, Worlington, Bury St Edmunds, Suffolk IP28 8SE *Livery,* 210. *Clerk,* Ralph Riley *Master,* Rear-Adm. Bob Mark

WAX CHANDLERS *(20)*. *Hall,* Wax Chandlers' Hall, 6 Gresham Street, London EC2V 7AD *Livery,* 120. *Clerk,* Georgina Brown *Master,* Graeme Marrs

WEAVERS *(42)*. Saddlers' House, Gutter Lane, London EC2V 6BR *Livery,* 125. *Clerk,* John Snowdon *Upper Bailiff,* John Pilling

WHEELWRIGHTS *(68)*. 7 Glengall Road, Bexleyheath, Kent DA7 4AL *Livery,* 220. *Clerk,* Brian François *Master,* Richard Proctor

WOOLMEN *(43)*. The Old Post Office, 56 Lower Way, Great Brickhill, Bucks MK17 9AG *Livery,* 141. *Clerk,* Gillian Wilson *Master,* Simon A. Bailey

WORLD TRADERS *(101)*. 13 Hall Gardens, Colney Heath, St. Albans, Herts AL4 0QF *Livery*, 240. *Clerk*, Mrs Gaye Duffy *Master*, Michael Wren

PARISH CLERKS *(No Livery*)*. Acreholt, 33 Medstead Road, Beech, Alton, Hants GU34 4AD *Members*, 95. *Clerk*, Alana Coombes *Master*, Stephen Priddle

WATERMEN AND LIGHTERMEN *(No Livery*)*. *Hall*, Watermen's Hall, 16 St Mary-at-Hill, London EC3R 8EF *Craft Owning Freemen*, 600. *Clerk*, Colin Middlemiss *Master*, Duncan Clegg

* Parish Clerks and Watermen and Lightermen have requested to remain with no livery

LONDON BOROUGH COUNCILS

Council	*Telephone*	*Population**	*Council Tax†*	*Chief Executive*
Barking and Dagenham	020-8592 4500	168,900	£1,326	David Woods
Barnet	020-8359 2000	331,500	£1,423	Nick Walkley
Bexley	020-8303 7777	223,300	£1,438	Will Tuckley
Brent	020-8937 1234	270,600	£1,369	Gareth Daniel
Bromley	020-8464 3333	302,600	£1,301	Doug Patterson
Camden	020-7974 4444	235,700	£1,332	Moira Gibb, CBE
CITY OF LONDON CORPORATION	020-7606 3030	7,900	£950	Chris Duffield
Croydon	020-8726 6000	341,800	£1,460	Jon Rouse
Ealing	020-8825 5000	309,000	£1,370	Martin Smith
Enfield	020-8379 1000	287,600	£1,410	Rob Leak
Greenwich	020-8854 8888	222,900	£1,291	Mary Ney
Hackney	020-8356 5000	212,200	£1,308	Tim Shields
Hammersmith and Fulham	020-8748 3020	172,200	£1,122	Geoff Alltimes
Haringey	020-8489 0000	226,200	£1,494	Kevin Crompton
Harrow	020-8863 5611	216,200	£1,496	Michael Lockwood
Havering	01708-434343	230,100	£1,505	Cheryl Coppell
Hillingdon	01895-250111	253,200	£1,423	Hugh Dunnachie
Hounslow	020-8583 2000	222,600	£1,400	Michael Frater
Islington	020-7527 2000	190,900	£1,272	John Foster
Kensington and Chelsea	020-7361 3000	180,300	£1,092	Derek Myers
Kingston upon Thames	020-8547 5757	160,100	£1,663	Bruce McDonald
Lambeth	020-7926 1000	274,500	£1,235	Derrick Anderson
Lewisham	020-8314 6000	261,600	£1,352	Barry Quirk, CBE
Merton	020-8543 2222	201,400	£1,416	Ged Curran
Newham	020-8430 2000	249,500	£1,255	Joe Duckworth
Redbridge	020-8554 5000	257,600	£1,405	Roger Hampson
Richmond upon Thames	020-8891 1411	180,100	£1,597	Gillian Norton
Southwark	020-7525 5000	278,000	£1,222	Annie Shepperd
Sutton	020-8770 5000	187,600	£1,451	Paul Martin
Tower Hamlets	020-7364 5000	220,500	£1,195	Dr. Kevan Collins *(acting)*
Waltham Forest	020-8496 3000	223,200	£1,462	Martin Esom *(acting)*
Wandsworth	020-8871 6000	284,000	£687	Gerald Jones
WESTMINSTER	020-7641 6000	236,000	£688	Mike More

* *Source:* ONS – *Mid-2008 Population Estimates* (Crown copyright)
† Average Band D council tax bill for 2010–11
Councils in CAPITAL LETTERS have city status

WALES

Cymru

The principality of Wales (Cymru) occupies the extreme west of the central southern portion of the island of Great Britain, with a total area of 20,778 sq. km (8,022 sq. miles): land 20,733 sq. km (8,005 sq. miles); inland water 45 sq. km (17 sq. miles). It is bordered in the north by the Irish Sea, in the south by the Bristol Channel, in the east by the English counties of Cheshire West and Chester, Shropshire, Herefordshire and Gloucestershire, and in the west by St George's Channel.

Across the Menai Straits is Ynys Mon (Isle of Anglesey) (715 sq. km/276 sq. miles), communication with which is facilitated by the Menai Suspension Bridge (305m/1,000ft long) built by Telford in 1826, and by the Britannia Bridge (351m/1,151ft), a two-tier road and rail truss arch design, rebuilt in 1972 after a fire destroyed the original tubular railway bridge built by Stephenson in 1850. Holyhead harbour, on Holy Isle (north-west of Anglesey), provides ferry services to Dublin (113km/70 miles).

POPULATION

The population at the 2001 census was 2,903,085 (men 1,403,782; women 1,499,303). The average density of population in 2001 was 140 persons per sq. km (362 per sq. mile).

RELIEF

Wales is a country of extensive tracts of high plateau and shorter stretches of mountain ranges deeply dissected by river valleys. Lower-lying ground is largely confined to the coastal belt and the lower parts of the valleys. The highest mountains are those of Snowdonia in the north-west (Snowdon, 1,085m/3,559ft and Aran Fawddwy, 906m/2,971ft). Snowdonia is also home to Cader Idris (Pen y Gadair, 892m/2,928ft). Other high peaks are to be found in the Cambrian range (Plynlimon, 752m/2,467ft), and the Black Mountains, Brecon Beacons and Black Forest ranges in the south-east (Pen y Fan, 886m/2,906ft; Waun Fâch, 811m/2,660ft; Carmarthen Van, 802m/2,630ft).

HYDROGRAPHY

The principal river in Wales is the Severn, which flows from the slopes of Plynlimon to the English border. The Wye (209km/130 miles) also rises in the slopes of Plynlimon. The Usk (90km/56 miles) flows into the Bristol Channel through Gwent. The Dee (113km/70 miles) rises in Bala Lake and flows through the Vale of Llangollen, where an aqueduct (built by Telford in 1805) carries the Pontcysyllte branch of the Shropshire Union Canal across the valley. The estuary of the Dee is the navigable portion, it is 23km (14 miles) in length and about 8km (5 miles) in breadth. The Towy (109km/68 miles), Teifi (80km/50 miles), Taff (64km/40 miles), Dovey (48km/30 miles), Taf (40km/25 miles) and Conway (39km/24 miles) are wholly Welsh rivers.

The largest natural lake is Bala (Llyn Tegid) in Gwynedd, nearly 7km (4 miles) long and 1.6km (1 mile) wide. Lake Vyrnwy is an artificial reservoir, about the size of Bala, it forms the water supply of Liverpool; Birmingham's water is supplied from reservoirs in the Elan and Claerwen valleys.

WELSH LANGUAGE

According to the 2001 census results, the percentage of people aged three years and over who are able to speak Welsh is:

Blaenau Gwent	9.1	Neath Port Talbot	17.8
Bridgend	10.6	Newport	9.6
Caerphilly	10.9	Pembrokeshire	21.5
Cardiff	10.9	Powys	20.8
Carmarthenshire	50.1	Rhondda Cynon Taf	12.3
Ceredigion	51.8	Swansea	13.2
Conwy	29.2	Torfaen	10.7
Denbighshire	26.1	Vale of Glamorgan	11.1
Flintshire	14.1	Wrexham	14.4
Gwynedd	67.8	Ynys Mon	
Merthyr Tydfil	10.0	(Isle of Anglesey)	59.8
Monmouthshire	9.0	*Total in Wales*	20.5

FLAG

The flag of Wales, the Red Dragon (*Y Ddraig Goch*), is a red dragon on a field divided white over green (per fess argent and vert a dragon passant gules). The flag was augmented in 1953 by a royal badge on a shield encircled with a riband bearing the words *Ddraig Goch Ddyry Cychwyn* and imperially crowned, but this augmented flag is rarely used.

EARLY HISTORY

The earliest inhabitants of whom there is any record appear to have been subdued or exterminated by the Goidels (a people of Celtic race) in the Bronze Age. A further invasion of Celtic Brythons and Belgae followed in the ensuing Iron Age. The Roman conquest of southern Britain and Wales was for some time successfully opposed by Caratacus (Caractacus or Caradog), chieftain of the Catuvellauni and son of Cunobelinus (Cymbeline). South-east Wales was subjugated and the legionary fortress at Caerleon-on-Usk established by around AD 75–7; the conquest of Wales was completed by Agricola around AD 78. Communications were opened up by the construction of military roads from Chester to Caerleon-on-Usk and Caerwent, and from Chester to Conwy (and thence to Carmarthen and Neath). Christianity was introduced in the fourth century, during the Roman occupation.

ANGLO-SAXON ATTACKS

The Anglo-Saxon invaders of southern Britain drove the Celts into the mountain stronghold of Wales, and into Strathclyde (Cumberland and south-west Scotland) and Cornwall, giving them the name of *Waelisc* (Welsh), meaning 'foreign'. The West Saxons' victory of Deorham (AD 577) isolated Wales from Cornwall and the battle of Chester (AD 613) cut off communication with Strathclyde and northern Britain. In the eighth century the boundaries of the Welsh were further restricted by the annexations of Offa, King of Mercia, and counter-attacks were largely prevented by the construction of an artificial boundary from the Dee to the Wye (Offa's Dyke).

In the ninth century Rhodri Mawr (844–878) united the country and successfully resisted further incursions of the Saxons by land and raids of Norse and Danish pirates by sea, but at his death his three provinces of Gwynedd (north), Powys (central) and Deheubarth (south) were divided among his three sons, Anarawd, Mervyn and Cadell. Cadell's son Hywel Dda ruled a large part of Wales and codified its laws but the provinces were not united again until the rule of Llewelyn ap Seisyllt (husband of the heiress of Gwynedd) from 1018 to 1023.

THE NORMAN CONQUEST

After the Norman conquest of England, William I created palatine counties along the Welsh frontier, and the Norman barons began to make encroachments into Welsh territory. The Welsh princes recovered many of their losses during the civil wars of Stephen's reign (1135–54), and in the early 13th century Owen Gruffydd, prince of Gwynedd, was the dominant figure in Wales. Under Llywelyn ap Iorwerth (1194–1240) the Welsh united in powerful resistance to English incursions and Llywelyn's privileges and *de facto* independence were recognised in the Magna Carta. His grandson, Llywelyn ap Gruffydd, was the last native prince; he was killed in 1282 during hostilities between the Welsh and English, allowing Edward I of England to establish his authority over the country. On 7 February 1301, Edward of Caernarvon, son of Edward I, was created Prince of Wales, a title subsequently borne by the eldest son of the sovereign.

Strong Welsh national feeling continued, expressed in the early 15th century in the rising led by Owain Glyndwr, but the situation was altered by the accession to the English throne in 1485 of Henry VII of the Welsh House of Tudor. Wales was politically annexed by England under the Act of Union of 1535, which extended English laws to the principality and gave it parliamentary representation for the first time.

EISTEDDFOD

The Welsh are a distinct nation, with a language and literature of their own; the national bardic festival (Eisteddfod), instituted by Prince Rhys ap Griffith in 1176, is still held annually.

PRINCIPAL CITIES

There are five cities in Wales (with date city status conferred): Bangor (pre-1900), Cardiff (1905), Newport (2002), St David's (1994) and Swansea (1969).

Cardiff and Swansea have also been granted Lord Mayoralities.

CARDIFF

Cardiff, at the mouth of the rivers Taff, Rhymney and Ely, is the capital city of Wales and at the 2001 census had a population of 305,353. The city has changed dramatically in recent years following the regeneration of Cardiff Bay and construction of a barrage, which has created a permanent freshwater lake and waterfront for the city. As the capital city, Cardiff is home to the National Assembly for Wales and is a major administrative, retail, business and cultural centre.

The city is home to many fine buildings including the City Hall, Cardiff Castle, Llandaff Cathedral, the National Museum of Wales, university buildings, law courts and the Temple of Peace and Health. The Millennium Stadium opened in 1999 and has hosted high-profile events since 2001.

SWANSEA

Swansea *(Abertawe)* is a seaport with a population of 223,293 at the 2001 census. The Gower peninsula was brought within the city boundary under local government reform in 1974.

The principal buildings are the Norman Castle (rebuilt *c.*1330), the Royal Institution of South Wales, founded in 1835 (including library), the University of Wales Swansea at Singleton and the Guildhall, containing Frank Brangwyn's British Empire panels. The Dylan Thomas Centre, formerly the old Guildhall, was restored in 1995. More recent buildings include the County Hall, the Maritime Quarter Marina, the Wales National Pool and the National Waterfront Museum.

Swansea was chartered by the Earl of Warwick (1158–84), and further charters were granted by King John, Henry III, Edward II, Edward III and James II, Oliver Cromwell and the Marcher Lord William de Breos. It was formally invested with city status in 1969 by HRH The Prince of Wales.

LORD-LIEUTENANTS AND HIGH SHERIFFS

Area	*Lord-Lieutenant*	*High Sheriff (2010–11)*
Clwyd	T. Jones, CBE	Lady Jones
Dyfed	Hon. Robin Lewis, OBE	David Lloyd
Gwent	S. Boyle	Wilfred Phillips
Gwynedd	His Hon. Huw Daniel	Griffith Evans
Mid Glamorgan	Kate Thomas, CVO	Beverley Humphreys
Powys	Hon. Mrs E. Legge-Bourke, LVO	Jennifer Thomas
South Glamorgan	Dr Peter Beck, MD, FRCP	Margaret Campbell
West Glamorgan	D. Byron Lewis	Rowland Jones

LOCAL COUNCILS

Council	*Administrative Headquarters*	*Telephone*	*Population**	*Council Tax†*	*Chief Executive*
Blaenau Gwent	Ebbw Vale	01495-350555	69,100	£1,382	Robin Morrison
Bridgend	Bridgend	01656-643643	134,800	£1,241	Dr Jo Farrar
Caerphilly	Hengoed	01443-815588	172,400	£1,089	Stuart Rosser
CARDIFF	Cardiff	029-2087 2000	324,800	£1,061	Jon House
Carmarthenshire	Carmarthen	01267-234567	180,500	£1,145	Mark James
Ceredigion	Aberaeron	01545-570881	78,000	£1,097	Bronwen Morgan
Conwy	Conwy	01492-574000	112,000	£1,050	K. W. Finch *(acting)*
Denbighshire	Ruthin	01824-706000	97,600	£1,232	Dr Mohammed Mehmet
Flintshire	Mold	01352-752121	151,000	£1,115	Colin Everett
Gwynedd	Caernarfon	01766-771000	118,200	£1,190	Harry Thomas
Merthyr Tydfil	Merthyr Tydfil	01685-725000	55,700	£1,299	Alistair Neill
Monmouthshire	Cwmbran	01633-644644	88,400	£1,189	Paul Matthews
Neath Port Talbot	Port Talbot	01639-763333	137,600	£1,343	S. Phillips
NEWPORT	Newport	01633-656656	140,700	£957	Tracey Lee
Pembrokeshire	Haverfordwest	01437-764551	118,800	£895	Bryn Parry-Jones
Powys	Llandrindod Wells	01597-826000	132,600	£1,103	Jeremy Patterson *(acting)*
Rhondda Cynon Taff	Tonypandy	01443-424000	234,100	£1,263	Keith Griffiths
SWANSEA	Swansea	01792-636000	229,100	£1,121	Paul Smith
Torfaen	Pontypool	01495-762200	91,100	£1,145	Alison Ward
Vale of Glamorgan	Barry	01446-700111	124,900	£1,086	John Maitland-Evans
Wrexham	Wrexham	01978-292000	132,900	£1,101	Isobel Garner
Ynys Mon (Isle of Anglesey)	Ynys Mon	01248-750057	69,000	£1,055	David Bowles

* *Source:* ONS – *Mid-2008 Population Estimates* (Crown copyright)
† Average Band D council tax bill 2010–11
Councils in CAPITAL LETTERS have city status

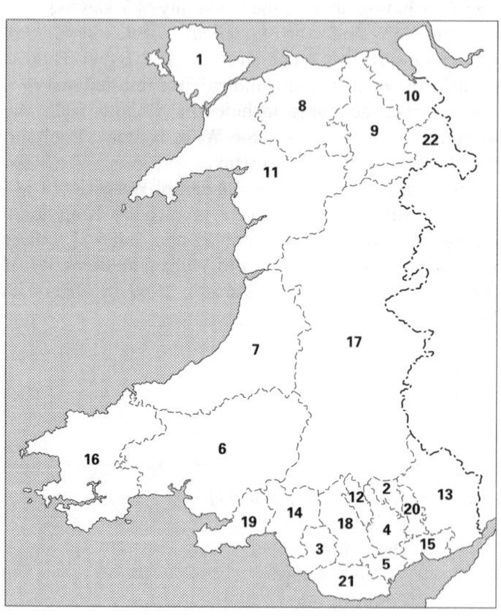

Key	*Council*	*Key*	*Council*
1	Anglesey (Ynys Mon)	12	Merthyr Tydfil
2	Blaenau Gwent	13	Monmouthshire
3	Bridgend	14	Neath Port Talbot
4	Caerphilly	15	Newport
5	Cardiff	16	Pembrokeshire
6	Carmarthenshire	17	Powys
7	Ceredigion	18	Rhondda Cynon Taff
8	Conwy	19	Swansea
9	Denbighshire	20	Torfaen
10	Flintshire	21	Vale of Glamorgan
11	Gwynedd	22	Wrexham

SCOTLAND

Scotland occupies the northern portion of the main island of Great Britain and includes the Inner and Outer Hebrides, Orkney, Shetland and many other islands. It lies between 60° 51′ 30″ and 54° 38′ N. latitude and between 1° 45′ 32″ and 6° 14′ W. longitude, with England to the south-east, the North Channel and the Irish Sea to the south-west, the Atlantic Ocean on the north and west, and the North Sea on the east.

The greatest length of the mainland (Cape Wrath to the Mull of Galloway) is 441km (274 miles), and the greatest breadth (Buchan Ness to Applecross) is 248km (154 miles). The customary measurement of the island of Great Britain is from the site of John o' Groats house, near Duncansby Head, Caithness, to Land's End, Cornwall, a total distance of 970km (603 miles) in a straight line and approximately 1,448km (900 miles) by road.

The total area of Scotland is 78,807 sq. km (30,427 sq. miles): land 77,907 sq. km (30,080 sq. miles), inland water 900 sq. km (347 sq. miles).

POPULATION

The population at the 2001 census was 5,062,011 (men 2,432,494; women 2,629,517). The average density of the population in 2001 was 64 persons per sq. km (166 per sq. mile).

RELIEF

There are three natural orographic divisions of Scotland. The southern uplands have their highest points in Merrick (843m/2,766ft), Rhinns of Kells (814m/2,669ft) and Cairnsmuir of Carsphairn (797m/2,614ft), in the west; and the Tweedsmuir Hills in the east (Broad Law 840m/2,756ft; Dollar Law 817m/2,682ft; Hartfell 808m/2,651ft).

The central lowlands, formed by the valleys of the Clyde, Forth and Tay, divide the southern uplands from the Highlands, which extend from close to the extreme north of the mainland to the central lowlands, and are divided into a northern and a southern system by the Great Glen.

The Grampian Mountains, the southern Highland system, include in the west Ben Nevis (1,343m/4,406ft), the highest point in the British Isles, and in the east the Cairngorm Mountains (Ben Macdui 1,309m/4,296ft; Braeriach 1,295m/4,248ft; Cairn Gorm 1,245m/4,084ft). The North West Highlands area contains the mountains of Wester and Easter Ross (Carn Eige 1,183m/3,880ft; Sgurr na Lapaich 1,151m/3,775ft).

Created, like the central lowlands, by a major geological fault, the Great Glen (97km/60 miles long) runs between Inverness and Fort William, and contains Loch Ness, Loch Oich and Loch Lochy. These are linked to each other and to the north-east and south-west coasts of Scotland by the Caledonian Canal, providing a navigable passage between the Moray Firth and the Inner Hebrides.

HYDROGRAPHY

The western coast is fragmented by peninsulas and islands, and indented by fjords (sea-lochs), the longest of which is Loch Fyne (68km/42 miles long) in Argyll. Although the east coast tends to be less fractured and lower, there are several great drowned inlets (firths), including the Firth of Forth, the Firth of Tay and the Moray Firth, as well as the Firth of Clyde in the west.

The lochs are the principal hydrographic feature. The largest in Scotland and in Britain is Loch Lomond (70 sq. km/27 sq. miles), in the Grampian valleys and the longest and deepest is Loch Ness (39km/24 miles long and 244m/800ft deep), in the Great Glen.

The longest river is the Tay (188km/117 miles), noted for its salmon. It flows into the North Sea, with Dundee on the estuary, which is spanned by the Tay Bridge (3,136m/10,289ft) opened in 1887 and the Tay Road Bridge (2,245m/7,365ft) opened in 1966. Other noted salmon rivers are the Dee (145km/90 miles) which flows into the North Sea at Aberdeen, and the Spey (177km/110 miles), the swiftest flowing river in the British Isles, which flows into Moray Firth. The Tweed, which gave its name to the woollen cloth produced along its banks, marks in the lower stretches of its 154km (96 mile) course the border between Scotland and England.

The most important river commercially is the Clyde (171km/106 miles), formed by the junction of the Daer and Portrail water, which flows through the city of Glasgow to the Firth of Clyde. During its course it passes over the picturesque Falls of Clyde, Bonnington Linn (9m/30ft), Corra Linn (26m/84ft), Dundaff Linn (3m/10ft) and Stonebyres Linn (24m/80ft), above and below Lanark. The Forth (106km/66 miles), upon which stands Edinburgh, the capital, is spanned by the Forth Railway Bridge (1890), which is 1,625m (5,330ft) long, and the Forth Road Bridge (1964), which has a total length of 1,876m (6,156ft) (over water) and a single span of 914m (3,000ft).

The highest waterfall in Scotland, and the British Isles, is Eas a'Chùal Aluinn with a total height of 201m (658ft), which falls from Glas Bheinn in Sutherland. The Falls of Glomach, on a head-stream of the Elchaig in Wester Ross, have a drop of 113m (370ft).

GAELIC LANGUAGE

According to the 2001 census, 1.2 per cent of the population of Scotland, mainly in Eilean Siar (Western Isles), were able to speak the Scottish form of Gaelic.

LOWLAND SCOTTISH LANGUAGE

Several regional lowland Scottish dialects, known variously as Scots, Lallans or Doric, are widely spoken. The General Register Office (Scotland) estimated in 1996 that 1.5 million people, or 30 per cent of the population, are Scots speakers. A question on Scots was not included in the 2001 census.

FLAG

The flag of Scotland is known as the Saltire. It is a white diagonal cross on a blue field (saltire argent in a field azure) and represents St Andrew, the patron saint of Scotland.

THE SCOTTISH ISLANDS

ORKNEY

The Orkney Islands (total area 972 sq. km/376 sq. miles) lie about 10km (six miles) north of the mainland, separated from it by the Pentland Firth. Of the 90 islands and islets (holms and skerries) in the group, about one-third are inhabited.

The total population at the 2001 census was 19,245; the 2001 populations of the islands shown here include those of smaller islands forming part of the same council district.

Mainland, 15,339
Burray, 357
Eday, 121
Flotta, 81
Hoy, 392
North Ronaldsay, 70
Papa Westray, 65
Rousay, 267
Sanday, 478
Shapinsay, 300
South Ronaldsay, 854
Stronsay, 358
Westray, 563

The islands are rich in prehistoric and Scandinavian remains, the most notable being the Stone Age village of Skara Brae, the burial chamber of Maes Howe, the many brochs (towers) and the 12th-century St Magnus Cathedral. Scapa Flow, between the Mainland and Hoy, was the war station of the British Grand Fleet from 1914 to 1919 and the scene of the scuttling of the surrendered German High Seas Fleet (21 June 1919).

Most of the islands are low-lying and fertile, and farming (principally beef cattle) is the main industry. Flotta, to the south of Scapa Flow, is the site of the oil terminal for the Piper, Claymore and Tartan fields in the North Sea.

The capital is Kirkwall (population 6,206) situated on Mainland.

SHETLAND

The Shetland Islands have a total area of 1,427 sq. km (551 sq. miles) and a population at the 2001 census of 21,988. They lie about 80km (50 miles) north of the Orkneys, with Fair Isle about half way between the two groups. Out Stack, off Muckle Flugga, 1.6km (one mile) north of Unst, is the most northerly part of the British Isles (60° 51′ 30″ N. lat.).

There are over 100 islands, of which 16 are inhabited. Populations at the 2001 census were:

Mainland, 17,575
Bressay, 384
East Burra, 66
Fair Isle, 69
Fetlar, 86
Housay, 76
Muckle Roe, 104
Trondra, 133
Unst, 720
West Burra, 784
Whalsay, 1,034
Yell, 957

Shetland's many archaeological sites include Jarlshof, Mousa and Clickhimin, and its long connection with Scandinavia has resulted in a strong Norse influence on its place names and dialect.

Industries include fishing, knitwear and farming. In addition to the fishing fleet there are fish processing factories, and the traditional handknitting of Fair Isle and Unst is now supplemented with machine-knitted garments. Farming is mainly crofting, with sheep being raised on the moorland and hills of the islands. Latterly the islands have become a centre of the North Sea oil industry, with pipelines from the Brent and Ninian fields running to the terminal at Sullom Voe, the largest of its kind in Europe.

The capital is Lerwick (population 6,830) situated on Mainland. Lerwick is the main centre for supply services for offshore oil exploration and development.

THE HEBRIDES

Until the late 13th century the Hebrides included other Scottish islands in the Firth of Clyde, the peninsula of Kintyre (Argyll), the Isle of Man, and the (Irish) Isle of Rathlin. The origin of the name is probably the Greek *Eboudai,* latinised as *Hebudes* by Pliny, and corrupted to its present form. The Norwegian name *Sudreyjar* (Southern Islands) was latinised as *Sodorenses,* a name that survives in the Anglican bishopric of Sodor and Man.

There are over 500 islands and islets, of which about 100 are inhabited, though mountainous terrain and extensive peat bogs mean that only a fraction of the total area is under cultivation. Stone, Bronze and Iron Age settlement has left many remains, including those at Callanish on Lewis, and Norse colonisation influenced language, customs and placenames. Occupations include farming (mostly crofting and stock-raising), fishing and the manufacture of tweeds and other woollens. Tourism is also an important part of the economy.

The Inner Hebrides lie off the west coast of Scotland and are relatively close to the mainland. The largest and best-known is Skye (area 1,665 sq. km/643 sq. miles; pop. 9,251; chief town, Portree), which contains the Cuillin Hills (Sgurr Alasdair 993m/3,257ft), Bla Bheinn (928m/3,046ft), the Storr (719m/2,358ft) and the Red Hills (Beinn na Caillich 732m/2,403ft). Other islands in the Highland council area include Raasay (pop. 194), Rum, Eigg (pop. 131) and Muck.

Further south the Inner Hebridean islands include Arran (pop. 5,058) containing Goat Fell (874m/2,868ft); Coll and Tiree (pop. 934); Colonsay and Oronsay (pop. 113); Easdale (pop. 58); Gigha (pop. 110); Islay (area 608 sq. km/235 sq. miles; pop. 3,457); Jura (area 414 sq. km/160 sq. miles; pop. 188) with a range of hills culminating in the Paps of Jura (Beinn-an-Oir, 785m/2,576ft, and Beinn Chaolais, 755m/2,477ft); Lismore (pop. 146); Luing (pop. 220); and Mull (area 950 sq. km/367 sq. miles; pop. 2,696; chief town Tobermory) containing Ben More (967m/3,171ft).

The Outer Hebrides, separated from the mainland by the Minch, now form the Eilean Siar (Western Isles) council area (area 2,897 sq. km/1,119 sq. miles; pop. 26,502). The main islands are Lewis with Harris (area 1,994 sq. km/770 sq. miles, pop. 19,918), whose chief town, Stornoway, is the administrative headquarters; North Uist (pop. 1,320); South Uist (pop. 1,818); Benbecula (pop. 1,249) and Barra (pop. 1,078). Other inhabited islands include Bernera (233), Berneray (136), Eriskay (133), Grimsay (201), Scalpay (322) and Vatersay (94).

EARLY HISTORY

There is evidence of human settlement in Scotland dating from the third millennium BC, the earliest settlers being Mesolithic hunters and fishermen. Early in the second millennium BC, Neolithic farmers began to cultivate crops and rear livestock; their settlements were on the west coast and in the north, and included Skara Brae and Maeshowe (Orkney). Settlement by the early Bronze Age 'Beaker Folk', so-called from the shape of their drinking vessels, in eastern Scotland dates from about 1800 BC. Further settlement is believed to have occurred from 700 BC onwards, as tribes were displaced from further south by new incursions from the Continent and the Roman invasions from AD 43.

Julius Agricola, the Roman governor of Britain AD 77–84, extended the Roman conquests in Britain by advancing into Caledonia, culminating with a victory at Mons Graupius, probably in AD 84; he was recalled to Rome shortly afterwards and his forward policy was not pursued. Hadrian's Wall, mostly completed by AD 30, marked the northern frontier of the Roman empire except for the period between about AD 144 and 190 when the frontier moved north to the Forth-Clyde isthmus and a turf wall, the Antonine Wall, was manned.

After the Roman withdrawal from Britain, there were centuries of warfare between the Picts, Scots, Britons, Angles and Vikings. The Picts, generally accepted to be descended from the indigenous Iron Age people of northern Scotland, occupied the area north of the Forth. The Scots, a Gaelic-speaking people of northern Ireland, colonised the area of Argyll and Bute (the kingdom of Dalriada) in the fifth century AD and then expanded eastwards and northwards. The Britons, speaking a Brythonic Celtic language, colonised Scotland from the south from the first century BC; they lost control of south-eastern Scotland (incorporated into the kingdom of Northumbria) to the Angles in the early seventh century but retained Strathclyde (south-western Scotland and Cumbria). Viking raids from the late eighth century were followed by Norse settlement in the western and northern isles, Argyll, Caithness and Sutherland from the mid-ninth century onwards.

UNIFICATION

The union of the areas which now comprise Scotland began in AD 843 when Kenneth mac Alpin, king of the Scots from *c.*834, also became king of the Picts, joining the two lands to form the kingdom of Alba (comprising Scotland north of a line between the Forth and Clyde rivers). Lothian, the eastern part of the area between the Forth and the Tweed, seems to have been leased to Kenneth II of Alba (reigned 971–995) by Edgar of England *c.*973, and Scottish possession was confirmed by Malcolm II's victory over a Northumbrian army at Carham *c.*1016. At about this time Malcolm II (reigned 1005–34) placed his grandson Duncan on the throne of the British kingdom of Strathclyde, bringing under Scots rule virtually all of what is now Scotland.

The Norse possessions were incorporated into the kingdom of Scotland from the 12th century onwards. An uprising in the mid-12th century drove the Norse from most of mainland Argyll. The Hebrides were ceded to Scotland by the treaty of Perth in 1266 after a Norwegian expedition in 1263 failed to maintain Norse authority over the islands. Orkney and Shetland fell to Scotland in 1468–9 as a pledge for the unpaid dowry of Margaret of Denmark, wife of James III, although Danish claims of suzerainty were relinquished only with the marriage of Anne of Denmark to James VI in 1590.

From the 11th century, there were frequent wars between Scotland and England over territory and the extent of England's political influence. The failure of the Scottish royal line with the death of Margaret of Norway in 1290 led to disputes over the throne which were resolved by the adjudication of Edward I of England. He awarded the throne to John Balliol in 1292 but Balliol's refusal to be a puppet king led to war. Balliol surrendered to Edward I in 1296 and Edward attempted to rule Scotland himself. Resistance to Scotland's loss of independence was led by William Wallace, who defeated the English at Stirling Bridge (1297), and Robert Bruce, crowned in 1306, who held most of Scotland by 1311 and routed Edward II's army at Bannockburn (1314). England recognised the independence of Scotland in the treaty of Northampton in 1328. Subsequent clashes include the disastrous battle of Flodden (1513) in which James IV and many of his nobles fell.

THE UNION

In 1603 James VI of Scotland succeeded Elizabeth I on the throne of England (his mother, Mary Queen of Scots, was the great-granddaughter of Henry VII), his successors reigning as sovereigns of Great Britain. Political union of the two countries did not occur until 1707.

THE JACOBITE REVOLTS

After the abdication (by flight) in 1688 of James VII and II, the crown devolved upon William III (grandson of Charles I) and Mary II (elder daughter of James VII and II). In 1689 Graham of Claverhouse roused the Highlands on behalf of James VII and II, but died after a military success at Killiecrankie.

After the death of Anne (younger daughter of James VII and II), the throne devolved upon George I (great-grandson of James VI and I). In 1715, armed risings on behalf of James Stuart (the Old Pretender, son of James VII and II) led to the indecisive battle of Sheriffmuir, and the Jacobite movement died down until 1745, when Charles Stuart (the Young Pretender) defeated the Royalist troops at Prestonpans and advanced to Derby (1746). From Derby, the adherents of 'James VIII and III' (the title claimed for his father by Charles Stuart) fell back on the defensive and were finally crushed at Culloden (16 April 1746) by an army led by by the Duke of Cumberland, son of George II.

PRINCIPAL CITIES

ABERDEEN

Aberdeen, 209km (130 miles) north-east of Edinburgh, received its charter as a Royal Burgh in 1124. Scotland's third largest city, Aberdeen lies between two rivers, the Dee and the Don, facing the North Sea; the city has a strong maritime history and is today a major centre for offshore oil exploration and production. It is also an ancient university town and distinguished research centre. Other industries include engineering, food processing, textiles, paper manufacturing and chemicals.

Places of interest include King's College, St Machar's Cathedral, Brig o' Balgownie, Duthie Park and Winter Gardens, Hazlehead Park, the Kirk of St Nicholas, Mercat Cross, Marischal College and Marischal Museum, Provost Skene's House, Aberdeen Art Gallery, Gordon Highlanders Museum, Satrosphere Science Centre, and Aberdeen Maritime Museum.

DUNDEE

The Royal Burgh of Dundee is situated on the north bank of the Tay estuary. The city's port and dock installations are important to the offshore oil industry and the airport also provides servicing facilities. Principal industries include textiles, biotechnology and digital media, lasers, printing, tyre manufacture, food processing, engineering and tourism.

The unique City Churches – three churches under one roof, together with the 15th-century St Mary's Tower – are the most prominent architectural feature. Dundee is home to two historic ships: the Dundee-built RRS *Discovery* which took Capt. Scott to the Antarctic lies alongside Discovery Quay, and the frigate *Unicorn,* the only British-built wooden warship still afloat, is moored in Victoria Dock. Places of interest include Mills Public Observatory, the Tay road and rail bridges, Dundee Contemporary Arts centre, McManus Galleries, Claypotts Castle, Broughty Castle, Verdant Works (textile heritage centre) and the Sensation Science Centre.

EDINBURGH

Edinburgh is the capital city and seat of government in Scotland. The new Scottish parliament building designed by Enric Miralles was completed in 2004 and is open to visitors. The city is built on a group of hills and both the Old and New Towns are inscribed on the UNESCO World Cultural and Natural Heritage List for their cultural significance.

Other places of interest include the castle, which houses the Stone of Scone and also includes St Margaret's Chapel, the oldest building in Edinburgh, and near it, the Scottish National War Memorial; the Palace of Holyroodhouse, the Queen's official residence in Scotland; Parliament House, the present seat of the judicature; Princes Street; three universities (Edinburgh, Heriot-Watt, Napier); St Giles' Cathedral; St Mary's (Scottish Episcopal) Cathedral (Sir George Gilbert Scott); the General Register House (Robert Adam); the National and Signet libraries; the National Gallery of Scotland; the Royal Scottish Academy; the Scottish National Portrait Gallery and the Edinburgh International Conference Centre.

GLASGOW

Glasgow, a Royal Burgh, is Scotland's largest city and its principal commercial and industrial centre. The city occupies the north and south banks of the Clyde, formerly one of the chief commercial estuaries in the world. The main industries include engineering, electronics, finance, chemicals and printing. The city is also a key tourist and conference destination.

The chief buildings are the 13th-century Gothic cathedral, the university (Sir George Gilbert Scott), the City Chambers, the Royal Concert Hall, St Mungo Museum of Religious Life and Art, Pollok House, the School of Art (Charles Rennie Mackintosh), Kelvingrove Art Gallery and Museum, the Gallery of Modern Art, the Burrell Collection museum and the Mitchell Library. The city is home to the Royal Scottish National Orchestra, Scottish Opera, Scottish Ballet and BBC Scotland and Scottish Television (STV).

INVERNESS

Inverness was granted city status in 2000. The city's name is derived from the Gaelic for 'the mouth of the Ness', referring to the river on which it lies. Inverness is recorded as being at the junction of the old trade routes since AD 565. Today the city is the main administrative centre for the north of Scotland and is the capital of the Highlands. Tourism is one of the city's main industries.

Among the city's most notable buildings is Abertarff House, built in 1593 and the oldest secular building remaining in Inverness. Balnain House, built as a town house in 1726, is a fine example of early Georgian architecture. The Old High Church, on St Michael's Mount, is the original parish church of Inverness and is built on the site of the earliest Christian church in the city. Parts of the church date back to the 14th century.

Stirling was granted city status in 2002. Aberdeen, Dundee, Edinburgh and Glasgow have also been granted Lord Mayoralty/Lord Provostship.

LORD-LIEUTENANTS

Title	*Name*
Aberdeen City*	Lord Provost Peter Stephen
Aberdeenshire	A. Farquharson, OBE
Angus	Mrs G. Osborne
Argyll and Bute	K. Mackinnon
Ayrshire and Arran	John Duncan, QPM
Banffshire	Clare Russell
Berwickshire	Maj. A. Trotter
Caithness	Miss M. Dunnett
Clackmannan	Mrs S. Cruickshank
Dumfries	Jean Tulloch
Dunbartonshire	Rear-Adm. Alexander Gregory, OBE
Dundee City*	Lord Provost John Letford
East Lothian	W. Garth Morrison, CBE
Edinburgh City*	Rt. Hon. Lord Provost George Grubb
Eilean Siar (Western Isles)	A. Matheson, OBE
Fife	Mrs C. Dean
Glasgow City*	Rt. Hon. Lord Provost Robert Winter
Inverness	Donald Angus Cameron of Lochiel
Kincardineshire	Carol Kinghorn
Lanarkshire	G. Cox, MBE
Midlothian	Patrick Prenter, CBE
Moray	Grenville Shaw Johnston, OBE, TD
Nairn	Ewen Brodie of Lethan
Orkney	Dr Anthony Trickett, MBE
Perth and Kinross	Brig. Melville Jameson, CBE
Renfrewshire	Guy Clark
Ross and Cromarty	Janet Bowen
Roxburgh, Ettrick and Lauderdale	Hon. Capt. Gerald Maitland-Carew
Shetland	J. Scott
Stirling and Falkirk	Mrs M. McLachlan
Sutherland	Dr Monica Maitland Main
The Stewartry of Kirkcudbright	Lt.-Col. Sir Malcolm Walter Hugh Ross, GCVO, OBE
Tweeddale	Capt. D. Younger
West Lothian	Mrs I. Brydie, MBE
Wigtown	Marion Brewis

* The Lord Provosts of the four cities of Aberdeen, Dundee, Edinburgh and Glasgow are Lord-Lieutenants *ex officio* for those districts

LOCAL COUNCILS

Council	*Administrative Headquarters*	*Telephone*	*Population**	*Council Tax*†	*Chief Executive*
ABERDEEN	Aberdeen	08456 08 09 10	210,400	£1,230	Sue Bruce
Aberdeenshire	Aberdeen	01467-620981	241,500	£1,141	Colin Mackenzie
Angus	Forfar	0845-277 7778	110,300	£1,072	David Sawers
Argyll and Bute	Lochgilphead	01546-602127	90,500	£1,178	Sally Loudon
Clackmannanshire	Alloa	01259-452000	50,500	£1,148	Angela Leitch
Dumfries and Galloway	Dumfries	01387-260000	148,600	£1,049	Gavin Stevenson
DUNDEE	Dundee	01382-434000	142,500	£1,211	David Dorward
East Ayrshire	Kilmarnock	01563-576000	119,900	£1,189	Fiona Lees
East Dunbartonshire	Kirkintilloch	0845-045 4510	104,700	£1,142	Gerry Cornes
East Lothian	Haddington	01620-827827	96,100	£1,118	Alan Blackie
East Renfrewshire	Giffnock	0141-577 3000	89,200	£1,126	Lorraine McMillan
EDINBURGH	Edinburgh	0131-200 2000	471,700	£1,169	Tom Aitchison, CBE
Eilean Siar (Western Isles)	Stornoway	01851-703773	26,200	£1,024	Malcolm Burr
Falkirk	Falkirk	01324-506070	151,600	£1,070	Mary Pitcaithly, OBE
Fife	Glenrothes	0845-555555	361,900	£1,118	Ronnie Hynde
GLASGOW	Glasgow	0141-287 2000	584,200	£1,213	George Black
Highland	Inverness	01463-702000	219,400	£1,163	Alistair Dodds
Inverclyde	Greenock	01475-717171	80,800	£1,198	John Mundell
Midlothian	Dalkeith	0131-270 7500	80,600	£1,210	Kenneth Lawrie
Moray	Elgin	01343-543451	87,800	£1,135	Alastair Keddie
North Ayrshire	Irvine	0845-603 0590	135,900	£1,152	Elma Murray
North Lanarkshire	Motherwell	01698-302222	325,500	£1,098	Gavin Whitefield
Orkney	Kirkwall	01856-873535	19,900	£1,037	Albert Tait
Perth and Kinross	Perth	01738-475000	144,200	£1,158	Bernadette Malone
Renfrewshire	Paisley	0141-842 5000	169,800	£1,165	David Martin
Scottish Borders	Melrose	01835-824000	112,400	£1,084	David Hume
Shetland	Lerwick	01595-693535	22,000	£1,053	vacant
South Ayrshire	Ayr	01292-612000	111,700	£1,154	David Anderson
South Lanarkshire	Hamilton	01698-454444	310,100	£1,101	Archie Strang
STIRLING	Stirling	0845-277 7000	88,400	£1,209	Bob Jack
West Dunbartonshire	Dumbarton	01389-737000	90,900	£1,163	David McMillan
West Lothian	Livingston	01506-775000	169,500	£1,128	Alex Linkston

* *Source:* ONS – *Mid-2008 Population Estimates* (Crown copyright)
† Average Band D council tax bill 2010–11
Councils in CAPITAL LETTERS have city status

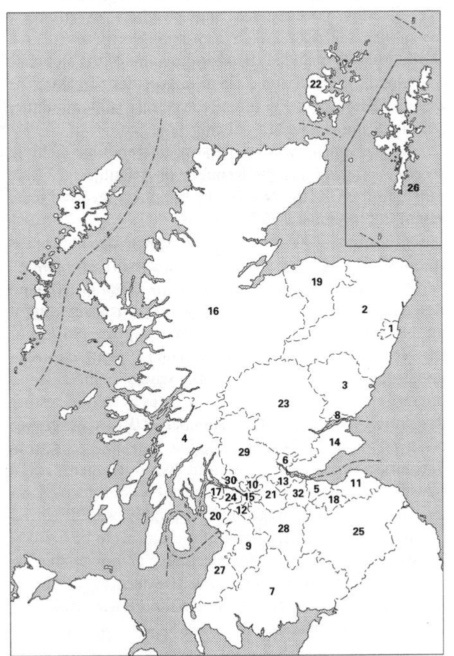

Key	*Council*	*Key*	*Council*
1	Aberdeen City	18	Midlothian
2	Aberdeenshire	19	Moray
3	Angus	20	North Ayrshire
4	Argyll and Bute	21	North Lanarkshire
5	City of Edinburgh	22	Orkney
6	Clackmannanshire	23	Perth and Kinross
7	Dumfries and Galloway	24	Renfrewshire
8	Dundee City	25	Scottish Borders
9	East Ayrshire	26	Shetland
10	East Dunbartonshire	27	South Ayrshire
11	East Lothian	28	South Lanarkshire
12	East Renfrewshire	29	Stirling
13	Falkirk	30	West Dunbartonshire
14	Fife	31	Western Isles (Eilean Siar)
15	Glasgow City	32	West Lothian
16	Highland		
17	Inverclyde		

NORTHERN IRELAND

Northern Ireland has a total area of 14,149 sq. km (5,463 sq. miles): land, 13,576 sq. km (5,242 sq. miles); inland water, 573 sq. km (221 sq. miles).

The population of Northern Ireland at the 2001 census was 1,685,267 (men 821,449; women 863,818). The average density of population in 2001 was 119 persons per sq. km (308 per sq. mile).

At the 2001 census, the number of persons in the various religious denominations (expressed as percentages of the total population) were: Catholic, 40.26%; Presbyterian, 20.69%; Church of Ireland, 15.30%; Methodist Church in Ireland, 3.51%; other Christian (including Christian related), 6.07%; other religions and philosophies, 0.3%; no religion or religion not stated, 13.88%.

FLAG

The official national flag of Northern Ireland is the Union Flag.

PRINCIPAL CITIES

In addition to Belfast and Londonderry, three other places in Northern Ireland have been granted city status: Armagh (1994), Lisburn (2002) and Newry (2002).

BELFAST

Belfast, the administrative centre of Northern Ireland, is situated at the mouth of the River Lagan at its entrance to Belfast Lough. The city grew to be a great industrial centre, owing to its easy access by sea to Scottish coal and iron.

The principal buildings are of a relatively young age and include the parliament buildings at Stormont, the City Hall, Waterfront Hall, the Law Courts, the Public Library and the Museum and Art Gallery.

Belfast received its first charter of incorporation in 1613 and was created a city in 1888; the title of lord mayor was conferred in 1892.

LONDONDERRY

Londonderry (originally Derry) is situated on the River Foyle, and has important associations with the City of London. The Irish Society was created by the City of London in 1610, and under its royal charter of 1613 it fortified the city and was for a long time closely associated with its administration. Because of this connection the city was incorporated in 1613 under the new name of Londonderry.

The city is famous for the great siege of 1688–9, when for 105 days the town held out against the forces of James II. The city walls are still intact and form a circuit of 1.6 km (one mile) around the old city.

Interesting buildings are the Protestant cathedral of St Columb's (1633) and the Guildhall, reconstructed in 1912 and containing a number of beautiful stained glass windows, many of which were presented by the livery companies of London.

CONSTITUTIONAL HISTORY

Northern Ireland is subject to the same fundamental constitutional provisions which apply to the rest of the UK. It had its own parliament and government from 1921 to 1972, but after increasing civil unrest the Northern Ireland (Temporary Provisions) Act 1972 transferred the legislative and executive powers of the Northern Ireland parliament and government to the UK parliament and a secretary of state. The Northern Ireland Constitution Act 1973 provided for devolution in Northern Ireland through an assembly and executive, but a power-sharing executive formed by the Northern Ireland political parties in January 1974 collapsed in May 1974. Following the collapse of the power-sharing executive Northern Ireland returned to direct rule governance under the provisions of the Northern Ireland Act 1974, placing the Northern Ireland department under the direction and control of the Northern Ireland secretary.

In December 1993 the British and Irish governments published the Joint Declaration complementing their political talks, and making clear that any settlement would need to be founded on principles of democracy and consent.

On 12 January 1998 the British and Irish governments issued a joint document, *Propositions on Heads of Agreement,* proposing the establishment of various new cross-border bodies; further proposals were presented on 27 January. A draft peace settlement was issued by the talks' chairman, US Senator George Mitchell, on 6 April 1998 but was rejected by the Unionists the following day. On 10 April agreement was reached between the British and Irish governments and the eight Northern Ireland political parties still involved in the talks (the Good Friday Agreement). The agreement provided for an elected Northern Ireland Assembly, a North/South Ministerial Council, and a British-Irish Council comprising representatives of the British, Irish, Channel Islands and Isle of Man governments and members of the new assemblies for Scotland, Wales and Northern Ireland. Further points included the abandonment of the Republic of Ireland's constitutional claim to Northern Ireland; the decommissioning of weapons; the release of paramilitary prisoners and changes in policing.

The agreement was ratified in referendums held in Northern Ireland and the Republic of Ireland on 22 May 1998. In the UK, the Northern Ireland Act received royal assent in November 1998.

On 28 April 2003 the secretary of state again assumed responsibility for the direction of the Northern Ireland departments on the dissolution of the Northern Ireland Assembly, following its initial suspension from midnight on 14 October 2002. In 2006, following the passing of the Northern Ireland Act, the secretary of state created a non-legislative fixed-term assembly which would cease to operate either when the political parties agreed to restore devolution, or on 24 November 2006 (whichever occurred first). In October 2006 a timetable to restore devolution was drawn up (St Andrews Agreement) and a transitional Northern Ireland Assembly was formed on 24 November. The transitional assembly was dissolved in January 2007 in preparation for elections to be held on 7 March; following the elections a power-sharing executive was formed and the new 108-member Northern Ireland Assembly became operational on 8 May 2007.

See also Regional Government.

LORD-LIEUTENANTS AND HIGH SHERIFFS

County	*Lord-Lieutenant*	*High Sheriff (2010)*
Antrim	Joan Christie	Steven Montgomery
Armagh	The Earl of Caledon	John Collen
Belfast City	Dame Mary Peters, DBE	Cllr Christopher Stalford
Down	David Lindsay	David Corbett
Fermanagh	The Earl of Erne	Kenneth Fisher
Londonderry	Denis Desmond, CBE	Trevor Magee
Londonderry City	Dr Donal Keegan, OBE	Hugh Hegarty
Tyrone	Robert Scott, OBE	Francis Shields

LOCAL COUNCILS

Council	*County Area*	*Map Key*	*Telephone*	*Population**	*Chief Executive*
Antrim	Down	1	028-9446 3113	53,200	David McCammick
Ards	Down	2	028-9182 4000	77,600	Ashley Boreland
ARMAGH	Armagh	3	028-3752 9600	58,200	John Briggs
Ballymena	Antrim	4	028-2566 0300	62,700	Anne Donaghy
Ballymoney	Antrim	5	028-2766 0200	30,100	John Dempsey
Banbridge	Down	6	028-4066 0600	47,000	Liam Hannaway
BELFAST	Antrim & Down	7	028-9032 0202	268,300	Peter McNaney
Carrickfergus	Antrim	8	028-9335 8000	40,000	Alan Cardwell
Castlereagh	Down	9	028-9046 4500	66,200	vacant
Coleraine	Londonderry	10	028-7034 7034	57,000	Roger Wilson
Cookstown	Tyrone	11	028-8676 2205	35,900	Michael McGuckin
Craigavon	Armagh	12	028-3831 2400	90,800	Michael Docherty *(acting)*
DERRY	Londonderry	13	028-7136 5151	109,100	Valerie Watts
Down	Down	14	028-4461 0800	69,800	John McGrillen
Dungannon & South Tyrone	Tyrone	15	028-8772 0300	55,400	Iain Frazer *(acting)*
Fermanagh	Fermanagh	16	028-6632 5050	62,000	Brendan Hegarty
Larne	Antrim	17	028-2827 2313	31,300	Geraldine McGahey
Limavady	Londonderry	18	028-7772 2226	34,100	Liam Flanigan
LISBURN	Antrim	19	028-9250 9250	114,800	Norman Davidson
Magherafelt	Londonderry	20	028-7939 7979	43,800	John McLaughlin
Moyle	Antrim	21	028-2076 2225	16,900	Richard Lewis
NEWRY & Mourne	Down & Armagh	22	028-3031 3031	97,300	Thomas McCall
Newtownabbey	Antrim	23	028-9034 0000	82,700	Jacqui Dickson
North Down	Down	24	028-9127 0371	78,900	Trevor Polley
Omagh	Tyrone	25	028 8224 5321	52,100	Daniel McSorley
Strabane	Tyrone	26	028-7138 2204	39,600	Philip Faithfull

* *Source:* ONS – *Mid-2008 Population Estimates* (Crown copyright)
Councils in CAPITAL LETTERS have city status

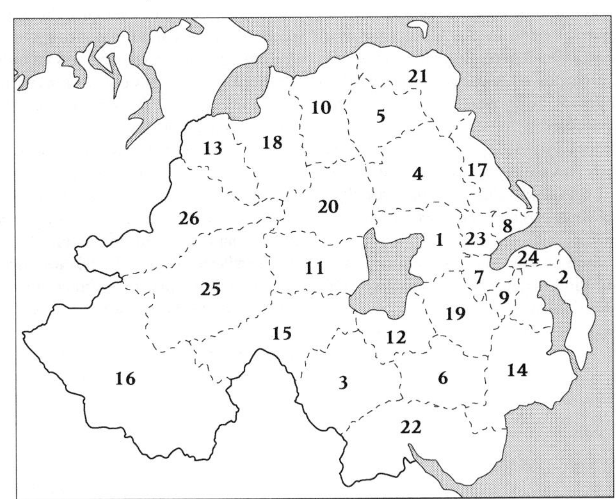

THE ISLE OF MAN

Ellan Vannin

The Isle of Man is an island situated in the Irish Sea, at latitude 54° 3′–54° 25′ N. and longitude 4° 18′–4° 47′ W., nearly equidistant from England, Scotland and Ireland. Although the early inhabitants were of Celtic origin, the Isle of Man was part of the Norwegian Kingdom of the Hebrides until 1266, when this was ceded to Scotland. Subsequently granted to the Stanleys (Earls of Derby) in the 15th century and later to the Dukes of Atholl, it was brought under the administration of the Crown in 1765. The island forms the bishopric of Sodor and Man.

The total land area is 572 sq. km (221 sq. miles). The 2006 census showed a resident population of 80,058 (men, 39,523; women, 40,535). The main language in use is English. Around 1,550 people are able to speak the Manx Gaelic language.

CAPITAL – ΨDouglas; population, 26,218 (2006). ΨCastletown (3,109) is the ancient capital; the other towns are ΨPeel (4,280) and ΨRamsey (7,309)

FLAG – A red flag charged with three conjoined armoured legs in white and gold

NATIONAL DAY – 5 July (Tynwald Day)

GOVERNMENT

The Isle of Man is a self-governing Crown dependency, with its own parliamentary, legal and administrative system. The British government is responsible for international relations and defence. Under the UK Act of Accession, Protocol 3, the island's relationship with the European Union is limited to trade alone and does not extend to financial aid. The Lieutenant-Governor is the Queen's personal representative on the island.

The legislature, Tynwald, is the oldest parliament in the world in continuous existence. It has two branches: the Legislative Council and the House of Keys. The council consists of the President of Tynwald, the Bishop of Sodor and Man, the Attorney-General (who does not have a vote) and eight members elected by the House of Keys. The House of Keys has 24 members, elected by universal adult suffrage. The branches sit separately to consider legislation and sit together, as Tynwald Court, for most other parliamentary purposes.

The presiding officer of Tynwald Court is the President of Tynwald, elected by the members, who also presides over sittings of the Legislative Council. The presiding officer of the House of Keys is the Speaker, who is elected by members of the house.

The principal members of the Manx government are the chief minister and nine departmental ministers, who comprise the Council of Ministers.

Lieutenant-Governor, HE Vice-Adm. Sir Paul Haddacks, KCB
President of Tynwald, Hon. Noel Cringle
Speaker, House of Keys, Hon. Steve Rodan, SHK
The First Deemster and Clerk of the Rolls, Michael Kerruish
Clerk of Tynwald, Secretary to the House of Keys and Counsel to the Speaker, Roger Phillips
Clerk of the Legislative Council and Deputy Clerk of Tynwald, Jonathan King
Attorney-General, John Corlett, QC
Chief Minister, Hon. Tony Brown, MHK
Chief Secretary, Mrs Mary Williams

ECONOMY

Most of the income generated in the island is earned in the services sector with financial and professional services accounting for just over half of the national income. Tourism and manufacturing are also major generators of income while the island's other traditional industries of agriculture and fishing now play a smaller role in the economy. Under the terms of protocol 3, the island has tariff-free access to EU markets for its goods.

In May 2010 the island's unemployment rate was 1.9 per cent and inflation (RPI) was 5.6 per cent.

FINANCE

The budget for 2010–11 provides for net revenue expenditure of £535m. The principal sources of government revenue are taxes on income and expenditure. Income tax is payable at a rate of 10 per cent on the first £10,500 of taxable income for single resident individuals and 20 per cent on the balance, after personal allowances of £9,300. These bands are doubled for married couples. The rate of income tax for trading companies is zero per cent except for income from banking and land and property, which is taxed at 10 per cent. By agreement with the British government, the island keeps most of its rates of indirect taxation (VAT and duties) the same as those in the UK. However, VAT on tourist accommodation, property, repairs and renovations is charged at 5 per cent. A reciprocal agreement on national insurance benefits and pensions exists between the governments of the Isle of Man and the UK. Taxes are also charged on property (rates), but these are comparatively low.

The major government expenditure items are health, social security, social services and education, which account for 65 per cent of the government budget. The island makes an annual contribution to the UK for defence and other external services.

The island has a special relationship with the European Union and neither contributes money to nor receives funds from the EU budget.

Ψ = sea port

THE CHANNEL ISLANDS

The Channel Islands, situated off the north-west coast of France (at a distance of 16km (10 miles) at their closest point), are the only portions of the Dukedom of Normandy still belonging to the Crown, to which they have been attached since the Norman Conquest of 1066. They were the only British territory to come under German occupation during the Second World War, following invasion on 30 June and 1 July 1940. The islands were relieved by British forces on 9 May 1945, and 9 May (Liberation Day) is now observed as a bank and public holiday.

The islands consist of Jersey (11,630ha/28,717 acres), Guernsey (6,340ha/15,654 acres), and the dependencies of Guernsey: Alderney (795ha/1,962 acres), Brecqhou (30ha/74 acres), Great Sark (419ha/1,035 acres), Little Sark (97ha/239 acres), Herm (130ha/320 acres), Jethou (18ha/44 acres) and Lihou (15ha/38 acres) – a total of 19,474ha/48,083 acres, or 194 sq. km/75 sq. miles. The most recent estimate of the population of Jersey from the States of Jersey Statistics Unit was 92,500. The 2001 census showed the population of Jersey as 87,186; Guernsey, 59,807 and Alderney, 2,294. Sark did not complete the same census but a recent informal census gave its population figure as 591. The official languages are English and French. In country districts of Jersey and Guernsey and throughout Sark a Norman-French *patois* is also in use, though to a lesser extent.

GOVERNMENT

The islands are Crown dependencies with their own legislative assemblies (the States in Jersey and Alderney, the States of Deliberation in Guernsey and the Chief Pleas in Sark), systems of local administration and law, and their own courts. Acts passed by the States require the sanction of the Queen-in-council. The UK government is responsible for defence and international relations. The Channel Islands are not part of the European Union but, under protocol 3, have trading rights with the free movement of goods within the EU.

In both Jersey and Guernsey bailiwicks the Lieutenant-Governor and Commander-in-Chief, who is appointed by the Crown, is the personal representative of the Queen and the channel of communication between the Crown (via the Privy Council) and the island's government.

The head of government in both Jersey and Guernsey is the Chief Minister. Jersey has a ministerial system of government; the executive comprises the Council of Ministers and consists of a chief minister and nine other ministers. The ministers are assisted by up to 13 assistant ministers. Members of the States who are not in the executive are able to sit on a number of scrutiny panels and the Public Accounts Committee to examine the policy of the executive and hold ministers to account. Guernsey has a consensus form of government. There are ten States departments with mandated responsibilities, each department is constituted of a minister and four members of the States. Each of the ministers has a seat on the Policy Council which is presided over by the Chief Minister. There are also five specialist committees, each led by a chair, responsible for scrutinising policy, finance and legislation, parliamentary procedural matters and public sector pay negotiations.

Justice is administered by the royal courts of Jersey and Guernsey, each consisting of the bailiff and 12 elected jurats. The bailiffs of Jersey and Guernsey, appointed by the Crown, are presidents of the states and of the royal courts of their respective islands.

Each bailiwick constitutes a deanery under the jurisdiction of the Bishop of Winchester.

ECONOMY

A mild climate and good soil have led to the development of intensive systems of agriculture and horticulture, which form a significant part of the economy. Equally important are earnings from tourism and banking and finance: the low rates of income and corporation tax and the absence of death duties make the islands an important offshore financial centre. The financial services sector contributes over 50 per cent of GDP in Jersey and around 40 per cent in Guernsey. In addition, there is no VAT or equivalent tax in Guernsey and only small goods and services tax in Jersey (set at 3 per cent for three years from 6 May 2008). The Channel Islands stock exchange is located in Guernsey, which also has a thriving e-gaming sector.

Principal exports are agricultural produce and flowers; imports are chiefly machinery, manufactured goods, food, fuel and chemicals. Trade with the UK is regarded as internal.

British currency is legal tender in the Channel Islands but each bailiwick issues its own coins and notes (*see* Currency section). They also issue their own postage stamps; UK stamps are not valid.

JERSEY

Lieutenant-Governor and Commander-in-Chief of Jersey, HE Lt.-Gen. Andrew Peter Ridgway, CB, CBE, *apptd* 2006
Secretary and ADC, Lt.-Col. A. Woodrow, OBE, MC
Bailiff of Jersey, Michael St J. Birt
Deputy Bailiff, W. Bailhache, QC
Attorney-General, Timothy Le Cocq, QC
Receiver-General, P. Lewin
Solicitor-General, Howard Sharp, QC
Greffier of the States, M. de la Haye
States Treasurer, I. Black
Chief Minister, Senator T. Le Sueur

FINANCE

	2008	*2009*
Revenue income	£872,075,000	£864,542,000
Revenue expenditure	£814,690,000	£789,021,000
Capital expenditure	£71,168,000	£123,531,000

CHIEF TOWN – ΨSt Helier, on the south coast
FLAG – A white field charged with a red saltire cross, and the arms of Jersey in the upper centre

GUERNSEY AND DEPENDENCIES

Lieutenant-Governor and Commander-in-Chief of the Bailiwick of Guernsey and its Dependencies,
HE Vice-Adm. Sir Fabian Malbon, KBE, *apptd* 2005
Presiding Officer, Bailiff Sir Geoffrey Rowland
Deputy Presiding Officer, Richard Collas
HM Procureur and Receiver-General, Howard Roberts, QC
HM Comptroller, Richard McMahon, QC

GUERNSEY

Chief Minister, Deputy Lyndon Trott
Chief Executive, Mike Brown

FINANCE

	2008	*2009*
Revenue	£349m	£341m
Expenditure	£297m	£326m

CHIEF TOWNS – ΨSt Peter Port, on the east coast of Guernsey; St Anne on Alderney
FLAG – White, bearing a red cross of St George, with a gold cross of Normandy overall in the centre

ALDERNEY

President of the States, Sir Norman Browse, OBE
Chief Executive, David Jeremiah, OBE, QC
Greffier, Sarah Kelly

SARK

Sark was the last European territory to abolish feudal parliamentary representation. Elections for a democratic legislative assembly took place in December 2008, with the *conseillers* taking their seats in the newly constituted Chief Pleas in January 2009.
Seigneur of Sark, John Beaumont, OBE
Seneschal, Lt.-Col. R Guille, MBE
Greffier, Trevor Hamon

OTHER DEPENDENCIES

Herm and Lihou are owned by the States of Guernsey; Herm is leased, Lihou is uninhabited. Jethou is leased by the Crown to the States of Guernsey and is sub-let by the States. Brecqhou is within the legislative and judicial territory of Sark.

Ψ = seaport

LAW COURTS AND OFFICES

HIERARCHY OF ENGLISH COURTS

Court	*Courts it binds*	*Courts it follows*
European court of justice	The court making the preliminary reference	None
Supreme court	All English courts	None
Court of appeal	Divisional courts High court Crown court County courts Magistrates' courts	Supreme court
Divisional courts	High court Crown court County courts Magistrates' courts	Supreme court Court of appeal
High court	County courts Magistrates' courts	Supreme court Court of appeal Divisional courts
Crown court	None	Supreme court
County courts	None	Court of appeal
Magistrates' courts	None	Divisional courts High court

JUDICATURE OF ENGLAND AND WALES

The legal system in England and Wales is divided into criminal law and civil law. Criminal law is concerned with acts harmful to the community and the rules laid down by the state for the benefit of citizens, whereas civil law governs the relationships and transactions between individuals. Administrative law is a kind of civil law usually concerning the interaction of individuals and the state, and most cases are heard in tribunals specific to the subject (*see* Tribunals section). Scotland and Northern Ireland possess legal systems that differ from the system in England and Wales in law, judicial procedure and court structure, but retain the distinction between criminal and civil law.

The supreme court of the United Kingdom is the highest judicial authority; it replaced the House of Lords in its judicial capacity on 1 October 2009. It is the ultimate court of appeal for all courts in Great Britain and Northern Ireland (except criminal courts in Scotland) for all cases except those concerning the interpretation and application of European Community law, including preliminary rulings requested by British courts and tribunals, which are decided by the court of justice of the European Union (*see* European Union section). The UK supreme court also assumed jurisdiction in relation to devolution matters under the Scotland Act 1998, the Northern Ireland Act 1988 and the Government of Wales Act 2006; these powers were transferred from the Judicial Committee of the Privy Council. Ten of the twelve Lords of Appeal in Ordinary from the House of Lords transferred to the 12-member supreme court when it came into operation (at the same time one law lord retired and another was appointed Master of the Rolls). All new justices of the supreme court will be appointed by an independent UK Supreme Court Appointments Commission, and will not be members of the House of Lords. The eleventh justice of the supreme court was appointed on 20 April 2009, and the twelfth justice was appointed on 23 March 2010, both through the appointments commission.

Under the provisions of the Criminal Appeal Act 1995, a commission was set up to direct and supervise investigations into possible miscarriages of justice and to refer cases to the appeal courts on the grounds of conviction and sentence; these functions were formerly the responsibility of the home secretary.

SENIOR COURTS OF ENGLAND AND WALES

The senior courts of England and Wales (until September 2009 known as the supreme court of judicature of England and Wales) comprise the high court, the crown court and the court of appeal. The President of the Courts of England and Wales, a new title given to the Lord Chief Justice under the Constitutional Reform Act 2005, is the head of the judiciary.

The high court was created in 1875 and combined many previously separate courts. Sittings are held at the royal courts of justice in London or at about 120 district registries outside the capital. It is the superior civil court and is split into three divisions – the chancery division, the Queen's bench division and the family division – each of which is further divided. The chancery division is headed by the Chancellor of the High Court and is concerned mainly with equity, trusts, tax and bankruptcy, while also including two specialist courts, the patents court and the companies court. The Queen's bench division (QBD) is the largest of the three divisions, and is headed by its own president, who is also Head of Criminal Justice. It deals with common law (ie tort, contract, debt and personal injuries), some tax law, eg VAT tribunal appeals, and encompasses the admiralty court and the commercial court. The QBD also administers the technology and construction court. The family division was created in 1970 and is headed by its own president, who is also Head of Family Justice, and hears cases concerning divorce, access to and custody of children, and other family matters. The divisional court of the high court sits in the family and chancery divisions, and hears appeals from the magistrates' courts and county courts.

The crown court was set up in 1972 and sits at 77 centres throughout England and Wales. It deals with more serious (indictable) criminal offences, which are triable before a judge and jury, including treason, murder, rape, kidnapping, armed robbery and Official Secrets Act offences. It also handles cases transferred from the magistrates' courts where the magistrate decides his or her own power of sentence is inadequate, or where someone appeals against a magistrate's decision, or in a case that is triable 'either way' where the accused has chosen a jury trial. The crown court centres are divided into three tiers: high court judges, and sometimes circuit judges and recorders (part-time circuit judges), sit in first-tier centres and deal with the most serious (Class 1) criminal offences (eg murder, treason) and with some civil high court cases; the second-tier centres are presided over by high court judges, circuit judges or recorders and deal with Class 2 criminal offences (eg rape, manslaughter); third-tier courts deal with Class 3 criminal offences, with circuit judges or recorders presiding.

The court of appeal hears appeals against both fact and law, and was last restructured in 1966 when it replaced the court of criminal appeal. It is split into the civil division (which hears appeals from the high court, tribunals and in certain cases, the county courts) and the criminal division (which hears appeals from the crown court). Cases are heard by Lord Justices of Appeal if deemed suitable for reconsideration.

The Constitutional Reform Act 2005 instigated several key changes to the judiciary in England and Wales. These included the establishment of an independent supreme court, which opened in October 2009; the reform of the post of Lord Chancellor, transferring its judicial functions to the President of the Courts of England and Wales; a duty on government ministers to uphold the independence of the judiciary by barring them from trying to influence judicial decisions through any special access to judges; the formation of a fully transparent and independent Judicial Appointments Commission that is responsible for selecting candidates to recommend for judicial appointment to the Secretary of State for Justice; and the creation of the post of Judicial Appointments and Conduct Ombudsman.

CRIMINAL CASES

In criminal matters the decision to prosecute (in the majority of cases) rests with the Crown Prosecution Service (CPS), which is the independent prosecuting body in England and Wales. The CPS is headed by the director of public prosecutions, who works under the superintendence of the Attorney-General. Certain categories of offence continue to require the Attorney-General's consent for prosecution.

Most minor criminal cases (summary offences) are dealt with in magistrates' courts, usually by a bench of three unpaid lay magistrates (justices of the peace) sitting without a jury and assisted on points of law and procedure by a legally trained clerk. There were 28,607 justices of the peace as at 1 April 2010. In busier courts a full-time, salaried and legally qualified district judge (magistrates' court) – formerly known as a stipendiary judge – presides alone. There were 143 district judges (magistrates' courts) as at 1 August 2010. Magistrates' courts oversee the completion of 95 per cent of all criminal cases. Magistrates' courts also house some family proceedings courts (which deal with relationship breakdown and childcare cases) and youth courts. Cases of medium seriousness (known as 'offences triable either way') where the defendant pleads not guilty can be heard in the crown court for a trial by jury, if the defendant so chooses. Preliminary proceedings in a serious case to decide whether there is evidence to justify committal for trial in the crown court are dealt with in the magistrates' courts.

The 77 centres that the crown court sits in are divided into seven regions; a case is presided over by high court judges, circuit judges or recorders. There are 1,233 recorders; they must sit a minimum of 15 days per year and are usually subject to a maximum of 30. A jury is present in all trials that are contested.

Appeals from magistrates' courts against sentence or conviction are made to the crown court, and appeals upon a point of law are made to the high court, which may ultimately be appealed to the supreme court. Appeals from the crown court, either against sentence or conviction, are made to the court of appeal (criminal division), presided over by the Lord Chief Justice. Again, these appeals may be brought to the supreme court if a point of law is contested, and if the house considers it is of sufficient importance.

CIVIL CASES

Most minor civil cases – including contract, tort (especially personal injuries), property, divorce and other family matters, bankruptcy etc – are dealt with by the county courts, of which there are 216 (*see* the Court Service website, W www.hmcourts-service.gov.uk, for further details). Cases are heard by circuit judges, recorders or district judges. For cases involving small claims (with certain exceptions, where the amount claimed is £5,000 or less) there are informal and simplified procedures designed to enable parties to present their cases themselves without recourse to lawyers. Where there are financial limits on county court jurisdiction, claims that exceed those limits may be tried in the county courts with the consent of the parties, subject to the court's agreement, or in certain circumstances on transfer from the high court. Outside London, bankruptcy proceedings can be heard in designated county courts. Magistrates' courts also deal with certain classes of civil case, and committees of magistrates license public houses, clubs and betting shops. For the implementation of the Children Act 1989, a new structure of hearing centres was set up in 1991 for family proceedings cases, involving magistrates' courts (family proceedings courts), divorce county courts, family hearing centres and care centres.

Appeals in certain family matters heard in the family proceedings courts go to the family division of the high court. Appeals against decisions made in magistrates' courts are heard in the crown court. Appeals from county courts may be heard in the court of appeal (civil division) or the high court, presided over by the Master of the Rolls, and may go on to the supreme court.

CORONERS' COURTS

The coroners' courts investigate violent and unnatural deaths or sudden deaths where the cause is unknown. Doctors, the police, various public authorities or members of the public may bring cases before a local coroner (a senior lawyer or doctor), in order to determine whether further criminal investigation is necessary. Where a death is sudden and the cause is unknown, the coroner may order a post-mortem examination to determine the cause of death rather than hold an inquest in court. An inquest must be held however if a person died in a violent or unnatural way, or died in prison or other unusual circumstances. If the coroner suspects murder, manslaughter or infanticide, he or she must summon a jury.

SUPREME COURT OF THE UNITED KINGDOM

President of the Supreme Court (£214,165), Rt. Hon. Lord Phillips of Worth Matravers, *born* 1938, *apptd* 2008
Deputy President of the Supreme Court (£206,857), Rt. Hon. Lord Hope of Craighead, KT, *born* 1938, *apptd* 1996

JUSTICES OF THE SUPREME COURT *as at August 2010* (each £206,857)
Style, The Rt. Hon. Lord/Lady–

Rt. Hon. Lord Saville of Newdigate, *born* 1936, *apptd* 1997
Rt. Hon. Lord Rodger of Earlsferry, *born* 1944, *apptd* 2001
Rt. Hon. Lord Walker of Gestingthorpe, *born* 1938, *apptd* 2002
Rt. Hon. Lady Hale of Richmond, *born* 1945, *apptd* 2004
Rt. Hon. Lord Brown of Eaton-under-Heywood, *born* 1937, *apptd* 2004
Rt. Hon. Lord Mance, *born* 1943, *apptd* 2005
Rt. Hon. Lord Collins of Mapesbury, *born* 1941, *apptd* 2009
Rt. Hon. Lord Kerr of Tonaghmore, *born* 1948, *apptd* 2009
Rt. Hon. Lord Clarke of Stone-cum-Ebony, *born* 1943, *apptd* 2009
Rt. Hon. Sir John Anthony Dyson, *born* 1943, *apptd.* 2010

UNITED KINGDOM SUPREME COURT
Parliament Square, London SW1P 3BD T 020-7960 1900
Chief Executive, Jenny Rowe

SENIOR JUDICIARY OF ENGLAND AND WALES

Lord Chief Justice of England and Wales (£239,845), Rt. Hon. Lord Judge, *born* 1941, *apptd* 2008
Master of the Rolls and Head of Civil Justice (£214,165), Rt. Hon. Lord Neuberger of Abbotsbury, *born* 1948, *apptd* 2009
President of the Queen's Bench Division (£206,857), Sir Anthony May, *born* 1940, *apptd* 2008
President of the Family Division and Head of Family Justice (£206,857), Rt. Hon. Sir Nicholas Wall, *born* 1945, *apptd* 2010
Chancellor of the High Court (£206,857), Rt. Hon. Sir Robert Morritt, CVO, *born* 1938, *apptd* 2000

SENIOR COURTS OF ENGLAND AND WALES

COURT OF APPEAL
Master of the Rolls (£214,165), Rt. Hon. Lord Neuberger of Abbotsbury, *born* 1948, *apptd* 2009
Secretary, Noella Roberts
Clerk, Graham Lister

LORD JUSTICES OF APPEAL *as at August 2010* (each £196,707)
Style, The Rt. Hon. Lord/Lady Justice [surname]

Rt. Hon. Sir Malcolm Pill, *born* 1938, *apptd* 1995
Rt. Hon. Sir Alan Ward, *born* 1938, *apptd* 1995
Rt. Hon. Sir Mathew Thorpe, *born* 1938, *apptd* 1995
Rt. Hon. Sir John Mummery, *born* 1938, *apptd* 1996
Rt. Hon. Sir John Laws, *born* 1945, *apptd* 1999
Rt. Hon. Sir Stephen Sedley, *born* 1939, *apptd* 1999
Rt. Hon. Sir Bernard Rix, *born* 1944, *apptd* 2000
Rt. Hon. Dame Mary Arden, DBE, *born* 1947, *apptd* 2000
Rt. Hon. Sir Andrew Longmore, *born* 1944, *apptd* 2001
Rt. Hon. Sir Robert Carnwath, CVO, *born* 1945, *apptd* 2002
Rt. Hon. Dame Janet Smith, DBE, *born* 1940, *apptd* 2002
Rt. Hon. Sir Roger Thomas, *born* 1947, *apptd* 2003
Rt. Hon. Sir Robin Jacob, *born* 1941, *apptd* 2003
Rt. Hon. Sir Maurice Kay, *born* 1942, *apptd* 2004
Rt. Hon. Sir Anthony Hooper, *born* 1937, *apptd* 2004
Rt. Hon. Sir Timothy Lloyd, *born* 1946, *apptd* 2005
Rt. Hon. Sir Martin Moore-Bick, *born* 1948, *apptd* 2005
Rt. Hon. Sir Nicholas Wilson, *born* 1945, *apptd* 2005
Rt. Hon. Sir Alan Moses, *born* 1945, *apptd* 2005
Rt. Hon. Sir Stephen Richards, *born* 1950, *apptd* 2005
Rt. Hon. Dame Heather Hallett, DBE, *born* 1949, *apptd* 2005
Rt. Hon. Sir Anthony Hughes, *born* 1948, *apptd* 2006
Rt. Hon. Sir Brian Leveson, *born* 1949, *apptd* 2006
Rt. Hon. Sir Roger Toulson, *born* 1946, *apptd* 2007
Rt. Hon. Sir Colin Rimer, *born* 1944, *apptd* 2007
Rt. Hon. Sir Stanley Burnton, *born* 1942, *apptd* 2007
Rt. Hon. Sir Terence Etherton, *born* 1951, *apptd* 2008
Rt. Hon. Sir Rupert Jackson, *born* 1948, *apptd* 2008
Rt. Hon. Sir John Goldring, *born* 1944, *apptd* 2008
Rt. Hon. Sir Richard Aikens, *born* 1948, *apptd* 2008
Rt. Hon. Sir Jeremy Sullivan, *born* 1945, *apptd* 2009
Rt. Hon. Sir Patrick Elias, *born* 1947, *apptd* 2009
Rt. Hon. Sir Nicholas Patten, *born* 1950, *apptd* 2009
Rt. Hon. Sir James Munby, *born* 1948, *apptd* 2009
Rt. Hon. Sir Christopher Pitchford, *born* 1947, *apptd* 2010
Rt. Hon. Dame Jill Black, DBE, *born* 1954, *apptd* 2010
Rt. Hon. Sir Stephen Tomlinson, *born* 1952, *apptd* 2010
Rt. Hon. Sir Peter Gross, *born* 1952, *apptd* 2010
Ex Officio Judges, Lord Chief Justice of England and Wales; Master of the Rolls; President of the Queen's Bench Division; President of the Family Division; and Chancellor of the High Court

COURT OF APPEAL (CIVIL DIVISION)
Vice-President, Rt. Hon. Sir Maurice Kay

COURT OF APPEAL (CRIMINAL DIVISION)
Vice-President, Rt. Hon. Sir Anthony Hughes
Judges, Lord Chief Justice of England and Wales; Master of the Rolls; Lord Justices of Appeal; and Judges of the High Court of Justice

COURTS-MARTIAL APPEAL COURT
Judges, Lord Chief Justice of England and Wales; Master of the Rolls; Lord Justices of Appeal; and Judges of the High Court of Justice

HIGH COURT OF JUSTICE

CHANCERY DIVISION

Chancellor of the High Court (£206,857), Rt. Hon. Sir Andrew Morritt, CVO, *born* 1938, *apptd* 2000
Secretary, Elaine Harbert
Clerk, Sheila Glasgow

JUDGES *as at August 2010* (each £172,753)
Style, The Hon. Mr/Mrs Justice [surname]

Hon. Sir Peter Smith, *born* 1952, *apptd* 2002
Hon. Sir Kim Lewison, *born* 1952, *apptd* 2003
Hon. Sir David Richards, *born* 1951, *apptd* 2003
Hon. Sir George Mann, *born* 1951, *apptd* 2004
Hon. Sir Nicholas Warren, *born* 1949, *apptd* 2005
Hon. Sir David Kitchin, *born* 1955, *apptd* 2005
Hon. Sir Michael Briggs, *born* 1954, *apptd* 2006
Hon. Sir Launcelot Henderson, *born* 1951, *apptd* 2006
Hon. Sir Paul Morgan, *born* 1952, *apptd* 2007
Hon. Sir Alastair Norris, *born* 1950, *apptd* 2007
Hon. Sir Gerald Barling, *born* 1949, *apptd* 2007
Hon. Sir Christopher Floyd, *born* 1951, *apptd* 2007
Hon. Sir Philip Sales, *born* 1962, *apptd* 2008
Hon. Dame Sonia Proudman, DBE, *born* 1949, *apptd* 2008
Hon. Sir Richard Arnold, *born* 1961, *apptd* 2008
Hon. Sir Peter Roth, *born* 1952, *apptd* 2009
Hon. Sir Geoffrey Vos, *born* 1955, *apptd* 2009
Hon. Sir Guy Newey, *born* 1959, *apptd* 2010

The Chancery Division also includes three specialist courts: the companies court, the patents court and the bankruptcy court.

QUEEN'S BENCH DIVISION

Lord Chief Justice of England and Wales (£239,845), Rt. Hon. Lord Judge, *born* 1941, *apptd* 2008
Secretary, Michèle Souris
Clerk, Linda Francis
President (£206,857), Rt. Hon. Sir Anthony May, *born* 1940, *apptd* 2008
Vice-President (£196,707), Rt. Hon. Sir Roger Thomas, *born* 1947, *apptd* 2008

JUDGES *as at August 2010* (each £172,753)
Style, The Hon. Mr/Mrs Justice [surname]

Hon. Sir Andrew Collins, *born* 1942, *apptd* 1994
Hon. Sir Alexander Butterfield, *born* 1942, *apptd* 1995
Hon. Sir David Eady, *born* 1943, *apptd* 1997
Hon. Sir David Steel, *born* 1943, *apptd* 1998
Hon. Sir Nicolas Bratza, *born* 1945, *apptd* 1998
Hon. Sir Michael Burton, *born* 1946, *apptd* 1998
Hon. Sir Stephen Silber, *born* 1944, *apptd* 1999
Hon. Dame Anne Rafferty, DBE, *born* 1950, *apptd* 2000
Hon. Sir Richard Henriques, *born* 1943, *apptd* 2000
Hon. Sir Andrew Smith, *born* 1947, *apptd* 2000
Hon. Sir Duncan Ouseley, *born* 1950, *apptd* 2000
Hon. Sir Richard McCombe, *born* 1952, *apptd* 2001
Hon. Sir Raymond Jack, *born* 1942, *apptd* 2001
Hon. Sir Robert Owen, *born* 1944, *apptd* 2001
Hon. Sir Colin Mackay, *born* 1943, *apptd* 2001
Hon. Sir John Mitting, *born* 1947, *apptd* 2001
Hon. Sir Roderick Evans, *born* 1946, *apptd* 2001
Hon. Sir Nigel Davis, *born* 1951, *apptd* 2001
Hon. Sir Brian Keith, *born* 1944, *apptd* 2001
Hon. Sir Jeremy Cooke, *born* 1949, *apptd* 2001
Hon. Sir Richard Field, *born* 1947, *apptd* 2002
Hon. Sir Colman Treacy, *born* 1949, *apptd* 2002
Hon. Sir Peregrine Simon, *born* 1950, *apptd* 2002
Hon. Sir Roger Royce, *born* 1944, *apptd* 2002
Hon. Dame Laura Cox, DBE, *born* 1951, *apptd* 2002
Hon. Sir Adrian Fulford, *born* 1953, *apptd* 2002
Hon. Sir Jack Beatson, *born* 1948, *apptd* 2003
Hon. Sir Michael Tugendhat, *born* 1944, *apptd* 2003
Hon. Dame Elizabeth Gloster, DBE, *born* 1949, *apptd* 2004
Hon. Sir David Bean, *born* 1954, *apptd* 2004
Hon. Sir Alan Wilkie, *born* 1947, *apptd* 2004
Hon. Dame Linda Dobbs, DBE, *born* 1951, *apptd* 2004
Hon. Sir Paul Walker, *born* 1954, *apptd* 2004
Hon. Sir David Calvert-Smith, *born* 1945, *apptd* 2005
Hon. Sir Christopher Clarke, *born* 1947, *apptd* 2005
Hon. Sir Charles Openshaw, *born* 1947, *apptd* 2005
Hon. Dame Caroline Swift, DBE, *born* 1955, *apptd* 2005
Hon. Sir Brian Langstaff, *born* 1948, *apptd* 2005
Hon. Sir David Lloyd Jones, *born* 1952, *apptd* 2005
Hon. Sir Vivian Ramsey, *born* 1950, *apptd* 2005
Hon. Sir Nicholas Underhill, *born* 1952, *apptd* 2006
Hon. Sir Stephen Irwin, *born* 1953, *apptd* 2006
Hon. Sir Nigel Teare, *born* 1952, *apptd* 2006
Hon. Sir Griffith Williams, *born* 1944, *apptd* 2007
Hon. Sir Wyn Williams, *born* 1951, *apptd* 2007
Hon. Sir Timothy King, *born* 1946, *apptd* 2007
Hon. Sir John Saunders, *born* 1959, *apptd* 2007
Hon. Sir Julian Flaux, *born* 1955, *apptd* 2007
Hon. Sir David Foskett, *born* 1949, *apptd* 2007
Hon. Sir Robert Akenhead, *born* 1949, *apptd* 2007
Hon. Sir Nicholas Stadlen, *born* 1950, *apptd* 2007
Hon. Sir Nicholas Blake, *born* 1949, *apptd* 2007
Hon. Sir Ross Cranston, *born* 1948, *apptd* 2007
Hon. Sir Peter Coulson, *born* 1958, *apptd* 2008
Hon. Sir David Maddison, *born* 1947, *apptd* 2008
Hon. Sir Richard Plender, *born* 1945, *apptd* 2008
Hon. Sir William Blair, *born* 1950, *apptd* 2008
Hon. Sir Alistair MacDuff, *born* 1945, *apptd* 2008
Hon. Sir Ian Burnett, *born* 1958, *apptd* 2008
Hon. Sir Nigel Sweeney, *born* 1954, *apptd* 2008
Hon. Dame Elizabeth Slade, DBE, *born* 1949, *apptd* 2008
Hon. Sir Nicholas Hamblen, *born* 1957, *apptd* 2008
Hon. Sir Gary Hickinbottom, *born* 1955, *apptd* 2009
Hon. Sir Timothy Holroyde, *born* 1955, *apptd* 2009
Hon. Dame Victoria Sharp, DBE, *born* 1956, *apptd* 2009
Hon. Sir Andrew Nicol, *born* 1951, *apptd* 2009
Hon. Sir Kenneth Parker, *born* 1945, *apptd* 2009
Hon. Sir Antony Edwards-Stuart, *born* 1946, *apptd* 2009
Hon. Dame Nicola Davies, DBE, *born* 1953, *apptd* 2010
Hon. Dame Kathryn Thirlwall, DBE, *born* 1957, *apptd* 2010
Hon. Sir Michael Supperstone, *born* 1950, *apptd* 2010
Hon. Sir Robin Spencer, *born* 1955, *apptd* 2010
Hon. Sir Keith Lindblom, *born* 1956, *apptd* 2010

The Queen's Bench Division also includes three specialist courts – the commercial court, the admiralty court and the administration court – and administers the technology and construction court.

FAMILY DIVISION

President (£206,857), Rt. Hon. Sir Nicholas Wall, *born* 1945, *apptd* 2010
Secretary, Mrs Sarah Leung
Clerk, John Curtis

JUDGES *as at August 2010* (each £172,753)
Style, The Hon. Mr/Mrs Justice [surname]

Hon. Sir Jan Singer, *born* 1944, *apptd* 1993
Hon. Sir Edward Holman, *born* 1947, *apptd* 1995

Hon. Dame Mary Hogg, DBE, *born* 1947, *apptd* 1995
Hon. Sir Arthur Charles, *born* 1948, *apptd* 1998
Hon. Sir David Bodey, *born* 1947, *apptd* 1999
Hon. Sir Paul Coleridge, *born* 1949, *apptd* 2000
Hon. Sir Mark Hedley, *born* 1946, *apptd* 2002
Hon. Dame Anna Pauffley, DBE, *born* 1956, *apptd* 2003
Hon. Sir Roderic Wood, *born* 1951, *apptd* 2004
Hon. Dame Florence Baron, DBE, *born* 1952, *apptd* 2004
Hon. Sir Ernest Ryder, *born* 1957, *apptd* 2004
Hon. Sir Andrew McFarlane, *born* 1954, *apptd* 2005
Hon. Dame Julia Macur, DBE, *born* 1957, *apptd* 2005
Hon. Sir Andrew Moylan, *born* 1953, *apptd* 2007
Hon. Dame Eleanor King, DBE, *born* 1957, *apptd* 2008
Hon. Dame Judith Parker, DBE, *born* 1950, *apptd* 2008
Hon. Sir Jonathan Baker, *born* 1955, *apptd* 2009
Hon. Sir Nicholas Mostyn, *born* 1957, *apptd* 2010

DEPARTMENTS AND OFFICES OF THE SENIOR COURTS OF ENGLAND AND WALES

Royal Courts of Justice, London WC2A 2LL
T 020-7947 6000

DIRECTOR'S OFFICE

T 020-7947 6159
Director, D. Thompson
Area Directors, S. Fash *(High Court Group)*; H. Smith *(Probate Service)*
Managers, K. Richardson *(Finance)*; A. Monsarrat *(Regional Change and Performance)*

ADMIRALTY, COMMERCIAL AND LONDON MERCANTILE COURT

T 020-7947 6112
Registrar (£102,921), J. Kay, QC
Admiralty Marshal and Court Manager, K. Houghton

BANKRUPTCY COURT REGISTRY

T 020-7947 6441
Chief Registrar (£128,296), S. Baister
Bankruptcy Registrars (£102,921), S. Barber; C. Derrett; G. W. Jaques; W. Nicholls; J. A. Simmonds
Court Manager, P. O'Brien

CENTRAL OFFICE OF THE QUEEN'S BENCH DIVISION

Senior Master, and Queen's Remembrancer (£128,296), S. D. Whitaker
Masters of the Queen's Bench Division (£102,921), R. Eastman; P. G. A. Eyre; B. J. F. Fontaine; I. H. Foster; R. Kay; H. J. Leslie; V. McCloud; R. Roberts; B. Yoxall
Court Manager, J. Ryan

CHANCERY CHAMBERS

T 020-7947 6754
Chief Master (£128,296), J. Winegarten
Masters of the Senior Courts (£102,921, T. J. Bowles; N. W. Bragge; J. A. Moncaster; N. S. Price; P. R. Teverson
Court Manager, P. O'Brien

COURT OF APPEAL CIVIL DIVISION

T 020-7947 6916
Court Manager, Kim Langan

COURT OF APPEAL CRIMINAL DIVISION

T 020-7947 6011
Registrar (£102,921), R. A. Venne
Deputy Registrar, Mrs L. G. Knapman
Court Manager, Miss C. Brownbill

ADMINISTRATIVE COURT OFFICE

T 020-7947 6655
Master of the Crown Office, and Queen's Coroner and Attorney (£102,921), R. A. Venne
Head of Crown Office, Mrs L. G. Knapman
Court Manager, Dave Brupbacher

EXAMINERS OF THE COURT

Empowered to take examination of witnesses in all divisions of the High Court.
Examiners, His Hon. M. W. M. Chism; A. G. Dyer; A. W. Hughes; Mrs G. M. Keene; R. M. Planterose

COSTS OFFICE

T 020-7947 6423
Senior Costs Judge (£128,296), P. T. Hurst
Masters of the Senior Courts (£102,921), C. D. N. Campbell; A. Gordon-Saker; P. Haworth; J. E. O'Hare; J. Simons; C. C. Wright
Court Manager, Helene Newman

COURT OF PROTECTION

11th Floor, Archway Tower, 2 Junction Road, London N19 5SZ
T 0300-456 4600
Senior Judge (£128,296), D. Lush

COURT OF PROTECTION VISITORS

Office of the Public Guardian, PO Box 15118, Birmingham B16 6GX T 0845-330 2900

The Mental Capacity Act 2005 came into force on 1 October 2007, and it makes provision for two panels of court of protection visitors (special visitors or general visitors).

ELECTION PETITIONS OFFICE

Room E13, Royal Courts of Justice, London WC2A 2LL
T 020-7947 7529

The office accepts petitions and deals with all matters relating to the questioning of parliamentary, European parliament, local government and parish elections, and with applications for relief under the 'representation of the people' legislation.
Prescribed Officer (£128,296), Senior Master and Queen's Remembrancer, S. D. Whitaker
Chief Clerk, Stuart Pycock

OFFICIAL RECEIVERS' DEPARTMENT (THE INSOLVENCY SERVICE)

21 Bloomsbury Street, London WC1B 3QW
T 020-7637 1110
Chief Executive, S. Speed
Head of Service, L. Gramp
Deputy Chief Executive, G. Hall

OFFICE OF COURT FUNDS, OFFICIAL SOLICITOR AND PUBLIC TRUSTEE

Court Funds, 22 Kingsway, London WC2B 6LE
T 0845-223 8500
Official Solicitor and Public Trustee, 81 Chancery Lane, London WC2A 1DD
T 020-7911 7127
Official Solicitor to the Senior Courts, A. Pitblado
Public Trustee and Head of the Court Funds Office, E. Bloomfield

PRINCIPAL REGISTRY (FAMILY DIVISION)
First Avenue House, 42–49 High Holborn, London WC1V 6NP
T 020-7947 6000
Senior District Judge (£128,296), P. Waller
District Judges (£102,921), Mrs A. Aitken; A. R. S. Bassett-Cross; M. C. Berry; Ms S. M. Bowman; Ms H. C. Bradley; Ms P. Cushing; Mrs L. Gordon-Saker; P. Greene; R. Harper; E. Hess; Ms H. MacGregor; K. Malik; C. Million; Ms C. Reid; Ms L. D. Roberts; R. Robinson; Ms S. Walker; K. J. White
Area Director, London Civil and Family, K. Launchbury
Head of Operations, London Family, J. Miller

PROBATE SERVICE
Thomas More Building, 8th Floor, Royal Courts of Justice, Strand, London WC2A 2LL
T 020-7947 6000
Area Director, H. Smith

DISTRICT PROBATE REGISTRARS
Probate Manager of London, T. Constantinou
Birmingham District, P. Walbeoff
Brighton District, S. Catt
Bristol District, R. Joyce
Ipswich District, H. Whitby
Leeds District, A. Parry
Liverpool District, K. Clark-Rimmer
Manchester District, K. Murphy
Newcastle District, M. C. Riley
Oxford District, R. D'Costa
Wales District, P. Curran
Winchester District, A. Butler

JUDGE ADVOCATES

The Judge Advocate General is the judicial head of the Service justice system, and the leader of the judges who provide over trials in the court martial and other Service courts. The defendants are service personnel from the Royal Navy, the army and the Royal Air Force, and civilians accompanying them overseas.

OFFICE OF THE JUDGE ADVOCATE-GENERAL OF THE FORCES
9th Floor, Thomas More Building, Royal Courts of Justice, Strand, London WC2A 2LL
T 020-7218 8095
Judge Advocate General (£138,548), His Hon. Judge Blackett
Vice Judge Advocate General (£120,785), Michael Hunter
Assistant Judge Advocates General (£106,921)*, C. R. Burn; J. P. Camp; M. R. Elsom; R. D. Hill; A. M. Large; A. J. B. McGrigor; E. Peters
Style, Judge [surname]

* Salary includes £2,000 London salary lead and a London allowance of £2,000

HIGH COURT AND CROWN COURT CENTRES

First-tier centres deal with both civil and criminal cases and are served by high court and circuit judges. Second-tier centres deal with criminal cases only and are served by high court and circuit judges. Third-tier centres deal with criminal cases only and are served only by circuit judges.

LONDON REGION
First-tier – None
Second-tier – Central Criminal Court
Third-tier – Blackfriars, Croydon, Harrow, Inner London, Isleworth, Kingston upon Thames, Snaresbrook, Southwark, Wood Green, Woolwich
Regional Director, Alan Eccles, 2nd Floor, Rose Court, 2 Southwark Bridge, London SE1 9HS T 020-7921 2010
Area Directors, Dave Weston *(Crime, Central and South);* Sandra Aston *(Crime, North East and West);* Kevin Launchbury *(Family and Civil)*

The high court in Greater London sits at the Royal Courts of Justice.

MIDLAND REGION
First-tier – Birmingham, Lincoln, Nottingham, Stafford, Warwick
Second-tier – Leicester, Northampton, Shrewsbury, Worcester, Wolverhampton
Third-tier – Coventry, Derby, Hereford, Stoke-on-Trent
Regional Director, Mark Swales, PO Box 11772, 6th Floor, Temple Court, Bull Street, Birmingham B4 6WF
T 0121-250 6162
Area Directors, Robin Lovell *(East Midlands);* Jacqui Grosvenor *(West Midlands and Warwickshire);* Richard Redgrave *(Staffordshire and West Mercia)*

NORTH-EAST REGION
First-tier – Leeds, Newcastle upon Tyne, Sheffield, Teesside
Second-tier – Bradford, York
Third-tier – Doncaster, Durham, Kingston-upon-Hull, Great Grimsby
Regional Director, S. Caven, 11th Floor, West Riding House, Albion Street, Leeds LS1 5AA T 0113-251 1200
Area Directors, Sheila Proudlock *(Cleveland, Durham and Northumbria);* Paul Bradley *(South Yorkshire and Humber);* Dyfed Foulkes *(North and West Yorkshire)*

NORTH-WEST REGION
First-tier – Carlisle, Chester, Liverpool, Manchester (Crown Square), Preston
Third-tier – Barrow-in-Furness, Bolton, Burnley, Knutsford, Lancaster, Manchester (Minshull Street), Warrington
Regional Director, Richard Knott, PO Box 4237, Manchester M60 1TE T 0161-240 5800
Area Directors, Geoffrey Appleton *(Cheshire and Merseyside);* Gill Hague *(Cumbria and Lancashire);* John Foley *(Greater Manchester)*

SOUTH-EAST REGION
First-tier – Cambridge, Chelmsford, Lewes, Norwich, Oxford
Second-tier – Guildford, Ipswich, Luton, Maidstone, Reading, St Albans
Third-tier – Aylesbury, Basildon, Canterbury, Chichester, Croydon, King's Lynn, Peterborough, Southend
Regional Director, Keith Budgen, 3rd Floor, Rose Court, 2 Southwark Bridge, London SE1 9HS T 020-7921 2061
Area Directors, Jonathan Lane *(Bedfordshire, Hertfordshire and Thames Valley);* Mike Littlewood *(Cambridgeshire, Essex, Norfolk and Suffolk);* Julia Eeles *(Kent, Surrey and Sussex);* Jonathan Lane *(Thames Valley)*

SOUTH-WEST REGION
First-tier – Bristol, Exeter, Truro, Winchester
Second-tier – Dorchester & Weymouth, Gloucester, Plymouth
Third-tier – Barnstaple, Bournemouth, Newport (IoW), Portsmouth, Salisbury, Southampton, Swindon, Taunton

Regional Director, Peter Risk, Spectrum, 3rd Floor, Suite A, Bond Street, Bristol BS1 3LG T 0117-300 6238
Area Directors, David Gentry *(Devon, Cornwall, Avon, Gloucester and Somerset);* Simon Townley *(Hampshire, Isle of Wight, Dorset, Gloucestershire and Wiltshire)*

WALES REGION
First-tier – Caernarfon, Cardiff, Merthyr Tydfil, Mold, Swansea
Second-tier – Carmarthen, Newport, Welshpool
Third-tier – Dolgellau, Haverfordwest
Regional Director, Miss C. Pillman, Churchill House, Churchill Way, Cardiff CF10 2HH T 029-2067 8302
Operations Director, Luigi Strinati

CIRCUIT JUDGES

Circuit judges are barristers of at least seven years' standing or recorders of at least five years' standing. Circuit judges serve in the county courts and the crown court.
Style, His/Her Hon. Judge [surname]
Senior Presiding Judge, Rt. Hon. Lord Justice Goldring
Senior Circuit Judges, each £138,548
Circuit Judges at the Central Criminal Court, London (Old Bailey Judges), each £138,548
Circuit Judges, each £128,296

MIDLAND REGION
Presiding Judges, Hon. Mr Justice Flaux; Hon. Mrs Justice Macur, DBE

NORTH-EASTERN REGION
Presiding Judges, Hon. Mr Justice Openshaw; Hon. Mr Justice Wilkie

NORTHERN REGION
Presiding Judges, Hon. Mr Justice Irwin; Hon. Mr Justice Ryder

SOUTH-EASTERN REGION
Presiding Judges, Hon. Mr Justice Bean; Hon. Mr Justice Cooke; Hon. Mr Justice Fulford; Hon. Mr Justice Saunders

WALES REGION
Presiding Judges, Hon. Mr Justice Lloyd Jones; Hon. Mr Justice Griffith-Williams

WESTERN REGION
Presiding Judges, Hon. Mr Justice Field; Hon. Mr Justice Royce

DISTRICT JUDGES

District judges, formerly known as registrars of the court, are solicitors of at least seven years' standing and serve in county courts.
District Judges, each £102,921

DISTRICT JUDGES (MAGISTRATES' COURTS)

District judges (magistrates' courts), formerly known as stipendiary magistrates, must be barristers or solicitors of at least seven years' standing (including at least two years' experience as a deputy district judge), and serve in magistrates' courts. All former provincial and metropolitan stipendiary magistrates can serve nationally within any district.
District Judges, each £106,921 (salary includes £4,000 inner London weighting)

CROWN PROSECUTION SERVICE

Rose Court, 2 Southwark Bridge, London SE1 9HS
T 020-7023 6539 E enquiries@cps.gsi.gov.uk
W www.cps.gov.uk

The Crown Prosecution Service (CPS) is responsible for prosecuting cases investigated by the police in England and Wales, with the exception of cases conducted by the Serious Fraud Office and certain minor offences.

The CPS is headed by the director of public prosecutions (DPP), who works under the superintendence of the attorney-general. The service comprises a headquarters and 43 areas (including two head offices in London and York), with each area corresponding to a police area in England and Wales. Each area is headed by a chief crown prosecutor, supported by an area business manager.
Director of Public Prosecutions, Keir Starmer, QC
Chief Executive, Peter Lewis
Directors, Mike Kennedy *(Business Development);* David Jones *(Business Information Systems);* Sue Hemming *(Counter-Terrorism);* Dale Simon *(Equality and Diversity);* John Graham *(Finance);* Ros McCool *(Human Resources);* Alun Milford *(Organised Crime);* Roger Daw *(Policy);* Alison Levitt *(Principal Legal Adviser);* Simon Clements *(Special Crime)*
Head of Strategic Communications, P. Teare

CPS AREAS ENGLAND
CPS DIRECT, 6th Floor, United House, Piccadilly, York YO1 9PQ T 01904-545400
Chief Crown Prosecutor, Martin Goldman
AVON AND SOMERSET, 2nd Floor, Froomsgate House, Rupert Street, Bristol BS1 2QJ T 0117-930 2800
Chief Crown Prosecutor, Barry Hughes
BEDFORDSHIRE, Sceptre House, 7–9 Castle Street, Luton LU1 3AJ T 01582-816600
Chief Crown Prosecutor, Richard Newcombe
CAMBRIDGESHIRE, Justinian House, Spitfire Close, Ermine Business Park, Huntingdon, Cambs PE29 6XY T 01480-825200
Chief Crown Prosecutor, Richard Crowley
CHESHIRE, 2nd Floor, Windsor House, Pepper Street, Chester CH1 1TD T 01244-408600
Chief Crown Prosecutor, Claire Lindley
CLEVELAND, 1 Hudson Quay, The Halyard, Middlehaven, Middlesbrough TS3 6RT T 01642-204500
Chief Crown Prosecutor, Gerry Wareham
CUMBRIA, 1st Floor, Stocklund House, Castle Street, Carlisle CA3 8SY T 01228-882900
Chief Crown Prosecutor, Christopher Long
DERBYSHIRE, 7th Floor, St Peter's House, Gower Street, Derby DE1 1SB T 01332-614000
Chief Crown Prosecutor, Brian Gunn
DEVON AND CORNWALL, Hawkins House, Pynes Hill, Rydon Lane, Exeter EX2 5SS T 01392-288000
Chief Crown Prosecutor, Tracy Easton
DORSET, Ground Floor, Oxford House, Oxford Road, Bournemouth BH8 8HA T 01202-498700
Chief Crown Prosecutor, Kate Brown
DURHAM, Elvet House, Hallgarth Street, Durham DH1 3AT T 0191-383 5800
Chief Crown Prosecutor, Chris Enzor
ESSEX, County House, 100 New London Road, Chelmsford CM2 0RG T 01245-455800
Chief Crown Prosecutor, Ken Caley

GLOUCESTERSHIRE, 2 Kimbrose Way, Gloucester GL1 2DB T 01452-872400
Chief Crown Prosecutor, Adrian Foster
GREATER MANCHESTER, PO Box 237, 5th Floor, Sunlight House, Quay Street, Manchester M60 3PS T 0161-827 4700
Chief Crown Prosecutor, Robert Marshall
HAMPSHIRE AND ISLE OF WIGHT, 3rd Floor, Black Horse House, 8–10 Leigh Road, Eastleigh, Hants SO50 9FH T 023-8067 3800
Chief Crown Prosecutor, Nick Hawkins
HERTFORDSHIRE, Queen's House, 58 Victoria Street, St Albans, Herts AL1 3HZ T 01727-798700
Chief Crown Prosecutor, David Robinson
HUMBERSIDE, Citadel House, 58 High Street, Kingston-upon-Hull HU1 1QD T 01482-621000
Chief Crown Prosecutor, Barbara Petchey
KENT, Priory Gate, 29 Union Street, Maidstone ME14 1PT T 01622-356300
Chief Crown Prosecutor, Roger Coe-Salazar
LANCASHIRE, 2nd Floor Podium, Unicentre, Lord's Walk, Preston PR1 1OH T 01772-208100
Chief Crown Prosecutor, Ian Rushton
LEICESTERSHIRE, Princes Court, 34 York Road, Leicester LE1 5TU T 0116-204 6700
Chief Crown Prosecutor, Kate Carty
LINCOLNSHIRE, Crosstrend House, 10A Newport, Lincoln LN1 3DF T 01522-585900
Chief Crown Prosecutor, vacant
LONDON, 7th Floor, CPS HQ, 50 Ludgate Hill, London, EC4M 7EX T 020-7796 8000
Chief Crown Prosecutor, Alison Saunders
MERSEYSIDE, 7th Floor (South), Royal Liver Building, Pier Head, Liverpool L3 1HN T 0151-239 6400
Chief Crown Prosecutor, Paul Whittaker
NORFOLK, Carmelite House, St James Court, Whitefriars, Norwich NR3 1SL T 01603-693000
Chief Crown Prosecutor, Andrew Baxter
NORTH YORKSHIRE, Athena House, Kettlestring Lane, Clifton Moor, York YO30 4XF T 01904-731700
Chief Crown Prosecutor (acting), Xanthe Tait
NORTHAMPTONSHIRE, Beaumont House, Cliftonville, Northampton NN1 5BE T 01604-823600
Chief Crown Prosecutor, Patricia Richardson
NORTHUMBRIA, St Ann's Quay, 122 Quayside, Newcastle upon Tyne NE1 3BD T 0191-260 4200
Chief Crown Prosecutor, Wendy Williams
NOTTINGHAMSHIRE, 2 King Edward Court, King Edward Street, Nottingham NG1 1EL T 0115-852 3300
Chief Crown Prosecutor, Judith Walker
SOUTH YORKSHIRE, Greenfield House, 32 Scotland Street, Sheffield S3 7DQ T 0114-229 8600
Chief Crown Prosecutor, Naheed Hussain
STAFFORDSHIRE, Building 3, Etruria Valley Office Village, Etruria, Stoke-on-Trent ST1 5RU T 01782-664560
Chief Crown Prosecutor, Ed Beltrami
SUFFOLK, 9th Floor, St Vincent's House, 1 Cutler Street, Ipswich IP1 1UL T 01473-282100
Chief Crown Prosecutor, Paula Abrahams
SURREY, Gateway, Power Close, Guildford, Surrey GU1 1EJ T 01483-468200
Chief Crown Prosecutor, Portia Ragnauth
SUSSEX, City Gates, 185 Dyke Road, Brighton BN3 1TL T 01273-765600
Chief Crown Prosecutor, Jaswant Narwal
THAMES VALLEY, Eaton Court, 112 Oxford Road, Reading RG1 7LL T 0118-951 3600
Chief Crown Prosecutor, Baljit Ubhey
WARWICKSHIRE, Rossmore House, 10 Newbold Terrace, Leamington Spa CV32 4EA T 01926-455000
Chief Crown Prosecutor, Zafar Siddique
WEST MERCIA, Artillery House, Heritage Way, Droitwich, Worcester WR9 8YB T 01905-825000
Chief Crown Prosecutor, Colin Chapman
WEST MIDLANDS, Colmore Gate, 2 Colmore Row, Birmingham B3 2QA T 0121-262 1300
Chief Crown Prosecutor, Harry Ireland
WEST YORKSHIRE, Oxford House, Oxford Row, Leeds LS1 3BE T 0113-290 2700
Chief Crown Prosecutor, Neil Franklin
WILTSHIRE, 2nd Floor, Fox Talbot House, Bellinger Close, Malmesbury Road, Chippenham SN15 1BN T 01249-766100
Chief Crown Prosecutor, Karen Harrold

CPS AREAS WALES
DYFED POWYS, Heol Penlanffos, Tanerdy, Carmarthen, Dyfed SA31 2EZ T 01267-242100
Chief Crown Prosecutor (acting), Iwan Jenkins
GWENT, Vantage Point, Ty Coch Way, Cwmbran NP44 7XX T 01633-261100
Chief Crown Prosecutor, Jim Brisbane
NORTH WALES, Bromfield House, Ellice Way, Wrexham LL13 7YW T 01978-346000
Chief Crown Prosecutor, vacant
SOUTH WALES, 20th Floor, Capital House, Greyfriars Road, Cardiff CF10 3PL T 029-2080 3905
Chief Crown Prosecutor (acting), Jim Brisbane

HER MAJESTY'S COURTS SERVICE

4th Floor, 102 Petty France, London SW1H 9AJ
T 0845-456 8770 W www.hmcourts-service.gov.uk

Her Majesty's Courts Service (HMCS) was launched on 1 April 2005, bringing together the Magistrates' Courts Service and the Court Service into a single organisation. It is responsible for managing the court of appeal, high court, magistrates' courts, the probate service, the crown court and county courts in England and Wales. HMCS is an executive agency of the Ministry of Justice.
Chief Executive, Mrs Chris Mayer, CBE

JUDICIAL APPOINTMENTS COMMISSION

Steel House, 11 Tothill Street, London SW1H 9LJ
T 020-3334 0453 E enquiries@jac.gsi.gov.uk
W www.judicialappointments.gov.uk

The Judicial Appointments Commission was established as an independent non-departmental public body in April 2006 by the Constitutional Reform Act 2005. Its role is to select judicial office holders independently of government (a responsibility previously held by the Lord Chancellor) for courts and tribunals in England and Wales, and for some tribunals whose jurisdiction extends to Scotland or Northern Ireland. It has a statutory duty to encourage diversity in the range of persons available for selection and is sponsored by the Ministry of Justice and accountable to parliament through the Lord Chancellor. It is made up of 15 commissioners, including a chair.
Chair, Baroness Prashar, CBE
Commissioners, Lady Justice Black, DBE; Dame Boreland-Kelly, DBE, FRSA; Dame Prof. Hazel Genn, DBE; Rt. Hon. Lady Justice Hallett, DBE; Sir Geoffrey Inkin, OBE; Her Hon. Judge Kirkham; Edward Nally;

Sara Nathan, OBE; Charles Newman; His Hon. Judge Pearl; Francis Plowden; Harriet Spicer; Jonathan Sumption, OBE, QC; Rt. Hon. Lord Justice Toulson
Chief Executive, Clare Pelham

DIRECTORATE OF JUDICIAL OFFICES

The Judicial Office for England and Wales was established in April 2006 following the implementation of the Constitutional Reform Act 2005, and incorporates the Judicial Office, the Judicial Communications Office and the Judicial Studies Board. It provides the Lord Chief Justice, the judicial executive board, the judges' council, and senior judges with the support they need to fulfil the responsibilities which transferred to the judiciary in April 2006. Although part of the office is based at the royal courts of justice (managed by HM Courts Service), the judicial office works independently from government departments and agencies.

CHIEF EXECUTIVE'S OFFICE
T 020-7947 7598
Chief Executive Officer, Anne Sharp
Personal Secretary, Maxine Fidler

JUDICIAL OFFICE
T 020-7073 4858
Head, Jonathan Creer
Secretary to the Judges' Council, Barbara Flaxman

JUDICIAL COMMUNICATIONS OFFICE
T 020-7947 7836
Head, Mike Wicksteed
Head of News, Stephen Ward
Head of Corporate Communications, Jane Holman

JUDICIAL STUDIES BOARD
Steel House, 11 Tothill Street, London SW1H 9LJ
T 020-7217 4708
Joint Executive Directors, Judith Killick; Maggy Pigott
Director of Studies, His Hon. Judge Phillips, CBE
Heads, Mark Shore *(Corporate Services);* Judith Lennard *(Judicial Training);* Lynne McGechie *(Training Advice);* John Gibbons *(Tribunals/ETAC/International);* Terry Hunter *(Magistrates' Courts Training)*

JUDICIAL COMMITTEE OF THE PRIVY COUNCIL

The Judicial Committee of the Privy Council is the final court of appeal for the United Kingdom overseas territories (*see* UK Overseas Territories section), crown dependencies and those independent Commonwealth countries which have retained this avenue of appeal (Antigua and Barbuda, Bahamas, Brunei, Cook Islands and Niue, Dominica, Grenada, Jamaica, Kiribati, Mauritius, St Christopher and Nevis, St Lucia, St Vincent and the Grenadines, Trinidad and Tobago, and Tuvalu) and the sovereign base areas of Akrotiri and Dhekelia in Cyprus. The committee also hears appeals against pastoral schemes under the Pastoral Measure 1983, and deals with appeals from veterinary disciplinary bodies.

Until October 2009, the Judicial Committee of the Privy Council was the final arbiter in disputes as to the legal competence of matters done or proposed by the devolved legislative and executive authorities in Scotland, Wales and Northern Ireland. This is now the responsibility of the new UK Supreme Court.

In 2009 the Judicial Committee dealt with a total of 40 appeals and 40 petitions for special leave to appeal.

The members of the Judicial Committee are the justices of the supreme court, and Privy Counsellors who hold or have held high judicial office in the United Kingdom or in certain designated courts of Commonwealth countries from which appeals are taken to committee.

JUDICIAL COMMITTEE OF THE PRIVY COUNCIL
Parliament Square, London SW1A 2AJ T 020-7960 1500
Registrar of the Privy Council (acting), Louise di Mambro
Chief Clerk, Jackie Lindsay

SCOTTISH JUDICATURE

Scotland has a legal system separate from, and differing greatly from, the English legal system in enacted law, judicial procedure and the structure of courts.

In Scotland the system of public prosecution is headed by the Lord Advocate and is independent of the police, who have no say in the decision to prosecute. The Lord Advocate, discharging his functions through the Crown Office in Edinburgh, is responsible for prosecutions in the high court, sheriff courts and district courts. Prosecutions in the high court are prepared by the Crown Office and conducted in court by one of the law officers, by an advocate-depute, or by a solicitor advocate. In the inferior courts the decision to prosecute is made and prosecution is preferred by procurators fiscal, who are lawyers and full-time civil servants subject to the directions of the Crown Office. A permanent legally qualified civil servant, known as the crown agent, is responsible for the running of the Crown Office and the organisation of the Procurator Fiscal Service, of which he or she is the head.

Scotland is divided into six sheriffdoms, each with a full-time sheriff principal. The sheriffdoms are further divided into sheriff court districts, each of which has a legally qualified resident sheriff or sheriffs, who are the judges of the court.

In criminal cases sheriffs principal and sheriffs have the same powers; sitting with a jury of 15 members, they may try more serious cases on indictment, or, sitting alone, may try lesser cases under summary procedure. Minor summary offences are dealt with in district courts which are administered by the district and the islands local government authorities and presided over by lay justices of the peace (of whom some 500 regularly sit in court) and, in Glasgow only, by stipendiary magistrates. Juvenile offenders (children under 16) may be brought before an informal children's hearing comprising three local lay people. The superior criminal court is the high court of justiciary which is both a trial and an appeal court. Cases on indictment are tried by a high court judge, sitting with a jury of 15, in Edinburgh and on circuit in other towns. Appeals from the lower courts against conviction or sentence are also heard by the high court, which sits as an appeal court only in Edinburgh. There is no further appeal to the supreme court in criminal cases.

In civil cases the jurisdiction of the sheriff court extends to most kinds of action. Appeals against decisions of the sheriff may be made to the sheriff principal and thence to the court of session, or direct to the court of session, which sits only in Edinburgh. The court of session is divided into the inner and the outer house. The outer house is a court of first instance in which cases are heard by judges sitting singly, sometimes with a jury of 12. The inner house, itself subdivided into two divisions of equal status, is mainly an appeal court. Appeals may be made to the inner house from the outer house as well as from the sheriff court. An appeal may be made from the inner house to the supreme court.

The judges of the court of session are the same as those of the high court of justiciary, with the Lord President of the court of session also holding the office of Lord Justice General in the high court. Senators of the College of Justice are Lords Commissioners of Justiciary as well as judges of the court of session. On appointment, a senator takes a judicial title, which is retained for life. Although styled The Hon./Rt. Hon. Lord, the senator is not a peer, although some judges are peers in their own right.

The office of coroner does not exist in Scotland. The local procurator fiscal inquires privately into sudden or suspicious deaths and may report findings to the crown agent. In some cases a fatal accident inquiry may be held before the sheriff.

COURT OF SESSION AND HIGH COURT OF JUSTICIARY

The Lord President and Lord Justice General (£214,165), Rt. Hon. Lord Hamilton, *born* 1942, *apptd* 2005
Private Secretary, A. Maxwell

INNER HOUSE

Lords of Session (each £196,707)

FIRST DIVISION

The Lord President

Rt. Hon. Lord Kingarth (Derek Emslie), *born* 1945, *apptd* 1997
Rt. Hon. Lord Eassie (Ronald Mackay), *born* 1945, *apptd* 2008
Rt. Hon. Lord Reed (Robert Reed), *born* 1956, *apptd* 2008
Rt. Hon. Lord Hardie (Andrew Hardie), *born* 1946, *apptd* 2009

SECOND DIVISION

Lord Justice Clerk (£206,857), Rt. Hon. Lord Gill (Brian Gill), *born* 1942, *apptd* 2001
Rt. Hon. Lord Osborne (Kenneth Osborne), *born* 1937, *apptd* 1990
Rt. Hon. Lady Paton (Ann Paton), *born* 1952, *apptd* 2000
Rt. Hon. Lord Carloway (Colin Sutherland), *born* 1954, *apptd* 2008
Rt. Hon. Lord Clarke (Matthew Clarke), *born* 1947, *apptd* 2008
Rt. Hon. Lord Mackay of Drumadoon (Donald Mackay), *born* 1946, *apptd* 2009

OUTER HOUSE

Lords of Session (each £172,753)
Hon. Lord Bonomy (Iain Bonomy), *born* 1946, *apptd* 1997
Hon. Lord Menzies (Duncan Menzies), *born* 1953, *apptd* 2001
Hon. Lord Drummond Young (James Drummond Young), *born* 1950, *apptd* 2001
Hon. Lord Emslie (Nigel Emslie), *born* 1947, *apptd* 2001
Hon. Lady Smith (Anne Smith), *born* 1955, *apptd* 2001
Hon. Lord Brodie (Philip Brodie), *born* 1950, *apptd* 2002
Hon. Lord Bracadale (Alastair Campbell), *born* 1949, *apptd* 2003
Hon. Lady Dorrian (Leona Dorrian), *born* 1959, *apptd* 2005
Hon. Lord Hodge (Patrick Hodge), *born* 1953, *apptd* 2005
Hon. Lord Glennie (Angus Glennie), *born* 1950, *apptd* 2005
Hon. Lord Kinclaven (Alexander F. Wylie), *born* 1951, *apptd* 2005
Hon. Lady Clark of Calton (Lynda Clark), *born* 1946, *apptd* 2006
Hon. Lord Turnbull (Alan Turnbull), *born* 1958, *apptd* 2006
Hon. Lord Brailsford (Sidney Brailsford), *born* 1954, *apptd* 2006
Hon. Lord Uist (Roderick Macdonald), *born* 1951, *apptd* 2006
Hon. Lord Malcolm (Colin M. Campbell), *born* 1953, *apptd* 2007
Hon. Lord Matthews (Hugh Matthews), *born* 1953, *apptd* 2007
Hon. Lord Woolman (Stephen Woolman), *born* 1953, *apptd* 2008
Hon. Lord Pentland (Paul Cullen), *born* 1957, *apptd* 2008
Hon. Lord Bannatyne (Iain Peebles), *born* 1954, *apptd* 2008
Hon. Lady Stacey (Valerie E. Stacey), *born* 1954, *apptd* 2009
Hon. Lord Tyre (Colin Tyre), *born* 1956, *apptd* 2010
Hon. Lord Doherty (Raymond Doherty), *born* 1958, *apptd* 2010

COURT OF SESSION AND HIGH COURT OF JUSTICIARY

Parliament House, Parliament Square, Edinburgh EH1 1HQ
T 0131-225 2595
Principal Clerk of Session and Justiciary, Graheme Marwick
Deputy Principal Clerk of Justiciary, G. Prentice
Deputy Principal Clerk of Session and Principal Extractor, R. Cockburn
Depute in Charge of Offices of Court, Y. Anderson
Keeper of the Rolls, A. Moffat
Depute Clerks of Session and Justiciary, J. Atkinson; R. Broome; D. Bruton; A. Corr; D. Cullen; L. Curran; E. Dickson; W. Dunn; P. Fiddes; A. Finlayson; H. Fraser; C. Fyffe; A. Galloway; R. Jenkins; T. Kell; A. Lynch; L. McLachlan; D. MacLeod; R. MacPherson; A. McArdle; L. McNamara; N. Marchant; I. Martin; N. McGinley; A. McKay; D. Morrison; R. Newlands; R. Philips; C. Reid; C. Richardson; N. Roberts; N. Robertson; C. Scott; R. Sinclair; G. Slater; K. Todd; C. Truby; P. Weir; E. Woods

SHERIFF COURT OF CHANCERY

27 Chambers Street, Edinburgh EH1 1LB
T 0131-225 2525

The court deals with service of heirs and completion of title in relation to heritable property.
Sheriff of Chancery, Edward F. Bowen, QC

HM COMMISSARY OFFICE

27 Chambers Street, Edinburgh EH1 1LB
T 0131-225 2525

The office is responsible for issuing confirmation, a legal document entitling a person to execute a deceased person's will, and other related matters.
Commissary Clerk, David Fyfe

SCOTTISH LAND COURT
126 George Street, Edinburgh EH2 4HH
T 0131-271 4360

The court deals with disputes relating to agricultural and crofting land in Scotland.
Chair (£138,548), Hon. Lord McGhie (James McGhie), QC
Deputy Chair, R. J. Macleod
Members, D. J. Houston; A. Macdonald *(part-time)*; J. A. Smith *(part-time)*
Principal Clerk, B. A. Brown, WS
Deputy Principal Clerk, M. I. E. Steel

SCOTTISH GOVERNMENT, CONSTITUTION, LAW AND COURTS DIRECTORATE
Legal System Division, Room 2W, St Andrew's House, Edinburgh EH1 3DG T 0131-244 2698

The Courts Directorate is responsible for the appointment of judges and sheriffs to meet the needs of the business of the supreme and sheriffs court in Scotland. It is also responsible for providing resources for the efficient administration of certain specialist courts and tribunals.
Deputy Director, C. McKay

JUDICIAL APPOINTMENTS BOARD FOR SCOTLAND
38–39 Drumsheugh Gardens, Edinburgh EH3 7SW
T 0131-528 5101

The board's remit is to provide the first minister with a list of candidates recommended for appointment to the posts of judge of the court of session chair of the Scottish Land Court, temporary judge, sheriff principal, sheriff and part-time sheriff.
Chair, Sir Muir Russell, KCB, FRSE

SCOTTISH COURT SERVICE
Saughton House, Broomhouse Drive, Edinburgh EH11 3XD
T 0131-444 3300 W www.scotcourts.gov.uk

The Scottish Court Service is responsible for the provision of staff, buildings and technology to support Scotland's courts, the independent judiciary, the courts' Rules Councils and the Office of the Public Guardian. On 1 April 2010 it was established by the Judiciary and Courts (Scotland) Act 2008 as an independent body, governed by a corporate board and chaired by the Lord President.
Chief Executive, Eleanor Emberson

JUDICIAL OFFICE FOR SCOTLAND
1A Parliament Square, Edinburgh EH1 1RQ
T 0131-240 6672 W www.scotcourts.gov.uk

The Judicial Office for Scotland came into being on 1 April 2010 as part of the changes introduced by the Judiciary and Courts (Scotland) Act 2008. It provides support for the Lord President in his role as head of the Scottish judiciary with responsibility for the training, welfare, deployment and conduct of judges and the efficient disposal of business in the courts.
Executive Director, Steve Humphreys

SHERIFFDOMS

SALARIES	
Sheriff Principal	£138,548
Sheriff	£128,296

GLASGOW AND STRATHKELVIN
Sheriff Principal, James A. Taylor
GRAMPIAN, HIGHLAND AND ISLANDS
Sheriff Principal, Sir Stephen S. T. Young, Bt., QC
LOTHIAN AND BORDERS
Sheriff Principal, E. F. Bowen, QC
NORTH STRATHCLYDE
Sheriff Principal, B. A. Kerr, QC
SOUTH STRATHCLYDE, DUMFRIES AND GALLOWAY
Sheriff Principal, B. A. Lockhart
TAYSIDE, CENTRAL AND FIFE
Sheriff Principal, R. A. Dunlop, QC

JUSTICE OF THE PEACE AND STIPENDIARY MAGISTRATES COURT

GLASGOW
R. B. Christie, *apptd* 1985; A. Findlay, *apptd* 2008; Ms J. Kerr, *apptd* 2008; Mrs J. A. M. MacLean, *apptd* 1990

CROWN OFFICE AND PROCURATOR FISCAL SERVICE

CROWN OFFICE
25 Chambers Street, Edinburgh EH1 1LA
T 0131-226 2626 W www.crownoffice.gov.uk
Crown Agent, Catherine Oyer
Deputy Crown Agent, John Dunn

PROCURATORS FISCAL

SALARIES	
Area Fiscals	£58,200–£162,500
District Procurator Fiscal	£48,899–£128,900

GRAMPIAN AREA
Area Procurator Fiscal, Mrs A. Currie *(Aberdeen)*
HIGHLAND AND ISLANDS AREA
Area Procurator Fiscal, A. Laing *(Inverness)*
LANARKSHIRE AREA
Area Procurator Fiscal, Ms J. Cameron *(Hamilton)*
CENTRAL AREA
Area Procurator Fiscal, Ms M. MacLeod *(Stirling)*
TAYSIDE AREA
Area Procurator Fiscal, T. Dysart *(Dundee)*
FIFE AREA
Area Procurator Fiscal, C. Ritchie *(Kirkcaldy)*
LOTHIAN AND BORDERS AREA
Area Procurator Fiscal, Ms M. McLaughlin *(Edinburgh)*
AYRSHIRE AREA
Area Procurator Fiscal, Mrs G. Watt *(Kilmarnock)*
ARGYLL AND CLYDE AREA
Area Procurator Fiscal, J. Watt *(Paisley)*
DUMFRIES AND GALLOWAY AREA
Area Procurator Fiscal, Ms R. McQuaid *(Dumfries)*
GLASGOW AREA
Area Procurator Fiscal, Ms L. Thomson *(Glasgow)*

COURT OF THE LORD LYON
HM New Register House, Edinburgh EH1 3YT
T 0131-556 7255
W www.lyon-court.com

The Court of the Lord Lyon is the Scottish Court of Chivalry (including the genealogical jurisdiction of the *Ri-Sennachie* of Scotland's Celtic kings). The Lord Lyon King of Arms has jurisdiction, subject to appeal to the

Court of Session and the House of Lords, in questions of heraldry and the right to bear arms. The court also administers the Public Register of All Arms and Bearings and the Public Register of All Genealogies in Scotland. Pedigrees are established by decrees of Lyon Court and by letters patent. As Royal Commissioner in Armory, the Lord Lyon grants patents of arms to virtuous and well-deserving Scots and to petitioners (personal or corporate) in the Queen's overseas realms of Scottish connection, and also issues birthbrieves. For information on Her Majesty's Officers of Arms in Scotland, *see* the Court of the Lord Lyon in the Public Bodies section.

Lord Lyon King of Arms, David Sellar, FSA SCOT, FRHISTS
Lyon Clerk and Keeper of the Records, Mrs C. G. W. Roads, MVO, FSA SCOT
Procurator Fiscal, vacant
Macer, H. M. Love

NORTHERN IRELAND JUDICATURE

In Northern Ireland the legal system and the structure of courts closely resemble those of England and Wales; there are, however, often differences in enacted law.

The court of judicature of Northern Ireland comprises the court of appeal, the high court of justice and the crown court. The practice and procedure of these courts is similar to that in England. The superior civil court is the high court of justice, from which an appeal lies to the Northern Ireland court of appeal; the UK supreme court is the final civil appeal court.

The crown court, served by high court and county court judges, deals with criminal trials on indictment. Cases are heard before a judge and, except those certified by the Director of Public Prosecutions under the Justice and Security Act 2007, a jury. Appeals from the crown court against conviction or sentence are heard by the Northern Ireland court of appeal; the supreme court is the final court of appeal.

The decision to prosecute in criminal cases in Northern Ireland rests with the director of public prosecutions.

Minor criminal offences are dealt with in magistrates' courts by a legally qualified district judge (magistrates' courts) and, where an offender is under the age of 18, by youth courts each consisting of a district judge and two lay magistrates (at least one of whom must be a woman). On 1 July 2009 there were 764 justices of the peace in Northern Ireland. Appeals from magistrates' courts are heard by the county court, or by the court of appeal on a point of law or an issue as to jurisdiction.

Magistrates' courts in Northern Ireland can deal with certain classes of civil case but most minor civil cases are dealt with in county courts. Judgments of all civil courts are enforceable through a centralised procedure administered by the Enforcement of Judgments Office.

SUPREME COURT OF JUDICATURE

The Royal Courts of Justice, Belfast BT1 3JF
T 028-9023 5111

Lord Chief Justice of Northern Ireland (£214,165), Rt. Hon. Sir Declan Morgan, *born* 1952, *apptd* 2009
Principal Secretary, S. T. A. Rogers

LORD JUSTICES OF APPEAL (£196,707)
Style, The Rt. Hon. Lord Justice [surname]

Rt. Hon. Sir Malachy Higgins, *born* 1944, *apptd* 2007
Rt. Hon. Sir Paul Girvan, *born* 1948, *apptd* 2007
Rt. Hon. Sir Patrick Coghlin, *born* 1945, *apptd* 2008

PUISNE JUDGES (£172,753)
Style, The Hon. Mr Justice [surname]

Hon. Sir John Gillen, *born* 1947, *apptd* 1999
Hon. Sir Richard McLaughlin, *born* 1947, *apptd* 1999
Hon. Sir Ronald Weatherup, *born* 1947, *apptd* 2001
Hon. Sir Reginald Weir, *born* 1947, *apptd* 2003
Hon. Sir Donnell Deeny, *born* 1950, *apptd* 2004
Hon. Sir Anthony Hart, *born* 1946, *apptd* 2005
Hon. Sir Seamus Treacy, *born* 1956, *apptd* 2007
Hon. Sir William Stephens, *born* 1954, *apptd* 2007
Hon. Sir Bernard McCloskey, *born* 1956, *apptd* 2008

MASTERS OF THE SUPREME COURT (£102,921)
Master, Queen's Bench and Appeals, C. J. McCorry
Master, Office of Care and Protection, H. Wells
Master, Chancery and Probate, R. A. Ellison
Master, Matrimonial, C. W. G. Redpath
Master, Queen's Bench and Matrimonial, E. Bell
Master, Taxing Office, J. Baillie
Master, Bankruptcy, F. Kelly

OFFICIAL SOLICITOR
Official Solicitor to the Supreme Court of Northern Ireland, Miss B. M. Donnelly

COUNTY COURTS

JUDGES (£138,548)
Style, His/Her Hon. Judge [surname]

Judge Babington; Judge Finnegan, QC; Judge Gibson, QC; Judge Grant; Her Hon. Judge Kennedy; Judge Lockie; Judge Loughran; Judge Lynch, QC; Judge McFarland; Judge McReynolds; Judge Martin *(Chief Social Security and Child Support Commissioner)*; Judge Miller, QC; Judge Philpott, QC; Judge Rodgers; Judge Smyth, QC; Her Hon. Judge Smyth

RECORDERS
Belfast (£149,631), Judge Burgess
Londonderry (£138,548), Judge Marrinan, QC

MAGISTRATES' COURTS

DISTRICT JUDGES (MAGISTRATES' COURTS) (£102,921)
There are 21 district judges (magistrates' courts) in Northern Ireland.

NORTHERN IRELAND COURTS AND TRIBUNALS SERVICE
Laganside House, 23–25 Oxford Street, Belfast BT1 3LA
T 028-9032 8594 W www.courtsni.gov.uk
Director, D. A. Lavery

CROWN SOLICITOR'S OFFICE
PO Box 410, Royal Courts of Justice, Belfast BT1 3JY
T 028-9054 6047
Crown Solicitor, J. Conn

PUBLIC PROSECUTION SERVICE
93 Chichester Street, Belfast BT1 3JR
T 028-9054 2444 W www.ppsni.gov.uk
Director of Public Prosecutions, Sir Alasdair Fraser, CB, QC

TRIBUNALS

THE TRIBUNALS SERVICE

5th Floor, 102 Petty France, London SW1H 9AJ
T 0845-600 0877 W www.tribunals.gov.uk

The Tribunals Service, launched in April 2006, is an executive agency within the Ministry of Justice that provides common administrative support to central government tribunals (plus the Adjudicator to HM Land Registry and the Gender Recognition Panel, which are not technically tribunals). The service also aims to deliver greater consistency in practice and procedure, to ensure tribunals are manifestly independent from those whose decisions are being reviewed, and to provide increased access to information for the public.

A new two-tier tribunal system was established on 3 November 2008 as a result of radical reform under the Tribunals, Courts and Enforcement Act 2007. The Tribunals Service now operates a First-tier Tribunal and an Upper Tribunal, both of which are split into chambers. The chambers group together individual tribunals (also known as 'jurisdictions') which deal with similar work or require similar skills. Cases start in the First-tier Tribunal and there is a right of appeal to the Upper Tribunal. Some tribunals transferred to the new two-tier system immediately and most tribunals are expected to transfer into it by the end of 2010. The exception is employment tribunals, which remain outside this structure. The Act also allowed legally qualified tribunal chairmen and adjudicators to swear the judicial oath and become judges.

Senior President, Lord Justice Carnwath
Deputy Senior President, Mr Justice Walker
Chief Executive, Kevin Sadler

FIRST-TIER TRIBUNAL

The main function of the First-tier Tribunal is to hear appeals by citizens against decisions of the government. In most cases appeals are heard by a panel made up of one judge and two non-legal members who are specialists in their field. Judges are appointed by the Lord Chancellor; other members are appointed by the Secretary of State relevant to the tribunal (or jurisdiction) in question. Most of the tribunals administered by central government are expected to become part of the First-tier Tribunal, with new chambers being created as this happens.

GENERAL REGULATORY CHAMBER

President (acting), Judge Angel

CHARITY TRIBUNAL

Tribunals Operational Support Centre, PO Box 9300, Leicester LE1 8DJ
T 0845-600 0877 E charitytribunal@tribunals.gsi.gov.uk
W www.charity.tribunals.gov.uk

The Charity Tribunal was established under the Charities Act 2006 to hear appeals against the decisions of the Charity Commission, to hear applications for the review of decisions made by the Charity Commission and to consider references from the Attorney General or the Charity Commission on points of law. It became part of the General Regulatory Chamber on 1 September 2009. The tribunal consists of the principal judge, five legal members and seven non-legal members. The tribunal currently only has jurisdiction in respect of Charity Commission decisions made on or after 18 March 2008.

Principal Judge, Alison McKenna

IMMIGRATION SERVICES TRIBUNAL

7th Floor, Victory House, 30–34 Kingsway, London WC2B 6EX
T 020-3077 5860 E imset@tribunals.gsi.gov.uk
W www.immigrationservicestribunal.gov.uk

The Immigration Services tribunal is an independent judicial body established in 2000 to provide a forum in which appeals against decisions of the Immigration Services Commissioner and complaints made by the Immigration Services Commissioner can be heard and determined. The cases exclusively concern people providing advice and representation services in connection with immigration matters.

The tribunal forms part of the Ministry of Justice. There is a principal judge, who is the judicial head; other judicial members, who must be legally qualified; lay members, who must have substantial experience in immigration services or in the law and procedure relating to immigration; and a secretary, who is responsible for administration. The tribunal can sit anywhere in the UK.

Principal Judge, His Hon. Judge the Lord Parmoor

INFORMATION RIGHTS TRIBUNAL

Arnhem House Support Centre, PO Box 9300, Leicester LE1 8DJ
T 0845-600 0877 E informationtribunal@tribunals.gsi.gov.uk
W www.informationtribunal.gov.uk

The Information Rights tribunal determines appeals against notices issued by the Information Commissioner. The principal judge and other judges are appointed by the Lord Chancellor and must be legally qualified. Members are appointed by the Lord Chancellor to represent the interests of data users or data subjects. A tribunal consists of the principal judge and one other judge sitting with two of the members.

Principal Judge, Judge Angel

TRANSPORT TRIBUNAL

7th Floor, Victory House, 30–34 Kingsway, London WC2B 6EX
T 020-3077 5860 E transport@tribunals.gsi.gov.uk
W www.transporttribunal.gov.uk

The Transport Tribunal has three jurisdictions: it hears appeals against decisions made by Traffic Commissioners at public inquiries, appeals against decisions of the Registrar of Approved Driving Instructors and is able to resolve disputes under the Postal Services Act 2000. The tribunal consists of a legally qualified principal judge, other judicial members, and lay members. The principal judge and legal members are appointed by the Lord Chancellor and the lay members by the transport secretary. Members of the Transport Tribunal also act as the London Service Permit Appeals Panel. Appeals from

decisions made by Traffic Commissioners are under the jurisdiction of the Upper Tribunal Administrative Appeals Chamber.
Principal Judge, Judge Brodrick

HEALTH, EDUCATION AND SOCIAL CARE CHAMBER
President, His Hon. Judge Sycamore

CARE STANDARDS
Mowden Hall, Staindrop Road, Darlington, Co Durham DL3 9BG
T 01325-392712 E cst@tribunals.gsi.gov.uk
W www.carestandardstribunal.gov.uk

The tribunal was established under the Protection of Children Act 1999 and considers appeals in relation to decisions made about the inclusion of individuals' names on the list of those considered unsuitable to work with children or vulnerable adults, restrictions from teaching and employment in schools/further education institutions, and the registration of independent schools. It also deals with general registration decisions made about care homes, children's homes, childcare providers, nurses' agencies, social workers, residential family centres, independent hospitals and fostering agencies. The tribunal's principal judge appoints the panels for each case.
Deputy Chamber President, Judge Aitken

MENTAL HEALTH
Secretariat: PO Box 8793, 5th Floor, Leicester LE1 8BN
T 0845-233 2022 W www.mhrt.org.uk

The tribunal is an independent judicial body which reviews the cases of patients compulsorily detained under the provisions of the Mental Health Act 1983 (amended by the Mental Health Act 2007). It has the power to discharge the patient, to recommend leave of absence, to recommend supervised community treatment, or to recommend transfer to another hospital. Judges are appointed by the Lord Chancellor, and non-legal members are appointed by the Secretary of State for Health or the Secretary of State for Wales. Each case is heard by three members including a judge and a medical specialist. There are separate mental health tribunals in Wales and Scotland.
Principal Judge, Judge Wright

PRIMARY HEALTH LISTS
York House, York Place, Leeds LS1 2ED
T 0113-389 6061 W www.fhsaa.tribunals.gov.uk

Primary Health Lists took over the role of the Family Health Services Appeal Authority on 18 January 2010. The tribunal is independent of the Department of Health and considers appeals against the decisions of primary care trusts (PCTs), including appeals by GPs, dentists, pharmacists and opticians regarding action taken against them. The tribunal allocates appeals and applications to panels normally consisting of a tribunal judge, a specialist member and a lay member. All members are appointed by the Lord Chancellor following recommendation from the Judicial Appointments Commission, or may be assigned from other areas of the tribunal.
Deputy Chamber President, Judge Aitken

SPECIAL EDUCATIONAL NEEDS AND DISABILITY
Ground Floor, Mowden Hall, Staindrop Road DL3 9BG
T 01325-392760 E sendistqueries@tribunals.gsi.gov.uk
W www.sendist.gov.uk

The Special Educational Needs and Disability tribunal considers parents' appeals against the decisions of local authorities (LAs) about children's special educational needs if parents cannot reach agreement with the LA. It also considers claims of disability discrimination in schools.
Deputy Chamber President, Judge Aitken

IMMIGRATION AND ASYLUM CHAMBER
PO Box 6987, Leicester LE1 6ZX
T 0845-606 0766 E customer.service@tribunals.gsi.gov.uk
W www.tribunals.gsi.gov.uk/ImmigrationAsylum

The Immigration and Asylum Chamber replaced the Asylum and Immigration tribunal in February 2010. It is an independent tribunal dealing with appeals against decisions made by the Home Office, such as the decision to refuse a person asylum, or the decision to refuse a person leave to remain in the UK. Judges and non-legal members are appointed by the Lord Chancellor. Appeals are heard by one or more immigration judges, sometimes accompanied by non-legal members.
President (acting), Judge Arfon-Jones

SOCIAL ENTITLEMENT CHAMBER
President, His Hon. Judge Martin

ASYLUM SUPPORT
Second Floor, Anchorage House, 2 Clove Crescent, London E14 2BE T 020-7538 6171
W www.asylum-support-tribunal.gov.uk

Asylum Support deals with appeals against decisions made by the UK Border Agency (UKBA). The UKBA decides whether asylum seekers and their dependants meet the test of destitution according to the Immigration and Asylum Act 1999, and determines what support, such as money or accommodation, should be provided. Asylum Support can only consider appeals against a refusal or termination of support, and can ask the Home Secretary to reconsider the matter, substitute the original decision with the tribunal's decision, or dismiss the appeal.
Principal Judge, Sehba Storey

CRIMINAL INJURIES COMPENSATION
Head Office, Wellington House, 134–136 Wellington Street, Glasgow G2 2XL T 0141-354 8555
Judicial Review Enquiries, 5th Floor, Fox Court, 14 Gray's Inn Road, London WC1X 8HN T 020-3206 0664
E enquiries-cicap@tribunals.gsi.gov.uk W www.cicap.gov.uk

The Criminal Injuries Compensation tribunal (previously known as the Criminal Injuries Compensation Appeals Panel) determines appeals against review decisions made by the Criminal Injuries Compensation Authority on applications for compensation made by victims of violent crime. It only considers appeals on claims made on or after 1 April 1996 under the Criminal Injuries Compensation Scheme.
Principal Judge, Anthony Summers

SOCIAL SECURITY AND CHILD SUPPORT

Administrative Support Centre, PO Box 14620, Birmingham B16 6FR **T** 0845-408 3500
W www.appeals-service.gov.uk

The Social Security and Child Support tribunal (SSCS) arranges and hears appeals on a range of decisions made by the Department for Work and Pensions, HM Revenue and Customs, and local authorities. Appeals considered include those concerned with income support, jobseeker's allowance, child support, child tax credit, retirement pensions, housing benefit, council tax benefit, disability living allowance, vaccine damage, tax credits and compensation recovery.

The tribunal is headed by the president of the Social Entitlement Chamber. The SSCS also contains an executive agency responsible for the administration of appeals, headed by the chief executive of the Tribunals Service.

Judicial Lead, His Hon. Judge Martin

TAX CHAMBER

45 Bedford Square, London WC1B 3DN
T 0845-223 8080 **E** taxappeals@tribunals.gsi.gov.uk
W www.tribunals.gov.uk/tax

The Tax Chamber, established on 1 April 2009, replaced four separate tax tribunals, the General Commissioners of Income Tax, the Special Commissioners, the VAT and Duties Tribunals, and section 706 tribunals. The chamber hears most appeals against decisions of Her Majesty's Revenue and Customs in relation to tax. The chamber listens to appeals about income tax; corporation tax; capital gains tax; inheritance tax; national insurance contributions; and VAT or duties, and appeals can be made by individuals or organisations, single taxpayers or large multinational companies. Appeals are heard by legally qualified judges, non-legally qualified expert members or a mix of the two. The chamber has jurisdiction throughout the UK.

President, His Hon. Sir Stephen Oliver, QC

WAR PENSIONS AND ARMED FORCES COMPENSATION CHAMBER

5th Floor, Fox Court, 14 Gray's Inn Road, London WC1X 8HN
T 020-3206 0705 **E** pensions.appeal@tribunals.gsi.gov.uk
W www.pensionsappealtribunals.gov.uk

The War Pensions and Armed Forces Compensation Chamber is the successor to the Pensions Appeal Tribunal which has existed in different forms since the War Pensions Act 1919. It hears appeals from ex-servicemen or women who have had claims in respect of a war pension rejected by the Secretary of State for Defence. The tribunal decides appeals under the war pensions legislation for injuries that occurred before 5 April 2005, and under the armed forces compensation scheme for injuries after that date. Under the war pensions legislation, the tribunal decides on entitlement to a war pension, the degree of disablement and entitlement to certain allowances (eg for mobility needs). Under the armed forces compensation scheme it decides entitlement to an award and the tariff level of the award. The tribunal's jurisdiction covers England and Wales.

President, Judge Bano

PENSIONS APPEAL TRIBUNALS FOR SCOTLAND

George House, 126 George Street, Edinburgh EH2 4HH
T 0131-271 4340 **E** info@patscotland.org.uk
W www.patscotland.org.uk

President, C. M. McEachran, QC

UPPER TRIBUNAL

The Upper Tribunal deals with appeals from, and enforcement of, decisions taken by the First-tier Tribunal. It has also assumed some of the supervisory powers of the courts to deal with the actions of tribunals, government departments and some other public authorities. All the decision-makers of the Upper Tribunal are judges or expert members sitting in a panel chaired by a judge, and are specialists in the areas of law they handle. Over time their decisions are expected to build comprehensive case law for each area covered by the tribunals.

ADMINISTRATIVE APPEALS CHAMBER

5th Floor, Chichester Rents, 81 Chancery Lane, London WC2A 1DD **T** 020-7911 7085
E adminappeals@tribunals.gsi.gov.uk
W www.administrativeappeals.tribunals.gov.uk

The Administrative Appeals Chamber deals with appeals from the Social Entitlement Chamber, the War Pensions and Armed Forces Compensation Chamber, the Health, Education and Social Care Chamber and the General Regulatory Chamber of the First-tier Tribunal, Forfeiture Act references and appeals in cases about safeguarding vulnerable groups. The Upper Tribunal in Northern Ireland deals with appeals from the Pensions Appeal Tribunal for Northern Ireland. There are 16 full-time judges and 17 deputy judges who sit part-time. Judges normally sit on their own to hear cases and most of their cases are decided without oral hearings.

President, Mr Justice Walker

OFFICE OF THE SOCIAL SECURITY COMMISSIONERS AND CHILD SUPPORT COMMISSIONERS FOR NORTHERN IRELAND

Bedford House, 3rd Floor, 16–22 Bedford Street, Belfast BT2 7FD
T 028-9072 8731
E socialsecuritycommissioners@courtsni.gov.uk
W www.courtsni.gov.uk

The role of Northern Ireland Social Security Commissioners and Child Support Commissioners is similar to that of the Administrative Appeals Chamber in England, Wales and Scotland; they also have jurisdiction to deal with questions arising under the Forfeiture (Northern Ireland) Order 1982. The commissioners are not part of the Tribunals Service. There are two commissioners for Northern Ireland.

Chief Commissioner, His Hon. Judge Martin, QC

IMMIGRATION AND ASYLUM CHAMBER

Arnhem Support Centre, PO Box 6987, Leicester LE1 6ZX
T 0845-6000 877 **E** customer.service@tribunals.gsi.gov.uk
W www.tribunals.gsi.gov.uk/ImmigrationAsylum/utiac

The Immigration and Asylum Chamber was created on 15 February 2010. It hears appeals against decisions made by the Immigration and Asylum Chamber in the First-tier Tribunal in matters of immigration, asylum and nationality. Judges and members are appointed by the Lord Chancellor. Appeals are heard by one or more senior

or designated immigration judges, sometimes accompanied by non-legal members.
President, Mr Justice Blake

LANDS CHAMBER
43–45 Bedford Square, London WC1B 3AS
T 020-7612 9710 E lands@tribunals.gsi.gov.uk
W www.landstribunal.gov.uk

The Lands tribunal determines questions relating to the valuation of land, rating appeals from valuation tribunals, appeals from leasehold valuation tribunals and residential property tribunals, applications to discharge or modify restrictions on the use of land, and compulsory purchase compensation. The tribunal may also arbitrate under references by consent. Cases are usually heard by a single member but they may sometimes be heard by two or three members.
President, George Bartlett, QC

LANDS TRIBUNAL FOR SCOTLAND
George House, 126 George Street, Edinburgh EH2 4HH
T 0131-271 4350 E mailbox@lands-tribunal-scotland.org.uk
W www.lands-tribunal-scotland.org.uk

The Lands Tribunal for Scotland has much the same remit as the tribunal for England and Wales but also covers questions relating to tenants' rights to buy their homes under the Housing (Scotland) Act 1987. It is not part of the Tribunals Service. The president is appointed by the Lord President of the Court of Session.
President, Hon. Lord McGhie, QC

TAX AND CHANCERY CHAMBER
45 Bedford Square, London WC1B 3DN
T 020-7612 9700 E financeandtaxappeals@tribunals.gsi.gov.uk
W www.tribunals.gov.uk/financeandtax

The Tax and Chancery Chamber decides applications for permissions to appeal and appeals on point of law from decisions of the Tax Chamber in the first-tier. The judiciary consists of high court judges and specialist tax judiciary, and the tribunal has jurisdiction throughout the UK. The jurisdiction of the former Financial Services and Markets tribunal transferred to the chamber in April 2010. As a result the chamber now hears appeals against decisions issued by the Financial Services Authority and from the Pensions Regulator.
President, Mr Justice Warren

EMPLOYMENT TRIBUNALS

ENGLAND AND WALES
3rd Floor, Alexandra House, 14–22 The Parsonage, Manchester M3 2JA T 0845-795 9775
W www.employmenttribunals.gov.uk

Employment Tribunals for England and Wales sit in 12 regions. The tribunals deal with matters of employment law, redundancy, dismissal, contract disputes, sexual, racial and disability discrimination and related areas of dispute which may arise in the workplace. A public register of judgments is held at 100 Southgate Street, Bury St Edmunds, Suffolk IP33 2AQ.

Chairs, who may be full-time or part-time, are legally qualified. They, along with the tribunal members, are appointed by the Ministry of Justice.
President, David John Latham

SCOTLAND
Central Office, Eagle Building, 215 Bothwell Street, Glasgow G2 7TS T 0141-204 0730

Tribunals in Scotland have the same remit as those in England and Wales. Employment judges are appointed by the Lord President of the Court of Session and lay members by the Lord Chancellor.
President, Shona Simon

EMPLOYMENT APPEAL TRIBUNAL
London Office: Audit House, 58 Victoria Embankment, London EC4Y 0DS
T 020-7273 1041 E londoneat@tribunals.gsi.gov.uk
Edinburgh Office: 52 Melville Street, Edinburgh EH3 7HF
T 0131-225 3963 E edinburgheat@tribunals.gsi.gov.uk
W www.employmentappeals.gov.uk

The Employment Appeal Tribunal hears appeals (on points of law only) arising from decisions made by employment tribunals. Hearings are conducted by a judge, either alone or accompanied by two lay members who have practical experience in employment relations.
President, Hon. Mr Justice Underhill
Registrar, Pauline Donleavy

SPECIAL IMMIGRATION APPEALS COMMISSION
PO Box 36469, London EC4A 1WR
T 0845-600 0877 E customer.service@tribunals.gsi.gov.uk
W www.siac.tribunals.gov.uk

The commission was set up under the Special Immigration Appeals Commission Act 1997. It remains separate from the First-tier and Upper Tribunal structure but is part of the Tribunals Service. Its main function is to consider appeals against orders for deportations in cases which involve, in the main, considerations of national security or the public interest. The commission also hears appeals against decisions to deprive persons of citizenship status. Members are appointed by the Lord Chancellor.
Chair, Hon. Mr Justice Mitting

INDEPENDENT TRIBUNALS

The following tribunals are not administered by the Tribunals Service.

AGRICULTURAL LAND TRIBUNALS
c/o DEFRA, Area 8E (Millbank), 17 Smith Square, London SW1P 3JR
T 0845-933 5577 E helpline@defra.gsi.gov.uk
W www.defra.gov.uk/foodfarm/farmmanage/alt/index.htm

Agricultural Land Tribunals settle disputes and other issues between landlords and tenants of agricultural holdings under the Agricultural Holdings Act 1986, mainly in relation to succession rights and notices to quit. The tribunals also settle drainage disputes between neighbours under the Land Drainage Act 1991.

There are seven tribunals covering England and one covering Wales. For each tribunal the Lord Chancellor appoints a chair and one or more deputies (barristers or solicitors of at least seven years' standing). The Lord Chancellor also appoints three panels of lay members: the 'landowners' panel, the 'farmers' panel and the 'drainage' panel.

Each tribunal is an independent statutory body with

jurisdiction only within its own geographical area. A separate tribunal is constituted for each case, and consists of a chair and two lay members nominated by the chair.
Chairs (England), Shirley Evans; His Hon. John Machin; George Newsom; Paul de la Piquerie; His Hon. Robert Taylor; Nigel Thomas; Martin Wood
Chair (Wales), James Buxton

CIVIL AVIATION AUTHORITY

CAA House, 45–59 Kingsway, London WC2B 6TE
T 020-7453 6162 **E** legal@caa.co.uk
W www.caa.co.uk

The Civil Aviation Authority (CAA) does not have a separate tribunal department as such, but for certain purposes the CAA must conform to tribunal requirements. For example, to deal with appeals against the refusal or revocation of aviation licences and certificates issued by the CAA, and the allocation of routes outside of the EU to airlines.

The chair and four non-executive members who may sit on panels for tribunal purposes are appointed by the Secretary of State for Transport.
Chair, Dame Deirdre Hutton, DBE

COMPETITION APPEAL TRIBUNAL

Victoria House, Bloomsbury Place, London WC1A 2EB
T 020-7979 7979 **E** info@catribunal.org.uk
W www.catribunal.org.uk

The Competition Appeal Tribunal (CAT) is a specialist tribunal established to hear certain cases in the sphere of UK competition and economic regulatory law. It hears appeals against decisions of the Office of Fair Trading (OFT) and their sectoral regulators, and also decisions of the OFT, Secretary of State for Business, Innovation and Skills and the Competition Commission. The CAT also has jurisdiction to award damages in respect of infringements of EC or UK competition law and to hear appeals against decisions of OFCOM.

Cases are heard before a panel consisting of three members: either the president or a member of the panel of chairmen and two ordinary members. The members of the panel of chairmen are judges of the Chancery Division of the high court and other senior lawyers. The ordinary members have expertise in law and/or related fields. The president and chairmen are appointed by the Lord Chancellor; the ordinary members are appointed by the secretary of state.
President, Hon. Mr Justice Barling

COPYRIGHT TRIBUNAL

21 Bloomsbury Street, London WC1B 3HF
T 020-7034 2836 **E** copyright.tribunal@ipo.gov.uk
W www.ipo.gov.uk/copy/tribunal

The Copyright Tribunal resolves disputes over the terms and conditions of licences offered by, or licensing schemes operated by, collective licensing bodies in the copyright and related rights area. Its decisions are appealable to the high court on points of law only.

The chair and two deputy chairs are appointed by the Lord Chancellor. Up to eight ordinary members are appointed by the Secretary of State for Business, Innovation and Skills. The tribunal operates on a panel basis and its members have wide expertise in business, public administration and the professions.
Chair, His Hon. Judge Fysh, QC

INDUSTRIAL TRIBUNALS AND THE FAIR EMPLOYMENT TRIBUNAL (NORTHERN IRELAND)

Killymeal House, 2 Cromac Quay, Ormeau Road, Belfast BT7 2JD
T 028-9032 7666 **E** mail@employmenttribunalsni.org
W www.employmenttribunalsni.co.uk

The industrial tribunal system in Northern Ireland was set up in 1965 and has a similar remit to the employment tribunals in the rest of the UK. There is also a Fair Employment Tribunal, which hears and determines individual cases of alleged religious or political discrimination in employment. Employers can appeal to the Fair Employment Tribunal if they consider the directions of the Equality Commission to be unreasonable, inappropriate or unnecessary, and the Equality Commission can make application to the tribunal for the enforcement of undertakings or directions with which an employer has not complied.

The president, vice-president and chairs of the Industrial Tribunal and the Fair Employment Tribunal are appointed by the Lord Chancellor. The panel members to both the industrial tribunals and the Fair Employment Tribunal were appointed by the Department for Employment and Learning, but any future appointments will be made through a full public appointment process.
President of the Industrial Tribunals and the Fair Employment Tribunal, Eileen McBride

INVESTIGATORY POWERS TRIBUNAL

PO Box 33220, London SW1H 9ZQ
T 020-7035 3711 **E** info@ipt-uk.com **W** www.ipt-uk.com

The Investigatory Powers Tribunal replaced the Interception of Communications Tribunal, the Intelligence Services Tribunal, the Security Services Tribunal and the complaints function of the commissioner appointed under the Police Act 1997.

The Regulation of Investigatory Powers Act 2000 (RIPA) provides for a tribunal made up of senior members of the legal profession, independent of the government and appointed by the Queen, to consider all complaints against the intelligence services and those against public authorities in respect of powers covered by RIPA; and to consider proceedings brought under section 7 of the Human Rights Act 1998 against the intelligence services and law enforcement agencies in respect of these powers.
President, Rt. Hon. Lord Justice Mummery

NATIONAL HEALTH SERVICE TRIBUNAL (SCOTLAND)

Fyfe Ireland LLP, 6 Blythswood Square, Glasgow G2 4AD
T 0141-222 2216

The Scottish National Health Service Tribunal considers representations that the continued inclusion of a family health service practitioner (eg a doctor, dentist, optometrist or pharmacist) on a health board's list would be prejudicial to the efficiency of the service concerned, by virtue either of fraudulent practices or unsatisfactory personal or professional conduct. If this is established, the tribunal has the power to disqualify practitioners from working in the NHS family health services. The tribunal sits when required and is composed of a chair, one lay member, and one practitioner member drawn from a representative professional panel. The chair is appointed by the Lord President of the Court of Session, and the lay

member and the members of the professional panel are appointed by the Scottish ministers.
Chair, J. Michael D. Graham

RESIDENTIAL PROPERTY TRIBUNAL SERVICE

10 Alfred Place, London WC1E 7LR
T 0845-600 3178 E rptscorporateunit@communities.gsi.gov.uk
W www.rpts.gov.uk

The Residential Property Tribunal Service provides members to sit on panels for the Rent Assessment Committees, Residential Property Tribunals and Leasehold Valuation Tribunals, and serves the private-rented and leasehold property market in England by resolving disputes between leaseholders, tenants and landlords. The president and chair are appointed by the Lord Chancellor and other members are appointed by the Department for Communities and Local Government and the Ministry of Justice.
Senior President, Siobhan McGrath

SOLICITORS' DISCIPLINARY TRIBUNAL

3rd Floor, Gate House, 1 Farringdon Street, London EC4M 7NS
T 020-7329 4808 E enquiries@solicitorsdt.com
W www.solicitorstribunal.org.uk

The Solicitors' Disciplinary Tribunal is an independent statutory body whose members are appointed by the Master of the Rolls. The tribunal considers applications made to it alleging either professional misconduct and/or a breach of the statutory rules by which solicitors are bound against an individually named solicitor, former solicitor, registered foreign lawyer, or solicitor's clerk. The tribunal has around 60 members, two-thirds are solicitor members and one-third are lay members.
President, Jeremy Barnecutt

SOLICITORS' DISCIPLINE TRIBUNAL (SCOTTISH)

Unit 3.5, The Granary Business Centre, Coal Road, Cupar, Fife KY15 5YQ T 01334-659088 W www.ssdt.org.uk

The Scottish Solicitors' Discipline Tribunal is an independent statutory body with a panel of 24 members, 12 of whom are solicitors; members are appointed by the Lord President of the Court of Session. Its principal function is to consider complaints of misconduct against solicitors in Scotland.
Chair, A. Cockburn

TRAFFIC PENALTY TRIBUNAL

Barlow House, Minshull Street, Manchester M1 3DZ
T 0161-242 5252 E info@trafficpenaltytribunal.gov.uk
W www.trafficpenaltytribunal.gov.uk

The Traffic Penalty Tribunal considers appeals from motorists against penalty charge notices issued by Civil Enforcement Authorities in England and Wales (outside London) under the Road Traffic Act 1991 and the Traffic Management Act 2004, and considers appeals against bus lane contraventions in England (outside London). Parking adjudicators are appointed with the express consent of the Lord Chancellor and must be lawyers of five years' standing. Cases are decided by a single adjudicator, either in a postal, telephone or a personal hearing.
Head of Service, Louise Hutchinson

VALUATION TRIBUNAL SERVICE

2nd Floor, Black Lion House, 45 Whitechapel Road, London E1 1DU T 020-7426 3900
W www.valuationtribunal.gov.uk

The Valuation Tribunal Service (VTS) was created as a corporate body by the Local Government Act 2003, and is responsible for providing or arranging the services required for the operation of the valuation tribunal for England. The VTS board consists of a chair and members appointed by the secretary of state. The VTS is funded by the Department for Communities and Local Government.
Chair, VTS Board, Anne Galbraith, OBE

VALUATION TRIBUNAL FOR ENGLAND

President's Office, 2nd Floor, Black Lion House,
45 Whitechapel Road, London E1 1DU
T 020-7246 3900 W www.valuationtribunal.gov.uk

The Valuation Tribunal for England (VTE) came into being on 1 October 2009, replacing 56 valuation tribunals in England. Provision for the VTE was made in the Local Government and Public Involvement in Health Act 2007. The Valuation Tribunal for England hears appeals concerning council tax and non-domestic rating and land drainage rates. A separate tribunal is constituted for each hearing, and consists of a chair and two or three other members. A clerk, who is a paid employee of the VTS, is present to advise on points of procedure and law. The national president is the judicial head of a volunteer membership. Members will in future be appointed by the Judicial Appointments Commission.
President, Prof. Graham Zellick

VALUATION TRIBUNAL SERVICE FOR WALES

Governing Council of VTSW, 22 Gold Tops, Newport,
South Wales NP20 4PG T 01633-266367
E eastwales.vt@vto.gsx.gov.uk

The Valuation Tribunal Service for Wales (VTSW) was created under the Valuation Tribunals (Wales) Regulations 2005, and is responsible for providing or arranging the services required for the operation of the four tribunals in Wales. The governing council of the VTSW is composed of four regional presidents, one of whom is elected director together with one member who is appointed by the National Assembly for Wales. The VTSW tribunals hear appeals concerning council tax and non-domestic rating, and land drainage rates in Wales. An individual tribunal, supported by a clerk, is constituted for each hearing and is normally serviced by three members, one of whom also chairs.
Chief Executive, Simon Hill

OMBUDSMAN SERVICES

The following section is a listing of selected ombudsman services. Ombudsmen are a free, independent and impartial means of resolving certain disputes outside of the courts. These disputes are, in the majority of cases, concerned with whether something has been badly or unfairly handled (for example owing to delay, neglect, inefficiency or failure to follow proper procedures). Most ombudsman schemes are established by statute; they cover various public and private bodies and generally examine matters only after the relevant body has been given a reasonable opportunity to deal with the complaint.

After conducting an investigation an ombudsman will usually issue a written report, which normally suggests a resolution to the dispute and often includes recommendations concerning the improvement of procedures.

BRITISH AND IRISH OMBUDSMAN ASSOCIATION (BIOA)

PO Box 308, Twickenham TW1 9BE
T 020-8894 9272 E secretary@bioa.org.uk
W www.bioa.org.uk

The BIOA was established in 1994 and exists to provide information to the government, public bodies, and the public about ombudsmen and other complaint-handling services. An ombudsman scheme must meet four criteria in order to attain full BIOA membership: independence from the organisations the ombudsman has the power to investigate, fairness, effectiveness and public accountability. Associate membership is open to complaint-handling bodies that do not meet these criteria in full. Ombudsmen schemes from the UK, Ireland, the Channel Islands, the Isle of Man and British overseas territories may apply to BIOA for membership.
Secretary, Ian Pattison

The following is a selection of organisations that are members of the BIOA.

FINANCIAL OMBUDSMAN SERVICE

South Quay Plaza, 183 Marsh Wall, London E14 9SR
T 020-7964 1000
E complaint.info@financial-ombudsman.org.uk
W www.financial-ombudsman.org.uk

The Financial Ombudsman Service settles individual disputes between businesses providing financial services and their customers. The service deals with around a million enquiries every year and settles over 100,000 disputes. The service examines complaints about most financial matters, including banking, insurance, mortgages, pensions, savings, loans and credit cards. *See also* Banking and Finance.
Chief Ombudsman and Chief Executive, Natalie Ceeney
Chair, Sir Christopher Kelly, KCB

HOUSING OMBUDSMAN SERVICE

81 Aldwych, London WC2B 4HN
T 0300-111 3000 E info@housing-ombudsman.org.uk
W www.housing-ombudsman.org.uk

The Housing Ombudsman Service, established in 1997, deals with complaints and disputes involving tenants and housing associations and social landlords, certain private sector landlords and managing agents. The ombudsman has a statutory jurisdiction over all registered social landlords in England. Private and other landlords can join the service on a voluntary basis. Complaints from council/local authority tenants have to be made to the Local Government Ombudsman.
Ombudsman, Dr Mike Biles
Deputy Ombudsman, Rafael Runco

INDEPENDENT POLICE COMPLAINTS COMMISSION (IPCC)

90 High Holborn, London WC1V 6BH
T 0845-300 2002 E enquiries@ipcc.gsi.gov.uk
W www.ipcc.gov.uk

The IPCC succeeded the Police Complaints Authority in 2004. It was established under the Police Reform Act 2002. The IPCC has teams of investigators headed by commissioners in each of its regions to assist with the supervision and management of some police investigations. They also carry out independent investigations into serious incidents or allegations of misconduct by persons serving with the police. The IPCC decides on appeals against complaints investigated by the police service. It also has responsibility for investigating complaints of serious incidents, including death or injury, made against staff of HM Revenue and Customs, the Serious Organised Crime Agency and the United Kingdom Border Agency. The 12 commissioners of the IPCC must not previously have worked for the police.
Chair, Nick Hardwick
Deputy Chairs, Deborah Glass; Len Jackson
Chief Executive, Jane Furniss

LEGAL OMBUDSMAN

2nd Floor, Baskerville House, Centenary Square, Broad Street, Birmingham B1 2ND
T 0121-503 2930 E enquiries@legalombudsman.org.uk
W www.legalombudsman.org.uk

The Legal Ombudsman was set up by the Office for Legal Complaints under the Legal Services Act 2007 and is the single body for all consumer legal complaints in England and Wales, replacing the Office of the Legal Services Ombudsman in 2010. The Legal Ombudsman aims to resolve disputes between individuals and authorised legal practitioners, including barristers, law costs draftsmen, legal executives, licensed conveyancers, notaries, patent attorneys, probate practitioners, registered European lawyers, solicitors and trade mark attorneys.
Chief Ombudsman, Adam Sampson

LOCAL GOVERNMENT OMBUDSMAN

Advice Team, PO Box 4771, Coventry CV4 0EH
T 0300-061 0614 W www.lgo.org.uk

The Local Government Ombudsman deals with complaints of injustice arising from maladministration by local authorities and certain other bodies.

There are three ombudsmen in England, each with responsibility for different regions; they aim to provide satisfactory redress for complainants and better administration for the authorities. The ombudsmen investigate complaints about most council matters, including housing, planning, education, social care, consumer protection, drainage and council tax. *See also* Local Government.

Local Government Ombudsmen, Tony Redmond; Anne Seex; Jane Martin

NORTHERN IRELAND OMBUDSMAN

Progressive House, 33 Wellington Place, Belfast BT1 6HN
T 028-9023 3821 E ombudsman@ni-ombudsman.org.uk
W www.ni-ombudsman.org.uk

The ombudsman (also known as the Assembly Ombudsman for Northern Ireland and the Northern Ireland Commissioner for Complaints) is appointed under legislation with powers to investigate complaints by people claiming to have sustained injustice arising from action taken by a Northern Ireland government department, or any other public body within his remit. The ombudsman can investigate all local councils, education and library boards, health and social services boards and trusts, as well as all government departments and their agencies. As commissioner for complaints, the ombudsman can investigate complaints about doctors, dentists, pharmacists, optometrists and other healthcare professionals.

Ombudsman, Dr Tom Frawley, CBE
Deputy Ombudsman, Marie Anderson

OFFICE OF THE PENSIONS OMBUDSMAN

6th Floor, 11 Belgrave Road, London SW1V 1RB
T 020-7630 2200 E enquiries@pensions-ombudsman.org.uk
W www.pensions-ombudsman.org.uk

The Pensions Ombudsman is appointed by the Secretary of State for Work and Pensions, under the Pension Schemes Act 1993 as amended by the Pensions Act 1995. He investigates and decides complaints and disputes about the way that personal and occupational pension schemes are run. As the Ombudsman for the Board of the Pension Protection Fund, he can deal with disputes about the decisions made by the board or the actions of their staff. He also deals with appeals against decisions made by the scheme manager under the Financial Assistance Scheme.

Pensions Ombudsman, Tony King
Deputy Pensions Ombudsman, Jane Irvine

PARLIAMENTARY AND HEALTH SERVICE OMBUDSMAN

Millbank Tower, Millbank, London SW1P 4QP
T 0345-015 4033 E phso.enquiries@ombudsman.org.uk
W www.ombudsman.org.uk

The Parliamentary Ombudsman (also known as the Parliamentary Commissioner for Administration) is independent of government and is an officer of parliament. She is responsible for investigating complaints referred to her by MPs from members of the public who claim to have sustained injustice in consequence of maladministration by or on behalf of government departments and certain non-departmental public bodies. In 1999 an additional 158 public bodies were brought within the jurisdiction of the Parliamentary Ombudsman. Certain types of action by government departments or bodies are excluded from investigation.

The Health Service Ombudsman for England is responsible for investigating complaints against National Health Service authorities and trusts that are not dealt with by those authorities to the satisfaction of the complainant. Complaints can be referred directly by the member of the public who claims to have sustained injustice or hardship in consequence of the failure in a service provided by a relevant body. The ombudsman's jurisdiction now covers complaints about family doctors, dentists, pharmacists and opticians, and complaints about actions resulting from clinical judgement.

The Health Service Ombudsman is also responsible for investigating complaints that information has been wrongly refused under the Code of Practice on Openness in the National Health Service 1995. The parliamentary and the health offices are presently held by the same person.

Parliamentary Ombudsman and Health Service Ombudsman, Ms A. Abraham
Deputy Ombudsman, Ms K. Hudson

PROPERTY OMBUDSMAN

Beckett House, 4 Bridge Street, Salisbury, Wiltshire SP1 2LX
T 01722-333306 E admin@tpos.co.uk
W www.tpos.co.uk

The Property Ombudsman service was established in 1998 and provides a service for dealing with disputes between estate agents and consumers who are actual or potential buyers or sellers of residential property, or residential letting agents, in the UK.

Complaints that the ombudsman considers include allegations of unfair treatment, maladministration and infringement of legal rights. The ombudsman's role is to resolve these complaints in full and final settlement and, where appropriate, make an award of financial compensation.

Ombudsman, Christopher Hamer

PUBLIC SERVICES OMBUDSMAN FOR WALES

1 Ffordd yr Hen Gae, Pencoed CF35 5LJ
T 01656-641150 E ask@ombudsman-wales.org.uk
W www.ombudsman-wales.org.uk

The office of Public Services Ombudsman for Wales was established, with effect from 1 April 2006, by the Public Services Ombudsman (Wales) Act 2005. The ombudsman, who is appointed by the Queen, investigates complaints of injustice caused by maladministration or service failure by the Assembly Commission (and public bodies sponsored by the assembly); Welsh Assembly Government; National Health Service bodies, including GPs, family health service providers and hospitals; registered social landlords; local authorities, including community councils; fire and rescue authorities; police authorities; national park authorities; and countryside and environmental organisations. Free leaflets explaining the process of making a complaint are available from the ombudsman's office.

Ombudsman, Peter Tyndall

REMOVALS INDUSTRY OMBUDSMAN SCHEME

Chess Chambers, 2 Broadway Court, Chesham, Bucks HP5 1EG
T 01753-888206 E ombudsman@removalsombudsman.co.uk
W www.removalsombudsman.org.uk

The Removals Industry Ombudsman Scheme was established to resolve disputes between removal companies that are members of the scheme and their clients, both domestic and commercial. The ombudsman investigates complaints such as breaches of contract, unprofessional conduct, delays, or breaches in the code of practice.
Ombudsman, Matti Alderson

SCOTTISH PUBLIC SERVICES OMBUDSMAN

Freepost EH641, Edinburgh EH3 0BR
T 0800-377 7330 E ask@spso.org.uk
W www.spso.org.uk

The Scottish Public Services Ombudsman (SPSO) was established in 2002. The ombudsman investigates complaints about Scottish government departments and agencies, councils, housing associations, the National Health Service (NHS), the Scottish Parliamentary Corporate Body and most other public bodies. The public bodies that the SPSO may consider investigating are contained in a list outlined in the Scottish Public Services Ombudsman Act 2002. The ombudsman's remit was extended in 2005 to cover Scotland's further education colleges and higher education institutions. Complaints considered by the ombudsman include complaints about poor service, failure to provide a service and administrative failure.
Scottish Public Services Ombudsman, Jim Martin

THE OMBUDSMAN SERVICE LTD

Wilderspool Park, Greenalls Avenue, Warrington WA4 6HL
W www.tosl.org.uk

The Ombudsman Service Limited (TOSL) is a not-for-profit private limited company that administers four ombudsman services – the Energy Ombudsman, Otelo (the Office of the Telecommunications Ombudsman), Ombudsman Services: Property, and the PRS for Music Ombudsman.

The Energy Ombudsman resolves disputes between domestic and small business customers and their gas and electricity companies.

Otelo deals with complaints from consumers concerning public communications providers (any company that provides an electronic communications network or service to members of the public or small businesses).

The Ombudsman Services: Property investigates complaints made about the service provided by chartered surveyors and estate agents, for example a breach of legal obligations, avoidable delays, discourtesy or incompetence.

The PRS for Music Ombudsman resolves disagreements between the PRS for Music service, which licenses the public performance of copyright music in the UK, and its users.
Chair, Peter Holland, CBE
Chief Ombudsman, Lewis Shand Smith
Ombudsmen, Gillian Fleming *(Property);* Dr Richard Sills *(Energy);* Andrew Walker *(Otelo)*

ENERGY OMBUDSMAN

PO Box 966, Warrington WA4 9DF
T 0330-440 1624
E enquiries@energy-ombudsman.org.uk
W www.energy-ombudsman.org.uk

OTELO

PO Box 730, Warrington WA4 6WU
T 0300-440 1614
E enquiries@otelo.org.uk W www.otelo.org.uk

OMBUDSMAN SERVICES: PROPERTY

PO Box 1021, Warrington WA4 9FE
T 0300-440 1634
E enquiries@os-property.org
W www.surveyors-ombudsman.org.uk

PRS FOR MUSIC OMBUDSMAN

PO Box 1124, Warrington WA4 9GH
T 0300-440 1601
E enquiries@prsformusic-ombudsman.org
W www.prsformusic-ombudsman.org

WATERWAYS OMBUDSMAN

PO Box 35, York YO60 6WW
T 01347-879075 E enquiries@waterways-ombudsman.org
W www.waterways-ombudsman.org

The Waterways Ombudsman considers complaints of maladministration or unfairness made against British Waterways or its subsidiaries, including British Waterways Marinas Limited. Complaints concerning the waterways responsibilities of the Environment Agency should be directed to the Parliamentary and Health Service Ombudsman.
Ombudsman, Hilary Bainbridge

THE POLICE SERVICE

There are 52 police forces in the United Kingdom: 43 in England and Wales, including the Metropolitan Police and the City of London Police, eight in Scotland and the Police Service of Northern Ireland. Most forces' areas are coterminous with one or more local authority areas. The Isle of Man, Jersey and Guernsey have their own forces responsible for policing in their respective islands and bailiwicks. The Serious Organised Crime Agency (SOCA) is responsible for the investigation of national and international serious organised crime.

Police authorities are independent bodies, responsible for the supervision of local policing. There are 43 police authorities in England and Wales, plus an additional one for British Transport Police. Most police authorities have 17 members, comprising nine local councillors and eight independent members, of whom at least one must be a magistrate. Authorities which are responsible for larger areas may have more members, such as the Metropolitan Police Authority, which has 23 members: 12 drawn from the London Assembly, 10 independent members and one magistrate. The Corporation of London acts as the police authority for the City of London Police. In Scotland, six of the forces are maintained by joint police boards, made up of local councillors from each council in the force area; the other two constabularies (Dumfries & Galloway and Fife) are directly administered by their respective councils. The Northern Ireland Policing Board is an independent public body consisting of 19 political and independent members.

Police forces in England, Scotland and Wales are financed by central and local government grants and a precept on the council tax. The Police Service of Northern Ireland is wholly funded by central government. The police authorities, subject to the approval of the home secretary (in England and Wales), the Northern Ireland secretary and to regulations, are responsible for appointing the Chief Constable. In England and Wales the latter are responsible for the force's budget, levying the precept on the council tax, publishing annual policing plans and reports, setting local objectives, monitoring performance targets and appointing or dismissing senior officers. In Scotland the police authorities are responsible for setting the force's budget, providing the resources necessary to police the area adequately and appointing officers of the rank of Assistant Chief Constable and above. In Northern Ireland, the Northern Ireland Policing Board exercises similar functions.

The home secretary, the Northern Ireland secretary and the Scottish government are responsible for the organisation, administration and operation of the police service. They regulate police ranks, discipline, hours of duty and pay and allowances. All police forces are subject to inspection by HM Inspectors of Constabulary, who report to the home secretary, Scottish government or the Northern Ireland secretary.

COMPLAINTS

The Independent Police Complaints Commission (IPCC) was established under the Police Reform Act 2002 and became operational on 1 April 2004. The IPCC is responsible for carrying out independent investigations into serious incidents or allegations of misconduct by those serving with the police in England and Wales, HM Revenue and Customs, SOCA and the UK Border Agency. It has the power to initiate, undertake and oversee investigations and is also responsible for the way complaints are handled by local police forces. Complaints regarding local operational issues or quality of service should be made directly to the Chief Constable of the police force concerned or to the local police authority.

If a complaint is relatively minor, the police force will attempt to resolve it internally and an official investigation might not be required. In more serious cases the IPCC or police force may refer the case to the Crown Prosecution Service, which will decide whether to bring criminal charges against the officer(s) involved. An officer who is dismissed, required to resign or reduced in rank, whether as a result of a complaint or not, can appeal to a police appeals tribunal established by the relevant police authority.

Under the Police, Public Order and Criminal Justice (Scotland) Act 2006, which came into force on 1 April 2007, the Police Complaints Commissioner for Scotland is responsible for providing independent scrutiny of the way Scottish police forces, authorities and policing agencies handle complaints from the public. The commissioner also has the power to direct police forces to re-examine any complaints which are not considered to have been dealt with satisfactorily. If there is a suggestion of criminal activity, the complaint is investigated by a procurator fiscal.

The Police Ombudsman for Northern Ireland provides an independent police complaints system for Northern Ireland, dealing with all stages of the complaints procedure. Complaints that cannot be resolved informally are investigated and the ombudsman recommends a suitable course of action to the Chief Constable of the Police Service of Northern Ireland or the Northern Ireland Policing Board based on the investigation's findings. The ombudsman may recommend that a police officer be prosecuted, but the decision to prosecute a police officer rests with the Director of Public Prosecutions.

INDEPENDENT POLICE COMPLAINTS COMMISSION, 90 High Holborn, London WC1V 6BH
T 0845-300 2002 E enquiries@ipcc.gsi.gov.uk
W www.ipcc.gov.uk

POLICE COMPLAINTS COMMISSIONER FOR SCOTLAND, Hamilton House, Hamilton Business Park, ML3 0QA T 0808-178 5577 E enquiries@pcc-scotland.org
W www.pcc-scotland.org
Police Complaints Commissioner for Scotland, John McNeill

POLICE OMBUDSMAN FOR NORTHERN IRELAND, New Cathedral Buildings, St Anne's Square, 11 Church Street, Belfast BT1 1PG T 028-9082 8600
E info@policeombudsman.org
W www.policeombudsman.org
Police Ombudsman, Al Hutchinson

POLICE SERVICES

FORENSIC SCIENCE SERVICE

Headquarters: Trident Court, 2920 Solihull Parkway, Birmingham Business Park, Birmingham B37 7YN
T 0121-329 5200 **W** www.forensic.gov.uk

The Forensic Science Service (FSS) is a government-owned company which is independent from the police service. It provides forensic science and technology services to police forces in England and Wales and other law enforcement agencies such as the Crown Prosecution Service, SOCA, MoD Police and Guarding Agency, British Transport Police and HM Revenue and Customs. Services are also available to defence lawyers and commercial companies. The FSS primarily covers England and Wales but can provide services worldwide.
Chair, Bill Griffiths

NATIONAL EXTREMISM TACTICAL COORDINATION UNIT

PO Box 525, Huntingdon PE29 9AL
T 01480-425091 **E** mailbox@netcu.pnn.police.uk
W www.netcu.org.uk

The National Extremism Tactical Coordination Unit (NETCU) provides the police service of England and Wales and other law enforcement agencies with tactical advice and guidance on policing domestic extremism and associated criminality. The unit also supports organisations and companies that are the targets of domestic extremism campaigns. NETCU is funded by the Home Office, is accountable to the National Coordinator for Domestic Extremism and forms part of the Association of Chief Police Officers' Terrorism and Allied Matters business unit.
National Coordinator for Domestic Extremism, Anton Setchell

NATIONAL POLICING IMPROVEMENT AGENCY

4th Floor, 10–18 Victoria Street, London SW1H 0NN
T 0800-496 3322 **E** enquiries@npia.pnn.police.uk
W www.npia.police.uk

Established under the Police and Justice Act 2006 the National Policing Improvement Agency (NPIA) is a non-departmental public body sponsored and funded by the Home Office, with its executive leadership drawn from the police service.The NPIA is owned and governed by the board which comprises representatives of the Association of Chief Police Officers, the Association of Police Authorities and the Home Office, in addition to the chair, chief executive and two independent members. The board is responsible for agreeing the budget and setting the objectives for the NPIA.

The NPIA's remit is to ensure that agreed programmes of reforms are implemented and good practice is applied throughout the police service. It is responsible for the procurement and deployment of information and communications technology systems to support and improve policing and works actively with police forces to develop a wide range of learning and professional development programmes. The NPIA is charged with improving policing in England and Wales but it is also connected to policing bodies in Scotland and Northern Ireland and collaborates with them on some initiatives.
Chief Executive, Peter Neyroud, QPM
Chair, Peter Holland, CBE

NPIA MISSING PERSONS BUREAU

Foxley Hall, Bramshill, Hook, Hampshire RG27 0JW
T 01256-602979
E missingpersonsbureau@npia.pnn.police.uk
W www.missingpersons.police.uk

The NPIA Missing Persons Bureau was launched in April 2008 within the National Policing Improvement Agency. The NPIA Missing Persons Bureau acts as the centre for the exchange of information connected with the search for missing persons nationally and internationally alongside the police and other related organisations. The unit focuses on cross-matching missing persons with unidentified persons or bodies by maintaining records, including a dental index of ante-mortem chartings of long-term missing persons and post-mortem chartings from unidentified bodies. The bureau also manages the missing children website (**W** www.missingkids.co.uk) and coordinates the child rescue alert services.

Information is supplied and collected for all persons who have been missing in the UK for over three days (or fewer where police deem appropriate), foreign nationals reported missing in the UK, UK nationals reported missing abroad and all unidentified bodies and persons found within the UK.

SERIOUS ORGANISED CRIME AGENCY

PO Box 8000, London SE11 5EN **T** 0370-496 7622
W www.soca.gov.uk

The Serious Organised Crime Agency (SOCA) is an executive non-departmental public body sponsored by, but operationally independent from, the Home Office. The agency was formed in April 2006 from the amalgamation of the National Crime Squad, National Criminal Intelligence Service, the part of HM Revenue and Customs responsible for dealing with drug trafficking and associated criminal finance and the part of the UK Immigration Service responsible for dealing with organised immigration crime. In April 2008 the Assets Recovery Agency merged with SOCA.

SOCA officers can have the combined powers of police, customs and immigration officers. The organisation uses intelligence-led investigation to tackle Class A drug trafficking and organised immigration crime. Other targeted criminal activities are fraud, high-technology crime, counterfeiting, firearms, serious robbery and investigating criminal profit and finances.
Chair, Sir Stephen Lander, KCB
Director-General (interim), Trevor Pearce

POLICE FORCES

ENGLAND*			
Force	*Telephone*	*Strength*†	*Chief Constable*
Avon and Somerset	0845-456 7000	3,362	C. Port
Bedfordshire	01234-841212	1,271	Gillian Parker, QPM
Cambridgeshire	0345-456 4564	1,397	Julie Spence, OBE, QPM
Cheshire	0845-458 0000	2,142	D. Whatton, QPM
Cleveland	01642-326326	1,727	Sean Price, QPM
Cumbria	0845-330 0247	1,284	Craig Mackey, QPM
Derbyshire	0345-123 3333	2,115	M. Creedon
Devon and Cornwall	0845-277 7444	3,500	Stephen Otter, QPM
Dorset	01202-222222	1,472	M. Baker, QPM
Durham	0345-606 0365	1,549	T. Stoddart, QPM
Essex	0300-333 4444	3,664	Jim Barker-McCardle, QPM
Gloucestershire	0845-090 1234	1,365	Tony Melville
Greater Manchester	0161-872 5050	8,119	Peter Fahy, QPM
Hampshire	0845-045 4545	3,698	Alex Marshall
Hertfordshire	0845-330 0222	2,088	Frank Whiteley, QPM
Humberside	0845-606 0222	2,099	Tim Hollis, QPM
Kent	01622-690690	3,847	Michael Fuller, QPM
Lancashire	01772-614444	3,720	Stephen Finnigan, QPM
Leicestershire	0116-222 2222	2,378	Chris Eyre
Lincolnshire	01522-532222	1,209	R. Crompton
Merseyside	0151-709 6010	4,504	B. Lawson
North Yorkshire	0845-606 0247	1,481	Grahame Maxwell
Norfolk	0845-456 4567	1,666	Ian McPherson, QPM
Northamptonshire	03000-111222	1,347	Adrian Lee
Northumbria	01661-872555	4,164	M. Craik, QPM
Nottinghamshire	0115-967 0900	2,410	J. Hodson, QPM
South Yorkshire	0114-220 2020	3,124	M. Hughes, QPM
Staffordshire	0300-123 4455	2,235	Mike Cunningham
Suffolk	01473-613500	1,359	Simon Ash
Surrey	0845-125 2222	1,817	Mark Rowley
Sussex	0845-607 0999	3,288	Martin Richards
Thames Valley	0845-850 5505	4,526	Sara Thornton, QPM
Warwickshire	01926-415000	995	Keith Bristow, QPM
West Mercia	0300-333 3000	2,440	Paul West, QPM
West Midlands	0845-113 5000	8,581	C. Sims, OBE, QPM
West Yorkshire	01924-375222	5,853	Sir Norman Bettison
Wiltshire	0845-408 7000	1,217	Brian Moore, QPM
WALES			
Dyfed-Powys	0845-330 2000	1,212	Ian Arundale
Gwent	01633-838111	1,418	M. Giannasi
North Wales	0845-607 1001	1,596	M. Polin, QPM
South Wales	01656-655555	3,105	Peter Vaughan
SCOTLAND			
Central Scotland	01786-456000	817	Kevin Smith
Dumfries and Galloway	0845-600 5701	503	Patrick Shearer, QPM
Fife	0845-600 5702	1,073	Norma Graham, QPM
Grampian	0845-600 5700	1,599	Colin McKerracher, CBE, QPM
Lothian and Borders	0131-311 3131	2,839	David Strang, QPM
Northern	0845-603 3388	791	Ian Latimer
Strathclyde	0141-532 2000	8,014	Stephen House, QPM
Tayside	0300-111 2222	1,209	Justine Curran
NORTHERN IRELAND			
Police Service of NI	0845-600 8000	7,299	Matt Baggott CBE, QPM
ISLANDS			
Isle of Man	01624-631212	236	Mike Langdon, QPM
States of Jersey	01534-612612	246	Graham Power, QPM
Guernsey	01481-725111	177	G. Le Page, QPM

* For the City of London Police and the Metropolitan Police Service *see* London Forces

† Size of force as at February 2010

Source: R. Hazell & Co. *Police and Constabulary Almanac 2010*

LONDON FORCES

CITY OF LONDON POLICE

37 Wood Street, London EC2P 2NQ **T** 020-7601 2222
W www.cityoflondon.police.uk
Strength (February 2010), 823

Though small, the City of London has one of the most important financial centres in the world and the force has particular expertise in areas such as fraud investigation. The force has a wholly elected police authority, the police committee of the Corporation of London, which appoints the commissioner.
Commissioner, Mike Bowron, QPM
Assistant Commissioner, Frank Armstrong
Commander, Patrick Rice

METROPOLITAN POLICE SERVICE

New Scotland Yard, 8–10 Broadway, London SW1H 0BG
T 020-7230 1212 **W** www.met.police.uk
Strength (February 2010), 33,298
Commissioner, Sir Paul Stephenson, QPM
Deputy Commissioner, Tim Godwin, OBE, QPM

The Metropolitan Police Service is divided into four main areas for operational purposes:

TERRITORIAL POLICING
Most of the day-to-day policing of London is carried out by 33 borough operational command units; 32 command units operate within the same boundaries as the London borough councils, plus there is an additional unit which is responsible for policing Heathrow airport.
Assistant Commissioner (acting), Rose Fitzpatrick, QPM

SPECIALIST CRIME DIRECTORATE
The Specialist Crime Directorate's main areas of focus are dismantling criminal networks of all levels, from neighbourhood street gangs to sophisticated international operations, and seizing their assets; safeguarding children and young people from physical, sexual and emotional abuse; and the investigation and prevention of homicide.
Assistant Commissioner, Cressida Dick, QPM

SPECIALIST OPERATIONS
Specialist Operations is divided into three commands:

- *Counter Terrorism Command* is responsible for the prevention and disruption of terrorist activity, domestic extremism and related offences both within London and nationally, providing an explosives disposal and chemical, biological, radiological and nuclear capability within London, assisting the security services in fulfilling their roles and providing a single point of contact for international partners in counter-terrorism matters
- *Protection Command* is responsible for the protection and security of high-profile persons; key public figures, including the royal family; official delegations in the UK and overseas; and others where it is in the national interest or intelligence suggests protection is necessary. It is also responsible for protecting royal residences and embassies, providing residential protection for visiting heads of state, heads of government and foreign ministers and advising the diplomatic community on security
- *Protective Security Command* works in conjunction with authorities at the Houses of Parliament to provide security for peers, MPs, employees and visitors to the palace of Westminster. It is also responsible for policing Heathrow and London City airports

Assistant Commissioner, John Yates, QPM

CENTRAL OPERATIONS
Central Operations consists of a number of specialised units with a broad range of policing functions which provide an integrated, community-focused service to London. Central Operations also has the remit for delivering the security arrangements for the 2012 London Olympic Games.
Assistant Commissioner, Chris Allison

SPECIALIST FORCES

BRITISH TRANSPORT POLICE

25–27 Camden Road, London NW1 9LN **T** 020-7388 7541
W www.btp.police.uk
Strength (February 2010), 2,835

British Transport Police is the national police force for the railways in England, Wales and Scotland, including the London Underground system, Docklands Light Railway, Glasgow Subway, Midland Metro Tram system and Croydon Tramlink. The chief constable reports to the British Transport Police Authority. The members of the authority are appointed by the transport secretary and include representatives from the rail industry as well as independent members. Officers are paid the same as other police forces.
Chief Constable, Andrew Trotter, OBE, QPM
Deputy Chief Constable, Paul Crowther

CIVIL NUCLEAR CONSTABULARY

Building F6, Culham Science Centre, Abingdon,
Oxfordshire OX14 3DB **T** 01235-466606 **W** www.cnc.police.uk
*Strength (March 2010), c.*900

The Civil Nuclear Constabulary (CNC) operates under the strategic direction of the Department of Energy and Climate Change. The CNC is a specialised armed force that protects civil nuclear sites and nuclear materials. The constabulary is responsible for policing UK civil nuclear industry facilities and for escorting nuclear material between establishments within the UK and worldwide.
Chief Constable, Richard Thompson
Deputy Chief Constable, John Sampson

MINISTRY OF DEFENCE POLICE

Ministry of Defence Police and Guarding Agency, Wethersfield, Braintree, Essex CM7 4AZ **T** 01371-854000
W www.mod.police.uk
Strength (March 2010), 3,490

Part of the Ministry of Defence Police and Guarding Agency, the Ministry of Defence Police is a statutory civil police force with particular responsibility for the security and policing of the MoD environment. It contributes to the physical protection of property and personnel within its jurisdiction and provides a comprehensive police service to the MoD as a whole.
Chief Constable/Chief Executive, Stephen Love
Deputy Chief Constable, G. McAuley

THE SPECIAL CONSTABULARY

The Special Constabulary is a force of trained volunteers who support and work with their local police force usually for a minimum of four hours a week (the

Metropolitan Police Special Constabulary usually asks for a minimum commitment of eight hours a week). Special Constables are thoroughly grounded in the basic aspects of police work, such as self-defence, powers of arrest, common crimes and preparing evidence for court, before they can begin to carry out any police duties. Once they have completed their training, they have the same powers as a regular officer and wear a similar uniform. Information on the Special Constabulary can be found at W www.policespecials.com.

RATES OF PAY

London weighting of £2,220 per annum is awarded to all police officers working in the capital irrespective of their ranks and in addition to the salaries listed below:

BASIC RATES OF PAY *from 1 September 2010*

Chief Constables of Greater Manchester, Strathclyde and West Midlands*	£173,994–£176,943
Chief Constable*	£123,858–£165,147
Deputy Chief Constable*	£106,167–£135,660
Assistant Chief Constable and Commanders*	£88,470–£103,218
Chief Superintendent	£72,543–£76,680
Superintendent Range 2†	£69,558–£74,022
Superintendent	£60,750–£70,779
Chief Inspector‡§	£50,502 (£52,515)–£52,578 (£54,588)
Inspector‡§	£45,624 (£47,625)–£49,488 (£51,504)
Sergeant‡	£35,610–£40,020
Constable‡	£22,680–£35,610
Metropolitan Police	
Commissioner	£253,620
Deputy Commissioner	£209,382
City of London Police	
Commissioner	£156,900
Assistant Commissioner	£129,414
Police Service of Northern Ireland	
Chief Constable	£188,736
Deputy Chief Constable	£153,348

* Chief Officers may receive a bonus of at least 5 per cent of pensionable pay if their performance is deemed exceptional

† For Superintendents who were not given the rank of Chief Superintendent on its re-introduction on 1 January 2002

‡ Officers who have been on the highest available salary for one year have access to a competence-related threshold payment of £1,182 per annum

§ London salary in parentheses (applicable only to officers in the Metropolitan and City of London police forces)

STAFF ASSOCIATIONS

Police officers are not permitted to join a trade union or to take strike action. All ranks have their own staff associations.

ASSOCIATION OF CHIEF POLICE OFFICERS OF ENGLAND, WALES AND NORTHERN IRELAND, 10 Victoria Street, London SW1H 0NN T 020-7084 8950
Chief Executive, Thomas Flaherty

ENGLAND AND WALES

POLICE FEDERATION OF ENGLAND AND WALES, Federation House, Highbury Drive, Leatherhead, Surrey KT22 7UY T 01372-352000 W www.polfed.org E gensec@polfed.org
General Secretary, Ian Rennie

POLICE SUPERINTENDENTS' ASSOCIATION OF ENGLAND AND WALES, 67A Reading Road, Pangbourne, Reading RG8 7JD T 0118-984 4005 E enquiries@policesupers.com W www.policesupers.com
National Secretary, Chief Supt. Patrick Stayt

SCOTLAND

ASSOCIATION OF CHIEF POLICE OFFICERS IN SCOTLAND, 26 Holland Street, Glasgow G2 4NH T 0141-435 1230 W www.acpos.police.uk
General Secretary, Caroline Scott

ASSOCIATION OF SCOTTISH POLICE SUPERINTENDENTS, *Secretariat,* 99 Main Street, Glasgow G62 6JM T 0141-532 4022 E secretariat@scottishpolicesupers.org.uk W www.scottishpolicesupers.org.uk
General Secretary, Carol Forfar

SCOTTISH POLICE FEDERATION, 5 Woodside Place, Glasgow G3 7QF T 0141-332 5234 W www.spf.org.uk
General Secretary and Treasurer, Calum Steele

NORTHERN IRELAND

POLICE FEDERATION FOR NORTHERN IRELAND, 77–79 Garnerville Road, Belfast BT4 2NX T 028-9076 4200 E office.pfni@btconnect.com W www.policefed-ni.org.uk
Secretary, Stevie McCann

SUPERINTENDENTS' ASSOCIATION OF NORTHERN IRELAND, PSNI College, Garnerville Road, Belfast BT4 2NX T 028-9092 2201 E mail@psani.org W www.psani.org
Secretary (interim), Wesley Wilson, QPM

THE PRISON SERVICE

The prison services in the United Kingdom are the responsibility of the Secretary of State for Justice, the Scottish Government Justice Department and the Minister of Justice in Northern Ireland. The chief directors-general (chief executive in Scotland, director-general in Northern Ireland), officers of the Prison Service, the Scottish Prison Service and the Northern Ireland Prison Service are responsible for the day-to-day running of the system.

There are 140 prison establishments in England and Wales, 16 in Scotland and three in Northern Ireland. Convicted prisoners are classified according to their assessed security risk and are housed in establishments appropriate to that level of security. There are no open prisons in Northern Ireland. Female prisoners are housed in women's establishments or in separate wings of mixed prisons. Remand prisoners are, where possible, housed separately from convicted prisoners. Offenders under the age of 21 are usually detained in a Young Offender Institution, which may be a separate establishment or part of a prison. Appellant and failed asylum seekers are held in Immigration Removal Centres, or in separate units of other prisons.

Eleven prisons are now run by the private sector in England and Wales, and in England, Wales and Scotland all escort services have been contracted out to private companies. In Scotland, two prisons (Kilmarnock and Addiewell) were built and financed by the private sector and are being operated by private contractors.

There are independent prison inspectorates in England, Wales and Scotland which report annually on conditions and the treatment of prisoners. The Chief Inspector of Criminal Justice in Northern Ireland and HM Chief Inspector of Prisons for England and Wales perform an inspectorate role for prisons in Northern Ireland. Every prison establishment also has an independent monitoring board made up of local volunteers.

Any prisoner whose complaint is not satisfied by the internal complaints procedures may complain to the prisons ombudsman for England and Wales, the Scottish public services ombudsman or the prisoner ombudsman in Northern Ireland.

The 11 private sector prisons in England and Wales are the direct responsibility of the chief executive of the National Offender Management Service (NOMS). NOMS was created in January 2004, in order to integrate prisons and probation into a system whereby end-to-end management of offenders is provided; this is expected to reduce re-offending and cut the growth rate of the prison population. In May 2007 NOMS was amalgamated into the Ministry of Justice; in 2008 it was restructured with responsibilities for running HM Prison Service, overseeing the contracts of privately run prisons, managing probation performance and creating probation trusts. The prisons and probation inspectors, the prisons ombudsman and the independent monitoring boards report to the home secretary and to the Minister of Justice in Northern Ireland.

PRISON STATISTICS

PRISON POPULATION (UK)
as at April 2010
The projected 'high scenario' prison population for 2015 in England and Wales is 93,900; the 'low scenario' is 83,300.

PRISON POPULATION (UK) *as at April 2010*

	Remand	*Sentenced*	*Other*
ENGLAND AND WALES			
Male	12,015	67,607	1,136
Female	799	3,484	45
Total	12,814	79,091	1,181
SCOTLAND			
Male	1,097	6,317	18
Female	71	344	—
Total	1,168	6,661	18
N. IRELAND			
Male	437	924	3
Female	20	22	—
Total	457	946	3
UK TOTAL	14,439	86,698	1,202

Sources: Home Office; Scottish Prison Service; Northern Ireland Prison Service

PRISON CAPACITY (ENGLAND AND WALES)
as at 4 June 2010

Male prisoners	80,763
Female prisoners	4,333
Number of prisoners held in police cells under Operation Safeguard and in court cells*	0
Total	85,096
Useable operational capacity	87,849
Number under home detention curfew supervision	2,385

* No places are currently activated under Operation Safeguard

SENTENCED PRISON POPULATION BY SEX AND OFFENCE (ENGLAND AND WALES)
as at April 2010

	Male	*Female*
Violence against the person	19,509	915
Sexual offences	9,225	75
Burglary	6,706	145
Robbery	8,577	288
Theft, handling	3,317	441
Fraud and forgery	1,386	202
Drugs offences	10,094	831
Motoring offences	880	12
Other offences	6,879	472
Offence not recorded	910	90
*Total**	67,483	3,471

* Figures do not include civil (non-criminal) prisoners or fine defaulters

Source: Home Office – *Research Development Statistics*

SENTENCED POPULATION BY LENGTH OF SENTENCE (ENGLAND AND WALES)
as at April 2010

	Adults	*Young offenders*
Less than 12 months	6,294	1,601
12 months to less than 4 years	16,833	4,268
4 years to less than life	21,614	2,040
Life	12,220	698
*Total**	56,961	8,607

* Figures do not include civil (non-criminal) prisoners or fine defaulters
Source: Home Office – *Research Development Statistics*

AVERAGE DAILY SENTENCED POPULATION BY LENGTH OF SENTENCE 2009–10 (SCOTLAND)

	Adults	*Young offenders*
Less than 4 years	2,887	544
4 years or over (including life)	2,839	175
Total	5,725	719

Source: Scottish Prison Service – *Annual Report and Accounts 2009–10*

SELF-INFLICTED DEATHS IN PRISON IN 2009 (ENGLAND AND WALES)

Men	57
Women	3
Total	60
Rate per 100,000 prisoners in custody	72

Source: www.justice.gov.uk

THE PRISON SERVICES

HM PRISON SERVICE

Cleland House, Page Street, London SW1P 4LN
T 0870-000 1397 E public.enquiries@hmps.gsi.gov.uk
W www.hmprisonservice.gov.uk

HM Prison Service became part of the National Offender Management Service on 1 April 2008 as part of the reorganisation of the Ministry of Justice.

SALARIES
from 1 April 2010

Senior manager a	£64,765–£82,892
Senior manager B	£60,980–£80,458
Senior manager C	£56,920–£72,451
Senior manager D	£45,700–£61,038
Manager E	£33,335–£46,024
Manager F	£29,685–£39,041
Manager G	£25,105–£32,140

THE NATIONAL OFFENDER MANAGEMENT SERVICE BOARD
Chief Executive Officer (SCS), Michael Spurr
Director of High Security Prisons (SCS), Danny McAllister
Director of Finance and Performance (SCS), Camilla Taylor
Director of Human Resources (SCS), Robin Wilkinson
Director of Information and Communications Technology, Martin Bellamy
Director of Service Development (SCS), Ian Poree
Director of Offender Health (SCS), Richard Bradshaw
Board Secretary and Head of Secretariat (SMB), Ken Everett

DIRECTORS OF OFFENDER MANAGEMENT
Beverley Shears *(East Midlands);* Trevor Williams *(East of England);* Digby Griffith *(London);* Phil Copple *(North-East);* Caroline Marsh *(North-West);* Roger Hill *(South-East);* Colin Allars *(South-West);* Yvonne Thomas *(Wales);* Gill Mortlock *(West Midlands);* Steve Wagstaffe *(Yorkshire and Humberside)*

OPERATING COSTS OF PRISON SERVICE IN ENGLAND AND WALES 2008–9

Staff costs	£2,527,161,000
Other operating costs	£2,801,631,000
Operating income	(£384,423,000)
Net operating costs for the year	£4,944,369,000

Source: HM Prison Service – *Annual Report and Accounts 2008–9*

SCOTTISH PRISON SERVICE (SPS)

Calton House, 5 Redheughs Rigg, Edinburgh EH12 9HW
T 0131-244 8747 E gaolinfo@sps.pnn.gov.uk
W www.sps.gov.uk

SALARIES 2010–11
Senior managers in the Scottish Prison Service, including governors and deputy governors of prisons, are paid across three pay bands:

Band I	£54,386–£67,755
Band H	£43,169–£56,142
Band G	£33,993–£46,682

SPS BOARD
Chief Executive, John Ewing
Directors, Willie Pretswell *(Finance and Business Services);* Dr Andrew Fraser *(Health and Care);* Stephen Swan *(Human Resources);* Eric Murch *(Partnerships and Commissioning);* Rona Sweeney *(Prisons)*
Non-Executive Directors, Allan Burns; Harry McGuigan; Jane Martin; Susan Matheson; Bill Morton; Zoe Van Zwanenberg

OPERATING COSTS OF SCOTTISH PRISON SERVICE 2009–10

Total income	£2,210,000
Total expenditure	£273,453,000
Staff costs	£137,343,000
Running costs	£153,973,000
Other current expenditure	£29,422,000
Operating cost	£271,243,000
Cost of capital charges	£19,848,000
Interest payable and similar charges	£8,432,000
Net operating cost	£299,723,000

Source: Scottish Prison Service – *Annual Report and Accounts 2009–10*

NORTHERN IRELAND PRISON SERVICE

Dundonald House, Upper Newtownards Road, Belfast BT4 3SU
T 028-9052 2922 E info@niprisonservice.gov.uk
W www.niprisonservice.gov.uk

SALARIES 2009–10

Governor 1	£74,006–£79,750
Governor 2	£67,307–£71,465
Governor 3	£58,240–£62,143
Governor 4	£50,648–£54,857
Governor 5	£44,488–£49,896

SENIOR STAFF

Director-General, Robin Masefield, CBE

Directors, Colin McConnell *(Operations);* Mark McGuckin *(Human Resources and Organisation Development);* Max Murray *(Programmes and Development);* Graeme Wilkinson *(Finance and Corporate Services)*

OPERATING COSTS OF NORTHERN IRELAND PRISON SERVICE 2009–10

Staff costs	£90,492,000
Net running costs	£26,939,000
Depreciation	£12,693,000
Finance charges	£7,248,000
Operating expenditure	£137,372,000
Net operating costs for the year	£140,058,000

Source: Northern Ireland Prison Service – *Annual Report and Accounts 2009–10*

PRISON ESTABLISHMENTS

as at April 2010

ENGLAND AND WALES

Prison	*Address*	*Prisoners*	*Governor/Director*
ACKLINGTON	Northumberland NE65 9XF	942	Neil Evans *(acting)*
ALBANY	Isle of Wight PO30 5RS	557	Barry Greenbury
ALTCOURSE (private prison)	Liverpool L9 7LH	1,265	John McLaughlin
†‡ASHFIELD (private prison)	Bristol BS16 9QJ	229	Wendy Sinclair
ASHWELL	Leics LE15 7LF	213	Dave Harding
*‡ASKHAM GRANGE	York YO23 3FT	108	Marion Mahoney
‡AYLESBURY	Bucks HP20 1EH	440	Kevin Leggett
BEDFORD	Bedford MK40 1HG	477	Frank Flynn
BELMARSH	London SE28 0EB	873	Phil Wragg
BIRMINGHAM	Birmingham B18 4AS	1,437	James Shanley
BLANTYRE HOUSE	Kent TN17 2NH	119	Jim Carmichael
BLUNDESTON	Suffolk NR32 5BG	519	Sue Doolan
†‡BRINSFORD	Wolverhampton WV10 7PY	500	Steph Roberts-Bibby
‡BRISTOL	Bristol BS7 8PS	614	Kenny Brown
‡BRIXTON	London SW2 5XF	767	Amy Rees
*BRONZEFIELD (private prison)	Middlesex TW15 3JZ	504	Helga Swidenbank
BUCKLEY HALL	Lancs OL12 9DP	377	Mick Regan
BULLINGDON	PO Box 50, Oxon OX25 1WD	1,091	Andy Lattimore
‡BULLWOOD HALL	Essex SS5 4TE	223	Steve Bradford
BURE	Norfolk NR10 5GB	375	Paul Cawkwell
CANTERBURY	Kent CT1 1PJ	302	Chris Bartlett
†CARDIFF	Cardiff CF24 0UG	815	Richard Booty
‡CASTINGTON	Northumberland NE65 9XG	252	Paddy Fox
CHANNINGS WOOD	Devon TQ12 6DW	725	Jeannine Hendrick
‡CHELMSFORD	Essex CM2 6LQ	656	Rob Davis
COLDINGLEY	Surrey GU24 9EX	510	Glenn Knight
‡COOKHAM WOOD	Kent ME1 3LU	118	Emily Thomas
DARTMOOR	Devon PL20 6RR	584	Tony Corcoran
‡DEERBOLT	Co. Durham DL12 9BG	505	Jenny Mooney
‡DONCASTER (private prison)	Doncaster DN5 8UX	1,105	Brian Anderson
†DORCHESTER	Dorset DT1 1JD	227	Serena Watts
DOVEGATE (private prison)	Staffs ST14 8XR	1,098	Wyn Jones
§DOVER	Kent CT17 9DR	307	Andy Bell
*DOWNVIEW	Surrey SM2 5PD	334	Louise Spencer
*‡DRAKE HALL	Staffs ST21 6LQ	292	Bridie Oaks-Richards
DURHAM	Durham DH1 3HU	972	Tim Allen *(acting)*
*‡EAST SUTTON PARK	Kent ME17 3DF	86	Jim Carmichael
*‡EASTWOOD PARK	Glos GL12 8DB	311	Andrea Whitfield
EDMUNDS HILL	Suffolk CB8 9YN	366	Kevin Reilly
ELMLEY	Kent ME12 4DZ	968	Sarah Coccia
ERLESTOKE	Wilts SN10 5TU	466	Andy Rogers
EVERTHORPE	E. Yorks HU15 1RB	678	Alec McCrystal
†‡EXETER	Devon EX4 4EX	529	Mark Flinton
FEATHERSTONE	Wolverhampton WV10 7PU	650	Deborah McGivern
†‡FELTHAM	Middx TW13 4ND	671	Cathy Robinson
FORD	W. Sussex BN18 0BX	512	Sharon Williams
‡FOREST BANK (private prison)	Manchester M27 8FB	1,370	Trevor Short
*FOSTON HALL	Derby DE65 5DN	245	Grey Riley-Smith
FRANKLAND	Durham DH1 5YD	815	Dave Thompson
FULL SUTTON	York YO41 1PS	583	Steve Tilley
GARTH	Preston PR26 8NE	828	Terry Williams

Prison	*Address*	*Prisoners*	*Governor/Director*
GARTREE	Leics LE16 7RP	673	Neil Richards
†‡GLEN PARVA	Leicester LE18 4TN	757	Michael Wood
†‡GLOUCESTER	Gloucester GL1 2JN	316	Mike Bolton
GRENDON	Bucks HP18 0TL	547	Dr Peter Bennett
‡GUYS MARSH	Dorset SP7 0AH	548	Julia Killick
§HASLAR	Hampshire PO12 2AW	116	Vicky Baker
HAVERIGG	Cumbria LA18 4NA	610	Martin Farquhar
HEWELL	Worcs B97 6QS	1,380	Kieron Taylor
HIGH DOWN	Surrey SM2 5PJ	1,073	Peter Dawson
HIGHPOINT	Suffolk CB8 9YG	934	Michelle Jarman-Howe
†‡HINDLEY	Lancs WN2 5TH	330	Peter Francis
‡HOLLESLEY BAY	Suffolk IP12 3JW	338	Declan Moore
*‡HOLLOWAY	London N7 0NU	439	vacant
HOLME HOUSE	Stockton-on-Tees TS18 2QU	1,131	Matt Spencer
‡HULL	Hull HU9 5LS	1,022	Paul Foweather
‡HUNTERCOMBE	Oxon RG9 5SB	149	Nigel Atkinson
ISLE OF WIGHT	Isle of Wight PO20 5RS	1,656	Barry Greenbury
KENNET	Merseyside L31 1HX	338	Derek Harrison
KINGSTON	Portsmouth PO3 6AS	198	Ian Telfer
KIRKHAM	Lancs PR4 2RN	587	John Hewitson
KIRKLEVINGTON GRANGE	Cleveland TS15 9PA	271	Gabrielle Lee *(acting)*
LANCASTER	Lancaster LA1 1YL	239	Derek Ross
†‡LANCASTER FARMS	Lancaster LA1 3QZ	499	Steve Lawrence
LATCHMERE HOUSE	Surrey TW10 5HH	206	Phil Taylor
LEEDS	Leeds LS12 2TJ	1,156	Rob Kellet
LEICESTER	Leicester LE2 7AJ	358	Karen Head *(acting)*
‡LEWES	E. Sussex BN7 1EA	479	Robin Eldridge
LEYHILL	Glos GL12 8BT	516	Mick Bell
LINCOLN	Lincoln LN2 4BD	650	Ian Thomas
§LINDHOLME	Doncaster DN7 6EE	1,104	Bob Mullen
LITTLEHEY	Cambs PE28 0SR	940	Danny Spencer
LIVERPOOL	Liverpool L9 3DF	1,295	John Illingsworth
LONG LARTIN	Worcs WR11 8TZ	618	Simon Cartwright
*‡LOW NEWTON	Durham DH1 5YA	277	Alan Richer
LOWDHAM GRANGE (private prison)	Notts NG14 7DA	825	John Biggin
MAIDSTONE	Kent ME14 1UZ	589	Andy Hudson
MANCHESTER	Manchester M60 9AH	1,215	Richard Vince
‡MOORLAND CLOSED	Doncaster DN7 6BW	1,016	Tom Wheatley
‡MOORLAND OPEN	Doncaster DN7 6EL	1,016	Tom Wheatley
*MORTON HALL	Lincoln LN6 9PT	306	Jamie Bennett
THE MOUNT	Herts HP3 0NZ	758	Damian Evans
*‡NEW HALL	W. Yorks WF4 4XX	369	Marion Mahoney
NORTH SEA CAMP	Lincs PE22 0QX	301	Graham Batchford
‡NORTHALLERTON	N. Yorks DL6 1NW	237	Norman Griffin
‡NORWICH	Norfolk NR1 4LU	741	Paul Baker
NOTTINGHAM	Nottingham NG5 3AG	701	Peter Wright
‡ONLEY	Warks CV23 8AP	702	John O'Sullivan
†‡PARC (private prison)	Bridgend CF35 6AR	1,187	Janet Wallsgrove
‡PENTONVILLE	London N7 8TT	1,177	Gary Monaghon
*†PETERBOROUGH (private prison)	Peterborough PE3 7PD	604	Mike Conway
‡PORTLAND	Dorset DT5 1DL	467	Steve Holland
‡PRESCOED	Monmouthshire NP4 0TB	426	Steve Cross
PRESTON	Lancs PR1 5AB	792	Paul Holland
RANBY	Notts DN22 8EU	1,058	Louise Taylor
†‡READING	Berks RG1 3HY	266	Dave Rogers
RISLEY	Cheshire WA3 6BP	1,076	Andrew Dickinson *(acting)*
‡ROCHESTER	Kent ME1 3QS	712	John Wilson
RYE HILL (private prison)	Warks CV23 8SZ	644	Cathy James
*SEND	Surrey GU23 7LJ	273	Louise Spencer
SHEPTON MALLET	Somerset BA4 5LU	188	Nick Evans
‡SHREWSBURY	Shropshire SY1 2HR	310	Gerry Hendry
SPRING HILL	Bucks HP18 0TL	547	Dr Peter Bennett
STAFFORD	Stafford ST16 3AW	728	Peter Small
STANDFORD HILL	Kent ME12 4AA	429	Nigel Foote
STOCKEN	Leics LE15 7RD	833	Steve Turner
‡STOKE HEATH	Shropshire TF9 2JL	623	John Huntington

Prison	*Address*	*Prisoners*	*Governor/Director*
*‡STYAL	Cheshire SK9 4HR	449	Clive Chatterton
SUDBURY	Derbys DE6 5HW	578	Ken Kan
SWALESIDE	Kent ME12 4AX	999	Jim Bourke
†‡SWANSEA	Swansea SA1 3SR	380	Neil Lavis
‡SWINFEN HALL	Staffs WS14 9QS	610	Tom Watson
‡THORN CROSS	Cheshire WA4 4RL	280	Sue Brown
USK	Monmouthshire NP15 1XP	426	Steve Cross
THE VERNE	Dorset DT5 1EQ	583	Denise Hodder
WAKEFIELD	West Yorks WF2 9AG	737	Susan Howard
WANDSWORTH	London SW18 3HS	1,628	David Taylor
‡WARREN HILL	Suffolk IP12 3JW	148	Roger Plant
WAYLAND	Norfolk IP25 6RL	1,005	Kevin Riley
WEALSTUN	W. Yorks LS23 7AZ	520	Norma Harrington
WELLINGBOROUGH	Northants NN8 2NH	601	Peter Siddons
‡WERRINGTON	Stoke-on-Trent ST9 0DX	123	Carl Hardwick
‡WETHERBY	W. Yorks LS22 5ED	322	Will Styles
WHATTON	Nottingham NG13 9FQ	816	Lynn Saunders
WHITEMOOR	Cambs PE15 0PR	442	vacant
WINCHESTER	Winchester SO22 5DF	691	David Ward
WOLDS (private prison)	E. Yorks HU15 2JZ	383	Dave McDonnell
WOODHILL	Bucks MK4 4DA	810	Nigel Smith
WORMWOOD SCRUBS	London W12 0AE	1,225	Phil Taylor
WYMOTT	Preston PR26 8LW	1,165	Paul Norbury

SCOTLAND

Prison	*Address*	*Prisoners*	*Governor/Director*
ABERDEEN	Aberdeen AB11 8FN	229	Audrey Mooney
ADDIEWELL(private prison)	West Lothian EH55 8GA	704	Audrey Park
†BARLINNIE	Glasgow G33 2QX	1,450	Bill McKinlay
CASTLE HUNTLY	Dundee DD2 5HL	264 (with Noranside)	Jim Farish
*†‡CORNTON VALE	Stirling FK9 5NU	333	Teresa Medhurst
†DUMFRIES	Dumfries DG2 9AX	192	Martyn Bettel
†EDINBURGH	Edinburgh EH11 3LN	885	Nigel Ironside
GLENOCHIL	Tullibody FK10 3AD	665	Dan Gunn
†‡GREENOCK	Greenock PA16 9AH	268	Jim Kerr
*†INVERNESS	Inverness IV2 3HH	144	David Abernethy
†‡KILMARNOCK (private prison)	Kilmarnock KA1 5AA	549	Sandy McEwan
NORANSIDE	Angus DD8 3QY	264 (with Castle Huntly)	Jim Farish
†PERTH	Perth PH2 8AT	595	Michael Stoney
PETERHEAD	Aberdeenshire AB42 2YY	305	Mike Hebden
†‡POLMONT	Falkirk FK2 0AB	722	Derek McGill
SHOTTS	Lanarkshire ML7 4LE	538	Malcolm McLennan

NORTHERN IRELAND

Prison	*Address*	*Prisoners*	*Governor/Director*
*†‡HYDEBANK WOOD	Belfast BT8 8NA	204	Gary Alcock *(acting)*
†§MAGHABERRY	Co. Antrim BT28 2NF	743	Pat Maguire
MAGILLIGAN	Co. Londonderry BT49 0LR	459	Tom Woods

PRISON ESTABLISHMENTS KEY

* Women's establishment or establishment with units for women
† Remand Centre or establishment with units for remand prisoners
‡ Young Offender Institution or establishment with units for young offenders
§ Immigration Removal Centre or establishment with units for immigration detainees

DEFENCE

The armed forces of the United Kingdom comprise the Royal Navy, the Army and the Royal Air Force (RAF). The Queen is Commander-in-Chief of all the armed forces. The Secretary of State for Defence is responsible for the formulation and content of defence policy and for providing the means by which it is conducted. The formal legal basis for the conduct of defence in the UK rests on a range of powers vested by statute and letters patent in the Defence Council, chaired by the Secretary of State for Defence. Beneath the ministers lies the top management of the Ministry of Defence (MoD), headed jointly by the Permanent Secretary and the Chief of Defence Staff. The Permanent Secretary is the government's principal civilian adviser on defence and has the primary responsibility for policy, finance, management and administration. He is also personally accountable to parliament for the expenditure of all public money allocated to defence purposes. The Chief of the Defence Staff is the professional head of the armed forces in the UK and the principal military adviser to the secretary of state and the government.

The Defence Board is the executive of the Defence Council. Chaired by the Permanent Secretary, it acts as the main executive board of the Ministry of Defence, providing senior level leadership and strategic management of defence.

The Central Staff, headed by the Vice-Chief of the Defence Staff and the Second Permanent Under-Secretary of State, is the policy core of the department. Defence Equipment and Support, headed by the Chief of Defence Materiel, is responsible for purchasing defence equipment and providing logistical support to the armed forces.

A permanent Joint Headquarters for the conduct of joint operations was set up at Northwood in 1996. The Joint Headquarters connects the policy and strategic functions of the MoD head office with the conduct of operations and is intended to strengthen the policy/executive division.

The UK pursues its defence and security policies through its membership of NATO (to which most of its armed forces are committed), the European Union, the Organisation for Security and Cooperation in Europe and the UN (*see* International Organisations section).

STRENGTH OF THE ARMED FORCES

	Royal Navy	*Army*	*RAF*	*All Services*
1975 strength	76,200	167,100	95,000	338,300
1990 strength	63,210	152,810	89,680	305,700
2001 strength	42,420	109,530	53,700	205,650
2002 strength	41,630	110,050	53,000	204,680
2003 strength	41,550	112,130	53,240	206,920
2004 strength	40,880	112,750	53,390	207,020
2005 strength	39,940	109,290	51,870	201,100
2006 strength	39,390	107,730	48,730	195,850
2007 strength	38,860	106,170*	45,370	190,400*
2008 strength	38,570*	105,090*	43,390*	187,060*
2009 strength	38,340*	106,460*	43,570*	188,370*
2010 strength	38,370*	108,870*	44,050*	191,660*

* Provisional figures

Source: MoD Defence Analytical Services Agency *National Statistics* (Crown copyright)

SERVICE PERSONNEL BY RANK AND GENDER*

	Officers		*Other ranks*	
	Males	*Females*	*Males*	*Females*
All services	28,040	3,890	145,300	14,430
Royal Navy	6,740	720	28,280	2,990
Army	12,980	1,660	87,320	6,910
RAF	8,310	1,510	29,690	4,540

* Provisional figures

Source: MoD Defence Analytical Services Agency *National Statistics* (Crown copyright)

UK regular forces include trained and untrained personnel and nursing services, but exclude Gurkhas, full-time reserve service personnel, mobilised reservists and naval activated reservists. As at 1 April 2010 these groups provisionally numbered:

All Gurkhas	3,840
Full-time reserve service	2,280
Mobilised reservists	
Army	1,420
RAF	120
Naval activated reservists	150

Source: MoD Defence Analytical Services Agency *National Statistics* (Crown copyright)

CIVILIAN PERSONNEL

1993 level	159,600
2000 level	121,300
2001 level	118,200
2002 level	110,100
2003 level	107,600
2004 level	108,990
2005 level	107,680
2006 level	102,970
2007 level	95,790
2008 level	88,690
2009 level	85,730
2010 level	85,180

Source: MoD Defence Analytical Services Agency *National Statistics* (Crown copyright)

UK REGULAR FORCES: DEATHS

In 2009 there were a total of 205 deaths among the UK regular armed forces, of which 23 were serving in the Royal Navy and Royal Marines, 158 in the Army and 24 in the RAF. The largest single cause of death was as a result of hostile action (killed in action and died of wounds), which accounted for 107 deaths (53 per cent of the total) in 2009. Land transport accidents accounted for 28 deaths (14 per cent) and other accidents accounted for a further 15 deaths (7 per cent). Suicides accounted for eight deaths or 4 per cent of the total.

NUMBER OF DEATHS AND MORTALITY RATES

	2002	2005	2007	2008	2009
Total number	147	160	204	137	205
Royal Navy	26	27	27	40	23
Army	94	93	145	79	158
RAF	27	40	32	18	24
Mortality rates per thousand					
Tri-service rate	0.74	0.81	1.06	0.72	1.06
Navy	0.72	0.70	0.71	1.09	0.55
Army	0.85	0.86	1.29	0.72	1.34
RAF	0.53	0.72	0.70	0.34	0.51

Source: MoD Defence Analytical Services Agency *National Statistics* (Crown copyright)

NUCLEAR FORCES

The Vanguard Class SSBN (ship submersible ballistic nuclear) provides the UK's strategic nuclear deterrent. Each Vanguard Class submarine is capable of carrying 16 Trident D5 missiles equipped with nuclear warheads.

There is a ballistic missile early warning system station at RAF Fylingdales in North Yorkshire.

ARMS CONTROL

The 1990 Conventional Armed Forces in Europe (CFE) Treaty, which commits all NATO and former Warsaw Pact members to limiting their holdings of five major classes of conventional weapons, has been adapted to reflect the changed geo-strategic environment and negotiations continue for its implementation. The Open Skies Treaty, which the UK signed in 1992 and entered into force in 2002, allows for the overflight of states parties by other states parties using unarmed observation aircraft.

The UN Convention on Certain Conventional Weapons (as amended 2001), which bans or restricts the use of specific types of weapons that are considered to cause unnecessary or unjustifiable suffering to combatants, or to affect civilians indiscriminately, was ratified by the UK in 1995. In 1968 the UK signed and ratified the Nuclear Non-Proliferation Treaty, which came into force in 1970 and was indefinitely and unconditionally extended in 1995. In 1996 the UK signed the Comprehensive Nuclear Test Ban Treaty and ratified it in 1998. The UK is a party to the 1972 Biological and Toxin Weapons Convention, which provides for a worldwide ban on biological weapons, and the 1993 Chemical Weapons Convention, which came into force in 1997 and provides for a verifiable worldwide ban on chemical weapons.

DEFENCE BUDGET DEPARTMENTAL EXPENDITURE LIMITS (DEL) *(£ billion)*

	Resource budget	*Capital budget*	*Total DEL*
2008–9 (outturn)	32.6	9.0	41.6
2009–10 (estimate)	35.2	9.2	44.4
2010–11 (projection)	36.0	10.1	46.1

Source: HM Treasury – *Budget 2010* (Crown copyright)

MINISTRY OF DEFENCE

Main Building, Whitehall, London SW1A 2HB
T 020-7218 9000 W www.mod.uk

Secretary of State for Defence, Rt. Hon. Liam Fox, MP
Private Secretary, Will Jessett
Special Advisers, Luke Coffey; Ollie Waghorn
Parliamentary Private Secretary, vacant
Minister of State, Nick Harvey, MP *(Armed Forces)*
Private Secretary, Hannah Lim
Parliamentary Private Secretary, vacant
Parliamentary Under-Secretary of State, Gerald Howarth, MP *(International Security Strategy)*
Private Secretary, Mark Selfridge
Parliamentary Under-Secretary of State, Andrew Robathan, MP *(Defence Personnel, Welfare and Veterans)*
Private Secretary, Alan Nisbett
Parliamentary Under-Secretary of State, Peter Luff, MP *(Defence Equipment, Support and Technology)*
Private Secretary, Dr Glenn Kelly
Parliamentary Under-Secretary of State for Defence and Lords Spokesman on Defence, Lord Astor
Private Secretary, vacant

CHIEFS OF STAFF

Chief of the Defence Staff, Gen. Sir David Richards, KCB, CBE, DSO, ADC
Vice Chief of the Defence Staff, Gen. Sir Nick Houghton, KCB, CBE
Chief of the Naval Staff and First Sea Lord, Adm. Sir Mark Stanhope, GCB, OBE, ADC
Assistant Chief of the Naval Staff, Rear-Adm. Philip Jones
Chief of the General Staff, Gen. Sir Peter Wall, KCB, CBE, ADC
Assistant Chief of the General Staff, Maj.-Gen. Richard Barrons, CBE
Chief of the Air Staff, Air Chief Marshal Sir Stephen Dalton, KCB, ADC
Assistant Chief of the Air Staff, Air Vice-Marshal Barry North, OBE

SENIOR OFFICIALS

Permanent Under-Secretary of State, vacant
Second Permanent Under-Secretary of State, Ursula Brennan
Chief of Defence Materiel, Gen. Sir Kevin O'Donoghue, KCB, CBE
Chief Scientific Adviser, Prof. Mark Welland, FRS, FRENG
Director-General Finance, Jon Thompson

THE DEFENCE COUNCIL

The Defence Council is the senior committee of the MoD, and was established by royal prerogative under letters patent in April 1964. The letters patent confer on the Defence Council the command over all of the armed forces and charge the council with such matters relating to the administration of the armed forces as the Secretary of State for Defence should direct them to execute. It is chaired by the Secretary of State for Defence and consists of the Secretary of State for Defence, the Minister of State for the Armed Forces, the Minister of State for International Security Strategy, the Minister of State for Defence Personnel, Welfare and Veterans, the Minister of State for Defence Equipment, Support and Technology, the Parliamentary Under-Secretary of State for Defence and Lords Spokesman on Defence, the Chief of Defence Staff, the Permanent Under-Secretary of State, the Chief of the Naval Staff and First Sea Lord, the Chief of the General Staff, the Chief of the Air Staff, the Vice-Chief of the Defence Staff, the Chief of Defence Materiel, the Chief Scientific Adviser, the Second Permanent Under-Secretary of State and the Director-General Finance.

CENTRAL STAFF

Vice-Chief of the Defence Staff, Gen. Sir Nick Houghton, KCB, CBE
Second Permanent Under-Secretary of State, Ursula Brennan

PERMANENT JOINT HQ
Chief of Joint Operations, Air Vice-Marshal Sir Stuart Peach, KCB, CBE
Chief of Staff (Operations), Rear-Adm. George Zambellas, DSC
Chief of Staff (Joint Warfare Development), Maj.-Gen. R. Porter, MBE

FLEET COMMAND
Commander-in-Chief Fleet, Adm. Sir Trevor Soar, KCB, OBE
Deputy Commander-in-Chief Fleet, Vice-Adm. Richard Ibbotson, CB, DSC

NAVAL HOME COMMAND
Second Sea Lord and Commander-in-Chief Naval Home Command, Adm. Alan Massey, CBE, ADC
Chief of Staff to Second Sea Lord and Commander-in-Chief Naval Home Command, Rear-Adm. David Steel, CBE

LAND FORCES
Commander-in-Chief Land Forces, Gen. Sir Nick Parker, KCB, CBE
Chief of Staff Land Forces, Maj.-Gen. Mark Poffley, OBE

AIR COMMAND
Commander-in-Chief Air Command, Air Chief Marshal Simon Bryant, CBE
Deputy Commander-in-Chief Operations, Air Marshal Iain McNicoll, CB, CBE
Deputy Commander-in-Chief Personnel, vacant

DEFENCE EQUIPMENT AND SUPPORT
Chief of Defence Materiel, Gen. Sir Kevin O'Donoghue, KCB, CBE
Chief Operating Officer, Dr Andrew Tyler
Chief of Corporate Services, Trevor Woolley
Chief of Materiel (Fleet), Vice-Adm. Andy Matthews, OBE
Chief of Materiel (Land), Lt.-Gen. Gary Coward, CB, OBE
Chief of Materiel (Air), Air Marshal Kevin Leeson, CBE

EXECUTIVE AGENCIES

DEFENCE SCIENCE AND TECHNOLOGY LABORATORY
Porton Down, Salisbury, Wiltshire SP4 0JQ **T** 01980-613121
E centralenquiries@dstl.gov.uk **W** www.dstl.gov.uk
Chief Executive, Dr Frances Saunders

DEFENCE SUPPORT GROUP
Building 203, Monxton Road, Andover, Hampshire SP11 8HT
T 01264-383295 **E** info@dsg.mod.uk **W** www.dsg.mod.uk
Chief Executive, Archie Hughes

DEFENCE VETTING AGENCY
Building 107, Imphal Barracks, Fulford Road, York YO10 4AS
T 01904–662644 **E** dvacustomersupport@land.mod.uk
Chief Executive, Jacky Ridley

MET OFFICE
Fitzroy Road, Exeter, Devon EX1 3PB **T** 0870-900 0100
E enquiries@metoffice.gov.uk **W** www.metoffice.gov.uk
Chief Executive, John Hirst

MINISTRY OF DEFENCE POLICE AND GUARDING AGENCY
Weathersfield, Braintree, Essex CM7 4AZ **T** 01371-854751
E corpcomms@mdpga.mod.uk
Chief Constable, Stephen Love

PEOPLE, PAY AND PENSIONS AGENCY
J Block Foxhill, Combe Down, Bath BA1 5AB **T** 0800-345 7772
E peopleservices@pppa.mod.uk
Chief Executive, Mark Hutchinson

SERVICE CHILDREN'S EDUCATION
HQ SCE, Wegberg Military Complex, BFPO 40 **T** (+49) (2161) 908 2294 **E** info@sceschools.com **W** www.sceschools.com
Chief Executive, Linda Fisher

SERVICE PERSONNEL AND VETERANS AGENCY (SPVA)
Norcross, Blackpool FY5 3WP **T** 0800-169 2277 (veterans' enquiries) **E** veterans.help@spva.gsi.gov.uk
W www.veterans-uk.info
Chief Executive, Kathy Barnes

UK HYDROGRAPHIC OFFICE
Admiralty Way, Taunton, Somerset TA1 2DN **T** 01823-337900
E customerservices@ukho.gov.uk **W** www.ukho.gov.uk
Chief Executive, Mike Robinson

ARMED FORCES TRAINING AND RECRUITMENT

In April 2006 the MoD removed agency status from the three armed forces training agencies which now function as an integral part of their respective service.

Flag Officer Sea Training (FOST) is responsible for all Royal Navy and Royal Fleet Auxiliary training. FOST's International Defence Training provides the focal point for all aspects of naval training. Training is divided into five streams: Naval Core Training (responsible for new entry, command, leadership and management training); Royal Marine; Submarine; Surface and Aviation.

The Army Recruiting and Training Division (ARTD) is responsible for the four key areas of army training: soldier initial training, at the School of Infantry or at one of the army's four other facilities; officer initial training at the Royal Military Academy Sandhurst; trade training at one of the army's specialist facilities; and resettlement training for those about to leave the army. Trade training facilities include: the Armour Centre; the Defence College of Logistics and Personnel Administration; the Royal School of Artillery; the Royal School of Military Engineering and the School of Army Aviation.

The Royal Air Force No. 22 (Training) Group exists to recruit RAF personnel and provide trained specialist personnel to the armed forces as a whole, such as providing the army air corps with trained helicopter pilots. The group is split into eight areas: RAF College Cranwell and Inspectorate of Recruiting; the Directorate of Flying Training (DFT); the Directorate of Joint Technical Training (DJTT); the Air Cadet Organisation (ACO); Core Headquarters; the Defence College of Aeronautical Engineering (DCAE); the Defence College of Communications and Information Systems (DCCIS) and the Defence College of Electro-Mechanical Engineering (DCEME).

USEFUL WEBSITES
W www.royalnavy.mod.uk
W www.army.mod.uk
W www.raf.mod.uk

THE ROYAL NAVY

In Order of Seniority

LORD HIGH ADMIRAL OF THE UNITED KINGDOM
HM The Queen

ADMIRALS OF THE FLEET
HRH The Prince Philip, Duke of Edinburgh, KG, KT, OM, GBE, AC, QSO, PC, *apptd* 1953
Sir Edward Ashmore, GCB, DSC, *apptd* 1977
Sir Henry Leach, GCB, *apptd* 1982
Sir Julian Oswald, GCB, *apptd* 1993
Sir Benjamin Bathurst, GCB, *apptd* 1995

ADMIRALS
(Former Chiefs or Vice Chiefs of Defence Staff and First Sea Lords who remain on the active list)
Slater, Sir Jock, GCB, LVO, *apptd* 1991
Boyce, Lord, GCB, OBE, *apptd* 1995
Abbott, Sir Peter, GBE, KCB, *apptd* 1995
Essenhigh, Sir Nigel, GCB, *apptd* 1998
West of Spithead, Lord, GCB, DSC, PC, *apptd* 2000
Band, Sir Jonathon, GCB, *apptd* 2002

ADMIRALS
HRH The Prince of Wales, KG, KT, GCB, OM, AK, QSO, PC, ADC
Stanhope, Sir Mark, KCB, OBE, ADC *(First Sea Lord and Chief of Naval Staff)*
Soar, Sir Trevor, KCB, OBE *(Commander-in-Chief Fleet)*

VICE-ADMIRALS
HRH The Princess Royal, KG, KT, GCVO, QSO *(Chief Commandant for Women in the Royal Navy)*
Ibbotson, Richard, CB, DSC *(Deputy Commander-in-Chief Fleet, Chief of Staff Navy Command HQ and Chief Naval Warfare Officer)*
Lambert, Paul, CB *(Deputy Chief of Defence Staff (Capability))*
Matthews, Andrew, CB *(Chief of Materiel (Fleet) and Chief of Fleet Support to the Navy Board)*
Cooling, Robert *(Chief of Staff to the Supreme Allied Commander Transformation)*
Montgomery, Charles, CBE, ADC *(Second Sea Lord and Commander-in-Chief Naval Home Command)*

REAR-ADMIRALS
HRH The Duke of York, KG, KCVO, ADC
Zambellas, George, DSC *(Chief of Staff (Operations), Permanent Joint HQ)*
Hussain, Amjad *(Director (Precision Attack) and Controller of the Navy)*
Johnstone-Burt, (Charles) Anthony, OBE *(Cdr Joint Helicopter Command)*
Snow, Christopher *(Flag Officer Sea Training and Rear-Adm. Surface Ships (Head of Fighting Arm))*
Love, Robert, OBE *(Director Ships and Chief Naval Engineering Officer)*
Richards, Alan *(Assistant Chief of Defence Staff (Strategy and Plans))*
Charlier, Simon *(Military Aviation Authority Operational Director)*
Jones, Philip *(Assistant Chief of Naval Staff)*
Lister, Simon, OBE *(Director Submarines)*
Alabaster, Martin *(Flag Officer Scotland, Northern England and Northern Ireland and Flag Officer Reserve Forces)*
Lloyd, Stephen *(Chief Strategic Systems Executive)*
Anderson, Mark *(Cdr (Operations) and Rear-Adm. Submarines (Head of Fighting Arm))*
Corder, Ian *(Deputy Cdr Striking Force NATO)*
Williams, Simon, OBE *(Senior Directing Staff (Navy), Royal College of Defence Studies)*
Hudson, Peter, CBE *(Cdr UK Maritime Forces)*
Williams, Bruce, CBE *(Chief of Staff to the Maritime Component Command Naples and Senior Naval Representative Naples)*
Cunningham, Thomas *(Chief of Staff (Aviation) and Rear-Adm. Fleet Air Arm (Head of Fighting Arm))*
Rymer, Alan *(Director Training, Education and Skills)*
Steel, David, CBE *(Naval Secretary and Chief of Staff (Personnel) and Chief Naval Logistics Officer)*
Lambert, Nicholas *(National Hydrographer and Deputy Chief Executive (Hydrography))*

MEDICAL
Raffaelli, Philip, QHP, FRCP *(Surgeon Vice-Adm., Surgeon General)*
Jarvis, Lionel, QHS *(Surgeon Rear-Adm. Assistant Chief of Defence Staff (Health) and Chief Naval Medical Officer)*

ROYAL MARINES

CAPTAIN-GENERAL
HRH The Prince Philip, Duke of Edinburgh, KG, KT, OM, GBE, AC, QSO, PC

MAJOR-GENERALS
Robison, Garry, CB *(Chief of Staff (Capability))*
Thomas, Jeremy, DSO *(Assistant Chief of Defence Staff (Intelligence Capability))*
Salmon, Andrew, OBE *(Deputy Chief of Staff Force Readiness)*
Capewell, David, OBE *(Assistant Chief of Defence Staff (Operations))*
Mason, Jeffrey, MBE *(Assistant Chief of Defence Staff (Logistic Operations))*
Messenger, Gordon, DSO, OBE *(Chief of Defence Staff Strategic Communications Officer)*
Howes, F. H., OBE *(Cdr UK Amphibious Forces and Commandant General Royal Marines)*

The Royal Marines were formed in 1664 and are part of the Naval Service. Their primary purpose is to conduct amphibious and land warfare. The principal operational units are:

- Three Commando Brigade, an amphibious all-arms brigade trained to operate in arduous environments (a core element of the UK's Joint Rapid Reaction Force). The commando units each have a strength of around 700 and are based in Taunton (40 Commando), Plymouth (42 Commando) and Arbroath (45 Commando)
- Fleet Protection Group, responsible for a wide range of tasks worldwide in support of the Royal Navy. The group is over 500 strong and is based at HM Naval Base Clyde on the west coast of Scotland
- Assault Group, which has its headquarters located in Devonport, Plymouth is responsible for ten landing craft training squadron at Poole, Dorset and 11 amphibious trials and training squadron at Instow, Devon

The Royal Marines also provide detachments for warships and land-based naval parties as required.

ROYAL MARINES RESERVES (RMR)

The Royal Marines Reserve is a commando-trained volunteer force with the principal role, when mobilised, of supporting the Royal Marines. The RMR consists of approximately 600 trained ranks who are distributed between the five RMR centres in the UK. Approximately 10 per cent of the RMR are working with the regular corps on long-term attachments within all of the Royal Marines regular units.

OTHER PARTS OF THE NAVAL SERVICE

FLEET AIR ARM

The Fleet Air Arm (FAA) provides the Royal Navy with a multi-role aviation combat capability able to operate autonomously at short notice worldwide in all environments, over the sea and land. The FAA numbers some 6,200 people, which comprises 11.5 per cent of the total Royal Naval strength. It operates some 200 combat aircraft and more than 50 support/training aircraft.

ROYAL FLEET AUXILIARY SERVICE (RFA)

The Royal Fleet Auxiliary Service is a civilian-manned flotilla of 16 ships. Its primary role is to supply the Royal Navy and host nations while at sea with fuel, ammunition, food and spares, enabling them to maintain operations away from their home ports. It also provides amphibious support and secure sea transport for military units and their equipment. The ships routinely support and embark Royal Naval Air Squadrons.

ROYAL NAVAL RESERVE (RNR)

The Royal Naval Reserve is an integral part of the Naval Service. It is a part-time force of 2,300 trained men and women who are deployed with the Royal Navy in times of tension, humanitarian crisis or conflict.

The Royal Naval Reserve has 22 units throughout the UK; 19 of these provide initial training while three other specialist units provide intelligence and aviation training. Basic training is provided at HMS Raleigh, Torpoint in Cornwall for ratings and at the Britannia Royal Naval College, Dartmouth in Devon for officers; both these and most other RNR courses are of two weeks' duration or less.

QUEEN ALEXANDRA'S ROYAL NAVAL NURSING SERVICE

The first nursing sisters were appointed to naval hospitals in 1884 and the Queen Alexandra's Royal Naval Nursing Service (QARNNS) gained its current title in 1902. Nursing ratings were introduced in 1960 and men were integrated into the service in 1982; QARNNS recruits qualified nurses as both officers and ratings, and student nurse training can be undertaken in the service.

Patron, HRH Princess Alexandra, the Hon. Lady Ogilvy, KG, GCVO

Director of Naval Nursing Services and Matron-in-Chief, Capt. H. Allkins, QARNNS

HM FLEET

as at 1 June 2010

Submarines	
Vanguard Class	Vanguard, Vengeance, Victorious, Vigilant
Swiftsure Class	Sceptre
Trafalgar Class	Talent, Tireless, Torbay, Trafalgar, Trenchant, Triumph, Turbulent
Aircraft Carriers	Ark Royal, Illustrious, Invincible*
Amphibious Assault Ships	Ocean, Albion, Bulwark
Destroyers	
Type 42 Batch 2	Liverpool
Type 42 Batch 3	Edinburgh, Gloucester, Manchester, York
Type 45	Daring†
Frigates	
Type 22	Campbeltown, Chatham, Cornwall, Cumberland
Type 23	Argyll, Iron Duke, Kent, Lancaster, Monmouth, Montrose, Northumberland, Portland, Richmond, St Albans, Somerset, Sutherland, Westminster
Minehunters	
Hunt Class	Atherstone, Brocklesby, Cattistock, Chiddingfold, Hurworth, Ledbury, Middleton, Quorn
Sandown Class	Bangor, Blyth, Grimsby, Pembroke, Penzance, Ramsey, Shoreham, Walney‡
Patrol Class	
Archer Class P2000 Training Boats	Archer, Biter, Blazer, Charger, Dasher, Example, Exploit, Explorer, Express, Puncher, Pursuer, Raider, Ranger, Smiter, Tracker, Trumpeter
Gibraltar Squadron 16m Fast Patrol Class	Sabre, Scimitar
River Class Patrol Vessels	Mersey, Severn, Tyne, Clyde
Survey Vessels	
Ice Patrol Ship	Endurance
Ocean Survey Vessel	Scott
Coastal Survey Vessel	Gleaner
Multi-Role Survey Vessels	Echo, Enterprise

* HMS Invincible is being held at very low readiness and is due to be withdrawn from service by the end of 2010

† HMS Daring is due to enter full service by the end of 2010

‡ HMS Walney is due to be withdrawn from service by the end of 2010

ROYAL FLEET AUXILIARY

Landing Ship Dock (Auxiliary)	RFA Cardigan Bay, RFA Mounts Bay, RFA Largs Bay, RFA Lyme Bay
Wave Class	RFA Wave Knight, RFA Wave Ruler
Rover Class	RFA Black Rover, RFA Gold Rover
Leaf Class	RFA Orangeleaf, RFA Bayleaf
Fort Class	RFA Fort Austin, RFA Fort George, RFA Fort Rosalie, RFA Fort Victoria
Forward Repair Ship	RFA Diligence
Joint Casualty Treatment Ship/Maritime Afloat Training Capability	RFA Argus

THE ARMY

*In Order of Seniority**

THE QUEEN

FIELD MARSHALS

HRH The Prince Philip, Duke of Edinburgh, KG, KT, OM, GBE, AC, QSO, PC, *apptd* 1953
Lord Bramall, KG, GCB, OBE, MC, *apptd* 1982
Lord Vincent of Coleshill, GBE, KCB, DSO, *apptd* 1991
Sir John Chapple, GCB, CBE, *apptd* 1992
HRH The Duke of Kent, KG, GCMG, GCVO, ADC, *apptd* 1993
Lord Inge, KG, GCB *apptd* 1994

FORMER CHIEFS OF STAFF

Gen. Lord Guthrie of Craigiebank, GCB, LVO, OBE, *apptd* 1994
Gen. Sir Roger Wheeler, GCB, CBE, *apptd* 1997
Gen. Lord Walker of Aldringham, GCB, CMG, CBE, *apptd* 2000
Gen. Sir Mike Jackson, GCB, CBE, DSO, *apptd* 2003
Gen. Sir Timothy Granville-Chapman, GBE, KCB, *apptd* 2005
Gen. Sir Richard Dannatt, GCB, CBE, MC, *apptd* 2006

GENERALS

O'Donoghue, Sir Kevin, KCB, CBE *(Chief of Defence Materiel, Defence Equipment and Support and Master General of Logistics)*
HRH The Prince of Wales, KG, KT, GCB, OM, AK, QSO, PC, ADC
McColl, Sir John, KCB, CBE, DSO *(Deputy Supreme Allied Cdr Europe)*
Richards, Sir David, KCB, CBE, DSO, ADC *(Chief of the Defence Staff)*
Houghton, Sir Nicholas, KCB, CBE *(Vice Chief of Defence Staff)*
Wall, Sir Peter, KCB, CBE *(Chief of the General Staff)*
Parker, Sir Nick, KCB, CBE *(Commander-in-Chief Land Forces)*

LIEUTENANT-GENERALS

Applegate, R., CB, OBE *(Defence Career Partner)*
Baxter, R., CBE *(Deputy Chief of the Defence Staff (Health))*
Rollo, Sir W., KCB, CBE *(Deputy Chief of the Defence Staff (Personnel))*
Shirreff, Sir A., KCB, CBE *(Cdr Allied Rapid Reaction Corps)*
Graham, A., CBE *(Director Defence Academy)*
Bill, D., CB *(UK Military Representative to NATO and the European Union)*
Brown, C., CBE *(Iraq Compendium Study Team Leader)*
Mayall, S., CB *(Deputy Chief of Defence Staff (Operations))*
White-Spunner, B., CBE *(Cdr Field Army)*
Coward, G., CB, OBE *(Chief of Materiel (Land), Defence Equipment and Support and Quartermaster General)*
Mans, M., CBE *(Adjutant-General)*

MAJOR-GENERALS

Howell, D., CB, OBE
Whitley, A., CMG, CBE *(Senior British Loan Service Officer, Oman)*
Wilson, C., CB, CBE *(Strategy Director Thales Land Defence)*
Newton, P., CBE *(Cdr Force Development and Training, HQ Land Forces)*
Gregory, A., CB *(Deputy Adjutant-General and Director-General Service Conditions (Army))*
Melvin, R., OBE *(Senior Army Member, Royal College of Defence Studies)*
Bucknall, J., CBE *(Deputy Cdr ISAF Afghanistan)*
Binns, G., CBE, DSO, MC
von Bertele, M., OBE, QHP *(Director-General Army Medical Services)*
Macklin, A. *(Armoured Fighting Vehicles Group Leader, Defence Equipment and Support)*
Berragan, G. *(Director-General Army Recruiting and Training)*
Shaw, J., CBE *(Assistant Chief of Defence Staff (International Security Policy))*
Lalor, S., CB, TD
Sykes, R. *(Defence Services Secretary)*
Page, J., CB, OBE *(MoD)*
Moore, W., CBE *(Director Battlespace Manoeuvre and Master General of the Ordnance)*
Cubitt, W., CBE *(GOC London District and Maj.-Gen. Commanding The Household Division)*
Rutherford-Jones, D., CB *(Military Secretary)*
Rutledge, M., OBE *(GOC 5th Division)*
Brealey, B., *(GOC Theatre Troops)*
Bradshaw, A., CB, OBE *(GOC 1st (UK) Armoured Division)*
Inshaw, T., *(Director Information Systems and Services, Defence Equipment and Support)*
Kennett, A., CBE *(Director-General Land Warfare)*
Caplin, N. *(GOC UK Support Command, Germany)*
Robbins, Ven. S., QHC *(Chaplain-General to HM Land Forces)*
Barrons, R., CBE *(Assistant Chief of the General Staff)*
Dale, I., CBE *(Director Land Equipment, Defence Equipment and Support)*
Porter, R., MBE *(Chief of Staff (Joint Warfare Development), Permanent Joint HQ, UK)*
Gordon, J., CBE *(Cdr British Forces Cyprus and Administrator of the Sovereign Base Areas of Akrotiri and Dhekelia)*
Deverell, C., MBE *(Director-General Logistics, Support and Equipment)*
Kirkland, R., CBE *(GOC 4th Division)*
Carter, N., CBE *(GOC 6th (UK) Division)*
Poffley, M., OBE *(Chief of Staff HQ Land Forces)*
Andrews, S., CBE *(Director Strategy, Defence Medical Services)*
Foster, A., MBE *(Deputy Force Cdr UN Mission, D. R. Congo)*
Everard, J., CBE *(GOC 3rd (UK) Division)*
Marriot, P., CBE *(Commandant Royal Military Academy Sandhurst)*
Beckett, T. *(Deputy Cdr NATO Rapid Redeployment Corps, Italy)*
Chapman, C. *(Senior British Military Advisor, US Central Command)*
Conway, M. *(Director-General Army Legal Services)*
Copeland, I. *(Director Joint Support Chain, Defence Equipment and Support)*
Evans, T. *(Chief of Staff HQ Allied Rapid Reaction Corps and ISAF Joint Command HQ, Afghanistan)*
Howes, F. *(Cdr, UK Amphibious Forces and Commandant General, Royal Marines)*

Jones, P. *(Director Force Reintegration, HQ ISAF, Afghanistan)*
Messenger, G. *(Chief of Staff (Operations), Permanent Joint HQ)*
Shaw, D. *(Cdr 2nd Division and Governor, Edinburgh Castle)*
Smith, G. *(Assistant Chief of the Defence Staff (Reserves and Cadets))*

* Owing to a lack of resources in the army disclosures branch, the army were unable to provide a list of senior army appointments for 2010. Some job descriptions may no longer be current and new appointments are not listed in order of seniority

CONSTITUTION OF THE ARMY

The army consists of the Regular Army, the Regular Reserve and the Territorial Army (TA). It is commanded by the Chief of the General Staff, who is the professional Head of Service and Chair of the Executive Committee of the Army Board, which provides overall strategic policy and direction to the Commander-in-Chief Land Forces. There are four subordinate commands that report to the Commander-in-Chief Land Forces: the Field Army; Personnel and Support Command, headed by the Adjutant-General; Force Development and Training Command and the Joint Helicopter Command. The army is divided into functional arms and services, subdivided into regiments and corps (listed below in order of precedence). During 2008, as part of the Future Army Structure (FAS) reform programme, the infantry was re-structured into large multi-battalion regiments, which involved amalgamations and changes in title for some regiments.

Members of the public can write for general information to Headquarters Adjutant General Secretariat, Trenchard Lines, Upavon, Wiltshire SN9 6BE. All enquiries with regard to records of serving personnel (Regular and Territorial Army) should be directed to The Army Personnel Centre Help Desk, Kentigern House, 65 Brown Street, Glasgow G2 8EX T 0141-224 2023/3303. Enquirers should note that the Army is governed in the release of personal information by various Acts of Parliament.

ORDER OF PRECEDENCE OF CORPS AND REGIMENTS OF THE BRITISH ARMY

ARMS

HOUSEHOLD CAVALRY
The Life Guards
The Blues and Royals (Royal Horse Guards and 1st Dragoons)

ROYAL HORSE ARTILLERY
(when on parade, the Royal Horse Artillery take precedence over the Household Cavalry)

ROYAL ARMOURED CORPS
1st the Queen's Dragoon Guards
The Royal Scots Dragoon Guards (Carabiniers and Greys)
The Royal Dragoon Guards
The Queen's Royal Hussars (The Queen's Own and Royal Irish)
9th/12th Royal Lancers (Prince of Wales')
The King's Royal Hussars
The Light Dragoons
The Queen's Royal Lancers
1st Royal Tank Regiment
2nd Royal Tank Regiment

ROYAL REGIMENT OF ARTILLERY
(with the exception of the Royal Horse Artillery (*see* above))

CORPS OF ROYAL ENGINEERS

ROYAL CORPS OF SIGNALS

REGIMENTS OF FOOT GUARDS
Grenadier Guards
Coldstream Guards
Scots Guards
Irish Guards
Welsh Guards

REGIMENTS OF INFANTRY
The Royal Regiment of Scotland
The Princess of Wales' Royal Regiment (Queen and Royal Hampshire's)
The Duke of Lancaster's Regiment (King's, Lancashire and Border)
The Royal Regiment of Fusiliers
The Royal Anglian Regiment
The Rifles
The Yorkshire Regiment
The Mercian Regiment
The Royal Welsh
The Royal Irish Regiment
The Parachute Regiment
The Royal Gurkha Rifles

SPECIAL AIR SERVICE

ARMY AIR CORPS

SERVICES

ROYAL ARMY CHAPLAINS' DEPARTMENT
THE ROYAL LOGISTIC CORPS
ROYAL ARMY MEDICAL CORPS
CORPS OF ROYAL ELECTRICAL AND MECHANICAL ENGINEERS
ADJUTANT-GENERAL'S CORPS
ROYAL ARMY VETERINARY CORPS
SMALL ARMS SCHOOL CORPS
ROYAL ARMY DENTAL CORPS
INTELLIGENCE CORPS
ARMY PHYSICAL TRAINING CORPS
QUEEN ALEXANDRA'S ROYAL ARMY NURSING CORPS
CORPS OF ARMY MUSIC
THE ROYAL MONMOUTHSHIRE ROYAL ENGINEERS (MILITIA) (TA)
THE HONOURABLE ARTILLERY COMPANY (TA)
REST OF THE TERRITORIAL ARMY (TA)

ARMY EQUIPMENT

Tanks	386
Challenger 2	386
Reconnaissance vehicles	475
Fuchs	11
Sabre	137
Scimitar	327
Reconnaissance aircraft	3
Armoured Infantry Fighting Vehicle	575
Armoured Personnel Carrier	2,718

ombat Personnel Vehicle	100
Jackal	100
rtillery pieces	877
nti-tank missile	800+
elicopters	299
Attack	165
Apache	66
Lynx	99
Observation	133
Gazelle	133
nmanned aerial vehicle*	192+
urface-to-air missile	339+
and radar	157
iscellaneous boats/craft	4
mphibious craft	4
ogistics and support vehicles	6

2008 figure

THE TERRITORIAL ARMY (TA)

he Territorial Army is part of the UK's reserve land orces and provides support to the regular army at home nd overseas. The TA is divided into three types of unit: ational, regional, and sponsored. TA soldiers serving in egional units complete a minimum of 27 days training a ear, comprising some evenings, weekends and an annual two-week camp. National units normally specialise in a specific role or trade, such as logistics, IT, communications or medical services. Members of national units have a lower level of training commitment and complete 19 days training a year. Sponsored reserves are individuals who will serve, as members of the workforce of a company contracted to the MoD, in a military capacity and have agreed to accept a reserve liability to be called up for active service in a crisis. As at 1 January 2010 the TA's total strength was around 34,000.

QUEEN ALEXANDRA'S ROYAL ARMY NURSING CORPS

The Queen Alexandra's Royal Army Nursing Corps (QARANC) was founded in 1902 as Queen Alexandra's Imperial Military Nursing Service and gained its present title in 1949. The QARANC has trained nurses for the register since 1950 and also trains and employs health care assistants to Level 2 NVQ, with the option to train to Level 3. The corps recruits qualified nurses as officers and other ranks and in 1992 male nurses already serving in the army were transferred to the QARANC.

Colonel-in-Chief, HRH The Countess of Wessex
Colonels Commandant, Col. Rosemary Kennedy, TD; Col. Bridget McEvilly, CBE

THE ROYAL AIR FORCE

In Order of Seniority

THE QUEEN

MARSHAL OF THE ROYAL AIR FORCE
HRH The Prince Philip, Duke of Edinburgh, KG, KT, OM, GBE, AC, QSO, PC, *apptd* 1953

FORMER CHIEFS OF THE AIR STAFF

MARSHALS OF THE ROYAL AIR FORCE
Sir Michael Beetham, GCB, CBE, DFC, AFC, *apptd* 1982
Sir Keith Williamson, GCB, AFC, *apptd* 1985
Lord Craig of Radley, GCB, OBE, *apptd* 1988

AIR CHIEF MARSHALS
Sir Michael Graydon, GCB, CBE, *apptd* 1991
Sir Richard Johns, GCB, KCVO, OBE, *apptd* 1994
Sir Peter Squire, GCB, DFC, AFC *apptd* 1999
Sir Glenn Torpy, GCB, CBE, DSO *apptd* 2006

AIR RANK LIST

AIR CHIEF MARSHALS
HRH The Prince of Wales, KG, KT, GCB, OM, AK, QSO, PC, ADC
Dalton, Sir Stephen, KCB, ADC *(Chief of the Air Staff)*
Bryant, Simon, CBE *(Commander-in-Chief, Air Command)*

AIR MARSHALS
Peach, Sir Stuart, KCB, CBE *(Chief of Joint Operations)*
Walker, D., CBE, AFC *(Deputy Cdr Allied Air Component Command, Ramstein)*
Nickols, C., CBE *(Chief of Defence Intelligence)*
Ruddock, P., CBE *(Director-General Saudi Arabia Armed Forces Project)*
Harper, C., CBE *(Deputy Commander Allied Joint Force Command, Brunssum)*
Leeson, K., CBE *(Chief of Materiel (Air)/Air Member for Materiel)*
Anderson, T., CB, DSO *(Director General of the Military Aviation Authority)*
Pulford, A., CBE *(Deputy Commander-in-Chief Personnel and Air Member for Personnel, Air Command)*
Garwood, E., CB *(Deputy Commander-in-Chief Operations, Air Command)*

AIR VICE-MARSHALS
Ness, C., CB *(Director of Technical Airworthiness in the Military Aviation Authority)*
Walker, D., OBE, MVO *(Master of the Royal Household)*
Kurth, N., CBE *(Chief of Staff (Support) Air Command)*
Bollom, S., *(Director Combat (Air) Defence Equipment and Support)*
Wiles, M., CBE, *(Director Joint Support Chain, Defence Equipment and Support)*
Dixon, C., CB, OBE *(Cdr Joint Helicopter Command)*
Evans, C., QHP *(Cdr Joint Medical Command)*
Hillier, S., CBE, DFC *(Director Information Superiority/Air Member for Equipment Capability)*
Harwood, M., CBE *(Head of the British Defence Staff, USA and Defence Attaché)*
Bagwell, G., CBE *(Air Officer Commanding No. 1 Group)*
Stacey, G., MBE *(Senior British Military Adviser, HQ USA Central Command)*
Lloyd, M., *(Chief of Staff Personnel and Air Secretary)*
North, B., OBE *(Assistant Chief of the Air Staff)*
Irvine, L., *(Director RAF Legal Services)*
Lamonte, J., *(Chief of Staff Strategy, Policy and Plans, Air Command)*
Bates, B., CBE *(Senior Directing Staff (Air), Royal College of Defence Studies)*
Young, J., OBE *(Director Defence Support Review)*
Morris, C., QHS *(Chief of Staff Health and Director General Medical Services (RAF))*
Pentland, R., QHC *(Chaplain Chief (RAF))*
Bushell, C., *(Director of the Oman Typhoon Project Team, UK Trade and Investment Defence and Security Organisation)*
Colley, M., OBE *(Assistant Chief of the Defence Staff Concepts and Doctrine)*
Green, M., CBE *(Air Officer Commanding, No. 22 Group/Chief of Staff Training)*
Murray, D., OBE *(Assistant Chief of the Defence Staff (Personnel) and Defence Services Secretary)*
Lock, R., CBE *(Commandant Joint Services Command and Staff College)*
Osborn, P., CBE *(Air Officer Commanding No.2 Group)*

CONSTITUTION OF THE RAF

The RAF consists of a single command, Air Command, based at RAF High Wycombe. RAF Air Command was formed on 1 April 2007 from the amalgamation of Strike Command and Personnel and Training Command.

Air Command consists of three groups, each organised around specific operational duties. No. 1 Group is the coordinating organisation for the tactical fast-jet forces responsible for attack, offensive support and air defence operations. No. 2 Group provides air combat support including air transport and air to air refuelling; intelligence surveillance; targeting and reconnaissance; and force protection. No. 22 (Training) Group recruits personnel and provides trained specialist personnel to the RAF, as well as to the Royal Navy and the Army (*see also* Armed Forces Training and Recruitment).

RAF EQUIPMENT

Aircraft	
BAe 125	6
BAe 146	2
Dominie	9
Firefly	38
Globemaster	6
Harrier	64
Hawk	123
Hercules	43
Islander	2
Nimrod	14
Sentinel	5
Sentry	7
Shadow	4
Super King Air (leased)	7
Tornado	149
Tristar	9
Tucano	95
Tutor	101
Typhoon	58
VC10	16

elicopters	
ninook	40
riffin	16
erlin	28
ıma	34
a King	25
quirrel	31

OYAL AUXILIARY AIR FORCE

ne Auxiliary Air Force was formed in 1924 to train an ite corps of civilians to serve their country in flying uadrons in their spare time. In 1947 the force was varded the prefix 'royal' in recognition of its stinguished war service and the Sovereign's Colour for e Royal Auxiliary Air Force (RAuxAF) was presented in 989. The RAuxAF continues to recruit civilians who ndertake military training in their spare time to support e Royal Air Force in times of emergency or war.

Air Commodore-in-Chief, HM The Queen
Honorary Inspector-General Royal Auxiliary Air Force, Air Vice-Marshal Lord Beaverbrook
Inspector Royal Auxiliary Air Force, Gp Capt. Gary Bunkell, QVRM, AE, ADC

PRINCESS MARY'S ROYAL AIR FORCE NURSING SERVICE

The Princess Mary's Royal Air Force Nursing Service (PMRAFNS) was formed on 1 June 1918 as the Royal Air Force Nursing Service. In June 1923, His Majesty King George V gave his royal assent for the Royal Air Force Nursing Service to be known as the Princess Mary's Royal Air Force Nursing Service. Men were integrated into the PMRAFNS in 1980.

Patron and Air Chief Commandant, HRH Princess Alexandra, The Hon. Lady Ogilvy, KG, GCVO
Director of Nursing Services and Matron-in-Chief, Gp Capt. Jacqueline Gross

SERVICE SALARIES

The following rates of pay apply from 1 April 2010 and are rounded to the nearest pound.

The pay rates shown are for army personnel. The rates also apply to personnel of equivalent rank and pay band in the other services (*see* below for table of relative ranks).

Rank	*Annual salary*
SECOND LIEUTENANT	£24,615
LIEUTENANT	
On appointment	£29,587
After 1 year in rank	£30,369
After 2 years in rank	£31,147
After 3 years in rank	£31,921
After 4 years in rank	£32,703
CAPTAIN	
On appointment	£37,916
After 1 year in rank	£38,932
After 2 years in rank	£39,959
After 3 years in rank	£40,991
After 4 years in rank	£42,011
After 5 years in rank	£43,039
After 6 years in rank	£44,059
After 7 years in rank	£44,579
After 8 years in rank	£45,090
MAJOR	
On appointment	£47,760
After 1 year in rank	£48,940
After 2 years in rank	£50,111
After 3 years in rank	£51,298
After 4 years in rank	£52,474
After 5 years in rank	£53,661
After 6 years in rank	£54,841
After 7 years in rank	£56,016
After 8 years in rank	£57,199
LIEUTENANT-COLONEL	
On appointment	£67,032
After 1 year in rank	£67,920
After 2 years in rank	£68,801
After 3 years in rank	£69,681
After 4 years in rank	£70,562
After 5 years in rank	£74,614
After 6 years in rank	£75,609
After 7 years in rank	£76,613
After 8 years in rank	£77,617
COLONEL	
On appointment	£81,310
After 1 year in rank	£82,321
After 2 years in rank	£83,336
After 3 years in rank	£84,347
After 4 years in rank	£85,357
After 5 years in rank	£86,368
After 6 years in rank	£87,379
After 7 years in rank	£88,394
After 8 years in rank	£89,408
BRIGADIER	
On appointment	£97,030
After 1 year in rank	£98,013
After 2 years in rank	£98,995
After 3 years in rank	£99,973
After 4 years in rank	£100,964

PAY SYSTEM FOR SENIOR MILITARY OFFICERS

Pay rates effective from 1 April 2010 for all militar officers of 2* rank and above (excluding medical an dental officers). All pay rates are rounded to the neares pound.

Rank	
MAJOR-GENERAL (2*)	*Annual salar*
Scale 1	£108,20
Scale 2	£110,31
Scale 3	£112,47
Scale 4	£114,67
Scale 5	£116,92
Scale 6	£119,21
LIEUTENANT-GENERAL (3*)	
Scale 1	£125,90
Scale 2	£132,08
Scale 3	£138,56
Scale 4	£144,01
Scale 5	£148,26
Scale 6	£152,64
GENERAL (4*)	
Scale 1	£165,28
Scale 2	£169,41
Scale 3	£173,65
Scale 4	£177,99
Scale 5	£181,55
Scale 6	£185,18

Field Marshal – appointments to this rank will not usuall be made in peacetime. The salary for holders of the ran is equivalent to the salary of a 5-star General, a salar created only in times of war. In peacetime, the equivalen rank to Field Marshal is the Chief of the Defence Staff From 1 April 2010, the annual salary range for the Chie of the Defence Staff is £238,123–£252,698.

OFFICERS COMMISSIONED FROM THE SENIOR RANKS

Rank	*Annual salar*
Level 15	£50,68
Level 14	£50,34
Level 13	£50,00
Level 12	£49,32
Level 11	£48,65
Level 10	£47,97
Level 9	£47,29
Level 8	£46,62
Level 7*	£45,77
Level 6	£45,25
Level 5	£44,73
Level 4†	£43,68
Level 3	£43,16
Level 2	£42,63
Level 1‡	£41,59

* Officers commissioned from the ranks with more than 15 years' service enter on level 7

† Officers commissioned from the ranks with between 12 and 15 years' service enter on level 4

‡ Officers commissioned from the ranks with less than 12 years' service enter on level 1

SOLDIERS' SALARIES

Under the Pay 2000 scheme, personnel are paid in either a high or low band in accordance with how their trade has been allocated to those bands at each rank. Pay is based on trade and rank, not on individual appointment, or in response to temporary changes in role.

Rates of pay effective from 1 April 2010 (rounded to the nearest pound) are:

Rank	*Lower band*	*Higher band*
PRIVATE		
Level 1	£17,015	£17,015
Level 2	£17,486	£18,342
Level 3	£17,957	£20,250
Level 4	£19,529	£21,773
LANCE CORPORAL (levels 5–7 also applicable to Privates)		
Level 5	£20,582	£24,075
Level 6	£21,442	£25,246
Level 7	£22,359	£26,405
Level 8	£23,383	£27,592
Level 9	£24,230	£28,940
CORPORAL		
Level 1	£26,405	£27,592
Level 2	£27,592	£28,940
Level 3	£28,940	£30,357
Level 4	£29,161	£31,065
Level 5	£29,390	£31,814
Level 6	£29,624	£32,474
Level 7	£29,840	£33,182
SERGEANT		
Level 1	£30,013	£32,756
Level 2	£30,799	£33,604
Level 3	£31,573	£34,456
Level 4	£31,892	£34,890
Level 5	£32,723	£35,570
Level 6	£33,854	£36,249
Level 7	£34,112	£36,929
STAFF SERGEANT		
Level 1	£33,223	£36,954
Level 2	£33,657	£37,846
Level 3	£34,750	£38,751
Level 4	£35,565	£39,648
WARRANT OFFICER II (levels 5–7 also applicable to Staff Sergeants)		
Level 5	£36,049	£40,549
Level 6	£37,678	£41,446
Level 7	£38,256	£42,044
Level 8	£38,751	£42,642
Level 9	£39,628	£43,252
WARRANT OFFICER I		
Level 1	£38,600	£42,080
Level 2	£39,349	£42,908
Level 3	£40,144	£43,645
Level 4	£40,938	£44,448
Level 5	£41,737	£45,242
Level 6	£42,908	£46,049
Level 7	£44,120	£46,753

RELATIVE RANK – ARMED FORCES

Royal Navy	*Army*	*Royal Air Force*
1 Admiral of the Fleet	1 Field Marshal	1 Marshal of the RAF
2 Admiral (Adm.)	2 General (Gen.)	2 Air Chief Marshal
3 Vice-Admiral (Vice-Adm.)	3 Lieutenant-General (Lt.-Gen.)	3 Air Marshal
4 Rear-Admiral (Rear-Adm.)	4 Major-General (Maj.-Gen.)	4 Air Vice-Marshal
5 Commodore (Cdre)	5 Brigadier (Brig.)	5 Air Commodore (Air Cdre)
6 Captain (Capt.)	6 Colonel (Col.)	6 Group Captain (Gp Capt.)
7 Commander (Cdr)	7 Lieutenant-Colonel (Lt.-Col.)	7 Wing Commander (Wg Cdr)
8 Lieutenant-Commander (Lt.-Cdr)	8 Major (Maj.)	8 Squadron Leader (Sqn Ldr)
9 Lieutenant (Lt.)	9 Captain (Capt.)	9 Flight Lieutenant (Flt Lt)
10 Sub-Lieutenant (Sub-Lt.)	10 Lieutenant (Lt.)	10 Flying Officer (FO)
11 Midshipman	11 Second Lieutenant (2nd Lt.)	11 Pilot Officer (PO)

SERVICE RETIRED PAY

on compulsory retirement

Those who leave the services having served at least five years, but not long enough to qualify for the appropriate immediate pension, now qualify for a preserved pension and terminal grant, both of which are payable at age 60. The tax-free resettlement grants shown below are payable on release to those who qualify for a preserved pension and who have completed nine years' service from age 21 (officers) or 12 years from age 18 (other ranks).

The annual rates for army personnel are given. The rates also apply to personnel of equivalent rank in the other services, including the nursing services.

OFFICERS

Applicable to officers who give full pay service on the active list on or after 31 March 2010. Pensionable earnings for senior officers (*) is defined as the total amount of basic pay received during the year ending on the day prior to retirement, or the amount of basic pay received during any 12-month period within 3 years prior to retirement, whichever is the higher. Figures for senior officers are percentage rates of pensionable earnings on final salary arrangements on or after 31 March 2010.

No. of years reckonable service	*Capt. and below*	*Major*	*Lt.-Col.*	*Colonel*	*Brigadier*	*Major-General**	*Lieutenant-General**	*General**
16	£12,557	£14,955	£19,608	£23,751	£28,214	—	—	—
17	£13,135	£15,665	£20,610	£24,840	£29,313	—	—	—
18	£13,714	£16,376	£21,612	£25,930	£30,413	—	—	—
19	£14,293	£17,086	£22,614	£27,019	£31,513	—	—	—
20	£14,872	£17,797	£23,616	£28,109	£32,613	—	—	—
21	£15,450	£18,507	£24,618	£29,199	£33,713	—	—	—
22	£16,029	£19,217	£25,620	£30,288	£34,813	—	—	—
23	£16,608	£19,928	£26,622	£31,378	£35,913	—	—	—
24	£17,187	£20,638	£27,624	£32,467	£37,013	38.5%	—	—
25	£17,765	£21,348	£28,626	£33,557	£38,113	39.7%	—	—
26	£18,344	£22,059	£29,628	£34,646	£39,213	40.8%	—	—
27	£18,923	£22,769	£30,630	£35,736	£40,313	42.0%	42.0%	—
28	£19,502	£23,480	£31,632	£36,826	£41,413	43.1%	43.1%	—
29	£20,080	£24,190	£32,634	£37,915	£42,513	44.3%	44.3%	—
30	£20,659	£24,900	£33,636	£39,005	£43,613	45.4%	45.4%	45.4%
31	£21,238	£25,611	£34,638	£40,094	£44,713	46.6%	46.6%	46.6%
32	£21,817	£26,321	£35,640	£41,184	£45,813	47.7%	47.7%	47.7%
33	£22,395	£27,031	£36,642	£42,273	£46,913	48.9%	48.9%	48.9%
34	£22,974	£27,742	£37,644	£43,363	£48,012	50.0%	50.0%	50.0%

WARRANT OFFICERS, NCOS AND PRIVATES

(Applicable to soldiers who give full pay service on or after 31 March 2010)

No. of years reckonable service	*Below Corporal*	*Corporal*	*Sergeant*	*Staff Sergeant*	*Warrant Officer Level II*	*Warrant Officer Level I*
22	£7,431	£9,586	£10,509	£11,971	£12,781	£13,590
23	£7,690	£9,920	£10,876	£12,389	£13,227	£14,065
24	£7,950	£10,255	£11,243	£12,807	£13,673	£14,539
25	£8,209	£10,590	£11,610	£13,225	£14,119	£15,014
26	£8,469	£10,924	£11,977	£13,643	£14,565	£15,488
27	£8,728	£11,259	£12,344	£14,061	£15,011	£15,962
28	£8,987	£11,593	£12,710	£14,479	£15,458	£16,437
29	£9,247	£11,928	£13,077	£14,896	£15,904	£16,911
30	£9,506	£12,263	£13,444	£15,314	£16,350	£17,385
31	£9,765	£12,597	£13,811	£15,732	£16,796	£17,860
32	£10,025	£12,932	£14,178	£16,150	£17,242	£18,334
33	£10,284	£13,266	£14,545	£16,568	£17,688	£18,809
34	£10,544	£13,601	£14,911	£16,986	£18,134	£19,283
35	£10,803	£13,935	£15,278	£17,404	£18,580	£19,757
36	£11,062	£14,270	£15,645	£17,821	£19,026	£20,232
37	£11,322	£14,605	£16,012	£18,239	£19,473	£20,706

GRANTS AND GRATUITIES

Terminal grants are in each case three times the rate of retired pay or pension. There are special rates of retired pay for certain other ranks not shown above. Lower rates are payable in cases of voluntary retirement.

A gratuity of £4,270 is payable for officers with short service commissions for each year completed. Resettlement grants are £10,302 for officers and for other ranks.

EDUCATION

THE UK EDUCATION SYSTEM

The structure of the education system in the UK is a devolved matter with each of the countries of the UK having separate systems under separate governments. There are differences between the school systems in terms of the curriculum, examinations and final qualifications and, at university level, in terms of the nature of some degrees and the matter of tuition fees. The systems in England, Wales and Northern Ireland are similar and have more in common with one another than the Scottish system which differs significantly.

Education in England is overseen by the Department for Education (DfE), formed by the new coalition government on 12 May 2010 to replace the former government's Department for Children, Schools and Families (DCSF), and by the Department for Business, Innovation and Skills (BIS).

In Wales, responsibility for education lies with the Department for Children, Education, Lifelong Learning and Skills (DCELLS) within the Welsh Assembly Government. Ministers in the Scottish Government are responsible for education in Scotland while in Northern Ireland responsibility lies with the Department of Education (DENI) and the Department for Employment and Learning (DELNI) within the Northern Ireland Government.

DEPARTMENT FOR EDUCATION
T 0870-000 2288 W www.education.gov.uk

DEPARTMENT FOR BUSINESS, INNOVATION AND SKILLS T 020-7215 5000 W www.bis.gov.uk

DEPARTMENT FOR CHILDREN, EDUCATION, LIFELONG LEARNING AND SKILLS (DCELLS)
T 0300-060 3300, 0845-010 3300
W www.wales.gov.uk/about/civilservice/departments/dcells

SCOTTISH GOVERNMENT – EDUCATION
T 08457-741741, 0131-556 8400
W www.scotland.gov.uk/Topics/Education

DEPARTMENT OF EDUCATION (NI)
T 028-9127 9279 W www.deni.gov.uk

DEPARTMENT FOR EMPLOYMENT AND LEARNING (NI)
T 028-9025 7777 W www.delni.gov.uk

RECENT DEVELOPMENTS

Changes have been made and will be taking place over coming months within many areas of the education sector in England as a result of policies of the new Conservative and Liberal Democrat coalition government which took office in May 2010.

- It was announced on 24 May 2010 that schools and education for 16- to 19-year-olds are protected from the £6.2bn cuts in government spending that are being made in order to tackle the UK's deficit during the 2010–11 financial year. The Department for Education is making savings of £670m by reducing waste and costs elsewhere in its budget. Some £80m of this is being saved by cutting costs in education quangos, including the Training and Development Agency for Schools and the National College for Leadership of Schools and Children's Services, and closing Becta, the government's technology agency for schools. The government has also confirmed that it intends to introduce legislation in autumn 2010 to close the Qualifications and Curriculum Development Agency and the General Teaching Council for England. It was also announced that £500m of the £6.2bn savings would be reinvested partly in targeted support for further education and apprenticeships.
- Legislation has been introduced to enable more schools in England, including primaries for the first time, to apply for academy status, which allows them to leave local authority control and have extra freedom over their curriculum and how much they pay their teachers. The change removes local authorities' previous power to veto a school becoming an academy. Parent and/or teacher groups who want to set up their own schools – known as 'free schools' – are also being encouraged to apply for academy status. Schools that have been deemed 'outstanding' by inspectors – more than 2,000 primaries and 600 secondaries – can fast-track the process.
- Legislation has been promised for autumn 2010 which will introduce: a 'pupil premium' allocating more money to the poorest pupils; a slimmer curriculum giving teachers more freedom in how and what they teach; a reading test for 6-year-olds; and powers for teachers and head teachers to improve behaviour and tackle bullying. Legislation will also reform the school inspection body Ofsted and other accountability frameworks to ensure head teachers are held accountable for the core educational goals of attainment and closing the gap between rich and poor.

STATE SCHOOL SYSTEM

PRE-SCHOOL

Pre-school education for children from 3 to 5 years of age is not compulsory. Parents may take as little or as much of their entitlement as they choose, although a free place is available for every 3- and 4-year-old whose parents want one. From September 2010 all 3- and 4-year-olds in England are entitled to 15 hours a week of free early education over 38 weeks of the year until they reach compulsory school age (the term following their fifth birthday). This is delivered flexibly over a minimum of three days each week during normal term times. Free places are funded by local authorities and are delivered by a range of providers in the maintained and non-maintained sectors – nursery schools; nursery classes in primary schools; private schools; private day nurseries; voluntary playgroups; pre-schools; and registered childminders. In order to receive funding, providers must be working towards the early learning goals and other features of the Early Years Foundation Stage curriculum, must be inspected on a regular basis by Ofsted and must meet any conditions set by the local authority.

In Wales, every child is entitled to receive free Foundation Phase education for a minimum of two hours a day from the term following their third birthday.

In Scotland, councils have a duty to provide a

pre-school education for all 3- and 4-year-olds whose parents request one. Education authorities must offer each child 475 hours of free pre-school education a year (less for children who start pre-school later in the year), although they may provide more if they choose. This is usually delivered as five 2.5 hour sessions a week.

In Northern Ireland, there are now free, part-time nursery places available for over 90 per cent of children in their final pre-school year. Most places offer 2.5 hours a day, five days a week for 38 weeks a year.

PRIMARY AND SECONDARY SCHOOLS

By law, full-time education starts at the age of five for children in England, Scotland and Wales and at the age of four in Northern Ireland. In practice, most children in the UK start school before their fifth birthday: in England from 2011 all children will be entitled to a primary school place from the September after their fourth birthday. In all parts of the UK, compulsory schooling ends at age 16, but children born between certain dates may leave school before their 16th birthday. Most young people stay in some form of education until 17 or 18. From 2013, all pupils in England will be required to continue in education or training to 17 years and from 2015, to 18 years.

Primary education consists mainly of infant schools for children aged 5 to 7, junior schools for those aged 7 to 11, and combined infant and junior schools for both age groups. First schools in some parts of England cater for ages 5 to 10 as the first stage of a three-tier system of first, middle and secondary schools. Scotland has only primary schools with no infant/junior division.

Children usually leave primary school and move on to secondary school at the age of 11 (or 12 in Scotland). In the few areas of England that have a three-tier system of schools, middle schools cater for children after they leave first schools for three to four years between the ages of 8 and 14, depending on the local authority.

Secondary schools cater for children aged 11 to 16 and, if they have a sixth form, for those who choose to stay on to age 17 or 18. From the age of 16, students may move instead to further education colleges or work-based training.

Most UK secondary schools are co-educational. The largest secondary schools have more than 1,500 pupils and around 60 per cent of pupils in the UK are in schools that take more than 1,000 pupils.

Most state-maintained secondary schools in England, Wales and Scotland are comprehensive schools, whose admission arrangements are made without reference to ability or aptitude. In England there remain some areas with grammar schools, catering for pupils aged 11 to 18, which select pupils on the basis of high academic ability. Northern Ireland continues to have many grammar schools, though this is changing – *see* below.

More than 90 per cent of pupils in the UK attend publicly funded schools and receive free education. The rest attend privately funded 'independent' schools, which charge fees, or are educated at home. No fees are charged by any publicly maintained school in England, Wales or Scotland. In Northern Ireland, fees may be charged in the preparatory classes of grammar schools.

The bulk of the UK government's expenditure on school education is through local authorities (Education and Library Boards in Northern Ireland), who pass on state funding to schools and other educational institutions.

SPECIAL EDUCATION

Schools and local authorities in England and Wales, Education and Library Boards (ELBs) in Northern Ireland and education authorities in Scotland are required to identify and secure provision for children with special educational needs and to involve parents in decisions. Where appropriate, and taking parents' wishes into account, children with special educational needs are educated in ordinary mainstream schools, sometimes with supplementary help from outside specialists. Parents of children with special educational needs (referred to as additional support needs in Scotland) have a right of appeal to independent tribunals if their wishes are not met.

Special educational needs provision may be made in maintained special schools, special units attached to mainstream schools or in mainstream classes themselves, all funded by local authorities. There are also non-maintained special schools run by voluntary bodies, mainly charities, who may receive grants from central government for capital expenditure and equipment but whose other costs are met primarily from the fees charged to local authorities for pupils placed in the schools. Some independent schools also provide education wholly or mainly for children with special educational needs.

ADDITIONAL SUPPORT NEEDS TRIBUNALS FOR SCOTLAND **T** 0845-120 2906 **W** www.asntscotland.gov.uk

SPECIAL EDUCATIONAL NEEDS AND DISABILITY TRIBUNAL **T** 01325-392760 **W** www.sendist.gov.uk

SPECIAL EDUCATIONAL NEEDS TRIBUNAL FOR WALES **T** 01597-829800 **W** www.sentw.gov.uk

HOME EDUCATION

In England and Wales parents have the right to educate their children at home and do not have to be qualified teachers to do so. Home-educated children do not have to follow the National Curriculum or take national tests nor do they need a fixed timetable, formal lessons or to observe school hours, days or terms. However, by law parents must ensure that the home education provided is full-time and suitable for the child's age, ability and aptitude and, if appropriate, to any special educational needs. Parents have no legal obligation to notify the local authority that a child is being educated at home, but if they take a child out of school, they must notify the school in writing and the school must report this to the local authority. Local authorities can make informal enquiries of parents to establish that a suitable education is being provided. For children in special schools, parents must seek the consent of the local authority before taking steps to educate them at home.

In Northern Ireland, Education and Library Boards monitor the quality of home provision and provide general guidance on appropriate materials and exam types through regular home visits.

The home schooling law in Scotland is similar to that of England. One difference, however, is that if parents wish to take a child out of school they must have permission from the local education authority.

HOME EDUCATION ADVISORY SERVICE **T** 01707-371854 **W** www.heas.org.uk

HOME EDUCATION IN NORTHERN IRELAND **W** www.hedni.org

SCHOOLHOUSE HOME EDUCATION ASSOCIATION (SCOTLAND) **T** 01307-463120 **W** www.schoolhouse.org.uk

FURTHER EDUCATION

In the UK further education (FE) is generally understood as post-secondary education; ie any education undertaken after an individual leaves school that is below higher education level. FE therefore embraces a wide range of general and vocational study undertaken by people of all ages from 16 upwards, full-time or part-time, who may be self funded, employer funded or state funded.

FE in the UK is often undertaken at further education colleges, although some takes place on employers' premises. Many of these colleges offer some courses at higher education level; and some FE colleges teach certain subjects to 14- to 16-year-olds under collaborative arrangements with schools. Colleges' income comes from public funding, student fees and work for and with employers.

HIGHER EDUCATION

Higher education (HE) in the UK describes courses of study, provided in universities, specialist colleges of higher education and in some FE colleges, where the level of instruction is above that of A-level or equivalent exams.

All UK universities and colleges that provide HE are autonomous bodies with their own internal systems of governance. They are not owned by the state. However, most receive a portion of their income from state funds distributed by the separate HE funding councils for England, Scotland and Wales, and the Department for Employment and Learning in Northern Ireland. The rest of their income comes from a number of sources including fees from home and overseas students, government funding for research and work with or for business.

EXPENDITURE

UK-MANAGED EXPENDITURE ON EDUCATION (REAL TERMS) *£bn*

2001–2	61.8	2006–7	76.9
2002–3	64.0	2007–8	80.1
2003–4	69.4	2008–9	82.6
2004–5	72.0	2009–10 (est)	86.7
2005–6	75.7		

Source: PESA *Public Expenditure Statistical Analyses* 2010

SCHOOLS

ENGLAND AND WALES

In England and Wales publicly funded schools are referred to as 'state schools'. The four main categories of state school – community, foundation, voluntary aided and voluntary controlled – are maintained by local authorities, who have a duty to ensure there is a suitable place for every school-age child resident in their area. Each school has a governing body, made up of volunteers elected or appointed by parents, staff, the community and the local authority, which is responsible for strategic management, ensuring accountability, monitoring school performance, setting budgets and appointing the headteacher and senior staff. The headteacher is responsible for the school's day-to-day management and operations and for decisions requiring professional teaching expertise.

In *Community schools,* which are non-denominational, local authorities are the employers of the staff, own the land and buildings and set the admissions criteria.

In *Foundation schools,* the governing body employs the staff and sets the admissions criteria. The land and buildings are usually owned by the governing body or a charitable foundation. A foundation school may have a religious character, although most do not. A *trust school* is a distinct type of foundation school that forms a charitable trust with an outside partner – for example, a business, a university, an educational charity, or simply another school – that shares the school's aspirations. The decision to become a trust school is taken by the governing body while taking account of parents' views. Community schools can take on foundation status and set up a trust in a single process.

Most *voluntary-aided schools* are religious schools founded by Christian denominations or other faiths. As with foundation schools, the governing body employs the staff and sets the admissions criteria, which may include priority for members of the faith or denomination. The school buildings and land are normally owned and provided by a charitable foundation, often a religious organisation, which appoints a majority of the school's governors and makes a small contribution to major building costs.

Voluntary-controlled schools are similar to voluntary-aided schools in that they often have a particular religious ethos, commonly Church of England, and the school land and buildings are normally owned by a charity. However, as with community schools, the local authority employs the school's staff, sets the admissions criteria and bears all the costs.

Among the local authority-maintained schools are some with particular characteristics.

Community and foundation special schools cater for children with specific special educational needs, which may include physical disabilities or learning difficulties.

Grammar schools are secondary schools catering for pupils aged 11 to 18 that select all of their pupils based on academic ability. In England there are 164 grammar schools, concentrated in certain local authority areas. Wales has none.

Maintained boarding schools are state funded and offer free tuition but charge fees for board and lodging.

In Wales, *Welsh-medium primary and secondary schools* were first established in the 1950s and 1960s, originally in response to the wishes of Welsh-speaking parents who wanted their children to be educated through the medium of the Welsh language. Now, many children who are not from Welsh-speaking homes also attend Welsh-medium and bilingual schools throughout Wales. Welsh language education has become increasingly important following the Welsh Assembly Government's vision of creating a bilingual Wales. The latest statistics show that Wales has 464 Welsh-medium primary schools, where the main or sole medium of instruction is in the Welsh language, and 55 Welsh-medium secondary schools, where more than a half of foundations subjects (other than English and Welsh) and religious education are taught wholly or partly in Welsh.

England now has increasing numbers of schools that are publicly funded and charge no fees but are not local authority-maintained. Almost all of these are *Academies,* sometimes called 'independent state schools'. Academies are all-ability schools set up by sponsors from business, faith or voluntary groups in partnership with the Department for Education. Together they fund the land and buildings, with the government covering the running costs at a level comparable to other local schools. The new coalition government has introduced legislation to enable more schools, including primaries for the first time, to apply for academy status in order to leave local authority control and have greater freedom over what they teach, the pay and conditions of their teachers and how they organise schooling. *See also* Recent Developments.

SCOTLAND

Most schools in Scotland, known as 'publicly funded' schools, are state funded and charge no fees. Funding is met from resources raised by the Scottish local authorities and from an annual grant from the Scottish government. Scotland does not have school governing bodies like the rest of the UK: local authorities retain greater responsibility for the management and performance of publicly funded schools. Headteachers manage at least 80 per cent of a school's budget, covering staffing, furnishings, repairs, supplies, services and energy costs. Expenditure on new buildings, modernisation projects and equipment is financed by the local authority within the limits set by the Scottish government.

Scotland has approaching 400 state-funded *faith schools,* the majority of which are Catholic. It has no grammar schools.

Integrated community schools form part of the Scottish government's strategy to promote social inclusion and to raise educational standards. They encourage closer and better joint working among education, health and social work agencies and professionals, greater pupil and parental involvement in schools, and improved support and service provision for vulnerable children and young people.

Scotland has a number of *grant-aided schools* that are independent of local authorities but supported financially by the Scottish government. These schools are managed by boards and most of them provide education for children and young people with special educational needs.

NORTHERN IRELAND

Most schools in Northern Ireland are maintained by the state and generally charge no fees, though fees may be charged in preparatory departments of some grammar schools. There are different types of state-funded schools, each under the control of management committees who also employ the teachers.

Controlled schools (nursery, primary, special, secondary and grammar schools) are managed by Northern Ireland's five Education and Library Boards (ELBs) through boards of governors which consist of teachers, parents, members of the ELB and transferor representatives (mainly from the Protestant churches).

Catholic maintained schools (nursery, primary, special and secondary) are under the management of boards of governors that consist of teachers, parents and members nominated by the employing authority, the Council for Catholic Maintained Schools (CCMS).

Other Maintained schools (primary, special and secondary) are, in the main, Irish-medium schools that provide education in an Irish-speaking environment. The Department of Education has a duty to encourage and facilitate the development of Irish-medium education. Northern Ireland has more than 20 standalone Irish-medium schools, most of them primary schools, and around a dozen Irish-medium units attached to English-medium host schools.

Voluntary schools are mainly grammar schools, which select pupils according to academic ability. They are managed by boards of governors consisting of teachers parents and, in most cases, representatives from the Department of Education and the ELB.

Integrated schools (primary and secondary) educate pupils from both the Protestant and Catholic communities as well as those of other faiths and no faith, each managed by a board of governors. There are at present 61 integrated schools maintained by the state, 23 of which are controlled schools.

In 2008 Northern Ireland's Minister for Education proposed a phased ending of grammar schools' academic selection over a three-year period, but these proposals did not attract the necessary level of support to become law. As a result, post-primary transfer arrangements for September 2010 admissions were unregulated, although informed by guidance from the Department of Education which did not recommend the use of academic admissions criteria. From 2013 new post-primary arrangements will guarantee all pupils access to a much wider range of courses, with a minimum of 24 courses at Key Stage 4, and 27 at post-16. At least one third of the courses on offer will be academic and another third will be vocational. Legislation is already in place to give effect to these changes and to enable schools to enter into collaborative arrangements with other schools, FE colleges or other providers.

INDEPENDENT SCHOOLS

Around 6.5 per cent of the UK's schoolchildren are educated by privately funded 'independent' schools that charge fees and set their own admissions policies. Independent schools are required to meet certain minimum standards but need not teach the National Curriculum. *See also* Independent Schools.

UK SCHOOLS BY CATEGORY (2008–9)

	England	*Wales*
Maintained nursery schools	440	28
Maintained primary and secondary schools (total):	20,289	1,701
Community	12,285	1,428
Voluntary aided	4,260	162
Voluntary controlled	2,625	99
Foundation	1,119	12
Pupil referral units	548	53
Maintained special schools	985	44
*Non-maintained special schools	73	–
†Academies, including City Technology Colleges	136	–
Independent schools	2,356	60
Total	24,737	1,886

Scotland	
Publicly funded schools (total):	2,708
Primary	2,151
Secondary	375
Special	182
Independent schools (total):	159
Primary	59
Secondary	55
Special	45
Total	2,867

* Excludes voluntary and private pre-school education centres
† Figure includes two hospital schools

Jorthern Ireland	
tate-maintained nursery schools	98
tate-maintained primary and secondary schools (total):	1,085
Controlled	463
Voluntary	66
Catholic maintained	470
Other maintained	25
Integrated	61
pecial schools	43
ıdependent schools	15
'otal	1,241

ource: DCSF 2009

NSPECTION

:NGLAND

'he Office for Standards in Education, Children's ;ervices and Skills (Ofsted) is the main body responsible or inspecting education in English schools. As well as ıspecting all publicly funded and some independent chools, Ofsted inspects a range of other services in :ngland, including childcare, children's homes, pupil eferral units, local authority children's services, further ducation, initial teacher training and publicly funded dult skills training.

Ofsted is an independent, non-ministerial government lepartment that reports directly to Parliament, headed by Her Majesty's Chief Inspector (HMCI). Ofsted is required o promote improvement in the public services it inspects; nsure that these services focus on the interests of their sers – children, parents, learners and employers; and see hat these services are efficient, effective and promote 'alue for money.

Ofsted publishes the findings of its inspection reports, ts recommendations and statistical information on its website.

)FFICE FOR STANDARDS IN EDUCATION, CHILDREN'S SERVICES AND SKILLS
T 0300-123 1231 W www.ofsted.gov.uk

WALES

:styn is the office of Her Majesty's Inspectorate for :ducation and Training in Wales. It is independent of, but 'unded by, the Welsh Assembly Government and is led by Her Majesty's Chief Inspector of Education and Training n Wales.

Estyn's role is to inspect quality and standards in :ducation and training in Wales, including in primary, secondary, special and independent schools and pupil 'eferral units, publicly funded nursery schools and settings, 'urther education, adult community-based and work-based earning, LAs and teacher education and training.

Estyn also provides advice on quality and standards in :ducation and training to the Welsh Assembly and others and its remit includes making public good practice based on inspection evidence. Estyn publishes the findings of its inspection reports, its recommendations and statistical information on its website.

HER MAJESTY'S INSPECTORATE FOR EDUCATION AND TRAINING IN WALES
T 029-2044 6446 W www.estyn.gov.uk

SCOTLAND

HM Inspectorate of Education (HMIE) in Scotland is an executive agency of the Scottish government. It operates independently and impartially while being directly accountable to Scottish ministers for the standards of its work. It is led by HM Senior Chief Inspector (HMSCI) who is accountable for the overall quality of HMIE's work.

The core business of HMIE is inspection and review and its stated core objective is to promote and contribute to sustainable improvements in standards, quality and achievements for all learners in a Scottish education system which is inclusive. HMIE combines inspection with self-evaluation in its drive to raise educational standards and works with schools, authorities and colleges to promote effective self-evaluation. Services it is responsible for inspecting or reviewing include all schools, pre-school centres, further education colleges, local authorities, teacher education and publicly funded training programmes.

HMIE publishes the findings of its inspection reports and reviews, its recommendations, examples of good practice and statistical information on its website.

HER MAJESTY'S INSPECTORATE OF EDUCATION IN SCOTLAND T 01506-600200 W www.hmie.gov.uk

NORTHERN IRELAND

The Education and Training Inspectorate (ETINI) provides inspection services for the Department of Education Northern Ireland, the Department for Employment and Learning and the Department of Culture, Arts and Leisure. Its role is to promote improvement in the interests of all learners, through inspections and the dissemination of its findings.

ETINI carries out inspections of all schools, pre-school services, special education, further education colleges, initial teacher training, training organisations, and curriculum advisory and support services.

The inspectorate provides evidence-based advice to ministers to assist in the formulation of policies. It publishes the findings of its inspection reports, its recommendations and statistical information on its website.

EDUCATION AND TRAINING INSPECTORATE
T 028-9127 9726 W www.etini.gov.uk

THE NATIONAL CURRICULUM

ENGLAND

The National Curriculum, first introduced in 1988, is mandatory in all state schools. It is organised into blocks of years called 'Key Stages' and sets out the core subjects that must be taught and the standards or attainment targets for each subject at each Key Stage. In addition, there is also a mandatory curriculum for the Early Years Foundation Stage (EYFS).

The National Curriculum has four Key Stages:

- The Early Years Foundation Stage covers children from birth to age 5, or the end of Reception Year in primary school
- Key Stage 1 covers Years 1 and 2 of primary school, for children aged 5–7
- Key Stage 2 covers Years 3 to 6 of primary school, for children aged 7–11
- Key Stage 3 covers Years 7 to 9 of secondary school, for children aged 11–14
- Key Stage 4 covers Years 10 and 11 of secondary school, for children aged 14–16.

Within the framework of the National Curriculum, schools may plan and organise teaching and learning in the way that best meets the needs of their pupils. Many schools have used the Qualifications and Curriculum Development Agency (QCDA) schemes of work to plan their curriculum, which help to translate the National

Curriculum's objectives into teaching and learning activities. QCDA is a non-departmental public body with a wide range of responsibilities for developing the curriculum, testing and reforming qualifications. However, the coalition government has stated its intention to introduce legislation in autumn 2010 to close QCDA.

The government also announced a review of the Early Years Foundation Stage. The EYFS learning and development requirement, which all schools, nurseries and other registered early years providers must deliver, has three elements: the early learning goals, educational programmes and assessment arrangements. It sets out six areas covered by the early learning goals and educational programmes: personal, social and emotional development; communication, language and literacy; problem-solving, reasoning and numeracy; knowledge and understanding of the world; physical development; and creative development.

KEY STAGES 1 AND 2 COMPULSORY SUBJECTS
English
Mathematics
Science
Design and technology
Information and Communication Technology (ICT)
History
Geography
Art and design
Music
Physical education

Schools must also provide religious education (RE), although parents have the right to withdraw children for all or part of the RE curriculum. Schools are also advised to teach personal, social and health education (PSHE) and citizenship, together with at least one modern foreign language.

The former Labour government intended to introduce, from September 2011, a new primary curriculum, which included a requirement for children to learn a modern foreign language from the age of seven. However, the new coalition government announced in June 2010 that it would not proceed with this. It plans instead to introduce legislation in autumn 2010 to alter the National Curriculum to ensure a focus on traditional, basic subjects and give teachers more freedom in what and how they teach. Schools have been advised that the existing primary curriculum will remain in force until 2012.

In Key Stage 3, compulsory subjects include those for Key Stages 1 and 2 plus modern foreign languages and citizenship. Sex and relationship education (SRE) and RE must also be provided, as must careers education and guidance during Year 9. Parents can choose to withdraw their children from all or part of the RE curriculum and from the non-statutory elements of SRE, but not from the statutory elements of SRE which form part of the National Curriculum for science.

Pupils in Key Stage 4 study a mix of compulsory and optional subjects in preparation for national examinations such as GCSEs.

KEY STAGE 4 COMPULSORY SUBJECTS
English
Mathematics
Science
Information and Communication Technology (ICT)
Physical education
Citizenship

Pupils also have to undertake careers education and work-related learning. Schools must also offer RE, SRE and at least one subject from each of four 'entitlement' areas: arts subjects (art and design, music, dance, drama and media arts); design and technology; humanities (history and geography); and modern foreign languages. Other subjects such as classical languages are taught where school resources permit.

For each National Curriculum subject, there is a programme of study that describes the subject knowledge, skills and understanding pupils are expected to develop during each key stage.

The programmes of study also map out a scale of attainment within the subject. In most subjects, these 'attainment targets' are split into eight levels plus an 'exceptional performance' level.

Schools inform parents what National Curriculum level their children have reached in any formal assessment. Parents can use these levels to get an idea of how their child is progressing compared to what is typical for their age. For example, by the end of Key Stage 2, most will be at level 4.

Statutory assessment takes place towards the end of the EYFS, when children's level of development is compared to and recorded against a Foundation Stage Profile. National tests and tasks take place in English and mathematics at the end of Key Stages 1 and 2; all pupils in publicly funded schools in the relevant years are expected to take these tests. At Key Stage 1 the results of tasks and tests are not reported, except to parents, but are used to underpin teachers' overall assessment of pupils. At Key Stages 2 and 3 separate teacher assessments of pupils' progress are made. In Key Stage 2 this is set alongside the test results. At Key Stage 4, national examinations are the main form of assessment.

Each year the DfE publishes on its website achievement and attainment tables, showing performance measures for every school and local authority. The tables for primary schools are based mainly on the results of the tests taken by children at the end of Key Stage 2 when they are usually aged 11, although the 2010 tables will include teacher assessment results. The tables for secondary schools rely on the results of national examinations.

QUALIFICATIONS AND CURRICULUM DEVELOPMENT AGENCY
T 0300-303 3010 W www.qcda.gov.uk

DEPARTMENT FOR EDUCATION
T 0870-000 2288 W www.education.gov.uk

WALES

Wales has introduced a Foundation Phase curriculum for 3- to 7-year-olds. Full implementation began for 3-year-olds from September 2008 and for 4-year-olds from September 2009, will begin for 5-year-olds in 2010 and for 6-year-olds from September 2011. Children's skills and knowledge are planned across seven areas of learning in the Foundation Phase. They are:

- Personal and social development, well-being and cultural diversity
- Language, literacy and communication skills
- Mathematical development
- Welsh language development
- Knowledge and understanding of the world
- Physical development
- Creative development

Full details of the Foundation Phase can be found in *Framework for Children's Learning for 3- to 7-year-olds in*

Wales, available on the Welsh Assembly Government website.

The National Curriculum exists for 7- to 16-year-olds. Originally it was broadly similar to that of England, with distinctive characteristics for Wales reflected in the programmes of study. From September 2008 a revised school curriculum was implemented, consisting of the National Curriculum subjects together with non-statutory frameworks for personal and social education, the world of work, religious education and skills.

The National Curriculum in Wales includes the following subjects:

- Key Stage 2 English, Welsh, mathematics, science, design & technology, information & communication technology (ICT), history, geography, art & design, music and physical education
- Key Stage 3 – as Key Stage 2, plus a modern foreign language
- Key Stage 4 English, Welsh, mathematics, science and physical education

Welsh is compulsory for pupils at all key stages, either as a first or as a second language. The proportion of pupils taught Welsh as a first language rose from 15.7 per cent in 2008 to 16 per cent in 2009.

Statutory testing was removed for pupils in Wales at the end of Key Stage 2 from 2004–5. Only statutory teacher assessment remains. It is also done at the end of Key Stage 1 (in future, the Foundation Phase) and Key Stage 3, and is being strengthened by moderation and accreditation arrangements.

THE WELSH ASSEMBLY GOVERNMENT – EDUCATION AND SKILLS
W http://wales.gov.uk/topics/educationandskills/curriculumassessment

SCOTLAND

The curriculum in Scotland is not prescribed by statute but is the responsibility of education authorities and individual schools. However, schools and authorities are expected to follow the Scottish Government's guidance on management and delivery of the curriculum.

Advice and guidance are provided by the Scottish Government primarily through Learning and Teaching Scotland (LTS), an executive non-departmental public body sponsored by the government. LTS provides advice to Scottish Ministers on all matters related to learning and teaching, the curriculum, assessment and ICT. It reviews and develops the curriculum, producing national guidelines on its structure and on assessment across the whole curriculum.

Scotland is pursuing its biggest education reform for a generation by introducing a new curriculum – Curriculum for Excellence – which aims to provide more autonomy for teachers, greater choice and opportunity for pupils and a single coherent curriculum for all children and young people aged 3 to 18.

The purpose of Curriculum for Excellence is encapsulated in 'the four capacities': to enable each child or young person to be a successful learner, a confident individual, a responsible citizen and an effective contributor. It focuses on providing a broad curriculum that develops skills for learning, skills for life and skills for work, with a sustained focus on literacy and numeracy. The period of education from pre-school through to the end of secondary stage 3, when pupils reach age 14, has the particular purpose of providing each young person in Scotland with this broad general education.

Curriculum for Excellence sets out 'experiences and outcomes', which describe broad areas of learning and what is to be achieved within them. They are:

- Expressive arts (including art & design, dance, drama, music)
- Health & wellbeing (including physical education, food & health, relationships & sexual health and mental, physical and social wellbeing)
- Languages
- Mathematics
- Religious and moral education
- Sciences
- Social studies (including history, geography, society and economy)
- Technologies (including business, computing, food & textiles, craft, design, engineering and graphics)

The experiences and outcomes are written at five levels with progression to examinations and qualifications during the senior phase, which covers secondary stages 4 to 6 when students are generally aged 14 to 17. The framework is designed to be flexible so that pupils can progress at their own pace.

Level	*Stage*
Early	The pre-school years and Primary 1 (ages 3–5), or later for some
First	To the end of Primary 4 (age 8), but earlier or later for some
Second	To the end of Primary 7 (age 11), but earlier or later for some
Third and Fourth	Secondary 1 to Secondary 3 (ages 12–14), but earlier for some. The fourth level experiences and outcomes are intended to provide possibilities for choice and young people's programmes will not include all of the fourth level outcomes.
Senior phase	Secondary 4 to Secondary 6 (ages 15–18), and college or other means of study

Under the new curriculum, assessment of students' progress and achievements from ages 3 to 15 is carried out by teachers who are required to base their assessment judgements on a range of evidence rather than single assessment instruments such as tests. From autumn 2010 teachers have access to a new online National Assessment Resource (NAR), which provides a range of assessment material and national exemplars across the curriculum areas.

In the senior phase, young people aged 16 to 18, including those studying outside schools, build up a portfolio of national qualifications, awarded by the Scottish Qualifications Authority (SQA).

Provision is made for teaching in Gaelic in many parts of Scotland and the number of pupils, from nursery to secondary, in Gaelic-medium education is growing. Full details of the new curriculum can be found on the LTS website.

LEARNING AND TEACHING SCOTLAND
T 0870-010 0297 W www.ltscotland.org.uk
SCOTTISH QUALIFICATIONS AUTHORITY
T 0845-279 1000 W www.sqa.org.uk

NORTHERN IRELAND

Since September 2007 Northern Ireland has been phasing in a revised statutory curriculum that places greater emphasis than before on developing skills and preparing young people for life and work. The new curriculum has now been in place across Years 1 to 12 since September 2009.

The revised curriculum includes a new Foundation Stage to cover years one and two of primary school. This is to allow a more appropriate learning style for the youngest pupils and to ease the transition from pre-school. Key Stage 1 now covers primary years 3 and 4, until children are 8, and Key Stage 2 covers primary years 5, 6 and 7, until children are 11. At post-primary, Key Stage 3 covers Years 8, 9 and 10 and Key Stage 4 Years 11 and 12.

The revised primary curriculum is made up of religious education (RE) and the following areas of learning:

- Language and literacy
- Mathematics and numeracy
- The arts
- The world around us
- Personal development and mutual understanding
- Physical education (PE)

The revised post-primary curriculum includes a new area of learning for life and work, made up of employability, personal development, local and global citizenship and home economics (at Key Stage 3). In addition, it is made up of RE and the following areas of learning:

- Language and literacy
- Mathematics and numeracy
- Modern languages
- The arts
- Environment and society
- PE
- Science and technology

At Key Stage 4, the statutory requirements have been significantly reduced to learning for life and work, PE, RE and developing skills and capabilities. The aim is to provide greater choice and flexibility for pupils and allow them access to a wider range of academic and vocational courses provided under the revised curriculum's 'entitlement framework' (EF). This should be fully in place by 2013.

From 2013, schools will be required to provide pupils with access to at least 24 courses at Key Stage 4 and at least 27 courses post-16. In both cases at least one-third of the courses must be academic and at least one-third applied (vocational/ professional/ technical). The remaining one-third of courses is at the discretion of each school. Individual pupils decide on the number and mix of courses they follow.

RE is a compulsory part of the Northern Ireland curriculum, although parents have the right to withdraw their children from part or all of RE or collective worship. Schools have to provide RE in accordance with a core syllabus drawn up by the province's four main churches (Church of Ireland, Presbyterian, Methodist and Roman Catholic) and specified by the Department of Education.

Revised assessment and reporting arrangements, expected to be fully in place by June 2012, are being introduced to support the revised curriculum. The focus from Foundation to Key Stage 3 is on 'assessment for learning'. This programme includes classroom-based teacher assessment, computer-based assessment of literacy and numeracy and pupils deciding on their strengths and weaknesses and how they might progress to achieve their potential. Assessment information is reported to parents using a new pupil profile. Pupils at Key Stage 4 and beyond continue to be assessed through public examinations.

The Council for the Curriculum, Examinations and Assessment (CCEA), a non-departmental public body reporting to the Department of Education in Northern Ireland, is unique in the UK in combining the functions of a curriculum advisory body, an awarding body and a qualifications regulatory body. It advises the government on what should be taught in Northern Ireland's schools and colleges, ensures that the qualifications and examinations offered by awarding bodies in Northern Ireland are of an appropriate quality and standard and, as the leading awarding body itself, offers a range of qualifications including GCSEs, A-levels and AS-levels.

The CCEA hosts a dedicated curriculum website covering all aspects of the revised curriculum, assessment and reporting – *see* below.

COUNCIL FOR THE CURRICULUM EXAMINATIONS AND ASSESSMENT
T 028-9026 1200 W www.ccea.org.uk

NORTHERN IRELAND CURRICULUM
T 028-9028 1200 W www.nicurriculum.org.uk

QUALIFICATIONS

ENGLAND, WALES AND NORTHERN IRELAND

There is a very wide range of public examinations and qualifications available, accredited by the Office of Qualifications and Examinations Regulation (OFQUAL) in England; the Department for Children, Education, Lifelong Learning and Skills (DCELLS) in Wales; and the Council for the Curriculum, Examinations and Assessment (CCEA) in Northern Ireland. Up-to-date information on all accredited qualifications and awarding bodies is available online at the National Database of Accredited Qualifications (NDAQ).

The National Qualifications Framework (NQF) establishes the level of all accredited qualifications in England, Wales and Northern Ireland. The NQF comprises nine levels (entry level to level 8) and, at each level, groups together qualifications that place similar demands on individuals as learners. Entry level, for example, covers basic knowledge and skills in English, maths and ICT not geared towards specific occupations, while level 3 includes qualifications such as A-levels which are appropriate for people who plan to go to university, and level 7 covers Masters degrees and vocational qualifications appropriate for senior professionals and managers.

Young people aged 14 to 19 in schools or (post-16) colleges or apprenticeships may gain academic qualifications such as GCSEs, AS-levels and A-levels; qualifications linked to particular career fields, like Diplomas; vocational qualifications such as BTECs and NVQs; and functional, key or basic skills qualifications – discussed in this order below.

COUNCIL FOR THE CURRICULUM, EXAMINATIONS AND ASSESSMENT (NORTHERN IRELAND) T 028-9026 1200
W www.ccea.org.uk

DEPARTMENT FOR CHILDREN, EDUCATION, LIFELONG LEARNING AND SKILLS (DCELLS)
T 0300-0603300, 0845-010 3300
W http://wales.gov.uk/about/civilservice/departments/dcells

DIRECTGOV W www.direct.gov.uk

NATIONAL DATABASE OF ACCREDITED QUALIFICATIONS (NDAQ) T 0300-303 3346
W www.accreditedqualifications.org.uk

OFFICE OF QUALIFICATIONS AND EXAMINATIONS REGULATION (OFQUAL)
T 0300-303 3344 W www.ofqual.gov.uk

GCSE
The vast majority of pupils in their last year of compulsory schooling in England, Wales and Northern Ireland take at least one General Certificate of Secondary Education (GCSE) exam; though GCSEs may be taken at any age. GCSEs assess the performance of pupils on a subject-specific basis and are mostly taken after a two-year course. They are available in more than 50 subjects, most of them academic subjects, though some, known as vocational or applied GCSEs, involve the study of a particular area of employment and the development of work-related skills. Some subjects are also offered as short-course qualifications, equivalent to half a standard GCSE, or as double awards, equivalent to two GCSEs.

GCSEs are usually assessed by exams at the end of the course and by coursework completed by students during the course. GCSE certificates are awarded on an eight-point scale from A* to G. In most subjects two different papers, foundation and higher, are provided for different ranges of ability with grades A*–D available from the higher tier and C–G available from the foundation tier.

All GCSE specifications, assessments and grading procedures are monitored by OFQUAL, DCELLS and CCEA in Northern Ireland, who are currently revising the qualification and subject criteria. A key change is that coursework is being replaced in nearly all subjects by 'controlled assessment'; extended tasks sat in exam conditions. The new specifications for many GCSE subjects were introduced in schools in September 2009 and those for English, ICT and mathematics will be taught from September 2010.

From September 2010 state schools will be allowed to offer pupils International GCSE (iGCSE) exams in key subjects including English, mathematics, science and ICT after the coalition government announced that it would allow state schools to offer the qualification, previously available only in independent schools. iGCSEs do not include coursework and are viewed by some experts as more rigorous than traditional GCSEs.

GCE A-LEVEL AND AS-LEVEL
GCE (General Certificate of Education) advanced levels (A-levels) are the qualifications that the majority of young people in England, Wales and Northern Ireland use to gain entry to university.

A-levels are subject-based qualifications mostly taken by UK students aged 16 to 19 over a two-year course in school sixth forms or at college, but they can be taken at any age. They are available in more than 45, mostly academic, subjects, though there are some A-levels in vocational areas, often termed 'applied A-levels'.

An A-level qualification consists of advanced subsidiary (AS) and A2 units. The AS is a standalone qualification and is worth half a full A-level qualification. It normally consists of two units, assessed at the standard expected for a learner half way through an A-level course, that together contribute 50 per cent towards the full A-level.

The A2 is the second half of a full A-level qualification. It normally consists of two units, assessed at the standard expected for a learner at the end of a full A-level course, that together are worth 50 per cent of the full A-level qualification. Most units are assessed by examination but some are by internal assessment. Each unit is graded A–E. Revised A-level specifications were introduced in September 2008, with a new A* grade awarded from 2010 to reward exceptional candidates.

An extended project was introduced in September 2008 as a separate qualification. It is a single piece of work on a topic of the student's own choosing that requires a high degree of planning, preparation, research and autonomous working. Awards are graded A–E and the extended project is accredited as half an A-level.

INTERNATIONAL BACCALAUREATE
The International Baccalaureate (IB) offers three educational programmes for students aged 3 to 19.

More than 100 schools and colleges in the UK, both state and independent, now offer the IB diploma programme for students aged 16 to 19. Based around detailed academic study of a wide range of subjects, including languages, the arts, science, maths, history and geography, this leads to a single qualification recognised by UK universities.

The IB diploma is made up of a compulsory 'core' plus six separate subjects where individuals have some choice over what they study. The compulsory core contains three elements: theory of knowledge; creativity, action and service; and a 4,000-word extended essay.

The diploma normally takes two years to complete and most of the assessment is done through externally marked examinations. Candidates are awarded points for each part of the programme, up to a maximum of 45. A candidate must score 24 points or more to achieve a full diploma.

Successfully completing the diploma earns points on the 'UCAS tariff', the UK system for allocating points to qualifications used for entry to higher education. An IB diploma total of 24 points is worth 260 UCAS points – the same as a 'B' and two 'C' grades at A-level. The maximum of 45 points earns 720 UCAS points – equivalent to six A-levels at grade 'A'.

WELSH BACCALAUREATE
The Welsh Baccalaureate (WBQ), available for 14- to 19-year-olds in Wales, combines a compulsory core, which incorporates personal development skills, with options from existing qualifications such as A-Levels, GCSEs and NVQs to make one broader award. The WBQ can be studied in English or Welsh, or a combination of the two. Following positive evaluation of pilots, the WBQ is being rolled out across the 14 to 19 age range at Advanced, Intermediate and Foundation levels. As at September 2010, centres in Wales offering the WBQ were set to rise from 167 to 217, catering for an estimated 37,000 learners.

DIPLOMAS
The Diploma is a new qualification for 14- to 19-year-olds that combines practical, hands-on experience with academic learning. It was introduced by the former Labour government to increase the qualification choices available to young people and to help them to develop the knowledge and skills employers and universities demand. Consequently, all Diplomas were developed in partnership with employers. The Diploma is a flexible 'umbrella' qualification that can be gained by accruing other qualifications at the relevant level, so young people studying for a Diploma can include GCSEs and A-levels within their Diploma programme.

Diplomas in ten subject areas were introduced in selected schools and colleges from September 2009.

- business administration and finance
- construction and the built environment
- creative and media
- engineering
- environmental and land-based studies
- hair and beauty studies
- hospitality
- information technology
- manufacturing and product design
- society, health and development

A further four Diplomas – travel and tourism; public services; retail business; and sport and active leisure – will be first taught from September 2010. However, the Diplomas the Labour government planned to introduce in science, languages and humanities, to be taught from September 2011, have been cancelled. There are three levels of Diploma, each taking two years to complete:

- Foundation Diploma – a level 1 qualification, equivalent to five GCSEs at grades D to G
- Higher Diploma – a level 2 qualification, equivalent to seven GCSEs at grades A* to C
- Advanced Diploma – a level 3 qualification for those over 16, equivalent to 3.5 A-levels

All Diploma students continue to study English, maths and ICT and have some work experience with an employer. Advanced Diplomas can lead either to university or to a career.

BTECS, OCR NATIONALS AND OTHER VOCATIONAL QUALIFICATIONS

Vocational qualifications can range from general qualifications where you learn skills relevant to a variety of jobs, to specialist qualifications designed for a particular sector. They are available from several awarding bodies, such as City & Guilds, Edexcel and OCR, and can be taken at many different levels.

BTEC qualifications and OCR Nationals are particular types of work-related qualifications, available in a wide range of subjects, including: art and design, business, health and social care, information technology, media, public services, science and sport. The qualifications offer a mix of theory and practice, can include work experience and can take the form of (or be part of) a technical certificate, one of the key components of an Apprenticeship. They can be studied full-time at college or school, or part-time at college. BTEC qualifications are available at various levels on the National Qualifications Framework (NQF), including Higher National Certificates and Diplomas (HNCs and HNDs), at higher education level; OCR Nationals are achieved at levels 1 to 3.

Learners complete a range of assignments, case studies and practical activities, as well as a portfolio of evidence that shows what work has been completed. Assessment is usually done by the teacher or trainer, sometimes externally. BTEC and OCR Nationals are graded as pass, merit or distinction. BTEC and OCR Nationals at Level 3 can qualify the learner for university entry.

BTECs and OCR Nationals are being updated and will be available as new vocational qualifications on the Qualifications and Credit Framework (QCF) by the end of 2010. The QCF is a new framework containing new vocational or work-related qualifications. These qualifications are made up of units that can be studied at each individual's own pace and built up to full qualifications over time.

When an individual takes vocational qualifications on the QCF, their learning is 'banked' over time and stored on their personal learner record, showing their completed units and how they can progress further. Every qualification and unit on the QCF has a credit value, showing how long it takes to complete. One credit is equivalent to ten hours.

There are more than 2,500 new vocational qualifications on the QCF, available in a broad range of subjects from a wide range of learning providers and some employers. Available in England, Northern Ireland and Wales, they are also recognised in Scotland.

NVQS

A National Vocational Qualification (NVQ) is a 'competence-based' qualification that is recognised by employers. Individuals learn practical, work-related tasks designed to help them develop the skills and knowledge to do a particular job effectively. They can be taken in school, at college or by people already in work. There are more than 1,300 different NVQs available from the vast majority of business sectors. NVQs exist at levels 1 to 5 on the National Qualifications Framework. By the end of 2010 they will be available as new vocational qualifications on the Qualifications and Credit Framework, though some will continue to be called NVQs. An NVQ qualification at level 2 or 3 can also be taken as part of an Apprenticeship.

FUNCTIONAL SKILLS

Functional skills are a new set of qualifications launching across England during 2010 and available for all learners aged 14 and above. They test practical skills in English, information and communication technology (ICT) and mathematics that allow people to work confidently, effectively and independently in life. These skills are an integral part of the secondary school curriculum and other qualifications including Diplomas and Apprenticeships and, from September 2010, individuals are able to take functional skills qualifications on their own, assessed mainly by a set of practical tasks completed within a given time limit. New ways of assessment such as electronic and online methods are also being considered. Functional skills replace previous skills for life qualifications and the three main key skills qualifications in England. In Wales these new qualifications are known as 'essential skills'.

APPRENTICESHIPS

An apprenticeship combines on-the-job training with nationally recognised qualifications, allowing individuals to gain skills and qualifications while working and earning a wage. Apprenticeships are available in more than 190 job roles across a wide variety of industry sectors and take between one and four years to complete. There are three levels available:

- Apprenticeships – sit at level 2 on the National Qualifications Framework (NQF) and are equivalent to five good GCSE passes
- Advanced Apprenticeships – sit at level 3 on the NQF and are equivalent to two A-level passes
- Higher Apprenticeships – lead to qualifications at NVQ Level 4 or, in some cases, a foundation degree

In England, the National Apprenticeship Service (NAS), launched in 2009, has responsibility for the delivery of apprenticeships including the provision of an online vacancy matching system. In England in 2008–9, 240,000 young people started an apprenticeship. The Welsh Assembly Government and the Department for Employment and Learning (DEL) are responsible for the apprenticeship programmes in Wales and Northern Ireland respectively.

NATIONAL APPRENTICESHIP SERVICE (NAS)
W www.apprenticeships.org.uk

SCOTLAND

Scotland has its own system of public examinations and qualifications. The Scottish Qualifications Authority (SQA) is Scotland's national body for qualifications, responsible for developing, accrediting, assessing and certificating all Scottish qualifications apart from university degrees and some professional body qualifications.

There are qualifications at all levels of attainment. Almost all school candidates gain SQA qualifications in the fourth year of secondary school and most obtain further qualifications in the fifth or sixth year or in further education colleges. Increasingly, people also take them in the workplace.

SQA, with partners such as Universities Scotland, has introduced the Scottish Credit and Qualifications Framework (SCQF) as a way of comparing and understanding Scottish qualifications. It includes qualifications across academic and vocational sectors and compares them by giving a level and credit points. There are 12 levels in the SCQF, level 1 being the least difficult and level 12 the most difficult. The number of SCQF credit points shows how much learning has to be done to achieve the qualification. For instance, one SCQF credit point equals about 10 hours of learning including assessment.

SQA is responsible for three main types of qualification: units, courses and group awards.

UNITS

NATIONAL UNITS

National Units can be taken at schools, colleges, and in other training centres. There are more than 3,500 units available in a wide range of subjects such as science, engineering, agriculture and care. Most units are designed to take 40 hours of teaching time to complete. National Units can be built up into national courses, National Progression Awards (NPAs) and National Certificates (NC) – *see* below. The names for the National Units at the various SCQF levels are:

- level 1 – Access 1
- level 2 – Access 2
- level 3 – Access 3
- level 4 – Intermediate 1
- level 5 – Intermediate 2
- level 6 – Higher
- level 7 – Advanced Higher

HIGHER NATIONAL UNITS

Higher National Units, which cover the skills and knowledge that people need in jobs at middle management and technician levels, are mainly taken at college. They are the building blocks of Higher National Certificates (HNCs) and Higher National Diplomas (HNDs) – *see* below, though they are also qualifications in their own right. These units can sit at various SCQF levels but are normally between levels 6 and 9 and are often used for progression to courses in higher education.

SVQ UNITS

SVQ units are based on national 'standards of competence' drawn up by government-sponsored bodies called 'sector skills councils', which are made up of trade bodies, employers and specialists. There are sector skills councils for most industries. Each SVQ unit defines one aspect of a job or a work-role, and says what it is to be competent in that aspect of the job. These units can be built into Scottish Vocational Qualifications (SVQs) – *see* below, and are sometimes used in wider schemes such as apprenticeships.

COURSES

STANDARD GRADES

Standard Grades are generally taken over two years of study in Years 3 and 4 at secondary school. These courses are made up of different parts called 'elements', usually with an exam at the end. There are Standard Grades at SCQF levels 3, 4 and 5 called:

- level 3 – Foundation
- level 4 – General
- level 5 – Credit

Candidates generally progress from Standard Grades to National Courses.

NATIONAL COURSES

National Courses are available at these levels:

- level 2 – Access 2
- level 3 – Access 3
- level 4 – Intermediate 1
- level 5 – Intermediate 2
- level 6 – Higher
- level 7 – Advanced Higher

Most National Courses are made up of three units plus an external assessment, usually an examination marked and checked by professional examiners appointed by the SQA. Candidates must pass all three units and are awarded grades A to D on the basis of how they did in their external assessment. Most young people who qualify for places at college and university do so on the basis of the Highers and Advanced Highers.

SKILLS FOR WORK COURSES

Skills for Work Courses are practical courses designed as an equivalent option to an existing qualification, such as Standard Grade, to help young people develop skills that are important to employment and life. These courses offer candidates practical experiences that are linked to particular careers and are normally delivered by a school and college working in partnership. They are assessed by the teacher or lecturer and have no final exam.

GROUP AWARDS

NPAs

National Progression Awards (NPAs) are designed to assess a defined set of skills and knowledge in specialist vocational areas and link to national occupational standards, the basis of SVQs. NPAs are at SCQF levels 2 to 6, and are mainly used in colleges for short programmes of study.

NATIONAL CERTIFICATES

National Certificates, also at SCQF levels 2 to 6, aim to develop a range of skills and knowledge, including transferable skills, such as core skills. Each National Certificate also has specific aims relating to a subject or occupational area and is designed to prepare candidates for further progression. They are primarily aimed at 16- to 18-year-olds and adults in full-time education, normally at a college. They prepare candidates for more advanced study at HNC/HND level or employment.

HNCs AND HNDs
Higher National Certificates (HNCs) and Higher National Diplomas (HNDs) are qualifications introduced in the mid-1920s that provide the skills and knowledge needed for training towards jobs at middle management and technician level. They are made up of Higher National Units and cover a wide range of occupations. Many HNDs allow the holder entry to the second or third year of a degree course. HNCs are at SCQF level 7 and HNDs at level 8.

SVQs
Scottish Vocational Qualifications (SVQs) are based on job competence, and recognise the skills and knowledge people need in employment. There are SVQs in most occupations, and they are available for all types and levels of jobs. Primarily delivered to candidates in full-time employment, they are available at SCQF levels 4 to 12.

PDAs
Professional Development Awards (PDAs) are qualifications for people who are already in a career or vocation and who wish to extend or broaden their skills. People often take a PDA after completing a degree or vocational qualification. There are PDAs at SCQF levels 6 to 12. Customised Awards are vocational qualifications specially designed by SQA to meet an organisation's specific needs for skills and expertise.

THE SCOTTISH QUALIFICATIONS AUTHORITY (SQA) T 0845-279 1000 W www.sqa.org.uk
SCOTTISH CREDIT AND QUALIFICATIONS FRAMEWORK (SCQF) T 0845-270 7371 W www.scqf.org.uk

FURTHER EDUCATION AND LIFELONG LEARNING

ENGLAND

The FE system in England provides a wide range of education and training opportunities for young people and adults. From the age of 16, young people who wish to remain in education, but not in a school setting, can undertake further education (including skills training) in a further education (FE) college. There are two main types of college in the FE sector: sixth form colleges and general further education (GFE) colleges. Some FE colleges focus on a particular area, such as art and design or agriculture and horticulture. Each institution decides its own range of subjects and courses. Students at FE colleges can study for a wide and growing range of academic and/or work-related qualifications, from entry level to higher education level.

Though the Department for Business, Innovation & Skills is responsible for the FE sector and for funding FE for adults (19 or over), the Department for Education funds all education and training for 16- to 18-year-olds.

The proportion of 16- to 18-year-olds in education or training has risen steadily over recent years: in 2008–9 there were nearly 1.5 million 16- to 18-year-olds in state-funded learning, of which 888,000 were in FE and 191,000 in apprenticeships, which often involve attending FE colleges; the rest were in school sixth forms. The percentage will reach 100 per cent by the time England's education-leaving age rises to 18 in 2015. It is assumed that most of the additional students will go into FE or work-based training rather than staying on at school.

The 'September Guarantee', introduced in 2007, offers a place in post-16 education or training to all 16- and 17-year-olds who want one. In 2009 more than 96 per cent of 16-year-olds and almost 90 per cent of 17-year-olds said they wanted to continue in learning and received an offer under the guarantee.

From April 2010, the statutory responsibility for 16 to 19 education and training in England was transferred from the Learning and Skills Council (LSC) to local authorities, supported by the Young People's Learning Agency (YPLA), a new, non-departmental public body. The agency's remit includes funding and supporting academies and providing direct support for young learners, in particular the Education Maintenance Allowance for 16- to 19-year-olds – *see* below.

The FE sector in England, as in other parts of the UK, also provides a range of opportunities for adults. The UK government is committed to lifelong learning to help improve opportunities for people at all stages of life and to ensure that people can access the skills training they need to play a part in growing a prosperous economy.

The Skills Funding Agency (SFA), part of the department for Business, Innovation and Skills (BIS), is presently responsible for funding and regulating education and training for adults; however, the Secretary of State has expressed a wish to change to a Further Education Funding Council. In 2008–9 BIS funded provision for more than 3.5 million adult learners (aged 19 or over): 1,450,000 individuals who chose their own FE; 1,160,000 people sponsored by their employers under the Train to Gain programme; 277,000 apprentices; 630,000 people with learning difficulties or disabilities on 'safeguarded learning' courses; and 4,000 on programmes for people unemployed for more than six months.

There are currently 16 employer-led, funded and designed centres of training excellence called National Skills Academies in various stages of development. Each academy operates in a key sector of the economy, from financial services to construction, and operates in partnership with colleges, schools and independent training providers to offer specialist training within their sector.

Among the many voluntary bodies providing adult education, the Workers' Educational Association (WEA) is the UK's largest, operating throughout England and Scotland. It provides part-time courses to adults in response to local need in community centres, village halls, schools, pubs or workplaces. Similar but separate WEA organisations operate in Wales and Northern Ireland.

The National Institute of Adult Continuing Education (NIACE), a charitable non-governmental organisation, promotes lifelong learning opportunities for adults in England and Wales.

NATIONAL INSTITUTE OF ADULT CONTINUING EDUCATION (NIACE) T 0116-204 4200 W www.niace.org.uk
THE SKILLS FUNDING AGENCY T 0845-377 5000 W www.skillsfundingagency.bis.gov.uk
WORKERS' EDUCATIONAL ASSOCIATION (WEA) T 020-7426 3450 W www.wea.org.uk
THE YOUNG PEOPLE'S LEARNING AGENCY T 0845-337 2000 W www.ypla.gov.uk

WALES

In Wales, the aims and makeup of the FE system are similar to those outlined for England. The Welsh Assembly Government funds a wide range of learning programmes for young people through colleges, local authorities and private organisations. Current thinking is outlined in *Skills That Work for Wales,* published in July 2008, which describes the 'One Wales' ambition for a highly educated, highly skilled and high-employment Wales, and *Transforming Education and Training Provision in Wales; Delivering Skills that Work for Wales,* published in November 2009. The Assembly Government has set out plans to improve learning opportunities for all post-16 learners in the shortest possible time, to increase the engagement of disadvantaged young people in the learning process, and to transform the learning network to increase learner choice, reduce duplication of provision and encourage higher quality learning and teaching in all post-16 provision. One goal is to ensure that, by 2015, 95 per cent of young people will be ready for high-skilled employment or higher education by the age of 25.

In Wales, responsibility for adult and continuing education lies with the Department for Children, Education, Lifelong Learning and Skills (DCELLS) within the Welsh Assembly Government. Wales operates a range of programmes to support skills development, including subsidised work-based training courses for employees and the Workforce Development Programme, where employers can use the free services of experienced skills advisers to develop staff training plans.

COLEG HARLECH WEA T 01248-353254
W www.harlech.ac.uk/en/

NIACE DYSGU CYMRU T 029-2037 0900
W www.niacedc.org.uk

WEA SOUTH WALES T 029-2023 5277
W www.swales.wea.org.uk

SCOTLAND

Scotland's 43 FE colleges (known simply as colleges) are at the forefront of lifelong learning, education, training and skills in Scotland. Colleges cater for the needs of learners both in and out of employment at all stages in their lives from middle secondary school and earlier to retirement. Colleges' curriculums span much of the range of learning needs, from specialised vocational education and training through to general educational programmes. The level of provision ranges from essential life skills and provision for students with learning difficulties to Higher National Certificates (HNCs) and Higher National Diplomas (HNDs). Some colleges, notably those in the Highlands and Islands, also deliver degrees and postgraduate qualifications.

The Scottish Funding Council (SFC) is the statutory body responsible for funding teaching and learning provision, research and other activities in Scotland's colleges. The 43 colleges were incorporated in 1993. Overall strategic direction for the sector is provided by the Lifelong Learning Directorate of the Scottish Government, which provides annual guidance to the SFC and liaises closely with bodies such as Scotland's Colleges, the Scottish Qualifications Authority and the FE colleges themselves to ensure that its policies remain relevant and practical.

The Scottish government takes responsibility for community learning and development in Scotland while Skills Development Scotland, a non-departmental public body, is charged with improving Scotland's skills performance by linking skills supply and demand and helping people and organisations learn, develop and make use of these skills to greater effect. ILA Scotland is a Scottish government scheme delivered by Skills Development Scotland that provides funding for training to individuals over the age of 16 with an income of less than £22,000 a year.

SCOTLAND'S COLLEGES
T 01786-892000 W www.scotlandscolleges.ac.uk

SCOTTISH FUNDING COUNCIL
T 0131-313 6500 W www.sfc.ac.uk

SKILLS DEVELOPMENT SCOTLAND
T 0141-285 6000 W www.skillsdevelopmentscotland.co.uk/

NORTHERN IRELAND

FE in Northern Ireland is provided through six multi-campus colleges. Most secondary schools also provide a sixth form where students can choose to attend for two additional years to complete their AS-levels and A-levels.

The Association of Northern Ireland Colleges (ANIC) acts as the representative body for the six FE colleges which, like their counterparts in the rest of the UK, are independent corporate bodies where management responsibility lies with each individual college's governing body. The range of courses they offer spans essential skills, a wide choice of vocational and academic programmes and higher education programmes. The majority of full-time enrolments in the six colleges are in the 16 to 19 age group, while most part-time students are over 19.

The Department for Employment and Learning (DELNI) is responsible for the policy, strategic development and financing of the statutory FE sector and for lifelong learning, and also provides support to a small number of non-statutory FE providers. The Educational Guidance Service for Adults (EGSA), an independent, not-for-profit organisation, has a network of local offices based across Northern Ireland which provide services to adult learners, learning advisers, providers, employers and others interested in improving access to learning for adults.

ASSOCIATION OF NORTHERN IRELAND COLLEGES (ANIC)
T 028-9090 0060 W www.anic.ac.uk

THE EDUCATIONAL GUIDANCE SERVICE FOR ADULTS
T 028-9024 4274 W www.egsa.org.uk

WEA NORTHERN IRELAND
T 028-9032 9718 W www.wea-ni.com

FINANCIAL SUPPORT

The *Education Maintenance Allowance* (EMA) in England is an income-assessed weekly allowance of £10, £20 or £30 paid directly to learners aged 16, 17 and 18 from households with incomes below £30,810 (2009–10 rates). To be eligible students must be about to leave, or have left, compulsory education and to have enrolled in a full-time FE course in a school or college, or a course that leads to an Apprenticeship or foundation learning programme. A full-time FE course is one involving an average of 12 hours or more study a week. EMA is not affected by any money the student may earn from part-time work.

There are similar EMA schemes in Scotland, Wales and Northern Ireland, but with slightly different eligibility conditions. Students must apply to the EMA scheme for the part of the UK where they intend to study.

The *Adult Learning Grant* (ALG) is similar to the EMA

but for those aged 19 and over. The ALG pays up to £30 a week during term-time to low-skilled, low-income adults studying full-time for any 'full level 2' qualification (ie any academic or vocational qualification or combination of qualifications equivalent in breadth and challenge to at least five GCSEs at grade C or above) or any 'full level 3' qualification (equivalent to at least two A-levels).

Care to Learn is available in England to help young parents under the age of 20 who are caring for their own child or children with the costs of childcare and travel while they are in some form of publicly funded learning (below higher education level). The scheme is not income assessed and pays up to £160 a week (£175 in London) to cover costs. The *Sixth Form College Childcare Scheme* is similar to *Care to Learn*, also for the under-20s, and pays the same rates, but is income-assessed and available only to those learning in a school sixth form or sixth-form college.

The *Free Childcare for Training and Learning for Work Scheme,* launched in April 2009, is for adults aged 20 years and over in England. Aimed at low-income, two-parent families where one parent is in work and the other is looking to enter learning leading to work, it pays childcare and transport costs of up to £175 a week per child (or up to £215 a week per child in London). The household income needs to be £20,000 or less in the previous tax year.

Dance and Drama Awards (DaDA) are state-funded scholarships for students over the age of 16 enrolled at one of 22 private dance and drama schools in England, who are taking specified courses at National Certificate or National Diploma level. Awards cover most but not all of a student's tuition fees but students also need to make a personal contribution – £1,275 for the 2010–11 academic year. DaDA is not income-assessed. Students from England, Scotland or Wales may get extra help with living costs and childcare if their family's annual income is below £33,000.

Young people studying away from home because their chosen course is not available locally may qualify for the *Residential Support Scheme* or *Residential Bursaries.*

Information and advice on applications for EMA, ALG and other schemes outlined above is available from the Learner Support helpline on the Directgov website.

Discretionary Support Funds (DSF) are available in colleges and school sixth forms to help students who have trouble meeting the costs of participating in further education.

In Wales, students aged 19 or over on further education courses may be eligible for the *Assembly Learning Grant for Further Education Scheme – ALG (FE).* This is a means-tested payment of up to £1,500 for full-time students and up to £750 for those studying part-time. *Discretionary Financial Contingency Funds* are also available to all students in Wales suffering hardship and are administered by the institutions themselves. *Individual Learning Accounts* in Wales provide adults with means-tested support of up to £200 to undertake a wide range of learning.

In Scotland, FE students can apply to their college for discretionary support in the form of *Further Education Bursaries.* These can include allowances for maintenance, travel, study, childcare and additional support needs.

In Northern Ireland, FE students may be eligible for *Further Education Awards,* non-refundable assistance administered on behalf of the five Education and Library Boards by the Western Education and Library Board.

UK FE students over 18 whose costs are not fully met from the grants described above may also be eligible for *Professional and Career Development Loans.* These loans – also available to HE students – cover up to 80 per cent of course fees (up to 100 per cent for those unemployed for three months); other course costs, such as books, travel and childcare; and living expenses, such as rent, food and clothing (for those who are unemployed or working fewer than 30 hours a week). The loans, of between £300 and £10,000, are available from participating high street banks – currently Barclays and the Co-operative. The Young People's Learning Agency (YPLA) pays the interest on the loan while the student is studying and for one month afterwards. Once students complete their courses, they must pay interest at the rate fixed when they took out the loan, which will be competitive with other commercially available 'unsecured' personal loans.

DIRECTGOV
W www.direct.gov.uk

STUDENT FINANCE WALES T 0845-602 8845
W www.studentfinancewales.co.uk

WESTERN EDUCATION AND LIBRARY BOARD
T 028-8241 1411 W www.welbni.org

HIGHER EDUCATION

Publicly funded higher education (HE) in the UK is provided in 116 universities; 51 higher education colleges and other specialist HE institutions; and a significant number of FE colleges which offer higher education courses.

The Higher Education Funding Council for England (HEFCE) funds teaching and research in 130 English higher education institutions (HEIs), of which 91 are universities, and also funds the HE courses in 123 FE colleges.

The Higher Education Funding Council for Wales (HEFCW) distributes funding for HE in Wales through Wales's 12 HEIs, of which 8 are universities, and some FE colleges.

The Scottish Funding Council (SFC) – which is also responsible for FE in Scotland – is the national, strategic body responsible for funding HE teaching and research in Scotland's 20 HEIs, of which 15 are universities.

In Northern Ireland HE is provided in two universities, two university colleges and six regional institutes of further and higher education. Unlike other parts of the UK, Northern Ireland has no higher education funding council: the Department for Employment and Learning fulfils that role.

All UK universities and a number of HE colleges award their own degrees and other HE qualifications. HE providers who do not have their own degree-awarding powers offer degrees under 'validation arrangements' with other institutions that do have those powers. The Open University (OU), for example, runs a validation service which enables a number of other institutions to award OU degrees, after the OU has assured itself that the academic standards of their courses are as high as the OU's own standards.

Each HE institution is responsible for the standards of the awards it makes and the quality of the education it provides to its students, and each has its own internal quality assurance procedures. External quality assurance for HE institutions throughout the UK is provided by the Quality Assurance Agency for Higher Education (QAA).

The QAA is independent of government, funded by subscriptions from all publicly funded UK universities and colleges of higher education. Its main role is to safeguard the standards of higher education qualifications. It does this by defining standards for higher education through a framework known as the academic infrastructure. QAA also carries out reviews of the quality of UK higher education institutions via a system known as 'institutional audits'. QAA also advises government on a range of higher education quality issues, including applications for the grant of degree-awarding powers. It publishes reports on its review activities on its website.

DEPARTMENT FOR EMPLOYMENT AND LEARNING T 028-9025 7777 W www.delni.gov.uk

HIGHER EDUCATION FUNDING COUNCIL FOR ENGLAND T 0117-931 7317 W www.hefce.ac.uk

HIGHER EDUCATION FUNDING COUNCIL FOR WALES T 029-2076 1861 W www.hefcw.ac.uk

SCOTTISH FUNDING COUNCIL T 0131-313 6500 W www.sfc.ac.uk

THE QUALITY ASSURANCE AGENCY FOR HIGHER EDUCATION T 01452-557000 W www.qaa.ac.uk

See also Universities for information on the Research Assessment Exercise and listings of universities in the UK.

STUDENTS IN HIGHER EDUCATION (2008–9)*

	Full-time	*Part-time*	*Total*
HE students	–	–	2,396,050
Postgraduate students	268,000	268,815	536,815
Undergraduate students	1,272,030	587,205	1,859,235

*Includes UK, EU and non-EU students

Source: HESA 2009

UK HIGHER EDUCATION QUALIFICATIONS AWARDED (2008–9)

	Full-time	*Part-time*
First degrees	296,870	36,855
Other undergraduate qualifications	58,670	77,465
Postgraduate Certificate in Education (PGCE)	19,135	1,565
Other postgraduate qualifications	13,165	29,725
Total higher degrees including doctorates	104,260	36,705

Source: HESA 2009

COURSES

Higher Education institutions in the UK mainly offer courses leading to the following qualifications. These qualifications go from Levels 4 to 8 on England's National Qualifications Framework, Levels 7 to 12 on Scotland's Credit and Qualifications Framework. Individual HEIs may not offer all of these.

Certificates of Higher Education (CertHE), awarded after one year's full-time study (or equivalent). If available to students on longer courses, they certify that students have reached a minimum standard in their first year.

Diplomas of Higher Education (DipHE) and other Higher Diplomas, awarded after two to three years' full-time study (or equivalent). They certify that a student has achieved a minimum standard in first- and second-year courses, and in the case of nursing, third-year courses. They can often be used for entry to the third year of a related degree course.

Foundation degrees, awarded after two years of full-time study (or equivalent). These degrees combine academic study with work-based learning, and have been designed jointly by universities, colleges and employers with a particular area of work in mind. They are usually accepted as a basis for entry to the third year of a related degree course.

Bachelors' degrees, also referred to as *first degrees.* There are different titles; Bachelor of Arts (BA) and Bachelor of Science (BSc) being the most common. In England, Wales and Northern Ireland most Bachelors' degree courses are typically 'with Honours' and awarded after three years of full-time study, although in some subjects the courses last longer. In Scotland, where young people often leave school and go to university a year younger, HE institutions typically offer Ordinary Bachelors degrees after three years' study and Bachelors' degrees with Honours after four years. Honours degrees are graded: first; upper-second (2:1); lower second (2:2); or third. HEIs in England, Wales and Northern Ireland may allow students who fail the first year of an Honours degree by a small margin to transfer to an Ordinary degree course, if they have one; Ordinary degrees may also be awarded to Honours degree students who do not finish an Honours degree course but complete enough of it to earn a pass.

Postgraduate or *Higher degrees.* Graduates may go on to take *Master's degrees,* which involve one or two years' work and can be taught or research-based. They may also take one-year postgraduate diplomas and certificates, often linked to a specific profession, such as the *Postgraduate Certificate in Education* (PGCE) required to become a state school teacher. A *doctorate,* leading to a qualification such as a Doctor of Philosophy – a PhD or D.Phil, usually involves at least three years of full-time research.

The framework for higher education qualifications in England, Wales and Northern Ireland (FHEQ) and the framework for qualifications of higher education institutions in Scotland, both found on the QAA website (W www.qaa.ac.uk/academicinfrastructure/FHEQ/SCQF/), describe the achievement represented by HE qualifications.

ADMISSIONS

When preparing to apply to a university or other HE college, individuals can compare facts and figures on institutions and courses using the government's Unistats website. This includes details of students' views from the annual National Student Survey.

For the vast majority of full-time undergraduate courses, individuals need to apply online through UCAS, the organisation responsible for managing applications to HE courses in the UK. More than half a million people wanting to study at a university or college each year use this UCAS service, which has useful online tools to help students find the right course.

UCAS also provides two specialist applications services used by more than 50,000 people each year: the Conservatoires UK Admissions Service (CUKAS), for those applying to UK music conservatoires, and the Graduate Teacher Training Registry (GTTR), for postgraduate applications for initial teacher training courses in England and Wales and some in Scotland. Details of initial teacher training courses in Scotland can also be obtained from Universities Scotland and from Teach in Scotland, the website created by the Scottish government to promote teaching.

Each university or college sets its own entry requirements. These can be in terms of particular exam grades or total points on the 'UCAS tariff' (UCAS's system for allocating points to different qualifications on a common basis), or be non-academic, like having a health check. HEIs will make 'firm offers' to candidates who have already gained the qualifications they present for entry, and 'conditional offers' to those who have yet to take their exams or obtain their results. Conditional offers often require a minimum level of achievement in a specified subject, for example '300 points to include grade A at A-level Chemistry'. If candidates' achievements are lower than specified in their conditional offers, the university or college may not accept them; then, if they still wish to go into higher education, they need to find another institution through the UCAS 'clearing' process.

The Open University conducts its own admissions. It is the UK's only university dedicated to distance learning and the UK's largest for part-time HE. Because it is designed to be 'open' to all, no qualifications are needed for entry to the majority of its courses

Individuals can search more than 58,000 UK postgraduate courses and research opportunities on UK graduate careers website Prospects. The application process for postgraduate places can vary between institutions. Most universities and colleges accept direct applications and many accept applications through UKPASS, a free, centralised online service run by UCAS that allows individuals to submit up to ten different applications, track their progress and attach supporting material, such as references. Applications for postgraduate social work courses must also be made through UCAS.

UNISTATS W http://unistats.direct.gov.uk
UCAS T 0871-468 0468 W www.ucas.com
UNIVERSITIES SCOTLAND T 0131-226 1111
W www.universities-scotland.ac.uk
TEACH IN SCOTLAND T 0131-244 7930
W www.teachinginscotland.com
PROSPECTS T 0161-277 5200 W www.prospects.ac.uk
UKPASS T 0871-334 4447 W http://ukpass.ac.uk

TUITION FEES AND STUDENT SUPPORT

HE institutions in England, Wales and Northern Ireland are allowed to charge variable tuition fees for full-time HE courses. Although students from outside the EU can be charged the full cost of their courses, the amount HEIs may charge students from the UK and other EU countries – whose tuition costs are subsidised by Funding Council payments to institutions – has been capped since 2006 at £3,000 a year plus inflationary increases. The maximum an institution can charge new UK and EU students for the 2010–11 academic year is £3,290. For 2009–10 the maximum was £3,225. The exact fee depends on the course studied and the institution attended. Students do not have to pay their fees before or during their course, as tuition fee loans to cover the full cost are available and do not have to be repaid until the student is working (*see* below).

Unlike in England, Northern Ireland and Wales, Scottish HE institutions charge a flat rate for fees set by the Scottish government. The fee level for new undergraduates entering in 2010 was £1,820 a year. Undergraduate students classed as being ordinarily resident in Scotland or another EU country outside the UK are not required to pay tuition fees at Scottish HE institutions. All tuition fees are paid on their behalf by the Scottish government through the Student Awards Agency for Scotland (SAAS); students must apply for this funding every year. Undergraduate students classed as being ordinarily resident in England, Wales or Northern Ireland are required to pay tuition fees for each year of their course in Scotland, though, as explained above, they can get repayable tuition fee loans to cover the cost.

STUDENT LOANS, GRANTS AND BURSARIES

ENGLAND

All students starting a full-time HE course in 2010–11 can apply through Student Finance England for financial support. Two student loans are available from the government: a *tuition fee loan* of up to £3,290 for 2010–11; and a *maintenance loan* to help with living expenses of up to £4,950 for those living away from home (£6,928 if studying away from home in London) and £3,838 for those living with their parents during term time.

The tuition fee loan is not affected by household income and is paid directly to the relevant HE institution. A proportion (currently 72 per cent) of the maximum maintenance loan is available irrespective of household income while the rest depends on an income assessment. Student Finance England usually pays the money into the student's own bank account in three instalments, one at the start of each term.

Repayment of both loans does not start until the April after the student has finished his or her course and is earning more than £15,000 a year. At this point the individual's employer will take 9 per cent of any salary above the £15,000 threshold through the Pay As You Earn (PAYE) system. The self-employed make repayments through their tax returns. Someone earning £18,000 a year (the average starting salary for a graduate-level job), will have to pay back around £5.19 a week. Student loans accrue interest from the date they are paid out, up until they are repaid in full. Generally, the interest rate for student loans is set in September each year. (The latest rate can be found at W www.studentloanrepayment.co.uk/interest)

Students can also apply for a *maintenance grant* towards living expenses which does not have to be repaid. The maximum grant available for 2010–11 is £2,906 for the academic year. This is available to full-time HE students with a household income of £25,000 or under. Those with a household income of £50,020 or under receive a partial grant. The exact amount paid depends upon income. For 2010–11, around 40 per cent of new students are expected to qualify for the full maintenance grant, with many more getting a partial grant. Students eligible for help through the maintenance grant receive some of it instead of the maintenance loan. The amount they are eligible for through the maintenance loan is reduced by 50p for every £1 of maintenance grant they are entitled to. This means that students from lower income households have less to repay when they finish studying and start work.

Certain groups of students who claim means-tested state benefits can get the *special support grant*, also worth up to £2,906, instead of the maintenance grant. Likely recipients include single parents and students with certain disabilities. If a student receives the special support grant, it does not affect the amount of maintenance loan he or she receives.

Bursaries are an additional source of help available from universities and colleges. They do not have to be repaid. Institutions in England must offer at least a minimum bursary payment to students paying maximum tuition fees and getting the full maintenance grant or special support grant.

Students can use the student finance calculator on the Student Finance England website to work out what financial support they may get.

PART-TIME HIGHER EDUCATION STUDENTS

Part-time HE students in England may be entitled to a grant towards their fees, and a grant towards their course costs. This help does not have to be repaid.

There are no regulations stating how much universities or colleges can charge in tuition fees for most part-time courses. The maximum *fee grant* is based on how 'intensive' the course is, or how long it takes to complete compared to the equivalent full-time course. For the most intensive courses, the maximum available for 2010–11 is £1,230. Students on certain state benefits qualify for the maximum automatically. Otherwise the amount awarded depends on the student's household income. The maximum *course grant* for 2010–11 is £265 and the amount awarded depends again on income. Separate applications for these grants must be made each academic year. Details are available on the Student Finance England website.

If the student's chosen HE institution runs the *additional fee support scheme*, it could provide extra financial help if the student is on a low income and in certain other circumstances. Help may also be available through the institution's *access to learning fund*, for students in financial difficulty.

STUDENT FINANCE ENGLAND T 0845-300 5090
W www.studentfinance.direct.gov.uk

WALES

Changes have been made to the Welsh system, affecting all Welsh students starting a full-time HE course in 2010–11. Such students can apply through Student Finance Wales for the forms of financial support described below.

A similar system of tuition fee loans and maintenance loans now operates in Wales as in England but with slightly lower maximum maintenance loans available: up to £4,745 for students living away from home (£6,648 if studying away from home in London) and £3,673 for those living with their parents during term time. Tuition fee loans of up to £3,290 are available to cover the exact amount that the institution charges for a course.

The Welsh Assembly Government has made a commitment that all new Welsh-domiciled students who take out a maintenance loan from academic year 2010–11, irrespective of where they study in the UK, will receive up to £1,500 debt relief when they start repayment.

Welsh-domiciled students may apply for an *assembly learning grant* (ALG) of up to £5,000 to help meet general living costs. This is paid in three instalments, one at the start of each term, like the student maintenance loan. The amount a student gets depends on household income. The maximum grant is available to those with a household income of £18,730 or under. Those with an income of £50,020 or under receive a partial grant.

Universities and colleges in Wales are committed to providing additional support for students under the *Welsh bursary scheme*. Every full-time HE student, regardless of where they live in the UK, may be considered for a means-tested bursary, which is paid in addition to other financial support received and is not offset by any reductions in other forms of support.

Institutions also hold *financial contingency funds* to provide discretionary assistance to students experiencing financial difficulties.

Students can use the student finance calculator on the Student Finance Wales website to work out what financial support they may get.

PART-TIME HIGHER EDUCATION STUDENTS

Part-time undergraduate students studying at least 50 per cent of an equivalent full-time course are entitled to receive a *fee grant*, depending on their household income. The rate depends on how intensive the course is. For 2010–11, the maximum fee grant, which applies to students who study at a rate equivalent to 75 per cent of a full-time course, is £975. Such students may also be entitled to receive *adult dependants' grant* (ADG), *childcare grant* (CCG) or *parents' learning allowance* (PLA). The amount received depends on the intensity of the course undertaken. The maximum grants paid to eligible students are: £1,985.25 ADG; £121.13 a week CCG (one child) or £205.55 (two or more children); and £1,131 PLA.

Part-time students can also apply for assistance with course-related costs worth up to £1,095. Students who already have a degree cannot normally apply for this support. Those on part-time teacher-training courses are not eligible for part-time grants but may qualify for full-time support.

STUDENT FINANCE WALES T 0845-602 8845
W www.studentfinancewales.co.uk

SCOTLAND

All students starting a full-time HE course in 2010–11 can apply through the Student Awards Agency for Scotland for financial support. Living cost support is mainly provided through a *student loan*, the majority of which is income-assessed. The maximum loan for 2010–11 paid to students living away from home is £5,067 and for those living with their parents £4,107 a year. If the family income is over approximately £58,300 a year, the student receives only the minimum loans of £915 and £605 respectively. Low-income students may also be eligible for an *additional loan* of up to £785 with the maximum lent to those whose household income is £18,300 or less a year.

The *young students' bursary* (YSB) is available to young students from low-income backgrounds and is non-repayable. Eligible students receive this bursary instead of part of the student loan, thus reducing their level of repayable debt. In 2010–11 the maximum annual support provided through YSB is £2,640 paid if household income is £19,310 or less a year.

The *Independent Students' Bursary* (ISB) similarly replaces part of the loan and reduces repayable debt for low-income students classed as 'independent' of parental support. The maximum paid is £1,000 a year to those whose household income is £19,310 or less a year.

An income-assessed *travel expenses grant* is available of up to £811 a year for students living in their parents' home and up to £462 for those living away from home. There are also *supplementary grants* available to certain categories of students such as lone parents and those with dependants. Extra help is also available to those who have a disability, learning difficulty or mental health problem.

STUDENT AWARDS AGENCY FOR SCOTLAND
T 0845-111 1711 W www.student-support-saas.gov.uk

NORTHERN IRELAND

All students starting a full-time HE course in 2010–11 can apply through Student Finance Northern Ireland for financial support. The arrangements for both full-time and part-time students are similar to those for England. The main difference is that the income-assessed *maintenance grant* (or *special support grant* for students on certain income-assessed benefits) for new full-time students studying at UK universities and colleges is worth

up to £3,475 while continuing students are eligible instead for a *higher education bursary* of up to £2,000.
STUDENT FINANCE NORTHERN IRELAND
T 0845-600 0662 W www.studentfinanceni.co.uk

Disabled Students' Allowances (DSAs) are grants available throughout the UK to help meet the extra course costs students can face as a direct result of a disability, ongoing health condition, mental health condition or specific learning difficulty. They help disabled people to study in HE on an equal basis with other students. They are paid on top of the standard student finance package and do not have to be repaid. The amount an individual gets depends on the type of extra help needed, not on household income. Eligible individuals should apply as early as possible to their relevant UK awarding authority.

POSTGRADUATE AWARDS
In general, postgraduate students do not qualify for mandatory support like student loans. An exception to this is students taking a Postgraduate Certificate in Education (PGCE), who can qualify for the finance package usually available only to undergraduates.

There is heavy competition for any postgraduate funding available. Individuals can search for postgraduate awards and scholarships on two websites: Hot Courses and Prospects. They can also search for grants available from educational trusts, often reserved for students from poorer backgrounds or for those who have achieved academic excellence, on the Educational Grants Advisory Service (EGAS) website. Otherwise they need to fund their own fees and living expenses.

Postgraduates from Scotland on certain full-time vocational courses can apply through the Student Awards Agency for Scotland for funding under the *postgraduate students' allowances scheme.* In Northern Ireland, the Department for Employment and Learning and the Education and Library Boards provide postgraduate funding for certain courses. Postgraduate students with an impairment, health condition or learning difficulty can apply for disabled students' allowances (*see* above) for both taught courses and research places.

DEPARTMENT FOR EMPLOYMENT AND LEARNING (NI) T 028-9025 7777 W www.delni.gov.uk
EDUCATIONAL GRANTS ADVISORY SERVICE (EGAS) T 020-7241 7459 W www.family-action.org.uk
HOT COURSES W www.scholarship-search.org.uk
PROSPECTS W www.prospects.ac.uk
STUDENT AWARDS AGENCY FOR SCOTLAND (SAAS) T 0845-111 0244 W www.student-support-saas.gov.uk

TEACHER TRAINING

See Professional Education

EMPLOYEES AND SALARIES

EMPLOYEES

FULL-TIME EQUIVALENT NUMBER OF QUALIFIED TEACHERS IN MAINTAINED SCHOOLS (2008–9), *thousands*

	England	*Wales*	*Scotland*	*NI*	*UK*
Nursery and primary schools	198.5	13.5	24.9	8.2	245.1
Secondary schools	222.5*	13.3	25.4	10.2	271.4
Special schools	14.9	0.7	2.0	0.8	18.4
Education elsewhere†	6.8	–	–	–	6.8
Total	442.8	27.5	52.3	19.2	541.8

* Includes academies in England
†Figure includes pupil referral units and is a separate statistic for England only

FULL-TIME EQUIVALENT NUMBER OF SUPPORT STAFF IN MAINTAINED SCHOOLS (2008–9), *thousands*

	England	*Wales*	*Scotland*	*Northern Ireland‡*
Teaching assistants	183.7	14.1	11.6	N/A
Other support staff	162.2§	5.0	10.5	N/A

‡ Figures are not collated centrally for Northern Ireland
§ Includes academies and city technology colleges in England

NUMBER OF ACADEMIC STAFF IN UK HIGHER EDUCATION INSTITUTIONS (2007–8)

	Full-time	*Part-time*	*Total*
Professors	16,180	2,110	18,290
Senior lecturers and researchers	31,505	5,450	36,960
Lecturers	29,180	22,710	51,890
Researchers	31,875	6,100	37,975
Other grades	7,750	22,075	29,830

Source: HESA 2009

SALARIES

State school teachers In England and Wales are employed by local authorities or the governing bodies of their schools, but their pay and conditions are set nationally. Classroom teachers start on the main pay scale which has different rates for different areas. Each September teachers move one point up on the main pay scale until they reach the maximum basic rate of pay (M6). Qualified teachers who reach the top of the main pay scale are eligible to apply and be assessed against national standards to 'cross the threshold' on to a three point upper pay scale. Progress along the upper pay scale is not automatic, but is based on performance recommendations made by the headteacher. Unqualified 'associate' teachers such as instructors are paid on a separate salary scale.

There are teaching and learning responsibility payments for specific posts, special needs work and recruitment and retention factors which may be awarded at the discretion of the school governing body or the local authority. An 'Excellent Teacher' scheme allows eligible teachers, who share their skills in classroom teaching for the benefit of professional development of other teachers within their own school, to access a higher salary. The Advanced Skills Teacher grade was introduced to enhance the prospects of the most able classroom teachers who disseminate good practice by working in other local schools. Advanced skills teachers have their own pay spine. Headteachers and other school leaders are paid on a separate leadership pay spine. All teachers are eligible for membership of the Teachers' Pension Scheme.

As at July 2010, salary scales for teachers in England and Wales were:

Headteacher	£41,426–£102,734
Excellent teachers	£38,304–£50,918
Advanced skills teacher	£36,618–£55,669
Classroom teacher (upper pay scale)	£33,412–£35,929
Classroom teacher (main pay scale)	£21,102–£30,842
Associate teachers	£15,461–£24,453
Inner London	
Headteacher	£48,353–£109,658
Excellent teachers	£47,188–£59,302
Advanced skills teacher	£43,538–£62,596
Classroom teacher (upper pay scale)	£40,288–£43,692
Classroom teacher (main pay scale)	£26,000–£35,568
Associate teachers	£19,445–£28,434

Pay structures for teachers in Scotland have been agreed up until April 2011. Teachers are paid on a seven-point scale where the entry point is for newly qualified teachers undertaking their probationary year. There is no equivalent in Scotland of the upper pay spine operated in England and Wales. Experienced, ambitious teachers who reach the top of the main pay scale are eligible to become chartered teachers and earn more on a separate pay spine. However, to do so they must study for further professional qualifications and finance these studies. Headteachers and deputies have a separate pay spine as do 'principals' or heads of department. Additional allowances are payable to teachers under a range of circumstances, such as working in distant islands and remote schools.

As at 1 April 2010, salary scales for teachers in Scotland were:

Headteacher/deputy headteacher	£42,288–£82,542
Principal teacher	£37,284–£48,120
Chartered teacher	£35,253–£41,925
Main grade	£21,438–£34,200

Teachers in Northern Ireland have broadly similar pay and working conditions to teachers in England and Wales, although there is neither an advanced skills teacher grade nor an excellent teacher scheme. Classroom teachers who take on teaching and learning responsibilities outside their normal classroom duties may be awarded one of five teaching allowances.

As at September 2009, salary scales for teachers in Northern Ireland were:

Principal (headteacher)	£41,426–£102,734
Classroom teacher (upper pay scale)	£33,412–£35,929
Classroom teacher (main pay scale)	£21,102–£30,842
Associate teachers	£13,425
Teaching allowances	£1,805–£11,643

Since 2007, most academic staff in higher education across the UK are paid on a single national pay scale as a result of a national framework agreement negotiated by the HE unions and HE institutions. The main features of the agreement are that all staff are paid according to rates on a 51-point national pay spine and that academic and academic-related staff are graded according to a national grading structure. Since August 2009 the pay spine has ranged from £13,150 to £55,535. As HE institutions are autonomous employers, precise job grades and salaries do vary to some extent from one institution to another but the following table gives a guide to the salaries that typically tally with certain job roles in HE.

Principal lecturer	£45,155–£52,347
Senior lecturer	£35,646–£43,840
Lecturer	£29,853–£34,607
Junior researcher	£23,566–£28,983

UNIVERSITIES

The following is a list of universities, which are those institutions that have been granted degree awarding powers by either a royal charter or an act of parliament, or have been permitted to use the word 'university' (or 'university college') by the Privy Council. There are other recognised bodies in the UK with degree awarding powers, as well as institutions offering courses leading to a degree from a recognised body. Further information is available at W www.dbis.gov.uk

Student figures represent the number of undergraduate and postgraduate students based on information available at May 2010.

For information on tuition fees and student loans, *see* The Education System.

RESEARCH ASSESSMENT EXERCISE

The research assessment exercise (RAE) gives a rating to each university department or specialist college put forward for evaluation, based on the quality of its research. It enables the higher education funding bodies to distribute public funds for research selectively on the basis of quality. Institutions conducting the best research receive a larger proportion of the available grant so that the infrastructure for the top level of research in the UK is protected and developed. The table below shows the top five universities or specialist colleges for each discipline based on the mean average ranking of the overall quality of their research. The next RAE is due at the end of 2012.

Subject	*Universities or university colleges*
Anthropology	LSE (1), SOAS (1), Cambridge (3), Roehampton (4), UCL (5)
Archaeology	Durham (1), Reading (2), Cambridge (3), Oxford (3), Liverpool (5)
Biological sciences	Institute of Cancer Research (1), Manchester (2), Oxford (2), Sheffield (2), Dundee (5), RHUL (5)
Business and management	London Business School (1), Imperial (2), Cambridge (3), Cardiff (4), Bath (5), King's (5), Lancaster (5), LSE (5), Oxford (5), Warwick (5)
Chemistry	Cambridge (1), Nottingham (2), Oxford (3), Bristol (4), Edinburgh (4), St Andrews (4)
Classics	Cambridge (1), Oxford (2), UCL (3), Durham (4), King's (4), Warwick (4)
Communication and media studies	Westminster (1), East Anglia (2), Goldsmiths (3), LSE (3), Cardiff (5)
Computer science	Cambridge (1), Edinburgh (2), Imperial (2), Southampton (2), Manchester (5), Oxford (5), UCL (5)
Dentistry	Manchester (1), Queen Mary (2), King's (3), Sheffield (4), Bristol (5), Cardiff (5)
Drama and performing arts	Queen Mary (1), St Andrews (1), Manchester (3), Warwick (4), Bristol (5), King's (5)
Economics	LSE (1), UCL (2), Essex (3), Oxford (3), Warwick (3)
Engineering (electronic)	Leeds (1), Bangor (2), Manchester (2), Surrey (2), Imperial (5)
Engineering (general)	Cambridge (1), Oxford (2), Leeds (3), Nottingham (3), Imperial (5), Swansea (5)
English	York (1), Edinburgh (2), Manchester (2), Queen Mary (2), Exeter (5), Nottingham (5), Oxford (5)
French	Oxford (1), King's (2), Warwick (2), Aberdeen (4), Cambridge (4), St Andrews (4)
Geography	Bristol (1), Cambridge (1), Durham (1), Oxford (1), Queen Mary (1)
German, Dutch and Scandinavian	Oxford (1), Cambridge (2), Durham (2), King's (2), Leeds (2), RHUL (2), St Andrews (2)
History	Imperial (1), Essex (2), Kent (2), Liverpool (2), Oxford (2), Warwick (2)
Law	LSE (1), UCL (2), Oxford (3), Durham (4), Nottingham (4)
Mathematics (applied)	Cambridge (1), Oxford (1), Bristol (3), Bath (4), Portsmouth (4), St Andrews (4)
Mathematics (pure)	Imperial (1), Warwick (2), Oxford (3), Cambridge (4), Bristol (5), Edinburgh (5), Heriot-Watt (5)
Music	RHUL (1), Birmingham (2), Manchester (2), Cambridge (4), King's (4), Sheffield (4), Southampton (4)
Philosophy	UCL (1), St Andrews (1), King's (3), Reading (3), Sheffield (3)
Physics	Lancaster (1), Bath (2), Cambridge (2), Nottingham (2), St Andrews (2)
Politics	Essex (1), Sheffield (1), Aberystwyth (3), Oxford (4), LSE (5)
Psychology	Cambridge (1), Oxford (2), Birmingham (3), UCL (4), Birkbeck (5), Cardiff (5)
Sociology	Essex (1), Goldsmiths (1), Manchester (1), York (1), Lancaster (5)
Sports-related subjects	Birmingham (1), Loughborough (1), Bristol (3), Liverpool John Moores (4), Stirling (5)

Subject	*Universities or university colleges*
Theology and religious studies	Durham (1), Aberdeen (2), Cambridge (3), Oxford (3), UCL (3)

UG= undergraduate PG= postgraduate

UNIVERSITY OF ABERDEEN (1495)
King's College, Aberdeen AB24 3FX **T** 01224-272000
E communications@abdn.ac.uk **W** www.abdn.ac.uk
Students: 10,760 UG; 4,095 PG
Chancellor, Lord Wilson of Tillyorn, KT, GCMG, FRSE
Principal and Vice-Chancellor, Prof. Ian Diamond
Academic Registrar, Dr Gillian Mackintosh

UNIVERSITY OF ABERTAY DUNDEE (1994)
Bell Street, Dundee DD1 1HG **T** 01382-308000
E enquiries@abertay.ac.uk **W** www.abertay.ac.uk
Students: 3,520 UG; 610 PG
Chancellor, Baron Cullen of Whitekirk, KT, PC, QC
Vice-Chancellor, Prof. Bernard King, CBE
Academic Registrar, Dr Colin Fraser

ANGLIA RUSKIN UNIVERSITY (1992)
Chelmsford Campus, Bishop Hall Lane, Chelmsford CM1 1SQ
T 0845-271 3333 **E** answers@anglia.ac.uk
W www.anglia.ac.uk
Students: 13,991 UG; 2,847 PG
Chancellor, Lord Ashcroft, KCMG
Vice-Chancellor, Prof. Michael Thorne, FRSA
The Secretary and Clerk, Stephen Bennett

UNIVERSITY OF THE ARTS LONDON (Formerly The London Institute (1986), University of the Arts London was formed in 2004)
272 High Holborn, London WC1V 7EY **T** 020-7514 6000
E info@arts.ac.uk **W** www.arts.ac.uk
Students: 22,051 UG; 2,061 PG
Chancellor, Lord Stevenson, CBE
Rector, Sir Michael Bichard, KCB
University Secretary, Martin Prince

COLLEGES

CAMBERWELL COLLEGE OF ARTS (1898)
Peckham Road, London SE5 8UF **T** 020-7514 6302
W www.camberwell.arts.ac.uk
Head of College, Chris Wainwright

CENTRAL SAINT MARTINS COLLEGE OF ART & DESIGN (1854)
Southampton Row, London WC1B 4AP **T** 020-7514 7022
W www.csm.arts.ac.uk
Head of College, Jane Rapley, OBE

CHELSEA COLLEGE OF ART & DESIGN (1895)
Millbank, London SW1P 4RJ **T** 020-7514 7751
W www.chelsea.arts.ac.uk
Head of College, Chris Wainwright

LONDON COLLEGE OF COMMUNICATION (1894)
Elephant & Castle, London SE1 6SB **T** 020-7514 6500
W www.lcc.arts.ac.uk
Head of College, Sandra Kemp

LONDON COLLEGE OF FASHION (1963)
20 John Princes Street, London W1G 0BJ **T** 020-7514 7500
W www.fashion.arts.ac.uk
Head of College, Dr Frances Corner

WIMBLEDON COLLEGE OF ART (1930)
Merton Hall Road, London SW19 3QA **T** 020-7514 9641
W www.wimbledon.arts.ac.uk
Head of College, Chris Wainwright

ASTON UNIVERSITY (1966)
Aston Triangle, Birmingham B4 7ET **T** 0121-204 3000
W www.aston.ac.uk
Students: 7,760 UG; 2,730 PG
Chancellor, Sir Michael Bett, CBE
Vice-Chancellor, Prof. Julia King, CBE, FRENG, FRSA
Chief Operating Officer, Richard Middleton

UNIVERSITY OF BATH (1966)
Bath BA2 7AY **T** 01225-388388 **W** www.bath.ac.uk
Students: 9,306 UG; 4,072 PG
Chancellor, Lord Tugendhat
Vice-Chancellor, Prof. Glynis Breakwell, FRSA
University Secretary, Mark Humphriss

BATH SPA UNIVERSITY (2005)
Newton Park, Newton St Loe, Bath BA2 9BN **T** 01225-875875
E enquiries@bathspa.ac.uk **W** www.bathspa.ac.uk
Students: 5,196 UG; 3,208 PG
Vice-Chancellor, Prof. Frank Morgan
Academic Registrar, Christopher Ellicott

UNIVERSITY OF BEDFORDSHIRE (1993)
Park Square, Luton LU1 3JU **T** 01234-400400
W www.beds.ac.uk
Students: 13,240 UG; 4,040 PG
Chancellor, Baroness Howells of St David, OBE
Vice-Chancellor, Prof. Les Ebdon, CBE
Registrar, Prof. Jim Franklin

UNIVERSITY OF BIRMINGHAM (1900)
Edgbaston, Birmingham B15 2TT **T** 0121-414 3344
W www.bham.ac.uk
Students: 16,696 UG; 8,060 PG
Chancellor, Sir Dominic Cadbury
Vice-Chancellor, Prof. David Eastwood
Registrar and Secretary, Mr Lee Sanders

BIRMINGHAM CITY UNIVERSITY (1992)
Franchise Street, Perry Barr, Birmingham B42 2SU
T 0121-331 5000 **E** choices@bcu.ac.uk **W** www.bcu.ac.uk
Students: 20,630 UG; 3,725 PG
Chancellor, Lord Mayor of Birmingham, Michael Wilkes
Vice-Chancellor, Prof. David H. Tidmarsh
University Secretary, Ms Christine Abbott

UNIVERSITY OF BOLTON (2005)
Deane Road, Bolton BL3 5AB **T** 01204-900600
E enquiries@bolton.ac.uk **W** www.bolton.ac.uk
Students: 10,681 UG; 2,360 PG
Chancellor, Rt. Hon. The Baroness of Bolton, OBE
Vice Chancellor, Dr George Holmes
Secetary and Clerk the Governors, Sue Duncan

BOURNEMOUTH UNIVERSITY (1992)
Fern Barrow, Poole BH12 5BB **T** 01202-524111
E enquiries@bournemouth.ac.uk **W** www.bournemouth.ac.uk
Students: 15,635 UG; 2,330 PG
Chancellor, Rt Hon. Lord Phillips of Worth Matravers, PC, QC
Vice-Chancellor, Prof. Paul Curran
Registrar, Noel Richardson

UNIVERSITY OF BRADFORD (1966)
Bradford BD7 1DP T 01274-232323 E vcp@bradford.ac.uk
W www.brad.ac.uk
Students: 9,485 UG; 3,255 PG
Chancellor, Imran Khan
Vice-Chancellor, Prof. Mark Cleary
Registrar, Adrian Pearce

UNIVERSITY OF BRIGHTON (1992)
Mithras House, Lewes Road, Brighton BN2 4AT
T 01273-600900 E postmaster@bton.ac.uk W www.bton.ac.uk
Students: 16,850 UG; 4,125 PG
Chairman, Lord Mogg
Vice-Chancellor, Prof. Julian Crampton
Registrar, Mrs Carol Burns

UNIVERSITY OF BRISTOL (1909)
Senate House, Tyndall Avenue, Bristol BS8 1TH
T 0117-928 9000 E public-relations@bristol.ac.uk
W www.bristol.ac.uk
Students: 12,963 UG; 5,181 PG
Chancellor, Baroness Hale of Richmond, DBE, PC
Vice Chancellor, Prof. Eric Thomas
Registrar, Derek Pretty

BRUNEL UNIVERSITY (1966)
Uxbridge UB8 3PH T 01895-274000
E admissions@brunel.ac.uk W www.brunel.ac.uk
Students: 10,837 UG; 4,041 PG
Chancellor, Lord Wakeham, PC
Vice-Chancellor and Principal, Prof. Chris Jenkins, FRSA
Interim Academic Registrar, Bob Westaway

UNIVERSITY OF BUCKINGHAM (1983)
Buckingham MK18 1EG T 01280-814080
E reception@buckingham.ac.uk W www.buckingham.ac.uk
Students: 776 UG; 277 PG
Chancellor, Lord Tanlaw of Tanlaw Hill
Vice-Chancellor, Dr Terence Kealey
Registrar, Prof. Len Evans

BUCKINGHAMSHIRE NEW UNIVERSITY (2007)
High Wycombe Campus, Queen Alexandra Road, High Wycombe HP11 2JZ T 0800-0565 660 E advice@bucks.ac.uk
W www.bucks.ac.uk
Students: 7,009 UG; 527 PG
Vice-Chancellor, Prof. Ruth Farwell
Academic Secretary, Ellie Smith

UNIVERSITY OF CAMBRIDGE (1209)
The Old Schools, Trinity Lane, Cambridge CB2 1TN
T 01223-337733 W www.cam.ac.uk
Students: 12,006 UG; 5,521 PG
Chancellor, HRH The Prince Philip, Duke of Edinburgh, KG, KT, OM, GBE, PC, FRS
Vice-Chancellor, Sir Leszek Borysiewicz, FRS (Wolfson)
High Steward, Lord Watson of Richmond, CBE (Jesus)
Deputy High Steward, Mrs A. Lonsdale, CBE (Murray Edwards)
Commissary, Lord Mackay of Clashfern, KT, PC, FRSE (Trinity)
Pro-Vice-Chancellors, Prof. I. H. White, FRE NG (Jesus); Prof. L. F. Gladden, CBE, FRS (Trinity); Dr J. C. Barnes (Murray Edwards); Prof. J. M. Rallison (Trinity); Prof. S. J. Young, FRENG (Emmanuel)
Proctors, J. A. Trevithick (King's); Dr J. P. Spencer (Sidney Sussex)
Orator, Dr R. J. E. Thompson (Selwyn)
Registrary, Dr J. W. Nicholls (Emmanuel)
Librarian, Mrs A. E. Jarvis (Wolfson)
Director of the Fitzwilliam Museum, Dr T. F. Potts (Clare)
Academic Secretary, G. P. Allen (Wolfson)
Director of Finance, A. M. Reid (Wolfson)

COLLEGES AND HALLS *with dates of foundation*
CHRIST'S (1505)
Master, Prof. F. P. Kelly, FRS
CHURCHILL (1960)
Master, Prof. Sir David Wallace, CBE, FRS
CLARE (1326)
Master, Prof. A. J. Badger
CLARE HALL (1966)
President, Prof. Sir Martin Harris, CBE
CORPUS CHRISTI (1352)
Master, Mr S. Laing
DARWIN (1964)
Master, Prof. W. A. Brown, CBE
DOWNING (1800)
Master, Prof. B. J. Everitt, FRS
EMMANUEL (1584)
Master, Lord Wilson of Dinton, GCB
FITZWILLIAM (1966)
Master, Prof. R. D. Lethbridge
GIRTON (1869)
Mistress, Prof. S. J. Smith, FBA
GONVILLE AND CAIUS (1348)
Master, Sir Christopher Hum, KCMG
HOMERTON (1824)
Principal, Dr K. B. Pretty, CBE
HUGHES HALL (1985)
President, Mrs S. L. Squire
JESUS (1496)
Master, Prof. R. Mair, CBE, FRS
KING'S (1441)
Provost, Prof. T. R. Harrison
LUCY CAVENDISH (1965)
President, Prof. J. M. Todd
MAGDALENE (1542)
Master, Mr D. D. Robinson, CBE
MURRAY EDWARDS (1954)
President, Dr J. C. Barnes
NEWNHAM (1871)
Principal, Dame Patricia Hodgson, DBE
PEMBROKE (1347)
Master, Sir Richard Dearlove, KCMG, OBE
PETERHOUSE (1284)
Master, Prof. A. K. Dixon, FRCP
QUEENS' (1448)
President, Prof. Lord Eatwell
ROBINSON (1977)
Warden, Prof. A. D. Yates
ST CATHARINE'S (1473)
Master, Prof. Dame Jean Thomas, DBE, FRS
ST EDMUND'S (1896)
Master, Prof. J. P. Luzio, FRCPATH
ST JOHN'S (1511)
Master, Prof. C. M. Dobson, FRS
SELWYN (1882)
Master, Prof. R. J. Bowring
SIDNEY SUSSEX (1596)
Master, Prof. A. F. Wallace-Hadrill, OBE
TRINITY (1546)
Master, Prof. Lord Rees of Ludlow, OM, PRS
TRINITY HALL (1350)
Master, Prof. M. J. Daunton, FBA

WOLFSON (1965)
President, Prof. R. J. Evans, FBA

CANTERBURY CHRIST CHURCH UNIVERSITY (2005)
North Holmes Road, Canterbury CT1 1QU **T** 01227-767700
W www.canterbury.ac.uk **E** admissions@canterbury.co.uk
Students: 12,618 UG; 4,137 PG
Vice-Chancellor and Principal, Prof. Michael Wright
Academic Registrar, Lorri Currie

CARDIFF UNIVERSITY (1883)
Cardiff CF10 3XQ **T** 029-2087 4000 **W** www.cardiff.ac.uk
Students: 20,089 UG; 7,438 PG
President, Prof. Sir Martin Evans, FRS
Vice-Chancellor, Dr David Grant, CBE, FRENG

UNIVERSITY OF CENTRAL LANCASHIRE (1992)
Preston PR1 2HE **T** 01772-201201 **W** www.uclan.ac.uk
E cenquiries@uclan.ac.uk
Students: 24,595 UG; 3,535 PG
Chancellor, Sir Richard Evans, CBE
Vice-Chancellor, Dr Malcolm McVicar

UNIVERSITY OF CHESTER (2005)
Parkgate Road, Chester CH1 4BJ **T** 01244-511000
E enquiries@chester.ac.uk **W** www.chester.ac.uk
Students: 11,836 UG; 3,759 PG
Chancellor, His Grace, The Duke of Westminster, KG, OBE, DL
Vice-Chancellor, Canon Prof. Tim Wheeler, DL
Director of Registry Services, Mr Jonathan Moores

UNIVERSITY OF CHICHESTER (2005)
Bishop Otter Campus, College Lane, Chichester PO19 6PE
T 01243-816000 **W** www.chiuni.ac.uk **E** info@chi.ac.uk
Students: 4,103 UG; 1,347 PG
Vice-Chancellor (acting), Prof. Clive Behagg
University Secretary, Isabel Cherrett

CITY UNIVERSITY (1966)
Northampton Square, London EC1V 0HB **T** 020-7040 5060
E enquiries@city.ac.uk **W** www.city.ac.uk
Students: 14,597 UG; 6,619 PG
Chancellor, Lord Mayor of the City of London Nick Anstee
Vice-Chancellor, Prof. Paul Curran

COVENTRY UNIVERSITY (1992)
Priory Street, Coventry CV1 5FB **T** 024-7688 7688
W www.coventry.ac.uk
Students: 14,832 UG; 3,257 PG
Chancellor, Sir John Egan
Vice-Chancellor, Prof. Madeleine Atkins
Academic Registrar and Secretary, Ms Kate Quantrell

CRANFIELD UNIVERSITY (1969)
Cranfield MK43 0AL **T** 01234-750111 **E** info@cranfield.ac.uk
W www.cranfield.ac.uk
Students: 5,320 PG (postgraduate only)
Chancellor, Baroness Young of Old Scone
Vice-Chancellor, Prof. Sir John O'Reilly
Secretary and Registrar, Prof. William Stephens

UNIVERSITY FOR THE CREATIVE ARTS (2008)
Falkner Road, Farnham GU9 7DS **T** 01252-722441
W www.ucreative.ac.uk
Students: 5,070 UG; 215 PG
Chancellor, Zandra Rhodes
Vice-Chancellor, Prof. Elaine Thomas
University Secretary, Marion Wilks

UNIVERSITY OF CUMBRIA (2007)
Fusehill Street, Carlisle CA1 2HH **T** 01228-616234
W www.cumbria.ac.uk
Students: 10,415 UG; 2,690 PG
Chancellor, Most Rev. and Rt Hon. Dr John Sentamu, Archbishop of York
Interim Vice-Chancellor, Prof. Graham Upton
University Secretary, Neil Harris

DE MONTFORT UNIVERSITY (1992)
The Gateway, Leicester LE1 9BH **T** 0845-945 4647
E enquiry@dmu.ac.uk **W** www.dmu.ac.uk
Students: 17,088 UG; 3,821 PG
Chancellor, Lord Waheed Alli
Vice-Chancellor, Prof. Dominic Shellard
Registrar, Eugene Critchlow

UNIVERSITY OF DERBY (1992)
Kedleston Road, Derby DE22 1GB **T** 01332-590500
E askadmissions@derby.ac.uk **W** www.derby.ac.uk
Students: 15,866 UG; 3,217 PG
Chancellor, The Duke of Devonshire, KCVO, CBE
Vice-Chancellor, Prof. John Coyne
Registrar, June Hughes

UNIVERSITY OF DUNDEE (1967)
Nethergate, Dundee DD1 4HN **T** 01382-383000
E university@dundee.ac.uk **W** www.dundee.ac.uk
Students: 10,550 UG; 4,970 PG
Chancellor, Lord Patel, KT, FRSE
Principal and Vice-Chancellor, Prof. Peter Downes, OBE, FRSE
Secretary, Dr Jim McGeorge

DURHAM UNIVERSITY (1832)
The University Office, Old Elvet, Durham DH1 3HP
T 0191-334 2000 **W** www.dur.ac.uk
Students: 11,370 UG; 5,475 PG
Chancellor, Bill Bryson
Vice-Chancellor and Warden, Prof. Christopher Higgins, FRSE
Registrar and Secretary, Carolyn Fowler

COLLEGES
COLLINGWOOD (1972)
Principal, Prof E. Corrigan, FRS
GREY
Master, Prof. J. M. Chamberlain, DPHIL
HATFIELD (1846)
Master, Prof. T. P. Burt, DSC
JOHN SNOW (2001)
Principal, Prof. Carolyn Summerbell
JOSEPHINE BUTLER (2006)
Principal, A. Simpson
ST AIDAN'S
Principal (acting), Dr Susan F. Frenk
ST CHAD'S (1904)
Principal, Revd Dr J. P. M. Cassidy
ST CUTHBERT'S SOCIETY (1888)
Principal, Prof. G. Towl
ST HILD AND ST BEDE (1975)
Principal, Prof. C. J. Hutchinson
ST JOHN'S (1909)
Principal, Revd Dr D. Wilkinson

ST MARY'S
Principal, Prof. P. Gilmartin
STEPHENSON (2001)
Principal, Prof. A. C. Darnell
TREVELYAN (1966)
Principal, Prof. H. M. Evans
UNIVERSITY (1832)
Master, Prof. M. E. Tucker
USHAW
President, Fr. J. Marsland
USTINOV
Principal, Penelope B. Wilson, DPHIL
VAN MILDERT (1965)
Master, Prof. P. O'Meara, DPHIL

UNIVERSITY OF EAST ANGLIA (1963)
Norwich NR4 7TJ **T** 01603-456161 **E** press@uea.ac.uk
W www.uea.ac.uk
Students: 10,988 UG; 3,260 PG
Chancellor, Sir Brandon Gough
Vice-Chancellor, Prof. Edward Acton
Registrar, Brian Summers

UNIVERSITY OF EAST LONDON (1898)
University Way, London E16 2RD **T** 020-8223 3333
E study@uel.ac.uk **W** www.uel.ac.uk
Students: 13,735 UG; 5,044 PG
Chancellor, Lord Rix
Vice-Chancellor, Prof. Patrick McGhee
Registrar, Jill Grinstead

EDGE HILL UNIVERSITY (2006)
St Helens Road, Ormskirk L39 4QP **T** 01695-575171
W www.edgehill.ac.uk
Students: 10,735 UG; 13,605 PG
Chancellor, Prof. Tanya Byron
Vice-Chancellor, Dr John Cater
University Secretary, Lesley Munroe

UNIVERSITY OF EDINBURGH (1583)
Old College, South Bridge, Edinburgh EH8 9YL
T 0131-650 1000 **E** communications.office@ed.ac.uk
W www.ed.ac.uk
Students: 17,285 UG; 7,235 PG
Chancellor, HRH The Prince Philip, Duke of Edinburgh, KG, KT, OM
Principal and Vice-Chancellor, Prof. Sir Timothy O'Shea, FRSE
University Secretary, Melvyn Cornish

EDINBURGH NAPIER UNIVERSITY (1992)
Craighouse Road, Edinburgh EH10 5LG **T** 0845-260 6040
E info@napier.ac.uk **W** www.napier.ac.uk
Students: 13,107 UG; 2,584 PG
Chancellor, Tim Waterstone
Vice-Chancellor, Prof. Dame Joan Stringer, CBE
Secretary, Dr Gerry Webber

UNIVERSITY OF ESSEX (1965)
Wivenhoe Park, Colchester CO4 3SQ **T** 01206-873333
W www.essex.ac.uk
Students: 6,376 UG; 2,786 PG
Chancellor, Lord Phillips of Sudbury, OBE
Vice-Chancellor, Prof. Colin Riordan
Academic Registrar, Dr Tony Rich

UNIVERSITY OF EXETER (1955)
The Queen's Drive, Exeter EX4 4QJ **T** 01392-661000
W www.exeter.ac.uk
Students: 11,356 UG; 4,167 PG
Chancellor, Floella Benjamin, OBE
Vice-Chancellor, Prof. Steve Smith
Registrar and Secretary, David Allen

UNIVERSITY OF GLAMORGAN (1992)
Pontypridd CF37 1DL **T** 0845-6434 030 **E** enquiries@glam.ac.uk
W www.glam.ac.uk
Students: 17,635 UG; 3,265 PG
Chancellor, Lord Morris of Aberavon, KG, PC, QC
Vice-Chancellor, Julie Lydon
Academic Registrar, William Callaway

UNIVERSITY OF GLASGOW (1451)
Gilbert Scott Building, University Avenue, Glasgow G12 8QQ
T 0141-330 2000 **E** communications@gla.ac.uk
W www.gla.ac.uk
Students: 16,558 UG; 5,366 PG
Chancellor, Prof. Sir Kenneth Calman, KCB, MD, FRCS
Vice-Chancellor, Prof. Anton Muscatelli, FRSE
Secretary of Court, David Newall

GLASGOW CALEDONIAN UNIVERSITY (1993)
City Campus, Cowcaddens Road, Glasgow G4 0BA
T 0141-331 3000 **E** helpline@gcal.ac.uk
W www.caledonian.ac.uk
Students: 15,135 UG; 3,275 PG
Chancellor, Lord Macdonald of Tradeston, PC, CBE
Vice-Chancellor and Principal, Prof. Pamela Gillies, FRSA
Secretary, Jan Hulme

UNIVERSITY OF GLOUCESTERSHIRE (2001)
The Park, Cheltenham GL50 2RH **T** 0844-801 0001
E marketing@glos.ac.uk **W** www.glos.ac.uk
Students: 7,641 UG; 1,588 PG
Chancellor, vacant
Acting Vice-Chancellor, Dr Paul Hartley
Academic Registrar, Julie Thackray

UNIVERSITY OF GREENWICH (1992)
Old Royal Naval College, Park Row, Greenwich, London SE10 9LS **T** 020-8331 8000 **E** courseinfo@gre.ac.uk
W www.gre.ac.uk
Students: 20,549 UG; 5,567 PG
Chancellor, Lord Hart of Chilton
Vice-Chancellor, Baroness Blackstone
Secretary and Registrar, Linda Cording

HERIOT-WATT UNIVERSITY (1966)
Edinburgh EH14 4AS **T** 0131-449 5111 **E** enquiries@hw.ac.uk
W www.hw.ac.uk
Students: 6,395 UG; 2,594 PG
Chancellor, Baroness Susan Greenfield, CBE, FRCP
Principal and Vice-Chancellor, Prof. Steve Chapman, FRSE
Secretary, Peter Wilson

UNIVERSITY OF HERTFORDSHIRE (1992)
College Lane, Hatfield AL10 9AB **T** 01707-284000
W www.herts.ac.uk
Students: 19,840 UG; 5,280 PG
Chancellor, Lord Salisbury, PC
Vice-Chancellor, Prof. Tim Wilson
Registrar, Philip Waters

UNIVERSITY OF HUDDERSFIELD (1992)
Queensgate, Huddersfield HD1 3DH **T** 01484-422288
W www.hud.ac.uk
Students: 17,735 UG; 3,421 PG
Chancellor, Prof. Sir Patrick Stewart, OBE

Vice-Chancellor, Prof. Bob Cryan
Head of Registry, Mrs Kathy Sherlock

UNIVERSITY OF HULL (1927)
Cottingham Road, Hull HU6 7RX **T** 01482-346311
W www.hull.ac.uk
Students: 19,045 UG; 3,325 PG
Chancellor, Baroness Bottomley, PC
Vice-Chancellor, Prof. Calie Pistorius, FRSA
Registrar and Secretary, Mrs Frances Owen

IMPERIAL COLLEGE LONDON (1907)
South Kensington SW7 2AZ **T** 020-7589 5111
W www.imperial.ac.uk
Students: 8,580 UG; 5,570 PG
Acting Rector, Sir Keith O'Nions
Deputy Rector, Prof. Stephen Richardson
Academic Registrar, Nigel Wheatley

KEELE UNIVERSITY (1962)
Keele ST5 5BG **T** 01782-732000 **W** www.keele.ac.uk
Students: 6,400 UG; 2,700 PG
Chancellor, Prof. Sir David Weatherall, DSC, MD, FRCP
Vice-Chancellor, Prof. Nick Foskett
Registrar and Secretary, Simon Morris

UNIVERSITY OF KENT (1965)
Canterbury CT2 7NZ **T** 01227-764000
E information@kent.ac.uk **W** www.kent.ac.uk
Students: 16,463 UG; 2,536 PG
Chancellor, Prof. Sir Robert Worcester, KBE
Vice-Chancellor, Prof. Julia Goodfellow, CBE
Academic Registrar, Jon Pink

KINGSTON UNIVERSITY (1992)
River House, 53–57 High Street, Kingston upon Thames
KT1 1LQ **T** 020-8417 9000 **E** admissions-info@kingston.ac.uk
W www.kingston.ac.uk
Students: 19,535 UG; 6,250 PG
Chancellor, Sir Peter Hall
Vice-Chancellor, Prof. Sir Peter Scott
Academic Registrar, Dr David Ashton

UNIVERSITY OF LANCASTER (1964)
Bailrigg, Lancaster LA1 4YW **T** 01524-65201
W www.lancs.ac.uk
Students: 9,430 UG; 3,265 PG
Chancellor, Sir Christian Bonington, CBE
Vice-Chancellor, Prof. Paul Wellings
University Secretary, Fiona Aiken

UNIVERSITY OF LEEDS (1904)
Leeds LS2 9JT **T** 0113-243 1751 **W** www.leeds.ac.uk
Students: 24,374 UG; 6,931 PG
Chancellor, Lord Bragg, LLD, DLITT, DCL
Vice-Chancellor, Prof. Michael Arthur, DM, FRCP
Secretary, Mr Roger Gair

LEEDS METROPOLITAN UNIVERSITY (1992)
Civic Quarter, Leeds LS1 3HE **T** 0113-812 0000
E course-enquiries@leedsmet.ac.uk **W** www.leedsmet.ac.uk
Students: 23,660 UG; 4,140 PG
Chancellor, vacant
Vice-Chancellor, Prof. Susan Price
Registrar, Stephen Denton

UNIVERSITY OF LEICESTER (1957)
University Road, Leicester LE1 7RH **T** 0116-252 2522
W www.le.ac.uk
Students: 10,971 UG; 10,657 PG
Chancellor, vacant
Vice-Chancellor, Prof. Sir Robert Burgess
Registrar, Dave Hall

UNIVERSITY OF LINCOLN (1992)
Brayford Pool, Lincoln LN6 7TS **T** 01522-882000
E enquiries@lincoln.ac.uk **W** www.lincoln.ac.uk
Students: 10,000 UG; 1,460 PG
Vice-Chancellor, Prof. Mary Stuart
Registrar, Mr Chris Spendlove

UNIVERSITY OF LIVERPOOL (1903)
Liverpool L69 7ZX **T** 0151-794 2000 **W** www.liv.ac.uk
Students: 14,049 UG; 3,036 PG
Chancellor, Prof. Sir David King, CH, PC, FRCP
Vice-Chancellor, Prof. Sir Howard Newby, FRSA
Chief Operating Officer, Patrick Hackett

LIVERPOOL HOPE UNIVERSITY (2005)
Hope Park, Liverpool L16 9JD **T** 0151-291 3000
E admission@hope.ac.uk **W** www.hope.ac.uk
Students: 5,570 UG; 1,375 PG
Chancellor, Baroness Cox
Vice-Chancellor, Prof. Gerald Pillay, FRSA
Registrar, Neil McLaughlin Cook

LIVERPOOL JOHN MOORES UNIVERSITY (1992)
Egerton Court, 2 Rodney Street, Liverpool L3 5UX
T 0151-231 2121 **E** recruitment@ljmu.ac.uk
W www.ljmu.ac.uk
Students: 21,074 UG; 4,923 PG
Chancellor, Dr Brian May, CBE
Vice-Chancellor, Prof. Michael Brown, CBE, DL
Secretary, Alison Wild

UNIVERSITY OF LONDON (1836)
Senate House, Malet Street, London WC1E 7HU **T** 020-7862 8000 **E** enquiries@london.ac.uk **W** www.london.ac.uk
Chancellor, HRH the Princess Royal, KG, GCVO, FRS
Vice-Chancellor, Prof. Sir Graeme Davies, FRENG, FRSE
Chair of the Board of Trustees, Dame Jenny Abramsky
Director of Administration, Catherine Swarbrick

COLLEGES

BIRKBECK COLLEGE
Malet Street, London WC1E 7HX
Students: 4,263 UG; 3,075 PG
President, Prof. Eric Hobsbawm
Master, Prof. David Latchman

CENTRAL SCHOOL OF SPEECH AND DRAMA
Embassy Theatre, Eton Avenue, London NW3 3HY
Students: 600 UG; 216 PG
President, Michael Grandage
Principal, Prof. Gavin Henderson, CBE

COURTAULD INSTITUTE OF ART
North Block, Somerset House, Strand, London WC2R 0RN
Students: 150 UG; 220 PG
Director, Dr Deborah Swallow

GOLDSMITHS COLLEGE
Lewisham Way, New Cross, London SE14 6NW
Students, 4,075 UG; 2,064 PG
Warden, Pat Loughrey

HEYTHROP COLLEGE
Kensington Square, London W8 5HQ
Students: 320 UG; 480 PG
Principal, Revd Dr John McDade, SJ, BD

INSTITUTE OF CANCER RESEARCH
123 Old Brompton Road, London SW7 3RP
Students: 300 PG (postgraduate only)
Chief Executive, Prof. Peter Rigby

INSTITUTE OF EDUCATION
20 Bedford Way, London WC1H 0AL
Students: 310 UG; 7,075 PG
Director, Prof. Geoff Whitty

KING'S COLLEGE LONDON (includes Guy's, King's and St Thomas's Schools of Medicine, Dentistry and Biomedical Sciences)
Strand, London WC2R 2LS
Students: 14,280 UG; 5,720 PG
Principal, Prof. Rick Trainor

LONDON BUSINESS SCHOOL
Regent's Park, London NW1 4SA
Students: 1,869 PG (postgraduate only)
Dean, Sir Andrew Likierman

LONDON SCHOOL OF ECONOMICS AND POLITICAL SCIENCE
Houghton Street, London WC2A 2AE
Students: 4,238 UG; 5,314 PG
Director, Sir Howard Davies

LONDON SCHOOL OF HYGIENE AND TROPICAL MEDICINE
Keppel Street, London WC1E 7HT
Students: 1,048 PG (postgraduate only)
Dean, Prof. Sir Andrew Haines

QUEEN MARY (incorporating St Bartholomew's and the Royal London School of Medicine and Dentistry)
Mile End Road, London E1 4NS
Students: 12,000 UG; 3,000 PG
Principal, Prof. Simon Gaskell

ROYAL ACADEMY OF MUSIC
Marylebone Road, London NW1 5HT
Students: 331 UG; 353 PG
Principal, Prof. Jonathan Freeman-Attwood

ROYAL HOLLOWAY
Egham Hill, Egham, Surrey TW20 0EX
Students: 6,560 UG; 1,825 PG
Acting Principal, Prof. Rob Kemp

ROYAL VETERINARY COLLEGE
Royal College Street, London NW1 0TU
Students: 1,533 UG; 351 PG
Principal and Dean, Prof. Quintin McKellar

ST GEORGE'S
Cranmer Terrace, London SW17 0RE
Students: 2,900 UG; 400 PG
Principal, Prof. Peter Kopelman, FRCGP

SCHOOL OF ORIENTAL AND AFRICAN STUDIES
Thornhaugh Street, Russell Square, London WC1H 0XG
Students: 2,421 UG; 1,847 PG
Director, Prof. Paul Webley

SCHOOL OF PHARMACY
29–39 Brunswick Square, London WC1N 1AX
Students: 700 UG; 135 PG
Dean, Prof. Anthony Smith

UNIVERSITY COLLEGE LONDON (including UCL Medical School)
Gower Street, London WC1E 6BT
Students: 12,600 UG; 8,500 PG
Provost and President, Prof. Malcolm Grant, CBE

INSTITUTES

UNIVERSITY OF LONDON INSTITUTE IN PARIS
9–11 rue de Constantine, 75340 Paris Cedex 07
Dean, Prof. Andrew Hussey

UNIVERSITY MARINE BIOLOGICAL STATION
Millport, Isle of Cumbrae KA28 0EG
Director, Prof. Jim Atkinson

SCHOOL OF ADVANCED STUDY
Senate House, Malet Street, London WC1E 7HU
Dean, Prof. Avrom Sherr

INSTITUTE OF ADVANCED LEGAL STUDIES
Charles Clore House, 17 Russell Square, London WC1B 5DR
Director, Prof. Avrom Sherr

INSTITUTE OF CLASSICAL STUDIES
Senate House, Malet Street, London WC1E 7HU
Director, Prof. M. Edwards

INSTITUTE OF COMMONWEALTH STUDIES
Senate House, Malet Street, London WC1E 7HU
Director, Prof. Philip Murphy

INSTITUTE OF ENGLISH STUDIES
Senate House, Malet Street, London WC1E 7HU
Director, Prof. Warwick Gould

INSTITUTE OF GERMANIC AND ROMANCE STUDIES
Senate House, Malet Street, London WC1E 7HU
Director, Prof. Naomi Segal

INSTITUTE OF HISTORICAL RESEARCH
Senate House, Malet Street, London WC1E 7HU
Director, Prof. Miles Taylor

INSTITUTE OF MUSICAL RESEARCH
Senate House, Malet Street, London WC1E 7HU
Director, Prof. John Irving

INSTITUTE OF PHILOSOPHY
Senate House, Malet Street, London WC1E 7HU
Director, Prof. Barry Smith

INSTITUTE FOR THE STUDY OF THE AMERICAS
Senate House, Malet Street, London WC1E 7HU
Director, Prof. Maxine Molyneux

WARBURG INSTITUTE
Woburn Square, London WC1H 0AB
Director, Prof. C. Hope

LONDON METROPOLITAN UNIVERSITY (2002)
31 Jewry Street, London EC3N 2EY **T** 020-7423 0000
W www.londonmet.ac.uk **E** admissions@londonmet.ac.uk
Students: 19,505 UG; 6,875 PG
Vice-Chancellor and Chief Executive, Prof. Malcolm Gillies
Academic Registrar, Dr Ray Smith

LONDON SOUTH BANK UNIVERSITY (1992)
103 Borough Road, London SE1 0AA T 020-7815 7815
W www.lsbu.ac.uk E enquiry@lsbu.ac.uk
Students: 13,705 UG; 5,809 PG
Chancellor, vacant
Vice-Chancellor, Martin Earwicker

LOUGHBOROUGH UNIVERSITY (1966)
Ashby Road, Loughborough LE11 3TU T 01509-263171
W www.lboro.ac.uk
Students: 11,963 UG; 4,176 PG
Chancellor, Sir John Jennings, CBE, FRSE, PHD
Vice-Chancellor, Prof. Shirley Pearce, CBE
Chief Operating Officer, Will Spinks

UNIVERSITY OF MANCHESTER (2004)
Oxford Road, Manchester M13 9PL T 0161-306 6000
W www.manchester.ac.uk
Students: 27,194 UG; 9,827 PG
Chancellor, Tom Bloxham, MBE
President and Vice-Chancellor, Prof. Dame Nancy Rothwell
Registrar and Secretary, Albert McMenemy

MANCHESTER METROPOLITAN UNIVERSITY (1992)
All Saints, Manchester M15 6BH T 0161-247 2000
E enquiries@mmu.ac.uk W www.mmu.ac.uk
Students: 27,669 UG; 7,008 PG
Chancellor, vacant
Vice-Chancellor, Prof. John Brooks, DSC
Registrar, Gwyn Arnold

MIDDLESEX UNIVERSITY (1992), Hendon Campus, The Burroughs, London NW4 4BT T 020-8411 5555
E admissions@mdx.ac.uk W www.mdx.ac.uk
Students: 16,450 UG; 4,895 PG
Chancellor, Lord Sheppard of Didgemere, KT, KCVO
Vice-Chancellor, Prof. Michael Driscoll
Academic Registrar, Colin Davis

NEWCASTLE UNIVERSITY (1963)
Newcastle upon Tyne NE1 7RU T 0191-222 6000
W www.ncl.ac.uk
Students: 14,155 UG; 4,723 PG
Chancellor, Prof. Sir Liam Donaldson
Vice-Chancellor, Prof. Chris Brink, FRS, DPHIL
Registrar, Dr John Hogan

UNIVERSITY OF NORTHAMPTON (2005)
Park Campus, Boughton Green Road, Northampton NN2 7AL
T 01604-735500 E study@northampton.ac.uk
W www.northampton.ac.uk
Students: 10,520 UG; 2,160 PG
Chancellor, Baroness Falkner
Vice-Chancellor, Ann Tate
Registrar, Jane Bunce

NORTHUMBRIA UNIVERSITY AT NEWCASTLE (1992)
Ellison Building, Ellison Place, Newcastle upon Tyne NE1 8ST
T 0191-232 6002 W www.northumbria.ac.uk
E ca.marketing@northumbria.ac.uk
Students: 27,541 UG; 5,225 PG
Chancellor, Lord Stevens of Kirkwhelpington, QPM, DCL
Vice-Chancellor, Prof. Andrew Wathey, FRS
Registrar, Paul Kelly

UNIVERSITY OF NOTTINGHAM (1948)
King's Meadow Campus, Lenton Lane, Nottingham NG7 2NR
T 0115-951 5151
E undergraduate-enquiries@nottingham.ac.uk
W www.nottingham.ac.uk
Students: 23,401 UG; 7,274 PG
Chancellor, Prof. Yang Fujia, LITTD
Vice Chancellor, Prof. David Greenaway
Registrar, Dr Paul Greatrix

NOTTINGHAM TRENT UNIVERSITY (1992)
Burton Street, Nottingham NG1 4BU T 0115-941 8418
E cor.web@ntu.ac.uk W www.ntu.ac.uk
Students: 20,245 UG; 4,660 PG
Chancellor, Sir Michael Parkinson, MBE
Vice-Chancellor, Prof. Neil Gorman
Registrar, David Samson

OPEN UNIVERSITY (1969)
Walton Hall, Milton Keynes MK7 6AA T 01908-274066
E general-enquiries@open.ac.uk W www.open.ac.uk
Students: 180,124 UG; 15,645 PG
Chancellor, Lord Puttnam
Vice-Chancellor, Mr Martin Bean
Director, Students, Will Swan

UNIVERSITY OF OXFORD (*c.*12th century)
University Offices, Wellington Square, Oxford OX1 2JD
T 01865-270000 E information.office@admin.ox.ac.uk
W www.ox.ac.uk
Students: 11,766 UG; 8,701 PG
Chancellor, Lord Patten of Barnes, CH, PC (Balliol, St Antony's)
High Steward, Lord Rodger of Earlsferry (Balliol, New, St Hugh's)
Vice-Chancellor, Prof. Andrew Hamilton
Pro-Vice-Chancellors, Dr Sally Mapstone (St Hilda's); Prof. E. G. McKendrick (Lady Margaret Hall); Prof. A. P. Monaco (Merton); Prof. M. J. Earl (Green Templeton); Prof. I. A. Walmsley (St. Hugh's)
Registrar, Dr J. K. Maxton (University)
Secretary of the Faculties and Academic Registrar, M. D. Sibly (St Anne's)
Public Orator, R. H. A. Jenkyns (Lady Margaret Hall)
Director of University Library Services and Bodley's Librarian, Dr S. E. Thomas (Balliol)
Director of the Ashmolean Museum, Dr C. Brown (Worcester)
Keeper of Archives, S. Bailey (Linacre)
Director of Estates, Ms J. Wood (Lincoln)
Director of Finance, G. F. B. Kerr (Keble)

COLLEGES AND HALLS *with dates of foundation*
ALL SOULS (1438)
Warden, Prof. Sir John Vickers, FBA
BALLIOL (1263)
Master, Andrew Graham
BLACKFRIARS (1221)
Regent, Revd Dr Richard Finn
BRASENOSE (1509)
Principal, Prof. Roger Cashmore, CMG, FRS
CAMPION HALL (1896)
Master, Revd Brendan Callaghan
CHRIST CHURCH (1546)
Dean, Very Revd Dr Christopher A. Lewis
CORPUS CHRISTI (1517)
President, Prof. Richard Carwardine, FBA

EXETER (1314)
Rector, Ms Frances Cairncross, CBE, FRSE
GREEN TEMPLETON (2008)
Principal, Prof. Sir David Watson
HARRIS MANCHESTER (1889)
Principal, Revd Dr Ralph Waller, FRSE
HERTFORD (1740)
Principal, Dr John Landers
JESUS (1571)
Principal, Lord Krebs, FRS
KEBLE (1870)
Warden, Sir Jonathan Phillips
KELLOGG (1990)
President, Prof. Jonathan M. Michie
LADY MARGARET HALL (1878)
Principal, Dr Frances Lannon
LINACRE (1962)
Principal, Dr Nick Brown
LINCOLN (1427)
Rector, Prof. Paul Langford, FBA
MAGDALEN (1458)
President, Prof. David Clary, FRS
MANSFIELD (1886)
Principal, Dr Diana Walford, CBE, FRCP
MERTON (1264)
Warden, Prof. Sir Martin Taylor
NEW COLLEGE (1379)
Warden, Prof. Sir Curtis Price
NUFFIELD (1958)
Warden, Prof. Stephen Nickell, CBE, FBA
ORIEL (1326)
Provost, Sir Derek Morris
PEMBROKE (1624)
Master, Giles Henderson, CBE
QUEEN'S (1341)
Provost, Prof. Paul Madden, FRS, FRSE
REGENT'S PARK (1810)
Principal, Revd Dr Robert Ellis
ST ANNE'S (1878)
Principal, Tim Gardam
ST ANTONY'S (1953)
Warden, Prof. Margaret MacMillan
ST BENET'S HALL (1897)
Master, Revd J. Felix Stephens
ST CATHERINE'S (1963)
Master, Prof. Roger Ainsworth
ST CROSS (1965)
Master, Prof. Andrew Goudie
ST EDMUND HALL (*C.*1278)
Principal, Prof. Keith Gull, CBE, FRS
ST HILDA'S (1893)
Principal, Sheila Forbes, CBE
ST HUGH'S (1886)
Principal, Andrew Dilnot, CBE
ST JOHN'S (1555)
President, Sir Michael Scholar, KCB
ST PETER'S (1929)
Principal, Mark Damazer
ST STEPHEN'S HOUSE (1876)
Principal, Revd Dr Robin Ward
SOMERVILLE (1879)
Principal, Dr Alice Prochaska
TRINITY (1554)
President, Sir Ivor Roberts, KCMG
UNIVERSITY (1249)
Master, Sir Ivor Crewe
WADHAM (1610)
Warden, Sir Neil Chalmers
WOLFSON (1981)
President, Prof. Hermione Lee, FBA, FRSL, CBE
WORCESTER (1714)
Provost, Richard Smethurst
WYCLIFFE HALL (1877)
Principal, Revd Dr Richard Turnbull

OXFORD BROOKES UNIVERSITY (1992)
Gipsy Lane, Oxford OX3 0BP **T** 01865-741111
E query@brookes.ac.uk **W** www.brookes.ac.uk
Students: 13,985 UG; 4,185 PG
Chancellor, Shami Chakrabarti, CBE
Vice-Chancellor, Prof. Janet Beer
Academic Registrar, Matthew P. Andrews

UNIVERSITY OF PLYMOUTH (1992)
Drake Circus, Plymouth PL4 8AA **T** 01752-600600
E publicrelations@plymouth.ac.uk **W** www.plymouth.ac.uk
Students: 27,107 UG; 4,907 PG
Vice-Chancellor and Chief Executive, Prof. Wendy Purcell
Academic Registrar and Secretary, Miss Jane Hopkinson

UNIVERSITY OF PORTSMOUTH (1992)
University House, Winston Churchill Avenue, Portsmouth
PO1 2UP **T** 023-9284 8484 **E** info.centre@port.ac.uk
W www.port.ac.uk
Students: 17,265 UG; 4,115 PG
Chancellor, Sheila Hancock, OBE
Vice-Chancellor, Prof. John Craven
Academic Registrar, Andrew Rees

QUEEN MARGARET UNIVERSITY (2007)
Queen Margaret University Drive, Musselburgh, Edinburgh
EH21 6UU **T** 0131-474 0000 **E** marketing@qmu.ac.uk
W www.qmu.ac.uk
Students: 4,525 UG; 1,376 PG
Chancellor, Sir Tom Farmer, CBE, KCSG
Vice Chancellor, Dr Petra Wend
Academic Registrar, Irene Hynd

QUEEN'S UNIVERSITY BELFAST (1908)
University Road, Belfast BT7 1NN **T** 028-9024 5133
W www.qub.ac.uk **E** comms.office@qub.ac.uk
Students: 17,512 UG; 5,299 PG
Chancellor, His Excellency Kamalesh Sharma
Vice-Chancellor, Prof. Peter Gregson, FRENG
Registrar, James O'Kane

UNIVERSITY OF READING (1926)
Whiteknights, PO Box 217, Reading RG6 6AH **T** 0118-987 5123
W www.reading.ac.uk
Students: 13,949 UG; 5,785 PG
Chancellor, Sir John Madejski, OBE, DL
Vice-Chancellor, Prof. Gordon Marshall, CBE, FBA
Secretary, Keith Hodgson

ROBERT GORDON UNIVERSITY (1992)
Schoolhill, Aberdeen AB10 1FR **T** 01224-262000
E admissions@rgu.ac.uk **W** www.rgu.ac.uk
Students: 9,866 UG; 5,713 PG
Chancellor, Sir Ian Wood, CBE
Vice-Chancellor (acting), Prof. John Harper
Academic Registrar, Hilary Douglas

ROEHAMPTON UNIVERSITY (2004)
Erasmus House, Roehampton Lane, London SW15 5PU
T 020-8392 3000 **E** enquiries@roehampton.ac.uk
W www.roehampton.ac.uk

Students: 6,560 UG; 2,345 PG
Chancellor, John Simpson, CBE
Vice-Chancellor, Prof. Paul O'Prey
Academic Secretary, Robin Geller

ROYAL COLLEGE OF ART (1967)
Kensington Gore, London SW7 2EU **T** 020-7590 4444
E admissions@rca.ac.uk **W** www.rca.ac.uk
Students: 880 PG
Provost, Sir Terence Conran
Rector and Vice-Provost, Dr Paul Thomson
Registrar, Alan Selby

ROYAL COLLEGE OF MUSIC (1882)
Prince Consort Road, London SW7 2BS **T** 020-7589 3643
E info@rcm.ac.uk **W** www.rcm.ac.uk
Students: 300 UG; 380 PG
President, HRH The Prince of Wales, KG, KT, GCB
Vice-Chancellor, Prof. Colin Lawson, DMUS, FRCM
Deputy Director, Kevin Porter

UNIVERSITY OF ST ANDREWS (1413)
College Gate, St Andrews KY16 9AJ **T** 01334-476161
E admissions@st-andrews.ac.uk **W** www.st-andrews.ac.uk
Students: 7,420 UG; 1,850 PG
Chancellor, Sir Menzies Campbell, CBE, QC, MP
Principal and Vice-Chancellor, Dr Louise Richardson
Registrar, Lorraine Fraser

UNIVERSITY OF SALFORD (1967)
Salford M5 4WT **T** 0161-295 5000 **W** www.salford.ac.uk
Students: 15,899 UG; 3,407 PG
Chancellor, Dr Irene Khan
Vice-Chancellor, Prof. Martin Hall
Registrar, Dr Adrian Graves

UNIVERSITY OF SHEFFIELD (1905)
Western Bank, Sheffield S10 2TN **T** 0114-222 2000
W www.sheffield.ac.uk **E** ask@sheffield.ac.uk
Students: 18,463 UG; 5,856 PG
Chancellor, Sir Peter Middleton, GCB
Vice-Chancellor, Prof. Keith Burnett, CBE, DPHIL, FRS
Registrar and Secretary, Philip Harvey

SHEFFIELD HALLAM UNIVERSITY (1992)
City Campus, Howard Street, Sheffield S1 1WB
T 0114-225 5555 **W** www.shu.ac.uk
Students: 25,555 UG; 8,270 PG
Chancellor, Prof. Lord Winston, DSC, FRCOG, FRCP
Vice-Chancellor, Prof. Philip Jones, LLB, LLM
Secretary and Registrar, Elizabeth Winders

UNIVERSITY OF SOUTHAMPTON (1952)
Building 37, Highfield, Southampton SO17 1BJ
T 023-8059 5000 **E** prospenq@soton.ac.uk
W www.soton.ac.uk
Students: 16,800 UG; 5,880 PG
Chancellor Sir John Parker
Vice-Chancellor, Prof. Don Nutbeam
Registrar and Chief Operating Officer, Simon Higman

SOUTHAMPTON SOLENT UNIVERSITY (2005)
East Park Terrace, Southampton SO14 0YN **T** 023-8031 9000
E ask@solent.ac.uk **W** www.solent.ac.uk
Students: 11,000 UG; 486 PG
Chancellor, Admiral the Lord West of Spithead, GCB, DSC
Vice-Chancellor, Prof. Van Gore

STAFFORDSHIRE UNIVERSITY (1992)
Federation House, Stoke-on-Trent ST4 2DE **T** 01782-294000
W www.staffs.ac.uk
Students: 13,385 UG; 3,605 PG
Chancellor, Lord Morris of Handsworth
Vice-Chancellor, Prof. Christine E. King, CBE, FRSA
University Secretary, Ken Sproston

UNIVERSITY OF STIRLING (1967)
Stirling FK9 4LA **T** 01786-473171 **E** externalrelations@stir.ac.uk
W www.external.stir.ac.uk
Students: 7,550 UG; 2,575 PG
Chancellor, Dr James Naughtie, OBE
Vice-Chancellor, Prof. Gerry McCormac, FRSE
Registrar, Mrs Joanna Morrow

UNIVERSITY OF STRATHCLYDE (1964)
16 Richmond Street, Glasgow G1 1XQ **T** 0141-552 4400
W www.strath.ac.uk **E** corporatecomms@strath.ac.uk
Students: 11,676 UG; 4,537 PG
Chancellor, Rt. Hon. Lord Hope of Craighead, FRSE
Vice-Chancellor, Prof. Jim McDonald, DPHIL, FRSC, FRSE
Chief Operating Officer, Hugh Hall

UNIVERSITY OF SUNDERLAND (1992)
Edinburgh Building, Chester Road, Sunderland SR1 3SD
T 0191-515 2000 **E** student.helpline@sunderland.ac.uk
W www.sunderland.ac.uk
Students: 17,160 UG; 2,870 PG
Chancellor, Steve Cram, MBE
Vice-Chancellor, Prof. Peter Fidler
Secretary, Mr John Pacey

UNIVERSITY OF SURREY (1966)
Guildford GU2 7XH **T** 01483-300800 **E** enquiries@surrey.ac.uk
W www.surrey.ac.uk
Students: 10,280 UG; 5,475 PG
Chancellor, HRH the Duke of Kent, KG, GCMG, GCVO
Vice-Chancellor, Prof. Christopher Snowden, FRS, FRENG
Registrar, Mr Philip Henry, TD

UNIVERSITY OF SUSSEX (1961)
Sussex House, Brighton BN1 9RH **T** 01273-606755
E information@sussex.ac.uk **W** www.sussex.ac.uk
Students: 9,635 UG; 2,725 PG
Chancellor, Sanjeev Bhaskar, OBE
Vice-Chancellor, Prof. Michael Farthing
Academic Registrar, Owen Richards

UNIVERSITY OF TEESSIDE (1992)
Middlesbrough TS1 3BA **T** 01642-218121 **E** registry@tees.ac.uk
W www.tees.ac.uk
Students: 24,883 UG; 3,071 PG
Chancellor, Lord Sawyer
Vice-Chancellor and Chief Executive, Prof. Graham Henderson
University Secretary and Registrar, Morgan McClintock

THAMES VALLEY UNIVERSITY (1993)
St Mary's Road, Ealing, London W5 5RF **T** 020-8579 5000
W www.tvu.ac.uk
Students: 15,035 UG; 2,075 PG
Chancellor, Lord Bilimoria, CBE
Vice-Chancellor, Prof. Peter John
Secretary and Registrar, Ann Marie Dalton

UNIVERSITY OF ULSTER (1984)
Cromore Road, Coleraine BT52 1SA T 0870-040 0700
W www.ulster.ac.uk
Students: 18,415 UG; 4,745 PG
Chancellor, James Nesbitt
Vice-Chancellor, Prof. Richard Barnett
Registrar, Norma Cameron

UNIVERSITY OF WALES (1893)
King Edward VII Avenue, Cathays Park, Cardiff CF10 3NS
T 029-2037 6999 E uniwales@wales.ac.uk W www.wales.ac.uk
Chancellor, HRH The Prince of Wales, KG, KT, GCB
Vice-Chancellor and Chief Executive, Prof. Marc Clement

ACCREDITED INSTITUTIONS
ABERYSTWYTH UNIVERSITY
Old College, King Street, Aberystwyth SY23 2AX
T 01970-623111
Students: 8,385 UG; 1,825 PG
Vice-Chancellor, Prof. N. G. Lloyd

BANGOR UNIVERSITY
Gwynedd LL57 2DG T 01248-351151
Students: 8,800 UG; 2,395 PG
Vice-Chancellor, Prof. M. Jones

GLYNDWR UNIVERSITY
Mold Road, Wrexham LL11 2AW
T 01978-293439
Students: 6,815 UG; 915 PG
Principal, Prof. M. Scott

UNIVERSITY OF WALES INSTITUTE, CARDIFF
Llandaff Campus, Western Avenue, Cardiff CF5 2YB
T 029-2041 6070
Students: 8,040 UG; 3,005 PG
Vice-Chancellor, Prof. A. J. Chapman

UNIVERSITY OF WALES, LAMPETER
Lampeter SA48 7ED T 01570-422351
Students: 4,840 UG; 1,320 PG
Vice-Chancellor, Dr Medwin Hughes

UNIVERSITY OF WALES, NEWPORT
Caerleon Campus, Newport NP18 3QT
T 01633-430088
Students: 7,360 UG; 1,705 PG
Vice-Chancellor, Dr P. Noyes

SWANSEA UNIVERSITY
Singleton Park SA2 8PP T 01792-205678
Students: 11,890 UG; 2,125 PG
Vice-Chancellor, Prof. R. B. Davies

SWANSEA METROPOLITAN UNIVERSITY
Mount Pleasant, Swansea SA1 6ED
T 01792-481000
Students: 4,725 UG; 1,150 PG
Vice-Chancellor, Prof. D. Warner

TRINITY COLLEGE, CARMARTHEN
Carmarthen SA31 3EP T 01267-676767
Students: 2,090 UG; 255 PG
Vice-Chancellor, Dr M. Hughes

UNIVERSITY OF WARWICK (1965)
Coventry CV4 7AL T 024-7652 3523 W www.warwick.ac.uk
Students: 12,510 UG; 9,088 PG
Chancellor, Richard Lambert
Vice-Chancellor, Prof. Nigel Thrift
Registrar, Jon Baldwin

UNIVERSITY OF WESTMINSTER (1992)
309 Regent Street, London W1B 2UW T 020-7911 5000
E course_enquiries@westminster.ac.uk
W www.westminster.ac.uk
Students: 16,430 UG; 6,730 PG
Chancellor, Lord Paul
Vice-Chancellor and Rector, Prof. Geoffrey Petts
Registrar and Secretary, Carole Mainstone

UNIVERSITY OF THE WEST OF ENGLAND (1992)
Frenchay Campus, Coldharbour Lane, Bristol BS16 1QY
T 0117-965 6261 E enquiries@uwe.ac.uk W www.uwe.ac.uk
Students: 23,535 UG; 6,595 PG
Chancellor, Rt. Hon. Baroness Elizabeth Butler-Sloss, GBE
Vice-Chancellor, Prof. Steven West, KB, CBE
Academic Registrar, Tessa Harrison

UNIVERSITY OF THE WEST OF SCOTLAND (1992)
Paisley PA1 2BE T 0141-848 3000 E uni-direct@uws.ac.uk
W www.uws.ac.uk
Students: 10,000 UG; 10,000 PG
Chancellor, Lord Smith of Kelvin, FSA, KT
Principal and Vice-Chancellor, Prof. Seamus McDaid
Secretary, Kenneth Alexander

UNIVERSITY OF WINCHESTER (2005)
Winchester SO22 4NR T 01962-841515
E course.enquiries@winchester.ac.uk W www.winchester.ac.uk
Students: 4,671 UG; 1,253 PG
Chancellor, Mary Fagan
Vice-Chancellor, Prof. Joy Carter
Registrar, Malcolm Willis

UNIVERSITY OF WOLVERHAMPTON (1992)
Wulfruna Street, Wolverhampton WV1 1LY T 01902-321000
W www.wlv.ac.uk
Students: 19,198 UG; 4,116 PG
Chancellor, Rt Hon. Lord Paul of Marylebone
Vice-Chancellor, Prof. Caroline Gipps
Academic Registrar, Mr Paul Travill

UNIVERSITY OF WORCESTER (2005)
Henwick Grove, Worcester WR2 6AJ T 01905-855000
E study@worc.ac.uk W www.worcester.ac.uk
Students: 6,664 UG; 1,655 PG
Chancellor, HRH The Duke of Gloucester, KG, GCVO
Vice-Chancellor and Chief Executive, Prof. David Green
Registrar and Secretary, John Ryan

UNIVERSITY OF YORK (1963)
Heslington, York YO10 5DD T 01904-430000
W www.york.ac.uk
Students: 9,699 UG; 3,310 PG
Chancellor, Greg Dyke
Vice-Chancellor, Prof. Brian Cantor, FRENG, FIM, FRMS
Registrar, Dr David Duncan

YORK ST JOHN UNIVERSITY (2006)
Lord Mayor's Walk, York YO31 7EX T 01904-624624
E admissions@yorksj.ac.uk W www.yorksj.ac.uk
Students: 4,815 UG; 766 PG
Chancellor, Most Revd and Rt Hon Dr John Sentamu, Archbishop of York, PC
Vice-Chancellor, Prof. David Fleming
Registrar, Pauline Aldous

PROFESSIONAL EDUCATION

The organisations selected below provide specialist training, conduct examinations or are responsible for maintaining a register of those with professional qualifications in their sector, thereby controlling entry into a profession.

EU RECOGNITION

It is possible for those with professional qualifications obtained in the UK to have these recognised in other European countries. Further information can be obtained from:

EUROPE OPEN UK NARIC, Oriel House, Oriel Road, Cheltenham, Glos GL50 1XP **T** 0871-226 2850 **W** www.europeopen.org.uk

ACCOUNTANCY

Salary range for chartered accountants:

Certified £14,500–£25,000 (starting) rising to £29,000–£52,000+ (qualified), £40,000–£100,000+ at senior levels

Management £23,000 (starting), £25,000–£57,000 (newly qualified), £62,000–£106,000+ at senior levels

Public finance £28,500–£34,000 (newly qualified) rising to £34,000–£150,000+

Most chartered accountancy trainees are graduates, although some contracts are available to school-leavers. The undergraduate degree is followed by a three-year training contract with an approved employer culminating in professional exams provided by the Institute of Chartered Accountants in England and Wales (ICAEW), the Institute of Chartered Accountants of Scotland (ICAS) or the Institute of Chartered Accountants in Ireland (ICAI). Success in the examination and membership of one of the institutes allows the use of the designation 'chartered accountant' and the letters ACA or CA.

The training route for chartered certified accountants is similar to that of chartered accountants and is taken by students in a range of business sectors and countries. The Association of Chartered Certified Accountants (ACCA) qualification involves up to 14 examinations and a minimum of three years of relevant supervised experience. Chartered certified accountants can use the designatory letters ACCA.

Chartered management accountants focus on accounting for businesses, and most do not work in accountancy practices but in industry, commerce, not-for-profit and public sector organisations. Graduates who have not studied a business or accounting undergraduate degree must gain the Chartered Institute of Management Accountants (CIMA) Certificate in Business Accounting (formerly known as the foundation level) before studying for the CIMA Professional Qualification. This qualification requires three years of practical experience combined with nine examinations and a pass in the Institute's Test of Professional Competence in Management Accounting (TOPCIMA).

Chartered public finance accountants usually work for public bodies, but they can also work in the private sector. To gain chartered public finance accountant status (CPFA), trainees must complete the three parts of the Chartered Institute of Public Finance and Accountancy (CIPFA) Professional Accountancy Qualification (PAQ), which takes approximately three years. The first stage is the certificate level, which leads to affiliate membership of CIPFA, the second is the diploma level which leads to associate membership, and finally completion of the Final Test of Professional Competence leads to full membership of CIPFA.

ASSOCIATION OF CHARTERED CERTIFIED ACCOUNTANTS (ACCA) 29 Lincoln's Inn Fields, London WC2A 3EE **T** 020-7059 5000 **E** info@accaglobal.com **W** www.accaglobal.com
Chief Executive, Helen Brand

CHARTERED INSTITUTE OF MANAGEMENT ACCOUNTANTS (CIMA) 26 Chapter Street, London SW1P 4NP **T** 020-8849 2251 **E** cima.contact@cimaglobal.com **W** www.cimaglobal.com
Chief Executive, Charles Tilley

CHARTERED INSTITUTE OF PUBLIC FINANCE AND ACCOUNTANCY (CIPFA) 3 Robert Street, London WC2N 6RL **T** 020-7543 5600 **E** corporate@cipfa.org.uk **W** www.cipfa.org.uk
Chief Executive, Steve Freer

INSTITUTE OF CHARTERED ACCOUNTANTS IN ENGLAND AND WALES (ICAEW) Chartered Accountants' Hall, PO Box 433, London EC2P 2BJ **T** 020-7920 8100 **W** www.icaew.com
Chief Executive, Michael Izza

INSTITUTE OF CHARTERED ACCOUNTANTS IN IRELAND (ICAI) The Linenhall, 32–38 Linenhall Street, Belfast BT2 8BG **T** 028-9043 5840 **E** ca@icai.ie **W** www.icai.ie
Chief Executive, Pat Costello

INSTITUTE OF CHARTERED ACCOUNTANTS OF SCOTLAND (ICAS) CA House, 21 Haymarket Yards, Edinburgh EH12 5BH **T** 0131-347 0100 **E** enquiries@icas.org.uk **W** www.icas.org.uk
Chief Executive, Anton Colella

ACTUARIAL SCIENCE

Salary range: £25,000–£35,000 for graduate trainees; £45,000–£55,000 after qualification; £60,000–£100,000+ for senior roles

Actuaries apply financial and statistical theories to solve business problems. These problems usually involve analysing future financial events in order to assess investment risks. Until July 2010 the actuarial profession was controlled by the Faculty of Actuaries in Edinburgh and the Institute of Actuaries in London. Following a vote of their respective memberships, the Faculty and Institute merged to form one professional body in the UK: the Institute and Faculty of Actuaries. This body develops actuarial techniques and sets examinations, professional codes and disciplinary standards. UK qualified actuaries are fellows and bear the designations FIA or FFA. On average, it takes five years to qualify as an actuary; examinations are held twice a year, and applicants to the profession must also have completed three years of actuarial work experience before gaining fellowship.

The Financial Reporting Council (FRC) is the unified

independent regulator for corporate reporting, auditing, actuarial practice, corporate governance and the professionalism of accountants and actuaries. The FRC's Board for Actuarial Standards sets and maintains technical actuarial standards independently of the profession while the Professional Oversight Board of the FRC oversees the regulation of the accountancy and actuarial professions by their respective professional bodies. The Accountancy and Actuarial Discipline Board operates an investigation and discipline scheme in relation to members of the profession who raise issues affecting UK public interest.

FINANCIAL REPORTING COUNCIL (FRC) 5th Floor, Aldwych House, 71–91 Aldwych, London WC2B 4HN
T 020-7492 2300 W www.frc.org.uk
Chief Executive, Stephen Haddrill

INSTITUTE AND FACULTY OF ACTUARIES
Staple Inn Hall, High Holborn, London WC1V 7QJ
T 020-7632 2100 E info@actuaries.org.uk
W www.actuaries.org.uk
Chief Executive, Caroline M. Instance

ARCHITECTURE

Salary range: £17,000–£30,000 during training; newly registered £25,000–£35,000; project architect and senior roles £35,000–£80,000+

It takes a minimum of seven years to become an architect, involving three stages: a three-year first degree, a two-year second degree or diploma and two years of professional experience followed by the successful completion of a professional practice examination.

The Architects Registration Board (ARB) is the independent regulator for the profession. It was set up by an act of parliament in 1997 and is responsible for maintaining the register of UK architects, prescribing qualifications that lead to registration as an architect, investigating complaints about the conduct and competence of architects, and ensuring only those who are registered with ARB offer their services as an architect. It is only following registration with ARB that an architect can apply for chartered membership of the Royal Institute of British Architects (RIBA). RIBA, the UK body for architecture and the architectural profession, received its royal charter in 1837 and validates courses at over 40 UK schools of architecture; it also validates overseas courses. RIBA provides support and guidance for its members in the form of training, technical services and events and sets standards for the education of architects.

The Chartered Institute of Architectural Technologists is the international qualifying body for chartered architectural technologists (MCIAT) and architectural technicians (TCIAT).

ARCHITECTS REGISTRATION BOARD (ARB)
8 Weymouth Street, London W1W 5BU T 020-7580 5861
E info@arb.org.uk W www.arb.org.uk
Registrar and Chief Executive, Alison Carr

CHARTERED INSTITUTE OF ARCHITECTURAL TECHNOLOGISTS 397 City Road, London EC1V 1NH
T 020-7278 2206 E info@ciat.org.uk W www.ciat.org.uk
Chief Executive, Francesca Berriman

ROYAL INCORPORATION OF ARCHITECTS IN SCOTLAND 15 Rutland Square, Edinburgh EH1 2BE
T 0131-229 7545 E info@rias.org.uk W www.rias.org.uk
Secretary and Treasurer, Neil Baxter

ROYAL INSTITUTE OF BRITISH ARCHITECTS (RIBA) 66 Portland Place, London W1B 1AD
T 020-7580 5533 E info@inst.riba.org W www.riba.org
Chief Executive, Harry Rich

ENGINEERING

Salary range:
Civil/structural £27,000–£34,000 (graduate); £32,000–£48,000 with experience, rising to £80,000+ in senior posts
Chemical £26,000 average (graduate); £44,000–£72,000+ (chartered)
Electrical £20,000–£23,000 (graduate); £45,000+ with experience

The Engineering Council sets standards of professional competence and ethics for engineers, technologists and technicians, and regulates the profession through the 36 institutions (Licensed Members) listed below who are licensed to put suitably qualified members on the Engineering Council's Register of Engineers. All candidates for registration as chartered engineer, incorporated engineer, engineering technician or information and communication technology technicians must satisfy the competence standards set by the Engineering Council and be members of the appropriate institution. Applicants must show that they have a satisfactory educational base, have undergone approved professional development, and, at interview, must demonstrate their professional competence against specific criteria.

ENGINEERING COUNCIL 246 High Holborn, London WC1V 7EX T 020-3206 0500 E info@engc.org.uk
W www.engc.org.uk
Chief Executive Officer, Andrew Ramsay

LICENSED MEMBERS
British Computer Society W www.bcs.org.uk
British Institute of Non-destructive Testing W www.bindt.org
Chartered Institution of Building Services Engineers W www.cibse.org
Chartered Institution of Highways and Transportation W www.ciht.org.uk
Chartered Institute of Plumbing and Heating Engineers W www.ciphe.org.uk
Chartered Institution of Water and Environmental Management W www.ciwem.org
Energy Institute W www.energyinst.org.uk
Institute of Acoustics W www.ioa.org.uk
Institute of Cast Metals Engineers W www.icme.org.uk
Institute of Healthcare Engineering and Estate Management W www.iheem.org.uk
Institute of Highway Engineers W www.ihie.org.uk
Institute of Marine Engineering, Science and Technology W www.imarest.org
Institute of Materials, Minerals and Mining W www.iom3.org
Institute of Measurement and Control W www.instmc.org.uk
Institute of Physics W www.iop.org
Institute of Physics and Engineering in Medicine W www.ipem.ac.uk
Institute of Water W www.instituteofwater.org.uk
Institution of Agricultural Engineers W www.iagre.org
Institution of Chemical Engineers W www.icheme.org
Institution of Civil Engineers W www.ice.org.uk
Institution of Diesel and Gas Turbine Engineers W www.idgte.org.uk
Institution of Engineering Designers W www.ied.org.uk
Institution of Engineering and Technology W www.theiet.org
Institution of Fire Engineers W www.ife.org.uk

Institution of Gas Engineers and Managers W www.igem.org.uk
Institution of Lighting Engineers W www.ile.org.uk
Institution of Mechanical Engineers W www.imeche.org
Institution of Railway Signal Engineers W www.irse.org
Institution of Royal Engineers W www.instre.org
Institution of Structural Engineers W www.istructe.org
Nuclear Institute W www.nuclearinst.com
Royal Aeronautical Society W www.raes.org.uk
Royal Institution of Naval Architects W www.rina.org.uk
Society of Environmental Engineers W www.environmental.org.uk
Society of Operations Engineers W www.soe.org.uk
Welding Institute W www.twi.co.uk

HEALTHCARE

CHIROPRACTIC
Salary range: £22,000–£40,000 starting salary; with own practice up to £70,000

Chiropractors diagnose and treat conditions caused by problems with joints, ligaments, tendons and nerves of the body. The General Chiropractic Council (GCC) is the independent statutory regulatory body for chiropractors and its role and remit is defined in the Chiropractors Act 1994. The GCC sets the criteria for the recognition of chiropractic degrees and for standards of proficiency and conduct. Details of the institutions offering degree programmes are available on the GCC website (*see* below). It is illegal for anyone in the UK to use the title 'chiropractor' unless registered with the GCC.

The British Chiropractic Association and the Scottish Chiropractic Association are two representative bodies for the profession and are sources of further information.

BRITISH CHIROPRACTIC ASSOCIATION 59 Castle Street, Reading RG1 7SN T 0118-950 5950 W www.chiropractic-uk.co.uk
Executive Director, Sue Wakefield

GENERAL CHIROPRACTIC COUNCIL 44 Wicklow Street, London WC1X 9HL T 020-7713 5155 E enquiries@gcc-uk.org W www.gcc-uk.org
Chief Executive, Margaret Coats

SCOTTISH CHIROPRACTIC ASSOCIATION 1 Chisholm Avenue, Bishopton, Renfrewshire PA7 5JH T 0141-404 0260 E admin@sca-chiropractic.org W www.sca-chiropractic.org
Administrator, Morag Cairns

DENTISTRY
Salary range: see Health: Employees and Salaries

The General Dental Council (GDC) is the organisation that regulates dental professionals in the United Kingdom. All dentists, dental hygienists, dental therapists, clinical dental technicians, dental nurses and orthodontic therapists must be registered with the GDC to work in the UK.

There are various different routes to qualify for registration as a dentist, including holding a degree from a UK university; completing the GDC's qualifying examination; or holding a relevant European Economic Area or overseas diploma. The GDC's purpose is to protect the public through the regulation of UK dental professionals. It keeps up-to-date registers of dental professionals, works to set standards of dental practice, behaviour and education, and helps to protect patients by hearing complaints and taking action against professionals where necessary.

The British Dental Association is a membership organisation that provides dentists with professional and educational services.

BRITISH DENTAL ASSOCIATION 64 Wimpole Street, London W1G 8YS T 020-7935 0875 E enquiries@bda.org W www.bda.org
Chief Executive, Peter Ward

GENERAL DENTAL COUNCIL 37 Wimpole Street, London W1G 8DQ T 020-7887 3800 E information@gdc-uk.org W www.gdc-uk.org
Chief Executive, Evlynne Gilvarry

MEDICINE
Salary range: see Health: Employees and Salaries

The General Medical Council (GMC) regulates medical education and training in the UK. This covers undergraduate study (usually five years), the two-year foundation programme taken by doctors directly after graduation, and all subsequent postgraduate study, including specialty and GP training.

All doctors must be registered with the GMC, which is responsible for protecting the public. It does this by setting standards for professional practice, overseeing medical education, keeping a register of qualified doctors and taking action where a doctor's fitness to practise is in doubt. Doctors are eligible for full registration upon successful completion of the first year of training after graduation.

Following the foundation programme, many doctors undertake specialist training (provided by the colleges and faculties listed below) to become either a consultant or a GP. Once specialist training has been completed, doctors are awarded the Certificate of Completion of Training (CCT) and are eligible to be placed on either the GMC's specialist register or its GP register.

GENERAL MEDICAL COUNCIL (GMC) 350 Euston Road, London NW1 3JN T 0845-357 8001 E gmc@gmc-uk.org W www.gmc-uk.org
Chief Executive, Niall Dickson

SOCIETY OF APOTHECARIES OF LONDON Black Friars Lane, London EC4V 6EJ T 020-7236 1189 E clerk@apothecaries.org W www.apothecaries.org
Master, Dr R. G. H. Bethel

SPECIALIST TRAINING COLLEGES AND FACULTIES
College of Emergency Medicine W www.collemergencymed.ac.uk
Faculty of Pharmaceutical Medicine W www.fpm.org.uk
Faculty of Public Health W www.fph.org.uk
Royal College of Anaesthetists W www.rcoa.ac.uk
Royal College of General Practitioners W www.rcgp.org.uk
Royal College of Obstetricians and Gynaecologists W www.rcog.org.uk
Royal College of Opthalmologists W www.rcophth.ac.uk
Royal College of Paediatrics and Child Health W www.rcpch.ac.uk
Royal College of Pathologists W www.rcpath.org
Royal College of Physicians, London W www.rcplondon.ac.uk
Royal College of Physicians and Surgeons of Glasgow W www.rcpsg.ac.uk
Royal College of Physicians of Edinburgh W www.rcpe.ac.uk
Royal College of Psychiatrists W www.rcpsych.ac.uk
Royal College of Radiologists W www.rcr.ac.uk
Royal College of Surgeons of Edinburgh W www.rcsed.ac.uk
Royal College of Surgeons of England W www.rcseng.ac.uk

MEDICINE, SUPPLEMENTARY PROFESSIONS

The standard of professional education for arts therapists, biomedical scientists, chiropodists and podiatrists, clinical scientists, dietitians, occupational therapists, operating department practitioners, orthoptists, paramedics, physiotherapists, practitioner psychologists, prosthetists and orthotists, radiographers, and speech and language therapists is regulated by the Health Professions Council (HPC), who only register those practitioners who meet certain standards of training, professional skills, behaviour and health. Other than biomedical science and clinical science, all the professions listed below are described by the NHS as 'allied health professions'. The HPC currently registers over 200,000 professionals.

HEALTH PROFESSIONS COUNCIL Park House, 184 Kennington Park Road, London SE11 4BU **T** 020-7582 0866 **E** info@hpc-uk.org **W** www.hpc-uk.org
Chief Executive and Registrar, Marc Seale

ART, DRAMA AND MUSIC THERAPIES
Salary range: £25,000–£39,000

An art, drama or music therapist encourages people to express their feelings and emotions through art, such as painting and drawing, drama or music. A postgraduate qualification in the relevant therapy is required. Details of accredited training programmes in the UK can be obtained from the following organisations:

ASSOCIATION OF PROFESSIONAL MUSIC THERAPISTS 24–27 White Lion Street, London N1 9PD **T** 020-7387 6100 **E** apmtoffice@aol.com **W** www.apmt.org
Chair, Stephen Sandford

BRITISH ASSOCIATION OF ART THERAPISTS 24–27 White Lion Street, London N1 9PD **T** 020-7686 4216 **E** info@baat.org **W** www.baat.org
Chief Executive, Val Huet

BRITISH ASSOCIATION OF DRAMA THERAPISTS Waverley, Battledown Approach, Cheltenham, Gloucestershire GL52 6RE **T** 01242-235 5155 **E** enquiries@badth.org.uk **W** www.badth.org.uk
Chair, Madeline Andersen-Warren

BIOMEDICAL SCIENCES
Salary range: £21,000–£66,000+

Biomedical scientists analyse specimens from patients in order to help make diagnoses. Qualifications from higher education establishments and training in medical laboratories are required for membership of the Institute of Biomedical Science, which sets the professional standards of competence for those who practise biomedical science.

INSTITUTE OF BIOMEDICAL SCIENCE 12 Coldbath Square, London EC1R 5HL **T** 020-7713 0214 **E** mail@ibms.org **W** www.ibms.org
Chief Executive, Alan Potter, MBE

CHIROPODY AND PODIATRY
Salary range: £21,000–£40,000

Chiropodists and podiatrists assess, diagnose and treat problems of the lower leg and foot. The Society of Chiropodists and Podiatrists is the professional body and trade union for the profession. Qualifications granted and degrees recognised by the society are approved by the Health Professions Council (HPC). HPC registration is required in order to use the titles chiropodist and podiatrist.

SOCIETY OF CHIROPODISTS AND PODIATRISTS 1 Fellmonger's Path, Tower Bridge Road, London SE1 3LY **T** 0845-450 3720 **E** enq@scpod.org **W** www.feetforlife.org
Chief Executive, Joanna Brown

CLINICAL SCIENCE
Salary range: £25,000–£95,000+

Clinical scientists conduct tests in laboratories in order to diagnose and manage disease. The Association of Clinical Scientists is responsible for setting the criteria for competence of applicants to the HPC's register and to present a Certificate of Attainment to candidates following a successful assessment. This certificate will allow direct registration with the HPC.

ASSOCIATION OF CLINICAL SCIENTISTS c/o Association for Clinical Biochemistry, 130–132 Tooley Street, London SE1 2TU **T** 020-7940 8960 **E** info@assclinsci.org **W** www.assclinsci.org
Chair, Dr Iain Chambers

DIETETICS
Salary range: £21,000–£40,000

Dietitians advise patients on how to improve their health and counter specific health problems through diet. The British Dietetic Association, established in 1936, is the professional association for dietitians. Full membership is open to UK-registered dietitians, who must also be registered with the Health Professions Council.

BRITISH DIETETIC ASSOCIATION 5th Floor, Charles House, 148–149 Great Charles Street Queensway, Birmingham B3 3HT **T** 0121-200 8080 **E** info@bda.uk.com **W** www.bda.uk.com
Chief Executive, Andy Burman

OCCUPATIONAL THERAPY
Salary range: £21,000–£40,000

Occupational therapists work with people who have physical, mental and/or social problems, either from birth or as a result of accident, illness or ageing, and aim to make them as independent as possible. The professional qualification and eligibility for registration may be obtained upon successful completion of a validated course in any of the educational institutions approved by the College of Occupational Therapists, which is the professional body for occupational therapy in the UK. The courses are normally degree-level courses based in higher education institutions.

COLLEGE OF OCCUPATIONAL THERAPISTS 106–114 Borough High Street, London SE1 1LB **T** 020-7357 6480 **W** www.cot.org.uk
Chief Executive, Julia Scott

MENTAL HEALTH
Salary range:
Clinical psychologist £25,000 rising to £30,000–£97,000+ in senior roles
Counsellor £18,000–£27,000 rising to £40,000–£50,000 with experience
Educational psychologist £21,000 rising to £31,000 when chartered and up to £56,000 in senior posts
Psychotherapist £21,000–£26,000 (starting) rising to £77,000+ in senior positions

Mental health professionals (other than psychiatrists, who are trained doctors) can work in a range of settings including prisons, schools and hospitals as well as businesses. The UK psychological profession is represented by the British Psychological Society (BPS), which has more than 49,000 members. It accredits qualifications in psychology, and offers support to members through continuing professional development. The Association of Educational Psychologists (AEP) represents the interests of educational psychologists, while the British Association for Counselling and Psychotherapy (BACP) sets educational standards and provides professional support to those psychologists working in psychotherapy or counselling-related roles. The BPS website provides more information on the different specialisations that may be pursued by psychologists.

ASSOCIATION OF EDUCATIONAL PSYCHOLOGISTS (AEP) 4 The Riverside Centre, Frankland Lane, Durham DH1 5TA T 0191-384 9512 E enquiries@aep.org.uk W www.aep.org.uk
General Secretary, Kate Fallon

BRITISH ASSOCIATION FOR COUNSELLING AND PSYCHOTHERAPY (BACP) BACP House, 15 St John's Business Park, Lutterworth, Leicestershire LE17 4HB T 01455-883300 E bacp@bacp.co.uk W www.bacp.co.uk
President, Laurie Clarke

BRITISH PSYCHOLOGICAL SOCIETY (BPS) St Andrews House, 48 Princess Road East, Leicester LE1 7DR T 0116-254 9568 E enquiries@bps.org.uk W www.bps.org.uk
President, Gerry Mulhern

ORTHOPTICS

Salary range: £21,000–£34,000 rising to £39,000–£67,000 in senior posts

Orthoptists undertake the diagnosis and treatment of all types of squint and other anomalies of binocular vision, working in close collaboration with ophthalmologists. The professional body is the British and Irish Orthoptic Society and training is at degree level.

BRITISH AND IRISH ORTHOPTIC SOCIETY Tavistock House North, Tavistock Square, London WC1H 9HX T 020-7387 7992 W www.orthoptics.org.uk
Chair, Rosemary Auld

PARAMEDICAL SERVICES

Salary range: £21,000–£34,000

Paramedics deal with accidents and emergencies, assessing patients and carrying out any specialist treatment and care needed in the first instance. The body that represents ambulance professionals is the College of Paramedics.

COLLEGE OF PARAMEDICS The Exchange, Express Park, Bristol Road, Bridgwater TA6 4RR T 01278-420014 E help@collegeofparamedics.net W www.collegeofparamedics.net
Chief Executive, Roland Furber

PHYSIOTHERAPY

Salary range: £21,000–£40,000

Physiotherapists are concerned with movement and function and deal with problems arising from injury, illness and ageing. Full-time three- or four-year degree courses are available at around 35 higher education institutions in the UK. Information about courses leading to state registration is available from the Chartered Society of Physiotherapy.

CHARTERED SOCIETY OF PHYSIOTHERAPY 14 Bedford Row, London WC1R 4ED T 020-7306 6666 W www.csp.org.uk
Chief Executive, Phil Gray

PROSTHETICS AND ORTHOTICS

Salary range: £21,000 on qualification up to £67,000 as a consultant

Prosthetists provide artificial limbs, while orthotists provide devices to support or control a part of the body. It is necessary to obtain an honours degree to become a prosthetist or orthotist. Training is centred at the universities of Salford and Strathclyde.

BRITISH ASSOCIATION OF PROSTHETISTS AND ORTHOTISTS Sir James Clark Building, Abbey Mill Business Centre, Paisley PA1 1TJ T 0141-561 7217 E enquiries@bapo.com W www.bapo.org
Chair, Peter Honeycombe

RADIOGRAPHY

Salary range: £21,000–£40,000

In order to practise both diagnostic and therapeutic radiography in the UK, it is necessary to have successfully completed a course of education and training recognised by the Health Professionals Council. Such courses are offered by universities throughout the UK and lead to the award of a degree in radiography. Further information is available from the Society and College of Radiographers.

SOCIETY AND COLLEGE OF RADIOGRAPHERS 207 Providence Square, Mill Street, London SE1 2EW T 020-7740 7200 E info@sor.org W www.sor.org
Chief Executive, Richard Evans

SPEECH AND LANGUAGE THERAPY

Salary range: £18,000 rising upwards of £40,000 in senior roles

Speech and language therapists (SLTs) work with people with communication, swallowing, eating and drinking problems. The Royal College of Speech and Language Therapists is the professional body for speech and language therapists and support workers. Alongside the Health Professions Council, it accredits education and training courses leading to qualification.

ROYAL COLLEGE OF SPEECH AND LANGUAGE THERAPISTS 2 White Hart Yard, London SE1 1NX T 020-7378 1200 E info@rcslt.org W www.rcslt.org
Chief Executive, Kamini Gadhok, MBE

NURSING

Salary range: see Health: Employees and Salaries

In order to practise in the UK all nurses and midwives must be registered with the Nursing and Midwifery Council (NMC). The NMC is a statutory regulatory body that establishes and maintains standards of education, training, conduct and performance for nursing and midwifery. Courses leading to registration are currently at a minimum of diploma in higher education, with some offered at degree level. All are a minimum of three years if undertaken full-time. From September 2011 diplomas will be phased out, and by 2013 all new entrants to the nursing profession will have to study a degree. These changes will not affect those studying or applying in 2010. The NMC approves programmes run jointly by higher education institutions with their healthcare service partners who offer clinical placements. The nursing part of the register has four fields of practice: adult, children's, learning disability and mental health nursing. During the first year of a nursing course, the common foundation programme, students are taught across all four fields of practice. In addition those studying to become adult nurses gain experience of nursing in relation to medicine, surgery, maternity care and nursing in the home. The NMC also sets standards for programmes leading to registration as a midwife and a range of post-registration courses including specialist practice programmes, nurse prescribing and those for teachers of nursing and midwifery. The NMC has a part of the register for specialist community public health nurses and approves programmes for health visitors, occupational health nurses and school nurses.

The Royal College of Nursing is the largest professional union for nursing in the UK, representing qualified nurses, healthcare assistants and nursing students in the NHS and the independent sector.

NURSING AND MIDWIFERY COUNCIL 23 Portland Place, London W1B 1PZ T 020-7333 9333 E advice@nmc-uk.org W www.nmc-uk.org
Chief Executive and Registrar, Dickon Weir-Hughes

ROYAL COLLEGE OF NURSING 20 Cavendish Square, London W1G 0RN T 020-740 3333 W www.rcn.org.uk
Chief Executive and General Secretary, Dr Peter Carter

OPTOMETRY AND DISPENSING OPTICS

Salary range:
Optometrist £23,000–£50,000 (up to £75,000 for consultant posts)
Dispensing Optician £18,000–£30,000+

There are various routes to qualification as a dispensing optician. Qualification takes three years in total, and can be completed by combining a distance learning course or day release while working as a trainee under the supervision of a qualified and registered optician. Alternatively, students can do a two-year full-time course followed by one year of supervised practice with a qualified and registered optician. Training must be done at a training establishment approved by the regulatory body – the General Optical Council (GOC). There are six training establishments which are approved by the GOC: the college of the Association of British Dispensing Opticians (ABDO), Anglia Ruskin University, Bradford College, the City and Islington College, City University and Glasgow Caledonian University. All routes are concluded by professional qualifying examinations, successful completion of which leads to registration with the GOC, which is compulsory for all practising dispensing opticians. After qualifying as a dispensing optician and completing training to fit contact lenses, students have the option to take a career progression course at the University of Bradford that allows them to graduate with a degree in optometry in one calendar year.

Optometrists must obtain an undergraduate optometry degree from one of the eight institutions approved by the GOC (Anglia Ruskin University, Aston University, the University of Bradford, Cardiff University, City University, Glasgow Caledonian University, the University of Manchester and the University of Ulster). Following graduation, trainees must complete a year of supervised salaried training with a registered optometrist after which they must pass a series of assessments set by the College of Optometrists. As with dispensing opticians, optometrists must be registered with the GOC in order to practise.

ASSOCIATION OF BRITISH DISPENSING OPTICIANS 199 Gloucester Terrace, London W2 6LD T 020-7298 5100 E general@abdolondon.org.uk W www.abdo.org.uk
General Secretary, Sir Anthony Garrett, CBE

COLLEGE OF OPTOMETRISTS 41–42 Craven Street, London WC2N 5NG T 020-7839 6000 E optometry@college-optometrists.org W www.college-optometrists.org
Chief Executive, Bryony Pawinska

GENERAL OPTICAL COUNCIL (GOC) 1 Harley Street, London W1G 8DJ T 020-7580 3898 E goc@optical.org W www.optical.org
Chief Executive, Dian Taylor

OSTEOPATHY

Salary Range: £16,000–£65,000

Osteopathy is a way of detecting and treating damage in areas of the body such as muscles, ligaments, nerves and joints. The General Osteopathic Council (GOsC) regulates the practice of osteopathy in the UK and maintains a register of those entitled to practise. It is a criminal offence for anyone to describe themselves as an osteopath unless they are registered with the GOsC.

To gain entry to the register, applicants must hold a recognised qualification from an osteopathic education institute accredited by the GOsC; this involves a four- to five-year honours degree programme combined with clinical training.

GENERAL OSTEOPATHIC COUNCIL Osteopathy House, 176 Tower Bridge Road, London SE1 3LU T 020-7357 6655 E info@osteopathy.org.uk W www.osteopathy.org.uk
Chief Executive and Registrar, Evlynne Gilvarry

PHARMACY

Salary range: £23,000–£68,000+

Pharmacists are involved in the preparation and use of medicines, from the discovery of their active ingredients to their use by patients. Pharmacists also monitor the effects of medicines, both for patient care and for research purposes.

The General Pharmaceutical Council (GPhC) is the independent regulatory body for pharmacists in England, Scotland and Wales, having taken over the regulating function of the Royal Pharmaceutical Society of Great Britain in 2010. The GPhC maintains the register of pharmacists, pharmacy technicians and pharmacy premises; it also sets national standards for training, ethics, proficiency and continuing professional development. The Pharmaceutical Society of Northern Ireland (PSNI) performs the same role in Northern Ireland. In order to register, students must complete a four-year degree in pharmacy that is accredited by either the GPhC or the PSNI followed by one year of pre-registration training at an approved pharmacy, and must then pass an entrance examination.

GENERAL PHARMACEUTICAL COUNCIL (GPHC) 129 Lambeth Road, London SE1 7BT T 020-3365 3400 E info@pharmacyregulation.org W www.pharmacyregulation.org
Chief Executive and Registrar, Duncan Rudkin

PHARMACEUTICAL SOCIETY OF NORTHERN IRELAND 73 University Street, Belfast BT7 1HL T 028-9032 6927 E info@psni.org.uk W www.psni.org.uk
Director, Trevor Patterson

ROYAL PHARMACEUTICAL SOCIETY OF GREAT BRITAIN (RPSGB) 1 Lambeth High Street, London SE1 7JN T 020-7735 9141 E enquiries@rpsgb.org W www.rpsgb.org
Chief Executive and Registrar, Jeremy Holmes

JOURNALISM

Salary range: starting salaries £12,000–£18,000; £22,000+ for established journalists, rising to £39,000–£85,000 for senior journalists/editors

The National Council for the Training of Journalists (NCTJ) accredits 70 courses for journalists run by 42 education providers; it also provides professional support to journalists.

The Broadcast Journalism Training Council (BJTC) is an association of the UK's main broadcast journalism employers and accredits courses in broadcast journalism.

BROADCAST JOURNALISM TRAINING COUNCIL (BJTC) 18 Miller's Close, Rippingale Nr. Bourne, Lincolnshire PE10 0TH T 01778-440025 E sec@bjtc.org.uk W www.bjtc.org.uk
Secretary, Jim Latham

NATIONAL COUNCIL FOR THE TRAINING OF JOURNALISTS (NCTJ) The New Granary, Station Road, Newport, Saffron Walden, Essex CB11 3PL T 01799-544014 E info@nctj.com W www.nctj.com
Chief Executive, Joanne Butcher

INFORMATION MANAGEMENT

Salary range:
Archivist £21,000–£30,000 (starting); £30,000–£55,000+ in senior posts
Information Officer £19,000–£23,000 (starting); £23,000–£41,000+ in senior posts
Librarian £19,000–£23,000 (newly qualified); £49,000+ in senior posts

The Chartered Institute of Library and Information Professionals (CILIP) is the professional body for librarians, information specialists and knowledge managers. CILIP accredits undergraduate and postgraduate librarianship and information courses. The Society of Archivists is the professional body for archivists and record managers. ASLIB provides training and advice on a wide range of topics relevant to the work of information professionals.

ARCHIVES AND RECORDS ASSOCIATION Prioryfield House, 20 Canon Street, Taunton, Somerset TA1 1SW T 01823-327030 E societyofarchivists@archives.org.uk W www.archives.org.uk
Executive Director, John Chambers

ASLIB Howard House, Wagon Lane, Bingley, West Yorkshire, BD16 1WA T 01274-777700 E support@aslib.com W www.aslib.com
Chief Executive, John Peters

CHARTERED INSTITUTE OF LIBRARY AND INFORMATION PROFESSIONALS (CILIP) 7 Ridgmount Street, London WC1E 7AE T 020-7255 0500 E info@cilip.org.uk W www.cilip.org.uk
President, Biddy Fisher

LAW

There are three types of practising lawyers: barristers, notaries and solicitors. Solicitors tend to work as a group in firms, and can be approached directly by individuals. They advise on a variety of legal issues and must decide the most appropriate course of action, if any. Notaries have all the powers of a solicitor other than the conduct of litigation. Most of them are primarily concerned with the preparation and authentication of documents for use abroad. Barristers are usually self-employed. If a solicitor believes that a barrister is required, he or she will instruct one on behalf of the client; the client will not have contact with the barrister without the solicitor being present.

When specialist expertise is needed, barristers give opinions on complex matters of law, and when clients require representation in the higher courts (crown courts, the high court, the court of appeal and the supreme court), barristers provide a specialist advocacy service. However, solicitors – who represent their clients in the lower courts such as tribunals, magistrates' courts and county courts – can also apply for advocacy rights in the higher courts instead of briefing a barrister.

THE BAR

Salary range: £10,000–£200,000+

The governing body of the Bar of England and Wales is the General Council of the Bar, also known as the Bar Council. Since January 2006, the regulatory functions of the Bar Council (including regulating the education and training requirements for those wishing to enter the profession) have been undertaken by the Bar Standards Board.

In the first (or 'academic') stage of training, aspiring barristers must obtain a law degree of a good standard (at least second class). Alternatively, those with a non-law degree (at least second class) may complete a one-year full-time or two-year part-time Common Professional Examination (CPE) or Graduate Diploma in Law (GDL).

The second (vocational) stage is the completion of the Bar Professional Training Course (BPTC), which is available at nine validated institutions in the UK and must be applied for around one year in advance (W www.barprofessionaltraining.org.uk). All barristers must join one of the four Inns of Court prior to commencing the BPTC.

Students are 'called to the Bar' by their Inn after completion of the vocational stage, but cannot practise as a barrister until completion of the third stage, which is called 'pupillage'. Call to the Bar does not entitle a person to practise as a barrister – successful completion of pupillage is now a pre-requisite. Pupillage lasts for two six-month periods: the 'non-practising six' and the 'practising six'. The former consists of shadowing an experienced barrister, while the latter involves appearing in court as a barrister.

Admission to the Bar of Northern Ireland is controlled by the Honorable Society of the Inn of Court of Northern Ireland; admission as an Advocate to the Scottish Bar is through the Faculty of Advocates.

BAR STANDARDS BOARD 289–293 High Holborn, London WC1V 7HZ T 020-7611 1444 E contactus@barstandardsboard.org.uk W www.barstandardsboard.org.uk
Director, Mandie Lavin

FACULTY OF ADVOCATES Parliament House, Edinburgh EH1 1RF T 0131-226 5071 W www.advocates.org.uk
Dean, Richard Keen, QC

GENERAL COUNCIL OF THE BAR 289–293 High Holborn, London WC1V 7HZ T 020-7242 0082 E contactus@barcouncil.org.uk W www.barcouncil.org.uk
Chief Executive, David Hobart

GENERAL COUNCIL OF THE BAR OF NORTHERN IRELAND The Bar Library, 91 Chichester Street, Belfast BT1 3JQ T 028-9056 2349
E chief.executive@barcouncil-ni.org.uk
W www.barlibrary.com
Chief Executive, Brendan Garland

HONOURABLE SOCIETY OF THE INN OF COURT OF NORTHERN IRELAND Bar Council Office, The Bar Library, 91 Chichester Street, Belfast BT1 3JQ
T 028-9056 2349 W www.actuaries.org.uk
Under-Treasurer, John P. B. Maxwell

THE INNS OF COURT

HONOURABLE SOCIETY OF GRAY'S INN
8 South Square, London WC1R 5ET T 020-7458 7800
W www.graysinn.org.uk
Under-Treasurer, Brig. Anthony Faith, CBE

HONOURABLE SOCIETY OF LINCOLN'S INN
Treasury Office, Lincoln's Inn, London WC2A 3TL
T 020-7405 1393 E mail@lincolnsinn.org.uk
W www.lincolnsinn.org.uk
Under-Treasurer, Col. D. Hills, MBE

HONOURABLE SOCIETY OF THE INNER TEMPLE
Inner Temple, London EC4Y 7HL T 020-7797 8250
E enquiries@innertemple.org.uk
W www.innertemple.org.uk
Sub-Treasurer, Patrick Maddams

HONOURABLE SOCIETY OF THE MIDDLE TEMPLE
Middle Temple Lane, London EC4Y 9AT T 020-7427 4800
E members@middletemple.org.uk
W www.middletemple.org.uk
Under-Treasurer, Air Cdre Peter Hilling

NOTARIES PUBLIC

Notaries are qualified lawyers with a postgraduate Cambridge University diploma in notarial practice. Once a potential notary has passed the postgraduate diploma they can petition the Court of Faculties for a 'faculty'. After the faculty is granted, the notary is able to practise; however, for the first two years this must be under the supervision of an experienced notary. The admission and regulation of notaries in England and Wales is a statutory function of the Faculty Office. This jurisdiction was confirmed by the Courts and Legal Services Act 1990. The Notaries Society of England and Wales is the representative body for practising notaries.

THE FACULTY OFFICE, 1 The Sanctuary, Westminster, London SW1P 3JT T 020-7222 5381
E faculty.office@1thesanctuary.com
W www.facultyoffice.org.uk
Registrar, Peter Beesley

THE NOTARIES SOCIETY OF ENGLAND AND WALES, PO Box 226, Melton Woodbridge IP12 1WX
T 01394-380436 E admin@the notariessociety.org.uk
W www.thenotariessociety.org.uk
Secretary, Christopher J. Vaughan

SOLICITORS

Salary range: £15,000–£23,000 (trainee); £42,000–£50,000 (associate or partner)

Graduates from any discipline can train to be a solicitor; however, if the undergraduate degree is not in law, a one-year conversion course – either the Common Professional Examination (CPE) or the Graduate Diploma in Law (GDL) – must be completed. The next stage, and the beginning of the vocational phase, is the Legal Practice Course (LPC), which takes one year and is obligatory for both law and non-law graduates. The LPC provides professional instruction for prospective solicitors and can be completed on a full-time or part-time basis. Trainee solicitors then enter the final stage, which is a paid period of supervised work that lasts two years for full-time contracts. The employer that provides the training contract must be authorised by the Solicitors Regulation Authority (SRA) (the regulatory body of the Law Society of England and Wales), the Law Society of Scotland, or the Law Society of Northern Ireland. The SRA also monitors the training contract to ensure that it provides the trainee with the expertise to qualify as a solicitor.

Conveyancers are specialist property lawyers, dealing with the legal processes involved in transferring buildings, land and associated finances from one owner to another. This was the sole responsibility of solicitors until 1987 but under current legislation it is now possible for others to train as conveyancers.

COUNCIL FOR LICENSED CONVEYANCERS (CLC)
16–17 Glebe Road, Chelmsford, Essex CM1 1QG
T 01245-349599 E clc@clc-uk.org W www.clc-uk.org
Chief Executive, Mr V. Olowe

THE LAW SOCIETY OF ENGLAND AND WALES
The Law Society's Hall, 113 Chancery Lane, London WC2A 1PL T 020-7242 1222 E enquiries@lawsociety.org.uk
W www.lawsociety.org.uk
Chief Executive, Des Hudson

LAW SOCIETY OF NORTHERN IRELAND Law Society House, 96 Victoria Street, Belfast BT1 3GN T 028-9023 1614
E info@lawsoc-ni.org W www.lawsoc-ni.org
Chief Executive and Secretary, Alan Hunter

LAW SOCIETY OF SCOTLAND 26 Drumsheugh Gardens, Edinburgh EH3 7YR T 0131-226 7411
E lawscot@lawscot.org.uk W www.lawscot.org.uk
Chief Executive, Lorna Jack

SOLICITORS REGULATION AUTHORITY Ipsley Court, Berrington Close, Redditch, Worcs B98 0TD
T 0870-606 2555 W www.sra.org.uk
Chief Executive, Antony Townsend

SOCIAL WORK

Salary range: £24,000–£30,000 (starting), rising to £42,000 as an experienced manager; £57,000+ at senior levels

Social workers tend to specialise in either adult or children's services. The General Social Care Council is responsible for setting standards of conduct and practice for social care workers and their employers; regulating the workforce and social work education and training. A degree or postgraduate qualification is needed in order to become a social worker. For more information *see* Social Welfare.

GENERAL SOCIAL CARE COUNCIL (GSCC) Goldings House, 2 Hay's Lane, London SE1 2HB T 020-7397 5100
E info@gscc.org.uk W www.gscc.org.uk
Chief Executive, Penny Thompson

SURVEYING

Salary range: £21,000–£24,000 (starting); £39,000+ (senior); £70,000+ (partner)

The Royal Institution of Chartered Surveyors (RICS) is the professional body that represents and regulates property professionals including land surveyors, valuers, auctioneers, quantity surveyors and project managers. Entry to the institution, following completion of a RICS-accredited degree, is through completion of the Assessment of Professional Competence (APC), which involves a period of practical training concluded by a final assessment of competence. Entry as a technical surveyor requires completion of the Assessment of Technical Competence (ATC), which mirrors the format of the APC. The different levels of RICS membership are MRICS (member) or FRICS (fellow) for chartered surveyors, and AssocRICS for associate members.

Relevant courses can also be accredited by the Chartered Institute of Building (CIOB), which represents managers working in a range of construction disciplines The CIOB offers four levels of membership to those who satisfy its requirements: FCIOB (fellow), MCIOB (member), ICIOB (incorporated) and ACIOB (associate).

CHARTERED INSTITUTE OF BUILDING Englemere, King's Ride, Ascot SL5 7TB T 01344-630700
E reception@ciob.org.uk W www.ciob.org.uk
Chief Executive, Chris Blythe

ROYAL INSTITUTION OF CHARTERED SURVEYORS (RICS) RICS Contact Centre, Surveyor Court, Westwood Way, Coventry CV4 8JE T 0870-333 1600
E contactrics@rics.org W www.rics.org
Chief Executive, Louis Armstrong

TEACHING

(*See also* Education)
Salary range: £21,000–£63,000; headteacher £37,000–£110,000

The General Teaching Councils (GTCs) for England, Northern Ireland, Scotland and Wales maintain registers of qualified teachers in their respective countries, and registration is a legal requirement in order to teach in local authority schools. The future of GTCs is uncertain under the new coalition government. The Graduate Teacher Training Registry (GTTR) processes applications for entry to postgraduate teaching courses in England, Wales and Scotland. All new entrants to the UK teaching profession must have qualified teacher status (QTS), which requires completing an initial teacher training (ITT) period. In order to gain QTS, individuals must be graduates.

Teachers in Further Education (FE) need not have QTS, though new entrants to FE are required to work towards a specified FE qualification recognised by Lifelong Learning UK. Similarly, academic staff in Higher Education require no formal teaching qualification, but are expected to obtain a qualification that meets standards set by the Higher Education Academy.

Details of routes to gaining QTS and funding for ITT are available in England from the Training and Development Agency for Schools (TDA), in Wales from the Teacher Training & Education Recruitment Forum Wales, in Scotland from Teach in Scotland, and in Northern Ireland from the Department of Education.

The College of Teachers, under the terms of its royal charter, provides professional qualifications and membership to teachers and those involved in education in the UK and overseas.

COLLEGE OF TEACHERS Institute of Education, 20 Bedford Way, London WC1H 0AL T 020-7911 5536
W www.cot.ac.uk
Chief Executive and Registrar, Matthew Martin

DEPARTMENT OF EDUCATION NORTHERN IRELAND Rathgael House, Balloo Road, Bangor BT19 7PR
T 028-9127 9279 E mail@deni.gov.uk W www.deni.gov.uk
Permanent Secretary, Paul Sweeney

GENERAL TEACHING COUNCIL FOR ENGLAND Whittington House, 19–30 Alfred Place, London WC1E 7EA
T 0370-001 0308 E info@gtce.org.uk W www.gtce.org.uk
Chief Executive, Keith Bartley

GENERAL TEACHING COUNCIL FOR NORTHERN IRELAND 4th Floor, Albany House, 73–75 Great Victoria Street, Belfast BT2 7AF T 028-9033 3390
E info@gtcni.org.uk W www.gtcni.org.uk
Chair, Sally McKee

GENERAL TEACHING COUNCIL FOR SCOTLAND Clerwood House, 96 Clermiston Road, Edinburgh EH12 6UT
T 0131-314 6000 E gtcs@gtcs.org.uk W www.gtcs.org.uk
Chief Executive, Anthony Finn

GENERAL TEACHING COUNCIL FOR WALES 4th Floor, Southgate House, Wood Street, Cardiff CF10 1EW
T 029-2055 0350 E information@gtcw.org.uk
W www.gtcw.org.uk
Chief Executive, Gary Brace

GRADUATE TEACHER TRAINING REGISTRY Rosehill, New Barn Lane, Cheltenham GL52 3LZ
T 0871-468 0469 E enquiries@gttr.ac.uk W www.gttr.ac.uk
Chief Executive, Mary Curnock Cook

HIGHER EDUCATION ACADEMY Innovation Way, York Science Park, Heslington, York YO10 5BR
T 01904-717500 E enquiries@heacademy.ac.uk
W www.heacademy
Chief Executive, Craig Mahoney

LIFELONG LEARNING UK 8th Floor, Centurion House, 24 Monument Street, London EC3R 8AQ T 0300-303 8077
E enquiries@lluk.org W www.lluk.org
Chief Executive (interim), Sue Dutton

TRAINING AND DEVELOPMENT AGENCY FOR SCHOOLS Piccadilly Gate, Store Street, Manchester, M1 2WD T 0870-496 0123 W www.tda.gov.uk
Chief Executive, Graham Holley

VETERINARY MEDICINE

Salary range: £30,000–£48,000

The regulatory body for veterinary surgeons in the UK is the Royal College of Veterinary Surgeons (RCVS), which keeps the register of those entitled to practise veterinary medicine as well as the list of qualified veterinary nurses. Holders of recognised degrees from any of the six UK university veterinary schools or from certain EU or overseas universities are entitled to be registered, and holders of certain other degrees may take a statutory membership examination. The UK's veterinary schools are located at the University of Bristol, the University of Cambridge, the University of Edinburgh, the University of Glasgow, the University of Liverpool and the Royal Veterinary College in London; all veterinary degrees last for five years except that offered at Cambridge, which lasts for six. A new course at the University of Nottingham's School of Veterinary Medicine and Science will produce its first veterinary graduates in 2011.

The British Veterinary Association is the professional body representing veterinary surgeons. The British Veterinary Nursing Association is the professional body representing veterinary nurses.

BRITISH VETERINARY ASSOCIATION 7 Mansfield Street, London W1G 9NQ T 020-7636 6541
E bvahq@bva.co.uk W www.bva.co.uk
Secretary General, Henrietta Alderman

BRITISH VETERINARY NURSING ASSOCIATION 82 Greenway Business Centre, Harlow Business Park, Harlow CM19 5QE T 01279-408644 E bvna@bvna.co.uk
W www.bvna.org.uk

ROYAL COLLEGE OF VETERINARY SURGEONS Belgravia House, 62–64 Horseferry Road, London SW1P 2AF
T 020-7222 2001 E admin@rcvs.org.uk W www.rcvs.org.uk
Registrar, Jane C. Hern

INDEPENDENT SCHOOLS

Independent schools (non-maintained mainstream schools) charge fees and are owned and managed under special trusts, with profits being used for the benefit of the schools concerned. In 2008–9 there were 2,547 non-maintained mainstream schools in the UK, educating over 627,000 pupils, or around 6.5 per cent of the total school-age population. The approximate number of pupils at non-maintained mainstream schools in 2008–9 was:

UK	627,700
England	587,000
Wales	9,300
Scotland	30,700
Northern Ireland	700

The Independent Schools Council (ISC), formed in 1974, acts on behalf of the eight independent schools' associations which constitute it. These associations are:

Association of Governing Bodies of Independent Schools (AGBIS)
Council of British International Schools (COBIS)
Girls' Schools Association (GSA)
Headmasters' & Headmistresses' Conference (HMC)
Independent Association of Prep Schools (IAPS)
Independent Schools Association (ISA)
Independent Schools' Bursars Association (ISBA)
Society of Headmasters & Headmistresses of Independent Schools (SHMIS)

In 2009–10 there were 511,886 pupils being educated in 1,260 schools in membership of associations within the Independent Schools Council (ISC). Most schools not in membership of an ISC association are likely to be privately owned. The Independent Schools Inspectorate (ISI) was demerged from ISC with effect from 1 January 2008 and is legally and operationally independent of ISC. ISI works as an accredited inspectorate of schools in membership of the ISC associations under a framework agreed with the DfE. A school must pass an ISI accreditation inspection to qualify for membership of an association within ISC.

In 2009 at GCSE 59.8 per cent of all exams taken by candidates in ISC associations' member schools achieved either an A* or A grade (compared to the national average of 21.6 per cent), and at A-level 77.9 per cent of entries were awarded an A or B grade (national average, 51.2 per cent). In 2009–10 over 142,000 pupils at schools in ISC associations received help with their fees in the form of bursaries and scholarships from the schools. These cost the schools more than £540m.

INDEPENDENT SCHOOLS COUNCIL
St Vincent House, 30 Orange Street, London WC2H 7HH
T 020-7766 7070 **W** www.isc.co.uk

The list of schools below was compiled from the *Independent Schools Yearbook 2010–11* (ed. Judy Mott, published by A&C Black) which includes schools whose heads are members of one of the ISC's five Heads' Associations. Further details are available online (**W** www.isyb.co.uk).

The fees shown below represent the upper limits payable as at September 2010 (fees noted with an * are for 2009–10) for UK pupils who do not qualify for any reduction; scholarships and bursaries are available at many of the schools listed.

School	*Web Address*	*Termly Fees* *Day*	*Board*	*Head*
ENGLAND				
Abbey Gate College, Cheshire	www.abbeygatecollege.co.uk	£3,275	–	Mrs L. M. Horner
The Abbey School, Berks	www.theabbey.co.uk	£4,020	–	Mrs B. Stanley
Abbots Bromley School for Girls, Staffs	www.abbotsbromley.staffs.sch.uk	£4,635	£7,625	M. A. Fisher
Abbot's Hill School, Herts	www.abbotshill.herts.sch.uk	£4,640	–	Mrs K. Lewis
Abbotsholme School, Derbys	www.abbotsholme.com	£6,040	£8,870	S. Fairclough
Abingdon School, Oxon	www.abingdon.org.uk	£4,635	£9,505	Miss O. Lusk
Ackworth School, W. Yorks	www.ackworthschool.com	£3,845	£6,294	Mrs K. Bell
Aldenham School, Herts	www.aldenham.com	£5,863	£8,523	J. Fowler
Alderley Edge School for Girls, Cheshire	www.aesg.info	£2,985	–	Mrs S. Goff
Alleyn's School, London SE22	www.alleyns.org.uk	£4,671	–	Dr G. Savage
Amberfield School, Suffolk	www.amberfield.suffolk.sch.uk	£3,345	–	Mrs L. Ingram
Ampleforth College, N. Yorks	www.college.ampleforth.org.uk	£5,755	£9,125	Rev C. Everitt
Ardingly College, W. Sussex	www.ardingly.com	£6,490	£8,650	P. Green
Arnold School, Lancs	www.arnoldschool.com	£2,975	–	B. Hughes
Ashford School, Kent	www.ashfordschool.co.uk	£4,704	£8,710	M. Buchanan
Ashville College, N. Yorks	www.ashville.co.uk	£3,660	£7,165	D. Lauder
Austin Friars St Monica's School, Cumbria	www.austinfriars.cumbria.sch.uk	£3,657	–	C. Lumb
Bablake School, W. Midlands	www.bablake.com	£2,880	–	J. Watson
Badminton School, Bristol	www.badminton.bristol.sch.uk	£5,120	£9,110	Mrs J. Scarrow
Bancroft's School, Essex	www.bancrofts.org	£4,186	–	Mrs M. Ireland
Barnard Castle School, Durham	www.barnardcastleschool.org.uk	£3,536	£6,259	A. Stevens

Batley Grammar School, W. Yorks	www.batleygrammar.co.uk	£2,949	–	Mrs B. Tullie
Bearwood College, Berks	www.bearwoodcollege.co.uk	£5,246	£9,001	S. Aiano
Bedales School, Hants	www.bedales.org.uk	£7,550	£9,605	K. Budge
Bedford Modern School, Beds	www.bedmod.co.uk	£3,432	–	M. Hall
Bedford School, Beds	www.bedfordschool.org.uk	£5,098	£8,257	J. Moule
Bedstone College, Shrops	www.bedstone.org	£3,965	£7,195	M. Symonds
Beechwood Sacred Heart School, Kent	www.beechwood.org.uk	£4,700	£7,800	N. Beesley
Benenden School, Kent	www.benenden.kent.sch.uk	–	£9,690	Mrs C. Oulton
Berkhamsted School, Herts	www.berkhamstedschool.org.uk	£5,400	£8,600	M. Steed
Bethany School, Kent	www.bethanyschool.org.uk	£4,893	£7,639	M. Healy
Birkdale School, S. Yorks	www.birkdaleschool.org.uk	£3,439	–	Dr P. Owen
Birkenhead School, Merseyside	www.birkenheadschool.co.uk	£3,142	–	D. Clark
Bishop's Stortford College, Herts	www.bishops-stortford-college.herts.sch.uk	£4,815	£6,853	J. Trotman
Blackheath High School, London SE3	www.blackheathhighschool.gdst.net	£4,002	–	Mrs E. Laws
Bloxham School, Oxon	www.bloxhamschool.com	£6,955	£8,993	M. Allbrook
Blundell's School, Devon	www.blundells.org	£5,605	£8,690	I. Davenport
Bolton School Boys' Division, Lancs	www.boltonschool.org/seniorboys	£3,200	–	P. Britton
Bolton School Girls' Division, Lancs	www.boltonschool.org/seniorgirls	£3,200	–	Mrs G. Richards
Bootham School, N. Yorks	www.boothamschool.com	£4,940	£8,300	J. Taylor
Bournemouth Collegiate School, Dorset	www.bournemouthcollegiateschool.co.uk	£4,707	£7,716	Stephen Duckitt
Box Hill School, Surrey	www.boxhillschool.com	£5,200	£8,750	M. Eagers
Bradfield College, Berks	www.bradfieldcollege.org.uk	£7,580	£9,475	P. Roberts
Bradford Girls' Grammar School, W. Yorks	www.bggs.com	£3,511	–	Mrs K. Matthews
Bradford Grammar School, W. Yorks	www.bradfordgrammar.com	£3,402	–	S. Davidson
Brentwood School, Essex	www.brentwoodschool.co.uk	£4,520	£8,115	D. Davies
Brighton and Hove High School, E. Sussex	www.bhhs.gdst.net	£3,232	–	Mrs L. Duggleby
Brighton College, E. Sussex	www.brightoncollege.net	£5,986	£10,326	R. Cairns
Brigidine School Windsor, Berks	www.brigidine.org.uk	£4,585	–	Mrs E. Robinson
Bristol Grammar School, Bristol	www.bristolgrammarschool.co.uk	£3,530	–	R. MacKinnon
Bromley High School, Kent	www.bromleyhigh.gdst.net	£4,002	–	Ms L. Simpson
Bromsgrove School, Worcs	www.bromsgrove-school.co.uk	£4,150	£8,145	C. Edwards
Bruton School for Girls, Somerset	www.brutonschool.co.uk	£4,170	£7,535	J. Burrough
Bryanston School, Dorset	www.bryanston.co.uk	£7,806	£9,520	Ms S. Thomas
Burgess Hill School for Girls, W. Sussex	www.burgesshill-school.com	£4,325	£7,625	Mrs A. Aughwane
Bury Grammar School Boys, Lancs	www.bgsboys.co.uk	£2,800	–	Revd S. Harvey
Bury Grammar School Girls, Lancs	www.bgsg.bury.sch.uk	£2,800	–	Mrs R. Georghiou
Canford School, Dorset	www.canford.com	£7,000	£8,990	J. Lever
Casterton School, Lancs	www.castertonschool.co.uk	£4,891	£8,200	Mrs M. Lucas
Caterham School, Surrey	www.caterhamschool.co.uk	£4,632	£8,642	J. Thomas
Central Newcastle High School, Tyne and Wear	www.newcastlehigh.gdst.net	£3,209	–	Mrs H. French
Channing School, London N6	www.channing.co.uk	£4,465	–	Mrs B. Elliott
Charterhouse, Surrey	www.charterhouse.org.uk	£8,110	£9,810	Revd J. Witheridge
Cheadle Hulme School, Cheshire	www.cheadlehulmeschool.co.uk	£3,052	–	Miss L. Pearson
Cheltenham College, Glos	www.cheltenhamcollege.org	£7,120	£9,505	Dr A. Peterken
The Cheltenham Ladies' College, Glos	www.cheltladiescollege.org	£6,208	£9,245	Mrs V. Tuck
Chetham's School of Music, Greater Manchester	www.chethams.com	sliding scale		Mrs C. Hickman
Chetwynde School, Cumbria	www.chetwynde.co.uk	£2,700	–	R. Collier
Chigwell School, Essex	www.chigwell-school.org	£4,844	£7,445	M. Punt
Christ's Hospital	www.christs-hospital.org.uk	sliding scale		J. Franklin
Churcher's College, Hants	www.churcherscollege.com	£3,705	–	S. Williams
City of London Freemen's School, Surrey	www.clfs.surrey.sch.uk	£4,794	£7,629	P. MacDonald
City of London School, London EC4	www.clsb.org.uk	£4,350	–	D. Levin
City of London School for Girls, London EC2	www.clsg.org.uk	£4,377	–	Miss D. Vernon

Claremont Fan Court School, Surrey	www.claremont-school.co.uk	£4,379	–	Mrs A. Stanley-Dervin
Clayesmore School, Dorset	www.clayesmore.com	£6,730	£9,199	M. Cooke
Clifton College, Bristol	www.cliftoncollegeuk.com	£6,450	£9,250	M. Moore
Clifton High School, Bristol	www.cliftonhigh.bristol.sch.uk	£3,635	£6,535	Dr A. Neill
Cobham Hall, Kent	www.cobhamhall.com	£5,800	£8,700	P. Mitchell
Cokethorpe School, Oxon	www.cokethorpe.org.uk	£4,795	–	D. Ettinger
Colfe's School, London SE12	www.colfes.com	£4,164	–	R. Russell
Colston's School, Bristol	www.colstons.bristol.sch.uk	£3,360	£6,580	P. Fraser
Combe Bank School, Kent	www.combebank.kent.sch.uk	£4,680	–	Mrs E. Abbotts
Concord College, Shrops	www.concordcollegeuk.com	£3,833	£8,300	N. Hawkins
Cranford House School, Oxon	www.cranford-house.org	£4,325	–	Mrs C. Hamilton
Cranleigh School, Surrey	www.cranleigh.org	£7,550	£9,265	G. Waller
Croydon High School, Surrey	www.croydonhigh.gdst.net	£4,002	–	Mrs D. Leonard
Culford School, Suffolk	www.culford.co.uk	£5,080	£8,220	J. Johnson-Munday
Dame Alice Harpur School, Beds	www.dahs.co.uk	£3,342*	–	Miss J. Mackenzie
Dame Allan's Boys' School, Tyne and Wear	www.dameallans.co.uk	£3,167	–	Dr J. Hind
Dame Allan's Girls' School, Tyne and Wear	www.dameallans.co.uk	£3,167	–	Dr J. Hind
Dauntsey's School, Wilts	www.dauntseys.org	£5,020	£8,460	S. Roberts
Dean Close School, Glos	www.deanclose.org.uk	£6,560	£9,290	J. Lancashire
Denstone College, Staffs	www.denstonecollege.org	£3,868	£6,735	D. Derbyshire
Derby High School, Derbys	www.derbyhigh.derby.sch.uk	£3,170	–	C. Callaghan
Dodderhill School, Worcs	www.dodderhill.co.uk	£3,050	–	Mrs J. Mumby
Dover College, Kent	www.dovercollege.org.uk	£4,195	£8,479	S. Jones
d'Overbroeck's College, Oxon	www.doverbroecks.com	£5,958	£9,023	S. Cohen
Downe House, Berks	www.downehouse.net	£6,965	£9,625	Mrs E. McKendrick
Dulwich College, London SE21	www.dulwich.org.uk	£4,728	£9,657	Dr J. Spence
Dunottar School, Surrey	www.dunottar.surrey.sch.uk	£4,025	–	Mrs N. Matthews
Durham High School for Girls, Durham	www.dhsfg.org.uk	£3,220	–	Mrs A. Templeman
Durham School, Durham	www.durhamschool.co.uk	£4,902	£7,138	E. George
Eastbourne College, E. Sussex	www.eastbourne-college.co.uk	£5,765	£8,710	S. Davies
Edgbaston High School, W. Midlands	www.edgbastonhigh.co.uk	£3,039	–	Dr R. Weeks
Ellesmere College, Shrops	www.ellesmere.com	£4,995	£8,262	B. Wignall
Eltham College, London SE9	www.eltham-college.org.uk	£4,175	–	P. Henderson
Emanuel School, London SW11	www.emanuel.org.uk	£4,713	–	M. Hanley-Browne
Epsom College, Surrey	www.epsomcollege.org.uk	£6,421	£9,400	S. Borthwick
Eton College, Berks	www.etoncollege.com	–	£9,954	A. Little
Ewell Castle School, Surrey	www.ewellcastle.co.uk	£3,900	–	A. Tibble
Exeter School, Devon	www.exeterschool.org.uk	£3,300	–	R. Griffin
Farlington School, W. Sussex	www.farlingtonschool.net	£4,484	£7,285	Mrs J. Goyer
Farnborough Hill, Hants	www.farnborough-hill.org.uk	£3,575	–	Mrs S. Buckle
Farringtons School, Kent	www.farringtons.org.uk	£3,840	£7,280	Mrs C. James
Felsted School, Essex	www.felsted.org	£6,160	£8,235	Dr M. Walker
Forest School, London E17	www.forest.org.uk	£4,470	–	Mrs S. Kerr-Dineen
Framlingham College, Suffolk	www.framlinghamcollege.co.uk	£5,079	£7,902	P. Taylor
Francis Holland School, London NW1	www.francisholland.org.uk	£4,630	–	Mrs V. Durham
Francis Holland School, London SW1	www.francisholland.org.uk	£4,735	–	Miss S. Pattenden
Frensham Heights, Surrey	www.frensham-heights.org.uk	£5,120	£7,720	A. Fisher
Friends' School, Essex	www.friends.org.uk	£4,675	£7,445	G. Wigley
Fulneck School, W. Yorks	www.fulneckschool.co.uk	£3,390	£6,300	T. Kernohan
Gateways School, W. Yorks	www.gatewayschool.co.uk	£3,445	–	Mrs Y. Wilkinson
Giggleswick School, N. Yorks	www.giggleswickschool.co.uk	£5,920	£8,650	G. Boult
The Godolphin and Latymer School, London W6	www.godolphinandlatymer.com	£4,950	–	Mrs R. Mercer
The Godolphin School, Wilts	www.godolphin.org	£5,486	£7,887	Mrs S. Price
The Grange School, Cheshire	www.grange.org.uk	£2,910	–	C. Jeffery
Greenacre School for Girls, Surrey	www.greenacre.surrey.sch.uk	£4,035	–	Mrs L. Redding
Gresham's School, Norfolk	www.greshams.com	£6,500	£8,465	P. John
Guildford High School, Surrey	www.guildfordhigh.surrey.sch.uk	£4,248	–	Mrs F. Boulton

The Haberdashers' Aske's Boys' School, Herts	www.habsboys.org.uk	£4,701	–	P. Hamilton
Haberdashers' Aske's School for Girls, Herts	www.habsgirls.org.uk	£3,830	–	Mrs E. Radice
Haileybury, Herts	www.haileybury.com	£6,607	£8,798	J. Davies
Halliford School, Middx	www.hallifordschool.co.uk	£3,678	–	P. Cottam
Hampshire Collegiate School, Hants	www.hampshirecs.org.uk	£4,308	£7,128	H. MacDonald
Hampton School, Middx	www.hamptonschool.org.uk	£4,670	–	B. Martin
Harrogate Ladies' College, N. Yorks	www.hlc.org.uk	£4,319	£7,542	Mrs R. Wilkinson
Harrow School, Middx	www.harrowschool.org.uk	–	£9,890	B. Lenon
Headington School, Oxon	www.headington.org	£4,295	£8,315	Mrs A. Coutts
Heathfield School, Berks	www.heathfieldschool.net	–	£9,299	Mrs J. Heywood
Heathfield School, Middx	www.heathfield.gdst.net	£4,002	–	Miss C. Juett
Hereford Cathedral School, Herefordshire	www.herefordcs.com	£3,660	–	P. Smith
Hethersett Old Hall School, Norfolk	www.hohs.co.uk	£3,775	£7,050	S. Crump
Highclare School, W. Midlands	www.highclareschool.co.uk	£3,250	–	Mrs M. Viles
Highgate School, London N6	www.highgateschool.org.uk	£5,040	–	A. Pettitt
Hipperholme Grammar School Foundation, W. Yorks	www.hgsf.org.uk	£3,150	–	Dr J. Scarth
Hollygirt School, Notts	www.hollygirt.co.uk	£3,073	–	Mrs P. Hutley
Hull Collegiate School, E. Yorks	www.hullcollegiateschool.co.uk	£3,089	–	R. Haworth
Hurstpierpoint College, W. Sussex	www.hppc.co.uk	£6,165	£9,250	T. Manly
Hymers College, E. Yorks	www.hymerscollege.co.uk	£2,772*	–	D. Elstone
Immanuel College, Herts	www.immanuelcollege.co.uk	£4,150	–	P. Skelker
Ipswich High School, Suffolk	www.ipswichhighschool.co.uk	£3,209	–	Ms E. Purves
Ipswich School, Suffolk	www.ipswich.suffolk.sch.uk	£3,747	£6,754	N. Weaver
James Allen's Girls' School (JAGS), London SE22	www.jags.org.uk	£4,325	–	Mrs M. Gibbs
The John Lyon School, Middx	www.johnlyon.org	£4,520	–	Miss K. Haynes
Kelly College, Devon	www.kellycollege.com	£4,700	£8,200	Dr G. Hawley
Kent College, Kent	www.kentcollege.com	£4,997	£8,717	D. Lamper
Kent College Pembury, Kent	www.kent-college.co.uk	£5,158	£8,315	Mrs S. Huang
Kimbolton School, Cambs	www.kimbolton.cambs.sch.uk	£3,995	£6,610	J. Belbin
King Edward VI. High School for Girls, W. Midlands	www.kehs.org.uk	£3,245	–	Miss S. Evans
King Edward VI. School, Hants	www.kes.hants.sch.uk	£3,745	–	A. Thould
King Edward VII. and Queen Mary School, Lancs	www.keqms.co.uk	£2,832	–	R. Karling
King Edward's School, Somerset	www.kesbath.com	£3,697	–	M. Boden
King Edward's School, W. Midlands	www.kes.org.uk	£3,300	–	J. Claughton
King Edward's School, Surrey	www.kesw.org	£5,770	£8,140	J. Attwater
King Henry VIII. School, W. Midlands	www.khviii.com	£2,974	–	J. Slack
King William's College, Isle of Man	www.kwc.im	£5,877	£8,559	M. Humphreys
Kingham Hill School, Oxon	www.kingham-hill.oxon.sch.uk	£4,860	£8,060	Revd Nick Seward
King's College School, London SW19	www.kcs.org.uk	£5,560	–	A. Halls
King's College, Somerset	www.kings-taunton.co.uk	£5,680	£8,390	R. Biggs
King's High School, Warwicks	www.kingshighwarwick.co.uk	£3,173	–	Mrs E. Surber
King's School, Somerset	www.kingsbruton.com	£6,162	£8,485	I. Wilmshurst
The King's School, Canterbury, Kent	www.kings-school.co.uk	£7,185	£9,725	M. Lascelles
The King's School, Chester, Cheshire	www.kingschester.co.uk	£3,391	–	C. Ramsey
The King's School, Cambs	www.kingsschoolely.co.uk	£5,465	£7,910	Mrs S. Freestone
The King's School, Glos	www.thekingsschool.co.uk	£5,100	–	A. Macnaughton
The King's School, Macclesfield, Cheshire	www.kingsmac.co.uk	£3,075	–	S. Coyne
King's School, Rochester, Kent	www.kings-school-rochester.co.uk	£5,140	£8,335	Dr I. Walker
The King's School, Tyne and Wear	www.kings-tynemouth.org.uk	£3,164	–	M. Heywood
The King's School, Worcs	www.ksw.org.uk	£3,598	–	T. Keyes
Kingsley School, Devon	www.kingsleyschoolbideford.co.uk	£3,770	£7,200	A. Waters
The Kingsley School, Warwicks	www.thekingsleyschool.com	£3,385	–	Ms H. Owens
Kingston Grammar School, Surrey	www.kgs.org.uk	£4,761	–	Mrs S. Fletcher

Kingswood School, Somerset	www.kingswood.bath.sch.uk	£3,740	£8,061	S. Morris
Kirkham Grammar School, Lancs	www.kirkhamgrammar.co.uk	£2,945	–	D. Walker
The Lady Eleanor Holles School, Middx	www.lehs.org.uk	£4,600	–	Mrs G. Low
Lancing College, W. Sussex	www.lancingcollege.co.uk	£6,465	£9,250	J. Gillespie
Langley School, Norfolk	www.langleyschool.co.uk	£3,615	£7,345	D. Findlay
Latymer Upper School, London W6	www.latymer-upper.org	£4,820	–	P. Winter
Lavant House, W. Sussex	www.lavanthouse.org.uk	£4,340	£6,830	Mrs K. Bartholomew
The Grammar School at Leeds, W. Yorks	www.gsal.org.uk	£3,453	–	M. Gibbons
Leicester Grammar School, Leics	www.leicestergrammar.org.uk	£3,348	–	C. King
Leicester High School for Girls, Leics	www.leicesterhigh.co.uk	£3,100	–	Mrs J. Burns
Leighton Park School, Berks	www.leightonpark.com	£5,776	£8,810	J. Dunston
Leweston School, Dorset	www.leweston.co.uk	£5,090	£7,875	A. Aylward
The Leys School, Cambs	www.theleys.net	£5,635	£8,470	M. Slater
The Licensed Victuallers' School, Berks	www.lvs.ascot.sch.uk	£4,470	£7,850	Mrs C. Cunniffe
Lincoln Minster School, Lincs	www.lincolnminsterschool.co.uk	£3,576	£6,920	C. Rickart
Liverpool College, Merseyside	www.liverpoolcollege.org.uk	£3,158	–	H. van Mourik Broekman
Lodge School, Surrey	www.lodgeschool.co.uk	£4,270	–	Miss P. Maynard
Longridge Towers School, Northumberland	www.lts.org.uk	£3,547	£7,226	T. Manning
Lord Wandsworth College, Hants	www.lordwandsworth.org	£6,040	£8,515	F. Livingstone
Loughborough Grammar School, Leics	www.lesgrammar.org	£3,320	£5,998	P. Fisher
Loughborough High School, Leics	www.leshigh.org	£3,093	–	Miss B. O'Connor
Luckley-Oakfield School, Berks	www.luckley.wokingham.sch.uk	£4,382	£7,596	Miss V. Davis
Magdalen College School, Oxon	www.mcsoxford.org	£4,356	–	T. Hands
Malvern College, Worcs	www.malcol.org	£6,464	£9,752	A. Clark
Malvern St James, Worcs	www.malvernstjames.co.uk	£4,695	£9,275	Mrs P. Woodhouse
The Manchester Grammar School	www.mgs.org	£3,220	–	C. Ray
Manchester High School for Girls	www.manchesterhigh.co.uk	£3,090	–	Mrs A. Hewitt
Manor House School, Surrey	www.manorhouseschool.org	£4,170	–	Miss Z. Axton
The Marist Senior School, Berks	www.themaristschools.com	£3,385	–	K. McCloskey
Marlborough College, Wilts	www.marlboroughcollege.org	£7,415	£9,770	N. Sampson
Marymount International School, Surrey	www.marymountlondon.com	£6,077	£10,200	Ms S. Gallagher
The Maynard School, Devon	www.maynard.co.uk	£3,429	–	Ms B. Hughes
Merchant Taylors' Boys' School, Merseyside	www.merchanttaylors.com	£2,976	–	D. Cook
Merchant Taylors' Girls' School, Merseyside	www.merchanttaylors.com	£2,976	–	Mrs L. Robinson
Merchant Taylors' School, Middx	www.mtsn.org.uk	£5,083	–	S. Wright
Mill Hill School, London NW7	www.millhill.org.uk	£5,375	£8,493	Dr D. Luckett
Millfield, Somerset	www.millfieldschool.com	£6,285	£9,340	C. Considine
Milton Abbey School, Dorset	www.miltonabbey.co.uk	£7,100	£9,450	G. Doodes
Moira House Girls School, E. Sussex	www.moirahouse.co.uk	£4,650	£8,185	Mrs L. Watson
Monkton Combe School, Somerset	www.monktoncombeschool.com	£5,552	£8,758	R. Backhouse
More House School, London SW1	www.morehouse.org.uk	£4,570	–	R. Carlysle
Moreton Hall, Shrops	www.moretonhall.org	£6,860*	£8,510	J. Forster
Mount St Mary's College, Derbys	www.msmcollege.com	£3,597	£7,200	L. McKell
The Mount School, London NW7	www.mountschool.com	£3,635		Ms C. Cozens
The Mount School, N. Yorks	www.mountschoolyork.co.uk	£4,665	£7,260	Mrs D. Gant
New Hall School, Essex	www.newhallschool.co.uk	£4,975	£7,520	Mrs K. Jeffrey
Newcastle School for Boys, Tyne and Wear	www.newcastleschool.co.uk	£3,305	–	C. Hutchinson
Newcastle-under-Lyme School, Staffs	www.nuls.org.uk	£3,061	–	N. Rugg
The Newcastle upon Tyne Church High School, Tyne and Wear	www.churchhigh.com	£3,452	–	Mrs J. Gatenby
North Cestrian Grammar School, Cheshire	www.ncgs.co.uk	£2,660	–	D. Vanstone
North London Collegiate School, Middx	www.nlcs.org.uk	£4,524	–	Mrs B. McCabe
Northampton High School	www.gdst.net/northamptonhigh	£3,545	–	Mrs S. Dixon

Northamptonshire Grammar School	www.ngs-school.com	£3,776	–	N. Toone
Northwood College, Middx	www.northwoodcollege.co.uk	£4,200	–	Miss J. Pain
Norwich High School, Norfolk	www.norwichhigh.gdst.net	£3,193	–	J. Morrow
Norwich School, Norfolk	www.norwich-school.org.uk	£3,865	–	J. Hawkins
Notre Dame Senior School, Surrey	www.notredame.co.uk	£4,000	–	Mrs B. Williams
Notting Hill and Ealing High School, London W13	www.nhehs.gdst.net	£4,021	–	Ms L. Hunt
Nottingham Girls' High School, Notts	www.nottinghamgirlshigh.gdst.net	£3,209	–	Mrs S. Gorham
Nottingham High School, Notts	www.nottinghamhigh.co.uk	£3,624	–	K. Fear
Oakham School, Rutland	www.oakham.rutland.sch.uk	£5,215	£8,730	N. Lashbrook
Ockbrook School, Derbys	www.ockbrook.derby.sch.uk	£2,805	£3,180	Mrs A. Steele
Oldham Hulme Grammar Schools, Lancs	www.hulme-grammar.oldham.sch.uk	£2,860	–	Dr P. Neeson
The Oratory School, Berks	www.oratory.co.uk	£6,265	£8,675	C. Dytor
Oswestry School, Shrops	www.oswestryschool.org.uk	£4,115	£7,030	D. Robb
Oundle School, Northants	www.oundleschool.org.uk	£5,925	£9,100	C. Bush
Our Lady of Sion School, W. Sussex	www.sionschool.org.uk	£3,250	–	M. Scullion
Our Lady's Abingdon Senior School, Oxon	www.olab.org.uk	£3,660	–	Mrs L. Renwick
Oxford High School, Oxon	www.oxfordhigh.gdst.net	£3,240	–	Mrs O. Curry
Padworth College, Berks	www.padworth.com	£3,650	£7,900	Mrs L. Melhuish
Palmers Green High School, London N21	www.pghs.co.uk	£3,785	–	Mrs C. Edmundson
Pangbourne College, Berks	www.pangbournecollege.com	£5,995*	£8,475*	T. Garnier
The Perse Upper School, Cambs	www.perse.co.uk	£4,421	–	E. Elliott
The Peterborough School, Cambs	www.thepeterboroughschool.co.uk	£3,833	£7,135	A. Meadows
Pipers Corner School, Bucks	www.piperscorner.co.uk	£4,225	£7,015	Mrs H. Ness-Gifford
Plymouth College, Devon	www.plymouthcollege.com	£4,065	£7,765	Dr S. Wormleighton
Pocklington School, E. Yorks	www.pocklingtonschool.com	£3,741	£6,697	M. Ronan
Polam Hall School, Durham	www.polamhall.com	£3,720	£7,135	Miss M. Green
Portland Place School, London W1	www.portland-place.co.uk	£4,995	–	R. Walker
The Portsmouth Grammar School, Hants	www.pgs.org.uk	£3,923	–	J. Priory
Portsmouth High School, Hants	www.portsmouthhigh.co.uk	£3,240	–	Mrs J. Clough
Princess Helena College, Herts	www.princesshelenacollege.co.uk	£5,490	£7,925	Mrs J-A. Duncan
Princethorpe College, Warwicks	www.princethorpe.co.uk	£3,000	–	E. Hester
Prior Park College, Somerset	www.priorparkschools.co.uk	£4,359	£7,861	J. Murphy-O'Connor
Prior's Field, Surrey	www.priorsfieldschool.com	£4,735	£7,660	Mrs J. Roseblade
The Purcell School, Herts	www.purcell-school.org	£8,259	£10,562	P. Crook
Putney High School, London SW15	www.putneyhigh.gdst.net	£4,021	–	Dr D. Lodge
Queen Anne's School, Berks	www.qas.org.uk	£5,865	£8,645	Mrs J. Harrington
Queen Elizabeth Grammar School, W. Yorks	www.wgsf.org.uk	£3,235	–	D. Craig
Queen Elizabeth's Grammar School, Lancs	www.qegs.blackburn.sch.uk	£3,153	–	S. Corns
Queen Elizabeth's Hospital (QEH), Bristol	www.qehbristol.co.uk	£3,460	–	S. Holliday
Queen Margaret's School, N. Yorks	www.queenmargarets.com	£5,152	£8,131	Dr P. Silverwood
Queen Mary's School, N. Yorks	www.queenmarys.org	£4,505	£5,945	R. McKenzie Johnston
Queen's College, London W1	www.qcl.org.uk	£4,825	–	Dr F. Ramsey
Queen's College, Somerset	www.queenscollege.org.uk	£4,700	£7,435	C. Alcock
Queen's Gate School, London SW7	www.queensgate.org.uk	£4,850	–	Mrs R. Kamaryc
The Queen's School, Cheshire	www.queens.cheshire.sch.uk	£3,450	–	Mrs E. Clark
Queenswood, Herts	www.queenswood.org	£6,995	£9,055	Mrs P. Edgar
Radley College, Oxon	www.radley.org.uk	£9,500	–	A. McPhail
Ratcliffe College, Leics	www.ratcliffecollege.com	£4,416	£6,654	G. Lloyd
The Read School, N. Yorks	www.readschool.co.uk	£2,941	£6,303	R. Hadfield
Reading Blue Coat School, Berks	www.rbcs.org.uk	£4,130	–	M. Windsor
The Red Maids' School, Bristol	www.redmaids.bristol.sch.uk	£3,335	–	Mrs I. Tobias
Redland High School for Girls, Bristol	www.redlandhigh.com	£3,200	–	Mrs C. Bateson
Reed's School, Surrey	www.reeds.surrey.sch.uk	£6,218	£8,225	D. Jarrett

Reigate Grammar School, Surrey	www.reigategrammar.org	£4,608	–	D. Thomas
Rendcomb College, Glos	www.rendcombcollege.org.uk	£5,970	£7,995	G. Holden
Repton School, Derbys	www.repton.org.uk	£6,715	£9,050	R. Holroyd
Rishworth School, W. Yorks	www.rishworth-school.co.uk	£3,415	£6,755	R. Baker
Roedean School, E. Sussex	www.roedean.co.uk	£5,600	£9,400	Mrs F. King
Rossall School, Lancs	www.rossallschool.org.uk	£3,900	£9,960	Dr S. Winkley
The Royal Grammar School, Surrey	www.rgs-guildford.co.uk	£4,341	–	J. Cox
Royal Grammar School, Tyne and Wear	www.rgs.newcastle.sch.uk	£3,249	–	B. St J. Trafford
RGS. Worcester, Worcs	www.rgsw.org.uk	£3,150	–	A. Rattue
The Royal High School, Bath, Somerset	www.gdst.net/royalhighbath	£3,209	£6,350	Mrs R. Dougall
The Royal Hospital School, Suffolk	www.royalhospitalschool.org	£3,959	£7,263	H. Blackett
The Royal Masonic School for Girls, Herts	www.royalmasonic.herts.sch.uk	£4,590	£7,340	Mrs D. Rose
Royal Russell School, Surrey	www.royalrussell.co.uk	£4,580	£9,060	J. Jennings
Royal School Hampstead, London NW3	www.royalschoolhampstead.net	£3,780	£7,450	Ms J. Ebner
The Royal Wolverhampton School, W. Midlands	www.theroyalschool.co.uk	£3,870	£7,925	S. Bailey
Rugby School, Warwicks	www.rugbyschool.net	£5,825	£9,350	P. Derham
Ryde School with Upper Chine, IOW	www.rydeschool.org.uk	£3,425	£6,700	Dr N. England
Rye St Antony, Oxon	www.ryestantony.co.uk	£3,820	£6,480	Miss A. Jones
St Albans High School, Herts	www.stahs.org.uk	£3,955	–	Mrs R. Martin
St Albans School, Herts	www.st-albans.herts.sch.uk	£4,430	–	A. Grant
St Andrew's School, Beds	www.standrewsschoolbedford.com	£3,390	–	S. Skehan
Saint Augustine's Priory School, London W5	www.saintaugustinespriory.org.uk	£3,570	–	Mrs F. Gumley-Mason
St Bede's College, Greater Manchester	www.stbedescollege.co.uk	£2,882	–	M. Barber
St Bede's School, E. Sussex	www.stbedesschool.org	£5,150	£8,575	Dr R. Maloney
St Bees School, Cumbria	www.st-bees-school.org	£4,853	£8,176	P. Capes
St Benedict's School, London W5	www.stbenedicts.org.uk	£4,010	–	C. Cleugh
St Catherine's School, Surrey	www.stcatherines.info	£4,560	£7,505	Mrs A. Phillips
St Catherine's School, Middx	www.stcatherineschool.co.uk	£3,665	–	Sister P. Thomas
St Christopher School, Herts	www.stchris.co.uk	£4,835	£8,490	R. Palmer
St Columba's College, Herts	www.stcolumbascollege.org	£3,628	–	D. Buxton
St Dominic's Priory School, Staffs	www.st-dominics.co.uk	£3,074	–	Mrs M. Adamson
St Dominic's School, Staffs	www.stdominicsschool.co.uk	£3,780	–	Mrs S. White
St Dunstan's College, London SE6	www.stdunstans.org.uk	£4,380	–	Mrs J. Davies
St Edmund's College, Herts	www.stedmundscollege.org	£4,675	£7,700	C. Long
St Edmund's School, Kent	www.stedmunds.org.uk	£5,520	£8,591	J. Gladwin
St Edward's, Oxford, Oxon	www.stedwards.oxon.sch.uk	£7,643	£9,553	A. Trotman
St Edward's School, Glos	www.stedwards.co.uk	£3,993	–	A. Nash
Saint Felix School, Suffolk	www.stfelix.co.uk	£4,300	£7,600	D. Ward
St Francis' College, Herts	www.st-francis.herts.sch.uk	£3,755	£7,385	Mrs D. MacGinty
St Gabriel's School, Berks	www.stgabriels.co.uk	£4,245	–	A. Jones
St George's College, Surrey	www.st-georges-college.co.uk	£4,770	–	J. Peake
St George's School, W. Midlands	www.sgse.co.uk	£3,255	–	Sir Robert Dowling
St George's School, Berks	www.stgeorges-ascot.org.uk	£5,995	£9,225	Mrs C. Jordan
The School of St Helen and St Katharine, Oxon	www.shsk.org.uk	£3,745	–	Miss R. Edbrooke
St Helen's School, Middx	www.sthn.co.uk	£4,276	–	Mrs M. Morris
St James Independent School for Senior Boys, Middx	www.stjamesboys.co.uk	£3,965	£5,520	D. Boddy
St James Senior Girls' School, London W14	www.stjamesgirls.co.uk	£4,055	–	Mrs L. Hyde
St John's College, Hants	www.stjohnscollege.co.uk	£2,965	£6,450	G. Best
St John's School, Surrey	www.stjohnsleatherhead.co.uk	£6,165	£8,475	N. Haddock
St Joseph's College, Suffolk	www.stjos.co.uk	£3,880	£6,710	Mrs S. Grant
St Lawrence College, Kent	www.slcuk.com	£4,894	£8,495	Revd M. Aitken
St Leonards-Mayfield School, E. Sussex	www.mayfieldgirls.org	£5,350	£8,130	Miss A. Beary
St Margaret's School, Herts	www.stmargaretsbushey.org.uk	£4,330	£7,890	Mrs L. Crighton
St Margaret's School, Devon	www.stmargarets-school.co.uk	£3,110*	–	Mrs S. Cooper

St Margaret's School, London NW3	www.st-margarets.co.uk	£3,473	–	M. Webster
St Martha's Senior School, Herts	www.st-marthas.co.uk	£3,275	–	J. Sheridan
Saint Martin's, W. Midlands	www.saintmartins-school.com	£3,365	–	Mrs J. Carwithen
St Mary's School Ascot, Berks	www.st-marys-ascot.co.uk	£6,700	£9,410	Mrs M. Breen
St Mary's Calne, Wilts	www.stmaryscalne.org	£7,000	£9,650	Mrs H. Wright
St Mary's School, Cambs	www.stmaryscambridge.co.uk	£4,155	£8,954	Miss C. Avery
St Mary's School, Essex	www.stmaryscolchester.org.uk	£3,100	–	Mrs H. Vipond
St Mary's College, Merseyside	www.stmaryscrosby.co.uk	£2,887	–	M. Kennedy
St Mary's School, Bucks	www.stmarysschool.co.uk	£4,135	–	Mrs J. Ross
St Mary's School, Dorset	www.st-marys-shaftesbury.co.uk	£5,190	£7,550	R. James
St Mary's, Worcs	www.stmarys.org.uk	£3,300	–	Mrs C. Jawaheer
St Nicholas' School, Hants	www.st-nicholas.hants.sch.uk	£3,480*	–	Mrs A. Whatmough
St Paul's Girls' School, London W6	www.spgs.org	£5,434	–	Ms C. Farr
St Paul's School, London SW13	www.stpaulsschool.org.uk	£5,976	£8,853	G. Stephen
St Peter's School York, N. Yorks	www.st-peters.york.sch.uk	£4,698	£7,564	L. Winkley
St Swithun's School, Hants	www.stswithuns.com	£4,990	£8,230	Ms J. Gandee
St Teresa's School, Surrey	www.stteresasschool.com	£4,480	£7,720	Mrs L. Falconer
Scarborough College, N. Yorks	www.scarboroughcollege.co.uk	£3,652	£5,989	Mrs I. Nixon
Seaford College, W. Sussex	www.seaford.org	£5,200	£8,025	T. Mullins
Sedbergh School, Cumbria	www.sedberghschool.org	£6,450	£8,755	A. Fleck
Sevenoaks School, Kent	www.sevenoaksschool.org	£5,690	£9,126	Mrs C. Ricks
Shebbear College, Devon	www.shebbearcollege.co.uk	£3,375	£6,280	R. Barnes
Sheffield High School, S. Yorks	www.sheffieldhighschool.org.uk	£3,177	–	Mrs V. Dunsford
Sherborne Girls, Dorset	www.sherborne.com	£6,703	£9,220	Mrs J. Dwyer
Sherborne School, Dorset	www.sherborne.org	£7,575	£9,355	C. Davis
Shiplake College, Oxon	www.shiplake.org.uk	£5,512	£8,175	A. Davies
Shrewsbury High School, Shrops	www.shrewsburyhigh.gdst.net	£3,209	–	Mrs M. Cass
Shrewsbury School, Shrops	www.shrewsbury.org.uk	£6,375	£9,100	M. Turner
Sibford School, Oxon	www.sibford.oxon.sch.uk	£3,773	£7,330	M. Goodwin
Silcoates School, W. Yorks	www.silcoates.org.uk	£3,800	–	D. Wideman
Solihull School, W. Midlands	www.solsch.org.uk	£3,255	–	D. Lloyd
South Hampstead High School, London NW3	www.shhs.gdst.net	£4,002	–	Mrs J. Stephen
Stafford Grammar School, Staffs	www.stafford-grammar.co.uk	£3,126	–	M. Darley
Stamford High School, Lincs	www.ses.lincs.sch.uk	£3,932	£7,180	S. Roberts
Stamford School, Lincs	www.ses.lincs.sch.uk	£3,932	£7,180	S. Roberts
Stanbridge Earls School, Hants	www.stanbridgeearls.co.uk	£6,089	£8,192	P. Trythall
The Stephen Perse Foundation, Cambs	www.stephenperse.com	£4,550	–	Miss P. Kelleher
Stockport Grammar School, Cheshire	www.stockportgrammar.co.uk	£2,961	–	A. Chicken
Stonar School, Wilts	www.stonarschool.com	£4,245	£7,480	Mrs S. Shayler
Stonyhurst College, Lancs	www.stonyhurst.ac.uk	£5,001	£7,320	A. Johnson
Stover School, Devon	www.stover.co.uk	£3,395	£6,885	Mrs S. Bradley
Stowe School, Bucks	www.stowe.co.uk	£6,800	£9,375	A. Wallersteiner
Streatham & Clapham High School, London SW16	www.gdst.net/streathamhigh	£4,002	–	Mrs S. Mitchell
Sunderland High School, Tyne and Wear	www.sunderlandhigh.co.uk	£2,671*	–	Dr A. Slater
Surbiton High School, Surrey	www.surbitonhigh.com	£4,082	–	Ms E. Haydon
Sutton High School, Surrey	www.suttonhigh.gdst.net	£4,002	–	S. Callaghan
Sutton Valence School, Kent	www.svs.org.uk	£5,600	£8,540	B. Grindlay
Sydenham High School, London SE26	www.sydenhamhighschool.gdst.net	£4,002	–	Mrs K. Pullen
Talbot Heath, Dorset	www.talbotheath.org	£3,486	£5,806	Mrs A. Holloway
Taunton School, Somerset	www.tauntonschool.co.uk	£5,000	£8,165	Dr J. Newton
Teesside High School, Cleveland	www.teessidehigh.co.uk	£3,414	–	T. Packer
Tettenhall College, W. Midlands	www.tettenhallcollege.co.uk	£3,976	£7,245	M. Long
Thetford Grammar School, Norfolk	www.thetgram.norfolk.sch.uk	£3,414	–	G. Price
Thornton College, Bucks	www.thorntoncollege.com	£3,205*	£5,250*	Miss A. Williams
Tonbridge School, Kent	www.tonbridge-school.co.uk	£7,445	£9,971	T. Haynes
Tormead School, Surrey	www.tormeadschool.org.uk	£3,970	–	Mrs C. Foord
Trent College, Notts	www.trentcollege.net	£4,490	£6,875	Mrs G. Dixon
Tring Park School for the Performing Arts, Herts	www.tringpark.com	£6,045	£8,835	S. Anderson
Trinity School, Surrey	www.trinity-school.org	£3,980	–	M. Bishop

Truro High School for Girls, Cornwall	www.trurohigh.co.uk	£3,440	£6,539	Mrs C. Pascoe
Truro School, Cornwall	www.truroschool.com	£3,590	£6,865	P. Smith
Tudor Hall, Oxon	www.tudorhallschool.com	£5,513	£8,500	Miss W. Griffiths
University College School, London NW3	www.ucs.org.uk	£5,155	–	K. Durham
Uppingham School, Rutland	www.uppingham.co.uk	£6,630	£9,467	R. Harman
Wakefield Girls' High School, W. Yorks	www.wgsf.org.uk	£3,235	–	Mrs P. Langham
Walthamstow Hall, Kent	www.walthamstow-hall.co.uk	£4,950	–	Mrs J. Milner
Warminster School, Wilts	www.warminsterschool.org.uk	£4,235	£7,435	M. Priestley
Warwick School, Warwicks	www.warwickschool.org	£3,369	£7,189	E. Halse
Wellingborough School, Northants	www.wellingboroughschool.org	£4,060	–	G. Bowe
Wellington College, Berks	www.wellingtoncollege.org.uk	£7,190	£9,595	Dr A. Seldon
Wellington School, Somerset	www.wellington-school.org.uk	£3,765	£6,685	M. Reader
Wells Cathedral School, Somerset	www.wells-cathedral-school.com	£4,750	£7,940	Mrs E. Cairncross
West Buckland School, Devon	www.westbuckland.devon.sch.uk	£3,900	£7,400	J. Vick
Westfield School, Tyne and Wear	www.westfield.newcastle.sch.uk	£3,378	–	Mrs M. Farndale
Westholme School, Lancs	www.westholmeschool.com	£2,767	–	Mrs L. Croston
Westminster School, London SW1	www.westminster.org.uk	£6,788	£9,802	M. S. Spurr
Westonbirt, Glos	www.westonbirt.gloucs.sch.uk	£6,272	£9,330	Mrs M. Henderson
Whitgift School, Surrey	www.whitgift.co.uk	£4,577	£4,577	C. Barnett
Wimbledon High School, London SW19	www.wimbledonhigh.gdst.net	£4,021	–	Mrs H. Hanbury
Winchester College, Hants	www.winchestercollege.org	£9,491	£9,990	R. Townsend
Windermere School, Cumbria	www.windermereschool.co.uk	£4,472	£8,006	I. Lavender
Wisbech Grammar School, Cambs	www.wgs.cambs.sch.uk	£3,425	–	N. Hammond
Withington Girls' School, Greater Manchester	www.withington.manchester.sch.uk	£3,100	–	Mrs S. Marks
Woldingham School, Surrey	www.woldinghamschool.co.uk	£5,539	£8,935	Mrs J. Triffitt
Wolverhampton Grammar School, W. Midlands	www.wgs.org.uk	£3,545*	–	J. Darby
Woodbridge School, Suffolk	www.woodbridge.suffolk.sch.uk	£4,339	£7,666	S. Cole
Woodhouse Grove School, W. Yorks	www.woodhousegrove.co.uk	£3,410	£6,800	D. Humphreys
Worksop College, Notts	www.worksopcollege.notts.sch.uk	£5,065	£7,540	R. Collard
Worth School, W. Sussex	www.worthschool.co.uk	£6,327	£8,542	G. Carminati
Wrekin College, Shrops	www.wrekincollege.com	£4,892	£8,075	S. Drew
Wychwood School, Oxon	www.wychwood-school.org.uk	£3,660	£5,955	Mrs S. Wingfield Digby
Wycliffe College, Glos	www.wycliffe.co.uk	£5,440	£8,360	Mrs M. Burnet Ward
Wycombe Abbey School, Bucks	www.wycombeabbey.com	£7,310	£9,750	Mrs C. Hall
Wykeham House School, Hants	www.wykehamhouse.com	£3,175	–	Mrs L. Clarke
Yarm School, Cleveland	www.yarmschool.org	£3,439	–	D. M. Dunn
The Yehudi Menuhin School, Surrey	www.yehudimenuhinschool.co.uk	sliding scale		Dr R. Hillier

WALES

Christ College, Brecon	www.christcollegebrecon.com	£4,630	£7,155	Mrs E. Taylor
Haberdashers' Monmouth School for Girls, Monmouth	www.habs-monmouth.org	£3,815	£7,166	Mrs H. Davy
Howell's School, Denbigh	www.howells.org	£3,900	£6,300	B. Routledge
Howell's School Llandaff, Cardiff	www.howells-cardiff.gdst.net	£3,210	–	Mrs S. Davis
Llandovery College, Llandovery	www.llandoverycollege.com	£4,495	£6,650	I. Hunt
Monmouth School, Monmouth	www.habs-monmouth.org	£4,115	£7,166	S. Connors
Rougemont School, Newport	www.rougemontschool.co.uk	£3,300	–	Dr J. Tribbick
Ruthin School, Ruthin	www.ruthinschool.co.uk	£3,859	£6,999	T. Belfield
Rydal Penrhos School, Colwyn Bay	www.rydal-penrhos.com	£4,330	£8,635	P. Lee-Browne
St David's College, Llandudno	www.stdavidscollege.co.uk	£5,421	£8,050	S. Hay

NORTHERN IRELAND

Bangor Grammar School, Bangor	www.bangorgrammarschool.org.uk	–	–	S. Connolly
Belfast Royal Academy, Belfast	www.belfastroyalacademy.com	£47	–	J. Dickson
Campbell College, Belfast	www.campbellcollege.co.uk	£710	£3,543	J. Piggot
Coleraine Academical Institution, Coleraine	www.coleraineai.com	£47	–	Dr D. Carruthers
Foyle and Londonderry College, Londonderry	www.foylenet.org/foyleandlondonderry	£40	–	W. Magill

The Royal Belfast Academical Institution, Belfast	www.rbai.org.uk	£265	–	Miss J. Williamson
The Royal School Dungannon, Dungannon	www.royaldungannon.com	£45	£2,212	D. Burnett

SCOTLAND

Dollar Academy, Dollar	www.dollaracademy.org.uk	£3,270	£7,461	D. Knapman
The High School of Dundee, Dundee	www.highschoolofdundee.co.uk	£3,280	–	Dr J. Halliday
The Edinburgh Academy, Edinburgh	www.edinburghacademy.org.uk	£3,660	–	M. Longmore
Fettes College, Edinburgh	www.fettes.com	£6,350	£8,620	M. Spens
George Heriot's School, Edinburgh	www.george-heriots.com	£3,144	–	A. Hector
The Glasgow Academy, Glasgow	www.theglasgowacademy.org.uk	£3,215	–	P. Brodie
The High School of Glasgow, Glasgow	www.glasgowhigh.com	£2,882	–	C. Mair
Glenalmond College, Perth	www.glenalmondcollege.co.uk	£5,966	£8,748	G. Woods
Hutchesons' Grammar School, Glasgow	www.hutchesons.org	£3,076	–	Dr K. Greig
Kelvinside Academy, Glasgow	www.kelvinsideacademy.org.uk	£3,299	–	Mrs L. Douglas
Kilgraston, Bridge of Earn	www.kilgraston.com	£4,530	£7,725	M. Farmer
Lomond School, Helensburgh	www.lomond-school.org	£3,040	£6,500	S. Mills
Loretto School, Musselburgh	www.loretto.com	£5,920	£8,710	P. Hogan
The Mary Erskine School, Edinburgh	www.esms.edin.sch.uk	£3,123	£5,930	J. Gray
Merchiston Castle School, Edinburgh	www.merchiston.co.uk	£5,980	£8,260	A. Hunter
Morrison's Academy, Crieff	www.morrisonsacademy.org	£3,225	–	G. Pengelley
Robert Gordon's College, Aberdeen	www.rgc.aberdeen.sch.uk	£3,255	–	H. Ouston
St Aloysius' College, Glasgow	www.staloysius.org	£2,916	–	J. Stoer
St Columba's School, Kilmacolm	www.st-columbas.org	£3,150	–	D. G. Girdwood
St Margaret's School for Girls, Aberdeen	www.st-margaret.aberdeen.sch.uk	£3,245	–	Dr J. Land
Stewart's Melville College, Edinburgh	www.esms.edin.sch.uk	£3,123	£5,930	J. Gray
Strathallan School, Perth	www.strathallan.co.uk	£5,754	£8,480	B. Thompson

CHANNEL ISLANDS

Elizabeth College, Guernsey	www.elizcoll.org	£2,600	–	G. Hartley
The Ladies' College, Guernsey	www.ladiescollege.com	£1,960	–	Ms J. Riches
Victoria College, Jersey	www.victoriacollege.je	£1,398	–	A. Watkins

NATIONAL ACADEMIES OF SCHOLARSHIP

The national academies are self-governing bodies whose members are elected as a result of achievement and distinction in the academy's field. Within their discipline, the academies provide advice, support education and exceptional scholars, stimulate debate, promote UK research worldwide and collaborate with international counterparts.

In addition to income from donations, membership contributions, trading and investments, the English academies receive grant-in-aid funding from the science budget, administered by the Department for Business, Innovation and Skills.

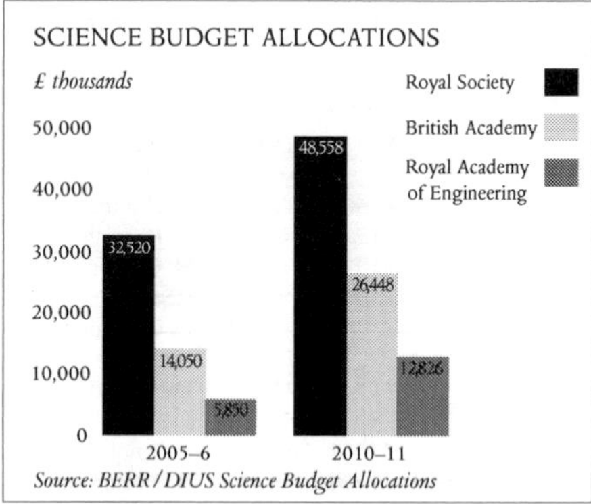

Source: BERR / DIUS Science Budget Allocations

ACADEMY OF MEDICAL SCIENCES (1998)

10 Carlton House Terrace, London SW1Y 5AH
T 020-7969 5288
W www.acmedsci.ac.uk

The Academy of Medical Sciences was established in 1998 to promote advances in medical science and to ensure these are converted into healthcare benefits for society. It campaigns for the development, protection and promotion of careers for academics in the biomedical sciences and encourages good practice in training and development.

The academy is independent and self-governing and receives funding from a variety of sources including the fellowship, charitable donations, government and industry.

Fellows are elected from a broad range of medical sciences: biomedical, clinical and population based. The academy includes in its remit veterinary medicine, dentistry, nursing, medical law, economics, sociology and ethics. Elections are from nominations put forward by existing fellows.

At June 2010 there were 983 fellows and 29 honorary fellows.

President, Prof. Sir John Bell, FRS, PMedSci
Vice-Presidents, Prof. Patrick Sissons FMedSci; Prof. Ronald Laskey FRS, FMedSci
Executive Director, Dr Helen Munn

BRITISH ACADEMY (1902)

10 Carlton House Terrace, London SW1Y 5AH
T 020-7969 5200
W www.britac.ac.uk

The British Academy is an independent, self-governing learned society for the promotion of the humanities and social sciences. It supports advanced academic research and is a channel for the government's support of research in those disciplines.

The fellows are scholars who have attained distinction in one of the branches of study that the academy exists to promote. Candidates must be nominated by existing fellows. There are 924 fellows, 21 honorary fellows and 314 corresponding fellows overseas.

President, Prof. Sir Adam Roberts, KCMG
Chief Executive, Dr R. Jackson

ROYAL ACADEMY OF ENGINEERING (197

3 Carlton House Terrace, London SW1Y 5DG
T 020-7766 0600
W www.raeng.org.uk

The Royal Academy of Engineering was established as the Fellowship of Engineering in 1976. It was granted a royal charter in 1983 and its present title in 1992. It is an independent, self-governing body whose object is the pursuit, encouragement and maintenance of excellence in the whole field of engineering, in order to promote the advancement of science, art and practice of engineering for the benefit of the public.

Election to the fellowship is by invitation only, from nominations supported by the body of fellows. At May 2010 there were 1,423 fellows. The Duke of Edinburgh is the senior fellow and the Duke of Kent is a royal fellow.

President, Lord Browne of Madingley, FRENG, FRS
Senior Vice-President, Prof. R. J. Mair, FRENG, FRS
Chief Executive, P. D. Greenish, CBE

ROYAL SOCIETY (1660)

6–9 Carlton House Terrace, London SW1Y 5AG
T 020-7451 2500
W www.royalsociety.org

The Royal Society is an independent academy promoting the natural and applied sciences. Founded in 1660, the society has three roles, as the UK academy of science, as a learned society and as a funding agency. It is an independent, self-governing body under a royal charter, promoting and advancing all fields of physical and biological sciences, of mathematics and engineering, medical and agricultural sciences and their application.

Fellows are elected for their contributions to science, both in fundamental research resulting in greater understanding, and also in leading and directing scientific and technological progress in industry and research establishments. A maximum of 44 new fellows, who must be citizens or residents of the British Commonwealth countries or Ireland, may be elected annually.

Up to eight foreign members, who are selected from those not eligible to become fellows because of citizenship or residency, are elected annually for their contributions to science.

One honorary fellow may be elected each year from those not eligible for election as fellows or foreign members. There are approximately 1,400 fellows and foreign members covering all scientific disciplines.

President, Prof. Lord Rees of Ludlow, PRS
Executive Secretary, S. Cox, CVO

ROYAL SOCIETY OF EDINBURGH (1783)

22–26 George Street, Edinburgh EH2 2PQ
T 0131-240 5000
W www.royalsoced.org.uk

The Royal Society of Edinburgh (RSE) is an educational charity and Scotland's National Academy. An independent body with charitable status, its multidisciplinary membership represents a knowledge resource for the people of Scotland. Granted its royal charter in 1783 for the 'advancement of learning and useful knowledge', the society organises conferences, debates and lectures; conducts independent inquiries; facilitates international collaboration and showcases the country's research and development capabilities; provides educational activities for primary and secondary school students and awards prizes and medals. The society also awards over £2m annually to Scotland's top researchers and entrepreneurs working in Scotland.

At May 2010 there were 1,529 fellows.

President, Lord Wilson of Tillyorn, KT, GCMG, PRS
Vice-Presidents, Prof. Jean Beggs CBE, Prof. Tariq Durrani, OBE, FRENG, FRSE, Prof. Hector MacQueen, FRSE, John McClelland CBE
General Secretary, Prof. Geoffrey Boulton, OBE, FRS, FRSE

PRIVATELY FUNDED ARTS ACADEMIES

The Royal Academy and the Royal Scottish Academy support the visual arts community in the UK, hold educational events and promote interest in the arts. They are entirely privately funded through contributions by 'friends' (regular donors who receive benefits such as free entry, previews and magazines), bequests, corporate donations and exhibitions.

ROYAL ACADEMY OF ARTS (1768)

Burlington House, Piccadilly, London W1J 0BD
T 020-7300 8000
W www.royalacademy.org.uk

The Royal Academy of Arts is an independent, self-governing society devoted to the encouragement and promotion of the fine arts.

Membership of the academy is limited to 80 academicians, all being painters, engravers, sculptors or architects. Candidates are nominated and elected by the existing academicians. There is also a limited class of honorary academicians, of whom as of May 2010 there were 20.

President, Sir Nicholas Grimshaw, CBE, PRA
Secretary and Chief Executive, Charles Saumarez Smith, CBE

ROYAL SCOTTISH ACADEMY (1838)

The Mound, Edinburgh EH2 2EL
T 0131-225 6671
W www.royalscottishacademy.org

Founded in 1826 and granted a Royal Charter in 1838, The Royal Scottish Academy is an independent institution led by prominent Scottish artists and architects. It promotes and supports the visual arts through an ongoing exhibitions programme, related educational events and through a series of awards, bursaries and scholarships for artists at all stages of their careers.

Members are elected from the disciplines of art and architecture and elections are from nominations put forward by the existing membership. At mid 2010 there were 34 honorary members and around 107 members.

President, Prof. Bill Scott, PRSA
Secretary, Arthur Watson, RSA

RESEARCH COUNCILS

The government funds basic and applied civil science research, mostly through seven research councils, which are established under royal charter and supported by the Department for Business, Innovation and Skills (BIS). Research Councils UK is the strategic partnership of these seven councils* (for further information *see* **W** www.rcuk.ac.uk). The councils support research and training in universities and other higher education and research establishments. The science budget, administered by BIS, contributes to public sector investment in research, with funding from other government departments (including higher education funding) and regional development making up the remaining investment. The councils also receive income for research commissioned by government departments and the private sector, in addition to income from charitable sources.

GOVERNMENT SCIENCE BUDGET
£ thousand

	2009–10	*2010–11*
Arts and Humanities Research Council	104,397	108,827
Biotechnology and Biological Sciences Research Council	452,563	471,057
Economic and Social Research Council	170,614	177,574
Engineering and Physical Sciences Research Council	814,528	843,465
Medical Research Council	658,472	707,025
Natural Environment Research Council	408,162	436,000
Science and Technology Facilities Council	630,337	651,636
Capital Investment Fund	184,860	189,851
Higher Education Innnovation Fund	99,000	113,000

Source: DIUS – *Science Budget Allocations 2008–9 to 2010–11*

ALCOHOL EDUCATION AND RESEARCH COUNCIL

Eliot House, 10–12 Allington Street, London SW1E 5EH
T 020-7808 7150 **W** www.aerc.org.uk

The AERC was established by act of parliament in 1982 to administer the Alcohol Education and Research Fund. The government fund is used in UK education and research projects to develop new ways to help those with drinking problems. The AERC funds up to five research projects of around £50,000 every year and awards a number of small research grants up to a maximum of £5,000. The AERC aims to increase awareness of alcohol issues, to reduce alcohol-related harm and to encourage best practice.
Chief Executive, Mr Dave Roberts
Director, Prof. Ray Hodgson

ARTS AND HUMANITIES RESEARCH COUNCIL*

Polaris House, North Star Avenue, Swindon SN2 1FL
T 01793-416000 **W** www.ahrc.ac.uk

Launched in April 2005 as the successor organisation to the Arts and Humanities Research Board, the AHRC provides funding for postgraduate training and research in the arts and humanities. In any one year, the AHRC makes approximately 700 research awards and around 1,300 postgraduate awards. Awards are made after a rigorous peer review process, which ensures the quality of applications.
Chair, Prof. Sir Alan Wilson
Chief Executive, Prof. Rick Rylance

BIOTECHNOLOGY AND BIOLOGICAL SCIENCES RESEARCH COUNCIL*

Polaris House, North Star Avenue, Swindon SN2 1UH
T 01793-413200 **W** www.bbsrc.ac.uk

Established by royal charter in 1994, the BBSRC is the UK funding agency for research in the life sciences. It funds research into how all living organisms function and behave, benefiting the agriculture, food, health, pharmaceutical and chemical sectors. To deliver its mission, the BBSRC supports research and training in universities and research centres throughout the UK, including providing strategic research grants to the institutes listed below.
Chair, Prof. Sir T. Blundell
Chief Executive, Prof. D. Kell

INSTITUTES

BABRAHAM INSTITUTE, Babraham Hall, Babraham, Cambridge CB2 3AT **T** 01223-496000
Director, Prof. M. Wakelam

GENOME ANALYSIS CENTRE, Norwich Research Park, Colney, Norwich NR4 7UH **T** 01603-450000
Director, Dr J. Rogers

INSTITUTE FOR ANIMAL HEALTH, Compton Laboratory, Compton, Newbury, Berks RG20 7NN **T** 01635-578411
Director, Prof. M. Shirley

INSTITUTE FOR BIOLOGICAL, ENVIRONMENTAL AND RURAL STUDIES (ABERYSTWYTH UNIVERSITY), Penglais, Aberystwyth, Ceredigion SY23 3DA **T** 01970-621904
Director, Prof. W. Powell

INSTITUTE OF FOOD RESEARCH, Norwich Research Park, Colney Lane, Norwich NR4 7UA **T** 01603-255000
Director, Prof. D. Boxer

JOHN INNES CENTRE, Norwich Research Park, Colney, Norwich NR4 7UH **T** 01603-450000
Director, Prof. C. Lamb

ROSLIN INSTITUTE (UNIVERSITY OF EDINBURGH), Roslin Biocentre, Roslin, Midlothian EH25 9PS **T** 0131-527 4200
Director, Prof. D. Hume

ROTHAMSTED RESEARCH, Rothamsted, Harpenden, Herts AL5 2JQ **T** 01582-763133
Director, Prof. M. Moloney

ECONOMIC AND SOCIAL RESEARCH COUNCIL*

Polaris House, North Star Avenue, Swindon SN2 1UJ
T 01793-413000 E comms@esrc.ac.uk
W www.esrcsocietytoday.ac.uk

The purpose of the ESRC is to promote and support research and postgraduate training in the social sciences. It also provides advice, disseminates knowledge and promotes public understanding in these areas. The ESRC provides core funding to the centres listed below. Further information can be obtained on the ESRC website, including details of centres it funds in collaboration with other research councils.

Chair, Dr Alan Gillespie
Chief Executive (interim), Astrid Wissenburg

RESEARCH CENTRES

CENTRE FOR BUSINESS RELATIONSHIPS, ACCOUNTABILITY, SUSTAINABILITY AND SOCIETY, University of Cardiff, 55 Park Place, Cardiff CF10 3AT T 029-2087 6562
Director, Prof. K. Peattie

CENTRE FOR CHARITABLE GIVING AND PHILANTHROPY, Cass Business School, 106 Bunhill Row, London EC1Y 8TZ T 020-7040 0136
Directors, Prof. J. Harrow; Prof. C. Pharoah

CENTRE FOR CLIMATE CHANGE, ECONOMICS AND POLICY, LSE, Houghton Street, London WC2 2AE T 020-7955 6228
Directors, Prof. J. Rees; Prof. A. Gouldson

CENTRE FOR COMPETITION POLICY, University of East Anglia, Norwich NR4 7TJ T 01603-593715
Director, Prof. C. Waddams

CENTRE FOR COMPETITIVE ADVANTAGE IN THE GLOBAL ECONOMY, Department of Economics, University of Warwick, Coventry, Warks CV4 7AL T 02476-523468
Director, Prof. Nick Crafts

CENTRE FOR ECONOMIC AND SOCIAL ASPECTS OF GENOMICS, Cardiff University, 6 Museum Place, CF10 3BG
Director, Prof. Ruth Chadwick

CENTRE FOR ECONOMIC PERFORMANCE, London School of Economics and Political Science, Houghton Street, London WC2A 2AE T 020-7955 7048
Director, Prof. J. Van Reenen

CENTRE FOR GENOMICS IN SOCIETY, Egenis Office, University of Exeter, Byrne House, St German's Road, Exeter EX4 4PJ T 01392-269127
Director, Prof. John Dupré

CENTRE FOR MARKET AND PUBLIC ORGANISATION, Bristol Institute of Public Affairs, 2 Priory Road, Bristol BS8 1TX T 0117-928 8436
Director, Prof. S. Burgess

CENTRE FOR MICRODATA METHODS AND PRACTICE, Department of Economics, UCL, Gower Street, London WC1E 6BT T 020-7679 5857
Director, Prof. Andrew Chesher

CENTRE FOR MICROECONOMIC ANALYSIS OF PUBLIC POLICY, Institute for Fiscal Studies, 7 Ridgmount Street, London WC1E 7AE T 020-7291 4820
Director, Prof. R. Blundell

CENTRE FOR POPULATION CHANGE, School of Social Sciences, University of Southampton SO17 1BJ T 023-8059 3192
Director, Prof. J. Falkingham

CENTRE FOR RESEARCH ON SOCIO-CULTURAL CHANGE, University of Manchester, 178 Waterloo Place, Oxford Road, Manchester M13 9PL T 0161-275 8985
Directors, Prof. M. Savage

CENTRE FOR SOCIAL AND ECONOMIC RESEARCH ON INNOVATION IN GENOMICS, Innogen Centre, University of Edinburgh, Old Surgeon's Hall, High School Yards, Edinburgh EH1 1LZ T 0131-650 6385
Director, Prof. D. Wield

CENTRE FOR SOCIAL, TECHNOLOGICAL AND ENVIRONMENTAL PATHWAYS TO SUSTAINABILITY, Institute of Development Studies, Brighton BN1 9RE T 01273-606261
Director, Prof. M. Leach

CENTRE FOR SPATIAL ECONOMICS, LSE, Houghton Street, London WC2A 2AE T 020-7955 6581
Director, Dr Henry Overman

CENTRE FOR THIRD SECTOR RESEARCH, Park House, 40 Edgbaston Park Road, University of Birmingham B15 2RT T 0121-414 3171
Director, Prof. Peter Alcock

CENTRE OF MICRO-SOCIAL CHANGE, University of Essex, Colchester, Essex CO4 3SQ T 01206-873789
Director, Prof. S. Pudney

CENTRE ON MIGRATION, POLICY AND SOCIETY, University of Oxford, 58 Banbury Road, Oxford OX2 6QS T 01865-274711
Director, Prof. M. Keith

CENTRE ON SKILLS, KNOWLEDGE AND ORGANISATIONAL PERFORMANCE, Department of Education, University of Oxford, 15 Norham Gardens, Oxford OX2 6PY T 01865-611030
Director, Mr K. Mayhew

ELECTRICITY POLICY RESEARCH GROUP, University of Cambridge, Trumpington Street CB2 1AG T 01223-335246
Director, Prof. D. Newbery

INNOVATION RESEARCH CENTRE, Judge Business School Building, Trumpington Street, Cambridge CB2 1AG T 01223-765335
Director, Prof. Alan Hughes

INTERNATIONAL CENTRE FOR LIFECOURSE STUDIES IN SOCIETY AND HEALTH, UCL Research Department of Epidemiology and Public Health, 1–19 Torrington Place, London WC1E 7HB T 020-7679 1708
Director, Prof. M. Bartley

LANGUAGE-BASED AREA STUDIES CENTRES T 01793-413089
Directors, Dr Robin Aizlewood; Dr Richard Berry; Prof. Anoush Ehteshami; Prof. Victor King; Dr Frank Pieke

LEARNING AND LIFE CHANCES IN KNOWLEDGE ECONOMIES AND SOCIETIES, Institute of Education, University of London, 20 Bedford Way, London WC1H 0AL T 020-7911 5464
Director, Prof. A. Green

RESEARCH GROUP ON LIFESTYLES, VALUES AND ENVIRONMENT, Centre for Environmental Strategy, University of Surrey, Guildford, Surrey GU2 7XH T 01483-689072
Director, Prof. T. Jackson

UK TRANSPORT RESEARCH CENTRE T 020-7679 0478
Director, Prof. P. Jones

ENGINEERING AND PHYSICAL SCIENCES RESEARCH COUNCIL*

Polaris House, North Star Avenue, Swindon SN2 1ET
T 01793-444000 W www.epsrc.ac.uk

The EPSRC is the UK government's main funding agency for research and training in engineering and the physical sciences in universities and other organisations throughout the UK. It also provides advice, disseminates knowledge and promotes public understanding in these areas.
Chair, John Armitt, CBE, FRENG
Chief Executive, Prof. David Delpy, FRS

HEALTH PROTECTION AGENCY

7th Floor, Holborn Gate, 330 High Holborn, London WC1V 7PP
T 020-7759 2700 **E** webteam@hpa.org.uk
W www.hpa.org.uk

The Health Protection Agency is a Special Health Authority, established in 2003 (merged with the National Radiological Protection Board in 2005), which gives advice to the public, health authorities and the government. It works to reduce the impact of infectious diseases and exposure to chemicals, poisons and radiation at local, national and regional levels and in emergency situations. The agency researches new ways to combat illness and to assess exposure to chemicals and radiation to determine whether treatment is needed.
Chairman, Sir William Stewart
Chief Executive, Justin McCracken

RESEARCH CENTRES

CENTRE FOR INFECTIONS, 61 Colindale Avenue, London NW9 5EQ **T** 020-8200 4400
Director, Prof. Peter Borriello

CENTRE FOR EMERGENCY PREPAREDNESS AND RESPONSE Porton Down, Salisbury, SP4 0JG
T 01980-612100
Director, Dr Stephen Chatfield

CENTRE FOR RADIATION, CHEMICAL AND ENVIRONMENTAL HAZARDS, Chilton, Didcot OX11 0RQ
T 01235-831600
Director, Dr Roger Cox

MEDICAL RESEARCH COUNCIL*

20 Park Crescent, London W1B 1AL **T** 020-7636 5422
W www.mrc.ac.uk

The purpose of the MRC is to promote medical and related biological research. The council employs its own research staff and funds research by other institutions and individuals, complementing the research resources of the universities and hospitals.
Chair, Sir John Chisholm
Chief Executive, Sir Leszek Borysiewicz
Chair, Neurosciences and Mental Health Board, Prof. C. Kennard
Chair, Molecular and Cellular Medicine Board, Prof. P. Luzio
Chair, Infections and Immunity Board, Prof. D. Cantrell
Chair, Population and Systems Medicine Board, Prof. S. Holgate

MRC UNITS, CENTRES AND INSTITUTES

MRC Anatomical Neuropharmacology Unit
W mrcanu.pharm.ox.ac.uk

MRC Biostatistics Unit
W www.mrc-bsu.cam.ac.uk

MRC Cancer Cell Unit
W www.hutchison-mrc.cam.ac.uk

MRC Cell Biology Unit
W www.ucl.ac.uk/lmcb

MRC Centre for Behavioural and Clinical Neuroscience Institute
W www.psychol.cam.ac.uk/bcni

MRC Centre for Brain Ageing and Vitality
W www.ncl.ac.uk

MRC Centre for Causal Analyses in Translational Epidemiology
W www.bristol.ac.uk/caite

MRC Centre for Cognitive Ageing and Cognitive Epidemiology
W www.ccace.ed.ac.uk

MRC Centre for Developmental and Biomedical Genetics
W cdbg.shef.ac.uk

MRC Centre for Developmental Neurobiology at King's College London
W www.kcl.ac.uk/depsta/biomedical/mrc

MRC Centre for Drug Safety Science
W www.liv.ac.uk/drug-safety/

MRC Centre for Genomics and Global Health
W www.cggh.ox.ac.uk

MRC/University of Birmingham Centre for Immune Regulation
W www.bham.ac.uk/mrcbcir

MRC/University of Edinburgh Centre for Inflammation Research
W www.cir.med.ed.ac.uk

MRC/UCL Centre for Medical Molecular Virology
T 020-7504 9343

MRC Centre for Neuromuscular Diseases
W www.cnmd.ac.uk

MRC Centre for Neurodegeneration Research
W cnr.iop.kcl.ac.uk

MRC Centre for Neuropsychiatric Genetics and Genomics
W http://medicine.cf.ac.uk/research/research-groups/cngg/

MRC Centre for Nutritional Epidemiology in Cancer Prevention and Survival
W www.srl.cam.ac.uk

MRC Centre for Obesity and Related Metabolic Diseases
W www.mrl.ims.cam.ac.uk

MRC Centre for Outbreak Analysis and Modelling
W www1.imperial.ac.uk

MRC Centre for Protein Engineering
W www.mrc-cpe.cam.ac.uk

MRC Centre for Regenerative Medicine
W www.scrm.ed.ac.uk

MRC Centre for Stem Cell Biology and Regenerative Medicine
W www.stemcells.cam.ac.uk

MRC/University of Bristol Centre for Synaptic Plasticity
W www.bris.ac.uk/depts/synaptic

MRC Centre for Transplantation
W http://transplantation.kcl.ac.uk

MRC/Asthma UK Centre in Allergic Mechanisms of Asthma
W www.asthma-allergy.ac.uk

MRC/University of Sussex Centre in Genome Damage and Stability
W www.sussex.ac.uk/gdsc

MRC Centre of Epidemiology for Child Health
W www.ich.ucl.ac.uk

MRC Clinical Sciences Centre
W www.csc.mrc.ac.uk

MRC/Cancer Research UK/BHF Clinical Trial Service Unit & Epidemiological Studies Unit
W www.ctsu.ox.ac.uk

MRC Clinical Trials Unit
W www.ctu.mrc.ac.uk

MRC Cognition and Brain Sciences Unit
W www.mrc-cbu.cam.ac.uk

MRC Collaborative Centre for Human Nutrition Research
W www.mrc-hnr.cam.ac.uk
MRC Epidemiology Resource Centre
W www.mrc.soton.ac.uk
MRC Epidemiology Unit
W www.mrc-epid.cam.ac.uk
MRC Functional Genomics Unit
W www.mrcfgu.ox.ac.uk
MRC General Practice Research Framework
W www.gprf.mrc.ac.uk
MRC Human Genetics Unit
W www.hgu.mrc.ac.uk
MRC Human Immunology Unit
W www.imm.ox.ac.uk/groups/mrc-hiu
MRC Human Reproductive Sciences Unit
W www.hrsu.mrc.ac.uk
MRC Institute of Hearing Research
W www.ihr.mrc.ac.uk
MRC Laboratory of Molecular Biology
W www2.mrc-lmb.cam.ac.uk
MRC Mammalian Genetics Unit
W www.mgu.har.mrc.ac.uk
MRC Mitochondrial Biology Unit
W www.mrc-mbu.cam.ac.uk
MRC Molecular Haemotology Unit
W www.imm.ox.ac.uk/groups/mrc_molhaem
MRC National Institute for Medical Research
W www.nimr.mrc.ac.uk
MRC Prion Unit
W www.prion.ucl.ac.uk
MRC Protein Phosphorylation Unit
W www.dundee.ac.uk/lifesciences/mrcppu
MRC Radiation Oncology and Biology Initiative
W www.rob.ox.ac.uk
MRC Social and Public Health Sciences Unit
W www.msoc-mrc.gla.ac.uk
MRC Social, Genetic and Developmental Psychiatry Research Centre
W www.iop.kcl.ac.uk/departments
MRC Toxicology Unit
W www.le.ac.uk/mrctox
MRC/UCL Crucible Centre
W www.ucl.ac.uk/crucible
MRC Unit for Lifelong Health and Ageing
W www.nhsd.mrc.ac.uk
MRC/UVRIUganda Research Unit on AIDS
T (+256) (41) 320272
MRC (UK), the Gambia
W www.mrc.gm
MRC Virology Unit
W www.mrcvu.gla.ac.uk

NATIONAL PHYSICAL LABORATORY

Hampton Road, Teddington, Middx TW11 0LW
T 020-8977 3222 E enquiry@npl.co.uk
W www.npl.co.uk

The National Physical Laboratory (NPL) was established in 1900 and is the UK's national measurement institute. It develops, maintains and disseminates national measurement standards for physical quantities such as mass, length, time, temperature, voltage and force. It also conducts underpinning research on engineering materials and information technology, and disseminates good measurement practice. It is government-owned but contractor-operated.
Managing Director, B. Bowsher

NATURAL ENVIRONMENT RESEARCH COUNCIL*

Polaris House, North Star Avenue, Swindon SN2 1EU
T 01793-411500 W www.nerc.ac.uk

The NERC funds and carries out impartial scientific research in the sciences relating to natural environment. Its work covers the full range of atmospheric, earth, biological, terrestrial and aquatic sciences, from the depths of the oceans to the upper atmosphere. Its mission is to gather and apply knowledge, create understanding and predict the behaviour of the natural environment and its resources.
Chair, Edmund Wallis
Chief Executive, Prof. Alan Thorpe

RESEARCH CENTRES

BRITISH ANTARCTIC SURVEY, High Cross, Madingley Road, Cambridge CB3 0ET
T 01223-221400
Director, Prof. Nick Owens
BRITISH GEOLOGICAL SURVEY, Kingsley Dunham Centre, Keyworth, Nottingham NG12 5GG T 0115-936 3100
Executive Director, Dr John Ludden
CENTRE FOR ECOLOGY AND HYDROLOGY, Maclean Building, Benson Lane, Crowmarsh Gifford, Wallingford OX10 8BB T 01491-838800
Director, Prof. Patricia Nuttall, OBE
NATIONAL OCEANOGRAPHY CENTRE, Joseph Proudman Building, 6 Brownlow Street, Liverpool L3 5DA
T 0151-795 4800
Director, Prof. Edward Hill

COLLABORATIVE CENTRES

CENTRE FOR EARTH OBSERVATION INSTRUMENTATION, NERC, Polaris House, North Star Avenue, Swindon SN2 1EU T 01793-411698
Director, Prof. Mick Johnson
CENTRE FOR POPULATION BIOLOGY, Imperial College London, Silwood Park Campus, Ascot SL5 7PY
T 020-7594 2475
Director, Prof. Georgina Mace, FRS
NATIONAL CENTRE FOR ATMOSPHERIC SCIENCE, NERC, Polaris House, North Star Avenue, Swindon SN2 1EU
T 0113-343 5158
Director, Prof. Stephen Mobbs
NATIONAL CENTRE FOR EARTH OBSERVATION, Department of Meteorology, University of Reading, Building 58, Earley Gate, Reading RG6 6BB T 0118-378 6728
Director, Prof. Alan O'Neill
NATIONAL INSTITUTE FOR ENVIRONMENTAL E-SCIENCE, Department of Earth Sciences, University of Cambridge, Downing Street, Cambridge CB2 3EQ
T 01223-764917
Director, Dr Martin Dove
PLYMOUTH MARINE LABORATORY, Prospect Place, Plymouth PL1 3DH T 01752-633100
Director, Prof. Steven de Mora
SCOTTISH ASSOCIATION FOR MARINE SCIENCE, Dunstaffnage Marine Laboratory, Oban PA37 1QA
T 01631-559000
Director, Prof. Laurence Mee
SEA MAMMAL RESEARCH UNIT, Gatty Marine Laboratory, University of St Andrews, St Andrews KY16 8LB
T 01334-462630
Director, Prof. Ian Boyd

TYNDALL CENTRE FOR CLIMATE CHANGE RESEARCH, School of Environmental Sciences, University of East Anglia, Norwich, Norfolk NR4 7TJ **T** 01603-593900
Executive Director, Prof. Kevin Anderson

UK ENERGY RESEARCH CENTRE, 58 Prince's Gate, Exhibition Road, London SW7 2PG **T** 020-7594 1574
Research Director, Prof. Jim Skea, OBE

SCIENCE AND TECHNOLOGY FACILITIES COUNCIL*

Polaris House, North Star Avenue, Swindon SN2 1SZ
T 01793-442000 **W** www.scitech.ac.uk

Formed by royal charter on 1 April 2007, through the merger of the Council for the Central Laboratory of the Research Councils and the Particle Physics and Astronomy Research Council, the STFC is a non-departmental public body reporting to the Department for Business, Innovation and Skills.

The STFC invests in large national and international research facilities, while delivering science, technology and expertise for the UK. The council is involved in research projects including the Diamond Light Source Synchrotron and the Large Hadron Collider, and develops new areas of science and technology. The EPSRC has transferred its responsibility for nuclear physics to the STFC.

Chair, Prof. Michael Sterling
Chief Executive, Prof. Keith Mason

CHILBOLTON OBSERVATORY, Chilbolton, Stockbridge, Hampshire SO20 6BJ **T** 01264-860391

DARESBURY LABORATORY, Daresbury Science and Innovation Campus, Warrington WA4 4AD **T** 01925-603000

RUTHERFORD APPLETON LABORATORY, Harwell Science and Innovation Campus, Didcot OX11 0QX
T 01235-445000

UK ASTRONOMY TECHNOLOGY CENTRE, Royal Observatory, Edinburgh, Blackford Hill, Edinburgh EH9 3HJ
T 0131-668 8100

RESEARCH AND TECHNOLOGY ORGANISATIONS

Over 30 industrial and technological research bodies are members of the Association of Independent Research and Technology Organisations Limited (AIRTO). Members' activities span a wide range of disciplines from life sciences to engineering. Their work includes basic research, development and design of innovative products or processes, instrumentation testing and certification, and technology and management consultancy. AIRTO publishes a directory to help clients identify the organisations that might be able to assist them. For a full list of members, *see* AIRTO's website.

AIRTO LTD, c/o CAMPDEN BRI, Station Road, Chipping Campden, Glos GL55 6LD **T** 01386-842247
E airto@campden.co.uk **W** www.airto.co.uk
President, Prof. R. Brook, OBE, FRENG

HEALTH

NATIONAL HEALTH SERVICE

The National Health Service (NHS) came into being on 5 July 1948 under the National Health Service Act 1946, covering England and Wales and, under separate legislation, Scotland and Northern Ireland. The NHS is now administered by the Secretary of State for Health (in England), the Welsh Assembly Government, the Scottish government and the Secretary of State for Northern Ireland.

The function of the NHS is to provide a comprehensive health service designed to secure improvement in the physical and mental health of the people and to prevent, diagnose and treat illness. It was founded on the principle that treatment should be provided according to clinical need rather than ability to pay, and should be free at the point of delivery.

Hospital, mental, dental, nursing, ophthalmic and ambulance services and facilities for the care of expectant and nursing mothers and young children are provided by the NHS to meet all reasonable requirements. Rehabilitation services such as occupational therapy, physiotherapy, speech therapy and surgical and medical appliances are supplied where appropriate. Specialists and consultants who work in NHS hospitals can also engage in private practice, including the treatment of their private patients in NHS hospitals.

STRUCTURE

The structure of the NHS remained relatively stable for the first 30 years of its existence. In 1974, a three-tier management structure comprising regional health authorities, area health authorities and district management teams was introduced in England, and the NHS became responsible for community health services. In 1979 area health authorities were abolished and district management teams were replaced by district health authorities.

The National Health Service and Community Care Act 1990 provided for more streamlined regional health authorities and district health authorities, and for the establishment of family health services authorities (FHSAs) and NHS trusts. The concept of the 'internal market' was introduced into health care, whereby care was provided through NHS contracts where health authorities or boards and GP fundholders (the purchasers) were responsible for buying health care from hospitals, non-fundholding GPs, community services and ambulance services (the providers). The Act also paved the way for the community care reforms, which were introduced in April 1993, and changed the way care is administered for older people, the mentally ill, the physically disabled and people with learning disabilities.

ENGLAND

Regional health authorities in England were abolished in April 1996 and replaced by eight regional offices which, together with the headquarters in Leeds, formed the NHS executive (which has since been merged with the Department of Health). In April 2002, as an interim arrangement, the eight regional offices were replaced by four directorates of health and social care (DHSCs). In April 2003, the DHSCs were abolished.

HEALTH AUTHORITIES

In April 1996 the district health authorities and family health service authorities were merged to form 100 unified health authorities (HAs) in England. In April 2002, 28 new health authorities were formed from the existing HAs. In October 2002, as part of the new arrangements set out in the NHS Reform and Health Care Professions Act 2002, these new health authorities were renamed strategic health authorities. The whole of England is now split into 10 strategic health authorities (SHAs), each of which is divided into various types of trusts that take responsibilty for running different NHS services locally. The different types of trusts comprise acute trusts and foundation trusts (which are responsible for the management of NHS hospitals), ambulance trusts, care trusts, mental health trusts and primary care trusts. SHAs are charged with improving and monitoring the performance of the trusts in their area.

PRIMARY CARE TRUSTS

The first 17 primary care trusts (PCTs) became operational on 1 April 2000 and there are now around 150 PCTs in England. PCTs were created to give primary care professionals greater control over how resources are best used to benefit patients. PCTs are free-standing statutory bodies responsible for securing the provision of services and integrating health and social care locally. PCTs receive most of their funding directly from the Department of Health and can use this to purchase hospital and other services from NHS trusts and other healthcare providers. They are also responsible for making payments to independent primary care contractors such as GPs and dentists.

Each PCT is overseen by a board, typically comprising a chair; at least five non-executive directors who are appointed by the Appointments Commission; at least five executive members, including the chief executive, finance director and director of public health; and at least two members of the PCT's professional executive committee (PEC), which is made up of health professionals. Clinical expertise is provided by the PEC with representation from local GPs, nurses, other health professionals and social services. The board concentrates on the overall strategies for the trust and ensures that the trust meets its statutory, financial and legal obligations.

ACUTE TRUSTS AND FOUNDATION TRUSTS

Hospitals are managed by acute trusts that are responsible for the quality of hospital health care and for spending funds efficiently. There are 167 acute NHS trusts and 58 mental health NHS trusts which oversee around 1,600 NHS hospitals and specialist care centres.

First introduced in April 2004, there are now 129 foundation trusts in England. NHS foundation trusts are NHS hospitals, but have their own accountability and governance systems, which function outside of the

Department of Health's framework, giving them greater freedom to run their own affairs. NHS foundation trusts treat patients according to NHS principles and standards and are regulated by the Care Quality Commission.

STRATEGIC HEALTH AUTHORITIES

EAST OF ENGLAND, Victoria House, Capital Park, Fulbourn, Cambridge CB21 5XB **T** 01223-597500 **W** www.eoe.nhs.uk
Chief Executive, Sir Neil McKay, CB

EAST MIDLANDS, Octavia House, Bostocks Lane, Sandiacre, Nottingham NG10 5QG **T** 0115-968 4444 **W** www.eastmidlands.nhs.uk
Chief Executive, Dame Barbara Hakin, DBE

LONDON, 4th Floor Southside, 105 Victoria Street, London SW1E 6QT **T** 020-7932 3700 **W** www.london.nhs.uk
Chief Executive, Ruth Carnall, CBE

NORTH EAST, Riverside House, Goldcrest Way, Newcastle upon Tyne NE15 8NY **T** 0191-210 6400 **W** www.northeast.nhs.uk
Chief Executive, Ian Dalton

NORTH WEST, 4th Floor, 3 Piccadilly Place, Manchester M1 3BN **T** 0845-050 0194 **W** www.northwest.nhs.uk
Chief Executive, Mike Farrar, CBE

SOUTH CENTRAL, Newbury Business Park, London Road, Newbury, Berks RG14 2PZ **T** 01635-275500 **W** www.southcentral.nhs.uk
Chief Executive, Andrea Young

SOUTH EAST, York House, 18–20 Masetts Road, Horley, Surrey RH6 7DE **T** 01293-778899 **W** www.southeastcoast.nhs.uk
Chief Executive, Candy Morris, CBE

SOUTH WEST, South West House, Blackbrook Park Avenue, Taunton, Somerset TA1 2PX **T** 01823-361000 **W** www.southwest.nhs.uk
Chief Executive, Sir Ian Carruthers, OBE

WEST MIDLANDS, St Chad's Court, 213 Hagley Road, Edgbaston, Birmingham B16 9RG **T** 0121-695 2222 **W** www.westmidlands.nhs.uk
Chief Executive, Ian Cumming, OBE

YORKSHIRE AND THE HUMBER, Blenheim House, Duncombe Street, Leeds LS1 4PL **T** 0113-295 2000 **W** www.yorksandhumber.nhs.uk
Chief Executive, Bill McCarthy

Contact details for PCTs and other NHS trusts in England can be found on the NHS Choices website (**W** www.nhs.uk).

WALES

The NHS Wales was reorganised according to Welsh Assembly commitments laid out in the *One Wales* strategy and came into effect in October 2009. There are now seven local health boards (LHBs) that are responsible for delivering all health care services within a geographical area, rather than the trust and local health board system that existed previously. Community health councils (CHCs) are statutory lay bodies that represent the public for the health service in their region. The number of CHCs is being reduced to seven, contiguous with the new LHBs. These seven CHCs are to be underpinned by 23 area associations with strong local links.

NHS TRUSTS

There are three NHS trusts in Wales. The Welsh Ambulance Services NHS Trust is for emergency services; the Velindre NHS Trust offers specialist services in cancer care and other national support services; while Public Health Wales serves as a unified public health organisation for Wales.

REGIONAL HEALTH BOARDS

The websites of the seven LHBs, and contact details for community health councils and NHS trusts, are available in the *NHS Wales Directory* on the NHS Wales website (**W** www.wales.nhs.uk).

ANEURIN BEVAN HEALTH BOARD, Mamhilad House, Block A, Mamhilad Park Estate, Pontypool, Torfaen NP4 0YP **T** 01873-732732
Chief Executive, Dr Andrew Goodall

ABERTAWE BRO MORGANNWG UNIVERSITY HEALTH BOARD, One Talbot Gateway, Baglan Energy Park, Baglan, Port Talbot SA12 7BR **T** 01639-683670
Chief Executive, David Sissling

BETSI CADWALADR UNIVERSITY HEALTH BOARD, Ysbyty Gwynedd, Penrhosgarnedd, Bangor, Gwynedd LL57 2PW **T** 01248-384384
Chief Executive, Mary Burrows

CARDIFF AND VALE UNIVERSITY HEALTH BOARD, Whitchurch Hospital, Park Road, Whitchurch, Cardiff CF14 7XB **T** 029-2074 7747
Chief Executive, Jan Williams

CWM TAF HEALTH BOARD, Ynysmeurig House, Navigation Park, Abercynon, Mid Glamorgan CF45 4SN **T** 01443-406834
Chief Executive, Margaret Foster

HYWEL DDA HEALTH BOARD, Merlin's Court, Winch Lane, Haverfordwest, Pembrokeshire SA61 1SB **T** 01437-771220
Chief Executive, Trevor Purt

POWYS TEACHING HEALTH BOARD, Mansion House, Bronllys, Brecon, Powys LD3 0LS **T** 01874-771661
Chief Executive, Rebecca Richards

SCOTLAND

The Scottish government Health Directorate is responsible both for NHS Scotland and for the development and implementation of health and community care policy. The chief executive of NHS Scotland leads the central management of the NHS, is accountable to ministers for the efficiency and performance of the service and heads the Health Department which oversees the work of the 14 regional health boards. These boards provide strategic management for the entire local NHS system and are responsible for ensuring that services are delivered effectively and efficiently.

In addition to the 14 regional health boards there are a further eight special boards which provide national services, such as the Scottish ambulance service and NHS National Services Scotland, which provides national screening programmes, blood transfusion services and monitors communicable diseases.

REGIONAL HEALTH BOARDS

AYRSHIRE AND ARRAN, Eglinton House, Ailsa Hospital, Dalmellington Road, Ayr KA6 6AB **T** 0800-169 1441 **W** www.nhsayrshireandarran.com
Chief Executive, Dr Wai-yin Hatton

BORDERS, Newstead, Melrose TD6 9DA **T** 01896-826000 **W** www.nhsborders.org.uk
Chief Executive, Calum Campbell

DUMFRIES AND GALLOWAY, Ryan North, Crichton Hall, Dumfries DG1 4TG **T** 01387-246246 **W** www.nhsdg.scot.nhs.uk
Chief Executive, John Burns

FIFE, Hayfield House, Hayfield Road, Kirkcaldy, Fife KY2 5AH T 01592-643355 W www.nhsfife.scot.nhs.uk
Chief Executive, George Brechin

FORTH VALLEY, Carseview House, Castle Business Park, Stirling FK9 4SW T 01786-463031 W www.nhsforthvalley.com
Chief Executive, Fiona Mackenzie

GRAMPIAN, Summerfield House, 2 Eday Road, Aberdeen AB15 6RE T 0845-456 6000 W www.nhsgrampian.org
Chief Executive, Richard Carey

GREATER GLASGOW AND CLYDE, Dalian House, 350 St Vincent Street, Glasgow G3 8YZ T 0141-201 4444 W www.nhsggc.org.uk
Chief Executive, Robert Calderwood

HIGHLAND, Assynt House, Beechwood Park, Inverness IV2 3BW T 01463-717123 W www.nhshighland.scot.nhs.uk
Chief Executive, Dr Roger Gibbins

LANARKSHIRE, 14 Beckford Street, Hamilton, Lanarkshire ML3 0BR T 0845-313 0130 W www.nhslanarkshire.org.uk
Chief Executive, Tim Davison

LOTHIAN, Waverley Gate, 2–4 Waterloo Place, Edinburgh EH1 3EG T 0131-536 9000 W www.nhslothian.scot.nhs.uk
Chief Executive, Prof. James Barbour, OBE

ORKNEY, Garden House, New Scapa Road, Kirkwall, Orkney KW15 1BH T 01856-888000 W www.ohb.scot.nhs.uk
Chief Executive, Cathie Cowan

SHETLAND, Brevik House, South Road, Lerwick ZE1 0TG T 01595-743063 W www.shb.scot.nhs.uk
Chief Executive, Sandra Laurenson

TAYSIDE, Kings Cross, Clepington Road, Dundee DD3 8EA T 01382-818479 W www.nhstayside.scot.nhs.uk
Chief Executive, Prof. Tony Wells

WESTERN ISLES, 37 South Beach Street, Stornoway, Isle of Lewis HS1 2BB T 01851-702997 W www.wihb.scot.nhs.uk
Chief Executive, Gordon Jamieson

NORTHERN IRELAND

On 1 April 2009 the four health and social services boards in Northern Ireland were replaced by a single health and social care board for the whole of Northern Ireland. The new board together with its local commissioning groups (whose boundaries are subject to review pending the outcome of local government reform) are responsible for improving the health and social wellbeing of people in the area for which they are responsible, planning and commissioning services, and coordinating the delivery of services in a cost-effective manner.

HEALTH AND SOCIAL CARE BOARD, 12–22 Linenhall Street, Belfast BT2 8BS T 028-9032 1313 W www.hscboard.hscni.net
Chief Executive, John Compton

NHS POLICY

In July 2000 the Labour government launched the NHS Plan, a ten-year strategy to modernise the health service. In June 2004 it also launched the NHS Improvement Plan, which set out the next stage of NHS reform, moving the focus from access to services towards the broader issues of public health and chronic disease management. The core aims were to sustain increased levels of investment in the NHS and to continue to focus on the improvements outlined in the NHS Plan, while delivering greater levels of choice and information to patients. In July 2004, the Department of Health published *National Standards, Local Action: Health and Social Care Standards and Planning Framework 2005/6–2007/8,* which cut the number of national targets from 62 to 20. The national targets, which covered areas such as waiting times for accident and emergency treatment, became national core standards which all providers of care were required to maintain from April 2005. Alongside this, NHS providers were given power to set more locally relevant targets.

In June 2010 the coalition government published a white paper, *Liberating the NHS,* which set out its intentions for NHS reforms. In the lead up to 2013 it is proposed that GPs will be given increased control over budgets, which at present are controlled by the primary care trusts. The *Revision to the Operating Framework for the NHS in England 2010/11,* also published in June 2010, announced immediate changes to performance targets and plans for further changes to targets in 2011–12. The framework and further information on planned changes is available on the Department for Health website (W www.dh.gov.uk).

FINANCE

The NHS is still funded mainly through general taxation, although in recent years more reliance has been placed on the NHS element of national insurance contributions, patient charges and other sources of income.

The budgeted departmental expenditure limit for the NHS in England was set at £99.5bn out of £101.5bn allocated to the Department of Health for 2010–11. Expenditure for the NHS in Wales, Scotland and Northern Ireland is set by the devolved governments.

PRIVATE FINANCE INITIATIVE

The Private Finance Initiative (PFI) was launched in 1992, and involves the private sector in designing, building, financing and operating new hospitals and primary care premises, which are then leased to the NHS. Partnerships for Health, a public-private venture between the Department of Health and Partnerships UK plc was established in September 2001. Its role was to support the development of NHS Local Improvement Finance Trusts (LIFTs) by implementing a standard approach to procurement as well as providing some equity. LIFTs were set up as limited companies with the local NHS Partnerships for Health and the private sector as shareholders to build and refurbish primary care premises, which the schemes own and then rent to GPs on a lease basis (as well as other parties such as chemists, opticians, dentists etc).

At the end of March 2008, 48 LIFT projects, in four waves, had been approved in England. The total capital cost of all LIFT schemes as at 31 March 2008 was £1,341.39m.

EMPLOYEES AND SALARIES

NHS HEALTH SERVICE STAFF 2009 (ENGLAND)
Full-time equivalent

All hospital, community and dental staff	431,996
Consultants	36,950
Registrars	37,108
Qualified nursing and midwifery staff	417,164
General practitioners	40,269
Qualified scientific, therapeutic and technical staff	149,596

Source: ONS – *Annual Abstract of Statistics 2010* (Crown copyright)

SALARIES

Many general practitioners (GPs) are self-employed and hold contracts, either on their own or as part of a partnership, with their local PCT. The profit of GPs varies according to the services they provide for their patients and the way they choose to provide these services. The pay range for salaried GPs employed directly by PCTs for 2010–11 is £53,781–£81,158, dependent on, among other factors, length of service and experience. Most NHS dentists are self-employed contractors. A contract for dentists was introduced on 1 April 2006 which provides dentists with an annual income in return for carrying out an agreed amount, or units, of work. A salaried dentist employed directly by a PCT earns between £37,714 and £80,674.

BASIC SALARIES FOR HOSPITAL MEDICAL AND DENTAL STAFF*
from 1 April 2010

Consultant (2003 contract)	£74,504–£100,446
Consultant (pre-2003 contract)	£61,859–£80,186
Specialist registrar	£30,992–£46,708
Speciality registrar (full)	£29,705–£46,708
Speciality registrar (fixed term)	£29,705–£39,300
Senior house officer	£27,798–£38,705
House officer	£22,412–£25,209

* These figures do not include merit awards, discretionary points or banding supplements

NURSES

From 1 December 2004 the *Agenda for Change* pay system was introduced throughout the UK for all NHS staff with the exception of medical and dental staff, doctors in public health medicine and the community health service. Nurses' salaries are incorporated in the *Agenda for Change* nine pay band structure, which provides additional payments for flexible working such as providing out-of-hours services, working weekends and nights and being 'on-call'.

SALARIES FOR NURSES AND MIDWIVES

Nurse/Midwife consultant	£38,851–£67,134
Modern matron	£38,851–£46,621
Nurse advanced/team manager	£30,460–£40,157
Midwife higher level	£30,460–£40,157
Nurse specialist/team leader	£25,472–£34,189
Hospital/community midwife	£25,472–£34,189
Registered nurse/entry level midwife	£21,176–£27,534

HEALTH SERVICES

PRIMARY CARE

Primary care comprises the services provided by general practitioners, community health centres, pharmacies, dental surgeries and opticians. Primary nursing care includes the work carried out by practice nurses, community nurses, community midwives and health visitors.

PRIMARY MEDICAL SERVICES

In England, primary medical services are the responsibility of PCTs, which contract with health care providers – GPs, dentists, pharmacists etc – to provide the service to the NHS.

In Wales, responsibility for primary medical services rests with local health boards (LHBs), in Scotland with the 14 regional health boards and in Northern Ireland with the health and social care board.

Any vocationally trained doctor may provide general or personal medical services. GPs may also have private fee-paying patients, but not if that patient is already an NHS patient on that doctor's patient list.

A person who is ordinarily resident in the UK is eligible to register with a GP (or PMS provider) for free primary care treatment. Should a patient have difficulty in registering with a doctor, he or she should contact the local PCT for help. When a person is away from home he/she can still access primary care treatment from a GP if they ask to be treated as a temporary resident. In an emergency any doctor in the service will give treatment and advice.

GPs or PCTs are responsible for the care of their patients 24 hours a day, seven days a week, but can fulfil the terms of their contract by delegating or transferring responsibility for out-of-hours care to an accredited provider.

Increasingly, some secondary care services, such as minor operations and consultations, can be provided in a primary care setting. The number of such practitioners is growing.

In addition there are around 93 NHS walk-in centres throughout England. Usually open seven days a week, from early in the morning until late in the evening, they are nurse-led and provide treatment for minor ailments and injuries, health information and self-help advice.

HEALTH COSTS

Some people are exempt from, or entitled to help with, health costs such as prescription charges, ophthalmic and dental costs, and in some cases help towards travel costs to and from hospital.

The following list is intended as a general guide to those who may be entitled to help, or who are exempt from some of the charges relating to the above:

- children under 16 and young people in full-time education who are under 19
- people aged 60 or over
- pregnant women and women who have had a baby in the last 12 months
- people, or their partners, who are in receipt of income support, income-based jobseeker's allowance and/or income-based employment and support allowance
- people in receipt of the pension credit guarantee credit
- diagnosed glaucoma patients, people who have been advised by an ophthalmologist that they are at risk of glaucoma and people aged 40 or over who have an immediate family member who is a diagnosed glaucoma patient
- NHS in-patients
- NHS out-patients for all prescribed contraceptives, medication given at a hospital, NHS walk-in centre, personally administered by a GP or supplied at a hospital or primary care trust clinic for the treatment of tuberculosis or a sexually transmissable infection
- patients of the Community Dental Service or an out-patient of the NHS Hospital Dental Service
- people registered blind or partially sighted
- people who need complex lenses
- war pensioners whose treatment/prescription is for their accepted disablement and who have a valid exemption certificate
- people who are entitled to, or named on, a valid NHS tax credit exemption or HC2 certificate

people who have a medical exemption (MedEx) certificate, including those with cancer or diabetes

eople in other circumstances may also be eligible for elp; *see* booklet HC12 (England) and HCS2 (Scotland) or further information.

VALES

Dn 1 April 2007 all prescription charges (including those or medical supports and appliances and wigs) for people ving in Wales were abolished. The above guide still pplies for NHS dental and optical charges although all eople aged under 25 living in Wales are also entitled to ree dental examinations.

HARMACEUTICAL SERVICES

atients may obtain medicines and appliances under the NHS from any pharmacy whose owner has entered into rrangements with the PCT to provide this service. There re also some suppliers who only provide special ppliances. In rural areas, where access to a pharmacy may e difficult, patients may be able to obtain medicines, etc, rom a dispensing doctor.

In England, a charge of £7.20 is payable for each item upplied (except for contraceptives for which there is no harge), unless the patient is exempt and the declaration n the back of the prescription form is completed. repayment certificates (£28.25 valid for three months, £104.00 valid for a year) may be purchased by those atients not entitled to exemption who require frequent rescriptions.

Since 1 April 2008 prescription charges in Scotland ave been different from England; a charge of £3 is ayable for each item supplied and prepayment ertificates are available for four months (£10) and 12 nonths (£28). It is planned that prescription charges will e abolished in Scotland from April 2011.

In Northern Ireland prescription charges were bolished on 1 April 2010.

In Wales NHS prescription charges were abolished on 1 April 2007.

DENTAL SERVICES

Dentists, like doctors, may take part in the NHS and also have private patients. Dentists are responsible to the local health provider in whose areas they provide services. Patients may go to any dentist who is taking part in the NHS and is willing to accept them. On 1 April 2006 the charging system for NHS dentistry in England and Wales was changed. There is now a three-tier payment system based on the individual course of treatment required.

COURSE OF TREATMENT COSTS 2010–11

	England/Wales
Examination, diagnosis, preventive care (A)* (eg x-rays, scale and polish)	£16.50/£12.00
A+ basic additional treatment (eg fillings and extractions)	£45.60/£39.00
A+ all other treatment (eg more complex procedures such as crowns, dentures etc)	£198.00/£177.00

* Urgent and out-of-hours treatment is also charged at this payment tier

The cost of individual treatment plans should be known prior to treatment and some dental practices may require payment in advance. There is no charge for writing a prescription or removing stitches and only one charge is payable for each course of treatment even if more than one visit to the dentist is required. If additional treatment is required within two months of visiting the dentist and this is covered by the course of treatment most recently paid for (eg payment was made for the second tier of treatment but an additional filling is required) then this will be provided free of charge.

SCOTLAND AND NORTHERN IRELAND

Scotland and Northern Ireland have yet to simplify their charging systems. NHS dental patients pay 80 per cent of the cost of the individual items of treatment provided up to a maximum of £384. Patients in Scotland are entitled to free basic and extensive examinations.

GENERAL OPHTHALMIC SERVICES

General ophthalmic services are administered by local health providers. Testing of sight may be carried out by any ophthalmic medical practitioner or ophthalmic optician (optometrist). The optician must give the prescription to the patient, who can take this to any supplier of glasses to have them dispensed. Only registered opticians can supply glasses to children and to people registered as blind or partially sighted.

Free eyesight tests and help towards the cost are available to people in certain circumstances. Help is also available for the purchase of glasses or contact lenses (*see* Health Costs section). In Scotland eye examinations, which include a sight test, are free to all. Help is also available for the purchase of glasses or contact lenses to those entitled to help with health costs in the same way it is available to those in England and Wales.

CHILD HEALTH SERVICES

Pre-school services at GP surgeries or child health clinics provide regular monitoring of children's physical, mental and emotional health and development and advise parents on their children's health and welfare.

NHS DIRECT AND NHS 24

NHS Direct is a 24-hour nurse-led advice telephone service for England and Wales. It provides medical advice as well as directing people to the appropriate part of the NHS for treatment if necessary (T 0845-4647).

NHS 24 provides an equivalent service for Scotland (T 0845-424 2424).

SECONDARY CARE AND OTHER SERVICES

HOSPITALS

NHS hospitals provide acute and specialist care services, treating conditions which normally cannot be dealt with by primary care specialists, and provide for medical emergencies.

NUMBER OF BEDS 2009–10*

	Average daily	
	available beds	*occupation of beds*
England	158,319	134,835
Wales	13,116	10,821
Scotland	26,300	20,900
Northern Ireland	7,706	6,342

* Figures for Scotland are for 2007–8; figures for Wales and Northern Ireland are for 2008–9

Sources: Department of Health; ONS; Welsh Assembly Government

HOSPITAL CHARGES

Acute or foundation trusts can provide hospital accommodation in single rooms or small wards, if not required for patients who need privacy for medical reasons. The patient is still an NHS patient, but there may be a charge for these additional facilities. Acute or foundation trusts can charge for certain patient services that are considered to be additional treatments over and above the normal hospital service provision. There is no blanket policy to cover this and each case is considered in the light of the patient's clinical need. However, if an item or service is considered to be an integral part of a patient's treatment by their clinician, then a charge should not be made.

In some NHS hospitals, accommodation and services are available for the treatment of private patients where it does not interfere with care for NHS patients. Income generated by treating private patients is then put back into local NHS services. Private patients undertake to pay the full costs of medical treatment, accommodation, medication and other related services. Charges for private patients are set locally.

WAITING LISTS

England

In July 2004 a target of an 18-week maximum wait, from start time (ie seeing a GP) to treatment, was introduced. For April 2010, 289,000 admitted patients and 841,000 non-admitted patients completed their referral to treatment. Of the admitted patients, 92.1 per cent were treated within 18 weeks, and for non-admitted patients 97.9 per cent were treated within 18 weeks. The *Revision to the Operating Framework for the NHS in England 2010/11,* published in June 2010, abolished the performance management of the 18-week waiting time target although referral to treatment data will continue to be published.

Wales

In Wales the main target is for referral to treatment to take no longer than 26 weeks. In May 2010, 64,350 patients were treated, of which 92 per cent had waited less than 26 weeks. There are also operational standards for maximum waiting times for first outpatient appointments and inpatient or day case treatment but these are not set targets. The standards are 14 weeks for inpatient or day case treatment, and ten weeks for a first outpatient appointment.

Scotland

In Scotland the national standard is for patients to be seen at an out-patient appointment within 12 weeks of referral by their GP or dentist. Before 31 March 2010, the national target was 15 weeks. During the quarter ending on 31 March 2010, 228,724 patients were seen, of which 3,084 had waited over 12 weeks and 305 over 15 weeks. During the quarter ending on 31 March 2009, of the 235,670 patients who were seen, 3,788 waited over 15 weeks.

Northern Ireland

From April 2009 the target is that no patient should wait more than nine weeks for a first out-patient appointment or 13 weeks for in-patient or day-case treatment. The total number of people waiting for a first out-patient appointment during the quarter ending 31 March 2010 was 86,501, of these, 8,581 had been waiting over nine weeks. The number of people waiting for in-patient treatment during the quarter ending 31 March 2010 was 36,052 – of these, 3,289 had been waiting for more than 13 weeks.

AMBULANCE SERVICE

The NHS provides emergency ambulance services free of charge via the 999 emergency telephone service. Air ambulances, provided through local charities and partially funded by the NHS, are used throughout the UK. They assist with cases where access may be difficult or heavy traffic could hinder road progress. Non-emergency ambulance services are provided free of charge to patients who are deemed to require them on medical grounds.

Since 1 April 2001 all services have had a system of call prioritisation. The prioritisation procedures require all emergency calls to be classified as either immediately life threatening (category A) or other emergency (category B). Services are expected to reach 75 per cent of Category A (life threatening) calls within eight minutes and 95 per cent of category B calls within 19 minutes.

AMBULANCE STAFF 2009

	Total staff	*Number of paramedics*
England	32,284	10,089
Wales	1,413*	847*
Scotland	3,836	1,323
Northern Ireland	1,033	635†

* 2008 figures

† Includes emergency medical technicians

Source: ONS – *Annual Abstract of Statistics 2009* (Crown copyright)

BLOOD AND TRANSPLANT SERVICES

There are four national bodies which coordinate the blood donor programme and transplant and related services in the UK. Donors give blood at local centres on a voluntary basis.

NHS BLOOD AND TRANSPLANT, Oak House, Reeds Crescent, Watford, Herts WD24 4QN **T** 01923-486800 **W** www.nhsbt.nhs.uk

WELSH BLOOD SERVICE, Ely Valley Road, Talbot Green, Pontyclun CF72 9WB **T** 01443-622000 **W** www.welsh-blood.org.uk

SCOTTISH NATIONAL BLOOD TRANSFUSION SERVICE, 21 Ellen's Glen Road, Edinburgh EH17 7QT **T** 0131-536 5700 **W** www.scotblood.co.uk

NORTHERN IRELAND BLOOD TRANSFUSION SERVICE, Lisburn Road, Belfast BT9 7TS **T** 028-9032 1414 **W** www.nibts.org

HOSPICES

Hospice or palliative care may be available for patients with life-threatening illnesses. It may be provided at the patient's home or in a voluntary or NHS hospice or in hospital, and is intended to ensure the best possible quality of life for the patient during their illness, and to provide help and support to both the patient and the patient's family. The National Council for Palliative Care coordinates NHS and voluntary services in England, Wales and Northern Ireland; the Scottish Partnership for Palliative Care performs the same function in Scotland.

NATIONAL COUNCIL FOR PALLIATIVE CARE, The Fitzpatrick Building, 188–194 York Way, London N7 9AS **T** 020-7697 1520 **W** www.ncpc.org.uk

SCOTTISH PARTNERSHIP FOR PALLIATIVE CARE, 1A Cambridge Street, Edinburgh EH1 2DY T 0131-229 0538 W www.palliativecarescotland.org.uk

COMPLAINTS

Firstly, an attempt must be made to resolve the complaint at a local level directly with the health care provider concerned. Patient advice and liaison services (PALS) have been established for every NHS and PCT in England. PALS are not part of the complaints procedure itself, but can give advice on local complaints procedure, or resolve concerns informally. For more information, *see* W www.pals.nhs.uk. If the case is not resolved locally or the complainant is not satisfied with the way a local NHS body or practice has dealt with their complaint, they may approach the Health Service Ombudsman in England, the Scottish Public Services Ombudsman, Public Services Ombudsman for Wales or the Commissioner for Complaints in Northern Ireland.

RECIPROCAL ARRANGEMENTS

The European Health Insurance Card (EHIC) allows UK residents access to state-provided health care that may become necessary while temporarily travelling in all European Economic Area countries and Switzerland either free of charge or at a reduced cost. A card is free, valid for up to five years and should be obtained before travelling. Applications can be made by telephone (T 0845-606 2030), online (W www.ehic.org.uk) or by post (a form is available from the post office).

The UK also has bilateral agreements with several other countries, including Australia and New Zealand, for the free provision of urgent medical treatment.

European Economic Area nationals visiting the UK and visitors from other countries with which the UK has bilateral health care agreements are entitled to receive emergency health care on the NHS on the same terms as it is available to UK residents.

SOCIAL WELFARE

SOCIAL SERVICES

The Secretary of State for Health (in England), the Welsh Assembly Government, the Scottish government and the Secretary of State for Northern Ireland are responsible, under the Local Authority Social Services Act 1970, for the provision of social services for older people, disabled people, families and children, and those with mental disorders. Personal social services are administered by local authorities according to policies, with standards set by central and devolved government. Each authority has a director and a committee responsible for the social services functions placed upon them. Local authorities provide, enable and commission care after assessing the needs of their population. The private and voluntary sectors also play an important role in the delivery of social services, and an estimated 6 million people in the UK provide substantial regular care for a member of their family.

The Care Quality Commission (CQC) was established in April 2009, bringing together the independent regulation of health, mental health and adult social care. Prior to 1 April 2009 this work was carried out by three separate organisations: the Healthcare Commission, the Mental Health Act Commission and the Commission for Social Care Inspection. The CQC is responsible for the registration of health and social care providers, the monitoring and inspection of all health and adult social care, issuing fines, public warnings or closures if standards are not met and for undertaking regular performance reviews. Since April 2007 the Office for Standards in Education, Children's Services and Skills (Ofsted) has been responsible for inspecting and regulating all care services for children and young people in England. Both Ofsted and CQC collate information on local care services and make this information available to the public.

The Care and Social Services Inspectorate Wales (CSSIW), an operationally independent part of the Welsh Assembly Government, is reponsible for the regulation and inspection of all social care services in Wales and the Scottish Commission for the Regulation of Care (the Care Commission), established in April 2002 under the Regulation of Care (Scotland) Act 2001, is the independent care services regulator for Scotland.

The Department of Health, Social Services and Public Safety is responsible for social care services in Northern Ireland.

CARE QUALITY COMMISSION (CQC), Citygate, Gallowgate, Newcastle upon Tyne NE1 4PA
T 0300-061 6161 **E** enquiries@cqc.org.uk
W www.cqc.org.uk

OFFICE FOR STANDARDS IN EDUCATION, CHILDREN'S SERVICES AND SKILLS (Ofsted), Royal Exchange Buildings, St Ann's Square, Manchester M2 7LA **T** 0300-123 1231 **E** enquiries@ofsted.gov.uk
W www.ofsted.gov.uk

CARE AND SOCIAL SERVICES INSPECTORATE WALES (CSSIW), Cathays Park, Cardiff CF10 3NQ
T 01443-848450 **E** cssiw@wales.gsi.gov.uk
W www.cssiw.org.uk

SCOTTISH COMMISSION FOR THE REGULATION OF CARE, Compass House, 11 Riverside Drive, Dundee DD1 4NY **T** 01382-207100
E enquiries@carecommission.com
W www.carecommission.com

DEPARTMENT OF HEALTH, SOCIAL SERVICES AND PUBLIC SAFETY, Castle Buildings, Stormont, Belfast BT4 3SJ **T** 028-9052 0500 **E** webmaster@dhsspsni.gov.uk
W www.dhsspsni.gov.uk

STAFF

Total Social Services Staff (England, full-time)	200,100
Area office/field work	111,700
Residential care staff	41,100
Day care staff	24,400
Central and strategic staff	21,100
Other staff	1,800

Source: Department of Health

OLDER PEOPLE

Services for older people are designed to enable them to remain living in their own homes for as long as possible. Local authority services include advice, domestic help, meals in the home, alterations to the home to aid mobility, emergency alarm systems, day and/or night attendants, laundry services and the provision of day centres and recreational facilities. Charges may be made for these services. Respite care may also be provided in order to allow carers temporary relief from their responsibilities.

Local authorities and the private sector also provide 'sheltered housing' for older people, sometimes with resident wardens.

If an older person is admitted to a residential home, charges are made according to a means test; if the person cannot afford to pay, the costs are met by the local authority.

DISABLED PEOPLE

Services for disabled people are designed to enable them to remain living in their own homes wherever possible. Local authority services include advice, adaptations to the home, meals in the home, help with personal care, occupational therapy, educational facilities and recreational facilities. Respite care may also be provided in order to allow carers temporary relief from their responsibilities.

Special housing may be available for disabled people who can live independently, and residential accommodation for those who cannot.

FAMILIES AND CHILDREN

Local authorities are required to provide services aimed at safeguarding the welfare of children in need and, wherever possible, allowing them to be brought up by their families. Services include advice, counselling, help in the home and the provision of family centres. Many authorities also provide short-term refuge accommodation for women and children.

DAY CARE

In allocating day care places to children, local authorities give priority to children with special needs, whether in terms of their health, learning abilities or social needs. Since September 2001 Ofsted has been responsible for the regulation and registration of all early years childcare and education provision in England (previously the responsibility of the local authorities). All day care and childminding services that care for children under eight years of age for more than two hours a day must register with Ofsted and are inspected at least every two years. As at 31 March 2010 there were 93,870 registered childcare providers in England.

CHILD PROTECTION

Children considered to be at risk of physical injury, neglect or sexual abuse are placed on the local authority's child protection register. Local authority social services staff, schools, health visitors and other agencies work together to prevent and detect cases of abuse. In England as at 31 March 2009 there were 34,100 children on child protection registers, of these, 15,800 were at risk of neglect, 4,400 of physical abuse, 2,000 of sexual abuse and 9,100 of emotional abuse. At 31 March 2009 there were 2,510 children on child protection registers in Wales, 2,682 in Scotland and 2,488 in Northern Ireland.

LOCAL AUTHORITY CARE

Local authorities are required to provide accommodation for children who have no parents or guardians or whose parents or guardians are unable or unwilling to care for them. A family proceedings court may also issue a care order where a child is being neglected or abused, or is not attending school; the court must be satisfied that this would positively contribute to the well-being of the child.

The welfare of children in local authority care must be properly safeguarded. Children may be placed with foster families, who receive payments to cover the expenses of caring for the child or children, or in residential care.

Children's homes may be run by the local authority or by the private or voluntary sectors; all homes are subject to inspection procedures. As at 31 March 2009, 60,900 children in the UK were in the care of local authorities, of these, 44,200 were in foster placements and 6,200 were in children's homes, hostels or secure units.

ADOPTION

Local authorities are required to provide an adoption service, either directly or via approved voluntary societies. In 2008–9, 2,500 children aged under 18 were entered in the adopted children register in the UK.

PEOPLE WITH LEARNING DISABILITIES

Services for people with learning disabilities are designed to enable them to remain living in the community wherever possible. Local authority services include short-term care, support in the home, the provision of day care centres, and help with other activities outside the home. Residential care is provided for the severely or profoundly disabled.

MENTALLY ILL PEOPLE

Under the care programme approach, mentally ill people should be assessed by specialist services and receive a care plan, and a key worker should be appointed for each patient. Regular reviews of the person's progress should be conducted. Local authorities provide help and advice to mentally ill people and their families, and places in day centres and social centres. Social workers can apply for a mentally disturbed person to be compulsorily detained in hospital. Where appropriate, mentally ill people are provided with accommodation in special hospitals, local authority accommodation, or at homes run by private or voluntary organisations. Patients who have been discharged from hospitals may be placed on a supervision register.

NATIONAL INSURANCE

The National Insurance (NI) scheme operates under the Social Security Contributions and Benefits Act 1992 and the Social Security Administration Act 1992, and orders and regulations made thereunder. The scheme is financed by contributions payable by earners, employers and others (*see* below). Money collected under the scheme is used to finance the National Insurance Fund (from which contributory benefits are paid) and to contribute to the cost of the National Health Service.

NATIONAL INSURANCE FUND

Estimated receipts, payments and statement of balances of the National Insurance Fund for 2010–11:

Receipts	*£ million*
Net national insurance contributions	78,015
Compensation from the Consolidated Fund for statutory sick, maternity, paternity and adoption pay recoveries	2,013
Income from investments	2,341
State scheme premiums	66
Other receipts	52
TOTAL RECEIPTS	82,486

Payments	*£ million*
Benefits	
At present rates	76,820
Increase due to proposed rate changes	1,423
Personal and stakeholder pensions contracted-out rebates	2,228
Age-related rebates for contracted-out money purchase schemes	204
Administration costs	1,414
Redundancy fund payments	418
Transfer to Northern Ireland	400
Other payments	100
TOTAL PAYMENTS	83,006

Balances	*£ million*
Opening balance	50,707
Excess of receipts over payments	(520)
BALANCE AT END OF YEAR	50,187

CONTRIBUTIONS

There are six classes of National Insurance contributions (NICs):

Class 1	paid by employees and their employers
Class 1A	paid by employers who provide employees with certain benefits in kind for private use, such as company cars
Class 1B	paid by employers who enter into a pay as you earn (PAYE) settlement agreement with HM Revenue and Customs
Class 2	paid by self-employed people
Class 3	voluntary contributions paid to protect entitlement to the state pension for those who do not pay enough NI contributions in another class
Class 4	paid by the self-employed on their taxable profits over a set limit. These are normally paid by self-employed people in addition to class 2 contributions. Class 4 contributions do not count towards benefits.

The lower and upper earnings limits and the percentage rates referred to below apply from April 2010 to April 2011.

CLASS 1

Class 1 contributions are paid where a person:

- is an employed earner (employee), office holder (eg company director) or employed under a contract of service in Great Britain or Northern Ireland
- is 16 or over and under state pension age
- earns at or above the earnings threshold of £110 per week (including overtime pay, bonus, commission, etc, without deduction of superannuation contributions)

Class 1 contributions are made up of primary and secondary contributions. Primary contributions are those paid by the employee and these are deducted from earnings by the employer. Since 6 April 2001 the employee's and employer's earnings thresholds have been the same and are referred to as the earnings threshold. Primary contributions are not paid on earnings below the earnings threshold of £110.00 per week. However, between the lower earnings limit of £97.00 per week and the earnings threshold of £110.00 per week, NI contributions are treated as having been paid to protect the benefit entitlement position of lower earners. Contributions are payable at the rate of 11 per cent on earnings between the earnings threshold and the upper earnings limit of £844.00 per week (9.4 per cent for contracted-out employment). Above the upper earnings limit 1 per cent is payable.

Some married women or widows pay a reduced rate of 4.85 per cent on earnings between the earnings threshold and upper earnings limits and 1 per cent above this. It is no longer possible to elect to pay the reduced rate but those who had reduced liability before 12 May 1977 may retain it for as long as certain conditions are met.

Secondary contributions are paid by employers of employed earners at the rate of 12.8 per cent on all earnings above the earnings threshold of £110.00 per week. There is no upper earnings limit for employers' contributions. Employers operating contracted-out salary related schemes pay reduced contributions of 9.1 per cent; those with contracted-out money-purchase schemes pay 11.4 per cent. The contracted-out rate applies only to that portion of earnings between the earnings threshold and the upper earnings limit. Employers' contributions below and above those respective limits are assessed at the appropriate not contracted-out rate.

CLASS 2

Class 2 contributions are paid where a person is self-employed and is 16 or over and under state pension age. Contributions are paid at a flat rate of £2.40 per week regardless of the amount earned. However, those with earnings of less than £5,075 a year can apply for small earnings exception. Those granted exemption from class 2 contributions may pay class 2 or class 3 contributions voluntarily. Self-employed earners (whether or not they pay class 2 contributions) may also be liable to pay class 4 contributions based on profits. There are special rules for those who are concurrently employed and self-employed.

Married women and widows can no longer choose not to pay class 2 contributions but those who elected not to pay class 2 contributions before 12 May 1977 may retain the right for as long as certain conditions are met.

Class 2 contributions are collected by the national insurance contributions department of HM Revenue and Customs (HMRC), by direct debit or quarterly bills.

CLASS 3
Class 3 contributions are voluntary flat-rate contributions of £12.05 per week payable by persons over the age of 16 who would otherwise be unable to qualify for retirement pension and certain other benefits because they have an insufficient record of class 1 or class 2 contributions. This may include those who are not working, those not liable for class 1 or class 2 contributions, or those excepted from class 2 contributions. Married women and widows who on or before 11 May 1977 elected not to pay class 1 (full rate) or class 2 contributions cannot pay class 3 contributions while they retain this right. Class 3 contributions are collected by HMRC by quarterly bills or direct debit.

CLASS 4
Self-employed people whose profits and gains are over £5,715 a year pay class 4 contributions in addition to class 2 contributions. This applies to self-employed earners over 16 and under the state pension age. Class 4 contributions are calculated at 8 per cent of annual profits or gains between £5,715 and £43,875 and 1 per cent above. Class 4 contributions are assessed and collected by HMRC. It is possible, in some circumstances, to apply for exceptions from liability to pay class 4 contributions or to have the amount of contribution reduced.

PENSIONS

Many people will qualify for a state pension; however, there are further pension choices available, such as personal and stakeholder pensions. There are also other non-pension savings and investment options. The following section provides background information on existing pension schemes.

STATE PENSION SCHEME

The state pension scheme consists of:

- basic state pension
- additional state pension

People may be able to get both or either when they reach state pension age and meet the qualifying conditions.

The state pension does not have to be claimed at state pension age, people can delay claiming it to earn extra weekly state pension or a lump sum payment.

Basic State Pension

The amount of basic state pension paid is dependent on the number of 'qualifying years' a person has established during their working life. In 2010–11, the full basic state pension is £97.65 a week *(see also* Benefits, State Pension: Categories A and B).

Working Life

Generally a working life is counted from the start of the tax year (6 April) in which a person reaches 16 to the end of the tax year (5 April) before the one in which they reach state pension age (*see* State Pension Age).

Qualifying Years

A 'qualifying year' is a tax year in which a person has enough earnings on which they have paid, are treated as having paid, or have been credited with national insurance (NI) contributions (*see* National Insurance Credits section). For people reaching state pension age before 6 April 2010, a person needs to have one qualifying year from NI contributions paid or from NI contributions treated as being paid to be eligible for any basic state pension. From 6 April 2010 a person will also be entitled to a basic state pension based on just one qualifying year of national insurance credits.

For people reaching state pension age before 6 April 2010, to get the full rate (100 per cent) basic state pension, a person must normally have qualifying years for about 90 per cent of their working life. To get the minimum basic state pension (25 per cent) a person normally needs ten or 11 qualifying years. The number of qualifying years can be reduced if a person qualifies for home responsibilities protection (*see* below). From 6 April 2010 a person reaching state pension age will be entitled to a full basic state pension if they have 30 qualifying years.

National Insurance Credits

Those in receipt of carer's allowance, working tax credit (with a disability element), jobseeker's allowance, incapacity benefit, employment support allowance, unemployability supplement, statutory sick pay, statutory maternity pay or statutory adoption pay may have class 1 NI contributions credited to them each week. People may also get credits if they are unemployed and looking for work or too sick to work, even if they have not paid enough contributions to receive benefit. Persons undertaking certain training courses or jury service or who have been wrongly imprisoned for a conviction which is quashed on appeal may also get class 1 NI credits for each week they fulfil certain conditions. Class 1 credits may also be available to men approaching state pension age. Until 5 April 2010, these credits were awarded for the tax years in which they reached age 60 and continued until age 64, if they were not liable to pay contributions and were not absent from the UK for more than six months in any tax year. Since 6 April 2010 these credits are being phased out in line with the increase in women's state pension age and men born after 1954 will no longer receive them. Class 1 NI credits count toward all future contributory benefits. A class 3 NI credit for basic state pension and bereavement benefit purposes is awarded, where required, for each week the working tax credit (without a disability element) has been received. Class 3 credits are also awarded automatically to young people aged 16 to 18 if they have not paid enough contributions to gain a qualifying year.

State Pension Age

State pension age is:

- 65 for men
- 60 for women born on or before 5 April 1950
- 65 for women born on or after 6 April 1955

Women born between 6 April 1950 and 5 April 1955 will have a state pension age between 60 and 65 depending on their date of birth. Further information can be obtained from the online state pension calculator (W www.thepensionservice.gov.uk/state-pension/age-calculator.asp).

Using the NI Contribution Record of Another Person to Claim a State Pension

Married women who are not entitled to a state pension on their own NI contributions may get a basic state pension calculated using their husband's NI contribution record. A basic state pension may be paid of up to 60 per cent of the husband's entitlement (up to £58.50 a week in 2010–11). From 6 April 2010, married men and civil partners are able to claim a basic state pension based on their wife or civil partner's NI record if better than one based on their own record and if their wife or civil partner was born after 6 April 1950. A state pension is also payable to widows, widowers, surviving civil partners, and people who are divorced or whose civil partnership has been dissolved, based on their late or ex-spouse's/civil partner's NI contributions.

Non-contributory State Pensions

A non-contributory state pension may be payable to those aged 80 or over who live in England, Scotland or Wales, and have done so for a total of ten years or more for any continuous period in the 20 years after their 60th birthday, if they are not entitled to another category of state pension, or are entitled to one below the rate of £58.50 a week in 2010–11 (*see also* Benefits, State Pension for people aged 80 and over).

Graduated Retirement Benefit

Graduated Retirement Benefit (GRB) is based on the amount of graduated NI contributions paid into the GRB scheme between April 1961 and April 1975 (*see also* Benefits, Graduated Retirement Benefit).

Home Responsibilities Protection

From 6 April 1978 until 5 April 2010, it was possible for people who had low income or were unable to work because they cared for children or a sick or disabled erson at home to reduce the number of qualifying years quired for basic state pension. Thus was called home sponsibilities protection (HRP); the number of years for hich HRP was given was deducted from the number of ualifying years needed. HRP could, in some cases, also ualify the recipient for additional state pension. From pril 2003 to April 2010 HRP was also available to pproved foster carers.

From 6 April 2010, HRP was replaced by weekly edits for parents and carers. A class 3 national insurance edit is given, where required, towards basic pension and ereavement benefits for spouses and civil partners. An arnings factor credit towards additional state pension is so awarded. Any years of HRP accrued before 6 April 010 have been converted into qualifying years of edits for people reaching state pension age after that ate, up to a maximum of 22 years for basic state pension urposes.

dditional State Pension

he amount of additional state pension paid depends on e amount of earnings a person has, or is treated as aving, between the lower and upper earnings limits rom April 2009, the upper accruals point replaced the pper earnings limit for additional pension) for each omplete tax year between 6 April 1978 (when the heme started) and the tax year before they reach ate pension age. The right to additional state pension oes not depend on the person's right to basic state ension.

From 1978 to 2002, additional state pension was alled the State Earnings-Related Pension Scheme SERPS). SERPS covered all earnings by employees from April 1978 to 5 April 1997 on which standard rate class NI contributions had been paid, and earnings between April 1997 and 5 April 2002 if the standard rate class 1 NI contributions had been contracted-in.

In 2002, SERPS was reformed through the state econd pension, by improving the pension available to w and moderate earners and extending access to certain arers and people with long-term illness or disability. If arnings on which class 1 NI contributions have been aid or can be treated as paid are above the annual NI wer earnings limit (£5,044 for 2010–11) but below the tatutory low earnings threshold (£14,100 for 2010–11), he state second pension regards this as earnings of 14,100 and it is treated as equivalent. Certain carers and eople with long-term illness and disability will be onsidered as having earned at the low earnings threshold or each complete tax year since 2002–3 even if they do ot work at all, or earn less than the annual NI lower arnings limit.

The amount of additional state pension paid also epends on when a person reaches state pension age; hanges phased in from 6 April 1999 mean that pensions re calculated differently from that date.

nheritance

Men or women widowed before 6 October 2002 can nherit all of their late spouse's SERPS pension. From 6 October 2002, the maximum percentage of SERPS ension that a person can inherit from a late spouse or ivil partner depends on their late spouse or civil partner's ate of birth:

Maximum SERPS entitlement	*d.o.b (men)*	*d.o.b (women)*
100%	5/10/37 or earlier	5/10/42 or earlier
90%	6/10/37 to 5/10/39	6/10/42 to 5/10/44
80%	6/10/39 to 5/10/41	6/10/44 to 5/10/46
70%	6/10/41 to 5/10/43	6/10/46 to 5/10/48
60%	6/10/43 to 5/10/45	6/10/48 to 5/7/50
50%	6/10/45 or later	6/7/50 or later

The maximum state second pension a person can inherit from a late spouse or civil partner is 50 per cent.

Pension Forecasts

The Pension, Disability and Carers Service provides a state pension forecasting service. A state pension forecast provides an estimate of the current value of an individual's state pension, based on information held on their NI record, and an estimate of what it may be worth when they reach state pension age. There is also an online state pension profiler that tells the user their state pension age, an estimate of their basic state pension and how they are affected by changes to the state pension (T 0845-300 0168 W www.direct.gov.uk/pensionsandretirementplanning).

PRIVATE PENSION SCHEMES

Contracted-Out Appropriate Personal Pension Schemes (including Appropriate Stakeholder Pension Schemes)

Since July 1988 an employee has been able to start a personal pension which, if it meets certain conditions, can be used in place of the additional state pension. These pensions are known as appropriate personal pensions (APPs) and employees who use them in place of the additional state pension are said to be 'contracted-out' of the state scheme.

At the end of the tax year HM Revenue and Customs pays an age-related rebate on contracted-out employees' NI contributions together with tax relief on the employee's share of the rebate directly into the scheme to be invested on behalf of the employee. These payments are known as 'minimum contributions'.

Age-related rebates are intended to provide benefits broadly equivalent to those given up in the additional state pension. At retirement, a contracted-out deduction will be made from additional state pension accrued from 6 April 1987 to 5 April 1997.

The rules for contracting out of the additional state pension are due to change in April 2012. Contracting out through defined contribution schemes (ie money purchase, personal pension and stakeholder arrangements) is to be abolished from 6 April 2012. Anyone contracted out on a defined contribution basis at that time will automatically be contracted back into the additional state pension.

Contracted-Out Salary-Related (COSR) Scheme

- these schemes (also known as contracted-out defined benefit (DB) schemes) provide a pension related to earnings and the length of pensionable service
- any notional additional state pension built up from 6 April 1978 to 5 April 1997 will be reduced by the amount of guaranteed minimum pension (GMP) accrued during that period (the contracted-out deduction)
- since 6 April 1997 these schemes no longer provide a GMP. Instead, as a condition of contracting out they have to satisfy a reference scheme test to ensure that the benefits provided are at least as good as a prescribed standard
- when someone contracts out of the additional state pension through a COSR scheme, both the scheme member and the employer pay a reduced rate of NI

contributions (known as the contracted-out rebate) to compensate for the additional state pension given up

Contracted-Out Money Purchase (COMP) Scheme

- these schemes (also known as contracted-out defined contribution (DC) schemes) provide a pension based on the value of the fund at retirement, ie the money paid in, along with the investment return
- the part of the COMP fund derived from protected rights (rights made up mainly from the contracted-out rebate and its investment return) is intended to provide benefits broadly equivalent to those given up in the additional state pension
- a contracted-out deduction, which may be more or less than that part of the pension derived from the protected rights, will be made from any notional additional pension built up from 6 April 1988 to 5 April 1997
- as with a COSR scheme, when someone contracts out of the additional state pension through a COMP scheme, both the scheme member and the employer pay a reduced rate of NI contributions (the contracted-out rebate) to compensate for the state pension given up. In addition, at the end of each tax year, HM Revenue and Customs pays an additional age-related rebate direct to the scheme for investment on behalf of the employee

Contracted-Out Mixed Benefit (COMB) Scheme

A mixed benefit scheme is a single scheme with both a salary-related section and a money purchase section. Scheme rules set out which section individual employees may join and the circumstances (if any), in which members may move between sections. Each section must satisfy the respective contracting-out conditions for COSR and COMP schemes.

For more information on contracted-out pension schemes *see* the Department for Work and Pensions' leaflet *Contracted-out Pensions* (PM7).

STAKEHOLDER PENSION SCHEMES

Introduced in 2001, stakeholder pensions are available to everyone but are principally for moderate earners who do not have access to a good value company pension scheme. Stakeholder pensions must meet a number of minimum standards to make sure they are flexible, portable and annual management charges are capped. The minimum contribution is £20.

As with personal pensions it is possible to invest up to £3,600 (including tax relief) into stakeholder pensions each year without evidence of earnings. Contributions can be made on someone else's behalf, for example a non-working partner.

Stakeholder pensions can also be used by employees to contract out of the additional state pension. For more information *see* Contracted-Out Appropriate Personal Pension Schemes (including Appropriate Stakeholder Pension Schemes).

COMPLAINTS

The Pensions Advisory Service provides information and guidance to members of the public, on state, company, personal and stakeholder schemes. They also help any member of the public who has a problem, complaint or dispute with their occupational or personal pensions.

There are two bodies for pension complaints. The Financial Ombudsman Service deals with complaints which predominantly concern the sale and/or marketing of occupational, stakeholder and personal pensions. The Pensions Ombudsman deals with complaints which predominantly concern the management (after sale or marketing) of occupational, stakeholder and personal pensions.

The Pensions Regulator is the UK regulator for work-based pension schemes; it concentrates its resources on schemes where there is the greatest risk to the security of members' benefits, promotes good administration practice for all work-based schemes and works with trustees, employers and professional advisers to put things right when necessary.

WAR PENSIONS AND THE ARMED FORCES COMPENSATION SCHEME

The Service Personnel and Veterans Agency (SPVA) is an executive agency of the Ministry of Defence. SPVA was formed on 1 April 2007 from the former Armed Forces Personnel Administration Agency and the Veterans Agency to provide services to both serving personnel and veterans.

SPVA is responsible for the administration of the war pensions scheme and the armed forces compensation scheme (AFCS) to members of the armed forces in respect of disablement or death due to service. There is also a scheme for civilians and civil defence workers in respect of the Second World War, and other schemes for groups such as merchant seamen and Polish armed forces who served under British command during the Second World War. The agency is also responsible for the administration of the armed forces pension scheme, which provides occupational pensions for ex-service personnel (*see* Defence).

THE WAR PENSIONS SCHEME

War disablement pension is awarded for the disabling effects of any injury, wound or disease which was the result of, or was aggravated by, service in the armed forces prior to 6 April 2005. Claims are only considered once the person has left the armed forces. The amount of pension paid depends on the severity of disablement, which is assessed by comparing the health of the claimant with that of a healthy person of the same age and sex. The person's earning capacity or occupation are not taken into account in this assessment. A pension is awarded if the person has a disablement of 20 per cent or more and a lump sum is usually payable to those with a disablement of less than 20 per cent. No award is made for noise-induced sensorineural hearing loss where the assessment of disablement is less than 20 per cent.

A pension is payable to war widows, widowers and surviving civil partners where the spouse's or civil partner's death was due to, or hastened by, service in the armed forces prior to 6 April 2005 or where the spouse or civil partner was in receipt of a war disablement pension constant attendance allowance (or would have been if not in hospital) at the time of death. A pension is also payable to widows, widowers or surviving civil partners if the spouse or civil partner was receiving the war disablement pension at the 80 per cent rate or higher in conjunction with unemployability supplement at the time of death. War widows, widowers and surviving civil partners receive a standard rank-related rate, but a lower weekly rate is payable to war widows, widowers and surviving civil partners of personnel of the rank of Major or below who are under the age of 40, without children and capable of maintaining themselves. This is increased to the tandard rate at age 40. Allowances are paid for children in addition to child benefit) and adult dependants. An age illowance is automatically given when the widow, widower or surviving civil partner reaches 65 and ncreased at ages 70 and 80.

Pensioners living overseas receive the same pension rates as those living in the UK. All war disablement pensions and allowances and pensions for war widows, widowers and surviving civil partners are tax-free in the UK; this does not always apply in overseas countries due to different tax laws.

SUPPLEMENTARY ALLOWANCES

A number of supplementary allowances may be awarded to a war pensioner and are intended to meet various needs. The principal supplementary allowances are unemployability supplement, allowance for lowered standard of occupation and constant attendance allowance. Others include exceptionally severe disablement allowance, severe disablement occupational allowance, treatment allowance, mobility supplement, comforts allowance, clothing allowance, age allowance and widow/widower/surviving civil partner's age allowance. Rent and children's allowances are also available on pensions for war widows, widowers and surviving civil partners.

ARMED FORCES COMPENSATION SCHEME

The armed forces compensation scheme (AFCS) became effective on 6 April 2005 and covers all regular (including Gurkhas) and reserve personnel whose injury, ill health or death is caused by service on or after 6 April 2005. Ex-members of the armed forces who served prior to this date or who are in receipt of any pension under the war pensions scheme will continue to receive their pension and any associated benefits in the normal way.

The AFCS provides compensation where service in the armed forces is the only or main cause of injury, illness or death. Compensation can also be paid in certain exceptional circumstances to off-duty personnel; for example, to victims of a terrorist attack targeted owing to their position in the armed forces. Under the terms of the scheme a lump sum is payable to service or ex-service personnel based on a 15-level tariff, graduated according to the seriousness of the condition. A guaranteed income payment (GIP), payable for life, is received by those who could be expected to experience a serious loss of earning capability. A GIP will also be paid to surviving spouses, civil partners and unmarried partners who meet certain criteria. GIP is calculated by multiplying the pensionable pay of the service person by a factor that depends on the age at the person's last birthday. The younger the person, the higher the factor, because there are more years to normal retirement age.

DEPARTMENT FOR WORK AND PENSIONS BENEFITS

Most benefits are paid in addition to those in receipt of payments under the AFCS and the war pensions scheme, but may be affected by any supplementary allowances in payment. Any state pension for which a war widow, widower or surviving civil partner qualifies for on their own NI contribution record can be paid in addition to monies received under the war pensions scheme.

CLAIMS AND QUESTIONS

Further information on the war pensions scheme, the armed forces compensation scheme and the nearest War Pensioners' Welfare Office can be obtained from the Service Personnel and Veterans Agency by telephone (T 0800-169 2277, if calling from the UK or, if living overseas, T (+44) (125) 386-6043).

SERVICE PERSONNEL AND VETERANS AGENCY, Norcross, Blackpool FY5 3WP
E veterans.help@spva.gsi.gov.uk W www.veterans-uk.info

TAX CREDITS

Tax credits are administered by HM Revenue and Customs (HMRC). They are based on an individual's or couple's household income and current circumstances and can be adjusted during the year to reflect changes in income or circumstances. Further information regarding the qualifying conditions for tax credits, how to claim and the rates payable is available online on the HMRC website (W www.hmrc.gov.uk/taxcredits).

WORKING TAX CREDIT

Working tax credit is a payment from the government to support people on low incomes. It may be claimed by those aged 25 or over who work at least 30 hours a week; those aged 50 or over who are returning to work after a period on benefits of at least six months; and those aged 16 or over who work at least 16 hours a week and are responsible for a child or young person or have a disability that puts them at a disadvantage of getting a job.

The system makes assumptions based on the national minimum wage and the number of hours worked per week. An annual income of £9,150 represents the 2010–11 income of an adult working 30 hours a week at the national minimum wage: six months at the 2009–10 rate of £5.80 per hour and six months at the rate of £5.93 per hour (national minimum wage from October 2010).

WORKING TAX CREDIT 2010–11

Annual Income/Status	*Tax Credit per annum*
£5,000*	
Single	–
Couple	–
Single adult with a disability	£4,495
£9,150†	
Single	£1,650
Couple	£3,540
Single adult with a disability	£4,220
£10,000	
Single	£1,315
Couple	£3,210
Single adult with a disability	£3,890
£15,000	
Single	–
Couple	£1,260
Single adult with a disability	£1,940

* Those with incomes of £5,000 a year are assumed to work part-time (working between 16 and 30 hours a week)

† Income of £9,150 represents the income of an adult working 30 hours per week at the national minimum wage rate (*see* above for explanation). In families with an income of £9,150 a year or more, at least one adult is assumed to be working 30 or more hours a week

CHILDCARE

In families with children where a lone parent or both partners in a couple work at least 16 hours a week, or where one partner works and the other is disabled, the family is entitled to the childcare element of working tax credit. This payment can contribute up to 80 per cent of childcare costs up to a maximum of £175 a week for one child and up to £300 a week for two or more children. Families can only claim if they use an approved or registered childcare provider.

CHILD TAX CREDIT

Child tax credit combines all income-related support for children and is paid direct to the main carer. The credit is made up of a main 'family' payment with additional payments for each extra child in the household, for children with a disability and an extra payment for children who are severely disabled. Child tax credit is available to households where:

- there is at least one dependant under 16
- there is at least one dependant under 20 who is in relevant education or training or is registered for work, education or training with an approved body

CHILD TAX CREDIT AND WORKING TAX CREDIT 2010–11 *(£ per year)*

	One Child		Two Children	
Annual Income	*No Childcare*	*Maximum Childcare*	*No Childcare*	*Maximum Childcare*
0	2,850	2,850	5,150	5,150
5,000*	6,660	13,940	8,965	21,445
9,150*	6,390	13,670	8,695	21,175
10,000†	6,060	13,340	8,360	20,840
15,000	4,110	11,390	6,410	18,890
20,000	2,160	9,440	4,460	16,940
25,000	545	7,490	2,510	14,990
30,000	545	5,540	560	13,040
35,000	545	3,590	545	11,090
40,000	545	1,640	545	9,140
45,000	545	545	545	7,190
50,000	545	545	545	5,240
60,000	–	–	–	1340
65,000	–	–	–	350
70,000	–	–	–	–

* At income levels of £5,000 and £9,150 awards are shown for lone parents. At an income level of £5,000 the award is shown for a lone parent working part-time (between 16 and 30 hours a week). At an income level of £9,150 the award is shown for a lone parent working 30 hours a week

† At an income level of £10,000 awards are shown for two parents working part-time (between 16 and 30 hours per week)

BENEFITS

The following is intended as a general guide to the benefits system. Conditions of entitlement and benefit rates change annually and all prospective claimants should check exact entitlements and rates of benefit directly with their local Jobcentre Plus office, pension centre or online (W www.direct.gov.uk). Leaflets relating to the various benefits and contribution conditions for different benefits are available from local Jobcentre Plus offices.

CONTRIBUTORY BENEFITS

Entitlement to contributory benefits depends on national insurance contribution conditions being satisfied either by the claimant or by someone on the claimant's behalf (depending on the kind of benefit). The class or classes of national insurance contribution relevant to each benefit are:

Jobseeker's allowance (contribution-based)	Class 1
Incapacity benefit	Class 1 or 2
Employment and Support Allowance (contributory)	Class 1 or 2
Widow's benefit and bereavement benefit	Class 1, 2 or 3
State pensions, categories A and B	Class 1, 2 or 3

The system of contribution conditions relates to yearly levels of earnings on which national insurance (NI) contributions have been paid.

JOBSEEKER'S ALLOWANCE

Jobseeker's allowance (JSA) replaced unemployment benefit and income support for unemployed people under state pension age from 7 October 1996. There are two routes of entitlement. Contribution-based JSA is paid at a personal rate (ie additional benefit for dependants is not paid) to those who have made sufficient NI contributions in two particular tax years. Savings and partner's earnings are not taken into account and payment can be made for up to six months. Rates of JSA correspond to income support rates.

Claims are made through Jobcentre Plus. A person wishing to claim JSA must generally be unemployed or working on average less than 16 hours a week, capable of work and available for any work which he or she can reasonably be expected to do, usually for at least 40 hours per week. The claimant must agree and sign a 'jobseeker's agreement', which will set out his or her plans to find work, and must actively seek work. If the claimant refuses work or training the benefit may be sanctioned for between one and 26 weeks.

A person will be sanctioned from JSA for up to 26 weeks if he or she has left a job voluntarily without just cause or through misconduct. In these circumstances, it may be possible to receive hardship payments, particularly where the claimant or the claimant's family is vulnerable, eg if sick or pregnant, or with children or caring responsibilities.

Weekly Rates from April 2010	
Person aged 16–24	£51.85
Person aged 25 to state pension age*	£65.45

* Since October 2003 people aged between 60 and state pension age can choose to claim pension credits instead of JSA

INCAPACITY BENEFIT

Employment and support allowance replaced incapacity benefit for new claimants from 27 October 2008. Those claiming incapacity benefit prior to this date will continue to receive it for as long as they qualify, although it is intended that remaining recipients of incapacity benefit will be moved to employment and support allowance by 2013. There are three rates of incapacity benefit:

- short-term lower rate for the first 28 weeks of sickness
- short-term higher rate from weeks 29 to 52
- long-term rate from week 53 onwards

The terminally ill and those entitled to the highest rate care component of disability living allowance are paid the long-term rate after 28 weeks. Incapacity benefit is taxable after 28 weeks.

An age addition payment may be available where incapacity for work commenced before the age of 45. Increases are also available for adult dependants caring for children.

The 'personal capability' assessment is the main test for incapacity benefit claims. Claimants are assessed on their ability to carry out a range of work-related activities and may also be required to attend a medical examination. Incapacity benefit claimants (excluding people who are severely disabled and those who are terminally ill) are invited back for work-focused interviews at intervals of not longer than three years. The interviews do not include medical tests, but if the claimant is due for a medical test around the same time, their local office will aim to schedule both together.

Weekly Rates from April 2010	
Short-term incapacity benefit lower rate	
Person under state pension age	£68.95
Person over state pension age	£87.75
Short-term incapacity benefit higher rate	
Person under state pension age	£81.60
Person over state pension age	£91.40
Long-term incapacity benefit	
Person under state pension age	£91.40
Person over state pension age	–

EMPLOYMENT AND SUPPORT ALLOWANCE

From 27 October 2008, employment and support allowance (ESA) replaced incapacity benefit and income support paid on the grounds of incapacity or disability. The benefit consists of two strands, contribution-based benefit and income-related benefit, so that people no longer need to make two claims for benefit in order to gain their full entitlement. Contributory ESA is available to those who have limited capability for work but cannot get statutory sick pay from their employer. Those over pensionable age are not entitled to ESA. Apart from those who qualify under the special provisions for people incapacitated in youth, entitlement to contributory ESA is based on a person's NI contribution record. In order to qualify for contributory ESA, two contribution conditions, based on the last three years before the tax year in which benefit is claimed, must be satisfied. The amount of contributory ESA payable may be reduced where the person receives more than a specified amount of occupational or personal pension. Contributory ESA is paid only in respect of the person claiming the benefit – there are no additional amounts for dependants.

At the outset, new claimants are paid a basic allowance (the same rate as jobseeker's allowance) for 13 weeks while their medical condition is assessed and a work capability assessment is conducted. Following the completion of the assessment phase those claimants capable of engaging in work-related activities will receive a work-related activity component on top of the basic rate. The work-related activity component can be subject to sanctions if the claimant does not engage in the conditionality requirements without good reason. The maximum sanction is equal to the value of the work-related activity component of the benefit.

Those with the most severe health conditions or disabilities will receive the support component, which is more than the work-related activity component. Claimants in receipt of the support component are not required to engage in work-related activities, although they can volunteer to do so or undertake permitted work if their condition allows.

Weekly Rates from April 2010

ESA plus work-related activity component	up to £91.40
ESA plus support component	up to £96.85

BEREAVEMENT BENEFITS

Bereavement benefits replaced widow's benefit on 9 April 2001. Those claiming widow's benefit before this date will continue to receive it under the old scheme for as long as they qualify. The new system provides bereavement benefits for widows, widowers and, from 5 December 2005, surviving civil partners (providing that their deceased spouse or civil partner paid NI contributions). The new system offers benefits in three forms:

- *Bereavement payment* – may be received by a man or woman who is under the state pension age at the time of their spouse or civil partner's death, or whose husband, wife or civil partner was not entitled to a category A retirement pension when he or she died. It is a single tax-free lump sum of £2,000 payable immediately on widowhood or loss of a civil partner
- *Widowed parent's allowance* – a taxable benefit payable to the surviving partner if he or she is entitled or treated as entitled to child benefit, or to a widow if she is expecting her husband's baby at the time of his death
- *Bereavement allowance* – a taxable weekly benefit paid for 52 weeks after the spouse or civil partner's death. If aged over 55 and under state pension age the full allowance is payable, if aged between 45 and 54 a percentage of the full rate is paid. A widow, widower or surviving civil partner may receive this allowance if his or her widowed parent's allowance ends before 52 weeks

It is not possible to receive widowed parent's allowance and bereavement allowance at the same time. Bereavement benefits and widow's benefit, in any form, cease upon remarriage or a new civil partnership or are suspended during a period of cohabitation as partners without being legally married or in a civil partnership.

Weekly Rates from April 2010

Bereavement payment (lump sum)	£2,000
Widowed parent's allowance (or widowed mother's allowance)	£95.25
Bereavement allowance (or widow's pension), full entitlement (aged 55 and over at time of spouse's or civil partner's death)	£95.25

Amount of bereavement allowance (or widow's pension) by age of widow/widower or surviving civil partner at spouse's or civil partner's death:

aged 54	£90.81
aged 53	£83.98
aged 52	£77.14
aged 51	£70.31
aged 50	£63.47
aged 49	£56.64
aged 48	£49.80
aged 47	£42.97
aged 46	£36.13
aged 45	£29.30

STATE PENSION: CATEGORIES A AND B

Category A pension is payable for life to men and women who reach state pension age, who satisfy the contributions conditions and who claim for it. Category B pension is payable for life to married women, widows, widowers and surviving civil partners and is based on their wife, husband or civil partner's contributions. It is payable to a married woman only when both the wife and husband have both reached state pension age. From 6 April 2010 a married man and civil partner became able to qualify for a category B pension from their wife's or civil partner's contributions providing the wife or civil partner were born on or after 6 April 1950. Category B pension is also payable to widows, widowers and surviving civil partners who are bereaved before state pension age if they were previously entitled to widowed parent's allowance or bereavement allowance based on their late spouse's or civil partner's NI contributions. Widows who are bereaved when over state pension age can qualify for a category B pension regardless of the age of their husband when he died; although at present, it is only paid to widowers and civil partners bereaved over state pension age if their wife or civil partner had reached state pension age when they died. Since 6 April 2010, widowers or surviving civil partners who reach state pension age on or after 6 April 2010 have been able to get a category B pension on the same terms as widows.

Where a person is entitled to both a category A and category B pension then they can be combined to give a composite pension, but this cannot be more than the full rate pension. Where a person is entitled to more than one category A or category B pension then only one can be paid. In such cases the person can choose which to get; if no choice is made, the most favourable one is paid.

A person may defer claiming their pension beyond state pension age. In doing so they may earn increments which will increase the weekly amount paid by 1 per cent per five weeks of deferral (equivalent to 10.4 per cent/year) when they claim their state pension. If a person delays claiming for at least 12 months they are given the option of a one-off taxable lump sum, instead of a pension increase, based on the weekly pension deferred, plus interest of at least 2 per cent above the Bank of England base rate. Historically, if a married man deferred his category A pension, his wife could not claim a category B pension on his contributions but could earn increments on her state pension during this time. Since 6 April 2010, a category B pension has been treated independently of the spouse's or partner's pension. It is possible to take a category B pension even if the spouse or partner has deferred theirs.

It is no longer possible to claim an increase on a state pension for another adult (known as adult dependency increase). Those who received the increase before April 2010 can keep receiving it until the conditions are no longer met or until 5 April 2020, whichever is first.

Provision for children is made through child tax

credits. An age addition of 25p per week is payable with a state pension if a pensioner is aged 80 or over.

Since 1989 pensioners have been allowed to have unlimited earnings without affecting their state pension. *See also* Pensions.

Weekly Rates from April 2010

Category A or B pension for a single person	£97.65
Maximum category B pension (married women)	£58.50
Increase for adult dependant	£58.50
Age addition at age 80	£0.25

GRADUATED RETIREMENT BENEFIT

Graduated retirement benefit (GRB) is based on the amount of graduated NI contributions paid into the GRB scheme between April 1961 and April 1975; however, it is still paid in addition to any state pension to those who made the relevant contributions. A person will receive graduated retirement benefit based on their own contributions, even if not entitled to a basic state pension. Widows, widowers and surviving civil partners may inherit half of their deceased spouse's or civil partner's entitlement, but none that the deceased spouse or civil partner may have been eligible for from a former spouse or civil partner. If a person defers making a claim beyond state pension age, they may earn an increase or a one-off lump sum payment in respect of their deferred graduated retirement benefit; calculated in the same way as for category A or B state pension.

NON-CONTRIBUTORY BENEFITS

These benefits are paid from general taxation and are not dependent on NI contributions.

JOBSEEKER'S ALLOWANCE (INCOME-BASED)

Those who do not qualify for contribution-based jobseeker's allowance (JSA), those who have exhausted their entitlement to contribution-based JSA or those for whom contribution-based JSA provides insufficient income may qualify for income-based JSA. The amount paid depends on age, whether they are single or a couple, number of dependants and amount of income and savings. Income-based JSA comprises three parts:

- a personal allowance for the jobseeker and his/her partner*
- premiums for people with special needs
- amounts for housing costs

* Since April 2003, child dependants have been provided for through the child tax credit system

The rules of entitlement are the same as for contribution-based JSA.

If one person in a couple was born after 28 October 1957 and neither person in the couple has responsibility for a child or children, then the couple will have to make a joint claim for JSA if they wish to receive income-based JSA.

Weekly Rates from April 2010

Person aged 16–24	£51.85
Person aged 25 to state pension age	£65.45
Couple with one or both under 18*	£51.85–£78.30
Couple aged 18 to state pension age	£102.75
Lone parents aged under 18	£51.85
Lone parents aged 18 to state pension age	£65.45

* depending on circumstances

MATERNITY ALLOWANCE

Maternity allowance (MA) is a benefit available for pregnant women who cannot get statutory maternity pay (SMP) from their employer or have been employed/self-employed during or close to their pregnancy. In order to qualify for payment, a woman must have been employed and/or self-employed for at least 26 weeks in the 66-week period up to and including the week before the baby is due (test period). These weeks do not have to be in a row and any part weeks worked will count towards the 26 weeks. She must also have an average weekly earning of at least £30 (maternity allowance threshold) over any 13 weeks of the woman's choice within the test period.

Self-employed women who pay class 2 NI contributions or who hold a small earnings exception certificate are deemed to have enough earnings to qualify for MA.

A woman can choose to start receiving MA from the 11th week before the week in which the baby is due (if she stops work before then) up to the day following the day of birth. The exact date MA starts will depend on when the woman stops work to have her baby or if the baby is born before she stops work. However, where the woman is absent from work wholly or partly due to her pregnancy in the four weeks before the week the baby is due to be born, MA will start the day following the first day of absence from work. MA is paid for a maximum of 39 weeks.

The woman may be entitled to get extra payments for her husband, civil partner or someone else who looks after her children.

Weekly Rate from April 2010

Standard rate	£124.88 or 90 per cent of the woman's average weekly earnings if less than £124.88

CHILD BENEFIT

Child benefit is payable for virtually all children aged under 16 and for those aged 16 and 17 if they are in relevant education or training or are registered for work, education or training with an approved body.

Weekly Rates from April 2010

Eldest/only child	£20.30
Each subsequent child	£13.40

GUARDIAN'S ALLOWANCE

Guardian's allowance is payable to a person who is bringing up a child or young person because the child's parents have died, or in some circumstances, where only one parent has died. To receive the allowance the person must be in receipt of child benefit for the child or young person, although they do not have to be the child's legal guardian.

Weekly Rate from April 2010

Each child	£14.30

HEALTH IN PREGNANCY GRANT

A one-off payment of £190 for each pregnancy to all women who meet the residency requirements, irrespective of income, from the 25th week of pregnancy. The grant has to be claimed from HM Revenue and Customs following authorisation by a doctor or midwife. The coalition government announced in July 2010 that this grant would be abolished from April 2011.

CARER'S ALLOWANCE

Carer's allowance (CA) is a benefit payable to people who spend at least 35 hours per week caring for a severely disabled person. To qualify for CA a person must be caring for someone in receipt of one of the following benefits:

- attendance allowance
- disability living allowance care component at the middle or highest rate
- constant attendance allowance, paid at not less than the normal maximum rate or basic (full-day) rate, under the industrial injuries or war pension schemes.

Weekly Rate from April 2010

Carer's allowance	£53.90

SEVERE DISABLEMENT ALLOWANCE

Since April 2001 severe disablement allowance (SDA) has not been available to new claimants. Those claiming SDA before that date will continue to receive it for as long as they qualify.

Weekly Rates from April 2010

Basic rate	£59.45
Age related addition*:	
Under 40	£15.00
40–49	£8.40
50–59	£5.45

* The age addition applies to the age when incapacity began

ATTENDANCE ALLOWANCE

This may be payable to people aged 65 or over who need help with personal care because they are physically or mentally disabled, and who have needed help for a period of at least six months. Attendance allowance has two rates: the lower rate is for day or night care, and the higher rate is for day and night care. People not expected to live for more than six months because of a progressive disease can receive the highest rate of attendance allowance straight away.

Weekly Rates from April 2010

Higher rate	£71.40
Lower rate	£47.80

DISABILITY LIVING ALLOWANCE

This may be payable to people aged under 65 who have had personal care and/or mobility needs because of an illness or disability for a period of at least three months and are likely to have those needs for a further six months or more. The allowance has two components: the care component, which has three rates, and the mobility component, which has two rates. The rates depend on the care and mobility needs of the claimant. People not expected to live for more than six months because of a progressive disease will automatically receive the highest rate of the care component.

Weekly Rates from April 2010

Care component	
Higher rate	£71.40
Middle rate	£47.80
Lowest rate	£18.95
Mobility component	
Higher rate	£49.85
Lower rate	£18.95

STATE PENSION FOR PEOPLE AGED 80 AND OVER

A state pension, also referred to as category D pension, is provided for people aged 80 and over if they are not entitled to another category of pension or are entitled to a state pension that is less than £58.50 a week. The person must also live in Great Britain and have done so for a period of ten years or more in any continuous 20-year period since their 60th birthday.

Weekly Rate from April 2010

Single person	£58.50

INCOME SUPPORT

Broadly speaking income support is a benefit for those aged 16 and over whose income is below a certain level, who work on average less than 16 hours a week and who are:

- bringing up children alone
- registered sick or disabled
- a student who is also a lone parent or disabled
- caring for someone who is sick or elderly

Pension credit replaced income support for people aged 60 or over on 6 October 2003.

Income support is not payable if the claimant, or claimant and partner, have capital or savings in excess of £16,000 – and deductions are made for capital and savings in excess of £6,000. For people permanently in residential care and nursing homes deductions apply for capital in excess of £10,000.

Sums payable depend on fixed allowances laid down by law for people in different circumstances. If both partners are eligible for income support, either may claim it for the couple. People receiving income support may be able to receive housing benefit, help with mortgage or home loan interest and help with healthcare. They may also be eligible for help with exceptional expenses from the Social Fund. Special rates may apply to some people living in residential care or nursing homes.

INCOME SUPPORT PREMIUMS

Income support premiums are extra weekly payments for those with additional needs. People qualifying for more than one premium will normally only receive the highest single premium for which they qualify. However, family premium, disabled child premium, severe disability premium and carer premium are payable in addition to other premiums.

Child tax credit replaced premiums for people with children for all new income support claims from 6 April 2004. People with children who were already in receipt of income support in April 2004 and have not claimed child tax credit may qualify for:

- the family premium if they have at least one child
- the disabled child premium if they have a child who receives disability living allowance or is registered blind
- the enhanced disability child premium if they have a child in receipt of the higher rate disability living allowance care component

Carers may qualify for:

- the carer premium if they or their partner are in receipt of carer's allowance

Long-term sick or disabled people may qualify for:

- the disability premium if they or their partner are receiving certain benefits because they are disabled or cannot work; are registered blind; or if the claimant has

been incapable of work or receiving statutory sick pay for at least 364 days (196 days if the person is terminally ill), including periods of incapacity separated by eight weeks or less
- the severe disability premium if the person lives alone and receives the middle or higher rate of disability living allowance care component and no one receives carer's allowance for caring for that person
- the enhanced disability premium if the person is in receipt of the higher rate disability living allowance care component

People with a partner aged over 60 may qualify for:
- the pensioner premium

WEEKLY RATES OF INCOME SUPPORT
from April 2010

Single person	
aged 16–24	£51.85
aged 25+	£65.45
aged under 18 and a single parent	£51.85
aged 18+ and a single parent	£65.45
Couples	
Both under 18	£51.85
Both under 18, in certain circumstances	£78.30
One under 18, one aged 18–24	£51.85
One under 18, one aged 25+	£65.45
Both aged 18+	£102.75
Premiums	
Carer premium	£30.05
Severe disability premium	£53.65
Enhanced disability premium	
Single person	£13.65
Couples	£19.65
Pensioner premium (couple)	£68.25–£99.65

PENSION CREDIT

Pension credit was introduced on 6 October 2003 and replaced income support for those aged 60 and over. Between April 2010 and April 2020 the pension credit qualifying age is increasing from 60 to 65 alongside the increase in women's state pension age.

There are two elements to pension credit:

THE GUARANTEE CREDIT

The guarantee credit guarantees a minimum income of £132.60 for single people and £202.40 for couples, with additional elements for people who have:
- eligible housing costs
- severe disabilities
- caring responsibilities

Income from state pension, private pensions, earnings, working tax credit and certain benefits are taken into account when calculating the pension credit. For savings and capital in excess of £10,000, £1 for every £500 or part of £500 held is taken into account as income when working out entitlement to pension credit.

People receiving the guarantee credit element of pension credit will be able to receive housing benefit, council tax benefit and help with healthcare costs.

Weekly Rates from April 2010

Additional amount for severe disability	
Single person	£53.65
Couple (one qualifies)	£53.65
Couple (both qualify)	£107.30
Additional amount for carers	£30.05

THE SAVINGS CREDIT

Single people aged 65 or over (and couples where one member is 65 or over) may be entitled to a savings credit which provides additional support for pensioners who have made modest provision towards their retirement. The savings credit is calculated by taking into account any qualifying income above the savings credit threshold. For 2010–11 the threshold is £98.40 for single people and £157.25 for couples. The savings credit gives pensioners a cash addition calculated at 60p for every pound of qualifying income they have between the savings credit threshold and the guarantee credit. After this, the maximum savings credit will be reduced by 40p for every pound of income above the guarantee level. The maximum savings credit is £20.52 per week (£27.09 a week for couples).

Income that qualifies towards the savings credit includes state pensions, earnings, second pensions and income taken into account from capital above £10,000.

Some people will be entitled to the guarantee credit, some to the savings credit and some to both.

Where only the savings credit is in payment, people need to claim standard housing benefit or council tax benefit. Although local authorities take any savings credit into account in the housing benefit or council tax benefit assessment, for people aged 65 and over housing benefit or council tax benefit is enhanced to ensure that gains in pension credit are not depleted.

HOUSING BENEFIT

Housing benefit is designed to help people with rent (including rent for accommodation in guesthouses, lodgings or hostels). It does not cover mortgage payments. The amount of benefit paid depends on:
- the income of the claimant, and partner if there is one, including earned income, unearned income (any other income including some other benefits) and savings
- number of dependants
- certain extra needs of the claimant, partner or any dependants
- number and gross income of people sharing the home who are not dependent on the claimant
- how much rent is paid

Housing benefit is not payable if the claimant, or claimant and partner, have savings in excess of £16,000. The amount of benefit is affected if savings held exceed £6,000 (£10,000 for people living in residential care and nursing homes). Housing benefit is not paid for meals, fuel or certain service charges that may be included in the rent. Deductions are also made for most non-dependants who live in the same accommodation as the claimant (and their partner).

The maximum amount of benefit (which is not necessarily the same as the amount of rent paid) may be paid where the claimant is in receipt of income support, income-based jobseeker's allowance, the guarantee element of pension credit or where the claimant's income is less than the amount allowed for their needs. Any income over that allowed for their needs will mean that their benefit is reduced.

LOCAL HOUSING ALLOWANCE

Local housing allowance (LHA), which was rolled out nationally from 7 April 2008, is a way of calculating the rent element of housing benefit based on the area in which a person lives and household size. It affects people in the deregulated private rented sector who make a new claim for housing benefit or existing recipients who move address. LHA ensures that tenants in similar circumstances in the same area receive the same amount of financial support for their housing costs. It does not affect the way a person's income or capital is taken into account. LHA is paid to the tenant rather than the landlord in most circumstances and tenants are able to keep any excess benefit up to a maximum of £15 per week that is over and above the cost of their rent. If their rent is higher than their LHA entitlement they must make up the difference from other sources of income.

COUNCIL TAX BENEFIT

Nearly all the rules that apply to housing benefit apply to council tax benefit, which helps people on low incomes to pay council tax bills. The amount payable depends on how much council tax is paid and who lives with the claimant. The benefit may be available to those receiving income support, income-based jobseeker's allowance, the guarantee element of pension credit or to those whose income is less than that allowed for their needs. Any income over that allowed for their needs will mean that their council tax benefit is reduced. Deductions are made for non-dependants.

The maximum amount that is payable for those living in properties in council tax bands A to E is 100 per cent of the claimant's council tax liability. This also applies to those living in properties in bands F to H who were in receipt of the benefit at 31 March 1998 if they have remained in the same property.

If a person shares a home with one or more adults (not their partner) who are on a low income, it may be possible to claim a second adult rebate. Those who are entitled to both council tax benefit and second adult rebate will be awarded whichever is the greater. Second adult rebate may be claimed by those not in receipt of or eligible for council tax benefit.

THE SOCIAL FUND

REGULATED PAYMENTS

Sure Start Maternity Grant

Sure start maternity grant (SSMG) is a one-off payment of £500 to help people on low incomes pay for essential items for new babies that are expected, born, adopted, the subject of a parental order (following a surrogate birth) or, in certain circumstances, the subject of a residency order. SSMG can be claimed any time from the 29th week of pregnancy up to three months after the birth, adoption or date of parental or residency order. Those eligible are people in receipt of income support, income-based jobseeker's allowance, pension credit, child tax credit at a rate higher than the family element or working tax credit where a disability or severe disability element is in payment.

Funeral Payments

Payable to help cover the necessary cost of burial or cremation, a new burial plot with an exclusive right of burial (where burial is chosen), certain other expenses, and up to £700 for any other funeral expenses, such as the funeral director's fees, the coffin or flowers. Those eligible are people receiving income support, income-based jobseeker's allowance, pension credit, child tax credit at a higher rate than the family element, working tax credit where a disability or severe disability element is in payment, council tax benefit or housing benefit who have good reason for taking responsibility for the funeral expenses. These payments are recoverable from any estate of the deceased.

Cold Weather Payments

A payment of £8.50 when the average temperature is recorded at or forecast to be 0°C or below over seven consecutive days in the qualifying person's area. Payments are made to people on pension credit or child tax credit with a disability element, those on income support whose benefit includes a pensioner or disability premium, and those on income-based jobseeker's allowance or employment and support allowance who have a child who is disabled or under the age of five. Payments are made automatically and do not have to be repaid.

Winter Fuel Payments

For 2010–11 the winter fuel payment is up to £250 for households with someone aged 60–79 and up to £400 for households with someone aged 80 or over. The rate paid is based on the person's age and circumstances in the 'qualifying week' between 20 and 26 September 2010. The majority of eligible people are paid automatically before Christmas, although a few need to claim. Payments do not have to be repaid.

Christmas Bonus

The Christmas bonus is a one-off tax-free £10 payment made before Christmas to those people in receipt of a qualifying benefit in the qualifying week.

DISCRETIONARY PAYMENTS

Community Care Grants

These are intended to help people in receipt of income support, income-based jobseeker's allowance or employment and support allowance, pension credit, or payments on account of such benefits (or those likely to receive these benefits within the next six weeks because they are leaving residential or institutional accommodation) to live as independently as possible in the community; ease exceptional pressures on families; care for a prisoner or young offender released on temporary licence; help people set up home as part of a resettlement programme and/or assist with certain travelling expenses. They do not have to be repaid.

Budgeting Loans

These are interest-free loans to people who have been receiving income support, income-based jobseeker's allowance or employment and support allowance, pension credit or payments on account of such benefits for at least 26 weeks, for intermittent expenses that may be difficult to budget for.

Crisis Loans

These are interest-free loans to anyone aged 16 or over, whether receiving benefits or not, who is without resources in an emergency or due to a disaster, where there is no other means of preventing serious damage or serious risk to their or their family members' health or safety.

SAVINGS

Savings over £500 (£1,000 for people aged 60 or over) are taken into account for community care grants and savings of £1,000 (£2,000 for people aged 60 or over) are taken into account for budgeting loans. All savings are taken into account for crisis loans. Savings are not taken into account for sure start maternity grant, funeral payments, cold weather payments, winter fuel payments or the Christmas bonus.

INDUSTRIAL INJURIES AND DISABLEMENT BENEFITS

The Industrial Injuries Scheme, administered under the Social Security Contributions and Benefits Act 1992, provides a range of benefits designed to compensate for disablement resulting from an industrial accident (ie an accident arising out of and in the course of an earner's employment) or from a prescribed disease due to the nature of a person's employment. Those who are self-employed are not covered by this scheme.

INDUSTRIAL INJURIES DISABLEMENT BENEFIT

A person may be able to claim industrial injuries disablement benefit if they are ill or disabled due to an accident or incident that happened at work or in connection with work in England, Scotland or Wales. The amount of benefit awarded depends on the person's age and the degree of disability as assessed by a doctor.

The benefit is payable whether the person works or not and those who are incapable of work are entitled to draw other benefits, such as statutory sick pay or incapacity benefit, in addition to industrial injuries disablement benefit. It may also be possible to claim the following allowances:

- reduced earnings allowance for those who are unable to return to their regular work or work of the same standard and who had their accident (or whose disease started) before 1 October 1990. At state pension age this is converted to retirement allowance
- constant attendance allowance for those with a disablement of 100 per cent who need constant care. There are four rates of allowance depending on how much care the person needs
- exceptionally severe disablement allowance can be claimed in addition to constant care attendance allowance at one of the higher rates for those who need constant care permanently

Weekly Rates of Benefit from April 2010

Degree of disablement	*Aged 18+ or with dependants*	*Aged under 18 with no dependants*
100 per cent	£145.80	£89.35
90	£131.22	£80.42
80	£116.64	£71.48
70	£102.06	£62.55
60	£87.48	£53.61
50	£72.90	£44.68
40	£58.32	£35.74
30	£43.74	£26.81
20	£29.16	£17.87
Unemployability supplement		£90.10
Reduced earnings allowance (maximum)		£58.32
Retirement allowance (maximum)		£14.58
Constant attendance allowance (normal maximum rate)		£58.40
Exceptionally severe disablement allowance		£58.40

OTHER BENEFITS

People who are disabled because of an accident or disease that was the result of work that they did before 5 July 1948 are not entitled to industrial injuries disablement benefit. They may, however, be entitled to payment under the Workmen's Compensation Scheme or the Pneumoconiosis, Byssinosis and Miscellaneous Diseases Benefit Scheme. People who suffer from certain industrial diseases caused by dust, or their dependants, can make a claim for an additional payment under the Pneumoconiosis Act 1979 if they are unable to get damages from the employer who caused or contributed to the disease.

Diffuse Mesothelioma Payment

Since 1 October 2008 any person suffering from the asbestos-related disease, diffuse mesothelioma, who is unable to make a claim under the Pneumoconiosis Act 1979, have not received payment in respect of the disease from an employer, via a civil claim or elsewhere, and are not entitled to compensation from a MoD scheme, can claim a one-off lump sum payment. The scheme covers people whose exposure to asbestos occurred in the UK and was not as a result of their work as an employee (ie they lived near a factory using asbestos). The amount paid depends on the age of the person when the disease was diagnosed, or the date of the claim if the diagnosis date is not known. From 1 October 2009 claims must be received within 12 months of the date of diagnosis. If the sufferer has died, their dependants may be able to claim, but must do so within 12 months of the date of death.

CLAIMS AND QUESTIONS

Entitlement to benefit and regulated Social Fund payments is determined by a decision maker on behalf of the Secretary of State for the Department for Work and Pensions. A claimant who is dissatisfied with that decision can ask for an explanation. He or she can dispute the decision by applying to have it revised or, in particular circumstances, superseded. The claimant can go to the Appeals Service where the case will be heard by an independent tribunal. There is a further right of appeal to a social security commissioner against the tribunal's decision but this is on a point of law only and leave to appeal must first be obtained.

Decisions on claims and applications for housing benefit and council tax benefit are made by local authorities. The explanation, dispute and appeals process is the same as for other benefits.

All decisions on applications to the discretionary Social Fund are made by Jobcentre Plus Social Fund decision makers. Applicants can ask for a review of the decision within 28 days of the date on the decision letter. The Social Fund review officer will review the case and there is a further right of review by an independent Social Fund inspector.

EMPLOYER PAYMENTS

STATUTORY MATERNITY PAY

Employers pay statutory maternity pay (SMP) to pregnant women who have been employed by them full or part-time continuously for at least 26 weeks into the 15th week before the week the baby is due, and whose earnings on average at least equal the lower earnings limit applied to NI contributions (£97 a week from April 2010). SMP can be paid for a maximum period of up to 39 weeks. If the qualifying conditions are met women will receive a payment of 90 per cent of their average earnings for the first six weeks, followed by 33 weeks at £124.88 or 90 per cent of the woman's average weekly earnings if this is less than £124.88. SMP can be paid, at the earliest, 11 weeks before the week in which the baby is due, up to the day following the birth. Women can decide when they wish their maternity leave and pay to start and can work until the baby is born. However, where the woman is absent from work wholly or partly due to her pregnancy in the four weeks before the week the baby is due to be born, SMP will start the day following the first day of absence from work.

Employers are reimbursed for 92 per cent of the SMP they pay. Small employers with annual gross NI payments of £45,000 or less recover 100 per cent of the SMP paid out plus 4.5 per cent in compensation for the secondary NI contributions paid on SMP.

STATUTORY PATERNITY PAY

Employers pay statutory paternity pay (SPP) to employees who are taking leave when a child is born or placed for adoption. To qualify the employee must:

- have responsibility for the child's upbringing
- be the biological father of the child (or the child's adopter), or the spouse/civil partner/partner of the mother or adopter
- have been employed by the same employer for at least 26 weeks ending with the 15th week before the baby is due (or the week in which the adopter is notified of having been matched with a child)
- continue working for the employer up to the child's birth (or placement for adoption)
- have earnings on average at least equal to the lower earnings limit applied to NI contributions (£97 a week from April 2010)

Employees who meet these conditions receive payment of £124.88 or 90 per cent of the employee's average weekly earnings if this is less than £124.88. The employee can choose to be paid for one or two consecutive weeks. The earliest the SPP period can begin is the date of the child's birth or placement for adoption. The SPP period must be completed within eight weeks of that date. SPP is not payable for any week in which the employee works. Employers are reimbursed in the same way as for statutory maternity pay.

ADDITIONAL PATERNITY LEAVE

Regulations introduced on 6 April 2010 give parents greater flexibility in how they use their maternity and paternity provisions. For births from 3 April 2010, additional paternity leave (APL) entitles eligible fathers to take up to 26 weeks' additional paternity leave, allowing for up to a total of one year's leave to be shared between the couple. APL entitlement requires the mother to have returned to work; it must also be taken between 20 weeks and one year after the child is born. APL may be paid if taken during the mother's statutory maternity pay period or maternity allowance period.

The APL entitlement will also apply to husbands, partners or civil partners who are not the child's father but expect to have the main responsibility (apart from the mother) for the child's upbringing.

Statutory paternity pay (*see* above) is due to be renamed ordinary paternity leave (OPL) but otherwise remains unchanged.

STATUTORY ADOPTION PAY

Employers pay statutory adoption pay (SAP) to employees taking adoption leave from their employers. To qualify for SAP the employee must:

- be newly matched with a child by an adoption agency
- have been employed by the same employer for at least 26 weeks ending the week in which they have been notified of being matched with a child
- have earnings at least equal to the lower earnings limit applied to NI contributions (£97 a week from April 2010)

Employees who meet these conditions receive payment of £124.88 or 90 per cent of their average weekly earnings if this is less than £124.88 for up to 39 weeks. The earliest SAP can be paid from is two weeks before the expected date of placement; the latest it can start is the date of the child's placement. Where a couple adopt a child, only one of them may receive SAP, the other may be able to receive statutory paternity pay (SPP) if they meet the eligibility criteria. Employers are reimbursed in the same way as for statutory maternity pay.

The additional paternity leave entitlement (*see* above) will also apply to adoptions where adoptive parents are notified of a match on or after 3 April 2011.

STATUTORY SICK PAY

Employers pay statutory sick pay (SSP) for up to a maximum of 28 weeks to any employee incapable of work for four or more consecutive days. Employees must have done some work under their contract of service and have average weekly earnings of at least £97 from April 2010. SSP is a daily payment and is usually paid for the days that an employee would normally work, these days are known as qualifying days. SSP is not paid for the first three qualifying days in a period of sickness. SSP is paid at £79.15 per week and is subject to PAYE and NI contributions. Employees who cannot obtain SSP may be able to claim incapacity benefit. Employers may be able to recover some SSP costs.

THE WATER INDUSTRY

Water services in England and Wales are provided by private companies. In Scotland and Northern Ireland there are single authorities, Scottish Water and Northern Ireland Water, that are publicly owned companies answerable to their respective governments. In the UK the water industry provides services to over 25 million properties and has an annual turnover of £9bn. It also manages assets that include over 1,500 water treatment and 9,300 wastewater treatment works, 550 impounding reservoirs, over 6,500 service reservoirs/water towers and 807,000km of water mains and sewers.

ENGLAND AND WALES

The water industry supplies around 17 billion litres a day of water to domestic and commercial customers and collects and treats more than 16 billion litres of wastewater a day. In quality tests carried out in 2009, the water industry in England and Wales achieved 99.95 per cent compliance with the standards required by the European Drinking Water Directive. In England and Wales the Secretary of State for Environment, Food and Rural Affairs and the National Assembly for Wales have overall responsibility for water policy and oversee environmental standards for the water industry.

Water UK is the industry association that represents all UK water and wastewater service suppliers at national and European level and is funded directly by its members, who are the service suppliers for England, Scotland, Wales and Northern Ireland; every member has a seat on the Water UK Council. The statutory consumer representative body for water services is the Consumer Council for Water.

CONSUMER COUNCIL FOR WATER, 1st Floor, Victoria Square House, Victoria Square, Birmingham B2 4AJ T 0845-039 2837 W www.ccwater.org.uk

WATER UK, 1 Queen Anne's Gate, London SW1H 9BT T 020-7344 1844 W www.water.org.uk
Chief Executive, Pamela Taylor

WATER SERVICE COMPANIES
*(*not a member of Water UK)*

*ALBION WATER LTD, 78 High Street, Harpenden, Herts AL5 2SP T 0845-604 2355 W www.albionwater.co.uk

ANGLIAN WATER SERVICES LTD, Customer Services, PO Box 10642, Harlow CM20 9HA T 0845-791 9155 W www.anglianwater.co.uk

BOURNEMOUTH & WEST HAMPSHIRE WATER PLC, George Jessel House, Francis Avenue, Bournemouth, Dorset BH11 8NX T 01202-590059 W www.bwhwater.co.uk

BRISTOL WATER PLC, PO Box 218, Bridgwater Road, Bristol BS99 7AU T 0117-966 5881 W www.bristolwater.co.uk

CAMBRIDGE WATER PLC, 90 Fulbourn Road, Cambridge CB1 9JN T 01223-706050 W www.cambridge-water.co.uk

*CHOLDERTON & DISTRICT WATER COMPANY, Estate Office, Cholderton, Salisbury, Wiltshire SP4 0DR T 01980-629203 W www.choldertonwater.co.uk

DEE VALLEY WATER PLC, Packsaddle, Wrexham Road, Rhostyllen, Wrexham LL14 4EH T 01978-846946 W www.deevalleywater.co.uk

DWR CYMRU (WELSH WATER), Pentwyn Road, Nelson, Treharris, Mid Glamorgan CF46 6LY T 0800-052 0145 W www.dwrcymru.co.uk

ESSEX & SUFFOLK WATER PLC (subsidiary of Northumbrian Water Ltd), Customer Centre, PO Box 292, Durham DH1 9TX T 0845-782 0999 W www.eswater.co.uk

NORTHUMBRIAN WATER LTD, Customer Centre, PO Box 300, Durham DH1 9WQ T 0845-717 1100 W www.nwl.co.uk

PORTSMOUTH WATER LTD, PO Box 8, West Street, Havant, Hampshire PO9 1LG T 023-9249 9888 W www.portsmouthwater.co.uk

SEVERN TRENT LTD, 2297 Coventry Road, Birmingham B26 3PU T 0121-722 4000 W www.severntrent.co.uk

SOUTH EAST WATER LTD, Rocfort Road, Snodland, Kent ME6 5AH T 0845-850 6060 W www.southeastwater.co.uk

SOUTH STAFFORDSHIRE WATER PLC, PO Box 63, Walsall WS2 7PJ T 0845-607 0456 W www.south-staffs-water.co.uk

SOUTH WEST WATER LTD, Peninsula House, Rydon Lane, Exeter EX2 7HR T 0800-169 1144 W www.southwestwater.co.uk

SOUTHERN WATER SERVICES LTD, Southern House, Yeoman Road, Worthing, W. Sussex BN13 3NX T 0845-278 0845 W www.southernwater.co.uk

SUTTON AND EAST SURREY WATER PLC, London Road, Redhill, Surrey RH1 1LJ T 01737-772000 W www.waterplc.com

THAMES WATER UTILITIES LTD, PO Box 286, Swindon SN38 2RA T 0845-920 0800 W www.thameswater.co.uk

UNITED UTILITIES WATER PLC, Haweswater House, Lingley Mere Business Park, Great Sankey, Warrington WA5 3LP T 0845-746 2200 W www.unitedutilities.com

VEOLIA WATER CENTRAL LTD, Tamblin Way, Hatfield, Herts AL10 9EZ T 01707-268111 W www.veoliawater.co.uk/central

VEOLIA WATER EAST LTD, Mill Hill, Manningtree, Essex CO11 2AZ T 01206-399333 W www.veoliawater.co.uk/east

VEOLIA WATER SOUTHEAST LTD, The Cherry Garden, Cherry Garden Lane, Folkestone, Kent CT19 4QB T 0845-888 5888 W www.veoliawater.co.uk/southeast

WESSEX WATER SERVICES LTD, Claverton Down Road, Bath BA2 7WW T 0845-600 4600 W wessexwater.co.uk

YORKSHIRE WATER SERVICES LTD, PO Box 52, Bradford BD3 7YD T 0845-124 2424 W www.yorkshirewater.com

ISLAND WATER AUTHORITIES
(not members of Water UK)

COUNCIL OF THE ISLES OF SCILLY, Town Hall, St Mary's, Isles of Scilly TR21 0LW T 01720-422537 W www.scilly.gov.uk

ISLE OF MAN WATER AUTHORITY, Tromode Road, Douglas, Isle of Man IM2 5PA T 01624-695949 W www.gov.im/water

JERSEY WATER, Mulcaster House, Westmount Road, St Helier, Jersey JE1 1DG T 01534-707300 W www.jerseywater.je

STATES OF GUERNSEY WATER BOARD, PO Box 30, South Esplanade, St Peter Port, Guernsey GY1 3AS T 01481-724552 W www.water.gg

REGULATORY BODIES

The Water Services Regulation Authority (OFWAT) was established under the Water Industry Act 1991 and is the independent economic regulator of the water and sewerage companies in England and Wales. Overall responsibility for water policy and overseeing environmental standards for the water industry lies with DEFRA and the Welsh Assembly. OFWAT's main duties are to ensure that the companies can finance and carry out their statutory functions and to protect the interests of water customers. OFWAT is a non-ministerial government department headed by a board following a change in legislation introduced by the Water Act 2003.

Under the Competition Act 1998, from 1 March 2000 the Competition Appeal Tribunal has heard appeals against the regulator's decisions regarding anti-competitive agreements and abuse of a dominant position in the marketplace. The Water Act 2003 placed a new duty on OFWAT to contribute to the achievement of sustainable development.

The Environment Agency has statutory duties and powers in relation to water resources, pollution control, flood defence, fisheries, recreation, conservation and navigation in England and Wales. They are also responsible for issuing permits, licences, consents and registrations such as industrial licences to extract water and fishing licences.

The Drinking Water Inspectorate (DWI) is the drinking water quality regulator for England and Wales, responsible for assessing the quality of the drinking water supplied by the water companies and investigating any incidents affecting drinking water quality, initiating prosecution where necessary. The DWI also provides scientific advice on drinking water policy issues to DEFRA and the Welsh Assembly.

OFWAT, Centre City Tower, 7 Hill Street, Birmingham B5 4UA T 0121-644 7500 E enquiries@ofwat.gsi.gov.uk W www.ofwat.gov.uk
Chair, Philip Fletcher, CBE
Chief Executive, Regina Finn

METHODS OF CHARGING

In England and Wales, most domestic customers still pay for domestic water supply and sewerage services through charges based on the rateable value of their property. OFWAT estimates that the proportion of household customers in England and Wales to have metered supplies will rise from 37 per cent in 2009–10 to about 50 per cent in 2014–15. Nearly all non-household customers are charged according to consumption.

Under the Water Industry Act 1999, water companies can continue basing their charges on the old rateable value of the property. Domestic customers can continue paying on an unmeasured basis unless they choose to pay according to consumption. After having a meter installed (which is free of charge), a customer can revert to unmeasured charging within 12 months. However, water companies may charge by meter for new homes, or homes where there is a high discretionary use of water. Domestic, school and hospital customers cannot be disconnected for non-payment.

Price limits for the period 2010–15 were set by OFWAT in November 2009.

On average, prices for 2010–11 will remain broadly flat, decreasing by around 0.8 per cent. This takes into account inflation of 0.3 per cent. Average bills for water

WATER SUPPLY AND CONSUMPTION 2008–9

	Supply		*Consumption*			
			Household (litres/head/day)		*Non-household (litres/property/day)*	
	Distribution Input (megalitres/day)	*Total Leakage (megalitres/day)*	*Unmetered*	*Metered*	*Unmetered*	*Metered*
WATER AND SEWERAGE COMPANIES						
Anglian	1,160.2	210	172.6	145.2	612.1	2,741.6
Dwr Cymru	828.8	195	168.0	134.4	536.0	1,971.8
Northumbrian (NE)	688.1	150	162.2	146.8	774.6	3,302.4
Northumbrian (Essex & Suffolk)	451.3	67	175.9	156.7	672.1	2,468.1
Severn Trent	1,843.8	490	148.6	125.6	854.5	2,002.1
South West	422.0	84	166.0	139.5	1,157.7	1,409.9
Southern	555.7	87	154.6	142.1	773.7	2,552.6
Thames	2,573.7	700	189.0	151.6	700.8	2,950.3
United Utilities	1,812.2	460	152.4	120.0	693.6	2,560.9
Wessex	345.7	72	166.7	145.2	3,227.9	1,916.6
Yorkshire	1,266.2	295	165.2	123.8	173.2	2,437.1
Total	11,947.6	2,811	—	—	—	—
Average	—	—	165.4	137.0	785.5	2,421.1
WATER ONLY COMPANIES						
Total	2,657.0	479	—	—	—	—
Average	—	—	180.3	149.1	929.6	2,394.2

Source: OFWAT

services range from £88 for Portsmouth Water to £205 for South West Water, with an overall average of £165. The average sewerage bill costs £174, ranging from £114 for Thames Water up to £282 for South West Water.

SCOTLAND

Overall responsibility for national water policy in Scotland rests with the Scottish ministers. Until the Local Government (Scotland) Act 1994, water supply and sewerage services were local authority responsibilities. The Central Scotland Water Development Board had the function of developing new sources of water supply for the purpose of providing water in bulk to water authorities whose limits of supply were within the board's area. Under the act, three new public water authorities, covering the north, east and west of Scotland respectively, took over the provision of water and sewerage services from April 1996. The Central Scotland Water Development Board was then abolished. The act also established the Scottish Water and Sewerage Customers Council representing consumer interests. It monitored the performance of the authorities; approved charges schemes; investigated complaints; and advised the secretary of state. The Water Industry Act 1999, whose Scottish provisions were accepted by the Scottish government, abolished the Scottish Water and Sewerage Customers Council and replaced it in November 1999 with a Water Industry Commissioner.

The Water Industry (Scotland) Act 2002 resulted from the Scottish government's proposal that a single authority was better placed than three separate authorities to harmonise changes across the Scottish water industry. In 2002 the three existing water authorities (East of Scotland Water, North of Scotland Water and West of Scotland Water) merged to form Scottish Water. Scottish Water is a public sector company, structured and managed like a private company, but remains answerable to the Scottish parliament. Scottish Water is regulated by the Water Industry Commission for Scotland, the Scottish Environment Protection Agency (SEPA), and the Drinking Water Quality Regulator for Scotland. The Water Industry Commissioner is responsible for regulating all aspects of economic and customer service performance, including water and sewerage charges. SEPA is responsible for environmental issues, including controlling pollution and promoting the cleanliness of Scotland's rivers, lochs and coastal waters. Waterwatch Scotland is the consumer representative body for the water industry and the national complaints handling authority for water customers in Scotland.

METHODS OF CHARGING

Scottish Water sets charges for domestic and non-domestic water and sewerage provision through charges schemes which are regulated by the Water Industries Commissioner for Scotland. In February 2004 the harmonisation of all household charges across the country was completed following the merger of the separate authorities under Scottish Water. In November 2009 the Water Industry Commission for Scotland published *The Strategic Review of Charges 2010–2015*, stating that annual price rises would be kept at 5 per cent below the rate of inflation during this five-year period.

SCOTTISH ENVIRONMENT PROTECTION AGENCY, Erskine Court, Castle Business Park, Stirling FK9 4TR **T** 01786-457700 **W** www.sepa.org.uk

SCOTTISH WATER, PO Box 8855, Edinburgh EH10 6YQ **T** 0845-601 8855 **W** www.scottishwater.co.uk

WATER INDUSTRY COMMISSION FOR SCOTLAND, Ochil House, Springkerse Business Park, Stirling FK7 7XE **T** 01786-430200 **W** www.watercommission.co.uk

WATERWATCH SCOTLAND, Corporate Office, Forrester Lodge, Inglewood, Alloa FK10 2HU **T** 0845-850 3344 **W** www.waterwatchscotland.org

NORTHERN IRELAND

Formerly an executive agency of the Department for Regional Development, Northern Ireland Water is a government-owned company set up as a result of government reform of water and sewerage services in April 2007. It is responsible for policy and coordination with regard to the supply, distribution and cleanliness of water, and the provision and maintenance of sewerage services. The Northern Ireland Authority for Utility Regulation (known as the Utility Regulator) is responsible for regulating the water services provided by Northern Ireland Water. The Drinking Water Inspectorate, a unit in the Northern Ireland Environment Agency (NIEA), regulates drinking water quality. Another NIEA unit, the Water Management Unit, has responsibility for the protection of the aquatic environment. The Consumer Council for Northern Ireland is the consumer representative body for water services.

METHODS OF CHARGING

The water and sewerage used by domestic customers in Northern Ireland is currently paid for by the Department for Regional Development (DRD), a system which will continue until at least March 2011. In March 2010, the Northern Ireland Assembly passed the Water and Sewerage Services (Amendment) Act (Northern Ireland) 2010, which ensured that Northern Ireland Water would continue to receive DRD subsidy until 2013. Whether domestic billing will be introduced before this date is yet to be decided. Non-domestic customers in Northern Ireland became subject to water and sewerage charges and trade effluent charges where applicable in April 2008.

CONSUMER COUNCIL FOR NORTHERN IRELAND, 116 Holywood Road, Belfast BT4 1NY **T** 028-9067 2488 **W** www.consumercouncil.org.uk

NORTHERN IRELAND AUTHORITY FOR UTILITY REGULATION, Queens House, 14 Queen Street, Belfast BT1 6ED **T** 028-9031 1575 **W** www.uregni.gov.uk

NORTHERN IRELAND WATER, PO Box 1026, Belfast BT1 9DJ **T** 0845-744 0088 **W** www.niwater.com

ENERGY

The main primary sources of energy in Britain are oil, natural gas, coal, nuclear power and renewables. The main secondary sources (ie sources derived from the primary sources) are electricity, coke and smokeless fuels and petroleum products. The UK was a net importer of fuels until the 1970s, when exports grew substantially as oil production from the North Sea began to come on line. The subsequent fuel surplus in 1981 was largely sustained until 2004. In the last five years, the UK has been a net importer of most fuels in both volume and value terms; total fuel deficit for 2009 was £6.4bn. The Department of Energy and Climate Change is responsible for promoting energy efficiency.

INDIGENOUS PRODUCTION OF PRIMARY FUELS
Million tonnes of oil equivalent

	2008	*2009*
Primary oils	78.6	74.7
Natural gas	69.7	59.7
Primary electricity	13.0	16.5
Coal	11.3	11.0
Renewable and waste	4.5	4.9
Total	177.0	166.9

Source: Department of Energy and Climate Change

INLAND ENERGY CONSUMPTION BY PRIMARY FUEL
Million tonnes of oil equivalent, seasonally adjusted

	2008	*2009*
Natural gas	93.0	85.9
Petroleum	75.1	71.2
Coal	38.0	31.2
Nuclear electricity	11.9	15.2
Renewables and waste	5.4	6.1
Hydro electricity	1.1	1.3
Net Imports	0.9	0.2
Total	225.4	211.2

Source: Department of Energy and Climate Change

TRADE IN FUELS AND RELATED MATERIALS (2009)

	Quantity, million tonnes of oil equivalent	*Value £m*
Imports		
Crude petroleum	55.4	14,520
Petroleum products	27.7	9,470
Natural gas	39.2	4,773
Coal and other solid fuel	25.2	2,676
Electricity	0.6	259
Total	148.1	31,698
Exports		
Crude petroleum	47.3	12,466
Petroleum products	38.3	11,370
Natural gas	11.8	1,218
Electricity	0.3	161
Coal and other solid fuel	0.5	108
Total	98.3	25,323

Source: DECC/ONS

OIL

Until the 1960s Britain imported almost all its oil supplies. In 1969 oil was discovered in the Arbroath field in the North Sea. The first oilfield to be brought into production was Argyll in 1975, and since the mid-1970s Britain has been a major producer of crude oil.

Licences for exploration and production are granted to companies by the Department of Energy and Climate Change. At the end of 2004, 565 seaward production licences and 101 onshore petroleum exploration and development licences had been awarded. At the end of 2009, there were a total of 317 offshore oil and gas fields in production. To date, the UK has produced around 26 billion barrels of oil. It is estimated that there are between 4 and 12 billion barrels remaining to be produced. Total UK oil production peaked in 1999 and is now declining. Profits from oil production are subject to a special tax regime with different taxes applying depending on the date of approval of each field.

DRILLING ACTIVITY (2009)
by number of wells started

	Offshore	*Onshore*
Exploration	23	13
Appraisal	42	2
Development	65	11

Source: Department of Energy and Climate Change

INDIGENOUS PRODUCTION AND REFINERY RECEIPTS
Thousand tonnes

	2008	*2009*
Indigenous production	71,665	68,199
Crude oil	65,487	62,820
NGLs*	6,168	5,378
Refinery receipts	75,844	79,037

* Natural Gas Liquids: condensates and petroleum gases derived at onshore treatment plants

Source: Department of Energy and Climate Change

DELIVERIES OF PETROLEUM PRODUCTS FOR INLAND CONSUMPTION BY ENERGY USE
Thousand tonnes

	2008	*2009*
Transport	51,924	49,614
Industry	5,446	4,939
Domestic	2,730	2,713
Other	1,305	1,148
Total	61,405	58,414

Source: Department of Energy and Climate Change

COAL

Mines were in private ownership until 1947 when they were nationalised and came under the management of the National Coal Board, later the British Coal Corporation. The corporation held a monopoly on coal production until 1994 when the industry was restructured. Under the Coal Industry Act 1994, the Coal Authority was established to take over ownership of coal reserves and to issue licences to private mining companies. The Coal Authority is also responsible for the physical legacy of mining, eg subsidence damage claims, and for holding and making available all existing records. It also publishes current data on the coal industry.

The mines owned by the British Coal Corporation were sold as five separate businesses in 1994 and coal production is now undertaken entirely in the private sector. Coal output was around 50 million tonnes a year in 1994 but has since declined to below 18 million tonnes. As at 31 March 2010 there were five large and ten small underground mines as well as 32 surface mines in production in the UK.

The main consumer of coal in the UK is the electricity supply industry. Coal still supplies a third of the UK's electricity needs but as indigenous production has declined, imports have risen to make up the shortfall and now represent around 66 per cent of feedstock, half of which is currently supplied from Russia.

Following the publication of an energy white paper in May 2007, the government set out its international and domestic energy strategy to meet the long-term challenges posed by climate change to ensure secure, clean and affordable energy. Coal's availability, flexibility and reliability compared to other sources mean that it is expected to continue to play an important role in the future generating mix, but there is a need to tackle carbon emissions through the introduction of abatement technologies and, in the long term, the introduction of carbon capture and storage (CCS).

CCS attempts to mitigate the effects of global warming by capturing the carbon dioxide emissions from power stations that burn fossil fuels, preventing the gas from being released into the atmosphere, and storing it in underground geological formations.

In April 2009 the government announced that all new combustion power stations would have to be Carbon Capture Ready and outlined proposals for a new regime for coal-fired power stations. On 17 March 2010 it launched the Office of Carbon Capture and Storage, simultaneously publishing a strategy for the industrial development of CCS. Funding for the first two design and development studies of CCS was awarded by the government in March 2010 and the subsequent Energy Act 2010 included:

- provision for up to four commercial-scale CCS demonstrations in Britain, covering a range of CCS technologies
- a requirement that any new coal power station in England and Wales demonstrates CCS on a defined area of its capacity
- a requirement for new coal power stations to retrofit CCS to their full station capacity by 2025

CCS is still in its infancy and only through its successful demonstration and development will it be possible for coal to remain a part of a low-carbon UK energy mix. To environmentalists, CCS remains an expensive and unproven technology with the potential for captured carbon to leak. There are also concerns that investment is being diverted from the development of renewable technologies.

INLAND COAL USE
Thousand tonnes

	2008	*2009*
Fuel producers		
Electricity generators	47,808	39,678
Coke manufacture	5,875	4,936
Blast furnaces	1,170	852
Heat generation	500	465
†Other conversion industries	322	340
Final consumption		
Industry	1,939	1,760
Domestic	684	686
Public administration	14	24
Commerce	10	49
Agriculture	10	–

† Mainly recycled products
Source: Department of Energy and Climate Change

COAL PRODUCTION AND FOREIGN TRADE
Thousand tonnes

	2008	*2009*
Opencast	9,509	9,854
Deep-mined	8,096	7,520
Imports	43,875	38,167
Exports	−599	−646
Total supply	58,219*	48,786*
TOTAL	58,346	48,805

* Includes an estimate for slurry and stock change
Source: Department of Energy and Climate Change

GAS

From the late 18th century gas in Britain was produced from coal. In the 1960s town gas began to be produced from oil-based feedstocks using imported oil. In 1965 gas was discovered in the North Sea in the West Sole field, which became the first gasfield in production in 1967, and from the late 1960s natural gas began to replace town gas. From October 1998 Britain was connected to the continental European gas system via a pipeline from Bacton, Norfolk to Zeebrugge, Belgium. Gas is transported through 275,000km of mains pipeline including 6,400km of high-pressure gas pipelines owned and operated in the UK by National Grid Gas plc.

The gas industry in Britain was nationalised in 1949 and operated as the Gas Council. The Gas Council was replaced by the British Gas Corporation in 1972 and the industry became more centralised. The British Gas Corporation was privatised in 1986 as British Gas plc. In 1993 the Monopolies and Mergers Commission found that British Gas's integrated business in Great Britain as a gas trader and the owner of the gas transportation system could operate against the public interest. In February 1997, British Gas demerged its trading arm to become two separate companies, BG plc and Centrica plc. BG Group, as the company is now known, is an international natural gas company whose principal business is finding and developing gas reserves and building gas markets. Its core operations are located in the UK, South America,

Egypt, Trinidad and Tobago, Kazakhstan and India. Centrica runs the trading and services operations under the British Gas brand name in Great Britain. In October 2000 BG demerged its pipeline business, Transco, which became part of Lattice Group, finally merging with the National Grid Group in 2002 to become National Grid Transco plc.

In July 2005 National Grid Transco plc changed its name to National Grid plc and Transco plc became National Grid Gas plc. In the same year National Grid Gas also completed the sale of four of its eight gas distribution networks. The distribution networks transport gas at lower pressures, which eventually supply the consumers such as domestic customers. The Scotland and south-east of England networks were sold to Scotia Gas Networks. The Wales and south-west network was sold to Wales & West Utilities and the network in the north-east to Northern Gas Networks. This was the biggest change in the corporate structure of gas infrastructure since privatisation in 1986.

Competition was gradually introduced into the industrial gas market from 1986. Supply of gas to the domestic market was opened to companies other than British Gas, starting in April 1996 with a pilot project in the West Country and Wales, with the rest of the UK following soon after. Since competition was introduced in domestic retail of gas, around 55 per cent of Britain's 22 million gas customers have changed their supplier.

Declines in UK indigenous gas production and increasing demand led to the UK becoming a net importer of gas once more in 2004. In 2009, gross natural gas production fell 14.3 per cent, and imports accounted for a third of gas input into the transmission system. As part of the Energy Act 2008, the government planned to strengthen regulation of the offshore gas supply infrastructure, to allow private sector investment to help maintain UK energy supplies.

BG GROUP PLC, Thames Valley Park, Reading RG6 1PT
T 0118-935 3222 W www.bg-group.com
Chair, Sir Robert Wilson
Chief Executive, Frank Chapman

CENTRICA PLC, Millstream, Maidenhead Road, Windsor, Berkshire SL4 5GD T 01753-494000 W www.centrica.co.uk
Chair, Roger Carr
Chief Executive, Sam Laidlaw

NATIONAL GRID PLC, Lakeside House, The Lakes, Northampton NN4 7HD T 0845-606 6677
W www.nationalgrid.com
Chair, Sir John Parker
Chief Executive, Steve Holliday

UK GAS CONSUMPTION BY INDUSTRY
GWh

	2007	*2008*
Domestic	349,943	363,315
Other industries	129,475	125,683
Public administration	44,589	47,288
Iron and steel industry	7,337	6,818
Agriculture	1,999	2,161
Miscellaneous	17,323	18,066
Total gas consumption	1,045,533	1,077,003

Source: Annual Abstract of Statistics 2010 (Crown copyright)

ELECTRICITY

The first power station in Britain generating electricity for public supply began operating in 1882. In the 1930s a national transmission grid was developed and it was reconstructed and extended in the 1950s and 1960s. Power stations were operated by the Central Electricity Generating Board.

Under the Electricity Act 1989, 12 regional electricity companies, responsible for the distribution of electricity from the national grid to consumers, were formed from the former area electricity boards in England and Wales. Four companies were formed from the Central Electricity Generating Board: three generating companies (National Power plc, Nuclear Electric plc and Powergen plc) and the National Grid Company plc, which owned and operated the transmission system in England and Wales. National Power and Powergen were floated on the stock market in 1991.

National Power was demerged in October 2000 to form two separate companies: International Power plc and Innogy plc, which manages the bulk of National Power's UK assets. Nuclear Electric was split into two parts in 1996 (*see* Nuclear Energy).

The National Grid Company was floated on the stock market in 1995 and formed a new holding company, National Grid Group. National Grid Group completed a merger with Lattice in 2002 to form National Grid Transco, a public limited company (*see* Gas).

Following privatisation, generators and suppliers in England and Wales traded via the Electricity Pool. A competitive wholesale trading market known as NETA (New Electricity Trading Arrangements) replaced the Electricity Pool in March 2001, and was extended to include Scotland via the British Electricity Transmissions and Trading Arrangements (BETTA) in 2005. As part of BETTA, National Grid became the system operator for all transmission. The introduction of competition into the domestic electricity market was completed in May 1999. Since competition was introduced, over 19 million of Britain's 28 million electricity customers have switched their supplier.

In Scotland, three new companies were formed under the Electricity Act 1989: Scottish Power plc and Scottish Hydro-Electric plc, which were responsible for generation, transmission, distribution and supply; and Scottish Nuclear Ltd. Scottish Power and Scottish Hydro-Electric were floated on the stock market in 1991. Scottish Hydro-Electric merged with Southern Electric in 1998 to become Scottish and Southern Energy plc. Scottish Nuclear was incorporated into British Energy in 1996. BETTA opened the Scottish market to the same competition that had applied in England and Wales.

In Northern Ireland, Northern Ireland Electricity plc was set up in 1993 under a 1991 Order in Council. In 1993 it was floated on the stock market and in 1998 it became part of the Viridian Group and is responsible for distribution and supply.

On 30 September 2003 the Electricity Association, the industry's main trade association, was replaced with three separate trade bodies:

ASSOCIATION OF ELECTRICITY PRODUCERS, Charles House, 5–11 Regent Street, London SW1Y 4LR
T 020-7930 9390 W www.aepuk.com

ENERGY NETWORKS ASSOCIATION, 6th floor, Dean Bradley House, 52 Horseferry Road, London SW1P 2AF
T 020-7706 5100 W www.energynetworks.org

ENERGY RETAIL ASSOCIATION, 1 Hobhouse Court, Suffolk Street, London SW1Y 4HH T 020-7104 4150 W www.energy-retail.org.uk

ELECTRICITY GENERATION, SUPPLY AND CONSUMPTION
GWh

	2007	2008
Electricity generated		
Conventional thermal and other*	144,404	127,763
Combined cycle gas turbine stations	139,826	158,734
Hydroelectric stations		
Natural flow	4,144	4,224
Pumped storage	3,859	4,089
Nuclear stations	63,028	52,486
Renewables other than hydro	2,991	7,988
Major power producers: total	358,252	355,284
Other generators total	38,205	34,365
Electricity used on works: total	18,087	16,317
Electricity supplied (gross)		
Conventional thermal and other*	136,399	120,707
Combined cycle gas turbine stations	137,561	156,225
Hydroelectric stations		
Natural flow	4,114	4,209
Pumped storage	3,846	4,075
Nuclear stations	57,249	47,673
Renewables other than hydro	2,574	7,724
Major power producers: total	341,742	340,613
Other generators total	36,628	32,719
Electricity used in pumping	5,071	5,371
Electricity consumed		
Fuel industries	8,048	8,377
Final users total	342,552	342,128
Industrial sector	118,340	114,124
Domestic sector	115,050	117,841
Other sectors	109,062	110,163
Total	350,601	350,505

* Includes electricity supplied by gas turbines, oil engines and plants producing electricity from renewable resources other than hydro

Source: Annual Abstract of Statistics 2010 (Crown copyright)

GAS AND ELECTRICITY SUPPLIERS

With the gas and electricity markets open, most suppliers offer their customers both services. The majority of gas/electricity companies have become part of larger multi-utility companies, often operating internationally.

As part of measures to reduce the UK's carbon output, the government has outlined plans to introduce 'smart meters' to all UK homes. Smart meters perform the traditional meter function of measuring energy consumption, in addition to more advanced functions such as allowing energy suppliers to communicate directly with their customers and removing the need for meter readings and bill estimates. The meters also allow domestic customers to have direct access to energy consumption information.

The following list comprises a selection of suppliers offering gas and electricity. Organisations in italics are subsidiaries of the companies listed in capital letters directly above.

ENGLAND, SCOTLAND AND WALES

CE ELECTRIC UK, W www.ceelectricuk.com

Northern Electric Distribution Ltd, Manor House, Station Road, New Penshaw, Houghton-le-Spring DH4 7LA T 0800-668877

Yorkshire Electricity Distribution, Manor House, Station Road, New Penshaw, Houghton-le-Spring DH4 7LA T 0800-375675

CENTRICA PLC, Millstream, Maidenhead Road, Windsor, Berkshire SL4 5GD T 01753-494000 W www.centrica.co.uk

BRITISH GAS/SCOTTISH GAS, PO Box 4805, Worthing BN11 9QW T 0800-048 0202 W www.britishgas.co.uk

EDF ENERGY, Osprey House, Osprey Road, Exeter, EX2 7WN T 0800-096 9000 W www.edfenergy.com

E.ON, 6th Floor, 100 Pall Mall, London SW1Y 5NQ T 024-7618 3843 W www.eon-uk.com

NPOWER, PO Box 93, Peterlee SR8 2XX T 0845-070 4851 W www.npower.com

SCOTTISH AND SOUTHERN ENERGY PLC, Inveralmond House, 200 Dunkeld Road, Perth PH1 3AQ T 01738-456000 W www.scottish-southern.co.uk

Scottish Hydro Electric, PO Box 7506, Perth PH1 3QR T 0845-300 2141 W www.hydro.co.uk

Southern Electric, PO Box 7506, Perth PH1 3QR T 0845-744 4555 W www.southern-electric.co.uk

SWALEC, PO Box 7506, Perth PH1 3QR T 0800-052 5252 W www.swalec.co.uk

SCOTTISHPOWER, PO Box 8729, Bellshill ML4 3YD T 0845-273 4444 W www.scottishpower.co.uk

NORTHERN IRELAND

VIRIDIAN GROUP PLC, 120 Malone Road, Belfast BT9 5HT T 028-9066 8416 W www.viridiangroup.co.uk

Energia, PO Box 1275, Belfast BT9 5WH T 1850-363744 W www.energia.ie

Northern Ireland Electricity, 120 Malone Road, Belfast BT9 5HT T 08457-643643 W www.nie.co.uk

REGULATION OF THE GAS AND ELECTRICITY INDUSTRIES

The Office of the Gas and Electricity Markets (OFGEM) regulates the gas and electricity industries in Great Britain. It was formed in 1999 by the merger of the Office of Gas Supply and the Office of Electricity Regulation. OFGEM's overriding aim is to protect and promote the interests of all gas and electricity customers by promoting competition and regulating monopolies. It is governed by an authority and its powers are provided for under the Gas Act 1986, the Electricity Act 1989, the Competition Act 1998, the Utilities Act 2000 and the Enterprise Act 2002. Energywatch is the independent gas and electricity watchdog, set up in November 2000 through the Utility Act to protect and promote the interests of gas and electricity consumers. In October 2008 Energywatch merged with Postwatch and the National Consumer Council to form a new advocacy body, Consumer Focus.

CONSUMER FOCUS, 4th Floor, Artillery House, Artillery Row, London SW1P 1RT T 020-7799 7900 W www.consumerfocus.org.uk

THE OFFICE OF THE GAS AND ELECTRCITY MARKETS (OFGEM), 9 Millbank, London SW1 3GE T 020-7901 7000 W www.ofgem.gov.uk

NUCLEAR POWER

Nuclear reactors began to supply electricity to the national grid in 1956. Nuclear power is currently generated in the UK at ten sites: two magnox reactors (shutdown expected in December 2010 and June 2011), seven advanced gas-cooled reactors (AGR) and one pressurised water reactor (PWR), Sizewell 'B' in Suffolk. The AGRs and PWR are owned by a private company, British Energy, while the two magnox reactors are state-owned under British Nuclear Fuels Ltd. The first of a series of new-generation plants is expected to come on-line around 2017; all but one of the current sites (Sizewell 'B') will be retired by 2023.

In April 2005 the responsibility for the decommissioning of civil nuclear reactors and other nuclear facilities used in research and development was handed to the Nuclear Decommissioning Authority (NDA). The NDA is a non-departmental public body, funded mainly by the Department of Energy and Climate Change (DECC). Until April 2007, UK Nirex was responsible for the disposal of intermediate and some low-level nuclear waste. After this date Nirex was integrated into the NDA and renamed the Radioactive Waste Management Directorate.

There are currently nine non-operational magnox power stations and four nuclear research facilities undergoing decommissioning by the NDA, including the world's first commercial power station at Calder Hall on the Sellafield site in Cumbria. The decommissioning of these sites is scheduled for completion within the next 15 to 20 years. In the case of the Dounreay research facility in Scotland, controls on access to contaminated land are expected to remain in place until around 2300.

In 2009 electricity supplied from nuclear sources had increased, accounting for 18 per cent of the total electricity supply. The 2008 Energy Bill paved the way for the construction of up to ten new nuclear power stations by 2020. A number of factors have led to government backing for nuclear power: domestic gas supplies are running low; oil and gas prices are high; carbon emissions must be cut to comply with EU legislation and meet global climate change targets; and a number of coal-fired power stations that fail to meet clean air requirements are due to be closed.

Nuclear power has its advantages: reactors emit virtually no carbon dioxide and uranium prices remain relatively steady. However, the advantages of low emissions are countered by the high costs of construction and difficulties in disposing of nuclear waste. Currently, the only method is to store it securely until it has slowly decayed to safe levels. Public distrust persists despite the advances in safety technology.

SAFETY AND REGULATION

The Nuclear Safety Directorate of the Health and Safety Executive is the nuclear industry's regulator. Operations at all UK nuclear power stations are governed by a site licence which is issued under the Nuclear Installations Act. The Nuclear Installations Inspectorate (NII) monitors compliance and has the jurisdiction to close down a reactor if the terms of the licence are breached. The DECC is responsible for security at all the UK's nuclear power stations, which are policed by the Civil Nuclear Constabulary, a specialised armed force created in April 2005. In 2009 Magnox Electric Ltd was found guilty of breaking the Radioactive Substances Act 2003: it had left a radioactive leak on a holding tank at Bradwell power station, Essex, unchecked for 14 years.

RENEWABLE SOURCES

Renewable sources of energy principally include biofuels, hydro, wind and solar. Renewable sources produced over 6.9 million tonnes of oil equivalent for primary energy usage in 2009; of this, about 4.9 million tonnes was used to generate electricity, 1.0 million tonnes to generate heat and 1.0 million tonnes was used as transport fuels. In 2009, the UK generated 6.7 per cent of its total energy production from renewable sources, up by 1.1 per cent from 2008.

The government's principal mechanism for developing renewable energy sources are Non-Fossil Fuel Obligation Renewables Orders. Under the terms of the orders, regional electricity companies are required to buy specified amounts of electricity from non-fossil fuel sources. The Renewables Obligation (RO) aims to increase the contribution of electricity from renewables in the UK, so that 9.1 per cent of licensed UK electricity sales should be from renewable sources eligible for the RO by 2009, and 15.4 per cent should be eligible by 2016. In 2009 renewables accounted for 6.7 per cent of sales on an RO basis, a rise on the 2008 figure of 5.3 per cent.

A renewables obligation has been in place in England and Wales since April 2002 to give incentives to generators to supply progressively higher levels of renewable energy over time. These measures included exempting renewable energy sources from the climate change levy, capital grants, enhanced research funding and regional planning to meet renewables targets. The government approved an EU-wide agreement in March 2007 to generate 20 per cent of energy production from renewable sources by 2020. It has since negotiated down the national share in this target to 15 per cent of energy production by 2020 (and 10 per cent by 2010), a figure many believe overly optimistic. In July 2009 the government published a Renewable Energy Strategy, which outlines policies that will help the UK to meet the 15 per cent target. Other impediments to the expansion of renewable energy production include planning restrictions, rising raw material prices, and the possible redirection of funds to develop CCS technology and nuclear energy sources. For further information on renewable energy sources *see* The Environment.

RENEWABLE ENERGY UTILISATION

By source, 2009

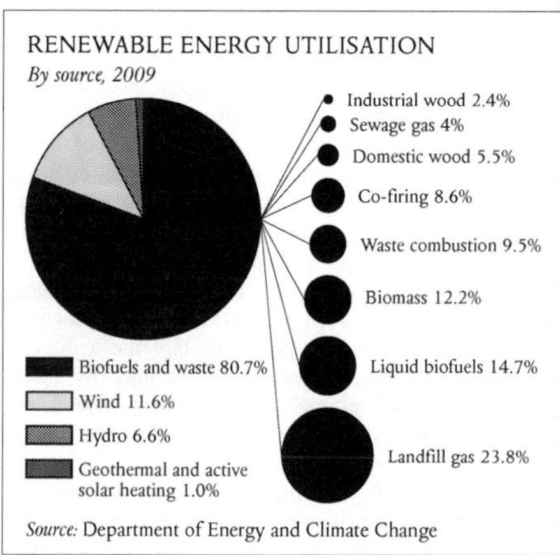

Source: Department of Energy and Climate Change

TRANSPORT

CIVIL AVIATION

Since the privatisation of British Airways in 1987, UK airlines have been operated entirely by the private sector. In 2009, total capacity of British airlines amounted to 49 billion tonne km, of which 39 billion tonne km was on scheduled services. British airlines carried around 124 million passengers; 102 million on scheduled services and 22 million on charter flights. Passenger traffic through UK airports decreased by 7.3 per cent, the largest annual decline for 65 years. Traffic at the five main London airports decreased by 4.9 per cent over 2009 and regional airports saw a decrease of 10.7 per cent. In spring 2010 an ash cloud resulting from the eruption of the Eyjafjallajokull volcano in Iceland caused major disruption to UK flights.

Leading British airlines include BMI, British Airways, EasyJet, Monarch, My Travel Airways, Thomas Cook Airlines, Thomson Airways and Virgin Atlantic. Irish airline Ryanair also operates frequent flights from Britain.

There are around 144 licensed civil aerodromes in Britain, with Heathrow and Gatwick handling the highest volume of passengers. BAA plc owns and operates six major airports: Heathrow, Stansted, Southampton, Glasgow, Edinburgh and Aberdeen. BAA sold Gatwick to an investment group in December 2009 for £1.5bn. Other airports are controlled by local authorities or private companies.

The Civil Aviation Authority (CAA), an independent statutory body, is responsible for the regulation of UK airlines. This includes economic and airspace regulation, air safety, consumer protection and environmental research and consultancy. All commercial airline companies must be granted an air operator's certificate, which is issued by the CAA to operators meeting the required safety standards. The CAA issues airport safety licences, which must be obtained by any airport used for public transport and training flights. All British-registered aircraft must be granted an airworthiness certificate, and the CAA issues professional licences to pilots, flight crew, ground engineers and air traffic controllers. The CAA also manages the Air Travel Organiser's Licence (ATOL), the UK's principal travel protection scheme. The CAA's costs are met entirely from charges on those whom it regulates; there is no direct government funding of the CAA's work.

The Transport Act, passed by parliament on 29 November 2000, separated the CAA from its subsidiary, National Air Traffic Services (NATS), which provides air traffic control services to aircraft flying in UK airspace and over the eastern part of the North Atlantic. In March 2001 the Airline Group, a consortium of seven UK airlines (British Airways, BMI, Virgin Atlantic, Britannia, Monarch, EasyJet and Airtours), was selected by the government as its strategic partner for NATS. Financial restructuring of NATS was completed in March 2003 with additional equity investment of £65m each from BAA and the government. The new structure enabled NATS to begin a ten-year £1bn investment programme, to increase its flight handling capability from two to three million flights per annum by 2012. NATS is a public private partnership between the Airline Group, which holds 42 per cent of the shares; NATS staff, who hold 5 per cent; BAA, which holds 4 per cent, and the government, which holds 49 per cent and a golden share. In 2009 NATS handled a total of 2,200,326 flights, a decrease of 9.6 per cent against 2008 figures.

AIR PASSENGERS 2009

All UK Airports: Total	221,857,419
Aberdeen (BAA)	2,984,445
Barra (HIAL)*	10,186
Belfast City	2,621,763
Belfast International	4,546,475
Benbecula (HIAL)*	33,025
Biggin Hill†	–
Birmingham	9,102,899
Blackpool	276,866
Bournemouth	870,754
Bristol	5,642,921
Cambridge	1,307
Campbeltown (HIAL)*	9,536
Cardiff	1,631,236
City of Derry (Eglinton)	345,857
Doncaster Sheffield	835,768
Dundee	72,495
Durham Tees Valley	289,464
Edinburgh (BAA)	9,049,355
Exeter	795,721
Gatwick (BAA)	32,392,520
Glasgow (BAA)	7,225,021
Gloucestershire	20,531
Hawarden (Chester)†	–
Heathrow (BAA)	66,036,937
Humberside	336,649
Inverness (HIAL)*	591,397
Islay (HIAL)*	26,325
Isle of Man	708,127
Isles of Scilly (St Mary's)	120,909
Isles of Scilly (Tresco)	34,485
Kent International	5,574
Kirkwall (HIAL)*	150,343
Lands End (St Just)	35,044
Leeds Bradford	2,574,426
Lerwick (Tingwall)	4,709
Liverpool	4,884,494
London City	2,796,890
Luton	9,120,546
Lydd	588
Manchester	18,724,889
Newcastle	4,587,883
Newquay	386,870
Norwich	430,594
Nottingham (East Midlands International)	4,658,151
Oxford (Kidlington)	1,297
Penzance Heliport	85,911
Plymouth	157,933
Prestwick	1,817,727
Scatsta	270,101
Shoreham	1,213
Southampton (BAA)	1,789,901

Southend	3,948
Stansted (BAA)	19,957,077
Stornoway (HIAL)*	123,199
Sumburgh (HIAL)*	140,714
Tiree (HIAL)*	8,350
Wick (HIAL)*	22,403
Channel Islands Airports: Total	3,211,777
Alderney	74,835
Guernsey	937,391
Jersey	1,491,424

* Highlands and Islands Airports Ltd (HIAL)
† Figure not supplied by airport
Source: Civil Aviation Authority

CAA, CAA House, 45–59 Kingsway, London WC2B 6TE T 020-7379 7311 W www.caa.co.uk

BAA, The Compass Centre, Nelson Road, London Heathrow Airport, Hounslow TW6 2GW T 020-8745 9800 W www.baa.com

Heathrow Airport	T 0844-335 1801
Southampton Airport	T 0844-481 7777
Stansted Airport	T 0844-335 1803
Aberdeen Airport	T 0844-481 6666
Edinburgh Airport	T 0844 481 8989
Glasgow Airport	T 0844 481 5555

BMI, Donington Hall, Castle Donington, Derby DE74 2SB T 01332-854000 W www.flybmi.com

BRITISH AIRWAYS, PO Box 365, Waterside, Harmondsworth UB7 0GB T 01805-266522 W www.britishairways.com

EASYJET, Hangar 89, London Luton Airport LU2 9PF T 0871-244 2366 W www.easyjet.com

MONARCH, Prospect House, Prospect Way, London Luton Airport LU2 9NU T 0871-225 0250 W www.monarch.co.uk

THOMAS COOK AIRLINES, Thomas Cook Business Park, Coningsby Road, Peterborough PE3 8SB T 0844-855 0515 W www.thomascookairlines.co.uk

THOMSON AIRWAYS, Wigmore House, Wigmore Place, Wigmore Lane, Luton, Bedfordshire LU2 9TN T 0844-871 1603 W www.thomson.co.uk

VIRGIN ATLANTIC, PO Box 747, Dunstable LU6 9AH T 0844-811 0000 W www.virgin-atlantic.com

RAILWAYS

The railway network in Britain was developed by private companies in the 19th century. In 1948 the main railway companies were nationalised and were run by a public authority, the British Transport Commission. The commission was replaced by the British Railways Board in 1963, operating as British Rail. On 1 April 1994, responsibility for managing the track and railway infrastructure passed to a newly formed company, Railtrack plc. In October 2001 Railtrack was put into administration under the Railways Act 1993 and Ernst and Young was appointed as administrator. In October 2002 Railtrack was taken out of administration and replaced by the not-for-profit company Network Rail. The British Railways Board continued as operator of all train services until 1996–7, when they were sold or franchised to the private sector.

The Strategic Rail Authority (SRA) was created to provide strategic leadership to the rail industry and formally came into being on 1 February 2001 following the passing of the Transport Act 2000. In January 2002 it published its first strategic plan, setting out the strategic priorities for Britain's railways over the next ten years. In addition to its coordinating role, the SRA was responsible for allocating government funding to the railways and awarding and monitoring the franchises for operating rail services.

On 15 July 2004 the transport secretary announced a new structure for the rail industry in the white paper *The Future of Rail*. These proposals were implemented under the Railways Act 2005, which abolished the Strategic Rail Authority, passing most of its functions to the Department for Transport; established the Rail Passengers Council (RPC) as a single national body, dissolving the regional committees; and gave devolved governments in Scotland and Wales more say in decisions at a local level. In addition, responsibility for railway safety regulation was transferred to the Office of Rail Regulation from the Health and Safety Executive.

OFFICE OF RAIL REGULATION

The Office of Rail Regulation (ORR) was established on 5 July 2004 by the Railways and Transport Safety Act 2003, replacing the Office of the Rail Regulator. As the railway industry's economic and safety regulator, the ORR's principal function is to regulate Network Rail's stewardship of the national network. The ORR also licenses operators of railway assets, approves agreements for access by operators to track, stations and light maintenance depots, and enforces domestic competition law. The ORR is led by a board appointed by the Secretary of State for Transport and chaired by Anna Walker.

SERVICES

For privatisation, under the Railways Act 1993, domestic passenger services were divided into 25 train operating units, which were franchised to private sector operators via a competitive tendering process. The train operators formed the Association of Train Operating Companies (ATOC) to act as the official voice of the passenger rail industry and provide its members with a range of services enabling them to comply with conditions imposed on them through their franchise agreements and operating licences.

As at June 2010 there were 29 passenger train operating companies: Arriva Trains Wales, c2c, Chiltern Railways, CrossCountry, East Midlands Trains, East Coast, Eurostar, First Capital Connect, First Great Western, First Hull Trains, First TransPennine Express, Gatwick Express, Grand Central, Heathrow Connect, Heathrow Express, Island Line Trains (Isle of Wight), London Midland, London Overground, London Underground, Merseyrail, National Express East Anglia, Northern Rail, ScotRail, South West Trains, Southeastern, Southern, Stansted Express, Virgin Trains and Wrexham & Shropshire.

Network Rail publishes a national timetable which contains details of rail services operated over the UK network and sea ferry services which provide connections with Ireland, the Isle of Man, the Isle of Wight, the Channel Islands and some European destinations.

The national rail enquiries service offers information about train times and fares for any part of the country, Transport for London (TfL) provides London-specific travel information for all modes of travel and Eurostar provides information for international channel tunnel rail services:

NATIONAL RAIL ENQUIRIES
T 0845-748 4950 W www.nationalrail.co.uk

TRANSPORT FOR LONDON
T 0843-222 1234 W www.tfl.gov.uk
EUROSTAR
T 08432-186186 W www.eurostar.com

PASSENGER FOCUS AND LONDON TRAVELWATCH

Passenger Focus is the operating name of the Rail Passengers' Council, a single national consumer body for rail, which is funded by the Department for Transport but whose independence is guaranteed by an act of parliament. Rail Users' Consultative Committees were set up under the Railways Act 1993 to protect the interests of users of the services and facilities provided on Britain's rail network. The Transport Act 2000 changed their name to Rail Passenger Committees (RPCs) and brought the committees under the overall sponsorship of the Strategic Rail Authority. There were eight RPCs nationwide, one for each of the six English regions and one each for Scotland and Wales. Under the Railways Act 2005, the eight regional committees were disbanded in June 2005 and their functions and duties transferred to the Rail Passengers' Council, the Strategic Rail Authority was abolished and sponsorship for the Rail Passengers' Council transferred to the Department for Transport.

Established in July 2000, London TravelWatch is the operating name of the official watchdog organisation representing the interests of transport users in and around the capital. Officially known as the London Transport Users' Committee, it is sponsored and funded by the London Assembly and is independent of the transport operators. London TravelWatch represents users of buses, the Underground, river and rail services in and around London, including Eurostar and Heathrow Express, Croydon Tramlink and the Docklands Light Railway. The interests of pedestrians, cyclists and motorists are also represented, as are those of taxi users.

FREIGHT

Rail freight services are provided by a small number of companies. On privatisation, British Rail's bulk freight operations were sold to English, Welsh and Scottish Railways (EWS). There are currently seven freight operating companies licensed to provide services for moving goods by rail: Colas Rail, Direct Rail Services, DB Schenker (formerly EWS), First GBRf (part of the First Group), Fastline and Freightliner Group and Freight Europe. The Department for Transport announced in June 2007 that £44m worth of funding would be awarded via the Rail Environmental Benefit Procurement Scheme over three years in order to encourage the movement of freight on rail that would otherwise be transported by road. In 2009–10 freight moved by rail amounted to 19.06 billion tonne-kilometres, a 7.6 per cent decrease from 2008–9.

NETWORK RAIL

Network Rail is responsible for the tracks, bridges, tunnels, level crossings, viaducts and 18 main stations that form Britain's rail network. In addition to providing the timetables for the passenger and freight operators, Network Rail is also responsible for all the signalling and electrical control equipment needed to operate the rail network and for monitoring and reporting performance across the industry.

Network Rail is a private company run as a commercial business; it is directly accountable to its members and regulated by the ORR. The members have similar rights to those of shareholders in a public company except they do not receive dividends or share capital and thereby have no financial or economic interest in Network Rail. All of Network Rail's profits are reinvested into maintaining and upgrading the rail infrastructure.

ASSOCIATION OF TRAIN OPERATING COMPANIES, 3rd Floor, 40 Bernard Street, London WC1N 1BY T 020-7841 8000 W www.atoc.org
LONDON TRAVELWATCH, 6 Middle Street, London EC1A 7JA T 020-7505 9000 W www.londontravelwatch.org.uk
NETWORK RAIL, Kings Place, 90 York Way, London N1 9AG T 020-7557 8000 W www.networkrail.co.uk
OFFICE OF RAIL REGULATION, 1 Kemble Street, London WC2B 4AN T 020-7282 2000 W www.rail-reg.gov.uk
PASSENGER FOCUS, Freepost (RRRE-ETTC-LEET), PO Box 4257, Manchester M60 3AR T 0300-123 2350 W www.passengerfocus.org.uk

RAIL SAFETY

On 1 April 2006 responsibility for health and safety policy and enforcement on the railways transferred from the Health and Safety Executive to the Office of Rail Regulation (ORR).

In 2008 a total of 28 passengers, railway staff and other members of the public were fatally injured in all rail incidents (excluding trespassers and suicides), compared with 27 in 2007.

ACCIDENTS ON RAILWAYS

	2007	*2008*
Train incident fatalities	5	4
Passengers	1	0
Railway employees	0	0
Others	4	4
Train incident injuries	110	27
Passengers	94	10
Railway staff	12	10
Others	3	7

TRESPASSERS, SUICIDES AND ATTEMPTED SUICIDES 2008

Fatalities	288
Injuries	156

Source: ORR – *National Rail Trends 2008–9 Yearbook*

OTHER RAIL SYSTEMS

Responsibility for the London Underground passed from the government to the Mayor and Transport for London on 15 July 2003, with a public-private partnership (PPP) already in place. Plans for a public-private partnership for London Underground were pushed through by the government in February 2002 despite opposition from the Mayor of London and a range of transport organisations. Under the PPP, long-term contracts with private companies were estimated to enable around £16bn to be invested in renewing and upgrading the Underground's infrastructure over 15 years. In July 2007, Metronet, which was responsible for two of three PPP contracts, went into administration; TfL took over both contracts. Responsibility for stations, trains, operations, signalling and safety remains in the public sector. In 2008–9 there were 1,089 million passenger journeys on the London Underground.

Britain has nine other light rail, tram or underground systems: Blackpool Trams, Croydon Tramlink, Docklands Light Railway (DLR), Glasgow Subway, Manchester

Metrolink, Midland Metro, Nottingham Express Transit (NET), Stagecoach Supertram in Sheffield and Tyne and Wear Metro.

Light rail and metro systems in Great Britain contributed to the growth in public transport, with 203 million passenger journeys in 2008–9, an increase of 1 per cent on the previous year. In England there were 189 million passenger journeys in 2008–9, compared with 124 million in 2000–1.

THE CHANNEL TUNNEL

The earliest recorded scheme for a submarine transport connection between Britain and France was in 1802. Tunnelling began simultaneously on both sides of the Channel three times: in 1881, in the early 1970s, and on 1 December 1987, when construction workers bored the first of the three tunnels which form the Channel Tunnel. Engineers 'holed through' the first tunnel (the service tunnel) on 1 December 1990 and tunnelling was completed in June 1991. The tunnel was officially inaugurated by the Queen and President Mitterrand of France on 6 May 1994.

The submarine link comprises two rail tunnels, each carrying trains in one direction, which measure 7.6m (24.93ft) in diameter. Between them lies a smaller service tunnel, measuring 4.8m (15.75ft) in diameter. The service tunnel is linked to the rail tunnels by 130 cross-passages for maintenance and safety purposes. The tunnels are 50km (31 miles) long, 38km (24 miles) of which is under the seabed at an average depth of 40m (132ft). The rail terminals are situated at Folkestone and Calais, and the tunnels go underground at Shakespeare Cliff, Dover, and Sangatte, west of Calais.

RAIL LINKS

The British Channel Tunnel Rail Link route runs from Folkestone to St Pancras station, London, with intermediate stations at Ashford and Ebbsfleet in Kent.

Construction of the rail link was financed by the private sector with a substantial government contribution. A private sector consortium, London and Continental Railways Ltd (LCR), comprising Union Railways and the UK operator of Eurostar, owns the rail link and was responsible for its design and construction. The rail link was constructed in two phases: phase one, from the Channel Tunnel to Fawkham Junction, Kent, began in October 1998 and opened to fare-paying passengers on 28 September 2003; phase two, from Southfleet Junction to St Pancras, was completed in November 2007.

There are direct services from the UK to Calais, Disneyland Paris, Lille and Paris in France and Brussels in Belgium. There are also direct services to Avignon in the south of France between July and September and during the winter months (December to April) to the French Alps. High-speed trains also run from Lille to the south of France.

Eurostar, the high-speed passenger train service, connects London with Paris in 2 hours 15 minutes, Brussels in 1 hour 51 minutes and Lille in 1 hour 20 minutes. There are Eurostar terminals at London St Pancras, Ashford and Ebbsfleet in Kent, Paris Gare Du Nord and Lille in France, and Brussels-South in Belgium.

ROADS

HIGHWAY AUTHORITIES

The powers and responsibilities of highway authorities in England and Wales are set out in the Highways Act 1980; for Scotland there is separate legislation.

Responsibility for motorways and other trunk roads in Great Britain rests in England with the Secretary of State for Transport, in Scotland with the Scottish government, and in Wales with the Welsh Assembly Government. The highway authority for non-trunk roads in England, Wales and Scotland is, in general, the local authority in whose area the roads lie. With the establishment of the Greater London Authority in July 2000, Transport for London became the highway authority for roads in London.

In Northern Ireland the Department of Regional Development is the statutory road authority responsible for public roads and their maintenance and construction; the Roads Service executive agency carries out these functions on behalf of the department.

FINANCE

In England all aspects of trunk road and motorway funding are provided directly by the government to the Highways Agency, which operates, maintains and improves a network of motorways and trunk roads around 7,050km (4,381 miles) long, on behalf of the secretary of state. Since 2001 the length of the network that the Highways Agency is responsible for has been decreasing owing to a policy of de-trunking, which transfers responsibility for non-core roads to local authorities. For the financial year 2010–11 the Highways Agency's total planned expenditure is £4,839m: £748m for maintenance, £1,348m for major improvements, £325m for traffic management and technology improvements and the remainder for other programmes and administration costs.

Government support for local authority capital expenditure on roads and other transport infrastructure is provided through grant and credit approvals as part of the Local Transport Plan (LTP). Local authorities bid for resources on the basis of a five-year programme built around delivering integrated transport strategies. As well as covering the structural maintenance of local roads and the construction of major new road schemes, LTP funding also includes smaller-scale safety and traffic management measures with associated improvements for public transport, cyclists and pedestrians.

For the financial year 2010–11, total allocated LTP funding amounted to £1,411m: £763m for formulaic maintenance, £602m for integrated transport measures and £46m for other maintenance.

Total expenditure by the Welsh Assembly Government on trunk roads, motorways, rail, bus and other transport services (including grants to local authorities) in 2009–10 was over £656m. Planned expenditure for 2010–11 is £615m.

Since 1 July 1999 all decisions on Scottish transport expenditure have been devolved to the Scottish government. Total expenditure on motorways and trunk roads in Scotland during 2009–10 was £1,182m (including cost of capital, depreciation and other annually managed expenditure charges). Planned expenditure for 2010–11 is £1,181m.

In Northern Ireland total expenditure by the Roads Service on all roads in 2009–10 was £226.7m, with £158.4m spent on trunk roads and motorways. Planned expenditure for 2010–11 is £265.7m, with £225.7m allocated for trunk roads and motorways.

The Transport Act 2000 gave English and Welsh local authorities (outside London) powers to introduce road-user charging or workplace parking levy schemes. The act requires that the net revenue raised is used to improve local transport services and facilities for at least ten years. The aim is to reduce congestion and encourage greater use of alternative modes of transport. Schemes developed by local authorities require government approval. The UK's first toll road, the M6 Toll, opened in December 2003 and runs for 43.5km (27 miles) around Birmingham from junction 3a to junction 11a on the M6.

Charging schemes in London are allowed under the 1999 Greater London Authority Act. The Central London Congestion Charge Scheme began on 17 February 2003 (*see also* Regional Government).

ROAD LENGTHS 2007
Kilometres

	England	*Wales*	*Scotland*	*Great Britain*
Motorways	3,011	141	407	3,559
Dual carriageway	6,604	549	783	7,936
Single carriageway	25,651	3,615	9,488	38,756
B roads	19,853	2,989	7,319	30,161
C roads	64,358	9,797	10,419	84,574
Unclassified roads	181,489	16,766	31,226	229,482
Total	300,967	33,858	59,642	394,467

Source: Department for Transport

FREIGHT TRANSPORT BY ROAD (GREAT BRITAIN) 2008
GOODS MOVED

By mode of working (billion tonne kilometres)	
All modes	151.7
Own account	48.9
Public haulage	102.9
By gross weight of vehicle (billion tonne kilometres)	
All vehicles	151.7
3.5–25 tonnes	14.1
Over 25 tonnes	137.6

GOODS LIFTED

By mode of working (million tonnes)	
All modes	1,734
Own account	748
Public haulage	986
By gross weight of vehicle (million tonnes)	
All vehicles	1,734
3.5–25 tonnes	230
Over 25 tonnes	1,504

Source: Department for Transport

ROAD TRAFFIC BY TYPE OF VEHICLE (GREAT BRITAIN) 2008
Million vehicle kilometres

All motor vehicles	508,900
Cars and taxis	401,700
Light vans	68,100
Other goods vehicles	28,700
Buses and coaches	5,200
Motorcycles	5,100
Pedal cycles	4,700

Source: Department for Transport

BUSES

The majority of bus services outside London are provided on a commercial basis by private operators. Local authorities have powers to subsidise services where needs are not being met by a commercial service.

The Transport Act 2000 outlines a ten-year transport plan intended to promote bus use, through agreements between local authorities and bus operators, and to improve the standard and efficiency of services. Funding for many new services has been made available through the rural bus grants and urban bus challenge schemes. In addition, the Bus Service Operators Grant (BSOG) is paid directly to bus operators by the government and reimburses the major part of the excise duty paid on the fuel used in operating locally registered bus services. In 2008–9 BSOG amounted to £504m.

Since April 2008 people aged 60 and over and disabled people who qualify under the categories listed in the Transport Act 2000 have been able to travel for free on any local bus across England between 9.30am and 11pm Monday to Friday and all day on weekends and bank holidays. Local authorities recompense operators for the reduced fare revenue. A similar scheme operates in Wales and within London, although there is no time restriction. In Scotland, people aged 60 and over and disabled people have been able to travel for free on any local or long-distance bus since April 2006.

In London, Transport for London (TfL) has overall responsibility for setting routes, service standards and fares for the bus network. Almost all routes are competitively tendered to commercial operators.

In Northern Ireland, passenger transport services are provided by Ulsterbus and Metro (formerly Citybus), two wholly owned subsidiaries of the Northern Ireland Transport Holding Company. Along with Northern Ireland Railways, Ulsterbus and Metro operate under the brand name of Translink and are publicly owned. Ulsterbus is responsible for virtually all bus services in Northern Ireland except Belfast city services, which are operated by Metro. People living in Northern Ireland aged 65 and over can travel on buses and trains for free once they have obtained a Senior SmartPass from Translink.

BUS PASSENGER JOURNEYS 2008–9 (LOCAL)
No. of journeys (millions)

England	4,555
London	2,149
Scotland	493
Wales	125
Total	5,174

Source: Department for Transport

TAXIS AND PRIVATE HIRE VEHICLES

A taxi is a public transport vehicle with fewer than nine passenger seats, which is licensed to 'ply for hire'. This distinguishes taxis from private hire vehicles which must be booked in advance through an operator. In London, taxis and private hire vehicles are licensed by the Public Carriage Office (PCO), part of TfL. Outside London, local authorities are responsible for the licensing of taxis and private hire vehicles operational in their respective administrative areas. At the end of March 2009 there were 71,000 licensed taxis in England.

ROAD SAFETY

In March 2000, the government published a new road safety strategy, *Tomorrow's Roads – Safer for Everyone,* which set casualty reduction targets for 2010. The targets included a 40 per cent reduction in the overall number of people killed or seriously injured in road accidents, a 50 per cent reduction in the number of children killed or seriously injured and a 10 per cent reduction in the slight casualty rate (per 100 million vehicle kilometres), all compared with the average for 1994–8.

There were just over 220,000 reported casualties on roads in Great Britain in 2009, 4 per cent fewer than in 2008. Child casualties overall fell by 6 per cent with 81 child fatalities, a reduction of more than a third compared to 2008 figures. Car user casualties decreased by 4 per cent on the 2008 level to 143,412 and fatalities decreased by 16 per cent to 1,059. Pedestrian casualties were 26,887 in 2009, 6 per cent less than 2008, while pedestrian deaths were 13 per cent lower compared to 2008 at 500. Compared to 2008, pedal cyclist casualties increased by 5 per cent to 17,064, although the number of pedal cyclists killed on British roads decreased by 10 per cent to 104.

ROAD ACCIDENT CASUALTIES 2009

	Fatal	*Serious*	*Slight*	*All Severities*
Average for 1994–8	3,578	44,078	272,272	319,928
England	1,880	21,320	173,534	196,734
Scotland	216	2,269	12,527	15,012
Wales	126	1,095	9,133	10,354
Great Britain	2,222	24,684	195,194	222,100

Source: Department for Transport

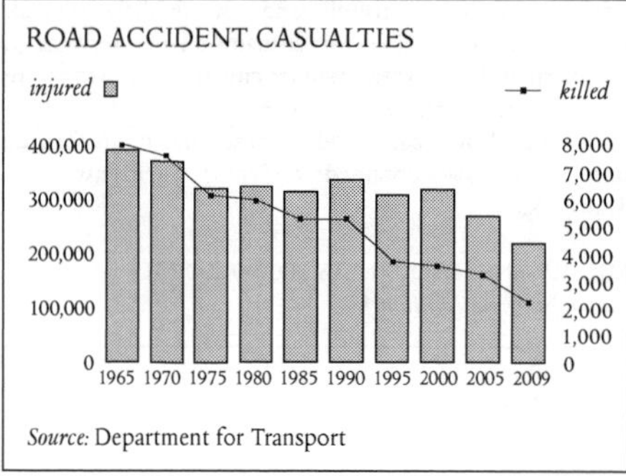

Source: Department for Transport

DRIVING LICENCES

It is necessary to hold a valid full licence in order to drive unaccompanied on public roads in the UK. Learner drivers must obtain a provisional driving licence before starting to learn to drive and must then pass theory and practical tests to obtain a full driving licence.

There are separate tests for driving motorcycles, cars, passenger-carrying vehicles (PCVs) and large goods vehicles (LGVs). Drivers must hold full car entitlement before they can apply for PCV or LGV entitlements.

The Driver and Vehicle Licensing Agency (DVLA) ceased the issue of paper licences in March 2000, but those currently in circulation will remain valid until they expire or the details on them change. The photocard driving licence was introduced to comply with the second EC directive on driving licences. This requires a photograph of the driver to be included on all UK licences issued from July 2001.

To apply for a first photocard driving licence, individuals are required to complete the form *Application for a Driving Licence* (D1).

The minimum age for driving motor cars, light goods vehicles up to 3.5 tonnes and motorcycles is 17 (moped, 16). Since June 1997, drivers who collect six or more penalty points within two years of qualifying lose their licence and are required to take another test. All forms and leaflets including *What You Need to Know About Driving Licences* (D100), are available from post offices, DVLA local offices and online (W www.dvla.gov.uk or W www.direct.gov.uk).

The DVLA is responsible for issuing driving licences, registering and licensing vehicles, and collecting excise duty in Great Britain. Driver and Vehicle Licensing Northern Ireland (DVLNI), part of the Driver and Vehicle Agency (DVA), has similar responsibilities in Northern Ireland.

DRIVING LICENCE FEES
As at June 2010

Provisional licence	
Car, motorcycle or moped	£50.00
Bus or lorry	Free
After disqualification until passing re-test	Free
Changing a provisional licence to a full licence	Free
Renewal	
Renewing the photo on the licence (must be renewed every 10 years)	£20.00
At age 70 and over	Free
For medical reasons	Free
Bus or lorry licence	Free
After disqualification	£65.00
After disqualification for some drink driving offences†	£90.00
After revocation	£50.00
Replacing a lost or stolen licence	£20.00
Adding an entitlement to a full licence	Free
Removing expired endorsements	
from a photocard licence	£20.00
from a paper licence (while exchanging it for a photocard licence)	£20.00
Exchanging	
a paper licence for a photocard licence	£20.00
a photocard for a photocard licence	£20.00
a full GB licence for a full Northern Ireland licence	Free
a full GB licence for a full EU/EEA or other foreign licence (including Channel Islands and Isle of Man)	Free
a full EU/EEA or other foreign licence (including Channel Islands and Isle of Man) for a full GB licence	£50.00
Change of name or address (existing licence must be surrendered)	Free

† For an alcohol-related offence where the DVLA needed to arrange medical enquiries

DRIVING TESTS

The Driving Standards Agency (DSA) is responsible for carrying out driving tests and approving driving instructors in Great Britain. Driver and Vehicle Testing, part of the Driver and Vehicle Agency, is responsible for testing drivers and vehicles in Northern Ireland.

DRIVING TESTS TAKEN AND PASSED
April 2009–March 2010

	Number Taken	*Percentage Passed*
Practical Test		
Car	1,532,780	46
Motorcycle Module 1*	50,778	61
Motorcycle Module 2*	37,866	70
Large goods vehicle	46,281	50
Passenger-carrying vehicle	9,021	52
Theory Test		
Car	1,348,123	64
Motorcycle	55,381	81
Large goods vehicle		
Multiple choice	25,782	80
Hazard perception	25,670	82
Passenger-carrying vehicle		
Multiple choice	7,593	79
Hazard perception	7,499	81

* Motorcycle tests are for the new style of testing and cover the period 27 April 2009 to 31 March 2010
Source: DSA

The theory and practical driving tests can be booked with a postal application, online (W www.direct.gov.uk/drivingtest) or by phone (T 0300-200 1122).

DRIVING TEST FEES (WEEKDAY/EVENING* AND WEEKEND)
As at June 2010

Theory tests	
Car and motorcycle	£31.00
Bus and lorry	
Multiple choice test	£35.00
Hazard perception test	£15.00
Driver Certificate of Professional Competence (CPC)	£30.00
Practical tests	
Car	£62.00/£75.00
Tractor and other specialist vehicles	£62.00/£75.00
Motorcycle	
Module 1	£15.50/£15.50
Module 2	£75.00/£88.50
Lorry and bus	£115.00/£141.00
Driver Certificate of Professional Competence (CPC)	£55.00/£63.00
Car and trailer	£115.00/£141.00
Extended tests for disqualified drivers	
Car	£124.00/£150.00
Motorcycle	
Module 1	£15.50/£15.50
Module 2	£150.00/£177.00

* After 4.30pm

VEHICLE LICENCES

Registration and first licensing of vehicles is through local offices of the DVLA in Swansea. Local facilities for relicensing are available at any post office which deals with vehicle licensing. Applicants will need to take their vehicle registration document (V5C) or, if this is not available, the applicant must complete form V62. Postal applications can be made to the post offices shown in the V100 booklet, which also provides guidance on registering and licensing vehicles. All forms and booklets are available at post offices, DVLA local offices and online (W www.dvla.gov.uk or W www.direct.gov.uk)

MOTOR VEHICLES LICENSED 2009 (GREAT BRITAIN)

	Thousands
All cars	28,459
Light goods vehicles	3,224
Motorcycles	1,292
Heavy goods vehicles	499
Buses and coaches	179
Other vehicles*	605
Total	34,258

* Includes rear diggers, lift trucks, rollers, ambulances, taxis, three-wheelers and agricultural vehicles
Source: Department for Transport

VEHICLE EXCISE DUTY

Details of the present duties chargeable on motor vehicles are available at DVLA local offices, post offices and online (W www.dvla.gov.uk or W www.direct.gov.uk). The Vehicle Excise and Registration Act 1994 provides *inter alia* that any vehicle kept on a public road but not used on roads is chargeable to excise duty as if it were in use. All non-commercial vehicles constructed before 1 January 1973 are exempt from vehicle excise duty. Any vehicle licensed on or after 31 January 1998, not in use and not kept on public roads must be registered as SORN (Statutory Off Road Notification) to be exempted from vehicle excise duty. From 1 January 2004 the registered keeper of a vehicle remains responsible for taxing a vehicle or making a SORN declaration until that liability is formally transferred to a new keeper.

RATES OF DUTY *from April 2010*

	12 months	6 months
Cars (private/light goods) registered before 1 March 2001		
Under 1,549cc	£125.00	£68.75
Over 1,549cc	£205.00	£112.75
Cars (private/light goods) registered on or after 1 March 2001	£200.00	£110.00
Euro 4 light goods vehicles registered between 1 March 2003 and 31 December 2006	£125.00	£68.75
Euro 5 light goods vehicles registered between 1 January 2009 and 31 December 2010	£125.00	£68.75
Motorcycles (with or without sidecar)		
Not over 150cc	£15.00	–
151–400cc	£33.00	–
401–600cc	£50.00	–
600cc+	£70.00	£38.50
Tricycles		
Not over 150cc	£15.00	–
All others	£70.00	£38.50
*Buses**		
Seating 10–17	£165.00	£90.75
Seating 18–36	£220.00	£121.00
Seating 37–61	£330.00	£181.50
Seating 62+	£500.00	£275.00

* Seating capacity includes driver. The 12-month rate for all reduced pollution buses is £165.00 and the 6-month rate is £90.75

RATES OF DUTY

Cars registered on or after 1 March 2001 and first-year rates*

Band	CO_2 Emissions 6 months (g/km)	Petrol and Diesel Car 12 months	6 months	Alternative Fuel Car 12 months	6 months
A	Up to 100	–	–	–	–
B	101–110	£20.00	–	£10.00	–
C	111–120	£30.00	–	£20.00	–
D	121–130	£90.00	£49.50	£80.00	£44.00
E	131–140	£110.00	£60.50	£100.00	£55.00
F	141–150	£125.00	£68.75	£115.00	£63.25
G	151–165	£155.00	£85.25	£145.00	£79.75
H	166–175	£180.00 (£250.00*)	£99.00	£170.00	£93.50
I	176–185	£200.00 (£300.00*)	£110.00	£190.00	£104.50
J	186–200	£235.00 (£425.00*)	£129.25	£225.00	£123.75
K†	201–225	£245.00 (£550.00*)	£134.75	£235.00	£129.25
L	226–255	£425.00 (£750.00*)	£233.75	£415.00	£228.25
M	255+	£435.00 (£950.00*)	£239.25	£425.00	£233.75

* From 1 April 2010, some new cars attracted a first-year rate for the first tax disc (figures in parentheses). From 1 April 2011 onwards, the standard rate applies

† Includes cars that have a CO_2 emission figure over 225g/km but were registered before 23 March 2006

MOT TESTING

Cars, motorcycles, motor caravans, light goods and dual-purpose vehicles more than three years old must be covered by a current MOT test certificate. However, some vehicles (ie minibuses, ambulances and taxis) may require a certificate at one year old. All certificates must be renewed annually. The MOT testing scheme is administered by the Vehicle and Operator Services Agency (VOSA) on behalf of the Secretary of State for Transport.

A fee is payable to MOT testing stations, which must be authorised to carry out tests. The current maximum fees are:

For cars, private hire and public service vehicles, motor caravans, dual purpose vehicles, ambulances and taxis (all up to eight passenger seats)	£54.85
For motorcycles	£29.65
For motorcycles with sidecar	£37.80
For three-wheeled vehicles (up to 450kg unladen weight)	£37.80
*Private passenger vehicles and ambulances with:	
9–12 passenger seats	£57.30 (£64.00)
13–16 passenger seats	£59.55 (£80.50)
16+ passenger seats	£80.65 (£124.50)
Goods vehicles (3,000–3,500kg)	£58.60

* Figures in parentheses include seatbelt installation check

SHIPPING AND PORTS

Sea trade has always played a central role in Britain's economy. By the 17th century Britain had built up a substantial merchant fleet and by the early 20th century it dominated the world shipping industry. Until the late 1990s the size and tonnage of the UK-registered trading fleet had been steadily declining. In December 1998 the government published *British Shipping: Charting a New Course,* which outlined strategies to promote the long-term interests of British shipping. By the end of 2009 the number of ships in the UK-flagged merchant fleet had increased by 79 per cent while gross tonnage had more than quadrupled since 1999. The UK-flagged merchant fleet now constitutes 1.3 per cent of the world merchant fleet in terms of vessels and 1.8 per cent in terms of gross tonnage.

Freight is carried by liner and bulk services, almost all scheduled liner services being containerised. About 95 per cent by weight of Britain's overseas trade is carried by sea; this amounts to 75 per cent of its total value. Passengers and vehicles are carried by roll-on, roll-off ferries, hovercraft, hydrofoils and high-speed catamarans. There were around 44 million ferry passengers in 2009, of whom 22 million travelled internationally.

Lloyd's of London provides the most comprehensive shipping intelligence service in the world. *Lloyd's Shipping Index,* published daily, lists some 25,000 ocean-going vessels and gives the latest known report of each.

PORTS

There are more than 650 ports in Great Britain for which statutory harbour powers have been granted. Of these about 120 are commercially significant ports. In 2009* the largest ports in terms of freight tonnage were Grimsby and Immingham (54.7 million tonnes), London (45.4 million tonnes), Milford Haven (39.3 million tonnes), Tees and Hartlepool (39.2 million tonnes), Southampton (37.2 million tonnes), Forth (36.7 million tonnes), Liverpool (29.9 million tonnes), Felixstowe (26.4 million tonnes), Dover (25.1 million tonnes) and Medway (13.1 million tonnes). Belfast is the principal freight port in Northern Ireland.

Broadly speaking, ports are owned and operated by private companies, local authorities or trusts. The largest operator is Associated British Ports which owns 21 ports. Provisional port traffic results show that 508.5 million tonnes were handled by UK ports in 2009, a decrease of 9.5 per cent on the previous year's figure of 562.2 million tonnes.

* Provisional data

MARINE SAFETY

The Maritime and Coastguard Agency is an executive agency of the Department for Transport. Working closely with the shipping industry and the public, it aims to:

- reduce accidents and accident-related deaths within UK search and rescue waters and coastline
- reduce accidents and accident-related deaths from UK-registered merchant ships and fishing vessels
- reduce the number of incidents of pollution from shipping activities in the UK pollution control zone

HM Coastguard maintains a 24-hour search and rescue response and coordination capability for the whole of the UK coast and the internationally agreed search and rescue region. HM Coastguard is responsible for mobilising and organising resources in response to people in distress at sea, or at risk of injury or death on the UK's cliffs or shoreline.

Locations hazardous to shipping in coastal waters are marked by lighthouses and other lights and buoys. The lighthouse authorities are the Corporation of Trinity House (for England, Wales and the Channel Islands), the Northern Lighthouse Board (for Scotland and the Isle of Man), and the Commissioners of Irish Lights (for Northern Ireland and the Republic of Ireland). Trinity House maintains 69 lighthouses, 10 light vessels/floats, 412 buoys, 19 beacons, 48 radar beacons and seven DGPS (Differential Global Positioning System) stations*. The Northern Lighthouse Board maintains 208 lighthouses, 165 buoys, 34 beacons, 27 radar beacons, eight AIS (automatic identification system) stations, four DGPS stations and one LORAN (long-range navigation) station; and Irish Lights looks after 80 lighthouses, 148 buoys, 45 beacons, 22 radar beacons, three DGPS stations, one LANBY (large automatic navigational buoy) with AIS in operation on ten lighthouses.

Harbour authorities are responsible for pilotage within their harbour areas; and the Ports Act 1991 provides for the transfer of lights and buoys to harbour authorities where these are used mainly for local navigation.

* DGPS is a satellite-based navigation system

UK-OWNED TRADING VESSELS

500 gross tons and over, as at end 2008

Type of vessel	*No.*	*Gross tonnage*
Tankers	145	5,827,000
Fully cellular container	104	4,886,000
Bulk carriers	70	3,214,000
Ro-Ro (passenger and cargo)	107	1,450,000
Passenger	25	1,360,000
Other general cargo	157	1,095,000
Specialised carriers	23	960,000
All vessels	631	18,792,000

Source: Department for Transport

UK SEA PASSENGER MOVEMENTS 2008

Type of journey	*No. of passenger movements*
International	
Ro-Ro Passengers on short sea routes	22,840,000
Passengers on cruises beginning or ending at UK ports*	1,341,000
Passengers on long sea journeys	72,000
Total	24,254,000

* Passengers are included at both departure and arrival if their journeys begin and end at a UK seaport

Source: Department for Transport

MARINECALL WEATHER FORECAST SERVICE

Marinecall offers a wide range of inshore, offshore and European forecasts from the Met Office which include gale and strong wind warnings, the general situation, wind speed and direction, probability and strength of gusts, developing weather conditions, visibility and sea state. Information is provided by various means including telephone, fax, SMS etc. Marinecall 10-day forecasts contain a 48-hour inshore waters forecast for the coastal area and up to 12 miles offshore, followed by a 1–5 day forecast for the local sea area, 6–10 day national forecast and an outlook for the month ahead. In addition fax forecasts provide an Atlantic surface pressure chart and 24-hour offshore forecast maps. Other services such as area specific, current weather reports and 48-hour forecasts are also available.

MARINECALL 10-DAY FORECAST

	By Phone	By Fax
INSHORE AREA	09068-500+	09065-300+
Cape Wrath – Rattray Head	451	251
Rattray Head – Berwick	452	252
Berwick – Whitby	453	253
Whitby – Gibraltar Point	454	254
Gibraltar Point – North Foreland	455	255
North Foreland – Selsey Bill	456	256
Selsey Bill – Lyme Regis	457	257
Lyme Regis – Hartland Point	458	258
Hartland Point – St David's Head	459	259
St David's Head – Great Ormes Head	460	260
Great Ormes Head – Mull of Galloway	461	261
Mull of Galloway – Mull of Kintyre	462	262
Mull of Kintyre – Ardnamurchan	463	263
Ardnamurchan – Cape Wrath	464	264
Lough Foyle – Carlingford Lough	465	265
Channel Islands	432	–
OFFSHORE AREA		
English Channel	992	270
Southern North Sea	991	271
Irish Sea	954	273
Biscay	953	274
North-west Scotland	955	275
Northern North Sea	985	276

Marinecall by UK landline is charged at 60p per minute and Marinecall by fax at £1.50 per minute. Calls from mobiles may be subject to network operator surcharges. Subscription packages are available.

UK SHIPPING FORECAST AREAS

Weather bulletins for shipping are broadcast daily on BBC Radio 4 at 00h 48m, 05h 20m, 12h 01m and 17h 54m. All transmissions are broadcast on long wave at 1515m (198kHz) and the 00h 48m and 05h 20m transmissions are also broadcast on FM. The bulletins consist of a gale warning summary, general synopsis, sea-area forecasts and coastal station reports. In addition, gale warnings are broadcast at the first available programme break after receipt. If this does not coincide with a news bulletin, the warning is repeated after the next news bulletin. Shipping forecasts and gale warnings are also available online (W www.bbc.co.uk/weather/coast/shipping).

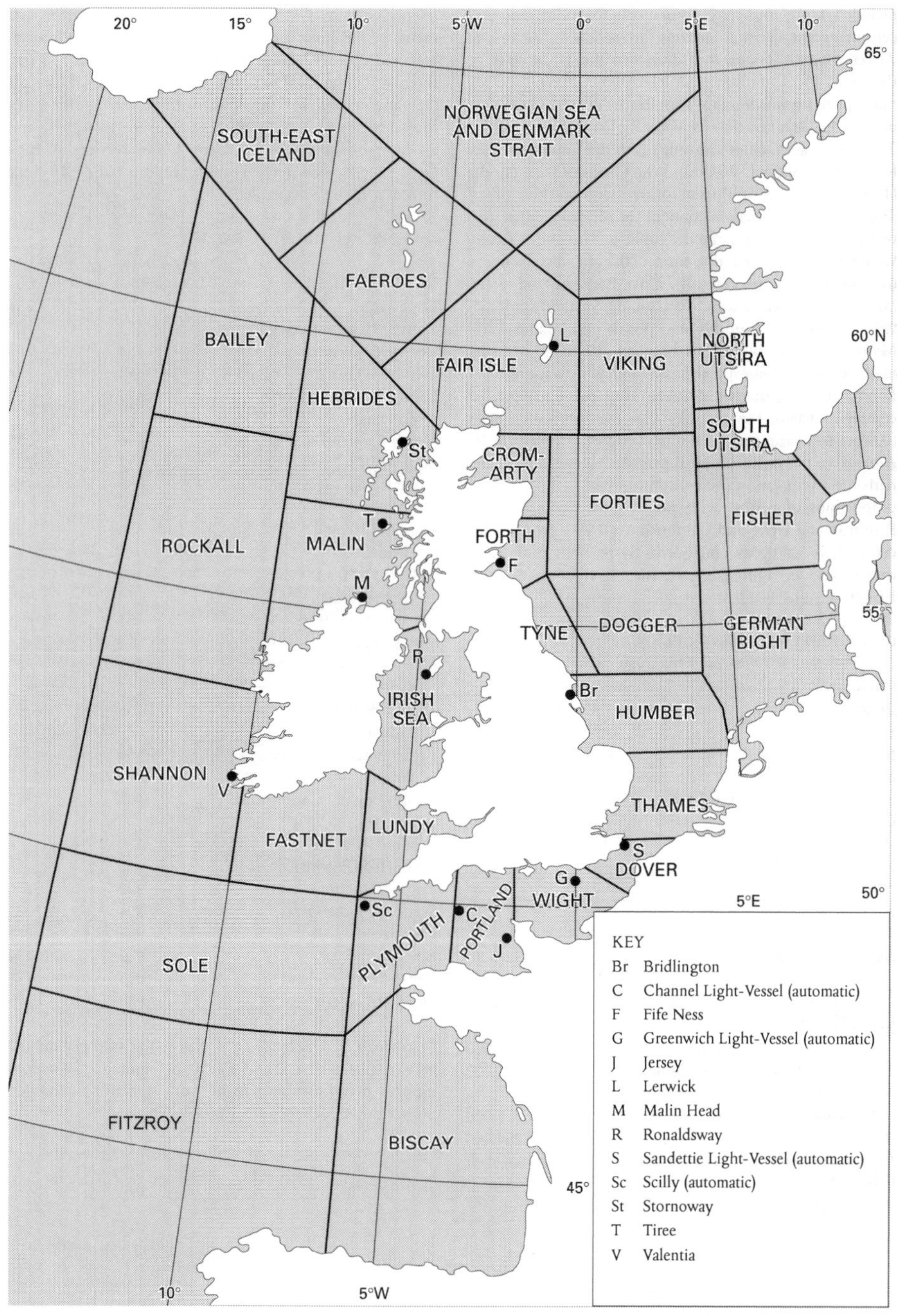

RELIGION IN THE UK

The 2001 census included a voluntary question on religion for the first time (although the question had been included in previous censuses in Northern Ireland); 92 per cent of people chose to answer the question. In the UK, 71.6 per cent of people in Britain identified themselves as Christian (42.1 million people). After Christianity, the next most prevalent faith was Islam with 2.7 per cent describing their religion as Muslim (1.6 million people). The next largest religious groups were Hindus (559,000), followed by Sikhs (336,000), Jews (267,000), Buddhists (152,000) and people from other religions (179,000). Together, these groups accounted for less than 3 per cent of the total UK population. People in Northern Ireland were most likely to say that they identified with a religion (86 per cent) compared with 77 per cent in England and Wales and 67 per cent in Scotland. The English counties with the highest proportion of Christians are Durham, Merseyside and Cumbria, each with 82 per cent or more; in Wales it is Ynys Mon (Isle of Anglesey) (79 per cent). London has the highest proportion of Muslims (8.5 per cent), Hindus (4.1 per cent), Jews (2.1 per cent), Buddhists (0.8 per cent) and people of other religions (0.5 per cent). Around 16 per cent of the UK population stated that they had no religion. The districts with the highest proportions of people with no religion were Norwich, Brighton and Hove and Cambridge, all with over 25 per cent. This category included those who identified themselves as agnostics, atheists, heathens and Jedi Knights.

CENSUS 2001 RESULTS — RELIGIONS IN THE UK

	thousands	*per cent*
Christian	42,079	71.6
Buddhist	152	0.3
Hindu	559	1.0
Jewish	267	0.5
Muslim	1,591	2.7
Sikh	336	0.6
Other religion	179	0.3
All religions	45,163	76.8
No religion	9,104	15.5
Not stated	4,289	7.3
All no religion/not stated	13,626	23.2
TOTAL	58,789	100

Source: Census 2001

INTER-CHURCH AND INTER-FAITH COOPERATION

The main umbrella body for the Christian churches in the UK is Churches Together in Britain and Ireland. There are also ecumenical bodies in each of the constituent countries of the UK: Churches Together in England, Action of Churches Together in Scotland, CYTUN (Churches Together in Wales), and the Irish Council of Churches. The Free Churches Group (formerly the Free Churches Council), which is closely associated with Churches Together in England, represents most of the free churches in England and Wales, and the Evangelical Alliance represents evangelical Christians.

The Inter Faith Network for the United Kingdom promotes cooperation between faiths, and the Council of Christians and Jews works to improve relations between the two religions. Churches Together in Britain and Ireland also has a commission on inter-faith relations.

ACTION OF CHURCHES TOGETHER IN SCOTLAND, Inglewood House, Alloa, Clackmannanshire FK10 2HU T 01259-216980 W www.acts-scotland.org
General Secretary, Brother Stephen Smyth

CHURCHES TOGETHER IN BRITAIN AND IRELAND, 39 Eccleston Square, London SW1V 1BX T 020-7901 4890 E info@ctbi.org.uk W www.ctbi.org.uk
General Secretary, Revd Bob Fyffe

CHURCHES TOGETHER IN ENGLAND, 27 Tavistock Square, London WC1H 9HH T 020-7529 8131 E office@cte.org.uk W www.churches-together.net
General Secretary, Revd Dr David Cornick

COUNCIL OF CHRISTIANS AND JEWS, 1st Floor, Camelford House, 87–89 Albert Embankment, London SE1 7TP T 020-7820 0090 E cjrelations@ccj.org.uk W www.ccj.org.uk
Chief Executive, David Gifford

CYTUN (CHURCHES TOGETHER IN WALES), 58 Richmond Road, Cardiff CF24 3UR T 029-2046 4375 E post@scytun.org.uk W www.cytun.org.uk
Chief Executive, Revd Aled Edwards, OBE

EVANGELICAL ALLIANCE, 186 Kennington Park Road, London SE11 4BT T 020-7207 2100 E info@eauk.org W www.eauk.org
General Director, Steve Clifford

FREE CHURCHES GROUP, 27 Tavistock Square, London WC1H 9HH T 020-7529 8131 E freechurch@cte.org.uk
Executive Secretary, Revd Mark Fisher

INTER-FAITH NETWORK FOR THE UK, 8A Lower Grosvenor Place, London SW1W 0EN T 020-7931 7766 E ifnet@interfaith.org.uk W www.interfaith.org.uk
Director, Dr Harriet Crabtree

IRISH COUNCIL OF CHURCHES, Inter-Church Centre, 48 Elmwood Avenue, Belfast BT9 6AZ T 028-9066 3145 E info@irishchurches.org W www.irishchurches.org
General Secretary, Michael Earle

RELIGIONS AND BELIEFS

BAHA'I FAITH

Mirza Husayn-'Ali, known as *Baha'u'llah* (Glory of God) was born in Iran in 1817 and became a follower of the *Bab,* a religious reformer and prophet who was imprisoned for his beliefs and executed on the grounds of heresy in 1850. Baha'u'llah was himself imprisoned in 1852, and in 1853 he had a vision that he was the 'promised one' foretold by the Bab. He was exiled after his release from prison and eventually arrived in Acre, now in Israel, where he continued to compose the Baha'i sacred scriptures. He died in 1892 and was succeeded by his son, Abdu'l-Baha, as spiritual leader, under whose guidance the faith spread to Europe and North America. He was followed by Shoghi Effendi, his grandson, who translated many of Baha'u'llah's works into English. Upon his death in 1957, a democratic system of leadership was brought into operation.

The Baha'i faith espouses the unity and relativity of religious truth and teaches that there is only one God, whose will has been revealed to mankind by a series of messengers, such as Zoroaster, Abraham, Moses, Buddha, Krishna, Christ, Muhammad, the Bab and Baha'u'llah, who were seen as the founders of separate religions, but whose common purpose was to bring God's message to mankind. It teaches that all races and both sexes are equal and deserving of equal opportunities and treatment, that education is a fundamental right and encourages a fair distribution of wealth. In addition, the faith exhorts mankind to establish a world federal system to promote peace and tolerance.

A feast is held every 19 days, which consists of prayer and readings of Baha'i scriptures, consultation on community business, and social activities. Music, food and beverages usually accompany the proceedings. There is no clergy; each local community elects a local assembly, which coordinates community activities, enrols new members, counsels and assists members in need, and conducts Baha'i marriages and funerals. A national assembly is elected annually by locally elected delegates, and every five years the national spiritual assemblies meet together to elect the Universal House of Justice, the supreme international governing body of the Baha'i Faith. Worldwide there are over 13,000 local spiritual assemblies; there are around five million members residing in about 235 countries, of which 179 have national organisations.

THE BAHA'I OFFICE OF PUBLIC INFORMATION, 27 Rutland Gate, London SW7 1PD **T** 020-7584 2566 **E** opi@bahai.org.uk **W** www.bahai.org.uk

Secretary of the National Spiritual Assembly, Dr Kishan Manocha

Director, Office of Public Information, Barney Leith

BUDDHISM

Buddhism originated in what is now the Bihar area of northern India in the teachings of Siddhartha Gautama, who became the *Buddha* (Enlightened One). In the Thai or Suriyakati calendar the beginning of the Buddhist era is dated from death of Buddha; the year 2011 is therefore 2554 by the Thai Buddhist reckoning.

Fundamental to Buddhism is the concept of rebirth, whereby each life carries with it the consequences of the conduct of earlier lives (known as the law of *karma*) and this cycle of death and rebirth is broken only when the state of *nirvana* has been reached. Buddhism steers a middle path between belief in personal continuity and the belief that death results in total extinction.

While doctrine does not have a pivotal position in Buddhism, a statement of four 'Noble Truths' is common to all its schools and varieties. These are: suffering is inescapable in even the most fortunate of existences; craving is the root cause of suffering; abandonment of the selfish mindset is the way to end suffering; and bodily and mental discipline, accompanied by the cultivation of wisdom and compassion, provides the spiritual path ('Noble Eightfold Path') to accomplish this. Buddhists deny the idea of a creator and prefer to emphasise the practical aspects of moral and spiritual development.

The schools of Buddhism can be broadly divided into three: *Theravada,* the generally monastic-led tradition practised in Sri Lanka and South-East Asia; *Mahayana,* the philosophical and popular traditions of the Far East; and *Esoteric,* the Tantric-derived traditions found in Tibet and Mongolia and, to a lesser extent, China and Japan. The extensive Theravada scriptures are contained in the *Pali Canon,* which dates in its written form from the first century BC. Mahayana and Esoteric schools have Sanskrit-derived translations of these plus many more additional scriptures as well as exegetical material.

In the East the new and full moons and the lunar quarter days were (and to a certain extent, still are) significant in determining the religious calendar. Most private homes contain a shrine where offerings, worship and other spiritual practices (such as meditation, chanting or mantra recitation) take place on a daily basis. Buddhist festivals vary according to local traditions within the different schools and there is little uniformity – even in commemorating the birth, enlightenment and death of the Buddha.

There is no governing authority for Buddhism in the UK. Communities representing all schools of Buddhism operate independently. The Buddhist Society was established in 1924; it runs courses, lectures and meditation groups, and publishes books about Buddhism. The Network of Buddhist Organisations was founded in 1993 to promote fellowship and dialogue between Buddhist organisations and to facilitate cooperation in matters of common interest.

There are estimated to be at least 300 million Buddhists worldwide. Of the 152,000 Buddhists in the UK (according to the 2001 census), 60,000 are white British (the majority are converts), 36,000 Chinese, 15,000 Asian and 36,000 'other ethnic'.

THE BUDDHIST SOCIETY, 58 Eccleston Square, London SW1V 1PH **T** 020-7834 5858 **E** info@thebuddhistsociety.org **W** www.thebuddhistsociety.org

FRIENDS OF THE WESTERN BUDDHIST ORDER, The London Buddhist Centre, 51 Roman Road, London E2 0HU **T** 0845-458 4716 **E** info@lbc.org.uk **W** www.fwbo.org

THE NETWORK OF BUDDHIST ORGANISATIONS, PO Box 4147, Maidenhead SL60 1DN **T** 0845-345 8978 **E** secretary@nbo.org.uk **W** www.nbo.org.uk

THE OFFICE OF TIBET, Tibet House, 1 Culworth Street, London NW8 7AF **T** 020-7722 5378 **E** samdup@tibet.com **W** www.tibet.com

Representative of HH the Dalai Lama, Thubten Samdup

SOKA GAKKAI INTERNATIONAL (UK), Taplow Court Grand Cultural Centre, Taplow, Berkshire SL6 0ER **T** 01628-773163 **W** www.sgi-uk.org

CHRISTIANITY

Christianity is a monotheistic faith based on the person and teachings of Jesus Christ, and all Christian denominations claim his authority. Central to its teaching is the concept of God and his son Jesus Christ, who was crucified and resurrected in order to enable mankind to attain salvation.

The Jewish scriptures predicted the coming of a *Messiah,* an 'anointed one', who would bring salvation. To Christians, Jesus of Nazareth, a Jewish rabbi (teacher) who was born in Palestine, was the promised Messiah. Jesus' birth, teachings, crucifixion and subsequent resurrection are recorded in the *Gospels,* which, together with other scriptures that summarise Christian belief, form the *New Testament.* This, together with the Hebrew scriptures – entitled the *Old Testament* by Christians – makes up the Bible, the sacred texts of Christianity.

Christians believe that sin distanced mankind from God, and that Jesus was the son of God, sent to redeem mankind from sin by his death. In addition, many believe that Jesus will return again at some future date, triumph over evil and establish a kingdom on earth, thus inaugurating a new age. The Gospel assures Christians that those who believe in Jesus and obey his teachings will be forgiven their sins and will be resurrected from the dead.

The Apostles were Jesus' first converts and are recognised by Christians as the founders of the Christian community. Early Christianity spread rapidly throughout the eastern provinces of the Roman Empire but was subjected to great persecution until AD 313, when Emperor Constantine's Edict of Toleration confirmed its right to exist. Christianity was established as the religion of the Roman Empire in AD 381.

Between AD 325 and 787 there were seven Oecumenical Councils at which bishops from the entire Christian world assembled to resolve various doctrinal disputes. The estrangement between East and West began after Constantine moved the centre of the Roman Empire from Rome to Constantinople, and it grew after the division of the Roman Empire into eastern and western halves. Linguistic and cultural differences between Greek East and Latin West served to encourage separate ecclesiastical developments which became pronounced in the tenth and early 11th centuries. Administration of the church was divided between five ancient patriarchates: Rome and all the West, Constantinople (the imperial city – the 'New Rome'), Jerusalem and all of Palestine, Antioch and all the East and Alexandria and all of Africa. Of these, only Rome was in the Latin West and after the schism in 1054, Rome developed a structure of authority centralised on the Papacy, while the Orthodox East maintained the style of localised administration. Papal authority over the doctrine and jurisdiction of the church in Western Europe was unrivalled after the split with the Eastern Orthodox Church until the Protestant Reformation in the 16th century.

Christian practices vary widely between different Christian churches, but prayer, charity and giving (for the maintenance of the church buildings, for the work of the church, and to those in need) are common to all. In addition, certain days of observance, ie the *Sabbath, Easter* and *Christmas,* are celebrated by most Christians. The Orthodox, Roman Catholic and Anglican churches celebrate many more days of observance, based on saints and significant events in the life of Jesus. The belief in sacraments, physical signs believed to have been ordained by Jesus Christ to symbolise and convey spiritual gifts, varies greatly between Christian denominations; *baptism* and the *Eucharist* are practised by most Christians. Baptism, symbolising repentance and faith in Jesus, is an act marking entry into the Christian community; the Eucharist, the ritual re-enactment of the Last Supper, Jesus' final meal with his disciples, is also practised by most denominations. Other sacraments, such as anointing the sick, the laying on of hands to symbolise the passing on of the office of priesthood or to heal the sick and speaking in tongues, where it is believed that the person is possessed by the Holy Spirit, are less common. In denominations where infant baptism is practised, confirmation (where the person confirms the commitments made on their behalf in infancy) is common. Matrimony and the ordination of priests are also widely believed to be sacraments. Many Protestants regard only baptism and the Eucharist to be sacraments; the Quakers and the Salvation Army reject the use of sacraments.

See Churches for contact details of the Church of England, the Roman Catholic Church and other Christian churches in the UK.

HINDUISM

Hinduism has no historical founder but had become highly developed in India by *c.*2500 BC. Its adherents originally called themselves Aryans; Muslim invaders first called the Aryans 'Hindus' (derived from 'Sindhu', the name of the river Indus) in the eighth century.

Most Hindus hold that *satya* (truthfulness), honesty, sincerity and devotion to God are essential for good living. They believe in one supreme spirit *(Brahman),* and in the transmigration of *atman* (the soul). Most Hindus accept the doctrine of *karma* (consequences of actions), the concept of *samsara* (successive lives) and the possibility of all atmans achieving *moksha* (liberation from samsara) through *jnana* (knowledge), *yoga* (meditation), *karma* (work or action) and *bhakti* (devotion).

Most Hindus offer worship to *murtis* (images of deities) representing different incarnations or aspects of Brahman, and follow their *dharma* (religious and social duty) according to the traditions of their *varna* (social class), *ashrama* (stage in life), *jaiti* (caste) and *kula* (family).

Hinduism's sacred texts are divided into *shruti* ('that which is heard'), including the *Vedas,* and *smriti* ('that which is remembered'), including the *Ramayana,* the *Mahabharata,* the *Puranas* (ancient myths), and the sacred law books. Most Hindus recognise the authority of the *Vedas,* the oldest holy books, and accept the philosophical teachings of the *Upanishads,* the *Vedanta Sutras* and the *Bhagavad-Gita.*

Hindus believe Brahman to be omniscient, omnipotent, limitless and all-pervading. Brahman is usually worshipped in its deity form. Brahma, Vishnu and Shiva are the most important deities or aspects of Brahman worshipped by Hindus; their respective consorts are Saraswati, Lakshmi and Durga or Parvati, also known as Shakti. There are believed to have been ten *avatars* (incarnations) of Vishnu, of whom the most important are Rama and Krishna. Other popular gods are Ganesha, Hanuman and Subrahmanyam. All Hindu gods are seen as aspects of the supreme spirit (Brahman), not as competing deities.

Orthodox Hindus revere all gods and goddesses equally, but there are many denominations, including the Hare-Krishna movement (ISKCon), the Arya Samaj and the Swaminarayan Hindu mission, in which worship is concentrated on one deity. The *guru* (spiritual teacher) is seen as the source of spiritual guidance.

Hinduism does not have a centrally trained and ordained priesthood. The pronouncements of the *shankaracharyas* (heads of monasteries) of Shringeri, Puri, Dwarka and Badrinath are heeded by the orthodox but may be ignored by the various sects.

The commonest form of worship is *puja,* in which water, flowers, food, fruit, incense and light are offered to the deity. Puja may be done either in a home shrine or a *mandir* (temple). Many British Hindus celebrate *samskars* (purification rites), to name a baby, for the sacred thread (an initiation ceremony), marriage and cremation.

The largest communities of Hindus in Britain are in Leicester, London, Birmingham and Bradford, and developed as a result of immigration from India, eastern Africa and Sri Lanka.

There are an estimated 800 million Hindus worldwide; there are around 559,000 adherents, according to the 2001 UK census, and over 140 temples in the UK.

ARYA SAMAJ LONDON, 69A Argyle Road, London W13 0LY T 020-8991 1732
E aryasamajlondon@yahoo.co.uk
General Secretary, Amrit Lal Bhardwaj

BHARATIYA VIDYA BHAVAN, Institute of Indian Art and Culture, 4A Castletown Road, London W14 9HE
T 020-7381 3086 E info@bhavan.net W www.bhavan.net
Executive Director, Dr M. N. Nandakumara

INTERNATIONAL SOCIETY FOR KRISHNA CONSCIOUSNESS (ISKCON), Bhaktivedanta Manor, Dharam Marg, Hilfield Lane, Aldenham, Watford, Herts WD25 8EZ T 01923-851000 E info@krishnatemple.com
W www.krishnatemple.com
Temple Chair, Sruti Dharma Das

NATIONAL COUNCIL OF HINDU TEMPLES (UK), 1 Hans Close, Stoke, Coventry CV2 4WA T 0780-505 4776
E sanjay.jagatia@ntlworld.com W www.nchtuk.org
General Secretary, Sanjay Jagatia

SWAMINARAYAN HINDU MISSION (SHRI SWAMINARAYAN MANDIR), 105–119 Brentfield Road, London NW10 8LD T 020-8965 2651 E info@mandir.org
W www.mandir.org

HUMANISM

Humanism traces its roots back to ancient times, with Indian, Chinese, Greek and Roman philosophers expressing Humanist ideas some 2,500 years ago. Confucius, the Chinese philosopher who lived *c.*500 BC, believed that religious observances should be replaced with moral values as the basis of social and political order and that 'the true way' is based on reason and humanity. He also stressed the importance of benevolence and respect for others, and believed that the individual situation should be considered rather than the global application of traditional rules.

Humanists believe that there is no God or other supernatural being, that humans have only one life (Humanists do not believe in an afterlife or reincarnation) and that humans can live ethical and fulfilling lives without religious beliefs through a moral code derived from a shared history, personal experience and thought. There are no sacred Humanist texts. Particular emphasis is placed on science as the only reliable source of knowledge of the universe. Many Humanists recognise a need for ceremonies to mark important occasions in life and the British Humanist Association has a network of celebrants who are trained and accredited to conduct baby namings, weddings and funerals. The British Humanist Association's campaigns for a secular society (a society based on freedom of religious or non-religious belief with no privileges for any particular set of beliefs) are based on equality and human rights. The association also campaigns for inclusive schools that meet the needs of all parents and pupils, regardless of their religious or non-religious beliefs.

BRITISH HUMANIST ASSOCIATION, 1 Gower Street, London WC1E 6HD T 020-7079 3580 F 020-7079 3588
E info@humanism.org.uk W www.humanism.org.uk
Chief Executive, Andrew Copson

ISLAM

Islam (which means 'peace arising from submission to the will of Allah' in Arabic) is a monotheistic religion which was taught in Arabia by the Prophet Muhammad, who was born in Mecca (Al-Makkah) in 570 AD. Islam spread to Egypt, north Africa, Spain and the borders of China in the century following the Prophet's death, and is now the predominant religion in Indonesia, the near and Middle East, northern and parts of western Africa, Pakistan, Bangladesh, Malaysia and some of the former Soviet republics. There are also large Muslim communities in other countries.

For Muslims (adherents of Islam), there is one God *(Allah)*, who holds absolute power. Muslims believe that Allah's commands were revealed to mankind through the prophets, who include Abraham, Moses and Jesus, but that Allah's message was gradually corrupted until revealed finally and in perfect form to Muhammad through the angel *Jibril* (Gabriel) over a period of 23 years. This last, incorruptible message is said to have been recorded in the *Qur'an* (Koran), which contains 114 divisions called *surahs,* each made up of *ayahs* of various lengths, and is held to be the essence of all previous scriptures. The *Ahadith* are the records of the Prophet Muhammad's deeds and sayings (the *Sunnah*) as practised and recounted by his immediate followers. A culture and a system of law and theology gradually developed to form a distinctive Islamic civilisation. Islam makes no distinction between sacred and worldly affairs and provides rules for every aspect of human life. The *Shariah* is the sacred law of Islam based primarily upon prescriptions derived from the *Qur'an* and the *Sunnah* of the Prophet.

The 'five pillars of Islam' are *shahadah* (a declaration of faith in the oneness and supremacy of Allah and the messengership of Muhammad); *salat* (formal prayer, to be performed five times a day facing the *Ka'bah* (the most sacred shrine in the holy city of Mecca)); *zakat* (welfare due, paid annually on all savings at the rate of 2.5 per cent); *sawm* (fasting during the month of Ramadan from dawn until sunset); and *hajj* (pilgrimage to Mecca made once in a lifetime if the believer is financially and physically able). Some Muslims would add *jihad* as the sixth pillar (striving for the cause of good and resistance to evil).

Two main groups developed among Muslims. *Sunni* Muslims accept the legitimacy of Muhammad's first four *caliphs* (successors as head of the Muslim community) and of the authority of the Muslim community as a whole. About 90 per cent of Muslims are Sunni Muslims.

Shi'ites recognise only Muhammad's son-in-law Ali as his rightful successor and the *Imams* (descendants of Ali, not to be confused with *imams,* who are prayer leaders or religious teachers) as the principal legitimate religious authority. The largest group within Shi'ism is *Twelver Shi'ism,* which has been the official school of law and theology in Iran since the 16th century; other subsects include the *Ismailis,* the *Druze* and the *Alawis,* the latter two differing considerably from the main body of Muslims. The *Ibadis* of Oman are neither Sunni nor Shia, deriving from the strictly observant *Khariji* (Seceeders). There is no organised priesthood, but learned men such as imams, *ulama,* and *ayatollahs* are accorded great respect. The *Sufis* are the mystics of Islam. Mosques are centres for worship and teaching and also for social and welfare activities.

Islam was first recorded in western Europe in the eighth century AD when 800 years of Muslim rule began in Spain. Later, Islam spread to eastern Europe. More recently, Muslims came to Europe from Africa, the Middle East and Asia in the late 19th century. Both the Sunni and Shi'a traditions are represented in Britain, but the majority of Muslims in Britain adhere to Sunni Islam. Efforts to establish a representative national body for Muslims in Britain resulted in the founding, in 1997, of the Muslim Council of Britain. In addition, there are many other Muslim organisations in the UK. There are around 1,200 million Muslims worldwide, with nearly two million adherents and about 1,650 mosques in the UK.

IMAMS AND MOSQUES COUNCIL, 20–22 Creffield Road, London W5 3RP T 020-8992 6636 E msraza@muslimcollege.ac.uk
Director, Moulana M. S. Raza

ISLAMIC CULTURAL CENTRE – THE LONDON CENTRAL MOSQUE, 146 Park Road, London NW8 7RG T 020-7725 2213 E info@iccuk.org W www.iccuk.org
Director, Dr Ahmad Al-Dubayan

MUSLIM COUNCIL OF BRITAIN, PO Box 57330, London E1 2WJ T 0845-262 6786 E admin@mcb.org.uk W www.mcb.org.uk

MUSLIM WORLD LEAGUE LONDON, 46 Goodge Street, London W1T 4LU T 020-7636 7568
Director, Dr Ahmad Makhoodom

UNION OF MUSLIM ORGANISATIONS OF THE UK AND IRELAND, 109 Campden Hill Road, London W8 7TL T 020-7581 9236
Secretary-General, Dr Syed A. Pasha

JAINISM

Jainism traces its history to Vardhamana Jnatriputra, known as *Tirthankara Mahavira* (the Great Hero) whose traditional dates were 599–527 BC. Jains believe he was the last of a series of 24 *Jinas* (those who overcome all passions and desires) or *Tirthankaras* (those who show a way across the ocean of life) stretching back to remote antiquity. Born to a noble family in north-eastern India (the state of Bihar), he renounced the world for the life of a wandering ascetic and after 12 years of austerity and meditation he attained enlightenment. He then preached his message until, at the age of 72, he left the mortal world and achieved total liberation *(moksha)* from the cycle of death and rebirth.

Jains declare that the Hindu rituals of transferring merit are not acceptable as each living being is responsible for its own actions. They recognise some of the minor deities of the Hindu pantheon, but the supreme objects of worship are the Tirthankaras. The pious Jain does not ask favours from the Tirthankaras, but seeks to emulate their example in his or her own life.

Jains believe that the universe is eternal and self-subsisting, that there is no omnipotent creator God ruling it and the destiny of the individual is in his or her own hands. *Karma,* the fruit of past actions, is believed to determine the place of every living being and rebirth may be in the heavens, on earth as a human, an animal or other lower being, or in the hells. The ultimate goal of existence for Jains is *moksha,* a state of perfect knowledge and tranquility for each individual soul, which can be achieved only by gaining enlightenment.

The Jainist path to liberation is defined by the three jewels: *Samyak Darshan* (right perception), *Samyak Jnana* (right knowledge) and *Samyak Charitra* (right conduct). Of the five fundamental precepts of the Jains, *Ahimsa* (non-injury to any form of being, in any mode: thought, speech or action) is the first and foremost, and was popularised by Gandhi as *Ahimsa paramo dharma* (non-violence is the supreme religion).

The largest population of Jains can be found in India but there are approximately 30,000 Jains in Britain, sizeable communities in North America, East Africa, Australia and smaller groups in many other countries.

INSTITUTE OF JAINOLOGY, Unit 18, Silicon Business Centre, 28 Wadsworth Road, Perivale, Greenford, Middx UB6 7JZ T 020-8997 2300 E enquiries@jainology.org W www.jainology.org
Hon. Secretary, Dr Harshad Sanghrajka

JUDAISM

Judaism is the oldest monotheistic faith. The primary text of Judaism is the Hebrew bible or *Tanakh,* which records how the descendants of Abraham were led by Moses out of their slavery in Egypt to Mount Sinai where God's law *(Torah)* was revealed to them as the chosen people. The *Talmud,* which consists of commentaries on the *Mishnah* (the first text of rabbinical Judaism), is also held to be authoritative, and may be divided into two main categories: the *halakah* (dealing with legal and ritual matters) and the *aggadah* (dealing with theological and ethical matters not directly concerned with the regulation of conduct). The *midrash* comprises rabbinic writings containing biblical interpretations in the spirit of the aggadah. The halakah has become a source of division: orthodox Jews regard Jewish law as derived from God and therefore unalterable; progressive Jews seek to interpret it in the light of contemporary considerations; and conservative Jews aim to maintain most of the traditional rituals but to allow changes in accordance with tradition. Reconstructionist Judaism, a 20th-century movement, regards Judaism as a culture rather than a theological system and accepts all forms of Jewish practice.

The family is the basic unit of Jewish ritual, with the synagogue playing an important role as the centre for public worship and religious study. A synagogue is led by a group of laymen who are elected to office. The Rabbi is primarily a teacher and spiritual guide. The *Sabbath* is the central religious observance. Most British Jews are descendants of either the *Ashkenazim* of central and eastern Europe or the *Sephardim* of Spain, Portugal and the Middle East.

The Chief Rabbi of the United Hebrew Congregations of the Commonwealth is appointed by a Chief Rabbinate Conference, and is the rabbinical authority of the mainstream Orthodox sector of the Ashkenazi Jewish community, the largest body of which is the United Synagogue. His formal ecclesiastical authority is not recognised by the Reform Synagogues of Great Britain (the largest progressive group), the Union of Liberal and Progressive Synagogues, the Sephardi community or the Assembly of Masorti Synagogues. He is, however, generally recognised both outside the Jewish community and within it as the public religious representative of the totality of British Jewry. The Chief Rabbi is President of the London *Beth Din* (Court of Judgement), a rabbinic court. The *Dayanim* (Assessors) adjudicate in disputes or on matters of Jewish law and tradition; they also oversee dietary law administration, marriage, divorce and issues of personal status.

The Board of Deputies of British Jews, established in 1760, is the representative body of British Jewry. The basis of representation is through the election of deputies by synagogues and communal organisations. It protects and promotes the interests of British Jewry, acts as the central voice of the community and seeks to counter anti-Jewish discrimination and anti-Semitic activities.

There are over 12.5 million Jews worldwide; in the UK there are an estimated 300,000 adherents and almost 400 synagogues.

OFFICE OF THE CHIEF RABBI, 305 Ballards Lane, London N12 8GB T 020-8343 6301 E info@chiefrabbi.org W www.chiefrabbi.org
Chief Rabbi, Lord Sacks

BETH DIN (COURT OF THE CHIEF RABBI), 305 Ballards Lane, London N12 8GB T 020-8343 6270 E info@bethdin.org.uk W www.theus.org.uk

Registrar, David Frei
Dayanim, Rabbi Chanoch Ehrentreu *(Consultant Dayan);* Menachem Gelley *(Senior Dayan);* Ivan Binstock; Yonason Abraham; Shmuel Simons

ASSEMBLY OF MASORTI SYNAGOGUES, Alexander House, 3 Shakespeare Road, London N3 1XE T 020-8349 6650 E enquiries@masorti.org.uk W www.masorti.org.uk
Executive Director, Michael Gluckman

BOARD OF DEPUTIES OF BRITISH JEWS, 6 Bloomsbury Square, London WC1A 2LP T 020-7543 5400 F 020-7543 0010 E info@bod.org.uk W www.bod.org.uk
President, Vivian Wineman

FEDERATION OF SYNAGOGUES, 65 Watford Way, London NW4 3AQ T 020-8202 2263 E info@federationofsynagogues.com W www.federationofsynagogues.com
President, Alan Finlay
Chief Executive, Dr Eli Kienwald

LIBERAL JUDAISM, The Montagu Centre, 21 Maple Street, London W1T 4BE T 020-7580 1663 E montagu@liberaljudaism.org W www.liberaljudaism.org
Chief Executive, Rabbi Danny Rich

THE MOVEMENT FOR REFORM JUDAISM, The Sternberg Centre for Judaism, 80 East End Road, London N3 2SY T 020-8349 5640 E admin@reformjudaism.org.uk W www.reformjudaism.org.uk
Head of Movement, Rabbi Dr Tony Bayfield

SPANISH AND PORTUGUESE JEWS' CONGREGATION, 2 Ashworth Road, London W9 1JY T 020-7289 2573 E howardmiller@spsyn.org.uk W www.sandp.org.uk
Chief Executive, Howard Miller

UNION OF ORTHODOX HEBREW CONGREGATIONS, 140 Stamford Hill, London N16 6QT T 020-8802 6226
Executive Coordinator, Chanoch Kesselman
Secretary, Chayim Schneck

UNITED SYNAGOGUE HEAD OFFICE, Adler House, 735 High Road, London N12 0US T 020-8343 8989 E info@theus.org.uk W www.theus.org.uk
Chief Executive, Jeremy Jacobs

PAGANISM

Paganism draws on the ideas of the Celtic people of pre-Roman Europe and is closely linked to Druidism. The first historical record of Druidry comes from classical Greek and Roman writers of the third century BC, who noted the existence of Druids among a people called the Keltoi who inhabited central and southern Europe. The word druid may derive from the Indo-European 'dreo-vid', meaning 'one who knows the truth'. In practice it was probably understood to mean something like 'wise-one' or 'philosopher-priest'.

Paganism is a pantheistic nature-worshipping religion which incorporates beliefs and ritual practices from ancient times. Pagans place much emphasis on the natural world and the ongoing cycle of life and death is central to their beliefs. Most Pagans believe that they are part of nature and not separate from, or superior to it, and seek to live in a way that minimises harm to the natural environment (the word Pagan derives from the Latin *Paganus,* meaning 'rural'). Paganism strongly emphasises the equality of the sexes, with women playing a prominent role in the modern Pagan movement and goddess worship featuring in most ceremonies. Paganism cannot be defined by any principal beliefs because it is shaped by each individual's experiences.

The Pagan Federation was founded in 1971 to provide information on Paganism, campaigns on issues which affect Paganism and provides support to members of the Pagan community. Within the UK the Pagan Federation is divided into 13 districts each with a district manager, regional and local coordinators. Local meetings are called 'moots' and take place in private homes, pubs or coffee bars. The Pagan Federation publishes a quarterly journal, *Pagan Dawn,* formerly *The Wiccan* (founded in 1968). The federation also publishes other material, arranges members-only and public events and maintains personal contact by letter with individual members and the wider Pagan community. Regional gatherings and conferences are held throughout the year.

THE PAGAN FEDERATION, BM Box 7097, London WC1N 3XX T 0798-603 4387 E secretary@paganfed.org W www.paganfed.org
President, John MacIntyre
Secretary, Lee-Anne Haye

SIKHISM

The Sikh religion dates from the birth of Guru Nanak in the Punjab in 1469. 'Guru' means teacher but in Sikh tradition has come to represent the divine presence of God giving inner spiritual guidance. Nanak's role as the human vessel of the divine guru was passed on to nine successors, the last of whom (Guru Gobind Singh) died in 1708. The immortal guru is now held to reside in the sacred scripture, Guru Granth Sahib, and so to be present in all Sikh gatherings.

Guru Nanak taught that there is one God and that different religions are like different roads leading to the same destination. He condemned religious conflict, ritualism and caste prejudices. The fifth Guru, Guru Arjan Dev, largely compiled the Sikh Holy scripture, a collection of hymns *(gurbani)* known as the *Adi Granth.* It includes the writings of the first five gurus and the ninth guru, and selected writings of Hindu and Muslim saints whose views are in accord with the gurus' teachings. Guru Arjan Dev also built the Golden Temple at Amritsar, the centre of Sikhism. The tenth guru, Guru Gobind Singh, passed on the guruship to the sacred scripture, *Guru Granth Sahib* and founded the *Khalsa,* an order intended to fight against tyranny and injustice. Male initiates to the order added 'Singh' to their given names and women added 'Kaur'. Guru Gobind Singh also made the wearing of five symbols obligatory: *kaccha* (a special undergarment), *kara* (a steel bangle), *kirpan* (a small sword), *kesh* (long unshorn hair, and consequently the wearing of a turban) and *kangha* (a comb). These practices are still compulsory for those Sikhs who are initiated into the Khalsa (the *Amritdharis*). Those who do not seek initiation are known as *Sehajdharis.*

There are no professional priests in Sikhism; anyone with a reasonable proficiency in the Punjabi language can conduct a service. Worship can be offered individually or communally, and in a private house or a *gurdwara* (temple). Sikhs are forbidden to eat meat prepared by ritual slaughter; they are also asked to abstain from smoking, alcohol and other intoxicants. Such abstention is compulsory for the Amritdharis.

There are about 20 million Sikhs worldwide and, according to the 2001 census, there are 336,000 adherents in the UK. Every gurdwara manages its own affairs; there is no central body in the UK. The Sikh Missionary Society provides an information service.

SIKH MISSIONARY SOCIETY UK, 10 Featherstone Road, Southall, Middx UB2 5AA **T** 020-8574 1902
E info@sikhmissionarysociety.org
W www.sikhmissionarysociety.org
Hon. General Secretary, Teja Singh Manget

ZOROASTRIANISM

Zoroastrians are followers of the Iranian prophet Spitaman Zarathushtra (or Zoroaster in its hellenised form) who lived *c.*1200 BC. Zoroastrians were persecuted in Iran following the Arab invasion of Persia in the seventh century AD and a group (who are known as Parsis) migrated to India in the eighth century AD to avoid harassment and persecution. Zarathushtra's words are recorded in five poems called the *Gathas,* which, together with other scriptures, forms the *Avesta.*

Zoroastrianism teaches that there is one God, *Ahura Mazda* (Wise Lord), and that all creation stems ultimately from God; the Gathas teach that human beings have free will, are responsible for their own actions and can choose between good and evil. It is believed that choosing *Asha* (truth or righteousness), with the aid of *Vohu Manah* (good mind), leads to happiness for the individual and society, whereas choosing evil leads to unhappiness and conflict. The *Gathas* also encourage hard work, good deeds and charitable acts. Zoroastrians believe that after death the immortal soul is judged by God, and is then sent to paradise or hell, where it will stay until the end of time to be resurrected for the final judgement.

In Zoroastrian places of worship, an urn containing fire is the central feature; the fire symbolises purity, light and truth and is a visible symbol of the *Fravashi* or *Farohar* (spirit), the presence of Ahura Mazda in every human being. Zoroastrians respect nature and much importance is attached to cultivating land and protecting air, earth and water.

The Zoroastrian Trust Funds of Europe is the main body for Zoroastrians in the UK. Founded in 1861 as the Religious Funds of the Zoroastrians of Europe, it disseminates information on the Zoroastrian faith, provides a place of worship and maintains separate burial grounds for Zoroastrians. It also holds religious and social functions and provides assistance to Zoroastrians as considered necessary, including the provision of loans and grants to students of Zoroastrianism.

There are approximately 140,000 Zoroastrians worldwide, of which around 7,000 reside in Britain, mainly in London and the South East.

ZOROASTRIAN TRUST FUNDS OF EUROPE, Zoroastrian Centre, 440 Alexandra Avenue, Harrow, Middx HA2 9TL **T** 020-8866 0765 **E** secretary@ztfe.com
W www.ztfe.com
President, Malcolm Deboo

CHURCHES

There are two established (ie state) churches in the United Kingdom: the Church of England and the Church of Scotland. There are no established churches in Wales or Northern Ireland, though the Church in Wales, the Scottish Episcopal Church and the Church of Ireland are members of the Anglican Communion.

CHURCH OF ENGLAND

The Church of England is divided into the two provinces of Canterbury and York, each under an archbishop. The two provinces are subdivided into 44 dioceses.

Legislative provision for the Church of England is made by the General Synod, established in 1970. It also discusses and expresses opinion on any other matter of religious or public interest. The General Synod has 467 members in total, divided between three houses: the House of Bishops, the House of Clergy and the House of Laity. It is presided over jointly by the Archbishops of Canterbury and York and normally meets twice a year. The synod has the power, delegated by parliament, to frame statute law (known as a 'measure') on any matter concerning the Church of England. A measure must be laid before both houses of parliament, who may accept or reject it but cannot amend it. Once accepted the measure is submitted for royal assent and then has the full force of law. In addition to the General Synod, there are synods at diocesan level. The entire General Synod is re-elected once every five years. It was dissolved in July 2010 and the election was held in the autumn. The new General Synod was due to be opened by the Queen on 23 November 2010.

The Archbishops' Council was established in January 1999. Its creation was the result of changes to the Church of England's national structure proposed in 1995 and subsequently approved by the synod and parliament. The council's purpose, set out in the National Institutions Measure 1998, is 'to coordinate, promote and further the work and mission of the Church of England'. It reports to the General Synod. The Archbishops' Council comprises the Archbishops of Canterbury and York, *ex officio*, the prolocutors elected by the convocations of Canterbury and York, the chair and vice-chair of the House of Laity, elected by that house, two bishops, two clergy and two lay persons elected by their respective houses of the General Synod, and up to six persons appointed jointly by the two archbishops with the approval of the General Synod.

There are also a number of national boards, councils and other bodies working on matters such as social responsibility, mission, Christian unity and education which report to the General Synod through the Archbishops' Council.

GENERAL SYNOD OF THE CHURCH OF ENGLAND, Church House, Great Smith Street, London SW1P 3NZ
T 020-7898 1000
Joint Presidents, Archbishops of Canterbury and York

ARCHBISHOPS' COUNCIL, Church House, Great Smith Street, London SW1P 3NZ T 020-7898 1000
Joint Presidents, Archbishops of Canterbury and York;
Secretary-General, William Fittall

THE ORDINATION OF WOMEN

The canon making it possible for women to be ordained to the priesthood was promulgated in the General Synod in February 1994 and the first 32 women priests were ordained on 12 March 1994.

PORVOO DECLARATION

The Porvoo Declaration was approved by the General Synod of the Church of England in July 1995. Churches that approve the declaration regard baptised members of each other's churches as members of their own, and allow free interchange of episcopally ordained ministers within the rules of each church.

MEMBERSHIP

In 2008, 139,100 people were baptised, 53,100 people were married in parish churches, the Church of England had an electoral roll membership of 1.2 million, and each week over 1.1 million people attended services.

As at December 2009 there were over 16,000 churches and places of worship; 358 dignitaries (including bishops, archdeacons and cathedral clergy); 7,544 full-time parochial stipendiary clergy; 326 full-time non parochial stipendiary clergy; 3,100 self-supporting ministers; 1,480 chaplains; 341 lay workers and Church Army evangelists; 7,501 licensed readers and 2,557 readers with permission to officiate and active emeriti; and approximately 4,610 active retired ordained clergy.

	Full-time Equivalent Diocesan Clergy 2009		*Electoral Roll Membership*
	Male	*Female*	*2008*
Bath and Wells	162	46	35,400
Birmingham	117	45	17,200
Blackburn	158	18	33,400
Bradford	86	16	11,300
Bristol	101	27	15,000
Canterbury	117	25	20,500
Carlisle	109	29	20,000
Chelmsford	303	79	46,100
Chester	207	51	43,700
Chichester	279	20	53,000
Coventry	95	21	16,600
Derby	119	28	18,100
Durham	150	45	21,900
Ely	104	42	18,600
Europe	128*	13*	10,700
Exeter	178	36	30,900
Gloucester	104	37	23,000
Guildford	140	38	28,800
Hereford	68	26	17,400
Leicester	106	38	16,000
Lichfield	250	65	43,300
Lincoln	140	37	26,500
Liverpool	158	52	27,500
London	456	76	68,700

Manchester	181	58	32,300
Newcastle	103	35	16,100
Norwich	157	38	20,000
Oxford	296	93	53,600
Peterborough	109	27	18,800
Portsmouth	87	21	16,800
Ripon and Leeds	90	38	16,800
Rochester	181	32	29,500
St Albans	181	76	38,000
St Edmundsbury and Ipswich	109	34	23,000
Salisbury	163	50	40,500
Sheffield	116	39	17,400
Sodor and Man	12	1	2,600
Southwark	268	83	45,800
Southwell and Nottingham	110	46	18,600
Truro	92	17	15,600
Wakefield	103	41	19,500
Winchester	182	23	38,300
Worcester	109	29	18,600
York	181	45	33,700
Total	6,659	1,734	1,179,000

* Full time figures

STIPENDS 2010–11†

Archbishop of Canterbury	£70,810‡
Archbishop of York	£60,690‡
Bishop of London	£55,630‡
Other diocesan bishops	£38,440‡
Suffragan bishops	£31,360‡
Assistant bishops (full-time)	£30,350‡
Deans	£31,360‡
Archdeacons (recommended)	£30,650
Residentiary canons	£24,280‡§
Incumbents and clergy of similar status	£22,470§

† For those appointed on or after 1 April 2004, transitional arrangements are in place for those appointed prior to this date.
‡ Same rate as 2009–10
§ Adjusted regionally to reflect variations in the cost of living

CANTERBURY

104TH ARCHBISHOP AND PRIMATE OF ALL ENGLAND
Most Revd and Rt. Hon. Rowan Williams, *cons.* 1992, *apptd* 2002; Lambeth Palace, London SE1 7JU
Signs Rowan Cantuar:

BISHOPS SUFFRAGAN
Dover, Rt. Revd Trevor Willmott, *cons.* 2002, *apptd* 2009; Upway, St Martin's Hill, Canterbury, Kent CT1 1PR
Maidstone, vacant
Ebbsfleet, Rt. Revd Andrew Burnham, *cons.* 2000, *apptd* 2000 (provincial episcopal visitor); Bishop's House, Dry Sandsford, Abingdon, Oxon OX13 6JP
Richborough, Rt. Revd Keith Newton, *cons.* 2002, *apptd* 2002 (provincial episcopal visitor); 6 Mellis Gardens, Woodford Green, Essex IG8 0BH

DEAN
Very Revd Robert Willis, *apptd* 2001

Organist, D. Flood, FRCO, *apptd* 1988

ARCHDEACONS
Canterbury, Ven. Sheila Watson *apptd* 2007
Maidstone, Ven. Philip Down, *apptd* 2002

Vicar-General of Province and Diocese, Chancellor Sheila Cameron, QC
Commissary-General, His Hon. Richard Walker
Joint Registrars of the Province, Canon John Rees; Stephen Slack
Diocesan Registrar and Legal Adviser, Owen Carew Jones
Diocesan Secretary, Julian Hills, Diocesan House, Lady Wootton's Green, Canterbury CT1 1NQ
T 01227-459401

YORK

97TH ARCHBISHOP AND PRIMATE OF ENGLAND
Most Revd and Rt. Hon. Dr John Sentamu, *cons.* 1996, *trans.* 2005; Bishopthorpe, York YO23 2GE
Signs Sentamu Ebor:

BISHOPS SUFFRAGAN
Hull, Rt. Revd Richard Frith, *cons.* 1998, *apptd* 1998; Hullen House, Woodfield Lane, Hessle, Hull HU13 0ES
Selby, Rt. Revd Martin Wallace, *cons.* 2003, *apptd* 2003; Bishop's House, Barton le Street, Malton, York YO17 6PL
Whitby, Rt. Revd Martin Warner, PHD, *cons.* 2010, *apptd* 2009; 60 West Green, Stokesley, Middlesbrough TS9 5BD

PRINCIPAL EPISCOPAL VISITOR
Rt. Revd Martyn Jarrett (*Bishop Suffragan of Beverley*), *cons.* 1994, *apptd* 2000; 3 North Lane, Roundhay, Leeds LS8 2QJ

DEAN
Very Revd Keith Jones, *apptd* 2004

Director of Music, Robert Sharpe, *apptd* 2008

ARCHDEACONS
Cleveland, Ven. Paul Ferguson, *apptd* 2001
East Riding, Ven. David Butterfield, *apptd* 2006
York, Ven. Richard Seed, *apptd* 1999

Chancellor of the Diocese, His Hon. Judge Peter Collier, QC, *apptd* 2006
Registrar and Legal Secretary, Lionel Lennox
Diocesan Secretary, Peter Warry, Diocesan House, Aviator Court, Clifton Moor, York YO30 4WJ
T 01904-699500

LONDON *(Canterbury)*

132ND BISHOP
Rt. Revd and Rt. Hon. Richard Chartres, KCVO, *cons.* 1992, *apptd* 1995; The Old Deanery, Dean's Court, London EC4V 5AA
Signs Richard Londin:

AREA BISHOPS
Edmonton, Rt. Revd Peter Wheatley, *cons.* 1999, *apptd* 1999; 27 Thurlow Road, London NW3 5PP
Kensington, Rt. Revd Paul Williams, *cons.* 2009, *apptd* 2008; Dial House, Riverside, Twickenham, Middlesex TW1 3DT
Stepney, vacant
Willesden, Rt. Revd Peter Broadbent, *cons.* 2001, *apptd* 2001; 173 Willesden Lane, London NW6 7YN

BISHOP SUFFRAGAN
Fulham, Rt. Revd John Broadhurst, *cons.* 1996, *apptd* 1996; 26 Canonbury Park South, London N1 2FN

DEAN OF ST PAUL'S
Rt. Revd Graeme Knowles, *apptd* 2007

Director of Music, Andrew Carwood, *apptd* 2007

ARCHDEACONS
Charing Cross, Ven. Dr William Jacob, *apptd* 1996
Hackney, vacant
Hampstead, vacant
London, Ven. David Meara, *apptd* 2009
Middlesex, Ven. Stephan Welch, *apptd* 2006
Northolt, Ven. Rachel Treweek, *apptd* 2006
Chancellor, Nigel Seed, QC, *apptd* 2002
Registrar and Legal Secretary, Paul Morris
Diocesan Secretary, Andrew Brookes, London Diocesan House, 36 Causton Street, London SW1P 4AU T 020-7932 1100

DURHAM *(York)*

72ND BISHOP
vacant

BISHOP SUFFRAGAN
Jarrow, Rt. Revd Mark Bryant, *cons.* 2007, *apptd* 2007; Bishop's House, 25 Ivy Lane, Low Fell, Gateshead NE9 6QD

DEAN
Very Revd Michael Sadgrove, *apptd* 2003

Organist, James Lancelot, FRCO, *apptd* 1985

ARCHDEACONS
Auckland, Ven. Nicholas Barker, *apptd* 2007
Durham, Ven. Ian Jagger, *apptd* 2006
Sunderland, Ven. Stuart Bain, *apptd* 2002
Chancellor, The Worshipful Revd Dr Rupert Bursell, QC, *apptd* 1989
Registrar and Legal Secretary, Hilary Monckton-Milnes
Diocesan Secretary, Ian Boothroyd, Diocesan Office, Auckland Castle, Bishop Auckland, Co. Durham DL14 7QJ T 01388-604515

WINCHESTER *(Canterbury)*

96TH BISHOP
Rt. Revd Michael C. Scott-Joynt, *cons.*1987, *trans.* 1995: Wolvesey, Winchester SO23 9ND
Signs Michael Winton:

BISHOPS SUFFRAGAN
Basingstoke, Rt. Revd Peter Hancock, *apptd* 2010, *cons.* 2010; Old Alresford Place, Alresford, Hants SO24 9DH
Southampton, Rt. Revd Jonathan Frost, *apptd* 2010, *cons.* 2010; Old Alresford Place, Alresford, Hants SO24 9DH

DEAN
Very Revd James Atwell, *apptd* 2005
Dean of Jersey (A Peculiar), Very Revd Robert Key, *apptd* 2005
Dean of Guernsey (A Peculiar), Very Revd Paul Mellor, *apptd* 2003
Director of Music, Andrew Lumsden, *apptd* 2002

ARCHDEACONS
Bournemouth, Ven. Adrian Harbidge, *apptd* 1998
Winchester, Ven. Michael Harley, *apptd* 2009

Chancellor, Christopher Clark, *apptd* 1993
Registrar and Legal Secretary, Peter White
Diocesan Secretary, Andrew Robinson, Old Alresford Place, Alresford, Hants SO24 9DH T 01962-737305

BATH AND WELLS *(Canterbury)*

78TH BISHOP
Rt. Revd Peter Price, *cons.* 1997, *apptd* 2002; The Palace, Wells BA5 2PD
Signs Peter Bath & Wells

BISHOP SUFFRAGAN
Taunton, Rt. Revd Peter Maurice, *cons.* 2006, *apptd* 2006; The Palace, Wells BA5 2PD

DEAN
Very Revd John Clarke, *apptd* 2004

Organist, Matthew Owens, *apptd* 2005

ARCHDEACONS
Bath, Ven. Andrew Piggott, *apptd* 2005
Taunton, Ven. John Reed, *apptd* 1999
Wells, Ven. Nicola Sullivan, *apptd* 2006

Chancellor, Timothy Briden, *apptd* 1993
Registrar and Legal Secretary, Tim Berry
Diocesan Secretary, Nicholas Denison, The Old Deanery, Wells, Somerset BA5 2UG T 01749-670777

BIRMINGHAM *(Canterbury)*

8TH BISHOP
Rt. Revd David Urquhart, *cons.* 2000, *apptd* 2006; Bishop's Croft, Old Church Road, Harborne, Birmingham B17 0BG
Signs David Birmingham:

BISHOP SUFFRAGAN
Aston, Rt. Revd Andrew Watson, *cons.* 2008, *apptd* 2008; 175 Harborne Park Road, Birmingham B17 0BH

DEAN
Very Revd Catherine Ogle, *apptd* 2010

Director of Music, Marcus Huxley, FRCO, *apptd* 1986

ARCHDEACONS
Aston, Ven. Dr Brian Russell, *apptd* 2005
Birmingham, Ven. Hayward Osborne, *apptd* 2001

Chancellor, His Hon. Judge Martin Cardinal, *apptd* 2005
Registrar and Legal Secretary, Hugh Carslake
Diocesan Secretary, Jim Drennan, 175 Harborne Park Road, Harborne, Birmingham B17 0BH T 0121-426 0400

BLACKBURN *(York)*

8TH BISHOP
Rt. Revd Nicholas Reade, *apptd* 2003, *cons.* March 2004; Bishop's House, Ribchester Road, Blackburn BB1 9EF
Signs Nicholas Blackburn

BISHOPS SUFFRAGAN
Burnley, Rt. Revd John Goddard, *cons.* 2000, *apptd* 2000; All Saints House, Padiham Road, Burnley BB12 6PA
Lancaster, Rt. Revd Geoffrey Pearson, *cons.* 2006, *apptd* 2006; The Vicarage, Whinney Brow Lane, Shireshead, Forton, Preston PR3 0AE

DEAN
Very Revd Christopher Armstrong, *apptd* 2001

Organist and Director of Music, Richard Tanner, *apptd* 1998

ARCHDEACON
Blackburn, Ven. John Hawley, *apptd* 2002

Chancellor, His Hon. Judge John Bullimore, *apptd* 1990
Registrar and Legal Secretary, Thomas Hoyle
Diocesan Secretary, Graeme Pollard, Diocesan Office, Cathedral Close, Blackburn BB1 5AA T 01254-503070

BRADFORD *(York)*

10TH BISHOP
vacant

DEAN
Very Revd Dr David Ison, *apptd* 2005

Organist, Andrew Teague, FRCO, *apptd* 2003

ARCHDEACONS
Bradford, Ven. David Lee, *apptd* 2004
Craven, Ven. Paul Slater, *apptd* 2005

Chancellor, His Hon. Judge John de G. Walford, *apptd* 1999
Registrar and Legal Secretary, Peter Foskett
Diocesan Secretary (acting), Debbie Child, Kadugli House, Elmsley Street, Steeton, Keighley BD20 6SE **T** 01535-650555

BRISTOL *(Canterbury)*

55TH BISHOP
Rt. Revd Michael Hill, *cons.* 1998, *apptd* 2003; 58A High Street, Winterbourne, Bristol BS36 1JQ
Signs Michael Bristol

BISHOP SUFFRAGAN
Swindon, Rt. Revd Dr Lee Rayfield, *cons.* 2005, *apptd* 2005; Mark House, Field Rise, Swindon, Wiltshire, SN1 4HP

DEAN
Very Revd David Hoyle, *apptd* 2010

Organist and Director of Music, Mark Lee, *apptd* 1998

ARCHDEACONS
Bristol, Ven. Tim McClure, *apptd* 1999
Malmesbury, Ven. Alan Hawker, *apptd* 1998

Chancellor, Dr James Behrens, *apptd* 2005
Registrar and Legal Secretary, Tim Berry
Diocesan Secretary, Lesley Farrall, Diocesan Church House, 23 Great George Street, Bristol BS1 5QZ **T** 0117-906 0100

CARLISLE *(York)*

66TH BISHOP
Rt. Revd James Newcome, *cons.* 2002, *apptd* 2009; Holm Croft, Castle Road, Kendal, Cumbria LA9 7AU
Signs James Carliol

BISHOP SUFFRAGAN
Penrith, vacant; Holm Croft, Castle Road, Kendal, Cumbria LA9 7AU

DEAN
Very Revd Mark Boyling, *apptd* 2004

Organist, Jeremy Suter, FRCO, *apptd* 1991

ARCHDEACONS
Carlisle, Ven. Kevin Roberts, *apptd* 2009
West Cumberland, Ven. Dr Richard Pratt, *apptd* 2009
Westmorland and Furness, Ven. George Howe, *apptd* 2000

Chancellor, Geoffrey Tattersall, QC, *apptd* 2003
Registrar and Legal Secretary, Jane Lowdon
Diocesan Secretary, Derek Hurton, Church House, West Walls, Carlisle CA3 8UE **T** 01228-522573

CHELMSFORD *(Canterbury)*

10TH BISHOP
Rt. Revd Stephen Cottrell, *cons.* 2004, *apptd.* 2010; Bishopscourt, Main Road, Margaretting, Ingatestone, Essex CM4 0HD
Signs Stephen Chelmsford

BISHOPS SUFFRAGAN
Barking, Rt. Revd David Hawkins, *cons.* 2002, *apptd* 2003; Barking Lodge, Verulam Avenue, London, E17 8ES
Bradwell, Rt. Revd Dr Laurence Green, *cons.* 1993, *apptd* 1993; Bishop's House, Orsett Road, Horndon-on-the-Hill, Stanford-le-Hope, Essex SS17 8NS
Colchester, Rt. Revd Christopher Morgan, *cons.* 2001, *apptd* 2001; 1 Fitzwalter Road, Colchester, Essex CO3 3SS

DEAN
Very Revd Peter S. M. Judd, *apptd* 1997

Master of Music, Peter Nardone, *apptd* 2000

ARCHDEACONS
Colchester, Ven. Annette Cooper, *apptd* 2004
Harlow, Ven. Martin Webster, *apptd* 2009
Southend, Ven. David Lowman, *apptd* 2001
West Ham, Ven. Elwin Cockett, *apptd* 2007

Chancellor, George Pulman QC, *apptd* 2001
Registrar and Legal Secretary, Brian Hood
Chief Executive, Steven Webb, 53 New Street, Chelmsford, Essex CM1 1AT **T** 01245-294400

CHESTER *(York)*

40TH BISHOP
Rt. Revd Peter Forster, PHD, *cons.* 1996, *apptd* 1996; Bishop's House, Abbey Square, Chester CH1 2JD
Signs Peter Cestr:

BISHOPS SUFFRAGAN
Birkenhead, Rt. Revd Keith Sinclair, *cons.* 2007, *apptd* 2007; Bishop's Lodge, 67 Bidston Road, Prenton CH43 6TR
Stockport, Rt. Revd Robert Atwell, *cons.* 2008, *apptd* 2008; Bishop's Lodge, Back Lane, Dunham Town, Altrincham WA14 4SG

DEAN
Very Revd Dr Gordon McPhate, *apptd* 2002

Organist and Director of Music, Philip Rushforth, FRCO, *apptd* 2008

ARCHDEACONS
Chester (acting), Revd Michael Walters
Macclesfield, Ven. Richard Gillings, *apptd* 1994

Chancellor, His Hon. Judge Turner, QC, *apptd* 1998
Registrar and Legal Secretary, Helen McFall
Diocesan Secretary, Dr John Mason, Church House, Lower Lane, Aldford, Chester CH3 6HP **T** 01244-681973

CHICHESTER *(Canterbury)*

102ND BISHOP
Rt. Revd Dr John Hind, *cons.* 1991, *apptd* 2001; The Palace, Chichester PO19 1PY
Signs John Cicestr:

BISHOPS SUFFRAGAN
Horsham, Rt. Revd Mark Sowerby, *cons.* 2009, *apptd* 2009
Lewes, Rt. Revd Wallace Benn, *cons.* 1997, *apptd* 1997; Bishop's Lodge, 16A Prideaux Road, Eastbourne, E. Sussex BN21 2NB

DEAN
Very Revd Nicholas Frayling, *apptd* 2002

Organist, Sarah Baldock, *apptd* 2007

ARCHDEACONS
Chichester, Ven. Douglas McKittrick, *apptd* 2002
Horsham, Ven. Roger Combes, *apptd* 2003
Lewes and Hastings, Ven. Philip Jones, *apptd* 2005

Chancellor, Mark Hill
Registrar and Legal Secretary, John Stapleton
Diocesan Secretary, Francesca Del Mese, Diocesan Church House, 211 New Church Road, Hove, E. Sussex BN3 4ED T 01273-421021

COVENTRY *(Canterbury)*

9TH BISHOP
Rt. Revd Dr Christopher Cocksworth, *cons.* 2008, *apptd* 2008; The Bishop's House, 23 Davenport Road, Coventry CV5 6PW
Signs Christopher Coventry

BISHOP SUFFRAGAN
Warwick, Rt. Revd John Stroyan, *cons.* 2005, *apptd* 2005; Warwick House, 139 Kenilworth Road, Coventry CV4 7AP

DEAN
Very Revd John Irvine, *apptd* 2001

Director of Music, Mr Kerry Beaumont, *apptd* 2006

ARCHDEACONS
Coventry, Ven. Ian Watson, *apptd* 2007
Warwick, Ven. Morris Rodham, *apptd* 2010

Chancellor, Stephen Eyre, *apptd* 2009
Registrar and Legal Secretary, Mary Allanson
Diocesan Secretary, Simon Lloyd, Cathedral & Diocesan Offices, 1 Hilltop, Coventry CV1 5AB T 024-7652 1200

DERBY *(Canterbury)*

7TH BISHOP
Rt. Revd Dr Alastair Redfern, *cons.* 1997, *apptd* 2005; The Bishop's House, 6 King Street, Duffield, Belper, Derbyshire, DE56 4EU
Signs Alastair Derby

BISHOP SUFFRAGAN
Repton, Rt. Revd Humphrey Southern, *cons.* 2007, *apptd* 2007; Repton House, Lea, Matlock, Derbyshire DE4 5JP

DEAN
Very Revd Dr John Davies, *apptd* 2010

Organist, Peter Gould, *apptd* 1982

ARCHDEACONS
Chesterfield, Ven. Christine Wilson, *apptd* 2010
Derby, Ven. Dr Christopher Cunliffe, *apptd* 2006

Chancellor, His Hon. Judge John Bullimore, *apptd* 1981
Registrar and Legal Secretary, Mrs Nadine Waldron
Diocesan Secretary, Bob Carey, Derby Church House, Full Street, Derby DE1 3DR T 01332-388650

ELY *(Canterbury)*

69TH BISHOP
vacant

BISHOP SUFFRAGAN
Huntingdon, Rt. Revd David Thomson, DPHIL, *cons.* 2008, *apptd* 2008; 14 Lynn Road, Ely, Cambs CB6 1DA

DEAN
Very Revd Dr Michael Chandler, *apptd* 2003

Director of Music, Paul Trepte, FRCO, *apptd* 1991

ARCHDEACONS
Cambridge, Ven. John Beer, *apptd* 2004
Huntingdon and Wisbech, Ven. Hugh McCurdy, *apptd* 2005

Chancellor, Rt. Hon. Sir William Gage, QC
Registrar, Peter Beesley
Diocesan Secretary, Dr Matthew Lavis, Bishop Woodford House, Barton Road, Ely, Cambs CB7 4DX T 01353-652700

EXETER *(Canterbury)*

70TH BISHOP
Rt. Revd Michael Langrish, *cons.* 1993, *apptd* 2000; The Palace, Exeter, EX1 1HY
Signs Michael Exon:

BISHOPS SUFFRAGAN
Crediton, Rt. Revd Robert Evens, *cons.* 2004, *apptd* 2004; 32 The Avenue, Tiverton EX16 4HW
Plymouth, Rt. Revd John Ford, *cons.* 2006, *apptd* 2005; 31 Riverside Walk, Tamerton Foliot, Plymouth PL5 4AQ

DEAN
Very Revd Jonathan Meyrick, *apptd* 2005

Director of Music, Andrew Millington, *apptd* 1999

ARCHDEACONS
Barnstaple, Ven. David Gunn-Johnson, *apptd* 2003
Exeter, Ven. Penny Driver, *apptd* 2006
Plymouth, vacant
Totnes, Ven. John Rawlings, *apptd* 2006

Chancellor, Hon. Sir Andrew McFarlane
Registrar and Legal Secretary, M. Follett
Diocesan Secretary, Mark Beedell, The Old Deanery, The Cloisters, Exeter EX1 1HS T 01392-272686

GIBRALTAR IN EUROPE *(Canterbury)*

3RD BISHOP
Rt. Revd Dr Geoffrey Rowell, *cons.* 1994, *apptd* 2001; Bishop's Lodge, Church Road, Worth, Crawley, West Sussex RH10 7RT

BISHOP SUFFRAGAN
In Europe, Rt. Revd David Hamid, *cons.* 2002, *apptd* 2002; 14 Tufton Street, London SW1P 3QZ
Dean, Cathedral Church of the Holy Trinity, Gibraltar, Very Revd Dr John Paddock

Chancellor, Pro-Cathedral of St Paul, Valletta, Malta, Canon Simon Godfrey
Chancellor, Pro-Cathedral of the Holy Trinity, Brussels, Belgium, Canon Dr Robert Innes

ARCHDEACONS
Eastern, Ven. Patrick Curran
North-West Europe, Ven. John de Wit
France, Ven. Kenneth Letts
Gibraltar, Ven. David Sutch
Italy, Ven. Jonathan Boardman

Scandinavia and Germany, Ven. Jonathan Lloyd
Switzerland, Ven. Peter Potter

Chancellor, Mark Hill
Registrar and Legal Secretary, Aiden Hargreaves-Smith
Diocesan Secretary, Adrian Mumford, 14 Tufton Street, London SW1P 3QZ T 020-7898 1155

GLOUCESTER *(Canterbury)*

40TH BISHOP
Rt. Revd Michael Perham, *cons.* 2004, *apptd* 2004; Bishopscourt, Pitt Street, Gloucester GL1 2BQ
Signs Michael Gloucestr

BISHOP SUFFRAGAN
Tewkesbury, Rt. Revd John Went, *cons.* 1995, *apptd* 1995; Bishop's House, Staverton, Cheltenham GL51 0TW

DEAN
vacant

Director of Music, Adrian Partington, *apptd* 2007

ARCHDEACONS
Cheltenham, Ven. Robert Springett, *apptd* 2010
Gloucester, Ven. Geoffrey Sidaway, *apptd* 2000

Chancellor and Vicar-General, June Rodgers, *apptd* 1990
Registrar and Legal Secretary, Chris Peak
Diocesan Secretary, Dr Kevin Brown, Church House, College Green, Gloucester GL1 2LY T 01452-410022

GUILDFORD *(Canterbury)*

9TH BISHOP
Rt. Revd Christopher Hill, *cons.* 1996, *apptd* 2004; Willow Grange, Woking Road, Guildford GU4 7QS
Signs Christopher Guildford

BISHOP SUFFRAGAN
Dorking, Rt. Revd Ian Brackley, *cons.* 1996, *apptd* 1995; Dayspring, 13 Pilgrims Way, Guildford GU4 8AD

DEAN
Very Revd Victor Stock, *apptd* 2002

Organist, Katherine Dienes-Williams, *apptd* 2007

ARCHDEACONS
Dorking, Ven. Julian Henderson, *apptd* 2005
Surrey, Ven. Stuart Beake, *apptd* 2005

Chancellor, Andrew Jordan
Registrar and Legal Secretary, Peter Beesley
Diocesan Secretary, Stephen Marriott, Diocesan House, Quarry Street, Guildford GU1 3AG T 01483-571826

HEREFORD *(Canterbury)*

104TH BISHOP
Rt. Revd Anthony Priddis, *cons.* 1996, *apptd* 2004; The Bishop's House, Hereford HR4 9BN
Signs Anthony Hereford

BISHOP SUFFRAGAN
Ludlow, Rt. Revd Alistair Magowan, *cons.* 2009, *apptd* 2009; Bishop's House, Corvedale Road, Craven Arms, Shropshire SY7 9BT

DEAN
Very Revd Michael Tavinor, *apptd* 2002

Organist and Director of Music, Geraint Bowen, FRCO, *apptd* 2001

ARCHDEACONS
Hereford, vacant
Ludlow, Rt. Revd Alistair Magowan, *apptd* 2009

Chancellor, His Hon. Judge Roger Kaye, QC
Registrar and Legal Secretary, Peter Beesley
Diocesan Secretary, John Clark, The Palace, Hereford HR4 9BL T 01432-373300

LEICESTER *(Canterbury)*

6TH BISHOP
Rt. Revd Timothy Stevens, *cons.* 1995, *apptd* 1999; Bishop's Lodge, 10 Springfield Road, Leicester LE2 3BD
Signs Timothy Leicester

DEAN
Very Revd Vivienne Faull, *apptd* 2000

Director of Music, vacant

ARCHDEACONS
Leicester, Ven. Richard Atkinson, *apptd* 2002
Loughborough, David Newman, *apptd* 2009

Chancellor, Dr James Behrens
Registrar and Legal Secretary, Trevor Kirkman
Diocesan Secretary, Jane Easton, Church House, 3–5 St Martin's East, Leicester LE1 5FX T 0116-248 7400

LICHFIELD *(Canterbury)*

98TH BISHOP
Rt. Revd Jonathan Gledhill *cons.* 1996, *apptd* 2003; Bishop's House, The Close, Lichfield WS13 7LG
Signs Jonathan Lichfield

BISHOPS SUFFRAGAN
Shrewsbury, Rt. Revd Mark Rylands, *cons.* 2009, *apptd* 2009; Athlone House, 66 London Road, Shrewsbury SY2 6PG
Stafford, vacant
Wolverhampton, Rt. Revd Clive Gregory, *cons.* 2007, *apptd* 2007; 61 Richmond Road, Wolverhampton WV3 9JH

DEAN
Very Revd Adrian Dorber, *apptd* 2005

Organist, Philip Scriven, *apptd* 2002

ARCHDEACONS
Lichfield, Ven. Christopher Liley, *apptd* 2001
Salop, Ven. John Hall, *apptd* 1998
Stoke-on-Trent, Ven. Godfrey Owen Stone, *apptd* 2002
Walsall, Ven. Christopher Sims, *apptd* 2009

Chancellor, His Hon. Judge Marten Coates
Registrar and Legal Secretary, N. Blackie
Diocesan Secretary, Julie Jones, St Mary's House, The Close, Lichfield, Staffs WS13 7LD T 01543-306030

LINCOLN *(Canterbury)*

71ST BISHOP
Rt. Revd Dr John Saxbee, *cons.* 1994, *apptd* 2002; Bishop's House, Eastgate, Lincoln LN2 1QQ
Signs John Lincoln

BISHOPS SUFFRAGAN
Grantham, Rt. Revd Dr Timothy Ellis, *cons.* 2006, *apptd* 2006; Saxonwell Vicarage, Church Street, Long Bennington, Newark NG23 5ES
Grimsby, Rt. Revd David D. J. Rossdale, *cons.* 2000, *apptd* 2000; Bishop's House, Church Lane, Irby-upon-Humber, Grimsby DN37 7JR

DEAN
Very Revd Philip Buckler, *apptd* 2007

Director of Music, A. Prentice, *apptd* 2003

ARCHDEACONS
Lincoln, Ven. Timothy Barker, *apptd* 2009
Lindsey and Stow, Ven. Jane Sinclair, *apptd* 2007

Chancellor, His Hon. Judge Mark Bishop, QC, *apptd* 2007
Registrar and Legal Secretary, Caroline Mockford, *apptd* 2008
Diocesan Secretary, Max Manin,The Old Palace, Lincoln LN2 1PU T 01522-504050

LIVERPOOL *(York)*

7TH BISHOP
Rt. Revd James Jones, *cons.* 1994, *apptd* 1998; Bishop's Lodge, Woolton Park, Liverpool L25 6DT
Signs James Liverpool

BISHOP SUFFRAGAN
Warrington, Rt. Revd Richard Blackburn, *cons.* 2009, *apptd* 2009; 34 Central Avenue, Eccleston Park, Liverpool L34 2QP

DEAN
Very Revd Justin Welby, *apptd* 2007

Director of Music, David Poulter, *apptd* 2008

ARCHDEACONS
Liverpool, Ven. Richard Panter, *apptd* 2002
Warrington, Ven. Peter Bradley, *apptd* 2001

Chancellor, Hon. Sir Mark Hedley
Registrar and Legal Secretary, vacant
Diocesan Secretary, Mike Eastwood, St James House, 20 St James Street, Liverpool L1 7BY T 0151-709 9722

MANCHESTER *(York)*

11TH BISHOP
Rt. Revd Nigel McCulloch, *cons.* 1986, *apptd* 2002, *trans.* 2002; Bishopscourt, Bury New Road, Manchester M7 4LE
Signs Nigel Manchester

BISHOPS SUFFRAGAN
Bolton, Rt. Revd Christopher Edmondson, *cons.* 2008, *apptd* 2008; Bishop's Lodge, Walkden Road, Worsley, Manchester M28 2WH
Middleton, Rt. Revd Mark Davies, *cons.* 2008, *apptd* 2008; The Hollies, Manchester Road, Rochdale OL11 3QY

DEAN
Revd Rogers Govender, *apptd* 2006

Organist, Christopher Stokes, *apptd* 1992

ARCHDEACONS
Bolton, Ven. David Bailey, *apptd* 2008
Manchester, Ven. Mark Ashcroft, *apptd* 2009
Rochdale, Cherry Vann, *apptd* 2008

Chancellor, Geoffrey Tattersall, QC
Registrar and Legal Secretary, Jane Monks
Chief Executive, John Beck, Diocesan Church House, 90 Deansgate, Manchester M3 2GH T 0161-828 1400

NEWCASTLE *(York)*

11TH BISHOP
Rt. Revd J. Martin Wharton, *cons.* 1992, *apptd* 1997; Bishop's House, 29 Moor Road South, Gosforth, Newcastle upon Tyne NE3 1PA
Signs Martin Newcastle

ASSISTANT BISHOP
Rt. Revd Frank White, *cons.* 2002, *apptd* 2010

DEAN
Very Revd Christopher C. Dalliston, *apptd* 2003

Director of Music, Michael Stoddart, *apptd* 2009

ARCHDEACONS
Lindisfarne, Ven. Dr Peter Robinson, *apptd* 2008
Northumberland, Ven. Geoffrey Miller, *apptd* 2004

Chancellor, His Hon. Judge David Hodson, *apptd* 2009
Registrar and Legal Secretary, Jane Lowdon
Diocesan Secretary, Graham Barnard, Church House, St John's Terrace, North Shields NE29 6HS T 0191-270 4100

NORWICH *(Canterbury)*

71ST BISHOP
Rt. Revd Graham R. James, *cons.* 1993, *apptd* 2000; Bishop's House, Norwich NR3 1SB
Signs Graham Norvic:

BISHOPS SUFFRAGAN
Lynn, vacant
Thetford, Rt. Revd Alan Winton PHD, *cons.* 2009, *apptd* 2009; The Red House, 53 Norwich Road, Stoke Holy Cross, Norwich NR14 8AB

DEAN
Very Revd Graham Smith, *apptd* 2004

Master of Music, David Lowe, *apptd* 2007

ARCHDEACONS
Lynn, Ven. John Ashe, *apptd* 2009
Norfolk, Ven. David Hayden, *apptd* 2002
Norwich, Ven. Jan McFarlane, *apptd* 2008

Chancellor, His Hon. Judge Paul Downes, *apptd* 2007
Registrar and Legal Secretary, Stuart Jones
Diocesan Secretary, Richard Butler, Diocesan House, 109 Dereham Road, Easton, Norwich, Norfolk NR9 5ES T 01603-880853

OXFORD *(Canterbury)*

42ND BISHOP
Rt. Revd John Pritchard *cons.* 2002, *apptd* 2007; Diocesan Church House, North Hinksey Lane, Oxford OX2 0NB
Signs John Oxon:

AREA BISHOPS
Buckingham, Rt. Revd Dr Alan Wilson *cons.* 2003, *apptd* 2003; Sheridan, Grimms Hill, Great Missenden, Bucks HP16 9BD
Dorchester, Rt. Revd Colin Fletcher, *cons.* 2000, *apptd* 2000; Arran House, Sandy Lane, Yarnton, Oxon OX5 1PB
Reading, vacant

DEAN OF CHRIST CHURCH
Very Revd Dr Christopher Lewis, *apptd* 2003

Organist, Dr Stephen Darlington, FRCO, *apptd* 1985

ARCHDEACONS
Berkshire, Ven. Norman Russell, *apptd* 1998
Buckingham, Ven. Karen Gorham, *apptd* 2007
Oxford, Ven. Julian Hubbard, *apptd* 2005

Chancellor, Revd Dr Rupert Bursell, *apptd* 2001
Registrar and Legal Secretary, Revd Canon John Rees
Diocesan Secretary, Rosemary Pearce, Diocesan Church House, North Hinksey, Oxford OX2 0NB T 01865-208202

PETERBOROUGH *(Canterbury)*

38TH BISHOP
Rt. Revd Donald Allister, *cons.* 2010, *apptd* 2009; Bishop's Lodging, The Palace, Peterborough PE1 1YA
Signs Donald Petriburg:

BISHOP SUFFRAGAN
Brixworth, vacant

DEAN
Very Revd Charles Taylor, *apptd* 2007

Director of Music, Andrew Reid, *apptd* 2004

ARCHDEACONS
Northampton, Ven. Christine Allsopp, *apptd* 2005
Oakham, Ven. David Painter, *apptd* 2000

Chancellor, David Pittaway, QC, *apptd* 2005
Registrar and Legal Secretary, Revd Raymond Hemingray
Diocesan Secretary, Canon Richard Pestell, Diocesan Office, The Palace, Peterborough PE1 1YB T 01733-887000

PORTSMOUTH *(Canterbury)*

9TH BISHOP
Rt. Revd Christopher Foster, *cons.* 2010, *apptd* 2010; Bishopsgrove, 26 Osborn Road, Fareham, Hants PO16 7DQ
Signs Christopher Portsmouth

DEAN
Very Revd David Brindley, *apptd* 2002

Organist, David Price, *apptd* 1996

ARCHDEACONS
Isle of Wight, Ven. Caroline Baston, *apptd* 2006
Portsdown, Ven. Trevor Reader, *apptd* 2006
The Meon, vacant

Chancellor, C. Clark, QC
Registrar and Legal Secretary, Hilary Tyler
Diocesan Secretary, Wendy Kennedy, Diocesan Offices, 1st Floor, Peninsular House, Wharf Road, Portsmouth PO2 8HB T 023-9289 9664

RIPON AND LEEDS *(York)*

12TH BISHOP
Rt. Revd John Packer, *cons.* 1996, *apptd* 2000; Hollin House, Weetwood Avenue LS16 5NG
Signs John Ripon and Leeds

BISHOP SUFFRAGAN
Knaresborough, Rt. Revd James Bell, *cons.* 2004, *apptd* 2004; Thistledown, Main Street, Exelby, Bedale DL8 2HD

DEAN
Revd Keith Jukes, *apptd* 2007

Director of Music, Andrew Bryden, *apptd* 2003

ARCHDEACONS
Leeds, Ven. Peter Burrows, *apptd* 2005
Richmond, Ven. Janet Henderson, *apptd* 2007

Chancellor, His Hon. Judge Simon Grenfell, *apptd* 1992
Registrars and Legal Secretaries, Nicola Harding; Christopher Tunnard
Diocesan Secretary, Philip Arundel, Diocesan Office, St Mary's Street, Leeds LS9 7DP T 0113-200 0540

ROCHESTER *(Canterbury)*

107TH BISHOP
Rt Revd James Langstaff, *cons.* 2004, *apptd* 2010; Bishopscourt, St Margaret's Street, Rochester ME1 1TS

BISHOP SUFFRAGAN
Tonbridge, Rt. Revd Dr Brian C. Castle, *cons.* 2002, *apptd* 2002; Bishop's Lodge, 48 St Botolph's Road, Sevenoaks TN13 3AG

DEAN
Very Revd Adrian Newman, *apptd* 2004

Director of Music, Scott Farrell, *apptd* 2008

ARCHDEACONS
Bromley, Ven. Paul Wright, *apptd* 2003
Rochester, Ven. Simon Burton-Jones, *apptd* 2010
Tonbridge, Ven. Clive Mansell, *apptd* 2002

Chancellor, John Gallagher, *apptd* 2006
Registrar and Legal Secretary, Owen Carew-Jones
Diocesan Secretary, Canon Louise Gilbert, St Nicholas Church, Boley Hill, Rochester ME1 1SL T 01634-560000

ST ALBANS *(Canterbury)*

10TH BISHOP
Rt. Revd Dr Alan Smith, *cons.* 2001, *apptd* 2009, *trans.* 2009; Abbey Gate House, St Albans AL3 4HD
Signs Alan St Albans

BISHOPS SUFFRAGAN
Bedford, Rt. Revd Richard N. Inwood, *cons.* 2003, *apptd* 2003; Bishop's Lodge, Bedford Road, Cardington, Bedford MK44 3SS
Hertford, vacant

DEAN
Very Revd Dr Jeffrey John, *apptd* 2004

Organist, Andrew Lucas, *apptd* 1998

ARCHDEACONS
Bedford, Ven. Paul Hughes, *apptd* 2004
Hertford, Ven. Trevor Jones, *apptd* 1997
St Albans, Ven. Jonathan Smith, *apptd* 2008

Chancellor, Roger Kaye, *apptd* 2002
Registrar and Legal Secretary, David Cheetham
Diocesan Secretary, Susan Pope, Holywell Lodge, 41 Holywell Hill, St Albans AL1 1HE T 01727-854532

ST EDMUNDSBURY AND IPSWICH *(Canterbury)*

10TH BISHOP
Rt. Revd Nigel Stock, *cons.* 2000, *apptd* 2007; Bishop's House, 4 Park Road, Ipswich IP1 3ST
Signs Nigel St Edum and Ipswich

BISHOP SUFFRAGAN
Dunwich, Rt. Revd Clive Young, *cons.* 1999, *apptd* 1999; 28 Westerfield Road, Ipswich IP4 2UJ

DEAN
Very Revd Frances Ward, *apptd* 2010

Director of Music, James Thomas, *apptd* 1997

ARCHDEACONS
Sudbury, Ven. Dr David Jenkins, *apptd* 2010
Suffolk, Ven. Dr Judy Hunt, *apptd* 2009

Chancellor, David Etherington, QC
Registrar and Legal Secretary, James Hall
Diocesan Secretary, Nicholas Edgell, Diocesan Office, St Nicholas Centre, 4 Cutler Street, Ipswich IP1 1UQ T 01473-298500

SALISBURY *(Canterbury)*

78TH BISHOP
vacant

BISHOPS SUFFRAGAN
Ramsbury, Rt. Revd Stephen Conway, *cons.* 2006, *apptd* 2006; Southbroom House, London Road, Devizes, Wiltshire SN10 1LT
Sherborne, Rt. Revd Graham Kings, PHD, *cons.* 2009, *apptd* 2009; Little Bailie, Dullar Lane, Sturminster Marshall, Wimborne, Dorset BH21 4AD

DEAN
Very Revd June Osborne, *apptd* 2004

Organist, David Halls, *apptd* 2005

ARCHDEACONS
Dorset, Ven. Stephen Waine, *apptd* 2010
Sarum, Ven. Alan Jeans, *apptd* 2003
Sherborne, Ven. Paul Taylor, *apptd* 2004
Wilts, Ven. John Wraw, *apptd* 2004

Chancellor, His Hon. Judge Samuel Wiggs, *apptd* 1997
Registrar and Legal Secretary, Andrew Johnson
Diocesan Secretary, Lucinda Herklots, Church House, Crane Street, Salisbury SP1 2QB T 01722-411922

SHEFFIELD *(York)*

7TH BISHOP
Rt. Revd Steven Croft, PHD, *cons.* 2009, *apptd* 2008; Bishopscroft, Snaithing Lane, Sheffield S10 3LG
Signs Steven Sheffield

BISHOP SUFFRAGAN
Doncaster, Rt. Revd Cyril Guy Ashton, *cons.* 2000, *apptd* 2000; Bishop's House, 3 Farrington Court, Wickersley, Rotherham S66 1JQ

DEAN
Very Revd Peter Bradley, *apptd* 2003

Master of Music, Neil Taylor, *apptd* 1997

ARCHDEACONS
Doncaster, Ven. Robert Fitzharris, *apptd* 2001
Sheffield and Rotherham, Ven. Martyn Snow, *apptd* 2010

Chancellor, Prof. David McClean, *apptd* 1992
Registrar and Legal Secretary, Andrew Vidler
Diocesan Secretary, Malcolm Fair, Diocesan Church House, 95–99 Effingham Street, Rotherham S65 1BL T 01709-309100

SODOR AND MAN *(York)*

81ST BISHOP
Rt. Revd Robert Paterson, *cons.* 2008, *apptd* 2008; The Bishop's House, The Falls, Tromode Road, Douglas, Isle of Man IM4 4PZ
Signs Robert Sodor and Man

ARCHDEACON OF MAN
Ven. Brian Smith, *apptd* 2005
Vicar-General and Chancellor, Clare Faulds
Registrar, Timothy Mann
Diocesan Secretary, Mrs S. Lawrinson, 8 Hilary Wharf, South Quay, Douglas, Isle of Man IM1 5BL T 01624-673477

SOUTHWARK *(Canterbury)*

10TH BISHOP
vacant

AREA BISHOPS
Croydon, Rt. Revd Nicholas Baines, *cons.* 2003, *apptd* 2003; St Matthew's House, 100 George Street, Croydon, Surrey CR0 1PE
Kingston upon Thames, Rt. Revd Richard Cheetham, *cons.* 2002, *apptd* 2002; Kingston Episcopal Area Office, 620 Kingston Road, London SW20 8DN
Woolwich, Rt. Revd Christopher Chessun (Bishop for Urban Life and Faith), *cons.* 2005, *apptd* 2005; Diocesan Office (*see* below)

DEAN
Very Revd Colin B. Slee, OBE, *apptd* 1994

Organist, Peter Wright, FRCO, *apptd* 1989

ARCHDEACONS
Croydon, Ven. Tony Davies, *apptd* 1994
Lambeth, Ven. Christopher Skilton, *apptd* 2003
Lewisham, Ven. Christine Hardman, *apptd* 2001
Reigate, Ven. Daniel Kajumba, *apptd* 2001
Southwark, Ven. Dr Michael Ipgrave, *apptd* 2004
Wandsworth, Ven. Stephen Roberts, *apptd* 2005

Chancellor, Philip Petchey
Registrar and Legal Secretary, Paul Morris
Diocesan Secretary, Simon Parton, Trinity House, 4 Chapel Court, Borough High Street, London SE1 1HW T 020-7939 9400

SOUTHWELL AND NOTTINGHAM *(York)*

11TH BISHOP
Rt. Revd Paul Butler, *cons.* 2004, *apptd* 2009; Bishop's Manor, Southwell NG25 0JR
Signs Paul Southwell and Nottingham

BISHOP SUFFRAGAN
Sherwood, Rt. Revd Anthony Porter, *cons.* 2006, *apptd* 2006; Dunham House, 8 Westgate, Southwell NG25 0JL

DEAN
Very Revd John Guille, *apptd* 2007

Organist, Paul Hale, *apptd* 1989

ARCHDEACONS
Newark, Ven. Nigel Peyton, *apptd* 1999
Nottingham, Ven. Peter Hill, *apptd* 2007

Chancellor, Linda Box, *apptd* 2005
Registrar and Legal Secretary, Christopher Hodson
Diocesan Secretary, Dunham House, Westgate, Southwell, Notts NG25 0JL T 01636-817204

TRURO *(Canterbury)*

15TH BISHOP

Rt. Revd Tim Thornton, *cons.* 2001, *apptd* 2008; Lis Escop, Truro TR3 6QQ
Signs Tim Truro

BISHOP SUFFRAGAN

St Germans, Rt. Revd Royden Screech, *cons.* 2000, *apptd;* 2000; 32 Falmouth Road, Truro, Cornwall TR1 2HX

DEAN

Very Revd Dr Christopher Hardwick, *apptd* 2005

Organist and Director of Music, Chris Gray, *apptd* 2008

ARCHDEACONS

Cornwall, Ven. Roger Bush, *apptd* 2006
Bodmin, Ven. Clive Cohen, *apptd* 2000

Chancellor, Timothy Briden, *apptd* 1998
Registrar and Legal Secretary, Martin Follett
Diocesan Secretary, Clive Cohen, Diocesan House, Kenwyn, Truro TR1 1JQ T 01872-274351

WAKEFIELD *(York)*

12TH BISHOP

Rt. Revd Stephen Platten, *cons.* 2003, *apptd* 2003; Bishop's Lodge, Woodthorpe Lane, Wakefield WF2 6JL
Signs Stephen Wakefield

BISHOP SUFFRAGAN

Pontefract, Rt. Revd Anthony William Robinson, *cons.* 2003, *apptd* 2002; Pontefract House, 181A Manygates Lane, Wakefield WF2 7DR

DEAN

Very Revd Jonathan Greener, *apptd* 2007

Organist, Thomas Moore, *apptd* 2010

ARCHDEACONS

Halifax, Ven. Robert Freeman, *apptd* 2003
Pontefract, Peter Townley, *apptd* 2008

Chancellor, Paul Downes, *apptd* 2006
Registrar and Legal Secretaries, Julian Gill; Julia Wilding
Diocesan Secretary, Ashley Ellis, Church House, 1 South Parade, Wakefield WF1 1LP T 01924-371802

WORCESTER *(Canterbury)*

113TH BISHOP

Rt. Revd Dr John Inge, *cons.* 2003, *apptd* 2007; The Bishop's Office, The Old Palace, Deansway, Worcester WR1 2JE
Signs John Wigorn

SUFFRAGAN BISHOP

Dudley, Rt. Revd Dr David S. Walker, *cons.* 2000, *apptd* 2000; The Bishop's House, Bishop's Walk, Cradley Heath B64 7JF

DEAN

Very Revd Peter Atkinson, *apptd* 2006

Organist, Dr Adrian Lucas, *apptd* 1996

ARCHDEACONS

Dudley, Ven. Fred Trethewey, *apptd* 2001
Worcester, Ven. Roger Morris, *apptd* 2008

Chancellor, Charles Mynors, *apptd* 1999
Registrar and Legal Secretary, Michael Huskinson
Diocesan Secretary, Robert Higham, The Old Palace, Deansway, Worcester WR1 2JE T 01905-20537

ROYAL PECULIARS

WESTMINSTER

The Collegiate Church of St Peter
Dean, Very Revd Dr John Hall
Sub Dean and Archdeacon, vacant
Chapter Clerk and Receiver-General, Sir Stephen Lamport, KCVO, Chapter Office, 20 Dean's Yard, London SW1P 3PA
Organist, James O'Donnell, *apptd* 1999
Registrar, Stuart Holmes, MVO
Legal Secretary, Christopher Vyse, *apptd* 2000

WINDSOR

The Queen's Free Chapel of St George within Her Castle of Windsor
Dean, Rt. Revd Sir David Conner, KCVO, *apptd* 1998
Chapter Clerk, Charlotte Manley, LVO, OBE, *apptd* 2003; Chapter Office, The Cloisters, Windsor Castle, Windsor, Berks SL4 1NJ
Director of Music, Timothy Byram-Wigfield, *apptd* 2004

OTHER ANGLICAN CHURCHES

THE CHURCH IN WALES

The Anglican Church was the established church in Wales from the 16th century until 1920, when the estrangement of the majority of Welsh people from Anglicanism resulted in disestablishment. Since then the Church in Wales has been an autonomous province consisting of six sees. The bishops are elected by an electoral college comprising elected lay and clerical members, who also elect one of the diocesan bishops as Archbishop of Wales.

The legislative body of the Church in Wales is the Governing Body, which has 143 members divided between the three orders of bishops, clergy and laity. Its president is the Archbishop of Wales and it meets twice annually. Its decisions are binding upon all members of the church. The church's property and finances are the responsibility of the Representative Body. There are about 65,644 members of the Church in Wales, with 536 stipendiary clergy and 944 parishes.

THE REPRESENTATIVE BODY OF THE CHURCH IN WALES, 39 Cathedral Road, Cardiff CF11 9XF T 029-2034 8200 *Secretary,* John Shirley

12th ARCHBISHOP OF WALES, Most Revd Dr Barry Morgan (Bishop of Llandaff), *elected* 2003
Signs Barry Cambrensis

BISHOPS

Bangor (81st), Rt. Revd Andrew John, *b.* 1964 *cons.* 2008, *elected* 2008; Ty'r Esgob, Upper Garth Road, Bangor, Gwynedd LL57 2SS *Signs* Andrew Bangor. *Stipendiary clergy,* 51

Llandaff (102nd), Most Revd Dr Barry Morgan (*also* Archbishop of Wales), *b.* 1947, *cons.* 1993, *trans.* 1999; Llys Esgob, The Cathedral Green, Llandaff, Cardiff CF5 2YE *Signs* Barry Cambrensis. *Stipendiary clergy,* 143

Monmouth (9th), Rt. Revd Dominic Walker, *b.* 1948, *cons.* 1997, *elected* 2003; Bishopstow, Stow Hill, Newport NP20 4EA *Signs* Dominic Monmouth. *Stipendiary clergy,* 90

St Asaph (76th), Rt. Revd Gregory Cameron, *b.* 1959, *cons.* 2009, *elected* 2009; Esgobty, Upper Denbigh Road,

St Asaph, Denbighshire LL17 0TW *Signs* Gregory Llanelwy. *Stipendiary clergy,* 102

St David's (128th), Rt. Revd (John) Wyn Evans, *b.* 1946, *cons.* 2008, *elected* 2008; Llys Esgob, Abergwili, Carmarthen SA31 2JG *Signs* Wyn St Davids. *Stipendiary clergy,* 126

Swansea and Brecon (9th), Rt. Revd John Davies, *b.* 1953, *cons.* 2008, *elected* 2008; Ely Tower, Castle Square, Brecon, Powys LD3 9DJ *Signs* John Swansea & Brecon. *Stipendiary clergy,* 71

The stipend for a diocesan bishop of the Church in Wales is £38,800 a year for 2010–11.

SCOTTISH EPISCOPAL CHURCH

The Scottish Episcopal Church was founded after the Act of Settlement (1690) established the presbyterian nature of the Church of Scotland. The Scottish Episcopal Church is a member of the worldwide Anglican Communion. The governing authority is the General Synod, an elected body of 140 members (70 from the clergy and 70 from the laity) which meets once a year. The bishop who convenes and presides at meetings of the General Synod is called the 'primus' and is elected by his fellow bishops.

There are 37,047 members of the Scottish Episcopal Church, seven bishops, 518 serving clergy and around 299 churches and places of worship.

THE GENERAL SYNOD OF THE SCOTTISH EPISCOPAL CHURCH, 21 Grosvenor Crescent, Edinburgh EH12 5EE T 0131-225 6357
W www.scotland.anglican.org
Secretary-General, John Stuart

PRIMUS OF THE SCOTTISH EPISCOPAL CHURCH, Most Revd David Chillingworth (Bishop of St Andrews, Dunkeld and Dunblane), *elected* 2009

BISHOPS

Aberdeen and Orkney, Rt. Revd Dr Bob Gillies, *b.* 1951, *cons.* 2007, *elected* 2007. *Clergy,* 54

Argyll and the Isles, vacant. *Clergy* 22

Brechin, Rt. Revd Dr John Mantle, *b.* 1946, *cons.* 2005, *elected* 2005. *Clergy,* 35

Edinburgh, Rt. Revd Brian Smith, *b.* 1943, *cons.* 1993, *elected* 2001. *Clergy,* 162

Glasgow and Galloway, Rt. Revd Dr Gregor Duncan, *b.* 1950, *cons.* 2010, *elected* 2010. *Clergy,* 99

Moray, Ross and Caithness, Rt. Revd Mark Strange, *b.* 1961, *cons.* 2007, *elected* 2007. *Clergy,* 31

St Andrews, Dunkeld and Dunblane, Most Revd David Chillingworth, *b.* 1951, *cons.* 2005, *elected* 2005. *Clergy,* 86

The minimum stipend of a diocesan bishop of the Scottish Episcopal Church for 2010 is £33,705 (ie 1.5 times the standard clergy stipend of £22,470).

CHURCH OF IRELAND

The Anglican Church was the established church in Ireland from the 16th century but never secured the allegiance of the majority and was disestablished in 1871. The Church of Ireland is divided into the provinces of Armagh and Dublin, each under an archbishop. The provinces are subdivided into 12 dioceses.

The legislative body is the General Synod, which has 660 members in total, divided between the House of Bishops (12 members) and the House of Representatives (216 clergy and 432 laity). The Archbishop of Armagh is elected by the House of Bishops; other episcopal elections are made by an electoral college.

There are around 390,000 members of the Church of Ireland, 275,000 in Northern Ireland and 115,000 in the Republic of Ireland. There are two archbishops, ten bishops and over 500 stipendiary clergy.

CENTRAL OFFICE, Church of Ireland House, Church Avenue, Rathmines, Dublin 6 T (+353) (1) 497 8422
Chief Officer and Secretary of the Representative Church Body, D. C. Reardon

PROVINCE OF ARMAGH

Archbishop of Armagh, Primate of all Ireland and Metropolitan, Most Revd Alan Harper, OBE, *b.* 1944, *cons.* 2002, *trans.* 2007. *Clergy,* 55

BISHOPS

Clogher, Rt. Revd Michael Jackson, PhD, DPHIL, *b.* 1956, *cons.* 2002, *apptd* 2002. *Clergy,* 32

Connor, Rt. Revd Alan Abernethy, *b.* 1957, *cons.* 2007, *apptd* 2007. *Clergy,* 106

Derry and Raphoe, Rt. Revd Kenneth Good, *b.* 1952, *cons.* 2002, *apptd* 2002. *Clergy,* 51

Down and Dromore, Rt. Revd Harold Miller, *b.* 1950, *cons.* 1997, *apptd* 1997. *Clergy,* 116

Kilmore, Elphin and Ardagh, Rt. Revd Kenneth Clarke, *b.* 1949, *cons.* 2001, *apptd* 2001. *Clergy,* 21

Tuam, Killala and Achonry, Rt. Revd Richard Henderson, DPHIL, *b.* 1957, *cons.* 1998, *apptd* 1998. *Clergy,* 13

PROVINCE OF DUBLIN

Archbishop of Dublin, Bishop of Glendalough, Primate of Ireland and Metropolitan, Most Revd John Neill, *b.* 1945, *apptd* 2002. *Clergy,* 86

BISHOPS

Cashel and Ossory, Most Revd Michael Burrows, *b.* 1961, *cons.* 2006, *apptd* 2006. *Clergy,* 42

Cork, Cloyne and Ross, Rt. Revd William Colton, *b.* 1960, *cons.* 1999, *apptd* 1999. *Clergy,* 30

Limerick, Killaloe and Ardfert, Rt. Revd Trevor Williams, *b.* 1948, *cons.* 2008. *Clergy,* 19

Meath and Kildare, Most Revd Richard Clarke, PhD, *b.* 1949, *cons.* 1996, *apptd* 1996. *Clergy,* 26

OVERSEAS

PRIMATES

Primate and Presiding Bishop of Aotearoa, New Zealand and Polynesia, Most Revd William Turei

Primate of Australia, Most Revd Phillip Aspinall

Primate of Brazil, Most Revd Maurício Araújo de Andrade

Archbishop of the Province of Burundi, Most Revd Bernard Ntahoturi

Archbishop and Primate of Canada, Most Revd Frederick Hiltz

Archbishop of the Province of Central Africa, vacant

Primate of the Central Region of America, Most Revd Martin de Jesus Barahona

Archbishop of the Province of Congo, Most Revd Henry Isingoma

Primate of the Province of Hong Kong Sheng Kung Hui, Most Revd Paul Kwong

Archbishop of the Province of the Indian Ocean, Most Revd Gerald Ernest

Primate of Japan (Nippon Sei Ko Kai), Most Revd Nathaniel Uematsu

President-Bishop of Jerusalem and the Middle East, Most Revd Dr Mouneer Anis
Archbishop of the Province of Kenya, Most Revd Eliud Wabukala
Archbishop of the Province of Korea, Rt. Revd Soloman Yoon
Archbishop of the Province of Melanesia, Most Revd David Vunagi
Archbishop of Mexico, Most Revd Carlos Touche-Porter
Archbishop of the Province of Myanmar, Most Revd Stephen Oo
Archbishop of the Province of Nigeria, Most Rt. Revd Nicholas Okoh
Archbishop of Papua New Guinea, Most Revd James Ayong
Prime Bishop of the Philippines, Rt. Revd Edward Malecdan
Archbishop of the Province of Rwanda, Most Revd Emmanuel Kolini
Primate of the Province of South East Asia, Most Revd Dr John Chew
Metropolitan of the Province of Southern Africa, Most Revd Thabo Makgoba
Presiding Bishop of the Southern Cone of America, Most Revd Gregory Venables
Archbishop of the Province of the Sudan, Most Revd Daniel Yak
Archbishop of the Province of Tanzania, Most Revd Valentino Mokiwa
Archbishop of the Province of Uganda, Most Revd Henry Orombi
Presiding Bishop and Primate of the USA, Most Revd Katharine Schori
Archbishop of the Province of West Africa, Most Revd Justice Ofei Akrofi
Archbishop of the Province of the West Indies, Most Revd Dr John Holder

OTHER CHURCHES AND EXTRA-PROVINCIAL DIOCESES

Anglican Church of Bermuda, extra-provincial to Canterbury
Bishop, Rt. Revd Patrick White
Church of Ceylon, extra-provincial to Canterbury
Bishop of Colombo, Rt. Revd Duleep de Chickera
Bishop of Kurunagala, Rt. Revd Kumara Illangasinghe
Episcopal Church of Cuba, Rt. Revd Miguel Zaldivar *(interim)*
Falkland Islands, extra-provincial to Canterbury
Episcopal Commissary, Rt. Revd Stephen Venner (Bishop to the Forces)
Lusitanian Church (Portuguese Episcopal Church), extra-provincial to Canterbury
Bishop, Rt. Revd Fernando Soares
Reformed Episcopal Church of Spain, extra-provincial to Canterbury
Bishop, Rt. Revd Carlos López-Lozano

MODERATION OF CHURCHES IN FULL COMMUNION WITH THE ANGLICAN COMMUNION

Church of Bangladesh, Rt. Revd Paul Sarkar
Church of North India, Most Revd Purely Lyngdoh
Church of South India, Most Revd Suputhrappa Kumar
Church of Pakistan, Rt. Revd Samuel Azariah

CHURCH OF SCOTLAND

The Church of Scotland is the national church of Scotland. The church is reformed in doctrine, and presbyterian in constitution; ie based on a hierarchy of courts of ministers and elders and, since 1990, of members of a diaconate. At local level the Kirk Session consists of the parish minister and ruling elders. At district level the presbyteries, of which there are 44 in Britain, consist of all the ministers in the district, one ruling elder from each congregation, and those members of the diaconate who qualify for membership. The General Assembly is the supreme authority, and is presided over by a Moderator chosen annually by the Assembly. The sovereign, if not present in person, is represented by a Lord High Commissioner who is appointed each year by the Crown.

The Church of Scotland has around 600,000 members, 1,200 parish ministers and 1,464 churches. There are about 20 ministers and other personnel working overseas.

Lord High Commissioner (2010–11), Rt. Hon. Lord Wilson of Tillyorn
Moderator of the General Assembly (2010–11), Rt. Revd John Christie
Principal Clerk, Revd John Chalmers
Depute Clerk, Revd Dr M. MacLean
Procurator, Miss L. Dunlop
Law Agent and Solicitor of the Church, Mrs J. Wilson
Parliamentary Officer, Ms C. Clemmons
General Treasurer, I. Grimmond
Secretary, Church and Society Council, Revd Ewan Aitken
CHURCH OFFICE, 121 George Street, Edinburgh EH2 4YN
T 0131-225 5722

PRESBYTERIES AND CLERKS

Aberdeen, Revd Dr I. McLean
Abernethy, Revd J. MacEwan
Annandale and Eskdale, Revd C. Haston
Angus, Revd M. Bickett
Ardrossan, Revd J. Mackay
Argyll, I. MacLagan
Ayr, Revd K. Elliott
Buchan, George Berstan
Caithness, J. Houston
Dumbarton, Revd C. Caskie
Dumfries and Kirkcudbright, Revd G. Savage
Dundee, Revd J. Wilson
Dunfermline, Revd E. Kenny
Dunkeld and Meigle, Revd J. Russell
Duns, P. Johnson
Edinburgh, Revd G. Whyte
England, Revd S. Brown
Europe, Revd J. Cowie
Falkirk, Revd J. O'Brien
Glasgow, Revd Dr A. Kerr
Gordon, Revd G. Glen
Greenock and Paisley, Revd A. Cherry
Hamilton, Revd S. Paterson
Inverness, Revd A. Younger
Irvine and Kilmarnock, Revd C. Brockie
Jedburgh, Revd W. Frank Campbell
Kincardine and Deeside, Revd Hugh Conkey
Kirkcaldy, Rosemary Frew
Lanark, Revd J. Cutler
Lewis, Revd T. Sinclair
Lochaber, Mrs E. Gill
Lochcarron-Skye, Revd A. MacArthur
Lothian, J. McCulloch

Melrose and Peebles, Jack Stewart
Moray, Revd Hugh Smith
Orkney, Revd T. Hunt
Perth, Revd D. Main
Ross, Ronald Gunstone
St Andrews, Revd K. MacKie
Shetland, Revd C. Greig
Stirling, Dorothy Kinloch
Sutherland, Mrs M. Stobo
Uist, Revd M. Smith
West Lothian, Revd D. Shaw
Wigtown and Stranraer, Revd D. Dutton

The stipends for ministers in the Church of Scotland in 2009 range from £23,139–£30,426, depending on length of service.

ROMAN CATHOLIC CHURCH

The Roman Catholic Church is one worldwide Christian church acknowledging as its head the Bishop of Rome, known as the Pope (Father). He leads a communion of followers of Christ, who believe they continue his presence in the world as servants of faith, hope and love to all society. The Pope is held to be the successor of St Peter and thus invested with the power which was entrusted to St Peter by Jesus Christ. A direct line of succession is therefore claimed from the earliest Christian communities. With the fall of the Roman Empire the Pope also became an important political leader. His territory is now limited to the 0.44 sq. km (0.17 sq. miles) of the Vatican City State, created to provide some independence to the Pope from Italy and other nations.

The Pope exercises spiritual authority over the church with the advice and assistance of the Sacred College of Cardinals, the supreme council of the church. He is also advised by bishops in communion with him, by a group of officers which form the Roman Curia and by his ambassadors, called Apostolic Nuncios, who liaise with the Bishops' Conference in each country.

Those members of the College of Cardinals who are under the age of 80 elect a successor of the Pope following his death. The assembly of the cardinals called to the Vatican for the election of a new Pope is known as the conclave. In complete seclusion the cardinals vote by a secret ballot; a two-thirds majority is necessary before the vote can be accepted as final. When a cardinal receives the necessary number of votes, the Dean of the Sacred College formally asks him if he will accept election and the name by which he wishes to be known. On his acceptance of the office of Supreme Pontiff, the conclave is dissolved and the first Cardinal Deacon announces the election to the assembled crowd in St Peter's Square.

The number of cardinals was fixed at 70 by Pope Sixtus V in 1586 but has been steadily increased since the pontificate of John XXIII and in February 2010 stood at 182. As at February 2010, 111 of the 182 cardinals were cardinal electors.

The Pope has full legislative, judicial and administrative power over the whole church. He is aided in his administration by the curia, which is made up of a number of departments. The Secretariat of State is the central office for carrying out the Pope's instructions and is presided over by the Cardinal Secretary of State. It maintains relations with the departments of the curia, with the episcopate, with the representatives of the Holy See in various countries, governments and private persons. The congregations and pontifical councils are the Pope's ministries and include departments such as the Congregation for the Doctrine of Faith, whose field of competence concerns faith and morals; the Congregation for the Clergy and the Congregation for the Evangelisation of Peoples, the Pontifical Council for the Family and the Pontifical Council for the Promotion of Christian Unity.

The Vatican State does not have diplomatic representatives. The Holy See, composed of the Pope and those who help him in his mission for the church, is recognised by the Conventions of Vienna as an international moral body. The representatives of the Holy See are known as Apostolic Nuncios. Where representation is only to the local churches and not to the government of a country, the papal representative is known as an apostolic delegate. The Roman Catholic Church has over one billion adherents under the care of some 2,500 diocesan bishops worldwide.

SOVEREIGN PONTIFF

His Holiness Pope Benedict XVI (Joseph Ratzinger), *born* Bavaria, Germany, 16 April 1927; *ordained priest* 1951; *appointed Archbishop* (of Munich), March 1977; *created Cardinal* June 1977; *assumed pontificate* 19 April 2005

SECRETARIAT OF STATE

Secretary of State, HE Cardinal Tarcisio Bertone
First Section (General Affairs), Most Revd Fernando Filoni (Titular Archbishop of Volturno)
Second Section (Relations with Other States), Most Revd Dominique Mamberti (Titular Archbishop of Sagona)

BISHOPS' CONFERENCE

The Catholic Church in England and Wales consists of a total of 22 dioceses. The Bishops' Conference, which coordinates common activity, includes the diocesan bishops, the Apostolic Exarch of the Ukrainians, the Bishop of the Forces and the auxiliary bishops. The conference is headed by the president (Most Revd Vincent Nichols, Archbishop of Westminster) and vice-president (the Most Revd Peter Smith, Archbishop of Southwark). There are six departments, each with an episcopal chair: the Department for Christian Life and Worship (the Bishop of Leeds), the Department for Dialogue and Unity (vacant), the Department for Catholic Education and Formation (the Bishop of Nottingham), the Department for Christian Responsibility and Citizenship (the Archbishop of Southwark), the Department for International Affairs (the Bishop of Clifton) and the Department for Evangelisation and Catechesis (the Bishop of Arundel and Brighton).

The Bishops' Conference Standing Committee is made up of two directly elected bishops in addition to the Metropolitan Archbishops and chairs from each of the above departments. The committee has general responsibility for continuity of policy between the plenary sessions of the conference, preparing the conference agenda and implementing its decisions.

The administration of the Bishops' Conference is funded by a levy on each diocese, according to income. A general secretariat in London coordinates and supervises the Bishops' Conference administration activities. There are also other agencies and consultative bodies affiliated to the conference.

The Bishops' Conference of Scotland is the

permanently constituted assembly of the bishops of Scotland. The conference is headed by the president (HE Cardinal Keith Patrick O'Brien, Archbishop of St. Andrews and Edinburgh). The conference establishes various agencies which have an advisory function in relation to the conference. The more important of these agencies are called commissions and each one has a bishop president who, with the other members of the commissions, are appointed by the conference.

The Irish Catholic Bishops' Conference (also known as the Irish Episcopal Conference) has as its president Cardinal Sean Brady of Armagh. Its membership comprises all 31 of the archbishops and bishops of Ireland. It appoints various commissions and agencies to assist with the work of the Catholic Church in Ireland.

The Catholic Church in the UK has an estimated 915,556 mass attendees, 5,599 priests and 4,583 churches.

Bishops' Conferences secretariats:

ENGLAND AND WALES, 39 Eccleston Square, London SW1V 1BX **T** 020-7630 8220 **E** secretariat@cbcew.org.uk **W** www.catholicchurch.org.uk
General Secretary, Mgr Andrew Summersgill

SCOTLAND, 64 Aitken Street, Airdrie ML6 6LT **T** 01236-764061 **W** www.bpsconfscot.com
General Secretary, Revd Paul Conroy

IRELAND, Columba Centre, Maynooth, County Kildare **T** (+353) (1) 505 3000 **E** info@catholicbishops.ie **W** www.catholicbishops.ie
Secretary, Most Revd William Lee (Bishop of Waterford and Lismore)
Executive Secretary, Revd Eamon Martin

GREAT BRITAIN

APOSTOLIC NUNCIO TO GREAT BRITAIN

Most Revd Faustino Sainz Muñoz, 54 Parkside, London SW19 5NE **T** 020-8944 7189

ENGLAND AND WALES

THE MOST REVD ARCHBISHOPS

Westminster, Vincent Nichols, *cons.* 1992, *apptd* 2009 *Archbishop Emeritus,* Cardinal Cormac Murphy-O'Connor, *cons.* 1977, *elevated* 2001 *Auxiliaries,* George Stack, *cons.* 2001; Alan Hopes *cons.* 2003; John Arnold *cons.* 2006. *Clergy,* 690. *Archbishop's Residence,* Archbishop's House, Ambrosden Avenue, London SW1P 1QJ **T** 020-7798 9033

Birmingham, Bernard Longley, *cons.* 2003, *apptd* 2009 *Auxiliaries,* David McGough, *cons.* 2005; William Kenney, *cons.* 1987; Philip Pargeter (retd), *cons.* 1990. *Clergy,* 430. *Archbishop's Residence,* Archbishop's House, 8 Shadwell Street, Birmingham B4 6EY **T** 0121-236 9090

Cardiff, vacant. *Clergy,* 93. *Archbishop's Residence,* Archbishop's House, 41–43 Cathedral Road, Cardiff CF11 9HD **T** 029-2022 0411

Liverpool, Patrick Kelly, *cons.* 1984, *apptd* 1996 *Auxiliary,* Thomas Williams, *cons.* 2003. *Clergy,* 449. *Diocesan Curia,* Archdiocese of Liverpool, Centre for Evangelisation, Croxteth Drive, Sefton Park, Liverpool L17 1AA **T** 0151-522 1000

Southwark, Peter Smith, *cons.* 1995, *apptd* 2010 *Auxiliaries,* John Hine, *cons.* 2001; Patrick Lynch, *cons.* 2006; Paul Hendricks, *cons.* 2006. *Clergy,* 546. *Diocesan Curia,* Archbishop's House, 150 St George's Road, London SE1 6HX **T** 020-7928 5592

THE RT. REVD BISHOPS

Arundel and Brighton, Kieran Conry, *cons.* 2001, *apptd* 2001. *Clergy,* 96. *Diocesan Curia,* Bishop's House, The Upper Drive, Hove, E. Sussex BN3 6NB **T** 01273-506387

Brentwood, Thomas McMahon, *cons.* 1980, *apptd* 1980. *Clergy,* 121. *Bishop's Office,* Cathedral House, Ingrave Road, Brentwood, Essex CM15 8AT **T** 01277-232266

Clifton, Declan Lang, *cons.* 2001, *apptd* 2001. *Clergy,* 251. *Bishop's House,* St Ambrose, North Road, Leigh Woods, Bristol BS8 3PW **T** 0117-973 3072

East Anglia, Michael Evans, *cons* 2003, *apptd* 2003. *Clergy,* 129. *Diocesan Curia,* The White House, 21 Upgate, Poringland, Norwich NR14 7SH **T** 01508-492202

Hallam, John Rawsthorne, *cons.* 1981, *apptd* 1997. *Clergy,* 75. *Bishop's House,* 75 Norfolk Road, Sheffield S2 2SZ **T** 0114-278 7988

Hexham and Newcastle, Seamus Cunningham, *cons.* 2009, *apptd* 2009. *Clergy,* 211. *Diocesan Curia,* Bishop's House, East Denton Hall, 800 West Road, Newcastle upon Tyne NE5 2BJ **T** 0191-228 0003

Lancaster, Michael Campbell, *cons.* 2008, *apptd* 2009. *Clergy,* 170. *Bishop's Office,* The Pastoral Centre, Balmoral Road, Lancaster LA1 3BT **T** 01524-596050

Leeds, Arthur Roche, *cons.* 2001, *apptd* 2004. *Clergy,* 193. *Diocesan Curia,* Hinsley Hall, 62 Headingley Lane, Leeds LS6 2BX **T** 0113-261 8022

Menevia (Wales), Thomas Burns, *cons.* 2002, *apptd* 2008. *Clergy,* 60. *Diocesan Curia,* 27 Convent Street, Swansea SA1 2BX **T** 01792-644017

Middlesbrough, Terence Drainey, *cons.* 2008, *apptd* 2007. *Clergy,* 98. *Diocesan Curia,* 50A The Avenue, Linthorpe, Middlesbrough TS5 6QT **T** 01642-850505

Northampton, Peter Doyle, *Clergy,* 178. *Diocesan Curia,* Bishop's House, Marriott Street, Northampton NN2 6AW **T** 01604-715635

Nottingham, Malcolm McMahon, *cons.* 2000, *apptd* 2000. *Clergy,* 162. *Bishop's House,* 27 Cavendish Road East, The Park, Nottingham NG7 1BB **T** 0115-947 4786

Plymouth, Christopher Budd, *cons.* 1986, *apptd* 1985. *Clergy,* 130. *Bishop's Residence,* Bishop's House, 31 Wyndham Street West, Plymouth PL1 5RZ **T** 01752-224414

Portsmouth, Crispian Hollis, *cons.* 1987, *apptd* 1989. *Clergy,* 282. *Bishop's Residence,* Bishop's House, Edinburgh Road, Portsmouth, Hants PO1 3HG **T** 023-9282 0894

Salford, Terence Brain, *cons.* 1991, *apptd* 1997. *Clergy,* 387. *Diocesan Curia,* Wardley Hall, Worsley, Manchester M28 2ND **T** 0161-794 2825

Shrewsbury, Brian Noble, *cons.* 1995, *apptd* 1995. *Clergy* 125. *Diocesan Curia,* 2 Park Road South, Prenton, Wirral CH43 4UX **T** 0151-652 9855
Coadjutor Bishop, Mark Davies

Wrexham (Wales), Edwin Regan, *cons.*1994, *apptd* 1994. *Clergy,* 45. *Diocesan Curia,* Bishop's House, Sontley Road, Wrexham LL13 7EW **T** 01978-262726

SCOTLAND

THE MOST REVD ARCHBISHOPS

St Andrews and Edinburgh, HE Cardinal Keith Patrick O'Brien, *cons.* 1985, *apptd* 1985, *elevated* 2003. *Clergy,* 170. *Diocesan Office,* 100 Strathearn Road, Edinburgh EH9 1BB **T** 0131-623 8900

Glasgow, Mario Joseph Conti, *cons.* 1977, *apptd* 2002. *Clergy,* 225. *Diocesan Curia,* 196 Clyde Street, Glasgow G1 4JY **T** 0141-226 5898

THE RT. REVD BISHOPS

Aberdeen, Peter Moran, *cons.* 2003, *apptd* 2003. *Clergy,* 43. *Diocesan Curia,* Bishop's House, 3 Queen's Cross, Aberdeen AB15 4XU T 01224-319154

Argyll and the Isles, Joseph Toal, *cons.* 2008, *apptd* 2008. *Clergy,* 32. *Bishop's House,* Esplanade, Oban, Argyll PA34 5AB T 01631-567436

Dunkeld, Vincent Logan, *cons.* 1981. *Clergy,* 50. *Diocesan Curia,* 24–28 Lawside Road, Dundee DD3 6XY T 01382-225453

Galloway, John Cunningham, *cons.* 2004, *apptd* 2004. *Clergy* 56. *Diocesan Curia,* 8 Corsehill Road, Ayr KA7 2ST T 01292-266750

Motherwell, Joseph Devine, *cons.* 1977, *apptd* 1983. *Clergy,* 123. *Diocesan Curia,* Coursington Road, Motherwell ML1 1PP T 01698-269114

Paisley, Philip Tartaglia, *cons.* 2005, *apptd* 2005. *Clergy,* 83. *Diocesan Curia,* Diocesan Centre, Cathedral Precincts, Incle Street, Paisley PA1 1HR T 0141-847 6130

BISHOPRIC OF THE FORCES

Rt. Revd Richard Moth, *cons.* 2009, *apptd* 2009. *Administration,* RC Bishopric of the Forces, Wellington House, St Omer Barracks, Thornhill Road, Aldershot, Hants GU11 2BG T 01252-348234

IRELAND

There is one hierarchy for the whole of Ireland. Several of the dioceses have territory partly in the Republic of Ireland and partly in Northern Ireland.

APOSTOLIC NUNCIO TO IRELAND

HE Most Revd Giuseppe Leanza (Titular Archbishop of Lilybaeum), 183 Navan Road, Dublin 7 T (+353) (1) 838 0577 F (+353) (1) 838 0276

THE MOST REVD ARCHBISHOPS

Armagh, Cardinal Seán Brady (*also* Primate of all Ireland), *cons.* 1995, *apptd* 1996. *Auxiliary Bishop,* Most Revd Gerard Clifford, *cons.* 1991. *Clergy,* 165. *Bishop's Residence,* Ara Coeli, Armagh BT61 7QY T 028-3752 2045

Cashel and Emly, Dermot Clifford, *cons.* 1986, *apptd* 1988. *Clergy,* 103. *Archbishop's House,* Thurles, Co. Tipperary T (+353) (504) 21512

Dublin, Diarmuid Martin, *cons.* 1999, *apptd Coadjutor Archbishop* 2003, *succeeded as Archbishop* 2004. *Archbishop Emeritus,* HE Cardinal Desmond Connell, *cons.* 1988, *elevated* 2001. *Auxiliary,* vacant. *Clergy,* 994. *Archbishop's House,* Drumcondra, Dublin 9 T (+353) (1) 837 3732

Tuam, Michael Neary, *cons.* 1992, *apptd* 1995. *Clergy,* 141. *Archbishop's House,* Tuam, Co. Galway T (+353) (93) 24166

THE RT. REVD BISHOPS

Achonry, Brendan Kelly, *cons.* 2008, *apptd* 2007. *Clergy,* 53. *Bishop's House,* Edmondstown, Ballaghaderreen, Co. Roscommon T (+353) (94) 986 0021

Ardagh and Clonmacnois, Colm O'Reilly, *cons.* 1983, *apptd* 1983. *Clergy,* 65. *Diocesan Office,* St Michael's, Longford, Co. Longford T (+353) (43) 46432

Clogher, Liam MacDaid *cons.* 2010, *apptd* 2010. *Clergy,* 74. *Bishop's House,* Monaghan T (+353) (47) 81019

Clonfert, John Kirby, *cons.* 1988 *apptd* 1988. *Clergy,* 40. *Bishop's Residence,* Coorheen, Loughrea, Co. Galway T (+353) (91) 841560

Cloyne, vacant. *Clergy,* 144. *Diocesan Centre,* Cobh, Co. Cork T (+353) (21) 481 1430

Cork and Ross, John Buckley, *cons.* 1984, *apptd* 1998. *Clergy,* 136. *Diocesan Office,* Cork and Ross Offices, Redemption Road, Cork T (+353) (21) 430 1717

Derry, Seamus Hegarty, *cons.* 1982, *apptd* 1994. *Auxiliary,* vacant. *Clergy,* 130. *Bishop's House,* St Eugene's Cathedral, Derry BT48 9YG T 028-7126 2302

Down and Connor, Noel Treanor, *cons.* 2008, *apptd* 2008. *Auxiliaries,* Anthony Farquhar, *cons.* 1983; Donal McKeown, *cons.* 2001. *Clergy,* 225. *Bishop's Residence,* Lisbreen, 73 Somerton Road, Belfast, Co. Antrim BT15 4DE T 028-9077 6185

Dromore, John McAreavey, *cons.* 1999, *apptd* 1999. *Clergy,* 43. *Bishop's House,* 44 Armagh Road, Newry, Co. Down BT35 6PN T 028-3026 2444

Elphin, Christopher Jones, *cons.* 1994, *apptd* 1994. *Clergy,* 70. *Bishop's Residence,* St Mary's, Sligo T (+353) (71) 916 2670

Ferns, Denis Brennan, *cons.* 2006, *apptd* 2006. *Clergy,* 122. *Bishop's House,* Summerhill, Wexford T (+353) (53) 912 2177

Galway, Kilmacduagh and Kilfenora, Martin Drennan, *cons.* 1997, *apptd* 2005. *Clergy,* 76. *Bishop's Residence,* Mount Saint Mary's, Taylor's Hill, Galway T (+353) (91) 563566

Kerry, William Murphy, *cons.* 1995, *apptd* 1995. *Clergy,* 124. *Bishop's House,* Killarney, Co. Kerry T (+353) (64) 663 1168

Kildare and Leighlin, vacant. *Clergy,* 110. *Bishop's House,* Carlow T (+353) (59) 917 6725

Killala, John Fleming, *cons.* 2002, *apptd* 2002. *Clergy,* 54. *Bishop's House,* Ballina, Co. Mayo T (+353) (96) 21518

Killaloe, Dr Keiran O'Reilly, *cons.* 2010, *apptd* 2010. *Clergy,* 130. *Diocesan Office,* Westbourne, Ennis, Co. Clare T (+353) (65) 682 8638

Kilmore, Leo O'Reilly, *cons.* 1997, *apptd* 1998. *Clergy,* 90. *Bishop's House,* Cullies, Co. Cavan T (+353) (49) 433 1496

Limerick, vacant. *Clergy,* 109. *Diocesan Office,* Social Service Centre, Henry Street, Limerick T (+353) (61) 315856

Meath, Michael Smith, *cons.* 1984, *apptd* 1990. *Clergy,* 141. *Bishop's House,* Dublin Road, Mullingar, Co. Westmeath T (+353) (44) 934 8841

Ossory, Séamus Freeman, *cons.* 2007, *apptd* 2007. *Clergy,* 79. *Bishop's Residence,* Sion House, Kilkenny T (+353) (56) 776 2448

Raphoe, Philip Boyce, *cons.* 1995, *apptd* 1995. *Clergy,* 82. *Bishop's Residence,* Ard Adhamhnáin, Letterkenny, Co. Donegal T (+353) (74) 912 1208

Waterford and Lismore, William Lee, *cons.* 1993, *apptd* 1993. *Clergy,* 114. *Bishop's House,* John's Hill, Waterford T (+353) (51) 874463

OTHER CHURCHES IN THE UK

AFRICAN AND CARIBBEAN CHURCHES

There are large numbers of African and Caribbean Christian churches or groups in the UK. Some of the larger churches or groups include: the Aladura Churches, the Beneficial Veracious Christ Church, the Cherubim and Seraphim Church, the Christ Embassy, the Deeper Life Bible Church, the Gospel Faith Mission International, Kingsway International Christian Centre, the New Covenant Church, the New Testament Assembly (pentecostal), the Progressive National Baptist Convention, the Redeemed Christian Church of God, the Ruach Ministries and the Universal Prayer Ministries.

African and Caribbean churches are among the fastest growing and largest churches in the UK. There are estimated to be around 135,000 members of African and Caribbean churches in the UK.

ASSOCIATED PRESBYTERIAN CHURCHES OF SCOTLAND

The Associated Presbyterian Churches came into being in 1989 as a result of a division within the Free Presbyterian Church of Scotland. The Associated Presbyterian Churches is reformed and evangelistic in nature and emphasises the importance of doctrine based primarily on the Bible and secondly on the Westminster Confession of Faith. There are congregations in Scotland and Canada, with an estimated 300 members, 6 ministers and 11 congregations in Scotland.

ASSOCIATED PRESBYTERIAN CHURCHES OF SCOTLAND, APC Manse, Polvinster Road, Oban PA34 5TN T 01631-567076 E archibald.mcphail@virgin.net W www.apchurches.org
Moderator of Presbytery, Revd Donald Macaskill
Clerk of Presbytery, Revd Archibald McPhail

BAPTIST CHURCH

Baptists trace their origins to John Smyth, who in 1609 in Amsterdam reinstituted the baptism of conscious believers as the basis of the fellowship of a gathered church. Members of Smyth's church established the first Baptist church in England in 1612. They came to be known as 'General' Baptists and their theology was Arminian, whereas a later group of Calvinists who adopted the baptism of believers came to be known as 'Particular' Baptists. The two sections of the Baptists were united into one body, the Baptist Union of Great Britain and Ireland, in 1891. In 1988 the title was changed to the Baptist Union of Great Britain.

Baptists emphasise the complete autonomy of the local church, although individual churches are linked in various kinds of associations. There are international bodies (such as the Baptist World Alliance) and national bodies, but some Baptist churches belong to neither. However, in Great Britain the majority of churches and associations belong to the Baptist Union of Great Britain. There are also Baptist Unions in Wales, Scotland and Ireland which are much smaller than the Baptist Union of Great Britain, and there is some overlap of membership.

There are currently around 140,000 members, 2,500 ministers and 2,000 churches associated with the Baptist Union of Great Britain. The Baptist Union of Great Britain is one of the founder members of the European Baptist Federation (1948) and the Baptist World Alliance (1905) which represents around 40 million members worldwide.

In the Baptist Union of Scotland there are 12,880 members, 140 pastors and 169 churches.

In the Baptist Union of Wales (Undeb Bedyddwyr Cymru) there are 13,858 members, 108 pastors and 431 churches, including those in England.

BAPTIST UNION OF GREAT BRITAIN, Baptist House, PO Box 44, 129 Broadway, Didcot, Oxon OX11 8RT T 01235-517700 E info@baptist.org.uk W www.baptist.org.uk
General Secretary, Revd Jonathan Edwards

BAPTIST UNION OF SCOTLAND, 14 Aytoun Road, Glasgow G41 5RT T 0141-423 6169 E director@scottishbaptist.org.uk
General Director, Revd A. J. Donaldson

BAPTIST UNION OF WALES, Y Llwyfan, Trinity College, College Road, Carmarthen SA31 3EQ T 01267-245660 E peter@bedyddwyrcymru.co.uk W www.buw.org.uk
President of the English Assembly (2010), Revd Steven Lee
President of the Welsh Assembly (2010–11), Vivian Williams
General Secretary of the Baptist Union of Wales, Revd Peter Thomas

THE BRETHREN

The Brethren was founded in Dublin in 1827–8, it rejected denominationalism and clericalism, and based itself on the structures and practices of the early church. Many groups sprang up; the group at Plymouth became the best known, resulting in the designation by others as the 'Plymouth Brethren'. Early worship had a prescribed form but quickly assumed an unstructured, non-liturgical format.

There are services devoted to worship, usually involving the breaking of bread, and separate preaching meetings. There is no salaried ministry.

A theological dispute led in 1848 to schism between the Open Brethren and the Closed or Exclusive Brethren, each branch later suffering further divisions.

Open Brethren churches are completely independent, but freely cooperate with each other and are run by appointed elders. Exclusive Brethren churches believe in a universal fellowship between congregations. They do not have appointed elders, but use respected members of their congregation to perform certain administrative functions.

The Brethren are established throughout the UK, Ireland, Europe, India, Africa and Australasia. In the UK there are an estimated 71,415 members, 1,268 assembly halls and around 207 full-time workers who are Bible teachers, evangelists and perform administrative functions. There are a number of publishing houses which publish Brethren-related literature. Chapter Two is the main supplier of such literature in the UK and also has a Brethren history archive which is available for use by appointment.

CHAPTER TWO, Conduit Mews, London SE18 7AP T 020-8316 5389 E info@chaptertwobooks.org.uk W www.chaptertwobooks.org.uk

CONGREGATIONAL FEDERATION

The Congregational Federation was founded by members of Congregational churches in England and Wales who did not join the United Reformed Church in 1972. There are also churches in Scotland and France affiliated to the federation. The federation exists to encourage congregations of believers to worship in free assembly, but it has no authority over them and emphasises their right to independence and self-governance.

The federation has 9,151 members, 80 accredited ministers and 295 churches in England, Wales and Scotland.

CONGREGATIONAL FEDERATION, 6 Castle Gate, Nottingham NG1 7AS T 0115-911 1460 E admin@congregational.org.uk W www.congregational.org.uk
President of the Federation (2010–11), Revd Sandra Turner
General Secretary, Revd M. Heaney

FELLOWSHIP OF INDEPENDENT EVANGELICAL CHURCHES

The Fellowship of Independent Evangelical Churches was founded by Revd E. J. Poole-Connor (1872–1962) in 1922. In 1923 the fellowship published its first register of non-denominational pastors, evangelists and congregations who had accepted the doctrinal basis for the fellowship.

Members of the fellowship have two primary convictions, firstly to defend the evangelical faith, and secondly that evangelicalism is the bond that unites the fellowship, rather than forms of worship or church government.

The Fellowship of Independent Evangelical Churches exists to promote the welfare of non-denominational Bible churches and to give expression to the fundamental doctrines of evangelical Christianity. It supports individual churches by gathering and disseminating information and resources, advising churches on current theological, moral, social and practical issues and seeking to uphold the quality and integrity of church leaders through the Pastors' Association.

More than 500 churches throughout the UK are linked through the fellowship. There are more than 350 pastors and approximately 38,000 people worship in fellowship churches every Sunday.

FELLOWSHIP OF INDEPENDENT EVANGELICAL CHURCHES, 39 The Point, Market Harborough, Leics LE16 7QU **T** 01858-434540 **E** admin@fiec.org.uk
W www.fiec.org.uk
Director, John Stevens

FREE CHURCH OF ENGLAND

The Free Church of England, otherwise called the Reformed Episcopal Church, is an independent church, constituted according to the historic faith, tradition and practice of the Church of England. Its roots lie in the 18th century, but most of its growth took place from the 1840s onwards, as clergy and congregations joined it from the established church in protest against the Oxford Movement. The historic episcopate was conferred on the English church in 1876 through bishops of the Reformed Episcopal Church (which had broken away from the Protestant Episcopal Church in the USA in 1873). A branch of the Reformed Episcopal Church was founded in the UK and this merged with the Free Church of England in 1927 to create the present church.

Worship is according to the *Book of Common Prayer* and some modern liturgy is permissable. Only men are ordained to the orders of deacon, presbyter and bishop.

The Free Church of England has around 1,155 members, 17 congregations and around 29 ministers, now mainly confined to England with one congregation in St Petersburg, Russia.

THE FREE CHURCH OF ENGLAND, St Andrews Church, Wolverhampton Road West, Bentley, Walsall WV13 2RL
T 01902-607335 **W** www.fcofe.org.uk
General Secretary, Rt. Revd Paul Hunt

FREE CHURCH OF SCOTLAND

The Free Church of Scotland was formed in 1843 when over 400 ministers withdrew from the Church of Scotland as a result of interference in the internal affairs of the church by the civil authorities. In 1900, all but 26 ministers joined with others to form the United Free Church (most of which rejoined the Church of Scotland in 1929). In 1904 the remaining 26 ministers were recognised by the House of Lords as continuing the Free Church of Scotland.

The church maintains strict adherence to the Westminster Confession of Faith (1648) and accepts the Bible as the sole rule of faith and conduct. Its general assembly meets annually. It also has links with reformed churches overseas. The Free Church of Scotland has about 12,000 members, 90 ministers and 100 congregations.

FREE CHURCH OF SCOTLAND, 15 North Bank Street, The Mound, Edinburgh EH1 2LS **T** 0131-226 5286
E offices@freechurchofscotland.org.uk
W www.freechurch.org
Chief Administrative Officer, Rod Morrison

FREE PRESBYTERIAN CHURCH OF SCOTLAND

The Free Presbyterian Church of Scotland was formed in 1893 by two ministers of the Free Church of Scotland who refused to accept a Declaratory Act passed by the Free Church General Assembly in 1892. The Free Presbyterian Church of Scotland is Calvinistic in doctrine and emphasises observance of the Sabbath. It adheres strictly to the Westminster Confession of Faith of 1648.

The church has about 1,000 members in Scotland and about 4,000 in overseas congregations. It has 20 ministers and 50 churches in the UK.

FREE PRESBYTERIAN CHURCH OF SCOTLAND, 133 Woodlands Road, Glasgow G3 6LE **T** 0141-332 9283
W www.fpchurch.org.uk
Moderator (2010–11), Revd Edward Rayner
Clerk of the Synod, Revd John MacLeod

HOLY APOSTOLIC CATHOLIC ASSYRIAN CHURCH OF THE EAST

The Holy Apostolic Catholic Assyrian Church of the East traces its beginnings to the middle of the first century. It spread from Upper Mesopotamia throughout the territories of the Persian Empire. The Assyrian Church of the East became theologically separated from the rest of the Christian community following the Council of Ephesus in 431. The church is headed by the Catholicos Patriarch and is episcopal in government. The liturgical language is Syriac (Aramaic). The Assyrian Church of the East and the Roman Catholic Church agreed a common Christological declaration in 1994 and a process of dialogue between the Assyrian Church of the East and the Chaldean Catholic Church, which is in communion with Rome but shares the Syriac liturgy, was instituted in 1996.

The church has about 400,000 members in the Middle East, India, Europe, North America and Australasia. In the UK there are around 7,000 members, three congregations and 15 priests.

The church in Great Britain forms part of the diocese of Europe under Mar Odisho Oraham.

HOLY APOSTOLIC CATHOLIC ASSYRIAN CHURCH OF THE EAST, St Mary's Church, Westminster Road, Hanwell, London W7 3TU **T** 020-8567 1814
Representative in Great Britain, Revd Tony

INDEPENDENT METHODIST CHURCHES

The Independent Methodist Churches were formed in 1805 and remained independent when the Methodist Church in Great Britain was formed in 1932. They are mainly concentrated in the industrial areas of the north of England.

The churches are Methodist in doctrine but their organisation is congregational. All the churches are members of the Independent Methodist Connexion of Churches. The controlling body of the Connexion is the Annual Meeting, to which churches send delegates. The Connexional President is elected annually. Between annual meetings the affairs of the Connexion are handled by departmental committees. Ministers are appointed by the churches and trained through the Connexion. The ministry is open to both men and women and is unpaid.

There are 1,900 members, 86 ministers and 84 churches in Great Britain.

INDEPENDENT METHODIST RESOURCE CENTRE, Fleet Street, Pemberton, Wigan WN5 0DS **T** 01942-223526 **E** resourcecentre@imcgb.org.uk **W** www.imcgb.org.uk
President, Eric Southwick
General Secretary, Brian Rowney

LUTHERAN CHURCH

Lutheranism is based on the teachings of Martin Luther, the German leader of the Protestant Reformation. The authority of the scriptures is held to be supreme over church tradition. The teachings of Lutheranism are explained in detail in 16th-century confessional writings, particularly the Augsburg Confession. Lutheranism is one of the largest Protestant denominations and it is particularly strong in northern Europe and the USA. Some Lutheran churches are episcopal, while others have a synodal form of organisation; unity is based on doctrine rather than structure. Most Lutheran churches are members of the Lutheran World Federation, based in Geneva.

Lutheran services in Great Britain are held in 18 languages to serve members of different nationalities. Services usually follow ancient liturgies. English-language congregations are members either of the Lutheran Church in Great Britain or of the Evangelical Lutheran Church of England. The Lutheran Church in Great Britain and other Lutheran churches in Britain are members of the Lutheran Council of Great Britain, which represents them and coordinates their common work.

There are over 70 million Lutherans worldwide; in Great Britain there are about 170,000 members, 45 clergy and 100 congregations.

THE LUTHERAN COUNCIL OF GREAT BRITAIN, 30 Thanet Street, London WC1H 9QH **T** 020-7554 2900 **E** enquiries@lutheran.org.uk **W** www.lutheran.org.uk
General Secretary, Revd Thomas Bruch

METHODIST CHURCH

The Methodist movement started in England in 1729 when the Revd John Wesley, an Anglican priest, and his brother Charles met with others in Oxford and resolved to conduct their lives and study by 'rule and method'. In 1739 the Wesleys began evangelistic preaching and the first Methodist chapel was founded in Bristol in the same year. In 1744 the first annual conference was held, at which the Articles of Religion were drawn up. Doctrinal emphases included repentance, faith, the assurance of salvation, social concern and the priesthood of all believers. After John Wesley's death in 1791 the Methodists withdrew from the established church to form the Methodist Church. Methodists gradually drifted into many groups, but in 1932 the Wesleyan Methodist Church, the United Methodist Church and the Primitive Methodist Church united to form the Methodist Church of Great Britain.

The governing body of the Methodist Church is the conference. The conference meets annually in June or July and consists of two parts: the ministerial and representative sessions. The Methodist Church is structured as a 'Connexion' of churches, circuits and districts: the circuit is formed from the local churches in a defined area; a number of circuits make up each of the 31 districts which provide the link between the conference and the circuits. There are around 70 million Methodists worldwide; at the last count in 2007 there were 267,257 members, 3,509 ministers, 226 Deacons and 6,402 churches in Great Britain.

THE METHODIST CHURCH OF GREAT BRITAIN, Methodist Church House, 25 Marylebone Road, London NW1 5JR **T** 020-7486 5502 **E** helpdesk@methodistchurch.org.uk **W** www.methodist.org.uk
President of the Conference (2010–11), Revd Alison Tomlin
Vice-President of the Conference (2010–11), Deacon Eunice Attwood
General Secretary and Secretary of the Conference, Revd Dr Martyn Atkins

THE METHODIST CHURCH IN IRELAND

The Methodist Church in Ireland is autonomous but has close links with British Methodism. It has a community roll of 51,843 members, 126 ministers, 235 lay preachers and 230 churches.

1 Fountainville Avenue, Belfast BT9 6AN **T** 028-9032 4554 **E** secretary@irishmethodist.org **W** www.irishmethodist.org
President (2010–11) and Secretary, Revd Paul Kingston

ORTHODOX CHURCHES

EASTERN ORTHODOX CHURCH

The Eastern (or Byzantine) Orthodox Church is a communion of self-governing Christian churches that recognises the honorary primacy of the Oecumenical Patriarch of Constantinople.

The position of Orthodox Christians is that the faith was fully defined during the period of the Oecumenical Councils. In doctrine it is strongly trinitarian, and stresses the mystery and importance of the sacraments. It is episcopal in government. The structure of the Orthodox Christian year differs from that of western churches.

Orthodox Christians throughout the world are estimated to number about 300 million; there are 300,000 in the UK.

GREEK ORTHODOX CHURCH (PATRIARCHATE OF ANTIOCH)

There are 19 parishes in the UK and Ireland. The Arch Diocese of Western and Central Europe is led by HE Metropolitan John (Yazigi), based in Paris.

St George's Cathedral, 1A Redhill Street, London NW1 4BG **T** 020-7383 0403 **E** fr.s.gholam@antiochgreekorth.co.uk **W** www.antiochgreekorth.co.uk
Priest, Fr. Samir Gholam

Antiochian Orthodox Parish, St Botolph's Church, Bishopsgate, London EC2M 3TL **T** 07745-478767 **E** alexander.tefft@yahoo.com **W** www.antiochan-london.org
Archpriest, Fr. Alexander Tefft

GREEK ORTHODOX CHURCH (PATRIARCHATE OF CONSTANTINOPLE)

The presence of Greek Orthodox Christians in Britain dates back at least to 1677 when Archbishop Joseph Geogirenes of Samos fled from Turkish persecution and came to London. The present Greek cathedral in Moscow Road, Bayswater, was opened for public worship in 1879 and the Diocese of Thyateira and Great Britain was established in 1922. There are now 116 parishes and other communities (including monasteries) in the UK, served by four bishops, 120 clergy, nine cathedrals and about 94 churches.

The Patriarchate Of Constantinople In Great Britain, Thyateira House, 5 Craven Hill, London W2 3EN
T 020-7723 4787 E mail@thyateira.org.uk
W www.thyateira.org.uk
Archbishop, Gregorios of Thyateira and Great Britain

THE RUSSIAN ORTHODOX CHURCH (PATRIARCHATE OF MOSCOW) AND THE RUSSIAN ORTHODOX CHURCH OUTSIDE RUSSIA

RUSSIAN ORTHODOX CHURCH

The records of Russian Orthodox Church activities in Britain date from the visit to England of Tsar Peter I in the early 18th century. Clergy were sent from Russia to serve the chapel established to minister to the staff of the Imperial Russian Embassy in London.

In 2007, after an 80-year division, the Russian Orthodox Church Outside Russia agreed to become an autonomous part of the Russian Orthodox Church, Patriarchate of Moscow. The reunification agreement was signed by Patriarch Alexy II, 15th Patriarch of Moscow and All Russia and Metropolitan Laurus, leader of the Russian Orthodox Church Outside Russia on 17 May at a ceremony at Christ the Saviour Cathedral in Moscow. Patriarch Alexy II died on 5 December 2008. Metropolitan Kirill of Smolensk and Kaliningrad was enthroned as the 16th Patriarch of Moscow and All Russia on 1 February 2009, having been elected by a secret ballot of clergy on 27 January 2009.

The diocese of Sourozh is the diocese of the Russian Orthodox Church in Great Britain and Ireland and is led by Archbishop Elisey of Sourozh.

Diocese of Sourozh, Diocesan Office, Cathedral of the Dormition and All Saints, 67 Ennismore Gardens, London SW7 1NH T 020-7584 0096 W www.sourozh.org
Diocesan Bishop, Most Revd Elisey (Ganaba) of Sourozh
Assistant Diocesan Bishop, Most Revd Anatoly (Kuznetsov) of Kerch

SERBIAN ORTHODOX CHURCH (PATRIARCHATE OF SERBIA)

There are around 4,000 members in the UK served by 12 clergy. The UK is part of the Diocese of Great Britain and Scandinavia under Bishop Dositej. The church can be contacted in the UK via the church of St Sava in London.

Serbian Orthodox Church in Great Britain, Saint Sava, 89 Lancaster Road, London W11 1QQ T 020-7727 8367
E crkva@spclondon.org W www.spclondon.org
Priest, Very Revd Milun Kostic

OTHER NATIONALITIES

The Patriarchates of Romania and Bulgaria (Diocese of Western Europe) have memberships estimated at 20,000 and 2,000 respectively, while the Georgian Orthodox Church has around 500 members. The Belarusian (membership estimated at 2,400) and Latvian (membership of around 100) Orthodox churches are part of the Patriarchate of Constantinople.

ORIENTAL ORTHODOX CHURCHES

The term 'Oriental Orthodox Churches' is now generally used to describe a group of six ancient eastern churches (Armenian, Coptic, Eritrean, Ethiopian, Indian (Malankara) and Syrian) which rejected the Christological definition of the Council of Chalcedon (AD 451). There are around 50 million members worldwide of the Oriental Orthodox Churches and about 20,075 in the UK.

ARMENIAN ORTHODOX CHURCH (CATHOLICOSATE OF ETCHMIADZIN)

The Armenian Orthodox Church is led by HH Karekin II, Catholicos of All Armenians. The Very Revd Dr Vahan Hovhanessian is the Primate of the Armenian Church of Great Britain and President of the Armenian Community and Church Council.

Armenian Church of Great Britain, The Armenian Vicarage, Iverna Gardens, London W8 6TP T 020-7937 0152
E information@armenianchurch.org.uk
W www.armenianchurch.co.uk
Primate, Very Revd Dr Vahan Hovhanessian

COPTIC ORTHODOX CHURCH

The Coptic Orthodox Church is led by HH Pope Shenouda III and is represented in Great Britain by Bishop Angaelos at the Coptic Orthodox Cathedral of St George at the Coptic Orthodox Church Centre. The Coptic Orthodox Church is the largest Oriental Orthodox community in Great Britain.

Coptic Orthodox Church Centre, Shephalbury Manor, Broadhall Way, Stevenage, Herts SG2 8NP T 01438-745232
E general@copticcentre.com W www.copticcentre.com
Bishop, Bishop Angaelos

BRITISH ORTHODOX CHURCH

The British Orthodox Church is canonically part of the Coptic Orthodox Patriarchate of Alexandria. As it ministers to British people all its services are in English.

The British Orthodox Church, 10 Heathwood Gardens, Charlton, London SE7 8EP T 020-8854 3090
E info@britishorthodox.org W www.britishorthodox.org
Metropolitan, Abba Seraphim

INDIAN ORTHODOX CHURCH

The Indian Orthodox Church, also known as the Malankara Orthodox Church, is part of the Diocese of Europe, UK and Canada under Metropolitan HG Dr Mathews Mar Thimotios. The church in the UK can be contacted via Fr John Samuel at St Gregorios Indian Orthodox Church.

Indian Orthodox Church, St Gregorios Indian Orthodox Church, Cranfield Road, Brockley, London SE4 1UF
T 020-8691 9456 E vicar@indian-orthodox.co.uk
W www.indian-orthodox.co.uk
Vicar, Fr. John Samuel
Hon. Secretary, Abraham Kurien

SYRIAN ORTHODOX CHURCH

The Patriarchate Vicariate of the Syrian Orthodox Church in the United Kingdom is represented by Fr Toma Hazim Dawood.

Syrian Orthodox Church in the UK, 5 Canning Road, Croydon CR0 6QA T 020-8654 7531
E enquiry-uk@syrianorthodoxchurch.net
W www.syrianorthodoxchurch.net
Patriarchal Vicar, Fr Toma Hazim Dawood

PENTECOSTAL CHURCHES

Pentecostalism is inspired by the descent of the Holy Spirit upon the apostles at Pentecost. The movement began in Los Angeles, USA, in 1906 and is characterised by baptism with the Holy Spirit, divine healing, speaking in tongues (glossolalia), and a literal interpretation of the scriptures.

The Pentecostal movement in Britain dates from 1907. Initially, groups of Pentecostalists were led by laymen and did not organise formally. However, in 1915 the Elim Foursquare Gospel Alliance (more usually called the Elim Pentecostal Church) was founded in Ireland by George Jeffreys and currently has about 550 churches, 68,500 adherents and 650 accredited ministers. In 1924 about 70 independent assemblies formed a fellowship, the Assemblies of God in Great Britain and Ireland, which now incorporates around 700 churches and is known as the Assemblies of God Incorporated.

The Apostolic Church grew out of the 1904–5 revivals in South Wales and was established in 1916. The Apostolic Church has around 109 churches, 5,400 adherents and 103 ministers in the UK. The New Testament Church of God was established in England in 1953 and has around 125 congregations, 28,137 members and 320 ministers across England and Wales. In recent years many aspects of Pentecostalism have been adopted by the growing charismatic movement within the Roman Catholic, Protestant and Eastern Orthodox churches. There are about 105 million Pentecostalists worldwide, with about 354,934 adherents in the UK.

THE APOSTOLIC CHURCH, International Administration Offices, PO Box 51298, London SE11 9AJ T 020-7587 1802
E admin@apostolic-church.org
National Leader, Emmanuel Mbakwe

THE ASSEMBLIES OF GOD INCORPORATED, PO Box 7634, Nottingham NG11 6ZY T 0115-921 7272
E info@aog.org.uk W www.aog.org.uk
National leader, John Partington

THE ELIM PENTECOSTAL CHURCH, De Walden House, De Walden Road, West Malvern, Worcestershire WR14 4DF T 0845-302 6750 E info@elimhq.net
W www.elim.org.uk
General Superintendent, Revd John Glass

THE NEW TESTAMENT CHURCH OF GOD, 3 Cheyne Walk, Northampton NN1 5PT T 01604-824222
W www.ntcg.org.uk
Administrative Bishop, Eric Brown

PRESBYTERIAN CHURCH IN IRELAND

The Presbyterian Church in Ireland is reformed in doctrine and presbyterian in constitution. Presbyterianism was established in Ireland as a result of the Ulster plantation in the early 17th century when English and Scottish Protestants mainly settled in the north of Ireland.

There are 21 presbyteries under the chief court known as the general assembly. The general assembly meets annually and is presided over by a moderator who is elected for one year. The ongoing work of the church is undertaken by 15 boards under which there are specialist committees.

There are around 255,557 members of Irish presbyterian churches in the UK and Ireland, forming 549 congregations.

THE PRESBYTERIAN CHURCH IN IRELAND, Church House, Belfast BT1 6DW T 028-9032 2284
E info@presbyterianireland.org
W www.presbyterianireland.org
Moderator (2010–11), Revd Norman Hamilton, OBE
Clerk of Assembly and General Secretary, Revd Dr Donald Watts

PRESBYTERIAN CHURCH OF WALES

The Presbyterian Church of Wales or Calvinistic Methodist Church of Wales is Calvinistic in doctrine and presbyterian in constitution. It was formed in 1811 when Welsh Calvinists severed the relationship with the established church by ordaining their own ministers. It secured its own confession of faith in 1823 and a Constitutional Deed in 1826, and since 1864 the General Assembly has met annually, presided over by a moderator elected for a year. The doctrine and constitutional structure of the Presbyterian Church of Wales was confirmed by act of parliament in 1931–2.

The Church has 28,687 members, 65 ministers and 676 congregations.

THE PRESBYTERIAN CHURCH OF WALES, Tabernacle Chapel, 81 Merthyr Road, Whitchurch, Cardiff CF14 1DD
T 029-2062 7465 E swyddfa.office@ebcpcw.org.uk
W www.ebcpcw.org.uk
Moderator (2010–11), Revd Iain B. Hodgins
General Secretary, Revd Ifan Roberts

RELIGIOUS SOCIETY OF FRIENDS (QUAKERS)

Quakerism is a religious denomination which was founded in the 17th century by George Fox and others in an attempt to revive what they saw as the original 'primitive Christianity'. The movement, at first called Friends of the Truth, started in the Midlands, Yorkshire and north-west England, but there are now Quakers all over Britain and in 36 countries around the world. The colony of Pennsylvania, founded by William Penn, was originally Quaker.

Emphasis is placed on the experience of God in daily life rather than on sacraments or religious occasions. There is no church calendar. Worship is largely silent and there are no appointed ministers; the responsibility for conducting a meeting is shared equally among those present. Religious tolerance and social reform have always been important to Quakers, together with a commitment to peace and non-violence in resolving disputes.

There are more than 25,300 'friends' or Quakers in Great Britain. There are about 500 places where Quaker meetings are held, many of them Quaker-owned Friends Meeting Houses. The Britain Yearly Meeting is the name given to the central organisation of Quakers in Britain.

THE RELIGIOUS SOCIETY OF FRIENDS (QUAKERS) IN BRITAIN, Friends House, 173–177 Euston Road, London NW1 2BJ T 020-7663 1000
E enquiries@quaker.org.uk W www.quaker.org.uk
Recording Clerk, Gillian Ashmore

SALVATION ARMY

The Salvation Army is an international Christian organisation working in 117 countries worldwide. As a church and registered charity, the Salvation Army is funded through donations from its members, the general public and, where appropriate, government grants.

The Salvation Army was founded by a Methodist

minister, William Booth, in the East End of London in 1865, and now has 709 local church and community centres, 57 residential centres for the homeless, 17 elderly care centres and six substance misuse centres. It also runs a clothing recycling programme, charity shops, a prison visiting service and a family tracing service. In 1878 it adopted a quasi-military command structure intended to inspire and regulate its endeavours and to reflect its view that the church was engaged in spiritual warfare. There are around 50,000 members and 1,350 Salvation Army officers (full-time ministers) in the UK. Salvationists emphasise evangelism and the provision of social welfare.

UK TERRITORIAL HEADQUARTERS, 101 Newington Causeway, London SE1 6BN T 020-7367 4500 E info@salvationarmy.org.uk W www.salvationarmy.org.uk
UK Territorial Commander, Commissioner John Matear

SEVENTH-DAY ADVENTIST CHURCH

The Seventh-day Adventist Church is a worldwide Christian church marked by its observance of Saturday as the Sabbath and by its emphasis on the imminent second coming of Jesus Christ. Adventists summarise their faith in '28 fundamental beliefs'.

The church grew out of the Millerite movement in the USA during the mid-19th century and was formally established in 1863. The church has an ethnically and culturally diverse worldwide membership of over 16 million, with a presence in more than 200 countries. In the UK and Ireland there are approximately 31,000 members worshipping in 289 churches and companies.

BRITISH UNION CONFERENCE OF SEVENTH-DAY ADVENTISTS, Stanborough Park, Watford WD25 9JZ T 01923-672251 W www.adventist.org.uk
President, Pastor D. McFarlane

THE (SWEDENBORGIAN) NEW CHURCH

The New Church is based on the teachings of the 18th-century Swedish scientist and theologian Emanuel Swedenborg (1688–1772), who believed that Jesus Christ appeared to him and instructed him to reveal the spiritual meaning of the Bible. He claimed to have visions of the spiritual world, including heaven and hell, and conversations with angels and spirits. He published several theological works, including descriptions of the spiritual world and a Bible commentary.

The second coming of Jesus Christ is believed to have already taken place and is still taking place, being not an actual physical reappearance of Christ, but rather his return in spirit. It is also believed that concurrent with our life on earth is life in a parallel spiritual world, of which we are usually unconscious until death. There are around 30,000 Swedenborgians worldwide, with 8,470 members, 21 Churches and 20 ministers in the UK.

THE GENERAL CONFERENCE OF THE NEW CHURCH, Swedenborg House, 20 Bloomsbury Way, London WC1A 2TH T 0845-686 0086
E enquiries@generalconference.org.uk
W www.generalconference.org.uk
Chief Executive, Michael Hindley

UNDEB YR ANNIBYNWYR CYMRAEG

Undeb Yr Annibynwyr Cymraeg, the Union of Welsh Independents, was formed in 1872 and is a voluntary association of Welsh Congregational churches and personal members. It is mainly Welsh-speaking. Congregationalism in Wales dates back to 1639 when the first Welsh Congregational church was opened in Gwent. Member churches are traditionally Calvinistic in doctrine, although a wide range of interpretations are permitted, and congregationalist in organisation. Each church has complete independence in the government and administration of its affairs.

The Union has 28,892 members, 98 ministers and 449 member churches.

UNDEB YR ANNIBYNWYR CYMRAEG, 5 Axis Court, Riverside Business Park, Swansea Vale, Swansea SA7 0AJ
T 01792-795888 E undeb@annibynwyr.org
W www.annibynwyr.org
President of the Union (2010–12), Revd Andrew Lenny
General Secretary, Revd Dr Geraint Tudur

UNITED REFORMED CHURCH

The United Reformed Church (URC) was first formed by the union of most of the Congregational churches in England and Wales with the Presbyterian Church of England in 1972. Congregationalism dates from the mid-16th century. It is Calvinistic in doctrine, and its followers form independent self-governing congregations bound under God by covenant, a principle laid down in the writings of Robert Browne (1550–1633). From the late 16th century the movement was driven underground by persecution, but the cause was defended at the Westminster Assembly in 1643 and the Savoy Declaration of 1658 laid down its principles. Congregational churches formed county associations for mutual support and in 1832 these associations merged to form the Congregational Union of England and Wales.

Presbyterianism in England also dates from the mid 16th century, and was Calvinistic and evangelical in its doctrine. It was governed by a hierarchy of courts.

In the 1960s there was close cooperation locally and nationally between congregational and presbyterian churches. This led to union negotiations and a Scheme of Union, supported by act of parliament in 1972. In 1981 a further unification took place, with the Reformed Association of Churches of Christ becoming part of the URC. In 2000 a third union took place, with the Congregational Union of Scotland. In its basis the United Reformed Church reflects local church initiative and responsibility with a conciliar pattern of oversight.

The United Reformed Church is divided into 13 synods, each with a synod moderator. There are around 1,600 congregations which serve around 75,000 adults and 70,000 children and young people. There are around 750 serving ministers.

The General Assembly is the central body, and comprises around 400 representatives, mainly appointed by the synods, of which half are lay persons and half are ministers. From 2010 the General Assembly will meet biennially to elect two moderators, both lay and ordained, who will then become the public representatives of the URC. This replaces the arrangement whereby one lay or ordained moderator was elected annually by the General Assembly.

UNITED REFORMED CHURCH, 86 Tavistock Place, London WC1H 9RT T 020-7916 2020 E info@urc.org.uk
W www.urc.org.uk
Moderators of the General Assembly (2010–12), Val Morrison; Revd Dr Kirsty Thorpe
General Secretary, Val Robinson

WESLEYAN REFORM UNION

The Wesleyan Reform Union was founded by Methodists who left or were expelled from Wesleyan Methodism in 1849 following a period of internal conflict. Its doctrine is conservative evangelical and its organisation is congregational, each church having complete independence in the government and administration of its affairs. The union has around 1,540 members, 20 ministers and 96 churches.

THE WESLEYAN REFORM UNION, Wesleyan Reform Church House, 123 Queen Street, Sheffield S1 2DU
T 0114-272 1938 E admin@thewru.co.uk
W www.thewru.com
President (2010–11), Cliff Darby
General Secretary, Revd Colin Braithwaite

NON-TRINITARIAN CHURCHES

CHRISTADELPHIAN

Christadelphians believe that the Bible is the word of God and that it reveals both God's dealings with mankind in the past and his plans for the future. These plans centre on the work of Jesus Christ, who it is believed will return to Earth to establish God's kingdom. Christadelphians have existed since the 1850s, beginning in the USA through the work of an Englishman, Dr John Thomas.

THE CHRISTADELPHIAN, 404 Shaftmoor Lane, Hall Green, Birmingham B28 8SZ T 0121-777 6328
E enquiries@thechristadelphian.com
W www.thechristadelphian.com

CHURCH OF CHRIST, SCIENTIST

The Church of Christ, Scientist was founded by Mary Baker Eddy in the USA in 1879 to 'reinstate primitive Christianity and its lost element of healing'. Christian Science teaches the need for spiritual regeneration and salvation from sin, but is best known for its reliance on prayer alone in the healing of sickness. Adherents believe that such healing is the result of divine laws, or divine science, and is in direct line with that practised by Jesus Christ (revered, not as God, but as the son of God) and by the early Christian church.

The denomination consists of The First Church of Christ, Scientist, in Boston, Massachusetts, USA ('The Mother Church') and its branch churches in almost 80 countries worldwide. The Bible and Mary Baker Eddy's book, *Science and Health with Key to the Scriptures,* are used for daily spiritual guidance and healing by all members and are read at services; there are no clergy. Those engaged in full-time healing are called Christian Science practitioners, of whom there are 1,500 worldwide. The church also publishes *The Christian Science Monitor.*

No membership figures are available, since Mary Baker Eddy felt that numbers are no measure of spiritual vitality and ruled that such statistics should not be published. There are almost 2,000 branch churches worldwide, including over 100 in the UK.

CHRISTIAN SCIENCE COMMITTEE ON PUBLICATION, Unit T10, Tideway Yard, 125 Mortlake High Street, London SW14 8SN T 020-8150 0245
E londoncs@csps.com W www.christianscience.com
District Manager for the UK and the Republic of Ireland, Tony Lobl

CHURCH OF JESUS CHRIST OF LATTER-DAY SAINTS

The Church of Jesus Christ of Latter-Day Saints (often referred to as 'Mormons') was founded in New York State, USA, in 1830, and came to Britain in 1837. The oldest continuous congregation of the church is in Preston, Lancashire.

Mormons are Christians who claim to belong to the 'restored church' of Jesus Christ. They believe that true Christianity died when the last original apostle died, but that it was given back to the world by God and Christ through Joseph Smith, the church's founder and first president. They accept and use the Bible as scripture, but believe in continuing revelation from God and use additional scriptures, including *The Book of Mormon: Another Testament of Jesus Christ.* The importance of the family is central to the church's beliefs and practices. Church members set aside Monday evenings as family home evenings when Christian family values are taught. Polygamy was formally discontinued in 1890.

The church has no paid ministry: local congregations are headed by a leader chosen from among their number. The world governing body, based in Utah, USA, is led by a president, believed to be the chosen prophet, and his two counsellors. There are more than 13 million members worldwide, with over 190,000 adherents and 411 congregations in the UK.

CHURCH OF JESUS CHRIST OF LATTER-DAY SAINTS, British Headquarters, 751 Warwick Road, Solihull, W. Midlands B91 3DQ T 0121-712 1200 W www.lds.org.uk

JEHOVAH'S WITNESSES

The movement now known as Jehovah's Witnesses grew from a Bible study group formed by Charles Taze Russell in 1872 in Pennsylvania, USA. In 1896 it adopted the name of the Watch Tower Bible and Tract Society, and in 1931 its members became known as Jehovah's Witnesses.

Jehovah's (God's) Witnesses believe in the Bible as the word of God, and consider it to be inspired and historically accurate. They take the scriptures literally, except where there are obvious indications that they are figurative or symbolic, and reject the doctrine of the Trinity. Witnesses also believe that the earth will remain forever and that all those approved of by Jehovah will have eternal life on a cleansed and beautified earth; only 144,000 will go to heaven to rule with Christ. They believe that the second coming of Christ began in 1914 and his thousand-year reign over the earth is imminent, and that armageddon (a final battle in which evil will be defeated) will precede Christ's rule of peace. They refuse to take part in military service and do not accept blood transfusions.

The nine-member world governing body is based in New York, USA. There is no paid ministry, but each congregation has elders assigned to look after various duties and every Witness is assigned homes to visit in their congregation. There are over 7.3 million Jehovah's Witnesses worldwide, with 133,000 Witnesses in the UK organised into more than 1,500 congregations.

BRITISH ISLES HEADQUARTERS, Watch Tower House, The Ridgeway, London NW7 1RN T 020-8906 2211
E opi@uk.jw.org W www.watchtower.org

UNITARIAN AND FREE CHRISTIAN CHURCHES

Unitarianism has its historical roots in the Judaeo-Christian tradition but rejects the deity of Christ and the doctrine of the Trinity. It allows the individual to embrace insights from all the world's faiths and philosophies, as there is no fixed creed. It is accepted that beliefs may evolve in the light of personal experience.

Unitarian communities first became established in Poland and Transylvania in the 16th century. The first avowedly Unitarian place of worship in the British Isles opened in London in 1774. The General Assembly of Unitarian and Free Christian Churches came into existence in 1928 as the result of the amalgamation of two earlier organisations.

There are around 5,000 Unitarians in Great Britain and about 76 Unitarian ministers. Nearly 200 self-governing congregations and fellowship groups, including a small number overseas, are members of the General Assembly.

GENERAL ASSEMBLY OF UNITARIAN AND FREE CHRISTIAN CHURCHES, Essex Hall, 1–6 Essex Street, London WC2R 3HY **T** 020-7240 2384
E ga@unitarian.org.uk **W** www.unitarian.org.uk
President (2010–11), Neville Kenyon
Vice-President (2010–11), Revd Dr Ann Peart

COMMUNICATIONS

POSTAL SERVICES

The Royal Mail Group plc operates Parcelforce Worldwide, General Logistics Systems (GLS), the Post Office and Royal Mail. Each working day Royal Mail processes and delivers more than 84 million items to 27 million addresses. The Postal Services Commission (Postcomm), an independent regulator accountable to parliament, oversees postal operations in the UK. It is responsible for promoting effective competition between postal operators after the market was opened to full competition in 2006. All 50 of the UK's current operators, including Royal Mail, are licensed by Postcomm to ensure that the mail they handle is secure and that they maintain certain standards. In October 2008 Postwatch merged with Energywatch and the National Consumer Council to form Consumer Focus, a new consumer representation and advocacy body. Consumer Focus is responsible for postal services and takes up complaints on behalf of consumers against any licensed provider of postal services.

CONSUMER FOCUS, 4th Floor, Artillery House, Artillery Row, London SW1P 1RT **T** 020-7799 7900 **W** www.consumerfocus.org.uk

POSTCOMM, Hercules House, 6 Hercules Road, London SE1 7DB **T** 020-7593 2100 **W** www.psc.gov.uk

PRICING IN PROPORTION

Since August 2006 Royal Mail has priced mail according to its size as well as its weight. The system is intended to reflect the fact that larger, bulkier items cost more to handle than smaller, lighter ones. There are three basic categories of correspondence:

LETTER
Length up to 240mm, *width* up to 165mm, *thickness* up to 5mm, *weight* up to 100g; eg most cards, postcards and bills

LARGE LETTER
Length up to 353mm, *width* up to 250mm, *thickness* up to 25mm, *weight* up to 750g; eg most A4 documents, CDs and magazines

PACKET
Length over 353mm, *width* over 250mm, *thickness* over 25mm, *weight* over 750g; eg books, clothes, gifts, prints and posters in cylindrical packaging

INLAND POSTAL SERVICES

Below are details of a number of popular postal services along with prices correct as at April 2010.

FIRST AND SECOND CLASS

Format	*Maximum weight*	*First class*	*Second class*†
Letter*	100g	£0.41	£0.32
Large letter	100g	£0.66	£0.51
	250g	£0.96	£0.81
	500g	£1.32	£1.11
	750g	£1.87	£1.59
Packet	100g	£1.39	£1.17
	250g	£1.72	£1.51
	500g	£2.24	£1.95
	750g	£2.75	£2.36
	1,000g‡	£3.35	£2.84

* Includes postcards
† First class post is normally delivered on the following working day and second class within three working days
‡ Packets heavier than 1,000g must be sent first class. For a full list of prices *see* **W** www.royalmail.com

STANDARD PARCEL RATES*

Maximum weight	*Standard tariff*
2kg	£4.41
4kg	£7.06
6kg	£9.58
8kg	£11.74
10kg	£12.61
20kg	£14.69

* Standard parcels may be up to 1.5m long and 20kg in weight with a combined length and width of less than 3m. They are normally delivered within three to five working days

OVERSEAS POSTAL SERVICES

Royal Mail divides the world into two zones: **Europe** (Albania, Andorra, Armenia, Austria, Azerbaijan, Azores, Balearic Islands, Belarus, Belgium, Bosnia and Hercegovina, Bulgaria, Canary Islands, Corsica, Croatia, Cyprus, Czech Republic, Denmark, Estonia, Faroe Islands, Finland, France, Georgia, Germany, Gibraltar, Greece, Greenland, Hungary, Iceland, Rep. of Ireland, Italy, Kazakhstan, Kosovo, Kyrgyzstan, Latvia, Liechtenstein, Lithuania, Luxembourg, Macedonia, Madeira, Malta, Moldova, Monaco, Montenegro, Netherlands, Norway, Poland, Portugal, Romania, Russia, San Marino, Serbia, Slovakia, Slovenia, Spain, Sweden, Switzerland, Tajikistan, Turkey, Turkmenistan, Ukraine, Uzbekistan, Vatican City State) and **Rest of the World** (all countries that are not listed under Europe).

OVERSEAS SURFACE MAIL RATES*
Letters

Maximum weight	*Standard tariff*	*Maximum weight*	*Standard tariff*
20g†	£0.58	450g	£5.31
60g	£1.00	500g	£5.86
100g	£1.41	750g	£8.62
150g	£1.99	1,000g	£11.36
200g	£2.54	1,250g	£14.11
250g	£3.11	1,500g	£16.87
300g	£3.65	1,750g	£19.34
350g	£4.20	2,000g	£21.64
400g	£4.76		

* Letters and postcards to Europe are sent by Airmail
† Includes postcards

Small packets and printed papers

Maximum weight	*Standard tariff*	*Maximum weight*	*Standard tariff*
100g	£0.99	450g	£3.33
150g	£1.32	500g	£3.65
200g	£1.66	750g	£5.32
250g	£2.00	1,000g	£6.98
300g	£2.32	1,500g	£10.31
350g	£2.65	2,000g*	£13.22
400g	£3.00		

* Maximum weight. For printed papers only: add £0.28 for each additional 50g up to a maximum weight of 5,000g

AIRMAIL LETTERS

Europe:

Maximum weight	*Standard tariff*	*Maximum weight*	*Standard tariff*
20g*	£0.60	300g	£4.19
40g	£0.88	320g	£4.35
60g	£1.14	340g	£4.51
80g	£1.39	360g	£4.67
100g	£1.65	380g	£4.83
120g	£1.92	400g	£4.99
140g	£2.19	420g	£5.15
160g	£2.46	440g	£5.31
180g	£2.73	460g	£5.47
200g	£2.97	480g	£5.63
220g	£3.22	500g	£5.79
240g	£3.47	1,000g	£10.04
260g	£3.71	2,000g	£17.54
280g	£3.94		

* Includes postcards

Rest of the World:

Maximum weight	*Standard tariff*
Postcards	£0.67
20g	£0.97
40g	£1.46
60g	£1.98
80g	£2.51
100g	£3.04
500g	£10.94
1,000g	£17.44
2,000g	£29.94

Note that there are different rates for small packets and printed matter, and that the latter has a greater maximum weight allowance. *See* W www.royalmail.com for further details.

SPECIAL DELIVERY SERVICES

INTERNATIONAL SIGNED FOR AND AIRSURE

Express airmail services (maximum weight 2kg) that include £41 compensation in case of loss or damage. The fee for International Signed For is £4.25 plus airmail postage. The fee for Airsure is £4.90 plus airmail postage.

RECORDED SIGNED FOR

Provides a record of posting and delivery of letters and ensures a signature on delivery. This service is recommended for items of little or no monetary value. All packets must be handed to the post office and a receipt issued as proof of posting. The charge is 74p plus the standard first or second class postage with up to £41 compensation in case of loss or damage.

SPECIAL DELIVERY NEXT DAY

A guaranteed next working day delivery service by 1pm to 99 per cent of the UK (maximum item weight is 10kg). Prices start at £5.05. There is also a service that guarantees delivery by 9am (maximum item weight is 2kg). Prices start at £11.35. There is also a Saturday guarantee for mail sent out on a Friday, which costs an additional £2.25 an item. Note that size restrictions apply on these services.

OTHER SERVICES

BUSINESS SERVICES

A range of postal services are available to businesses including business collection, freepost, business reply services, secure mail opening, international bulk and sustainable mailing options. Smartstamp allows businesses to print postage directly from a computer using a pre-pay system.

COMPENSATION

Compensation for loss or damage to an item sent varies according to the service used to send the item.

KEEPSAFE

Mail is held for up to two months while the addressee is away, and is delivered when the addressee returns. Prices start at £8.95 for 17 days. Recorded items are held for a week before being returned to the sender, and special delivery items for three weeks beyond the Keepsafe expiry date.

PASSPORT APPLICATIONS

Many post offices process passport applications. To find your nearest post office offering this service and for further information, *see* W www.postoffice.co.uk

POST OFFICE BOX

A PO Box provides a short and memorable alternative address. Mail is held at a local delivery office until the addressee is ready to collect it, or delivered to a street address for an extra fee. Prices start at £60 for six months or £95 for a year.

POSTCODE FINDER

Customers can search an online database to find UK postcodes and addresses. For more information *see* Royal Mail's postcode finder W http://postcode.royalmail.com

REDIRECTION

Customers may arrange the redirection of their mail via phone, post, at the Post Office or online, subject to verification of their identity. A fee is payable for each different surname on the application form, and the service may be renewed up to a maximum of two years. The charges are, one month, £7.64 (abroad via airmail, £21.85); three months, £16.82 (£47.75); six months, £25.96 (£73.45); 12 months, £38.99 (£110.00).

TRACK AND TRACE

An online service for customers to track the progress of items sent using special delivery. It is accessible from W www.royalmail.com and W www.postoffice.co.uk.

CONTACTS

Parcelforce Worldwide
T 08708-501150 W www.parcelforce.com

Post Office enquiries
T 08457-223344 W www.postoffice.co.uk
Postcode enquiry line
T 0906-302 1222 / 08457-111222
Royal Mail business enquiries
T 08457-950950
Royal Mail general enquiries
T 08457-740740 W www.royalmail.com

TELECOMMUNICATIONS

The 1984 Telecommunications Act set the framework for a competitive market for telecommunications by abolishing British Telecom's (BT) exclusive right to provide services. The early 1990s saw the market open up and a number of new national public telecommunications operators (PTOs) received licences. This ended the duopoly that had existed in the 1980s when only BT and Mercury were licensed to provide fixed-line telecoms networks in the UK.

Four EU directives were agreed in March 2002 with the aim of further developing a pro-competitive regulatory structure. These directives were provided for in the Communications Act which came into force in July 2003. Under the act, licences are no longer required for providing communications networks or services in the UK. All persons providing such networks and services are subject to 'general conditions of entitlement', which constitute a set of rules they are obliged to observe.

Mobile network technology has improved dramatically since the launch in 1985 of the first-generation global system for mobile communications (GSM), which offered little or no data capability. In 1992 Vodafone launched a new GSM network, usually referred to as 2G or second generation, which used digital encoding and allowed voice and low-speed data communications. This technology has now been extended, via the enhanced data transfer rate of 2.5G, to 3G – a family of mobile standards that provide high bandwidth support to applications such as voice- and video-calling, high-speed data transfer, television streaming and full internet access.

RECENT DEVELOPMENTS

The four GSM operators, namely Orange, O2, T-Mobile and Vodafone, were joined in March 2003 by the first 3G operator, '3' (Hutchison 3UK). Orange, T-Mobile and Vodafone all launched their own 3G services in 2004, and O2 in February 2005. The number of 3G subscriptions grew by 5.4 million during 2008, with 23 per cent of mobile users using 3G at the end of the year compared to 17 per cent in 2007. During 2008 Vodafone overtook '3' as the UK's largest provider of 3G subscriptions.

In August 2009 the European Commission announced it would invest €18m (£15.3m) in researching the deployment of 4G technology throughout Europe, and the International Telecommunication Union (ITU) has set minimum speed standards for this technology. Research has so far yielded an intermediate '3.9G' service, available in Oslo and Stockholm, which allows for enhanced television streaming, gaming and conferencing capability. True 4G technology is expected to be confirmed by the ITU in October 2010.

The use of Wi-Fi (wireless fidelity) continues to grow, with over 27,000 public Wi-Fi hotspots active in the UK and around 4,500 in London alone. Deregulation has allowed public network operators to use certain parts of the spectrum, which are exempt from licensing, for wireless LAN (Wi-Fi) type systems. Initially only personal use was permitted in these bands, but this has been expanded to a full commercial service. Twelve city centres offer continuous Wi-Fi coverage using a network, or 'mesh', of 300m-range Wi-Fi signals.

FIXED-LINE COMMUNICATIONS

In the year to December 2008 customers spent £9bn on fixed-line telephony and there was a slight drop in the number of fixed exchange lines to 33.2 million (from 33.5 million in 2007), mainly resulting from a rise in the business sector's use of mobile phones, email and voice over internet protocol (VoIP). Due to local loop unbundling – which enables operators to connect directly to the consumer using BT lines, then add their own equipment to offer broadband and other services – a growing proportion of consumers are buying voice services from an operator other than BT. At the end of 2008, 38 per cent of UK landlines were taking a voice service from an alternative network provider, a rise of nearly 5 per cent from 2007.

The number of residential and small/medium business internet connections reached 19.2 million at the end of 2008, a 0.5 million increase from 2007; of this total, the number of broadband connections grew from 15.6 million to 17.3 million.

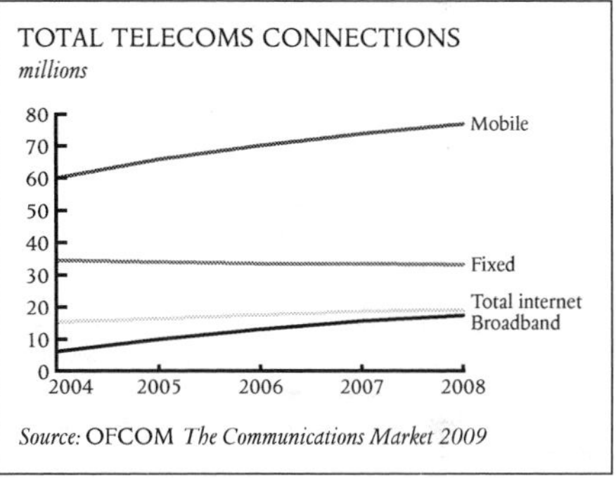

Source: OFCOM *The Communications Market 2009*

MOBILE COMMUNICATIONS

In *The Communications Market 2009* report, UK regulator OFCOM revealed that year-on-year growth in mobile revenues continued during 2008, with income from users totalling £15.4bn and representing 50 per cent of all retail telecoms revenue. OFCOM attributed this drop in revenue growth to the increasing popularity of cheaper SIM-only contracts. At the end of 2008 there were 76.8 million active mobile connections in the UK, equating to approximately 1.26 connections per head of population. This is due to the take-up of devices such as mobile data cards and 3G dongles for business purposes, and to many consumers having more than one phone to take advantage of call rates from different suppliers.

With various technologies converging, the structure of the mobile communications industry is becoming increasingly complex, but it can broadly be divided into two types of players: network operators, such as BT and Vodafone, who own the infrastructure, set tariffs and bill customers, and mobile virtual network operators (MVNOs), who lease network capacity from the operators.

MOBILE SUBSCRIPTIONS

There are two basic types of mobile subscription: contracts and pre-pay or 'pay as you go'. The proportion of contract to pay-as-you-go customers in the UK has remained relatively constant over the last few years. At the end of 2008 there were 29.9 million active contract subscribers and 46.9 million pre-pay customers.

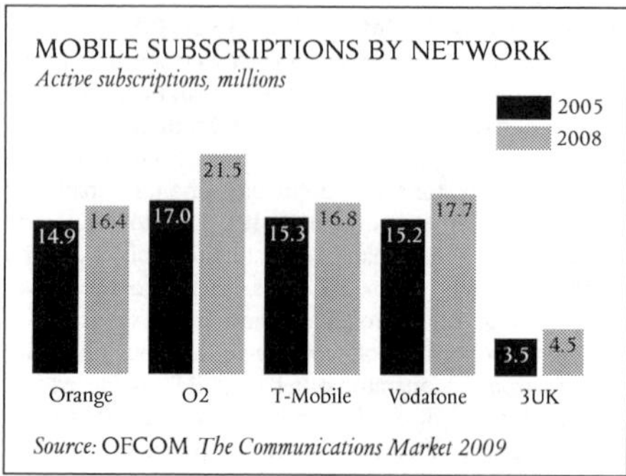

Source: OFCOM *The Communications Market 2009*

HEALTH

In 1999 the Independent Expert Group on Mobile Phones (IEGMP) was established to examine the possible effects on health of mobile phones, base stations and transmitters. The main findings of the IEGMP's report *Mobile Phones and Health,* published in May 2000, were:

- exposure to radio frequency radiation below guideline levels did not cause adverse health effects to the general population
- the use of mobile phones by drivers of any vehicle can increase the chance of accidents
- the widespread use of mobile phones by children for non-essential calls should be discouraged because if there are unrecognised adverse health effects children may be more vulnerable
- there is no general risk to the health of people living near to base stations on the basis that exposures are expected to be much lower than guidelines set by the International Commission on Non-Ionising Radiation Protection (ICNIRP)

As part of its response to the research recommendations contained in the IEGMP's report, the government set up the Mobile Telecommunications Health and Research (MTHR) programme in 2001 to undertake independent research into the possible health risks from mobile telephone technology. The MTHR programme published its report in September 2007 concluding that, in the short term, neither mobile phones nor base stations have been found to be associated with any biological or adverse health effects. An international cohort study into the possible long-term health effects of mobile phone use was launched by the MTHR in April 2010. The study is known as COSMOS and aims to follow the health of 250,000 mobile phone users from five countries over 20 to 30 years. The full 2007 report and details of COSMOS can be found on the MTHR website (W www.mthr.org.uk).

A national measurement programme, to ensure that emissions from mobile phone base stations do not exceed the ICNIRP guideline levels, is overseen by OFCOM and annual audits of these levels can be found on the sitefinder part of its website. The Health Protection Agency is responsible for providing information and advice in relation to the health effects of electromagnetic fields, including those emitted from mobile phones and base stations (W www.hpa.org.uk).

SAFETY WHILE DRIVING

Under legislation that came into effect in December 2003 it is illegal for drivers to use a hand-held mobile phone while driving. Since February 2007, under the Road Safety Act 2006, the fixed penalty for using a hand-held mobile while driving is £60 and three penalty points. The same fixed penalty can also be issued to a driver for not having proper control of a vehicle while using a hands-free device. If the police or driver chooses to take the case to court rather than issue or accept a fixed penalty notice, the maximum fine is £1,000 for car drivers and £2,500 for drivers of buses, coaches or heavy goods vehicles.

REGULATION

Under the Communications Act 2003, OFCOM is the independent regulator and competition authority for the UK communications industries, with responsibilities across television, radio, telecommunications and wireless communications services. Competition in the communications market is also regulated by the Office of Fair Trading, although OFCOM takes the lead in competition investigations in the UK market. The Competition Appeal Tribunal hears appeals against OFCOM's decisions, and price-related appeals are referred to the Competition Commission.

CONTACTS

DEPARTMENT FOR BUSINESS, INNOVATION AND SKILLS, 1 Victoria Street, London SW1H 0ET
T 020-7215 5000 W www.bis.gov.uk

OFCOM, Riverside House, 2A Southwark Bridge Road, London SE1 9HA T 020-7981 3000 W www.ofcom.org.uk

INTERNATIONAL DIRECT DIALLING

When dialling add two zeros before the IDD code, followed by the area code and the telephone number. Also add two zeros before the IDD code when dialling into the UK unless otherwise indicated.

* No extra zeros should be added
† Varies depending on area and/or carrier
‡ used to dial between Ireland and Northern Ireland; cheaper than using the UK code

	IDD from UK	*IDD to UK*
Afghanistan	93	44
Albania	355	44
Algeria	213	44
American Samoa	1 684	011 44*
Andorra	376	44
Angola	244	44
Anguilla	1 264	011 44*
Antigua and Barbuda	1 268	011 44*
Argentina	54	44
Armenia	374	44
Aruba	297	44
Ascension Island	247	44
Australia	61	11 44
Austria	43	44
Azerbaijan	994	44
Azores	351	44
Bahamas	1 242	011 44*
Bahrain	973	44
Bangladesh	880	44
Barbados	1 246	011 44*
Belarus	375	810 44*

Belgium	32	44
Belize	501	44
Benin	229	44
Bermuda	1 441	011 44*
Bhutan	975	44
Bolivia	591	10 44†
		11 44†
		12 44†
		13 44†
Bosnia and Hercegovina	387	44
Botswana	267	44
Brazil	55	14 44†
		15 44†
		21 44†
		23 44†
		31 44†
British Virgin Islands	1 284	011 44*
Brunei	673	44
Bulgaria	359	44
Burkina Faso	226	44
Burundi	257	44
Cambodia	855	1 44
Cameroon	237	44
Canada	1	011 44*
Cape Verde	238	44
Cayman Islands	1 345	011 44*
Central African Republic	236	44
Chad	235	15 44*
Chile	56	44
China	86	44
Colombia	57	5 44†
		7 44†
		9 44†
The Comoros	269	44
Congo, Dem. Rep. of	243	44
Congo, Rep. of	242	44
Cook Islands	682	44
Costa Rica	506	44
Côte d'Ivoire	225	44
Croatia	385	44
Cuba	53	119 44*
Cyprus	357	44
Czech Rep.	420	44
Denmark	45	44
Djibouti	253	44
Dominica	1 767	011 44*
Dominican Rep.	1 809	011 44*
	1 829	
Ecuador	593	44
Egypt	20	44
El Salvador	503	44
Equatorial Guinea	240	44
Eritrea	291	44
Estonia	372	44
Ethiopia	251	44
Falkland Islands	500	44
Faeroe Islands	298	44
Fiji	679	44
Finland	358	44
France	33	44
French Guiana	594	44
French Polynesia	689	44
Gabon	241	44
The Gambia	220	44
Georgia	995	810 44*
Germany	49	44
Ghana	233	44
Gibraltar	350	44
Greece	30	44
Greenland	299	44
Grenada	1 473	011 44*
Guadeloupe	590	44
Guam	1 671	011 44*
Guatemala	502	44
Guinea	224	44
Guinea-Bissau	245	44
Guyana	592	1 44
Haiti	509	44
Honduras	504	44
Hong Kong	852	1 44
Hungary	36	44
Iceland	354	44
India	91	44
Indonesia	62	1 44†
		8 44†
Iran	98	44
Iraq	964	44
Ireland	353	44
		048*‡
Israel	972	44†
		012*†
		013*†
		014*†
Italy	39	44
Jamaica	1 876	011 44*
Japan	81	1 44†
		010 44*†
		41 44†
		61 44†
Jordan	962	44
Kazakhstan	7	810 44*
Kenya	254	0 44
Kiribati	686	44
Korea, Dem. People's Rep. Of	850	44
Korea, Republic Of	82	1 44†
		2 44†
Kuwait	965	44
Kyrgyzstan	996	44
Laos	856	44
Latvia	371	44
Lebanon	961	44
Lesotho	266	44
Liberia	231	44
Libya	218	44
Liechtenstein	423	44
Lithuania	370	44
Luxembourg	352	44
Macao	853	44
Macedonia	389	44
Madagascar	261	44
Madeira	351	44
Malawi	265	44
Malaysia	60	44
Maldives	960	44
Mali	223	44
Malta	356	44
Marshall Islands	692	011 44*
Martinique	596	44
Mauritania	222	44
Mauritius	230	44
Mayotte	262	44
Mexico	52	44
Micronesia, Federated States of	691	011 44*
Midway Island	1 808	011 44*

Moldova	373	44	Serbia	381	44
Monaco	377	44	Seychelles	248	44
Mongolia	976	1 44	Sierra Leone	232	44
Montenegro	382	44	Singapore	65	1 44†
Montserrat	1 664	011 44*			2 44†
Morocco	212	44			8 44†
Mozambique	258	44	Slovakia	421	44
Myanmar	95	44	Slovenia	386	44
Namibia	264	44	Solomon Islands	677	44
Nauru	674	44	Somalia	252	44
Nepal	977	44	South Africa	27	44
The Netherlands	31	44	Spain	34	44
Netherlands Antilles	599	44	Sri Lanka	94	44
New Caledonia	687	44	Sudan	249	44
New Zealand	64	44	Suriname	597	44
Nicaragua	505	44	Swaziland	268	44
Niger	227	44	Sweden	46	44
Nigeria	234	9 44	Switzerland	41	44
Niue	683	44	Syria	963	44
Norfolk Island	672	44	Taiwan	886	2 44
Northern Mariana Islands	1 670	011 44*	Tajikistan	992	810 44*
Norway	47	44	Tanzania	255	0 44
Oman	968	44	Thailand	66	1 44
Pakistan	92	44	Timor-Leste	670	44
Palau	680	011 44*	Togo	228	44
Panama	507	44	Tokelau	690	44
Papua New Guinea	675	44	Tonga	676	44
Paraguay	595	44	Trinidad and Tobago	1 868	011 44*
Peru	51	44	Tristan de Cunha	290	44
The Philippines	63	44	Tunisia	216	44
Poland	48	44	Turkey	90	44
Portugal	351	44	Turkmenistan	993	810 44*
Puerto Rico	1 787	011 44*	Turks and Caicos Islands	1 649	011 44*
	1 939		Tuvalu	688	44
Qatar	974	44	Uganda	256	0 44
Réunion	262	44	Ukraine	380	44
Romania	40	44	United Arab Emirates	971	44
Russia	7	810 44*	United States of America	1	011 44*
Rwanda	250	44	Uruguay	598	44
St Christopher and Nevis	1 869	011 44*	Uzbekistan	998	810 44*
St Helena	290	44	Vanuatu	678	44
St Lucia	1 758	011 44*	Vatican City State	39	44
St Pierre and Miquelon	508	44		379	
St Vincent and the Grenadines	1 784	011 44*	Venezuela	58	44
			Vietnam	84	44
Samoa	685	0 44*	Virgin Islands	1 340	011 44*
San Marino	378	44	Yemen	967	44
Sao Tome and Principe	239	44	Zambia	260	44
Saudi Arabia	966	44	Zimbabwe	263	44
Senegal	221	44			

INTERNET DOMAIN NAMES

The domain name system (DNS) helps users to find their way around the internet. Just as a telephone line has an identifying number attached to it, each computer connected to the internet has a unique numerical address known as its IP address. The DNS means users seldom need to recall the string of numbers in an IP address, as they can instead access internet content via the more memorable domain names (for example, whitakersalmanack.com).

Top-level domains (TLDs) are the rightmost element of an internet domain name (in the above example .com is the website's TLD) and their management is delegated by the Internet Corporation for Assigned Names and Numbers (ICANN). There are two types of TLD: generic top-level domains (gTLDs) and country code top-level domains (ccTLDs).

Generic TLDs designate general categories of organisation, such as .org for public interest or .jobs for human resources. Some gTLDs, such as .com and .net, can be registered without restriction while others, such as .edu and .gov, have limited purposes.

Country code TLDs are usually two letters long and identify the website's country or territory of origin. In May 2010 the first ccTLDs using characters outside of the basic Latin alphabet were implemented by ICANN for sites in Egypt, Saudi Arabia and the UAE. This means that users in these countries can apply to register domain names ending with ccTLDs composed of native script. The rules and policies for registering domain names within a ccTLD vary significantly, although registration of a ccTLD is always limited to citizens of the corresponding country.

The list below is of active two-letter domain names for countries only.

ad	Andorra
ae	United Arab Emirates
af	Afghanistan
ag	Antigua and Barbuda
al	Albania
am	Armenia
ao	Angola
ar	Argentina
at	Austria
au	Australia
az	Azerbaijan
ba	Bosnia and Hercegovina
bb	Barbados
bd	Bangladesh
be	Belgium
bf	Burkina Faso
bg	Bulgaria
bh	Bahrain
bi	Burundi
bj	Benin
bn	Brunei
bo	Bolivia
br	Brazil
bs	The Bahamas
bt	Bhutan
bw	Botswana
by	Belarus
bz	Belize
ca	Canada
cd	Congo, Dem. Republic of
cf	Central African Republic
cg	Congo, Republic of
ch	Switzerland
ci	Côte d'Ivoire
cl	Chile
cm	Cameroon
cn	China
co	Colombia
cr	Costa Rica
cu	Cuba
cv	Cape Verde
cy	Cyprus
cz	Czech Republic
de	Germany
dj	Djibouti
dk	Denmark
dm	Dominica
do	Dominican Republic
dz	Algeria
ec	Ecuador
ee	Estonia
eg	Egypt
er	Eritrea
es	Spain
et	Ethiopia
fi	Finland
fj	Fiji
fm	Micronesia, Federated States of
fr	France
ga	Gabon
gd	Grenada
ge	Georgia
gh	Ghana
gm	The Gambia
gn	Guinea
gq	Equatorial Guinea
gr	Greece
gt	Guatemala
gw	Guinea-Bissau
gy	Guyana
hn	Honduras
hr	Croatia
ht	Haiti
hu	Hungary
id	Indonesia
ie	Ireland
il	Israel
in	India
iq	Iraq
ir	Iran
is	Iceland
it	Italy
jm	Jamaica
jo	Jordan
jp	Japan
ke	Kenya
kg	Kyrgyzstan
kh	Cambodia
ki	Kiribati
km	The Comoros
kn	St Christopher and Nevis
kp	Korea, Democratic People's Republic of
kr	Korea, Republic of
kw	Kuwait
kz	Kazakhstan
la	Laos
lb	Lebanon
lc	St Lucia
li	Liechtenstein
lk	Sri Lanka
lr	Liberia
ls	Lesotho
lt	Lithuania
lu	Luxembourg
lv	Latvia
ly	Libya
ma	Morocco
mc	Monaco
md	Moldova
me	Montenegro
mg	Madagascar
mh	Marshall Islands
mk	Macedonia
ml	Mali
mm	Myanmar
mn	Mongolia
mr	Mauritania
mt	Malta
mu	Mauritius
mv	Maldives
mw	Malawi
mx	Mexico
my	Malaysia
mz	Mozambique
na	Namibia
ne	Niger
ng	Nigeria
ni	Nicaragua
nl	The Netherlands
no	Norway
np	Nepal
nr	Nauru
nz	New Zealand
om	Oman
pa	Panama
pe	Peru
pg	Papua New Guinea
ph	The Philippines
pk	Pakistan
pl	Poland
pt	Portugal
pw	Palau
py	Paraguay
qa	Qatar
ro	Romania
rs	Serbia
ru	Russian Federation
rw	Rwanda
sa	Saudi Arabia
sb	Solomon Islands
sc	Seychelles
sd	Sudan
se	Sweden
sg	Singapore
si	Slovenia
sk	Slovakia
sl	Sierra Leone
sm	San Marino
sn	Senegal
so	Somalia
sr	Suriname
st	São Tomé and Príncipe
sv	El Salvador
sy	Syria
sz	Swaziland
td	Chad
tg	Togo
th	Thailand
tj	Tajikistan
tl	Timor-Leste
tm	Turkmenistan
tn	Tunisia
to	Tonga
tp	Timor-Leste*
tr	Turkey
tt	Trinidad and Tobago
tv	Tuvalu
tw	Taiwan
tz	Tanzania
ua	Ukraine
ug	Uganda
uk	United Kingdom
us	United States of America
uy	Uruguay
uz	Uzbekistan
va	Vatican City State (Holy See)
vc	St Vincent and the Grenadines
ve	Venezuela
vn	Vietnam
vu	Vanuatu
ws	Samoa
ye	Yemen
za	South Africa
zm	Zambia
zw	Zimbabwe

* No new registrations are being accepted for the code .tp, which is active but being phased out in favour of .tl

THE ENVIRONMENT

The past two decades have witnessed a reduction in the production of chemicals that damage the ozone layer by 95 per cent, the establishment of a greenhouse gas emissions reduction treaty and carbon trading, and the introduction of much legislation. However, there remain persistent and intractable problems. Climate change continues to be a threat to the planet, according to the United Nations Environment Programme's *Global Environment Outlook (GEO-4)* report, which assessed the current state of the global atmosphere, land, water and biodiversity and evaluated changes since 1987.

Global average temperatures are about 0.7 per cent higher than in the pre-industrial era, while the rate of global average temperature change has increased from 0.1°C per decade over the last 100 years, to 0.16°C in the past 10 years. The decade 2000–9 was the warmest since records began in the mid-19th century, according to the *UNEP Year Book 2010*.

A best estimate for temperature rise in the 21st century is between 1.8°C and 4°C. A rise of more than 2°C above pre-industrial levels is the level at which major, irreversible damage becomes more likely. Climate change is a challenge for Europe, with related areas of concern including biodiversity, marine ecosystems, land and water resources, air pollution and health.

Past legislation has been effective, according to the European Environment Agency. Water and air have been cleaned up, ozone-depleting substances have been phased out and more waste is recycled. However, this is potentially being undermined by changes in individual consumption patterns. Europeans are living longer and more of them live alone, increasing the demand on living space. They typically travel longer distances, more frequently, than previous generations, and are estimated to consume the planet's natural resources at twice the world's average rate.

UK GREENHOUSE GAS EMISSIONS FROM TRANSPORT
By sector, 2007

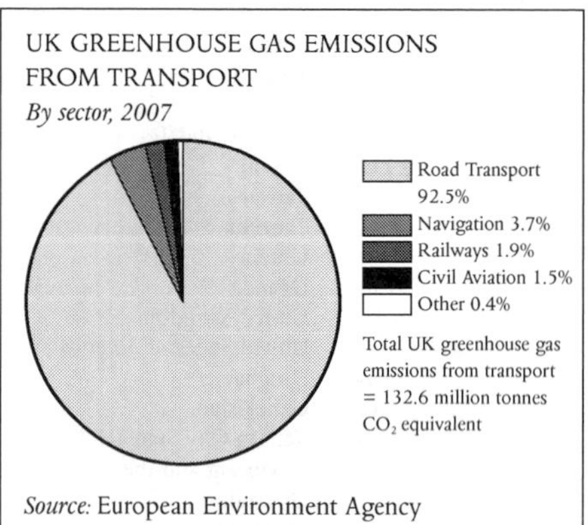

Source: European Environment Agency

Transport is the fastest-growing contributor to greenhouse gas emissions and is likely to be so for the foreseeable future. It is one of the few sectors where emissions continue to rise rapidly, currently accounting for 22 per cent of total European greenhouse gas emissions. Greenhouse gas emissions from air transport used by UK households doubled between 1992 and 2006, as passengers passing through UK airports rose by 126 per cent. Road transport produces about 28 per cent of UK carbon dioxide emissions. In 2008, average emissions from new cars fell 3.3 per cent to 153.5g per kilometre, and new EU legislation aims to reduce this further to 130g per kilometre by 2012 (the UK aims to meet this target by 2011).

Interest in biofuels is also increasing. By 2020, 10 per cent of transport fuel must be from renewable sources. Biodiesel is the most common biofuel in Europe, while ethanol is the most common worldwide. The usage of biofuels helps to reduce fossil fuel use, decrease greenhouse gas emissions and promote rural development. But there are also downsides such as higher prices for food crops such as corn, pressure on farmland biodiversity, soil erosion and deforestation. With these issues in mind, governments prefer and support sustainable biofuel production. Any rewards under the EU fuel rules after 2011 will be given only for biofuels that meet sustainability standards, which use criteria for monitoring land-use change, biodiversity conservation, soil conservation, water use and workers' rights. Twenty per cent of UK biofuels meet sustainability standards, which is 10 per cent below the government target.

UK CO_2 EMISSIONS
By end-user, 2008

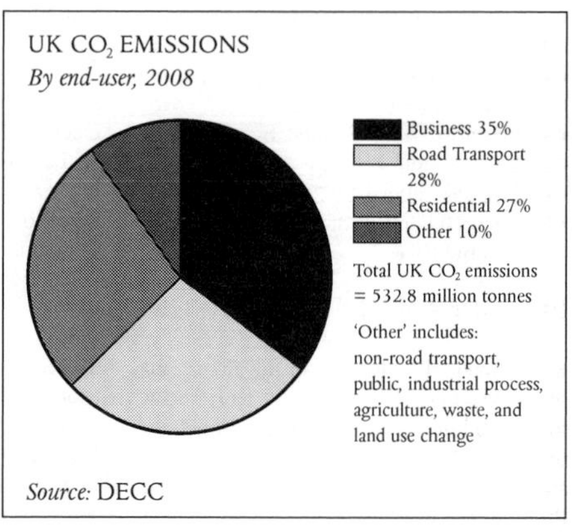

Source: DECC

Attention is turning to individuals and what they can do to reduce their carbon footprint. This is a measure of the amount of carbon dioxide emitted by the fossil fuels burned as part of a person's daily life or, in the case of an organisation, as part of its everyday operations. More than 40 per cent of the UK's carbon dioxide emissions come from people's homes and travel, and 80 per cent of the energy used in homes is for heating.

The UK emitted 532.8 million tonnes of carbon dioxide in 2008 and has a carbon footprint ranging from a high in the north-east of 12.5 tonnes per person to a low of 6 tonnes per person in greater London. To put this into context, the average American generates 20 tonnes of carbon dioxide a year, against a global average of about 4 tonnes.

SELECTED UK TARGETS

CLIMATE CHANGE
- Reduce carbon dioxide emissions to 20 per cent below 1990 levels by 2010, 34 per cent by 2020, and 80 per cent by 2050
- UK to reduce greenhouse gas emissions to 12.5 per cent below 1990 levels by 2008–12
- Carbon dioxide emissions from new cars to be 130g per kilometre by 2015 and 95g per kilometre by 2020
- By 2010, an average new car in the UK to emit 40 per cent less carbon than in 2009

WASTE
- Recycle or compost 40 per cent of household waste by 2010 and 50 per cent by 2020
- Reduce amount of household waste not reused, recycled or composted from 22.2 million tonnes in 2000 to 12.2 million tonnes by 2020, a reduction of 45 per cent
- Reduce biodegradable municipal waste sent to landfill to 75 per cent of 1995 levels by 2010, 50 per cent by 2013 and 35 per cent by 2020
- Recycle or compost 60 per cent of municipal waste in Scotland by 2020 and 70 per cent by 2025

ENERGY
- Provide 10 per cent of UK electricity from renewable sources by 2010 and 15 per cent by 2020
- Scotland to generate 31 per cent of electricity from renewable sources by 2011, rising to 50 per cent by 2020
- Around 40 per cent of UK electricity to be from low carbon sources (ie renewable, nuclear or clean coal) by 2020
- Produce around 30 per cent of UK electricity from renewable sources by 2020
- Reduce fossil fuel demand by around 10 per cent by 2020
- Reduce gas imports by 20 to 30 per cent by 2020
- Produce 10 per cent of transport energy from renewable sources by 2020

EUROPEAN UNION MEASURES

Environmental legislation in the EU is based around the principle that the polluter pays and policies are formulated at the level of international conventions and protocols, European directives, and national legislation and strategies. The interlinked Sixth Environment Action Programme, EU Sustainable Development Strategy and the Cardiff Process (which aims to integrate environmental concerns into other policies) are being developed as a framework for more detailed strategies.

The first environment action programme began in the 1970s and the EU adopted the sixth programme, *Environment 2010: Our Future, Our Choice,* in January 2001. Focusing on the topics of climate change, nature and biodiversity, environment and health, and natural resources and waste, it is the cornerstone of EU policy.

The European Commission (EC) is also using more diverse methods, in particular market-based instruments such as environmental taxes and voluntary measures. These are increasingly being adopted across Europe. Taxing energy consumption and selling the right to emit greenhouse gases are key ways of tackling climate change, and both follow the 'polluter pays' principle. Items subject to environmental taxes in Europe include plastic bags (Belgium, Ireland and Italy), plastic mineral water bottles (Italy), milk and fruit juice cartons (Norway), tyres (Denmark and Finland), disposable cutlery (Belgium) and paper and cardboard (France).

SUSTAINABLE DEVELOPMENT

The environmental agenda is part of a wider move to address sustainability that incorporates social, environmental and economic development. During the World Summit on Sustainable Development, held in Johannesburg in 2002, governments agreed on a series of commitments in five priority areas: water and sanitation, energy, health, agriculture and biodiversity. Approved targets and timetables included halving the number of people who lack access to clean water or proper sanitation by 2015, and reducing biodiversity loss by 2010. Following the summit, the United Nations Commission on Sustainable Development agreed its programme for the next 15 years. In addition, 2005–15 has been named as the 'Water for Life' decade.

The EU's sustainable development strategy stresses the importance of education, research and public funding to achieve sustainable development and consumption. The focus is now on putting policy into practice. The UK also has a sustainable development strategy, *Securing the Future,* alongside a framework for sustainable development across the UK, *Our Future – Different Paths,* shared between the government, the devolved administrations and the Northern Ireland Office.

CLIMATE CHANGE AND AIR POLLUTION

Temperature in central England has risen by about 1°C since the 1970s, with 2008 being the warmest year on record. Severe wind storms have become more frequent over recent decades, but are not more commonplace than they were in the 1920s. Sea levels around the UK rose by 1mm a year in the 20th century, although the rate for the 1990s and 2000s is higher.

The government's response to climate change has been driven by the UN framework convention on climate change. This is a binding agreement that aims to reduce the risks of global warming by limiting greenhouse gas emissions.

Global carbon dioxide emissions increased by 29 per cent between 2000 and 2009. The annual growth of atmospheric carbon dioxide was 1.8ppm (parts per million) in 2008. The average growth rate for the previous 20 years was about 1.5ppm a year, bringing the concentration of carbon dioxide in the atmosphere to 385ppm in 2008. There is an international campaign focusing on a target of 350ppm (or 400ppm of carbon dioxide equivalents).

Progress towards the UN framework convention's targets is assessed at regular conferences. At Kyoto in 1997, the Kyoto protocol was adopted. It covers the six main greenhouse gases: carbon dioxide, methane, nitrous oxide, hydrofluorocarbons (HFCs), perfluorocarbons (PFCs) and sulphur hexafluoride. Under the protocol, industrialised countries agreed to a legally binding target of cutting emissions of greenhouse gases to 5.2 per cent below 1990 levels by 2008–12. The protocol came into force in February 2005 after it was ratified by Russia. The USA has not ratified the treaty, while the UK set its own target at a 12.5 per cent reduction on 1990.

A legally binding post-Kyoto agreement was expected at the Copenhagen climate change conference in

December 2009. However, no consensus was reached. Instead, a political agreement was drawn up – known as the Copenhagen Accord – that recognises the objective to cap the global temperature rise to below 2°C (445–490ppm carbon dioxide equivalents) and outlines developed countries' commitments for additional funding to help the developing world address climate change. Countries have made pledges to cut emissions, but the UN says these are unlikely to keep temperatures below the target of a 2°C temperature rise by 2050. The challenge is to turn this into an effective and legally binding agreement by the conference in Mexico in 2010.

The EU wants to limit global warming to less than 2°C above pre-industrial temperatures. To achieve this, global emissions need to peak before 2020 and be reduced to less than 50 per cent of 1990 levels by 2050. The EU has proposed that developed countries as a group cut their greenhouse gas emissions to 25–40 per cent below 1990 levels by 2020. It also wants developing countries, particularly the big emerging economies, to limit the growth in their emissions to 15–30 per cent below 'business as usual' levels by the same deadline.

In 2007, the EU heads of state and government agreed a firm target of cutting 20 per cent of the EU's greenhouse gas emissions by 2020, rising to 30 per cent if the USA, Canada and India make similar commitments. Greenhouse gas emissions in the 27 EU member states are decreasing. Between 1990 and 2008, they dropped by 10.7 per cent. For the 15 original EU members, emissions are now 6.2 per cent below 1990 levels.

UK emissions are now 19.4 per cent below 1990 levels without emissions trading and 22 per cent below including emissions trading. In 2008, the UK already had a goal to reduce its carbon dioxide emissions to 20 per cent below 1990 levels by 2010. However, the Climate Change Act proposed two further goals: an interim target of a 34 per cent reduction in carbon dioxide emissions below 1990 levels by 2020 and a legally binding target of an 80 per cent reduction by 2050. The government must also set binding limits on carbon dioxide emissions during five-year budget periods; budgets have been set until 2022 and the UK is on track to meet the first.

Measures to tackle climate change in the UK are also covered by the climate change programme, launched in March 2006. It targets every sector of the economy and includes: a stricter emissions cap for industry; measures to encourage the uptake of biofuels in petrol; tighter building regulations; measures to improve household energy efficiency; a renewed emphasis on encouraging and enabling the general public, businesses and public authorities to help achieve the government's targets; and increased levels of microgeneration.

The UK has a voluntary greenhouse gas emissions trading scheme that allows businesses to buy an emission allowance to meet emission targets, or to sell surplus emission allowances. A new UK-wide emissions trading scheme, the Carbon Reduction Commitment (CRC), started in April 2010 and is aimed at organisations such as supermarkets and banks.

A mandatory EU emissions trading scheme for carbon dioxide applies at a company level. The companies covered by the ruling account for almost half of the EU's total carbon dioxide emissions. From 2012, airlines will be included in the scheme, covering emissions from all domestic and international flights arriving at, or departing from, an EU airport. Ticket prices are expected to rise by around €40 (£35) for long-haul and €9 (£8) for short-haul return flights.

Emissions of other pollutants are also regulated within the EU. Countries have legally binding targets for emissions of sulphur dioxide, nitrogen oxides, non-methane volatile organic compounds and ammonia, which harm both human health and the environment. These targets must be met by 2010. However projections indicate that the 27 EU countries, as a whole, will be above the targets for emissions of nitrogen oxides. The situation is better for the other three pollutants, with most EU member states expected to reduce their emissions below target level.

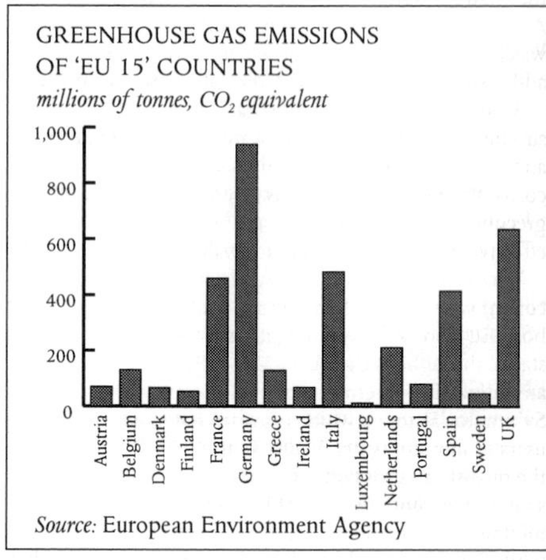

Source: European Environment Agency

WASTE

By 2020 the EU could be generating 45 per cent more waste than in 1995. In the UK the uncoupling of waste growth from economic growth is a key objective along with placing greater emphasis on prevention and reuse, putting less non-municipal waste into landfill and investing in the infrastructure necessary to divert waste from landfill. The principles informing this thinking are: the waste hierarchy of reduce, reuse, recycle, dispose; the 'proximity principle' of disposing of waste close to its generation; and national self-sufficiency.

In 2008 the UK generated about 565kg of municipal waste per person compared with an average across Europe of 524kg, ranging from a low of 306kg per person in the Czech Republic to a high of 802kg in Denmark. The majority of municipal waste across Europe went into landfill (41 per cent); the rest is recycled (22 per cent), incinerated (20 per cent) or composted (17 per cent). In the UK, the proportion of household waste recycled or composted has been increasing steadily, reaching 38 per cent in the year to June 2009 in contrast to 6 per cent in 1995–6. The UK is still behind Austria, Belgium, Germany and the Netherlands, who recycle or compost around 60 per cent of their municipal waste. Bulgaria, Cyprus, the Czech Republic, Greece, Latvia, Lithuania and Malta all landfill over 80 per cent. The UK has a longterm goal of becoming a zero waste nation.

EU directives help to shape UK policy, particularly in relation to commercial and industrial waste. For instance, the EU's European Integrated Products Policy aims to minimise the environmental impact of a product by looking at all phases of its life-cycle and encouraging each one to improve its environmental performance. A series of directives on packaging waste, vehicles, waste electrical and electronic equipment and batteries is intended to promote greater responsibility for products at the end of their life. The EU is also examining the issue of bio-waste (ie biodegradable garden, kitchen and food waste) which accounts for around one third of municipal waste.

WATER

Climate change alters rainfall patterns in ways that can put pressure on water resources, resulting in certain regions having more droughts. The EU flagship water legislation, the Water Framework Directive, takes this into account. Among its policy suggestions is the pricing of water in ways that would encourage efficient water use, thereby addressing water scarcity and drought.

Water strategy in the UK tackles similar issues: the sustainable delivery of secure water supplies; an improved and protected water environment; fair, affordable and cost-reflective water charges; reduced water industry greenhouse gas emissions; and more sustainable and effective management of surface water.

For drinking water, wastewater discharges, rivers, coastal water and bathing water, quality targets are set at both EU and UK level: the aim is to achieve 'good water status' throughout the EU by 2015. The EU has launched an interactive internet tool, WISE (Water Information System for Europe), which provides water data and allows users to monitor water quality in their neighbourhood. In the quality tests for bathing water in 2009, 98 per cent of swimming spots in the UK met the EU directive's minimum requirements, compared to two-thirds in 1988, while 70 per cent achieved a newer, tighter standard.

ENERGY

Energy used in the home is responsible for 27 per cent of the UK's carbon dioxide emissions. The Climate Change Act 2008 sets out four energy policy goals for the UK: cutting carbon dioxide emissions by 80 per cent by 2050, maintaining reliable energy supplies, promoting competitive energy markets, and ensuring homes are adequately and affordably heated. In terms of renewable energy, the UK target is to increase the contribution of renewables to 10 per cent of electricity by 2010, with a further target (set by the EU) of 15 per cent by 2020. As part of the UK's Low Carbon Transition Plan, launched July 2009, a tougher goal of around 30 per cent of electricity from renewables by 2020 was set.

The EU has also adopted a number of targets. These are to improve energy efficiency by 20 per cent by 2020; increase the level of renewables used in transport fuel to 10 per cent by 2020 (the target was originally just for biofuels); and for 20 per cent of the EU's energy consumption to come from renewables by 2020. In 2007, renewable energy accounted for 7.8 per cent of EU primary energy consumption.

Global renewable energy capacity (excluding hydro-electric power which supplies approximately 20 per cent of world electricity) was 280GW in 2008, a 16 per cent rise from 2007, and for the first time more renewable energy than conventional power capacity was added in both the EU and the USA. Global wind energy capacity grew by 31 per cent in 2009, to bring total installations up to 157.9GW. Solar photovoltaic technology grew to 20GW in 2009 (from 15GW in 2008).

The UK intends to turn more food waste into power; it produces more than 100 million tonnes of organic waste, which could be turned into heat and power for over 2 million homes. The government is also consulting on energy efficiency standards that would result in the worst performing products being taken off the market. Meanwhile, 16GW of new nuclear capacity is planned.

The capacity for renewables is increasing and the UK Renewable Energy Strategy was published in July 2009. Renewables accounted for 6.8 per cent of electricity generated in the UK in 2009, an increase from 5.5 per cent in 2008. The UK is one of only a few countries with more than 3GW of wind power capacity. In 2008, it became the world number one for installed offshore wind capacity and it has the potential for a further 32GW. Energy capacity from biofuel and waste is growing. A UK bioethanol plant with a capacity matching the largest in the world is scheduled for 2010 and will produce 420 million litres a year of bioethanol from wheat. Wave and tidal technologies are still at the experimental stage.

ENVIRONMENT AND HEALTH

Particulate matter in the air, noise and ground-level ozone damages the health of thousands of people each year. Environmental pollutants, including pesticides, endocrine disruptors, dioxins and PCBs persist in the environment and their long-term effect on health is not fully understood. There are concerns about the effects of electromagnetic fields on human health and whether the use of nanotechnology in food could be dangerous for the human body. In 2008, the EU set binding limits on emissions of fine particles. Under the new law, which takes effect in 2011, countries will have to reduce exposure to fine particles in urban areas by an average of 20 per cent by 2020, based on 2010 levels.

Concerns about pollution's impact on health are addressed by the EU environment and health strategy and its Environment and Health Action Plan 2004–10. The plan outlines an integrated approach involving closer cooperation between the health, environment and research areas. It builds on an assessment of the current baseline knowledge in the areas of: integrated monitoring of dioxins and PCBs, heavy metals and endocrine disrupters; childhood cancer, neurodevelopmental disorders and respiratory health; human biomonitoring, environment and health indicators; and research needs.

A chemicals policy, under which industry has to provide information on the effects of chemicals on human health and the environment, as well as on safe ways of handling them, has also been set up.

CONTACTS

DEPARTMENT FOR ENVIRONMENT, FOOD AND RURAL AFFAIRS, Eastbury House, 30–34 Albert Embankment, London SE1 7TL **T** 0845-933 5577 **W** www.defra.gov.uk

DEPARTMENT OF ENERGY AND CLIMATE CHANGE, 3 Whitehall Place, London SW1A 2AW **T** 0300-060 4000 **W** www.decc.gov.uk

ENVIRONMENT AGENCY, National Consumer Contact Centre, PO Box 544, Rotherham S60 4UD **T** 0870-850 6506 **W** www.environment-agency.gov.uk

EUROPEAN ENVIRONMENT AGENCY, Kongens Nytorv 6, DK-1050 Copenhagen K, Denmark **T** +45 3336 7100 **W** www.eea.europa.eu

ROYAL COMMISSION ON ENVIRONMENTAL POLLUTION, Room 108, 55 Whitehall, London SW1A 2EY **T** 0300-068 6474 **W** www.rcep.org.uk

SCOTTISH EXECUTIVE, ENVIRONMENT DIRECTORATE, Victoria Quay, Edinburgh EH6 6QQ **T** 0131-556 8400 **W** www.scotland.gov.uk

CONSERVATION AND HERITAGE

NATIONAL PARKS

© *Natural England – material is reproduced with the permission of Natural England*

ENGLAND AND WALES

There are now nine national parks in England and three in Wales. In addition, the Norfolk and Suffolk Broads are considered to have equivalent status to a national park. Under the provisions of the National Parks and Access to the Countryside Act 1949, as clarified by the Natural Environment and Rural Communities Act 2006, areas designated as national parks have a statutory requirement to conserve and protect scenic landscapes from inappropriate development and to provide access to the land for public enjoyment.

Natural England is the statutory body that has the power to designate national parks in England, and the Countryside Council for Wales is responsible for national parks in Wales. Designations in England are confirmed by the Secretary of State for Environment, Food and Rural Affairs and those in Wales by the Welsh Assembly Government. The designation of a national park does not affect the ownership of the land or remove the rights of the local community. The majority of the land in the national parks is owned by private landowners (74 per cent) or by bodies such as the National Trust (7 per cent) and the Forestry Commission (7 per cent). The national park authorities own only around 2 per cent of the land.

The Environment Act 1995 replaced the existing national park boards and committees with free-standing national park authorities (NPAs). NPAs are the sole local planning authorities for their areas and as such influence land use and development, and deal with planning applications. Their duties include conserving and enhancing the natural beauty, wildlife and cultural heritage of the parks; promoting opportunities for public understanding and enjoyment; and fostering the economic and social well-being of the communities within national parks. The NPAs publish management plans as statements of their policies and appoint their own officers and staff.

The Broads Authority was established under the Norfolk and Suffolk Broads Act 1998 and meets the requirement for the authority to have a navigation function in addition to a regard for the needs of agriculture, forestry and the economic and social interests of those who live or work in the Broads.

MEMBERSHIP

Membership of English NPAs comprises local authority appointees, members directly appointed by the environment secretary of state and members appointed by her after a consultation with local parishes. Under the Natural Environment and Rural Communities Act 2006 every district, county or unitary authority with land in a national park is entitled to appoint at least one member unless it chooses to opt out. The total number of local authority and parish members must exceed the number of national members. Since 1 April 2007 NPAs have between 22 and 30 members.

The Broads Authority has 21 members: nine appointed by the constituent local authorities, two appointed by the Navigation Committee and ten appointed by the secretary of state. The secretary of state's appointees include at least three which are appointed after consultation with representatives of boating interests and at least two which are appointed after consultation with representatives of landowning and farming interests.

In Wales two-thirds of NPA members are appointed by the constituent local authorities and one-third by the Welsh Assembly Government, advised by the Countryside Council for Wales.

FUNDING

The English NPAs and the Broads Authority are funded by central government. In the financial year 2010–11 a core grant totalling £48.9m was allocated between the authorities.

In Wales, national parks are funded via a grant from the National Assembly. National park grant for 2010–11 amounted to £11.2m. The three NPAs in Wales receive further funding from relevant local authorities.

All NPAs and the Broads Authority can take advantage of grants from other bodies including lottery and European grants.

The national parks (with date designation confirmed) are:

BRECON BEACONS (1957), Powys (66 per cent)/ Carmarthenshire/Rhondda, Cynon and Taff/Merthyr

Tydfil/Blaenau Gwent/Monmouthshire, 1,344 sq. km/519 sq. miles – The park is centred on the Brecon Beacons mountain range, which includes the three highest mountains in southern Britain (Pen y Fan, Corn Du and Cribyn), but also includes the valley of the rivers Usk and Wye, the Black Mountains to the east and the Black Mountain to the west. There are information centres at the national park visitor centre at Libanus (near Brecon), Abergavenny, Llandovery and Pontneddfechan.
National Park Authority, Plas y Ffynnon, Cambrian Way, Brecon, Powys LD3 7HP **T** 01874-624437
E enquiries@breconbeacons.org **W** www.breconbeacons.org
Chief Executive, John Cook

BROADS (1989), Norfolk/Suffolk, 305 sq. km/118 sq. miles – The Broads are located between Norwich and Great Yarmouth on the flood plains of the six rivers flowing through the area to the sea. The area is one of fens, winding waterways, woodland and marsh. The 60 or so broads are man-made, and many are connected to the rivers by dykes, providing over 200km of navigable waterways. There are information centres at Beccles, Hoveton, Potter Heigham, Ranworth, Whitlingham and Toad Hole Cottage at How Hill.
Broads Authority, Dragonfly House, 2 Gilders Way, Norwich NR3 1UB **T** 01603-610734
E broads@broads-authority.gov.uk
W www.broads-authority.gov.uk
Chief Executive, Dr John Packman

DARTMOOR (1951), Devon, 953 sq. km/368 sq. miles – The park consists of moorland and rocky granite tors, and is rich in prehistoric remains. There are information centres at Haytor, Princetown (main visitor centre) and Postbridge.
National Park Authority, Parke, Bovey Tracey, Devon TQ13 9JQ **T** 01626-832093 **E** hq@dartmoor-npa.gov.uk
W www.dartmoor-npa.gov.uk
Chief Executive, Kevin Bishop

EXMOOR (1954), Somerset (71 per cent)/Devon, 694 sq. km/268 sq. miles – Exmoor is a moorland plateau inhabited by wild Exmoor ponies and red deer. There are many ancient remains and burial mounds. There are national park centres at Dunster, Dulverton and Lynmouth.
National Park Authority, Exmoor House, Dulverton, Somerset TA22 9HL **T** 01398-323665
E info@exmoor-nationalpark.gov.uk
W www.exmoor-nationalpark.gov.uk
Chief Executive/National Park Officer, Dr Nigel Stone

LAKE DISTRICT (1951), Cumbria, 2,292 sq. km/885 sq. miles – The Lake District includes England's highest mountains (Scafell Pike, Helvellyn and Skiddaw) but it is most famous for its glaciated lakes. There are national park information centres at Bowness Bay, Keswick, Ullswater and a visitor centre at Brockhole, Windermere.
National Park Authority, Murley Moss, Oxenholme Road, Kendal, Cumbria LA9 7RL **T** 01539-724555
E hq@lakedistrict.gov.uk **W** www.lakedistrict.gov.uk
National Park Officer, Richard Leafe

NEW FOREST (2005), Hampshire, 570 sq. km/220 sq. miles – The forest has been protected since 1079 when it was declared a royal hunting forest. The area consists of forest, ancient woodland and heathland. Much of the forest is managed by the Forestry Commission, which provides several campsites. The main villages are Brockenhurst, Burley and Lyndhurst, which has a visitor centre.
National Park Authority, South Efford House, Milford Road, Lymington, Hants SO41 0JD **T** 01590-646600
E enquiries@newforestnpa.gov.uk
W www.newforestnpa.gov.uk
Chief Executive, Alison Barnes

NORTH YORK MOORS (1952), North Yorkshire (96 per cent)/Redcar and Cleveland, 1,434 sq. km/554 sq. miles – The park consists of woodland and moorland, and includes the Hambleton Hills and the Cleveland Way. There are information centres at Danby and Sutton Bank.
National Park Authority, The Old Vicarage, Bondgate, Helmsley, York YO62 5BP **T** 01439-770657
E info@northyorkmoors-npa.gov.uk
W www.northyorkmoors.org.uk
Chief Executive, Andrew Wilson

NORTHUMBERLAND (1956), Northumberland, 1,048 sq. km/405 sq. miles – The park is an area of hill country stretching from Hadrian's Wall to the Scottish border. There are information centres at Ingram, Once Brewed and Rothbury.
National Park Authority, Eastburn, South Park, Hexham, Northumberland NE46 1BS **T** 01434-605555
E enquiries@nnpa.org.uk
W www.northumberlandnationalpark.org.uk
Chief Executive, Tony Gates

PEAK DISTRICT (1951), Derbyshire (64 per cent)/Staffordshire/South Yorkshire/Cheshire/West Yorkshire/Greater Manchester, 1,437 sq. km/555 sq. miles – The Peak District includes the gritstone moors of the 'Dark Peak' and the limestone dales of the 'White Peak'. There are information centres at Bakewell, Castleton, Edale and Upper Derwent.
National Park Authority, Aldern House, Baslow Road, Bakewell, Derbyshire DE45 1AE **T** 01629-816200
E customer.service@peakdistrict.gov.uk
W www.peakdistrict.gov.uk
Chief Executive, Jim Dixon

PEMBROKESHIRE COAST (1952 and 1995), Pembrokeshire, 621 sq. km/240 sq. miles – The park includes cliffs, moorland and a number of islands, including Skomer and Ramsey. There are information centres in Newport and Tenby and a gallery and visitor centre, Oriel y Parc, in St Davids.
National Park Authority, Llanion Park, Pembroke Dock, Pembrokeshire SA72 6DY **T** 0845-345 7275
E info@pembrokeshirecoast.org.uk
W www.pembrokeshirecoast.org.uk
Chief Executive/National Park Officer, Tegryn Jones

SNOWDONIA/ERYRI (1951), Gwynedd/Conwy, 2,176 sq. km/840 sq. miles – Snowdonia is an area of deep valleys and rugged mountains. There are information centres at Aberdyfi, Beddgelert, Betws y Coed, Dolgellau and Harlech.
National Park Authority, Penrhyndeudraeth, Gwynedd LL48 6LF **T** 01766-770274 **E** parc@snowdonia-npa.gov.uk
W www.snowdonia-npa.gov.uk
Chief Executive, Aneurin Phillips

THE SOUTH DOWNS (2010), West Sussex/Hampshire,1,624 sq. km/627 sq. miles – The South Downs contains a diversity of natural habitats, including flower-studded chalk grassland, ancient woodland, flood meadow, lowland heath and rare chalk heathland. The South Downs National Park Authority is due to acquire statutory powers and begin work in April 2011.

South National Park Authority, Rosemary's Parlour, North Street, Midhurst, W. Sussex GU29 9SB
T 0300-303 1053 E info@southdowns.gov.uk
W www.southdowns.gov.uk
Chair, Margaret Paren

YORKSHIRE DALES (1954), North Yorkshire (88 per cent)/Cumbria, 1,769 sq. km/683 sq. miles – The Yorkshire Dales is composed primarily of limestone overlaid in places by millstone grit. The three peaks of Ingleborough, Whernside and Pen-y-ghent are within the park. There are information centres at Grassington, Hawes, Aysgarth Falls, Malham and Reeth.
National Park Authority, Yoredale, Bainbridge, Leyburn, N. Yorks DL8 3EL T 0300-456 0030
E info@yorkshiredales.org.uk W www.yorkshiredales.org.uk
Chief Executive, David Butterworth

SCOTLAND

On 9 August 2000 the national parks (Scotland) bill received royal assent, giving parliament the ability to create national parks in Scotland. The first two Scottish national parks became operational in 2002 and 2003 respectively. The Act gives Scottish parks wider powers than in England and Wales, including statutory responsibilities for the economy and rural communities. The board of each Scottish NPA consists of 25 members, of which five are directly elected by a postal ballot of the local electorate. The remaining 20 members, ten of which are nominated by the constituent local authorities, are chosen by the Scottish ministers. In Scotland, the national parks are central government bodies and are wholly funded by the Scottish government. Funding for 2010–11 totals £12.9m.

CAIRNGORMS (2003), North-East Scotland, 3,800 sq. km/1,466 sq. miles – The Cairngorms national park is the largest in the UK. It displays a vast collection of landforms, including five of the six highest mountains in the UK. The near natural woodlands contain remnants of the original ancient Caledonian pine forest.
National Park Authority, 14 The Square, Grantown-on-Spey, Morayshire PH26 3HG T 01479-873535
E enquiries@cairngorms.co.uk W www.cairngorms.co.uk
Chief Executive, Jane Hope

LOCH LOMOND AND THE TROSSACHS (2002), Argyll and Bute/Perth and Kinross/Stirling/West Dunbartonshire, 1,865 sq. km/720 sq. miles – The park boundaries encompass lochs, rivers, forests, 20 mountains above 3,000ft including Ben More and a further 20 mountains between 2,500ft and 3,000ft.
National Park Authority, Carrochan, Carrochan Road, Balloch G83 8EG T 01389-722600
E info@lochlomond-trossachs.org
W www.lochlomond-trossachs.org
Chief Executive, Fiona Logan

NORTHERN IRELAND

There is a power to designate national parks in Northern Ireland under the Nature Conservation and Amenity Lands Order (Northern Ireland) 1985, but there are currently no national parks in Northern Ireland.

AREAS OF OUTSTANDING NATURAL BEAUTY

ENGLAND AND WALES

Under the National Parks and Access to the Countryside Act 1949, provision was made for the designation of areas of outstanding natural beauty (AONBs). Natural England is responsible for AONBs in England and the Countryside Council for Wales for the Welsh AONBs. Designations in England are confirmed by the Secretary of State for Environment, Food and Rural Affairs and those in Wales by the National Assembly for Wales. The Countryside and Rights of Way (CROW) Act 2000 placed greater responsibility on local authorities to protect AONBs and made it a statutory duty for relevant authorities to produce a management plan for their AONB area. The CROW Act also provided for the creation of conservation boards for larger and more complex AONBs. The first two conservation boards for the Cotswolds and Chilterns AONBs were established in July 2004.

The primary objective of the AONB designation is to conserve and enhance the natural beauty of the area. Where an AONB has a conservation board, it has the additional purpose of increasing public understanding and enjoyment of the special qualities of the area; the board has greater weight should there be a conflict of interests between the two. In addition, the board is also required to foster the economic and social well-being of the local communities but without incurring significant expenditure in doing so. Overall responsibility for AONBs lies with the relevant local authorities or conservation board. To coordinate planning and management responsibilities between local authorities in whose area they fall, AONBs are overseen by a joint advisory committee (or similar body) which includes representatives from the local authorities, landowners, farmers, residents and conservation and recreation groups. Core funding for AONBs is provided by central government through Natural England and the Countryside Council for Wales.

The 40 Areas of Outstanding Natural Beauty (with date designation confirmed) are:

ARNSIDE AND SILVERDALE (1972), Cumbria/Lancashire, 75 sq. km/29 sq. miles
BLACKDOWN HILLS (1991), Devon/Somerset, 370 sq. km/143 sq. miles
CANNOCK CHASE (1958), Staffordshire, 68 sq. km/26 sq. miles
CHICHESTER HARBOUR (1964), Hampshire/West Sussex, 74 sq. km/29 sq. miles
CHILTERNS (1965; extended 1990), Bedfordshire/Buckinghamshire/Herefordshire/Oxfordshire, 833 sq. km/322 sq. miles
CLWYDIAN RANGE (1985), Denbighshire/Flintshire, 157 sq. km/61 sq. miles
CORNWALL (1959; Camel Estuary 1983), 958 sq. km/370 sq. miles
COTSWOLDS (1966; extended 1990), Gloucestershire/Oxfordshire/Warwickshire/Wiltshire/Worcestershire, 2,038 sq. km/787 sq. miles
CRANBORNE CHASE AND WEST WILTSHIRE DOWNS (1983), Dorset/Hampshire/Somerset/Wiltshire, 983 sq. km/380 sq. miles
DEDHAM VALE (1970; extended 1978, 1991), Essex/Suffolk, 90 sq. km/35 sq. miles
DORSET (1959), Dorset/Somerset, 1,129 sq. km/436 sq. miles
EAST DEVON (1963), 268 sq. km/103 sq. miles
EAST HAMPSHIRE (1962), 383 sq. km/148 sq. miles
FOREST OF BOWLAND (1964), Lancashire/North Yorkshire, 802 sq. km/310 sq. miles
GOWER (1956), Swansea, 188 sq. km/73 sq. miles
HIGH WEALD (1983), East Sussex/Kent/Surrey/West Sussex, 1,460 sq. km/564 sq. miles

HOWARDIAN HILLS (1987), North Yorkshire, 204 sq. km/79 sq. miles
ISLE OF WIGHT (1963), 189 sq. km/73 sq. miles
ISLES OF SCILLY (1976), 16 sq. km/6 sq. miles
KENT DOWNS (1968), 878 sq. km/339 sq. miles
LINCOLNSHIRE WOLDS (1973), 558 sq. km/215 sq. miles
LLYN (1957), Gwynedd, 161 sq. km/62 sq. miles
MALVERN HILLS (1959), Gloucestershire/Worcestershire, 150 sq. km/58 sq. miles
MENDIP HILLS (1972; extended 1989), Somerset, 198 sq. km/76 sq. miles
NIDDERDALE (1994), North Yorkshire, 603 sq. km/233 sq. miles
NORFOLK COAST (1968), 451 sq. km/174 sq. miles
NORTH DEVON (1960), 171 sq. km/66 sq. miles
NORTH PENNINES (1988), Cumbria/Durham/North Yorkshire/Northumberland, 1,983 sq. km/766 sq. miles
NORTH WESSEX DOWNS (1972), Hampshire/Oxfordshire/Wiltshire, 1,730 sq. km/668 sq. miles
NORTHUMBERLAND COAST (1958), 135 sq. km/52 sq. miles
QUANTOCK HILLS (1957), Somerset, 99 sq. km/38 sq. miles
SHROPSHIRE HILLS (1959), 804 sq. km/310 sq. miles
SOLWAY COAST (1964), Cumbria, 115 sq. km/44 sq. miles
SOUTH DEVON (1960), 337 sq. km/130 sq. miles
SUFFOLK COAST AND HEATHS (1970), 403 sq. km/156 sq. miles
SURREY HILLS (1958), 419 sq. km/162 sq. miles
SUSSEX DOWNS (1966), 983 sq. km/379 sq. miles
TAMAR VALLEY (1995), Cornwall/Devon, 195 sq. km/75 sq. miles
WYE VALLEY (1971), Gloucestershire/Herefordshire/Monmouthshire, 326 sq. km/126 sq. miles
YNYS MON (ISLE OF ANGLESEY) (1967), 221 sq. km/85 sq. miles

NORTHERN IRELAND

The Department of the Environment for Northern Ireland, with advice from the Council for Nature Conservation and the Countryside, designates Areas of Outstanding Natural Beauty in Northern Ireland. At present there are eight and these cover a total area of 2,849 sq. km (1,100 sq. miles). Dates given are those of designation.

ANTRIM COAST AND GLENS (1988), Co. Antrim, 706 sq. km/272 sq. miles
BINEVENAGH (2006), Co. Londonderry, 166 sq. km/64 sq. miles
CAUSEWAY COAST (1989), Co. Antrim, 42 sq. km/16 sq. miles
LAGAN VALLEY (1965), Co. Down, 39 sq. km/15 sq. miles
MOURNE (1986), Co. Down, 570 sq. km/220 sq. miles
RING OF GULLION (1991), Co. Armagh, 154 sq. km/59 sq. miles
SPERRIN (1968; extended 2008), Co. Tyrone/Co. Londonderry, 1,182 sq. km/456 sq. miles
STRANGFORD LOUGH AND LECALE (2010)*, Co. Down, 528 sq. km/204 sq. miles

*Strangford Lough (1972) and Lecale Coast (1967) merged in 2010

NATIONAL SCENIC AREAS

In Scotland, national scenic areas have a broadly equivalent status to AONBs. Scottish Natural Heritage recognises areas of national scenic significance. At the end of May 2010 there were 40, covering a land area of 1,020,500 hectares (2,521,710 acres) and a marine area of 357,900 hectares (884,390 acres).

Development within national scenic areas is dealt with by local authorities, who are required to consult Scottish Natural Heritage concerning certain categories of development. Disagreements between Scottish Natural Heritage and local authorities are referred to the Scottish government. Land management uses can also be modified in the interest of scenic conservation.

ASSYNT-COIGACH, Highland, 90,200ha/222,884 acres
BEN NEVIS AND GLEN COE, Highland, 101,600ha/251,053 acres
CAIRNGORM MOUNTAINS, Highland/Aberdeenshire/Moray, 67,200ha/166,051 acres
CUILLIN HILLS, Highland, 21,900ha/54,115 acres
DEESIDE AND LOCHNAGAR, Aberdeenshire, 40,000ha/98,840 acres
DORNOCH FIRTH, Highland, 7,500ha/18,532 acres
EAST STEWARTRY COAST, Dumfries and Galloway, 4,500ha/11,119 acres
EILDON AND LEADERFOOT, Borders, 3,600ha/8,896 acres
FLEET VALLEY, Dumfries and Galloway, 5,300ha/13,096 acres
GLEN AFFRIC, Highland, 19,300ha/47,690 acres
GLEN STRATHFARRAR, Highland, 3,800ha/9,390 acres
HOY AND WEST MAINLAND, Orkney Islands, 14,800ha/36,571 acres
JURA, Argyll and Bute, 21,800ha/53,868 acres
KINTAIL, Highland, 15,500ha/38,300 acres
KNAPDALE, Argyll and Bute, 19,800ha/48,926 acres
KNOYDART, Highland, 39,500ha/97,604 acres
KYLE OF TONGUE, Highland, 18,500ha/45,713 acres
KYLES OF BUTE, Argyll and Bute, 4,400ha/10,872 acres
LOCH NA KEAL, Mull, Argyll and Bute, 12,700ha/31,382 acres
LOCH LOMOND, Argyll and Bute, 27,400ha/67,705 acres
LOCH RANNOCH AND GLEN LYON, Perthshire and Kinross, 48,400ha/119,596 acres
LOCH SHIEL, Highland, 13,400ha/33,111 acres
LOCH TUMMEL, Perthshire and Kinross, 9,200ha/22,733 acres
LYNN OF LORN, Argyll and Bute, 4,800ha/11,861 acres
MORAR, MOIDART AND ARDNAMURCHAN, Highland, 13,500ha/33,358 acres
NITH ESTUARY, Dumfries and Galloway, 9,300ha/22,980 acres
NORTH ARRAN, North Ayrshire, 23,800ha/58,810 acres
NORTH-WEST SUTHERLAND, Highland, 20,500ha/50,655 acres
RIVER EARN, Perthshire and Kinross, 3,000ha/7,413 acres
RIVER TAY, Perthshire and Kinross, 5,600ha/13,838 acres

ST KILDA, Eilean Siar (Western Isles), 900ha/2,224 acres
SCARBA, LUNGA AND THE GARVELLACHS, Argyll and Bute, 1,900ha/4,695 acres
SHETLAND, Shetland Isles, 11,600ha/28,664 acres
SMALL ISLANDS, Highland, 15,500ha/38,300 acres
SOUTH LEWIS, HARRIS AND NORTH UIST, Eilean Siar (Western Isles), 109,600ha/270,822 acres
SOUTH UIST MACHAIR, Eilean Siar (Western Isles), 6,100ha/15,073 acres
THE TROSSACHS, Stirling, 4,600ha/11,367 acres
TROTTERNISH, Highland, 5,000ha/12,355 acres
UPPER TWEEDDALE, Borders, 10,500ha/25,945 acres
WESTER ROSS, Highland, 145,300ha/359,036 acres

THE NATIONAL FOREST

The National Forest is being planted across 517 sq. km (200 sq. miles) of Derbyshire, Leicestershire and Staffordshire. Seven million trees, of mixed species but mainly broadleaved, covering over 5,400 hectares (13,300 acres) have been planted. The aim is to eventually cover about one-third of the designated area.

The project was developed in 1992–5 by the Countryside Commission and is now run by the National Forest Company, which was established in April 1995. The National Forest Company is responsible for the delivery of the government-approved National Forest Strategy and is funded by DEFRA.

NATIONAL FOREST COMPANY, Enterprise Glade, Bath Lane, Moira, Swadlincote, Derbyshire DE12 6BD
T 01283-551211 E enquiries@nationalforest.org
W www.nationalforest.org
Chief Executive, Sophie Churchill

SITES OF SPECIAL SCIENTIFIC INTEREST

Site of special scientific interest (SSSI) is a legal notification applied to land in England, Scotland or Wales which Natural England (NE) (formerly English Nature), Scottish Natural Heritage (SNH) or the Countryside Council for Wales (CCW) identifies as being of special interest because of its flora, fauna, geological, geomorphological or physiographical features. In some cases, SSSIs are managed as nature reserves.

NE, SNH and CCW must notify the designation of an SSSI to the local planning authority, every owner/occupier of the land, and the environment secretary, the Scottish ministers or the National Assembly for Wales. Forestry and agricultural departments and a number of other interested parties are also formally notified.

Objections to the notification of an SSSI can be made and ultimately considered at a full meeting of the Council of NE or CCW. In Scotland an objection will be dealt with by the main board of SNH or an appropriate subgroup, depending on the nature of the objection.

The protection of these sites depends on the cooperation of individual landowners and occupiers. Owner/occupiers must consult NE, SNH or CCW and gain written consent before they can undertake certain listed activities on the site. Funds are available through management agreements and grants to assist owners and occupiers in conserving sites' interests. Sites can also be protected by management schemes, management notices and other enforcement mechanisms. As a last resort a site can be purchased.

The number and area of SSSIs in Britain as at May 2010 was:

	Number	*Hectares*	*Acres*
England	4,118	1,077,168	2,661,740
Scotland	1,453	1,035,884	2,559,634
Wales	1,025	258,612	639,057

NORTHERN IRELAND

In Northern Ireland 305 Areas of Special Scientific Interest (ASSIs) have been declared by the Department of the Environment for Northern Ireland.

NATIONAL NATURE RESERVES

National nature reserves are defined in the National Parks and Access to the Countryside Act 1949 as modified by the Natural Environment and Rural Communities Act 2006. National nature reserves may be managed solely for the purpose of conservation, or for both the purposes of conservation and recreation, providing this does not compromise the conservation purpose.

Natural England (NE), Scottish Natural Heritage (SNH) or the Countryside Council for Wales (CCW) can declare as a national nature reserve land which is held and managed as a nature reserve under an agreement; land held and managed by NE, SNH or CCW; or land held and managed as a nature reserve by an approved body. NE, SNH or CCW can make by-laws to protect reserves from undesirable activities; these are subject to confirmation by the Secretary of State for Environment, Food and Rural Affairs, the National Assembly for Wales or the Scottish ministers in Scotland.

The number and area of national nature reserves in Britain as at May 2010 was:

	Number	*Hectares*	*Acres*
England	225	96,664	238,861
Scotland	64	136,042	336,155
Wales	72	25,623	63,316

NORTHERN IRELAND

Nature reserves are established and managed by the Department of the Environment for Northern Ireland, with advice from the Council for Nature Conservation and the Countryside. Nature reserves are declared under the Nature Conservation and Amenity Lands (Northern Ireland) order 1985; to date, 49 nature reserves have been declared.

LOCAL NATURE RESERVES

Local nature reserves are defined in the National Parks and Access to the Countryside Act 1949 (as amended by the Natural Environment and Rural Communities Act 2006) as land designated for the study and preservation of flora and fauna, or of geological or physiographical features. Local nature reserves also have a statutory obligation to provide opportunities for the enjoyment of nature or open air recreation, providing this does not compromise the conservation purpose of the reserve. Local authorities in England, Scotland and Wales have the power to acquire, declare and manage reserves in consultation with Natural England, Scottish Natural Heritage and the Countryside Council for Wales. There is similar legislation in Northern Ireland where the consulting organisation is the Environment and Heritage Service.

Any organisation, such as water companies, educational trusts, local amenity groups and charitable nature conservation bodies, such as wildlife trusts, may manage local nature reserves, provided that a local authority has a legal interest in the land. This means that the local authority must either own it, lease it or have a management agreement with the landowner.

The number and area of designated local nature reserves in Britain as at May 2010 was:

	Number	*Hectares*	*Acres*
England	1,475	35,527	87,751
Scotland	56	10,001	24,712
Wales	79	5,819	14,379

There are 11 local nature reserves in Northern Ireland.

FOREST RESERVES

The Forestry Commission is the government department responsible for forestry policy throughout Great Britain. Forestry is a devolved matter, with the separate Forestry Commissions for England, Scotland and Wales reporting directly to their appropriate minister. The equivalent body in Northern Ireland is the Forest Service, an agency of the Department of Agriculture and Rural Development for Northern Ireland. The Forestry Commission in each country is led by a director who is also a member of the GB Board of Commissioners. As at March 2010, UK woodland certified by the Forestry Commission (including Forestry Commission-managed woodland) amounted to around 1,288,000 hectares: 343,000 hectares in England, 124,000 hectares in Wales, 757,000 hectares in Scotland and 64,000 hectares in Northern Ireland. For more information, *see* W www.forestry.gov.uk

There are 34 forest nature reserves in Northern Ireland, covering 1,512 hectares (3,736 acres), designated and administered by the Forest Service. There are also 16 national nature reserves on Forest Service-owned property.

MARINE NATURE RESERVES

Marine protected areas provide protection for marine flora and fauna, and geological and physiographical features on land covered by tidal waters or parts of the sea in or adjacent to the UK. These areas also provide opportunities for study and research. The 2009 Marine and Coastal Access Act created a new kind of statutory protection to replace marine protected areas (MPAs). Marine conservation zones (MCZs) increase the protection of species and habitats deemed to be of national importance over a wider area. Individual MCZs can have varying levels of protection: some restrict specific activities, while others prohibit all damaging activities. The act converted former MPA Lundy to MCZ status and it is expected that Skomer and Strangford Lough will follow by 2012.

The Secretary of State for Environment, Food and Rural Affairs, the National Assembly for Wales and the Scottish government have the power to designate MCZs. Natural England, Scottish Natural Heritage and the Countryside Council for Wales select and manage these reserves. Marine nature reserves may be established in Northern Ireland under a 1985 order.

Marine conservation zone:

LUNDY (1986), Bristol Channel

Marine nature reserves:

SKOMER (1990), Pembrokeshire, Wales

STRANGFORD LOUGH (1995), Northern Ireland

CONSERVATION OF WILDLIFE AND HABITATS

The UK is party to a number of international conventions.

BERN CONVENTION

The 1979 Bern Convention on the Conservation of European Wildlife and Natural Habitats came into force in the UK in June 1982. Currently there are 50 contracting parties and a number of other states attend meetings as observers.

The aims are to conserve wild flora and fauna and their natural habitats, especially where this requires the cooperation of several countries, and to promote such cooperation. The convention gives particular emphasis to endangered and vulnerable species.

All parties to the convention must promote national conservation policies and take account of the conservation of wild flora and fauna when setting planning and development policies. Reports on contracting parties' conservation policies must be submitted to the standing committee every four years.

SECRETARIAT OF THE BERN CONVENTION STANDING COMMITTEE, Council of Europe, 67075 Strasbourg-Cedex, France T (+33) (3) 8841 2000 W www.coe.int

BIODIVERSITY

The UK ratified the Convention on Biological Diversity in June 1994. As at May 2010 there were 193 parties to the convention.

The objectives are the conservation of biological diversity, the sustainable use of its components and the fair and equitable sharing of the benefits arising out of the use of genetic resources. There are seven thematic work programmes addressing agricultural biodiversity, marine and coastal biodiversity and the biodiversity of inland waters, dry and sub-humid lands, islands, mountains and forests. The Conference of the Parties to the Convention on Biological Diversity adopted a supplementary agreement to the convention known as the Cartagena Protocol on Biosafety on 29 January 2000. The protocol seeks to protect biological diversity from potential risks that may be posed by introducing modified living organisms, resulting from biotechnology, into the environment. As at May 2010, 158 countries were party to the protocol; the UK joined on 17 February 2004.

The UK Biodiversity Action Plan (UKBAP) is the UK government's response to the Convention on Biological Diversity and constitutes a record of UK biological resources and a detailed plan for their protection. The list of priority species and habitats under the UKBAP covers 1,150 species and 65 habitats. The UK Biodiversity Partnership Standing Committee guides and supports the UK Biodiversity Partnership in implementing UKBAP; it also coordinates between the four UK country groups which form the partnership and are responsible for implementing UKBAP at a national level. In addition, the UK Biodiversity Partnership includes two support groups: the Biodiversity Research Advisory Group and the Biodiversity Reporting and Information Group.

BIODIVERSITY POLICY UNIT, Zone 1/07, Temple Quay House, 2 The Square, Temple Quay, Bristol BS1 6EB T 0845-933 5577 W www.ukbap.org.uk

BONN CONVENTION

The 1979 Convention on Conservation of Migratory Species of Wild Animals (also known as CMS or Bonn Convention) came into force in the UK in October 1979. As at 1 January 2010, 113 countries were party to the convention.

It requires the protection of listed endangered migratory species and encourages international agreements covering these and other threatened species. International agreements can range from legally binding treaties to less formal memorandums of understanding.

Seven agreements have been concluded to date under the convention. They aim to conserve seals in the Wadden Sea; bat populations in Europe; small cetaceans of the Baltic and North Seas; African-Eurasian migratory waterbirds; cetaceans of the Mediterranean Sea, Black Sea and contiguous Atlantic area; albatrosses and petrels; and Wadden sea seals. A further 17 memorandums of understanding have been agreed for the Siberian crane, slender-billed curlews, marine turtles of the Atlantic coast of Africa, Indian Ocean and South-East Asia, the middle-European population of the great bustard, bukhara deer, aquatic warblers, West African populations of the African elephant, the saiga antelope, cetaceans of the Pacific Islands, dugongs (large marine mammals), Mediterranean monk seals, the ruddy-headed goose, grassland birds of southern South America, birds of prey, aquatic mammals of West Africa, and high Andean flamingoes.

UNEP/CMS SECRETARIAT, United Nations Premises, Hermann-Ehlers-Str. 10, 53113 Bonn, Germany T (+49) (228) 815 2426 E secretariat@cms.int W www.cms.int

CITES

The 1973 Convention on International Trade in Endangered Species of Wild Fauna and Flora (CITES) is an agreement between governments to ensure that international trade in specimens of wild animals and plants does not threaten their survival. The UK became party to the convention in July 1975 and there are currently 175 member countries. Countries party to the convention ban commercial international trade in an agreed list of endangered species and regulate and monitor trade in other species that might become endangered. The convention accords varying degrees of protection to more than 30,000 species of animals and plants whether they are traded as live specimens or as products derived from them, such as fur coats and dried herbs.

The Conference of the Parties to CITES meets every two to three years to review the convention's implementation. The Wildlife Species Conservation Division at the Department for Environment, Food and Rural Affairs carries out the government's responsibilities under CITES.

CITES SECRETARIAT, International Environment House, Chemin des Anémones, CH-1219 Châtelaine, Geneva, Switzerland T (+41) (22) 917 8139/8140 E info@cites.org W www.cites.org

EUROPEAN WILDLIFE TRADE REGULATION

The Council (EC) Regulation on the Protection of Species of Wild Fauna and Flora by Regulating Trade Therein came into force in the UK on 1 June 1997. It is intended to standardise wildlife trade regulations across Europe and to improve the application of CITES.

RAMSAR CONVENTION

The 1971 Ramsar Convention on Wetlands of International Importance especially as Waterfowl Habitat entered into force in the UK in May 1976. As at May 2010, 159 countries were party to the convention.

The aim of the convention is the conservation and wise use of wetlands and their resources. Governments that are party to the convention must designate wetlands and include wetland conservation considerations in their land-use planning. 1,889 wetland sites, totalling 186 million hectares, have been designated for inclusion in the list of wetlands of international importance. The UK currently has 168 designated sites covering 1,274,323 hectares. The member countries meet every three years to assess the progress of the convention and the next meeting is scheduled for May 2012.

The UK has set targets under the Ramsar Strategic Plan, 2009–15. Progress towards these is monitored by the UK Ramsar Committee, known as the Joint Working Party. The UK and the Republic of Ireland have established a formal protocol to ensure common monitoring standards for waterbirds in the two countries.

RAMSAR CONVENTION SECRETARIAT,
rue Mauverney 28, CH-1196 Gland, Switzerland
T (+41) (22) 999 0170 **W** www.ramsar.org

UK LEGISLATION

The Wildlife and Countryside Act 1981 gives legal protection to a wide range of wild animals and plants. Every five years the statutory nature conservation agencies (Natural England, Countryside Council for Wales and Scottish Natural Heritage) are required to review schedules 5 (animals, other than birds) and 8 (plants) of the Wildlife and Countryside Act 1981. They make recommendations to the Secretary of State for Environment, Food and Rural Affairs, the National Assembly for Wales and the Scottish government for changes to these schedules. The most recent variation of schedule 5 for England came into effect in February 2008 (the fourth quinquennial review recommended no changes to schedule 8; the fifth is currently under way).

Under section 9 of the act it is an offence to kill, injure, take, possess or sell (whether alive or dead) any wild animal included in schedule 5 of the act and to disturb its place of shelter and protection or to destroy that place. However certain species listed on schedule 5 are protected against some, but not all, of these activities.

Under section 13 of the act it is illegal without a licence to pick, uproot, sell or destroy plants listed in schedule 8. Since January 2001, under the Countryside and Rights of Way Act 2000, persons found guilty of an offence under part 1 of the Wildlife and Countryside Act 1981 face a maximum penalty of up to £5,000 and/or up to six months custodial sentence per specimen.

BIRDS

The act lays down a close season for birds (listed on Schedule 2, part 1) from 1 February to 31 August inclusive, each year. Exceptions to these dates are made for:

Capercaillie and (except Scotland) Woodcock – 1 February to 30 September
Snipe – 1 February to 11 August
Birds listed on schedule 2, part 1 (below high water mark) (*see* below) – 21 February to 31 August
Wild duck and wild geese, in or over any area below the high-water mark of ordinary spring tides – 21 February to 31 August
Birds listed on schedule 2, part 1, which may be killed or taken outside the close season are: capercaillie; coot; certain wild duck (gadwall, goldeneye, mallard, pintail, pochard, shoveler, teal, tufted duck, wigeon); certain wild geese (Canada, greylag, pink-footed, white-fronted (in England and Wales only); golden plover; moorhen; snipe; and woodcock.

Section 16 of the 1981 act allows licences to be issued on either an individual or general basis, to allow the killing, taking and sale of certain birds for specified reasons such as public health and safety. All other wild birds are fully protected by law throughout the year.

ANIMALS PROTECTED BY SCHEDULE 5

Adder *(Vipera berus)*
Allis Shad *(Alosa alosa)*
Anemone, Ivell's Sea *(Edwardsia ivelli)*
Anemone, Starlet Sea *(Nematosella vectensis)*
Bat, Horseshoe, all species *(Rhinolophidae)*
Bat, Typical, all species *(Vespertilionidae)*
Beetle *(Hypebaeus flavipes)*
Beetle, Lesser Silver Water *(Hydrochara caraboides)*
Beetle, Mire Pill *(Curimopsis nigrita)*
Beetle, Rainbow Leaf *(Chrysolina cerealis)*
Beetle, Spangled Water *(Graphoderus zonatus)*
Beetle, Stag *(Lucanus cervus)*
Beetle, Violet Click *(Limoniscus violaceus)*
Beetle, Water *(Paracymus aeneus)*
Burbot *(Lota lota)*
Butterfly, Adonis Blue *(Lysandra bellargus)*
Butterfly, Black Hairstreak *(Strymonidia pruni)*
Butterfly, Brown Hairstreak *(Thecla betulae)*
Butterfly, Chalkhill Blue *(Lysandra coridon)*
Butterfly, Chequered Skipper *(Carterocephalus palaemon)*
Butterfly, Duke of Burgundy Fritillary *(Hamearis lucina)*
Butterfly, Glanville Fritillary *(Melitaea cinxia)*
Butterfly, Heath Fritillary *(Mellicta athalia* or *Melitaea athalia)*
Butterfly, High Brown Fritillary *(Argynnis adippe)*
Butterfly, Large Blue *(Maculinea arion)*
Butterfly, Large Copper *(Lycaena dispar)*
Butterfly, Large Heath *(Coenonympha tullia)*
Butterfly, Large Tortoiseshell *(Nymphalis polychloros)*
Butterfly, Lulworth Skipper *(Thymelicus acteon)*
Butterfly, Marsh Fritillary *(Eurodryas aurinia)*
Butterfly, Mountain Ringlet *(Erebia epiphron)*
Butterfly, Northern Brown Argus *(Aricia artaxerxes)*
Butterfly, Pearl-bordered Fritillary *(Boloria euphrosyne)*
Butterfly, Purple Emperor *(Apatura iris)*
Butterfly, Silver Spotted Skipper *(Hesperia comma)*
Butterfly, Silver-studded Blue *(Plebejus argus)*
Butterfly, Small Blue *(Cupido minimus)*
Butterfly, Swallowtail *(Papilio machaon)*
Butterfly, White Letter Hairstreak *(Stymonida w-album)*
Butterfly, Wood White *(Leptidea sinapis)*
Cat, Wild *(Felis silvestris)*
Cicada, New Forest *(Cicadetta montana)*
Crayfish, Atlantic Stream *(Austropotamobius pallipes)*
Cricket, Field *(Gryllus campestris)*
Cricket, Mole *(Gryllotalpa gryllotalpa)*
Cricket, Wart-biter *(Decticus verrucivorus)*
Damselfly, Southern *(Coenagrion mercuriale)*
Dolphin, all species *(Cetacea)*
Dormouse *(Muscardinus avellanarius)*

Dragonfly, Norfolk Aeshna *(Aeshna isosceles)*
Frog, Common *(Rana temporaria)*
Goby, Couch's *(Gobius couchii)*
Goby, Giant *(Gobius cobitis)*
Hatchet Shell, Northern *(Thyasira gouldi)*
Hydroid, Marine *(Clavopsella navis)*
Lagoon Snail *(Paludinella littorina)*
Lagoon Snail, De Folin's *(Caecum armoricum)*
Lagoon Worm, Tentacled *(Alkmaria romijni)*
Leech, Medicinal *(Hirudo medicinalis)*
Lizard, Sand *(Lacerta agilis)*
Lizard, Viviparous *(Lacerta vivipara)*
Marten, Pine *(Martes martes)*
Moth, Barberry Carpet *(Pareulype berberata)*
Moth, Black-veined *(Siona lineata* or *Idaea lineata)*
Moth, Essex Emerald *(Thetidia smaragdaria)*
Moth, Fiery Clearwing *(Bembecia chrysidiformis)*
Moth, Fisher's Estuarine *(Gortyna borelii)*
Moth, New Forest Burnet *(Zygaena viciae)*
Moth, Reddish Buff *(Acosmetia caliginosa)*
Moth, Sussex Emerald *(Thalera fimbrialis)*
Mussel, Fan *(Atrina fragilis)*
Mussel, Freshwater Pearl *(Margaritifera margaritifera)*
Newt, Great Crested (or Warty) *(Triturus cristatus)*
Newt, Palmate *(Triturus helveticus)*
Newt, Smooth *(Triturus vulgaris)*
Otter, Common *(Lutra lutra)*
Porpoise, all species *(Cetacea)*
Sandworm, Lagoon *(Armandia cirrhosa)*
Sea Fan, Pink *(Eunicella verrucosa)*
Sea Slug, Lagoon *(Tenellia adspersa)*
Sea-mat, Trembling *(Victorella pavida)*
Seahorse, Short Snouted (England only) *(Hippocampus hippocampus)*
Seahorse, Spiny (England only) *(Hippocampus guttulatus)*
Shad, Twaite *(Alosa fallax)*
Shark, Angel (England only) *(Squatina squatina)*
Shark, Basking *(Cetorhinus maximus)*
Shrimp, Fairy *(Chirocephalus diaphanus)*
Shrimp, Lagoon Sand *(Gammarus insensibilis)*
Shrimp, Tadpole (Apus) *(Triops cancriformis)*
Slow-worm *(Anguis fragilis)*
Snail, Glutinous *(Myxas glutinosa)*
Snail, Roman (England only) *(Helix pomatia)*
Snail, Sandbowl *(Catinella arenaria)*
Snake, Grass *(Natrix natrix* or *Natrix helvetica)*
Snake, Smooth *(Coronella austriaca)*
Spider, Fen Raft *(Dolomedes plantarius)*
Spider, Ladybird *(Eresus niger)*
Squirrel, Red *(Sciurus vulgaris)*
Sturgeon *(Acipenser sturio)*
Toad, Common *(Bufo bufo)*
Toad, Natterjack *(Bufo calamita)*
Turtle, Flatback *(Cheloniidae/Natator Depressus)*
Turtle, Green Sea *(Chelonia mydas)*
Turtle, Hawksbill *(Eretmochelys imbricate)*
Turtle, Kemp's Ridley Sea *(Lepidochelys kempii)*
Turtle, Leatherback Sea *(Dermochelys coriacea)*
Turtle, Loggerhead Sea *(Caretta caretta)*
Turtle, Olive Ridley *(Lepidochelys olivacea)*
Vendace *(Coregonus albula)*
Vole, Water *(Arvicola terrestris)*
Walrus *(Odobenus rosmarus)*
Whale, all species *(Cetacea)*
Whitefish *(Coregonus lavaretus)*

PLANTS PROTECTED BY SCHEDULE 8
Adder's Tongue, Least *(Ophioglossum lusitanicum)*
Alison, Small *(Alyssum alyssoides)*
Anomodon, Long-leaved *(Anomodon longifolius)*
Beech-lichen, New Forest *(Enterographa elaborata)*
Blackwort *(Southbya nigrella)*
Bluebell *(Hyacinthoides non-scripta)*
Bolete, Royal *(Boletus regius)*
Broomrape, Bedstraw *(Orobanche caryophyllacea)*
Broomrape, Oxtongue *(Orobanche loricata)*
Broomrape, Thistle *(Orobanche reticulata)*
Cabbage, Lundy *(Rhynchosinapis wrightii)*
Calamint, Wood *(Calamintha sylvatica)*
Caloplaca, Snow *(Caloplaca nivalis)*
Catapyrenium, Tree *(Catapyrenium psoromoides)*
Catchfly, Alpine *(Lychnis alpina)*
Catillaria, Laurer's *(Catellaria laureri)*
Centaury, Slender *(Centaurium tenuiflorum)*
Cinquefoil, Rock *(Potentilla rupestris)*
Cladonia, Convoluted *(Cladonia convoluta)*
Cladonia, Upright Mountain *(Cladonia stricta)*
Clary, Meadow *(Salvia pratensis)*
Club-rush, Triangular *(Scirpus triquetrus)*
Colt's-foot, Purple *(Homogyne alpina)*
Cotoneaster, Wild *(Cotoneaster integerrimus)*
Cottongrass, Slender *(Eriophorum gracile)*
Cow-wheat, Field *(Melampyrum arvense)*
Crocus, Sand *(Romulea columnae)*
Crystalwort, Lizard *(Riccia bifurca)*
Cudweed, Broad-leaved *(Filago pyramidata)*
Cudweed, Jersey *(Gnaphalium luteoalbum)*
Cudweed, Red-tipped *(Filago lutescens)*
Cut-grass *(Leersia oryzoides)*
Diapensia *(Diapensia lapponica)*
Dock, Shore *(Rumex rupestris)*
Earwort, Marsh *(Jamesoniella undulifolia)*
Eryngo, Field *(Eryngium campestre)*
Fern, Dickie's Bladder *(Cystopteris dickieana)*
Fern, Killarney *(Trichomanes speciosum)*
Flapwort, Norfolk *(Leiocolea rutheana)*
Fleabane, Alpine *(Erigeron borealis)*
Fleabane, Small *(Pulicaria vulgaris)*
Fleawort, South Stack *(Tephroseris integrifolia ssp maritima)*
Frostwort, Pointed *(Gymnomitrion apiculatum)*
Fungus, Hedgehog *(Hericium erinaceum)*
Galingale, Brown *(Cyperus fuscus)*
Gentian, Alpine *(Gentiana nivalis)*
Gentian, Dune *(Gentianella uliginosa)*
Gentian, Early *(Gentianella anglica)*
Gentian, Fringed *(Gentianella ciliata)*
Gentian, Spring *(Gentiana verna)*
Germander, Cut-leaved *(Teucrium botrys)*
Germander, Water *(Teucrium scordium)*
Gladiolus, Wild *(Gladiolus illyricus)*
Goblin Lights *(Catolechia wahlenbergii)*
Goosefoot, Stinking *(Chenopodium vulvaria)*
Grass-poly *(Lythrum hyssopifolia)*
Grimmia, Blunt-leaved *(Grimmia unicolor)*
Gyalecta, Elm *(Gyalecta ulmi)*
Hare's-ear, Sickle-leaved *(Bupleurum falcatum)*
Hare's-ear, Small *(Bupleurum baldense)*
Hawk's-beard, Stinking *(Crepis foetida)*
Hawkweed, Northroe *(Hieracium northroense)*
Hawkweed, Shetland *(Hieracium zetlandicum)*
Hawkweed, Weak-leaved *(Hieracium attenuatifolium)*
Heath, Blue *(Phyllodoce caerulea)*
Helleborine, Red *(Cephalanthera rubra)*
Helleborine, Young's *(Epipactis youngiana)*

Horsetail, Branched *(Equisetum ramosissimum)*
Hound's-tongue, Green *(Cynoglossum germanicum)*
Knawel, Perennial *(Scleranthus perennis)*
Knotgrass, Sea *(Polygonum maritimum)*
Lady's-slipper *(Cypripedium calceolus)*
Lecanactis, Churchyard *(Lecanactis hemisphaerica)*
Lecanora, Tarn *(Lecanora archariana)*
Lecidea, Copper *(Lecidea inops)*
Leek, Round-headed *(Allium sphaerocephalon)*
Lettuce, Least *(Lactuca saligna)*
Lichen, Arctic Kidney *(Nephroma arcticum)*
Lichen, Ciliate Strap *(Heterodermia leucomelos)*
Lichen, Coralloid Rosette *(Heterodermia propagulifera)*
Lichen, Ear-lobed Dog *(Peltigera lepidophora)*
Lichen, Forked Hair *(Bryoria furcellata)*
Lichen, Golden Hair *(Teloschistes flavicans)*
Lichen, Orange-fruited Elm *(Caloplaca luteoalba)*
Lichen, River Jelly *(Collema dichotomum)*
Lichen, Scaly Breck *(Squamarina lentigera)*
Lichen, Starry Breck *(Buellia asterella)*
Lily, Snowdon *(Lloydia serotina)*
Liverwort, Lindenberg's Leafy *(Adelanthus lindenbergianus)*
Marsh-mallow, Rough *(Althaea hirsuta)*
Marshwort, Creeping *(Apium repens)*
Milk-parsley, Cambridge *(Selinum carvifolia)*
Moss *(Drepanocladius vernicosus)*
Moss, Alpine Copper *(Mielichoferia mielichoferi)*
Moss, Baltic Bog *(Sphagnum balticum)*
Moss, Blue Dew *(Saelania glaucescens)*
Moss, Blunt-leaved Bristle *(Orthotrichum obtusifolium)*
Moss, Bright Green Cave *(Cyclodictyon laetevirens)*
Moss, Cordate Beard *(Barbula cordata)*
Moss, Cornish Path *(Ditrichum cornubicum)*
Moss, Derbyshire Feather *(Thamnobryum angustifolium)*
Moss, Dune Thread *(Bryum mamillatum)*
Moss, Flamingo *(Desmatodon cernuus)*
Moss, Glaucous Beard *(Barbula glauca)*
Moss, Green Shield *(Buxbaumia viridis)*
Moss, Hair Silk *(Plagiothecium piliferum)*
Moss, Knothole *(Zygodon forsteri)*
Moss, Large Yellow Feather *(Scorpidium turgescens)*
Moss, Millimetre *(Micromitrium tenerum)*
Moss, Multi-fruited River *(Cryphaea lamyana)*
Moss, Nowell's Limestone *(Zygodon gracilis)*
Moss, Polar Feather *(Hygrohypnum polare)*
Moss, Rigid Apple *(Bartramia stricta)*
Moss, Round-leaved Feather *(Rhyncostegium rotundifolium)*
Moss, Schleicher's Thread *(Bryum schleicheri)*
Moss, Slender Green Feather *(Drepanocladus vernicosus)*
Moss, Triangular Pygmy *(Acaulon triquetrum)*
Moss, Vaucher's Feather *(Hypnum vaucheri)*
Mudwort, Welsh *(Limosella austeralis)*
Naiad, Holly-leaved *(Najas marina)*
Naiad, Slender *(Najas flexilis)*
Orache, Stalked *(Halimione pedunculata)*
Orchid, Early Spider *(Ophrys sphegodes)*
Orchid, Fen *(Liparis loeselii)*
Orchid, Ghost *(Epipogium aphyllum)*
Orchid, Lapland Marsh *(Dactylorhiza lapponica)*
Orchid, Late Spider *(Ophrys fuciflora)*
Orchid, Lizard *(Himantoglossum hircinum)*
Orchid, Military *(Orchis militaris)*
Orchid, Monkey *(Orchis simia)*
Pannaria, Caledonia *(Panneria ignobilis)*
Parmelia, New Forest *(Parmelia minarum)*
Parmentaria, Oil Stain *(Parmentaria chilensis)*
Pear, Plymouth *(Pyrus cordata)*
Penny-cress, Perfoliate *(Thlaspi perfoliatum)*
Pennyroyal *(Mentha pulegium)*
Pertusaria, Alpine Moss *(Pertusaria bryontha)*
Petalwort *(Petallophyllum ralfsi)*
Physcia, Southern Grey *(Physcia tribacioides)*
Pigmyweed *(Crassula aquatica)*
Pine, Ground *(Ajuga chamaepitys)*
Pink, Cheddar *(Dianthus gratianopolitanus)*
Pink, Childing *(Petroraghia nanteuilii)*
Pink, Deptford (England and Wales only) *(Dianthus armeria)*
Polypore, Oak *(Buglossoporus pulvinus)*
Pseudocyphellaria, Ragged *(Pseudocyphellaria lacerata)*
Psora, Rusty Alpine *(Psora rubiformis)*
Puffball, Sandy Stilt *(Battarraea phalloides)*
Ragwort, Fen *(Senecio paludosus)*
Ramping-fumitory, Martin's *(Fumaria martinii)*
Rampion, Spiked *(Phyteuma spicatum)*
Restharrow, Small *(Ononis reclinata)*
Rock-cress, Alpine *(Arabis alpina)*
Rock-cress, Bristol *(Arabis stricta)*
Rustwort, Western *(Marsupella profunda)*
Sandwort, Norwegian *(Arenaria norvegica)*
Sandwort, Teesdale *(Minuartia stricta)*
Saxifrage, Drooping *(Saxifraga cernua)*
Saxifrage, Tufted *(Saxifraga cespitosa)*
Saxifrage, Yellow Marsh *(Saxifrage hirulus)*
Solenopsora, Serpentine *(Solenopsora liparina)*
Solomon's-seal, Whorled *(Polygonatum verticillatum)*
Sow-thistle, Alpine *(Cicerbita alpina)*
Spearwort, Adder's-tongue *(Ranunculus ophioglossifolius)*
Speedwell, Fingered *(Veronica triphyllos)*
Speedwell, Spiked *(Veronica spicata)*
Spike-rush, Dwarf *(Eleocharis parvula)*
Star-of-Bethlehem, Early *(Gagea bohemica)*
Starfruit *(Damasonium alisma)*
Stonewort, Bearded *(Chara canescens)*
Stonewort, Foxtail *(Lamprothamnium papulosum)*
Strapwort *(Corrigiola litoralis)*
Sulphur-tresses, Alpine *(Alectoria ochroleuca)*
Threadmoss, Long-leaved *(Bryum neodamense)*
Turpswort *(Geocalyx graveolens)*
Violet, Fen *(Viola persicifolia)*
Viper's-grass *(Scorzonera humilis)*
Water-plantain, Floating *(Luronium natans)*
Water-plantain, Ribbon-leaved *(Alisma gramineum)*
Wood-sedge, Starved *(Carex depauperata)*
Woodsia, Alpine *(Woodsia alpina)*
Woodsia, Oblong *(Woodsia ilvenis)*
Wormwood, Field *(Artemisia campestris)*
Woundwort, Downy *(Stachys germanica)*
Woundwort, Limestone *(Stachys alpina)*
Yellow-rattle, Greater *(Rhinanthus serotinus)*

WORLD HERITAGE SITES

The Convention Concerning the Protection of the World Cultural and Natural Heritage was adopted by the United Nations Educational Scientific and Cultural Organisation (UNESCO) in 1972 and ratified by the UK in 1984. As at 10 June 2010 187 states were party to the convention. The convention provides for the identification, protection and conservation of cultural and natural sites of outstanding universal value.

Cultural sites may be:

- sites representing architectural and technological innovation or cultural interchange
- sites of artistic, historic, aesthetic, archaeological, scientific, ethnologic or anthropologic value
- 'cultural landscapes', ie sites whose characteristics are marked by significant interactions between human populations and their natural environment
- exceptional examples of traditional settlement or land- or sea-use; especially those threatened by irreversible change

Natural sites may be:

- those with remarkable physical, biological or geological formations
- those with outstanding universal value from the point of view of science, conservation or natural beauty
- the habitat of threatened species and plants

Governments which are party to the convention nominate sites in their country for inclusion in the World Cultural and Natural Heritage List. Nominations are considered by the World Heritage Committee, an inter-governmental committee composed of 21 representatives of the parties to the convention. The committee is advised by the International Council on Monuments and Sites (ICOMOS), the International Centre for the Study of the Preservation and Restoration of Cultural Property (ICCROM) and the World Conservation Union (IUCN). ICOMOS evaluates and reports on proposed cultural and mixed sites, ICCROM provides expert advice and training on how to conserve and restore cultural property and IUCN provides technical evaluations of natural heritage sites and reports on the state of conservation of listed sites. The Department for Culture, Media and Sport represents the UK government in matters relating to the convention.

A prerequisite for inclusion in the World Heritage List is the existence of an effective legal protection system in the country in which the site is situated and a detailed management plan to ensure the conservation of the site. Inclusion in the list does not confer any greater degree of protection on the site than that offered by the national protection framework.

If a site is considered to be in serious danger of decay or damage, the committee may add it to the World Heritage in Danger List. Sites on this list may benefit from particular attention or emergency measures to allay threats and allow them to retain their world heritage status, or in extreme cases of damage or neglect they may lose their world heritage status completely.

Financial support for the conservation of sites on the World Cultural and Natural Heritage List is provided by the World Heritage Fund, administered by the World Heritage Committee. The fund's income is derived from compulsory and voluntary contributions from the states party to the convention and from private donations.

DESIGNATED SITES

As at 3 August 2010, following the 34th session of the World Heritage Committee, 911 sites were inscribed on the World Cultural and Natural Heritage List. Of these, 25 are in the United Kingdom and three in British overseas territories; 23 are listed for their cultural significance (†), four for their natural significance (*) and one for both cultural and natural significance. The year in which sites were designated appears in parentheses. In 2005 Hadrian's Wall, a World Heritage Site in its own right since 1987, was joined by the upper German-Raetian Limes to form the first section of a trans-national world heritage site, Frontiers of the Roman Empire.

UNITED KINGDOM

†Bath – the city (1987)
†Blaenarvon industrial landscape, Wales (2000)
†Blenheim Palace and Park, Oxfordshire (1987)
†Canterbury Cathedral, St Augustine's Abbey, St Martin's Church, Kent (1988)
†Castle and town walls of King Edward I, north Wales – Beaumaris, Caernarfon Castle, Conwy Castle, Harlech Castle, Ynys Mon (Isle of Anglesey) (1986)
†Cornwall and west Devon mining landscape (2006)
†Derwent Valley Mills, Derbyshire (2001)
*Dorset and east Devon coast (2001)
†Durham Cathedral and Castle (1986)
†Edinburgh old and new towns (1995)
†Frontiers of the Roman Empire, Hadrian's Wall, northern England (1987, 2005)
*Giant's Causeway and Causeway coast, Co. Antrim (1986)
†Greenwich, London – maritime Greenwich, including the Royal Naval College, Old Royal Observatory, Queen's House, town centre (1997)
†Heart of Neolithic Orkney (1999)
†Ironbridge Gorge, Shropshire – the world's first iron bridge and other early industrial sites (1986)
†Liverpool – six areas of the maritime mercantile city (2004)
†New Lanark, South Lanarkshire, Scotland (2001)
†Pontcysyllte Aqueduct and Canal, Wrexham, Wales (2009)
†Royal Botanic Gardens, Kew (2003)
†*St Kilda, Eilean Siar (Western Isles) (1986)
†Saltaire, West Yorkshire (2001)
†Stonehenge, Avebury and related megalithic sites, Wiltshire (1986)
†Studley Royal Park, Fountains Abbey, St Mary's Church, N. Yorkshire (1986)
†Tower of London (1988)
†Westminster Abbey, Palace of Westminster, St Margaret's Church, London (1987)

BRITISH OVERSEAS TERRITORIES

*Henderson Island, Pitcairn Islands, South Pacific Ocean (1988)
*Gough Island and Inaccessible Island (part of Tristan da Cunha), South Atlantic Ocean (1995)
†St George town and related fortifications, Bermuda (2000)

WORLD HERITAGE CENTRE, UNESCO 7 Place de Fontenoy, 75352 Paris 07 SP, France
W http://whc.unesco.org

HISTORIC BUILDINGS AND MONUMENTS

ENGLAND

Under the Planning (Listed Buildings and Conservation Areas) Act 1990, the Secretary of State for Culture, Media and Sport has a statutory duty to approve lists of buildings or groups of buildings in England which are of special architectural or historic interest. In November 2009 responsibility for compiling the list of buildings was passed to English Heritage. Under the Ancient Monuments and Archaeological Areas Act 1979 as amended by the National Heritage Act 1983, the secretary of state is also responsible for compiling a schedule of ancient monuments. Decisions are taken on the advice of English Heritage. On 1 April 2005 responsibility for the administration of the listing system was transferred from the secretary of state to English Heritage. This marked the start of a programme of changes designed to increase the involvement and awareness of the property owner and make the listing process more straightforward and more accountable.

LISTED BUILDINGS

Listed buildings are classified into Grade I, Grade II* and Grade II. There are around 374,300 individual listed buildings in England, of which approximately 92 per cent are Grade II listed. Almost all pre-1700 buildings are listed, as are most buildings of 1700 to 1840. English Heritage carries out thematic surveys of particular types of buildings with a view to making recommendations for listing, and members of the public may propose a building for consideration. The main purpose of listing is to ensure that care is taken in deciding the future of a building. No changes which affect the architectural or historic character of a listed building can be made without listed building consent (in addition to planning permission where relevant). Applications for listed building consent are normally dealt with by the local planning authority, although English Heritage is always consulted about proposals affecting Grade I and Grade II* properties. It is a criminal offence to demolish a listed building, or alter it in such a way as to affect its character, without consent.

SCHEDULED MONUMENTS

There are around 19,700 scheduled monuments in England. English Heritage is carrying out a Monuments Protection Programme assessing archaeological sites with a view to making recommendations for scheduling, and members of the public may propose a monument for consideration. All monuments proposed for scheduling are considered to be of national importance. Where buildings are both scheduled and listed, ancient monuments legislation takes precedence. The main purpose of scheduling a monument is to preserve it for the future and to protect it from damage, destruction or any unnecessary interference. Once a monument has been scheduled, scheduled monument consent is required before any works can be carried out. The scope of the control is more extensive and more detailed than that applied to listed buildings, but certain minor works, as detailed in the Ancient Monuments (Class Consents) Order 1994, may be carried out without consent. It is a criminal offence to carry out unauthorised work to scheduled monuments.

WALES

Under the Planning (Listed Buildings and Conservation Areas) Act 1990 and the Ancient Monuments and Archaeological Areas Act 1979, the National Assembly for Wales is responsible for listing buildings and scheduling monuments in Wales on the advice of Cadw (the Welsh Assembly's historic environment division), the Historic Buildings Advisory Council for Wales, the Ancient Monuments Advisory Board for Wales and the Royal Commission on the Ancient and Historical Monuments of Wales (RCAHMW). The criteria for evaluating buildings are similar to those in England and the same listing system is used. There are approximately 29,900 listed buildings and approximately 4,100 scheduled monuments in Wales.

SCOTLAND

Under the Planning (Listed Buildings and Conservation Areas) (Scotland) Act 1997 and the Ancient Monuments and Archaeological Areas Act 1979, Scottish ministers are responsible for listing buildings and scheduling monuments in Scotland on the advice of Historic Scotland, the Historic Environment Advisory Council for Scotland (HEACS) and the Royal Commission on the Ancient and Historical Monuments of Scotland (RCAHMS). The criteria for evaluating buildings are similar to those in England but an A, B, C(S) categorisation is used. There are approximately 47,500 listed buildings and 8,100 scheduled monuments in Scotland.

NORTHERN IRELAND

Under the Planning (Northern Ireland) Order 1991 and the Historic Monuments and Archaeological Objects (Northern Ireland) Order 1995, the Northern Ireland Environment Agency (part of the Department of the Environment of the Northern Ireland) is responsible for listing buildings and scheduling monuments. The Historic Buildings Council for Northern Ireland and the relevant district council must be consulted on listing proposals, and the Historic Monuments Council for Northern Ireland must be consulted on scheduling proposals. The criteria for evaluating buildings are similar to those in England but an A, B+, B1 and B2 categorisation is used. There are approximately 8,500 listed buildings and 1,845 scheduled monuments in Northern Ireland.

ENGLAND

For more information on English Heritage properties, including those listed below, the official website is www.english-heritage.org.uk
For more information on National Trust properties in England, including those listed below, the official website is www.nationaltrust.org.uk
(EH) English Heritage property
(NT) National Trust property

A LA RONDE (NT), Exmouth, Devon EX8 5BD
T 01395-265514
Unique 16-sided house completed *c.*1796
ALNWICK CASTLE, Alnwick, Northumberland NE66 1NQ
T 01665-510777 W www.alnwickcastle.com
Seat of the Dukes of Northumberland since 1309; Italian Renaissance-style interior; gardens with spectacular water features
ALTHORP, Northants NN7 4HQ T 01604-770107
W www.althorp.com
Spencer family seat; Diana, Princess of Wales memorabilia
ANGLESEY ABBEY (NT), Lode, Cambs CB25 9EJ
T 01223-810080 W www.angleseyabbey.org
House built *c.*1600; houses many paintings and a unique clock collection; gardens and Lode Mill
APSLEY HOUSE (EH), London W1J 7NT T 020-7499 5676
Built by Robert Adam 1771–8, home of the Dukes of Wellington since 1817 and known as 'No. 1 London'; collection of fine and decorative arts
ARUNDEL CASTLE, Arundel, W. Sussex BN18 9AB
T 01903-882173 W www.arundelcastle.org
Castle dating from the Norman Conquest; seat of the Dukes of Norfolk
AVEBURY (NT), Wilts SN8 1RF T 01672-539250
Remains of stone circles constructed 4,000 years ago surrounding the later village of Avebury
BANQUETING HOUSE, Whitehall, London SW1A 2ER
T 0844-482 7777 W www.hrp.org.uk
Designed by Inigo Jones; ceiling paintings by Rubens; site of the execution of Charles I
BASILDON PARK (NT), Reading, Berks RG8 9NR
T 0118-984 3040
Palladian mansion built in 1776–83 by John Carr
BATTLE ABBEY (EH), Battle, E. Sussex TN33 0AD
T 01424-775705
Remains of the abbey founded by William the Conqueror on the site of the Battle of Hastings
BEAULIEU, Brockenhurst, Hants SO42 7ZN T 01590-612345
W www.beaulieu.co.uk
House and gardens; Beaulieu Abbey and exhibition of monastic life; National Motor Museum
BEESTON CASTLE (EH), Cheshire CW6 9TX
T 01829-260464
Built in the 13th century by Ranulf, sixth Earl of Chester
BELTON HOUSE (NT), Grantham, Lincs NG32 2LS
T 01476-566116
17th-century house; formal gardens in landscaped park
BELVOIR CASTLE, Grantham, Lincs NG32 1PE
T 01476-871002 W www.belvoircastle.com
Seat of the Dukes of Rutland; 19th-century Gothic-style castle
BERKELEY CASTLE, Glos GL13 9BQ T 01453-810332
W www.berkeley-castle.com
Completed 1153; site of the murder of Edward II (1327)
BIRDOSWALD FORT (EH), Cumbria CA8 7DD
T 01697-747602
Stretch of Hadrian's Wall with Roman wall fort, turret and milecastle
BLENHEIM PALACE, Woodstock, Oxon OX20 1PX
T 01993-810500 W www.blenheimpalace.com
Seat of the Dukes of Marlborough and Winston Churchill's birthplace; designed by Vanbrugh
BLICKLING HALL (NT), Blickling, Norfolk NR11 6NF
T 01263-738030
Jacobean house with state rooms; temple and 18th-century orangery
BODIAM CASTLE (NT), Bodiam, E. Sussex TN32 5UA
T 01580-830196
Well-preserved medieval moated castle built in 1385
BOLSOVER CASTLE (EH), Bolsover, Derbys S44 6PR
T 01246-822844
17th-century buildings on site of medieval castle
BOSCOBEL HOUSE (EH), Bishops Wood, Staffs ST19 9AR
T 01902-850244
Timber-framed 17th-century hunting lodge; refuge of fugitive Charles II
BOUGHTON HOUSE, Kettering, Northants NN14 1BJ
T 01536-515731 W www.boughtonhouse.org.uk
A 17th-century house with French-style additions; home of the Dukes of Buccleuch and Queensbury
BOWOOD HOUSE, Calne, Wilts SN11 0LZ
T 01249-812102 W www.bowood-house.co.uk
An 18th-century house in Capability Brown park, with lake, temple and arboretum
BRONTË PARSONAGE, Haworth, W. Yorks BD22 8DR
T 01535-642323 W www.bronte.org.uk
Home of the Brontë sisters; museum and memorabilia
BUCKFAST ABBEY, Buckfastleigh, Devon TQ11 0EE
T 01364-645500 W www.buckfast.org.uk
Benedictine monastery on medieval foundations
BUCKINGHAM PALACE, London SW1A 1AA
T 020-7766 7300 W www.royalcollection.org.uk
Purchased by George III in 1761, and the Sovereign's official London residence since 1837; 18 state rooms, including the Throne Room, and Picture Gallery
BUCKLAND ABBEY (NT), Yelverton, Devon PL20 6EY
T 01822-853607
13th-century Cistercian monastery; home of Sir Francis Drake
BURGHLEY HOUSE, Stamford, Lincs PE9 3JY
T 01780-752451 W www.burghley.co.uk
Late Elizabethan house built by William Cecil, first Lord Burghley
CALKE ABBEY (NT), Ticknall, Derbys DE73 7LE
T 01332-863822
Baroque 18th-century mansion
CARISBROOKE CASTLE (EH), Newport, Isle of Wight PO30 1XY T 01983-522107
W www.carisbrookecastlemuseum.org.uk
Norman castle; museum; prison of Charles I 1647–8
CARLISLE CASTLE (EH), Carlisle, Cumbria CA3 8UR
T 01228-591922
Medieval castle; prison of Mary Queen of Scots
CARLYLE'S HOUSE (NT), Chelsea, London SW3 5HL
T 020-7352 7087
Home of Thomas Carlyle
CASTLE ACRE PRIORY (EH), Swaffham, Norfolk PE32 2XD T 01760-755394
Remains include 12th-century church and prior's lodgings
CASTLE DROGO (NT), Drewsteignton, Devon EX6 6PB
T 01647-433306
Granite castle designed by Lutyens

CASTLE HOWARD, N. Yorks YO60 7DA T 01653-648333 W www.castlehoward.co.uk
Designed by Vanbrugh 1699–1726; mausoleum designed by Hawksmoor

CASTLE RISING CASTLE (EH), King's Lynn, Norfolk PE31 6AH T 01553-631330 W www.castlerising.co.uk
12th-century keep in a massive earthwork with gatehouse and bridge

CHARLES DARWIN'S HOUSE (EH), Down House, Luxted Road, Downe, Kent BR6 7JT T 01689-859119
The family home where Darwin wrote *On the Origin of Species*

CHARTWELL (NT), Westerham, Kent TN16 1PS T 01732-866368
Home of Sir Winston Churchill

CHATSWORTH, Bakewell, Derbys DE45 1PP T 01246-565300 W www.chatsworth.org
Tudor mansion set in magnificent parkland

CHESTERS ROMAN FORT (EH), Chollerford, Northumberland NE46 4EU T 01434-681379
Roman cavalry fort built to guard Hadrian's Wall

CHYSAUSTER ANCIENT VILLAGE (EH), Penzance, Cornwall TR20 8XA T 07831-757934
Remains of Celtic settlement; eight stone-walled homesteads

CLANDON PARK (NT), West Clandon, Guildford, Surrey GU4 7RQ T 01483-222482 W www.clandonpark.co.uk
18th-century Palladian mansion and gardens, which contain a Maori meeting house, removed from New Zealand in 1892

CLIFFORD'S TOWER (EH), York YO1 9SA T 01904-646940 W www.cliffordstower.com
13th-century tower built on a mound; remains of a castle built by William the Conqueror

CLIVEDEN (NT), Taplow, Berks SL6 0JA T 01494-755562
Former home of the Astors, now a hotel set in garden and woodland

CORBRIDGE ROMAN SITE (EH), Corbridge, Northumberland NE45 5NT T 01434-632349
Excavated central area of a Roman town and successive military bases

CORFE CASTLE (NT), Wareham, Dorset BH20 5EZ T 01929-481294
Ruined former royal castle dating from the 11th century

CROFT CASTLE AND PARKLAND (NT), Herefordshire HR6 9PW T 01568-780246
Pre-Conquest border castle with Georgian-Gothic interior

DEAL CASTLE (EH), Deal, Kent CT14 7BA T 01304-372762
Largest of the coastal defence forts built by Henry VIII

DICKENS HOUSE, Doughty Street, London WC1N 2LX T 020-7405 2127 W www.dickensmuseum.com
House occupied by Dickens 1837–9; manuscripts, furniture and portraits

DOVE COTTAGE, Grasmere, Cumbria LA22 9SH T 01539-435544 W www.wordsworth.org.uk
Wordsworth's home 1799–1808; museum

DOVER CASTLE (EH), Dover, Kent CT16 1HU T 01304-211067
Castle with Roman, Saxon and Norman features; wartime operations rooms

DR JOHNSON'S HOUSE, Gough Square, London EC4A 3DE T 020-7353 3745 W www.drjohnsonshouse.org
Home of Samuel Johnson 1748–59

DUNSTANBURGH CASTLE (NT), Craster, nr Alnwick, Northumberland NE66 3TT T 01665-576231
14th-century castle ruins on a cliff with a substantial gatehouse-keep

ELTHAM PALACE (EH), Eltham, London SE9 5QE T 020-8294 2548
Combines an Art Deco country house and remains of medieval palace set in moated gardens

FARLEIGH HUNGERFORD CASTLE (EH), Somerset BA2 7RS T 01225-754026
Late 14th-century castle with two courts; chapel with tomb of Sir Thomas Hungerford

FARNHAM CASTLE KEEP (EH), Farnham, Surrey GA9 0JA T 01252-713393 W www.farnhamcastle.com
Large 12th-century castle keep with motte and bailey wall

FISHBOURNE ROMAN PALACE, Salthill Road, Fishbourne, Chichester, W. Sussex PO19 3QR T 01243-785859 W www.sussexpast.co.uk
Excavated Roman palace with largest collection of in-situ mosaics in Britain

FOUNTAINS ABBEY (NT), nr Ripon, N. Yorks HG4 3DY T 01765-608888 W www.fountainsabbey.org.uk
Deer park; St Mary's Church; ruined Cistercian monastery; Georgian water garden

FRAMLINGHAM CASTLE (EH), Woodbridge, Suffolk IP13 9BP T 01728-724189
Castle (*c.*1200) with high curtain walls enclosing an almshouse (1639)

FURNESS ABBEY (EH), Barrow-in-Furness, Cumbria LA13 0PJ T 01229-823420
Remains of church and cloister buildings founded in 1123

GLASTONBURY ABBEY, Glastonbury, Somerset BA6 9EL T 01458-832267 W www.glastonburyabbey.com
Ruins of a 12th-century abbey rebuilt after fire; site of an early Christian settlement

GOODRICH CASTLE (EH), Ross-on-Wye, Herefordshire HR9 6HY T 01600-890538
Remains of 13th-century castle with 12th-century keep

GREENWICH, London SE10 9NF W www.greenwichwhs.org.uk
Former Royal Observatory (founded 1675) housing the time ball and zero meridian of longitude; the Queen's House, designed for Queen Anne, wife of James I, by Inigo Jones; Painted Hall and Chapel (Old Royal Naval College)

GRIMES GRAVES (EH), Brandon, Norfolk IP26 5DE T 01842-810656
Neolithic flint mines; one shaft can be descended

GUILDHALL, London EC2P 2EJ T 020-7606 3030 W www.cityoflondon.gov.uk
Centre of civic government of the City built *c.* 1441; facade built 1788–9

HADDON HALL, Bakewell, Derbys DE45 1LA T 01629-812855 W www.haddonhall.co.uk
Well-preserved 12th-century manor house

HAILES ABBEY (EH), Cheltenham, Glos GL54 5PB T 01242-602398
Ruins of a 13th-century Cistercian monastery

HAM HOUSE (NT), Richmond-upon-Thames, Surrey TW10 7RS T 020-8940 1950
Stuart house with lavish interiors and formal gardens

HAMPTON COURT PALACE, East Molesey, Surrey KT8 9AU T 0844-482 7777 W www.hrp.org.uk
16th-century palace with additions by Wren

HARDWICK HALL (NT), Chesterfield, Derbys S44 5QJ T 01246-850430
Built 1591–7 for Bess of Hardwick

HARDY'S COTTAGE (NT), Higher Bockhampton, Dorset DT2 8QJ T 01297-489481
Birthplace and home of Thomas Hardy

HAREWOOD HOUSE, Harewood, W. Yorks LS17 9LG
T 0113-218 1010 W www.harewood.org
18th-century house designed by John Carr and Robert Adam; park by Capability Brown

HATFIELD HOUSE, Hatfield, Herts AL9 5NQ
T 01707-287010 W www.hatfield-house.co.uk
Jacobean house built by Robert Cecil; surviving wing of Royal Palace of Hatfield (*c.*1485)

HELMSLEY CASTLE (EH), Helmsley, N. Yorks YO62 5AB
T 01439-770442
12th-century keep and curtain wall with 16th-century buildings; spectacular earthwork defences

HEVER CASTLE, nr Edenbridge, Kent TN8 7NG
T 01732-865224 W www.hevercastle.co.uk
13th-century double-moated castle; childhood home of Anne Boleyn

HOLKER HALL, Cumbria LA11 7PL T 01539-558328
W www.holker.co.uk
Former home of the Dukes of Devonshire; award-winning gardens

HOLKHAM HALL, Wells-next-the-Sea, Norfolk NR23 1AB
T 01328-710227 W www.holkham.co.uk
Palladian mansion; notable fine art collection

HOUSESTEADS ROMAN FORT (EH), Hexham, Northumberland NE47 6NN T 01434-344363
Excavated infantry fort on Hadrian's Wall with museum

HUGHENDEN MANOR (NT), High Wycombe, Bucks HP14 4LA T 01494-755565
Home of Disraeli; small formal garden

JANE AUSTEN'S HOUSE, Chawton, Hants GU34 1SD
T 01420-83262
W www.jane-austens-house-museum.org.uk
Jane Austen's home from 1809 to 1817

KEDLESTON HALL (NT), Derbys DE22 5JH
T 01332-842191
Classical Palladian mansion built 1759–65; complete Robert Adam interiors

KELMSCOTT MANOR, nr Lechlade, Glos GL7 3HJ
T 01367-252486 W www.kelmscottmanor.org.uk
Summer home of William Morris, with products of Morris and Co.

KENILWORTH CASTLE (EH), Kenilworth, Warks CV8 1NE
T 01926-852078
Largest castle ruin in England

KENSINGTON PALACE, Kensington Gardens, London W8 4PX T 0870-482 7777 W www.hrp.org.uk
Built in 1605 and enlarged by Wren; birthplace of Queen Victoria; Royal Ceremonial Dress collection

KENWOOD HOUSE (EH), Hampstead Lane, London NW3 7JR T 020-8348 1286
Neo-classical villa housing the Iveagh bequest of paintings and furniture

KEW PALACE, Richmond-upon-Thames, Surrey TW9 3AB
T 0870-482 7777 W www.hrp.org.uk
Includes Queen Charlotte's Cottage, used by King George III and family as a summerhouse

KINGSTON LACY (NT), Wimborne Minster, Dorset BH21 4EA T 01202-883402
17th-century house with 19th-century alterations; important art collection

KNEBWORTH HOUSE, Knebworth, Herts SG3 6PY
T 01438-812661 W www.knebworthhouse.com
Tudor manor house concealed by 19th-century Gothic decoration; Lutyens gardens

KNOLE (NT), Sevenoaks, Kent TN15 0RP T 01732-450608
House dating from 1456 set in parkland; fine art collection; birthplace of Vita Sackville-West

LAMBETH PALACE, London SE1 7JU T 020-7898 1200
W www.archbishopofcanterbury.org
Official residence of the Archbishop of Canterbury; partly dating from the 12th century

LANERCOST PRIORY (EH), Brampton, Cumbria CA8 2HQ
T 01697-73030
The nave of the Augustinian priory church, *c.*1166, is still used; remains of other claustral buildings

LANHYDROCK (NT), Bodmin, Cornwall PL30 5AD
T 01208-265950
House dating from the 17th century; 50 rooms, including kitchen and nursery

LEEDS CASTLE, nr Maidstone, Kent ME17 1PL
T 01622-765400 W www.leeds-castle.com
Castle dating from the 12th century, on two islands in lake

LEVENS HALL, Kendal, Cumbria LA8 0PD T 01539-560321
W www.levenshall.co.uk
Elizabethan house with unique topiary garden (1694); steam engine collection

LINCOLN CASTLE, Lincoln, Lincs LN1 3AA
T 01522-511068 W www.lincolnshire.gov.uk
Built by William the Conqueror in 1068

LINDISFARNE PRIORY (EH), Holy Island, Northumberland TD15 2RX T 01289-389200
Founded in AD 635; re-established in the 12th century as a Benedictine priory, now ruined

LITTLE MORETON HALL (NT), Congleton, Cheshire CW12 4SD T 01260-272018
Timber-framed moated Tudor manor house with knot garden

LONGLEAT HOUSE, Warminster, Wilts BA12 7NW
T 01985-844400 W www.longleat.co.uk
Elizabethan house in Italian Renaissance style; safari park

LULLINGSTONE ROMAN VILLA (EH), Eynsford, Kent DA4 0JA T 01322-863467
Large villa occupied for much of the Roman period; fine mosaics

MARBLE HILL HOUSE (EH), Twickenham, Middx TW1 2NL T 020-8892 5115
English Palladian villa with Georgian paintings and furniture

MICHELHAM PRIORY, Hailsham, E. Sussex BN27 3QS
T 01323-844224 W www.sussexpast.co.uk
Tudor house built onto an Augustinian priory

MIDDLEHAM CASTLE (EH), Leyburn, N. Yorks DL8 4QJ
T 01969-623899
12th-century keep within later fortifications; childhood home of Richard III

MONTACUTE HOUSE (NT), Montacute, Somerset TA15 6XP T 01935-823289
Elizabethan house with National Portrait Gallery collection of portraits from the period

MOUNT GRACE PRIORY (EH), Northallerton, N. Yorks DL6 3JG T 01609-883494
Carthusian priory with remains of monastic buildings

OLD SARUM (EH), Salisbury, Wilts SP1 3SD
T 01722-335398
Earthworks enclosing remains of Norman castle and cathedral

ORFORD CASTLE (EH), Orford, Suffolk IP12 2ND
T 01394-450472
Circular keep of *c.*1170 and remains of coastal defence castle built by Henry II

OSBORNE HOUSE (EH), East Cowes, Isle of Wight PO32 6JX T 01983-200022
Queen Victoria's seaside residence

OSTERLEY PARK (NT), Isleworth, Middx TW7 4RB
T 020-8232 5050 W www.osterleypark.org.uk
Elizabethan mansion set in parkland

PENDENNIS CASTLE (EH), Falmouth, Cornwall TR11 4LP
T 01326-316594
Well-preserved 16th-century coastal defence castle

PENSHURST PLACE, Penshurst, Kent TN11 8DG
T 01892-870307 W www.penshurstplace.com
House with medieval Baron's Hall and 14th-century gardens

PETWORTH HOUSE (NT), Petworth, W. Sussex GU28 0AE
T 01798-343929
Late 17th-century house set in Capability Brown landscaped deer park

PEVENSEY CASTLE (EH), Pevensey, E. Sussex BN24 5LE
T 01323-762604
Walls of a fourth-century Roman fort; remains of an 11th-century castle

PEVERIL CASTLE (EH), Castleton, Derbys S33 8WQ
T 01433-620613
12th-century castle defended on two sides by precipitous rocks

POLESDEN LACEY (NT), nr Dorking, Surrey RH5 6BD
T 01372-458203
Regency villa remodelled in the Edwardian era; fine paintings and furnishings

PORTCHESTER CASTLE (EH), Portchester, Hants PO16 9QW T 02392-378291
Walls of a late Roman fort enclosing a Norman keep and an Augustinian priory church

POWDERHAM CASTLE, Kenton, Devon EX6 8JQ
T 01626-890243 W www.powderham.co.uk
Medieval castle with 18th- and 19th-century alterations

RABY CASTLE, Staindrop, Co. Durham DL2 3AH
T 01833-660202 W www.rabycastle.com
14th-century castle with walled gardens

RAGLEY HALL, Alcester, Warks B49 5NJ T 01789-762090
W www.ragleyhall.com
17th-century house with gardens, park and lake

RICHBOROUGH ROMAN FORT (EH), Richborough, Kent CT13 9JW T 01304-612013
Landing-site of the Claudian invasion in AD 43

RICHMOND CASTLE (EH), Richmond, N. Yorks DL10 4QW T 01748-822493
12th-century keep with 11th-century curtain wall

RIEVAULX ABBEY (EH), nr Helmsley, N. Yorks YO62 5LB
T 01439-798228
Remains of a Cistercian abbey founded *c.*1132

ROCHESTER CASTLE (EH), Rochester, Kent ME1 1SW
T 01634-402276
11th-century castle partly on the Roman city wall, with a square keep of *c.* 1130

ROCKINGHAM CASTLE, Market Harborough, Leics LE16 8TH T 01536-770240 W www.rockinghamcastle.com
Built by William the Conqueror

ROYAL PAVILION, Brighton BN1 1EE T 03000-290900
W www.royalpavilion.org.uk
Palace of George IV, in Chinese style with Indian exterior and Regency gardens

RUFFORD OLD HALL (NT), nr Ormskirk, Lancs L40 1SG
T 01704-821254
16th-century hall with unique screen

ST AUGUSTINE'S ABBEY (EH), Canterbury, Kent CT1 1TF
T 01227-378100
Remains of Benedictine monastery founded AD 597

ST MAWES CASTLE (EH), St Mawes, Cornwall TR2 5DE
T 01326-270526
Coastal defence castle built by Henry VIII

ST MICHAEL'S MOUNT (NT), Cornwall TR17 0HT
T 01736-710507 W www.stmichaelsmount.co.uk
12th-century castle with later additions, off the coast at Marazion

SANDRINGHAM, Norfolk PE35 6EN T 01553-612908
W www.sandringhamestate.co.uk
The Queen's private residence; a neo-Jacobean house built in 1870

SCARBOROUGH CASTLE (EH), Scarborough, N. Yorks YO11 1HY T 01723-372451
Remains of 12th-century keep and curtain walls

SHERBORNE CASTLE, Sherborne, Dorset DT9 3PY
T 01935-813182 W www.sherbornecastle.com
16th-century castle built by Sir Walter Raleigh set in landscaped gardens

SHUGBOROUGH ESTATE (NT), Milford, Staffs ST17 0XB
T 01889-881388 W www.shugborough.org.uk
House set in 18th-century park with monuments, temples and pavilions in the Greek Revival style; arboretum; seat of the Earls of Lichfield

SKIPTON CASTLE, Skipton, N. Yorks BD23 1AW
T 01756-792442 W www.skiptoncastle.co.uk
D-shaped castle with six round towers and inner courtyard

SMALLHYTHE PLACE (NT), Tenterden, Kent TN30 7NG
T 01580-762334
Half-timbered 16th-century house; home of Ellen Terry 1899–1928; the Barn Theatre

STONEHENGE (EH), nr Amesbury, Wilts SP4 7DE
T 0870-333 1181
Prehistoric monument consisting of concentric stone circles surrounded by a ditch and bank

STONOR PARK, Henley-on-Thames, Oxon RG9 6HF
T 01491-638587 W www.stonor.com
Medieval house with Georgian facade; centre of Roman Catholicism after the Reformation

STOURHEAD (NT), Stourton, Wilts BA12 6QD
T 01747-841152
English 18th-century Palladian mansion with landscape gardens

STRATFIELD SAYE HOUSE, Hants RG7 2BT
T 01256-882694 W www.stratfield-saye.co.uk
House built 1630–40; home of the Dukes of Wellington since 1817

STRATFORD-UPON-AVON, Warks T 01789-204016
W www.shakespeare.org.uk
Shakespeare's Birthplace Trust with Shakespeare Centre; Anne Hathaway's Cottage, home of Shakespeare's wife; Mary Arden's House, home of Shakespeare's mother; grammar school attended by Shakespeare; Holy Trinity Church, where Shakespeare is buried; Royal Shakespeare Theatre (burnt down 1926, rebuilt 1932) and Swan Theatre (opened 1986)

SUDELEY CASTLE, Winchcombe, Glos GL54 5JD
T 01242-602308 W www.sudeleycastle.co.uk
Castle built in 1442; restored in the 19th century

SULGRAVE MANOR, nr Banbury, Oxon OX17 2SD
T 01295-760205 W www.sulgravemanor.org.uk
Home of George Washington's family

SUTTON HOUSE (NT), 2 & 4 Homerton High Street, Hackney, London E9 6JQ T 020-8986 2264
Tudor house, built in 1535 by Sir Ralph Sadleir

SYON HOUSE, Brentford, Middx TW8 8JF T 020-8560 0881
W www.syonpark.co.uk
Built on the site of a former monastery; Robert Adam interior; Capability Brown park

TILBURY FORT (EH), Tilbury, Essex RM18 7NR
T 01375-858489
17th-century coastal fort

TINTAGEL CASTLE (EH), Tintagel, Cornwall PL34 0HE T 01840-770328
13th-century cliff-top castle and Dark Age settlement site; linked with Arthurian legend

TOWER OF LONDON, London EC3N 4AB T 0870-482 7777 W www.hrp.org.uk
Royal palace and fortress begun by William the Conqueror in 1078; houses the Crown Jewels

TRERICE (NT), nr Newquay, Cornwall TR8 4PG T 01637-875404
Elizabethan manor house

TYNEMOUTH PRIORY AND CASTLE (EH), Tyne and Wear NE30 4BZ T 0191-257 1090
Remains of a Benedictine priory, founded *c.* 1090, on Saxon monastic site

UPPARK (NT), South Harting, W. Sussex GU31 5QR T 01730-825857
Late 17th-century house, completely restored after fire; Fetherstonhaugh art collection

WALMER CASTLE (EH), Walmer, Kent CT14 7LJ T 01304-364288
One of Henry VIII's coastal defence castles, now the residence of the Lord Warden of the Cinque Ports

WARKWORTH CASTLE (EH), Warkworth, Northumberland NE65 0UJ T 01665-711423
14th-century keep amid earlier ruins, with hermitage upstream

WHITBY ABBEY (EH), Whitby, N. Yorks YO22 4JT T 01947-603568
Remains of Norman church on the site of a monastery founded in AD 657

WILTON HOUSE, nr Salisbury, Wilts SP2 0BJ T 01722-746714 W www.wiltonhouse.co.uk
17th-century house on the site of a Tudor house and ninth-century nunnery

WINDSOR CASTLE, Windsor, Berks SL4 1NJ T 020-7766 7304 W www.royalcollection.org.uk
Official residence of the Queen; oldest royal residence still in regular use; largest inhabited castle in the world. Also St George's Chapel

WOBURN ABBEY, Woburn, Beds MK17 9WA T 01525-290333 W www.woburn.co.uk
Built on the site of a Cistercian abbey; seat of the Dukes of Bedford; art collection; antiques centre

WROXETER ROMAN CITY (EH), nr Shrewsbury, Shropshire SY5 6PH T 01743-761330
Second-century public baths and part of the forum of the Roman town of Viroconium

WALES

For more information on Cadw properties, including those listed below, the official website is www.cadw.wales.gov.uk

For more information on National Trust properties in Wales, including those listed below, the official website is www.nationaltrust.org.uk

(C) Property of Cadw: Welsh Historic Monuments
(NT) National Trust property

BEAUMARIS CASTLE (C), Anglesey LL58 8AP T 01248-810361
Concentrically planned castle, still virtually intact

CAERLEON ROMAN BATHS AND AMPHITHEATRE (C), Newport NP18 1AE T 01633-422518
Rare example of a legionary bath-house and late first-century arena surrounded by bank for spectators

CAERNARFON CASTLE (C), Gwynedd LL55 2AY T 01286-677617 W www.caernarfon.com
Castle built between 1283 and 1330, initially for King Edward I of England; setting for the investiture of Prince Charles in 1969

CAERPHILLY CASTLE (C), Caerphilly CF83 1JD T 029-2088 3143
Concentrically planned castle (*c.* 1270) notable for its scale and use of water defences

CARDIFF CASTLE, Cardiff CF10 3RB T 029-2087 8100 W www.cardiffcastle.com
Castle built on the site of a Roman fort

CASTELL COCH (C), Tongwynlais, Cardiff CF15 7JS T 029-2081 0101
'Fairytale castle' rebuilt 1875–90 on medieval foundations

CHEPSTOW CASTLE (C), Monmouthshire NP16 5EZ T 01291-624065
Rectangular keep amid extensive fortifications; developed throughout the Middle Ages

CONWY CASTLE (C), Gwynedd LL32 8AY T 01492-592358
Built for Edward I, 1283–7, on a narrow rocky outcrop

CRICCIETH CASTLE (C), Gwynedd LL55 0DP T 01766-522227
Native Welsh 13th-century castle, altered by Edward I and Edward II

DENBIGH CASTLE (C), Denbighshire LL16 3NB T 01745-813385
Remains of the castle (begun 1282), including triple-towered gatehouse

HARLECH CASTLE (C), Gwynedd LL46 2YH T 01766-780552
Well-preserved Edwardian castle, constructed 1283–9, on an outcrop above the former shoreline

PEMBROKE CASTLE, Pembrokeshire SA71 4LA T 01646-684585 W www.pembrokecastle.co.uk
Castle founded in 1093; Great Tower built in late 12th century; birthplace of King Henry VII

PENRHYN CASTLE (NT), Bangor, Gwynedd LL57 4HN T 01248-371337
Neo-Norman castle built in the 19th century; railway museum; private art collection

PORTMEIRION, Gwynedd LL48 6ER T 01766-770000 W www.portmeirion-village.com
Village in Italianate style built by Clough Williams-Ellis

POWIS CASTLE (NT), Welshpool, Powys SY21 8RF T 01938-551944
Medieval castle with interior in variety of styles; 17th-century gardens; Clive of India museum

RAGLAN CASTLE (C), Monmouthshire NP15 2BT T 01291-690228
Remains of 15th-century castle with moated hexagonal keep

ST DAVIDS BISHOP'S PALACE (C), Pembrokeshire SA62 6PE T 01437-720517
Remains of residence of Bishops of St Davids built 1328–47

TINTERN ABBEY (C), nr Chepstow, Monmouthshire NP16 6SE T 01291-689251
Remains of 13th-century church and conventual buildings of a 12th-century Cistercian monastery

TRETOWER COURT AND CASTLE (C), nr Crickhowell, Powys NP8 1RF T 01874-730279
Medieval house rebuilt in the 15th century, with remains of 12th-century castle nearby

SCOTLAND

For more information on Historic Scotland properties, including those listed below, the official website is www.historic-scotland.gov.uk

For more information on National Trust for Scotland properties, including those listed below, the official website is www.nts.org.uk

(HS) Historic Scotland property

(NTS) National Trust for Scotland property

ABBOTSFORD HOUSE, Melrose, Roxburghshire TD6 9BQ
T 01896-752043 W www.scottsabbotsford.co.uk
Home of Sir Walter Scott

ANTONINE WALL, between the Clyde and the Forth
W www.antoninewall.org
Built around AD 142; consists of ditch, turf rampart, road and forts at regular intervals

BALMORAL CASTLE, Ballater, Aberdeenshire AB35 5TB
T 01339-742534 W www.balmoralcastle.com
Baronial-style castle built for Victoria and Albert; the Queen's private residence

BLACKHOUSE, ARNOL (HS), Lewis, Western Isles HS2 9DB T 01851-710395
Traditional Lewis thatched house

BLAIR CASTLE, Blair Atholl, Perthshire PH18 5TL
T 01796-481207 W www.blair-castle.co.uk
Mid-18th-century mansion with 13th-century tower; seat of the Dukes and Earls of Atholl

BONAWE IRON FURNACE (HS), Taynuilt, Argyll PA35 1JQ T 01866-822432
Charcoal-fuelled ironworks founded in 1753

BOWHILL, Selkirkshire TD7 5ET T 01750-22204
W www.bowhill.org
Seat of the Dukes of Buccleuch and Queensberry; fine collection of paintings

BROUGH OF BIRSAY (HS), Orkney KW17 2NH
T 01856-841815
Remains of Norse and Pictish village on the tidal island of Birsay

BURNS NATIONAL HERITAGE PARK (NTS), Alloway, Ayrshire KA7 4PQ T 01292-443700
W www.burnsheritagepark.com
Contains Burns Cottage, birthplace of the poet, and a museum

CAERLAVEROCK CASTLE (HS), Glencaple, Dumfriesshire DG1 4RU T 01387-770244
Triangular 13th-century castle with classical Renaissance additions

CAIRNPAPPLE HILL (HS), Torphichen, West Lothian
T 01506-634622
Neolithic and Bronze Age ceremonial site and burial chambers

CALANAIS STANDING STONES (HS), Lewis, Western Isles HS2 9DY T 01851-621422
Standing stones in a cross-shaped setting, dating from *c.* 3000 BC

CATERTHUNS (BROWN AND WHITE) (HS), Menmuir, nr Brechin, Angus
Two large Iron Age hill forts

CAWDOR CASTLE, Nairn, Moray IV12 5RD
T 01667-404401 W www.cawdorcastle.com
14th-century keep with 15th- and 17th-century additions

CLAVA CAIRNS (HS), nr Inverness, Inverness-shire
T 01667-460232
Bronze Age cemetery complex of cairns and standing stones

CRATHES CASTLE (NTS), nr Banchory, Aberdeenshire AB31 5QJ T 08444-932166
16th-century baronial castle in woodland, fields and gardens

CULZEAN CASTLE (NTS), Maybole, Ayrshire KA19 8LE
T 08444-932149 W www.culzeanexperience.org
18th-century Robert Adam castle with oval staircase and circular saloon

DRYBURGH ABBEY (HS), nr Melrose, Roxburghshire TD6 0RQ T 01835-822381
12th-century abbey containing the tomb of Sir Walter Scott

DUNVEGAN CASTLE, Skye IV55 8WF T 01470-521206
W www.dunvegancastle.com
13th-century castle with later additions; home of the chiefs of the Clan MacLeod

EDINBURGH CASTLE (HS) EH1 2NG T 0131-225 9846
W www.edinburghcastle.gov.uk
Includes the Scottish Crown Jewels, Scottish National War Memorial, Scottish United Services Museum and historic apartments

EDZELL CASTLE (HS), nr Brechin, Angus DD9 7UE
T 01356-648631
16th-century tower house on medieval foundations; walled garden

EILEAN DONAN CASTLE, Dornie, Ross and Cromarty IV40 8DX T 01599-555202 W www.eileandonancastle.com
13th-century castle with Jacobite relics at the meeting point of three sea lochs

ELGIN CATHEDRAL (HS), Moray IV30 1HU
T 01343-547171
13th-century cathedral and chapterhouse

FLOORS CASTLE, Kelso, Roxburghshire TD5 7SF
T 01573-223333 W www.floorscastle.com
Largest inhabited castle in Scotland; seat of the Dukes of Roxburghe; built 1721 by William Adam

FORT GEORGE (HS), Ardersier, Inverness-shire IV2 7TD
T 01667-460232
18th-century fort; still a working army barracks

GLAMIS CASTLE, Forfar, Angus DD8 1RJ T 01307-840393
W www.glamis-castle.co.uk
Seat of the Lyon family (later Earls of Strathmore and Kinghorne) since 1372

GLASGOW CATHEDRAL (HS), Lanarkshire G4 0QZ
T 0141-552 6891 W www.glasgow-cathedral.com
Medieval cathedral with elaborately vaulted crypt

GLENELG BROCHS (HS), Shielbridge, Ross and Cromarty
T 01667-460232
Two broch towers (Dun Telve and Dun Troddan) with well-preserved structural features

HOPETOUN HOUSE, South Queensferry, W. Lothian EH30 9SL T 0131-331 2451 W www.hopetounhouse.com
House designed by Sir William Bruce, enlarged by William Adam, built 1699

HUNTLY CASTLE (HS), Aberdeenshire AB54 4SH
T 01466-793191
Ruin of a 16th- and 17th-century baronial residence

INVERARAY CASTLE, Argyll PA32 8XE T 01499-302203
W www.inveraray-castle.com
Gothic-style 18th-century castle; seat of the Dukes of Argyll

IONA ABBEY (HS), Iona, Inner Hebrides PA76 6SQ
T 01681-700512
Monastery founded by St Columba in AD 563

JARLSHOF (HS), Sumburgh Head, Shetland ZE3 9JN
T 01950-460112
Prehistoric and Norse settlement

JEDBURGH ABBEY (HS), Scottish Borders TD8 6JQ T 01835-863925
Romanesque and early Gothic church founded *c.*1138

KISIMUL CASTLE (HS), Castlebay, Barra, Western Isles HS9 5UZ T 01871-810313
Medieval home of the Clan MacNeil

LINLITHGOW PALACE (HS), Kirkgate, Linlithgow, W. Lothian EH49 7AL T 01506-842896
Ruin of royal palace in park setting; birthplace of James V and Mary, Queen of Scots

MAESHOWE (HS), Stenness, Orkney KW16 3HA T 01856-761606
Neolithic chambered tomb

MEIGLE SCULPTURED STONES (HS), Meigle, Perthshire PH12 8SB T 01828-640612
Twenty-six carved stones dating from the eighth to the 10th centuries

MELROSE ABBEY (HS), Melrose, Roxburghshire TD6 9LG T 01896-822562
Ruin of Cistercian abbey founded *c.*1136 by David I

MOUSA BROCH (HS), Island of Mousa, Shetland T 01856-841815
Finest surviving Iron Age broch tower

NEW ABBEY CORN MILL (HS), Dumfriesshire DG2 8BX T 01387-850260
Working water-powered mill; operates in summer months

PALACE OF HOLYROODHOUSE, Edinburgh EH8 8DX T 0131-556 5100 W www.royalcollection.org.uk
The Queen's official Scottish residence; main part of the palace built 1671–9

RING O' BRODGAR (HS), nr Stromness, Orkney T 01856-841815
Neolithic circle of upright stones with an enclosing ditch

ROSSLYN CHAPEL, Roslin, Midlothian EH25 9PU T 0131-440 2159 W www.rosslynchapel.org.uk
Historic church with unique stone carvings

RUTHWELL CROSS (HS), Ruthwell, Dumfriesshire T 0131-550 7612
Seventh-century Anglo-Saxon cross, open by arrangement

ST ANDREWS CASTLE AND CATHEDRAL (HS), Fife KY16 9QL T 01334-477196 (castle); 01334-472563 (cathedral)
Ruins of 13th-century castle and remains of the largest cathedral in Scotland

SCONE PALACE, Perth, Perthshire PH2 6BD T 01738-552300 W www.scone-palace.net
House built 1802–13 on the site of a medieval palace

SKARA BRAE (HS), nr Stromness, Orkney KW16 3LR T 01856-841815
Stone Age village with adjacent replica house

SMAILHOLM TOWER (HS), nr Kelso, Roxburghshire TD5 7PG T 01573-460365
Well-preserved 15th-century tower-house

STIRLING CASTLE (HS), Stirlingshire FK8 1EJ T 01786-450000 W www.stirlingcastle.gov.uk
Great Hall and gatehouse of James IV, palace of James V, Chapel Royal remodelled by James VI

TANTALLON CASTLE (HS), North Berwick, E. Lothian EH39 5PN T 01620-892727
Fortification with earthwork defences; 14th-century curtain wall with towers

THREAVE CASTLE (HS), Castle Douglas, Kirkcudbrightshire DG7 1TJ T 07711-223101
Late 14th-century tower on an island; accessible only by boat

URQUHART CASTLE (HS), Drumnadrochit, Inverness-shire IV63 6XJ T 01456-450551
13th-century castle remains on the banks of Loch Ness

NORTHERN IRELAND

For the Northern Ireland Environment and Heritage Service, the official website is www.ni-environment.gov.uk
For more information on National Trust properties in Northern Ireland, including those listed below, the official website is www.nationaltrust.org.uk
(EHS) Property in the care of the Northern Ireland Environment and Heritage Service
(NT) National Trust property

CARRICKFERGUS CASTLE (EHS), Carrickfergus, Co. Antrim BT38 7BG T 028-9335 1273
Castle begun in 1180 and garrisoned until 1928

CASTLE COOLE (NT), Enniskillen, Co. Fermanagh BT74 6JY T 028-6632 2690
18th-century mansion by James Wyatt in parkland

CASTLE WARD (NT), Strangford, Co. Down BT30 7LS T 028-4488 1204
18th-century house with Classical and Gothic facades

DEVENISH MONASTIC SITE (EHS), nr Enniskillen, Co. Fermanagh
Island monastery founded in the sixth century by St Molaise

DOWNHILL DEMESNE (NT), Castlerock, Co. Londonderry BT51 4RP T 028-2073 1582
Ruins of palatial house in landscaped estate including Mussenden Temple

DUNLUCE CASTLE (EHS), Bushmills, Co. Antrim BT57 8UY T 028-2073 1938
Ruins of 16th-century stronghold of the McDonnells

FLORENCE COURT (NT), Enniskillen, Co. Fermanagh BT92 1DB T 028-6634 8249
Mid-18th-century house with Rococo decoration

GREY ABBEY (EHS), Greyabbey, Co. Down BT22 2NQ T 028-9181 1491
Substantial remains of a Cistercian abbey founded in 1193

HILLSBOROUGH COURTHOUSE (EHS), Hillsborough, Co. Down BT26 6AG T 028-9054 3030
Built in the 18th century; Hillsborough Fort is nearby

MOUNT STEWART (NT), Newtownards, Co. Down BT22 2AD T 028-4278 8387
18th-century house; childhood home of Lord Castlereagh; Temple of the Winds

NENDRUM MONASTERY (EHS), Mahee Island, Co. Down T 028-9054 3037
Island monastery founded in the fifth century by St Machaoi

PATTERSON'S SPADE MILL (NT), Templepatrick, Co. Antrim BT39 0AP T 028-9443 3619
An authentic water-driven spade mill

TULLY CASTLE (EHS), Co. Fermanagh T 028-6862 1588
Fortified house and bawn built in 1613

MUSEUMS AND GALLERIES

There are approximately 2,500 museums and galleries in the United Kingdom. Around 1,400 of these are accredited by the Museums, Libraries and Archives Council (MLA), which indicates that they have an appropriate constitution, are soundly financed, have adequate collection management standards and public services, and have access to professional curatorial advice. A further 400 museums and galleries have applied for, or are in the process of obtaining accreditation, and these applications are assessed by either the relevant regional agency in England; Museums, Archives and Libraries Wales (CyMAL); Museums Galleries Scotland or the Northern Ireland Museums Council.

The following is a selection of museums and art galleries in the United Kingdom. Opening hours and admission charges vary. Further information about museums and galleries in the UK is available from the Museums Association (W www.museumsassociation.org T 020-7426 6910)

W www.culture24.org.uk includes a database of all the museums and galleries in the UK.

ENGLAND

* England's national museums and galleries, which receive funding from a government department, such as the DCMS or MOD. These institutions are deemed to have collections of national importance, and the government is able to call upon their staff for expert advice

BARNARD CASTLE

The Bowes Museum, Co. Durham DL12 8NP T 01833-690606 W www.thebowesmuseum.org.uk
European art from the late medieval period to the 19th century; music and costume galleries; English period rooms from Elizabeth I to Victoria; local archaeology

BATH

American Museum, Claverton Manor BA2 7BD T 01225-460503 W www.americanmuseum.org
American decorative arts from the 17th to 19th centuries; American heritage exhibition

Fashion Museum, Bennett Street BA1 2QH T 01225-477173 W www.museumofcostume.co.uk
Fashion from the 18th century to the present day

Roman Baths Museum, Pump Room, Stall Street BA1 1LZ T 01225-477785 W www.romanbaths.co.uk
Museum adjoins the remains of a Roman baths and temple complex

Victoria Art Gallery, Bridge Street BA2 4AT T 01225-477233 W www.victoriagal.org.uk
European Old Masters and British art since the 15th century

BEAMISH

The North of England Open Air Museum, Co. Durham DH9 0RG T 0191-370 4000 W www.beamish.org.uk
Northern town recreated in 1825 and 1913

BEAULIEU

National Motor Museum, Hants SO42 7ZN T 01590-614650 W www.nationalmotormuseum.org.uk
Displays of over 250 vehicles dating from 1895 to the present day

BIRMINGHAM

Aston Hall, Trinity Road B6 6JD T 0121-675 4722 W www.bmag.org.uk
Jacobean House containing paintings, furniture and tapestries from the 17th to 19th centuries

Barber Institute of Fine Arts, University of Birmingham, Edgbaston B15 2TS T 0121-414 7333 W www.barber.org.uk
Fine arts, including Old Masters

Birmingham Museum and Art Gallery, Chamberlain Square B3 3DH T 0121-303 2834 W www.bmag.org.uk
Includes notable collection of Pre-Raphaelite art

Museum of the Jewellery Quarter, Vyse Street, Hockley B18 6HA T 0121-554 3598 W www.bmag.org.uk
Built around a real jewellery workshop

BOVINGTON

Tank Museum, Dorset BH20 6JG T 01929-405096 W www.tankmuseum.org
Collection of 300 tanks from the earliest days of tank warfare to the present

BRADFORD

Bradford Industrial Museum and Horses at Work, Moorside Road, Eccleshill BD2 3HP T 01274-435900 W www.bradfordmuseums.org
Engineering, textiles, transport and social history exhibits

Cartwright Hall Art Gallery, Lister Park BD9 4NS T 01274-431212 W www.bradfordmuseums.org
British 19th- and 20th-century fine art

**National Media Museum,* Princes Way BD1 1NQ T 0870-701 0200 W www.nationalmediamuseum.org.uk
Photography, film and television interactive exhibits; features an IMAX cinema and the only public Cinerama screen in the world

BRIGHTON

Booth Museum of Natural History, Dyke Road BN1 5AA T 03000-290900 W www.booth.virtualmuseum.info
Zoology, botany and geology collections; British birds in recreated habitats

Brighton Museum and Art Gallery, Royal Pavilion Gardens BN1 1EE T 03000-290900 W www.brighton.virtualmuseum.info
Includes fine art and design, fashion, non-Western art; Brighton history

BRISTOL

Arnolfini, Narrow Quay BS1 4QA T 0117-917 2300 W www.arnolfini.org.uk
Contemporary visual arts, dance, performance, music, talks and workshops

Blaise Castle House Museum, Henbury BS10 7QS T 0117-903 9818 W www.bristol-city.gov.uk/museums
Agricultural and social history collections in an 18th-century mansion

City Museum and Art Gallery, Queen's Road BS8 1RL T 0117-922 3571 W www.bristol-city.gov.uk/museums
Includes fine and decorative art, oriental art, Egyptology and Bristol ceramics and paintings

CAMBRIDGE

Fitzwilliam Museum, Trumpington Street CB2 1RB T 01223-332900 W www.fitzmuseum.cam.ac.uk

Antiquities, fine and applied arts, clocks, ceramics, manuscripts, furniture, sculpture, coins and medals
**Imperial War Museum Duxford,* Duxford CB22 4QR T 01223-835000 W duxford.iwm.org.uk
Displays of military and civil aircraft, tanks, guns and naval exhibits
Sedgwick Museum of Earth Sciences, Downing Street CB2 3EQ T 01223-333456 W www.sedgwickmuseum.org
Extensive geological collection
University Museum of Archaeology and Anthropology, Downing Street CB2 3DZ T 01223-333516 W www.maa.cam.ac.uk
Extensive global archaeological and anthropological collections
University Museum of Zoology, Downing Street CB2 3EJ T 01223-336650 W www.museum.zoo.cam.ac.uk
Extensive zoological collection
Whipple Museum of the History of Science, Free School Lane CB2 3RH T 01223-330906 W www.hps.cam.ac.uk/whipple
Scientific instruments from the 14th century to the present

CARLISLE

Tullie House Museum and Art Gallery, Castle Street CA3 8TP T 01228-618718 W www.tulliehouse.co.uk
Prehistoric archaeology, Hadrian's Wall, Viking and medieval Cumbria, and the social history of Carlisle

CHATHAM

The Historic Dockyard, ME4 4TZ T 01634-823800 W www.chdt.org.uk
Maritime attractions including HMS *Cavalier,* the UK's last Second World War destroyer
Royal Engineers Museum and Library, Prince Arthur Road, Gillingham ME4 4UG T 01634-822839 W www.remuseum.org.uk
Regimental history, ethnography, decorative art and photography

CHELTENHAM

Art Gallery and Museum, Clarence Street GL50 3JT T 01242-237431 W www.cheltenhammuseum.org.uk
Paintings, arts and crafts

CHESTER

Grosvenor Museum, Grosvenor Street CH1 2DD T 01244-402033 W www.grosvenormuseum.co.uk
Roman collections, natural history, art, Chester silver, local history and costume

CHICHESTER

Weald and Downland Open Air Museum, Singleton PO18 0EU T 01243-811363 W www.wealddown.co.uk
Rebuilt vernacular buildings from south-east England; includes medieval houses, agricultural and rural craft buildings and a working watermill

COLCHESTER

Colchester Castle Museum, Castle Park CO1 1TJ T 01206-282939 W www.colchestermuseums.org.uk
Largest Norman keep in Europe standing on foundations of the Roman Temple of Claudius; tours of the Roman vaults, castle walls and chapel

COVENTRY

Coventry Transport Museum, Hales Street CV1 1JD T 024-7623 4270 W www.transport-museum.com
Hundreds of motor vehicles and bicycles
Herbert Art Gallery and Museum, Jordan Well CV1 5QP T 024-7683 2386 W www.theherbert.org
Local history, archaeology and industry, and fine and decorative art

DERBY

Derby Museum and Art Gallery, The Strand DE1 1BS T 01332-641901 W www.derby.gov.uk/museums
Includes paintings by Joseph Wright of Derby and Derby porcelain
Pickford's House Museum, Friar Gate DE1 1DA T 01332-255363 W www.derby.gov.uk/museums
Georgian town house by architect Joseph Pickford; museum of Georgian life and costume
The Silk Mill, Derby's Museum of Industry and History, Full Street DE1 3AF T 01332-255308 W www.derby.gov.uk/museums
Rolls-Royce aero engine collection and railway engineering gallery; on the site of two silk mills built in the early 1700s

DEVIZES

Wiltshire Heritage Museum, Long Street SN10 1NS T 01380-727369 W www.wiltshireheritage.org.uk
Natural and local history; art gallery; archaeological finds from prehistoric, Roman and Saxon sites

DORCHESTER

Dorset County Museum, High West Street DT1 1XA T 01305-262735 W www.dorsetcountymuseum.org
Includes a collection of Thomas Hardy's manuscripts, books, notebooks and drawings; local history

DOVER

Dover Museum, Market Square CT16 1PB T 01304-201066 W www.dovermuseum.co.uk
Contains the Dover Bronze Age Boat Gallery and archaeological finds from Bronze Age, Roman and Saxon sites

GATESHEAD

Baltic Centre for Contemporary Art, South Shore Road NE8 3BA T 0191-478 1810 W www.balticmill.com
Contemporary art exhibitions and events
Shipley Art Gallery, Prince Consort Road NE8 4JB T 0191-477 1495 W www.twmuseums.org.uk/shipley
Contemporary crafts

GAYDON

Heritage Motor Centre, Banbury Road, Warks CV35 0BJ T 01926-641188 W www.heritage-motor-centre.co.uk
History of British motor industry from 1895 to present; classic vehicles; engineering gallery; Corgi and Lucas collections

GLOUCESTER

National Waterways Museum, Gloucester Docks GL1 2EH T 01452-318200 W www.nwm.org.uk
Two-hundred-year history of Britain's canals and inland waterways

GOSPORT

Royal Navy Submarine Museum, Haslar Jetty Road, Hants PO12 2AS T 023-9251 0354 W www.rnsubmus.co.uk
Underwater warfare, including the submarine *Alliance;* first Royal Navy submarine

GRASMERE

Dove Cottage and the *Wordsworth Museum,* Cumbria LA22 9SH T 01539-435544 W www.wordsworth.org.uk
William Wordsworth's manuscripts, home and garden

HULL

Ferens Art Gallery, Queen Victoria Square HU1 3RA T 01482-300300 W www.hullcc.gov.uk
European art, especially Dutch 17th-century paintings, British portraits from 17th to 20th centuries, and marine paintings
Hull Maritime Museum, Queen Victoria Square HU1 3DX T 01482-300300 W www.hullcc.gov.uk
Whaling, fishing and navigation exhibits

HUNTINGDON

The Cromwell Museum, Grammar School Walk PE29 3LF T 01480-375830 W www.cambridgeshire.gov.uk/cromwell
Portraits and memorabilia relating to Oliver Cromwell

IPSWICH

Christchurch Mansion and *Wolsey Art Gallery,* Christchurch Park IP4 2BE T 01473-433554 W www.ipswich.gov.uk
Tudor house with paintings by Gainsborough, Constable and other Suffolk artists; furniture and 18th-century ceramics; temporary exhibitions

LEEDS

Armley Mills, Leeds Industrial Museum, Canal Road, Armley LS12 2QF T 0113-263 7861
W www.leeds.gov.uk/armleymills
World's largest woollen mill, now a museum for textiles, clothing and engine manufacture

Leeds City Art Gallery, The Headrow LS1 3AA
T 0113-247 8256 W www.leeds.gov.uk/artgallery
Includes English watercolours; modern sculpture; Henry Moore gallery; print room

Lotherton Hall, Aberford LS25 3EB T 0113-281 3259
W www.leeds.gov.uk/lothertonhall
Costume, ceramics and furniture collections in furnished Edwardian house; deer park and bird garden

**Royal Armouries Museum,* Armouries Drive LS10 1LT
T 0113-220 1999 W www.royalarmouries.org
National collection of arms and armour from BC to present; demonstrations of foot combat in museum's five galleries; falconry and mounted combat in the tiltyard

Temple Newsam, LS15 0AE T 0113-264 5535
W www.leeds.gov.uk/templenewsam
Old Masters and 17th- and 18th-century decorative art in furnished Jacobean/Tudor house

LEICESTER

Jewry Wall Museum, St Nicholas Circle LE1 4LB
T 0116-225 4971 W www.leicester.gov.uk
Archaeology; Roman Jewry Wall and baths; mosaics

New Walk Museum and Art Gallery, New Walk LE1 7EA
T 0116-255 4900 W www.leicester.gov.uk
Natural history and geology; ancient Egypt gallery; European art and decorative arts

LINCOLN

The Collection, Danes Terrace LN2 1LP T 01522-550990
W www.lincolnshire.gov.uk
Artefacts from the Stone Age to the Viking and Medieval eras; adjacent art gallery with decorative and contemporary visual arts

Museum of Lincolnshire Life, Burton Road LN1 3LY
T 01522-528448 W www.lincolnshire.gov.uk
Social history and agricultural collection

LIVERPOOL

**International Slavery Museum,* Albert Dock L3 4AX
T 0151-478 4499 W www.liverpoolmuseums.org.uk/ism
Explores historical and contemporary aspects of slavery

**Lady Lever Art Gallery,* Wirral CH62 5EQ T 0151-478 4136
W www.liverpoolmuseums.org.uk/ladylever
Paintings, furniture and porcelain

**Merseyside Maritime Museum,* Albert Dock L3 4AQ
T 0151-478 4499
W www.liverpoolmuseums.org.uk/maritime
Floating exhibits, working displays and craft demonstrations; incorporates *HM Customs and Excise National Museum*

**Museum of Liverpool,* Pier Head L3 1PZ
T 0151-478 4499 W www.liverpoolmuseums.org.uk/mol
Due to reopen in 2011, formerly known as the *Museum of Liverpool Life*

**Sudley House,* Mossley Hill Road L18 8BX T 0151-724 3245
W www.liverpoolmuseums.org.uk/sudley
Late 18th- and 19th-century paintings in former shipowner's home

**Tate Liverpool,* Albert Dock L3 4BB T 0151-702 7400
W www.tate.org.uk/liverpool
Twentieth-century paintings and sculpture

**Walker Art Gallery,* William Brown Street L3 8EL
T 0151-478 4199 W www.liverpoolmuseums.org.uk/walker
Paintings from the 14th to 20th centuries

**World Museum Liverpool,* William Brown Street L3 8EN
T 0151-478 4393 W www.liverpoolmuseums.org.uk/wml
Includes Egyptian mummies, weapons and classical sculpture; planetarium, aquarium, vivarium and natural history centre

LONDON: GALLERIES

Barbican Art Gallery, Barbican Centre, Silk Street EC2Y 8DS
T 020-7638 4141 W www.barbican.org.uk
Temporary exhibitions

Courtauld Institute of Art Gallery, Somerset House, Strand WC2R 0RN T 020-7848 2526 W www.courtauld.ac.uk
Impressionist and post-impressionist paintings

Dulwich Picture Gallery, Gallery Road, Dulwich Village SE21 7AD T 020-8693 5254
W www.dulwichpicturegallery.org.uk
England's first public art gallery; designed by Sir John Soane to house 17th- and 18th-century paintings

Estorick Collection of Modern Italian Art, Canonbury Square N1 2AN T 020-7704 9522 W www.estorickcollection.com
Early 20th-century Italian drawings, paintings, sculptures and etchings, with an emphasis on Futurism

Hayward Gallery, Belvedere Road SE1 8XX T 020-7960 4200
W www.southbankcentre.co.uk
Temporary exhibitions

**National Gallery,* Trafalgar Square WC2N 5DN
T 020-7747 2885 W www.nationalgallery.org.uk
Western painting from the 13th to 20th centuries; early Renaissance collection in the Sainsbury Wing

**National Portrait Gallery,* St Martin's Place WC2H 0HE
T 020-7306 0055 W www.npg.org.uk
Portraits of eminent people in British history

Percival David Foundation of Chinese Art
see British Museum

Photographers' Gallery, Ramillies Street W1F 7LW
T 0845-262 1618 W www.photonet.org.uk
Temporary exhibitions

The Queen's Gallery, Buckingham Palace SW1A 1AA
T 020-7766 7301 W www.royalcollection.org.uk
Art from the Royal Collection

Royal Academy of Arts, Burlington House, Piccadilly W1J 0BD
T 020-7300 8000 W www.royalacademy.org.uk
British art since 1750 and temporary exhibitions; annual Summer Exhibition

Saatchi Gallery, Duke of York's HQ, King's Road, SW3 4SQ
T 020-7823 2363 W www.saatchi-gallery.co.uk
Contemporary art including paintings, photographs, sculpture and installations

Serpentine Gallery, Kensington Gardens W2 3XA
T 020-7402 6075 W www.serpentinegallery.org
Temporary exhibitions of British and international contemporary art

**Tate Britain,* Millbank SW1P 4RG T 020-7887 8888
W www.tate.org.uk/britain
British painting and 20th-century painting and sculpture

**Tate Modern,* Bankside SE1 9TG T 020-7887 8888
W www.tate.org.uk/modern
International modern art from 1900 to the present

**Wallace Collection,* Manchester Square W1U 3BN
T 020-7563 9500 W www.wallacecollection.org

Paintings and drawings, French 18th-century furniture, armour, porcelain, clocks and sculpture

Whitechapel Art Gallery, Whitechapel High Street E1 7QX T 020-7522 7888 W www.whitechapel.org
Temporary exhibitions of modern art

LONDON: MUSEUMS

Bank of England Museum, Threadneedle Street EC2R 8AH (entrance on Bartholomew Lane) T 020-7601 5545 W www.bankofengland.co.uk/museum
History of the Bank of England since 1694

**British Museum,* Great Russell Street WC1B 3DG T 020-7323 8000 W www.thebritishmuseum.org
Antiquities, coins, medals, prints and drawings; temporary exhibitions; home of the Sir Percival David collection of Chinese ceramics

Brunel Museum, Rotherhithe SE16 4LF T 020-7231 3840 W www.brunel-museum.org.uk
Explores the engineering achievements of Isambard Kingdom Brunel and his father, Marc Brunel

**Cabinet War Rooms,* King Charles Street SW1A 2AQ T 020-7930 6961 W cwr.iwm.org.uk
Underground rooms used by Churchill and the government during the Second World War

Design Museum, Shad Thames SE1 2YD T 020-7940 8790 W www.designmuseum.org
The development of design and the mass-production of consumer objects

Firepower, the Royal Artillery Museum, Royal Arsenal, Woolwich SE18 6ST T 020-8855 7755 W www.firepower.org.uk
The history and development of artillery over the last 700 years including the collections of the Royal Regiment of Artillery

Geffrye Museum, Kingsland Road E2 8EA T 020-7739 9893 W www.geffrye-museum.org.uk
English urban domestic interiors from 1600 to the present day; also paintings, furniture, decorative arts, walled herb garden and period garden rooms

**HMS Belfast,* Morgan's Lane, Tooley Street SE1 2JH T 020-7940 6300 W hmsbelfast.iwm.org.uk
Life on a Second World War cruiser

**Horniman Museum,* London Road SE23 3PQ T 020-8699 1872 W www.horniman.ac.uk
Museum of anthropology, musical instruments and natural history; aquarium; reference library; gardens

**Imperial War Museum,* Lambeth Road SE1 6HZ T 020-7416 5320 W www.iwm.org.uk
All aspects of the two World Wars and other military operations involving Britain and the Commonwealth since 1914

Jewish Museum, Albert Street NW1 7NB T 020-7284 7384 W www.jewishmuseum.org.uk
Jewish life, history and religion

London Metropolitan Archives , Northampton Road EC1R 0HB T 020-7332 3820 W www.cityoflondon.gov.uk/lma
Material on the history of London and its people dating 1067–2006

London Transport Museum, Covent Garden Piazza WC2E 7BB T 020-7379 6344 W www.ltmuseum.co.uk
Vehicles, photographs and graphic art relating to the history of transport in London

MCC Museum, Lord's, St John's Wood NW8 8QN T 020-7616 8656 W www.lords.org/mcc
Cricket museum; guided tours by appointment

Museum in Docklands, West India Quay, Hertsmere Road E14 4AL T 020-7001 9844 W www.museumindocklands.org.uk
Explores the story of London's river, port and people over 2,000 years, from Roman times through to the recent regeneration of London's Docklands

**Museum of Childhood at Bethnal Green (V&A),* Cambridge Heath Road E2 9PA T 020-8983 5200 W www.vam.ac.uk/moc
Toys, games and exhibits relating to the social history of childhood

Museum of Garden History, Lambeth Palace Road SE1 7LB T 020-7401 8865 W www.museumgardenhistory.org
History and development of gardens and gardening; recreated 17th-century garden

**Museum of London,* London Wall EC2Y 5HN T 020-7001 9844 W www.museumoflondon.org.uk
History of London from prehistoric times to the present day

National Archives Museum, Kew TW9 4DU T 020-8876 3444 W www.nationalarchives.gov.uk
Displays treasures from the archives, including the Domesday Book

**National Army Museum,* Royal Hospital Road SW3 4HT T 020-7730 0717 W www.national-army-museum.ac.uk
Five-hundred-year history of the British soldier; exhibits include model of the Battle of Waterloo and recreated First World War trench

**National Maritime Museum,* Greenwich SE10 9NF T 020-8858 4422 W www.nmm.ac.uk
Maritime history of Britain; collections include globes, clocks, telescopes and paintings; comprises the main building, the Royal Observatory and the Queen's House

**Natural History Museum,* Cromwell Road SW7 5BD T 020-7942 5000 W www.nhm.ac.uk
Natural history collections

Petrie Museum of Egyptian Archaeology, University College London, Malet Place WC1E 6BT T 020-7679 2884 W www.petrie.ucl.ac.uk
Egyptian archaeology collection

**Royal Air Force Museum,* Hendon NW9 5LL T 020-8205 2266 W www.rafmuseum.org.uk
Aviation from before the Wright brothers to the present-day RAF

Royal Mews, Buckingham Palace SW1A 1AA T 020-7766 7302 W www.royalcollection.org.uk
State vehicles, including the Queen's gold state coach; home to the Queen's horses

**Science Museum,* Exhibition Road SW7 2DD T 0870 870 4868 W www.sciencemuseum.org.uk
Science, technology, industry and medicine collections; children's interactive gallery; IMAX cinema

Shakespeare's Globe Exhibition, Bankside SE1 9DT T 020-7902 1400 W www.shakespeares-globe.org
Recreation of Elizabethan theatre using 16th-century techniques; includes a tour of the theatre

**Sir John Soane's Museum,* Lincoln's Inn Fields WC2A 3BP T 020-7405 2107 W www.soane.org
Art and antiquities collected by Soane throughout his lifetime; house designed by Soane

Tower Bridge Experience, SE1 2UP T 020-7403 3761 W www.towerbridge.org.uk
History of the bridge and display of Victorian steam machinery; panoramic views from walkways

**Victoria and Albert Museum,* Cromwell Road SW7 2RL T 020-7942 2000 W www.vam.ac.uk
Includes National Art Library and Print Room; fine and applied art and design; furniture, glass, textiles, theatre and dress collections

Wellington Museum, Apsley House, Hyde Park Corner W1J 7NT T 020-7499 5676

W www.english-heritage.org.uk/apsleyhouse
Home of the first Duke of Wellington; art pieces including part of the Spanish Royal Collection
Wimbledon Lawn Tennis Museum, Church Road SW19 5AE T 020-8946 6131 W www.wimbledon.org/museum
Tennis trophies, fashion and memorabilia; view of Centre Court

MALTON
Eden Camp, N. Yorks YO17 6RT T 01653-697777 W www.edencamp.co.uk
Restored POW camp and Second World War memorabilia

MANCHESTER
Gallery of Costume, Platt Hall, Rusholme M14 5LL T 0161-245 7245 W www.manchestergalleries.org
Exhibits from the 17th century to the present day
**Imperial War Museum North,* Trafford Wharf, Trafford Park M17 1TZ T 0161-836 4000 W north.iwm.org.uk
History of war in the 20th and 21st centuries
Manchester Art Gallery, Mosley Street M2 3JL T 0161-235 8888 W www.manchestergalleries.org
Six centuries of European fine and decorative art
Manchester Museum, Oxford Road M13 9PL T 0161-275 2634 W www.museum.manchester.ac.uk
Collections include archaeology, decorative arts, Egyptology, natural history and zoology
**Museum of Science and Industry,* Liverpool Road, Castlefield M3 4FP T 0161-832 2244 W www.mosi.org.uk
On site of world's oldest passenger railway station; galleries relating to space, energy, power, transport, aviation, textiles and social history
People's History Museum, Left Bank, Spinningfields M3 3ER T 0161-838 9190 W www.phm.org.uk
British political and working life history
Whitworth Art Gallery, Oxford Road M15 6ER T 0161-275 7450 W www.whitworth.manchester.ac.uk
Watercolours, drawings, prints, textiles, wallpapers and British art

MILTON KEYNES
Bletchley Park National Codes Centre, Bucks MK3 6EB T 01908-640404 W www.bletchleypark.org.uk
Home of British codebreaking during the Second World War; Enigma machine; computer museum; wartime toys and memorabilia

MONKWEARMOUTH
Monkwearmouth Station Museum, North Bridge Street, Sunderland SR5 1AP T 0191-567 7075 W www.twmuseums.org.uk/monkwearmouth
Victorian train station; interactive galleries

NEWCASTLE UPON TYNE
Discovery Museum, Blandford Square NE1 4JA T 0191-232 6789 W www.twmuseums.org.uk/discovery
Science and industry, local history, fashion; Tyneside's maritime history; *Turbinia* (first steam-driven vessel) gallery
Great North Museum: Hancock, Barras Bridge NE2 4PT T 0191-222 6765 W www.twmuseums.org.uk/greatnorthmuseum
Natural history and ancient history
Laing Art Gallery, New Bridge Street NE1 8AG T 0191-232 7734 W www.twmuseums.org.uk/laing
18th- and 19th-century collection; watercolour gallery

NEWMARKET
National Horseracing Museum, High Street CB8 8JH T 01638-667333 W www.nhrm.co.uk
The story of people and horses involved in racing; temporary exhibitions

NORTH SHIELDS
Stephenson Railway Museum, Middle Engine Lane NE29 8DX T 0191-200 7146 W www.twmuseums.org.uk/stephenson
Locomotive engines and rolling stock

NOTTINGHAM
Castle Museum and Art Gallery, Friar Lane NG1 6EL T 0115-915 3700 W www.nottinghamcity.gov.uk
Paintings, ceramics, silver and glass; history of Nottingham
Museum of Nottingham Life, Brewhouse Yard, Castle Boulevard NG7 1FB T 0115-915 3600 W www.nottinghamcity.gov.uk
Social history from the 17th to 20th centuries
Natural History Museum, Wollaton Hall, Wollaton NG8 2AE T 0115-915 3900 W www.nottinghamcity.gov.uk
Local natural history and wildlife dioramas

OXFORD
Ashmolean Museum, Beaumont Street OX1 2PH T 01865-278000 W www.ashmolean.org
European and Oriental fine and applied arts, archaeology, Egyptology and numismatics
Modern Art Oxford, Pembroke Street OX1 1BP T 01865-722733 W www.modernartoxford.org.uk
Temporary exhibitions
Museum of the History of Science, Broad Street OX1 3AZ T 01865-277280 W www.mhs.ox.ac.uk
Displays include early scientific instruments, chemical apparatus, clocks and watches
Oxford University Museum of Natural History, Parks Road OX1 3PW T 01865-272950 W www.oum.ox.ac.uk
Entomology, geology, mineralogy and zoology
Pitt Rivers Museum, South Parks Road OX1 3PP T 01865-270927 W www.prm.ox.ac.uk
Ethnographic and archaeological artefacts

PLYMOUTH
City Museum and Art Gallery, Drake Circus PL4 8AJ T 01752-304774 W www.plymouthmuseum.gov.uk
Local and natural history; ceramics; silver; Old Masters; world artefacts; temporary exhibitions

PORTSMOUTH
Charles Dickens Birthplace, Old Commercial Road PO1 4QL T 023-9282 7261 W www.charlesdickensbirthplace.co.uk
Dickens memorabilia
D-Day Museum, Clarence Esplanade, Southsea PO5 3NT T 023-9282 7261 W www.ddaymuseum.co.uk
Includes the Overlord embroidery
Portsmouth Historic Dockyard, HM Naval Base PO1 3LJ T 023-9283 9766 W www.historicdockyard.co.uk
Incorporates the **Royal Naval Museum* (PO1 3NH T 023-9272 7562 W www.royalnavalmuseum.org), *HMS Victory* (PO1 3NH T 023-9272 3111 W www.hms-victory.com), *HMS Warrior* (PO1 3QX T 023-9277 8600 W www.hmswarrior.org), the *Mary Rose* (PO1 3LX T 023-9281 2931 W www.maryrose.org) and *Action Stations* (PO1 3LJ T 023-9289 3316 W www.actionstations.org)
History of the Royal Navy and of the dockyard; warships and technology spanning 500 years

PRESTON
Harris Museum and Art Gallery, Market Square PR1 2PP T 01772-258248 W www.harrismuseum.org.uk
British art since the 18th century; ceramics, glass, costume and local history; contemporary exhibitions
National Football Museum, Sir Tom Finney Way PR1 6PA T 01772-908442 W www.nationalfootballmuseum.com
Home to the FIFA, FA and Football League collections on long-term loan

ST ALBANS

Verulamium Museum, St Michael's Street AL3 4SW T 01727-751810 W www.stalbansmuseums.org.uk
Remains of Iron Age settlement and the third-largest city in Roman Britain; exhibits include Roman wall plasters, jewellery, mosaics and room reconstructions

ST IVES

**Tate St Ives,* Porthmeor Beach, Cornwall TR26 1TG T 01736-796226 W www.tate.org.uk/stives
Modern art, much by artists associated with St Ives; includes the Barbara Hepworth Museum and Sculpture Garden

SALISBURY

Salisbury & South Wiltshire Museum, The Close SP1 2EN T 01722-332151 W www.salisburymuseum.org.uk
Archaeology collection

SHEFFIELD

Graves Art Gallery, Surrey Street S1 1XZ T 0114-278 2600 W www.museums-sheffield.org.uk
Twentieth-century British art, Grice Collection of Chinese ivories

Millennium Galleries, Arundel Gate S1 2PP T 0114-278 2600 W www.museums-sheffield.org.uk
Incorporates four different galleries: the Special Exhibition Gallery, the Craft and Design Gallery, the Metalwork Gallery and the Ruskin Gallery, which houses John Ruskin's collection of paintings, drawings, books and medieval manuscripts

Weston Park Museum, Western Bank S10 2TP T 0114-278 2600 W www.museums-sheffield.org.uk
World history for families

SOUTHAMPTON

City Art Gallery, Commercial Road SO14 7LP T 023-8083 2277 W www.southampton.gov.uk/art
Fine art collection spanning six centuries of European art

God's House Tower Museum of Archaeology, Winkle Street SO14 2NY T 023-8091 5732 W www.southampton.gov.uk
Roman, Saxon and medieval archaeology

Maritime Museum, Town Quay Road SO14 2NY T 023-8083 2705 W www.southampton.gov.uk
Southampton maritime history; Titanic exhibition

SOUTH SHIELDS

Arbeia Roman Fort, Baring Street NE33 2BB T 0191-456 1369 W www.twmuseums.org.uk/arbeia
Excavated ruins; reconstructions of original buildings

South Shields Museum and Art Gallery, Ocean Road NE33 2JA T 0191-456 8740 W www.twmuseums.org.uk/southshields
South Tyneside history; interactive art gallery

STOKE-ON-TRENT

Etruria Industrial Museum, Lower Bedford Street ST4 7AF T 01782-233144 W www.stokemuseums.org.uk/eim
Britain's sole surviving steam-powered potter's mill

Gladstone Pottery Museum, Longton ST3 1PQ T 01782-237777 W www.stokemuseums.org.uk/gpm
A working Victorian pottery

Potteries Museum and Art Gallery, Hanley ST1 3DW T 01782-232323 W www.stokemuseums.org.uk/pmag
Pottery, china and porcelain collections and a Mark XVI Spitfire

The Wedgwood Museum, Barlaston ST12 9ER T 01782-371900 W www.wedgwoodmuseum.org.uk
The story of Josiah Wedgwood and the company he founded

SUNDERLAND

Sunderland Museum & Winter Gardens, Burdon Road SR1 1PP T 0191-553 2323 W www.twmuseums.org.uk/sunderland
Fine and decorative art, local history and gardens

TELFORD

Ironbridge Gorge Museums, TF8 7DQ T 01952-884391 W www.ironbridge.org.uk
World's first iron bridge; Blists Hill (late Victorian working town); Museum of Iron; Jackfield Tile Museum; Coalport China Museum; Tar Tunnel; Broseley Pipeworks

WAKEFIELD

National Coal Mining Museum for England, Overton WF4 4RH T 01924-848806 W www.ncm.org.uk
Includes underground tours of one of Britain's oldest working mines

Yorkshire Sculpture Park, West Bretton WF4 4LG T 01924-832631 W www.ysp.co.uk
Open-air sculpture gallery including works by Moore, Hepworth, Frink and others in 202 hectares (500 acres) of parkland

WEYBRIDGE

Brooklands Museum, KT13 0QN T 01932-857381 W www.brooklandsmuseum.com
Birthplace of British motorsport; world's first purpose-built motor racing circuit

WILMSLOW

Quarry Bank Mill, Styal SK9 4LA T 01625-527468 W www.quarrybankmill.org.uk
Working mill owned by the National Trust illustrating history of cotton industry; costumed guides at restored Apprentice House

WINCHESTER

INTECH, Telegraph Way, Hampshire SO21 1HZ T 01962-863791 W www.intech-uk.com
Interactive science centre and planetarium

WORCESTER

City Museum and Art Gallery, Foregate Street WR1 1DT T 01905-25371 W www.worcestercitymuseums.org.uk
Includes a military museum, 19th-century chemist shop and changing art exhibitions

Museum of Worcester Porcelain, Severn Street WR1 2NE T 01905-21247 W www.worcesterporcelainmuseum.org.uk
Worcester porcelain from 1751 to the present day

YEOVIL

Fleet Air Arm Museum, Royal Naval Air Station, Yeovilton, Somerset BA22 8HT T 01935-840565 W www.fleetairarm.com
History of naval aviation; historic aircraft, including Concorde 002

YORK

Beningbrough Hall, Beningbrough YO30 1DD T 01904-472027 W www.nationaltrust.org.uk
18th-century house with portraits from the National Portrait Gallery

JORVIK Viking Centre, Coppergate YO1 9WT T 01904-543400 W www.jorvik-viking-centre.co.uk
Reconstruction of Viking York based on archaeological evidence

**National Railway Museum,* Leeman Road YO26 4XJ T 0844-815 3139 W www.nrm.org.uk
Includes locomotives, rolling stock and carriages

York Art Gallery, Exhibition Square YO1 7EW T 01904-687687 W www.yorkartgallery.org.uk
European and British painting spanning seven centuries; modern pottery; decorative arts

York Castle Museum, Eye of York YO1 9RY T 01904-687687 W www.yorkcastlemuseum.org.uk
Reconstructed streets and rooms; costume and military collections

Yorkshire Museum & Gardens, Museum Gardens YO1 7FR T 01904-687687 W www.yorkshiremuseum.org.uk
Yorkshire life from Roman to medieval times; geology and biology; York observatory

WALES

* Members of National Museum Wales, a public body that receives its funding through grant-in-aid from the Welsh Assembly

ABERYSTWYTH
Ceredigion Museum, Terrace Road SY23 2AQ T 01970-633087 W www.ceredigion.gov.uk
Local history, housed in a restored Edwardian theatre
Llywernog Silver-Lead Mine, Ponterwyd SY23 3AB T 01970-890620 W www.silverminetours.co.uk
Tours of an 18th-century silver mine, exhibitions containing artefacts used therein
BLAENAFON
**Big Pit National Coal Museum,* Torfaen NP4 9XP T 01495-790311 W www.museumwales.ac.uk
Colliery with underground tour
BODELWYDDAN
Bodelwyddan Castle, Denbighshire LL18 5YA T 01745-584060 W www.bodelwyddan-castle.co.uk
Portraits from the National Portrait Gallery; furniture from the Victoria and Albert Museum; sculptures from the Royal Academy
CAERLEON
**National Roman Legion Museum,* NP18 1AE T 01633-423134 W www.museumwales.ac.uk
Material from the site of the Roman fortress of Isca and its suburbs
CARDIFF
**National Museum Cardiff,* Cathays Park CF10 3NP T 029-2039 7951 W www.museumwales.ac.uk
Includes natural sciences, archaeology and Impressionist paintings
**St Fagans: National History Museum,* St Fagans CF5 6XB T 029-2057 3500 W www.museumwales.ac.uk
Open-air museum with re-erected buildings, agricultural equipment and costume
TECHNIQUEST, Stuart Street CF10 5BW T 029-2047 5475 W www.techniquest.org
Interactive science exhibits, planetarium and science theatre
CRICCIETH
Lloyd George Museum, Llanystumdwy LL52 0SH T 01766-522071 W www.gwynedd.gov.uk
Childhood home of David Lloyd George; museum commemorates his life
DRE-FACH FELINDRE
**National Wool Museum,* nr Llandysul SA44 5UP T 01559-370929 W www.museumwales.ac.uk
Exhibitions, a working woollen mill and craft workshops
LLANBERIS
**National Slate Museum,* Gwynedd LL55 4TY T 01286-870630 W www.museumwales.ac.uk
Former slate quarry with original machinery and plant; slate crafts demonstrations; working waterwheel
LLANDRINDOD WELLS
National Cycle Collection, Automobile Palace, Temple Street LD1 5DL T 01597-825531 W www.cyclemuseum.org.uk
Over 200 bicycles on display, from 1819–present
PRESTEIGNE
Judge's Lodging Museum, Broad Street LD8 2AD T 01544-260650 W www.judgeslodging.org.uk
Restored apartments, courtroom, cells and servants' quarters
SWANSEA
Glynn Vivian Art Gallery, Alexandra Road SA1 5DZ T 01792-516900 W www.swansea.gov.uk/glynnvivian
Paintings, ceramics, Swansea pottery and porcelain, clocks, glass and Welsh art
**National Waterfront Museum,* Oystermouth Road SA1 3RD T 01792-638950 W www.museumwales.ac.uk
Wales during the Industrial Revolution
Swansea Museum, Victoria Road SA1 1SN T 01792-653763 W www.swansea.gov.uk/swanseamuseum
Archaeology, social history, Swansea pottery
TENBY
Tenby Museum and Art Gallery, Castle Hill SA70 7BP T 01834-842809 W www.tenbymuseum.org.uk
Local archaeology, history, geology and art

SCOTLAND

* Members of National Museums of Scotland or National Galleries of Scotland, which are non-departmental public bodies funded by, and accountable to, the Scottish government

ABERDEEN
Aberdeen Art Gallery, Schoolhill AB10 1FQ T 01224-523700 W www.aagm.co.uk
Impressionists, Scottish Colourists, decorative art and modern art
Aberdeen Maritime Museum, Shiprow AB11 5BY T 01224-337700 W www.aagm.co.uk
Maritime history, including shipbuilding and North Sea oil
DUMFRIES
**National Museum of Costume,* New Abbey DG2 8HQ T 0131-247 4030 W www.nms.ac.uk/costume
History of fashion from the 1850s to the 1950s
EDINBURGH
Britannia, Leith EH6 6JJ T 0131-555 5566 W www.royalyachtbritannia.co.uk
Former royal yacht with royal barge and royal family picture gallery
City Art Centre, Market Street EH1 1DE T 0131-529 3993 W www.cac.org.uk
Scottish late 19th- and 20th-century art and temporary exhibitions
**Dean Gallery,* Belford Road EH4 3DS T 0131-624 6200 W www.nationalgalleries.org
Dada, Surrealism and sculpture – particularly works by Sir Eduardo Paolozzi
Museum of Childhood, High Street EH1 1TG T 0131-529 4142 W www.cac.org.uk
Toys, games, clothes and exhibits relating to the social history of childhood
Museum of Edinburgh, Canongate EH8 8DD T 0131-529 4143 W www.cac.org.uk
Local history, silver, glass and Scottish pottery
**Museum of Flight,* East Fortune Airfield, East Lothian EH39 5LF T 0131-247 4238 W www.nms.ac.uk/flight
Display of aircraft
**Museum of Scotland,* Chambers Street EH1 1JF T 0131-225 7534 W www.nms.ac.uk/scotland
Scottish history from prehistoric times to the present
**National Gallery of Scotland,* The Mound EH2 2EL T 0131-624 6200 W www.nationalgalleries.org
Paintings, drawings and prints from the early Renaissance to the end of the 19th century

**National War Museum of Scotland,* Edinburgh Castle EH1 2NG T 0131-247 4413 W www.nms.ac.uk/war
History of Scottish military and conflicts

**Royal Museum,* Chambers Street EH1 1JF T 0131-247 4422 W www.nms.ac.uk
Decorative arts, natural history, science and industry; closed for major refurbishment until 2011

**Scottish National Gallery of Modern Art,* Belford Road EH4 3DR T 0131-624 6200 W www.nationalgalleries.org
20th-century painting, sculpture and graphic art

**Scottish National Portrait Gallery,* Queen Street EH2 1JD T 0131-624 6200 W www.nationalgalleries.org
Due to reopen in late 2011: portraits of eminent people in Scottish history; the national collection of photography

The Writers' Museum, Lawnmarket EH1 2PA T 0131-529 4901 W www.cac.org.uk
Exhibitions relating to Robert Louis Stevenson, Walter Scott and Robert Burns

FORT WILLIAM

West Highland Museum, Cameron Square PH33 6AJ T 01397-702169 W www.westhighlandmuseum.org.uk
Includes tartan collections and exhibits relating to 1745 uprising

GLASGOW

Burrell Collection, Pollokshaws Road G43 1AT T 0141-287 2550 W www.glasgowmuseums.com
Paintings, textiles, furniture, ceramics, stained glass and silver from classical times to the 19th century

Gallery of Modern Art, Royal Exchange Square G1 3AH T 0141-287 3050 W www.glasgowmuseums.com
Collection of contemporary Scottish and world art

Hunterian Museum & Art Gallery, University of Glasgow G12 8QQ T 0141-330 4221 W www.hunterian.gla.ac.uk
Rennie Mackintosh and Whistler collections; Old Masters; Scottish paintings; archaeology; medicine; zoology

Kelvingrove Art Gallery & Museum, Argyle Street G3 8AG T 0141-276 9599 W www.glasgowmuseums.com
Includes Old Masters, 19th-century French paintings and armour collection

Museum of Piping, McPhater Street G4 0HW T 0141-353 0220 W www.thepipingcentre.co.uk
The history and origins of bagpiping

**Museum of Rural Life,* East Kilbride G76 9HR T 0131-247 4369 W www.nms.ac.uk
History of rural life and work

Museum of Transport, Bunhouse Road G3 8DP T 0141-287 2720 W www.glasgowmuseums.com
Includes a reproduction of a 1938 Glasgow street, cars since the 1930s, trams and a Glasgow subway station

People's Palace and Winter Gardens, Glasgow Green G40 1AT T 0141-276 0788 W www.glasgowmuseums.com
Social history of Glasgow since 1750

St Mungo Museum of Religious Life and Art, Castle Street G4 0RH T 0141-276 1625 W www.glasgowmuseums.com
Explores universal themes through objects from the main world religions

NORTHERN IRELAND

* Members of National Museums Northern Ireland, a non-departmental public body of the Northern Ireland Office

ARMAGH

**Armagh County Museum,* The Mall East BT61 9BE T 028-3752 3070 W www.nmni.com/acm
Local history; archaeology; crafts

BANGOR

North Down Museum, Castle Park Avenue BT20 4BT T 028-9127 1200 W www.northdown.gov.uk/heritage
Presents the history of North Down, including its early-Christian monastery

BELFAST

**W5,* Odyssey, Queen's Quay BT3 9QQ T 028-9046 7700 W www.w5online.co.uk
Interactive science and technology centre

HOLYWOOD

**Ulster Folk and Transport Museum,* Cultra, Co. Down BT18 0EU T 028-9042 8428 W www.nmni.com/uftm
Open-air museum with original buildings from Ulster town and rural life *c.*1900; indoor galleries including Irish rail and road transport and *Titanic* exhibitions

LONDONDERRY

The Tower Museum, Union Hall Place BT48 6LU T 028-7137 2411 W www.derrycity.gov.uk/museums
Tells the story of Ireland through the history of Londonderry

Workhouse Museum, Glendermott Road BT48 6BG T 028-7131 8328 W www.derrycity.gov.uk/museums
Exhibitions on the Second World War, workhouse life, 19th-century poverty and the famine

NEWTOWNARDS

The Somme Heritage Centre, Whitespots Country Park BT23 7PH T 01247-823202 W www.irishsoldier.org
Commemorates the part played by Irish forces in the First World War

OMAGH

**Ulster American Folk Park,* Castletown, Co. Tyrone BT78 5QU T 028-8224 3292 W www.nmni.com/uafp
Open-air museum telling the story of Ulster's emigrants to America; restored or recreated dwellings and workshops; ship and dockside gallery

**Ulster Museum,* Botanic Gardens BT9 5AB T 0845-608 0000 W www.nmni.com/um
Irish antiquities; natural and local history; fine and applied arts

SIGHTS OF LONDON

For historic buildings, museums and galleries in London, *see* the Historic Buildings and Monuments and Museums and Galleries sections.

BRIDGES

The bridges over the Thames in London, from east to west, are:

Queen Elizabeth II Bridge (2,872m/9,423ft), engineer: William Halcrow and partners, opened 1991

Tower Bridge (268m/880ft by 18m/60ft), architect: Horace Jones, engineer: John Wolfe Barry, opened 1894

London Bridge (262m/860ft by 32m/105ft), original 13th-century stone bridge rebuilt and opened 1831 (engineer: John Rennie), reconstructed in Arizona when current London Bridge opened 1973 (architect: Lord Holford, engineer: Mott, Hay and Anderson)

Cannon Street Railway Bridge (261m/855ft), engineers: John Hawkshaw and John Wolfe Barry, originally named the Alexandra Bridge, opened 1866; renovated 1979–82

Southwark Bridge (244m/800ft by 17m/55ft), engineer: John Rennie, opened 1819; rebuilt 1912–21 (architect: Ernest George, engineer: Mott, Hay and Anderson)

Millennium Bridge (325m/1,066ft by 4m/13ft), architect: Foster and Partners, engineer: Ove Arup and Partners, opened 2000; reopened after modification 2002

Blackfriars Railway Bridge (284m/933ft), engineers: John Wolfe Barry and Henri Marc Brunel, opened 1886

London, Chatham and Dover Railway Bridge (234m/933ft), engineer: Joseph Cubitt, opened in 1864; only the columns remain, the rest of the structure was removed in 1985

Blackfriars Bridge (294m/963ft by 32m/105ft), engineer: Robert Mylne, opened 1769; rebuilt 1869 (engineer: Joseph Cubitt); widened 1909

Waterloo Bridge (366m/1,200ft by 24m/80ft), engineer: John Rennie, opened 1817; rebuilt 1945 (architect: Sir Giles Gilbert Scott, engineer: Rendel, Palmer and Triton)

Golden Jubilee Bridges (325m/1,066ft by 4.7m/15ft), architect: Lifschutz Davidson, engineer: WSP Group, opened 2002; commonly known as the Hungerford Footbridges

Hungerford Railway Bridge (366m/1,200ft), engineer: Isambard Kingdom Brunel, suspension bridge opened 1845; present railway bridge opened 1864 (engineer: John Hawkshaw); widened in 1886

Westminster Bridge (228m/748ft by 26m/85ft), engineer: Charles Labelye, opened 1750; rebuilt 1862 (architect: Charles Barry, engineer: Thomas Page)

Lambeth Bridge (237m/776ft by 18m/60ft), engineer: Peter W. Barlow, original suspension bridge opened 1862; current structure opened 1932 (architect: Reginald Blomfield, engineer: George W. Humphreys)

Vauxhall Bridge (231m/759ft by 24m/80ft), engineer: James Walker, opened 1816; redesigned and opened 1906 (architect: William Edward Riley, engineers: Alexander Binnie and Maurice Fitzmaurice)

Grosvenor Railway Bridge (213m/700ft), engineer: John Fowler, opened 1860; rebuilt 1965; also known as the Victoria Railway Bridge

Chelsea Bridge (213m/698ft by 25m/83ft), original suspension bridge opened 1858 (engineer: Thomas Page); rebuilt 1937 (architects: George Topham Forrest and E. P. Wheeler, engineer: Rendel, Palmer and Triton)

Albert Bridge (216m/710ft, by 12m/40ft) engineer: Rowland M. Ordish, opened 1873; restructured 1884 (engineer: Joseph Bazalgette); strengthened 1971–3

Battersea Bridge (204m/670ft by 17m/55ft), engineer: Henry Holland, opened 1771; rebuilt 1890 (engineer: Joseph Bazalgette)

Battersea Railway Bridge (204m/670ft), engineer: William Baker, opened 1863, also known as Cremorne Bridge

Wandsworth Bridge (189m/619ft by 18m/60ft), engineer: Julian Tolmé, opened 1873; rebuilt 1940 (architect: E. P. Wheeler, engineer: T. Peirson Frank)

Putney Railway Bridge (229m/750ft), engineers: W. H. Thomas and William Jacomb and opened 1889, also known as the Fulham Railway Bridge or the Iron Bridge – it has no official name

Putney Bridge (213m/700ft by 23m/74ft), architect: Jacob Ackworth, original wooden bridge opened 1729; current granite structure completed in 1886 (engineer: Joseph Bazalgette)

Hammersmith Bridge (210m/688ft by 10m/33ft), engineer: William Tierney Clarke; the first suspension bridge in London, originally built 1827; rebuilt 1887 (engineer: Joseph Bazalgette)

Barnes Railway Bridge (also footbridge, 110m/360ft), engineer: Joseph Locke, opened 1849; rebuilt 1895 (engineers: London and South Western Railway); the original structure stands unused

Chiswick Bridge (137m/450ft by 21m/70ft), architect: Herbert Baker, engineer: Alfred Dryland, opened 1933

Kew Railway Bridge (175m/575ft), engineer: W. R. Galbraith, opened 1869

Kew Bridge (110m/360ft by 17m/56ft), engineer: Robert Tunstall, original timber bridge built 1759; replaced by a Portland stone structure in 1789 (engineer: James Paine); current granite bridge renamed King Edward VII Bridge in 1903, but still known as Kew Bridge (engineers: John Wolfe Barry and Cuthbert Brereton)

Richmond Lock (91m/300ft by 11m/36ft), engineer: F. G. M. Stoney, lock and footbridge opened 1894

Twickenham Bridge (85m/280ft by 21m/70ft), architect: Maxwell Ayrton, engineer: Alfred Dryland, opened 1933

Richmond Railway Bridge (91m/300ft), engineer: Joseph Locke, opened 1848; rebuilt 1906–8 (engineer: J. W. Jacomb-Hood)

Richmond Bridge (85m/280ft by 10m/36ft), architect: James Paine, engineer: Kenton Couse, built 1777; widened 1939

Teddington Lock (198m/650ft), engineer: G. Pooley, two footbridges opened 1889; marks the end of the tidal reach of the Thames

Kingston Railway Bridge, architects: J. E. Errington and W. R. Galbraith, engineer: Thomas Brassey, opened 1863

Kingston Bridge (116m/382ft), engineer: Edward Lapidge,

built 1825–8; widened 1911–14 (engineers: Basil Mott and David Hay) and 1999–2001

Hampton Court Bridge engineers: Samuel Stevens and Benjamin Ludgator, built 1753; replaced by iron bridge 1865; present bridge opened 1933 (architect: Edwin Lutyens, engineer: W. P. Robinson)

CEMETERIES

In 1832, in response to the overcrowding of burial grounds in London, the government authorised the establishment of seven non-denominational cemeteries that would encircle the city. These large cemeteries, known as the 'magnificent seven', were seen by many Victorian families as places in which to demonstrate their wealth and stature, and as a result there are some highly ornate graves and tombs.

THE MAGNIFICENT SEVEN

Abney Park, Stamford Hill, N16 (13ha/32 acres), established 1840; tomb of General Booth, founder of the Salvation Army, and memorials to many nonconformists and dissenters

Brompton, Old Brompton Road, SW10 (16ha/40 acres), established 1840; graves of Sir Henry Cole, Emmeline Pankhurst, John Wisden. Managed by the Royal Parks, it is the only Crown cemetery.

Highgate, Swains Lane, N6 (15ha/38 acres), established 1839; graves of Douglas Adams, George Eliot, Michael Faraday, Karl Marx, Christina Rossetti and Radclyffe Hall; western side only accessible as part of a guided tour

Kensal Green, Harrow Road, W10 (31.5ha/79 acres), established 1832; tombs of William Makepeace Thackeray, Anthony Trollope, Sydney Smith, Wilkie Collins, Tom Hood, George Cruikshank, Leigh Hunt, Isambard Kingdom Brunel and Charles Kemble

Nunhead, Linden Grove, SE15 (21ha/52 acres), established 1840; closed in 1969, subsequently restored and opened for burials

Tower Hamlets, Southern Grove, E3 (11ha/27 acres), established 1841; bombed heavily during the Second World War and closed to burials in 1966; now a nature reserve

West Norwood Cemetery and Crematorium, Norwood High Street, SE27 (17ha/42 acres), established 1837; tombs of Sir Henry Bessemer, Mrs Beeton, Sir Henry Tate and Joseph Whitaker *(Whitaker's Almanack)*

OTHER CEMETERIES

Bunhill Fields, City Road, EC1 (1.6ha/4 acres), 17th-century nonconformist burial ground containing the graves of William Blake, John Bunyan and Daniel Defoe

City of London Cemetery and Crematorium, Aldersbrook Road, E12 (81ha/200 acres), established 1856

Golders Green Crematorium, Hoop Lane, NW11 (5ha/12 acres), established 1902; retains the ashes of Kingsley Amis, Peter Sellers, Marc Bolan, Sigmund Freud, Ivor Novello, Bram Stoker, H. G. Wells, Anna Pavlova and Joe Orton

Hampstead, Fortune Green Road, NW6 (10.5ha/26 acres), established 1876; graves of Kate Greenaway, Lord Lister, Marie Lloyd

MARKETS

Billingsgate (fish), a market site for over 1,000 years, with the Lower Thames Street site dating from 1876; moved to the Isle of Dogs (Trafalgar Way, E14) in 1982; owned and run by the Corporation of London

Borough, Southwark Street, SE1 (vegetables, fruit, gourmet food, flowers), established on present site in 1756; privately owned and run

Brick Lane, E1 (jewellery, vintage clothes, bric-a-brac, food), open Sunday

Brixton, SW8 (African-Caribbean food, music, clothes), open Monday to Saturday

Broadway, E8 (food, fashion, crafts), re-established in 2004, open Saturday

Camden Lock, NW1 (second-hand clothing, jewellery, alternative fashion, crafts), established in 1973

Columbia Road, E2 (flowers), dates from 19th century; became dedicated flower market in the 20th century

Covent Garden, WC2 (antiques, handicrafts, jewellery, clothing, food), originally a fruit and vegetable market (*see* New Covent Garden market), it has been trading in its current form since 1980

Greenwich, SE10 (crafts, fashion, food), market revived in the 1980s

Grays, Davies Street, W1 (antiques), indoor market in listed building, established 1977

Leadenhall, Leadenhall Street, EC3 (meat, poultry, fish, etc), site of market since 14th century; present hall built 1881; owned and run by the Corporation of London

New Covent Garden (wholesale vegetables, fruit and flowers) owned and run by the Covent Garden Market Authority, whose board is appointed by DEFRA; established in 1670 under a charter of Charles II; in 1974 it relocated from central London to Nine Elms, SW8

Petticoat Lane, Middlesex Street, E1, a market has existed on the site for over 500 years, now a Sunday morning market selling almost anything

Portobello Road, W11, originally for herbs and horse-trading from 1870; became famous for antiques after the closure of the Caledonian Market in 1948

Smithfield, EC1 (meat, poultry), built 1866–8, refurbished 1993–4; the site of St Bartholomew's Fair from 12th to 19th century; owned and run by the Corporation of London

New Spitalfields, E10 (vegetables, fruit), established 1682, modernised 1928, moved out of the City to Leyton in 1991

Old Spitalfields, E1, continues to trade on the original Spitalfields site on Commercial Street, selling arts, crafts, books, clothes, organic food and antiques on Sundays

MONUMENTS

CENOTAPH

Whitehall, SW1. The Cenotaph (from the Greek meaning 'empty tomb') was built to commemorate 'The Glorious Dead' and is a memorial to all ranks of the sea, land and air forces who gave their lives in the service of the Empire during the First World War. Designed by Sir Edwin Lutyens and constructed in plaster as a temporary memorial in 1919, it was replaced by a permanent structure of Portland stone and unveiled by George V on 11 November 1920, Armistice Day. An additional inscription was made in 1946 to commemorate those who gave their lives in the Second World War

FOURTH PLINTH

Trafalgar Square, WC2. The fourth plinth (1841) was designed for an equestrian statue that was never built due to lack of funds. From 1999 temporary works have been displayed on the plinth including *Ecce Homo* (Mark Wallinger), *Regardless of History* (Bill Woodrow), *Monument* (Rachel Whiteread), *Alison Lapper Pregnant* (Marc Quinn) and *Model for a Hotel* (Thomas Schütte). Antony Gormley's project *One & Other* occupied the plinth from July–October 2009. This was followed in November 2009 by a memorial statue to Second World War hero Air Chief Marshal Sir Keith Park and from May 2010 by *Nelson's Ship in a Bottle* by Yinka Shonibare

LONDON MONUMENT

(Commonly called the Monument), Monument Street, EC3. Built to designs by Sir Christopher Wren and Robert Hooke between 1671 and 1677, the Monument commemorates the Great Fire of London, which broke out in Pudding Lane on 2 September 1666. The fluted Doric column is 36.6m (120ft) high, the moulded cylinder above the balcony supporting a flaming vase of gilt bronze is an additional 12.8 m (42ft), and the column is based on a square plinth 12.2m (40ft) high (with fine carvings on the west face), making a total height of 61.6m (202ft) – the tallest isolated stone column in the world, with views of London from a gallery at the top (311 steps)

OTHER MONUMENTS

(sculptor's name in parentheses):

7 July Memorial (Carmody Groarke), Hyde Park
Viscount Alanbrooke (Roberts-Jones), Whitehall
Albert Memorial (Scott), Kensington Gore
Battle of Britain (Day), Victoria Embankment
Beatty (Wheeler), Trafalgar Square
Belgian Gratitude (setting by Blomfield, statue by Rousseau), Victoria Embankment
Boadicea (or Boudicca), *Queen of the Iceni* (Thornycroft), Westminster Bridge
Brunel (Marochetti), Victoria Embankment
Burghers of Calais (Rodin), Victoria Tower Gardens, Westminster
Burns (Steell), Embankment Gardens
Canada Memorial (Granche), Green Park
Carlyle (Boehm), Chelsea Embankment
Cavalry (Jones), Hyde Park
Edith Cavell (Frampton), St Martin's Place
Charles I (Le Sueur), Trafalgar Square
Charles II (Gibbons), Royal Hospital, Chelsea
Churchill (Roberts-Jones), Parliament Square
Cleopatra's Needle (20.9m/68.5ft high, *c.*1500BC, erected in London in 1878; the sphinxes are Victorian), Thames Embankment
Clive (Tweed), King Charles Street
Captain Cook (Brock), The Mall
Oliver Cromwell (Thornycroft), outside Westminster Hall
Cunningham (Belsky), Trafalgar Square
Gen. Charles de Gaulle (Conner), Carlton Gardens
Diana, Princess of Wales Memorial Fountain (Gustafson Porter), Hyde Park
Disraeli, Earl of Beaconsfield (Raggi), Parliament Square
Lord Dowding (Winter), Strand
Duke of Cambridge (Jones), Whitehall
Duke of York (37.8m/124ft column, with statue by Westmacott), Carlton House Terrace
Edward VII (Mackennal), Waterloo Place
Elizabeth I (Kerwin, 1586, oldest outdoor statue in London; from Ludgate), Fleet Street
Eros (Shaftesbury Memorial) (Gilbert), Piccadilly Circus
Marechal/Marshall Foch (Mallisard, copy of one in Cassel, France), Grosvenor Gardens
Charles James Fox (Westmacott), Bloomsbury Square
George III (Cotes Wyatt), Cockspur Street
George IV (Chantrey), Trafalgar Square
George V (Reid Dick and Scott), Old Palace Yard
George VI (McMillan), Carlton Gardens
Gladstone (Thornycroft), Strand
Guards' (Crimea) (Bell), Waterloo Place
Guards Division (Ledward, figures, Bradshaw, cenotaph), Horse Guards' Parade
Haig (Hardiman), Whitehall
Sir Arthur (Bomber) Harris (Winter), Strand
Gen. Henry Havelock (Behnes), Trafalgar Square
International Brigades Memorial (Spanish Civil War) (Ian Walters), Jubilee Gardens, South Bank
Irving (Brock), north side of National Portrait Gallery
Isis (Gudgeon), Hyde Park
James II (Gibbons), Trafalgar Square
Jellicoe (McMillan), Trafalgar Square
Samuel Johnson (Fitzgerald), opposite St Clement Danes
Kitchener (Tweed), Horse Guards' Parade
Abraham Lincoln (Saint-Gaudens, copy of one in Chicago), Parliament Square
Mandela (Walters), Parliament Square
Milton (Montford), St Giles, Cripplegate
Mountbatten (Belsky), Foreign Office Green
Gen. Charles James Napier (Adams), Trafalgar Square
Nelson (Railton), Trafalgar Square, with Landseer's lions (cast from guns recovered from the wreck of the *Royal George*)
Florence Nightingale (Walker), Waterloo Place
Palmerston (Woolner), Parliament Square
Peel (Noble), Parliament Square
Pitt (Chantrey), Hanover Square
Portal (Nemon), Embankment Gardens
Prince Albert (Bacon), Holborn Circus
Queen Elizabeth Gate (Lund and Wynne), Hyde Park Corner
Queen Mother (Jackson), Carlton Gardens
Raleigh (McMillan), Greenwich
Richard I (Coeur de Lion) (Marochetti), Old Palace Yard
Roberts (Bates), Horse Guards' Parade
Royal Air Force (Blomfield), Victoria Embankment
Franklin D. Roosevelt (Reid Dick), Grosvenor Square
Royal Artillery (Great War) (Jagger and Pearson), Hyde Park Corner
Royal Artillery (South Africa) (Colton), The Mall; *Captain Scott* (Lady Scott), Waterloo Place; *Shackleton* (Jagger), Kensington Gore
Shakespeare (Fontana, copy of one by Scheemakers in Westminster Abbey), Leicester Square
Smuts (Epstein), Parliament Square
Sullivan (Goscombe John), Victoria Embankment
Trenchard (McMillan), Victoria Embankment
Victoria Memorial (Webb and Brock), in front of Buckingham Palace
Raoul Wallenberg (Jackson), Great Cumberland Place
George Washington (Houdon copy), Trafalgar Square
Wellington (Boehm), Hyde Park Corner
Wellington (Chantrey), outside Royal Exchange
John Wesley (Adams Acton), City Road
Westminster School (Crimea) (Scott), Broad Sanctuary
William III (Bacon), St James's Square
Wolseley (Goscombe John), Horse Guards' Parade

PARKS, GARDENS AND OPEN SPACES

CORPORATION OF LONDON OPEN SPACES

W www.cityoflondon.gov.uk

Ashtead Common (202ha/500 acres), Surrey

Burnham Beeches and *Fleet Wood* (219ha/540 acres), Bucks. Purchased by the Corporation for the benefit of the public in 1880, Fleet Wood (26ha/65 acres) being presented in 1921
Coulsdon Common (51ha/127 acres), Surrey
Epping Forest (2,476ha/6,118 acres), Essex. Purchased by the Corporation and opened to the public in 1882. The Queen Elizabeth Hunting Lodge, built for Henry VIII in the mid-16th century lies at the edge of the forest. The present forest is 19.3km (12 miles) long by around 3km (2 miles) wide, approximately one-tenth of its original area
**Epping Forest Buffer Land* (718ha/1,774 acres), Waltham Abbey/Epping
Farthing Downs and New Hill (95ha/235 acres), Surrey
Hampstead Heath (275ha/680 acres), NW3 Including Golders Hill (15ha/36 acres) and Parliament Hill (110ha/271 acres)
Highgate Wood (28ha/70 acres), N6/N10
Kenley Common (56ha/139 acres), Surrey
Queen's Park (12ha/30 acres), NW6
Riddlesdown (43ha/107 acres), Surrey
Spring Park (21ha/51 acres), Kent
Stoke Common (83ha/206 acres), Bucks. Ownership was transferred to the Corporation in 2007
West Ham Park (31ha/77 acres), E15
West Wickham Common (11ha/26 acres), Kent
Also over 150 smaller open spaces within the City of London, including *Finsbury Circus* and *St Dunstan-in-the-East*

* Includes Copped Hall Park, Woodredon Estate and Warlies Park

OTHER PARKS AND GARDENS

CHELSEA PHYSIC GARDEN, 66 Royal Hospital Road SW3 4HS T 020-7352 5646 W www.chelseaphysicgarden.co.uk A garden of general botanical research and education, maintaining a wide range of rare and unusual plants; established in 1673 by the Society of Apothecaries
HAMPTON COURT PARK AND GARDENS (303.5ha/750 acres), Surrey KT8 9AU T 0844-482 7777 W www.hrp.org.uk Also known as Home Park, the park lies beyond the palace's formal gardens. It contains a herd of deer and a 1,000-year-old oak tree from the original park
KEW, ROYAL BOTANIC GARDENS (120ha/300 acres), Richmond, Surrey TW9 3AB T 020-8332 5655 W www.kew.org Officially inscribed on the UNESCO list of World Heritage Sites
THAMES BARRIER PARK (9ha/22acres), North Woolwich E16 2HP T 020-7476 3741 W www.thamesbarrierpark.org.uk Opened in 2000, landscaped gardens with spectacular views of the Thames Barrier

ROYAL PARKS

W www.royalparks.gov.uk

Bushy Park (450ha/1,099 acres), Middx. Adjoins Hampton Court; contains an avenue of horse-chestnuts enclosed in a fourfold avenue of limes planted by William III
Green Park (19ha/47 acres), W1 Between Piccadilly and St James's Park, with Constitution Hill leading to Hyde Park Corner
Greenwich Park (74ha/183 acres), SE10 Enclosed by Humphrey, Duke of Gloucester, and laid out by Charles II from the designs of Le Nôtre. On a hill in Greenwich Park is the Royal Observatory (founded 1675). Its buildings are now managed by the National Maritime Museum T 020-8858 4422 W www.nmm.ac.uk and the earliest building is named Flamsteed House, after John Flamsteed (1646–1719), the first astronomer royal
Hyde Park (142ha/350 acres), W1/W2 From Park Lane to Kensington Gardens and incorporating the Serpentine lake, Apsley House, the Achilles Statue, Rotten Row and the Ladies' Mile; fine gateway at Hyde Park Corner. To the north-east is Marble Arch, originally erected by George IV at the entrance to Buckingham Palace and re-erected in the present position in 1851
Kensington Gardens (111ha/275 acres), W2/W8 From the western boundary of Hyde Park to Kensington Palace; contains the Albert Memorial, Serpentine Gallery and Peter Pan statue
Regent's Park and *Primrose Hill* (197ha/487 acres), NW1 From Marylebone Road to Primrose Hill surrounded by the Outer Circle; divided by the Broad Walk leading to the Zoological Gardens
Richmond Park (1,000ha/2,500 acres), Surrey. Designated a National Nature Reserve, a Site of Special Scientific Interest and a Special Area of Conservation
St James's Park (23ha/58 acres), SW1 From Whitehall to Buckingham Palace; ornamental lake of 4.9ha (12 acres); the Mall leads from Admiralty Arch to Buckingham Palace, Birdcage Walk from Storey's Gate to Buckingham Palace

PLACES OF HISTORICAL AND CULTURAL INTEREST

1 Canada Square
Canary Wharf E14 5DY T 020-7418 2000
W www.canarywharf.com
Also known as 'Canary Wharf', the steel and glass skyscraper is the tallest structure in London and the tallest habitable building in the UK

30 St Mary Axe
EC3A 8EP W www.30stmaryaxe.com
Completed in 2004 and commonly known as the 'Gherkin', it is the second-tallest building in the City of London

Alexandra Palace
Alexandra Palace Way, Wood Green N22 7AY
T 020-8365 2121 W www.alexandrapalace.com
The Victorian palace was severely damaged by fire in 1980 but was restored, and reopened in 1988. Alexandra Palace now provides modern facilities for exhibitions, conferences, banquets and leisure activities. There is a winter ice rink, a boating lake, the Phoenix Bar and a conservation area

Barbican Centre
Silk Street EC2Y 8DS T 020-7638 4141
W www.barbican.org.uk
Owned, funded and managed by the Corporation of London, the Barbican Centre opened in 1982 and houses the Barbican Theatre, a studio theatre called The Pit and the Barbican Hall; it is also home to the London Symphony Orchestra. There are three cinemas, seven conference rooms, two art galleries, a sculpture court, a lending library, trade and banqueting facilities, a conservatory, shops, restaurants, cafes and bars

British Library
St Pancras, 96 Euston Road NW1 2DB T 0843-208 1144
W www.bl.uk
The largest building constructed in the UK in the 20th century with basements extending 24.5m underground. Holdings include the *Magna Carta*, the *Lindisfarne Gospels*, Mozart manuscripts and the world's

earliest dated printed book, the *Diamond Sutra*. Holds temporary exhibitions on a range of topics

Central Criminal Court
Old Bailey EC4M 7EH T 020-7248 3277
W www.cityoflondon.gov.uk
The highest criminal court in the UK, the 'Old Bailey' is located on the site of the old Newgate Prison. Trials held here have included those of Oscar Wilde, Dr Crippen and the Yorkshire Ripper. The courthouse has been rebuilt several times since 1674; Edward VII officially opened the current neo-baroque building in 1907

Charterhouse
Charterhouse Square EC1M 6AN T 020-7253 9503
W www.thecharterhouse.org
A Carthusian monastery from 1371 to 1538, purchased in 1611 by Thomas Sutton, who endowed it as a residence for aged men 'of gentle birth' and a school for poor scholars (removed to Godalming in 1872)

Cutty Sark
Greenwich SE10 T 020-8858 2698 W www.cuttysark.org.uk
The last of the famous tea clippers, it was moved into a specially constructed dry dock in 1954 and opened to the public in 1957. Damaged by fire in 2007, the ship is closed to the public and restoration work is ongoing

Downing Street SW1
Number 10 Downing Street is the official town residence of the Prime Minister, number 11 of the Chancellor of the Exchequer and number 12 is the office of the Government Whips. The street was named after Sir George Downing, Bt., soldier and diplomat, who was MP for Morpeth 1660–84

George Inn
Borough High Street SE1 1NH T 020-7407 2056
W www.nationaltrust.org.uk
The last galleried inn in London, built in 1677. Now owned by the National Trust and run as an ordinary public house

Horse Guards, Whitehall, SW1
Archway and offices built about 1753. The changing of the guard takes place daily at 11am (10am on Sundays) and the inspection at 4pm. Only those with the Queen's permission may drive through the gates and archway into *Horse Guards' Parade,* where the colour is 'trooped' on the Queen's official birthday

HOUSES OF PARLIAMENT

House of Commons, Westminster SW1A 0AA T 020-7219 4272
W www.parliament.uk

House of Lords, Westminster SW1A 0PW T 020-7219 3107
W www.parliament.uk
The royal palace of Westminster, originally built by Edward the Confessor, was the normal meeting place of Parliament from about 1340. St Stephen's Chapel was used from about 1550 for the meetings of the House of Commons, which had previously been held in the Chapter House or Refectory of Westminster Abbey. The House of Lords met in an apartment of the royal palace. The fire of 1834 destroyed much of the palace, and the present Houses of Parliament were erected on the site from the designs of Sir Charles Barry and Augustus Welby Pugin between 1840 and 1867. The chamber of the House of Commons was destroyed by bombing in 1941, and a new chamber designed by Sir Giles Gilbert Scott was used for the first time in 1950. *Westminster Hall and the Crypt Chapel* was the only part of the old palace of Westminster to survive the fire of 1834. It was built by William II from 1097 to 1099 and altered by Richard II between 1394 and 1399. The hammerbeam roof of carved oak dates from 1396–8. The Hall was the scene of the trial of Charles I. *The Victoria Tower* of the House of Lords is 98.5m (323ft) high, and when Parliament is sitting, the Union flag flies by day from its flagstaff. *The Clock Tower* of the House of Commons is 96.3m (316ft) high and contains 'Big Ben', the hour bell said to be named after Sir Benjamin Hall, First Commissioner of Works when the original bell was cast in 1856. This bell, which weighed 16 tons 11 cwt, was found to be cracked in 1857. The present bell (13.5 tons) is a recasting of the original and was first brought into use in 1859. The dials of the clock are 7m (23ft) in diameter, the hands being 2.7m (9ft) and 4.3m (14ft) long (including balance piece). A light is displayed from the Clock Tower at night when parliament is sitting.

During session, tours of the Houses of Parliament are only available to UK residents who have made advance arrangements through an MP or peer. Overseas visitors are no longer provided with permits to tour the Houses of Parliament during session, although they can tour during the summer opening and attend debates for both houses in the Strangers' Galleries. During the summer recess tickets for tours of the Houses of Parliament can be booked by telephone (T 0870-906 3773) or bought on site at the ticket office on Abingdon Green opposite Parliament and the Victoria Tower Gardens. The Strangers' Gallery of the House of Commons is open to the public when the house is sitting. To acquire tickets in advance UK residents should write to their local MP and overseas visitors should apply to their embassy or high commission in the UK for a permit. If none of these arrangements has been made, visitors should join the public queue outside St Stephen's Entrance, where there is also a queue for entry to the House of Lords Gallery

INNS OF COURT

The Inns of Court are ancient unincorporated bodies of lawyers which for more than five centuries have had the power to call to the Bar those of their members who have qualified for the rank or degree of Barrister-at-Law. There are four Inns of Court as well as many lesser inns

Lincoln's Inn, Chancery Lane/Lincoln's Inn Fields WC2A 3TL T 020-7405 1393 W www.lincolnsinn.org.uk
The most ancient of the inns with records dating back to 1422. The hall and library buildings are from 1845, although the library is first mentioned in 1474; the old hall (late 15th century) and the chapel were rebuilt *c.*1619–23

Inner Temple, King's Bench Walk EC4Y 7HL
T 020-7797 8250 W www.innertemple.org.uk

Middle Temple, Middle Temple Lane EC4Y 9AT
T 020-7427 4800 W www.middletemple.org.uk
Records for the Middle and Inner Temple date back to the beginning of the 16th century. The site was originally occupied by the Order of Knights Templar *c.*1160–1312. The two inns have separate halls thought to have been formed *c.*1350. The division between the two societies was formalised in 1732 with Temple Church and the Masters House remaining in common. The Inner Temple Garden is normally open to the public on weekdays between 12.30pm and 3pm

Temple Church, EC4Y 7BB T 020-7353 8559
W www.templechurch.com

The nave forms one of five remaining round churches in England

Gray's Inn, South Square WC1R 5ET T 020-7458 7800 W www.graysinn.info

Founded early 14th century; Hall 1556–8

No other 'Inns' are active, but there are remains of *Staple Inn,* a gabled front on Holborn (opposite Gray's Inn Road). *Clement's Inn* (near St Clement Danes Church), *Clifford's Inn,* Fleet Street, and *Thavies Inn,* Holborn Circus, are all rebuilt. *Serjeants' Inn,* Fleet Street, and another (demolished 1910) of the same name in Chancery Lane, were composed of Serjeants-at-Law, the last of whom died in 1922

Institute of Contemporary Arts

The Mall SW1Y 5AH T 020-7930 3647 W www.ica.org.uk

Exhibitions of modern art in the fields of film, theatre, new media and the visual arts

Lloyd's

Lime Street EC3M 7HA T 020-7327 1000

W www.lloyds.com

International insurance market which evolved during the 17th century from Lloyd's Coffee House. The present building was opened for business in May 1986, and houses the Lutine Bell. Underwriting is on three floors with a total area of 10,591 sq. m (114,000 sq. ft). The Lloyd's building is not open to the general public

London Central Mosque and the Islamic Cultural Centre

Park Road NW8 7RG T 020-7725 2213 W www.iccuk.org

The focus for London's Muslims; established in 1944 but not completed until 1977, the mosque can accommodate about 5,000 worshippers; guided tours are available

London Eye

South Bank SE1 7PB T 0870-990 8883

W www.londoneye.com

Opened in March 2000 as London's millennium landmark, this 450ft observation wheel is the tallest cantilevered observation wheel in the world. The wheel provides a 30-minute ride offering panoramic views of the capital

London Zoo

Regent's Park NW1 4RY T 020-7722 3333

W www.londonzoo.org

Madame Tussauds

Marylebone Road NW1 5LR T 0871-894 3000

W www.madametussauds.com

Waxwork exhibition

Marlborough House

Pall Mall SW1Y 5HX T 020-7747 6500

W www.thecommonwealth.org

Built by Wren for the first Duke of Marlborough and completed in 1711, the house reverted to the Crown in 1835. In 1863 it became the London house of the Prince of Wales and was the London home of Queen Mary until her death in 1953. In 1959 Marlborough House was given by the Queen as the headquarters for the Commonwealth Secretariat and it was opened as such in 1965. The Queen's Chapel, Marlborough Gate, was begun in 1623 from the designs of Inigo Jones for the Infanta Maria of Spain, and completed for Queen Henrietta Maria. Marlborough House is not open to the public

Mansion House

Cannon Street EC4N 8BH T 020-7626 2500

W www.cityoflondon.gov.uk

The official residence of the Lord Mayor. Built in the 18th century in the Palladian style. Open to groups by appointment only

Neasden Temple

BAPS Shri Swaminarayan Mandir, 105–119 Brentfield Road, Neasden NW10 8LD T 020-8965 2651 W www.mandir.org

The first and largest traditional Hindu Mandir outside of India; opened in 1995

Port of London

Port of London Authority, Bakers' Hall, 7 Harp Lane EC3R 6LB T 01474-562200 W www.pla.co.uk

The Port of London covers the tidal section of the river Thames from Teddington to the seaward limit (the outer Tongue buoy and the Sunk light vessel), a distance of 150km. The governing body is the Port of London Authority (PLA). Cargo is handled at privately operated riverside terminals between Fulham and Canvey Island, including the enclosed dock at Tilbury, 40km below London Bridge. Passenger vessels and cruise liners can be handled at moorings at Greenwich, Tower Bridge and Tilbury

Roman Remains

The city wall of Roman *Londinium* was largely rebuilt during the medieval period but sections may be seen near the White Tower in the Tower of London; at Tower Hill; at Coopers' Row; at All Hallows, London Wall, its vestry being built on the remains of a semi-circular Roman bastion; at St Alphage, London Wall, showing a succession of building repairs from the Roman until the late medieval period; and at St Giles, Cripplegate. Sections of the great forum and basilica, more than 165 sq. m, have been encountered during excavations in the area of Leadenhall, Gracechurch Street and Lombard Street. Traces of Roman activity along the river include a massive riverside wall built in the late Roman period, and a succession of Roman timber quays along Lower and Upper Thames Street. Finds from these sites can be seen at the Museum of London.

Other major buildings are the amphitheatre at Guildhall, remains of bath-buildings in Upper and Lower Thames Street, and the temple of Mithras in Walbrook

Royal Albert Hall

Kensington Gore SW7 2AP T 020-7589 8212

W www.royalalberthall.com

The elliptical hall, one of the largest in the world, was completed in 1871; since 1941 it has been the venue each summer for the Promenade Concerts founded in 1895 by Sir Henry Wood. Other events include pop and classical music concerts, dance, opera, sporting events, conferences and banquets

Royal Courts of Justice

Strand WC2A 2LL T 020-7947 6000

W www.hmcourts-service.gov.uk

Victorian Gothic building that is home to the high court. Visitors are free to watch proceedings

Royal Hospital, Chelsea

Royal Hospital Road SW3 4SR T 020-7881 5200

W www.chelsea-pensioners.co.uk

Founded by Charles II in 1682, and built by Wren; opened in 1692 for old and disabled soldiers. The extensive grounds include the former Ranelagh Gardens and are the venue for the Chelsea Flower Show each May

Royal Naval College

Greenwich SE10 9LW T 020-8269 4747

W www.oldroyalnavalcollege.org

The building was the Greenwich Hospital until 1869.

It was built by Charles II, largely from designs by John Webb, and by Queen Mary II and William III, from designs by Wren. It stands on the site of an ancient abbey, a royal house and Greenwich Palace, which was constructed by Henry VII. Henry VIII, Mary I and Elizabeth I were born in the royal palace and Edward VI died there

Royal Opera House
Covent Garden WC2E 9DD **T** 020-7240 1200
W www.roh.org.uk
Home of The Royal Ballet (1931) and The Royal Opera (1946). The Royal Opera House is the third theatre to be built on the site, opening 1858; the first was opened in 1732

St James's Palace
Pall Mall SW1A 1BQ **T** 020-7930 4832
W www.royal.gov.uk
Built by Henry VIII, only the Gatehouse and Presence Chamber remain; later alterations were made by Wren and Kent. Representatives of foreign powers are still accredited 'to the Court of St James's'. *Clarence House* (1825), the official London residence of the Prince of Wales and his sons, stands within the St James's Palace estate

St Paul's Cathedral
St Paul's Churchyard EC4M 8AD **T** 020-7236 4128
E chapter@stpaulscathedral.org.uk **W** www.stpauls.co.uk
Built 1675–1710. The cross on the dome is 111m (365ft) above ground level, the inner cupola 66.4m (218ft) above the floor. 'Great Paul' in the south-west tower weighs nearly 17 tons. The organ by Father Smith (enlarged by Willis and rebuilt by Mander) is in a case carved by Grinling Gibbons, who also carved the choir stalls

Somerset House
Strand WC2R 1LA **T** 020 7845 4600
W www.somersethouse.org.uk
The river facade (183m/600ft long) was built in 1776–1801 from the designs of Sir William Chambers; the eastern extension, which houses part of King's College, was built by Smirke in 1829–35. Somerset House was the property of Lord Protector Somerset, at whose attainder in 1552 the palace passed to the Crown, and it was a royal residence until 1692. Somerset House has recently undergone extensive renovation and is home to the Gilbert Collection, Embankment Galleries and the Courtauld Institute Gallery. Open-air concerts and ice-skating (Dec–Jan) are held in the courtyard

SOUTH BANK, SE1
Arts complex on the south bank of the river Thames which consists of:
The *Royal Festival Hall* **T** 020-7960 4200
W www.southbankcentre.co.uk
Opened in 1951 for the Festival of Britain, adjacent are the *Queen Elizabeth Hall,* the *Purcell Room,* and the *Hayward Gallery*
BFI Southbank **T** 020-7633 0274 **W** www.bfi.org.uk
Opened in 1952 and is administered by the British Film Institute, has three auditoria and an IMAX cinema. The London Film Festival is held here every November
The *Royal National Theatre,* **T** 020-7452 3000
W www.nationaltheatre.org.uk
Opened in 1976; comprises the Olivier, the Lyttelton and the Cottesloe theatres

Southwark Cathedral
London Bridge SE1 9DA **T** 020-7367 6700
W www.cathedral.southwark.anglican.org
Mainly 13th century, but the nave is largely rebuilt. The tomb of John Gower (1330–1408) is between the Bunyan and Chaucer memorial windows in the north aisle; Shakespeare's effigy, backed by a view of Southwark and the Globe Theatre, is in the south aisle; the tomb of Bishop Andrewes (*d.*1626) is near the screen. The Lady Chapel was the scene of the consistory courts of the reign of Mary (Gardiner and Bonner) and is still used as a consistory court. John Harvard, after whom Harvard University is named, was baptised here in 1607, and the chapel by the north choir aisle is his memorial chapel

Thames Embankments
Sir Joseph Bazalgette (1819–91) constructed the *Victoria Embankment,* on the north side from Westminster to Blackfriars for the Metropolitan Board of Works, 1864–70; (the seats, of which the supports of some are a kneeling camel, laden with spicery, and of others a winged sphinx, were presented by the Grocers' Company and by W. H. Smith, MP, in 1874); the *Albert Embankment,* on the south side from Westminster Bridge to Vauxhall, 1866–9, and the Chelsea Embankment, 1871–4. The total cost exceeded £2m. Bazalgette also inaugurated the London main drainage system, 1858–65. A medallion *(Flumini vincula posuit)* has been placed on a pier of the *Victoria Embankment* to commemorate the engineer

Thames Flood Barrier
W www.environment-agency.gov.uk
Officially opened in May 1984, though first used in February 1983, the barrier consists of ten rising sector gates which span approximately 570 yards from bank to bank of the Thames at Woolwich Reach. When not in use the gates lie horizontally, allowing shipping to navigate the river normally; when the barrier is closed, the gates turn through 90 degrees to stand vertically more than 50 feet above the river bed. The barrier took eight years to complete and can be raised within about 30 minutes

Trafalgar Tavern
Park Row, Greenwich SE10 9NW **T** 020-8858 2909
W www.trafalgartavern.co.uk
Regency-period riverside public house built in 1837. Charles Dickens and William Gladstone were patrons

Westminster Abbey
Broad Sanctuary SW1P 3PA **T** 020-7222 5152
E info@westminster-abbey.org
W www.westminster-abbey.org
Founded as a Benedictine monastery over 1,000 years ago, the church was rebuilt by Edward the Confessor in 1065 and again by Henry III in the 13th century. The abbey is the resting place for monarchs including Edward I, Henry III, Henry V, Henry VII, Elizabeth I, Mary I and Mary Queen of Scots, and has been the setting of coronations since that of William the Conqueror in 1066. In Poets' Corner there are memorials to many literary figures, and many scientists and musicians are also remembered here. The grave of the Unknown Warrior is to be found in the nave

Westminster Cathedral
Francis Street SW1P 1QW **T** 020-7798 9055
W www.westminstercathedral.org.uk
Roman Catholic cathedral built 1895–1903 from the designs of J. F. Bentley. The campanile is 284ft high

LONDON THEATRES

For contact details for individual theatres and information on shows, *see* W www.londontheatre.co.uk

Adelphi Theatre, Strand, WC2R 0NS ⊖ Charing Cross
Aldwych Theatre, Aldwych, WC2B 4DF ⊖ Covent Garden/Holborn
Almeida Theatre, Almeida Street, N1 1TA ⊖ Angel/Highbury & Islington
Ambassadors Theatre, West Street, WC2H 9ND ⊖ Leicester Square
Apollo Theatre, Shaftesbury Avenue, W1D 7EZ ⊖ Piccadilly Circus
Apollo Victoria Theatre, Wilton Road, SW1 1LL ⊖ Victoria
Arcola Theatre, Arcola Street, ED2 DJ6 ⊖ Highbury and Islington/Liverpool Street
Barbican Theatre, Barbican Centre, EC2Y 8DS ⊖ Barbican/Moorgate
Bloomsbury Theatre, Gordon Street, WC1H 0AH ⊖ Euston/Euston Square
Cambridge Theatre, Earlham Street, WC2 9HU ⊖ Covent Garden/Leicester Square
Chelsea Theatre, World's End Place, SW10 0DR ⊖ Sloane Square
Comedy Theatre, Panton Street, SW1Y 4DN ⊖ Leicester Square/Piccadilly Circus
Criterion Theatre, Jermyn Street, SW1Y 4XA ⊖ Piccadilly Circus
Dominion Theatre, Tottenham Court Road, W1T 7AQ ⊖ Tottenham Court Road
Donmar Warehouse, Earlham Street, WC2H 9LX ⊖ Covent Garden
Duchess Theatre, Catherine Street, WC2B 5LA ⊖ Covent Garden
Duke Of York's Theatre, St Martin's Lane, WC2N 4BG ⊖ Leicester Square/Piccadilly Circus
Fortune Theatre, Russell Street, WC2B 5HH ⊖ Covent Garden
Garrick Theatre, Charing Cross Road, WC2H 0HH ⊖ Charing Cross/Leicester Square
Gielgud Theatre, Shaftesbury Avenue, W1D 6AR ⊖ Piccadilly Circus
Globe Theatre, New Globe Walk, SE1 9DT ⊖ Mansion House
Hackney Empire, Mare Street, E8 1EJ ⊖ Bethnal Green
Her Majesty's Theatre, Haymarket, SW1Y 4QL ⊖ Piccadilly Circus
Jermyn Street Theatre, Jermyn Street, SW1Y 6ST ⊖ Piccadilly Circus
Leicester Square Theatre, Leicester Place, WC2H 7BX ⊖ Leicester Square
London Coliseum, St Martin's Lane, WC2N 4ES ⊖ Charing Cross
London Palladium, Argyll Street, W1F 7TF ⊖ Oxford Circus
Lyceum Theatre, Wellington Street, WC2E 7RQ ⊖ Covent Garden
Lyric Theatre, Shaftesbury Avenue, W1D 7ES ⊖ Piccadilly Circus
Lyric Theatre Hammersmith, King Street, W6 0QL ⊖ Hammersmith
National Theatre, South Bank, SE1 9PX ⊖ Waterloo
New London Theatre, Drury Lane, WC2B 5PW ⊖ Holborn
Noël Coward (formerly Albery), St Martin's Lane, WC2N 4AA ⊖ Leicester Square
Novello Theatre, Aldwych, WC2B 4LD ⊖ Charing Cross
Old Vic Theatre, The Cut, SE1 8NB ⊖ Waterloo
Palace Theatre, Shaftesbury Avenue, W1V 8AY ⊖ Leicester Square/Piccadilly Circus
Phoenix Theatre, Charing Cross Road, WC2H 0JP ⊖ Tottenham Court Road
Piccadilly Theatre, Denman Street, W1D 7DY ⊖ Piccadilly Circus
Playhouse Theatre, Northumberland Avenue, WC2N 5DE ⊖ Embankment
Prince Edward Theatre, Old Compton Street, W1D 4HS ⊖ Leicester Square
Prince of Wales Theatre, Coventry Street, W1D 6AS ⊖ Piccadilly Circus
Queen's Theatre, Shaftesbury Avenue, W1D 6BA ⊖ Piccadilly Circus
Riverside Studios, Crisp Road, W6 9RL ⊖ Hammersmith
Royal Albert Hall, Kensington Gore, SW7 2AP ⊖ South Kensington
Royal Court Theatre, Sloane Square, SW1W 8AS ⊖ Sloane Square
Royal Festival Hall, South Bank SE1 8XX ⊖ Waterloo
Sadler's Wells, Rosebery Avenue, EC1R 4TN ⊖ Angel
St Martin's Theatre, West Street, WC2H 9NZ ⊖ Leicester Square
Savoy Theatre, Strand, WC2R 0ET ⊖ Charing Cross
Shaftesbury Theatre, Shaftesbury Avenue, WC2H 8DP ⊖ Holborn/Tottenham Court Road
Soho Theatre, Dean Street, W1D 3NE ⊖ Tottenham Court Road
Southwark Playhouse, Shipwright Yard, SE1 2TF ⊖ Southwark
Theatre Royal Drury Lane, Catherine Street, WC2B 5JF ⊖ Covent Garden
Theatre Royal Haymarket, Haymarket, SW1Y 4HT ⊖ Piccadilly Circus
Trafalgar Studios, Whitehall, SW1A 2DY ⊖ Charing Cross/Embankment
Tricycle Theatre, Kilburn High Road, NW6 7JR ⊖ Kilburn
Unicorn Theatre, Tooley Street SE1 2HZ ⊖ London Bridge
Vaudeville Theatre, Strand, WC2R 0NH ⊖ Charing Cross
Victoria Palace Theatre, Victoria Street, SW1E 5EA ⊖ Victoria
Wyndham's Theatre, Charing Cross Road, WC2H 0DA ⊖ Leicester Square
Young Vic, The Cut, SE1 8LZ ⊖ Waterloo

HALLMARKS

Hallmarks are the symbols stamped on gold, silver, palladium or platinum articles to indicate that they have been tested at an official Assay Office and that they conform to one of the legal standards. The marking of gold and silver articles to identify the maker was instituted in England in 1363 under a statute of Edward III. In 1478 the Assay Office in Goldsmiths' Hall was established and all gold and silversmiths were required to bring their wares to be date-marked by the Hall, hence the term 'hallmarked'.

With certain exceptions, all gold, silver, palladium or platinum articles are required by law to be hallmarked before they are offered for sale. Current hallmarking requirements come under the UK Hallmarking Act 1973 and subsequent amendments. The act is built around the principle of description, where it is an offence for any person to apply to an unhallmarked article a description indicating that it is wholly or partly made of gold, silver, palladium or platinum. There is an exemption by weight: compulsory hallmarks are not needed on gold and palladium under 1g, silver under 7.78g and platinum under 0.5g. Also, some descriptions, such as rolled gold and gold plate, are permissible. The British Hallmarking Council is a statutory body created as a result of the Hallmarking Act. It ensures adequate provision for assaying and hallmarking, supervises the assay offices and ensures the enforcement of hallmarking legislation. The four assay offices at London, Birmingham, Sheffield and Edinburgh operate under the act.

BRITISH HALLMARKING COUNCIL Secretariat, 1 Colmore Square, Birmingham B4 6AA **T** 0800-763 1414 **W** www.britishhallmarkingcouncil.gov.uk

COMPULSORY MARKS

Since January 1999 UK hallmarks have consisted of three compulsory symbols – the sponsor's mark, the millesimal fineness (purity) mark and the assay office mark. The distinction between UK and foreign articles has been removed, and more finenesses are now legal, reflecting the more common finenesses elsewhere in Europe.

SPONSOR'S MARK

Formerly known as the maker's mark, the sponsor's mark was instituted in England in 1363. Originally a device such as a bird or fleur-de-lis, now it consists of a combination of at least two initials (usually a shortened form of the manufacturer's name) and a shield design. The London Assay Office offers 45 standard shield designs but other designs are possible by arrangement.

MILLESIMAL FINENESS MARK

The millesimal fineness (purity) mark indicates the number of parts per thousand of pure metal in the alloy. The current finenesses allowed in the UK are:

Gold	999	
	990	
	916.6	(22 carat)
	750	(18 carat)
	585	(14 carat)
	375	(9 carat)
Silver	999	
	958.4	(Britannia)
	925	(sterling)
	800	
Palladium	999	
	950	
	500	
Platinum	999	
	950	
	900	
	850	

ASSAY OFFICE MARK

This mark identifies the particular assay office at which the article was tested and marked. The British assay offices are:

LONDON, Goldsmiths' Hall, Gutter Lane, London EC2V 8AQ **T** 020-7606 8971 **W** www.thegoldsmiths.co.uk

BIRMINGHAM, PO Box 151, Newhall Street, Birmingham B3 1SB **T** 0121-236 6951 **W** www.theassayoffice.co.uk

SHEFFIELD, Guardians' Hall, Beulah Road, Hillsborough, Sheffield S6 2AN **T** 0114-275 5111 **W** www.assayoffice.co.uk

EDINBURGH, Goldsmiths' Hall, 24A Broughton Street, Edinburgh EH1 3RH **T** 0131-556 1144 **W** www.assayofficescotland.com

Assay offices formerly existed in other towns, eg Chester, Exeter, Glasgow, Newcastle, Norwich and York, each having its own distinguishing mark.

OPTIONAL MARKS

Since 1999 traditional pictorial marks such as a crown for gold, the Britannia for 958 silver, the lion passant for 925 silver (lion rampant in Scotland) and the orb for 950 platinum may be added voluntarily to the millesimal mark. In 2010 a pictorial mark for 950 palladium was introduced.

Gold – a crown

Britannia silver

Sterling silver (England)

Sterling silver (Scotland)

Platinum – an orb

Palladium – the Greek goddess Pallas Athene

DATE LETTER

The date letter shows the year in which an article was assayed and hallmarked. Each alphabetical cycle has a distinctive style of lettering or shape of shield. The date letters were different at the various assay offices and the particular office must be established from the assay office mark before reference is made to tables of date letters. Date letter marks became voluntary from 1 January 1999.

The table which follows shows one specimen shield and letter used by the London Assay Office on silver articles for each alphabetical cycle from 1498. The same letters are found on gold articles but the surrounding shield may differ. Until 1 January 1975 two calendar years are given for each specimen date letter as the letter changed annually in May on St Dunstan's Day (the patron saint of silversmiths). Since 1 January 1975, each date letter has indicated a calendar year from January to December and each office has used the same style of date letter and shield for all articles:

LONDON (GOLDSMITHS' HALL) DATE LETTERS FROM 1498

from	*to*
1498–9	1517–18
1518–19	1537–8
1538–9	1557–8
1558–9	1577–8
1578–9	1597–8
1598–9	1617–1
1618–19	1637–8
1638–9	1657–8
1658–9	1677–8
1678–9	1696–7
1697	1715–16
1716–17	1735–6
1736–7	1738–9
1739–40	1755–6
1756–7	1775–6
1776–7	1795–6
1796–7	1815–16
1816–17	1835–6
1836–7	1855–6
1856–7	1875–6
1876–7 (A to M square shield, N to Z as shown)	1895–6
1896–7	1915–16
1916–17	1935–6
1936–7	1955–6
1956–7	1974
1975	1999
2000	

OTHER MARKS

FOREIGN GOODS

Foreign goods imported into the UK are required to be hallmarked before sale, unless they already bear a convention mark (*see* below) or a hallmark struck by an independent assay office in the European Economic Area which is deemed to be equivalent to a UK hallmark.

The following are the assay office marks used for gold imported articles until the end of 1998. For silver and platinum the symbols remain the same but the shields differ in shape.

 *London*  *Sheffield*

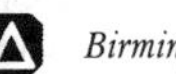 *Birmingham*  *Edinburgh*

CONVENTION HALLMARKS

Special marks at authorised assay offices of the signatory countries of the International Convention on Hallmarking (Austria, the Czech Republic, Denmark, Finland, Hungary, Ireland, Latvia, Lithuania, the Netherlands, Norway, Poland, Portugal, Sweden, Switzerland, UK and Ukraine) are legally recognised in the United Kingdom as approved hallmarks. These consist of a sponsor's mark, a common control mark, a fineness mark (arabic numerals showing the standard in parts per thousand), and an assay office mark. There is no date letter.

The common control marks are:

GOLD SILVER PALLADIUM PLATINUM

COMMEMORATIVE MARKS

There are other marks to commemorate special events: the silver jubilee of King George V and Queen Mary in 1935, the coronation of Queen Elizabeth II in 1953, and her silver jubilee in 1977. During 1999 and 2000 there was a voluntary additional Millennium Mark. A mark to commemorate the golden jubilee of Queen Elizabeth II was available during 2002.

BRITISH CURRENCY

The unit of currency is the pound sterling (£) of 100 pence. The decimal system was introduced on 15 February 1971.

COIN

Gold Coins
One hundred pounds £100*
Fifty pounds £50*
Twenty-five pounds £25*
Ten pounds £10*
Five pounds £5
Two pounds £2
Sovereign £1
Half-sovereign 50p

Silver Coins (Britannia coins)*
Two pounds £2
One pound £1
Fifty pence 50p
Twenty pence 20p

Maundy Money†
Fourpence 4p
Threepence 3p
Twopence 2p
Penny 1p

Bi-colour Coins‡
Two pounds £2

Nickel-Brass Coins
Two pounds £2 (pre-1997)§
One pound £1

Cupro-Nickel Coins
Crown £5 (since 1990)§
Fifty pence 50p
Crown 25p (pre-1990)§
Twenty pence 20p
Ten pence 10p
Five pence 5p

Bronze Coins
Two pence 2p
One penny 1p

Copper-plated Steel Coins¶
Two pence 2p
One penny 1p

* Britannia coins: gold bullion coins introduced 1987; silver coins introduced 1997
† Gifts of special money distributed by the sovereign annually on Maundy Thursday to the number of elderly men and women corresponding to the sovereign's own age
‡ Cupro-nickel centre and nickel-brass outer ring
§ Commemorative coins; not intended for general circulation
¶ Since September 1992, although in 1998 the 2p was struck in both copper-plated steel and bronze

GOLD COIN

Gold ceased to circulate during the First World War. Since then controls on buying, selling and holding gold coins have been imposed at various times but have subsequently been revoked. Under the Exchange Control (Gold Coins Exemption) Order 1979, gold coins may now be imported and exported without restriction, except gold coins which are more than 50 years old and valued at a sum in excess of £8,000; these cannot be exported without specific authorisation from the Department for Business, Innovation and Skills.

Value Added Taxation on the sale of gold coins was revoked in 2000.

SILVER COIN

Prior to 1920 silver coins were struck from sterling silver, an alloy of which 925 parts in 1,000 were silver. In 1920 the proportion of silver was reduced to 500 parts. Since 1947 all 'silver' coins, except Maundy money, have been struck from cupro-nickel, an alloy of 75 parts copper and 25 parts nickel, except for the 20p, composed of 84 parts copper, 16 parts nickel. Maundy coins continue to be struck from sterling silver.

BRONZE COIN

Bronze, introduced in 1860 to replace copper, is an alloy consisting mainly of copper with small amounts of zinc and tin. Bronze was replaced by copper-plated steel in September 1992 with the exception of 1998 when the 2p was made in both copper-plated steel and bronze.

LEGAL TENDER

Gold (dated 1838 onwards, if not below least current weight)	to any amount
£5 (Crown since 1990)*	to any amount
£2	to any amount
£1	to any amount
50p	up to £10
25p (Crown pre-1990)*	up to £10
20p	up to £10
10p	up to £5
5p	up to £5
2p	up to 20p
1p	up to 20p

* Only redeemable at the Post Office

The £1 coin was introduced in 1983 to replace the £1 note. The following coins have ceased to be legal tender:

Farthing	31 Dec 1960
Halfpenny (½d)	31 Jul 1969
Half-crown	31 Dec 1969
Threepence	31 Aug 1971
Penny (1d)	31 Aug 1971
Sixpence	30 Jun 1980
Halfpenny (½p)	31 Dec 1984
Old 5 pence	31 Dec 1990
Old 10 pence	30 Jun 1993
Old 50 pence	28 Feb 1998

The Channel Islands and the Isle of Man issue their own coinage, which is legal tender only in the island of issue.

COIN STANDARDS

	Metal	*Standard weight (g)*	*Standard diameter (mm)*
1p	bronze	3.56	20.3
1p	copper-plated steel	3.56	20.3
2p	bronze	7.13	25.9
2p	copper-plated steel	7.13	25.9
5p	cupro-nickel	3.25	18.0
10p	cupro-nickel	6.5	24.5
20p	cupro-nickel	5.0	21.4
25p Crown	cupro-nickel	28.28	38.6
50p	cupro-nickel	8.00	27.3
£1	nickel-brass	9.5	22.5
£2	nickel-brass	15.98	28.4
£2	cupro-nickel, nickel-brass	12.00	28.4
£5 Crown	cupro-nickel	28.28	38.6

The 'remedy' is the amount of variation from standard permitted in weight and fineness of coins when first issued from the Royal Mint.

THE TRIAL OF THE PYX

The Trial of the Pyx is the examination by a jury to ascertain that coins made by the Royal Mint, which have been set aside in the pyx (or box), are of the proper weight, diameter and composition required by law. The trial is held annually, presided over by the Queen's Remembrancer, with a jury of freemen of the Company of Goldsmiths.

BANKNOTES

Bank of England notes are issued in denominations of £5, £10, £20 and £50 for the amount of the fiduciary note issue, and are legal tender in England and Wales. No £1 notes have been issued since 1984 and in March 1998 the outstanding notes were written off in accordance with the provision of the Currency Act 1983.

The current E series of notes was introduced from June 1990, replacing the D series (*see* below). A new-style £20 note, the first in series F, was introduced on 13 March 2007. The historical figures portrayed in these series are:

£5	May 2002–date	Elizabeth Fry
£5	Jun 1990–2003	George Stephenson*
£10	Nov 2000–date	Charles Darwin
£10	Apr 1992–2003	Charles Dickens*
£20	Mar 2007–date	Adam Smith
£20	Jun 1999–2010	Sir Edward Elgar*
£20	Jun 1991–2001	Michael Faraday*
£50	Apr 1994–date	Sir John Houblon

* These notes have been withdrawn from circulation: George Stephenson on 21 Nov 2003; Charles Dickens on 31 Jul 2003; Michael Faraday on 28 Feb 2001; Sir Edward Elgar on 30 Jun 2010

NOTE CIRCULATION

Note circulation is highest at the two peak spending periods of the year: around Christmas and during the summer holiday period.

The value of notes in circulation (£ million) at the end of February 2009 and 2010 was:

	2009	*2010*
£5	1,302	1,245
£10	6,304	6,399
£20	28,089	30,048
£50	8,691	9,248
Other notes*	4,222	3,280
TOTAL	48,608	50,220

* Includes higher value notes used internally in the Bank of England, eg as cover for the note issues of banks in Scotland and Northern Ireland in excess of their permitted issue

LEGAL TENDER

Banknotes which are no longer legal tender are payable when presented at the head office of the Bank of England in London.

The white notes for £10, £20, £50, £100, £500 and £1,000, which were issued until April 1943, ceased to be legal tender in May 1945, and the white £5 note in March 1946.

The white £5 note issued between October 1945 and September 1956, the £5 notes issued between 1957 and 1963 (bearing a portrait of Britannia) and the first series to bear a portrait of the Queen, issued between 1963 and 1971, ceased to be legal tender in March 1961, June 1967 and September 1973 respectively.

The series of £1 notes issued during the years 1928 to 1960 and the 10 shilling notes issued from 1928 to 1961 (those without the royal portrait) ceased to be legal tender in May and October 1962 respectively. The £1 note first issued in March 1960 (bearing on the back a representation of Britannia) and the £10 note first issued in February 1964 (bearing a lion on the back), both bearing a portrait of the Queen on the front, ceased to be legal tender in June 1979. The £1 note first issued in 1978 ceased to be legal tender on 11 March 1988. The 10 shilling note was replaced by the 50p coin in October 1969, and ceased to be legal tender on 21 November 1970.

The D series of banknotes was introduced from 1970 and ceased to be legal tender from the dates shown below. The predominant identifying feature of each note was the portrayal on the back of a prominent figure from British history:

£1	Feb 1978–Mar 1988	Sir Isaac Newton
£5	Nov 1971–Nov 1991	Duke of Wellington
£10	Feb 1975–May 1994	Florence Nightingale
£20	Jul 1970–Mar 1993	William Shakespeare
£50	Mar 1981–Sep 1996	Sir Christopher Wren

The £1 coin was introduced on 21 April 1983 to replace the £1 note.

OTHER BANKNOTES

Scotland – Banknotes are issued by three Scottish banks. The Royal Bank of Scotland issues notes for £1, £5, £10, £20, £50 and £100. Bank of Scotland and the Clydesdale Bank issue notes for £5, £10, £20, £50 and £100. Scottish notes are not legal tender in the UK but they are an authorised currency.

Northern Ireland – Banknotes are issued by four banks in Northern Ireland. The Bank of Ireland, the Northern Bank and the Ulster Bank issue notes for £5, £10, £20, £50 and £100. The First Trust Bank issues notes for £10, £20, £50 and £100. Northern Ireland notes are not legal tender in Northern Ireland but they circulate widely and enjoy a status comparable to that of Bank of England notes.

Channel Islands – The States of Guernsey issues its own currency notes and coinage. The notes are for £1, £5, £10, £20 and £50, and the coins are for 1p, 2p, 5p, 10p, 20p, 50p, £1, £2 and £5. The States of Jersey issues its own currency notes and coinage. The notes are for £1, £5, £10, £20 and £50, and the coins are for 1p, 2p, 5p, 10p, 20p, 50p, £1 and £2.

The Isle of Man – The Isle of Man government issues notes for £1, £5, £10, £20 and £50. Although these notes are only legal tender in the Isle of Man, they are accepted at face value in branches of the clearing banks in the UK. The Isle of Man issues coins for 1p, 2p, 5p, 10p, 20p, 50p, £1, £2 and £5.

Although none of the series of notes specified above is legal tender in the UK, they are generally accepted by banks irrespective of their place of issue. At one time banks made a commission charge for handling Scottish and Irish notes but this was abolished some years ago.

BANK FAMILY TREE

Includes the major retail banks operating in the UK as at April 2010. Financial results for these banks are given on the following page. Building societies are only included in instances where they demutualised to become a bank.

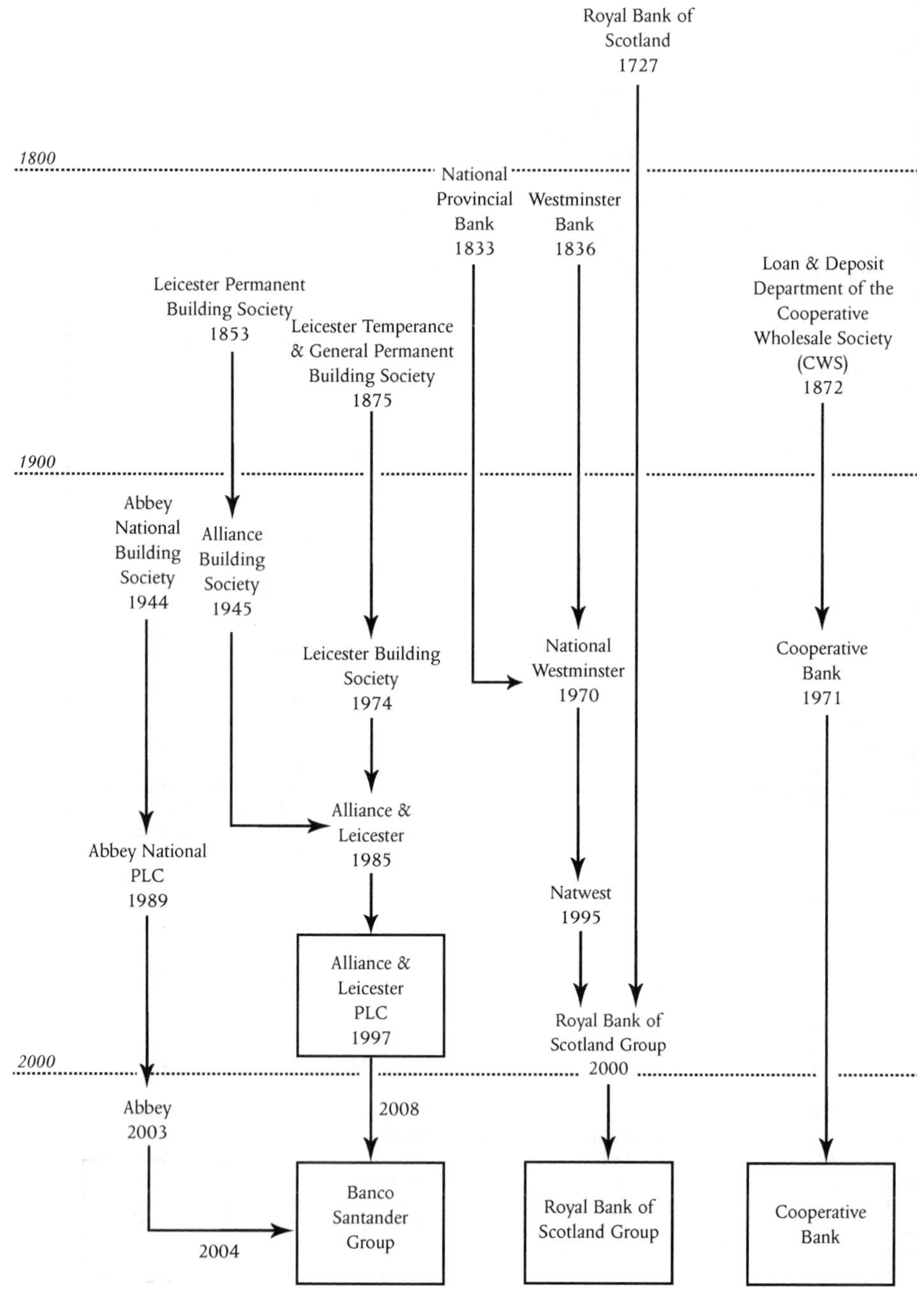

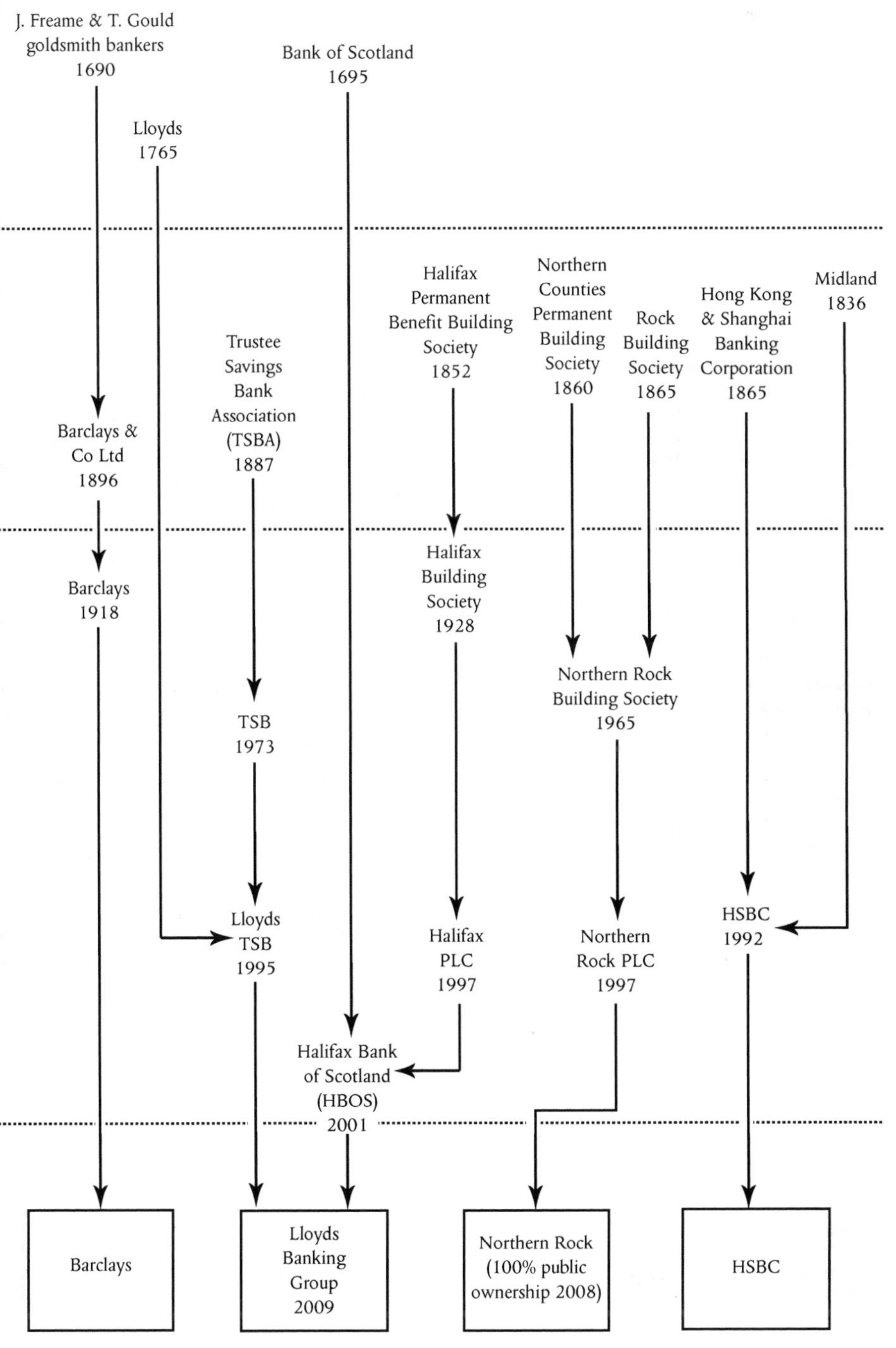
J. Freame & T. Gould
goldsmith bankers
1690
Bank of Scotland
1695
Lloyds
1765
Halifax
Permanent
Benefit Building
Society
1852
Northern
Counties
Permanent
Building
Society
1860
Rock
Building
Society
1865
Hong Kong
& Shanghai
Banking
Corporation
1865
Midland
1836
Trustee
Savings
Bank
Association
(TSBA)
1887
Barclays &
Co Ltd
1896
Barclays
1918
Halifax
Building
Society
1928
Northern Rock
Building Society
1965
TSB
1973
Lloyds
TSB
1995
Halifax
PLC
1997
Northern
Rock PLC
1997
HSBC
1992
Halifax Bank
of Scotland
(HBOS)
2001
Barclays
Lloyds
Banking
Group
2009
Northern Rock
(100% public
ownership 2008)
HSBC

BANKING AND PERSONAL FINANCE

There are two main types of deposit-taking institutions: banks and building societies, although National Savings and Investments also provides savings products. Banks and building societies are supervised by the Financial Services Authority and National Savings and Investments is accountable to the Treasury. As a result of the conversion of several building societies into banks in the 1990s, the size of the banking sector, which was already substantially greater than the non-bank deposit-taking sector, increased further.

The main institutions within the British banking system are the Bank of England (the central bank), retail banks, investment banks and overseas banks. In its role as the central bank, the Bank of England acts as banker to the government and as a note-issuing authority; it also oversees the efficient functioning of payment and settlement systems.

Since May 1997, the Bank of England has had operational responsibility for monetary policy. At monthly meetings of its monetary policy committee the Bank sets the interest rate at which it will lend to the money markets.

OFFICIAL INTEREST RATES 2005–10

4 August 2005	4.50%
3 August 2006	4.75%
9 November 2006	5.00%
11 January 2007	5.25%
10 May 2007	5.50%
5 July 2007	5.75%
6 December 2007	5.50%
7 February 2008	5.25%
10 April 2008	5.00%
8 October 2008	4.50%
6 November 2008	3.00%
4 December 2008	2.00%
8 January 2009	1.50%
5 February 2009	1.00%
5 March 2009	0.50%

RETAIL BANKING

Retail banks offer a wide variety of financial services to individuals and companies, including current and deposit accounts, loan and overdraft facilities, credit and debit cards, investment services, pensions, insurance and mortgages. All banks offer telephone and internet banking facilities in addition to traditional branch services.

The Financial Ombudsman Service provides independent and impartial arbitration in disputes between banks and their customers (*see* Financial Services Regulation).

PAYMENT CLEARINGS

The UK Payments Administration Ltd (UKPA) is a trade body that brings together the organisations responsible for delivering payment services. It also provides information on payment issues such as card fraud, cheques, plastic cards, electronic payments and cash. The Payments Council sets strategy for UK payments to ensure they meet the needs of users, payment service providers and the wider economy. Membership of the Payments Council is open to any member of a payment scheme that is widely used or significant in the UK. As at April 2010 the Payments Council had 28 members, comprising banks, financial services providers, one building society and Royal Mail Group.

There are three separate companies that manage the majority of payment clearings in the UK:

- BACS manages the schemes under which electronic payments are made, processing direct debits, direct credits and standing orders (W www.bacs.co.uk)
- CHAPS Clearing Company provides electronic same-day clearing and real-time settlement services for sterling payments (W www.chapsco.co.uk)
- The Cheque and Credit Clearing Company manages the cheque clearing system in Great Britain (W www.chequeandcredit.co.uk)

PAYMENTS COUNCIL/UKPA, Mercury House, Triton Court, 14 Finsbury Square, London EC2A 1LQ
T 020-7711 6200 W www.ukpayments.org.uk

GLOSSARY OF FINANCIAL TERMS

AER (ANNUAL EQUIVALENT RATE) – A notional rate quoted on savings and investment products which demonstrates the return on interest, when compounded and paid annually.

APR (ANNUAL PERCENTAGE RATE) – Calculates the total amount of interest payable over the whole term of a product (such as investment or loan), allowing

MAJOR RETAIL BANKS' FINANCIAL RESULTS 2009

Bank group	*Profit/(loss) before taxation £ million*	*Profit/(loss) after taxation £ million*	*Total assets £ million*
Banco Santander Group*	10,322	7,847	974,378
Barclays	11,642	10,288	1,378,929
Cooperative Bank	203	141	46,119
HSBC	4,601	4,351	1,536,894
Lloyds Banking Group†	1,042	2,953	1,027,255
Northern Rock‡	(258)	(277)	75,569
RBS Group	(1,928)	(1,589)	1,522,481

* Incorporates Abbey National and Alliance & Leicester PLC
† Includes Lloyds TSB and Halifax Bank of Scotland (HBOS)
‡ In February 2008 Northern Rock was taken into public ownership

consumers to compare rival products on a like-for-like basis. Companies offering loans, credit cards, mortgages or overdrafts are required by law to provide the APR rate. Where typical APR is shown, it refers to the company's typical borrower and so is given as a best example; rate and costs may vary depending on individual circumstances.

ANNUITY – A type of insurance policy that provides regular income in exchange for a lump sum. The annuity can be bought from a company other than the existing pension provider.

ASU – Accident, sickness and unemployment insurance taken out by a borrower to protect against being unable to work for these reasons. The policy will usually pay a percentage of the normal monthly mortgage repayment if the borrower is unable to work.

ATM (AUTOMATED TELLER MACHINES) – Commonly referred to as cash machines. Users can access their bank accounts using a card for simple transactions such as withdrawing and depositing cash. Some banks and independent ATM deployers charge for transactions.

BANKER'S DRAFT – A cheque drawn on a bank against a cash deposit. Considered to be a secure way of receiving money in instances where a cheque could 'bounce' or where it is not desirable to receive cash.

BASE RATE – The interest rate set by the Bank of England at which it will lend to financial institutions. This acts as a benchmark for all other interest rates.

BASIS POINT – Unit of measure (usually one-hundredth of a percentage point) used to express movements in interest rates, foreign rates or bond yields.

BUY-TO-LET – The purchase of a residential property for the sole purpose of letting to a tenant. Not all lenders provide mortgage finance for this purpose. Buy-to-let lenders assess projected rental income (typical expectations are between 125 and 130 per cent of the monthly interest payment) in addition to, or instead of, the borrower's income. Buy-to-let mortgages are available as either interest only or repayment.

CAPITAL GAIN/LOSS – Increase/decrease in the value of a capital asset when it is sold or transferred compared to its initial worth.

CAPPED RATE MORTGAGE – The interest rate applied to a loan is guaranteed not to rise above a certain rate for a set period of time; the rate can therefore fall but will not rise above the capped rate. The level at which the cap is fixed is usually higher than for a fixed rate mortgage for a comparable period of time. The lender normally imposes early redemption penalties within the first few years.

CASH CARD – Issued by banks and building societies for withdrawing cash from ATMs.

CHARGE CARD – Charge cards, eg American Express and Diners Club, can be used in a similar way to credit cards but the debt must be settled in full each month.

CHIP AND PIN CARD – A credit/debit card which incorporates an embedded chip containing unique owner details. When used with a PIN, such cards offer greater security as they are less prone to fraud. Since 14 February 2006, most card transactions in the UK have required the use of a chip and pin card.

CREDIT CARD – Normally issued with a credit limit, credit cards can be used for purchases until the limit is reached. There is normally an interest-free period on the outstanding balance of up to 56 days. Charges can be avoided if the balance is paid off in full within the interest-free period. Alternatively part of the balance can be paid and in most cases there is a minimum amount set by the issuer (normally a percentage of the outstanding balance) which must be paid on a monthly basis. Some card issuers charge an annual fee and most issuers belong to a least one major credit card network, eg Mastercard or Visa.

CREDIT RATING – Overall credit worthiness of a borrower based on information from a credit reference agency, such as Experian or Equifax, which holds details of credit agreements, payment records, county court judgements etc for all adults in the UK. This information is supplied to lenders who use it in their credit scoring or underwriting systems to calculate the risk of granting a loan to an individual and the probability that it will be repaid. Each lender sets their own criteria for credit worthiness and may accept or reject a credit application based on an individual's credit rating.

CRITICAL ILLNESS COVER – Insurance that covers borrowers against critical illnesses such as stroke, heart attack or cancer and is designed to protect mortgage or other loan payments.

DEBIT CARD – Debit cards were introduced on a large scale in the UK in the mid-1980s, replacing cash and cheques to purchase goods and services. They can be used to withdraw cash from ATMs in the UK and abroad and may also function as a cheque guarantee card. Funds are automatically withdrawn from an individual's bank account after making a purchase and no interest is charged.

DIRECT DEBIT – An instruction from a customer to their bank, which authorises the payee to charge costs to the customer's bank account.

DISCOUNTED MORTGAGE – Discounted mortgages guarantee an interest rate set at a margin below the standard variable rate for a period of time. The discounted rate will move up or down with the standard variable rate, but the payment rate will retain the agreed differential below the standard variable rate. The lender normally imposes early redemption penalties within the first few years.

EARLY REDEMPTION PENALTY – *see* Redemption Penalty

ENDOWMENT MORTGAGE – Only the interest on a property loan is paid back to the lender each month as long as an endowment life insurance policy is taken out for an agreed amount of time, typically 25 years. When the policy matures the lender will take repayment of the money owed on the property loan and any surplus goes to the policyholder. If the endowment policy shows a shortfall on projected returns, the policy holder must make further provision to pay off the mortgage.

EQUITY – When applied to real estate, equity is the difference between the value of a property and the amount outstanding on any loan secured against it. Negative equity occurs when the loan is greater than the market value of the property.

FIXED RATE MORTGAGE – A repayment mortgage where the interest rate on the loan is fixed for a set amount of time, normally a period of between one and ten years. The interest rate does not vary with changes to the base rate resulting in the monthly mortgage payment remaining the same for the duration of the fixed period. The lender normally imposes early redemption penalties within the first few years.

INTEREST ONLY MORTGAGE – Only interest is paid by the borrower and capital remains constant for the term of the loan. The onus is on the borrower to make provision to repay the capital at the end of the term. This is usually achieved through an investment vehicle such as an endowment policy or pension.

ISA – The individual savings account is a means by which investors can save and invest without paying any tax on the proceeds. Money can be invested across three investment elements: cash, stocks and shares and life insurance products. There are limits on the amount that can be invested during any given tax year.

LOAN TO VALUE (LTV) – This is the ratio between the size of a mortgage loan sought and the mortgage lender's valuation. On a loan of £55,000, for example, on a property valued at £100,000 the loan to value is 55 per cent. This means that there is sufficient equity in the property for the lender to be reassured that if interest or capital repayments were stopped, it could sell the property and recoup the money owed. Fewer options are available to borrowers requiring high LTV.

LONDON INTERBANK OFFERED RATE (LIBOR) – Is the interest rate that London banks charge when lending to one another on the wholesale money market. LIBOR is set by supply and demand of money as banks lend to each other in order to balance their books on a daily basis.

MIG (MORTGAGE INDEMNITY GUARANTEE) – An insurance for the lender paid by the borrower on high LTV mortgages (typically more than 90 per cent). It is a policy designed to protect the lender against loss in the event of the borrower defaulting or ceasing to repay a mortgage and is usually paid as a one-off premium or can be added to the value of the loan. It offers no protection to the borrower. Not all lenders charge MIG premiums.

PERSONAL PENSION PLAN (PPP) – Designed for the self-employed or those in non-pensionable employment. Contributions made to a PPP are exempt from tax and the retirement age may be selected at any time from age 50 to 75. Up to 25 per cent of the pension fund may be taken as a tax-free cash sum on retirement.

PHISHING – A fraudulent attempt to obtain bank account details and security codes through an email. The email purports to come from a *bona fide* bank or building society and attempts to steer the recipient, usually under the pretext that the banking institution is updating its security arrangements, to a website which requests personal details.

PIN (PERSONAL IDENTIFICATION NUMBER) – A PIN is issued alongside a cash card to allow the user to access a bank account via an ATM. PINs are also issued with smart, credit and debit cards and, since 14 February 2006, have been requested in the majority of shops and restaurants as a security measure when making a purchase.

PORTABLE MORTGAGE – A mortgage product that can be transferred to a different property in the event of a house move. Preferable where early redemption penalties are charged.

REDEMPTION PENALTY – A charge levied for paying off a loan, debt balance or mortgage before a date agreed with the lender.

REPAYMENT MORTGAGE – In contrast to the interest only mortgage, the monthly repayment includes an element of the capital sum borrowed in addition to the interest charged.

SELF-CERTIFICATION – Some lenders allow borrowers to self-certify their income. This type of scheme is useful to the self-employed who may not have accounts available or any other person who has difficulty proving their regular income.

SHARE – A share is a divided-up unit of the value of a company. If a company is worth £100m, and there are 50 million shares in issue, then each share is worth £2 (usually listed as pence). As the overall value of the company fluctuates so does the share price.

SMART CARD – *see* chip and pin card

STANDING ORDER – An instruction made by the customer to their bank, which allows the transfer of a set amount to a payee at regular intervals.

TELEPHONE BANKING – Banking facilities which can be accessed via the telephone.

UNIT TRUST – A 'pooled' fund of assets, usually shares, owned by a number of individuals. Managed by professional, authorised fund-management groups, unit trusts have traditionally delivered better returns than average cash deposits, but do rise and fall in value as their underlying investment varies in value.

VARIABLE RATE MORTGAGE – Repayment mortgages where the interest rate set by the lender increases or decreases in relation to the base interest rate which can result in fluctuating monthly repayments.

WITH-PROFITS – Usually applies to pensions, endowments, savings schemes or bonds. The intention is to smooth out the rises and falls in the stock market for the benefit of the investor. Actuaries working for the insurance company, or fund managers, hold back some profits in good years in order to make up the difference in years when shares perform badly.

FINANCIAL SERVICES REGULATION

FINANCIAL SERVICES AUTHORITY

The FSA has been the single regulator for financial services in the UK since 1 December 2001, when the Financial Services and Markets Act 2000 (FSMA) came into force. As at May 2010, the FSA is required to pursue five statutory objectives:

- maintaining market confidence
- contributing to financial stability
- raising public awareness
- protecting consumers
- reducing financial crime

The legislation also requires the FSA to have regard to the following principles while carrying out its general functions:

- using its resources in an economic and efficient way
- the responsibilities of regulated firms' own management
- being proportionate in imposing burdens or restrictions on the industry
- facilitating innovation
- the international character of financial services and the competitive position of the UK
- not impeding or distorting competition unnecessarily

ORGANISATION AND STRUCTURE

The FSA is a company limited by guarantee and financed by levies on the industry. It receives no funds from the public purse. It is accountable to treasury ministers and, through them, to parliament. The FSA must report annually on the achievement of its statutory objectives to the Treasury, which is required to lay the report before parliament. The FSA's budget for 2010–11 is £458m.

FSA REGISTER

The FSA register is a public record of financial services firms, individuals and other bodies who come under the FSA's regulatory jurisdiction as defined in the FSMA. The register has information on all authorised firms currently doing business in the UK. It includes firms that are UK registered as well as those authorised in other European economic area states that conduct business in the UK. Each entry outlines exactly what regulated activities the firm or individual is authorised to carry out.

FINANCIAL SERVICES AUTHORITY, 25 The North Colonnade, Canary Wharf, London E14 5HS **T** 020-7066 1000
W www.fsa.gov.uk
Chair, Lord Turner of Ecchinswell
Chief Executive, Hector Sants

COMPENSATION

Created under the FSMA, the Financial Services Compensation Scheme (FSCS) is the UK's statutory fund of last resort for customers of authorised financial services firms. It provides compensation if a firm authorised by the FSA is unable, or likely to be unable, to pay claims against it. In general this is when a firm has stopped trading and has insufficient assets to meet claims, or is in insolvency. The FSCS covers deposits, insurance policies, insurance broking, investment business and mortgage advice and arranging. The FSCS is independent of the FSA, with separate staff and premises. However, the FSA appoints the board of the FSCS and sets its guidelines. The FSCS is funded by levies on authorised firms.

The Pension Protection Fund (PPF) is a statutory fund established under the Pensions Act 2004 and became operational on 6 April 2005. The fund was set up to pay compensation to members of eligible defined benefit pension schemes, where there is a qualifying insolvency event in relation to the employer and where there are insufficient assets in the pension scheme to cover PPF levels of compensation. Compulsory annual levies are charged on all eligible schemes to help fund the PPF, in addition to investment of PPF assets.

FINANCIAL SERVICES COMPENSATION SCHEME, 7th Floor, Lloyds Chambers, Portsoken Street, London E1 8BN
T 020-7892 7300/0800-678 1100 **E** enquiries@fscs.org.uk
W www.fscs.org.uk
Chair, David Hall
Chief Executive, Mark Neale

PENSION PROTECTION FUND, Knollys House, 17 Addiscombe Road, Croydon, Surrey CR0 6SR **T** 0845-600 2541
E information@ppf.gsi.gov.uk
W www.pensionprotectionfund.org.uk
Chair, Lady Barbara Judge
Chief Executive, Alan Rubenstein

DESIGNATED PROFESSIONAL BODIES

Professional firms are exempt from requiring direct regulation by the FSA if they carry out only certain restricted activities that arise out of, or are complementary to, the provision of professional services, such as arranging the sale of shares on the instructions of executors or trustees, or providing services to small, private companies. These firms are, however, supervised by designated professional bodies (DPBs). There are a number of safeguards to protect consumers dealing with firms that do not require direct regulation. These arrangements include:

- the FSA's power to ban a specific firm from taking advantage of the exemption and to restrict the regulated activities permitted to the firms
- rules which require professional firms to ensure that their clients are aware that they are not authorised persons
- a requirement for the DPBs to supervise and regulate the firms and inform the FSA on how the professional firms carry on their regulated activities

See Professional Education section for details of the following DPBs:
Association of Chartered Certified Accountants
Council for Licensed Conveyancers
Institute and Faculty of Actuaries
Institute of Chartered Accountants in England and Wales
Institute of Chartered Accountants in Ireland
Institute of Chartered Accountants of Scotland

Law Society of England and Wales
Law Society of Northern Ireland
Law Society of Scotland
Royal Institution of Chartered Surveyors

RECOGNISED INVESTMENT EXCHANGES

The FSA currently supervises six recognised investment exchanges (RIEs) in the UK; under the FSMA, recognition confers an exemption from the need to be authorised to carry out regulated activities in the UK. The RIEs are organised markets on which member firms can trade investments such as equities and derivatives. As a regulator the FSA must focus on the impact of changes brought about by the continued growth in electronic trading by exchanges and other organisations. Issues such as how these changes affect market quality, reliability and access are important and the FSA works with the exchanges to ensure that new systems meet regulatory requirements. The RIEs are listed with their year of recognition in parentheses:

EUROPEAN DERIVATIVES EXCHANGE (EDX) LONDON (2003), 10 Paternoster Square, London EC4M 7LS **T** 020-7797 4683 **W** www.londonstockexchange.com/edx (*see also* London Stock Exchange)

INTERCONTINENTAL EXCHANGE (ICE) FUTURES EUROPE (2001), 5th Floor, Milton Gate, 60 Chiswell Street, London EC1Y 4SA **T** 020-7065 7700 **W** www.theice.com

LONDON INTERNATIONAL FINANCIAL FUTURES (LIFFE) ADMINISTRATION AND MANAGEMENT (2001), Cannon Bridge House, 1 Cousin Lane, London EC4R 3XX **T** 020-7623 0444 **W** www.liffe.com

LONDON METAL EXCHANGE (2001), 56 Leadenhall Street, London EC3A 2BJ **T** 020-7264 5555 **W** www.lme.co.uk

LONDON STOCK EXCHANGE (LSE) (2001), 10 Paternoster Square, London EC4M 7LS **T** 020-7797 1000 **W** www.londonstockexchange.com

PLUS MARKETS (2007), Standon House, 21 Mansell Street, London E1 8AA **T** 020-7553 2046 **W** www.plusmarketsgroup.com

RECOGNISED CLEARING HOUSES

The FSA is also responsible for recognising and supervising recognised clearing houses (RCHs), which organise the settlement of transactions on recognised investment exchanges. There are currently four RCHs in the UK:

EUROCLEAR UK AND IRELAND (2001), Watling House, 33 Cannon Street, London EC4M 5SB **T** 020-7849 0000 **W** www.crestco.co.uk

EUROPEAN CENTRAL COUNTERPARTY (2008), Broadgate West, 1 Snowdon Street, London EC2A 2DQ **T** 020-7650 1401 **W** www.euroccp.co.uk

ICE CLEAR EUROPE (2008), 5th Floor, Milton Gate, 60 Chiswell Street, London EC1Y 4SA **T** 020-7265 3648 **W** www.theice.com/clear_europe

LONDON CLEARING HOUSE (LCH) CLEARNET (2001), Aldgate House, 33 Aldgate High Street, London EC3N 1EA **T** 020-7426 7000 **W** www.lchclearnet.com

OMBUDSMAN SCHEMES

The Financial Ombudsman Service was set up by the Financial Services and Markets Act 2000 to provide consumers with a free, independent service for resolving disputes with authorised financial firms. The Financial Ombudsman Service can consider complaints about most financial matters including: banking; credit cards and store cards; financial advice; hire purchase and pawnbroking; insurance; loans and credit; mortgages; pensions; savings and investments; stocks, shares, unit trusts and bonds.

Complainants must first complain to the firm involved. They do not have to accept the ombudsman's decision and are free to go to court if they wish, but if a decision is accepted, it is binding for both the complainant and the firm.

The Pensions Ombudsman can investigate and decide complaints and disputes about the way that occupational and personal pension schemes are administered and managed. The Pensions Ombudsman is also the Ombudsman for the Pension Protection Fund (PPF) and the Financial Assistance Scheme (which offers help to those who were a member of an under-funded defined benefit pension scheme that started to wind-up in specific financial circumstances between 1 January 1997 and 5 April 2005).

FINANCIAL OMBUDSMAN SERVICE, South Quay Plaza, 183 Marsh Wall, London E14 9SR Helpline 0845-080 1800 **T** 020-7964 1000
E complaint.info@financial-ombudsman.org.uk
W www.financial-ombudsman.org.uk
Chief Executive and Chief Ombudsman, Natalie Ceeney
Principal Ombudsmen, Tony Boorman; David Thomas

PENSIONS OMBUDSMAN, 11 Belgrave Road, London SW1V 1RB **T** 020-7630 2200 **E** enquiries@pensions-ombudsman.org.uk
W www.pensions-ombudsman.org.uk
Pensions Ombudsman, Tony King
Deputy Pensions Ombudsman, Jane Irvine

PANEL ON TAKEOVERS AND MERGERS

The Panel on Takeovers and Mergers is an independent body, established in 1968, whose main functions are to issue and administer the City code and to ensure equality of treatment and opportunity for all shareholders in takeover bids and mergers. The panel's statutory functions are set out in the Companies Act 2006.

The panel comprises up to 34 members drawn from major financial and business institutions. The chair, deputy chair and up to 20 independent members are nominated by the panel's own nomination committee. The remaining members are nominated by professional bodies representing the banking, insurance, investment, pension and accountancy industries and the CBI.

PANEL ON TAKEOVERS AND MERGERS, 10 Paternoster Square, London EC4M 7DY **T** 020-7382 9026
W www.thetakeoverpanel.org.uk
Chair, Sir Gordon Langley

NATIONAL SAVINGS AND INVESTMENTS

NS&I (National Savings and Investments) is an executive agency of HM Treasury and one of the UK's largest financial providers, with almost 27 million customers and over £98bn invested. NS&I offers savings and investment products to personal savers and investors and the money is used to manage the national debt. When people invest in NS&I they are lending money to the government which pays them interest or prizes in return. All products are financially secure because they are guaranteed by HM Treasury.

TAX-FREE PRODUCTS

SAVINGS CERTIFICATES

Index-linked Saving Certificates
Otherwise known as inflation-beating savings, index-linked saving certificates are fixed rate investments that pay tax-free returns guaranteed to be above inflation. They are available in three- and five-year terms and are sold in issues. The minimum investment for each issue is £100 and the maximum £15,000.

Fixed Interest Saving Certificates
Fixed interest saving certificates are fixed rate investments that pay tax-free returns. They are available in two- and five-year terms and are sold in issues for which the minimum investment is £100 and the maximum £15,000.

NS&I withdrew index-linked and fixed interest saving certificates from sale on 19 July 2010, as sales had exceeded the level anticipated. Existing customers could continue their investment on the same terms.

PREMIUM BONDS

Introduced in 1956, premium bonds enable savers to enter a regular draw for tax-free prizes, while retaining the right to get their money back. A sum equivalent to interest on each bond is put into a prize fund and distributed by monthly prize draws. The prizes are drawn by ERNIE (electronic random number indicator equipment) and are free of all UK income tax and capital gains tax. A £1m jackpot is drawn each month in addition to other tax-free prizes ranging in value from £25 to £100,000.

Bonds are in units of £1, with a minimum purchase of £100; above this, purchases must be in multiples of £10, up to a maximum holding limit of £30,000 per person. Bonds become eligible for prizes once they have been held for one clear calendar month following the month of purchase. Each £1 unit can win only one prize per draw, but it will be awarded the highest for which it is drawn. Bonds remain eligible for prizes until they are repaid.

The scheme offers a facility to reinvest prize wins automatically. Upon completion of an automatic prize reinvestment mandate, holders receive new bonds which are immediately eligible for future prize draws. Bonds can only be held in the name of an individual and not by organisations.

As at March 2010, over 205 million prizes totalling £12bn had been distributed since the first prize draw in 1957.

CHILDREN'S BONUS BONDS

Children's bonus bonds were introduced in 1991. The bonds are sold in five-year issues at multiples of £25. For each issue the minimum holding is £25 and the maximum holding is £3,000 per child. They can be bought for any child under 16, but must be held by a parent or guardian. All returns are totally exempt from UK income tax and a bonus is payable if the bond is held for the full five years.

OTHER PRODUCTS

GUARANTEED EQUITY BONDS

Guaranteed equity bonds are five-year investments where the returns are linked to the performance of the FTSE-100 index with a guarantee that the original capital invested will be returned even if the FTSE-100 index fell over the five years. They are sold in limited issues with a minimum investment of £1,000 and a maximum of £1m. The returns are subject to income tax on maturity, unless they are held in a self-invested pension plan (SIPP).

SAVINGS AND INVESTMENT ACCOUNTS

The direct saver account was launched in March 2010. Customers are able to invest between £1 and £2m per person. The account can be managed online or by telephone. Interest is paid without deduction of tax at source.

The easy access savings account offers access to savings via Post Office counters, an ATM card, telephone and online. It can be opened with a minimum balance of £100 and has a maximum limit of £2m (£4m jointly). The interest is paid without deduction of tax at source.

The investment account is a passbook account which pays tiered rates of interest. It can be opened with a minimum balance of £20 and has a maximum limit of £100,000. The interest is paid without deduction of tax at source.

Since April 1999 NS&I has offered cash individual savings accounts (ISAs). Its Direct ISA, launched in April 2006, can be opened and managed online and by telephone with a minimum investment of £100. Interest for the Direct ISA is calculated daily and is free of tax.

INCOME BONDS

NS&I income bonds were introduced in 1982. They are suitable for those who want to receive regular monthly payments of interest while preserving the full cash value of their capital. The bonds are sold in multiples of £500. The minimum holding is £500 and the maximum £1m (sole or joint holding). A variable rate of interest is calculated on a day-to-day basis and paid monthly. Interest is taxable but is paid without deduction of tax at source.

GUARANTEED INCOME BONDS

Guaranteed income bonds were introduced in February 2008. They are designed for those who want to receive regular monthly payments of interest while preserving the full cash value of their capital. The minimum holding is £500 and the maximum £1m, including any amount held in guaranteed growth bonds and fixed rate savings bonds (the latter was closed to new investment in 2008). A fixed rate of interest is calculated on a day-to-day basis and paid monthly on these bonds. Interest is taxable and tax is deducted at source.

GUARANTEED GROWTH BONDS
Guaranteed growth bonds were introduced in February 2008. They are suitable for those who want to receive regular monthly payments of interest while preserving the full cash value of their capital. The minimum holding is £500 and the maximum £1m, including any amount held in guaranteed income bonds and fixed rate savings bonds (the latter was closed to new investment in 2008). A fixed rate of interest is calculated on a day-to-day basis and is paid annually on the anniversary of the date of investment. Interest is taxable and tax is deducted at source.

FURTHER INFORMATION
Further information can be obtained online (W www.nsandi.com), by telephone (T 0500-007007) or at Post Office counters.

NATIONAL DEBT

The UK Debt Management Office (DMO), an executive agency of HM Treasury, was created in April 1998 following the transfer of operational responsibility for monetary policy from HM Treasury to the Bank of England. Initially the DMO was responsible only for the management of government marketable debt and for issuing gilts. In April 2000 responsibility for exchequer cash management and for issuing Treasury bills (short-dated securities with maturities of less than one year) was transferred from the Bank of England to the DMO. The national debt also includes the (non-marketable) liabilities of National Savings and Investments and other public sector and foreign currency debt.

In 2002 the operations of the long-standing statutory functions of the Public Works Loan Board, which lends capital to local authorities, and the Commissioners for the Reduction of National Debt, which manages the investment portfolios of certain public funds, were integrated within the DMO (*see also* Government Departments).

Since 2008 the DMO has undertaken a range of activities at the request of HM Treasury to help stabilise the financial markets and support the UK banking sector. These include administering aspects of the government's credit guarantee scheme and the provision of Treasury bills for use in the special liquidity scheme. Since November 2008, the DMO has also undertaken auctions of EU allowances on behalf of the Department of Energy and Climate Change as part of the emissions trading system.

UK NATIONAL DEBT

	£ billion	*Per cent of GDP*
2008–9 (outturn)	617.0	43.8
2009–10 (estimate)	776.6	54.1
2010–11 (projection)	952.0	63.6

Source: HM Treasury: *Budget 2010* (Crown copyright)

THE LONDON STOCK EXCHANGE

The London Stock Exchange serves the needs of companies and investors by providing facilities for raising capital and a central marketplace for securities trading. This marketplace covers UK and overseas company shares and other instruments such as: exchange traded funds (ETFs) and exchange traded commodities (ETCs), Russian and Scandinavian equity derivative products (through EDX London) and both corporate and government bonds.

Over 400 member firms trading on the London Stock Exchange buy and sell securities on behalf of the public, as well as institutions such as pension funds or insurance companies.

The London Stock Exchange is a subsidiary, along with Borsa Italiana, of the London Stock Exchange Group (LSEG).

HISTORY

The London Stock Exchange is one of the world's oldest stock exchanges dating back more than 300 years when it began in the coffee houses of 17th-century London. It was formally established as a membership organisation in 1801.

RECENT DEVELOPMENTS

'BIG BANG'
What has come to be known as 'Big Bang' was a package of reforms in 1986 that transformed the Exchange and the City, liberalising the way in which banks and stock-broking firms operated and bringing in foreign investment. The Exchange ceased granting voting rights to individual members and became a private company. Big Bang also saw the start of a move towards fully electronic trading and the closure of the trading floor.

INTRODUCTION OF SETS
In October 1997, the Exchange introduced SETS, its electronic order book. The system enhanced the efficiency and transparency of trading on the Exchange, allowing trades to be executed automatically and anonymously rather than negotiated by telephone.

DEMUTALISATION AND LISTING
The London Stock Exchange became demutualised in 2000 and listed on its own main market in 2001 in order to allow further commercialisation.

EDX LONDON
In 2003 the London Stock Exchange created EDX London (European derivatives exchange), a recognised investment exchange for international equity derivatives. It now also offers trading in Russian and Scandinavian equity derivatives.

MERGER WITH BORSA ITALIANA
On 1 October 2007 the Exchange merged with the Italian stock exchange Borsa Italiana and London Stock Exchange Group PLC replaced the London Stock Exchange as the listed entity.

PRIMARY MARKETS

The London Stock Exchange enables UK and overseas companies to raise capital for development and growth through the issue of securities. For a company entering the market the Exchange offers a choice of four differently regulated markets, depending upon the size, history and requirements of the company:

- the main market enables established companies to raise capital, widen their investor base and have their shares traded on a global stock market. The market is regulated by the FSA's UK Listing Authority (UKLA). The FTSE 100 index is based on main market stocks
- the Alternative Investment Market (AIM), established in June 1995, is specially designed to meet the needs of small, young and growing companies, enabling them to raise capital, broaden their investor base and benefit from being traded on an internationally recognised market. AIM is regulated by the London Stock Exchange and quoted companies must adhere to the AIM rules and retain a Nominated Adviser (or 'Nomad') at all times, who is responsible for ensuring the company's suitability for the market. The AIM model has been extended to AIM Italia, launched in Italy at the end of 2008, and AIM Tokyo, launched in collaboration with the Tokyo Stock Exchange in spring 2009
- the Professional Securities Market (PSM), established in July 2005 and regulated by the FSA, offers international companies that wish to access an exclusively institutional investor base an option to list equity and debt securities in London on a market that offers greater flexibility in accounting standards
- the Specialist Fund Market (SFM), established in November 2007, is the Exchange's market for highly specialised investment entities, such as hedge funds or private equity funds, that wish to target institutional investors. This market is regulated by the FSA in accordance with standards set out in EU directives

At April 2010 there were 2,736 companies quoted on the London Stock Exchange: 1,121 on the UK main market, with a combined market capitalisation of £1,807.5bn; 324 on the international main market, with a combined market capitalisation of £1,952.6bn; 1,253 on AIM, with a combined market capitalisation of £64.5bn; 32 on the PSM, with a combined market capitalisation of £8.4bn; and six companies listed on the SFM.

LONDON STOCK EXCHANGE, 10 Paternoster Square, London EC4M 7LS **T** 020-7797 1000
W www.londonstockexchange.com
Chair, Dr Christopher Gibson-Smith
Chief Executive, Xavier Rolet

ECONOMIC STATISTICS

THE BUDGET (JUNE 2010)

GOVERNMENT EXPENDITURE

The budgets for departmental expenditure limits (DELs) below reflect policy decisions of the coalition government and reductions to the 2010–11 projections based on the £6.2bn savings package announced in June 2010.

DEPARTMENTAL EXPENDITURE LIMITS *£ billion*

	Outturn 2008–9	*Estimate 2009–10*	*Projection 2010–11*
Resource DEL			
Education	46.8	49.6	50.9
Health	90.3	97.6	101.5
of which NHS England	88.8	96.0	99.5
Transport	5.8	7.0	6.4
Business, Innovation and Skills	17.9	19.2	19.2
Communities	4.1	4.3	3.8
Local Government	24.7	25.5	26.0
Home Office	9.2	9.5	9.4
Justice	9.2	9.6	9.1
Law Officers' Departments	0.7	0.7	0.7
Defence	32.6	35.2	36.0
Foreign and Commonwealth Office	2.0	2.2	2.0
International Development	4.8	5.3	6.1
Energy and Climate Change	0.3	1.2	1.2
Environment, Food and Rural Affairs	2.4	2.5	2.4
Culture, Media and Sport	1.5	1.6	1.5
Work and Pensions	7.9	9.1	8.8
Scotland	24.1	25.1	25.7
Wales	12.8	13.6	13.9
Northern Ireland Executive	7.9	8.8	8.6
Northern Ireland Office	1.2	1.1	1.2
Chancellor's departments	4.5	4.5	4.1
Cabinet Office	2.0	2.2	2.3
Independent bodies	0.8	0.8	1.0
Modernisation funding	0.0	0.0	0.2
Reserve	0.0	0.0	0.6
Allowance for shortfall	0.0	(1.4)	0.0
TOTAL RESOURCE DEL	313.5	334.8	342.7
Capital DEL			
Education	5.5	7.5	6.7
Health	4.4	5.4	4.9
of which NHS England	4.2	5.2	4.7
Transport	7.3	8.3	7.2
Business, Innovation and Skills	2.1	3.0	2.0
Communities	7.1	9.2	6.2
Local Government	0.1	0.2	0.0
Home Office	0.8	1.0	0.8
Justice	0.9	0.9	0.6
Law Officers' Departments	0.0	0.0	0.0
Defence	9.0	9.2	10.1
Foreign and Commonwealth Office	0.2	0.2	0.2
International Development	0.9	1.3	1.6
Energy and Climate Change	1.7	1.9	1.9
Environment, Food and Rural Affairs	0.6	0.7	0.5
Culture, Media and Sport	0.8	0.6	0.5
Work and Pensions	0.1	0.3	0.2
Scotland	3.3	3.9	3.2
Wales	1.6	1.9	1.7
Northern Ireland Executive	1.2	1.2	1.1
Northern Ireland Office	0.1	0.1	0.1
Chancellor's departments	0.3	0.4	0.3
Cabinet Office	0.4	0.5	0.3
Independent bodies	0.0	0.0	0.1
Reserve	0.0	0.0	1.5
Allowance for shortfall	0.0	(1.2)	0.0
TOTAL CAPITAL DEL	48.5	56.6	51.6
Less depreciation	(11.6)	(13.3)	(14.3)
TOTAL DEL	350.4	378.0	380.0

Source: HM Treasury – *Budget 2010* (Crown copyright)

TOTAL MANAGED EXPENDITURE *£ billion*

	Outturn 2008–9	*Estimate 2009–10*	*Projection 2010–11*
Current Expenditure			
Resource Annually Managed Expenditure	251.3	265.8	294.6
Implied Resource DELs	313.5	334.8	342.7
Public sector current expenditure	564.7	600.6	637.3
Capital Expenditure			
Capital Annually Managed Expenditure (AME)	16.6	12.1	7.8
Implied Capital DELs	48.5	56.6	51.6
Public sector gross investment	65.1	68.7	59.5
Less public sector depreciation	(18.7)	(19.7)	(20.6)
Public sector net investment	46.4	49.0	38.9
TOTAL MANAGED EXPENDITURE	629.8	669.3	696.8

Source: HM Treasury – *Budget 2010* (Crown copyright)

THE BUDGET (MARCH 2010)

GOVERNMENT RECEIPTS

£ billion	Outturn 2008–9	Estimate 2009–10	Projection 2010–11
HM Revenue and Customs (HMRC)			
Income tax (gross of tax credits)	153.4	144.4	146.4
Income tax credits	(5.6)	(5.6)	(5.9)
National insurance contributions (NIC)	96.9	94.9	97.0
Value added tax	78.4	70.0	78.0
Corporation tax[1]	43.7	36.0	42.1
Corporation tax credits[2]	(0.6)	(0.7)	(0.8)
Petroleum revenue tax	2.6	0.8	1.6
Fuel duties	24.6	26.2	27.5
Capital gains tax	7.8	2.5	2.7
Inheritance tax	2.8	2.4	2.3
Stamp duties	8.0	7.7	9.8
Tobacco duties	8.2	8.8	8.8
Spirits duties	2.4	2.6	2.6
Wine duties	2.7	3.0	3.1
Beer and cider duties	3.4	3.5	3.6
Betting and gaming duties	1.5	1.4	1.4
Air passenger duty	1.9	1.9	2.4
Insurance premium tax	2.3	2.3	2.3
Landfill tax	1.0	0.8	1.1
Climate change levy	0.7	0.7	0.7
Aggregates levy	0.3	0.3	0.3
Customs duties and levies	2.7	2.6	2.6
Temporary bank payroll tax[3]	0.0	0.0	2.0
TOTAL HMRC	439.1	406.5	431.8
Vehicle excise duties	5.6	5.7	6.0
Business rates	22.9	23.7	24.7
Council tax[4]	24.4	24.8	25.8
Other taxes and royalties[5]	16.0	15.7	18.7
NET TAXES AND NIC[6]	507.9	476.4	507.0
Accruals adjustments on taxes	(4.2)	1.4	4.0
Less own resources contribution to European Union (EU) budget	(5.1)	(3.8)	(4.6)
Less private company corporation tax payments	(0.2)	(0.2)	(0.2)
Tax credits adjustment[7]	0.7	0.7	0.8
Interest and dividends	7.7	4.2	4.4
Other receipts[8]	26.8	28.7	29.5
CURRENT RECEIPTS	533.5	507.5	540.8
North Sea revenues[9]	12.9	6.4	8.5

1 National accounts measure: gross of enhanced and payable tax credits

2 Includes enhanced company tax credits

3 Bank payroll tax on a cash basis

4 Council tax increases are projections determined annually by local authorities, not by the government

5 Includes VAT refunds and money paid into the National Lottery Distribution Fund

6 Includes VAT and 'traditional own resources' contributions to EU budget

7 Tax credits which are scored as negative tax in the calculation of net taxes and NIC but expenditure in the national accounts

8 Includes gross operating surplus, rent and business rate payments by local authorities

9 Consists of North Sea corporation tax and petroleum revenue tax

Source: HM Treasury – *Budget 2010: Securing the Recovery* (Crown copyright)

GOVERNMENT EXPENDITURE

The 1998 Economic and Fiscal Strategy Report introduced changes to the public expenditure control regime. Three-year departmental expenditure limits (DELs) now apply to most government departments. Spending which cannot easily be subject to three-year planning is reviewed annually in the budget as annually managed expenditure (AME). Current and capital expenditure are treated separately.

DEPARTMENTAL EXPENDITURE LIMITS

£ billion	Outturn 2008–9	Estimate 2009–10	Projection 2010–11
Resource DEL			
Children, Schools and Families	46.8	49.6	51.5
Health	92.3	99.6	104.1
of which NHS England	90.7	98.0	102.1
Transport	5.7	6.9	7.0
Business, Innovation and Skills	18.0	19.5	19.6
Communities	4.2	4.5	4.4
Local Government	24.7	25.5	26.3
Home Office	9.2	9.5	9.8
Justice	9.1	9.9	9.4
Law Officers' Departments	0.7	0.7	0.7
Defence	36.7	39.1	40.4
Foreign and Commonwealth Office	2.1	2.3	2.2
International Development	4.8	5.4	6.2
Energy and Climate Change	0.4	1.2	1.2
Environment, Food and Rural Affairs	2.6	2.7	2.7
Culture, Media and Sport	1.5	1.7	1.7
Work and Pensions	8.0	9.1	9.3
Scotland	24.6	25.6	26.2
Wales	12.9	14.0	14.0
Northern Ireland Executive	8.0	9.0	8.7
Northern Ireland Office	1.3	1.2	1.2
Chancellor's departments	4.5	4.5	4.3
Cabinet Office	2.1	2.2	2.4
Independent bodies	0.8	0.9	1.0
Modernisation funding	0.0	0.0	0.2
Reserve	0.0	0.0	0.8
Allowance for shortfall	0.0	(1.2)	0.0
TOTAL RESOURCE DEL	321.1	343.5	355.1
Capital DEL			
Children, Schools and Families	5.5	7.5	6.7
Health	4.4	5.4	4.7
of which NHS England	4.2	5.2	4.5
Transport	7.2	8.3	7.7
Business, Innovation, and Skills	2.1	3.0	2.4

Communities	7.1	9.1	6.4
Local Government	0.1	0.2	0.1
Home Office	0.8	1.0	0.8
Justice	0.9	0.9	0.7
Law Officers' Departments	0.0	0.0	0.0
Defence	8.7	9.2	10.1
Foreign and Commonwealth Office	0.2	0.2	0.2
International Development	0.9	1.3	1.6
Energy and Climate Change	1.7	1.9	2.0
Environment, Food and Rural Affairs	0.6	0.7	0.6
Culture, Media and Sport	0.9	0.6	0.6
Work and Pensions	0.1	0.3	0.3
Scotland	3.3	3.9	3.2
Wales	1.6	2.0	1.7
Northern Ireland Executive	1.2	1.2	1.1
Northern Ireland Office	0.1	0.1	0.1
Chancellor's departments	0.3	0.4	0.3
Cabinet Office	0.4	0.5	0.4
Independent bodies	0.0	0.0	0.1
Reserve	0.0	0.0	1.5
Allowance for shortfall	0.0	(1.2)	0.0
TOTAL CAPITAL DEL	48.1	56.6	53.0
Less depreciation	(11.6)	(13.5)	(14.7)
TOTAL DEL	357.6	386.7	393.4

Source: HM Treasury – *Budget 2010: Securing the Recovery* (Crown copyright)

ANNUALLY MANAGED EXPENDITURE *£ billion*

	Outturn 2008–9	*Estimate 2009–10*	*Projection 2010–11*
Resource AME			
Social security benefits[1]	149.7	163.7	170.0
Tax credits[1]	19.9	22.9	23.6
Net public service pensions[2]	3.1	3.4	4.4
National Lottery	1.0	0.9	0.9
BBC domestic services	3.4	3.5	3.7
Other departmental expenditure	1.3	(0.1)	1.3
Net expenditure transfers to EU institutions[3]	3.1	6.4	7.6
Locally financed expenditure[4]	26.8	26.8	28.1
Central government gross debt interest	30.5	30.8	41.6
AME margin	0.0	0.0	0.9
Accounting adjustments	3.9	2.8	6.8
TOTAL RESOURCE AME	242.6	261.1	288.9
Capital AME			
National Lottery	0.5	1.0	0.9
Locally financed expenditure[4]	7.5	6.5	5.1
Public corporations' own-financed capital expenditure	7.8	7.0	7.6
Central government grants to public sector banks	9.4	4.5	0.0
Other capital expenditure	0.2	1.8	2.5
AME margin	0.0	0.0	0.1
Accounting adjustments	(7.6)	(8.0)	(9.2)
TOTAL CAPITAL AME	17.8	12.8	7.0

[1] Child allowances in income support and jobseeker's allowance are included under tax credits
[2] Reported on a national accounts basis
[3] AME spending component only
[4] This expenditure is mainly financed by council tax revenues
Source: HM Treasury – *Budget 2010: Securing the Recovery* (Crown copyright)

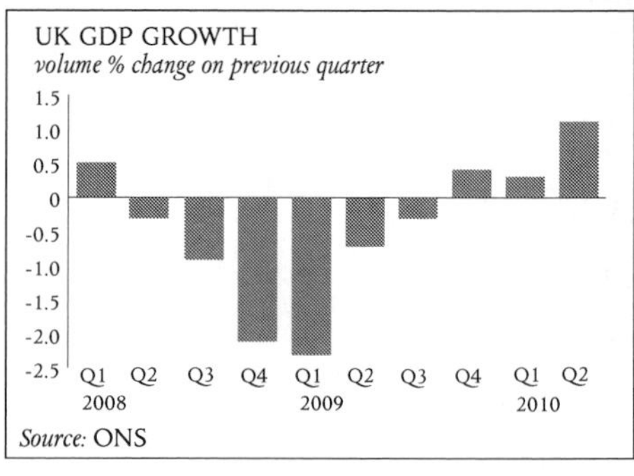

Source: ONS

TRADE

TRADE IN GOODS

	Exports	*Imports*	*£ million Balance*
1999	166,166	195,217	(29,051)
2000	187,936	220,912	(32,976)
2001	189,093	230,305	(41,212)
2002	186,524	234,229	(47,705)
2003	188,320	236,927	(48,607)
2004	190,874	251,774	(60,900)
2005	211,608	280,197	(68,589)
2006	243,635	319,947	(76,312)
2007	220,858	310,612	(89,754)
2008	251,643	345,024	(93,381)
2009	227,670	309,460	(81,790)

Source: ONS – *Annual Abstract of Statistics 2010* (Crown copyright)

BALANCE OF PAYMENTS, 2009

Current Account	*£ million*
Trade in goods and services	
Trade in goods	(81,790)
Trade in services	49,313
Total trade in goods and services	(32,477)
Income	
Compensation of employees	(688)
Investment income	29,344
Total income	28,656
Total current transfers	(14,614)
TOTAL (CURRENT BALANCE)	(18,435)

Source: ONS – *Annual Abstract of Statistics 2010* (Crown copyright)

EMPLOYMENT

DISTRIBUTION OF THE WORKFORCE

	2008	2009
Claimant count	905,100	1,531,800
Workforce jobs	31,661,000	30,987,000
HM forces	193,000	197,000
Self-employment jobs	4,181,000	4,222,000
Employees jobs	27,232,000	26,522,000
Government-supported trainees	54,000	46,000

Source: ONS – *Annual Abstract of Statistics 2010* (Crown copyright)

EMPLOYMENT, 2009

Thousands

Age	*Male*	*Female*
16–17	196	234
18–24	1,788	1,661
25–34	3,404	2,818
35–49	5,744	5,171
50–64(m)/59(f)	3,922	2,658
65+(m)/60+(f)	443	940
All aged 16+	15,497	13,482

m = male, f = female

Source: ONS – *Annual Abstract of Statistics 2010* (Crown copyright)

UNEMPLOYMENT, 2009

Thousands

Age	*Male*	*Female*
16–17	110	90
18–24	444	271
25–34	313	198
35–49	336	260
50–64(m)/59(f)	246	90
65+(m)/60+(f)	16	20
All aged 16+	1,465	930

Source: ONS – *Annual Abstract of Statistics 2010* (Crown copyright)

UNEMPLOYMENT RATES BY REGION

per cent

	2008	*2009*
North East	7.6	9.2
North West	6.7	8.4
Yorkshire and The Humber	6.1	8.6
East Midlands	5.8	7.2
West Midlands	6.7	9.8
East	4.8	6.3
London	7.1	8.8
South East	4.4	5.9
South West	4.1	6.3
Wales	6.0	8.2
Scotland	4.6	7.0
Northern Ireland	4.5	6.5

Source: ONS – *Annual Abstract of Statistics 2010* (Crown copyright)

DURATION OF UNEMPLOYMENT, 2009

	Thousands
All unemployed	2,395
Duration of unemployment	
Less than 6 months	1,325
6 months–1 year	483
1 year +	587
1 year + as percentage of total	24.5

Source: ONS – *Annual Abstract of Statistics 2010* (Crown copyright)

MEDIAN* EARNINGS AND HOURS OF FULL-TIME EMPLOYEES, 2009

	All	*Male*	*Female*
Median gross weekly earnings (£)	488.7	531.1	426.4
Median total paid hours	37.5	38.7	37.0
Median hourly earnings (£)			
Including overtime	12.43	13.09	11.42
Excluding overtime	12.34	12.97	11.40

* Median values are less affected by extremes of earnings at either end of the scale

Source: ONS – *Annual Abstract of Statistics 2010* (Crown copyright)

NUMBER OF TAXPAYERS BY ANNUAL INCOME*, 2009

	Number of taxpayers (thousands)
£6,475†–£7,499	990
£7,500–£9,999	2,650
£10,000–£14,999	6,290
£15,000–£19,999	5,060
£20,000–£29,999	6,680
£30,000–£49,999	5,270
£50,000–£99,999	1,800
£100,000–£149,999	304
£150,000–£199,999	117
£200,000–£499,999	134
£500,000–£999,999	26
£1,000,000+	11
All incomes	29,300

* Includes investment income

† Basic personal tax-free allowance for 2009–10

Source: ONS – *Social Trends 2010* (Crown copyright)

LABOUR DISPUTES BY DURATION, 2008

Under 5 days	136
5–10 days	5
10–20 days	1
20–30 days	–
30–50 days	1
50+ days	1

Source: ONS – *Annual Abstract of Statistics 2010* (Crown copyright)

WORKING DAYS LOST THROUGH LABOUR DISPUTES BY INDUSTRY, 2008

Mining, quarrying, electricity, gas and water	1,000
Manufacturing	7,000
Construction	3,000
Transport, storage and communication	25,000
Public administration and defence	614,000
Education	103,000
Health and social work	2,000
Other community, social and personal services	3,000
All other industries and services	2,000

Source: ONS – *Annual Abstract of Statistics 2010* (Crown copyright)

TRADE UNIONS

Year	*No. of unions*	*Total membership*
2000–1	237	7,897,519
2001–2	226	7,779,393
2002–3	216	7,750,990
2003–4	213	7,735,983
2004–5	206	7,559,062
2005–6	193	7,473,000
2006–7	192	7,602,842
2007–8	193	7,627,693
2008–9	185	7,656,156

Source: ONS – *Annual Abstract of Statistics 2010* (Crown copyright)

HOUSEHOLD INCOME AND EXPENDITURE

AVERAGE HOUSEHOLD INCOME, 2008

Income by source	*£ per week*	*Percentage of total*
Wages and Salaries	476.30	67
Self-employment	66.10	9
Investments	27.80	4
Annuities and pensions	48.70	7
Social security benefits*	88.70	12
Other sources	5.50	1
Total	713.10	100

* Excluding housing and council tax benefit

Source: ONS – *Annual Abstract of Statistics 2010* (Crown copyright)

AVERAGE HOUSEHOLD EXPENDITURE, 2008

Commodity or service	*£ per week*	*Percentage of total*
Housing	94.00	20
Fuel and power	18.90	4
Food and non-alcoholic drinks	74.50	16
Alcoholic drink	13.40	3
Tobacco	4.60	1
Clothing and footwear	21.20	5
Household goods	34.00	7
Household services	27.30	6
Personal goods and services	17.20	4
Motoring	63.60	14
Fares and other travel costs	14.20	3
Leisure goods	19.00	4
Leisure services	65.90	14
Miscellaneous	2.00	–
Total	469.70	100

Source: ONS – *Annual Abstract of Statistics 2010* (Crown copyright)

HOUSEHOLD OWNERSHIP OF SELECTED DURABLE GOODS

Percentages

	2000–1	*2008*
Car/van	72	74
One	44	43
Two	22	25
Three+	6	6
Central heating (full or partial)	91	95
Washing machine	92	96
Tumble dryer	53	59
Fridge/freezer or deep freezer	94	97
Dishwasher	25	38
Microwave	84	92
Telephone	93	90
Mobile phone	47	79
Home computer	44	72
Video recorder	87	70
DVD player	–	88
CD player	77	86
Digital television service	40	82
Internet connection	32	66

Source: ONS – *Annual Abstract of Statistics 2010* (Crown copyright)

INDIVIDUAL INSOLVENCIES

	2000	*2005*	*2009*
England and Wales	29,528	67,584	134,142
Scotland	5,766	11,846	23,482
Northern Ireland	616	1,454	1,959
Total	35,910	80,884	159,583

Source: ONS – *Annual Abstract of Statistics 2010* (Crown copyright)

COST OF LIVING AND INFLATION RATES

The first cost of living index to be calculated took July 1914 as 100 and was based on the pattern of expenditure of working-class families in 1914. The cost of living index was superseded in 1947 by the general index of retail prices (RPI), although the older term is still popularly applied.

The Harmonised Index of Consumer Prices (HICP) was introduced in 1997 to enable comparisons within the European Union using an agreed methodology. In 2003 the National Statistician renamed the HICP as the Consumer Prices Index (CPI) to reflect its role as the main target measure of inflation for macroeconomic purposes. The RPI and indices based on it continue to be published alongside the CPI. Pensions, benefits and index-linked gilts continue to be calculated with reference to RPI or its derivatives.

CPI AND RPI

The CPI and RPI measure the changes month by month in the average level of prices of goods and services purchased by households in the UK. The indices are compiled using a selection of around 650 goods and services, and the prices charged for these items are collected at regular intervals at about 150 locations throughout the country. The Office for National Statistics (ONS) reviews the components of the indices once every year to reflect changes in consumer preferences and the establishment of new products. The table below shows changes made by the ONS to the CPI 'shopping basket' in 2010.

CPI excludes a number of items that are included in RPI, mainly related to housing such as council tax and a range of owner-occupier housing costs, such as mortgage payments. The CPI covers all private households, whereas RPI excludes the top 4 per cent by income and pensioner households who derive at least three-quarters of their income from state benefits. The two indices use different methodologies to combine the prices of goods and services, which means that since 1996 the CPI inflation measure is less than the RPI inflation measure.

INFLATION RATE

The 12-monthly percentage change in the 'all items' index of the RPI or CPI is referred to as the rate of inflation. As the most familiar measure of inflation, RPI is often referred to as the 'headline rate of inflation'. CPI is the main measure of inflation for macroeconomic purposes and forms the basis for the government's inflation target, which is currently 2 per cent. The percentage change in prices between any two months/years can be obtained using the following formula:

$$\frac{\text{Later date RPI/CPI} - \text{Earlier date RPI/CPI}}{\text{Earlier date RPI/CPI}} \times 100$$

eg to find the CPI rate of inflation for 2006, using the annual averages for 2005 and 2006:

$$\frac{102.3 - 100.0}{100.0} \times 100 = 2.3$$

CHANGES TO THE 2010 'SHOPPING BASKET' OF GOODS AND SERVICES

The table below shows changes to the 2010 CPI* basket of goods and services made by the ONS in order to reflect changes in consumer preferences and the establishment of new products.

Goods and services group	*Removed items*	*New items*
Audio-visual equipment and related products	disposable camera	blu-ray disc player
Food	baby food; pitta bread	cereal bars; frozen fish (in breadcrumbs/batter); garlic bread; powdered baby formula
Footwear	men's training shoe	–
Insurance	–	household services maintenance policy
Maintenance and repair services	gas call-out charge; gas service charge	–
Medical products and services	eyesight test charge	allergy tablets
Personal care	bar of soap; hairdryer; lipstick	electrical hair straighteners/tongs; lip gloss; liquid soap
Recreation and culture	squash court hire	computer games with accessory
Soft drinks	fizzy drink (can); fruit drink (carton)	fruit drink (bottle); still mineral water (small bottle)

* RPI goods and services are grouped together under different classifications

From 14 February 2006 the reference year for CPI was re-based to 2005=100 to improve price comparison clarity across the EU. None of the underlying data, from which the re-referenced series was calculated, was revised. Historical rates of change (such as annual inflation figures), calculated from the re-based rounded index levels, were revised due to the effect of rounding. The CPI rate of inflation figure given in the table below may differ by plus or minus 0.1 percentage points from the figure calculated by the above equation. The change of reference period and revision due to rounding does not apply to the RPI which remains unchanged.

The RPI and CPI figures are published by the Office for National Statistics on either the second or third Tuesday of each month in an Indices bulletin and electronically on the National Statistics website (W www.statistics.gov.uk).

PURCHASING POWER OF THE POUND

Changes in the internal purchasing power of the pound may be defined as the 'inverse' of changes in the level of prices: when prices go up, the amount which can be purchased with a given sum of money goes down. To find the purchasing power of the pound in one month or year, given that it was 100p in a previous month or year, the calculation would be:

$$100\text{p} \times \frac{\text{Earlier month/year RPI}}{\text{Later month/year RPI}}$$

Thus, if the purchasing power of the pound is taken to be 100p in 1975, the comparable purchasing power in 2000 would be:

$$100\text{p} \times \frac{34.2}{170.3} = 20.1\text{p}$$

For longer term comparisons, it has been the practice to use an index which has been constructed by linking together the RPI for the period 1962 to date; an index derived from the consumers' expenditure deflator for the period from 1938 to 1962; and the pre-war 'cost of living' index for the period 1914 to 1938. This long-term index enables the internal purchasing power of the pound to be calculated for any year from 1914 onwards. It should be noted that these figures can only be approximate.

	Annual average RPI (1987 = 100)	*Purchasing power of £ (1998 = 1.00)*	*Annual average CPI (2005 = 100)**	*Rate of inflation (RPI/CPI)*
1914	2.8	58.18		
1915	3.5	46.54		
1920	7.0	23.27		
1925	5.0	32.58		
1930	4.5	36.20		
1935	4.0	40.72		
1938	4.4	37.02		
There are no official figures for 1939–45				
1946	7.4	22.01		
1950	9.0	18.10		
1955	11.2	14.54		
1960	12.6	12.93		
1965	14.8	11.00		
1970	18.5	8.80		
1975	34.2	4.76		
1980	66.8	2.44	18.0	
1985	94.6	1.72	6.1	
1990	126.1	1.29	71.5	9.5/7.0
1995	149.1	1.09	86.0	3.5/2.6
1998	162.9	1.00	91.1	3.4/1.6
2000	170.3	0.96	93.1	3.0/0.8
2005	192.0	0.85	100.0	2.8/2.1
2006	198.1	0.82	102.3	3.2/2.3
2007	206.6	0.79	104.7	4.3/2.3
2008	214.8	0.76	108.5	4.0/3.6
2009	213.7	0.76	110.8	–0.5/2.2

* In accordance with an EU Commission regulation all published CPI figures were re-based to 2005 = 100 with effect from 14 February 2006, replacing the 1996 = 100 series

INSURANCE

AUTHORISATION AND REGULATION OF INSURANCE COMPANIES

Since 2001, the Financial Services Authority (FSA) has been the authorising, enforcement, supervisory and rule-making body of insurers. Since 2005, this has also included insurance brokers and intermediaries.

The FSA's powers are primarily conferred by the Financial Services and Markets Act 2000, which unified the previous sectoral arrangements and regulators.

AUTHORISATION

The FSA's role is to ensure that firms to which it grants authorisation satisfy the necessary financial criteria, that the senior management of the company are 'fit and proper persons' and that unauthorised firms are not permitted to trade. This part of the FSA's role was previously undertaken by HM Treasury under the Insurance Companies Act 1982, which was repealed when the Financial Services and Markets Act came fully into force. At the end of 2009 there were over 1,400 insurance organisations and friendly societies with authorisation from the FSA to transact one or more classes of insurance business in the UK. However, the single European insurance market, established in 1994, gave insurers authorised in any other European Union country automatic UK authorisation without further formality. This means a potential market of over 4,000 insurers.

REGULATION

All life insurers, general insurers, re-insurers, insurance and reinsurance brokers, financial advisers and composite firms are statutorily regulated. This is achieved through the formulation (after consultation) by the FSA of rules and guidance for regulated organisations. The FSA is also responsible for consumer education and the reduction of financial crime, particularly money laundering.

FINANCIAL SERVICES AUTHORITY, 25 The North Colonnade, London E14 5HS T 020-7066 1000 W www.fsa.gov.uk
Chair, Lord Turner of Ecchinswell
Chief Executive, Hector Sants

COMPLAINTS

Disputes between policyholders and insurers can be referred to the Financial Ombudsman Service (FOS). Policyholders with a complaint against their financial services provider must firstly take the matter to the highest level within the company. Thereafter, if it remains unresolved and it involves an amount below £100,000, they can refer, free of charge, to the Ombudsman Service, which examines the facts of a complaint and delivers a decision binding on the provider (but not the policyholder). Small businesses with a turnover of up to €2m (£1.7m) and fewer than ten employees also have access to the scheme. The Financial Ombudsman Service also covers other areas of the financial services industry including banks, building societies and investment firms. In 2009 the FOS handled around 150,000 complaints about financial services companies.

FINANCIAL SERVICES OMBUDSMAN SERVICE, South Quay Plaza, 183 Marsh Wall, London E14 9SR T 020-7964 1000 W www.fos.org.uk
Chair, Sir Christopher Kelly, KBE
Chief Ombudsman, Natalie Ceeney

ASSOCIATION OF BRITISH INSURERS

Over 90 per cent of the domestic business of UK insurance companies is transacted by the 340 members of the Association of British Insurers (ABI). ABI is a trade association which protects and promotes the interests of all its insurance company members. Only insurers authorised in the EU are eligible for membership. Brokers, intermediaries, financial advisers and claims handlers may not join ABI but may have their own trade associations.

ASSOCIATION OF BRITISH INSURERS (ABI), 51 Gresham Street, London EC2V 7HQ W www.abi.org.uk
Chair, Tim Breedon
Director-General (acting), Margaret Craig

BALANCE OF PAYMENTS

The financial services industry contributes 6.8 per cent to the UK's gross domestic product (GDP). In 2008 insurance companies' net exports rose to £8bn, a 48 per cent increase on 2007.

WORLDWIDE MARKET

The UK insurance industry is the third largest in the world behind the USA and Japan.

Market	*Premium Income ($bn)*	*Percentage of total*
United States	1,241	29
Japan	473	11
United Kingdom	450	10

TAKEOVERS AND MERGERS

The expected sales of the insurance arms of Royal Bank of Scotland and Lloyds Banking Group did not materialise in 2009. The only major activity was the takeover of Friends Provident by Resolution, the closed fund specialists.

INDUSTRY ISSUES

The fall-out from the banking crisis in 2008 continued to be felt throughout the year but the insurance industry appeared to have won the argument that banks should be regulated differently from other sectors of financial services.

In March 2009 Lord Turner of Echinswell published his review of regulation which included a range of reforms such as a pan-European regulator, better prudential supervision and a review of remuneration policies. Before the general election in 2010 the Conservative party pledged to reform financial services regulation and replace the FSA so implementation of the

Turner report looked unlikely. It is not clear how the new coalition government will approach this issue.

Another issue facing the incoming government is the danger of more insurers deciding to move away from the UK. Since 2006 a number of major insurers including Hiscox, Kiln Beazley and BRIT have relocated to Bermuda, Ireland or the Netherlands arguing that the countries' tax rates, stability and friendly attitude to business made them more attractive than the UK. Insurance remains one of the few sectors where the UK is a world leader, but this could change if the trend for relocation is not halted.

GENERAL INSURANCE

A number of ongoing or unresolved issues continued to cause concern for general insurers during 2009. The year began with news of a massive rise in payment protection insurance claims. This was scarcely a surprise given increasing unemployment figures, but the size of the rise (up 118 per cent year-on-year) still proved a shock. Fire and theft claims also continued at record levels, with arson, which tends to increase during a recession, accounting for half of all commercial fires. Socially deprived areas and schools were particularly vulnerable, with arson rates being 30 times higher in poorer areas and 20 schools a week suffering an arson attack.

The weather is never far from a list of insurers' concerns. Heavy snow and freezing temperatures in February and December 2009, and January 2010, together with heavy rain and flooding in November 2009, pushed the total payouts for weather damage from these events to around £1bn.

In October 2009, four trade associations representing the financial services industry (the Association of British Insurers, the British Bankers' Association, the Building Societies Association and the Council of Mortgage Lenders) agreed with the UK regulator, the Financial Services Authority, on an overhaul and review of mortgage payment protection insurance. This was instigated following criticism by FSA chairman Lord Turner about premium increases and reductions in cover during the recession. The review of individual policies and action arising from the findings were said to be on track for completion by the FSA's deadline of June 2010.

The issue surrounding the medical condition known as pleural plaques continued during 2009. Pleural plaques is a blood condition which insurers, backed by medical opinion, say is symptomless and victims are therefore not entitled to compensation. The case went to the House of Lords in 2007 who found for the insurers. Subsequently, in March 2009 the Scottish parliament passed the Damages (Asbestos-Related Conditions) (Scotland) Act 2009 which reimposed a right to compensation. In April 2009 four major insurance companies launched a judicial review of this act but early in 2010 this review failed. The insurers concerned have now lodged an appeal, with the outcome expected in autumn 2010.

In July 2009 the ABI published research that supported the widely held theory that insurance fraud increases during a recession. ABI estimated that undetected general insurance claims fraud now totals £1.9bn a year, which adds around £44 to the annual costs individual policyholders face, on average, each year. This is up from around £1.6bn when the research was last conducted in 2006. The more encouraging news is that the detection of general insurance fraud has improved significantly over the last five years. Over £730m worth of fraudulent claims were detected and prevented in 2008 by the increased use of databases and better insurer/police cooperation.

LONDON INSURANCE MARKET

The London Insurance Market is a unique wholesale marketplace and a distinct, separate sector of the UK insurance and reinsurance industry. It is the world's leading market for internationally traded insurance and reinsurance, its business comprising mainly overseas non-life large and high-exposure risks. It is the only place in the world where all 20 of the world's largest insurance companies have an office. The market is centred on the square mile of the City of London, which provides the required financial, banking, legal and other support services. Around 58 per cent of London market business is transacted at Lloyd's of London, 30 per cent through insurance companies and the remainder through protection and indemnity clubs. In 2008 the market had a written gross premium income of over £24.7bn. Around 170 Lloyd's brokers service the market.

The trade association for the international insurers and reinsurers writing primarily non-marine insurance and all classes of reinsurance business in the London market is the International Underwriting Association (IUA).

INTERNATIONAL UNDERWRITING ASSOCIATION, London Underwriting Centre, 3 Mincing Lane, London EC3R 7DD **W** www.iua.co.uk
Chair, Stephen Riley
Chief Executive, Dave Matcham

BRITISH INSURANCE COMPANIES

The following insurance company figures refer to members and certain non-members of the ABI.

WORLDWIDE GENERAL BUSINESS UNDERWRITING RESULTS *(£m)*

	2007			*2008*		
	UK	*Overseas*	*Total*	*UK*	*Overseas*	*Total*
Motor						
Premiums	10,527	3,471	13,998	10,676	4,086	14,783
Profit (loss)	(267)	250	(17)	(503)	264	(240)
Percentage of premiums	2.5	7.2	0.1	4.7	6.5	1.6
Non-motor						
Premiums	20,770	6,875	27,644	20,949	8,708	29,653
Profit (loss)	(667)	461	(206)	1,076	160	1,236
Percentage of premiums	3.2	6.7	0.8	5.1	1.8	4.2

CLAIMS STATISTICS *(£m)*

	2005	*2006*	*2007*	*2008*	*2009*
Theft	475	517	525	531	555
Fire	1,128	1,139	1,102	1,273	1,205
Weather	735	475	2,459	904	662
Domestic subsidence	225	302	162	137	175
Business interruption	267	168	320	193	128
Total	2,851	2,601	4,568	3,038	2,725

WORLDWIDE GENERAL BUSINESS TRADING RESULTS *(£m)*

	2007	*2008*
Net written premiums	43,698	47,213
Underwriting results	104	1,115
Investment income	5,374	3,368
Overall trading profit	5,478	4,483
Profit as percentage of premium income	12.5	9.5

NET PREMIUM INCOME BY SECTOR 2008 *(£m)*

	UK	*Overseas*
Motor	10,676	4,086
Non-motor	20,949	8,708
Marine, aviation and transport	795	339
Reinsurance	1,234	280
Total general business	33,654	13,413
Ordinary long-term	131,049	36,948
Industrial long-term	166	–
Total long-term business	131,215	36,948

LLOYD'S OF LONDON

Lloyd's of London is an international market for almost all types of general insurance. Lloyd's currently has a capacity to accept insurance premiums of around £16.9bn. Much of this business comes from outside the UK and makes a valuable contribution to the balance of payments.

A policy is underwritten at Lloyd's by a mixture of private and corporate members; corporate members having been admitted for the first time in 1992. Specialist underwriters accept insurance risks at Lloyd's on behalf of members (referred to as 'Names') grouped in syndicates. There are currently 80 syndicates of varying sizes, each managed by one of the 51 underwriting agents approved by the Council of Lloyd's.

Members divide into three categories: corporate organisations, individuals who have no limit to their liability for losses, and those who have an agreed limit (known as NameCos).

Lloyd's is incorporated by an act of parliament (Lloyd's Acts 1871 onwards) and is governed by an 18-person council, made up of six working, six external and six nominated members. The structure immediately below this changed when, in 2002, Lloyd's members voted at an extraordinary general meeting to implement a new franchise system for the market with the aim of improving profitability. The first move was the introduction of a new governance structure, replacing the Lloyd's Market Board and the Lloyd's Regulatory Board with an 11-person Lloyd's Franchise Board. Four main committees report to this board.

The corporation is a non-profit making body chiefly financed by its members' subscriptions. It provides the premises, administrative staff and services enabling Lloyd's underwriting syndicates to conduct their business. It does not, however, assume corporate liability for the risks accepted by its members. Individual members are responsible to the full extent of their personal means for their underwriting affairs unless they have converted to limited liability companies.

Lloyd's syndicates have no direct contact with the public. All business is transacted through insurance brokers accredited by the Corporation of Lloyd's. In addition, non-Lloyd's brokers in the UK, when guaranteed by Lloyd's brokers, are able to deal directly with Lloyd's motor syndicates, a facility that has made the Lloyd's market more accessible to the insuring public.

The FSA has ultimate responsibility for the regulation of the Lloyd's market. However, in situations where Lloyd's internal regulatory and compensation arrangements are more far-reaching – as for example with the Lloyd's Central Fund which safeguards claim payments to policyholders – the regulatory role is delegated to the Council of Lloyd's.

Lloyd's also provides the most comprehensive shipping intelligence service in the world. The shipping and other information received from Lloyd's agents, shipowners, news agencies and other sources throughout the world is collated and distributed to the media as well as to the maritime and commercial sectors in general. *Lloyd's List* is London's oldest daily newspaper and contains news of general commercial interest as well as shipping information. It has been independent of Lloyd's since a management buy-out in 1992. *Lloyd's Shipping Index,* published weekly, lists some 23,000 ocean-going merchant vessels in alphabetical order and gives the latest known report of each.

DEVELOPMENTS IN 2009

The Lloyd's market recorded a healthy profit before tax of £3,868m for 2009. This was partly due to a quiet hurricane season in the Gulf of Mexico, which saw the lowest number of substantial storms since 1997. The five major claims events (where losses were over US$1bn) were due to severe weather incidents in the USA and Europe.

The aviation market did suffer a number of losses, the largest being the loss of an Air France A330-200 over the Atlantic Ocean in June 2009.

Overall the Lloyd's market, like the other sectors of the UK financial services industry, has so far weathered the economic storm. Continued profitability will only come as long as underwriting discipline and conservative investment strategies are maintained.

LLOYD'S OF LONDON, One Lime Street, London EC3M 7HA **T** 020-7327 1000 **W** www.lloyds.com
Chair, Lord Levene of Portsoken
Chief Executive, Richard Ward

LLOYD'S MEMBERSHIP

	2009	*2010*
Individual	773	700
Corporate	1,238	1,443

LLOYD'S SEGMENTAL RESULTS 2009 *(£m)*

	Gross premiums written	*Net earned premium*	*Result*
Reinsurance	7,989	5,763	1,245
Casualty	4,320	3,430	316
Property	4,954	3,859	292
Marine	1,606	1,303	157
Motor	1,118	984	(83)
Energy	1,371	985	157
Aviation	551	344	10
Life	60	53	1
Total from syndicate operations	21,969	16,721	2,095

LIFE AND LONG-TERM INSURANCE AND PENSIONS

Discussions on the Financial Services Authority's (FSA) Retail Distribution Review continued during 2009. The review was launched in June 2006 and the FSA issued an interim report in April 2008. In June 2009 a paper on delivering the results of the review was published. This is due to have a fundamental effect on the way financial products are marketed and sold. The main features are a switch to a system of 'independent advice' or 'restricted advice'. This introduces the possibility of advisers being able to offer the products of more than one provider. The other main feature is an end to the payment of commission to advisers. The alternative will be a fee-based system called 'adviser charging' which will eliminate any possibility – real or perceived – of advisers offering products because they earn them the highest commission levels. A policy statement and final rules was expected from the FSA in 2010 with implementation in 2012. The financial services industry has largely welcomed the proposals. There is however a fear that the new regime might be extended to include protection products with no investment element which providers believe should be outside these changes.

An analysis of new business for the year shows the recession having an effect on the sales of most life and long-term products. There was a 9 per cent decrease in year-on-year sales of regular premium savings and protection products in 2009, mainly because of reduced sales of individual pensions. Single premium savings and protection product sales also decreased by 33 per cent year-on-year. Almost every product in this category recorded a drop in sales.

One area to buck the trend was regular premium individual protection contracts where sales increased on average by 4 per cent year-on-year, driven mainly by a 33 per cent increase in group life insurances.

These falls are to be expected given the economic climate, low interest rates and the lack of any real incentive to save.

PAYMENTS TO POLICYHOLDERS *(£m)*

	2007	*2008*
Payments to UK policyholders	170,154	180,757
Payments to overseas policyholders	22,327	31,981
Total	192,481	212,738

WORLDWIDE LONG-TERM PREMIUM INCOME *(£m)*

	2004	*2005*	*2006*	*2007*	*2008*
UK Life Insurance					
Regular Premium	10,507	10,585	9,414	8,927	8,187
Single Premium	20,516	25,421	32,088	40,256	27,600
Total	31,023	36,032	41,502	49,183	35,787
Individual Pensions					
Regular Premium	8,974	8,548	8,628	8,714	9,632
Single Premium	12,361	12,311	24,906	24,368	18,724
Total	21,335	20,859	33,534	33,082	28,356
Other Pensions					
Regular Premium	4,183	4,577	5,752	5,687	5,907
Single Premium	42,509	54,383	59,410	93,020	57,048
Total	46,692	58,960	60,162	98,707	62,735
Other (eg Income protection, Annuities)	5,277	4,343	9,852	4,425	4,337
TOTAL UK PREMIUM INCOME	104,327	120,194	145,050	183,772	131,215
Overseas Premium Income					
Regular Premium	7,692	8,171	8,191	7,877	10,370
Single Premium	16,084	16,814	21,104	25,693	26,728
Total	23,775	24,985	29,295	33,571	37,098
TOTAL WORLDWIDE PREMIUM INCOME	128,102	145,178	174,345	218,968	168,313

PRIVATE MEDICAL INSURANCE

	2004	*2005*	*2006*	*2007*	*2008*
Number of people covered (thousand)	5,820	5,820	5,879	6,004	6,224
Corporate	4,084	4,125	4,188	4,341	4,571
Personal	1,736	1,695	1,691	1,663	1,653
Gross Earned Premiums (£m)	2,855	2,942	3,070	3,241	3,468
Corporate	1,433	1,493	1,561	1,696	1,831
Personal	1,422	1,449	1,509	1,545	1,631
Gross Claims Incurred (£m)	2,188	2,255	2,376	2,501	2,653

INVESTMENTS OF INSURANCE COMPANIES 2008

Investment of funds	*Long-term business (£m)*	*General business (£m)*
Index-linked British government securities	52,966	279
Non-index-linked British government securities	125,6784	9,363
Other UK public sector debt securities	6,756	631
Overseas government, provincial and municipal securities	64,033	16,563
Debentures, loan shares, preference and guaranteed stocks and shares		
UK	142,470	10,881
Overseas	196,029	25,190
Ordinary stocks and shares UK	206,924	3,900
Overseas	198,296	7,652
Unit trusts		
Equities	132,106	5,457
Fixed interest	49,710	669
Loans secured on property	29,474	11,740
Real property and ground rents	56,496	5,824
Other invested assets	123,430	24,407
Total invested assets	1,384,370	111,642
NET INVESTMENT INCOME	29,249	3,384

NEW BUSINESS

	2005	*2006*	*2006*	*2008*	*2009*
New regular premiums					
Investment and savings	117	92	88	75	77
Individual protection	894	905	867	858	883
Group protection	387	311	318	290	313
Individual pension	2,127	3,024	3,273	3,363	2,805
Group pension	766	753	821	989	962
Offshore business	26	22	21	19	21
TOTAL REGULAR	4,319	5,107	5,388	5,594	5,060
New single premiums					
Investments and savings	24,121	30,540	38,903	23,769	12,444
Individual protection	1,698	1,634	1,266	1,019	236
Individual pensions	12,164	18,758	22,165	18,389	14,811
Retirement income products	9,307	12,157	14,061	13,916	12,673
Occupational pensions	6,544	10,796	10,986	12,097	10,039
Offshore business	4,804	7,150	7,594	7,777	4,267
TOTAL SINGLE	58,638	81,034	94,970	76,967	54,830

TAXATION

The government raises money to pay for public services such as education, health and the social security system through tax. Each year the Chancellor of the Exchequer's budget sets out how much it will cost to provide these services and how much tax is therefore needed to pay for them. HM Revenue and Customs (HMRC) is the government department that collects it. There are several different types of tax. The varieties that individuals may have to pay include income tax payable on earnings, pensions, state benefits, savings and investments; capital gains tax (CGT) payable on the disposal of certain assets; inheritance tax (IHT) payable on estates upon death and certain lifetime gifts; stamp duty payable when purchasing property and shares; and value added tax (VAT) payable on goods and services, plus certain other duties such as fuel duty on petrol and excise duty on alcohol and tobacco. Government funds are also raised from companies and small businesses through corporation tax.

In July 2010 the Chancellor of the Exchequer launched the Office of Tax Simplification, an independent office of the Treasury which draws together expertise from across the tax and legal professions to provide the government with independent advice on simplifying the UK tax system with the objective of reducing compliance burdens on both businesses and individual taxpayers. The office is due to produce a report with recommendations ahead of the 2011 budget.

HELP AND INFORMATION ON TAXATION

For detailed information on any aspect of taxation individuals may contact their local tax office or enquiry centre. The HMRC website (W www.hmrc.gov.uk) provides wide-ranging information online. All HMRC forms, leaflets and guides are listed on, and can be downloaded from, the website or ordered by telephone. A list of all HMRC telephone helplines and order lines is also on the website. Those most relevant to topics covered in this section on taxation are included at pertinent points throughout. Information on taxation is also available in the Money, Tax and Benefits section of the government's public information website for individuals W www.direct.gov.uk, and the Taxes, Returns and Payroll section of the equivalent information website for companies W www.businesslink.gov.uk.

INCOME TAX

Income tax is levied on different sorts of income. Not all types of income are taxable, however, and individuals are only taxed on their 'taxable income' above a certain level. Reliefs and allowances can also reduce or, in some cases, cancel out an individual's income tax bill.

An individual's taxable income is assessed each tax year, starting on 6 April and ending on 5 April the following year. The information below relates specifically to the year of assessment 2010–11, ending on 5 April 2011, and has only limited application to earlier years. Changes due to come into operation at a later date are briefly mentioned where information is available. Types of income that are taxable include:

- earnings from employment or self-employment
- most pensions income including state, company and personal pensions
- interest on most savings
- income (dividends) from shares
- income from property
- income received from a trust
- certain state benefits
- an individual's share of any joint income

There are certain sorts of income on which individuals never pay tax. These are ignored altogether when working out how much income tax an individual may need to pay. Types of income that are not taxable include:

- certain state benefits and tax credits such as child benefit, working tax credit, child tax credit, pension credit, attendance allowance, disability living allowance, income support, housing benefit and the first 28 weeks of incapacity benefit
- winter fuel payments
- income from tax-free National Savings and Investments, such as savings certificates
- interest and terminal bonuses under Save As You Earn schemes
- interest, dividends and other income from various tax-free investments, notably individual savings accounts (ISAs)
- premium bond, national lottery and gambling prizes

PERSONAL ALLOWANCE

Every individual resident in the UK for tax purposes has a 'personal allowance'. This is the amount of taxable income that an individual can earn or receive each year tax-free. This tax year (2010–11) the basic personal allowance or tax-free amount is £6,475. Individuals may be entitled to a higher personal allowance if they are 65 or over. Income tax is only due on an individual's taxable income that is above his or her tax-free allowance. Husbands and wives are taxed separately, with each entitled to his or her personal allowance. Each spouse may obtain other allowances and reliefs where the required conditions are satisfied.

The amount of personal allowance depends on an individual's age on 5 April 2010 and, if he or she is 65 or over, the total income received from all taxable sources. There are three age-related levels of personal allowance – *see* table below. If an individual became 65 or 75 during the year to 5 April 2010, he or she is entitled to the allowance for that age group.

If an individual's income is over the 'income limit', the age-related allowance reduces by half the amount (£1 for every £2) he or she has over that limit, until the basic rate allowance is reached. For a 66-year-old with an income of £23,300 (£400 over the limit), for example, the age-related allowance would reduce by £200 to £22,700.

In the past, all those entitled to the basic personal allowance received the same amount of tax-free income regardless of income, currently £6,475. However, from 2010–11, the basic personal allowance is subject to a single income limit of £100,000, meaning that its value is restricted for individuals with an 'adjusted net income' (*see* below) over £100,000.

If an individual's adjusted net income is below or equal to the £100,000 limit, he or she is entitled to the full amount of basic personal allowance. However, where an individual's adjusted net income exceeds the income limit of £100,000, the amount of the personal allowance will be reduced by £1 for every £2 above the limit. The personal allowance is reduced to nil from this income limit.

'Adjusted net income' is the measure of an individual's income that is used for the calculation of the existing income-related reductions to personal allowances for those aged between 65 and 74 and for those 75 and over. It is calculated in a series of steps. The starting point is 'net income', which is the total of the individual's income subject to income tax less specified deductions such as payments made gross to pension schemes. This net income is then reduced by the grossed-up amount of the individual's Gift Aid contributions to charities and the grossed-up amount of the individual's pension contributions that have received tax relief at source. The final step is to add back any relief for payments to trade unions or police organisations deducted in arriving at the individual's net income. The result is the individual's adjusted net income.

LEVELS OF PERSONAL ALLOWANCE FOR 2010–11

	Personal allowance	*Income limit*
Age under 65	£6,475	£100,000
Age 65–74	£9,490	£22,900
Age 75 and over	£9,640	£22,900

BLIND PERSON'S ALLOWANCE

If an individual is registered blind or is unable to perform any work for which eyesight is essential, he or she can claim blind person's allowance, an extra amount of tax-free income added to the personal allowance. In 2010–11 the blind person's allowance is £1,890. It is the same for everyone who can claim it, whatever his or her age or level of income. If an individual is married or in a civil partnership and cannot use all of his or her blind person's allowance because of insufficient income, the unused part of the allowance can be passed to the spouse or civil partner.

Other deductible allowances and reliefs that have the effect of reducing an income tax bill are available to taxpayers in certain circumstances and will be explained in more detail later in this section.

CALCULATING INCOME TAX DUE

Individuals' liability to pay income tax is determined by establishing their level of taxable income for the year. For married couples and civil partners income must be allocated between the couple by reference to the individual who is beneficially entitled to that income. Where income arises from jointly held assets, it is normally apportioned equally between the partners. If, however, the beneficial interests in jointly held assets are not equal, in most cases couples can make a special declaration to have income apportioned by reference to the actual interests in that income.

To work out an individual's liability for tax, his or her taxable income must be allocated between three different types: earned income (excluding income from savings and dividends); income from savings; and company dividends from shares and other equity-based investments.

After the tax-free allowance plus any deductible allowances and reliefs have been taken into account, the amount of tax an individual pays is calculated using different tax rates and a series of tax bands. The tax band applies to an individual's income after tax allowances and any reliefs have been taken into account. Individuals are not taxed on all of their income.

There were significant changes to income tax rates for 2008–9. The basic rate of income tax was reduced from 22 per cent to 20 per cent and a previous 10 per cent starting rate was removed for earned income and pensions. This created a simpler structure of two rates: a 20 pence (in the pound) basic rate and a 40 pence (in the pound) higher rate. From 2010–11 the main rates of income tax remain at 20 per cent and 40 per cent. However, an additional income tax rate of 50 per cent has been introduced, which applies on both savings and non-savings income over £150,000.

The 10 per cent starting rate continues to be available for savings income only, with a limit of £2,440. If an individual's taxable non-savings income is above £2,440, the 10 per cent savings rate is not applicable.

It was announced in the coalition government's budget on 22 June 2010 that from April 2011 the personal allowance for people aged under 65 will be increased by £1,000 in cash terms to £7,475 for the tax year 2011–12. The basic rate band above which tax is payable at the higher rate of 40 per cent will also be reduced to ensure that higher rate taxpayers do not benefit from this change.

INCOME TAX RATES (PER CENT) AND TAX BANDS FOR 2010–11

Band	*Earned income*	*Band*	*Savings*	*Dividends*
£0–£37,400	20%	£0–£2,440*	10%	10%
£37,400+	40%	£2,440–£37,400	20%	10%
£150,000+	50%	£37,400+	40%	32.5%
		£150,000+	50%	42.5%

* If an individual's taxable non-savings income is above £2,440 the 20 per cent tax band applies to savings income from £0–£37,400

The first calculation is applied to earned income which includes income from employment or self-employment, most pension income and rental income plus the value of a wide range of employee fringe benefits such as company cars, living accommodation and private medical insurance (for more information on fringe benefits, *see* later section on payment of income tax). In working out the amount of an individual's net taxable earnings, all expenses incurred 'wholly, exclusively and necessarily' in the performance of his or her work duties, together with the cost of business travel, may be deducted. Fees and subscriptions to certain professional bodies may also be deducted. Redundancy payments and other sums paid on the termination of an employment are assessable income, but the first £30,000 is normally tax-free provided the payment is not linked with the recipient's retirement or performance.

The first £37,400 of taxable income remaining after the tax-free allowance plus any deductible allowances and reliefs have been taken into account, is taxed at the basic rate of 20 per cent. Taxable income between £37,400 and £150,000 is taxed at the higher rate of 40 per cent. Taxable income above £150,000 is taxed at a new rate of 50 per cent.

Savings and dividends income is added to an individual's other taxable income and taxed last. This means that tax on such sorts of income is based on an individual's highest income tax band.

SAVINGS INCOME

The second calculation is applied to any income from savings received by an individual. The appropriate rate at which it must be taxed is determined by adding income from savings to an individual's other taxable income, excluding dividends.

There is a 10 per cent starting rate for savings income only, with a limit of £2,440. If an individual's taxable non-savings income exceeds this limit, the 10 per cent savings rate is not applicable. Savings income above £2,440 and below the £37,400 basic rate limit is taxable at 20 per cent. Savings income between £37,400 and £150,000 is taxable at 40 per cent. Savings income over £150,000 is taxed at 50 per cent. If savings income falls on both sides of a tax band, the relevant amounts are taxed at the rates for each tax band.

Most savings income, such as interest paid on bank and building society accounts, already has tax at a rate of 20 per cent deducted from it 'at source' – that is, before it is paid out to individuals. This is confirmed by the entry 'net interest' on bank and building society statements.

Higher rate taxpayers whose income is sufficient to pay 40 or 50 per cent tax on their savings income must let their tax office know what savings income they have received so that the extra tax they owe can be collected.

Non taxpayers – ie individuals, including most children, whose taxable income is less than their tax allowances – can register to have their savings interest paid 'gross' without any tax being deducted from it at source. To do this, they must complete form R85, available at all banks and building societies. Parents or guardians need to fill in this form on behalf of those under 16. For individuals who are unsure whether they qualify as non taxpayers and, therefore, whether they are able to register to have their savings interest paid gross, HMRC offers an 'R85 checker' on its website at W www.hmrc.gov.uk/calcs/r85/

Non taxpayers who have already had tax deducted from their savings interest can claim it back from HMRC by filling in form R40. For help or information about registering to get interest paid tax-free or to claim tax back on savings interest, individuals may visit W www.hmrc.gov.uk/taxon/bank.htm or call a dedicated savings helpline on T 0845-980 0645. Further information is available in the leaflet *IR111: Bank and building society interest – Are you paying tax when you don't need to?*

DIVIDEND INCOME

The third and final income tax calculation is on UK dividends, which means income from shares in UK companies and other share-based investments including unit trusts and open-ended investment companies (OEICs).

Dividend tax rates differ from those on savings income. The rate that an individual pays on his or her dividends depends on the amount of his or her overall taxable income (after allowances). Dividend income at or below the £37,400 basic rate tax limit is taxable at 10 per cent, between £37,400 and £150,000 at 32.5 per cent, and above £150,000 at a new 42.5 per cent rate.

When dividends are paid, a voucher is sent that shows the dividend paid and the amount of associated 'tax credit'. Companies pay dividends out of profits on which they have already paid or are due to pay tax. The tax credit takes account of this and is available to the shareholder to offset against any income tax that may be due on their dividend income. The dividend paid represents 90 per cent of their dividend income. The remaining 10 per cent is made up of the tax credit. In other words the tax credit represents 10 per cent of the dividend income.

Individuals who pay tax at the basic rate have no tax to pay on their dividend income because the tax liability is 10 per cent – the same amount as the tax credit. Higher rate taxpayers pay a total of 32.5 per cent tax on dividend income above the £37,400 basic rate income tax limit, but because the first 10 per cent of the tax due on their dividend income is already covered by the tax credit, in practice they owe only 22.5 per cent. For the same reason, additional rate taxpayers who pay a total of 42.5 per cent on dividend income above the £150,000 additional rate tax limit, owe only 32.5 per cent in practice.

Non taxpayers cannot claim the 10 per cent tax credit. This is because income tax has not been deducted from the dividends paid to them. The view is that they have simply been given a 10 per cent credit against any income tax due.

If there is significant change to an individual's savings or other income, whatever his or her current tax bracket, it is the individual's responsibility to contact the relevant tax office immediately, even if he or she does not normally complete a tax return. This enables the tax office to work out whether extra or less tax should be paid.

INDIVIDUAL SAVINGS ACCOUNTS (ISAS)

There is a small selection of savings and investment products that is tax-free. This means that there is no tax to pay on any income generated in the form of interest or dividends nor on any increase in the value of the capital invested. Their tax-efficient status has been granted by the government in order to give people an incentive to save more. For this reason there are usually limits and restrictions on the amount of money an individual may invest in such savings and investments. Individual savings accounts (ISAs) are the best known among tax-efficient savings and investments. They were introduced in 1999 to replace other similar schemes called PEPs and TESSAs. Individuals can use an ISA to save cash, or invest in stocks and shares.

Changes were made to the ISA rules which took effect from April 2008. These reforms removed the distinction between what were previously known as maxi and mini ISAs and simplified an individual's options.

Since 6 April 2010 individuals have been able to save up to £10,200 each tax year in an ISA and receive all profits free of tax provided that they are UK residents and are over 18 (over 16 for cash ISAs). An ISA must be in an individual's name and cannot be held jointly with another person.

Individuals may invest in two separate ISAs each tax year: a cash ISA and a stocks and shares ISA (an umbrella term covering investments in unit trusts, company shares, bonds, investment-type life insurance and so on). Up to £5,100 of an individual's ISA allowance may be saved in one cash ISA with one provider. The remainder of the £10,200 can be invested in one stocks and shares ISA with either the same or a different provider. Alternatively an individual may open a single stocks and shares ISA and invest the full £10,200 into it. Various non-cash assets can be held in a stocks and shares ISA including unit trusts, company shares, bonds, investment-type life insurance and investment trusts.

It was announced in the March 2010 budget that, from 6 April 2011 and annually over the course of the next parliament, the ISA limits (currently £10,200 and £5,100 as above) will increase in line with the Retail Prices Index (RPI). Each September's RPI figure will be used to set the ISA limits for the following tax year. The limits will be rounded each year to the nearest multiple of £120 to enable savers to plan monthly savings more easily.

Under the simplified ISA regime, what used to be known as mini cash ISAs, TESSA-only ISAs (TOISAs) and the cash component of a maxi ISA have become cash ISAs. Similarly, mini stocks and shares ISAs, the stocks and shares component of a maxi ISA and all Personal Equity Plans (PEPs) have become stocks and shares ISAs.

ISA savers have the option to transfer some or all of the money they have saved in previous tax years in cash ISAs to their stocks and shares ISA without affecting their annual ISA investment allowance. They may also choose to transfer all the money they have saved to date in a cash ISA in the current tax year to a stocks and shares ISA. However, the rules do not allow the reverse; that is, the transfer of monies saved in a stocks and shares ISA to a cash ISA.

Further details are available via HMRC's savings helpline on T 0845-604 1701.

DEDUCTIBLE ALLOWANCES AND RELIEF

Income taxpayers may be entitled to certain tax-deductible allowances and reliefs as well as their personal allowances. Examples include the married couple's allowance and maintenance payments relief, both of which are explained below. Unlike the tax-free allowances, these are not amounts of income that an individual can receive tax-free but amounts by which their tax bill can be reduced.

MARRIED COUPLE'S ALLOWANCE

A married couple's allowance (MCA) is available to taxpayers who are married or are in a civil partnership only where one or other partner was born before 6 April 1935. Eligible couples can start to claim the MCA from the year of marriage or civil partnership registration.

The MCA is restricted to give relief at a fixed rate of 10 per cent, which means that – unlike the personal allowance – it is not income that can be received without paying tax. Instead, it reduces an individual's tax bill by up to a fixed amount calculated as 10 per cent of the amount of the allowance to which they are entitled.

In 2010–11, the MCA is £6,965 at 10 per cent, worth up to £696.50 off a couple's tax bill. The MCA is made up of two parts. There is a minimum amount (£2,670 in 2010–11) which will always be due. The remaining amount (£4,295 in 2010–11) can be reduced if the husband's income exceeds certain limits.

The husband will normally receive the allowance, but the couple can jointly decide which of them will get the minimum amount of the allowance. Alternatively, they can decide to have the minimum amount of the allowance split equally between them. They must inform their tax office of their decision before the start of the new tax year in which they want the decision to take effect. Once this is done, the change will apply until the couple decides to alter it. The remaining part of the allowance must go to the husband unless he lacks sufficient income to use it.

If an individual does not have enough income to use all his or her share of the married couple's allowance, the tax office can transfer the unused part of it to his or her spouse or civil partner.

Like the personal allowance, the MCA can be gradually reduced at the rate of £1 of the allowance for every £2 of income above the income limit (£22,900 in 2010–11). The amount of MCA can only be affected by the husband's income, and it only starts to be affected if his personal allowance has already been reduced back to the basic level for people under 65. The wife's income never affects the amount of MCA. It does not matter whether all or part of the minimum amount of the allowance has been transferred to her. Whatever the level of the husband's income, the MCA can never be reduced below the minimum amount: in 2010–11 this is £2,670 at 10 per cent.

The same system of allowance allocation applies to civil partners based on the income of the highest earner.

MAINTENANCE PAYMENTS RELIEF

An allowance is available to reduce an individual's tax bill for maintenance payments he or she makes to his or her ex spouse or former civil partner in certain circumstances. To be eligible one or other partner must have been born before 6 April 1935; the couple must be legally separated or divorced; the maintenance payments being made must be under a court order; and the payments must be for the maintenance of an ex spouse or former civil partner (provided he or she is not now remarried or in a new civil partnership) or for children who are under 21. For the tax year 2010–11, this allowance can reduce an individual's tax bill by:

- 10 per cent of £2,670 (maximum £267) – this applies where an individual makes maintenance payments of £2,670 or more a year
- 10 per cent of the amount the individual has actually paid – this applies where an individual makes maintenance payments of less than £2,670 a year

An individual cannot claim a tax reduction for any voluntary payments he or she makes for a child, ex-spouse or former civil partner. To claim maintenance payments relief, individuals should contact their tax office.

CHARITABLE DONATION

A number of charitable donations qualify for tax relief. Individuals can increase the value of regular or one-off charitable gifts of money, however small, by using the Gift Aid scheme that allows charities or community amateur sports clubs (CASCs) to reclaim 20 per cent basic rate tax relief on donations they receive.

The way the scheme works means that if a taxpayer gives £10 using Gift Aid, for example, the donation is worth £12.50 to the charity or CASC. For donations between 6 April 2008 and 5 April 2011 the charity or CASC also receives a separate government supplement of 3 pence on every £1 given. This extra government top-up has no effect on the cost of the gift to the donor.

Individuals who pay 40 per cent higher rate income tax can claim back the difference between the 40 per cent and the 20 per cent basic rate of income tax on the total (gross) value of their donations. For example, a 40 per cent tax payer donates £100. The total value of this donation to the charity or CASC is £125, of which the individual can claim back 20 per cent (£25) for themself. Similarly, those who pay 50 per cent additional rate income tax can claim back the difference between the 50 per cent and the 20 per cent basic rate on the total (gross) value of their donations. On a £100 donation, this means they can claim back £37.50.

Individuals who claim the age-related personal allowance, married couple's allowance or tax credits should tell HMRC about any Gift Aid donations they make because these can sometimes increase the amount of allowance or tax credit to which they are entitled.

In order to make a Gift Aid donation, individuals need to make a Gift Aid declaration. The charity or CASC will normally ask an individual to complete a simple form. One form can cover every gift made to the same charity or CASC for whatever period chosen, including both gifts made in the past and in the future.

Individuals can use Gift Aid provided the amount of income tax and/or capital gains tax they have paid in the tax year in which their donations are made is at least equal to the amount of basic rate tax the charity or CASC is reclaiming on their gifts. It is the responsibility of the individual to make sure this is the case. If an individual makes Gift Aid donations and has not paid sufficient tax, they may have to pay the shortfall to HMRC. The Gift Aid scheme is not suitable for non taxpayers.

Individuals who complete a tax return and are due a tax refund can ask HMRC to treat all or part of it as a Gift Aid donation.

For employees or those in receipt of an occupational pension, a tax-efficient way of making regular donations to charities is to use the Payroll Giving scheme. It allows the donations to be paid from a salary or pension before income tax is deducted. This effectively reduces the cost of giving for donors, which may allow them to give more.

For example, it costs a basic-rate taxpayer only £8 in take-home pay to give £10 to charity from their pre-tax pay. Where a donor pays 40 per cent higher rate tax, that same £10 donation costs the taxpayer £6 and for donors who pay the additional 50 per cent rate tax, it costs £5.

Anyone who pays tax through the PAYE system can give to any charity of their choosing in this way, providing their employer or pension provider offers a payroll giving scheme, and there is no limit to the amount individuals can donate.

Details of tax-efficient charitable giving methods can be found at W www.direct.gov.uk/en/MoneyTaxAndBenefits/ManagingMoney and W www.hmrc.gov.uk/individuals/giving

TAX RELIEF ON PENSION CONTRIBUTIONS

Pensions are long-term investments designed to help ensure that people have enough income in retirement. The government encourages individuals to save towards a pension by offering tax relief on their contributions. Tax relief reduces an individual's tax bill or increases their pension fund.

The way tax relief is given on pension contributions depends on whether an individual pays into a company, public service or personal pension scheme.

For employees who pay into a company or public service pension scheme, most employers take the pension contributions from the employee's pay before deducting tax, which means that the individual – whether they pay income tax at the basic or higher rate – gets full tax relief straight away. Some employers, however, use the same method of paying pension contributions as that used by personal pension scheme payers described below.

Individuals who pay into a personal pension scheme make contributions from their net salary; that is, after tax has been deducted. For each pound that individuals contribute to their pension from net salary, the pension provider claims tax back from the government at the basic rate of 20 per cent and reinvests it on behalf of the individual into the scheme. In practice this means that for every £80 an individual pays into their pension, they receive £100 in their pension fund.

All higher rate taxpayers currently get 40 per cent tax relief on money they put into a pension. On contributions made from net salary, the first 20 per cent is claimed back from HMRC by the pension scheme in the same way as for a lower rate taxpayer. It is then up to individuals to claim back the other 20 per cent from their tax office, either when they fill in their annual tax return or by telephone or letter.

Under certain circumstances, individuals who are subject to the 50 per cent additional rate of income tax introduced from April 2010 can get 50 per cent tax relief on contributions they make to a pension in the tax year 2010–11. This applies, for example, where an individual makes regular, ongoing annual contributions of £20,000 or less. However, 50 per cent taxpayers cannot get 50 per cent tax relief on all and any pension contributions made in 2010–11 because of new government rules (*see* below).

Most providers of retirement annuities, which are a type of personal pension scheme set up before July 1988, do not offer a 'tax relief at source' scheme whereby they claim back tax at the basic rate as is the case with more modern personal pensions. In such cases, contributing individuals need to claim the tax relief they are due through their tax return or by telephoning or writing to HMRC.

Non taxpayers can still pay into a personal pension scheme and benefit from 20 per cent basic rate relief on the first £2,880 a year they contribute. In practice this means that the government tops up their £2,880 contribution to make it £3,600 which is the current universal pension allowance. Such pension contributions may be made on behalf of a non taxpayer by another individual. An individual may, for example, contribute to a pension on behalf of a husband, wife, civil partner, child or grandchild. Tax relief will be added to their contribution at the basic rate, again on up to £2,880 a year benefiting the recipient, but their own tax bill will not be affected.

In any one tax year, individuals can get tax relief on pension contributions made into any number and type of registered pension schemes of 100 per cent of their annual earnings, irrespective of age, up to a maximum 'annual allowance'. For the tax year 2010–11 the annual allowance is £255,000. Individuals pay tax at 40 per cent on any contributions they make above the annual allowance. Everyone now also has a 'lifetime allowance' (£1.8m for 2010–11) which means taxpayers can save up to a total of £1.8m in their pension fund and still get tax relief at their highest income tax rate on all their contributions.

It was announced in the Labour government's 2009 Budget that, from April 2011, tax relief on pension contributions would be restricted for those on high incomes. For individuals with gross income between £150,000 and £180,000, tax relief on pension contributions (including the value of employer contributions for those in employment) would reduce gradually from marginal rate to basic rate as income increases. Where gross income was £180,000 or more, tax relief on pension contributions would be restricted to 20 per cent. The change would raise £3.5 billion of revenues.

To provide more certainty for individuals about whether they would be affected in 2011, the then government set an income floor such that individuals with pre-tax incomes of £130,000 (including an individual's own pension contributions and charitable donations) would be unaffected.

Anti-forestalling legislation was also introduced to stop high income individuals making substantial additional pension contributions and getting full tax relief prior to the 2011 restriction taking effect. Again, individuals who had never earned in excess of £130,000 would be unaffected.

However, the new coalition government said in its budget on 22 June 2010 that the previous government's plan to reduce pension tax relief for people on high incomes (outlined above) was too complex. It said it would work on alternative ways of raising the same £3.5bn revenue to be announced at a later date.

Individuals are therefore advised to seek advice before taking any action to change their pension contributions. More detail is available from the HMRC helpline T 0845-600 3622.

For information on pensions and tax relief visit W www.direct.gov.uk/en/Pensionsandretirementplanning Another useful source of information and advice is The Pensions Advisory Service (TPAS), an independent voluntary organisation grant-aided by the Department for Work and Pensions at W www.pensionsadvisoryservice.org.uk; its Pensions Helpline is on T 0845-601 2923.

PAYMENT OF INCOME TAX

Employees have their income tax deducted from their wages throughout the year by their employer who sends it on to HMRC. Those in receipt of a company pension have their due tax deducted in the same way by their pension provider. This system of collecting income tax is known as 'pay as you earn' (PAYE).

BENEFITS IN KIND

The PAYE system is also used to collect tax on certain fringe benefits or 'benefits in kind' that employees or directors receive from their employer but that are not included in their salary cheque or wages. These include company cars, private medical insurance paid for by the employer or cheap or free loans from the employer. Some fringe benefits are tax-free, including employer-paid contributions into an employee's pension fund, cheap or free canteen meals, works buses, in-house sports facilities, reasonable relocation expenses, provision of a mobile phone, workplace nursery places provided for the children of employees, and certain other employer-supported childcare up to £55 a week.

For taxable fringe benefits tax is paid on the 'taxable value' of the benefit. The way it is calculated depends on whether or not the benefit is given to a director or 'higher-paid' employee, defined as an individual earning £8,500 gross or more a year including the value of his or her taxable fringe benefits. Company directors normally count as higher-paid, however much they earn.

Employers submit returns for individual employees to the tax office on the form P11D, with details of any fringe benefits they have been given. Employees should get a copy of this form by 6 July following the end of the tax year and must enter the value of the fringe benefits they have received on their tax return for the relevant year, even if tax has already been paid on them under PAYE. Fringe benefits may be taxed under PAYE by being offset against personal tax allowances in an individual's PAYE code. Otherwise tax will be collected after the end of the tax year by the issue of an assessment on the fringe benefits.

SELF-ASSESSMENT

Individuals who are not on PAYE, notably the self-employed, need to complete a self-assessment tax return each year, in paper form or online at the HMRC website (W www.hmrc.gov.uk), and pay any income tax owed in twice-yearly instalments. Some individuals with more complex tax affairs such as those who earn money from rents or investments above a certain level may also need to fill out a self-assessment return, even if they are on PAYE. HMRC uses the figures supplied on the tax return to work out the individual's tax bill, or they can choose to work it out themselves. It is called 'self-assessment' because individuals are responsible for making sure the details they provide are correct.

Tax returns are usually sent out in early April, following the end of the tax year to which they apply. They may also go out at other times, for example if an individual wants to claim an allowance or repayment or to register for self-assessment for the first time.

Individuals with simple tax affairs, including employees, pensioners and the self-employed with turnovers below £30,000, may receive a short four-page return. Those with more complex affairs must fill out a full return that has 12 core pages plus extra pages, depending on the sorts of income received.

Central to the self-assessment system is the requirement for individuals to contact their tax office if they do not receive a self-assessment return but think they should or if their financial circumstances change. Individuals have six months from when the tax year ends to report any new income, for example. If an individual becomes self-employed, they have three months after the calendar month in which they began self-employed work to let HMRC know. This can be done by telephoning the helpline number for the newly self-employed on T 0845-915 4515.

TAX RETURN FILING AND PAYMENT DEADLINES

There are also key deadlines for filing (sending in) completed tax returns and paying the tax due. Failure to do so can incur penalties, interest charges and surcharges. The deadlines are more generous for individuals who do not want to calculate the tax due themselves and file their tax return online.

KEY FILING DATES FOR SELF-ASSESSMENT RETURNS ISSUED ON OR AFTER 6 APRIL 2010

Date	*Why the deadline is important*
31 Oct	Deadline for filing paper returns for tax year ended the previous 5 April. Late filing incurs an automatic £100 penalty. This deadline applies whether the taxpayer calculates his or her own tax liability or whether he or she wants HMRC to calculate it on their behalf.
31 Jan	Deadline for online filing of returns received by the previous 31 October. Late filing incurs an automatic £100 penalty.
30 Dec	Where a taxpayer files the return online, he or she must do so by this date if HMRC is to collect tax through his or her tax code (if possible) where the amount owed is less than £2,000. Otherwise it can be filed up to 31 January.

KEY SELF-ASSESSMENT DATES

Date	*What payments or penalties are due?*
31 Jan	If a tax return was sent by the previous 31 October, this is the deadline for paying the

balance of any tax owed – the 'balancing payment'. HMRC will charge daily interest after this date until it receives the payment. It is also the date by which a taxpayer must make any first 'payment on account' for the current tax year. For example on 31 January 2010 a taxpayer may have to pay both the balancing payment for the year 2009–10 and the first payment on account for 2010–11.

28 Feb If the balancing payment is not paid by 31 January, a 5 per cent surcharge incurred on top of the amount outstanding may be charged. This is in addition to any interest payments.

31 Jul The deadline for making a second payment on account for tax owing for the preceding tax year. If tax is still owed that was due by the previous 31 January, a second 5 per cent surcharge levied on top of the amount owed may be charged.

TAX CREDITS

Child tax credit and working tax credit are paid to qualifying individuals. Although the title of both credits incorporates the word 'tax', neither affects the amount of income tax payable or repayable. Both are forms of social security benefits. *See* the Social Welfare section.

CAPITAL GAINS TAX

Capital gains tax (CGT) is a tax on the gain or profit that an individual makes when they sell, give away or otherwise dispose of an asset – that is, something they own such as shares, land or buildings. An individual potentially has to pay CGT on gains they make from any disposal of assets during a tax year. There is, however, a tax-free allowance and some additional reliefs that may reduce an individual's CGT bill. The following information relates to the tax year 2010–11 ending on 5 April 2011.

CGT is paid by individuals who are either resident or ordinarily resident in the UK for the tax year, executors or administrators – 'personal representatives' – responsible for a deceased person's financial affairs and trustees of a settlement. Non-residents are not usually liable to CGT unless they carry on a business in the UK through a branch or agency. Special CGT rules may apply to individuals who used to live and work in the UK but have since left the country.

CAPITAL GAINS CHARGEABLE TO CGT

Typically, individuals have made a gain if they sell an asset for more than they paid for it. It is the gain that is taxed, not the amount the individual receives for the asset. For example, a man buys shares for £1,000 and later sells them for £3,000. He has made a gain of £2,000 (£3,000 less £1,000). If someone gives an asset away, the gain will be based on the difference between what the asset was worth when originally acquired compared with its worth at the time of disposal. The same is true when an asset is sold for less than its full worth in order to give away part of the value. For example, a woman buys a property for £120,000 and three years later, when the property's market value has risen to £180,000, she gives it to her son. The son may pay nothing for the property or pay less than its true worth, eg £100,000. Either way, she has made a gain of £60,000 (£180,000 less £120,000).

If an individual disposes of an asset he or she received as a gift, the gain is worked out according to the market value of the asset when it was received. For example, a man gives his sister a painting worth £8,000. She pays nothing for it. Later she sells the painting for £10,000. For CGT purposes, she is treated as making a gain of £2,000 (£10,000 less £8,000). If an individual inherits an asset, the estate of the person who died does not pay CGT at the time. If the inheritor later disposes of the asset, the gain is worked out by looking at the market value at the time of the death. For example, a woman acquires some shares for £5,000 and leaves them to her niece when she dies. No CGT is payable at the time of death when the shares are worth £8,000. Later the niece sells the shares for £10,000. She has made a gain of £2,000 (£10,000 less £8,000).

Individuals may also have to pay CGT if they dispose of part of an asset or exchange one asset for another. Similarly, CGT may be payable if an individual receives a capital sum of money from an asset without disposing of it, for example where he or she receives compensation when an asset is damaged.

Assets that may lead to a CGT charge when they are disposed of include:

- shares in a company
- units in a unit trust
- land and buildings (though not normally an individual's main home – *see* 'disposal of a home' section for details)
- higher value jewellery, paintings, antiques and other personal effects assets used in business such as goodwill

EXEMPT GAINS

Certain kinds of assets do not give rise to a chargeable gain when they are disposed of. Assets exempt from CGT include:

- an individual's private car
- an individual's main home, provided certain conditions are met
- tax-free investments such as assets held in an individual savings account (ISA)
- UK government gilts or 'bonds'
- personal belongings including jewellery, paintings, antiques individually worth £6,000 or less
- cash in sterling or foreign currency held for an individual or his/her family's own personal use
- betting, lottery or pools winnings
- personal injury compensation

DISPOSAL OF A HOME: PRIVATE RESIDENCE RELIEF

Individuals do not have to pay CGT when they sell their main home if all the following conditions are met:

- they bought it and made any expenditure on it, primarily for use as their home rather than with a view to making a profit
- the property was their only home throughout the period they owned it (ignoring the last three years of ownership)
- the property was actually used as their home all the time that they owned it and, throughout the period, it was not used for any purpose other than as a home for the individual, his or her family and no more than one lodger
- the garden and area of grounds sold with the property does not exceed 5,000 sq. m (1.24 acres) including the site of the property

Even if all these conditions are not met, individuals may still be entitled to CGT relief when they sell the home. They may, for example, qualify for relief if they lived away from home temporarily while working abroad. Married couples or couples in a civil partnership may have relief from CGT on only one home. There is a special exception, however, where the spouse or partner each had a qualifying home before marriage or civil partnership and both live together in one of these homes after marriage or civil partnership and sell the other. Provided that it is sold within three years of marriage or the civil partnership, they may not have to pay any CGT (subject to the normal rules for this relief). If they sell it after more than three years it may qualify for partial relief. There are special rules on divorce and separation.

Certain other kinds of disposal similarly do not give rise to a chargeable gain. For example, individuals who are married or in a civil partnership and who live together may sell or give assets to their spouse or civil partner without having to pay CGT. Individuals may not, however, give or sell assets cheaply to their children without having to consider CGT. There is no CGT to pay on assets given to a registered charity.

CALCULATING CGT

CGT is worked out for each tax year and is charged on the total of an individual's taxable gains after taking into account certain costs and reliefs that can reduce or defer chargeable gains, allowable losses made on assets to which CGT normally applies and an annual exempt (tax-free) amount that applies to every individual. If the total of an individual's net gains in a tax year is less than the annual exempt amount (AEA), the individual will not have to pay CGT. For the tax year 2010–11 the AEA is £10,100. If an individual's net gains are more than the AEA, they pay CGT on the excess. Should any part of the exemption remain unused, this cannot be carried forward to a future year. A smaller exemption amount (£5,050 for 2010–11) applies to most trusts.

There are certain reliefs available that may eliminate, reduce or defer CGT. Some reliefs are available to many people while others are available only in special circumstances. Some reliefs are given automatically while others are given only if they are claimed. Some of the costs of buying, selling and improving assets may be deducted from total gains when working out an individual's chargeable gain.

RATES OF TAX

The net gains remaining, if any, calculated after subtracting the AEA, deducting costs and taking into account all CGT reliefs, incur liability to capital gains tax. There was a single rate of CGT of 18 per cent for individuals, trustees and personal representatives on taxable gains until the coalition government's budget on 22 June 2010 when it was announced that, from 23 June 2010, CGT would rise to 28 per cent for higher and additional rate taxpayers. Basic rate taxpayers continue to pay CGT at a rate of 18 per cent.

CGT for 2010–11 falls due for payment in full on 31 January 2012. If payment is delayed, interest or surcharges may be imposed. A husband and wife or registered civil partners who live together are separately assessed to CGT. Each partner must independently calculate his or her gains and losses with each entitled to the AEA of £10,100 for 2010–11.

VALUATION OF ASSETS

The disposal proceeds – ie the amount received as consideration for the disposal of an asset – are the sum used to establish the gain or loss once certain allowable costs have been deducted. In most cases this is straightforward because the disposal proceeds are the amount actually received for disposing of the asset. This may include cash payable now or in the future and the value of any asset received in exchange for the asset disposed of. However, in certain circumstances, the disposal proceeds may not accurately reflect the value of the asset and the individual may be treated as disposing of an asset for an amount other than the actual amount (if any) that they received. This applies, in particular, where an asset is transferred as a gift or sold for a price known to be below market value. Disposal proceeds in such transactions are deemed to be equal to the market value of the asset at the time it was disposed of rather than the actual amount (if any) received for it.

Market value represents the price that an asset might reasonably be expected to fetch upon sale in the open market. In the case of unquoted shares or securities, it is to be assumed that the hypothetical purchaser in the open market would have available all the information that a prudent prospective purchaser of shares or securities might reasonably require if that person were proposing to purchase them from a willing vendor by private treaty and at arm's length. The market value of unquoted shares or securities will often be established following negotiations with the specialist HM Revenue and Customs Shares & Assets Valuation department. The valuation of land and interests in land in the UK is dealt with by the Valuation Office Agency. Special rules apply to determine the market value of shares quoted on the London Stock Exchange.

ALLOWABLE COSTS

When working out a chargeable gain, once the actual or notional disposal proceeds have been determined, certain allowable costs may be deducted. There is a general rule that no costs that could be taken into account when working out income or losses for income tax purposes may be deducted. Subject to this, allowable costs are:

- acquisition costs – the actual amount spent on acquiring the asset or, in certain circumstances, the equivalent market value
- incidental costs of acquiring the asset such as fees paid for professional advice, valuation costs, stamp duty and advertising costs to find a seller
- enhancement costs – incurred for the purpose of enhancing the value of the asset (not including normal maintenance and repair costs)
- expenditure on defending or establishing a person's rights over the asset
- incidental costs of disposing of the asset such as fees paid for professional advice, valuation costs, stamp duty and advertising costs to find a buyer

If an individual disposes of part of his or her interest in an asset, or part of a holding of shares of the same class in the same company, or part of a holding of units in the same unit trust, he or she can deduct part of the allowable costs of the asset or holding when working out the chargeable gain. Allowable costs may also be reduced by some reliefs.

ENTREPRENEURS' RELIEF

Introduced in April 2008, Entrepreneurs' Relief allows individuals in business and some trustees to claim relief on the first £5m of gains (£2m prior to 23 June 2010) made on the disposal of any of the following: all or part of a business; the assets of a business after it has ceased; and shares in a company. The relief is available to taxpayers as individuals if they are in business, for example as a sole trader or as a partner in a trading business, or if they hold shares in their own personal trading company. This relief is not available for companies.

Depending on the type of disposal, certain qualifying conditions need to be met throughout a qualifying one-year period. For example, if an individual is selling all or part of their business, they must have owned the business during a one-year period that ends on the date of the disposal.

The relief reduces gains liable to CGT by four-ninths on all qualifying gains up to £5m, resulting in an effective 10 per cent rate. An individual can make claims for this relief on more than one occasion as long as the lifetime total of all their claims does not exceed £5m of gains qualifying for relief.

BUSINESS ASSET ROLL-OVER RELIEF

When certain types of business asset are sold or disposed of and the proceeds reinvested in new qualifying trading assets, business asset roll-over relief makes it possible to 'roll-over' or postpone the payment of any CGT that would normally be due. The gain is deducted from the base cost of the new asset and only becomes chargeable to CGT on the eventual disposal of that replacement asset unless a further roll-over situation then develops. Full relief is available if all the proceeds from the original asset are reinvested in the qualifying replacement asset.

For example, a trader sells a freehold office for £75,000 and makes a gain of £30,000. All of the proceeds are reinvested in a new freehold business premises costing £90,000. The trader can postpone the whole of the £30,000 gain made on the sale of the old office, as all of the proceeds have been reinvested. When the trader eventually sells the new business premises and the CGT bill becomes payable, the cost of the new premises will be treated as £60,000 (£90,000 less the £30,000 gain).

If only part of the proceeds from the disposal of an old asset is reinvested in a new one, it may still be possible to postpone paying tax on part of the gain until the eventual disposal of the new asset.

Relief is only available if the acquisition of the new asset takes place within a period between 12 months before, and 36 months after, the disposal of the old asset. However, HMRC may extend this time limit at their discretion where there is a clear intention to acquire a replacement asset. The most common types of business assets that qualify for roll-over relief are land, buildings occupied and used for the purposes of trade, fixed plant and machinery. Assets used for the commercial letting of furnished holiday accommodation qualify if certain conditions are satisfied.

An HMRC help sheet on business asset roll-over relief can be found at W www.hmrc.gov.uk/helpsheets/hs290.pdf

GIFTS HOLD-OVER RELIEF

The gift of an asset is treated as a disposal made for a consideration equal to market value, with a corresponding acquisition by the transferee at an identical value. In the case of gifts of business assets made by individuals and a limited range of trustees, a form of hold-over relief may be available. This relief, which must be claimed, in effect enables liability for CGT to be deferred and passed to the person to whom the gift is made. Relief is limited to the transfer of certain assets including the following:

- gifts of assets used for the purposes of a business carried on by the donor or his or her personal company
- gifts of shares in trading companies that are not listed on a stock exchange
- gifts of shares or securities in the donor's personal trading company
- gifts of agricultural land and buildings that would qualify for inheritance tax agricultural property relief
- gifts that are chargeable transfers for inheritance tax purposes
- certain types of gifts that are specifically exempted from inheritance tax

Hold-over relief is automatically due on certain sorts of gifts including gifts to charities and community amateur sports clubs, and gifts of works of art where certain undertakings have been given. There are certain rules to prevent gifts hold-over relief being used for tax-avoidance purposes. For example, restrictions may apply where an individual gifts assets to trustees administering a trust in which the individual retains an interest or the assets transferred comprise a dwelling-house. Subject to these exceptions, the effect of a valid claim for hold-over relief is similar to that following a claim for roll-over relief on the disposal of business assets. An HMRC helpsheet on gifts hold-over relief can be found at W www.hmrc.gov.uk/helpsheets/hs295.pdf

OTHER CGT RELIEFS

There are certain other CGT reliefs available on the disposal of property, shares and business assets. For detailed information on these reliefs and for more general guidance on CGT, see the capital gains tax pages on the HMRC website (W www.hmrc.gov.uk/cgt).

REPORTING AND PAYING CGT

Individuals are responsible for telling HMRC about capital gains on which they they have to pay tax. Individuals who receive a self-assessment tax return may report capital gains by filling in the capital gains supplementary pages – the return explains how to obtain these pages if needed.

Individuals who do not normally complete a tax return but who need to report capital gains or losses should contact their local tax office. If an individual has CGT to pay, they must tell their tax office in writing by 5 October after the end of the tax year for which the CGT is due.

There is a time limit for claiming capital losses. The deadline is five years from 31 January after the end of the tax year in which the loss was made.

INHERITANCE TAX

Inheritance tax (IHT) is a tax on the value of a person's estate on death and on certain gifts made by an individual during his or her lifetime, usually payable within six months of death. Broadly speaking, a person's estate is everything he or she owned at the time of death including property, possessions, money and investments, less his or her debts. Not everyone pays IHT. It only applies if the taxable value of an estate is above the current inheritance tax threshold. If an estate, including any assets held in trust and gifts made within seven years of death, is less than the threshold, no IHT will be due. See table for the lower threshold limit, known as the nil rate band.

It was announced in the 2009 pre-Budget report that the nil rate band for 2010–11 would be frozen at £325,000 and it was further announced in the 2010 Budget that this freeze would extend until 2014–15.

2007–8	£300,000
2008–9	£312,000
2009–10	£325,000
2010–11	£325,000

A claim can be made to transfer any unused IHT nil-rate band on a person's death to the estate of their surviving spouse or civil partner. This applies where the IHT nil-rate band of the first deceased spouse or civil partner was not fully used in calculating the IHT liability of their estate. When the surviving spouse or civil partner dies, the unused amount may be added to their own nil-rate band (*see* below for details).

IHT used to be something only very wealthy individuals needed to consider. This is no longer the case. The fact that the IHT threshold has not kept pace with house price inflation in recent years means that the estates of some 'ordinary' taxpayers, who would not consider themselves wealthy, are now liable for IHT purely because of the value of their home. However, there are a number of ways that individuals – while still alive – can legally reduce the IHT bill that will apply to their estates on death. Several valuable IHT exemptions are available (explained further below) which allow individuals to pass on assets during their lifetime or in their will without any IHT being due. Detailed information on IHT is available on the HMRC website (W www.hmrc.gov.uk/inheritancetax/index.htm). Further help is also available from the IHT & Probate Helpline on T 0845-302 0900.

DOMICILE

Liability to IHT depends on an individual's domicile at the time of any gift or on death. Domicile is a complex legal concept and what follows explains some of the main issues. An individual is domiciled in the country where he or she has a permanent home. Domicile is different from nationality or residence, and an individual can only have one domicile at any given time.

A 'domicile of origin' is normally acquired from the individual's father on birth, though this may not be the country in which he or she is born. For example, a child born in Germany while his or her father is working there, but whose permanent home is in the UK, will have the UK as his or her domicile of origin. Until a person legally changes his or her domicile, it will be the same as that of the person on whom they are legally dependent.

Individuals can legally acquire a new domicile – a 'domicile of choice' – from the age of 16 by leaving the current country of domicile and settling in another country and providing strong evidence of intention to live there permanently or indefinitely. Women who were married before 1974 acquired their husband's domicile and still retain it until they legally acquire a new domicile.

For IHT purposes, there is a concept of 'deemed domicile'. This means that even if a person is not domiciled in the UK under general law, he or she is treated as domiciled in the UK at the time of a transfer (ie at the time of a lifetime gift or on death) if he or she (a) was domiciled in the UK within the three years immediately before the transfer, or (b) was 'resident' in the UK in at least 17 of the 20 income tax years of assessment ending with the year in which a transfer is made. Where a person is domiciled, or treated as domiciled, in the UK at the time of a gift or on death, the location of assets is immaterial and full liability to IHT arises. A non-UK domiciled individual is also liable to IHT but only on chargeable property in the UK.

The assets of husband and wife and registered civil partners are not merged for IHT purposes, except that the IHT value of assets owned by one spouse or civil partner may be affected if the other also owns similar assets (eg shares in the same company or a share in their jointly owned house). Each spouse or partner is treated as a separate individual entitled to receive the benefit of his or her exemptions, reliefs and rates of tax.

IHT EXEMPTIONS

There are some important exemptions that allow individuals to legally pass assets on to others, both before and after their death – without being subject to IHT.

Exempt beneficiaries

Assets can be given away to certain people and organisations without any IHT having to be paid. These gifts, which are exempt whether individuals make them during their lifetime or in their will, include gifts to:

- a husband, wife or civil partner, even if the couple is legally separated (but not if they are divorced or the civil partnership has dissolved), as long as both partners have a permanent home in the UK. Note that gifts to an unmarried partner or a partner with whom the donor has not formed a civil partnership are not exempt
- UK charities
- some national institutions, including national museums, universities and the National Trust
- UK political parties

Annual exemption

The first £3,000 of gifts made each tax year by each individual is exempt from IHT. If this exemption is not used, or not wholly used in any year, the balance may be carried forward to the following year only. A couple, therefore, may give away a total of £6,000 per tax year between them or £12,000 if they haven't used their previous year's annual exemptions.

Wedding gifts/civil partnership ceremony gifts

Some gifts are exempt from IHT because of the type of gift or reason for making it. Wedding or civil partnership ceremony gifts made to either of the couple are exempt from IHT up to certain amounts:

- gifts by a parent, £5,000
- gifts by a grandparent or other relative, £2,500
- gifts by anyone else, £1,000

The gift must be made on or shortly before the date of the wedding or civil partnership ceremony. If the ceremony is called off but the gift is made, this exemption will not apply.

Small gifts

An individual can make small gifts, up to the value of £250, to any number of people in any one tax year without them being liable for IHT. However, a larger sum such as £500 cannot be given and exemption claimed for the first £250. In addition, this exemption cannot be used with any other exemption when giving to the same person. For example, a parent cannot combine a 'small gifts exemption' with a 'wedding/civil partnership ceremony gift exemption' to give a child £5,250 when he or she gets married or forms a civil partnership. Neither may an individual combine a 'small gifts exemption' with the 'annual exemption' to give someone £3,250. Note that it is possible to use the 'annual exemption' with any other exemption, such as the 'wedding/civil partnership ceremony gift exemption'. For example, if a child marries or forms a civil partnership, the parent can give him or her a total IHT-free gift of £8,000 by combining £5,000 under the wedding/civil partnership gift exemption and £3,000 under the annual exemption.

Normal expenditure

Any gifts made out of individuals' after-tax income (not capital) are exempt from IHT if they are part of their normal expenditure and do not result in a fall in their standard of living. These can include regular payments to someone, such as an allowance or gifts for Christmas or a birthday and regular premiums paid on a life insurance policy for someone else.

Maintenance gifts

An individual can make IHT-free maintenance payments to his or her spouse or registered civil partner, ex spouse or former civil partner, relatives dependent because of old age or infirmity, and children (including adopted children and step-children) who are under 18 or in full-time education.

POTENTIALLY EXEMPT TRANSFERS

If an individual makes a gift to either another individual or certain types of trust and it is not covered by one of the above exemptions, it is known as a 'potentially exempt transfer' (PET). A PET is only free of IHT on two strict conditions: (a) the gift must be made at least seven years before the donor's death. If the donor does not survive seven years after making the gift, it will be liable for IHT and (b) the gift must be made as a true gift with no strings attached (technically known as a 'gift with reservation of benefit'). This means that the donor must give up all rights to the gift and stop benefiting from it in any way.

If a gift is made and the donor does retain some benefit from it then it will still count as part of his or her estate no matter how long he or she lives after making it. For example, a father could make a lifetime gift of his home to his child. HMRC would not accept this as a true gift, however, if the father continued to live in the home (unless he paid his child a full commercial rent to do so) because he would be considered to still have a material interest in the gifted home. Its value, therefore, would still be liable for IHT.

In some circumstances a gift with strings attached might give rise to an income tax charge on the donor based on the value of the benefit he or she retains. In this case the donor can choose whether to pay the income tax or have the gift treated as a gift with reservation.

CHARGEABLE TRANSFERS

Any remaining lifetime gifts that are not (potentially or otherwise) exempt transfers are chargeable transfers or 'chargeable gifts', meaning that they incur liability to IHT. Chargeable transfers comprise mainly gifts to or from companies and gifts to particular types of trust. There is an immediate claim for IHT on chargeable gifts, and additional tax may be payable if the donor dies within seven years of making a chargeable gift.

DEATH

Immediately before the time of death an individual is deemed to make a transfer of value. This transfer will comprise the value of assets forming part of the deceased's estate after subtracting most liabilities. Any exempt transfers may be excluded such as transfers for the benefit of a surviving spouse or civil partner, and charities. Death may also trigger three additional liabilities:

- a PET made within the seven years before the death loses its potential status and becomes chargeable to IHT
- the value of gifts made with reservation may incur liability if any benefit was enjoyed within the seven years before the death
- additional tax may become payable for chargeable lifetime transfers made within the seven years before the death

The 'personal representative' (the person nominated to handle the affairs of the deceased person) arranges to value the estate and pay any IHT that is due. One or more personal representatives can be nominated in a person's will, in which case they are known as the 'executors'. If a person dies without leaving a will a court can nominate the personal representative, who is then known as the 'administrator'. Valuing the deceased person's estate is one of the first things his or her personal representative needs to do. The representative will not normally be able to take over management of the estate (called 'applying for probate') until all or some of any IHT that is due has been paid.

VALUATIONS

When valuing a deceased person's estate all assets (property, possessions and money) owned at the time of death and certain assets given away during the seven years before death must be included. The valuation must accurately reflect what those assets would reasonably fetch in the open market at the date of death. The value of all of the assets that the deceased owned should include:

- his or her share of any assets owned jointly with someone else, for example a house owned with a partner
- any assets that are held in a trust, from which the deceased had the right to benefit
- any assets given away, but in which he or she kept an interest (gifts with reservation)
- PETs given away within the last seven years

Most estate assets can be valued quite easily, for example money in bank accounts or stocks and shares. In other instances the help of a professional valuer may be needed. Advice on how to value different assets including joint or trust assets is available at W www.hmrc.gov.uk. When valuing an estate, special relief is made available for certain assets. The two main reliefs are business relief and agricultural property relief outlined below. Once all assets have been valued, the next step is to deduct from the total assets everything that the deceased person owed such as unpaid bills, outstanding mortgages and other loans plus their funeral expenses. The value of all of the assets, less the deductible debts, is their estate. IHT is only payable on any value above £325,000 for the tax year 2010–11 at the current rate of 40 per cent.

RELIEF FOR SELECTED ASSETS

Agricultural Property
Relief from IHT is available on the agricultural value of agricultural property that is transferred. Agricultural property generally includes land or pasture used in the growing of crops or intensive rearing of animals for food consumption. It can also include farmhouses and farm cottages. The agricultural property can be owner-occupied or let. Relief is only due if the transferor has owned the property and it has been occupied for agricultural purposes for a minimum period.

The chargeable value transferred, either on a lifetime gift or on death, must be determined. This value may then be reduced by a percentage. Under current rates, a 100 per cent deduction will be available if the transferor retained vacant possession or could have obtained that possession within a period of 12 months following the transfer. In other cases, notably including land let to tenants, a lower deduction of 50 per cent is usually available. However, this lower deduction may be increased to 100 per cent if the letting was made after 31 August 1995.

To qualify for the relief, the agricultural property must either have been occupied by the transferor for the purposes of agriculture throughout a two-year period ending on the date of the transfer, or have been owned by the transferor throughout a period of seven years ending on that date and also occupied for agricultural purposes.

Business Relief
Business relief is available on transfers of certain types of business and of business assets if they qualify as relevant business property and the transferor has owned them for a minimum period. The relief can be claimed for transfers made during the person's lifetime and on death and on chargeable occasions arising on relevant business property held in trust. Where the chargeable value transferred is attributable to relevant business property, the business relief reduces that value by a percentage. Business relief may be claimed on relevant business property including:

- a business or an interest in a business such as a partnership
- unquoted shares and securities
- shares or securities of a quoted company which themselves or with other listed shares or securities give the transferor control of a company
- any land, buildings, plant or machinery owned by a partner or controlling shareholder and used wholly or mainly in the business of the partnership or company immediately before the transfer; this applies only if the partnership interest or shareholding would itself, if it were transferred, qualify for business relief
- any land, buildings, machinery or plant that were used wholly or mainly for the purpose of a business carried on by the transferor

If an asset qualifies for business relief, the rates at which it is currently allowed are as follows:

A business or interest in a business	100%
A holding of shares in an unquoted company	100%
Control holding of shares in a quoted company (more than 50 per cent of the voting rights)	50%
Land, buildings or plant and machinery used in a business of which the deceased was a partner at the date of death or used by a company controlled by the deceased	50%
Land, buildings, plant and machinery held in a trust where the deceased had the right to benefit from the trust and the asset was used in a business carried on by the deceased	50%

It is a general requirement that the property must have been retained for a period of two years before the transfer or death, and restrictions may be necessary if the property has not been used wholly for business purposes. The same property cannot obtain both business property relief and the relief available for agricultural property.

CALCULATION OF TAX PAYABLE

The calculation of IHT payable adopts the use of a cumulative or 'running' total. Looking back seven years from the death the chargeable value of gifts in that period is added to the total value of the estate at death. The gifts will use up all or part of the inheritance tax threshold (the 'nil-rate band' above which IHT becomes payable) first.

Lifetime Chargeable Transfers
The value transferred by lifetime chargeable transfers must be added to the seven-year running total to calculate whether any IHT is due. If the nil-rate band is exceeded, tax will be imposed on the excess at the rate of 20 per cent. However, if the donor dies within a period of seven years from the date of the chargeable lifetime transfer, additional tax may be due. This is calculated by applying tax at the full rate of 40 per cent in substitution for the rate of 20 per cent previously used. The amount of tax is then reduced to a percentage by applying tapering relief. This percentage is governed by the number of years from the date of the lifetime gift to the date of death, as follows:

PERIOD OF YEARS BEFORE DEATH

Not more than 3	100%
More than 3 but not more than 4	80%
More than 4 but not more than 5	60%
More than 5 but not more than 6	40%
More than 6 but not more than 7	20%

Should this exercise produce liability greater than that previously paid at the 20 per cent rate on the lifetime transfer, additional tax, representing the difference, must be paid. Where the calculation shows an amount falling below tax paid on the lifetime transfer, no additional liability can arise nor will the shortfall become repayable.

Tapering relief is, of course, only available if the calculation discloses a liability to IHT. There is no liability if the lifetime transfer falls within the nil-rate band.

Potentially Exempt Transfers
Where a PET loses immunity from liability to IHT because the donor dies within seven years of making the transfer, the value transferred enters into the running total. Any liability to IHT will be calculated by applying the full rate of 40 per cent, reduced to the percentage governed by tapering relief if the original transfer occurred more than three years before death. Again, liability to IHT can only arise if the nil-rate band is exceeded.

Death
On death, IHT is due on the value of the deceased's estate plus the running total of gifts made in the seven years

before death if they come to more than the nil-rate band. IHT is then charged at the full rate of 40 per cent on the amount in excess of the nil-rate band.

Settled Property and Trusts
Trusts are special legal arrangements that can be used by individuals to control how their assets are distributed to their beneficiaries and minimise their IHT liability. Complex rules apply to establish IHT liability on settled property which includes property held in trust, and individuals are advised to take expert legal advice when setting up trusts.

RATES OF TAX
Previously there were several rates of IHT that progressively increased as the value transferred grew in size. However, since 1988 there have been only three rates:

- a nil rate
- a lifetime rate of 20 per cent
- a full rate of 40 per cent

The nil-rate band usually changes on an annual basis, and for events taking place after 5 April 2010 applies to the first £325,000. Any excess over this level is taxable at 20 per cent or 40 per cent as the case may be.

TRANSFER OF NIL-RATE BAND
Transfers of property between spouses or civil partners are generally exempt from IHT. This means that someone who dies leaving some or all of their property to their spouse or civil partner may not have fully used up their nil-rate band. Under rules introduced in autumn 2007, any nil-rate band unused on the first death can be used when the surviving spouse or civil partner dies. A transfer of unused nil-rate band from a deceased spouse or civil partner (no matter what the date of their death) may be made to the estate of their surviving spouse or civil partner who dies on or after 9 October 2007.

Where a valid claim to transfer unused nil-rate band is made, the nil-rate band that is available when the surviving spouse or civil partner dies is increased by the proportion of the nil-rate band unused on the first death. For example, if on the first death the chargeable estate is £150,000 and the nil-rate band is £300,000, 50 per cent of the nil-rate band would be unused. If the nil-rate band when the survivor dies is £325,000, then that would be increased by 50 per cent to £487,500. The amount of the nil-rate band that can be transferred does not depend on the value of the first spouse or civil partner's estate. Whatever proportion of the nil-rate band is unused on the first death is available for transfer to the survivor.

The amount of additional nil-rate band that can be accumulated by any one surviving spouse or civil partner is limited to the value of the nil-rate band in force at the time of their death. This may be relevant, for example, where a person dies having survived more than one spouse or civil partner.

Where these rules have effect, personal representatives do not have to claim for unused nil-rate band to be transferred at the time of the first death. Any claims for transfer of unused nil-rate band amounts are made by the personal representatives of the estate of the second spouse or civil partner to die when they make an IHT return.

Detailed guidance on how to transfer the nil-rate band can be found on the HMRC website.

PAYMENT OF TAX
IHT is normally due six months after the end of the month in which the death occurs or the chargeable transaction takes place. This is referred to as the 'due date'. Tax on some assets such as business property, certain shares and securities and land and buildings (including the deceased person's home) can be deferred and paid in equal instalments over ten years, though interest will be charged in most cases. If IHT is due on lifetime gifts and transfers, the person or transferee who received the gift or assets is normally liable to pay the IHT, though any IHT already paid at the time of a transfer into a trust or company will be taken into account. If tax owed is not paid by the due date, interest is charged on any unpaid IHT, no matter what caused the delay in payment.

CORPORATION TAX

Corporation tax is a tax on a company's profits, including all its income and gains. This tax is payable by UK resident companies and by non-resident companies carrying on a trade in the UK through a permanent establishment. The following comments are confined to companies resident in the UK. The word 'company' is also used to include:

- members' clubs, societies and associations
- trade associations
- housing associations
- groups of individuals carrying on a business but not as a partnership (for example, cooperatives)

A company's taxable income is charged by reference to income or gains arising in its 'accounting period', which is normally 12 months long. In some circumstances accounting periods can be shorter than 12 months, but never longer. The accounting period is also normally the period for which a company's accounts are drawn up, but the two periods do not have to coincide.

If a company is liable to pay corporation tax on its profits, several things must be done. HMRC must be informed that the company exists and is liable for tax. A self-assessment company tax return plus full accounts and calculation of tax liability must be filed by the statutory filing date, normally 12 months after the end of the accounting period. Companies have to work out their own tax liability and have to pay their tax without prior assessment by HMRC. Records of all company expenditure and income must be kept in order to work out the tax liability correctly. Companies are liable to penalties if they fail to carry out these obligations.

Extensive corporation tax information is available on the HMRC website at W www.hmrc.gov.uk/businesses and companies may file their company tax returns online at W www.hmrc.gov.uk/ct/ct-online/file-return/online.htm

RATE OF TAX
The rate of corporation tax is fixed for a financial year starting on 1 April and ending on the following 31 March. If a company's accounting period does not coincide with the financial year, its profits must be apportioned between the financial years and the tax rates for each financial year applied to those profits. The corporation tax liability is the total tax for both financial years.

The main rate of corporation tax for 2010–11 is 28 per cent. North Sea oil and gas ringfence activities but retain a main corporation tax rate of 30 per cent. The main rate of corporation tax applies when profits (including ringfence profits) are at a rate exceeding £1.5m, or where there is no claim to another rate, or where another rate does not apply.

It was announced in the 22 June 2010 budget that the main rate of corporation tax will be reduced to 27 per cent in 2011–12, with further reductions to 26 per cent in 2012–13, 25 per cent in 2013–14 and 24 per cent in 2014–15.

SMALL COMPANIES' RATE

Where the profits of a company do not exceed stated limits, corporation tax becomes payable at the small companies' rate. It is the amount of profits and not the size of the company that governs the application of the small companies' rate.

The small companies rate for 2010–11 is 21 per cent. It was announced in the 22 June 2010 budget that this rate will fall to 20 per cent from April 2011. North Sea oil and gas ringfence activities retain a small companies' rate of 19 per cent.

A company can make profits of up to £300,000 without losing the benefit of the small companies' rate. If, however, its profits exceed £300,000 but fall below £1.5m, then marginal small companies' rate relief applies to ease the transition. The effect of marginal relief is that the average rate of corporation tax imposed on all profits steadily increases from the lower small companies' rate of 21 per cent to the main rate of 28 per cent, with tax being imposed on profits in the margin at an increased rate. HMRC has produced an easy-to-use corporation tax marginal relief rate calculator at W www.hmrc.gov.uk/calcs/mrr.htm

Where a change in the rate of tax is introduced and the accounting period of a company overlaps 31 March, profits must be apportioned to establish the appropriate rate for each part of those profits.

The lower limit of £300,000 and the upper limit of £1.5m apply to a period of 12 months and must be proportionately reduced for shorter periods. Some restriction in the small companies' rate and the marginal rate may be necessary if there are two or more associated companies, namely companies under common control.

CORPORATION TAX ON PROFITS

£ per year	*2010–11*	*2011–12*
£0–£300,000	21%	20%
£300,001–£1,500,000	Marginal relief	Marginal relief
£1,500,001 or more	28%	27%

CAPITAL ALLOWANCES

Businesses can claim tax allowances, called capital allowances, on certain purchases or investments. This means that a proportion of these costs can be deducted from a business' taxable profits and reduce its tax bill. Capital allowances are currently available on plant and machinery, buildings and research and development. The amount of the allowance depends on what is being claimed for.

Detailed information on capital allowances is available from the Enhanced Capital Allowances website (W www.eca.gov.uk).

PAYMENT OF TAX

Corporation tax liabilities are normally due and payable in a single lump sum not later than nine months and one day after the end of the accounting period. For 'large' companies – those with profits over £1.5m which pay corporation tax at the main rate – there is a requirement to pay corporation tax in four quarterly instalments. Where a company is a member of a group, the profits of the entire group must be merged to establish whether the company is large.

In November 2008 HMRC launched a Business Payment Support Service (BPSS) which allows businesses facing temporary financial difficulties more time to pay their tax bills. Traders concerned about their ability to meet corporation tax, VAT or other payments owed to HMRC can call the Business Payment Support Line on T 0845-302 1435 seven days a week. This helpline is for new enquiries only, not for traders who have already been contacted by HMRC about an overdue payment. For details of the service visit W www.hmrc.gov.uk/pbr2008/business-payment.htm

CAPITAL GAINS

Chargeable gains arising to a company are calculated in a manner similar to that used for individuals. However, companies are not entitled to the CGT annual exemption. Companies do not suffer capital gains tax on chargeable gains but incur liability to corporation tax instead. Tax is due on the full chargeable gain of an accounting period after subtracting relief for losses, if any.

GROUPS OF COMPANIES

Each company within a group is separately charged to corporation tax on profits, gains and income. However, where one group member realises a loss for which special rules apply, other than a capital loss, a claim may be made to offset the deficiency against profits of some other member of the same group. The transfer of capital assets from one member of a group to a fellow member will usually incur no liability to tax on chargeable gains.

SPORTS CLUBS

Though corporation tax is payable by unincorporated associations including most clubs, a substantial exemption from liability to corporation tax, introduced in April 2002, is available to qualifying registered community amateur sports clubs (CASCs). Sports clubs that are registered as CASCs are exempt from liability to corporation tax on:

- profits from trading where the turnover of the trade is less than £30,000 in a 12-month period
- income from letting property where the gross rental income is less than £20,000 in a 12-month period
- bank and building society interest received
- chargeable gains

All of the exemptions depend upon the club having been a registered CASC for the whole of the relevant accounting period and the income or gains being used only for qualifying purposes. If the club has only been a registered CASC for part of an accounting period the exemption amounts of £30,000 (for trading) and £20,000 (for income from property) are reduced proportionately. Only interest and gains received after the club is registered are exempted.

Among other advantages available to registered clubs is that donations may be received under the Gift Aid arrangements. Charities are also generally exempt from corporation tax where they operate through a company structure.

VALUE ADDED TAX

Value added tax (VAT) is a tax on consumer expenditure charged when an individual buys goods and services in the European Union including the UK. It is normally included in the sale price of goods and services and paid at the point of purchase. Each EU country has its own rate of VAT. From a business point of view, VAT is charged on most business transactions involving the supply of goods and services by a registered trader in the UK and Isle of Man. It is also charged on goods and some services imported from places outside the EU and on goods and some services coming into the UK from the other EU countries. VAT is administered by HM Revenue and Customs. A wide range of information on VAT, including VAT forms, is available online at W www.hmrc.gov.uk/vat/index. HMRC also runs a VAT and Excise helpline on T 0845-010 9000.

RATES OF TAX

There are three rates of VAT in the UK. The standard rate, payable on most goods and services in the UK, is 17.5 per cent until 4 January 2011 when it rises to 20 per cent. This increase was announced in the coalition government's budget on 22 June 2010.

The reduced rate – currently 5 per cent – is payable on certain goods and services including, for example, domestic fuel and power, children's car seats, women's sanitary products, contraceptive products and the installation of energy-saving materials such as wall insulation and solar panels. Since 1 January 2008 renovations and alterations to residential properties that have been empty for at least two years have been eligible for the 5 per cent rate.

A zero, or nil, rate applies to certain items including, for example, children's clothes, books, newspapers, most food and drink, and drugs and aids for disabled people. There are numerous exceptions to the zero-rated categories however. While most food and drink is zero-rated, items including ice creams, chocolates, sweets, potato crisps and alcoholic drinks are not. Neither are drinks or items sold for consumption in a restaurant or cafe. Takeaway cold items such as sandwiches are zero-rated, while takeaway hot foods like fish and chips are not.

REGISTRATION

All traders, including professional persons and companies, must register for VAT if they are making 'taxable supplies' of a value exceeding stated limits. All goods and services that are VAT-rated are defined as 'taxable supplies' including zero-rated items which must be included when calculating the total value of a trader's taxable supplies – his or her 'taxable turnover'. The limits that govern mandatory registration are amended periodically.

An unregistered trader must register for VAT if:

- at the end of any month the total value of his or her taxable turnover (not just profit) for the past 12 months or less is more than the current VAT threshold of £70,000 – *and*
- at any time he or she has reasonable grounds to expect that his or her taxable turnover will be more than the current registration threshold of £70,000 in the next 30 days alone

To register for VAT, one or more forms must be completed and sent to HMRC within 30 days of any of the above. Basic VAT registration can currently be completed online (W https://online.hmrc.gov.uk/registration/). Traders who do not register at the correct time can be fined. Traders must charge VAT on their taxable supplies from the date they first need to be registered. Traders who only supply zero-rated goods may not have to register for VAT even if their taxable turnover goes above the registration threshold. However, a trader in this position must inform HMRC first and apply to be 'exempt from registration'. A trader whose taxable turnover does not reach the mandatory registration limit may choose to register for VAT voluntarily if what he or she does counts as a business for VAT purposes. This step may be thought advisable to recover input tax (*see* below) or to compete with other registered traders. Registered traders may submit an application for deregistration if their taxable turnover subsequently falls. An application for deregistration can be made if the taxable turnover for the year beginning on the application date is not expected to exceed £68,000.

INPUT TAX

Registered traders suffer input tax when buying in goods or services for the purposes of their business. It is the VAT that traders pay out to their suppliers on goods and services coming *in* to their business. Relief can usually be obtained for input tax suffered, either by setting that tax against output tax due or by repayment. Most items of input tax can be relieved in this manner. Where a registered trader makes both exempt supplies and taxable supplies to his customers or clients, there may be some restriction in the amount of input tax that can be recovered.

OUTPUT TAX

When making a taxable supply of goods or services, registered traders must account for output tax, if any, on the value of that supply. Output tax is the term used to describe the VAT on the goods and services that they supply or sell – the VAT on supplies going *out* of the business and collected from customers on each sale made. Usually the price charged by the registered trader will be increased by adding VAT, but failure to make the required addition will not remove liability to account for output tax. The liability to account for output tax, and also relief for input tax, may be affected where a trader is using a special secondhand goods scheme.

EXEMPT SUPPLIES

VAT is not chargeable on certain goods and services because the law deems them 'exempt' from VAT. These include the provision of burial and cremation facilities, insurance, loans of money, certain types of education and training and some property transactions. The granting of a lease to occupy land or the sale of land will usually comprise an exempt supply, for example, but there are numerous exceptions. Exempt supplies do not enter into the calculation of taxable turnover that governs liability to mandatory registration (*see* above). Such supplies made by a registered trader may, however, limit the amount of input tax that can be relieved. It is for this reason that the exemption may be useful.

COLLECTION OF TAX

Registered traders submit VAT returns for accounting periods usually of three months in duration, but arrangements can be made to submit returns on a monthly basis. Very large traders must account for tax on a monthly basis, but this does not affect the three-monthly return. The return will show both the output tax due for supplies made by the trader in the accounting period and also the input tax for which relief is claimed. If the output tax exceeds input tax the balance must be remitted with the VAT return. Where input tax suffered exceeds the output tax due, the registered trader may claim the excess from HMRC.

This basis for collecting tax explains the structure of VAT. Where supplies are made between registered traders the supplier will account for an amount of tax that will usually be identical to the tax recovered by the person to whom the supply is made. However, where the supply is made to a person who is not a registered trader there can be no recovery of input tax and it is on this person that the final burden of VAT eventually falls. Where goods are acquired by a UK trader from a supplier within the EU, the trader must also account for the tax due on acquisition. There are a number of simplified arrangements to make VAT accounting easier for businesses, particularly small businesses, and there is advice on the HMRC website about how to choose the most appropriate scheme for a business:

Cash accounting
This scheme allows businesses to only pay VAT on the basis of payments received from their customers rather than on invoice dates or time of supply. It can therefore be useful for businesses with cash flow problems that cannot pay their VAT as a result. Businesses may use the cash accounting scheme if taxable turnover is under £1.35m. There is no need to apply for the scheme – eligible businesses may start using it at the beginning of a new tax period. If a trader opts to use this scheme, he or she can do so until the taxable turnover reaches £1.6m.

Annual accounting
If taxable turnover is under £1.35m a year, the trader may join the annual accounting scheme which allows them to make nine monthly or three quarterly instalments during the year based on an estimate of their total annual VAT bill. At the end of the year they submit a single return and any balance due. The advantages of this scheme for businesses are easier budgeting and cash flow planning because fixed payments are spread regularly throughout the year. Once a trader has joined the annual accounting scheme, membership may continue until the annual taxable turnover reaches £1.6m.

Flat rate scheme
First introduced in the 2002 budget, this scheme allows small businesses with an annual taxable turnover of less than £150,000 to save on administration by paying VAT as a set flat percentage of their annual turnover instead of accounting internally for VAT on each individual 'in and out'. The percentage rate used is governed by the trade sector into which the business falls. The scheme can no longer be used once annual income exceeds £225,000 (rising to £230,000 from 4 January 2011).

Retail schemes
There are special schemes that offer retailers an alternative if it is impractical for them to issue invoices for a large number of supplies direct to the public. These schemes include a provision to claim relief from VAT on bad debts where goods or services are supplied to a customer who does not pay for them.

VAT FACT SUMMARY
from 1 April 2010

Standard rate	15%
Reduced rate	5%
Registration (last 12 months or next 30 days)	£70,000
Deregistration (next 12 months under)	£68,000
Cash accounting scheme – up to	£1,350,000
Flat rate scheme – up to	£150,000
Annual accounting scheme – up to	£1,350,000

STAMP DUTY

For the majority of people, contact with stamp duty arises when they buy a property. Stamp duty is payable by the buyer as a way of raising revenue for the government based on the purchase price of a property, stocks and shares. This section aims to provide a broad overview of stamp duty as it may affect the average person.

STAMP DUTY LAND TAX

Stamp duty land tax was introduced on 1 December 2003 and covers the purchase of houses, flats and other land, buildings and certain leases in the UK.

Before 1 December 2003 property purchasers had to submit documents providing all details of the purchase to the Stamp Office for 'stamping'. The purchaser's solicitor or licensed conveyancer would then send the stamped documentation to the appropriate land registry to register ownership of the property. Under stamp duty land tax, purchasers do not have to send documents for stamping. Instead, a land transaction return form SDLT1, which contains all information regarding the purchase that is relevant to HMRC, is signed by the purchaser. Buyers of property are responsible for completing the land transaction return and payment of stamp duty, though the solicitor or licensed conveyancer acting for them in a land transaction will normally complete the relevant paperwork. Once HMRC has received the completed land transaction return and the payment of any stamp duty due, a certificate will be issued that enables a solicitor or licensed conveyancer to register the property in the new owner's name at the Land Registry.

The threshold for notification of residential property went up from £1,000 to £40,000 on 12 March 2008. This means that taxpayers entering into a transaction involving residential or non-residential property where the chargeable consideration is less than £40,000 no longer need to notify HMRC about the transaction.

RATES OF STAMP DUTY LAND TAX
Stamp duty is charged at different rates and has thresholds for different types of property and different values of transaction. The tax rate and payment threshold can vary according to whether the property is in residential or non-residential use and whether it is freehold or leasehold.

Below a certain threshold, currently £125,000, no stamp duty is payable on residential property purchases. A two-year holiday period from stamp duty for first-time property buyers was announced by the Labour government in its 2010 Budget. The relief is equivalent to a reduction in the average deposit for first-time buyers of £1,500 and is available where:

- an individual or individuals jointly purchase a major interest in land which is wholly residential, and

- the consideration is more than £125,000 but not more than £250,000, and
- that individual (or all of them) intends to occupy the property as their only or main residence, and
- that individual (or all of them) has not previously purchased such an interest, or its equivalent, anywhere in the world, and
- the effective date of the transaction is on or after 25 March 2010 and before 25 March 2012

In order to fund this first-time buyer stamp duty holiday, it was also announced in the 2010 Budget that a new 5 per cent rate of stamp duty would apply to purchases of residential property over £1m from April 2011.

The coalition government announced in its 22 June 2010 budget that it is considering further changes to the rules on stamp duty on high value property transactions in order to prevent tax avoidance in this area.

The following table shows the rates of stamp duty and payment thresholds that apply on residential property purchase prices during 2010–11:

Purchase price	*Rate of tax (% of purchase price)*
up to £125,000*	0%
over £125,000 to £250,000**	1%
over £250,000 to £500,000	3%
over £500,000	4%

* Or over £150,000 for residential property transactions in certain designated disadvantaged areas, a full list of which can be found at W www.hmrc.gov.uk. For transactions of non-residential land and property, the zero per cent rate applies for purchases up to £150,000. A 1 per cent rate is payable for transactions of £150,001–£250,000; thereafter, rates are as per residential property transactions

** First-time buyers can claim relief from stamp duty on residential transactions up to £250,000 between 25 March 2010 and 25 March 2012

When assessing how much stamp duty is payable, the entire purchase price must be taken into account so the relevant stamp duty rate is paid on the whole sum, not just on the amount over each tax threshold. For example, on a property bought for £250,000, 1 per cent (£2,500) is payable in stamp duty. On a property bought for £250,001, however, 3 per cent of the whole price (£7,500) is payable.

RELIEF FOR NEW ZERO CARBON HOMES

A relief from stamp duty land tax was introduced on 1 October 2007 for the vast majority of new-build 'zero carbon' homes in the UK. The relief is time limited for five years and therefore expires on 30 September 2012. Qualifying criteria for the relief require zero carbon emissions from all energy use in the home over a year. To achieve this, the fabric of the home is required to reach a very high energy efficiency standard and to be able to provide onsite renewable heat and power. New homes which are liable to stamp duty land tax on the first sale are eligible to qualify. The relief provides complete removal of stamp duty liabilities for all homes up to a purchase price of £500,000. Where the purchase price is in excess of £500,000 then the stamp duty liability is reduced by £15,000. The balance of the stamp duty is due in the normal way. Relief is not available on second and subsequent sales of new-build zero carbon homes.

FIXTURES AND CHATTELS

As well as buying a property a purchaser may buy items inside the property. Some things inside a property are, in law, part of the land. These are called 'fixtures'. Examples are fitted kitchen units and bathroom suites. Because these fixtures are part of the land, any price paid for them must be taken into account for stamp duty purposes. Other things inside a property are not part of the land. These are called 'chattels'. Examples are free-standing cookers, curtains and fitted carpets. The purchase of chattels is not chargeable to stamp duty. However, where both a property and chattels are purchased, the amount shown on the land transaction return as the purchase price of the property must be a 'just and reasonable' apportionment of the total amount paid. As with other entries on the form, the purchaser is responsible for the accuracy of this information. HMRC pays especial attention to residential property purchases just below stamp duty thresholds to prevent arrangements between buyer and seller to hand over cash so that the purchase price on paper looks lower or to pay unreasonably high amounts to buy chattels.

STAMP DUTY RESERVE TAX

Stamp duty or stamp duty reserve tax (SDRT) is payable at the rate of 0.5 per cent when shares are purchased. Stamp duty is payable when the shares are transferred using a stock transfer form, whereas SDRT is payable on 'paperless' share transactions where the shares are transferred electronically without using a stock transfer form. Most share transactions nowadays are paperless and settled by stockbrokers through CREST (the electronic settlement and registration system). SDRT therefore now accounts for the majority of taxation collected on share transactions effected through the London Stock Exchange.

The flat rate of 0.5 per cent is based on the amount paid for the shares, not what they are worth. If, for example, shares are bought for £2,000, £10 SDRT is payable, whatever the value of the shares themselves. If shares are transferred for free, no SDRT is payable.

A higher rate of 1.5 per cent is payable if shares are transferred into a 'depositary receipt scheme' or a 'clearance service'. These are special arrangements where the shares are held by a third party.

CREST automatically deducts the SDRT and sends it to the HMRC. A stockbroker will settle up with CREST for the cost of the shares and the SDRT and then bill the purchaser for these and the broker's fees. If shares are not purchased through CREST, the stamp duty must be paid by the purchaser to HMRC.

UK stamp duty or SDRT is not payable on the purchase of foreign shares, though there may be foreign taxes to pay. SDRT is already accounted for in the price paid for units in unit trusts or shares in open-ended investment companies.

HELP AND INFORMATION

Further information on stamp duty land tax is available via the stamp taxes helpline on T 0845-603 0135 (open 8.30am to 5pm Monday to Friday) or the HMRC website (W www.hmrc.gov.uk), where a stamp duty calculator for both shares and land and property can be found.

LEGAL NOTES

These notes outline certain aspects of the law as they might affect the average person. They are intended only as a broad guideline and are by no means definitive. The law is constantly changing so expert advice should always be taken. In some cases, sources of further information are given in these notes.

It is always advisable to consult a solicitor without delay. Anyone who does not have a solicitor can contact the following for assistance in finding one: Citizens Advice (W www.citizensadvice.org.uk), the Community Legal Advice service (W www.communitylegaladvice.gov.uk) or the Law Society of England and Wales. For assistance in Scotland, contact Citizens Advice Scotland (W www.cas.org.uk) or the Law Society of Scotland.

Legal aid schemes exist to make the help of a lawyer available to those who would not otherwise be able to afford one. Entitlement for most types of legal aid depends on an individual's means but a solicitor or Citizens Advice will be able to advise on this.

LAW SOCIETY OF ENGLAND AND WALES
113 Chancery Lane, London WC2A 1PL T 020-7242 1222
W www.lawsociety.org.uk

LAW SOCIETY OF SCOTLAND
26 Drumsheugh Gardens, Edinburgh EH3 7YR
T 0131-226 7411 W www.lawscot.org.uk

ABORTION

Abortion is governed by the Abortion Act 1967. Under its provisions, a legally induced abortion must be:

- performed by a registered medical practitioner
- carried out in an NHS hospital or other approved premises
- certified by two registered medical practitioners as justified on one or more of the following grounds:
  (a) that the pregnancy has not exceeded its 24th week and that the continuance of the pregnancy would involve risk, greater than if the pregnancy were terminated, of injury to the physical or mental health of the pregnant woman or any existing children of her family
  (b) that the termination is necessary to prevent grave permanent injury to the physical or mental health of the pregnant woman
  (c) that the continuance of the pregnancy would involve risk to the life of the pregnant woman, greater than if the pregnancy were terminated
  (d) that there is a substantial risk that if the child were born it would suffer from such physical or mental abnormalities as to be seriously handicapped.

In determining whether the continuance of a pregnancy would involve such risk of injury to health as is mentioned in grounds (a) or (b), account may be taken of the pregnant woman's actual or reasonably foreseeable environment.

The requirements relating to the opinion of two registered medical practitioners and to the performance of the abortion at an NHS hospital or other approved place cease to apply in circumstances where a registered medical practitioner is of the opinion, formed in good faith, that a termination is immediately necessary to save the life, or to prevent grave permanent injury to the physical or mental health, of the pregnant woman.

The Abortion Act 1967 does not apply to Northern Ireland, where abortion is not legal.

FAMILY PLANNING ASSOCIATION (UK)
50 Featherstone Street, London EC1Y 8QU T 020-7608 5240
W www.fpa.org.uk

BRITISH PREGNANCY ADVISORY SERVICE (BPAS)
T 0845-730 4030 W www.bpas.org

ADOPTION OF CHILDREN

The Adoption and Children Act 2002 reformed the framework for domestic and intercountry adoption in England and Wales and some parts of it extend to Scotland and Northern Ireland. The Children and Adoption Act 2006 introduces further provisions for adoptions involving a foreign element.

WHO MAY APPLY FOR AN ADOPTION ORDER

A couple (whether married or two people living as partners in an enduring family relationship) may apply for an adoption order where both of them are over 21 or where one is only 18 but the natural parent and the other is 21. An adoption order may be made for one applicant where that person is 21 and: a) the court is satisfied that person is the partner of a parent of the person to be adopted; or b) they are not married and are not civil partners; or c) married or in a civil partnership but they are separated from their spouse or civil partner and living apart with the separation likely to be permanent; or d) their spouse/civil partner is either unable to be found, or their spouse/civil partner is incapable by reason of ill-health of making an application. There are certain qualifying conditions an applicant must meet eg residency in the British Isles.

ARRANGING AN ADOPTION

Adoptions may generally only be arranged by an adoption agency or by way of an order from the high court; breach of the restrictions on who may arrange an adoption would constitute a criminal offence. When deciding whether a child should be placed for adoption, the court or adoption agency must consider all the factors set out in the 'welfare checklist' – the paramount consideration being the child's welfare, throughout his or her life. These factors include the child's wishes, needs, age, sex, background and any harm which the child has suffered or is likely to suffer. At all times, the court or adoption agency must bear in mind that delay is likely to prejudice a child's welfare.

ADOPTION ORDER

Once an adoption has been arranged, a court order is necessary to make it legal; this may be obtained from the high court, county court or magistrates' court (including family proceedings court). An adoption order may not be given unless the court is satisfied that the consent of the child's natural parents (or guardians) has correctly been given. Consent can be dispensed with on two grounds: where the parent or guardian cannot be found or is incapable of giving consent, or where the welfare of the child so demands.

An adoption order in effect extinguishes the parental responsibility that a person other than the adopters (or adopter) has for the child; although where an order is made on the application of the partner of the parent, that parent keeps parental responsibility. Once adopted the child has the same status as a child born to the adoptive parents, but may lose rights to the estates of those losing their parental responsibility.

REGISTRATION AND CERTIFICATES

All adoption orders made in England and Wales are required to be registered in the Adopted Children Register which also contains particulars of children adopted under registrable foreign adoptions. The General Register Office keeps this register from which certificates may be obtained in a similar way to birth certificates. The General Register Office also has equivalents in Scotland and Northern Ireland.

TRACING NATURAL PARENTS OR CHILDREN WHO HAVE BEEN ADOPTED

An adult adopted person may apply to the Registrar-General to obtain a certified copy of his/her birth certificate. For those adopted before 12 November 1975 it is obligatory to receive counselling services before this information is given. In any event, adoption agencies and adoption support agencies should provide services to adopted persons to assist them in obtaining information about their adoption and facilitate contact with their relatives. There is an Adoption Contact Register which provides a safe and confidential way for birth parents and other relatives to assure an adopted person that contact would be welcome. The BAAF (*see* below) can provide addresses of organisations which offer advice, information and counselling to adopted people, adoptive parents and people who have had their children adopted.

BRITISH ASSOCIATION FOR ADOPTION AND FOSTERING (BAAF)
Saffron House, 6–10 Kirkby Street, London EC1N 8TS
T 020-7421 2600 **W** www.baaf.org.uk

SCOTLAND

The relevant legislation is the Adoption and Children (Scotland) Act 2007. Previously adoption was governed in Scotland by the Adoption (Scotland) Act 1978, as amended by the Children (Scotland) Act 1995. In September 2009, the 2007 act made further amendments to the 1995 act and repealed the 1978 act – but for Part IV – when its final provisions took effect. The provisions of the 2007 act are similar to those described above. In Scotland, petitions for adoption are made to the sheriff court or the court of session.

BRITISH ASSOCIATION FOR ADOPTION AND FOSTERING (BAAF)
BAAF Scottish Centre, 113 Rose Street, Edinburgh EH2 3DT
T 0131-226 9270

BIRTHS (REGISTRATION)

It is the duty of the parents of a child born in England or Wales to register the birth within 42 days of the date of birth at the register office in the district in which the baby was born. If it is inconvenient to go to the district where the birth took place, the information for the registration may be given to a registrar in another district, who will send your details to the appropriate register office. Failure to register the birth within 42 days without reasonable cause may leave the parents liable to a penalty. If a birth has not been registered within 12 months of its occurrence it is possible for the late registration of the birth to be authorised by the Registrar-General, provided certain requirements can be met.

If the parents of the child were married to each other at the time of the birth (or conception), either the mother or the father may register the birth. If the parents were not married to each other at the time of the child's birth (or conception), the father's particulars may be entered in the register only where he attends the register office with the mother and they sign the birth register together. Where an unmarried parent is unable to attend the register office either parent may submit to the registrar a statutory declaration on Form 16 (or Form 16W for births which took place in Wales) acknowledging the father's paternity (this form may be obtained from any registrar in England or Wales); alternatively a parental responsibility agreement or appropriate court order may be produced to the registrar.

If the parents do not register the birth of their child the following people may do so:

- the occupier of the house or hospital where the child was born
- a person who was present at the birth
- a person who is responsible for the child

Upon registration of the birth a short certificate is issued.

BIRTHS ABROAD

There are certain countries where birth registrations may be made for British citizens overseas (for more details on British citizenship *see* below). The British consul or high commission may register the births and issue certificates which are then sent to the General Register Office. If a birth is registered by the British consul or high commission, the registration would show the person's claim to British citizenship, British overseas territories citizenship or British overseas citizenship.

SCOTLAND

In Scotland the birth of a child must be registered within 21 days at the register office of either the district in which the baby was born or the district in which the mother was resident at the time of the birth.

If the child is born, either in or out of Scotland, on a ship, aircraft or land vehicle that ends its journey at any place in Scotland, the child, in most cases, will be registered as if born in that place.

CERTIFICATES OF BIRTHS, DEATHS OR MARRIAGES

Certificates of births, marriages and deaths that have taken place in England and Wales since 1837 can be obtained from the General Register Office.

Marriage or death certificates may also be obtained from the minister of the church in which the marriage or funeral took place. Any register office can advise about the best way to obtain certificates.

The fees for certificates are:

Online application:

- full certificate of birth, marriage, death or adoption, £9.25
- full certificate of birth, marriage, death or adoption with GRO reference supplied, £9.25

By postal/phone/fax application:

- full certificate of birth, marriage, death or adoption, £9.25

- full certificate of birth, marriage, death or adoption with GRO reference supplied, £9.25
- extra copies of the same birth, marriage or death certificate issued at the same time, £9.25

A priority service is available for an additional fee.

A complete set of the GRO indexes including births, deaths and marriages, civil partnerships, adoptions and provisional indexes for births and deaths for 2009 is available at City of Westminster Archives Centre, London Metropolitan Archives, Greater Manchester County Record Office, Birmingham Central Library, Bridgend Reference and Information Centre and Plymouth Central Library. These are also available at the National Archives at Kew and the British Library. Copies of GRO indexes may also be held at some libraries, family history societies, local records offices and The Church of Jesus Christ of Latter Day Saints family history centres. Some organisations may not hold a complete record of indexes and a small fee may be charged by some of these organisations. GRO indexes are also available online.

The Society of Genealogists has many records of baptisms, marriages and deaths prior to 1837.

SCOTLAND

Certificates of births, deaths or marriages that have taken place in Scotland since 1855 can be obtained from the General Register Office for Scotland or from the appropriate local registrar.

Applicable fees – local registrar:

- each extract or abbreviated certificate of birth, death, marriage, civil partnership or adoption within the year of registration, £9.00
- each extract or abbreviated certificate of birth, death, marriage, civil partnership or adoption outwith the current year of registration, £14.00

A priority service is available for an additional fee.

The General Register Office for Scotland also keeps the Register of Divorces (including decrees of declaration of nullity of marriage), and holds parish registers dating from before 1855.

Applicable fees – General Register Office for Scotland:

- personal application: £11.00
- postal, telephone or fax order: £13.00

A priority service for a response within 24 hours is available for an additional fee of £10.00.

General search in the indexes to the statutory registers and parochial registers, per day or part thereof:

- full or part-day search pass: £10.00
- Quarterly search pass: £440.00
- annual search pass: £1,250.00

Online searching is also available. For more information, visit W www.scotlandspeople.gov.uk.

THE GENERAL REGISTER OFFICE
General Register Office, Trafalgar Road, Southport PR8 2HH
T 0845-603 7788 W www.gro.gov.uk/gro/content/certificates

THE GENERAL REGISTER OFFICE FOR SCOTLAND
New Register House, 3 West Register Street, Edinburgh EH1 3YT T 0131-334 0380 W www.gro-scotland.gov.uk

THE SOCIETY OF GENEALOGISTS
14 Charterhouse Buildings, Goswell Road, London EC1M 7BA
T 020-7251 8799 W www.societyofgenealogists.com

BRITISH NATIONALITY

Principally, there are six types of British nationality status, the most widely held being British citizenship. Almost everyone who was a citizen of the UK and colonies before 1 January 1983 and had a right of abode in the UK became a British citizen when the British Nationality Act 1981 came into force. British citizens have the right to live permanently in the UK and are free to leave and re-enter the UK at any time.

A person born on or after 1 January 1983 in the UK (including, for this purpose, the Channel Islands and the Isle of Man) is entitled to British citizenship if he/she falls into one of the following categories:

- he/she has a parent who is a British citizen
- he/she has a parent who is settled in the UK
- he/she is a newborn infant found abandoned in the UK
- his/her parents subsequently settle in the UK or become British citizens and an application is made before he/she is 18
- he/she lives in the UK for the first ten years of his/her life and is not absent for more than 90 days in each of those years
- he/she is adopted in the UK and one of the adopters is a British citizen
- the home secretary consents to his/her registration while he/she is a minor
- if he/she has always been stateless and lives in the UK for a period of five years before his/her 22nd birthday

A person born outside the UK may acquire British citizenship if he/she falls into one of the following categories:

- he/she has a parent who is a British citizen otherwise than by descent, eg a parent who was born in the UK
- he/she has a parent who is a British citizen serving the crown overseas
- the home secretary consents to his/her registration while he/she is a minor
- he/she is a British overseas territories citizen, a British overseas citizen, a British subject or a British protected person and has been lawfully resident in the UK for five years
- he/she is a British overseas territories citizen who acquired that citizenship from a connection with Gibraltar
- he/she is adopted or naturalised

Where parents are married, the status of either may confer citizenship on their child. Where parents are not married, the status of the mother determines the child's citizenship.

Under the 1981 act, Commonwealth citizens and citizens of the Republic of Ireland were entitled to registration as British citizens before 1 January 1983. In 1983, citizens of the Falkland Islands were granted British citizenship.

Renunciation of British citizenship must be registered with the home secretary and will be revoked if no new citizenship or nationality is acquired within six months. If the renunciation was required in order to retain or acquire another citizenship or nationality, the citizenship may be reacquired only once. The secretary of state may deprive a person of a citizenship status if he or she is satisfied that the person has done anything seriously prejudicial to the vital interests of the UK, or a British overseas territory, unless making the order would have the effect of rendering such a person stateless. A person may also be deprived of a citizenship status which results from his registration or naturalisation if the secretary of state is satisfied that the registration or naturalisation was obtained by fraud, false representation or concealment of a material fact.

BRITISH DEPENDENT TERRITORIES CITIZENSHIP
Since 26 February 2006, this category of nationality no longer exists and has been replaced by British overseas territory citizenship.

If a person had this class of nationality only by reason of a connection to the territory of Hong Kong, they lost it automatically when Hong Kong was returned to the People's Republic of China. However, if after 30 June 1997, they had no other nationality and would have become stateless, or were born after 30 June 1997 and would have been born stateless (but had a parent who was a British national (overseas) or a British overseas citizen), they became a British overseas citizen.

BRITISH OVERSEAS CITIZENSHIP
Under the 1981 act, as amended by the British Overseas Territories Act 2002, this type of citizenship was conferred on any UK and colonies citizens who did not become either a British citizen or a British overseas territories citizen on 1 January 1983 and as such is now, for most purposes, only acquired by persons who would otherwise be stateless.

BRITISH OVERSEAS TERRITORIES CITIZENSHIP
This category of nationality replaced British dependent territories citizenship. Most commonly, this form of nationality is acquired where, after 31 December 1982, a person was a citizen of the UK and colonies and did not become a British citizen, and that person, and their parents or grandparents, were born, registered or naturalised in the specified British overseas territory. However, on 21 May 2002, people became British citizens if they had British overseas territories citizenship by connection with any British overseas territory except for the sovereign base areas of Akrotiri and Dhekelia in Cyprus.

RESIDUAL CATEGORIES
British subjects, British protected persons and British nationals (overseas) may be entitled to registration as British citizens on completion of five years' legal residence in the UK.

Citizens of the Republic of Ireland who were also British subjects before 1 January 1949 can retain that status if they fulfil certain conditions.

EUROPEAN UNION CITIZENSHIP
British citizens (including Gibraltarians who are registered for this purpose) are also EU citizens and are entitled to travel freely to other EU countries to work, study, reside and set up a business. EU citizens have the same rights with respect to the UK.

NATURALISATION
Naturalisation is granted at the discretion of the home secretary. The basic requirements are five years' residence (three years if the applicant is married to, or is the civil partner of a British citizen), good character, adequate knowledge of the English, Welsh or Scottish Gaelic language, passing the UK citizenship test and an intention to reside permanently in the UK.

STATUS OF ALIENS
Aliens, being persons without any of the above forms of British nationality, may not hold public office or vote in Britain and they may not own a British ship or aircraft. Citizens of the Republic of Ireland are not deemed to be aliens. Certain provisions of the Immigration and Asylum Act 1999 make provision about immigration and asylum and about procedures in connection with marriage by superintendent registrar's certificate.

CONSUMER LAW

SALE OF GOODS
A sale of goods contract is the most common type of contract. It is governed by the Sale of Goods Act 1979 (as amended by the Sale and Supply of Goods Act 1994). The act provides protection for buyers by implying terms into every sale of goods contract. These terms include:

- an implied term that the seller will pass good title to the buyer (unless it appears from the contract or is to be inferred from the circumstances that there is an intention that the seller should transfer only such title as he has)
- where the seller sells goods by reference to a description, an implied term that the goods will match that description and, where the sale is by sample and description, it will not be sufficient that the bulk of the goods corresponds with the sample if the goods do not also correspond with the description
- where goods are sold by a business seller, an implied term that the goods will be of satisfactory quality if they meet the standard that a reasonable person would regard as satisfactory, taking into account any description of the goods, the price, and all other relevant circumstances. The quality of the goods includes their state and condition, relevant aspects being whether they are fit for all the purposes for which such goods are commonly supplied, their appearance and finish, freedom from minor defects and their safety and durability. This term will not be implied, however, if a buyer has examined the goods (including in a sale by sample) and should have noticed the defect or if the seller specifically drew the buyer's attention to the defect
- where goods are sold by a business seller, an implied term that the goods are reasonably fit for any purpose made known to the seller by the buyer (either expressly or by implication), unless it is shown that the buyer does not rely on the seller's judgment, or it is not reasonable for him/her to do so
- where goods are sold by sample, implied terms that the bulk of the sample will correspond with the sample in quality, and that the goods are free from any defect rendering them unsatisfactory which would have been apparent on a reasonable examination of the sample

Some of the above terms can be excluded from contracts by the seller. The seller's right to do this is, however, restricted by the Unfair Contract Terms Act 1977. The act offers more protection to a buyer who 'deals as a consumer' (that is where the seller is selling in the course of a business, the goods are of a type ordinarily bought for private use and the goods are bought by a buyer who is not a business buyer, though not allowing any liability for breach of the implied terms described above to be excluded). In a sale of secondhand goods by auction (at which individuals have the opportunity of attending the sale in person), a buyer does not deal as a consumer.

HIRE-PURCHASE AGREEMENTS
Terms similar to those implied in contracts of sales of goods are implied into contracts of hire-purchase, under the Supply of Goods (Implied Terms) Act 1973. The 1977 act limits the exclusion of these implied terms as before.

SUPPLY OF GOODS AND SERVICES

Under the Supply of Goods and Services Act 1982, similar terms are also implied in other types of contract under which ownership of goods passes, and contracts for the hire of goods (though not hire-purchase agreements). These types of contracts have additional implied terms:

- that the supplier will use reasonable care and skill in carrying out the service
- that the supplier will carry out the service in a reasonable time (unless the time has been agreed)
- that the supplier will make a reasonable charge (unless the charge has already been agreed)

The 1977 act limits the exclusion of these implied terms in a similar manner as before.

UNFAIR TERMS

The Unfair Terms in Consumer Contracts Regulations 1999 apply to contracts between business sellers (or suppliers of goods and services) and consumers. Where the terms have not been individually negotiated (ie where the terms were drafted in advance so that the consumer was unable to influence those terms), a term will be deemed unfair if it operates to the detriment of the consumer (ie causes a significant imbalance in the parties' rights and obligations arising under the contract). An unfair term does not bind the consumer but the contract may continue to bind the parties if it is capable of existing without the unfair term. The regulations contain a non-exhaustive list of terms that are regarded as potentially unfair. When a term does not fall into such a category, whether it will be regarded as fair or not will depend on many factors, including the nature of the goods or services, the surrounding circumstances (such as the bargaining strength of both parties) and the other terms in the contract.

CONSUMER PROTECTION

The Consumer Protection from Unfair Trading Regulations 2008 (CPRs) replaced much previous consumer protection regulation including the majority of the Trade Descriptions Act 1968. CPRs prohibit 31 specific practices, which include false claims of membership of trade associations, pyramid schemes and aggressive sales. In addition CPRs prohibit business sellers from making misleading actions and misleading omissions, which cause, or are likely to cause, the average consumer to take a different transactional decision. There is also a general duty not to trade unfairly.

Under the Consumer Protection Act 1987, producers of goods are liable for any injury, death or damage to any property exceeding £275 caused by a defect in their product (subject to certain defences).

Consumers are also afforded protection under the Consumer Protection (Distance Selling) Regulations 2000 and the Cancellation of Contracts made in a Consumer's Home or Place of Work etc Regulations 2008 in relation to cancellation rights.

CONSUMER CREDIT

In matters relating to the provision of credit (or the supply of goods on hire or hire-purchase), consumers are also protected by the Consumer Credit Act 1974 (as amended by the Consumer Credit Act 2006). Under this act a licence, issued by the Office of Fair Trading, is required in order to conduct a consumer credit or consumer hire business or an ancillary credit business, subject to certain exemptions. Any 'fit' person as defined within the act may apply to the Director-General of Fair Trading for a licence. The provisions of the act only apply to 'regulated' agreements: there are a number of exemptions under which consumer credit agreements are not regulated by the Act (such as first charge mortgages which are regulated instead by the FSA). Provisions include:

- in order for a creditor to enforce a regulated agreement, the agreement must comply with certain formalities and must be properly executed. An improperly executed regulated agreement is enforceable only on an order of the court. The debtor must also be given specified information by the creditor or his/her broker or agent during the negotiations which take place before the signing of the agreement. The agreement must state information such as the rights and duties conferred or imposed on the debtor and the protection and remedies available to him/her under the act
- if a contract is made during or after a solicited or unsolicited visit by a trader to a person's home or place of work and the total payment is more than £35, a cooling-off period of at least seven days applies. The cancellation rights must be clearly and prominently displayed in any written contract or provided in writing if there is no written contract
- if the debtor is in breach of the agreement, the creditor must serve a default notice before taking any action such as repossessing the goods
- if the agreement is a hire-purchase or conditional sale agreement, the creditor cannot repossess the goods without a court order if the debtor has paid one third of the total price of the goods
- in agreements where the relationship between the creditor and the debtor is unfair to the debtor, the court may alter or set aside some of the terms of the agreement. The agreement can also be reopened during enforcement proceedings by the court itself

Where a credit reference agency has been used to check the debtor's financial standing, the creditor must give the agency's name to the debtor, who is entitled to see the agency's file on him. A fee of £2 is payable to the agency.

The Consumer Credit Act 1974 and associated regulations will be altered as a result of the Consumer Credit (EU Directive) Regulations, which are due to come into force on 1 February 2011.

SCOTLAND

The legislation governing the sale and supply of goods applies to Scotland as follows:

- the Sale of Goods Act 1979 applies with some modifications and it has been amended by the Sale and Supply of Goods Act 1994
- the Supply of Goods (Implied Terms) Act 1973 applies
- the Supply of Goods and Services Act 1982 does not extend to Scotland but some of its provisions were introduced by the Sale and Supply of Goods Act 1994
- only Parts II and III of the Unfair Contract Terms Act 1977 apply
- the Trade Descriptions Act 1968 applies with minor modifications
- the Consumer Credit Act 1974 applies
- the Consumer Protection Act 1987 applies
- the General Product Safety Regulations 2005 apply
- the Unfair Terms in Consumer Contracts Regulations 1999 apply
- the Unfair Terms in Consumer Contracts (Amendment) Regulations 2001 apply
- the Consumer Protection (Distance Selling) Regulations 2000 apply

- the Sale and Supply of Goods to Consumers Regulations 2002 apply
- the Consumer Protection from Unfair Trading Regulations 2008 apply

PROCEEDINGS AGAINST THE CROWN

Until 1947, proceedings against the Crown were generally possible only by a procedure known as a petition of right, which put the private litigant at a considerable disadvantage. The Crown Proceedings Act 1947 placed the Crown (not the sovereign in his/her private capacity, but as the embodiment of the state) largely in the same position as a private individual and made proceedings in the high court involving the Crown subject to the same rules as any other case. The act did not, however, extinguish or limit the Crown's prerogative or statutory powers, and it continued the immunity of HM ships and aircraft. It also left certain Crown privileges unaffected. The act largely abolished the special procedures which previously applied to civil proceedings by and against the Crown. Civil proceedings may be initiated against the appropriate government department or if there is doubt regarding which is the appropriate department, against the attorney-general.

In Scotland proceedings against the Crown founded on breach of contract could be taken before the 1947 act and no special procedures applied. The Crown could, however, claim certain special pleas. The 1947 act applies in part to Scotland and brings the practice of the two countries as closely together as the different legal systems permit. As a result of the Scotland Act 1998 actions against government departments should be raised against the Lord Advocate or the advocate-general. Actions should be raised against the Lord Advocate where the department involved administers a devolved matter. Devolved matters include agriculture, education, housing, local government, health and justice. Actions should be raised against the advocate-general where the department is dealing with a reserved matter. Reserved matters include defence, foreign affairs and social security.

DEATHS

WHEN A DEATH OCCURS

If the death (including stillbirth) was expected, the doctor who attended the deceased during their final illness should be contacted. If the death was sudden or unexpected, the family doctor (if known) and police should be contacted. If the cause of death is quite clear the doctor will provide:

- a medical certificate that shows the cause of death
- a formal notice that states that the doctor has signed the medical certificate and that explains how to get the death registered
- if the death was known to be caused by a natural illness but the doctor wishes to know more about the cause of death, he/she may ask the relatives for permission to carry out a post-mortem examination

In England and Wales a coroner is responsible for investigating deaths occurring when:

- there is no doctor who can issue a medical certificate of cause of death
- no doctor has treated the deceased during his or her last illness or when the doctor attending the patient did not see him or her within 14 days before death, or after death
- the death occurred during an operation or before recovery from the effect of an anaesthetic
- the death was sudden and unexplained or attended by suspicious circumstances
- the death might be due to an industrial injury or disease, or to accident, violence, neglect or abortion, attended by suspicious circumstances
- the death occurred in prison or in police custody

The doctor will write on the formal notice that the death has been referred to the coroner; if the post-mortem shows that death was due to natural causes, the coroner may issue a notification which gives the cause of death so that the death can be registered. If the cause of death was violent or unnatural, the coroner must hold an inquest.

In Scotland the office of coroner does not exist. The local procurator fiscal inquires into sudden or suspicious deaths. A fatal accident inquiry will be held before the sheriff where the death has resulted from an accident during the course of the employment of the person who has died, or where the person who has died was in legal custody, or where the Lord Advocate deems it in the public interest that an inquiry be held.

REGISTERING A DEATH

In England and Wales the death must be registered by the registrar of births and deaths for the district in which it occurred. Information concerning a death can be given before any registrar of births and deaths in England and Wales. The registrar will pass the relevant details to the registrar for the district where the death occurred, who will then register the death.

In England and Wales the death must normally be registered within five days; in Scotland within eight days. If the death has been referred to the coroner/local procurator fiscal it cannot be registered until the registrar has received authority from the coroner/local procurator fiscal to do so. Failure to register a death involves a penalty in England and Wales and may lead to a court decree being granted by a sheriff in Scotland.

If the death occurred at a house or hospital, the death may be registered by:

- any relative of the deceased
- any person present at the death
- the occupier or any inmate of the house or hospital if he/she knew of the occurrence of the death
- any person making the funeral arrangements
- an official from the hospital
- in Scotland, the deceased's executor or legal representative

For deaths that took place elsewhere, the death may be registered by:

- any relative of the deceased
- someone present at the death
- someone who found the body
- a person in charge of the body
- any person making the funeral arrangements

The majority of deaths are registered by a relative of the deceased. The registrar would normally allow one of the other listed persons to register the death only if there were no relatives available.

The person registering the death should take the medical certificate of the cause of death with them; it is also useful, though not essential, to take the deceased's birth and marriage/civil partnership certificates, NHS medical card, pension documentation and life assurance details. The details given to the registrar must be absolutely correct, otherwise it may be difficult to change them later. The person registering the death should check the entry carefully before it is signed. The registrar will issue a certificate for burial or cremation, a certificate of registration of death and a certificate for social security purposes – all free of charge. A death certificate is a certified copy of the entry in the death register; these can be provided on payment of a fee and may be required for the following purposes:

- the will
- bank and building society accounts
- savings bank certificates and premium bonds
- insurance policies
- pension claims

If the death occurred abroad or on a foreign ship or aircraft, the death should be registered according to the local regulations of the relevant country and a death certificate should be obtained. In many countries the death can also be registered with the British consulate in that country and a record will be kept at the General Register Office. This avoids the expense of bringing the body back.

After 12 months (three months in Scotland) of death or the finding of a dead body, no death can be registered without the consent of the registrar-general.

BURIAL AND CREMATION

In most circumstances in England and Wales a certificate for burial or cremation must be obtained from the registrar before the burial or cremation can take place. If the death has been referred to the coroner, an order for burial or a certificate for cremation must be obtained. In Scotland a body may be buried (but not cremated) before the death is registered.

Funeral costs can normally be repaid out of the deceased's estate and will be given priority over any other claims. If the deceased has left a will it may contain directions concerning the funeral; however, these directions need not be followed by the executor.

The deceased's papers should also indicate whether a grave space had already been arranged. This information will be contained in a document known as a 'Deed of Grant'. Most town churchyards and many suburban churchyards are no longer open for burial because they are full. Most cemeteries are non-denominational and may be owned by local authorities or private companies; fees vary.

If the body is to be cremated, an application form, two cremation certificates (for which there is a charge) or a certificate for cremation if the death was referred to the coroner, and a certificate signed by the medical referee must be completed in addition to the certificate for burial or cremation (the form is not required if the coroner has issued a certificate for cremation). All the forms are available from the funeral director or crematorium. Most crematoria are run by local authorities; the fees usually include the medical referee's fee and the use of the chapel. Ashes may be scattered, buried in a churchyard or cemetery, or kept.

The registrar must be notified of the date, place and means of disposal of the body within 96 hours (England and Wales) or three days (Scotland).

If the death occurred abroad or on a foreign ship or aircraft, a local burial or cremation may be arranged. If the body is to be brought back to England or Wales, a death certificate from the relevant country or an authorisation for the removal of the body from the country of death from the coroner or relevant authority will be required. To arrange a funeral in England or Wales, an authenticated translation of a foreign death certificate or a death certificate issued in Scotland or Northern Ireland which must show the cause of death, is needed, together with a certificate of no liability to register from the registrar in England and Wales in whose sub-district it is intended to bury or cremate the body. If it is intended to cremate the body, a cremation order will be required from the Home Office or a certificate for cremation.

THE GENERAL REGISTER OFFICE
General Register Office, PO Box 2, Southport PR8 2JD
T 0845-603 7788 **W** www.gro.gov.uk/gro/content/certificates

THE GENERAL REGISTER OFFICE FOR SCOTLAND
New Register House, 3 West Register Street, Edinburgh EH1 3YT **T** 0131-334 0380 **W** www.gro-scotland.gov.uk

DIVORCE AND RELATED MATTERS

There are three types of matrimonial suit: annulment of marriage, judicial separation and divorce. To obtain an annulment, judicial separation or divorce in England and Wales (provided a European Union court (except Denmark) has jurisdiction) the one commencing the proceedings (the petitioner) and the one defending the proceedings (the respondent) must be habitually resident in England and Wales; or the petitioner and the respondent must have last been habitually resident in England and Wales and one of them must continue to reside there; or the respondent must be habitually resident in England and Wales; or the petitioner must have been habitually resident in England and Wales throughout the period of at least one year ending with the start of proceedings; or the petitioner must be domiciled in England and Wales and must have been habitually resident in England and Wales throughout the period of at least six months, ending with the start of the proceedings; or both parties must be domiciled in England and Wales. If no European Union court (except Denmark) has jurisdiction, one or both parties must be domiciled in England and Wales. All cases are commenced in a divorce county court or in the Principal Registry in London. If a suit is defended, it may be transferred to the high court.

ANNULMENT OF MARRIAGE

Various circumstances have the potential to render a marriage void or voidable in annulment proceedings including: if there has been wilful non-consummation of the marriage; one partner has a venereal disease at the time of the marriage and the other did not know about it; the female partner was pregnant at the time of the marriage with another person's child and the male partner did not know of the pregnancy; the parties were within prohibited degrees of consanguinity, affinity or adoption; the parties were not male and female; either of the parties was already married or had entered a civil partnership; either of the parties was under the age of 16; the formalities of the marriage were defective, eg the marriage did not take place in an authorised building and both parties knew of the defect.

SEPARATION

A couple may enter into a private agreement to separate by consent without getting divorced but for the agreement to be valid it must be followed by an immediate separation; a solicitor should be contacted.

Another form of separation is judicial separation. Judicial separation does not dissolve a marriage and it is not necessary to prove that the marriage has irretrievably broken down. Either party can petition for a judicial separation at any time; the grounds listed below as grounds for divorce are also grounds for judicial separation. To petition for judicial separation, the parties do not have to prove that they have been married for 12 months or more.

A financial settlement between spouses in a separation agreement or which accompanies a judicial separation is not binding on the court and will not necessarily be upheld by the court after the start of divorce proceedings.

DIVORCE

Neither party can petition for divorce until at least one year after the date of the marriage. The sole ground for divorce is the irretrievable breakdown of the marriage; this must be proved on one or more of the following facts:

- the respondent has committed adultery and the petitioner finds it intolerable to live with him/her; however, the petitioner cannot rely on an act of adultery by the respondent if they have lived together as husband and wife for more than six months after the discovery of the adultery
- the respondent has behaved in such a way that the petitioner cannot reasonably be expected to continue living with him/her
- the respondent has deserted the petitioner for two years immediately before the petition
- the petitioner and the respondent have lived separately for two years immediately before the petition and the respondent consents to the divorce
- the petitioner and the respondent have lived separately for five years immediately before the petition

A total period of less than six months during which the parties have resumed living together is disregarded in determining whether the prescribed period of separation or desertion has been continuous (but may not be included as part of the period of separation).

The Matrimonial Causes Act 1973 requires the solicitor for the petitioner to certify whether the possibility of a reconciliation has been discussed with the petitioner.

THE DECREE NISI

A decree nisi does not dissolve or annul the marriage, but must be obtained before a divorce or annulment can take place.

Where the suit is undefended, the evidence normally takes the form of a sworn written statement made by the petitioner which is considered by a district judge. If the judge is satisfied that the petitioner has proved the contents of the petition, a date will be set for the pronouncement of the decree nisi in open court: neither party need attend.

If the suit is defended, the petition will be heard in open court with parties giving oral evidence.

THE DECREE ABSOLUTE

The decree nisi is capable of being made absolute on the application of the petitioner six weeks after the decree nisi. If the petitioner does not apply, the respondent must wait for a further three months before application may be made. In exceptional circumstances the granting of the decree absolute may be delayed, for example if matters regarding children are not capable of resolution. A decree absolute is unlikely to be applied for until the financial matters have been resolved. The decree absolute dissolves or annuls the marriage. Where the couple have been married in accordance with Jewish or other religious usages, the court may require them to produce a declaration that they have taken such steps as are required to dissolve the marriage in accordance with those usages before the decree absolute is issued.

MAINTENANCE

Either party may be liable to make financial payments as maintenance to a spouse or former spouse. If there are any children of the marriage, both parties have a legal responsibility to support them financially if they can afford to do so.

The courts are responsible for assessing maintenance for a spouse or former spouse, taking into account each party's income and essential outgoings and other aspects of the case. The court can also deal with any maintenance for a child that has been treated by the spouses as a child of the family, such as a step-child.

The Child Maintenance and Other Payments Act 2008 changed the law with regards to child maintenance and set up a new commission, the Child Maintenance and Enforcement Commission (CMEC). Since October 2008, all parents have been able to choose either a private or statutory maintenance arrangement, thereby removing the compulsion for benefit claimants to use the Child Support Agency (CSA).

Since April 2010 the amount of child maintenance that the parent with care receives will not affect their benefits.

At the time of writing the CSA is still responsible for assessing the maintenance that non-resident parents shall pay for their natural or adopted children (whether or not a marriage has taken place). The CSA accepts applications only when all the people involved are habitually resident in the UK; the courts will continue to deal with cases where one of the individuals lives abroad (and does not work for a UK-based employer, the armed forces or the civil service).

A formula is used to work out how much child maintenance is payable under CSA jurisdiction. The basic rate formula requires the non-resident parent to pay 15 per cent net of income post-tax, national insurance and pension contributions for one child, 20 per cent for two and 25 per cent for more than two children. An earnings cap of £104,000 net a year applies. Deductions are applied for staying in contact and for further children in the non-resident parent's household. In court jurisdiction cases, the CSA formula is adopted as a guideline only.

Some cases involving unusual circumstances are treated as special cases and the assessment is modified, and in some cases the court retains jurisdiction (for educational costs and high income cases, for example). Where there is financial need (eg because of disability or continual education) maintenance may be ordered by the court for children beyond the age of 18.

Either parent can report a change of circumstances and request a review at any time but appeals must be made within one month of the letter informing the parents of the CSA's decision. There is an independent complaints examiner for the CSA.

If the non-resident parent does not pay CSA maintenance, the CSA may make an order for payments to be deducted directly from his/her salary; if all other methods fail, the CSA may take court action to enforce payment.

OTHER FINANCIAL RELIEF

Unlike in some other jurisdictions, there is no formula for division of assets on divorce. The courts must exercise their powers so as to achieve an outcome which is fair between the parties. In determining what is 'fair' the court must have regard to all the circumstances of the case, first consideration being given to the welfare of any minor child(ren) of the family. Beyond this, the court must have particular regard to a prescribed list of statutory factors:

- the income, earning capacity, property and other financial resources which each of the parties to the marriage has or is likely to have in the foreseeable future, including in the case of earning capacity, any increase in that capacity which it would, in the opinion of the court, be reasonable to expect a party to the marriage to take steps to acquire
- the financial needs, obligations and responsibilities which each of the parties to the marriage has or is likely to have in the foreseeable future
- the standard of living enjoyed by the family before the breakdown of the marriage
- the age of each party to the marriage and the duration of the marriage
- any physical or mental disability of either of the parties to the marriage
- the contribution which each of the parties has made or is likely in the foreseeable future to make to the welfare of the family, including any contribution by looking after the home or caring for the family
- the conduct of each of the parties, if that conduct is such that it would, in the opinion of the court, be inequitable to disregard it
- in the case of proceedings for divorce or nullity of marriage, the value to each of the parties to the marriage of any benefit (for example a pension) which by reason of the dissolution of the marriage that party will lose the chance of acquiring.

The court also has a duty to consider making an order which will settle once and for all the parties financial responsibilities towards each other. This is known as a financial 'clean break'. Where a clean break is not possible, the court will combine provision of capital via a lump sum and/or property adjustment order and/or pension sharing/attachment order with an ongoing income order, known as maintenance (alimony).

Maintenance can be for a 'term' (ie for a limited period only) or it can be for the joint lives of the parties. In some cases, the courts use nominal maintenance to leave a party's income claims open. It is possible for either party to apply to court to vary the amount or duration of the maintenance at a future date.

Prior to 2000, in considering the above factors, the courts considered the 'reasonable financial requirements' of the applicant, usually the wife, and treated this as determinative of the extent of the applicant's award. In the landmark case of *White v White* in 2000 the House of Lords re-evaluated the court's approach to dividing assets on divorce. The law lords enunciated three key principles. Firstly, the outcome has to be as fair as possible in all the circumstances with each party being entitled to a fair share of the available property. Secondly, in seeking to achieve a fair outcome there is no space for discriminating between the breadwinner and the homemaker in their respective roles. Thirdly, having considered all the circumstances of the case, and the statutory checklist, the judge should consider his view against the 'yardstick of equality of division'.

More recently, the law lords have offered further guidance as to how to achieve a fair division of assets on divorce in the cases of *Miller* and *McFarlane*. In determining fairness, the court must now consider three strands or principles, being each party's respective needs, the possibility of compensating the financially weaker party for any 'relationship' generated disadvantage, which will be relevant where one party has given up a career, and 'equal sharing' of family assets, which is applicable as much to short marriages as to long marriages, and which will apply unless there is good reason to the contrary.

In the recent 'huge money' divorce case of *Charman* the presumption of 50:50 in assessing financial awards on divorce emerged undamaged. Those with trust interests must be aware that the court will ignore the trust structure if it takes the view that the assets will be made available to the party on request.

In assessing whether there is a good reason to depart from the concept of equal sharing, the court will consider the nature of property and whether the property was acquired during the marriage otherwise than by inheritance or gift, known as matrimonial property, such as the matrimonial home, or other property to which the other spouse has not contributed. Whilst the yardstick of equality will apply to matrimonial assets to give full effect to the sharing entitlement, it will apply less readily to non-matrimonial assets, particularly in short marriages. Additionally, conduct and special contributions will be relevant in assessing whether there should be a departure from equality, but only in exceptional cases, where such conduct or contribution is 'gross and obvious'.

The Law Commission's Marital Property Agreements project began in October 2009. The project is examining the status and enforceability of agreements made between spouses or civil partners (or those contemplating marriage or civil partnership) concerning their property or finances.

COHABITING COUPLES

Rights of unmarried couples are not the same as for married couples. Agreements, whether express or inferred by conduct, often determine interest in money and property. Reliance upon inferences is problematic, therefore it is advisable to consider entering into a contract, or 'cohabitation agreement', which establishes how money and property should be divided in the event of a relationship breakdown.

This area of the law is still developing. In July 2007, the Law Commission published its report to parliament, recommending a scheme to provide remedies for eligible candidates. The Cohabitation Bill was subsequently introduced to parliament in December 2008 and the first day of the committee stage took place in April 2009. The next day of the committee stage is yet to be scheduled. In the meantime, cohabitation agreements continue to be governed by the general principles of contract law.

CIVIL PARTNERSHIP

The Civil Partnership Act 2004 came into force on 5 December 2005; it has UK-wide status. Same-sex couples, by registering as civil partners, are able to gain legal recognition of their relationship and thereby obtain rights and obligations broadly equivalent to those of married couples. These rights and responsibilities include a duty to provide reasonable maintenance for your civil partner and any children of the family, equitable treatment in respect of life assurance and pension benefits, recognition under intestacy rules and domestic violence protection. In addition, inheritance tax is waived as with married couples and there is a right of succession for tenancy. A civil partnership which has irretrievably broken down may be dissolved by the court on the application of either civil partner. The irretrievable breakdown of the partnership must be proved on one of four grounds. These grounds are the same as those for divorce (*see* above), save for a civil partner may not seek dissolution of the partnership on the basis of the other's adultery.

DOMESTIC VIOLENCE
The Domestic Violence, Crime and Victims Act 2004 is intended to provide greater protection for victims of domestic violence. If one spouse has been subjected to violence at the hands of the other, it is possible to obtain an order from court to restrain further violence and if necessary to have the other spouse excluded from the home. Such orders also apply to civil partnerships and cohabiting couples (including same sex couples), and may also apply to a range of other relationships including parents and children and, to a lesser extent, non-cohabiting couples

SCOTLAND

Although some provisions are similar to those for England and Wales, there is separate legislation for Scotland covering nullity of marriage, judicial separation, divorce and ancillary matters. The principal legislation in relation to family law in Scotland is the Family Law (Scotland) Act 1985. The Family Law (Scotland) Act 2006 came in to force on 4 May 2006, and introduced reforms to various aspects of Scottish family law. The following is confined to major points on which the law in Scotland differs from that of England and Wales.

An action for judicial separation or divorce may be raised in the court of session; it may also be raised in the sheriff court if either party was resident in the sheriffdom for 40 days immediately before the date of the action or for 40 days ending not more than 40 days before the date of the action. The fee for starting a divorce petition in the sheriff court is £125.

The grounds for raising an action of divorce in Scotland have been subject to reform in terms of the 2006 act. The current grounds for divorce are:

- the defender has committed adultery. When adultery is cited as proof that the marriage has broken down irretrievably, it is not necessary in Scotland to prove that it is also intolerable for the pursuer to live with the defender
- the defender's behaviour is such that the pursuer cannot reasonably be expected to cohabit with the defender
- there has been no cohabitation between the parties for one year prior to the raising of the action for divorce, and the defender consents to the granting of decree of divorce
- there has been no cohabitation between the parties for two years prior to the raising of the action for divorce

The previously available ground of desertion was abolished by the 2006 act.

A simplified procedure for 'do-it-yourself divorce' was introduced in 1983 for certain divorces. If the action is based on one or two years' separation and will not be opposed, and if there are no children under 16 and no financial claims, and there is no sign that the applicant's spouse is unable to manage his or her affairs through mental illness or handicap, the applicant can write directly to the local sheriff court or to the court of session for the appropriate forms to enable him or her to proceed. The fee is £95, unless the applicant receives income support or legal advice and assistance, in which case there may be no fee.

Where a divorce action has been raised, it may be put on hold for a variety of reasons. In all actions for divorce an extract decree, which brings the marriage to an end, will be made available 14 days after the divorce has been granted. Unlike in England, there is no decree nisi, only a final decree of divorce. Parties must ensure that all financial issues have been resolved prior to divorce, as it is not possible to seek further financial provision after divorce has been granted.

FINANCIAL PROVISION
In relation to financial provision on divorce, the first, and most important, principle is fair sharing of the matrimonial property. In terms of Scots law matrimonial property is defined as all property acquired by either spouse from the date of marriage up to the date of separation. Property acquired before the marriage is not deemed to be matrimonial unless it was acquired for use by the parties as a family home or as furniture for that home. Property acquired after the date of separation is not matrimonial property. Any property acquired by either of the parties by way of gift or inheritance during the marriage is excluded and does not form part of the matrimonial property.

When considering whether to make an award of financial provision a court shall also take account of any economic advantage derived by either party to the marriage as a result of contributions, financial or otherwise, by the other, and of any economic disadvantage suffered by either party for the benefit of the other party. The court must also ensure that the economic burden of caring for a child under the age of 16 is shared fairly between the parties.

A court can also consider making an order requiring one party to pay the other party a periodical allowance for a certain period of time following divorce. Such an order may be appropriate in cases where there is insufficient capital to effect a fair sharing of the matrimonial property. Orders for periodical allowance are uncommon, as courts will favour a 'clean break' where possible.

CHILDREN
The court has the power to award a residence order in respect of any children of the marriage or to make an order regulating the child's contact with the non-resident parent. The court will only make such orders if it is deemed better for the child to do so than to make no order at all, and the welfare of the children is of paramount importance. The fact that a spouse has caused the breakdown of the marriage does not in itself preclude him/her from being awarded residence.

NULLITY
An action for 'declaration of nullity' can be brought if someone with a legitimate interest is able to show that the marriage is void or voidable. The action can only be brought in the court of session. Although the grounds on which a marriage may be void or voidable are similar to those on which a marriage can be declared invalid in England, there are some differences. Where a spouse is capable of sexual intercourse but refuses to consummate the marriage, this is not a ground for nullity in Scots law, though it could be a ground for divorce. Where a spouse was suffering from venereal disease at the time of marriage and the other spouse did not know, this is not a ground for nullity in Scots law, neither is the fact that a wife was pregnant by another man at the time of marriage without the knowledge of her husband.

COHABITING COUPLES

The law in Scotland now provides certain financial and property rights for cohabiting couples in terms of the Family Law (Scotland) Act 2006, or 'the 2006 Act'. The relevant 2006 act provisions do not place cohabitants in Scotland on an equal footing with married couples or civil partners, but provide some rights for cohabitants in the event that the relationship is terminated by separation or death. The provisions relate to couples who cease to cohabit after 4 May 2006.

The legislation provides for a presumption that any contents of the home shared by the cohabitants are owned in equal shares. A former cohabitant can also seek financial provision on termination of the relationship in the form of a capital payment if they can successfully demonstrate that they have been financially disadvantaged, and that conversely the other cohabitant has been financially advantaged, as a consequence of contributions made (financial or otherwise). Such a claim must be made no later than one year after the day on which the cohabitants cease to cohabit.

The 2006 act also provides that a cohabitant may make a claim on their partner's estate in the event of that partner's death, providing that there is no will. A claim of this nature must be made no later than six months after the date of the partner's death.

THE PRINCIPAL REGISTRY
First Avenue House, 42–49 High Holborn, London WC21 6NP
THE COURT OF SESSION
Parliament House, Parliament Square, Edinburgh EH1 1RQ
T 0131-225 2595 W www.scotcourts.gov.uk
THE CHILD SUPPORT AGENCY
T 08457-133133 W www.csa.gov.uk

EMPLOYMENT LAW

EMPLOYEES

A fundamental distinction in UK employment law is that drawn between an employee and someone who is self-employed. Further, there is an important, intermediate category introduced by legislation: 'workers' covers all employees but also catches some of those who are self-employed. An 'employee' is someone who has entered into or works under a contract of employment, while a 'worker' has entered into or works under a contract whereby he undertakes to do or perform personally any work or services for another party whose status is not that of a client or customer. Whether or not someone is an employee or a worker as opposed to being genuinely self-employed is an important and complex question, for it determines that person's statutory rights and protections.

The greater the level of control that the employer has over the work carried out, the greater the depth of integration of the employee in the employer's business, and the closer the obligations to provide and perform work between the parties, the more likely it is that the parties will be employer and employee.

PAY AND CONDITIONS

The Employment Rights Act 1996 consolidated the statutory provisions relating to employees' rights. Employers must give each employee employed for one month or more a written statement containing the following information:

- names of employer and employee
- date when employment began and the date on which the employee's period of *continuous* employment began (taking into account any employment with a previous employer which counts towards that period)
- the scale, rate or other method of calculating remuneration and intervals at which it will be paid
- job title or description of job
- hours and the permitted place(s) of work and, where there are several such places, the address of the employer
- holiday entitlement and holiday pay
- provisions concerning incapacity for work due to sickness and injury, including provisions for sick pay
- details of pension scheme(s)
- length of notice period that employer and employee need to give to terminate employment
- if the employment is not intended to be permanent, the period for which it is expected to continue or, if it is for a fixed term, the end date of the contract
- details of any collective agreement (including the parties to the agreement) which affects the terms of employment
- details of disciplinary and grievance procedures (including the individual to whom a complaint should be made and the process of making that complaint)
- if the employee is to work outside the UK for more than one month, the period of such work and the currency in which payment is made
- a note stating whether a contracting out certificate is in force

This must be given to the employee within two months of the start of their employment.

If the employer does not provide the written statement within two months (or a statement of any changes to these particulars within one month of the changes being made) then the employee can complain to an employment tribunal, which can specify the information that the employer should have given. When, in the context of an employee's successful tribunal claim, the employer is also found to have been in breach of the duty to provide the written statement at the time proceedings were commenced, the tribunal must award the employee two weeks' pay, and may award four weeks' pay, unless it would be unjust or inequitable to do so.

The Working Time Regulations 1998, the National Minimum Wage Act 1998, the Employment Rights (Dispute Resolution) Act 1998, Employment Relations Act 1999, the Employment Act 2002 and the Employment Act 2008 now supplement the 1996 act.

FLEXIBLE WORKING

The Employment Act 2002 (and regulations made under it) gives employees who are responsible for the upbringing of a child the right to apply for flexible working for the purpose of caring for that child. The right has been extended to carers of adults. Whether or not an employee has this right depends on both the employee and the child/adult cared for meeting a number of criteria. If an application under the act is rejected, the employee may complain to an employment tribunal.

SICK PAY

Employees absent from work through illness or injury are entitled to receive Statutory Sick Pay (SSP) from the employer for a maximum period of 28 weeks in any three-year period.

MATERNITY AND PARENTAL RIGHTS

Under the Employment Relations Act 1999, the Employment Act 2002, the Maternity and Parental Leave

Regulations 1999 (as amended in 2002 and 2006) and the Paternity and Adoption Leave Regulations 2002 and 2003, both men and women are entitled to take leave when they become a parent. Women are protected from discrimination, detriment or dismissal by reason of their pregnancy. Men are protected from suffering a detriment or dismissal for taking paternity or parental leave.

Any woman who needs to attend an antenatal appointment on the advice of a registered medical professional is entitled to paid leave from work to attend the appointment. All pregnant women are entitled to a maximum period of maternity leave of 52 weeks. This comprises 26 weeks' ordinary maternity leave, followed immediately by 26 weeks' additional maternity leave. A woman who takes ordinary maternity leave normally has the right to return to the job in which she was employed before her absence. If she takes additional maternity leave, she is entitled to return to the same job or, if that is not reasonably practicable, to another job that is suitable and appropriate for her to do. There is a two-week period of compulsory maternity leave, immediately following the birth of the child, wherein the employer is not permitted to allow the mother to work.

A woman will qualify for Statutory Maternity Pay (SMP), which is payable for up to 39 weeks, if she has been continuously employed for not less than 26 weeks prior to the 15th week before the expected week of childbirth. For further information *see* Social Welfare, Employer Payments.

Employees are entitled to adoption leave and adoption pay (at the same rates as SMP) subject to fulfilment of similar criteria to those in relation to maternity leave and pay, but note that there is a 26-week qualifying period for adoption leave. Where a couple is adopting a child, either one (but not both) of the parents may take adoption leave, and the other may take paternity leave.

Certain employees are entitled to paternity leave on the birth or adoption of a child. To be eligible, the employee must be the child's father, or the partner of the mother or adopter, and meet other conditions. These conditions are, firstly, that they must have been continuously employed for not less than 26 weeks prior to the 15th week before the expected week of childbirth (or, in the case of adoptions, 26 weeks ending with the week in which notification of the adoption match is given) and, secondly, that the employee must have or expect to have responsibility for the upbringing of the child. The employee may take either one week's leave, or two consecutive weeks' leave. This leave may be taken at any time between the date of the child's birth (or placement for adoption) and 56 days later.

For births and adoptions from 3 April 2011, an eligible employee may take additional paternity leave at the end of the mother's or adopter's leave period. For more information *see* Social Welfare, Employer Payments.

Any employee with one year's service who has, or expects to have, responsibility for a child may take parental leave to care for the child. Each parent is entitled to a total of 13 weeks' parental leave for each of their children (or 18 weeks if the child is disabled). This leave must be taken (at the rate of no more than four weeks a year, and in blocks of whole weeks only) before the child's fifth birthday (18th birthday if the child is disabled) or before the fifth anniversary of the date of placement of an adopted child.

SUNDAY TRADING

The Sunday Trading Act 1994 allows shops to open on Sunday for serving retail customers. The Employment Rights Act 1996 gives shop workers and betting workers the right not to be dismissed, selected for redundancy or to suffer any detriment (such as the denial of overtime, promotion or training) if they refuse to work on Sundays. This does not apply to those who, under their contracts, are employed to work on Sundays.

TERMINATION OF EMPLOYMENT

An employee may be dismissed without notice if guilty of gross misconduct but in other cases a period of notice must be given by the employer. The minimum periods of notice specified in the Employment Rights Act 1996 are:

- one week if the employee has been continuously employed for one month or more but for less than two years
- an additional week for each complete year of continuous employment from and including two to 12 years (making the maximum statutory notice period 12 weeks after 12 years' continuous employment)
- longer periods apply if these are specified in the contract of employment

If an employee is dismissed with less notice than he/she is entitled to by statute, or under their contract if longer, he/she will have a wrongful dismissal claim (unless the employer paid the employee in lieu of notice in accordance with a contractual provision entitling it to do so). This claim for wrongful dismissal can be brought by the employee either in the civil courts or the employment tribunal, but if brought in the tribunal the maximum amount that can be awarded is £25,000.

REDUNDANCY

An employee dismissed because of redundancy may be entitled to redundancy pay. This applies if:

- the employee has at least two years' continuous service
- the employee is dismissed by the employer (this can include cases of voluntary redundancy)
- dismissal is due to redundancy.

Redundancy can mean closure of the entire business, closure of a particular site of the business, or a reduction in the need for employees to carry out work of a particular kind.

An employee may not be entitled to a redundancy payment if offered a suitable alternative job by the same employer. The amount of statutory redundancy pay depends on the length of service, age, and their earnings, subject to a weekly maximum of (currently) £380. The maximum payment that can be awarded is £11,400. The redundancy payment is guaranteed by the government in cases where the employer becomes insolvent.

UNFAIR DISMISSAL

Complaints of unfair dismissal are dealt with by an employment tribunal. Any employee with one year's continuous service (subject to exceptions, including in relation to whistleblowers – *see* below) can make a complaint to the tribunal. At the tribunal, it is for the employer to prove that the dismissal was due to one or more potentially fair reasons: a legal restriction preventing the continuation of the employee's contract; the employee's capability or qualifications for the job he/she was employed to do; the employee's conduct; redundancy; retirement; or some other substantial reason.

If the employer succeeds in showing this, the tribunal must then decide whether the employer acted reasonably in dismissing the employee for that reason. If the employee is found to have been unfairly dismissed, the tribunal can order that he/she be reinstated, re-engaged or compensated. Any person believing that they may have been unfairly dismissed should contact their local Citizens Advice bureau or seek legal advice. A claim must be brought within three months of the date of termination of employment.

The normal maximum compensatory award for unfair dismissal is £65,300 (as at 1 February 2010). If the dismissal occurred after 6 April 2009 and the employer unreasonably failed to follow the ACAS Code of Practice on Disciplinary and Grievance Procedures in carrying out the dismissal, the tribunal may increase the employee's compensation by up to 25 per cent.

WHISTLEBLOWING

Under the whistleblowing legislation (Public Interest Disclosure Act 1998, which inserted provisions into the Employment Rights Act 1996) dismissal of an employee is automatically unfair if the reason or principal reason for the dismissal is that the employee has made a protected disclosure. The legislation also makes it unlawful to subject workers (a broad category that includes employees and certain other individuals, such as agency workers) who have made a protected disclosure to any detriment on the ground that they have done so.

For a disclosure to qualify for protection, the claimant must show that he has disclosed information, which in his reasonable belief tends to show one or more of the following six categories of wrongdoing: criminal offences; breach of any legal obligation; miscarriages of justice; danger to the health and safety of any individual; damage to the environment; or the deliberate concealing of information about any of the other categories. The malpractices can be past, present, prospective or merely alleged.

A qualifying disclosure will only be protected if the manner of the disclosure fulfills certain conditions, including being made in good faith and being made to a defined category of persons, which varies according to the type of disclosure.

Any whistleblower claim in the employment tribunal must normally be brought within three months of the date of dismissal or other act leading to a detriment.

An individual does not need to have been working with the employer for any particular period of time to be able to bring such a claim and compensation is uncapped (and can include an amount for injury to feelings).

DISCRIMINATION

Discrimination in employment on the grounds of sex (including gender reassignment), sexual orientation, race, colour, nationality, ethnic or national origins, religion or belief, marital or civil partnership status, age or disability is unlawful. Discrimination legislation generally covers direct discrimination, indirect discrimination, harassment and victimisation. Only in limited circumstances can such discrimination be justified (rendering it lawful).

An individual does not need to be employed for any particular period of time to be able to claim discrimination (discrimination can be alleged at the recruitment phase), and discrimination compensation is uncapped (and can include an amount for injury to feelings). These features distinguish the discrimination laws from, for example, the unfair dismissal laws.

The Equality Act 2010 was passed on 8 April 2010 and many of its key provisions are due to come into force in late 2010. The Act unifies separate pieces of discrimination legislation, providing one definition of direct discrimination, indirect discrimination, harassment and victimisation. At the time of writing the following legislation remains in force and applies to those employed in Great Britain but not to employees in Northern Ireland or (subject to EC exceptions) to those who work mainly abroad:

- the Sex Discrimination Act 1975 (as amended) makes it unlawful to discriminate on the grounds of sex or marital/civil partner status. This covers all aspects of employment (including advertising for jobs), but there are some limited exceptions, such as where the essential nature of the job requires it to be given to someone of a particular sex, or where decency and privacy requires it. The Equal Pay Act 1970 (as amended) entitles men and women to equality of remuneration for equivalent work or work of the same value
- the Race Relations Act 1976 gives individuals the right not to be discriminated against on the grounds of race, colour, nationality, or ethnic or national origins. It applies to all aspects of employment
- the Disability Discrimination Act 1995 makes discrimination against a disabled person in all aspects of employment unlawful. In certain circumstances, the employer may show that the less favourable treatment is justified and so does not constitute discrimination. The act also imposes a duty on employers to make 'reasonable adjustments' to the arrangements and physical features of the workplace if these place disabled people at a substantial disadvantage compared with those who are not disabled. The definition of a 'disabled person' is wide and includes people diagnosed with HIV, cancer and multiple sclerosis
- the Employment Equality (Religion or Belief) Regulations 2003 make discrimination against a person on the grounds of religion or belief, in all aspects of employment, unlawful
- the Employment Equality (Sexual Orientation) Regulations 2003 make discrimination against an individual on the grounds of sexual orientation, in all aspects of employment, unlawful
- the Employment Equality (Age) Regulations 2006 outlaw age discrimination in the workplace. Currently, an employer may dismiss an employee by reason of retirement once they have reached the age of 65, provided the employer follows the correct procedures set out in statute. However, the government has announced its intention to phase out the default retirement age

The responsibility for monitoring equality in society rests with the Equality and Human Rights Commission.

In Northern Ireland similar provisions exist but are contained in separate legislation (although the Disability Discrimination Act does extend to Northern Ireland).

In Northern Ireland there is one combined body working towards equality and eliminating discrimination, the Equality Commission for Northern Ireland.

WORKING TIME

The Working Time Regulations 1998 impose rules that limit working hours and provide for rest breaks and holidays. The regulations apply to workers and so cover not only employees but also other individuals who undertake to perform personally any work or services (eg freelancers). The regulations are complex and subject to various exceptions and qualifications but the basic provisions relating to adult day workers are as follows:

- No worker is permitted to work more than an average of 48 hours per week (unless they have made a genuine voluntary opt-out of this limit – it is not sufficient to make it a term of the contract that the worker opts out), and a worker is entitled to, but is not required to take, the following breaks:
- 11 consecutive hours' rest in every 24-hour period
- an uninterrupted rest period of at least 24 hours in each 7-day period or 48 hours in each fortnight (in addition to the daily rest period)
- 20 minutes' rest break provided that the working day is longer than 6 hours
- 5.6 weeks' paid annual leave (28 days full-time). This equates to 4 weeks plus public holidays

There are specific provisions relating to night work, young workers (ie those over school leaving age but under 18) and a variety of workers in specialised sectors (such as off-shore oil rig workers).

HUMAN RIGHTS

On 2 October 2000 the Human Rights Act 1998 came into force. This act incorporates the European Convention on Human Rights into the law of the UK. The main principles of the act are as follows:

- all legislation must be interpreted and given effect by the courts as compatible with the Convention so far as it is possible to do so. Before the second reading of a new bill the minister responsible for the bill must provide a statement regarding its compatibility with the Human Rights Act
- subordinate legislation (eg statutory instruments) which are incompatible with the Convention can be struck down by the courts
- primary legislation (eg an act of parliament) which is incompatible with the Convention cannot be struck down by a court, but the higher courts can make a declaration of incompatibility which is a signal to parliament to change the law
- all public authorities (including courts and tribunals) must not act in a way which is incompatible with the Convention
- individuals whose Convention rights have been infringed by a public authority may bring proceedings against that authority, but the act is not intended to create new rights as between individuals

The main human rights protected by the Convention are the right to life (article 2); protection from torture and inhuman or degrading treatment (article 3); protection from slavery or forced labour (article 4); the right to liberty and security of the person (article 5); the right to a fair trial (article 6); the right not to be subject to retrospective criminal offences (article 7); the right to respect for private and family life (article 8); freedom of thought, conscience and religion (article 9); freedom of expression (article 10); freedom of peaceful association and assembly (article 11); the right to marry and found a family (article 12); protection from discrimination (article 14); the right to property (article 1 protocol No.1); the right to education (article 2 protocol No.1); and the right to free elections (article 3 protocol No.1). Most of the Convention rights are subject to limitations which deem the breach of the right acceptable on the basis it is 'necessary in a democratic society'.

Human rights are also enshrined in the common law (of tort). Although this is of historical significance, the common law (for example the duty of confidentiality) remains especially important regarding violations of human rights that occur between private parties, where the Human Rights Act 1998 does not apply.

PARENTAL RESPONSIBILITY

The Children Act 1989 gives both the mother and father parental responsibility for the child if the parents are married to each other at the time of the child's birth. If the parents are not married, only the mother has parental responsibility. The father may acquire it in accordance with the provisions of section 4 of the Children Act 1989. He can do this in one of four ways: a) by being registered as the father on the child's birth certificate with the consent of the mother (only for fathers of children born after 1 December 2003, following changes to the Adoption and Children Act 2002); b) by applying to the court for a parental responsibility order; c) by entering into a parental responsibility agreement with the mother which must be in the prescribed form; or d) by obtaining a residence order from the court. Otherwise, a father can gain parental responsibility by marrying the mother of the child.

Where a child is adopted, parental responsibility will be given to the adopter of a child. However, before an order for adoption can be made, the court must be satisfied that every parent or guardian consents. The consent of a father without parental responsibility is not required, although adoption agencies and local authorities must be careful to establish, if possible, the identity of the father and satisfy themselves that any person claiming to be the father either has no intention to apply for parental responsibility or that if he did apply, the application would be likely to be refused.

In Scotland, the relevant legislation is the Children (Scotland) Act 1995, which also gives the mother parental responsibility for her child whether or not she is married to the child's father. A father who is married to the mother, either at the time of the child's conception or subsequently, will also have automatic parental rights. Section 23 of the 2006 act provides that an unmarried father will obtain automatic parental responsibilities and rights if he is registered as the father on the child's birth certificate. For unmarried fathers who are not named on the birth certificate, or whose children were born before the 2006 act came into force, it is possible to acquire parental responsibilities and rights by applying to the court or by entering into a parental responsibilities and rights agreement with the mother. The father of any child, regardless of parental rights, has a duty to aliment that child until he/she is 18 (25 if the child is still at an educational establishment).

LEGITIMATION

Under the Legitimacy Act 1976, an illegitimate person automatically becomes legitimate when his/her parents marry. This applies even where one of the parents was married to a third person at the time of the birth. In such cases it is necessary to re-register the birth of the child. In Scotland, the status of illegitimacy has been abolished by section 21 of the 2006 act. The Law Reform Act 1987 reformed the law so as to remove so far as possible the legal disadvantages of illegitimacy.

JURY SERVICE

In England and Wales a person charged with serious criminal offences is entitled to have their trial heard by a jury in a crown court, except in some complex fraud cases or where there is a real risk of jury tampering, in which case a judge may be entitled to order a trial by judge alone. No such right exists in Scotland, although more serious offences are heard before a jury. In England and Wales there must be at least nine, and not more than 12 members of a jury in a criminal case and eight members in a civil case. In Scotland there are 12 members of a jury in a civil case in the court of session (the civil jury being confined to the court of session and a restricted number of actions), and 15 in a criminal trial in the high court of justiciary. Jurors are normally asked to serve for ten working days, during which time they could sit on more than one case. Jurors selected for longer cases are expected to sit for the duration of the trial.

Every 'registered' parliamentary or local government elector between the ages of 18 and 70 who has lived in the UK (including, for this purpose, the Channel Islands and the Isle of Man) for any period of at least five years since reaching the age of 13 is qualified to serve on a jury unless he/she is 'mentally disordered' or disqualified. Those disqualified from jury service include:

- those who have at any time been sentenced by a court in the UK (including, for this purpose, the Channel Islands and the Isle of Man) to a term of imprisonment or youth custody of five years or more
- those who have been imprisoned for life, detained at Her Majesty's pleasure, detained for a period of at least five years, or imprisoned or detained for public protection
- those who have within the previous ten years served any part of a sentence of imprisonment, youth custody or detention, been detained in a young offenders' institution, received a suspended sentence of imprisonment or order for detention, or received a community service order
- those who are on bail in criminal proceedings

The court has the discretion to excuse a juror from service, or defer the date of service, if the juror can show there is good reason why he/she should be excused from attending or good reason why his attendance should be deferred. It is an offence to fail to attend when summoned, to serve knowing that you are disqualified from service, or to make false representations in an attempt to evade service. In criminal cases the defendant can object to any juror if he/she can show cause.

An individual juror (or the entire jury) can be discharged if it is shown that they or any of their number have, among other things, separated from the rest of the jury without the leave of the court; talked to any person out of court who is not a member of the jury; determined the verdict of the trial by drawing lots; been drunk, or otherwise incapacitated, while carrying out their duties as a juror; exerted improper pressure on the other members of the jury (eg harassment or bullying); declined to take part in the jury's functions; displayed actual or apparent bias (eg racism, sexism or other discriminatory or deliberate hostility); or inadvertently possessed knowledge of the bad character of a party to the proceedings which has not been adduced as evidence in the proceedings.

A jury's verdict need not be unanimous. In criminal proceedings the agreement of 10 jurors will suffice when there are not fewer than 11 people on the jury (or 9 in a jury of 10). In civil proceedings the agreement of seven jurors will suffice. However the court must be satisfied that the jury had reasonable time to consider its verdict based on the nature and complexity of the case. In criminal proceedings this must be no less than two hours.

A juror may claim travelling expenses, a subsistence allowance and an allowance for other financial loss (eg loss of earnings or benefits, fees paid to carers or child-minders) up to a stated limit. It is a contempt of court for a juror to disclose what happened in the jury room even after the trial is over.

SCOTLAND

Qualification criteria for jury service in Scotland are similar to those in England and Wales, except that the maximum age for a juror is 65, members of the judiciary are ineligible for ten years after ceasing to hold their post, and others concerned with the administration of justice are only eligible for service five years after ceasing to hold office. Certain persons who have the right to be excused include full-time members of the medical, dental, nursing, veterinary and pharmaceutical professions, full-time members of the armed forces, ministers of religion, persons who have served on a jury within the previous five years, members of the Scottish parliament, members of the Scottish government and junior Scottish ministers. Those convicted of a serious crime are automatically disqualified. Those who are incapable by reason of a mental disorder may also be excused. The maximum fine for a person serving on a jury knowing himself/herself to be ineligible is £1,000. The maximum fine for failing to attend without good cause is also £1,000.

THE COURT SERVICE
Southside, 105 Victoria Street, London SW1E 6QT
T 020-7210 2266

SCOTTISH COURTS SERVICE
Courts of Session, Parliament House, Parliament Square, Edinburgh EH1 1RQ T 0131-225 2595
W www.scotcourts.gov.uk

THE CLERK OF JUSTICIARY
High Court of Justiciary, Lawnmarket, Edinburgh EH2 2NS
T 0131-240 6900

LANDLORD AND TENANT

RESIDENTIAL LETTINGS

The provisions outlined here apply only where the tenant lives in a separate dwelling from the landlord and where the dwelling is the tenant's only or main home. It does not apply to licensees such as lodgers, guests or service occupiers.

The 1996 Housing Act radically changed certain aspects of the legislation referred to below; in particular, the grant of assured and assured shorthold tenancies under the Housing Act 1988.

ASSURED SHORTHOLD TENANCIES

If a tenancy was granted on or after 15 January 1989 and before 28 February 1997, the tenant would have an assured tenancy unless the landlord served notice under section 20 in the prescribed form prior to the commencement of the tenancy, stating that the tenancy is to be an assured shorthold tenancy and the tenancy is for a minimum fixed term period of six months (*see* below). An assured tenancy gives that tenant greater security. The tenant could, for example, stay in possession of the dwelling for as long as the tenant observed the terms of the tenancy. The landlord cannot obtain possession from such a tenant unless the landlord can establish a specific ground for possession (set out in the Housing Act 1988) and obtains a court order. The rent payable is that agreed with the landlord at the start of the tenancy. The landlord has the right to increase the rent annually by serving a notice. If that happens the tenant can apply to have the rent fixed by the rent assessment committee of the local authority. The tenant or the landlord may request that the committee sets the rent in line with open market rents for that type of property.

Under the Housing Act 1996, all new lettings (below an annual rent threshold of £100,000 since October 2010) entered into on or after 28 February 1997 (for whatever term) will be assured shorthold tenancies unless the landlord serves a notice stating that the tenancy is not to be an assured shorthold tenancy. This means that the landlord is entitled to possession at the end of the tenancy provided he serves a notice under section 21 Housing Act 1988 and commences the proceedings in accordance with the correct procedure. The landlord must obtain a court order, however, to obtain possession if the tenant refuses to vacate at the end of the tenancy. If the tenancy is an assured shorthold tenancy, the court must grant the order. For both assured and assured shorthold tenancies, if the tenant is more than eight weeks in arrears, the landlord can serve notice and, if the tenant is still in arrears at the date of the hearing, the court must make an order for possession.

REGULATED TENANCIES

Before the Housing Act 1988 came into force on 15 January 1989 there were regulated tenancies; some are still in existence and are protected by the Rent Act 1977. Under this act it is possible for the landlord or the tenant to apply to the local rent officer to have a 'fair' rent registered. The fair rent is then the maximum rent payable.

SECURE TENANCIES

Secure tenancies are generally given to tenants of local authorities, housing associations (before 15 January 1989) and certain other bodies. This gives the tenant security of tenure unless the terms of the agreement are broken by the tenant and it is reasonable to make an order for possession. Those with secure tenancies may have the right to buy their property. In practice this right is generally only available to council tenants.

AGRICULTURAL PROPERTY

Tenancies in agricultural properties are governed by the Agricultural Holdings Act 1986, the Agricultural Tenancies Act 1995 (both amended by the Regulatory Reform (Agricultural Tenancies) (England and Wales) Order 2006), the Tribunals, Courts and Enforcement Act 2007, the Legal Services Act 2007 and the Rent (Agriculture) Act 1976, which give similar protections to those described above, eg security of tenure, right to compensation for disturbance, etc. The Agricultural Holdings (Scotland) Act 1991 along with Agricultural Holdings (Scotland) Act 2003 and the Housing (Scotland) Act 2006 apply similar provisions to Scotland.

EVICTION

The Protection from Eviction Act 1977 (as amended by the Housing Act 1988 and Nationality, Immigration and Asylum Act 2002) sets out the procedure a landlord must follow in order to obtain possession of property. It is unlawful for a landlord to evict a tenant otherwise than in accordance with the law. For common law tenancies and for Rent Act tenants a notice to quit in the prescribed form giving 28 days is required. For secure and assured tenancies a notice seeking possession must be served. It is unlawful for the landlord to evict a person by putting their belongings on to the street, by changing the locks and so on. It is also unlawful for a landlord to harass a tenant in any way in order to persuade him/her to give up the tenancy. The tenant may be able to obtain an injunction to restrain the actions of the landlord and get back into the property and be awarded damages.

LANDLORD RESPONSIBILITIES

Under the Landlord and Tenant Act 1985, where the term of the lease is less than seven years, the landlord is responsible for maintaining the structure and exterior of the property, for sanitation, for heating and hot water, and all installations for the supply of water, gas and electricity.

LEASEHOLDERS

Strictly speaking, leaseholders have bought a long lease rather than a property and in certain limited circumstances the landlord can end the tenancy. Under the Leasehold Reform Act 1967 (as amended by the Housing Acts 1969, 1974, 1980 and 1985), leaseholders of houses may have the right to buy the freehold or to take an extended lease for a term of 50 years. This applies to leases where the term of the lease is over 21 years, at a low rent, and where the leaseholder has occupied the house as his/her only or main residence for the last two years, or for a total of two years over the last ten. The tenant must give the landlord written notice of his desire to acquire the freehold or extend the leasehold.

The Leasehold Reform, Housing and Urban Development Act came into force in 1993 and allows the leaseholders of flats in certain circumstances to buy the freehold of the building in which they live.

Responsibility for maintenance of the structure, exterior and interior of the building should be set out in the lease. Usually the upkeep of the interior of his/her part of the property is the responsibility of the leaseholder, and responsibility for the structure, exterior and common interior areas is shared between the freeholder and the leaseholder(s).

If leaseholders are dissatisfied with charges made in respect of lease extensions, they are entitled to have their situation evaluated by the Leasehold Valuation Tribunal.

The Commonhold and Leasehold Reform Act 2002 makes provision for the freehold estate in land to be registered as commonhold land and for the legal interest in the land to be vested in a 'commonhold association' ie a private limited company.

BUSINESS LETTINGS

The Landlord and Tenant acts 1927 and 1954 (as amended) give security of tenure to the tenants of most business premises. The landlord can only evict the tenant on one of the grounds laid down in the 1954 act, and in some cases where the landlord repossesses the property the tenant may be entitled to compensation.

SCOTLAND

In Scotland assured and short assured tenancies exist for lettings after 2 January 1989 and are similar to assured tenancies in England and Wales. The relevant legislation is the Housing (Scotland) Act 1988.

Most tenancies created before 2 January 1989 were regulated tenancies and the Rent (Scotland) Act 1984 still applies where these exist. The act defines, among other things, the circumstances in which a landlord can increase the rent when improvements are made to the property.

The provisions of the Rent Act do not apply to tenancies where the landlord is the Crown, a local authority or a housing corporation.

The Housing (Scotland) Acts of 1987 and 2001 relate to local authority responsibilities for housing, the right to buy, and local authority secured tenancies. The provisions are broadly similar to England and Wales. The Housing (Scotland) Bill was introduced to the Scottish parliament on 13 January 2010 and, if enacted, will reform the existing right-to-buy provisions, modernise social housing regulation and replace the regulatory framework established by the 1988 and 2001 acts.

In Scotland, business premises are not controlled by statute to the same extent as in England and Wales, although the Tenancy of Shops (Scotland) Act 1949 gives some security to tenants of shops. Tenants of shops can apply to the sheriff, within 21 days of being served a notice to quit, for a renewal of tenancy if threatened with eviction. This application may be dismissed on various grounds including where the landlord has offered to sell the property to the tenant at an agreed price or, in the absence of agreement as to price, at a price fixed by a single arbiter appointed by the parties or the sheriff. The act extends to properties where the Crown or government departments are the landlords or the tenants.

Under the Leases Act 1449 the landlord's successors (either purchasers or creditors) are bound by the agreement made with any tenants so long as the following conditions are met:

- the lease, if for more than one year, must be in writing
- there must be a rent
- there must be a term of expiry
- the tenant must have entered into possession
- the subjects of the lease must be land
- the landlord, if owner, must be the proprietor with a recorded title, ie the title deeds recorded in the Register of Sasines or registered in the Land Register

The Antisocial Behaviour etc (Scotland) Act 2004 provides that all landlords letting property in Scotland must register with the local authority in which the let property is situated. Exceptions apply to holiday lets, owner-occupied accommodation and agricultural holdings. The act applies to partnerships, trusts and companies as well as to individuals.

LEGAL AID

The Access to Justice Act 1999 has transformed what used to be known as the Legal Aid system. The Legal Aid Board has been replaced by the Legal Services Commission, which is responsible for the development and administration of two legal funding schemes in England and Wales, namely the Criminal Defence Service and the Community Legal Service. The Criminal Defence Service assists people who are under police investigation or facing criminal charges. The Community Legal Service is designed to increase access to legal information and advice by involving a much wider network of funders and providers in giving publicly funded legal services. In Scotland, provision of legal aid is governed by the Legal Aid (Scotland) Act 1986 and administered by the Scottish Legal Aid Board.

LEGAL SERVICES COMMISSION

4 Abbey Orchard Street, London SW1P 2BS **T** 020-7783 7000
W www.legalservices.gov.uk

CIVIL LEGAL AID

From 1 January 2000, only organisations (such as solicitors or Citizens Advice) with a contract with the Legal Services Commission have been able to give initial help in any civil matter. Moreover, from that date decisions about funding were devolved from the Legal Services Commission to contracted organisations in relation to any level of publicly funded service in family and immigration cases. For other types of case, applications for public funding are made through a solicitor (or other contracted legal services providers) in much the same way as the former Legal Aid. On 1 April 2001 the so-called civil contracting scheme was extended to cover all levels of service for all types of cases.

Under the civil funding scheme there are broadly six levels of service available:

- legal help
- help at court
- family help – either family help (lower) or family help (higher)
- legal representation – either investigative help or full representation
- family mediation
- such other services as authorised by specific orders

ELIGIBILITY

Eligibility for funding from the Community Legal Service depends broadly on five factors:

- the level of service sought (*see* above)
- whether the applicant qualifies financially
- the merits of the applicant's case
- a costs-benefits analysis (if the costs are likely to outweigh any benefit that might be gained from the proceedings, funding may be refused)
- whether there is any public interest in the case being litigated (ie whether the case has a wider public interest beyond that of the parties involved – for example, a human rights case)

The limits on capital and income above which a person is not entitled to public funding vary with the type of service sought.

CONTRIBUTIONS

Some of those who qualify for Community Legal Service funding will have to contribute towards their legal costs. Contributions must be paid by anyone who has a disposable income or disposable capital exceeding a prescribed amount. The rules relating to applicable contributions are complex and detailed information can be obtained from the Legal Services Commission.

STATUTORY CHARGE

A statutory charge is made if a person keeps or gains money or property in a case for which they have received legal aid. This means that the amount paid by the Community Legal Service fund on their behalf is deducted from the amount that the person receives. This does not apply if the court has ordered that the costs be paid by the other party (unless the amount paid by the other party does not cover all of the costs). In certain circumstances, the Legal Services Commission may waive or postpone payment.

CONTINGENCY OR CONDITIONAL FEES

This system was introduced by the Courts and Legal Services Act 1990. It can offer legal representation on a 'no win, no fee' basis. It provides an alternative form of assistance, especially for those cases which are ineligible for funding by the Community Legal Service. The main area for such work is in the field of personal injuries.

Not all solicitors offer such a scheme and different solicitors may well have different terms. The effect of the agreement is that solicitors may not make any charges, or may waive some of their charges, until the case is concluded successfully. If a case is won then the losing party will usually have to pay towards costs, with the winning party contributing around one third.

SCOTLAND

Civil legal aid is available for cases in the following:

- the sheriff courts
- the court of session
- the House of Lords
- the lands valuation appeal court
- the Scottish land court
- the Lands Tribunal for Scotland
- the Employment Appeal Tribunals
- the Judicial Committee of the Privy Council
- the Proscribed Organisations Appeal Commissioner
- proceedings before the Social Security Commissioners
- proceedings before the Child Support Commissioners

Civil legal aid is not available for defamation actions, small claims or simplified divorce procedures or petitions by a debtor for his own sequestration.

Eligibility for civil legal aid is assessed in a similar way to that in England and Wales, though the financial limits differ in some respects. A person shall be eligible for civil legal aid if their disposable income does not exceed £25,450 a year. A person may be refused civil aid if their disposable capital exceeds £12,626 and it appears to the Legal Aid board that they can afford to pay without legal aid. Additionally:

- if disposable income is between £3,416 and £11,193, a contribution of one third of the difference between £3,416 and the disposable income may be payable
- if disposable income is between £11,194 and £15,270, one third of the difference between £3,416 and £11,193 plus half the difference between £11,194 and the disposable income may be payable
- if disposable income is between £15,271 and £25,450, a contribution of the following: one third of the difference between £3,416 and £11,193, plus half the difference between £11,194 and £15,270, plus all the remaining disposable income between £15,271 and £25,450 – will be payable

CRIMINAL LEGAL AID

The Legal Services Commission provides defendants facing criminal charges with free legal representation if they pass a merits test and a means test.

Criminal legal aid covers the cost of preparing a case and legal representation in criminal proceedings. It is also available for appeals against verdicts or sentences in magistrates' courts, the crown court or the court of appeal. It is not available for bringing a private prosecution in a criminal court.

If granted criminal legal aid, either the person may choose their own solicitor or the court will assign one. Contributions to the legal costs may be required. The rules relating to applicable contributions are complex and detailed information can be obtained from the Legal Services Commission.

DUTY SOLICITORS

The Legal Aid Act 1988 also provides free advice and assistance to anyone questioned by the police (whether under arrest or helping the police with their enquiries). No means test or contributions are required for this.

SCOTLAND

Legal advice and assistance operates in a similar way in Scotland. A person is eligible:

- if disposable income does not exceed £238 a week. If disposable income is between £102 and £238 a week, contributions are payable
- if disposable capital does not exceed £1,664 (if the person has dependent relatives, the savings allowance is higher)
- if receiving income support or income-related job seeker's allowance they qualify automatically provided they have no savings over the limit

The procedure for application for criminal legal aid depends on the circumstances of each case. In solemn cases (more serious cases, such as murder) heard before a jury, a person is automatically entitled to criminal legal aid until they are given bail or placed in custody. Thereafter, it is for the court to decide whether to grant legal aid. The court will do this if the person accused cannot meet the expenses of the case without undue hardship on him or his dependants. In less serious cases the procedure depends on whether the person is in custody:

- anyone taken into custody has the right to free legal aid from the duty solicitor up to and including the first court appearance
- if the person is not in custody and wishes to plead guilty, they are not entitled to criminal legal aid but may be entitled to legal advice and assistance, including assistance by way of representation
- if the person is not in custody and wishes to plead not guilty, they can apply for criminal legal aid. This must be done within 14 days of the first court appearance at which they made the plea

The criteria used to assess whether or not criminal legal aid should be granted is similar to the criteria for England and Wales. When meeting with your solicitor, take evidence of your financial position such as details of savings, bank statements, pay slips, pension book or benefits book.

THE SCOTTISH LEGAL AID BOARD
44 Drumsheugh Gardens, Edinburgh EH3 7SW
T 0131-226 7061 W www.slab.org.uk

MARRIAGE

Any two persons may marry provided that:

- they are at least 16 years old on the day of the marriage (in England and Wales persons under the age of 18 must generally obtain the consent of their parents; if consent is refused an appeal may be made to the high court, the county court or a court of summary jurisdiction)
- they are not related to one another in a way which would prevent their marrying
- they are unmarried (a person who has already been married must produce documentary evidence that the previous marriage has been ended by death, divorce or annulment)
- they are not of the same sex (though same sex couples can register a civil partnership instead)
- they are capable of understanding the nature of a marriage ceremony and of consenting to marriage

The parties should check the marriage will be recognised

as valid in their home country if either is not a British citizen.

DEGREES OF RELATIONSHIP

A marriage between persons within the prohibited degrees of consanguinity, affinity or adoption is void.

A man may not marry his mother, daughter, grandmother, granddaughter, sister, aunt, niece, great-grandmother, adoptive mother, former adoptive mother, adopted daughter or former adopted daughter.

A woman may not marry her father, son, grandfather, grandson, brother, uncle, nephew, great-grandfather, adoptive father, former adoptive father, adopted son or former adopted son. Under the Marriage (Prohibited Degrees of Relationship) Act 1986, some exceptions to the law permit a man or a woman to marry certain step-relatives or in-laws.

All references to brothers/sisters include half-brothers/sisters.

ENGLAND AND WALES

TYPES OF MARRIAGE CEREMONY

It is possible to marry by either religious or civil ceremony. A religious ceremony can take place at a church or chapel of the Church of England or the Church in Wales, or at any other place of worship which has been formally registered by the Registrar-General.

A civil ceremony can take place at a register office, a registered building or any other premises approved by the local authority.

An application for an approved premises licence must be made by the owners or trustees of the building concerned; it cannot be made by the prospective marriage couple. Approved premises must be regularly open to the public so that the marriage can be witnessed; the venue must be deemed to be a permanent and immovable structure. Open-air ceremonies are prohibited.

Non-Anglican marriages may also be solemnised following the issue of a Registrar-General's licence in unregistered premises where one of the parties is seriously ill, is not expected to recover, and cannot be moved to registered premises. Detained and housebound persons may be married at their place of residence.

MARRIAGE IN THE CHURCH OF ENGLAND OR THE CHURCH IN WALES

Marriage by banns

The marriage can take place in a parish in which one of the parties lives, or in a church in another parish if it is the usual place of worship of either or both of the parties. New regulations introduced in October 2008 also allow marriages to take place in a parish where one of the parties was baptised or prepared for confirmation; a parish where one of the parties lived for six months or more; a parish where one of the parents of either of the parties lived for six months or more; in a parish where one of the parents of either of the parties has attended public worship for six months or more in the child's lifetime; or a parish where the parents or grandparents of either of the parties were married. The banns (ie the announcement of the marriage ceremony) must be called in the parish in which the marriage is to take place on three Sundays before the day of the ceremony; if either or both of the parties lives in a different parish the banns must also be called there. After three months the banns are no longer valid. The minister will not perform the marriage unless satisfied that the banns have been properly called.

Marriage by common licence

The vicar who is to conduct the marriage will arrange for a common licence to be issued by the diocesan bishop; this dispenses with the necessity for banns. One of the parties must have lived in the parish for 15 days immediately before the issuing of the licence or must usually worship at the church. Eligibility requirements vary from diocese to diocese, but it is not normally required that the parties should have been baptised. The licence is valid for three months.

Marriage by special licence

A special licence is granted by the Archbishop of Canterbury in special circumstances for the marriage to take place at any place, with or without previous residence in the parish, or at any time. Application must be made to the registrar of the Faculty Office: 1 The Sanctuary, London SW1P 3JT **T** 020-7222 5381.

Marriage by certificate

The marriage can be conducted on the authority of the superintendent registrar's certificate, provided that the vicar's consent is obtained (the vicar is not obliged to accept the certificate). One of the parties must live in the parish or must usually worship at the church.

MARRIAGE BY OTHER RELIGIOUS CEREMONY

One of the parties must normally live in the registration district where the marriage is to take place. In addition to giving notice to the superintendent registrar it may also be necessary to book a registrar to be present at the ceremony.

CIVIL MARRIAGE

A marriage may be solemnised at any register office, registered building or approved premises in England and Wales. The superintendent registrar of the district should be contacted, and, if the marriage is to take place at approved premises, the necessary arrangements at the venue must also be made.

NOTICE OF MARRIAGE

Unless it is to take place by banns or under common or special licence in the Church of England or the Church in Wales, a notice of the marriage must be given in person to the superintendent registrar. Notice of marriage may be given in the following ways:

- by certificate. Both parties must have lived in a registration district in England or Wales for at least eight days immediately before giving notice at the local register office. If they live in different registration districts, notice must be given in both districts. The marriage can take place in any register office or other approved premises in England and Wales no sooner than 15 days after notice has been given, when the superintendent registrar issues a certificate.
- by licence (often known as 'special licence'). One of the parties must have lived in a registration district in England or Wales for at least 15 days before giving notice at the register office; the other party need only be a resident of, or be physically in, England and Wales on the day notice is given. The marriage can take place one clear day (other than a Sunday, Christmas Day or Good Friday) after notice has been given.

A notice of marriage is valid for 12 months, unless it is for the marriage of a detained or housebound person, when it will usually only be accepted within three months of publication. Notice for marriages taking place within the Church of England or Church of Wales should also only be valid within three months of publication. It should be possible to make an advance (provisional) booking 12 months before the ceremony. In this case it is still necessary to give formal notice three months before the marriage. When giving notice of the marriage it is necessary to produce official proof, if relevant, that any previous marriage has ended in divorce or death by producing a decree absolute or death certificate; it is also necessary to provide proof of age, identity and nationality for each of the parties, for example, with a passport. If either party is under 18 years old, evidence of consent by their parent or guardian is required. There are special procedures for those wishing to get married in the UK that are subject to immigration control; the register office will be able to advise on these.

SOLEMNISATION OF THE MARRIAGE

On the day of the wedding there must be at least two other people present who are prepared to act as witnesses and sign the marriage register. A registrar of marriages must be present at a marriage in a register office or at approved premises, but an authorised person may act in the capacity of registrar in a registered building.

If the marriage takes place at approved premises, the room must be separate from any other activity on the premises at the time of the ceremony, and no food or drink can be sold or consumed in the room during the ceremony or for one hour beforehand.

The marriage must be solemnised between 8am and 6pm, with open doors. At some time during the ceremony the parties must make a declaration that they know of no legal impediment to the marriage and they must also say the contracting words; the declaratory and contracting words may vary according to the form of service. A civil marriage cannot contain any religious aspects, but it may be possible for non-religious music and/or readings to be included. It may also be possible to embellish the marriage vows taken by the couple.

CIVIL FEES

Notice and registration of Marriage at a Register Office

By superintendent registrar's certificate, £33.50 per person for the notice of the marriage (which is not refundable if the marriage does not in fact take place) and £40 for the registration of the marriage.

Marriage at a Register Office/Approved Premises

Fees for marriage at a register office are set by the local authority responsible. An additional fee will also be payable for the superintendent registrar's and registrar's attendance at the marriage on an approved premises. This is also set locally by the local authority responsible. A further charge is likely to be made by the owners of the building for the use of the premises. For marriages taking place in a religious building other than the Church of England or Church of Wales, an additional fee of £80 is payable for the registrar's attendance at the marriage unless an 'Authorised Person' appointed by the trustees of the building has agreed to register the marriage. Additional fees may be charged by the trustees of the building for the wedding and by the person who performs the ceremony.

ECCLESIASTICAL FEES

(Church of England and Church in Wales)

Marriage by banns

For publication of banns, £22*

For certificate of banns issued at time of publication, £12.00*

For marriage service, £260*

For marriage certificate at registration if required £3.50**

* These fees are revised from 1 January each calendar year. Some may not apply to the Church in Wales

** This fee is revised from 1 April each calendar year

SCOTLAND

REGULAR MARRIAGES

A regular marriage is one which is celebrated by a minister of religion or authorised registrar or other celebrant. Each of the parties must complete a marriage notice form and return it to the district registrar for the area in which they are to be married, irrespective of where they live, within the three month period prior to the date of the marriage and not later than 15 days prior to that date. The district registrar must then enter the date of receipt and certain details in a marriage book kept for this purpose, and must also enter the names of the parties and the proposed date of marriage in a list which is displayed in a conspicuous place at the registration office until the date of the marriage has passed. All persons wishing to enter into a regular marriage in Scotland must follow the same preliminary procedure regardless of whether they intend to have a religious or civil ceremony. Before the marriage ceremony takes place any person may submit an objection in writing to the district registrar.

A marriage schedule, which is prepared by the registrar, will be issued to one or both of the parties in person up to seven days before a religious marriage; for a civil marriage the schedule will be available at the ceremony. The schedule must be handed to the celebrant before the ceremony starts; it must be signed immediately after the wedding and the marriage must be registered within three days.

The authority to conduct a religious marriage is deemed to be vested in the authorised celebrant rather than the building in which it takes place; open-air religious ceremonies are therefore permissible in Scotland.

From 10 June 2002 it has been possible, under the Marriage (Scotland) Act 2002, for venues or couples to apply to the local council for a licence to allow a civil ceremony to take place at a venue other than a registration office. To obtain further information, a venue or couple should contact the district registrar in the area they wish to marry. A list of licensed venues is also available on the General Register Office for Scotland website.

MARRIAGE BY COHABITATION WITH HABIT AND REPUTE

Prior to the enactment of the 2006 act, if two people had lived together constantly as husband and wife and were generally held to be such by the neighbourhood and among their friends and relations, a presumption could arise from which marriage could be inferred. Before such a marriage could be registered, however, a decree of declarator of marriage had to be obtained from the court of session. Section 3 of the 2006 act provides that it will no longer be possible for a marriage to be constituted by cohabitation with habit and repute, but it will still be possible for couples whose period of cohabitation began before commencement of the 2006 act to seek a declarator under the old rule of law.

CIVIL FEES

The fee for submitting a notice of marriage to the district registrar is £30.00 a person. Solemnisation of a civil marriage costs £55.00, while the extract of the entry in the register of marriages attracts a fee of £9.00. The costs of religious marriage ceremonies can vary.

THE GENERAL REGISTER OFFICE
PO Box 2, Southport PR8 2JD
T 0845-603 7788 **W** www.gro.gov.uk/gro/content/certificates

THE GENERAL REGISTER OFFICE FOR SCOTLAND
New Register House, 3 West Register Street, Edinburgh EH1 3YT **T** 0131-314 4452 **W** www.gro-scotland.gov.uk

TOWN AND COUNTRY PLANNING

The planning system can help to protect the environment and assist individuals in assessing their land rights. There are a number of acts governing the development of land and buildings in England and Wales and advice should always be sought from Citizens Advice or the local planning authority before undertaking building works on any land or to property. If development takes place which requires planning permission without permission being given, enforcement action may take place and the situation may need to be rectified. Planning law in Scotland is similar but certain Scotland-specific legislation applies so advice should always be sought.

PLANNING PERMISSION

Planning permission is needed if the work involves:

- making a material change in use, such as dividing off part of the house or garden so that it can be used as a separate home or dividing off part of the house for commercial use, eg for a workshop
- going against the terms of the original planning permission, eg there may be a restriction on fences in front gardens on an open-plan estate
- building, engineering for mining, except for the permissions below
- new or wider access to a main road
- additions or extensions to flats or maisonettes
- work which might obstruct the view of road users

Planning permission is not needed to carry out internal alterations or work which does not affect the external appearance of the building, and are not works for making good damage or works begun after 5 December 1968 for the alteration of a building by providing additional space in it underground.

Under regulations which came into effect on 1 October 2008, there are certain types of development for which the Secretary of State for the Environment, Food and Rural Affairs has granted general permissions (permitted development rights). These include house extensions and additions, outbuildings and garages, other ancillary garden buildings such as swimming pools or ponds, and laying patios, paths or driveways for domestic use. All developments are subject to a number of conditions (for more information, *see* **W** www.planningportal.gov.uk).

Before carrying out any of the above permitted developments you should contact your local authority to find out whether the general permission has been modified in your area.

OTHER RESTRICTIONS

It may be necessary to obtain other types of permissions before carrying out any development. These permissions are separate from planning permission and apply regardless of whether or not planning permission is needed, eg:

- building regulations will probably apply if a new building is to be erected, if an existing one is to be altered or extended, or if the work involves building over a drain or sewer. The building control department of the local authority will advise on this
- any alterations to a listed building or the grounds of a listed building must be approved by the local authority. Listing will include not only the main building but everything in the curtilage of the building
- local authority approval is necessary if a building (or, in some circumstances, gates, walls, fences or railings) in a conservation area is to be demolished; each local authority keeps a register of all local buildings that are in conservation areas
- many trees are protected by tree preservation orders and must not be pruned or taken down without local authority consent
- bats and many other species are protected, and Natural England, the Countryside Council for Wales or Scottish Natural Heritage must be notified before any work is carried out that will affect the habitat of protected species, eg timber treatment, renovation or extensions of lofts
- any development in areas designated as a national park, an AONB, a national scenic area or in the Norfolk or Suffolk Broads is subject to greater restrictions. The local planning authority will advise or refer enquirers to the relevant authority

The local authority should be contacted if planning permission is required. There may also be restriction on development contained in the title to the property which should be considered when works are planned.

VOTERS' QUALIFICATIONS

Those entitled to vote at parliamentary, and local government elections are those who, at the date of taking the poll, are:

- on the electoral roll
- aged 18 years or older
- British citizens, Commonwealth citizens or citizens of the Irish Republic who are resident in the UK
- those who suffer from no other legal bar to voting (eg prisoners)
- in Northern Ireland electors must have been resident in Northern Ireland during the whole of the three-month period prior to the relevant date
- citizens of any EU member state may vote in local elections if they meet the criteria listed above

British citizens resident abroad are entitled to vote for 15 years after leaving Britain, as overseas electors in domestic parliamentary elections in the constituency in which they were last resident if they are on the electoral roll of the relevant constituency. Members of the armed forces, Crown servants and employees of the British Council who are overseas and their spouses are entitled to vote regardless of how long they have been abroad. British citizens who had never been registered as an elector in the UK are not eligible to register as an overseas voter unless they left the UK before they were 18, providing they left the country no more than 15 years ago.

The main categories of people who are not entitled to vote at general elections are:

- sitting peers in the House of Lords
- convicted persons detained in pursuance of their sentences (though remand prisoners, unconvicted prisoners and civil prisoners can vote if on the electoral register)

- those convicted within the previous five years of corrupt or illegal election practices
- EU citizens (who may only vote in EU and local government elections)

Under the Representation of the Peoples Act 2000, several new groups of people are permitted to vote for the first time. These include: people who live on barges; people in mental health hospitals (other than those with criminal convictions) and homeless people who have made a 'declaration of local connection'.

REGISTERING TO VOTE

Voters must be entered on an electoral register. The Electoral Registration Officer (ERO) for each council area is responsible for preparing and publishing the register for his area by 1 December each year. Names may be added to the register to reflect changes in people's circumstances as they occur and each month during December to August, the ERO publishes a list of alterations to the published register.

A registration form is sent to all households in the autumn of each year and the householder is required to provide details of all occupants who are eligible to vote, including ones who will reach their 18th birthday in the year covered by the register. Anyone failing to supply information to the ERO when requested, or supplying false information, may be fined by up to £1,000. Application forms and more information are available from the Electoral Commission (W www.electoralcommision.org.uk. or at W www.aboutmyvote.co.uk).

VOTING

Voting is not compulsory in the UK. Those who wish to vote do so in person at the allotted polling station. Postal votes are now available to anyone on request and you do not need to give a reason for using a postal vote.

For the appointment of an indefinite or long-term proxy (whereby the voter nominates someone to vote in person on their behalf), the voter needs to specify physical employment or study reasons as to why they are making an application. With proxy votes where a particular election is specified, the voter needs to provide details of the circumstances by which they cannot reasonably be expected to go to the polling station. Overseas electors who wish to vote must do so by proxy.

Further information can be obtained from the local authority's ERO in England and Wales or the electoral registration office in Scotland, or the Chief Electoral Officer in Northern Ireland.

WILLS

A will is used to appoint executors (who will administer the estate), give directions as to the disposal of the body, appoint guardians for children, and determine how and to whom property is to be passed. A well-drafted will can operate to reduce the level of inheritance tax which the estate pays. It is best to have a will drawn up by a solicitor, but if a solicitor is not employed the following points must be taken into account:

- if possible the will must not be prepared on behalf of another person by someone who is to benefit from it or who is a close relative of a major beneficiary
- the language used must be clear and unambiguous and it is better to avoid the use of legal terms where the same thing can be expressed in plain language
- it is better to rewrite the whole document if a mistake is made. If necessary, alterations can be made by striking through the words with a pen, and the signature or initials of the testator and the witnesses must be put in the margin opposite the alteration. No alteration of any kind should be made after the will has been executed
- if the person later wishes to change the will or part of it, it is better to write a new will revoking the old. The use of codicils (documents written as supplements or containing modifications to the will) should be left to a solicitor
- the will should be typed or printed, or if handwritten be legible and preferably in ink. Commercial will forms can be obtained from some stationers

The form of a will varies to suit different cases – a solicitor will be able to advise as to wording, however, 'DIY' will-writing kits can be purchased from good stationery shops and many banks offer a will-writing service.

LAPSED LEGATEES

If a person who has been left property in a will dies before the person who made the will, the gift fails and will pass to the person entitled to everything not otherwise disposed of (the residuary estate).

If the person left the residuary estate dies before the person who made the will, their share will pass to the closest relative(s) of the testator under the intestacy rule. It is always better to draw up a new will if a beneficiary predeceases the person who made the will.

EXECUTORS

It is usual to appoint two executors, although one is sufficient. No more than four persons can deal with the estate of the person who has died. The name and address of each executor should be given in full (the addresses are not essential but including them adds clarity to the document). Executors should be 18 years of age or over. An executor may be a beneficiary of the will.

WITNESSES

A person who is a beneficiary of a will, or the spouse of a beneficiary at the time the will is signed, must not act as a witness or else he/she will be unable to take his/her gift. Husband and wife can both act as witnesses provided neither benefits from the will.

It is better that a person does not act as an executor and as a witness, as he/she can take no benefit under a will to which he/she is witness. The identity of the witnesses should be made as explicit as possible.

EXECUTION OF A WILL

The person making the will should sign his/her name at the foot of the document, in the presence of the two witnesses. The witnesses must then sign their names while the person making the will looks on. If this procedure is not adhered to, the will may be considered invalid. There are certain exceptional circumstances where these rules are relaxed, eg where the person may be too ill to sign.

CAPACITY TO MAKE A WILL

Anyone aged 18 or over can make a will. However, if there is any suspicion that the person making the will is not, through reasons of infirmity or age, fully in command of his/her faculties, it is advisable to arrange for a medical practitioner to examine the person making the will at the time it is to be executed (to verify his/her mental capacity and to record that medical opinion in writing), and to ask the examining practitioner to act as a witness. If a person is not mentally able to make a will, the court may do this for him/her by virtue of the Mental Health Act 2005.

REVOCATION

A will may be revoked or cancelled in a number of ways:

- a later will revokes an earlier one if it says so; otherwise the earlier will is by implication revoked by the later one to the extent that it contradicts or repeats the earlier one
- a will is also revoked if the physical document on which it is written is destroyed by the person whose will it is. There must be an intention to revoke the will and it may not be sufficient to obliterate the will with a pen
- a will is revoked when the person marries or forms a civil partnership, unless it is clear from the will that the person intended the will to stand after the marriage or civil partnership
- where a marriage or civil partnership ends in divorce or dissolution or is annulled or declared void, gifts to the spouse or civil partner and the appointment of the spouse or civil partner as executor fail unless the will says that this is not to happen. A former spouse or civil partner is treated as having predeceased the testator. A separation does not change the effect of a married person's will.

PROBATE AND LETTERS OF ADMINISTRATION

Probate is granted to the executors named in a will and once granted, the executors are obliged to carry out the instructions of the will. Letters of administration are granted where no executor is named in a will or is willing or able to act or where there is no will or no valid will; this gives a person, often the next of kin, similar powers and duties to those of an executor.

Applications for probate or for letters of administration can be made to the Principal Registry of the Family Division, to a district probate registry or to a probate sub-registry. Applicants will need the following documents: the Probate Application Form; the original will (if any); a certificate of death; oath for executors or administrators; and the appropriate tax form (an 'IHT 205' if no inheritance tax is owed; otherwise an 'IHT 400'). Certain property, up to the value of £5,000, may be disposed of without a grant of probate or letters of administration.

WHERE TO FIND A PROVED WILL

Since 1858 wills which have been proved, that is wills on which probate or letters of administration have been granted, must have been proved at the Principal Registry of the Family Division or at a district probate registry. The Lord Chancellor has power to direct where the original documents are kept but most are filed where they were proved and may be inspected there and a copy obtained. The Principal Registry also holds copies of all wills proved at district probate registries and these may be inspected at First Avenue House, High Holborn. An index of all grants, both of probate and of letters of administration, is compiled by the Principal Registry and may be seen either at the Principal Registry or at a district probate registry.

It is also possible to discover when a grant of probate or letters of administration is issued by requesting a standing search. In response to a request and for a small fee, a district probate registry will supply the names and addresses of executors or administrators and the registry in which the grant was made, of any grant in the estate of a specified person made in the previous 12 months or following six months. This is useful for creditors of the deceased and for applicants who may be beneficiaries to a will but who have lost contact with the deceased.

INTESTACY

Intestacy occurs when someone dies without leaving a will or leaves a will which is invalid or which does not take effect for some reason. Intestacy can be partial, for instance, if there is a will which disposes of some but not all of the testator's property. In such cases the person's estate (property, possessions, other assets following the payment of debts) passes to certain members of the family. If a will has been written that disposes of only part of a person's property, these rules apply to the part which is undisposed of.

If the person (intestate) leaves a spouse or a civil partner who survives for 28 days and children (legitimate, illegitimate and adopted children and other descendants), the estate is divided as follows:

- the spouse or civil partner takes the 'personal chattels' (household articles, including cars, but nothing used for business purposes), £250,000 and a life interest in half of the rest of the estate (which can be capitalised by the spouse or civil partner if he/she wishes)
- the rest of the estate goes to the children*

If the person leaves a spouse or civil partner who survives for 28 days but no children:

- the spouse or civil partner takes the personal chattels, £450,000 tax-free (interest payable as before) and full ownership of half of the rest of the estate
- the other half of the rest of the estate goes to the parents (equally, if both alive) or, if none, to the brothers and sisters of the whole blood*
- if there are no parents or brothers or sisters of the whole blood or their children, the spouse or civil partner takes the whole estate
- if the estate is worth less than £250,000, the surviving spouse or civil partner takes it in its entirety

If there is no surviving spouse or civil partner, the estate is distributed among those who survive the intestate as follows:

- to surviving children*, but if none to
- parents (equally, if both alive), but if none to
- brothers and sisters of the whole blood* (including issue of deceased ones), but if none to
- brothers and sisters of the half blood* (including issue of deceased ones), but if none to
- grandparents (equally, if more than one), but if none to
- aunts and uncles of the whole blood*, but if none to
- aunts and uncles of the half blood*, but if none to
- the crown, Duchy of Lancaster or the Duke of Cornwall (*bona vacantia*)

* To inherit, a member of these groups must survive the intestate and attain the age of 18, or marry under that age. If they die under the age of 18 (unless married under that age), their share goes to others, if any, in the same group. If any member of these groups predeceases the intestate leaving children, their share is divided equally among their children.

In England and Wales the provisions of the Inheritance (Provision for Family and Dependants) Act 1975 may allow other people to claim provision from the deceased's assets. This act also applies to cases where a will has been made and allows a person to apply to the court if they feel that the will or rules of intestacy or both do not make adequate provision for them. The court can order payment from the deceased's assets or the transfer of property from them if the applicant's claim is accepted. The application must be made within six months of the grant of probate or letters of administration and the following people can make an application:

- the spouse or civil partner
- a former spouse or civil partner who has not remarried or formed a subsequent civil partnership
- a child of the deceased
- someone treated as a child of the deceased's family
- someone maintained by the deceased
- someone who has cohabited for two years before the death in the same household as the deceased and as the husband or wife or civil partner of the deceased

SCOTLAND

In Scotland any person over 12 and of sound mind can make a will. The person making the will can only freely dispose of the heritage and what is known as the 'dead's part' of the estate because:

- the spouse or civil partner has the right to inherit one-third of the moveable estate if there are children or other descendants, and one-half of it if there are not
- children are entitled to one-third of the moveable estate if there is a surviving spouse or civil partner, and one-half of it if there is not

The remaining portion is the dead's part, and legacies and bequests are payable from this. Debts are payable out of the whole estate before any division.

From August 1995, wills no longer needed to be 'holographed' and it is now only necessary to have one witness. The person making the will still needs to sign each page. It is better that the will is not witnessed by a beneficiary although the attestation would still be sound and the beneficiary would not have to relinquish the gift.

Subsequent marriage or civil partnership does not revoke a will but the birth of a child who is not provided for may do so. A will may be revoked by a subsequent will, either expressly or by implication, but in so far as the two can be read together both have effect. If a subsequent will is revoked, the earlier will is revived.

Wills may be registered in the sheriff court Books of the Sheriffdom in which the deceased lived or in the Books of Council and Session at the Registers of Scotland.

CONFIRMATION

Confirmation (the Scottish equivalent of probate) is obtained in the sheriff court of the sheriffdom in which the deceased was resident at the time of death. Executors are either 'nominate' (named by the deceased in the will) or 'dative' (appointed by the court in cases where no executor is named in a will or in cases of intestacy). Applicants for confirmation must first provide an inventory of the deceased's estate and a schedule of debts, with an affidavit. In estates under £30,000 gross, confirmation can be obtained under a simplified procedure at reduced fees, with no need for a solicitor. The local sheriff clerk's office can provide assistance.

PRINCIPAL REGISTRY (FAMILY DIVISION)
First Avenue House, 42–49 High Holborn, London WC1 6NP
T 020-7947 6000

REGISTERS OF SCOTLAND
Erskine House, 68 Queen Street, Edinburgh, EH2 4NF
T 0845-607 0161

INTESTACY

The rules of distribution are contained in the Succession (Scotland) Act 1964 and are extended to include civil partners by the Civil Partnership Act 2004.

A surviving spouse or civil partner is entitled to 'prior rights'. This means that the spouse or civil partner has the right to inherit:

- the matrimonial or family home up to a value of £300,000, or one matrimonial or family home if there is more than one, or, in certain circumstances, the value of the home
- the furnishings and contents of that home, up to the value of £24,000
- a cash sum of £42,000 if the deceased left children or other descendants, or £75,000 if not

These figures are increased from time to time by regulations.

Once prior rights have been satisfied legal rights are settled. Legal rights are:

- *Jus relicti(ae) and rights under the section 131 of the Civil Partnership Act 2004* – the right of a surviving spouse or civil partner to one-half of the net moveable estate, after satisfaction of prior rights, if there are no surviving children; if there are surviving children, the spouse or civil partner is entitled to one-third of the net moveable estate
- *Legitim and rights under the section 131 of the Civil Partnership Act 2004* – the right of surviving children to one-half of the net moveable estate if there is no surviving spouse or civil partner; if there is a surviving spouse or civil partner, the children are entitled to one-third of the net moveable estate after the satisfaction of prior rights

Where there is no surviving spouse, civil partner or children, half of the estate is taken by the parents and half by the brothers and sisters. Failing that, the lines of succession, in general, are:

- to descendants
- if no descendants, then to collaterals (ie brothers and sisters) and parents
- surviving spouse or civil partner
- if no collaterals, parents, spouse or civil partner, then to ascendants collaterals (ie aunts and uncles), and so on in an ascending scale
- if all lines of succession fail, the estate passes to the Crown. Relatives of the whole blood are preferred to relatives of the half blood. The right of representation, ie the right of the issue of a person who would have succeeded if he/she had survived the intestate, also applies.

INTELLECTUAL PROPERTY

Intellectual property is a broad term covering a number of legal rights provided by the government to help people protect their creative works and encourage further innovation. By using these legal rights people can own the things they create and control the way in which others use their innovations. Intellectual property owners can take legal action to stop others using their intellectual property, they can license their intellectual property to others or they can sell it on. Different types of intellectual property utilise different forms of protection including copyright, designs, patents and trade marks, which are all covered below in more detail.

COPYRIGHT

Copyright protects all original literary, dramatic, musical and artistic works, as well as sound and film recordings and broadcasts. Among the works covered by copyright are novels, computer programs, newspaper articles, sculptures, technical drawings, websites, maps and photographs. Under copyright the creators of these works can control the various ways in which their material may be exploited, the rights broadly covering copying, adapting, issuing (including renting and lending) copies to the public, performing in public, and broadcasting the material. The transfer of copyright works to formats accessible to visually impaired persons without infringement of copyright was enacted in 2002.

Copyright protection in the United Kingdom is automatic and there is no official registration system. The creator of a work can help to protect it by including the copyright symbol (©), the name of the copyright owner, and the year in which the work was created. In addition, steps can be taken by the work's creator to provide evidence that he/she had the work at a particular time (eg by depositing a copy with a bank or solicitor). The main legislation is the Copyright, Designs and Patents Act 1988 (as amended). As a result of an EU directive effective from January 1996, the term of copyright protection for literary, dramatic, musical (including song lyrics and musical compositions) and artistic works lasts for 70 years after the death of the creator. For film, copyright lasts for 70 years after the death of the last to survive of the director, authors of the screenplay and dialogue, or the composer of any music specially created for the film. Sound recordings are protected for 50 years after their publication (or their first performance if they are not published), and broadcasts for 50 years from the end of the year in which the broadcast/transmission was made. The typographical arrangement of published editions remains under copyright protection for 25 years from the end of the year in which the edition was published.

The main international treaties protecting copyright are the Berne Convention for the Protection of Literary and Artistic Works (administered by the World Intellectual Property Organisation (WIPO)), the Rome Convention for the Protection of Performers, Producers of Phonograms and Broadcasting Organisations (administered by UNESCO, the International Labour Organisation and WIPO), the Geneva Phonograms Convention (administered by WIPO), and the Universal Copyright Convention (developed by UNESCO); the UK is a signatory to these conventions. Copyright material created by UK nationals or residents is protected in each country that is a member of the conventions by the national law of that country. A list of participating countries may be obtained from the UK Intellectual Property Office. The World Trade Organisation's Trade-Related Aspects of Intellectual Property Rights (TRIPS) agreement, signed in 1995, may also provide copyright protection abroad.

Two treaties which strengthen and update international standards of protection, particularly in relation to new technologies, were agreed in December 1996: the WIPO copyright treaty, and the WIPO performances and phonograms treaty. In May 2001 the European Union passed a new directive (which in 2003 became law in the UK) aimed at harmonising copyright law throughout the EU to take account of the internet and other technologies. More information can be found online (W www.ipo.gov.uk).

LICENSING

Use of copyright material without seeking permission in each instance may be permitted under 'blanket' licences available from national copyright licensing agencies. The International Federation of Reproduction Rights Organisations facilitates agreements between its member licensing agencies and on behalf of its members with organisations such as WIPO, UNESCO, the European Union and the Council of Europe. More information can be found online (W www.ifrro.org).

DESIGN PROTECTION

Design protection covers the outward appearance of an article and in the UK takes two forms: registered design and design right, which are not mutually exclusive. Registered design protects the aesthetic appearance of an article, including shape, configuration, pattern or ornament, although artistic works such as sculptures are excluded, being generally protected by copyright. In order to qualify for protection, a design must be new and materially different from earlier UK published designs. The owner of the design must apply to the UK Intellectual Property Office. Initial registration lasts for five years and can be extended in five-year increments to a maximum of 25 years. The current legislation is the Registered Designs Act 1949 which has been amended several times, most recently by the Regulatory Reform Order 2006.

UK applicants wishing to protect their designs in the EU can do so by applying for a Registered Community Design with the Office for Harmonisation in the Internal Market. Outside the EU separate applications must be made in each country in which protection is sought.

Design right is an automatic right which applies to the shape or configuration of articles and does not require registration. Unlike registered design, two-dimensional designs do not qualify for protection but designs of semiconductor chips (topographies) are protected by design right. Designs must be original and non-commonplace. The term of design right is ten years from first marketing of the design, or 15 years after the creation of the design, whichever is earlier. The right is effective only in the UK. After five years anyone is entitled to apply for a licence of right, which allows others to make and sell products copying the design. The current legislation is Part 3 of the Copyright, Designs and Patents Act 1988, amended on 9 December 2001 to incorporate the European designs directive, and again in 2006.

PATENTS

A patent is a document issued by the UK Intellectual Property Office relating to an invention and giving the proprietor the right for a limited period to stop others from making, using, importing or selling the invention without the inventor's permission. In return the patentee pays a fee to cover the costs of processing the patent and publicly discloses details of the invention.

To qualify for a patent an invention must be new, must be functional or technical, must exhibit an inventive step, and must be capable of industrial application. The patent is valid for a maximum of 20 years from the date on which the application was filed, subject to payment of annual fees from the end of the fifth year.

The UK Intellectual Property Office, established in 1852, is responsible for ensuring that all stages of an application comply with the Patents Act 1977, and that the invention meets the criteria for a patent.

WIPO is responsible for administering many of the international conventions on intellectual property. The Patent Cooperation Treaty allows inventors to file a single application for patent rights in some or all of the contracting states. This application is searched by an International Searching Authority and published by the International Bureau of WIPO. It may also be the subject of an (optional) international preliminary examination. Applicants must then deal directly with the patent offices in the countries where they are seeking patent rights. The European Patent Convention allows inventors to obtain patent rights in all the contracting states by filing a single application with the European Patent Office. More information can be found online (W www.ipo.gov.uk).

RESEARCH DISCLOSURES

Research disclosures are publicly disclosed details of inventions. Once published, an invention is considered no longer novel and becomes prior art. Publishing a disclosure is significantly cheaper than applying for a patent; however unlike a patent, it does not entitle the author to exclusive rights to use or license the invention. Instead, research disclosures are primarily published to ensure the inventor freedom to use the invention. This works because publishing legally prevents other parties from patenting the disclosed innovation and in the UK, patent law dictates that by disclosing, even the inventor relinquishes their right to a patent.

In theory, publishing details of an invention anywhere should be enough to make a research disclosure. However to be effective a research disclosure needs to be published in a location which patent examiners will include in their prior art searches. To ensure global legal precedent it must be included in a publication with a recognised date stamp and made publicly available across the world.

The *Research Disclosure* journal established in 1960, published by KMP Ltd, is the primary publisher of research disclosures. It is the only disclosure service recognised by the Patent Cooperation Treaty as a mandatory search resource which must be consulted by the international search authorities. More information can be found online (W www.researchdisclosure.com).

TRADE MARKS

Trade marks are a means of identification, whether words or a logo or a combination of both, which enables traders to make their goods or services readily distinguishable from those supplied by others. Registration prevents other traders using the same or similar trade marks for similar products or services for which the mark is registered.

In the UK trade marks are registered at the UK Intellectual Property Office. In order to qualify for registration a mark must be capable of distinguishing its proprietor's goods or services from those of other undertakings; it should be non-deceptive, should not describe the goods and services or any characteristics of them, should not be contrary to law or morality and should not be similar or identical to any earlier marks for the same or similar goods or services. The owner of a registered trade mark may include an fi symbol next to it, and must renew their registration every ten years to keep it in force. The relevant current legislation is the Trade Marks Act 1994 (as amended).

It is possible to obtain an international trade mark registration, effective in 84 countries, under the Madrid system for the international registration of marks, to which the UK is party. British companies can obtain international trade mark registration in those countries party to the system through a single application to WIPO.

EU trade mark regulation is administered by the Office for Harmonisation in the Internal Market (Trade Marks and Designs) in Alicante, Spain. The office registers Community trade marks, which are valid throughout the European Union. The national registration of trade marks in member states continues in parallel with EU trade mark standards.

DOMAIN NAMES

An internet domain name (eg acblack.com) has to be registered separately from a trade mark, and this can be done through a number of registrars which charge varying rates and compete for business. For each top-level domain name (eg .uk, .com), there is a central registry to store the unique internet names and addresses using that suffix. A list of accredited registrars can be found online (W www.icann.org).

CONTACTS

COPYRIGHT LICENSING AGENCY LTD, Saffron House, 6–10 Kirby Street, London EC1N 8TS
T 020-7400 3100 W www.cla.co.uk

EUROPEAN PATENT OFFICE, Headquarters, Erhardtstrasse 27, 80469, Munich 2, Germany
T (+49) 89 2399 4636 W www.epo.org

THE UK INTELLECTUAL PROPERTY OFFICE, Concept House, Cardiff Road, Newport NP10 8QQ
T 0845-950 0505 W www.ipo.gov.uk

WORLD INTELLECTUAL PROPERTY ORGANISATION, 34 chemin des Colombettes, CH-1211 Geneva 20, Switzerland T (+41) 22 338 9111
W www.wipo.int

THE MEDIA

CROSS-MEDIA OWNERSHIP

The rules surrounding cross-media ownership were overhauled as part of the 2003 Communications Act. The act simplified and relaxed existing rules to encourage dispersion of ownership and new market entry while preventing the most influential media in any community being controlled by too narrow a range of interests. However, transfers and mergers are not solely subject to examination on competition grounds by the competition authorities. The Secretary of State for Culture, Olympics, Media and Sport has a broad remit to decide if a transaction is permissible and can intervene on public interest grounds (relating both to newspapers and cross-media criteria, if broadcasting interests are also involved). The Office of Communications (OFCOM) has an advisory role in this context. Government and parliamentary assurances were given that any intervention into local newspaper transfers would be rare and exceptional. In June 2010 the Secretary of State for Culture, Olympics, Media and Sport requested that OFCOM consider the case for removing all restrictions from the ownership of local media.

REGULATION

OFCOM is the regulator for the communication industries in the UK and has responsibility for television, radio, telecommunications and wireless communications services. It replaced the Broadcasting Standards Commission, the Independent Television Commission, the Radio Authority, the Radio Communications Agency and OFTEL. OFCOM is required to report annually to parliament and exists to further the interests of consumers by balancing choice and competition with the duty to foster plurality; protect viewers and listeners and promote cultural diversity in the media; and to ensure full and fair competition between communications providers.

OFFICE OF COMMUNICATIONS (OFCOM)
Riverside House, 2A Southwark Bridge Road, London SE1 9HA
T 020-7981 3000 W www.ofcom.org.uk
Chief Executive, Ed Richards

COMPLAINTS

Under the Communications Act 2003 OFCOM's licensees are obliged to adhere to the provisions of its codes (including advertising, programme standards, fairness, privacy and sponsorship). Complainants should contact the broadcaster in the first instance (details can be found on OFCOM's website); however, if the complainant wishes the complaint to be considered by OFCOM, it will do so. Complaints should be made within a reasonable time, as broadcasters are only required to keep recordings for the following periods: radio, 42 days; television, 90 days; and cable and satellite, 60 days. OFCOM can fine a broadcaster, revoke a licence or take programmes off the air. Since November 2004 complaints relating to individual advertisements on TV or radio have been dealt with by the Advertising Standards Authority.

ADVERTISING STANDARDS AUTHORITY
Mid City Place, 71 High Holborn, London WC1V 6QT
T 020-7492 2222 E enquiries@asa.org.uk W www.asa.org.uk
Chief Executive, Guy Parker

TELEVISION

There are six major television broadcasters operating in the UK. Four of these – the BBC, ITV, Channel 4 and Channel 5 – launched as free-to-air analogue terrestrial networks. BSkyB and Virgin Media Television provide satellite television services.

The BBC is the oldest broadcaster in the world. The corporation began a London-only television service from Alexandra Palace in 1936 and achieved nationwide coverage 15 years later. A second station, BBC Two, was launched in 1964. The BBC's digital services comprise BBC Three, BBC Four, BBC News and BBC Parliament; the children's channels, CBeebies and CBBC; and the interactive channel BBCi. The services are funded by the licence fee. The corporation also has a commercial arm, BBC Worldwide, which was formed in 1994 and exists to maximise the value of the BBC's programme and publishing assets for the benefit of the licence payer. Its businesses include international programming distribution, magazines, other licensed products, live events and media monitoring.

The ITV (Independent Television) network was set up on a regional basis in 1955 to provide competition for the BBC. It comprised a number of independent licensees, the majority of which have now merged to form ITV plc. The network generates funds through broadcasting television advertisements. Its flagship analogue channel was renamed ITV1 in 2001 as part of a rebranding exercise to coincide with the creation of a number of digital-only channels. These now include ITV2, ITV3, ITV4 and CiTV. ITV Network Centre is wholly owned by the ITV companies and undertakes commissioning and scheduling of programmes shown across the ITV network and, as with the other terrestrial channels, 25 per cent of programmes must come from independent producers.

Channel 4 and S4C were launched in 1982 to provide programmes with a distinctive character that appeal to interests not catered for by ITV. Although state-owned, Channel 4 receives no public funding and is financed by commercial activities, including advertising. It has expanded to create the digital stations E4, More4, Film4 and 4Music. S4C receives annual funding from the Department for Culture, Olympics, Media and Sport. In March 2010 the S4C analogue service was closed and its digital service, S4C Digidol, became the default S4C channel across Wales, broadcasting entirely in the Welsh language.

Channel 5 began broadcasting in 1997. It was rebranded Five in 2002 but reverted to its original name, Channel 5, after the station was acquired by Northern & Shell in July 2010. Digital stations Five USA and Fiver (originally Five Life) were launched in October 2006.

BSkyB was formed after the merger in 1990 of Sky Television and British Sky Broadcasting. The company operates a satellite television service and has around 40 television channels, including Sky One and the Sky Sports and Sky Movies ranges. It is part-owned by Rupert Murdoch's News Corporation. Sky Digital was launched in 1998 and offers access to over 500 channels. With the 2005 acquisition of Easynet, an internet access provider and network operator, BSkyB now offers voice over IP (VoIP) telephony, video on demand and internet-based TV. With a special box, Sky+ allows viewers to pause and rewind live TV and record up to 40 hours of programming. In July 2010 BSkyB acquired Virgin Media Television, including its portfolio of channels such as Bravo, Challenge and Virgin1. It was subsequently rebranded as the Living TV Group.

VIEWING TRENDS, TERRESTRIAL TELEVISION

- 35 per cent of programmes watched on BBC One are current affairs or national news and weather
- Sport makes up 16 per cent of BBC Two's viewing
- Soap operas and dramas account for nearly half of ITV's peak-time viewing (46 per cent)
- 70 per cent of viewing on Channel 4 is factual and entertainment programming
- Films make up 30 per cent of programmes watched on Channel 5

Source: OFCOM Public Service Broadcasting Annual Report 2010

THE TELEVISION LICENCE

In the UK and its dependencies, a television licence is required to receive any publicly broadcast television service, regardless of its source, including commercial, satellite and cable programming.

The TV licence is classified as a tax, therefore non-payment is a criminal offence. A fine of up to £1,000 can be imposed on those successfully prosecuted. The Broadcasting Act 1990 made the BBC responsible for licence administration. TV Licensing is the name of the agent contracted to collect the licence fee on behalf of the BBC. Total licence fee income for 2009–10 was £3,446.8m. In 2010 an annual colour television licence cost £145.50 and a black and white licence £49. Concessions are available for the elderly and people with disabilities. Further details can be found at W www.tvlicensing.co.uk/information.

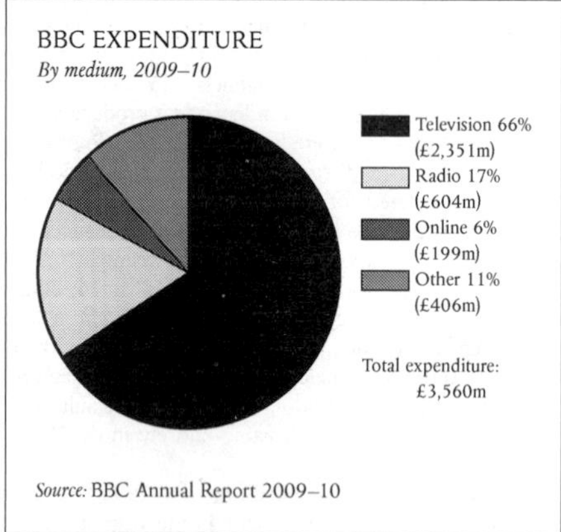

Source: BBC Annual Report 2009–10

DIGITAL TELEVISION

Digital broadcasting has dramatically increased the number and reception quality of television channels. Sound and pictures are converted into a digital format and compressed, using as few bits as possible to convey the information on a digital signal. This technique enables several television channels to be carried in the space used by the current analogue signals to carry one channel. Digital signals can be received by standard aerials using Freeview (*see* below), satellite dishes or cable. The signals are decoded and turned back into sound and pictures by either a set-top box or a decoder built into the television set (iDTV). A basic package of channels is available without charge and services are also offered by cable and satellite companies.

The Broadcasting Act 1996 provided for the licensing of 20 or more digital terrestrial television channels (on six frequency channels or 'multiplexes'). The first digital services went on air in autumn 1998.

In June 2002, following the collapse of ITV Digital, the digital terrestrial television licence was awarded to a consortium made up of the BBC, BSkyB and transmitter company Crown Castle by the Independent Television Commission. Freeview was launched on 30 October 2002: it offers around 50 digital channels and requires the purchase of a set-top box, but is subsequently free of charge.

At the end of March 2010, 92 per cent of British homes had access to multi-channel TV. The digital channels combined have a greater share of viewing than any of the five main channels and continue to increase this lead.

DIGITAL SWITCHOVER

The digital switchover involves the turning off of the analogue terrestrial transmissions network that has been in place since the 1930s and replacing it with an all-digital terrestrial network. Viewers who receive television through an aerial will need to upgrade their sets with a set-top box (typically costing between £20 and £100) or use integrated digital television (iDTV), cable or satellite digital services. The switchover has started and is due to be completed in 2012. The old analogue frequencies are likely to be sold to mobile telephone companies. For more information, *see* W www.digitaluk.co.uk.

Region	*Expected switchover date*
Border, West Country, Granada	Complete
Wales, West, STV North	Complete
STV Central	2010–11
Central, Yorkshire, Anglia	2011
London, Meridian, Tyne Tees, UTV	2012

Source: Digital UK

RECENT DEVELOPMENTS

The advent of digital television has coincided with the emergence of the internet as a viable alternative means of watching TV. Channel 4's 4oD (4 On Demand) service allows viewers to revisit and download programmes from the previous 28 days and access an archive of older footage using their PC. The BBC launched its iPlayer on Christmas Day 2007, enabling viewers to watch programmes broadcast in the previous seven days via the streaming option or download and store programmes for up to 30 days on their computer. An integrated service, launched in June 2008, allows viewers to access BBC radio programmes in addition to televisual output. In 2009 iPlayer was extended to more than 20 devices, including mobile phones, televisions and games consoles. A high definition (HD) service was launched in the same year. ITV has a similar service called Catch Up, and Channel 5's service is called Demand Five. Online streaming of TV has been a major success, especially with a younger demographic. In 2009–10, iPlayer alone received 18 million requests a week from around 5.5 million users.

HD TV is the latest development in TV picture quality, providing more vibrant colours, greater detail and picture clarity in addition to improved sound quality. While a standard television picture is made up of 576 lines of pixels, an HD television screen uses either 720 or 1,080 lines. Sky Digital, ITV and the BBC all provide HD channels, with a growing number becoming available. To access HD channels, viewers need an 'HD ready' TV set and HD TV decoder, available through satellite services or a cable connection. It is expected that four HD channels will become nationally available through Freeview by 2012. In April 2010 Samsung released the first consumer 3D TV; in the same month Sky launched the UK's first dedicated 3D channel.

In June 2010 the BBC Trust gave permission for the BBC to participate in the development of Project Canvas, a proposed standard for internet protocol television (IPTV) in partnership with ITV, BT, Channel 4, Talk Talk and Arqiva. Through the IPTV platform, viewers will be able to watch programmes (including on-demand), browse the internet and listen to digital radio via a special set-top box connected to a broadband connection. The service is likely to begin in April 2011.

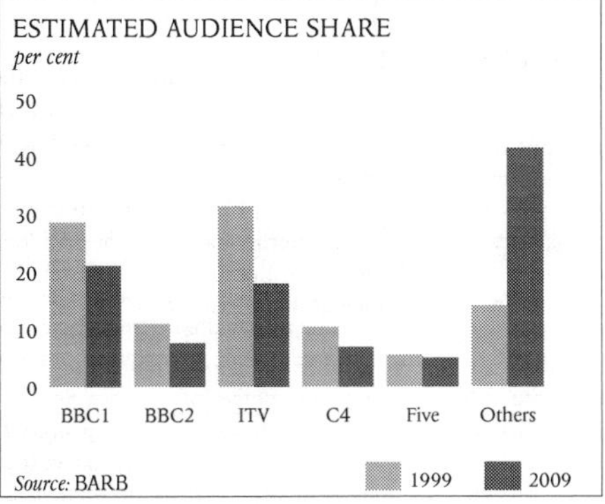

CONTACTS

THE BRITISH BROADCASTING CORPORATION
BBC TV Centre, Wood Lane, London W12 8QT
T 020-8743 8000 W www.bbc.co.uk
Chair, Sir Michael Lyons

BBC Worldwide Ltd, 201 Wood Lane, London W12 7TQ
T 020-8433 2000 W www.bbcworldwide.com

INDEPENDENT TELEVISION NETWORK
ITV Network Centre, 200 Gray's Inn Road, London WC1X 8HF
T 020-7156 6000 W www.itv.com
Chair, Archie Norman

INDEPENDENT TELEVISION NETWORK REGIONS AND COMPANIES
Anglia (eastern England), Anglia House, Norwich NR1 3JG T 0844-881 6900 W www.itv.com/anglia
Border (Borders and the Isle of Man), Television House, The Watermark, Gateshead NE11 9SZ T 0844-881 51000 W www.itv.com/border
Central (east, west and south Midlands), Gas Street, Birmingham B1 2JT T 0844-881 4121 W www.itv.com/central
Channel (Channel Islands), The Television Centre, St Helier, Jersey JE1 3ZD T 01534-816816 W www.channelonline.tv
Granada (north-west England), Quay Street, Manchester M60 9EA T 0161-952 6018 W www.itv.com/granada
London, 200 Gray's Inn Road, London WC1X 8HF T 020-7156 6762 W www.itv.com/london
Meridian (south and south-east England), Parkway Solent Business Park, Whiteley, Hants PO15 7PA T 0844-881 2000 W www.itv.com/meridian
STV (Scotland), Pacific Quay, Glasgow G51 1PQ T 0141-300 3704 W www.stv.tv
Tyne Tees (north-east England), Television House, The Watermark, Gateshead, Tyne and Wear NE11 9SZ T 0844-881 51000 W www.itv.com/tynetees
Ulster (Northern Ireland), Ormeau Road, Belfast BT7 1EB T 028-9032 8122 W www.u.tv
Wales, Media Centre, Culverhouse Cross, Cardiff CF5 6XJ T 0844-881 0100 W www.itv.com/wales
West, Television Centre, Bath Road, Bristol BS4 3HG T 0844-881 2345 W www.itv.com/west
Westcountry (south-west England), Bath Road, Bristol BS4 3HG T 0844-881 2301 W www.itv.com/westcountry
Yorkshire, 104 Kirkstall Road, Leeds LS3 1JS T 0845-121 1000 W www.itv.com/yorkshire

OTHER TELEVISION COMPANIES
Channel 4 Television, PO Box 1058, Belfast BT1 9DU T 0845-076 0191 W www.channel4.com
Channel 5 Broadcasting Ltd, 22 Long Acre, London WC2E 9LY T 020-7421 7270 W www.five.tv
GMTV, The London Television Centre, Upper Ground, London SE1 9TT T 0870-243 4333 W www.gm.tv
Owned by ITV, GMTV provides breakfast television and sells its own advertising.
Independent Television News (ITN), 200 Gray's Inn Road, London WC1X 8XZ T 020-7833 3000 W www.itn.co.uk
Provides news programming for ITV and Channel 4.
Sianel Pedwar Cymru (S4C), Parc Ty Glas, Llanishen, Cardiff CF14 5DU T 0870-600 4141 W www.s4c.co.uk
S4C schedules Welsh language programmes.
Teletext Ltd, Building 10, Chiswick Park, 566 Chiswick High Road, London W4 5TS T 020-8323 5000 W www.teletext.co.uk
Its analogue news service closed in 2009, but Teletext Ltd continues to offer holiday and other commercial services on digital channels.

DIRECT BROADCASTING BY SATELLITE TELEVISION
British Sky Broadcasting Group, Grant Way, Isleworth, Middx TW7 5QD T 020-7705 3000 W www.sky.com
Chief Executive, Jeremy Darroch
LIVING TV Group Ltd, 160 Great Portland Street, London W1W 5QA T 020-7299 5500 W www.livingtvgroup.co.uk
Chair, James Murdoch

RADIO

UK domestic radio services are broadcast across three wavebands: FM, medium wave and long wave (used by BBC Radio 4). In the UK the FM waveband extends in frequency from 87.5MHz to 108MHz and the medium waveband from 531kHz to 1602kHz. A number of radio stations are broadcast in both analogue and digital as well as a growing number in digital alone. As at March 2010, the BBC Radio network controlled just under 57 per cent of the listening market (*see* BBC Radio section), and the independent sector (*see* Independent Radio section) just over 41 per cent.

ESTIMATED AUDIENCE SHARE

			Percentage
	Jan–Mar 2008	Jan–Mar 2009	Jan–Mar 2010
BBC Radio 1	10.0	10.3	9.5
BBC Radio 2	16.0	15.9	17.2
BBC Radio 3	1.2	1.1	1.2
BBC Radio 4	12.0	12.5	12.2
BBC Radio Five Live	4.6	4.7	4.6
Five Live Sports Extra	0.2	0.1	0.2
6 Music	0.3	0.4	0.8
BBC Radio 7	0.4	0.5	0.6
Asian Network	0.3	0.2	0.2
1Xtra	0.3	0.3	0.3
BBC Local/Regional	9.6	9.4	9.3
BBC World Service	0.7	0.8	0.6
All BBC	55.5	56.3	56.5
All independent	42.4	41.6	41.3
All national independent	11.2	10.2	10.3
All local independent	31.2	31.3	31.1
Other	2.1	2.1	2.2

Source: RAJAR/Ipsos-MORI

DIGITAL RADIO

DAB (digital audio broadcasting) allows more services to be broadcast to a higher technical quality and provides the data facility for text and pictures. It improves the robustness of high fidelity radio services, especially compared with current FM and AM radio transmissions. It was developed in a collaborative research project under the pan-European Eureka 147 initiative and has been adopted as a world standard by the International Telecommunication Union for new digital radio systems. The frequencies allocated for terrestrial digital radio in the UK are 174 to 239MHz. Additional spectrum (in the 'L-Band' range: 1452–1478MHz) was introduced in 2007.

Digital radios are available as standalone portable units, hi-fi stacks, car radios and PC cards, or inbuilt within a mobile phone. Newer DAB radios allow the listener to rewind, pause and record broadcasts and then upload them to a computer using a USB cable. Some portable sets now combine MP3 playback with DAB. An alternative method is to listen to digital radio through television sets via Freeview, cable or satellite.

The possibility of a switchover to entirely digital radio services remains uncertain as takeup is still proportionately low. Twenty-four per cent of listening is now on a digital platform. DAB accounts for 63 per cent of total digital listening, 12 per cent is on the internet and 17 per cent on digital TV. In June 2009 the government published the white paper *Digital Britain*, which recommended that most services carried on the national and local DAB multiplexes should cease broadcasting on analogue radio by 2015. Ultra-local radio, consisting of small independent and community stations, would continue to broadcast on FM. There are two criteria that must be met for digital migration to occur:

- at least 50 per cent of radio listening is digital
- national DAB coverage is comparable to FM coverage, and local DAB reaches 90 per cent of the population and all major roads

LICENSING

The Broadcasting Act 1996 provided for the licensing of digital radio services (on multiplexes, where a number of stations share one frequency to transmit their services). To allocate the multiplexes, OFCOM advertises licences for which interested parties can bid. Once the licence has been awarded, the new owner seeks out services to broadcast on the multiplex. The BBC has a separate national multiplex for its services. There are local multiplexes around the country, each broadcasting an average of seven services, plus the local BBC station. There are also several regional multiplexes covering a wider area and broadcasting up to 11 services each.

INNOVATIONS

As with television, the opportunities offered by digital services and the internet have made important changes to radio. The internet offers a number of advantages compared to other digital platforms such as DAB including higher sound quality, a greater range of channel availability and flexibility in listening opportunity. Listeners can tune in to the majority of radio stations live on the internet or listen again online for seven days after broadcast. DAB radio does not allow the same interactivity: the data is only able to travel one-way from broadcaster to listener whereas the internet allows a two-way flow of information.

Since 2005 increasing numbers of radio stations offer all or part of their programmes as downloadable files, known as podcasts, to listen to on computers or mobile devices such as mp3 players or phones. Podcasting technology allows listeners to subscribe in order to receive automatically the latest episodes of regularly transmitted programmes as soon as they become available.

The relationship between radio stations and their audiences is also undergoing change. The quantity and availability of music on the internet has led to the creation of shows dedicated entirely to music sent in by listeners. Another new development in internet-based radio has been personalised radio stations, such as last.fm and Spotify. Last.fm 'recommends' songs based on the favourite artists and previous choices of the user. Spotify allows listeners access to the track, artist or genre of their choice, or to share and create playlists; either advertisements are played at set intervals or there is a subscription charge. WiFi technology is also making changes to radio-listening behaviour. WiFi internet radios and media adaptors (which plug into a hi-fi) mean that people are not limited to listening to internet radio stations, podcasts or on-demand programmes solely when using their computer.

BBC RADIO

BBC Radio broadcasts network services to the UK, Isle of Man and the Channel Islands. There is also a tier of national services in Wales, Scotland and Northern Ireland and 40 local radio stations in England and the Channel Islands. In Wales and Scotland there are also dedicated language services in Welsh and Gaelic respectively. The frequency allocated for digital BBC broadcasts is 225.648MHz.

Broadcasting House, Portland Place, London W1A 1AA
T 020-7580 4468

BBC NETWORK RADIO STATIONS

Radio 1 (contemporary pop music and entertainment news) – 24 hours a day, *frequencies:* 97–99 FM and digital

Radio 2 (popular music, entertainment, comedy and the arts) – 24 hours a day, *frequencies:* 88–91 FM and digital

Radio 3 (classical music, classic drama, documentaries and features) – 24 hours a day, *frequencies:* 90–93 FM and digital

Radio 4 (news, documentaries, drama, entertainment and cricket on long wave in season) – 5.20am–1am daily, with BBC World Service overnight, *frequencies:* 92–95 FM and 198 LW and digital
Radio Five Live (news and sport) – 24 hours a day, *frequencies:* 693/909 MW and digital
Five Live Sports Extra (live sport) – schedule varies, digital only
6 Music (contemporary and classic pop and rock music) – 24 hours a day, digital only
Radio 7 (comedy, drama and children's) – 24 hours a day, digital only
Asian Network (news, music and sport) – 24 hours a day Friday and Saturday; 5am–1am Sunday–Thursday, with Radio Five Live overnight, *frequencies:* various MW frequencies in Midlands and digital
1Xtra (urban music: drum & bass, garage, hip hop, R&B) – 24 hours a day, digital only

BBC NATIONAL RADIO STATIONS

Radio Cymru (Welsh-language), *frequencies:* 92–105 FM and digital
Radio Foyle, frequencies: 93.1 FM and 792 MW and digital
Radio Nan Gaidheal (Gaelic service), *frequencies:* 103.5–105 FM and 990 MW and digital
Radio Scotland, frequencies: 585/810 MW and 92.4–94.7 FM and digital. Local programmes for Highlands and Islands; North East; Borders; South West; Orkney; and Shetland
Radio Ulster, frequencies: 873/1341 MW and 92.4–95.4 FM and digital. Local programmes on Radio Foyle
Radio Wales, frequencies: 882/1125/657 MW and 93.9–95.9 FM and digital

BBC LOCAL RADIO STATIONS

In England, BBC local radio has an average weekly reach of 7.7 million listeners. There are 40 local stations serving England and the Channel Islands, all of which are available via the internet:

Berkshire, PO Box 1044, Reading RG4 8FH T 0118-946 4200 *Frequencies:* 95.4/104.1 FM and digital
Bristol, PO Box 194, Bristol, BS99 7QT T 0117-974 1111 *Frequencies:* 94.9/104.6/103.6 FM, 1548 AM and digital
Cambridgeshire, 104 Hills Road, Cambridge CB2 1LQ T 01223-259696 *Frequencies:* 95.7/96 FM and digital
Cornwall, Phoenix Wharf, Truro TR1 1UA T 01872-275421 *Frequencies:* 95.2/103.9 FM and digital
Coventry and Warwickshire, Priory Place, Coventry CV1 5SQ T 024-7655 1000 *Frequencies:* 94.8/103.7 FM and digital
Cumbria, Annetwell Street, Carlisle CA3 8BB T 01228-592444 *Frequencies:* 95.6/96.1 FM
Derby, 56 St Helen's Street, Derby DE1 3HY T 01332-361111 *Frequencies:* 95.3/96.0/104.5 FM
Devon, PO Box 5, Broadcasting House, Seymour Road, Plymouth PL3 5YQ T 01752-229201 *Frequencies:* 95.7/103.4 FM, 801 AM and digital
Essex, 198 New London Road, Chelmsford CM2 9XB T 01245-616000 *Frequencies:* 95.3/103.5 FM, 765 AM and digital
Gloucestershire, London Road, Gloucester GL1 1SW T 01452-308585 *Frequencies:* 95.0/95.8/104.7 FM, 1413 AM
Guernsey, Broadcasting House, Bulwer Avenue, St Sampson's GY2 4LA T 01481-200373 *Frequencies:* 93.2/99.0 FM, 1116 AM
Hereford and Worcester, Hylton Road, Worcester WR2 5WW T 01905-748485 *Frequencies:* 94.7/104.0/104.4/104.6 FM, 738 AM
Humberside, Queen's Court, Hull HU1 3RH T 01482-323232 *Frequencies:* 95.9 FM, 1485 AM and digital
Jersey, 18 Parade Road, St Helier JE2 3PL T 01534-720255 *Frequencies:* 88.8 FM, 1026 AM
Kent, The Great Hall, Mount Pleasant Road, Tunbridge Wells TN1 1QQ T 01892-670000 *Frequencies:* 96.7/97.6/104.2 FM, 774 AM and digital
Lancashire, 20–26 Darwen Street, Blackburn BB2 2EA T 01254-583583 *Frequencies:* 95.5/103.9/104.5 FM, 1557 AM and digital
Leeds, 2 St Peter's Square, Leeds LS9 8AH T 0113-244 2131 *Frequencies:* 92.4/95.3/102.7/103.9 FM, 774 AM and digital
Leicester, 9 St Nicholas Place, Leicester LE1 5LB T 0116-251 1049 *Frequency:* 104.9 FM and digital
Lincolnshire, PO Box 219, Newport, Lincoln LN1 3XY T 01522-511411 *Frequencies:* 94.9/104.7 FM
London, 2nd Floor, Egton Wing, BBC Broadcasting House, Portland Place, London W1A 1AA T 020-7224 2424 *Frequency:* 94.9 FM and digital
Manchester, G100, New Broadcasting House, Oxford Road, Manchester M60 1SJ T 0161-200 2000 *Frequencies:* 95.1/104.6 FM and digital
Merseyside, PO Box 95.8, Liverpool L69 1ZJ T 0151-708 5500 *Frequencies:* 95.8 FM, 1485 AM and digital
Newcastle, Broadcasting Centre, Barrack Road, Newcastle upon Tyne NE99 1RN T 0191-232 4141 *Frequencies:* 95.4/96.0/103.7/104.4 FM, 1458 AM and digital
Norfolk, The Forum, Millennium Plain, Norwich NR2 1BH T 01603-617321 *Frequencies:* 95.1/95.6/104.4 FM, 855 AM and digital
Northampton, Broadcasting House, Abington Street, Northampton NN1 2BH T 01604-239100 *Frequencies:* 103.6/104.2 FM
Nottingham, London Road, Nottingham NG2 4UU T 0115-955 0500 *Frequencies:* 95.1/95.5/103.8 FM, 1584 AM and digital
Oxford, PO Box 95.2, Oxford OX2 7YL T 0845-931 1444 *Frequency:* 95.2 FM
Sheffield, 54 Shoreham Street, Sheffield S1 4RS T 0114-273 1177 *Frequencies:* 88.6/94.7/104.1 FM, 1035 AM and digital
Shropshire, 2–4 Boscobel Drive, Shrewsbury, Shrewsbury SY1 3TT T 01743-248484 *Frequencies:* 90.0/95.0/96.0/104.1 FM and digital
Solent, Havelock Road, Southampton SO14 7PW T 023-8063 1311 *Frequencies:* 96.1/103.8 FM, 999 AM and digital
Somerset, Broadcasting House, Park Street, Taunton TA1 4DA T 01823-323956 *Frequencies:* 95.5 FM,1566 AM
Stoke, Cheapside, Hanley, Stoke-on-Trent ST1 1JJ T 01782-208080 *Frequencies:* 94.6/104.1 FM and digital
Suffolk, Broadcasting House, St Matthew's Street, Ipswich IP1 3EP T 01473-250000 *Frequencies:* 95.5/95.9/103.9/104.6 FM
Surrey, Broadcasting Centre, Guildford, Surrey GU2 7AP T 03704-111046 *Frequencies:* 104/104.6 FM, 1368 AM
Sussex, Broadcasting House, Queens Road, Brighton, East Sussex BN1 3XB T 0845-957 0057 *Frequencies:* 95.0/95.1/95.3/104.5/104.8 FM, 1161 AM and digital
Tees, PO Box 95FM, Broadcasting House, Newport Road, Middlesborough TS1 5DG T 01642-225211 *Frequency:* 95 FM and digital

Three Counties, PO Box 3CR, Luton LU1 5XL
T 01582-637400 *Frequencies:* 95.5/103.8/104.5 FM, 630/1161 AM
Wiltshire, PO Box 1234, Swindon SN1 3RW
T 01793-513626 *Frequencies:* 103.5/104.3 FM, 1332 AM and digital
WM (West Midlands), The Mailbox, Birmingham B1 1RF
T 0121-567 6000 *Frequency:* 95.6 FM and digital
York, 20 Bootham Row, York YO30 7BR
T 01904-641351 *Frequencies:* 95.5/103.7/104.3 FM, 666 AM

BBC WORLD SERVICE

The BBC World Service broadcasts to an estimated weekly audience of 180 million worldwide, in 32 languages including English, and is now available in 154 capital cities. It no longer broadcasts in Dutch, French for Europe, German, Hebrew, Italian, Japanese or Malay because it was found that most speakers of these languages preferred to listen to the English broadcasts. In 2006 services in ten languages (Bulgarian, Croatian, Czech, Greek, Hungarian, Kazakh, Polish, Slovak, Slovene and Thai) were terminated to provide funding for a new Arabic television channel, which was launched in March 2008. In August 2008 the BBC's Romanian World Service broadcasts were discontinued after 68 years. The BBC World Service website offers interactive news services in English, Arabic, Chinese, Hindi, Persian, Portuguese for Brazil, Russian, Spanish and Urdu with audiostreaming available in 32 languages.

LANGUAGES

Albanian, Arabic, Azeri, Bengali, Burmese, Caribbean-English, Chinese, French for Africa, Hausa, Hindi, Indonesian, Kinyarwanda, Kirundi, Kyrgyz, Macedonian, Mandarin, Nepali, Pashto, Persian, Portuguese, Russian, Serbian, Sinhala, Somali, Spanish, Swahili, Tamil, Turkish, Ukrainian, Urdu, Uzbek and Vietnamese.

UK frequencies: digital and 648 MW in southern England; overnight on BBC Radio 4 and BBC Radio Wales.
BBC Learning English teaches English worldwide through radio, television and a wide range of published and online courses.
BBC Monitoring tracks the global media for the latest news reports emerging around the world.
BBC World Service Trust is a registered charity established in 1999 by BBC World Service. It promotes development through the innovative use of the media in the developing world. The trust presently works in over 40 countries worldwide, and focuses on health, education and good governance.
BBC WORLD SERVICE, Bush House, Strand, London WC2B 4PH T 020-7240 3456

INDEPENDENT RADIO

Until 1973, the BBC had a legal monopoly on radio broadcasting in the UK. During this time, the corporation's only competition came from pirate stations located abroad, such as Radio Luxembourg. Christopher Chataway, Minister for Post and Telecommunications in Edward Heath's government, changed this by creating the first licences for commercial radio stations. The Independent Broadcasting Authority (IBA) awarded the first of these licences to the London Broadcasting Company (LBC) to provide London's news and information service. LBC was followed by Capital Radio, to offer the city's entertainment service, Radio Clyde in Glasgow and BRMB in Birmingham.

The IBA was dissolved when the Broadcasting Act of 1990 de-regulated broadcasting, to be succeeded by the less rigid Radio Authority (RA). The RA began advertising new licences for the development of independent radio in January 1991. It awarded national and local radio, satellite and cable services licences, and long-term restricted service licences for stations serving non-commercial establishments such as hospitals and universities. The first national commercial digital multiplex licence was awarded in October 1998 and a number of local digital multiplex licences followed.

At the end of 2003 the RA was replaced by OFCOM, which now carries out the licensing administration.

The RadioCentre was formed in July 2006 as a result of the merger between the Radio Advertising Bureau (RAB) and the Commercial Radio Companies Association (CRCA), the former non-profit trade body for commercial radio companies in the UK, to operate essentially as a union for commercial radio stations. According to a 2008 audit, it is possible to listen to 93 per cent of independent radio stations online, while 48 per cent can be listened to on DAB radios.

THE RADIOCENTRE, 4th Floor, 5 Golden Square, London W1F 9BS T 020-3206 7800 W www.radiocentre.org
Chief Executive, Andrew Harrison

INDEPENDENT NATIONAL RADIO STATIONS

Absolute Radio, 1 Golden Square, London W1F 9DJ
T 020-7434 1215 – 24 hours a day, *Frequencies:* 105.8 FM, 1197/1215/1233/1242/1260 AM and digital
Amazing Radio, 19 Grey Street, Newcastle NE1 6EE – 24 hours a day, *Frequencies:* digital only
BFBS Radio UK, Chalfont Grove, Narcot Lane, Chalfont St Peter, Bucks SL9 8TN T 01494-878703 *Frequencies:* digital only
Classic FM, 30 Leicester Square, London WC2H 7LA
T 020-7343 9000 – 24 hours a day, *Frequencies:* 100–102 FM and digital
Planet Rock, 54 Lisson Street, London NW1 5DF
T 020-7453 1600 – 24 hours a day, *Frequency:* digital only
Talk Sport, 18 Hatfields, London SE1 8DJ T 020-7959 7800 – 24 hours a day, *Frequencies:* 1053/1071/1089/1107 AM and digital

INDEPENDENT LOCAL RADIO STATIONS ENGLAND

2BR, Imex Spaces, Nelson, Lancs BB9 7DR T 01282-690000 *Frequency:* 99.8 FM
3FM, 45 Victoria Street, Douglas, Isle of Man IM1 3RS
T 01624-616333 *Frequencies:* 104–106 FM
95.8 Galaxy Radio, 30 Leicester Square, London WC2H 7LA
T 020-7766 6000 *Frequency:* 95.8 FM and digital
96 Trent FM, Maid Marian Way, Nottingham NG1 6JR
T 0115-873 1500 *Frequencies:* 96.2/96.5 FM and digital
96.2 The Revolution, Sarah Moor Studios, Henshaw Street, Oldham OL1 3JF T 0161-621 6500 *Frequency:* 96.2 FM
96.2 Touch Radio (Coventry), Holly Farm Business Park, Honiley, Kenilworth, Warks CV8 1NP T 01926-485600 *Frequency:* 96.2 FM
96.3 Radio Aire, 51 Burley Road, Leeds LS3 1LR
T 0113-283 5500 *Frequency:* 96.3 FM and digital

96.4 Eagle Radio, Dolphin House, North Street, Guildford, Surrey GU1 4AA T 01483-300964 *Frequency:* 96.4 FM

96.4 FM BRMB, Nine Brindleyplace, 4 Oozells Square, Birmingham B1 2DJ T 0121-566 5200 *Frequency:* 96.4 FM

96.9 Viking FM, The Boathouse, Commercial Road, Hull, E. Yorks HU1 2SG T 01482-325141 *Frequency:* 96.9 FM and digital

97 FM Plymouth Sound, Earl's Acre, Plymouth PL3 4HX T 01752-275600 *Frequencies:* 96.6/97 FM and digital

97.2 Stray FM, The Hamlet, Hornbeam Park Avenue, Harrogate HG2 8RE T 01423-522972 *Frequency:* 97.2 FM

97.4 Rock FM, PO Box 974, St. Paul's Square, Preston, Lancs PR1 1YE T 01772-477700 *Frequency:* 97.4 FM and digital

99.9 Radio Norwich, Stanton House, 29 Yarmouth Road, Norwich, NR7 0SA T 0845-365 6999 *Frequency:* 99.9 FM

102 Touch FM, Holly Farm Business Park, Honiley, Kenilworth, Warks CV8 1NP T 01926-485600 *Frequency:* 102 FM

102.4 Wish FM, Orrell Lodge, Orrell Road, Wigan, Lancs WN5 8HJ T 01942-761024 *Frequency:* 102.4 FM

103.2 Alpha FM, Radio House, 11 Woodland Road, Darlington, Co Durham DL3 7BJ T 01325-255552 *Frequency:* 103.2 FM

103.4 Sun FM, PO Box 1034, Sunderland, Tyne and Wear SR5 2YL T 0191-548 1034 *Frequency:* 103.4 FM

106.5 Central Radio, 9–10 Eastway Business Village, Olivers Place, Fulwood, Preston PR2 9WT T 01772-708001 *Frequency:* 106.5 FM

107 The Bee, 8 Dalton Court, Darwen, Lancs BB3 0DG T 01254-778000 *Frequency:* 107 FM

107.2 The Wyre, Foley House, 123 Stourport Road, Kidderminster DY11 7BW T 01562-641072 *Frequency:* 107.2 FM

107.4 Telford FM, c/o The Shropshire Star, Waterloo Road, Ketley TF1 5HU T 01952-280011 *Frequency:* 107.4 FM

107.4 The Quay, Media House, Tipner Wharf, Twyford Avenue, Portsmouth PO2 8PE T 023-9236 4141 *Frequency:* 107.4 FM

107.5 Sovereign Radio, 14 St Mary's Walk, Hailsham, E. Sussex BN27 1AF T 01323-442700 *Frequency:* 107.5 FM

107.6 FM Juice Liverpool, 27 Fleet Street, Liverpool L1 4AR T 0151-707 3107 *Frequency:* 107.6 FM

107.6 Touch Banbury, Unit 9A, Manor Park, Banbury, Oxfordshire OX16 3TB T 0129-566 1076 *Frequency:* 107.6 FM

107.7 Splash FM, The Guildbourne Centre, Worthing, W. Sussex BN11 1LZ T 01903-233005 *Frequency:* 107.7 FM

107.7 The Wolf, 2nd Floor, Mander House, Wolverhampton WV1 3NB T 01902-571070 *Frequency:* 107.7 FM

107.8 Arrow FM, Priory Meadow Centre, Hastings, E. Sussex TN34 1PJ T 01424-461177 *Frequency:* 107.8 FM

107.8 Radio Jackie, 110–112 Tolworth Broadway, Surbiton, Surrey KT6 7JD T 020-8288 1300 *Frequency:* 107.8 FM

107.9 Dune FM, The Power Station, Victoria Way, Southport, Merseyside PR8 1RR T 01704-502500 *Frequency:* 107.9 FM

1548 AM Capital Gold, 30 Leicester Square, London WC2H 7LA T 020-7766-6000 *Frequency:* 1548 AM

Absolute 80s, 1 Golden Square, London W1F 9DJ T 020-7434 1215 *Frequency:* digital only

Absolute Radio Classic Rock, 1 Golden Square, London W1F 9DJ T 020-7434 1215 *Frequency:* digital only

Absolute Radio London, 1 Golden Square, London W1F 9DJ T 020-7434 1215 *Frequency:* 105.8 FM and digital

The Arrow, 1 The Square, 111 Broad Street, Birmingham, West Midlands B15 1AS T 0121-695 0000 *Frequency:* digital only

Asian Sound Radio, Globe House, Southall Street, Manchester M3 1LG T 0161-288 1000 *Frequencies:* 963/1377 AM and digital

Atlantic FM, Unit 10, Wheal Kitty Workshops, St Agnes, Cornwall TR5 0RD T 01872-554400 *Frequencies:* 105/107 FM

The Bay, PO Box 969, St George's Quay, Lancaster LA1 3LD T 0871-200 0747 *Frequencies:* 96.9/102.3/103.2 FM

The Beach, PO Box 1034, Lowestoft, Suffolk NR32 2TL T 0845-345 1035 *Frequencies:* 97.4/103.4 FM and digital

Beacon Radio, 267 Tettenhall Road, Wolverhampton WV6 0DE T 01902-461300 *Frequencies:* 97.2/103.1 FM and digital

Big L, 8 Manchester Park, Tewkesbury Road, Cheltenham GL51 9EJ T 01242-699555 *Frequency:* digital only

Bright 106.4, 11A The Market Place Shopping Centre, Burgess Hill, W. Sussex RH15 9NP T 01444-248127 *Frequency:* 106.4 FM

Brighton's Juice, 107.2, 170 North Street, Brighton BN1 1EA T 01273-386107 *Frequency:* 107.2 FM and digital

BRMB, Nine Brindleyplace, 4 Oozells Square, Birmingham B1 2DJ T 0121-566 5200 *Frequency:* 96.4 FM and digital

CFM (Carlisle and West Cumbria), PO Box 964, Carlisle, Cumbria CA1 3NG T 01228-818964 *Frequencies:* 96.4/102.5 FM (Carlisle); 102.2/103.4 FM (West Cumbria)

Chelmsford Radio 107.7, Icon Building, Western Esplanade, Southend-on-Sea, Essex SS1 1EE T 0845-365 1078 *Frequency:* 107.7 FM

Cheshire's 106.9 Silk FM, 140 Moss Lane, Macclesfield, Cheshire SK11 7XE T 01625 268000 *Frequency:* 106.9 FM

Choice 96.9/107.1 FM, 30 Leicester Square, London WC2H 7LA T 020-7766 6810 *Frequency:* 96.9/107.1 FM and digital

Club Asia, Asia House, 227–247 Gascoigne Road, Barking, Essex IG11 7LN T 020-8594 6662 *Frequencies:* 963/972 AM

Compass FM, 26A Wellowgate, Grimsby, Lincs DN32 0RA T 01472-346666 *Frequency:* 96.4 FM

Connect FM, 2nd Floor, 5 Church Street, Peterborough PE1 1XB T 0844-800 1769 *Frequencies:* 97.2/107.4 FM

County Sound Radio 1566 AM, Dolphin House, North Street, Guildford, Surrey GU1 4AA T 01483-300964 *Frequency:* 1566 AM

Dabbl, 1 Golden Square, London W1F 9DJ T 020-7434 1215 *Frequency:* digital only

Dearne FM, Unit 7, Network Centre, Zenith Park, Whaley Road, Barnsley S75 1HT T 01226-321733 *Frequencies:* 97.1/102 FM

Dee 106.3, 2 Chantry Court, Chester CH1 4QN T 01244-391000 *Frequency:* 106.3 FM

Delta FM, Tindle House, High Street, Bordon, Hants GU35 0AY T 01420-473473 *Frequencies:* 97.1/101.6/101.8/102 FM

Dream 100 FM, Northgate House, St Peter's Street, Colchester, Essex CO1 1HT T 01206-764466 *Frequency:* 100.2 FM

Energy FM, 100 Market Street, Douglas, Isle of Man IM1 2PH T 01624-611936 *Frequencies:* 91.2 FM (Laxey); 93.4 FM (north Isle of Man); 98.4 FM (Ramsey); 98.6 FM

Fire 107.6 FM, The Picture House, 307 Holden Hurst Road, Bournemouth, Dorset BH8 8BX T 01202-443600 *Frequency:* 107.6 FM

Fresh Radio, Firth Mill, Firth Street, Skipton, N. Yorks BD23 2PT T 01756-799991 *Frequencies:* 936/1413/1431 AM; 102.6/107.1/107.8 FM

Galaxy Birmingham, 1 The Square, 111 Broad Street, Birmingham, West Midlands B15 1AS T 0121-695 0000 *Frequency:* 102.2 FM and digital

Galaxy Manchester, Suite 1.1, 4 Exchange Quay, Salford, Manchester M5 3EE T 0161-662 4700 *Frequency:* 102 FM and digital

Galaxy North East, Kingfisher Way, Silverlink Business Park, Wallsend, Tyne and Wear NE28 9NX T 0191-206 8000 *Frequencies:* 105.3/105.6/105.8/106.4 FM and digital

Galaxy South Coast, Segensworth West, Fareham, Hampshire PO15 5SX T 01489-587600 *Frequency:* 103.2 FM and digital

Galaxy Yorkshire, Joseph's Well, Hanover Walk, Leeds LS3 1AB T 0113-213 0105 *Frequencies:* 105.1/105.6/105.8 FM and digital

Gaydar Radio, 6th Floor, Queens House, 2 Holly Road, Twickenham, Middlesex TW1 4EG T 020-8744 1287 *Frequency:* digital only

Gold (Berkshire and North Hampshire), The Chase, Calcot, Reading, Berks RG3 7RB T 0118-945 4400 *Frequencies:* 1431/1485 AM and digital

Gold (Birmingham), Nine Brindleyplace, 4 Oozells Square, Birmingham B1 2DJ T 0121-245 5000 *Frequency:* 1152 AM and digital

Gold (Bristol and Bath), PO Box 2000, One Passage Street, Bristol BS99 7SN T 0117-984 3200 *Frequency:* 1260 AM and digital

Gold (Cambridgeshire), PO Box 225, Queensgate Centre, Peterborough, Cambridge PE1 1XJ T 01733-460460 *Frequency:* 1332 AM and digital

Gold (Devon), Hawthorn House, Exeter Business Park, Exeter EX1 3QS T 01392-444444 *Frequencies:* 666/954 AM and digital

Gold (Dorset and Hampshire), 5–7 Southcote Road, Bournemouth, Dorset BH1 3LR T 01202-234900 *Frequency:* 828 AM and digital

Gold (East Midlands), Chapel Quarter, Maid Marian Way, Nottingham NG1 6JR T 01245-524549 *Frequencies:* 1359/1431 AM and digital

Gold (Essex), 31 Glebe Road, Chelmsford, Essex CM1 1QG T 01245-524549 *Frequencies:* 1359/1431 AM and digital

Gold (Gloucester and Cheltenham), Bridge Studios, Eastgate Centre, Gloucester GL1 1SS T 01452-572400 *Frequency:* 774 AM

Gold (Hampshire), Radio House, Whittle Avenue, Segensworth West, Farnham, Hants PO15 5SH T 01489-587610 *Frequencies:* 1170/1557 AM and digital

Gold (Herts, Beds and Bucks), Chiltern Road, Dunstable, Beds LU6 1HQ T 01582-676200 *Frequencies:* 792/828 AM and digital

Gold (Kent), Radio House, John Wilson Business Park, Whitstable, Kent CT5 3QX T 01227-772004 *Frequencies:* 603/1242 AM and digital

Gold (London), 30 Leicester Square, London WC2H 7LA T 020-7776 6000 *Frequency:* 1548 AM and digital

Gold (Manchester), Laser House, Waterfront Quays, Manchester M5 2XW T 0161-662 4700 *Frequency:* 1458 AM and digital

Gold (Norfolk), St George's Plain, 47–49 Colegate, Norwich NR3 1DB T 01603-630621 *Frequency:* 1152 AM and digital

Gold (Northamptonshire), 19–21 St Edmunds Road, Northampton NN1 5DY T 01604-795600 *Frequency:* 1557 AM and digital

Gold (Plymouth), Earl's Acre, Plymouth PL3 4HX T 01752-275600 *Frequency:* 1152 AM and digital

Gold (Suffolk), Alpha Business Park, 6–12 White House Road, Ipswich IP1 5LT T 01473-461000 *Frequencies:* 1170/1251 AM

Gold (Sussex), Radio House, PO Box 2000, Brighton BN41 2SS T 01273-430111 *Frequencies:* 945/1323 AM and digital

Gold (Sussex and Surrey), 9 The Stanley Centre, Kelvin Way, Crawley, W. Sussex RH10 9SE T 01293-519161 *Frequency:* 1521 AM and digital

Gold (Warwickshire), Hertford Place, Coventry CV1 3TT T 024-7686 8200 *Frequency:* 1359 AM and digital

Gold (Wiltshire), 1st Floor, Chiseldon House, Stonehill Green, Westlea, Swindon, Wilts SN5 7HB T 01793-663000 *Frequencies:* 936/1161 AM and digital

Gold (Wolverhampton and Shropshire), 267 Tettenhall Road, Wolverhampton WV6 0DQ T 01902-461200 *Frequencies:* 990/1017 AM and digital

Hallam FM, Radio House, 900 Herries Road, Sheffield S6 1RH T 0114-209 1000 *Frequencies:* 97.4/102.9/103.4 FM and digital

Heart (Bath), PO Box 2000, One Passage Street, Bristol BS99 7SN T 0117-984 3200 *Frequency:* 103 FM and digital

Heart (Bedfordshire) 5 Abbey Court, Fraser Road, Priory Business Park, Bedford MK44 3WH T 01234-235010 *Frequency:* 96.9 FM

Heart (Berkshire and North Hampshire), PO Box 2020, Reading, Berks RG31 7FG T 0118-945 4400 *Frequencies:* 97/102.9/103.4 FM and digital

Heart (Bristol and South Gloucester), PO Box 2000, One Passage Street, Bristol BS99 7SN T 0117-984 3200 *Frequencies:* 96.3/103 FM and digital

Heart (Cambridgeshire), Enterprise House, The Vision Park, Chivers Way, Histon, Cambridge CB24 9ZR T 01223-235255 *Frequencies:* 97.4/103 FM and digital

Heart (Colchester), Abbeygate Two, 9 Whitewell Road, Colchester, Essex CO2 7DE T 01206-216140 *Frequency:* 96.1 FM

Heart (Dorset and The New Forest), 5–7 Southcote Road, Bournemouth BH1 3LR T 01202-234900 *Frequency:* 102.3 FM and digital

Heart (East Midlands), City Link, Nottingham NG2 4NG T 0115-910 6100 *Frequency:* 106 FM and digital

Heart (Essex), Radio House, 31 Glebe Road, Chelmsford, Essex CM1 1QG T 01245-524500 *Frequencies:* 96.3/102.6 FM and digital

Heart (Exeter and East Devon), Hawthorn House, Exeter Business Park, Exeter EX1 3QS T 01392-444444 *Frequencies:* 97/103 FM and digital

Heart (Gloucester and Cheltenham), The Mall, Gloucester GL1 1SS T 01452-572400 *Frequencies:* 102.4/103 FM

Heart (Hampshire and West Sussex), Radio House, Apple Industrial Estate, Whittle Avenue, Fareham PO15 5SH T 01489-589911 *Frequencies:* 96.7/97.5 FM and digital

Heart (Herts, Beds and Bucks), Chiltern Road, Dunstable LU6 1HQ T 01582-676200 *Frequency:* 97.6 FM

Heart (Kent), Radio House, PO Box 100, Whitstable, Kent CT5 3QX T 01227-772004 *Frequencies:* 102.8/103.1 FM and digital

Heart (London), 30 Leicester Square, London WC2H 7LA T 020-7766 6222 *Frequency:* 106.2 FM and digital

Heart (Milton Keynes), 14 Vincent Avenue, Crownhill, Milton Keynes MK8 0AB T 01908-269111 *Frequency:* 103.3 FM

Heart (Norfolk and North Suffolk), 47–49 Colegate, Norwich NR3 1DB T 01603-630621 *Frequency:* 102.4 FM and digital

Heart (North Devon), Unit 2B, Lauder Lane, Roundswell Business Park, Barnstaple EX31 3TA T 01271-342342 *Frequencies:* 96.2/97.3 FM

Heart (Northamptonshire), 19–22 St Edmunds Road, Northampton NN1 5DY T 01604-795600 *Frequency:* 96.6 FM

Heart (Oxfordshire), Brush House, Pony Road, Oxford OX4 2XR T 01865-871000 *Frequencies:* 97.4/102.6 FM

Heart (Peterborough), Queensgate Centre, Peterborough PE1 1XJ T 01733-460460 *Frequency:* 102.7 FM and digital

Heart (Plymouth), Earls Acre, Plymouth PL3 4HX T 01752-275600 *Frequencies:* 96.6/97 FM and digital

Heart (Somerset), Haygrove House, Shoreditch Road, Taunton, Somerset TA3 7BT T 01823-338448 *Frequency:* 102.6 FM

Heart (South Devon), Unit 1G, South Hams Business Park, Churchstow, Kingsbridge, Devon TQ7 3QH T 01548-854595 *Frequencies:* 100.5/100.8/101.2/101.9 FM

Heart (Suffolk), Alpha Business Park, 6–12 White House Road, Ipswich, Suffolk IP1 5LT T 01473-461000 *Frequencies:* 96.4/97.1 FM

Heart (Sussex), Franklin Road, Brighton BN41 1AF T 01273-430111 *Frequencies:* 102.4/103.5 FM and digital

Heart (Torbay and South Devon), Harbourpoint, Victoria Parade, Torquay, Devon TQ1 2RA T 01803-201444 *Frequency:* 96.4 FM

Heart (Birmingham and West Midlands), 1 The Square, 111 Broad Street, Birmingham B15 1AS T 0121-695 0000 *Frequency:* 100.7 FM and digital

Heart (Wiltshire), Chiseldon House, Stonehill Green, Westlea, Swindon, Wilts SN5 7HB T 01793-842600 *Frequencies:* 96.5/97.2/102.2 FM and digital

Heart (Wirral), Pacific Road Arts Centre, Pacific Road, Birkenhead CH41 1LJ T 0151-650 1700 *Frequency:* 97.1 FM

Hertbeat FM, The Pump House, Knebworth Park, Herts SG3 6HQ T 01438-810900 *Frequencies:* 106.7/106.9 FM

Hertfordshire's Mercury, Unit 5, The Metro Centre, Dwight Road, Watford WD18 9UP T 01923-205470 *Frequency:* 96.6 FM

High Peak Radio, The Studios, Smithbrook Close, Chapel-en-le-Frith, High Peak, Derbys SK23 0QD T 01298-813144 *Frequencies:* 103.3/106.4 FM

Imagine FM, Regent House, Heaton Lane, Stockport, Cheshire, SK4 1BX T 0161-609 1400 *Frequency:* 104.9 FM

Isle Of Wight Radio, Dodnor Park, Newport, IOW PO30 5XE T 01983-822557 *Frequencies:* 102/107 FM

Jack FM (Bristol), County Gates, Ashton Road, Bristol BS3 2JH T 0117-966 1065 *Frequency:* 106.5 FM

Jack FM (Hertfordshire), The Pump House, Knebworth Park, Hertfordshire SG3 6HQ T 01438-810900 *Frequency:* 106 FM

Jack FM (Oxfordshire), 270 Woodstock Road, Oxford, Oxfordshire OX2 7NW T 01865-315980 *Frequency:* 106.8/106.4 FM

Kerrang! 105.2 FM, Aqua House, 20 Lionel Street, Birmingham B3 1AQ T 0845-053 1052 *Frequency:* 105.2 FM and digital

Kestrel FM, 2nd Floor, Paddington House, Festival Place, Basingstoke, Hants RG21 7LJ T 01256-694000 *Frequency:* 107.6 FM

Key 103, Castle Quay, Castlefield, Manchester M15 4PR T 0161-288 5000 *Frequency:* 103 FM and digital

Kick FM, The Studios, 42 Bone Lane, Newbury, Berks RG14 5SD T 01635-841600 *Frequencies:* 105.6/107.4 FM

Kismat, Radio House, Bridge Road, Southall, Middx UB2 4AT T 020-8574 6666 *Frequency:* 1035 AM and digital

Kiss 100 FM, Mappin House, 4 Winsley Street, London W1W 8HF T 020-7975 8100 *Frequency:* 100 FM and digital

Kiss 101 FM, 26 Baldwin Street, Bristol BS1 1SE T 0117-901 0101 *Frequencies:* 97.2/101 FM and digital

Kiss FM 105–108, Reflection House, Western Way, Olding Road, Bury St Edmunds, Suffolk IP33 3TA T 01284-715300 *Frequencies:* 105.6/106.1/106.4/107.7 FM and digital

KL.FM 96.7, 18 Blackfriars Street, King's Lynn, Norfolk PE30 1NN T 01553-772777 *Frequency:* 96.7 FM

KMFM for Ashford, 34–36 North Street, Ashford, Kent TN24 8JR T 01233-623232 *Frequency:* 107.7 FM

KMFM for Canterbury, 9 St George's Place, Canterbury, Kent CT1 1UU T 01227-475950 *Frequency:* 106 FM

KMFM for Maidstone, 6–8 Mill Street, Maidstone, Kent ME15 6XH T 01622-662500 *Frequency:* 105.5 FM

KMFM for Medway, Medway House, Ginsbury Close, Sir Thomas Longley Road, Medway City Estate, Strood, Rochester, Kent ME2 4DU T 01634-711079 *Frequencies:* 100.4/107.9 FM

KMFM for Shepway and White Cliffs Country, 93–95 Sandgate Road, Folkestone, Kent CT20 2BQ T 01303-220303 *Frequencies:* 96.4/106.8 FM

KMFM for Thanet, 183 Northdown Road, Cliftonville, Margate, Kent CT9 2TA T 01843-220222 *Frequency:* 107.2 FM

KMFM for West Kent, 1 East Street, Tonbridge, Kent TN9 1AR T 01732-369200 *Frequencies:* 96.2/101.6 FM

Lakeland Radio, Unit 4, Lakelands Food Park, Plumgarths, Crook Road, Kendal, Cumbria LA8 8QJ T 01539-737380 *Frequencies:* 100.1/100.8 FM

LBC 97.3 FM, The Chrysalis Building, 13 Bramley Road, London W10 6SP T 020-7314 7300 *Frequency:* 97.3 FM and digital

LBC News 1152 AM, The Chrysalis Building, 13 Bramley Road, London W10 6SP T 020-7314 7308 *Frequency:* 1152 AM and digital

Leicester Sound, 6 Dominus Way, Meridian Business Park, Leicester LE19 1RP T 0116-256 1300 *Frequency:* 105.4 FM and digital

Lincs FM, Witham Park, Waterside South, Lincoln LN5 7JN T 01522-549900 *Frequencies:* 96.7/102.2/97.6 FM and digital

London Greek Radio, LGR House, 437 High Road, London N12 0AP T 020-8349 6950 *Frequency:* 103.3 FM

London Turkish Radio, 185B High Road, Wood Green, London N22 6BA T 020-8881 0606 *Frequency:* 1584 AM

Magic 105.4 FM, Mappin House, 4 Winsley Street, London W1W 8HF T 020-7182 8000 *Frequency:* 105.4 FM and digital

Magic 828, 51 Burley Road, Leeds LS3 1LR T 0113-283 5500 *Frequency:* 828 AM and digital

Magic 999, St Paul's Square, Preston, Lancs PR1 1YE T 01772-477700 *Frequency:* 999 AM and digital

Magic 1152 (Tyne & Wear), 55 Degrees North, Pilgrim Street, Newcastle upon Tyne NE1 6BF T 0191-230 6100 *Frequency:* 1152 AM and digital

Magic 1161 AM, The Boathouse, Commercial Road, Hull, E. Yorks HU1 2SG T 01482-325141 *Frequency:* 1161 AM and digital

Magic 1170, Radio House, Yale Crescent, Thornaby, Stockton-on-Tees TS17 6AA T 01642-888222 *Frequency:* 1170 AM and digital

Magic 1548 AM, St John's Beacon, 1 Houghton Street, Liverpool L1 1RL T 0151-472 6800 *Frequency:* 1548 AM and digital

Magic AM, Radio House, 900 Herries Road, Sheffield S6 1RH T 0114-209 1000 *Frequencies:* 990/1305/1548 AM and digital

Manchester's Magic 1152, Castle Quay, Castlefield, Manchester M15 4AW T 0161-288 5000 *Frequency:* 1152 AM and digital

Mansfield 103.2 FM, The Media Suite, Brunts Business Centre, Samuel Brunts Way, Mansfield, Notts NG18 2AH T 01623-646666 *Frequency:* 103.2 FM

Manx Radio, PO Box 1368, Broadcasting House, Douglas, Isle of Man IM99 1SW T 01624-682600 *Frequencies:* 89.0/97.2/103.7 FM, 1368 AM

Mercia, Hertford Place, Coventry CV1 3TT T 024-7686 8200 *Frequencies:* 97/102.9 FM and digital

Mercury FM, 9 The Stanley Centre, Kelvin Way, Crawley, West Sussex RH10 9SE T 01293-636000 *Frequencies:* 97.5/102.7 FM

Metro Radio, 55 Degrees North, Pilgrim Street, Newcastle upon Tyne NE1 6BF T 0191-230 6100 *Frequencies:* 97.1/102.6/103/103.2 FM and digital

Midwest Radio (Blandford & The Vale) Longmead Studios, Shaftesbury, Dorset SP7 8QQ T 01747-855711 *Frequencies:* 96.6/97.4 FM

Midwest Radio (Somerset & West Dorset), The Studios, Middle Street, Yeovil, Somerset BA20 1DJ T 01935-848488 *Frequencies:* 105.6/106.6 FM

Minster FM, PO Box 123, Dunnington, York YO1 5ZX T 01904-488888 *Frequencies:* 104.7 FM

Mix 96, Friars Square Studios, 11 Bourbon Street, Aylesbury, Bucks HP20 2PZ T 01296-399396 *Frequency:* 96.2 FM

NME, B2 Blue Fin Building, 110 Southwark Street, London SE1 0SU T 0207-922 1991 *Frequency:* digital only

North Norfolk Radio, The Studio, Breck Farm, Stody, Norfolk NR24 2ER T 01263-860808 *Frequencies:* 96.2/103.2 FM

Oak FM, 3 Martins Court, Telford Way, Coalville LE67 3HD T 01530-835107 *Frequencies:* 107/107.9 FM

Oxford's FM 1079, 270 Woodstock Road, Oxford OX2 7NW T 01865-315980 *Frequency:* 107.9 FM

Palm (105.5), Marble Court, Lymington Road, Torquay TQ1 4FB T 01803-321 055 *Frequency:* 105.5 FM

Passion Radio, PO Box 4738, Worthing, West Sussex BN11 9LR T 01903-685555 *Frequency:* digital only

Peak 107 FM, Radio House, Foxwood Road, Chesterfield, Derbys S41 9RF T 01246-267138 *Frequencies:* 102/107.4 FM

Pirate FM, Carn Brea Studios, Wilson Way, Redruth, Cornwall TR15 3XX T 01209-314400 *Frequencies:* 102.2/102.8 FM and digital

Polish Radio London, Unit 6, King Street Cloisters, Clifton Walk, London W6 0GY T 020-8846 3619 *Frequency:* digital only

Premier Christian Radio, 22 Chapter Street, London SW1P 4NP T 020-7316 1300 *Frequencies:* 1305/1332/1413 AM and digital

Pulse of West Yorkshire, Forster Square, Bradford, W. Yorks BD1 5NE T 01274-203040 *Frequencies:* 97.5/102.5 FM and digital

Pulse 2, Forster Square, Bradford, W. Yorks BD1 5NE T 01274-203040 *Frequencies:* 1278/1530 AM and digital

Radio City 96.7, St John's Beacon, 1 Houghton Street, Liverpool L1 1RL T 0151-472 6800 *Frequency:* 96.7 FM and digital

Radio Wave 96.5 FM, 965 Mowbray Drive, Blackpool, Lancs FY3 7JR T 01253-650300 *Frequency:* 96.5 FM

Radio XL 1296 AM, KMS House, Bradford Street, Birmingham B12 0JD T 0121-753 5353 *Frequency:* 1296 AM and digital

Ram FM, 35/36 Irongate, Derby DE1 3GA T 01332-324000 *Frequency:* 102.8 FM

Reading 107 FM, Radio House, Madejski Stadium, Reading, Berks RG2 0FN T 0118-986 2555 *Frequency:* 107 FM

Real Radio (Northeast), Marquis Court, Team Valley, Trading Estate, Gateshead NE11 0RU T 0191-440 7500 *Frequencies:* 100–102 FM and digital

Real Radio (Northwest), Laser House, Waterfront Quays, Manchester M50 3XW T 0161-886 8800 *Frequency:* 105.4 FM and digital

Real Radio (Yorkshire), 1 Sterling Court, Capitol Park, Leeds WF3 1EL T 0113-238 1114 *Frequencies:* 106–108 FM and digital

Ridings FM, 2 Thornes Office Park, Monckton Road, Wakefield WF2 7AN T 01924-367177 *Frequency:* 106.8 FM and digital

Rother FM, Aspen Court, Bessemer Way, Rotherham S60 1FB T 01709-369991 *Frequency:* 96.1 FM

Rugby FM, Holly Farm Business Park, Honiley, Kenilworth CV8 1NP T 01926-485 600 *Frequency:* 107.1 FM

Rutland Radio, 40 Melton Road, Oakham, Rutland, Leics LE15 6AY T 01572-757868 *Frequencies:* 97.4/107.2 FM

Sabras Radio, Radio House, 63 Melton Road, Leicester LE4 6PN T 0116-261 0666 *Frequency:* 1260 AM and digital

The Severn, MNA Broadcasting, Shropshire Newspapers, Waterloo Road, Ketley, Telford TF1 5HU T 0333-456 0777 *Frequencies:* 106.5/107.1 FM

Signal 1, Stoke Road, Stoke-on-Trent ST4 2SR T 01782-441300 *Frequencies:* 96.4/96.9/102.6 FM and digital

Signal 2, Stoke Road, Stoke-on-Trent ST4 2SR T 01782-441300 *Frequency:* 1170 AM and digital

Smooth Radio East Midlands, PO Box 1066, East Midlands NG2 1RX T 0115-986 1066 *Frequency:* 106.6 FM and digital

Smooth Radio London, 26–27 Castlereagh Street, London W1H 5DL T 020-7706 4100 *Frequency:* 102.2 FM and digital

Smooth Radio Northeast, Marquis Court, Team Valley Trading Estate, Gateshead NE11 0RU T 0191-440 7500 *Frequencies:* 95.7FM /107.7 FM and digital

Smooth Radio Northwest, Laser House, Waterfront Quay, Salford Quays, Manchester M50 3XW T 0845-050 1004 *Frequency:* 100.4 FM and digital

Smooth Radio West Midlands, 3rd Floor, Crown House, 123 Hagley Road, Birmingham B16 8LD T 0121-452 1057 *Frequency:* 105.7 FM and digital

Southend Radio 105.1, The Icon Building, Western Esplanade, Southend-on-Sea, Essex SS1 1EE T 01702-455080 *Frequency:* 105.1 FM and digital

Spectrum Radio, 4 Ingate Place, Battersea, London SW8 3NS T 020-7627 4433 *Frequency:* 558 AM and digital

Spire FM, City Hall Studios, Malthouse Lane, Salisbury, Wilts SP2 7QQ T 01722-416644 *Frequency:* 102 FM

Spirit FM, 9–10 Dukes Court, Bognor Road, Chichester, W. Sussex PO19 8FX T 01243-773600 *Frequencies:* 96.6/102.3/106.6 FM

Star Radio in Bristol, County Gates, Ashton Road, Bristol BS3 2JH T 0117-966 1065 *Frequency:* 107.2 FM

Star Radio in Cambridge, 20 Mercers Row, Cambridge CB5 8HY T 01223-305107 *Frequencies:* 107.1/107.9 FM

Sunshine Radio, PO Box 262, Worcester, Worcs WR6 5ZE T 01905-740600 *Frequencies:* 954/1530 AM

Sunrise FM, Sunrise House, 55 Leeds Road, Little Germany, Bradford BD1 5AF T 01274-735043 *Frequency:* 103.2 FM and digital

Sunrise Radio, Sunrise House, Sunrise Road, Southall, Middx UB2 4AT T 020-8574 6666 *Frequency:* 1458 AM and digital

Telford FM, MNA Broadcasting, Shropshire Newspapers, Waterloo Road, Ketley TF1 5HU T 01952-280011 *Frequency:* 107.4 FM

TFM, Radio House, Yale Crescent, Thornaby, Stockton-on-Tees TS17 6AA T 01642-888222 *Frequency:* 96.6 FM and digital

Time 106.6, Radio House, Southall, Middlesex UB2 4AT T 0845-194 1066 *Frequency:* 106.6 FM

Time 107.5, 7th Floor, Lambourne House, 7 Western Road, Romford, Essex RM1 3LD T 01708-731 643 *Frequency:* 107.5 FM

Total Star Gloucestershire, 8 Manchester Park, Tewkesbury Road, Cheltenham GL51 9EJ T 01242-252333 *Frequency:* 107.5 FM

Total Star Somerset, 8 Manchester Park, Tewkesbury Road, Cheltenham GL51 9EJ T 01242-252333 *Frequencies:* 100.8/102.4/107.4 FM

Tower FM, The Mill, Brownlow Way, Bolton BL1 2RA T 01204-387000 *Frequency:* 107.4 FM

Town FM, First Floor, Radio House Orion Court, Great Blakenham, Ipswich, Suffolk IP6 0LW T 0845-365 1102 *Frequency:* 102 FM

Touch FM, 5–6 Aldergate, Tamworth, Staffordshire B79 7DJ T 01827-318000 *Frequencies:* 101.6/102.4 FM and digital

Trax FM, 5 Sidings Court, White Rose Way, Doncaster DN4 5NU T 01302-341166 *Frequencies:* 107.1/107.9 FM and digital

Wave 105 FM, PO Box 105, Fareham, Hampshire PO15 5YF T 01489-481050 *Frequencies:* 105.2/105.8 FM and digital

Wessex FM, Radio House, Trinity Street, Dorchester, Dorset DT1 1DJ T 01305-250333 *Frequencies:* 96/97.2 FM

Wire FM, Warrington Business Park, Long Lane, Warrington WA2 8TX T 01925-445545 *Frequency:* 107.2 FM

Wyvern FM, First Floor, Kirkham House, John Comyn Drive, Worcester WR3 7NS T 01905-545510 *Frequencies:* 96.7/97.6/102.8 FM

XFM Manchester, Suite 1.1, 4 Exchange Quay, Manchester M5 3EE T 0161-662 4700 *Frequency:* 97.7 FM and digital

XFM UK, 30 Leicester Square, London WC2H 7LA T 020-7054 8000 *Frequency:* 104.9 FM and digital

Yorkshire Coast Radio, PO Box 962, Scarborough, N. Yorks YO11 3ZP T 01723-581700 *Frequencies:* 96.2/102.4/103.1 FM

Yorkshire Radio, Elland Road, Leeds LS11 0ES T 0871-521 2288 *Frequency:* digital only

WALES

96.4 FM The Wave, PO Box 964, Elizabeth Road, Gowerton, Swansea SA4 3AB T 01792-511964 *Frequency:* 96.4 FM and digital

97.1 Radio Carmarthenshire, PO Box 971, Llanelli, Carmarthenshire SA15 1YH T 0845-890 7000 *Frequencies:* 97.1/97.5 FM

97.5 Scarlet FM, PO Box 971, Llanelli, Carmarthenshire SA15 1YH T 0845-890 7000 *Frequency:* 97.5 FM

102.5 Radio Pembrokeshire, Unit 14, The Old School Estate, Station Road, Narberth, Pembrokeshire SA67 7DU T 01834-869384 *Frequencies:* 102.5/107.5 FM

106.3 Bridge FM, PO Box 1063, Bridgend CF35 6WF T 0845-890 4000 *Frequency:* 106.3 FM

Afan FM, AquaDome, Hollywood Park, Princess Margaret Way, Port Talbot SA12 6QW T 01639-894600 *Frequencies:* 97.4/107.9 FM

Gold (North Wales and Cheshire), Mold Road, Gwersyllt, Wrexham LL11 4AF T 01987-752202 *Frequency:* 1260 AM

Gold (South Wales), Red Dragon Centre, Atlantic Wharf, Cardiff CF10 4DJ T 029-2066 2066 *Frequencies:* 1305/1359 AM and digital

Heart 103 (Cymru), Unit D1, Llys-Y-Dderwen, Parc Menai, Bangor, Gwynedd LL57 4BN T 01248-673400 *Frequency:* 103 FM

Heart (North West and Wales), The Studios, Mold Road, Gwersyllt, Wrexham LL11 4AF T 01978-722 200 *Frequencies:* 96.3/103.4 FM

Nation Radio, Newby House, Neath Abbey Business Park, Neath SA10 7DR T 0845-025 1000 *Frequencies:* 106.8/107.3 FM and digital

Radio Ceredigion, Yr Hen Ysgol Gymraeg, Aberystwyth, Ceredigion SY23 1LF T 01970-627999 *Frequencies:* 96.6/97.4/103.3/FM

Radio Maldwyn, The Studios, The Park, Newtown, Powys SY16 2NZ T 01686-623555 *Frequency:* 756 AM

Real Radio (Wales), Unit 1, Ty-Nant Court, Ty-Nant Road, Morganstown, Cardiff CF15 8LW T 029-2031 5100 *Frequencies:* 105.2/105.4/105.7/105.9/106/106.2 FM and digital

Red Dragon FM, Atlantic Wharf, Cardiff CF10 4DJ T 029-2066 2066 *Frequencies:* 97.4/103.2 FM and digital

Swansea Bay Radio, Newby House, Neath Abbey Industrial Estate, Neath SA10 7DR T 0845-890 4000 *Frequency:* 102.1 FM

Swansea Sound, Victoria Road, Gowerton, Swansea SA4 3AB T 01792-511170 *Frequency:* 1170 AM and digital

SCOTLAND

Argyll FM, 27–29 Longrow, Campbelltown, Argyll PA28 6ER T 01586-551800 *Frequencies:* 106.5/107.1/107.7 FM

Central 103.1 FM, 201–203 High Street, Falkirk FK1 1DU T 01324-611164 *Frequency:* 103.1 FM

Clyde 1, Clydebank Business Park, Clydebank, Glasgow G81 2RX T 0141-565 2200 *Frequencies:* 97/102.5/103.3 FM and digital

Clyde 2, Clydebank Business Park, Clydebank, Glasgow G81 2RX T 0141-565 2200 *Frequency:* 1152 AM and digital

Cuillin FM, Stormyhill Road, Portree, Isle of Skye IV51 9DY T 01478-611797 *Frequencies:* 102.7/106.2 FM

Forth One, Forth House, Forth Street, Edinburgh EH1 3LE T 0131-556 9255 *Frequencies:* 97.3/97.6/102.2 FM and digital

Forth 2, Forth House, Forth Street, Edinburgh EH1 3LE T 0131-556 9255 *Frequency:* 1548 AM and digital

Heartland FM, 9 Alba Place, Pitlochry, Perthshire PH16 5BU T 01796-474040 *Frequency:* 97.5 FM

Isles FM, PO Box 333, Stornoway, Isle of Lewis HS1 2PU T 01851-703333 *Frequency:* 103 FM

Kingdom FM, Haig House, Haig Business Park, Balgonie Road, Markinch, Fife KY7 6AQ T 01592-753753 *Frequencies:* 95.2/96.1/96.6/105.4/106.3 FM

Lanarkshire's L107, Radio House, 69 Bothwell Road, Hamilton, Lanarkshire ML3 0DW T 01698-303420 *Frequencies:* 107.5/107.9 FM

Lochbroom FM, Radio House, Mill Street, Ullapool, Ross-shire IV26 2UN T 01854-613131 *Frequencies:* 96.8/102.2 FM

Moray Firth Radio (MFR), Scorguie Place, Inverness IV3 8UJ T 01463-224433 *Frequencies:* 97.4 FM/1107 AM and digital

NECR, The Shed, School Road, Kintore, Iveruie, Aberdeenshire AB51 0UX T 01467-632909 *Frequencies:* 97.1/101.9/102.1/102.6/103.2/106.4 FM and digital

Nevis Radio, Ben Nevis Estate, Claggan, Fort William PH33 6PR T 01397-700007 *Frequencies:* 96.6/97/102.3/102.4 FM

Northsound 1, Abbotswell Road, West Tullos, Aberdeen AB12 3AJ T 01224-337000 *Frequencies:* 96.9/97.6/103 FM and digital

Northsound 2, Abbotswell Road, West Tullos, Aberdeen AB12 3AJ T 01224-337000 *Frequency:* 1035 AM and digital

Oban FM, 132 George Street, Oban, Argyll PA34 5NT T 01631-570057 *Frequency:* 103.3 FM

Original 106, Craigshaw Road, West Tullos, Aberdeen AB12 3AR T 01224-294860 *Frequency:* 106 FM

Radio Borders, Tweedside Park, Galashiels TD1 3TD T 01896-759444 *Frequencies:* 96.8/102.3/103.1/103.4 FM

Real Radio (Scotland), Parkway Court, Glasgow Business Park, Glasgow G69 6GA T 0141-781 1011 *Frequencies:* 100.3/101.1 FM and digital

RNA FM, Rosemount Road, Arbroath, Angus DD11 2AT T 01241-879660 *Frequencies:* 96.6/87.7 FM and digital

Rock Radio, Unit 1130, Glasgow Business Park, Glasgow G69 6GA T 0141-781 1011 *Frequency:* 96.3 FM and digital

SIBC, Market Street, Lerwick, Shetland ZE1 0JN T 01595-695299 *Frequencies:* 96.2/102.2 FM

Smooth 105.2, PO Box 105, Glasgow G69 1AQ T 0141-781 1011 *Frequency:* 105.2 FM and digital

South West Sound FM, Unit 40, The Loreburne Centre, High St, Dumfries DG1 2BD T 01387-250999 *Frequencies:* 96.5/97/103 FM

Tay AM, 6 North Isla Street, Dundee DD3 7JQ T 01382-200800 *Frequencies:* 1161/1584 AM and digital
Tay FM, 6 North Isla Street, Dundee DD3 7JQ T 01382-200800 *Frequencies:* 96.4/102.8 FM and digital
Two Lochs Radio, Gairloch, Ross-shire IV21 2LR T 01445-712106 *Frequencies:* 106/106.6 FM
Wave 102, 8 South Tay Street, Dundee DD1 1PA T 01382-901000 *Frequency:* 102 FM and digital
Waves Radio, 7 Blackhouse Circle, Blackhouse Industrial Estate, Peterhead, Aberdeenshire AB42 1BN T 01779-491012 *Frequency:* 101.2 FM and digital
West FM, Radio House, 54A Holmston Road, Ayr KA7 3BE T 01292-283662 *Frequencies:* 96.7/97.5 FM and digital
West Sound AM, Radio House, 54A Holmston Road, Ayr KA7 3BE T 01292-283662 *Frequency:* 1035 AM and digital
Yourradio, Pioneer Park Studios, Unit 3, 80 Castlegreen Street, Dumbarton G82 1JB T 01389-734444 *Frequencies:* 103 FM (Dumbarton), 106.9 FM (Helensburgh)

NORTHERN IRELAND

Citybeat 96.7 FM, 2nd Floor, Arena Building, 85 Ormeau Road, Belfast, Antrim BT7 1SH T 028-9023 4967 *Frequency:* 96.7 FM and digital
Cool FM, Kiltonga Industrial Estate, Newtownards, Belfast BT23 4ES T 028-9181 7181 *Frequency:* 97.4 FM and digital
Downtown Radio, Newtownards, Co. Down BT23 4ES T 028-9181 5555 *Frequencies:* 96.4 FM (Limavady); 96.6 FM (Enniskillen); 97.1 FM (Larne); 102.3 FM (Ballymena); 102.4 FM (Londonderry) and digital
Q97.2 FM (Causeway Coast), 24 Cloyfin Road, Coleraine, Co. Londonderry BT52 2NU T 028-7035 9100 *Frequency:* 97.2 FM
Q101.2 West FM, 42A Market Street, Omagh, Co. Tyrone BT78 1EH T 028-8224 5777 *Frequency:* 101.2 FM
Q102.9 FM Northwest, The Riverview Suite, 87 Rossdowney Road, Waterside, Londonderry BT47 5SU T 028-7134 4449/346666 *Frequency:* 102.9 FM and digital
Seven FM, 1 Millennium Park, Woodside Industrial Estate, Woodside Road, Ballymena, Co Antrim BT42 4PT T 028-2564 8777 *Frequency:* 107 FM
Six FM, 2C Park Avenue, Cookstown, Co. Tyrone BT80 8AH T 028-8675 8696 *Frequencies:* 106/107.2 FM
U105, UTV, Ormeau Road, Belfast BT7 1EB T 028-9033 2105 *Frequency:* 105.8 FM

CHANNEL ISLANDS

Channel 103 FM, 6 Tunnell Street, St Helier, Jersey JE2 4LU T 01534-888103 *Frequency:* 103.7 FM
Island FM, 12 Westerbrook, St Sampsons, Guernsey GY2 4QQ T 01481-242000 *Frequencies:* 93.7/104.7 FM

THE PRESS

The newspaper and periodical press in the UK is large and diverse, catering for a wide variety of views and interests. There is no state control or censorship of the press; however, it is subject to the laws on publication, and the Press Complaints Commission (PCC) was set up by the industry as a means of self-regulation.

The press is not state-subsidised and receives few tax concessions. The income of most newspapers and periodicals is derived largely from sales and from advertising; the press is the largest advertising medium in Britain, although its market share is dropping as the proportion of online advertising grows.

SELF-REGULATION

The PCC was founded by the newspaper and magazine industry in January 1991 to replace the Press Council (established in 1953). It is a voluntary, non-statutory body set up to operate the press' self-regulation system following the Calcutt report in 1990 on privacy and related matters, when the industry feared that failure to regulate itself might lead to statutory regulation of the press. The performance of the PCC was reviewed in February 2010 by the Culture, Media and Sport Select Committee, which concluded in favour of continuing self-regulation. In July 2010 an independent review into the commission's governance made 75 recommendations for enhancing the system of press self-regulation. The commission is funded by the industry through the Press Standards Board of Finance.

COMPLAINTS

The PCC's aims are to consider, adjudicate, conciliate, and resolve complaints of unfair treatment by the press; and to ensure that the press maintains the highest professional standards and shows respect for generally recognised freedoms, including freedom of expression, the public's right to know, and the right of the press to operate free from improper pressure. The commission judges newspaper and magazine conduct by a code of practice drafted by editors, agreed by the industry and ratified by the commission.

The PCC has three classes of members: the chairman, public members and press members. Although a number of the commision's members are newspaper or magazine editors, the majority of the 17 members have no connection with the press in order to ensure that the PCC maintains independence from the newspaper industry. In 2009 the PCC processed 738 'complaints with merit', an increase of 9 per cent from 2008, and received around 37,000 complaints in total. The number of complaints was significantly higher than usual, owing largely to an article by Jan Moir in the *Daily Mail*. The article, concerning the death of the pop star Stephen Gately, incited over 25,000 complaints – more than five times as many as for the whole of 2008.

PRESS COMPLAINTS COMMISSION
Halton House, 20–23 Holborn, London EC1N 2JD
T 020-7831 0022 E complaints@pcc.org.uk
W www.pcc.org.uk
Chair, Baroness Peta Buscombe

NEWSPAPERS

Newspapers are mostly financially independent of any political party, though most adopt a political stance in their editorial comments, usually reflecting proprietorial influence. Ownership of the national and regional daily newspapers is concentrated in the hands of large corporations whose interests cover publishing and communications, although *The Guardian* and *The Observer* are owned by the *Scott Trust*, formed in 1936 to protect the financial and editorial independence of *The Guardian* in perpetuity. The rules on cross-media ownership, as amended by the Broadcasting Act 1996, which limited the extent to which newspaper organisations may become involved in broadcasting, have been relaxed by the Communications Act 2003: newspapers with over a 20 per cent share of national circulation may own national and/or local radio licences.

There are around 15 daily and 15 Sunday national papers and several hundred local papers that are published daily, weekly or twice-weekly. Scotland, Wales and Northern Ireland all have at least one daily and one Sunday national paper.

UK CIRCULATION

National Daily Newspapers	*June 2009*	*June 2010*
The Sun	2,860,159	2,797,972
Daily Mail	2,025,338	1,924,051
Daily Mirror	1,205,197	1,119,135
Daily Star	753,460	703,365
The Daily Telegraph	781,774	635,719
Daily Express	687,555	624,288
The Times	560,258	463,177
Daily Record	347,195	307,574
The Guardian	292,854	261,738
The Independent	152,932	162,232
Financial Times	112,111	110,684
The Herald	57,754	53,228
The Scotsman	47,559	44,315
National Sunday Newspapers	*June 2009*	*June 2010*
News of the World	2,796,589	2,610,900
The Mail on Sunday	1,802,623	1,676,088
Sunday Mirror	1,155,776	1,052,230
The Sunday Times	1,039,625	920,681
Sunday Express	595,859	524,699
The Sunday Telegraph	576,219	475,995
The People	533,896	471,681
Sunday Mail	394,437	368,978
Sunday Post	345,527	323,742
The Observer	363,431	299,492
Daily Star Sunday	319,048	287,478
The Independent on Sunday	117,498	127,730
Scotland on Sunday	62,653	55,657
Sunday Herald	37,335	40,715

Source: Audit Bureau of Circulations Ltd

Newspapers are usually published in either broadsheet or smaller, tabloid format. The 'quality' daily papers – ie those providing detailed coverage of a wide range of public matters – have traditionally been broadsheets, the more populist newspapers tabloid. In 2004 this correlation between format and content was redefined when three traditionally broadsheet newspapers, *The Times, The Independent* and *The Scotsman*, switched to tabloid-sized editions, while *The Guardian* launched a 'Berliner' format in September 2005. In October 2005 *The Independent on Sunday* became the first Sunday broadsheet to be published in the tabloid (or 'compact') size, and *The Observer*, like its daily counterpart *The Guardian*, began publishing in the Berliner format in January 2006.

NATIONAL DAILY NEWSPAPERS

DAILY EXPRESS
Northern & Shell Building, 10 Lower Thames Street, London EC3R 6EN **T** 0208-612 7000 **W** www.express.co.uk
Editor, Peter Hill

DAILY MAIL
Northcliffe House, 2 Derry Street, London W8 5TT **T** 020-7938 6000 **W** www.dailymail.co.uk
Editor, Paul Dacre

DAILY MIRROR
1 Canada Square, Canary Wharf, London E14 5AP **T** 020-7293 3000 **W** www.mirror.co.uk
Editor, Richard Wallace

DAILY RECORD
1 Central Quay, Glasgow G3 8DA **T** 0141-309 3000 **W** www.record-mail.co.uk
Editor, Bruce Waddell

DAILY SPORT
19 Great Ancoats Street, Manchester M60 4BT **T** 0161-236 4466 **W** www.dailysport.co.uk
Editor, Pam McVitie

DAILY STAR
Express Newspapers, Northern & Shell Building, 10 Lower Thames Street, London EC3R 6EN **T** 020-8612 7000 **W** www.dailystar.co.uk
Editor, Dawn Neesom

THE DAILY TELEGRAPH
111 Buckingham Palace Road, London SW1W 0DT **T** 020-7931 2000 **W** www.telegraph.co.uk
Editor, Tony Gallagher

FINANCIAL TIMES
1 Southwark Bridge, London SE1 9HL **T** 020-7873 3000 **W** www.ft.com
Editor, Lionel Barber

THE GUARDIAN
King's Place, 90 York Way, London N1 9GU **T** 020-3353 2000 **W** www.guardian.co.uk, commentisfree.com
Editor, Alan Rusbridger

THE HERALD
Herald & Times Group, 200 Renfield Street, Glasgow G2 3QB **T** 0141-302 7000 **W** www.theherald.co.uk
Editor, Jonathan Russell

THE INDEPENDENT
Northcliffe House, 2 Derry Street, London W8 5TT **T** 020-7005 2000 **W** www.independent.co.uk
Editor-in-Chief, Simon Kelner

MORNING STAR
People's Press Printing Society Ltd, William Rust House, 52 Beachey Road, London E3 2NS **T** 020-8510 0815 **W** www.morningstaronline.co.uk
Editor, Bill Benfield

THE SCOTSMAN
Barclay House, 108 Holyrood Road, Edinburgh EH8 8AS **T** 0131-620 8620 **W** www.scotsman.com
Editor, John McLellan

THE SUN
News Group Newspapers Ltd, 1 Virginia Street, London E1 9XP **T** 020-7782 4000 **W** www.the-sun.co.uk
Editor, Dominic Mohan

THE TIMES
1 Pennington Street, London E98 1TT **T** 020-7782 5000 **W** www.timesonline.co.uk
Editor, James Harding

WEEKLY NEWSPAPERS

DAILY STAR SUNDAY
Express Newspapers, The Northern and Shell Building, 10 Lower Thames Street, London EC3R 6EN **T** 0871-520 7424 **W** www.dailystarsunday.co.uk
Editor, Gareth Morgan

INDEPENDENT ON SUNDAY
Northcliffe House, 2 Derry Street, London W8 5TT **T** 020-7005 2000 **W** www.independent.co.uk
Executive Editor, Lisa Markwell

MAIL ON SUNDAY
Northcliffe House, 2 Derry Street, London W8 5TT **T** 020-7938 6000 **W** www.mailonsunday.co.uk
Editor, Peter Wright

NEWS OF THE WORLD
1 Virginia Street, London E98 1NW **T** 020-7782 4000 **W** www.newsoftheworld.co.uk, www.notw.co.uk
Editor, Colin Myler

THE OBSERVER
Kings Place, 90 York Way, London N1 9GU **T** 020-3353 2000 **W** www.observer.co.uk
Editor, John Mulholland

THE PEOPLE
1 Canada Square, Canary Wharf, London E14 5AP **T** 020-7293 3000 **W** www.people.co.uk
Editor, Lloyd Embley

SCOTLAND ON SUNDAY
108 Holyrood Road, Edinburgh EH8 8AS **T** 0131-620 8620 **W** www.scotlandonsunday.co.uk
Editor, Ian Stewart

SUNDAY EXPRESS
Northern & Shell Building, 10 Lower Thames Street, London EC4R 6EN **T** 020-8612 7000 **W** www.express.co.uk/Sunday
Editor, Martin Townsend

SUNDAY HERALD
200 Renfield Street, Glasgow G2 3QB **T** 0141-302 7800 **W** www.sundayherald.com
Editor, Richard Walker

SUNDAY MAIL
1 Central Quay, Glasgow G3 8DA **T** 0141-309 3000 **W** www.sundaymail.com
Editor, Allan Rennie

SUNDAY MIRROR
1 Canada Square, Canary Wharf, London E14 5AP **T** 020-7293 3000 **W** www.sundaymirror.co.uk
Editor, Tina Weaver

SUNDAY POST
D.C. Thomson & Co. Ltd, 144 Port Dundas Road, Glasgow G4 0HZ **T** 0141-332 9933 **W** www.sundaypost.com
Editor, Donald Martin

SUNDAY TELEGRAPH
111 Buckingham Palace Road, London SW1W 0DT **T** 020-7931 2000 **W** www.telegraph.co.uk
Editor, Ian MacGregor

THE SUNDAY TIMES
1 Pennington Street, London E98 1ST **T** 020-7782 5000 **W** www.sunday-times.co.uk
Editor, John Witherow

THE SUNDAY TIMES SCOTLAND
6th Floor, Guildhall, 57 Queen Street, Glasgow G1 3EN **T** 0141-420 5100 **W** www.timesonline.co.uk
Editor, Carlos Alba

WALES ON SUNDAY
6 Park Street, Cardiff CF10 1XR **T** 029-2024 3600
W www.icwales.co.uk
Editor, Tim Gordon

REGIONAL DAILY NEWSPAPERS

EAST ANGLIA

CAMBRIDGE EVENING NEWS
Winship Road, Milton, Cambs. CB24 6PP **T** 01223-434437
W www.cambridge-news.co.uk
Group Editor-in-Chief, Colin Grant

EAST ANGLIAN DAILY TIMES
30 Lower Brook Street, Ipswich, Suffolk IP4 1AN
T 01473-230023 **W** www.eadt.co.uk
Editor, Terry Hunt

EASTERN DAILY PRESS
Prospect House, Rouen Road, Norwich NR1 1RE
T 01603-628311 **W** www.edp24.co.uk
Editor, Peter Waters

EVENING STAR
Archant Regional, Press House, 30 Lower Brook Street, Ipswich, Suffolk IP4 1AN **T** 01473-230023 **W** www.eveningstar.co.uk
Editor, Nigel Pickoner

NORWICH EVENING NEWS
Prospect House, Rouen Road, Norwich NR1 1RE
T 01603-628311 **W** www.eveningnews24.co.uk
Editor, Tim Williams

EAST MIDLANDS

BURTON MAIL
Burton Daily Mail Ltd, 65–68 High Street, Burton on Trent DE14 1LE **T** 01283-524855 **W** www.burtonmail.co.uk
Editor, Andy Parker

CHRONICLE & ECHO, NORTHAMPTON
Northamptonshire Newspapers Ltd, Upper Mounts, Northampton NN1 3HR **T** 01604-467000
Editor, David Summers

DERBY EVENING TELEGRAPH
Northcliffe House, Meadow Road, Derby DE1 2BH
T 01332-291111 **W** www.thisisderbyshire.co.uk
Editor, Steve Hall

THE LEICESTER MERCURY
St George Street, Leicester LE1 9FQ **T** 0116-251 2512
W www.thisisleicestershire.co.uk
Editor, Keith Perch

LINCOLNSHIRE ECHO
Brayford Wharf East, Lincoln LN5 7AT **T** 01522-820000
W www.thisislincolnshire.co.uk
Editor, Jon Grubb

NOTTINGHAM EVENING POST
Castle Wharf House, Nottingham NG1 7EU **T** 0115-948 2000
W www.thisisnottingham.co.uk
Editor, Malcolm Pheby

LONDON

EVENING STANDARD
Northcliffe House, 2 Derry Street, London W8 5EE
T 020-3367 7000 **W** www.thisislondon.com
Editor, Geordie Greig

METRO
Northcliffe House, 2 Derry Street, London W8 5TT
T 020-7651 5200 **W** www.metro.co.uk
Editor, Sarah Getty

NORTH EAST

EVENING CHRONICLE
ncjMedia Ltd, Groat Market, Newcastle upon Tyne NE1 1ED
T 0191-232 7500 **W** www.chroniclelive.co.uk
Editor, Paul Robertson

EVENING GAZETTE
Gazette Media Company Ltd, 105–111 Borough Road, Middlesbrough TS1 3AZ **T** 01642-245401
W www.gazettelive.co.uk
Editor, Darren Thwaites

HARTLEPOOL MAIL
Northeast Press Ltd, New Clarence House, Wesley Square, Hartlepool TS24 8BX **T** 01429-239333
W www.hartlepoolmail.co.uk, www.peterleemail.co.uk
Editor, Joy Yates

THE JOURNAL
Groat Market, Newcastle upon Tyne NE1 1ED **T** 0191-232 7500
W www.journallive.co.uk
Editor, Brian Aitken

THE NORTHERN ECHO
Priestgate, Darlington, Co. Durham DL1 1NF **T** 01325-381313
W www.thenorthernecho.co.uk
Editor, Peter Barron

THE SHIELDS GAZETTE
Chapter Row, South Shields, Tyne & Wear NE33 1BL
T 0191-427 4800 **W** www.shieldsgazette.com
Editor, John Szymanski

THE SUNDAY SUN
Groat Market, Newcastle upon Tyne NE1 1ED **T** 0191-201 6201
W www.sundaysun.co.uk
Editor, Colin Patterson

SUNDERLAND ECHO
Echo House, Pennywell, Sunderland, Tyne & Wear SR4 9ER
T 0191-501 5800 **W** www.sunderlandecho.com
Editor, Rob Lawson

NORTH WEST

THE BLACKPOOL GAZETTE
Blackpool Gazette & Herald Ltd, Avroe House, Avroe Crescent, Blackpool Business Park, Squires Gate, Blackpool FY4 2DP
T 01253-400888 **W** www.blackpoolgazette.co.uk
Editor, David Helliwell

THE BOLTON NEWS
Newspaper House, Churchgate, Bolton, Lancs. BL1 1DE
T 01204-537270 **W** www.thisisbolton.co.uk
Editor-in-Chief, Ian Savage

CARLISLE NEWS AND STAR
CN Group, Newspaper House, Dalston Road, Carlisle CA2 5UA
T 01228-612600 **W** www.newsandstar.co.uk
Editorial Director, Neil Hodgkinson

LANCASHIRE EVENING POST
Oliver's Place, Preston PR2 9ZA **T** 01772-254841
W www.lep.co.uk
Editor, Simon Reynolds

LANCASHIRE TELEGRAPH
Newspaper House, High Street, Blackburn, Lancs. BB1 1HT **T** 01254-678678
W www.lancashiretelegraph.co.uk
Editor, Kevin Young

LIVERPOOL DAILY POST
PO Box 48, Old Hall Street, Liverpool L69 3EB **T** 0151-227 2000
W www.liverpooldailypost.co.uk
Editor, Mark Thomas

LIVERPOOL ECHO
PO Box 48, Old Hall Street, Liverpool L69 3EB **T** 0151-227 2000
W www.liverpoolecho.co.uk
Editor, Alastair Machray

MANCHESTER EVENING NEWS
1 Scott Place, Hardman Street, Manchester M3 3RN
T 0161-832 7200 W www.manchestereveningnews.co.uk
Editor, Paul Horrocks

NORTH-WEST EVENING MAIL
Newspaper House, Abbey Road, Barrow-in-Furness, Cumbria LA14 5QS T 01229-840150 W www.nwemail.co.uk
Editor, Jonathan Lee

OLDHAM EVENING CHRONICLE
PO Box 47, Union Street, Oldham, Lancs. OL1 1EQ
T 0161-633 2121 W www.oldham-chronicle.co.uk
Editor, Jim Williams

SOUTH

THE ARGUS
Argus House, Crowhurst Road, Hollingbury, Brighton BN1 8AR
T 01273-544544 W www.theargus.co.uk
Group Editor, Michael Beard

ECHO
Newspaper House, Chester Hall Lane, Basildon, Essex SS14 3BL
T 01268-522792 W www.echo-news.co.uk
Editor, Martin McNeill

MEDWAY MESSENGER
Medway House, Ginsbury Close, Sir Thomas Longley Road, Medway City Estate, Strood, Kent ME2 4DU
T 01634-227800 W www.kentonline.co.uk
Editor, Bob Bounds

THE NEWS, PORTSMOUTH
The News Centre, London Road, Hilsea, Portsmouth PO2 9SX
T 023-9266 4488 W www.portsmouth.co.uk
Editor, Mark Waldron

OXFORD MAIL
Newspaper House, Osney Mead, Oxford OX2 0EJ
T 01865-425262 W www.oxfordmail.co.uk
Editor, Simon O'Neill

READING EVENING POST
8 Tessa Road, Reading, Berks. RG1 8NS T 0118-918 3000
W www.getreading.co.uk
Editor, Andy Murrill

THE SOUTHERN DAILY ECHO
Newspaper House, Test Lane, Redbridge, Southampton SO16 9JX T 023-8042 4777 W www.dailyecho.co.uk
Editor, Ian Murray

SOUTH WEST

BRISTOL EVENING POST
Temple Way, Old Market, Bristol BS99 7HD T 0117-934 3000
W www.thisisbristol.co.uk
Editor-in-chief, Mike Norton

THE CITIZEN
1 Clarence Parade, Cheltenham GL50 3NY T 01452-420621
W www.thisisgloucestershire.co.uk
Editor, Ian Mean

DAILY ECHO
Richmond Hill, Bournemouth BH2 6HH T 01202-554601
W www.bournemouthecho.co.uk
Editor, Neal Butterworth

DORSET ECHO
Fleet House, Hampshire Road, Weymouth, Dorset DT4 9XD
T 01305-830930 W www.thisisweymouth.co.uk
Editor, Toby Granville

EXPRESS & ECHO
Express & Echo News & Media, Heron Road, Sowton, Exeter EX2 7NF T 01392-442211 W www.thisisexeter.co.uk
Editor, Marc Astley

GLOUCESTERSHIRE ECHO
1 Clarence Parade, Cheltenham, Glos. GL50 3NY
T 01242-271900 W www.thisisgloucestershire.co.uk
Editor, Kevan Blackadder

THE HERALD
17 Brest Road, Derriford Business Park, Plymouth PL6 5AA
T 01752-765500 W www.thisisplymouth.co.uk
Editor, Bill Martin

HERALD EXPRESS
Harmsworth House, Barton Hill Road, Torquay, Devon TQ2 8JN
T 01803-676000 W www.thisissouthdevon.co.uk
Editor, Andy Phelan

SUNDAY INDEPENDENT
The Sunday Independent Newspapers Ltd, Webbs House, Tindle Suite, Liskeard, Cornwall PL14 6AH
T 01579-342174
Editor, John Noble

SWINDON ADVERTISER
100 Victoria Road, Old Town, Swindon SN1 3BE
T 01793-528144 W www.swindonadvertiser.co.uk
Editor, Dave King

WESTERN DAILY PRESS
Bristol Evening Post and Press Ltd, Temple Way, Bristol BS99 7HD T 0117-934 3000
W www.westerndailypress.co.uk
Editor, Tim Dixon

THE WESTERN MORNING NEWS
17 Brest Road, Derriford, Plymouth PL6 5AA T 01752-765500
W www.thisiswesternmorningnews.co.uk
Editor, Alan Qualtrough

WEST MIDLANDS

BIRMINGHAM MAIL
6th Floor, Fort Dunlop, Fort Parkway, Birmingham B24 9FF
T 0121-236 3366 W www.birminghammail.net
Editor, David Brookes

THE BIRMINGHAM POST
6th Floor, Fort Dunlop, Fort Parkway, Birmingham B24 9FF
T 0121-234 5301 W www.birminghampost.net
Editor, David Brookes

COVENTRY TELEGRAPH
Corporation Street, Coventry CV1 1FP T 024-7663 3633
W www.coventrytelegraph.net
Editor, Darren Parkin

EXPRESS & STAR
Queen Street, Wolverhampton WV1 1ES T 01902-313131
W www.expressandstar.com
Editor, Adrian Faber

THE SENTINEL
Staffordshire Sentinel News & Media Ltd, Sentinel House, Etruria, Stoke-on-Trent ST1 5SS
T 01782-602525 W www.thisisthesentinel.co.uk
Editor, Michael Sassi

SHROPSHIRE STAR
Waterloo Road, Ketley, Telford TF1 5HU T 01952-242424
W www.shropshirestar.com
Editor, Sarah Jane Smith

WORCESTER NEWS
Berrows House, Hylton Road, Worcester WR2 5JX
T 01905-748200 W www.worcesternews.co.uk
Editor, Kevin Ward

YORKSHIRE AND HUMBERSIDE

EVENING COURIER
PO Box 19, King Cross Street, Halifax HX1 2SF T 01422-260200
W www.halifaxcourier.co.uk
Editor, John Furbisher

EVENING NEWS
17–23 Aberdeen Walk, Scarborough, North Yorkshire YO11 1BB T 01723-363636
W www.scarborougheveningnews.co.uk
Editor, Ed Asquith

GRIMSBY TELEGRAPH
80 Cleethorpe Road, Grimsby, North East Lincolnshire DN31 3EH **T** 01472-360360 **W** www.thisisgrimsby.co.uk
Editor, Michelle Lalor

THE HUDDERSFIELD DAILY EXAMINER
Trinity Mirror Huddersfield Ltd, Queen Street South, Huddersfield HD1 3DU **T** 01484-430000 **W** www.examiner.co.uk
Editor, Roy Wright

HULL DAILY MAIL
Blundell's Corner, Beverley Road, Hull HU3 1XS **T** 01482-327111 **W** www.thisishullandeastriding.co.uk
Editor, John Meehan

THE PRESS
Newsquest York, PO Box 29, 76–86 Walmgate, York YO1 9YN **T** 01904-653051 **W** www.yorkpress.co.uk
Managing Editor, Steve Hughes

SHEFFIELD STAR
York Street, Sheffield S1 1PU **T** 0114-276 7676 **W** www.thestar.co.uk
Editor, Alan Powell

TELEGRAPH & ARGUS
Hall Ings, Bradford BD1 1JR **T** 01274-729511 **W** www.thetelegraphandargus.co.uk
Editor, Perry Austin-Clarke

YORKSHIRE EVENING POST
PO Box 168, Wellington Street, Leeds LS1 1RF **T** 0113-2432701 **W** www.yorkshireeveningpost.co.uk
Editor, Paul Napier

YORKSHIRE POST
Wellington Street, Leeds LS1 1RF **T** 0113-243 2701 **W** www.yorkshirepost.co.uk
Editor, Peter Charlton

SCOTLAND

THE COURIER AND ADVERTISER
D.C. Thomson & Co. Ltd, 80 Kingsway East, Dundee DD4 8SL **T** 01382-223131 **W** www.thecourier.co.uk
Editor, Bill Hutcheon

DUNDEE EVENING TELEGRAPH AND POST
80 Kingsway East, Dundee DD4 8SL **T** 01382-223131 **W** www.eveningtelegraph.co.uk

EVENING EXPRESS
Aberdeen Journals Ltd, PO Box 43, Lang Stracht, Mastrick, Aberdeen AB15 6DF **T** 01224-690222 **W** www.eveningexpress.co.uk
Editor, Damian Bates

EVENING NEWS
108 Holyrood Road, Edinburgh EH8 8AS **T** 0131-620 8620 **W** www.edinburghnews.com
Editor, Tom Little

GLASGOW EVENING TIMES
200 Renfield Street, Glasgow G2 3QB **T** 0141-302 7000 **W** www.eveningtimes.co.uk
Editor, Tony Carlin

INVERNESS COURIER
New Century House, Stadium Road, Inverness IV1 1FG **T** 01463-233059 **W** www.inverness-courier.co.uk
Editor, Robert Taylor

PAISLEY DAILY EXPRESS
Scottish and Universal Newspapers Ltd, 14 New Street, Paisley, Renfrewshire PA1 1YA **T** 0141-887 7911 **W** www.paisleydailyexpress.co.uk
Editor, Anne Dalrymple

THE PRESS AND JOURNAL
Lang Stracht, Aberdeen AB15 6DF **T** 01224-690222 **W** www.pressandjournal.co.uk
Editor, Derek Tucker

WALES

THE LEADER
NWN Media Ltd, Mold Business Park, Wrexham Road, Mold, Flintshire CH7 1XY **T** 01352-707707 **W** www.leaderlive.co.uk
Editor, Barrie Jones

SOUTH WALES ARGUS
South Wales Argus, Cardiff Road, Maesglas, Newport, Gwent NP20 3QN **T** 01633-810000 **W** www.southwalesargus.co.uk
Editor, Gerry Keighley

SOUTH WALES ECHO
6 Park Street, Cardiff CF10 1XR **T** 02920-223333 **W** www.walesonline.co.uk
Editor, Mike Hill

SOUTH WALES EVENING POST
PO Box 14, Adelaide Street, Swansea SA1 1QT **T** 01792-510000 **W** www.thisissouthwales.co.uk
Editor-in-Chief, Spencer Feeney

WESTERN MAIL
6 Park Street, Cardiff CF10 1XR **T** 029-2022 3333 **W** www.walesonline.co.uk
Editor, Alan Edmunds

NORTHERN IRELAND

BELFAST TELEGRAPH
124–144 Royal Avenue, Belfast BT1 1EB **T** 028-9026 4000 **W** www.belfasttelegraph.co.uk
Editor, Mike Gilson

IRISH NEWS
113–117 Donegall Street, Belfast BT1 2GE **T** 028-9032 2226 **W** www.irishnews.com
Editor, Noel Doran

NEWS LETTER
2 Esky Drive, Portadown, Craigavon, Belfast BT63 5YY **T** 028-9089 7720 **W** www.newsletter.co.uk
Editor, Darwin Templeton

SUNDAY LIFE
124–144 Royal Avenue, Belfast BT1 1EB **T** 028-9026 4000 **W** www.sundaylife.co.uk
Editor, Martin Breen

CHANNEL ISLANDS

GUERNSEY PRESS AND STAR
PO Box 57, Braye Road, Vale, Guernsey GY1 3BW **T** 01481-240240 **W** www.guernseypress.com
Editor, Richard Digard

JERSEY EVENING POST
PO Box 582, Five Oaks, St Saviour, Jersey JE4 8XQ **T** 01534-611611 **W** www.thisisjersey.com
Editor, Chris Bright

PERIODICALS

ACCOUNTANCY AGE
Incisive Media, 32–34 Broadwick Street, London W1A 2HG **T** 020-7316 9000 **W** www.accountancyage.com
Editor, Gavin Hinks

ACCOUNTING & BUSINESS
Association of Chartered Certified Accountants, 29 Lincolns Inn Fields, London WC2A 3EE **T** 020-7059 5000 **W** www.accaglobal.com
Editor, Chris Quick

AEROPLANE MONTHLY
IPC Media Ltd, The Blue Fin Building, 110 Southwark Street, London SE1 0SU **T** 020-3148 4100 **W** www.aeroplanemonthly.com
Editor, Michael Oakey

AESTHETICA MAGAZINE
PO Box 371, York YO23 1WL **T** 01904-479168
W www.aestheticamagazine.com
Editor, Cherie Federico

AFRICA CONFIDENTIAL
Asempa Ltd, 73 Farringdon Road, London EC1M 3JQ
T 020-7831 3511 **W** www.africa-confidential.com
Editor, Patrick Smith

ALL OUT CRICKET
Unit 3–23 Kennington Court, 1–3 Brixton Road, London SW9 6DE **T** 020-3176 0187
W www.alloutcricket.com
Editor, Andy Afford

AMATEUR PHOTOGRAPHER
IPC Media, The Blue Fin Building, 110 Southwark Street, London SE1 0SU **T** 020-3148 5000
W www.amateurphotographer.co.uk
Editor, Damien Demolder

AMBIT
17 Priory Gardens, London N6 5QY **T** 020-8340 3566
W www.ambitmagazine.co.uk
Editor, Martin Bax

ANGLING TIMES
Bauer Consumer Media, Bushfield House, Orton Centre, Peterborough PE2 5UW **T** 01733-395106
W www.gofishing.co.uk/Angling-Times
Editor, Richard Lee

APOLLO
22 Old Queen Street, London SW1H 9HP **T** 020-7961 0150
W www.apollo-magazine.com
Editor, Oscar Humphries

THE ARCHITECTS' JOURNAL
EMAP Construct, Greater London House, Hampstead Road, London NW1 7EJ **T** 020-7728 5000
W www.architectsjournal.co.uk
Editor, Kieran Long

THE ARCHITECTURAL REVIEW
EMAP Construct, Greater London House, Hampstead Road, London NW1 7EJ **T** 020-7728 4591
W www.arplus.com
Editor-in-Chief, Kieran Long

ART MONTHLY
4th Floor, 28 Charing Cross Road, London WC2H 0DB
T 020-7240 0389 **W** www.artmonthly.co.uk
Editor, Patricia Bickers

THE ART NEWSPAPER
70 South Lambeth Road, London SW8 1RL **T** 020-7735 3331
W www.theartnewspaper.com
Editor, Jane Morris

ART QUARTERLY
The Art Fund, Millais House, 7 Cromwell Place, London SW7 2JN **T** 020-7225 4800 **W** www.artfund.org
Editor, Caroline Bugler

ARTISTS & ILLUSTRATORS
26–30 Old Church Street, London SW3 5BY **T** 020-7349 3150
W www.artistsandillustrators.co.uk
Editor, Steve Pill

ASTRONOMY NOW
Pole Star Publications, PO Box 175, Tonbridge, Kent TN10 4ZY
T 01732-446110 **W** www.astronomynow.com
Editor, Keith Cooper

ATTITUDE
Ground Floor, 211 Old Street, London EC1V 9NR
T 020-7608 6446 **W** www.attitude.co.uk
Editor, Matthew Todd

THE BEANO
D.C. Thomson & Co. Ltd, 80 Kingsway East, Dundee DD4 8SL
Editor, Alan Digby

THE BIG ISSUE
1–5 Wandsworth Road, London SW8 2LN **T** 020-7526 3200
W www.bigissue.com
Editor-in-Chief, Charles Howgego

BIKE
Bauer Consumer Media, Media House, Lynchwood, Peterborough PE2 6EA **T** 01733-468181
W www.bikemagazine.co.uk
Editor, Tim Thompson

BIRDWATCH
Solo Publishing Ltd, The Chocolate Factory, 5 Clarendon Road, London N22 6XJ **T** 020-8881 0550 **W** www.birdwatch.co.uk
Editor, Dominic Mitchell

THE BOOKSELLER
VNU Entertainment Media Ltd, 5th Floor, Endeavour House, 189 Shaftesbury Avenue, London WC2H 8TJ
T 020-7420 6006 **W** www.thebookseller.com
Editor-in-Chief, Neill Denny

BRITISH CHESS MAGAZINE
44 Baker Street, London W1U 7RT **T** 020-7486 8222
W www.bcmchess.co.uk
Editor, John Saunders

THE BRITISH JOURNAL OF PHOTOGRAPHY
32–34 Broadwick Street, London W1A 2HG **T** 020-7316 9000
W www.bjp-online.com
Editor, Simon Bainbridge

BRITISH JOURNALISM REVIEW
Sage Publications, 1 Oliver's Yard, 55 City Road, London EC1Y 1SP **T** 020-7324 8500 **W** www.bjr.org.uk
Editor, Bill Hagerty

BRITISH MEDICAL JOURNAL
BMJ Publishing Group, BMA House, Tavistock Square, London WC1H 9JR **T** 020-7387 4499 **W** www.bmj.com
Editor, Dr Fiona Godlee

BRITISH PHILATELIC BULLETIN
Royal Mail, 35–50 Rathbone Place, London W1T 1HQ
W www.royalmail.com/stamps
Editor, J. R. Holman

BUILDING DESIGN
UBM Information Ltd, Ludgate House, 245 Blackfriars Road, London SE1 9UY **T** 020-7921 5000 **W** www.bdonline.co.uk
Editor, Amanda Baillieu

CANALS & RIVERS
PO Box 618, Norwich NR7 0QT **T** 01603-708930
W www.canalsandrivers.co.uk
Editor, Chris Cattrall

CAR
Bauer Consumer Media, 3rd Floor, Media House, Lynchwood, Peterborough PE2 6EA **T** 01733-468379
Editor, Phil McNamara

CARING BUSINESS
CMP Information, Ludgate House, 245 Blackfriars Road, London SE1 9UY **T** 020-7921 8502
W www.caringbusiness.co.uk
Editor, Olufunmi Majekodunmi

CHURCH TIMES
13–17 Long Lane, London EC1A 9DJ **T** 020-7776 1060
W www.churchtimes.co.uk
Editor, Paul Handley

CLASSIC CARS
Bauer Consumer Media, Media House, Lynchwood, Peterborough Business Park, Peterborough PE2 6EA
T 01733-468000 **W** www.classiccarsmagazine.co.uk
Editor, Phil Bell

CLASSIC ROCK
Future Publishing Ltd, 30 Monmouth Street, Bath BA1 2BW
T 01225-442244 **W** www.classicrockmagazine.com
Editor in Chief, Scott Rowley

CLASSICAL MUSIC
Rhinegold Publishing Ltd, 241 Shaftesbury Avenue, London WC2H 8TF **T** 020-7333 1742 **W** www.rhinegold.co.uk
Editor, Keith Clarke

CLIMB MAGAZINE
PO Box 21, Buxton, Derbyshire SK17 9BR **T** 01298-72801 **W** www.climbmagazine.com
Editor, Neil Pearsons

COIN NEWS
Token Publishing Ltd, Orchard House, Duchy Road, Heathpark, Honiton, Devon EX14 1YD **T** 01404-46972
Editor, John W. Mussell

COMMUNITY CARE
Reed Business Information Ltd, Quadrant House, The Quadrant, Sutton, Surrey SM2 5AS **T** 020-8652 3500 **W** www.communitycare.co.uk
Editor, Bronagh Miskelly

CONDÉ NAST TRAVELLER
Vogue House, Hanover Square, London W1S 1JU **T** 020-7499 9080 **W** www.cntraveller.com
Editor, Sarah Miller

CONTEMPORARY
Studio 56, 4 Montpelier Street, London SW7 1EE **T** 020-7019 6205 **W** www.contemporary-magazine.com
Editor, Brian Muller

CONTEMPORARY REVIEW
Contemporary Review Co. Ltd, PO Box 1242, Oxford OX1 4FJ **T** 01865-201529 **W** www.contemporaryreview.co.uk
Editor, Dr Richard Mullen

COSMOPOLITAN
National Magazine House, 72 Broadwick Street, London W1F 9EP **T** 020-7439 5000
Editor-in-Chief, Louise Court

COUNTRY LIFE
IPC Media Ltd, The Blue Fin Building, 110 Southwark Street, London SE1 0SU **T** 020-3148 5000 **W** www.countrylife.co.uk
Editor, Mark Hedges

CYCLING WEEKLY
IPC Media, Leon House, 233 High Street, Croydon CR9 1HZ **T** 020-8726 8462 **W** www.cyclingweekly.co.uk
Editor, Robert Garbutt

DANCING TIMES
The Dancing Times Ltd, 45–47 Clerkenwell Green, London EC1R 0EB **T** 020-7250 3006 **W** www.dancing-times.co.uk
Editor, Jonathan Gray

THE DANDY
D.C. Thomson & Co. Ltd, Albert Square, Dundee DD1 9QJ **T** 01382-223131
Editor, Craig Graham

DARTS WORLD
MB Graphics, 25 Orlestone View, Ham Street, Ashford, Kent TN26 2LB **T** 01233-733558 **W** www.dartsworld.com
Editor, Michael Beeken

DIGITAL CAMERA
Future Publishing Ltd, 30 Monmouth Street, Bath BA1 2BW **W** www.dcmag.co.uk
Editor, Geoff Harris

DISABILITY NOW
6 Market Road, London N7 9PW **T** 020-7619 7323 **W** www.disabilitynow.org.uk
Editor, Ian Macrae

THE ECOLOGIST
Unit 102, Lana House Studios, 116–118 Commercial Street, London E1 6NF **T** 020-7422 8100 **W** www.theecologist.org
Editor, Mark Anslow

THE ECONOMIST
25 St James's Street, London SW1A 1HG **T** 020-7830 7000 **W** www.economist.com
Editor, John Micklethwait

EMPIRE
Bauer Consumer Media, Mappin House, 4 Winsley Street, London W1W 8HF **T** 020-7182 8000 **W** www.empireonline.com
Editor, Mark Dinning

THE ENGINEER
Centaur Communications Ltd, St Giles House, 50 Poland Street, London W1F 7AX **T** 020-7970 4437 **W** www.theengineer.com
Editor, Jon Excell

ESQUIRE
National Magazine House, 72 Broadwick Street, London W1F 9EP **T** 020-7439 5000 **W** www.esquire.co.uk
Editor, Jeremy Langmead

ESSENTIALS
IPC Media, The Blue Fin Building, 110 Southwark Street, London SE1 0SU **T** 020-3148 7211
Editor, Jules Barton-Breck

FAMILY TREE
61 Great Whyte, Ramsey, Huntingdon, Cambs PE26 1HJ **T** 01487-814050 **W** www.family-tree.co.uk
Editor, Helen Tovey

FARMERS WEEKLY
Reed Business Information, Quadrant House, The Quadrant, Sutton, Surrey SM2 5AS **T** 020-8652 4911 **W** www.fwi.co.uk
Editor, Jane King

THE FEMINIST REVIEW
Palgrave Macmillan Ltd, Brunel Road, Houndmills, Basingstoke, Hants RG21 6XS **T** 01256-329242 **W** www.feminist-review.com
Editors, a collective

FHM (FOR HIM MAGAZINE)
Bauer Consumer Media, Endeavour House, 189 Shaftesbury Avenue, London WC2H 8JG **T** 020-7182 8000 **W** www.fhm.com
Editor, Anthony Noguera

THE FIELD
IPC Inspire, The Blue Fin Building, 110 Southwark Street, London SE1 0SU **T** 020-3148 5000 **W** www.thefield.co.uk
Editor, Jonathan Young

FOLIO
2nd Floor, Bristol News and Media, Temple Way, Bristol BS99 7HD **T** 0117-942 8491 **W** www.foliomagazine.co.uk
Editor, Mike Gartside

FORTEAN TIMES
Box 2409, London NW5 4NP **T** 020-7907 6235 **W** www.forteantimes.com
Editor, David Sutton

FORTNIGHT
11 University Road, Belfast BT7 1NA **T** 028-9023 2353 **W** www.fortnight.org
Editor, Rudie Goldsmith

FOURFOURTWO
Haymarket, Teddington Studios, Broom Road, Teddington, Middlesex TW11 9BE **T** 020-8267 5848 **W** www.fourfourtwo.magazine.co.uk
Editor, David Hall

FRIEZE
81 Rivington Street, London EC2A 3AY **T** 020-3372 6111 **W** www.frieze.com

GAMESMASTER
Future Publishing Ltd, 30 Monmouth Street, Bath BA1 2BW T 01225-442244
Editor-in-Chief, Robin Alway

GAY TIMES – GT
Spectrum House, 32–34 Gordon House Road, London NW5 1LP T 020-7424 7400 W www.gaytimes.co.uk
Editor, Joseph Galliano

GEOGRAPHICAL JOURNAL
1 Kensington Gore, London SW7 2AR T 020-7591 3026
Editor, Prof. Klaus Dodds

GLAMOUR
6–8 Old Bond Street, London W1S 4PH T 020-7499 9080 W www.glamourmagazine.com
Editor, Jo Elvin

GOLF WORLD
Bauer Media, Media House, Lynchwood, Peterborough Business Park, Peterborough PE2 6EA T 01733-468000 W www.golf-world.co.uk
Editor, Chris Jones

GOOD HOUSEKEEPING
National Magazine House, 72 Broadwick Street, London W1F 9EP T 020-7439 5000 W www.goodhousekeeping.co.uk
Editor, Rosemary Ellis

GQ
Condé Nast Publications, Vogue House, Hanover Square, London W1S 1JU T 020-7499 9080 W www.gq-magazine.co.uk
Editor, Dylan Jones

GRANTA
12 Addison Avenue, London W11 4QR T 020-7605 1360 W www.granta.com
Editor, John Freeman

GREEN FUTURES
Overseas House, 19–23 Ironmonger Row, London EC1V 3QN W www.greenfutures.org.uk
Editor-in-Chief, Martin Wright

GROW YOUR OWN
25 Phoenix Court, Hawkins Road, Colchester CO2 8JY T 01206-505979 W www.growfruitandveg.co.uk
Editor, Lucy Halsall

GUITARIST
Future Publishing UK, 30 Monmouth Street, Bath BA1 2BW T 01225-442244 W www.futurenet.co.uk
Editor, Mick Taylor

HARPER'S BAZAAR
National Magazine House, 72 Broadwick Street, London W1F 9EP T 020-7439 5000 W www.natmags.co.uk
Editor, Lucy Yeomans

HEALTHY
1 Neal Street, London WC2H 9QL T 020-7306 0304 W www.healthy-magazine.co.uk
Editor, Jane Druker

HEAT
Bauer Consumer Media, Endeavour House, 189 Shaftesbury Avenue, London WC2H 8JG T 020-7437 9011 W www.heatworld.com
Editor, Sam Delaney

HELLO!
Wellington House, 69–71 Upper Ground, London SE1 9PQ T 020-7667 8700
Editor-in-Chief, Eduardo Sanchez Perez

HISTORY TODAY
20 Old Compton Street, London W1D 4TW T 020-7534 8000 W www.historytoday.com
Editor, Paul Lay

HOMES AND GARDENS
IPC Magazines Ltd, The Blue Fin Building, 110 Southwark Street, London SE1 0SU T 020-3148 5000 W www.homesandgardens.com
Editor, Deborah Barker

HORSE & HOUND
IPC Inspire, 9th Floor, The Blue Fin Building, 110 Southwark Street, London SE1 0SU T 020-3148 4562 W www.horseandhound.co.uk
Editor, Lucy Higginson

HOUSE & GARDEN
Vogue House, 1 Hanover Square, London W1S 1JU T 020-7499 9080
Editor, Susan Crewe

ICON MAGAZINE
Media 10, National House, High Street, Epping, Essex CM16 4BD T 01992-570030 W www.iconeye.com
Editor, Justin McGuirk

IN STYLE
IPC Southbank, The Blue Fin Building, 110 Southwark Street, London SE1 0SU T 020-3148 5000
Editor, Eilidh MacAskill

INTERNATIONAL AFFAIRS
The Royal Institute of International Affairs, Chatham House, 10 St James's Square, London SW1Y 4LE T 020-7957 5728
Editor, Caroline Soper

JEWISH CHRONICLE
25 Furnival Street, London EC4A 1JT T 020-7415 1500 W www.thejc.com
Editor, Stephen Pollard

KERRANG!
Bauer Consumer Media, Mappin House, 4 Winsley Street, London W1W 8HF T 020-7182 8406 W www.kerrang.com
Editor, Nichola Browne

LANCET
32 Jamestown Road, London NW1 7BY T 020-7424 4910 W www.thelancet.com
Editor, Dr Richard Horton

THE LAWYER
Centaur Communications Group, St Giles House, 50 Poland Street, London W1F 7AX T 020-7970 4000 W www.thelawyer.com
Editor, Catrin Griffiths

LEGAL WEEK
32–34 Broadwick Street, London W1A 2HG T 020-7316 9000 W www.legalweek.com
Editor, Alex Novarese

THE LIST
14 High Street, Edinburgh EH1 1TE T 0131-550 3050 W www.list.co.uk
Editor, Claire Sawyer

THE LITERARY REVIEW
44 Lexington Street, London W1F 0LW T 020-7437 9392 W www.literaryreview.co.uk
Editor, Nancy Sladek

THE LONDON MAGAZINE: A REVIEW OF LITERATURE AND THE ARTS
Administration Flat 5, 11 Queen's Gate, London SW7 5EL W www.thelondonmagazine.net
Editor, Steven O'Brien

LONDON REVIEW OF BOOKS
28 Little Russell Street, London WC1A 2HN T 020-7209 1101
Editor, Mary-Kay Wilmers

MACWORLD
101 Euston Road, London NW1 2RA T 020-7756 2877 W www.macworld.co.uk
Editor, Karen Haslam

MARIE CLAIRE
European Magazines Ltd, 7th Floor, The Blue Fin Building, 110 Southwark Street, London SE1 0SU **T** 020-3148 7513 **W** www.marieclaire.co.uk
Editor, Trish Halpin

MEDIA WEEK
Haymarket Publishing Ltd, 174 Hammersmith Road, London W6 7JP **T** 020-8267 5000
Editor, Steve Barrett

MEN'S HEALTH
Natmag Rodale Ltd, 33 Broadwick Street, London W1F 0DQ **T** 020-7339 4400 **W** www.menshealth.co.uk
Editor, Morgan Rees

MILITARY MODELLING
PO Box 6017, Leighton Buzzard LU7 2FA **T** 01525-370389 **W** www.militarymodelling.com
Editor, Ken Jones

MOJO
Bauer Consumer Media, Mappin House, 4 Winsley Street, London W1W 8HF **T** 020-7182 8616 **W** www.mojo4music.com
Editor, Phil Alexander

MONEYWISE
Standon House, 21 Mansell Street, London E1 8AA **T** 020-7680 3600 **W** www.moneywise.co.uk
Editor, Johanna Gornitzki

MOTHER & BABY
Endeavour House, 189 Shaftsbury Avenue, London WC2H 8JG **T** 020-7347 1869 **W** www.motherandbabymagazine.com
Editor, Miranda Levy

MSLEXIA
PO Box 656, Newcastle upon Tyne NE99 1PZ **T** 0191-233 3860 **W** www.mslexia.co.uk
Editor, Daneet Steffens

MUSIC WEEK
CMPi, 1st Floor, Ludgate House, 245 Blackfriars Road, London SE1 9UY **W** www.musicweek.com
Editor, Paul Williams

THE NATIONAL TRUST MAGAZINE
The National Trust, Heelis, Kemble Drive, Swindon SN2 2NA **T** 01793-817716 **W** www.nationaltrust.org.uk
Editor, Sue Herdman

NATURE
Macmillan Magazines Ltd, The Macmillan Building, 4 Crinan Street, London N1 9XW **T** 020-7833 4000 **W** www.nature.com/nature
Editor, Philip Campbell

NB MAGAZINE
RNIB, 105 Judd Street, London WC1H 9NE **T** 020-7391 2070
Editor, Ann Lee

NEW HUMANIST
1 Gower Street, London WC1E 6HD **T** 020-7436 1171 **W** www.newhumanist.org.uk
Editor, Caspar Melville

NEW INTERNATIONALIST
55 Rectory Road, Oxford OX4 1BW **T** 01865-811400 **W** www.newint.org
Editors, Vanessa Baird, Chris Bozier, Hadari Ditmars, Dinyar Godrej and Jess Worth

NEW LAW JOURNAL
Lexis Nexis Butterworths, Halsbury House, 35 Chancery Lane, London WC2A 1EL **T** 020-7400 2580 **W** www.newlawjournal.co.uk
Editor, Jan Miller

NEW MUSICAL EXPRESS (NME)
IPC Ignite, The Blue Fin Building, 110 Southwark Street, London SE1 0SU **T** 020-3148 5000
Editor, Krissi Murison

NEW SCIENTIST
Lacon House, 84 Theobalds Road, London WC1X 8NS **T** 020-7611 1200 **W** www.newscientist.com
Editor, Jeremy Webb

NEW STATESMAN
7th Floor, John Carpenter House, John Carpenter Street, London EC4Y 0AN **T** 020-7730 3444 **W** www.newstatesman.co.uk
Editor, Jason Cowley

THE NEWSPAPER
Young Media Holdings Ltd, PO Box 400, Bridgwater TA6 9DT **T** 0845-094 0646 **W** www.thenewspaper.org.uk
Managing Editor, Phil Wood

NOW
IPC Connect, The Blue Fin Building, 110 Southwark Street, London SE1 0SU **T** 020-3148 5000 **W** www.nowmagazine.co.uk
Editor, Abigail Blackburn

OK!
Northern & Shell Building, 10 Lower Thames Street, London EC3R 6EN **T** 0871-434 1010 **W** www.ok-magazine.com
Editor, Lisa Byrne

THE OLDIE
65 Newman Street, London W1T 3EG **T** 020-7436 8801 **W** www.theoldie.co.uk
Editor, Richard Ingrams

OPERA
36 Black Lion Lane, London W6 9BE **T** 020-8563 8893 **W** www.opera.co.uk
Editor, John Allison

OPERA NOW
241 Shaftesbury Avenue, London WC2H 8TF **T** 020-7333 1740 **W** www.rhinegold.co.uk
Editor, Ashutosh Khandekar

PC PRO
Dennis Publishing Ltd, 30 Cleveland Street, London W1T 4JD **T** 020-7907 6000 **W** www.pcpro.co.uk
Editor, Tim Danton

PEACE NEWS
5 Caledonian Road, London N1 9DY **T** 020-7278 3344 **W** www.peacenews.info
Editors, Emily Johns and Milan Rai

THE PHOTOGRAPHER
PO Box 9337, Witham, Essex CM8 2UT **T** 01279-503871 **W** www.bipp.com
Editor, Jonathan Briggs

POETRY LONDON
81 Lambeth Walk, London SE11 6DX **T** 020-7735 8880 **W** www.poetrylondon.co.uk
Editors, Colette Bryce, Tim Dooley, Martha Kapos and Scott Verner

POETRY REVIEW
22 Betterton Street, London WC2H 9BX **T** 020-7420 9883 **W** www.poetrysociety.org.uk
Editor, Fiona Sampson

THE POLITICAL QUARTERLY
Wiley-Blackwell, 9600 Garsington Road, Oxford OX4 2DQ **T** 01865-776868 **W** www.wiley.com
Editors, Andrew Gamble and Tony Wright MP

PRACTICAL PARENTING
Magicalia Limited, 15–18 White Lion Street, Islington, London N1 9PD **T** 020-7843 8800 **W** www.practicalparenting.co.uk
Editor, Daniella Delaney

PRESS GAZETTE
John Carpenter House, John Carpenter Street, London EC4Y 0AN **T** 020-7936 6432 **W** www.pressgazette.co.uk
Editor, Dominic Ponsford

PRIDE
Pride House, 55 Battersea Bridge Road, London SW11 3AX T 020-7228 3110 W www.pridemagazine.com
Publisher, C. Cushnie

PRIVATE EYE
6 Carlisle Street, London W1D 3BN T 020-7437 4017 W www.private-eye.co.uk
Editor, Ian Hislop

PROSPECT MAGAZINE
Prospect Publishing Ltd, 2 Bloomsbury Place, London WC1A 2QA T 020-7255 1281 W www.prospect-magazine.co.uk
Editor, David Goodhart

PSYCHOLOGIES
Hachette Filipacchi UK Ltd, 64 North Row, London W1K 7LL T 020-7150 7000 W www.psychologies.co.uk
Editor, Louise Chunn

PULSE
CMP Medica Ltd, Ludgate House, 245 Blackfriars Road, London SE1 9UY T 020-7921 8102 W www.pulsetoday.co.uk
Editor, Jo Haynes

Q MAGAZINE
Bauer Consumer Media, Mappin House, 4 Winsley Street, London W1W 8HF T 020-7436 1515 W www.q4music.com
Editor, Paul Rees

RA MAGAZINE
Royal Academy of Arts, Burlington House, Piccadilly, London W1J 0BD T 020-7300 5820 W www.ramagazine.org.uk
Acting Editor, Nigel Billen

RACING POST
Floor 23, 1 Canada Square, Canary Wharf, London E14 5AP T 020-7293 3000 W www.racingpost.com
Editor, Bruce Millington

RADIO TIMES
BBC Worldwide Ltd, 201 Wood Lane, London W12 7TQ T 020-8433 3400 W www.radiotimes.com
Editor, Ben Preston

RAILWAY MAGAZINE
IPC Inspire, The Blue Fin Building, 110 Southwark Street, London SE1 0SU T 020-3148 5000 W www.railwaymagazine.co.uk
Editor, Nick Pigott

READER'S DIGEST
The Reader's Digest Association Ltd, 11 Westferry Circus, Canary Wharf, London E14 4HE T 020-7715 8000 W www.readersdigest.co.uk
Editor-in-Chief, Gill Hudson

RED
Hachette Filipacchi UK Ltd, 64 North Row, London W1K 7LL T 020-7150 7600 W www.redmagazine.co.uk
Editor-in-chief, Sam Baker

RED PEPPER
Socialist Newspaper (Publications) Ltd, 1B Waterlow Road, London N19 5NJ W www.redpepper.org.uk
Co-editors, Michael Calderbank, James O'Nions and Hilary Wainwright

RUGBY WORLD
IPC Media Ltd, 9th Floor, The Blue Fin Building, 110 Southwark Street, London SE1 0SU T 020-3148 5000
Editor, Paul Morgan

RUNNER'S WORLD
Natmag Rodale Ltd, 33 Broadwick Street, London W1F 0DG T 020-7339 4400 W www.runnersworld.co.uk
Editor, Andy Dixon

RUSI JOURNAL
Whitehall, London SW1A 2ET T 020-7747 2600 W www.rusi.org
Editor, Dr Ian Kerns

SAGA MAGAZINE
Saga Publishing Ltd, The Saga Building, Enbrook Park, Sandgate, Folkestone, Kent CT20 3SE T 01303-771523
Editor, Katy Bravery

SCREEN INTERNATIONAL
EMAP Media, Greater London House, 1 Hampstead Road, London NW1 7EJ T 020-7728 5000 W www.screendaily.com
Editor, Conor Dignam

SFX MAGAZINE
Future Publishing Ltd, 30 Monmouth Street, Bath BA1 2BW T 01225-442244 W www.sfx.co.uk
Editor, Dave Bradley

SHOOTING TIMES AND COUNTRY MAGAZINE
IPC Inspire, The Blue Fin Building, 110 Southwark Street, London SE1 0SU T 020-3148 4741 W www.shootingtimes.co.uk
Editor, Camilla Clark

SIGHT AND SOUND
BFI, 21 Stephen Street, London W1T 1LN T 020-7255 1444 W www.bfi.org.uk/sightandsound
Editor, Nick James

SNOOKER SCENE
Hayley Green Court, 130 Hagley Road, Halesowen, West Midlands B63 1DY T 0121-585 9188 W www.snookerscene.com
Editor, Clive Everton

SOLICITORS' JOURNAL
Waterlow Professional Publishing, 6–14 Underwood Street, London N1 7JQ T 020-7490 0049 W www.solicitorsjournal.com
Editor, Jean-Yves Gilg

THE SPECTATOR
22 Old Queen Street, London SW1H 9HP T 020-7961 0200 W www.spectator.co.uk
Editor, Fraser Nelson

SPIRIT & DESTINY
H. Bauer Publishing, Academic House, 24–28 Oval Road, London NW1 7DT T 020-7241 8000
Editor, Rhiannon Powell

THE STAGE
Stage House, 47 Bermondsey Street, London SE1 3XT T 020-7403 1818 W www.thestage.co.uk
Editor, Brian Attwood

STAR TREK MAGAZINE
Titan Magazines, Titan House, 144 Southwark Street, London SE1 0UP T 020-7620 0200
Editor, Paul Simpson

STUFF
Haymarket Ltd, Teddington Studios, Broom Road, Teddington, Middlesex TW11 9BE T 020-8267 5036 W www.stuff.tv
Editor, Fraser Macdonald

THE TABLET
1 King Street Cloisters, Clifton Walk, London W6 0GY T 020-8748 8484 W www.thetablet.co.uk
Editor, Catherine Pepinster

TAKE A BREAK
H. Bauer Publishing Ltd, Academic House, 24–28 Oval Road, London NW1 7DT T 020-7241 8000 W www.bauer.com
Editor, John Dale

TATE ETC
20 John Islip Street, London SW1P 4RG T 020-7887 8724 W www.tate.org.uk/tateetc
Editor, Simon Grant

TATLER
Vogue House, Hanover Square, London W1S 1JU T 020-7499 9080 W www.tatler.co.uk
Editor, Catherine Ostler

THE TEACHER
National Union of Teachers, Hamilton House, Mabledon Place, London WC1H 9BD **T** 020-7380 4708
Editor, Elyssa Campbell-Barr

TEMPO
Cambridge University Press, The Edinburgh Building, Shaftesbury Road, Cambridge CB2 8RU
Editor, Calum MacDonald

THE TES
26 Red Lion Square, Holborn WC1R 4HQ **T** 020-3194 3000 **W** www.tes.co.uk
Editor, Gerard Kelly

TGO (THE GREAT OUTDOORS) MAGAZINE
Newsquest, 200 Renfield Street, Glasgow G2 3QB **T** 0141-302 7700 **W** www.tgomagazine.co.uk
Editor, Cameron McNeish

THIRD WAY
13–17 Long Lane, London EC1A 9PN **T** 020-7776 1071 **W** www.thirdway.org.uk
Editor, Simon Jones

TIME OUT
Time Out Group Ltd, Universal House, 251 Tottenham Court Road, London W1T 7AB **T** 020-7813 3000 **W** www.timeout.com
Editor, Mark Frith

TLS (THE TIMES LITERARY SUPPLEMENT)
Times House, 1 Pennington Street, London E98 1BS **T** 020-7782 5000 **W** www.the-tls.co.uk
Editor, Peter Stothard

TOTAL FILM
2 Balcombe Street, London NW1 6NW **T** 020-7042 4000 **W** www.totalfilm.com
Editor, Aubrey Day

TRIBUNE
9 Arkwright Road, London NW3 6AN **T** 020-7433 6410
Editor, Chris McLaughlin

VANITY FAIR
The Condé Nast Publications Ltd, Vogue House, Hanover Square, London W1S 1JU **T** 020-7499 9080 **W** www.vanityfair.co.uk
Editor-in-Chief, Graydon Carter

VENUE
Venue Publishing, Bristol News & Media, Temple Way, Bristol BS99 7HD **T** 0117-942 8491 **W** www.venue.co.uk
Editor, Joe Spurgeon

VIZ
Dennis Publishing, 30 Cleveland Street, London W1T 4JD **T** 020-7907 6000 **W** www.viz.co.uk
Editor, Joel Enos

VOGUE
Vogue House, 1 Hanover Square, London W1S 1JU **T** 020-7499 9080 **W** www.vogue.co.uk
Editor, Alexandra Shulman

THE VOICE
6th Floor, Northern & Shell Tower, 4 Selsdon Way, London E14 9GL **T** 020-7510 0340 **W** www.voice-online.co.uk
Editor, Steve Pope

WALK
The Ramblers' Association, 2nd Floor, Camelford House, 87–90 Albert Embankment, London SE1 7TW **T** 020-7339 8540 **W** www.walkmag.co.uk
Editor, Dominic Bates

WALLPAPER
IPC Media, The Blue Fin Building, 110 Southwark Street, London SE1 0SU **T** 020-3148 5000 **W** www.wallpaper.com
Editor-in-Chief, Tony Chambers

WANDERLUST
PO Box 1832, Windsor SL4 1YT **T** 01753-620426 **W** www.wanderlust.co.uk
Editor, Dan Linstead

WATERWAYS WORLD
Waterways World Ltd, 151 Station Street, Burton-on-Trent DE14 1BG **T** 01283-742950 **W** www.waterwaysworld.com
Editor, Richard Fairhurst

WEDDING MAGAZINE
IPC Southbank, 7th Floor, The Blue Fin Building, 110 Southwark Street, London SE1 0SU **T** 020-3148 7790
Editor, Catherine Westwood

THE WEEK
The Week Ltd, 6th Floor, Compass House, 22 Redan Place, London W2 4SA **T** 020-7907 6180 **W** www.theweek.co.uk
Editor-in-chief, Jeremy O'Grady

WEIGHT WATCHERS MAGAZINE
River Publishing Ltd, 1 Neal Street, London WC2H 9QL **T** 020-7306 0304
Editor, Mary Frances

WHAT CAR?
Haymarket Motoring Magazines Ltd, Teddington Studios, Broom Road, Teddington, Middlesex TW11 9BE **T** 020-8267 5688 **W** www.whatcar.com
Group Editor, Steve Fowler

THE WISDEN CRICKETER
2nd Floor, 123 Buckingham Palace Road, London SW1W 9SL **T** 020-7705 4911 **W** www.wisdencricketer.com
Editor, John Stern

WOMAN'S OWN
IPC Connect Ltd, The Blue Fin Building, 110 Southwark Street, London SE1 0SU **T** 020-3148 5000
Editor (acting), Jayne Marsden

WOMAN'S WEEKLY
IPC Connect, The Blue Fin Building, 110 Southwark Street, London SE1 0SU **T** 020-3148 5000
Editor, Diane Kenwood

THE WORD
Development Hell Ltd, 90–92 Pentonville Road, London N1 9HS **T** 020-7520 8625 **W** www.wordmagazine.co.uk
Editor, Mark Ellen

THE WORLD OF INTERIORS
The Condé Nast Publications Ltd, Vogue House, 1 Hanover Square, London W1S 1JU **T** 020-7499 9080 **W** www.worldofinteriors.co.uk
Editor, Rupert Thomas

WORLD SOCCER
IPC Inspire, The Blue Fin Building, 110 Southwark Street, London SE1 0SU **T** 020-3148 5000 **W** www.worldsoccer.com
Editor, Gavin Hamilton

THE WORLD TODAY
Chatham House, 10 St James's Square, London SW1Y 4LE **T** 020-7957 5712 **W** www.theworldtoday.org
Editor, Graham Walker

YACHTING WORLD
IPC Inspire, The Blue Fin Building, 110 Southwark Street, London SE1 0SU **T** 020-3148 5000 **W** www.yachtingworld.com
Editor, Andrew Bray

YOGA & HEALTH
PO Box 16969, London E1W 1FY **T** 020-7480 5456 **W** www.yogaandhealthmag.co.uk
Editor, Jane Sill

ZEST
National Magazine House, 72 Broadwick Street, London W1F 9EP **T** 020-7439 5000
Editor, Mandie Gower

INTERNET

INTERNET TRENDS

In keeping with global trends, the UK's internet usage continued to rise in 2009: the number of connected households reached 70 per cent (18.3 million), and nine out of ten of these had broadband.

Encouraged by the proliferation of ways to connect, UK adults increasingly accessed the internet via mobile technology: of those who connected during January to March 2009, 26 per cent had used a laptop 'on the go' and a further 26 per cent used mobile phones. The number of people connecting to the internet via wi-fi hotspots tripled between 2007 and 2009.

TOP 10 BROADBAND SUBSCRIBERS BY COUNTRY

Country (2008 position)	*2009*
1. China (1)	88,088,000
2. USA (2)	83,968,547
3. Japan (3)	30,631,900
4. Germany (4)	24,144,350
5. France (5)	18,009,500
6. UK (6)	17,661,100
7. South Korea (7)	15,709,771
8. Italy (8)	12,447,533
9. Brazil (9)	10,065,200
10. Canada (10)	9,533,500

Source: www.point-topic.com

In 2009, the internet celebrated its 40th anniversary and the World Wide Web turned 20 – appropriate milestones for a year that saw advances in broadband delivery. Virgin Media and BT both trialled broadband services with the potential to deliver improved speeds to residential customers. In April 2009, around 100 residents in Ashford, Kent, received Virgin Media's 200Mbit/s service as part of an ongoing pilot: such a speed allows users to download around 200 mp3 files a minute, or the complete digitised works of Charles Dickens in just over two. Copyright and piracy issues continued to concern the creative industries and government alike.

Communicating online proved the UK's most popular internet activity: 90 per cent of users sent or received email in 2009, and the number posting messages to social networking sites doubled from 2008 to 40 per cent. The average time spent on sites such as Facebook and Twitter was up from three hours a month in 2008 to five and a half in 2009, and half of all UK users had a profile page. For many, this socialising bore fruit: in 2009 over a third of internet users met someone online they did not know before. The ill-effects were also evident: 36 per cent felt they spent too much time online.

- The number of UK adults who have never accessed the internet continued to decrease, with the figure down to 10.2 million, or 21 per cent of the adult population, in 2009
- An increasing number of UK broadcasters made their TV and radio content available on the web in 2009; 42 per cent of web users watched or listened online
- Interest in the 2010 FIFA World Cup gained momentum in 2009: Google's end-of-year zeitgeist survey indicated that 'fifa 10' was one of the fastest growing sports-related UK searches

Sources: CIBER *Digital Consumers in the online age,* Google *Zeitgeist 2009,* OFCOM *Communications Market Report 2009,* ONS, Oxford Internet Institute

GLOSSARY OF TERMS

The following is a list of selected internet terms. It is by no means exhaustive but is intended to cover those that the average computer user might encounter.

AJAX: Asynchronous JavaScript and XML – a more interactive way of including content in a web page, achieved by exchanging small amounts of data with the server behind the scenes so that an entire web page does not have to be reloaded each time the user makes a change.

BANNER AD: An advertisement on a web page that links to a corresponding website when clicked.

BLOG: Short for 'web log' – an online personal journal that is frequently updated and intended to be read by the public. Blogs are kept by 'bloggers' and are commonly available as RSS feeds.

BROWSER: Typically refers to a 'web browser' program that allows a computer user to view web page content on their computer, eg Firefox, Internet Explorer or Safari.

CLICK-THROUGH: The number of times a web user 'clicks through' a paid advertisement link to the corresponding website.

COOKIE: A piece of information placed on a user's hard disk by a web server. Cookies contain data about the user's activity on a website, and are returned to the server whenever a browser makes further requests. They are important for remembering information such as login and registration details, 'shopping cart' data, user preferences etc, and are often set to expire after a fixed period.

CSS: Cascading Style Sheet – a standard for specifying the appearance of text. It provides a single 'library' of styles that are used throughout a large number of related documents.

DOMAIN: A set of words or letters, separated by dots, used to identify an internet server, eg www.whitakersalmanack.co.uk, where 'www' denotes a web (http) server, 'whitakersalmanack' denotes the organisation name, 'co' denotes that the organisation is a company and 'uk' indicates United Kingdom. (For a complete list of country suffixes *see* Internet Domain Names section.)

FTP: File Transfer Protocol – a set of network rules enabling a user to exchange files with a remote server.

HACKER: A person who attempts to break or 'hack' into websites. Motives typically involve the desire to procure personal information such as addresses, passwords or credit card details. Hackers may also delete code or incorporate traces of malicious code to damage the functionality of a website. The malicious activities of a hacker might be simulated by a 'penetration tester', someone legitimately employed to test the security of information systems.

HIT: A single request from a web browser for a single item from a web server. In order for a web browser to display a page that contains three graphics, four 'hits' would occur at the server: one for the HTML page and one for each of the three graphics. Therefore the number of hits on a website is not synonymous with the number of visitors.

HTML: HyperText Mark-up Language – a programming language used to denote or mark up how an internet page should be presented to a user from an HTTP server via a web browser.

HTTP: HyperText Transfer Protocol – an internet protocol whereby a web server sends web pages, images and files to a web browser.

HYPERLINK: A piece of specially coded text that users can click on to navigate to the web page, or element of a web page, associated with that link's code. Links are typically distinguished through the use of bold, underlined, or differently coloured text.

MALWARE: A combination of the words 'malicious' and 'software'. Malware is software designed with the specific intention of infiltrating a computer and damaging its system.

META TAG: A type of HTML tag that contains information not normally displayed to the user. Meta tags are typically used to include information for search engines to help them categorise a page.

MP3: A popular audio compression format allowing quicker transmission of files for later playback on personal computers and music players.

MPEG: Motion Picture Encoding Group – a popular format standard for compressing video and audio information for transmission over the internet and later playback on personal computers and hand-held devices.

OPEN CONTENT: Copyrighted information that is made available by the owner to the general public under licence terms that allow reuse of the material, often with the requirement that the reuser grant the public the same rights to the modified version. Information that is in the 'public domain' might also be considered a form of open content.

OPEN-SOURCE: Describes a computer program that has its source code (the instructions that make up a program) freely available for viewing and modification.

P2P: Peer to peer – the act of a computer on one network communicating to a computer on a different network. The communication usually involves the sharing of files between computers.

PAGERANK: A link analysis algorithm used by search engines that assigns a numerical value based on a website's relevance and reputation. In general, a site with a higher pagerank has more traffic than a site with a lower one.

PODCASTING: A form of audio and video broadcasting using the internet. Although the word is a portmanteau of 'iPod' and broadcasting, podcasting does not require the use of an iPod. A podcaster creates a list of files and makes it available in the RSS 2.0 format. The list can then be obtained using podcast 'retriever' software which makes the files available to digital devices (including, but not limited to, iPods); users may then listen or watch at their convenience.

RSS FEED: Rich Site Summary or RDF Site Summary or Real Simple Syndication – a commonly used protocol for syndication and sharing of content, originally developed to facilitate the syndication of news articles, now widely used to share the content of blogs.

SEO: Search engine optimisation – the process of optimising the content of a web page to ensure that a website is properly set up and structured to be indexed by search engines.

SERVER: A node on a network that provides service to the terminals on the network. These computers have higher hardware specifications, ie more resources and greater speed, in order to handle large amounts of data.

SOCIAL NETWORKING: The practice of using a web-hosted service such as Facebook or MySpace to upload and share content and build friendship networks.

SPAM: A term used for unsolicited, generally junk, email. Junk email is becoming a major issue, with some estimates suggesting that spam is becoming more prevalent than legitimate email. Many legislatures around the globe are taking steps to ban or regulate spam.

SPOTIFY: A peer-to-peer music streaming service that allows users to share songs and playlists.

TRAFFIC: The number of visitors to a website.

TROLL: Someone who posts controversial, inflammatory or irrelevant messages on a blog or other online discussion forum in order to disrupt on-topic discussion or provoke other users into an emotional response.

TWITTER: An online microblogging service that allows users to stay connected through the exchange of 140-character posts, known as 'tweets'.

URL: Uniform Resource Locator – address of a file accessible on the internet, eg http://www.whitakersalmanack.com

USER-GENERATED CONTENT (UGC): Refers to various media content produced or primarily influenced by end-users, as opposed to traditional media producers such as licensed broadcasters and production companies. These forms of media include digital video, blogging, podcasting, mobile phone photography and wikis.

VISIBILITY: How visible a website is to search engines and browsers.

VOIP: Voice Over Internet Protocol – various technologies used to make telephone calls over computer networks, especially the internet. Just as modems allow computers to connect to the internet over regular telephone lines, VOIP technology allows telephone calls to take place over internet connections. Costs for VOIP calls are usually much lower than for traditional telephone calls.

WEB 2.0: Generally refers to a second generation of services available on the web that lets people collaborate and share information online. In contrast to the static web pages of the first generation, Web 2.0 gives users an experience closer to that of desktop applications. Web 2.0 applications often use a combination of techniques, including AJAX and web syndication.

WIDGET: A piece of software that provides access to online information items or to functions which the user accesses on a regular basis.

WIKI: Software that allows users to freely create and edit web page content using any web browser. Theoretically this encourages the democratic use of the internet and promotes content composition by non-technical users.

BOOK PUBLISHERS

This is a selection of UK publishers and is not an exhaustive list. For more information refer to the *Writers' & Artists' Yearbook*, published by A&C Black.

ANDERSEN PRESS LTD
20 Vauxhall Bridge Road, London SW1V 2SA **T** 020-7840 8701 **W** www.andersenpress.co.uk
Children's books: picture books, junior and teenage fiction. Founded 1976

ANVIL PRESS POETRY
Neptune House, 70 Royal Hill, London SE10 8RF **T** 020-8469 3033 **W** www.anvilpresspoetry.com
Poetry. Founded 1968

ARCADIA BOOKS LTD
15–16 Nassau Street, London W1W 7AB **T** 020-7436 9898 **W** www.arcadiabooks.co.uk
Fiction, fiction in translation, autobiography, biography, travel, gender studies, gay books. Founded 1996

ATLANTIC BOOKS
Ormond House, 26–27 Boswell Street, London WC1N 3JZ **T** 020-7269 1610
Literary fiction, thrillers; history, current affairs, politics, reference, biography, memoir. Founded 2000

BERG PUBLISHERS
1st Floor, Angel Court, 81 St Clements Street, Oxford OX4 1AW **T** 01865-245104 **W** www.bergpublishers.com
Fashion studies, design studies, food studies, cultural studies, visual culture, social anthropology, film studies. Founded 1983

A&C BLACK PUBLISHERS LTD
36 Soho Square, London W1D 3QY **T** 020-7758 0200 **W** www.acblack.com
Children's and educational books, ceramics, art and craft, drama, ornithology, reference, sport, theatre, books for writers, dictionaries. Founded 1807

BLACK DOG PUBLISHING LONDON UK
10A Acton Street, London WC1X 9NG **T** 020-7713 5097 **W** www.blackdogonline.com
Contemporary art, architecture, design, photography

BLOODAXE BOOKS LTD
Highgreen, Tarset, Northumberland NE48 1RP **T** 01434-240500 **W** www.bloodaxebooks.com
Poetry. Founded 1978

BLOOMSBURY PUBLISHING PLC
36 Soho Square, London W1D 3QY **T** 020-7494 2111 **W** www.bloomsbury.com
Fiction, biography, illustrated, travel, children's, trade paperbacks and mass market paperbacks. Founded 1986

BRITISH MUSEUM COMPANY LTD
38 Russell Square, London WC1B 3QQ **T** 020-7323 1234 **W** www.britishmuseum.co.uk
Adult and children's books on art history, archaeology, history and world cultures. Founded 1973

CAMBRIDGE UNIVERSITY PRESS
The Edinburgh Building, Shaftesbury Road, Cambridge CB2 8RU **T** 01223-312393 **W** www.cambridge.org
Academic books. Founded 1534

CANONGATE BOOKS LTD
14 High Street, Edinburgh EH1 1TE **T** 0131-557 5111 **W** www.canongate.net
Adult general non-fiction and fiction: literary fiction, translated fiction, memoir, pop science, humour, travel, popular culture, history and biography. Founded 1973

CONSTABLE & ROBINSON LTD
3 The Lanchesters, 162 Fulham Palace Road, London W6 9ER **T** 020-8741 3663 **W** www.constablerobinson.com
Literary and crime fiction; current affairs, health, history, self-help. Founded 1795 (Constable); 1983 (Robinson)

THE CONTINUUM INTERNATIONAL PUBLISHING GROUP LTD
The Tower Building, 11 York Road, London SE1 7NX **T** 020-7922 0880 **W** www.continuumbooks.com
Serious non-fiction, academic and professional

GERALD DUCKWORTH & CO. LTD
First Floor, 90–93 Cowcross Street, London EC1M 6BF **T** 020-7490 7300 **W** www.ducknet.co.uk
General trade publishers; strong academic division. Founded 1898

EARTHSCAN
Dunston House, 14A St Cross Street, London EC1N 8XA **T** 020-7841 1930 **W** www.earthscan.co.uk
Academic and professional: sustainable development, climate, energy, natural resource management, cities, built environment, business, economics, design and technology

EDINBURGH UNIVERSITY PRESS
22 George Square, Edinburgh EH8 9LF **T** 0131-650 4218 **W** www.euppublishing.com
Academic publishers of scholarly books and journals

EGMONT BOOKS
103 Westerhill Road, Bishopbriggs, Glasgow G64 2QT **T** 08445-768113 **W** www.egmont.co.uk
Children's books. Founded 1878

ENCYCLOPAEDIA BRITANNICA (UK) LTD
2nd Floor, Unity Wharf, 13 Mill Street, London SE1 2BH **T** 020-7500 7800 **W** www.britannica.co.uk

FABER AND FABER LTD
Bloomsbury House, 74–77 Great Russell Street, London WC1B 3DA **T** 020-7927 3800 **W** www.faber.co.uk
High-quality general fiction and non-fiction, children's fiction and non-fiction, drama, film, music, poetry

FABIAN SOCIETY
11 Dartmouth Street, London SW1H 9BN **T** 020-7227 4900
W www.fabians.org.uk
Current affairs, political thought, economics, education, environment, foreign affairs, social policy. Founded 1884

SAMUEL FRENCH LTD
52 Fitzroy Street, London W1T 5JR **T** 020-7387 9373, 020-7255 4300 **W** www.samuelfrench-london.co.uk
Plays. Founded 1830

GRANTA PUBLICATIONS
12 Addison Avenue, London W11 4QR **T** 020-7605 1360
W www.granta.com
Literary fiction, memoir, political non-fiction, travel, history etc. Founded 1982

GUINNESS WORLD RECORDS
3rd Floor, 184–192 Drummond Street, London NW1 3HP
T 020-7891 4567 **W** www.guinnessworldrecords.com
Founded 1954

HACHETTE UK
338 Euston Road, London NW1 3BH **T** 020-7873 6000
W www.hachette.co.uk
Fiction and non-fiction

HARLEQUIN MILLS & BOON LTD
Eton House, 18–24 Paradise Road, Richmond, Surrey TW9 1SR **T** 020-8288 2800
W www.millsandboon.co.uk
Founded 1908

HARPERCOLLINS PUBLISHERS
77–85 Fulham Palace Road, London W6 8JB
T 020-8741 7070 **W** www.harpercollins.co.uk
Popular fiction and non-fiction. Founded 1819

THE HISTORY PRESS LTD
The Mill, Briscombe Port, Stroud, Glos. GL5 2QG
T 01453-883300 **W** www.thehistorypress.co.uk

HODDER & STOUGHTON
338 Euston Road, London NW1 3BH **T** 020-7873 6000
W www.hodder.co.uk
Autobiography, biography, fiction, humour, lifestyle

ICON BOOKS LTD
The Omnibus Business Centre, 39–41 North Road, London N7 9DP **T** 020-7697 9695 **W** www.iconbooks.co.uk
Popular non-fiction: *Introducing* series, literature, history, philosophy, politics. Founded 1991

LAURENCE KING PUBLISHING LTD
361–373 City Road, London EC1V 1LR **T** 020-7841 6900
W www.laurenceking.co.uk
Illustrated books: design, contemporary architecture, art, interiors, fashion. Founded 1976

LETTS AND LONSDALE
PO Box 113, Holme, Carnforth, Lancs. LA6 1WL
T 01539-564911 **W** www.lettsandlonsdale.com
Study and revision guides for children of all ages

LITTLE, BROWN BOOK GROUP
100 Victoria Embankment, London EC4Y 0DY
T 020-7911 8000 **W** www.littlebrown.co.uk
Fiction and general non-fiction. Founded 1988

LONELY PLANET
2nd Floor, 186 City Road, London EC1V 2NT
T 020-7106 2100
W www.lonelyplanet.com
Country and regional guidebooks, city guides

MCGRAW-HILL EDUCATION
McGraw-Hill House, Shoppenhangers Road, Maidenhead, Berks. SL6 2QL **T** 01628-502500
W www.mcgraw-hill.co.uk
Higher education and professional

MACMILLAN PUBLISHERS LTD
The Macmillan Building, 4 Crinan Street, London N1 9XW
T 020-7833 4000 **W** www.macmillan.com

METHUEN PUBLISHING LTD
8 Artillery Row, London SW1P 1RZ **T** 020-7802 0018
W www.methuen.co.uk
Literary fiction and non-fiction

JOHN MURRAY (PUBLISHERS)
338 Euston Road, London NW1 3BH **T** 020-7873 6000
W www.johnmurray.co.uk
Commercial fiction and non-fiction: travel, history, entertainment, reference, biography and memoir

NATURAL HISTORY MUSEUM PUBLISHING
Cromwell Road, London SW7 5BD **T** 020-7942 5336
W www.nhm.ac.uk/publishing
Natural sciences. Founded 1881

W. W. NORTON & COMPANY
Castle House, 75–76 Wells Street, London W1T 3QT **T** 020-7323 1579
W www.wwnorton.co.uk
English and American literature. Founded 1980

OBERON BOOKS
521 Caledonian Road, London N7 9RH **T** 020-7607 3637
W www.oberonbooks.com
New and classic play texts, programme texts and general theatre and performing arts books. Founded 1986

OMNIBUS PRESS
14–15 Berners Street, London W1T 3LJ **T** 020-7612 7400
W www.omnibuspress.com
Rock music biographies, general music. Founded 1976

ONEWORLD PUBLICATIONS
185 Banbury Road, Oxford OX2 7AR **T** 01865-310597
W www.oneworld-publications.com
Fiction and general non-fiction: current affairs, politics, history, popular science, philosophy. Founded 1986

THE ORION PUBLISHING GROUP LTD
Orion House, 5 Upper St Martin's Lane, London WC2H 9EA
T 020-7240 3444 **W** www.orionbooks.co.uk
Fiction, non-fiction and audio. Founded 1992

OXFORD UNIVERSITY PRESS
Great Clarendon Street, Oxford OX2 6DP **T** 01865-556767
W www.oup.com
Academic, literature, reference. Founded 1478

PEARSON UK
Edinburgh Gate, Harlow, Essex CM20 2JE **T** 0845-313 6666
W www.pearsoned.co.uk

continued on page 634

PUBLISHERS' FAMILY TREE

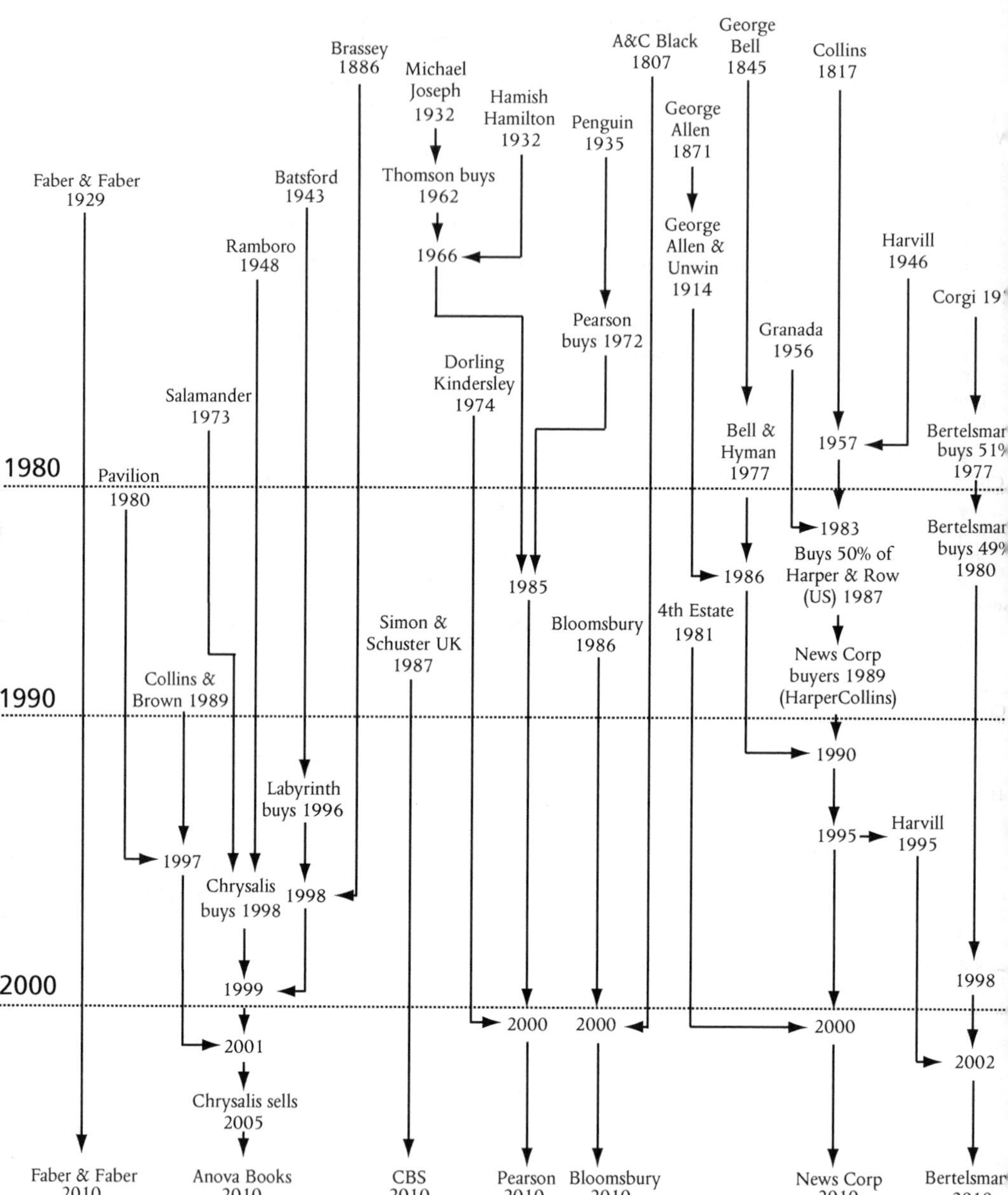

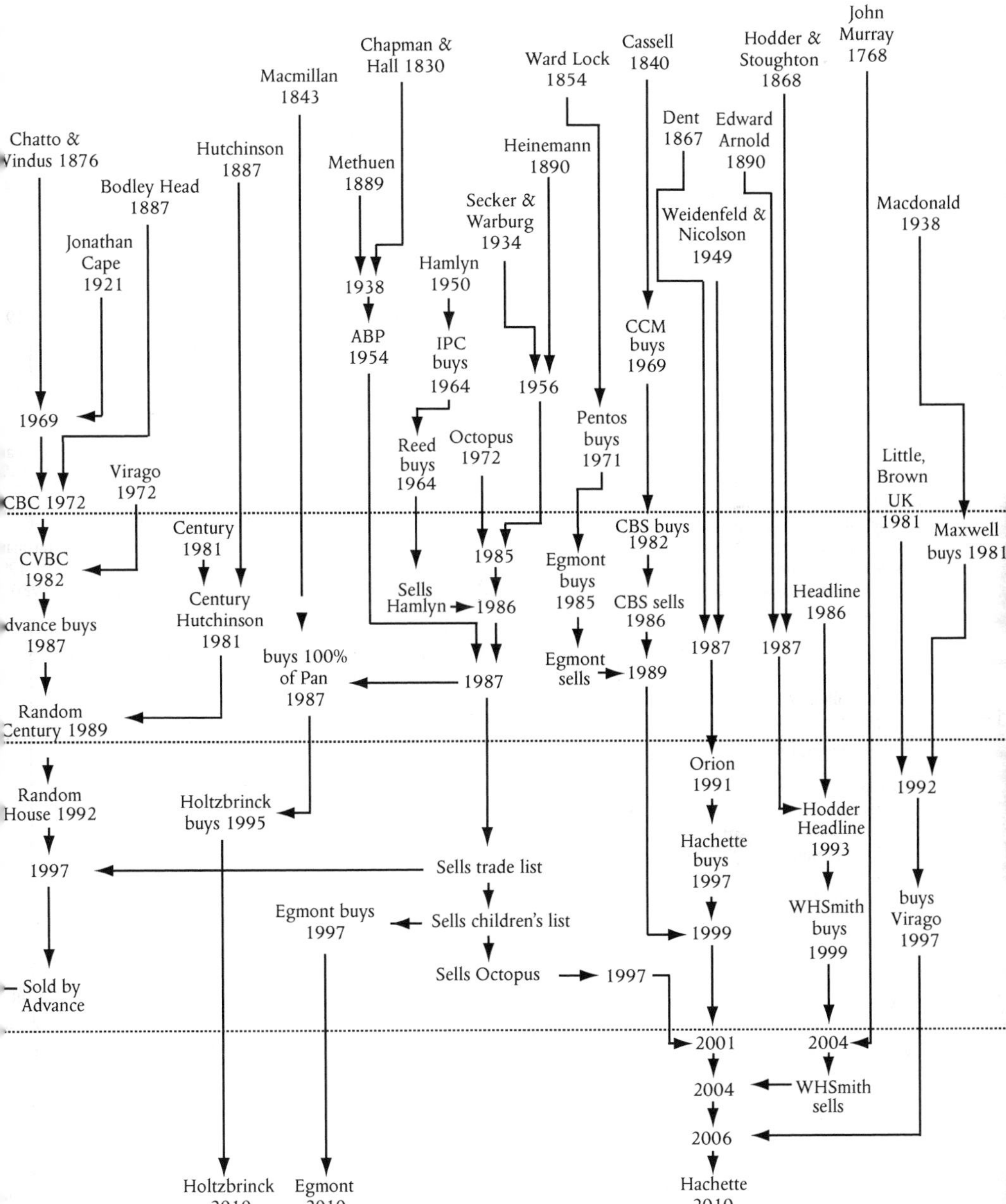
Chatto & Windus 1876
Bodley Head 1887
Jonathan Cape 1921
Hutchinson 1887
Macmillan 1843
Chapman & Hall 1830
Methuen 1889
1938
ABP 1954
Hamlyn 1950
IPC buys 1964
Reed buys 1964
Secker & Warburg 1934
Heinemann 1890
1956
Octopus 1972
Ward Lock 1854
Pentos buys 1971
Cassell 1840
CCM buys 1969
Dent 1867
Weidenfeld & Nicolson 1949
Edward Arnold 1890
Hodder & Stoughton 1868
John Murray 1768
Macdonald 1938
1969
CBC 1972
Virago 1972
CVBC 1982
Century 1981
Century Hutchinson 1981
Advance buys 1987
Random Century 1989
Random House 1992
1997
Sold by Advance
buys 100% of Pan 1987
Holtzbrinck buys 1995
Holtzbrinck 2010
1985
Sells Hamlyn
1986
1987
Sells trade list
Sells children's list
Sells Octopus
Egmont buys 1997
Egmont 2010
1997
Egmont buys 1985
Egmont sells
CBS buys 1982
CBS sells 1986
1989
1987
1987
Orion 1991
Hachette buys 1997
1999
2001
2004
2006
Hachette 2010
Headline 1986
Hodder Headline 1993
WHSmith buys 1999
2004
WHSmith sells
Little, Brown UK 1981
Maxwell buys 1981
1992
buys Virago 1997

PENGUIN GROUP
80 Strand, London WC2R 0RL **T** 020-7010 3000
W www.penguin.co.uk
Children's books; adult subjects include biography, fiction, current affairs, leisure, health, history, humour, literature, politics, relationships, spirituality, sports, travel

PHAIDON PRESS LTD
Regent's Wharf, All Saints Street, London N1 9PA
T 020-7843 1000 **W** www.phaidon.com
Visual arts, lifestyle and culture

PLUTO PRESS
345 Archway Road, London N6 5AA **T** 020-8348 2724
W www.plutobooks.com
Politics, anthropology, development, media, cultural, economics, history, Irish studies, Black studies, Islamic studies, Middle East, international relations

PROFILE BOOKS LTD
3A Exmouth House, Pine Street, London EC1R 0JH
T 020-7841 6300 **W** www.profilebooks.com
Non-fiction: history, biography, current affairs, popular science, politics. Founded 1996

PUSHKIN PRESS
12 Chester Terrace, London NW1 4ND **T** 020-7730 0750
W www.pushkinpress.com
Continental European literature in translation. Founded 1997

THE QUARTO GROUP, INC.
226 City Road, London, EC1V 2TT **T** 020-7700 9000
W www.quarto.com
Independent publishing group encompassing traditional and co-edition publishing

QUERCUS PUBLISHING PLC
21 Bloomsbury Square, London WC1A 2NS **T** 020-7291 7200
W www.quercusbooks.co.uk
Fiction and non-fiction. Founded 2005

THE RANDOM HOUSE GROUP LTD
20 Vauxhall Bridge Road, London SW1V 2SA **T** 020-7840 8400
W www.randomhouse.co.uk
Fiction and non-fiction

SIMON & SCHUSTER UK LTD
222 Gray's Inn Road, London WC1X 8HB **T** 020-7316 1900
W www.simonandschuster.co.uk
Commercial and literary fiction; general and serious non-fiction; children's. Founded 1986

TASCHEN UK LTD
5th Floor, 1 Heathcock Court, 415 Strand, London WC2R 0NS
T 020-7845 8585 **W** www.taschen.com
Art, architecture, design, film, lifestyle, photography, popular culture. Founded 1980

THAMES & HUDSON LTD
181A High Holborn, London WC1V 7QX **T** 020-7845 5000
W www.thamesandhudson.com
Illustrated non-fiction: archaeology, architecture, art, fashion, garden and landscape design, graphic design, history, mythology, photography, religion

TITAN BOOKS
144 Southwark Street, London SE1 0UP **T** 020-7620 0200
W www.titanbooks.com
Graphic novels, film and TV tie-ins and cinema reference books. Founded 1981

USBORNE PUBLISHING LTD
Usborne House, 83–85 Saffron Hill, London EC1N 8RT
T 020-7430 2800 **W** www.usborne.com
Children's books: reference, practical, craft, natural history, science, languages, history, geography, preschool, fiction. Founded 1973

V&A PUBLISHING
Victoria and Albert Museum, South Kensington, London SW7 2RL **T** 020-7942 2696
W www.vandashop.com
Popular and scholarly books on fine and decorative arts, architecture, contemporary design, fashion and photography. Founded 1980

VERSO LTD
6 Meard Street, London W1V 3HR **T** 020-7437 3546
W www.verso.com
Current affairs, politics, sociology, economics, history, philosophy, cultural studies. Founded 1970

WALKER BOOKS LTD
87 Vauxhall Walk, London SE11 5HJ **T** 020-7793 0909
W www.walker.co.uk
Children's: picture books, non-fiction and novelty titles; junior and teenage fiction. Founded 1980

WILEY-BLACKWELL
9600 Garsington Road, Oxford OX4 2DQ **T** 01865-776868
W www.wiley.com
Books and journals in medicine, science, social sciences, business and humanities

THE WOMEN'S PRESS
27 Goodge Street, London W1T 2LD **T** 020-7636 3992
W www.the-womens-press.com
Books by women in the areas of literary and crime fiction, biography and autobiography, health, culture, politics. Founded 1978

WORDSWORTH EDITIONS LTD
8B East Street, Ware, Herts. SG12 9HJ **T** 01920-465167
W www.wordsworth-editions.com
Reprints of classic books: literary, children's; poetry; reference. Founded 1987

YALE UNIVERSITY PRESS LONDON
47 Bedford Square, London WC1B 3DP **T** 020-7079 4900
W www.yalebooks.co.uk
Art, architecture, history, economics, political science, religion, history of science, biography, current affairs and music. Founded 1961

ZED BOOKS LTD
7 Cynthia Street, London N1 9JF **T** 020-7837 4014
W www.zedbooks.co.uk
Social sciences on international issues. Founded 1976

TRADE AND PROFESSIONAL BODIES

The following is a list of employers' and trade associations and other professional bodies in the UK. It does not represent a comprehensive list. For further professional bodies *see* Professional Education.

ASSOCIATIONS

ADVERTISING ASSOCIATION 7th Floor North, Artillery House, 11–19 Artillery Row, London SW1P 1RT **T** 020-7340 1100 **E** aa@adassoc.org.uk **W** www.adassoc.org.uk
Chief Executive, Tim Lefroy

AGRICULTURAL ENGINEERS ASSOCIATION Samuelson House, 62 Forder Way, Hampton, Peterborough PE7 8JB **T** 08456-448748 **E** ab@aea.uk.com **W** www.aea.uk.com
Chief Executive Officer, Roger Lane-Nott

ASBESTOS REMOVAL CONTRACTORS ASSOCIATION ARCA House, 237 Branston Road, Burton upon Trent DE14 3BT **T** 01283-531126 **E** info@arca.org.uk **W** www.arca.org.uk
Chair, Steve Watts

ASSOCIATION FOR CONSULTANCY AND ENGINEERING Alliance House, 12 Caxton Street, London SW1H 0QL **T** 020-7222 6557 **E** consult@acenet.co.uk **W** www.acenet.co.uk
Chief Executive, Nelson Ogunshakin

ASSOCIATION OF ACCOUNTING TECHNICIANS 140 Aldersgate Street, London EC1A 4HY **T** 020-7397 3000 **E** aat@aat.org.uk **W** www.aat.org.uk
Chief Executive, Jane Scott Paul

ASSOCIATION OF ANAESTHETISTS OF GREAT BRITAIN AND IRELAND 21 Portland Place, London W1B 1PY **T** 020-7631 1650 **E** info@aagbi.org **W** www.aagbi.org
President, Dr Richard Birks

ASSOCIATION OF BRITISH INSURERS 51 Gresham Street, London EC2V 7HQ **T** 020-7600 3333 **E** info@abi.org.uk **W** www.abi.org.uk
Director-General, Kerrie Kelly

ASSOCIATION OF BRITISH TRAVEL AGENTS (ABTA) 30 Park Street, London SE1 9EQ **T** 020-3117 0500 **E** abta@abta.co.uk **W** www.abta.com
Chief Executive, Mark Tanzer

ASSOCIATION OF BUILDING ENGINEERS Lutyens House, Billing Brook Road, Weston Favell, Northampton NN3 8NW **T** 01604-404121 **E** building.engineers@abe.org.uk **W** www.abe.org.uk
Chief Executive, David Gibson

ASSOCIATION OF BUSINESS RECOVERY PROFESSIONALS 8th Floor, 120 Aldersgate Street, London EC1A 4JQ **T** 020-7566 4200 **E** association@r3.org.uk **W** www.r3.org.uk
Chief Executive, Graham Rumney

ASSOCIATION OF CONSULTING SCIENTISTS 5 Willow Heights, Cradley Heath B64 7PL **T** 0121-602 3515 **E** secretary@consultingscientists.co.uk **W** www.consultingscientists.co.uk
Director, Dr Stuart Guy

ASSOCIATION OF CONVENIENCE STORES LTD Federation House, 17 Farnborough Street, Farnborough GU14 8AG **T** 01252-515001 **E** acs@acs.org.uk **W** www.acs.org.uk
Chief Executive, James Lowman

ASSOCIATION OF CORPORATE TREASURERS 51 Moorgate, London EC2R 6BH **T** 020-7847 2540 **E** enquiries@treasurers.org **W** www.treasurers.org
Chief Executive, Stuart Siddall

ASSOCIATION OF COUNCIL SECRETARIES AND SOLICITORS 64 Smithbrook Kilns, Cranleigh GU6 8JJ **T** 01483-277888 **E** admin@acses.org.uk **W** www.acses.org.uk
President, Mirza Ahmad

ASSOCIATION OF DRAINAGE AUTHORITIES 12 Cranes Drive, Surbiton KT5 8AL **T** 0844-209 0089 **E** admin@ada.org.uk **W** www.ada.org.uk
Chief Executive, Jean Venables, OBE FRENG

ASSOCIATION OF ELECTRICITY PRODUCERS Charles House, 5–11 Regent Street, SW1Y 4LR **T** 020-7930 9390 **E** enquiries@aepuk.com **W** www.aepuk.com
Chief Executive, David Porter

BAR ASSOCIATION FOR LOCAL GOVERNMENT AND THE PUBLIC SERVICE c/o Birmingham City Council, Ingleby House, 11–14 Cannon Street, Birmingham B2 5EN **T** 0121-303 9991 **E** chairman@balgps.org.uk **W** www.balgps.org.uk
Chair, Dr Mirza Ahmad

BOOKSELLERS ASSOCIATION OF THE UK & IRELAND LTD Minster House, 272 Vauxhall Bridge Road, London SW1V 1BA **T** 020-7802 0802 **E** mail@booksellers.org.uk **W** www.booksellers.org.uk
Chief Executive, T. E. Godfray

BRITISH ANTIQUE DEALERS' ASSOCIATION 20 Rutland Gate, London SW7 1BD **T** 020-7589 4128 **E** info@bada.org **W** www.bada.org
Chair, Ian H. Walker

BRITISH ASSOCIATION OF SOCIAL WORKERS 16 Kent Street, Birmingham B5 6RD **T** 0121-622 3911 **E** info@basw.co.uk **W** www.basw.co.uk
Chief Executive, Hilton Dawson

BRITISH BANKERS' ASSOCIATION Pinners Hall, 105–108 Old Broad Street, London EC2N 1EX **T** 020-7216 8800 **E** info@bba.org.uk **W** www.bba.org.uk
Chief Executive, Angela Knight, CBE

BRITISH BEER AND PUB ASSOCIATION Market Towers, 1 Nine Elms Lane, London SW8 5NQ **T** 020-7627 9191 **E** web@beerandpub.com **W** www.beerandpub.com
Chief Executive, Brigid Simmonds, OBE

BRITISH CHAMBERS OF COMMERCE 65 Petty France, St James Park, London SW1H 9EU **T** 020-7654 5800 **E** info@britishchambers.org.uk **W** www.britishchambers.org.uk
Director-General, David Frost

BRITISH ELECTROTECHNICAL AND ALLIED MANUFACTURERS ASSOCIATION (BEAMA) Westminster Tower, 3 Albert Embankment, London SE1 7SL **T** 020-7793 3000 **E** info@beama.org.uk **W** www.beama.org.uk
Chief Operating Officer, Dr Howard Porter

BRITISH HOROLOGICAL INSTITUTE Upton Hall, Upton, Newark NG23 5TE **T** 01636-813795 **E** clocks@bhi.co.uk **W** www.bhi.co.uk
Chair, Ken Lloyd Jones

BRITISH HOSPITALITY ASSOCIATION Queens House, 55–56 Lincoln's Inn Fields, London WC2A 3BH **T** 0845-880 7744 **E** bha@bha.org.uk **W** www.bha.org.uk
Chief Executive, Robert Cotton, OBE

BRITISH INSTITUTE OF PROFESSIONAL PHOTOGRAPHY 1 Prebendal Court, Oxford Road, Aylesbury HP19 8EY **T** 01296-718530 **E** info@bipp.com **W** www.bipp.com
Chief Executive, Chris Harper

BRITISH INSURANCE BROKERS' ASSOCIATION 8th Floor, John Stow House, 18 Bevis Marks, London EC3A 7JB **T** 0870-950 1790 **E** enquiries@biba.org.uk **W** www.biba.org.uk
Chief Executive, Eric Galbraith

BRITISH MARINE FEDERATION Marine House, Thorpe Lea Road, Egham TW20 8BF **T** 01784-473377 **E** info@britishmarine.co.uk **W** www.britishmarine.co.uk
Chief Executive, Rob Stevens, CB

BRITISH MEDICAL ASSOCIATION BMA House, Tavistock Square, London WC1H 9JP **T** 020-7387 4499 **W** www.bma.org.uk
Chief Executive, Tony Bourne

BRITISH OFFICE SUPPLIES AND SERVICES (BOSS) FEDERATION Farringdon Point, 29–35 Farringdon Road, EC1M 3JF **T** 0845-450 1565 **E** info@bossfederation.co.uk **W** www.bossfederation.co.uk
Chief Executive, Michael Gardner

BRITISH PHONOGRAPHIC INDUSTRY Riverside Building, County Hall, Westminster Bridge Road, London SE1 7JA **T** 020-7803 1300 **E** general@bpi.co.uk **W** www.bpi.co.uk
Chief Executive, Geoff Taylor

BRITISH PLASTICS FEDERATION 5–6 Bath Place, Rivington Street, London EC2A 3JE **T** 020-7457 5000 **E** reception@bpf.co.uk **W** www.bpf.co.uk
Director-General, Peter Davis, OBE

BRITISH PORTS ASSOCIATION 4th Floor Carthusian Court, 12 Carthusian Street, London EC1M 6EZ **T** 020-7260 1780 **E** info@britishports.org.uk **W** www.britishports.org.uk
Director, David Whitehead

BRITISH PRINTING INDUSTRIES FEDERATION Farringdon Point, 29–35 Farringdon Road, London EC1M 3JF **T** 020-7915 8300 **W** www.britishprint.com
Chief Executive, Michael Johnson

BRITISH PROPERTY FEDERATION 5th Floor, St Albans House, 57–59 Haymarket, London SW1Y 4QX **T** 020-7828 0111 **E** info@bpf.org.uk **W** www.bpf.org.uk
Chief Executive, Liz Peace

BRITISH RETAIL CONSORTIUM 2nd Floor, 21 Dartmouth Street, London SW1H 9BP **T** 020-7854 8900 **E** info@brc.org.uk **W** www.brc.org.uk
Director-General, Stephen Robertson

BRITISH TYRE MANUFACTURERS' ASSOCIATION LTD 5 Berewyk Hall Court, White Colne, Colchester EC2A 3JE **T** 01787-226995 **E** mail@btmauk.com **W** www.btmauk.com
Chief Executive, Mr G. C. Willson

BUILDING SOCIETIES ASSOCIATION York House, 23 Kingsway, London WC2B 6UJ **T** 020-7520 5900 **E** simon.rex@bsa.org.uk **W** www.bsa.org.uk
Director-General, Adrian Coles

CHAMBER OF SHIPPING LTD Carthusian Court, 12 Carthusian Street, London EC1M 6EZ **T** 020-7417 2800 **E** postmaster@british-shipping.org **W** www.british-shipping.org
Director-General, Mark Brownrigg

CHARTERED INSTITUTE OF ENVIRONMENTAL HEALTH Chadwick Court, 15 Hatfields, London SE1 8DJ **T** 020-7928 6006 **E** information@cieh.org **W** www.cieh.org
Chief Executive, Graham Jukes

CHARTERED INSTITUTE OF JOURNALISTS 2 Dock Offices, Surrey Quays Road, London SE16 2XU **T** 020-7252 1187 **E** memberservices@cioj.co.uk **W** www.cioj.co.uk
General Secretary, Dominic Cooper

CHARTERED INSTITUTE OF PURCHASING AND SUPPLY Easton House, Easton on the Hill, Stamford PE9 3NZ **T** 01780-756777 **E** info@cips.org **W** www.cips.org
Chief Executive, David Noble

CHARTERED INSTITUTE OF TAXATION 1st Floor, 11–19 Artillery Row, London SW1P 1RT **T** 020-7340 6700 **E** post@ciot.org.uk **W** www.tax.org.uk
Chief Executive, Peter Fanning

CHARTERED INSURANCE INSTITUTE 42–48 High Road, South Woodford, London E18 2JP **T** 020-8989 8464 **E** customer.serv@cii.co.uk **W** www.cii.co.uk
Chief Executive, Dr Alexander Scott

CHARTERED MANAGEMENT INSTITUTE Management House, Cottingham Road, Corby NN17 1TT **T** 01536-204222 **E** enquiries@managers.org.uk **W** www.managers.org.uk
Chief Executive, Ruth Spellman, OBE

CHARTERED QUALITY INSTITUTE 12 Grosvenor Crescent, London SW1X 7EE **T** 020-7245 6722 **E** cqi@thecqi.org **W** www.thecqi.org
Chair, Peter Bennett

CHEMICAL INDUSTRIES ASSOCIATION Kings Buildings, Smith Square, London SW1P 3JJ **T** 020-7834 3399 **E** enquiries@cia.org.uk **W** www.cia.org.uk
Chief Executive, Steve Elliott

CONFEDERATION OF PAPER INDUSTRIES 1 Rivenhall Road, Swindon SN5 7BD **T** 01793-889600 **E** cpi@paper.org.uk **W** www.paper.org.uk
Director-General, Dr Martin Oldman

CONFEDERATION OF PASSENGER TRANSPORT UK Drury House, 34–43 Russell Street, London WC2B 5HA **T** 020-7240 3131 **E** admin@cpt-uk.org **W** www.cpt-uk.org
Chief Executive, Simon Posner

CONSTRUCTION PRODUCTS ASSOCIATION 26 Store Street, London WC1E 7BT **T** 020-7323 3770 **E** enquiries@constructionproducts.org.uk **W** www.constructionproducts.org.uk
Chief Executive, Michael Ankers, OBE

DAIRY UK 93 Baker Street, London W1U 6QQ **T** 020-7486 7244 **E** info@dairyuk.org **W** www.dairyuk.org
Director-General, Jim Begg

EEF, THE MANUFACTURERS' ORGANISATION Broadway House, Tothill Street, London SW1H 9NQ **T** 020-7222 7777 **E** enquiries@eef.org.uk **W** www.eef.org.uk
Chief Executive, Terry Scuoler

FEDERATION OF BAKERS 6 Catherine Street, London WC2B 5JW **T** 020-7420 7190 **E** info@bakersfederation.org.uk **W** www.bakersfederation.org.uk
Director, Gordon Polson

FEDERATION OF MASTER BUILDERS Gordon Fisher House, 14–15 Great James Street, London WC1N 3DP **T** 020-7242 7583 **E** central@fmb.org.uk **W** www.fmb.org.uk
Director-General, Richard Diment

FEDERATION OF SPORTS AND PLAY ASSOCIATIONS Federation House, Stoneleigh Park, CV8 2RF **T** 024-7641 4999 **E** info@sportsandplay.com **W** www.sportsandplay.com
Managing Director, Jane Montgomery

FINANCE AND LEASING ASSOCIATION 2nd Floor, Imperial House, 15–19 Kingsway, London WC2B 6UN **T** 020-7836 6511 **E** info@fla.org.uk **W** www.fla.org.uk
Director-General, Stephen Sklaroff

FOOD AND DRINK FEDERATION 6 Catherine Street, London WC2B 5JJ T 020-7836 2460 E generalenquiries@fdf.org.uk W www.fdf.org.uk
Director-General, Melanie Leech

FREIGHT TRANSPORT ASSOCIATION LTD Hermes House, St John's Road, Tunbridge Wells TN4 9UZ T 01892-526171 E enquiries@fta.co.uk W www.fta.co.uk
Chief Executive, Theo de Pencier

GLASGOW CHAMBER OF COMMERCE 30 George Square, Glasgow G2 1EQ T 0141-204 2121 E chamber@glasgowchamber.org W www.glasgowchamber.org
President, James Andrew

INSTITUTE FOR ARCHAEOLOGISTS School of Human and Environmental Science, Whiteknights, University of Reading, PO Box 227, RG6 6AB T 0118-378 6446 E admin@archaeologists.net W www.archaeologists.net
Chief Executive, Peter Hinton, FRSA, FSA

INSTITUTE OF ADMINISTRATIVE MANAGEMENT 6 Graphite Square, Vauxhall Walk, London SE11 5EE T 020-7091 2600 E info@instam.org W www.instam.org
Chief Executive, Jenny Hewell

INSTITUTE OF BREWING AND DISTILLING 33 Clarges Street, London W1J 7EE T 020-7499 8144 E enquiries@ibd.org.uk W www.ibd.org.uk
Executive Director, Simon Jackson

INSTITUTE OF BRITISH ORGAN BUILDING 13 Ryefields, Thurston, Bury St Edmunds IP31 3TD T 01359-233433 E administrator@ibo.co.uk W www.ibo.co.uk
President, Martin Goetze

INSTITUTE OF CHARTERED FORESTERS 59 George Street, Edinburgh EH2 2JG T 0131-240 1425 E icf@charteredforesters.org W www.charteredforesters.org
Executive Director, Shireen Chambers

INSTITUTE OF CHARTERED SECRETARIES AND ADMINISTRATORS 16 Park Crescent, London W1B 1AH T 020-7580 4741 E info@icsa.co.uk W www.icsa.org.uk
Chief Executive, Roger Dickinson

INSTITUTE OF CHARTERED SHIPBROKERS 85 Gracechurch Street, London EC3V 0AA T 020-7623 1111 E info@ics.org.uk W www.ics.org.uk
Director, Alan Phillips

INSTITUTE OF DIRECTORS 116 Pall Mall, London SW1Y 5ED T 020-7766 8866 E enquiries@iod.com W www.iod.com
Chief Operating Officer, Andrew Main Wilson

INSTITUTE OF EXPORT Export House, Minerva Business Park, Lynch Wood, Peterborough PE2 6FT T 01733-404400 E institute@export.org.uk W www.export.org.uk
Chair, Lesley Batchelor

INSTITUTE OF FINANCIAL ACCOUNTANTS Burford House, 44 London Road, Sevenoaks TN13 1AS T 01732-458080 E mail@ifa.org.uk W www.ifa.org.uk
Chief Executive, David Woodgate

INSTITUTE OF HEALTHCARE MANAGEMENT 18–21 Morley Street, London SE1 7QZ T 020-7620 1030 E enquiries@ihm.org.uk W www.ihm.org.uk
Chief Executive, Susan Hodgetts

INSTITUTE OF HOSPITALITY Trinity Court, 34 West Street, Sutton, Surrey SM1 1SH T 020-8661 4900 E info@instituteofhospitality.org W www.instituteofhospitality.org
Chief Executive, Philippe Rossiter

INSTITUTE OF INTERNAL COMMUNICATION Suite GA2, Oak House, Woodlands Business Park, Breckland, Linford Wood West MK14 6EY T 01908-313755 E enquiries@cib.uk.com W www.cib.uk.com
Chief Executive, Kathie Jones

INSTITUTE OF MANAGEMENT SERVICES Brooke House, 24 Dam Street, Lichfield WS13 6AA T 01543-266 909 E admin@ims-stowe.fsnet.co.uk W www.ims-productivity.com
Chair, David Blanchflower

INSTITUTE OF QUARRYING 7 Regent Street, Nottingham NG1 5BS T 0115-945 3880 E mail@quarrying.org W www.quarrying.org
Executive Director, Jack Berridge

INSTITUTE OF ROAD SAFETY OFFICERS Pin Point, 1–2 Rosslyn Crescent, Harrow HA1 2SU T 0870-010 4442 E irso@dbda.co.uk W www.irso.org.uk
Acting Chair, Darren Divall

INSTITUTE OF THE MOTOR INDUSTRY Fanshaws, Brickendon, Hertford SG13 8PQ T 01992-511521 E imi@motor.org.uk W www.motor.org.uk
Executive Chair, Sarah Sillars, OBE

INSTITUTION OF OCCUPATIONAL SAFETY AND HEALTH The Grange, Highfield Drive, Wigston LE18 1NN T 0116-257 3100 E techinfo@iosh.co.uk W www.iosh.co.uk
Chief Executive, Rob Strange, OBE

IP FEDERATION 5th Floor, 63–66 Hatton Garden, London EC1N 8LE T 020-7242 3923 E admin@ipfederation.com W www.ipfederation.com
President, James R. Hayles

MAGISTRATES' ASSOCIATION 28 Fitzroy Square, London W1T 6DD T 020-7387 2353 E information@magistrates-association.org.uk W www.magistrates-association.org.uk
Chief Executive and Secretary, Sally Dickinson

MANAGEMENT CONSULTANCIES ASSOCIATION 60 Trafalgar Square, London WC2N 5DS T 020-7321 3990 E info@mca.org.uk W www.mca.org.uk
Chief Executive, Alan Leaman, OBE

MASTER LOCKSMITHS ASSOCIATION 5D Great Central Way, Wood Halse, Daventry, Northants NN11 3PZ T 01327-262 255 E enquiries@locksmiths.co.uk W www.locksmiths.co.uk
Chair, Roger Barratt

NATIONAL ASSOCIATION OF BRITISH MARKET AUTHORITIES The Guildhall, Oswestry, Shrops SY11 1PZ T 01691-680713 E nabma@nabma.com W www.nabma.com
Chief Executive, Graham Wilson

NATIONAL ASSOCIATION OF ESTATE AGENTS Arbon House, 6 Tournament Court, Edgehill Drive, Warwick CV34 6LG T 01926-496800 E info@nfopp.co.uk W www.naea.co.uk
President, Peter Bolton King

NATIONAL CATTLE ASSOCIATION (DAIRY) Brick House, Risbury, Leominster HR6 0NQ T 01568-760632 E timbrigstocke@hotmail.com
Executive Secretary, Tim Brigstocke, MBE

NATIONAL FARMERS' UNION (NFU) Agriculture House, Stoneleigh Park, Stoneleigh CV8 2TZ T 024-7685 8500 E nfu@nfuonline.com W www.nfuonline.com
President, Peter Kendall

NATIONAL FEDERATION OF RETAIL NEWSAGENTS Yeoman House, Sekforde Street, London EC1R 0HF T 020-7253 4225 E service@nfrnonline.com W www.nfrnonline.com
General Manager, Paul Chambers

NATIONAL LANDLORDS ASSOCIATION 22–26 Albert Embankment, London SE1 7TJ T 020-7840 8900 E info@landlords.org.uk W www.landlords.org.uk
Chair, David Salusbury

NATIONAL MARKET TRADERS FEDERATION Hampton House, Hawshaw Lane, Hoyland, Barnsley S74 0HA T 01226-749021 E genoffice@nmtf.co.uk W www.nmtf.co.uk
Chief Executive, Joe Harrison

NATIONAL PHARMACY ASSOCIATION Mallinson House, 38–42 St Peter's Street, St Albans, Herts AL1 3NP T 01727-858687 E npa@npa.co.uk W www.npa.co.uk
Chief Executive, John Turk

NEWSPAPER SOCIETY St Andrew's House, 18–20 St Andrew Street, London EC4A 3AY T 020-7632 7400 E ns@newspapersoc.org.uk W www.newspapersoc.org.uk
Director, David Newell

OIL AND GAS UK 2nd Floor, 232–242 Vauxhall Bridge Road, London SW1V 1AU T 020-7802 2400 E info@oilandgasuk.co.uk W www.oilandgasuk.co.uk
Chief Executive, Bob Keiller

PROPERTY CARE ASSOCIATION Lakeview Court, Ermine Business Park, Huntingdon PE29 6XR T 0844-375 4301 E pca@property-care.org W www.property-care.org
Executive Director, Yasmin Chopin

PUBLISHERS ASSOCIATION 29B Montague Street, London WC1B 5BW T 020-7691 9191 E mail@publishers.org.uk W www.publishers.org.uk
Chief Executive, Simon Juden

RADIOCENTRE 4th Floor, 5 Golden Square, London W1F 9BS T 020-3206 7800 E info@radiocentre.org W www.radiocentre.org
Chief Executive, Andrew Harrison

ROAD HAULAGE ASSOCIATION LTD Roadway House, Bretton PE3 8DD T 01733-261131 E southern-eastern@rha.uk.net W www.rha.uk.net
Chief Executive, Geoff Dunning

ROYAL ASSOCIATION OF BRITISH DAIRY FARMERS Dairy House, Unit 31, Abbey Park, Stareton, Kenilworth CV8 2LY T 0845-458 2711 E office@rabdf.co.uk W www.rabdf.co.uk
Chief Executive, Nick Everington

ROYAL FACULTY OF PROCURATORS IN GLASGOW 12 Nelson Mandela Place, Glasgow G2 1BT T 0141-332 3593 E library@rfpg.org W www.rfpg.org
Chief Executive, John McKenzie

SHELLFISH ASSOCIATION OF GREAT BRITAIN Fishmongers' Hall, London Bridge, London EC4R 9EL T 020-7283 8305 E sagb@shellfish.org.uk W www.shellfish.org.uk
Director, Dr Tom Pickerell

SOCIETY OF BRITISH AEROSPACE COMPANIES LTD Salamanca Square, 9 Albert Embankment, London SE1 7SP T 020-7091 4500 E post@sbac.co.uk W www.sbac.co.uk
Chief Executive, Rees Ward

SOCIETY OF LOCAL AUTHORITY CHIEF EXECUTIVES AND SENIOR MANAGERS Hope House, 45 Great Peter Street, London SW1P 3LT T 0845-652 4010 E hope.house@solace.org.uk W www.solace.org.uk
Director-General, David Clark

SOCIETY OF MOTOR MANUFACTURERS AND TRADERS LTD Forbes House, Halkin Street, London SW1X 7DS T 020-7235 7000 W www.smmt.co.uk
Chief Executive, Paul Everitt

TIMBER TRADE FEDERATION The Building Centre, 26 Store Street, London WC1E 7BT T 020-3205 0067 E ttf@ttf.co.uk W www.ttf.co.uk
Chief Executive, John White

TRADING STANDARDS INSTITUTE 1 Sylvan Court, Sylvan Way, Southfields Business Park, Basildon SS15 6TH T 0845-608 9400 E institute@tsi.org.uk W www.tradingstandards.gov.uk
Chief Executive, Ron Gainsford

UK FASHION AND TEXTILE INDUSTRY 5 Portland Place, London W1B 1PW T 020-7636 7788 E info@ukft.org.uk W www.ukft.org
Director-General, John Wilson, OBE

UK LEATHER FEDERATION Leather Trade House, Kings Park Road, Moulton Park, Northampton NN3 6JD T 01604-679917 E info@uklf.org W www.ukleather.org
Director, Paul Pearson

UK PETROLEUM INDUSTRY ASSOCIATION LTD Quality House, Quality Court, London WC2A 1HP T 020-7269 7600 E info@ukpia.com W www.ukpia.com
Director-General, Chris Hunt

ULSTER FARMERS' UNION 475 Antrim Road, Belfast BT15 3DA T 028-9037 0222 E info@ufuhq.com W www.ufuni.org
Chief Executive, Clarke Black

WINE AND SPIRIT TRADE ASSOCIATION International Wine and Spirit Centre, 39–45 Bermondsey Street, London SE1 3XF T 020-7089 3877 E info@wsta.co.uk W www.wsta.co.uk
Chief Executive, Jeremy Beadles

CBI

Centre Point, 103 New Oxford Street, London WC1A 1DU T 020-7379 7400 W www.cbi.org.uk

The CBI was founded in 1965 and is an independent non-party political body financed by industry and commerce. It works with the UK government, international legislators and policymakers to help UK businesses compete effectively. It is the recognised spokesman for the business viewpoint and is consulted as such by the government.

The CBI speaks for some 240,000 businesses that together employ approximately one-third of the private sector workforce. Member companies, which decide all policy positions, include 80 of the FTSE 100 index, some 200,000 small and medium-size firms, more than 20,000 manufacturers and over 150 sectoral associations.

The CBI board meets four times a year in London under the chairmanship of the president. It is assisted by 16 expert standing committees which advise on the main aspects of policy. There are 13 regional councils and offices, covering the administrative regions of England, Wales, Scotland and Northern Ireland. There are also offices in Beijing, Brussels, Delhi and Washington.

President, Helen Alexander

WALES: 2 Caspian Point, Caspian Way, Cardiff Bay, Cardiff CF10 4DQ T 029-2097 7600
Regional Director, David Rosser

SCOTLAND: 16 Robertson Street, Glasgow G2 8DS T 0141-222 2184
Regional Director, Iain McMillan

NORTHERN IRELAND: Scottish Amicable Building, 11 Donegall Square, Belfast BT1 5JE T 028-9010 1100
Regional Director, Nigel Smyth

TRADE UNIONS

A trade union is an organisation of workers formed (historically) for the purpose of collective bargaining over pay and working conditions. Today, trade unions may also provide legal and financial advice, sickness benefits and education facilities to their members. Legally any employee has the right to join a trade union, but not all employers recognise all or any trade unions. Conversely an employee also has the right not to join a trade union, in particular since the practice of a 'closed shop' system, where all employees have to join the employer's preferred union, is no longer permitted. Below is a list of key dates in the development of the British trade unionist movement.

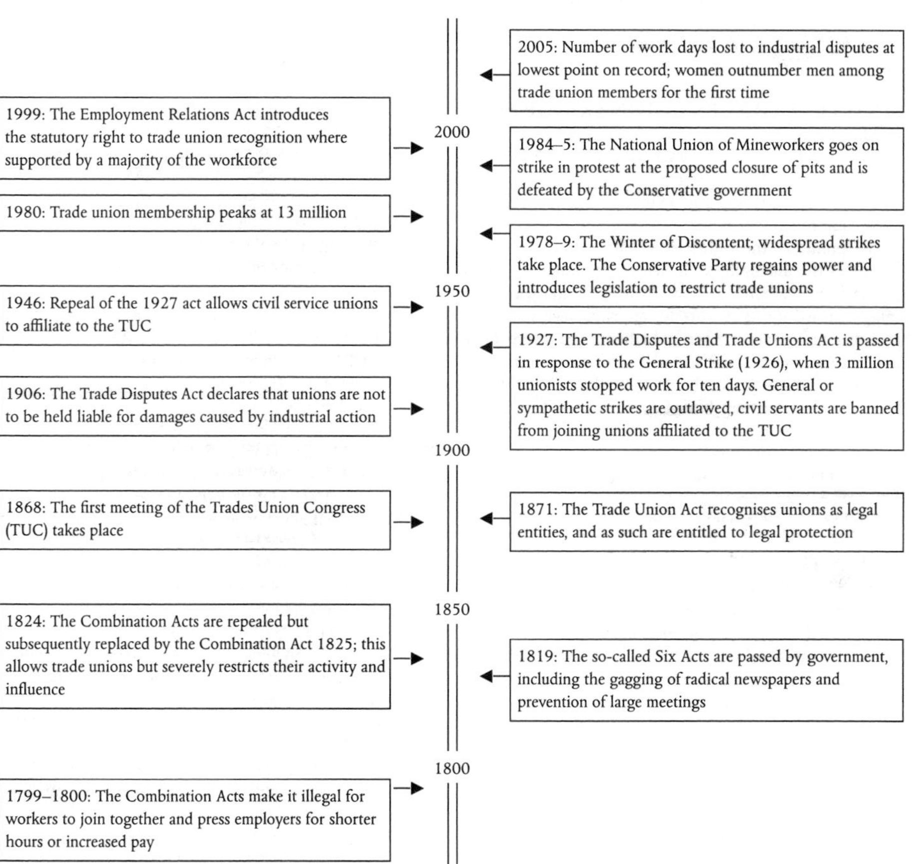

THE CENTRAL ARBITRATION COMMITTEE

22nd Floor, Euston Tower, 286 Euston Road, London NW1 3JJ
T 020-7904 2300 E enquiries@cac.gov.uk
W www.cac.gov.uk

The Central Arbitration Committee's main role is concerned with requests for trade union recognition and de-recognition under the statutory procedures of Schedule A1 of the Employment Rights Act 1999. It also determines disclosure of information complaints under the Trade Union and Labour Relations (Consolidation) Act 1992, considers applications and complaints under the Information and Consultation Regulations 2004, and performs a similar role in relation to European works councils, European companies, European cooperative societies and cross-border mergers. It also provides voluntary arbitration in industrial disputes.

Chair, Sir Michael Burton
Chief Executive, Graeme Charles

TRADES UNION CONGRESS (TUC)

Congress House, 23–28 Great Russell Street, London WC1B 3LS T 020-7636 4030
E info@tuc.org.uk W www.tuc.org.uk

The Trades Union Congress, founded in 1868, is an independent association of trade unions. The TUC promotes the rights and welfare of those in work and helps the unemployed. It helps its member unions promote membership in new areas and industries, and campaigns for rights at work for all employees, including part-time and temporary workers, whether union members or not. TUC representatives sit on many public bodies at national and international level such as government, political parties, employers and the European Union.

The governing body of the TUC is the annual congress. Between congresses, business is conducted by a general council, which meets five times a year, and an executive committee, which meets monthly. The full-time staff is headed by the general secretary who is elected by congress and is a permanent member of the general council.

There are 58 affiliated unions, with a total membership of nearly 6,300,000.

President (2009–10), Dougie Rooney
General Secretary, Brendan Barber

SCOTTISH TRADES UNION CONGRESS (STUC)

333 Woodlands Road, Glasgow G3 6NG **T** 0141-337 8100
E info@stuc.org.uk **W** www.stuc.org.uk

The congress was formed in 1897 and acts as a national centre for the trade union movement in Scotland. The STUC promotes the rights to welfare of those in work and helps the unemployed. It helps its member unions to promote membership in new areas and industries, and campaigns for rights at work for all employees, including part-time temporary workers, whether union members or not. It also makes representations to government and employers. In April 2010 it consisted of 37 affiliated unions with a membership of more than 650,000 and 24 trades union councils.

The annual congress in April elects a 36-member general council on the basis of six sections.

President, Martin Keenan
General Secretary, Grahame Smith

WALES TUC

1 Cathedral Road, Cardiff CF11 9SD **T** 029-2034 7010
E wtuc@tuc.org.uk **W** www.wtuc.org.uk

The Wales TUC was established in 1974 to ensure that the role of the TUC was effectively undertaken in Wales. Its structure reflects the four economic regions of Wales and matches the regional committee areas of the National Assembly of Wales. The regional committees oversee the delivery of Wales TUC policy and campaigns in the relevant regions, and liaise with local government, training organisations and regional economic development bodies. The Wales TUC seeks to reduce unemployment, increase the levels of skill and pay, and eliminate discrimination.

The governing body of Wales TUC is the conference, which meets annually in May and elects a general council (usually of around 50 people) which oversees the work of the TUC throughout the year.

There are over 50 affiliated unions, with a total membership of around 500,000.

President, Sian Wiblin
General Secretary, Martin Mansfield

TUC-AFFILIATED UNIONS

As at April 2010

ACCORD Simmons House, 46 Old Bath Road, Charvil RG10 9QR **T** 0118-934 1808 **E** info@accordhq.org **W** www.accord-myunion.org
General Secretary, Ged Nichols *Membership:* 32,745

ADVANCE (FORMERLY ANGU) 2nd Floor, 16–17 High Street, Tring HP23 5AH **T** 01442-891122 **E** info@advance-union.org **W** www.advance-union.org
General Secretary, Linda Rolph *Membership:* 7,200

AEP (ASSOCIATION OF EDUCATIONAL PSYCHOLOGISTS) Unit 4, The Riverside Centre, Frankland Lane, Durham DH1 5TA **T** 0191-384 9512 **E** sao@aep.org.uk **W** www.aep.org.uk
General Secretary, Charles Ward *Membership:* 3,200

AFA COUNCIL 7 (ASSOCIATION OF FLIGHT ATTENDANTS) United Airlines Cargo Centre, Shoreham Road East, Heathrow Airport TW6 3UA **T** 020-8276 6723 **E** afalhr@unitedafa.org **W** www.afalhr.org.uk
President, Saad Bhatkar *Membership:* 610

AMIE (ASSOCIATION FOR MANAGERS IN EDUCATION) 35 The Point, Market Harborough LE16 7QU **T** 01858-461110 **E** admin@amie.uk.com **W** www.amie.uk.com
General Secretary, Peter Pendle *Membership:* 3,555

ASLEF (ASSOCIATED SOCIETY OF LOCOMOTIVE ENGINEERS AND FIREMEN) 9 Arkwright Road, Hampstead, London NW3 6AB **T** 020-7317 8600 **E** info@aslef.org.uk **W** www.aslef.org.uk
General Secretary, Keith Norman *Membership:* 18,200

ASPECT (FORMERLY NAEIAC) Woolley Hall, Woolley WF4 2JR **T** 01226-383428 **E** info@aspect.org.uk **W** www.aspect.org.uk
General Secretary, John Chowcat *Membership:* 4,000

ATL (ASSOCIATION OF TEACHERS AND LECTURERS) 7 Northumberland Street, London WC2N 5RD **T** 020-7930 6441 **E** info@atl.org.uk **W** www.atl.org.uk
General Secretary, Mary Bousted *Membership:* 122,372

BACM-TEAM (BRITISH ASSOCIATION OF COLLIERY MANAGEMENT – TECHNICAL, ENERGY AND ADMINISTRATIVE MANAGEMENT) Danum House, 6A South Parade, Doncaster DN1 2DY **T** 01302-815551 **E** enquiries@bacmteam.org.uk **W** www.bacmteam.org.uk
General Secretary, Patrick Carragher *Membership:* 2,664

BALPA (BRITISH AIRLINE PILOTS ASSOCIATION) BALPA House, 5 Heathrow Boulevard, 278 Bath Road, West Drayton UB7 0DQ **T** 020-8476 4000 **E** balpa@balpa.org **W** www.balpa.org.uk
General Secretary, Jim McAuslan *Membership:* 14,000

BDA (BRITISH DIETETIC ASSOCIATION) 5th Floor, Charles House, 148–149 Great Charles Street, Birmingham B3 3HT **T** 0121-200 8080 **E** info@bda.uk.com **W** www.bda.uk.com
Chief Executive, Andy Burman *Membership:* 6,500

BECTU (BROADCASTING, ENTERTAINMENT, CINEMATOGRAPH AND THEATRE UNION) 373–377 Clapham Road, London SW9 9BT **T** 020-7346 0900 **E** info@bectu.org.uk **W** www.bectu.org.uk
General Secretary, Gerry Morrissey *Membership:* 25,044

BFAWU (BAKERS, FOOD AND ALLIED WORKERS' UNION) Stanborough House, Great North Road, Stanborough, Welwyn Garden City AL8 7TA **T** 01707-260150 **E** info@bfawu.org **W** www.bfawu.org
General Secretary, Joe Marino *Membership:* 30,000

BIOS (BRITISH AND IRISH ORTHOPTIC SOCIETY) Tavistock House North, Tavistock Square, London WC1H 9HX **T** 020-7387 7992 **E** bios@orthoptics.org.uk **W** www.orthoptics.org.uk
Executive Officer, Rosie Auld *Membership:* 1,299

BSU (BRITANNIA STAFF UNION) Court Lodge, Leonard Street, Leek ST13 5JP **T** 01538-399627 **E** staff.union@britannia.co.uk **W** www.britanniasu.org.uk
General Secretary, John Stoddard *Membership:* 3,240

CDNA (COMMUNITY AND DISTRICT NURSING ASSOCIATION) c/o GMB, 22–24 Worpole Road SW19 4GG **T** 020-8971 4268 **E** info@cdnaonline.org **W** www.cdnaonline.org
Chief Executive, Anne Duffy *Membership:* 2,900

CGSU (CHESHIRE GROUP STAFF UNION) 26 High Street, Mold CH7 1AZ **T** 01352-751512 **E** karen.hughes@thecheshire.org.uk
General Secretary, Karen Hughes *Membership:* 310

COMMUNITY 67–68 Long Acre, Covent Garden, London WC2E 9FA **T** 020-7420 4000 **E** info@community-tu.org **W** www.community-tu.org
General Secretary, Michael Leahy, OBE *Membership:* 30,000

CSP (CHARTERED SOCIETY OF PHYSIOTHERAPY) 14 Bedford Row, London WC1R 4ED **T** 020-7306 6666 **E** enquiries@csp.org.uk **W** www.csp.org.uk
Chief Executive, Phil Gray *Membership:* 49,000

CWU (COMMUNICATION WORKERS UNION) 150 The Broadway, Wimbledon, London SW19 1RX **T** 020-8971 7200 **E** info@cwu.org **W** www.cwu.org
General Secretary, W. Hayes *Membership:* 220,000

DGSU (DERBYSHIRE GROUP STAFF UNION) The Lodge, Duffield Hall, DE56 1AG **T** 01332-844396 **E** dgsu@thederbyshire.co.uk **W** www.dgsu.org.uk
Chair, Sue Burgess *Membership:* 394

EIS (EDUCATIONAL INSTITUTE OF SCOTLAND) 46 Moray Place, Edinburgh EH3 6BH **T** 0131-225 6244 **E** enquiries@eis.org.uk **W** www.eis.org.uk
General Secretary, Ronald A. Smith *Membership:* 60,110

EQUITY Guild House, Upper St Martin's Lane, London WC2H 9EG **T** 020-7379 6000 **E** info@equity.org.uk **W** www.equity.org.uk
General Secretary, Christine Payne *Membership:* 35,500

FBU (FIRE BRIGADES UNION) Bradley House, 68 Coombe Road, Kingston upon Thames KT2 7AE **T** 020-8541 1765 **E** office@fbu.org.uk **W** www.fbu.org.uk
General Secretary, Matt Wrack *Membership:* 50,000

FDA 8 Leake Street, London SE1 7NN **T** 020-7401 5555 **E** info@fda.org.uk **W** www.fda.org.uk
General Secretary, Jonathan Baume *Membership:* 17,977

GMB 22–24 Worple Road, London SW19 4DD **T** 020-8947 3131 **E** info@gmb.org.uk **W** www.gmb.org.uk
General Secretary, Paul Kenny *Membership:* 610,000

HCSA (HOSPITAL CONSULTANTS' AND SPECIALISTS' ASSOCIATION) 1 Kingsclere Road, Overton, Basingstoke RG25 3JA **T** 01256-771777 **E** conspec@hcsa.com **W** www.hcsa.com
Chief Executive, Stephen Campion *Membership:* 3,250

MU (MUSICIANS' UNION) 60–62 Clapham Road, London SW9 0JJ **T** 020-7582 5566 **E** info@musiciansunion.org.uk **W** www.musiciansunion.org.uk
General Secretary, John F. Smith *Membership:* 32,000

NACODS (NATIONAL ASSOCIATION OF COLLIERY OVERMEN, DEPUTIES AND SHOTFIRERS) Wadsworth House, 130–132 Doncaster Road, Barnsley S70 1TP **T** 01226-203743 **E** natnacods@googlemail.com **W** www.nacods.org.uk
General Secretary, Rowland Soar *Membership:* 330

NACO (NATIONAL ASSOCIATION OF COOPERATIVE OFFICIALS) 6A Clarendon Place, Hyde SK14 2QZ **T** 0161-351 7900 **E** info@nacoco-op.org **W** www.naco.coop
President, Ann Breen *Membership:* 2,120

NAPO (TRADE UNION AND PROFESSIONAL ASSOCIATION FOR FAMILY COURT AND PROBATION STAFF) 4 Chivalry Road, London SW11 1HT **T** 020-7223 4887 **E** info@napo.org.uk **W** www.napo.org.uk
General Secretary, Jonathan Ledger *Membership:* 9,500

NASS (NATIONAL ASSOCIATION OF STABLE STAFF) 74A High Street, Swadlincote DE11 8HS **T** 01283-211522 **E** office@naoss.co.uk **W** www.naoss.co.uk
Chief Executive, Jim Cornelius *Membership:* 1,703

NASUWT (NATIONAL ASSOCIATION OF SCHOOLMASTERS/UNION OF WOMEN TEACHERS) Hillscourt Education Centre, Rose Hill, Rednal, Birmingham B45 8RS **T** 0121-453 6150 **E** nasuwt@mail.nasuwt.org.uk **W** www.nasuwt.org.uk
General Secretary, Ms Chris Keates *Membership:* 279,145

NAUTILUS INTERNATIONAL Oceanair House, 750–760 High Road, Leytonstone, London E11 3BB **T** 020-8989 6677 **E** enquiries@nautilusint.org **W** www.nautilusint.org
General Secretary, Mark Dickinson *Membership:* 25,000

NGSU (NATIONWIDE GROUP STAFF UNION) Middleton Farmhouse, 37 Main Road, Middleton Cheney OX17 2QT **T** 01295-710767 **E** ngsu@ngsu.org.uk **W** www.ngsu.org.uk
President, Bill Blumsom *Membership:* 12,643

NUJ (NATIONAL UNION OF JOURNALISTS) Headland House, 308–312 Gray's Inn Road, London WC1X 8DP **T** 020-7843 3709 **E** info@nuj.org.uk **W** www.nuj.org.uk
General Secretary, Jeremy Dear *Membership:* 36,900

NUM (NATIONAL UNION OF MINEWORKERS) Miners' Offices, 2 Huddersfield Road, Barnsley S70 2LS **T** 01226-215555 **E** chris.kitchen@num.org.uk **W** www.num.org.uk
President, I. Lavery *Membership:* 1,600

NUT (NATIONAL UNION OF TEACHERS) Hamilton House, Mabledon Place, London WC1H 9BD **T** 020-7388 6191 **W** www.teachers.org.uk
General Secretary, Christine Blower *Membership:* 376,797

PCS (PUBLIC AND COMMERCIAL SERVICES UNION) 160 Falcon Road, London SW11 2LN **T** 020-7924 2727 **E** editor@pcs.org.uk **W** www.pcs.org.uk
General Secretary, Mark Serwotka *Membership:* 300,000

PFA (PROFESSIONAL FOOTBALLERS' ASSOCIATION) 20 Oxford Court, Bishopsgate, Manchester M2 3WQ **T** 0161-236 0575 **E** info@thepfa.co.uk **W** www.givemefootball.com
Chief Executive, Gordon Taylor, OBE *Membership:* 4,000

POA (PROFESSIONAL TRADE UNION FOR PRISON, CORRECTIONAL AND SECURE PSYCHIATRIC WORKERS) Cronin House, 245 Church Street, London N9 9HW **T** 020-8803 0255 **E** general@poauk.org.uk **W** www.poauk.org.uk
General Secretary, Brian Caton *Membership:* 36,000

PROSPECT New Prospect House, 8 Leake Street, London SE1 7NN **T** 020-7902 6600 **E** enquiries@prospect.org.uk **W** www.prospect.org.uk
President, Catherine Donaldson *Membership:* 122,000

RMT (NATIONAL UNION OF RAIL, MARITIME AND TRANSPORT WORKERS) Unity House, 39 Chalton Street, London NW1 1JD **T** 020-7387 4771 **E** info@rmt.org.uk **W** www.rmt.org.uk
General Secretary, Bob Crow *Membership:* 80,000

SCP (SOCIETY OF CHIROPODISTS AND PODIATRISTS) 1 Fellmonger's Path, Tower Bridge Road, London SE1 3LY T 020-7234 8620 E enq@scpod.org W www.feetforlife.org
Chief Executive, Joanna Brown *Membership:* 10,000

SOR (SOCIETY OF RADIOGRAPHERS) 207 Providence Square, Mill Street, London SE1 2EW T 020-7740 7200 E info@sor.org W www.sor.org
Chief Executive, Richard Evans *Membership:* 20,500

TSSA (TRANSPORT SALARIED STAFFS' ASSOCIATION) Walkden House, 10 Melton Street, London NW1 2EJ T 020-7387 2101 E enquiries@tssa.org.uk W www.tssa.org.uk
General Secretary, Gerry Doherty *Membership:* 30,000

UCAC (UNDEB CENEDLAETHOL ATHRAWON CYMRU) (NATIONAL UNION OF THE TEACHERS OF WALES) Prif Swyddfa UCAC, Ffordd Penglais, Aberystwyth SY23 2EU T 01970-639950 E ucac@athrawon.com W www.athrawon.com
General Secretary, Elaine Edwards *Membership:* 4,500

UCATT (UNION OF CONSTRUCTION, ALLIED TRADES AND TECHNICIANS) UCATT House, 177 Abbeville Road, London SW4 9RL T 020-7622 2442 E info@ucatt.org.uk W www.ucatt.org.uk
General Secretary, Alan Ritchie *Membership:* 125,000

UCU (UNIVERSITY AND COLLEGE UNION) Carlow Street, London NW1 7LH T 020-7756 2500 E hq@ucu.org.uk W www.ucu.org.uk
General Secretary, Sally Hunt *Membership:* 118,000

UNISON 1 Mabledon Place, London WC1H 9AJ T 0845-355 0845 W www.unison.org.uk
General Secretary, Dave Prentis *Membership:* 1,400,000

UNITE (FORMERLY AMICUS AND T&G)* 35 King Street, London WC2E 8JG T 020-7420 8900 W www.unitetheunion.org
General Secretaries, Derek Simpson; Tony Woodley *Membership:* 2,000,000

UNITY Hillcrest House, Garth Street, Hanley, Stoke-on-Trent ST1 2AB T 01782-272755 E geoffbagnall@unitytheunion.org.uk W www.unitytheunion.org.uk
General Secretary, Geoff Bagnall *Membership:* 5,000

URTU (UNITED ROAD TRANSPORT UNION) Almond House, Oak Green, Stanley Green Business Park, Cheadle Hulme SK8 6QL T 0800-526639 E info@urtu.com W www.urtu.com
General Secretary, Robert Monks *Membership:* 13,000

USDAW (UNION OF SHOP, DISTRIBUTIVE AND ALLIED WORKERS) 188 Wilmslow Road, Manchester M14 6LJ T 0161-224 2804 E enquiries@usdaw.org.uk W www.usdaw.org.uk
General Secretary, John Hannett *Membership:* 387,055

WRITERS' GUILD OF GREAT BRITAIN (WGGB) 40 Rosebery Avenue, London EC1R 4RX T 020-7833 0777 E admin@writersguild.org.uk W www.writersguild.org.uk
President, David Edgar *Membership:* 2,258

YORKSHIRE INDEPENDENT STAFF ASSOCIATION (YISA) c/o Yorkshire Building Society, Yorkshire House, Yorkshire Drive, Rooley Lane, Bradford BD5 8LJ T 01274-472453 E kmwatson@ybs.co.uk
Chair, Karen Watson *Membership:* 1,500

* In July 2008 Unite agreed an accord with United Steelworkers (of the USA) to begin preparations for the creation of the first transatlantic trade union, Workers Uniting, which will represent over 3 million members in the UK, Ireland, USA and Canada

NON-AFFILIATED UNIONS

As at April 2010

ASCL (ASSOCIATION OF SCHOOL AND COLLEGE LEADERS) 130 Regent Road, Leicester LE1 7PG T 0116-299 1122 E info@ascl.org.uk W www.ascl.org.uk
General Secretary, Brian Lightman *Membership:* 15,000

BDA (BRITISH DENTAL ASSOCIATION) 64 Wimpole Street, London W1G 8YS T 020-7935 0875 E enquiries@bda.org W www.bda.org
Chief Executive, Peter Ward *Membership:* 23,349

CIOJ (CHARTERED INSTITUTE OF JOURNALISTS) 2 Dock Offices, Surrey Quays Road, London SE16 2XU T 020-7252 1187 E memberservices@cioj.co.uk W www.cioj.co.uk
General Secretary, Dominic Cooper *Membership:* 2,000

NAHT (NATIONAL ASSOCIATION OF HEAD TEACHERS) 1 Heath Square, Boltro Road, Haywards Heath RH16 1BL T 01444-472472 E info@naht.org.uk W www.naht.org.uk
General Secretary, Russell Hobby *Membership:* 28,400

NSEAD (NATIONAL SOCIETY FOR EDUCATION IN ART AND DESIGN) 3 Mason's Wharf, Potley Lane, Corsham SN13 9FY T 01225-810134 E info@nsead.org W www.nsead.org
General Secretary, Dr John Steers *Membership:* 2,066

RBA (RETAIL BOOK ASSOCIATION) 22 Borough Fields Shopping Centre, Wootton Bassett, Swindon SN4 7AX T 01793-841414 E info@the-rba.org W www.the-rba.org
President, David Pickles *Membership:* 3,500

RCM (ROYAL COLLEGE OF MIDWIVES) 15 Mansfield Street, London W1G 9NH T 020-7312 3535 E info@rcm.org.uk W www.rcm.org.uk
General Secretary, Prof. Cathy Warwick, CBE *Membership:* 38,000

SOCIETY OF AUTHORS 84 Drayton Gardens, London SW10 9SB T 020-7373 6642 E info@societyofauthors.org W www.societyofauthors.org
General Secretary, Mark Le Fanu, OBE *Membership:* 8,500

SSTA (SCOTTISH SECONDARY TEACHERS' ASSOCIATION) West End House, 14 West End Place, Edinburgh EH11 2ED T 0131-313 7300 E info@ssta.org.uk W www.ssta.org.uk
General Secretary, Ann Ballinger *Membership:* 8,500

SPORTS BODIES

SPORTS COUNCILS

CENTRAL COUNCIL OF PHYSICAL RECREATION Burwood House, 14–16 Caxton Street, London SW1H 0QT T 020-7976 3900 E info@ccpr.org.uk W www.ccpr.org.uk
Chief Executive, Tim Lamb

SPORT ENGLAND 3rd Floor, Victoria House, Bloomsbury Square, London WC1B 4SE T 0845-850 8508 E info@sportengland.org W www.sportengland.org
Chief Executive, Jennie Price

SPORT NORTHERN IRELAND House of Sport, 2A Upper Malone Road, Belfast BT9 5LA T 028-9038 1222 E info@sportni.net W www.sportni.net
Chief Executive, Prof. Eamonn McCartan

SPORTSCOTLAND Doges, Templeton on the Green, 62 Templeton Street, Glasgow G40 1DA T 0141-534 6500 E sportscotland.enquiries@sportscotland.org.uk W www.sportscotland.org.uk
Chief Executive, Stewart Harris

SPORTS COUNCIL FOR WALES Sophia Gardens, Cardiff CF11 9SW T 0845-045 0904 E info@sportwales.org.uk W www.sports-council-wales.org.uk
Chief Executive, Dr Huw Jones

UK SPORT 40 Bernard Street, London WC1N 1ST T 020-7211 5100 E info@uksport.gov.uk W www.uksport.gov.uk
Chief Executive, John Steele

AMERICAN FOOTBALL

BRITISH AMERICAN FOOTBALL ASSOCIATION West House, Hedley on the Hill, Stocksfield NE43 7SW T 01661-843179 E chairman@bafa.org.uk W www.bafa.org.uk
Chair, Gary Marshall

ANGLING

ANGLING TRUST Eastwood House, 6 Rainbow Street, Leominster, Herefordshire HR6 8DQ T 0844-770 0616 E admin@anglingtrust.net W www.anglingtrust.net
Chief Executive, Mark Lloyd

ARCHERY

GRAND NATIONAL ARCHERY SOCIETY Lilleshall National Sports Centre, Newport TF10 9AT T 01952-677888 E enquiries@archerygb.org W www.gnas.org
Chief Executive, David Sherratt

ASSOCIATION FOOTBALL

FOOTBALL ASSOCIATION Wembley Stadium, PO Box 1966, SW1P 9EQ T 020-7745 4545 W www.thefa.com
Acting Chief Executive, Alex Horne

FOOTBALL ASSOCIATION OF WALES 11–12 Neptune Court, Vanguard Way, Cardiff CF24 5PJ T 029-2043 5830 E info@faw.org.uk W www.faw.org.uk
Chief Executive, Jonathan Ford

FOOTBALL LEAGUE Edward VII Quay, Navigation Way, Preston PR2 2YF T 0844-463 1888 E fl@football-league.co.uk W www.football-league.co.uk
Chief Operating Officer, A. G. Williamson

IRISH FOOTBALL ASSOCIATION 20 Windsor Avenue, Belfast BT9 6EG T 028-9066 9458 E info@irishfa.com W www.irishfa.com
Chief Executive, Patrick Nelson

IRISH PREMIER LEAGUE Benmore House, Unit 2, 343–353 Lisburn Road, Belfast BT9 7EN T 028-9066 9559 E enquiries@irishpremierleague.com W www.irishpremierleague.com
General Secretary, Craig Stanfield

PREMIER LEAGUE 30 Gloucester Place, London W1U 8PL T 020-7864 9190 E info@premierleague.com W www.premierleague.com
Chief Executive, Richard Scudamore

SCOTTISH FOOTBALL ASSOCIATION Hampden Park, Glasgow G42 9AY T 0141-616 6000 E info@scottishfa.co.uk W www.scottishfa.co.uk
Chief Executive, Gordon Smith

SCOTTISH FOOTBALL LEAGUE The National Stadium, Hampden Park, Glasgow G42 9EB T 0141-620 4160 E info@scottishfootballleague.com W www.scottishfootballleague.com
Chief Executive, David A. Longmuir

ATHLETICS

ATHLETICS NORTHERN IRELAND Athletics House, Old Coach Road, Belfast BT9 5PR T 028-9060 2707 E info@niathletics.org W www.niathletics.org
Hon. Secretary, John Allen

SCOTTISH ATHLETICS Caledonia House, South Gyle, Edinburgh EH12 9DQ T 0131-539 7320 E admin@scottishathletics.org.uk W www.scottishathletics.org.uk
Chief Executive, Nigel Holl

UK ATHLETICS Athletics House, Central Boulevard, Blythe Valley Park, Solihull B90 8AJ T 0121-713 8400 W www.uka.org.uk
Chief Executive, Niels de Vos

WELSH ATHLETICS Cardiff International Sports Stadium, Leckwith Road, Cardiff CF11 8AZ T 029-2064 4870 E office@welshathletics.org W www.welshathletics.org
Chief Executive Officer, Matt Newman

BADMINTON

BADMINTON ENGLAND National Badminton Centre, Milton Keynes MK8 9LA T 01908-268400 E enquiries@badmintonengland.co.uk W www.badmintonengland.co.uk
Chief Executive, Adrian Christy

BADMINTON SCOTLAND Cockburn Centre, 40 Bogmoor Place, Glasgow G51 4QT T 0141-445 1218 E enquiries@badmintonscotland.org.uk W www.badmintonscotland.org.uk
Chief Executive, Anne Smillie

WELSH BADMINTON UNION Sport Wales National Centre, Sophia Gardens, Cardiff CF11 9SW T 0845-045 4301 E wbu@welshbadminton.net W www.welshbadminton.net
Chief Executive, Eddie O'Neill

BASEBALL

BASEBALLSOFTBALL UK Ariel House, 74A Charlotte Street, London W1T 4QJ T 020-7453 7055 W www.baseballsoftballuk.com
Head of Operations, Jenny Fromer

BASKETBALL

BASKETBALL SCOTLAND Caledonia House, South Gyle, Edinburgh EH12 9DQ **T** 0131-317 7260 **E** enquiries@basketball-scotland.com **W** www.basketball-scotland.com
Chair, Colin Pearson

ENGLAND BASKETBALL PO Box 3971, Sheffield S9 9AZ **T** 0114-284 1060 **E** info@englandbasketball.co.uk **W** www.englandbasketball.com
Chief Executive, Keith Mair

BILLIARDS AND SNOOKER

WORLD LADIES BILLIARDS AND SNOOKER ASSOCIATION 231 Ramnoth Road, Wisbech, PE13 2SN **T** 01945-589589 **E** worldladiessnooker@ntlworld.com **W** www.worldladiessnooker.co.uk
Chair, Mandy Fisher

WORLD SNOOKER 2nd Floor, Albert House, 111–117 Victoria Street, Bristol BS1 6AX **T** 0117-317 8200 **E** enq@worldsnooker.com **W** www.worldsnooker.com
Chair, Barry Hearn

BOBSLEIGH

BRITISH BOBSLEIGH AND SKELETON ASSOCIATION 9 Looke Lane, Puncknowle, Dorchester DP2 9BD **T** 01403-221844 **E** hq@bobteamgb.org **W** www.bobteamgb.org
Chair, Martin Allison

BOWLS

BOWLS ENGLAND Lyndhurst Road, Worthing BN11 2AZ **T** 01903-820222 **E** enquiries@bowlsengland.com **W** www.bowlsengland.com
Chief Executive, A. Allcock, MBE

BRITISH ISLES BOWLS COUNCIL 23 Leysland Avenue, Countesthorpe LE8 5XX **T** 0116-277 3234 **E** michaelswatland@btinternet.com **W** www.britishislesbowls.com
Hon. Secretary, Michael Swatland

ENGLISH INDOOR BOWLING ASSOCIATION LIMITED David Cornwell House, Bowling Green, Leicester Road, Melton Mowbray LE13 0FA **T** 01664-481900 **E** enquiries@eiba.co.uk **W** www.eiba.co.uk
Chief Operating Executive, Peter Thompson

BOXING

AMATEUR BOXING ASSOCIATION OF ENGLAND English Institute of Sport, Coleridge Road, Sheffield S9 5DA **T** 0114-223 5654 **E** membership@abae.org.uk **W** www.abae.org.uk
Company Secretary, Paul King

BRITISH BOXING BOARD OF CONTROL 14 North Road, Trinity Street, Cardiff CF10 3DY **T** 029-2036 7000 **E** admin@bbbofc.com **W** www.bbbofc.com
Chair, Charles Giles

CANOEING

BRITISH CANOE UNION 18 Market Place, Bingham, Nottingham NG13 8AP **T** 0845-370 9500 **E** info@bcu.org.uk **W** www.bcu.org.uk
Chief Executive, Paul Owen

CHESS

ENGLISH CHESS FEDERATION The Watch Oak, Chain Lane, Battle TN33 0YD **T** 01424-775222 **E** office@englishchess.org.uk **W** www.englishchess.org.uk
Chief Executive, Chris Majer

CRICKET

ENGLAND AND WALES CRICKET BOARD Lord's Cricket Ground, London NW8 8QZ **T** 020-7432 1200 **E** feedback@ecb.co.uk **W** www.ecb.co.uk
Chief Executive, David Collier

MCC Lord's Cricket Ground, St John's Wood, London NW8 8QN **T** 020-7616 8500 **W** www.lords.org
Secretary and Chief Executive, Keith Bradshaw

CROQUET

CROQUET ASSOCIATION Cheltenham Croquet Club, Old Bath Road, Cheltenham GL53 7DF **T** 01242-242318 **E** caoffice@croquet.org.uk **W** www.croquet.org.uk
President, Quiller Barrett

CURLING

BRITISH CURLING ASSOCIATION 51 Atholl Road, Pitlochry, Perthshire PH16 5BU **T** 01463-242922 **E** info@britishcurling.co.uk **W** www.britishcurling.co.uk
Chair, Chris L. Hildrey

ROYAL CALEDONIAN CURLING CLUB Cairnie House, Avenue K, Ingliston Showground, Newbridge EH28 8NB **T** 0131-333 3003 **E** office@royalcaledoniancurlingclub.org **W** www.royalcaledoniancurlingclub.org
Chief Executive Officer, Colin T. Grahamslaw

CYCLING

BRITISH CYCLING FEDERATION National Cycling Centre, Stuart Street, Manchester M11 4DQ **T** 0161-274 2000 **E** info@britishcycling.org.uk **W** www.britishcycling.org.uk
Chief Executive, Ian Drake

CYCLING TIME TRIALS 77 Arlington Drive, Pennington, Leigh WN7 3QP **T** 01942-603976 **E** phil.heaton@cyclingtimetrials.org.uk **W** www.cyclingtimetrials.org.uk
Chair, Sheila Hardy

DARTS

BRITISH DARTS ORGANISATION 2 Pages Lane, Muswell Hill, London N10 1PS **T** 020-8883 5544 **E** britishdartsorg@btconnect.com **W** www.bdodarts.com
Chair, Dave Alderman

EQUESTRIANISM

BRITISH EQUESTRIAN FEDERATION Stoneleigh Park, Kenilworth CV8 2RH **T** 024-7669 8871 **E** info@bef.co.uk **W** www.bef.co.uk
Chief Executive, Andrew Finding

BRITISH EVENTING Stoneleigh Park, Kenilworth CV8 2RN **T** 0845-262 3344 **E** info@britisheventing.com **W** www.britisheventing.com
Chief Executive, Mike Etherington-Smith

ETON FIVES

ETON FIVES ASSOCIATION 45 Sandhills Crescent, Hillfield, Solihull B91 3UE **T** 07833-600230 **E** efa@etonfives.co.uk **W** www.etonfives.co.uk
Chair, Richard Barber, OBE

FENCING

BRITISH FENCING ASSOCIATION 1 Baron's Gate, 33–35 Rothschild Road, London W4 5HT **T** 020-8742 3032 **E** headoffice@britishfencing.com **W** www.britishfencing.com
Chief Executive Officer, Piers Martin

GLIDING

BRITISH GLIDING ASSOCIATION 3rd Floor, Kimberley House, Vaughan Way, Leicester LE1 4SE
T 0116-253 1051 E office@gliding.co.uk
W www.gliding.co.uk
Chief Executive, Pete Stratten

GOLF

ENGLISH GOLF UNION The National Golf Centre, Woodhall Spa LN10 6PU T 01526-354500
E info@englishgolfunion.org
W www.englishgolfunion.org
Chief Executive, John Petrie

LADIES' GOLF UNION The Scores, St Andrews KY16 9AT T 01334-475811 W www.lgu.org
Chief Executive, Shona Malcolm

THE R&A Golf Place, St Andrews KY16 9JD
T 01334-460000 E thesecretary@randagc.org
W www.randa.org
Secretary, Peter Dawson

GYMNASTICS

BRITISH GYMNASTICS Ford Hall, Lilleshall National Sports Centre, Newport TF10 9NB T 0845-129 7129
E information@british-gymnastics.org
W www.british-gymnastics.org
Chief Executive, vacant

HANDBALL

BRITISH HANDBALL ASSOCIATION
40 Newchurch Road, Rawtenstall, Rossendale BB4 7QX
T 020-3086 9676 E office@britishhandball.com
W http://britishhandball.worldhandball.com
Chief Executive, Paul Goodwin

HOCKEY

ENGLAND HOCKEY Bisham Abbey National Sports Centre, Marlow SL7 1RR T 01628-897500
E info@englandhockey.org
W www.englandhockey.co.uk
Chief Executive, Sally Munday

SCOTTISH HOCKEY UNION 589 Lanark Road, Edinburgh EH14 5DA T 0131-453 9070
E info@scottish-hockey.org.uk
W www.scottish-hockey.org.uk
Chief Executive, Brent Deans

WELSH HOCKEY UNION Sport Wales National Centre, Sophie Gardens, Cardiff CF11 9SW
T 029-2078 0730 E info@welsh-hockey.co.uk
W www.welsh-hockey.co.uk
Chief Executive, Helen Bushell

HORSERACING

BRITISH HORSERACING AUTHORITY
75 High Holborn, London WC1V 6LS T 020-7152 0000
E info@britishhorseracing.com
W www.britishhorseracing.com
Chief Executive, Nic Coward

THE JOCKEY CLUB 75 High Holborn, London WC1V 6LS T 020-7611 1800 E info@thejockeyclub.co.uk
W www.thejockeyclub.co.uk
Chief Executive, Simon Bazalgette

ICE HOCKEY

ICE HOCKEY UK 19 Heather Avenue, Rise Park, Romford RM1 4SL T 07917-194264
E ihukoffice@yahoo.co.uk W www.icehockeyuk.co.uk
Chair, Eamon Convery

ICE SKATING

NATIONAL ICE SKATING ASSOCIATION OF THE UK Grains Building, High Cross Street, Hockley, Nottingham NG1 3AX T 0115-988 8060
W www.iceskating.org.uk
General Secretary, Keith Horton

LACROSSE

ENGLISH LACROSSE ASSOCIATION Belle Vue Athletics Centre, Pink Bank Lane, Manchester M12 5GL
T 0161-227 3626 E info@englishlacrosse.co.uk
W www.englishlacrosse.co.uk
Chief Executive Officer, David Shuttleworth

LAWN TENNIS

LAWN TENNIS ASSOCIATION National Tennis Centre, 100 Priory Lane, London SW15 5JQ
T 020-8487 7000 E info@lta.org.uk W www.lta.org.uk
Chief Executive, Roger Draper

MARTIAL ARTS

BRITISH JUDO ASSOCIATION Suite B, Loughborough Technology Park, Epinal Way, Loughborough LE11 3GE T 01509-631670 E bja@britishjudo.org.uk
W www.britishjudo.org.uk
Chief Executive, Scott McCarthy

BRITISH JU JITSU ASSOCIATION 5 Avenue Parade, Accrington BB5 6PN T 01254-396 806
E chairman@bjjagb.com W www.bjjagb.com
Chair, Martin Dixon

BRITISH TAEKWONDO COUNCIL Yiewsley Leisure Centre, Otterfield Road, West Drayton UB7 8PE
T 01895-427359 E admin@tkdcouncil.com
W www.britishtaekwondocouncil.org
Chair, M. Prewett

MODERN PENTATHLON

PENTATHLON GB Wessex House, University of Bath, Claverton Down, Bath BA2 7AY T 01225-386808
E skip.peacey@pentathlongb.org W www.pentathlongb.org
Chief Executive, Peter Hart

MOTOR SPORTS

AUTO-CYCLE UNION ACU House, Wood Street, Rugby CV21 2YX T 01788-566400 E admin@acu.org.uk
W www.acu.org.uk
General Secretary, Gary Thompson, MBE

MOTOR SPORTS ASSOCIATION Motor Sports House, Riverside Park, Colnbrook, SL3 0HG
T 01753-765000 W www.msauk.org
Chief Executive, Colin Hilton

SCOTTISH AUTO CYCLE UNION 28 West Main Street, Uphall EH52 5DW T 01506-858354
E office@sacu.co.uk W www.sacu.co.uk
President, Andy Russell

MOUNTAINEERING

BRITISH MOUNTAINEERING COUNCIL The Old Church, 177–179 Burton Road, Manchester M20 2BB
T 0161-445 6111 E office@thebmc.co.uk
W www.thebmc.co.uk
Chief Executive, Dave Turnbull

MULTI-SPORTS BODIES

BRITISH OLYMPIC ASSOCIATION 60 Charlotte Street, London W1T 2NU T 020-7842 5700
E boa@boa.org.uk W www.olympics.org.uk
Chief Executive, Andy Hunt

BRITISH PARALYMPIC ASSOCIATION 60 Charlotte Street, London W1T 2NU T 020-7842 5789 E info@paralympics.org.uk W www.paralympics.org.uk
Chair, Tim Reddish, OBE

BRITISH UNIVERSITIES AND COLLEGES SPORT 20–24 Kings Bench Street, London SE1 0QX T 020-7633 5080 E info@bucs.org.uk W www.bucs.org.uk
Chief Executive, Karen Rothery

COMMONWEALTH GAMES COUNCIL FOR ENGLAND Jubilee Stand, Crystal Palace, National Sports Centre, London SE19 2YY T 020-8676 3543 E info@weareengland.org W www.weareengland.org
Chief Executive, Ann Hogbin, CBE

COMMONWEALTH GAMES FEDERATION 2nd Floor, 138 Piccadilly, London W1J 7NR T 020-7491 8801 E info@thecgf.com W www.thecgf.com
Chief Executive Officer, Michael Hooper

ENGLISH FEDERATION OF DISABILITY SPORT Manchester Metropolitan University, Alsager Campus, Hassall Road, Alsager ST7 2HL T 0161-247 5294 E federation@efds.co.uk W www.efds.co.uk
Chief Executive, Colin Chaytors

NETBALL

ALL ENGLAND NETBALL ASSOCIATION Netball House, 9 Paynes Park, Hitchin SG5 1EH T 01462-442344 E info@englandnetball.co.uk W www.englandnetball.co.uk
Chief Executive, Paul Clark

NETBALL NI 36 Belfast Road, Lisburn BT27 4AS T 028-9266 8412 E netballni@btconnect.com W www.netballni.org
President, Lorraine Lindsay

NETBALL SCOTLAND Suite 296, 3rd Floor, Central Chambers, 93 Hope Street, Glasgow G2 6LD T 0141-572 0114 E membership@netballscotland.com W www.netballscotland.com
Chair, Patricia Osborne

WELSH NETBALL ASSOCIATION Welsh Institute of Sport, Sophia Gardens, Cardiff CF11 9SW T 0845-045 4302 E welshnetball@welshnetball.com W www.welshnetball.co.uk
Chief Executive Officer, M. Fatkin

ORIENTEERING

BRITISH ORIENTEERING 8A Stancliffe House, Whitworth Road, Darley Dale, Matlock DE4 2HJ T 01629-734042 E info@britishorienteering.org.uk W www.britishorienteering.org.uk
Chief Executive, Mike Hamilton

POLO

THE HURLINGHAM POLO ASSOCIATION Manor Farm, Little Coxwell, Faringdon SN7 7LW T 01367-242828 E enquiries@hpa-polo.co.uk W www.hpa-polo.co.uk
Chief Executive, David Woodd

RACKETS AND REAL TENNIS

TENNIS AND RACKETS ASSOCIATION c/o The Queen's Club, Palliser Road, London W14 9EQ T 020-7835 6937 E office@tennisandrackets.com W www.tennisandrackets.com
Chief Executive, J. G. Walton

ROWING

BRITISH ROWING 6 Lower Mall, Hammersmith, London W6 9DJ T 020-8237 6700 E info@britishrowing.org W www.britishrowing.org
National Manager, Rosemary Napp

HENLEY ROYAL REGATTA Regatta Headquarters, Henley-on-Thames RG9 2LY T 01491-572153 W www.hrr.co.uk
Secretary, D. G. M. Grist

RUGBY LEAGUE

BRITISH AMATEUR RUGBY LEAGUE ASSOCIATION West Yorkshire House, 4 New North Parade, Huddersfield HD1 5JP T 01484-510682 E info@barla.org.uk W www.barla.org.uk
Chair, Spen Allison

RUGBY FOOTBALL LEAGUE Red Hall, Red Hall Lane, Leeds LS17 8NB T 0844-477 7113 E enquiries@rfl.uk.com W www.therfl.co.uk
Chair, Richard Lewis

RUGBY UNION

IRISH RUGBY FOOTBALL UNION 10–12 Lansdowne Road, Ballsbridge, Dublin 4 T (+353) 1647 3800 E info@irishrugby.ie W www.irishrugby.ie
Chief Executive, Philip Browne

RUGBY FOOTBALL UNION Rugby House, Twickenham Stadium, 200 Whitton Road, Twickenham TW2 7BA T 0871-222 2120 E enquiries@therfu.com W www.rfu.com
Chief Executive, vacant

RUGBY FOOTBALL UNION FOR WOMEN Rugby House, Rugby Road, Twickenham TW1 1DS T 020-8831 7996 E rfuw@therfu.com W www.rfu.com
Chair, Deborah Griffin

SCOTTISH RUGBY UNION Murrayfield, Roseburn Street, Edinburgh EH12 5PJ T 0131-346 5000 E feedback@sru.org.uk W www.scottishrugby.org
Chief Executive, Gordon McKie

SCOTTISH WOMEN'S RUGBY UNION Scottish Rugby Union, Murrayfield, Edinburgh EH12 5PJ T 0131-346 5000 W www.swru.org.uk
Chair, Kath Vass

WELSH RUGBY UNION Westgate Terrace, Millennium Stadium, Westgate Street, Cardiff CF10 1NS T 0870-013 8600 E info@wru.co.uk W www.wru.co.uk
Chief Executive, Roger Lewis

SHOOTING

BRITISH SHOOTING Edmonton House, Bisley Camp, Brookwood, Woking GU24 0NP T 01483-486948 E admin@britishshooting.org.uk W www.britishshooting.org.uk
Chair, vacant

CLAY PIGEON SHOOTING ASSOCIATION Edmonton House, National Shooting Centre, Brookwood, Woking GU24 0NP T 01483-485400 E info@cpsa.co.uk W www.cpsa.co.uk
National Director and Chair, Terry Bobbett

NATIONAL RIFLE ASSOCIATION Bisley, Brookwood, Woking GU24 0PB T 01483-797777 W www.nra.org.uk
Chair, Dr Robin Pizer

NATIONAL SMALL-BORE RIFLE ASSOCIATION Lord Robert's Centre, Bisley Camp, Brookwood, Woking GU24 0NP T 01483-485505 W www.nsra.co.uk
Chief Executive, Allan Boosey

SNOWBOARDING

BRITISH SNOWBOARDING ASSOCIATION c/o Snowboard Club UK (SCUK), B5, Enterprise Point, Melbourne Street, Brighton BN2 3LH **T** 0131-335 5678 **E** bsa@snowboardclub.co.uk **W** www.snowboardclub.co.uk/bsa
Chair, John O'Grady

SPEEDWAY

BRITISH SPEEDWAY ACU Headquarters, Wood Street, Rugby CV21 2YX **T** 01788-560648 **E** office@speedwaygb.com **W** www.speedwaygb.com
Chair, Alex Harkess

SQUASH

ENGLAND SQUASH AND RACKETBALL National Squash Centre, Sportcity, Manchester M11 3FF **T** 0161-231 4499 **E** enquiries@englandsquashandracketball.com **W** www.englandsquashandracketball.com
Chief Executive, Nick Rider

SCOTTISH SQUASH Caledonia House, South Gyle, Edinburgh EH12 9DQ **T** 0131-625 4425 **E** info@scottishsquash.org **W** www.scottishsquash.org
Chief Executive Officer, vacant

SQUASH WALES Sport Wales National Centre, Sophia Gardens, Cardiff CF11 9SW **T** 0845-846 0027 **E** squashwales@squashwales.co.uk **W** www.squashwales.co.uk
Chair, Phil Brailey

SUB-AQUA

BRITISH SUB-AQUA CLUB Telford's Quay, South Pier Road, Ellesmere Port CH65 4FL **T** 0151-350 6200 **E** info@bsac.com **W** www.bsac.com
Chief Executive, Mary Tetley

SWIMMING

AMATEUR SWIMMING ASSOCIATION Harold Fern House, Derby Square, Loughborough LE11 5AL **T** 01509-618700 **E** customerservices@swimming.org **W** www.swimming.org
Chief Executive, D. Sparkes

SCOTTISH SWIMMING National Swimming Academy, University of Stirling, Stirling, FK9 4LA **T** 01786-466520 **E** info@scottishswimming.com **W** www.scottishswimming.com
Chair, Maureen Campbell

SWIM WALES Wales National Pool, Sketty Lane, Swansea SA2 8QG **T** 01792-513636 **W** www.welshasa.co.uk
Chief Executive, Robert James

TABLE TENNIS

ENGLISH TABLE TENNIS ASSOCIATION Queensbury House, 3rd Floor, Havelock Road, Hastings TN34 1HF **T** 01424-722525 **E** admin@etta.co.uk **W** www.englishtabletennis.org.uk
Chief Executive, Richard Yule

TABLE TENNIS ASSOCIATION OF WALES c/o Old Oak House, 49–51 Lammas Street, Carmarthen, SA31 3AL **T** 01454-417491 **E** admin@ttaw.co.uk **W** www.ttaw.co.uk
Chair, John Fraser

TABLE TENNIS SCOTLAND Caledonia House, South Gyle, Edinburgh EH12 9DQ **T** 0131-317 8077 **E** graham@ttscotland.com **W** www.ttscotland.com
Chair, Jonathan Whitaker

TRIATHLON

BRITISH TRIATHLON PO Box 25, Loughborough LE11 3WX **T** 01509-226161 **E** info@britishtriathlon.org **W** www.britishtriathlon.org
Chief Executive, Zara Hyde Peters

VOLLEYBALL

ENGLISH VOLLEYBALL ASSOCIATION Suite B, Loughborough Technology Centre, Epinal Way, Loughborough LE11 3GE **T** 01509-227722 **E** info@volleyballengland.org **W** www.volleyballengland.org
President, Richard Callicott

NORTHERN IRELAND VOLLEYBALL ASSOCIATION UUJ Sports Centre, Shore Road, Newtownabbey BT37 0QB **T** 028-9036 6373 **E** mark@nivb.com **W** www.nivb.com
General Secretary, Mark Fulton

SCOTTISH VOLLEYBALL ASSOCIATION 48 The Pleasance, Edinburgh EH8 9TJ **T** 0131-556 4633 **E** info@scottishvolleyball.org **W** www.scottishvolleyball.org
Chief Executive, Margaret Ann Fleming

VOLLEYBALL WALES 13 Beckgrove Close, Pengam Green, Cardiff CF24 2SE **T** 029-2041 6537 **E** mail@volleyballwales.org **W** www.volleyballwales.org
Chair, Yvonne Saker

WALKING

RACE WALKING ASSOCIATION Hufflers, Heard's Lane, Shenfield, Brentwood CM15 0SF **T** 01277-220687 **E** racewalkingassociation@btinternet.com **W** www.racewalkingassociation.btinternet.co.uk
Hon. General Secretary, Peter Cassidy

WATER SKIING

BRITISH WATER SKI FEDERATION The Forum, Hanworth Lane, Chertsey, KT16 9JX **T** 01932-560007 **E** info@bwsf.co.uk **W** www.britishwaterski.org.uk
Chief Executive Officer, Patrick Donovan

WEIGHTLIFTING

BRITISH WEIGHTLIFTERS ASSOCIATION (BWLA) Lilleshall National Sports Centre, Nr. Newport TF10 9AT **T** 01952-604201 **E** lorraine.fleming@bwla.co.uk **W** www.bwla.co.uk
Chief Executive, Steve Cannon

WRESTLING

BRITISH WRESTLING ASSOCIATION 12 Westwood Lane, Chesterfield S43 1PA **T** 01246-236443 **E** admin@britishwrestling.org **W** www.britishwrestling.org
Chief Executive, Colin Nicholson

YACHTING

ROYAL YACHTING ASSOCIATION RYA House, Ensign Way, Hamble, Southampton SO31 4YA **T** 023-8060 4100 **W** www.rya.org.uk
Chief Executive, Sarah Treseder

CLUBS

Originally called gentlemen's clubs, these organisations are permanent institutions with a fixed clubhouse, which usually includes restaurants, bars, a library and overnight accommodation. Members are fee-paying and typically vetted for their suitability.

Gentlemen's clubs were created for males of the English upper class and grew out of the 17th-century fashion for coffee houses which enjoyed enormous popularity, despite opposition from Charles II, who believed they encouraged the spreading of royal disaffection. The first of the London clubs – White's – was founded in 1693 by Francesco Bianco in St James's Street, in the area that quickly became known as 'clubland' (*see* map below). Membership to the first of the clubs was a matter of hereditary privilege or special favour, a deliberately exclusionary measure which prompted an enormous growth in the number of clubs throughout the 19th century, fed by a burgeoning and aspirational middle class.

At the turn of the 20th century, there were more than 200 gentlemen's clubs in London alone, half of which had been founded since 1870. Inevitably, this level of competition could not be sustained, particularly given the number of men killed in two world wars. Financial restrictions necessitated greater provision for women and the relaxation of the social qualifications needed for membership. Nevertheless, waiting lists still exist for the leading clubs and a recommendation from at least one current member is almost always required to join.

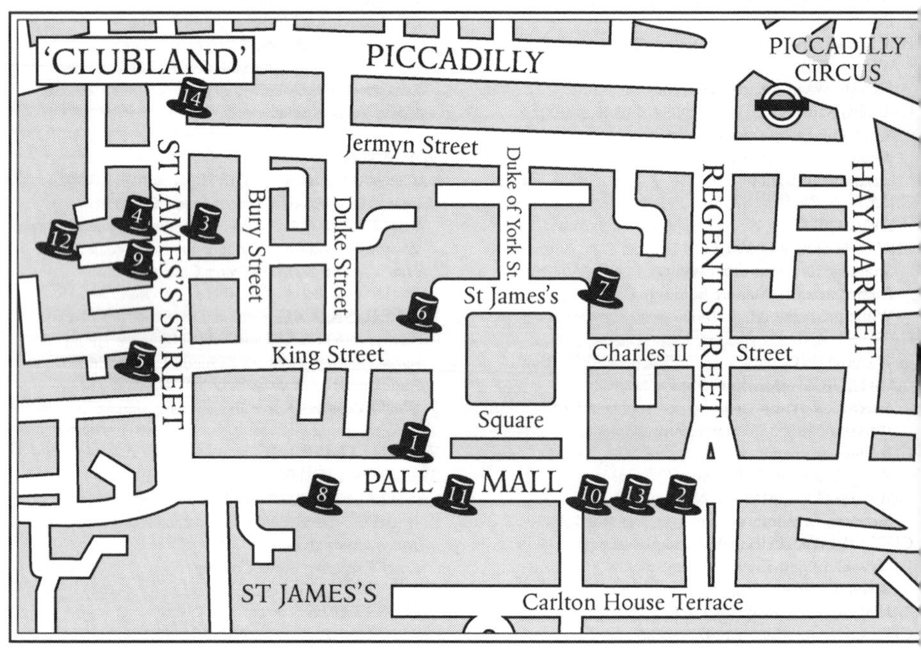

1 Army and Navy Club
2 Athenaeum
3 Boodle's
4 Brooks's
5 Carlton Club
6 East India Club
7 Naval and Military Club
8 Oxford and Cambridge Club
9 Pratt's Club
10 Reform Club
11 Royal Automobile Club
12 Royal Over-Seas League
13 Travellers Club
14 White's

* Men only † Women only

ARMY AND NAVY CLUB (1837), 36 Pall Mall, London SW1Y 5JN T 020-7930 9721 E secretary@therag.co.uk W www.armynavyclub.co.uk
Chief Executive and Secretary, Cdr. R. W. W. Craig, RN
Former members: The Duke of Wellington

ARTS CLUB (1863), 40 Dover Street, London W1S 4NP T 020-7499 8581 E secretary@theartsclub.co.uk W www.theartsclub.co.uk
Managing Director, Brian Clivaz
Former members: Charles Dickens, Algernon Charles Swinburne, Ivan Turgenev

ATHENAEUM (1824), 107 Pall Mall, London SW1Y 5ER T 020-7930 4843 E library@hellenist.org.uk W www.athenaeumclub.co.uk
Secretary, J. H. Ford
Former members: Matthew Arnold, Michael Faraday, Anthony Trollope

ATHENAEUM (1797), Church Alley, Liverpool L1 3DD T 0151-709 7770 E reception@theathenaeum.org.uk W www.theathenaeum.org.uk
Honorary Secretary, Geoffrey Appleton

AUTHORS' CLUB (1891), 40 Dover Street, London

W1S 4NP T 020-7499 8581 W www.theauthorsclub.co.uk
Secretary, Stella Kane
Former members: E. M. Forster, Jerome K. Jerome, George Meredith

BATH AND COUNTY CLUB (1858), Queen's Parade, Bath BA1 2NJ T 01225-423732
E secretary@bathandcountyclub.com
W www.bathandcountyclub.com
President, Sir Alec Morris, KBE, CB

BEEFSTEAK CLUB* (1876), 9 Irving Street, London WC2H 7AH T 020-7930 5722 E beefsteakclub@tiscali.co.uk
Secretary, Maria Hibbert
Former members: John Betjeman, Rudyard Kipling, Harold Macmillan

BOODLE'S* (1762), 28 St James's Street, London SW1A 1HJ T 020-7930 7166 E secretary@boodles.org
Secretary, Andrew Phillips
Former members: Winston Churchill, Ian Fleming

BROOKS'S* (1764), St James's Street, London SW1A 1LN T 020-7493 4411 E secretary@brooksclub.org
Secretary, Graham Snell
Former members: Edward Gibbon, Roy Jenkins, William Pitt

BUCK'S CLUB* (1919), 18 Clifford Street, London W1S 3RF T 020-7734 2337 E secretary@bucksclub.co.uk
Secretary, Maj. Rupert Lendrum

CALEDONIAN CLUB (1891), 9 Halkin Street, London SW1X 7DR T 020-7235 5162 E admin@caledonianclub.com
W www.caledonianclub.com
Secretary, Ian Campbell

CARLTON CLUB (1832), 69 St James's Street, London SW1A 1PJ T 020-7493 1164 E info@carltonclub.co.uk
W www.carltonclub.co.uk
Secretary, Jonathan Orr-Ewing
Former members: Stanley Baldwin, Benjamin Disraeli, William Gladstone

CAVALRY AND GUARDS CLUB (1890), 127 Piccadilly, London W1J 7PX T 020-7499 1261
E secretary@cavgds.co.uk W www.cavgds.co.uk
Secretary, David J Cowdery
Former members: Lawrence Oates

CHELSEA ARTS CLUB (1891), 143 Old Church Street, London SW3 6EB T 020-7376 3311
W www.chelseaartsclub.com
Secretary, D. Winterbottom

CITY LIVERY CLUB (1914), 38 St. Mary Axe, London EC3A 8EX T 020-7369 1672 E postbox@cityliveryclub.com
W www.cityliveryclub.com
Hon. Secretary, Roger T. Hacker, FCCA

CITY OF LONDON CLUB* (1832), 19 Old Broad Street, London EC2N 1DS T 020-7588 7991
E secretary@cityoflondonclub.com
W www.cityoflondonclub.com
Secretary, Ian Faul
Former members: Robert Peel

CITY UNIVERSITY CLUB (1895), 50 Cornhill, London EC3V 3PD T 020-7626 8571
E secretary@cityuniversityclub.co.uk
W www.cityuniversityclub.co.uk
Secretary, Miss R. C. Graham

THE COBDEN CLUB (1996), 170–172 Kensal Road, London W10 5BN T 020-8960 4222
E info@thecobden.co.uk W www.thecobden.co.uk
Membership Secretary, Lesley Young

THE COMMONWEALTH CLUB (1868), 25 Northumberland Avenue, London WC2N 5AP
T 020-7766 9200 E info@thercs.org W www.thercs.org
Membership Manager, Kerrie Fuller

DEN NORSKE KLUB LTD (1887), In & Out, 4 St James's Square, London SW1Y 4JU T 020-7839 6242
W www.dennorskeklub.co.uk
Secretary, Jenifer Andersen

DURHAM COUNTY CLUB (1890), 52 Old Elvet, Durham DH1 3HN T 0191-384 8156
Hon. Secretary, S. Smith

EAST INDIA CLUB* (1849), 16 St James's Square, London SW1Y 4LH T 020-7930 1000
E secretary@eastindiaclub.co.uk
W www.eastindiaclub.co.uk
Secretary, A. Bray

FARMERS CLUB (1842), 3 Whitehall Court, London SW1A 2EL T 020-7930 3557
E reception@thefarmersclub.com
W www.thefarmersclub.com
Secretary, Air Cdre Stephen Skinner

FOX CLUB, 46 Clarges Street, London W1J 7ER
T 020-7495 3656 E bethan@foxclublondon.com
W www.foxclublondon.com
General Manager, Bethan Seaton

FREWEN CLUB* (1869), 98 St Aldate's, Oxford OX1 1BT T 01865-243816
Hon. General Secretary, M. J. Dean

GARRICK CLUB* (1831), 15 Garrick Street, London WC2E 9AY T 020-7379 6478 E office@garrickclub.co.uk
W www.garrickclub.co.uk
Secretary, Olaf Born
Former members: Charles Dickens, Henry Irving, William Thackeray

GROUCHO CLUB (1985), 45 Dean Street, London W1D 4QB T 020-7439 4685 E info@thegrouchoclub.com
W www.thegrouchoclub.com
Secretary, Miriam Brown

THE HURLINGHAM CLUB (1869), Ranelagh Gardens, London SW6 3PR T 020-7736 8411
E membership@hurlinghamclub.org.uk
W www.hurlinghamclub.org.uk
Chief Executive, Rear-Adm. Niall Kilgour, CB
Former members: King Edward VII

LONDON PRESS CLUB (1882), St Bride Foundation, 14 Bride Lane, London EC4Y 8EQ T 020-7353 7086
E info@londonpressclub.co.uk
W www.londonpressclub.co.uk
Secretary, Peter Durrant
Former members: Lord Astor, Lord Rothermere, Edgar Wallace

NATIONAL CLUB (1845), c/o The Carlton Club,
T 01225-480606 E secretary@thenationalclub.org.uk
W www.thenationalclub.org.uk
Hon. Secretary, The Revd R. J. R. Paice
Former members: Lord Coggan

NATIONAL LIBERAL CLUB (1882), 1 Whitehall Place, London SW1A 2HE T 020-7930 9871
W www.nlc.org.uk
Secretary, S. J. Roberts
Former members: Ramsay MacDonald, George Bernard Shaw, H. G. Wells

NAVAL AND MILITARY CLUB (1862), 4 St James's Square, London SW1Y 4JU T 020-7827 5757
E club@navalandmilitaryclub.co.uk
W www.navalandmilitaryclub.co.uk
Secretary, Ian Gregory

THE NEW CLUB (1874), 2 Montpellier Parade, Cheltenham GL50 1UD T 01242-541121
E secretary@thenewclub.co.uk
W www.thenewclub.co.uk
Hon. Secretary, Peter Walsh

THE NEW CLUB (1787), 86 Princes Street, Edinburgh EH2 2BB **T** 0131-226 4881 **E** info@newclub.co.uk **W** www.newclub.co.uk
Secretary, Col. A. P. W. Campbell
Former members: Alec Douglas-Home, Walter Scott

NEW CAVENDISH CLUB (1920), 44 Great Cumberland Place, London W1H 8BS **T** 020-7723 0391 **E** info@newcavendishclub.co.uk **W** www.newcavendishclub.co.uk
Chair, Sue Ann Dowle

NORFOLK CLUB (1770), 17 Upper King Street, Norwich NR3 1RB **T** 01603-626767 **E** secretary@thenorfolkclub.co.uk **W** www.thenorfolkclub.co.uk
Secretary, Peter Lawrence

NORTHERN COUNTIES CLUB (1829), 11 Hood Street, Newcastle upon Tyne NE1 6LH **T** 0191-232 2744 **E** secretary@northerncountiesclub.co.uk **W** www.northerncountiesclub.co.uk
General Manager, D. J. Devennie

ORIENTAL CLUB (1824), Stratford House, Stratford Place, London W1C 1ES **T** 020-7629 5126 **W** www.orientalclub.org.uk
Secretary, Capt. D. M. Swain, RN

OXFORD AND CAMBRIDGE CLUB (1830), 71 Pall Mall, London SW1Y 5HD **T** 020-7930 5151 **E** club@oandc.uk.com **W** www.oxfordandcambridgeclub.co.uk
Secretary, Alistair E. Telfer
Former members: Clement Attlee, William Gladstone, The Duke of Wellington

PORTLAND CLUB (1816), 69 Brook Street, London W1Y 4ER **T** 020-7499 1523
Secretary, J. Burns, CBE

PRATT'S CLUB* (1841), 14 Park Place, London SW1A 1LP **T** 020-7493 0397 **E** secretary@prattsclub.org
Secretary, Graham Snell
Former members: Winston Churchill

REFORM CLUB (1836), 104–105 Pall Mall, London SW1Y 5EW **T** 020-7930 9374 **E** generaloffice@reformclub.com **W** www.reformclub.com
Secretary, M. D. B. McKerchar
Former members: Isambard Kingdom Brunel, Guy Burgess, Arthur Conan Doyle, Henry James, David Lloyd George

ROYAL AIR FORCE CLUB (1918), 128 Piccadilly, London W1J 7PY **T** 020-7399 1000 **E** admin@rafclub.org.uk **W** www.rafclub.org.uk
Secretary, P. N. Owen

ROYAL ANGLO-BELGIAN CLUB (1955), 8 Northumberland Avenue, London WC2N 5BY **T** 020-7127 5139 **E** membership@ra-bc.com **W** www.ra-bc.com
Chair, Michel Vanhoonacker

ROYAL AUTOMOBILE CLUB (1897), Pall Mall Clubhouse, 89 Pall Mall, London SW1Y 5HS **T** 020-7930 2345 **E** members@royalautomobileclub.co.uk **W** www.royalautomobileclub.co.uk
Secretary, A. I. G. Kennedy, CB, CBE
Former members: Winston Churchill, Charles Rolls

ROYAL NORTHERN & UNIVERSITY CLUB* (1854), 9 Albyn Place, Aberdeen AB10 1YE **T** 01224-583292 **E** secretary@rnuc.org.uk **W** www.rnuc.org.uk
Secretary, Rosemary Black

ROYAL OVER-SEAS LEAGUE (1910), Over-Seas House, Park Place, St James's Street, London SW1A 1LR **T** 020-7408 0214 **E** info@rosl.org.uk **W** www.rosl.org.uk
Director-General, Robert F. Newell, LVO

ST STEPHEN'S CLUB (1870), 34 Queen Anne's Gate, London SW1H 9AB **T** 020-7222 1382 **E** info@ststephensclub.co.uk **W** www.ststephensclub.co.uk
General Manager, Bernard Moray
Former members: Benjamin Disraeli

SAVAGE CLUB* (1857), 1 Whitehall Place, London SW1A 2HD **T** 020-7930 8118 **E** info@savageclub.com **W** www.savageclub.com
Hon. Secretary, Adrian MacIntosh
Former members: Edward Elgar, Alexander Fleming, Harry Secombe, Dylan Thomas, Mark Twain, Peter Ustinov

SAVILE CLUB* (1868), 69 Brook Street, London W1K 4ER **T** 020-7629 5462 **W** www.savileclub.co.uk
Secretary, Julian Malone-Lee
Former members: Max Beerbohm, Thomas Hardy, Robert Louis Stevenson

SCOTTISH ARTS CLUB (1872), 24 Rutland Square, Edinburgh EH1 2BW **T** 0131-229 8157 **W** www.scottishartsclub.co.uk
House Convenor, Hilary Mounfield

SLOANE CLUB (1976), Lower Sloane Street, London SW1W 8BS **T** 020-7730 9131 **E** reservations@sloaneclub.co.uk **W** www.sloaneclub.co.uk
Membership Secretary, Fran Bremner

SOHO HOUSE (1995), 40 Greek Street, London W1D 4EB **T** 020-7734 5188 **W** www.sohohouse.com

THE CANNING CLUB (1910), 4 St James's Square, London SW1Y 4JU **T** 020-7827 5730 **E** canningclub@navalandmilitaryclub.co.uk
Secretary, Fiona Sedgwick

THREE ALBION PLACE (1849), 3 Albion Place, Leeds LS1 6JL **T** 0113-388 2800 **E** info@3albionplace.com **W** www.3albionplace.com
Membership Director, Caron Munro

TRAVELLERS CLUB* (1819), 106 Pall Mall, London SW1Y 5EP **T** 020-7930 8688 **E** secretary@thetravellersclub.org.uk **W** www.thetravellersclub.org.uk
Secretary, David Broadhead
Former members: Arthur Balfour, Alec Douglas-Home, Anthony Powell

TURF CLUB (1868), 5 Carlton House Terrace, London SW1Y 5AQ **T** 020-7930 8555 **E** mail@turfclub.co.uk
Secretary, Lt.-Col. O. R. StJ. Breakwell, MBE

ULSTER REFORM CLUB (1885), 4 Royal Avenue, Belfast BT1 1DA **T** 028-9032 3411 **E** info@ulsterreformclub.com **W** www.ulsterreformclub.com
Chief Executive, A. W. Graham

UNIVERSITY WOMEN'S CLUB† (1886), 2 Audley Square, London W1K 1DB **T** 020-7499 2268 **E** uwc@uwc-london.com **W** www.universitywomensclub.com
Secretary, Ms S. McCue

VINCENT'S* (1863), 1A King Edward Street, Oxford OX1 4HS **T** 01865-722984 **E** secretary@vincents.org **W** www.vincents.org
Secretary, Adam Healy
Former members: Roger Bannister, King Edward VIII

WESTERN CLUB (1825), 32 Royal Exchange Square, Glasgow G1 3AB **T** 0141-221 2016 **E** secretary@westernclub.co.uk **W** www.westernclub.co.uk
Secretary, Douglas H. Gifford

WHITE'S* (1693), 37–38 St James's Street, London SW1A 1JG **T** 020-7493 6671
Secretary, D. A. Anderson
Former members: Beau Brummel, Horace Walpole, Evelyn Waugh

CHARITIES AND SOCIETIES

The following is a selection of charities, societies and non-profit organisations in the UK and does not represent a comprehensive list. For professional and employment-related organisations, *see* Professional Education and Trade and Professional Bodies.

ABBEYFIELD SOCIETY (1956), Abbeyfield House, 53 Victoria Street, St Albans AL1 3UW **T** 01727-857536 **E** post@abbeyfield.com **W** www.abbeyfield.com
Chief Executive, Paul Allen

ACTIONAID (1972), Hamlyn House, Macdonald Road, Archway, London N19 5PG **T** 020-7561 7561 **E** mail@actionaid.org.uk **W** www.actionaid.org.uk
Chair, Andrew Purkis

ACTION FOR BLIND PEOPLE (1857), 14–16 Verney Road, London SE16 3DZ **T** 0800-915 4666 **W** www.actionforblindpeople.org.uk
Chief Executive, Stephen Remington

ACTION MEDICAL RESEARCH (1952), Vincent House, Horsham RH12 2DP **T** 01403-210406 **E** info@action.org.uk **W** www.action.org.uk
Chief Executive, Julie Buckler

ACTORS' BENEVOLENT FUND (1882), 6 Adam Street, London WC2N 6AD **T** 020-7836 6378 **E** office@abf.org.uk **W** www.actorsbenevolentfund.co.uk
General Secretary, Willie Bicket

ACTORS' CHARITABLE TRUST (1896), 58 Bloomsbury Street, London WC1B 3QT **T** 020-7636 7868 **E** robert@tactactors.org **W** www.tactactors.org
General Secretary, Robert Ashby

ADAM SMITH INSTITUTE (1977), 23 Great Smith Street, London SW1P 3BL **T** 020-7222 4995 **E** info@adamsmith.org **W** www.adamsmith.org
President, Dr Madsen Pirie

ADDACTION (1967), 67–69 Cowcross Street, London EC1M 6BP **T** 020-7017 5860 **E** info@addaction.org.uk **W** www.addaction.org.uk
Chief Executive, Simon Antrobus

ADVERTISING STANDARDS AUTHORITY (1962), Mid City Place, 71 High Holborn, London WC1V 6QT **T** 020-7492 2222 **E** enquiries@asa.org.uk **W** www.asa.org.uk
Chief Executive, Guy Parker

AFASIC (1968), 1st Floor, Olive House, 20 Bowling Green Lane, London EC1R 0BD **T** 020-7490 9410 **E** info@afasic.org.uk **W** www.afasic.org.uk
Chief Executive, Linda Lascelles

AGE UK (2010), 1268 London Road, London SW16 4ER **T** 020-8765 7200 **E** info@ageuk.org **W** www.ageuk.org.uk
Chief Executive, Tom Wright, CBE

ALCOHOLICS ANONYMOUS (1947), PO Box 1, 10 Toft Green, York YO1 7NJ **T** 01904-644026, **Helpline** 0845-769 7555 **E** help@alcoholics-anonymous.org.uk **W** www.alcoholics-anonymous.org.uk
General Secretary, Ann Napier

ALEXANDRA ROSE CHARITIES (1912), 5 Mead Lane, Farnham GU9 7DY **T** 01252-726171 **E** enquiries@alexandrarose.org.uk **W** www.alexandrarosecharities.org.uk
National Director, Margaret Stock

ALZHEIMER'S SOCIETY (1979), Devon House, 58 St Katharine's Way, London E1W 1JX **T** 020-7423 3500 **E** enquiries@alzheimers.org.uk **W** www.alzheimers.org.uk
Chief Executive (acting), Ruth Sutherland

AMNESTY INTERNATIONAL UNITED KINGDOM (1961), The Human Rights Action Centre, 17–25 New Inn Yard, London EC2A 3EA **T** 020-7033 1500 **E** sct@ammnesty.org.uk **W** www.amnesty.org.uk
UK Director, Kate Allen

AMREF UK (1957), Clifford's Inn, Fetter Lane, London EC4A 1BZ **T** 020-7269 5520 **E** info@amrefuk.org **W** www.amref.org/uk
Chief Executive, Grace Mukasa

ANCIENT MONUMENTS SOCIETY (1924), St Ann's Vestry Hall, 2 Church Entry, London EC4V 5HB **T** 020-7236 3934 **E** office@ancientmonumentssociety.org.uk **W** www.ancientmonumentssociety.org.uk
Secretary, M. J. Saunders, MBE

ANGLO-BELGIAN SOCIETY (1982), 5 Hartley Close, Bickley BR1 2TP **T** 020-8467 8442 **E** secretary@anglo-belgiansoc.com **W** www.anglo-belgiansoc.com
Chair, David Colvin, CMG

ANGLO-DANISH SOCIETY (1924), 43 Maresfield Gardens, London NW3 5TF **T** 020-7794 8781 **E** info@anglo-danishsociety.org.uk **W** www.anglo-danishsociety.org.uk
Chair, Simon Freeman

ANGLO-NORSE SOCIETY (1918), 25 Belgrave Square, London SW1X 8QD **T** 020-7235 9529 **E** secretariat@anglo-norse.org.uk **W** www.anglo-norse.org.uk
Chair, Sir Richard Dales

ANIMAL CONCERN (1876), PO Box 5178, Dumbarton G82 5YJ **T** 01389-841639 **E** animals@jfrobins.force9.co.uk **W** www.animalconcern.com
Secretary, John F Robins

ANIMAL HEALTH TRUST (1942), Lanwades Park, Kentford, Newmarket CB8 7UU **T** 01638-751000 **E** info@aht.org.uk **W** www.aht.org.uk
Chief Executive, Dr Peter Webbon

ANTHONY NOLAN TRUST (1974), 2–3 Heathgate Place, 75–87 Agincourt Road, London NW3 2NU **T** 0303-303 0303 **E** info@anthonynolan.org.uk **W** www.anthonynolan.org.uk
Chief Executive, Henny Braund

ANTHROPOSOPHICAL SOCIETY IN GREAT BRITAIN (1923), Rudolf Steiner House, 35 Park Road, London NW1 6XT **T** 020-7723 4400 **E** rsh-office@anth.org.uk **W** www.rsh.anth.org.uk
General Secretary, Philip Martyn

ANTI-SLAVERY INTERNATIONAL (1839), Thomas Clarkson House, The Stableyard, Broomgrove Road, London SW9 9TL **T** 020-7501 8920 **E** info@antislavery.org **W** www.antislavery.org
Director, Aidan McQuade

ARCHITECTS BENEVOLENT SOCIETY (1850), 43 Portland Place, London W1B 1QH **T** 020-7580 2823 **E** help@absnet.org.uk **W** www.absnet.org.uk
Company Secretary, Keith Robinson

ARCHITECTURAL HERITAGE FUND (1976), Alhambra House, 27–31 Charing Cross Road, London WC2H 0AU **T** 020-7925 0199 **E** ahf@ahfund.org.uk **W** www.ahfund.org.uk
Chief Executive, Ian Lush

ARLIS/UK AND IRELAND (1969), The National Art Library, Word & Image Department, Victoria & Albert Museum, Cromwell Road, London SW7 2RL **T** 020-7942 2317 **E** arlis@vam.ac.uk **W** www.arlis.org.uk
Chair, Pat Christie

ART FUND (1903), Millais House, 7 Cromwell Place, London SW7 2JN **T** 020-7225 4800 **E** info@artfund.org **W** www.artfund.org
Director, Dr Stephen Deuchar

ARTHRITIS CARE (1947), 18 Stephenson Way, London NW1 2HD **T** 020-7380 6500 **E** info@arthritiscare.org.uk **W** www.arthritiscare.org.uk
Chief Executive, Neil Betteridge

ASSOCIATION FOR LANGUAGE LEARNING (1990), University of Leicester, University Road, Leicester LE1 7RH **T** 0116-229 7453 **E** info@all-languages.org.uk **W** www.all-languages.org.uk
Director, Linda Parker

ASSOCIATION FOR SCIENCE EDUCATION (1901), College Lane, Hatfield AL10 9AA **T** 01707-283000 **E** info@ase.org.uk **W** www.ase.org.uk
Chief Executive, Annette Smith

ASSOCIATION FOR THE PROTECTION OF RURAL SCOTLAND (1926), 3rd Floor, Gladstone's Land, 483 Lawnmarket, Edinburgh EH1 2NT **T** 0131-225 7012 **E** info@ruralscotland.org **W** www.ruralscotland.org
Director, John Mayhew

ASSOCIATION OF FINANCIAL MUTUALS (1995), PO Box 21, Altrincham, Cheshire WA14 4PD **T** 0161-952 5083 **E** martin@financialmutuals.org **W** www.financialmutuals.org
Chief Executive, Martin Shaw

ASSOCIATION OF GENEALOGISTS AND RESEARCHERS IN ARCHIVES (1968), 120 North Gate, Newark upon Trent NG24 1HY **E** agra@agra.org.uk **W** www.agra.org.uk
Company Secretary, Jeremy Goldsmith

ASSOCIATION OF ROYAL NAVY OFFICERS (1920), 70 Porchester Terrace, London W2 3TP **T** 020-7402 5231 **E** osec@arno.org.uk **W** www.arno.org.uk
Director, Cdr. W. K. Ridley

ASSOCIATION OF SPEAKERS CLUBS (1971), 36 Pemberton Road, Winstanley, Wigan WN3 6DA **T** 01942-222815 **E** national.secretary@the-asc.org.uk **W** www.the-asc.org.uk
National President, David Grainger

ASTHMA UK (1927), Summit House, 70 Wilson Street, London EC2A 2DB **T** 020-7786 4900 **E** info@asthma.org.uk **W** www.asthma.org.uk
Chief Executive, Neil Churchill

AUDIT BUREAU OF CIRCULATIONS LTD (1931), Saxon House, 211 High Street, Berkhamsted HP4 1AD **T** 01442-870800 **E** info@abc.co.uk **W** www.abc.org.uk
Chair, Sally Cartwright, OBE

AUTISM INITIATIVES (1971), 7 Chesterfield Road, Liverpool L23 9XL **T** 0151-330 9500 **E** information@autisminitiatives.org **W** www.autisminitiatives.org
Chair, Brian Williams

AUTOMOBILE ASSOCIATION (1905), Lambert House, Stockport Road, Cheadle SK8 2DY **T** 0800-085 2721 **E** customer.services@theaa.com **W** www.theaa.com
Chief Executive, Andrew Strong

BALTIC EXCHANGE (1744), 38 St Mary Axe, London EC3A 8BH **T** 020-7623 5501 **E** enquiries@balticexchange.com **W** www.balticexchange.com
Chief Executive, Jeremy Penn

BARNARDO'S (1866), Tanners Lane, Barkingside, Ilford IG6 1QG **T** 020-8550 8822 **E** info@barnardos.org.uk **W** www.barnardos.org.uk
Chief Executive, Martin Narey

BARRISTERS' BENEVOLENT ASSOCIATION (1873), 14 Gray's Inn Square, London WC1R 5JP **T** 020-7242 4761 **E** enquiries@the-bba.com **W** www.the-bba.com
Director, Janet South

BBC WORLD SERVICE TRUST (1999), Bush House, PO Box 76, Strand, London WC2B 4PH **T** 020-7557 2462 **E** ws.trust@bbc.co.uk **W** www.bbcworldservicetrust.org

BCS, THE CHARTERED INSTITUTE FOR IT (1957), 1st Floor, Block D, North Star House, North Star Avenue SN2 1FA **T** 01793-417417 **W** www.bcs.org
Chief Executive, David Clarke

BEAT, Wensum House, 103 Prince of Wales Road, Norwich NR1 1DW **T** 0300-123 3355, **Helpline** 0845-634 1414, **Youthline** 0845-634 7650 **E** info@b-eat.co.uk **W** www.b-eat.co.uk
Chief Executive, Mrs Susan Ringwood

BEVIN BOYS ASSOCIATION (1989), 23 Great Cranford Street, Poundbury, Dorchester DT1 3SQ **T** 01305-261269
Vice President & Chair, Warwick Taylor, MBE

BIBLIOGRAPHICAL SOCIETY (1892), c/o University of London, Institute of English Studies, Senate House, Malet Street, London WC1E 7HU
T 020-7862 8679 E secretary@bibsoc.org.uk
W www.bibsoc.org.uk
Hon. Secretary, Margaret Ford

BLISS (1979), 9 Holyrood Street, London SE1 2EL
T 020-7378 1122, Helpline 0500-618140
E information@bliss.org.uk W www.bliss.org.uk
Chief Executive, Andy Cole

BLUE CROSS (1897), Shilton Road, Burford OX18 4PF
T 01993-822651 E info@bluecross.org.uk
W www.thebluecross.org.uk
Chief Executive, Kim Hamilton

BOOK AID INTERNATIONAL (1954), 39–41 Coldharbour Lane, London SE5 9NR
T 020-7733 3577 E info@bookaid.org
W www.bookaid.org
Director, Clive Nettleton

BOOK TRADE CHARITY (BTBS) (1837), The Foyle Centre, The Retreat, Kings Langley WD4 8LT
T 01923-263128 E david@btbs.org
W www.booktradecharity.org
Chief Executive, David Hicks

BOOKTRUST (1926), Book House, 45 East Hill, London SW18 2QZ T 020-8516 2977
E query@booktrust.org.uk W www.booktrust.org.uk
Chief Executive, Vivian Bird

BOTANICAL SOCIETY OF SCOTLAND (1836), c/o Royal Botanic Garden Edinburgh, 20A Inverleith Row, Edinburgh EH3 5LR T 0131-552 7171
W www.botanical-society-scotland.org.uk
Hon. General Secretary, Dr B. A. Harvie

BOTANICAL SOCIETY OF THE BRITISH ISLES (1836), c/o Department of Botany, The Natural History Museum, Cromwell Road, London SW7 5BD
T 020-7942 5002 E coordinator@bsbi.org.uk
W www.bsbi.org.uk
Director of Research and Development, K. Walker

BOYS' BRIGADE (1883), Felden Lodge, Felden, Hemel Hempstead HP3 0BL T 01442-231681
E enquiries@boys-brigade.org.uk
W www.boys-brigade.org.uk
Brigade Secretary, Steven Dickinson

BRITISH ACADEMY OF FORENSIC SCIENCES (1960), Haematology Department, ICMS, Barts and The London, 4 Newark Street, London E1 2AT
T 020-7882 2276 E y.d.syndercombe-court@qmul.ac.uk
W www.bafs.org.uk
Secretary-General, Dr Denise Syndercombe Court

BRITISH AND FOREIGN BIBLE SOCIETY (1804), Stonehill Green, Westlea, Swindon SN5 7DG
T 01793-418222 E contactus@biblesociety.org.uk
W www.biblesociety.org.uk
Chief Executive, James Catford

BRITISH ASSOCIATION FOR EARLY CHILDHOOD EDUCATION (1923), 136 Cavell Street, London E1 2JA T 020-7539 5400
E office@early-education.org.uk
W www.early-education.org.uk
Chief Executive, Megan Pacey

BRITISH ASSOCIATION FOR LOCAL HISTORY, PO Box 6549, Somersal Herbert DE6 5WH T 01283-585947
E mail@balh.co.uk W www.balh.co.uk
Business Manager, Annmarie Jones

BRITISH ASTRONOMICAL ASSOCIATION (1890), Burlington House, Piccadilly, London W1J 0DU
T 020-7734 4145 E office@britastro.org
W www.britastro.org
President, Dr David Boyd

BRITISH BEEKEEPERS' ASSOCIATION (1874), National Beekeeping Centre, Stoneleigh Park, Kenilworth CV8 2LG T 024-7669 6679
E bbka@britishbeekeepers.com
W www.britishbeekeepers.com
General Secretary, Mike Harris

BRITISH BOARD OF FILM CLASSIFICATION (1912), 3 Soho Square, London W1D 3HD T 020-7440 1570
E contact_the_bbfc@bbfc.co.uk W www.bbfc.co.uk
Director, David Cooke

BRITISH CATTLE BREEDERS CLUB (1946), Lake Villa, Bradworthy, Holsworthy, Devon EX22 7SQ
T 01409-241579 E lesley.lewin@cattlebreeders.org.uk
W www.cattlebreeders.org.uk
Chair, Rob Wills

BRITISH COPYRIGHT COUNCIL (1965), 29–33 Berners Street, London W1T 3AB T 01986-788122
E info@britishcopyright.org W www.britishcopyright.org
Secretary, Janet Ibbotson

BRITISH DEAF ASSOCIATION (1890), 10th Floor, Coventry Point, Market Way, Coventry CV1 1EA
T 02476-550936 E headoffice@bda.org.uk
W www.bda.org.uk
Chair, Terry Riley

BRITISH DRIVING SOCIETY LTD (1957), 83 New Road, Helmingham, Stowmarket IP14 6EA
T 01473-892001 E email@britishdrivingsociety.co.uk
W www.britishdrivingsociety.co.uk
Chair, John Parker

BRITISH ECOLOGICAL SOCIETY (1913), Charles Darwin House, 12 Roger Street, London WC1N 2JU
T 020-7685 2500 E info@britishecologicalsociety.org
W www.britishecologicalsociety.org
Executive Director, Dr Hazel Norman

BRITISH EYE RESEARCH FOUNDATION (1965), 36–38 Botolph Lane, London EC3R 8DE T 020-7929 7755
W www.fightforsight.org.uk

BRITISH FALSE MEMORY SOCIETY (1993), Bradford on Avon BA15 1NF T 01225-868682
E bfms@bfms.org.uk W www.bfms.org.uk
Director, M. Greenhalgh

BRITISH FEDERATION OF WOMEN GRADUATES (1907), 4 Mandeville Courtyard, 142 Battersea Park Road, London SW11 4NB **T** 020-7498 8037 **E** office@bfwg.org.uk **W** www.bfwg.org.uk
President, Marianne Haslegrave

BRITISH HEALTH CARE ASSOCIATION (1930), Unit 8, Cherry Hall Road, Noth Kettering Business Park, Kettering NN14 1UE **T** 01536-519960 **E** steve.fritz@bhcaservices.co.uk **W** www.bhca.org.uk
Chief Executive, Stephen Fritz

BRITISH HEART FOUNDATION (1961), Greater London House, 180 Hampstead Road, London NW1 7AW **T** 020-7554 0000 **W** www.bhf.org.uk
Chief Executive, Peter Hollins

BRITISH HEDGEHOG PRESERVATION SOCIETY (1982), Hedgehog House, Dhustone, Ludlow SY8 3PL **T** 01584-890801 **E** info@britishhedgehogs.org.uk **W** www.britishhedgehogs.org.uk
Chief Executive, Fay Vass

BRITISH HERPETOLOGICAL SOCIETY (1947), 11 Strathmore Place, Montrose DD10 8LQ **T** 01674-671676 **E** info@thebhs.org **W** www.thebhs.org
President, Prof. Trevor J. C. Beebee

BRITISH HORSE SOCIETY (1947), Abbey Park, Stareton, Kenilworth CV8 2XZ **T** 01926-707700 **E** enquiry@bhs.org.uk **W** www.bhs.org.uk
Chief Executive, Graham Cory

BRITISH HUMANIST ASSOCIATION (1896), 1 Gower Street, London WC1E 6HD **T** 020-7079 3580 **E** info@humanism.org.uk **W** www.humanism.org.uk
Chief Executive, Andrew Copson

BRITISH INSTITUTE IN EASTERN AFRICA (1959), 10 Carlton House Terrace, London SW1Y 5AH **T** 020-7969 5201 **E** biea@britac.ac.uk **W** www.biea.ac.uk
Director, Dr Ambreena Manji

BRITISH INTERPLANETARY SOCIETY (1933), 27–29 South Lambeth Road, London SW8 1SZ **T** 020-7735 3160 **E** mail@bis-spaceflight.com **W** www.bis-spaceflight.com
Executive Secretary, Suszann Parry

BRITISH-ISRAEL-WORLD FEDERATION (1919), 121 Low Etherley, Bishop Auckland, Co Durham DL14 0HA **T** 01388-834395 **E** admin@britishisrael.co.uk **W** www.britishisrael.co.uk
President, M. A. Clark

BRITISH LUNG FOUNDATION (1985), 73–75 Goswell Road, London EC1V 7ER **T** 08458-505020 **E** enquiries@blf-uk.org **W** www.lunguk.org
Chief Executive, Dame Helena Shovelton, DBE

BRITISH MANAGEMENT DATA FOUNDATION (1979), Highfield, Longridge, Sheepscombe GL6 7QU **T** 01452-812837 **E** bmdfstroud@aol.com **W** www.bmdf.co.uk; www.eurotreaties.com
Director, Andrew Cowgill, MBE

BRITISH MENSA LTD (1946), St John's House, St John's Square, Wolverhampton WV2 4AH **T** 01902-772771 **E** enquiries@mensa.org.uk **W** www.mensa.org.uk
Chief Executive, John Stevenage

BRITISH MUSIC HALL SOCIETY (1963), 45 Mayflower Road, Park Street, St Albans AL2 2QN **T** 01727-768878 **W** www.music-hall-society.com
President, Roy Hudd

BRITISH NATURALISTS' ASSOCIATION (1905), 1 Bracken Mews, London E4 7UT **E** info@bna-naturalists.org **W** www.bna-naturalists.org
Hon. Membership Secretary, Yvonne Griffiths

BRITISH NUTRITION FOUNDATION (1967), High Holborn House, 52–54 High Holborn, London WC1V 6RQ **T** 020-7404 6504 **E** postbox@nutrition.org.uk **W** www.nutrition.org.uk
Director-General, Prof. Judith Buttriss

BRITISH ORNITHOLOGISTS' UNION (1858), PO Box 417, Peterborough PE7 3FX **T** 01733-844 820 **E** bou@bou.org.uk **W** www.bou.org.uk
Senior Administrator, S. P. Dudley

BRITISH PHARMACOLOGICAL SOCIETY (1931), 16 Angel Gate, City Road, London EC1V 2PT **T** 020-7417 0110 **E** info@bps.ac.uk **W** www.bps.ac.uk
President, Prof. Ray Hill

BRITISH PIG ASSOCIATION (1884), Trumpington Mews, 40B High Street, Trumpington, Cambridge CB2 2LS **T** 01223-845100 **E** bpa@britishpigs.org **W** www.britishpigs.org.uk
Chief Executive, Marcus Bates

BRITISH POLIO FELLOWSHIP (1939), Eagle Office Centre, The Runway, South Ruislip HA4 6SE **T** 0800-018 0586 **E** info@britishpolio.org.uk **W** www.britishpolio.org.uk
Chief Executive, Dr John Hooper

BRITISH RED CROSS (1870), 44 Moorfields, London EC2Y 9AL **T** 0844-871 1111 **E** information@redcross.org.uk **W** www.redcross.org.uk
Chief Executive, Sir Nicholas Young

BRITISH REFUGEE COUNCIL, 240–250 Ferndale Road, London SW9 8BB **T** 020-7346 6700 **E** philippa.mcintyre@refugeecouncil.org.uk **W** www.refugeecouncil.org.uk
Chair, Douglas Board

BRITISH SAFETY COUNCIL (1957), 70 Chancellors Road, London W6 9RS **T** 020-8741 1231 **E** mail@britsafe.org **W** www.britishsafetycouncil.org
Chief Executive, Julie Nerney

BRITISH SCIENCE ASSOCIATION (1831), Wellcome Wolfson Building, 165 Queen's Gate, London SW7 5HD **T** 0870-770 7101 **E** info@britishscienceassociation.org **W** www.britishscienceassociation.org
Chief Executive, Sir Roland Jackson

BRITISH TRUST FOR ORNITHOLOGY (1933), The Nunnery, Thetford IP24 2PU **T** 01842-750050 **E** info@bto.org **W** www.bto.org
Director, Dr Andy Clements

BRITISH UNION FOR THE ABOLITION OF VIVISECTION (1898), 16A Crane Grove, London N7 8NN T 020-7700 4888 E info@buav.org W www.buav.org
Chief Executive, Michelle Thew

BTCV (1959), Sedum House, Mallard Way, Doncaster DN4 8DB T 01302-388888 E information@btcv.org.uk W www.btcv.org
Chief Executive, Tom Flood, CBE

BUCKINGHAMSHIRE ARCHAEOLOGICAL SOCIETY (1847), County Museum, Church Street, Aylesbury HP20 2QP T 01296-387341 E bucksas@buckscc.gov.uk W www.bucksas.org.uk
Hon. Secretary, Sue Fox

BUDGERIGAR SOCIETY (1930), Spring Gardens, Northampton NN1 1DR T 01604-624549 W www.budgerigarsociety.com
General Secretary, David Whittaker

BUILD AFRICA (1978), 27 Church Road, Tunbridge Wells TN1 1HT T 0800-652 6294 E hello@build-africa.org.uk W www.build-africa.org
Chief Executive, Susanne Niedrum

BUSINESS AND PROFESSIONAL WOMEN UK LTD (1938), 74 Fairfield Rise, Billericay CM12 9NU T 01277-623867 E hq@bpwuk.co.uk W www.bpwuk.co.uk
President, Sue Ashmore

CAFOD (CATHOLIC FUND FOR OVERSEAS DEVELOPMENT) (1962), 55 Westminster Bridge Road, London SE1 7JB T 020-7733 7900 E hqcafod@cafod.org.uk W www.cafod.org.uk
Director, Chris Bain

CALOUSTE GULBENKIAN FOUNDATION (1956), 50 Hoxton Square, Hoxton, London N1 6PB T 020-7012 1400 E info@gulbenkian.org.uk W www.gulbenkian.org.uk
Director, Andrew Barnett

CAMBRIAN ARCHAEOLOGICAL ASSOCIATION (1847), Braemar, Llangunnor Road, SA31 2PB T 01248-364865 E h.james443@btinternet.com W www.cambrians.org.uk
General Secretary, Heather James

CAMBRIDGE ANTIQUARIAN SOCIETY (1840), 86 Harvey Goodwin Court, French's Road, Cambridge CB4 3JR E secretary@camantsoc.org W www.camantsoc.org
Hon. Secretary, Chris Michaelides

CAMERON FUND (1970), Tavistock House North, Tavistock Square, London WC1 9HR T 020-7388 0796 E info@cameronfund.org.uk W www.cameronfund.org.uk
Chief Executive, David Harris

CAMPAIGN FOR COURTESY (1986), 240 Tolworth Rise South, Surbiton, Surrey KT5 9NB T 020-8330 3707 E peter.foot1@btinternet.com W www.campaignforcourtesy.org
Chairman, Peter G. Foot

CAMPAIGN FOR FREEDOM OF INFORMATION (1984), Suite 102, 16 Baldwins Gardens, London EC1N 7RJ T 020-7831 7477 E admin@cfoi.demon.co.uk W www.cfoi.org.uk
Director, Maurice Frankel

CAMPAIGN FOR NUCLEAR DISARMAMENT (1958), 162 Holloway Road, London N7 8DQ T 020-7700 2393 E enquiries@cnduk.org W www.cnduk.org
Chair, Kate Hudson

CAMPAIGN FOR THE PROTECTION OF RURAL WALES (1928), Ty Gwyn, 31 High Street, Welshpool SY21 7YD T 01938-552525 E info@cprwmail.org.uk W www.cprw.org.uk
Director, Peter Ogden

CANCER RESEARCH UK (2002), PO Box 123, Lincoln's Inn Fields, London WC2A 3PX T 020-7242 0200 W www.cancerresearchuk.org
Chief Executive, Harpal S. Kumar

CAREERS RESEARCH AND ADVISORY CENTRE, 2nd Floor, Sheraton House, Castle Park, Cambridge CB3 0AX T 01223-460277 E website@crac.org.uk W www.crac.org.uk
Chief Executive, Jeffrey Defries

CARERS UK (1965), 20 Great Dover Street, Southwark, London SE1 4LX T 020-7378 4999 E info@carersuk.org W www.carersuk.org
Chief Executive, Imelda Redmond, CBE

CARNEGIE UNITED KINGDOM TRUST (1913), Andrew Carnegie House, Pittencrieff Street, Dunfermline KY12 8AW T 01383-721445 E info@carnegieuk.org W www.carnegieuktrust.org.uk
Chair, Melanie Leech

CATHEDRALS FABRIC COMMISSION FOR ENGLAND (1991), Church House, Great Smith Street, London SW1P 3NZ T 020-7898 1863 E enquiries@c-of-e.org.uk
Secretary, Janet Gough

CATHOLIC UNION OF GREAT BRITAIN (1872), St Maximillian Kolbe House, 63 Jeddo Road, London W12 9EE T 020-8749 1321 E info@catholicunion.org W www.catholicunion.org
President, Lord Brennan, QC

CENTRAL AND CECIL HOUSING TRUST (1927), 266 Waterloo Road, London, Richmond SE1 8RQ T 020-7922 5300 E enquiries@ccht.org.uk W www.ccht.org.uk
Chief Executive, Dorry McLaughlin

CENTRAL COUNCIL OF CHURCH BELL RINGERS (1891), 11 Bullfields, Sawbridgeworth, CM21 9DB T 01279-726159 E secretary@cccbr.org.uk W www.cccbr.org.uk
Hon. Secretary, Mary Bone

CENTREPOINT (1969), Central House, 25 Camperdown Street, London E1 8DZ T 0845-466 3400 E info@centrepoint.org W www.centrepoint.org.uk
Chief Executive, Seyi Obakin

CEREDIGION HISTORICAL SOCIETY, Abermagwr, Aberystwyth, SY23 4AR T 01974-261222 E ymholiadau@cymdeithashanesceredigion.org W www.ceredigionhistoricalsociety.org
Hon. Secretary, Mrs E. Baskerville

CHANGING FACES (1992), The Squire Centre, 33–37 University Street, London WC1E 6JN T 0845-450 0275 E info@changingfaces.org.uk W www.changingfaces.org.uk
Chief Executive, James Partridge

CHARITIES AID FOUNDATION (1924), 25 Kings Hill Avenue, West Malling ME19 4TA T 0300-012 3000 E enquiries@cafonline.org W www.cafonline.org
Chief Executive, Dr John Low, CBE

CHARTERED INSTITUTE OF ARBITRATORS (1915), International Arbitration and Mediation Centre, 12–14 Bloomsbury Square, London WC1A 2LP T 020-7421 7444 E info@ciarb.org W www.ciarb.org
Director-General, Michael Forbes Smith

CHARTERED INSTITUTE OF LINGUISTS (1910), Saxon House, 48 Southwark Street, London SE1 1UN T 020-7940 3100 E info@iol.org.uk W www.iol.org.uk
Chief Executive, John Hammond

CHATHAM HOUSE (1920), Chatham House, 10 St James's Square, London SW1Y 4LE T 020-7957 5700 E contact@chathamhouse.org.uk W www.chathamhouse.org.uk
Director, Dr Robin Niblett

CHILD POVERTY ACTION GROUP (1965), 94 White Lion Street, London N1 9PF T 020-7837 7979 E staff@cpag.org.uk W www.cpag.org.uk
Chief Executive, Kate Green

CHILDREN 1ST (1884), 83 Whitehouse Loan, Edinburgh EH9 1AT T 0131-446 2300 E info@children1st.org.uk W www.children1st.org.uk
Chief Executive, Anne Houston

CHILDREN'S SOCIETY (1881), Edward Rudolf House, Margery Street, London WC1X 0JL T 0845-300 1128 E supportercare@childrenssociety.org.uk W www.childrenssociety.org.uk
Chief Executive, Bob Reitemeier

CHOICE SUPPORT (1987), 100 Westminster Bridge Road, London SE1 7XA T 020-7261 4100 E choicesupport@choicesupport.org.uk W www.choicesupport.org.uk
Chief Executive, Steven Rose

CHRISTIAN AID (1945), 35 Lower Marsh, London SE1 7RL T 020-7620 4444 E info@christian-aid.org W www.christianaid.org.uk
Director, Loretta Minghella

CHRISTIAN AID SCOTLAND (1945), The Pentagon Centre, 36 Washington Street, Glasgow G3 8AZ T 0141-221 7475 E glasgow@christian-aid.org W www.christianaid.org.uk
Head of Team for Scotland, Kathy Galloway

CHRISTIAN EDUCATION (2001), 1020 Bristol Road, Selly Oak, Birmingham B29 6LB T 0121-472 4242 E enquiries@christianeducation.org.uk W www.christianeducation.org.uk
Chief Executive, Peter Fishpool

CHURCHILL CENTRE UK (1968), PO Box 1915, Quarley, Andover, Hants SP10 9EE T 01264-889627 E ndege@tiscali.co.uk W www.winstonchurchill.org
UK Chair, P. H. Courtenay

CHURCHILL SOCIETY – LONDON (1990), Ivy House, 18 Grove Lane, Ipswich IP4 1NR T 01473-413533 E dutysecretary@churchill-society-london.org.uk W www.churchill-society-london.org.uk
General Secretary, J. H. Rogers

CHURCH LADS' AND CHURCH GIRLS' BRIGADE (1891), 2 Barnsley Road, Wath-upon-Dearne, Rotherham S63 6PY T 01709-876535 E brigadesecretary@clcgb.org.uk W www.clcgb.org.uk
Brigade Secretary, A. Millward

CHURCH MISSION SOCIETY (1799), Watlington Road, Oxford OX4 6BZ T 0845-620 1799 E info@cms-uk.org W www.cms-uk.org
Executive Director, Revd Canon Tim Dakin

CHURCH MONUMENTS SOCIETY (1979), Moor View, Exbourne EX20 3SA T 01837-851483 E churchmonuments@aol.com W www.churchmonumentssociety.org
Secretary, Dr Amy Harris

CHURCH UNION (1859), 2A, The Cloisters, Gordon Square, London WC1H 0AG E secretary@churchunion.co.uk W www.churchunion.co.uk
Chair, David Morgan

CITIZENS ADVICE (1939), Myddelton House, 115–123 Pentonville Road, London N1 9LZ T 0845-126 4264 W www.citizensadvice.org.uk
Chief Executive, David Harker

CITY BUSINESS LIBRARY (1970), City Business Library, Aldermanbury, London EC2V 7HH T 020-7332 1812 E cbl@cityoflondon.gov.uk W www.cityoflondon.gov.uk/citybusinesslibrary
Business Librarian, Goretti Considine

CITY OF COVENTRY FREEMEN'S GUILD (1946), 1 Trossachs Road, Coventry CV5 7BJ T 024-7646 3203 W www.coventryfreemensguild.co.uk
Hon. Clerk, George Wilkinson

CLASSICAL ASSOCIATION (1903), Senate House, Malet Street, London WC1E 7HU T 020-7862 8706 E office@classicalassociation.org W www.classicalassociation.org
Secretary, Claire Davenport

CLIMATE CHANGE ORGANISATION (2004), The Tower Building, 3rd Floor, 11 York Road, London SE1 7NX T 020-7960 2970 E info@theclimategroup.org W www.theclimategroup.org
Chief Executive, Steve Howard

COMMONWEALTH SOCIETY FOR THE DEAF 'SOUND SEEKERS' (1959), 34 Buckingham Palace Road, London SW1W 0RE **T** 020-7233 5700
E sound.seekers@btinternet.com
W www.sound-seekers.org.uk
Chief Executive, Gary Williams

COMMUNITY INTEGRATED CARE (1988), 2 Old Market Court, Miners Way, Widnes WA8 7SP
T 0151 420 3637 **E** information@c-i-c.co.uk
W www.c-i-c.co.uk
Chief Executive, Phil Edgington

CONCERN WORLDWIDE (1968), 13–14 Calico House, Clove Hitch Quay, London SW11 3TN
T 020-7801 1850 **E** info@concern.net **W** www.concern.net
Chief Executive, Tom Arnold

CONTEMPORARY APPLIED ARTS (1948), 2 Percy Street, London W1T 1DD **T** 020-7436 2344
E sales@caa.org.uk **W** www.caa.org.uk
Director, Sarah Edwards

COOPERATIVE PARTY (1917), 77 Weston Street, London SE1 3SD **T** 020-7367 4150 **E** mail@party.coop
W www.party.coop
General Secretary, Michael Stephenson

COOPERATIVES UK (1869), Holyoake House, Hanover Street, Manchester M60 0AS **T** 0161-246 2900
E info@cooperatives-uk.coop **W** www.cooperatives-uk.coop
Secretary General, Ed Mayo

CORAM FAMILY (1739), 49 Mecklenburgh Square, London WC1N 2QA **T** 020-7520 0300
E reception@coram.org.uk **W** www.coram.org.uk
Chief Executive, Dr Carol Homden

CORONERS' SOCIETY OF ENGLAND AND WALES (1846), The Court House, Bewdley Road, Stourport on Severn, Worcs DY13 8XE **T** 0151-233 5708
W www.coroner.org.uk
Hon. Secretary, André Joseph Anthony Rebello

CORPORATION OF CHURCH HOUSE (1888), Church House, Great Smith Street, London SW1P 3AZ
T 020-7898 1000 **E** info@churchhouse.org.uk
W www.churchhouse.org.uk
Secretary, Colin D. L. Menzies

COUNCIL FOR AWARDS OF ROYAL AGRICULTURAL SOCIETIES (1970), Springvale, Orchard Close, Shaldon, TQ14 0HF **T** 01626-873159
E ejwibberley@btinternet.com
Hon. Secretary, Prof. John Wibberley

COUNCIL FOR BRITISH ARCHAEOLOGY (1944), St Mary's House, 66 Bootham, York YO30 7BZ
T 01904-671417 **E** info@britarch.ac.uk
W www.britarch.ac.uk
Director, Dr Mike Heyworth, MBE

COUNCIL FOR THE CARE OF CHURCHES (1921), Church House, Great Smith Street, London SW1P 3NZ **T** 020-7898 1866 **E** enquiries.ccb@c-of-e.org.uk
W www.churchcare.co.uk
Secretary, Janet Gough

COUNCIL FOR WORLD MISSION (1977), Ipalo House, 32–34 Great Peter Street, London SW1P 2DB
T 020-7222 4214 **E** council@cwmission.org.uk
W www.cwmission.org.uk
General Secretary, Revd Dr D. van der Water

COUNCIL OF CHRISTIANS AND JEWS (1942), Godliman House, 21 Godliman Street, London EC4V 5BD
T 020-7015 5160 **E** cjrelations@ccj.org.uk
W www.ccj.org.uk
Chief Executive, David Gifford

COUNCIL OF UNIVERSITY CLASSICAL DEPARTMENTS (1972), Faculty of Classics, Sidgwick Avenue, Cambridge CB3 9DA **T** 01223-335158
E ro225@cam.ac.uk **W** www.rhul.ac.uk/classics/cucd
Chair, Prof Robin G. Osborne, FBA

COUNSEL AND CARE (1954), Twyman House, 16 Bonny Street, London NW1 9PG **T** 020-7241 8555
E advice@counselandcare.org.uk
W www.counselandcare.org.uk
Chief Executive, Stephen Burke

COUNTRY HOUSES FOUNDATION (2005), Steephouse Farm, Uley Road, Dursley GL11 5AD
T 0845-402 4102 **E** info@countryhousesfoundation.org.uk
W www.countryhousesfoundation.org.uk
Chief Executive, David Price

COUNTRY LAND & BUSINESS ASSOCIATION (1907), 16 Belgrave Square, London SW1X 8PQ
T 020-7235 0511 **E** mail@cla.org.uk **W** www.cla.org.uk
President, William Worsely

COUNTRYSIDE ALLIANCE (1997), Old Town Hall, 367 Kennington Road, London SE11 4PT **T** 020-7840 9200
W www.countryside-alliance.org.uk
Chief Executive, Simon Hart

CPRE (CAMPAIGN TO PROTECT RURAL ENGLAND) (1926), 128 Southwark Street, London SE1 0SW **T** 020-7981 2800 **E** info@cpre.org.uk
W www.cpre.org.uk
Chief Executive, Shaun Spiers

CRAFTS COUNCIL (1971), 44A Pentonville Road, London N1 9BY **T** 020-7806 2500
E reference@craftscouncil.org.uk
W www.craftscouncil.org.uk
Executive Director, Rosy Greenlees

CRANSTOUN DRUG SERVICES (1969), 1st Floor, St Andrews House, 26–27 Victoria Road, Surbiton KT6 4JZ
T 020-8335 1830 **E** info@cranstoun.org.uk
W www.cranstoun.org.uk
Chief Executive, Steve Rossell

CRISIS UK (1967), 66 Commercial Street, London E1 6LT **T** 0844-251 0111 **E** enquiries@crisis.org.uk
W www.crisis.org.uk
Chief Executive, Leslie Morphy

CRUSE BEREAVEMENT CARE (1959), Unit 01, One Victoria Villas, Richmond TW9 2GW **T** 020-8939 9530,
Helpline 0844-477 9400 **E** info@cruse.org.uk
W www.cruse.org.uk
Chief Executive, Debbie Kerslake

CSV (1962), 237 Pentonville Road, London N1 9NJ T 020-7278 6601 E information@csv.org.uk W www.csv.org.uk
Chief Executive, Dame Elisabeth Hoodless

CTC (THE UK'S NATIONAL CYCLISTS' ORGANISATION) (1878), Parklands, Railton Road, Guildford GU2 9JX T 01483-238337 E cycling@ctc.org.uk W www.ctc.org.uk
Director, Kevin Mayne

CYSTIC FIBROSIS TRUST (1964), 11 London Road, Bromley BR1 1BY T 020-8464 7211 E enquiries@cftrust.org.uk W www.cftrust.org.uk
Chief Executive, Rosie Barnes

DAY ONE CHRISTIAN MINISTRIES (1831), Ryelands Road, Leominster HR6 8NZ T 01568-613740 E sales@dayone.co.uk W www.dayone.co.uk
Managing Director, Mark Roberts

DEMOS, Third Floor, Magdalen House, 136 Tooley Street, London SE1 2TU T 0845-458 5949 E hello@demos.co.uk W www.demos.co.uk
Director, Richard Reeves

DESIGN AND TECHNOLOGY ASSOCIATION (1989), 16 Wellesbourne House, Walton Road, Wellesbourne CV35 9JB T 01789-470007 E info@data.org.uk W www.data.org.uk
Chief Executive, Richard Green

DIABETES UK (1934), Macleod House, 10 Parkway, London NW1 7AA T 020-7424 1000 E info@diabetes.org.uk W www.diabetes.org.uk
Chief Executive, Douglas Smallwood

DITCHLEY FOUNDATION (1958), Ditchley Park, Enstone, Chipping Norton OX7 4ER T 01608-677346 E mail@ditchley.co.uk W www.ditchley.co.uk
Director, Sir John Holmes, GCVO, KBE, CMG

DOWN'S SYNDROME ASSOCIATION (1970), The Langdon Down Centre, 2A Langdon Park, Teddington TW11 9PS T 0845-230 0372 E info@downs-syndrome.org.uk W www.downs-syndrome.org.uk
Chief Executive Officer, Carol Boys

DUKE OF EDINBURGH'S AWARD (1956), Gulliver House, Madeira Walk, Windsor SL4 1EU T 01753-727400 E info@DofE.org W www.DofE.org
Chief Executive, Peter Westgarth

DYSLEXIA ACTION (2006), Park House, Wick Road, Egham TW20 0HH T 01784-222300 E info@dyslexiaaction.org.uk W www.dyslexiaaction.org.uk
Chief Executive, Shirley Cramer

EAST HERTFORDSHIRE ARCHAEOLOGICAL SOCIETY (1898), 11 St Leonard's Close, Bengeo, Hertford SG14 3LL T 01992-423433 E EHASoc@googlemail.com W www.ehas.org.uk
Hon. Secretary, Mrs G. R. Pollard

EAST OF ENGLAND AGRICULTURAL SOCIETY (1797), East of England Showground, Peterborough PE2 6XE T 01733-234451 E info@eastofengland.org.uk W www.eastofengland.org.uk
Chief Executive, Andrew Mercer

ECCLESIOLOGICAL SOCIETY (1879), 38 Rosebery Avenue, New Malden KT3 4JS E info@ecclsoc.org W www.ecclsoc.org
Chair, Trevor Cooper

ELECTORAL REFORM SOCIETY (1884), 6 Chancel Street, London SE1 0UU T 020-7928 1622 E ers@electoral-reform.org.uk W www.electoral-reform.org.uk
Chief Executive, Dr Ken Ritchie

ELGAR FOUNDATION (1935), The Elgar Birthplace Museum, Lower Broadheath, Worcester WR2 6RH T 01905-333224 E birthplace@elgarmuseum.org W www.elgarmuseum.org
Museum Director, Catherine Sloan

EMERGENCY PLANNING SOCIETY (1993), The Media Centre, Culverhouse Cross, Cardiff CF6 6XJ T 0845-600 9587 E manager@the-eps.org W www.the-eps.org

ENERGY INSTITUTE (2003), 61 New Cavendish Street, London W1G 7AR T 020-7467 7100 E info@energyinst.org W www.energyinst.org
Chief Executive, Louise Kingham

ENGLISH ASSOCIATION (1906), University of Leicester, University Road, Leicester LE1 7RH T 0116-252 3982 E engassoc@le.ac.uk W www.le.ac.uk/engassoc
Chief Executive, Ms H. Lucas

ENGLISH CHESS FEDERATION (1904), The Watch Oak, Chain Lane, Battle TN33 0YD T 01424-775222 E office@englishchess.org.uk W www.englishchess.org.uk
Chief Executive, Christopher Majer

ENGLISH FOLK DANCE AND SONG SOCIETY (1932), Cecil Sharp House, 2 Regent's Park Road, London NW1 7AY T 020-7485 2206 E info@efdss.org W www.efdss.org
Chief Executive, K. Spicer

ENGLISH-SPEAKING UNION OF THE COMMONWEALTH (1918), Dartmouth House, 37 Charles Street, London W1J 5ED T 020-7529 1550 E esu@esu.org W www.esu.org
Director-General, Mike Lake, CBE

ENVIRONMENT COUNCIL (1970), 212 High Holborn, London WC1V 7BF T 020-7836 2626 E info@envcouncil.org.uk W www.the-environment-council.org.uk
Chief Executive, Mrs Winsome MacLaurin

EPILEPSY ACTION (1950), New Anstey House, Gate Way Drive, Yeadon, Leeds LS19 7XY T 0113-210 8800, Helpline 0808-800 5050 E helpline@epilepsy.org.uk W www.epilepsy.org.uk
Chief Executive, Philip Lee

ESPERANTO ASSOCIATION OF BRITAIN (1976), Esperanto House, Station Road, Barlaston, Stoke-on-Trent ST12 9DE T 0845-230 1887 E eab@esperanto-gb.org W www.esperanto-gb.org
President, Prof. John Wells

FABIAN SOCIETY (1884), 11 Dartmouth Street, London SW1H 9BN T 020-7227 4900 E info@fabian-society.org.uk W www.fabian-society.org.uk
General Secretary, S. Katwala

FAMILY WELFARE ASSOCIATION (1869), 501–505 Kingsland Road, London E8 4AU **T** 020-7254 6251 **W** www.fwa.org.uk
Chief Executive, Helen Dent

FEDERATION OF BRITISH ARTISTS (1961), 17 Carlton House Terrace, London SW1Y 5BD **T** 020-7930 6844 **E** info@mallgalleries.com **W** www.mallgalleries.org.uk
Director, Lewis McNaught

FEDERATION OF FAMILY HISTORY SOCIETIES (1974), PO Box 8857, Lutterworth LE17 9BJ **T** 01455-293133 **E** info@ffhs.org.uk **W** www.ffhs.org.uk
Administrator, Philippa McCray

FEDERATION OF SMALL BUSINESSES (1974), 2 Catherine Place, Westminster, London SW1E 6HF **T** 020-7592 8100 **E** holly.lee@fsb.org.uk **W** www.fsb.org.uk
Head of Public Affairs, Stephen Alambritis

FIELDS IN TRUST (1925), Ground Floor South, 100 Christian Street, London E1 1RS **T** 020-7264 2400 **E** info@fieldsintrust.org **W** www.fieldsintrust.org
Chief Executive, Alison Moore-Gwyn

FIELD STUDIES COUNCIL (1943), Preston Montford, Montford Bridge, Shrewsbury SY4 1HW **T** 01743-852100 **E** fsc.headoffice@field-studies-council.org **W** www.field-studies-council.org
Chief Executive, Rob Lucas

FIRE FIGHTERS CHARITY (1943), Level 6, Belvedere House, Basing View, Basingstoke RG21 4HG **T** 01256-366566 **E** info@firefighterscharity.org.uk **W** www.firefighterscharity.org.uk
Chief Executive, Jan Barlow

FIRE PROTECTION ASSOCIATION (1946), London Road, Moreton in Marsh, Glos GL56 0RH **T** 01608-812500 **E** fpa@thefpa.co.uk **W** www.thefpa.co.uk
Managing Director, Jonathan O'Neill

FLAG INSTITUTE (1971), 38 Hill Street, Mayfair, London W1J 5NS **E** membership@flaginstitute.org **W** www.flaginstitute.org
President, Capt. Malcolm Farrow, OBE, FFI, RN

FLEET AIR ARM OFFICERS' ASSOCIATION (1957), 4 St James's Square, London SW1Y 4JU **T** 020-7930 7722 **E** faaoa@fleetairarmoa.org **W** www.fleetairarmoa.org
Chair, Rear-Adm. S. Lidbetter

FORENSIC SCIENCE SOCIETY (1959), Clarke House, 18A Mount Parade, Harrogate HG1 1BX **T** 01423-506068 **E** info@forensic-science-society.org.uk **W** www.forensic-science-society.org.uk
Chief Executive, Dr Carol Ostell

FOUNDATION FOR CREDIT COUNSELLING (1993), 11th Floor, Wade House, Merrion Centre, Leeds LS2 8NG **T** 0113-297 0107 **E** contactus@cccs.co.uk **W** www.cccs.co.uk
Chief Executive, Gordon Bell

FOUNDATION FOR THE STUDY OF INFANT DEATHS (1971), 11 Belgrave Road, London SW1V 1RB **T** 020-7802 3200 **E** office@fsid.org.uk **W** www.fsid.org.uk
Director, Mrs J. Epstein

FPA (1930), 50 Featherstone Street, London EC1Y 8QU **T** 020-7608 5240 **E** library&information@fpa.org.uk **W** www.fpa.org.uk
Chief Executive, Ms Julie Bentley

FRANCO-BRITISH SOCIETY (1924), 2 Dovedale Studios, 465 Battersea Park Road, London SW11 4LR **T** 020 7924 3511 **E** execsec@francobritishsociety.org.uk **W** www.francobritishsociety.org.uk
Executive Secretary, Mrs Kate Brayn

FRIENDS OF CATHEDRAL MUSIC (1956), 21 Bradford Road, Trowbridge BA14 9AL **T** 0845-644 3721 **E** info@fcm.org.uk **W** www.fcm.org.uk
Secretary, Roger Bishton

FRIENDS OF FRIENDLESS CHURCHES (1957), St Ann's Vestry Hall, 2 Church Entry, London EC4V 5HB **T** 020-7236 3934 **E** office@friendsoffriendlesschurches.org.uk **W** www.friendsoffriendlesschurches.org.uk
Hon. Director, Matthew Saunders, MBE

FRIENDS OF THE EARTH SCOTLAND (1978), Thorn House, 5 Rose Street, Edinburgh EH2 2PR **T** 0131-243 2700 **E** info@foe-scotland.org.uk **W** www.foe-scotland.org.uk
Chief Executive Officer, Duncan McLaren

FRIENDS OF THE NATIONAL LIBRARIES (1931), c/o Department of Manuscripts, The British Library, 96 Euston Road, London NW1 2DB **T** 020-7412 7559 **W** www.friendsofnationallibraries.org.uk
Chairman, Lord Egremont, FRSL

FURNITURE HISTORY SOCIETY (1964), 1 Mercedes Cottages, St John's Road, Haywards Heath RH16 4EH **T** 01444-413845 **E** furniturehistorysociety@hotmail.com **W** www.furniturehistorysociety.org
Membership Secretary, Dr Brian Austen

GALLIPOLI ASSOCIATION (1969), Earleydene Orchard, Earleydene, Ascot SL5 9JY **T** 01344-626523 **E** webmaster@gallipoli-association.org **W** www.gallipoli-association.org
Hon. Secretary, J. C. Watson Smith

GAME AND WILDLIFE CONSERVATION TRUST (1969), Fordingbridge SP6 1EF **T** 01425-652381 **E** info@gwct.org.uk **W** www.gwct.org.uk
Chief Executive, Teresa Dent

GARDEN HISTORY SOCIETY (1965), 70 Cowcross Street, London EC1M 6EJ **T** 020-7608 2409 **E** enquiries@gardenhistorysociety.org **W** www.gardenhistorysociety.org
Chair, Dominic Cole

GEMMOLOGICAL ASSOCIATION OF GREAT BRITAIN (1931), 27 Greville Street (Saffron Hill entrance), London EC1N 8TN **T** 020-7404 3334 **E** information@gem-a.com **W** www.gem-a.com
Chief Executive, Dr Jack Ogden

GENERAL MEDICAL COUNCIL (1858), Regent's Place, 350 Euston Road, London NW1 3JN **T** 0845-357 8001 **E** gmc@gmc-uk.org **W** www.gmc-uk.org
Chief Executive, Niall Dickson

GENERAL OPTICAL COUNCIL (1959), 41 Harley Street, London W1G 8DJ **T** 020-7580 3898 **E** goc@optical.org **W** www.optical.org
Chief Executive and Registrar, Dian Taylor

GEOGRAPHICAL ASSOCIATION (1893), 160 Solly Street, Sheffield S1 4BF **T** 0114-296 0088 **E** info@geography.org.uk **W** www.geography.org.uk
Chief Executive, David Lambert

GIRLGUIDING UK (1910), 17–19 Buckingham Palace Road, London SW1W 0PT **T** 020-7834 6242 **E** chq@girlguiding.org.uk **W** www.girlguiding.org.uk
Chief Guide, Liz Burnley

GIRLS' BRIGADE ENGLAND AND WALES, PO Box 196, 129 The Broadway, Didcot OX11 8XN **T** 01235-510425 **E** gbco@girlsbrigadeew.org.uk **W** www.girlsb.org
National Director, Ruth Gilson

GIRLS' VENTURE CORPS AIR CADETS (1964), 1 Bawtry Gate, Sheffield, S9 1WD **T** 0114-2448405 **E** gvcac@toucansurf.com **W** www.gvcac.org.uk
Corps Director, Mrs Brenda Layne, MBE

GREENPEACE UK (1979), Canonbury Villas, London N1 2PN **T** 020-7865 8100 **E** info@uk.greenpeace.org **W** www.greenpeace.org.uk
Executive Director, John Sauven

GUIDE DOGS FOR THE BLIND ASSOCIATION (1934), Hillfields, Burghfield Common, Reading RG7 3YG **T** 0118-983 5555 **E** guidedogs@guidedogs.org.uk **W** www.guidedogs.org.uk
Chief Executive, Richard Leaman

GUILD OF AID FOR GENTLEPEOPLE (1904), 10 St Christopher's Place, London W1U 1HZ **T** 020-7935 0641 **E** admin@pcac.org.uk **W** www.pcac.uk

GUILD OF FREEMEN OF THE CITY OF LONDON (1908), 4 Dowgate Hill, London EC4R 2SH **T** 020-8541 1435 **E** clerk@guild-freemen-london.co.uk **W** www.guild-freemen-london.co.uk
Clerk to the Guild, Brigadier M. I. Keun

GUILD OF GLASS ENGRAVERS (1975), 87 Nether Street, Finchley, London N12 7NP **T** 020-8446 4050 **E** enquiries@gge.org.uk **W** www.gge.org.uk
Secretary, Christine Reyland

GURKHA WELFARE TRUST (1969), PO Box 2170, 22 Queen Street, Salisbury SP2 2EX **T** 01722-323955 **E** staffassistant@gwt.org.uk **W** www.gwt.org.uk
Chief Executive, Col. William Shuttlewood, OBE

GUY'S AND ST THOMAS' CHARITY (1553), West Wing, Counting House, Guy's Hospital, Great Maze Pond, London SE1 9RT **T** 020-7188 7700 **E** info@gsttcharity.org.uk **W** www.gsttcharity.org.uk
Chief Executive, Peter Hewitt

HAEMOPHILIA SOCIETY (1950), First Floor, Petersham House, 57A Hatton Garden, London EC1N 8JG **T** 020-7831 1020, **Helpline** 0800-018 6068 **E** info@haemophilia.org.uk **W** www.haemophilia.org.uk
Chief Executive, Chris James

HAIG HOMES (1929), Alban Dobson House, Green Lane, Morden SM4 5NS **T** 020-8685 5777 **E** haig@haighomes.org.uk **W** www.haighomes.org.uk
Chief Executive, Maj.-Gen. P. V. R. Besgrove, CBE

HALIFAX ANTIQUARIAN SOCIETY (1900), 356 Oldham Road, Sowerby Bridge, Halifax HX6 4QU **T** 01422-823966 **W** www.halifaxhistory.org.uk
Hon. Secretary, Anne Kirker

HANSARD SOCIETY FOR PARLIAMENTARY GOVERNMENT (1944), 40–43 Chancery Lane, London WC2A 1JA **T** 020-7438 1222 **E** hansard@hansard.lse.ac.uk **W** www.hansardsociety.org.uk
Chief Executive, Fiona Booth

HARVEIAN SOCIETY OF LONDON (1831), Lettsom House, 11 Chandos Street, London W1G 9EB **T** 020-7580 1043 **E** harveiansoclondon@btconnect.com
Executive Secretary, Cdr R. C. Ireland, MBE

HAWICK ARCHAEOLOGICAL SOCIETY (1856), 8 Melgund Place, Hawick TD9 9HY **T** 01450-376220 **E** info@airchieoliver.co.uk **W** www.airchieoliver.co.uk
Hon. Secretary, Gerald M. Graham

HEARING CONCERN (1947), 19 Hartfield Road, Eastbourne BN21 2AR **T** 01323-638230 **E** info@hearingconcernlink.org **W** www.hearingconcernlink.org
Chief Executive, Dr Lorraine Gailey

HERALDRY SOCIETY (1947), PO Box 772, Guildford GU3 3ZX **T** 01483-237373 **E** memsec@theheraldrysociety.com **W** www.theheraldrysociety.com
Honorary Secretary, John Tunesi of Liongam

HISPANIC AND LUSO BRAZILIAN COUNCIL (1943), Canning House, 2 Belgrave Square, London SW1X 8PJ **T** 020-7235 2303 **E** enquiries@canninghouse.org **W** www.canninghouse.org
Director, Nigel McCollum

HISTORICAL ASSOCIATION (1906), 59A Kennington Park Road, London SE11 4JH **T** 020-7735 3901 **E** enquiry@history.org.uk **W** www.history.org.uk
Chief Executive, Rebecca Sullivan

HISTORIC HOUSES ASSOCIATION (1973), 2 Chester Street, London SW1X 7BB **T** 020-7259 5688 **E** info@hha.org.uk **W** www.hha.org.uk
Director-General, Nick Way

HONG KONG ASSOCIATION (1961), Swire House, 59 Buckingham Gate, London SW1E 6AJ **T** 020-7963 9445/47 **E** communications@hkas.org.uk **W** www.hkas.org.uk
Executive Director, R. L. Guy

HONOURABLE SOCIETY OF CYMMRODORION (1751), PO Box 55178, London N12 2AY **T** 020-7631 0502 **E** aelodau1751we@yahoo.co.uk **W** www.cymmrodorion1751.org.uk
Hon. Secretary, Peter Jeffreys

HOSTELLING INTERNATIONAL NORTHERN IRELAND (1931), 22–32 Donegall Road, Belfast BT12 5JN T 028-9032 4733 E info@hini.org.uk W www.hini.org.uk
General Secretary, Ken Canavan

HOUSING JUSTICE (1956), 209 Old Marylebone Road, London NW1 5QT T 020-7920 6600 E info@housingjustice.org.uk W www.housingjustice.org.uk
Director, Alison Gelder

HR SOCIETY LTD (1970), 1–5 Stud Offices, Redenham Park, Redenham, Andover SP11 9AQ T 01264-774004 E network@hrsociety.co.uk W www.hrsociety.co.uk
President, Andrew Mayo

HUMANE RESEARCH TRUST (1962), Brook House, 29 Bramhall Lane South, Bramhall, Stockport SK7 2DN T 0161-439 8041 E info@humaneresearch.org.uk W www.humaneresearch.org.uk
Chair, K. Cholerton

HYMN SOCIETY OF GREAT BRITAIN AND IRELAND (1936), 99 Barton Road, Lancaster LA1 4EN T 01524-66740 E robcanham@haystacks.fsnet.co.uk W www.hymnsocietygbi.org.uk
Hon. Secretary, Revd Robert A. Canham

I CAN (1888), 8 Wakely Street, London EC1V 7QE T 0845-225 4073 E info@ican.org.uk W www.ican.org.uk
Chief Executive, Virginia Beardshaw

IMMIGRATION ADVISORY SERVICE (1970), 3rd Floor, County House, 190 Great Dover Street, London SE1 4YB T 0844-974 4000 E advice@iasuk.org W www.iasuk.org
Chief Executive (acting), Margaret McKinlay

INCORPORATED SOCIETY OF MUSICIANS (1882), 10 Stratford Place, London W1C 1AA T 020-7629 4413 E membership@ism.org W www.ism.org
Chief Executive, Deborah Annetts

INDEPENDENTAGE (1863), 6 Avonmore Road, London W14 8RL T 020-7605 4200 E charity@independentage.org.uk W www.independentage.org.uk
Chief Executive, Janet Morrison

INDEPENDENT SCHOOLS' BURSARS ASSOCIATION (1932), Unit 11–12, Manor Farm, Cliddesden RG25 2JB T 01256-330369 E office@theisba.org.uk W www.theisba.org.uk
General Secretary, Jonathan Cook

INDUSTRY AND PARLIAMENT TRUST (1977), Suite 101, 3 Whitehall Court, London SW1A 2EL T 020-7839 9400 E admin@ipt.org.uk W www.ipt.org.uk
Chief Executive, Sally Muggeridge

INSTITUTE FOR PUBLIC POLICY RESEARCH (1988), 30–32 Southampton Street, London WC2E 7RA T 020-7470 6100 W www.ippr.org E info@ippr.org
Chair, John Makinson

INSTITUTE OF BIOLOGY (2009), 9 Red Lion Court, London EC4A 3EF T 020-7936 5900 E info@societyofbiology.org W www.societyofbiology.org
Chief Executive, Dr Mark Downs

INSTITUTE OF CANCER RESEARCH (1909), 123 Old Brompton Road, London SW7 3RP T 020-7352 8133 W www.icr.ac.uk
Chief Executive, Prof. Peter Rigby

INSTITUTE OF ECONOMIC AFFAIRS (1955), 2 Lord North Street, London SW1P 3LB T 020-7799 8900 E iea@iea.org.uk W www.iea.org.uk
Director-General, Mark Littlewood

INSTITUTE OF HEALTH PROMOTION AND EDUCATION, School of Dentistry, University of Manchester, Higher Cambridge Street, Manchester M15 6FH T 0161-275 6610 E honsec@ihpe.org.uk W www.ihpe.org.uk
Hon. Secretary, Kathy Lewis

INSTITUTE OF HERALDIC AND GENEALOGICAL STUDIES (1961), 79–82 Northgate, Canterbury CT1 1BA T 01227-768664 E ihgs@ihgs.ac.uk W www.ihgs.ac.uk
Principal, Dr Richard Baker

INSTITUTE OF MASTERS OF WINE (1953), Mapfre House, 2–3 Philpot Lane, London EC3M 8AN T 020-7621 2830 W www.mastersofwine.org
Executive Director, Siobhan Turner

INSTITUTE OF MATHEMATICS AND ITS APPLICATIONS (1964), Catherine Richards House, 16 Nelson Street, Southend-on-Sea SS1 1EF T 01702-354020 E post@ima.org.uk W www.ima.org.uk
Executive Director, David Youdan

INTERCONTINENTAL CHURCH SOCIETY (1823), 1 Athena Drive, Tachbrook Park CV34 6NL T 01926-430347 E enquiries@ics-uk.org W www.ics-uk.org
General Manager, David Healey

INTERNATIONAL AFRICAN INSTITUTE (1926), SOAS, Thornhaugh Street, Russell Square, London WC1H 0XG T 020-7898 4420 E iai@soas.ac.uk W www.internationalafricaninstitute.org
Hon. Director, Prof. Philip Burnham

INTERNATIONAL INSTITUTE FOR CONSERVATION OF HISTORIC AND ARTISTIC WORKS (1950), 6 Buckingham Street, London WC2N 6BA T 020-7839 5975 E iic@iconservation.org W www.iiconservation.org
Secretary-General, Josephine Kirby Atkinson

INTERNATIONAL PEN (1921), Brownlow House, 50–51 High Holborn, London WC1V 6ER T 020-7405 0338 E info@internationalpen.org.uk W www.internationalpen.org.uk
Executive Director, Caroline McCormick

INTERNATIONAL POLICE ASSOCIATION (BRITISH SECTION) (1950), Arthur Troop House, 1 Fox Road, West Bridgford, Nottingham NG2 6AJ T 0115-981 3638 E mail@ipa-uk.org W www.ipa-uk.org
Business Operations Manager, Michele Rai

INTERNATIONAL STUDENTS HOUSE (1962), 229 Great Portland Street, Regent's Park, London W1W 5PN T 020-7631 8300 E info@ish.org.uk W www.ish.org.uk
Executive Director, Peter Anwyl

INTERSERVE (1852), 5–6 Walker Avenue, Wolverton Hill MK12 5TW T 01908-552700 E enquiries@isewi.org W www.interserve.org.uk
National Director, Steve Bell

IRAN SOCIETY (1935), 2 Belgrave Square, London SW1X 8PJ T 020-7235 5122 E info@iransociety.org W www.iransociety.org
Chair, Antony Wynn

ISLE OF WIGHT NATURAL HISTORY AND ARCHAEOLOGICAL SOCIETY (1919), Unit 16, Prospect Business Centre, Prospect Road, Cowes PO31 7AD T 01983-282596 W www.iwnhas.org
President, Mrs J. Jones

JACQUELINE DU PRÉ MUSIC BUILDING LTD (1995), St Hilda's College, Oxford OX4 1DY T 01865-276821 E jdp@st-hildas.ox.ac.uk W www.st-hildas.ox.ac.uk/jdp
Administrator, Miss Anna-Andrea

JAPAN SOCIETY (1891), Swire House, 59 Buckingham Gate, London SW1E 6AJ T 020-7828 6330 E info@japansociety.org.uk W www.japansociety.org.uk
Chief Executive, Heidi Potter

JERUSALEM AND THE MIDDLE EAST CHURCH ASSOCIATION (1929), 1 Hart House, The Hart, Farnham GU9 7HJ T 01252-726994 E secretary@jmeca.eclipse.co.uk W www.jmeca.org.uk
Chair, John Clark

JOHN STUART MILL INSTITUTE (1992), 1 Whitehall Place, London SW1A 2HE T 07973-752473 E jsmi@cyberstar.uk.com W www.jsmillinstitute.org.uk
Convenor, Dr Alan Butt Philip

JOURNALISTS' CHARITY (1864), Dickens House, 35 Wathen Road, Dorking RH4 1JY T 01306-887511 E enquiries@journalistscharity.org.uk W www.journalistscharity.org.uk
Director, David Ilott

JUSTICE (1957), 59 Carter Lane, London EC4V 5AQ T 020-7329 5100 E admin@justice.org.uk W www.justice.org.uk
Director, Roger Smith, OBE

KENT ARCHAEOLOGICAL SOCIETY (1857), Maidstone Museum, St Faiths Street, Maidstone ME14 1LH T 01303-262425 E secretary@kentarchaeology.org.uk W www.kentarchaeology.org.uk
Hon. General Secretary, Dr P. Stutchbury

KIPLING SOCIETY (1927), 6 Clifton Road, London W9 1SS T 020-7286 0194 E jmkeskar@btinternet.com W www.kipling.org.uk
Hon. Secretary, Jane Keskar

LCIA (LONDON COURT OF INTERNATIONAL ARBITRATION) (1892), 70 Fleet Street, London EC4Y 1EU T 020-7936 7007 E lcia@lcia.org W www.lcia.org
Director-General, Adrian Winstanley

LEAGUE OF THE HELPING HAND (1908), PO Box 342, Burgess Hill, RH15 5AQ T 01444-236099 E secretary@lhh.org.uk W www.lhh.org.uk
Executive Secretary, Moira Parrott

LEPROSY MISSION, ENGLAND, WALES, THE CHANNEL ISLANDS AND THE ISLE OF MAN (1874), Goldhay Way, Orton Goldhay, Peterborough PE2 5GZ T 01733-370505 E post@tlmew.org.uk W www.leprosymission.org.uk
National Director, Rupert Haydock

LEUKAEMIA AND LYMPHOMA RESEARCH (1960), 43 Great Ormond Street, London WC1N 3JJ T 020-7405 0101 E info@llresearch.org.uk W www.llresearch.org.uk
Chief Executive, Cathy Gilman

LIBERTY (NATIONAL COUNCIL FOR CIVIL LIBERTIES) (1934), 21 Tabard Street, London SE1 4LA T 020-7403 3888 W www.liberty-human-rights.org.uk
Director, Shami Chakrabarti, CBE

LINNEAN SOCIETY OF LONDON (1788), Burlington House, Piccadilly, London W1J 0BF T 020-7434 4479 E info@linnean.org W www.linnean.org
Executive Secretary, Dr Ruth Temple

LISTENING BOOKS (1959), 12 Lant Street, London SE1 1QH T 020-7407 9417 E info@listening-books.org.uk W www.listening-books.org.uk
Director, Bill Dee

LIVABILITY (*c.*1840), 50 Scrutton Street, London EC2A 4XQ T 020-7452 2000 E info@livability.org.uk W www.livability.org.uk
Chief Executive, Tim Fallon

LOCAL GOVERNMENT ASSOCIATION (1997), Local Government House, Smith Square, London SW1P 3HZ T 020-7664 3000 E info@lga.gov.uk W www.lga.gov.uk
Chief Executive, John Ransford

LONDON COUNCILS (2000), 59½ Southwark Street, London SE1 0AL T 020-7934 9999 E info@londoncouncils.gov.uk W www.londoncouncils.gov.uk
Chief Executive, John O'Brien

LONDON LIBRARY (1841), 14 St James's Square, London SW1Y 4LG T 020-7930 7705 E enquiries@londonlibrary.co.uk W www.londonlibrary.co.uk
Librarian, Inez Lynn

LONDON PLAYING FIELDS FOUNDATION (1890), 73 Collier Street, London N1 9BE T 0845-026 2292 E enquiries@lpff.org.uk W www.lpff.org.uk
Chief Executive, Alex Welsh

LONDON SOCIETY (1912), Mortimer Wheeler House, 46 Eagle Wharf Road, London N1 7ED T 020-7253 9400 E info@londonsociety.org.uk W www.londonsociety.org.uk
Hon. Secretary, John D. Hill

MACMILLAN CANCER SUPPORT (1911), 89 Albert Embankment, London SE1 7UQ T 0808-808 0000 E contactus@macmillan.org.uk W www.macmillan.org.uk
Chief Executive, Ciarán Devane

MAKING MUSIC, THE NATIONAL FEDERATION OF MUSIC SOCIETIES (1935), 2–4 Great Eastern Street, London EC2A 3NW **T** 020-7422 8280 **E** info@makingmusic.org.uk **W** www.makingmusic.org.uk
Chief Executive, Robin Osterley

MANORIAL SOCIETY OF GREAT BRITAIN (1906), 104 Kennington Road, London SE11 6RE **T** 020-7735 6633 **E** manorial@msgb.co.uk **W** www.msgb.co.uk
Chairman, Robert Smith

MARIE CURIE CANCER CARE (1948), 89 Albert Embankment, London SE1 7TP **T** 020-7599 7777 **W** www.mariecurie.org.uk
Chief Executive, Thomas Hughes-Hallett

MARINE BIOLOGICAL ASSOCIATION OF THE UK (1884), Citadel Hill, Plymouth PL1 2BP **T** 01752-633207 **E** sec@mba.ac.uk **W** www.mba.ac.uk
President, Sir Geoffrey Holland

MARINE SOCIETY AND SEA CADETS (1756), 202 Lambeth Road, London SE1 7JW **T** 020-7654 7000 **E** info@ms-sc.org **W** www.ms-sc.org
Chief Executive, Michael J. Cornish

MARRIAGE CARE (1946), 1 Blythe Mews, Blythe Road, London W14 0NW **T** 020-7371 1341 **E** info@marriagecare.org.uk **W** www.marriagecare.org.uk
Chief Executive, Terry Prendergast

MATHEMATICAL ASSOCIATION (1871), 259 London Road, Leicester LE2 3BE **T** 0116-221 0013 **E** office@m-a.org.uk **W** www.m-a.org.uk
President, Dr David Acheson

MDF THE BIPOLAR ORGANISATION (1983), Castle Works, 21 St George's Road, London SE1 6ES **T** 020-7793 2600 **E** mdf@mdf.org.uk **W** www.mdf.org.uk
Charity Manager, Jean Wit

ME ASSOCIATION (1976), 7 Apollo Office Court, Radclive Road, Gawcott MK18 4DF **T** 0870-444 1836, **Helpline** 0844-576 5326 **E** meconnect@meassociation.org.uk **W** www.meassociation.org.uk
Chair, Neil Riley

MEDIAWATCH-UK (1965), 3 Willow House, Kennington Road, Ashford TN24 0NR **T** 01233-633936 **E** info@mediawatchuk.org **W** www.mediawatchuk.org
Director, Vivienne Pattison

MEDICAL SOCIETY OF LONDON (1773), Lettsom House, 11 Chandos Street, London W1G 9EB **T** 020-7580 1043 **E** medicalsoclondon@btconnect.com **W** www.medsoclondon.org
Registrar, Cdr Roger Ireland, MBE

MEDICAL WOMEN'S FEDERATION (1917), Tavistock House North, Tavistock Square, London WC1H 9HX **T** 020-7387 7765 **E** admin.mwf@btconnect.com **W** www.medicalwomensfederation.org.uk
President, Dr Clarissa Fabre

MENCAP (ROYAL MENCAP SOCIETY) (1946), 123 Golden Lane, London EC1Y 0RT **T** 020-7454 0454 **E** information@mencap.org.uk **W** www.mencap.org.uk
Chief Executive, Mark Goldring, CBE

MENTAL HEALTH FOUNDATION, Sea Containers House, 20 Upper Ground, London SE1 9QB **T** 020-7803 1100 **E** mhf@mhf.org.uk **W** www.mentalhealth.org.uk
Chief Executive, Andrew McCulloch

MERCHANT NAVY WELFARE BOARD (1948), 30 Palmerston Road, Southampton SO14 1LL **T** 023-8033 7799 **E** enquiries@mnwb.org.uk **W** www.mnwb.org
Chief Executive, Capt. D. A. Parsons

MHA CARE GROUP (1943), Epworth House, 3 Stuart Street, Derby DE1 2EQ **T** 01332-296200 **E** enquiries@mha.org.uk **W** www.mha.org.uk
Chief Executive, Roger Davies

MIDDLE EAST ASSOCIATION (1961), Bury House, 33 Bury Street, London SW1Y 6AX **T** 020-7839 2137 **E** info@the-mea.co.uk **W** www.the-mea.co.uk
Director-General, Michael Thomas

MIGRAINE ACTION ASSOCIATION (1958), 27 East Street, LE1 6NB **T** 0116-275 8317 **E** info@migraine.org.uk **W** www.migraine.org.uk
Director, Ms Lee Tomkins

MILITARY HISTORICAL SOCIETY (1948), National Army Museum, Royal Hospital Road, London SW3 4HT **T** 01252-621056 **E** m.h.s@hotmail.co.uk **W** www.militaryhistsoc.plus.com
Chair, Tim Wright

MIND (NATIONAL ASSOCIATION FOR MENTAL HEALTH) (1946), 15–19 Broadway, London E15 4BQ **T** 020-8519 2122, **Infoline** 0845-766 0163 **E** contact@mind.org.uk **W** www.mind.org.uk
Chief Executive, Paul Farmer

MINERALOGICAL SOCIETY (1876), 12 Baylis Mews, Amyand Park Road, Twickenham TW1 3HQ **T** 020-8891 6600 **E** info@minersoc.org **W** www.minersoc.org
Executive Director, Kevin Murphy

MISSING PEOPLE (1993), 284 Upper Richmond Road West, London SW17 7JE **T** 020-8392 4590 **E** info@missingpeople.org.uk **W** www.missingpeople.org.uk
Chief Executive, Martin Houghton-Brown

MISSION TO SEAFARERS (1856), St Michael Paternoster Royal, College Hill, London EC4R 2RL **T** 020-7248 5202 **E** general@missiontoseafarers.org **W** www.missiontoseafarers.org
Secretary-General, Revd Tom Heffer

MULTIPLE SCLEROSIS SOCIETY (1953), MS National Centre, 372 Edgware Road, Staples Corner, London NW2 6ND **T** 020-8438 0700 **W** www.mssociety.org.uk
Chief Executive, Simon Gillespie

MUSEUMS ASSOCIATION (1889), 24 Calvin Street, London E1 6NW **T** 020-7426 6910 **E** info@museumsassociation.org **W** www.museumsassociation.org
Director, Mark Taylor

MUSICIANS BENEVOLENT FUND (1921), 7–11 Britannia Street, London WC1X 9JS **T** 020-7239 9100 **E** info@mbf.org.uk **W** www.mbf.org.uk
Chief Executive, David Sulkin

NABS (1916), 47–50 Margaret Street, London W1W 8SB **T** 020-7462 3150 **E** nabs@nabs.org.uk **W** www.nabs.org.uk
Chief Executive, Zoe Osmond

NACRO, THE CRIME REDUCTION CHARITY (1966), Park Place, 10–12 Lawn Lane, London SW8 1UD **T** 020-7840 7200 **E** debbie.john@nacro.org.uk **W** www.nacro.org.uk
Chief Executive, Paul McDowell

NATIONAL AIDS TRUST (1987), New City Cloisters, 196 Old Street, London EC1V 9FR **T** 020-7814 6767 **E** info@nat.org.uk **W** www.nat.org.uk
Chief Executive, Deborah Jack

NATIONAL ASSOCIATION FOR COLITIS AND CROHN'S DISEASE, 4 Beaumont House, Sutton Road, St Albans AL1 5HH **T** 01727-830038 **E** nacc@nacc.org.uk **W** www.nacc.org.uk
Director, Richard Driscoll

NATIONAL ASSOCIATION FOR GIFTED CHILDREN (1967), Suite 14, Challenge House, Bletchley, Milton Keynes MK3 6DP **T** 0845-450 0295 **E** amazingchildren@nagcbritain.org.uk **W** www.nagcbritain.org.uk
Chief Executive, Denise Yates

NATIONAL ASSOCIATION OF CLUBS FOR YOUNG PEOPLE (1925), 371 Kennington Lane, London SE11 5QY **T** 020-7793 0787 **E** office@clubsforyoungpeople.org.uk **W** www.clubsforyoungpeople.org.uk
Chief Executive, Simon Antrobus

NATIONAL ASSOCIATION OF PRISON VISITORS (1924), PO Box 6396, London, W1A 2HR **E** info@naopv.com **W** www.naopv.com
Chair, David Crompton

NATIONAL BENEVOLENT INSTITUTION (1812), Peter Herve House, Eccles Court, Tetbury GL8 8EH **T** 01666-505500 **E** office@nbi.org.uk **W** www.nbicharity.org.uk
Chief Executive, Paul Rossi

NATIONAL CAMPAIGN FOR THE ARTS LTD (1985), 1 Kingly Street, London W1B 5PA **T** 020-7287 3777 **E** nca@artscampaign.org.uk **W** www.artscampaign.org.uk
Director, Louise de Winter

NATIONAL CHILDBIRTH TRUST (1956), Alexandra House, Oldham Terrace, London W3 6NH **T** 0300-330 0770 **E** enquiries@nct.org.uk **W** www.nct.co.uk
Chief Executive, Ms B. Phipps

NATIONAL CHILDMINDING ASSOCIATION (1971), Royal Court, 81 Tweedy Road, Bromley BR1 1TG **T** 0845 880 0044 **E** info@ncma.org.uk **W** www.ncma.org.uk
Chief Executives, Andrew Fletcher and Catherine Farrell

NATIONAL COUNCIL OF WOMEN OF GREAT BRITAIN (1895), 72 Victoria Road, Darlington DL1 5JG **T** 01325-367375 **E** info@ncwgb.org **W** www.ncwgb.org
President, Sheila Eaton

NATIONAL EXTENSION COLLEGE (1963), Michael Young Centre, Purbeck Road, Cambridge CB2 8HN **T** 01223-400200 **E** info@nec.ac.uk **W** www.nec.ac.uk
Chief Executive, Gavin Teasdale

NATIONAL FEDERATION OF WOMEN'S INSTITUTES (1915), 104 New Kings Road, London SW6 4LY **T** 020-7371 9300 **E** hq@nfwi.org.uk **W** www.thewi.org.uk
General Secretary, Mrs J. Osborne

NATIONAL FOUNDATION FOR EDUCATIONAL RESEARCH IN ENGLAND AND WALES (1946), The Mere, Upton Park, Slough SL1 2DQ **T** 01753-574123 **E** enquiries@nfer.ac.uk **W** www.nfer.ac.uk
Chief Executive, Sue Rossiter

NATIONAL GARDENS SCHEME CHARITABLE TRUST (1927), Hatchlands Park, East Clandon, Guildford GU4 7RT **T** 01483-211535 **E** ngs@ngs.org.uk **W** www.ngs.org.uk
Chief Executive, Julia Grant

NATIONAL HEALTH SERVICE CONFEDERATION (1997), 29 Bressenden Place, London SW1E 5DD **T** 020-7074 3200 **E** enquiries@nhsconfed.org **W** www.nhsconfed.org
Chief Executive, Steve Barnett

NATIONAL OPERATIC AND DRAMATIC ASSOCIATION (1899), NODA House, 58–60 Lincoln Road, Peterborough PE1 2RZ **T** 01733-865790 **E** info@noda.org.uk **W** www.noda.org.uk
Chief Executive, Tony Gibbs

NATIONAL OSTEOPOROSIS SOCIETY (1986), Camerton, Bath BA2 0PJ **T** 01761-471771, **Helpline** 0845-450 0230 **E** info@nos.org.uk **W** www.nos.org.uk
Chief Executive, Claire Severgnini

NATIONAL SOCIETY FOR EPILEPSY (1892), Chesham Lane, Chalfont St Peter SL9 0RJ **T** 01494-601300, **Helpline** 01494-601400 **W** www.epilepsysociety.org.uk
Chief Executive, Graham Faulkner

NATIONAL TRUST (1895), Heelis, Kemble Drive, Swindon SN2 2NA **T** 0844-800 1895 **E** enquiries@thenationaltrust.org.uk **W** www.nationaltrust.org.uk
Director-General, Fiona Reynolds

NATIONAL UNION OF STUDENTS (1922), 2nd Floor, Centro 3, 19 Mandela Street, London NW1 0DU **T** 020-7380 6600 **E** nusuk@nus.org.uk **W** www.nus.org.uk
President, Aaron Porter

NATIONAL WOMEN'S REGISTER (1966), 3A Vulcan House, Vulcan Road North, Norwich NR6 6AQ **T** 08454-500287 **E** office@nwr.org.uk **W** www.nwr.org.uk
Membership Coordinator, Kathryn Buckman

NAVY RECORDS SOCIETY (1893), c/o Pangbourne College, Pangbourne, Berks RG8 8LA **T** 01189-842101 **E** honsec@navyrecords.org.uk **W** www.navyrecords.org.uk
Hon. Secretary, Robin Brodhurst

NOISE ABATEMENT SOCIETY (1959), Flat 2, 26 Brunswick Terrace, Hove BN3 1HJ **T** 01273-823850 **E** info@noise-abatement.org **W** www.noiseabatementsociety.com
Chief Executive, Gloria Elliott

NSPCC (1884), Weston House, 42 Curtain Road, London EC2A 3NH **T** 020-7825 2500 **E** info@nspcc.org.uk **W** www.nspcc.org.uk
Chief Executive, Andrew Flanagan

NUFFIELD FOUNDATION (1943), 28 Bedford Square, London WC1B 3JS **T** 020-7631 0566 **E** info@nuffieldfoundation.org **W** www.nuffieldfoundation.org
Director, Anthony Tomei

NUFFIELD TRUST (1940), 59 New Cavendish Street, London W1G 7LP **T** 020-7631 8450 **E** info@nuffieldtrust.org.uk **W** www.nuffieldtrust.org.uk
Director, Dr Jennifer Dixon

NUTRITION SOCIETY (1941), 10 Cambridge Court, 210 Shepherds Bush Road, London W6 7NJ **T** 020-7602 0228 **E** office@nutsoc.org.uk **W** www.nutritionsociety.org
Chief Executive, Frederick Wentworth-Bowyer

OFFICERS' ASSOCIATION (1919), Mountbarrow House, 6–20 Elizabeth Street, London SW1W 9RB **T** 0845-873 7140 **E** s.haughton@officersassociation.org.uk **W** www.officersassociation.org.uk
General Secretary, Maj.-Gen. J. C. B. Sutherell, CBE

OPEN SPACES SOCIETY (1865), 25A Bell Street, Henley-on-Thames RG9 2BA **T** 01491-573535 **E** hq@oss.org.uk **W** www.oss.org.uk
General Secretary, Kate Ashbrook

ORAL HISTORY SOCIETY (1971), PO Box 64, Berkhamsted **T** 01442-879097 **W** www.ohs.org.uk
Secretary, Robert Perks

ORDERS AND MEDALS RESEARCH SOCIETY (1942), PO Box 1233, High Wycombe HP11 9BW **T** 01494-441207 **E** generalsecretary@omrs.org **W** www.omrs.org.uk
General Secretary, P. M. R. Helmore

OVERSEAS DEVELOPMENT INSTITUTE (1960), 111 Westminster Bridge Road, London SE1 7JD **T** 020-7922 0300 **E** odi@odi.org.uk **W** www.odi.org.uk
Director, Dr Alison Evans

OVERSEAS SERVICE PENSIONERS' ASSOCIATION (1960), 138 High Street, Tonbridge TN9 1AX **T** 01732-363836 **E** mail@ospa.org.uk **W** www.ospa.org.uk
Secretary, D. F. B. Le Breton, CBE

OXFAM GREAT BRITAIN (1942), Oxfam House, John Smith Drive, Cowley, Oxford OX4 2JY **T** 0300-200 1300 **W** www.oxfam.org.uk
Chief Executive, Barbara Stocking, CBE

OXFORD PRESERVATION TRUST (1927), 10 Turn Again Lane, St Ebbes, Oxford OX1 1QL **T** 01865-242918 **E** info@oxfordpreservation.org.uk **W** www.oxfordpreservation.org.uk
Director, Debbie Dance

PALAEONTOLOGICAL ASSOCIATION (1957), c/o Institute of Geography & Earth Sciences, University of Wales Aberystwyth, Ceredigion, SY23 3BD **E** palass@palass.org **W** www.palass.org
Chief Executive, Dr T. J. Palmer

PARLIAMENTARY AND SCIENTIFIC COMMITTEE (1939), 3 Birdcage Walk, Westminster, London SW1H 9JJ **T** 020-7222 7085 **E** secretariat@pandsctte.demon.co.uk **W** www.scienceinparliament.org.uk
Scientific Secretary, Prof. Peter Simpson

PATIENTS ASSOCIATION (1963), PO Box 935, Harrow HA1 3YJ **T** 020-8423 9111, **Helpline** 0845-608 4455 **E** helpline@patients-association.com **W** www.patients-association.com
Chair, Roswyn Hakesley-Brown, CBE

PEABODY TRUST (1862), Minster Court, 45 Westminster Bridge Road, London SE1 7JB **T** 020-7021 4000 **W** www.peabody.org.uk
Chief Executive, Steve Howlett

PENSIONS ADVISORY SERVICE (1983), 11 Belgrave Road, London SW1V 1RB **T** 0845-601 2923 **E** enquiries@pensionsadvisoryservice.org.uk **W** www.pensionsadvisoryservice.org.uk
Chief Executive, M. Phillips, OBE

PERENNIAL (1839), Bridge House, 115–117 Kingston Road, Leatherhead KT22 7SU **T** 0845-230 1839 **E** info@perennial.org.uk **W** www.perennial.org.uk
Chief Executive, Richard Capewell

PHILOLOGICAL SOCIETY (1842), Department of the Languages and Cultures of Africa, School of Oriental and African Studies, Thornhaugh Street, London WC1H 0XG **T** 020-7898 4653 **E** secretary@philsoc.org.uk **W** www.philsoc.org.uk
Hon. Secretary, Dr Lutz Marten

PILGRIMS OF GREAT BRITAIN (1902), Allington Castle, Maidstone ME16 0NB **T** 01622-606404 **E** sec@pilgrimsociety.org
Chair, Sir Robert Worcester, KBE, DL

PLAIN ENGLISH CAMPAIGN (1979), PO Box 3, New Mills, High Peak SK22 4QP **T** 01663-744409 **E** info@plainenglish.co.uk **W** www.plainenglish.co.uk
Director, Ms C. Maher

POETRY SOCIETY (1909), 22 Betterton Street, London WC2H 9BX **T** 020-7420 9880 **E** info@poetrysociety.org.uk **W** www.poetrysociety.org.uk
Director, Judith Palmer

POWYSLAND CLUB (1867), Cartref, 14 Berriew Road, Welshpool SY21 7SS T 01938-552161
W www.powyslandclub.co.uk
Hon. Secretary, Dr Roger L. Brown

PRAYER BOOK SOCIETY (1975), The Studio, Copyhold Farm, Goring Heath, Reading RG8 7RT
T 0118-984 2582 E pbs.admin@pbs.org.uk
W www.pbs.org.uk
Chair, Prudence Dailey

PRE-SCHOOL LEARNING ALLIANCE (1961), The Fitzpatrick Building, 188 York Way, London N7 9AD T 020-7697 2500
E info@pre-school.org.uk
W www.pre-school.org.uk
Chief Executive, Steve Alexander

PRINCE'S TRUST (1976), 18 Park Square East, London NW1 4LH T 0800-842842
E webinfops@princes-trust.org.uk
W www.princes-trust.org.uk
Chief Executive, Martina Milburn

PRINCESS ROYAL TRUST FOR CARERS (1991), Unit 14, Bourne Court, Southend Road, Woodford Green IG8 8HD T 0844 800 4361 E info@carers.org
W www.carers.org
Chair, Ian Robertson

PRISONERS ABROAD (1978), 89–93 Fonthill Road, London N4 3JH T 020-7561 6820
E info@prisonersabroad.org.uk
W www.prisonersabroad.org.uk
Chief Executive, Pauline Crowe

PRIVATE LIBRARIES ASSOCIATION (1956), Ravelston, South View Road, Pinner HA5 3YD
E dchambers@aol.com W www.plabooks.org
Chair, David Chambers

PRS FOR MUSIC, 29–33 Berners Street, London W1T 3AB T 020-7580 5544 E enquiry@prsformusic.com
W www.prsformusic.com
Chief Executive, Robert Ashcroft

PSORIASIS ASSOCIATION (1968), Dick Coles House, 2 Queensbridge, Northampton NN4 7BF T 08456-760076
E mail@psoriasis-association.org.uk
W www.psoriasis-association.org.uk
Chief Executive, Helen McAteer

QUAKER PEACE AND SOCIAL WITNESS (2000), Friends House, 173–177 Euston Road, London NW1 2BJ
T 020-7663 1000 E qpsw@quaker.org.uk
W www.quaker.org.uk
General Secretary, Helen Drewery

QUEEN ELIZABETH'S FOUNDATION FOR DISABLED PEOPLE (1934), Leatherhead Court, Woodlands Road, Leatherhead KT22 0BN
T 01372-841100 E info@qef.org.uk
W www.qef.org.uk
Chief Executive, Jonathan Powell

QUEEN'S ENGLISH SOCIETY (1973), 1 Oban Gardens, Woodley, Reading RG5 3RG T 07979-474826
E enquiries@queens-english-society.com
W www.queens-english-society.com
Hon. Secretary, Sidney Callis

QUEEN'S NURSING INSTITUTE (1887), 3 Albemarle Way, London EC1V 4RQ T 020-7549 1400
E mail@qni.org.uk W www.qni.org.uk
Director, Rosemary Cook, CBE

QUEEN VICTORIA CLERGY FUND (1897), Church House, Great Smith Street, London SW1P 3AZ
T 020-7898 1000 E info@churchhouse.org.uk
Chief Executive, Colin Menzies

QUIT (1926), 63 St Marys Axe, London EC3A 8AA
T 020-7469 0400, Quitline 0800-002 200
E info@quit.org.uk W www.quit.org.uk
Chief Executive, Steve Crone

RAILWAY AND CANAL HISTORICAL SOCIETY (1954), 3 West Court, West Street, Oxford OX2 0NP
T 01865-240514 E secretary@rchs.org.uk
W www.rchs.org.uk
Hon. Secretary, M. Searle

RAILWAY BENEFIT FUND (1858), Electra Way, Crewe Business Park, Crewe CW1 6HS
T 01270-251316
E director@railwaybenefitfund.org.uk
W www.railwaybenefitfund.org.uk
Director & Secretary, Keith Alldread

RAMBLERS' ASSOCIATION (1935), 2nd Floor, Camelford House, 87–90 Albert Embankment, London SE1 7TW T 020-7339 8500 E ramblers@ramblers.org.uk
W www.ramblers.org.uk
Chief Executive, Tom Franklin

RARE BREEDS SURVIVAL TRUST (1973), Stoneleigh Park, Nr. Kenilworth CV8 2LG T 024-7669 6551
W www.rbst.org.uk
Executive Chairman, Tim Brigstocke

REFUGEE COUNCIL (1981), 240–250 Ferndale Road, London SW9 8BB T 020-7346 6709
E info@refugeecouncil.org.uk
W www.refugeecouncil.org.uk
Chief Executive, Donna Covey

REGIONAL STUDIES ASSOCIATION (1965), PO Box 2058, Seaford BN25 4QU T 01323-899698
E info@rsa-ls.ac.uk W www.regional-studies-assoc.ac.uk
Chief Executive, Sally Hardy

REGULAR FORCES EMPLOYMENT ASSOCIATION LTD (1885), 1st Floor, Mountbarrow House, 6–20 Elizabeth Street, London SW1W 9RB
T 0845-873 7162 E adminrfea@ctp.org.uk
W www.rfea.org.uk
Chief Executive, Brig. Stephen Gledhill

RELATE (1938), Premier House, Carolina Court, Lakeside, Doncaster DN4 5RA T 0300-100 1234
E enquiries@relate.org.uk W www.relate.org.uk
Chief Executive, Claire Tyler

RETIRED NURSES' NATIONAL HOME (1934), Riverside Avenue, Bournemouth BH7 7EE **T** 01202-396418 **E** rnnhoffice1@btconnect.com **W** www.rnnh.co.uk
Chair, Mrs S. Young

RICHARD III SOCIETY (1924), 23 Ash Rise, Halstead, Essex CO9 1RD **E** wells4r3@btinternet.com **W** www.richardiii.net
Chair, Dr P. T. Stone

RNIB NATIONAL LIBRARY SERVICE (1868), Far Cromwell Road, Bredbury, Stockport SK6 2SG **T** 0303-123 9999 **E** helpline@rnib.org.uk **W** www.rnib.org.uk/reading
Head of National Library Service, Helen Brazier

RNID (ROYAL NATIONAL INSTITUTE FOR DEAF PEOPLE) (1911), 19–23 Featherstone Street, London EC1Y 8SL **T** 0808-808 0123, **Textphone** 0808-808 9000 **E** informationline@rnid.org.uk **W** www.rnid.org.uk
Chief Executive, Jackie Ballard

ROADS AND ROAD TRANSPORT HISTORY ASSOCIATION (1992), c/o Kithead Trust, De Salis Drive, Hampton Lovett, Droitwich WR9 0QE **E** enquiries@rrtha.org.uk **W** www.rrtha.org.uk
Chair, Grahame Boyes

ROTARY INTERNATIONAL IN GREAT BRITAIN AND IRELAND (1922), Kinwarton Road, Alcester B49 6PB **T** 01789-765411 **E** secretary@ribi.org **W** www.rotary-ribi.org
Chief Executive, Annemarie Harte

ROYAL AGRICULTURAL BENEVOLENT INSTITUTION (1860), Shaw House, 27 West Way, Oxford OX2 0QH **T** 01865-724931 **E** info@rabi.org.uk **W** www.rabi.org.uk
Chief Executive, W. A. McMahon, CVO, AFC

ROYAL AGRICULTURAL SOCIETY OF THE COMMONWEALTH (1957), c/o Royal Highland Centre, Ingliston, Edinburgh EH28 8NF **T** 0131-335 6200 **E** rasc@commagshow.org **W** www.commagshow.org
Hon. Secretary, W. H. Yarr, OBE

ROYAL AIR FORCES ASSOCIATION (1943), 117½ Loughborough Road, Leicester LE4 5ND **T** 0116-266 5224 **E** enquiries@rafa.org.uk **W** www.rafa.org.uk
Secretary General, G. Jones

ROYAL ARTILLERY ASSOCIATION (1920), Artillery House, Royal Artillery Barracks, Larkhill, Salisbury SP4 8QT **T** 01980-845895 **E** ARTYCEN-RHQRA-RACF-RAA-GenSecPA@mod.uk **W** www.theraa.co.uk
General Secretary, Lt.-Col. I. A. Vere Nicoll, MBE

ROYAL ASSOCIATION FOR DEAF PEOPLE (1841), 18 Westside Centre, London Road, Stanway CO3 8PH **T** 0845-688 2525 **E** info@royaldeaf.org.uk **W** www.royaldeaf.org.uk
Chief Executive, Tom Fenton

ROYAL ASSOCIATION FOR DISABILITY AND REHABILITATION (1977), 12 City Forum, 250 City Road, London EC1V 8AF **T** 020-7250 3222 **E** radar@radar.org.uk **W** www.radar.org.uk
Chair, Liz Sayce, OBE

ROYAL BIRMINGHAM SOCIETY OF ARTISTS (1814), 4 Brook Street, Birmingham B3 1SA **T** 0121-236 4353 **E** secretary@rbsa.org.uk **W** www.rbsa.org.uk
Gallery Director, Marie Considine

ROYAL BRITISH LEGION (1921), 199 Borough High Street, London SE1 1AA **T** 020-3207 2100 **E** info@britishlegion.org.uk **W** www.britishlegion.org.uk
Director-General, Chris Simpkins

ROYAL CAMBRIAN ACADEMY (1882), Crown Lane, Conwy LL32 8AN **T** 01492-593413 **E** rca@rcaconwy.org **W** www.rcaconwy.org
President, Maurice Cockrill

ROYAL CELTIC SOCIETY (1820), 23 Rutland Street, Edinburgh EH1 2RN **T** 0131-228 6449 **E** gcameron@stuartandstuart.co.uk **W** www.royalcelticsociety.org.uk
Secretary, J. Gordon Cameron, WS

ROYAL HIGHLAND AND AGRICULTURAL SOCIETY OF SCOTLAND (1784), Royal Highland Centre, Ingliston, Edinburgh EH28 8NB **T** 0131-335 6200 **E** info@rhass.org.uk **W** www.rhass.org.uk
Chief Executive, R. Jones

ROYAL HISTORICAL SOCIETY (1868), University College London, Gower Street, London WC1E 6BT **T** 020-7387 7532 **E** royalhistsoc@ucl.ac.uk **W** www.royalhistoricalsociety.org
President, Prof. Colin Jones

ROYAL HORTICULTURAL SOCIETY (1804), 80 Vincent Square, London SW1P 2PE **T** 0845-260 5000 **E** info@rhs.org.uk **W** www.rhs.org.uk
Director-General, Gordon Seabright

ROYAL HOSPITAL FOR NEURO-DISABILITY (1854), West Hill, Putney, London SW15 3SW **T** 020-8780 4500 **E** info@rhn.org.uk **W** www.rhn.org.uk
Chief Executive, Angus Somerville

ROYAL HUMANE SOCIETY (1774), 50–51 Temple Chambers, 3–7 Temple Avenue, London EC4Y 0HP **T** 020-7936 2942 **E** info@royalhumanesociety.org.uk **W** www.royalhumanesociety.org.uk
Secretary, Dick Wilkinson, TD

ROYAL INSTITUTE OF NAVIGATION (1947), 1 Kensington Gore, London SW7 2AT **T** 020-7591 3130 **E** admin@rin.org.uk **W** www.rin.org.uk
Director, Capt. P. Chapman-Andrews

ROYAL INSTITUTE OF OIL PAINTERS (1882), 17 Carlton House Terrace, London SW1Y 5BD **T** 020-7930 6844 **E** info@mallgalleries.com **W** www.mallgalleries.org.uk
President, Peter Wileman

ROYAL INSTITUTE OF PAINTERS IN WATER COLOURS (1831), 17 Carlton House Terrace, London SW1Y 5BD **T** 020-7930 6844 **E** info@mallgalleries.com **W** www.mallgalleries.org.uk
President, Ronald Maddox

ROYAL INSTITUTE OF PHILOSOPHY (1925), 14 Gordon Square, London WC1H 0AG **T** 020-7387 4130 **W** www.royalinstitutephilosophy.org
Secretary, Dr James Garvey

ROYAL INSTITUTION OF GREAT BRITAIN (1799), 21 Albemarle Street, London W1S 4BS **T** 020-7409 2992 **E** ri@ri.ac.uk **W** www.rigb.org
Chief Executive, Mr Chris Rofe

ROYAL LIFE SAVING SOCIETY UK (1891), River House, High Street, Broom B50 4HN **T** 01789-773994 **E** lifesavers@rlss.org.uk **W** www.lifesavers.org.uk
Chief Executive, D. Standley

ROYAL LITERARY FUND (1790), 3 Johnson's Court, off Fleet Street, London EC4A 3EA **T** 020-7353 7159 **E** egunnrlf@globalnet.co.uk **W** www.rlf.org.uk
Chief Executive, Eileen Gunn

ROYAL LONDON SOCIETY FOR THE BLIND (1838), Dorton House, Seal, Sevenoaks TN15 0ED **T** 01732-592500 **E** ceo@rlsb.org.uk **W** www.rlsb.org.uk
Chief Executive, Brian J. Cooney

ROYAL MASONIC TRUST FOR GIRLS AND BOYS (1982), 60 Great Queen Street, London WC2B 5AZ **T** 020-7405 2644 **E** info@rmtgb.org **W** www.rmtgb.org
Chief Executive, L. Hutchinson

ROYAL MICROSCOPICAL SOCIETY (1839), 37–38 St Clements, Oxford OX4 1AJ **T** 01865-254760 **E** info@rms.org.uk **W** www.rms.org.uk
Administrator, Karen Lonsdale

ROYAL MUSICAL ASSOCIATION (1874), 4 Chandos Road, Chorlton-cum-Hardy, Manchester M21 0ST **T** 0161-861 7542 **E** jeffrey.dean@stingrayoffice.com **W** www.rma.ac.uk
President, Philip Olleson

ROYAL NATIONAL COLLEGE FOR THE BLIND (1872), College Road, Hereford HR1 1EB **T** 01432-265725 **E** info@rncb.ac.uk **W** www.rncb.ac.uk
Principal, Mr Geoff Draper

ROYAL NATIONAL INSTITUTE OF BLIND PEOPLE (1868), 105 Judd Street, London WC1H 9NE **T** 020-7388 1266, **Helpline** 0303-123 9999 **E** helpline@rnib.org.uk **W** www.rnib.org.uk
Chief Executive, Lesley-Anne Alexander

ROYAL NATIONAL LIFEBOAT INSTITUTION (1824), West Quay Road, Poole BH15 1HZ **T** 0845-122 6999 **E** info@rnli.org.uk **W** www.rnli.org.uk
Chief Executive, Paul Boissier

ROYAL NAVAL ASSOCIATION (1949), Room 209, Royal Semaphore Tower, PP70, HM Naval Base, Portsmouth PO1 3LT **T** 02392-723823 **W** www.royal-naval-association.co.uk
President, Vice-Adm. John McAnally, CB, LVO

ROYAL NAVY OFFICERS' CHARITY (1739), 70 Porchester Terrace, London W2 3TP **T** 020-7402 5231 **E** rnoc@arno.org.uk
Chair, Rear-Adm. D. J. Anthony, MBE

ROYAL PHILATELIC SOCIETY LONDON (1869), 41 Devonshire Place, London W1G 6JY **T** 020-7486 1044 **E** secretary@rpsl.org.uk **W** www.rpsl.org.uk
President, A. N. Moorcroft

ROYAL PHILHARMONIC SOCIETY (1813), 10 Stratford Place, London W1C 1BA **T** 020-7491 8110 **E** admin@royalphilharmonicsociety.org.uk **W** www.royalphilharmonicsociety.org.uk
Executive Director, Rosemary Johnson

ROYAL PHOTOGRAPHIC SOCIETY (1853), Fenton House, 122 Wells Road, Bath BA2 3AH **T** 01225-325733 **E** reception@rps.org **W** www.rps.org
Director General, Stuart Blake

ROYAL SCHOOL OF CHURCH MUSIC (1927), 19 The Close, Salisbury SP1 2EB **T** 01722-424848 **E** enquiries@rscm.com **W** www.rscm.com
Director, Mr Lindsay Gray

ROYAL SCHOOL OF NEEDLEWORK (1872), Apartment 12A, Hampton Court Palace KT8 9AU **T** 020-3166 6932 **E** enquiries@royal-needlework.org.uk **W** www.royal-needlework.org.uk
Chief Executive, Dr Susan Kay-Williams

ROYAL SOCIETY FOR ASIAN AFFAIRS (1901), 2 Belgrave Square, London SW1X 8PJ **T** 020-7235 5122 **E** sec@rsaa.org.uk **W** www.rsaa.org.uk
Chairman of Council, Sir David John, KCMG

ROYAL SOCIETY FOR THE ENCOURAGEMENT OF ARTS, MANUFACTURES AND COMMERCE (1754), 8 John Adam Street, London WC2N 6EZ **T** 020-7930 5115 **E** general@rsa.org.uk **W** www.thersa.org
Chief Executive, Matthew Taylor

ROYAL SOCIETY FOR THE PREVENTION OF ACCIDENTS (1917), 27–28 Calthorpe Road, Edgbaston, Birmingham B15 1RP **T** 0121-248 2000 **E** help@rospa.com **W** www.rospa.com
Chief Executive, Tom Mullarkey, MBE

ROYAL SOCIETY FOR THE PREVENTION OF CRUELTY TO ANIMALS (1824), Wilberforce Way, Horsham RH13 9RS **T** 0300-123 4555 **W** www.rspca.org.uk
Chief Executive, Mark Watts

ROYAL SOCIETY FOR THE PROTECTION OF BIRDS (1889), The Lodge, Sandy SG19 2DL **T** 01767-680551 **W** www.rspb.org.uk
Chief Executive, Mike Clarke

ROYAL SOCIETY OF LITERATURE (1820), Somerset House, Strand, London WC2R 1LA **T** 020-7845 4676 **E** info@rslit.org **W** www.rslit.org
President, Colin Thubron

ROYAL SOCIETY OF MARINE ARTISTS (1939), 17 Carlton House Terrace, London SW1Y 5BD **T** 020-7930 6844 **E** info@mallgalleries.com **W** www.mallgalleries.org.uk
President, David Howell

ROYAL SOCIETY OF MEDICINE (1805), 1 Wimpole Street, London W1G 0AE **T** 020-7290 2900 **E** membership@rsm.ac.uk **W** www.rsm.ac.uk
Chief Executive, Ian Balmer

ROYAL SOCIETY OF MINIATURE PAINTERS, SCULPTORS AND GRAVERS (1895), 3 Briar Walk, London SW15 6UD **T** 020-8785 2338 **E** info@royal-miniature-society.org.uk **W** www.royal-miniature-society.org.uk
Executive Secretary, Phyllis Rennell

ROYAL SOCIETY OF MUSICIANS OF GREAT BRITAIN (1738), 10 Stratford Place, London W1C 1BA **T** 020-7629 6137 **W** www.royalsocietyofmusicians.co.uk
Secretary, Mrs M. Gibb

ROYAL SOCIETY OF PAINTER-PRINTMAKERS (1880), Bankside Gallery, 48 Hopton Street, London SE1 9JH **T** 020-7928 7521 **E** info@banksidegallery.com
President, Hilary Paynter

ROYAL SOCIETY OF PORTRAIT PAINTERS (1891), 17 Carlton House Terrace, London SW1Y 5BD **T** 020-7930 6844 **E** info@mallgalleries.com **W** www.mallgalleries.org.uk
President, Alastair Adams

ROYAL SOCIETY OF ST GEORGE (1894), 127 Sandgate Road, Folkstone CT20 2BH **T** 01303-241795 **E** info@royalsocietyofstgeorge.com **W** www.royalsocietyofstgeorge.com
Chair, James E. Newton

ROYAL SOCIETY OF TROPICAL MEDICINE AND HYGIENE (1907), 50 Bedford Square, London WC1B 3DP **T** 020-7580 2127 **E** info@rstmh.org **W** www.rstmh.org
Chief Executive, Ms. G. McHugh

ROYAL THEATRICAL FUND (1839), 11 Garrick Street, London WC2E 9AR **T** 020-7836 3322 **E** admin@trtf.com **W** www.trtf.com
President, Sir Donald Sinden, CBE, FRSA

ROYAL WATERCOLOUR SOCIETY (1804), Bankside Gallery, 48 Hopton Street, London SE1 9JH **T** 020-7928 7521 **E** info@banksidegallery.com **W** www.royalwatercoloursociety.co.uk
President, David Paskett

RSABI (1897), The Rural Centre, West Mains of Ingliston, Newbridge, Edinburgh EH28 8LT **T** 0131-472 4166 **E** rsabi@rsabi.org.uk **W** www.rsabi.org.uk
Chief Executive, Dr Maurice S. Hankey

ST DEINIOL'S RESIDENTIAL LIBRARY (1894), Church Lane, Hawarden CH5 3DF **T** 01244-532350 **E** enquiries@st-deiniols.org **W** www.st-deiniols.org
Warden and Chief Librarian, Revd Peter Francis

ST DUNSTAN'S (1915), 12–14 Harcourt Street, London W1H 4HD **T** 020-7723 5021 **E** enquiries@st-dunstans.org.uk **W** www.st-dunstans.org.uk
Chief Executive, Robert Leader

ST JOHN AMBULANCE (1877), 27 St John's Lane, London EC1M 4BU **T** 020-7324 4000 **E** info@sja.org.uk **W** www.sja.org.uk
Chief Executive, Sue Killen

SANE (1986), 1st Floor, Cityside House, 40 Adler Street, London E1 1EE **T** 020-7375 1002, **Helpline** 0845-767 8000 **E** info@sane.org.uk **W** www.sane.org.uk
Chief Executive, Ms M. Wallace, MBE

SAVE BRITAIN'S HERITAGE (1975), 70 Cowcross Street, London EC1M 6EJ **T** 020-7253 3500 **E** office@savebritainsheritage.org **W** www.savebritainsheritage.org
President, Marcus Binney, OBE

SAVE THE CHILDREN UK (1919), 1 St John's Lane, London EC1M 4AR **T** 020-7012 6400 **E** supporter.care@savethechildren.org.uk **W** www.savethechildren.org.uk
Chief Executive, Jasmine Whitbread

SCHOOL LIBRARY ASSOCIATION (1937), Unit 2, Lotmead Business Village, Lotmead Farm, Wanborough, nr Swindon SN4 0UY **T** 01793-791787 **E** info@sla.org.uk **W** www.sla.org.uk
Chief Executive, Mrs T. Adams

SCOPE (1952), 6 Market Road, London N7 9PW **T** 020-7619 7100, **Helpline** 0808-800 3333 **E** response@scope.org.uk **W** www.scope.org.uk
Chief Executive, Richard Hawkes

SCOTTISH ASSOCIATION FOR MARINE SCIENCE (1884), Scottish Marine Institute, Oban, Argyll PA37 1QA **T** 01631-559000 **E** info@sams.ac.uk **W** www.sams.ac.uk
Director, Prof. Laurence Mee

SCOTTISH ASSOCIATION FOR MENTAL HEALTH (1923), Cumbrae House, 15 Carlton Court, Glasgow G5 9JP **T** 0141-568 7000 **E** enquire@samh.org.uk **W** www.samh.org.uk
Chief Executive, Billy Watson

SCOTTISH CHAMBERS OF COMMERCE (1948), 30 George Square, Glasgow G2 1EQ **T** 0141-204 8316 **E** admin@scottishchambers.org.uk **W** www.scottishchambers.org.uk
Chief Executive, Liz Cameron

SCOTTISH COUNCIL FOR VOLUNTARY ORGANISATIONS (1943), Mansfield Traquair Centre, 15 Mansfield Place, Edinburgh EH3 6BB **T** 0131-556 3882 **E** enquiries@scvo.org.uk **W** www.scvo.org.uk
Chief Executive, M. Sime

SCOTTISH GENEALOGY SOCIETY (1953), Library and Family History Centre, 15 Victoria Terrace, Edinburgh EH1 2JL **T** 0131-220 3677 **E** info@scotsgenealogy.com **W** www.scotsgenealogy.com
Hon. Secretary, Kenneth A. M. Nisbet

SCOTTISH NATIONAL WAR MEMORIAL (1927), The Castle, Edinburgh EH1 2YT **T** 0131-226 7393 **E** info@snwm.org **W** www.snwm.org
Secretary to the Trustees, Lt.-Col. R. J. Binks

SCOTTISH NATURAL HISTORY LIBRARY (1970), Foremount House, Kilbarchan PA10 2EZ **T** 01505-702419
Director, Dr J. A. Gibson

SCOTTISH RURAL PROPERTY AND BUSINESS ASSOCIATION, Stuart House, Eskmills Business Park, Musselburgh EH21 7PB **T** 0131-653 5400 **E** info@srpba.com **W** www.srpba.com
Chief Executive, Douglas McAdam

SCOTTISH SOCIETY FOR THE PREVENTION OF CRUELTY TO ANIMALS (1839), Kingseat Road, Halbeath, Dunfermline KY11 8RY **T** 03000-999999 **E** info@scottishspca.org **W** www.scottishspca.org
Chief Executive, Stuart Earley

SCOTTISH SOCIETY FOR THE PROTECTION OF WILD BIRDS (1927), Foremount House, Kilbarchan PA10 2EZ **T** 01505-702419
Hon. Secretary, Dr J. A. Gibson

SCOTTISH WILDLIFE TRUST (1964), Cramond House, Cramond Glebe Road, Edinburgh EH4 6NS **T** 0131-312 7765 **E** enquiries@swt.org.uk **W** www.swt.org.uk
Chief Executive, Simon Milne

SCOUT ASSOCIATION (1907), Gilwell Park, Chingford, London E4 7QW **T** 020-8443 7100 **E** scout.association@scouts.org.uk **W** www.scouts.org.uk
Chief Executive, D. M. Twine, CBE

SEEABILITY (1799), SeeAbility House, Hook Road, Epsom KT19 8SQ **T** 01372-755000 **E** enquiries@seeability.org **W** www.seeability.org
Chief Executive, D. Scott-Ralphs

SELDEN SOCIETY (1887), School of Law, Queen Mary, Mile End Road, London E1 4NS **T** 020-7882 3968 **E** selden-society@qmul.ac.uk **W** www.selden-society.qmul.ac.uk
Secretary, V. Tunkel

SENSE (THE NATIONAL DEAFBLIND AND RUBELLA ASSOCIATION) (1955), 101 Pentonville Road, London N1 9LG **T** 0845-127 0060 **E** info@sense.org.uk **W** www.sense.org.uk
Chief Executive, Richard Brook

SHELTER (NATIONAL CAMPAIGN FOR HOMELESS PEOPLE) (1966), 88 Old Street, London EC1V 9HU **T** 0300-330 1234, **Helpline** 0808-800 4444 **E** info@shelter.org.uk **W** www.shelter.org.uk
Director, Campbell Robb

SHIRE HORSE SOCIETY (1878), East of England Showground, Peterborough PE2 6XE **T** 01733-234451 **E** info@shire-horse.org.uk **W** www.shire-horse.org.uk
Chief Executive Officer, Andrew Mercer

SIGHTSAVERS (ROYAL COMMONWEALTH SOCIETY FOR THE BLIND) (1950), Grosvenor Hall, Bolnore Road, Haywards Heath RH16 4BX **T** 01444-446600 **E** info@sightsavers.org **W** www.sightsavers.org
Chief Executive, Dr Caroline Harper, OBE

SIMPLIFIED SPELLING SOCIETY (1908), 4 Valetta Way, Wellesbourne, Warwick CV35 9TB **E** membership@spellingsociety.org **W** www.spellingsociety.org
Membership Secretary, John Gledhill

SOCIALIST PARTY OF GREAT BRITAIN (1904), 52 Clapham High Street, London SW4 7UN **T** 020-7622 3811 **E** spgb@worldsocialism.org **W** www.worldsocialism.org
General Secretary, Tristan Miller

SOCIÉTÉ JERSIAISE (1873), 7 Pier Road, St Helier JE2 4XW **T** 01534-758314 **E** societe@societe-jersiaise.org **W** www.societe-jersiaise.org
Executive Director, Mrs P. Syvret

SOCIETY FOR NAUTICAL RESEARCH (1910), 6 Ashmeadow Road, Arnside, via Carnforth LA5 0AE **T** 01524-761616 **E** honsec@snr.org.uk **W** www.snr.org.uk
Hon. Secretary, Peter Winterbottom

SOCIETY FOR PROMOTING CHRISTIAN KNOWLEDGE (1698), 36 Causton Street, London SW1P 4ST **T** 020-7592 3900 **E** spck@spck.org.uk **W** www.spck.org.uk
General Secretary, Simon Kingston

SOCIETY FOR PSYCHICAL RESEARCH (1882), 49 Marloes Road, London W8 6LA **T** 020-7937 8984 **E** secretary@spr.ac.uk **W** www.spr.ac.uk
Secretary, Peter Johnson

SOCIETY FOR THE PROMOTION OF ROMAN STUDIES (1910), Senate House, Malet Street, London WC1E 7HU **T** 020-7862 8727 **E** office@romansociety.org **W** www.romansociety.org
Secretary, Dr Fiona Haarer

SOCIETY FOR THE PROTECTION OF ANCIENT BUILDINGS (1877), 37 Spital Square, London E1 6DY **T** 020-7377 1644 **E** info@spab.org.uk **W** www.spab.org.uk
Secretary, Philip Venning

SOCIETY OF ANTIQUARIES OF LONDON (1707), Burlington House, Piccadilly, London W1J 0BE **T** 020-7479 7080 **E** admin@sal.org.uk **W** www.sal.org.uk
General-Secretary, Dr David Gaimster, FSA

SOCIETY OF ANTIQUARIES OF NEWCASTLE UPON TYNE (1813), Great North Museum: Hancock, Barras Bridge, Newcastle upon Tyne NE2 4PT **T** 0191-231 2700 **E** admin@newcastle-antiquaries.org.uk **W** www.newcastle-antiquaries.org.uk
Hon. Secretary, Dr N. Hodgson

SOCIETY OF BOTANICAL ARTISTS (1985), 1 Knapp Cottages, Wyke, Gillingham SP8 4NQ **T** 01747-825718 **E** pam@soc-botanical-artists.org **W** www.soc-botanical-artists.org
Executive Secretary, Pam Henderson

SOCIETY OF EDITORS, University Centre, Granta Place, Mill Lane, Cambridge CB2 1RU **T** 01223-304080 **E** info@societyofeditors.org **W** www.societyofeditors.co.uk
Executive Director, Bob Satchwell

SOCIETY OF GENEALOGISTS (1911), 14 Charterhouse Buildings, Goswell Road, London EC1M 7BA **T** 020-7251 8799 **E** librarian@sog.org.uk **W** www.sog.org.uk
Chief Executive, June Perrin

SOCIETY OF GLASS TECHNOLOGY (1917), Unit 9, Twelve O'Clock Court, 21 Attercliffe Road, Sheffield S4 7WW **T** 0114-263 4455 **E** info@sgt.org **W** www.sgt.org
Managing Editor, David Moore

SOCIETY OF INDEXERS (1957), Woodbourn Business Centre, 10 Jessell Street, Sheffield S9 3HY
T 0114-244 9561 E info@indexers.org.uk
W www.indexers.org.uk
Chair, Ann Kingdom

SOCIETY OF LEGAL SCHOLARS (1908), School of Law, Southampton University, Southampton SO17 1BJ
T 023-8059 4039 E s.j.thomson@soton.ac.uk
W www.legalscholars.ac.uk
Hon. Secretary, Prof. Stephen Bailey

SOCIETY OF SCHOOLMASTERS AND SCHOOLMISTRESSES (1798), c/o L. I. Baggott, SGBI Office, Queen Mary House, Manor Park Road, Chistlehurst BR7 5PY T 020-8468 7997 E sgbi@fsmail.net
Secretary (acting), Laurence Baggott, FCA

SOCIETY OF SCRIBES AND ILLUMINATORS (1921), 6 Queen Square, London WC1N 3AT
T 01524-251534 E scribe@calligraphyonline.org
W www.calligraphyonline.org
Chairman, Sylvie Gokulsing

SOCIETY OF SOLICITORS IN THE SUPREME COURT OF SCOTLAND (1784), SSC Library, Parliament House, 11 Parliament Square, Edinburgh EH1 1RF
T 0131-225 6268 E enquiries@ssclibrary.co.uk
W www.ssclibrary.co.uk
Secretary, I. L. S. Balfour

SOCIETY OF WOMEN ARTISTS (1855), 1 Knapp Cottages, Wyke, Gillingham SP8 4NQ T 01747-825718
E pamhenderson@dsl.pipex.com
W www.society-women-artists.org.uk
Executive Secretary, Pam Henderson

SOCIETY OF WRITERS TO HM SIGNET (1594), The Signet Library, Parliament Square, Edinburgh EH1 1RF
T 0131-220 3249 E enquiries@wssociety.co.uk
W www.wssociety.co.uk
Chief Executive, Robert Pirrie

SOIL ASSOCIATION (1946), South Plaza, Marlborough Street, Bristol BS1 3NX T 0117-314 5000
W www.soilassociation.org
Director, Patrick Holden

SOUND AND MUSIC (1967), 3rd Floor, South Wing, Somerset House, London WC2R 1LA T 020-7759 1800
E info@soundandmusic.org W www.soundandmusic.org
Director, Matthew Greenall

SOUTH AMERICAN MISSION SOCIETY IRELAND (1844), 1 Irwin Crescent, Lurgan BT66 7EZ
T 028-3831 0144 E info@samsireland.com
W www.samsireland.com
General Secretary, Denis Johnston

SPORT HORSE BREEDING OF GREAT BRITAIN (1886), 96 High Street, Edenbridge TN8 5AR
T 01732-866277 E office@sporthorsegb.co.uk
W www.sporthorsegb.co.uk
General Secretary, Catherine Burdock

SPURGEONS (1867), 74 Wellingborough Road, Rushden NN10 9TY T 01933-412412 E info@spurgeons.org
W www.spurgeons.org
Chief Executive, T. Jeffery

STANDING COUNCIL OF SCOTTISH CHIEFS, Hope Chambers, 52 Leith Walk, Edinburgh EH6 5HW
T 0131-553 2232 E romilly.squire@virgin.net
Hon. Secretary, Romilly Squire of Rubislaw

STANDING COUNCIL OF THE BARONETAGE (1903), Forestside, Martin's Corner, Hambledon, Waterlooville PO7 4RA T 023-9263 2672
E secretary@baronetage.org W www.baronetage.org
Chair, Sir Ian Lowson, BT, OSTJ

SUZY LAMPLUGH TRUST (1986), National Centre for Personal Safety, 218 The Strand, London WC2 R1AT
T 020-7091 0014 E info@suzylamplugh.org
W www.suzylamplugh.org
Joint Chief Executives (acting), Ann Elledge and Sarah Haddon

SWEDENBORG SOCIETY (1810), 20–21 Bloomsbury Way, London WC1A 2TH
T 020-7405 7986 E richard@swedenborg.org.uk
W www.swedenborg.org.uk
Secretary, Richard Lines

TEACHER SUPPORT NETWORK (1870), 40A Drayton Park, London N5 1EW T 0800-056 2561
E enquiries@teachersupport.info
W www.teachersupport.info
Chief Executive, Julian Stanley

THEATRES TRUST (1976), 22 Charing Cross Road, London WC2H 0QL T 020-7836 8591
E info@theatrestrust.org.uk W www.theatrestrust.org.uk
Director, Mhora Samuel

THORESBY SOCIETY (1889), Claremont, 23 Clarendon Road, Leeds LS2 9NZ T 0113-247 0704
E secretary@thoresby.org.uk W www.thoresby.org.uk
President, Mr C. J. Morgan

TOGETHER: WORKING FOR WELLBEING (1879), 12 Old Street, London EC1V 9BE T 020-7780 7300
E contact-us@together-uk.org W www.together-uk.org
Chief Executive, Liz Felton

TOWN AND COUNTRY PLANNING ASSOCIATION, 17 Carlton House Terrace, London SW1Y 5AS T 020-7930 8903 (1899), W www.tcpa.org.uk
E tcpa@tcpa.org.uk
Interim Chief Executive, Kate Henderson

TREE COUNCIL (1974), 71 Newcomen Street, London SE1 1YT T 020-7407 9992
E info@treecouncil.org.uk W www.treecouncil.org.uk
Director-General, Pauline Buchanan Black

TURNER SOCIETY (1975), BCM Box Turner, London WC1N 3XX W www.turnersociety.org.uk
Chair, Andrew Wilton

UNDERSTANDING ANIMAL RESEARCH (2008), 25 Shaftesbury Avenue, London W1D 7EG
T 020-7287 2818 E office@uar.org.uk W www.uar.org.uk
Chief Executive, Dr S. Festing

UNITED GRAND LODGE OF ENGLAND (1717), Freemasons' Hall, Great Queen Street, London WC2B 5AZ
T 020-7831 9811 E enquiries@ugle.org.uk
W www.ugle.org.uk
Grand Master, HRH The Duke of Kent, KG, GCMG, GCVO

UNITED KINGDOM RESERVE FORCES ASSOCIATION (1972), Holderness House, 51–61 Clifton Street, London EC2A 4EY T 020-7426 8361 E co-rfa@co.rfca.mod.uk W www.ukrfa.org
President, Air Vice-Marshal B. H. Newton, CB, CVO, OBE

UNITED REFORMED CHURCH HISTORY SOCIETY (1972), Westminster College, Madingley Road, Cambridge CB3 0AA T 01223-741300 E mt212@cam.ac.uk
Hon. Secretary, Revd E. J. Brown

UNIVERSITIES FEDERATION FOR ANIMAL WELFARE (1926), The Old School, Brewhouse Hill, Wheathampstead AL4 8AN T 01582-831818 E ufaw@ufaw.org.uk W www.ufaw.org.uk
Chief Executive and Scientific Director, Dr J. K. Kirkwood

UNIVERSITIES UK (2000), Woburn House, 20 Tavistock Square, London WC1H 9HQ T 020-7419 4111 E info@universitiesuk.ac.uk W www.universitiesuk.ac.uk
Chief Executive, Ms Nicola Dandridge

VEGAN SOCIETY (1944), Donald Watson House, 21 Hylton Street, Hockley B18 6HJ T 0845-458 8244 E info@vegansociety.com W www.vegansociety.com
Chief Executive, Nigel Winter

VEGETARIAN SOCIETY OF THE UNITED KINGDOM LTD (1847), Parkdale, Dunham Road, Altrincham, Cheshire WA14 4QG T 0161-925 2000 E info@vegsoc.org W www.vegsoc.org
Chief Executive, Dr Annette Pinner

VICTIM SUPPORT (1979), Hannibal House, Elephant and Castle Shopping Centre, London SE1 6TB T 020-7448 9898, Helpline 0845-303 0900 W www.victimsupport.org.uk
Chief Executive, Gillian Guy

VICTORIA CROSS AND GEORGE CROSS ASSOCIATION (1956), Horse Guards, Whitehall, London SW1A 2AX T 020-7930 3506
Secretary, Mrs D. Grahame, OBE, MVO

VICTORIAN SOCIETY (1958), 1 Priory Gardens, Bedford Park, London W4 1TT T 020-8994 1019 E admin@victoriansociety.org.uk W www.victoriansociety.org.uk
Director, Dr Ian Dungavell

VSO (VOLUNTARY SERVICE OVERSEAS) (1958), 27A Carlton Drive, Putney, London SW15 2BS T 020-8780 7500 E enquiry@vso.org.uk W www.vso.org.uk
Chief Executive, Derrick Anderson

WAR WIDOWS ASSOCIATION OF GREAT BRITAIN (1971), 199 Borough High Street, SE1 1AA T 0845-241 2189 E info@warwidowsassociation.org.uk W www.warwidowsassociation.org.uk
Chair, Gill Grigg, MBE

WELLBEING OF WOMEN (1965), 27 Sussex Place, Regent's Park, London NW1 4SP T 020-7772 6400 E wellbeingofwomen@rcog.org.uk W www.wellbeingofwomen.org.uk
Directors, Liz Campbell

WESLEY HISTORICAL SOCIETY (1893), 7 Haugh Shaw Road, Halifax, West Yorkshire HX1 3AH T 01422-250780 E johnahargreaves@blueyonder.co.uk W www.wesleyhistoricalsociety.org.uk
General Secretary, Dr John A. Hargreaves, FSA

WESTMINSTER FOUNDATION FOR DEMOCRACY (1992), Artillery House, 11–19 Artillery Row, London SW1P 1RT T 020-7799 1311 E wfd@wfd.org W www.wfd.org
Chief Executive, Linda Duffield

WILDFOWL AND WETLANDS TRUST (1946), Slimbridge GL2 7BT T 01453-891900 E enquiries@wwt.org.uk W www.wwt.org.uk
Chief Executive, Martin Spray

WOMEN'S ENGINEERING SOCIETY (1919), c/o The IET, Michael Faraday House, Six Hills Way, Stevenage SG1 2AY T 01438-765506 E info@wes.org.uk W www.wes.org.uk
President, Dr Jan Peters

WOODLAND TRUST (1972), Autumn Park, Dysart Road, Grantham NG31 6LL T 01476-581111 E enquiries@woodlandtrust.org.uk W www.woodlandtrust.org.uk
Chief Executive, Sue Holden

WORCESTERSHIRE ARCHAEOLOGICAL SOCIETY (1854), 26 Albert Park Road, Malvern WR14 1HN T 01299-250416 E museum@worcestershire.gov.uk W www.communigate.co.uk/worcs
Hon. Secretary, Dr J. W. Dunleavey

WORKING FAMILIES (2003), 1–3 Berry Street, London EC1V 0AA T 020-7253 7243 E office@workingfamilies.org.uk W www.workingfamilies.org.uk
Chief Executive, Sarah Jackson

YMCA (1844), National Council of YMCAs, 640 Forest Road, London E17 3DZ T 020-8520 5599 E enquiries@ymca.org.uk W www.ymca.org.uk
Chief Executive, Ian Green

YOUTH HOSTELS ASSOCIATION (ENGLAND & WALES) (1930), Trevelyan House, Dimple Road, Matlock DE4 3YH T 01629-592600 E customerservices@yha.org.uk W www.yha.org.uk
Chief Executive, Caroline White

YWCA ENGLAND & WALES (1855), Clarendon House, 52 Cornmarket Street, Oxford OX1 3EJ T 01865-304200 E info@ywca.org.uk W www.ywca.org.uk
Chief Executive, Sarah Payne

ZOOLOGICAL SOCIETY OF LONDON (1826), Regent's Park, London NW1 4RY T 020-7722 3333 W www.zsl.org
Director-General, Ralph Armond, FRS

THE WORLD

THE WORLD IN FIGURES

THE EARTH

The shape of the Earth is that of an oblate spheroid or solid of revolution whose meridian sections are ellipses, while the sections at right angles are circles.

DIMENSIONS

Equatorial diameter = 12,756.27km (7,926.38 miles)
Polar diameter = 12,713.50km (7,899.80 miles)
Equatorial circumference = 40,075.01km (24,901.46 miles)
Polar circumference = 40,007.86km (24,859.73 miles)
Mass = 5,974,000,000,000,000,000,000 tonnes (5.879×10^{21} tons)

The equatorial circumference is divided into 360 degrees of longitude, which is measured in degrees, minutes and seconds east or west of the Greenwich meridian (0°) to 180°, the meridian 180° E. coinciding with 180° W. This dateline was internationally ratified on 13 October 1884. The position of the dateline has been modified on occasions, most recently on 1 January 1995 when it was moved to the east of Kiribati. *See also* Astronomy.

Distance north and south of the equator is measured in degrees, minutes and seconds of latitude. The equator is 0°, the North Pole is 90°N. and the South Pole is 90°S. The tropics lie at 23° 27′ N. (tropic of cancer) and 23° 27′ S. (tropic of capricorn). The Arctic Circle lies at 66° 33′ N. and the Antarctic Circle at 66° 33′ S. (Note the tropics and the Arctic and Antarctic circles are affected by the slow decrease in obliquity of the ecliptic, of about 0.47 arcseconds per year. The effect of this is that the Arctic and Antarctic circles are currently moving towards their respective poles by about 14m per annum, while the tropics move towards the equator by the same amount.)

AREA ETC

The surface area of the Earth is 510,069,120km² (196,938,800 miles²), of which the water area is 70.92 per cent and the land area is 29.08 per cent.

The radial velocity on the Earth's surface at the equator is 1,669.79km per hour (1,037.56mph). The Earth's mean velocity in its orbit around the Sun is 107,229km per hour (66,629mph). The Earth's mean distance from the Sun is 149,597,870km (92,955,807 miles).

OCEANS

AREA

	km²	*miles²*
Pacific	155,557,000	59,270,000
Atlantic	76,762,000	29,638,000
Indian	68,556,000	26,467,000
Southern	20,327,000	7,848,300
Arctic	14,056,000	5,427,000

The equator divides the Pacific into the North and South Pacific and the Atlantic into the North and South Atlantic. In 2000 the International Hydrographic Organisation approved the description of the 20,327,000km² (7,848,300 miles²) of circum-Antarctic waters up to 60°S. as the Southern Ocean.

GREATEST OCEAN DEPTHS

Greatest depth	*Location*	*metres*	*feet*
Mariana Trench*	Pacific	10,911	35,798
Puerto Rico Trench	Atlantic	8,605	28,232
South Sandwich Trench	Southern	7,235	23,737
Java (Sunda) Trench	Indian	7,125	23,376
Molloy Deep	Arctic	5,680	18,400

* On 23 January 1960, Jacques Piccard (Swiss) and Don Walsh (USA) descended in the bathyscaphe *Trieste* to the floor of the Mariana Trench, a depth later calculated as 10,916m (35,814ft). The current depth was calculated by the Japanese remote-controlled probe *Kaiko* on 24 March 1995. On 1 June 2009, sonar mapping of the Challenger Deep in the Mariana Trench by the US oceanographic research vessel *Kilo Moana* indicated a possible depth of 10,971m (35,994ft).

SEAS

LARGEST BY AREA

	km²	*miles²*
South China	2,974,600	1,148,500
Caribbean	2,515,900	971,400
Mediterranean	2,509,900	969,100
Bering	2,261,000	873,000
Gulf of Mexico	1,507,600	582,100
Okhotsk	1,392,000	537,500
Japan	1,012,900	391,100
Hudson Bay	730,100	281,900
East China	664,600	256,600
Andaman	564,880	218,100
Black Sea	507,900	196,100
Red Sea	453,000	174,900
North Sea	427,100	164,900

GREATEST DEPTHS

	metres	*feet*
Caribbean	8,605	28,232
East China (Ryu Kyu Trench)	7,507	24,629
South China	7,258	23,812
Mediterranean (Ionian Basin)	5,150	16,896
Andaman	4,267	14,000
Bering	3,936	12,913
Gulf of Mexico	3,504	11,496
Okhotsk	3,365	11,040
Japan	3,053	10,016
Red Sea	2,266	7,434
Black Sea	2,212	7,257
North Sea	439	1,440

THE CONTINENTS

There are six geographic continents, although America is often divided politically into North and Central America, and South America, making seven.

AFRICA is surrounded by sea except for the narrow isthmus of Suez in the north-east, through which was cut the Suez Canal (opened 17 November 1869). Its extreme longitudes are 17° 20′ W. at Cape Verde, Senegal, and 51° 24′ E. at Raas Xaafunn, Somalia. The extreme latitudes are 37° 20′ N. at Cape Blanc, Tunisia, and 34° 50′ S. at Cape Agulhas, South Africa, about 7,081km (4,400 miles) apart. The Equator passes across Gabon, Republic of the Congo, Uganda, Kenya and Somalia in the middle of the continent.

NORTH AMERICA, including Mexico, is surrounded by ocean except in the south, where the isthmian states of Central America link North America with South America. Its extreme longitudes are 168° 5′ W. at Cape Prince of Wales, Alaska, and 55° 40′ W. at Cape Charles, Newfoundland. The extreme continental latitudes are the tip of the Boothia peninsula, NW Territories, Canada (71° 51′ N.) and 14° 22′ N. in southern Mexico near La Victoria, Guatemala.

SOUTH AMERICA lies mostly in the southern hemisphere, the equator passing across Ecuador, Colombia and Brazil in the north of the continent. It is surrounded by ocean except where it is joined to Central America in the north by the narrow isthmus through which was cut the Panama Canal (opened 15 August 1914). Its extreme longitudes are 34° 47′ W. at Cape Branco in Brazil and 81° 20′ W. at Punta Pariña, Peru. The extreme continental latitudes are 12° 25′ N. at Punta Gallinas, Colombia, and 53° 54′ S. at the southernmost tip of Peninsula de Brunswick, Chile. Cape Horn, on Cape Island, Chile, lies in 55° 59′ S.

ANTARCTICA lies almost entirely within the Antarctic Circle (66° 33′ S.) and is the largest of the world's glaciated areas. Ninety-eight per cent of the continent is permanently covered in ice. The ice amounts to some 30 million km³ (7.2 million miles³) and represents more than 70 per cent of the world's fresh water. The ice sheet is on average 1.6km (1 mile) thick; if it were to melt, the world's seas would rise by more than 60m (197ft). The environment is too hostile for unsupported human habitation.

ASIA is the largest continent and occupies 29.6 per cent of the world's land surface. The extreme longitudes are 26° 05′ E. at Baba Buran, Turkey, and 169° 40′ W. at Mys Dezhneva (East Cape), Russia, a distance of about 9,656km (6,000 miles). Its extreme northern latitude is 77° 45′ N. at Mys Chelyuskin, Russia, and it extends over 8,046km (5,000 miles) south to Tanjong Piai, Malaysia.

AUSTRALIA is the smallest of the continents and lies in the southern hemisphere. It is entirely surrounded by ocean. Its extreme longitudes are 113° 11′ E. at Steep Point, Western Australia, and 153° 11′ E. at Cape Byron, New South Wales. The extreme latitudes are 10° 42′ S. at Cape York, Queensland, and 39°S. at South East Point, Tasmania. Australia, together with New Zealand (Australasia), Papua New Guinea and the Pacific Islands, comprises Oceania.

EUROPE, including European Russia, is the smallest continent in the northern hemisphere. Its extreme latitudes are 71° 11′ N. at Nord Kapp in Norway, and 36° 23′ N. at Akra Tainaron (Matapas) in southern Greece, a distance of about 3,862km (2,400 miles). Its breadth from Cabo Carvoeiro in Portugal (9° 34′ W.) in the west to the Kara River, north of the Urals (66° 30′ E.) in the east is about 5,310km (3,300 miles). The division between Europe and Asia is generally regarded as the watershed of the Ural Mountains; down the Ural river to Atyrau, Kazakhstan; across the Caspian Sea to Apsheronskiy Poluostrov, near Baku; along the watershed of the Caucasus Mountains to Anapa and then across the Black Sea to the Bosporus in Turkey; across the Sea of Marmara to Canakkale Bogazi (Dardanelles).

Continent	*Area*	
	km²	miles²
Asia	43,998,000	16,988,000
America*	41,918,000	16,185,000
Africa	29,800,000	11,506,000
Antarctica	13,209,000	5,100,000
Europe†	9,699,000	3,745,000
Australia	7,618,493	2,941,526

* North and Central America has an area of 24,255,000km² (9,365,000 miles²)

† Includes 5,571,000km² (2,151,000 miles²) of former USSR territory, including the Baltic states, Belarus, Moldova, Ukraine and the part of Russia west of the Ural Mountains and Kazakhstan west of the Ural river. European Turkey (24,378km²/9,412 miles²) comprises territory to the west and north of the Bosporus and the Dardanelles

GLACIATED AREAS

It is estimated that 14,800,000km² (5,712,800 miles²) or 10 per cent of the world's land surface is permanently covered with ice. Glacial retreat and thinning occurs where glaciers melt faster than they are created. The phenomenon has been observed since the mid-19th century but has accelerated since about 1980 as a result of global warming. It is most notable in the Antarctic: a 2005 report by the American Association for the Advancement of Science indicated that 87 per cent of the continent's 244 marine glaciers have retreated over the past 50 years. The largest glacier is the 515km (320 miles) long Lambert-Fisher Ice Passage, Mac Robertson Land, Eastern Antarctica.

Location	*Area*	
	km²	miles²
South Polar regions	13,830,000	5,340,000
North Polar regions (incl. Greenland)	1,965,000	758,500
Alaska-Canada	58,800	22,700
Asia	37,800	14,600
South America	11,900	4,600
Europe	10,700	4,128
New Zealand	1,015	391
Africa	238	92

PENINSULAS

Peninsula	*Area*	
	km²	miles²
Arabian	3,250,000	1,250,000
Southern Indian	2,072,000	800,000
Alaskan	1,500,000	580,000
Labradorian	1,300,000	500,000
Scandinavian	800,300	309,000
Iberian	584,000	225,500

LARGEST ISLANDS

Island and ocean	*Area*	
	km²	miles²
Greenland (Kalaallit Nunaat), Arctic	2,175,500	840,000
New Guinea, Pacific	792,500	306,000

Borneo, Pacific	725,450	280,100
Madagascar, Indian	587,041	226,674
Baffin Island, Arctic	507,451	195,928
Sumatra, Indian	427,350	165,000
Honshu, Pacific	227,413	87,805
Great Britain, Atlantic*	218,077	84,200
Victoria Island, Arctic	217,292	83,897
Ellesmere Island, Arctic	196,236	75,767

* Mainland only

LARGEST DESERTS

Desert and location	*Area (approx)*	
	km^2	$miles^2$
Sahara, N. Africa	9,000,000	3,500,000
Gobi, Mongolia/China	1,300,000	500,000
Arabian (Eastern) Desert, Egypt	1,000,000	385,000
Kalahari Desert, Botswana/Namibia/S. Africa	570,000	220,000
Great Victoria, Australia	350,000	135,000
Taklimakan Shamo, Mongolia/China	320,000	125,000
Kara Kum, Turkmenistan*	310,000	120,000
Great Sandy, Australia	270,000	100,000
Thar Desert, India/Pakistan	260,000	100,000
Somali Desert, Somalia	260,000	100,000

* Together with the Kyzyl Kum 259,000km^2 (100,000 miles^2) known as the Turkestan Desert

DEEPEST DEPRESSIONS

Depression and location	*Maximum depth below sea level*	
	metres	feet
Dead Sea, Jordan/Israel	408	1,338
Lake Assal, Djibouti	156	511
Turfan depression, Sinkiang, China	153	505
Qattara depression, Egypt	132	436
Mangyshlak peninsula, Kazakhstan	131	433
Danakil depression, Ethiopia	116	383
Death Valley, California, USA	86	282
Salton Sink, California, USA	71	235
West of Ustyurt plateau, Kazakhstan	70	230
Prikaspiyskaya Nizmennost', Russia/Kazakhstan	67	220
Lake Sarykamysh, Uzbekistan/Turkmenistan	45	148
El Faiyum, Egypt	44	147
Peninsula Valdes, Chubut, Argentina	40	131
Lake Eyre, South Australia	16	52

The world's largest exposed depression is the Prikaspiyskaya Nizmennost' covering the hinterland of the northern third of the Caspian Sea, which is itself 28m (92ft) below sea level.

Western Antarctica and central Greenland largely comprise crypto-depressions under ice burdens. The Antarctic Bentley subglacial trench has a bedrock 2,538m (8,326ft) below sea level. In Greenland (lat. 73° N., long. 39° W.) the bedrock is 365m (1,197ft) below sea level.

Nearly one quarter of the area of the Netherlands lies marginally below sea level, an area of more than 10,000km^2 (3,860 miles^2).

No part of the Maldives is higher than 2.4m (8ft) and nowhere in Lesotho is lower than 1,381m (4,531ft).

CAVES

DEEPEST CAVES

The world's deepest cave was discovered in January 2001 by a team of Ukrainian cave explorers in the Arabikskaya system in the western Caucasus mountains of Georgia. It is a branch of the Voronya or 'Crow's Cave'.

Cave system/location	*Depth*	
	metres	feet
Krubera (Voronya), Georgia	2,191	7,188
Illyuzia-Mezhonnogo-Snezhnaya, Georgia	1,753	5,751
Lamprechtsofen Vogelschacht, Austria	1,632	5,354
Gouffre Mirolda, France	1,626	5,335
Réseau Jean Bernard, France	1,602	5,256
Torca del Cerro del Cuevon/Torca de las Saxifragas, Spain	1,589	5,213
Sarma, Georgia	1,543	5,062
Shakta Vyacheslav, Georgia	1,508	4,947
Sima de la Cornisa (Torca Magali), Spain	1,507	4,944
Cehi 2, Slovenia	1,502	4,928
Sistema Cheve (Cuicateco), Mexico	1,484	4,868
Sistema Huautla, Mexico	1,475	4,839

LONGEST CAVE SYSTEMS

Cave system/location	*Total known length*	
	km	miles
Mammoth Cave System, Kentucky, USA	590.6	367
Jewel Cave, South Dakota, USA	241.6	150
Optimisticheskaya, Ukraine	230.1	143
Wind Cave, South Dakota, USA	214.4	133
Lechuguilla Cave, New Mexico, USA	206.9	129
Hölloch, Switzerland	195.9	122
Fisher Ridge System, Kentucky, USA	182.1	113
Sistema Ox Bel Ha, Mexico (submerged)	180.0	112
Sistema Sac Actun, Mexico (submerged)	175.7	109
Gua Air Jernih, Malaysia	175.6	109
Siebenhengste-hohgant, Switzerland	156.0	97
Schoenbergsystem, Austria	130.2	81

LONGEST MOUNTAIN RANGES

Range and location	*Length*	
	km	miles
Cordillera de Los Andes, South America	7,200	4,500
Rocky Mountains, North America	4,800	3,000
Himalaya-Karakoram-Hindu Kush, Central Asia	3,850	2,400
Great Dividing Range, Australia	3,620	2,250
Trans-Antarctic Mts, Antarctica	3,540	2,200
Atlantic Coast Range, Brazil	3,050	1,900
West Sumatran-Javan Range, Indonesia	2,900	1,800
Aleutian Range, Alaska and N.W. Pacific	2,650	1,650
Tien Shan, Central Asia	2,250	1,400
Central New Guinea Range, Papua New Guinea	2,010	1,250

HIGHEST MOUNTAINS

The world's twelve 8,000m (26,247ft) mountains (with five subsidiary peaks) are all in the Himalaya-Karakoram-Hindu Kush ranges.

Mountain (first ascent)	*Height*	
	metres	feet
Mt Everest* (Qomolangma) (29 May 1953)	8,848	29,028
K2 (Qogir)† (31 July 1954)	8,611	28,251
Kangchenjunga (25 May 1955)	8,597	28,208
Lhotse I (18 May 1956)	8,510	27,923
Makalu I (15 May 1955)	8,480	27,824
Lhotse Shar (II) (12 May 1979)	8,400	27,560
Dhaulagiri I (13 May 1960)	8,171	26,810
Manaslu I (Kutang I) (9 May 1956)	8,156	26,760
Cho Oyu (19 October 1954)	8,153	26,750
Nanga Parbat (Diamir) (3 July 1953)	8,125	26,660

* Named after Sir George Everest (1790–1866), Surveyor-General of India 1830–43, in 1863. He pronounced his name Eve-rest

† Formerly named after Col. Henry Haversham Godwin-Austen (1834–1923), who worked on the Trigonometrical Survey of India, which established the heights of the Himalayan peaks, including Everest

The culminating summits in the other major mountain ranges are:

Mountain, by range or country	*Height*	
	metres	feet
Pik Pobedy, Tien Shan	7,439	24,406
Cerro Aconcagua, Cordillera de Los Andes	6,960	22,834
Mt McKinley (S. Peak), Alaska Range	6,194	20,320
Kilimanjaro (Kibo), Tanzania	5,894	19,340
Hkakabo Razi, Myanmar	5,881	19,296
Citlaltépetl (Orizaba), Mexico	5,655	18,555
El'brus, (W. Peak), Caucasus	5,642	18,510
Vinson Massif, Antarctica	4,897	16,066
Puncak Jaya, Central New Guinea Range	4,884	16,023
Mt Blanc, Alps	4,807	15,771

HIGHEST ACTIVE VOLCANOES

Although it displays fumarolic activity, emitting steam and gas, no major eruption has ever been observed of the world's highest volcano and second highest peak in the western hemisphere, the 6,893m (22,615ft) Ojos del Salado, in the Andes on the Argentina/Chile border. For comparison, Eyjafjallajokull, the Icelandic volcano which erupted in 2010 causing air transport chaos, has an elevation of 1,666m (5,466ft).

The volcanoes listed below include only those that have had activity recorded since 1960.

Volcano and location (most recent activity)	*Height*	
	metres	feet
San Pedro, Andes, Chile (1960)	6,145	20,161
Aracar, Andes, Argentina (1993)	6,082	19,954
Volcan Guallatiri, Andes, Chile (1960)	6,069	19,882
Sabancaya, Andes, Peru (2003)	5,967	19,577
San José, Andes, Argentina/Chile (1960)	5,856	19,213
Tupungatito, Andes, Chile (1987)	5,640	18,504
Lascar, Andes, Chile (2007)	5,591	18,346
Popocatepetl, Mexico (2010)	5,426	17,802
Nevado del Ruiz, Colombia (1991)	5,321	17,457
Sangay, Andes, Ecuador (2008)	5,230	17,159
Irruputuncu, Chile (1995)	5,163	16,939
Tungurahua, Ecuador	5,023	16,480
Klyuchevskaya Sopka, Kamchatka peninsula, Russia (2010)	4,835	15,863

LAKES

LARGEST LAKES

The areas of some of the lakes listed are subject to seasonal variation. The most voluminous lakes are the Caspian Sea (saline) with 78,700km^3 (18,880 miles^3) and Baikal (fresh water) with 23,000km^3 (5,518 miles^3). Baikal is also the world's deepest lake (*see* below). It is estimated that it contains as much water as the entire Great Lakes system in North America – more than 20 per cent of the world's fresh water and some 90 per cent of all the fresh water in Russia.

The Aral was once the fifth largest in the world, with an area of 68,000km^2 (26,255 miles^2), but since the 1960s many of its feeder rivers have been diverted for irrigation, as a result of which its area shrank to 17,160km^2 (6,626 miles^2). Its salinity was almost three times that of seawater, and pollution led to the extinction of many aquatic species. Since the construction of the Kok-Aral dam (2005), water levels are rising again, especially in the north.

Lake and location	*Area*		*Length*	
	km^2	miles^2	km	miles
Caspian Sea, Iran/Azerbaijan/Russia/Turkmenistan/Kazakhstan	371,000	143,000	1,171	728
Michigan–Huron, USA/Canada*	117,610	45,300	1,010	627
Superior, Canada/USA	82,100	31,700	563	350
Victoria, Uganda/Tanzania/Kenya	69,500	26,828	362	225
Tanganyika, Dem. Rep. of Congo/Tanzania/Zambia/Burundi	32,900	12,665	725	450
Great Bear, Canada	31,328	12,096	309	192
Baikal, Russia†	30,500	11,776	620	385
Malawi (Nyasa), Tanzania/Malawi/Mozambique	28,900	11,150	580	360
Great Slave, Canada	28,570	11,031	480	298
Erie, Canada/USA	25,670	9,910	388	241

* Lakes Michigan and Huron may be regarded as lobes of the same lake. The Michigan lobe has an area of 57,750km^2 (22,300 miles^2) and the Huron lobe an area of 59,570km^2 (23,000 miles^2)

† World's deepest lake (1,637m/5,371ft)

UNITED KINGDOM (BY COUNTRY)

Lake and location	*Area*		*Length*	
	km^2	miles^2	km	miles
Lough Neagh, Northern Ireland	381.73	147.39	28.90	18.00
Loch Lomond, Scotland	71.12	27.46	36.44	22.64
Windermere, England	14.74	5.69	16.90	10.50
Lake Vyrnwy, Wales (artificial)	4.53	1.75	7.56	4.70
Llyn Tegid (Bala), Wales (natural)	4.38	1.69	5.80	3.65

LARGEST MANMADE LAKES

*Dam/lake**	*Volume*	
	km^3	miles^3
Owen Falls, Uganda/Kenya/Tanzania (1954)	204.80	49.13
Bratskoye, Russia (1967)	169.27	40.61
Nasser, Egypt (1970)	168.90	40.52
Kariba, Zimbabwe/Zambia (1959)	160.30	38.46

Volta, Ghana (1965)	148.00	35.51
Manicouagan (Daniel Johnson dam), Canada (1968)	141.85	34.03
Guri (Raul Leoni), Venezuela (1986)	136.30	33.11
Krasnoyarskoye, Russia (1967)	73.30	17.58
Wadi-Tatar, Iraq (1967)	72.80	17.46
Williston (W. A. C. Bennett dam), Canada (1967)	70.31	16.87

* Formed as a result of dam construction

The UK's largest reservoir is Kielder Water, Northumberland (1975) with a volume of 0.2km^3 (0.048 miles^3)

DEEPEST LAKES

Lake and location	*Greatest depth*	
	metres	feet
Baikal, Russia	1,637	5,371
Tanganyika, Burundi/Tanzania/ Dem. Rep. of Congo/Zambia	1,470	4,825
Caspian Sea, Azerbaijan/Iran/ Kazakhstan/Russia/Turkmenistan	1,025	3,363
O'Higgins, Chile/San Martin, Argentina	836	2,743
Malawi, Malawi/Mozambique/ Tanzania	706	2,316
Issyk Kul, Kyrgyzstan	702	2,303
Great Slave, Canada	614	2,015
Quesnel, Canada	610	2,001
Crater, Oregon, USA	594	1,949
Danau Matano, South Sulawesi, Indonesia	590	1,936
Lago Buenos Aires, Argentina/Lago General Carrera, Chile	586	1,923
Hornindalsvastnet, Norway	514	1,686
Danau Toba, Sumatra, Indonesia	505	1,657
Sarezskoye Ozero, Tajikistan	505	1,657
Tahoe, California/Nevada, USA	501	1,645
Lago Argentina, Argentina	500	1,640

Loch Morar, Highland, Scotland is the UK's deepest lake at 310m (1,017ft).

LONGEST RIVERS

River, source and outflow	*Length*	
	km	miles
Nile (Bahr-el-Nil), R. Luvironza, Burundi–E. Mediterranean Sea	6,725	4,180
Amazon (Amazonas), Lago Villafro, Peru–S. Atlantic Ocean	6,448	4,007
Yangtze-Kiang (Chang Jiang), Kunlun Mts, W. China–Yellow Sea	6,380	3,964
Mississippi-Missouri-Red Rock, Montana–Gulf of Mexico	5,970	3,710
Yenisey-Angara, W. Mongolia–Kara Sea	5,536	3,440
Huang He (Yellow River), Bayan Har Shan range, Central China–Yellow Sea	5,463	3,395
Ob'-Irtysh, W. Mongolia–Kara Sea	5,410	3,362
Zaire (Congo), R. Lualaba, Dem. Rep. of Congo-Zambia–S. Atlantic Ocean	4,665	2,900
Amur-Argun, R. Argun, Khingan Mts, N. China–Sea of Okhotsk	4,416	2,744
Lena-Kirenga, R. Kirenga, W. of Lake Baikal–Laptev Sea, Arctic Ocean	4,400	2,734

BRITISH ISLES

River, source and outflow	*Length*	
	km	miles
Shannon, Co. Cavan, Rep. of Ireland–Atlantic Ocean	386	240
Severn, Powys, Wales–Bristol Channel	354	220
Thames, Gloucestershire, England–North Sea	346	215
Tay, Perthshire, Scotland–North Sea	188	117
Clyde, Lanarkshire, Scotland–Firth of Clyde	158	98.5
Tweed, Scottish Borders–North Sea	155	96.5
Bann (Upper and Lower), Co. Down, N. Ireland–Atlantic Ocean	122	76

WATERFALLS

GREATEST BY HEIGHT

Waterfall, river and location	*Total drop*		*Greatest single leap*	
	metres	feet	metres	feet
Salto Angel, Carrao Auyan Tepui, Venezuela	979	3,212	807	2,648
Tugela, Tugela, S. Africa (5 leaps)	948	3,110	410	1,350
Ramnefjellsfossen, Jostedal Glacier, Norway	800	2,625	600	1,970
Mongefossen, Monge, Norway	773	2,535	—	—
Gocta, Cocahuayco, Peru	771	2,531	—	—
Mutarazi, Mutarazi, Zimbabwe	762	2,499	479	1,572
Yosemite, Yosemite Creek, USA	739	2,425	435	1,430
Ostre Mardola Foss, Mardals, Norway*	655	2,149	296	974
Tyssestrengene, Tysso, Norway*	646	2,120	289	948
Cuquenán, Arabopo, Venezuela	610	2,000	—	—

* Volume much affected by hydroelectric harnessing

BRITISH ISLES, BY HEIGHT

Waterfall, river and location	*Total drop*	
	metres	feet
Eas a' Chual Aluinn, Glas Bheinn, Sutherland, Scotland	200	656
Powerscourt Falls, Dargle, Co. Wicklow, Rep. of Ireland	121	398
Pistyll-y-Llyn, Powys/Dyfed border, Wales (cascades)	91	300
Pistyll Rhaeadr, Clwyd/Powys border, Wales (single leap)	71.5	235
Cauldron Snout, Tees, Cumbria/Durham, England (cascades)	61	200

GREATEST BY VOLUME

*Waterfall, river and location**	*Mean annual flow* m^3/sec
Khone, Mekong, Laos	11,610
Para, Caura, Venezuela	3,540
Paulo Afonso, Sao Francisco, Brazil	2,832
Niagara (Horseshoe), Niagara/Lake Erie–Lake Ontario, Canada	2,407
Salto de Iguaçu, Parana, Argentina/Brazil	1,746
Victoria (Mosi-oa-Tunya), Zambezi, Zimbabwe/Zambia	1,088
Virginia, Nahanni, Canada	1,000
Sivasamudram, Kaveri (Cauvery), India	934
Kongou, Ivindo, Gabon	900
Willamette, Willamette, Oregon, USA	874

* Excludes waterfalls that have been submerged as a result of dam construction or consist of rapids or cascades with individual vertical drops of less than 6m (20ft)

DAMS

TALLEST DAMS

Dam and location	*Height*	
	metres	feet
Jinping-I, China (2014)*	305	1,001
Nurek, Tajikistan (1980)	300	984
Xiaowan, China (2010)	292	960
Grande Dixence, Switzerland (1965)	285	935
Inguri, Georgia (1987)	272	892
Vaiont, Italy (1959)†	262	859
Manuel Moreno Torres, Mexico (1981)	261	856
Tehri, India (2006)	261	856

* Scheduled completion date
† Disused

TALLEST ...

All heights are in accordance with the Council on Tall Buildings and Urban Habitat's regulations, which measure from the ground level of the main entrance to the architectural tip of the building and include spires but not antennae, signage or flag poles.

INHABITED BUILDINGS

Building and location	*Height*	
	metres	feet
Burj Khalifa, Dubai, UAE (2010)	828	2,717
Abraj Al-Bait Tower, Mecca, Saudi Arabia (2010)	591	1,939
Taipei 101, Taipei, Taiwan (2003)	509	1,671
Federation Tower, Moscow, Russia (2011)*	506	1,660
Shanghai World Finance Centre, Shanghai, China (2008)	492	1,613
International Commerce Centre, Hong Kong, China (2010)	483	1,584
Petronas Towers I and II, Kuala Lumpur, Malaysia (1998)	452	1,482
Nangjing Greenland Financial Centre, China (2010)	450	1,475
Willis Tower, Chicago, USA (1974)†	442	1,450
Guangzhou West Tower, China (2010)	440	1,444
Trump International Hotel and Tower, Chicago, USA (2010)	423	1,388
Jin Mao Tower, Shanghai, China (1998)	421	1,380
Two International Finance Centre, Hong Kong, China (2003)	416	1,362
Princess Tower, Dubai, UAE (2011)†	414	1,357
Al Hamra Tower, Kuwait (2011)†	412	1,352

* Scheduled completion date
† With TV antennae, 520m (1,707ft)

STRUCTURES

Structure and location	*Height*	
	metres	feet
Tokyo Skytree, Tokyo, Japan (2011)*	634	2,080
KVLY (formerly KTHI)-TV Mast, North Dakota (guyed), USA (1963)†	629	2,063
Guangzhou TV & Sightseeing Tower, Guangzhou, China (2010)	610	2,001
CN Tower, Toronto, Canada (1975)	555	1,822
Ostankino Tower, Moscow, Russia (1967)	540	1,772

* Scheduled completion date
† The USA has numerous other guyed TV towers above 600m (1,969ft)

TWIN TOWERS

Structure and location	*Storeys*	*Height*	
		metres	feet
Petronas Towers, Kuala Lumpur, Malaysia (1997)	96	452	1,482
Emirates Park Towers, Dubai, UAE (2010)	77	365	1,296
The Cullinan, Hong Kong, China (2008)	68	270	885
Al Kazim Towers, Dubai, UAE (2008)	53	265	870
Grand Gateway, Shanghai, China (2005)	52	262	860
Dual Towers, Manama, Bahrain (2007)	53	260	855
Abraj Al Bait Towers, Mecca, Saudi Arabia (2008)	55	260	855
The Imperial, Mumbai, India (2009)	60	249	817
Al Fattan Towers, Dubai, UAE (2006)	60	245	802
Destroyed 2001			
World Trade Center One, New York City, USA (1972)	110	417	1,368
World Trade Center Two, New York City, USA (1973)	110	415	1,362

CHURCHES

Structure and location	*Height*	
	metres	feet
Sagrada Família, Barcelona, Spain (2026)*	170	558
Ulm Cathedral, Ulm, Germany (1890)	162	530
Notre-Dame Cathedral, Rouen, France (1876)	158	518
Cologne Cathedral, Cologne, Germany (1880)	157	516
Our Lady of Peace Basilica, Yamoussoukro, Côte d'Ivoire (1990)	149	489
St Nicholas Church, Hamburg, Germany (1847)	147	482
Notre-Dame Cathedral, Strasbourg, France (1439)	144	472
Queen of Peace Shrine and Basilica, Lichen, Poland (2002)	140	459
Basilica of St Peter, Rome, Italy (1626)	138	452
St Stephen's Cathedral, Vienna, Austria (1570)	137	448

* Scheduled completion date, the 100th anniversary of the death of its architect, Antoni Gaudí; open for worship following its consecration by Pope Benedict XVI in 2010

The Chicago Methodist Temple, Chicago, USA (completed 1924) is 173m (568ft) high, but is sited atop a 25-storey, 100m (328ft) building. Salisbury Cathedral (1521), at 123m (404ft), is the UK's tallest religious building. St Paul's Cathedral, London, and Liverpool Anglican Cathedral are the only others in the UK over

100m (328ft) tall. At 94m (309ft) the Church of St Walburge, Preston, Lancashire is the tallest church in Britain that is not a cathedral.

TALLEST STRUCTURES — A CHRONOLOGY

Structure and location	Year	Height metres	Height feet
Djoser's Step Pyramid, Saqqara, Egypt	c.2650 BC	61	200
Pyramid of Meidum, Egypt	c.2600 BC	92	302
Snefru's Bent Pyramid, Dahshur, Egypt	c.2600 BC	102	336
Red Pyramid, Dahshur, Egypt	c.2590 BC	105	345
Great Pyramid, Giza, Egypt*	c.2580 BC	146	479
Liuhe (Six Harmonies) Pagoda, Hangzhou, China†	AD 970	150	492
Lincoln Cathedral, Lincoln, England‡	1311–1400	160	525
St Paul's Cathedral, London, England§¶	1315	149	489
St Olaf's Church, Tallinn, Estonia**	1438–1519	159	522
St Mary's Church, Stralsund, Germany§	1384–1478	151	495
Notre-Dame, Strasbourg, France§	1439	143	469
St Nicholas Church, Hamburg, Germany§	1847	147	482
Rouen Cathedral, Rouen, France	1876	148	485
Cologne Cathedral, Cologne, Germany	1880	157	515
Washington Monument, Washington DC, USA	1884	169	555
Eiffel Tower, Paris, France	1889	300	984
Chrysler Building, New York, USA	1930	319	1,046
Empire State Building, New York, USA	1930	381	1,250
KWTV Mast, Oklahoma City, USA	1954	479	1,572
KOBR-TV Tower, Caprock, USA	1960	490	1,608
KFVS TV Mast, Egypt Mills, USA	1960	511	1,677
Nexstar Broadcasting Tower Vivian, Vivian, USA	1961	534	1,752
KVLY (formerly KTHI)-TV Mast, Blanchard, USA§	1963	629	2,063
Warszawa Radio Mast, Konstantynow, Poland††	1974	646	2,118
Burj Khalifa, Dubai, UAE	2010	828	2,717

* Later reduced through loss of topstone to 137m (449ft)
† Destroyed in 1121
‡ Destroyed in 1549
§ The collapse of taller structures enabled these runners-up to gain or regain the status of 'world's tallest'
¶ Destroyed in 1561
** Spire burned down in 1625; renovated in 1931 to present height of 123m (403ft)
†† Collapsed in 1991 during renovation

BRIDGES

The longest stretch of bridging of any kind is that carrying the Interstate 55 and Interstate 10 highways at Manchac, Louisiana, USA (1979), on twin concrete trestles over 55.21km (34.31 miles). The 'floating' bridging at Evergreen Point, Seattle, Washington, USA (1963), is 3,839m (12,596ft) long, of which 2,310m (7,578ft) floats.

LONGEST SUSPENSION SPANS

Bridge and location	Length metres	Length feet
Akashi-Kaikyo, Japan (1998)	1,991	6,532
Xihoumen, China (2008)	1,650	5,413
Storebaelt East Bridge, Denmark (1998)	1,624	5,328
Gwangyang, South Korea (2012)*	1,545	5,069
Runyang (Yangtze), China (2005)	1,490	4,888
Nanjing Fourth (Yangtze), China (2013)*	1,418	4,652
Humber Estuary, England (1981)	1,410	4,626
Jiangyin (Yangtze), China (1999)	1,385	4,544
Tsing Ma, Hong Kong, China (1997)	1,377	4,518
Hardanger, Norway (2013)*	1,310	4,298

* Scheduled completion date

LONGEST CANTILEVER SPANS

Bridge and location	Length metres	Length feet
Pont de Québec (rail-road), St Lawrence, Canada (1917)	548.6	1,800
Firth of Forth (rail), Scotland (two spans of 1,710ft each) (1890)	521.2	1,710
Minato (Nanko), Japan (1974)	510.0	1,673
Commodore Barry, New Jersey/Pennsylvania, USA (1974)	494.3	1,622
Greater New Orleans, Louisiana, USA (I 1958, II 1988)*	480.0	1,575
Howrah (rail-road), India (1936–43)	457.2	1,500
Veterans Memorial, Louisiana, USA (1995)	445.0	1,460
San Francisco Oakland Bay, California, USA (1936)	426.7	1,400
Horace Wilkinson, Louisiana, USA (1969)	376.0	1,235
Tappan Zee, New York, USA (1955)	369.0	1,212

* Also known as Crescent City Connection

LONGEST STEEL ARCH SPANS

Bridge and location	Length metres	Length feet
Chaotianmen, China (2009)	552.0	1,811
Lupu, China (2003)	550.0	1,804
New River Gorge, West Virginia, USA (1977)	518.0	1,700
Bayonne (Kill van Kull), New Jersey/New York, USA (1931)	510.5	1,675
Sydney Harbour, Australia (1932)	502.9	1,650
Chenab, India (2012)*	467.0	1,532
Wushan, China (2005)	460.0	1,509
Yongjiang, China (2011)*	450.0	1,476
Zhijinghe, China (2009)	430.0	1,410
Xinguang, China (2008)	428.0	1,404

* Scheduled completion date

TALLEST BRIDGE TOWERS

Bridge and location	*Height*	
	metres	feet
Millau, France (2004)	336	1,102
Sutong, China (2008)	306	1,004
Akashi-Kaikyo, Japan (1998)	298	978
Stonecutters, Hong Kong, China (2008)	298	978
Gwangan, South Korea (2002)	270	886
Jingsha, China (2009)	267	876
East Bridge, Great Belt Fixed Link, Denmark (1997)	254	833
Edong, China (2010)	243	797
Mezcala, Mexico (1993)	242	794
Incheon, South Korea (2010)	230	755
Golden Gate, California, USA (1937)	227	754
Tatara, Japan (1999)	226	741
Jambatan Pulau Pinang, Malaysia (1985)	225	739
Le Ponte de Normandie, France (1994)	215	705
Runyang, China	215	705
Verrazano Narrows, New York, USA (1964)	211	692
Xihoumen, China	211	692
Tsing Ma, China (1997)	206	675

LONGEST VEHICULAR TUNNELS

Tunnel and location	*Length*	
	km	miles
*Seikan (rail), Tsugaru Channel, Japan (1988)	53.85	33.46
*Channel tunnel, (rail) Cheriton, Kent, UK–Sangatte, Calais, France (1994)	50.45	31.35
Moscow metro, Serpukhovsko–Timiryazevskaya line, Moscow, Russia (2002)	41.50	25.79
Lötschberg (rail), Switzerland (2007)	34.58	21.49
Berlin U-Bahn (U7 line) (rail) (1984)	31.76	19.74
Guadarrama (rail), Spain (2007)	28.38	17.63
Taihang, China (rail) (2008)	27.85	17.31
London Underground Northern Line, East Finchley–Morden (1939)	27.84	17.30
Hakkoda (rail), Japan (2010)	26.46	16.43
Iwate-Ichinoe (rail), Japan (2002)	25.81	16.03
Pajares (rail), Spain (2010)	24.67	15.32
Laerdal–Aurland Road Link, Norway (2000)	24.51	15.22
*Oshimizu (rail), Honshu, Japan (1982)	22.17	13.78
Wushaoling (rail), China (2007)	21.05	13.08
Simplon II (rail), Brigue, Switzerland–Iselle, Italy (1922)	19.82	12.31

* Sub-aqueous

The longest non-vehicular tunnelling in the world is the Delaware Aqueduct in New York State, USA, constructed in 1937–44 to a length of 168.9km (105 miles).
St Gotthard (rail) tunnel in Switzerland will be 57.07km (35.46 miles) long when completed in 2018.

BRITISH RAIL TUNNELS

	Length	
	km	miles
Severn, Bristol–Newport	6.88	4.28
Totley, Manchester–Sheffield	5.70	3.54
Standedge, Manchester–Huddersfield	4.89	3.04
Sodbury, Swindon–Bristol	4.06	2.53
Strood, Medway, Kent	3.61	2.24
Disley, Stockport–Sheffield	3.54	2.20
Ffestiniog, Llandudno–Blaenau Ffestiniog	3.53	2.19
Bramhope, Leeds–Harrogate	3.44	2.14
Cowburn, Manchester–Sheffield	3.39	2.10

The longest road tunnel in Britain is the Mersey Queensway Tunnel (1934), 3.43km (2.13 miles) long. The longest canal tunnel, at Standedge, W. Yorks, is 5.03km (3.13 miles) long; it was completed in 1811, closed in 1944 and reopened in 2001.

LONGEST SHIP CANALS

Canal	*Length*		*Min. depth*	
	km	miles	metres	feet
White Sea–Baltic (formerly Stalin) (1933), of which canalised river 51.5km (32 miles)	235	146.02	5.0	16.5
Rhine–Main–Danube, Germany (1992)	171	106.25	4.0	13.1
*Suez (1869), links Red and Mediterranean Seas	162	100.60	12.9	42.3
V. I. Lenin Volga–Don, Russia (1952), links Black and Caspian Seas	100	62.20	3.6	11.8
Kiel (or North Sea), Germany (1895), links North and Baltic Seas	98	60.90	13.7	45.0
*Houston, USA (1940), links inland city with Gulf of Mexico	91	56.70	10.4	34.0
Alphonse XIII, Spain (1926), gives Seville access to Atlantic Ocean	85	53.00	7.6	25.0
Panama (1914), links Pacific Ocean and Caribbean Sea; lake chain, 78.9km (49 miles) dug	82	50.71	12.5	41.0
Danube–Black Sea, Romania (1984)	64.4	40.02	7.0	23.0
Manchester Ship, UK (1894), links city with Irish Channel	64	39.70	8.5	28.0
Welland (1932), circumvents Niagara Falls and Rapids	43.5	27.00	8.8	29.0
Brussels (Rupel Sea), Belgium (1922), renders Brussels an inland port	32	19.80	6.4	21.0

* Has no locks

The first section of China's Grand Canal, running 1,782km (1,107 miles) from Beijing to Hangzhou, was opened in AD 610 and completed in 1283. Today it is limited to 2,000-tonne vessels.

The St Lawrence Seaway comprises the Beauharnois, Welland and Welland Bypass and Seaway 54–59 canals, and allows access to Duluth, Minnesota, USA via the Great Lakes from the Atlantic end of Canada's Gulf of St Lawrence, a distance of 3,769km (2,342 miles). The St Lawrence Canal, completed in 1959, is 293km (182 miles) long.

DISTANCES FROM LONDON BY AIR

The following list details the distances from Heathrow Airport in London to various airports worldwide. Airport name, if different from its location, and the International Air Transport Association (IATA) airport codes are given in brackets.

To	*Km*	*Miles*
Abu Dhabi (AUH)	5,512	3,425
Acapulco (Gen. Juan N. Álvarez, ACA)	9,177	5,702
Accra (Kotoka, ACC)	5,097	3,167
Addis Ababa (Bole, ADD)	5,915	3,675
Adelaide (ADL)	16,283	10,111
Aden (ADE)	5,907	3,670
Alexandria (Borg El Arab, HBE)	3,365	2,091
Algiers (Houari Boumediene, ALG)	1,666	1,035
Amman (Queen Alia, AMM)	3,681	2,287
Amsterdam (Schiphol, AMS)	370	230
Anchorage (Ted Stevens, ANC)	7,196	4,472
Ankara (Esenboga, ESB)	2,848	1,770
Atlanta (Hartsfield-Jackson, ATL)	6,756	4,198
Auckland (AKL)	18,353	11,404
Bali (Ngurah Rai, DPS)	12,518	7,779
Bangkok (Suvarnabhumi, BKK)	9,540	5,928
Barcelona (El Prat, BCN)	1,146	712
Beijing (Capital, PEK)	8,148	5,063
Beirut (Rafic Hariri, BEY)	3,478	2,161
Belfast (BFS)	524	325
Belgrade (Nikola Tesla, BEG)	1,700	1,056
Belize City (Philip S. W. Goldson, BZE)	8,340	5,182
Benghazi (Benina, BEN)	2,734	1,699
Berlin (Tegel, TXL)	947	588
Bogotá (El Nuevo Dorado, BOG)	8,468	5,262
Boston (Logan, BOS)	5,239	3,255
Brasilia (Presidente Juscelino Kubitschek, BSB)	8,775	5,452
Bratislava (M. R. Stefanika, BTS)	1,315	817
Brazzaville (Maya Maya, BZV)	6,368	3,957
Bridgetown (Grantley Adams, BGI)	6,748	4,193
Brisbane (BNE)	16,533	10,273
Brussels (BRU)	349	217
Bucharest (Henri Coanda, OTP)	2,103	1,307
Budapest (Ferihegy, BUD)	1,486	923
Buenos Aires-Ezeiza (Ministro Pistarini, EZE)	11,129	6,915
Cairo (CAI)	3,531	2,194
Calgary (YYC)	7,012	4,357
Canberra (CBR)	16,999	10,563
Cape Town (CPT)	9,675	6,011
Caracas (Simón Bolívar, CCS)	7,466	4,639
Cardiff (CWL)	200	124
Casablanca (Mohammed V, CMN)	2,092	1,300
Chennai (MAA)	8,229	5,113
Chicago (O'Hare, ORD)	6,343	3,941
Cologne/Bonn (Konrad Adenauer, CGN)	533	331
Colombo (Bandaranaike, CMB)	8,708	5,411
Copenhagen (Kastrup, CPH)	978	608
Dallas/Fort Worth (DFW)	7,622	4,736
Damascus (DAM)	3,577	2,223
Dar es Salaam (Julius Nyerere, DAR)	7,502	4,662
Darwin (DRW)	13,861	8,613
Denver (DEN)	7,492	4,655
Dhaka (Zia, DAC)	8,008	4,976
Doha (DOH)	5,235	3,253
Douala (DLA)	5,356	3,328
Dresden (DRS)	987	613
Dubai (DXB)	5,494	3,414
Dublin (DUB)	449	279
Dubrovnik (DBV)	1,727	1,073
Dundee (DND)	579	359
Durban (DUR)	9,555	5,937
Düsseldorf (DUS)	500	310
Edmonton (YEG)	6,805	4,229
Frankfurt (am Main, FRA)	653	406
Gaborone (Sir Seretse Khama, GBE)	8,842	5,494
Geneva (Cointrin, GVA)	754	468
Glasgow (GLA)	555	345
Gothenburg (Landvetter, GOT)	1,071	666
Gran Canaria (Las Palmas, LPA)	2,897	1,800
Guatemala City (La Aurora, GUA)	8,745	5,435
Hamburg (HAM)	745	463
Hannover (HAJ)	703	437
Harare (HRE)	8,298	5,156
Havana (José Martí, HAV)	7,479	4,647
Helsinki (Vantaa, HEL)	1,847	1,147
Hobart (HBA)	17,430	10,833
Ho Chi Minh City (Tan Son Nhat, SGN)	10,211	6,345
Hong Kong (HKG)	9,640	5,990
Honolulu (HNL)	11,619	7,220
Houston (George Bush Intercontinental, IAH)	7,759	4,821
Islamabad (Benazir Bhutto, ISB)	6,062	3,767
Isle of Man (Ronaldsway, IOM)	403	250
Istanbul (Ataturk, IST)	2,510	1,560
Jakarta (Soekarno-Hatta, CGK)	11,712	7,277
Jeddah (King Abdulaziz, JED)	4,743	2,947
Johannesburg (O. R. Tambo, JNB)	9,068	5,634
Kabul (Khwaja Rawash, KBL)	5,726	3,558
Karachi (Jinnah, KHI)	6,334	3,935
Kathmandu (Tribhuvan, KTM)	7,354	4,570
Khartoum (KRT)	4,943	3,071
Kiev (Boryspil, KBP)	2,184	1,357
Kigali (KGL)	6,600	4,101
Kilimanjaro (JRO)	7,055	4,384
Kingston, Jamaica (Norman Manley, KIN)	7,513	4,668
Kinshasa (N'Djili, FIH)	6,387	3,969
Kolkata (Netaji Subhas Chandra Bose, CCU)	7,979	4,958
Krakow (John Paul II, KRK)	1,425	886
Kuala Lumpur (KUL)	10,552	6,557
Kuwait (KWI)	4,671	2,903
Lagos (Murtala Muhammed, LOS)	5,000	3,107
Larnaca (LCA)	3,276	2,036
Lisbon (Portela, LIS)	1,564	972
Ljubljana (Joze Pucnik, LJU)	1,233	767
Lomé-Tokoin (Gnassingbe Eyadema, LFW)	5,036	3,129
Los Angeles (LAX)	8,753	5,439
Luanda (Quatro de Fevereiro, LAD)	6,830	4,243
Lusaka (LUN)	7,933	4,929

Luxor (LXR)	3,999	2,485
Lyon-Saint Exupéry (LYS)	759	472
Madrid (Barajas, MAD)	1,244	773
Málaga (AGP)	1,675	1,041
Malé (MLE)	8,533	5,302
Malmo (MMX)	1,017	632
Malta (MLA)	2,100	1,305
Manila (Ninoy Aquino, MNL)	10,758	6,685
Maputo (MPM)	9,184	5,707
Marrakech-Menara (RAK)	2,292	1,424
Marseille (Provence, MRS)	988	614
Melbourne (Tullamarine, MEL)	16,897	10,499
Memphis (MEM)	7,005	4,353
Menorca (Mahon, MAH)	1,339	832
Mexico City (Benito Juárez, MEX)	8,899	5,529
Miami (MIA)	7,104	4,414
Milan (Malpensa, MXP)	979	609
Minneapolis-St Paul (MSP)	6,439	4,001
Minsk (Minsk 2, MSQ)	1,893	1,176
Mombasa (Moi, MBA)	7,236	4,497
Montego Bay (Sangster, MBJ)	7,544	4,687
Montevideo (Carrasco, MVD)	11,010	6,841
Montréal (Pierre Elliott Trudeau, YUL)	5,213	3,239
Moscow (Domodedovo, DME)	2,543	1,580
Mumbai (Chhatrapati Shivaji, BOM)	7,207	4,478
Munich (Franz Josef Strauss, MUC)	940	584
Muscat (MCT)	5,828	3,621
Nairobi (Jomo Kenyatta, NBO)	6,837	4,249
Naples (Capodichino, NAP)	1,628	1,011
Nassau (Lynden Pindling, NAS)	6,973	4,333
Natal (Augusto Severo, NAT)	7,180	4,462
N'Djamena (NDJ)	4,588	2,851
Newark (Liberty, EWR)	5,558	3,454
New Delhi (Indira Gandhi, DEL)	6,727	4,180
New York (John F. Kennedy, JFK)	5,536	3,440
Nice (Côte d'Azur, NCE)	1,039	645
Novosibirsk (Tolmachevo, OVB)	5,216	3,241
Orlando (MCO)	6,954	4,321
Osaka (Kansai, KIX)	9,555	5,938
Oslo (Gardermoen, OSL)	1,206	749
Ostend-Bruges (OST)	232	144
Ottawa (Macdonald-Cartier, YOW)	5,344	3,321
Ouagadougou (OUA)	4,348	2,702
Palma de Mallorca (PMI)	1,347	836
Panama City (Tocumen, PTY)	8,448	5,249
Paris (Charles de Gaulle, CDG)	346	215
Penang (PEN)	10,277	6,386
Perth, Australia (PER)	14,497	9,008
Philadelphia (PHL)	5,686	3,533
Pisa (Galileo Galilei, PSA)	1,184	736
Port of Spain (Piarco, POS)	7,088	4,404
Prague (Ruzyne, PRG)	1,043	649
Québec (Jean Lesage, YQB)	4,979	3,093
*Quito (Mariscal Sucre, UIO)	9,188	5,709
Rabat (Sale, RBA)	2,001	1,243
Reykjavik (Keflavik, KEF)	1,895	1,177
Rhodes (Diagoras, RHO)	2,805	1,743
Riga (RIX)	1,695	1,054
Rimini (Federico Fellini, RMI)	1,275	793
Rio de Janeiro-Galeao (Antonio Carlos Jobim, GIG)	9,245	5,745
Riyadh (King Khaled, RUH)	4,936	3,067
Rome (Leonardo da Vinci-Fiumicino, FCO)	1,441	895
St Lucia (Hewanorra, UVF)	6,785	4,216
St Petersburg (Pulkovo, LED)	2,114	1,314
Salt Lake City (SLC)	7,806	4,850
Salzburg (W. A. Mozart, SZG)	1,048	651
San Diego (Lindbergh Field, SAN)	8,802	5,469
San Francisco (SFO)	8,610	5,351
Sao Paulo (Congonhas, CGH)	9,483	5,892
Sarajevo (SJJ)	1,636	1,017
Seoul (Incheon, ICN)	8,855	5,503
Seychelles (SEZ)	8,169	5,076
Shannon (SNN)	594	369
Shetland Islands (Sumburgh, LSI)	936	582
Singapore (Changi, SIN)	10,873	6,756
Skopje (Alexander the Great, SKP)	1,963	1,220
Sofia (Vrazhdebna, SOF)	2,038	1,266
Split-Kastela (SPU)	1,530	951
Stockholm (Arlanda, ARN)	1,461	908
Strasbourg (Entzheim, SXB)	663	412
Stuttgart (STR)	754	469
Suva (Nausori, SUV)	16,285	10,119
Sydney (Kingsford Smith, SYD)	17,008	10,568
Tahiti (Faa'a, PPT)	15,361	9,545
Taipei (Taiwan Taoyuan, TPE)	9,775	6,074
Tbilisi (TBS)	3,571	2,219
Tehran (Imam Khomeini, IKA)	4,420	2,747
Tel Aviv (Ben Gurion, TLV)	3,585	2,227
Thessaloniki (Macedonia, SKG)	2,164	1,345
Tokyo (Narita, NRT)	9,585	5,956
Toronto (Pearson, YYZ)	5,704	3,544
Tripoli (TIP)	2,362	1,468
Trondheim (Vaernes, TRD)	1,490	926
Tunis-Carthage (TUN)	1,830	1,137
Turin (Sandro Pertini, TRN)	917	570
Ulaanbaatar (Chinggis Khaan, ULN)	6,984	4,340
Vancouver (YVR)	7,574	4,707
Venice (Marco Polo, VCE)	1,150	715
Vienna (Schwechat, VIE)	1,272	790
Vladivostok (VVO)	8,526	5,298
Warsaw (Fryderyk Chopin, WAW)	1,468	912
Washington (Dulles, IAD)	5,898	3,665
Wellington (WLG)	18,817	11,692
Yangon (Mingaladon, RGN)	8,984	5,582
Zagreb (Pleso, ZAG)	1,365	848
Zürich-Kloten (ZRH)	787	490

* Quito Mariscal Sucre is due to be replaced in October 2010 by New Quito International Airport

TIME ZONES

Standard time differences from the Greenwich meridian

+ hours ahead of GMT
– hours behind GMT
* may vary from standard time at some part of the year (Summer Time or Daylight Saving Time)
† some areas may keep another time zone
‡ unofficial time zone
h hours
m minutes

	h	*m*
Afghanistan	+ 4	30
*Albania	+ 1	
Algeria	+ 1	
*Andorra	+ 1	
Angola	+ 1	
Antigua and Barbuda	– 4	
*†Argentina	– 3	
*Armenia	+ 4	
*Australia		
*ACT, NSW (except Broken Hill area and Lord Howe Island), Tas, Vic, Whitsunday Islands	+ 10	
Northern Territory	+ 9	30
Queensland	+ 10	
*South Australia	+ 9	30
*†Western Australia	+ 8	
Christmas Island (Indian Ocean)	+ 7	
Cocos (Keeling) Islands	+ 6	30
Norfolk Island	+ 11	30
*Austria	+ 1	
*Azerbaijan	+ 4	
*Bahamas	– 5	
Bahrain	+ 3	
*Bangladesh	+ 6	
Barbados	– 4	
*Belarus	+ 2	
*Belgium	+ 1	
Belize	– 6	
Benin	+ 1	
Bhutan	+ 6	
Bolivia	– 4	
*Bosnia and Hercegovina	+ 1	
Botswana	+ 2	
*Brazil		
*central states	– 4	
*N. and N. E. coastal states	– 2	
*S. and E. coastal states, including Brasilia	– 3	
*Fernando de Noronha Island	– 2	
Brunei	+ 8	
*Bulgaria	+ 2	
Burkina Faso	0	
Burundi	+ 2	
Cambodia	+ 7	
Cameroon	+ 1	
*Canada		
*Alberta	– 7	
*†British Columbia	– 8	
*Manitoba	– 6	
*New Brunswick	– 4	
*†Newfoundland and Labrador	– 3	30
*†Northwest Territories	– 7	
*Nova Scotia	– 4	
*Nunavut		
central	– 6	
eastern	– 5	
mountain	– 7	
*Ontario		
east of 90° W.	– 5	
west of 90° W.	– 6	
*Prince Edward Island	– 4	
*Québec		
east of 63° W.	– 4	
*west of 63° W.	– 5	
*†Saskatchewan	– 6	
*Yukon	– 8	
Cape Verde	– 1	
Central African Republic	+ 1	
Chad	+ 1	
*Chile	– 4	
*Easter Island	– 6	
China (inc. Hong Kong and Macau)	+ 8	
Colombia	– 5	
The Comoros	+ 3	
Congo, Dem. Rep. of		
eastern	+ 2	
western	+ 1	
Congo, Republic of	+ 1	
Costa Rica	– 6	
Côte d'Ivoire	0	
*Croatia	+ 1	
*Cuba	– 5	
*Cyprus	+ 2	
*Czech Republic	+ 1	
*Denmark	+ 1	
*Faeroe Islands	0	
*Greenland	– 3	
Danmarks Havn, Mesters Vig	0	
*Scoresby Sund	– 1	
Thule area	– 4	
Djibouti	+ 3	
Dominica	– 4	
Dominican Republic	– 4	
Ecuador	– 5	
Galápagos Islands	– 6	
*Egypt	+ 2	
El Salvador	– 6	
Equatorial Guinea	+ 1	
Eritrea	+ 3	
*Estonia	+ 2	
Ethiopia	+ 3	
Fiji	+ 12	
*Finland	+ 2	
*France	+ 1	
French Guiana	– 3	
†French Polynesia	– 10	
Guadeloupe	– 4	
Martinique	– 4	
Mayotte	+ 3	
New Caledonia	+ 11	
St Barthélemy	– 4	
Réunion	+ 4	
*St Pierre and Miquelon	– 3	
Wallis and Futuna	+ 12	
Gabon	+ 1	
The Gambia	0	
Georgia	+ 4	
*Germany	+ 1	
Ghana	0	
*Greece	+ 2	
Grenada	– 4	
Guatemala	– 6	
Guinea	0	
Guinea-Bissau	0	
Guyana	– 4	
Haiti	– 5	
Honduras	– 6	
*Hungary	+ 1	
Iceland	0	
India	+ 5	30
Indonesia		
Java, Kalimantan (west and central), Madura, Sumatra	+ 7	
Bali, Flores, Kalimantan (south and east), Lombok, Sulawesi, Sumbawa, West Timor	+ 8	
Irian Jaya, Maluku	+ 9	
*Iran	+ 3	30
Iraq	+ 3	
*Ireland, Republic of	0	
*Israel	+ 2	
*Italy	+ 1	
Jamaica	– 5	
Japan	+ 9	
*Jordan	+ 2	
Kazakhstan		
western	+ 5	
eastern	+ 6	
Kenya	+ 3	
Kiribati	+ 12	
Line Islands	+ 14	
Phoenix Islands	+ 13	
Korea, Dem. People's Rep. of	+ 9	
Korea, Republic of	+ 9	
Kosovo	+ 1	

	h m
Kuwait	+ 3
Kyrgyzstan	+ 6
Laos	+ 7
*Latvia	+ 2
*Lebanon	+ 2
Lesotho	+ 2
Liberia	0
Libya	+ 2
*Liechtenstein	+ 1
*Lithuania	+ 2
*Luxembourg	+ 1
*Macedonia	+ 1
Madagascar	+ 3
Malawi	+ 2
Malaysia	+ 8
Maldives	+ 5
Mali	0
*Malta	+ 1
Marshall Islands	+ 12
Mauritania	0
*Mauritius	+ 4
*Mexico	– 6
*Chihuahua, Nayarit, Sinaloa, S. Baja California	– 7
*N. Baja California	– 8
Sonora	– 7
Micronesia, Fed. States of	
Chuuk, Yap	+ 10
Kosrae, Pingelap, Pohnpei	+ 11
*Moldova	+ 2
*Monaco	+ 1
†Mongolia	+ 8
*Montenegro	+ 1
Morocco	0
Mozambique	+ 2
Myanmar	+ 6 30
*Namibia	+ 1
Nauru	+ 12
Nepal	+ 5 45
*The Netherlands	+ 1
Aruba	– 4
Netherlands Antilles	– 4
*New Zealand	+ 12
*Chatham Islands	+ 12 45
Cook Islands	– 10
Niue	– 11
Tokelau Island	– 10
Nicaragua	– 6
Niger	+ 1
Nigeria	+ 1
*Norway	+ 1
*Svalbard, Jan Mayen	+ 1
Oman	+ 4
Pakistan	+ 5
Palau	+ 9
*Palestinian Autonomous Areas	+ 2
Panama	– 5
Papua New Guinea	+ 10
*Paraguay	– 4
Peru	– 5
The Philippines	+ 8
*Poland	+ 1
*Portugal	0
*Azores	– 1
*Madeira	0
Qatar	+ 3
*Romania	+ 2
*Russia	
*Zone 1	+ 2
*Zone 2	+ 3
*Zone 3	+ 4
*Zone 4	+ 5
*Zone 5	+ 6
*Zone 6	+ 7
*Zone 7	+ 8
*Zone 8	+ 9
*Zone 9	+ 10
*Zone 10	+ 11
*Zone 11	+ 12
Rwanda	+ 2
St Kitts and Nevis	– 4
St Lucia	– 4
St Vincent and the Grenadines	– 4
*Samoa	– 11
*San Marino	+ 1
Sao Tome and Príncipe	0
Saudi Arabia	+ 3
Senegal	0
*Serbia	+ 1
Seychelles	+ 4
Sierra Leone	0
Singapore	+ 8
*Slovakia	+ 1
*Slovenia	+ 1
Solomon Islands	+ 11
Somalia	+ 3
South Africa	+ 2
*Spain	+ 1
*Canary Islands	0
Sri Lanka	+ 5 30
Sudan	+ 3
Suriname	– 3
Swaziland	+ 2
*Sweden	+ 1
*Switzerland	+ 1
*Syria	+ 2
Taiwan	+ 8
Tajikistan	+ 5
Tanzania	+ 3
Thailand	+ 7
Timor–Leste	+ 9
Togo	0
Tonga	+ 13
Trinidad and Tobago	– 4
Tunisia	+ 1
*Turkey	+ 2
Turkmenistan	+ 5
Tuvalu	+ 12
Uganda	+ 3
*Ukraine	+ 2
United Arab Emirates	+ 4
*United Kingdom	0
Anguilla	– 4
*Bermuda	– 4
†‡British Antarctic Territory	– 3
British Indian Ocean Territory	+ 6
British Virgin Islands	– 4
Cayman Islands	– 5
*Channel Islands	0
*Falkland Islands	– 4
*Gibraltar	+ 1
Montserrat	– 4
Pitcairn Islands	– 8
St Helena and Dependencies	0
South Georgia and South Sandwich Islands	– 2
*Turks and Caicos Islands	– 5
*United States of America	
*Alaska	– 9
Aleutian Islands, east of 169′ 30′ W.	– 9
Aleutian Islands, west of 169′ 30′ W.	– 10
*central time	– 6
*eastern time	– 5
Guam	+ 10
Hawaii	– 10
*mountain time	– 7
Northern Mariana Islands	+ 10
*Pacific time	– 8
Puerto Rico	– 4
Samoa, American	– 11
Virgin Islands	– 4
*Uruguay	– 3
Uzbekistan	+ 5
Vanuatu	+ 11
*Vatican City State	+ 1
Venezuela	– 4 30
Vietnam	+ 7
Western Sahara	0
Yemen	+ 3
Zambia	+ 2

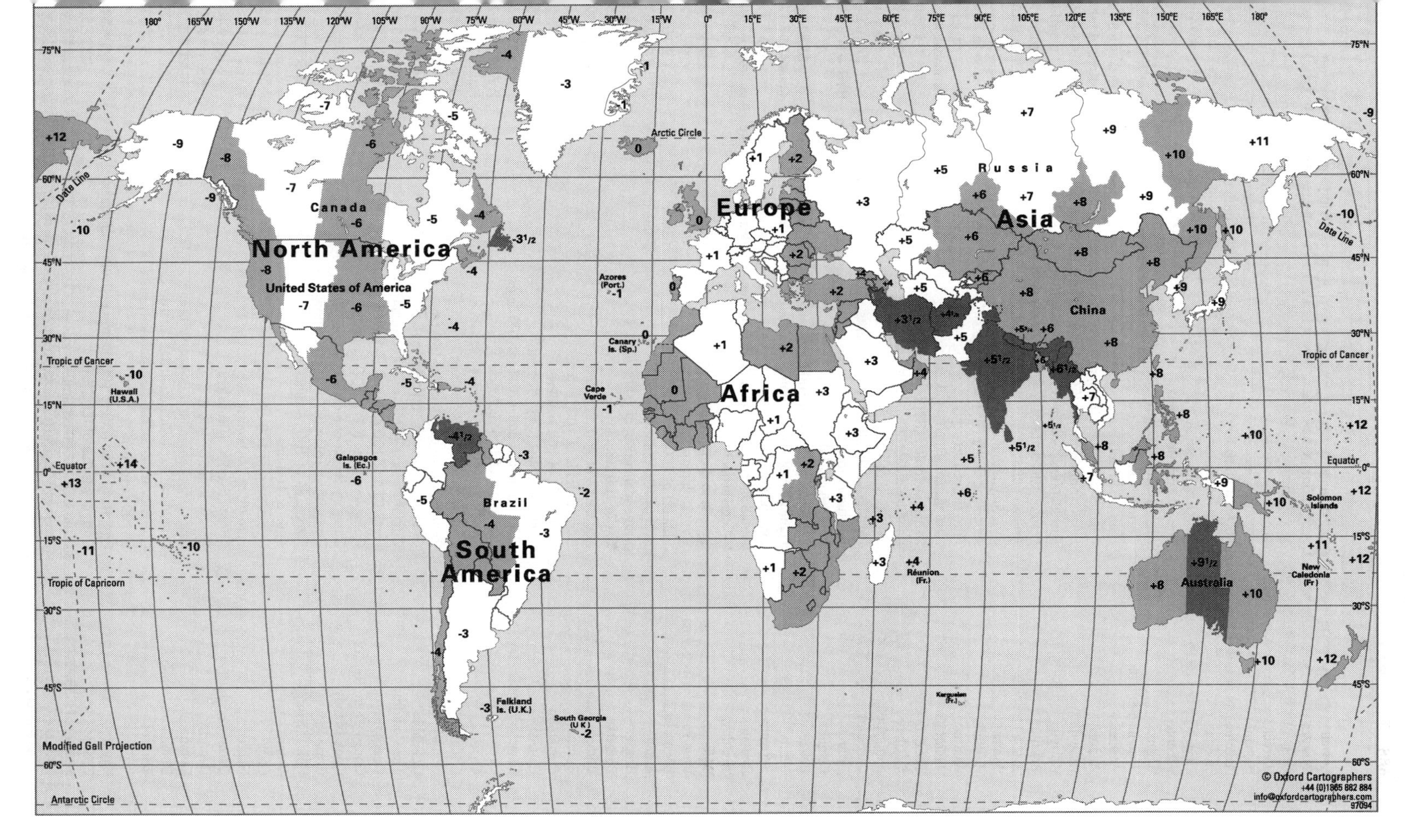
North America
Canada
United States of America
South America
Brazil
Europe
Africa
Asia
Russia
China
Australia
Arctic Circle
Tropic of Cancer
Equator
Tropic of Capricorn
Antarctic Circle
Date Line
Hawaii (U.S.A.)
Galapagos Is. (Ec.)
Azores (Port.)
Canary Is. (Sp.)
Cape Verde
Falkland Is. (U.K.)
South Georgia (U.K.)
Réunion (Fr.)
Kerguelen (Fr.)
Solomon Islands
New Caledonia (Fr.)
Modified Gall Projection
© Oxford Cartographers
+44 (0)1865 882 884
info@oxfordcartographers.com
97094

CURRENCIES AND EXCHANGE RATES

Average rate against £1 sterling on 30 April 2010

COUNTRY/TERRITORY	CURRENCY	VALUE
Albania	Lek (Lk) of 100 qindarka	Lk 158.61
Algeria	Algerian dinar (DA) of 100 centimes	DA 112.37
American Samoa	Currency is that of the USA	US$1.53
Andorra	Euro (€) of 100 cents	€1.15
Angola	Readjusted kwanza (Krzl) of 100 centimos	Kzrl 143.09
Anguilla	East Caribbean dollar (EC$) of 100 cents	EC$4.13
Antigua and Barbuda	East Caribbean dollar (EC$) of 100 cents	EC$4.13
Argentina	Peso of 100 centavos	Pesos 5.95
Aruba	Aruban guilder	Guilder 2.74
Ascension Island	Currency is that of St Helena	—
Australia	Australian dollar ($A) of 100 cents	$A1.64
Austria	Euro (€) of 100 cents	€1.15
Azerbaijan	New manat of 100 gopik	New manat 1.23
The Bahamas	Bahamian dollar (B$) of 100 cents	B$1.53
Bahrain	Bahraini dinar (BD) of 1,000 fils	BD 0.58
Bangladesh	Taka (Tk) of 100 poisha	Tk 106.02
Barbados	Barbados dollar (BD$) of 100 cents	BD$3.06
Belarus	Belarusian rouble of 100 kopeks	BYR 4,533.79
Belgium	Euro (€) of 100 cents	€1.15
Belize	Belize dollar (BZ$) of 100 cents	BZ$2.98
Benin	Franc CFA of 100 centimes	Francs 755.12
Bermuda	Bermuda dollar of 100 cents	$1.53
Bhutan	Ngultrum of 100 chetrum (Indian currency is also legal tender)	Ngultrum 67.90
Bolivia	Boliviano ($b) of 100 centavos	$b10.75
Bosnia and Hercegovina	Convertible marka of 100 fenings	Mark 2.25
Botswana	Pula (P) of 100 thebe	P 10.41
Brazil	Real of 100 centavos	Real 2.65
Brunei	Brunei dollar (B$) of 100 sen	B$2.10
Bulgaria	Lev of 100 stotinki	Leva 2.25
Burkina Faso	Franc CFA of 100 centimes	Francs 755.12
Burundi	Burundi franc of 100 centimes	Francs 1,882.86
Cameroon	Franc CFA of 100 centimes	Francs 755.12
Canada	Canadian dollar (C$) 100 cents	C$1.55
Cayman Islands	Cayman Islands dollar (CI$) of 100 cents	CI$1.26
Central African Republic	Franc CFA of 100 centimes	Francs 755.12
Chad	Franc CFA of 100 centimes	Francs 755.12
Chile	Chilean peso of 100 centavos	Pesos 790.58
China	Renminbi yuan of 10 jiao or 100 fen	Yuan 10.45
Colombia	Colombian peso of 100 centavos	Pesos 2,986.83
The Comoros	Comorian franc (KMF) of 100 centimes	Francs 566.34
Congo, Rep. of	Franc CFA of 100 centimes	Francs 755.12
Congo, Dem. Rep. of	Congolese franc (CFr) of 100 cents	CFr 1,370.43
Cook Islands	Currency is that of New Zealand	NZ$2.10
Costa Rica	Costa Rican colón (C) of 100 céntimos	C782.12
Côte d'Ivoire	Franc CFA of 100 centimes	Francs 755.12
Croatia	Kuna of 100 lipa	Kuna 8.35
Cuba	Cuban peso of 100 centavos	Pesos 1.53
Cyprus	Euro (€) of 100 cents	€1.15
Czech Republic	Koruna (Kcs) of 100 haleru	Kcs 29.46
Denmark	Danish krone of 100 ore	Kroner 8.57
Dominica	East Caribbean dollar (EC$) of 100 cents	EC$4.13
Dominican Republic	Dominican Republic peso (RD$) of 100 centavos	RD$56.30
Ecuador	Currency is that of the USA (formerly sucre of 100 centavos)	US$1.53
Egypt	Egyptian pound (£E) of 100 piastres or 1,000 millièmes	£E8.51
El Salvador	Currency is that of the USA	US$1.53
Equatorial Guinea	Franc CFA of 100 centimes	Francs 755.12
Estonia	Kroon of 100 senti (expected to introduce the euro in Jan 2011)	Kroons 18.01

Ethiopia	Ethiopian birr (EB) of 100 cents	EB 20.68
Faeroe Islands	Currency is that of Denmark	Kroner 8.57
Falkland Islands	Falkland pound of 100 pence	£1.00
Fiji	Fiji dollar (F$) of 100 cents	F$2.94
Finland	Euro (€) of 100 cents	€1.15
France	Euro (€) of 100 cents	€1.15
French Guiana	Euro (€) of 100 cents	€1.15
French Polynesia	Franc CFP of 100 centimes	Francs 137.28
Gabon	Franc CFA of 100 centimes	Francs 755.12
Gambia	Dalasi (D) of 100 butut	D 41.33
Georgia	Lari of 100 tetri	Lari 2.71
Germany	Euro (€) of 100 cents	€1.15
Ghana	Cedi of 100 pesewas	Cedi 2.17
Gibraltar	Gibraltar pound of 100 pence	£1.00
Greece	Euro (€) of 100 cents	€1.15
Greenland	Currency is that of Denmark	Kroner 8.57
Grenada	East Caribbean dollar (EC$) of 100 cents	EC$4.13
Guadeloupe	Euro (€) of 100 cents	€1.15
Guam	Currency is that of the USA	US$1.53
Guatemala	Quetzal (Q) of 100 centavos	Q 12.28
Guinea	Guinea franc of 100 centimes	Francs 7,691.53
Guinea-Bissau	Franc CFA of 100 centimes	Francs 755.12
Haiti	Gourde of 100 centimes	Gourdes 60.84
Honduras	Lempira of 100 centavos	Lempiras 28.92
Hong Kong	Hong Kong (HK$) of 100 cents	HK$11.88
Hungary	Forint of 100 filler	Forints 308.21
Iceland	Icelandic krona (Kr) of 100 aurar	Kr 195.75
India	Indian rupee (Rs) of 100 paise	Rs 67.90
Indonesia	Rupiah (Rp) of 100 sen	Rp 13,797.28
Ireland, Republic of	Euro (€) of 100 cents	€1.15
Israel	Shekel of 100 agora	Shekels 5.69
Italy	Euro (€) of 100 cents	€1.15
Jamaica	Jamaican dollar (J$) of 100 cents	J$135.42
Japan	Yen of 100 sen	Yen 143.90
Jordan	Jordanian dinar (JD) of 10 dirhams	JD 1.08
Kazakhstan	Tenge of 100 tiyn	Tenge 224.15
Kenya	Kenyan shilling (Ksh) of 100 cents	Ksh 118.09
Kiribati	Currency is that of Australia	$A1.64
Korea, Republic of	Won of 100 jeon	Won 1,696.50
Kuwait	Kuwaiti dinar (KD) of 1,000 fils	KD 0.44
Kyrgyzstan	Som of 100 tyiyn	Som 69.25
Latvia	Lats of 100 santims	Lats 0.81
Lebanon	Lebanese pound (L£) of of 100 piastres	L£2,297.51
Lesotho	Loti (M) of 100 lisente	M 11.26
Liechtenstein	Currency is that of Switzerland	Francs 1.65
Lithuania	Litas of 100 centas	Litas 3.97
Luxembourg	Euro (€) of 100 cents	€1.15
Macao	Pataca of 100 avos	Pataca 12.24
Macedonia	Denar of 100 deni	Den 70.87
Madagascar	Ariary of 5 iraimbilanja	MGA 3,137.84
Malawi	Kwacha (K) of 100 tambala	MK 230.78
Malaysia	Malaysian ringgit (dollar) (RM) of 100 sen	RM 4.87
Maldives	Rufiyaa of 100 laaris	Rufiyaa 19.59
Mali	Franc CFA of 100 centimes	Francs 755.12
Malta	Euro (€) of 100 cents	€1.15
Marshall Islands	Currency is that of the USA	US$1.53
Martinique	Currency is that of France	€1.15
Mauritania	Ouguiya (UM) of 5 khoums	UM 412.51
Mauritius	Mauritius rupee of 100 cents	Rs 47.11
Mayotte	Currency is that of France	€1.15
Mexico	Peso of 100 centavos	Pesos 18.75
Micronesia, Federated States of	Currency is that of the USA	US$1.53
Moldova	Moldovan leu of 100 bani	MDL 19.38
Monaco	Euro (€) of 100 cents	€1.15
Mongolia	Tugrik of 100 mongo	Tugriks 2,099.29
Montenegro	Euro (€) of 100 cents	€1.15
Montserrat	East Caribbean dollar (EC$) of 100 cents	EC$4.13
Morocco	Dirham (DH) of 100 centimes	DH 12.84

Mozambique	New metical (MT) of 100 centavos	MT 51.85
Namibia	Namibian dollar of 100 cents	$11.26
Nauru	Currency is that of Australia	$A1.64
Nepal	Nepalese rupee of 100 paisa	Rs 108.64
The Netherlands	Euro (€) of 100 cents	€1.15
Netherlands Antilles	Netherlands Antilles guilder of 100 cents	Guilders 2.74
New Caledonia	Franc CFP of 100 centimes	Francs 137.28
New Zealand	New Zealand dollar (NZ$) of 100 cents	NZ$2.10
Nicaragua	Córdoba (C$) of 100 centavos	C$32.42
Niger	Franc CFA of 100 centimes	Francs 755.12
Nigeria	Naira (N) of 100 kobo	N 231.05
Niue	Currency is that of New Zealand	NZ$2.10
Norfolk Island	Currency is that of Australia	$A1.64
Northern Mariana Islands	Currency is that of the USA	US$1.53
Norway	Krone of 100 ore	Kroner 9.04
Oman	Rial Omani (OR) of 1,000 baisas	OR 0.59
Pakistan	Pakistan rupee of 100 paisa	Rs 128.57
Palau	Currency is that of the USA	US$1.53
Panama	Balboa of 100 centésimos (US notes are in circulation)	Balboa 1.53
Papua New Guinea	Kina (K) of 100 toea	K 4.21
Paraguay	Guaraní (Gs) of 100 céntimos	Gs 7,224.68
Peru	New Sol of 100 centimos	New Sol 4.36
The Philippines	Philippine peso (P) of 100 centavos	P 68.05
Pitcairn Islands	Currency is that of New Zealand	NZ$2.10
Poland	Zloty of 100 groszy	Zlotych 4.51
Portugal	Euro (€) of 100 cents	€1.15
Puerto Rico	Currency is that of the USA	US$1.53
Qatar	Qatar riyal of 100 dirhams	Riyals 5.57
Réunion	Currency is that of France	€1.15
Romania	New leu of 100 bani	Lei 4.75
Russian Federation	Rouble of 100 kopeks	Rbl 44.73
Rwanda	Rwanda franc of 100 centimes	Francs 882.24
St Helena	St Helena pound (£) of 100 pence	£1.00
St Kitts and Nevis	East Caribbean dollar (EC$) of 100 cents	EC$4.13
St Lucia	East Caribbean dollar (EC$) of 100 cents	EC$4.13
St Pierre and Miquelon	Currency is that of France	€1.15
St Vincent and the Grenadines	East Caribbean dollar (EC$) of 100 cents	EC$4.13
Samoa	Tala (S$) of 100 sene	S$3.79
San Marino	Euro (€) of 100 cents	€1.15
Saudi Arabia	Saudi riyal (SR) of 100 halala	SR 5.74
Senegal	Franc CFA of 100 centimes	Francs 755.12
Serbia	New dinar of 100 paras	New dinars 114.29
Seychelles	Seychelles rupee of 100 cents	Rs 18.32
Sierra Leone	Leone (Le) of 100 cents	Le 5,982.87
Singapore	Singapore dollar (S$) of 100 cents (fully interchangeable with Brunei currency)	S$2.10
Slovakia	Euro (€) of 100 cents	€1.15
Slovenia	Euro (€) of 100 cents	€1.15
Solomon Islands	Solomon Islands dollar (SI$) of 100 cents	SI$12.05
South Africa	Rand (R) of 100 cents	R 11.26
Spain	Euro (€) of 100 cents	€1.15
Sri Lanka	Sri Lankan rupee of 100 cents	Rs 174.42
Suriname	Surinamese dollar of 100 cents	Dollar 4.20
Swaziland	Lilangeni (E) of 100 cents (South African currency is also in circulation)	E 11.26
Sweden	Swedish krona of 100 ore	Kronor 11.10
Switzerland	Swiss franc of 100 rappen (or centimes)	Francs 1.65
Taiwan	New Taiwan dollar (NT$) of 100 cents	NT$47.97
Tanzania	Tanzanian shilling of 100 cents	Shillings 2,120.72
Thailand	Baht of 100 satang	Baht 49.52
Timor–Leste	Currency is that of the USA	US$1.53
Togo	Franc CFA of 100 centimes	Francs 755.12
Tokelau	Currency is that of New Zealand	NZ$2.10
Tonga	Pa'anga (T$) of 100 seniti	T$2.98
Trinidad and Tobago	Trinidad and Tobago dollar (TT$) of 100 cents	TT$9.72
Tristan da Cunha	Currency is that of the UK	—
Tunisia	Tunisian dinar of 1,000 millimes	Dinars 2.19
Turkey	New Turkish lira (TL) of 100 kurus	TL 2.27

Turks and Caicos Islands	Currency is that of the USA	US$1.53
Tuvalu	Currency is that of Australia	$A1.64
Uganda	Uganda shilling of 100 cents	Shillings 3,248.04
Ukraine	Hryvna of 100 kopiykas	UAH 12.13
United Arab Emirates	UAE dirham (Dh) of 100 fils	Dirham 5.62
United States of America	US dollar (US$) of 100 cents	US$1.53
Uruguay	Uruguayan peso of 100 centésimos	Pesos 29.47
Uzbekistan	Sum of 100 tiyin	Sum 2,397.67
Vanuatu	Vatu	Vatu 152.41
Vatican City State	Euro (€) of 100 cents	€1.15
Venezuela	Bolívar fuerte (Bs. F) of 100 céntimos	Bs. F 6.57
Vietnam	Dong of 10 hao or 100 xu	Dong 29,047.92
Virgin Islands, British	Currency is that of the USA (£ sterling and EC$ also circulate)	US$1.53
Virgin Islands, US	Currency is that of the USA	US$1.53
Wallis and Futuna Islands	Franc CFP of 100 centimes	Francs 137.28
Yemen	Riyal of 100 fils	Riyals 344.85
Zambia	Kwacha (K) of 100 ngwee	K 7,262.94
Zimbabwe	Zimbabwe dollar (Z$) suspended April 2009; US dollar now base currency	US$1.53

Source: WM/Reuters Closing Spot Rates

TRAVEL OVERSEAS

PASSPORT REGULATIONS

Application forms for United Kingdom passports can be obtained from the UK Identity and Passport Service's (IPS) telephone advice line or website, regional passport offices, or from main post offices.

UK IDENTITY AND PASSPORT SERVICE
T 0300-222 0000
W www.direct.gov.uk/en/travelandtransport/passports

REGIONAL OFFICES

- Hampton House, 47–53 High Street, Belfast BT1 2QS
- Millburngate House, Durham DH97 1PA
- 3 Northgate, 96 Milton Street, Cowcaddens, Glasgow G4 0BT
- 101 Old Hall Street, Liverpool L3 9BD
- Globe House, 89 Eccleston Square, London SW1V 1PN
- Olympia House, Upper Dock Street, Newport, Gwent NP20 1XA
- Aragon Court, Northminster Road, Peterborough PE1 1QG

The passport offices are open Monday to Saturday on an appointment-only basis (appointments should be arranged by calling the central telephone number listed above). For an additional fee, passport offices provide either a guaranteed same-day service (for renewals and minor amendments only) or a one-week fast-track service (all except new adult applications).

Standard postal applications are processed within three weeks. The completed application form should be posted, with the appropriate supporting documents and fee, to the regional passport office indicated on the addressed envelope which is provided with each application form. Accompanying cheques and postal orders should be made payable to 'Identity and Passport Service', or to 'Post Office Ltd' when using the Check & Send service. For online applications, the completed online form will be printed out by the Passport Office and posted to the applicant for them to sign and return. After the paper copy has been received, online applications are also returned within three weeks.

Applications can also be submitted through Check & Send outlets at selected main post offices, who, for a small handling charge, will forward the application form to the relevant regional passport office after having checked that it has been completed correctly and has the appropriate documents attached. These applications take a minimum of two weeks.

A passport cannot be issued or extended on behalf of a person already abroad; such persons should apply to the nearest British High Commission or Consulate.

UK passports are granted to:

- British citizens
- British nationals (overseas)
- British overseas territories citizens
- British subjects
- British protected persons

UK passports are generally available for travel to all countries. The possession of a passport does not exempt the holder from compliance with any immigration regulations in force in British or foreign countries, or from the necessity of obtaining a visa where required (*see* below for a list of countries for which UK citizens do not require a visa).

Biometric passports were introduced in 2006. The new design and security features, including a chip containing the biometrics (the facial image and biographical data of the holder), render the passport more secure against forgery and aid border controls.

ADULTS

A passport granted to a person over 16 will normally be valid for ten years. Thereafter, or if at any time the passport contains no further space for visas, a new passport must be obtained.

The issue of passports including details of the holder's spouse was discontinued in 1988.

British nationals born on or before 2 September 1929 are eligible for a free standard passport.

CHILDREN

Since 5 October 1998 all children under the age of 16 are required to have their own passport. This is primarily to help prevent child abductions. The passports are initially valid for five years, but can be renewed for a further five years at the end of this period. Any adult passport which includes children will have expired in or before 2008: the parent will need to renew their passport and apply for a separate first child passport for any children.

COUNTERSIGNATURES

A countersignature is needed if the application is for a first passport, to replace a lost, stolen or damaged passport, or to renew a passport for a child aged 11 or under. A countersignature is also needed for renewals if the applicant's appearance has significantly changed and the photograph in their previous passport is unrecognisable. The signatory must be willing to enter their own passport number on to the form. The list of acceptable countersignatories includes: MP; justice of the peace; minister of religion; a professionally qualified person (eg doctor, engineer, lawyer, teacher); bank officer; military officer; civil servant; police officer; or a person of similar standing who has known the applicant for at least two years, who lives in the UK and who holds a British or Irish passport. A relative or partner, someone living at the same address as the applicant, or an employee of the IPS must not countersign the application.

If the application is for a child under the age of 16, the countersignature should be by someone of relevant standing who has known the parent or person with parental responsibility who signs the declaration of consent, rather than the child.

PHOTOGRAPHS

Two identical, unmounted, recent colour photographs of the applicant must be sent. These photographs should measure 45mm by 35mm, be printed on plain white photographic paper and should be taken full face against a plain cream or light grey background. The photo must show the applicant's full face, looking straight at the camera, with a neutral expression and with their mouth closed. If a countersignature is required for the application, the person who countersigned the form should also certify one photograph as a true likeness of the applicant.

DOCUMENTATION

The applicant's birth certificate or previous British passport, and other documents in support of the statements made in the application, must be produced at the time of applying. Details of which documents are required are set out in the notes accompanying the application form.

If the passport applicant is a British national by naturalisation or registration, the certificate proving this must be produced with the application, unless the applicant holds a previous British passport issued after registration or naturalisation.

INTERVIEWS

Interviews for adults applying for their first passport (not including those who held their own passport as a child) were introduced on 1 June 2007 to combat passport fraud and forgery. After applying for a passport, applicants will be sent a letter asking them to book an interview at one of the 66 offices in the UK. Interviews last for approximately 30 minutes and applicants are asked to confirm facts about themselves that someone attempting to steal their identity would not know. The IPS recommends that new applicants now allow six weeks to receive their passport. There is no one-week fast-track service for first adult passports.

48-PAGE PASSPORTS

The 48-page 'jumbo' passport is intended to meet the needs of frequent travellers who fill standard passports well before the validity has expired. It is valid for ten years but is not available for children.

PASSPORT FEES*	
First adult passport	£77.50
First child passport	£49
Renewal or amendment of adult passport	£77.50
Renewal or amendment of child passport	£49
48-page passport	£90.50

* Standard postal applications only. A charge is added for applications made in person at a partner office in the UK, currently £8 for Check & Send at a post office

HEALTH ADVICE

The NHS Choices website provides health advice for those travelling abroad, including information on immunisations and reciprocal health agreements with other countries. *See* W www.nhs.uk/livewell/travelhealth

VISA REQUIREMENTS

The countries listed below do not require British citizens to hold a valid visa or tourist card before arrival on short visits. For longer visits – or for countries not listed – it is advisable to check specific visa requirements with the appropriate embassy before making final travel arrangements (*see* Countries of the World section for foreign embassy contact details).

All EU member states and their overseas territories (*see* The European Union) except Ascension Island and Tristan da Cunha, Albania, Andorra, Antigua and Barbuda, Argentina, Barbados, Belize, Bolivia, Bosnia and Hercegovina, Botswana, Brazil, Brunei, Canada, Chile, Colombia, Costa Rica, Cyprus, Dominica, Ecuador, El Salvador, Fiji, Gambia, Georgia, Grenada, Guatemala, Haiti, Hong Kong, Iceland, Israel, Jamaica, Japan, Kiribati, Republic of Korea (South Korea), Lebanon*, Liechtenstein, Macao, Macedonia, Malawi*, Malaysia, Marshall Islands, Mauritius, Mexico, Micronesia (Federated States of)*, Moldova, Monaco, Montenegro, Morocco, Namibia, Nicaragua, New Zealand, Norway, Palau, Panama, Paraguay, Peru, Philippines, Saint Lucia, Samoa, San Marino, Senegal, Serbia, Seychelles, Singapore, Solomon Islands, South Africa, St Kitts and Nevis, St Vincent and the Grenadines, Swaziland, Switzerland, Taiwan, Thailand†, Tonga, Trinidad and Tobago, Tunisia, Tuvalu, United Arab Emirates*, Uruguay, USA‡, Vanuatu, Vatican City, Venezuela†, Western Sahara.

* Upon entry to these countries a visa or tourist card will be issued at no extra charge

† Only applicable when arriving by air; those arriving at overland crossings or by sea should arrange documentation in advance

‡ Those travelling to the USA under the Visa Waiver Programme must provide details online at least 72 hours in advance of travel

The following countries bar entry to travellers with HIV or AIDS:

The Bahamas, Brunei, Equatorial Guinea, Iraq, Jordan, Papua New Guinea, Qatar, Russia, Singapore, Solomon Islands, Sudan, UAE and Yemen.

Residents of the following countries must hold a valid visa for every entry to the UK:

Afghanistan, Albania, Algeria, Angola, Armenia, Azerbaijan, Bahrain, Bangladesh, Belarus, Benin, Bhutan, Bolivia, Bosnia and Hercegovina, Burkina Faso, Burundi, Cambodia, Cameroon, Cape Verde, Central African Republic, Chad, China, Colombia, Comoros, Dem. Rep. of Congo, Rep. of Congo, Côte d'Ivoire, Cuba, Djibouti, Dominican Republic, Ecuador, Egypt, Equatorial Guinea, Eritrea, Ethiopia, Fiji, Gabon, Gambia, Georgia, Ghana, Guinea, Guinea-Bissau, Guyana, Haiti, India, Indonesia, Iran, Iraq, Jamaica, Jordan, Kazakhstan, Kenya, Dem. People's Republic of Korea, Kosovo, Kuwait, Kyrgyzstan, Laos, Lebanon, Lesotho, Liberia, Libya, Macedonia, Madagascar, Malawi, Mali, Mauritania, Moldova, Mongolia, Montenegro, Morocco, Mozambique, Myanmar, Nepal, Niger, Nigeria, Oman, Pakistan, Palestinian Authority, Peru, Philippines, Qatar, Russian Federation, Rwanda, Sao Tome and Príncipe, Saudi Arabia, Senegal, Serbia, Sierra Leone, Somalia, South Africa, Sri Lanka, Sudan, Suriname, Swaziland, Syria, Tajikistan, Tanzania, Thailand, Togo, Tunisia, Turkey (including northern Cyprus), Turkmenistan, Uganda, Ukraine, United Arab Emirates, Uzbekistan, Vatican City (holders of Holy See Service and Emergency Passports), Venezuela, Vietnam, Yemen, Zambia, Zimbabwe.

BAGGAGE RESTRICTIONS

As of April 2010, the Department for Transport no longer sets a maximum size for items of hand baggage. Individual airlines may set their own limits, and travellers should check these before arriving at the airport: oversize baggage may have to be checked in as hold luggage, which often incurs a fee. Since January 2008, some airports have allowed passengers to take more than one item into the aircraft cabin. Other airports in the UK still have a one-bag restriction in place, and individual airlines may operate their own policies. *See* W www.direct.gov.uk for more information on baggage restrictions.

THE EUROPEAN UNION

MEMBER STATE	ACCESSION DATE	POPULATION (2009)	COUNCIL VOTES	EP SEATS†
Austria	1 Jan 1995	8,355,260	10	17
Belgium	1 Jan 1958	10,750,000*	12	22
Bulgaria	1 Jan 2007	7,606,551	10	17
Cyprus	1 May 2004	796,875	4	6
Czech Republic	1 May 2004	10,467,542	12	22
Denmark	1 Jan 1973	5,511,451	7	13
Estonia	1 May 2004	1,340,415	4	6
Finland	1 Jan 1995	5,326,314	7	13
France	1 Jan 1958	64,350,759	29	72
Germany	1 Jan 1958	82,002,356	29	99
Greece	1 Jan 1981	11,260,402	12	22
Hungary	1 May 2004	10,030,975	12	22
Ireland	1 Jan 1973	4,450,014	7	12
Italy	1 Jan 1958	60,045,068	29	72
Latvia	1 May 2004	2,261,294	4	8
Lithuania	1 May 2004	3,349,872	7	12
Luxembourg	1 Jan 1958	493,500	4	6
Malta	1 May 2004	413,609	3	5
The Netherlands	1 Jan 1958	16,485,787	13	25
Poland	1 May 2004	38,135,876	27	50
Portugal	1 Jan 1986	10,627,250	12	22
Romania	1 Jan 2007	21,498,616	14	33
Slovakia	1 May 2004	5,412,254	7	13
Slovenia	1 May 2004	2,032,362	4	7
Spain	1 Jan 1986	45,828,172	27	50
Sweden	1 Jan 1995	9,256,347	10	18
United Kingdom	1 Jan 1973	61,634,599*	29	72

* Provisional figures

† The treaty of Lisbon allows for 18 additional MEPs distributed among 12 member states, but they cannot take their seats until all member states have ratified the change.

Sources: Eurostat; www.europa.eu

CHRONOLOGY

1950 Robert Schuman (French foreign minister) proposes that France and West Germany pool their coal and steel industries under a supranational authority (Schuman Plan)
1951 Paris treaty, signed by France, West Germany, Belgium, Italy, Luxembourg and the Netherlands, establishes the European Coal and Steel Community (ECSC)
1952 ECSC treaty enters into force
1957 Treaty of Rome, signed by the six ECSC member countries, establishes the European Economic Community (EEC) and the European Atomic Energy Authority (EURATOM). Treaty aims to create a customs union; remove obstacles to free movement of capital, goods, people and services; establish common external trade policy and common agricultural and fisheries policies; coordinate economic policies; harmonise social policies; and promote cooperation in nuclear research
1958 EEC and EURATOM begin operation. Joint parliament and Court of Justice established for all three communities, and the Commission, Council of the European Union, Economic and Social Committee and Investment Bank for the EEC established
1962 Common Agricultural Policy (CAP) agreed
1967 EEC, ECSC and EURATOM merge to form the European Communities (EC), with a single Council of the European Union and Commission
1968 EEC customs union completed
Implementation of CAP completed
1973 UK joins the European Communities
1974 Regular heads of governments summits begin
1975 'Own resources' funding of EC budget introduced
UK renegotiates its terms of accession
European Regional Development Fund created
1979 European Monetary System (EMS) comes into operation
First direct elections to European parliament
1984 Fontainebleau summit settles UK annual budget rebate and agrees first major CAP reform
1986 Single European Act (SEA) signed
European Political Cooperation (EPC) established
1991 Maastricht treaty agreed
1992 Single internal market programme completed
1993 The exchange rate mechanism (ERM) of the EMS effectively suspended
Maastricht treaty enters into force, establishing the European Union (EU)
1994 European Economic Area (EEA) agreement comes into operation
Norway rejects EU membership in referendum
1997 Amsterdam treaty agreed
1998 Eleven states chosen to enter first round of European Monetary Union (EMU)
1999 Euro launched
Amsterdam treaty enters into force
2000 Treaty of Nice agreed
ECSC treaty expires following transfer of coal and steel sectors to the treaty of Rome
2004 Cyprus, Czech Republic, Estonia, Hungary, Latvia, Lithuania, Malta, Poland, Slovakia and Slovenia become members of the EU
The European constitution is signed in Rome
2005 France and the Netherlands reject the European constitution
2007 Bulgaria and Romania join the EU
The EU celebrates its 50th birthday
EU leaders agree to the Lisbon treaty to replace the 2004 constitution
2008 Ireland votes against the treaty of Lisbon
2009 Ireland holds a second referendum in October – 67 per cent vote for the Lisbon treaty. The treaty enters into force on 1 December

LEGISLATIVE PROCESS

The core of the EU policy-making process is a dialogue between the European Commission, which initiates and implements policy, and the Council of the European Union and the European parliament, which take policy decisions.

The original legislative process is known as the consultation procedure. The commission drafts a proposal which it submits to the council and to the parliament. The council then consults the Economic and Social Committee, the parliament and the Committee of the Regions; the parliament may request that amendments are made. With or without these amendments, the proposal is then adopted by the council and becomes law. The consultation procedure now only applies to cases not specifically subject to one of the other procedures.

The Single European Act introduced the assent procedure (now the consent procedure), whereby an absolute majority of the parliament must vote to approve laws in certain fields before they are passed. Issues covered by the procedure include uniform procedure for elections, some international agreements, violation of human rights and the accession of new member states.

The Maastricht treaty introduced the co-decision procedure as an extension of the cooperation procedure; if, after the parliament's second reading of a proposal, the council and parliament fail to agree, a conciliation committee of the two will reach a compromise. If a compromise is not reached, the parliament can reject the legislation by the vote of an absolute majority of its members. The Amsterdam treaty extended the co-decision procedure to all areas covered by qualified majority voting, with the exception of measures related to the European Monetary Union.

The Lisbon treaty extended the use of the co-decision procedure to several new fields, and renamed it the ordinary legislative procedure. The treaty strengthens the role of the European parliament so that it is involved in almost all new legislation. The changes give the European parliament equal powers in areas such as legal immigration, crime prevention and police cooperation. As a result of the Lisbon treaty, the Council of the European Union must now vote in public on any new legislation, and if one third of national parliaments disagree with a proposal then it can be sent back to be reviewed.

The council, commission and parliament can issue the following legislation:

- regulations, which are binding in their entirety and directly applicable to all member states; they do not need to be incorporated into national law to come into effect

- directives, which are less specific, binding as to the result to be achieved but leaving the method of implementation open to member states; a directive thus has no force until it is incorporated into national law
- decisions, which are also binding but are addressed solely to one or more member states or individuals in a member state
- recommendations or opinions, which are merely persuasive

The council and parliament also have certain budgetary powers and determine all expenditure together. The final decision on whether the budget should be adopted or rejected lies with the parliament.

The European Central Bank has legislative powers within its field of competence. The commission also has limited legislative powers, where it has been delegated the power to implement or revise legislation by the council.

RECENT LEGISLATION

SCHENGEN AGREEMENT

The Schengen agreement was signed by France, Germany, Belgium, Luxembourg and the Netherlands in 1985. The agreement committed the five states to abolishing internal border controls, erecting external frontiers against illegal immigrants, drug traffickers, terrorists and organised crime, and implementing the Schengen Information System to enable police stations and consular agents from Schengen member states to access data on specific individuals or vehicles and objects which are lost or stolen.

Subsequently signed by Spain and Portugal, the agreement was ratified by the seven signatory states and entered into force in March 1995 with the removal of internal frontier, passport, customs and immigration controls. Italy and Austria became full members of the agreement in 1997; Greece in 2000; and Denmark, Sweden and Finland in 2001. The Czech Republic, Estonia, Hungary, Latvia, Lithuania, Malta, Poland, Slovakia and Slovenia joined in 2007. Although not members of the EU, Norway and Iceland joined the agreement in 2001 and Switzerland in 2008. The UK and the Republic of Ireland have not signed the agreement and are only partial participants, since their border controls have been maintained. In May 2009 Sweden blocked Liechtenstein's accession to the Schengen agreement on financial grounds. There is no date set for Cyprus, Bulgaria or Romania to join.

The Schengen agreement originated as an intergovernmental agreement but became part of the EU following the signing of the Amsterdam treaty. A second generation Schengen Information System (SIS II), which will cater for the newest member states, is under development, but with delays due to legal and technical problems.

MAASTRICHT TREATY

Agreed in Maastricht, the Netherlands, in 1991, the treaty came into effect in November 1993 following ratification by the member states. Three pillars formed its basis:

- the European Community (EC) (removing Economic from its name) with its established institutions and decision-making processes
- a common foreign and security policy (*see* below) with the Western European Union as the potential defence component of the EU
- cooperation in justice and home affairs, with the Council of the European Union coordinating policies on asylum, immigration, conditions of entry, cross-border crime, drug trafficking and terrorism

The treaty established a common European citizenship for nationals of all member states and introduced the principle of subsidiarity, whereby decisions are taken at the most appropriate level (national, regional or local). It extended EC competency into the areas of environmental and industrial policies, consumer affairs, health, and education and training, and extended qualified majority voting in the Council of the European Union to some areas which had previously required a unanimous vote. The powers of the European parliament over the budget and over the European Commission were also enhanced, and a co-decision procedure enabled the parliament to override decisions made by the council in certain policy areas. A separate protocol to the Maastricht treaty on social policy was agreed by 11 states and was incorporated into the Amsterdam treaty in 1997 following adoption by the UK.

COMMON FOREIGN AND SECURITY POLICY

The common foreign and security policy (CFSP) was created as a pillar of the EU by the Maastricht treaty (*see* above). It adopted the machinery of the European political cooperation framework, which it replaced, and was charged with providing a forum for member states and EU institutions to consult on foreign affairs.

The CFSP system is headed by the European Council, which provides general lines of policy. Specific policy decisions are taken by the General Affairs and External Relations Council, which meets at least once a month to determine areas for joint action. The high representative of the CFSP initiates action, manages the CFSP and represents it abroad. The Council of the European Union is supported by the Political and Security Committee, which meets monthly, or within 48 hours if there is a crisis, to prepare for ministerial discussions. A group of correspondents, designated diplomats in each member's foreign ministry, provides day-to-day contact.

As part of the CFSP the EU also created the common security and defence policy (CSDP), originally named the European security and defence policy, with the potential, if agreed later on, for creating a common defence structure. In the recent past, missions have been deployed in Kosovo, Georgia and the Democratic Republic of the Congo. The member states agreed at the Helsinki summit in 1999 to establish a capability for military crisis-management operations, known as the rapid reaction force, which would have a credible intervention capability and be able to undertake peacemaking missions independently of NATO. The force was declared operational at the Laeken summit in 2001.

The Amsterdam treaty introduced qualified majority voting for foreign affairs and created a high representative of CFSP to act as a spokesperson. It also established a new planning and early warning unit to monitor international developments and provide the opportunity for the EU to react to these developments with a cohesive response. The Lisbon treaty merged the three pillars of the EU. It created a high representative of the union for foreign affairs and security policy to replace the high representative of CFSP, and will lead to the dissolution of the Western European Union (*see* International Organisations).

AMSTERDAM TREATY

The treaties of Rome and Maastricht were amended through the Amsterdam treaty, which was signed in 1997 and came into effect on 1 May 1999. It extended the scope of qualified majority voting and the powers of the European parliament. It also included a formal commitment to fundamental human rights, gave additional powers to the European Court of Justice and provided for the reform of the CFSP.

LISBON TREATY

The treaty of Lisbon was drawn up to replace the original European constitution, which was rejected in referendums in France and the Netherlands in 2005. It amends, rather than replaces, existing European Union and European Community treaties. Ireland, the only country to hold a referendum on the Lisbon treaty, voted against ratification on 12 June 2008. It held a second referendum on 2 October 2009 where 67 per cent voted in favour, and – as a result of all EU countries approving the treaty – it came into force on 1 December 2009.

The Lisbon treaty granted 'legal personality' (the right under international law to adopt laws and treaties) to the European Union. The three pillars created by the Maastricht treaty (*see* above) merged to make the European Union a single legal entity, replacing the European Community. The Lisbon treaty introduced a number of changes to the EU: a new president was appointed to the European Council for a two-and-a-half year term to replace the previous system of a six-month rotating presidency (this still exists in a reduced capacity for the Council of the European Union). The position of High Representative of the Union for Foreign Affairs and Security Policy was created, to enhance the EU's relations with other countries. The European parliament was strengthened and given more legislative and budgetary powers, and the number of MEPs was set at 751 from the 2014 election onwards. The system of qualified majority voting was extended to new policy areas and from 2014 will be based on a double majority of member states and people; a decision must be agreed by 55 per cent of member states representing at least 65 per cent of the EU population. The treaty establishes the principle of 'mutual recognition', where each member state acknowledges that legal decisions by other member states are valid; the UK has an opt-out clause with regard to some policies such as external borders, asylum and immigration.

ENLARGEMENT AND EXTERNAL RELATIONS

The procedure for accession to the EU is laid down in the treaty of Rome; states must be stable European democracies governed by the rule of law with free-market economies. A membership application is studied by the European Commission, which produces an 'opinion'. If the opinion is positive, negotiations may be opened leading to an accession treaty that must be approved by all member state governments and parliaments, the European parliament, and the applicant state's government and parliament.

Cyprus, the Czech Republic, Estonia, Hungary, Latvia, Lithuania, Malta, Poland, Slovakia and Slovenia became full members of the EU on 1 May 2004. Bulgaria and Romania joined the EU on 1 January 2007. The European Council recalled the offer of an accession partnership to Turkey in 2002, following the commission's conclusion that Turkey did not yet fully meet the required political criteria. However, at its December 2004 meeting in Brussels, the council decided that Turkey sufficiently met the Copenhagen political criteria, and accession negotiations began in October 2005. Accession talks with Croatia, scheduled to start in March 2005 but postponed due to the lack of full cooperation with the UN war crimes tribunal, began in October 2005. Macedonia was granted candidate status in December 2005. There are currently six potential candidates for membership of the EU.

The EU has several types of agreements with other European and non-European states. Association agreements can include commitments to reforming the country's trade, human rights, economy or political system in exchange for financial assistance or trade agreements. Countries that have signed agreements include Algeria, Egypt, Israel, Morocco and Turkey. Partnership and cooperation agreements (PCAs) are legal frameworks, based on the respect of democratic principles and human rights, setting out the political, economic and trade relationship between the EU and its partner countries. Each PCA is a ten-year bilateral treaty signed and ratified by the EU and the individual state. After the ten-year period expires the agreements are automatically renewed annually unless one of the parties objects. Agreements have been implemented with Russia (1997), Ukraine and Moldova (1998), Armenia, Azerbaijan, Georgia, Kazakhstan, Kyrgyzstan and Uzbekistan (1999). PCAs have also been signed with Belarus (1995), Turkmenistan (1998) and Tajikistan (2004) but are not yet in force. In 2003 the PCA council summit decreed to strengthen EU cooperation with the Russian Federation by establishing a permanent partnership council (PPC). At the council's first meeting in April 2004 a protocol was signed, extending the PCA with the Russian Federation to the ten new member states of the EU; the agreement currently in place also covers Romania and Bulgaria.

Trade and cooperation agreements are intended to foster trade and economic relations, and include a commitment to respect the human rights and democratic principles of both parties. The European Commission has negotiated around 120 agreements worldwide. The European neighbourhood policy was developed in 2004 and applies to the enlarged EU's immediate neighbours. It aims to strengthen stability and security through economic integration and deeper political relationships based on a mutual commitment to common values (democracy, human rights, rule of law, good governance and market economy).

A stabilisation and association agreement (SAA) – which is tailored towards the western Balkan states and is similar to the earlier Europe agreements held with previous candidate countries, in that it provides the contractual framework for relations that will lead to accession to the EU – entered into force with Macedonia in April 2004, Croatia in February 2005, Albania in April 2009, and with Montenegro in May 2010. SAA negotiations were launched with Kosovo in November 2006; SAA agreements were signed by Serbia in April 2008 and Bosnia and Hercegovina in June 2008, which will enter into force following ratification.

TREATY OF NICE

The treaty of Nice was signed in 2001 and came into effect in 2003. It enabled the EU to accommodate up to 13 new member states, and extended qualified majority voting to 30 further articles of the treaties that previously required unanimity. The weighting of votes in the EU

Council was altered from 1 January 2005 for the new member states. To obtain a qualified majority, a decision requires a specified number of votes (to be reviewed following each accession); the decision has to be approved by a majority of member states and represent at least 62 per cent of the total population of the EU. The treaty also set the number of MEPs that both existing and new member states would have following enlargement.

The Maastricht treaty established the right of groups of member states to work together without requiring the participation of all members (enhanced cooperation); the treaty of Nice removed the right of individual member states to veto the launch of enhanced cooperation.

The European Commission has been limited to one member per member state since 2005, with a maximum of 27 commissioners; a rotation system is to be introduced once EU membership exceeds 27 states. The treaty also added to the powers of the president of the commission and amended the rules of operation of the court of Justice.

ECONOMY

BUDGET OF THE EUROPEAN UNION

The principles of funding the European Union budget (formerly known as the European Community budget) were established by the treaty of Rome and remain, with modifications, to this day. There is a legally binding limit on the overall level of resources (known as 'own resources') that the European Union can raise from its member states; this limit is defined as a percentage of gross national income (GNI). Budget revenue and expenditure must balance, and there is therefore no deficit financing. The 'own resources' decision, which came into effect in 1975 and has been regularly updated, states that there are four sources of funding under which each member state makes contributions: duties charged on agricultural imports into the EU from non-member states; customs duties on imports from non-member states; contributions based on member states' shares of a notional EU-harmonised VAT base; and contributions based on member states' shares of total GNI. The latter is the budget-balancing item and covers the difference between total expenditure and the revenue from the other three sources.

EU BUDGET 2010

	*Billion euro**
Sustainable growth	64.3
Natural resources	59.5
Global activities	8.1
Citizenship, freedom, security and justice	1.7
Administration	7.9
Total	141.5

* 1 euro = £0.85 as at 6 May 2010
Source: Publications Office of the European Union

The framework budget for 2007–13 (formally known as the Financial Perspective) was completed at the end of the UK's presidency of the EU in December 2005. A figure of €862.36bn (£682.21bn) was agreed, which is equal to 1.045 per cent of the EU's combined gross national income.

From 1984 up until 2005, the UK had received an annual rebate equivalent to 66 per cent of the difference between UK contributions to the budget and its receipts. This was introduced to compensate the UK for disproportionate contributions caused by its high share of agricultural and non-agricultural imports from non-member states and its relatively small receipts from the Common Agricultural Policy, the most important portion of EU expenditure. Before the budget for 2007–13 was finalised, the UK conceded €10.5bn (£8.3bn) (approximately 20 per cent) of its rebate over the six-year period, in return for a wide-ranging review of EU spending.

SINGLE MARKET

Even after the removal of tariffs and quotas between member states in the 1970s and 1980s, the European Community (EC) was still separated into a number of national markets by a series of non-tariff barriers. It was to overcome these internal barriers to trade that the concept of the single market was developed. The measures to be undertaken were codified in the commission's 1985 white paper on completing the internal market.

The white paper included articles removing obstacles distorting the internal market: the elimination of frontier controls; the mutual recognition of professional qualifications; the harmonisation of product specifications, largely by the mutual recognition of national standards; open tendering for public procurement contracts; the free movement of capital; the harmonisation of VAT and excise duties; and the reduction of state aid to particular industries. The Single European Act (SEA) aided the completion of the single market by changing the legislative process within the EC, particularly with the introduction of qualified majority voting in the Council of the European Union for some policy areas, and the introduction of the assent procedure in the European parliament. The SEA also extended EC competence into the fields of technology, the environment, regional policy, monetary policy and external policy. The single market came into effect on 1 January 1993, though full implementation of the elimination of frontier controls and the harmonisation of taxes have been repeatedly delayed. A fundamental review of the single market was completed in 2007, which resulted in an operational set of initiatives intended to modernise single market policy. Following the abolition of the EC in 2009 as a result of the Lisbon treaty, the single market policy now applies to the EU.

EUROPEAN ECONOMIC AREA

The single market programme spurred European non-member states to open negotiations with the EC on preferential access for their goods, services, labour and capital to the single market. Principal among these states were European Free Trade Association (EFTA) members who opened negotiations on extending the single market to EFTA by the formation of the European Economic Area (EEA), encompassing all 19 EC and EFTA states. Agreement was reached in 1992, but the operation of the EEA was delayed by its rejection in a Swiss referendum, necessitating an additional protocol agreed by the remaining 18 states. The EEA came into effect in 1994 after ratification by 17 member states (Liechtenstein joined in 1995 after adapting its customs union with Switzerland).

Austria, Finland and Sweden joined the EU on 1 January 1995, leaving only Norway, Iceland and Liechtenstein as the non-EU EEA members. Under the EEA agreement, the three states are to adopt the EU's *acquis communautaire,* apart from in the fields of agriculture, fisheries, and coal and steel.

The EEA is controlled by regular ministerial meetings and by a joint EU-EFTA committee which extends relevant EU legislation to EEA states. Apart from single market measures, there is cooperation in several areas, including education, civil protection, research and development, consumer policy and tourism. An EFTA Court has been established in Luxembourg and an EFTA surveillance authority in Brussels to supervise the implementation of the EEA Agreement.

The EEA Enlargement Agreement came into force on 1 May 2004, which allowed the simultaneous expansion of both the EU and the EEA without disruption of the internal market. A similar process took place to ensure that Bulgaria and Romania could become contracting parties to the EEA upon joining the EU in 2007.

EUROPEAN MONETARY SYSTEM AND THE SINGLE CURRENCY

The European Monetary System (EMS) began operation in March 1979 with three main purposes. The first was to establish monetary stability in Europe, initially in exchange rates between EC member state currencies through the Exchange Rate Mechanism (ERM), and in the longer term to be part of a wider stabilisation process, overcoming inflation and budget and trade deficits. The second purpose was to overcome the constraints resulting from the interdependence of EC economies, and the third was to aid the long-term process of European monetary integration.

The Maastricht treaty set in motion timetables for achieving economic and monetary union (EMU) and a single currency (the euro). At the Brussels summit in May 1998, 11 member states were judged to fulfil or be close to fulfilling the necessary convergence criteria for participation in the first stage of EMU: Austria, Belgium, Finland, France, Germany, Ireland, Italy, Luxembourg, the Netherlands, Portugal and Spain. The criteria were that:

- the budget deficit should be 3 per cent or less of gross domestic product (GDP)
- total national debt must not exceed 60 per cent of GDP
- inflation should be no more than 1.5 per cent above the average rate of the three best performing economies in the EU
- long-term interest rates should be no more than 2 per cent above the average of the three best performing economies in the EU in the previous 12 months
- applicants must have been members of the ERM for two years without having realigned or devalued their currency

Under the terms of a stability and growth pact agreed in Dublin in December 1996 and revised in 2005, penalties may be imposed on EMU members with high budget deficits. Governments with deficits exceeding 3 per cent of GDP will receive a warning and will be obliged to pay up to 0.5 per cent of their GDP into a fund after ten months. This will become a fine if the budget deficit is not rectified within two years. A member state with negative growth will be allowed to apply for an exemption from the fine by referring to a number of relevant factors outlined in the pact.

As a result of the global economic downturn, by May 2010 24 out of 27 countries in the European Union had a deficit exceeding 3 per cent of GDP. The European Commission revised its existing recommendations in November 2009 and proposed extended deadlines for each country to correct its budget deficit. In the case of the UK, a deadline of 2014–15 was proposed, the longest deadline given to any of the EMU nations.

On 1 January 1999 the qualifying member states adopted the euro at irrevocably fixed exchange rates, the European Central Bank (ECB) took charge of the single monetary policy, and the euro replaced the ECU (an artificial currency adopted by European Community member states in 1979 as an internal accounting unit for the EMS) on a one-for-one basis.

In 2000 Greece was judged to have fulfilled the criteria for participation and adopted the euro on 1 January 2001. Referendums on the adoption of the euro have been held in Denmark and Sweden, but participation was rejected. In June 2003 Britain announced that the euro would not be adopted at present on the grounds that the country was not economically ready to join the single currency, though a future joining of the eurozone was not ruled out.

The euro is now the legal currency in the participating states. Euro notes and coins were introduced on 1 January 2002 and circulated alongside national currencies for a period of up to two months, after which time national notes and coins ceased to be legal tender. The new EU member states are expected to adopt the euro when the necessary economic conditions have been met; Slovenia joined the eurozone on 1 January 2007, Cyprus and Malta on 1 January 2008, and Slovakia on 1 January 2009.

The ECB meets twice a month to set the following month's monetary policy applicable to the countries participating in the euro. Its governing council has 22 members, being the six members of the ECB's executive board and the 16 governors of the national central banks of the participating states.

COMMON AGRICULTURAL POLICY

The Common Agricultural Policy (CAP) was established to increase agricultural production, provide a fair standard of living for farmers and ensure the availability of food at reasonable prices. This aim was achieved by a number of mechanisms, including import levies, intervention purchase and export subsidies.

These measures stimulated production but also placed increasing demands on the European Community (EC) budget, which were exacerbated by the increase in EC members and yields enlarged by technological innovation; CAP now accounts for over 40 per cent of EU expenditure. To surmount these problems reforms were agreed in 1984, 1988, 1992, 1997, 1999, 2003 and 2008.

REFORMS

The 1984 reforms created the system of co-responsibility levies: farm payments to the EC by volume of product sold. This system was supplemented by national quotas for particular products, such as milk. The 1988 reforms emphasised 'set-aside', whereby farmers are given direct grants to take land out of production as a means of reducing surpluses. The set-aside reforms were extended in 1993 for another five years and to every farm in the EC. The 1999 reforms further reduced surpluses of cereals, beef and milk by cutting the intervention prices by up to 20 per cent and compensating producers by making area payments. Under the reforms, CAP rules were also simplified, eliminating inconsistencies between policies.

In June 2003, EU farm ministers adopted a fundamental reform of the CAP, which included the following provisions:

- a single farm payment for EU farmers, independent of production (begun in 2005)
- payment to be linked to the respect of environmental, food safety, animal and plant health and animal welfare standards, and the requirement to keep all farmland in good condition
- a strengthened rural development policy with more EU money to help farmers meet EU production standards (begun in 2005)
- a reduction in direct payments for bigger farms
- a mechanism for financial discipline to ensure that the farm budget fixed until 2013 is not exceeded

The ten EU members that joined in 2004 were also given access to a special €5.8bn (£3.9bn) three-year funding package. The 2007–13 EU budget stipulated that no extra money would be made available to pay farm subsidies to Romania and Bulgaria.

A CAP 'health check' was carried out in 2008 and resulted in a set of proposals intended to further modernise and streamline EU agricultural policy, and to allow farmers to follow market signals by breaking the link between direct payments and production. These include abolishing the requirement for farmers to leave 10 per cent of their arable land fallow; a gradual increase in milk quotas before their abolition in 2015 and a general reduction in market intervention.

THE UK AND THE EU IN 2010

- Economy: The European Commission announced that the economic recession in the EU came to an end in the third quarter of 2009, but predicted that recovery would be gradual. The commission forecast a peak EU unemployment rate of 10 per cent and a public deficit reaching 7.25 per cent of GDP in 2010.
- Economy: The Eurozone countries and the IMF agreed on €500bn (£430bn) of emergency funding in May 2010 in order to prevent a crisis in the Greek economy affecting other countries; the package included a combination of loan guarantees for countries using the euro and emergency European Commission funding.
- Treaty of Lisbon: UK peer Baroness Ashton of Upholland was appointed as the new High Representative of the Union for Foreign Affairs and Security Policy.
- The environment: representatives of the European Union attended the UN climate change conference in December 2009. The EU formally agreed to the resulting Copenhagen Accord in January 2010, and pledged to reduce emissions by 20 per cent by 2020. The EU is also committed to creating a legally binding international agreement to begin upon the expiry of the Kyoto protocol in 2013.

INSTITUTIONS

EUROPEAN PARLIAMENT

E eplondon@europarl.europa.eu W www.europarl.europa.eu; www.europarl.org.uk

The European parliament (EP) originated as the common assembly of the ECSC, acquiring its present name in 1962. The parliament now comprises 736 seats. Members (MEPs), initially appointed from the membership of national parliaments, have been directly elected at five-year intervals since 1979. Elections to the parliament are held on differing bases throughout the EU; British MEPs have been elected by a regional list system of proportional representation since June 1999. The most recent elections were held in June 2009.

MEPs serve on committees which scrutinise draft EU legislation and the activities of the European Commission. A minimum of 12 plenary sessions a year are held in Strasbourg and six additional shorter plenary sessions a year are held in Brussels; committees meet in Brussels, and the secretariat's headquarters is in Luxembourg.

The influence of the EP has gradually expanded within the EU since the Single European Act of 1985, which introduced the cooperation procedure; the Maastricht treaty, which extended the cooperation procedure and introduced the co-decision (now ordinary legislative) procedure (*see* Legislative Process); the Amsterdam treaty, which effectively extended the ordinary legislative procedure to all areas except economic and monetary union, and taxation; and the Lisbon treaty, which gave parliament legislative powers comparable with the Council of the European Union. Parliament has general powers of supervision over the European Commission, and powers of consultation and co-decision with the Council of the European Union; it votes to approve a newly appointed commission and can dismiss it at any time by a two-thirds majority. Under the Maastricht treaty it has the right to be consulted on the appointment of the new commission, and can also veto its appointment. Under the Lisbon treaty, parliament elects the president of the commission on the proposal of the European Council. The EP has equal right to decide on budgetary matters as the Council of the European Union, and they work together to approve and adopt the entire annual budget. In accordance with the Maastricht treaty the EP appoints the European Ombudsman, to provide citizens with redress against maladministration by EU institutions.

The EP's organisation is deliberately biased in favour of multinational political groupings; recognition of a political grouping in the parliament entitles it to offices, funding, representation on committees and influence in debates and legislation. A political group must be composed of a minimum of 25 MEPs elected in at least seven member states. For a list of UK MEPs, *see* European Parliament section.

PARLIAMENT, Allée du Printemps, BP 1024/F, F-67070 Strasbourg Cedex, France
T (+33) (3) 8817 4001 F (+33) (3) 8817 5184
Wiertzstraat, Postbus 1047, B-1047 Brussels, Belgium
T (+32) (2) 284 2111 F (+32) (2) 284 6974

SECRETARIAT, Centre Européen, Plateau du Kirchberg, BP 1601, L-2929 Luxembourg
T (+352) 43001 F (+352) 4300 29393/29292
President, Jerzy Buzek (Poland)

OMBUDSMAN, 1 Avenue du Président Robert Schuman, CS 30403, F-67001 Strasbourg Cedex, France
E euro-ombudsman@europarl.europa.eu
W www.euro-ombudsman.europa.eu
Ombudsman, Nikiforos Diamandouros (Greece)

EUROPEAN PARLIAMENT UK OFFICE
2 Queen Anne's Gate, London SW1H 9AA
E eplondon@europarl.europa.eu W www.europarl.org.uk

EUROPEAN PARLIAMENT OFFICE IN SCOTLAND
The Tun, Holyrood Road, Edinburgh EH8 8PJ
E epedinburgh@europarl.europa.eu

COUNCIL OF THE EUROPEAN UNION

Rue de la Loi, 175 B-1048 Brussels, Belgium
W www.consilium.europa.eu

The Council of the European Union (Council of Ministers) is the main decision-making body of the

European Union, and formally comprises the ministers of the member states. Depending on the issue on the agenda, each country will be represented by the minister responsible for that subject. It passes laws, usually legislating jointly with the European parliament; coordinates the broad economic policies of the member states; approves the EU's budget jointly with the European parliament; defines and implements the EU's common foreign and security policy; concludes agreements between the EU and other states or international organisations; and coordinates the actions of member states and adopts measures in the area of police and judicial cooperation. Council decisions are taken by qualified majority vote (in which members' votes are weighted), by a simple majority, or by unanimity.

Unanimity votes are taken on sensitive issues such as taxation and defence; the treaty of Lisbon otherwise extended areas where qualified majority votes may be taken, making this procedure the norm. Member states have weighted votes in the council loosely proportional to their relative population sizes (*see* introductory table), with a total of 345 votes. The acts of the council can take the form of regulations, directives, decisions, common actions or common positions, recommendations or opinions. The council can also adopt conclusions, declarations or resolutions. The number of votes each member state can cast is set by the treaties. The treaties also define cases in which a simple majority, qualified majority or unanimity are required. A qualified majority will be reached if the following two conditions are met:

- a majority of member states approve (in some cases a two-thirds majority)
- a minimum of 255 votes is cast in favour of the proposal, ie 73.9 per cent of the total

In addition, a member state may ask for confirmation that the votes in favour represent at least 62 per cent of the total population of the EU. If this is found not to be the case, the decision will not be adopted.

The presidency of the Council of the European Union is held in rotation for six-month periods, setting the agenda for and chairing council meetings in all policy areas except foreign affairs. The holders of the presidency for the years 2010–11 are:

2010 Jan–Jun, Spain
2010 Jul–Dec, Belgium
2011 Jan–Jun, Hungary
2011 Jul–Dec, Poland

In the area of foreign affairs, council meetings are chaired by the High Representative of the Union for Foreign Affairs and Security Policy.

High Representative of the Union for Foreign Affairs and Security Policy, Baroness Ashton of Upholland (United Kingdom)

GENERAL SECRETARIAT OF THE COUNCIL OF THE EUROPEAN UNION

Wetstraat, rue de la Loi, 175 B-1048 Brussels, Belgium
W www.consilium.europa.eu

Secretary-General of the Council of the European Union, Pierre de Boissieu (France)

EUROPEAN COUNCIL

The European council, formed in 1974, was given formal recognition by the Single European Act in 1987; under the treaty of Lisbon it has become a fully fledged institution of the EU with a permanent president. It normally meets four times a year and consists of the heads of state or government for each of the member states of the EU, and the president of the European Commission. Meetings are chaired by a full-time president of the European council.

The primary function of the European council is to give political guidance in all areas of European Union activities at both European and national levels. The European council can issue declarations and resolutions expressing the opinions of the heads of state and governments, but its decisions are not legally binding.

President of the European Council, Herman Van Rompuy (Belgium)

EUROPEAN COMMISSION

Wetstraat 200, rue de la Loi, B-1049 Brussels, Belgium

The European Commission consists of 27 commissioners, one per member state. The members of the commission are appointed for five-year renewable terms by the agreement of the member states; the terms run concurrently with the terms of the European parliament. The president and the other commissioners are nominated by the governments of the member states, and, under the terms of the Lisbon treaty, the appointments are approved by the European parliament. The commissioners pledge sole allegiance to the EU. The commission initiates and implements EU legislation and is the guardian of the EU treaties. It is the exponent of community-wide interests rather than the national preoccupations of the council. Each commissioner is supported by advisers and oversees the departments assigned to them, known as directorates-general and services.

President Jose Manuel Barroso was re-elected for a second mandate by the European parliament on 16 September 2009. He announced the new commission on 27 November 2009, which officially took office on 10 February 2010.

The commission has a total staff of around 26,000 permanent civil servants.

COMMISSIONERS *as at February 2010*

President, Jose Manuel Barroso (Portugal)
Vice-President, High Representative of the Union for Foreign Affairs and Security Policy, Baroness Ashton of Upholland (United Kingdom)
Vice-President, Competition, Joaquín Almunia (Spain)
Vice-President, Digital Agenda, Neelie Kroes (The Netherlands)
Vice-President, Industry and Entrepreneurship, Antonio Tajani (Italy)
Vice-President, Institutional Relations and Administration, Marcos Sefcovic (Slovakia)
Vice-President, Justice, Fundamental Rights and Citizenship, Viviane Reding (Luxembourg)
Vice-President, Transport, Siim Kallas (Estonia)
Agriculture and Rural Development, Dacian Ciolos (Romania)
Climate Action, Connie Hedegaard (Denmark)
Development, Andris Piebalgs (Latvia)
Economic and Monetary Affairs, Olli Rehn (Finland)
Education, Culture, Multilingualism and Youth, Androulla Vassiliou (Cyprus)
Employment, Social Affairs and Inclusion, Laszlo Andor (Hungary)
Energy, Günther Oettinger (Germany)
Enlargement and European Neighbourhood Policy, Stefan Fule (Czech Republic)

Environment, Janez Potocnik (Slovenia)
Financial Programming and Budget, Janusz Lewandowski (Poland)
Fisheries and Maritime Affairs, Maria Damanaki (Greece)
Health and Consumer Policy, John Dalli (Malta)
Home Affairs, Cecilia Malmstrom (Sweden)
Internal Market and Services, Michel Barnier (France)
International Cooperation, Humanitarian Aid and Crisis Response, Kristalina Giorgieva (Bulgaria)
Regional Policy, Johannes Hahn (Austria)
Research and Innovation, Maire Geoghegan-Quinn (Ireland)
Taxation and Customs Union, Audit and Anti-Fraud, Algirdas Semeta (Lithuania)
Trade, Karel De Gucht (Belgium)

COURT OF JUSTICE OF THE EUROPEAN UNION
Palais de la Cour de Justice, Boulevard Konrad Adenauer, Kirchberg, L–2925 Luxembourg **W** www.curia.europa.eu

The treaty of Lisbon gave a new framework to the EU court system. The court of justice of the European Union is now composed of three courts: the court of justice, the general court and the civil service tribunal.

COURT OF JUSTICE
Rue du Fort Niedergrünewald, L 2925 Luxembourg

The court of justice exists to safeguard the law in the interpretation and application of European Union treaties, to decide on the legality of decisions of the Council of the European Union or the European Commission, and to determine infringements of the treaties. Cases may be brought to it by the member states, EU institutions, firms or individuals. Its decisions are directly binding in the member countries, and the Maastricht treaty enhanced the court's powers by permitting it to impose fines on member states. The 27 judges and eight advocates-general of the court are appointed for renewable six-year terms by the member governments in concert. During 2008, 592 new cases were lodged at the court and 567 cases were concluded.
President, Vassilios Skouris (Greece)
First Advocate-General, Paolo Mengozzi (Italy)

GENERAL COURT
Rue du Fort Niedergrünewald, L 2925 Luxembourg

Established under powers conferred by the Single European Act, the general court (known as the Court of First Instance until 1 December 2009) has jurisdiction to hear and determine all actions brought by natural or legal persons, and all direct actions against any of the institutions or offices of the European Union, except those reserved for the court of justice. It is composed of 27 judges, appointed for renewable six-year terms by the governments of the member states.
President, Marc Jaeger (Luxembourg)

CIVIL SERVICE TRIBUNAL
35A, Avenue J. F. Kennedy, L 1855 Luxembourg

The civil service tribunal has jurisdiction to hear disputes between civil servants and the European Union in matters such as pay, disciplinary measures and accidents at work. It does not deal with disputes between national governments and their employees. There are seven judges, appointed for renewable six-year terms.
President, Paul J. Mahoney (United Kingdom)

EUROPEAN COURT OF AUDITORS
12 rue Alcide de Gasperi, L–1615 Luxembourg
E euraud@eca.europa.eu **W** www.eca.europa.eu

The European Court of Auditors, established in 1977, examines the accounts of all revenue and expenditure of the European Union. It evaluates whether all revenue has been received and all expenditure incurred in a lawful and regular manner and in accordance with the principles of sound financial management. The court issues an annual report and a statement of assurance as to the reliability of the accounts and the legality and regularity of the underlying transactions. It also publishes special reports on specific topics and delivers opinions on financial matters. The court has one member from each member state appointed for a six-year term by the Council of the European Union following consultation with the European parliament.
President, Vitor Caldeira (Portugal)

FINANCIAL BODIES

EUROPEAN CENTRAL BANK
Kaiserstrasse 29, D-60311 Frankfurt am Main, Germany
E info@ecb.europa.eu **W** www.ecb.europa.eu

The European Central Bank (ECB), which superseded the European Monetary Institute, became fully operational on 1 January 1999 and defines and implements the single monetary policy for the euro area. The ECB's main task is to maintain the euro's purchasing power and price stability in the 16 EU countries that have introduced the currency since 1999. Its decision-making bodies are the executive board, the governing council and the general council. The executive board consists of the president, the vice-president and four other members. All members are appointed by the governments of the states participating in the single currency, at the level of heads of state and government. The governing council, the main decision-making body of the ECB, comprises the six members of the executive board and the governors of the national central banks of the 16 euro area states. The general council comprises the president and vice-president and the 27 governors of the national central banks of all the member states of the European Union, the other members of the executive board being entitled to participate but not to vote. The ECB is independent of national governments and of all other EU institutions.
President, Jean-Claude Trichet (France)
Vice-President, Lucas Papademos (Greece)

EUROPEAN INVESTMENT BANK
100 Boulevard Konrad Adenauer, L-2950 Luxembourg
E info@eib.org **W** www.eib.org

The European Investment Bank (EIB) was set up in 1958 under the terms of the treaty of Rome and is the financing arm of the European Union. The EIB's main activity is to provide long-term loans in support of investments undertaken by private or public promoters, for projects furthering European integration.

The EIB also operates outside the EU, in support of EU development and cooperation policies in partner countries including the enlargement area of Europe (both candidate and potential candidate countries), the Mediterranean, Russia and the Southern Caucasus, Africa, the Caribbean and the Pacific, Asia and Latin America.

The EIB assesses and selects the projects it finances independently and usually only finances up to 50 per cent of the total cost of a project. Each EIB-financed project must be financially, technically and environmentally viable.

The bank is not dependent on the EU budget, and raises its own resources on the capital markets. It is the biggest supranational bond issuer and lender in the world with an AAA credit rating. In 2009 it raised €79.4bn and lent a total of €79.1bn, of which 89 per cent was lent within the EU.

The shareholders of the EIB are the 27 member states, whose ministers of economy and finance constitute its board of governors. This body lays down general directives on the credit policy of the bank and appoints members to the board of directors. The board of directors consists of 27 members nominated by the member states, and one by the European Commission. It takes decisions on the granting and raising of loans and the fixing of interest rates. A management committee, composed of the bank's president and eight vice-presidents and also appointed by the board of governors, is responsible for the day-to-day operations of the bank.

President, Philippe Maystadt (Belgium)

ADVISORY BODIES

COMMITTEE OF THE REGIONS

Bâtiment Jacques Delors, rue Belliard 99–101, B-1040 Brussels, Belgium **E** pressecdr@cor.europa.eu **W** www.cor.europa.eu

The Committee of the Regions (CoR) was established in 1994 and is the political assembly which provides local and regional authorities with a voice within the European Union. The EU treaties oblige the European Commission and Council of the European Union to consult the Committee of the Regions whenever new proposals are made in areas which have repercussions at regional or local level. The CoR issues opinions on proposals for EU laws, which directly affect local and regional authorities. It can also draw up opinions on its own initiative, which enables it to put issues on the EU agenda, as well as resolutions on topical political issues. The treaty of Lisbon gave the CoR the right to challenge new EU laws in the European court of justice in certain instances.

The committee has 344 full members and the same number of alternate members. They are proposed by the member states to the Council of the European Union, which appoints them for a four-year renewable term of office. Members must hold a regional or local authority electoral mandate or be politically accountable to an elected assembly. They participate in the work of six specialist commissions which are responsible for drafting the CoR's opinions and resolutions on a wide range of topics.

President, Mercedes Bresso (Italy)
Secretary-General, Gerhard Stahl (Germany)

EUROPEAN ECONOMIC AND SOCIAL COMMITTEE

Rue Belliard 99, B-1040 Brussels, Belgium
W www.eesc.europa.eu

The European Economic and Social Committee (EESC) is an advisory and consultative body, which has 344 members appointed by the governments of the 27 member states for a five-year renewable term. It is divided into three groups: employers, workers, and other interest groups such as consumers, farmers and the self-employed. Every two-and-a-half years the EESC elects a bureau made up of 39 members, and a president and two vice-presidents chosen from each of the three groups in rotation. The EESC issues opinions on draft EC legislation and can bring matters to the attention of the commission, council and parliament. The EESC's competencies have increased as a result of revisions to the treaty of Rome, and the treaty of Nice formally recognised the importance of the opinions of the EU's economic and social partners.

President, Mario Sepi (Italy)

AGENCIES

EUROPEAN ENVIRONMENT AGENCY

Kongens Nytorv 6, DK–1050 Copenhagen K, Denmark
T (+45) 3336 7100 **W** www.eea.europa.eu

The European Environment Agency (EEA) aims to support sustainable development and to help achieve significant and measurable improvement in Europe's environment, through the provision of information to policy-making agents and the public. The EEA has been operational since 1994, and now has 32 member countries. It is a European Union body but is open to non-EU countries that share its objectives. The management board consists of representatives of the member countries, two representatives of the European Commission and two representatives designated by the European parliament.

Chair, Karsten Sach (Germany)

EUROPEAN JUDICIAL COOPERATION UNIT (EUROJUST)

Maanweg 174, 2516 AB The Hague, The Netherlands
E info@eurojust.europa.eu **W** www.eurojust.europa.eu

The European Union's Judicial Cooperation Unit (Eurojust) was established in 2002 with the aim of enhancing the development of Europe-wide cooperation in criminal justice cases involving serious cross-border and organised crime. Eurojust improves cooperation between the authorities of member states, in particular by facilitating the execution of international mutual legal assistance and through the implementation of extradition requests; it is the first permanent network of judicial authorities to be established anywhere in the world. It is a key interlocutor with the European parliament, the Council of the European Union and the European Commission.

The college of Eurojust is composed of 27 national members, one nominated by each member state. The national members are experienced prosecutors or judges.

President of the College, Aled Williams (United Kingdom)

EUROPEAN POLICE OFFICE (EUROPOL)

PO Box 90850, NL-2509 LW, The Hague, The Netherlands
W www.europol.europa.eu

The European Police Office (Europol) came into being on 1 October 1998 and assumed its full powers on 1 July 1999. It superseded the Europol Drugs Unit and exists to improve police cooperation between member states and to combat terrorism, illicit traffic in drugs and other serious forms of organised international crime. It is ultimately responsible to the Council of the European Union. Each

member state has a national unit to liaise with Europol, and the units send at least one liaison officer to represent its interests at Europol headquarters. Europol maintains a computerised information system, designed to facilitate the exchange of information between member states, and has a management board comprising one senior representative from each member state. An independent joint supervisory body monitors the content and use of all personal data held by Europol, to ensure that the rights of the individual are upheld.
Director, Rob Wainwright (United Kingdom)

EUROPEAN UNION INFORMATION

EUROPEAN COMMISSION REPRESENTATION OFFICES

UK, 8 Storey's Gate, London SW1P 3AT **T** 020-7973 1992
WALES, 2 Caspian Point, Caspian Way, Cardiff CF10 4QQ **T** 029-2089 5020
SCOTLAND, 9 Alva Street, Edinburgh EH2 4PH **T** 0131-225 2058
NORTHERN IRELAND, 74–76 Dublin Road, Belfast BT2 7HP **T** 028-9024 0708

EUROPEAN COMMISSION DELEGATIONS

AUSTRALIA AND NEW ZEALAND, 18 Arkana Street, Yarralumla, ACT 2600, Canberra
CANADA, 150 Metcalfe Street, Suite 1900, Ottawa, Ontario K2P 1P1
UK OFFICE OF THE EUROPEAN PARLIAMENT, 2 Queen Anne's Gate, London SW1H 9AA **T** 020-7227 4300
USA, 2300 M Street, NW Washington DC 20037

UK REPRESENTATIVE TO THE EUROPEAN UNION

OFFICE OF THE UNITED KINGDOM PERMANENT REPRESENTATIVE TO THE EUROPEAN UNION
Ave d'Auderghem 10, B-1040 Brussels, Belgium
E ukrep@fco.gov.uk **W** http://ukeu.fco.gov.uk
Ambassador and UK Permanent Representative, Kim Darroch, CMG, *apptd* 2007

EUROPEAN PARLIAMENT

POLITICAL GROUPINGS
as at August 2010

	EPP	S&D	ALDE	Greens/EFA	ECR	GUE/NGL	EFD	NA	Total
Austria	6	4	–	2	–	–	–	5	17
Belgium	5	5	5	4	1	–	–	2	22
Bulgaria	6	4	5	–	–	–	–	2	17
Cyprus	2	2	–	–	–	2	–	–	6
Czech Republic	2	7	–	–	9	4	–	–	22
Denmark	1	4	3	2	–	1	2	–	13
Estonia	1	1	3	1	–	–	–	–	6
Finland	4	2	4	2	–	–	1	–	13
France	29	14	6	14	–	5	1	3	72
Germany	42	23	12	14	–	8	–	–	99
Greece	8	8	–	1	–	3	2	–	22
Hungary	14	4	–	–	1	–	–	3	22
Ireland	4	3	4	–	–	1	–	–	12
Italy	35	21	7	–	–	–	9	–	72
Latvia	3	1	1	1	1	1	–	–	8
Lithuania	4	3	2	–	1	–	2	–	12
Luxembourg	3	1	1	1	–	–	–	–	6
Malta	2	3	–	–	–	–	–	–	5
The Netherlands	5	3	6	3	1	2	1	4	25
Poland	28	7	–	–	15	–	–	–	50
Portugal	10	7	–	–	–	5	–	–	22
Romania	14	11	5	–	–	–	–	3	33
Slovakia	6	5	1	–	–	–	1	–	13
Slovenia	3	2	2	–	–	–	–	–	7
Spain	23	21	2	2	–	1	–	1	50
Sweden	5	5	4	3	–	1	–	–	18
UK	–	13	12	5	25	1	11	5	72
Total	265	184	85	55	54	35	30	28	736

EPP – European People's Party (Christian Democrats)
W www.eppgroup.eu

S&D – Progressive Alliance of Socialists and Democrats in the European Parliament
W www.socialistsanddemocrats.eu

ALDE – Alliance of Liberals and Democrats for Europe
W www.alde.eu

Greens/EFA – Greens/European Free Alliance
W www.greens-efa.org

ECR – European Conservatives and Reformists
W www.ecrgroup.eu

GUE/NGL – Confederal Group of the European United Left/Nordic Green Left
W www.guengl.eu

EFD – Europe of Freedom and Democracy
W www.efdgroup.eu

NA – Non-Attached

INTERNATIONAL ORGANISATIONS

International organisations are intergovernmental organisations, whose membership can only include either sovereign states or other international organisations. They are subject to international law and are capable of entering into agreements among themselves or with states. They do not include private non-governmental organisations with an international scope. International organisations are usually established by a treaty providing them with legal recognition, which distinguishes them from collections of states such as the G8.

AFRICAN UNION

PO Box 3243, Addis Ababa, Ethiopia
T (+251) (1) 1551 7700 **E** webmaster@africa-union.org
W www.africa-union.org

The African Union (AU) was launched in 2002 as a successor to the amalgamated Organisation of African Unity (OAU) and the African Economic Community. It currently has 53 members, representing every African country except Morocco, which left the OAU in 1984 in protest at the admission of Saharan Arab Democratic Republic, representing Western Sahara, as a member. The AU aims to further African unity and solidarity, to coordinate political, economic, social and defence policies, and eventually to create an African single currency.

Chief AU governing organs include the assembly of heads of state or government, the ultimate decision-making body; the executive council, composed of foreign ministers from member states and which advises the assembly; the African Commission, which is the AU secretariat and consists of ten commissioners, each with a separate portfolio, who elect a chair to a four-year term; the peace and security council, modelled on that of the UN and capable of military intervention; and the pan-African parliament, established in 2004 to debate and advise heads of state.

Substantial budgetary arrears due to delays in the payment of national contributions have presented the AU with difficulties in achieving its objectives. Since 2004, the AU has deployed a peacekeeping force in the Darfur region of Sudan which, in December 2007, amalgamated into a joint UN-AU operation (UNAMID). In March 2010 UNAMID had a strength of 21,800 uniformed personnel.
Chair, Col. Muammar al-Gaddafi (Libya)

ANDEAN COMMUNITY

General Secretariat, Paseo de la República 3895, esq. Aramburú, San Isidro, Lima 27, Peru
T (+51) (1) 411 1400 **E** contacto@comunidadandina.org
W www.comunidadandina.org

The Andean Community, known as the Andean Pact until 1996, began operating formally on 21 November 1969 when its commission was established. It comprises four member states – Bolivia, Colombia, Ecuador and Peru – and the organisations and institutions of the Andean Integration System (AIS). Mexico and Panama hold observer status, while Argentina, Brazil, Chile, Paraguay and Uruguay are associated states.

The community's objectives are to facilitate economic growth, create jobs and facilitate regional integration towards the goal of a Latin American common market. It also aims to reduce the inequalities in development between member states. It pursues its objectives through a programme of trade liberalisation, a common external tariff, the relaxation of border controls, coordination between national legislatures and the promotion of industrial, agricultural and technological development.

The general secretariat of the Andean Community is its executive body, responsible for administration and dispute resolution. The general secretariat operates under the direction of the secretary-general, who is elected for a five-year term by the Andean council of foreign ministers (ACFM). It can propose decisions or suggestions to the ACFM; it also manages the integration process, ensures that community commitments are fulfilled, and maintains relations with the member countries and the executive bodies of other international organisations.

The Andean presidential council is the highest-level body of the AIS and comprises the presidents of the member states. Its responsibilities include setting new policies, evaluating the integration process and communicating with other bodies. The chairmanship is rotated among the members of the council each calendar year.

In 2001 the organisation introduced Andean passports for member states and since 2005 a policy of free flow of persons has enabled citizens to travel throughout the area without a visa.
Secretary-General, Freddy Ehlers Zurita (Ecuador)

ARAB MAGHREB UNION

14 rue Zalagh, Agdal, Rabat, Morocco
T (+212) (3) 767 1274 **E** sg.uma@maghrebarabe.org
W www.maghrebarabe.org

The treaty establishing the Arab Maghreb Union (AMU) was signed on 17 February 1989 by the heads of state of the five member states: Algeria, Libya, Mauritania, Morocco and Tunisia. The AMU aims to strengthen ties between the member countries by developing agriculture and commerce, working towards a customs union and economic common market, and establishing joint projects and economic cooperation programmes.

Decisions must be unanimous and are made by a council of heads of state, which is briefed by a council of foreign affairs ministers. The council of heads of state has not assembled since 1994 because of a dispute over the status of Western Sahara. A consultative assembly – consisting of 30 representatives from each member state – is based in Algiers; the secretariat is in Rabat; and the court of justice, with two judges from each country, operates in Nouakchott, Mauritania.
Secretary-General, Habib Ben Yahia (Tunisia)

ARCTIC COUNCIL

Polarmiljosenteret, 9296 Tromso, Norway
T (+47) 7775 0140 **E** ac-chair@arctic-council.org
W www.arctic-council.org

The Arctic Council was founded in 1996 in Ottawa, Canada, and is a regional forum for socio-economic development and scientific research within the Arctic region. It comprises eight states: Canada, Denmark (including Greenland and the Faeroe Islands), Finland, Iceland, Norway, Russia, Sweden and the USA. A further six organisations representing indigenous peoples are granted permanent participatory status and include the Saami Council, Inuit Circumpolar Conference and the Arctic Athabaskan Council. Six states (France, Germany, the Netherlands, Poland, Spain and the UK) have observer status.

Decisions within the Arctic Council are taken at biennial ministerial meetings attended by foreign ministers or designates of the member states. The chairmanship of the council and secretariat also rotate on a biennial basis. Between these meetings, the operation of the council is administered by the Committee of Senior Arctic Officials, which meets biannually.

The main scientific work of the Arctic Council is carried out by six working groups, each focusing on specific issues such as the monitoring and prevention of pollution; climate change; biodiversity; and public health.

Chair, Denmark (2009–11); Sweden (2012–13)

ASIA COOPERATION DIALOGUE

E acd@mfa.go.th W www.acddialogue.com

The Asia Cooperation Dialogue (ACD) was initiated by the former prime minister of Thailand, Thaksin Shinawatra, and inaugurated in June 2002. It currently has 31 members, with Morocco granted development partner status.

Its purpose is to provide a continent-wide forum to assist development in every Asian nation, with the ultimate goal to create an Asian community capable of equal interaction with the rest of the world. It aims to achieve these objectives through promoting interdependence among Asian countries, improving quality of life and expanding the continent's trade and financial markets.

Representatives from each of the member states (typically foreign ministers) meet annually to discuss ACD developments, issues of regional cooperation and methods of enhancing Asian unity. In addition, ministers also meet during the annual UN general assembly to discuss the implementation of policy and a common approach to international issues.

ASIAN-AFRICAN LEGAL CONSULTATIVE ORGANISATION

29-C, Rizal Marg, Diplomatic Enclave, Chanakyapuri,
New Delhi 110021, India
T (+91) (11) 2419 7000
E mail@aalco.int W www.aalco.int

The Asian-African Legal Consultative Organisation (AALCO), founded as a result of the Bandung Conference of 1955, was previously known as both the Asian Legal Consultative Committee and the Asian-African Legal Consultative Committee before its name was changed again in 2001. It was initially established as a non-permanent committee for a five-year term which was repeatedly extended until 1981, when its was granted permanent status. It has 47 member states.

The functions of the AALCO include serving as an advisory body to its member states in the field of international law, operating as a forum for common concerns among its members and making recommendations to governments and other international organisations.

Representatives from member states meet for the annual session which is hosted on a rotational basis and is attended by members of government, observers from other organisations and members of the International Court of Justice and International Law Commission.

The secretariat is located in New Delhi and is responsible for the day-to-day functioning of the organisation. It is headed by a secretary-general, elected to a four-year term. Other infrastructure includes four regional arbitration centres, located in Egypt, Iran, Malaysia and Nigeria; plans have been agreed for a fifth centre to be established in Kenya.

Secretary-General, Prof Dr Ramat bin Mohamad (Malaysia)

ASIAN DEVELOPMENT BANK

PO Box 789, 0980 Manila, The Philippines
T (+632) 632 4444 W www.adb.org

The Asian Development Bank (ADB) was founded in 1966 and is a multilateral financial institution dedicated to reducing poverty in Asia and the Pacific. It has 67 member countries from across the world. The ADB extends loans, equity investments and technical assistance to governments and public and private enterprises in its member countries, and promotes the investment of public and private capital for development. The bank's programmes prioritise economic growth, human development, good governance, environmental protection, private sector growth and regional cooperation.

The ADB is controlled by its board of governors, which meets annually and consists of a representative from each of the member states. It elects and delegates its powers to a board of directors which is responsible for administration and policy review.

The ADB raises funds through members' contributions and issuing bonds on the world's capital markets. In 2008, the ADB provided loans totalling US$13,230m (£8,534m) and technical assistance costing US$267m (£172.2m).

President, Haruhiko Kuroda (Japan)

ASIA-PACIFIC ECONOMIC COOPERATION

35 Heng Mui Keng Terrace, Singapore 119616
T (+65) 6891 9600 E info@apec.org W www.apec.org

Asia-Pacific Economic Cooperation (APEC) is an economic forum for Pacific Rim countries to discuss regional economy, cooperation, trade and investment. APEC was founded in 1989 in response to the growing interdependence among Asia-Pacific economies. The 1994 Declaration of Common Resolve envisaged free and open trade between member states with industrialised economies by 2010, extending to members with developing economies by 2020. Its 21 members define and fund work programmes for APEC's four committees, 11 working groups and other task forces.

APEC's chairmanship rotates annually among member states and the chair is responsible for hosting the annual leaders' meeting, as well as meetings of foreign affairs and trade ministers. The permanent secretariat, based in Singapore, is responsible for implementing policy, and is headed by an executive director selected by member states to serve a three-year term.

Executive Director, HE Muhamad Noor Yacob (Malaysia)

ASSOCIATION OF SOUTH-EAST ASIAN NATIONS

Jalan Sisingamangaraja 70a, Jakarta 12110, Indonesia
T (+62) (21) 726 2991/724 3372 E public@aseansec.org
W www.aseansec.org

The Association of South-East Asian Nations (ASEAN) is a geo-political and economic organisation formed in

1967 with the aim of accelerating economic growth, social progress and cultural development, and ensuring regional stability. It currently has ten member states.

The ASEAN summit, a biannual meeting of the heads of government, is the organisation's highest authority. The biannual ASEAN foreign ministers' meeting is responsible for preparing summit meetings, implementing their policies, and coordinating ASEAN's activities. The ASEAN economic ministers meet annually to coordinate economic policy.

An ASEAN free trade area was implemented in 2003, while a common preferential tariff was introduced in 1993. At the ASEAN summit in 1995, a south-east Asia nuclear weapon-free zone was declared. In December 2008 a new charter came into force which gave ASEAN legal status and a new institutional framework, committed it to the promotion of democracy, and provided for the establishment of the intergovernmental commission on human rights – in October 2009.

The secretary-general of ASEAN is appointed on merit by the heads of government and can initiate, advise on, coordinate and implement ASEAN activities. In addition to the ASEAN secretariat based in Jakarta, each member state has a national secretariat in its foreign ministry which organises and implements activities at a national level.

Secretary-General, Dr Surin Pitsuwan (Thailand)

BALTIC ASSEMBLY

Room 616, 2 Citadeles Street, Riga, LV-1010, Latvia
T (+371) 6722 5178 E baltasam@baltasam.org
W www.baltasam.org

Established in November 1991, the Baltic Assembly (BA) is an international organisation for cooperation between the parliaments of Estonia, Latvia and Lithuania. Each member state appoints between 12 and 20 parliamentarians to the assembly, including a head and deputy head of the national delegation. The political allegiances of the appointees reflect party proportions in each of the domestic parliaments. The BA holds an annual session in each of the member states in rotation. Several permanent and *ad hoc* committees also meet at least three times a year. The Baltic council of ministers, which comprises the heads of government and ministers of the member states, meets with the BA once a year and promotes intergovernmental and regional cooperation between the Baltic states; the joint sessions are known as the Baltic council.

President, Erika Zommere (Latvia)

CAB INTERNATIONAL

Nosworthy Way, Wallingford, Oxon OX10 8DE
T 01491-832111 E enquiries@cabi.org W www.cabi.org

Founded in 1910, CAB International (CABI) (formerly the Commonwealth Agricultural Bureau) is a non-profit organisation which provides scientific expertise to assist sustainable development and environmental protection. The organisation consists of 39 countries and five British overseas territories; each is represented on both the executive council, which meets biannually, and the review conference, held every five years to appraise policy and set future goals. A governing board provides guidance on policy issues.

CABI has three divisions: publishing, development projects and research, and microbial services. Each division undertakes research and provides consultancy aimed at raising agricultural productivity, conserving biological resources, protecting the environment and controlling disease. Any country is eligible to apply for membership.

Chief Executive Officer, Dr Trevor Nicholls (UK)

CARIBBEAN COMMUNITY AND COMMON MARKET

Turkeyen, Greater Georgetown, Guyana
T (+592) 222 0001/ 0075 E registry@caricom.org
W www.caricom.org

The Caribbean Community and Common Market (CARICOM) was established in 1973 with the signing of the Treaty of Chaguaramas. The objectives of CARICOM are to improve member states' working and living standards, boost employment levels, promote economic development and competitiveness, coordinate foreign and economic policies and enhance cooperation in the delivery of services such as health and education.

The supreme organ is the conference of heads of government, which determines policy and resolves conflict. The community council of ministers consists of ministers of government assigned to CARICOM affairs and is responsible for economic and strategic planning. The principal administrative arm is the secretariat, based in Guyana. The bureau of the conference of heads of government is the executive body; it comprises the chair of the conference, the outgoing chair and the secretary-general, who are all authorised to initiate proposals and to secure the implementation of decisions. In addition, there are five ministerial councils dealing with trade and economic development, foreign and community relations, human and social development, finance and planning, and national security and law enforcement.

Thirteen member states are committed to the CARICOM single market and economy, agreed in 2006. Twelve member states now issue CARICOM passports.

CARICOM has 15 member states and five associate members.

Secretary-General, Edwin W. Carrington (Trinidad and Tobago)

THE COMMONWEALTH

The Commonwealth is a voluntary association of 54 sovereign and independent states together with their associated states and dependencies. All of the states were formerly parts of the British Empire or League of Nations (later the UN) mandated territories, except for Mozambique and Rwanda which were admitted because of their history of cooperation with neighbouring Commonwealth nations.

The status and relationship of member nations were first defined by the inter-imperial relations committee of the 1926 Imperial Conference, when the six existing dominions (Australia, Canada, the Irish Free State, Newfoundland, New Zealand and South Africa) were described as 'autonomous communities within the British Empire, equal in status, in no way subordinate one to another in any aspect of their domestic or external affairs, though united by a common allegiance to the Crown and freely associated as members of the British Commonwealth of Nations'. This formula was given legal substance by the statute of Westminster in 1931.

This concept of a group of countries owing allegiance to a single crown changed in 1949 when India decided to become a republic. Her continued membership of the

Commonwealth was agreed by the other members on the basis of her 'acceptance of the monarch as the symbol of the free association of its independent member nations and as such the head of the Commonwealth'. This enabled subsequent new republics to join the association. Member nations agreed at the time of the accession of Queen Elizabeth II to recognise Her Majesty as the new head of the Commonwealth. However, the position is not vested in the British Crown.

THE MODERN COMMONWEALTH

As the UK's former colonies joined, after India and Pakistan in 1947, the Commonwealth was transformed from a grouping of all-white dominions into a multiracial association of equal nations. It increasingly focused on promoting development and racial equality. South Africa withdrew in 1961 when it became clear that its reapplication for membership on becoming a republic would be rejected over its policy of apartheid.

The new goals of advocating democracy, the rule of law, good government and social justice were enshrined in the Harare Commonwealth Declaration (1991), which formed the basis of new membership guidelines agreed in Cyprus in 1993. Following the adoption of measures at the New Zealand summit in 1995 against serious or persistent violations of these principles, Nigeria was suspended in 1995 and Sierra Leone was suspended in 1997 for anti-democratic behaviour. Sierra Leone's suspension was revoked the following year when a legitimate government was returned to power. Similarly, Nigeria's suspension was lifted in 1999, the day a newly elected civilian president took office. A heads of government meeting in 1997 established a set of economic principles for the Commonwealth, promoting economic growth while protecting smaller member states from the negative effects of globalisation. Zimbabwe was suspended from the councils of the Commonwealth in March 2002, and in 2003 the Zimbabwean government officially confirmed its departure from the association. Following President Pervez Musharraf's imposition of emergency rule in Pakistan in November 2007, the country was briefly suspended from the Commonwealth's councils. The suspension was lifted after successful democratic elections in February 2008. Fiji's Commonwealth membership was suspended in September 2009 after its military government refused to commit to elections in 2010.

MEMBERSHIP

Membership of the Commonwealth involves acceptance of the association's basic principles and is subject to the approval of existing members. There are 54 members at present, of which 16 have Queen Elizabeth II as head of state, 32 are republics and six have national monarchies. (The date of joining the Commonwealth is shown in parentheses.)

*Antigua and Barbuda (1981)
*Australia (1931)
*The Bahamas (1973)
Bangladesh (1972)
*Barbados (1966)
*Belize (1981)
Botswana (1966)
Brunei (1984)
Cameroon (1995)
*Canada (1931)
Cyprus (1961)
Dominica (1978)
‡Fiji (1970)
The Gambia (1965)
Ghana (1957)
*Grenada (1974)
Guyana (1966)
India (1947)
*Jamaica (1962)
Kenya (1963)
Kiribati (1979)
Lesotho (1966)
Malawi (1964)
Malaysia (1957)
Maldives (1982)
Malta (1964)
Mauritius (1968)
Mozambique (1995)
Namibia (1990)
†Nauru (1968)
*New Zealand (1931)
Nigeria (1960)
Pakistan (1947)
*Papua New Guinea (1975)
Rwanda (2009)
*St Kitts and Nevis (1983)
*St Lucia (1979)
*St Vincent and the Grenadines (1979)
Samoa (1970)
Seychelles (1976)
Sierra Leone (1961)
Singapore (1965)
*Solomon Islands (1978)
South Africa (1931)
Sri Lanka (1948)
Swaziland (1968)
Tanzania (1961)
Tonga (1970)
Trinidad and Tobago (1962)
*Tuvalu (1978)
Uganda (1962)
*United Kingdom
Vanuatu (1980)
Zambia (1964)

* Realms of Queen Elizabeth II
† Nauru is a member in arrears
‡ Currently suspended from the Commonwealth

COUNTRIES WHICH HAVE LEFT THE COMMONWEALTH

Republic of Ireland (1949)
South Africa (1961, rejoined 1994)
Pakistan (1972, rejoined 1989; suspended 1999, suspension lifted 2004; suspended 2007, suspension lifted 2008)
Zimbabwe (2003)

In each of the realms where Queen Elizabeth II is head of state (except for the UK), she is personally represented by a governor-general, who holds in all essential respects the same position in relation to the administration of public affairs in the realm as is held by Her Majesty in the UK. The governor-general is appointed by the Queen on the advice of the government of the state concerned.

INTERGOVERNMENTAL AND OTHER LINKS

The main forum for consultation is the Commonwealth heads of government meetings, held biennially to discuss international developments and to consider cooperation among members. Decisions are reached by consensus, and the views of the meeting are set out in a communiqué. There are also annual meetings of finance ministers and frequent meetings of ministers and officials in other fields, such as education, health, gender and youth affairs. Intergovernmental links are complemented by the activities of some 90 Commonwealth non-governmental organisations linking professionals, sportsmen and sportswomen, and interest groups. The Commonwealth Games take place every four years.

COMMONWEALTH SECRETARIAT

The Commonwealth has a secretariat, established in 1965 in London, which is funded by member governments. This is the main agency for multilateral communication between member governments on issues relating to the Commonwealth as a whole. It promotes consultation and cooperation, disseminates information on matters of common concern, organises meetings including the biennial summits, coordinates Commonwealth activities and provides technical assistance for economic and social development through the Commonwealth fund for technical cooperation.

The Commonwealth Foundation was established by

Commonwealth governments in 1965 as an autonomous body with a board of governors representing Commonwealth governments that fund the foundation. It promotes and funds exchanges and other activities aimed at strengthening the skills and effectiveness of professionals and non-governmental organisations. It also promotes culture, rural development, social welfare, human rights and gender equality.

COMMONWEALTH SECRETARIAT, Marlborough House, Pall Mall, London SW1Y 5HX T 020-7747 6500 E info@commonwealth.int W www.thecommonwealth.org
Secretary-General, Kamalesh Sharma (India)

COMMONWEALTH FOUNDATION, Marlborough House, Pall Mall, London SW1Y 5HY T 020-7930 3783 E geninfo@commonwealth.int W www.commonwealthfoundation.com
Chair, Prof. Guido de Marco (Malta)

COMMONWEALTH INSTITUTE, New Zealand House, 80 Haymarket, London SW1Y 4TQ T 020-7024 9822 E info@commonwealth-institute.org W www.commonwealth-institute.org

COMMONWEALTH OF INDEPENDENT STATES

Ulitsa Kirova 17, Minsk 220030, Belarus
T (+375) (17) 222 35 17 E postmaster@cis.minsk.by
W www.cis.minsk.by

The Commonwealth of Independent States (CIS) is a multilateral grouping of 11 former Soviet republics. It was formed in 1991 and its charter was signed by ten states in 1993–4. The CIS acts as a coordinating mechanism for foreign, defence and economic policies and as a forum for addressing problems arising from the break-up of the USSR. These matters are addressed in more than 70 inter-state, intergovernmental coordinating and consultative statutory bodies.

The two supreme CIS organs are the council of heads of state, which meets twice a year, and the council of heads of government. The executive committee, based in Minsk and Moscow, provides administrative support. There are also numerous ministerial, parliamentary, economic and security councils.

On becoming members of the CIS, the member states agreed to recognise their existing borders, respect one another's territorial integrity and reject the use of military force or coercion to settle disputes. A treaty on collective security was signed in 1992 by six states, and a joint peacemaking force, to intervene in CIS conflicts, was agreed upon by nine states. Russia concluded bilateral and multilateral agreements with other CIS states under the supervision of the council of heads of collective security (established 1993). These were gradually upgraded into CIS agreements under the umbrella of the collective security treaty, enabling Russia to station troops in eight of the other 11 CIS states (not Moldova, Turkmenistan or Ukraine), and giving Russian forces *de facto* control of virtually all of the former USSR's external borders. Only Ukraine and Moldova remained outside the defence cooperation framework and did not sign the treaty. In 1999, Azerbaijan, Georgia and Uzbekistan withdrew from the treaty and formed a new defensive with Moldova and Ukraine. Georgia withdrew from the organisation entirely effective from August 2009, following the country's war with Russia in 2008.

In 1991, 11 republics signed a treaty forming an economic community. Members agreed to refrain from economic actions that would damage each other and to coordinate economic and monetary policies. A coordinating consultative committee, an economic arbitration court and an inter-state bank were established. A single monetary unit, the rouble, was agreed upon by all member states, though the 'rouble zone' gradually collapsed during 1992–3. Members also affirmed the principles of private ownership, free enterprise and competition as the basis for economic recovery.

The 11 CIS members who signed the Establishment of an Economic Union treaty in September 1993 (of which Ukraine remains an associate member) committed themselves to a common economic space with free movement of goods, services, capital and labour. Belarus, Kazakhstan, Kyrgyzstan and Russia signed a treaty on the establishment of a customs union in 1996; the treaty was later signed by Tajikistan. In 2000 the presidents of the five countries approved a treaty establishing the Eurasian Economic Community, and in July 2010 Russia, Belarus and Kazakhstan were due to complete the formation of a customs union.

Executive Secretary, Sergey Lebedev (Russian Federation)

COOPERATION COUNCIL FOR THE ARAB STATES OF THE GULF

PO Box 7153, Riyadh 11-462, Saudi Arabia
T (+966) (1) 482 7777 W www.gcc-sg.org

The Cooperation Council for the Arab States of the Gulf, or Gulf Cooperation Council (GCC), was established on 25 May 1981. Its main objectives are increasing coordination and integration, harmonising economic, commercial, educational and social policies and promoting scientific and technical innovation among its member states. It established a common market in 2008, and set up a customs union in 2003 which is yet to be fully enforced. The GCC has six members: Oman, the United Arab Emirates, Bahrain, Kuwait, Qatar, and Saudi Arabia; the latter four plan to adopt a common currency with a central bank based in Riyadh.

The highest authority of the GCC is the supreme council, whose presidency rotates among members' heads of states. It holds one regular session every year, but extraordinary sessions may be convened if necessary.

The ministerial council, which ordinarily meets every three months, consists of the foreign ministers of the member states or other delegated ministers. It is authorised to propose policies and recommendations and ensure that resolutions are implemented.

Secretary-General, Abdul-Rahman bin Hamad al-Attiyah (Qatar)

COUNCIL OF EUROPE

Avenue de l'Europe, F-67075 Strasbourg-Cedex, France
T (+33) (3) 8841 2000 W www.coe.int

The Council of Europe was founded in 1949. Its aim is to achieve greater unity between its members, to safeguard their European heritage and to facilitate their progress in economic, social, cultural, educational, scientific, legal and administrative matters, and to further pluralist democracy, human rights and fundamental freedoms. It has 47 member states.

The organs are the committee of ministers, consisting of the foreign ministers of member countries, and the parliamentary assembly of 318 members (and 318 substitutes), elected or chosen by the national parliaments of member countries in proportion to the relative strength of political parties.

The committee of ministers is the executive organ. The majority of its conclusions take the form of international agreements (known as European conventions) or recommendations to governments. Decisions of the ministers may also be embodied in partial agreements to which a limited number of member governments are party.

One of the principal achievements of the Council of Europe is the European Convention on Human Rights (1950) under which the European Commission of Human Rights and the European Court of Human Rights were established; the two merged in 1998. The reorganised European Court of Human Rights sits in chambers of seven judges or, exceptionally, as a grand chamber of 17 judges. Litigants must exhaust legal processes in their own country prior to bringing cases before the court.

Among other conventions and agreements are the European Social Charter, the European Cultural Convention, the European Code of Social Security, the European Convention on the Protection of National Minorities, and conventions on extradition, the legal status of migrant workers, torture prevention, conservation and the transfer of sentenced prisoners. In 1990 the Venice Commission, an independent legal advisory body, was set up to assist in developing legislative, administrative and constitutional reforms in both European and non-European countries; it currently has 57 member states.

Non-member states take part in certain Council of Europe activities, such as educational, cultural and sports activities on a regular or *ad hoc* basis. The council's ordinary budget for 2010 totalled €218m (£192.5m).

Secretary-General, Thorbjorn Jagland (Norway)

COUNCIL OF THE BALTIC SEA STATES

PO Box 2010, Stromsborg, S-103 11 Stockholm, Sweden
T (+46) 8440 1920 **E** cbss@cbss.org **W** www.cbss.org

The Council of the Baltic Sea States was established in 1992 with the aim of creating a regional forum to increase cooperation and coordination among the states that border on the Baltic Sea. The organisation focuses mainly on the environment, economic development, energy security, civil security and education and culture; members also cooperate on health, humanitarian aid, tourism, transportation and communication issues, and in assisting new democratic institutions. It currently has 12 members (11 countries and the European Commission) while a further ten countries (including the UK and the USA) hold observer status.

The council consists of the foreign ministers of each member state and a member of the European Commission. Chairmanship of the council rotates on an annual basis, and the annual session is held in the country currently in the chair. The foreign minister of the presiding country is responsible for coordinating activities between the sessions. Since 1998 a permanent international secretariat has been established in Stockholm, Sweden.

Chair, Norway (2010–11)

ECONOMIC COMMUNITY OF WEST AFRICAN STATES

60 Yakubu Gowon Crescent, Asokoro District, PMB 401, Abuja, Nigeria
T (+234) (9) 314 7647 **E** info@ecowas.int **W** www.ecowas.int

The Economic Community of West African States (ECOWAS) was founded in 1975 and came into operation in 1977. It aims to promote the economic, social and cultural development of West Africa through mutual cooperation, and to prevent and control regional conflicts.

The supreme authority of ECOWAS is vested in the annual summit of heads of government of all 15 member states. A council of ministers meets biannually to monitor the organisation and make recommendations to the summit. Since restructuring in 2007, ECOWAS has been managed by a commission, headed by the president. The ECOWAS parliament was inaugurated in November 2000 and judges for the court of justice were appointed in January 2001.

Five member states of ECOWAS (The Gambia, Ghana, Guinea, Nigeria and Sierra Leone) plan to introduce the eco as a single common currency in January 2015. Eight other states currently use the CFA franc – it is planned eventually to amalgamate the two currencies. An ECOWAS travel certificate is issued allowing free movement within the community, and nine countries have a common passport.

An ECOWAS peacekeeping force has been involved in attempts to restore peace in Liberia (1990–6), in Guinea-Bissau (1998–9) and in Sierra Leone (1997–9). Niger was suspended from the organisation in October 2009 after it proceeded to hold legislative elections which violated an ECOWAS protocol on democracy and good governance.

President, Victor Gbeho (Ghana)

EUROPEAN BANK FOR RECONSTRUCTION AND DEVELOPMENT

One Exchange Square, London EC2A 2JN
T 020-7338 6000 **W** www.ebrd.com

The European Bank for Reconstruction and Development (EBRD), established in 1991, is an international institution whose membership comprises 61 member states, the European Union and the European Investment Bank.

Currently operating in 29 countries from central Europe to central Asia, the EBRD aims to aid the development of market economies and democracies. It provides project financing for banks, industries and businesses. It also works with publicly owned companies to support privatisation, the restructuring of state-owned firms and the improvement of public services.

The main forms of EBRD financing are loans, equity investments and guarantees, and its charter stipulates that at least 60 per cent of lending must contribute to the privatisation of state-owned enterprises. The EBRD pays particular attention to strengthening the financial sector and to promoting small and medium-sized businesses. It works in cooperation with national governments, private companies and international organisations such as the OECD, the IMF, the World Bank and the UN specialised agencies. The EBRD is also able to borrow on world capital markets.

The EBRD's reported annual business volume for 2009 was €7.9bn (£7bn), an increase of around 55 per cent on 2008, reflecting the support given to the countries in which the EBRD operates in response to the financial crisis; 61 per cent of the EBRD's business volume in 2009 was classified as 'crisis response'. For the second consecutive year the EBRD recorded a loss in 2009; the net loss before transfers of net income was €746m

(£659m), compared with a net loss of €602 (£531.5m) in 2008.

The EBRD's highest authority is the board of governors; each member appoints one governor and one alternate. The governors delegate most powers to a 23-member board of directors; the directors are responsible for the EBRD's operations and budget, and are elected by the governors for three-year terms. The governors also elect the president of the board of directors, who acts as the bank's president for a four-year term.

President, Dr Thomas Mirow (Germany)

EUROPEAN FREE TRADE ASSOCIATION

9–11 rue de Varembé, CH-1211 Geneva 20, Switzerland
T (+41) (22) 332 2626 **E** mail.gva@efta.int **W** www.efta.int

The European Free Trade Association (EFTA) was established in 1960 by Austria, Denmark, Norway, Portugal, Sweden, Switzerland and the UK, and was subsequently joined by Finland, Iceland and Liechtenstein. Six members have left to join what is now the European Union: Denmark and the UK (1972), Portugal (1985), Austria, Finland and Sweden (1995). EFTA's remaining members are Iceland, Liechtenstein, Norway and Switzerland.

The first objective of EFTA was to establish free trade in industrial products between members; this was achieved in 1966. Its second goal was the creation of a single market in Western Europe and in 1972 EFTA signed free trade agreements with the EC covering trade in industrial goods. The remaining tariffs on industrial products were abolished in 1977, and the Luxembourg Declaration on broader cooperation between EFTA and the EC was signed in 1984.

An agreement on the creation of the European Economic Area (EEA), an extension of the EC single market to the EFTA states, was signed in 1992 and entered into force in January 1994. Switzerland rejected EEA membership in a referendum in 1992 and Liechtenstein joined in May 1995 after adapting its customs union with Switzerland.

Since 2002, free trade area agreements have been signed between the EFTA states and Albania, Canada, Chile, Colombia, Egypt, the Gulf Cooperation Council, Lebanon, the Republic of Korea, Serbia, Singapore, the Southern African Customs Union (SACU) and Tunisia. Negotiations on free trade agreements with Algeria, India, Peru and Ukraine are ongoing.

The EFTA council is the principal organ. Member states' permanent delegations to the EFTA hold monthly meetings in Geneva.

Secretary-General, Kare Bryn (Norway)

EUROPEAN ORGANISATION FOR NUCLEAR RESEARCH (CERN)

CH-1211 Geneva 23, Switzerland
T (+41) (22) 767 6111 **E** cern.reception@cern.ch
W www.cern.ch

The convention establishing the European Organisation for Nuclear Research (CERN) came into force in 1954. CERN promotes European collaboration in high-energy physics with scientific goals and no military implication. It has 20 member states and eight members with observer status, including the European Commission and UNESCO.

The council, which is the highest policy-making body, comprises two delegates from each member state and is chaired by the president, who is elected by the council in session. The council also elects a director-general, who is responsible for the internal organisation of CERN. The director-general heads a workforce of approximately 2,400, including physicists, craftsmen, technicians and administrative staff. At present nearly 10,000 physicists use CERN's facilities.

Tim Berners-Lee developed the World Wide Web while working at CERN in 1990, and in 2008 CERN completed construction work on the Large Hadron Collider, the world's largest and most powerful particle accelerator.

Director-General, Dr Rolf-Dieter Heuer (Germany)

EUROPEAN SPACE AGENCY

8–10 rue Mario Nikis, F-75738 Paris Cedex 15, France
T (+33) (1) 5369 7155 **W** www.esa.int

The European Space Agency (ESA) was created in 1975 by the merger of the European Space Research Organisation and the European Launcher Development Organisation. Its aims include the advancement of space research and technology and the implementation of European space policy. ESA has 18 member states and one cooperating state, with five other nations participating in the Plan for European Cooperating States. ESA's mandatory activities are funded by contributions from all member states and calculated in accordance with each country's gross national income. In 2010, ESA's budget amounted to around €3,700m (£3,267m).

The agency is directed by a council composed of the representatives of its member states; its chief officer is the director-general who is elected by the council every four years. ESA has liaison offices in Belgium (for the EU), the United States of America and Russia, while a launch base is stationed in French Guiana.

Director-General, Jean-Jacques Dordain (France)

EUROPEAN UNION

See European Union section

FOOD AND AGRICULTURE ORGANISATION OF THE UNITED NATIONS

Viale delle Terme di Caracalla, 00153 Rome, Italy
T (+39) (06) 57051 **E** fao-hq@fao.org **W** www.fao.org

The Food and Agriculture Organisation (FAO) is a specialised UN agency, established in 1945. It assists rural populations by raising levels of nutrition and living standards, and by encouraging greater efficiency in food production and distribution. It analyses and publishes information on agriculture and natural resources. The FAO also advises governments on national agricultural policy and planning through its investment centre and collaboration with the World Bank and other financial institutions. The FAO's field programme covers a range of activities, including strengthening crop production, rural and livestock development and conservation.

The FAO's priorities are sustainable agriculture, rural development and food security. The organisation monitors potential famine areas, channels emergency aid from governments and other agencies, assists in rehabilitation, and responds to urgent or unforeseen requests for technical assistance.

The FAO has 193 members (192 states plus the European Union). It is governed by a biennial conference of its members which sets a programme and budget. The budget for 2009–10 was US$1.005bn (£648m), funded by member countries in proportion to their gross national income. The FAO is also funded by donor governments and other institutions.

The conference elects a director-general and a 49-member council which governs between conferences. The regular and field programmes are administered by a secretariat, headed by the director-general. Five regional, nine sub-regional and 74 national offices help administer the field programme.

Director-General, Jacques Diouf (Senegal)

INTERNATIONAL ATOMIC ENERGY AGENCY

PO Box 100, Wagramer Strasse 5, A-1400 Vienna, Austria
T (+43) (1) 26000 E official.mail@iaea.org W www.iaea.org

The International Atomic Energy Agency (IAEA) was established in 1957. It is an intergovernmental organisation that reports to, but is not a specialised agency of, the UN.

The IAEA aims to enhance the contribution of atomic energy to peace, health and prosperity. It does not advocate the use of atomic energy for military purposes. It establishes atomic energy safety standards and offers services to its member states to upgrade safety and security measures for their nuclear installations and material, and for radioactive sources, material and waste. It is the focal point for international conventions on the early notification of a nuclear accident, accident assistance, civil liability for nuclear damage, physical protection of nuclear material, and the safety of spent fuel and radioactive waste management. The IAEA also encourages research and training in nuclear power. It is additionally charged with drawing up safeguards and verifying their enforcement in accordance with several international nuclear weapons treaties.

The IAEA has 151 members that meet annually in a general conference. The conference decides policy, a programme and a budget – €315.4m (£278.5m) in 2010 – as well as electing a director-general and a 35-member board of governors. The board meets five times a year to review and formulate policy, which is implemented by the secretariat.

Director-General, Yukiya Amano (Japan)

INTERNATIONAL CIVIL AVIATION ORGANISATION

999 University Street, Montréal, Québec, Canada H3C 5H7
T (+1) (514) 954 8221 E icaohq@icao.int W www.icao.int

The International Civil Aviation Organisation (ICAO) was founded with the signing of the Chicago Convention on International Civil Aviation in 1944 and became a specialised agency of the UN in 1947. It sets international technical standards and regulations for aviation safety, security and efficiency, as well as environmental protection.

ICAO has 190 members and is governed by an assembly. A council of 36 members is elected, which represents leading air transport nations as well as less developed countries. The council elects the president, appoints the secretary-general and supervises the organisation through subsidiary committees, serviced by a secretariat.

President of the Council, Roberto Kobeh González (Mexico)

INTERNATIONAL CRIMINAL POLICE ORGANISATION (INTERPOL)

200 Quai Charles de Gaulle, F-69006 Lyon, France
E compr@interpol.int W www.interpol.int

Interpol was set up in 1923 to establish an international criminal records office and to harmonise extradition procedures. In 2010, the organisation comprised 188 member states. Interpol's aims are to promote cooperation between criminal police authorities and to support government agencies concerned with combating crime, while respecting national sovereignty. It is financed by annual contributions from the governments of member states.

Interpol policy is formulated by the general assembly which meets annually and is composed of delegates appointed by the member states. The 13-member executive committee is elected by the general assembly from the member states' delegates and is chaired by the president, who serves a four-year term of office. The permanent administrative organ is the general secretariat, headed by the secretary-general, who is appointed by the general assembly.

The UK Interpol National Central Bureau is operated by the Serious Organised Crime Agency (SOCA).

Secretary-General, Ronald K. Noble (USA)

INTERNATIONAL ENERGY AGENCY

9 rue de la Fédération, F-75739 Paris, France
T (+33) (1) 4057 6500/01 E info@iea.org W www.iea.org

The International Energy Agency (IEA), founded in 1974, is an autonomous agency within the framework of the Organisation for Economic Cooperation and Development (OECD). The IEA's objectives include the improvement of energy cooperation worldwide, development of alternative energy sources and the promotion of relations between oil-producing and oil-consuming countries. The IEA also maintains an emergency system to alleviate the effects of severe oil supply disruptions.

The main decision-making body is the governing board, composed of senior energy officials from member countries. The IEA secretariat, with a staff of energy experts, carries out the work of the governing board and its subordinate bodies. The executive director is appointed by the board. The IEA has 28 member states; the European Commission also participates in its work.

Executive Director, Nobuo Tanaka (Japan)

INTERNATIONAL FRANCOPHONE ORGANISATION

Cabinet du Secrétaire général, 28 rue de Bourgogne, F-75007 Paris, France
T (+33) (1) 4411 1250 W www.francophonie.org

The International Francophone Organisation (known as La Francophonie) is an intergovernmental organisation founded in 1970 by 21 French-speaking countries. It aims to prevent conflict and promote development and cooperation, represent its member states internationally and promote French culture and language.

The conference of heads of state and government of countries with French as a common language – also known as the Francophone summit – takes place biennially. Other institutions include the ministerial conference, the permanent council and the secretariat.

The ministerial conference, which consists of the

foreign ministers or the ministers responsible for Francophone affairs of each member state, implements decisions made at the summits and puts forward prospective new members. The permanent council, which is chaired by the secretary-general and consists of representatives of the member states, oversees the execution of decisions made by the ministerial conference, allocates funds, and reviews and approves projects.

La Francophonie has 56 members, three associate member states and 14 observers.
Secretary-General, Abdou Diouf (Senegal)

INTERNATIONAL FUND FOR AGRICULTURAL DEVELOPMENT

44 Via Paolo di Dono, 00142 Rome, Italy
T (+39) (06) 54591 E ifad@ifad.org W www.ifad.org

The International Fund for Agricultural Development (IFAD) began operations as a UN specialised agency in 1978. It develops and finances agricultural and rural projects in developing countries and aims to promote employment and additional income for poor farmers, reduce malnutrition and improve food security systems.

IFAD has 165 members and membership is divided into three lists: List A (OECD countries), List B (OPEC countries), and List C (developing countries) which is subdivided into C1 (Africa), C2 (Europe, Asia and the Pacific) and C3 (Latin America and the Caribbean). All powers are vested in a governing council of all member countries, which meets annually. It elects an 18-member executive board responsible for IFAD's operations, and a president who chairs the executive board. The president serves a four-year term that can be renewed once.

Since its establishment, IFAD has committed almost $12bn (£7.7bn) in loans and grants for 829 approved projects and programmes. It has also mobilised close to $18bn (£11.6bn) in cofinancing and funding for rural development from domestic sources.
President, Kanayo F. Nwanze (Nigeria)

INTERNATIONAL HYDROGRAPHIC ORGANISATION

4 Quai Antoine 1er, B.P. 445, 98011, Monaco
T (+377) 9310 8100 E info@ihb.mc W www.iho.int

The International Hydrographic Organisation began operating in 1921 with 19 member states and headquarters in the Principality of Monaco. In 1970 its name was changed from the International Hydrographic Bureau. The IHO is an intergovernmental organisation that has a purely consultative role and aims to support safety in international navigation, set policy for marine conservation and improve coordination between national hydrographic institutions. The IHO has a membership of 80 states that meet at five-yearly conferences to set policy, approve budget, review progress and adopt programmes of work. Each member is represented at these conferences by their most senior hydrographer. All member states have an opportunity to initiate new proposals for IHO consideration. Outside of its membership, the IHO acts to promote hydrography and facilitate the exchange of technology with developing countries. It is also the source that defines the boundaries between seas and oceans.
President, Vice-Adm. Alexandros Maratos (Greece)

INTERNATIONAL LABOUR ORGANISATION

4 route des Morillons, CH-1211 Geneva 22, Switzerland
T (+41) (22) 799 6111 E ilo@ilo.org W www.ilo.org

The International Labour Organisation (ILO) was established in 1919 as an autonomous body of the League of Nations and became the UN's first specialised agency in 1946. The ILO aims to increase employment, improve working conditions, extend social protection and promote dialogue between government, workers' and employers' organisations.

It sets minimum international labour standards through the drafting of international conventions. Member countries are obliged to submit these to their domestic authorities for ratification, and thus undertake to bring their domestic legislation in line with the conventions. Members must report to the ILO periodically on how these regulations are being implemented. The ILO is also a principal resource centre for information, analysis and guidance on labour and employment.

The ILO has 183 member states and is composed of the International Labour Conference, the governing body and the International Labour Office. The conference of members meets annually, and is attended by national delegations. It adopts international labour conventions and recommendations, provides a forum for discussion of world employment and social issues and approves the ILO's programme and budget.

The 56-member governing body is composed of 28 government, 14 worker and 14 employer members and acts as the ILO's executive council. Ten governments, including the UK, hold permanent seats on the governing body because of their industrial importance. There are also various regional conferences and advisory committees. The ILO acts as a secretariat and as a centre for operations, publishing and research.
Director-General, Juan Somavia (Chile)

INTERNATIONAL MARITIME ORGANISATION

4 Albert Embankment, London SE1 7SR
T 020-7735 7611 E info@imo.org W www.imo.org

Originally named the Inter-Governmental Maritime Consultative Organisation, the International Maritime Organisation (IMO) was established as a UN specialised agency in 1948. Owing to delays in treaty ratification it did not commence operations until 1958.

The IMO fosters intergovernmental cooperation in technical matters relating to international shipping, particularly regarding safety and security at sea, efficiency in navigation and protecting the marine environment from pollution caused by shipping. The IMO is responsible for convening maritime conferences and drafting marine conventions. It also provides technical aid to countries wishing to develop their activities at sea.

In 2010, the IMO had 169 members and three associate members. It is governed by an assembly comprising delegates of all its members. It meets biennially to formulate policy, set a budget (£61.1m for 2009–10), to vote on specific recommendations on pollution, maritime safety and security, and to elect the council. The council, which meets twice a year, fulfils the functions of the assembly between sessions and appoints a secretary-general. It consists of 40 members: ten from the world's largest shipping nations, ten from the nations most dependent on seaborne trade and 20 other members

to ensure a fair geographical representation. The IMO acts as the secretariat for the London convention (1972) which regulates the disposal of land-generated waste at sea.
Secretary-General, Efthimios E. Mitropoulos (Greece)

INTERNATIONAL MONETARY FUND

700 19th Street NW, Washington DC 20431, USA
T (+1) (202) 623 7300 E publicaffairs@imf.org W www.imf.org

The International Monetary Fund (IMF) was established at the UN Monetary and Financial Conference at Bretton Woods, New Hampshire, in 1944. Its articles of agreement entered into force in 1945 and it began operations in 1947.

The IMF exists to promote international monetary cooperation, the expansion of world trade and exchange stability. It advises members on their economic and financial policies; promotes policy coordination among the major industrial countries; and gives technical assistance in central banking, balance of payments accounting, taxation and other financial matters. The IMF serves as a forum for members to discuss monetary policy issues and seeks the balanced growth of international trade. It has 187 members; Kosovo joined in June 2009, and Tuvalu in June 2010.

Upon joining the IMF, a member is assigned a quota based on that member's relative standing in the world economy and its balance of payments position. The quota determines the size of the member's capital subscription to the fund, access to IMF resources, voting power and share in the allocation of special drawing rights (SDRs). Quotas are reviewed every five years and adjusted accordingly. The 13th general review in 2008 determined that no general quota increase was necessary, but in April 2008 the IMF board of governors adopted a reform package which would introduce a new quota formula, grant *ad hoc* quota increases to 54 countries found to be underrepresented at present, and allocate triple the number of basic votes to members in order to increase the voting power of low-income countries. It was also agreed that future reviews should consider voting and quota share adjustments to ensure that they reflect members' relative positions in the world economy. The reforms will become effective when 85 per cent of member countries formally give their approval.

The SDR, the reserve currency created by the IMF in 1969, is calculated daily on a basket of usable currencies and is the IMF's unit of account; on 26 April 2010, 1 SDR equalled US$1.51 (£1.00). SDRs are allocated at intervals to supplement members' reserves and thereby improve international financial liquidity. Total quotas as at April 2009 stood at SDR217.4bn, or around US$329bn (£217.9bn).

The IMF is not a bank and does not lend money; it provides temporary financial assistance by selling a member's SDRs or other members' currencies in exchange for the member's own currency. The member can then use the purchased currency to alleviate its balance of payments difficulties. IMF financial resources derive primarily from members' capital subscriptions, which are equivalent to their quotas. In addition, the IMF is authorised to borrow from official lenders. It may also draw on a line of credit of SDR18.5bn from 12 countries under the so-called general arrangements to borrow (GAB); the ten-fold expansion of another set of credit arrangements, the new arrangements to borrow (NAB), from SDR34bn to SDR367.5bn was approved by the IMF's executive board in April 2010. A further 13 countries are expected to be added to the 26 currently participating in the NAB.

Benign market conditions between 2004 and 2008 prompted many countries to start repaying their outstanding loans, and demand for the fund's resources dropped dramatically; however, in 2008 the IMF increased its lending in response to the global financial crisis. In March 2009 the IMF announced a number of reforms to its lending framework, intended to provide greater speed and flexibility in lending arrangements, double access limits on loans and more closely tailor the conditionality of loans to fit the recipient state's needs and strengths. In February 2010 a defined poverty line (a gross national income of $1,135 per capita) was introduced under which countries would qualify to access low-cost concessional loans under the poverty reduction and growth trust, whose resources would thus be reserved for those most in need. On 31 March 2010, total outstanding IMF credits amounted to SDR46.2bn, or US$70.2bn (£45.3bn).

The IMF supports long-term efforts at economic reform and transformation as well as medium-term programmes under the extended fund facility, which runs for three to four years and is aimed at overcoming balance of payments difficulties stemming from macroeconomic and structural problems. Typically, measures are introduced to reform taxation and the financial sector, to privatise state-owned enterprises and to make labour markets more flexible.

The IMF is headed by a board of governors, comprising representatives of each member state, which meets annually. The governors delegate powers to 24 executive directors, who are appointed or elected by member countries. The executive directors operate the fund on a daily basis under a managing director, whom they elect.
Managing Director, Dominique Strauss-Kahn (France)

INTERNATIONAL ORGANISATION FOR MIGRATION

17 route des Morillons, CH-1211 Geneva 19, Switzerland
T (+41) 22717 9111 E hq@iom.int W www.iom.int

The International Organisation for Migration (IOM) was founded in 1951 to resettle European displaced persons and refugees. During the 1960s and 1970s the IOM developed links with the United Nations High Commissioner for Refugees (UNHCR) and began a programme of assistance and reintegration outside of Europe. There are currently 127 member states and 17 observer countries. Internally, the IOM is led by a director-general who is elected for a five-year term. The director-general's office has the constitutional authority to manage the organisation, carry out the activities within its mandate and develop current policies, procedures and strategies. The office of the inspector-general (OIG) incorporates the functions of evaluation, internal audit and assessment of projects.

The role of the IOM has recently expanded to cover migration health services, counter-trafficking measures, emergency and post-crisis management and assisted voluntary returns. It currently employs more than 7,000 staff and is present in 450 field locations.
Director-General, William Lacy Swing (USA)

INTERNATIONAL RED CROSS AND RED CRESCENT MOVEMENT

19 avenue de la Paix, CH-1202 Geneva, Switzerland
T (+41) 2273 46001 W www.icrc.org

The International Red Cross and Red Crescent Movement is composed of three elements – the International Committee of the Red Cross, the International Federation of Red Cross and Red Crescent Societies, and the National Red Cross and Red Crescent Societies.

The International Committee of the Red Cross (ICRC), the organisation's founding body, was formed in 1863. It aims to protect and assist victims of armed conflict. It also seeks to ensure the application of the Geneva Conventions regarding prisoners of war and detainees.

The International Federation of Red Cross and Red Crescent Societies was founded in 1919 to assist the humanitarian activities of national societies, coordinate their relief operations for victims of natural disasters and care for refugees outside areas of conflict. There are Red Cross and Red Crescent societies in 186 countries; it has 60 field delegations internationally and runs over 80 relief operations a year.

The international conference of the Red Cross and Red Crescent meets every four years, bringing together delegates of the ICRC, the International Federation and the national societies, as well as representatives of signatory states to the Geneva Conventions.
President, Jakob Kellenberger (Switzerland)

INTERNATIONAL TELECOMMUNICATION UNION

Place des Nations, CH-1211 Geneva 20, Switzerland
T (+41) (22) 730 5111 E itumail@itu.int W www.itu.int

The International Telecommunication Union (ITU) was founded in Paris in 1865 as the International Telegraph Union and became a UN specialised agency in 1947.

ITU is an intergovernmental organisation for the development of telecommunications and the harmonisation of national telecommunication policies. It comprises 191 member states, 561 sector members and 156 associates who represent public and private organisations involved in telecommunications. Its mission is to promote the development of information and communication technologies, and to offer technical assistance to developing countries.

ITU operates initiatives aimed at promoting the growth and expansion of electronic commerce. These include a programme of strategic workshops; the adoption of international regulations, treaties and technical standards to foster global interactivity; and the provision of policy advice and technical assistance. ITU also organises worldwide and regional exhibitions and forums to exchange ideas, knowledge and technology.
Secretary-General, Dr Hamadoun Touré (Mali)

INTERNATIONAL TRADE UNION CONFEDERATION

5 Boulevard du Roi Albert II, 5 B 1, B-1210 Brussels, Belgium
T (+32) (2) 224 0211 E info@ituc-csi.org W www.ituc-csi.org

The International Trade Union Confederation (ITUC) was created in 2006 by the merger between the International Confederation of Free Trade Unions (ICFTU), the World Confederation of Labour (WCL) and other independent unions. Through public and industrial advocacy work it seeks to assert and defend the rights and interests of workers, and to foster international cooperation between trade unions. In February 2010 the ITUC represented 176 million workers in 155 countries and territories and had 312 national affiliates.

The congress, the supreme authority of the ITUC, meets once every four years to review and propose policy and to elect the 78-member general council. Council members are apportioned according to population-weighted geographical regions, with six seats reserved for nomination by the women's committee, and two by the youth committee. The council, and the general secretary elected at each congress, govern the organisation. It also elects a 27-member executive bureau from among its members which deals with urgent issues and those delegated to it by the council; it also makes decisions on finances and formulates the annual budget for council approval.

The ITUC has regional organisations for Asia-Pacific (ITUC-AP), Africa (ITUC-AF), the Americas (TUCA) and Europe (the pan-European regional council, or PERC). It also cooperates closely with the Global Union Federations, the Trade Union Advisory Committee to the Organisation for Economic Cooperation and Development (OECD), the European Trade Union Confederation, the International Labour Organisation, a number of other UN specialised agencies, and national and regional unions and organisations.
General Secretary, Guy Ryder (UK)

INTERNATIONAL WHALING COMMISSION

The Red House, 135 Station Road, Impington, Cambridge CB24 9NP
T 01223-233971 E secretariat@iwcoffice.org
W www.iwcoffice.org

The International Whaling Commission (IWC) was set up under the International Convention for the Regulation of Whaling, signed in Washington DC in 1946. It has 88 member states as of April 2010. The purpose of the IWC is to provide for the conservation of whale stocks, enabling the development of the whaling industry. The organisation reviews and revises the schedule to the convention that decrees the complete protection of certain species, sets limits for when and where whaling can take place, coordinates and funds whale research, and publishes and promotes scientific studies.

The IWC has four main committees, responsible for scientific, technical, conservation and finance matters. There are further sub-committees and working groups concerned with aboriginal subsistence whaling, infractions, small cetaceans, whalewatching, whale-killing methods and animal welfare issues.
Chair, HE Cristián Maquieira (Chile)

LATIN UNION

131 rue du Bac, F-75007 Paris, France
T (+33) (1) 4549 6060 E ulsg@unilat.org W www.unilat.org

The Latin Union is an international organisation whose member states use a Romance language. It was created in 1954 with the signing of a constituent agreement in Madrid and has existed as a functioning institution since 1983. The aims of the organisation are to protect, project and promote the common heritage and to unify identities of the Latin and Latin-influenced world. It has 37 member states and 3 members with observer status.

The senior body of the organisation, the congress,

consists of representatives from each of the member states and meets every two years. It is responsible for approving the budget and setting the agenda for the Union's activities. The executive council is made up of representatives from 12 member states who are elected for a four-year term by congress, as is the secretary-general who is responsible for the implementation of policy through the general secretariat.

The official languages of the Latin Union are Catalan, French, Italian, Portuguese, Castillian (Spanish) and Romanian, although Catalan and Romanian are not used as working languages.

Secretary-General, José Luis Dicenta (Spain)

LEAGUE OF ARAB STATES

Al-Tahrir Square, PO Box 11642, Cairo, Egypt
T (+20) (2) 2575 0511 W www.arableagueonline.org

The League of Arab States was founded in 1945 to protect the independence and sovereignty of its member states, supervise the affairs and interests of Arab countries and promote the process of integration among them. The organisation has 22 member states. The League itself has observer status at the United Nations.

The heads of member states meet annually at the Arab League summit, while foreign ministers convene every six months as part of the Arab League council. Member states participate in various specialised agencies which develop specific areas of cooperation between Arab states. These include the Arab Monetary Fund; the Arab Satellite Communications Organisation; the Arab Academy for Science, Technology and Maritime Transport; the Arab Bank for Economic Development in Africa; the Arab League Educational, Cultural and Scientific Organisation and the Council of Arab Economic Unity.

Secretary-General, Amr Moussa (Egypt)

MERCOSUR

Luis Piera 1992, piso 1, 11200-Montevideo, Uruguay
T (+598) (2) 412 9024 E divulgacion@mercosur.org.uy
W www.mercosur.int

MERCOSUR (the Southern Common Market) was created by the treaty of Asunción, signed by Argentina, Brazil, Paraguay and Uruguay on 26 March 1991. Venezuela signed an adhesion protocol in 2006, but its full incorporation into MERCOSUR has yet to receive final ratification from the Paraguayan parliament. Five other countries have associate member status.

The Common Market Council (CMC) is the highest-level agency of MERCOSUR, with authority to formulate policy and enforce member states' compliance with the treaty of Asunción. The CMC comprises ministers of foreign affairs and economic ministers of the member states and meets at least once a year.

The Common Market Group is the executive body of MERCOSUR and is coordinated by the foreign ministries of the member states. Its function is to implement decisions made by the CMC and resolve disputes. It can establish subgroups to work on particular issues and comprises four permanent members and four substitutes from each country. Other bodies include a joint parliamentary committee, a trade commission and a socio-economic advisory forum.

In 2005, Argentina, Brazil, Paraguay and Uruguay became associate members of the Andean Community, reciprocating MERCOSUR's action to grant associate membership to all Andean Community nations. In December 2005, the Columbian president ratified a free trade agreement (FTA) with MERCOSUR giving Columbian products preferential access to MERCOSUR countries. MERCOSUR signed an FTA with Israel in December 2007, the bloc's first such agreement outside Latin America; negotiations with the EU over a possible FTA were relaunched in May 2010.

President, Carlos Álvarez (Argentina)

NORDIC COUNCIL

Store Strandstraede 18, 1255 Copenhagen K, Denmark
T (+45) 3396 0400 E nordisk-rad@norden.org
W www.norden.org

The Nordic Council was established in March 1952 as an advisory body on economic and social cooperation, comprising parliamentary delegates from Denmark, Iceland, Norway and Sweden. It was subsequently joined by Finland (1955), and representatives from the Faroes (1970), the Aland Islands (1970), and Greenland (1984).

Cooperation is regulated by the Helsinki agreement, signed in 1962. This was amended in 1971 to create a Nordic council of ministers, which discusses all matters except defence and foreign affairs. Decisions of the council of ministers, which are taken by consensus, are binding, although if ratification by member parliaments is required, decisions only become effective following parliamentary approval. The council of ministers is advised by the Nordic Council, to which it reports annually. There are ministers for Nordic cooperation in every member government.

The Nordic Council comprises 87 voting delegates nominated from member parliaments and about 80 non-voting government representatives. It meets at least once a year in plenary sessions. The full council chooses a 13-member presidium, which conducts business between sessions. A secretariat, headed by a secretary-general, provides administrative support. The presidency of the Nordic Council rotates between the five countries, and the presiding country always hosts the annual council session.

President, Helgi Hjorvar (Iceland)

NORTH AMERICAN FREE TRADE AGREEMENT

NAFTA Secretariat, Canadian Section, 90 Sparks Street, Suite 705, Ottawa, Ontario K1P 5B4, Canada
T (+1) (613) 992 9388 E canada@nafta-sec-alena.org

NAFTA Secretariat, Mexican Section, Blvd. Adolfo López Mateos 3025, 2° Piso, Col. Héroes de Padierna, C.P. 10700, Mexico, D.F.
T (+52) (55) 5629 9630 E naftamexico@nafta-sec-alena.org

NAFTA Secretariat, US Section, Room 2061, 14th Street and Constitution Avenue, NW, Washington DC, 20230, USA
T (+1) (202) 482 5438 E usa@nafta-sec-alena.org
W www.nafta-sec-alena.org

The leaders of Canada, Mexico and the USA signed the North American Free Trade Agreement (NAFTA) on 17 December 1992 in their respective capitals; it came into force in January 1994 after being ratified by the legislatures of the three member states.

NAFTA aims to eliminate barriers to trade in goods and services, promote fair competition within the free trade area, protect and enforce intellectual property rights and create a framework for further cooperation. To achieve these aims, import tariffs, quotas and limits on cross-border investment are being removed.

The NAFTA secretariat is composed of Canadian, Mexican and US sections. It is responsible for administering the dispute settlement provisions of the agreement, providing assistance to the Free Trade Commission and support for various committees and working groups, and facilitating the operation of the agreement.

NORTH ATLANTIC TREATY ORGANISATION

Bvld Leopold III, Brussels B-1110, Belgium
T (+32) (2) 707 4111 E natodoc@hq.nato.int W www.nato.int

NATO is a political and military alliance designed to provide common security for its members through cooperation and consultation in political, military and economic as well as scientific and other non-military fields.

The North Atlantic treaty (treaty of Washington) was signed in 1949 by Belgium, Canada, Denmark, France, Iceland, Italy, Luxembourg, the Netherlands, Norway, Portugal, the UK and the USA. Greece and Turkey acceded to the treaty in 1952, the Federal Republic of Germany in 1955 (the reunited Germany acceded in October 1990), Spain in 1982, and the Czech Republic, Hungary and Poland in 1999. Bulgaria, Estonia, Latvia, Lithuania, Romania, Slovakia and Slovenia signed membership protocols in March 2003 and officially joined the North Atlantic Treaty Organisation (NATO) in March 2004. Albania and Croatia became official members in April 2009, having signed membership accords in September 2008.

STRUCTURE

The North Atlantic council (NAC), chaired by the secretary-general, is the highest authority of the alliance and is composed of permanent representatives of the 28 member countries. It meets weekly, but also holds meetings at higher levels involving foreign and defence ministers and heads of government. The permanent representatives (ambassadors) head national delegations of advisers and experts. The defence planning committee (DPC) is composed of all member countries, as is the nuclear planning group (NPG), with the exception of France. Both the DPC and the NPG also meet at ministerial level at least twice a year. The NATO secretary-general chairs the council, the DPC and the NPG. Much of the NAC policy is prepared and drafted by the senior political committee, a group of deputy permanent representatives and policy advisers.

The senior military authority in NATO, which advises the council and DPC, is the military committee, composed of the chief of defence staffs of each member country except Iceland, which has no military forces and is represented by a civilian. The military committee, which is assisted by an integrated international military staff, also meets in permanent session with permanent military representatives and is responsible for making recommendations to the council and DPC on measures considered necessary for the common defence of the NATO area and for supplying guidance on military matters to the NATO strategic commanders. The chair of the military committee, elected for a period of two to three years, represents the committee on the council.

The alliance's military command structure is divided between two functional strategic commands: Allied Command Operations (ACO) is responsible for all NATO military operations, whereas Allied Command Transformation (ACT) is charged with training and restructuring NATO military forces and capabilities. The headquarters of ACO is at the Supreme Headquarters of the Allied Powers Europe (SHAPE) at Mons, Belgium, and comes under the command of the Supreme Allied Commander Europe (SACEUR). The headquarters of ACT is at Norfolk, Virginia, USA, and is under the command of the Supreme Allied Commander, Transformation (SACT). There is also a regional planning group for Canada and the USA.

POST COLD WAR DEVELOPMENTS

The Euro-Atlantic partnership council (EAPC) was established in 1997 to develop closer security links with Eastern European and former Soviet states. Replacing the North Atlantic cooperation council (NACC) as the first institutional framework for cooperation between NATO member countries and former adversaries from Central and Eastern Europe, the EAPC focuses on defence planning, defence industry conversion, defence management and force structuring. Its membership comprises the 28 NATO members and Armenia, Austria, Azerbaijan, Belarus, Bosnia and Hercegovina, Finland, Georgia, Ireland, Kazakhstan, Kyrgyzstan, Macedonia, Malta, Moldova, Montenegro, Russia, Serbia, Sweden, Switzerland, Tajikistan, Turkmenistan, Ukraine and Uzbekistan. The EAPC provides the multilateral, political framework for the partnership for peace programme (PFP) in which each of its member countries participates. The PFP is the basis for practical, bilateral security cooperation between NATO and individual partner countries in the fields of defence planning and budgeting, military exercises and civil emergency operations. It also works to improve the interoperability between the forces of partner and member countries to enable them to undertake joint operations and has provided the context for cooperation by many of the partner countries in NATO-led peacekeeping and peace-support operations in Bosnia and Hercegovina, Kosovo and Afghanistan.

NATO and Russia committed themselves to helping build a stable, secure and undivided continent on the basis of partnership and mutual interest when they signed the 1997 Founding Act on mutual relations, cooperation and security, which provided for the creation of a NATO-Russia permanent joint council (PJC). In 2002 it was replaced by the NATO-Russia council (NRC), which cooperates on security issues and other areas of common interest. The NRC usually meets every month at ambassadorial level and twice each year at ministerial level to address issues of joint concern such as terrorist threats and the narcotics trade, and to pursue bilateral programmes in defence reform, search and rescue, and civil emergency planning. NATO suspended formal NRC meetings, and cooperation in many areas, in response to Russia's military action in Georgia in August 2008, and its subsequent recognition of South Ossetia and Abkhazia as independent states. Although the two sides resumed normal relations in April 2009, the status of these areas remains in dispute.

The establishment of the NATO-Ukraine commission (NUC) in 1997 committed both parties to developing their relationship under a programme of consultation and cooperation on political and security issues. The NUC meets at least twice a year. The NATO-Georgia commission, created in 2008, is pursuing political dialogue between NATO and Georgia, and helping to supervise Georgia's progress towards membership of NATO. The commission is also co-ordinating support to help the country recover from the summer 2008 conflict.

NATO's Mediterranean dialogue, launched in 1994, aims to improve trust and understanding of NATO's goals and objectives among the countries of the southern Mediterranean area: Algeria, Egypt, Israel, Jordan, Mauritania, Morocco and Tunisia. At its summit meeting in 2004, the alliance launched the Istanbul cooperation initiative (ICI), promoting practical cooperation with the Gulf cooperation council (GCC) and other interested countries in the Middle East. To date Bahrain, Qatar, Kuwait and the United Arab Emirates have joined the ICI.

The development of a European security and defence identity, which would strengthen NATO's European pillar, was agreed at the 1999 NATO summit meeting in Washington. Subsequent developments have served to strengthen cooperation between NATO and the European Union and to establish a strategic partnership. This has led, among other developments, to the transfer of responsibility from NATO to the European Union, for continuing peace-support operations in the Former Yugoslav Republic of Macedonia and in Bosnia and Hercegovina, in accordance with the 'Berlin plus' arrangements providing for NATO support for EU-led military operations of this kind.

At the Washington summit a defence capabilities initiative was also launched which aimed to improve defence interoperability among NATO forces. At the 2002 Prague summit, further measures to improve capabilities were taken on the basis of a new capabilities commitment, in which member countries agreed to specific targets and time frames for improvements. A military concept for defence against terrorism was also agreed, and additional initiatives taken in the areas of nuclear, biological and chemical weapons defence, and protection against cyber attacks. The NATO response force, a rapid-reaction unit comprising land, sea and air special forces, was officially launched at the Prague summit and became fully operational in 2006.

AFGHANISTAN

From January 2001, following the establishment of the Afghan Transitional Authority, an international security assistance force (ISAF) was created on the basis of a UN mandate to provide the security required to allow infrastructure reconstruction and create a stable democratic government. In 2002, NATO began providing support for ISAF at the request of the lead nations and, in August 2003, assumed full responsibility for the leadership of ISAF. In accordance with an October 2003 UN security council mandate, ISAF gradually extended its authority from the capital, Kabul, to assume responsibility for the security, reconstruction and development of the entire country in October 2006. ISAF is responsible for provincial reconstruction teams which provide security for aid workers and help with reconstruction work across the country; it also provides training and mentoring for the Afghan National Army and support for the Afghan National Police. In February 2010 there were approximately 85,785 ISAF troops serving in Afghanistan from 43 NATO and non-NATO countries.

IRAQ

Following a summit meeting in Istanbul in 2004, NATO agreed to establish an Iraq training mission. This included the foundation of a joint staff college, tasked with the training of mid- to senior-level Iraqi military officers, which opened at Ar-Rustamiyah, near Baghdad, in September 2005. In 2007, NATO also initiated a programme of Gendarmerie-type training for the Iraqi police, and introduced further training schemes for the navy, airforce and other areas of national security in December 2008; training for Iraqi customs and border police was introduced in 2010.

AFRICA

NATO counter-piracy operations were active between October and December 2008, and again between March and July 2009, in response to the growing threat presented by piracy in the Horn of Africa region. Currently, Operation Ocean Shield – approved by the North Atlantic council in August 2009 – is focused on at-sea operations, but also offers assistance to regional states in developing their capacity to combat piracy.

At the request of the African Union (AU) NATO is providing support to the AU mission in Sudan. It is also providing airlift assistance to the AU mission in Somalia, and capacity-building support to the AU's long-term peace-keeping capabilities, in particular the African standby force.

Secretary-General and Chair of the North Atlantic Council, of the DPC and of the NPG, Anders Fogh Rasmussen (Denmark)

ORGANISATION FOR ECONOMIC COOPERATION AND DEVELOPMENT

2 rue André-Pascal, F-75775 Paris, France
T (+33) (1) 4524 8200 **E** webmaster@oecd.org
W www.oecd.org

The Organisation for Economic Cooperation and Development (OECD) was formed in 1961 to replace the Organisation for European Economic Cooperation. It is the instrument for international cooperation among industrialised member countries on economic and social policies. Its objectives are to assist its member governments in creating policies designed to achieve high, sustained economic growth and maintain financial stability, to contribute to world trade on a multilateral basis and to stimulate members' aid to developing countries. OECD has 30 members, most of which have developed, high-income economies. The European Commission is involved in the work of the OECD but is not a member of the organisation.

The council is the supreme body of the organisation. It is composed of one representative for each member country and meets at permanent representative level under the chairmanship of the secretary-general, and at ministerial level (usually once a year) under the chair of a minister, elected annually. Decisions and recommendations are adopted by the unanimous agreement of all members. Most of the OECD's work is undertaken by over 150 specialised committees and working parties. These are serviced by an international secretariat headed by a secretary-general.

Chile, Estonia, Israel, the Russian Federation and Slovenia are negotiating accession to the OECD. The organisation has links to many other non-member states and in 2007 launched a programme of enhanced engagement with Brazil, China, India, Indonesia and South Africa. The funding of the OECD is divided according to a member state's economy and population size; the USA, the largest contributor, supplies almost 25 per cent of the organisation's budget.

Secretary-General, Angel Gurría (Mexico)

ORGANISATION FOR SECURITY AND COOPERATION IN EUROPE

6 Wallnerstrasse, 1010 Vienna, Austria
T (+43) (1) 51436 6000 E info@osce.org W www.osce.org

The Organisation for Security and Cooperation in Europe (OSCE) was launched in 1975 as the Conference on Security and Cooperation in Europe (CSCE) under the Helsinki Final Act. This established agreements between NATO members, Warsaw Pact members, and neutral and non-aligned European countries covering security, cooperation and human rights. It was renamed in 1995.

The Charter of Paris for a New Europe, signed in November 1990, committed members to support multiparty democracy, free-market economics, the rule of law and human rights. The signatories also agreed to regular meetings of heads of government, ministers and officials. The first CSCE summit was held in Helsinki in December 1992, at which the Helsinki Document was adopted. This declared the CSCE to be a regional organisation under the UN charter and defined the structures of the organisation.

Three structures have been established: the ministerial council, which comprises the foreign ministers of participating states and meets at least once a year; the permanent council, which is the main regular body for political consulation, meeting weekly in Vienna; and the forum for security cooperation, also meeting weekly. The chairmanship of the OSCE rotates annually and the post of chair-in-office is held by the foreign minister of a participating state.

The OSCE is also underpinned by four permanent institutions: a secretariat (Vienna); an office for democratic institutions and human rights (Warsaw), which is charged with furthering human rights, democracy and the rule of law; an office of the high commissioner on national minorities (The Hague), which identifies ethnic tensions that might endanger peace and promotes their resolution; and a representative on freedom of the media (Vienna), which is responsible for assisting governments in the furthering of free, independent and pluralistic media.

The OSCE has 18 field operations in Europe, the Caucasus and Central Asia. Since 1996, the OSCE has observed more than 150 elections and supervised all elections in Bosnia and Hercegovina between 1996 and 2000 and in Kosovo between 2000 and 2004. In 1999, the charter on European security committed the OSCE to cooperating with other organisations and institutions concerned with the promotion of security within the OSCE area. The OSCE has 56 participating states and in 2010 its budget was €150.8m (£133.1m).
Chair, Kazakhstan (2010)
Chair-in-office, Kanat Saudabayev (Kazakhstan)

ORGANISATION OF AMERICAN STATES

17th Street and Constitution Avenue, NW, Washington
DC 20006, USA
T (+1) (202) 458 3000 W www.oas.org

Originally founded in 1890 for largely commercial purposes, the Organisation of American States (OAS) adopted its present name and charter in 1948. The charter entered into force in 1951 and was amended in 1970, 1988, 1996 and 1997. OAS has 35 member states, though the membership of Honduras was suspended in July 2009 following a coup against President Jose Zelaya. The European Union and 63 non-American states have permanent observer status.

The OAS aims to strengthen the peace and security of the Americas; to promote and consolidate representative democracy; to prevent or resolve any political, judicial or economic issues which may arise among member states; to promote their economic, social and cultural development; and to achieve an effective limitation of conventional weapons.

Policy is determined by the annual general assembly, the organisation's supreme authority, which elects the secretary-general for a five-year term. The meeting of consultation of ministers of foreign affairs considers urgent problems on an *ad hoc* basis. The permanent council, comprising one ambassador from each member state, implements the policies approved by the general assembly, acts as an intermediary in cases of disputes arising between states and oversees the general secretariat, the main administrative body. The inter-American council for integral development was created in 1996 by the ratification of the protocol of Managua to promote sustainable development.
Secretary-General, José Miguel Insulza (Chile)

ORGANISATION OF ARAB PETROLEUM EXPORTING COUNTRIES

PO Box 20501, Safat 13066, Kuwait
T (+965) 2495 9000 E oapec@oapecorg.org
W www.oapecorg.org

The Organisation of Arab Petroleum Exporting Countries (OAPEC) was founded in 1968. Its objectives are to promote cooperation in economic activities, unite efforts to ensure the flow of oil to consumer markets, and create a favourable climate for capital investment and the development of the petroleum industry. OAPEC has 11 member states, although Tunisia's membership has been inactive since 1987.

The ministerial council is composed of oil ministers from the member countries and meets twice a year to determine policy and approve the budgets and accounts of the general secretariat and the judicial tribunal. The judicial tribunal is composed of seven judges who rule on disputes between member countries and between countries and oil companies. The executive organ of OAPEC is the general secretariat.

The active members are Algeria, Bahrain, Egypt, Iraq, Kuwait, Libya, Qatar, Saudi Arabia, Syria and the United Arab Emirates.
Secretary-General, Abbas Ali Naqi (Kuwait)

ORGANISATION OF THE BLACK SEA ECONOMIC COOPERATION

Sakip Sabanci Caddesi, Musir Fuad Pasa Yalisi, Eski Tersane, 34460 Istanbul, Turkey
T (+90) (212) 229 6330/6335 E info@bsec-organization.org
W www.bsec-organization.org

The Black Sea Economic Cooperation (BSEC) resulted from the Istanbul Summit Declaration and the adoption of the Bosphorus statement on 25 June 1992; it acquired a permanent secretariat in 1994. A charter was inaugurated to found the Organisation of the Black Sea Economic Cooperation in May 1999, following the Yalta Summit of the heads of state or government in June 1998. It has 12 member states.

The organisation aims to promote closer political and economic cooperation between the countries in the Black Sea region and to foster greater security, foreign investment, and good governance.

The council of the ministers of foreign affairs is the highest decision-making authority and meets twice-yearly. The meetings rotate among the member states and the chair is the foreign minister of the state in which the meeting is held. There is also a committee of senior officials, and a number of working groups which deal with specific areas of cooperation. BSEC has a permanent secretariat based in Istanbul.

Chair, Georgia (May–October 2010); Greece (November 2010–April 2011)

ORGANISATION OF THE ISLAMIC CONFERENCE

PO Box 178, Jeddah 21411, Saudi Arabia
T (+966) (2) 651 5222 E cabinet@oic-oci.org
W www.oic-oci.org

The Organisation of the Islamic Conference (OIC) was established in 1969 with the purpose of promoting solidarity and cooperation between its member states. It also has the specific aims of supporting the formation of a Palestinian state, coordinating the views of member states in international forums such as the UN, and improving cooperation in the fields of economics, culture and science.

The OIC has three main bodies: the Islamic summit, the organisation's supreme authority composed of the heads of member states, which meets triennially; the annual conference of foreign ministers; and the general secretariat, which implements policy and is headed by a secretary-general elected by the conference of foreign ministers for a once-renewable five-year term.

In addition to this structure, the OIC has several subsidiary bodies, institutions, and standing committees. These include the international Islamic court of justice; the Islamic Solidarity Fund, to aid Islamic institutions in member countries; the Islamic Development Bank, to finance development projects in member states and the Islamic Educational, Scientific and Cultural Organisation.

Since 1991, the OIC has spoken out in protest of violence against Muslims in India, the Occupied Territories and Bosnia-Hercegovina. From 1993 to 1995 the OIC coordinated the offering of troops to the UN by Muslim states to protect Muslim areas of Bosnia-Hercegovina. The OIC is currently focused on issues arising from the situations in Iraq, Somalia, Sudan, and the Jammu and Kashmir dispute, and those of terrorism, human rights abuse and anti-Muslim discrimination.

The organisation has 57 members (27 states in Africa; 24 in the Middle East, central and south-east Asia plus the Palestinian Authority; three in Europe, and two in South America) and five observer states.

Secretary-General, Prof. Ekmeleddin Ihsanoglu (Turkey)

ORGANISATION OF THE PETROLEUM EXPORTING COUNTRIES

Helferstorferstrasse 17, A-1010 Vienna, Austria
T (+43) (1) 2111 20 E prid@opec.org W www.opec.org

The Organisation of the Petroleum Exporting Countries (OPEC) was created in 1960 as a permanent intergovernmental organisation with the principal aims of unifying and coordinating the petroleum policies of its members, and stabilising prices and supply in international oil markets. Since 1982 OPEC has attempted, with mixed success, to impose overall production limits and production quotas to maintain stable oil prices.

The supreme authority is the conference of ministers of oil, mining and energy of member countries, which meets at least twice a year. The board of governors, nominated by member countries, directs the management of OPEC and implements conference resolutions. The secretariat carries out executive functions under the direction of the board of governors.

According to BP's annual statistical review, OPEC's 12 member countries held 76 per cent of the world's oil reserves at the end of 2008, and that year accounted for 44.8 per cent of the world's oil production. Indonesia suspended its membership of OPEC from January 2009, after declining production caused it to become a net importer of oil.

Secretary-General, Abdalla Salem El-Badri (Libya)

PACIFIC ISLANDS FORUM

Secretariat, Private Mail Bag, Suva, Fiji
T (+679) 331 2600 E info@forumsec.org.fj
W www.forumsec.org

The Pacific Islands Forum (PIF), formerly the South Pacific Forum, was established in 1971 and represents heads of governments of 16 independent and self-governing Pacific island countries. It aims to foster cooperation between its governments and to represent the interests of the region in international organisations. The PIF meets annually, after which a dialogue is conducted at ministerial level with 13 forum partner states and the European Union.

The PIF secretariat is governed by the forum officials committee (FOC), composed of senior figures from each member country. It comprises divisions dealing with development and economic policy, trade and investment, political and international affairs and services, and is responsible for implementing the forum's decisions.

In 2006, French Polynesia and New Caledonia became associate members. Tokelau, Wallis and Futuna, the Commonwealth, the Asia Development Bank and the United Nations currently hold observer status, with Timor–Leste as a special observer. Fiji's membership was suspended in May 2009 over the failure of its military government to commit to a timeframe for a return to democratic government.

Secretary-General, Gregory Tuiloma Neroni Slade (Samoa)

PARTNERS IN POPULATION AND DEVELOPMENT

IPH Building, Mohakhali, 1212 Dhaka, Bangladesh
T (+88) (2) 988 1882 E partners@ppdsec.org
W www.partners-popdev.org

Partners in Population and Development (PPD) is an intergovernmental organisation launched at the UN International Conference on Population and Development in Cairo in 1994. It has 25 member states. PPD is dedicated to forming partnerships between and among individuals, organisations and the governments of developing countries. It provides a platform for its members to share successful experiences in education, migration, sexual health and combating infant mortality.

PPD is controlled by a board of directors consisting of a single representative from each member state. The responsibilities of the board include setting policy, promoting cooperation among members and providing advice to the secretariat. The secretariat is based in Dhaka,

Bangladesh, and is mandated to serve as the administrative centre of the organisation. It ensures policies are implemented and identifies new areas for collaboration. PPD also has an international advisory committee consisting of specialists who advise the board and secretariat on current trends in population, development and reproductive health.

PPD is a permanent observer at the United Nations.

Chair, HE Ghulam Nabi Azad (India)

SECRETARIAT OF THE PACIFIC COMMUNITY

BP D5, Nouméa Cedex, 98848, New Caledonia
T (+687) 262 000 E spc@spc.int W www.spc.int

The Secretariat of the Pacific Community (SPC) (formerly the South Pacific Commission) was established in 1947 by Australia, France, the Netherlands, New Zealand, the UK and the USA with the aim of promoting the economic and social stability of the islands in the region. The community now numbers 26 member states and territories: the four remaining founder states (the Netherlands and the UK have withdrawn) and the other 22 states and territories of Melanesia, Micronesia and Polynesia.

The SPC is a technical assistance agency with programmes in marine and land development and health and social policy. The governing body is the conference of the Pacific community, which meets every two years.

Director-General, Dr Jimmie Rodgers (Solomon Islands)

SHANGHAI COOPERATION ORGANISATION

41 Liangmaqiao Road, Chaoyang District, 100600 Beijing, China
T (+86) (10) 6532 9807 E sco@sectsco.org W www.sectsco.org

The Shanghai Cooperation Organisation (SCO) is a permanent intergovernmental organisation. It was established in 1996 as the Shanghai Five, when China, Kazakhstan, Kyrgyzstan, Russia and Tajikistan signed an agreement on cooperating to resolve disputes along the former Sino-Soviet border. It was renamed in 2001 when Uzbekistan became an official member.

The main principle of the SCO is strengthening cooperation among member states across a range of fields, including politics, economics, science, culture, energy, transportation, environment protection and tourism.

The heads of state council is the organisation's supreme body and meets annually to formulate SCO policy. The heads of government council also holds annual meetings to discuss cooperation strategies and approve budgets. The SCO has two permanent bodies: a secretariat based in Beijing and a regional anti-terrorist structure in Tashkent. The secretary-general and the director of the executive committee are appointed by the council of heads of state for a period of three years.

Secretary-General, Muratbek Imanaliev (Kyrgyzstan)

SOUTH ASIAN ASSOCIATION FOR REGIONAL COOPERATION

PO Box 4222, Tridevi Marg, Kathmandu, Nepal
T (+977) (1) 422 1785/ 6350 E saarc@saarc-sec.org
W www.saarc-sec.org

The South Asian Association for Regional Cooperation (SAARC) was established in 1985 by Bangladesh, Bhutan, India, the Maldives, Nepal, Pakistan and Sri Lanka; Afghanistan was admitted as its eighth member in 2007. Its primary objective is the acceleration of economic and social development in member states through collective action in agreed areas of cooperation. These include agricultural and environmental development, science and technology, health and communications.

A SAARC preferential trading arrangement, designed to reduce tariffs on trade between SAARC member states, was signed in 1993 and entered into force in 1995. The South Asian free trade area (SAFTA) was agreed in 2004, and came into effect in 2006, with the aim of abolishing practically all trade tarriffs by the end of 2016. Agreement was reached in 2002 to work towards the establishment of a South Asian economic union.

The highest authority rests with the heads of state or government of each member state. The council of ministers, which meets twice a year, is made up of the foreign ministers of the member states and is responsible for formulating policy. The standing committee is composed of the foreign secretaries of the member states and monitors and coordinates SAARC programmes; it meets twice a year. Technical committees are assigned to individual areas of SAARC's activities. Its secretariat monitors, facilitates and promotes SAARC's activities and serves as a channel of communication between the association and other regional and intergovernmental institutions.

In 2005, as the only country in South Asia not to be a member of SAARC, Iran declared its wish to join and has since become an observer member, along with seven other states and the European Union.

Secretary-General, HE Dr Sheel Kant Sharma (India)

SOUTHERN AFRICAN DEVELOPMENT COMMUNITY

Private Bag 0095, Gaborone, Botswana
T (+267) 395 1863 E registry@sadc.int W www.sadc.int

The Southern African Development Community (SADC) was formed in 1992 by the members of its predecessor, the Southern African Development Coordination Conference. The latter was founded in 1980 to harmonise economic development among southern Africa's 'majority ruled' countries and reduce their dependence on then apartheid South Africa. The SADC now comprises 15 countries, including South Africa, though Madagascar's membership remains suspended following a coup in March 2009.

The SADC aims to evolve common political values, promote economic growth, regional security, sustainable development and the interdependence of member states. An annual summit attended by members' heads of state is the SADC's supreme authority, and its policies are implemented by a secretariat.

Executive Secretary, Tomaz Augusto Salomao (Mozambique)

UNITED NATIONS

UN Plaza, New York, NY 10017, USA
T (+1) (212) 963 1234 W www.un.org

The United Nations (UN) is an intergovernmental organisation dedicated, through signature of the UN charter, to the maintenance of international peace and security and the solution of economic, social and political problems through international cooperation.

The UN was founded as a successor to the League of Nations and inherited many of its procedures and institutions. The name United Nations was first used in the Washington Declaration of 1942 to describe the 26 states that had allied to fight the Axis powers. The UN charter developed from discussions at the Moscow conference of the foreign ministers of China, the Soviet Union, the UK and the USA in 1943. Further progress was made at Dumbarton Oaks, Washington, in 1944 during talks involving the same states. The role of the security council was formulated at the Yalta conference in 1945. The charter was formally drawn up by 50 allied nations at the San Francisco conference between April and June 1945, when it was signed. Following ratification, the UN came into effect on 24 October 1945, which is celebrated annually as United Nations Day. The UN flag is light blue with the UN emblem centred in white.

The principal organs of the UN are the general assembly, the security council, the economic and social council, the secretariat and the international court of justice. The economic and social council is an auxiliary, charged with assisting and advising the general assembly, security council and member states, and coordinating the economic and social aspects of the work of UN agencies and commissions. The official languages used are Arabic, Chinese, English, French, Russian and Spanish; the working languages of the secretariat and the international court of justice are English and French.

MEMBERSHIP

Membership is open to all countries that accept the charter and its principle of peaceful co-existence. New members are admitted by the general assembly on the recommendation of the security council. The original membership of 51 states has grown to 192 (*see* below).

Members of the UN

Afghanistan
Albania
Algeria
Andorra
Angola
Antigua and Barbuda
Argentina*
Armenia
Australia*
Austria
Azerbaijan
Bahamas
Bahrain
Bangladesh
Barbados
Belarus*
Belgium*
Belize
Benin
Bhutan
Bolivia*
Bosnia and Hercegovina
Botswana
Brazil*
Brunei
Bulgaria
Burkina Faso
Burundi
Cambodia
Cameroon
Canada*
Cape Verde
Central African Republic
Chad
Chile*
China*
Colombia*
Comoros
Congo, Dem. Rep. of the
Congo, Republic of the
Costa Rica*
Côte d'Ivoire
Croatia
Cuba*
Cyprus
Czech Republic
Denmark*
Djibouti
Dominica
Dominican Republic*
East Timor
Ecuador*
Egypt*
El Salvador*
Equatorial Guinea
Eritrea
Estonia
Ethiopia*
Fiji
Finland
France*
FYR Macedonia
Gabon
The Gambia
Georgia
Germany
Ghana
Greece*
Grenada
Guatemala*
Guinea
Guinea-Bissau
Guyana
Haiti*
Honduras*
Hungary
Iceland
India*
Indonesia
Iran*
Iraq*
Ireland
Israel
Italy
Jamaica
Japan
Jordan
Kazakhstan
Kenya
Kiribati
Korea, Dem. People's Rep. of
Korea, Rep. of
Kuwait
Kyrgyzstan
Laos
Latvia
Lebanon*
Lesotho
Liberia*
Libya
Liechtenstein
Lithuania
Luxembourg*
Madagascar
Malawi
Malaysia
Maldives
Mali
Malta
Marshall Islands
Mauritania
Mauritius
Mexico*
Micronesia, Federated States of
Moldova
Monaco
Mongolia
Montenegro
Morocco
Mozambique
Myanmar
Namibia
Nauru
Nepal
The Netherlands*
New Zealand*
Nicaragua*
Niger
Nigeria
Norway*
Oman
Pakistan
Palau
Panama*
Papua New Guinea
Paraguay*
Peru*
The Philippines*
Poland*
Portugal
Qatar
Romania
Russian Federation*
Rwanda
St Kitts and Nevis
St Lucia
St Vincent and the Grenadines
Samoa
San Marino
São Tomé and Princípe
Saudi Arabia*
Senegal
Serbia
Seychelles
Sierra Leone
Singapore
Slovakia
Slovenia
Solomon Islands
Somalia
South Africa*
Spain
Sri Lanka
Sudan
Suriname
Swaziland
Sweden
Switzerland
Syria*
Tajikistan
Tanzania
Thailand
Togo
Tonga
Trinidad and Tobago
Tunisia
Turkey*
Turkmenistan
Tuvalu
Uganda
Ukraine*
United Arab Emirates
United Kingdom*
United States of America*
Uruguay*
Uzbekistan
Vanuatu
Venezuela*
Vietnam
Yemen
Zambia
Zimbabwe

* Original member (ie from 1945). Czechoslovakia, Yugoslavia and the USSR were all original members until their dissolution.

OBSERVERS
Permanent observer status is held by the Holy See. The Palestinian Authority has special observer status.

THE GENERAL ASSEMBLY

UN Plaza, New York, NY 10017, USA

The general assembly is the main deliberative organ of the UN. It consists of all members, each entitled to five representatives but having only one vote. The annual session begins on the third Tuesday of September, when the president is elected, and usually continues until mid-December. Special sessions are held on specific issues and emergency special sessions can be called within 24 hours.

The assembly is empowered to discuss any matter within the scope of the charter, except when it is under consideration by the security council, and to make recommendations. Under the peace resolution, adopted in 1950, the assembly may also take action to maintain international peace and security when the security council fails to do so because of a lack of unanimity of its permanent members. Important decisions, such as those on peace and security, the election of officers, the budget, etc, need a two-thirds majority. Others need a simple majority. The assembly has effective power only over the internal operations of the UN itself; external recommendations are not legally binding.

The work of the general assembly is divided among a number of committees, on each of which every member has the right to be represented. Subjects include human rights, the use of torture, peacekeeping, assistance to developing countries and discrimination. In addition, the general assembly appoints *ad hoc* committees to consider more specific issues. All committees consider items referred to them by the assembly and recommend draft resolutions to its plenary meeting.

The assembly is assisted by a number of functional committees. The general committee coordinates its proceedings and operations, while the credentials committee verifies the representatives.

President of the General Assembly, HE Father Miguel d'Escoto Brockmann (Nicaragua)

SPECIALISED BODIES

The assembly has created a large number of specialised bodies, some of which are supervised jointly with the economic and social council. They are supported by UN and voluntary contributions from governments, non-governmental organisations and individuals. These organisations include:

CONFERENCE ON DISARMAMENT
Palais des Nations, CH-1211 Geneva 10, Switzerland

The Conference on Disarmament (CD) was established in 1979 as the international community's multilateral disarmament negotiating forum. Originally comprising 40 member states, the CD has expanded to 65 members. The non-proliferation of nuclear weapons treaty entered into force on 5 March 1970 and has so far been ratified by 190 states. A chemical weapons convention was agreed in Paris in 1993 and came into force in April 1997 after being ratified by 87 countries. Currently 135 states participate in the convention, which bans the use, production, stockpiling and transfer of all chemical weapons. A convention which prohibits the use of cluster munitions, agreed in Dublin in 2008 and ratified by 32 states, will enter into force on 1 August 2010.

UNITED NATIONS CHILDREN'S FUND (UNICEF)
3 UN Plaza, New York, NY 10017, USA **T** (+1) 212 326 7000
W www.unicef.org

Established in 1946 to assist children and mothers in the immediate post-war period, UNICEF now concentrates on developing countries. It provides primary healthcare and health education, and conducts programmes in oral hydration, immunisation against common diseases, HIV/AIDS treatment and prevention and child growth monitoring. It also works to provide children with equal access to quality education.

UNITED NATIONS DEVELOPMENT PROGRAMME (UNDP)
1 UN Plaza, New York, NY 10017, USA **T** (+1) 212 906 5000
W www.undp.org

Established in 1966 from the merger of the UN expanded programme of technical assistance and the UN special fund, UNDP is the central funding agency for economic and social development projects around the world. Much of its annual expenditure is channelled through UN specialised agencies, governments and non-governmental organisations.

UNITED NATIONS HIGH COMMISSIONER FOR REFUGEES (UNHCR)
Case Postale 2500, CH-1211 Geneva 2 Depot, Switzerland
T (+41) 22 739 8111 **W** www.unhcr.org

Established in 1950 to protect the rights and interests of refugees, UNHCR organises emergency relief and longer-term solutions, such as voluntary repatriation, local integration or resettlement.

UNITED NATIONS RELIEF AND WORKS AGENCY FOR PALESTINE REFUGEES IN THE NEAR EAST (UNRWA)
HQ Gaza PO Box 140157, Amman 11814, Jordan
T (+972) 8 677 7333 **W** www.unrwa.org

The UNRWA was established in 1949 to bring relief to the Palestinians displaced by the Arab-Israeli conflict. The UN general assembly has repeatedly voted every three years to extend its mandate, most recently until June 2011.

UNITED NATIONS HUMAN RIGHTS COUNCIL (UNHRC)
Palais des Nations, CH-1211 Geneva 10, Switzerland
T (+22) 917 9000 **E** infodesk@ohchr.org **W** www.ohchr.org

The UNHRC is a 47-member council, established in 2006, replacing the United Nations Commission on Human Rights (UNCHR). The UNHRC has a mandate to promote and prevent violations of human rights by engaging in dialogue with governments and international organisations. It is also responsible for the coordination of all UN human rights activities and reports to, and is directly elected by, the general assembly.

THE SECURITY COUNCIL

UN Plaza, New York, NY 10017, USA
T (+41) (22) 917 9000 **W** www.un.org/docs/sc

The security council is the senior arm of the UN and has the primary responsibility for maintaining world peace and security. It consists of 15 members, each with one representative and one vote. There are five permanent members – China, France, Russia, the UK and the USA – and ten non-permanent members. Each of the non-permanent members is elected for a two-year term by a two-thirds majority of the general assembly and is ineligible for immediate re-election. Five of the elective seats are allocated to Africa and Asia, one to eastern Europe, two to Latin America and two to western Europe and remaining countries. Procedural questions are determined by a majority vote. Other matters require a majority inclusive of the votes of the permanent members; they thus have a right of veto. The abstention of a permanent member does not constitute a veto. The presidency rotates each month by state in (English) alphabetical order. Parties in a dispute, other non-members and individuals can be invited to participate in security council debates but are not permitted to vote.

The security council is empowered to settle or adjudicate in disputes or situations which threaten international peace and security. It can adopt political, economic and military measures to achieve this end. Any matter considered to be a threat to or breach of the peace or an act of aggression can be brought to the security council's attention by any member state or by the secretary-general. The charter envisaged members placing at the disposal of the security council armed forces and other facilities which would be coordinated by the military staff committee, composed of military representatives of the five permanent members. The security council is also supported by a committee of experts, to advise on procedural and technical matters, and a committee on admission of new members.

Owing to superpower disunity, the security council has rarely played the decisive role set out in the charter; the military staff committee was effectively suspended from 1948 until 1990, when a meeting was convened during the Gulf crisis on the formation and control of UN-supervised armed forces. In 1992, heads of government laid plans to transform the UN in light of the changed post-Cold War world. The secretary-general produced *An Agenda for Peace,* a report which centred on the establishment of a UN army composed of national contingents on permanent standby, as envisaged at the time of the UN's formation. However, enthusiasm for UN intervention waned during the rest of the decade after a problematic mission in Somalia during which 42 UN personnel were killed. The security council has since been criticised for its failure to intervene in subsequent conflicts, including the genocide in Rwanda and the ongoing situation in Darfur. More recently it has applied sanctions to Iran, North Korea and Pakistani militant group Lashkar-e-Taiba.

The security council also has the power to elect judges to the international court of justice and to recommend to the general assembly the election of a secretary-general.

PEACEKEEPING FORCES

The security council has established a number of peacekeeping forces since its foundation, comprising contingents provided mainly by neutral and non-aligned UN members. As at 28 February 2010, current operations were:

Continent	*UN Code*	*Year implemented*	*Personnel deployed*
Africa			
Western Sahara	MINURSO	1991	224
Democratic Republic of the Congo	MONUC	1999	20,573
Liberia	UNMIL	2003	10,427
Côte d'Ivoire	UNOCI	2004	8,544
Sudan	UNMIS	2005	10,541
Darfur, Sudan	UNAMID	2007	21,800
Central African Republic and Chad	MINURCAT	2007	3,814
The Americas			
Haiti	MINUSTAH	2004	9,087
Asia			
India and Pakistan	UNMOGIP	1949	44
Timor–Leste	UNMIT	2006	1,521
Europe			
Cyprus	UNFICYP	1964	919
Kosovo	UNMIK	1999	16
Middle East			
Egypt, Israel, Jordan, Lebanon and Syria	UNTSO	1948	153
Israel and Syria	UNDOF	1978	1,044
Lebanon	UNIFIL	1974	11,504

TOP FIVE CONTRIBUTORS TO UN PEACEKEEPING MISSIONS (*as at* April 2010)

Country	*Number of Troops*
Pakistan	10,742
Bangladesh	10,212
India	8,771
Nigeria	5,941
Egypt	5,457

Source: www.un.org/en/peacekeeping/

INTERNATIONAL CRIMINAL TRIBUNAL FOR THE FORMER YUGOSLAVIA

Churchillplein 1, 2517 JW The Hague, The Netherlands
T (+31) 7051 28591 W www.icty.org

In February 1993, the security council voted to establish the International Criminal Tribunal for the Former Yugoslavia (ICTFY) a war crimes tribunal to hear cases covering breaches of the Geneva Conventions and crimes against humanity during the Balkans conflict of the 1990s. The court was inaugurated in November 1993 in The Hague with 11 judges elected by the UN general assembly from 11 states. There are currently 16 permanent judges, divided into three trial chambers of three judges each and an appeal chamber of the remaining seven. The court is reliant upon states to arrest suspects to stand trial, but is empowered to pass verdicts in the absence of suspects and can put suspects under an 'act of accusation' which prevents them from leaving their own country. As well as running and managing a detention unit based at The Hague and a witness protection and assistance programme, the ICTFY also has powers to interview witnesses and seize evidence. The total biannual budget for 2008–9 is US$301.9m (£194.7m) and 1,050 staff representing 83 nations are currently employed by the tribunal.

President, Patrick L. Robinson (Jamaica)

INTERNATIONAL CRIMINAL TRIBUNAL FOR RWANDA
Churchillplein 1, 2517 JW The Hague, The Netherlands
T (+31) 7051 25027 E ictr-press@un.org W www.ictr.org

Following serious violations of humanitarian law in Rwanda, the UN security council created the International Criminal Tribunal for Rwanda on 8 November 1994 in order to contribute to the process of national reconciliation and the maintenance of peace in the region. Its remit is to prosecute persons responsible for genocide and other serious international humanitarian law violations committed in the territory of Rwanda between 1 January 1994 and 31 December 1994, and by Rwandan citizens in the territory of neighbouring states during the same period. The biannual budget for 2010–11 is US$245.3m (£158.2m) and 693 staff representing 77 nations are currently employed by the tribunal.
President, Judge Charles Michael Dennis Byron (St Christopher and Nevis)

THE ECONOMIC AND SOCIAL COUNCIL

UN Plaza, New York, NY 10017, USA
E ecosocinfo@un.org W www.un.org/ecosoc

The economic and social council is responsible under the general assembly for the economic and social work of the UN and for the coordination of the activities of the 14 specialised agencies and other UN bodies. It makes reports and recommendations on economic, social, cultural, educational, health and related matters, often in consultation with non-governmental organisations, passing the reports to the general assembly and other UN bodies. It also drafts conventions for submission to the assembly and calls conferences on matters within its remit.

The council consists of 54 members, 18 of whom are elected annually by the general assembly for overlapping three-year terms. Each member has one vote and can be immediately re-elected. The council elects a president and four vice-presidents each year: this five-member bureau proposes the council's agenda, draws up a programme of work and organises the substantive session. This session is held each July, and decisions are reached by a simple majority vote of those present.

The council has established a number of functional commissions and standing committees on particular issues. These include commissions on social development, sustainable development, population and development, the status of women, crime prevention and criminal justice, narcotic drugs, science and technology for development and the status of women, as well as five regional economic commissions.
President, HE Hamidon Ali (Malaysia)

THE SECRETARIAT

UN Plaza, New York, NY 10017, USA

The secretariat services the other principle UN organs and administers their programmes and policies. It is headed by a secretary-general elected by a majority vote of the general assembly on the recommendation of the security council. He is assisted by 39,978 staff worldwide, who represent all 192 member nationalities (as at June 2009). The secretary-general is charged with bringing to the attention of the security council any matter which he considers poses a threat to international peace and security. He may also bring other matters to the attention of the general assembly and other UN bodies and may be entrusted by them with additional duties. As chief administrator to the UN, the secretary-general is present in person or via representatives at all meetings of the other five main organs of the UN. He may also act as a mediator in disputes between member states.

The power and influence of the secretary-general has been determined largely by the character of the office-holder and by the state of relations between the superpowers. The thaw in these relations since the mid-1980s has increased the effectiveness of the UN, particularly in its attempts to intervene in international disputes. It helped to end the Iran-Iraq War and sponsored peace in Central America. Following Iraq's invasion of Kuwait in 1990, the UN took its first collective security action since the Korean War. Conflicts in Cyprus, Timor–Leste, Libya, Nigeria and Western Sahara were successfully prevented from escalating or spreading during the administration of Kofi Annan. However, the UN was heavily criticised for its failure to act in the Rwandan genocide of 1994 and its inability to halt the continuing conflict in Darfur, while the invasion of Iraq by the USA and UK in 2003 without a UN mandate, illegal under the organisation's charter, seriously undermined its authority.
Secretary-General, Ban Ki-moon (South Korea)
Deputy Secretary-General, Dr Asha-Rose Migiro (Tanzania)

FORMER SECRETARIES-GENERAL	
1946–52	Trygve Lie (Norway)
1953–61	Dag Hammarskjöld (Sweden)
1961–71	U Thant (Myanmar)
1972–81	Kurt Waldheim (Austria)
1982–91	Javier Pérez de Cuéllar (Peru)
1992–96	Boutros Boutros-Ghali (Egypt)
1997–2006	Kofi Annan (Ghana)

UK MISSION TO THE UN
1 Dag Hammarskjld Plaza, 885 Second Avenue, New York, NY 10017, USA T (+1) (212) 745 9200 E uk@un.int
W www.ukun.fco.gov.uk
Permanent Representative to the United Nations and Representative on the Security Council, Sir Mark Lyall Grant, *apptd* 2009

UK MISSION TO THE UN AND OTHER INTERNATIONAL ORGANISATIONS IN GENEVA
58 Avenue Louis Casai, 1216 Cointrin GE Geneva, Switzerland
T (+41) (22) 918 2300 E geneva_un@fco.gov.uk
Permanent UK Representative, Peter Gooderham, *apptd* 2008

UK MISSION TO THE UN IN VIENNA
Jaurèsgasse 12, A-1030 Vienna, Austria
T (+43) (1) 716 130 E ukmis.vienna@fco.gov.uk
W ukinaustria.fco.gov.uk
Permanent UK Representative, HE Simon Smith, *apptd* 2007

REGIONAL UN INFORMATION CENTRE
Block C2, Level 7, 155 rue de la Loi, Brussels 1040, Belgium
T (+32) 2788 8484 E info@unric.org W www.unric.org

THE INTERNATIONAL COURT OF JUSTICE

The Peace Palace, NL-2517 KJ, The Hague, The Netherlands
T (+31) 7030 22323 W www.icj-cij.org

The international court of justice is the principal judicial organ of the UN, and its statute is an integral part of the UN charter; all members of the UN are *ipso facto* parties to it. The court is composed of 15 judges, elected by both the general assembly and the security council for nine-year terms which are renewable. Judges may deliberate over cases in which their country is involved. If no judge on the bench is from a country which is a party to a dispute under consideration, that party may designate a judge to participate *ad hoc* in that particular deliberation. If any party to a case fails to adhere to the judgement of the court, the other party may have recourse to the security council.

President, Hisashi Owada (Japan)
Vice-President, Peter Tomka (Slovakia)
Judges, Antonio A. Cancado Trindade (Brazil); Shi Jiuyong (China); Ronny Abraham (France); Bruno Simma (Germany); Awn Shawkat al-Khasawneh (Jordan); Bernardo Sepúlveda-Amor (Mexico); Mohamed Bennouna (Morocco); Kenneth Keith (New Zealand); Leonid Skotnikov (Russian Federation); Abdul G. Koroma (Sierra Leone); Abdulqawi Ahmed Yusuf (Somalia); Christopher Greenwood (UK); Thomas Buergenthal (USA)

UNITED NATIONS EDUCATIONAL, SCIENTIFIC AND CULTURAL ORGANISATION

7 place de Fontenoy, F-75352 Paris, France
T (+33) (01) 4568 1000 E bpi@unesco.org W www.unesco.org

The United Nations Educational, Scientific and Cultural Organisation (UNESCO) was established in 1945. It promotes collaboration among its member states in education, science, culture and communication. It aims to promote a universal respect for human rights, justice and the rule of law, without distinction of race, sex, language or religion, in accordance with the UN charter.

UNESCO runs a number of programmes to improve education and extend access to it. It provides assistance to ensure the free flow of information and its wider dissemination without any barriers to freedom of expression, to safeguard cultural heritages and encourage sustainable development. It fosters research and study in the social and environmental sciences. The UNESCO world heritage list, decided upon by a 21-member committee of state representatives, includes 890 cultural and natural sites of 'outstanding universal value'.

UNESCO has 193 member states and seven associate members. The general conference, consisting of representatives of all the members, meets biennially to decide the programme and the budget. It elects the 58-member executive board, which supervises operations, and appoints a director-general who heads a secretariat responsible for carrying out the organisation's programmes. In most member states national commissions liaise with UNESCO to execute its policies.

Director-General, Irina Bokova (Bulgaria)

UNITED NATIONS INDUSTRIAL DEVELOPMENT ORGANISATION

Vienna International Centre, Wagramerstrasse 5, PO Box 300, A-1400 Vienna, Austria T (+43) (1) 260 260 E unido@unido.org W www.unido.org

The United Nations Industrial Development Organisation (UNIDO) was established in 1966 by the UN general assembly to act as the central coordinating body for industrial activities within the UN. It became a UN specialised agency in 1985. UNIDO aims to help countries with developing and transitional economies by increasing the productivity and competitiveness of their agricultural industries.

UNIDO has 172 members. It is funded by regular and operational budgets, together with contributions for technical cooperation activities. The regular budget is derived from member states' contributions. Technical cooperation is funded mainly through voluntary contributions from donor countries and institutions and by intergovernmental and non-governmental organisations. A general conference of all the members meets biennially to discuss strategy and policy, approve the budget – €381.6m (£308m) in 2008–9 – and elect the director-general. The industrial development board is composed of representatives from 53 member states and reviews the work programme and the budget, which is prepared by the programme and budget committee of 27 member states.

Director-General, Kandeh K. Yumkella (Sierra Leone)

UNIVERSAL POSTAL UNION

4 Weltpoststrasse, CH-3000 Bern 15, Switzerland
T (+41) (31) 350 3111 E info@upu.int W www.upu.int

The Universal Postal Union (UPU) was established by the treaty of Bern 1874, taking effect from 1875, and became a UN specialised agency in 1948. The UPU exists to form and regulate a single postal territory of all member countries for the reciprocal exchange of correspondence without discrimination. With a total of 191 members, it also assists and advises on the improvement of postal services.

The universal postal congress is the UPU's supreme authority and meets every four years. The council of administration meets annually to supervise the union's work between congresses, to investigate regulatory developments and policy issues, to approve the budget and to examine proposed treaty changes. The consultative committee was set up in 2004 to further the interests of the wider postal sector. It brings together representative bodies of customers, service providers, manufacturers and suppliers, and provides a forum for dialogue between postal industry stakeholders. The three UPU bodies are served by the international bureau, a secretariat headed by a director-general.

Funding is provided by members according to a scale of contributions drawn up by the congress. The council of administration sets the budget which amounts to approximately SFr37m (£21.7m) per year.

Director-General, Edouard Dayan (France)

UNREPRESENTED NATIONS AND PEOPLES ORGANISATION

PO Box 85878, 2508 CN, The Hague, The Netherlands
T (+31) (0) 70 364 6504 E unpo@unpo.org W www.unpo.org

The Unrepresented Nations and Peoples Organisation (UNPO) was founded in 1991 to offer an international forum for occupied nations, indigenous peoples and national minorities who are not represented in other international organisations.

The UNPO does not aim to represent these nations and peoples, but rather to assist and empower them to represent themselves more effectively, and provides professional services and facilities as well as education and training in the fields of diplomacy, international and human rights law, democratic processes, institution building, conflict management and resolution, and environmental protection.

Participation is open to all nations and peoples who are inadequately represented at the UN and who declare allegiance to five principles relating to the right of self-determination of all peoples: human rights, democracy, tolerance, non-violence and protection of the natural environment. Applicants must show that they constitute a nation or people and that the organisation applying for membership is representative of that nation or people.

As at April 2010, UNPO had 54 full members.

General Secretary, Marino Busdachin (Italy)

WESTERN EUROPEAN UNION

15 rue de l'Association, 1000 Brussels, Belgium
T (+32) (2) 500 4412 E secretariatgeneral@weu.int
W www.weu.int

Western European Union (WEU) is a defence and security organisation. It began as the Brussels Treaty Organisation (BTO), based on the Brussels treaty signed in 1948 by Belgium, France, Luxembourg, the Netherlands and the UK. The BTO was designed to provide collective self-defence and economic and social collaboration among its signatories. The treaty was modified to become the WEU in 1954 with the admission of West Germany and Italy.

In 1991, the EU Maastricht treaty committed the European Community to the establishment of a common foreign and security policy. The WEU was designated as the future defence component of the European Union and member states of the EU who were not already members of the WEU were invited to join or become observers. In 1992, the WEU's role as the common security dimension of the EU was enhanced when WEU ministers signed a declaration with remaining European NATO members to give them various forms of WEU membership.

In 1999, NATO and the EU decided to establish a direct relationship; the EU committed itself to ensuring that it was able to take decisions on conflict prevention and crisis management and NATO agreed to give the EU access to its collective assets and capabilities for operations in which NATO as a whole was not engaged. The WEU's crisis management functions were transferred to the EU in 2001, and the Lisbon Treaty which entered into force in December 2009 introduced provisions for the collective self-defence of all EU member states, and the creation of *ad hoc* interparliamentary groups. Thus superseded, in March 2010 the Brussels treaty was terminated and the WEU announced that it would cease operations by June 2011.

The WEU currently has ten member states, six associate members, and five observers, and a further seven countries are associate partners.

Presidency, Spain, Belgium (2010); Italy, Luxembourg (2011)

Acting Secretary-General, Arnaud Jacomet (France)

WORLD BANK GROUP

1818 H Street NW, Washington DC 20433, USA
T (+1) (202) 473 1000 E pic@worldbank.org
W www.worldbank.org

The World Bank Group was founded in 1944 and is one of the world's largest sources of development assistance. It has 187 member states. Originally directed towards post-war reconstruction in Europe, the bank subsequently turned towards assisting less-developed countries worldwide, and in 2009 funded 303 projects across the developing world. It works with government agencies, non-governmental organisations and the private sector to formulate assistance strategies. Its local offices implement the bank's programme in each country.

The World Bank is owned by the governments of member countries and its capital is subscribed by its members. It finances its lending primarily from borrowing in world capital markets, and derives a substantial contribution to its resources from its retained earnings and the repayment of loans. The interest rate on its loans is calculated in relation to its cost of borrowing.

The World Bank Group consists of two institutions and three affiliates. The International Bank for Reconstruction and Development (IBRD) provides loans and development assistance to middle-income countries and creditworthy poorer countries (total loans for 2009 US$32.9bn (£21.2bn)). The International Development Association (IDA) performs the same function as the IBRD but primarily to less-developed countries and on terms that bear less heavily on their balance of payments than IBRD loans (total loans for 2009 US$14bn (£9bn)).

The three affiliates are the International Finance Corporation (IFC), which has 182 members and promotes private sector investment in developing countries by mobilising domestic and foreign capital; the Multilateral Investment Guarantee Agency (MIGA), which promotes foreign direct investment in developing states by insuring investors against political risk and helping member countries to improve their investment climates; and the International Centre for Settlement of Investment Disputes, which has 144 full members (known as contracting states) and provides facilities for resolving disputes between foreign investors and their host countries.

The IBRD, IDA and the affiliates are financially and legally distinct but share headquarters. The IBRD is headed by a board of governors, which meets annually and consists of one governor and one alternate governor appointed by each member country; most IBRD governors also serve on the separate boards of the IDA, IFC and MIGA. Twenty-four executive directors exercise all powers of the World Bank (except those reserved to the board of governors); their number will rise to 25 in November 2010. The president, elected by the board of governors, conducts the business of the bank, assisted by an international staff. Membership in both the IFC and the IDA is open to all IBRD countries. The IDA is administered by the same staff as the bank; the IFC has its own personnel but can draw on the IBRD for administrative and other support. All share the same president.

President, Robert B. Zoellick (USA)

WORLD CUSTOMS ORGANISATION

30 rue de Marché, B-1210, Brussels, Belgium
T (+32) 2209 9211 E information@wcoomd.org
W www.wcoomd.org

The World Customs Organisation (WCO) is an independent body that works to enhance the effectiveness and efficiency of customs administrations worldwide. By developing a harmonised commodity description and coding system, the WCO introduced a universal goods classification and revenue collection method. The WCO also administers the WTO agreements on customs valuation and rules of origin.

Comprising 176 customs administrations, its members process around 98 per cent of international trade. The WCO is governed by a council which meets annually and

in which each member has one representative and one vote. The council elects and is assisted by a 24-member policy commission, a 17-member finance committee, and a permanent secretariat which implements the council's policies.
Secretary-General, Kuniyo Mikuriya (Japan)

WORLD HEALTH ORGANISATION

Avenue Appia 20, 1211 Geneva 27, Switzerland
T (+41) (22) 791 2111 **E** info@who.int **W** www.who.int

The UN International Health Conference, held in 1946, established the World Health Organisation (WHO) as a UN specialised agency, with effect from 1948. It is dedicated to attaining the highest possible level of health for all. It collaborates with member governments, UN agencies and other bodies to improve health standards, control communicable diseases and promote all aspects of family and environmental health. It seeks to raise the standards of health teaching and training and promotes research through collaborating with research centres worldwide.

WHO has 193 members and is governed by an annual assembly of members which sets policy, approves the budget, appoints a director-general, and adopts health conventions and regulations. It also elects 34 member states to each designate one expert to serve on the executive board. The board sets the assembly's agenda, suggests initiatives, implements its policies, and is empowered to deal with emergencies. A secretariat, headed by the director-general, supervises the activities of six regional offices.
Director-General, Dr Margaret Chan (China)

WORLD INTELLECTUAL PROPERTY ORGANISATION

34 chemin des Colombettes, CH-1211, Geneva 20, Switzerland
T (+41) (22) 338 9111 **E** information.centre@wipo.int
W www.wipo.int

The World Intellectual Property Organisation (WIPO) was established in 1967 by the Stockholm Convention, which entered into force in 1970. WIPO administers 24 treaties that deal with different legal and administrative aspects of intellectual property, notably the Paris Convention for the protection of industrial property and the Bern Convention for the protection of literary and artistic works. WIPO became a UN specialised agency in 1974.

Intellectual property falls into two main branches: industrial property (inventions, trademarks, industrial designs and geographical indications) and copyright (literary, musical, photographic, audiovisual and artistic works, etc). WIPO helps ensure that creative intellectual activity is rewarded, and facilitates technology transfer, particularly to developing countries.

WIPO's mission is to promote the protection of intellectual property rights worldwide. The organisation's activities fall into three broad categories: the progressive development of international intellectual property law, assistance to developing countries, and the provision of services which facilitate the process of obtaining intellectual property rights in multiple countries.

WIPO had 184 members as at April 2010. The biennial session of the general assembly, the conference and the coordination committee set policy, a programme and a budget. A separate agency, the International Union for the Protection of New Varieties of Plants, established by convention in 1961, is linked to WIPO and has 68 members.
Director-General, Francis Gurry (Australia)

WORLD METEOROLOGICAL ORGANISATION

7 bis, avenue de la Paix, PO Box 2300, CH-1211 Geneva 2, Switzerland **T** (+41) (22) 730 8111 **E** wmo@wmo.int
W www.wmo.int

The World Meteorological Organisation (WMO) was established in 1950 and became a UN specialised agency in 1951, succeeding the International Meteorological Organisation founded in 1873. It facilitates cooperation in the establishment of networks for making, processing and exchanging meteorological, climatological, hydrological and geophysical observations. It also fosters collaboration between meteorological and hydrological services, and furthers the application of meteorology to aviation, shipping, environment, water problems, agriculture and the mitigation of natural disasters.

In March 2010, the WMO had 183 member states and six member territories. Six regional associations are responsible for the coordination of activities within their own regions. There are also eight technical commissions, which study meteorological and hydrological problems, establish methodology and procedures, and make recommendations to the executive council and the congress. The supreme authority is the world meteorological congress, which meets every four years to determine general policy and set the budget (SFr269.8m (£136m) for 2008–11). It also elects 27 members of the 37-member executive council which supervises the implementation of congress decisions, initiates studies and makes recommendations on matters requiring international action. The secretariat is headed by a secretary-general, appointed by the congress.
Secretary-General, Michel Jarraud (France)

WORLD TOURISM ORGANISATION

Capitán Haya 42, 28020 Madrid, Spain
T (+34) 9156 78100 **E** omt@unwto.org **W** www.unwto.org

The World Tourism Organisation (UNWTO) was officially launched in 1975 to act as an executing agency of the United Nations Development Programme. Primarily concerned with developing public and private sector partnerships, the UNWTO also promotes the global code of ethics for tourism, a framework of policy aimed at tour operators, governments, labour organisations and travellers. There are 154 member states and seven associate member states.

The general assembly is the principal gathering of the UNWTO and meets every two years in order to approve policy and budget. Every four years, the assembly elects a secretary-general. The executive council is UNWTO's governing board and meets twice a year to ensure the organisation adheres to policy and budget. It is composed of 31 members of the general assembly. As host country of UNWTO's headquarters, Spain has a permanent seat on the executive council.
Secretary-General, Taleb Rifai (Jordan)

WORLD TRADE ORGANISATION

Centre William Rappard, 154 rue de Lausanne, CH-1211 Geneva 21, Switzerland **T** (+41) (22) 739 5111
E enquiries@wto.org **W** www.wto.org

The World Trade Organisation was established on 1 January 1995 as the successor to the General Agreement on Tariffs and Trade (GATT).

GATT was dedicated to the expansion of non-discriminatory international trade and progressively extended free trade via 'rounds' of multilateral negotiations. The final act of the comprehensive Uruguay round of negotiations was signed by trade ministers from the 128 GATT negotiating states and the EU in Marrakesh, Morocco, in 1994. New talks on agriculture and services began in 2000 and were incorporated into a broader agenda launched at the 2001 ministerial conference in Doha, Qatar.

The WTO is the legal and institutional foundation of the multilateral trading system. It provides the contractual obligations determining how governments frame and implement trade policy, and provides the forum for the debate, negotiation and adjudication of trade issues. The WTO's principal aims are to liberalise world trade and place it on a secure basis, and it seeks to achieve this through the combination of an agreed set of trade rules and market access agreements and further trade liberalisation negotiations. The WTO also administers and implements multilateral agreements in fields such as agriculture, industrial goods, services, government procurement, rules of origin and intellectual property.

The highest authority of the WTO is the ministerial conference composed of all members, which usually meets once every two years. The general council meets as required and acts on behalf of the ministerial conference in regard to the regular working of the WTO. The general council also convenes in two particular forms: as the dispute settlement body, dealing with disagreements between members arising from WTO agreements or commitments; and as the trade policy review body, conducting regular reviews of the trade policies of members. A secretariat of 629 staff, headed by a director-general, services WTO bodies and provides trade performance and trade policy analysis.

As at March 2010, there were 153 WTO members and 30 observers. The WTO budget for 2009 was SFr189.3m (£113.9m), with members' contributions calculated on the basis of their share of international trade. The official languages of the WTO are English, French and Spanish.

Director-General, Pascal Lamy (France)

COUNTRIES OF THE WORLD A–Z

DEFINITIONS AND ABBREVIATIONS

est = estimate
(m) = male; (f) = female
BIRTH RATE – figures are per 1,000 population. The birth rate is usually the dominant factor in determining the rate of population growth. It depends on both the level of fertility and the age structure of the population
CORRUPTION PERCEPTIONS INDEX (CPI) SCORE – the perception of the degree of public sector corruption as seen by business people and country analysts; ranging between 10 (highly clean) and 0 (highly corrupt). © Transparency International
DEATH PENALTY:
abolished for all crimes – countries whose laws do not provide for the death penalty for any crime
retained (not used) – countries which retain the death penalty for ordinary crimes such as murder but can be considered to have abolished it in practice, as they have not executed anyone during the last decade, are believed to have a policy against carrying out executions, or have made a commitment not to use the death penalty
retained for certain crimes – countries whose laws provide for the death penalty only for exceptional crimes such as those committed under military law or in exceptional circumstances. ('Last used' = date of last execution.)
retained – countries that retain the death penalty for ordinary crimes
GROSS ENROLMENT RATIO – the ratio of total enrolment, regardless of age, to the total population of the relevant age group expressed as a percentage; this figure can be above 100 per cent where, for example, where a greater number of children are attending classes designed for six-year-olds than there are six-year-olds in the country, owing to some children starting school late or skipping a year
GROSS NATIONAL INCOME (GNI) – the total incomes earned by a country's residents, regardless of where the assets are located; the second figure is GNI divided by the population to give a per capita figure
HEALTH EXPENDITURE – where a period of years is given (eg 2002–7), data is for the most recent year available
HIV/AIDS ADULT PREVALENCE – estimate of the percentage of the total adult population (aged 15–49) infected with HIV/AIDS. A year-on-year percentage rise may indicate a higher survival rate due to advances in treatment, or the provision of treatment, rather than an increased rate of infection
INFANT MORTALITY RATE – averages for male and female infants under one year old and per 1,000 live births
LIFE EXPECTANCY – averages for men and women aged between 15 and 49 years
MORTALITY RATE – figures are per 1,000 population. This indicator is significantly affected by age distribution, and most countries will eventually show a rise in the overall death rate, in spite of continued decline in mortality at all ages, as declining fertility results in an ageing population
PARAMILITARIES – not included in the total military personnel figure for each country
POPULATION BELOW POVERTY LINE – although strict definitions of poverty vary considerably between nations, this figure most commonly represents the percentage of the adult population whose income is less than US$1 per day
TOTAL EXTERNAL DEBT – the total public and private debt owed to non-residents repayable in foreign currency, goods, or services

AFGHANISTAN

Jomhuri-ye Eslami-ye Afghanestan – Islamic Republic of Afghanistan

Area – 652,230 sq. km
Capital – Kabul; population, 3,572,960 (2009 est)
Major cities – Herat, Jalalabad, Kandahar, Mazar-e-Sharif
Currency – Afghani (Af) of 100 puls
Population – 28,396,000 rising at 2.63 per cent a year (2009 est); Pashtun (42 per cent), Tajik (27 per cent), Hazara (9 per cent), Uzbek (9 per cent), Aimak (4 per cent), Turkmen (3 per cent), Baloch (2 per cent) (est)
Religion – Muslim (Sunni 80 per cent, Shia 19 per cent) (est); Islam is the state religion
Language – Dari (a dialect of Persian), Pashto (both official), Uzbek, Turkmen
Population density – 44 per sq. km (2008 est)
Urban population – 24 per cent (2007 est)
Median age (years) – 17.6 (2009 est)
National anthem – 'Milli Tharana' ['National Anthem']
National day – 19 August (Independence Day)
Life expectancy (years) – 44.64 (2009 est)
Mortality rate – 19.18 (2009 est)
Birth rate – 45.46 (2009 est)
Infant mortality rate – 151.95 (2009 est)
Death penalty – Retained
CPI score – 1.3 (2009)

CLIMATE AND TERRAIN

Mountains, chief among which are the Hindu Kush, cover three-quarters of the landlocked country, with plains in the north and south-west. Elevation extremes range from 7,485m at the highest point (Nowshak, a peak in the Hindu Kush) to 258m at the lowest (Amu Dar'ya). There are three great river basins: the Amu Dar'ya (Oxus), Helmand and Kabul. Natural hazards are flooding, drought and earthquakes. The climate is arid to semi-arid, with extreme temperatures. Summers are hot and dry, and the winters cold with heavy snowfalls, particularly in the mountains. Average annual rainfall is around 240mm per year. Temperatures in Kabul average −8°C to 2°C in January and 16°C to 33°C in July.

HISTORY AND POLITICS

Afghanistan first became a nation in 1747 under Ahmad Shah Durrani. Britain and Russia vied for influence over the region in the 19th and early 20th centuries, but the country remained independent. The monarchy was overthrown in 1973 and a republic was declared. After a coup in 1978 a communist government took power, and armed resistance by conservative Muslim elements began. The government was overthrown in a further coup in 1979 that prompted an invasion by the Soviet Union, which installed a pro-Soviet government. The guerrilla resistance (mujahidin), with foreign backing, fought against Soviet forces, which withdrew in 1989, and against Afghan government forces until the government collapsed in 1992. Factionalism led to ongoing civil conflict until the rise of the Taliban which, between 1994–8, extended its power across more than 90 per cent of the country and imposed strict Shariah law.

The Taliban allowed the al-Qaida network to base terrorist training camps in Afghanistan, and its refusal to hand over al-Qaida leaders after the 11 September 2001 terrorist attacks on the USA led to the regime's overthrow by a US-led international coalition and the Northern Alliance, a grouping of the four main mujahidin factions. A multi-ethnic interim government under Hamid Karzai was installed in December 2001 and, following a *Loya Jirga* (tribal council) in 2002, a transitional government was installed until presidential and parliamentary elections were held in 2004 and 2005.

The government's authority, although still tenuous in the provinces and largely dependent on the presence of foreign troops, is increasingly being asserted by the Afghan army and police. However, the power vacuum after 2001 allowed corruption and local infighting to become endemic, while conflict has escalated owing to the resurgence of the Taliban since 2005, particularly in the south and east, and to opposition to NATO-led drug-eradication programmes.

Hamid Karzai was elected president in 2004. Elections to the lower house of the legislature and to the provincial seats in the upper house were held in September 2005 and the new legislature was inaugurated in December. President Karzai was re-elected in 2009 in controversial circumstances; the first round of voting was marred by widespread electoral fraud, and the second-placed candidate withdrew from the second round as too little had been done to prevent a recurrence of fraud in the run-off. Legislative elections scheduled for May 2010 were postponed to September 2010. There is international concern about the management of these elections after President Karzai took control of the Electoral Complaints Commission in February 2010.

POLITICAL SYSTEM

Under the 2004 constitution, the executive president, who is directly elected for a five-year term, appoints the government, subject to the approval of the lower house of the legislature. The bicameral National Assembly, the *Jirga*, comprises the House of the People *(Wolesi Jirga)*, the lower house, and the House of Elders *(Meshrano Jirga)*. The House of the People has 249 members directly elected for a five-year term; ten seats are reserved for the Kuchi ethnic group and at least 65 seats for women. The House of Elders has 102 members: 34 elected by provincial councils for a three-year term, 34 elected by district councils for a four-year term, and 34 appointed by the president for a five-year term. There are no formal political parties at present.

HEAD OF STATE

President, Hamid Karzai, *elected* 9 October 2004, *sworn in* 7 December 2004, *re-elected* 2009
First Vice-President, Mohammad Qasim Fahim
Vice-President, Karim Khalili

SELECTED GOVERNMENT MEMBERS *as at May 2010*

Defence, Gen. Abdul Raheem Wardak
Foreign Affairs, Rangeen Dadfar Spanta
Finance, Zalmai Rasul
Interior (acting), Gen. Munir Mangal

EMBASSY OF THE ISLAMIC REPUBLIC OF AFGHANISTAN

31 Prince's Gate, London SW7 1QQ
T 020-7589 8891
Ambassador Extraordinary and Plenipotentiary, HE Mohammad Homayoun Tandar, *apptd* 2009

BRITISH EMBASSY

PO Box 334, 15th Street, Roundabout Wazir Akbar Khan, Kabul
T (+93) (70) 0102 000 E britishembassy.kabul@fco.gov.uk
W http://ukinafghanistan.fco.gov.uk
Ambassador Extraordinary and Plenipotentiary, HE Sir William Patey, KCMG, *apptd* 2010

BRITISH COUNCIL

House 15–17, Kart-e-Parwan, Kabul
T (+93) (79) 000 0130 E info.afghanistan@britishcouncil.org
W www.britishcouncil.org/afghanistan
Director, Tony Jones

DEFENCE

The Afghan government and the international community aim to bolster security by developing the national army and police force, with the intention of handing over responsibility for security from late 2010. The national army has 90,800 troops and is rapidly expanding. NATO's International Security Assistance Force has approximately 102,155 troops in Afghanistan.
Military expenditure – US$180m (2008)

ECONOMY AND TRADE

The economy, devastated by 30 years of conflict, is improving with international assistance, agricultural recovery and service sector growth. Although security problems, weak governance, corruption and inadequate infrastructure continue to hamper reconstruction, there has been sustained economic growth since 2001 and this has continued despite the global downturn, albeit at a slower rate. However, living conditions remain poor for the majority of the population. The illegal drug trade and smuggling underpin a large black economy, although the amount of land under poppy cultivation was reduced by about a quarter between 2008 and 2009. Eradication of the opium trade (which constitutes about 60 per cent of the economy) and exploration for oil and gas in the north are two major long-term policy objectives.

Over 70 per cent of the workforce is engaged in

agriculture, both subsistence and commercial, which accounts for 31 per cent of GDP. The main agricultural products are opium, wheat, fruit, nuts, wool, meat, sheepskins and lambskins. Natural gas, coal and copper are exploited. The main trading partners are Pakistan, the USA and India. Principal exports are agricultural products, handwoven carpets and gemstones. Imports are chiefly capital goods, food, textiles and petroleum products.
GNI – US$10,600m; US$370 per capita (2008)
Annual average growth of GDP – 3.4 per cent (2009 est)
Inflation rate – 26.8 per cent (2008 est)
Population below poverty line – 53 per cent (2003)
Unemployment – 40 per cent (2008 est)
Total external debt – US$8,000m (2004)

BALANCE OF PAYMENTS
Trade – US$4,487m deficit (2000)
Current Account – US$188m deficit (2008)

Trade with UK	*2008*	*2009*
Imports from UK	£85,825,513	£132,932,668
Exports to UK	£1,582,244	£1,134,183

COMMUNICATIONS

There are two international airports, at Kabul and Kandahar, and a further four major and 16 smaller regional airports servicing internal flights. The Amu Dar'ya river makes up most of the 1,200km of inland waterways and carries barge traffic; the main river ports are Kheyrabad and Shir Khan. There is no railway system, although there are railheads on the Pakistan border, and a railway is under construction from Mashhad, in Iran, to Herat. Much of the road system is in disrepair, although many of the main highways between Kabul, Kandahar and Herat have been reconstructed. The fixed-line telephone network is limited in extent (460,000 fixed lines in 2008), and mobile phone distribution has grown rapidly (8.5 million subscribers in 2008). Internet access is scarce, even in urban areas; there were 500,000 subscribers in 2008.

EDUCATION AND HEALTH

Education is free and nominally compulsory, elementary schools having been established in most centres. In 2002, schools reopened to 1.5 million children, many of whom had not received schooling under the Taliban. However, militants have targeted education facilities for girls.
Literacy rate – 28.0 per cent (2007 est)
Gross enrolment ratio (percentage of relevant age group) – primary 106 per cent; secondary 39 per cent (2008 est)
Health expenditure (per capita) – US$42 (2007)
Hospital beds (per 1,000 people) – 0.4 (2003–8)

MEDIA AND CULTURE

The media was severely restricted under the Taliban, which banned television broadcasting. Since 2001, radio and television stations and newspapers, both state-run and privately owned, have proliferated. National Radio-TV Afghanistan is the state broadcaster. Private TV stations are popular in urban areas, and provide imported Indian and Western-style programming. Relays of foreign radio stations, and stations funded by foreign governments and NGOs, are available in Kabul. The press enjoys freedom of expression and a growing readership. However, media laws prohibit content which offends Islamic law.

Much of Afghanistan's cultural heritage has been lost during its decades of conflict. The Kabul Museum was looted during the early 1990s, and treasures such as the Kunduz Hoard (silver Greek-style coins) were stolen. Its collection was further depleted by the Taliban's systematic iconoclasm, which included the demolition in 2001 of the giant Bamiyan Buddhas, carved in the fourth to sixth centuries; however, adjacent caves in Bamiyan were proven by scientists in 2008 to contain the oldest known examples of oil painting in the world, dating from the seventh century.

ALBANIA

Republika e Shqiperise – Republic of Albania

Area – 28,748 sq. km
Capital – Tirana; population, 432,652 (2009 est)
Major towns – Durres, Elbasan, Shkoder, Vlore
Currency – Lek (Lk) of 100 qindarka
Population – 3,639,453 rising at 0.55 per cent a year (2009 est); Albanian (95 per cent), Greek (3 per cent) (1989 est)
Religion – Muslim 70 per cent (Sunni, and Bektashi form of Shia Sufism), Christian 30 per cent (Albanian Orthodox and Roman Catholic) (est). Religious observance was banned in 1967; private religious practice has been permitted since 1990
Language – Albanian (official), Greek, Vlach, Romani, Slavic dialects
Population density – 115 per sq. km (2008)
Urban population – 46 per cent (2007 est)
Median age (years) – 29.9 (2009 est)
National anthem – 'Hymni i Flamurit' ['Hymn to the Flag']
National day – 28 November (Independence Day)
Life expectancy (years) – 77.96 (2009 est)
Mortality rate – 5.55 (2009 est)
Birth rate – 15.29 (2009 est)
Infant mortality rate – 18.62 (2009 est)
Death penalty – Abolished for all crimes (since 2007)
CPI score – 3.2 (2009)

CLIMATE AND TERRAIN

About two-thirds of the country is mountainous, and almost 40 per cent is covered by forest. The plain that runs the length of the Adriatic coastline is home to most of the population. The highest point of elevation is 2,764m (Maja e Korabit, a peak on the Macedonian border) and the lowest is 0m (Adriatic Sea). Albania shares Lake Scutari with Montenegro, and lakes Ohrid and Prespa with Macedonia. The climate is Mediterranean on the coast and continental in the interior. The average daily temperature in Tirana ranges between 2°C to 12°C in January and 17°C to 31°C in July.

HISTORY AND POLITICS

Albania was under Ottoman rule from 1468 until 1912, when independence was declared after the first Balkan War. After a period of unrest, a republic was declared in 1925 and in 1928 a monarchy. The country was occupied by the Italians in 1939 and by the Germans in 1943. Albania was liberated by mostly communist partisans led by Enver Hoxha in 1944. Elections in 1945 resulted in a communist-controlled assembly; the king was deposed *in absentia* and a republic declared in 1946.

From 1946 to 1990 Albania was a one-party communist state. Aligned with the USSR until 1961 and with China from 1961 to 1978, it pursued an isolationist policy from 1978 until Hoxha's death in 1985. Gradual moves towards democratisation and westernisation began in the late 1980s, and in 1991 and 1992 democratic elections took place, the Communists losing power in 1992.

Anti-government protests following the collapse of several 'pyramid' investment schemes in early 1997 resulted in near-anarchy for some months, the government losing control of large areas of the country until a change of government and an EU peacekeeping force restored order. The country remained stable in 1999 despite the pressures caused by the influx of 480,000 refugees fleeing from Serbian attacks on ethnic Albanians in Kosovo; the government supported NATO's moves to deal with the crisis and by the end of 1999 nearly all the refugees had left Albania.

Talks with the EU began in 2003 and, following progress on political and economic reform, a stabilisation and association agreement was signed in 2006. Albania became a member of NATO in 2009.

Bamir Topi, of the Democratic Party (PD), was elected president in July 2007 in the fourth round of voting. The incumbent PD and its allies won a narrow victory in the 2009 legislative election, and formed a new coalition with a minor party to secure an overall majority.

POLITICAL SYSTEM

Under the 1998 constitution, the president is elected by the legislature for a five-year term, renewable only once. The unicameral legislature, the People's Assembly, has 140 members (100 directly elected, 40 by proportional vote) who serve four-year terms. The president appoints the prime minister, who must be approved by the People's Assembly. The assembly elects the council of ministers.

HEAD OF STATE

President, Bamir Topi, *elected* 20 July 2007, *took office* 24 July 2007

SELECTED GOVERNMENT MEMBERS *as at May 2010*

Prime Minister, Sali Berisha
Deputy Prime Minister, Foreign Affairs, Ilir Meta
Defence, Arben Imami
Interior, Lulzim Basha
Finance, Ritvan Bode

EMBASSY OF THE REPUBLIC OF ALBANIA

33 St George's Drive, London SW1V 4DG
T 020-7828 8897 E embassy.london@mfa.gov.al
W www.albanianembassy.co.uk
Ambassador Extraordinary and Plenipotentiary, HE Zef Mazi, *apptd* 2007

BRITISH EMBASSY

Rruga Skenderbeg 12, Tirana
T (+355) (4) 223 4973 W ukinalbania.fco.gov.uk
Ambassador Extraordinary and Plenipotentiary, HE Fiona McIlwham, MBE, *apptd* 2009

BRITISH COUNCIL

Rruga Perlat Rexhepi, Pallati 197 Ana, Tirana
T (+355) (4) 224 0856/7 W www.britishcouncil.org/albania
Director, Clare Sears

DEFENCE

The Albanian armed forces (AAF) is a joint force. The land element has 3 main battle tanks and 6 armoured personnel carriers. The navy element has 27 patrol and coastal combatant vessels at two bases, Durres and Vlore. The air element has 16 helicopters.

Military budget – US$254m (2009)
Military personnel – 14,295: joint force command 8,150, support command 4,300, training and doctrine command 1,000, MoD and general staff 795; paramilitary 500
Conscription duration – 12 months

ECONOMY AND TRADE

Albania is one of the poorest countries in Europe. Communist isolationism resulted in dilapidated infrastructure, antiquated equipment and practices, and widespread corruption. Liberalisation measures have resulted in sustained growth since 2004, and inflation is under control. Nevertheless, the economy is still heavily dependent on remittances from expatriate workers, worth about 15 per cent of GDP, and overseas aid, primarily from the EU. Infrastructure and energy supply inadequacies, organised crime and corruption have deterred foreign investment, and tackling these is a government priority. A new thermal power plant and improved transmission lines from neighbouring countries should relieve energy shortages.

Agriculture accounts for 58 per cent of employment but only 20.6 per cent of GDP. The main crops are wheat, maize, vegetables, fruit, sugar beet and livestock products. The principal industries are food processing, textiles and clothing, timber, oil, cement, chemicals, mining (base metals) and hydro-electric power.

Trade is mainly with Italy, Greece and China. Exports include textiles and footwear, asphalt, metals and metal ores, crude oil, tobacco, fruit and vegetables. Imports include machinery and equipment, foodstuffs, textiles and chemicals.

GNI – US$12,100m; US$3,840 per capita (2008)
Annual average growth of GDP – 2.1 per cent (2009 est)
Inflation rate – 2.1 per cent (2009 est)
Population below poverty line – 25 per cent (2004 est)
Unemployment – 12 per cent (2009 est)
Total external debt – US$1,550m (2004)
Imports – US$5,300m (2008)
Exports – US$1,400m (2008)

BALANCE OF PAYMENTS

Trade – US$3,405m deficit (2009)
Current Account – US$1,975m deficit (2008)

Trade with UK	*2008*	*2009*
Imports from UK	£14,683,136	£17,667,897
Exports to UK	£1,143,684	£1,776,531

EDUCATION AND HEALTH

Literacy rate – 99 per cent (2007 est)
Gross enrolment ratio (percentage of relevant age group) – primary 105 per cent; secondary 77 per cent; tertiary 19 per cent (2006 est)

Health expenditure (per capita) – US$244 (2007)
Hospital beds (per 1,000 people) – 2.9 (2003–8)

MEDIA

The public broadcaster Albanian Radio and TV (RTSh) faces increasing competition from dozens of private television channels and radio stations, many of which were established within the last ten years. Political parties, trade unions, religious groups and state bodies are prohibited from owning private television and radio stations, but many publish their own newspapers.

ALGERIA

Al-Jumhuriyah al-Jaza'iriyah ad Dimuqratiyah ash Sha'biyah – People's Democratic Republic of Algeria

Area – 2,381,741 sq. km
Capital – Algiers (El Djazair, Al Jaza'ir); population, 2,740,070 (2009 est)
Major cities – El Djelfa, Batna, Constantine (Qacentina), Oran (Wahran)
Currency – Algerian dinar (DA) of 100 centimes
Population – 34,178,188 rising at 1.2 per cent a year (2009 est); Arab-Berber (99 per cent) (est)
Religion – Muslim (Sunni 99 per cent) (est)
Language – Arabic (official), French, Berber dialects
Population density – 14 per sq. km (2008)
Urban population – 65 per cent (2007 est)
Median age (years) – 26.6 (2009 est)
National anthem – 'Kassaman' ['We Pledge']
National day – 1 November (Revolution Day)
Life expectancy (years) – 74.02 (2009 est)
Mortality rate – 4.64 (2009 est)
Birth rate – 16.9 (2009 est)
Infant mortality rate – 27.73 (2009 est)
Death penalty – Retained (not used since 1993)
CPI score – 2.8 (2009)

CLIMATE AND TERRAIN

Algeria, the second largest country in Africa after Sudan, is dominated by the Sahara desert, which covers 80 per cent of its territory. The eastern part of the Atlas mountain range crosses the north of the country, separating the coastal plain, where the majority of the population lives, from the desert plateaux of the interior. The highest point of elevation is 3,003m (Mt Tahat) and the lowest is −40m (Chott Melrhir, a salt lake). The mountains are subject to earthquakes, and to flooding and mudslides during the rainy season (November to March). The temperate northern coastal areas receive the greatest and most frequent rainfall, whereas the interior plateaux are drier and experience cold winters and hot summers.

HISTORY AND POLITICS

Algeria was a Roman province with a Berber population that was conquered by Arabs in the seventh century and converted to Islam. It was part of the Ottoman Empire from the 16th century until its annexation by France in 1830. It gained independence in 1962, following an eight-year guerrilla war by the socialist Front de Libération Nationale (FLN). The FLN was the only permitted political party for many years until political pluralism was introduced in 1989.

The 1991–2 legislative elections were abandoned after the first round in anticipation of a victory by the opposition Islamic Salvation Front (FIS), which had campaigned on a radical Islamist platform. The FIS was banned in 1992, triggering civil unrest and conflict between Islamic groups (the FIS-backed Islamic Salvation Army and the more extreme Armed Islamic Group) and the military. A state of emergency was declared in 1992, and the country suffered an insurgency that claimed an estimated 100,000 lives. The level of violence started to fall in 1999, when the newly elected president Abdelaziz Bouteflika initiated a policy of reconciliation with the Islamists, and his 'civil concord' was approved by referendum in 1999. In 2005 a referendum approved a second amnesty for militants and the military, but since 2006 a group aligning itself with al-Qaida has carried out a series of bombings.

Another divisive issue is the ethnic Berber population's campaign since 2001 for greater political and cultural recognition. Following occasionally violent demonstrations and a Berber boycott of the 2002 and 2004 elections, negotiations led to an agreement in 2005 that promised greater government investment in the Berber-populated Kabylie region and greater recognition for the Berber language. The Berber protests also reflected the wider population's discontent with social conditions and living standards.

In the 2007 legislative election, the ruling FLN-led coalition won the most seats; the elections were blighted by violence, a low turnout and a high number of spoilt ballots. In 2009, President Bouteflika was re-elected for a third term with 90.2 per cent of the vote.

POLITICAL SYSTEM

The 1976 constitution was amended in 1989 to reintroduce political pluralism, and was revised in 2008, most notably to remove the limit on presidential terms. The president is directly elected for a five-year term, which may be renewed. The bicameral *Barlaman* comprises the National People's Assembly, the lower house, and the National Council. The assembly has 389 members, directly elected for a five-year term. The National Council has 144 members; 48 are appointed by the president, and 96 are indirectly elected for a six-year term by electoral colleges formed by local councils; half of these elected members are re-elected every three years. Although Algeria is no longer a one-party state, parties based on religion, including the FIS, or on race, language, gender or region, are banned under the constitution.

HEAD OF STATE

President, Defence, Abdelaziz Bouteflika, *elected* 15 April 1999, *re-elected* 2004, 2009

SELECTED GOVERMENT MEMBERS *as at May 2010*

Prime Minister, Ahmed Ouyahia
Finance, Karim Djoudi
Foreign Affairs, Mourad Medelci
Interior, Noureddine Yazid Zerhouni

ALGERIAN EMBASSY
54 Holland Park, London W11 3RS
T 020-7221 7800 E info@algerianembassy.org.uk
W www.algerianembassy.org.uk
Ambassador Extraordinary and Plenipotentiary, HE Mohamed Salah Dembri, *apptd* 2005

BRITISH EMBASSY
3 Chemin Capitaine Hocine Slimane, Ex Chemin des Glycines, Algiers
T (+213) (770) 085 000 E britishembassy.algiers@fco.gov.uk
W http://ukinalgeria.fco.gov.uk
Ambassador Extraordinary and Plenipotentiary, HE Martyn Roper, *apptd* 2010

BRITISH COUNCIL
BP 452 Ben Aknoun RP, Algiers 16028
T (+213) (21) 916 891 W www.britishcouncil.org/algeria
Director, Jeremy Jacobson

DEFENCE

The army has 1,082 main battle tanks, 1,040 armoured infantry fighting vehicles and 750 armoured personnel carriers. The navy has 2 submarines, 3 frigates, 6 corvettes and 20 patrol and coastal vessels. There are bases at Mers el Kebir, Algiers, Annaba and Jijel. The air force has 197 combat aircraft and 33 armed helicopters.
Military budget – US$5,300m (2009)
Military personnel – 147,000: army 127,000, navy 6,000, air force 14,000; paramilitary 187,200
Conscription duration – 18 months

ECONOMY AND TRADE

In 1994 the government embarked on the liberalisation of the centrally planned economy, and in 1997 initiated a privatisation programme. These reforms, combined with recent high oil prices, have resulted in trade surpluses, record foreign exchange reserves and the reduction of foreign debt. However, diversification away from the energy sector and development of the banking system and infrastructure is slow because of difficulty in attracting investment, inefficiency and corruption. Greater economic buoyancy has had little impact on the high levels of poverty and unemployment.

Algeria has substantial oil and gas reserves and the hydrocarbon industry accounts for 30 per cent of GDP, nearly 60 per cent of government revenue and over 95 per cent of export earnings. Services provide 29.4 per cent of GDP, industry 62.5 per cent and agriculture 8.1 per cent. Industries other than oil and gas production and processing include mining, electrical goods, food processing and light industries.

Algeria's main trading partners are the USA, France, Italy, other EU countries and China. The chief imports are capital goods, foodstuffs and consumer goods.
GNI – US$144,200m; US$4,190 per capita (2008)
Annual average growth of GDP – 3.4 per cent (2009 est)
Inflation rate – 4.1 per cent (2009 est)
Population below poverty line – 23 per cent (2006 est)
Unemployment – 12.4 per cent (2009 est)
Total external debt – US$3,389m (2009 est)
Imports – US$39,200m (2008)
Exports – US$78,200m (2008)

BALANCE OF PAYMENTS
Trade – US$32,513m surplus (2009)
Current Account – US$34,452m surplus (2008)

Trade with UK	*2008*	*2009*
Imports from UK	£268,158,352	£327,251,377
Exports to UK	£842,040,367	£511,253,376

EDUCATION AND HEALTH

Literacy rate – 75.4 per cent (2007 est)
Gross enrolment ratio (percentage of relevant age group) – primary 108 per cent; tertiary 24 per cent (2008 est)
Health expenditure (per capita) – US$173 (2007)
Hospital beds (per 1,000 people) – 1.7 (2003–8)

MEDIA

The television (Entreprise Nationale de Télévision) and radio stations (Radio-Télévision Algérienne) are state-controlled. Their output is supplemented by satellite television received on domestic dishes; French and European channels are popular, and some actively target Algerian viewers. There are several main daily newspapers, some published in Arabic and some in French. There is no direct censorship but defamation laws are used to rein in press criticism.

ANDORRA

Principat d'Andorra – Principality of Andorra

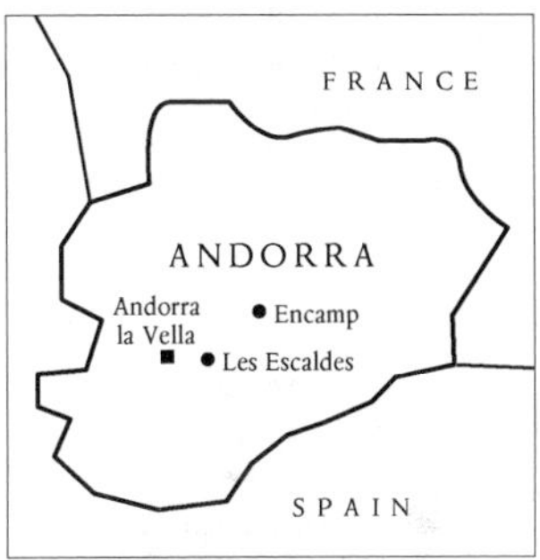

Area – 468 sq. km
Capital – Andorra la Vella; population, 24,864 (2009 est)
Major cities – Encamp, Les Escaldes
Currency – Euro (€) of 100 cents
Population – 83,888 rising at 1.14 per cent a year (2009 est); Spanish (43 per cent), Andorran (33 per cent), Portuguese (11 per cent), French (7 per cent) (1998)
Religion – Christian (Roman Catholic 90 per cent) (est)
Language – Catalan (official), French, Spanish (Castilian), Portuguese
Population density – 178 per sq. km (2008)
Urban population – 89 per cent (2007 est)
Median age (years) – 39.4 (2009 est)
National anthem – 'El Gran Carlemany' ['The Great Charlemagne']
National day – 8 September (Our Lady of Meritxell Day)
Life expectancy (years) – 82.51 (2009 est)
Mortality rate – 5.89 (2009 est)
Birth rate – 10.35 (2009 est)
Infant mortality rate – 3.76 (2009 est)
Death penalty – Abolished for all crimes (since 1990)

CLIMATE AND TERRAIN

Located in the Pyrenees, on the border between France and Spain, Andorra is a landlocked country of dramatic mountains interspersed by narrow valleys. Over a third of the country is forested. The highest point of elevation is

2,946m (Coma Pedrosa) and the lowest is 840m (Riu Runer). The climate is alpine, with heavy snowfall in winter and warm summers. Average temperature ranges from −1°C to 6°C in January and 12°C to 26°C in July.

HISTORY AND POLITICS

Liberated from Moorish rule by Charlemagne in 803, Andorra is a small, neutral principality that was formed by a *paréage* (a type of feudal treaty) in 1278 and since then has owed dual allegiance to two co-princes, the Spanish Bishop of Urgel and the head of state of France. Andorra became an independent democratic parliamentary co-principality in 1993. The first elections under the new constitution were held in 1993, and on 20 January 1994 the first sovereign government of Andorra took office. The country subsequently formalised its links with the EU and joined the UN and the Council of Europe.

In the 2009 legislative election, the opposition Social Democratic Party won 14 of the 28 seats, and formed a government under Jaime Bartumeu.

POLITICAL SYSTEM

Under the 1993 constitution, the heads of state are two co-princes, the President of France and the Bishop of Urgel, Spain. They are represented in Andorra by the permanent delegates (the Spanish vicar-general of the diocese of Urgel and the French prefect of the Pyrénées Orientales department), but their powers now relate solely to relations with France and Spain. The constitution established an independent judiciary and allows Andorra to conduct its own foreign policy, while its people may now join political parties and trade unions.

Andorra has a unicameral legislature, the General Council of the Valleys *(Consell General de las Valls)*, whose 28 members are directly elected for a four-year term by proportional representation. The council appoints the president of the executive council, who nominates government members.

HEADS OF STATE

The President of France, Nicolas Sarkozy
The Bishop of Urgell, Joan Enric Vives i Sicília
Permanent French Delegate, Christian Frémont
Permanent Episcopal Delegate, Nemesi Marqués Oste

SELECTED GOVERNMENT MEMBERS *as at May 2010*

President of the Executive Council, Jaume Bartumeu
Economy and Finance, Pere Lopez
Foreign Affairs, Xavier Espot Miro
Interior, Victor Naudi

BRITISH CONSULATE-GENERAL

Ambassador, HE Giles Paxman, *apptd* 2009, resident at Madrid, Spain

ECONOMY AND TRADE

The economy is largely based on tourism (80 per cent of GDP, with 11 million visitors annually and skiing especially popular), banking and commerce (due in part to a liberal tax regime), tobacco products, forestry, furniture-making and sheep-farming. Most of Andorra's food and electricity has to be imported. Andorra has been a member of the EU customs union since 1991.

Annual average growth of GDP – 2 per cent (2007 est)
Inflation rate – 3.9 per cent (2007)

Trade with UK	*2008*	*2009*
Imports from UK	£8,505,771	£17,477,363
Exports to UK	£391,409	£51,597

COMMUNICATIONS

There are 320km of roads but no railways, airports or waterways. A road into Andorra from Spain is open all year round, and that from France is closed only occasionally in winter. Mobile telephones are nearly twice as widespread as fixed-line connections.

MEDIA

The media is influenced by France and Spain and Andorrans have access to broadcasts from both countries. There is a state-owned radio station and a number of privately owned stations, as well as a state-owned television channel and two major daily newspapers *(Diari d'Andorra* and *El Periodic)*.

ANGOLA

Republica de Angola – Republic of Angola

Area – 1,246,700 sq. km; includes the exclave of Cabinda
Capital – Luanda; population, 4,510,690 (2009 est)
Major cities – Cabinda, Huambo, Lubango
Currency – Kwanza (Kzrl) of 100 centimos
Population – 12,799,293 rising at 2.1 per cent a year (2009 est); Ovimbundu (37 per cent), Kimbundu (25 per cent), Bakongo (13 per cent) (est)
Religion – Christian (predominantly Roman Catholic; indigenous African Christian denominations 25 per cent, Protestant denominations 10 per cent) (est). Some of the rural population practises animism or indigenous religions
Language – Portuguese (official), Bantu and other African languages
Population density – 14 per sq. km (2008)
Urban population – 56 per cent (2007 est)
Median age (years) – 18 (2009 est)
National anthem – 'Angola Avante' ['Forward Angola']
National day – 11 November (Independence Day)
Life expectancy (years) – 38.2 (2009 est)
Mortality rate – 24.08 (2009 est)
Birth rate – 43.69 (2009 est)
Infant mortality rate – 180.21 (2009 est)
HIV/AIDS adult prevalence – 2 per cent (2007 est)
Death penalty – Abolished for all crimes (since 1992)
CPI score – 1.9 (2009)
Literacy rate – 67.4 per cent (2007 est)
Gross enrolment ratio (percentage of relevant age group) – tertiary 3 per cent (2008 est)
Health expenditure (per capita) – US$86 (2007)
Hospital beds (per 1,000 people) – 0.8 (2003–8)

CLIMATE AND TERRAIN

The land rises from a narrow coastal plain to a vast interior plateau. On the plateau rise the Cunene, Cubango and Cuanza rivers, and further east are the sources of the

Zambezi and several tributaries of the Congo river. Some of these are dry except in the rainy season, when flooding may occur. The south is desert. The highest point of elevation is 2,620m (Morro do Moco) and the lowest is 0m (Atlantic Ocean). The climate is tropical in the north – with a cool, dry season from May to October and a hot, rainy season from November to April – and sub-tropical in the south and along the coast to Luanda.

HISTORY AND POLITICS

A Portuguese colony was established in the region in the 15th century and its territory expanded over the centuries, the current boundaries being defined in the 19th century. An anti-colonial war began in 1961, which developed into a civil war between three independence movements shortly before Angola became independent on 11 November 1975. At this point, the Popular Movement for the Liberation of Angola (MPLA) declared itself the government and introduced a one-party Marxist-Leninist regime, establishing its control over the towns. The National Union for the Total Independence of Angola (UNITA) led by Jonas Savimbi, and the Front for the Liberation of Angola (FNLA) conducted a guerrilla war in rural areas. The FNLA ceased operations in the 1980s and foreign support for the MPLA and UNITA was withdrawn after 1988, but the civil war between the government and UNITA continued until 2002. Following the death of Jonas Savimbi in February of that year, UNITA and the government signed a formal ceasefire agreement in April and pledged to adhere to the 1994 peace agreement. UNITA gradually demobilised its forces and transformed itself into a political party, electing Isaias Samakuva as leader in 2003.

Political pluralism was introduced under the 1991 peace agreement and multiparty elections were held in 1992, though UNITA refused to accept the results. The first legislative elections since 1992 were held in September 2008; the MPLA won, with 191 seats to UNITA's 16 seats, and formed a new government. A presidential election has not been held since 1992; the new constitution introduced in February 2010 ended direct election of the president, created the office of vice-president and abolished the post of prime minister.

SECESSION

In the oil-rich northern exclave of Cabinda, separatists have conducted a low-level guerrilla war since the mid-1970s. The government has been unable to end the fighting either through negotiation or by military means. A ceasefire and peace agreement reached in 2006 has not been observed by all parties.

POLITICAL SYSTEM

A new constitution was introduced in February 2010. Under this, the leader of the party with the largest number of seats in the legislature will automatically become president. The unicameral National Assembly has 223 members, elected by proportional representation for a four-year term.

HEAD OF STATE

President, Jose Eduardo dos Santos, *re-elected* 30 September 1992
Vice-President, Fernando da Piedade dos Santos

SELECTED GOVERNMENT MEMBERS *as at May 2010*

Defence, Candido Pereira dos Santos Van-Dunem
Finance, Carlos Alberto Lopez
Foreign Affairs, Assuncao Afonso dos Anjos
Interior, Gen. Roberto Leal Monteiro

EMBASSY OF THE REPUBLIC OF ANGOLA

22 Dorset Street, London W1U 6QY
T 020-7299 9850 E embassy@angola.org.uk
W www.angola.org.uk
Ambassador Extraordinary and Plenipotentiary, HE Ana Maria Teles Carreira, *apptd* 2005

BRITISH EMBASSY

Rua Diogo Cao 4 (Caixa Postal 1244), Luanda
T (+244) (22) 233 4582 E postmaster.luand@fco.gov.uk
W http://ukinangola.fco.gov.uk
Ambassador Extraordinary and Plenipotentiary, HE Richard Wildash, *apptd* 2010

DEFENCE

The army has an estimated 300 main battle tanks, 250 armoured infantry fighting vehicles and 170 armoured personnel carriers. The navy is based at Luanda and has 9 patrol and coastal combatant vessels. The air force has 85 combat aircraft and 16 armed helicopters.
Military budget – US$2,770m (2000)
Military personnel – 107,000: army 100,000, navy 1,000, air force 6,000; paramilitary 10,000

ECONOMY AND TRADE

The economy is still recovering from decades of mismanagement, corruption and war, but liberalisation and stabilisation are being achieved. Post-war increases in oil, diamond and agricultural production have driven strong economic growth, although the economy contracted in 2009 as the global downturn reduced demand for exports. The extractive industries and infrastructure projects have attracted foreign investment despite the corruption and stifling bureaucracy that have deterred investors in other sectors.

Angola, especially Cabinda, is rich in natural resources. The main industries involve extracting and processing oil (oil production and related activities account for over half of GDP), diamonds, metals and other minerals, forestry, fishing, food processing and the manufacture of cement, metal products, tobacco products and textiles, and ship repair. Angola has large areas of good farmland, but the prevalence of unexploded landmines has reduced the area under cultivation and forced many areas back to subsistence agriculture, although coffee, sisal and cotton are produced for export. Despite rising production, the country still imports half of its food.

The main trading partners are China, the USA, Portugal and Brazil. The principal exports are crude oil, diamonds, refined petroleum products, coffee, sisal, fish, timber and cotton. The main imports are machinery and electrical equipment, vehicles and spare parts, medicines, foodstuffs, textiles and military goods.
GNI – US$60,200m; US$3,340 per capita (2008)
Annual average growth of GDP – –0.2 per cent (2009 est)
Inflation rate – 13.1 per cent (2009 est)
Population below poverty line – 40.5 per cent (2006 est)
Total external debt – US$12,830m (2009 est)
Exports – US$66,300m (2008)

BALANCE OF PAYMENTS

Trade – US$20,960m surplus (2009)
Current Account – US$6,408m surplus (2008)

Trade with UK	*2008*	*2009*
Imports from UK	£287,821,273	£332,609,518
Exports to UK	£579,632,236	£270,034,371

COMMUNICATIONS

Land transport difficulties, caused by war damage to road and rail infrastructure, are compounded by uncleared landmines and security problems. Reconstruction began in 2005 with foreign aid, provided largely by China, and several projects have been completed. There are over 51,400km of roads and 2,764km of railway. Most internal travel takes place by air between the country's 192 airports and airfields. The main ports are Luanda, Lobito and Namibe. The fixed-line telephone system is poor, with fewer than one fixed line for 100 people; mobile phone use is growing rapidly, and was about 50 per 100 people in 2008.

MEDIA

The only national daily newspapers and television and radio broadcasters are government-owned and rarely critical. There are several commercial radio stations and private newspapers, one private television station, and some subscription services that include Brazilian and Portuguese channels; their coverage is confined to urban areas. Although freedom of speech is enshrined in the constitution, the private media is liable to harassment.

ANTIGUA AND BARBUDA

Antigua and Barbuda

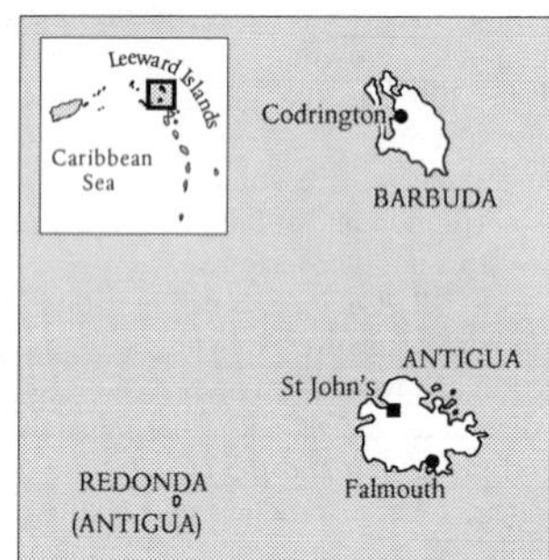

Area – 442.6 sq. km; Antigua 280 sq. km; Barbuda 161 sq. km; Redonda 1.6 sq. km
Capital – St John's; population, 26,580 (2009 est)
Currency – East Caribbean dollar (EC$) of 100 cents
Population – 85,632; rising at 1.3 per cent a year (2009 est)
Religion – Christian (Anglican 26 per cent, Evangelical 25 per cent, Jehovah's Witness 1 per cent), Rastafarian 1 per cent (est)
Language – English (official)
Population density – 197 per sq. km (2008)
Urban population – 31 per cent (2007 est)
Median age (years) – 29.7 (2009 est)
National anthem – 'Fair Antigua, We Salute Thee'
National day – 1 November (Independence Day)
Life expectancy (years) – 74.76 (2009 est)
Mortality rate – 5.94 (2009 est)
Birth rate – 16.59 (2009 est)
Infant mortality rate – 16.25 (2009 est)
Death penalty – Retained
Literacy rate – 90.0 per cent (2007 est)

CLIMATE AND TERRAIN

Antigua is part of the Leeward Islands in the eastern Caribbean. Unlike most other Leeward Islands, it has few high hills and little forest cover. Its elevation extremes range from 402m (Boggy Peak) to 0m (Caribbean Sea).

Barbuda, 48km north of Antigua, is a flat coral island with a large lagoon. Both islands are tropical, but drier than most of the West Indies. They lie within the hurricane belt and are subject to tropical storms and hurricanes between August and October.

HISTORY AND POLITICS

Prehistoric settlers were succeeded by the Arawaks, then the Caribs. Although discovered by Columbus in 1493, the European (English) settlement of Antigua began only in 1632. Barbuda was colonised from Antigua in 1661. Administered as part of the Leeward Islands Federation from 1871 to 1956, it became internally self-governing in 1967 and fully independent on 1 November 1981.

The United Progressive Party defeated the Antigua Labour Party, which had been in office since 1976, in the 2004 election and was re-elected in 2009.

POLITICAL SYSTEM

The head of state is Queen Elizabeth II, represented by the governor-general. The bicameral parliament comprises a senate of 17 members, appointed by the governor-general on the advice of the prime minister and opposition leader, and a House of Representatives of 17 directly elected members; both chambers serve a five-year term.

Governor-General, HE Dame Louise Lake-Tack, GCMG, *apptd* 2007

SELECTED GOVERNMENT MEMBERS *as at May 2010*

Prime Minister, Foreign Affairs, Baldwin Spencer
Minister of Finance and Economy, Harold Lovell
National Security, Leon Errol Cort

HIGH COMMISSION FOR ANTIGUA AND BARBUDA

2nd Floor, 45 Crawford Place, London W1H 4LP
T 020-7258 0070 E enquiries@antigua-barbuda.com
W www.antigua-barbuda.com
High Commissioner, HE Dr Carl Roberts, *apptd* 2004

BRITISH HIGH COMMISSION

HE Paul Brummell, *apptd* 2009, resident at Bridgetown, Barbados

DEFENCE

The navy has 3 patrol and coastal combatant vessels at a base at St Johns.
Military budget – US$7.8m (2009)
Military personnel – 170: army 125, navy 45 (combined Antigua and Barbuda Defence Force)

ECONOMY AND TRADE

The economy is largely based on tourism and related services (contributing about half of GDP), with light manufacturing (bedding, handicrafts, electronic components) for export, and agriculture (livestock, sea island cotton, market gardening, fishing) for local consumption. Economic growth in 2004–7 enabled the government to reduce public debt. However, in 2009, a decline in tourism caused by the global economic downturn and the collapse of Alan Stanford's Antigua-based financial group (which included Antigua's major financial institution) hit the economy badly and public debt is rising again.
GNI – US$1,143m; US$13,200 per capita (2008)
Annual average growth of GDP – –6.5 per cent (2009 est)

Inflation rate – 1.5 per cent (2008 est)
Unemployment – 11 per cent (2001 est)
Total external debt – US$359.8m (2006)

BALANCE OF PAYMENTS
Trade – US$723m deficit (2009)
Current Account – US$354m deficit (2008)

Trade with UK	*2008*	*2009*
Imports from UK	£12,280,799	£24,019,586
Exports to UK	£46,099,108	£281,994

MEDIA AND CULTURE

The Antigua Labour Party owns or controls many of the country's television and radio stations. Antigua's first independent radio station, Observer Radio, began broadcasting in 2001.

Antiguan culture is dominated by cricket and the country has produced several illustrious players, including former West Indies captains Viv Richards (*b.* 1952) and Richie Richardson (*b.* 1962) and bowler Curtly Ambrose (*b.* 1963).

ARGENTINA

República Argentina – Argentine Republic

Area – 2,780,400 sq. km
Capital – Buenos Aires; population, 12,987,800 (2009)
Major cities – Córdoba, La Plata, Mar del Plata, Mendoza, Rosario, Salta, San Miguel de Tucumán, Santa Fé
Currency – Peso of 100 centavos
Population – 40,913,584 rising at 1.05 per cent a year (2009 est)
Religion – Christian (Roman Catholic 76 per cent, Pentecostal 8 per cent, Muslim 1 per cent (of which Sunni 70 per cent, Shia 30 per cent) (est)
Language – Spanish (official), Italian, English, German, French
Population density – 15 per sq. km (2008)
Urban population – 92 per cent (2007 est)
Median age (years) – 30 (2009 est)
National anthem – 'Marcha de la Patria' ['March of the Fatherland']
National day – 25 May (Revolution Day)
Life expectancy (years) – 76.56 (2009 est)
Mortality rate – 7.41 (2009 est)
Birth rate – 17.94 (2009 est)
Infant mortality rate – 11.44 (2009 est)
Death penalty – Abolished for all crimes (since 2008)
CPI score – 2.9 (2009)

CLIMATE AND TERRAIN

The Andes mountain range runs the full length of the country, along its western border with Chile, and the area is prone to earthquakes. East of the Andes, the north is mostly subtropical rainforest, the centre contains the vast grasslands of the pampas (which experienced extreme drought in 2008–9), and the southern Patagonian plateau is arid and desolate, with glaciers in the far south. The highest point of elevation is 6,960m (Cerro Aconcagua) and the lowest is −105m (Laguna del Carbon). Temperatures range from subtropical in the north to subantarctic in the south. In Buenos Aires temperatures are between 17°C and 29°C in January and between 6°C and 14°C in July.

HISTORY AND POLITICS

The estuary of La Plata was discovered in 1515 by Juan Díaz de Solís and the region was subsequently colonised by the Spanish. Spain ruled the territory, which formed part of the United Provinces of the Rio Plata, from the 16th century until a revolution against Spain began in 1810. Independence was declared in 1816. During the following century power swung, often violently, between conservative and liberal factions, and between civil and military regimes.

A 1943 coup introduced a period of military rule before Juan Perón became president in 1946, establishing an authoritarian regime. His overthrow in 1955 instigated 18 years of political instability until 1973, when he was recalled from exile. Perón died within a year and was succeeded by the vice-president, his widow María ('Isabelita'), but she was overthrown in a coup in 1976 that established a military junta. The junta conducted a campaign known as the 'dirty war' in which over 8,000 people were allegedly murdered. The failure of Argentina's attempt to annex the Falkland Islands in 1982 discredited the junta and led to the restoration of civilian rule in 1983. In 2009 Argentina submitted to the UN a formal claim to an area of the South Atlantic Ocean that includes several island groups governed by Britain.

The 2007 presidential election was won in the first round by Cristina Fernández de Kirchner, wife of the outgoing president Néstor Kirchner. The Judicialist Party, a Peronist grouping including the Front for Liberty and the Front for Victory, lost its absolute majorities in both chambers in the 2009 legislative elections, but remained in power.

POLITICAL SYSTEM

After the constitutional amendments agreed in 1994, the executive president is directly elected for a four-year term, renewable only once. The bicameral National Congress consists of a 72-member senate (three members for each province and three for Buenos Aires) and a 257-member Chamber of Deputies. Deputies are directly elected for a four-year term, with half of the seats renewable every two years. Senators are directly elected for a six-year term, with one-third of seats renewable every two years.

HEAD OF STATE
President, Cristina Fernández de Kirchner, *sworn in* 10 December 2007
Vice-President, Julio Cobos

SELECTED GOVERNMENT MEMBERS *as at May 2010*
Cabinet Chief, Anibal Fernandez
Defence, Nilda Garré
Economy, Amado Boudou

Foreign Relations, Jorge Taiana
Interior, Anibal Randazzo

EMBASSY OF THE ARGENTINE REPUBLIC
65 Brook Street, London W1K 4AH
T 020-7318 1300 E info@argentine-embassy-uk.org
W www.argentine-embassy-uk.org
Ambassador Extraordinary and Plenipotentiary, vacant

BRITISH EMBASSY
Dr Luis Agote 2412, 1425 Buenos Aires
T (+54) (11) 4808 2200 W http://ukinargentina.fco.gov.uk
Ambassador Extraordinary and Plenipotentiary, HE Shan Morgan, *apptd* 2008

BRITISH COUNCIL
4th Floor, Marcelo T. de Alvear 590, C1058AAF Buenos Aires
T (+54) (11) 4114 8600 W www.britishcouncil.org/argentina
Director, Huw Jones

FEDERAL STRUCTURE
The republic is a federation of 23 provinces, each with an elected governor and legislature, plus the federal district of Buenos Aires, which has an elected mayor and autonomous government.

DEFENCE

The army has 213 main battle tanks, 263 armoured infantry fighting vehicles and 294 armoured personnel carriers. The navy has 3 submarines, 5 destroyers, 9 frigates, 15 patrol and coastal vessels and 23 combat aircraft. There are bases at Ushuaia, Mar del Plata, Buenos Aires, Puerto Belgrano and Zarate. The air force has 121 combat aircraft.
Military budget – US$2,220m (2009)
Military personnel – 73,100: army 38,500, navy 20,000, air force 14,600; paramilitary 31,240

ECONOMY AND TRADE

The economy recovered rapidly from the economic collapse of 2001–2, experiencing strong growth from 2003. Argentina restructured its defaulted debt in 2005 and repaid its IMF loan in 2006. Inflation rose sharply in 2007–8, pushing up food prices, and the economy contracted in 2008–9 owing to the global downturn. A shortfall in energy supplies remains a problem.

The country is rich in natural resources, particularly lead, zinc, tin, copper, iron ore, manganese, uranium, oil and coal. The fertile pampas supports a strong and export-orientated agricultural sector; the main crops are cereals, oil-bearing seeds, fruit, tea, tobacco and livestock products, especially beef, mutton and wool.

The main industrial activities are food processing (meat-packing, flour-milling, sugar-refining, wine production) and the production of motor vehicles, consumer durables, textiles, chemicals, petrochemicals, printing, metallurgy and steel.

The main trading partners are Brazil, China and the USA. The principal exports include soyabeans and derivatives, petroleum and gas, motor vehicles and cereals. The major imports are machinery, motor vehicles, oil and natural gas, chemicals and plastics.
GNI – US$286,600m; US$7,190 per capita (2008)
Annual average growth of GDP – –2.5 per cent (2009 est)
Inflation rate – 22 per cent (2008 est)
Population below poverty line – 23.4 per cent (January–June 2007)
Unemployment – 9.6 per cent (2009 est)
Total external debt – US$108,600m (2009)
Imports – US$57,400m (2008)
Exports – US$70,600m (2008)

BALANCE OF PAYMENTS
Trade – US$16,980m surplus (2009)
Current Account – US$8,651m surplus (2009)

Trade with UK	*2008*	*2009*
Imports from UK	£295,349,254	£235,064,496
Exports to UK	£531,733,655	£588,187,659

COMMUNICATIONS

The road and rail networks are extensive in the north and centre of the country; in Patagonia, roads are fewer and there are no railways. All 31,400km of railway is state owned. The combined national and provincial road network totals approximately 231,400km, of which 69,400km are surfaced. Internal long-distance travel is mainly by air and there are over 1,000 airports and airfields; the principal airports are at Buenos Aires, Córdoba, Salta and Rio Gallegos. There are many ports on the long coastline and the 11,000km of inland waterways formed by the major rivers; Buenos Aires, Ensenada (La Plata) and Bahía Blanca are the main seaports. The telecommunications system has been modernised and extended since the late 1990s. There were about 9.6 million fixed telephone lines in use and 46.5 million mobile phone subscriptions in 2008.

EDUCATION AND HEALTH

Education is compulsory until the age of 18.
Literacy rate – 97.6 per cent (2007 est)
Gross enrolment ratio (percentage of relevant age group) – primary 115 per cent; secondary 85 per cent; tertiary 68 per cent (2008 est)
Health expenditure (per capita) – US$663 (2007)
Hospital beds (per 1,000 people) – 4.0 (2003–8)

MEDIA AND CULTURE

Argentina's media is prolific, with over 150 daily newspapers (mainly in Spanish, with some in English and German), including seven major dailies published in Buenos Aires. There are hundreds of commercial radio stations (many unlicensed), over 40 television stations and widespread access to cable television.

Most Argentines are of European origin, particularly from Spain and Italy, and Patagonia also has a Welsh-speaking Argentine-Welsh community. The short story writer and poet Jorge Luis Borges (1899–1986) is one of Latin America's most eminent literary figures, and the world's first animated films were made in Argentina by Quirino Cristani (1896–1984). The tango, an African-influenced dance style set to music of diverse European origin, first became popular among European immigrants in Buenos Aires in the late 19th century.

Argentina has historically had a vibrant sporting culture, with successes in football, motor racing and polo. Its football team is a double World Cup winner and has held the Copa America trophy 14 times; noted Argentine players include Alfredo di Stefano (*b.* 1926) and Diego Maradona (*b.* 1960).

ARGENTINE ANTARCTIC TERRITORY

The Argentine Antarctic Territory consists of the Antarctic Peninsula and a triangular section extending to the South Pole, defined as the area between 25°W and 74° W and 60°S. This overlaps with both Britain's and Chile's claimed areas (*see also* The North and South Poles). Administratively, the territory is a department of the province of Tierra del Fuego, Antarctica and South Atlantic Islands. The population varies seasonally between approximately 150 and 300 people, all of whom are scientific researchers.

ARMENIA

Hayastani Hanrapetut'yun – Republic of Armenia

Area – 29,743 sq. km
Capital – Yerevan; population, 1,110,190 (2009 est)
Major cities – Gyumri, Vanadzor
Currency – Dram of 100 luma
Population – 2,967,004 falling at 0.03 per cent a year (2009 est); Armenian (97.9 per cent), Yezidi (1.3 per cent). The Armenian diaspora numbers at least 4,700,000
Religion – Christian (Armenian Apostolic 90 per cent) (est). The kingdom of Armenia was the first state to adopt Christianity as its official religion, in AD 301
Language – Armenian, Yezidi, Russian
Population density – 109 per sq. km (2008)
Urban population – 64 per cent (2007 est)
Median age (years) – 31.5 (2009 est)
National anthem – 'Mer Hayrenik' ['Our Fatherland']
National day – 21 September (Independence Day)
Life expectancy (years) – 72.68 (2009 est)
Mortality rate – 8.39 (2009 est)
Birth rate – 12.65 (2009 est)
Infant mortality rate – 20.21 (2009 est)
Death penalty – Abolished for all crimes (since 2003)
CPI score – 2.7 (2009)

CLIMATE AND TERRAIN

Landlocked Armenia is situated in the south-western part of the Caucasus region between the Black and Caspian seas. It lies at a high altitude and consists of vast plateaux surrounded by mountain ranges. The elevation extremes range from 4,095m (the highest peak of Mt Aragats) to 400m at the lowest (Debed river). The climate is continental, with hot summers, cold winters and low rainfall. Armenia experiences occasional droughts and severe earthquakes.

HISTORY AND POLITICS

The first Armenian state was founded *c.*190 BC and became part of the Roman Empire in 64 BC. It subsequently experienced short periods of autonomy interspersed with rule by successive empires and invasion by the Seljuk Turks, Mongols and other Central Asian tribes. In the 16th century most of Armenia was incorporated into the Ottoman Empire. The remaining eastern areas fell under the Persian Empire; these were later forcibly incorporated into the Russian Empire, which concluded wars with the Persians in 1813 and 1828. The part of Armenia that remained under Ottoman rule experienced pogroms from 1894 onwards, and from 1915 to 1918 over 1.5 million Armenians were deported, starved or killed.

Armenia declared its independence on 28 May 1918, but was invaded in 1920 by Soviet forces and declared a Soviet Socialist Republic. The Soviet government was overthrown by a nationalist revolt in 1921, but reinstated by the Red Army a few months later. In early 1922 Armenia acceded to the USSR.

An Armenian nationalist movement gained power in national elections in mid-1990. In a referendum in 1991, 99 per cent of the electorate voted for independence, which was declared on 21 September 1991.

In the 2007 legislative election, the Republican Party of Armenia (HHK) remained the largest party in the legislature, with 65 seats, and its leader, Serzh Sargsyan, continued in office at the head of a four-party coalition government. Sargsyan won the February 2008 presidential election in the first round with 52.9 per cent of the vote; protests by opposition supporters continued for some weeks, causing a state of emergency to be imposed in March. After his inauguration President Sargsyan nominated Tigran Sargsyan as prime minister.

FOREIGN RELATIONS

There is a longstanding dispute with Azerbaijan over the predominantly Armenian-populated Azeri region of Nagorny-Karabakh; Armenia claims this territory as historically native land arbitrarily granted to Soviet Azerbaijan by Stalin in 1921–2. The territory's government voted to transfer to Armenia in 1988 but this was rejected by the USSR. When the USSR collapsed in 1991, the territory declared independence. Azeri attempts to reassert control were met with resistance which escalated into a war that lasted from 1992 until a ceasefire was agreed between Armenia, Azerbaijan and Nagorny-Karabakh in 1994. By this time, Nagorno-Karabakh forces, supported by Armenia, had captured all of Nagorny-Karabakh, all Azeri territory that separated Nagorny-Karabakh from Armenia and all mountainous Azeri territory around the enclave. Talks mediated by the Organisation for Security and Cooperation in Europe failed to make any progress towards a peaceful resolution until 2008, when Azerbaijan and Armenia agreed to intensify efforts, and talks in 2009 were more productive.

POLITICAL SYSTEM

The 1995 constitution was amended by referendum in 2005. The president is directly elected for a five-year term, renewable only once. The unicameral National Assembly (*Azgayin Joghov*) has 131 members who are directly elected for a four-year term.

HEAD OF STATE
President, Serzh Sargsyan, *elected* 19 February 2008, *inaugurated* 9 April 2008

SELECTED GOVERNMENT MEMBERS *as at May 2010*
Prime Minister, Tigran Sargsyan
Deputy Prime Minister, Armen Gevorgyan
Defence, Seyran Ohanyan
Economy, Nerses Yeritsyan
Foreign Affairs, Eduard Nalbandyan

EMBASSY OF THE REPUBLIC OF ARMENIA
25A Cheniston Gardens, London W8 6TG
T 020-7938 5435 E armemb@armenianembassyuk.com
W www.armenianembassy.org.uk
Ambassador Extraordinary and Plenipotentiary, HE Dr Vahe Gabrielyan, *apptd* 2003

BRITISH EMBASSY
34 Baghramyan Avenue, Yerevan 0019
T (+374) (10) 264 301 E Enquiries.Yerevan@fco.gov.uk
W http://ukinarmenia.fco.gov.uk
Ambassador Extraordinary and Plenipotentiary, HE Charles Lonsdale, *apptd* 2008

BRITISH COUNCIL
24 Baghramyan Avenue, Yerevan 0019
T (+374) (56) 9923 W www.britishcouncil.org/armenia
Director, Arevik Saribekyan

DEFENCE

The army has 110 main battle tanks, 104 armoured infantry fighting vehicles and 136 armoured personnel carriers. The air force has 16 combat aircraft and 8 armed helicopters.

Russia maintains 3,214 army personnel in Armenia. An agreement on military cooperation with Russia was signed in 1996 which paved the way for joint military exercises. A protocol was also signed on the establishment of coalition troops in Transcaucasia and the planned use of Russian and Armenian armed forces as part of coalition troops in cases of mutual interest. In 2001 Russian president Vladimir Putin signed a federal law relating to an agreement between the Russian Federation and the Republic of Armenia on the joint planning of the use of troops in the interests of joint security provision. This stipulates measures to prevent the use by third countries of the territory of Armenia for purposes that may inflict damage on Russian national interests.

Military budget – US$376m (2009)
Military personnel – 46,684: army 43,772, air and air defence forces 2,912; paramilitary 4,748
Conscription duration – 24 months

ECONOMY AND TRADE

The economy experienced a severe decline following the break-up of the USSR in 1991, adding to existing problems arising from the 1988 earthquake and subsequently exacerbated by the Nagorny-Karabakh conflict and the consequent trade embargos imposed by Azerbaijan and Turkey, both of which are still in place. Economic liberalisation from 1994 brought sustained high growth and falls in inflation and poverty levels until the global economic crisis. This triggered a severe recession, largely owing to declines in construction and remittances, despite loans from Russia and international institutions such as the IMF.

The agricultural sector produces fruit, vegetables and livestock as cash crops, and grain. There are large mineral deposits, including iron and copper ore and non-ferrous metals. Industry is diversified and most small and medium-sized enterprises are now privatised. The main activities are diamond-processing, the production of industrial machinery, vehicles and parts, textiles and clothing, chemicals, instruments, microelectronics, jewellery, and software development and food processing. The severe energy shortages of the mid-1990s were overcome by the reopening of the nuclear power plant at Metsamor in 1995. This has enabled Armenia to become an electricity exporter, but there is international pressure to close the plant because of the earthquake risks in the area.

The main trading partners are Russia, EU countries, other former Soviet bloc states, China and the USA. Principal exports are pig iron, copper, non-ferrous metals, diamonds, mineral products, food and energy. The main imports are natural gas, petrol, tobacco products, foodstuffs and diamonds.

GNI – US$10,300m; US$3,350 per capita (2008)
Annual average growth of GDP – –15 per cent (2009 est)
Inflation rate – 4.2 per cent (2009 est)
Population below poverty line – 26.5 per cent (2006 est)
Unemployment – 7.1 per cent (2007 est)
Total external debt – US$4,470m (2009)
Imports – US$4,400m (2008)
Exports – US$1,100m (2008)

BALANCE OF PAYMENTS
Trade – US$2,522m deficit (2009)
Current Account – US$1,205m deficit (2009)

Trade with UK	*2008*	*2009*
Imports from UK	£9,737,220	£8,503,500
Exports to UK	£942,511	£1,690,476

EDUCATION AND HEALTH

State education is free and compulsory for all children aged six to 14. Children attend primary school until the age of nine, then secondary school until the age of 14. At the end of intermediate school a certificate of basic education is awarded. Senior secondary school may be attended from the ages of 14 to 16.

Literacy rate – 99.5 per cent (2007 est)
Gross enrolment ratio (percentage of relevant age group) – primary 80 per cent; secondary 88 per cent; tertiary 34 per cent (2008 est)
Health expenditure (per capita) – US$133 (2007)
Hospital beds (per 1,000 people) – 4.1 (2003–8)

MEDIA

Armenia has more than 40 private television stations, which operate alongside two public networks. The main Russian television channels are also available. Censorship is banned under a 2004 media law, but journalists have been imprisoned for libel and defamation offences. Newspapers have limited influence, often owing to small print runs, and tend to be owned by wealthy individuals and political parties.

AUSTRALIA

Commonwealth of Australia

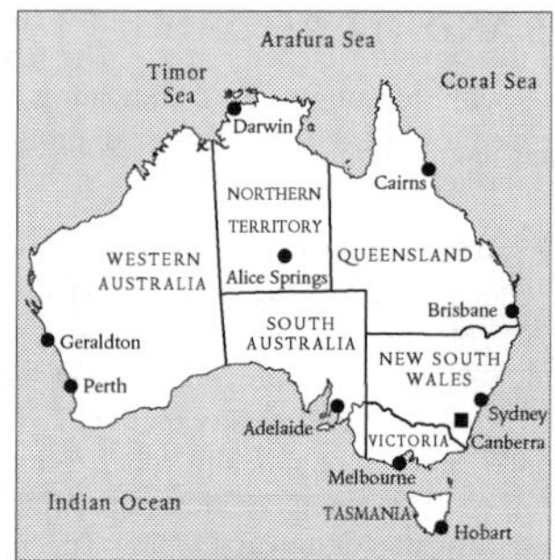

Area – 7,692,024 sq. km
Capital – Canberra, in the Australian Capital Territory; population, 384,091 (2009 est)
Major cities – Adelaide, Brisbane, Melbourne, Perth, Sydney
Currency – Australian dollar ($A) of 100 cents
Population – 21,262,641 rising at 1.2 per cent a year (2009 est)
Religion – Christian (Roman Catholic 26 per cent, Anglican 19 per cent, other 19 per cent), Buddhist 2 per cent, Muslim 2 per cent, Hindu 1 per cent (est)
Language – English, Chinese, Italian, Aboriginal languages
Population density – 3 per sq. km (2008)
Urban population – 89 per cent (2007 est)
Median age (years) – 37.3 (2009 est)
National anthem – 'Advance Australia Fair'
National day – 26 January (Australia Day)
Life expectancy (years) – 81.63 (2009 est)
Mortality rate – 6.74 (2009 est)
Birth rate – 12.47 (2009 est)
Infant mortality rate – 4.75 (2009 est)
Death penalty – Abolished for all crimes (since 1985)
CPI score – 8.7 (2009)

CLIMATE AND TERRAIN

Australia is the world's sixth-largest country and home to a wide variety of landscapes and weather conditions. Most of the country is a plateau, with hills, low mountain ranges and sparsely populated deserts in the interior, and tropical wetlands and rainforest in the north-east. Mountain ranges running down the east coast are the source of the rivers that flow across the densely populated fertile plain in the south-east. Off the north- east coast is the Great Barrier Reef, the world's largest coral reef. The highest point of elevation is 2,229m (Mt Kosciuszko) and the lowest is −15m (Lake Eyre). The climate is arid or semi-arid in the interior, tropical in the north and temperate in the south and east. The summer begins in December and the winter in June.

HISTORY AND POLITICS

The Aboriginals are thought to have arrived in Australia from south-east Asia *c.*40,000 years ago. Europeans first discovered Australia in the 17th century. Its eastern coast was claimed by Captain James Cook on behalf of Britain in 1770 and became a penal colony from 1788. The discovery of gold sparked several gold rushes in the 1850s that helped to attract free settlers, and the population trebled in a decade. The colonies of Tasmania, Western Australia, South Australia, Victoria and Queensland were established between 1825 and 1859, and became self-governing from the 1850s onwards. They were federated as the Commonwealth of Australia on 1 January 1901, and Australia was granted dominion status within the British Empire. Australia became independent within the British Commonwealth under the 1931 Statute of Westminster. Following a referendum in 1967, the Aboriginal population was granted full political rights. In 1986, the Australia Act abolished the remaining legislative, executive and judicial links to the UK while retaining the British monarch as head of state. Debate over whether to sever constitutional links with the British monarchy led to a national referendum in 1999; the proposal to make Australia a republic was defeated, with 45.3 per cent voting in favour and 54.7 per cent against.

The Australian Labor Party's resounding victory in the 2007 general election ended 11 years of government by a Liberal Party–National Party coalition. The ALP leader, Kevin Rudd, became prime minister and reversed many of the previous government's policies, signing the Kyoto protocol on climate change, apologising for past abuses of Aborigines and promising an end to the detention of asylum seekers on small Pacific island states. Mr Rudd stood down as Labor Party leader in June 2010 in anticipation of losing a planned party leadership ballot; his challenger, deputy prime minister Julia Gillard, became Australia's first female prime minister. A general election was due to be held in August 2010 (*see* Stop Press).

POLITICAL SYSTEM

Under the 1901 constitution, the Commonwealth of Australia is a federation of six states. The constitution defines the powers of the federal government, and residuary legislative power remains with the states. A degree of self-government was granted to the Northern Territory in 1978 and the Australian Capital Territory in 1988, and both tend to be treated as states.

The head of state is Queen Elizabeth II, represented by the governor-general, who is appointed on the advice of the Australian prime minister. The bicameral parliament consists of the senate and the House of Representatives. The constitution provides that the number of members of the House of Representatives shall be proportionate to the population of each state, with a minimum of five members for each state, and that the number of senators shall be, as nearly as practicable, half the number of representatives. There are currently 150 members, including two members for the Northern Territory and two for the Australian Capital Territory; they are directly elected for a three-year term. There are 76 senators; each state returns 12 senators, who are directly elected for a six-year term, with half retiring every third year. The Australian Capital Territory and the Northern Territory each return two senators, who are directly elected for a three-year term.

Governor-General, Quentin Bryce, *apptd* 2008

STATES AND TERRITORIES

	Area (sq. km)	*Population (2009 est)*	*Capital*	*Premier (2010)*
Australian Capital Territory (ACT)	2,349	353,600	Canberra	Jon Stanhope†
New South Wales (NSW)	801,349	7,165,400	Sydney	Kristina Keneally
Northern Territory (NT)	1,352,158	227,000	Darwin*	Paul Henderson†
Queensland (Qld)	1,734,157	4,450,400	Brisbane	Anna Bligh
South Australia (SA)	985,335	1,629,500	Adelaide	Mike Rann
Tasmania (Tas.)	67,914	504,400	Hobart	David Bartlett
Victoria (Vic.)	227,594	5,473,300	Melbourne	John Brumby
Western Australia (WA)	2,534,483	2,259,500	Perth	Colin Barnett

* Seat of administration † Chief Minister

SELECTED GOVERNMENT MEMBERS *as at June 2010*
Prime Minister, Julia Gillard
Deputy Prime Minister, Treasurer, Wayne Swan
Defence, John Faulkner
Foreign Affairs, Stephen Smith

AUSTRALIAN HIGH COMMISSION
Australia House, Strand, London WC2B 4LA
T 020-7379 4334 **W** www.uk.embassy.gov.au
High Commissioner, HE John Dauth, LVO, *apptd* 2008

BRITISH HIGH COMMISSION
Commonwealth Avenue, Yarralumla, Canberra, ACT 2600
T (+61) (2) 6270 6666 **E** ukinaustralia@fco.gov.uk
W http://ukinaustralia.fco.gov.uk
High Commissioner, HE Rt. Hon Baroness Amos, *apptd* 2009

BRITISH COUNCIL
Suite 403, 203–233 New South Head Road, Edgecliff, NSW 2027
T (+61) (2) 9326 2022 **W** www.britishcouncil.org/au
Director, Rebecca Matthews

FEDERAL STRUCTURE
Each of the six states has its own constitution, executive, legislature and judicature. Executive authority is vested in a governor (appointed by the Crown), assisted by a council of ministers or executive council headed by a state premier. There are ten territories, and three – the Australian Capital Territory, Northern Territory and Norfolk Island – have limited self-government, with an executive authority headed by an administrator (appointed by the governor-general), and legislative assembly led by a chief minister. The other territories are directly administered by the federal government.

DEFENCE

The army has 149 main battle tanks, 257 armoured infantry fighting vehicles, 774 armoured personnel carriers and 22 armed helicopters. The navy has 6 submarines, 12 frigates, 14 patrol and coastal vessels and 40 armed helicopters. There are bases at Sydney, Cairns, Darwin, Garden Island, Flinders, Jervis Bay and Nowra. The air force has 109 combat aircraft.
Military expenditure – US$27,600m (2009)
Military personnel – 54,747: army 27,461, navy 13,230, air force 14,056

ECONOMY AND TRADE

Australia has a highly diversified and internationally competitive market economy that saw sustained strong growth from the early 1990s until 2008, although agricultural output, a key export sector, dropped by about 20 per cent in 2006 owing to the worst drought in a century. A government fiscal stimulus package and low interest rates helped the economy to weather the global downturn better than most developed countries, avoiding recession. The service sector contributes 71.3 per cent of GDP and employs 75 per cent of the workforce; industry accounts for 24.9 per cent of GDP and 21.1 per cent of labour; and agriculture contributes 3.8 per cent of GDP and employs 3.6 per cent of the workforce.

A wide range of crops can be grown owing to the diversity of climatic and soil conditions, although most are confined to specific regions. Scant or erratic rainfall, limited scope for irrigation and unsuitable soils or topography have restricted intensive agriculture, although wheat is a major export and sugar cane and fruit are important crops. Cattle and sheep ranching is widespread, providing meat, meat derivatives, wool and dairy products.

Significant natural resources include bauxite, coal, copper, diamonds, gold, iron ore, lead, mineral salts, nickel, silver, tin, tungsten, uranium, zinc, oil and natural gas. The main industrial activities are mining, the production of industrial and transport equipment, chemicals and steel, and food processing. Production and processing of hydrocarbons are expected to increase once the oil and gas fields in the Timor Sea begin production.

Over the past 20 years, the focus of Australia's trade, like its foreign policy, has shifted from Europe to Asia and the Pacific region. It is a leading member of the Asia-Pacific Economic Cooperation forum, and a free-trade agreement (FTA) between Australia and the ASEAN countries entered into force in January 2010; it is also negotiating for FTAs with China, Japan and South Korea. Major trading partners include China, Japan, USA, the UK, South Korea, Singapore, India and New Zealand. The chief exports are coal, iron ore, gold, meat, wool, alumina, wheat, machinery and transport equipment. The main imports are machinery and transport equipment, computers, office and telecommunications equipment, crude oil and petroleum products.
GNI – US$862,500m; US$40,240 per capita (2008)
Annual average growth of GDP – 0.8 per cent (2009 est)
Inflation rate – 1.9 per cent (2009 est)
Unemployment – 5.7 per cent (2009 est)
Total external debt – US$920,000m (2009)
Imports – US$200,200m (2008)
Exports – US$187,000m (2008)

BALANCE OF PAYMENTS
Trade – US$6,274m deficit (2009)
Current Account – US$46,683m deficit (2008)

Trade with UK	*2008*	*2009*
Imports from UK	£2,960,974,813	£2,948,910,238
Exports to UK	£2,296,012,952	£3,676,666,367

COMMUNICATIONS

Most long-distance internal travel is by air or road. There are 464 airports and airfields. Road and rail networks are concentrated in the more densely populated areas of the east and south, and around Perth in the west. Elsewhere, roads are more widespread than railways, and both skirt the deserts of the interior, apart from a few transcontinental routes. There are six government-owned railway systems, and 37,900km of railway track. Most heavy freight is moved by road trains (trucks hauling two or three trailers) which measure up to 45m in length. There are 813,000km of roads. The 11 major ports and terminals include all the state capitals except Hobart, and there are private mining ports at Gove and Groote Eylandt in the Northern Territory. Mobile telephone distribution has grown rapidly to about 22.1 million in 2008, a density exceeding 100 per 100 people.

EDUCATION AND HEALTH

Education is administered by each state and territory, and is compulsory between the ages of five and 16 (15 in New South Wales and the Northern Territory, 17 in Western Australia). It is available at government schools and at private or independent schools, some of which are denominational.

Gross enrolment ratio (percentage of relevant age group) – primary 105 per cent; secondary 148 per cent; tertiary 75 per cent (2008 est)
Health expenditure (per capita) – US$3,986 (2007)
Hospital beds (per 1,000 people) – 4.0 (2003–8)

MEDIA

Eighty per cent of print and broadcast media ownership is concentrated in the hands of four privately owned groups, including Consolidated Media Holdings and Rupert Murdoch's News Corporation. Australia's leading newspapers are *The Sydney Morning Herald, Herald Sun, The Australian* and *The Daily Telegraph*. The Australian Broadcasting Corporation and the Special Broadcasting Service provide public service radio and television broadcasting, while the Seven, Nine and Ten networks dominate commercial television. Commercial broadcasters are required to transmit a minimum percentage of Australian programming and some of these home-made programmes are sold overseas.

CULTURE

Australia's diverse indigenous communities continue to practise traditional music and art forms, which for thousands of years have been used as the media for relating a community's history and folklore. In recent years these have also been adapted to modern materials and technology, and influenced by western cultural forms. Painting, carvings and sculpture are sources of income for many communities. Influential artists include Johnny Warangkula Tjupurrula (*c.* 1925–2001), pioneer of the commercially successful Aboriginal dot painting technique, and Rover Thomas (1926–98).

Since the colonial era, Australia has been dominated by European, and latterly US, culture. Prominent literary figures include novelist and travel writer Bruce Chatwin (1940–89), Nobel Prize winner Patrick White (1912–90), and double Booker Prize winner Peter Carey (*b.* 1943). Germaine Greer (*b.* 1939) and Clive James (*b.* 1939) are internationally respected cultural commentators.

The country's cinema industry enjoyed a renaissance in the 1980s with success for both art-house films and mass-market franchises such as *Mad Max* and *Crocodile Dundee*. Director Baz Luhrmann (*b.* 1962) and actors Russell Crowe (*b.* 1964) and Nicole Kidman (*b.* 1967) are established figures in Hollywood.

Sport is an integral part of the culture. Cricket and Australian rules football are the most popular sports and Australia is successful at international level in most major team sports, as well as producing individual participants such as swimmer Ian Thorpe (*b.* 1982), athlete Cathy Freeman (*b.* 1973) and tennis players Rod Laver (*b.* 1938) and Roy Emerson (*b.* 1936).

EXTERNAL TERRITORIES

Most of the territories are administered by the federal government through the Attorney-General's Department; the Australian Antarctic Territory and the Territory of Heard Island and McDonald Islands are administered through the Australian Antarctic Division of the Department of the Environment, Water, Heritage and the Arts.

ASHMORE AND CARTIER ISLANDS

The Ashmore Islands (comprising Middle, East and West Islands) and Cartier Island are situated in the Indian Ocean 320km off Australia's north-west coast. There is a nature reserve on Ashmore Reef and a marine reserve around Cartier Island. The islands became an Australian territory in 1933.

THE AUSTRALIAN ANTARCTIC TERRITORY

The Australian Antarctic Territory was established in 1933 and comprises all the islands and territories, other than Adélie Land, that are situated south of latitude 60° S. and lying between 160° E. longitude and 45° E. longitude. (*See also* The North and South Poles).

CHRISTMAS ISLAND

Area – 135 sq. km
Population – 1,402 (2009 est)

Christmas Island is situated in the Indian Ocean about 1,565km north-west of Northwest Cape in Western Australia. The island was annexed by Britain in 1888. Sovereignty was transferred to Australia in 1958. The Shire of Christmas Island (SOCI) is responsible for local government services on the island; its council has nine members directly elected for a four-year term. The main activities are phosphate mining (though this is in decline), tourism and the government sector. Plans to build a space satellite launching facility have not progressed.
Administrator, Brian Lacy

COCOS (KEELING) ISLANDS

Area – 14 sq. km
Population – 596 (2009 est)

The Cocos (Keeling) Islands are two separate atolls (North Keeling Island and, 24km to the south, the main atoll) comprising 27 small coral islands, situated in the Indian Ocean, about 2,950km north-west of Perth. The two inhabited islands of the southern atoll are West Island and Home Island, where around 80 per cent of the population lives, including most of the Cocos Malay community.

The islands were declared a British possession in 1857. In 1886 Queen Victoria granted all land in the islands to George Clunies-Ross and his heirs, who established coconut plantations worked by imported Malay labour. Sovereignty was transferred to Australia in 1955, and the government purchased the Clunies-Ross land and property in 1978, 1984 and 1993. The land is held in trust for the residents, with the local government body, the Shire of the Cocos (Keeling) Islands, as trustee. In 1984 the Cocos community, in a UN-supervised Act of Self-Determination, voted to integrate with Australia. The seven-member Shire Council of Cocos (Keeling) Islands is responsible for local government services. The public sector is the main employer and there is a little tourism; coconuts are the only cash crop.
Administrator, Brian Lacy

CORAL SEA ISLANDS TERRITORY

The Coral Sea Islands Territory lies east of Queensland between the Great Barrier Reef and longitude 156° 06′ E., and between latitudes 12° and 24° S. It comprises scattered islands, spread over a sea area of 780,000 sq. km. The islands are formed mainly of coral and sand, and most are extremely small. There is a manned meteorological station on Willis Island but the remaining islands are uninhabited. The territory was established in 1969. Much of it is nature reserve, administered jointly by the Department of the Environment, Water, Heritage and the Arts and the Department of Agriculture, Fisheries and Forestry.

HEARD ISLAND AND MCDONALD ISLANDS

The Territory of Heard Island and the McDonald Islands, about 4,100km south-west of Perth, comprises all the islands and rocks lying between 52° 30′ and 53° 30′ S. latitude and 72° and 74° 30′ E. longitude. The subantarctic islands were discovered in the 1850s and sovereignty was transferred from Britain to Australia in 1947. The islands are now part of a marine reserve established in 2002.

JERVIS BAY TERRITORY

Area – 67 sq. km
Population – 611 (2001 census)

The territory consists of 65 sq. km of land on the southern shore of Jervis Bay, 8 sq. km of marine waters and Bowen Island (0.5 sq. km), and lies about 200km south of Sydney. Originally part of New South Wales, the territory was acquired by the federal government in 1915 to provide Canberra with access to the sea. Much of the land and water now comprises Booderee National Park, leased from the Wreck Bay Aboriginal Community who since the 1980s have been granted 90 per cent of the land. The main economic activity is tourism.

NORFOLK ISLAND

Area – 36 sq. km
Population – 2,141 rising at 0.01 per cent per year (2009 est)
Seat of government – Kingston
National day – 8 June (Bounty Day)

Norfolk Island is situated in the South Pacific Ocean, about 1,600km north-east of Sydney. It is around 8km long by 5km wide. The climate is mild and subtropical. Discovered by Captain Cook in 1774, the island served as a penal colony from 1788 to 1814 and from 1825 to 1855. In 1856, 194 descendants of the *Bounty* mutineers accepted an invitation to leave Pitcairn and settle on Norfolk Island.

The island became a territory in 1914 and has been internally self-governing since 1979. The nine-member legislative assembly is directly elected for a three-year term, and elects the five-member executive council. This advises the Administrator, who represents the federal government and reports to the Attorney-General. The economy is dependent on tourism; other economic activities include the sale of postage stamps and pine and palm seeds, livestock-rearing and agriculture.
Administrator, Owen Walsh

AUSTRIA

Republik Österreich – Republic of Austria

Area – 83,871 sq. km
Capital – Vienna (Wien); population, 1,693,430 (2009 est)
Major cities – Graz, Innsbruck, Klagenfurt, Linz, Salzburg
Currency – Euro (€) of 100 cents
Population – 8,210,281 rising at 0.05 per cent a year (2009 est); Austrian (91.1 per cent), former Yugoslav (4 per cent), Turkish (1.6 per cent)
Religion – Christian (Roman Catholic 74 per cent, Lutheran and Presbyterian 5 per cent, Eastern Orthodox 2 per cent), Muslim 4 per cent (est)
Language – German (official), Croatian and Hungarian (official in Burgenland), Slovene (official in Carinthia), Turkish, Serbian
Population density – 101 per sq. km (2008)
Urban population – 67 per cent (2007 est)
Median age (years) – 42.2 (2009 est)
National anthem – 'Land der Berge, Land am Strome' ['Land of Mountains, Land on the River']
National day – 26 October
Life expectancy (years) – 79.5 (2009 est)
Mortality rate – 9.98 (2009 est)
Birth rate – 8.65 (2009 est)
Infant mortality rate – 4.42 (2009 est)
Death penalty – Abolished for all crimes (since 1968)
CPI score – 7.9 (2009)

CLIMATE AND TERRAIN

The north and east of the landlocked country feature rolling hills in the river Danube basin, while the west and south contain the eastern Alps, which cover nearly two-thirds of the country. The highest peak is 3,798m (Grossglockner) and the lowest point of elevation is 115m (Lake Neusiedl). Around 47 per cent of the land area is forested. The lowland climate is continental, and alpine in the mountains, with temperature averages ranging from 2°C in January to 20°C in July.

HISTORY AND POLITICS

The Austrian state dates back to the eighth century AD when Charlemagne conquered the territory, which had been settled from the sixth century onwards by Germanic tribes, and founded the *Ostmark,* the eastern march of the Holy Roman Empire. It became a duchy and in 1282 passed to the Habsburg dynasty, which established an empire that united much of central Europe, including present-day Austria and Hungary. Hegemony was lost to Prussia in the 19th century, when growing Hungarian nationalism also led to the establishment of the dual monarchy of Austria–Hungary. The assassination of the heir to the throne in 1914 triggered the First World War, towards the end of which the Austro-Hungarian Empire collapsed and most of the German-speaking lands became the Republic of Austria in November 1918. In March 1938, Austria was incorporated into Nazi Germany (the *Anschluss*) under the name *Ostmark.* After the Second World War, the Republic of Austria was reconstituted within its 1937 frontiers and a freely elected government took office in December 1945. The country was divided into four zones, occupied by the UK, USA, USSR and France, while Vienna was jointly occupied by the four powers.

In 1955 the occupying powers withdrew, recognising Austria as a sovereign, independent and democratic state with the same frontiers as on 1 January 1938. Austria joined the EU in 1995.

The 2004 presidential election was won by Heinz

Fischer of the Social Democrats (SPÖ); he was re-elected in April 2010. A snap legislative election was held in 2008 after the SPÖ-led coalition collapsed. The SPÖ and the Austrian People's Party (ÖVP) remained the largest parties after this election, but both lost ground to far-right parties. No party had an outright majority, and a new SPÖ–ÖVP coalition was formed under the new SPÖ leader, Werner Faymann.

POLITICAL SYSTEM

Under the 1955 constitution, the federal president is directly elected for a six-year term, renewable only once. There is a bicameral legislature, the *Parlament*, consisting of the National Council *(Nationalrat)*, which has 183 members directly elected for a four-year term, and the Federal Council *(Bundesrat)*, which has 62 members elected for terms of five to six years by the provincial assemblies. There is a 4 per cent qualification for parliamentary representation. Some powers may only be exercised by both houses acting together as the Federal Assembly *(Bundesversammlung)*. The executive is headed by the federal chancellor, who is appointed by the president.

HEAD OF STATE

Federal President, Heinz Fischer, *took office* 8 July 2004, *re-elected* 2010

SELECTED GOVERNMENT MEMBERS *as at May 2010*

Chancellor, Werner Faymann
Vice-Chancellor, Finance, Josef Pröll
Defence, Norbert Darabos
Foreign Affairs, Michael Spindelegger
Interior, Maria Fekter

EMBASSY OF AUSTRIA

18 Belgrave Mews West, London SW1X 8HU
T 020-7344 3250 E london-ob@bmeia.gv.at
W www.bmeia.gv.at/en/embassy/london
Ambassador Extraordinary and Plenipotentiary, HE Emil Brix, *apptd* 2010

BRITISH EMBASSY

Jaurèsgasse 12, 1030 Vienna
T (+43) (1) 716 130 E viennaconsularenquiries@fco.gov.uk
W http://ukinaustria.fco.gov.uk
Ambassador Extraordinary and Plenipotentiary, HE Simon Smith *apptd* 2007

BRITISH COUNCIL

Siebensterngasse 21, 1070 Vienna
T (+43) (1) 533 2616 W www.britishcouncil.org/austria
Regional Director, Michael Bird, OBE

FEDERAL STRUCTURE

There are nine provinces *(Länder)*: Burgenland, Carinthia, Lower Austria, Salzburg, Styria, Tyrol, Upper Austria, Vienna and Vorarlberg. Each has its own assembly and government.

DEFENCE

The army has 114 main battle tanks, 112 armoured infantry fighting vehicles and 458 armoured personnel carriers. The air force has 37 combat aircraft.
Military expenditure – US$3,190m (2008)
Military personnel – 27,300: army 13,600, air force 2,300, support 11,400
Conscription duration – 6 months (9–10 months for officers, NCOs and specialists)

ECONOMY AND TRADE

Austria has a well-developed market economy which is closely linked to other EU states. Its strong commercial links with central, eastern and south-eastern Europe, an attraction for foreign investors in the past, increased its vulnerability in the global economic downturn and its financial sector has required state support. The economy went into recession in 2008 but started to recover slightly in late 2009.

The services sector contributes most to GDP (65.8 per cent in 2009), followed by industry (32.3 per cent) and the small but highly developed agricultural sector (1.7 per cent). The main industries include tourism (about 16 per cent of GDP), construction, manufacturing of machinery, vehicles and parts, food processing, timber and wood processing, production of metals and metal goods, chemicals, paper and cardboard and communications equipment.

Austria's main trading partners are Germany, Italy and Switzerland. Principal exports include the goods produced by the main industries, iron and steel, and textiles. The main imports are machinery and equipment, vehicles, chemical products, metal goods, oil and oil products, and foodstuffs.
GNI – US$382,700m; US$45,900 per capita (2008)
Annual average growth of GDP – –3.6 per cent (2009 est)
Inflation rate – 0.1 per cent (2009 est)
Population below poverty line – 5.9 per cent (2004)
Unemployment – 4.7 per cent (2009 est)
Total external debt – US$832,400m (2009)
Imports – US$176,200m (2008)
Exports – US$173,400m (2008)

BALANCE OF PAYMENTS

Trade – US$3,123m deficit (2009)
Current Account – US$5,332m surplus (2009)

Trade with UK	*2008*	*2009*
Imports from UK	£1,429,878,595	£1,235,724,751
Exports to UK	£2,297,487,341	£2,245,891,818

COMMUNICATIONS

Although landlocked, Austria is strategically located in central Europe because of the navigability of the river Danube and the presence of traversable passes over the Alps. Of the 425km of waterways, 358km are navigable and there is considerable trade through the Danube ports (Vienna, Krems, Enns, Linz) from both local and foreign shipping. There are 107,262 km of roads and a network of 1,677km of *Autobahn* between major cities that also links up with German and Italian networks. The railways are state-owned and comprise 6,399km of track. The main airports are at Vienna, Graz, Innsbruck, Klagenfurt, Linz and Salzburg. Mobile telephone subscriptions overtook fixed-line in the 1990s and totalled 10.8 million in 2008, and there are 5.9 million internet users.

EDUCATION AND HEALTH

Education is free and compulsory from six to 15.
Gross enrolment ratio (percentage of relevant age group) – primary 101 per cent; secondary 100 per cent; tertiary 50 per cent (2008 est)
Health expenditure (per capita) – US$4,523 (2007)
Hospital beds (per 1,000 people) – 7.8 (2003–8)

MEDIA

The public broadcaster Österreichischer Rundfunk (ÖRF) has dominated Austrian television and radio for many years, but the number of private broadcasters is now increasing. Austria's print media is largely privately owned, and there are five main daily titles, including *Der Standard* and *Neue Kronenzeitung*.

CULTURE

From the 18th to the 20th centuries Vienna was one of Europe's greatest cultural centres. Musicians included Haydn (1732–1809), Mozart (1756–91), Beethoven (1770–1827), the Strauss family, Mahler (1860–1911) and Schoenberg (1874–1951). The late 19th century produced the writers Rainer Maria Rilke (1875–1926) and Robert Musil (1880–1942), the pioneering psychoanalyst Sigmund Freud (1856–1939), and the notable scientists Gregor Mendel (1822–84), whose research laid the foundations of modern genetics, and Erwin Schrödinger (1887–1961), who contributed to the development of quantum mechanics.

In art, the symbolist paintings of Gustav Klimt (1862–1918) are among the most recognisable of the Art Nouveau period. Director Fritz Lang (1890–1976) produced two of the earliest film classics: *Metropolis* (1927) and *M* (1931).

AZERBAIJAN

Azerbaycan Respublikasi – Republic of Azerbaijan

Area – 86,600 sq. km
Capital – Baku (Baki); population, 1,950,030 (2009 est)
Major cities – Ganca, Sumqayit
Currency – New Manat of 100 gopik
Population – 8,238,672 rising at 0.76 per cent a year (2009 est); Azeri (90.6 per cent), Dagestani (2.2 per cent), Russian (1.8 per cent), Armenian (1.5 per cent). There are more Azeris in Iran than in Azerbaijan. Almost all of the Armenian population lives in the Nagorny-Karabakh enclave
Religion – Muslim 96 per cent (of which Shia 65 per cent, Sunni 35 per cent) (est)
Language – Azeri (official), Lezgi, Russian, Armenian
Population density – 105 per sq. km (2008)
Urban population – 52 per cent (2007 est)
Median age – 28.2 years (2009 est)
National anthem – 'Azerbaijan Marsi' ['March of Azerbaijan']
National day – 28 May (Founding of the Democratic Republic of Azerbaijan, 1918)
Life expectancy – 66.66 (2009 est)
Mortality rate – 8.3 (2009 est)
Birth rate – 17.62 (2009 est)
Infant mortality rate – 54.6 (2009 est)
Death penalty – Abolished for all crimes (since 1998)
CPI score – 2.3 (2009)

CLIMATE AND TERRAIN

Azerbaijan lies on the western shore of the Caspian Sea, in the eastern part of the Caucasus region. It includes the exclave of Nakhichevan, separated from it by Armenia. The north-east of Azerbaijan rises to the south-eastern end of the main Great Caucasus mountain range; to the country's south-west lie the lower Caucasus hills, and in its south-eastern corner the spurs of the Talysh Ridge. Central Azerbaijan lies in a low plain irrigated by the river Kura and the lower reaches of its tributary the Araks. The highest point of elevation is 4,485m (Mt Bazarduzu) while the lowest is −28m (Caspian Sea). The climate and landscape vary greatly, but rainfall is generally low.

HISTORY AND POLITICS

The Turkic Azeri people formed an independent state in the first century BC. This was invaded in the seventh century AD by Muslim Arabs, who introduced Islam and secured the region as a province of the Muslim caliphate. Azerbaijan was invaded by Persia in the 16th century. The country was divided in 1828, the north (present-day Azerbaijan) becoming part of the Russian Empire and the south remaining Persian and subsequently Iranian.

In 1918 an independent Azerbaijani republic was established, which was overthrown in 1920 by a Soviet Red Army invasion supported by Azeri communist sympathisers. Azerbaijan acceded to the USSR in 1922.

In 1990, the Azeri Popular Front took power from the local communist party and declared independence from the Soviet Union. Soviet troops restored the communist regime, which declared Azerbaijan's independence in August 1991 after the failed coup in Moscow. The president elected in 1992 was overthrown in a coup in 1993 and replaced by Heydar Aliyev, the former communist party leader, who retained power despite a number of coup attempts in the mid-1990s. Aliyev won the presidential elections in 1993 and 1998, but withdrew from the 2003 race owing to health problems (he died in December 2003) and endorsed the campaign of his son, Ilham, who was successfully elected. His regime has been as authoritarian as that of his father.

The 2005 legislative election was won by the ruling New Azerbaijan Party by a large margin; as with all other presidential and legislative elections since independence, external monitors judged that the poll failed to meet international democratic standards. President Aliyev was re-elected in October 2008. A legislative election was scheduled for 7 November 2010.

SECESSION

There is a longstanding dispute with Armenia over the predominantly Armenian-populated Azeri region of Nagorny-Karabakh, which was transferred to Azerbaijan by Stalin in 1921–2. The territory's government voted to transfer to Armenia in 1988 but this was rejected by the USSR. When the USSR collapsed in 1991, the territory declared independence. Azeri attempts to reassert control were met with fierce resistance which escalated into a war that lasted from 1992 until a ceasefire was agreed between Azerbaijan, Armenia and Nagorny-Karabakh in 1994. By this time, Nagorno-Karabakh forces, supported by Armenia, had captured all of Nagorny-Karabakh, all Azeri territory that separated Nagorny-Karabakh from Armenia and all mountainous Azeri territory around the territory. Around 16 per cent of Azeri territory remains under separatist control and Azerbaijan has had to absorb nearly a million Azeris displaced from the territory. Talks mediated by the OSCE failed to make any progress towards a peaceful resolution until 2008, when Azerbaijan and Armenia agreed to intensify efforts and talks in 2009 were more productive.

POLITICAL SYSTEM

The 1995 constitution was amended in 2002 and 2009, when the limit on presidential terms of office was amended to two terms (2002) and then abolished (2009). The executive president is directly elected for a five-year term, which is renewable. The unicameral National Assembly *(Milli Majlis)* has 125 members directly elected for a five-year term. The president appoints the prime minister and the cabinet.

HEAD OF STATE

President, Ilham Aliyev, *sworn in* 31 October 2003, *re-elected* 15 October 2008

SELECTED GOVERNMENT MEMBERS *as at May 2010*

Prime Minister, Artur Rasizade
First Deputy Prime Minister, Yagub Abdulla Eyyubov
Deputy Prime Ministers, Elchin Efendiyev; Ali Hasanov; Abid Sarifov
Defence, Col.-Gen. Safar Abiyev
Finance, Samir Sharifov
Foreign Affairs, Elmar Muharram Mammadyarov

EMBASSY OF THE REPUBLIC OF AZERBAIJAN

4 Kensington Court, London W8 5DL
T 020-7938 3412 E london@mission.mfa.gov.az
W www.azembassy.org.uk
Ambassador Extraordinary and Plenipotentiary, HE Fakhraddin Gurbanov, *apptd* 2007

BRITISH EMBASSY

45 Khagani Street, Baku AZ 1010
T (+994) (12) 497 51 88 E generalenquiries.baku@fco.gov.uk
W http://ukinazerbaijan.fco.gov.uk
Ambassador Extraordinary and Plentipotentiary, HE Carolyn Browne, *apptd* 2007

BRITISH COUNCIL

8th Floor, Landmark III Building, 96 Nizami Street, Baku AZ1010
T (+994) (12) 497 1593 W www.britishcouncil.org/azerbaijan
Regional Director, Paul Doubleday

DEFENCE

The army has 320 main battle tanks, 127 armoured infantry fighting vehicles and 469 armoured personnel carriers. The navy is based at Baku, with a share of the former Soviet Caspian Fleet Flotilla, comprising 1 corvette and 5 patrol and coastal vessels. The air force has 57 combat aircraft and 15 armed helicopters.

Military budget – US$1,500m (2009)
Military personnel – 66,940: army 56,840, navy 2,200, air force 7,900; paramilitary 15,000
Conscription duration – 17 months, but can be extended for ground forces

ECONOMY AND TRADE

Azerbaijan's transition from a command to a market economy is slow, exacerbated by its failure to attract foreign investment in sectors other than energy, widespread corruption and systemic inefficiencies. The economy is dominated by oil and natural gas extraction and related industries, centred in Baku and Sumqayit, and exploited through co-production deals with foreign companies. Oil pipelines (1,424km) link the Azeri oilfields to Black Sea ports in Russia, Georgia and Turkey. The economy has avoided recession in the global economic downturn, but has contracted owing to the fall in world oil prices and transfers from the State Oil Fund were needed to make up the 2009 budget shortfall.

Although agriculture contributes only 6 per cent of GDP, it employs nearly 40 per cent of the workforce. The main crops are cotton, cereals, rice, fruit, vegetables, tea, tobacco and livestock. Around 90 per cent of agricultural land has been privatised. Industry produces oil, natural gas, petroleum products, oilfield equipment, steel, iron ore, cement, chemicals, petrochemicals and textiles.

Russia and other former Soviet republics are increasingly being replaced as trade partners by Turkey, the USA, and various European and Middle Eastern countries. Oil and gas constitute 90 per cent of exports, which also include machinery, cotton and foodstuffs. Principal imports are machinery and equipment, oil products, foodstuffs, metals and chemicals.

GNI – US$33,200m; US$3,830 per capita (2008)
Annual average growth of GDP – 3.2 per cent (2009 est)
Inflation rate – 2.2 per cent (2009 est)
Population below poverty line – 24 per cent (2005 est)
Unemployment – 1 per cent (2009 est)
Total external debt – US$2,411m (2009 est)
Imports – US$7,200m (2008)
Exports – US$30,600m (2008)

BALANCE OF PAYMENTS

Trade – US$21,992m surplus (2009)
Current Account – US$10,173m surplus (2009)

Trade with UK	*2008*	*2009*
Imports from UK	£304,005,279	£271,289,551
Exports to UK	£122,219,561	£397,690,847

COMMUNICATIONS

There are 2,900km of railway track, about 1,300km of it electrified, and over 59,000km of roads, although only half are paved. Azerbaijan is one of 12 participants in the Transport Corridor Europe–Caucasus–Asia (TRACEA) programme, which aims to construct an integrated multimodal transport system through the region by 2015. There are 27 airports, of which three (at Baku, Ganca and Nakhichevan) accept international flights. There are ferry links to Turkmenistan.

The telephone system is run by a state-owned monopoly so modernisation is slow. Greater competition in the mobile telephone market has led to rapid growth and in 2008 density was 80 per 100 people, compared to 15 fixed lines per 100 people. There were almost 1.5 million internet users in 2008.

EDUCATION AND HEALTH

Education up to university level is free.
Literacy rate – 99.5 per cent (2007 est)
Gross enrolment ratio (percentage of relevant age group) – primary 116 per cent; secondary 106 per cent; tertiary 16 per cent (2007 est)
Health expenditure (per capita) – US$140 (2007)
Hospital beds (per 1,000 people) – 7.9 (2003–8)

MEDIA

There are state-run and public press, television and radio outlets, competing with a growing private sector. Media outlets critical of the government have been subjected to harassment, despite the guarantee of freedom of speech in the constitution. As a requirement of the country's membership of the Council of Europe, editorially independent public television and radio services were launched in 2005.

THE BAHAMAS

Commonwealth of the Bahamas

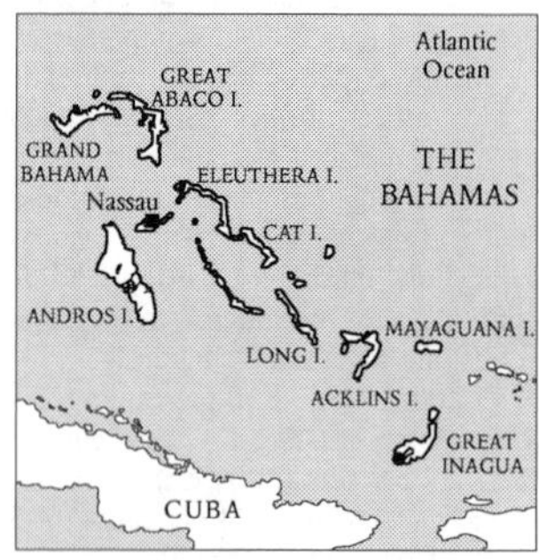

Area – 13,940 sq. km
Capital – Nassau, on New Providence; population, 247,659 (2009 est)
Major city – Freeport, on Grand Bahama
Currency – Bahamian dollar (B$) of 100 cents
Population – 309,156 rising at 0.54 per cent a year (2009 est)
Religion – Christian (Baptist 35 per cent, Anglican 15 per cent, Roman Catholic 14 per cent, Pentecostal 8 per cent, Church of God 5 per cent, Seventh-day Adventist 5 per cent, Methodist 4 per cent) (est)
Language – English (official), Creole
Population density – 34 per sq. km (2008)
Urban population – 83 per cent (2007 est)
Median age (years) – 28.7 (2009 est)
National anthem – 'March on, Bahamaland'
National day – 10 July (Independence Day)
Life expectancy (years) – 65.78 (2009 est)
Mortality rate – 9.32 (2009 est)
Birth rate – 16.81 (2009 est)
Infant mortality rate – 23.17 (2009 est)
HIV/AIDS adult prevalence – 2.5 per cent (2007 est)
Death penalty – Retained

CLIMATE AND TERRAIN

The Bahamas extend in a chain running from the coast of Florida in the north-west almost to Hispaniola in the south-east. The group consists of more than 700 islands and 2,400 cays, all low-lying. The highest point is 63m (Mt Alvernia, on Cat Island) and the lowest 0m (Atlantic Ocean). The principal islands include: Abaco, Acklins, Andros, Berry Islands, Bimini, Cat Island, Crooked Island, Eleuthera, Exuma, Grand Bahama, Harbour Island, Inagua, Long Island, Mayaguana, New Providence, Ragged Island, Rum Cay, San Salvador and Spanish Wells. The 14 major islands are inhabited, as are a few of the smaller islands. The climate is semitropical. The hurricane season is June to November.

HISTORY AND POLITICS

The islands were discovered by Columbus in 1492, settled by the British from the 17th century and became a crown colony in 1717. The Bahamas became internally self-governing in 1964 and gained independence on 10 July 1973.

The Progressive Liberal Party (PLP) held power for 25 years until the Free National Movement (FNM) won an absolute majority in the 1992 general election. Power has subsequently alternated between the two parties, and the PLP was defeated in the 2007 legislative election, which the FNM won with 23 seats.

POLITICAL SYSTEM

The head of state is Queen Elizabeth II, who is represented by a governor-general. The bicameral parliament has a senate of 16 appointed members and a House of Assembly of 41 members; both chambers serve a five-year term. A proposal that the country should become a republic is under consideration.
Governor-General, HE Sir Arthur Foulkes, *apptd* 2010

SELECTED GOVERNMENT MEMBERS *as at May 2010*
Prime Minister, Finance, Hubert Ingraham
Deputy Prime Minister, Foreign Affairs, Brent Symonette
National Security, Tommy Turnquest
Attorney-General, John Delaney

HIGH COMMISSION OF THE COMMONWEALTH OF THE BAHAMAS
10 Chesterfield Street, London W1J 5JL
T 020-7408 4488 E information@bahamashclondon.net
W www.bahamashclondon.net
High Commissioner, HE Paul Farquharson *apptd* 2008

BRITISH HIGH COMMISSION
High Commissioner, Howard Drake, *apptd* 2010, resident in Kingston, Jamaica

DEFENCE

The Royal Bahamian Defence Force has 13 patrol and coastal combatant vessels based at Coral Harbour, New Providence Island.
Military budget – US$46m (2009)
Military personnel – 860

ECONOMY AND TRADE

The economy is dominated by tourism and offshore financial services, which together contribute about 90 per cent of GDP. A tightening of financial regulations in 2000 caused a number of international businesses to relocate elsewhere, and visitor numbers from the USA (over 80 per cent of all visitors) declined from 2006; the effects of the global economic downturn caused the economy to contract further.

Manufacturing and agriculture account for 10 per cent of GDP and employment. Agriculture produces mainly fresh vegetables, fruit, meat and eggs. Mineral reserves produce aragonite and salt for export. Other industrial products include cement, rum, pharmaceuticals, steel pipes and the provision of oil trans-shipment services.

The main trading partners are the USA, Singapore, Japan, South Korea and Poland. The chief exports are mineral products and salt, animal products, rum, chemicals, fruit and vegetables. Imports are chiefly machinery and transport equipment, manufactured articles, chemicals, fuel, foodstuffs and livestock.
GNI – US$4,700m (2003); US$15,110 per capita (2003)
Annual average growth of GDP – –4 per cent (2009 est)
Inflation rate – 2.4 per cent (2007 est)
Population below poverty line – 9.3 per cent (2004)
Unemployment – 7.6 per cent (2006 est)

Total external debt – US$342.6m (2004 est)
Imports – US$3,300m (2008)
Exports – US$900m (2008)

BALANCE OF PAYMENTS
Trade – US$1,773m deficit (2009)
Current Account – US$1,165m deficit (2008)

Trade with UK	*2008*	*2009*
Imports from UK	£43,680,582	£18,797,494
Exports to UK	£36,282,640	£6,228,025

COMMUNICATIONS
The main ports are Nassau (New Providence), Freeport and South Riding Point (Grand Bahama). The Bahamas is a major ship registry, and 1,150 of the 1,223 ships registered in 2008 were foreign-owned. International air services are operated from Andros, Chubb Cay, Eleuthera, Exuma, Grand Bahama and New Providence. Nearly 60 smaller airports and landing strips facilitate services between the islands, mainly provided by Bahamasair, the national carrier. The Bahamas have some 2,717km of roads, 1,560km of which are paved. There are no railways.

BAHRAIN

Mamlakat al-Bahrayn – Kingdom of Bahrain

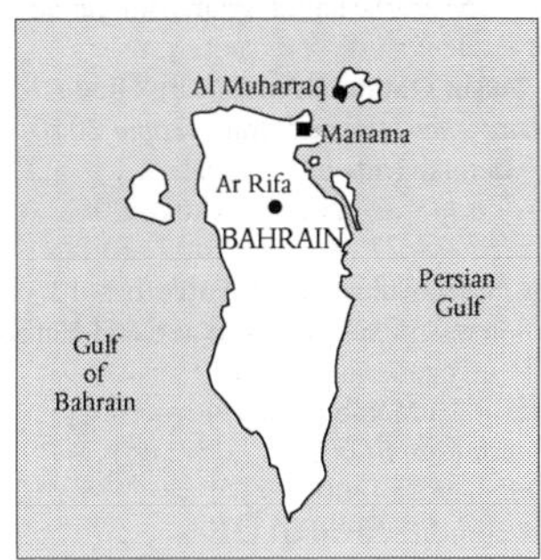

Area – 741 sq. km
Capital – Manama; population, 163,311 (2009 est)
Major towns – Al Muharraq, Ar Rifa
Currency – Bahraini dinar (BD) of 1,000 fils
Population – 727,785 rising at 1.29 per cent a year (2009 est); Bahraini (62.4 per cent). The non-Bahraini population includes large numbers of Europeans and South Asians
Religion – Muslim 99 per cent (of which Shia 60 per cent, Sunni 40 per cent) (est); Islam is the state religion
Language – Arabic (official), English, Farsi, Urdu
Population density – 1,092 per sq. km (2008)
Urban population – 88 per cent (2007 est)
Median age (years) – 30.1 (2009 est)
National anthem – 'Bahrainona' ['Our Bahrain']
National day – 16 December
Life expectancy (years) – 75.16 (2009 est)
Mortality rate – 4.37 (2009 est)
Birth rate – 17.02 (2009 est)
Infant mortality rate – 15.25 (2009 est)
Death penalty – Retained
CPI score – 5.1 (2009)
Literacy rate – 88.8 per cent (2007 est)

CLIMATE AND TERRAIN
Bahrain consists of an archipelago of 36 low-lying islands situated approximately halfway down the Persian Gulf, some 32km off the east coast of Saudi Arabia. The largest of these, Bahrain Island, is about 48km long and 16km wide at its broadest. The population is concentrated around the capital, Manama, on the north shore. The elevation extremes range from 122m (Jabal ad Dukhan) at the highest point to 0m at sea level. The climate is arid, hot and humid, with maximum average temperatures ranging from 20°C to 38°C.

HISTORY AND POLITICS
Bahrain was ruled by Persia (Iran) from 1602 until it was ousted in 1783 by the al-Khalifa family, who remain in power. The emirate was a British protectorate from 1820 until 1971, when it became independent. In 1975 the legislature was suspended and the emir assumed virtually absolute power after clashes between Sunni and Shia factions. Moves to return to democratic rule were made only in response to civil agitation in the 1990s, until Shaikh Hamad succeeded to the throne and initiated the transition to a constitutional monarchy. A new constitution was introduced in 2002 which established Bahrain as a kingdom and a constitutional monarchy, and legalised elections. There is ongoing agitation for further democratisation.

The legislative election in 2002, the first since 1973, was boycotted by Shia opposition groups, but in the 2006 election, a radical Shia group became the largest bloc, with 17 of the 40 seats. Although some Shia ministers were appointed, the majority of the cabinet are Sunnis.

POLITICAL SYSTEM
Under the 2002 constitution, the country is a hereditary constitutional monarchy with the king as head of state. The king appoints the cabinet. The bicameral National Assembly consists of a lower house, *Majlis al-Nuwab* (Council of Representatives), and an upper house, *Majlis al-Shura* (Consultative Council). The *Nuwab* has 40 members directly elected for a four-year term, and the *Shura* has 40 members appointed by the king for a four-year term. The 2002 constitution granted women the right to vote and to stand for election.

HEAD OF STATE
HH The King of Bahrain, Shaikh Hamad bin Isa al-Khalifa, KCMG *succeeded as emir* 6 March 1999, *proclaimed king* 14 February 2002
Crown Prince, Chair of the National Economic Development Council, Shaikh Salman bin Hamad al-Khalifa

SELECTED GOVERNMENT MEMBERS *as at May 2010*
Prime Minister, HH Shaikh Khalifa bin Salman al-Khalifa
Deputy Prime Ministers, Shaikh Mohammed bin Mubarak al-Khalifa; Shaikh Ali bin Khalifa al-Khalifa; Jawad bin Salem al Oraied
Foreign Affairs, Shaikh Khalid bin Ahmed bin Mohammed al-Khalifa
Defence, Shaikh Mohammad bin Abdullah al-Khalifa
Finance, Shaikh Ahmed bin Mohammed al-Khalifa
Interior, Lt.-Gen. Shaikh Rashid bin Abdulla bin Ahmed al-Khalifa

EMBASSY OF THE KINGDOM OF BAHRAIN
30 Belgrave Square, London SW1X 8QB
T 020-7201 9170 E info@bahrainembassy.co.uk
W www.bahrainembassy.co.uk
Ambassador Extraordinary and Plenipotentiary, HE Shaikh Khalifa bin Ali bin Rashid al-Khalifa, *apptd* 2008

BRITISH EMBASSY
PO Box 114, 21 Government Avenue, Manama 306
T (+973) 1757 4100 E british.embassy@batelco.com.bh
W http://ukinbahrain.fco.gov.uk
Ambassador Extraordinary and Plenipotentiary, HE Jamie Bowden, *apptd* 2007

BRITISH COUNCIL
PO Box 452, AMA Centre, 146 Shaikh Salman Highway, Manama 356
T (+973) 17 261 555 W www.britishcouncil.org/me-bahrain
Director, Brendan McSharry

DEFENCE

The army has 180 main battle tanks, 25 armoured infantry fighting vehicles and over 235 armoured personnel carriers. The navy, based at Mina Salman, has 1 frigate, 2 corvettes and 8 patrol and coastal vessels. The air force has 33 combat aircraft and 22 armed helicopters.
Military budget – US$697m (2009)
Military personnel – 8,200: army 6,000, navy 700, air force 1,500; paramilitary 11,260

ECONOMY AND TRADE

Bahrain was one of the first Gulf states to discover oil, in the 1930s, but reserves and production are lower than in neighbouring countries. It has diversified its economy, developing particularly as a regional financial and business centre, and as a tourist destination. Petroleum production and refining still accounts for an estimated 11 per cent of GDP, 70 per cent of government revenue and 60 per cent of total exports. Other industries include petrochemicals, aluminium smelting, and shipbuilding and repair. Bahrain's main trading partners are Saudi Arabia, Japan and the USA.
GNI – US$19,713m; US$25,420 per capita (2008)
Annual average growth of GDP – 2.9 per cent (2009 est)
Inflation rate – 3 per cent (2009 est)
Unemployment – 15 per cent (2005 est)
Total external debt – US$10,870m (2009 est)
Imports – US$12,500m (2008)
Exports – US$18,900m (2008)

BALANCE OF PAYMENTS
Trade – US$5,678m surplus (2009)
Current Account – US$2,256m surplus (2008)

Trade with UK	*2008*	*2009*
Imports from UK	£277,872,805	£241,271,444
Exports to UK	£76,289,626	£11,960,822

COMMUNICATIONS

Bahrain International airport is one of the main air traffic centres of the Gulf; it is the headquarters of Gulf Air, and a stopover point for other airlines on routes between Europe and Australia and the Far East. The four main islands are connected by causeways, and a 25km causeway links Bahrain Island to Saudi Arabia; the construction of an extension linking Bahrain to Qatar was approved in 2005. Of the 3,800km of road, 3,100km is paved. There are no railways. Khalifa bin Salman Port, opened in 2009, is the main terminal. There are modern telecommunications systems, and rapid growth in mobile telephone distribution to 1.4 million subscribers in 2008.

MEDIA

Most domestic television and radio services are provided by the state-run Bahrain Radio and Television Corporation. Most households also have a satellite receiver. Bahrain has a free press but self-censorship is widely practised. There are five main daily newspapers, including two published in English.

BANGLADESH

Gana Prajatantri Banladesh – People's Republic of Bangladesh

Area – 143,998 sq. km
Capital – Dhaka; population, 14,251,300 (2009 est)
Major cities – Chittagong, Khulna, Narayanganj
Currency – Taka (Tk) of 100 paisa
Population – 156,050,883 rising at 1.29 per cent a year (2009 est); Bengali (98 per cent) (est)
Religion – Muslim (Sunni 90 per cent), Hindu 9 per cent (est); Islam is the state religion
Language – Bengali (official), English
Population density – 1,229 per sq. km (2008)
Urban population – 27 per cent (2007 est)
Median age (years) – 23.3 (2009 est)
National anthem – 'Amar Shonar Bangla' ['My Golden Bengal']
National day – 26 March (Independence Day)
Life expectancy (years) – 60.25 (2009 est)
Mortality rate – 9.23 (2009 est)
Birth rate – 24.68 (2009 est)
Infant mortality rate – 59.02 (2009 est)
Death penalty – Retained
CPI score – 2.4 (2009)

CLIMATE AND TERRAIN

Although hilly in the south-east and north-east, over 75 per cent of the country is less than 3m above sea-level, situated on the alluvial plain and delta of the Ganges (Padma)–Brahmaputra (Jamuna)–Meghna river system, which empties into the Bay of Bengal, the largest estuarine delta in the world. The highest elevation is 1,230m (Keokradong) and the lowest 0m at the Indian Ocean. The climate is tropical, with a monsoon season (June to September) during which heavy rainfall causes flooding in around one third of the country each year; annual rainfall in most of the country is up to 2,500mm.

HISTORY AND POLITICS

Bangladesh consists of what was the eastern part of Bengal province and the Sylhet district of Assam province in British India. On independence in 1947, these territories acceded to Pakistan, forming the province of East Bengal (renamed East Pakistan in 1955). Tensions between East and West Pakistan (separated by over 1,600km) caused the East to secede in 1971. After months of civil war, and following the intervention of India, Bangladesh achieved independence from Pakistan on 16 December 1971.

The late 1970s and 1980s were marked by political instability, with a number of coups and attempted coups, the assassinations of President Mujibar Rahman in 1975 and President Zia in 1981, and periods of government under martial law (1975–8, 1982–6) or a state of emergency (1987–8, 2007–8). Mass protests forced the resignation in 1990 of Gen. Ershad (assumed power in 1982, elected president in 1986); and the Bangladesh Nationalist Party (BNP) won the subsequent parliamentary elections. In 1991 a constitutional amendment returned Bangladesh to parliamentary government.

Parliamentary government has remained in place since this date, despite occasional boycotts of parliament. Governments have been formed, or coalition governments led, by one of the two main parties: the BNP, led by Khaleda Zia (widow of President Zia), in 1991–6 and 2001–6; and the Awami League, led by Sheikh Hasina Wajed (daughter of President Mujibar Rahman), in 1996–2001 and since January 2009.

The BNP-led coalition government headed by Khaleda Zia stepped down in 2006 when its term of office expired. Following violent protests over the choice of an interim government and the impartiality of election preparations, President Iajuddin Ahmed declared a state of emergency and appointed a caretaker administration. President Ahmed's term of office expired in September 2007 but he continued in the post until a new parliament was convened after the December 2008 legislative election. The election was won by the Awami League, with 230 of the 345 seats. Zillur Rahman was elected president in February 2009.

POLITICAL SYSTEM

The head of state is the president, elected by the legislature for a five-year term. The unicameral parliament, *Jatiya Sangsad,* has 345 members directly elected for a five-year term; under a 2004 constitutional amendment, 45 seats are reserved for women. The president appoints the prime minister, and the cabinet on the advice of the prime minister.

HEAD OF STATE

President, Zillur Rahman, *elected* 11 February 2009

SELECTED GOVERNMENT MEMBERS *as at May 2010*

Prime Minister, Defence, Sheikh Hasina Wajed
Finance, Abu Maal Abdul Muhit
Foreign Affairs, Dipu Moni
Law, Justice and Parliamentary Affairs, Shafiq Ahmed

HIGH COMMISSION FOR THE PEOPLE'S REPUBLIC OF BANGLADESH
28 Queen's Gate, London SW7 5JA
T 020-7584 0081 E info@bhclondon.org.uk
W www.bhclondon.org.uk
High Commissioner, HE Dr Mohammad Sayeedur Rahman Khan, *apptd* 2009

BRITISH HIGH COMMISSION
PO Box 6079, United Nations Road, Baridhara, Dhaka 1212
T (+880) (2) 882 2705
E consular.bangladesh@fconet.fco.gov.uk
W http://ukinbangladesh.fco.gov.uk
High Commissioner, HE Stephen Evans, CMG OBE, *apptd* 2008

BRITISH COUNCIL
PO Box 161, 5 Fuller Road, Dhaka 1000
T (+880) (2) 861 8905 W www.britishcouncil.org/bangladesh
Director, Charles Nuttall

DEFENCE

The army has 232 main battle tanks and 226 armoured personnel carriers. The navy has 5 frigates and 39 patrol and coastal vessels. There are bases at Chittagong, Dhaka, Kaptai, Khulna and Mangla. The air force has 75 combat aircraft.

Military expenditure – US$1,190m (2008)
Military personnel – 157,053: army 126,153, navy 16,900, air force 14,000; paramilitaries 63,900

ECONOMY AND TRADE

Bangladesh is a poor country, highly dependent on foreign aid. Although poverty has been reduced by 1–2 per cent a year since 1990, over a third of the population lives below the poverty line. Many migrate to the Gulf states and south-east Asia to find work, and their remittances and garment manufacturing are the mainstay of the economy. These have fuelled the steady growth of 5–6 per cent a year since the mid-1990s, which has continued throughout the global downturn. However, inefficient state-owned enterprises, slow implementation of economic reforms, corruption and unreliable power supplies are obstacles to greater growth.

The service and industrial sectors account for 52.6 per cent and 28.7 per cent of GDP respectively. Although the smallest contributor to GDP (18.7 per cent), agriculture is the primary occupation of 45 per cent of the workforce. The chief industries are based on processing agricultural and fisheries products such as cotton, jute, tea, sugar, fish and seafood, the manufacture of textiles, garments, newsprint, cement and fertiliser, and light engineering. Most exports are to the USA and EU countries; imports come mainly from China, India and other Asian countries.

GNI – US$83,400m; US$520 per capita (2008)
Annual average growth of GDP – 5.7 per cent (2009 est)
Inflation rate – 5.1 per cent (2009 est)
Population below poverty line – 36.3 per cent (2008 est)
Unemployment – 2.5 per cent (2009 est)
Total external debt – US$23,220m (2009 est)
Imports – US$22,500m (2008)
Exports – US$11,800m (2008)

BALANCE OF PAYMENTS
Trade – US$6,873m deficit (2009)
Current Account – US$1,619m surplus (2008)

Trade with UK	*2008*	*2009*
Imports from UK	£64,230,556	£68,076,584
Exports to UK	£843,368,816	£1,052,185,943

COMMUNICATIONS

The principal seaports are Chittagong and Mongla. A state enterprise, the Bangladesh Shipping Corporation, operates the Bangladesh merchant fleet. Armed robbery of shipping in Bangladesh's territorial waters is growing. The 8,370km of internal waterways are a key element of the transport infrastructure, although reduced to 5,200km in the dry season. There are three international airports (at Dhaka, Chittagong and Sylhet) and 14 other airports and airfields. The international airline, Bangladesh Biman, provides international and internal flights. There are 2,768km of rail track, and rail links with India. The country's 239,226km of roads include only 22,726km which are surfaced. The telephone network is limited, with fewer than 1 fixed line per 100 people, and has been overtaken by mobile telephone distribution, which had a density of 30 per 100 people by 2008.

EDUCATION AND HEALTH

Primary education is compulsory and free, but drop-out rates are high.

Literacy rate – 53.5 per cent (2007 est)
Gross enrolment ratio (percentage of relevant age group) – primary 94 per cent; secondary 44 per cent; tertiary 7 per cent (2008 est)
Health expenditure (per capita) – US$15 (2007)
Hospital beds (per 1,000 people) – 0.4 (2003–8)

MEDIA

The main broadcasters (Radio Bangladesh and Bangladesh Television) are state-owned and pro-government. Television is the most popular medium, especially in urban areas, and foreign stations as well as domestic broadcasters have large audiences. Newspapers are privately owned and editorially independent, but journalists are liable to harassment despite the constitution guaranteeing press freedom. The four main daily newspapers are the Bengali-language *Dainik Ittefaq* and *Daily Prothom Alo,* and English-language publications *The Daily Star* and *The New Nation.*

BARBADOS

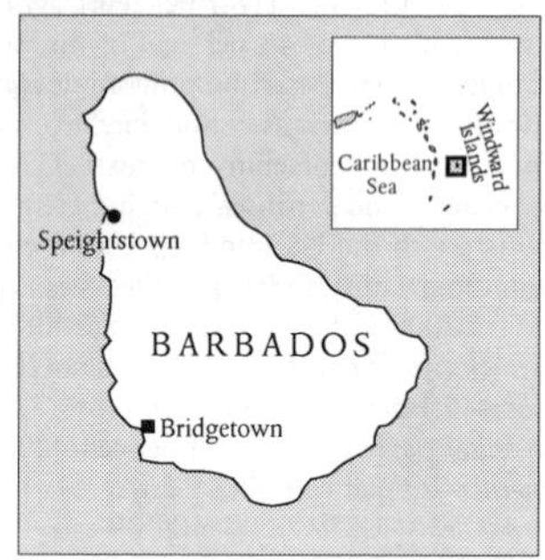

Area – 430 sq. km
Capital – Bridgetown, in the parish of St Michael; population, 112,154 (2009)
Currency – Barbados dollar (BD$) of 100 cents
Population – 284,589 rising at 0.38 per cent a year (2009 est)
Religion – Christian 95 per cent (predominantly Protestant denominations, of which the largest is Anglican), Muslim 1 per cent (est)
Language – English (official)
Population density – 594 per sq. km (2008)
Urban population – 39 per cent (2007)
Median age (years) – 35.8 (2009 est)
National anthem – 'In Plenty and in Time of Need'
National day – 30 November (Independence Day)
Life expectancy (years) – 73.94 (2009 est)
Mortality rate – 8.41 (2009 est)
Birth rate – 12.55 (2009 est)
Infant mortality rate – 12.29 (2009 est)
Death penalty – Retained
CPI score – 7.4 (2009)

CLIMATE AND TERRAIN

Barbados is the most easterly of the Caribbean islands. The land rises gently to central highlands, and elevation extremes range from 336m (Mt Hillaby) at the highest point to 0m (Atlantic Ocean) at the lowest. The climate is tropical with a wet season from July to November, and the island is subject to occasional hurricanes.

HISTORY AND POLITICS

Early settlers were succeeded by the Arawaks and then the Caribs. The island was uninhabited when settled by the English in 1627 and was a crown colony from 1652, achieving self-government in 1961. It became an independent state on 30 November 1966.

Since independence, power has alternated between the two main political parties, the Barbados Labour Party (BLP) and the Democratic Labour Party (DLP). In the 2008 general election the BLP was defeated by the DLP, which won 20 of the 30 seats and took office under David Thompson.

POLITICAL SYSTEM

The head of state is Queen Elizabeth II, represented by the governor-general. The bicameral parliament consists of a senate of 21 appointed members and a House of Assembly of 30 directly elected members; both chambers serve a five-year term.

There are 11 administrative areas (parishes): St Michael, Christ Church, St Andrew, St George, St James, St John, St Joseph, St Lucy, St Peter, St Philip and St Thomas.

Governor-General, HE Sir Clifford Husbands, GCMG, *apptd* June 1996

SELECTED GOVERNMENT MEMBERS *as at May 2010*

Prime Minister, Finance, David Thompson
Deputy Prime Minister, Attorney-General, Home Affairs, Freundel Stuart
Foreign Affairs, Maxine McClean

BARBADOS HIGH COMMISSION

1 Great Russell Street, London WC1B 3ND
T 020-7631 4975 E london@foreign.gov.bb
High Commissioner, HE Hugh Arthur, *apptd* 2008

BRITISH HIGH COMMISSION

PO Box 676, Lower Collymore Rock, Bridgetown
T (+1) (246) 430 7800 E britishhc@sunbeach.net
W http://ukinbarbados.fco.gov.uk
High Commissioner, HE Paul Brummell, *apptd* 2009

DEFENCE

The navy has 9 patrol and coastal combatant vessels located at Bridgetown.

Military budget – US$32.5m (2009 est)
Military personnel – 610: army 500, navy 110

ECONOMY AND TRADE

Historically, Barbados' chief products were sugar, rum and molasses. Since independence, tourism, offshore finance and information services, and light industry (especially the assembly of components for re-export) have become more significant. The global economic downturn has affected tourism in particular, causing the economy to contract in 2009.

The main trading partners are Trinidad and Tobago and the USA. Chief exports are manufactured goods, sugar and molasses, rum, other food and beverages, chemicals and electronic components.

GNI – US$2,500m (2003); US$9,270 per capita (2003)

Annual average growth of GDP – −2.8 per cent (2009 est)
Inflation rate – 5.5 per cent (2007 est)
Unemployment – 10.7 per cent (2003 est)
Total external debt – US$668m (2003)
Imports – US$2,000m (2008)
Exports – US$500m (2008)

BALANCE OF PAYMENTS
Trade – US$1,177m deficit (2009)
Current Account – US$184m deficit (2008)

Trade with UK	*2008*	*2009*
Imports from UK	£38,007,483	£40,813,526
Exports to UK	£20,656,858	£15,146,150

COMMUNICATIONS

Barbados has around 1,600km of roads, all of which are surfaced. The Grantley Adams International airport near Bridgetown is a hub for connections to other Caribbean islands and the USA. Bridgetown, the only port of entry, has a deep-water harbour with berths for nine; there are also five tanker terminals. Mobile phone ownership is high, at nearly 150 per 100 persons.

EDUCATION

Education is free in government schools at primary (ages four to 11) and secondary (ages 11 to 18) levels, and is compulsory until the age of 16.
Literacy rate – 99.7 per cent (2004 est)

MEDIA

Barbados has two daily newspapers, both privately owned. The sole television station is run by the state-owned Caribbean Broadcasting Corporation. There are both public and privately owned radio stations. The media broadcast a range of opinions and are free to criticise the authorities.

BELARUS

Respublika Byelarus' – Republic of Belarus

Area – 207,600 sq. km
Capital – Minsk (the administrative centre of the CIS); population, 1,836,880 (2009 est)
Major cities – Brest, Homyel, Hrodna, Mahilyow, Vitsyebsk
Currency – Belarusian rouble of 100 kopeks
Population – 9,648,533 falling at 0.38 per cent a year (2009 est); Belarusian (81.2 per cent), Russian (11.4 per cent), Polish (3.9 per cent), Ukrainian (2.4 per cent)
Religion – Christian (Belarusian Orthodox 48 per cent, Roman Catholic 8 per cent, Protestant denominations 1 per cent) (est)
Language – Belarusian, Russian (both official)
Population density – 48 per sq. km (2008)
Urban population – 73 per cent (2007 est)
Median age (years) – 38.6 (2009 est)
National anthem – 'My Belarusy' ['We, the Belarusians']
National day – 3 July (Independence Day)
Life expectancy (years) – 70.63 (2009 est)
Mortality rate – 13.86 (2009 est)
Birth rate – 9.71 (2009 est)
Infant mortality rate – 6.43 (2009 est)
Death penalty – Retained
CPI score – 2.4 (2009)

CLIMATE AND TERRAIN

Belarus is a landlocked country in eastern Europe, and was formerly part of the USSR. Much of the land is a plain, with many lakes, swamps and marshes, and forest cover is around 38 per cent. Its main rivers are the upper reaches of the Dnieper, the Nyoman and the Western Dvina. Elevation extremes range from 346m (Dzyarzhynskaya Hara) at the highest point to 90m (river Nyoman) at the lowest. The climate is continental, with cold winters and warm, humid summers.

HISTORY AND POLITICS

In the 13th century the area was absorbed into the grand duchy of Lithuania, which entered into the Polish Commonwealth from the 16th until the 18th centuries. Following the partitions of Poland in the late 18th century it became part of the expanding Russian Empire. It was the site of fierce fighting during the First World War, but its brief period of independence in 1918 ended, after a war over the territory, in partition between Poland and the USSR. The Polish territory was largely regained by the USSR after the Second World War, which devastated Belarus; over a quarter of the population was killed.

Belarus declared its independence from the USSR after a failed coup in Moscow in 1991. Stanislav Shuskevich became Belarusian leader at the head of a coalition of Communists and Democrats, but he was forced to resign in 1994. He was replaced by Gen. Mecheslav Grib, who pursued closer political, economic and trade relations with Russia.

Alexander Lukashenko was elected to the newly created post of president in 1994. Since coming to power, President Lukashenko has opposed privatisation and economic liberalisation (precipitating economic collapse), subverted political processes and repressed opposition and the media, creating a virtual dictatorship. Elections since 2000 have been condemned as neither free nor fair by opposition groups and international observers. The EU and USA have imposed sanctions several times because of the regime's poor human rights record and obstructiveness towards international election monitors. In the 2006 presidential election, President Lukashenko was returned with 82.6 per cent of the vote. Popular protests at the outcome of these polls, and other public expressions of opposition to the regime, were suppressed by the police. In the 2008 legislative elections, all the seats were won by the president's party.

FOREIGN RELATIONS

Belarus was a founder member of the Commonwealth of Independent States (CIS) in 1991. President Lukashenko, who opposed the break-up of the Soviet Union, has sought closer relations with Russia. In 1997 a treaty was signed with Russia providing for closer political and economic integration, and in 1999 the two countries signed a treaty on the creation of a union state, which committed them to eventually becoming a confederal state. However, there has been little progress towards integration, and Russia has increasingly condemned Belarus' poor economic development. Belarus agreed in 2009 to form a customs union with Kazakhstan and Russia; it entered into force in July 2010 despite Russia's refusal to abolish export taxes on oil and oil products within the union.

POLITICAL SYSTEM
Under the 1994 constitution, the president is directly elected for a five-year term; this was renewable only once until a 2004 constitutional amendment removed the two-term limit. The legislature is the bicameral National Assembly, comprising a 110-member House of Representatives (lower chamber), directly elected for a four-year term, and a Council of the Republic, with 56 members elected by regional *soviets* (councils) and eight members appointed by the president, for a four-year term.

The president may appoint half the members of the constitutional court and the electoral commission.

HEAD OF STATE
President, Alexander Lukashenko, *elected* 10 July 1994, *re-elected* September 2001, March 2006

SELECTED GOVERNMENT MEMBERS *as at May 2010*
Prime Minister, Sergei Sidorsky
First Deputy Prime Minister, Vladimir Semashko
Deputy Prime Ministers, Ivan Bambiza; Viktor Burya; Andrei Kobyakov; Vladimir Potupchik
Finance, Andrei Kharkovets
Economy, Nikolay Snopkov
Foreign Affairs, Sergei Martynov

EMBASSY OF THE REPUBLIC OF BELARUS
6 Kensington Court, London W8 5DL
T 020-7937 3288 E uk@belembassy.org
W www.uk.belembassy.org
Ambassador Extraordinary and Plenipotentiary, HE Aleksandr Mikhnevich, *apptd* 2006

BRITISH EMBASSY
37 Karl Marx Street, 220030 Minsk
T (+375) (172) 105 920 E britinfo@nsys.by
W http://ukinbelarus.fco.gov.uk
Ambassador Extraordinary and Plenipotentiary, HE Rosemary Thomas, *apptd* 2009

DEFENCE
The army has 1,586 main battle tanks, 1,588 armoured infantry fighting vehicles and 916 armoured personnel carriers. The air force has 175 combat aircraft and 50 armed helicopters.
Military budget – US$611m (2009)
Military personnel – 72,940: army 29,600, air force 18,170, joint staff 25,170; paramilitary 110,000
Conscription duration – 9–12 months

ECONOMY AND TRADE
Although prosperous under the Soviet regime, the country experienced a dramatic decline after independence and over a quarter of the population now lives below the poverty line. Since 1994, President Lukashenko has resisted structural reform of the economy and reimposed state control of prices and currency exchange rates. Some privatised businesses have been renationalised, and the small private sector is subject to pressure and intervention by the state, circumstances which continue to discourage foreign investment. The country is highly dependent on Russia for its energy needs, and economic growth in recent years was largely based on the re-export at market prices of heavily discounted oil and natural gas from Russia. This revenue stream is being reduced by sharp increases in oil and gas prices from 2007 (increasing to world prices by 2011), Russia's introduction of an export duty on oil shipped to Belarus, and Belarus' obligation to share with Russia its duties on re-exported oil. The drop in revenue and the effects of the global downturn pushed the economy into recession in 2009, leading to a devaluation of the rouble.

The main economic activities are oil-refining and the manufacture of heavy machinery and equipment, vehicles, domestic appliances, chemicals and textiles. These commodities, along with oil, mineral products, metals and foodstuffs, constitute the main exports and the main imports. The main trading partner is Russia.
GNI – US$51,900m; US$5,360 per capita (2008)
Average annual growth of GDP – –3.3 per cent (2009 est)
Inflation rate – 12.5 per cent (2009 est)
Population below poverty line – 27.1 per cent (2003 est)
Unemployment – 1.6 per cent (2005)
Total external debt – US$17,080m (2009)
Imports – US$39,500m (2008)
Exports – US$32,900m (2008)

BALANCE OF PAYMENTS
Trade – US$5,431m deficit (2009)
Current Account – US$6,326m deficit (2009)

Trade with UK	*2008*	*2009*
Imports from UK	£86,880,984	£76,366,405
Exports to UK	£98,748,220	£29,928,297

COMMUNICATIONS
Belarus has an extensive 2,500km canal and river system, but its use is limited by shallowness or remoteness. There is an international airport at Minsk and seven other major domestic airports, plus over 50 smaller airports and airfields. Most of the 94,800km of roads are surfaced but many are in bad repair. There are 5,538km of railways. The telephone system is state-operated; the network is being modernised but is not extensive in rural areas and fixed-line density is about 35 per 100 people. Mobile phone density is about 90 per 100 people. There were 3 million internet users in 2008.

EDUCATION AND HEALTH
The education system comprises pre-school, general secondary, out-of-school, vocational training and trade schools, secondary specialised and higher education. Education is compulsory between the ages of six and 15.
Literacy rate – 99.7 per cent (2007 est)
Gross enrolment ratio (percentage of relevant age group) – primary 99 per cent; secondary 95 per cent; tertiary 73 per cent (2008 est)
Health expenditure (per capita) – US$302 (2007)
Hospital beds (per 1,000 people) – 11.2 (2003–8)

MEDIA
A Soviet-era attitude towards press freedom remains; the government controls media content and the appointment of senior editors in the print and broadcast media. State-run newspapers and television channels receive

large subsidies and support government policies, while opposition publications are subject to harassment. The Belarusian National State Teleradio Company operates domestic radio and TV channels. A few private broadcasters target Belarusian audiences but operate from outside the country.

BELGIUM

Koninkrijk Belgie/Royaume de Belgique/Königreich Belgien – Kingdom of Belgium

Area – 30,528 sq. km
Capital – Brussels; population, 1,892,000 (2009 est)
Major cities – Antwerp, Bruges, Charleroi, Ghent, Liège
Currency – Euro (€) of 100 cents
Population – 10,414,336 rising at 0.09 per cent a year (2009 est); Fleming (58 per cent), Walloon (31 per cent) (est)
Religion – Christian (Roman Catholic 46 per cent, Protestant denominations 1 per cent, Orthodox 1 per cent), Muslim 4 per cent (est). An estimated 9 per cent of the population is laic (belonging to a non-confessional philosophical organisation)
Language – Dutch (Flemish), French, German (all official)
Population density – 354 per sq. km (2008)
Urban population – 97 per cent (2007 est)
Median age (years) – 41.7 (2009 est)
National anthem – 'La Brabançonne' ['The Song of Brabant']
National day – 21 July (Accession of King Leopold I, 1831)
Life expectancy (years) – 79.22 (2009 est)
Mortality rate – 10.44 (2009 est)
Birth rate – 10.15 (2009 est)
Infant mortality rate – 4.44 (2009 est)
Death penalty – Abolished for all crimes (since 1996)
CPI score – 7.1 (2009)

CLIMATE AND TERRAIN

There are two distinct regions; the west is generally low-lying and fertile, while in the east the forested hills of the Ardennes are more rugged with poorer soil. Elevation extremes range from sea level on the North Sea coast to 694m at the highest point (Signal de Botrange). The polders near the coast, which are protected by dykes against floods, cover an area of around 500 sq. km. The principal rivers are the Schelde and the Meuse (Maas). The climate is temperate. Average temperatures range from 2°C in January to 18°C in July.

HISTORY AND POLITICS

Part of the Roman Empire until the second century, the area was invaded by Germanic tribes and then became part of the Frankish Empire until much of the area was absorbed by the duchy of Burgundy from 1385. It was under the rule of the Spanish Habsburgs from 1477 until 1713 and the Austrian Habsburgs until 1794, when the area was conquered and held by Revolutionary France. After the collapse of the Napoleonic regime in 1814, it united with the kingdom of the Netherlands. The Belgian Revolution in 1830 led to the declaration of independence on 14 October 1830 and in 1831 the country became a constitutional monarchy. In the 20th century Belgium was invaded and occupied by Germany in both world wars; Eupen and Malmédy were ceded to Belgium by Germany under the treaty of Versailles in 1919.

Tensions between the Flemings (Flemish speakers in the north of the country) and the Walloons (French speakers in the south) have caused political instability throughout the post-war period. Inter-communal disputes led in 1980 to the establishment of regional assemblies, and in 1989 the country adopted a federal constitution. Belgium was a founder member of the EU in 1957 and joined the eurozone in 2002.

In the 2007 election, the Christian Democrats won the most seats but not an outright majority. After months of negotiations a five-party government led by the Christian Democrats took office in March 2008 under Yves Leterme. He resigned in December 2008 and was replaced by Herman Van Rompuy, but was reappointed prime minister in November 2009 after Van Rompuy was appointed president of the European Council. Mr Leterme resigned in April 2010 after the coalition collapsed, though his government continued in an interim capacity until elections held in June 2010. The New Flemish Alliance, a Flemish separatist party, emerged from this poll as the largest party in the Chamber of Representatives; it entered coalition negotiations with 27 parliamentary seats, while closest rivals the francophone Socialist party held 26.

POLITICAL SYSTEM

Belgium is a constitutional monarchy with a hereditary monarch as head of state. The bicameral legislature, the Federal Chambers, consists of a senate and a Chamber of Representatives. The latter has 150 members, directly elected by proportional representation for a four-year term. The senate has 71 members, who serve a four-year term; 40 are directly elected, the Flemish and French communities receive ten members each and the German community one, with the remaining ten co-opted by the elected members.

Amendments to the constitution since 1968 have devolved power to the regions. The national government retains competence only in foreign and defence policies, the national budget and monetary policy, social security, and the judicial, legal and penal systems.

HEAD OF STATE

HM The King of the Belgians, King Albert II, *born* 6 June 1934; *acceded* 9 August 1993
Heir, HRH Prince Philippe Léopold Louis Marie, *born* 15 April 1960

SELECTED GOVERNMENT MEMBERS *as at May 2010*

Prime Minister, Yves Leterme

Deputy Prime Ministers, Didier Reynders *(Finance);* Laurette Onkelinx; Guy Vanhengel; Steven Vanackere *(Foreign Affairs);* Joëlle Milquet
Defence, Pieter De Crem
Interior, Annemie Turtelboom

EMBASSY OF BELGIUM
17 Grosvenor Crescent, London SW1X 7EE
T 020-7470 3700 E london@diplobel.fed.be
W www.diplomatie.be/london
Ambassador Extraordinary and Plenipotentiary, HE Johan Verbeke, *apptd* 2010

BRITISH EMBASSY
Avenue d'Auderghem 10, Oudergemlaan, 1040 Brussels
T (+32) (2) 287 6211 E info@britain.be
W http://ukinbelgium.fco.gov.uk
Ambassador Extraordinary and Plenipotentiary, HE Dr Rachel Aronn, *apptd* 2007

BRITISH COUNCIL
Leopold Plaza, Rue de Trône 108/Troonstraat 108, 1050 Brussels
T (+32) (2) 227 0840 W www.britishcouncil.org/belgium
Director, Martin Hope

FEDERAL STRUCTURE
There are three language communities: Flemish, Francophone and Germanophone. Each community has its own assembly, which elects the community government. At this level, Flanders is covered by the Flemish community assembly; most of Wallonia is covered by the Francophone community assembly, and areas of Wallonia lying in the German-speaking communities of Eupen and Malmédy are covered by the Germanophone community assembly; Brussels is covered by a joint community commission of the Flemish and Francophone community assemblies.

At regional level, Belgium is divided into the three regions of Wallonia, Brussels and Flanders. Each region has its own directly elected assembly and government.

The ten provinces of Belgium are: Antwerp, East Flanders, Flemish Brabant, Hainaut, Liège, Limburg, Luxembourg, Namur, Walloon Brabant and West Flanders. In addition, 589 communes form the lowest level of local government.

Minister-President of the Brussels Capital Government, Charles Picqué
Minister-President of the Flemish Community and Flemish Region, Kris Peeters
Minister-President of the Walloon Region and of the French Community, Rudy Demotte
Minister-President of the German-speaking Community, Karl-Heinz Lambertz

DEFENCE
The army has 40 main battle tanks, 30 armoured infantry fighting vehicles and 226 armoured personnel carriers. The navy is based at Zeebrugge and has 2 frigates and 10 patrol and coastal vessels. The air force has 60 combat aircraft and 6 air bases.

The headquarters of NATO, and of its Supreme Headquarters Allied Powers Europe, are in Belgium; 1,274 US personnel (EUCOM) are stationed in the country.

Military expenditure – US$5,550m (2008)
Military personnel – 38,452: army 14,013, navy 1,605, air force 7,203, medical and joint services 15,631

ECONOMY AND TRADE
Belgium has a free-market economy with highly diversified industrial and commercial sectors. With no natural resources (coal production having now ceased), industry is based largely on the processing of imported raw materials for export. This makes the economy dependent on the state of world markets; rates of growth have been low in recent years and GDP contracted sharply in 2009. The banking sector was severely affected by the international banking crisis and government bail-outs caused the budget deficit to worsen. Principal industries are engineering and metal products, vehicle assembly, transport equipment, scientific instruments, food processing and beverages, chemicals, base metals, textiles, glass, petroleum and diamonds.

Industry accounts for 24.5 per cent of GDP and 25 per cent of employment. There is a large service sector, partly owing to the location in Brussels of EU institutions, NATO headquarters and a number of other international organisations. The service sector accounts for 74.7 per cent of GDP and 73 per cent of employment. There is a small agricultural sector (0.8 per cent of GDP and 2 per cent of employment).

Around three-quarters of trade is with other EU states, especially Germany, France and the Netherlands. External trade statistics relate to Luxembourg as well as Belgium as the two countries formed an economic union in 1921.

GNI – US$477,300m; US$44,570 per capita (2008)
Annual average growth of GDP – –3.4 per cent (2009 est)
Inflation rate – 0 per cent (2009 est)
Population below poverty line – 15.2 per cent (2007 est)
Unemployment – 8.3 per cent (2009 est)
Total external debt – US$1,354,000m (2008)
Imports – US$470,800m (2008)
Exports – US$477,400m (2008)

BALANCE OF PAYMENTS
Trade – US$24,241m surplus (2009)
Current Account – US$12,855 deficit (2008)

Trade with UK	*2008*	*2009*
Imports from UK	£12,643,598,115	£10,456,785,304
Exports to UK	£15,910,041,823	£14,783,451,915

COMMUNICATIONS
There are 2,043km of inland waterways, of which 1,528km are in regular commercial use; ship canals link Ostend and Zeebrugge with Bruges and Ghent, Ghent with Terneuzen in the Netherlands, Brussels with Charleroi and Willebroek Rupel, and Liège with Antwerp. The Meuse (Maas), Sambre and Schelde rivers form an integral part of the network. The main seaports are Antwerp, Ghent, Ostend and Zeebrugge, with major inland ports at Brussels and Liège. The main airports are at Antwerp, Brussels, Liège and Ostend. The rail system is run by Belgian National Railways and at 3,233km the network is one of the densest in the world. There are 152,256km of roads, including 1,763km of motorways. Mobile phone ownership was 11.8 million in 2008, and there were 7.3 million internet users.

EDUCATION AND HEALTH
Nursery schools provide free education for children from two-and-a-half to six years of age. There are over 4,000 primary schools (six to 12 years) and more than 1,000 secondary schools offering a general academic education, slightly over half of which are free institutions

(predominantly Roman Catholic and subsidised by the state) and the remainder state-run institutions. The official school-leaving age is 18.

Gross enrolment ratio (percentage of relevant age group) – primary 102 per cent; secondary 110 per cent; tertiary 62 per cent (2008 est)
Health expenditure (per capita) – US$4,056 (2007)
Hospital beds (per 1,000 people) – 5.3 (2003–8)

MEDIA AND CULTURE

The media reflects the multilingual nature of the population, with the community governments responsible for regulating broadcasting. There are two public broadcasters, each providing radio, TV and external broadcasting in a different language: RTBF in French, and VRT in Flemish. There are also French and Flemish commercial television channels and a German-language radio broadcaster. Cable television is popular, with 95 per cent of the population subscribing to domestic and foreign channels. A small number of media groups own and run the main news publications.

Belgium has produced some significant names in art, including Pieter Bruegel, the Elder (*c.*1525–69) and two key figures of the Baroque period, Peter Paul Rubens (1577–1640) and Anthony van Dyck (1599–1641); notable late-modern artists include James Ensor (1860–1949) and surrealist René Magritte (1898–1967). During the 20th century a rich comic-strip culture took root in Belgium, producing popular characters such as Tintin (Hergé, 1907–81) and the Smurfs (Peyo, 1928–92). The prolific and critically lauded detective novelist Georges Simenon (1903–89) was widely translated from his original French. The country's chocolate and beer are considered to be among the world's finest. Six of the world's seven Trappist breweries are based in Belgium.

BELIZE

Area – 22,966 sq. km
Capital – Belmopan; population, 19,717 (2009 est)
Major towns – Belize City (the former capital), Orange Walk, San Ignacio
Currency – Belize dollar (BZ$) of 100 cents. The Belize dollar is tied to the US dollar
Population – 307,899 rising at 2.15 per cent a year (2009 est); mestizo (48.7 per cent), Creole (24.9 per cent), Maya (10.6 per cent), Garifuna (6.1 per cent) (est)
Religion – Christian (Roman Catholic 50 per cent, Pentecostal 7 per cent, Anglican 5 per cent, Seventh-day Adventist 5 per cent, Baptist 4 per cent, Methodist 4 per cent, Mennonite 4 per cent, Nazarene 3 per cent) (est)
Language – English (official), Spanish, Creole, Mayan dialects, Garifuna, German
Population density – 14 per sq. km (2008)
Urban population – 51 per cent (2007 est)
Median age (years) – 20.4 (2009 est)
National anthem – 'Land of the Free'
National day – 21 September (Independence Day)
Life expectancy (years) – 68.2 (2009 est)
Mortality rate – 5.8 (2009 est)
Birth rate – 27.33 (2009 est)
Infant mortality rate – 23.07 (2009 est)
HIV/AIDS adult prevalence rate – 1.9 per cent (2007 est)
Death penalty – Retained
CPI score – 2.9 (2008)

CLIMATE AND TERRAIN

Belize comprises a large coastal plain, swamps in the north, fertile land in the south, and the Maya Mountains in the south-west. The highest point of elevation is 1,160m (Doyle's Delight), the lowest is at 0m (Caribbean Sea). Part of the Mesoamerican barrier reef system, the western hemisphere's longest, runs nearly the entire length of the coastline. The climate is subtropical but is cooled by trade winds. The hurricane season is from June to November.

HISTORY AND POLITICS

Numerous ruins in the area indicate that Belize was heavily populated by the Maya. The first British settlement was established in 1638 but was subject to repeated attacks by the Spanish, who claimed sovereignty until their defeat by the British navy and settlers in 1798. In 1862 the settlement was given colonial status as British Honduras. The colony became self-governing in 1964. In 1973 it was renamed Belize and it was granted independence on 21 September 1981.

Since independence, power has alternated between the two main politicial parties, the People's United Party (PUP) and the United Democratic Party (UDP). The PUP, in power since 1998, lost the 2008 legislative election to the UDP, which won 25 of the 31 assembly seats and took office under Dean Barrow.

FOREIGN RELATIONS

There is a longstanding territorial dispute with Guatemala, which claims the southern part of Belize. In 2002 Belize and Guatemala agreed a draft settlement brokered by the the Organisation of American States, but Guatemala rejected the terms of the settlement in 2003. In 2008 both countries agreed to an OAS recommendation that the dispute be referred to the International Court of Justice.

POLITICAL SYSTEM

Under the 1981 constitution, the head of state is Queen Elizabeth II, represented by a governor-general. There is a bicameral National Assembly, comprising a House of Representatives with 31 members directly elected for a five-year term, and a senate of 13 members appointed by the governor-general, including six on the advice of the prime minister, three on the advice of the opposition leader, and three representing various sectors of society; a referendum in 2008 approved the reform of the senate into an elected chamber effective from the next elections due in 2013. The prime minister is appointed by the governor-general and is responsible to the legislature.

Governor-General, HE Sir Colville Young, GCMG, *apptd* 17 November 1993

SELECTED GOVERNMENT MEMBERS *as at May 2010*
Prime Minister, Finance, Dean Barrow
Deputy Prime Minister, Gaspar Vega
Foreign Affairs, Wilfred Elrington
Attorney-General, Bernard Pitts

BELIZE HIGH COMMISSION
3rd Floor, 45 Crawford Place, London W1H 4LP
T 020-7723 3603 E bzhc-lon@btconnect.com
W www.belizehighcommission.com
High Commissioner, HE Kamela Palma, *apptd* 2008

BRITISH HIGH COMMISSION
PO Box 91, Belmopan
T (+501) 822 2146 E brithicom@btl.net
W http://ukinbelize.fco.gov.uk
High Commissioner, HE Patrick Ashworth, *apptd* 2009

DEFENCE

Military budget – US$19m (2008 est)
Military personnel – 1,050 (all army) (est)

ECONOMY AND TRADE

The economy grew steadily from 1999 to 2007, bolstered from 2006 by commercial exploitation of oil reserves, but it contracted sharply in 2009 owing to the global downturn, natural disasters and the drop in international oil prices. There is a high level of foreign debt, which was restructured in 2007. About one-third of the population lives below the poverty line.

The services sector has grown as tourism has developed, and accounts for around 54 per cent of GDP; industry contributes around 17 per cent, and agriculture and fisheries around 29 per cent. The main industries apart from tourism are garment manufacturing, food processing, construction and oil production. The chief trading partners are the USA, the UK and Mexico. The major exports are sugar, bananas, citrus fruits and juice, garments, shrimp, fish products, molasses, timber and crude oil. Imports are primarily machinery and transport equipment, manufactured goods, fuel, chemicals, pharmaceuticals, food, beverages and tobacco.
GNI – US$1,205m; US$3,740 per capita (2008)
Annual average growth of GDP – −1.5 per cent (2009)
Inflation rate – 0.3 per cent (2009 est)
Unemployment – 8.1 per cent (2008)
Total external debt – US$954.1m (2008 est)
Imports – US$900m (2008)
Exports – US$300m (2008)

BALANCE OF PAYMENTS
Trade – US$548m deficit (2009)
Current Account – US$137m deficit (2008)

Trade with UK	*2008*	*2009*
Imports from UK	£13,439,766	£7,566,079
Exports to UK	£54,011,924	£67,120,553

COMMUNICATIONS

Although there are 825km of waterways, these are only accessible by small craft. The main port is Belize City, which has deep water quays. There are around 40 airports and airfields, including the international airport at Belize City. There are 3,000 km of roads, 575 km of which are surfaced, but no railway system. Mobile phone distribution has reached a density of about 55 per 100 people, exceeding fixed-line connections of 10 per 100 people.

EDUCATION

Education is free and compulsory for nine years. The government maintains some schools but most are run by churches. The government is the main provider of health services.
Literacy rate – 75.1 per cent (2007 est)

MEDIA

The state-run radio service was privatised in 1998 and broadcasts are now provided by a number of commercial radio stations. There are no daily newspapers but there are a number of privately owned weekly news publications. There are three main television stations (Channels 5, 7 and 9), all of which are commercial.

BENIN

République du Bénin – Republic of Benin

Area – 112,622 sq. km
Capital – Porto Novo; population, 275,993 (2009 est). Cotonou is the seat of government; population 815,041 (2009 est)
Major cities – Abomey-Calavi, Djougou, Parakou
Currency – Franc CFA of 100 centimes
Population – 8,791,832 rising at 2.98 per cent a year (2009 est); Fon (39.2 per cent), Adja (15.2 per cent), Yoruba (12.3 per cent), Bariba (9.2 per cent), Fulani (7 per cent), Ottamari (6.1 per cent), Yoa-Lokpa (4 per cent), Dendi (2.5 per cent)
Religion – Christian (Roman Catholic 27 per cent, Celestial Christian 5 per cent, Methodist 3 per cent, other Protestant 2 per cent), Muslim 24 per cent (predominantly Sunni), Vodun (voodoo) 17 per cent, other traditional indigenous religions 6 per cent. Many Christians and Muslims also practise voodoo, which originated in this region of Africa, or other indigenous religions
Language – French (official), Fon, Yoruba and other African languages
Population density – 78 per sq. km (2008)
Urban population – 41 per cent (2007 est)
Median age (years) – 17.2 (2009 est)
National anthem – 'L'Aube Nouvelle' ['The Dawn of a New Day']
National day – 1 August
Life expectancy – 59 (2009 est)
Mortality rate – 9.45 (2009 est)
Birth rate – 39.22 (2009 est)
Infant mortality rate – 64.64 (2009 est)
HIV/AIDS adult prevalence – 1.2 per cent (2007 est)
Death penalty – Retained (not used since 1987)
CPI score – 2.9 (2009)

Literacy rate – 40.5 per cent (2007 est)
Gross enrolment ratio (percentage of relevant age group) – primary 117 per cent; tertiary 6 per cent (2008 est)
Health expenditure (per capita) – US$32 (2007)
Hospital beds (per 1,000 people) – 0.5 (2003–8)

CLIMATE AND TERRAIN

Benin has a short coastline of 121km on the Gulf of Guinea, but extends northwards inland for over 700km. The coast is a sandbar backed by lagoons that are fed by rivers. The land rises to a central plateau with the Atacora massif in the north-west, and falls to plains in the Niger basin in the north-east. Elevation extremes range from 658m (Mt Sokbaro) at the highest point to 0m (Atlantic Ocean) at the lowest. The climate is tropical in the south and semi-arid in the north.

HISTORY AND POLITICS

Dahomey, on the site of modern-day Benin, was a west African kingdom founded in the 11th to 12th centuries that rose to prominence during the 15th and 16th centuries. The first Europeans to visit the country were the Portuguese in 1472. Slavery became the region's primary trade, hence the area's historical name of the Slave Coast.

After a war between the French and the Dahomey kingdom, the French established a protectorate over the south in 1893 and gradually extended this to include the north by 1898. Dahomey was incorporated into French West Africa in 1904. It became an independent republic within the French Community in 1958 and independence was proclaimed on 1 August 1960.

Between 1960 and 1972 there was acute political instability, with frequent switches from civil to military rule and regional ethnic conflicts, until a military coup in 1972 brought to power Lt.-Col. Mathieu Kérékou, who declared the country a Marxist-Leninist state and in 1975 changed its name to Benin.

Civil rule was restored in 1977 (though Kérékou remained president) and, in response to popular discontent, Marxist-Leninism was abandoned in 1989 for economic liberalisation, and a pluralistic constitution was adopted in 1990, with legislative and presidential elections being held in 1991. The transition to fully democratic government was effected smoothly and has operated successfully, making Benin one of the most stable countries in Africa.

The 2006 presidential election was won in the second round by Yayi Boni, an independent candidate. In the 2007 legislative election, the Cauri Forces for an Emerging Benin, which supports the president, won the most seats. Presidential and legislative elections are due in March 2011.

POLITICAL SYSTEM

Under the 1990 constitution, the executive president is directly elected for a five-year term, renewable only once. The unicameral National Assembly has 83 members, directly elected for a four-year term. The president appoints and chairs the council of ministers.

HEAD OF STATE

President and Head of the Armed Forces, Boni Yayi, *elected* 19 March 2006

SELECTED GOVERNMENT MEMBERS *as at May 2010*

Foreign Affairs, Jean-Marie Ehouzou
Defence, Issifou Kogui N'douro
Economy, Finance, Idrissou Daouda
Interior, Security, Armand Zinzindohoue

EMBASSY OF THE REPUBLIC OF BENIN

87 Avenue Victor Hugo, 75116 Paris, France
T (+33) (1) 4500 9882 E ambassade.benin@gofornet.com
Ambassador Extraordinary and Plenipotentiary, HE Albert Agossou, *apptd* 2009

BRITISH AMBASSADOR

HE Robert Dewar, CMG, *apptd* 2007, resident at Abuja, Nigeria

DEFENCE

The army has 18 light tanks. The navy has 2 patrol and coastal combatant vessels.
Military budget – US$79m (2009 est)
Military personnel – 4,750: army 4,300, navy 200, air force 250; paramilitary 2,500
Conscription duration – 18 months

ECONOMY AND TRADE

The economy is underdeveloped, with over a third of the population below the poverty line; economic growth has been steady since 2000, but its effects have been outweighed by rapid population growth. Although still burdened by foreign debt, Benin has benefited from debt reduction and relief since its economic restructuring began to meet the criteria of international aid donors. Privatisation of industries, including utilities, began in 2001. The economy is based on agriculture, particularly cotton production, and re-export trade with neighbouring countries; customs receipts provide about half of government revenue, but much of the re-export trade operates outside the official economy and is unrecorded.

Agriculture is mostly at subsistence level and contributes 33.2 per cent to GDP, declining recently as industry (14.5 per cent) and services (52.3 per cent) have developed. The main cash crops are cotton, cashew nuts, shea butter, palm products and seafood, and the principal industrial activities are textiles and food processing. The main trading partners are China (15 per cent of exports; 36 per cent of imports), the USA and India, to which textiles and some of the cash crops are exported. The principal imports are food, capital goods and fuel.
GNI – US$6,100m; US$700 per capita (2008)
Annual average growth of GDP – 3.2 per cent (2009 est)
Inflation rate – 4 per cent (2009 est)
Population below poverty line – 37.4 per cent (2007 est)
Total external debt – US$1,200m (2007)
Imports – US$2,000m (2008)
Exports – US$1,100m (2008)

BALANCE OF PAYMENTS

Trade – US$1,452m deficit (2009)
Current Account – US$430m deficit (2008)

Trade with UK	*2008*	*2009*
Imports from UK	£45,417,016	£76,754,972
Exports to UK	£682,996	£461,364

MEDIA

Free speech is guaranteed by the constitution and the media is generally free from interference, although journalists are wary of stringent libel laws. There are over 50 newspapers and periodicals, including six daily newspapers, five of which are privately owned. The state runs a television channel and a radio network, and there are a handful of other commercial broadcasters. Radio is the main information medium, especially in rural areas.

BHUTAN

Druk Gyalkhap – Kingdom of Bhutan

Area – 38,394 sq. km
Capital – Thimphu; population, 89,454 (2009 est)
Major towns – Geylegphug, Paro, Phuentsholing
Currency – Ngultrum of 100 chetrum (Indian currency is also legal tender)
Population – 691,141 rising at 1.27 per cent a year (2009 est); Bhote (50 per cent), ethnic Nepalese (35 per cent), indigenous or migrant tribes (15 per cent) (est)
Religion – Buddhist 66 per cent (predominately Tibetan school of Mahayana), Hindu 25 per cent (est)
Language – Dzongkha (official), English, Nepali, Tibetan
Population density – 17.9 per sq. km (2008)
Urban population – 33 per cent (2007 est)
Median age (years) – 23.9 (2009 est)
National anthem – 'Druk Tsendhen' ['The Thunder Dragon Kingdom']
National day – 17 December
Life expectancy (years) – 66.13 (2009 est)
Mortality rate – 7.39 (2009 est)
Birth rate – 20.07 (2009 est)
Infant mortality rate – 49.36 (2009 est)
Death penalty – Abolished for all crimes (since 2004)
CPI score – 5 (2009)
Literacy rate – 52.8 per cent (2007 est)

CLIMATE AND TERRAIN

Bhutan is a landlocked Himalayan country lying between China and India. There is a mountainous northern region that is infertile and sparsely populated, central highlands, and densely forested foothills in the south, which are mainly inhabited by Nepalese settlers and indigenous tribespeople. The country is crossed by numerous rivers, and most of the population and cultivated land is found in the deep, fertile valleys of the highlands. Around 70 per cent of the land is forested. Extremes of elevation range from 7,553m (K'ula Kangri) at the highest point to 97m (Drangme Chhu) at the lowest. The climate is determined by altitude, varying from subtropical in the south to alpine in the north. There is heavy annual rainfall of up to 1,000mm in the central valleys and 5,000mm in the south.

HISTORY AND POLITICS

Bhutan's remoteness limited outside contact until modern times, although it signed a treaty of cooperation with Britain in 1774. Another treaty was signed with Britain in 1865 after Britain had annexed the south of the country. Bhutan's external relations were under the guidance of Britain from the 19th century until 1947, and of India from 1947 until 2007; a 2007 revision of the friendship treaty between the two countries left Bhutan free to manage its external relations without India's advice.

Although the country has opened up since the 1970s, the monarchy has taken measures to preserve its indigenous culture and the environment, including the compulsory wearing of national dress and restrictions on tourism. The emphasis on the majority culture has caused tension with the sizeable Nepali minority. Many were denied citizenship in the 1990s and obliged to leave, which resulted in over 100,000 becoming refugees in Nepal, where most remain, living in refugee camps.

Bhutan's transition from an absolute monarchy to a democracy began in the 1950s, with the establishment of an elected legislature in 1953, and the transfer of powers from the king to the legislature in 1969 and 1989. A new constitution was endorsed by the legislature and king in July 2008, formally establishing Bhutan as a parliamentary democracy with a constitutional monarchy, and providing for universal suffrage. King Jigme Singye Wangchuk abdicated in 2006 in favour of the Crown Prince.

The elections to the National Assembly in March 2008 resulted in an overwhelming majority for the pro-monarchy Bhutan Harmony Party (DPT), which won 45 of the 47 seats; the DPT leader, Jigme Thinley, was appointed prime minister and formed a government.

POLITICAL SYSTEM

Under the 2008 constitution, the head of state is a hereditary constitutional monarch, who must retire at the age of 65 and who may be required to abdicate by a two-thirds majority of both legislatures. The bicameral parliament comprises a National Assembly with 47 directly elected members and a National Council with 25 members: 20 directly elected and five appointed by the king. Both chambers serve a fixed five-year term. The cabinet is appointed by the king on the recommendation of the prime minister, who may serve two parliamentary terms.

HEAD OF STATE
HM The King of Bhutan, Jigme Khesar Namgyal Wangchuk, *born* 21 February 1980, *acceded* 14 December 2006, *crowned* 6 November 2008

SELECTED GOVERNMENT MEMBERS *as at May 2010*
Prime Minister, Jigme Thinley
Finance, Wangdi Norbu
Foreign Affairs, Ugyen Tshering
Home and Cultural Affairs, Minjur Dorji

HONORARY CONSULATE
2 Windacres, Warren Road, Guildford GU1 2HG
T 01483-538189 E rutland.michael@gmail.com
Honorary Consul, Michael R. Rutland

BRITISH DEPUTY HIGH COMMISSION
Vice Consul, Sanjay Wadvani, OBE, resident at Kolkata, India

ECONOMY AND TRADE

The economy is being cautiously modernised but is still based on agriculture (22.3 per cent of GDP in 2006) in what is largely a self-sufficient rural society. Industry (37.9 per cent of GDP) is on a small scale, and the growing services sector (39.8 per cent of GDP) is mostly the result of increased tourism. Agriculture and animal husbandry, much at subsistence level, engage over 60 per cent of the workforce, although the mountainous terrain and heavy forest cover limit the area under cultivation. The principal food crops are rice, cereals, vegetables and fruit. Bhutan is the world's third largest producer of cardamom.

Industries include forestry, mining (limestone, gypsum, dolomite, graphite, coal), cement and calcium carbide production, food processing, distilling, hydro-electric power generation and tourism. The main trading partner is India, which also provides most of Bhutan's development funding. The principal exports are electricity (to India), ferrosilicon, cement, calcium carbide, copper wire, manganese and vegetable oil; the main imports are fuel and lubricants, passenger vehicles, machinery and parts, fabrics and rice.

GNI – US$1,307m; US$1,900 per capita (2008)
Annual average growth of GDP – 5 per cent (2009 est)
Inflation rate – 8 per cent (2008 est)
Population below poverty line – 31.7 per cent (2003)
Unemployment – 4 per cent (2009)
Total external debt – US$836m (2009)
Imports – US$600m (2008)
Exports – US$600m (2008)

BALANCE OF PAYMENTS
Trade – US$183m surplus (2008)
Current Account – US$132m surplus (2007)

Trade with UK	*2008*	*2009*
Imports from UK	£618,520	£806,802
Exports to UK	£23,318	£49,597

MEDIA

Fear that outside influences would undermine Bhutanese culture meant that radio broadcasting began only in 1973, and television broadcasting and internet access in 1999; the country's first daily newspaper, *Bhutan Today*, privately owned and published in English, was launched in 2008. Radio and television services are provided by the state-owned Bhutan Broadcasting Service (BBS). Media freedom is restricted by the government and there are no private broadcasters, although cable TV relays from India are very popular.

BOLIVIA

Estado Plurinacional de Bolivia – Plurinational State of Bolivia

Area – 1,098,581 sq. km
Capital – La Paz, the seat of government; population, 1,641,950 (2009 est); Sucre, the legal capital and seat of the judiciary; population, 280,925 (2009 est)
Major cities – Cochabamba, El Alto, Oruro, Potosí, Santa Cruz
Currency – Boliviano ($b) of 100 centavos
Population – 9,775,246 rising at 1.77 per cent a year (2009 est); Quechua (30 per cent), mestizo (30 per cent), Aymara (25 per cent) (est)
Religion – Christian (Roman Catholic 78 per cent, Protestant denominations 16 per cent, other 3 per cent) (est)
Language – Spanish, 36 indigenous languages (all official); Quechua and Aymara are the main indigenous languages
Population density – 9 per sq. km (2008)
Urban population – 65 per cent (2007 est)
Median age (years) – 21.9 (2009 est)
National anthem – 'Himno Nacional de la República de Bolivia' ['National Anthem of the Republic of Bolivia']
National day – 6 August (Independence Day)
Life expectancy (years) – 66.89 (2009 est)
Mortality rate – 7.05 (2009 est)
Birth rate – 25.82 (2009 est)
Infant mortality rate – 44.66 (2009 est)
Death penalty – Retained for certain crimes (last used 1974)
CPI score – 2.7 (2009)

CLIMATE AND TERRAIN

Landlocked Bolivia's main topographical feature is its great central plateau, the Altiplano. Over 800km in length and at an average altitude of 3,750m above sea level, this plateau lies between two great chains of the Andes that traverse the country from north to south. Lake Titicaca, shared with Peru, lies on the Antiplano. Elevation extremes range from 6,542m (Nevado Sajama) at the highest point to 90m (Rio Paraguay) at the lowest. The land falls from the Andean ridges in the west through forested foothills to the plains of the north and east which lie in the Amazon basin. The plains are drained by the principal rivers, the Itenez, Beni, Mamoré and Madre de Dios. There is an average temperature of 26°C throughout most of the country but the south is prone to droughts. Temperatures become subpolar at an altitude of 500m. The wet season is November to March.

HISTORY AND POLITICS

The area of present-day Bolivia was assimilated into the Inca Empire *c.*1450, and was then conquered by the Spanish in 1525. Bolivia won its independence from Spain in 1825 after a war of liberation led by Simón Bolívar (1783–1830), from whom the country takes its name. Much of its territory was lost after wars with neighbouring countries, including a devastating defeat in the Chaco War (1932–5) against Paraguay.

Bolivia was ruled by military juntas from 1936 to 1952 and from 1964 to 1982, when civilian rule was restored amid worsening economic conditions as the tin market collapsed and inflation rose dramatically. Austerity measures introduced in 1983 succeeded over the next decade in curbing inflation and attracting foreign investment, but the measures widened social divisions and created great social unrest. Protests centred on coca crop eradication programmes, which were essential to attract overseas aid but caused economic hardship among the poor. The civil unrest also reflected the frustration of the mainly indigenous poor at their exclusion from political decision-making and failure to benefit from natural gas revenues. This led to a swing away from the traditional parties towards newer, more left-wing groupings.

Evo Morales, the country's first indigenous president and a former coca growers' leader, dealt with these issues by renationalising the energy industry and promising to relax restrictions on coca cultivation. He also sought to give greater political power to the indigenous population through constitutional changes. These were strongly opposed by many Bolivians, especially those in the wealthier regions in the east of the country who are seeking greater autonomy, provoking a political crisis in 2008, when President Morales faced a recall referendum. The president won that vote and the draft constitution was approved in a referendum in January 2009.

President Morales, leader of the Movement Towards Socialism (MAS), took office in 2006 after winning the 2005 presidential elections; he was re-elected in December 2009. After the 2005 legislative elections, the MAS had an outright majority in the lower chamber of the legislature but the Social and Democratic Power party was the largest party in the upper chamber. The MAS won a majority in both chambers in the 2009 legislative elections.

POLITICAL SYSTEM

The 1967 constitution was revised in 1994 and 2009. It provides for an executive president who is directly elected for a five-year term, which may be renewed once. The bicameral Plurinational Legislative Assembly consists of a 36-member Chamber of Senators and a 130-member Chamber of Deputies; members of both chambers are directly elected for a five-year term.

HEAD OF STATE

President, Evo Morales Ayma, *elected* 18 December 2005, *sworn in* 22 January 2006, *re-elected* 2009

President of the Senate, Vice-President, Alvaro Garcia Linera

SELECTED GOVERNMENT MEMBERS *as at May 2010*

Defence, Ruben Saavedra Soto

Economy and Public Finance, Luis Alberto Arce Catacora

Foreign Affairs, David Choquehuanca Cespedes

Interior, Sacha Sergio Llorenti Solis

BOLIVIAN EMBASSY

106 Eaton Square, London SW1W 9AD

T 020-7235 2257 E info@embassyofbolivia.co.uk

Ambassador Extraordinary and Plenipotentiary, HE Maria Beatriz Souviron, *apptd* 2006

BRITISH EMBASSY

PO Box 694, Avenida Arce 2732, La Paz

T (+591) (2) 243 3424 E ppa@megalink.com

W http://ukinbolivia.fco.gov.uk

Ambassador Extraordinary and Plenipotentiary, HE Nigel Baker, MVO, *apptd* 2007

DEFENCE

The army has 54 light tanks and over 115 armoured personnel carriers. The navy has 54 patrol and coastal vessels at 12 bases. The air force has 33 combat aircraft and 15 armed helicopters.

Military budget – US$243m (2009)

Military personnel – 46,100: army 34,800, navy 4,800, air force 6,500; paramilitary 37,100

ECONOMY AND TRADE

The country is one of the poorest and least developed in South America, with over half of the population living below the poverty line. The steady growth of the 1990s slowed in the 2000s owing to lower commodity prices and political instability, and the economy contracted in 2009 because of the global downturn. The renationalised energy industry is the mainstay of the economy but development is hampered by lack of investment. There are plans, some already implemented, to nationalise other key industries and utilities.

Mining (principally for zinc, tin and gold) and smelting, natural gas and oil production, agriculture and textiles are the principal industries. Industry contributes 36.9 per cent of GDP, agriculture 11.3 per cent and services 51.8 per cent.

The main trading partners are Brazil, Argentina and the USA. Principal exports are natural gas, soya beans and soya products, crude oil, zinc ore and tin. The main imports are petroleum products, plastics, paper, aircraft and aircraft parts, processed food, vehicles and insecticides.

GNI – US$14,100m; US$1,460 per capita (2008)

Annual average growth of GDP – 2.8 per cent (2009 est)

Inflation rate – 4.3 per cent (2009 est)

Population below poverty line – 60 per cent (2006 est)

Unemployment – 8.5 per cent (2009)

Total external debt – US$5,349m (2009 est)

Imports – US$5,000m (2008)

Exports – US$6,400m (2008)

BALANCE OF PAYMENTS

Trade – US$498m surplus (2009)

Current Account – US$2,015m surplus (2008)

Trade with UK	*2008*	*2009*
Imports from UK	£14,205,376	£14,575,941
Exports to UK	£9,554,352	£17,063,308

COMMUNICATIONS

Although landlocked, Bolivia has 10,000km of commercially navigable waterways, with an inland port on the river Paraguay at the border with Brazil. It has free port privileges at seaports in Argentina, Brazil, Chile and Paraguay, and a lease on a free-trade zone at the Peruvian port of Ilo. Bolivia has 952 airports and airfields, including four international airports serving the major cities. The 3,504km of railways form an eastern network and an Andean network; plans to link the two were initiated in 2004 (the link would complete a transcontinental railway line between the Brazilian and Chilean coasts). Of the 62,479km of roads, fewer than 4,000km are surfaced. The fixed-line telephone system is largely confined to the cities. Mobile phone use is growing rapidly, exceeding 50 per 100 persons by 2008.

EDUCATION AND HEALTH

Elementary education is compulsory and free from the ages of six to 13.

Literacy rate – 90.7 per cent (2007 est)

Gross enrolment ratio (percentage of relevant age group) – primary 108 per cent; secondary 82 per cent; tertiary 38 per cent (2008 est)

Health expenditure (per capita) – US$69 (2007)

Hospital beds (per 1,000 people) – 1.1 (2003–8)

MEDIA

Radio is historically the most important news medium owing to low literacy levels, particularly in rural areas. The media is largely privately owned and operated. Journalists practise self-censorship, avoiding sensitive topics such as drug-trafficking and political corruption.

There are six daily newspapers, each with limited influence. Television is mostly commercial, with one government-run channel.

BOSNIA AND HERCEGOVINA

Bosna i Hercegovina – Bosnia and Hercegovina

Area – 51,197 sq. km
Capital – Sarajevo; population, 391,870 (2009 est)
Major towns – Banja Luka, Bijeljina, Bosanski Samac, Mostar, Tuzla, Zenica
Currency – Convertible mark of 100 fenings
Population – 4,613,414 rising at 0.34 per cent a year (2009 est); Bosniak (48 per cent), Serb (37.1 per cent), Croat (14.3 per cent) (est)
Religion – Muslim 45 per cent (predominantly Sunni), Christian (Serb Orthodox 36 per cent, Roman Catholic 15 per cent, Protestant denominations 1 per cent) (est)
Language – Bosnian, Croatian, Serbian (all official)
Population density – 74 per sq. km (2008)
Urban population – 47 per cent (2007 est)
Median age (years) – 39.8 (2009 est)
National anthem – 'Drzavna Himna Bosne i Hercegovine' ['National Anthem of Bosnia and Hercegovina']
National day – 25 November
Life expectancy (years) – 78.5 (2009 est)
Mortality rate – 8.63 (2009 est)
Birth rate – 8.85 (2009 est)
Infant mortality rate – 9.1 (2009 est)
Death penalty – Abolished for all crimes (since 2001)
CPI score – 3 (2009)
Literacy rate – 96.7 per cent (2007 est)
Gross enrolment ratio (percentage of relevant age group) – primary 111 per cent; secondary 89 per cent; tertiary 62 per cent (2008 est)
Health expenditure (per capita) – US$397 (2007)
Hospital beds (per 1,000 people) – 3.0 (2003–8)

CLIMATE AND TERRAIN

The country is nearly landlocked, apart from a 20km coastline on the Adriatic. The Dinaric Alps lie along the western border. The mountainous centre is split by deep valleys, while the north is lower-lying, falling to the basin of the river Sava, which forms the northern border with Croatia. The highest point of elevation is 2,386m (Maglic), the lowest point is 0m (Adriatic Sea). Average temperatures in Sarajevo range from −1°C in January to 20°C in July.

HISTORY AND POLITICS

The area was settled by Slavs in the seventh century and conquered by the Ottoman Turks in 1463. Ruled by the Turks for over 400 years, the country came under Austro-Hungarian control in 1878. The assassination of the heir to the Austro-Hungarian throne in Sarajevo in 1914 precipitated the First World War, after which Bosnia-Hercegovina became part of the Kingdom of Serbs, Croats and Slovenes (renamed Yugoslavia in 1929). It was occupied by Axis forces between 1941 and 1945. After the end of the Second World War, Bosnia-Hercegovina formed part of the Socialist Federal Republic of Yugoslavia. This collapsed in 1991–2 following the secession of Slovenia, Croatia and Macedonia in 1991 and Bosnia-Hercegovina on 5 March 1992; its independence was recognised internationally in May 1992.

Federal attempts to prevent the various republics' secessions resulted in a number of mainly short-lived conflicts with nationalist paramilitary groups. But in Bosnia-Hercegovina the conflict quickly developed into a three-sided civil war in which predominantly Muslim Bosnians (Bosniaks) loyal to the government attempted to resist first Bosnian Serbs (in the east) and later Bosnian Croats (in the west and north) who had declared independence and were fighting to partition the country along ethnic lines. The Bosniak–Croat conflict continued until March 1994, when the two forces then united against the Serbs. All sides, but particularly the Serbs, expelled people of different ethnicity from the areas they seized ('ethnic cleansing'). UN forces, deployed from 1992, were unable to prevent ethnic cleansing or the many atrocities, such as the Srebrenica massacre (1995).

In August 1995, NATO intervention against Serb forces forced their leaders to participate in negotiations. These produced the Dayton Accord, which brought the war to an end in December 1995. An estimated 100,000 people died between 1992 and 1995 and a further two million were displaced.

The Dayton Accord preserved Bosnia as a single state with an almost equal division of territory between two self-governing entities, the Federation of Bosnia-Hercegovina (Bosniak/Croat) and the Republika Srpska (Bosnian Serbs), with a national government, presidency and democratically elected institutions. The Office of the High Representative was created to oversee the implementation of the civil aspects of the accord, and remains the state's highest authority. Since 1995 international peacekeeping duties have been undertaken by, successively, the UN (1995), NATO (1995–2005) and the EU (2005–).

Although stable under international administration, the country's ethnic divisions remain strong and hamper political and economic development. Constitutional reforms intended to strengthen central government and end ethnic separatism, under negotiation since 2005, have made little progress despite the incentive of eventual EU and NATO membership.

The latest legislative and collective presidential elections were held in 2006. In the federal legislature, the largest party remained the Bosniak-dominated Party for Democratic Action (SDA). It became a partner in a five-party coalition government led by Nikola Spiric. The SDA also retained its majority in the Bosniak-Croat legislature and formed a new government under Nedzad Brankovic; he resigned in June 2009 and was replaced by Mustafa Mujezinovic. In the Republika Srpska, the Alliance of Independent Social Democrats won the most seats and formed a government under Milorad Dodik. Milan Jelic, elected president of Republika Srpska in 2006, died in September 2007; Rajko Kuzmanovic was elected to replace him in December. The 2007 presidential election in the Bosniak-Croat Federation was won by Borjana Kristo. Federal legislative and presidential elections were due in October 2010.

POLITICAL SYSTEM

Under the Dayton Peace Accord, the Bosnian republican (national) government is responsible for foreign affairs, currency, citizenship and immigration. The head of state is a collective presidency comprising a representative from each of the three main ethnic groups, all directly elected for a four-year term; the chairmanship of the presidency rotates among its members every eight months. Legislative authority is vested in the bicameral Parliamentary Assembly of Bosnia and Hercegovina, comprising a House of Peoples and a House of Representatives. Both houses have four-year terms. The House of Peoples has 15 members – ten from the Federation and five from the Republika Srpska, who are appointed from the House of Representatives. The House of Representatives has 42 members who are directly elected to the two constituent chambers, the Chamber of Deputies of the Federation, which has 28 members, and the Chamber of Deputies of the Republika Srpska, which has 14 members.

In the Bosniak-Croat Federation, the president and vice-president are elected by the Bosniak and Croat members of the House of Peoples for a four-year term; a second vice-president is elected to represent the Serb population. There is a bicameral Assembly comprising a 58-member House of Peoples elected on an ethnic basis and a House of Representatives with 98 directly elected members.

In the Republika Srpska, the president is directly elected for a four-year term. There is a unicameral People's Assembly with 83 members directly elected for a four-year term.

There is a national council of ministers and each of the entities also has its own executive. All appointments to the executives are in consultation with the UN High Representative and may be vetoed by him.

REPUBLIC OF BOSNIA AND HERCEGOVINA

HEADS OF STATE

Presidency Members, Nebojsa Radmanovic (Serb), Zeljko Komsic (Croat), Haris Silajdzic (Bosniak)

SELECTED GOVERNMENT MEMBERS *as at May 2010*

Chair of the Council of Ministers, Nikola Spiric
Finance, Dragan Vrankic
Foreign Affairs, Sven Alkalaj
Defence, Selmo Cikotic

FEDERATION OF BOSNIA AND HERCEGOVINA

President, Borjana Kristo
Vice-Presidents, Mirsad Kebo; Spomenka Micic

SELECTED GOVERNMENT MEMBERS *as at May 2010*

Prime Minister, Mustafa Mujezinovic
Deputy Prime Minister, Vjekoslav Bevanda *(Finance)*

REPUBLIKA SRPSKA

President, Rajko Kuzmanovic
Vice-Presidents, Davor Cordas; Adil Osmanovic

SELECTED GOVERNMENT MEMBERS *as at May 2010*

Prime Minister, Milorad Dodik
Deputy Prime Ministers, Jasna Brkic *(Economy);* Anton Kasipovic
Interior, Stanislav Cadjo

OFFICE OF THE UN HIGH REPRESENTATIVE / EU SPECIAL REPRESENTATIVE

UN High Representative, Dr Valentin Inzko, *apptd* 2009

EMBASSY OF BOSNIA AND HERCEGOVINA

5–7 Lexham Gardens, London W8 5JJ
T 020-7373 0867 E embassy@bhembassy.co.uk
W www.bhembassy.co.uk
Ambassador Extraordinary and Plenipotentiary, HE Jadranka Negodic, *apptd* 2008

BRITISH EMBASSY

Tina Ujevica 8, 71000 Sarajevo
T (+387) (33) 282 200 E britemb@bih.net.ba
W http://ukinbih.fco.gov.uk
Ambassador Extraordinary and Plenipotentiary, HE Michael Tatham, *apptd* 2008

BRITISH COUNCIL

Ljubljanska 9, 71000 Sarajevo
T (+387) (33) 250 220 W www.britishcouncil.org/bih
Director, Michael Moore

DEFENCE

A reform process completed in 2006 united the separate armies of the Republika Sprska and the Federation of Bosnia Hercegovina into a single entity. The armed forces have 325 main battle tanks, 134 armoured infantry fighting vehicles and 142 armoured personnel carriers. The air wing has 19 combat capable aircraft and 13 attack helicopters.

Military budget – US$281m (2009)
Military personnel – 11,099: armed forces 10,712, Joint Operational Command 144, State Joint Staff 243

ECONOMY AND TRADE

When the civil war broke out, the structure of the economy (dominated by state-owned industries, mainly of a military nature) still reflected the central planning of the communist era. Since the war, growth has been largely generated by reconstruction, funded by external aid. Economic restructuring, such as privatisation, has been slow and uneven, although the financial sector is now largely privatised and stable. The economy contracted in 2009 owing to the global economic downturn and unemployment rose to a very high level, although many might be involved in unofficial economic activity. The difficulties inherent in tackling these problems are exacerbated by the duplication of administrative functions and reluctant cooperation between the different national and local political and administrative entities.

Most agricultural products are for domestic consumption and foodstuffs also have to be imported. The main industrial activities include mining (metals, minerals and coal), production of steel, textiles, tobacco products, wooden furniture and domestic appliances, assembly of vehicles, tanks and aircraft, and oil refining. The country has enough hydroelectric power for its needs and exports electricity. The main trading partners are Croatia, Slovenia and EU states, particularly Italy and Germany. Principal exports are metals, clothing and wood products, and the main imports are machinery and equipment, chemicals, fuels and foodstuffs.

GNI – US$17,100m; US$4,520 per capita (2008)
Annual average growth of GDP – –2.9 per cent (2009 est)
Inflation rate – 0.6 per cent (2009 est)
Population below poverty line – 25 per cent (2004 est)
Unemployment – 40 per cent (2009 est)
Total external debt – US$8,415m (2009 est)

BALANCE OF PAYMENTS
Trade – US$6,186m deficit (2009)
Current Account – US$2,765m deficit (2008)

Trade with UK	*2008*	*2009*
Imports from UK	£20,539,787	£19,779,817
Exports to UK	£22,586,475	£11,220,188

COMMUNICATIONS

Although the country has 20km of coastline on the Adriatic Sea, there are no seaports. There are four river ports on the river Sava, which is navigable by shipping but its use is limited. The 25 airports and airfields include international airports at Sarajevo, Banja Luka, Mostar and Tuzla. There are 1,000km of railways and 21,846km of roads, 11,425km of which are paved. Reconstruction of the telephone network has resulted in a rapid growth in fixed lines, to 1 million, while mobile subscriptions increased to almost 3.2 million in 2008.

MEDIA

During the war most media outlets became, to various degrees, propagandists for particular factions or centres of power; efforts since the 1995 peace accord to develop multi-ethnic outlets have had limited success. A national broadcasting service is being developed under the aegis of the Office of the High Representative. The public radio and television stations in the two entities are the most influential broadcasters but are not wholly independent, being subject to both government and party political pressure. There are more than 200 commercial television and radio stations, but a weak advertising market has limited their development.

BOTSWANA

Republic of Botswana

Area – 581,730 sq. km
Capital – Gaborone; population, 195,894 (2009 est)
Major cities – Francistown, Molepolole, Selebi-Phikwe
Currency – Pula (P) of 100 thebe
Population – 1,990,876 rising at 1.94 per cent a year (2009 est); Tswana (79 per cent), Kalanga (11 per cent), Basarwa (3 per cent) (est)
Religion – Christian 70 per cent (predominantly Protestant) (est)
Language – English (official), Setswana, Kalanga, Sekgalagadi
Population density – 3 per sq. km (2008)
Urban population – 59 per cent (2007 est)
Median age (years) – 21.7 (2009 est)
National anthem – 'Fatshe Leno La Rona' ['Blessed Be This Noble Land']
National day – 30 September (Botswana Day)
Life expectancy (years) – 61.85 (2009 est)
Mortality rate – 8.52 (2009 est)
Birth rate – 22.89 (2009 est)
Infant mortality rate – 12.59 (2009 est)
HIV/AIDS adult prevalence – 22.8 per cent (2007)
Death penalty – Retained
CPI score – 5.6 (2009)

CLIMATE AND TERRAIN

A landlocked country in southern Africa, Botswana lies on an undulating plateau. The Kalahari desert covers about three-quarters of the country, in the south and west. To the east, streams run into the Marico, Notwani and Limpopo rivers. In the north lies a flat region comprising the Makgadikgadi salt pans and the swampland of the Okavango delta. Elevation extremes range from 1,489m (Tsodilo Hills) at the highest point to 513m (junction of the Limpopo and Shashe rivers) at the lowest. The climate is subtropical in the north, arid in the south and west, and more temperate in the east, which has regular rain. Average temperatures range from 26°C in January to 13°C in July.

HISTORY AND POLITICS

The Tswana people were predominant in the area from the 17th century. In 1885, at the request of indigenous chiefs fearing invasion by the Boers, Britain formally took control of Bechuanaland, and the northern part of the territory was declared the Bechuanaland Protectorate, while land to the south of the Molopo river became British Bechuanaland, which was later incorporated into the Cape Colony. In 1964, the British Protectorate of Bechuanaland became self-governing, and on 30 September 1966 it became an independent republic under the name Botswana. Since independence, Botswana has been stable and relatively prosperous owing to the diamond mining industry. There is a high level of HIV/AIDS among the population, and although an advanced treatment programme in place since 2001 is reducing the level of infection, the country faces serious demographic and social problems.

President Festus Mogae stood down in 2008, having completed two terms of office, and was succeeded by the vice-president, Lt.-Gen. Ian Khama, son of the country's first president. The legislative election in October 2009 was won by the Botswana Democratic Party, with 45 seats. President Khama was elected president two days later.

POLITICAL SYSTEM

Under the 1966 constitution, the executive president is elected by the legislature for a five-year term, renewable only once. He appoints the vice-president and the cabinet. The unicameral National Assembly has 57 members directly elected for a five-year term, plus a variable number of members (currently four) nominated by the president and elected by the assembly. A 15-member House of Chiefs advises on tribal matters and constitutional changes.

HEAD OF STATE

President, Lt.-Gen. (retd) Ian Khama, *sworn in* 1 April 2008, *elected* 18 October 2009
Vice-President, Lt.-Gen. Mompati Merafhe

SELECTED GOVERNMENT MEMBERS *as at May 2010*

Finance and Development Planning, Kenneth Matambo

Foreign Affairs, Phandu Skelemani
Defence, Dikgakgamatso Seretse

BOTSWANA HIGH COMMISSION
6 Stratford Place, London W1C 1AY
T 020-7499 0031 E bohico@govbw.com
High Commissioner, HE Roy Blackbeard, *apptd* 1998

BRITISH HIGH COMMISSION
Private Bag 0023, Plot 1079-1084 Main Mall, off Queens Road, Gaborone
T (+267) 395 2841 E bhc@botsnet.bw
W http://ukinbotswana.fco.gov.uk
High Commissioner, HE Jennifer Anderson, *apptd* 2010

BRITISH COUNCIL
PO Box 439, British High Commission Building, 1079–1084 Main Mall, Gaborone
T (+267) 395 3602 W www.britishcouncil.org/africa
Director, Tanya Dunne

DEFENCE
The army has 55 light tanks and 156 armoured personnel carriers. The air wing has 31 combat capable aircraft.
Military budget – US$293m (2008 est)
Military personnel – 9,000: army 8,500, air force 500; paramilitary 1,500

ECONOMY AND TRADE
Botswana has been relatively prosperous since independence because of its mining industry, political stability and sound economic management. Despite this, about 30 per cent of the population lives below the poverty line. Longer-term problems are the impact of the high levels of HIV/AIDS among the workforce and the levelling off of diamond production, which usually accounts for 70 to 80 per cent of export earnings; diamond exports have declined owing to the global downturn, causing the economy to contract sharply in 2009. The government has sought to reduce the economy's dependence on the diamond industry by diversifying; safari tourism and financial services in particular have grown in recent years, and the services sector now contributes 45.8 per cent of GDP. The industrial sector contributes 52.6 per cent of GDP, of which 36 per cent is from mining diamonds, copper, nickel, salt, soda ash, potash and coal. Agriculture is predominantly pastoral and accounts for 1.6 per cent of GDP. Cattle-rearing represents over 80 per cent of agricultural production.

The main trading partners are EU and southern African countries. Principal exports are diamonds, copper, nickel, soda ash, meat and textiles. The main imports are foodstuffs, machinery, electrical goods, transport equipment, textiles, energy and fuel.
GNI – US$12,800m; US$6,640 per capita (2008)
Annual average growth of GDP – –12 per cent (2009 est)
Inflation rate – 7.3 per cent (2009 est)
Population below poverty line – 30.3 per cent (2003)
Unemployment – 7.5 per cent (2007)
Total external debt – US$1,651m (2009 est)
Imports – US$5,200m (2008)
Exports – US$5,000m (2008)

BALANCE OF PAYMENTS
Trade – US$547m deficit (2009)
Current Account – US$664m surplus (2008)

Trade with UK	*2008*	*2009*
Imports from UK	£15,348,712	£11,574,345
Exports to UK	£493,700,480	£227,663,305

COMMUNICATIONS
Because of its landlocked position, Botswana's trade is dependent on its international rail and road links. The only railway is the 888km line from Zimbabwe to South Africa, which passes through eastern Botswana. There are 25,800km of roads, of which 8,410km are paved. These include a highway connecting all the main towns and district capitals. The network links at the borders with the road networks of South Africa and Namibia. A major link is the 595km Trans-Kalahari Highway which connects Botswana with Namibia's capital (Windhoek) and its port at Walvis Bay. There are over 70 airports and airfields, including the international airport at Gaborone. Telecommunications systems are being expanded, although fixed-line connections have declined in recent years, while mobile phone distribution is growing rapidly; there were about 80 mobile phones per 100 people in 2008.

EDUCATION AND HEALTH
Botswana does not have a compulsory education policy. Many children receive ten years of education, though the government announced in 2004 that efforts would be made to increase this to 12 years (seven years of primary education, three years of junior secondary, and two years of senior secondary). In 2006 fees were reintroduced for state secondary schools, which had been free of charge for over 20 years.
Literacy rate – 82.9 per cent (2007 est)
Gross enrolment ratio (percentage of relevant age group) – primary 110 per cent; secondary 80 per cent (2008 est)
Health expenditure (per capita) – US$372 (2007)
Hospital beds (per 1,000 people) – 1.8 (2003–8)

MEDIA
Botswana has a good record on press transparency and respect for freedom of expression. Newspaper circulation is almost entirely limited to urban areas, and radio is the most important news medium. There are state-run and private commercial radio stations, and programmes are broadcast in both English and Setswana. State-run television (Botswana Television) was established in 2000, and commercial and satellite services are also available.

BRAZIL

Republica Federativa do Brasil – Federative Republic of Brazil

Area – 8,514,877 sq. km
Capital – Brasilia; population, 3,788,820 (2009 est)
Major cities – Belo Horizonte, Fortaleza, Porto Alegre, Recife, Rio de Janeiro (the former capital), Salvador, Sao Paulo
Currency – Real of 100 centavos
Population – 198,739,269 rising at 1.2 per cent a year (2009 est)
Religion – Christian (Roman Catholic 74 per cent, Protestant denominations 18 per cent) (est)
Language – Portuguese (official), Spanish, German, Italian, Japanese, English, Amerindian languages
Population density – 23 per sq. km (2008)
Urban population – 85 per cent (2007 est)
Median age (years) – 28.6 (2009 est)
National anthem – 'Hino Nacional Brasileiro' ['Brazilian National Anthem']
National day – 7 September (Independence Day)
Life expectancy (years) – 71.99 (2009 est)
Mortality rate – 6.35 (2009 est)
Birth rate – 18.43 (2009 est)
Infant mortality rate – 22.58 (2009 est)
Death penalty – Retained for certain crimes (last used 1855)
CPI score – 3.7 (2009)

CLIMATE AND TERRAIN

Brazil is South America's biggest country, taking up almost half of the continent. It has five distinct topographical areas: the Amazon basin (north and west of the country), the Parana-Paraguay river basin (south; the Parana drains the Pantanal, the world's largest freshwater wetland), the Guiana Highlands (north of the Amazon), the Mato Grosso plateau (centre) and Brazilian Highlands (south of the Amazon) and the coastal strip. Elevation extremes range from 2,994m (Pico da Neblina) at the highest point to 0m (Atlantic Ocean) at the lowest. Brazil has the world's largest rainforest, as well as expanses of savannah and wetlands. The climate is mostly tropical, with the equator passing through the north and the Tropic of Capricorn through the south-east. The Amazon basin sees annual rainfall of up to 2,000mm a year and there is no dry season (average temperature 30°C). The north-east is the driest area of the country and can experience long periods of drought (maximum average temperature 38°C). The southern states have a seasonal temperate climate (average temperatures between 17°C and 19°C).

HISTORY AND POLITICS

Brazil was claimed by the Portuguese navigator Pedro Cabral in 1500 and colonised by Portugal in the early 16th century, becoming a viceroyalty in 1572. During the Napoleonic Wars the Portuguese court took refuge in Brazil. In 1822 Pedro I, son of King Joao VI of Portugal, declared Brazil an independent monarchy. In 1889, Pedro II was overthrown in a coup, and a federal republic was proclaimed. Brazil was a dictatorship from 1930 to 1945 and under military rule from 1964 to 1985, when civilian rule was restored after several years of gradual democratisation. Governments since then have faced difficult economic conditions, and exploitation of the Amazon basin has attracted controversy because it threatens the environmentally important rainforest.

Luis ('Lula') da Silva of the Workers' Party (PT) was elected president in 2001, and was re-elected in 2006. In the 2006 legislative election, the Party of the Brazilian Democratic Movement (PMDB) became the largest party in the lower house and increased its seats in the senate, although the largest party in that house remained the Liberal Front Party (now the Democrats). After the elections, the coalition government, dominated by the PT and including the PMDB, continued in office. Presidential and legislative elections were scheduled for 3 October 2010.

POLITICAL SYSTEM

Under the 1988 constitution (as amended), the executive president is directly elected for a four-year term and, since 1997, may serve a second term. The National Congress consists of an 81-member federal senate (three senators per state, directly elected for an eight-year term) and a 513-member Chamber of Deputies which is directly elected every four years; the number of deputies per state depends upon the state's population.

HEAD OF STATE

President, Luis Inacio 'Lula' da Silva, *sworn in* 1 January 2003, *re-elected* October 2006
Vice-President, Jose Alencar Gomes de Silva

SELECTED GOVERNMENT MEMBERS *as at May 2010*

Defence, Nelson Jobim
Foreign Affairs, Celso Amorim
Finance, Guido Mantega
Attorney-General, Luis Inacio Lucena Adams

EMBASSY OF BRAZIL

32 Green Street, London W1K 7AT
T 020-7399 9000 E info@brazil.org.uk W www.brazil.org.uk
Ambassador Extraordinary and Plenipotentiary, HE Carlos Augusto Santos-Neves, *apptd* 2008

BRITISH EMBASSY

Setor de Embaixadas Sul, Quadra 801, Lote 8, CEP 70408-900, Brasilia DF
T (+55) (61) 3329 2300 E contact@uk.org.br
W http://ukinbrazil.fco.gov.uk
Ambassador Extraordinary and Plenipotentiary, HE Alan Charlton, CMG, *apptd* 2008

BRITISH COUNCIL

Edificio Centro Empresarial Varig, SCN Quadra 04, Bloco B, Torre Oeste Conjunto 202, 70714-900 Brasilia DF
T (+55) (61) 2106 7500 W www.britishcouncil.org/brazil
Director, Jim Scarth

FEDERAL STRUCTURE

The Federative Republic of Brazil is composed of the federal district in which the capital lies and 26 states: Acre, Alagoas, Amapa, Amazonas, Bahia, Ceara, Federal District of Brasilia, Espirito Santo, Goias, Maranhao, Mato Grosso, Mato Grosso do Sul, Minas Gerais, Para, Paraiba, Parana, Pernambuco, Piaui, Rio de Janeiro, Rio Grande do Norte, Rio Grande do Sul, Rondonia, Roraima, Santa Catarina, Sao Paulo, Sergipe and Tocantins. Each state has its own governor and legislative assembly.

DEFENCE

The army has 219 main battle tanks, 807 armoured personnel carriers and 63 armed helicopters. The navy is equipped with 5 submarines, 1 aircraft carrier, 5 corvettes, 10 frigates and 35 patrol and coastal vessels. Naval aviation consists of 23 combat aircraft and 16 armed helicopters; the Marines have 18 light tanks and 35 armoured personnel carriers. The air force has 334 combat aircraft.

Military expenditure – US$27,780m (2009)
Military personnel – 327,710: army 190,000, navy 67,000, air force 70,710; paramilitary 395,000
Conscription duration – 12 months (can be extended to 18)

ECONOMY AND TRADE

Historically subject to boom and bust cycles, the economy was stabilised by reforms in the 1990s. Tight fiscal management, IMF programmes, a growth in output and an expanding export base have produced steady growth since 2003, although poverty is still widespread. Brazil's economy, based on well-developed agriculture, mining, manufacturing and service sectors, is now the tenth largest in the world, giving the country growing global importance. Although the economy contracted in the global downturn, it weathered the crisis better than other countries and is recovering quickly.

The country is rich in mineral deposits, including iron ore (haematite), bauxite, gold, manganese, nickel, platinum and uranium. It produces oil, gas and hydroelectricity, and is close to self-sufficiency in oil. Brazil is the world's largest producer of coffee; the other main agricultural products are soya beans, wheat, rice, maize, sugar cane, cocoa, citrus fruit and beef. The expansion of agriculture and forestry threaten the rainforest, although recent governments' attempts to prevent further depredations by loggers and farmers have slowed the rate of deforestation considerably. Tourism is a growing industry. In 2009, services generated 67.7 per cent of GDP, industry 25.8 per cent and agriculture 6.5 per cent.

Brazil's main trading partners are the USA, China, Argentina and Germany. Principal exports are transport equipment, iron ore, soya beans, footwear, coffee and vehicles. The main imports are machinery, electrical and transport equipment, chemical products, oil, vehicle parts and electronics.

GNI – US$1,401,300m; US$7,300 per capita (2008)
Annual average growth of GDP – 0.1 per cent (2009)
Inflation rate – 4.2 per cent (2009 est)
Population below poverty line – 31 per cent (2005)
Unemployment – 7.4 per cent (2009 est)
Total external debt – US$216,100m (2009)
Imports – US$182,400m (2008)
Exports – US$197,900m (2008)

BALANCE OF PAYMENTS
Trade – US$24,637m surplus (2009)
Current Account – US$24,344m deficit (2009)

Trade with UK	*2008*	*2009*
Imports from UK	£1,618,112,599	£1,727,355,122
Exports to UK	£2,721,321,392	£3,028,158,395

COMMUNICATIONS

The 1,751,868km road network and 28,857km rail network are concentrated in the more densely populated south and east of the country. The railways are used primarily for transporting minerals to the ports; most passenger and freight traffic is on the roads. The Trans-Amazonian Highway connects the Amazon region with the rest of the country, although it is mostly unpaved and often becomes impassable in the rainy season. In remote regions, transport is primarily by air or water, utilising the 50,000km of navigable waterways and the 4,000 airports and airfields; international flights operate to the major cities. Rio de Janeiro and Santos are the two leading seaports but there are also another 14 fully equipped ports. Piracy and armed robbery against ships in territorial and offshore waters is a growing problem. The fixed-line telephone system is extensive. Mobile phone distribution has grown rapidly, reaching a density of 80 per 100 people by 2008; there were 65 million internet users in 2008.

EDUCATION AND HEALTH

The education system includes both public and private institutions. Public education is free at all levels, and is compulsory between the ages of seven and 14.
Literacy rate – 90.0 per cent (2007 est)
Gross enrolment ratio (percentage of relevant age group) – primary 130 per cent; secondary 100 per cent; tertiary 30 per cent (2008 est)
Health expenditure (per capita) – US$606 (2007)
Hospital beds (per 1,000 people) – 2.4 (2003–8)

MEDIA AND CULTURE

Brazil has South America's biggest media industry, with Brazilian-made soap operas, game shows and dramas exported all over the world. There are thousands of radio stations and hundreds of television channels. Domestic conglomerates, most notably Globo, dominate the market and run television and radio networks, newspapers and subscription television stations. The constitution guarantees a free press and media debate is vigorous.

The country is a melting pot of races, cultures, religious traditions, music and dance; the samba, bossa nova and lambada are world-famous. Luis de Camoes (1525–80) is widely regarded as Brazil's national poet, while Paolo Coelho (*b.* 1947) is its most commercially successful author. The film industry is thriving, with two directors, Walter Salles *(The Motorcycle Diaries)* and Fernando Meirelles *(City of God)*, achieving international recognition in recent years.

Football is central to contemporary culture and Brazil has won a record five World Cups as well as producing some of the world's most gifted players, including Pele (*b.* 1940), Ronaldo (*b.* 1976) and Ronaldinho (*b.* 1980).

BRUNEI

Negara Brunei Darussalam – Brunei Darussalam

Area – 5,765 sq. km
Capital – Bandar Seri Begawan; population, 22,228 (2009 est)
Major towns – Kuala Belait, Seria, Tutong
Currency – Brunei dollar (B$) of 100 sen (fully interchangeable with Singapore currency)

Population – 388,190 rising at 1.76 per cent a year (2009 est); Malay (66.3 per cent), Chinese (11.2 per cent) (2004 est)
Religion – Muslim 52 per cent (predominantly Shafi'i, a school of Sunni Islam), Buddhist 4 per cent, Christian 2 per cent (est); Islam is the state religion
Language – Malay (official), English, Chinese
Population density – 74 per sq. km (2007)
Urban population – 74 per cent (2008 est)
Median age (years) – 27.8 (2009 est)
National anthem – 'Allah Peliharakan Sultan' ['God Bless the Sultan']
National day – 23 February
Life expectancy (years) – 75.74 (2009 est)
Mortality rate – 3.29 (2009 est)
Birth rate – 18.2 (2009 est)
Infant mortality rate – 12.27 (2009 est)
Death penalty – Retained (no known use since 1957)
CPI score – 5.5 (2009)

CLIMATE AND TERRAIN

The country lies on the north-west coast of the island of Borneo. It is surrounded and divided in two by the Malaysian state of Sarawak. The terrain is mostly rainforest (over half of the country, although current estimates vary), with extensive mangrove swamps along the coastal plain. There are mountains on the border with Sarawak. Elevation extremes range from 1,850m (Bukit Pagon) at the highest point to 0m (South China Sea) at the lowest. The climate is tropical, with high humidity, an annual average daily temperature of 27°C and about 2,900mm of rain per year.

HISTORY AND POLITICS

Formerly a powerful Muslim sultanate that controlled Borneo and parts of the Philippines, Brunei was reduced to its present size by the mid-19th century and came under British protection in 1889. It chose to remain a British dependency in 1963 rather than joining the Federation of Malaysia. Internally self-governing from 1959, Brunei gained full independence on 1 January 1984.

In 1962 the legislative election was annulled after it was won by a party that sought to remove the sultan; a state of emergency was declared and the sultan has ruled by decree ever since. A ministerial system of government was introduced in 1984. Some political liberalisation and modernisation has taken place since 2004, when the legislature was reconvened after 20 years.

POLITICAL SYSTEM

Parts of the 1959 constitution have been suspended since the state of emergency began in 1962. Supreme executive authority is vested in the sultan, a hereditary monarch who presides over and is advised by a privy council, a religious council and the council of cabinet ministers. The legislative council was reconvened in 2004 with 21 members appointed by the sultan; it has passed constitutional amendments to increase its size to 45 members, 15 of whom will be directly elected. No date has been set for an election.

HEAD OF STATE

HM The Sultan of Brunei, Prime Minister, Defence, Finance, HM Hassanal Bolkiah, GCB, *acceded 5 October* 1967, *crowned* 1 August 1968
HM Crown Prince, Senior Minister in the Prime Minister's Office, Prince Al-Muhtadee Billah

SELECTED GOVERNMENT MEMBERS *as at May 2010*

Foreign Affairs, Prince Mohamed Bolkiah
Home Affairs, Pehin Dato Adanan Yusof

BRUNEI DARUSSALAM HIGH COMMISSION

19–20 Belgrave Square, London SW1X 8PG
T 020-7581 0521 E london.uk@mfa.gov.bn
High Commissioner, HE Pengiran Dato Maidin Hashim, *apptd* 2006

BRITISH HIGH COMMISSION

2.01, 2nd Floor, Block D, Kompleks Yayasan Sultan Haji Hassanal Bolkiah, Bandar Seri Begawan, BS 8711
T (+673) (2) 222 231 E brithc@brunet.bn
W http://ukinbrunei.fco.gov.uk
High Commissioner, Robert Fenn, *apptd* 2009

DEFENCE

The army has 20 light tanks and 39 armoured personnel carriers. The navy has over 16 patrol and coastal vessels. The air force has 5 support helicopters. There are 550 UK troops currently stationed in Brunei.
Military budget – US$395m (2009)
Military personnel – 7,000: army 4,900, navy 1,000, air force 1,100; paramilitaries 2,250

ECONOMY AND TRADE

The economy is based on the production of oil and natural gas and the income from overseas investments. Royalties and taxes from these operations form the bulk of government revenue and have enabled the construction of free health, education and welfare services. However, oil and gas reserves are declining and Brunei is now trying to diversify its economy, developing financial services and tourism.

Agriculture accounts for 0.7 per cent of GDP, industry 74.1 per cent and services 25.3 per cent. The main trading partners are the Japan, Singapore, Indonesia and Malaysia. Principal exports are crude oil, natural gas, refined products and clothing. The main imports are machinery and transport equipment, manufactured goods, food (over 80 per cent of domestic requirements is imported) and chemicals.
GNI – US$10,287m; US$26,930m per capita (2007)
Annual average growth of GDP – −1.9 per cent (2009 est)
Inflation rate – 0.3 per cent (2007)
Unemployment – 3.7 per cent (2008)

BALANCE OF PAYMENTS

Trade – US$3,823m surplus (2007)
Current Account – US$8,346m surplus (2008)

Trade with UK	*2008*	*2009*
Imports from UK	£62,676,177	£61,023,110
Exports to UK	£27,897,600	£22,819,339

COMMUNICATIONS

There are ports at Kuala Belait, Muara and Tanjong Salirong, and terminals at Lumut and Seria. Seria is the location of one of Brunei's two airports, the other being the international airport at Bandar Seri Begawan. The 209km of waterways is navigable only by shallow craft. There is a road network of 2,971km, most of which is paved, but no railway. The telephone system is extensive and modern. Mobile phone distribution is very high, at 376,000 in 2008.

EDUCATION

All levels of education are free. Children undertake six years of primary education, three of lower secondary and two to four years of upper secondary, which can be in a secondary school, vocational school or technical college.
Literacy rate – 94.9 per cent (2007 est)

MEDIA

The media is mostly privately owned, but tightly controlled; laws against reporting 'false news' carry heavy punishments, therefore criticism of the government is rare. The only broadcast media organisation, Radio Television Brunei (RTB), is state-owned. It broadcasts television in Malay and English and radio in Malay, English, Mandarin Chinese and Gurkhali. Foreign television channels are available via cable, and internet access is unrestricted.

BULGARIA

Republika Balgariya – Republic of Bulgaria

Area – 110,879 sq. km
Capital – Sofia; population, 1,191,890 (2009 est)
Major cities – Burgas, Plovdiv, Varna
Currency – Lev of 100 stotinki
Population – 7,204,687 falling at 0.79 per cent a year (2009 est); Bulgarian (83.9 per cent), Turkish (9.4 per cent), Roma (4.7 per cent)
Religion – Christian (Orthodox 85 per cent, Protestant 2 per cent, Catholic 1 per cent), Muslim 13 per cent (predominantly Sunni) (est)
Language – Bulgarian (official), Turkish, Romani
Population density – 70 per sq. km (2008)
Urban population – 71 per cent (2007 est)
Median age (years) – 41.4 (2009 est)
National anthem – 'Mila Rodino' ['Dear Motherland']
National day – 3 March (Liberation Day)
Life expectancy (years) – 73.09 (2009 est)
Mortality rate – 14.31 (2009 est)
Birth rate – 9.51 (2009 est)
Infant mortality rate – 17.87 (2009 est)
Death penalty – Abolished for all crimes (since 1998)
CPI score – 3.8 (2009)

CLIMATE AND TERRAIN

The country is dominated by mountains: the Balkan Mountains cross the country from west to east, averaging 2,000m in height; and the Rhodope Mountains in the south-west climb to almost 3,000m. Elevation extremes range from 2,925m (Musala) at the highest point to 0m (Black Sea) at the lowest. The lowland plains of the north and south-east are in the basins of the main rivers: the Danube in the north, which forms much of the border with Romania, and the Maritsa, which divides the Balkan and Rhodope ranges. The climate is temperate, with cold, damp winters and hot, dry summers. Average temperatures in Sofia range from −1°C in January to 22°C in July.

HISTORY AND POLITICS

Bulgarians are descended from Slavs and Bulgars, who migrated into the Balkans in the fifth century and the seventh century AD respectively. The first Bulgarian kingdom was founded in 681 but fell to the Ottoman Empire in the 1390s. The treaty of San Stefano, which concluded the Russo-Turkish war of 1877–8, envisaged Bulgaria as an independent principality; however, this agreement was revised by the treaty of Berlin in July 1878, under which Bulgaria's territory was substantially reduced and part remained subject to Ottoman suzerainty. In 1908 the country regained its lost territory and was declared a kingdom.

Bulgaria was allied with Germany in both world wars but switched sides in September 1944 after a coup brought to power the Fatherland Front, a left-wing coalition that came to be dominated by the communists. A referendum in 1946 led to the abolition of the monarchy and the establishment of a republic. The Communist Party (BCP), which had won the 1946 election, in 1947 established a one-party state and a centralised economy.

From the mid-1980s cautious reforms were introduced in line with the Soviet policies of *perestroika* and *glasnost*, and Bulgaria became a multiparty democracy in 1990. Political and economic liberalisation progressed slowly in the early 1990s, causing economic difficulties and political unrest. The political volatility had calmed by the late 1990s, when more radical economic reforms were introduced. After that, progress was sufficient for Bulgaria to join NATO in 2006 and the EU in 2007.

Georgi Parvanov, president since 2002, was re-elected in 2006. In the 2009 legislative election, the new centre-right party Citizens for European Development of Bulgaria (GERB) won the most seats, but without an overall majority, and formed a minority government with support in the legislature from small right-wing parties.

POLITICAL SYSTEM

Under the 1991 constitution, the president is directly elected for a five-year term, renewable once only. The head of government is the prime minister, who is appointed by the president, and is usually the leader of the largest party in the legislature. There is a unicameral National Assembly of 240 members who are directly elected for a four-year term.

HEAD OF STATE

President, Georgi Parvanov, *elected* 18 November 2001, *re-elected* 2006
Vice-President, Angel Marin

SELECTED GOVERNMENT MEMBERS *as at May 2010*

Prime Minister, Boiko Borisov
Deputy Prime Ministers, Anyu Angelov *(Defence)*, Tsvetan Tsvetanov *(Interior)*
Finance, Simeon Djankov
Foreign Affairs, Nikolay Mladenov

EMBASSY OF THE REPUBLIC OF BULGARIA

186–188 Queen's Gate, London SW7 5HL
T 020-7584 9400 E info@bulgarianembassy.org.uk
W www.bulgarianembassy-london.org
Ambassador Extraordinary and Plenipotentiary, HE Lyubomir Kyuchukov, *apptd* 2009

BRITISH EMBASSY
9 Moskovska Street, Sofia 1000
T (+359) (2) 933 9222 E britembsof@mbox.cit.bg
W http://ukinbulgaria.fco.gov.uk
Ambassador Extraordinary and Plenipotentiary, HE Steve Williams, *apptd* 2007

BRITISH COUNCIL
7 Krakra Street, 1504 Sofia
T (+359) 2942 4344 E bc.sofia@britishcouncil.bg
W www.britishcouncil.org/bulgaria
Director, Tony Buckby

DEFENCE

The army has 362 main battle tanks, 185 armoured infantry fighting vehicles and 1,393 armoured personnel carriers. The navy has 1 submarine, 4 frigates, 19 patrol and coastal vessels, and 6 armed helicopters. There are bases at Atya, Balchik, Vidin, Sozopol, Burgas and Varna. The air force has 62 combat aircraft and 18 armed helicopters.

Military expenditure – US$1,310m (2008)
Military personnel – 34,975: army 16,268, navy 3,471, air force 6,706, central staff 8,530; paramilitary 34,000
Conscription duration – 9 months

ECONOMY AND TRADE

The government adopted radical economic reforms in 1996 and the economy achieved stability and attracted a great deal of foreign investment, although administrative corruption and organised crime remain potential deterrents. Despite steady economic growth in 2004–8 and responsible fiscal management, the economy has contracted in the global economic downturn as industrial production and exports have declined.

Natural resources include copper, lead, zinc, other minerals, coal and timber. Fertile arable land produces vegetables, fruit, tobacco, wine, wheat, barley, sunflowers and livestock. About 7.5 per cent of the workforce is engaged in agriculture, which accounted for 7.5 per cent of GDP in 2009. Industries include energy generation, food processing, beverages, tobacco, machinery and equipment, base metals, chemicals, mining and oil refining. Tourism is growing. One of the main exports is electricity generated at the controversial Kozloduy nuclear power plant. Bulgaria has decommissioned two reactors in response to EU concerns about safety.

The main trading partners are Turkey, EU countries and Russia. Principal exports are clothing and footwear, iron and steel, machinery and equipment, and fuels. The main imports are predominantly raw materials for the industrial sector.

GNI – US$41,800m; US$5,490 per capita (2008)
Annual average growth of GDP – –4.8 per cent (2009 est)
Inflation rate – 2.7 per cent (2009 est)
Population below poverty line – 14.1 per cent (2003 est)
Unemployment – 9.1 per cent (2009 est)
Total external debt – US$49,280m (2009)
Imports – US$37,400m (2008)
Exports – US$22,600m (2008)

BALANCE OF PAYMENTS
Trade – US$6,619m deficit (2009)
Current Account – US$4,458m deficit (2009)

Trade with UK	*2008*	*2009*
Imports from UK	£246,314,694	£194,015,598
Exports to UK	£211,975,979	£177,906,639

COMMUNICATIONS

The main ports are Burgas and Varna on the Black Sea. There are 470km of waterways, and inland ports include Vidin, Lom and Ruse on the river Danube. The main airports are at Sofia, Plovdiv, Burgas and Varna. There are 4,294km of railways and 40,231km of roads, including 331km of motorways. The telephone system is extensive but needs modernising. Mobile phone distribution is high, at 10.6 million in 2008. There were 2.3 million fixed lines in use in 2008, and 2.6 million internet users.

EDUCATION AND HEALTH

Education is free and compulsory from seven to 16 years.
Literacy rate – 98.3 per cent (2007 est)
Gross enrolment ratio (percentage of relevant age group) – primary 101 per cent; secondary 105 per cent; tertiary 50 per cent (2008 est)
Health expenditure (per capita) – US$384 (2007)
Hospital beds (per 1,000 people) – 6.4 (2003–8)

MEDIA AND CULTURE

Public service broadcasters Bulgarian National Radio and Bulgarian National Television share the market with a vigorous commercial sector that provides national and regional broadcasting. However, pressure from organised crime and political and business interests causes many journalists to self-censor; those who do not often risk harassment or even violence. Some major publications are also known to charge or extort money in return for favourable coverage, or the suppression of negative stories.

Bulgaria's Roman and Byzantine ruins are culturally significant, as are its churches and monasteries. Notable Bulgarian writers include Stoyan Mikhaylovski (1856–1927) and Iordan Iovkov (1884–1938).

BURKINA FASO

Area – 274,200 sq. km
Capital – Ouagadougou; population, 1,776,910 (2009 est)
Major city – Bobo-Dioulasso
Currency – Franc CFA of 100 centimes
Population – 15,746,232 rising at 3.1 per cent a year (2009 est); 63 ethnic groups, of which Mossi (40 per cent) (est) is the largest
Religion – Muslim 61 per cent (predominantly Sunni), Christian (Roman Catholic 19 per cent, Protestant denominations 4 per cent), traditional indigenous religions 15 per cent (est); many Christians and Muslims also practise indigenous religious beliefs
Language – French (official), various African languages
Population density – 56 per sq. km (2008)
Urban population – 19 per cent (2007 est)

Median age (years) – 16.8 (2009 est)
National anthem – 'Une Seule Nuit' ['One Single Night']
National day – 11 December (Republic Day)
Life expectancy – 52.95 (2009 est)
Mortality rate – 13.3 (2009 est)
Birth rate – 44.33 (2009 est)
Infant mortality rate – 84.49 (2009 est)
HIV/AIDS adult prevalence – 1.5 per cent (2007 est)
Death penalty – Retained (not used since 1988)
CPI score – 3.6 (2009)

CLIMATE AND TERRAIN

The landlocked state occupies a plateau dissected by the White, Black and Red Volta rivers. There are tropical savannahs in the south and the north is semi-desert. Elevation extremes range from 749m (Tena Kourou) at the highest point to 200m (Mouhoun, or Black Volta, river) at the lowest. The climate is tropical, with a wet season from June to October; there are recurring droughts. Average temperatures range from 24°C in January to 28°C in July.

HISTORY AND POLITICS

Burkina Faso (Upper Volta until 1983) was part of the Mossi Empire in the 18th and 19th centuries. It was annexed by France in 1896 and between 1932 and 1947 was administered as part of other French colonies. In 1947 its original borders were reconstituted, and in 1958 it became autonomous within the French Community; independence was achieved on 5 August 1960.

In the three decades after independence there was a succession of military regimes; the last military coup, in 1987, brought to power Capt. Blaise Compaoré. Military rule ended in 1991 when a new constitution was adopted, and multiparty elections were held in 1992. Despite the constitutional restriction on the number of terms a president may serve, President Compaoré was re-elected for a third term in 2005. The 2007 legislative election was won by the governing Congress for Democracy and Progress (CDP) with a large overall majority. A presidential election is scheduled for 21 November 2010.

POLITICAL SYSTEM

Under the 1991 constitution, the president is directly elected; in 2000 the presidential term was reduced from seven to five years, renewable only once. The unicameral National Assembly has 111 deputies, who are directly elected for a five-year term. Executive power is vested jointly in the president and the council of ministers, both responsible to the legislature.

HEAD OF STATE

President, Capt. Blaise Compaoré, *assumed office* 1987, *elected* 1991, *re-elected* 1998, 2005

SELECTED GOVERNMENT MEMBERS *as at May 2010*

Prime Minister, Tertius Zongo
Defence, Yero Boli
Economy and Finance, Lucien Marie Noël Bembamba
Foreign Affairs, Alain Bedouma Yoda

EMBASSY OF THE REPUBLIC OF BURKINA FASO

16 Place Guy d'Arezzo, 1180 Brussels, Belgium
T (+32) (2) 345 9912 E ambassade.burkina@skynet.be
W www.ambassadeduburkina.be
Ambassador Extraordinary and Plenipotentiary, HE Kadré Désiré Ouedraogo, *apptd* 2001

BRITISH HIGH COMMISSIONER

Dr Nicholas Westcott, CMG, *apptd* 2008, resident at Accra, Ghana

DEFENCE

The army has 13 armoured personnel carriers. The air force has 2 armed helicopters.
Military budget – US$123m (2009 est)
Military personnel – 11,200: army 6,400, air force 600, Gendarmerie 4,200; Paramilitary 250

ECONOMY AND TRADE

The country is one of the poorest in the world, with around 90 per cent of the population engaged in subsistence agriculture and animal husbandry, which are vulnerable to periodic droughts. The economy is heavily dependent on cotton exports and therefore exposed to the vagaries of global price fluctuations. The civil war in neighbouring Cote d'Ivoire harmed trade by cutting off transport routes, and caused many expatriate Burkinabes to return home, adding to the unemployment problem and depriving the economy of their remittances.

Agriculture contributes 29.4 per cent of GDP; the main produce apart from cotton is livestock. Although there are few natural resources, a growing quantity of gold is mined and exploration for other minerals has begun. The processing of cotton and other agricultural products, gold mining and manufacturing of beverages, soap, cigarettes and textiles are the main industries, contributing 20.1 per cent to GDP. Services account for 50.5 per cent of GDP. The main trading partners are Côte d'Ivoire, France, Singapore and Belgium. Principal exports are cotton, livestock and gold. The chief imports are capital goods, foodstuffs and fuel.

GNI – US$7,300m; US$480 per capita (2008)
Annual average growth of GDP – 5.2 per cent (2009 est)
Inflation rate – 3.7 per cent (2009 est)
Population below poverty line – 46.4 per cent (2004)
Unemployment – 77 per cent (2004)
Total external debt – US$1,840m (2009)
Imports – US$1,800m (2008)
Exports – US$600m (2008)

BALANCE OF PAYMENTS

Trade – US$1,144m deficit (2009)
Current Account – US$972m deficit (2008)

Trade with UK	*2008*	*2009*
Imports from UK	£9,015,336	£6,395,809
Exports to UK	£302,895	£46,875

COMMUNICATIONS

There are over 20 airports and airfields; the two main airports are at Ouagadougou, which receives international flights, and Bobo-Dioulasso. There are 15,272km of roads, of which 4,000km are surfaced; an estimated 60 per cent of the country's villages are further than 3km from a main road and unpaved roads are often impassable during the wet season. There is 622km of railway track in operation. Fixed-line telephone connections are fewer than one per 100 people; mobile phone distribution is growing rapidly, with 2.6 million subscribers in 2008.

EDUCATION AND HEALTH

Literacy rate – 28.7 per cent (2007 est)
Gross enrolment ratio (percentage of relevant age group) – primary 79 per cent; secondary 20 per cent; tertiary 3 per cent (2009 est)
Health expenditure (per capita) – US$29 (2007)
Hospital beds (per 1,000 people) – 0.9 (2003–8)

MEDIA

Radio is the country's most popular medium, with dozens of private and community radio stations and several private television channels operating alongside state-run broadcasters. All media outlets are government regulated, but criticism is still expressed.

BURUNDI

Republika y'u Burundi/République du Burundi – Republic of Burundi

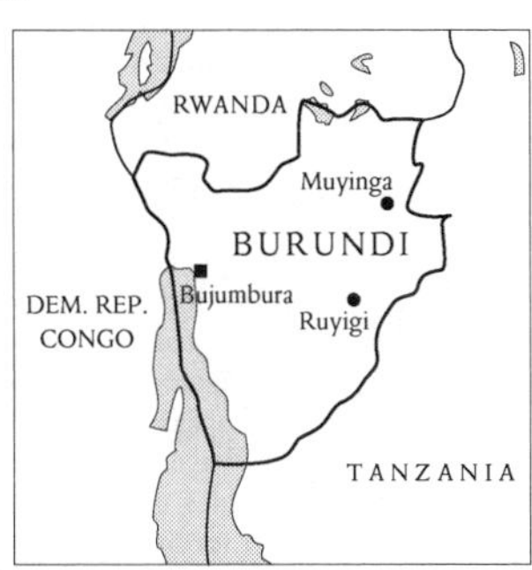

Area – 27,830 sq. km
Capital – Bujumbura; population, 454,866 (2009 est)
Major towns – Muyinga, Ruyigi
Currency – Burundi franc of 100 centimes
Population – 8,988,091 rising at 3.28 per cent a year (2009 est); Hutu (85 per cent), Tutsi (14 per cent), Twa (1 per cent) (est)
Religion – Christian (Roman Catholic 60 per cent, Protestant denominations 15 per cent), traditional indigenous beliefs 20 per cent, Muslim 2 per cent (predominantly Sunni) (est)
Language – Kirundi, French (both official), Swahili
Population density – 314 per sq. km (2008)
Urban population – 10 per cent (2007 est)
Median age (years) – 16.7 (2009 est)
National anthem – 'Burundi Bwacu' ['Our Burundi']
National day – 1 July (Independence Day)
Life expectancy – 52.09 (2009 est)
Mortality rate – 12.67 (2009 est)
Birth rate – 41.42 (2009 est)
Infant mortality rate – 59.64 (2009 est)
HIV/AIDS adult prevalence – 1.9 per cent (2007 est)
Death penalty – Abolished for all crimes (since 2009)
CPI score – 1.8 (2009)
Literacy rate – 59.3 per cent (2007 est)
Gross enrolment ratio (percentage of relevant age group) – primary 136 per cent; secondary 18 per cent; tertiary 3 per cent (2008 est)
Health expenditure (per capita) – US$17 (2007)
Hospital beds (per 1,000 people) – 0.7 (2003–8)

CLIMATE AND TERRAIN

The landlocked country lies across the Nile–Congo watershed in central Africa. A hilly interior rises from an average altitude of 1,700m to the country's highest point at 2,670m (Heha) and falls to a plateau in the east. The river Ruzizi forms part of the north-western border with the Democratic Republic of the Congo, along with Lake Tanganyika (the lowest elevation in the country at 772m) in the south-west. The climate is equatorial, moderated by altitude; average temperatures vary between 17°C and 23°C. There are two rainy seasons: March to May and October to December.

HISTORY AND POLITICS

From the 16th century the area was ruled by Tutsi kings who dominated a majority Hutu population. Germany annexed the area in 1890 and included it in German East Africa. After the First World War it was part of the League of Nations-mandated territory (later UN trusteeship) of Ruanda-Urundi, administered by Belgium. Burundi broke the union with Rwanda in 1962, and became independent as a constitutional monarchy on 1 July 1962. The monarchy was overthrown in 1966 and the country became a republic and a one-party state under a series of brutal regimes dominated by the Tutsi minority. This Tutsi domination of the majority Hutu population led to intercommunal tensions that often resulted in ethnic conflict.

Following a coup in 1987 and a five-year transition to democracy, the first multiparty elections in 1993 ended Tutsi political dominance with the election of a Hutu president, Melchior Ndadaye, and a Hutu majority in the legislature. Ndadaye was killed a few months later in a coup by the Tutsi-dominated army; although the coup was suppressed, ethnic conflict left more than 100,000 dead. In 1994 Nadadaye's successor, Cyprien Ntaryamira (also a Hutu), was killed when the plane in which he was travelling with the Rwandan president was shot down. These deaths sparked off fierce ethnic conflict which degenerated into civil war. Most of the belligerants signed a peace accord at Arusha (Tanzania) in 2000, and the four remaining rebel groups signed ceasefire agreements with the government in 2003 and 2006. The 2006 ceasefire with the FLN did not hold and there was renewed fighting from late 2007 until a new ceasefire was agreed in May 2008. In 2007 the UN ended its peacekeeping mission and redirected its operations to help with reconstruction.

The Arusha accord was ratified by a transitional assembly in 2000, and after a period of transitional government, legislative elections took place in 2005. The National Council for the Defence of Democracy–Forces for the Defence of Democracy (CNDD-FDD), a Hutu party, won a majority of seats in both chambers of the legislature. Pierre Nkurunziza of the CNDD-FDD was elected president by the newly elected legislature; Mr Nkurunziza was re-elected in the country's first direct presidential election in June 2010, though all opposition candidates boycotted the poll in protest at the alleged rigging of local elections held in May 2010. For this reason most opposition parties also boycotted legislative elections held in July 2010, in which the CNDD-FDD retained its majorities in both chambers.

POLITICAL SYSTEM

Under the 2005 constitution, the executive president is directly elected for a five-year term, renewable only once. The bicameral *Parlement* comprises the National Assembly and the senate; members of both serve a five-year term. The National Assembly has 100 directly elected members, three co-opted members from the Twa ethnic group, and up to 21 members (currently 15) co-opted to ensure a 60 per cent Hutu and 40 per cent Tutsi split and that 30 per cent of the total are women. The senate has 49 members: 34 directly elected members (one Hutu and one Tutsi from each province); three co-opted Twa members; all former presidents (currently four); and enough women (currently eight) to make the number of women senators up to 30 per cent of the total. The constitution also specifies the proportion of Hutu, Tutsi and female members of the council of ministers.

HEAD OF STATE
President, Pierre Nkurunziza, *sworn in* 26 August 2005, *re-elected 28 June 2010*
First Vice-President, Yves Sahinguvu
Second Vice-President, Gabriel Ntisezerana

SELECTED GOVERNMENT MEMBERS *as at May 2010*
Defence, Maj.-Gen. Germain Niyoyankana
Finance, Clotilde Nizigama
Interior, Edouard Nduwimana

EMBASSY OF THE REPUBLIC OF BURUNDI
46 Sq. Marie Louise, 1000 Brussels, Belgium
T (+32) (2) 230 4535 E ambassade.burundi@skynet.be
W www.ambassade-burundi.be
Ambassador Extraordinary and Plenipotentiary, HE Laurent Kavakure, *apptd* 2006

BRITISH AMBASSADOR
HE Nicholas Cannon, OBE, *apptd* 2008, resident at Kigali, Rwanda

DEFENCE

The army has 57 armoured personnel carriers. The air wing has 2 combat capable aircraft and 2 armed helicopters.
Military budget – US$82m (2009)
Military personnel – army 20,000 (including air wing 200); paramilitary 31,050

ECONOMY AND TRADE

Economic activity has increased since the civil war ended, but reform and reconstruction are hampered by a lack of administrative capacity, a poorly educated workforce, corruption and poor law enforcement. Agriculture is the mainstay of the economy, contributing 33.3 per cent of GDP and engaging 93.6 per cent of the population, although subsistence agriculture has contracted recently owing to continued insecurity, population growth and soil erosion. Exports of coffee and tea account for over 90 per cent of foreign exchange earnings, leaving the economy vulnerable to the effects of global price fluctuations and weather conditions. Industry is relatively small-scale and employs only 2.3 per cent of the workforce but contributes 21 per cent of GDP. The main activities are light manufacturing, food processing, the assembly of imported components and public sector construction.

Most trade is with Switzerland, Saudi Arabia, Belgium and the UK, but it is constrained by the poor transport infrastructure and landlocked location. The main exports are coffee, tea, sugar, cotton and hides. The principal imports are capital goods, petroleum products and food.
GNI – US$1,100m; US$140 per capita (2008)
Annual average growth of GDP – 3.8 per cent (2009 est)
Inflation rate – 14.1 per cent (2009 est)
Population below poverty line – 68 per cent (2002 est)
Total external debt – US$1,200m (2003)
Imports – US$400m (2008)
Exports – US$100m (2008)

BALANCE OF PAYMENTS
Trade – US$361m deficit (2009)
Current Account – US$153m deficit (2007)

Trade with UK	*2008*	*2009*
Imports from UK	£1,052,065	£2,213,264
Exports to UK	£87,995	£191,502

COMMUNICATIONS

There are no railways at present, but the feasibility of including Burundi in a project to expand the rail network in this region of central Africa is being investigated. Movement is currently either by water, on Lake Tanganyika, by road or by air. Bujumbura is the only port, the location of the only airport with a surfaced runway, and the main focus of the limited road network of 12,322km, only 1,286km of which is paved. The telephone system is rudimentary and limited. Mobile phone distribution is growing but was still only five per 100 people in 2008.

MEDIA

Low literacy levels mean that radio is the dominant news medium. The government-controlled *Radiodiffusion et Television Nationale de Burundi* (RTNB) runs the only television station and the only radio station with national coverage; the only newspaper to publish regularly is also government owned. Several radio stations are funded by international agencies or civil groups. Self-censorship is common because of the political climate, and occasional official censorship means that publication of opposition newspapers can be sporadic.

CAMBODIA

Preahreacheanachakr Kampuchea – Kingdom of Cambodia

Area – 181,035 sq. km
Capital – Phnom Penh; population, 1,519,330 (2009 est)
Major towns – Battambang, Siem Reap, Sihanoukville (Kompong Saom)
Currency – Riel of 100 sen; the US dollar is widely used
Population – 14,494,293 rising at 1.77 per cent a year (2009 est); Khmer (90 per cent), Vietnamese (5 per cent), Chinese (1 per cent) (est)
Religion – Buddhist (Theravada 93 per cent), Muslim 4 per cent (predominantly Shafi'i, a school of Sunni Islam), Christian 2 per cent (predominantly Protestant) (est)
Language – Khmer (official), French, English
Population density – 82 per sq. km (2008)
Urban population – 21 per cent (2007 est)
Median age (years) – 22.1 (2009 est)
National anthem – 'Nokoreach' ['Royal Kingdom']
National day – 9 November (Independence Day)
Life expectancy (years) – 62.1 (2008 est)
Mortality rate – 8.08 (2009 est)
Birth rate – 25.73 (2009 est)
Infant mortality rate – 54.79 (2009 est)
Death penalty – Abolished for all crimes (since 1989)
CPI score – 2 (2009)

Literacy rate – 76.3 per cent (2007 est)
Gross enrolment ratio (percentage of relevant age group) – primary 116 per cent; secondary 40 per cent; tertiary 7 per cent (2008 est)
Health expenditure (per capita) – US$36 (2007)
Hospital beds (per 1,000 people) – 0.1 (2003–8)

CLIMATE AND TERRAIN

Cambodia is a mostly flat country, apart from the Cardamom Mountains in the south-west and the uplands of the north-east. The fertile central plains are drained by rivers that run into Tonle Sap, the largest lake in south-east Asia, and into the Mekong river, which flows through the country from north to south. The highest point of elevation is at 1,810m (Phnum Aoral) while the lowest is 0m (Gulf of Thailand). The climate is tropical, with a monsoon season from May to November.

HISTORY AND POLITICS

Although the Khmer people have inhabited the region for almost 2,000 years, the Khmer kingdom was at its strongest in the 10th and 11th centuries, its territory covering modern-day Laos, Thailand and Vietnam. The kingdom lost power and territory from 1432 onwards.

Cambodia became a French protectorate in 1863 and part of French Indochina in 1887. It became an associate state within the French Union in 1949, and gained full independence in 1953 as the Kingdom of Cambodia. From the late 1960s there was a growing insurgency led by the left-wing Khmer Rouge, and in 1970 the monarchy was overthrown in a right-wing coup and the country was renamed the Khmer Republic. Fighting throughout the country involved forces from North and South Vietnam and the USA. In 1975, the regime was overthrown by the North Vietnamese-backed Khmer Rouge. During Khmer Rouge rule under Pol Pot (1975–9), extreme Marxist policies were brutally implemented and famine, disease and maltreatment caused the deaths of an estimated 1.7 million people. In 1978, Vietnamese troops invaded Cambodia, ousting Pol Pot, and in 1979 established a government in Phnom Penh. Guerrilla warfare between the Vietnamese-backed government, the Khmer Rouge and Prince Sihanouk's nationalist forces continued until Vietnamese forces withdrew from Cambodia in 1987–9.

Under a UN peace plan agreed in 1991, multiparty elections were held in 1993, a new constitution was adopted and Prince Sihanouk was elected king. The premiership was shared between the two main parties, the Cambodian People's Party (CPP), headed by Hun Sen and other former leaders of the Vietnamese-backed regime, and Funcinpec, formed by supporters of the king and led by Prince Ranariddh. Ranariddh was ousted as co-prime minister in 1997 in an effective coup by Hun Sen, who became the sole prime minister. The CPP won the 1998 and 2003 elections, but without the two-thirds majority needed to form a government on its own, and the coalition with Funcinpec continued.

King Sihanouk abdicated in 2004 and was succeeded by one of his sons, Prince Norodom Sihamoni. In the 2008 election, the CPP won 90 seats, giving it a large enough majority to form a government without a coalition (though the arrangement with Funcinpec, reduced to only two seats, continued).

INSURGENCIES

The Khmer Rouge was outlawed in 1994 but continued to fight a guerrilla war until 1996, when it was weakened by internal divisions. Pol Pot was tried by the Khmer Rouge in 1997 and died in captivity in 1998. The remaining Khmer Rouge soldiers surrendered in 1999. A UN-backed tribunal, established to try former leaders of the Khmer Rouge regime for atrocities committed during its rule, brought its first defendant to trial in 2009.

POLITICAL SYSTEM

Under the 1993 constitution, Cambodia is a pluralist liberal democracy with a hereditary constitutional monarchy. The monarch is chosen from eligible royal males by a Council of the Throne elected by parliament. Executive power rests with the government, which is responsible to parliament. The bicameral parliament comprises the National Assembly, which has 123 members directly elected for a five-year term, and the senate, which has 61 members, 57 of whom are elected for a six-year term by the National Assembly and commune councils, with two members appointed by the king and two appointed by the National Assembly.

HEAD OF STATE

HM The King of Cambodia, Norodom Sihamoni, *crowned* 29 October 2004
President of the National Assembly, Heng Samrin

SELECTED GOVERNMENT MEMBERS *as at May 2010*

Prime Minister, Hun Sen
Deputy Prime Ministers, Hor Namhong *(Foreign Affairs);* Sar Kheng *(Interior);* Gen. Tea Banh *(Defence);* Keat Chhon *(Economy and Finance);* Sok An; Gen. Nhoek Bunchhai; Yim Chhay Ly; Bin Chhin; Men Sam An; Ke Kim Yan

ROYAL EMBASSY OF CAMBODIA

64 Brondesbury Park, London NW6 7AT
T 020-8451 7850 E cambodianembassy@btconnect.com
W www.cambodianembassy.org.uk
Ambassador Extraordinary and Plenipotentiary, HE Hor Nambora, *apptd* 2004

BRITISH EMBASSY

27–29 Street 75, Sangat Srah Chak, Khan Daun Penh, Phnom Penh
T (+855) (23) 427 124 E britemb@online.com.kh
W http://ukincambodia.fco.gov.uk
Ambassador Extraordinary and Plenipotentiary, HE Andrew Mace, *apptd* 2008

DEFENCE

The army has 150 main battle tanks, 70 armoured infantry fighting vehicles and over 190 armoured personnel carriers. The navy has 11 patrol and coastal vessels with bases at Phnom Penh and Ream. The air force has 24 combat aircraft.

Military budget – US$222m (2009)
Military personnel – 124,300: army 75,000, navy 2,800, air force 1,500, provincial forces 45,000; paramilitaries 67,000

ECONOMY AND TRADE

Since 1999 the government has made progress with economic reform and development but the country remains very poor, with over a third of the population living below the poverty line and an absence of basic infrastructure in rural areas. The demographic imbalance (over half the population is under 21) and lack of education and skills also pose serious problems. Economic growth has been driven by the expansion of garment manufacturing, construction and tourism, but the benefits are limited to urban areas and all sectors have contracted owing to the global downturn. The discovery of oil and gas deposits in territorial waters promises additional revenue once exploitation begins. Recent international aid has been made conditional on the government tackling widespread corruption.

The service sector contributes 41 per cent of GDP, industry 30 per cent and agriculture 29 per cent. Agriculture still engages 68 per cent of the workforce; the main crops are rice, rubber, maize, vegetables, cashew nuts and tapioca. The main industrial activities are tourism, garment and textiles manufacturing, processing of agricultural and forestry products, fishing and mining gemstones. Exports go mostly to the USA (55 per cent) and EU countries; imports come mainly from Thailand (27 per cent) and other countries in the region.

GNI – US$9,300m; US$640 per capita (2008)
Annual average growth of GDP – −1.5 per cent (2009 est)
Inflation rate – −1 per cent (2009 est)
Population below poverty line – 35 per cent (2004)
Unemployment – 3.5 per cent (2007)
Total external debt – US$4,157m (2009 est)
Imports – US$6,500m (2008)
Exports – US$4,300m (2008)

BALANCE OF PAYMENTS
Trade – US$2,387m deficit (2009)
Current Account – US$1,149m deficit (2008)

Trade with UK	*2008*	*2009*
Imports from UK	£3,393,542	£4,028,420
Exports to UK	£124,104,647	£205,852,501

COMMUNICATIONS

There are 2,400km of navigable waterways, mostly on the Mekong river, and ships of up to 2,500 tonnes can sail as far as Phnom Penh all year round. The deep-water port at Sihanoukville (Kompong Saom) on the Gulf of Thailand can receive ships of up to 10,000 tonnes. The port is linked to Phnom Penh by a modern highway. The main airports are at Phnom Penh, Siem Reap and Sihanoukville, the latter two having been upgraded to deal with increasing tourist traffic. The country has about 38,100km of roads, although only 3,000km are surfaced and many are in a state of disrepair. There are 602km of railway lines, mostly in a poor condition. Rail services are infrequent; in response, improvised and unofficial 'bamboo trains' have arisen as a major mode of passenger and freight transport in some parts of the country.

With fixed-line connections scarce outside the cities, and connections at fewer than 1 per 100 people, mobile phone distribution continues to expand rapidly, having reached a density of about 30 per 100 people in 2008.

MEDIA

Much of the media relies on political parties, but Prime Minister Hun Sen has expressed his support for press freedom. There are state television and radio broadcasters, as well as six other major commercial and privately owned television channels and three commercial radio stations. There are no restrictions on the ownership and use of private satellite dishes, and foreign radio is also easily received and widely accessed.

CAMEROON

République du Cameroun – Republic of Cameroon

Area – 475,440 sq. km
Capital – Yaoundé; population, 1,739,010 (2009 est)
Major cities – Bamenda, Douala, Garoua, Maroua
Currency – Franc CFA of 100 centimes
Population – 18,879,301 rising at 2.19 per cent a year (2009 est); Cameroon Highlanders (31 per cent), Equatorial Bantu (19 per cent), Kirdi (11 per cent), Fulani (10 per cent), Northwestern Bantu (8 per cent), Eastern Nigritic (7 per cent) (est)
Religion – Christian (Roman Catholic 27 per cent, Protestant denominations 13 per cent), indigenous religions 40 per cent, Muslim 20 per cent (est)
Language – English, French (both official), about 250 African languages from 24 major language groups
Population density – 40 per sq. km (2008)
Urban population – 56 per cent (2007 est)
Median age (years) – 19.2 (2009 est)
National anthem – 'Chant de Ralliement' ['Rallying Song']
National day – 20 May (Republic Day)
Life expectancy (years) – 53.69 (2009 est)
Mortality rate – 12.2 (2009 est)
Birth rate – 34.1 (2009 est)
Infant mortality rate – 63.34 (2009 est)
HIV/AIDS adult prevalence – 4.6 per cent (2007 est)
Death penalty – Retained (not used since 1997)
CPI score – 2.2 (2009)
Literacy rate – 67.9 per cent (2007 est)
Gross enrolment ratio (percentage of relevant age group) – primary 111 per cent; secondary 37 per cent; tertiary 8 per cent (2008 est)
Health expenditure (per capita) – US$54 (2007)
Hospital beds (per 1,000 people) – 1.5 (2003–8)

CLIMATE AND TERRAIN

There are three main geographic zones: desert plains and savannah in the north (the Lake Chad basin), mountains and plateau in the central region, and tropical rainforests in the south and east. Elevation extremes range from 4,095m (Mt Cameroon, an active volcano) at the highest point to 0m (Atlantic Ocean) at the lowest. The climate varies from tropical in the south to arid in the north. There is a wet season from June to September in the north and from May to November in the south.

HISTORY AND POLITICS

The Bakas (Pygmies) and Bantu speakers of the Cameroonian highlands were probably the area's earliest inhabitants. Cameroon was explored by the Portuguese from 1472 and later by Spanish, Dutch and English traders. The Fulani people of the western Sahel conquered northern Cameroon between the 1770s and early 1800s.

The German protectorate of Kamerun was established in 1884. After the First World War it was divided into the League of Nations-mandated territories (later UN trusteeships) of East Cameroon (French-administered), and North and South Cameroons (British-administered). On 1 January 1960 East Cameroon became independent as the Republic of Cameroon. This was joined on 1 October 1961 by South Cameroon after a plebiscite held under the auspices of the UN; North Cameroon voted to join Nigeria. Cameroon became a federal republic comprising East Cameroon and West (formerly South) Cameroon, each with its own state government; the federal system was abolished in 1972. From 1966 to 1992, the country was ruled by one party, the National Union of Cameroon (renamed the Cameroon People's Democratic Movement (RDPC) in 1984), with Paul Biya as president from 1982.

Sharp economic decline in 1990 provoked widespread civil unrest and agitation for political pluralism. In the 1992 multiparty elections, the ruling RDPC won the legislative election, and Paul Biya the presidential. The result was challenged by the opposition, which alleged vote-rigging; similar allegations have been made after all subsequent elections, and in 1997 the opposition boycotted the presidential election altogether.

In 2004 President Biya was returned to office with 70.8 per cent of the vote. In the 2007 legislative election, the RDPC retained its overwhelming majority in the legislature, although elections were re-run in a number of seats where the original results were annulled because of suspected fraud.

INTERNATIONAL RELATIONS

A long-running dispute with Nigeria over their joint border, including the oil-rich Bakassi peninsula, was settled in Cameroon's favour in 2002 after being referred to the International Court of Justice. Nigeria's phased withdrawal from Bakassi was completed in 2008.

Cameroon joined the Commonwealth in 1995, becoming the first member to have been only partially under British rule in colonial times.

POLITICAL SYSTEM

The 1972 constitution was amended in 1990 to enable a return to multiparty rule, in 1996 to extend the president's term of office and to provide for the establishment of a second legislative chamber (yet to be implemented), and in 2008 to remove the limit on the number of presidential terms.

The president is directly elected for a seven-year term, and appoints the prime minister and cabinet. The unicameral National Assembly has 180 members, directly elected for a five-year term.

HEAD OF STATE

President, Paul Biya, *took power* 6 November 1982, *elected* 14 January 1984, *re-elected* 1988, 1992, 1997, 2004

SELECTED GOVERNMENT MEMBERS *as at May 2010*

Prime Minister, Philemon Yang
Deputy Prime Ministers, Amadou Ali; Jean Nkuete
Economy, Louis Paul Motaze
Foreign Affairs, Henri Ayissi Eyebe

HIGH COMMISSION FOR THE REPUBLIC OF CAMEROON

84 Holland Park, London W11 3SB
T 020-7727 0771 E info@cameroonhighcommission.co.uk
W www.cameroonhighcommission.co.uk
High Commissioner, HE Nkwelle Ekaney, *apptd* 2008

BRITISH HIGH COMMISSION

PO Box 547, Avenue Winston Churchill, Yaoundé
T (+237) (2) 2220 545 E bhc.yaounde@fco.gov.uk
W http://ukincameroon.fco.gov.uk
High Commissioner, HE Bharat Joshi, *apptd* 2009

BRITISH COUNCIL

Immeuble Christo, Avenue Charles de Gaulle, BP 818, Yaoundé
T (+237) (2) 2211 696/203 172
W www.britishcouncil.org/africa
Director, Paul Norton

DEFENCE

The army has 22 armoured infantry fighting vehicles and 33 armoured personnel carriers. The navy has 11 patrol and coastal combatant vessels at 3 bases. The air force has 15 combat capable aircraft and 7 armed helicopters.
Military budget – US$306m (2008)
Military personnel – 14,100: army 12,500, navy 1,300, air force 300; paramilitary 9,000

ECONOMY AND TRADE

Political stability and natural resources such as oil and timber have enabled agricultural, industrial and infrastructure development, although the economy is vulnerable to commodity price changes and has contracted for this reason in the global downturn. Cameroon also has a large and top-heavy public sector and endemic corruption, and recent IMF funding and debt relief have been conditional on progress towards privatisation and greater financial transparency.

Agriculture contributes 19.8 per cent to GDP, industry 29.7 per cent and services 50.4 per cent. Around 70 per cent of the workforce is engaged in agriculture. The main industrial activity is oil production and refining. Revenue is also earned from the oil pipeline passing through the country from Chad.

The main trading partners are EU countries, Nigeria, China and the USA. Principal exports are crude oil and petroleum products, timber, cocoa, aluminium, coffee and cotton. Imports are chiefly machinery, electrical equipment, transport equipment, fuel and food.
GNI – US$21,900m; US$1,150 per capita (2008)
Annual average growth of GDP – –1.5 per cent (2009 est)
Inflation rate – 2.5 per cent (2009 est)
Unemployment – 30 per cent (2001 est)
Total external debt – US$2,929m (2009 est)
Imports – US$4,400m (2008)
Exports – US$4,400m (2008)

BALANCE OF PAYMENTS

Trade – US$50m surplus (2009)
Current Account – US$427m deficit (2007)

Trade with UK	*2008*	*2009*
Imports from UK	£29,948,777	£29,671,662
Exports to UK	£80,702,700	£108,555,035

COMMUNICATIONS

The main seaports are at Douala and the Limboh terminal. Some inland navigation is also possible on the river

Benue. There are 36 airports and airfields; the main ones are at Yaoundé, Douala and Garoua. The 50,000km of roads include 5,000km of surfaced roads linking the main population centres. A rail network of 987km links the coast with the capital and the central highlands.

The fixed-line telephone network is antiquated and unreliable, with fewer than one line per 100 people. Mobile phone distribution has grown rapidly since 2002 and there were 33 per 100 people by 2008.

MEDIA

The state-run Cameroon Radio-Television Corporation (CRTV), which operates national television and radio networks as well as provincial stations, held a monopoly on broadcast media until liberalisation in 2000 allowed a commercial television station and several radio stations to be set up. Newspapers, the main source of news, are also subject to government restrictions, and stringent libel laws are used against government critics.

CANADA

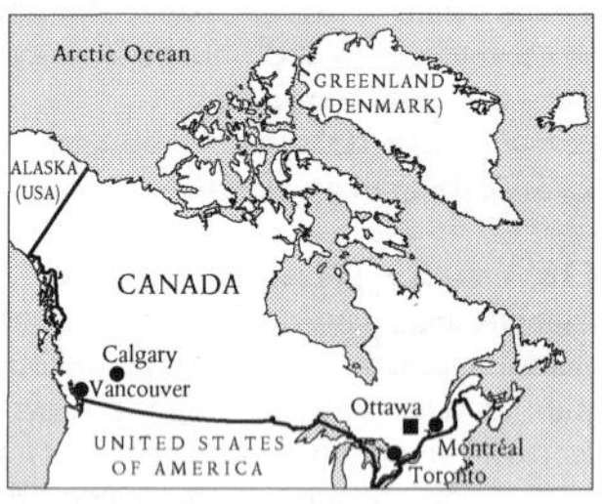

Area – 9,984,670 sq. km
Capital – Ottawa; population, 1,170,310 (2009 est; includes Gatineau)
Major cities – Calgary, Edmonton, Hamilton, Montréal, Québec, Toronto, Vancouver, Winnipeg
Currency – Canadian dollar (C$) of 100 cents
Population – 33,487,208 rising at 0.82 per cent a year (2009 est)
Religion – Christian (Roman Catholic 44 per cent, Protestant denominations 29 per cent, other 4 per cent), Muslim 2 per cent, Jewish 1 per cent, Buddhist 1 per cent, Hindu 1 per cent, Sikh 1 per cent (est)
Language – English, French (both official)
Population density – 4 per sq. km (2008)
Urban population – 80 per cent (2007 est)
Median age (years) – 40.4 (2009 est)
National anthem – 'O Canada'
National day – 1 July (Canada Day)
Life expectancy (years) – 81.23 (2009 est)
Mortality rate – 7.74 (2009 est)
Birth rate – 10.28 (2009 est)
Infant mortality rate – 5.04 (2009 est)
Death penalty – Abolished for all crimes (since 1998)
CPI score – 8.7 (2009)

CLIMATE AND TERRAIN

Canada occupies the entire northern part of the North American continent except for Alaska. The most southerly point is Middle Island in Lake Erie. The six main geographic divisions are: the Appalachian-Acadian region; the Canadian Shield, which comprises more than half the country; the St Lawrence-Great Lakes lowland; the interior plains; the Cordilleran region, and the Arctic archipelago, which lies under continuous permafrost. Elevation extremes range from 5,959m (Mt Logan) at the highest point to 0m (Atlantic Ocean) at the lowest. The climate varies from temperate in the south to subarctic and arctic in the north. The east and centre experience greater extremes than in corresponding latitudes in Europe, but the climate is milder in the south-western part of the prairie region and the southern parts of the Pacific slope. The tornado season is May to September, peaking in June and early July in southern Ontario, Alberta and Québec, Saskatchewan and Manitoba through to Thunder Bay. The interior of British Columbia and western New Brunswick are also tornado zones.

HISTORY AND POLITICS

The land was settled by peoples from Asia, who spread throughout the continent, including the Arctic regions. The first European contact was probably from Greenland c.1000, but the first recorded landing was by John Cabot in 1497. St John's, Newfoundland, was established as a shore base for English fisheries in 1504 and claimed for England in 1583. The French explored the St Lawrence Seaway from the 1530s, and founded Québec in 1608. The Hudson's Bay Company, founded in 1670, was significant in exploring and opening up the interior. From the 17th century the territory was a pawn in the power struggles of the main colonial powers. Britain gained large areas of the country under the treaty of Utrecht (1713), and after the Seven Years' War, the treaty of Paris (1763) awarded almost all of France's North American possessions to Britain. The American War of Independence caused many British loyalists to migrate to southern Canada, exacerbating existing tensions between British and French colonists. In the mid-19th century, Canadian territory still under Hudson's Bay Company control was brought under government control.

The British North America Act of 1867 formed a dominion under the name of Canada, comprising four provinces: Ontario, Québec, New Brunswick and Nova Scotia. Other provinces and territories were subsequently admitted to this federation: Manitoba and Northwest Territories (1870), British Columbia (1871), Prince Edward Island (1873), Yukon (1898), Alberta and Saskatchewan (1905) and Newfoundland (1949). The Territory of Nunavut ('our land') was created for the Inuit peoples in 1999 by partitioning the Northwest Territories.

The constitution was patriated (severed from the British parliament) in 1982. In 1985, following years of French-Canadian separatist agitation, the federal prime minister and the provincial premiers concluded the Meech Lake accord, which provided for Québec to be recognised as a distinct society within Canada. However, two provincial legislatures withheld approval and the accord did not come into force. A referendum in Québec calling for sovereignty and a new political and economic partnership was defeated in 1995, and support for independence has declined. In 1997, Québec was recognised as having a 'unique character' by leaders of the other provinces and territories, and in 2006 the federal parliament passed a motion recognising the Québecois as a nation within a united Canada.

A parliamentary vote of no confidence ended 12 years of Liberal government in 2005. In a snap general election in 2006 the Conservative Party won the most seats, but not a majority, and formed a minority government under Stephen Harper. In an early general election in October 2008, the Conservatives won 16 more seats but remained a minority government.

POLITICAL SYSTEM

Under the 1982 constitution, the head of state is Queen Elizabeth II, represented by a governor-general appointed on the advice of the Canadian prime minister.

The bicameral parliament consists of a senate and a House of Commons. The senate comprises 105 members, appointed by the governor-general on the recommendation of the prime minister, who serve until the age of 75; seats are assigned on a regional basis. The House of Commons has 308 members, directly elected for a five-year term; from 2009 the term will be fixed at four years. Representation is proportional to the population of each province.

Each province is largely self-governing, with its own lieutenant-governor and unicameral legislative assembly. The territories are administered by the federal government.

GOVERNOR-GENERAL

Governor-General, HE David Johnston

SELECTED GOVERNMENT MEMBERS *as at May 2010*

Prime Minister, Stephen Harper
Finance, James Flaherty
Foreign Affairs, Lawrence Cannon
Defence, Peter MacKay

CANADIAN HIGH COMMISSION

Macdonald House, 1 Grosvenor Square, London W1K 4AB
T 020-7258 6600 E ldn@international.gc.ca
W www.unitedkingdom.gc.ca
High Commissioner, HE James R. Wright, *apptd* 2006

BRITISH HIGH COMMISSION

80 Elgin Street, Ottawa, Ontario K1P 5K7
T (+1) (613) 237 1530 W http://ukincanada.fco.gov.uk
High Commissioner, HE Anthony Cary, CMG, *apptd* 2007

BRITISH COUNCIL

c/o British High Commission
T (+1) (613) 364 6233/6236 W www.britishcouncil.org/canada
Director, Martin Rose

DEFENCE

The Canadian armed forces are unified and organised into three functional commands: land force command, maritime command and air command.

The army (land forces) has 121 main battle tanks and 1,142 armoured personnel carriers. The navy (maritime command) has 4 submarines, 3 destroyers, 12 frigates and 12 patrol and coastal vessels. There are bases at Esquimalt, Halifax, Ottawa and Québec City. The air force has 97 combat aircraft.

Military expenditure – US$19,830m (2008)
Military personnel – 65,722: army 34,775, navy 11,025, air force 19,922

ECONOMY AND TRADE

Canada has a highly developed, industrialised and diversified market economy, which was transformed from a predominantly rural to an industrial economy in the second half of the 20th century by the growth of mining, manufacturing and services. Tight management of government finances resulted in balanced budgets from the late 1990s until 2007, and free-trade agreements with the USA in 1989 and 1994 (NAFTA) stimulated trade. However, the economy went into recession in 2008 owing to the global downturn, although the financial sector has proved more stable than that of many other major economies.

Canada's wealth of natural resources make it the world's largest exporter of timber, pulp and newsprint (nearly half the land is forested), and it is one of the world's largest exporters of minerals, particularly uranium (of which it is the world's second largest single producer) and diamonds (of which it is the world's third largest producer). About 5 per cent of the land area is farmed, of which 4.6 per cent is under cultivation, mostly in the prairie region of western Canada. The country is one of the world's leading food producers, particularly of wheat, barley, oilseed, tobacco, fruit, vegetables and dairy products. The fishing industry is also significant but has declined in recent years because of restrictions introduced to protect stocks after decades of overfishing. Oil, natural gas and hydroelectricity production is high enough for Canada to be a net exporter of energy. The shrinking of the Arctic ice cap is opening up access to offshore oil and gas reserves, new fishing grounds and shipping routes in the region. The government has development plans for the area but the assertion of its sovereignty has attracted criticism from other Arctic countries and is complicated by the lack of international agreement on countries' territorial claims.

In 2008, the services sector contributed 69.6 per cent of GDP, industry 28.4 per cent and agriculture 2 per cent.

The USA is Canada's main trading partner, taking 78 per cent of exports and providing 52 per cent of imports. The main exports are motor vehicles and parts, industrial machinery, aircraft, telecommunications equipment, chemicals, plastics, fertilisers, forestry products, energy

FEDERAL STRUCTURE

Provinces or Territories (with official contractions)	*Population (2009)*	*Area (sq. km)*	*Capital*	*Premier*
Alberta (AB)	3,687,700	661,848	Edmonton	Ed Stelmach
British Columbia (BC)	4,455,200	944,735	Victoriat	Gordon Campbell
Manitoba (MB)	1,222,000	747,797	Winnipeg	Greg Selinger
New Brunswick (NB)	749,500	72,908	Fredericton	Shawn Graham
Newfoundland and Labrador (NL)	508,900	405,212	St John's	Danny Williams
Northwest Territories (NT)	43,400	1,346,106	Yellowknife	Floyd Roland
Nova Scotia (NS)	938,200	55,284	Halifax	Darrell Dexter
Nunavut (NU)	32,200	2,093,190	Iqaluit	Eva Aariak
Ontario (ON)	13,069,200	1,076,395	Toronto	Dalton McGinley
Prince Edward Island (PE)	141,000	5,660	Charlottetown	Robert Ghiz
Québec (QC)	7,828,900	1,542,056	Québec City	Jean Charest
Saskatchewan (SK)	1,030,100	651,036	Regina	Brad Wall
Yukon Territory (YT)	33,700	482,443	Whitehorse	Dennis Fentie

products (including crude oil, natural gas and electricity) and aluminium.
GNI – US$1,453,800m; US$43,640 per capita (2008)
Annual average growth of GDP – -2.4 per cent (2009 est)
Inflation rate – 0.2 per cent (2009 est)
Unemployment – 8.5 per cent (2009 est)
Total external debt – US$833,800m (2009)
Imports – US$417,400m (2008)
Exports – US$452,200m (2008)

BALANCE OF PAYMENTS
Trade – US$8,341m deficit (2009)
Current Account – US$36,132m deficit (2009)

Trade with UK	*2008*	*2009*
Imports from UK	£3,595,847,073	£3,957,008,681
Exports to UK	£6,251,298,733	£8,076,735,617

COMMUNICATIONS

Canada has a coastline on three oceans, the Atlantic, the Arctic and the Pacific. In addition, the Great Lakes/St Lawrence Seaway system, the world's longest inland waterway, provides ocean-going shipping with access to the North American interior. There are over 300 ports, the most significant of which are Vancouver and Prince Rupert on the Pacific coast and Montréal, Halifax, Port Cartier, Sept-Iles/Pointe Noire, Saint John and Québec in the east. Most deep-water ports are open all year, and Churchill, on Hudson's Bay, is ice-free for longer periods as a result of climate change.

There are over 1,300 airports and airstrips, of which 26 serve national and provincial capitals and other major cities. The national carriers are Air Canada and Canadian Airlines International. The 46,700km railway network transports over 270 million tonnes of freight a year; the main service providers are Canadian National Railways and Canadian Pacific Railways, which also own several US lines. There are 1.04 million kilometres of roads. The 7,300km Trans-Canadian Highway links all ten provinces.

The usage of fixed telephone lines has declined as mobile phone distribution has grown. There were 18 million fixed lines in use, 21 million mobile phone subscribers and 25 million internet users in 2008.

EDUCATION AND HEALTH

Education is under the control of the provincial governments, the cost of the publicly controlled schools being met by local taxation and aided by provincial grants. Education is compulsory from ages six to 16 (18 in Ontario and New Brunswick).
Gross enrolment ratio (percentage of relevant age group) – primary 99 per cent; secondary 101 per cent (2007 est)
Health expenditure (per capita) – US$4,409 (2007)
Hospital beds (per 1,000 people) – 3.4 (2003–8)

MEDIA

The public broadcaster, the Canadian Broadcasting Corporation (CBC), was established in the 1930s and operates two television and four radio networks, transmitting programmes in English and French. It also operates television channels and radio services for indigenous peoples in the north of the country. Société Radio-Canada is the French-language public broadcasting service. There are several commercial television channels and around 2,000 licensed radio stations. The broadcasting regulator enforces quotas of Canadian material (30–35 per cent) on Canadian radio and television.

CULTURE

Canadian culture was originally influenced by the British and French heritage of its settlers, but is now dominated by the neighbouring USA. Canada has produced a number of successful actors, directors and comedians, including Jim Carrey (*b.* 1962), David Cronenberg (*b.* 1943), Mike Myers (*b.* 1963) and Donald (*b.* 1935) and Kiefer (*b.* 1966) Sutherland.

The country is also one of the world's largest exporters of popular music. Leonard Cohen (*b.* 1934), Joni Mitchell (*b.* 1943) and Neil Young (*b.* 1945) are all internationally successful, as were the Band (1967–76), while the Montreal International Jazz Festival is the largest of its kind in the world. Writers include the Nobel laureate Saul Bellow (1915–2005), International Booker prize winner Alice Munro (*b.* 1931), Carol Shields (1935–2003), who won the Pulitzer prize, and the Booker prize winner Margaret Atwood (*b.* 1939).

CAPE VERDE

Republica de Cabo Verde – Republic of Cape Verde

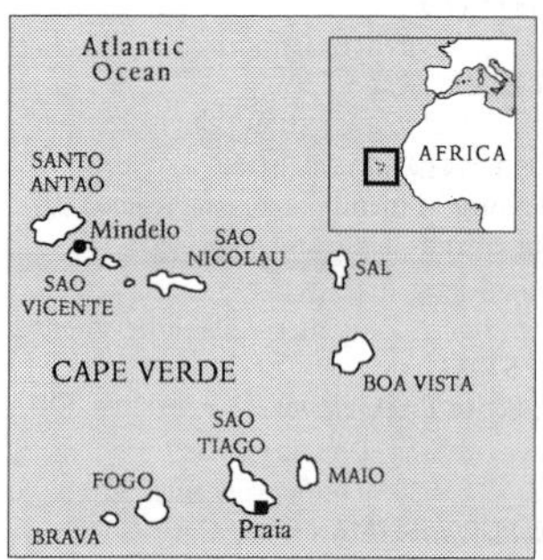

Area – 4,033 sq. km. Comprises the Windward Islands (Santo Antao, Sao Vicente, Santa Luzia, Sao Nicolau, Boa Vista and Sal) and Leeward Islands (Maio, Sao Tiago, Fogo and Brava)
Capital – Praia, on Sao Tiago; population, 125,148 (2009)
Major town – Mindelo
Currency – Escudo Caboverdiano of 100 centavos
Population – 429,474 rising at 0.56 per cent a year (2009 est)
Religion – Christian (Roman Catholic 85 per cent) (est)
Language – Portuguese (official), Creole
Population density – 124 per sq. km (2008)
Urban population – 59 per cent (2007 est)
Median age (years) – 21.1 (2009 est)
National anthem – 'Cantico da Liberdade' ['Song of Liberty']
National day – 5 July (Independence Day)
Life expectancy – 71.61 (2009 est)
Mortality rate – 6.22 (2009 est)
Birth rate – 23.5 (2009 est)
Infant mortality rate – 41.35 (2009 est)
Death penalty – Abolished for all crimes (since 1981)
CPI score – 5.1 (2009)
Literacy rate – 83.8 per cent (2007)

CLIMATE AND TERRAIN

The archipelago of ten islands of volcanic origin lies 600km off the west African coast. Elevation extremes range from 2,829m (Mt Fogo) at the highest point to 0m

(Atlantic Ocean) at the lowest. The climate is hot and dry, with periodic droughts.

HISTORY AND POLITICS

The islands were first discovered and colonised *c.*1460 by Portugal. Administered with Portuguese Guinea until 1879, they became an overseas province in 1951. The country achieved independence on 5 July 1975 after a campaign by the African Party for the Independence of Guinea Bissau and Cape Verde (PAIGC).

The republic was a one-party state under the African Party for the Independence of Cape Verde (PAICV) until 1990. Multiparty elections in 1991 were won by the opposition Movement for Democracy (MPD), and the MPD candidate Antonio Mascarenhas Monteiro was elected president. The MPD and President Monteiro served two terms before the 2001 legislative elections returned the PAICV to power, and its candidate, Pedro Pires, narrowly won the second round of the presidential election. In the 2006 elections, the PAICV retained its overall majority, with 41 seats, and President Pires was re-elected in the first round of voting. The next legislative and presidential elections are due in January and February 2011 respectively.

POLITICAL SYSTEM

Under the 1992 constitution, the president is directly elected for a five-year term. There is a unicameral National Assembly with 72 members directly elected for a five-year term. The prime minister appoints the council of ministers.

HEAD OF STATE

President, Pedro Pires, *elected* 25 February 2001, *re-elected* 2006

SELECTED GOVERNMENT MEMBERS *as at May 2010*

Prime Minister, Jose Maria Neves
Economy, Fatima Fialho
Finance and Planning, Cristina Duarte
Foreign Affairs, Jose Brito
Defence, Christina Fontes Lima

EMBASSY OF THE REPUBLIC OF CAPE VERDE

Avenue Jeane 29, 1050 Brussels, Belgium
T (+32) (2) 643 6270
Ambassador Extraordinary and Plenipotentiary, HE Fernando Jorge Wahnon Ferreira, *apptd* 2007

BRITISH AMBASSADOR

HE Christopher Trott, *apptd* 2007, resident at Dakar, Senegal

DEFENCE

The coastguard has 3 patrol and coastal combatant vessels.
Military budget – US$8.8m (2008)
Military personnel – 1,200: army 1,000, coastguard 100, air force 100

ECONOMY AND TRADE

The islands have few natural resources, little fresh water and are subject to periods of prolonged drought. Although well-managed, the economy is dependent on foreign aid; reforms are intended to attract foreign investment to aid diversification and development of the private sector. Due to large-scale emigration the expatriate population is larger than the resident one, and remittances are equivalent to 10–20 per cent of GDP. The service sector dominates, with commerce, tourism, transport and public services accounting for 74.3 per cent of GDP. Industry contributed 16.5 per cent and agriculture 9.2 per cent; fishing resources are not fully exploited.

The main industries are the production of food, beverages, garments and footwear, fishing and fish processing, salt mining and ship repair. The main trading partners are Portugal, Japan and Spain. Exports are fuel, footwear, garments, fish and hides. Imports include foodstuffs (over 80 per cent of food is imported), industrial products, transport equipment and fuel.
GNI – US$1,399m; US$2,800 per capita (2008)
Annual average growth of GDP – 1.8 per cent (2009 est)
Inflation rate – 4 per cent (2009 est)
Unemployment – 21 per cent (2000 est)
Total external debt – US$325m (2002)
Imports – US$750m (2007)
Exports – US$20m (2007)

BALANCE OF PAYMENTS

Trade – US$799m deficit (2009)
Current Account – US$216m deficit (2008)

Trade with UK	*2008*	*2009*
Imports from UK	£32,013,592	£4,950,194
Exports to UK	£216,228	£141,923

COMMUNICATIONS

The main ports are Praia, Mindelo and Tarrafal. Ferry services operate between the islands. There are ten airports, including international airports at Praia and on Sal, and regular internal flights between the islands. The national carrier, Cape Verde Airlines, is being privatised. The islands have no railways. There are 1,350km of roads; most of these are cobbled but a programme to resurface the roads with asphalt began in 2007.

The telephone system extends to all the islands, providing internet access and broadband services. Mobile phone services, introduced in 1998, had 278,000 subscribers in 2008.

MEDIA

Freedom of the media is guaranteed in the constitution, and this is generally upheld. There are growing private print and broadcast sectors, but much of the media remains state-run. Portuguese African services and Radio France Internationale are both available, as are a range of Portuguese and Brazilian newspapers.

CENTRAL AFRICAN REPUBLIC

République Centrafricaine – Central African Republic

Area – 622,984 sq. km
Capital – Bangui; population, 701,597 (2009 est)
Major cities – Berbérati, Bimbo, Mbaiki
Currency – Franc CFA of 100 centimes
Population – 4,511,488 rising at 1.49 per cent a year (2009 est); Baya (33 per cent), Banda (27 per cent), Mandja (13 per cent), Sara (10 per cent), Mboum (7 per ent), M'Baka (4 per cent), Yakoma (4 per cent) (est)
Religion – Christian (Protestant denominations 51 per cent, Roman Catholic 29 per cent), Muslim 10 per cent (est). Some also practise animism, although these beliefs are often integrated into Christian and Muslim worship
Language – French (official), Sangho
Population density – 7 per sq. km (2008)
Urban population – 38 per cent (2007 est)
Median age (years) – 18.8 (2009 est)
National anthem – 'La Renaissance' ['The Rebirth']
National day – 1 December (Republic Day)
Life expectancy – 44.47 (2009 est)
Mortality rate – 17.84 (2009 est)
Birth rate – 32.75 (2009 est)
Infant mortality rate – 80.62 (2009 est)
HIV/AIDS adult prevalence – 5.6 per cent (2007 est)
Death penalty – Retained (not used since 1981)
CPI score – 2 (2009)
Literacy rate – 48.6 per cent (2007 est)
Gross enrolment ratio (percentage of relevant age group) – primary 77 per cent; tertiary 2 per cent (2008 est)
Health expenditure (per capita) – US$16 (2007)
Hospital beds (per 1,000 people) – 1.2 (2003–8)

CLIMATE AND TERRAIN

This landlocked state lies on a plateau between the Chad and Congo river basins, with hills in the north-east and the north-west. It is mostly savannah in the north and rainforest in the south. The main river is the Oubangui, which is the lowest point of elevation (335m). The highest point is Mt Ngaoui (1,420m). The climate is tropical, with a wet season in the north from June to September and in the south from May to October. The north can experience temperatures of up to 40°C between February and May, and the humidity can be extreme. The south has a more equatorial climate.

HISTORY AND POLITICS

The area was annexed by France in the 1880s and, as the territory of Oubangui-Chari, became part of French Equatorial Africa. In 1958 it elected to remain within the French Community and adopted the title of the Central African Republic. The country became fully independent on 17 August 1960. Since independence it has been politically unstable, experiencing several coups. The 1966 coup brought to power the despotic Jean-Bedel Bokassa, who proclaimed himself emperor in 1976 and renamed the country the Central African Empire. Bokassa was deposed in a bloodless coup in 1979 and the country reverted to a republic. After a period under military rule (1981–5) and as a one-party state (1986–93), political pluralism and a civilian government were restored in 1993. This government was undermined by mutinies, financial crises and unrest in some neighbouring countries which caused large influxes of refugees and border incursions. It was overthrown in 2003 in a coup led by Gen. François Bozizé, who declared himself president and appointed a transitional government until elections were held in 2005.

In the 2005 elections, Gen. Bozizé was elected president in the second round of voting. The National Convergence–Kwa Na Kwa, which supports the president, won most seats in the legislature and became the main party in a coalition government that included seven parties and a number of independents. The government has struggled to maintain control outside the capital, faced with lawlessness, banditry and an insurgency in the north since 2005 as well as the problems that beset the previous administration. It has been supported by a central African peacekeeping force since 2007; an EU force deployed in 2008 to protect refugees in the north-east was replaced by a larger UN mission in 2009 (due to be withdrawn by the end of 2010). A peace agreement with the main rebel groups was signed in 2008 and their leaders were included in the national unity government appointed in January 2009. Presidential and legislative elections called for April and May 2010 were postponed to allow more time for preparations.

POLITICAL SYSTEM

Under the 2004 constitution, the president is elected for a five-year term, renewable only once. There is a unicameral National Assembly, which has 109 members, directly elected for a five-year term. The prime minister is appointed by the president, who also appoints the ministers.

HEAD OF STATE

President, Defence, Gen. François Bozizé, *took power* 15 March 2003, *elected* May 2005

SELECTED GOVERNMENT MEMBERS *as at May 2010*

Prime Minister, Faustin Archange Touadera
Finance and Budget, Albert Bessé
Foreign Affairs, Gen. Antoine Gambi
National Security, Gen. Jules Ouandé

EMBASSY OF THE CENTRAL AFRICAN REPUBLIC

30 rue des Perchamps, 75016 Paris, France
(+33) (1) 4224 4256
Ambassador Extraordinary and Plenipotentiary, Jean Willybiro Sako

BRITISH AMBASSADOR

HE Bharat Joshi, *apptd* 2009, resident at Yaoundé, Cameroon

DEFENCE

The army has 3 main battle tanks, 18 armoured infantry fighting vehicles, over 39 armoured personnel carriers and 9 patrol and coastal combatant vessels.
Military budget – US$22m (2009 est)
Military personnel – 3,150: army 2,000, air force 150, Gendarmerie 1,000
Conscription duration – 24 months

ECONOMY AND TRADE

The economy is largely undeveloped owing to decades of instability and misrule. Development is still hindered by political factionalism, a landlocked location, poor transport infrastructure, an unskilled workforce and corruption. The country is dependent on international aid. Natural resources include diamonds, gold, uranium and timber; diamond and gold mining and forestry are among the main industrial activities but the economy still depends mostly on agriculture, which accounts for over 50 per cent of GDP. Most production is at subsistence level but cotton, coffee and tobacco form the main

exports along with diamonds and timber. The main imports are food, textiles, fuels and machinery. Trade is mainly with Japan, South Korea and France.
GNI – US$1,800m; US$410 per capita (2008)
Annual average growth of GDP – 2.4 per cent (2009 est)
Inflation rate – 0.9 per cent (2007 est)
Unemployment – 8 per cent (2001 est)
Total external debt – US$1,153m (2007 est)
Imports – US$300m (2008)
Exports – US$200m (2008)

BALANCE OF PAYMENTS
Trade – US$134m deficit (2009)
Current Account – US$106m deficit (2007 est)

Trade with UK	*2008*	*2009*
Imports from UK	£829,165	£796,679
Exports to UK	£68,998	£108,315

COMMUNICATIONS

The infrastructure is poor: little of the 24,300km road network is surfaced, making many roads unusable in the wet season, and there is no railway system. There are 2,800km of waterways, mostly on the Oubangui and Sangha rivers, that are navigable all year and are important passenger and freight transport routes. The principal airport is at Bangui, and there are about 40 other airports and airfields. Fixed-line and mobile telephone networks are largely limited to the Bangui area, with density fewer than one per 100 people for fixed lines and three per 100 people for mobile phones.

MEDIA

The radio and television stations with a national reach are state run. There are a number of private radio and television stations; of these, the UN-sponsored Radio Ndeke Luka provides the most balanced output. There are a number of privately owned newspapers which freely criticise the government, but low literacy levels mean that they have little influence. Legislation passed in 2004 abolished prison terms for press offences.

CHAD

République du Tchad/Jumhuriyat Tshad – Republic of Chad

Area – 1,284,000 sq. km
Capital – N'Djamena; population, 808,442 (2009 est)
Major cities – Abéché, Moundou, Sarh
Currency – Franc CFA of 100 centimes
Population – 10,329,208 rising at 2.07 per cent a year (2009 est)
Religion – Muslim 53 per cent (predominantly Tijaniyah, a local order of Sufism), Christian 34 per cent (est), traditional indigenous religions
Language – French, Arabic (both official), Sara (in the south), Ouadi, Toubon (in the north)
Population density – 9 per sq. km (2008)
Urban population – 26 per cent (2007 est)
Median age (years) – 16.5 (2009 est)
National anthem – 'La Tchadienne' ['Song of Chad']
National day – 11 August (Independence Day)
Life expectancy– 47.7 (2009 est)
Mortality rate – 16.09 (2009 est)
Birth rate – 40.86 (2009 est)
Infant mortality rate – 98.69 (2009 est)
HIV/AIDS adult prevalence – 3.1 per cent (2007 est)
Death penalty – Retained
CPI score – 1.6 (2009)
Literacy rate – 31.8 per cent (2007 est)
Gross enrolment ratio (percentage of relevant age group) – primary 83 per cent; secondary 19 per cent; tertiary 2 per cent (2008 est)
Health expenditure (per capita) – US$32 (2007)
Hospital beds (per 1,000 people) – 0.4 (2003–8)

CLIMATE AND TERRAIN

The population of this landlocked country is concentrated in the fertile lowlands of the south, away from the arid central and northern desert areas. The highest point of elevation is 3,415m (Emi Koussi) and the lowest is 160m (the Djourab depression). The climate is desert in the north and tropical in the south, with a wet season from July to September.

HISTORY AND POLITICS

Chad was colonised by France from the 1890s and became part of French Equatorial Africa. It became self-governing after the Second World War and independent on 11 August 1960. A one-party state was declared in 1963 by the president, a southerner, which in 1965 prompted a rebellion in the north against a perceived pro-southern bias in the government. Regional and ethnic tensions, most notably between the Muslim Arab north and the Christian and animist African south, underlie the series of rebellions and coups that have made the country politically unstable since independence. Chad's instability was exacerbated from the 1970s to the 1990s by Libya's support for some rebels and its annexation of territory in northern Chad, and since 2004 by the overspill of the conflict in Sudan.

Idriss Déby seized power in 1990 after leading a rebellion in eastern Chad, and initiated a transition to democracy. A new constitution was introduced in 1996, and the first multiparty elections were held. However, Déby's hold on power remains tenuous; he has faced rebellions in the north and east since the late 1990s.

Déby won the first multiparty presidential election in 1996 and was re-elected in 2001 and 2006, despite doubts over the integrity of the polls. The 2002 legislative election was won by Déby's Patriotic Salvation Movement (MPS). The legislative election due in 2006 was twice postponed until 2009 and then scheduled for 23 November 2010.

INSURGENCIES
The series of insurgencies over the decades since independence means that no government has ever controlled the whole of the country. There are currently insurgencies in the north and east; rebels hold large areas of northern Chad, and rebel offensives reached the capital

in 2006 and 2008 before being repulsed. In 2009, eight rebel groups united to form the Union of Resistance Forces alliance.

Since 2004 the east and south-east have been further destabilised by the overspill of fighting from Sudan's Darfur region, with some militias mounting cross-border incursions to attack the estimated 250,000 Sudanese refugees taking shelter in Chad. An estimated 185,000 Chadians have also been displaced by the incursions, the insurgencies and Chadian ethnic violence. An EU peacekeeping force deployed in 2008 to protect Darfurian refugees in Chad was replaced by a larger UN mission in 2009, but this was due to be withdrawn by the end of 2010.

POLITICAL SYSTEM
The 1996 constitution was amended in 2005 to remove the limit on the number of terms a president may serve. The president is directly elected for a five-year term. The unicameral National Assembly of 155 members is directly elected for a four-year term. The prime minister is appointed by the president.

HEAD OF STATE
President, Idriss Déby, *took power* December 1990, *elected* 3 July 1996, *re-elected* 2001, 2006

SELECTED GOVERNMENT MEMBERS *as at May 2010*
Prime Minister, Emmanuel Nadingar
Economy, Mahamat Ali Hassan
Finance, Ngata Ngoulou
Foreign Affairs, Moussa Faki Mahamat
Interior, Ahmat Mahamat Bachir
Defence, Gen. Kamougue Wadal Abdelkader

EMBASSY OF THE REPUBLIC OF CHAD
Boulevard Lambermont 52, 1030 Brussels, Belgium
T (+32) (2) 215 1975 E ambassade.tchad@chello.be
Ambassador Extraordinary and Plenipotentiary, HE Ahmat Abderaman Hagger, *apptd* 2006

BRITISH AMBASSADOR
HE Bharat Joshi, *apptd* 2009, resident at Yaoundé, Cameroon

DEFENCE
The army has 60 main battle tanks, 89 armoured infantry fighting vehicles and 52 armoured personnel carriers. The air force has 6 combat-capable aircraft and 7 armed helicopters.
Military budget – US$151m (2009)
Military personnel – 25,350: army 17,000–20,000, air force 350, Republican Guard 5,000; paramilitary 9,500

ECONOMY AND TRADE
Economic development has been limited by political instability, a landlocked location and poor transport infrastructure. About 80 per cent of the workforce is occupied in subsistence agriculture, herding and fishing, which contributed 57.2 per cent of GDP in 2008. The main focus of development, funded by foreign investment and international aid, is the exploitation of oil deposits in the Doba basin in the south, which came into production in 2003; the oil is exported via a pipeline through Cameroon. The use of the oil revenue is subject to restrictions imposed by the World Bank. Other industries include cotton processing (the main industry before oil), other agricultural products and light manufacturing. Industry generated 7.5 per cent of GDP in 2008.

Chad's main trading partners are the USA (90 per cent of exports), France, Cameroon and China. Principal exports are oil, cattle, cotton and gum arabic. The main imports are machinery and transport equipment, industrial goods, food and textiles.
GNI – US$5,900m; US$540 per capita (2008)
Annual average growth of GDP – –1 per cent (2009 est)
Inflation rate – 6 per cent (2009 est)
Total external debt – US$1,600m (2005 est)
Imports – US$1,700m (2008)
Exports – US$4,800m (2008)

BALANCE OF PAYMENTS
Trade – US$2,113m surplus (2009)
Current Account – US$568m deficit (2006)

Trade with UK	*2008*	*2009*
Imports from UK	£12,592,105	£14,503,525
Exports to UK	£871,489	£565,512

COMMUNICATIONS
There are over 4,000km of waterways, although only 2,000km are navigable all year round. Of the 33,400km of roads, only 267km are surfaced, so many are unusable in the wet season. The principal airport is at N'Djamena and there are more than 50 other airports and airfields. There are no railways. The fixed-line telephone system is primitive, and mobile phone distribution is growing rapidly but was less than 20 per 100 people in 2008.

MEDIA
Low levels of literacy make radio the most important news medium. Radiodiffusion Nationale Tchadienne is the state-controlled radio station; private radio stations are closely monitored by the government. There is only one television station, Télétchad, and it is state-owned and controlled. Privately owned newspapers circulate in the capital and are often critical of the government.

CHILE

República de Chile – Republic of Chile

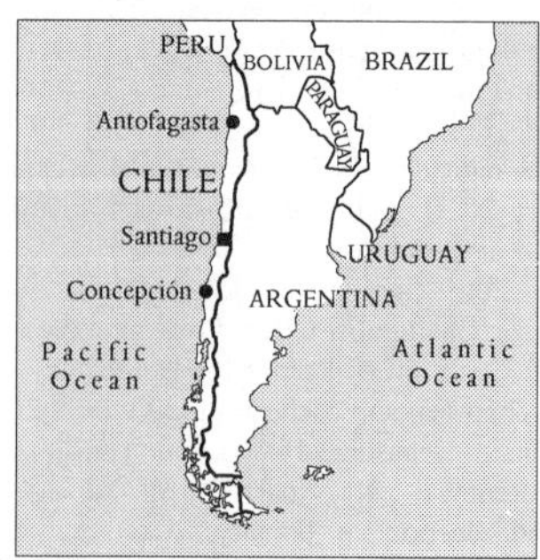

Area – 756,102 sq. km
Capital – Santiago; population, 5,883,040 (2009 est)
Major cities – Antofagasta, Arica, Concepción, Iquique, Punta Arenas, Temuco, Valparaíso
Currency – Chilean peso of 100 centavos
Population – 16,601,707 rising at 0.88 per cent a year (2009 est)

Religion – Christian (Roman Catholic 70 per cent, Protestant denominations 15 per cent) (est)
Language – Spanish (official), Mapudungun, German, English
Population density – 23 per sq. km (2008)
Urban population – 88 per cent (2007 est)
Median age (years) – 31.4 (2009 est)
National anthem – 'Himno Nacional de Chile' ['National Anthem of Chile']
National day – 18 September (Independence Day)
Life expectancy (years) – 77.34 (2009 est)
Mortality rate – 5.84 (2009 est)
Birth rate – 14.64 (2009 est)
Infant mortality rate – 7.71 (2009 est)
Death penalty – Retained for certain crimes (last used 1985)
CPI score – 6.7 (2009)
Literacy rate – 96.5 per cent (2007 est)

CLIMATE AND TERRAIN

Chile lies between the shores of the South Pacific Ocean and the Andes (1,524m to 4,572m above sea level), extending 4,480km, from the arid north around Arica to Cape Horn; the average breadth, north of 41°, is 160km. The Atacama desert lies in the north. In the central zone there is a fertile valley between the Andes and the low coastal range of mountains, with a Mediterranean climate; two-thirds of the population lives here. Chilean Patagonia, in the south, extends into subantarctic terrain, with glaciers and icefields; the climate is cool with high precipitation. Elevation extremes range from 6,880m (Nevado Ojos del Salado) at the highest point to 0m (Pacific Ocean) at the lowest. Its island possessions include the Juan Fernández group and Easter Island, both in the Pacific.

HISTORY AND POLITICS

Chile was conquered in the 16th century by the Spanish, who subjugated the indigenous population. It remained under Spanish rule until 1810, when the first autonomous government was established. Independence was achieved in 1818 after a revolutionary war.

A military coup in 1973 overthrew the Marxist president Salvador Allende. General Augusto Pinochet, the coup leader, assumed the presidency and retained the office until elections were held in 1989, beginning the transition to full democracy. Between 1998 and his death in 2006, a number of unsuccessful attempts were made to bring Gen. Pinochet to trial for human rights atrocities committed during his time in office. A massive earthquake, registering 8.8 in magnitude, hit central Chile in February 2010, killing about 500 people and causing widespread devastation.

In the 2009 legislative elections, the right-wing Coalition for Change (APC) won one more seat than the incumbent Coalition of Parties for Democracy (CPD) in the lower chamber, and each grouping won half the seats in the senate. Sebastián Piñera, the candidate of the National Renewal party (part of the APC), won the presidential election in January 2010 and formed a government consisting of members of the APC and independents.

POLITICAL SYSTEM

The 1981 constitution was amended in 1989 and 2005. The executive president is directly elected for a four-year term that is not renewable. The bicameral National Congress comprises a senate of 38 members elected for an eight-year term (half renewed every four years) and a Chamber of Deputies of 120 members directly elected for a four-year term.

HEAD OF STATE

President, Sebastián Piñera, *elected* 17 January 2010, *sworn in* 11 March 2010

SELECTED GOVERNMENT MEMBERS *as at May 2010*

Defence, Jaime Ravinet
Economy, Juan Andrés Fontaine
Finance, Felipe Larrain
Foreign Affairs, Alfredo Moreno
Interior, Rodrigo Hinzpeter

EMBASSY OF CHILE

37-41 Old Queen Street, London SW1H 9JA
T 020-7222 2361 E contacto@chileabroad.gov.cl
W www.chileabroad.gov.cl/reino-unido
Ambassador Extraordinary and Plenipotentiary, HE Rafael Moreno, *apptd* 2006

BRITISH EMBASSY

Avda. El Bosque Norte 0125, Las Condes, Santiago
T (+56) (2) 370 4100 E embsan@britemb.cl
W http://ukinchile.fco.gov.uk
Ambassador Extraordinary and Plenipotentiary, HE Jon Benjamin, *apptd* 2009

BRITISH COUNCIL

Eliodoro Yáñez 832, 750-0651 Providencia, Santiago
T (+56) (2) 410 6900 W www.britishcouncil.org/chile
Director, Sarah Barton

DEFENCE

The army has 309 main battle tanks, 309 armoured infantry fighting vehicles and 526 armoured personnel carriers. The navy has 4 submarines, 8 frigates, 13 patrol and coastal vessels and 17 combat aircraft. There are bases at Valparaíso, Talcahuano, Puerto Montt, Puerto Williams, Iquique and Punta Arenas. The marines have 16 light tanks and 25 armoured personnel carriers. The air force has 77 combat aircraft.
Military expenditure – US$5,230m (2009)
Military personnel – 60,560: army 35,000, navy 17,800, air force 7,760; paramilitary 41,500

ECONOMY AND TRADE

Economic reforms in the late 1970s and the 1980s and sound management of government finances and financial institutions have made Chile one of the most successful economies in Latin America. GDP growth is based on high copper prices, a strong export base and growing domestic demand. Although the economy contracted in 2009 owing to the global downturn, it is recovering quickly.

Chile is the world's largest producer of copper, and the world's only commercial producer of nitrate of soda (Chile saltpetre) from natural resources. The chief industries are mining, forestry, fishing, food and fish processing, and wine-making. Agriculture, which contributes 4.8 per cent of GDP, produces fruit, vegetables, cereals, meat and wool.

The main trading partners are the USA, China, Brazil, Japan and Argentina. Principal exports are copper, fruit, fish products, paper and pulp, chemicals and wine. The main imports are petrol and petroleum products, chemicals, electrical and telecommunications equipment, industrial machinery, vehicles and natural gas.

GNI – US$157,500m; US$9,370 per capita (2008)
Annual average growth of GDP – –1.5 per cent (2009 est)
Inflation rate – 1.7 per cent (2009 est)
Population living below poverty line – 18.2 per cent (2005)
Unemployment – 10 per cent (2009 est)
Total external debt – US$60,900m (2009)
Imports – US$61,900m (2008)
Exports – US$66,500m (2008)

BALANCE OF PAYMENTS
Trade – US$10,901m surplus (2009)
Current Account – US$2,522m deficit (2009)

Trade with UK	*2008*	*2009*
Imports from UK	£272,430,117	£478,163,896
Exports to UK	£549,374,436	£535,933,078

COMMUNICATIONS

The main ports are San Antonio, Valparaíso, San Vicente, Antofagasta and Iquique. There is a 5,500km railway system, but lines in some areas are not in use as rail travel is increasingly superseded by road and air travel; services are run by a state-owned company. The road network is about 80,500km in length, of which 16,700km is surfaced. There are over 350 airports and airfields; the principal airport is at Santiago. The national air carrier is LAN Airlines, with Sky Airline and Principal Airlines also providing domestic flights. Mobile phone distribution is growing rapidly, reaching 90 per 100 people in 2008, and fixed-line connections are decreasing as a result.

EDUCATION AND HEALTH

Education is free and compulsory for 12 years, although the education system has suffered from underinvestment and mismanagement. In response to massive student demonstrations and strikes in 2006, the government introduced a limited education reform package in 2009. Student protests have since continued, focusing on inequality in education provision.
Literacy rate – 96.5 per cent (2007 est)
Gross enrolment ratio (percentage of relevant age group) – primary 105 per cent; secondary 94 per cent; tertiary 50 per cent (2008 est)
Health expenditure (per capita) – US$615 (2007)
Hospital beds (per 1,000 people) – 2.3 (2003–8)

MEDIA AND CULTURE

Television is a combination of national and local, private and state-run, cable and terrestrial channels. Radio is the country's most important news medium, with 800 stations nationwide. Chile's constitution provides for press freedom, and the last remaining media restrictions from the Pinochet era were lifted in 2001.

Chile has a vibrant arts culture and is considered the most European of the Latin American countries. Chilean Nobel Prize winners for literature include the writers Gabriela Mistral (1889–1957) in 1945, and poet Pablo Neruda (1904–73) in 1971. The first English translation of a work by novelist Roberto Bolaño (1953–2003) was published in 2003.

One of the islands in the Juan Fernández group, about 576km from Valparaíso, was reputedly the scene of Alexander Selkirk's shipwreck in 1704, which inspired Daniel Defoe's novel *Robinson Crusoe*. Easter Island, about 3,200km away in the South Pacific Ocean, contains stone platforms and hundreds of mysterious stone figures, *moai*, thought to be carved from volcanic ash by Polynesian colonisers between 1100 and 1600.

CHILEAN ANTARCTIC TERRITORY

The Chilean Antarctic Territory covers the Antarctic peninsula and an area of the landmass that extends from 53°W to 90°W along a latitude of 60°S. This area is also claimed by the UK and Argentina, although the Antarctic treaty has frozen all disputes over territory. (*See also* The North and South Poles.)

CHINA

Zhonghua Renmin Gongheguo – People's Republic of China

Area – 9,596,961 sq. km
Capital – Beijing; population, 12,213,900 (2009 est)
Major cities – Changchun, Chengdu, Chongqing, Guangzhou, Harbin, Nanjing, Shanghai, Shenyang, Tianjin, Taiyuan, Wuhan, Xi'an
Currency – Renminbi (RMB) or yuan (Y) of 10 jiao or 100 fen
Population – 1,338,612,968 rising at 0.66 per cent a year (2009 est); Han Chinese (91.5 per cent), around 55 ethnic minorities 8.5 per cent (est)
Religion – officially atheist, but permits five state-registered religions: Buddhism, Taoism, Islam, Catholicism and Protestantism. It is difficult to estimate numbers, as many congregations worship in private; Mahayana Buddhism and Taoism are the predominant faiths but Christianity is growing rapidly
Language – Mandarin (official), Cantonese, Shanghainese, Fuzhou, Xiang, Gan, Taiwanese
Population density – 142 per sq. km (2008)
Urban population – 43 per cent (2007 est)
Median age (years) – 34.1 (2009 est)
National anthem – 'Yiyongjun Jinxingqu' ['The March of the Volunteers']
National day – 1 October (Founding of People's Republic)
Life expectancy (years) – 73.47 (2009 est)
Mortality rate – 7.06 (2009 est)
Birth rate – 14 (2009 est)
Infant mortality rate – 20.25 (2009 est)
Death penalty – Retained
CPI score – 3.6 (2009)

CLIMATE AND TERRAIN

China is twice the size of western Europe and contains a vast range of landscapes and climates. Two-thirds of the country is hilly or mountainous. The highest mountains are on the Tibetan plateau, in the west of the country, where the highest elevation is 8,848m (Mt Everest). To the north of the Tibetan plateau, the land drops to the arid, semi-desert steppes bisected by the Tian Shan mountains; the country's lowest elevation is −154m at Turpan Pendi. The southern plains and east coast have the most fertile land, irrigated by the Huang He (Yellow), Chang Jiang (Yangtze) and Xi Jiang (West) rivers, and are the most heavily populated areas.

There are seven climate zones. The north-east has cold winters, fierce winds, hot and humid summers and erratic rainfall. The mountainous south-west has mild winters and warm summers. Inner Mongolia has cold winters and hot summers. Central China has hot and humid summers with occasional tropical cyclones. South China is partly tropical with heavy rainfall. The high Tibet plateau is subject to harsh winters. Xinjiang and the west have a desert climate, with cold winters and little rain.

HISTORY AND POLITICS

China was ruled by imperial dynasties from the second millennium BC. The last emperor of the Qing dynasty abdicated in 1912 after a revolution broke out in 1911. Central authority collapsed, leading to a period of chaos and regional warlord domination, as neither the Guomindang (KMT), led by Sun Yat-sen, nor the Chinese Communist Party (CCP), founded in 1921, were able to unify the whole country. The KMT established a government in Nanjing in 1927 but the CCP broke with it in the mid-1930s and fled into the interior (the Long March, 1934–5). The conflict between them also hindered their individual and joint efforts to resist Japanese encroachment; Japan occupied Manchuria in 1932, and most northern and coastal areas of China by 1939. Japan's occupation was ended by its defeat by the Allies in 1945. Despite Allied support after 1941 for the KMT, now led by Chiang Kai-shek, the Communists established control over large areas of China in the early 1940s, seizing the territory abandoned by Japan in 1945. Following a civil war (1946–9) won by the Communists, the CCP inaugurated the People's Republic of China (PRC), and the KMT went into exile in Taiwan. The USA continued to recognise the Chiang Kai-shek regime as the rightful government of China until 1971, when the PRC took over China's membership of the UN from Taiwan.

Under Mao Zedong, political and economic restructuring was undertaken, including the collectivisation of agriculture and industry, the establishment of communes and the redistribution of land. Mao's 'Great Leap Forward' (1958–61), an attempt to industrialise rural areas, resulted in a famine in which 30–40 million people died. China was plunged into chaos during the Cultural Revolution (1966–70), when the Red Guards were formed to rid the country of 'rightist elements'.

Following Mao Zedong's death in 1976, the ousted Deng Xiaoping was recalled and he became the dominant force within the party; from 1978 he promoted an 'open door' policy in foreign relations, economic modernisation and social liberalisation. The party congresses of 1982 and 1987 reaffirmed Deng's policies, and in 1987 most of the revolutionary generation was replaced in the most senior posts by younger, more liberal supporters of reform.

Liberalisation suffered a setback in April–May 1989, when student-led pro-democracy demonstrations, centred on Tiananmen Square in Beijing, were brutally repressed by the army; some estimate that up to 3,000 protesters died. The events strengthened the position of conservatives within the leadership, who readopted policies of centralisation based on Marxist ideology.

Although Deng retired from his last official post in 1989, he retained effective control until late 1994 and, at his instigation, the emphasis shifted back to economic reform in 1992. The 1992 party congress endorsed Deng's calls for faster, bolder economic reforms and a socialist market economy. Following Deng's death in 1997 the government continued to promote economic growth, and also sought to improve China's standing in the international community.

In 2003 Hu Jintao was elected by the National People's Congress as the new state president and Wen Jaibao was elected as premier; both were re-elected to their posts at the 2008 party congress. Hu is pursuing policies in health, education, the environment and other areas which are intended to address the social inequalities created by the economic growth of recent years.

HUMAN RIGHTS

Liberalisation has allowed ordinary people greater personal choice: they can now travel freely, for example, or change professions. However, freedom of expression, religion and association are still tightly controlled, and the regime firmly suppresses dissent by ethnic minorities or other groups that it perceives as a threat to its authority. This has led to moves against separatists from the Uygur Muslim minority group in Xinjiang Autonomous Region since the 1990s, the banning of the Falun Gong spiritual movement in 1999 and the violent suppression of demonstrations in Tibet in 2008. Religious gatherings that have not been approved by the state-sanctioned religious bodies are broken up by the authorities and their leaders harassed; despite this, all religions are experiencing a revival throughout China, and underground Protestant churches in particular are growing rapidly.

POLITICAL SYSTEM

The Communist Party of China is the dominant political party, and all elements of the political system are subordinate to it. A party congress is held every five years and elects the Politburo and its standing committee. This standing committee is the policy- and decision-making body and the *de facto* government.

Under the 1982 constitution, the National People's Congress is the highest organ of state power. It has 2,987 members, indirectly elected for a five-year term, and holds only one full session a year; between sessions, its work is delegated to its standing committee. The congress elects the premier and, on his nomination, the State Council. The head of state is the president, also elected by the congress, who serves a five-year term, renewable only once.

Deputies to people's congresses at the primary level are directly elected by the voters from a list of approved candidates. These congresses elect the deputies to the congress at the next higher level. Deputies to the National People's Congress are elected by the provincial and municipal people's congresses, and by the armed forces.

Local government is conducted through people's governments at provincial/municipal, prefecture/city, county/district, township and village levels. There are 22 provinces (Taiwan is claimed as a 23rd province), four municipalities directly under the central government, five autonomous regions, and two special administrative areas; provinces may contain autonomous counties or towns for ethnic minorities.

HEAD OF STATE

President, Hu Jintao, *elected* 15 March 2003, *re-elected* March 2008
Vice-President, Xi Jinping

STATE COUNCIL *as at May 2010*
Premier, Wen Jiabao
Vice-Premiers, Li Keqiang; Zhang Dejiang; Hui Liangyu; Wang Qishan
State Councillors, Dai Bingguo; Liang Guanglie *(National Defence);* Meng Jianzhu *(Public Security);* Ma Kai *(Secretary-General of the State Council);* Liu Yandong

SELECTED GOVERNMENT MEMBERS *as at May 2010*
Civil Affairs, Li Xueju
Finance, Xie Xuren
Foreign Affairs, Yang Jiechi
State Security, Geng Huichang

EMBASSY OF THE PEOPLE'S REPUBLIC OF CHINA
49–51 Portland Place, London W1B 1JL
T 020-7299 4049 W www.chinese-embassy.org.uk
Ambassador Extraordinary and Plenipotentiary, HE Liu Xiaoming, *apptd* 2010

BRITISH EMBASSY
11 Guang Hua Lu, Jian Guo Men Wai, Beijing 100600
T (+86) (10) 5192 4000 E consular.beijing@fco.gov.uk
W http://ukinchina.fco.gov.uk
Ambassador, HE Sebastian Wood, *apptd* 2010

BRITISH COUNCIL
Cultural and Education Section, British Embassy, 4th Floor Landmark Building Tower 1, 8 North Dongsanhuan Road, Chaoyang District, Beijing 100004
T (+86) (10) 6590 6903 W www.britishcouncil.org/china
Director, Joanna Burke

DEFENCE

All three military arms are parts of the People's Liberation Army (PLA). China has at least 66 intercontinental, 204 short range and 118 intermediate ballistic missiles, and 3 nuclear-capable strategic submarines. The army has over 6,550 main battle tanks, 1,000 light tanks, 1,140 armoured infantry fighting vehicles, over 3,300 armoured personnel carriers and 126 armed helicopters.

The navy has 65 submarines (3 strategic), 28 destroyers, 52 frigates, 253 patrol and coastal vessels and 290 combat aircraft. The marines have 100 light tanks and 180 armoured personnel carriers. The air force has 1,617 combat aircraft.

Military budget – US$70,300m (2009 est)
Military personnel – 2,285,000: army 1,600,000, navy 255,000, air force 300,000; paramilitary 700,000
Conscription duration – 24 months (selective)

ECONOMY AND TRADE

Liberalisation since the 1980s has transformed the economy, developing a more autonomous state sector, a rapidly growing private sector and a leading presence in global trade and investment. A massive industrial base and transport infrastructure have been constructed, especially in the coastal regions, and the economy has become a free market in all but name, with several stock markets and Shanghai's emergence as a financial centre. China attracts considerable foreign investment and has become a major investor overseas. GDP has grown more than tenfold since 1978, and by some measures China's economy is now the second-largest in the world.

Although some 200 million people who migrated to urban areas have been lifted out of poverty in the past two decades, the effects of the rapid transformation have been unevenly distributed. There are wide income differences between urban and rural areas, poor healthcare provision, lack of access to public services for migrant workers, rampant official corruption, and environmental degradation of land, water and air; officials estimate that pollution costs China between 8 and 15 per cent of GDP, and the current five-year plan (2006–11) makes environmental protection a priority. The government is also keen to increase domestic consumption, and so reduce the economy's reliance on exports for growth, especially as foreign demand slowed in 2008 owing to the global economic downturn and plummeted in 2009. A drop in production caused a sharp rise in unemployment (over 10 million jobs were lost in 2008), but the government used subsidies, stimulus packages, training and infrastructure projects to cushion the impact until growth resumed in late 2009.

China's expansion boosted its need for oil and coal, met initially by imports but increasingly by domestic production. However, to achieve its aim of reducing environmental degradation, China is looking more to nuclear power (the government has contracted to buy five nuclear power generators) and alternative energy generation, such as hydroelectric power from the Three Gorges Dam (a full capacity of 18.2 million kilowatts per hour is projected by 2011).

Although rural areas have seen few benefits from the economic transformation and are suffering the effects of rural depopulation and pollution, agriculture remains important; it contributes 10.9 per cent of GDP but employs 39.5 per cent of the workforce. The size of the country, and the variations in terrain and climate, allow a wide variety of produce to be grown. The main crops are rice, cereals, vegetables, peanuts, tea, fruit, cotton and oilseed crops. Livestock is raised in large numbers. Silk farming is one of the oldest industries. Cotton, woollen and silk textiles are manufactured in large quantities.

The highly diversified industrial sector, encompassing heavy industry, manufacturing and construction, contributes 48.6 per cent of GDP and employs 27.2 per cent of the workforce. The services sector accounts for 40.5 per cent of GDP and 33.2 per cent of employment. Tourism is a major industry, and experienced a boom in 2008 with the Beijing Olympic Games. Exports include machinery, electrical equipment, data processing equipment, garments, textiles, iron and steel, and optical and medical equipment. The principal imports are electrical and other machinery, oil and mineral fuels, optical and medical equipment, metal ores, plastics and organic chemicals. The main trading partners are the USA, Japan, Hong Kong, South Korea, Germany and Taiwan, although trade with Latin America and Africa is growing.

GNI – US$3,888,100m; US$2,940 per capita (2008)
Annual average growth of GDP – 8.4 per cent (2009 est)
Inflation rate – –0.8 per cent (2009 est)
Population below poverty line – 8 per cent (2006 est)
Unemployment – 9 per cent (2009 est)
Total external debt – US$347,100m (2009 est)
Imports – US$1,131,600m (2008)
Exports – US$1,428,700m (2008)

BALANCE OF PAYMENTS
Trade – US$198,040m surplus (2009)
Current Account – US$426,107m surplus (2008)

Trade with UK	*2008*	*2009*
Imports from UK	£4,869,710,975	£5,130,435,040
Exports to UK	£21,967,681,506	£27,790,721,887

COMMUNICATIONS

The infrastructure created after the civil war has been greatly expanded and modernised since the 1980s. In the past, the principal means of internal communication was by river, the most important of which are the Huang He (Yellow), Chang Jiang (Yangtze) and Xi Jiang (West). These, together with the network of canals connecting them, are still much used, but their overall importance has declined. Coastal port facilities are being improved and the merchant fleet expanded. The main seaports are Shanghai and Dalian in the north, and Guangzhou in the south; Nanjing is the largest river port.

Long-distance internal travel is mostly by air and rail. The length of civil air routes has more than tripled in the past two decades. There are 482 airports and airfields and several national air carriers. The rail system has 77,800km of track, although only 24,400km is electrified; completion of the Qinghai–Tibet railway in 2006 is opening up the remote western provinces. The road network has been expanded to over 3.5 million km, making all towns and villages accessible, and the major cities are linked by 53,900km of modern highways. Motor vehicle ownership is growing rapidly, leading to the growing problems of congestion, road safety and pollution.

The telecommunications infrastructure is also expanding, although facilities for personal subscribers are unevenly distributed, concentrated in the cities, industrial centres and major towns. Mobile phone distribution is growing rapidly and, at 634 million in 2008, is nearly double fixed-line subscriptions. There were 298 million internet users in 2008.

EDUCATION AND HEALTH

Primary education lasts six years and secondary education six years (three years in junior middle school and three optional years in senior middle school).

Literacy rate – 93.3 per cent (2007 est)

Gross enrolment ratio (percentage of relevant age group) – primary 112 per cent; secondary 74 per cent; tertiary 22 per cent (2008 est)

Health expenditure (per capita) – US$108 (2007)

Hospital beds (per 1,000 people) – 2.1 (2003–8)

MEDIA

The Communist Party maintains a firm grip on the media and the internet through surveillance and censorship. It restricts access to foreign news media by blocking websites, radio broadcasts and satellite receivers, limiting rebroadcasting of foreign programming and the distribution of overseas newspapers, and curtailing blogs. Foreign journalists were allowed greater freedom to travel and interview before the 2008 Olympic Games and this has been retained in new regulations issued since. However, Chinese journalists exercise self-censorship; official corruption may be criticised but not the party's monopoly on power.

China's media industry is huge, with television a particularly popular medium. State-run stations offer over 2,000 freeview channels, and the take-up of subscription services was expected to reach 128 million by late 2010. Every city has its own newspaper, as well as a local Communist Party publication.

CULTURE

The Chinese language has many dialects, notably Cantonese, Hakka, Amoy, Foochow, Changsha, Nanchang, Wu (Shanghai) and the northern dialect. The common speech, or *putonghua* (often referred to as Mandarin), is based on the northern dialect. The Communists have promoted it as the national language and it is taught throughout the country. As *putonghua* encourages the use of the spoken language in writing, the old literary style and ideographic form of writing has fallen into disuse. Since 1956 simplified characters have been introduced to make reading and writing easier. In 1958 the National People's Congress adopted a system of romanisation known as *pinyin.*

Chinese literature is one of the oldest in the world. Paper has been employed for writing and printing for nearly 2,000 years. The Confucian classics, which formed the basis of traditional Chinese culture, date from the Warring States period (fourth to third centuries BC), as do the earliest texts of Taoism. Histories, philosophical and scientific works, poetry, literary and art criticism, novels and romances survive from most periods.

TIBET

Area – 1,199,164 sq. km
Population – 2,610,000 (2001 est)
Capital – Lhasa

Tibet is a plateau, seldom lower than 3,000m, in south-west China which forms the frontier with India (boundary imperfectly demarcated), from which it is separated by the Himalayas from Kashmir to Myanmar; Nepal and Bhutan also border it to the south. The Indus, Brahmaputra, Mekong and Yangtze rivers all rise on the Tibet plateau.

Tibet was under Mongol rule almost continuously from the 13th to the 17th centuries. Chinese control grew from the 18th century and direct rule began in 1910, but with the collapse of the Chinese Empire in 1911, Tibet declared its independence and the Dalai Lama ruled undisturbed until Communist rule was established in China. In 1950 Chinese Communist forces invaded Tibet, and in 1951 the Tibetan authorities signed a treaty agreeing joint Chinese-Tibetan rule. A series of revolts against Chinese rule culminated in a 1959 uprising in the capital, which was crushed after several days of fighting and military rule was imposed. The Dalai Lama fled to India where he and his followers were granted political asylum and established a government in exile. Tibet became an Autonomous Region of China in 1965. Martial law was declared in Tibet in 1989.

The Panchen Lama, the second-highest Lama, remained in Lhasa after 1959; when he died in 1989, China rejected the Dalai Lama's choice of successor and enthroned its own candidate. Subsequent appointments have been handled in a similar manner, increasing tension between the Chinese authorities and the Tibetan government-in-exile. Despite occasional talks between the Chinese government and representatives of the Dalai Lama, relations remain poor.

Another source of tension is the large number of Chinese migrants who have settled in Tibet since the 1970s, a development that the Tibetan government-in-exile regards as an attempt to eradicate the culture of the Tibetan people. Chinese now considerably outnumber Tibetans and have benefited disproportionately from the economic development of recent years.

Peaceful anti-Chinese demonstrations in Tibet increased in early 2008 as the imminence of the Beijing Olympics put China's human rights record under greater international scrutiny. The violence of the Chinese crackdown was condemned worldwide, and pro-Tibet activists abroad disrupted the Olympic torch relay in several countries. Resistance and unrest continued into 2009 when, in a show of passive resistance, farmers in Tibet and neighbouring provinces with large Tibetan populations refused to till the fields or plant crops.

SPECIAL ADMINISTRATIVE REGIONS

HONG KONG

Xianggang Tebie Xingzhengqu – Hong Kong Special Administrative Region
Area – 1,104 sq. km
Currency – Hong Kong dollar (HK$) of 100 cents
Population – 7,055,071, rising at 0.50 per cent a year (2009 est)
Population density – 6,696 per sq. km (2008)
Flag – Red, with a white bauhinia flower of five petals each containing a red star
National day – 1 July (Establishment Day)
Life expectancy (years) – 81.86 (2009 est)
Birth rate – 7.42 (2009 est)
Mortality rate – 6.76 (2009 est)
Infant mortality rate – 2.92 (2009 est)
Death penalty – Abolished for all crimes (since 2003)
CPI score – 8.2 (2009)

CLIMATE AND TERRAIN
Hong Kong consists of Hong Kong Island, Kowloon and the New Territories (on a peninsula of the mainland in Guangdong province) and over 260 islands, including Lantau Island. It is situated on the south-east coast of China, on the eastern side of the mouth of the Pearl river. Hong Kong Island is about 18km long and 3–8km wide. It is separated from the mainland by a narrow strait. The highest point is Tai Mo Shan (958m). The climate is subtropical, with hot, wet summers and cool, dry winters. Mean monthly temperatures range from 16°C to 29°C. Tropical cyclones occur between May and November, and nearly 80 per cent of the average annual rainfall of 2,214mm falls between May and September.

HISTORY AND POLITICS
Hong Kong developed as a major regional trading port because of its location on the main Far Eastern trade routes. Hong Kong Island was first occupied by Britain in 1841 and formally ceded to Britain in 1842. Kowloon was acquired in 1860, and the New Territories by a 99-year lease signed in 1898.

In 1984, the UK and China agreed that China would resume sovereignty over Hong Kong in 1997, and on 1 July 1997, Hong Kong became a Special Administrative Region (SAR) of the People's Republic of China. The 1984 joint declaration and the Basic Law (1990) guarantee that the SAR's social and economic systems will remain unchanged for 50 years and grant it a high degree of autonomy.

Although the Basic Law provides for the development of democratic processes, political reform has been slow, prompting frequent demonstrations to demand full democracy or to oppose measures perceived to be repressive. In 2007 the Chinese government said that the chief executive could be directly elected from 2017 and the legislature members from 2020.

Tung Chee-hwa resigned as chief executive in 2005 and Donald Tsang was elected to serve out the rest of his term of office; Tsang was re-elected in 2007. In the 2008 legislative elections, pro-China parties won 35 seats and pro-democracy parties won 23, sufficient for the pro-democracy parties to veto constitutional changes.

POLITICAL SYSTEM
The Basic Law, approved in 1990, has served as Hong Kong's constitution since 1997. Its government is headed by the chief executive, who is elected by a 800-member electoral committee and serves a five-year term. The chief executive is aided by an executive council consisting of 15 principal officials, who are the heads of administrative departments, and 14 non-official members. The legislative council consists of 60 members, 30 directly elected by geographic constituencies, and 30 elected by functional, occupation-based constituencies. They serve a four-year term. The government has proposed to expand the legislative council to 70 members, and the electoral committee to 1,200.
Chief Executive, Donald Tsang, *elected* 16 June 2005, *sworn in* 24 June 2005, *re-elected* 2007

SELECTED GOVERNMENT MEMBERS *as at May 2010*
Chief Secretary for Administration, Henry Tang
Financial Secretary, John Tsang
Secretary for Security, Ambrose Lee

BRITISH CONSULATE-GENERAL
PO Box 528, 1 Supreme Court Road, Central Hong Kong
T (+852) 2901 3000 E consular@bcg.org.hk
W http://ukinhongkong.fco.gov.uk
Consul-General, Andrew Seaton, *apptd* 2008

BRITISH COUNCIL
3 Supreme Court Road, Admiralty, Hong Kong
T (+852) 2913 5100 W www.britishcouncil.org/hongkong
Director, Peter Upton

ECONOMY AND TRADE
The economy has moved away from manufacturing (which has mostly relocated to mainland China) and is now service-based, with a high reliance on international trade and re-exports. It has developed into a regional corporate and banking centre, and has benefited in recent years from closer integration with China through increased trade, tourism and financial links. Although badly affected by the global economic downturn in 2008–9, the strength of the Chinese economy helped it recover quickly.

The economy is dominated by the service sector, which accounts for 92 per cent of GDP. The main contributors to this are tourism, financial services and shipping. Industry contributes 8 per cent of GDP. Principal products are textiles, clothing, electronics, plastics, toys, and clocks and watches.

The principal export markets are China (51 per cent), the USA and Japan. China is Hong Kong's principal supplier of imported goods (46 per cent).
GNI – US$219,255m; US$31,420 per capita (2008)
Annual average growth of GDP – –3 per cent (2009 est)
Inflation rate – –0.5 per cent (2009 est)
Unemployment – 5.3 per cent (2009 est)
Imports – US$388,500m (2008)
Exports – US$362,700m (2008)

BALANCE OF PAYMENTS
Trade – US$27,043m deficit (2009)
Current Account – US$23,373m surplus (2009)

Trade with UK	*2008*	*2009*
Imports from UK	£3,470,107,106	£3,558,215,474
Exports to UK	£7,658,663,673	£5,710,218,660

EDUCATION
Education is free of charge and compulsory for children up to the age of 15.
Gross enrolment ratio (percentage of age group) – secondary 83 per cent (2008 est)

COMMUNICATIONS
Hong Kong has one of the world's finest natural harbours, and is the third busiest container port in the world. Dockyard facilities include eight floating drydocks; the largest is capable of docking vessels of up to 150,000 tonnes deadweight. There are two airports, one accommodating international flights. Modern telecommunications systems supported 4.1 million fixed lines, 11.4 million mobile phone subscribers and 4.1 million internet users in 2008.

MACAU (AOMEN)
Aomen Tebie Xingzhengqu – Macau Special Administrative Region
Area – 28.2 sq. km
Currency – Pataca of 100 avos
Population – 559,846 rising at 2 per cent a year (2009 est)
Flag – Green, with a white lotus flower above a white stylised bridge and water, under a large gold five-point star and four gold stars in crescent
National day – 20 December (Establishment Day)
CPI score – 5.3 (2009)

CLIMATE AND TERRAIN
Macau consists of the Macau peninsula and the islands of Coloane and Taipa. It is situated at the western side of the mouth of the Pearl river, bordering Guangdong province in south-east China. It is 64km from Hong Kong. Its area has nearly doubled since the 19th century due to land reclamation. The highest point is Coloane Alto (172m). The climate is subtropical.

HISTORY AND POLITICS
The first Portuguese ship arrived at Macau in 1513 and trade with China commenced in 1553. Macau became a Portuguese colony in 1557; China recognised Portugal's sovereignty over Macau by treaty in 1887. An agreement to transfer the administration of Macau to China was signed in 1987, and Macau became the Macau Special Administrative Region (MSAR) of China on 19 December 1999. A new chief executive was elected in June 2009, and a legislative election was held in September 2009.

The Basic Law (1993) has served as Macao's constitution since 1999. The chief executive is elected by a 300-member election committee and serves a five-year term of office, which may be renewed once. The chief executive is assisted by the ten-member executive council. The legislative assembly has 29 members, who serve for four years; 12 are directly elected, ten are indirectly elected by corporate constituencies and seven are appointed by the chief executive.
Chief Executive, Fernando Chui, *elected* July 2009, *sworn in* 20 December 2009

SELECTED GOVERNMENT MEMBERS *as at May 2010*
Economy and Finance, Francis Tam Pak Yuen
Secretary for Administration and Justice, Florinda da Rosa Silva Chan

CONSUL-GENERAL
Andrew Seaton, resident at Hong Kong

ECONOMY AND TRADE
The economy is based on tourism and gambling, which have grown rapidly since 2001, and garment and textile manufacturing, which is in decline. Visitors totalled over 21 million in 2009, the majority coming from mainland China, where gambling is illegal. The service sector contributes about 97 per cent of GDP and industry 3 per cent. The principal products and exports are clothing, textiles, electronics, footwear and toys. The main trading partners are Hong Kong, China and the USA.
Annual average growth of GDP – 13.2 per cent (2009)
Inflation rate – 1.2 per cent (2009)
Imports – US$5,400m (2008)
Exports – US$2,000m (2008)

BALANCE OF PAYMENTS
Trade – US$3,564m deficit (2009)
Current Account – US$4,163m surplus (2004)

Trade with UK	*2008*	*2009*
Imports from UK	£21,554,890	£25,556,719
Exports to UK	£17,888,896	£18,486,074

COLOMBIA

República de Colombia – Republic of Colombia

Area – 1,138,914 sq. km
Capital – Bogotá; population, 8,261,650 (2009 est)
Major cities – Barranquilla, Cali, Cartagena, Medellín
Currency – Colombian peso of 100 centavos
Population – 45,644,023 rising at 1.38 per cent a year (2009 est)
Religion – Christian (Roman Catholic 80 per cent, other denominations 14 per cent) (est)
Language – Spanish (official)
Population density – 41 per sq. km (2008)
Urban population – 74 per cent (2007 est)
Median age (years) – 27.1 (2009 est)
National anthem – 'Himno Nacional de la República de Colombia' ['National Anthem of the Republic of Colombia']
National day – 20 July (Independence Day)
Life expectancy (years) – 72.81 (2009 est)
Mortality rate – 5.54 (2009 est)
Birth rate – 19.57 (2009 est)
Infant mortality rate – 18.9 (2009 est)
Death penalty – Abolished for all crimes (since 1910)
CPI score – 3.7 (2009)

CLIMATE AND TERRAIN

Colombia has a coastline on both the Caribbean Sea and the Pacific Ocean. The western, central and eastern ranges of the Andes run from south-west to north-east, separating the arid north-eastern peninsula and the tropical coastal regions in the north and west from the vast tablelands in the east. This region, having a temperate climate, is the most densely populated part of the country. Elevation extremes range from 5,775m (Pico Cristobal Colon) at the highest point to 0m (Pacific Ocean) at the lowest. The principal rivers are the Magdalena, which flows into the Caribbean; the Guaviare and Meta, tributaries of the Orinocco; and the Caquetá and Putumayo, which drain into the Amazon basin. The predominantly tropical climate is moderated by altitude in the interior.

HISTORY AND POLITICS

Spanish settlement of the region began in 1525, and Colombia was ruled as part of a vice-royalty until 1810, when independence was declared. In 1819, Simón Bolivar established the Republic of Gran Colombia, consisting of the territories now known as Colombia, Panama, Venezuela and Ecuador, after finally defeating the Spanish. In 1829–30 Venezuela and Ecuador withdrew, and in 1831 the remaining territories formed a separate state, which adopted the name of Colombia in 1866; Panama seceded in 1903.

Power alternated between the Conservative and Liberal parties from the mid 19th century. In 1949, a civil war broke out which lasted until 1957, when the Conservative and Liberal parties formed a coalition government known as the National Front. This arrangement continued until 1974 and was revived in 1978 in an attempt to maintain the rule of law in the face of violence by drugs cartels, a left-wing insurgency and counter-attacks by right-wing paramilitaries. Despite foreign assistance and increased military spending, drug trafficking continues to be widespread, although less of a threat to civil order than hitherto, but the government has been unable to suppress or reach a negotiated settlement with insurgents' leaders despite sporadic peace talks.

In legislative elections in March 2010, parties that supported President Uribe won the majority of seats in both chambers. The 2010 presidential election was won by former defence minister Juan Manuel Santos in the second round in June.

INSURGENCIES

Colombia has been dogged by violence since the 1960s, initially from insurgency by left-wing guerrilla groups, mainly the Revolutionary Armed Forces of Colombia (FARC) and the National Liberation Army (ELN), countered by right-wing paramilitaries affiliated with the United Self-Defence Forces of Colombia (AUC), which was suspected of having links with the security forces. In the 1980s, lawlessness increased with the rise of drug-producing and trafficking cartels. The guerrillas and paramilitaries became involved in drugs trafficking, kidnapping and other crime, and act to protect these sources of funding as much as to further their political aims.

Action against the insurgents and drug cartels since 2002 has extended state control so that the government now has a presence in every municipality. Talks between the government and the FARC and ELN have made little headway, but talks with the AUC from 2004 led to demobilisation of most units in 2006. The level of violence has dropped but drug-eradication programmes are aggressively resisted.

Neighbouring countries are affected by the overspill from the violence in Colombia, and cross-border incursions by Colombian forces in pursuit of the FARC, ELN or AUC have affected relations with both Ecuador and Venezuela in recent years. Venezuela also strongly opposes the USA's military presence in Colombia to counter drug-trafficking.

POLITICAL SYSTEM

Under the 1991 constitution, the executive president is directly elected for a four-year term; a 2005 amendment allows an incumbent president to stand for a second term. The bicameral congress comprises the House of Representatives, with 166 members directly elected for a four-year term, and the senate, with 102 members directly elected for a four-year term; two senate seats are reserved for representatives of indigenous people.

HEAD OF STATE

President, Juan Manuel Santos, *elected* 20 June 2010, *sworn in* 7 August 2010
Vice-President, Angelino Garzón

SELECTED GOVERNMENT MEMBERS *as at May 2010*

Defence, Gabriel Silva Luján
Finance, Oscar Ivan Zuluaga
Foreign Affairs, Jaime Bermúdez Merizalde
Interior, Justice, Fabio Valencia Cossio

EMBASSY OF COLOMBIA

3 Hans Crescent, London SW1X 0LN
T 020-7589 9177 E elondres@cancilleria.gov.co
W www.colombianembassy.co.uk
Ambassador Extraordinary and Plenipotentiary, HE Mauricio Rodriguez, *apptd* 2009

BRITISH EMBASSY

Carrera 9, No 76–49, Piso 8, Edificio ING Barings, Bogotá D.C.
T (+57) (1) 326 8300 E inquiries.bogota@fco.gov.uk
W http://ukincolombia.fco.gov.uk
Ambassador Extraordinary and Plenipotentiary, HE John Dew, *apptd* 2008

BRITISH COUNCIL

c/o British Embassy
T (+57) (1) 325 9090 W www.britishcouncil.org/colombia
Director, Robert Ness

DEFENCE

The army has 194 armoured personnel carriers. The navy has 4 submarines, 4 corvettes, and 86 patrol and coastal vessels at 9 bases. The air force has 90 combat aircraft and 26 armed helicopters.
Military expenditure – US$10,070m (2009)
Military personnel – 285,220: army 237,466, navy 34,620, air force 13,134; paramilitary 144,097

ECONOMY AND TRADE

The improving security situation, economic liberalisation and international investment aided economic growth from 2002 to 2008, although the economy contracted in 2009 owing to the global downturn. The government has encouraged diversification to reduce dependence on a limited range of commodities and markets, and this has led to the growth of new export-orientated industries, particularly textiles, clothing and footwear, and a broader range of export markets.

Services accounted for around 52.8 per cent of GDP, industry 38.2 per cent and agriculture 9.1 per cent in 2009. Coal, oil, natural gas and hydroelectricity resources are exploited, and Colombia is a net exporter of electricity and oil. Hydrocarbons account for about half of mining output, with iron ore, nickel, gold, emeralds, copper and other minerals accounting for the remainder. Major cash crops are coffee, bananas and cut flowers. Cattle are raised in large numbers, and forestry is also important.

The principal trading partners are the USA, Venezuela and China. Main exports are oil, coffee, coal, nickel, emeralds, garments, bananas and cut flowers. Imports include industrial and transport equipment, consumer goods, chemicals, paper products and fuels.

GNI – US$207,900m; US$4,620 per capita (2008)
Annual average growth of GDP – –0.1 per cent (2009 est)
Inflation rate – 3 per cent (2009 est)
Population below poverty line – 49.2 per cent (2005)
Unemployment – 12 per cent (2009 est)
Total external debt – US$47,330m (2009)
Imports – US$39,300m (2008)
Exports – US$38,300m (2008)

BALANCE OF PAYMENTS
Trade – US$426m surplus (2009)
Current Account – US$4,232m deficit (2009)

Trade with UK	*2008*	*2009*
Imports from UK	£156,285,579	£165,772,165
Exports to UK	£651,429,550	£527,676,582

COMMUNICATIONS

The terrain has always hampered internal transport, and historically travel was largely along the rivers, especially the Magdalena. This is still used for some bulk cargo but most long-distance internal travel is now by air. The growing road network (164,000km) is the main means of freight transport, superseding the 3,800km rail system as well as the 18,000km of waterways. There are 992 airports and airstrips, although only 116 have surfaced runways. The principal airports are at Bogotá, Barranquilla and Cali. The main seaports are Barranquilla, Cartagena and Santa Marta on the Caribbean Sea and Buenaventura on the Pacific coast. A modern telephone system covers the entire country, but falling mobile phone costs have seen fixed-line density decline to 15 per 100 people, while mobile phone density has risen to 90 per 100 people.

EDUCATION AND HEALTH

Elementary education is free of charge and compulsory for nine years. Most primary schools are run by the Roman Catholic Church and courses in Roman Catholicism are compulsory. There are some Protestant church schools (mainly in the capital). The government finances secondary and university level education.

Literacy rate – 92.7 per cent (2007 est)
Gross enrolment ratio (percentage of relevant age group) – primary 120 per cent; secondary 91 per cent; tertiary 35 per cent (2008 est)
Health expenditure (per capita) – US$284 (2007)
Hospital beds (per 1,000 people) – 1.0 (2003–8)

MEDIA

There are are both state-owned television and radio stations and private commercial networks. There are six main daily newspapers, but television remains the most popular medium. Colombia is one of the most dangerous countries in the world for journalists, who are often targeted by drug traffickers, guerrillas and paramilitary groups. More than 120 Colombian journalists were killed in the 1990s.

THE COMOROS

Udzima wa Komori/Jumhuriyat al Qamar al Muttahidah/ Union des Comores – Union of the Comoros

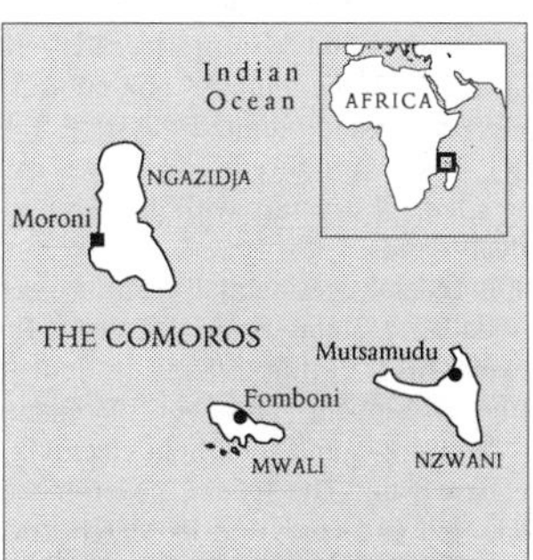

Area – 1,862 sq. km (excluding Mayotte). The Comoros includes the islands of Ngazidja (formerly Grande Comore), Nzwani (Anjouan), Mwali (Moheli) and certain islets in the Indian Ocean. Mayotte, the easternmost island of the archipelago, is a French dependency
Capital – Moroni, on Ngazidja; population, 48,629 (2009 est)
Major towns – Domoni, Fomboni, Mutsamudu
Currency – Comorian franc (KMF) of 100 centimes. The Franc CFA of 100 centimes is also used
Population – 752,438 rising at 2.77 per cent a year (2009 est)
Religion – Muslim (Sunni 99 per cent) (est). Islam is the state religion
Language – Comoran (Shikomoro, a blend of Swahili and Arabic), Arabic, French (all official)
Population density – 346 per sq. km (2008)
Urban population – 28 per cent (2007 est)
Median age (years) – 18.8 (2009 est)
National anthem – 'Udzima wa ya Masiwa' ['The Union of the Great Islands']
National day – 6 July (Independence Day)
Life expectancy (years) – 63.47 (2009 est)
Mortality rate – 7.57 (2009 est)
Birth rate – 35.23 (2009 est)
Infant mortality rate – 66.57 (2009 est)
Death penalty – Retained
CPI score – 2.3 (2009)
Literacy rate – 75.1 per cent (2007 est)

CLIMATE AND TERRAIN

Located in the Mozambique Channel between Africa and Madagascar, Njazidja, Nzwani and Mwali are mountainous volcanic islands in the Comoros archipelago. The highest point is Karthala (2,360m) on Njazidja, an active volcano that last erupted in 2005, and the lowest is 0m (Indian Ocean). The climate is tropical, with a hot, rainy season from November to April. The average temperature ranges from 25°C on the coasts to 22°C in the highlands. The islands are prone to cyclones during the rainy season.

HISTORY AND POLITICS

The islands were settled by a variety of peoples before becoming part of the trading empire of the Shirazis of Persia, who established sultanates in the 15th to 16th centuries. In 1886, France established protectorates over the islands, making them a colony in 1912. They achieved internal self-government in 1961. In a 1974 referendum, the residents of three of the main islands voted in favour of independence, which was declared on 6 July 1975; Mayotte voted to remain part of France. The republic experienced about 18 coups or attempted coups between 1975 and 1999, some supported by European mercenaries. Nzwani and Mwani seceded in 1997 but, after a coup in 1999, the military took control of all the islands' governments and reunited the state. Talks on the secessionist crisis produced a new constitution, introducing a federal structure with greater autonomy for the individual islands.

The 2006 federal presidential election was won by Ahmed Abdallah Sambi from Nzwani. Presidential elections were held in the islands in June 2007; in Nzwani, the incumbent president, Mohamed Bacar, refused to stand down and then held elections which he claimed to have won. The federal government declared the elections null and void, and in March 2008 federal troops, supported by African Union forces, ousted Bacar. The Nzwani presidential election in June 2008 was won by Moussa Toybou. Elections to the union parliament and the islands' legislatures were held in December 2009; in the union elections, supporters of President Sambi won 20 of the 24 seats.

POLITICAL SYSTEM

The 2002 constitution created a federal structure. Under this, the union president is elected from each of the three islands in turn and serves a four-year term. The executive president appoints the union ministers. The unicameral Assembly of the Union has 33 members; three are appointed by each of the three island parliaments and 24 are directly elected for a five-year term.

Constitutional amendments put to a referendum in May 2009 proposed to harmonise presidential and legislative terms, end the rotation of the presidency among the islands, downgrade the islands' presidents to governors and extend President Sambi's term to 2011; the result is disputed.

Each island has its own president and legislative assembly, and each island president may appoint eight ministers to form a government. The islands' governments deal with local issues; foreign affairs, finance, defence, judicial and religious matters remain the responsibility of the union government. There are still areas of dispute, principally over security, budget control and customs revenue.

HEAD OF STATE

President of the Union, Ahmed Abdallah Sambi, *elected* 14 May 2006, *sworn in* 25 May 2006

SELECTED GOVERNMENT MEMBERS *as at May 2010*

Vice-Presidents, Idi Nadhoim, Ikililou Dhoinine
Foreign Relations and Cooperation, Francophone and Arab Affairs, Fahami Said Ibrahim
Finance, Budget and Investment, Mohamed Bacar Dossar
Defence, Interior, Ibrahim Mhoumadi Sidi
Economy, Oubeid Mze Chei

HONORARY CONSULATE

Flat 6, 24–26 Avenue Road, London, NW8 6BU
T 020 7491 2098 E comorosuk@googlemail.com
Honorary Consul, Khaleb Chehabi

BRITISH AMBASSADOR

HE Nick Leake, *apptd* 2010, resident at Port Louis, Mauritius

ECONOMY AND TRADE

The Comoros is very poor and heavily dependent on foreign aid and technical assistance. It has few natural resources, an uneducated workforce and poor transport infrastructure. Continuing political tensions hinder government attempts to reform and develop the economy and social welfare provision. Unemployment is high and over 20 per cent of the workforce is employed abroad; remittances are a valuable contribution to the economy. Agriculture, fishing and forestry account for about 40 per cent of GDP and employ 80 per cent of the population; service industries account for 56 per cent and the manufacturing industry 4 per cent. The principal exports are vanilla, perfume essence, copra and cloves; coconuts, bananas and cassava are also cultivated. The main industries are fishing, tourism and perfume distillation.
GNI – US$483m; US$750 per capita (2008)
Annual average growth of GDP – 1 per cent (2009 est)
Inflation rate – 3 per cent (2007 est)

BALANCE OF PAYMENTS

Trade – US$181m deficit (2009)
Current Account – US$62m deficit (2008)

Trade with UK	*2008*	*2009*
Imports from UK	£80,077	£177,260
Exports to UK	£88,433	£28,120

MEDIA

Radio is the primary source of information. National radio and television broadcasting is provided by state-run networks, and some island governments run radio and television stations. There are also privately owned stations, and some areas receive programmes broadcast in Mayotte. Most newspapers are published weekly and have small circulations owing to a weak advertising market and poor distribution. They practise self-censorship to avoid harsh government sanctions over material deemed offensive.

DEMOCRATIC REPUBLIC OF THE CONGO

République Démocratique du Congo – Democratic Republic of the Congo

Area – 2,344,858 sq. km
Capital – Kinshasa; population, 8,401,390 (2009 est)
Major cities – Boma, Kananga, Kisangani, Kolwezi, Likasi, Lubumbashi, Mbuji-Mayi
Currency – Congolese franc of 100 centimes
Population – 68,692,542 rising at 3.21 per cent a year (2009 est). The population is composed of over 200 ethnic groups, including Bantu, Hamitic, Nilotic, Sudanese and Pygmoid; the four largest tribes – Mongo, Luba, Kongo (all Bantu) and Mangbtu-Azande (Hamitic) – make up around 45 per cent of the population
Religion – Christian (Roman Catholic 50 per cent, Protestant 20 per cent, Kimbanguist 9 per cent), Muslim 9 per cent (est)
Language – French (official), Lingala, Kingwana (a Swahili dialect), Kikongo, Tshiluba
Population density – 28 per sq. km (2008)
Urban population – 33 per cent (2007 est)
Median age (years) – 16.4 (2009 est)
National anthem – 'Debout Congolais' ['Stand Up, Congolese']
National day – 30 June (Independence Day)
Life expectancy (years) – 54.36 (2009 est)
Mortality rate – 11.63 (2009 est)
Birth rate – 42.63 (2009 est)
Infant mortality rate – 81.21 (2009 est)
HIV/AIDS adult prevalence – 2.9 per cent (2005 est)
Death penalty – Retained
CPI score – 1.9 (2009)
Literacy rate – 67.2 per cent (2007 est)
Gross enrolment ratio (percentage of relevant age group) – primary 90 per cent; secondary 35 per cent; tertiary 5 per cent (2008 est)
Health expenditure (per capita) – US$9 (2007)
Hospital beds (per 1,000 people) – 0.8 (2003–8)

CLIMATE AND TERRAIN

The Democratic Republic of the Congo is Africa's third largest country. The state lies on the equator, most of it in the basin of the river Congo and its principal tributaries, the Lualaba and the Kasai. A chain of mountains and lakes (Albert, Edward, Kivu and Tanganyika) run along the eastern border. Elevation extremes range from 5,110m (Mt Ngaliema, also known as Mt Stanley) at the highest point to 0m (Atlantic Ocean) at the lowest. The climate is tropical, though cooler in the eastern and southern highlands. There are different climatic cycles either side of the equator, which passes through the north of the country, with a wet season in the north from April to November and in the south from October to May.

HISTORY AND POLITICS

The state of the Congo, founded in 1885 by King Leopold II of Belgium, became a Belgian colony in 1908 and gained its independence in 1960. Mobutu Sésé Seko came to power in a military coup in 1965 and was elected president in 1970. The *Mouvement Populaire de la Révolution* (MPR) was the sole legal political party until the late 1980s, when the regime began moves towards a multiparty system, but progress was hindered by army revolts and political disagreements.

In 1996 ethnic conflict in the country's east, largely the aftermath of the Rwandan genocide in 1994, sparked a civil war in which the army found itself outgunned by anti-Mobutu rebels, who were backed by the Rwandan and Ugandan governments. Under the leadership of Laurent Kabila, the Alliance of Democratic Forces for the Liberation of Congo-Zaire (AFDL) captured Kinshasa in May 1997 and President Mobutu fled. The country, which had been known as Zaire since 1971, was renamed the Democratic Republic of the Congo.

In 1998 a rebellion against Kabila's government began in the east, initiating years of fighting between government forces and a shifting alliance of rebel groups, with neighbouring countries lending support to either the government (Angola, Chad, Kenya, Namibia, Zimbabwe) or the rebels (Rwanda, Uganda). All parties to the conflict plundered the country's rich natural resources and left an estimated 3.5 million dead from violence, famine and disease. A number of ceasefires were negotiated and broken, but by December 2000 the government and rebel groups had signed a disengagement agreement, and withdrew their troops 15km from their frontline positions by the end of March 2001. UN-sponsored peace talks in 2002 concluded in a power-sharing agreement between the government and the main rebel groups.

In 2003 a transitional government was established under the incumbent president, Maj.-Gen. Joseph Kabila (successor to his father Laurent, who was assassinated in 2001) and an interim legislature was inaugurated. Despite a number of coup attempts and occasional clashes with errant rebels, a fragile peace has held in much of the country, apart from the eastern provinces. The insurgency in the east halted for several months in 2008 after rebels signed a peace agreement with the government, but fighting broke out again. Violence against the civilian population is also perpetrated by Rwandan and Ugandan insurgents, and Congolese troops joined with those of neighbouring countries and UN forces in joint operations against the rebels in 2008 and 2009. A UN peacekeeping operation, established in 1999, had 20,819 uniformed personnel in the country in April 2010; the mission's mandate was due to expire mid-2010.

A new constitution came into effect in 2006 and presidential and legislative elections were held on 30 July 2006. The presidential election was won in the second round in October 2006 by Joseph Kabila. His People's Party for Reconstruction and Development (PPRD) won the largest number of seats in both legislative chambers. The PPRD became the major partner in the coalition government formed in February 2007. Fresh legislative elections are due in July 2011.

POLITICAL SYSTEM

Under the 2006 constitution, the executive president is directly elected for a five-year term, renewable only once. The bicameral *Parlement* consists of the National Assembly, which has 500 members directly elected for a five-year term, and the senate, which has 108 members elected by provincial assemblies to serve a five-year term, plus former elected presidents, who are senators for life.

HEAD OF STATE

President, Maj.-Gen. Joseph Kabila, *sworn in* 26 January 2001, *sworn in as president of the transitional government* 7 April 2003, *elected* 29 October 2006
Vice-President, Abdoulaye Yerodia Ndombasi

SELECTED GOVERNMENT MEMBERS *as at May 2010*

Prime Minister, Adolphe Muzito
Deputy Prime Ministers, Mobuto Nzanga, Adolphe N'sefu *(Interior)*
Finance, Matata Ponyo Mapon
Foreign Affairs and International Cooperation, Alexis Thambwe Mwamba

EMBASSY OF THE DEMOCRATIC REPUBLIC OF THE CONGO
281 Gray's Inn Road, London WC1X 8QF
T 020-7278 9825
Ambassador Extraordinary and Plenipotentiary, HE Barnabé Kikaya Bin Karubi, *apptd* 2009

BRITISH EMBASSY
83 Avenue du Roi Baudouin, Gombe, Kinshasa
T (+243) 81 715 0761 E ambrit@ic.cd
W http://ukindrc.fco.gov.uk
Ambassador Extraordinary and Plenipotentiary, HE Neil Wigan, *apptd* 2010

DEFENCE

The army has 49 main battle tanks, 20 armoured infantry fighting vehicles and 138 armoured personnel carriers. The navy has 3 patrol and coastal combatant vessels. The air force has 5 combat capable aircraft and 4 armed helicopters.
Military budget – US$168m (2008)
Military personnel – 139,251 (est): Central Staffs: 14,000 (est), army 110,000 (est), navy 6,703, air force 2,548, Republican Guard 6,000 (est)

ECONOMY AND TRADE

The country has immense natural resources, including copper, diamonds, gold, silver, uranium, other minerals, coal, oil, timber and hydroelectric power, and so great potential wealth. However a decade of civil war left the country with a huge external debt, little infrastructure, widespread corruption and an environment that discourages foreign investment. Improved stability from 2003 allowed some economic growth, but the economy contracted in 2008–9 as the global downturn caused a sharp drop in demand for minerals. The government has obtained financing from international organisations and donors and begun reforms. It was also granted US$10bn (£5bn) of debt relief by the IMF in 2003.

About half of GDP is contributed by agriculture, 35 per cent by the services sector and 11 per cent by industry. Apart from mining and mineral processing, the main industrial activities are the production of textiles, footwear, cigarettes, processed food, beverages and cement, and ship repair. Oil deposits are exploited off the Congo estuary, and hydroelectric schemes on the river Congo supply power to the major cities.

The main trading partners are China, South Africa, Belgium and Zambia. Principal exports are diamonds, gold, copper, cobalt, wood products, crude oil and coffee. The main imports are foodstuffs, mining and other machinery, transport equipment and fuels.
GNI – US$9,800m; US$150 per capita (2008)
Annual average growth of GDP – 3 per cent (2009 est)
Inflation rate – 16.7 per cent (2007 est)
Total external debt – US$10,000m (2007 est)

BALANCE OF PAYMENTS
Trade – US$442m deficit (2009)
Current Account – US$1,839m deficit (2008)

Trade with UK	*2008*	*2009*
Imports from UK	£14,119,235	£12,925,732
Exports to UK	£2,659,113	£17,885,141

COMMUNICATIONS

The transport infrastructure is undeveloped owing to the terrain, poverty and warfare. The river Congo and its main tributaries provide 15,000km of waterways, and the 4,000km rail system links the interior to the rivers and to the great lakes in the east. The system also connects with neighbouring states, through which east and south African ports can be accessed. There are approximately 153,000km of roads, of which 3,000km are surfaced. The country has over 190 airports and airfields, the principal airports being at Kinshasa, Kananga, Goma, Gemena and Mbandaka. The principal seaports are at Matadi and Boma. Following a 2009 trade agreement, China will build roads and railways in the country in return for mineral concessions.

The telecommunications infrastructure is poor, with limited coverage in and between urban areas. Fixed-line connections are fewer than one per 1,000, but mobile phone distribution is growing rapidly, achieving a density of 15 per 100 people by 2008.

MEDIA

The state-controlled Radio-Télévision Nationale Congolaise (RTNC) and La Voix du Congo have the greatest influence and broadcast reach. There are dozens of other private and commercial television stations and over 100 radio stations; the UN- and Swiss-sponsored Radio Okapi has become one of the most popular. Around 15 newspapers are published regularly in Kinshasa.

REPUBLIC OF THE CONGO

République du Congo – Republic of the Congo

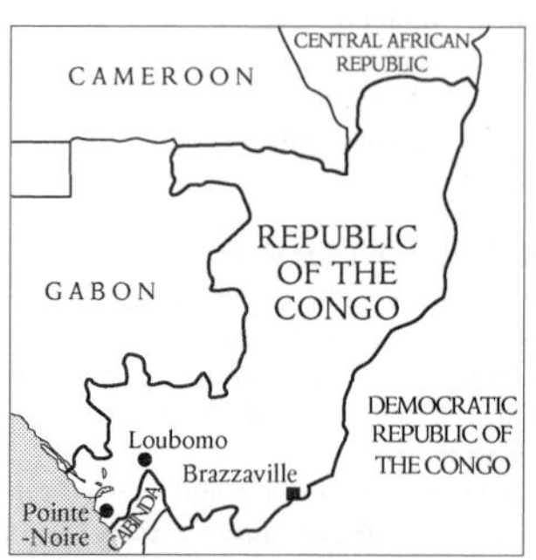

Area – 342,000 sq. km
Capital – Brazzaville; population, 1,292,390 (2009 est)
Major cities – Loubomo, Pointe-Noire
Currency – Franc CFA of 100 centimes
Population – 4,012,809 rising at 2.75 per cent a year (2009 est); Kongo (48 per cent), Sangha (20 per cent), Teke (17 per cent) and M'Bochi (12 per cent) (est) are the largest of the 15 main Bantu groups
Religion – Christian 50 per cent (Roman Catholic 45 per cent), Muslim 2 per cent (est). Other believers practise indigenous religious beliefs, or belong to messianic groups
Language – French (official), Lingala, Monokutuba, Kikongo
Population density – 11 per sq. km (2008)
Urban population – 61 per cent (2007 est)
Median age (years) – 16.8 (2009 est)
National anthem – 'La Congolaise' ['The Congolese']
National day – 15 August (Independence Day)
Life expectancy (years) – 54.15 (2009 est)
Mortality rate – 12.01 (2009 est)
Birth rate – 41.37 (2009 est)

Infant mortality rate – 79.78 (2009 est)
HIV/AIDS adult prevalence – 3.3 per cent (2007 est)
Death penalty – Retained (not used since 1982)
CPI score – 1.9 (2009)

CLIMATE AND TERRAIN

The republic, which lies on the equator, is covered by grassland, mangrove and dense rainforest. The land rises from the narrow Atlantic coastal plain to a central plateau; in the north and east it falls to the northern part of the basin of the river Congo, which forms part of the border with the Democratic Republic of the Congo, and to the valleys of the Sangha and Alima rivers in the north. Elevation extremes range from 903m (Mt Berongou) at the highest point to 0m at the lowest (Atlantic Ocean). The climate is tropical. The annual daily temperature in Brazzaville is between 28°C and 33°C and humidity is high. Outside of the main dry season between June and September, the country is prone to flooding.

HISTORY AND POLITICS

The first European visitors to the area were the Portuguese, who established slave trading in the 16th century. The French established a colonial presence in the area in the 1880s and, as Middle Congo, it was part of French Equatorial Africa from 1910. It became independent as the Republic of the Congo on 17 August 1960.

One-party socialism was introduced in 1964; the Congolese Labour Party (PCT) was set up shortly after a military coup in 1968, and continued to rule until 1990, when Marxism was renounced and, after popular pressure, the PCT abandoned its monopoly of power. Elections in 1993 left the PCT a minority party, and the power shift destabilised the country, with factional fighting after the 1993 election, a civil war between 1997 and 1999 following Denis Sassou-Nguesso's deposition of the elected president, and a renewed insurgency by opponents of the PCT over the manipulation of the 2002 elections. A peace accord ended the insurgency in 2003 but the peace remains fragile and remnants of the rebel militias are still active in the south of the country, where many have turned to banditry.

In the 2002 presidential election, Sassou-Nguesso was elected with nearly 90 per cent of the vote, although his victory was criticised after his candidature was unopposed owing to the barring of his main rivals. In the 2007 legislative election, which was boycotted by about 40 opposition parties, the PCT and its allies retained their large majority. The legitimacy of Sassou-Nguesso's overwhelming re-election victory in the presidential election in July 2009 was also disputed by opponents.

POLITICAL SYSTEM

Under the 2002 constitution, parties organised on regional, ethnic or religious lines are banned. The executive president is directly elected for a once-renewable seven-year term, and appoints the cabinet. The bicameral *Parlement* comprises the National Assembly, with 137 members directly elected for a five-year term, and the senate, which has 66 members indirectly elected for a six-term term, half of the members retiring every three years.

HEAD OF STATE

President, Denis Sassou-Nguesso, *took power* October 1997, *elected* 10 March 2002, re-elected 2009

SELECTED GOVERNMENT MEMBERS *as at May 2010*

Prime Minister, Isidore Mvouba
Economy, Pierre Moussa
Finance, Gilbert Ondongo
Foreign Affairs, Basil Ikouebe
Defence, Charles Zacharie Bowao

EMBASSY OF THE REPUBLIC OF THE CONGO

37 bis rue Paul Valéry, 75116 Paris, France
T (+33) (1) 4500 6057
Ambassador Extraordinary and Plenipotentiary, HE Henri Lopes, *apptd* 1999

BRITISH AMBASSADOR

HE Neil Wigan, *apptd* 2010, resident at Kinshasa, DR of Congo

DEFENCE

The army has 40 main battle tanks and 68 armoured personnel carriers. The navy has 3 patrol and coastal combatant vessels at a base at Pointe-Noire. The air force has 2 armed helicopters.
Military budget – US$112m (2008 est)
Military personnel – 10,000: army 8,000, navy 800, air force 1,200; paramilitary 2,000

ECONOMY AND TRADE

A decade of civil conflict has left the country with a high external debt, a devastated infrastructure and widespread poverty. Since 2003 the government has made efforts to address these problems and in 2006 qualified for debt relief under the IMF–World Bank heavily indebted poor countries initiative; most of Congo's debt was cancelled in 2007, and a further $1.9bn (£1.3bn) in debt relief was approved by the IMF and World Bank in January 2010.

Oil production is the backbone of the economy and the recent recovery in oil prices has boosted GDP. Mining, particularly of diamonds, forestry, brewing, agricultural processing and cement production are the other main industries. Agriculture, which is mostly at subsistence level, accounts for 5.6 per cent of GDP, industry for 57.1 per cent and services for 37.3 per cent.

The main markets are China, the USA and France. Principal exports are oil, timber, plywood, sugar, cocoa, coffee and diamonds. Imports are mainly capital equipment, construction materials and foodstuffs.
GNI – US$6,500m; US$1,790 per capita (2008)
Annual average growth of GDP – 7.5 per cent (2009 est)
Inflation rate – 4 per cent (2009 est)
Imports – US$2,900m (2008)
Exports – US$9,100m (2008)

BALANCE OF PAYMENTS

Trade – US$4,962m surplus (2009)
Current Account – US$148m deficit (2008)

Trade with UK	*2008*	*2009*
Imports from UK	£52,332,138	£76,447,225
Exports to UK	£9,709,170	£7,774,670

COMMUNICATIONS

Pointe-Noire is the main seaport and also the centre of the offshore oil industry. It is linked to Brazzaville by rail and road. Brazzaville is the main river port, lying on the river Congo which, with the river Oubangui, provides 1,120km of commercially navigable waterways. There are 795km of railways and 17,289km of roads, 864km of which are surfaced. Six of the 25 airports and airfields have surfaced runways. The fixed-line telephone network inadequate and unreliable. Mobile phone distribution has grown rapidly, and density in 2008 was 50 per 100 people.

EDUCATION AND HEALTH

Literacy rate – 81.1 per cent (2007 est)
Gross enrolment ratio (percentage of relevant age group) – primary 114 per cent (2008 est)
Health expenditure (per capita) – US$52 (2007)
Hospital beds (per 1,000 people) – 1.6 (2003–8)
HIV/AIDS adult prevalence – 3.3 per cent (2007 est)

MEDIA

Brazzaville is the centre of the country's print media, with five privately owned newspapers regularly published there. TV Congo is the only television station and is controlled by the state-run Radiodiffusion Télévision Congolaise. Radio Congo is also state-controlled. Prison sentences for libel and insult were abolished in 2001, but incitement to violence or racism remains an offence.

COSTA RICA

República de Costa Rica – Republic of Costa Rica

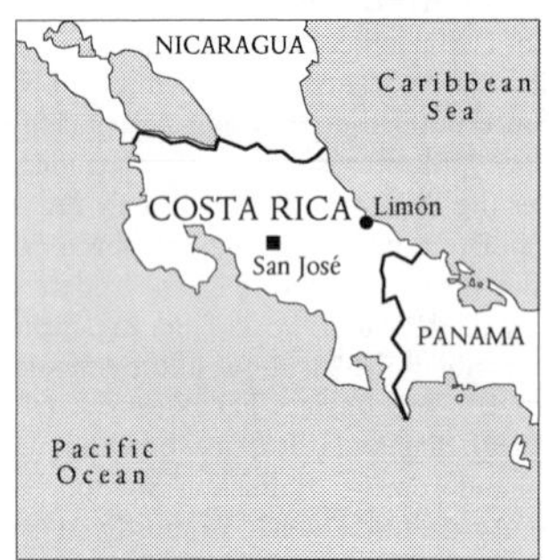

Area – 51,100 sq. km
Capital – San José; population, 1,415,510 (2009 est)
Major towns – Alajuela, Liberia, Limón, Paraíso, San Francisco
Currency – Costa Rican colón of 100 céntimos
Population – 4,253,877 rising at 1.36 per cent a year (2009 est)
Religion – Christian (Roman Catholic 75 per cent, Evangelical Protestant 15 per cent) (est)
Language – Spanish (official), English
Population density – 89 per sq. km (2008)
Urban population – 63 per cent (2007 est)
Median age (years) – 27.5 (2009 est)
National anthem – 'Noble Patria, Tu Hermosa Bandera' ['Noble Fatherland, Your Beautiful Flag']
National day – 15 September (Independence Day)
Life expectancy (years) – 77.58 (2009 est)
Mortality rate – 4.34 (2009 est)
Birth rate – 17.43 (2009 est)
Infant mortality rate – 8.77 (2009 est)
Death penalty – Abolished for all crimes (since 1877)
CPI score – 5.3 (2009)
Literacy rate – 95.9 per cent (2007 est)
Gross enrolment ratio (percentage of relevant age group) – primary 110 per cent; secondary 89 per cent (2008 est)
Health expenditure (per capita) – US$488 (2007)
Hospital beds (per 1,000 people) – 1.3 (2003–8)

CLIMATE AND TERRAIN

The Cordillera de Guanacaste (north-west), Cordillera de Talamanca and Cordillera Central (south-east) form a chain of volcanic mountain ranges that traverse the country from north to south. A central valley lies between the ranges, and the land slopes to plains on the Pacific and Caribbean coasts. Elevation extremes range from 3,810m (Chirripó Grande) to 0m (Pacific Ocean) at the lowest. The climate is tropical, with an average annual temperature of 26°C, and a wet season from May to November. The area is subject to occasional earthquakes, hurricanes, flooding and landslides.

HISTORY AND POLITICS

Visited by Columbus in 1502, Costa Rica was colonised by the Spanish from the 1560s and remained under Spanish rule until Central America gained its independence in 1821. Costa Rica was part of a Central American federation of former Spanish provinces from 1823 until its secession in 1838. Political unrest in the mid-20th century led to a brief civil war in 1948, after which the army was abolished and replaced with a national guard. Since then power has alternated between the two main political parties, the Social Christian Unity Party (PUSC) and the National Liberation Party (PLN).

In the 2010 legislative elections, the PLN remained the largest party with 23 seats but failed to win an outright majority. The simultaneous presidential election was won by the PLN candidate Laura Chinchilla, who became the country's first female president.

POLITICAL SYSTEM

Under the 1949 constitution, the executive president is directly elected for a four-year term. The unicameral legislative assembly has 57 members directly elected for a four-year term.

HEAD OF STATE

President, Laura Chinchilla, *elected* 7 February 2010, *sworn in* 8 May 2010
First Vice-President, Alfio Piva
Second Vice-President, Luis Liberman

SELECTED GOVERNMENT MEMBERS *as at May 2010*

Finance, Fernando Herrero
Foreign Affairs, René Castro
Economy, Mayi Antillón

EMBASSY OF COSTA RICA

14 Lancaster Gate, London W2 3LH
T 020-7706 8844 E costarica@btconnect.com
Ambassador Extraordinary and Plenipotentiary, HE Pilar Saborio de Rocafort, *apptd* 2007

BRITISH EMBASSY

Apartado 815–1007, Edificio Centro Colón (11th Floor), San José 1007
T (+506) 2258 2025 E britemb@racsa.co.cr
W http://ukincostarica.fco.gov.uk
Ambassador Extraordinary and Plenipotentiary, HE Tom Kennedy, LVO, *apptd* 2006

DEFENCE

Costa Rica maintains a national guard of 9,800 paramilitaries. The coastguard has 20 patrol and coastal vessels at 6 bases.
Security Budget – US$180m (2009)

Military personnel – 9,800: Civil Guard 4,500, Border Police 2,500, Coast Guard Unit 400, Air Surveillance Unit 400, Rural Guard 2,000

ECONOMY AND TRADE

Sixty years of political stability allowed economic growth, the creation of a social welfare system and a reduction in poverty; less than 20 per cent of the population is below the poverty line. However, the economy contracted in 2008 owing to the global downturn; the impact of this on government spending was tempered by reductions in the internal and external debt since 2006.

Tourism is the largest single industry, and with one-third of the country now national parkland or nature reserve, eco-tourism is on the increase. The manufacturing industry accounts for around 25.5 per cent of GDP, the principal products being microprocessors, foodstuffs, medical equipment, textiles, clothing, construction materials, fertiliser and plastic goods. The agricultural sector contributes 6.5 per cent of GDP; the principal products are tropical fruit, coffee, ornamental plants, sugar, rice, vegetables, meat and timber.

The main trading partners are the USA, China, the Netherlands and Mexico. The chief exports are tropical fruit, coffee, plants, sugar, seafood, electrical components and medical equipment. The chief imports are raw materials, consumer goods, capital equipment, oil and construction materials.

GNI – US$27,400m; US$6,060 per capita (2008)
Annual average growth of GDP – –2.5 per cent (2009 est)
Inflation rate – 8.3 per cent (2009 est)
Population below poverty line – 16 per cent (2006 est)
Unemployment – 6.4 per cent (2009 est)
Total external debt – US$8,057m (2009)
Imports – US$15,400m (2008)
Exports – US$9,600m (2008)

BALANCE OF PAYMENTS
Trade – US$2,587m deficit (2009)
Current Account – US$2,754m deficit (2008)

Trade with UK	*2008*	*2009*
Imports from UK	£47,671,817	£24,779,401
Exports to UK	£458,801,820	£250,523,715

COMMUNICATIONS

The chief seaports are Limón on the Atlantic coast, through which the majority of exported coffee passes, and Puntarenas on the Pacific coast. There are 151 airports and airfields, 38 of which have surfaced runways; the principal ones are at San José and Limón. The national air carrier is LACSA. There are 278km of railways, none of which is in use, and 35,330km of roads, 8,621km of which are surfaced. The telephone system is modern and efficient, although mobile phone coverage is restricted.

CÔTE D'IVOIRE

République de Côte d'Ivoire – Republic of Côte d'Ivoire

Area – 322,463 sq. km
Capital – Yamoussoukro (since 1983); population, 808,093 (2009 est); slow progress in transferring functions means that the former capital, Abidjan, remains the seat of government at present
Major cities – Abidjan, Bouaké, Daloa, Korhogo
Currency – Franc CFA of 100 centimes
Population – 20,617,068 rising at 2.13 per cent a year (2009 est); over 60 ethnic groups, including the Akan (42.1 per cent), Voltaiques or Gur (17.6 per cent), Northern Mandes (16.5 per cent), Krous (11 per cent), Southern Mandes (10 per cent) (est)
Religion – Christian 35 per cent, Muslim 35 per cent, indigenous religions 25 per cent (est). Many Christians and Muslims incorporate indigenous beliefs into their worship
Language – French (official), around 60 African languages of which Dioula is the most widely spoken
Population density – 65 per sq. km (2008)
Urban population – 48 per cent (2007 est)
Median age (years) – 19.2 (2009 est)
National anthem – 'L'Abidjanaise' ['Song of Abidjan']
National day – 7 August (Independence Day)
Life expectancy (years) – 55.45 (2009 est)
Mortality rate – 10.78 (2009 est)
Birth rate – 32.11 (2009 est)
Infant mortality rate – 68.06 (2009 est)
HIV/AIDS adult prevalence – 3.7 per cent (2007 est)
Death penalty – Abolished for all crimes (since 2000)
CPI score – 2.1 (2009)
Literacy rate – 48.7 per cent (2007 est)
Gross enrolment ratio (percentage of relevant age group) – primary 74 per cent; tertiary 8 per cent (2008 est)
Health expenditure (per capita) – US$41 (2007)
Hospital beds (per 1,000 people) – 0.4 (2003–8)

CLIMATE AND TERRAIN

The land rises from a coastal plain to a large interior plateau with mountains in the north and west. Coastal lagoons give way to central tropical rainforest and savannah in the north; deforestation means that the area of savannah is increasing. The country is dissected by the Sassandra, Bandama and Komoé rivers, the first two forming large central lakes. Elevation extremes range from 1,752m (Mt Nimba) at the highest point to 0m (Gulf of Guinea) at the lowest. The climate is tropical in the south and semi-arid in the north. The south has two rainy seasons (May to July, October to November) and the north one (June to September). Average temperatures range from 24°C in August to 27°C in March.

HISTORY AND POLITICS

The first European visitors were Portuguese navigators in the 1460s, and Europeans established the ivory trade and some slave trading in the 16th century. The area came under French influence from 1842, and Côte d'Ivoire became a protectorate in 1889 and a colony in 1893, although it was not entirely pacified until 1912. It achieved self-government in 1958, and became independent on 7 August 1960 as a one-party state with Felix Houphouët-Boigny as president. A multiparty system was introduced in 1990.

The post-independence period of stability ended after President Houphouët-Boigny's death in 1993. The adoption of xenophobia as a political tool in the late 1990s opened up religious and ethnic divisions, particularly between the Muslim north and the Christian south and west of the country. These emerged in factional violence following the 2000 presidential election, won by Laurent Gbagbo of the Ivorian Popular Front. Reconciliation moves were progressing when a mutiny in 2002 developed into a rebellion that plunged the country into civil war.

The civil war ended in 2003 with a ceasefire that left the country divided between the government-controlled south and the rebel-held north, with international peacekeeping troops deployed in 2003 to maintain a buffer zone between the two. Despite the ceasefire, clashes continued, drawing in UN peacekeepers in late 2004. The government of national unity formed in 2003 collapsed in 2004, but further talks in 2006–7 resulted in a new power-sharing agreement in March 2007, with rebel leader Guillaume Soro becoming prime minister of the transitional government. Although the country was officially reunited in April 2007, difficulties in preparing electoral registers have delayed the presidential and legislative elections originally due in 2005; elections were expected in 2010.

POLITICAL SYSTEM

Under the 2000 constitution, the executive president is directly elected for a five-year term, renewable only once. The president appoints the prime minister and the other ministers, who are nominated by the prime minister; under the current power-sharing agreement, the president and prime minister share authority to appoint ministers. The unicameral National Assembly has 225 members, directly elected for a five-year term.

HEAD OF STATE

President, Laurent Gbagbo, *elected* 22 October 2000, *sworn in* 26 October 2000, *term extended* November 2006

SELECTED GOVERNMENT MEMBERS *as at May 2010*

Prime Minister, Guillaume Soro
Defence, Michel Amani N'guessan
Interior, Desire Tagro Assegnini
Foreign Affairs, Jean-Marie Kacou Gervais
Finance and Economy, Charles Koffi Diby

EMBASSY OF THE REPUBLIC OF CÔTE D'IVOIRE

2 Upper Belgrave Street, London SW1X 8BJ
T 020-7235 6991 E info@ambaci-uk.org
W www.ambaci-uk.org
Ambassador Extraordinary and Plenipotentiary, HE Philippe Djangoné-Bi, *apptd* 2007

BRITISH HIGH COMMISSIONER

HE Dr Nicholas Westcott, CMG, *apptd* 2008, resident at Accra, Ghana

DEFENCE

The army has 10 main battle tanks, 10 armoured infantry fighting vehicles and 41 armoured personnel carriers. The navy has 3 patrol and coastal combatant vessels. Little of the air force is combat capable; it may have 1 armed helicopter.

Military budget – US$360m (2009 est)
Military personnel – 17,050: army 6,500, navy 900, air force 700, Presidential Guard 1,350, Gendarmerie 7,600; paramilitary 1,500

ECONOMY AND TRADE

The country was one of the most prosperous in the region, attracting large numbers of migrant workers from neighbouring countries until the political turbulence of the late 1990s caused many to return home. The civil war particularly damaged the economy in the north (the cotton-growing area), but recovery is beginning. Diversification away from agriculture, which makes the economy vulnerable to fluctuations in world prices of its key exports, has been hampered by the civil war and its aftermath. However, since 2006, revenue from oil, gas and refined products has outstripped earnings from cocoa, and offshore exploration for other deposits continues.

Agriculture accounts for 28 per cent of GDP, industry for 21.2 per cent and services for 50.8 per cent. Agriculture employs around 68 per cent of the workforce, producing cocoa (of which Côte d'Ivoire is the world's largest producer and exporter), coffee, cotton, bananas, pineapples and palm oil for export. The principal industries are food processing, forestry, oil refining, vehicle assembly, textiles, fishing and the production of oil, natural gas and hydroelectric power; the country is a net exporter of electricity. The main trading partners are Nigeria, France, other EU and west African states, and the USA.

GNI – US$20,300; US$980 per capita (2008)
Annual average growth of GDP – 3.2 per cent (2009 est)
Inflation rate – 2 per cent (2009 est)
Population below poverty line – 42 per cent (2006 est)
Total external debt – US$12,080m (2009 est)
Imports – US$7,200m (2008)
Exports – US$10,100m (2008)

BALANCE OF PAYMENTS

Trade – US$2,680m surplus (2009)
Current Account – US$135m deficit (2007)

Trade	*2008*	*2009*
Imports from UK	£68,045,470	£55,486,550
Exports to UK	£93,677,747	£168,874,087

COMMUNICATIONS

Côte d'Ivoire has 660km of railways and 80,000km of roads, 6,500km of which are surfaced. There are 980km of navigable rivers, canals and lagoons. The main seaports are Abidjan and San Pedro. There are 28 airports and airfields, the principal international airport being at Abidjan. The telephone system is well developed, and fixed-line density has quadrupled since the late 1990s. Mobile phone distribution has risen rapidly, reaching 55 per 100 people in 2008.

MEDIA

The state broadcaster, Radiodiffusion Télévision Ivoirienne (RTI), operates two national radio stations and two television channels; all were used as propaganda tools during the civil war. There are no private terrestrial television stations but subscription services are available.

Radio is the most popular medium for news, provided by dozens of non-commercial community radio stations and a UN radio station, Onuci FM, set up in 2004 and now nationally available.

There are two government-owned and around 20 privately owned daily newspapers; several opposition publications have been closed by the government.

CROATIA

Republika Hrvatska – Republic of Croatia

Area – 56,594 sq. km
Capital – Zagreb; population, 685,128 (2009 est)
Major cities – Dubrovnik, Osijek, Rijeka (Fiume), Split
Currency – Kuna of 100 lipa
Population – 4,489,409 falling at 0.05 per cent a year (2009 est); Croat (89.6 per cent), Serb (4.5 per cent)
Religion – Christian (Roman Catholic 85 per cent, Serbian Orthodox 6 per cent), Muslim 1 per cent (est)
Language – Croatian (official), Serbian
Population density – 82 per sq. km (2008)
Urban population – 57 per cent (2007 est)
Median age (years) – 41 (2009 est)
National anthem – 'Lijepa Nasa Domovina' ['Our Beautiful Homeland']
National day – 8 October (Independence Day)
Life expectancy (years) – 75.35 (2009 est)
Mortality rate – 11.75 (2009 est)
Birth rate – 9.64 (2009 est)
Infant mortality rate – 6.37 (2009 est)
Death penalty – Abolished for all crimes (since 1990)
CPI score – 4.1 (2009)

CLIMATE AND TERRAIN

There are three major geographic areas: the plains of the Pannonian region in the north, the central mountain belt, and the Adriatic coast region of Istria and Dalmatia, which has 1,185 islands and islets and 1,777km of coastline. Elevation extremes range from 1,830m (Dinara) at the highest point to 0m (Adriatic Sea) at the lowest. The climate varies significantly between the Dalmatian coast, where the winters are mild and the summers hot, and inland areas, which are more typical of eastern Europe with colder temperatures and rain in the summer. Average temperatures in Zagreb range from 2°C in January to 20°C in July.

HISTORY AND POLITICS

The area was part of the Roman provinces of Pannonia and Dalmatia, and was occupied by Croats in the sixth to seventh centuries. By the 16th century the area was under the rule of the Hapsburgs (Pannonia), the Ottomans (Slavonia) and Venice (Dalmatia). Slavonia was restored to the Hapsburgs in 1699 and Dalmatia passed to Austria in 1815; the whole area was part of the Austro-Hungarian Empire until its collapse in 1918. Croatia declared its independence in October 1918 but soon after joined with Slovenia, Bosnia-Hercegovina, Serbia and Montenegro to form the Kingdom of Serbs, Croats and Slovenes (renamed Yugoslavia in 1929). From 1941 to 1945, Yugoslavia was occupied by the Axis powers; Italy and Hungary annexed parts of Croatia and a pro-Nazi puppet state was established in the remainder of Croatia and Bosnia-Hercegovina. At the end of the Second World War, Croatia became a republic within the Socialist Federal Republic of Yugoslavia, which gradually disintegrated following the death of President Tito in 1980.

In October 1991 Croatia declared its independence from the Yugoslav federation. The efforts of the Federal Yugoslav Army (JNA) and ethnic Serbs in Croatia to prevent Croatia's secession led to civil war until January 1992, when a ceasefire was declared. Fighting restarted the following year as Croatian forces set out to retake the ethnic Serb areas of the country that had seceded; Krajina and Western Slavonia were recaptured in 1995, and Eastern Slavonia agreed in 1995 to reintegration by 1998. From 1992 to 1995 Croatian forces were also involved in the war in Bosnia-Hercegovina. Croatia signed the Dayton Accord in 1995.

Post-independence politics was dominated by the authoritarian President Franjo Tudjman, who was first elected president in 1990. Since Tudjman's death in 1999, Croatia has become more outward-looking; it normalised relations with its neighbours, joined NATO in 2009 and began EU accession negotiations in 2005.

In the 2007 legislative election, the Croatian Democratic Union (HDZ) remained the largest party in the legislature but without an overall majority. It formed a coalition government with the Croatian Social Liberal Party, the Independent Democratic Serb Party and the Croatian Peasant Party under Ivo Sanader. He resigned in 2009 and was replaced by Jadranka Kosor. The 2010 presidential election was won by Ivo Josipovic.

POLITICAL SYSTEM

The 1990 constitution was amended in 2000 to increase the powers of the legislature, making the presidency a largely ceremonial role, and in 2001 to abolish the upper house of the legislature. The head of state is a president, who is directly elected for a five-year term. The legislature, the Croatian Assembly, has one chamber, the House of Representatives, which has 153 members directly elected for a four-year term. The prime minister is appointed by the legislature and appoints the cabinet.

HEAD OF STATE

President, Ivo Josipovic, *elected* 10 January 2010, *sworn in* 18 February 2010

SELECTED GOVERNMENT MEMBERS *as at May 2010*

Prime Minister, Jadranka Kosor
Deputy Prime Ministers, Djurdja Adlesic; Slobodan Uzelac; Darko Milinovic; Ivan Suker *(Finance)*
Defence, Branko Vukelic

Foreign Affairs, Gordan Jandrokovic
Interior, Tomislav Karamarko

EMBASSY OF THE REPUBLIC OF CROATIA
21 Conway Street, London W1T 6BN
T 020-7387 2022 E croemb.london@mvp.hr
W uk.mfa.hr
Ambassador Extraordinary and Plenipotentiary, HE Dr Ivica Tomic, *apptd* 2009

BRITISH EMBASSY
ul Ivana Lucica 4, 10000 Zagreb
T (+385) 600 9100 E british.embassyzagreb@fco.gov.uk
W http://ukincroatia.fco.gov.uk
Ambassador Extraordinary and Plenipotentiary, HE David Blunt, *apptd* 2008

BRITISH COUNCIL
Illica 12, PP 55, 10001 Zagreb
T (+385) 1489 9500 W www.britishcouncil.org/croatia
Director, Les Dangerfield

DEFENCE

The armed forces are subject to an arms limitation regime established under the Dayton Accord. The army has 261 main battle tanks, 103 armoured infantry fighting vehicles and 38 armoured personnel carriers. The navy has 2 submarines, 2 corvettes and 7 patrol and coastal combatant vessels at five major bases. The air force has 12 combat aircraft.
Military budget – US$1,020m (2009)
Military personnel – 18,600: army 11,390, navy 1,850, air force 3,500, joint staff 1,860; paramilitary 3,000
Conscription duration – 6 months

ECONOMY AND TRADE

As part of Yugoslavia, Croatia was a prosperous and industrialised area, but the conflict in 1991–5 damaged its infrastructure, large areas of farmland, industrial productivity and the tourist industry. From 2000 to 2007 there was steady economic growth, led by a recovery in tourism, banking and public investment. However, a growing trade deficit and high unemployment are longer-term problems which caused the economy to contract in the global economic downturn; the large public sector also crowds out private investment in some industries. There is a lack of political will to address these issues.

The service sector accounts for 61.4 per cent of GDP, industry for 31.6 per cent, and agriculture for 7 per cent; tourism is a major contributor to GDP. Industry produces chemicals and plastics, machine tools, metals and metal products, electronics, wood products, construction materials and textiles, and includes food processing, shipbuilding and oil refining. Agricultural production includes cereals, pulses, fruit and vegetables, livestock and dairy products. Most trade is with EU and neighbouring countries.
GNI – US$60,200m; US$13,580 per capita (2008)
Annual average growth of GDP – –5.5 per cent (2009 est)
Inflation rate – 2.5 per cent (2009 est)
Population below poverty line – 11 per cent (2003)
Unemployment – 15.2 per cent (2009 est)
Total external debt – US$55,500m (2009)
Imports – US$30,700m (2008)
Exports – US$14,100m (2008)

BALANCE OF PAYMENTS
Trade – US$13,053m deficit (2009)
Current Account – US$6,397m deficit (2008)

Trade with UK	*2008*	*2009*
Imports from UK	£205,531,218	£205,952,270
Exports to UK	£85,033,259	£76,375,229

COMMUNICATIONS

Those parts of the transport infrastructure destroyed in fighting in the 1990s have mostly been reconstructed, and parts of the rail and road networks have been modernised and expanded. There are 2,722km of railways and 29,248km of roads, including 877km of motorway. The principal airports are at Zagreb and Split. The national carrier is Croatia Airlines. There are 785km of inland waterways, including a stretch of the river Danube, and frequent ferry services to the many Adriatic islands. The main seaports are Rijeka, Zadar, Split, Sibenik and Dubrovnik. The telephone system is being modernised and extended. There were 5.9 million mobile phone subscribers in 2008, compared to 1.9 million fixed-line users.

EDUCATION AND HEALTH

Literacy rate – 98.7 per cent (2007 est)
Gross enrolment ratio (percentage of relevant age group) – primary 99 per cent; secondary 94 per cent; tertiary 47 per cent (2008 est)
Health expenditure (per capita) – US$1,009 (2007)
Hospital beds (per 1,000 people) – 5.3 (2003–8)

MEDIA

The constitution guarantees freedom of the press, although on occasion the government has used libel laws against the media. Croatian Radio-Television (HRT) is the national state-owned public service broadcaster and is the main source of news. There are a growing number of private national radio and television networks. There are three main news publications: *Vecernji List* (daily), *Jutarnji List* (daily) and *Nacional* (weekly).

CUBA

República de Cuba – Republic of Cuba

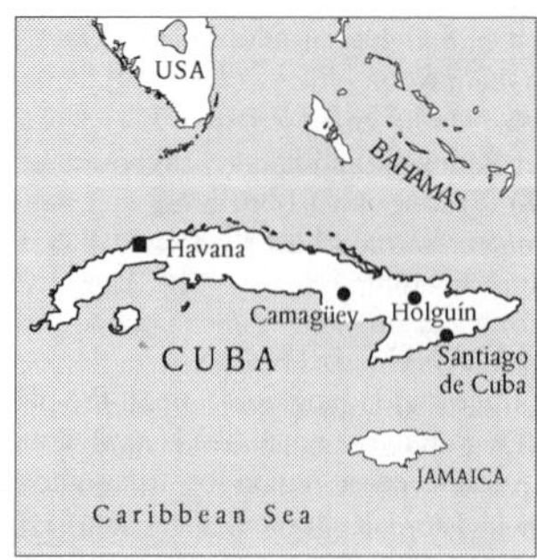

Area – 110,860 sq. km
Capital – Havana; population, 2,139,800 (2009 est)
Major cities – Camagüey, Guantánamo, Holguín, Santa Clara, Santiago de Cuba
Currency – Cuban peso of 100 centavos
Population – 11,451,652 rising at 0.23 per cent a year (2009 est)

Religion – Christian (Roman Catholic 60 per cent, Protestant denominations 5 per cent) (est); many practise Santería (African religions syncretised with Christianity). Religious activity is tightly controlled; house churches must be state-registered
Language – Spanish (official)
Population density – 102 per sq. km (2008)
Urban population – 76 per cent (2007 est)
Median age (years) – 37.3 (2009 est)
National anthem – 'El Himno de Bayamo' ['The Anthem of Bayamo']
National day – 1 January (Triumph of the Revolution)
Life expectancy (years) – 77.45 (2009 est)
Mortality rate – 7.24 (2009 est)
Birth rate – 11.13 (2009 est)
Infant mortality rate – 5.82 (2009 est)
Death penalty – Retained
CPI score – 4.4 (2009)

CLIMATE AND TERRAIN

Cuba, the largest island in the Caribbean, is part of an archipelago that also includes Isla de la Juventud and 1,600 other islets and cays. The island of Cuba has three mountainous ranges running from east to west. Elevation extremes range from 2,005m (Pico Turquino) at the highest point to 0m (Caribbean Sea) at the lowest. The climate is subtropical, with an average annual temperature of 25°C.

HISTORY AND POLITICS

The island was visited by Columbus in 1492. In the early 16th century the island was settled by the Spanish and remained under Spanish rule until a war of independence was won in 1898. Spain's defeat in Cuba coincided with its defeat in the Spanish–American War, and it ceded Cuba to the USA, which occupied the island in 1899. Cuba became independent in 1902, albeit with a condition allowing the USA to retain naval bases on the island.

The dictatorship of Gen. Batista (1933–44, 1952–9) was overthrown in 1959 in a revolution led by Fidel Castro. A communist state was established in 1961 which quickly became allied with the USSR. The regime's policies and its alignment with the Soviet bloc on the one hand, and the USA's support of exiled Cuban dissidents on the other, created great friction in US–Cuban relations; the USA has maintained an economic and trade embargo since 1961, although some restrictions were lifted after President Obama took office.

When the USSR collapsed in 1991, Cuba lost the economic, commercial and military support it had enjoyed since 1960. Faced with severe economic deterioration, the government introduced rationing and relaxed state controls on economic activity. The latter resulted in increased overseas investment and a growth in tourism, although state control has been reasserted in recent years. From 2003–8, the EU restricted its political and cultural contacts with Cuba over its poor human rights record.

Fidel Castro, who had been president since 1959, announced in February 2008 that he would not accept another term of office owing to ill-health. His brother, Raúl Castro, who had been acting president since July 2006, was elected head of state and head of government later that month by the national assembly. The most recent legislative election was in January 2008.

POLITICAL SYSTEM

The Communist Party of Cuba (PCC) is the only authorised political party. The 1976 constitution was amended in 1991 to allow direct election of the National Assembly by secret ballot, and in 2002 to enshrine socialism in the constitution. The president is elected by the legislature for a five-year term. The unicameral National Assembly of the People's Power has 614 members directly elected for a five-year term; all candidates are approved by the PCC and stand unopposed. Between its sessions, the assembly is represented by the Council of State, whose members are elected by the assembly.

HEAD OF STATE

President of Council of State and Council of Ministers, Gen. Raúl Castro Ruz, *elected* 24 February 2008
First Vice President of Council of State, José Ramón Machado Ventura

SELECTED GOVERNMENT MEMBERS *as at May 2009*

Vice Presidents of Council of Ministers, José Ramón Machado Ventura; José Ramón Fernández Álvarez; Osmany Cienfugos Gorriarán; Ricardo Cabrisas Ruiz; Div.-Gen. Ulises Rosales del Toro; Ramiro Valdés Menéndez; Marino Murillo Jorge *(Economy and Planning);* Gen. Antonio Enrique Lusson Batlle
Finance and Prices, Lina Pedraza Rodriguez
Foreign Relations, Bruno Rodriguez Parrilla
Interior, Gen. Abelardo Colome Ibarra

EMBASSY OF THE REPUBLIC OF CUBA

167 High Holborn, London WC1V 6PA
T 020-7240 2488 E embacuba@cubaldn.com
W www.cubaldn.com
Ambassador Extraordinary and Plenipotentiary, HE René Juan Mujica Cantelar, *apptd* 2005

BRITISH EMBASSY

Calle 34, No 702, Miramar, Playa, Havana
T (+53) (0) 7214 2200 E embrit@ceniai.inf.cu
W http://ukincuba.fco.gov.uk
Ambassador Extraordinary and Plenipotentiary, HE Dianna Melrose, *apptd* 2008

BRITISH COUNCIL

c/o British Embassy
T (+53) (0) 7214 2200 W www.britishcouncil.org/cuba
Director, Frank Fitzpatrick

DEFENCE

The army has around 900 main battle tanks, 50 armoured infantry fighting vehicles and 500 armoured personnel carriers. The navy has 7 patrol and coastal vessels and 7 bases. The air force has 45 combat aircraft and 4 armed helicopters.

The USA has 609 joint task force personnel at Guantánamo Bay Naval Base, which has been leased since 1902.

Military expenditure – US$2,290m (2008 est)
Military personnel – 49,000: army 38,000, navy 3,000, air force 8,000; paramilitary 26,500
Conscription duration – 24 months

ECONOMY AND TRADE

After the revolution virtually all land and industrial and commercial enterprises were nationalised. With the collapse of communism in Europe in 1989–91, the economy deteriorated sharply, necessitating rationing of energy, food and consumer goods, and obliging the government to introduce reforms. Since 1993, the government has permitted private enterprise, cut subsidies to loss-making state industries, allowed prices for some goods and services to rise, and introduced income tax. Since some ownership of property and business enterprises was opened to foreign investors in 1995, foreign companies have started to operate, especially in the oil and mining industries. The reforms, some now reversed, resulted in steady growth but, although basic food rations are provided by the state, accommodation is largely rent-free and utilities are heavily subsidised, the standard of living for most Cubans is still below the pre-1991 level.

State farms have been transformed into privately run cooperatives and are permitted to sell 20 per cent of their produce on the open market. However, production of cash crops for export means that food production is insufficient for domestic needs, and Cuba imports over 80 per cent of its food. Agriculture contributes 4.3 per cent of GDP but employs about 20 per cent of the workforce. Industrial activities include sugar refining, oil production, tobacco processing, construction, nickel mining and production of steel, cement, agricultural machinery and pharmaceuticals. Tourism is now a key industry, with over 2 million visitors a year. Industry contributes 20.9 per cent of GDP, and the service sector 74.8 per cent. About 78 per cent of the workforce is employed in the state sector.

The main trading partners are China, Canada and Venezuela; Venezuela provides oil on preferential terms. Principal exports are sugar, nickel, tobacco, fish, medical products, citrus fruits and coffee. The main imports are oil, food, machinery and equipment, and chemicals.

Annual average growth of GDP – 1 per cent (2009 est)
Inflation rate – 4.3 per cent (2009 est)
Unemployment – 1.6 per cent (2009 est)
Total external debt – US$19,440m (2009 est)

BALANCE OF PAYMENTS
Trade – US$10,098m deficit (2009)

Trade with UK	*2008*	*2009*
Imports from UK	£13,890,181	£8,886,817
Exports to UK	£11,175,734	£9,763,553

COMMUNICATIONS

The transport system has suffered as a result of recent economic difficulties, although the growth in tourism has stimulated and paid for some remedies. Even so, public transport is poor, and car ownership and freedom to travel are very limited. There are 4,000km of railways, with an additional 4,500km of track used exclusively by the sugar plantations. There are 60,858km of roads, 29,820km of which are surfaced, including 638km of motorway. Air services link the major cities and offshore islands; the islands are also served by ferries. There are 136 airports and airfields, of which 65 are surfaced; the main international airport is at Havana. The main ports are Havana, Cienfuegos and Matanzas.

The telephone system has been improved since 2000 but fixed-line density is low, with fewer than 10 lines per 100 residents. Mobile phone ownership has been permitted since 2008 but the cost is prohibitive. Ownership of computers and other electrical consumer goods has also been permitted since 2008, but internet access is largely restricted to foreigners and the government elite.

EDUCATION AND HEALTH

Education is free of charge and compulsory at all levels. In some rural areas children attend boarding schools where agricultural tasks are compulsory in addition to schoolwork. After basic education, students can choose to go to a pre-collegiate school or a technical school. The pre-collegiate school is free to graduates. Healthcare is free.

Literacy rate – 99.8 per cent (2007 est)
Gross enrolment ratio (percentage of relevant age group) – primary 102 per cent; secondary 91 per cent; tertiary 122 per cent (2008 est)
Health expenditure (per capita) – US$585 (2007)
Hospital beds (per 1,000 people) – 6.0 (2003–8)

MEDIA

The media is tightly controlled by the government; criticism of the government or its officials can be punished by a prison term of up to three years. Private ownership of electronic media is prohibited, and foreign news agencies are permitted to hire local journalists only through government offices. The official Communist Party newspaper is *Granma*. The main television stations are Cubavision, Tele-Rebelde and CHTV. The main radio stations are Radio Rebelde and Radio Reloj. Radio-TV Marti, a US government-backed station, transmits from Florida.

CULTURE

Cuba is known for its music, a vibrant mix of Spanish traditional guitar melodies and African rhythms. Rumba, mambo, bolero, salsa and cha-cha-cha all evolved from *son,* a type of Cuban music that originated in the hills of Oriente at the turn of the 20th century. Cuban music returned to the world stage with the success of the Buena Vista Social Club (publicised by the film of the same name) in the late 1990s. Writers of international standing include Cirilo Villaverde y de la Paz (1812–94), José Martí (1853–95), Nicolás Guillén (1902–89), Alejo Carpentier (1904–80) and Guillermo Cabrera Infante (1929–2005).

CYPRUS

Kypriaki Dimokratía/Kibris Cumhuriyeti – Republic of Cyprus

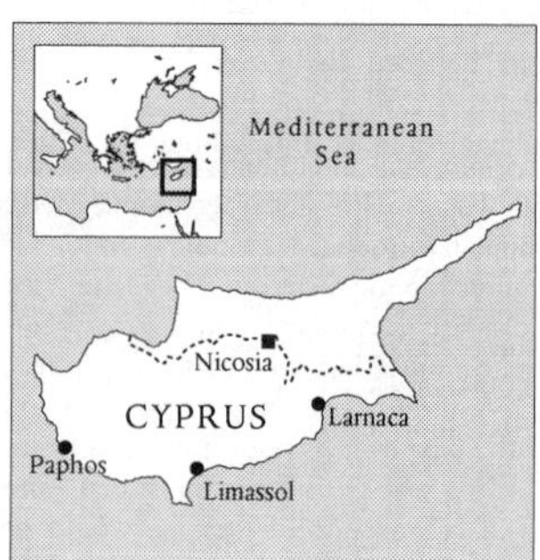

Area – 9,251 sq. km, of which 3,355 sq. km are in the Turkish Cypriot-administered area
Capital – Nicosia; population 239,859 (2009 est)
Major cities – Larnaca, Limassol, Paphos (south of the partition); Famagusta, Kyrenia (north)
Currency – Euro (€) of 100 cents (south), Turkish lira (north)

Population – 796,740 rising at 0.52 per cent a year (2009 est); Greek (77 per cent), Turkish (18 per cent)
Religion – Christian (Greek Orthodox 95 per cent) south of the partition; Sunni Muslim (98 per cent) in the north
Language – Greek, Turkish (both official), English
Population density – 93 per sq. km (2008)
Urban population – 70 per cent (2007 est)
Median age (years) – 35.5 (2009 est)
National anthem – 'Ymnos eis tin Eleftherian' ['Hymn to Freedom']
National day – 1 October (Independence Day)
Life expectancy (years) – 78.33 (2009 est)
Mortality rate – 7.8 (2009 est)
Birth rate – 12.57 (2009 est)
Infant mortality rate – 6.6 (2009 est)
Death penalty – Abolished for all crimes (since 2002)
CPI score – 6.6 (2009)
Literacy rate – 97.7 per cent (2007 est)

CLIMATE AND TERRAIN

Cyprus is the third largest island in the Mediterranean. It has two mountain ranges, the Pentadaktylos along the north coast, and the Troodos in the centre and west. Plains lie between the two ranges and on parts of the south coast. Elevation extremes range from 1,951m (Mt Olympus, Troodos range) at the highest point to 0m (Mediterranean Sea) at the lowest. The climate is Mediterranean, with very warm summers.

HISTORY AND POLITICS

Cyprus has a recorded history of over 4,000 years, and its rulers have included the Greeks, Phoenicians, Ptolemaic Egyptians, Romans, Byzantines, Arabs, Franks, Venetians, Turks and the British. Administration of Cyprus was taken over by Britain from Turkey in 1878, then Cyprus was formally annexed by Britain in 1914, and became a crown colony in 1925. Greek Cypriot demands for union with Greece *(enosis)* led to guerrilla warfare against the British administration in the 1950s and a four-year state of emergency (1955–9). An agreement was signed in 1959 between Britain, Greece, Turkey and the Greek and Turkish Cypriots which stipulated that Cyprus would become an independent republic; the island became independent on 16 August 1960, with Britain retaining sovereignty over two military bases (*see* below).

Tensions between the Greek and Turkish Cypriots caused power-sharing to break down and led to intercommunal conflict throughout the 1960s and in 1971. The UN Peacekeeping Force in Cyprus was deployed in 1964. In 1974, a coup against the Cypriot government backed by the Greek government led Turkey, which feared *enosis,* to invade. It occupied the northern third of the island, partitioning the island and displacing over 160,000 Greek Cypriots. Talks on reunification in the 1980s and 1990s were unsuccessful, and a UN-sponsored reunification plan, put to simultaneous referenda in the north and south in April 2004, was rejected by Greek Cypriots; only the southern part of the island joined the EU in May 2004. Relations improved markedly after the 2008 presidential election, and UN-facilitated talks began in September 2008.

In the 2006 legislative election, the Progressive Party of the Working People (AKEL) and the Democratic Rally (DISY) each won 18 seats. AKEL formed a coalition government with DIKO and another smaller party. Demetris Christofias, the AKEL candidate, was elected president in 2008. Legislative elections are due in May 2011.

POLITICAL SYSTEM

The 1960 constitution provides for power-sharing between the Greek and Turkish Cypriots but some of these provisions have been in abeyance since 1963, when the Turkish Cypriots withdrew from the power-sharing arrangements. The executive president is directly elected for a five-year term. The unicameral legislature, the House of Representatives, has 80 members, directly elected for a five-year term; elections to the 24 seats reserved for Turkish Cypriots have not taken place since 1963.

HEAD OF STATE

President, Demetris Christofias, *elected* 24 February 2008, *sworn in* 28 February 2008

SELECTED GOVERNMENT MEMBERS *as at May 2010*

Defence, Costas Papacostas
Finance, Kharilaos Stavrakis
Foreign Affairs, Markos Kyprianou
Interior, Neoclis Sylikiotis

HIGH COMMISSION FOR THE REPUBLIC OF CYPRUS

13 St James's Square, London SW1Y 4LB
T 020-7321 4100 E cyphclondon@dial.pipex.com
High Commissioner, HE Alexandros Zenon, *apptd* 2008

BRITISH HIGH COMMISSION

PO Box 21978, Alexander Pallis Street, 1587 Nicosia
T (+357) 2286 1100 E infobhc@cylink.cy
W http://ukincyprus.fco.gov.uk
High Commissioner, HE Peter Millett, apptd 2005

BRITISH COUNCIL

1–3 Aristotelous Street, 1011 Nicosia
T (+357) 2258 5000 W www.britishcouncil.org/cyprus
Director, Richard Law

BRITISH SOVEREIGN BASE AREAS

The Sovereign Base Areas (SBAs) of Akrotiri and Dhekelia are those parts of the island that remained under British sovereignty and jurisdiction when Cyprus became independent in 1960, and have the status of a British overseas territory. They are around 253 sq. km in size. There are approximately 14,800 residents: 7,000 Cypriots and 7,800 military and UK-based civilian personnel and their dependants.

Administrator of the British Sovereign Base Areas, Major-General Jamie Gordon, CBE, *apptd* 2008

DEFENCE

The National Guard has 147 main battle tanks, 43 armoured infantry fighting vehicles and 294 armoured personnel carriers. Turkey has around 36,000 troops in northern Cyprus.

A military airfield in Paphos provides a base for Greek military aircraft, as Cyprus does not possess its own air force.

Military budget – US$562m (2009)
Military personnel – national guard 10,050; paramilitaries 750; Northern Cyprus Army around 5,000, paramilitaries 150
Conscription duration – 24 months

ECONOMY AND TRADE

The Greek Cypriot economy is dominated by the service sector, which accounted for 78.9 per cent of GDP in

2009; this was derived mainly from tourism and financial services. Tourism represents around 20 per cent of GDP, making the economy vulnerable to fluctuations, and reduced visitor numbers owing to the global economic downturn contributed to the economy entering recession in 2009. Shipping services are also important; about 20 per cent of the world's shipping is Cypriot-registered. Industry contributes 19 per cent of GDP and agriculture 2.1 per cent. The main products for export are citrus fruits, potatoes, pharmaceuticals, cement and garments. Imports are primarily consumer goods, fuel and lubricants, intermediate goods, machinery and transport equipment. Over 50 per cent of trade is with other EU countries.

The Turkish Cypriot economy suffers from a small domestic market, international isolation and a bloated public sector. It is heavily dependent on financial support from the Turkish government. Services accounted for about 69 per cent of GDP in 2006, industry for 22 per cent and agriculture for 9 per cent. The main products for export are citrus fruits, dairy products, potatoes and textiles. The main imports are vehicles, fuel, cigarettes, food, minerals, chemicals and machinery. The tourist industry is small because the only international transport links are via Turkey, but a drop in tourist numbers and the global downturn had a serious impact on the economy in 2009.

GNI – US$21,366m; US$24,940 per capita (2008)
Annual average growth of GDP – –0.8 per cent (2009 est)
Inflation rate – 0.9 per cent (2009 est)
Unemployment – 4.8 per cent (2009 est)
Total external debt – US$32,860m (2008 est)
Imports – US$10,600m (2008)
Exports – US$1,600m (2008)

BALANCE OF PAYMENTS
Trade – US$6,508m deficit (2009)
Current Account – US$4,484m deficit (2008)

Trade with UK	*2008*	*2009*
Imports from UK	£515,146,160	£581,141,711
Exports to UK	£128,225,239	£72,467,280

COMMUNICATIONS

There are no railways. The road network (12,320km in the Greek part of the island and 2,350km in the Turkish part) serves the main population centres; crossings between the Greek and Turkish areas have all reopened or had some restrictions eased in recent years. In the Greek area, the main airports are at Larnaca and Paphos, and the principal ports are Limassol, Larnaca and Paphos. In the Turkish area, the main ports are Famagusta and Kyrenia; there is an airport but flight connections are with Turkey only.

MEDIA

The state-run Cyprus Broadcasting Corporation competes with a number of privately owned television and radio stations. The Turkish north operates its own services and broadcasts, and relays of mainland Greek and Turkish stations are available across the island. Newspapers on both sides of the divide are free to criticise the authorities.

TURKISH REPUBLIC OF NORTHERN CYPRUS

In 1974, a coup against the Cypriot government backed by the Greek government led Turkey, fearing the coup was a precursor to the union of Cyprus with Greece, to invade northern Cyprus and occupy over a third of the island. The following year, a Turkish Federated State of Cyprus was declared, and in 1983 a declaration of statehood was issued which purported to establish the Turkish Republic of Northern Cyprus. The declaration was condemned by the UN security council and only Turkey has recognised the republic. Presidential and legislative elections were held in 1985 and at regular intervals since.

Reunification talks were unsuccessful in the 1980s and 1990s, and although Turkish Cypriots approved a UN-sponsored reunification plan put to simultaneous referenda in 2004, it was rejected by Greek Cypriots. Since 2004, the EU has given aid to the area to promote and ease reunification, and UN-facilitated talks began in September 2008.

Dervis Eroglu won the 2010 presidential election, replacing Mehmet Ali Talat. The 2009 legislative election was won by the National Unity Party, which favours unification with Turkey.

DE FACTO HEAD OF STATE
President, Dervis Eroglu, *elected* 18 April 2010, *sworn in* 23 April 2010
Prime Minister, Irsen Kucuk

CZECH REPUBLIC

Ceska Republika – Czech Republic

Area – 78,867 sq. km
Capital – Prague (Praha); population, 1,161,770 (2009 est)
Major cities – Brno (Brünn), Ostrava, Plzen (Pilsen)
Currency – Koruna (Kcs) of 100 haleru
Population – 10,211,904 falling at 0.09 per cent a year (2009 est); Czech (90.4 per cent), Moravian (3.7 per cent), Slovak (1.9 per cent) (est)
Religion – Christian (Roman Catholic 33 per cent, Protestant denominations 3 per cent, Czech Hussite 1 per cent)
Language – Czech (official), Slovak
Population density – 135 per sq. km (2008)
Urban population – 73 per cent (2007 est)
Median age (years) – 40.1 (2009 est)
National anthem – 'Kde Domov Muj?' ['Where is My Motherland?']
National day – 28 October (Founding Day)
Life expectancy (years) – 76.81 (2009 est)
Mortality rate – 10.74 (2009 est)
Birth rate – 8.83 (2009 est)
Infant mortality rate – 3.79 (2009 est)
Death penalty – Abolished for all crimes (since 1990)
CPI score – 4.9 (2009)

CLIMATE AND TERRAIN

The landlocked republic is composed of Bohemia (the west and centre) and Moravia (the east). Bohemia contains the fertile plains of the river Elbe and the surrounding low mountains, while the hilly region of Moravia extends towards the basin of the river Danube. Roughly a third of the country is covered by forest. Elevation extremes range from 1,602m (Snezka) at the highest point to 115m (river Elbe) at the lowest. The climate is continental, with warm, humid summers and cold, dry winters. The average temperature in Prague ranges from −1°C in January to 19°C in July.

HISTORY AND POLITICS

The medieval kingdom of Bohemia (which included Moravia) came under the rule of the Habsburg dynasty in 1526 and, despite the rise of Czech nationalism in the 19th century, remained part of the Austro-Hungarian Empire until 1918. The collapse of the empire led to the creation of Czechoslovakia, an amalgamation of Bohemia, Moravia, Slovakia and Ruthenia. Its independence was declared on 28 October 1918 and confirmed at the Versailles Peace Conference of 1919.

Czechoslovakia was forced to cede the ethnic German Sudetenland to Nazi Germany in 1938 after the Munich agreement. German forces invaded the Czech lands in 1939 and incorporated them into Germany, while Slovakia became a puppet state. The republic was liberated by Soviet and US forces in 1945. The pre-war democratic Czechoslovak state was re-established in 1945, having ceded Ruthenia to the Soviet Union, but Communists took power in a coup in 1948.

In 1968, the Communist Party under Alexander Dubcek embarked on a political and economic reform programme known as the Prague Spring. The reforms were suppressed following an invasion by Soviet and Eastern bloc troops on 20 August 1968, and were abandoned when Gustav Husak became leader of the Communist Party in 1969.

After mass protests in November 1989, the Communist Party was forced to concede its monopoly on power. Free elections were held in 1990 in which the Communist Party was defeated.

In late 1992, the leaders of the Czech and Slovak republics agreed to dissolve the federation and form two sovereign states; this took effect on 1 January 1993. The Czech Republic joined NATO in 1999 and the EU in 2004.

Vaclav Klaus of the Civic Democrat Party (ODS) was elected president at the third attempt in February 2003; he was narrowly re-elected in 2008. The centre-right coalition government formed in January 2007 resigned in March 2009 after losing a vote of confidence; an interim government then took office. Legislative elections in May 2010 gave a combined majority to three centre-right parties – the ODS, Top09 and the Public Affairs party – which at the time of going to press were close to forming a coalition government under ODS leader Petr Necas, who was sworn in as prime minister on 28 June (*see also* Events of the Year).

POLITICAL SYSTEM

The 1992 constitution provided for the separation of the Czech Republic and Slovakia; federal laws remain in place unless superseded by Czech ones. The president is elected by a joint session of both chambers of the legislature for a five-year term, with a maximum of two consecutive terms. The bicameral *Parlament* comprises a 200-member Chamber of Deputies, directly elected for a four-year term, and an 81-member senate directly elected for a six-year term, one-third being elected every two years. The council of ministers is appointed by the president on the recommendation of the prime minister.

HEAD OF STATE

President, Vaclav Klaus, *elected* 28 February 2003, *sworn in* 7 March 2003, *re-elected* 2008

SELECTED GOVERNMENT MEMBERS *as at July 2010*

Prime Minister, Petr Necas
Foreign Affairs, Karel Schwartzenburg
Defence, Alexandr Vondra
Interior, Radek John
Finance, Miroslav Kalousek

EMBASSY OF THE CZECH REPUBLIC

26–30 Kensington Palace Gardens, London W8 4QY
T 020-7243 1115 E london@embassy.mzv.cz
W www.mzv.cz/london
Ambassadoor Extraordinary and Plenipotentiary, HE Michael Zantovska, *apptd* 2009

BRITISH EMBASSY

Thunovska 14, 11800 Prague 1
T (+420) (2) 5740 2111 E info@britain.cz
W http://ukinczechrepublic.fco.gov.uk
Ambassador Extraordinary and Plenipotentiary, HE Sian MacLeod, *apptd* 2009

BRITISH COUNCIL

Bredovsky dvur, Politickych veznu 13, 11000 Prague 1
T (+420) 221 991 111 W www.britishcouncil.org/czechrepublic
Director (acting), Paul Hilder

DEFENCE

The army has 175 main battle tanks, 525 armoured infantry fighting vehicles and 78 armoured personnel carriers. The air force has 48 combat aircraft and 24 armed helicopters.
Military expenditure – US$3,160m (2008)
Military personnel – 17,932: army 12,656, air force 5,276; paramilitary 3,100

ECONOMY AND TRADE

Economic reforms since 1990 have produced a stable and prosperous market economy. Accession to the EU has encouraged further reform and restructuring, as well as contributing to the steady growth by expanding export markets and encouraging investment. However, the global economic downturn caused the economy to contract in 2009 as its major export markets went into recession.

Services account for 62.3 per cent of GDP, industry for 35 per cent and agriculture for 2.8 per cent. The principal agricultural products are sugar beet, potatoes and cereal crops; the timber industry is also important. Having been the major industrial area of the Austro-Hungarian Empire, the country has long been industrialised, and metals, machinery, vehicles, glass and armaments are major products. Electricity is also exported. The principal trading partners are EU countries, especially Germany, and Taiwan and Russia.
GNI – US$173,600m; US$16,650 per capita (2008)
Annual average growth of GDP – −4.2 per cent (2009 est)
Inflation rate – 1.1 per cent (2009 est)
Unemployment – 9.3 per cent (2009 est)
Total external debt – US$76,830m (2009)
Imports – US$141,800m (2008)
Exports – US$146,100m (2008)

BALANCE OF PAYMENTS
Trade – US$8,745m surplus (2009)
Current Account – US$1,942m deficit (2009)

Trade with UK	*2008*	*2009*
Imports from UK	£1,499,722,839	£1,395,477,771
Exports to UK	£3,504,872,566	£3,331,378,324

COMMUNICATIONS

Extensive road (128,600km) and rail (9,620km) networks link the main population centres. Navigable inland waterways include 664km on the Elbe, Vltava, and Oder and other rivers, lakes and canals. The principal airport is at Prague and the national carrier is Czech Airlines, which operates international and domestic services. The telecommunications system was privatised recently and is being modernised. Mobile phone distribution has grown rapidly, to 13.8 million subscriptions in 2008.

EDUCATION AND HEALTH

Education is free of charge and compulsory for all children from the age of six to 15. Primary education lasts for nine years, divided into two stages of five and four years respectively. Secondary education comprises three main types of school: general, technical and vocational.
Gross enrolment ratio (percentage of relevant age group) – primary 102 per cent; secondary 95 per cent; tertiary 54 per cent (2008 est)
Health expenditure (per capita) – US$1,141 (2007)
Hospital beds (per 1,000 people) – 8.1 (2003–8)

MEDIA AND CULTURE

The public broadcaster Ceska Televize (CT) runs two networks and a 24-hour news channel. There are several private television stations. Czech public radio, Cesky Rozhlas (CRo), operates three national networks and local services alongside over 70 private radio stations throughout the country.

Prague is famous for its Art Nouveau architecture, cobbled streets and squares and thriving cultural life (particularly its contemporary jazz scene). The best-known Czech composers include Bedrich Smetana (1824–84), Antonin Dvorak (1841–1904) and Leos Janacek (1854–1928). Among its important writers are Franz Kafka (1883–1924), Milan Kundera (*b.* 1929), Ivan Klima (*b.* 1931) and Vaclav Havel (*b.* 1936).

DENMARK

Kongeriget Danmark – Kingdom of Denmark

Area – 43,094 sq. km (excluding the Faeroe Islands and Greenland)
Capital – Copenhagen; population, 1,173,680 (2009 est)
Major cities – Aalborg, Aarhus, Esbjerg, Odense
Currency – Danish krone (DKr) of 100 ore
Population – 5,500,510 rising at 0.28 per cent a year (2009 est)
Religion – Christian (Lutheran 82 per cent, Catholic 1 per cent), Muslim 4 per cent (est). The Evangelical Lutheran Church is the state church
Language – Danish (official), Faroese, Greenlandic, German. English is widely spoken as a second language
Population density – 129 per sq. km (2008)
Urban population – 86 per cent (2007 est)
Median age (years) – 40.5 (2009 est)
National anthem – 'Det er et Yndigt Land' ['There is a Lovely Land']
National day – 5 June (Constitution Day)
Life expectancy (years) – 78.3 (2009 est)
Mortality rate – 10.22 (2009 est)
Birth rate – 10.54 (2009 est)
Infant mortality rate – 4.34 (2009 est)
Death penalty – Abolished for all crimes (since 1978)
CPI score – 9.3 (2009)

CLIMATE AND TERRAIN

Denmark consists of most of the Jutland peninsula and 406 islands, mainly in the Baltic Sea or among the northern Frisian Islands in the North Sea. The largest islands are Sjaelland (Zealand), Fyn, Lolland, Faister and Bornholm. It is a low-lying country, indented by fjords on its east coast and with lagoons and sand dunes along the west coast; Lim Fjord nearly bisects the north of Jutland. Elevation extremes range from 173m (Yding Skovhoej) at the highest point to −7m (Lammefjord) at the lowest. The climate is temperate, with cold winters and warm summers. Average temperatures range from 0°C in January to 17°C in July.

HISTORY AND POLITICS

The Danes were at the forefront of Viking expansionism from the eighth century. Denmark was unified in the tenth century and was the centre of the short-lived empire, also including Norway and England, created by Cnut (Canute) in the 11th century. The Union of Kalmar (1397) brought Norway and Sweden (including Finland) under Danish rule. Danish power waned during the 16th century, enabling Sweden to re-establish its independence in 1523. In 1814 Norway was ceded to Sweden under the Treaty of Kiel, and in 1864 Schleswig and Holstein, which had been subsumed in 1460, were lost to Germany; northern Schleswig was returned in 1920 after a plebiscite. Denmark was neutral during the First World War, but in the Second World War it was invaded and occupied by Germany until May 1945.

Iceland declared its independence from Denmark in 1944 and the Faeroe Islands were granted home rule in 1948. Greenland, which previously had the status of a colony, was integrated into Denmark in 1953 and granted home rule in 1979.

Denmark joined the European Community in 1973. In a 2000 referendum, it rejected adopting the euro.

Social Democrat-led coalitions held office in the post-war era until the 1982 election, but were in power again from 1993 to 2001. In the 2001 legislative election, the Liberal Party became the largest party in parliament, and formed a coalition government with the Conservative People's Party. This coalition retained power in the 2005 and 2007 general elections. In 2009, Anders Fogh Rasmussen resigned as prime minister following his appointment as NATO secretary-general; he was replaced by Lars Loekke Rasmussen.

POLITICAL SYSTEM

The country is a constitutional monarchy, with a hereditary monarch as head of state. The head of government is the prime minister, who appoints the cabinet. The unicameral legislature, the *Folketing*, has 179 members, including two for the Faeroes and two for Greenland; members are elected for a four-year term by proportional representation.

HEAD OF STATE

HM The Queen of Denmark, Queen Margrethe II, KG, *born* 16 April 1940, *acceeded* 14 January 1972
Heir, HRH Crown Prince Frederik, *born* 26 May 1968

SELECTED GOVERNMENT MEMBERS *as at May 2010*

Prime Minister, Lars Loekke Rasmussen
Deputy Prime Minister, Lene Espersen *(Foreign Affairs)*
Defence, Gitte Lillelund Bech
Finance, Claus Hjort Frederiksen
Interior, Bertel Haarder

ROYAL DANISH EMBASSY

55 Sloane Street, London SW1X 9SR
T 020-7333 0200 E lonamb@um.dk
W www.amblondon.um.dk
Ambassador Extraordinary and Plenipotentiary, HE Birger Riis-Jorgensen, *apptd* 2006

BRITISH EMBASSY

Kastelsvej 36–40, 2100 Copenhagen O
T (+45) 3544 5200 E enquiry.copenhagen@fco.gov.uk
W http://ukindenmark.fco.gov.uk
Ambassador Extraordinary and Plenipotentiary, Nicholas Archer, MVO, *apptd* 2008

BRITISH COUNCIL

Gammel Mont 12.3, 1117 Copenhagen K
T (+45) (33) 369 400 W www.britishcouncil.org/denmark
Director, Hans Meir Anderson

DEFENCE

The army has 167 main battle tanks and 487 armoured personnel carriers. The navy has 49 patrol and coastal vessels at 2 bases. The air force has 48 combat aircraft.
Military expenditure – US$4,460m (2008)
Military personnel – 26,585: army 10,570, navy 3,498, air force 3,446, joint staff 9,071
Conscription duration – 4–12 months

ECONOMY AND TRADE

Denmark has a diversified and industrialised market economy with a high dependence on export trade. It is a net exporter of food and energy (oil, natural gas and electricity). Growth started to slow in 2007 and, exacerbated by the global downturn, the economy went into recession in 2009. The service sector contributes 64.7 per cent of GDP, industry 30.7 per cent and the highly efficient agricultural sector 4.6 per cent.

The main trading partners are other EU countries, especially Germany and Sweden. Principal exports are machinery and instruments, meat and meat products, dairy products, fish, pharmaceuticals, furniture and windmills. The main imports are machinery and equipment, industrial raw materials and semi-manufactures, chemicals, grain and foodstuffs, and consumer goods.
GNI – US$323,000m; US$58,800 per capita (2008)
Annual average growth of GDP – –3.6 per cent (2009 est)
Inflation rate – 1.3 per cent (2009 est)
Unemployment – 3.6 per cent (2009 est)
Total external debt – US$607,400m (2009)
Imports – US$111,300m (2008)
Exports – US$115,800m (2008)

BALANCE OF PAYMENTS

Trade – US$10,433m surplus (2009)
Current Account – US$12,363m surplus (2009)

Trade with UK	*2008*	*2009*
Imports from UK	£2,562,195,985	£2,396,508,316
Exports to UK	£3,845,104,444	£3,690,195,469

COMMUNICATIONS

The main ports are Aarhus, Odense, Copenhagen, Aalborg and Esbjerg. The principal airports are at Copenhagen, Aarhus, Aalborg and near Vejle. There are 2,667km of railway, of which 640km is electrified. A rail tunnel and a bridge link the islands of Sjaelland (Zealand) and Fyn, and a road and rail tunnel and a bridge across the Oresund link Copenhagen with Malmo, Sweden. There are 73,200km of roads, including 1,100km of motorways. The telecommunications network is modern and extensive; mobile phone distribution is over 100 per cent.

EDUCATION AND HEALTH

Education is free of charge and compulsory for nine years. Vocational educational programmes are numerous, with commercial, technical and agricultural training predominating.
Gross enrolment ratio (percentage of relevant age group) – primary 99 per cent; secondary 119 per cent; tertiary 80 per cent (2008 est)
Health expenditure (per capita) – US$5,551 (2007)
Hospital beds (per 1,000 people) – 3.5 (2003–8)

MEDIA

The public broadcaster is Danmarks Radio, which operates two television networks and national and regional radio stations. Private television stations can be obtained via satellite and cable. There are around 250 local commercial and community radio stations in operation. The country's commitment to a free press was demonstrated in 2006 following the publication of satirical cartoons of the Prophet Muhammad in the *Jyllands-Posten* daily newspaper, which led to violent protests in a number of countries.

CULTURE

Denmark has made significant contributions to science and its Nobel laureates include atomic physicist Niels Bohr (1885–1962), who collaborated on the Manhattan project to develop the first atomic bomb during the Second World War, and medical researcher Niels Finsen (1860–1904). Notable contributions have been made in music by Carl Nielsen (1865–1931), in design by Georg Jensen (1866–1935) and Arne Jacobsen (1902–71), in philosophy by Soren Kierkegaard (1813–55), and in literature by Hans Christian Andersen (1805–75) and Karen Blixen (1885–1962). Eminent film directors Lars von Trier (*b.* 1956) and Thomas Vinterburg (*b.* 1969) co-founded the avant-garde filmmaking movement Dogme 95 in the 1990s.

THE FAEROE ISLANDS

Area – 1,393 sq. km
Capital – Torshavn; population, 20,082 (2009 est)
Population – 48,856 rising at 0.4 per cent per year (2009 est)
National day – 29 July (Olaifest)

The Faeroe (Sheep) Islands are a group of 18 rugged islands (17 inhabited) and a few islets in the North Atlantic Ocean, between the Shetland Islands and Iceland. First settled in the ninth century, the islands were a Norwegian province and, with Norway, came under Danish rule in the 14th century. Since 1948 the Faeroes have been self-governing; they are not part of the EU.

The sovereign is represented in the islands by a high commissioner. The government *(Landsstyri)* is responsible for internal affairs. The parliament *(Loegting)* has 33 members, elected for a four-year term. The islands send two representatives to the *Folketing* at Copenhagen. In the 2008 election to the *Loegting*, the Republican Party won most seats but the coalition government of the Social Democrats, Union Party and People's Party formed in 2004 retained its overall majority and continued in office.
Prime Minister, Kaj Leo Johannesen

ECONOMY AND TRADE
The economy has grown steadily in recent years, but remains highly dependent on fishing and fish processing; fish and fish products account for 95 per cent of exports. Offshore oil discoveries raise the possibility of future diversification.

BALANCE OF PAYMENTS
Trade – US$90m deficit (2003)
Current Account – US$7m deficit (2003)

Trade with UK	*2008*	*2009*
Imports from UK	£20,537,517	£13,816,524
Exports to UK	£101,728,694	£102,341,731

BRITISH CONSULATE
P/F Damfar, PO Box 1154, Niels Finsengota 5, FR-110 Torshavn
T (+298) 35 00 77
Honorary Consul, Tummas H. Dam

GREENLAND (KALAALLIT NUNAAT)

Area – 2,166,086 sq. km
Capital – Nuuk (Godthab); population 15,182 (2009 est)
Population – 57,600 rising at 0.06 per cent per year (2009 est)
National day – 21 June (longest day)

Greenland, the world's largest island, lies between the Atlantic and Arctic oceans, to the east of Canada and to the west of Iceland. Most of Greenland is within the Arctic Circle, with permafrost covering about 80 per cent of the island. Elevation extremes range from 3,700m (Gunnbjorn) at the highest point to 0m (Atlantic Ocean) at the lowest.

Greenland was first discovered by small groups of hunters and nomadic groups who migrated from Canada *c.*500 BC. In the late tenth century, Icelanders established settlements along the south-eastern coast, but these colonies had died out by the 16th century. Danish colonisation began in the 18th century. Greenland was integrated into Denmark in 1953 and was granted internal autonomy in 1979; after a 2008 referendum, Greenlanders received greater autonomy from Denmark in 2009. Greenland negotiated its withdrawal from the EU, without discontinuing relations with Denmark, and left in 1985. The USA maintains air bases in Greenland.

The sovereign is represented by a high commissioner. The government *(Landsstyre)* is elected by the parliament *(Landsting)*, which has 31 members, elected for a four-year term. Greenland sends two representatives to the *Folketing* at Copenhagen. In the 2009 election to the *Landsting*, the Siumut (Forward) party, in power since the 1970s, was defeated by the Inuit Ataqatigiit (Brotherhood of the People) party, which won 14 seats.
Prime Minister, Kuupik Kleist

ECONOMY AND TRADE
The economy is dependent on Danish subsidies and fishing; fish and fish products comprise 82 per cent of exports. Natural resources include zinc, iron ore, lead, coal, molybdenum, gold, platinum and uranium, some of which are mined. Mineral exploration and mining operations are being extended as the ice cap shrinks. This is also benefiting offshore oil exploration, and global warming is extending the growing season. Tourism is being encouraged.

Trade with UK	*2008*	*2009*
Imports from UK	£21,571,440	£997,106
Exports to UK	£315,849	£4,103,882

DJIBOUTI

Jumhuriyat Jibuti/République de Djibouti – Republic of Djibouti

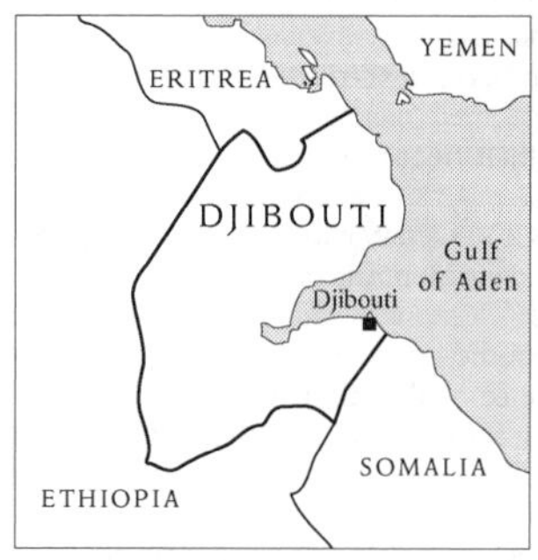

Area – 23,200 sq. km
Capital – Djibouti; population, 566,681
Currency – Djibouti franc of 100 centimes
Population – 516,055 rising at 1.9 per cent a year (2009 est); Somali (Issa) 60 per cent, Afar 35 per cent (est)
Religion – Sunni Muslim 99 per cent (est). This number may be inflated as citizens are officially presumed to be Muslim if they do not specifically identify with another faith
Language – French, Arabic (both official), Somali, Afar
Population density – 37 per sq. km (2008)
Urban population – 87 per cent (2007 est)
Median age (years) – 18.1 (2009 est)
National anthem – 'Djibouti'
National day – 27 June (Independence Day)
Life expectancy – 43.37 (2009 est)
Mortality rate – 19.1 (2009 est)

Birth rate – 38.13 (2009 est)
Infant mortality rate – 97.51 (2009 est)
HIV/AIDS adult prevalence – 2.9 per cent (2007 est)
Death penalty – Abolished for all crimes (since 1995)
CPI score – 2.8 (2009)

CLIMATE AND TERRAIN

Djibouti is situated on the strait linking the Gulf of Aden with the Red Sea, close to busy shipping lanes. The coastal plain is separated from an inland plateau by the central mountains. Elevation extremes range from 2,028m (Moussa Ali) at the highest point to −155m (Lake Assal) at the lowest. Although the climate is semi-arid with a hot season between May and September, occasional heavy rains can cause flash floods. The country is also prone to cyclones, drought and earthquakes.

HISTORY AND POLITICS

Settled by the Afars (Ethiopian) and Issas (Somali) about 2,000 years ago, the area was annexed by the French in 1888 and became French Somaliland; in 1967 it was renamed the French Territory of the Afars and the Issas. The territory became independent as Djibouti on 27 June 1977, under President Hassan Gouled Aptidon (an Issa), the leader of the *Rassemblement Populaire pour le Progrès* (RPP) party, which became the only legal political party in 1981.

In 1991, Afar discontent with the Issa domination of government under one-party rule led to civil war between the government and the *Front pour la Restauration de l'Unité et de la Démocratie* (FRUD), an alliance of rebel groups. A multiparty constitution was introduced and multiparty elections were held in 1992, but fighting continued until a power-sharing agreement was reached in 1994. The civil war ended with the signing of a peace accord in 1996, although a breakaway faction of the FRUD continued its armed opposition to the government until 2001.

Djibouti has a long-running dispute with Eritrea over an area of their common border. There were clashes between their troops in 2008, and the situation remains tense.

In the 2005 presidential election, President Guelleh was re-elected unopposed for a second term. In the 2008 legislative elections, which were boycotted by the opposition, the Union for a Presidential Majority (UMP) – an alliance of the RPP, FRUD and two other parties supporting President Guelleh – retained all 65 seats in the legislature.

POLITICAL SYSTEM

Under the 1992 constitution, the president was directly elected for a six-year term, renewable only once; in April 2010 the National Assembly unanimously adopted a constitutional amendment which abolished the presidential term limit and shortened that term to five years, effective from the next presidential election due in April 2011. The unicameral National Assembly has 65 members, directly elected for a five-year term. The president appoints the council of ministers.

HEAD OF STATE

President, Ismail Omar Guelleh, *elected* 9 April 1999, *re-elected* 8 April 2005

SELECTED GOVERNMENT MEMBERS *as at May 2010*

Prime Minister, Dileita Muhammad Dileita
Defence, Ougoureh Kifleh Ahmed
Interior, Yacin Elmi Bouh
Economy and Finance, Ali Farah Assoweh
Foreign Affairs, Mahamoud Ali Youssouf

EMBASSY OF THE REPUBLIC OF DJIBOUTI

26 rue Emile Ménier, 75116 Paris, France
T (+33) (1) 4727 4922 E webmaster@ambdjibouti.org
Ambassador Extraordinary and Plenipotentiary, HE Rachad Farah, *apptd* 2005

BRITISH AMBASSADOR

HE Norman Ling, *apptd* 2008, resident at Addis Ababa, Ethiopia

DEFENCE

The army has 20 armoured personnel carriers. The navy has 8 patrol and coastal combatant vessels. The Gendarmerie has 1 patrol and coastal combatant vessel.
Military budget – US$13m (2009)
Military personnel – 10,450: army 8,000, navy 200, air force 250, National Security Force 2,500, Gendarmerie 2,000

ECONOMY AND TRADE

A barren country with few natural resources and little industry, Djibouti's chief asset is its location on major shipping lanes. It is a transit port for neighbouring landlocked countries (especially Ethiopia, 90 per cent of whose trade passes through Djibouti), an international trans-shipment and refuelling centre, and a military base for US and EU forces because of its strategic position. The service sector accounts for 81.9 per cent of GDP, agriculture for 3.2 per cent, and industry for 14.9 per cent. The country is dependent on foreign aid and has fallen behind with external debt servicing in recent years. High unemployment is another major problem.

The main trading partners are Somalia (which takes 80 per cent of exports), Ethiopia, Saudi Arabia, India and China. Principal exports are re-exports, hides and skins, and coffee (in transit). The main imports are food, beverages, transport equipment, chemicals and petroleum products.
GNI – US$956m; US$1,130 per capita (2008)
Annual average growth of GDP – 6.5 per cent (2009 est)
Inflation rate – 5 per cent (2007 est)
Population below poverty line – 42 per cent (2007 est)
Unemployment – 59 per cent (2007 est)
Total external debt – US$428m (2006 est)
Imports – US$600m (2008)
Exports – US$100m (2008)

BALANCE OF PAYMENTS

Trade – US$622m deficit (2009)
Current Account – US$205m deficit (2007)

Trade with UK	*2008*	*2009*
Imports from UK	£7,384,691	£6,270,592
Exports to UK	£4,506,381	£437,256

COMMUNICATIONS

Djibouti city is the hub of the transport system, the location of the main port and the principal airport. The 100km Djibouti section of the Addis Ababa–Djibouti railway is controlled by both Djibouti and Ethiopia. The government is keen to expand the rail network into neighbouring countries to improve trade. Of the 3,065km of roads, 1,226km are now surfaced. There is a high risk of piracy and kidnapping for ransom in territorial waters.

Telecommunications systems, though adequate, are largely confined to the capital city and its environs.

MEDIA

The main newspaper, *La Nation,* and the national radio and television stations, operated by Radiodiffusion-Télévision de Djibouti, are government-owned. There are no private broadcasters, and the government exercises tight control of electronic media. A number of privately owned newspapers circulate freely, but journalists practise self-censorship.

DOMINICA

Commonwealth of Dominica

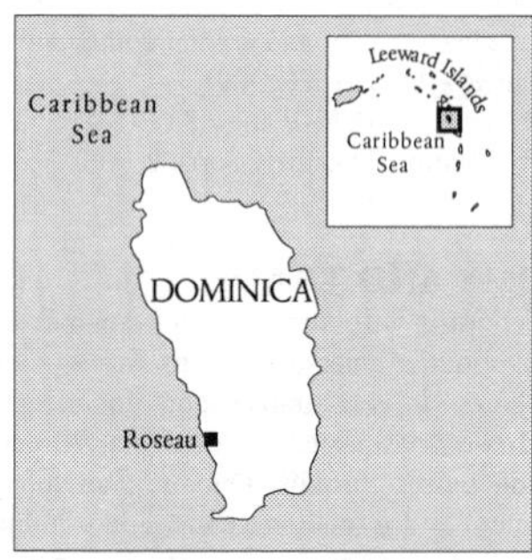

Area – 751 sq. km
Capital – Roseau; population, 14,266 (2009 est)
Currency – East Caribbean dollar (EC$) of 100 cents
Population – 72,660 rising at 0.21 per cent a year (2009 est)
Religion – Christian (Roman Catholic 61 per cent, Pentecostal 6 per cent, Seventh-day Adventist 6 per cent, Baptist 4 per cent, Methodist 4 per cent) (est)
Language – English (official), Creole
Population density – 98 per sq. km (2008)
Urban population – 74 per cent (2007 est)
Median age (years) – 29.8 (2009 est)
National anthem – 'Isle of Beauty, Isle of Splendour'
National day – 3 November (Independence Day)
Life expectancy – 75.55 (2009 est)
Mortality rate – 8.2 (2009 est)
Birth rate – 15.73 (2009 est)
Infant mortality rate – 13.65 (2009 est)
Death penalty – Retained
CPI score – 5.9 (2009)
Literacy rate – 88.0 per cent (2007 est)

CLIMATE AND TERRAIN

Dominica, the most northerly of the Windward Islands, is 46km long and 25km wide, with a mountainous and forested centre. Its peaks include volcanic craters, one of which contains Boiling Lake, the world's second-largest thermally active lake. Elevation extremes range from 1,447m (Morne Diablatins) at the highest point to 0m (Caribbean Sea) at the lowest. The climate is tropical, with average daily temperatures ranging from 25°C to 32°C. The island is located within the hurricane zone.

HISTORY AND POLITICS

Dominica was discovered by Columbus in 1493, when it was a stronghold of the Caribs, the sole inhabitants of the island until the French founded settlements in the 18th century. It was ceded to the British in 1763 but passed back and forth between France and Britain until 1805, after which British possession was unchallenged. From 1871 until the 1960s Dominica was administered by Britain as part of various federations of West Indian islands. Internal self-government from 1967 was followed on 3 November 1978 by independence as a republic.

President Nicholas Liverpool was the sole candidate nominated in the 2008 presidential election and was returned for a second term. The Dominica Labour Party (DLP), in power since 2000, won the legislative election in December 2009 and continued in government.

POLITICAL SYSTEM

Under the 1978 constitution, the president is elected by the legislature for a five-year term, renewable only once. The unicameral House of Assembly has 30 members, 21 directly elected, and nine appointed senators; all members serve a five-year term.

HEAD OF STATE

President, Nicholas Liverpool, *elected* 2003, *re-elected* 26 July 2008

SELECTED GOVERNMENT MEMBERS *as at May 2010*

Prime Minister, Finance, Foreign Affairs, Roosevelt Skerrit
National Security, Charles Savarin
Attorney-General, Francine Baron-Royer

OFFICE OF THE HIGH COMMISSIONER FOR THE COMMONWEALTH OF DOMINICA

1 Collingham Gardens, London SW5 0HW
T 020-7370 5194 E info@dominicahighcommission.co.uk
W www.dominicahighcommission.co.uk
High Commissioner (acting), Agnes Adonis

BRITISH HIGH COMMISSIONER

HE Paul Brummell, *apptd* 2009, resident at Bridgetown, Barbados

ECONOMY AND TRADE

The economy, traditionally dependent on banana exports, struggled in the early 2000s as EU preferential access for the fruit was phased out; the industry also suffered serious hurricane damage in 2007. Economic restructuring from 2003 led to steady growth, with an emphasis on eco-agriculture and eco-tourism, until the global downturn caused the economy to contract in 2009. Diversification into offshore financial services and light industry is also being encouraged, and exploitation of geothermal energy, fishing and forestry resources is planned.

Agriculture is the principal occupation, employing 40 per cent of the workforce but producing only 17.7 per cent of GDP. Services contribute 49.5 per cent of GDP and industry 32.8 per cent. The main trading partners are Japan, China, the USA and other Caribbean countries. Principal exports are bananas, soap, bay oil, vegetables and citrus fruits. The main imports are manufactured goods, machinery and equipment, food and chemicals.

GNI – US$348m; US$4,750 per capita (2008)
Annual average growth of GDP – 1.1 per cent (2009 est)
Inflation rate – 2.7 per cent (2007 est)
Total external debt – US$213m (2004)
Imports – US$200m (2008)

BALANCE OF PAYMENTS

Trade – US$189m deficit (2009)
Current Account – US$1116m deficit (2008)

Trade with UK	*2008*	*2009*
Imports from UK	£5,124,993	£7,879,014
Exports to UK	£5,667,364	£20,554,225

MEDIA

Although there is no national television service, a private cable network covers part of the island. There are no daily newspapers but there are several weekly publications. Private and public radio stations are in operation throughout the country.

DOMINICAN REPUBLIC

República Dominicana – Dominican Republic

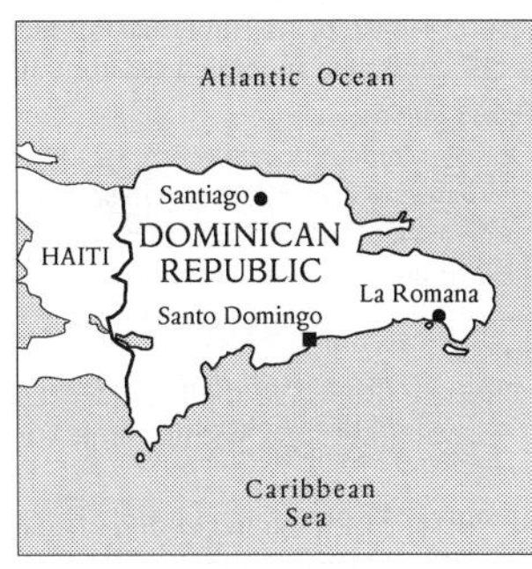

Area – 48,670 sq. km
Capital – Santo Domingo; population, 2,138,420 (2009 est)
Major cities – La Romana, San Pedro de Macorís, Santiago de los Caballeros
Currency – Dominican Republic peso (RD$) of 100 centavos
Population – 9,650,054 rising at 1.49 per cent a year (2009 est)
Religion – Christian (Roman Catholic 69 per cent, Protestant denominations 18 per cent) (est). Many also practise Santería (a syncretisation of Christianity and African religions), brujería (witchcraft) or Vodou (voodoo)
Language – Spanish (official)
Population density – 206 per sq. km (2008)
Urban population – 68 per cent (2007 est)
Median age (years) – 24.9 (2009 est)
National anthem – 'Quisqueyanos Valientes' ['Valiant Sons of Quisqueya']
National day – 27 February (Independence Day)
Life expectancy (years) – 73.7 (2009 est)
Mortality rate – 5.28 (2009 est)
Birth rate – 22.39 (2009 est)
Infant mortality rate – 25.96 (2009 est)
Death penalty – Abolished for all crimes (since 1966)
CPI score – 3 (2009)
Literacy rate – 89.1 per cent (2007 est)
Gross enrolment ratio (percentage of relevant age group) – primary 104 per cent; secondary 75 per cent (2008 est)
Health expenditure (per capita) – US$224 (2007)
Hospital beds (per 1,000 people) – 1.0 (2003–8)

CLIMATE AND TERRAIN

The republic forms the eastern two-thirds of the island of Hispaniola and is crossed from the north-west to the south-east by the Cordillera Central mountain range, which has a number of peaks at over 3,000m. Elevation extremes range from 3,175m (Pico Duarte) at the highest point to –46m (Lake Enriquillo) at the lowest. The climate is maritime tropical, with average temperatures ranging between 23°C and 27°C.

HISTORY AND POLITICS

The island was discovered by Columbus in 1492, and a Spanish colony was established in 1496. The eastern province of Santo Domingo remained under Spanish rule after the partition of Hispaniola in 1697, but was ceded to France in 1795. It was restored to Spain in 1809, but rebelled in 1821 and achieved independence briefly before being annexed by Haiti in 1822. Haitian rule ended in 1844 when independence was declared as the Dominican Republic, although the country was voluntarily under Spanish rule again from 1861 to 1865. A long dictatorship at the end of the 19th century was followed by revolution and bankruptcy, which led to occupation by US forces from 1916 until 1924. A military coup in 1930 established the dictatorship of Gen. Rafael Trujillo, whose corrupt rule continued until his assassination in 1961. After a period of political instability, a new constitution was adopted in 1966 and democracy was restored.

The 2004 presidential election was won by Leonel Fernández (president 1996–2000) of the Dominican Liberation Party (PLD), and he was re-elected in 2008. In legislative elections held in May 2010 the ruling PLD increased their majorities in both houses.

POLITICAL SYSTEM

Under the 1966 constitution (amended in 2002), the executive president is directly elected for a four-year term, renewable only once. The bicameral National Congress comprises the Chamber of Deputies, which has 183 members, and the senate, with 32 members, one for each province and one for Santo Domingo; both chambers are directly elected for a four-year term.

HEAD OF STATE

President, Leonel Fernández, *elected* 2004, *sworn in* August 2004, *re-elected* 17 May 2008
Vice-President, Rafael Alburquerque

SELECTED GOVERNMENT MEMBERS *as at May 2010*

Foreign Affairs, Carlos Morales Troncoso
Armed Forces, Maj.-Gen. Pedro Pena
Finance, Vincente Bengoa
Interior, Franklin Almeyda

EMBASSY OF THE DOMINICAN REPUBLIC

139 Inverness Terrace, London W2 6JF
T 0905 677 0054 **E** embassy@dominicanembassy.org.uk
W www.dominicanembassy.org.uk
Ambassador Extraordinary and Plenipotentiary, HE Anibal de Castro, *apptd* 2005

BRITISH EMBASSY

Edificio Corominas Pepín, 7th–8th Floor, Ave 27 de Febrero No 233, Santo Domingo
T (+1) (829) 472 7111 **E** brit.emb.sadom@codetel.net.do
W http://ukindominicanrepublic.fco.gov.uk
Ambassador Extraordinary and Plenipotentiary, HE Steven Fisher, *apptd* 2009

DEFENCE

The army has 12 light tanks and 8 armoured personnel carriers. The navy has 16 patrol and coastal combatant vessels at two bases.

Military budget – US$318m (2009)
Military personnel – 49,910: army 40,410, navy 4,000, air force 5,500; paramilitary 15,000

ECONOMY AND TRADE

In recent years, tourism and the free trade zones have overtaken agriculture as the mainstay of the economy, and services now account for 68.2 per cent of GDP. Agriculture accounts for 10.5 per cent of GDP, industry for 21.3 per cent. The main crops are sugar, coffee, cotton, cocoa, tobacco, rice, vegetables and bananas, and the main industrial activities are tourism, sugar processing, mining and the production of textiles, cement and tobacco products. Remittances from expatriate workers represent nearly 10 per cent of GDP but, like tourism, have been affected by the global economic downturn. A free-trade agreement with Central American states in 2007 has boosted trade, but unemployment and fluctuations in nickel prices remain problems.

The main trading partner is the USA, which takes 58 per cent of exports and provides 39 per cent of imports. Principal exports are ferro-nickel, sugar, gold, silver, coffee, cocoa, tobacco, meats and consumer goods. The chief imports are foodstuffs, fuel, cotton and fabrics, chemicals and pharmaceuticals.

GNI – US$43,100m; US$4,330 per capita (2008)
Annual average growth of GDP – –0.3 per cent (2009 est)
Inflation rate – 1.4 per cent (2009 est)
Population below poverty line – 42.2 per cent (2004)
Unemployment – 15.1per cent (2009 est)
Total external debt – US$11,850m (2009 est)
Imports – US$16,100m (2008)
Exports – US$2,400m (2008)

BALANCE OF PAYMENTS
Trade – US$11,447m deficit (2009)
Current Account – US$2,337m deficit (2009)

Trade with UK	*2008*	*2009*
Imports from UK	£61,506,890	£80,202,598
Exports to UK	£80,747,927	£101,987,984

COMMUNICATIONS

Santo Domingo and Rio Haina are the main seaports. There are 35 airports and airfields, ten of which handle international flights; the principal airport is at Santo Domingo. There are over 19,700km of roads, 9,900km of which are surfaced. There is 558km of railway, plus a further 1,226km operated by sugar companies. Santo Domingo's metro system was inaugurated in 2009.

Mobile phone distribution, at 75 per 100 people in 2008, is over seven times greater than fixed-line density, at 10 per 100 people. There are over 2.1 million internet users.

MEDIA

There are several terrestrial commercial broadcasting stations and around 30 multi-channel cable TV operators. The state-owned broadcaster is Corporacion Estatal de Radio y Television (CERTV). There are more than 200 commercial radio stations as well as two government stations. Press freedom is guaranteed by law.

ECUADOR

República del Ecuador – Republic of Ecuador

Area – 283,561 sq. km
Capital – Quito; population, 1,800,850 (2009 est)
Major cities – Cuenca, Guayaquil, Machala, Manta, Santo Domingo de los Colorados
Currency – US dollar (US$) of 100 cents
Population – 14,573,101 rising at 1.5 per cent a year (2009 est)
Religion – Christian (Roman Catholic 85 per cent) (est)
Language – Spanish (official), Quechua, other Amerindian languages
Population density – 49 per sq. km (2008)
Urban population – 65 per cent (2007 est)
Median age (years) – 25 (2009 est)
National anthem – 'Salve, Oh Patria' ['We Salute You, Our Homeland']
National day – 10 August (Independence Day)
Life expectancy (years) – 75.3 (2009 est)
Mortality rate – 4.99 (2009 est)
Birth rate – 20.77 (2009 est)
Infant mortality rate – 20.9 (2009 est)
Death penalty – Abolished for all crimes (since 1906)
CPI score – 2.2 (2009)

CLIMATE AND TERRAIN

Ecuador is an equatorial state lying on the north-west coast of South America. Its territory includes the Galápagos Islands in the Pacific Ocean. The Andes run north to south through the centre of the country, dividing the coastal plain in the west from the low-lying rainforest in the east, and between two local Andean chains lie the central highlands. Elevation extremes range from 0m (Pacific Ocean) at the lowest point to 6,267m (Chimborazo) at the highest. Other Andean peaks include Cotopaxi (5,896m) and Cayambe (5,790m) in the Eastern Cordillera. Ecuador is located in an earthquake zone and five of its volcanoes have erupted since 2000 – most recently Tungurahua in May 2010. The country has four different climatic zones, and is one of the most bio-diverse countries on earth. The average annual temperature in Quito is 15°C.

HISTORY AND POLITICS

The kingdom of the Caras, around Quito, was conquered by the Incas of Peru in the 15th century. After the Spanish defeated the Incas in Peru, Ecuador was conquered in 1534 and added to the Spanish viceroyalty of Peru. Independence from Spain was achieved in a revolutionary war that culminated in the battle of Mt Pichincha (1822). Ecuador then formed part of Gran Colombia with Colombia, Panama and Venezuela, but left this union to become a fully independent state in 1830. After independence, the country experienced periods of political instability interspersed with dictatorships and military rule. Democratic rule under civilian government was restored in 1979.

The exploitation of oil reserves funded economic and social transformation from the 1970s onwards but also caused rapid inflation and increased foreign debt. In recent years, these problems have worsened because of economic recession, leading to strikes and demonstrations. The most notable of these were by indigenous people, who have benefited least from the oil boom but been hardest hit by the economic downturn. Civil unrest forced three presidents from office between 1997 and 2003.

Presidential and legislative elections were held in April 2009 after a new constitution was approved by a national referendum in 2008. President Correa was re-elected in the first round of voting, and his party, the Country Alliance (AP), won the most seats in the new legislature.

POLITICAL SYSTEM

The 2008 constitution provides for an executive president who is directly elected for a four-year term, renewable only once. The unicameral National Assembly has 124 members elected on a party-list proportional representation basis for a four-year term. The republic is divided into 24 provinces.

HEAD OF STATE

President, Rafael Correa *took office* 15 January 2007, *re-elected* April 2009

Vice-President, Lenin Moreno

SELECTED GOVERNMENT MEMBERS *as at May 2010*

Finance, Patricio Rivera Yanez

Foreign Affairs, Ricardo Patino

National Defence, Javier Ponce Cevallos

EMBASSY OF ECUADOR

Flat 3B, 3 Hans Crescent, London SW1X 0LS

T 020-7584 1367 E eecugranbretania@mmrree.gov.ec

W www.consuladoecuador.org.uk

Ambassador Extraordinary and Plenipotentiary, vacant

BRITISH EMBASSY

PO Box 17-17-830, Citiplaza Building, Av. Naciones Unidas y Republica de El Salvador, Piso 14, Quito

T (+593) (2) 2970 800 E britembq@interactive.net.ec

W http://ukinecuador.fco.gov.uk

Ambassador Extraordinary and Plenipotentiary, HE Linda Cross, *apptd* 2008

DEFENCE

The army has 24 light tanks, 123 armoured personnel carriers and 18 armed helicopters. The navy has 2 submarines, 2 frigates, 6 corvettes, and 3 patrol and coastal combatant vessels at two bases. The air force has over 60 combat aircraft.

Military budget – US$1,100m (2009)

Military personnel – 57,983: army 46,500, navy 7,283, air force 4,200; paramilitary 400

Conscription duration – 12 months (selective)

ECONOMY AND TRADE

Oil is Ecuador's principal export, accounting for half of export earnings and a quarter of government revenue in recent years. The economy has recovered from the severe economic crisis in 1999 owing to structural reforms in 2000, including the adoption of the US dollar in place of the sucre. Growth was strong from 2002 to 2006 and the poverty rate declined, although it remains high. However, growth started to slow after 2006 owing to the uncertainty created by windfall taxes imposed on foreign oil companies, a fall in oil production since 2007, the government defaulting on 80 per cent of private external debt in 2008, and the cancellation of a number of bilateral investment treaties in 2009. The global downturn has further reduced oil revenue, remittances from expatriate workers (who number nearly one million) and export earnings.

After oil, agriculture, fishing and forestry are the most important activities, providing products both for export and for the food and wood processing industries. The main exports are oil, bananas, cut flowers, fish, cacao, coffee, hemp and timber. The main imports are industrial materials, fuels and lubricants and consumer goods. Principal trading partners are the USA and other South American countries.

GNI – US$49,800m; US$3,690 per capita (2008)

Annual average growth of GDP – –2 per cent (2009 est)

Inflation rate – 5.4 per cent (2009 est)

Population below poverty line – 38.3 per cent (2006)

Unemployment – 9.8 per cent (2009 est)

Total external debt – US$13,310m (2009)

Imports – US$18,700m (2008)

Exports – US$18,500m (2008)

BALANCE OF PAYMENTS

Trade – US$1,366m deficit (2009)

Current Account – US$1,205m surplus (2008)

Trade with UK	*2008*	*2009*
Imports from UK	£40,079,625	£54,346,174
Exports to UK	£99,249,433	£86,549,384

COMMUNICATIONS

There are 43,670km of roads, 6,470km of which are surfaced, and there are 965km of railways. The road and rail networks are largely to the west of the Andes. Travel to the east is mostly by air, with internal services between all major towns. There are 420 airports and airfields, of which 103 have surfaced runways, and international flights operate to Quito and Guayaquil. The main ports are Guayaquil and Esmeraldas. The fixed-line telephone system is being expanded but the service is limited. Mobile phone distribution has grown quickly, and in 2008 stood at 85 per 100 people.

EDUCATION AND HEALTH

Elementary education is free of charge and compulsory until age 14.

Literacy rate – 91.0 per cent (2007 est)

Gross enrolment ratio (percentage of relevant age group) – primary 118 per cent; secondary 70 per cent; tertiary 35 per cent (2008 est)

Health expenditure (per capita) – US$200 (2007)

Hospital beds (per 1,000 people) – 0.6 (2003–8)

MEDIA AND CULTURE

Most media outlets are in private ownership, including the six daily newspapers, television stations and radio stations. By law, the media must provide the government with free space or air time on demand, so programmes by the state are occasionally broadcast.

Quito has been a UNESCO World Heritage Site since

1978. South America's oldest market, which predates the Inca period, can be found in the small town of Otavalo.

GALÁPAGOS ISLANDS

The Galápagos (Giant Tortoise) Islands, about 960km from the mainland, were annexed by Ecuador in 1832. The 12 large and several hundred smaller islands lie on the equator, and most form part of a national park where unique marine birds, iguanas and the giant tortoises are conserved. This wildlife provided naturalist Charles Darwin (1809–82) with inspiration and research material for his theory of evolution by natural selection, expounded in *On the Origin of Species* (1859). The islands were declared a UNESCO World Heritage Site in 1978.

EGYPT

Jumhuriyat Misr al-Arabiyah – Arab Republic of Egypt

Area – 1,001,450 sq. km
Capital – Cairo; population, 10,902,500 (2009 est); stands on the Nile about 22 km from the head of the delta
Major cities – Alexandria (founded 332 BC by Alexander the Great; the capital for over 1,000 years), Giza, Port Said, Suez
Currency – Egyptian pound (£E) of 100 piastres or 1,000 millièmes
Population – 83,082,869 rising at 1.64 per cent a year (2009 est); Egyptian (including Berber and Bedouin) 99.6 per cent. The Bedouin of the Western and Eastern deserts are traditionally semi-sedentary tent-dwellers. The Nubians of the Nile Valley are of mixed Arab and African blood
Religion – Muslim (Sunni 90 per cent, Shia 1 per cent), Christian 8 per cent (predominantly Coptic) (est)
Language – Arabic (official), English, French
Population density – 82 per sq. km (2008)
Urban population – 43 per cent (2007 est)
Median age (years) – 24.8 (2009 est)
National anthem – 'Biladi, Biladi, Biladi' ['My Homeland, My Homeland, My Homeland']
National day – 23 July (Revolution Day)
Life expectancy (years) – 72.33 (2009 est)
Mortality rate – 5.08 (2009 est)
Birth rate – 21.7 (2009 est)
Infant mortality rate – 27.26 (2009 est)
Death penalty – Retained
CPI score – 2.8 (2009)

CLIMATE AND TERRAIN

There are four broad regions: the Western Desert, which covers nearly two-thirds of the country to the west of the Nile valley; the Eastern Desert, which lies between the Nile and the mountains along the Red Sea coast; the fertile Nile valley and delta, where most of the population lives; and the Sinai peninsula, where a coastal plain on the Mediterranean rises to mountains in the south. The deserts are arid plateaux, with depressions in the Western Desert whose springs irrigate oases, while the Eastern Desert is dissected by wadis (dry watercourses). Elevation extremes range from 2,629m (Mt Catherine, Sinai) at the highest point to −133m (Qattara depression) at the lowest. The country has a desert climate, with hot, dry summers and mild winters. Temperatures increase further south, and rainfall increases nearer the coast. Average daily temperatures range from 18°C to 30°C.

HISTORY AND POLITICS

The unification of the kingdoms of Lower Egypt and Upper Egypt *c*.3100 BC marked the establishment of the Egyptian state, with Memphis as its capital. Egypt was ruled for nearly 2,800 years by a succession of 31 pharaonic dynasties, which built the pyramids at Giza. Egypt's independence was lost to the Assyrians in *c*.669 BC, and it was conquered by the Persians in 525 BC and then by Alexander the Great in 332 BC. Subsequently ruled by Alexander's general Ptolemy and his descendants, it was conquered and ruled by Rome (30 BC to AD 324) and then by the Byzantine Empire. In AD 640 Egypt was subjugated by Arab Muslim invaders. In 1517 the country was incorporated into the Ottoman Empire, under which it remained, nominally, until the early 20th century. Britain occupied Egypt in 1882, and a British protectorate over Egypt lasted from 1914 to 1922, when Sultan Ahmed Fuad was proclaimed King of Egypt and the country became independent. In 1952 the monarchy was deposed and in 1953 Egypt was declared a republic. Egypt joined with Syria to form a short-lived single state, the United Arab Republic (UAR), between 1958 and 1961, when Syria seceded; Egypt retained the name of UAR until 1971.

Egypt was involved in the Arab-Israeli wars in 1948, 1967 and 1973. In the 1967 war (the Six Day War), the Sinai peninsula was lost to Israel. Sinai was returned to Egypt in 1982 under the 1979 treaty that resulted from the Camp David talks (1978–9) and formally terminated the 31-year-old state of war between the two countries. The treaty led to strained relations with other Arab nations until the mid-1980s.

President Hosni Mubarak, who took office after the assassination of President Sadat in 1981, played an active part in the Middle East peace process in the 1990s but was unable to suppress internal terrorism by Islamic fundamentalists. A state of emergency has been in force continuously since 1981 and was extended in May 2010 for a further two years. Frustration and resentment at the lack of political freedom has found expression in public demonstrations in recent years. Opposition politicians and media critics are subject to harassment.

President Mubarak was re-elected for his fifth successive term in 2005, in the first contested presidential election; the second is due in 2011. In the 2005 elections to the People's Assembly, the ruling National Democratic Party (NDP) won an overall majority; 20 per cent of the seats were won by members of the Muslim Brotherhood standing as independents because of the ban on religious political parties. The NDP also held the majority of seats in the Consultative Council after the 2007 elections.

INSURGENCIES
Militant Islamic fundamentalists emerged in the 1980s. Their campaign against the government became increasingly violent from the early 1990s, and was eventually directed against foreign tourists as well as domestic targets. Although the largest fundamentalist organisation, Gamaat-i-Islamiya, renounced violence in 1999, attacks continue, often targeting foreigners.

POLITICAL SYSTEM
The 1971 constitution was amended in 2005 to allow for direct elections to the presidency, and in 2007 to introduce changes increasing the president's powers. It provides for an executive president who appoints the council of ministers and determines government policy. Since 2005, the president has been directly elected from multiple candidates (who must meet strict criteria) to serve a six-year term. The unicameral People's Assembly currently has 454 members, who serve a five-year term; 444 members are directly elected and ten appointed by the president. After elections in November 2010 the chamber will be expanded by the addition of 64 seats reserved for female members. The Consultative Council has an advisory role; its 264 members include 176 who are directly elected and 88 presidential appointees, all serving a six-year term. Religious political parties are banned.

HEAD OF STATE
President, Mohammed Hosni Mubarak, *elected* 1981, *re-elected* 1987, 1993, 1999, 2005

SELECTED GOVERNMENT MEMBERS *as at May 2010*
Prime Minister, Ahmed Nazif
Defence, Field Marshal Mohammad Hussein Tantawi
Finance, Youssef Boutros Ghali
Foreign Affairs, Ahmed Aboul Gheit
Interior, Maj.-Gen. Habib al-Adli

EMBASSY OF THE ARAB REPUBLIC OF EGYPT
26 South Street, London W1K 1DW
T 020-7499 3304 E eg.emb_london@mfa.gov.eg
W www.egyptembassyuk.org
Ambassador Extraordinary and Plenipotentiary, HE Hatem Seif el-Nasr, *apptd* 2008

BRITISH EMBASSY
7 Ahmed Ragheb Street, Garden City, Cairo
T (+20) (2) 2791 6000 E info@britishembassy.org.eg
W http://ukinegypt.fco.gov.uk
Ambassador Extraordinary and Plenipotentiary, HE Dominic Asquith, CMG, *apptd* 2007

BRITISH COUNCIL
192 El Nil Street, Agouza, Cairo
T (+20) (2) 219 789 W www.britishcouncil.org/egypt
Director, Paul Smith

DEFENCE
The army has 3,723 main battle tanks, 610 armoured infantry fighting vehicles and 4,160 armoured personnel carriers. The navy has 4 submarines, 10 frigates, 41 patrol and coastal vessels and 5 armed helicopters at 8 bases. The air force has 461 combat aircraft and 105 armed helicopters.
Military budget – US$3,270m (2008 est)
Military personnel – 468,500: army 340,000, navy 18,500, air force 30,000, Air Defence Command 80,000; paramilitary 397,000
Conscription duration – 12–36 months

ECONOMY AND TRADE
Economic liberalisation in recent years has attracted foreign investment and promoted exports, producing strong growth in GDP. However living standards for most of the population remain low, with over a third living below the poverty line. There is a growing budget deficit, partly owing to price subsidies for basic necessities, and high public debt. Although the dams on the Nile have expanded the area of land under cultivation, other factors, such as population growth, put resources under pressure.

The services sector contributes 49.2 per cent to GDP and employs 51 per cent of the workforce. Tourism is the largest component of this sector (visitor numbers have increased by over 50 per cent since the late 1990s), along with Suez Canal revenues and expatriate remittances. Industry accounts for 37.7 per cent of GDP and 17 per cent of employment, but despite increasing industrialisation, agriculture still employs 32 per cent of the workforce, contributing 13.1 per cent of GDP. Egypt is a net importer of foodstuffs, especially grain, and a food security programme has been set up with the aim of achieving self-sufficiency. The main cash crop is cotton, of which Egypt is one of the world's main producers. Other important crops are rice, maize, wheat, vegetables, fruit and livestock. Industry is centred on oil and gas extraction, processing hydrocarbons, cotton and other agricultural products, producing textiles, chemicals and pharmaceuticals. Oil is the backbone of the economy and helps, alongside considerable reserves of natural gas and the hydroelectric power produced by the Aswan and High dams, to make Egypt self-sufficient in energy.

The main trading partners are the USA, Italy, Germany and China. Principal exports are crude oil and petroleum products, cotton, textiles, metal products, chemicals and processed food. The main imports are machinery and equipment, foodstuffs, chemicals, wood products and fuels.
GNI – US$146,800m; US$1,800 per capita (2008)
Annual average growth of GDP – 4.5 per cent (2009 est)
Inflation rate – 10.1 per cent (2009 est)
Population below poverty line – 38.3 per cent (2006 est)
Unemployment – 9.7 per cent (2009 est)
Total external debt – US$28,450m (2009)
Imports – US$48,800m (2008)
Exports – US$26,200m (2008)

BALANCE OF PAYMENTS
Trade – US$21,673m deficit (2009)
Current Account – US$888m surplus (2008)

Trade with UK	*2008*	*2009*
Imports from UK	£909,341,623	£945,413,153
Exports to UK	£616,596,474	£562,674,292

COMMUNICATIONS
Egypt has 3,500km of waterways, including the River Nile and Lake Nasser, the Alexandria–Cairo waterway, numerous small canals in the Nile delta and the Suez Canal (opened 1869; closed 1967–75). The main seaports are Alexandria, Damietta and Port Said on the Mediterranean Sea and Suez on the Red Sea. A road network of 65,000km and a rail network of 5,500km link the Nile valley and delta with the main development areas east and west of the river, but there are few routes in the interior. There are 85 airports and airfields; the principal airports are at Cairo, Luxor, Alexandria, Aswan and Hurgadah. The telephone system was modernised in the 1990s; there were 9.6 million fixed-line, 55.4 million

mobile phone and 11.4 million internet subscribers in 2008.

EDUCATION AND HEALTH

Education is free between the ages of six and 15.
Literacy rate – 66.4 per cent (2007 est)
Gross enrolment ratio (percentage of relevant age group) – primary 100 per cent (2008 est)
Health expenditure (per capita) – US$101 (2007)
Hospital beds (per 1,000 people) – 2.1 (2003–8)

MEDIA

The Egyptian media plays a central role in the Arab world; its newspapers are some of the most influential in the region, and the products of its film and television studios are shown in most Arab-speaking countries. Two state-run national television channels and six regional channels compete with the country's thriving satellite television industry, which is watched throughout the Arab-speaking world. The state's monopoly on radio broadcasting ended in 2003. The government has actively encouraged foreign media to base themselves in Egypt by establishing a free media zone in 2000 that offers economic incentives and access to its media infrastructure. The media are frequently critical of public figures, though in recent years defamation laws and provisions of the emergency law have been used to harass and detain bloggers, who are increasingly instrumental in mobilising political opposition.

CULTURE

Egyptian culture dates back five thousand years to one of the earliest-known civilisations on Earth; ancient Egyptian hieroglyphic scripts provide some of the world's oldest records of written communication. The country has experienced periods of Hellene, Christian, Arab and Islamic culture, and remains most famous for the pyramids of Giza, the library of Alexandria and the art and architecture of its ancient periods (beginning in the fourth millennium BC and waning around 31 BC). Modern Egypt has the highest number of Nobel laureates in Africa, including author Naguib Mahfouz (1911–2006) and diplomat Mohamed ElBaradei (*b.* 1942); actor Omar Sharif (*b.* 1932) is an Academy Award winner, while Cairo is home to Al-Ahly, the most widely supported football club in Africa.

EL SALVADOR

República de El Salvador – Republic of El Salvador

Area – 21,041 sq. km
Capital – San Salvador; population, 1,533,960 (2009 est)
Major cities – Apopo, San Miguel, Santa Ana
Currency – US dollar (US$) of 100 cents
Population – 7,185,218 rising at 1.66 per cent a year (2009 est)
Religion – Christian (Roman Catholic 53 per cent, Protestant denominations 28 per cent) (est)
Language – Spanish (official), Nahua
Population density – 296 per sq. km (2008)
Urban population – 60 per cent (2007 est)
Median age (years) – 22.5 (2009 est)
National anthem – 'Himno Nacional de El Salvador' ['National Anthem of El Salvador']
National day – 15 September (Independence Day)
Life expectancy (years) – 72.33 (2009 est)
Mortality rate – 5.47 (2009 est)
Birth rate – 25.31 (2009 est)
Infant mortality rate – 22.52 (2009 est)
Death penalty – Retained for certain crimes (last known use 1973)
CPI score – 3.4 (2009)

CLIMATE AND TERRAIN

El Salvador lies on the west coast of Central America. The country is mountainous (much of the interior has an average altitude of 600m), with narrow coastal plains and a central plateau. Many of its peaks are volcanoes; most are extinct, but Ilamatepec (or Santa Ana) erupted in 2005. There are also numerous volcanic lakes. Elevation extremes range from 2,730m (Cerro El Pital) at the highest point to 0m (Pacific Ocean) at the lowest. The climate is tropical on the coast but more temperate at higher altitudes. The average annual temperature in San Salvador is 23°C. Earthquakes and volcanic activity are common, and the country is also susceptible to hurricanes and tropical storms.

HISTORY AND POLITICS

El Salvador was part of the Aztec kingdom conquered in 1524 by Pedro de Alvarado, and formed part of the Spanish viceroyalty of Guatemala until 1821. It was part of a Central American federation of former Spanish provinces from 1823 until the federation's dissolution in 1838, becoming fully independent in 1840.

There was political unrest in the 1970s, and guerrilla activity by the left-wing Farabundo Martí National Liberation Front (FMLN), which intensified from 1977 amid reports of human rights abuses by government troops and right-wing death squads. Decades of military rule ended in 1979, but elections in 1982 were boycotted by left-wing parties and the right-wing National Republican Alliance (ARENA) took office. The civil war between the FMLN and the US-backed government lasted throughout the 1980s, until a UN-sponsored peace agreement was signed in 1992. The FMLN was recognised as a political party, and it won a few seats in the 1994 election, steadily increasing its share of the vote in subsequent elections. Although the FMLN has often been the largest party in parliament, ARENA remained in office continuously until 2009 as it held the presidency and formed coalition governments with smaller right-wing parties.

In the January 2009 legislative elections, the FMLN again won the most seats in the legislature, and the March 2009 presidential election was won by FMLN candidate Mauricio Funes.

POLITICAL SYSTEM

Under the 1983 constitution, the executive president is directly elected for a five-year term. The unicameral legislative assembly has 84 members, who are directly elected for a three-year term. The president appoints the Council of State. The country is divided into 14 departments.

HEAD OF STATE
President, Mauricio Funes, *elected* 15 March 2009, *took office* 1 June 2009
Vice-President, Sánchez Cerén

SELECTED GOVERNMENT MEMBERS *as at May 2010*
Defence, Col. David Munguía
Economy, Héctor Dada
Foreign Affairs, Hugo Martínez

EMBASSY OF EL SALVADOR
8 Dorset Square, London NW1 6PU
T 020-7224 9800 E embajadalondres@rree.gob.sv
Ambassador Extraordinary and Plenipotentiary, HE Werner Matías Romero, *apptd* 2010

BRITISH AMBASSADOR
HE Julie Chappell, OBE, *apptd* 2009, resident at Guatemala City, Guatemala

DEFENCE
The army has 38 armoured personnel carriers. The navy has 39 patrol and coastal combatant vessels. The air force has 19 combat aircraft.
Military budget – US$132m (2009)
Military personnel – 15,500: army 13,850, navy 700, air force 950; paramilitary 17,000
Conscription duration – 18 months voluntary

ECONOMY AND TRADE
The country is one of the most industrialised in Central America and has the region's third largest economy despite being its smallest country and having few natural resources. Recovery after the civil war was set back by a series of natural disasters, but the economy has been transformed from a mainly agricultural to a service-based economy with a growing manufacturing sector. Government diversification efforts have promoted textile production, international port services and tourism. Even so, the value of remittances from El Salvadoreans working abroad is equivalent to nearly all export earnings, and 30 per cent of the population lives below the poverty line. The economy contracted in 2009 with both exports and remittances adversely affected by the global downturn.

Agriculture contributes 11.1 per cent to GDP and employs 19 per cent of the workforce. The principal agricultural products are coffee, sugar, maize, rice, beans, oilseed, cotton, sorghum, beef and dairy products. Industry contributes 28.2 per cent of GDP, mostly through assembly for re-export, food processing, beverages, oil, chemicals, fertiliser, textiles, furniture and light metals. Services, through tourism, commerce and financial services, contribute 60.7 per cent of GDP.

The main trading partners are the USA and other Central American states. Principal exports are offshore assembly products, coffee, sugar, textiles, garments, gold, ethanol, chemicals and electricity. The chief imports are raw materials, consumer goods, capital goods, fuels, foodstuffs, oil and electricity.
GNI – US$21,200m; US$3,460 per capita (2008)
Annual average growth of GDP – –2.3 per cent (2009 est)
Inflation rate – 1 per cent (2009 est)
Population below poverty line – 30.7 per cent (2006 est)
Unemployment – 7.2 per cent (2009 est)
Total external debt – US$11,510m (2009)
Imports – US$9,800m (2008)
Exports – US$4,600m (2008)

BALANCE OF PAYMENTS
Trade – US$3,519m deficit (2009)
Current Account – US$373m deficit (2009)

Trade with UK	*2008*	*2009*
Imports from UK	£9,496,678	£8,220,360
Exports to UK	£5,847,286	£4,811,137

COMMUNICATIONS
The principal ports are Cutuco and Acajutla, and ports in Honduras and Guatemala are also used. There are 10,886km of roads, of which 2,827km are surfaced. The Pan-American Highway from the Guatemalan frontier passes through Santa Ana and San Salvador, continuing to the Honduran frontier. The rail network has not been in operation since 2005 because of lack of maintenance. There are 65 airports and airfields, although only four have surfaced runways. There is an international airport at San Salvador. Mobile phone density has grown rapidly, reaching nearly 100 per 100 people in 2007; this growth has slowed demand for fixed-line services.

EDUCATION AND HEALTH
Primary education is state-run, compulsory and free of charge.
Literacy rate – 82.0 per cent (2007 est)
Gross enrolment ratio (percentage of relevant age group) – primary 115 per cent; secondary 64 per cent; tertiary 25 per cent (2008 est)
Health expenditure (per capita) – US$24 (2007)
Hospital beds (per 1,000 people) – 0.8 (2003–8)

MEDIA
Television is dominated by a small number of large private broadcasters, but there are hundreds of private radio stations. Press freedom is guaranteed by the country's constitution.

EQUATORIAL GUINEA

República de Guinea Ecuatorial / Republique de Guinee equatoriale – Republic of Equatorial Guinea

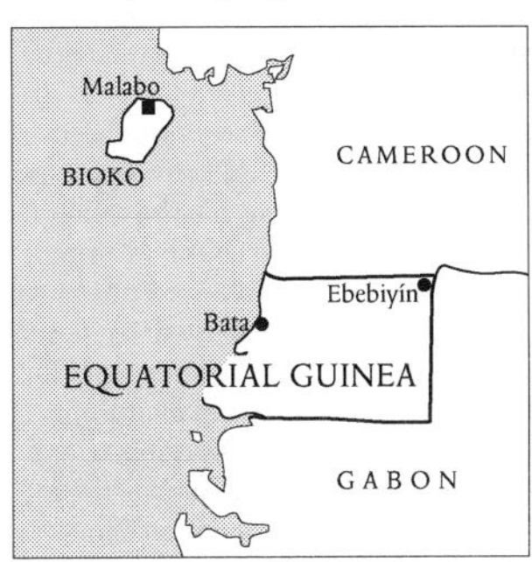

Area – 28,051 sq. km
Capital – Malabo, on Bioko; population, 127,743 (2009 est)
Major towns – Bata, the principal town and port of Río Muni; Ebebiyín

Currency – Franc CFA of 100 centimes
Population – 633,441 rising at 2.7 per cent a year (2009 est); predominantly Fang; indigenous Bubi now a minority on Bioko
Religion – Christian (Roman Catholic 87 per cent, other denominations 6 per cent), traditional indigenous religions 5 per cent (est). Many Catholics also follow traditional beliefs
Language – Spanish, French (both official), Fang, Bubi
Population density – 24 per sq. km (2008)
Urban population – 39 per cent (2007 est)
Median age (years) – 18.9 (2009 est)
National anthem – 'Caminemos Pisando la Senda' ['Let Us Tread the Path']
National day – 12 October (Independence Day)
Life expectancy – 61.61 (2009 est)
Mortality rate – 9.49 (2009 est)
Birth rate – 36.52 (2009 est)
Infant mortality rate – 81.58 (2009 est)
HIV/AIDS adult prevalence – 3.3 per cent (2007 est)
Death penalty – Retained
CPI score – 1.8 (2009)
Literacy rate – 87.0 per cent (2007 est)

CLIMATE AND TERRAIN

The country consists of several islands off the Cameroon coast and a small area on the mainland, Río Muni, where 80 per cent of the population lives. The islands, of which Bioko is the largest, are of volcanic origin. The mainland rises from a narrow coastal plain to a mountainous interior plateau, and is covered in dense vegetation. Elevation extremes range from 3,008m (Pico Basile) at the highest point to 0m (Atlantic Ocean) at the lowest. The climate is tropical, with a rainy season from July to January on Bioko, and from April to May and October to December on the mainland.

HISTORY AND POLITICS

The island of Fernando Po (Bioko) was claimed by the Portuguese in 1494 and held until 1777, when it was ceded to Spain. The mainland territory of Río Muni came under Spanish rule in 1844, and the two territories became one colony, subsequently known as Spanish Guinea, in 1904. The colony became autonomous in 1963, and independent in 1968 under its present name.

The first president, Francisco Macías Nguema, established a one-party state in 1970. His brutal regime was overthrown in 1979 in a military coup led by his nephew, Col. Obiang Nguema. A military regime was established after the coup, and only presidential nominees were allowed to stand in the 1983 and 1988 elections. Constitutional amendments were introduced in 1991 to allow multiparty elections, and ten opposition parties were legalised, operating alongside the ruling Democratic Party of Equatorial Guinea (PDGE). However, President Nguema and the PDGE have retained power since 1992; most elections have been boycotted by the opposition parties because of election irregularities and intimidation. The regime has been accused of human rights abuses and the suppression of political opposition, and in 2003 opposition leaders set up a 'government-in-exile' in Spain. There is also a separatist movement on Bioko.

In the 2008 legislative election, the PDGE retained its overwhelming majority in parliament. President Nguema won the 2009 presidential election with 96 per cent of the vote.

POLITICAL SYSTEM

The 1991 constitution introduced a multiparty system. The president is directly elected for a seven-year term. The unicameral House of Representatives of the People has 100 members, who are directly elected for a five-year term.

HEAD OF STATE

President, Brig.-Gen. Teodoro Obiang Nguema Mbasogo, *took power* August 1979, *re-elected* 1989, 1996, 2002, 2009

SELECTED GOVERNMENT MEMBERS *as at May 2010*

Prime Minister, Ignacio Milam Tang
Economy, Pedro Ondo Nguema
Foreign Affairs, Pastor Micha Ondo Bile
Interior, Clemente Engonga Nguema Onguene
Defence, Gen. Antonio Mba Nguema Mikwe

EMBASSY OF THE REPUBLIC OF EQUATORIAL GUINEA

13 Park Place, London SW1A 1LP
T 020-7499 6867 E embarege-londres@embarege-londres.org
W www.embarege-londres.org
Ambassador Extraordinary and Plenipotentiary, HE Agustin Nze Nfumu, *apptd* 2005

BRITISH AMBASSADOR

HE Robert Dewar, CMG, *apptd* 2007, resident at Abuja, Nigeria

DEFENCE

The army has 10 armoured personnel carriers and 20 armoured infantry fighting vehicles. The navy has 5 patrol and coastal combatant vessels at 2 bases. The coastguard has 1 patrol and coastal combatant vessel. The air force has 4 combat capable aircraft and 3 armed helicopters.
Military budget – US$11m (2008 est)
Military personnel – 1,320: army 1,100, navy 120, air force 100

ECONOMY AND TRADE

Large oil and natural gas deposits discovered off Bioko in the 1990s have transformed the economy, which has grown dramatically since production began in 1996, but contracted in 2009 owing to the fall in oil prices during the global downturn. The country has the reputation of being one of the most corrupt in the world; oil exploitation has not benefited much of the population as most businesses are owned by government officials or their families and, despite the oil revenues, the country has a large external debt.

Industry contributes 93.3 per cent of GDP, agriculture 2.4 per cent and services 4.2 per cent. The oil-driven growth in the GDP masks stagnation in other sectors; agriculture, once the mainstay of the economy, has declined to subsistence level owing to neglect and lack of investment. The main crops are coffee, cocoa, rice, fruit, nuts, livestock and timber. Industrial activities other than oil and natural gas production include fishing and timber processing. The main trading partners are the USA, China, Spain and France. Principal exports are petroleum, methanol, timber and cocoa. The main imports are oil industry and other industrial equipment.
GNI – US$9,875m; US$14,980 per capita (2008)
Annual average growth of GDP – −1.8 per cent (2009 est)
Inflation rate – 4.5 per cent (2009 est)
Total external debt – US$174m (2009 est)
Imports – US$3,200m (2008)
Exports – US$18,800m (2008)

BALANCE OF PAYMENTS
Trade – US$9,221m surplus (2009)
Current Account – US$1,684m deficit (2008)

Trade with UK	*2008*	*2009*
Imports from UK	£42,953,377	£43,598,988
Exports to UK	£8,803,240	£41,989,285

MEDIA

Television and radio broadcasts are state-controlled; the government owns the only television station and – other than a private station owned by President Nguema's son – the only radio station. The main newspaper, *Ebano,* is also state-owned. A few privately owned publications appear sporadically. Criticism of the authorities is extremely rare as the government has legal powers of censorship.

ERITREA

Hagere Ertra – State of Eritrea

Area – 117,600 sq. km
Capital – Asmara; population, 648,961 (2009 est)
Major towns – Assab, Keren, Massawa
Currency – Nakfa of 100 cents
Population – 5,647,168 rising at 2.58 per cent a year (2009 est); Tigrinya (50 per cent), Tigre and Kunama (40 per cent), Afar (4 per cent), Saho (3 per cent) (est)
Religion – Sunni Muslim 50 per cent, Christian (Eritrean Orthodox 30 per cent, Roman Catholic 13 per cent), indigenous religions 2 per cent (est). Only Christians of the Eritrean Orthodox, Catholic and Lutheran churches and Muslims may meet freely
Language – Tigrinya, Tigre, Arabic, Afar, Kunama
Population density – 49 per sq. km (2008)
Urban population – 20 per cent (2007 est)
Median age (years) – 18.4 (2009 est)
National anthem – 'Ertra, Ertra, Ertra' ['Eritrea, Eritrea, Eritrea']
National day – 24 May (Independence Day)
Life expectancy – 61.78 (2009 est)
Mortality rate – 8.43 (2009 est)
Birth rate – 34.2 (2009 est)
Infant mortality rate – 43.33 (2009 est)
HIV/AIDS adult prevalence – 1.3 per cent (2007 est)
Death penalty – Retained (not used since 1989)
CPI score – 2.6 (2009)
Literacy rate – 64.2 per cent (2007 est)
Gross enrolment ratio (percentage of relevant age group) – primary 52 per cent; secondary 30 per cent (2008 est); tertiary 2 per cent (2009 est)
Health expenditure (per capita) – US$9 (2007 est)
Hospital beds (per 1,000 people) – 1.2 (2003–8)

CLIMATE AND TERRAIN

The northern end of the Ethiopian Highlands extends into central Eritrea, where the average altitude is over 2,000m. The mountains fall in the west to a plateau, then rise to the hills on the Sudanese border. To the east of the mountains, the land falls to the narrow coastal plain. The coastal strip extending to the Djibouti border is low-lying, the border with Ethiopia running along the edge of the Danakil desert. Elevation extremes range from 3,018m (Soira) at the highest point to –75m (Danakil depression) at the lowest. The climate varies according to altitude, with temperatures averaging 16°C in the mountains, which are also wetter, and 30°C on the arid coastal plain.

HISTORY AND POLITICS

Part of the Axum empire from the first century AD, the area came under the control of the Ottoman Empire in the mid-16th century. It was occupied by Italy in the late 19th century and was the base for Italy's 1936 invasion of Abyssinia (now Ethiopia). After the Italian defeat in North Africa in 1941, Eritrea became a British protectorate until 15 September 1952, when a federation with Ethiopia was established by the UN. In 1962, Ethiopia annexed Eritrea outright.

The Eritrean Liberation Front (ELF) fought a guerrilla war for independence from 1961, and the Eritrean People's Liberation Front (a breakaway faction of the ELF) emerged in the 1970s, becoming the dominant rebel group in the 1980s. The EPLF joined with Ethiopian resistance groups to fight the Mengistu regime, which was overthrown in 1991. The EPLF secured the whole of Eritrea and formed an autonomous provisional government. The new Ethiopian government agreed to an Eritrean referendum on independence, which was held in April 1993 and recorded a 99.89 per cent vote in favour. Independence was declared on 24 May 1993.

Following independence, a transitional government for a four-year period was formed under Issaias Afwerki, and the EPLF became the ruling political party, renaming itself the People's Front for Democracy and Justice (PFDJ) in 1994. The post-independence regime has become increasingly authoritarian, and since 2001 has dealt harshly with anyone openly critical of the government. Although a new constitution was adopted in 1997, no presidential election has taken place since independence, and legislative elections scheduled for 2001 were postponed and have not been rescheduled.

FOREIGN RELATIONS

Since independence, Eritrea has been involved in disputes with Yemen, Ethiopia and Djibouti over territory, while Sudan has accused Eritrea of supporting rebels in eastern Sudan. The dispute with Yemen was over the Hanish and Mohabaka islands in the Red Sea; possession was divided between Yemen and Eritrea by international arbitration.

There has been fighting with Ethiopia in disputes over border territory, especially in the Tigray region, since 1998. Though usually sporadic, fighting escalated in 1999–2000 into a war that left thousands of people dead. An independent boundary commission defined the international border between the two countries in 2002, but both countries have failed to abide by the original demarcation or a revised ruling in 2006, and Ethiopia rejected the 2007 virtual demarcation. The UN peacekeeping mission deployed in 2000 was withdrawn in 2008, largely owing to the obstructiveness of the Eritrean government.

Fighting broke out on the part of the border disputed with Djibouti in 2008 after alleged incursions by Eritrean troops. Eritrea has repulsed international efforts to monitor a withdrawal or negotiate a settlement, denying that it has any troops in Djibouti territory.

In December 2009, the UN imposed sanctions on Eritrea owing to its alleged support for Islamist insurgents in Somalia.

POLITICAL SYSTEM

Although a new constitution was adopted in 1997, few of its provisions have been enacted and no presidential or legislative elections have been held, so the transitional president, state council (cabinet) and legislature remain in place. Under the constitution, the president is elected for a five-year term by the legislature, and the 150-member unicameral National Assembly is directly elected for a four-year term. The People's Front for Democracy and Justice (PFDJ) is the only legal political party.

HEAD OF STATE

President, Chairman of the State Council and of the National Assembly, Issaias Afewerki, *elected by the National Assembly* 22 May 1993

SELECTED GOVERNMENT MEMBERS *as at May 2010*

Defence, Gen. Sebhat Ephrem

Foreign Affairs, Osman Saleh

Finance, Berhane Abrehe

EMBASSY OF THE STATE OF ERITREA

96 White Lion Street, London N1 9PF

T 020-7713 0096 E eriemba@eriembauk.com

Ambassador Extraordinary and Plenipotentiary, HE Tesfamicael Gerahtu Ogbaghiorghis, *apptd* 2007

BRITISH EMBASSY

PO Box 5584, 66–68 Mariam Ghimbi Street, Asmara

T (+291) (1) 120 145 E asmara.enquiries@fco.gov.uk

W ukineritrea.fco.gov.uk

Ambassador Extraordinary and Plenipotentiary, HE Sandra Tyler-Haywood, *apptd* 2010

BRITISH COUNCIL

PO Box 997, 175-11 Street No 23, Asmara

T (+291) (1) 123 415/120 529 W www.britishcouncil.org/africa

Director, Angus Bjarnason

DEFENCE

The army has 270 main battle tanks, 15 armoured infantry fighting vehicles and 25 armoured personnel carriers. The navy has 13 patrol and coastal combatant vessels at 3 bases. The air force has 31 combat aircraft and 1 armed helicopter.

Military personnel – 201,750: army 200,000, navy 1,400, air force 350

Conscription duration – 16 months

ECONOMY AND TRADE

Over 30 years of conflict left the country's economy devastated, and the restrictive policies of the post-independent regime have hampered recovery. The command economy has concentrated business ownership in military and party hands, while agricultural output is restricted by lack of labour owing to the failure to demobilise the large army, the conflict with Ethiopia and the frequent droughts and ensuing famines. Currently, agriculture and herding are the means of subsistence of around 80 per cent of the population, but food production is insufficient and emergency food aid is needed for two-thirds of the people. The industrial sector has contracted since trade with Ethiopia halted in 1998, and the principal ports have suffered from the loss of the Ethiopian transit trade.

Mineral reserves include zinc, potash, gold, copper and possibly oil; these are not fully exploited at present, although mining production should begin in 2010. Industries include food processing, beverages, clothing and textiles, salt, cement and light manufacturing. The opening of a free trade zone at Massawa in 2008 may boost revenues, currently heavily dependent on remittances from expatriates.

The main trade partners are India, Italy, China, Saudi Arabia and Sudan. Principal exports are livestock, sorghum, textiles, food and light manufactures. The main imports are machinery, petroleum products, food and manufactured goods.

GNI – US$1,500m; US$300 per capita (2008)

Annual average growth of GDP – 2.5 per cent (2009 est)

Inflation rate – 15.5 per cent (2009 est)

Population below poverty line – 50 per cent (2004 est)

BALANCE OF PAYMENTS

Current Account – US$75m deficit (2008)

Trade with UK	*2008*	*2009*
Imports from UK	£1,681,370	£2,942,251
Exports to UK	£178,958	£91,165

COMMUNICATIONS

Infrastructure reconstruction has focused on the ports of Massawa and Assab, the roads from these ports to Ethiopia, and the railway from Massawa to Sudan via Asmara. There are 306km of railways and 4,010km of roads, of which 874km are surfaced. There are 14 airports and airfields, of which four have surfaced runways; the main international airport is at Asmara. The fixed-line telephone system is poor and largely confined to Asmara; mobile phone subscriptions are more than double the number of fixed-line subscribers, at 108,600 in 2008, but the combined density of both types of subscriber is only three per 100 people.

MEDIA

Eritrea is the only country in Africa without any privately owned news media. Existing organisations were closed down by the government in 2001, helping Eritrea supplant North Korea as the worst country in the world for press freedom in 2007 and 2009 according to Reporters Without Borders. Journalists have been detained without charge for publishing views critical of the government.

ESTONIA

Eesti Vabariik – Republic of Estonia

Area – 45,228 sq. km
Capital – Tallinn; population, 399,027 (2009 est)
Major towns – Kohtla-Jarve, Narva, Parnu, Tartu
Currency – Kroon of 100 senti
Population – 1,299,371 falling at 0.63 per cent a year (2009 est); Estonian (67.9 per cent), Russian (25.6 per cent), Ukrainian (2.1 per cent), Belarusian (1.3 per cent), Finn (0.9 per cent)
Religion – Christian (Orthodox 17 per cent, Lutheran 13 per cent) (est)
Language – Estonian (official), Russian
Population density – 32 per sq. km (2008)
Urban population – 69 per cent (2007 est)
Median age (years) – 39.9 (2009 est)
National anthem – 'Mu Isamaa, Mu Onn Ja Room' ['My Native Land, My Joy and Delight']
National day – 24 February (Independence Day)
Life expectancy (years) – 72.82 (2009 est)
Mortality rate – 13.42 (2009 est)
Birth rate – 10.37 (2009 est)
Infant mortality rate – 7.32 (2009 est)
Death penalty – Abolished for all crimes (since 1998)
CPI score – 6.6 (2009)

CLIMATE AND TERRAIN

The country is mostly a plain of lakes, marshes and forests, with a range of low hills in the south-east. Elevation extremes range from 318m (Suur Munamagi) at the highest point to 0m (Baltic Sea) at the lowest. Part of the border with Russia runs through the large Lake Peipsi. The climate is maritime, with average temperatures ranging from −6°C in January to 17°C in July.

HISTORY AND POLITICS

The area came under Swedish control between 1561 and 1629, and was ceded to the Russian Empire in 1721. An Estonian nationalist movement developed in the late 19th century and fought against occupying German forces during the First World War. Estonia declared its independence in February 1918 and defended it against Soviet forces until 1920, when independence was recognised by the USSR. However, the USSR annexed Estonia in 1940, and the country was subsequently occupied by German forces when they invaded the USSR in 1941. In 1944 the USSR expelled the Germans and reannexed the country, beginning a process of 'Sovietisation'.

There was a resurgence of nationalist sentiment in the 1980s, and in 1989 the Estonian Supreme Soviet declared the republic to be sovereign and its 1940 annexation by the USSR to be illegal. In 1990, the Communist Party's monopoly of power was abolished and, following multiparty elections in which pro-independence candidates won the majority of seats, a period of transition to independence was inaugurated, culminating in its declaration on 20 August 1991. The last Russian troops withdrew in 1994. Since independence, Estonia has pursued pro-Western policies. It joined NATO and the EU in 2004.

In 2006 Toomas Hendrik Ilves was elected president by an electoral assembly. In the 2007 legislative election, the Reform Party (ER), the main partner in the coalition government since 2005, became the largest party and formed a new coalition with the Union of Pro Patria and Res Publica (IRL) and the Estonian Social Democratic Party (SDE). The next legislative election is due in March 2011.

POLITICAL SYSTEM

Under the 1992 constitution, the president is elected for a five-year term by the legislature by a two-thirds majority or, if no candidate receives this majority after three rounds of voting, by an electoral assembly composed of the legislature members and local government representatives. The unicameral legislature, the *Riigikogu,* has 101 members, directly elected for a four-year term. The prime minister is appointed by the president and nominates the government. Members of the government need not be members of the *Riigikogu.*

HEAD OF STATE

President, Toomas Hendrik Ilves, *elected by electoral assembly* 23 September 2006, *sworn in* 9 October 2006

SELECTED GOVERNMENT MEMBERS *as at May 2010*

Prime Minister, Andrus Ansip
Defence, Jaak Aaviksoo
Finance, Jurgen Ligi
Foreign Affairs, Urmas Paet
Internal Affairs, Marko Pomerants

EMBASSY OF THE REPUBLIC OF ESTONIA

16 Hyde Park Gate, London SW7 5DG
T 020-7589 3428 E london@mfa.ee W www.estonia.gov.uk
Ambassador Extraordinary and Plenipotentiary, HE Dr Margus Laidre, *apptd* 2006

BRITISH EMBASSY

Wismari 6, Tallinn 10136
T (+372) 667 4700 E information@britishembassy.ee
W http://ukinestonia.fco.gov.uk
Ambassador Extraordinary and Plenipotentiary, HE Peter Carter, *apptd* 2007

BRITISH COUNCIL

Vana–Posti 7, Tallinn 10146
T (+372) 625 7788 W www.britishcouncil.org/estonia
Country Manager, Hede Kerstin Luik

DEFENCE

The army has 88 armoured personnel carriers. The navy has 1 principal surface combatant vessel. The paramilitary Border Guard was merged into the Police and Border Guard Board from January 2010. Operates joint naval unit BALTRON (*see* Latvia: Defence).
Military expenditure – US$450m (2008)
Military personnel – 4,750: army 4,200, navy 300, air force 250
Conscription duration – 8–11 months

ECONOMY AND TRADE

Economic reforms and restructuring since 1992 have resulted in a market economy, the growth of which was boosted by the country's accession to the EU. Estonia entered recession in 2008 after an investment and consumption slump and a drop in demand for exports. Nevertheless, it reined in persistently high inflation and turned its current account deficit into a surplus in 2009, meeting the accession criteria for the eurozone, which it is expected to join from 1 January 2011.

Agriculture engages 2.8 per cent of the workforce and accounts for 3 per cent of GDP, the main products being potatoes, vegetables, livestock and dairy products, and fish. Industry accounts for 22.7 per cent of employment and 24.4 per cent of GDP, concentrating on engineering, electronics, wood and wood products, textiles, information technology and telecommunications; electronics and telecommunications are particularly strong. The services sector accounts for 74.5 per cent of employment and 72.6 per cent of GDP.

The main trading partners are other EU countries, particularly Finland, and Russia. Principal exports are machinery and equipment, wood and paper, metals, food products, textiles and chemicals. The main imports are machinery and equipment, textiles, fuels, chemical products and foodstuffs. Estonia remains dependent on Russian natural gas supplies, but it is a net exporter of electricity.

GNI – US$19,500m; US$14,570 per capita (2008)
Annual average growth of GDP – –13.7 per cent (2009 est)
Inflation rate – –0.4 per cent (2009 est)
Population below poverty line – 5 per cent (2003)
Unemployment – 14.3 per cent (2009 est)
Total external debt – US$22,540m (2009)
Imports – US$16,000m (2008)
Exports – US$12,400m (2008)

BALANCE OF PAYMENTS
Trade – US$1,117m deficit (2009)
Current Account – US$880m surplus (2009)

Trade with UK	*2008*	*2009*
Imports from UK	£214,368,548	£146,180,808
Exports to UK	£2143,781,026	£123,472,598

EDUCATION AND HEALTH

Primary and secondary level education is compulsory between the ages of seven and 15. The country's best known university is Tartu, founded in 1632.

Literacy rate – 99.8 per cent (2007 est)
Gross enrolment ratio (percentage of relevant age group) – primary 99 per cent; secondary 100 per cent; tertiary 65 per cent (2008 est)
Health expenditure (per capita) – US$837 (2007)
Hospital beds (per 1,000 people) – 5.6 (2003–8)

MEDIA AND CULTURE

Freedom of the press is guaranteed in the constitution, and the state monopoly on television and radio ended soon after independence. All newspapers are privately owned, and public broadcasting channels compete with private-sector companies. Russian-language news and programmes are provided on Estonian television, as are channels in Swedish, Finnish and Latvian.

The old town area of Tallinn is a UNESCO World Heritage Site. The city has suffered many occupations but, apart from a Soviet bombing raid in 1944, its medieval and 18th-century architecture has never been harmed. Estonia's heritage is rich in traditional folk songs and poetry, which influences much of its contemporary culture. Novelist and poet Jaan Kross (1920–2007) has been the country's most eminent fiction writer of modern times. Well-known names in modern classical music include conductors Neeme Jarvi (*b.* 1937) and Tonu Kaljuste (*b.* 1953), and composers Arvo Part (*b.* 1935) and Veljo Tormis (*b.* 1930).

ETHIOPIA

Ityop'iya Federalawi Demokrasiyawi Ripeblik – Federal Democratic Republic of Ethiopia

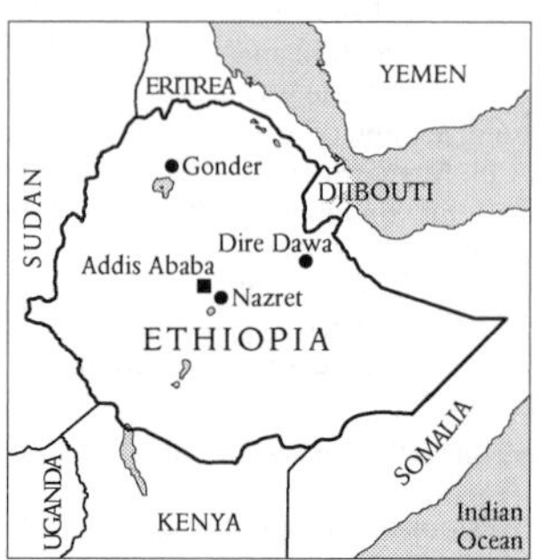

Area – 1,104,300 sq. km
Capital – Addis Ababa; population, 2,863,150 (2009 est)
Major cities – Bahir Dar, Dese, Dire Dawa, Gonder, Mek'ele, Nazret
Currency – Birr (EB) of 100 cents
Population – 85,237,338 rising at 3.21 per cent a year (2009 est); Oromo (34 per cent), Amhara (27 per cent), Somali (6 per cent), Tigray (6 per cent), Sidama (4 per cent) (2007 census)
Religion – Christian (Ethiopian Orthodox 44 per cent, Evangelical and Pentecostal denominations 19 per cent), Sunni Muslim 34 per cent (of which the majority are Sufi) (est)
Language – Amharic (official), Oromigna, Tigrinya, Somali, Arabic, English, Guaragigna, Sidamo
Population density – 81 per sq. km (2008)
Urban population – 17 per cent (2007 est)
Median age (years) – 16.9 (2009 est)
National anthem – 'Wodefit Gesgeshi Widd Innat Ityopp'ya' ['March Forward, Dear Mother Ethiopia']
National day – 28 May
Life expectancy (years) – 55.41 (2009 est)
Mortality rate – 11.55 (2009 est)
Birth rate – 43.66 (2009 est)
Infant mortality rate – 80.8 (2009 est)
HIV/AIDS adult prevalence – 1.9 per cent (2007 est)
Death penalty – Retained
CPI score – 2.7 (2009)

CLIMATE AND TERRAIN

Ethiopia is a landlocked country dominated by a central plateau, rising to the mountains of the Ethiopian Highlands, which are divided by the Great Rift Valley. The western mountains are the source of the Blue Nile. The land drops to desert plains in the east (Ogaden) and north-east (Danakil desert). Elevation extremes range from 4,533m (Ras Dejen) at the highest point to –125m (Danakil depression) at the lowest. There is a tropical monsoon climate, with variations according to altitude. The wet season is from April to September.

HISTORY AND POLITICS

The area's Hamitic culture was influenced by Semitic immigration in the centuries before the time of Christ. The coastal trading empire based at Axum was established in the first century AD and reached its zenith in the sixth century. Coptic Christianity was introduced in the fourth century. The independent kingdom of Abyssinia emerged in the 11th century. Modern Ethiopia dates from 1855 when Theodros established supremacy over the various tribes. Menelik II repulsed an Italian invasion in 1896, but Italy conquered Abyssinia in 1936 and occupied the country until its liberation and the return of the emperor, Haile Selassie, in 1941. Ethiopia was federated with Eritrea by the UN in 1952 and annexed the area in 1962.

Emperor Haile Selassie was deposed in a military coup in 1974 and a military government was installed. By 1977 Lt.-Col. Mengistu Haile Mariam had become head of state and his single-party Marxist regime initiated reforms based on the Soviet model, brutally suppressing opposition. War with Somalia over the predominently ethnic Somali and Muslim territory of Ogaden (1977–8), internal conflict with Ethiopian resistence and Eritrean separatist forces, drought and famine (1984–5), and government mismanagement and corruption undermined the regime, and it was overthrown in 1991. A transitional administration comprising the Ethiopian People's Revolutionary Democratic Front (EPRDF) and other opposition groups governed until a new federal constitution was adopted in 1994. The Federal Democratic Republic of Ethiopia was proclaimed on 22 August 1995.

There is a continuing low-level insurgency by separatists in the predominantly Somali regions.

Electoral fraud in the 2005 legislative election led to reruns of polls in over 30 seats. Popular protests against these polling irregularities were violently suppressed amid a crackdown on the opposition and the media. Since 2005 there has been a decline in respect for human rights, which has attracted international criticism and caused foreign donors to cut aid. Foreign agencies engaged in human rights or conflict resolution work were banned in 2009, and the activities of local agencies were restricted.

Lt. Girma Wolde Giorgis, the EPRDF candidate, was elected president in 2001 and re-elected in 2007. Meles Zenawi, prime minister since 1994, was re-appointed for a third term in 2005. In the legislative election in May 2010, the EPRDF won an overwhelming majority of seats; observers considered the polls flawed and opposition leaders called for a rerun, alleging government intimidation.

FOREIGN RELATIONS

There has been fighting with Eritrea in disputes over border territory, especially in Tigray, since 1998. Though usually sporadic, fighting escalated in 1999–2000 into a war in which thousands of people died. An independent boundary commission defined the international border between the two countries in 2002 but both countries have failed to abide by the original demarcation or a revised ruling in 2006, and Ethiopia rejected a 2007 virtual demarcation.

Ethiopia intervened in Somalia in 2006 in support of the Somali transitional government. Ethiopia formally withdrew its forces in January 2009, in accordance with a 2008 peace agreement between the Somali government and rebels. However, Ethiopian forces appear to have been in action in Somalia since the withdrawal.

POLITICAL SYSTEM

The 1994 constitution provides for a federal government responsible for foreign affairs, defence and economic policy, and nine ethnically based states. The president is elected by both houses of the legislature for a six-year term, renewable only once. The prime minister is appointed by the lower chamber of the legislature and appoints the government. The Federal Parliamentary Assembly is bicameral. The lower chamber, the House of People's Representatives, has 547 members, directly elected for a five-year term. The House of the Federation has 110 members, elected for a five-year term by the government councils of the nine states in the federation. These regional administrations have considerable autonomy and the right to secede.

HEAD OF STATE

President, Lt. Girma Wolde Giorgis, *elected* 8 October 2001, *re-elected* 2007

SELECTED GOVERNMENT MEMBERS *as at May 2010*

Prime Minister, C.-in-C. of the National Armed Forces, Meles Zenawi
Deputy Prime Minister, Addisu Legesse
Finance and Economic Development, Sufian Ahmed
Foreign Affairs, Seyoum Mesfin
Defence, Siraj Fegisa

EMBASSY OF THE FEDERAL DEMOCRATIC REPUBLIC OF ETHIOPIA

17 Princes Gate, London SW7 1PZ
T 020-7589 7212 E info@ethioembassy.org.uk
W www.ethioembassy.org.uk
Ambassador Extraordinary and Plenipotentiary, HE Berhanu Kebede, *apptd* 2006

BRITISH EMBASSY

PO Box 858, Comoros Street, Addis Ababa
T (+251) (11) 661 2354
E britishembassy.addisababa@fco.gov.uk
W http://ukinethiopia.fco.gov.uk
Ambassador Extraordinary and Plenipotentiary, HE Norman Ling, *apptd* 2008

BRITISH COUNCIL

PO Box 1043, Artistic Building, Adwa Avenue, Addis Ababa
T (+251) (11) 662 0338 W www.britishcouncil.org/africa
Director, Barbara Wickham

DEFENCE

The army has over 246 main battle tanks and around 450 armoured infantry fighting vehicles and armoured personnel carriers. The air force has 42 combat aircraft and 20 armed helicopters.

Military budget – US$317m (2009)
Military personnel – 138,000: army 135,000, air force 3,000

ECONOMY AND TRADE

The economy is highly dependent on agriculture, and therefore reliant on the rains; recurring droughts led to famine conditions in 1984–5, 1992, 1997, 2000, 2002 and 2009. In 2004, the government began to move more than two million people from the drought-stricken and overworked highlands to the east of the country, claiming that this would be a long-term solution to food shortages, but food aid is still required at times of drought. Although most foreign debt was cancelled in 2005 and economic growth has been steady, emergency IMF funding has been needed to cushion the country from the effects of the global downturn.

Agriculture and herding account for approximately 43.8 per cent of GDP, and 85 per cent of the population is dependent upon the land for a living. The main crops are cereals, pulses, coffee, oilseed, cotton, sugar, potatoes, qat, cut flowers, livestock products and fish. Natural resources, including gold, platinum, copper, potash, oil and natural gas, are largely unexploited; most industrial activity involves the processing of agricultural products, gold mining and metalworking, and textiles.

The main trade partners are China, Saudi Arabia, Germany and Italy. Principal exports are coffee (which normally provides over 20 per cent of foreign exchange earnings), qat (or khat, a flowering plant chewed for its stimulant properties), gold, leather products, livestock and oilseeds. The main imports are food, livestock, petroleum and petroleum products, chemicals, machinery, vehicles, cereals and textiles.

GNI – US$22,400m; US$280 per capita (2008)
Annual average growth of GDP – 6.8 per cent (2009 est)
Inflation rate – 11 per cent (2009 est)
Population below poverty line – 38.7 per cent (2005/6 est)
Total external debt – US$4,229m (2009 est)
Imports – US$7,600m (2008)
Exports – US$1,500m (2008)

BALANCE OF PAYMENTS
Trade – US$7,575m deficit (2009)
Current Account – US$1,620m deficit (2009)

Trade with UK	*2008*	*2009*
Imports from UK	£53,421,875	£77,243,170
Exports to UK	£29,928,327	£25,980,607

COMMUNICATIONS

Since Eritrea became independent, Ethiopia has been landlocked. Most trade is via Djibouti, although Ethiopia also uses the port of Berbera in northern Somalia. A network of roads links the major cities with each other and with neighbouring countries; there are 36,469km of roads, 6,980km of which are surfaced. The only railway line, 681km in length, links Addis Ababa to Djibouti but is largely inoperable. There are over 60 airports and airfields, including the international airport at Addis Ababa. Ethiopian Airlines maintains regular services throughout Africa and to Europe. A number of infrastructure construction projects are being undertaken with foreign assistance and funding. There is a limited telephone service, and although access is growing, especially for mobile phones, only about five per 100 people have access to either type of telephone.

EDUCATION AND HEALTH

Non-compulsory elementary and secondary education are provided by government schools in the main centres of population; there are also mission schools. The National University (founded 1961) coordinates the institutions of higher education.

Literacy rate – 35.9 per cent (2007 est)
Gross enrolment ratio (percentage of relevant age group) – primary 91 per cent; secondary 30 per cent; tertiary 3 per cent (2007 est)
Health expenditure (per capita) – US$7 (2006)
Hospital beds (per 1,000 people) – 0.2 (2002–7)

MEDIA

Radio is the most popular medium and although state-owned Radio Ethiopia is the main broadcaster, two private stations were granted licences in 2006. State-owned Ethiopian Television is the only television station. Over 50 privately owned newspapers are published in addition to the state-owned daily *Addis Zemen*. The media has experienced harassment and repression since 2005. In spring 2010, Voice of America's Amharic Service was jammed; according to prime minister Meles Zenawi, it was engaging in destabilising propaganda.

FIJI

Matanitu ko Viti – Republic of the Fiji Islands

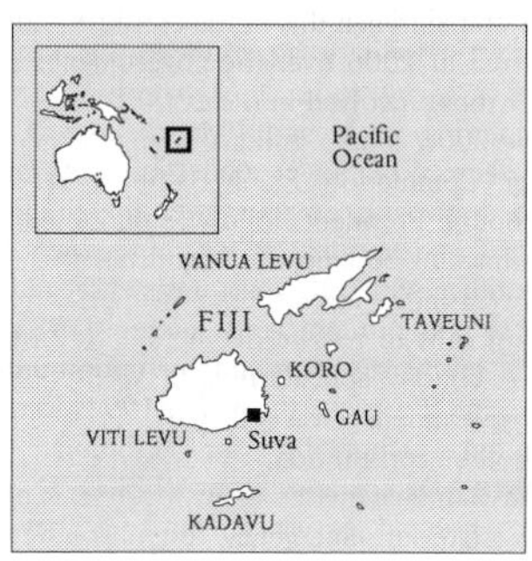

Area – 18,274 sq. km
Capital – Suva, on Viti Levu; population, 174,066 (2009 est)
Major towns – Lautoka, Nasinu, Nausori
Currency – Fiji dollar (F$) of 100 cents
Population – 944,720 rising at 1.38 per cent a year (2009 est); Fijian (57.3 per cent), Indian (37.6 per cent), Rotuman (1.2 per cent)
Religion – Christian 52 per cent (predominantly Methodist), Hindu 30 per cent, Muslim 7 per cent (predominantly Sunni) (est)
Language – English, Fijian, Hindustani (all official)
Population density – 46 per sq. km (2008)
Urban population – 52 per cent (2007 est)
Median age (years) – 25.5 (2009 est)
National anthem – 'Meda Dau Doka' ['God Bless Fiji']
National day – second Monday of October (Independence Day)
Life expectancy (years) – 70.73 (2009 est)
Mortality rate – 5.66 (2009 est)
Birth rate – 21.92 (2009 est)
Infant mortality rate – 11.58 (2009 est)
Death penalty – Retained for certain crimes (last used 1964)

CLIMATE AND TERRAIN

Fiji is a group of about 330 islands (around 110 are permanently inhabited) and over 500 islets in the South Pacific, about 1,770km north of New Zealand. The group extends 480km from east to west and 480km north to south. The International Date Line has been diverted to the east of the island group. The largest islands are Viti Levu and Vanua Levu. The terrain is mountainous and volcanic, with tropical rainforest and grassland, and most islands are surrounded by coral reefs. Elevation extremes range from 1,324m (Tomaniivi, on Viti Levu) at the highest point to 0m (Pacific Ocean) at the lowest. Fiji has a tropical maritime climate with high humidity and an average annual temperature of 27°C.

HISTORY AND POLITICS

The islands were settled by Melanesian peoples. European contact began with the visit of the Dutch explorer Abel Tasman in 1643; later visitors included Captain Cook in 1774. The islands became a British colony in 1874, and sugar plantations, employing more than 60,000 indentured Indian labourers, were established. Fiji became independent as a constitutional monarchy on 10 October 1970, and became a republic after the 1987 coups.

The growing size and political strength of the ethnic Indian population caused political instability in the late 1980s. There were two coups in 1987 and one in 2000 as indigenous Fijians attempted to reassert their political dominance and entrench this in the constitution. A fourth coup occurred in 2006 over the government's proposed amnesty for those involved in the 2000 coup.

Since the 2006 coup a military regime headed by the coup leader, Commodore Frank Bainimarama, has held power. Although President Iloilo was reinstated in 2007, when Bainimarama became prime minister, the regime has become increasingly authoritarian, suppressing dissent and resisting calls to restore democratic government. In response to a court of appeal ruling in April 2009 that the military government was illegal, President Iloilo suspended the constitution, dismissed the judiciary, reappointed Bainimarama as interim prime minister and declared a state of emergency, establishing a virtual dictatorship. The president has said that democracy will be restored through elections by 2014.

President Iloilo retired in 2009 and was replaced by the vice-president, Ratu Epeli Nailatikau.

POLITICAL SYSTEM

Under the 1997 constitution, suspended in 2006, the head of state is the president, appointed for a five-year term by the Great Council of Chiefs. The lower house of the bicameral parliament, which was dissolved in 2006, is the House of Representatives, with 71 members directly elected for a five-year term; 25 seats are open to all races and elected in single-member constituencies, while the other 46 are allocated for election by the country's various ethnic communities. The upper house, the senate, has 32 members, who are appointed for a five-year term by the president on the recommendation of the political parties (in proportion to their representation in the lower house) and the Great Council of Chiefs.

HEAD OF STATE

President, Ratu Epeli Nailatikau, *sworn in* 5 November 2009

SELECTED GOVERNMENT MEMBERS *as at May 2010*

Prime Minister, Finance, Commodore Voreqe ('Frank') Bainimarama
Attorney-General, Aiyaz Sayed-Khaiyum
Defence, Ratu Epeli Ganilau
Foreign Affairs, Ratu Inoke Kabuabola

HIGH COMMISSION OF THE REPUBLIC OF THE FIJI ISLANDS

34 Hyde Park Gate, London SW7 5DN
T 020-7584 3661 E mail@fijihighcommission.org.uk
W www.fijihighcommission.org.uk
High Commissioner, HE Pio Bosco Tikoisuva, *apptd* 2008

BRITISH HIGH COMMISSION

PO Box 1355, Victoria House, 47 Gladstone Road, Suva
T (+679) 322 9100 E publicdiplomacysuva@fco.gov.uk
W http://ukinfiji.fco.gov.uk
High Commissioner, HE Malcolm McLachlan, MBE, *apptd* 2009

DEFENCE

The navy has 7 patrol and coastal combatant vessels at 2 bases.
Military budget – US$52m (2009 est)
Military personnel – 3,500: army 3,200, navy 300

ECONOMY AND TRADE

Fiji has abundant natural resources and one of the more developed economies in the region. However, the economy suffered after the 1987 coups because of the mass emigration of Indian Fijians, and is now contracting owing to structural problems, inefficiency and continuing political instability. Tourism, the mainstay of the economy, has declined since 2006; in addition, remittances from expatriate Fijians have decreased significantly, and development aid has largely been reduced or suspended until the interim government moves to restore democracy.

Agriculture, much of it at subsistence level, accounts for 8.9 per cent of GDP and employs 70 per cent of the workforce. The principal cash crop is sugar cane, but revenue has been affected by a recent cut in EU subsidies. The other main crops are coconuts, cassava, rice, sweet potatoes, bananas, livestock and fish. The main industries are tourism, sugar processing, garment manufacturing, copra production, gold and silver mining, forestry and small cottage industries. The main trade partners are Australia, Singapore, New Zealand, the USA and the UK. Principal exports are sugar, garments, gold, timber, fish, molasses and coconut oil. The chief imports are manufactured goods, machinery and transport equipment, petroleum products, food and chemicals.
GNI – US$3,382m; US$4,010 per capita (2008)
Annual average growth of GDP – –1 per cent (2009 est)
Inflation rate – 4.8 per cent (2007)
Total external debt – US$127m (2004 est)
Imports – US$2,200m (2008)
Exports – US$900m (2008)

BALANCE OF PAYMENTS

Trade – US$870m deficit (2009)
Current Account – US$584m deficit (2007)

Trade with UK	*2008*	*2009*
Imports from UK	£6,418,119	£6,168,515
Exports to UK	£85,696,401	£79,152,775

COMMUNICATIONS

Fiji is one of the main aerial crossroads in the Pacific, providing services to New Zealand, Australia and other Pacific states; the 28 airports and airfields include international airports at Suva and Nadi. The main seaports are Suva and Lautoka. There are 3,440km of roads, 1,692km of which are surfaced. There are 597km of railway track, principally used by the sugar industry. The telephone system is modern and covers most of the islands.

MEDIA

Strict media censorship was imposed in April 2009 which prevents the publication of any material critical of the government. Fiji's privately owned newspapers are published in English, Fijian and Hindi; government-owned newspapers are also multilingual. Radio (both public and private) is the main source of news, particularly on the more remote outer islands. There are two main television networks, operated by Fiji Television Ltd: Fiji 1, a national channel, and Sky Fiji, accessed via subscription.

FINLAND

Suomen tasavalta / Republiken Finland – Republic of Finland

Area – 338,145 sq. km
Capital – Helsinki (Helsingfors); population, 1,106,910 (2009 est)
Major cities – Espoo (Esbo), Oulu (Uleaborg), Tampere (Tammerfors), Turku (Aabo), Vantaa (Vanda)
Currency – Euro (€) of 100 cents
Population – 5,250,275 rising at 0.1 per cent a year (2009 est); Finnish (93.4 per cent), Swedish (5.6 per cent), Sami (0.1 per cent) (2006)
Religion – Christian (Lutheran 82 per cent, Orthodox 1 per cent), Muslim 1 per cent (predominantly Sunni) (est)
Language – Finnish, Swedish (both official)
Population density – 17 per sq. km (2008)
Urban population – 63 per cent (2007 est)
Median age (years) – 42.1 (2009 est)
National anthem – 'Maamme'/'Vart Land' ['Our Land']
National day – 6 December (Independence Day)
Life expectancy (years) – 78.97 (2009 est)
Mortality rate – 10.07 (2009 est)
Birth rate – 10.38 (2009 est)
Infant mortality rate – 3.47 (2009 est)
Death penalty – Abolished for all crimes (since 1972)
CPI score – 8.9 (2009)

CLIMATE AND TERRAIN

Most of the country is a glaciated plain of forests (about 73 per cent of the land area) and over 60,000 lakes, with low hills along the eastern border with Russia and in the far north. Elevation extremes range from 1,328m (Haltiatunturi, or Halti) at the highest point to 0m (Baltic Sea) at the lowest. A quarter of the country lies north of the Arctic Circle; temperatures there can range from −20°C in January to 10°C in July. Average temperatures in Helsinki range from −6°C in January to 17°C in July.

Owing to isostatic uplift (the rise of land mass no longer depressed by the weight of glaciers), the surface area of Finland is growing by around 7 sq. km a year.

HISTORY AND POLITICS

Finland was part of the Swedish Empire from the 12th century until it was ceded to Russia in 1809, when it became an autonomous grand duchy of the Russian Empire. After the Russian Revolution in 1917, Finland declared its independence. An attempted coup by Finnish Bolsheviks led to a short civil war that ended in their defeat in 1918, and in 1919 a republic was established. It resisted the 1939 invasion by the USSR but was defeated in 1940 and forced to cede territory; in the hope of recovering this territory it joined Germany's attack on the USSR in 1941. After agreeing an armistice with the USSR in 1944, Finland concluded a peace treaty in 1947 that conceded further territory to the USSR and obliged it to pay reparations. A Soviet-Finnish cooperation treaty in 1948 forced Finland to demilitarise its Soviet border and to adopt a stance of neutrality; these terms lasted until the demise of the USSR in 1991.

Since the mid-1960s the majority of Finnish governments have been coalitions of centre and moderate left-wing parties, with the Social Democratic Party (SDP) or the Centre Party (KESK) leading coalitions. Finland joined the EU in 1995 and the European Monetary Union in 1998.

Tarja Halonen of the SDP became Finland's first woman president in 2000 and was re-elected in 2006. Following the 2007 legislative election, KESK remained the largest party and formed a new coalition government with the National Coalition Party, the Greens and the Swedish People's Party; fresh legislative elections are due in March 2011.

POLITICAL SYSTEM

Under the 2000 constitution, the president is directly elected for a six-year term. There is a unicameral legislature, the *Eduskunta,* with 200 members directly elected for a four-year term. The prime minister is elected by the *Eduskunta* and appointed by the president.

HEAD OF STATE

President, Tarja Halonen, *elected* 6 February 2000, *inaugurated* 1 March 2000, *re-elected* 2006

SELECTED GOVERNMENT MEMBERS *as at May 2010*

Prime Minister, Matti Vanhanen
Deputy Prime Minister; Finance, Jyrki Katainen
Defence, Jyri Hakamies
Foreign Affairs, Alexander Stubb
Interior, Anne Holmlund

EMBASSY OF FINLAND

38 Chesham Place, London SW1X 8HW
T 020-7838 6200 E sanomat.lon@formin.fi
W www.finemb.org.uk
Ambassador Extraordinary and Plenipotentiary, HE Pekka Huhtaniemi, *apptd* 2010

BRITISH EMBASSY

Itainen Puistotie 17, 00140 Helsinki
T (+358) (9) 2286 5100 E info@ukembassy.fi
W http://ukinfinland.fco.gov.uk
Ambassador Extraordinary and Plenipotentiary, HE Valerie Caton, *apptd* 2006

BRITISH COUNCIL

Urho Kekkosen Katu 2 C, 00100 Helsinki
T (+358) (9) 774 3330 W www.britishcouncil.fi
Director, Marjo Somari

DEFENCE

The army has 100 main battle tanks, 212 armoured infantry fighting vehicles and 990 armoured personnel carriers. The navy has 8 patrol and coastal vessels. The air force has 63 combat aircraft.

Military expenditure – US$3,630m (2008)
Military personnel – 22,600: army 16,000, navy 3,800, air force 2,750; paramilitary 2,950
Conscription duration – 6–12 months

ECONOMY AND TRADE

The country has a highly industrialised market economy which has thrived as a result of its telecommunications and electronics industries, particularly the manufacture of mobile phones, as well as its traditional timber and metals industries. However, the drop in exports and domestic demand owing to the global economic downturn pushed the economy into recession in 2009. The economy is particularly vulnerable to fluctuations in trade with Russia, both its own trade (Russia is its leading supplier of imports and a major export market) and foreign trade, for which Finland is a major transit point.

The main trade partners are Russia, Germany and Sweden. Principal exports are electrical and optical equipment, machinery, transport equipment, paper and pulp, chemicals, base metals and timber. The main imports are foodstuffs (especially grain), petroleum and petroleum products, chemicals, transport equipment, iron and steel, machinery, textile yarn and fabrics, and components for manufactured goods. Finland is a net importer of energy.

GNI – US$252,900m; US$47,600 per capita (2008)
Annual average growth of GDP – –6.7 per cent (2009 est)
Inflation rate – 0 per cent (2009 est)
Unemployment – 8.6 per cent (2009 est)
Total external debt – US$364,900m (2009)
Imports – US$92,100m (2008)
Exports – US$96,900m (2008)

BALANCE OF PAYMENTS
Trade – US$3,264m surplus (2009)
Current Account – US$3,297m surplus (2009)

Trade with UK	*2008*	*2009*
Imports from UK	£1,860,357,960	£1,322,505,684
Exports to UK	£2,726,579,113	£2,460,085,158

COMMUNICATIONS

The road and rail networks are concentrated in the southern half of the country, where most of the population and industry are located. There are 78,100km of roads, 50,900km of which are surfaced. There are 5,800km of railways. The main seaports are Helsinki, Kotka, Rauma and Turku, and there are passenger services to Sweden, Estonia and Germany as well as countries outside the Baltic. The principal airports are at Helsinki, Turku and Tampere. Mobile phone distribution, at 6.8 million subscribers in 2008, is over 100 per cent.

EDUCATION AND HEALTH

Primary education is free of charge and compulsory for children from seven to 16 years.

Gross enrolment ratio (percentage of relevant age group) – primary 98 per cent; secondary 111 per cent; tertiary 94 per cent (2008 est)
Health expenditure (per capita) – US$3,809 (2007)
Hospital beds (per 1,000 people) – 6.8 (2003–8)

MEDIA

Finland is highly rated for press freedom by Reporters Without Borders; every citizen has the right to publish and is guaranteed a right of reply. Newspapers are privately owned and offer a wide spectrum of political views. There are both commercial and state-owned broadcasters; the state broadcaster, Yleisradio Oy (YLE), is funded by licence fees and provides radio and television services in Swedish and Finnish, with radio in Sa'mi (Lappish). The analogue television signal was switched off in 2007. Newspapers, books, plays and films appear in both Finnish and Swedish.

FRANCE

République française – French Republic

Area – 551,500 sq. km (excluding overseas territories)
Capital – Paris; population, 10,410,000 (2009 est)
Major cities – Bordeaux, Lille, Lyon, Marseille, Montpellier, Nantes, Nice, Reims, Rennes, Strasbourg, Toulouse. The chief towns of Corsica are Ajaccio and Bastia
Currency – Euro (€) of 100 cents
Population – 62,150,775 (excluding overseas territories), rising at 0.55 per cent a year (2009 est)
Religion – Christian (Roman Catholic 65 per cent, Protestant denominations 2 per cent), Muslim 8 per cent, Jewish 1 per cent, Buddhist 1 per cent (est)
Language – French (official)
Population density – 114 per sq. km (2008) (excluding overseas territories)
Urban population – 77 per cent (2007 est)
Median age (years) – 39.4 (2009 est)
National anthem – 'La Marseillaise' ['Song of Marseille']
National day – 14 July (Fête de la Federation/Fête Nationale)
Life expectancy (years) – 80.98 (2009 est)
Mortality rate – 8.56 (2009 est)
Birth rate – 12.57 (2009 est)
Infant mortality rate – 3.33 (2009 est)
Death penalty – Abolished for all crimes (since 1981)
CPI score – 6.9 (2009)

CLIMATE AND TERRAIN

The north and west consist of flat plains, particularly in the basins of the Somme, Seine, Loire and Garonne rivers, with some low hills. The centre of the south is occupied by the Massif Central plateau, which is divided by the valley of the Rhone and Soane rivers from the mountains – the French Alps, the Jura and the Vosges – on the eastern border. The Pyrenees range lies along the southern border with Spain. Elevation extremes range from 4,807m (Mt Blanc, Alps) at the highest point to –2m (Rhône delta) at the lowest. The climate is generally temperate, though the south has a Mediterranean climate and the east a continental climate.

HISTORY AND POLITICS

The area that is now France was conquered by the Romans in the first century BC and, as the province of Gaul, remained part of the Roman Empire until the Frankish invasions of the fifth and sixth centuries. The treaty of Verdun (AD 843) divided the Frankish Empire created by Charlemagne into three parts, of which the western part, *Francia Occidentalis,* became the basis of modern France. Weak central government allowed the great nobles to form virtually independent duchies, and the assertion of royal power over these nobles was not completed until the 16th century. France's attempts to establish itself as the supreme European power from the 16th century were hindered by civil and religious wars (1562–98), but by the early 18th century this ambition was attained, along with a large overseas empire.

The *ancien régime* was overthrown in the French Revolution (1789), a republic was declared in 1792 and the king, Louis XVI, was executed. The republic was overthrown by Napoléon Bonaparte, who established the first French Empire (1804–14). After Bonaparte's defeat, the congress of Vienna restored the monarchy, but in 1848 the Second Republic was declared, which lasted only until 1852, when the Second Empire was proclaimed under Napoléon III. He was forced to abdicate following the defeat of France in the Franco-Prussian war (1870–71), after which the Third Republic (1870–1940) was established.

France was one of the victors in the First World War (1914–18), when German offensives in the north and east of the country were held and eventually defeated. However, the country was invaded in the Second World War and the north was occupied by Germany from 1940 until 1944, with a pro-German government in the south. The Fourth Republic was declared in 1946, but collapsed in 1958, when a new constitution was adopted and the Fifth Republic was proclaimed. France granted most of its colonies independence between 1954 and 1962.

France was a founder member of the EEC in 1958, and joined the European Monetary Union in 1999. In a 2005 referendum, the population rejected the EU constitution, stalling progress towards its introduction.

The 2007 presidential election was won in the second round by Nicolas Sarkozy, the Rally for the Republic (RPR) candidate. In the 2007 legislative elections, the RPR-led Union for a Popular Movement (UMP) won 313 seats in the National Assembly, and the UMP-dominated coalition government continued in office after a reshuffle. The UMP has also held a majority of the senate seats since the 2008 elections, but was heavily defeated in the 2010 regional elections.

INSURGENCIES

Corsican separatists pursued a campaign of bombings and shootings from the 1970s until 2003, when the main separatist faction declared a ceasefire; it observed this until 2005, since when minor bomb attacks have occurred. The French government's proposals to combine the island's two departments and to give the Corsican regional parliament greater autonomy were narrowly rejected in a 2003 referendum.

POLITICAL SYSTEM

Under the 1958 constitution, the head of state is a president directly elected for a five-year term, which is renewable only once. The legislature, the *Parlement,* consists of the National Assembly and the senate. The National Assembly has 577 deputies, 555 for metropolitan France and 22 for the overseas departments and territories; members are directly elected for a five-year term. The senate currently has 343 senators (321 for metropolitan France and overseas departments, ten for overseas collectivities and territories, and 12 for French nationals abroad); these are elected by an electoral college to serve a six-year term, with half elected every three years. Representation will be adjusted at the 2011 elections, when 348 senators will be elected (326 for metropolitan France and the overseas departments, ten for overseas collectivities and territories, and 12 for French nationals abroad).

The prime minister is nominated by the National Assembly and appointed by the president, as is the council of ministers. They are responsible to the legislature, but as the executive is constitutionally separate from the legislature, ministers may not sit in the legislature and must hand over their seats to a substitute.

A government plan for decentralisation of power from Paris was initiated in 2002, and constitutional amendments in 2003 paved the way for the devolution to the 22 regions and 96 departments of powers over economic development, transport, tourism, culture and further education.

HEAD OF STATE

President of the French Republic, Nicolas Sarkozy, *elected* 6 May 2007

SELECTED GOVERNMENT MEMBERS *as at May 2010*

Prime Minister, François Fillon
Defence, Hervé Morin
Economy, Christine Lagarde
Foreign Affairs, Bernard Kouchner
Interior, Brice Hortefeux

EMBASSY OF FRANCE

58 Knightsbridge, London SW1X 7JT
T 020-7073 1000 **E** presse.londres-amba@diplomatie.gouv.fr
W www.ambafrance-uk.org
Ambassador Extraordinary and Plenipotentiary, HE Maurice Gourdault-Montagne, *apptd* 2007

BRITISH EMBASSY

35 rue du Faubourg St Honoré, 75383 Paris Cédex 08
T (+33) (1) 4451 3100 **E** public.paris@fco.gov.uk
W http://ukinfrance.fco.gov.uk
Ambassador Extraordinary and Plenipotentiary, HE Sir Peter Westmacott, KCMG, LVO, *apptd* 2007

BRITISH COUNCIL

9 rue de Constantine, 75340 Paris Cédex 07
T (+33) (1) 4955 7300 **W** www.britishcouncil.org/france
Director, Chris Hickey

DEFENCE

The army has 637 main battle tanks, over 709 armoured infantry fighting vehicles, 3,894 armoured personnel carriers and 298 armed helicopters.

The navy has 9 submarines including 3 strategic submarines, 2 aircraft carriers, 11 destroyers, 20 frigates and 25 patrol and coastal vessels, 87 combat aircraft and

70 armed helicopters. The navy has 4 domestic and 6 overseas bases. The air force has 277 combat aircraft. There are currently 2 military satellites in service.

Military expenditure – US$67,100m (2008)

Military personnel – 352,771: army 134,000, navy 43,995, air force 57,600, central staff 5,200, Service de Santé 8,600, Gendarmerie 103,376

ECONOMY AND TRADE

The economy is in transition from a state of extensive government ownership and intervention to one which is more liberal and market-oriented; reform was initiated in response to poor economic growth and high unemployment. Implementation has been slow because of the constraints of eurozone membership, and strong resistance to the government's plans for privatisation and reform of labour, pensions and welfare – particularly by the trade unions and the large public sector – which have provoked demonstrations and strikes. Implementation was suspended in some areas as the government increased public investment in 2009 to alleviate the effects of the global downturn on the economy.

Over one third of the land area of metropolitan France is utilised for agricultural production and a further quarter is covered by forests. Viniculture is extensive, though France has lost market share to other countries in recent years. Cognac, liqueurs and cider are also produced. Other important agricultural products include cereals, sugar beet, potatoes, beef, dairy products and fish. Agriculture employs 3.8 per cent of the workforce and contributes 2.1 per cent of GDP.

Oil is produced from fields in the Landes area, but France is a net importer of crude oil, for processing by its oil-refining industry. Natural gas is produced in the foothills of the Pyrenees.

Industry contributes 19 per cent of GDP, employing 24.3 per cent of the workforce. The sector is highly diversified and includes the production of machinery, iron, steel, aluminium, chemicals, vehicles, aircraft, electronic goods, textiles and processed food. The service sector contributes 78.9 per cent of GDP and employs 71.8 per cent of the workforce. Tourism is an important contributor to GDP.

The main trading partners are other EU countries. Principal exports are machinery, vehicles, aircraft, plastics, chemicals, pharmaceutical products, iron and steel, and beverages. The main imports are raw materials for industry (eg crude oil, chemicals, plastics), machinery and equipment, vehicles and aircraft.

GNI – US$2,695,600m; US$42,000 per capita (2008)

Annual average growth of GDP – –2.1 per cent (2009 est)

Inflation rate – 0.1 per cent (2009 est)

Population below poverty line – 6.2 per cent (2004)

Unemployment – 9.7 per cent (2009 est)

Total external debt – US$5,021,000m (2009)

Imports – US$706,000m (2008)

Exports – US$606,000m (2008)

BALANCE OF PAYMENTS

Trade – US$59,392m deficit (2009)

Current Account – US$38,841m deficit (2009)

Trade with UK	*2008*	*2009*
Imports from UK	£18,698,002,970	£17,881,656,406
Exports to UK	£23,086,125,838	£21,140,965,776

COMMUNICATIONS

There are extensive road and rail networks covering the whole country, with approximately 1 million km of roads, including 11,000km of motorways, and around 29,200km of railways. The world's tallest road bridge was opened at Millau in 2004.

The principal seaports are Marseille on the Mediterranean Sea, Bordeaux and Nantes on the Atlantic coast, and Le Havre, Calais and Dunkirk on the Channel coast. There are 8,500km of navigable inland waterways, 1,600km navigable by large vessels, and Paris, Rouen and Strasbourg are significant river ports. The French mercantile marine consisted in 2008 of 138 ships of 1,000 gross tonnage or over, 127 of which are registered overseas. There are two international airports serving Paris, and many regional airports capable of accepting international flights.

In 2008, there were 35 million fixed telephone lines in use, 58 million mobile phone users and 42.3 million internet users.

EDUCATION AND HEALTH

Education is compulsory, free of charge and secular from the ages of six to 16. Schools may be single-sex or co-educational. Primary education is given in nursery schools and elementary schools. Lower secondary education is provided at *collèges d'enseignement général* (four-year secondary modern course), and higher secondary education in *collèges d'enseignement technique, collèges d'enseignement secondaire* and *lycées* (a seven-year course leading to one of the five *baccalauréats)*. Specialist schools are numerous.

There are many *grandes écoles* in France which award diplomas in subjects not taught at university, especially applied science and engineering. Most of these are state institutions but have a competitive system of entry, unlike the universities.

Gross enrolment ratio (percentage of relevant age group) – primary 110 per cent; secondary 113 per cent; tertiary 55 per cent (2008 est)

Health expenditure (per capita) – US$4,627 (2007)

Hospital beds (per 1,000 people) – 7.2 (2003–8)

MEDIA

France has over 100 daily newspapers, including *Le Monde, Le Figaro* and *Libération*. The press is mostly privately owned and not linked to political parties. State radio broadcasting caters for both domestic (Radio France) and overseas (Radio France Internationale) audiences. TV5 is an international French-language television channel co-financed by Belgium, Canada, France and Switzerland. The main domestic channel, TF1, was privatised in 1987. A global news channel, France 24, was launched in 2006 and broadcasts in both French and English.

CULTURE

Two of the earliest masterpieces of French literature are the medieval *Song of Roland* and *The Romance of the Rose*. Literature flowered particularly in the 19th century with the novels of Victor Hugo (1802–85), Alexandre Dumas (1802–70), Gustave Flaubert (1821–80), Jules Verne (1828–1905) and Émile Zola (1840–1902). Marcel Proust's (1871–1922) seven-volume *A la recherche du temps perdu* (1913–27) was one of the most influential works of modernist literature. Philosophers Voltaire (1694–1778) and Rousseau (1712–78) also used fiction to illustrate their thought, in *Candide* (1759) and *Julie*

(1761), respectively. The French contribution to philosophy and critical theory in the 20th century included the influential works of Jean-Paul Sartre (1905–80), Simone de Beauvoir (1908–86), Albert Camus (1913–60), Michel Foucault (1926–84) and Jacques Derrida (1930–2004).

France's artistic movements range from the classicism of Nicholas Poussin (1594–1665) and the Romanticism typified by Eugène Delacroix (1798–1863) to Impressionism, one of France's most productive artistic movements whose prominent figures include Édouard Manet (1832–83), Edgar Degas (1834–1917), Claude Monet (1840–1924), Pierre-Auguste Renoir (1841–1919) and Mary Cassatt (1844–1926). The work of Post-Impressionists Paul Cézanne (1839–1906) and Paul Gauguin (1848–1903) informed later movements such as Fauvism, which includes the early work of Henri Matisse (1869–1954), and Cubism, developed by Georges Braque (1882–1963) in collaboration with Pablo Picasso. Eminent French sculptors include Auguste Rodin (1840–1917) and Marcel Duchamp (1887–1968).

French cinema is characterised by experimental auteurs such as Jean-Luc Godard (*b.* 1930) and François Truffaut (1932–1984) while actors such as Brigitte Bardot (*b.* 1934), Catherine Deneuve (*b.* 1943) and Juliette Binoche (*b.* 1964) succeeded in Hollywood as well as France. In music, Edith Piaf (1915–63) and Serge Gainsbourg (1928–91) are the best-known proponents of the French musical form *chanson.* In classical music, Hector Berlioz (1803–69), Georges Bizet (1838–75) and Claude Debussy (1862–1918) are among the country's best-known composers.

OVERSEAS DEPARTMENTS/REGIONS

French Guiana, Guadeloupe, Martinique and Réunion have had departmental status since 1946. They were given regional status with greater powers of self-government and elected assemblies in 1982, and were redesignated as Overseas Regions in 2003. Their regional and departmental status is identical to that of regions and departments of metropolitan France, and they can choose to replace these with a single structure by merging their regional and departmental assemblies. The French government is represented by a *prefect* in each. In referendums held in January 2010 both French Guiana and Martinique rejected proposals for granting greater autonomy to their local governments.

FRENCH GUIANA

Area – 83,534 sq. km
Capital – Cayenne; population, 62,437 (2009 est)
Population – 199,000 (2006 est)

Situated on the north-eastern coast of South America, French Guiana is flanked by Suriname on the west and by Brazil on the south and east. Under the administration of French Guiana is the Îles du Salut group of islands (St Joseph, Île Royal and Île du Diable). The European Space Agency rocket launch site is situated at Kourou, and accounts for 25 per cent of GDP. Fishing, forestry and mining are the main activities, and the economy is dependent on government subsidies. The main exports are timber, shrimp and gold. Tourism is restricted by the lack of infrastructure, as much of the interior is only accessible by river.
Prefect, Daniel Ferey, *apptd* 2009

GUADELOUPE

Area – 1,705 sq. km
Capital – Basse-Terre; population 12,000 (2007 est), on Guadeloupe
Population – 405,000 (2006 est. adjusted for separation of St Bartelemy and St Martin)

Consists of a number of islands in the Leeward Islands group in the West Indies, including Guadeloupe (or Basse-Terre), Grande-Terre, Marie-Galante, La Désirade and the Îles des Saintes. The main towns are Les Abymes, Pointe-à-Pitre (Grande-Terre) and Grand Bourg (Marie-Galante). The main industries are tourism, agriculture, sugar refining and rum distilling. Bananas, sugar, rum and vanilla are the main exports.
Prefect, Jean-Luc Fabre, *apptd* 2009

MARTINIQUE

Area – 1,128 sq. km
Capital – Fort-de-France; population, 87,787 (2009 est)
Population – 399,700 (2008 est)

An island in the Windward Islands group in the West Indies, between Dominica in the north and St Lucia in the south, dominated by Mt Pelée (1,397m), an active volcano that last erupted in 1902. Tourism is a major industry. The main exports are bananas, rum and petroleum products.
Prefect, Ange Mancini, *apptd* 2007

RÉUNION

Area – 2,513 sq. km
Capital – St-Denis; population 140,906 (2009 est)
Population – 787,000 (2006 est)

A French possession since 1638, Réunion lies in the Indian Ocean, about 650km east of Madagascar and 180km south-west of Mauritius. The main industries are tourism and sugar and rum production.
Prefect, Michel Lalande, *apptd* 2010

TERRITORIAL COLLECTIVITIES

Overseas collectivities are administrative divisions with a degree of autonomy but without the status of a similar administrative division in metropolitan France; each has its own laws and an elected assembly and president. The French government is represented by a *prefect* or high commissioner in each. Constitutional changes in 2003 redesignated most of the former overseas territories as collectivities; New Caledonia is treated in this category because this is its *de facto* status at present, but its official designation depends upon the outcome of independence referendums to be held between 2014 and 2019.

FRENCH POLYNESIA

Area – 4,167 sq. km
Capital – Papeete, on Tahiti; population, 132,980 (2009 est)
Population – 287,032; rising at 1.39 per cent per year (2009 est)

French Polynesia consists of over 118 volcanic or coral islands and atolls in the South Pacific. There are five archipelagos: the Society Islands (Windward Islands group includes Tahiti, Moorea, Makatea, Mehetia, Tetiaroa, Tubuai Manu; Leeward Islands group includes Huahine, Raiatea, Tahaa, Bora-Bora, Maupiti), the

Tuamotu Islands (Rangiroa, Hao, Turéia etc), the Gambier Islands (Mangareva etc), the Tubuai Islands (Rimatara, Rurutu, Tubuai, Raivavae, Rapa etc) and the Marquesas Islands (Nuku-Hiva, Hiva-Oa, Fatu-Hiva, Tahuata, Ua Huka etc). Some of the atolls were used by France for testing nuclear weapons between 1966 and 1996. The main industries are tourism, pearl-farming, fishing, coconut products and vanilla production.
High Commissioner, Adolphe Colrat, *apptd* 2008

MAYOTTE

Area – 374 sq. km
Capital – Mamoudzou; population, 53,022 (2007 est)
Population – 223,765 rising at 3.32 per cent per year (2009 est)

Part of the Comoros archipelago, Mayotte remained a French dependency when the other three islands became independent as the Comoros Republic in 1975, and became a *collectivité territoriale* in 1976. The population voted in 2009 in favour of Mayotte becoming an overseas department of France from 2011. The main products are vanilla, ylang-ylang (perfume essence), coffee, copra, lobster and shrimp. The economy is dependent on French subsidies.
Prefect, Hubert Derache, *apptd* 2009

NEW CALEDONIA

Area – 18,575 sq. km
Capital – Nouméa; population, 143,577 (2009 est)
Population – 227,436 rising at 1.14 per cent per year (2009 est)

New Caledonia is a large island in the western Pacific, 1,120km off the eastern coast of Australia. Its dependencies are the Isle of Pines, the Loyalty Islands (Mahé, Lifou, Urea, etc), the Bélep Archipelago, the Chesterfield Islands, the Huon Islands and Walpole. New Caledonia was discovered in 1774 and annexed by France in 1853. Agitation for independence from the 1980s ended with the Nouméa accord in 1998, under which an increasing degree of autonomy will be transferred to the territory up to 2018, with referendums on independence to be held between 2014 and 2018. The territory is divided into three provinces, each with a provincial assembly; these combine to form the territorial assembly.

A quarter of the world's nickel deposits are found in the territory, and nickel mining and smelting are the main industries, along with tourism and fishing. Ferronickel, nickel ore and fish are the main exports.
High Commissioner, Yves Dassonville, *apptd* 2007

ST BARTHÉLEMY

Area – 21 sq. km
Capital – Gustavia
Population – 7,448 (2009 est)

The island lies in the Caribbean Sea about 240km north-west of Guadeloupe. It was settled by the French from 1648. France sold the island to Sweden in 1784 but bought it back again in 1878 and placed it under the administration of Guadeloupe. In 2003 the population voted to secede from Guadeloupe and in 2007 the island became a *collectivité territoriale.* The economy is based on luxury tourism and duty-free commerce in luxury goods. Freshwater sources are limited, so all food and energy and most manufactured goods are imported.
Prefect, Jacques Simonnet, *apptd* 2009

ST MARTIN

Area – 54.4 sq. km
Capital – Marigot
Population – 29,820 (2009 est)

The territory occupies the northern part of the island of St Martin, 250km to the north-west of Guadeloupe; the southern part is a territory of the Netherlands. The island was claimed for Spain by Columbus in 1493 but the Spanish relinquished it in 1648 to the Dutch and French, who divided the island between them. The French part was administered from Guadeloupe until, after its population voted to secede in 2003, it was made a *collectivité territoriale* in 2007. The economy is dependent on tourism, which employs 85 per cent of the workforce. Nearly all food, energy and manufactured goods are imported.
Deputy Prefect, Jacques Simonnet, *apptd* 2009

ST PIERRE AND MIQUELON

Area – 242 sq. km
Capital – St-Pierre; population, 5,476 (2009)
Population – 7,051 rising at 0.09 per cent a year (2009 est)

These two small groups of eight islands off the south coast of Newfoundland became a *collectivité territoriale* in 1985. The main industry of fishing and servicing fishing fleets has declined in step with the decline in cod stocks, and fish farming, crab fishing and agriculture are being developed. Tourism is of growing importance, but the economy is dependent on government subsidies.
Prefect, Jean-Régis Borius, *apptd* 2009

WALLIS AND FUTUNA ISLANDS

Area – 142 sq. km
Capital – Mata-Utu, on Uvea, the main island of the Wallis group; population, 1,112 (2009 est)
Population – 15,289 (2009 est)

The two groups of islands (the Wallis Archipelago and the Îles de Horne) lie in the South Pacific, north-east of Fiji. They became a French protectorate from the 1840s and were administered from New Caledonia until 1961. The main products are copra, vegetables, bananas, livestock products, fish and timber.
Administrator, Philippe Paolantoni, *apptd* 2008

OVERSEAS TERRITORIES

TERRITORY OF THE FRENCH SOUTHERN AND ANTARCTIC LANDS

Created in 1955 from former Réunion dependencies, the territory comprises the islands of Amsterdam (55 sq. km) and St Paul (7 sq. km), the Kerguelen Islands (7,215 sq. km) and Crozet Islands (352 sq. km) archipelagos, Adélie Land (302,500 sq. km) in the Antarctic continent and, since 2007, the islands of Bassas da India (80 sq. km), Europa (28 sq. km), les Glorieuses (5 sq. km), Juan de Nova (4.4 sq. km) and Tromelin (1 sq. km). The population consists only of staff of the meteorological and scientific research stations.
Prefect, Rollon Mouchel-Blaisot, *apptd* 2008

THE FRENCH COMMUNITY OF STATES

The 1958 constitution envisaged the establishment of a French Community of States. A number of former French colonies in Africa have seceded from the community but for all practical purposes continue to enjoy the same close links with France as do those that remain formal members. Most former French African colonies are closely linked to France by financial, technical and economic agreements.

GABON

République Gabonaise – Gabonese Republic

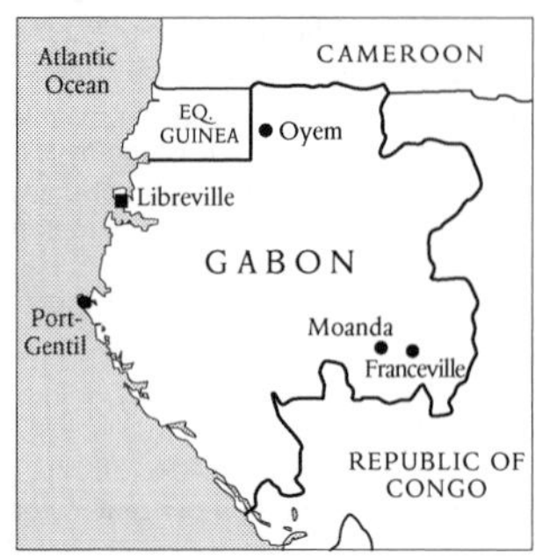

Area – 267,667 sq. km
Capital – Libreville; population, 618,957 (2009 est)
Major towns – Franceville (Masuku), Moanda, Oyem, Port-Gentil
Currency – Franc CFA of 100 centimes
Population – 1,514,993 rising at 1.93 per cent a year (2009 est); over 40 predominantly Bantu tribes, of which the Fang, Bapounou, Nzebi and Obamba are the largest tribal groupings
Religion – Christian 73 per cent (predominantly Roman Catholic), Muslim 12 per cent (mostly non-Gabonese), animism 10 per cent (est); many people combine elements of Christian and indigenous beliefs
Language – French (official), Fang, Myene, Nzebi, Bapounou, Bandjabi
Population density – 6 per sq. km (2008)
Urban population – 85 per cent (2007 est)
Median age (years) – 18.6 (2009 est)
National anthem – 'La Concorde' ['The Concord']
National day – 17 August (Independence Day)
Life expectancy (years) – 53.11 (2009 est)
Mortality rate – 12.76 (2009 est)
Birth rate – 35.57 (2009 est)
Infant mortality rate – 51.78 (2009 est)
HIV/AIDS adult prevalence – 5.3 per cent (2007 est)
Death penalty – Abolished for all crimes (since 2007)
CPI score – 2.9 (2009)
Literacy rate – 86.2 per cent (2007 est)
Gross enrolment ratio (percentage of relevant age group) – primary 152 per cent (2006 est)
Health expenditure (per capita) – US$373 (2007 est)
Hospital beds (per 1,000 people) – 1.3 (2003–8)

CLIMATE AND TERRAIN

The country lies on the equator. It rises from a narrow coastal plain to a hilly interior; approximately 85 per cent of the land is rainforest, with savannah in the east and south, although by 2006 as much as half of the country's forest was being leased for timber. In 2002, 10 per cent of the country was designated as national park. Elevation extremes range from 1,575m (Mt Iboundji) at the highest point to 0m (Atlantic Ocean) at the lowest. The climate is tropical, with an average temperature of 27°C. There are two wet seasons each year, from February to May and from October to December.

HISTORY AND POLITICS

The first Europeans to visit the region were the Portuguese in the 15th century; Dutch, French and English traders arrived soon after. Sovereignty was signed over to the French in 1839 by a local Mpongwe ruler. In 1849, slaves freed by the French formed a settlement which they called Libreville, now the capital. The country was occupied by the French in 1885 and became part of French Equatorial Africa in 1910. Gabon became autonomous within the French Community in 1958 and gained independence on 17 August 1960.

Omar Bongo succeeded to the presidency in 1967 after the death of the first president, and in 1968 he established a one-party state with the *Parti Démocratique Gabonais* (PDG) as the only party. By the late 1980s, the deteriorating economy was provoking unrest and demands for greater democracy, and in 1991 a multiparty system was reintroduced.

Under the multiparty system, the PDG has remained in power (amid allegations of electoral fraud) although it has included opposition party members in coalition governments since 1994. The 2006 legislative elections were again won by the PDG, which formed a coalition government with two smaller parties. President Bongo was re-elected for a sixth term of office in 2005; he died in June 2009, and was succeeded by his son, Ali-Ben Bongo, who was elected president in August 2009 amid allegations of vote-rigging.

POLITICAL SYSTEM

The 1991 constitution, amended in 1995, 1997 and 2003, provides for a president who is directly elected for a seven-year term; since 2003, there has been no limit on the number of terms a president may serve. The president appoints the prime minister, who then appoints the council of ministers. There is a bicameral *Parlement*, comprising the 120-member National Assembly (111 directly elected and nine appointed by the president for a five-year term) and the senate, which has 102 members elected for a six-year term by municipal and regional councillors.

HEAD OF STATE

President, Ali-Ben Bongo, *elected* 30 August 2009, *sworn in* 16 October 2009
Vice-President, Didjob Divungi di Ndinge

SELECTED GOVERNMENT MEMBERS *as at June 2010*

Prime Minister, Paul Biyoghe-Mba
Defence, Angélique Ngoma
Finance, Blaise Louembé
Economy, Magloire Ngambia
Interior, Jean-François Ndongou
Foreign Affairs, Paul Toungui

EMBASSY OF THE GABONESE REPUBLIC

27 Elvaston Place, London SW7 5NL
T 020-7823 9986
Ambassador Extraordinary and Plenipotentiary, Omer Piankali, *apptd* 2009

BRITISH AMBASSADOR

HE Bharat Joshi, *apptd* 2009, resident at Yaoundé, Cameroon

DEFENCE

The army has 12 armoured infantry fighting vehicles and 28 armoured personnel carriers. The navy has 9 patrol and coastal combatant vessels at a base at Port-Gentil. The air force has 14 combat capable aircraft and 5 armed helicopters.

Military budget – US$134m (2008 est)
Military personnel – 4,700: army 3,200, navy 500, air force 1,000; paramilitary 2,000

ECONOMY AND TRADE

Gabon is one of the most stable and prosperous countries in Africa, largely owing to its small population and abundance of oil and mineral resources. The economy is heavily dependent on oil (which contributes over 50 per cent of GDP) and other mineral resources, including manganese and uranium, and timber, but the government is investing in diversification to reduce economic vulnerability; falling commodity prices and a drop in export demand during the global downturn has caused the economy to contract. Despite the country's wealth, a large proportion of the population remains poor, and weak fiscal management has resulted in a high foreign debt which has had to be rescheduled several times.

Agriculture is largely at subsistence level, employing 60 per cent of the workforce but contributing only 5.4 per cent of GDP. It is restricted by the forest cover and lack of suitable land. The main products include cocoa, coffee, sugar, palm oil, rubber, cattle, timber and fish. Industry contributes 56.7 per cent of GDP and employs 15 per cent of the workforce, mainly in oil and mineral extraction, oil refining, chemicals, ship repair, textiles, and processing agricultural and forestry products.

The main trading partners are the USA, France and China. Principal exports are crude oil (70 per cent), timber, manganese and uranium. The main imports are machinery and equipment, food, chemicals and construction materials.

GNI – US$10,600m; US$7,320 per capita (2008)
Annual average growth of GDP – –2.8 per cent (2009 est)
Inflation rate – 3 per cent (2009 est)
Unemployment – 21 per cent (2006 est)
Total external debt – US$3,065m (2009 est)
Imports – US$2,600m (2008)
Exports – US$8,400m (2008)

BALANCE OF PAYMENTS
Trade – US$4,362m surplus (2009)
Current Account – US$1,283m surplus (2009 est)

Trade with UK	*2008*	*2009*
Imports from UK	£46,617,865	£43,511,082
Exports to UK	£4,085,861	£2,691,438

MEDIA

The state-controlled broadcaster, Radiodiffusion-Télévision Gabonaise, operates two television channels and two radio networks, and the only daily newspaper, *L'Union*, is also government-run. There are two other television channels and several privately owned newspapers that usually publish on a weekly basis. Radio is an important news medium because of low literacy rates in rural areas. Reporters Without Borders has expressed concern at the apparent harassment of journalists during and following the August 2010 election, and at suspensions imposed on several media outlets in subsequent months on questionable grounds. Africa No1, a pan-African radio broadcaster, is based in Gabon.

THE GAMBIA

Republic of The Gambia

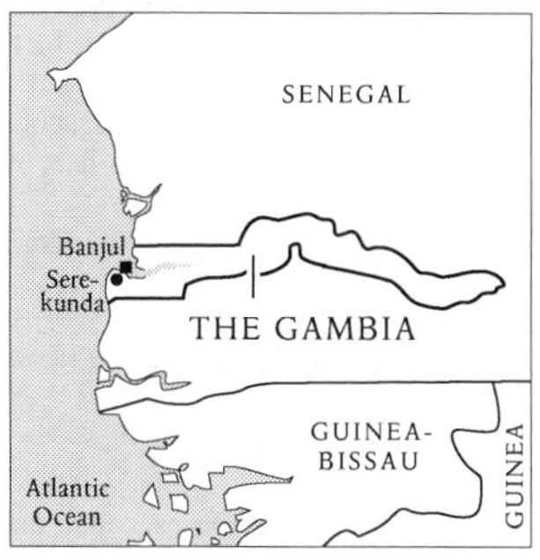

Area – 11,295 sq. km
Capital – Banjul; population, 436,447 (2009 est)
Major towns – Bakau, Brikama, Farafenni, Serekunda
Currency – Dalasi (D) of 100 butut
Population – 1,782,893 rising at 2.67 per cent a year (2009 est); Mandinka (42 per cent), Fulani (18 per cent), Wolof (16 per cent), Jola (10 per cent), Serahuli (Soninke) (9 per cent)
Religion – Sunni Muslim 90 per cent (majority Malikite Sufi), Christian 9 per cent (predominantly Roman Catholic), animist 1 per cent (est)
Language – English (official), Mandinka, Wolof, Fula
Population density – 166 per sq. km (2008)
Urban population – 56 per cent (2007 est)
Median age (years) – 17.9 (2009 est)
National anthem – 'For The Gambia Our Homeland'
National day – 18 February (Independence Day)
Life expectancy (years) – 55.35 (2009 est)
Mortality rate – 11.49 (2009 est)
Birth rate – 37.87 (2009 est)
Infant mortality rate – 67.33 (2009 est)
Death penalty – Retained (not used since 1981)
CPI score – 2.9 (2009)

CLIMATE AND TERRAIN

The Gambia consists of a narrow strip of land along the river Gambia, mostly comprising the basin and flood plain of the river, flanked by savannah and low hills. Elevation extremes range from 53m at the highest point to 0m (Atlantic Ocean) at the lowest. The climate is tropical, with a wet season from June to November.

HISTORY AND POLITICS

The Gambia river basin was part of an area dominated from the 10th to 16th centuries by the Mali and Songhai kingdoms. The Portuguese reached the river Gambia in 1447 and, later followed by other European merchants, established trading posts along the river. In 1816 a British garrison was stationed on an island at the river mouth that became the capital of a small British colony; this became a crown colony in 1843. The boundaries of the country were agreed by France and Britain in 1889; British territory would extend ten kilometres from the upper river on either bank. The Gambia became independent on 18 February 1965 and a republic in 1970.

The post-independence prime minister, Sir Dawda Jawara, was president from 1970 until 1994, when he was overthrown in a military coup. The coup leader, Lt. (later Capt.) Yahya Jammeh, assumed the presidency and a civilian-military government was formed to govern in conjunction with the ruling military council. Civilian government was restored after elections were held in 1996 and 1997 following the approval by referendum of a new constitution. Jammeh was elected president and his Alliance for Patriotic Reorientation and Construction (APRC) won an overall majority of the legislative seats. Jammeh and the APRC have won all subsequent elections; the opposition and media are subject to harassment and detention without charge.

In the 2006 presidential election, Jammeh was re-elected with 67 per cent of the vote; a fresh presidential election is due in 2011. The 2007 legislative election was won by the APRC, with 42 of the 48 elected seats.

POLITICAL SYSTEM
Under the 1996 constitution, the executive president is directly elected for a five-year term; there is no limit on re-election. The unicameral National Assembly has 53 members, of whom 48 are directly elected and five are appointed by the president, for a five-year term.

HEAD OF STATE
President, Defence, Agriculture, Col. Yahya Jammeh, *took power* July 1994, *elected* September 1996, *re-elected* 2001, 2006
Vice-President, Women and Social Affairs, Ajaratou Isatou Njie-Saidy

SELECTED GOVERNMENT MEMBERS *as at May 2010*
Foreign Affairs, Mamadou Tangara
Finance and Economic Affairs, Momodou Foon
Interior, Ousman Sonko
Justice, Attorney-General, Edward Gomez

THE GAMBIA HIGH COMMISSION
57 Kensington Court, London W8 5DG
T 020-7937 6316 E gambiahighcomuk@btconnect.com
High Commissioner, HE Elizabeth Ya Eli Harding, *apptd* 2007

BRITISH HIGH COMMISSION
PO Box 507, 48 Atlantic Road, Fajara, Banjul
T (+220) 449 5133 E bhcbanjul@fco.gov.uk
W http://ukingambia.fco.gov.uk
High Commissioner, HE Philip Sinkinson, *apptd* 2006

DEFENCE
The Marine Unit has 3 patrol and coastal combatant vessels at a base at Banjul.
Military budget – US$7m (2009)
Military personnel – army 800

ECONOMY AND TRADE
The country has limited natural resources and agricultural land. Historically, the mainstay of the economy was re-export trade with neighbouring countries, but this has fluctuated since the late 1990s, subject to the vagaries of government policies and trade and transport disputes with Senegal. There are high levels of public and foreign debt and the country is dependent on financial and technical aid from foreign donors. An important revenue source is remittances from Gambians working abroad.

About 75 per cent of the population is dependent on subsistence agriculture, which contributes 33.5 per cent of GDP. The chief product, peanuts, is also the main export and the basis of the main industrial activity, leaving the economy vulnerable to market fluctuations and the weather. Industry contributes 8.5 per cent to GDP, chiefly through processing peanuts, fish and hides, assembling agricultural machinery, metalworking, woodworking and the production of beverages and clothing. The services sector employs only 6 per cent of the workforce but contributes 58 per cent of GDP, largely owing to the growing tourism industry.

The main trade partners are China, India, Japan and Senegal. Principal exports are peanut products, fish, cotton lint, palm kernels and re-exports. The main imports are foodstuffs, manufactures, fuel, machinery and transport equipment.
GNI – US$700m; US$400 per capita (2008)
Annual average growth of GDP – 3.5 per cent (2009 est)
Inflation rate – 6 per cent (2009 est)
Total external debt – US$628.8m (2003 est)
Imports – US$310m (2007)
Exports – US$13m (2007)

BALANCE OF PAYMENTS
Trade – US$280m deficit (2009)
Current Account – US$131m deficit (2008)

Trade with UK	*2008*	*2009*
Imports from UK	£16,146,939	£15,586,743
Exports to UK	£1,569,471	£2,888,868

EDUCATION AND HEALTH
Education is compulsory until the age of eight.
Gross enrolment ratio (percentage of relevant age group) – primary 86 per cent; secondary 51 per cent (2008 est)
Health expenditure (per capita) – US$22 (2007)
Hospital beds (per 1,000 people) – 1.1 (2009)

MEDIA
Since 2002 private newspapers and radio stations have been tightly regulated by a government-run commission that has the power to imprison journalists and suspend publication or transmission licences, which are expensive to obtain; a 2004 law introduced jail terms for journalists convicted of libel or sedition. The state operates the only national television station, although there is also a private satellite channel. State-run Radio Gambia produces carefully controlled news broadcasts, which are relayed by private radio stations.

GEORGIA

Sak'art'velo – Georgia

Area – 69,700 sq. km
Capital – Tbilisi; population, 1,114,960 (2009 est)
Major cities – Batumi, Kutaisi, Poti, Rustavi

Currency – Lari of 100 tetri
Population – 4,615,807 falling at 0.33 per cent a year (2009 est); Georgian (83.8 per cent), Azeri (6.5 per cent), Armenian (5.7 per cent), Russian (1.5 per cent)
Religion – Christian (Orthodox 84 per cent, Armenian Apostolic 4 per cent, Catholic 1 per cent), Muslim 10 per cent (est)
Language – Georgian (official), Russian, Armenian, Azeri, Abkhaz (official in Abkhazia)
Population density – 62 per sq. km (2008)
Urban population – 53 per cent (2007 est)
Median age (years) – 38.6 (2009 est)
National anthem – 'Tavisupleba' ['Freedom']
National day – 26 May (Independence Day, 1918)
Life expectancy (years) – 76.72 (2009 est)
Mortality rate – 9.65 (2009 est)
Birth rate – 10.66 (2009 est)
Infant mortality rate – 16.22 (2009 est)
Death penalty – Abolished for all crimes (since 1997)
CPI score – 4.1 (2009)
Literacy rate – 100.0 per cent (2007 est)
Gross enrolment ratio (percentage of relevant age group) – primary 107 per cent; secondary 90 per cent; tertiary 34 per cent (2008 est)
Health expenditure (per capita) – US$191 (2007)
Hospital beds (per 1,000 people) – 3.3 (2003–8)

CLIMATE AND TERRAIN

Georgia lies in the western part of the Caucasus region, on the eastern shore of the Black Sea. It is mountainous, with the Great Caucasus mountain range in the north and the Lesser Caucasus in the south. These are divided by the Kolkhida lowland in the west and the Mtkvari (Kura) river basin in the east, between which runs the valley of the river Mtkvari. Elevation extremes range from 5,201m (Mt Shkhara) at the highest point to 0m (Black Sea) at the lowest. The climate is almost tropical in summer, while cold winters affect both the mountains and valleys. Average temperatures in Tbilisi range from a minimum of −1°C in January to a maximum of 31°C in July.

HISTORY AND POLITICS

The ancient kingdoms of the Georgian region came under Roman influence in the first century AD and converted to Christianity in the fourth century. After domination by Persians, Arabs and Turks, an independent kingdom was established that experienced a golden age from the 11th century until the Mongols invaded in 1236. The Ottoman and Persian empires competed for influence from the 16th to the 18th centuries; the Georgians increasingly turned to Russia for protection and were absorbed into the Russian Empire in 1801–4.

In the late 19th century, nationalist and Marxist movements competed for limited political influence under autocratic Russian rule. One of the most prominent Marxist activists was Iosif Dzhugashvili (Joseph Stalin). After the Russian Revolution of 1917, an independent nationalist government came to power in Georgia that was recognised by Soviet Russia shortly before its forces invaded and occupied the country in 1921. Georgia joined the USSR as part of the Transcaucasian Soviet Socialist Republic in 1922, becoming a separate republic in 1936.

Resurgent nationalism in the 1980s led to growing demands for autonomy, and in 1990 the Communist Party's monopoly on power was abolished and multiparty elections were held. Georgia declared its independence from the USSR in May 1991.

A coup in 1992 overthrew the increasingly authoritarian President Zviad Gamsakhurdia, who was replaced by Eduard Shevardnadze. A pro-Gamsakhurdia uprising in 1993, when most government forces were engaged in Abkhazia, forced Georgia to accept Russian armaments and troops to defeat the rebels; in return Georgia agreed to join the Commonwealth of Independent States, and remained a member until 2009.

President Shevardnadze was forced out of office in 2003 by mass demonstrations over alleged electoral fraud in the parliamentary elections. Mikheil Saakashvili, leader of the National Movement, was elected president in January 2004, and he was re-elected in 2008 with 53 per cent of the vote in the first round; despite opposition allegations of fraud, international monitors considered the election democratic. The United National Movement for a Victorious Georgia won 120 seats in the May 2008 legislative elections.

Relations between Russia and Georgia have been fraught since the 1990s owing to Russia's support for the secessionists in South Ossetia and Abkhazia, Georgia's increasingly pro-Western stance, and Russia's use of trade embargos and disruption of energy supplies. Georgia's application to join NATO's membership programme was deferred in April 2008 but antagonised Russia into increasing its support for the secessionists. After a series of clashes with secessionist forces, Georgia tried to retake South Ossetia by force in August 2008 and was repulsed by counter-attacking Russian troops. Russia expelled Georgian troops from South Ossetia and Abkhazia, and started to move further into Georgia before the EU brokered a ceasefire and a withdrawal to the positions held before fighting began. Russia has not fully complied with the ceasefire agreement, maintaining a considerable military presence in the secessionist areas and in a 'buffer zone' around them. It has also recognised both South Ossetia and Abkhazia as independent republics, attracting international condemnation for doing so.

SECESSION

Fears that Georgian independence would deprive them of their own autonomy led to unilateral declarations of independence by the central region of South Ossetia (1991) and the north-western region of Abkhazia (1992). The Georgian government resisted these moves and there was conflict with South Ossetia until 1992, while in Abkhazia, Georgian forces were forced to withdraw in 1993. In August 2008, clashes between Georgian troops and South Ossetian separatists escalated into a brief war between Georgia and Russia, which expelled Georgian forces from both separatist areas. Both regions remain outside Georgian control; their unilateral declarations of independence in August 2008 were recognised only by Russia. In both regions the economy and infrastructure are in ruins and the secessionists are dependent on Russia, which maintains peacekeeping forces in both and has stepped up its economic support. The UN operated a military observer mission in Abkhazia from 1993 to 2009, when Russia vetoed the renewal of its mandate.

Relations between Georgia and Ajaria, a semi-autonomous region in the south-west and a key trade hub, deteriorated briefly in 2004 when Aslan Abashidze, Ajaria's leader since 1991, refused to recognise the authority of the newly elected President Saakashvili, and accused Georgia of planning to invade Ajaria. Public demonstrations against Abashidze forced him to resign. The Georgian parliament granted the Ajarian assembly powers over local affairs but the

Georgian president retains the power to nominate the region's head of government and to dissolve its government and assembly.

POLITICAL SYSTEM

The 1995 constitution provides for a federal republic with a unicameral legislature, to become bicameral 'following the creation of appropriate conditions'. The president is directly elected for a five-year term, renewable only once. The unicameral parliament has 150 members, 75 elected in single-member constituencies and 75 by proportional representation, who serve for a four-year term.

HEAD OF STATE

President, Mikheil Saakashvili, *elected* 4 January 2004, *sworn in* 25 January 2004, *re-elected* 5 January 2008

SELECTED GOVERNMENT MEMBERS *as at June 2010*

Prime Minister, Nika Gilauri
First Deputy Prime Minister, David Tkeshelashvili
Deputy Prime Ministers, Giorgi Baramidze, Temur Iakobashvili
Defence, Bacho Akhalaia
Finance, Kakha Baindurashvili
Foreign Affairs, Grigol Vashadze

EMBASSY OF GEORGIA

4 Russell Gardens, London W14 8EZ
T 020-7348 1941 E london.emb@mfa.gov.ge
W www.uk.mfa.gov.ge
Ambassador Extraordinary and Plenipotentiary, HE Giorgi Badridze, *apptd* 2009

BRITISH EMBASSY

GMT Plaza, 4 Freedom Square, 0105 Tbilisi
T (+995) (32) 274 747 E british.embassy.tbilisi@fco.gov.uk
W http://ukingeorgia.fco.gov.uk
Ambassador Extraordinary and Plenipotentiary, HE Judith Gough, *apptd* 2010

BRITISH COUNCIL

34 Rustaveli Avenue, 0108 Tbilisi
T (+995) (32) 250 407/ 988 014 W www.britishcouncil.org.ge
Director, Paul Doubleday

DEFENCE

The army has 66 main battle tanks, 66 armoured infantry fighting vehicles and 46 armoured personnel carriers. The navy has 4 patrol and coastal combatant vessels, based at Tbilisi and Poti, while the coastguard has 11 patrol and coastal combatant vessels. The air force has 11 combat aircraft.

Military budget – US$537m (2009)
Military personnel – 21,150: army 17,767, navy 495, air force 1,310, National Guard 1,578; paramilitaries 11,700
Conscription duration – 18 months

ECONOMY AND TRADE

The economy grew rapidly from 2003, making good progress towards recovery following the near-collapse of the 1990s. Reform of the tax system nearly quadrupled government revenue, and added impetus in privatisation and anti-corruption programmes attracted foreign investment. However, the economy slowed in 2008 following the war with Russia and contracted in 2009 as the global economic downturn affected the regional economy and led to a decline in foreign investment and expatriates' remittances. The fuel crises in 2005–6 prompted the renovation of hydroelectric power plants and the repair of a pipeline from Azerbaijan which now brings in gas supplies. The government is also looking to diversify its export markets since Russia imposed an embargo on key exports, and it hopes Georgia's position as a transit state for oil and gas pipelines and for trade between central Asia and Europe will stimulate economic growth.

Agriculture employs 55.6 per cent of the workforce and generates 12.1 per cent of GDP, with a concentration on grapes for wine-making, tea, citrus fruits and hazelnuts. Industry, which contributes 25.9 per cent of GDP, produces steel, aircraft, machine tools, electrical appliances, manganese, copper, chemicals, wood products and wine.

The main trading partners are Turkey, Azerbaijan and Ukraine. Principal exports are scrap metal, wine, mineral water, mineral ores, vehicles, fruit and nuts. The main imports are fuels, vehicles, machinery and parts, food (especially grain) and pharmaceuticals.

GNI – US$10,800m; US$2,500 per capita (2008)
Annual average growth of GDP – –4.9 per cent (2009 est)
Inflation rate – 1 per cent (2009 est)
Population below poverty line – 31 per cent (2006)
Unemployment – 13.6 per cent (2006 est)
Total external debt – US$7,711m (2008)
Imports – US$6,100m (2008)
Exports – US$1,500m (2008)

BALANCE OF PAYMENTS

Trade – US$3,255m deficit (2009)
Current Account – US$1,312m deficit (2009)

Trade with UK	*2008*	*2009*
Imports from UK	£38,145,056	£25,558,806
Exports to UK	£101,230,427	£83,156,383

MEDIA

The law on broadcasting adopted in 2004 transformed the state-owned Television-Radio Corporation into a public broadcaster, Georgian Public Broadcasting, which provides television and radio services and is government funded. The state has also given up control of other media outlets, including newspapers and news agencies; there are now over 200 privately owned newspapers, although readership is generally low. Slander and libel were decriminalised in 2004, but the suspension of several private publications and a private television station during a state of emergency in 2007 cast doubt on the government's commitment to media freedom.

GERMANY

Bundesrepublik Deutschland – Federal Republic of Germany

Area – 357,022 sq. km
Capital – Berlin; population, 3,437,780 (2009 est)
Major cities – Bremen, Cologne, Dortmund, Dresden, Düsseldorf, Essen, Frankfurt, Hamburg, Hannover, Leipzig, Munich, Nuremberg, Stuttgart
Currency – Euro (€) of 100 cents
Population – 82,329,758 falling at 0.05 per cent a year (2009 est); German (91.5 per cent), Turkish (2.4 per cent) (est)
Religion – Christian (Roman Catholic 31 per cent, Evangelical Church in Germany federation 30 per cent, other Protestant denominations 1 per cent), Muslim 5 per cent (predominantly Sunni) (est)
Language – German (official)
Population density – 236 per sq. km (2007)
Urban population – 74 per cent (2007 est)
Median age (years) – 43.8 (2009 est)
National anthem – 'Das Deutschlandlied' ['The Song of Germany']
National day – 3 October (Unity Day)
Life expectancy (years) – 79.26 (2009 est)
Mortality rate – 10.9 (2009 est)
Birth rate – 8.18 (2009 est)
Infant mortality rate – 3.99 (2009 est)
Death penalty – Abolished for all crimes (since 1949 in FRG and 1987 in GDR)
CPI score – 8 (2009)

CLIMATE AND TERRAIN

The north of the country is low-lying, rising in the centre to uplands and Alpine foothills, then to the Bavarian Alps in the south. Elevation extremes range from 2,963m (Zugspitze, Bavaria) at the highest point to −3.54m (Neuendorf bei Wilster) at the lowest. The Rhine, Weser and Elbe rivers flow from the south to the North Sea, the Oder and Neisse rivers flow north to the Baltic Sea, and the Danube flows east from its source in the south of the country to the Austrian border. Nearly a third of the land is covered by forest or woodland. The climate is temperate, with average temperatures in Berlin ranging from lows of −3°C in January to highs of 24°C in July.

HISTORY AND POLITICS

Charlemagne extended Frankish authority over the Germanic tribes in the eighth century, and took the title of Holy Roman Emperor. The treaty of Verdun (843) divided this empire into three, the eastern part (corresponding to modern Germany) comprising hundreds of small dukedoms and principalities that enjoyed virtual independence under the hegemony of a nominally elective Holy Roman Emperor. Although a number of dynasties succeeded at times in centralising power between 962 and 1806, shifting allegiances and alliances enabled the states to challenge the authority of the emperor, which was never sufficient to achieve unification into a single nation state.

The empire was replaced in 1806 by a loose association of sovereign states known as the German Confederation, which was dissolved in 1866 and replaced by the Prussian-dominated North German Federation. The south German principalities united with the northern federation to form a second German Empire in 1871 and the King of Prussia was proclaimed emperor.

Defeat in the First World War led to the abdication of the emperor, and the country became a republic. The treaty of Versailles (1919) ceded Alsace-Lorraine to France, and large areas in the east were lost to Poland. The world economic crisis of 1929 contributed to the collapse of the Weimar Republic and the subsequent rise to power of the National Socialist movement led by Adolf Hitler, who became chancellor in 1933.

After concluding a treaty of non-aggression with the Soviet Union in August 1939, Germany invaded Poland (1 September 1939), precipitating the Second World War, which lasted until 1945. Hitler committed suicide on 30 April 1945. On 8 May 1945, Germany unconditionally surrendered.

Germany was divided into American, French, British and Soviet zones of occupation. The Federal Republic of Germany (FRG) was created out of the three Western zones in 1949. A Communist government was established in the Soviet zone, known as the German Democratic Republic (GDR). In 1961 the Soviet zone of Berlin was sealed off, and the Berlin Wall was built along the zonal boundary, partitioning the city, to prevent an exodus of citizens from east to west.

Soviet-initiated reform in eastern Europe during the late 1980s led to unrest in the GDR, culminating in the opening of the Berlin Wall in November 1989 and the collapse of the Communist government. The 'treaty on the final settlement with respect to Germany' concluded between the FRG, GDR and the four former occupying powers in September 1990 unified Germany, with effect from 3 October 1990, as a single sovereign state. Constitutionally, unification entailed the accession of Berlin and the five reformed *Länder* (states) of the GDR to the FRG, which remains in being. Berlin was declared the capital of the unified Germany and the legislature and government departments were transferred from Bonn.

West Germany was a founder member of the EEC in 1958 and Germany joined the eurozone in 1999.

President Horst Köhler, who was first elected in 2004 and re-elected in May 2009, resigned in May 2010, having made controversial remarks regarding the motivations of Germany's foreign military deployments; Christian Wulff was elected to succeed him in June 2010. Following the 2005 legislative election, a coalition of the incumbent Social Democratic Party (SDP) and the Christian Democratic Union/Christian Social Union (CDU/CSU) was formed under the CDU/CSU leader Angela Merkel, who became Germany's first female chancellor in November 2005. At the 2009 elections, the CDU increased its number of seats, while the SDP lost ground, and Angela Merkel was re-elected Chancellor at the head of a CDU/CSU coalition with the Free Democrats (FDP).

POLITICAL SYSTEM

The Basic Law (constitution) provides for a president, elected for a five-year term by the *Bundesversammlung* (an electoral college comprising the members of the *Bundestag* and an equal number of representatives elected by the state legislatures), and a bicameral legislature. The lower house, the Federal Assembly (*Bundestag*), has 622 members elected by a mixed constituency and proportional representation system for a four-year term. The Federal Council (*Bundesrat*), has 69 members appointed by the governments of the states (*Länder*) in proportion to *Länder* populations; their term of office is determined by their *Land*'s constitution. The head of government is the chancellor, who is proposed by the president and elected by the *Bundestag*.

HEAD OF STATE

Federal President, Christian Wulff *elected and sworn in* 30 June 2010

SELECTED GOVERNMENT MEMBERS *as at May 2010*
Federal Chancellor, Angela Merkel
Foreign Affairs, Guido Westerwelle
Defence, Karl-Theodor Zu Guttenberg
Interior, Thomas de Maizière
Finance, Wolfgan Schäuble

EMBASSY OF THE FEDERAL REPUBLIC OF GERMANY
23 Belgrave Square, London SW1X 8PZ
T 020-7824 1300 E info@london.diplo.de
W www.london.diplo.de
Ambassador Extraordinary and Plenipotentiary, HE Georg Boomgaarden, *apptd* 2008

BRITISH EMBASSY
Wilhelmstrasse 70, 10117 Berlin
T (+49) (30) 204 570 W http://ukingermany.fco.gov.uk
Ambassador Extraordinary and Plenipotentiary, HE Sir Michael Arthur, KCMG, *apptd* 2007

BRITISH COUNCIL
Alexanderplatz 1, 10178 Berlin
T (+49) (30) 311 0990 W www.britishcouncil.de
Director, Dr Patrick Hart

FEDERAL STRUCTURE
Germany is a federal republic composed of 16 states *(Länder)* (ten from the former FRG, five from the former GDR, and Berlin). Each *Land* has its own directly elected legislature and government led by a Minister-President (prime minister) or equivalent. The 1949 Basic Law vests executive power in the *Länder* governments except in those areas reserved for the federal government.

State	*Capital*	*Population (millions) (2005 est)*
Baden-Württemberg	Stuttgart	10.7
Bavaria	Munich	12.5
Berlin	—	3.4
Brandenburg	Potsdam	2.6
Bremen	—	0.7
Hamburg	—	1.7
Hesse	Wiesbaden	6.1
Lower Saxony	Hannover	8.0
Mecklenburg-West Pomerania	Schwerin	1.7
North Rhine-Westphalia	Düsseldorf	18.1
Rhineland-Palatinate	Mainz	4.1
Saarland	Saarbrücken	1.1
Saxony	Dresden	4.3
Saxony-Anhalt	Magdeburg	2.5
Schleswig-Holstein	Kiel	2.8
Thuringia	Erfurt	2.3

DEFENCE

The army has 1,385 main battle tanks, 2,307 armoured personnel carriers, 2,044 armoured infantry fighting vehicles and 159 armed helicopters. The navy has 12 submarines, 15 frigates, 3 corvettes, 10 patrol and coastal vessels and 22 armed helicopters at 6 bases. The air force has 303 combat aircraft.
Military expenditure – US$46,900m (2008)
Military personnel – 250,613: army 163,962, navy 24,407, air force 62,244.
Conscription duration – 9 months

ECONOMY AND TRADE

Germany has one of the world's largest economies but decades of strong economic performance gave way in the 1990s to a severe recession, largely an aftermath of reunification and of macroeconomic stagnation. Although the economy as a whole began to grow again in 2006, in the east it remains weak despite costly modernisation and integration measures. However, the revival was largely export-led and a decline in demand owing to the global economic downturn caused a recession in 2008–9. The government's economic stimulus measures have pushed the budget deficit slightly beyond the eurozone's 3 per cent threshold.

The country has a modern, diverse, highly industrialised and technologically advanced market economy. The services sector contributes 72 per cent of GDP, industry 27.1 per cent and agriculture 0.9 per cent. The industrial sector is among the world's largest producers of iron, steel, coal, cement, chemicals, machinery, vehicles, machine tools, electronics, food and beverages, ships and textiles. Germany depends on imports to meet its oil and natural gas needs; it remains a net exporter of electricity, despite the policy of successive governments since 1998 of phasing out the country's 17 nuclear power stations (which supply about 25 per cent of its electricity) by 2032. This threatened to create an electricity supply problem, and the policy was suspended by the coalition elected in 2009.

The main trading partners are other EU countries, the USA and China. Machinery, vehicles, chemicals, metals and manufactures, foodstuff and textiles are the principal imports and exports.
GNI – US$3,506,900m; US$42,710 per capita (2008)
Annual average growth of GDP – −5 per cent (2009 est)
Inflation rate – 0 per cent (2009 est)
Unemployment – 8.2 per cent (2009 est)
Total external debt – US$5,208,000m (2009)
Imports – US$1,199,000m (2008)
Exports – US$1,463,900m (2008)

BALANCE OF PAYMENTS
Trade – US$199,703m surplus (2009)
Current Account – US$160,627m surplus (2009)

Trade with UK	*2008*	*2009*
Imports from UK	£28,503,613,968	£24,802,785,867
Exports to UK	£44,349,808,916	£39,654,119,835

COMMUNICATIONS

There is an extensive road network of around 644,500km, including 12,600km of motorways *(autobahn)*. There are 41,900km of railways. Around 20 per cent of domestic freight is carried on the 7,500km of inland waterways. The Rhine and the Danube are linked by the Rhine-Maine-Danube canal, creating a through route from the North Sea to the Black Sea. The Kiel canal links the North Sea and the Baltic Sea. The main river ports are Duisburg, Frankfurt, Karlsruhe and Mainz; the main seaports are Hamburg, Kiel, Bremen, Bremerhaven, Rostock and Wilhemshaven. The busiest airport is at Frankfurt, other principal airports include Berlin, Munich and Bonn.

The telephone system in the east has been modernised and integrated with the rest of the country. Mobile phone distribution is widespread, with 107 million subscribers in 2008. There were 61.9 million internet users in 2008.

EDUCATION AND HEALTH

Education is free of charge and compulsory between the ages of six and 18. It comprises nine years of full-time education at primary and secondary schools and three years of vocational education on a part-time basis. The secondary school leaving examination *(Abitur)* entitles the holder to a place at a university or another institution of higher education.

Children below the age of 18 who are not attending a general secondary or a full-time vocational school have compulsory day-release at a vocational school.

The largest universities are in Munich, Berlin, Hamburg, Bonn, Frankfurt and Cologne. Germany's oldest university is Heidelberg, founded in 1386.

Gross enrolment ratio (percentage of relevant age group) – primary 106 per cent; secondary 101 per cent (2008 est)
Health expenditure (per capita) – US$4,209 (2007)
Hospital beds (per 1,000 people) – 8.3 (2003–8)

MEDIA

Each of the country's 16 states regulates broadcasting, both private and public, its own area. National and regional public television competes with a large private sector, with about 90 per cent of households having access to cable or satellite stations. Analogue radio and television services ended in 2010. Germany also has a considerable press industry, though this is stronger at regional than national level, and is home to many international media companies.

CULTURE

Germany has produced a wealth of composers, including Johann Sebastian Bach (1685–1750), Beethoven (1770–1827), Schubert (1797–1828), Wagner (1813–83) and Brahms (1833–97). Philosophers include Immanuel Kant (1724–1804), Karl Marx (1818–83), Friedrich Engels (1820–95) and Friedrich Nietzsche (1844–1900). The work of playwrights Goethe (1749–1832) and Friedrich Schiller (1759–1805) had a European-wide influence. Novelists Thomas Mann (1875–1955), Hermann Hesse (1877–1962) and Günter Grass (*b.* 1927) have all received the Nobel prize for literature.

Key figures in the visual arts are Albrecht Dürer (1471–1528), Hans Holbein the Younger (1497–1543), surrealist Max Ernst (1891–1976) and Joseph Beuys (1921–86). Film directors Friedrich Murnau (1888–1931), Leni Riefenstahl (1902–2003), Werner Herzog (*b.* 1942) and Wim Wenders (*b.* 1945), and actor Klaus Kinski (1926–91) all gained Hollywood recognition.

Physicist Albert Einstein (1879–1955) is perhaps the world's best-known modern scientist, having introduced his theory of relativity to the wider world in 1905. Other notable German scientists include Wilhelm Röntgen (1845–1923), Max Planck (1858–1947) and Hans Geiger (1882–1945).

GHANA

Republic of Ghana

Area – 238,533 sq. km
Capital – Accra; population, 2,268,500 (2009 est)
Major cities – Kumasi, Sekondi-Takoradi, Tamale
Currency – Cedi of 100 pesewas
Population – 23,832,495 rising at 1.88 per cent a year (2009 est); Akan (45.3 per cent), Mole-Dagomba (15.2 per cent), Ewe (11.7 per cent), Ga-Dangme (7.3 per cent), Guan (4 per cent), Gurma (3.6 per cent), Grusi (2.6 per cent)
Religion – Christian 69 per cent, Muslim 16 per cent (predominantly Sunni), indigenous religions and other groups 15 per cent (est)
Language – English (official), Asante, Ewe, Fante, Boron, Dagomba, Dangme, Dagarte, Akyem, Ga, Akuapem
Population density – 103 per sq. km (2008)
Urban population – 49 per cent (2007 est)
Median age (years) – 20.7 (2009 est)
National anthem – 'God Bless Our Homeland Ghana'
National day – 6 March (Independence Day)
Life expectancy (years) – 59.85 (2009 est)
Mortality rate – 9.24 (2009 est)
Birth rate – 28.58 (2009 est)
Infant mortality rate – 51.09 (2009 est)
HIV/AIDS adult prevalence – 1.7 per cent (2007 est)
Death penalty – Retained (not used since 1993)
CPI score – 3.9 (2009)

CLIMATE AND TERRAIN

Ghana consists mostly of plains dissected by the Volta river basin and the great central Lake Volta, and rising to the Ashanti plateau in the west. There is dense rainforest in the south and west and forested hills in the north, with savannah in the east and far north. Elevation extremes range from 880m (Mt Afadjato) at the highest point to 0m (Atlantic Ocean) at the lowest. The climate is tropical but with cooler temperatures on the south-east coast, and less rainfall in the south-east and north. Temperatures in Accra average between 23°C and 31°C.

HISTORY AND POLITICS

First reached by Europeans in the 15th century, after which it became a centre for gold and slave trading, the constituent parts of Ghana came under British administration at various times. The original Gold Coast colony was constituted in 1874 and Ashanti and the Northern Territories Protectorate in 1901. Trans-Volta-Togoland, part of the former German colony of Togo, was mandated to Britain by the League of Nations after the First World War and was integrated with the Gold Coast colony in 1956 following a plebiscite. The colony became independent as Ghana on 6 March 1957. It was proclaimed a republic in 1960, and became a one-party state in 1964.

Since 1966, Ghana has experienced long periods of military rule (1966–9, 1972–9, 1981–91) interspersed with short-lived civilian governments (1969–72, 1979–81). Flt. Lt. Jerry Rawlings, who had ousted the military regime in 1979 and deposed the civilian government in 1981, was elected president in 1992 after a referendum approved a new multiparty constitution . A reconciliation commission, set up in 2002 to investigate human rights violations during the period of military rule, reported in 2004.

Since the mid-1990s there have been intermittent clashes over land ownership between ethnic groups in the north. A state of emergency was in place for two years after the last major outbreak of ethnic violence in 2002.

In the 2008 elections, John Atta Mills, the candidate of

the National Democratic Congress (NDC), was elected president with 50.2 per cent of the vote, and the NDC became the largest party in the legislature, winning half the seats.

POLITICAL SYSTEM
Under the 1993 constitution, the executive president is directly elected for a four-year term, renewable only once. The president appoints members of the council of ministers subject to approval by the legislature. The unicameral parliament has 230 members who are directly elected for a four-year term.

HEAD OF STATE
President, National Security, John Atta Mills, *elected* 28 December 2008, *sworn in* 7 January 2009
Vice-President, John Dramani Mahama

SELECTED GOVERNMENT MEMBERS *as at June 2010*
Defence, Joseph Smith
Finance, Kabwena Duffuor
Foreign Affairs, Mohammed Mumuni
Interior, Martin Amidu

OFFICE OF THE HIGH COMMISSION FOR GHANA
13 Belgrave Square, London SW1X 8PN
T 020-7201 5900
E information@ghanahighcommissionuk.com
W www.ghanahighcommissionuk.com
High Commissioner, Prof. Kwaku Danso-Boafo, *apptd* 2009

BRITISH HIGH COMMISSION
PO Box 296, Osu Link, off Gamel Abdul Nasser Avenue, Accra
T (+233) (21) 221 665 E high.commission.accra@fco.gov.uk
W http://ukinghana.fco.gov.uk
High Commissioner, HE Dr Nicholas Westcott, CMG, *apptd* 2008

BRITISH COUNCIL
PO Box GP 771, Liberia Road, Accra
T (+233) (21) 610 090 W www.britishcouncil.org/ghana
Director, Moses Anibaba

DEFENCE
The army has 39 armoured infantry fighting vehicles and 50 armoured personnel carriers. The navy has 7 patrol and coastal combatant vessels at 2 bases. The air force has 11 combat capable aircraft.
Military budget – US$264m (2009)
Military personnel – 15,500: army 11,500, navy 2,000, air force 2,000

ECONOMY AND TRADE
Ghana has abundant natural resources, but high foreign debt and budget and trade deficits make it dependent on international financial and technical aid to fund its economic and social development programmes. It has benefited from tighter government management of the economy since 2001, and from debt relief in 2002 and 2006.

Gold, cocoa and expatriate remittances are the main foreign exchange earners. Agriculture, mostly subsistence, forms the basis of the economy, along with forestry and fishing. The sector employs 56 per cent of the workforce and generates 37.3 per cent of GDP. The main cash crops are cocoa, timber and tuna. Industry employs 15 per cent of the workforce and contributes 25.3 per cent of GDP, mainly from mining (gold, manganese, bauxite, diamonds), forestry, light manufacturing, aluminium smelting, food processing and shipbuilding. Services employ 29 per cent and account for 37.5 per cent of GDP. Hydroelectric power is generated at dams on Lake Volta and is transmitted to most of Ghana, and to Togo and Benin. Oil was discovered offshore in 2007 and production is expected to begin in 2010–11.

The main export markets are EU countries, Ukraine and the USA. Principal exports are gold, cocoa, timber, tuna, metals, minerals and diamonds. Imports are provided mainly by China, Nigeria, India, the USA and the EU. The main imports are capital equipment, fuel and foodstuffs.
GNI – US$14,700m; US$630 per capita (2008)
Annual average growth of GDP – 4.7 per cent (2009 est)
Inflation rate – 19.6 per cent (2009 est)
Population below poverty line – 28.5 per cent (2007 est)
Total external debt – US$5,840m (2009 est)
Imports – US$10,400m (2008)
Exports – US$5,700m (2008)

BALANCE OF PAYMENTS
Trade – US$4,416m deficit (2009)
Current Account – US$791m deficit (2008)

Trade with UK	*2008*	*2009*
Imports from UK	£265,572,807	£259,140,634
Exports to UK	£203,007,472	£186,391,219

EDUCATION AND HEALTH
The government provides nine years of compulsory basic education for all children free of charge. Ghana has one of Africa's oldest universities, at Legon in Accra (established in 1948).
Literacy rate – 65.0 per cent (2007 est)
Gross enrolment ratio (percentage of relevant age group) – primary 102 per cent; secondary 54 per cent; tertiary 6 per cent (2008 est)
Health expenditure (per capita) – US$54 (2007)
Hospital beds (per 1,000 people) – 0.9 (2009)

MEDIA
The Ghana Broadcasting Corporation (GBC) is the state-owned broadcaster, and runs national radio and television networks. TV3 is a private television channel, Multichoice is a cable television operator and Metro TV is jointly owned by the government and private backers. Radio is the country's most popular medium and there are hundreds of private stations. Ghana's private press and broadcasters operate without significant restrictions.

GREECE

Elliniki Dhimokratia – Hellenic Republic

Area – 131,957 sq. km
Capital – Athens; population, 3,252,250 (2009 est)
Major cities – Iraklion (Heraklion) on Crete, Larisa, Patrai (Patras), Piraeus, Thessaloniki (Salonika)
Currency – Euro (€) of 100 cents
Population – 10,737,428 rising at 0.13 per cent a year (2009 est)
Religion – Christian (Greek Orthodox 97 per cent) (est)
Language – Greek (official)
Population density – 87 per sq. km (2008)
Urban population – 61 per cent (2007 est)
Median age (years) – 41.8 (2009 est)
National anthem – 'Imnos eis tin Eleftherian' ['Hymn to Liberty']
National day – 25 March (Independence Day)
Life expectancy (years) – 79.66 (2009 est)
Mortality rate – 10.51 (2009 est)
Birth rate – 9.45 (2009 est)
Infant mortality rate – 5.16 (2009 est)
Death penalty – Abolished for all crimes (since 2004)
CPI score – 3.8 (2009)

CLIMATE AND TERRAIN

The main areas of Greece are: Macedonia, Thrace, Epirus, Thessaly, Continental Greece, the Peloponnese and Attica on the mainland and the island of Crete. The main island groups are the Sporades, the Dodecanese or Southern Sporades and the Cyclades in the Aegean Sea, and the Ionian islands, including Corfu, to the west of the mainland. Low-lying coastal areas rise to a hilly or mountainous interior on the mainland and the islands. The Pindos mountains form a spine down the centre of the mainland, continuing down the Peloponnese, which is divided from the mainland by the Gulf of Corinth, the largest of the gulfs and bays indenting the coast. Elevation extremes range from 2,917m (Mt Olympus) at the highest point to 0m (Mediterranean Sea) at the lowest. The climate is temperate; the coastline and islands have a Mediterranean climate but the weather is cooler at higher altitudes. The average temperature in Athens ranges from a minimum of 6°C in January to a maximum 33°C in July and August.

HISTORY AND POLITICS

Successive civilisations flourished in ancient Greece from the second millennium BC until it was conquered by Philip II of Macedon in the fourth century BC and then by the Romans in 146 BC. When the western Roman Empire fell, the eastern part continued as the Byzantine Empire until it was conquered by the Turks in the mid-15th century. Turkish rule was overthrown in a war of independence (1821–7) that led to the establishment of a Greek kingdom in the Peloponnese and the south in 1829. Other islands and territories were added gradually over the next century, but the country's political and economic stability was precarious.

After the German Nazi occupation of 1941–4 ended, a civil war broke out between monarchist and communist groups that lasted from 1944 to 1949, and although it resulted in the restoration of democracy, tension between right- and left-wing groups continued. In 1967, a right-wing faction of the army seized power and established a military regime (the Greek Colonels), and the king went into exile. The Colonels' regime was toppled following its involvement in an unsuccessful coup against President Makarios of Cyprus in July 1974 and democratic rule was restored, although the restoration of the monarchy was rejected in a referendum and Greece became a republic. Political life since has been dominated by the conservative New Democracy (ND) party and the left-wing Panhellenic Socialist Party (PASOK).

Greece joined the European Community in 1981 and adopted the euro in 2001.

Karolos Papoulias was elected president in 2005, and was re-elected in February 2010. A legislative election was held in October 2009, nearly two years early, and PASOK returned to government after winning an outright majority of seats.

POLITICAL SYSTEM

Under the 1975 constitution, the head of state is the president, elected by the legislature for a five-year term, renewable only once. The unicameral legislature, the *Vouli,* has 300 members directly elected for a four-year term.

HEAD OF STATE

President of the Hellenic Republic, Karolos Papoulias, *elected* 8 February 2005, *sworn in* 12 March 2005, *re-elected* 2010

SELECTED GOVERNMENT MEMBERS *as at June 2010*

Prime Minister, Foreign Affairs George Papandreou
Interior, Yiannis Ragoussis
Defence, Evangelos Venizelos
Finance, Georgios Papaconstantinou

EMBASSY OF GREECE

1A Holland Park, London W11 3TP
T 020-7229 3850 E political@greekembassy.org.uk
W www.greekembassy.org.uk
Ambassador Extraordinary and Plenipotentiary, Aristidis Sandis, *apptd* 2010

BRITISH EMBASSY

1 Ploutarchou Street, 106 75 Athens
T (+30) (210) 727 2600 E information.athens@fco.gov.uk
W http://ukingreece.fco.gov.uk
Ambassador Extraordinary and Plenipotentiary, HE Dr David Landsman, OBE, *apptd* 2009

BRITISH COUNCIL

17 Kolonaki Square (Plateia Philikis Etairias), 106 73, Athens
T (+30) (210) 369 2333 W www.britishcouncil.org/greece
Director, Richard Walker

DEFENCE

The army has 1,688 main battle tanks, 2,105 armoured personnel carriers, 377 armoured infantry fighting vehicles and 32 armed helicopters. The navy has 8 submarines, 14 frigates, 3 corvettes, 40 patrol and coastal vessels and 11 armed helicopters, with bases at Salamis, Patras and Soudha Bay. The air force has a total of 242 combat aircraft.

Greece maintains 950 army personnel in Cyprus.
Military expenditure – US$10,100m (2008)
Military personnel – 156,600: army 93,500, navy 20,000, air force 31,500, joint staff 11,600; paramilitary 4,000
Conscription duration – Up to 12 months

ECONOMY AND TRADE

Greece has a capitalist economy, although with a large public sector which accounts for 40 per cent of GDP. It experienced rapid economic growth in the final quarter of the 20th century, owing largely to increased tourism and its accession to the EC. But in the 2000s, high government spending, low fiscal revenue and recession contributed to a growing budget deficit, which soared to over 13 per cent of GDP in 2009 and left the country particularly vulnerable in the global economic downturn. The New Democracy government's persistent failure to address the public finances crisis contributed to its international debt rating being downgraded in late 2009, amid fears of an imminent default on its debt. In its first six months in office the PASOK government pushed through austerity measures, in the face of strikes and demonstrations led by powerful trade unions, and in May 2010 it agreed a three-year programme of economic reforms with the IMF and other EU countries in return for financial assistance.

Although there was substantial industrialisation in the 20th century, agriculture still employs 12 per cent of the workforce, contributing 3.4 per cent of GDP. The most important agricultural products are cereals, vegetables, fruit, tobacco, beef and dairy products. Industrial activities, which contribute 20.8 per cent of GDP, include food and tobacco processing, textiles, chemicals, metal products, mining and petroleum production. The service sector employs 65 per cent of the workforce and generates 75.8 per cent of GDP; much of this is derived from tourism, which accounts for about 15 per cent of GDP, and shipping. Greece is a net importer of energy, including oil for refining and re-export.

The main trading partners are other EU countries (especially Germany and Italy), Russia and China. Principal exports are food and wine, manufactured goods, petroleum products, chemicals and textiles. The main imports are machinery, transport equipment, fuels and chemicals.

GNI – US$319,200m; US$28,400 per capita (2008)
Annual average growth of GDP – −2.5 per cent (2009 est)
Inflation rate – 1 per cent (2009 est)
Unemployment – 8.9 per cent (2009 est)
Total external debt – US$552,800m (2009)
Imports – US$77,800m (2008)
Exports – US$25,200m (2008)

BALANCE OF PAYMENTS
Trade – US$40,083m deficit (2009)
Current Account – US$37,104m deficit (2009)

Trade with UK	*2008*	*2009*
Imports from UK	£1,611,467,119	£1,568,037,397
Exports to UK	£626,506,435	£537,898,962

COMMUNICATIONS

There are extensive rail and road networks. The 2,500km of railways are state-owned, with the exception of the Athens–Piraeus Electric Railway; the sale of a 49 per cent stake in the loss-making state-controlled rail network operator TrainOSE to a strategic investor, who would also take over management, is planned under the economic reform programme agreed in May 2010. There are 117,500km of roads, including 880km of motorways. The main seaports are Piraeus, Thessaloniki and Patrai on the mainland and Iraklion on Crete. An extensive ferry system connects the islands to one another and to the mainland. The 6km Corinth canal across the Corinth isthmus shortens the sea journey by 325km. There are 81 airports and airfields, of which 67 have surfaced runways; the main airports are at Athens, Thessaloniki, Iraklion (Crete) and Corfu town (Corfu), although several other islands, especially tourist destinations, have airports. In 2008 there were 6 million fixed-line and 13.8 million mobile telephone subscribers, and 4.3 million internet users.

EDUCATION AND HEALTH

Education is free of charge and compulsory between the ages of six and 15, and is maintained by state grants.
Literacy rate – 97.1 per cent (2007 est)
Gross enrolment ratio (percentage of relevant age group) – primary 101 per cent; secondary 102 per cent; tertiary 91 per cent (2008 est)
Health expenditure (per capita) – US$2,679 (2007)
Hospital beds (per 1,000 people) – 4.8 (2003–8)

MEDIA

Although the Greek media is largely free from regulation, editors and publishers risk prosecution should their material be considered offensive to religious beliefs or to the president. The state-run broadcasters had a near-monopoly of the market until the late 1980s, but have since lost the majority of market share to commercial services. A sizeable proportion of the country's roughly 1,700 private radio and television stations are unlicensed.

CULTURE

Greek civilisation emerged *c.*1300 BC and underpins the philosophy, politics, literature, art and mathematics of the Western world. The epic poems of Homer, the *Iliad* and the *Odyssey*, are thought to date from *c.*800 BC, making them the earliest recorded works in Western literature. Dramatists whose work has survived include Aeschylus (*c.*525–*c.*456 BC), who is credited with inventing modern drama, Euripedes (480–406 BC) and Aristophanes (446–388 BC), author of the earliest known comedies. Socrates (470–399 BC), Plato (*c.*428–*c.*348 BC) and Aristotle (384–322 BC), whose *Poetics* is the earliest work of literary criticism, are considered the founders of philosophy. Hippocrates (*c.*460 –370 BC) was the first to separate medicine from philosophy and religion; his theory of the body being ruled by four humours persisted until late medieval times.

The spoken language of modern Greece is descended from the common Greek of Alexander the Great's empire. *Katharevousa,* a conservative literary dialect evolved by Adamantios Korais (1748–1833), which was used for official and technical matters, has been phased out. Novels and poetry are mostly written in *dimotiki,* a progressive literary dialect which owes much to Yannis Psycharis (1854–1929). Giorgos Seferis (1900–71) and Odysseus Elytis (1911–96) won the Nobel prize for literature, in 1963 and 1979 respectively.

GRENADA

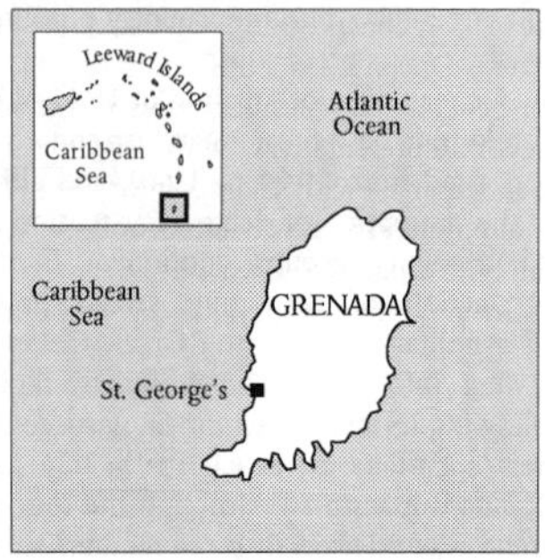

Area – 344 sq. km
Capital – St George's; population, 40,400 (2009 est)
Currency – East Caribbean dollar (EC$) of 100 cents
Population – 90,739 rising at 0.47 per cent a year (2009 est)
Religion – Christian (Roman Catholic 44 per cent, Anglican 12 per cent, Pentecostal 11 per cent, Seventh-day Adventist 11 per cent) (est)
Language – English (official), Creole (small minority)
Population density – 305 per sq. km (2008)
Urban population – 31 per cent (2007 est)
Median age (years) – 22.8 (2009 est)
National anthem – 'Hail Grenada'
National day – 7 February (Independence Day)
Life expectancy (years) – 65.95 (2009 est)
Mortality rate – 6.09 (2009 est)
Birth rate – 21.32 (2009 est)
Infant mortality rate – 13.23 (2009 est)
Death penalty – Retained (not used since 1978)
CPI score – 3.4 (2007)
Literacy rate – 96.0 per cent (2007 est)

CLIMATE AND TERRAIN

The most southerly of the Windward Islands, Grenada comprises three islands: Grenada (the largest at 18km in length and 34km in width), Carriacou and Petite Martinique. Elevation extremes range from 840m (Mt St Catherine) at the highest point to 0m (Caribbean Sea) at the lowest. The climate is subtropical, with a wet season from June to December. Grenada lies in a hurricane zone.

HISTORY AND POLITICS

Discovered by Columbus in 1498 and named Concepción, Grenada was colonised from the mid-17th century by the French, who subdued the native Caribs; the island was ceded to Britain in 1763. It became a crown colony in 1877, a self-governing associated state in 1967 and an independent nation on 7 February 1974.

The government was overthrown in 1979 by the New Jewel Movement led by Maurice Bishop, and a People's Revolutionary Government (PRG) was set up with Bishop as prime minister. In 1983, disagreements within the PRG led to the deposition and execution of Bishop, whose government was replaced by a revolutionary military council. These events prompted the intervention of Caribbean and US forces. After a period of interim government, democracy was restored and a general election held in 1984. Since the restoration of democracy, power has alternated between the New National Party (NNP) and the National Democratic Congress (NDC).

In the 2008 general election the NDC won a small overall majority, defeating the NNP, which had held power since 1995.

POLITICAL SYSTEM

Under the 1974 constitution, reinstated in 1984, the head of state is Queen Elizabeth II, represented locally by a governor-general. The bicameral parliament consists of the House of Representatives, with 15 directly elected members, and a senate with 13 appointed members, ten of which are appointed by the government and three by the opposition; both chambers serve a five-year term.
Governor-General, HE Sir Carlyle Glean, GCMG, *apptd* 2008

SELECTED GOVERNMENT MEMBERS *as at June 2010*

Prime Minister, National Security, Tillman Thomas
Finance, Nazim Burke
Foreign Affairs, Peter David

HIGH COMMISSION FOR GRENADA

The Chapel, Archel Road, London W14 9QH
T 020-7385 4415 E grenada@high-commission.demon.co.uk
High Commissioner, HE Ruth Rouse, *apptd* 2008

BRITISH HIGH COMMISSIONER

HE Paul Brummell, *apptd* 2009, resident at Bridgetown, Barbados

ECONOMY AND TRADE

The economy has grown considerably in recent decades owing to diversification into tourism and offshore financial services. Tourism and agriculture have recovered from severe hurricane damage in 2004 and 2005, but reconstruction has burdened the country with considerable debt and the global downturn's effect on tourism and remittances caused the economy to contract in 2009.

Agriculture now employs only 24 per cent of the workforce and produces 5.4 per cent of GDP. Industry consists of processing agricultural products, textile manufacturing, light assembly operations and construction, and contributes 18 per cent of GDP. The service sector, including tourism and financial services, accounts for 62 per cent of employment and 76.6 per cent of GDP.

The main trading partners are Trinidad and Tobago (43 per cent of imports), the USA, other Caribbean states and the UK. Principal exports are bananas, cocoa, nutmeg, fruit, vegetables, clothing and mace. Imports include food, manufactured goods, machinery, chemicals and fuels.
GNI – US$609m; US$5,880 per capita (2008)
Annual average growth of GDP – –4 per cent (2009 est)
Inflation rate – 3.7 per cent (2007 est)
Unemployment – 12.5 per cent (2004 est)
Total external debt – US$347m (2004)
Imports – US$280m (2006)
Exports – US$20m (2006)

BALANCE OF PAYMENTS

Trade – US$348m deficit (2009)
Current Account – US$263m deficit (2008)

Trade with UK	*2008*	*2009*
Imports from UK	£6,845,750	£5,285,737
Exports to UK	£4,101,876	£321,720

MEDIA

Grenadian law guarantees a free media. Of the two available television stations, GBN TV is operated by the public broadcaster Grenada Broadcasting Network, and MTV is US-owned. There are several radio stations jointly owned by the public and private sectors. There are no daily newspapers but several private weekly publications.

GUATEMALA

República de Guatemala – Republic of Guatemala

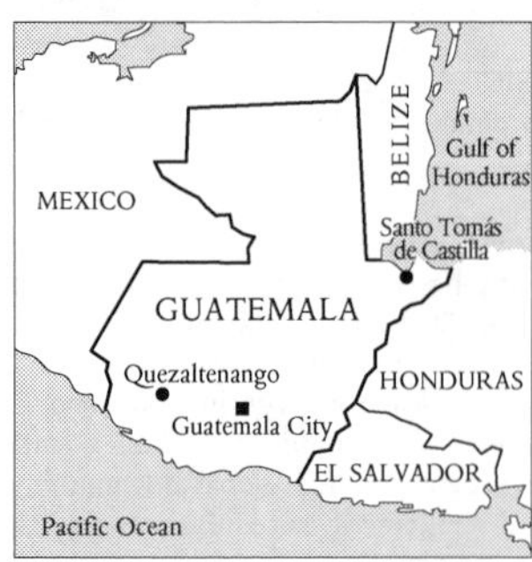

Area – 108,899 sq. km
Capital – Guatemala City; population, 1,074,870 (2009 est)
Major cities – Mixco, Quezaltenango, Villa Nueva
Currency – Quetzal (Q) of 100 centavos
Population – 13,276,517 rising at 2.07 per cent a year (2009 est); mestizo and European (59.4 per cent), K'iche (9.1 per cent), Kaqchikel (8.4 per cent), Mam (7.9 per cent), Q'eqchi (6.3 per cent)
Religion – Christian (Roman Catholic 57 per cent, Evangelical Protestant 31 per cent) (est)
Language – Spanish, 23 Amerindian languages (all official)
Population density – 128 per sq. km (2008)
Urban population – 48 per cent (2007 est)
Median age (years) – 19.4 (2009 est)
National anthem – 'Himno Nacional de Guatemala' ['National Anthem of Guatemala']
National day – 15 September (Independence Day)
Life expectancy (years) – 70.29 (2009 est)
Mortality rate – 5.11 (2009 est)
Birth rate – 27.98 (2009 est)
Infant mortality rate – 27.84 (2009 est)
Death penalty – Retained
CPI score – 3.4 (2009)

CLIMATE AND TERRAIN

Narrow tropical plains on both the north (Caribbean) and south (Pacific) coasts rise to a mountainous interior in the centre and south. The mountains fall in the north to lowlands covered in tropical jungle. Elevation extremes range from 4,211m (Tajumulco volcano) at the highest point to 0m (Pacific Ocean) at the lowest. There are 37 volcanoes, three active, in the central plateau. The climate is tropical but is cooler in the highlands. The wet season runs from May to October, when mudslides and hurricanes can occur. There are also frequent minor earth tremors and some earthquakes.

HISTORY AND POLITICS

Mayan and Aztec civilisations flourished in the area until the Spanish conquest in 1523–4, after which the area became a Spanish colony. It gained its independence in 1821, and formed part of a Central American federation of former Spanish provinces from 1823 to 1839. After independence, the country was ruled by a series of dictatorships and military regimes, interspersed with periods of democratic government. In 1960 a civil war began between military governments, right-wing vigilantes and left-wing guerrillas that lasted for 36 years and during which over 200,000 people died or disappeared.

In 1996 the democratically elected, civilian government concluded a peace agreement with the left-wing Guatemalan Revolutionary National Unity guerrillas that ended the civil war, and began a reduction in the size and political influence of the army that has been continued by its successors. In 1999, an independent commission found that 93 per cent of human rights abuses during the war had been instigated by the security forces, and in 2000 and 2004 the state formally admitted guilt in several human rights crimes, paying damages to the victims. Only a small number of the military personnel found to be responsible for the atrocities have been so far been prosecuted

In the 2007 legislative election, the National Unity of Hope party (UNE) won the most seats, but without an overall majority. The 2007 presidential election was won in the second round by the UNE candidate Alvaro Colom. The next legislative and presidential elections are scheduled in August 2011.

POLITICAL SYSTEM

Under the 1986 constitution, the executive president is directly elected for a four-year term, which is not renewable. He is responsible to the congress and appoints the cabinet. The unicameral Congress of the Republic has 158 members, who are directly elected for a four-year term.

HEAD OF STATE

President, Alvaro Colom Caballeros, *elected* 4 November 2007, *sworn in* 14 January 2008
Vice-President, Rafael Espada

SELECTED GOVERNMENT MEMBERS *as at June 2010*

Defence, Marco Tulio Garcia Franco
Economy, Rubén Morales
Foreign Affairs, Haroldo Rodas
Interior, Carlos Menocal

EMBASSY OF GUATEMALA

13A Fawcett Street, London SW10 9HN
T 020-7351 3042 **E** inglaterra@minex.gob.gt
Ambassador Extraordinary and Plenipotentiary, HE Acisclo Valladares Molina, *apptd* 2010

BRITISH EMBASSY

Edificio Torre Internacional, Nivel 11, 16 Calle 0-55, Zona 10, Guatemala City
T (+502) 2380 7300 **E** embassy@intelnett.com
W http://ukinguatemala.fco.gov.uk
Ambassador Extraordinary and Plenipotentiary, Julie Chappel, OBE, *apptd* 2009

DEFENCE

The army has 52 armoured personnel carriers. The navy has over 39 patrol and coastal combatant vessels at 2 bases. The air force has 9 combat capable aircraft.
Military budget – US$156m (2009)
Military personnel – 15,212: army 13,444, navy 897, air force 871; paramilitary 18,536

ECONOMY AND TRADE

The country suffers from a huge imbalance in wealth, and a civic structure and infrastructure still recovering from the civil war. IMF funding and foreign aid have underpinned the government's economic reforms and stabilisation programmes, but the trade deficit and high levels of corruption and violence remain problems. Remittances from expatriates, equivalent to nearly two-thirds of export revenue, are vital to the economy. Half of the population is dependent on agriculture, which contributes 13.5 per cent of GDP and accounts for over 40 per cent of exports. Industry accounts for 24.4 per cent of GDP, and the services sector, which includes tourism, for 62 per cent of GDP.

The main trading partners are the USA, El Salvador and Mexico. The principal exports are coffee, sugar, petroleum, garments, bananas, fruit, vegetables and cardamom. The chief imports are fuels, machinery and transport equipment, construction materials, grain, fertilisers and electricity.

GNI – US$36,600m; US$2,680 per capita (2008)
Annual average growth of GDP – –0.5 per cent (2009 est)
Inflation rate – 2.3 per cent (2009 est)
Population below poverty line – 56.2 per cent (2004 est)
Unemployment – 3.2 per cent (2005 est)
Total external debt – US$7,489m (2009 est)
Imports – US$12,800m (2008)
Exports – US$5,400m (2008)

BALANCE OF PAYMENTS
Trade – US$5,162m deficit (2009)
Current Account – US$1,773m deficit (2008)

Trade with UK	*2008*	*2009*
Imports from UK	£30,196,399	£24,524,502
Exports to UK	£21,317,842	£25,956,118

EDUCATION AND HEALTH

There are six years of compulsory education.
Literacy rate – 73.2 per cent (2007 est)
Gross enrolment ratio (percentage of relevant age group) – primary 114 per cent; secondary 57 per cent; tertiary 18 per cent (2008 est)
Health expenditure (per capita) – US$186 (2007)
Hospital beds (per 1,000 people) – 0.6 (2003–8)

MEDIA AND CULTURE

Freedom of the press is enshrined in the constitution, but journalists who pursue controversial stories are often subjected to threats. There are four major daily newspapers, including *Prensa Libre* and *El Periodico*. Four privately run television channels under the same ownership monopolise Guatemalan television.

The ruins of the Mayan civilisation dot the country, while the influence of African culture is evident along the Caribbean coast. Distinguished Guatemalans include the writers Miguel Angel Asturias (1899–1974), who won the Nobel prize for literature in 1967; Luis Cardoza y Aragon (1901–92), who edited the influential periodical *Revista de Guatemala* after the 1944 revolution; and Rigoberta Menchu (*b.* 1959), who won the Nobel peace prize in 1992.

GUINEA

République de Guinée – Republic of Guinea

Area – 245,857 sq. km
Capital – Conakry; population, 1,597,420 (2009 est)
Major cities – Guéckédou, Kankan, Nzérékoré
Currency – Guinea franc of 100 centimes
Population – 10,057,975 rising at 2.57 per cent a year (2009 est); Fulani (40 per cent), Malinke (30 per cent), Susu (20 per cent) (est)
Religion – Muslim 85 per cent (predominantly Sunni), Christian 10 per cent, traditional indigenous religions 5 per cent (est); some combine Islam or Christianity with indigenous beliefs
Language – French (official), eight African languages
Population density – 26 per sq. km (2008)
Urban population – 34 per cent (2007 est)
Median age (years) – 18.5 (2009 est)
National anthem – 'Liberté' ['Liberty']
National day – 2 October (Independence Day)
Life expectancy – 57.09 (2009 est)
Mortality rate – 11 (2009 est)
Birth rate – 37.52 (2009 est)
Infant mortality rate – 65.22 (2009 est)
HIV/AIDS adult prevalence – 1.5 per cent (2007 est)
Death penalty – Retained
CPI score – 1.8 (2009)
Literacy rate – 29.5 per cent (2007 est)
Gross enrolment ratio (percentage of relevant age group) – primary 90 per cent; secondary 36 per cent; tertiary 9 per cent (2008 est)
Health expenditure (per capita) – US$26 (2007)
Hospital beds (per 1,000 people) – 0.3 (2003–8)

CLIMATE AND TERRAIN

Guinea has a flat coastal plain that rises to the hilly Fouta Djallon plateau in the north-west, where the Gambia and Senegal rivers rise. East of the plateau is the central savannah, the source of the River Niger, with rainforest in the south-east. Elevation extremes range from 1,752m (Mt Nimba) at the highest point to 0m at the lowest (Atlantic Ocean). The climate is tropical, with a wet season from June to November; the average daily temperature is 27°C.

HISTORY AND POLITICS

Susi kingdoms were established in the area by the 13th century, and in the 16th century the north-east of the country was part of the Mali Empire. The Portuguese established ivory and slave trading in the region from the mid-15th century. In 1849 the French established a protectorate over the coastal areas, and the country was governed with Senegal until the 1890s, when it was renamed French Guinea, becoming part of French West Africa in 1904.

Guinea became independent on 2 October 1958 under President Ahmed Sekou Touré, who established a one-party socialist state and governed throughout the 1960s and 1970s. Touré's death in 1984 was followed by a military coup that brought Lansana Conté to power. Conté introduced greater economic liberalisation and, following strikes and mass protests in 1991, reintroduced a multiparty system. President Conté and his Party of Unity and Progress (PUP) won all subsequent elections, amid allegations of electoral fraud and intimidation of opponents.

The civil wars in neighbouring Sierra Leone, Liberia and Côte d'Ivoire caused an influx of refugees (about 700,000 over 15 years) that strained the economy, exacerbating already poor conditions. Low pay, poor living standards and price rises contributed to the growing unpopularity of Conté's government and led to strikes and violent protests, including by the army, between 2006 and 2008.

The day after President Conté's death in December 2008, a military coup occurred and Capt. Moussa Dadis Camara became president at the head of a National Council for Democracy and Development (CNDD), which appointed a predominantly civilian transitional government. After Camara was injured in an assassination attempt in December 2009, his deputy became acting president and negotiated a new power-sharing government with the opposition in January 2010. A presidential election was held in June 2010, with a run-off vote scheduled for September; a legislative election was expected in late 2010.

POLITICAL SYSTEM

Under the 1991 constitution (which is currently suspended), the executive president is directly elected for a five-year term, renewable only once; a 2001 amendment allowed the president to stand for a third term, lasting seven years, in 2003. The unicameral National Assembly has 114 members, who are directly elected for a five-year term. The president appoints the council of ministers.

HEAD OF STATE

President, Capt. Moussa Dadis Camara, *took power* 23 December 2008

Acting President, Defence, Gen. Sékouba Konaté

SELECTED GOVERNMENT MEMBERS *as at June 2010*

Prime Minister, Jean-Marie Doré

Finance and Economy, Kerfalla Yansane

Foreign Affairs, Bakary Fofana

Security, Maj.-Gen. Mamadou Ba Toto Camara

EMBASSY OF THE REPUBLIC OF GUINEA

258 Belsize Road, London, NW6 4BT

T 020-7316 1861 E ambaguineeuk@yahoo.co.uk

Ambassador Extraordinary and Plenipotentiary, HE Lansana Keita, *apptd* 2005

BRITISH EMBASSY

BP 6729, Conakry

T (+224) 6335 5329 E britembconakry@hotmail.com

Ambassador Extraordinary and Plenipotentiary, HE Ian Felton, *apptd* 2008

DEFENCE

The army has 38 main battle tanks and 40 armoured personnel carriers. The navy has 2 patrol and coastal combatant vessels at 2 bases. The air force has 7 combat capable aircraft and 5 attack helicopters.

Military budget – US$55m (2009 est)

Military personnel – 12,300: army 8,500, navy 400, air force 800, Gendarmerie 1,000, Republican Guard 1,600; paramilitary 7,000

Conscription duration – 24 months

ECONOMY AND TRADE

Despite an abundance of natural resources, including 30 per cent of the world's known bauxite reserves, decades of mismanagement have left the economy undeveloped, and nearly half the population is below the poverty line; some basic necessities are now unaffordable for many. There is a large foreign debt, and budget and trade deficits, but little foreign aid as most IMF and World Bank aid was suspended after the coup. Agriculture, much of it at subsistence level, employs 76 per cent of the population and contributes 23.8 per cent of GDP. Industry accounts for 37.9 per cent of GDP, mostly through mining and the processing of minerals and agricultural produce.

The main trading partners are India, China, France and Spain. Principal exports are bauxite, alumina, gold, diamonds, coffee, fish and other agricultural products. The main imports are petroleum products, metals, machinery, transport equipment, textiles, grain and other foodstuffs.

GNI – US$3,500m; US$350 per capita (2008)

Annual average growth of GDP – –1 per cent (2009 est)

Inflation rate – 9 per cent (2009 est)

Population below poverty line – 47 per cent (2006 est)

Total external debt – US$3,072m (2009 est)

Imports – US$1,600m (2008)

Exports – US$1,300m (2008)

BALANCE OF PAYMENTS

Trade – US$372m deficit (2009)

Current Account – US$517m deficit (2008)

Trade with UK	*2008*	*2009*
Imports from UK	£22,296,718	£85,418,006
Exports to UK	£2,107,767	£478,579

COMMUNICATIONS

Guinea has almost 1,200km of railways, 44,300km of roads (only 10 per cent of which are surfaced) and 1,300km of inland waterways navigable by shallow-draught craft. The major seaports are Conakry and Kamsar. Guinea has 17 airports, including five with surfaced runways; the principal airport is at Conakry. The fixed-line telephone system is limited in extent, with fixed-line density of less than one per 100 people. Mobile phone distribution is growing more quickly, with nearly 40 per 100 people. There were 90,000 internet users in 2008.

MEDIA

The state-run Radiodiffusion-Television Guineenne provides national radio and television broadcasting. The only daily national newspaper is also state-run. Private radio station licences became available in 2006, but the civil unrest of 2007 caused the government to tighten its control of the media, closing some radio stations and cybercafes. Although publishing is stifled by strict censorship laws and prohibitative printing costs, more than a dozen private publications are printed on a weekly, or less regular, basis.

GUINEA-BISSAU

Republica da Guine-Bissau – Republic of Guinea-Bissau

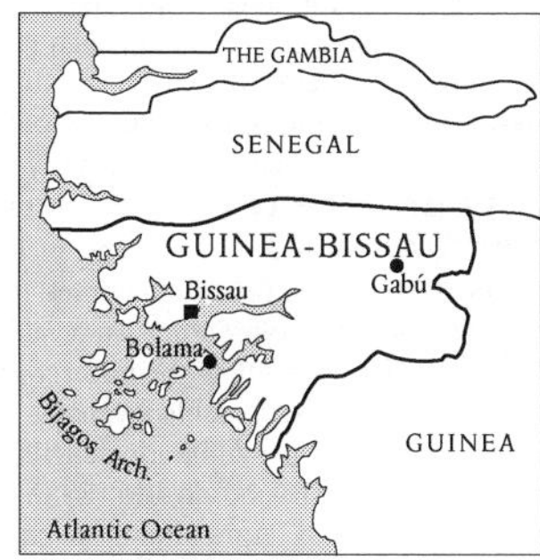

Area – 36,125 sq. km
Capital – Bissau; population, 301,839 (2009 est)
Currency – Franc CFA of 100 centimes
Population – 1,533,964 rising at 2.02 per cent a year (2009 est); Balanta (30 per cent), Fulani (20 per cent), Manjaca (14 per cent), Mandinga (13 per cent), Papel (7 per cent) (est)
Religion – Traditional indigenous beliefs 50 per cent, Muslim 40 per cent (predominantly Sunni), Christian 5 per cent (est)
Language – Portuguese (official), Creole
Population density – 56 per sq. km (2008)
Urban population – 30 per cent (2007 est)
Median age (years) – 19.3 (2009 est)
National anthem – 'Esta e a Nossa Patria Bem Amada' ['This is Our Beloved Country']
National day – 24 September (Independence Day)
Life expectancy (years) – 47.9 (2009 est)
Mortality rate – 15.79 (2009 est)
Birth rate – 35.97 (2009 est)
Infant mortality rate – 99.82 (2009 est)
HIV/AIDS adult prevalence – 1.7 per cent (2007 est)
Death penalty – Abolished for all crimes (since 1993)
CPI score – 1.9 (2009)
Literacy rate – 64.6 per cent (2007 est)
Gross enrolment ratio (percentage of relevant age group) – primary 120 per cent; secondary 36 per cent; tertiary 3 per cent (2008)
Health expenditure (per capita) – US$16 (2007 est)
Hospital beds (per 1,000 people) – 1.0 (2009)

CLIMATE AND TERRAIN

Guinea-Bissau has a low coastal plain that rises to savannah in the east. The coast is heavily indented and covered with mangrove swamps. Elevation extremes range from 300m (in the north-east) at the highest point to 0m (Atlantic Ocean) at the lowest. The climate is tropical, with a wet season from June to October. Mean temperatures range from 25°C in January to 28°C in October.

HISTORY AND POLITICS

A part of the ancient African empire of Mali, Guinea-Bissau was once the kingdom of Gabu, which became independent of the empire in 1546 and survived until 1867. In 1446, Portuguese traders discovered the coast and established slave trading there, subsequently administering Guinea-Bissau with the Cape Verde islands; it became a separate colony in 1879. After a guerrilla war led by the left-wing African Party for the Independence of Guinea and Cape Verde (PAIGC), Guinea-Bissau declared independence unilaterally in 1973 and Portugal recognised this in 1974.

After independence Guinea-Bissau became a one-party socialist state under the PAIGC, led by Luis Cabral. He was deposed in 1980, in a military coup led by General Joao Vieira, and the country was under military rule until 1994. A multiparty system was introduced in 1991 after popular agitation, but the following 15 years saw a short civil war (1998–9) and two more military coups (1999, 2003). Guinea-Bissau's political turbulence has been exacerbated by the unrest in Senegal's Casamance region since the 1990s, and the country's increasing use as a staging post by drug-smugglers and people-traffickers threatens to destabilise it further.

After a period of civilian-led transitional government, democratic government was restored in 2004–5. In the November 2008 legislative election, the PAIGC won an overall majority and formed a government in January 2009. The PAIGC candidate, Malam Bacai Sanha, was elected president in July 2009, succeeding Joao Vieira (president 1980–99, 2005–9), who had been assassinated in March.

POLITICAL SYSTEM

Under the 1999 constitution, the executive president is directly elected for a five-year term, which is renewable without limit. The president appoints the council of ministers. The unicameral National People's Assembly has 102 members, who are directly elected for a four-year term.

HEAD OF STATE

President, Malam Bacai Sanha, *elected* July 2009, *sworn in* 8 September 2009

SELECTED GOVERNMENT MEMBERS *as at May 2009*

Prime Minister, Carlos Gomes Jr
Economy, Helena Nosolini Embalo
Foreign Affairs, Adelino Mano Queita
Defence, Aristides Ocante da Silva
Interior, Adja Satu Camara Pinto

EMBASSY OF THE REPUBLIC OF GUINEA-BISSAU

94 rue St Lazare, 75009 Paris, France
T (+33) (1) 4526 1851
Ambassador Extraordinary and Plenipotentiary, vacant

BRITISH CONSULATE

Ambassador Extraordinary and Plenipotentiary, HE Christopher Trott, *apptd* 2007, resident in Dakar, Senegal

DEFENCE

The army has 10 main battle tanks and 55 armoured personnel carriers. The navy has 2 patrol and coastal combatant vessels at a base at Bissau. The air force has 2 combat capable aircraft.
Military budget – US$20m (2009 est)
Military personnel – 6,458 (est): army 4,000 (est), navy 350, air force 100, Gendarmerie 2,000

ECONOMY AND TRADE

The economy is in a poor state owing to decades of mismanagement and corruption, the devastating effects of the 1998–9 civil war and ongoing political instability. There is a massive foreign debt and the country is heavily dependent on foreign aid; emergency aid provided over 80 per cent of the national budget in 2004.

Although Guinea-Bissau has mineral resources,

including oil, the high cost of exploiting these inhibits development and the economy is based almost exclusively on agriculture and fishing. This sector employs 82 per cent of the population and contributes 62 per cent of GDP. The small industrial sector generates 12 per cent of GDP, mainly through the processing of agricultural products and beer and soft drink production.

The main trading partners are India (64 per cent of exports), Nigeria, Portugal and Senegal. Principal exports include cashew nuts, fish, peanuts, palm kernels and timber. The main imports are foodstuffs, machinery and transport equipment, and fuels.

GNI – US$400m; US$250 per capita (2008)
Annual average growth of GDP – 3.5 per cent (2009 est)
Inflation rate – 3.8 per cent (2007 est)
Imports – US$200m (2008)
Exports – US$100m (2008)

BALANCE OF PAYMENTS
Trade – US$55m deficit (2009)
Current Account – US$20m surplus (2008)

Trade with UK	*2008*	*2009*
Imports from UK	£603,122	£510,846
Exports to UK	£2,992	£12,795

COMMUNICATIONS

The infrastructure, already rudimentary, was badly damaged in the civil war. Guinea-Bissau has 3,455km of roads, of which only 965km are surfaced, and no railways. There are nine airports and airfields, two of which have surfaced runways; the principal airport is at Bissau. The main rivers are navigable for part of their lengths, and shallow-draught craft can access much of the interior via creeks and inlets. Bissau is the main seaport. The fixed-line telephone system is small, with fewer than one per 100 people in 2008, while mobile phone density was 35 per 100 people. There were 37,100 internet users in 2008.

MEDIA

Since the 2003 military coup, media organisations have been able to operate with greater freedom; government interference is often less of a concern now than reliable power supplies. Guinea-Bissau's principal television station and national radio broadcaster are state-run, and there are a number of commercial radio stations. One state-owned and three privately owned national newspapers are published, although the sector is limited by financial restraints.

GUYANA

Cooperative Republic of Guyana

Area – 214,969 sq. km
Capital – Georgetown; population, 131,660 (2009 est)
Major towns – Linden, New Amsterdam
Currency – Guyana dollar (G$) of 100 cents
Population – 772,298 rising at 0.18 per cent a year (2009 est); East Indian 43.5 per cent, black/African 30.2 per cent, mixed 16.7 per cent, Amerindian 9.1 per cent
Religion – Christian 57 per cent (predominantly Protestant), Hindu 28 per cent, Muslim 7 per cent (predominantly Sunni) (est)
Language – English (official), Amerindian dialects, Creole, Caribbean Hindustani (a dialect of Hindi), Urdu
Population density – 4 per sq. km (2008)
Urban population – 28 per cent (2008 est)
Median age (years) – 28.7 (2009 est)
National anthem – 'Dear Land of Guyana, of Rivers and Plains'
National day – 23 February (Republic Day)
Life expectancy (years) – 66.68 (2009 est)
Mortality rate – 8.31 (2009 est)
Birth rate – 17.56 (2009 est)
Infant mortality rate – 29.65 (2009 est)
HIV/AIDS adult prevalence – 2.4 per cent (2007 est)
Death penalty – Retained
CPI score – 2.6 (2009)

CLIMATE AND TERRAIN

The land rises from a narrow coastal plain to forested highlands in the west and savannah on the southern border; about 90 per cent of the population lives on the coastal plain, which constitutes 5 per cent of the land area. Much of the interior is covered in rainforest, with elevation extremes ranging from 2,835m (Mt Roraima) at the highest point to 0m (Atlantic Ocean) at the lowest. The climate is tropical, with an average daily temperature of between 27°C and 32°C and two wet seasons, from May to July and from December to January.

HISTORY AND POLITICS

Carib and Arawak peoples inhabited the coastal region of Guyana when Dutch merchants founded the first European settlement in the late 16th century. Guyana became an important producer of sugar, grown on plantations worked first by African slaves and then, after the abolition of slavery in 1834, by indentured labourers, mostly from India. Several areas were ceded to Britain in 1815, and consolidated as British Guiana in 1831. The country became independent, as Guyana, on 26 May 1966, and became a republic in 1970.

Guyana's first political party, the People's Progressive Party (PPP), split along ethnic lines in the 1950s; the PPP continued as a predominantly Indian party under Cheddi Jagan, while those of African descent formed the People's National Congress (PNC), led by Forbes Burnham. Burnham dominated political life after independence, first as prime minister (1966–80) and then as executive president until his death in 1985. Under his autocratic rule, politics became characterised by suspect elections and a disregard for civil liberties and human rights. The PPP's electoral victory in 1992 ended the PNC's monopoly of power but persistent ethnic tensions continue to destabilise politics.

Bharrat Jagdeo of the PPP, interim president from 1999 to 2001, was elected president in 2001. His presidency has seen attempts to encourage joint action between the government and the private sector, and reconciliation between the PPP and Guyana's other political parties in order to prevent further political violence.

The 2006 legislative election was won by the PPP, securing its fourth consecutive term of office and the re-election of President Jagdeo for a second term. Fresh legislative elections are due by August 2011.

POLITICAL SYSTEM
Under the 1980 constitution, the executive president is nominated by the majority party in the legislature after legislative elections, and serves a five-year term. The unicameral National Assembly has 65 members, of whom 40 are elected by proportional representation and 25 are regional representatives; they serve a five-year term.

HEAD OF STATE
President, Bharrat Jagdeo, *succeeded* 11 August 1999, *elected* 2001, *re-elected* 28 August 2006

SELECTED GOVERNMENT MEMBERS *as at June 2010*
Prime Minister, Samuel Hinds
Finance, Ashni Kumar Singh
Foreign Affairs, Carolyn Rodrigues-Burkett
Home Affairs, Clement Rohee

HIGH COMMISSION FOR GUYANA
3 Palace Court, Bayswater Road, London W2 4LP
T 020-7229 7684 E guyanahc1@btconnect.com
W www.guyanahc.com
High Commissioner, HE Laleshwar Singh, *apptd* 1993

BRITISH HIGH COMMISSION
PO Box 10849, 44 Main Street, Georgetown
T (+592) 226 5881 E bhcguyana@networksgy.com
W http://ukinguyana.fco.gov.uk
High Commissioner, HE Fraser Wheeler, *apptd* 2006

DEFENCE
The navy has 5 patrol and coastal combatant vessels at 3 bases. The air force has 2 utility helicopters.
Military budget – US$67m (2008)
Military personnel – 1,100: army 900, navy 100, air force 100; paramilitary 1,500

ECONOMY AND TRADE
The economy grew from 2001 to 2008 owing to expansion in agriculture and mining, the cancellation of over one-third of Guyana's external debt, and increases in foreign direct investment and remittances from expatriate workers. Poor infrastructure and skills shortages inhibit growth, especially attempts to develop tourism. The economy contracted in 2009 owing to the global downturn and lower commodity prices.

Agriculture accounts for 25.1 per cent of GDP and provides the raw materials for the major industries of sugar processing and rice milling. Non-agricultural activities include bauxite and gold mining, forestry, fishing and textile manufacturing; industry accounts for 24 per cent of GDP.

The main trading partners are the USA, Trinidad and Tobago, Canada and the UK. Principal exports include sugar, gold, bauxite, alumina, rice, shrimp, molasses, rum and timber. The main imports are manufactured goods, machinery, fuel and food.
GNI – US$1,107m; US$1,450 per capita (2008)
Annual average growth of GDP – –1.2 per cent (2009 est)
Inflation rate – 5.2 per cent (2009 est)
Unemployment – 11 per cent (2007 est)
Total external debt – US$804.3m (2008)
Imports – US$1,300m (2008)
Exports – US$800m (2008)

BALANCE OF PAYMENTS
Trade – US$543m deficit (2009)
Current Account – US$254m deficit (2008)

Trade with UK	*2008*	*2009*
Imports from UK	£21,408,109	£24,906,039
Exports to UK	£75,691,097	£72,293,260

COMMUNICATIONS
Roads and navigable waterways (the Berbice, Demerara and Essequibo rivers) form the main arteries of communication, though only 590km of roads, out of a total of 7,970km, are surfaced. Georgetown is the main seaport and the location of the principal airport. There are 99 airports and airfields in total, though only ten have surfaced runways. The Takutu bridge, completed in 2009, has opened up cross-border transport and trade links with Brazil that are expected to bring economic benefits to the south. Many areas lack fixed-line telephone services; density was about 15 per 100 people in 2005. Mobile phone distribution has grown quickly and density was 37 per 100 people in 2005.

MEDIA
The Guyanese government operates one television and two radio stations, and there are numerous private competitors. There are three daily newspapers, one of which is state-owned. Journalists operate freely but often practise self-censorship.

HAITI

République d'Haïti/Repiblik d'Ayiti – Republic of Haiti

Area – 27,750 sq. km
Capital – Port-au-Prince; population, 2,642,760 (2009 est)
Major cities – Cap-Haïtien, Gonaïves, Pétionville
Currency – Gourde of 100 centimes
Population – 9,035,536 rising at 1.84 per cent a year (2009 est)
Religion – Christian (Roman Catholic 55 per cent, Baptist 15 per cent, Pentecostal 8 per cent, Seventh-day Adventist 3 per cent), Vodou (voodoo) (as primary religion) 2 per cent (est); many Christians also practise voodoo, recognised as an official religion in 2003.
Language – French, Creole (both official)
Population density – 358 per sq. km (2008)
Urban population – 46 per cent (2007 est)
Median age (years) – 20.2 (2009 est)
National anthem – 'La Dessalinienne' ['Song of Dessalines']
National day – 1 January (Independence Day)
Life expectancy (years) – 60.78 (2009 est)

Mortality rate – 8.65 (2009 est)
Birth rate – 29.1 (2009 est)
Infant mortality rate – 59.69 (2009 est)
HIV/AIDS adult prevalence – 1.8 per cent (2007 est)
Death penalty – Abolished for all crimes (since 1987)
CPI score – 1.8 (2009)
Literacy rate – 62.1 per cent (2007 est)
Health expenditure (per capita) – US$35 (2007)
Hospital beds (per 1,000 people) – 1.3 (2003–8)

CLIMATE AND TERRAIN

The country occupies the western third of the island of Hispaniola (the remainder is the Dominican Republic). The terrain is mountainous, with coastal plains and a large central plateau. Elevation extremes range from 2,680m (Châine de la Selle) at the highest point to 0m (Caribbean Sea) at the lowest. The climate is tropical, and semi-arid where the eastern mountains block the trade winds, with two wet seasons (April–June, August–October) and a hurricane season from June to November.

HISTORY AND POLITICS

Columbus landed on Hispaniola in 1492 and it was colonised by the Spanish from the late 1490s. In 1697 the western part of Hispaniola was ceded to France and named Saint Domingue. It became probably the richest colony in the French Empire through its sugar cane and coffee plantations, worked by African slaves. In 1791, a slave rebellion expelled the French from the northern part of the colony and instigated a long war between freed slaves and colonists. By 1804 the Republic of Haiti was founded, marking the inception of the world's first black republic and, after the USA, the oldest republic in the western hemisphere. Separate post-independence regimes in the north and south were united in 1820.

Haiti has experienced very little stability since. The country endured 22 changes of government between 1843 and 1915. The resultant disorder led the USA to intervene in 1915, the beginning of 19 years of US occupation. Sovereign rule was restored in 1934.

In 1956, the Duvalier family gained control of the country and began a dictatorial rule which lasted 29 years. A series of transitional governments followed before Jean-Bertrand Aristide won the 1990 presidential election. Aristide was deposed the following year in a coup that instigated a period of military rule, but was restored in 1994 after the severity of the military's repression prompted the UN to authorise international intervention. Flawed elections in 1997 and 2000 led to several years of political turmoil until an armed rebellion in 2004 ousted Aristide, who had been re-elected in 2000. An interim government was sworn in and a UN-led multinational stabilisation force was deployed. UN peacekeepers' joint operations with the national police force were slowly having an impact on the widespread violence, lawlessness and corruption, but these have increased in the aftermath of the massive earthquake in January 2010. This left 230,000 dead, 300,000 injured and 1.2 million homeless, and damaged the country's political structure as well as its infrastructure.

The 2006 presidential election was won by René Préval (president 1996–2000) of the Front for Hope (Lespwa) party. In the 2006 legislative election, the Lespwa party won the most seats but not an overall majority, and headed a six-party coalition government. President Préval announced in June 2010 that overdue legislative elections, and a simultaneous presidential poll, would go ahead in November 2010.

POLITICAL SYSTEM

Under the 1987 constitution, the president is directly elected for a five-year term that may not be renewed immediately. The bicameral National Assembly comprises a lower house, the Chamber of Deputies, with 99 members directly elected for a four-year term, and the senate, with 30 members directly elected for a six-year term; one-third of the senators is elected every two years. The president appoints the prime minister, who must be approved by the legislature.

HEAD OF STATE

President, René Préval, *elected* February 2006, *sworn in* 14 May 2006

SELECTED GOVERNMENT MEMBERS *as at June 2010*

Prime Minister, Jean-Max Bellerive
Foreign Affairs, Mari Michèle Rey
Economy and Finance, Ronald Baudin
Interior, Paul Antoine Bien-Aime

BRITISH AMBASSADOR

HE Steven Fisher, *apptd* 2009, resident at Santo Domingo, Dominican Republic

ECONOMY AND TRADE

The country is the poorest in the western hemisphere, with most of the population living below the poverty line and over half in abject poverty. Its economy, devastated by years of political instability, violence and corruption as well as the natural disasters to which it is vulnerable, experienced moderate growth from 2005 and Haiti had around US$525 million of its foreign debt written off in 2009. But the 2010 earthquake reversed these gains, devastating the infrastructure and continuing the government's complete dependence on foreign aid. Remittances from the estimated one in six Haitians who live abroad, principally in the USA, are the main source of foreign revenue, worth nearly a quarter of GDP. About half of the population depends on agriculture – predominantly small-scale subsistence farming – which contributes 29 per cent of GDP. Industrial activities include sugar refining, flour milling, textiles and garments, and assembly of goods, especially vehicle parts, for re-export.

The main trading partners are the USA and Dominican Republic. Principal exports are garments (two-thirds of exports), manufactured goods, essential oils, cocoa, mangoes and coffee. The main imports are food, manufactured goods, machinery and transport equipment, fuels and raw materials.

GNI – US$5,000m; US$520 per capita (2007)
Annual average growth of GDP – –0.5 per cent (2009 est)
Inflation rate – 0.4 per cent (2009 est)
Population below poverty line – 80 per cent (2003 est)
Total external debt – US$428m (2009 est)
Imports – US$2,300m (2008)
Exports – US$500m (2008)

BALANCE OF PAYMENTS

Trade – US$1,091m deficit (2009)
Current Account – US$296m deficit (2008)

Trade with UK	*2008*	*2009*
Imports from UK	£6,868,327	£6,339,379
Exports to UK	£2,245,301	£4,041,794

COMMUNICATIONS

Less than a quarter of the country's 4,160km of highways are surfaced. There are 14 airports, four of which have surfaced runways; the international airports are at Port-au-Prince and Cap-Haitien. Cap-Haitien is the main port. The international airports and the main port are operable again following the repair of earthquake damage, but many roads remain impassable.

The telephone system is poor, with only 108,000 fixed lines in use; mobile phone distribution has grown rapidly, to 3.2 million subscribers in 2008.

MEDIA

Low literacy levels mean that radio is Haiti's most important medium, with more than 250 radio stations broadcasting in French and Creole. A single state broadcaster, Télévision Nationale d'Haiti, provides four television channels; these have been joined by two privately owned French-language stations.

HONDURAS

República de Honduras – Republic of Honduras

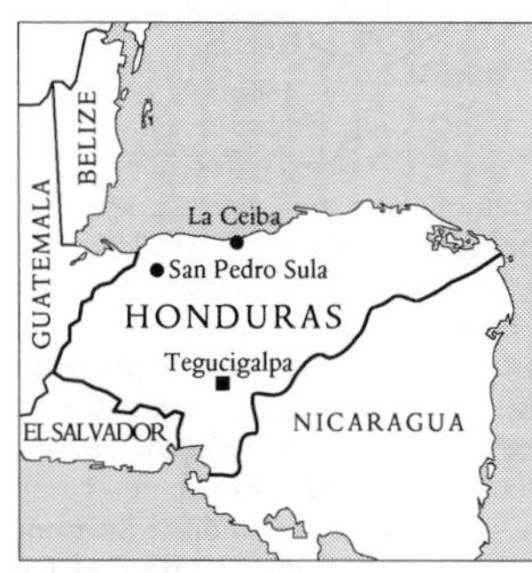

Area – 112,090 sq. km
Capital – Tegucigalpa; population, 1,000,080 (2009 est)
Major cities – Choloma, La Ceiba, El Progreso, San Pedro Sula
Currency – Lempira of 100 centavos
Population – 7,792,854 rising at 1.96 per cent a year (2009 est); mainly mestizo, with Amerindian and black minorities
Religion – Christian (Roman Catholic 47 per cent, Protestant denominations 36 per cent) (est)
Language – Spanish (official)
Population density – 65 per sq. km (2008)
Urban population – 47 per cent (2007 est)
Median age (years) – 20.3 (2009 est)
National anthem – 'Tu Bandera es un Lampo de Cielo' ['Your Flag is a Heavenly Light']
National day – 15 September (Independence Day)
Life expectancy – 69.4 (2009 est)
Mortality rate – 5.41 (2009 est)
Birth rate – 26.27 (2009 est)
Infant mortality rate – 24.03 (2009 est)
Death penalty – Abolished for all crimes (since 1956)
CPI score – 2.5 (2009)

CLIMATE AND TERRAIN

Honduras has a mountainous interior, falling to narrow coastal plains. Elevation extremes range from 2,870m (Cerro Las Minas) at the highest point to 0m (Caribbean Sea) at the lowest. The climate is subtropical in the lowlands and temperate in the mountains. Average temperatures in Tegucigalpa range from lows of 14°C in January and February to highs of 30°C in April and May.

HISTORY AND POLITICS

Honduras was home to part of the Mayan civilisation between the fourth and ninth centuries AD. Christopher Columbus first set foot on the American mainland at Trujillo in Honduras in 1502, but it was 1525 before Spanish colonisation began. In 1821, the country gained independence from Spain, and it was part of a Central American federation of former Spanish colonies from 1823 until it became fully independent in 1839. Thereafter the country underwent periods of political instability interspersed with military rule until 1982, when a civilian government took office. During the civil wars in Nicaragua and El Salvador, Honduras acted as a base for US forces and anti-Sandinista Contras, and there was a marked decline in its respect for human rights. The end of the civil wars led to a decline in the power of the army, which was brought under civilian control in 1999, but there are still very high levels of violent crime.

President Manuel Zelaya of the Liberal Party (PLH), elected in 2005, was deposed in June 2009 after going ahead with a constitutional referendum that had been declared illegal. There was international condemnation of Zelaya's deposition and several months of mass protests within the country by his supporters, but the interim government, upheld by the courts, rejected his reinstatement. In November 2009, the National Party of Honduras (PNH) candidate, Porfirio Lobo, defeated the PLH candidate in the presidential election, and the PLH also lost the legislative election to the PNH, which won 71 of the 128 seats.

POLITICAL SYSTEM

Under the 1982 constitution, the executive president is directly elected for a four-year term, which is not renewable, and appoints the government. The unicameral National Congress has 128 members, directly elected for a four-year term.

HEAD OF STATE

President, Porfirio Lobo, *elected* 29 November 2009, *took office* 27 January 2010
Vice-President, Aristides Mejia Carranza

SELECTED GOVERNMENT MEMBERS *as at June 2010*

Defence, Marlon Pascual
Finance, William Chong Wong
Foreign Relations, Mario Canahuati
Interior, Justice, Africo Madrid

EMBASSY OF HONDURAS

115 Gloucester Place, London W1U 6JT
T 020-7486 4880 E hondurasuk@lineone.net
Ambassador Extraordinary and Plenipotentiary, HE Ivan Romero-Martinez, *apptd* 2008

BRITISH AMBASSADOR

HE Julie Chappell, OBE, *apptd* 2009, resident at Guatemala City, Guatemala

DEFENCE

The army has 12 light tanks. The navy has 35 patrol and coastal combatant vessels at 3 bases. The air force has 16 combat capable aircraft.
Military budget – US$102m (2009)

Military personnel – 12,000: army 8,300, navy 1,400, air force 2,300; paramilitary 8,000

ECONOMY AND TRADE

The country has a huge imbalance in wealth and high levels of corruption and violent crime, often connected with drug-trafficking. Its narrow range of exports is vulnerable to natural disasters and commodity price changes, and economic activity is heavily dependent on the USA; a drop in exports and remittances owing to the global economic downturn contributed to the economy's contraction in 2009. Remittances from expatriate workers are equivalent to nearly a quarter of GDP.

Although still dependent on agriculture, fishing and forestry, whose products form the basis of industrial activity and are the main exports, the economy is gradually diversifing into offshore assembly for re-export and tourism. Agriculture employs 39.2 per cent of the workforce and contributes 12.2 per cent of GDP. Industry accounts for 27.1 per cent of GDP and 20.9 per cent of employment, and the services sector for 60.6 per cent of GDP and 39.8 per cent of employment.

The main trading partner is the USA, which takes 62 per cent of exports and provides 50 per cent of imports. Principal exports are garments, coffee, shrimp, wire harnessing, cigars, bananas, gold, palm oil, fruit, lobster and timber. The main imports are machinery and transport equipment, industrial raw materials, chemical products, fuels and foodstuffs.

GNI – US$12,700m; US$1,740 per capita (2008)
Annual average growth of GDP – −3.1 per cent (2009 est)
Inflation rate – 5.2 per cent (2009 est)
Population below poverty line – 50.7 per cent (2004)
Total external debt – US$3,315m (2009 est)
Imports – US$8,800m (2008)
Exports – US$2,600m (2008)

BALANCE OF PAYMENTS
Trade – US$3,712m deficit (2009)
Current Account – US$457m deficit (2009)

Trade with UK	*2008*	*2009*
Imports from UK	£8,567,699	£7,811,797
Exports to UK	£36,693,047	£70,685,611

COMMUNICATIONS

Honduras has ports on its Caribbean (Puerto Castilla, Puerto Cortes, Tela) and Pacific (San Lorenzo) coasts. There are 699km of railway and 13,600km of roads, 2,775km of which are surfaced. The mountainous interior has led to the development of a large number of airports, though only 12 of the 106 have surfaced runways; the principal airports are at Tegucigalpa, La Ceiba and San Pedro Sula. The fixed-line telephone system is expanding but density is only about 10 per 100 people. Mobile phone distribution has grown rapidly and is now over 80 per 100 people.

EDUCATION AND HEALTH

Primary and secondary education is free of charge and primary education is compulsory between the ages of seven and 12.

Literacy rate – 83.6 per cent (2007 est)
Gross enrolment ratio (percentage of relevant age group) – primary 116 per cent; secondary 65 per cent; tertiary 19 per cent (2008 est)
Health expenditure (per capita) – US$107 (2007)
Hospital beds (per 1,000 people) – 0.7 (2003–8)

MEDIA

Honduras has a state-owned radio station as well as several privately run broadcasters and newspapers. Televicentro operates several television channels. Harsh defamation laws are in place and journalists, who are often the target of threats and assault, tend to practise self-censorship. The interim government of June 2009 to January 2010 reportedly censored and sabotaged numerous media outlets critical of its policies.

HUNGARY

Magyar Koztarsasag – Republic of Hungary

Area – 93,028 sq. km
Capital – Budapest; population, 1,704,710 (2009 est)
Major cities – Debrecen, Gyor, Miskolc, Pecs, Szeged
Currency – Forint of 100 filler
Population – 9,905,596 falling at 0.26 per cent a year (2009 est); Hungarian (92.3 per cent), Roma (1.9 per cent). There are also smaller groups of ethnic Germans, Serbs, Romanians and Slovaks
Religion – Christian (Roman Catholic 55 per cent, Calvinist 15 per cent, Lutheran 3 per cent, Greek Catholic 3 per cent), Jewish (1 per cent) (est)
Language – Hungarian (official)
Population density – 112 per sq. km (2008)
Urban population – 67 per cent (2007 est)
Median age (years) – 39.4 (2009 est)
National anthem – 'Himnusz' ['Hymn']
National day – 20 August (St Stephen's Day)
Life expectancy (years) – 73.44 (2009 est)
Mortality rate – 12.94 (2009 est)
Birth rate – 9.51 (2009 est)
Infant mortality rate – 7.86 (2009 est)
Death penalty – Abolished for all crimes (since 1990)
CPI score – 5.1 (2009)

CLIMATE AND TERRAIN

Landlocked Hungary lies mostly on the vast plain created by the Danube and Tisza rivers, with hills and mountains along the northern border. Elevation extremes range from 1,014m (Mt Kekes) at the highest point to 78m (river Tisza) at the lowest. Lake Balaton lies in the west. The climate is temperate, with average temperatures ranging from −1°C in January to 21°C in July.

HISTORY AND POLITICS

Magyar tribes (the ancestors of modern Hungarians) settled on the Hungarian plains in the ninth century, and became a Christian kingdom under St Stephen in 1000. Most of the kingdom was conquered by Ottoman Turks in 1526, but the Turks were expelled in 1699 by the

Habsburgs and Hungary became a province of the dynasty's central European empire. Following years of Hungarian agitation, a dual monarchy was created in 1867, giving Hungary control of its internal affairs in return for the continued union of the Austrian and Hungarian crowns. This period is remembered as a time of cultural achievement and economic success. An ally of Germany in the First World War, the defeated Austro-Hungarian Empire collapsed in 1918.

Initially a communist republic after the war, in 1920 the country became a kingdom, with Admiral Horthy as regent. Hungary remained neutral when the Second World War began, but joined the conflict in 1941 on the side of the Axis powers. Horthy was deposed in 1944 after seeking an armistice with advancing Soviet troops, who drove out German forces in 1945.

The Communists came to power in the 1947 elections, and in 1949 Hungary became a communist state aligned with the Soviet Union. A national uprising broke out in 1956, with protesters demanding the withdrawal of Soviet forces from the country, but this was brutally suppressed. In the 1960s Janos Kadar introduced limited liberalisation, which encouraged the development of the most prosperous and permissive regime in the Soviet bloc.

The opening of Hungary's border with Austria in 1989 triggered the developments that led to the fall of communism throughout eastern Europe. Communist rule ended shortly afterwards in Hungary, which began the transition to a free-market democracy. The country joined NATO in 1999 and the EU in 2004.

The legislative election in April 2010 was won by the Fidesz party with an overwhelming majority and it formed a government under Viktor Orban (prime minister 1998–2002). The presidential election held in June 2010 was won convincingly by Pal Schmitt, a senior figure in the Fidesz party.

POLITICAL SYSTEM

The 1949 constitution has been amended several times, most radically in 1989 to allow a return to a multiparty democracy. The president is elected by the legislature for a five-year term, renewable only once; the post is largely ceremonial but powers include the appointment of the prime minister. The unicameral National Assembly has 386 members directly elected for a four-year term.

HEAD OF STATE

President, Pal Schmitt, *elected* 29 June 2010, *sworn in* 6 August 2010

SELECTED GOVERNMENT MEMBERS *as at June 2010*

Prime Minister, Viktor Orban
Deputy Prime Ministers, Tibor Navracsics, Zsolt Semjen
Economy, Gyorgy Matolcsy
Foreign Affairs, Janos Martonyi
Defence, Csaba Hende

EMBASSY OF THE REPUBLIC OF HUNGARY

35 Eaton Place, London SW1X 8BY
T 020-7201 3440 E office.lon@kum.hu
W www.mfa.gov.hu/emb/london
Ambassador Extraordinary and Plenipotentiary, HE Borbala Czako, *apptd* 2007

BRITISH EMBASSY

Harmincad Utca 6, 1051 Budapest
T (+36) (1) 266 2888 E info@britemb.hu
W http://ukinhungary.fco.gov.uk
Ambassador Extraordinary and Plenipotentiary, HE Gregory Dorey, *apptd* 2007

BRITISH COUNCIL

Madach Trade Center, Madach Imre ut 13–14, B epulet 4. emelet, 1075 Budapest
T (+36) (1) 478 2020 W www.britishcouncil.org/hungary
Director, Simon Ingram-Hill

DEFENCE

Hungary's armed forces have been reorganised into a joint force. The land component has 30 main battle tanks, 164 armoured infantry fighting vehicles and 164 armoured personnel carriers. The air component has 27 combat aircraft and 12 armed helicopters.
Military expenditure – US$1,860m (2008)
Military personnel – 29,450: army 10,936, air force 5,664, joint staff 12,850; paramilitary 12,000
Conscription duration – 6 months

ECONOMY AND TRADE

Hungary made a successful transition to a market economy after 1989, attracting high levels of foreign direct investment, and over 80 per cent of GDP is now generated by the private sector. The strong economic growth of the post-Communist years started to slow in 2006–7, partly as a result of a government austerity programme intended to reduce the budget deficit and public debt. The global economic downturn left Hungary unable to service this debt and the government had to obtain IMF assistance in 2008. The economy went into recession in 2009.

Nearly half the land is under cultivation, but agriculture accounts for only 3.4 per cent of GDP; the main crops are cereals, sunflower seeds, vegetables, livestock and dairy products. Industry contributes 34.3 per cent of GDP; the main activities include mining, metallurgy, food processing, and the production of construction materials, textiles, chemicals (especially pharmaceuticals) and motor vehicles. The main trading partners are Germany, other EU countries, Taiwan, Russia and China. Machinery and manufactured goods account for 90 per cent of exports and 82 per cent of imports. The country is a net importer of fuels and electricity.
GNI – US$128,600m; US$12,810 per capita (2008)
Annual average growth of GDP – –6.4 per cent (2009 est)
Inflation rate – 4.3 per cent (2009 est)
Unemployment – 11 per cent (2009 est)
Total external debt – US$150,300m (2009)
Imports – US$106,400m (2008)
Exports – US$107,500m (2008)

BALANCE OF PAYMENTS

Trade – US$6,473m surplus (2009)
Current Account – US$11,172m deficit (2008)

Trade with UK	*2008*	*2009*
Imports from UK	£982,379,073	£822,619,289
Exports to UK	£2,490,921,269	£2,122,988,188

COMMUNICATIONS

Hungary has 160,057km of roads, 70,539 of which are surfaced, and 8,057km of railways (including a cross-border line to Austria jointly managed by the two countries). There are 1,622km of permanently navigable waterways, mainly on the river Danube, and several major river ports and harbours on the Danube, including Budapest. There are 46 airports and airfields, 20 of which have surfaced runways; the principal airport is at Budapest. Fixed-line telephone subscriptions have declined as mobile phone use has risen rapidly since 2000, to 12.2 million subscribers in 2008. There were 5.9 million internet users in 2008.

EDUCATION AND HEALTH

Hungarians have ten years of compulsory education until age 16; a further two years at secondary level is optional.
Literacy rate – 98.9 per cent (2007 est)
Gross enrolment ratio (percentage of relevant age group) – primary 98 per cent; secondary 97 per cent; tertiary 67 per cent (2008 est)
Health expenditure (per capita) – US$1,019 (2007)
Hospital beds (per 1,000 people) – 7.1 (2003–8)

MEDIA AND CULTURE

The state-run broadcasters, Magyar Televizio and Hungarian Radio, compete with a number of privately owned television and radio stations. Hungary has a wide range of weekly and daily newspapers, some of which are owned by foreign investors.

The strong folk music tradition has influenced many native composers of classical music, including Franz Liszt (1811–86), Bela Bartok (1881–1945), Zoltan Kodaly (1882–1967) and Gyorgy Ligeti (1923–2006). Hungary's best known author is Imre Kertesz (*b.* 1929), who won the Nobel prize for literature in 2002.

ICELAND

Lydveldid Island – Republic of Iceland

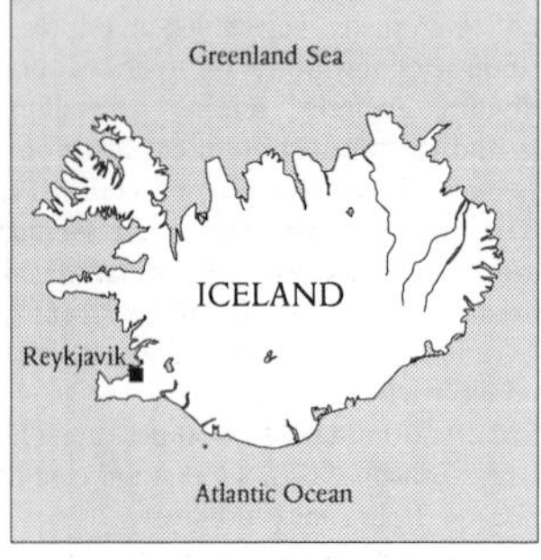

Area – 103,000 sq. km
Capital – Reykjavik; population, 198,093 (2009 est)
Major towns – Hafnarfjordur, Kopavogur
Currency – Icelandic krona (Kr) of 100 aurar
Population – 306,694 rising at 0.74 per cent a year (2009 est)
Religion – Christian (Lutheran 84 per cent, Roman Catholic 4 per cent) (est)
Language – Icelandic (official), English, German
Population density – 3 per sq. km (2008)
Urban population – 92 per cent (2007 est)
Median age (years) – 35.1 (2009 est)
National anthem – 'Lofsongur' ['Hymn']
National day – 17 June (Independence Day)
Life expectancy (years) – 80.67 (2009 est)
Mortality rate – 6.85 (2009 est)
Birth rate – 13.43 (2009 est)
Infant mortality rate – 3.23 (2009 est)
Death penalty – Abolished for all crimes (since 1928)
CPI score – 8.7 (2009)
Military budget – US$44.5m (2008 est)
Military personnel – paramilitary (coastguard) 130

CLIMATE AND TERRAIN

Iceland is a volcanic island in the North Atlantic Ocean, to the east of Greenland and to the west of Norway, and its northernmost point reaches the Arctic Circle. Some parts of the coastline have narrow strips of low-lying land, others are sheer cliffs. An inland plateau of glaciers, lakes and lava fields covers 79 per cent of the interior, with mountainous areas in the north and at the four glaciers in the centre and south. Elevation extremes range from 2,110m (Hvannadalshnukur) at the highest point to 0m (North Atlantic Ocean) at the lowest. There are geysers and hot springs owing to the numerous active volcanoes, which can create new islands, such as Surtsey in 1963; activity at the volcano under the Eyjafjallajokull glacier from March 2010 produced ash clouds that disrupted air travel in Europe. It is estimated that over the past 500 years, Iceland has emitted a third of the earth's total lava flow. The climate is influenced by the Gulf Stream and is therefore temperate in spite of the country's location. Average temperatures range from −3°C in January to 11°C in July.

HISTORY AND POLITICS

The first major settlement occurred from around AD 870 onwards, as turmoil in Scandinavia drove migrants to seek new homelands. Iceland hosted a flourishing Viking culture in the ninth and tenth centuries, becoming a fully Christian country in 1000. Iceland recognised Norwegian sovereignty in 1263, and with Norway came under Danish rule in 1397. When Norway was ceded to Sweden in 1814, Iceland remained Danish territory, achieving autonomy in domestic affairs in 1874. Though it became an independent state with the same sovereign as Denmark in 1918, Copenhagen continued to control its foreign policy and defence. The treaty of union with Denmark expired in 1943, while Denmark was under German occupation, and in a referendum Icelanders voted to become a fully independent republic, proclaimed on 17 June 1944.

The country's dependence on the fishing industry has led occasionally to fraught foreign relations. The introduction and extensions of an exclusive fishing limit around Iceland in 1958, 1972 and 1975 caused the so-called 'Cod War' disputes with the UK, with clashes between Icelandic patrol boats and British trawlers and navy vessels. Subsequent restrictions on fishing in Icelandic waters in the 1990s were less controversial.

Post-independence politics was dominated by the conservative Independence Party (SSF) until January 2009, when the country's economic crisis forced the government first to call an early election for April, then to resign with immediate effect. The Social Democratic Alliance, the junior party in the outgoing coalition, formed a new coalition with the Left-Green Movement (VGF) which then won the legislative election in April. Iceland formally applied for EU membership in July 2009.

POLITICAL SYSTEM

Under the 1944 constitution, the head of state is the president, who is directly elected for a four-year term, which is renewable. The unicameral legislature, the *Althing*, has 63 members, who are directly elected for a four-year term. Founded in AD 930, the *Althing* is the world's oldest functioning parliament.

HEAD OF STATE
President, Olafur Ragnar Grimsson, *elected* 29 June 1996, *re-elected* 2000, 2004, 2008

SELECTED GOVERNMENT MEMBERS *as at June 2010*
Prime Minister, Johanna Sigurdardottir
Finance, Steingrimur Sigfusson
Foreign Affairs, Ossur Skarphedinsson
Social Affairs, Arni Pall Arnason

EMBASSY OF ICELAND
2A Hans Street, London SW1X 0JE
T 020-7259 3999 E icemb.london@utn.stjr.is
W www.iceland.org/uk
Ambassador Extraordinary and Plenipotentiary, HE Benedikt Jonsson, *apptd* 2009

BRITISH EMBASSY
PO Box 460, Laufasvegur 31, 101 Reykjavik
T (+354) 550 5100 E britemb@centrum.is
W http://ukiniceland.fco.gov.uk
Ambassador Extraordinary and Plenipotentiary and Consul-General, HE Ian Whitting, *apptd* 2008

ECONOMY AND TRADE

Iceland has a market economy with an extensive welfare system. While it remains heavily dependent on the fishing industry, which accounts for 12 per cent of GDP and 40 per cent of export earnings, there has been recent diversification into aluminium smelting, ferrosilicon production, software production, biotechnology and tourism, encouraged by the plentiful supply of geothermal power. A major area of diversification was into banking, but aggressive expansion in the 2000s led to over-exposure in foreign markets. When global financial conditions worsened in 2008, the three largest banks collapsed and the government required over $10bn in loans to stabilise its currency and financial system. The economy has contracted sharply, causing widespread unemployment and rapid inflation, and the recession is expected to be protracted.

The main trading partners are EU countries, Norway, the USA and Japan. Principal exports are fish and fish products, aluminium, animal products, ferrosilicon and diatomite. The main imports are machinery, petroleum products, foodstuffs and textiles.
GNI – US$12,839m; US$40,450 per capita (2008)
Annual average growth of GDP – –6.3 per cent (2009 est)
Inflation rate – 12 per cent (2009 est)
Unemployment – 8.8 per cent (2009 est)
Total external debt – US$122,571m (2009 est))
Imports – US$5,600m (2008)
Exports – US$5,200m (2008)

BALANCE OF PAYMENTS
Trade – US$422m surplus (2009)
Current Account – US$460m surplus (2009)

Trade with UK	*2008*	*2009*
Imports from UK	£181,094,293	£124,501,001
Exports to UK	£440,244,040	£409,675,556

COMMUNICATIONS

Iceland has no railways and no navigable waterways. Although the country has 13,000km of roads, about two-thirds are unsurfaced and in winter these are often blocked by snow. Consequently much internal travel is by air or sea. Iceland has 99 airports and airfields, the principal ones being at Keflavik, near Reykjavik, in the south and Akureyri in the north. The national carrier, Icelandair, is a major employer. There are nine major ports and the capital, Reykjavik, operates shipping services to the USA and Europe. The landline telephone system has 187,000 fixed lines in use; in 2008 there were 342,000 mobile phone subscribers and 250,000 internet users.

MEDIA AND CULTURE

The state provides public service broadcasting on television and radio via the Icelandic National Broadcasting Service (RUV). There are several commercial stations and a variety of newspapers. Reporters Without Borders ranked the country the joint highest for press freedom in 2007.

Iceland enjoys a rich literary tradition. The Icelandic sagas, dating from the 12th to 14th centuries, are among the major works of medieval European literature. One of Iceland's best-known modern writers is Halldor Laxness (1902–98), winner of the Nobel prize for literature in 1955. The country is also known for popular music groups the Sugarcubes (whose singer Bjork has enjoyed worldwide success) and Sigur Ros.

INDIA

Bharatiya Ganarajya – Republic of India

Area – 3,287,263 sq. km
Capital – New Delhi; population, 294,783 (2001 est). Delhi urban agglomeration; population, 21,719,700 (2009 est)
Major cities – Ahmadabad, Bengaluru (Bangalore), Chennai (Madras), Hyderabad, Jaipur, Kanpur, Kolkata (Calcutta), Mumbai (Bombay), Pune, Surat
Currency – Indian rupee (Rs) of 100 paise
Population – 1,166,079,217 rising at 1.55 per cent a year (2009 est); Indo-Aryan (72 per cent), Dravidian (25 per cent) (est)
Religion – Hindu 81 per cent, Muslim 13 per cent (of which Sunni 85 per cent, Shia 15 per cent), Christian 2 per cent, Sikh 2 per cent (est)
Language – Hindi (official national language), English, Assamese, Bengali, Bodo, Dogri, Gujurati, Kannada, Kashmiri, Konkani, Maithili, Malayalam, Manipuri, Marathi, Nepali, Oriya, Punjabi, Sanskrit, Santhali, Sindhi, Tamil, Telugu, Urdu (all official)
Population density – 383 per sq. km (2008)
Urban population – 29 per cent (2007 est)
Median age (years) – 25.3 (2009 est)
National anthem – 'Jana Gana Mana' ['Thou Art the Ruler of the Minds of all People']
National day – 26 January (Republic Day)

Life expectancy (years) – 69.89 (2009 est)
Mortality rate – 6.23 (2009 est)
Birth rate – 21.76 (2009 est)
Infant mortality rate – 30.15 (2009 est)
Death penalty – Retained
CPI score – 3.4 (2009)

CLIMATE AND TERRAIN

India has three well-defined regions: the mountain range of the Himalayas, the Indo-Gangetic plain, and the southern peninsula. The Himalayas along the northern border reach 8,598m (Kanchenjunga) at the highest point of elevation, then drop to the northern plains formed by the basins of the Indus, Ganges and Brahmaputra rivers before rising to low hills running east to west that mark the division with the southern, Deccan peninsula. The peninsula has narrow coastal plains rising to a central plateau, with the Western Ghats and Eastern Ghats ranges of hills lying along the west and east coasts respectively. The Thar Desert lies in the north-west. The climate varies from tropical in the south to temperate in the north. It is influenced by the south-west monsoon; the main rainy season is June to October. During the drier season from December to May, the weather is cooler until February and then becomes increasingly hot until the monsoon breaks. The average temperature in New Delhi ranges from 14°C in January to 34°C in June.

HISTORY AND POLITICS

The Indus civilisation emerged in the Indus valley region *c*.2500 BC, and the beginnings of Hinduism date from this period. This civilisation was destroyed by Aryan tribes from central Asia between 1500 and 200 BC. Buddhism emerged in India from *c*.500 BC and was embraced by the Emperor Ashoka; it spread to the rest of eastern Asia via trade routes, but a Hindu revival from AD 40 onwards caused Buddhism to decline in the subcontinent.

The first Muslim advances into India occurred in the 10th and 11th centuries. Incursions swept across the north of the country, where large Muslim communities were established. Europeans arrived in India in the 15th century and had established territorial holdings by the 18th century, though it was not until 1803, when the British East India Company consolidated its influence, that a single power came to dominate the entire subcontinent. In 1857, rule passed from the company to the British government. From the late 19th century, opposition to British rule, led by the Indian National Congress (INC), latterly under the leadership of Mahatma Gandhi, became a concerted nationwide movement, and India achieved its independence in 1947. Against a backdrop of intercommunal violence, its predominantly Muslim regions were partitioned off to become the separate state of Pakistan. India became a republic in 1950.

The INC has been the dominant party in Indian politics in the decades since independence, holding power almost continuously for four decades, with periods in opposition in 1977–80, 1989–91 and 1996–2004. Jawaharlal Nehru's appointment as prime minister at independence began the rise of the Gandhi family, which has dominated the INC. Nehru was succeeded by his daughter, Indira Gandhi, who was succeeded after her assassination in 1984 by her son Rajiv until he too was assassinated in 1991; Rajiv's widow Sonia became president of the party in 1998. The INC's dominance was challenged in the early 1990s by the Hindu nationalist Bharatiya Janata Party (BJP), which formed a series of coalition governments between 1998 and 2004. The INC returned to power with a surprise victory in the 2004 parliamentary election and formed an INC-dominated coalition government called the United Progressive Alliance. The 2007 presidential election was won by Pratibha Patil, who became the country's first female head of state. In the 2009 legislative elections, the INC and its coalition partners won the most seats in the *Lok Sabha*, and were only ten seats short of an outright majority. A new INC-led coalition government was formed under Manmohan Singh, prime minister since 2004.

INTERNAL UNREST

Tensions between India's Hindu majority and large Muslim minority have never been fully resolved. Violence between the two at the time of partition in 1947 is thought to have cost up to one million lives. The rise of Hindu nationalism in the 1990s accompanied a rise in communal clashes. In 1992, a mosque in the town of Ayodhya was destroyed by Hindus who claimed it was built on the birthplace of the Hindu god Rama. Anti-Muslim mobs rampaged through many parts of India and the army was called upon to restore order. Intercommunal violence flared up again in 2002 when the massacre of pilgrims returning from Ayodhya prompted revenge killings.

There have been separatist campaigns or insurgencies in Manipur, Meghalaya, Mizoram, Nagaland and Tripura since 1947; in Assam since 1979; by Islamists in Kashmir since 1989; and by ethnic Gurkhas in Darjeeling in 1986–8 and since 2008. Sikh separatist agitation for an independent state in the Punjab became increasingly violent in the 1980s. The suppression of Sikh militants, and in particular the Indian army assault on the militant-occupied Golden Temple at Amritsar in 1984, led to the assassination of Indira Gandhi by her Sikh bodyguards later that year.

A peasant uprising in Naxalbari, West Bengal, in 1967 has developed into a Maoist uprising with the declared aim of overthrowing the government by 2050. By 2010 the insurgency affected 223 districts in 20 states, and the Maoists controlled a 'red corridor' between the east coast and the Nepalese border. A nationwide federal operation to tackle the insurgents, launched in 2009, has been met by a series of attacks by the Maoists.

FOREIGN RELATIONS

Since partition, sovereignty over the predominantly Muslim state of Jammu and Kashmir has been disputed by India and Pakistan. A short war in 1947–8 resulted in the state being partitioned between the two countries; its status remains unresolved, despite further outbreaks of war in 1965 and 1971, low-level conflict for control of the Siachen glacier since 1985 and occasional increases in military exchanges, most recently in 1999–2002 and 2003. Tension was exacerbated by Pakistan's support of the Muslim insurgency in the Indian part of the state, which began in the late 1980s and has included terrorist attacks in Indian cities, and by both countries' acquisition of nuclear weapons. Moves towards a peaceful settlement began in 2003, when diplomatic missions were reopened and the resumption of transport links was initiated. Formal diplomatic talks began in 2004 and have achieved several accords intended to reduce tension between the two countries (although the status of Kashmir has yet to be addressed). Talks were temporarily suspended by the Indian government after the Mumbai attacks in 2008 but resumed in early 2010.

In the Sino-Indian war in 1962, India lost territory to China. In addition, China claims Arunachal Pradesh and does not recognise Indian sovereignty over Sikkim. Talks between India and China in 2003 resulted in India's formal recognition of the Tibetan Autonomous Region as a part of China and a cross-border trade agreement on Sikkim.

POLITICAL SYSTEM

Under the 1950 constitution, the president is elected for a five-year term by an electoral college consisting of members of both chambers of the legislature. The president appoints the prime minister, who is responsible to the legislature. The vice-president, who is elected by both chambers for a five-year term, is *ex-officio* chair of the upper chamber. The legislature, the *Sansad,* consists of two chambers. The upper chamber, the *Rajya Sabha* (Council of States), has up to 250 members, who serve a six-year term; up to 238 members are elected by the state legislative assemblies as individual terms expire, and the rest are nominated by the president. The *Lok Sabha* (House of the People) has 545 members; 543 are directly elected for a five-year term, and two representatives of the Anglo-Indian community are nominated by the president.

HEAD OF STATE

President, Pratibha Patil, *elected* 19 July 2007, *took office* 25 July 2007
Vice-President, Hamid Ansari

SELECTED GOVERNMENT MEMBERS *as at June 2010*

Prime Minister, Manmohan Singh
Defence, A. K. Antony
Finance, Pranab Mukherjee
Home Affairs, Palaniappan Chidambaram
External Affairs, S. M. Krishna

OFFICE OF THE HIGH COMMISSIONER FOR INDIA

India House, Aldwych, London WC2B 4NA
T 020-7836 8484 E administration@hcilondon.in
W www.hcilondon.in
High Commissioner, HE Nalin Surie, *apptd* 2009

BRITISH HIGH COMMISSION

Chanakyapuri, New Delhi 21 1100-21
T (+91) (11) 2419 2100 E postmaster.newdelhi@fco.gov.uk
W www.ukinindia.fco.gov.uk
High Commissioner, Sir Richard Stagg, KCMG, CMG, *apptd* 2007

BRITISH COUNCIL

17 Kasturba Gandhi Marg, New Delhi 110001
T (+91) (11) 2371 1401/2371 0111
W www.britishcouncil.org/india
Regional Director, Ruth Gee

FEDERAL STRUCTURE

There are 28 states and seven union territories (including the national capital territory). Each state has its own executive, comprising a governor, who is appointed by the president for a five-year term, and a council of ministers. All states have a legislative assembly, and some also have a legislative council, elected directly for a maximum period of five years. The states have considerable autonomy, although the union government controls such matters as foreign policy, defence and external trade.

The union territories are administered, except where otherwise provided by parliament, by a lieutenant-governor or an administrator appointed by the president.

DEFENCE

The army has 4,047 main battle tanks, over 1,455 armoured infantry fighting vehicles, 12 combat helicopters and more than 317 armoured personnel carriers. The navy has 16 submarines, 1 aircraft carrier, 8 destroyers, 12 frigates, 24 corvettes, 28 patrol and coastal vessels, 23 combat aircraft and 54 armed helicopters. The air force has 632 combat aircraft and 20 armed helicopters.

India has had nuclear weapon technology since the mid-1970s, and by the mid-1990s had also successfully developed intermediate-range ballistic missiles.

Military expenditure – US$35,880m (2009)
Military personnel – 1,325,000: army 1,129,900, navy 58,350, air force 127,200, coastguard 9,550; paramilitary 1,300,586

ECONOMY AND TRADE

The economy was closed for several decades after independence, with high import tariffs and limits on foreign investment to stimulate domestic growth. Since 1991, economic liberalisation and more foreign investment have generated rapid expansion, with GDP growing by an average 7 per cent a year since 1997. Growth slowed owing to the global economic downturn, and the government announced two economic stimulus packages in 2008–9.

India's large skilled workforce has enabled it to develop knowledge-based industries, and become a global centre for manufacturing and services. Pharmaceuticals is another area of growth, as are tourism and the provision of services to the burgeoning urban middle class. The service sector now accounts for 62.6 per cent of GDP and industry for 20 per cent, employing 34 per cent and 14 per cent of the workforce respectively.

Although about 1 per cent of the population has been lifted out of poverty each year since 1997, rural areas have benefited disproportionately little from the economic growth. Since 2004 the government has initiated schemes intended to reduce rural poverty, which has been exacerbated by prolonged drought in some areas and the effects of the Indian Ocean tsunami of 2004. Agriculture, forestry and fishing support 52 per cent of the population and contribute 17.5 per cent of GDP. The main food crops are rice, cereals (principally wheat) and pulses. The major cash crops include cotton, jute, tea and sugar cane. Agriculture and forestry are threatened by deforestation, soil erosion, over-grazing and desertification.

Despite recent advances, the economy faces a number of problems, chief among which is the rapid growth in population. Economic constraints on continued growth include underinvestment in infrastructure (especially transport and power supply), excessive regulation and corruption. Shortfalls in energy generation cause frequent power cuts, and output is not expected to meet demand for some years.

The main trading partners are the UAE, the USA, China and Saudi Arabia. Principal exports include petroleum products, precious stones, machinery, iron and steel, chemicals, vehicles and garments. Its main imports are crude oil, precious stones, machinery, fertiliser, iron and steel, and chemicals.

GNI – US$1,186,700m; US$1,040 per capita (2008)
Annual average growth of GDP – 6.1 per cent (2009 est)
Inflation rate – 9.8 per cent (2009 est)
Population below poverty line – 25 per cent (2007 est)
Unemployment – 9.5 per cent (2009 est)
Total external debt – US$232,500m (2009)
Imports – US$292,700m (2008)
Exports – US$176,900m (2008)

BALANCE OF PAYMENTS
Trade – US$86,142m deficit (2009)
Current Account – US$26,621m deficit (2009)

Trade with UK	*2008*	*2009*
Imports from UK	£4,118,820,030	£2,943,446,125
Exports to UK	£4,267,816,130	£4,181,713,411

COMMUNICATIONS

India has over 64,000km of railways and 3.3 million km of roads, although fewer than half are surfaced. There are 349 airports and airfields, the principal ones being at Delhi, Mumbai, Chennai and Kolkata. The chief seaports are Mumbai, Kolkata, Haldia, Chennai, Cochin, Visakhapatnam, Mangalore and Tuticorin. The merchant fleet includes 501 ships of over 1,000 tonnes. There are 485km of canals and the great rivers provide over 5,200km of navigable waterways.

There were 545 million mobile phone subscribers in 2010, compared to 166 million in 2006. This has caused a decline in fixed-line use, to 36.8 million fixed lines in use in 2010. There were 81 million internet users in 2008, and 3.6 million internet hosts in 2009.

EDUCATION AND HEALTH

Education is free of charge, and became compulsory for children aged six to 14 years in April 2010.
Literacy rate – 66.0 per cent (2007 est)
Gross enrolment ratio (percentage of relevant age group) – primary 113 per cent; secondary 57 per cent; tertiary 13 per cent (2008 est)
Health expenditure (per capita) – US$40 (2007)
Hospital beds (per 1,000 people) – 0.9 (2003–8)

MEDIA

The state's monopoly of television broadcasting ended in 1992, since when the number of channels has increased rapidly. Satellite and cable channels are also popular. Commercial radio has expanded in recent years, but stations tend to aim programming at urban audiences, and only the public broadcaster All India Radio can broadcast the news. The private press is a thriving and diverse industry, often outspoken and critical of the government; circulations have grown in step with the growth of the urban middle class.

CULTURE

Bengali writer, polymath and social reformist Rabindranath Tagore (1861–1941) won the Nobel prize for literature in 1913, becoming Asia's first Nobel laureate. Contemporary writers of international standing include Vikram Seth (*b.* 1952), Salman Rushdie (*b.* 1947) and Arundhati Roy (*b.* 1961); Kiran Desai (*b.* 1971) and Aravind Adiga (*b.* 1974) won the 2006 and 2008 Booker prizes respectively. The Mumbai-based film industry, known as Bollywood, produces over 800 films a year. The influence of Bollywood in the West is growing, as shown by the success of films such as *Bride and Prejudice* (2004) and eight-time Oscar winner *Slumdog Millionaire* (2008).

Cricket, the most popular sport in India, was introduced by the British and matches have been played in the country since 1721. Notable players include spin bowlers Bishan Singh Bedi (*b.* 1946) and Anil Kumble (*b.* 1970), batsman Sachin Tendulkar (*b.* 1973) and *Wisden's* Indian Cricketer of the Century Kapil Dev (*b.* 1959).

INDONESIA

Republik Indonesia – Republic of Indonesia

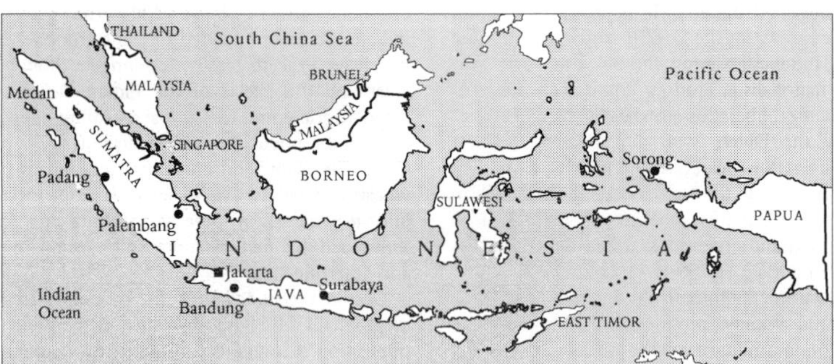

Area – 1,904,569 sq. km
Capital – Jakarta; population, 9,120,730 (2009 est)
Major cities – Bandung, Bekasi, Depok, Makasar, Medan, Palembang, Semarang, Surabaya, Tangerang
Currency – Rupiah (Rp) of 100 sen
Population – 240,271,522 rising at 1.14 per cent a year (2009 est); Javanese (40.6 per cent), Sundanese (15 per cent), Madurese (3.3 per cent), Minangkabau (2.7 per cent), Betawi (2.4 per cent), Bugis (2.4 per cent), Banten (2 per cent), Banjar (1.7 per cent) (est)
Religion – Muslim 88 per cent (predominantly Sunni), Christian (Protestant denominations 6 per cent, Roman Catholic 3 per cent), Hindu 2 per cent (est)
Language – Bahasa Indonesia (official), English, Dutch, Javanese, over 580 languages and dialects
Population density – 125 per sq. km (2008)
Urban population – 50 per cent (2007 est)
Median age (years) – 27.6 (2009 est)
National anthem – 'Indonesia Raya' ['Great Indonesia']
National day – 17 August (Independence Day)

Life expectancy (years) – 70.76 (2009 est)
Mortality rate – 6.25 (2009 est)
Birth rate – 18.84 (2009 est)
Infant mortality rate – 29.97 (2009 est)
Death penalty – Retained
CPI score – 2.8 (2009)
Literacy rate – 92.0 per cent (2007 est)
Gross enrolment ratio (percentage of relevant age group) – primary 121 per cent; secondary 76 per cent; tertiary 18 per cent (2008 est)
Health expenditure (per capita) – US$42 (2007)

CLIMATE AND TERRAIN

Indonesia is an archipelago of over 17,500 islands, of which about 6,000 are inhabited. They include the islands of Sumatra, Java, Madura, Bali, Lombok, Sumbawa, Sumba, Flores, the Riouw-Lingga archipelago, Bangka and Billiton, part of the island of Borneo (Kalimantan), Sulawesi (formerly Celebes), the Maluku (formerly Moluccas) archipelago and others comprising the provinces of East and West Nusa Tenggara, and the western halves of the islands of New Guinea (Papua; formerly Irian Jaya) and Timor. Many of the islands have narrow coastal plains with hilly or mountainous interiors, and over half of the country is covered by tropical rainforest. Elevation extremes range from 5,030m (Puncak Jaya, in Papua) at the highest point to 0m (Indian Ocean) at the lowest. The climate is tropical; temperatures in Jakarta range between 23°C and 31°C all year round, but rainfall peaks in January and February and is lowest in August.

The country is located near to an intersection of tectonic plates, making it susceptible to seismic activity such as earthquakes and volcanic eruptions. Its weather patterns are being affected by climate change.

HISTORY AND POLITICS

Hindu and Buddhist kingdoms existed in some parts of the Indonesian islands until the 14th century. Islam was introduced in the 13th century and spread over the next three centuries. Trading by the Portuguese began in the 16th century, but the Portuguese were displaced by the Dutch who, lured by the rich spice trade, came to dominate Indonesia by the early 20th century. Opposition to Dutch rule grew in the 1920s and the Japanese occupation of Indonesia during the Second World War strengthened nationalism, leading to a declaration of independence after liberation in 1945. This was not recognised by the Dutch, who attempted to reassert control, but after four years of guerrilla warfare they granted independence to the Netherlands Indies in 1949. Irian Jaya (now Papua) was annexed in 1963. Timor–Leste was invaded and annexed in 1975 but gained its independence in 2002.

Achmed Soekarno, the foremost proponent of self-rule since the 1920s, became president in 1949 but was deposed in 1966 in a military coup suppressed by General Suharto, who subsequently became president. Suharto remained in power until 1998 when, amid economic and social upheaval, he was succeeded by his deputy B. J. Habibie. Habibie's cautious introduction of social and economic reforms led to him being defeated in 1999 by Abdurrahman Wahid, in the first democratic elections for 44 years. President Wahid was impeached for alleged financial corruption and in 2001 the legislature appointed Megawati Soekarnoputri (daughter of Achmed Soekarno) to replace him.

In the 2009 legislative elections, the Democratic Party won the greatest number of seats but without an overall majority, and a coalition government was appointed by President Susilo Bambamg Yudhoyono. In the presidential election a few months later, Yudhoyono was re-elected in the first round with 60 per cent of the vote.

INSURGENCIES

Separatist movements developed in several parts of Indonesia after independence, including Maluku, which fought an unsuccessful separatist war in the 1950s; Irian Jaya (now Papua), which was granted greater autonomy in 2002, although separatist agitation continues; Timor–Leste, from its annexation in 1975 until independence in 2002; and Aceh province in Sumatra, which was granted a degree of autonomy after a peace accord between the separatist movement and the government in 2005.

Since the fall of Suharto in 1998, tensions between different ethnic and religious groups have surfaced, and there has been intercommunal violence in Kalimantan (1996–7, 1999, 2001), Sulawesi (1998–2000, 2001, 2005) and Maluku (1999–2002, 2004).

At least two Muslim extremist groups are based in Indonesia and claim links with al-Qaida. They have been held responsible for bombings in Bali in 2002 and 2005 and Jakarta in 2003, 2004 and 2009.

POLITICAL SYSTEM

The 1959 constitution was amended in 2001 to provide for the establishment of the upper chamber of the legislature, and in 2002 to provide for the direct election of the president and the abolition of parliamentary seats reserved for the armed forces. The executive president is directly elected for a five-year term of office, renewable only once, and appoints the cabinet. The bicameral People's Consultative Assembly is the state's highest authority, and makes decisions on the constitution. It comprises the House of Representatives, which has 560 members directly elected for a five-year term, and the House of Representatives of the Regions; this upper house, which deals with regional matters, has 132 members, four for each province, directly elected on a non-partisan basis for a five-year term.

HEAD OF STATE

President, Susilo Bambang Yudhoyono, *sworn in* 20 October 2004, *re-elected* 2009
Vice-President, Boediono

SELECTED GOVERNMENT MEMBERS *as at June 2010*

Defence, Purnomo Yusgiantoro
Finance, Agus Martowardojo
Foreign Affairs, Marty Muliana Natalegawa
Home Affairs, Gamawan Fauzi

EMBASSY OF THE REPUBLIC OF INDONESIA

38 Grosvenor Square, London W1K 2HW
T 020-7499 7661 **E** kbri@btconnect.com
W www.indonesianembassy.org.uk
Ambassador Extraordinary and Plenipotentiary, Yuri Octavian Thamrin, *apptd* 2008

BRITISH EMBASSY

Jalan M. H. Thamrin 75, Jakarta 10310
T (+62) (21) 2356 5200 **E** consulate.jakarta@fco.gov.uk
W http://ukinindonesia.fco.gov.uk
Ambassador Extraordinary and Plenipotentiary, HE Martin Hatfull, *apptd* 2008

BRITISH COUNCIL
Jakarta Stock Exchange, Tower II, 16th Floor, Jalan Jenderal Sudirman Kav. 52–53, Jakarta 12190
T (+62) (021) 515 5561 W www.britishcouncil.org/indonesia
Director, Keith Davies

DEFENCE

The army has 356 armoured personnel carriers, 11 armoured infantry fighting vehicles and 6 armed helicopters. The navy has 2 submarines, 7 frigates, 23 corvettes, 41 patrol and coastal vessels and 9 armed helicopters. There are 5 principal naval bases. The air force has 96 combat aircraft.

Military expenditure – US$5,100m (2008 est)
Military personnel – 302,000: army 233,000, navy 45,000, air force 24,000; paramilitaries 280,000
Conscription duration – 24 months (selective)

ECONOMY AND TRADE

The economy struggled from the late 1990s until recent years, hit in succession by the Asian financial crisis, the political turmoil following the fall of Suharto, a downturn in tourism following the Bali bombings, and a series of devastating natural disasters since 2004. President Yudhoyono's government introduced significant economic reforms which reduced debt, unemployment and inflation and boosted growth. Although growth slowed owing to the rises in global food and fuel prices in 2008, government stimulus measures countered the effect of the global downturn in 2009. Poverty, poor infrastructure, corruption, a complex regulatory regime and inequitable resource distribution among its regions continue to present problems.

Natural resources include oil, tin, natural gas, nickel, timber, bauxite, copper, coal, gold and silver. However, a lack of investment in prospecting for new sources of oil has led to a decline in oil production and Indonesia has been a net importer since 2004. The exploitation and processing of mineral assets, production of textiles, clothing, wood products, chemicals and rubber, and tourism are the main industrial activities; industry accounts for 47.1 per cent of GDP and services 38.5 per cent, employing 19 per cent and 39 per cent of the workforce respectively. Agriculture contributes only 14.4 per cent of GDP but employs 42 per cent of the workforce. The main crops are rice, cassava, peanuts, rubber, cocoa, coffee, palm oil, copra and livestock products.

The main trading partners are Japan, Singapore, China, the USA, South Korea and other Pacific Rim nations. Principal exports are oil and natural gas, electrical appliances, plywood, textiles and rubber. The main imports are machinery and equipment, chemicals, fuel and foodstuffs.

GNI – US$426,800m; US$1,880 per capita (2008)
Annual average growth of GDP – 4.4 per cent (2009 est)
Inflation rate – 5 per cent (2009 est)
Population below poverty line – 17.8 per cent (2006)
Unemployment – 7.7 per cent (2009 est)
Total external debt – US$150,700m (2009)
Imports – US$129,800m (2008)
Exports – US$147,600m (2008)

BALANCE OF PAYMENTS
Trade – US$27,058m surplus (2009)
Current Account – US$10,581m surplus (2009)

Trade with UK	*2008*	*2009*
Imports from UK	£390,877,855	£350,183,691
Exports to UK	£1,143,519,633	£1,196,969,843

COMMUNICATIONS

Indonesia has 437,800km of roads, 8,500km of railways and 21,600km of navigable waterways. An extensive network of ferry services links the islands. There are 683 airports and airfields, of which 164 have surfaced runways; each of the main islands has a major airport, with most capable of accepting international flights. There are nine major ports, usually the chief towns of the major islands, and the merchant fleet contains 971 ships of over 1,000 tonnes. The Strait of Malacca and the South China Sea are busy shipping lanes with high risks of piracy and armed robbery.

The telephone system covers the whole country, and access has improved with the installation of over 200,000 kiosks, many in remote areas. Mobile phone distribution is growing quickly and, at 140 million subscribers in 2008, exceeds fixed-line use at 30 million lines.

MEDIA

Media freedom has grown since the end of the Suharto regime, although defamation laws are used to deter media criticism. The dominant medium is television; the public-service broadcaster, Televisi Republik Indonesia, competes with several major commercial stations. A public-service radio broadcaster operates six networks, and there are many commercial radio stations, as well as several daily newspapers.

IRAN

Jomhuri-ye Eslami-ye Iran – Islamic Republic of Iran

Area – 1,648,195 sq. km
Capital – Tehran; population 7,190,400 (2009 est)
Major cities – Ahvaz, Esfahan, Karaj, Mashhad, Qom, Shiraz, Tabriz
Currency – Iranian rial of 100 dinar
Population – 66,429,284 rising at 0.88 per cent a year (2009 est); Persian (51 per cent), Azeri (24 per cent), Gilaki and Mazandarani (8 per cent), Kurdish (7 per cent), Arab (3 per cent), Lur (2 per cent), Baloch (2 per cent), Turkmen (2 per cent) (est)
Religion – Muslim (Shia 89 per cent, Sunni 9 per cent) (est); small Zoroastrian, Jewish, Christian and Baha'i minorities; Sufism is growing, but Shia orders of Sufism are being persecuted by the state
Language – Persian (official), Turkic, Kurdish, Luri, Balochi, Arabic, Turkish
Population density – 44 per sq. km (2008)

Urban population – 68 per cent (2007 est)
Median age (years) – 27 (2009 est)
National anthem – 'Sorud-e Melli-e Jomhuri-ye Eslami-ye Iran' ['Anthem of the Islamic Republic of Iran']
National day – 1 April (Republic Day)
Life expectancy (years) – 71.14 (2009 est)
Mortality rate – 5.72 (2009 est)
Birth rate – 17.17 (2009 est)
Infant mortality rate – 35.78 (2009 est)
Death penalty – Retained
CPI score – 1.8 (2009)

CLIMATE AND TERRAIN

Apart from narrow coastal plains on the Gulf coasts and the shores of the Caspian Sea, the interior is a plateau consisting of barren desert in the centre and east. This is enclosed by high mountains in the west and north, with smaller ranges on the eastern border and the southern coast. Elevation extremes range from 5,671m (Kuh-e Damavand) at the highest point to −28m (Caspian Sea) at the lowest. Earthquakes are frequent. The climate is arid or semi-arid in the interior, and subtropical on the Caspian shores. Average temperatures in Tehran are 3°C in January and 30°C in July.

HISTORY AND POLITICS

Iran is part of the Middle East's so-called fertile crescent, an area associated with the development of sophisticated agriculture in prehistoric times. In the sixth century BC, the Achaemenian king Cyrus the Great gained control of the area. His dynasty founded the Persian Empire, in which Zoroastrianism was the main religion. Two hundred years later, Persia was conquered by Alexander the Great. Alexander's death led to a period of economic turbulence, civil conflict and foreign invasion until the Sassanian Persian Empire was founded in the second century AD. This was destroyed in AD 637 by Arab conquerors who introduced Islam, converting the majority of the population and initiating a cultural revolution. The area was ruled by Arabs, Turks and Mongols until the accession of the Safavid dynasty, which ruled between the 16th and 18th centuries, a time recognised as a cultural golden age; it was followed by the Qajar dynasty in the 19th and 20th centuries.

The Qajar dynasty was overthrown in 1921 by Reza Khan, who became prime minister in 1923 and was crowned Shah in 1925. He was succeeded in 1941 by his son, Mohammad Reza Shah Pahlavi, who began a programme of economic modernisation, Westernisation and secularisation in the 1960s. Opposition to reform and popular protests against the Shah's regime in the 1970s led to a revolution in 1978. The Shah went into exile and in 1979 a non-party theocratic Islamic republic was proclaimed under Ayatollah Khomeini.

Since Ayatollah Khomeini's death in 1989, there has been a struggle for political dominance between conservatives and more liberal reformers. Although the reformers were generally in the ascendancy until 2004, liberalisation has been blocked by the religious authorities and the conservative judiciary, which also constitute the membership of the Council of Guardians and so are able to influence the selection of parliamentary candidates. There is a vocal popular pro-democracy movement.

At the 2008 legislative election, many pro-reform candidates were disqualified from standing by the Council of Guardians; conservatives won more than two-thirds of the seats. The incumbent president Mahmoud Ahmadinejad was declared the outright winner after the first round of voting in the presidential election in June 2009, but the result was challenged by the other candidates, who alleged electoral fraud. Following massive protest rallies, the Council of Guardians confirmed Ahmadinejad's victory and ruled out an annulment; further popular protests were suppressed. Since the protests in summer 2009, the regime has ruthlessly suppressed opposition (the Green Movement) and purged liberals from official positions. (*See also* Events of the Year.)

FOREIGN RELATIONS

Between 1980 and 1988, Iran was engaged in a bitter war with Iraq; ostensibly a boundary dispute over the Shatt-al-Arab waterway, it was fuelled by Iran's fear that Iraq was encouraging demands for autonomy by Arabs in its westernmost province. Fighting ended in 1988 and a peace settlement was agreed in 1990. Iran remained neutral in the Gulf War (1991) and the Iraq War (2003), but it has been accused since of subverting reconstruction in Iraq by arming Shia insurgents.

Since the 1978 revolution, Iran's relations with the West, and especially the USA, have been strained. It has not cooperated with international efforts to achieve peace in the Middle East, and has long been suspected of sponsoring terrorism by Islamic fundamentalists, especially in Lebanon and Palestine, and now is believed to be supplying arms to the Taliban.

Since 2002 international relations have deteriorated further because of concerns over Iran's nuclear and ballistic missile programmes, especially its acquisition of the ability to enrich uranium. Iran insists that this is for power generation and is not a precursor to developing nuclear weapons, but refuses to halt the programme or co-operate with the IAEA. The UN has passed six resolutions since 2006 calling on Iran to suspend uranium enrichment and reprocessing and to comply with its IAEA obligations and responsibilities; four of the resolutions imposed and extended sanctions on trade and travel.

POLITICAL SYSTEM

Under the 1979 constitution, overall authority rests with the spiritual leader of the republic, who is elected by the Assembly of Experts; this consists of 86 clerics who are directly elected for an eight-year term and decide religious and spiritual matters. The executive president is directly elected for a four-year term, renewable only once. Ministers are nominated by the president but must be approved by the legislature. The unicameral Consultative Council *(Majlis al-Shoura)* has 290 members who are directly elected for a four-year term on a non-party basis; five seats are reserved for religious minorities. Laws passed by the legislature must be approved by the Council of Guardians of the Constitution, six theologians appointed by the spiritual leader and six jurists whose nominations by the judiciary are approved by the legislature; it also has a supervisory role in elections. In 1997, the Constitutional Surveillance Council, a five-member body, was established to supervise the proper application of constitutional laws.

Spiritual Leader of the Islamic Republic and C.-in-C. of Armed Forces, Ayatollah Seyed Ali Khamenei, *appointed* June 1989
President, Mahmoud Ahmadinejad, *elected* 24 June 2005, *re-elected* 2009
First Vice-President, Mohammad Reza Rahimi

SELECTED GOVERNMENT MEMBERS *as at June 2010*
Defence, Ahmad Vahidi
Economic Affairs and Finance, Shamseddin Hosseini
Foreign Affairs, Manouchehr Mottaki
Interior, Mostafa Mohammad Najjar

EMBASSY OF THE ISLAMIC REPUBLIC OF IRAN
16 Prince's Gate, London SW7 1PT
T 020-7225 3000 E info@iran-embassy.org.uk
W www.iran-embassy.org.uk
Ambassador Extraordinary and Plenipotentiary, HE Rasoul Movahedian Attar, *apptd* 2006

BRITISH EMBASSY
PO Box 11365–4474, 198 Ferdowsi Avenue, Tehran 11344
T (+98) (21) 6405 2000 E britishembassytehran@fco.gov.uk
W http://ukiniran.fco.gov.uk
Ambassador Extraordinary and Plenipotentiary, HE Simon Gass, CMG, CVO, *apptd* 2009

BRITISH COUNCIL
Operations suspended indefinitely from 31 January 2009.
W www.britishcouncil.org/iran

DEFENCE

The army has over 1,613 main battle tanks, 640 armoured personnel carriers, 610 armoured infantry fighting vehicles and 50 armed helicopters. The navy has 3 submarines, 4 frigates, 2 corvettes, over 146 patrol and coastal vessels, 3 combat aircraft and 10 armed helicopters. There are 8 naval bases. The air force has 312 combat aircraft.
Military budget – US$9,590m (2008)
Military personnel – 523,000: army 350,000, Islamic Revolutionary Guard Corps 125,000, navy 18,000, air force 30,000; paramilitary 40,000

ECONOMY AND TRADE

Iran was one of the best-performing economies in the Middle East owing to its vast reserves of oil and natural gas, but its performance is deteriorating; the predominantly state-controlled economy is inefficient, with little progress made on liberalisation and diversification. Unemployment and inflation are serious problems, and there is a flourishing unofficial economy. Since 2008, falling oil prices and UN sanctions have increased Iran's economic problems.

Oil and gas extraction and processing dominate the economy, but other activities include petrochemicals, mining, textiles, construction materials, food processing, mineral products, metal fabrication and armaments. Agricultural production includes wheat, rice, other grains, sugar beet and sugar cane, fruit, nuts, cotton, dairy products, wool and caviar.

The main trading partners are China, the UAE, Japan, South Korea, the EU and India. Principal exports are petroleum (80 per cent), chemical and petrochemical products, fruit and nuts, and carpets. The main imports are industrial raw materials and intermediate goods, capital goods, foodstuffs, consumer goods and technical services.
GNI – US$251,500m; US$3,540 per capita (2008)
Annual average growth of GDP – 2.6 per cent (2009 est)
Inflation rate – 16.8 per cent (2009 est)
Population below poverty line – 18 per cent (2007 est)
Unemployment – 11.8 per cent (2009)
Total external debt – US$18,730m (2009 est)
Imports – US$57,200m (2008)
Exports – US$116,400m (2008)

BALANCE OF PAYMENTS
Trade – US$60,859m surplus (2009)
Current Account – US$23,987m surplus (2008)

Trade with UK	*2008*	*2009*
Imports from UK	£412,061,351	£374,036,961
Exports to UK	£66,645,984	£206,359,213

COMMUNICATIONS

Iran's seaports include Asaluyeh, Bushehr and Abadan (largely destroyed in the 1980–8 war with Iraq) on the Persian Gulf and Bandar Abbas on the Strait of Hormuz. The 850km of navigable waterways are mainly on the river Karun and Lake Urmia. There are a total of 173,000km of roads, of which 126,000km are surfaced, and 8,400km of railways. There are over 300 airports and airfields; the principal airports are at Tehran and Shiraz.

The state-owned telephone system is being modernised and expanded to include rural as well as urban areas. The fixed-line network more than doubled in capacity, to 24.8 million users, between 2000 and 2008. Mobile phone distribution and internet use have grown dramatically; there were 43 million mobile subscribers and 23 million internet users in 2008.

EDUCATION AND HEALTH

Since 1943 primary education has been compulsory and free of charge.
Literacy rate – 82.3 per cent (2007 est)
Gross enrolment ratio (percentage of relevant age group) – primary 128 per cent; secondary 80 per cent; tertiary 36 per cent (2008 est)
Health expenditure (per capita) – US$253 (2007)
Hospital beds (per 1,000 people) – 1.4 (2003–8)

MEDIA

The relative freedom of the media has been increasingly challenged in recent years, and since the protests in summer 2009 there has been a sustained crackdown on all independent media; western journalists have been expelled from or denied entry to the country, some domestic media workers have been dismissed or imprisoned, and several foreign-based radio stations have been banned. Viewing of satellite television was widespread and tolerated by the authorities but foreign channels are now frequently jammed. The internet is the main forum for expressing dissident opinions, but websites and blogs are subject to government censorship.

CULTURE

Iran is rich in Islamic and pre-Islamic architecture. Persepolis, constructed by Darius in the sixth century BC and the capital of the Achaemenian Empire, lies 644km south of Tehran. It was declared a UNESCO World Heritage Site in 1979.

The film industry was boosted in 1998 by the government's decision to subsidise productions. Director Abbas Kiarostami (*b.* 1940), whose films include Palme d'Or winner *Taste of Cherry* and *Ten*, has received much critical acclaim, while author and filmmaker Marjane Satrapi (*b.* 1969) received widespread acclaim for her graphic novel and film *Persepolis*.

IRAQ

Jumhuriyat al-Iraq – Republic of Iraq

Area – 438,317 sq. km
Capital – Baghdad; population, 5,751,210 (2009 est)
Major cities – Arbil, Basra, Kirkuk, Mosul, Najaf, Sulaymaniyah
Currency – New Iraqi dinar (NID) of 1,000 fils
Population – 28,945,657 rising at 2.51 per cent a year (2009 est); Arab (75–80 per cent), Kurdish (15–20 per cent) (est)
Religion – Muslim 97 per cent (of which Shia 65 per cent, Sunni 35 per cent), Christian 2 per cent (predominantly Chaldean Catholic) (est)
Language – Arabic (official), Kurdish (official in Kurdish Autonomous Region), Turkoman, Assyrian, Armenian
Population density – 70 per sq. km (2008 est)
Urban population – 67 per cent (2007 est)
Median age (years) – 20.4 (2009 est)
National anthem – 'Mawtini' ['My Homeland']
National day – 14 July (Republic Day)
Life expectancy (years) – 69.94 (2009 est)
Mortality rate – 5.03 (2009 est)
Birth rate – 30.1 (2009 est)
Infant mortality rate – 43.82 (2009 est)
Death penalty – Retained
CPI score – 1.5 (2009)

CLIMATE AND TERRAIN

The north-west and south of Iraq consist of an almost barren desert plain. The area between the Euphrates and Tigris rivers, which run across the country from north-west to south-east, is fertile, irrigated and heavily cultivated. The rivers run through marshland to their outflow in the Persian Gulf, on which Iraq has a 56km coastline. In the north-east the land rises to the Kurdistan mountains. Elevation extremes range from 3,611m at the highest point to 0m (Persian Gulf) at the lowest. The climate is mostly desert, though colder and wetter in the mountains. Average temperatures in Baghdad range from 9°C in January to 35°C in July.

HISTORY AND POLITICS

The Sumerians, the world's oldest civilisation, were the first people to populate the areas around the Tigris and Euphrates rivers. From around 3000 BC they began to build city-states, of which Ur, Lagash and Eridu are the earliest examples; the city-states were unified into an empire *c.*2350 BC. In the seventh century BC, the area became part of the Assyrian Empire until this was destroyed by the Babylonians and the Medes. Apart from 150 years of Roman rule (AD 114–266), Iraq was under Persian rule from the mid-sixth century BC until Persia's conquest by Arab Muslims in AD 637. The battle of Karbala in AD 680 marked the split between Sunnis and Shias, a decisive moment in Islamic history.

Iraq came under the control of the Ottoman Empire from 1533 until 1916, when the Ottomans, weakened by the First World War, ceded control to the British. A provisional government was set up in 1920, and in 1921 the Emir Faisal was elected king of Iraq. The monarchy was overthrown in 1958, and after a coup in 1968 Iraq came under the control of the socialist Ba'ath Party. In 1979, Saddam Hussein became president.

Under Saddam Hussein's regime, Iraq was at war three times; it fought a bitter war with Iran from 1980–8; in January 1991, a US-led alliance of NATO and Middle East countries launched a military offensive to liberate Kuwait, which Iraq had invaded and occupied in August 1990, ignoring international demands for it to withdraw; and in March 2003, US-led forces invaded Iraq after Saddam Hussein had for over a decade obstructed attempts to verify the decommissioning of its weapons of mass destruction. Saddam Hussein was captured in December 2003, and was convicted and executed in 2006 for crimes against humanity.

Following the invasion and occupation between March and May 2003, a coalition provisional authority became the occupying authority in Iraq before handing over sovereignty in June 2004 to the Iraqi interim governing council. Responsibility for security in many provinces has been transferred to Iraqi forces and police, and foreign troops are being withdrawn from the country; US troops are scheduled to leave in 2010–11.

Legislative elections took place in December 2005, but as no party or bloc commanded an outright majority, there were four months of political deadlock before Jalal Talabani, the Kurdish president of the transitional government, was re-elected president in April 2006 and asked Nouri al-Maliki (leader of a Shia party) to form a government. Maliki's coalition government, including the four main parliamentary blocs and one minor party, was sworn in on 20 May. In the 2010 legislative elections, scheduled for January but postponed to March, the Iraqiya bloc led by former prime minister Iyad Allawi won the most seats, but only by a narrow margin over the State of Law bloc led by incumbent prime minister Nouri al-Maliki. Both of the main blocs had started coalition negotiations with smaller parties at the time of going to press. (*See also* Events of the Year.)

INSURGENCIES

There are about four million Kurds in north-east Iraq, in areas adjoining the predominantly Kurdish areas in Iran and Turkey. Iraq's Kurdish nationalists have demanded an autonomous homeland, Kurdistan, since the 1960s, and turned to militant tactics in the 1970s. Their demands were opposed by Saddam Hussein's regime with great brutality. An uprising after the Gulf War (1991) was suppressed by Iraqi troops, prompting the creation of UN safe havens which enabled the Kurds to set up a semi-autonomous region in the north. An air exclusion zone was also established, but there was further conflict with Iraqi forces and between the two main Kurdish parties in the 1990s. During the war in 2003, Kurdish fighters fought alongside US troops in the north, taking control of the northern cities and establishing an administration in the area, which is now autonomous. The boundary of the autonomous area has yet to be defined, and its precise location will decide control of Kirkuk and of oilfields in the region; this issue is the cause of tension and some intercommunal violence between Arabs and Kurds in the area.

The Shias in southern Iraq also rebelled after the Gulf War and were brutally suppressed. The UN established an air exclusion zone over southern Iraq in 1992 to protect the population, but persecution continued until 2003.

After May 2003, there was insurgent activity throughout the country, particularly in the Baghdad area, the predominantly Sunni-populated towns in the centre and west of the country, and in and around Mosul. Initially the targets were foreign troops, Iraqi military and police, and foreign aid and reconstruction workers, but from early 2005 the attacks became increasingly sectarian in nature. The level of violence has dropped since 2007 because of the US military 'surge', a ceasefire by one of the main militias, the Mahdi Army, from August 2007, and a key Sunni militia, the Awakening movement, turning against al-Qaeda. There was an upsurge of violence in 2008 as the government mounted offensives against militias in Basra, Mosul and parts of Baghdad, and another upsurge in 2009–10 in the run-up to the legislative election and in the weeks following its inconclusive result. The approximate number of deaths as at May 2010 was estimated at: Iraqi civilians 96,000–105,000, US troops 4,400, other coalition troops 318.

POLITICAL SYSTEM

Under the 2005 constitution, the president is elected by the legislature for a four-year term, renewable only once. The president nominates the prime minister, subject to the approval of the legislature. The unicameral Council of Representatives *(Majlis al-Nuwab)* has 325 members (increased from 275 at the 2010 election), of whom 82 (formerly 69) must be women; members are directly elected for a four-year term.

HEAD OF STATE

President, Jalal Talabani, *elected* 6 April 2005, *re-elected* 22 April 2006

Vice-Presidents, Tariq al-Hashimi; Adil Abd al-Mahdi

SELECTED GOVERNMENT MEMBERS *as at June 2010*

Prime Minister, Nouri Jawad al-Maliki

Deputy Prime Ministers, Roj Nouri Shawis *(Economic Affairs);* Rafaa al-Esawi

Foreign Affairs, Hoshyar al-Zebari

Defence, Gen. Abdel Qader al-Obeidi

Interior, Jawad Kadem al-Bolani

EMBASSY OF THE REPUBLIC OF IRAQ

3 Elvaston Place, London SW7 5QH

T 020-7590 9220 E lonemb@iraqmofamail.net

W www.iraqembassy.org.uk

Ambassador Extraordinary and Plenipotentiary, Abdulmuhaimen al-Oraibi

BRITISH EMBASSY

International Zone, Baghdad

T (+964) 790 192 6280 E britembbaghdad@fco.gov.uk

W http://ukiniraq.fco.gov.uk

Ambassador Extraordinary and Plenipotentiary, HE Dr John Jenkins, CMG, LVO, *apptd* 2009

BRITISH COUNCIL

c/o British Embassy, International Zone, Baghdad *(post should be sent to Amman, Jordan office)*

T (+962) 790 191 1971 W www.britishcouncil.org/iraq

Director, Tony Reilly

DEFENCE

Iraq's armed forces were officially disbanded by the coalition provisional authority in May 2003. Since then, new Iraqi security forces have been recruited and trained by coalition troops. As at February 2010 the Iraqi security forces numbered 578,269: army 186,957, navy 2,000, air 3,000, Ministry of Interior forces 386,312 (est). The army has more than 149 main battle tanks and 1,479 armoured personnel carriers. The navy has over 38 patrol and coastal combatant vessels, based at Umm Qasr.

ECONOMY AND TRADE

The economy suffered three decades of state intervention, mismanagement, corruption, militarisation, war and international sanctions as well as the looting, insurgency and sabotage that followed the 2003 allied invasion. However, with the improvement in the security situation, economic activity has increased, the institutions required to implement economic policy are being put in place and a debt reduction programme has been arranged. Although unemployment remains high (15–30 per cent), inflation has been reduced considerably.

Oil is the main resource and export, and production has returned to pre-2003 levels; government contracts signed in 2009–10 with several major oil companies have the potential to increase production further, although regulatory restrictions and inadequate infrastructure hamper economic development. Other industries include chemicals, textiles, construction materials, food processing and metal fabrication. The main trading partners are the USA (39 per cent of exports), Syria (26 per cent of imports), Turkey and India. Principal exports are crude oil (84 per cent), other crude materials, food and livestock. The main imports are food, medicine and manufactured goods.

Annual average growth of GDP – 5.8 per cent (2009 est)

Inflation rate – 3.5 per cent (2009 est)

Total external debt – US$50,290m (2009 est)

BALANCE OF PAYMENTS

Trade – US$44,662m surplus (2009)

Current Account – US$13,886m surplus (2008)

Trade with UK	*2008*	*2009*
Imports from UK	£155,889,915	£163,433,684
Exports to UK	£2,208,951	£620,704

COMMUNICATIONS

The transport infrastructure was severely damaged during the wars in 1991 and 2003 and reconstruction has been slow because of security problems. Key bridges, airports and ports, including the main seaport at Basra, have been repaired and reopened. The main international airport is at Baghdad; the national carrier, Iraqi Airways, was dissolved by the government in May 2010 in an attempt to end a dispute with Kuwait Airways over reparations claimed for the alleged theft of planes and spare parts during Iraq's invasion of the country in 1990. Railway services between Baghdad and Basra resumed in 2008. There are 5,279km of waterways, primarily on the Tigris and Euphrates rivers.

The telephone system was badly disrupted in 2003 but is being repaired with greater capacity. Mobile phone services are expanding rapidly. There were 1.1 million fixed lines in use and 300,000 internet users in 2008, and 20 million mobile phone subscribers in 2009.

EDUCATION AND HEALTH

Since 2003 the country's education system has been reviewed, and over 2,500 schools have been refurbished. Primary education is compulsory.

Literacy rate – 74.1 per cent (2007 est)
Gross enrolment ratio (percentage of relevant age group) – primary 98 per cent; secondary 45 per cent; tertiary 15 per cent (2005 est)
Health expenditure (per capita) – US$62 (2007; excludes northern Iraq)
Hospital beds (per 1,000 people) – 1.3 (2003–8)

MEDIA

Once strictly controlled, the media has begun to flourish since 2003, although dozens of media workers have been killed in the insurgency and by coalition military actions. However, regulations introduced in November 2009 require media workers to obtain work permits and introduced $5,000 (£3,000) licence fees for all broadcast media, measures that raised concern about the government's attitude to media freedom. There are more than 100 newspapers and periodicals, many with an ethnic or religious affiliation, and private radio and television stations have also begun to thrive. The television and radio stations set up by the coalition provisional authority now form part of the publicly funded Iraqi Public Broadcasting Service. Satellite television is very popular, attracting around 70 per cent of Iraqi viewers. In the autonomous Kurdish areas, rival factions operate their own media.

IRELAND

Eire – Ireland

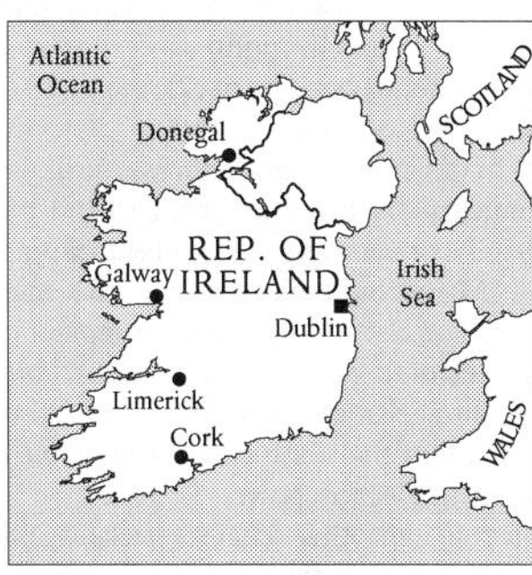

Area – 70,273 sq. km
Capital – Dublin *(Baile Átha Cliath)*; population, 1,084,160 (2009 est)
Major cities – Cork (Corcaigh), Galway (Gaillimh), Limerick (Liumneach), Swords (Sord Cholm Cille), Waterford (Port Láirge)
Currency – Euro (€) of 100 cents
Population – 4,203,200 rising at 1.12 per cent a year (2009 est)
Religion – Christian (Roman Catholic 87 per cent, Anglican 3 per cent, Presbyterian 1 per cent), Muslim 1 per cent (est)
Language – English, Irish (Gaelic) (both official)
Population density – 64 per sq. km (2008)
Urban population – 61 per cent (2007 est)
Median age (years) – 35 (2009 est)
National anthem – 'Amhran na bhFiann' ['The Soldier's Song']
National day – 17 March (St Patrick's Day)
Life expectancy (years) – 78.24 (2009 est)
Mortality rate – 7.75 (2009 est)
Birth rate – 14.23 (2009 est)
Infant mortality rate – 5.05 (2009 est)
Death penalty – Abolished for all crimes (since 1990)
CPI score – 8 (2009)

CLIMATE AND TERRAIN

The greatest length of the island of Ireland is 486km, from Torr Head in the north-east to Mizen Head in the south-west, and the greatest breadth is 280km, from Dundrum Bay in the east to Annagh Head in the west. Northern Ireland, in the north-east, is part of the UK. The republic has a central plain broken by hills and numerous lakes and bogs. It is surrounded by low mountains, including the Wicklow, Knockmealdown, Galty and Boggeragh mountains, and drained by the principal river, the Shannon (386km), which flows into the Atlantic Ocean. On the north coast of Achill Island (Co. Mayo) are the highest cliffs in the British Isles, 609m above sea level. Elevation extremes range from 1,041m (Carrauntoohil, Co. Kerry) at the highest point to 0m (Irish Sea) at the lowest.

HISTORY AND POLITICS

Settled by the Celts around 300 BC, Ireland developed a flourishing and distinct culture that remained largely intact until Christianity was introduced in the fifth century AD, after which Christian Ireland established itself as a centre of learning and high culture. Viking raiders began sustained attacks *c.*800 and established settlements from the mid-ninth century. In the 12th century, Anglo-Norman barons, invited to Ireland by a Gaelic king seeking allies, brought much of the south of the island under their own control, and Henry II of England declared himself Lord of Ireland in 1171. The island was unified under English control during Elizabeth I's reign. From the early 17th century, England began to promote the settlement of Protestant Scots in the north-eastern kingdom of Ulster, the last stronghold of Celtic power. This policy produced a long-standing antagonism between the north's Protestant and Catholic populations.

In the mid-17th century, widespread support in Ireland for the royalist side in the English Civil War prompted bloody reprisals from Oliver Cromwell, who invaded Ireland and reasserted English control in 1649–50. Catholic Irish support for the deposed Catholic king James II was defeated by William III at the Battle of the Boyne (1690) and penal laws passed in 1695 suppressed Catholic wealth and power. Popular discontent in the late 18th century and a rebellion in 1798 led to the abolition of the Irish parliament by the Act of Union (1800), which united Britain and Ireland. Simultaneously, Catholic opposition to English rule became increasingly organised with the formation of the Catholic Association, but agitation for home rule failed until 1912, when legislation was passed but did not come into effect because of the First World War.

By 1916, demands in some quarters had shifted from home rule to independence from Britain, and a rebellion broke out in Dublin. Known as the Easter Rising, it was repressed by the British but inspired Irish nationalists to contest the 1918 elections and, on gaining a majority of the Irish seats, to declare Irish independence under the leadership of Eamon de Valera. The British response was an attempt at violent suppression of the nationalists. The ensuing Anglo-Irish War lasted from 1919 to 1921, when the two sides negotiated a treaty giving Ireland internal self-government as the Irish Free State, with dominion status within the Commonwealth, but leaving as part of the UK the six predominantly Protestant counties in the north-east. This partition was not accepted by all nationalists and opposition developed into civil war in 1922–3. In 1937, the Irish Free State declared itself independent and sovereign, and in 1948 it left the Commonwealth and became a republic.

The status of Northern Ireland remained divisive, with the partition unacknowledged by the Irish constitution of 1937. The Anglo-Irish agreement in 1985 gave the Irish government a consultative role in the government of Northern Ireland, and in 1993 the Downing Street declaration set out a joint Anglo-Irish peace proposal to end the conflict in the north. The Irish government was involved in the negotiation of the 1998 Good Friday agreement; its proposals, including Irish recognition of the partition and the right of the north to self-determination, were approved in a referendum by 94 per cent of voters in the Irish Republic.

Ireland joined the EC in 1973 and the eurozone in 1999. In a 2008 referendum, the majority voted against ratification of the Lisbon treaty reforming EU institutions, though the electorate reversed this decision in a second referendum on the issue in October 2009.

The 1997 presidential election was won by Mary McAleese, and she was confirmed in office unopposed in 2004. In the 2007 elections to the House of Representatives, Fianna Fail (FF), led by Bertie Ahern (prime minister since 1997), remained the largest party but without an overall majority. The coalition government of the FF and the Progressive Democrats (PD) was expanded to include the Green Party. Bertie Ahern stood down as prime minister in May 2008 and was replaced as party leader and prime minister by Brian Cowen, previously the deputy prime minister, who appointed a reshuffled cabinet.

POLITICAL SYSTEM

Under the 1937 constitution, the president *(Uachtaran na Eireann)* is directly elected for a seven-year term, renewable only once. The bicameral National Parliament *(Oireachtas)* consists of the *Dail Eireann* (House of Representatives) and the *Seanad Eireann* (senate). The *Dail* has 166 members, elected for a five-year term by proportional representation. The *Seanad* has 60 members, who serve a five-year term; of these, 11 are nominated by the *Taoiseach* (prime minister) and 49 are elected, six by institutions of higher education and 43 from panels of candidates representing various sectoral interests.

The *Taoiseach* is appointed by the president on the nomination of the *Dail,* while other members of the government are appointed by the president on the nomination of the *Taoiseach* with the previous approval of the *Dail.* The *Taoiseach* appoints a member of the government to be the *Tanaiste* (deputy prime minister).

HEAD OF STATE

President, Mary McAleese, *elected* 30 October 1997, *confirmed in office* 1 October 2004, *sworn in* 11 November 2004

SELECTED GOVERNMENT MEMBERS *as at June 2010*

Taoiseach (Prime Minister), Brian Cowen
Tanaiste (Deputy PM), Mary Coughlan
Defence, Tony Killeen
Finance, Brian Lenihan
Foreign Affairs, Michael Martin

EMBASSY OF IRELAND

17 Grosvenor Place, London SW1X 7HR
T 020-7235 2171 W www.embassyofireland.co.uk
Ambassador Extraordinary and Plenipotentiary, HE Bobby McDonagh, *apptd* 2009

BRITISH EMBASSY

29 Merrion Road, Ballsbridge, Dublin 4
T (+353) (1) 205 3700
W http://britishembassyinireland.fco.gov.uk
Ambassador Extraordinary and Plenipotentiary, HE Julian King, CMG, *apptd* 2009

BRITISH COUNCIL

Newmount House, 22/24 Lower Mount Street, Dublin 2
T (+353) (1) 676 4088 W www.britishcouncil.org/ireland
Director, Matt Burney

DEFENCE

The army has 67 armoured personnel carriers. The navy has 8 patrol and coastal combatant vessels at 2 bases. The air force has 10 utility helicopters.
Military budget – US$1,530m (2009 est)
Military personnel – 10,460: army 8,500, navy 1,100, air force 850

ECONOMY AND TRADE

In the past few decades Ireland's economy has been transformed from a mainly agricultural to a modern, export-led economy that experienced strong growth from the mid-1990s until 2008, when the global economic crisis caused a sharp drop in economic activity and a recession began. The government acted to stabilise the financial system, and introduced economic stimulus measures and austerity budgets in 2009 and 2010.

Agriculture now accounts for only 5 per cent of GDP and 6 per cent of employment; services contributes 49 per cent and industry 46 per cent of GDP, and the sectors account for 67 per cent and 27 per cent of employment respectively. Major industries include the mining and processing of metals and gypsum, computer software, information technology, food and drink production, chemicals, pharmaceuticals and tourism. Although the Kinsale gas field off the south coast meets some of its gas needs, and hydroelectric power is generated from the Shannon barrage and other schemes, Ireland still imports over half the fuel needed for power generation.

The main trading partners are other EU countries and the USA. Principal exports are machinery, computers, chemicals, pharmaceuticals, livestock and livestock products. The main imports are data processing equipment, other machinery, chemicals, petroleum and petroleum products, textiles and clothing.
GNI – US$220,3000m; US$49,770 per capita (2008)
Annual average growth of GDP – –7.3 per cent (2009 est)
Inflation rate – –3.9 per cent (2009 est)
Population below poverty line – 7 per cent (2005 est)
Unemployment – 12.6 per cent (2009 est)
Total external debt – US$2,387,000m (2009)
Imports – US$82,700m (2008)
Exports – US$126,100m (2008)

BALANCE OF PAYMENTS

Trade – US$53,902m surplus (2009)
Current Account – US$6,705m deficit (2009)

Trade with UK	*2008*	*2009*
Imports from UK	£18,526,534,141	£15,295,838,653
Exports to UK	£12,034,201,552	£12,246,224,617

COMMUNICATIONS
Ireland has 96,036km of roads and 3,237km of railways. There are over 950km of waterways, although these are used only by leisure craft. The main ports are Cork, Dun Laoghaire, Galway, Limerick and Waterford. The principal airport is at Dublin, with others at Shannon, Waterford, Cork, Killarney, Galway and Knock. There were 2.2 million fixed telephone lines in use, 5 million mobile subscribers and 2.8 million internet users in 2008.

EDUCATION AND HEALTH
Primary education is directed by the state, with the exception of several private primary schools. Education is compulsory until age 16.

Gross enrolment ratio (percentage of relevant age group) – primary 105 per cent; secondary 113 per cent; tertiary 61 per cent (2008 est)
Health expenditure (per capita) – US$4,556 (2007)
Hospital beds (per 1,000 people) – 5.3 (2003–8)

MEDIA
Irish broadcasting is regulated by a commission appointed by the Department of Communications. The main radio and television broadcaster is the state-run Radio Telefis Eireann (RTE), whose competitors include a handful of Irish commercial stations and British terrestrial and satellite services. There are three national newspapers: the *Irish Times, Irish Independent* and *Irish Examiner*.

CULTURE
Given its size, Ireland has a disproportionately rich literary history, having produced four Nobel prize-winners: poets W. B. Yeats (1865–1939) and Seamus Heaney (*b.* 1939) and dramatists George Bernard Shaw (1856–1950) and Samuel Beckett (1906–89). Other great writers include Jonathan Swift (1667–1745), Oscar Wilde (1854–1900) and James Joyce (1882–1941).

Traditional forms of sport and music remain popular. Hurling and Gaelic football are passionately supported, as are rugby and football. Similarly, musicians adopting and adapting traditional music, such as the Pogues, Clannad and Enya (*b.* 1961), have achieved international success, alongside rock groups U2 and Thin Lizzy and boybands Westlife and Boyzone.

ISRAEL AND PALESTINIAN TERRITORIES

Medinat Yisra'el/Dawlat Isra'il – State of Israel

Area – 20,072 sq. km (includes Jerusalem and the Golan Heights)
Capital – The legislature and most government departments are in Jerusalem; population 767,634 (2009 est). A resolution proclaiming Jerusalem as the capital of Israel was adopted by the *Knesset* in 1950. It is not, however, recognised as the capital by the UN because East Jerusalem is part of the Occupied Territories captured in 1967. The UN and international law continues to consider the pre-1950 capital Tel Aviv (population, 392,500) to be the capital.
Major cities – Haifa; Rishon Le'Zion
Currency – New Israeli Shekel (NIS) of 100 agora
Population – 7,233,701 rising at 1.67 per cent a year (2009 est); includes about 384,000 settlers in the occupied areas. Since independence Israel has had a policy of granting an immigration visa to every Jew who expresses a desire to settle in the country. Between 1948 and 1992, 2.3 million immigrants entered Israel from over 100 different countries.
Religion – Jewish 76 per cent (of which secular 44 per cent, 'traditional religious' or 'traditional non-religious' 39 per cent, Orthodox 10 per cent, *Haredi* 7 per cent), Muslim 16.5 per cent (predominantly Sunni; Druze 2 per cent), Christian 2 per cent (predominantly Eastern Orthodox denominations) (est)
Language – Hebrew, Arabic (both official), English
Population density – 338 per sq. km (2008)
Urban population – 92 per cent (2007 est)
Median age (years) – 29.1 (2009 est)
National anthem – 'Hatikvah' ['The Hope']
National day – fifth day of Jewish month of Iyar (anniversary of Independence Day 1948); falls on 9 May in 2011
Life expectancy (years) – 80.73 (2009 est)
Mortality rate – 5.43 (2009 est)
Birth rate – 19.77 (2009 est)
Infant mortality rate – 4.22 (2009 est)
Death penalty – Retained for certain crimes (last used 1962)
CPI score – 6.1 (2009)

CLIMATE AND TERRAIN
Israel comprises the partly forested hill country of Galilee and parts of Judea and Samaria, the coastal plain from the Gaza Strip to north of Acre (including the plain of Esdraelon running from Haifa Bay to the south-east); the Negev, a triangular-shaped rocky desert in the south; and parts of the Jordan valley, including the Hula region, Lake Tiberias and the south-western part of the Dead Sea. Elevation extremes range from 1,208m (Har Meron) at the highest point to –408m (Dead Sea) at the lowest, which is the Earth's deepest depression. The climate is temperate, with hotter, drier conditions in the south and east. Average temperatures in Tel Aviv range from 14°C in January to 27°C in August.

HISTORY AND POLITICS
Regarded by Jews as their homeland since the Israelite settlement in Old Testament times, Palestine was conquered by the Babylonians, the Greeks and the Romans between the sixth and first centuries BC, beginning the diaspora. Conquered by Muslim Arabs in the seventh century AD, the area was contested between Muslims and Christians during the Crusades before becoming part of the Ottoman Empire in the 16th century.

Zionist settlement in Palestine began in the 1880s and

the British declared support for a Jewish homeland there in 1917 after capturing much of the Middle East from the Ottoman Empire during the First World War. Britain administered the area under a League of Nations mandate from 1918 to 1948, during which period Jewish immigration from Europe was encouraged, but this resulted in tension with the Arab population of Palestine, who had also been promised recognition of an Arab state by the British.

After the Second World War, the British mandate became increasingly untenable and they withdrew in 1948. The UN voted to partition Palestine, creating a Jewish and an Arab state, but the proposal was rejected by the Arabs, prompting the Jews to announce the creation of the independent State of Israel on 14 May 1948. This led to a ten-month war, the first of a series of conflicts between Israel and neighbouring Arab states, which created a large number of Palestinian refugees. Further conflict occurred in 1956, when Israel attacked Egypt's Suez Canal zone; in 1967 (the Six-Day War) when Israel gained control of the Gaza Strip, the Sinai peninsula, the West Bank and east Jerusalem, and the Golan Heights in Syria (the 'Occupied Territories'); in 1973, when Egypt and Syria attempted to regain their lost territory; and in 1982, when Israel invaded Lebanon to drive Palestinian guerrillas out of Beirut, occupying a buffer zone in the south until 2000. Southern Lebanon was the scene of further conflict in 2006, when Israeli forces attempted to dislodge Hezbollah guerrillas. The 1978 Camp David talks led to a peace treaty with Egypt in 1979, as a result of which Israel withdrew from Sinai. A peace treaty was signed with Jordan in 1994.

Israel has also experienced decades of internal violence by Palestinians seeking to recover land and property lost in 1948, and to end Israeli occupation of the territories taken in 1967. The Palestine Liberation Organisation (PLO), under Yasser Arafat, began a guerrilla war and terrorist campaign in the 1960s. A more widespread popular uprising *(intifada)* in the Gaza Strip and West Bank began in 1987 and lasted until 1993, when talks between Israel and the PLO resulted in the Oslo accords, which set out interim self-government arrangements for Palestinian areas until a final settlement was reached. Implementation began with the establishment of the Palestinian Autonomous Areas in 1994 and their extension in 1995. The security situation deteriorated again from the mid-1990s, with further violence and suicide bombings evoking an increasingly hard line from a new Israeli government already critical of the peace accords. Implementation of the Oslo accords stalled and negotiations on outstanding issues reached deadlock. A second *intifada* began in 2000, and in 2002 Israel began building a security wall between Jewish and Palestinian areas despite international protests at this *de facto* partitioning of the country.

In 2003, the USA, Russia, the EU and the UN proposed a 'road map' for peace which envisioned a two-state solution to the conflict, but little progress was made until after the death of Yasser Arafat in 2004. The Israeli government fulfilled a key undertaking – the evacuation and dismantling of Jewish settlements in, and military disengagement from, the Gaza Strip in 2005 – but refused to negotiate with the militant Palestinian government elected in January 2006. After a Palestinian power struggle in 2007 led to the creation of rival administrations in Gaza and the West Bank, Israel resumed talks with the West Bank administration headed by President Abbas, but it has continued its tight blockade of Gaza and its retaliation to attacks from the territory; this included a military invasion from December 2008 to January 2009.

The 2007 presidential election was won by Shimon Peres. In September 2008, Tzipi Livni was elected head of the governing Kadima party but her attempts to form a new coalition were unsuccessful and an election was called for February 2009. Although Kadima won 28 seats to Likud's 27 seats, Likud succeeded in forming a coalition government with the Labour party and three smaller parties under Benjamin Netanyahu; the government took office in March 2009.

POLITICAL SYSTEM

There is no written constitution; most constitutional provision is set out in the basic law on government. The head of state is the president, elected by the legislature for a seven-year term, which is not renewable. The unicameral *Knesset* has 120 members elected by proportional representation for a four-year term. The prime minister is responsible to the *Knesset,* and appoints the cabinet, subject to the approval of the *Knesset.*

HEAD OF STATE

President, Shimon Peres, *elected* 13 June 2007, *sworn in* 15 July 2007

SELECTED GOVERNMENT MEMBERS *as at June 2010*

Prime Minister, Benjamin Netanyahu
Vice Prime Ministers, Silvan Shalom, Moshe Ya'alon
Deputy Prime Ministers, Ehud Barak *(Defence),* Avigdor Liberman *(Foreign Affairs),* Eliyahu Yishai *(Interior);* Dan Meridor
Finance, Yuval Steinitz

EMBASSY OF ISRAEL

2 Palace Green, London W8 4QB
T 020-7957 9500 E info@london.mfa.gov.il
W http://london.mfa.gov.il
Ambassador Extraordinary and Plenipotentiary, HE Ron Prosor, *apptd* 2007

BRITISH EMBASSY

192 Hayarkon Street, Tel Aviv 63405
T (+972) (3) 725 1222 E webmaster.telaviv@fco.gov.uk
W http://ukinisrael.fco.gov.uk
Ambassador Extraordinary and Plenipotentiary, HE Matthew Gould, MBE, *apptd* 2010

BRITISH COUNCIL

PO Box 3302, Crystal House, 12 Hahilazon Street, Ramat Gan 52136
T (+972) (3) 611 3600 W www.britishcouncil.org/israel
Director, Jim Buttery

DEFENCE

Israel is believed to have a nuclear capability of around 200 warheads, which could be delivered by aircraft or *Jericho* I and II missiles. The army has 3,501 main battle tanks and around 10,419 armoured personnel carriers. The navy has 3 submarines, 3 corvettes and 61 patrol and coastal vessels at 4 bases. The air force has 461 combat aircraft and 81 armed helicopters.

Military expenditure – US$12,960m (2009)
Military personnel – 176,500: army 133,000, navy 9,500, air force 34,000; paramilitary 8,050
Conscription duration – 24–48 months (Jews and Druze only; Christians, Circassians and Muslims may volunteer)

ECONOMY AND TRADE

Israel has a technically advanced market economy, having developed its agriculture and industry intensively since the 1970s despite limited natural resources. After a short recession in the early 2000s, structural reforms and tighter fiscal control were implemented, resulting in steady growth from 2003 to 2007, increased foreign investment and a rising demand for exports. Despite the high level of external debt, the economy proved resilient in the global downturn, although it contracted in 2008–9 because of reduced demand for exports. Its debt and deficits are covered by foreign aid and loans; the USA is the main source of economic and military aid and is Israel's main creditor, owed about half of its external debt.

Israel has developed a strong technology sector, central to which are the aviation, electronics, biotechnology, communications and software industries. Other important industries include timber and paper, mineral and metal products, cement, chemicals, plastics, textiles, diamond cutting and tourism, which is reviving. The country is also an important producer of citrus fruits, vegetables, cotton, beef, poultry and dairy products. Service industries account for 65.4 per cent of GDP, industry for 32 per cent and agriculture for 2.6 per cent.

The main trading partners are the USA (32 per cent of exports), Belgium, other EU states and China. Principal exports are high-technology machinery and equipment, software, cut diamonds, agricultural products, chemicals, textiles and clothing. The main imports are raw materials, military equipment, investment goods, rough diamonds, fuels, grain and consumer goods.

GNI – US$180,600m; US$24,720 per capita (2008)
Annual average growth of GDP – –0.3 per cent (2009 est)
Inflation rate – 3.4 per cent (2009 est)
Population below poverty line – 21.6 per cent (2005; defined as less than $7.30 per day)
Unemployment – 8 per cent (2009 est)
Total external debt – US$84,690m (2009)
Imports – US$67,700m (2008)
Exports – US$60,800m (2008)

BALANCE OF PAYMENTS
Trade – US$5,091m deficit (2009)
Current Account – US$7,191m surplus (2009)

Trade with UK	*2008*	*2009*
Imports from UK	£1,282,502,735	£1,098,885,933
Exports to UK	£1,134,291,273	£974,263,067

COMMUNICATIONS

Israel State Railways operates a network of 949km, serving the main cities and towns. There are 18,096km of roads, including 146km of motorway. A major road-building programme has been under way in the West Bank since 1992. The chief seaports are Haifa and Ashdod on the Mediterranean, and Eilat on the Red Sea; Acre has an anchorage for small vessels. There are 47 airports and airfields; the chief international airport is Ben Gurion, between Tel Aviv and Jerusalem. The highly developed telephone system provides services for 3.1 million fixed-line users, 9.5 million mobile phone subscribers and 2.1 million internet users.

EDUCATION AND HEALTH

Education is compulsory between the ages of five and 16 and is free of charge.
Literacy rate – 97.1 per cent (2007 est)
Gross enrolment ratio (percentage of relevant age group) – primary 111 per cent; secondary 91 per cent; tertiary 60 per cent (2008 est)
Health expenditure (per capita) – US$1,893 (2007)
Hospital beds (per 1,000 people) – 5.8 (2003–8)

MEDIA AND CULTURE

The Israeli Broadcasting Authority (IBA) is a public broadcaster operating television and radio services funded largely by a licence fee. It competes with two main terrestrial commercial channels and a number of satellite and cable stations. The IBA's radio stations have faced commercial competition since 1995; there are also a large number of unlicensed radio stations. There are five national daily newspapers.

In Palestinian areas, the Palestinian Broadcasting Corporation runs television and radio services in competition with dozens of domestic and foreign private stations. There are two private daily newspapers and one published by the Palestinian Authority. Palestinian media workers face restrictions imposed by the Israeli authorities and can be the target of harassment, violence or arrest in Palestinian areas.

Jerusalem has a vast number of historic sites, including the Church of the Holy Sepulchre, sacred to Christians, and the al-Aqsa Mosque, which stands on the Temple Mount. The Israel Museum in the city houses the Dead Sea Scrolls.

PALESTINIAN AUTONOMOUS AREAS

Area – The total area is 6,231 sq. km. The area which is fully autonomous is 412 sq. km, of which the Gaza Strip is 352 sq. km and the Jericho enclave 60 sq. km
Capital – Although Palestinians claim East Jerusalem as their capital, the administrative capital was established in 1994 in Gaza City; population 479,400 (2005 est); since 2007 the president and transitional government have been located in Ramallah, on the West Bank; population, 69,479 (2009 est)
Major towns – Jabalia, Khan Yunis, Rafah in the Gaza Strip; Hebron, Jericho, Nablus and Ramallah on the West Bank
Population – 4,119,083 (2003 est)
Religion – Muslim 98 per cent (predominantly Sunni); small Jewish and Christian minorities (est)
Flag – Three horizontal stripes of black, white, green with a red triangle based on the hoist (the PLO flag)
National anthem – 'Fidai, Fidai' ['Freedom Fighter, Freedom Fighter']
Death penalty – Retained
Literacy rate – 93.8 per cent (2007 est)

HISTORY AND POLITICS

Since 1967 the West Bank and Gaza Strip have been under Israeli occupation and until 1994 were administered by the Israeli ministry of defence. Frustration at continued Israeli occupation led to a popular Palestinian uprising *(intifada)* from 1987 until the mid 1990s, when talks between Israel and the Palestinian Liberation Organisation (PLO) resulted in the Oslo accords (1993–5), which set out interim self-government arrangements for Palestinian areas until a final settlement was reached; the 1993 provisions were intended to be for a five-year interim period during which the final status of the West Bank, Gaza and Jerusalem was to be resolved.

The Gaza Strip and the town of Jericho on the West Bank were handed over to the Palestinian National

Authority (PNA) in 1994, and six West Bank towns and most of Hebron in 1995. The final status talks opened in 1996, but stalled in the late 1990s and broke down in 2001. Efforts to restart negotiations were hindered by the election of Israeli governments critical of the peace accords and the outbreak of the second *intifada* in 2000.

In 2003, the USA, Russia, the EU and the UN proposed the 'road map' peace plan, a staged process leading to the establishment of an autonomous Palestinian state by 2005, which also sought political reforms in the PNA. Although endorsed by most parties, implementation of the peace plan made little progress because of the continuing *intifada,* internal power struggles within the Palestinian administration and the refusal of Israel and the USA to negotiate with the Palestinian president Yasser Arafat. This stalemate was broken only by the death of Arafat in November 2004 and the election of a moderate as his successor. Talks with Israel resumed but the peace process continued to be jeopardised by the Palestinian authorities' inability to rein in the violence of extremists, and it stalled in early 2006 with the victory of the Islamist group Hamas in the Palestinian legislative election; Hamas refused to renounce violence, to recognise Israel's right to exist or to abide by existing peace agreements with Israel, which led international donors to cut off funding, causing increasingly severe hardship, especially in Gaza.

The 2005 presidential election was won by the Fatah candidate Mahmoud Abbas. In the 2006 legislative election, the Hamas movement, regarded by many countries as a terrorist organisation, won the most seats and formed the new government. Relations between Hamas and the more moderate Fatah, always tense, often became violent in 2006–7 and in June 2007 descended into a near civil war that left Hamas in control of the Gaza Strip and Fatah in control of the West Bank areas. In June 2007, President Abbas declared a state of emergency and dissolved the unity government appointed in March 2007, subsequently appointing a new, transitional government. Hamas politicians rejected the dissolution of the unity government and called for further talks. Although President Abbas ruled out negotiations until Hamas restored Gaza to the control of the Palestinian Authority and recognised the transitional government, talks were held in spring 2009 but made no progress and were discontinued. The presidential and legislative elections scheduled for January 2010 were postponed; the mandates of the president and parliament have been extended until elections are held.

Talks between President Abbas and the Israeli government resumed in 2007, although there was a break in early 2010 because of continued Israeli settlement in the West Bank. In the Hamas-controlled Gaza Strip, confrontation with Israel escalated and resulted in an Israeli aerial bombardment and military invasion from December 2008 to January 2009. The Israeli blockade of Gaza was tightened further, and the population of Gaza is experiencing extreme hardship.

POLITICAL SYSTEM

The Interim Agreement of 1995 invested the Palestinian Authority with executive, legislative and judicial authority, but not sovereignty, in the autonomous areas.

The president is directly elected for a four-year term. The unicameral Palestinian Legislative Council has one seat reserved for the president and 132 seats for members who are elected from party lists for a four-year term. The president appoints the prime minister, who appoints the council of ministers, which must be approved by the legislature.

SELECTED GOVERNMENT MEMBERS *as at June 2010*
President, Mahmoud Abbas
Prime Minister, Finance, Salam Khaled Abdallah Fayyad
Interior, Sa'id Abu Ali
Foreign Affairs, Riyad Najib Abd-al-Rahman al-Maliki

PALESTINIAN GENERAL DELEGATION
5 Galena Road, London W6 0LT
T 020-8563 0008 **E** 106323.3367@compuserve.com
W www.palestiniangd.org.uk
General Delegate, Prof. Manuel Hassassian

BRITISH CONSULATE-GENERAL
PO Box 19690, 19 Nashashibi Street, Sheikh Jarrah Quarter, East Jerusalem 97200
T (+972) (2) 541 4100 **E** british.jerusalem@fco.gov.uk
W http://ukinjerusalem.fco.gov.uk
Consul-General, Richard Makepeace, *apptd* 2006

BRITISH COUNCIL
PO Box 19136, 31 Nablus Road, East Jerusalem 97200
T (+972) (2) 626 7111 **W** www.britishcouncil.org/ps
Director, Sandra Hamrouni

ECONOMY AND TRADE

The *intifada,* and Israeli security restrictions in response to it, have damaged infrastructure and severely constrained economic activity in the Palestinian areas and external trade since 2000. Incomes had dropped and poverty risen sharply even before 2006, when the policies of the new Hamas government led to an embargo by international funding providers, and Israel stopped remitting customs dues collected on behalf of the Palestinian Authority. Emergency aid, provided through channels that bypass the Hamas government, was resumed in late 2006. The effects were and remain most severe in Gaza, where the population is dependent on food aid. On the West Bank, some Israeli restrictions have been eased since 2007, and the president's economic and structural reforms since 2008, underpinned by foreign aid donors, have stimulated economic development.

Most economic activity consists of small family businesses engaged in farming, quarrying and small-scale manufacturing of construction materials and textiles, metal goods and agricultural produce. The main exports are stone, fruit, olives and vegetables, and the main trading partners are Israel, Jordan and Egypt.

Inflation rate – 9.9 per cent (2009 est)
Population below poverty line – West Bank 46 per cent (2007 est); Gaza Strip 70 per cent (2009 est)

Trade with UK	*2008*	*2009*
Imports from UK	£2,971,598	£1,670,663
Exports to UK	£1,002,713	£656,319

ITALY

Repubblica Italiana – Italian Republic

Area – 301,340 sq. km
Capital – Rome; population, 3,357,470 (2009 est). The 'Eternal City' was founded, according to legend, by Romulus in 753 BC. It was the centre of the Latin civilisation and capital of the Roman republic and empire
Major cities – Bari, Bologna, Florence, Genoa, Milan, Naples, Turin, Venice, Verona. The chief town of Sicily is Palermo, and of Sardinia is Cagliari
Currency – Euro (€) of 100 cents
Population – 58,126,212 falling at 0.05 per cent a year (2009 est)
Religion – Christian (Roman Catholic 87 per cent) (est)
Language – Italian (official), German, French, Slovene
Population density – 203 per sq. km (2008)
Urban population – 68 per cent (2007 est)
Median age (years) – 43.3 (2009 est)
National anthem – 'L'Inno di Mameli' ['Mameli's Hymn']
National day – 2 June (Republic Day)
Life expectancy (years) – 80.2 (2009 est)
Mortality rate – 10.72 (2009 est)
Birth rate – 8.18 (2009 est)
Infant mortality rate – 5.51 (2009 est)
Death penalty – Abolished for all crimes (since 1994)
CPI score – 4.3 (2009)

CLIMATE AND TERRAIN

Italy consists of a peninsula, the islands of Sicily, Sardinia, Elba and about 70 smaller islands. The smaller islands include Pantelleria, the Pelagian islands, the Aeolian islands, Capri, the Flegrean islands, the Pontine archipelago, the Tremiti islands and the Tuscan archipelago. Most of the islands are mountainous.

The peninsula is also largely mountainous, but between the spine of the Apennines and the eastern coastline are two large fertile plains: Emilia-Romagna in the north and Apulia in the south. Italy is divided from France and Switzerland by the Alps, and from Austria and Slovenia by both the Alps and the Dolomites. Three volcanoes, Vesuvius, Etna and Stromboli, are still active. Elevation extremes range from 4,748m (Mt Bianco di Courmayeur) at the highest point to 0m (Mediterranean Sea) at the lowest. At the foot of the Alps lie the great lakes of Como, Maggiore and Garda. The chief rivers are the Po (651km) and the Adige, flowing through the northern plain to the Adriatic Sea, and the Arno (Florentine plain) and the Tiber (flowing through Rome to Ostia), which flow to the west coast. The climate is Mediterranean, with warm dry summers and mild winters.

HISTORY AND POLITICS

In pre-Roman times, the Italian peninsula was inhabited by the Etruscans in the north, the Latins in the centre and Greeks in the south, but by the third century BC most of it was part of the Roman Empire. At the height of its power, the Roman Empire had spread from Italy across Europe, Asia Minor and North Africa. Conquered and settled by a variety of invaders after the fall of Rome, the Italian peninsula developed into a number of competing city states. These, with their powerful and wealthy merchant classes, became the locations (and provided the capital) for the Renaissance. The country was divided between Austria, the Papal States, Naples, Sardinia and four duchies when Italian nationalists began to agitate for a unified Italy in the 19th century. The *Risorgimento* from 1848 united the northern states, culminating in the declaration of the Kingdom of Italy in 1861; unification was completed with the conquest of the Papal States in 1870. The major figures in Italian unification were Mazzini (1805–72), Garibaldi (1807–82) and Cavour (1810–61).

In 1923, the Fascist leader Benito Mussolini seized power and promised a firm rule to end political instability. He committed Italy to an alliance with Nazi Germany and thus led Italy into the Second World War on the Axis side. The Allied invasion of Sicily in 1943 led to the deposition of Mussolini; he was subsequently killed by partisans in April 1945, shortly before the end of the war. Italy became a republic in 1946 after voters narrowly approved the abolition of the monarchy by referendum; the country's new constitution came into force in 1948.

A post-war economic boom lasted until the late 1970s, when high inflation and unemployment ensued. This was a time of serious civil unrest, with unions opposed to often corrupt governments, and extreme right- and left-wing groups conducting violent campaigns. In the early 1990s, there was a drive to reform the political establishment after links were exposed between the government and organised crime; many politicians were arrested. In 1993, the electoral system was changed from proportional representation to majority voting in 75 per cent of the seats, helping to remedy the political instability that had resulted in 45 governments in 47 years. Although governments have continued to be coalitions, those of the past ten years have generally lasted longer. Corruption in public administration and business remains a problem.

Italy was a founding member of the EEC in 1957 and of the eurozone in 1999.

The 2006 presidential election was won, after four rounds of voting, by Giorgio Napolitano. Romano Prodi's centre-left coalition government, in power since the 2006 election, resigned in January 2008 after losing a vote of confidence. In the ensuing legislative election in April, the People of Freedom party (PdL) won the most seats in both chambers, achieving a majority through the support of the Northern League and the Movement for Autonomy. The PdL and Northern League formed a coalition government under PdL leader Silvio Berlusconi (prime minister 1994, 2001–6, 2008–).

POLITICAL SYSTEM

The 1948 constitution has been amended several times, notably in 2001 to provide for greater autonomy for the 20 regions in tax, education and environment matters. The president, who must be over 50 years of age, is elected for a seven-year term by an electoral college consisting of both chambers of the legislature and 58 regional representatives. The bicameral *Parlamento* comprises a 630-member Chamber of Deputies and a senate with 315 members directly elected on a regional basis and a variable number of life senators, who are past presidents and senators appointed by incumbent presidents. Members of both chambers serve a five-year term.

HEAD OF STATE
President, Giorgio Napolitano, *elected* 11 May 2006, *took office* 15 May 2006

SELECTED GOVERNMENT MEMBERS *as at June 2010*
Prime Minister, Silvio Berlusconi
Foreign Affairs, Franco Frattini
Defence, Ignazio La Russa
Economy and Finance, Giulio Tremonti
Interior, Roberto Maroni

ITALIAN EMBASSY
14 Three Kings Yard, Davies Street, London W1K 4EH
T 020-7312 2200 E ambasciata.londra@esteri.it
W www.amblondra.esteri.it
Ambassador Extraordinary and Plenipotentiary, HE Alain Economides

BRITISH EMBASSY
Via XX Settembre 80, 00187 Rome
T (+39) (6) 4220 0001 E info@rome.mail.foc.gov.uk
W http://ukinitaly.fco.gov.uk
Ambassador Extraordinary and Plenipotentiary, HE Edward Chaplin, *apptd* 2006

BRITISH COUNCIL
Palazzo del Drago, Via Quattro Fontane 20, 00184 Rome
T (+39) (6) 478 141 W www.britishcouncil.org/italy
Director, Christine Melia

DEFENCE

The army has 320 main battle tanks, 254 armoured infantry fighting vehicles and 1,752 armoured personnel carriers. The navy has 6 submarines, 2 aircraft carriers, 4 destroyers, 12 frigates, 8 corvettes, 14 patrol and coastal vessels, 17 combat aircraft and 41 armed helicopters. The air force has 245 combat aircraft.
Military expenditure – US$30,900m (2008)
Military personnel – 293,202: army 108,300, navy 34,000, air force 42,935, carabinieri 107,967; paramilitary 142,933
Conscription duration – 10 months

ECONOMY AND TRADE

Economically, Italy is divided between a prosperous and industrially developed north and a largely agricultural and welfare-dependent south that has high unemployment levels. There is a large unofficial economy that is estimated to be worth 15 per cent of GDP, but measures to tackle this and wider structural reforms have made slow progress because of political opposition and sluggish economic performance. The growth rate has been low in recent years, and the global economic downturn pushed the economy into recession in 2008. The government's response to recession is constrained by a budget deficit that is above the 3 per cent limit set by eurozone rules and public debt of over 100 per cent of GDP. A tax amnesty in late 2009 that repatriated untaxed assets held abroad raised over US$135,000 million (£94,000 million).

Tourism is the largest industry. Other major industries include precision machinery, iron and steel, chemicals, pharmaceuticals, motor vehicles, textiles, fashion clothing, footwear, ceramics and electrical goods. The services sector contributes 72.9 per cent of GDP, industry 25 per cent and agriculture 2.1 per cent. The main trading partners are other EU states, especially Germany. Principal exports are the products of the main industries, plus food, beverages, minerals and non-ferrous metals. The main imports are industrial raw materials and energy and fuel.
GNI – US$2,121,600m; US$35,460 per capita (2008)
Annual average growth of GDP – –5 per cent (2009 est)
Inflation rate – 0.6 per cent (2009 est)
Unemployment – 7.5 per cent (2009 est)
Total external debt – US$2,328,000m (2009)
Imports – US$558,500m (2008)
Exports – US$548,800m (2008)

BALANCE OF PAYMENTS
Trade – US$6,323m deficit (2009)
Current Account – US$71,270m deficit (2009)

Trade with UK	*2008*	*2009*
Imports from UK	£9,267,775,478	£8,251,001,265
Exports to UK	£14,017,900,493	£12,324,551,575

COMMUNICATIONS

A 6,700km network of motorways *(autostrade)* covers the country but there are 487,700km of roads in total. There are 19,729km of railways; the main railway system is run by the state-owned *Ferrovia dello Stato.* In 2001, Italy and France agreed plans to build a 52km rail tunnel through the Alps as part of a high-speed rail link between Turin and Lyons; commissioning of the project is scheduled for 2012. Alitalia, Italy's state-owned international and domestic airline, went bankrupt in 2008, but was restructured and relaunched in 2009 under private ownership. There are 132 airports and airfields, the major ones being at Rome, Milan, Naples and Venice, Palermo and Catania (Sicily) and Cagliari (Sardinia). The main seaports are Naples, Genoa, Livorno, Trieste, Venice, Palermo and Catania. In 2008, there were 20 million fixed telephone lines in use, 88.6 million mobile phone subscribers and 25 million internet users.

EDUCATION AND HEALTH

Education is free of charge and compulsory between the ages of six and 16. Pupils who obtain a middle school certificate may seek admission to any senior secondary school, which may be a lyceum with a classical or scientific or artistic bias, or an institute directed at technology, trade or industry, or teacher training. Courses at the lyceums and technical institutes usually last five years and success in the final examination qualifies students for admission to university. The universities at Bologna, Modena, Parma and Padua were established in the 12th century.
Literacy rate – 98.9 per cent (2007 est)
Gross enrolment ratio (percentage of relevant age group) – primary 104 per cent; secondary 100 per cent; tertiary 67 per cent (2008 est)
Health expenditure (per capita) – US$3,136 (2007)
Hospital beds (per 1,000 people) – 3.9 (2003–8)

MEDIA

Rai is Italy's public radio and television broadcaster and competes with a number of private television broadcasters, the leading one being Mediaset, part of the media empire of prime minister Silvio Berlusconi.

News Corp's Sky Italia has a virtual monopoly on the cable subscriptions market. The press is highly regionalised, although there are five national dailies, including *La Stampa* and *La Repubblica*, but readership is generally low, with television the primary source of news.

CULTURE

Florence, the capital of Tuscany, was the 'cradle' of the Renaissance in the 14th to 16th centuries; many of the greatest names in Italian art flourished there, including Donatello (1386–1466), Botticelli (1445–1510), Michelangelo (1475–1564) and Leonardo da Vinci (1452–1519), often under the patronage of the Medici family. Significant non-Florentine artists include Titian (*c*.1490–1576), Caravaggio (1571–1610) and Modigliani (1884–1920).

Italy's wealth of composers include Monteverdi (1567–1643), whose *Orfeo* (1607) is the oldest opera still regularly performed, Vivaldi (1678–1741), Verdi (1813–1901) and Puccini (1858–1924).

Dante Alighieri (1265–1321) and Boccaccio (1313–75) were two of the earliest Europeans to write in the vernacular. The works of the poet Petrarch (1304–74), politician Niccoló Machiavelli (1469–1527) and diplomat Baldassare Castiglione (1478–1529) strongly influenced other European writers. Notable modern writers include Primo Levi (1919–1987), Italo Calvino (1923–1985), Dario Fo (*b*. 1926), winner of the Nobel prize for literature in 1997, and Umberto Eco (*b*. 1932).

Italian cinema has produced world-renowned auteurs such as Luchino Visconti (1906–76), Federico Fellini (1920–93) and Michelangelo Antonioni (1912–2007). Director Sergio Leone (1929–89) and composer Ennio Morricone (*b*. 1928) are famed for their work on spaghetti westerns.

Sport has been an integral part of Italian life since the days of the Roman Empire. Football is the most popular sport and the country's national team has won the World Cup four times. Formula 1 motor racing also attracts significant interest and Ferrari has won more world championships than any other constructor.

JAMAICA

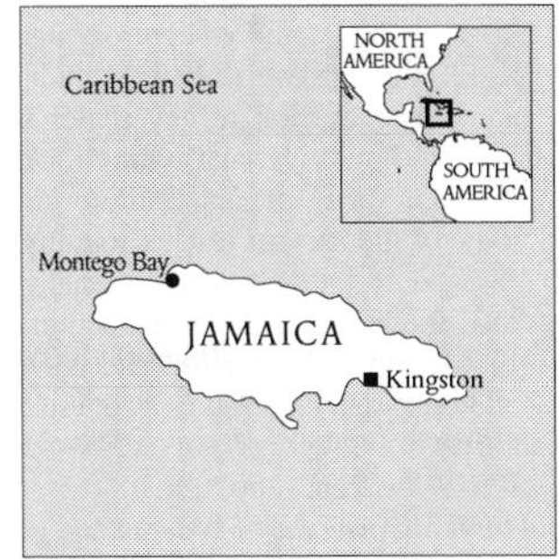

Area – 10,991 sq. km
Capital – Kingston; population, 579,642 (2009 est)
Major towns – Montego Bay, Portmore, Spanish Town
Currency – Jamaican dollar (J$) of 100 cents
Population – 2,825,928 rising at 0.76 per cent a year (2009 est)
Religion – Christian (Church of God 24 per cent, Seventh-day Adventist 11 per cent, Pentecostal 10 per cent, Baptist 7 per cent, Anglican 4 per cent, Roman Catholic 2 per cent, United Church 2 per cent, Methodist 2 per cent, Jehovah's Witness 2 per cent, Moravian 1 per cent, Brethren 1 per cent), Rastafarian 1 per cent (est)
Language – English (official), Jamaican patois
Population density – 248 per sq. km (2008)
Urban population – 53 per cent (2007 est)
Median age (years) – 23.7 (2009 est)
National anthem – 'Jamaica, Land We Love'
National day – 6 August (Independence Day)
Life expectancy (years) – 73.53 (2009 est)
Mortality rate – 6.43 (2009 est)
Birth rate – 19.68 (2009 est)
Infant mortality rate – 15.22 (2009 est)
HIV/AIDS adult prevalence – 1.4 per cent (2007 est)
Death penalty – Retained
CPI score – 3 (2009)

CLIMATE AND TERRAIN

An island in the Caribbean Sea, south of Cuba and west of Hispaniola, Jamaica is mostly mountainous and forested, with a narrow coastal plain. Elevation extremes range from 2,256m (Blue Mountain Peak) at the highest point to 0m (Caribbean Sea) at the lowest. The climate is tropical, although more temperate inland, with average temperatures ranging from lows of 19°C in January and February to highs of 32°C from June to September.

HISTORY AND POLITICS

Jamaica was visited by Columbus in 1494 and settled by the Spanish from 1509. Captured by the British in 1655, it became a crown colony in 1865. Jamaica became internally self-governing in 1959 and independent in 1962.

Post-independence politics has been dominated by the conservative Jamaican Labour Party (JLP) and social-democratic People's National Party (PNP). Relations between the two parties, often fraught, degenerated in the 1970s into violence that marred elections and political life for some years. Despite the current political stability, there is widespread lawlessness which is often connected to drug-trafficking.

In the 2007 legislative election, the PNP, which had been in power since 1989, was narrowly defeated by the JLP, which won 33 of the 60 seats. The JLP formed a government under Bruce Golding.

POLITICAL SYSTEM

Under the 1962 constitution, the head of state is Queen Elizabeth II, represented locally by a governor-general. The bicameral parliament consists of the House of Representatives, with 60 directly elected members, and the senate of 21 appointed members, 13 nominated by the prime minister and eight by the leader of the opposition; both chambers serve five-year terms. The prime minister is the leader of the majority party in the elected chamber.

Governor-General, HE Patrick Allen, *apptd* 2009

SELECTED GOVERNMENT MEMBERS *as at June 2010*

Prime Minister, Defence, Bruce Golding
Finance and Public Service, Audley Shaw
Foreign Affairs, Kenneth Baugh
National Security, Dwight Nelson

JAMAICAN HIGH COMMISSION

1–2 Prince Consort Road, London SW7 2BZ
T 020-7823 9911 E jamhigh@jhcuk.com W http://jhcuk.org
High Commissioner, HE Anthony Johnson, *apptd* 2010

BRITISH HIGH COMMISSION
PO Box 575, 28 Trafalgar Road, Kingston 10
T (+1) (876) 510 0700 E bhc.kingston@fco.gov.uk
W http://ukinjamaica.fco.gov.uk
High Commissioner, HE Howard Drake, *apptd* 2010

BRITISH COUNCIL
c/o British High Commission
T (+1) (876) 929 6915 W www.britishcouncil.org/jamaica
Manager, Pauline Samuels

DEFENCE

The army has 4 armoured personnel carriers. The coastguard has 18 patrol and coastal combatant vessels at 3 bases.

Military budget – US$90m (2009 est)
Military personnel – 2,830: army 2,500, coastguard 190, air force 140

ECONOMY AND TRADE

The economy is weak owing to high interest rates, increased foreign competition, unemployment, growing internal and external debt, and hurricane damage in 2004 and 2007. It depends on foreign aid and remittances from expatriates; remittances were worth nearly 20 per cent of GDP but have declined since the global downturn began. This hit the economy badly, and IMF support was needed in 2010. Economic growth is hindered by the high level of violent crime and corruption. Tourism, the main foreign exchange earner, remains strong, though discounted prices offered to maintain visitor numbers during the downturn have hurt the sector's profitability.

The economy is dominated by the service sector, which makes up 63.9 per cent of GDP; industry accounts for 30.1 per cent, and agriculture for 6 per cent. Industries include alumina and bauxite extraction (the main industry after tourism), processing of agricultural produce and light manufacturing.

The main trading partners are the USA, Trinidad and Tobago, Canada, Venezuela and the EU. Principal exports are alumina, bauxite, sugar, bananas, rum, coffee, yams, beverages, chemicals and clothing. The main imports are food, consumer goods, industrial supplies, fuel, and parts and accessories for capital goods.

GNI – US$12,900m; US$4,800 per capita (2008)
Annual average growth of GDP – –4 per cent (2009 est)
Inflation rate – 8.6 per cent (2009 est)
Population below poverty line – 14.8 per cent (2003 est)
Unemployment – 14.5 per cent (2009 est)
Total external debt – US$11,550m (2009 est)
Imports – US$7,700m (2008)
Exports – US$2,500m (2008)

BALANCE OF PAYMENTS
Trade – US$3,111m deficit (2009)
Current Account – US$2,534m deficit (2008)

Trade with UK	*2008*	*2009*
Imports from UK	£53,668,970	£46,186,968
Exports to UK	£124,077,478	£93,090,564

COMMUNICATIONS

There are several harbours, Kingston being the main seaport. The principal airports are at Kingston and Montego Bay. The island has 21,600km of roads, of which 15,900km are surfaced. The rail network is no longer in use. The number of fixed telephone lines has declined as mobile phone usage has grown; mobile phone density was 110 per cent by 2008.

EDUCATION AND HEALTH

In 2010 the Inter-American Development Bank provided US$45m in funding to enable the government to make improvements to the education system and expand compulsory schooling from age 16 to 18.

Literacy rate – 86.0 per cent (2007 est)
Gross enrolment ratio (percentage of relevant age group) – primary 90 per cent; secondary 90 per cent (2008 est)
Health expenditure (per capita) – US$224 (2007)
Hospital beds (per 1,000 people) – 1.7 (2003–8)

MEDIA

The state broadcaster was privatised in 1997 and now operates as Television Jamaica Ltd. It competes with a commercial and a religious broadcaster, and several local cable channels. There are a large number of commercial radio stations and four privately owned newspapers. The press operates independently and freely criticises the establishment.

CULTURE

Jamaica is widely regarded as the birthplace of reggae, and is also the home of ska, dub and dancehall. Significant musicians include reggae pioneer Bob Marley (1945–81), Jimmy Cliff (*b.* 1948) and Desmond Dekker (1941–2006). Closely connected to reggae is the Rastafari religious movement, which originated in the 1930s among descendants of slaves brought from Africa.

Major literary figures include the poets Claude McKay (1890–1948), a leading voice of the Harlem Renaissance, and Louis Simpson (*b.* 1923), who won the Pulitzer prize in 1964 after emigrating to the USA.

JAPAN

Nihon-koku/Nippon-koku – Japan

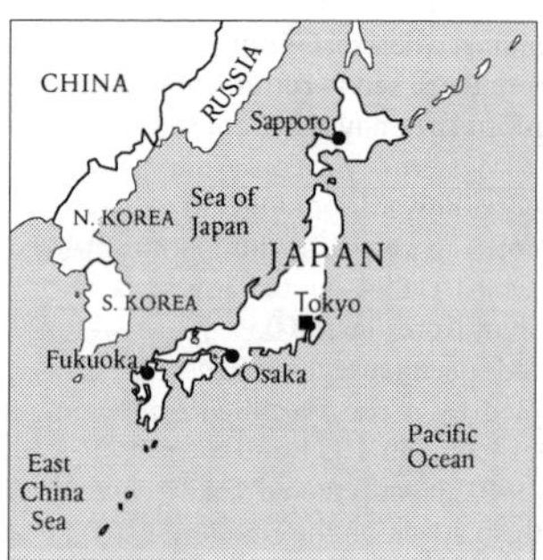

Area – 377,915 sq. km
Capital – Tokyo; population, 36,506,600 (2009 est)
Major cities – Fukuoka, Hiroshima, Kawasaki, Kobe, Kyoto (the ancient capital), Nagoya, Osaka, Saitama, Sapporo, Yokohama
Currency – Yen of 100 sen
Population – 127,078,679 falling at 0.19 per cent a year (2009 est)
Religion – Shinto 84 per cent, Buddhist 70 per cent, Christian 2 per cent (est); much of the population adheres to more than one religion, most commonly combining Shinto and Buddhist beliefs
Language – Japanese (official)
Population density – 350 per sq. km (2008)
Urban population – 66 per cent (2007 est)
Median age (years) – 44.2 (2009 est)

National anthem – 'Kimi ga Yo' ['May Your Reign Last Forever']
National day – 23 December (Birthday of Emperor Akihito)
Life expectancy (years) – 82.12 (2009 est)
Mortality rate – 9.54 (2009 est)
Birth rate – 7.64 (2009 est)
Infant mortality rate – 2.79 (2009 est)
Death penalty – Retained
CPI score – 7.7 (2009)

CLIMATE AND TERRAIN

Japan consists of four large islands: Honshu (or Mainland), Shikoku, Kyushu and Hokkaido, and many smaller islands. Typically, the islands have coastal plains and wooded, mountainous interiors. The mountains running across the mainland from the Sea of Japan to the Pacific Ocean include a number of volcanoes, mainly extinct or dormant. Elevation extremes range from 3,776m (Mt Fuji) at the highest point to –4m (Hachiro-gata) at the lowest. The climate varies from temperate in the north to tropical in the south. Average temperatures in Tokyo range from 4°C in January to 27°C in August.

The islands are located at the intersection of three tectonic plates and are prone to seismic activity; 20 per cent of the world's earthquakes occur in this area.

HISTORY AND POLITICS

A centralised state had been established in what is now Japan by the fifth century AD. In the 12th century, the country was plunged into centuries of rivalry and conflict between different *samurai* (feudal warrior class) families, who were subdued and ruled by successive dynasties of *shoguns* (military overlords) nominally appointed by the emperor. Imperial control was re-established in 1868 after long periods of civil warfare.

Contact with the West was severely restricted until the 19th century, when the visit of a US naval officer, Commodore Perry, led to the Japanese opening their ports to foreign trade. Industrialisation followed and Japan adopted a Western-style constitution in 1889. Policies became more outward-looking and, in the case of foreign policy, more aggressive, with successful wars against imperial China (1894–5) and Russia (1904–5), and the annexation of Korea in 1910.

A period of intense nationalism in the 1920s was accompanied by a rise in militarism, leading to Japan's invasion of China in 1931 and a pact with Germany and Italy in 1940. Japan entered the Second World War in 1941 with an attack on the US naval base at Pearl Harbor, Hawaii, and occupied British, French and Dutch colonial possessions in south-east Asia in 1941–2. Pushed back by Allied forces in 1943–5, Japan surrendered after atomic bombs were dropped on Hiroshima and Nagasaki in 1945. Political, social and economic reforms were introduced during the post-war Allied occupation; Japan's independence was restored in 1952.

The Liberal Democrat Party (LDP) has dominated post-war politics, holding power continuously from 1955 to 1993, and then – usually as the main party in coalition governments – from 1994 to 2009. In 2007, it lost control of the upper house of the legislature to the Democratic Party of Japan (DPJ), and the DPJ won an overwhelming majority of seats in elections to the lower house of the legislature in August 2009. The DPJ formed a coalition government with two minor parties under DPJ leader Yukio Hatoyama. Hatoyama resigned in June 2010 and was replaced as party leader and prime minister by Naoto Kan. The DPJ lost its majority in the upper house in an election in July 2010.

POLITICAL SYSTEM

The 1947 constitution established Japan as a constitutional monarchy with a hereditary emperor as head of state. The bicameral Diet comprises the House of Representatives (the lower house) and the House of Councillors. The House of Representatives has 480 members directly elected for a four-year term, including 180 by proportional representation. The House of Councillors has 242 members, including 96 elected by proportional representation, who serve six-year terms, with half elected every three years; unlike the lower house it cannot be dissolved by the prime minister. The prime minister is formally elected by the House of Representatives and appoints the cabinet.

HEAD OF STATE

HIM The Emperor of Japan, Akihito, *born* 23 December 1933, *succeeded* 8 January 1989, *enthroned* 12 November 1990
Heir, HRH Crown Prince Naruhito Hironomiya, *born* 23 February 1960

SELECTED GOVERNMENT MEMBERS *as at June 2010*

Prime Minister, Naoto Kan
Finance, Yoshihiko Noda
Foreign Affairs, Katsuya Okada
Defence, Toshimi Kitazawa
Internal Affairs, Kazuhiro Haraguchi

EMBASSY OF JAPAN

101–104 Piccadilly, London W1J 7JT
T 020-7465 6500 E info@ld.mofa.go.jp
W www.uk.emb-japan.go.jp
Ambassador Extraordinary and Plenipotentiary, HE Shin Ebihara, *apptd* 2008

BRITISH EMBASSY

No. 1 Ichiban-cho, Chiyoda-ku, Tokyo 102–8381
T (+81) (3) 5211 1100 E embassy.tokyo@fco.gov.uk
W http://ukinjapan.fco.gov.uk
Ambassador Extraordinary and Plenipotentiary, HE David Warren, *apptd* 2008

BRITISH COUNCIL

1–2 Kagurazaka, Shinjuku-ku, Tokyo 162–0825
T (+81) (3) 3235 8031 W www.britishcouncil.org/japan
Director, Jason James

DEFENCE

The constitution prohibits the maintenance of armed forces, although internal security forces were created in the 1950s and their mission was extended in 1954 to include the defence of Japan against aggression. In the 1990s, legislation was passed permitting limited participation by the armed forces in UN peacekeeping missions and allowing them to enter foreign conflicts in order to rescue Japanese nationals. A revision to the USA–Japan defence cooperation guidelines agreed in 1997 permits Japan to play a supporting role in US military operations in areas surrounding Japan; Japanese troops were also deployed in Iraq to assist with post-war reconstruction between 2003 and 2006.

The Ground Self-Defence Force (GSDF) has 880 main battle tanks, 780 armoured personnel carriers, 70 armoured infantry fighting vehicles, 10 aircraft and 200

armed helicopters. The Maritime Self-Defence Force (MSDF) has 16 submarines, 44 destroyers, 8 frigates, 7 patrol and coastal vessels, 80 combat aircraft and 91 armed helicopters at five bases. The Air Self-Defence Force (ASDF) has 260 combat aircraft.
Military budget – US$52,600m (2009)
Military personnel – 230,300: GSDF 138,400, MSDF 42,400, ASDF 34,760, central staff 2,200; paramilitary 12,250

ECONOMY AND TRADE

Japan has the third-largest economy in the world after the USA and China. Its rapid post-war economic growth, based largely on car and consumer electronics manufacturing, experienced a marked contraction from 1990. Exacerbated by the 1997 Asian economic crisis, the recession lasted 14 years, causing unprecedented levels of bankruptcy, unemployment and homelessness and a huge public debt (estimated at 192 per cent of GDP in 2009). Reforms introduced from 2001, particularly to the corporate and public sectors, improved economic growth from 2002 to 2007, but the economy went into recession again in 2008 owing to the global downturn. Government stimulus packages and an increase in global demand spurred the start of a recovery in late 2009.

High-technology industries remain the mainstay of the economy, producing vehicles, electronic equipment, machine tools, steel and other metals, ships, chemicals, textiles and processed food. Financial services is also a major sector, supplying a global market. Agriculture is constrained by the mountainous terrain but intensive cultivation produces high yields, and there is a large fishing industry. The service sector contributes 75.4 per cent of GDP, industry 23.1 per cent and agriculture 1.6 per cent.

The main trading partners are China, the USA, other Pacific Rim countries and the Gulf states. Principal exports include transport equipment, motor vehicles, semiconductors, electrical machinery and chemicals. The main imports are machinery and equipment, fuels, foodstuffs, chemicals, textiles and raw materials.
GNI – US$4,869,100m; US$38,130 per capita (2008)
Annual average growth of GDP – −5.7 per cent (2009 est)
Inflation rate – −1.3 per cent (2009 est)
Unemployment – 5.6 per cent (2009 est)
Total external debt – US$2,132,000m (2009)
Imports – US$762,600m (2008)
Exports – US$786,400m (2008)

BALANCE OF PAYMENTS
Trade – US$30,170m surplus (2009)
Current Account – US$141,656m surplus (2009)

Trade with UK	*2008*	*2009*
Imports from UK	£3,684,629,066	£3,372,530,776
Exports to UK	£8,106,131,485	£7,247,201,664

COMMUNICATIONS

Japan has a large merchant fleet, with 683 ships of over 1,000 tonnes in 2008. The main seaports are Tokyo, Osaka, Nagoya, Yokohama, Kobe and Kawasaki. There are 176 airports and airfields; the principal airports include Haneda (Tokyo), Narita, Kansai and Chubu. There are 26,400km of railway track and 1,203,700km of roads. *Shinkansen* (bullet train) tracks are currently being expanded. The Seikan rail tunnel and the Seto Ohashi rail bridge link the four major islands. In 2008, there were 47.6 million fixed telephone lines in use, 110.3 million mobile phone subscribers and 90.9 million internet users.

EDUCATION AND HEALTH

Elementary education is free of charge, and compulsory at elementary level (six-year course) and lower secondary (three-year course).
Gross enrolment ratio (percentage of relevant age group) – primary 102 per cent; secondary 101 per cent; tertiary 58 per cent (2008 est)
Health expenditure (per capita) – US$2,751 (2007)
Hospital beds (per 1,000 people) – 14.0 (2003–8)

MEDIA

A public broadcaster, NHK, provides radio and television services, competing with a number of national radio and terrestrial television companies, and a growing number of satellite and cable providers. Satellite and cable television is widespread and digital broadcasting is expanding. Around 80 per cent of the population reads a daily newspaper, creating huge markets for publications such as *Asahi Shimbun, Nikkei Net* and the English language title *The Japan Times*.

CULTURE

The popularity of technology in Japan has not obliterated traditional culture, instead creating a mixture of the old and new. Traditional woodblock printing and imported Western cartoons have been combined into Manga, a form of comic book illustration. Animated Manga, known as 'anime', are broadcast on television, included in computer games and have spawned a number of internationally successful films, most notably *Spirited Away* (2002) directed by Hayao Miyazaki (*b.* 1941), the first anime film to win an Academy Award. Akira Kurosawa (1910–98), awarded an Oscar for Lifetime Achievement, directed *Rashomon* (1950), *Seven Samurai* (1954) and many other films.

Japan has responded with enthusiasm to imported sports such as football and baseball. The country co-hosted the 2002 football World Cup with South Korea, while the national baseball league has existed since 1936. However, sumo remains the quintessential Japanese sport. Its roots are lost, but references to its earlier name, Sumai, exist in texts from the eighth century. The sport is immersed in ceremony, which has largely survived despite its huge commercial success.

JORDAN

Al-Mamlakah al-Urduniyah al-Hashimiyah – Hashemite Kingdom of Jordan

Area – 89, 342 sq. km
Capital – Amman; population, 1,087,910 (2009 est)
Major cities – Al Aqaba, Az Zarqa, Irbid
Currency – Jordanian dinar (JD) of 10 dirhams
Population – 6,342,948 rising at 2.26 per cent a year (2009 est); Arab (98 per cent), Circassian (1 per cent), Armenian (1 per cent) (est)
Religion – Muslim (Sunni 92 per cent), Christian denominations 2 per cent (est)
Language – Arabic (official), English
Population density – 67 per sq. km (2008)
Urban population – 78 per cent (2007 est)
Median age (years) – 24.3 (2009 est)
National anthem – 'As-Salam al-Malaki al-Urdoni' ['Long Live the King']
National day – 25 May (Independence Day)
Life expectancy (years) – 78.87 (2009 est)
Mortality rate – 2.75 (2009 est)
Birth rate – 19.55 (2009 est)
Infant mortality rate – 14.97 (2009 est)
Death penalty – Retained
CPI score – 5 (2009)

CLIMATE AND TERRAIN

Most of the country is a desert plateau, with the valley of the River Jordan and the Dead Sea in the west marking the border with Israel. The Jordan Valley and its extension from the Dead Sea to the Gulf of Aqaba are part of the Great Rift Valley in Africa. The only hills lie in the south, along the edge of the Great Rift Valley, although there is a hilly outcrop in the centre of the desert. Elevation extremes range from 1,734m (Jabal Ram) at the highest point to −408m (Dead Sea) at the lowest. The climate is arid, but with a rainy season in the west from November to April. Summers are very hot, and temperatures in the Jordan Valley have been known to reach 49°C. Winters can be cold, with frost and snow on the plateau.

HISTORY AND POLITICS

The area was part of the Roman Empire and subsequently of the Byzantine Empire. It came under Arab control in the seventh century, and in the 16th century became part of the Ottoman Empire until its collapse in 1918. The emirate of Transjordan was created in 1921 and administered by the British under a League of Nations mandate. When the mandate ended in 1946, Transjordan became independent as the Hashemite Kingdom of Jordan.

During the first Arab–Israeli War of 1948, Jordan seized the West Bank and part of Jerusalem, but these areas were recaptured by Israel in the Six Day War of 1967, resulting in an influx of Palestinian refugees into Jordan; the descendants of these refugees now constitute the majority of the Jordanian population. Jordan attempted to expel Palestinian guerrillas from the West Bank in 1970–1, causing a brief civil war. Jordan recognised the Palestinian Liberation Organisation (PLO) as the sole representative of the Palestinian people in the Occupied Territories in 1974, but severed links with the PLO and expelled its personnel in 1986. Jordan formally renounced sovereignty over the West Bank and East Jerusalem in 1999, having signed a peace agreement with Israel in 1994.

The economy declined in the 1980s and internal stability became increasingly precarious. Riots in 1989 forced the government to initiate a process of political, social and economic reform. The country's first free elections under universal suffrage took place in 1989, and a ban on political parties was lifted in 1992. Real power, however, effectively rests with the king, with parliament amending or approving legislation that originates with the monarch and his government. Although support for Islamist parties has grown, the system favours people's tribal loyalties over their religious affiliation; consequently there has been little constitutionally expressed opposition to the peace treaty with Israel or the close ties with the USA, both generally unpopular.

In the 2007 legislative election, over 90 per cent of the legislative seats were won by tribal leaders and other pro-government candidates; the Islamist share of the vote dropped to 5.5 per cent. The legislature was dissolved halfway through its term in November 2009; a legislative election was expected in November 2010, following the introduction of electoral reforms.

POLITICAL SYSTEM

The 1952 constitution provides for a constitutional monarchy with a hereditary king as head of state. The bicameral National Assembly comprises a House of Deputies and a senate or House of Notables. Under the new election law unveiled in May 2010, the House of Deputies has 120 members (raised from 110 members), directly elected for a four-year term; 12 seats (formerly six seats) are now reserved for women. The senate has 55 members, who are appointed by the king for a four-year term. The king appoints the prime minister, who chooses the council of ministers.

HEAD OF STATE

HM The King of Jordan, Abdullah II, *born* 30 January 1962, *succeeded* 7 February 1999
Crown Prince, Hamzeh ibn al-Hussein, *born* 29 March 1982

SELECTED GOVERNMENT MEMBERS *as at June 2010*

Prime Minister, Defence, Samir Rifai
Deputy Prime Ministers, Rajai Muasher; Nayif al-Qadi *(Interior)*
Finance, Mohammad Abu Hammour
Foreign Affairs, Nasir Judah

EMBASSY OF THE HASHEMITE KINGDOM OF JORDAN

6 Upper Phillimore Gardens, London W8 7HA
T 020-7937 3685 **E** london@fm.gov.jo
W www.jordanembassyuk.org
Ambassador Extraordinary and Plenipotentiary, HE Dr Alia Hatoug-Bouran, *apptd* 2006

BRITISH EMBASSY

PO Box 87, Abdoun, Amman 11118
T (+962) (6) 592 3100 **E** info@britain.org.jo
W http://ukinjordan.fco.gov.uk
Ambassador Extraordinary and Plenipotentiary, HE James Watt, *apptd* 2006

BRITISH COUNCIL

PO Box 634, Rainbow Street, First Circle, Jebel Amman, Amman 11118
T (+962) (6) 460 3420 **W** www.britishcouncil.org/jordan
Director, Marc Jessel

DEFENCE

The army has 1,182 main battle tanks, 1,391 armoured personnel carriers and 303 armoured infantry fighting vehicles. The navy has 13 patrol and coastal vessels at its base at Aqaba. The air force has 102 combat aircraft and 25 armed helicopters.

Military budget – US$2,310m (2009)
Military personnel – 100,500: army 88,000, navy 500, air force 12,000; paramilitary 10,000

ECONOMY AND TRADE

Jordan's economic development has been hindered by its lack of natural resources, influxes of refugees from the West Bank in 1967 and Iraq since 2003, and the impact of conflict on its trade with Israel and Iraq. High levels of poverty, unemployment and government debt are long-term problems. Since 1999, King Abdullah has implemented economic reforms, and these measures have increased productivity and exports, begun to attract foreign direct investment, and won agreement to debt rescheduling from international donors. Even so, the economy is still dependent on foreign aid, of which the USA is the largest provider, and a drop in this aid in 2009 exacerbated the effects of the global downturn on the already depressed economy.

Jordan has no oil reserves of its own and few water resources. Since 2003, several Gulf states have temporarily extended aid to Jordan in order to compensate for the loss of its usual oil supplies from Iraq. The country imports natural gas as well as oil but aims to become a net exporter of electricity via its national grid's links with those of Syria and Egypt. It is currently considering nuclear power generation to ensure an adequate future supply. Jordan has also begun joint ventures with Israel and Syria to guarantee water supplies.

The service sector, including tourism, accounts for 66.5 per cent of GDP. Industry generates 29.9 per cent, from activities that include garment manufacturing, fertilisers, potash and phosphate mining, pharmaceuticals, oil refining, cement, inorganic chemicals and light manufacturing. Agriculture, which accounts for 3.7 per cent of GDP, produces citrus and stone fruits, tomatoes, cucumbers, olives, sheep, poultry and dairy products.

The main export markets are India, Iraq and the USA, and the main sources of imports are Saudi Arabia, China and Germany. Principal exports are clothing, fertilisers, potash, phosphates, vegetables and pharmaceuticals. The main imports are crude oil, machinery, transport equipment, iron and cereals.

GNI – US$20,500m; US$3,470 per capita (2008)
Annual average growth of GDP – 3.1 per cent (2009 est)
Inflation rate – 1.7 per cent (2009 est)
Unemployment – 13.5 per cent (2009 est)
Total external debt – US$6,715m (2009 est)
Imports – US$16,800m (2008)
Exports – US$7,800m (2008)

BALANCE OF PAYMENTS
Trade – US$7,848m deficit (2009)
Current Account – US$1,276m deficit (2009)

Trade with UK	*2008*	*2009*
Imports from UK	£210,138,839	£245,401,706
Exports to UK	£20,931,799	£15,156,160

COMMUNICATIONS

Jordan has 8,000km of roads; Amman is linked to Jordan's seaport at Aqaba, the Saudi Arabian port of Jeddah and the Syrian and Iraqi capitals by roads which are of considerable importance in the overland trade of the Middle East. The 507km of rail track includes the former Hejaz Railway, used mainly for freight between Amman and Damascus, and the railway carrying phosphate rock from the mines of al-Hasa and al-Abiad to Aqaba. There are 17 airports and airfields; the principal airports are at Amman and Aqaba. The telephone system is modern and growing, but fixed-line subscriptions are declining as mobile phone use grows. Mobile phone subscribers numbered 5.9 million in 2010, and there were 503,000 fixed lines in use and 1.5 million internet users in 2008.

EDUCATION AND HEALTH

Literacy rate – 91.1 per cent (2007 est)
Gross enrolment ratio (percentage of relevant age group) – primary 96 per cent; secondary 86 per cent; tertiary 38 per cent (2008 est)
Health expenditure (per capita) – US$248 (2007; includes contributions from the UN Relief and Works Agency for Palestinian refugees)
Hospital beds (per 1,000 people) – 1.8 (2003–8)

MEDIA

There is strict media censorship, and scrutiny extends to internet usage. Jordan Radio and Television, the state-run broadcaster, operates three terrestrial television channels and a satellite channel as well as radio services in Arabic, English and French. A number of private radio stations also operate.

KAZAKHSTAN

Qazaqstan Respublikasy – Republic of Kazakhstan

Area – 2,724,900 sq. km
Capital – Astana (previously known as Akmola and Tselinograd); population, 649,818 (2009 est)
Major cities – Almaty (the former capital), Oskemen, Pavlodar, Qaraghandy, Semey, Shymkent, Taraz
Currency – Tenge of 100 tiyn
Population – 15,399,437 rising at 0.39 per cent a year (2009 est); Kazakh (53.4 per cent), Russian (30 per cent), Ukrainian (3.7 per cent), Uzbek (2.5 per cent), German (2.4 per cent), Tatar (1.7 per cent), Uygur (1.4 per cent). The Russian population is concentrated in the north of the country, where it forms a significant majority, and in Almaty
Religion – Muslim 65 per cent (predominantly Sunni), Christian 31 per cent (mostly Russian Orthodox) (est)
Language – Kazakh, Russian (both official)
Population density – 6 per sq. km (2008)
Urban population – 58 per cent (2007 est)
Median age (years) – 29.6 (2009 est)
National anthem – 'Menin Qazaqstanym' ['My Kazakhstan']
National day – 16 December (Independence Day)
Life expectancy (years) – 67.87 (2009 est)

Mortality rate – 9.39 (2009 est)
Birth rate – 16.6 (2009 est)
Infant mortality rate – 25.73 (2009 est)
Death penalty – Retained for certain crimes
CPI score – 2.7 (2009)
Gross enrolment ratio (percentage of relevant age group) – primary 109 per cent; secondary 95 per cent; tertiary 41 per cent (2009 est)
Literacy rate – 99.6 per cent (2007 est)
Health expenditure (per capita) – US$253 (2007)
Hospital beds (per 1,000 people) – 7.7 (2003–8)

CLIMATE AND TERRAIN

Landlocked Kazakhstan stretches from the basin of the river Volga and the Caspian Sea in the west to the Altai and Tien Shan mountains in the east. The terrain consists of arid steppes and semi-deserts, flat in the west, hilly in the east and mountainous in the south-east. Elevation extremes range from 6,995m (Khan Tangiri Shyngy) at the highest point to −132m (Vpadina Kaundy) at the lowest. The west of the country lies on the shores of the Caspian Sea, and it contains the northern part of the Aral Sea in the south-west, and Lake Balkhash and Lake Zaysan in the east. The climate is continental, and while arid in much of the country, it can be Siberian in the north. Average yearly temperatures in Astana range from −16°C in January to 22°C in July.

HISTORY AND POLITICS

Kazakhstan was inhabited by nomadic tribes before being invaded by Genghis Khan and incorporated into his empire in 1218. After this empire disintegrated, feudal towns emerged based on large oases and the nomadic tribes formed federations led by khans. The towns affiliated in the late 15th century and established a Kazakh state which engaged in almost continuous warfare with the marauding khanates on its southern border. After turning to Russia for protection in the 1730s, the Kazakh khanates were formally incorporated into the Russian Empire in the early 19th century.

The 1917 Bolshevik revolution in Russia was followed by civil war in Kazakhstan, which became an autonomous republic within the USSR in 1920 and a full union republic in 1936. Kazakhstan suffered severely under Stalin's policies of agricultural collectivisation and 'sedentarisation', which forced nomadic tribes to become farmers; around 1.5 million people died of famine or disease. Later Soviet rule saw the country used as a testing ground for nuclear weapons.

Growing nationalism in the 1980s and a reformist leader led to economic and cultural reforms in 1989 and a declaration of sovereignty in 1990. Kazakhstan declared its independence in December 1991, and became a founding member of the Commonwealth of Independent States. It entered an economic, social and military union with Kyrgyzstan and Uzbekistan in 1994, and an economic and military pact with Russia in 1995, when it achieved nuclear-free status. It agreed in 2009 to form a customs union with Belarus and Russia from July 2010. Despite economic reforms and considerable foreign investment since the 1990s, the country has serious economic, social and environmental problems, while its international standing is tarnished by political illiberalism and corruption.

Nursultan Nazarbayev, the reformist communist leader of 1989, became head of state in 1990 and was re-elected in 1991, 1999 and 2005; the 2005 election, in which he received over 90 per cent of the vote, was considered seriously flawed by the Organisation for Security and Cooperation in Europe (OSCE). A 2007 constitutional reform allows him to serve for an unlimited number of terms. He has been criticised for concentrating power in the presidency and suppressing political and media freedom.

In 2006, three pro-government parties merged with Nazarbayev's Fatherland Republican Party (Otan), which subsequently changed its name to Nur-Otan. Nur-Otan won every seat in the lower legislative chamber in the 2007 legislative elections, which observers said were better conducted than the 2004 elections but still did not meet international standards of fairness.

POLITICAL SYSTEM

The 1995 constitution was amended in 1998 to extend the presidential term from five to seven years, in 2000 to give President Nazarbayev special powers for life, and in 2007 to reduce the presidential term to five years, renewable only once, but exempting Nazarbayev from this restriction. The president is directly elected. The bicameral *Parlament* is composed of the assembly *(Majlis)* and the senate. The assembly has 107 members, 98 directly elected on a single constituency basis and nine seats reserved for ethnic groups; all serve a five-year term. The senate has 47 members, of whom 32 are indirectly elected and 15 are appointed for a six-year term, with half elected every three years. The president appoints the prime minister and other senior ministers.

HEAD OF STATE

President, Nursultan Nazarbayev, *elected* 1 December 1991, *confirmed in office by referendum* 1995, *re-elected* 1999, 2005

SELECTED GOVERNMENT MEMBERS *as at June 2010*

Prime Minister, Karim Masimov
First Deputy Prime Minister, Umirzak Shukeev
Deputy Prime Ministers, Yerbol Orynbayev; Serik Akhmetov; Aset Isekeshev
Defence, Adilbek Dzhaksybekov
Foreign Affairs, Kanat Saudabayev
Internal Affairs, Serik Baimaganbetov
Finance, Bolat Zhamishev

EMBASSY OF THE REPUBLIC OF KAZAKHSTAN

33 Thurloe Square, London SW7 2SD
T 020-7581 4646 E london@kazembassy.org.uk
W www.kazembassy.org.uk
Ambassador Extraordinary and Plenipotentiary, HE Kairat Abusseitov, *apptd* 2008

BRITISH EMBASSY

6th Floor, Renco Building, 62 Kosmonavtov Street, Astana 010000
T (+7) (317) 255 6200 E britishembassyastana@gmail.com
W http://ukinkz.fco.gov.uk
Ambassador Extraordinary and Plenipotentiary, HE David Moran, *apptd* 2009

BRITISH COUNCIL

13 Republic Square, Almaty 050013
T (+7) (327) 272 0111 W www.britishcouncil.org/kazakhstan
Director, Lena Milosevic

DEFENCE

The CIS mutual defence treaty of 1993, to which Kazakhstan is a signatory, retains a common air defence force, and Kazakh forces also take part in the CIS peacekeeping force on the Tajikistan–Afghanistan border. An agreement signed with Russia in 1995 provides for eventual reunification of the two states' armed forces. By 1996, all nuclear warheads had been returned to Russia, although Kazakhstan retained 48 SS-18 intercontinental ballistic missiles. Kazakhstan participates in the NATO partnership for peace programme.

The army has 980 main battle tanks, 370 armoured personnel carriers and 1,520 armoured infantry fighting vehicles. The navy has 14 patrol and coastal combatant vessels. The Caspian Sea Flotilla, which Kazakhstan shares with Russia and Turkmenistan, operates under Russian command. The air force has 162 combat aircraft and over 40 armed helicopters.

Military budget – US$1,330m (2009 est)
Military personnel – 49,000: army 30,000, navy 3,000, air force 12,000, MoD 4,000; paramilitary 31,500
Conscription duration – 24 months

ECONOMY AND TRADE

Economic reforms and privatisation in the 1990s enabled GDP to grow by at least 8 per cent a year from 2002 to 2007, although lower commodity prices and banking sector problems caused the economy to contract in 2008–9. Growth has largely been achieved through exploitation of vast oil and natural gas reserves, particularly since the opening of export pipelines to Black Sea ports (2001) and China (2005), and its use of the Azerbaijan–Turkey pipeline (2008); it is also part of a four-country consortium developing another pipeline to China. As a result of the boom, the government has eliminated the budget deficit, but it is also trying to stimulate growth in other industries to reduce dependency on oil. A fund was set up in 2001 to manage state finances and protect the economy from volatile oil prices. Despite these revenues, poverty remains widespread.

Other mineral resources are considerable and there is a significant mining industry exploiting coal, iron ore, manganese, chrome, lead, zinc, copper, titanium, bauxite, silver, gold and phosphate deposits. A large and well-developed agricultural industry produces grain, wool, cotton and livestock as cash crops. The main industries are mineral extraction and processing and machine-building, especially agricultural machinery and electric motors. Services contribute 55.5 per cent of GDP, industry 38.1 per cent and agriculture 6.4 per cent, although agriculture employs over 30 per cent of the workforce.

The main trading partners are Russia, China, Germany, other EU states and Ukraine. Principal exports are oil and oil products (59 per cent), ferrous metals, chemicals, machinery, grain, wool, meat and coal. The main imports are machinery and equipment, metal products and foodstuffs.

GNI – US$96,600m; US$6,160 per capita (2008)
Annual average growth of GDP – –1.8 per cent (2009 est)
Inflation rate – 7.3 per cent (2009 est)
Population below poverty line – 13.8 per cent (2007 est)
Unemployment – 7.5 per cent (2009 est)
Total external debt – US$93,210m (2009)
Imports – US$39,000m (2008)
Exports – US$77,200m (2008)

BALANCE OF PAYMENTS
Trade – US$14,030m surplus (2009)
Current Account – US$6,279m surplus (2008)

Trade with UK	*2008*	*2009*
Imports from UK	£209,418,900	£260,089,846
Exports to UK	£111,930,588	£202,700,953

COMMUNICATIONS

Because of Kazakhstan's size, long-distance internal travel is usually by air, and the country has 99 airports and airfields; the principal airports are at Astana, Almaty and Atyrau. There are extensive rail and road networks (15,000km of railways and 93,600km of roads), although the roads are concentrated in the more populous east. There are important ports on the Caspian and Aral seas which permit international trade (albeit significantly reduced on the drained and diminished Aral sea), while the Syr Darya and Irtysh rivers provide 4,000km of navigable waterways.

The telephone system is antiquated. Fixed-line services are being extended and density is now around 20 per 100 people. Mobile phone services have grown rapidly and were about 100 per 100 people by 2008. There were 2.3 million internet users in 2008.

MEDIA

There are several public television broadcasters, as well as a few private stations. Both sectors provide some Russian-language programmes. There is a public radio broadcaster as well as private stations, and government-backed and private-sector newspapers published in Kazakh and Russian. Although freedom of the press is protected by the constitution, opposition and privately owned media are subject to censorship and harassment; insulting the president or government officials is a criminal offence.

KENYA

Jamhuri ya Kenya – Republic of Kenya

Area – 580,367 sq. km
Capital – Nairobi; population, 3,375,460 (2009 est)
Major cities – Eldoret, Kisumu, Mombasa, Nakuru
Currency – Kenyan shilling (Ksh) of 100 cents
Population – 39,002,772 rising at 2.69 per cent a year (2009 est); Kikuyu (22 per cent), Luhya (14 per cent), Luo (13 per cent), Kalenjin (12 per cent), Mukamba (11 per cent), Kisii (6 per cent), Ameru (6 per cent) (est)
Religion – Christian 80 per cent (of which Protestant 58 per cent, Roman Catholic 42 per cent), Muslim 10 per cent (est). Most of the remainder follow traditional indigenous religions
Language – English, Kiswahili (both official), indigenous languages

Population density – 68 per sq. km (2008)
Urban population – 21 per cent (2007 est)
Median age (years) – 18.7 (2009 est)
National anthem – 'Ee Mungu Nguvu Yetu' ['Oh God of All Creation']
National day – 12 December (Independence Day)
Life expectancy (years) – 57.86 (2009 est)
Mortality rate – 9.72 (2009 est)
Birth rate – 36.64 (2009 est)
Infant mortality rate – 54.7 (2009 est)
HIV/AIDS adult prevalence – 6.1 per cent (2005 est)
Death penalty – Retained (not used since 1987)
CPI score – 2.2 (2009)

CLIMATE AND TERRAIN

The coastal plain and semi-desert plains in the east rise to mountainous highlands in the centre and west that are divided by the Great Rift Valley. Elevation extremes range from 5,199m (Mt Kenya) at the highest point to 0m (Indian Ocean) at the lowest. The country includes part of Lake Victoria in the south-west and most of Lake Turkana (Rudolph) in the north. An equatorial country, the climate is tropical on the coast and arid in the interior, tempered by altitude; average temperatures in Nairobi reach highs of 26°C in February and lows of 11°C between July and September.

HISTORY AND POLITICS

Fossils of early hominids found in the Lake Turkana region suggest that the area was inhabited some 2.6 million years ago. Arabs and Persians settled on the Kenyan coast from the eighth century AD. The Portuguese gained control of coastal areas in the 16th century but Arab overlordship was reasserted in the 18th century.

European exploration of the interior began in the 19th century and in 1895, Kenya became part of Britain's East African Protectorate, becoming a colony in 1920. Demands for internal self-government by white settlers were rejected in 1923, but from 1944 a nationalist group, the Kenya African Union (KAU), was founded to campaign for African rights. The Mau Mau rebellion of 1952–6, intended to drive white settlers from African tribal lands, resulted in a state of emergency that lasted until 1960, when preparations for majority African rule began. Kenya became independent in 1963, and a republic in 1964. President Jomo Kenyatta's death in 1978 brought Daniel arap Moi to power, and he remained president until 2002, when he was barred from standing for re-election.

Kenya was a one-party state ruled by the Kenya African National Union (KANU) between 1964 (in effect, though this was not formally declared until 1982) and 1991. A multiparty system was reintroduced after violent agitation and international pressure in the early 1990s but KANU maintained its grip on power until the 2002 elections, which were won by the National Rainbow Coalition (NARC). Despite the NARC coalition's anti-corruption electoral platform, once in government it made little headway against endemic corruption, and government ministers were implicated in corruption scandals in 2005 and 2006. It is estimated that up to US$1,000m (£500m) of official funds were misappropriated in 2002–7, and some aid donors suspended funding to pressurise the government into addressing the problem.

After decades of stability, intercommunal violence and conflict over land and water rights have become more frequent since the 1990s, exacerbated by a rural food crisis since 2004 following persistent drought and crop failures. In 2009 the president declared the food crisis a national disaster and asked for international food aid.

The 2007 legislative elections were won by the Orange Democratic Movement (ODM), led by Raila Odinga. The announcement that President Kibaki had won the simultaneous presidential election was greeted with accusations of electoral fraud by the opposition and triggered weeks of serious rioting; this developed into ethnic violence that left over 1,000 dead and 600,000 displaced. After international mediation, a power-sharing agreement was signed in February 2008; under this, Kibaki remained president and the post of prime minister was created for Raila Odinga. After several weeks of further negotiation, a coalition government was formed and took office in April. Disputes between the two coalition parties have virtually paralysed government business and prevented implementation of reforms.

POLITICAL SYSTEM

The 1963 constitution was amended in 2008 to create the post of prime minister and assigned some of the president's power to this post. A new constitution, which reduced the powers of the president and transferred some powers to the provinces, was approved by referendum and signed into law in August 2010.

The president is directly elected for a five-year term. The unicameral national assembly, the *Bunge*, has 224 members, of whom 210 are directly elected for a five-year term, 12 are nominated by the president, and two, the attorney-general and the speaker, are *ex-officio* members.

HEAD OF STATE

President, Mwai Kibaki, *elected* 27 December 2002, *took office* 30 December 2002, *re-elected* 2007
Vice-President, Home Affairs, Stephen Musyoka

SELECTED GOVERNMENT MEMBERS *as at June 2010*

Prime Minister, Raila Odinga
Deputy Prime Ministers, Uhuru Kenyatta *(Finance)*, Wycliffe Mudavadi
Foreign Affairs, Moses Wetangula
Defence, Yussuf Haji

KENYA HIGH COMMISSION

45 Portland Place, London W1B 1AS
T 020-7636 2371 **W** www.kenyahighcommission.net
High Commissioner, HE Ephraim Ngare, *apptd* 2009

BRITISH HIGH COMMISSION

PO Box 30465, Upper Hill Road, Nairobi
T (+254) (20) 284 4000 **E** bhcinfo@jambo.co.ke
W http://ukinkenya.fco.gov.uk
High Commissioner, HE Robert Macaire, *apptd* 2008

BRITISH COUNCIL

PO Box 40751, Upper Hill Road, Nairobi
T (+254) (20) 283 6000 **W** www.britishcouncil.org.uk/africa
Director, Liliana Biglou

DEFENCE

The army has 188 main battle tanks and 94 armoured personnel carriers. The navy has 11 patrol and coastal combatant vessels based at Mombasa. The air force has 42 combat aircraft and 11 armed helicopters.
Military budget – US$696m (2009)
Military personnel – 24,120: army 20,000, navy 1,620, air force 2,500; paramilitary 5,000

ECONOMY AND TRADE

Kenya acts as a regional trade and finance hub for its landlocked neighbours. However, its own economy is weak owing to endemic corruption, low commodity prices, low investor confidence and the frequent suspension of international aid because of successive governments' failure to tackle corruption. These problems are exacerbated by occasional severe droughts, and in 2008–9 the economy contracted owing to the post-election violence and the global downturn, which reduced tourism, exports and expatriates' remittances. There are high budget and trade deficits, a huge foreign debt, widespread unemployment and extreme poverty, with 50 per cent of the population living below the poverty line.

The country is overwhelmingly agricultural, with 75 per cent of the population engaged in agricultural and horticultural production; this sector contributes 21.4 per cent of GDP. The world's third largest producer of tea, it also grows coffee, maize, wheat, sugar cane, fruit and vegetables. Natural resources include gold, limestone, soda ash, salt, rubies, garnets and hydroelectric power, which makes it self-sufficient in energy.

The industrial sector has grown over the past two decades, developing a manufacturing base in consumer goods (such as textiles) and agricultural products (such as dehydrated vegetables), as well as oil refining, commercial ship repair and the production of steel, aluminium, lead and cement. Tourism is an important source of income. Industry contributes 16.3 per cent to GDP and the service sector 62.3 per cent.

The main export markets are the UK, the Netherlands, Uganda, Tanzania, the USA and Pakistan, while imports come mainly from the UAE, India, China and Saudi Arabia. Principal exports are tea, horticultural products, coffee, petroleum products, fish and cement. The main imports are machinery and transport equipment, petroleum products, vehicles, iron and steel, resins and plastics.

GNI – US$28,400m; US$730 per capita (2008)
Annual average growth of GDP – 1.8 per cent (2009 est)
Inflation rate – 20.5 per cent (2008 est)
Unemployment – 40 per cent (2008 est)
Total external debt – US$7,729m (2009 est)
Imports – US$11,100m (2008)
Exports – US$5,000m (2008)

BALANCE OF PAYMENTS
Trade – US$6,625m deficit (2009)
Current Account – US$2,106m deficit (2008)

Trade with UK	*2008*	*2009*
Imports from UK	£193,972,822	£261,536,671
Exports to UK	£315,597,814	£333,889,381

COMMUNICATIONS

The Kenya Railways Corporation operates 2,778km of railways. There are 177,800km of roads, of which 63,600km connect urban areas. The principal seaport is Mombasa, operated by the Kenya Ports Authority, and Lake Victoria also provides transport and trade routes. There are 181 airports and airfields; the international airports are at Nairobi, Mombasa and Eldoret.

The telephone system is antiquated and limited in extent. Mobile phone distribution has grown rapidly and there were 40 subscribers per 100 people in 2008. There were 3.4 million internet users in 2008.

EDUCATION AND HEALTH

The state provides eight years of free primary education. A free secondary education programme was initiated in 2008.

Literacy rate – 73.6 per cent (2007 est)
Gross enrolment ratio (percentage of relevant age group) – primary 111 per cent; secondary 58 per cent (2008 est); tertiary 4 per cent (2009 est)
HIV/AIDS adult prevalence – 6.7 per cent (2003 est)
Health expenditure – US$34 per capita (2007)
Hospital beds (per 1,000 people) – 1.4 (2003–8)

MEDIA

Kenya has a diverse and liberal media, but government action against media outlets has caused alarm in recent years, and legislation introduced in 2009 gave the government powers to control some content on security grounds. Most people rely on broadcast media, especially radio, for news. The state-run Kenya Broadcasting Corporation (KBC) competes with a range of commercial television and radio stations. There are six national newspapers that report a range of political views; five are published in English and one in Kiswahili.

KIRIBATI

Republic of Kiribati

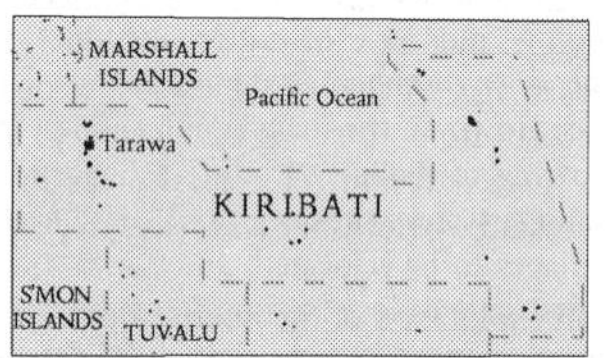

Area – 811 sq. km
Capital – Tarawa, on Bairiki; population, 42,925 (2009 est)
Currency – Australian dollar ($A) of 100 cents
Population – 112,850 rising at 2.24 per cent a year (2009 est); Micronesian (98.8 per cent) (est)
Religion – Christian (Roman Catholic 55 per cent, Kiribati Protestant Church 36 per cent, Mormon 3 per cent, Seventh-day Adventist 2 per cent), Baha'i 2 per cent (est)
Language – English, Kiribati (Gilbertese) (both official)
Population density – 119 per sq. km (2008)
Urban population – 44 per cent (2007 est)
Median age (years) – 20.8 (2009 est)
National anthem – 'Teirake Kaini Kiribati' ['Stand up, Kiribati']
National day – 12 July (Independence Day)
Life expectancy (years) – 63.22 (2009 est)
Mortality rate – 7.85 (2009 est)
Birth rate – 30.2 (2009 est)
Infant mortality rate – 43.48 (2009 est)
Death penalty – Abolished for all crimes (since 1979)
CPI score – 2.8 (2009)

CLIMATE AND TERRAIN

Kiribati (pronounced Kiri-bas) comprises 32 atolls and one island - about 20 are inhabited: Banaba island; the Kiribati (Gilbert) group (17); the Rawaki (Phoenix) Islands (8); and some of the Line Islands (11), including Kiritimati (Christmas Island). They are situated in the southern central Pacific Ocean, crossed by the Equator;

the area was also crossed by the international date line until 1995, when the government unilaterally moved the date line eastwards so that the whole country shared the same day. The atolls are coral, and few are more than 800m wide or more than 3m high, making the the country particularly vulnerable to rising sea levels. The highest elevation is 81m (on Banaba) and the lowest is 0m (Pacific Ocean). The climate is tropical.

HISTORY AND POLITICS

The islands were settled by Austronesian-speaking peoples in the first millennium BC and Samoans, Fijians and Tongans migrated there in the 11th to 14th centuries. British settlers arrived in the islands in the early 19th century. In 1892, the Gilbert (Kiribati) and Ellice (Tuvalu) islands were proclaimed a British protectorate and in 1916 became a British colony which subsequently incorporated the Line Islands and Phoenix Islands. During the Second World War, Banaba and the Gilbert islands were occupied by the Japanese and were the scene of fierce fighting between Japanese and US troops. Some of the Line Islands were used for British nuclear weapons tests in the 1950s and 1960s. In 1975, the territories separated and the Gilbert, Phoenix and Line Islands became independent as the Republic of Kiribati in July 1979.

Open-cast phosphate mining left Banaba unfit for human habitation and the population was evacuated in 1945, to be relocated to a northern island of Fiji. Overcrowding and lack of infrastructure have caused more general environmental degradation, especially in urban areas. However, the main problem is the rise in the sea level owing to global warming; salination is already contaminating water supplies and agricultural land, causing villages to be relocated, and Kiribati is expected to be the first state to lose land territory. The government is seeking permanent refugee status for its citizens in neighbouring countries.

Following the 2007 legislative elections, the Pillars of Truth grouping was the largest in the legislature, although still fewer in number than the other independent members. The incumbent president, Anote Tong, was re-elected in the 2007 presidential election.

POLITICAL SYSTEM

Under the 1979 constitution, the executive president is directly elected for a four-year term, with a maximum of three terms; presidential candidates are selected by and from members of the legislature. The unicameral legislature, the House of Assembly, has 46 members: 44 members directly elected for a four-year term, an appointed representative of the Banaban community in Fiji, and the attorney-general. There are no formal political parties but since the 1980s some associations of politicians formed for elections have proved durable enough to be given names.

HEAD OF STATE

President, Foreign Affairs, Anote Tong, *elected* 4 July 2003, *sworn in* 6 July 2003, *re-elected* 2007
Vice-President, Teima Onorio

SELECTED GOVERNMENT MEMBERS *as at June 2010*

Internal Affairs, Amberoti Nikora
Finance, Naatan Teewe

KIRIBATI HIGH COMMISSION

c/o Office of the President, PO Box 68, Bairiki, Tarawa, Kiribati
High Commissioner (acting), Makurita Baaro

BRITISH HIGH COMMISSIONER

HE Malcolm McLachlan, MBE, *apptd* 2009, resident at Suva, Fiji

ECONOMY AND TRADE

Since the phosphate deposits on Banaba ran out in 1979, the economy has been weak, dependent on coconuts, fish and tourism (over 20 per cent of GDP) as the main economic activities; tourism is hampered by remoteness, poor transport connections and the lack of funding, infrastructure and skills. Additional revenue comes from international aid (over 20 per cent of GDP), the sale of fishing licences, remittances from expatriates and monies from the trust fund established with phosphate mining revenues. A financial sector is being developed. The main trading partners are Pacific Rim countries and EU states. The principal exports are copra (62 per cent), coconuts, seaweed and fish. The principal imports are foodstuffs, machinery and transport equipment, manufactured goods and fuel.

GNI – US$197m; US$2,040 per capita (2008)
Annual average growth of GDP – 1.5 per cent (2009)
Inflation rate – 0.2 per cent (2007 est)

BALANCE OF PAYMENTS

Trade – US$36m deficit (2009)
Current Account – US$5m deficit (2009 est)

Trade with UK	*2008*	*2009*
Imports from UK	£1,008,762	£1,230,700
Exports to UK	£4,597	£163,609

COMMUNICATIONS

Air communication exists between most of the islands and is operated by the state-owned Air Kiribati; Coral Sun Airways, founded in 2009, provides additional services between the Gilbert islands. Flights to Fiji are provided by Air Kiribati and Air Pacific. There are 19 airports and airfields on the islands; the international airport is on Tarawa. Inter-island shipping is operated by the state-owned Shipping Corporation of Kiribati. The main seaport is Betio, on Tarawa. There are no railways, and only 670km of roads.

The telephone system provides good national and international services. Mobile phones are not widespread.

MEDIA

Kiribati has no domestic television, so radio forms the islands' main source of communication. There are two weekly newspapers, one state-owned and one private.

KOREA

Independent kingdoms and city states in the Korean peninsula were united by the Buddhist Silla dynasty in AD 668. The Silla were succeeded by the Koryo dynasty in 935 and the Yi dynasty from 1395 to 1910, during which period Korea became a vassal of China and Confucianism replaced Buddhism. Contact with outside cultures was discouraged by successive Korean rulers until 1876, when Japan forced the country to open up to foreign trade. Subsequently, Japan, China and Russia competed for influence, with Japan emerging as the dominant state, formally annexing Korea in 1910.

Japanese rule ended with its Second World War defeat in 1945, when Korea was divided along the 38th parallel by the occupying armies of liberation: US troops in the south and Soviet troops in the north. The Republic of Korea was founded in the south on 15 August 1948, following a general election and the adoption of a constitution. The Democratic People's Republic of Korea was established in the north on 9 September 1948; a Supreme People's Soviet was elected and a Soviet-style constitution was adopted.

UN plans to reunify the country after nationwide elections in 1950 were defied by North Korea. After elections in the south, South Korea declared its independence, which prompted its invasion by North Korea. A multinational UN force, with a large US contingent, intervened and pushed the North Korean troops back almost to the Chinese frontier. This brought China into the war in support of North Korea and their combined forces pushed back the UN troops, occupying Seoul. A UN counter-attack retook all territory south of the 38th parallel by the time an armistice was signed in 1953; a demilitarised border zone was established. The war devastated the entire peninsula, particularly North Korea, and left over two million people dead.

Talks between North and South Korea have taken place since the 1970s, although they were intermittent until 2000, when a summit ended with a joint declaration on normalisation measures; at a second summit in 2007 both sides agreed on the need for a peace treaty and expansion of economic cooperation. However, relations since 2002 have been complicated by international condemnation of North Korea's nuclear programme and the erratic nature of North Korea's attitude towards relations with South Korea, alternating between detente and aggression. Its attitude deteriorated steadily from early 2009, and inter-Korean relations reached a nadir in May 2010 after South Korea accused North Korea of sinking a South Korean warship in March 2010 and imposed financial and trade sanctions; North Korea repudiated the accusation and severed all ties with South Korea, threatening retaliation if sanctions were imposed. (*See also* Events of the Year.)

DEMOCRATIC PEOPLE'S REPUBLIC OF KOREA

Choson-minjujuui-inmin-konghwaguk – Democratic People's Republic of Korea

Area – 120,538 sq. km
Capital – Pyongyang; population, 2,827,640 (2009 est)
Major cities – Chongjin, Hamhung-Hungnam, Nampo
Currency – Won of 100 chon
Population – 22,665,345 rising at 0.42 per cent a year (2009 est)
Religion – Religious activity is almost non-existent outside government-sponsored religious groups, although many believers are thought to worship in private. Historically, the main religions were Buddhism and Confucianism; Buddhism, Christianity and Chondo (a syncretic religion) are officially recognised.
Language – Korean (official)
Population density – 198 per sq. km (2008)
Urban population – 62 per cent (2007 est)
Median age (years) – 33.5 (2009 est)
National anthem – 'Aegukka' ['The Patriotic Song']
National day – 9 September (Founding of the Democratic People's Republic of Korea)
Life expectancy (years) – 63.81 (2009 est)
Mortality rate – 10.52 (2009 est)
Birth rate – 14.82 (2009 est)
Infant mortality rate – 51.34 (2009 est)
Death penalty – Retained
Health expenditure (per capita) – $22 (2007)

CLIMATE AND TERRAIN

The republic occupies the northern half of the Korean peninsula. The land rises from coastal plains in the west to mountains and hills that occupy 80 per cent of the land area. Elevation extremes range from 2,744m (Paektu-san) at the highest point to 0m (Sea of Japan) at the lowest. The climate is temperate, though more extreme than in South Korea. Temperatures in January can fall to −13°C in Pyongyang, where the average temperature in July is 25°C.

HISTORY AND POLITICS

After the Korean war ended in 1953, Kim Il-sung continued the process of Soviet-style reform begun in 1946. He also developed *Juche* (self-reliance), an ideology demanding total economic independence. North Korea pursued an isolationist foreign policy for several decades, only signing a mutual assistance treaty with China in 1961 and improving relations with the USSR in 1985. It established diplomatic contacts with South Korea and Japan in 1990, raising hopes that it was abandoning its isolationism, but it remains a secretive, closed country under rigid state control.

This situation has had serious consequences domestically and internationally. The economy has suffered a long decline, and a series of natural disasters in the 1990s caused severe famine, obliging the government to request international aid. It is estimated that three million people have died since the 1990s as a result of the acute food shortages, which continue despite international food and fuel aid. International relations over the past two decades have been marked by alternating bouts of tension and detente, especially over the country's nuclear development programme (*see* below).

Kim Il-sung died in 1994. His son, Kim Jong-il, became chairman of the National Defence Commission, designated as the highest post of the state, and general secretary of the Korean Workers' Party in 1997. The most recent elections to the Supreme People's Assembly took place in March 2009. In June 2009 it was reported that Kim Jong-il's third son, Kim Jong-un, had been designated as his father's successor and had acted as head of state during his father's illness in 2008.

INTERNATIONAL RELATIONS

North Korea's relations with other countries have been erratic over the past 20 years, largely owing to its nuclear ambitions and international reaction to these. It first agreed to freeze its nuclear development programme in return for fuel and development aid in 1994, only to restart the programme in 2002, claiming that other parties to the agreement had reneged on it. This pattern of confrontation, negotiation and non-compliance has been repeated several times, with the regime using the discontinuation of its nuclear and missile development programmes to bargain for aid from international agencies and regional powers. Six-nation talks to resolve the nuclear issues began in 2003 after North Korea withdrew from the Nuclear Non-proliferation Treaty, but North Korea has never fully complied with any of the agreements concluded at the talks. The consequent suspension of aid by other nations, and UN censure and sanctions after North Korea test-fired ballistic missiles and nuclear devices in 2006 and 2009, have been interpreted as acts of aggression by North Korea and met with a bellicose response from the regime. Its attitude towards South Korea deteriorated steadily from early 2009, and inter-Korean relations reached a nadir in May 2010 after it was accused of sinking a South Korean warship in March 2010; North Korea repudiated the accusation and severed all ties with South Korea, threatening retaliation for its imposition of sanctions. (*See also* Events of the Year.)

POLITICAL SYSTEM

The communist Korean Workers' Party, founded in 1946 by Kim Il-sung, is the only permitted political party. However, political control and leadership is maintained by the cult of personality created by Kim Il-sung and continued by his son and successor Kim Jong-il.

The 1972 constitution was amended in 1998 to designate leading state posts; it made Kim Il-sung the Eternal President and the chairmanship of the National Defence Commission (NDC), held by Kim Jong-il, the highest post in the state, while providing that the chairman of the Presidium of the Supreme People's Assembly would represent the state on formal occasions. A further constitutional amendment in 2009 explicitly named the NDC chairman the 'supreme leader of the state', apparently strengthening Mr Kim's position; it also removed all references to communism, and established the *songun* principle of military responsibility for all internal affairs. There is a unicameral legislature, the Supreme People's Assembly, which has 687 members directly elected from a single list of candidates for a five-year term. The assembly elects a presidium and the premier, appointing the government on the recommendation of the premier. The Central People's Committee, which is also elected by the assembly, directs the administrative council (government), which implements the policy formulated by the committee.

HEAD OF STATE

Eternal President, Kim Il-sung (deceased)
Chair of the National Defence Commission, Kim Jong-il
Chair of the Presidium of the Supreme People's Assembly, Kim Yong-nam

SELECTED GOVERNMENT MEMBERS *as at June 2010*

Premier, Choe Yong-rim
Deputy Premiers, Ro Tu-cho, Thae Jong-su, Jon Ha-choi, Kang Nung-su, Kim Rak-hui, Ri Thae-nam, Jo Pyong-ju
Finance, Pak Su-gil
Foreign Affairs, Pak Ui-chun

EMBASSY OF THE DEMOCRATIC PEOPLE'S REPUBLIC OF KOREA
73 Gunnersbury Avenue, London W5 4LP
T 020-8992 4965 E dprkrepmission@yahoo.co.uk
Ambassador Extraordinary and Plenipotentiary, HE Ja Song-nam, *apptd* 2007

BRITISH EMBASSY
Munsu Dong, Pyongyang
T (+850) (2) 381 7980 E postmaster.pyonx@fco.gov.uk
Ambassador Extraordinary and Plenipotentiary, HE Peter Hughes, *apptd* 2008

DEFENCE

The army has about 3,500 main battle tanks and over 2,500 armoured personnel carriers. The navy has 63 submarines, 3 frigates, 5 corvettes and over 329 patrol and coastal vessels at 15 bases. The air force has 620 combat aircraft and 20 armed helicopters.
Military budget – US$2,300m (2006 est)
Military personnel – 1,106,000: army 950,000, navy 46,000, air force 110,000; paramilitary 189,000
Conscription duration – 3–12 years

ECONOMY AND TRADE

Although North Korea is rich in natural resources and had developed a heavy industry base in the first half of the 20th century, the economy is stagnant after decades of mismanagement, underinvestment and low export levels. Its long decline was compounded by the loss of Soviet support with the collapse of European communism in the 1990s. A redenomination of its currency in December 2009, with a cap on the amount that could be exchanged for new notes, wiped out many people's savings, disrupted the nascent private sector, triggered rapid inflation and was met with unprecedented public protests that lasted some weeks. South Korea's imposition of sanctions in May 2010 will put the economy under even greater pressure.

Industrial output is centred on mining, steel, chemicals and machine building, but antiquated machinery and fuel shortages have limited output to a fraction of pre-1990 levels. Agriculture is in an equally parlous state, as collective farming, lack of arable land and chronic shortages of fertilisers and agricultural machinery prevent the country from producing enough to feed its population. It has been dependent on massive amounts of food aid since the mid-1990s to avert a repeat of the 1995 famine, but chronic malnutrition is widespread. A relaxation of restrictions on private farming and markets in 2003 was partially rescinded in 2005 and a centralised rationing system was reinstated. South Korean assistance in developing infrastructure, industry, the Kaesong Industrial Zone and tourism has been limited by North Korea's restrictions, and was reduced or ended when South Korea imposed sanctions on the North in May 2010.

The main trading partners are China and South Korea. Principal exports are minerals, metallurgical products, armaments, textiles, and agricultural and fish products. The main imports are petroleum, coal, machinery and equipment, textiles and grain.
Annual average growth of GDP – 3.7 per cent (2008 est)
Imports – US$431m (2002)
Exports – US$298m (2002)

BALANCE OF PAYMENTS

Trade – US$3,597m deficit (2009)
Current Account – US$82m deficit (2002)

Trade with UK	*2008*	*2009*
Imports from UK	£192,887	£115,938
Exports to UK	£2,799,309	£911,478

COMMUNICATIONS

North Korea has 5,235km of railways and 25,554km of roads, although few are surfaced. There are some 2,250km of waterways but these are navigable only by small craft. The main seaports are Chongjin, Nampo and Wonsan. There are 79 airports and airfields; the principal airport is at Pyongyang.

MEDIA

There are no independent media in North Korea. All televisions and radios are pre-tuned to government stations and the four national newspapers are all government organs. Foreign and dissident radio stations are jammed and anyone found listening to foreign broadcasts is harshly punished. In 2008 Reporters Without Borders rated the country as the worst in the world for press freedom.

REPUBLIC OF KOREA

Taehan-min'guk – Republic of Korea

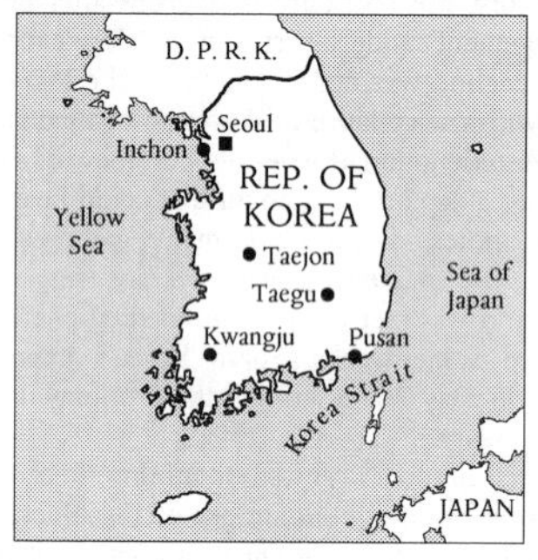

Area – 99,720 sq. km
Capital – Seoul; population, 9,777,720 (2009 est)
Major cities – Inchon, Koyang, Kwangju, Pusan, Songnam, Suwon, Taegu, Taejon
Currency – Won of 100 jeon
Population – 48,508,972 rising at 0.27 per cent a year (2009 est)
Religion – Christian (Protestant 18 per cent, Roman Catholic 11 per cent), Buddhist (23 per cent; predominantly the Jogye order of the Seon (Zen) school) (est)
Language – Korean (official), English
Population density – 502 per sq. km (2008)
Urban population – 81 per cent (2007 est)
Median age (years) – 37.3 (2009 est)
National anthem – 'Aegukka' ['The Patriotic Song']
National day – 15 August (Liberation Day)
Life expectancy (years) – 78.72 (2009 est)
Mortality rate – 5.94 (2009 est)
Birth rate – 8.93 (2009 est)
Infant mortality rate – 4.26 (2009 est)
Death penalty – Retained (not used since 1997)
CPI score – 5.5 (2009)

CLIMATE AND TERRAIN

The country occupies the southern part of the mountainous Korean peninsula, with highlands and mountains accounting for around 70 per cent of the land area. Elevation extremes range from 1,950m (Halla-san) at the highest point to 0m (Sea of Japan) at the lowest. The climate is temperate, although winters are very cold for the latitude. Temperatures in Seoul range from from −5°C in January to 27°C in August. The rainy season runs from June to September.

HISTORY AND POLITICS

From 1948, South Korea experienced over 40 years of mostly authoritarian, often military, rule and great industrial development. Syngman Rhee, president from 1948, resigned in 1960 in the face of popular protests at corruption and electoral fraud. A military coup in 1961 brought General Park Chung-hee to power and he instigated a programme of industrial development; by the time of his assassination in 1979 Korea was a leading shipbuilding nation and producer of electronic goods.

Following riots against the interim government, General Chun Do-hwan assumed power in 1980 after martial law was declared. Pro-democracy agitation in the mid-1980s led to constitutional changes in 1987 and the first multiparty legislative elections in 1988, but despite the anti-corruption campaign of the new democratically elected president Roh Tae-woo, politics continued to be plagued by allegations of corruption and fraud, and was subject to military influence. The first civilian president and the first wholly civilian government since 1961 were appointed in 1993. Kim Dae-jung's inauguration as president in 1998 saw the adoption of the 'sunshine policy' of engagement with North Korea.

The 2007 presidential election was won by Lee Myung-bak, the Grand National Party (GNP) candidate. In the 2008 legislative election, the GNP won a majority of seats in the legislature. Lee Myung-bak's government reversed the 'sunshine policy' in 2008, and imposed sanctions on North Korea in May 2010, blaming North Korea for the sinking of one of its warships in March 2010. (*See also* Events of the Year.)

POLITICAL SYSTEM

A new constitution was adopted when the Sixth Republic was inaugurated in 1988. Under this, the president is directly elected for a five-year term, which is not renewable. He appoints the prime minister with the approval of the legislature and members of the state council (cabinet) on the recommendation of the prime minister. The president is also empowered to take wide-ranging measures in an emergency, including the declaration of martial law, but must obtain the agreement of the legislature. The unicameral National Assembly has 299 members who are directly elected for a four-year term.

HEAD OF STATE
President, Lee Myung-bak, *elected* 19 December 2007, *sworn in* 25 February 2008

SELECTED GOVERNMENT MEMBERS *as at June 2010*
Prime Minister, Chung Un-chan
Finance, Yoon Jeung-hyun
Defence, Gen. Kim Tae-young
Foreign Affairs, Yu Myung-hwan
Justice, Lee Kwi-nam

EMBASSY OF THE REPUBLIC OF KOREA
60 Buckingham Gate, London SW1E 6AJ
T 020-7227 5500 **E** koreanembinuk@mofat.go.kr
W http://gbr.mofat.go.kr

Ambassador Extraordinary and Plenipotentiary, HE Choo Kyu-ho, *apptd* 2010

BRITISH EMBASSY
Taepyeongno 40, 4 Jeong-dong, Jung-gu, Seoul 100-120
T (+82) (2) 3210 5500 **E** postmaster.seoul@fco.gov.uk
W http://ukinrok.fco.gov.uk
Ambassador Extraordinary and Plenipotentiary, HE Martin Uden, *apptd* 2008

BRITISH COUNCIL
4F Hungkuk Life Insurance Building, 226 Shinmunro 1-ga, Jongro-gu, Seoul 110-786
T (+82) (2) 3702 0600 **W** www.britishcouncil.org/korea
Director, Roland Davies

DEFENCE

The army has 2,750 main battle tanks, 2,780 armoured personnel carriers, 40 armoured infantry fighting vehicles and 60 armed helicopters. The navy has 13 submarines, 10 destroyers, 9 frigates, 28 corvettes, around 76 patrol and coastal vessels, 8 combat aircraft, 24 armed helicopters and 60 main battle tanks. There are 8 naval bases. The air force has 490 combat aircraft.
Military budget – US$24,510m (2009)
Military personnel – 687,000: army 560,000, navy 68,000, air force 64,000; paramilitary 4,500
Conscription duration – 26 months

ECONOMY AND TRADE

Industrialisation from the 1960s transformed South Korea from a predominantly agrarian country into one of the Asian 'miracle' economies by the 1980s. Initially based on shipbuilding and electrical goods, production shifted towards electronics and IT goods in the 1980s. By 1997 South Korea was the world's eleventh largest economy, with an annual GDP growth rate of 8 per cent. However, the dominating conglomerates *(chaebols)* were experiencing difficulties which, exacerbated by the Asian financial crisis in 1997, caused a number to collapse in the late 1990s and the economy to contract sharply. Corporate and financial reforms were introduced and GDP growth resumed, on a more modest scale, from the early 2000s. The global downturn in 2008 caused another contraction, leading the government to introduce economic stimulus measures.

Services contribute 57.6 per cent to GDP, industry 39.4 per cent and agriculture 3 per cent. Major manufacturing industries include electronics, telecommunications, motor vehicles, chemicals, shipbuilding and steel. Tourism is of growing importance.

The main trading partners are China, Japan and the USA. Principal exports are semiconductors, telecommunications equipment, motor vehicles, computers, steel, ships and petrochemicals. The main imports are machinery, electronics and electronic equipment, oil, steel, transport equipment, organic chemicals and plastics.
GNI – US$1,046,300m; US$21,530 per capita (2008)
Annual average growth of GDP – –0.8 per cent (2009 est)
Inflation rate – 2.8 per cent (2009 est)
Population below poverty line – 15 per cent (2003 est)
Unemployment – 4.1 per cent (2009 est)
Total external debt – US$333,600m (2009)
Imports – US$435,300m (2008)
Exports – US$422,000m (2008)

BALANCE OF PAYMENTS
Trade – US$56,128m surplus (2009)
Current Account – US$42,668m surplus (2009)

Trade with UK	*2008*	*2009*
Imports from UK	£2,406,749,709	£2,025,098,462
Exports to UK	£3,329,373,703	£2,474,153,942

COMMUNICATIONS

There are 3,380km of railway in commercial operation, of which 1,840km are electrified. A high-speed railway line is being constructed between Seoul and Pusan and there are plans to build high-speed rail links from Seoul to Mokp'o and to Kangnung. There are 103,000km of roads, of which 3,400km are motorways. There are 116 airports and airfields, including international airports at Seoul (Kimpo), Kimhae (near Pusan), Taegu, Cheju city and Inchon. Pusan, Inchon and P'ohang are the major ports, although development and operations at Inchon are hampered by tidal variations of 9–10m.

Modern telecommunications systems served 21.3 million fixed-line users, 45.6 million mobile phone subscribers and 37.5 million internet users in 2008.

EDUCATION AND HEALTH

Primary education is free of charge and compulsory for nine years from the age of six. Secondary and higher education is extensive, with the option of middle school to age 15 and high school to age 18.
Gross enrolment ratio (percentage of relevant age group) – primary 104 per cent; secondary 97 per cent; tertiary 96 per cent (2008 est)
Health expenditure (per capita) – US$1,362 (2007)
Hospital beds (per 1,000 people) – 8.6 (2003–8)

MEDIA

Korea has a number of public radio and television broadcasters, including Korea Broadcasting System and Munhwa Broadcasting Corporation (MBC), as well as a diversified commercial sector. There is a high rate of subscription to cable and satellite services. Newspaper readership is very high and a number of dailies, many of which are owned by industrial conglomerates, are in English.

KOSOVO

Republika e Kosoves – Republic of Kosovo

Area – 10,887 sq. km
Capital – Pristina; population 500,000 (2009 est)
Major towns – Kosovska Mitrovica; Pec; Prizren
Currency – Euro (€) of 100 cents; the Serbian dinar is also in circulation

Population – 1,804,838 (2009 est); Albanian (88 per cent), Serb (7 per cent); small Bosniak, Turk, Ashkali, Egyptian, Roma and Gorani minorities
Religion – Muslim, Christian (Serbian Orthodox, Roman Catholic)
Language – Albanian, Serbian (both official), Bosnian, Turkish, Romany
National day – 17 February (Independence Day)

CLIMATE AND TERRAIN

The landlocked country has a hilly central region which divides plains in the east and west. Mountains lie along the borders with Albania, Macedonia and Montenegro, and along much of the border with Serbia. Elevation extremes range from 2,656m (Gjeravica) to 297m (Drini i Bardhe river in the west). The main rivers are the Drini i Bardhe and the Iberi in the north. The climate is continental.

HISTORY AND POLITICS

Kosovo was at the centre of the medieval kingdom of Serbia and was the location of the Serbian defeat by the Ottoman Turks in 1389 that led to the kingdom becoming part of the Ottoman Empire; the historic and cultural resonances of these events underlie Serbia's refusal to countenance the independence of what it views as the heartland of its nation. Kosovo was under Ottoman rule from 1389 until 1913, when Serbia regained control following the First Balkan War. As a province of Serbia, Kosovo became part of the Kingdom of Serbs, Croats and Slovenes (subsequently Yugoslavia) in 1918.

Under Ottoman rule, migration gradually altered the population's ethnicity, and Albanians had become the dominant ethnic group by the end of the 19th century. After the Second World War, the Yugoslav federal government made Kosovo an autonomous republic within Serbia, granting autonomy almost equivalent to that of one of the constituent republics in 1974. The Serbian republican government stripped the province of its autonomy in 1989 and progressively excluded the Albanian majority from public life, suppressing their culture. The Kosovans' decisive vote in a 1991 referendum for independence from both Serbia and Yugoslavia was declared illegal by the Serbian government, which tightened its control further.

An insurgency by the Kosovan Liberation Army (KLA) from the mid 1990s provoked Serbian military reprisals that from 1998 developed into systematic ethnic cleansing. Over 800,000 people sought refuge in Albania, Macedonia or Montenegro, and over 500,000 were internally displaced. NATO intervened in March 1999, and Serbia accepted a peace plan proposed by NATO and Russia in June 1999 and withdrew its forces. The UN then placed Kosovo under transitional administration, establishing autonomous democratic institutions to which it gradually devolved administrative responsibilities.

UN-sponsored talks on Kosovo's future began in 2005 but failed to make any progress. After further talks in 2007 proved fruitless, the Kosovan government unilaterally declared independence from Serbia on 17 February 2008. The UN completed its hand-over of administrative powers in June 2008, when the constitution came into force; that month the Serb minority set up its own assembly in Mitrovica, which has been a flashpoint for intercommunal tension. The UN's interim administration mission remains in Kosovo to maintain stability and protect the Serb minority, along with the EU (police and rule of law mission) and the International Civilian Office, headed by the EU's special representative.

Kosovo's declaration of independence has been recognised by 69 countries as of June 2010, but not by the UN. Serbia refuses to accept the declaration, and the UN referred consideration of its legality to the International Court of Justice in October 2008.

Fatmir Sejdiu, elected president in February 2006, was re-elected in January 2008. In the 2007 legislative election, the Democratic Party of Kosovo, led by Hashim Thaci, became the largest party in the legislature and formed a coalition government with the president's Democratic League of Kosovo and two smaller parties, under the leadership of Mr Thaci.

POLITICAL SYSTEM

Under the constitution which came into effect in June 2008, the president is elected by the legislature for a five-year term and can be re-elected once. The unicameral legislature, the Assembly of the Republic of Kosovo, has 120 members, elected for a four-year term; 100 seats have directly elected members, ten seats are reserved for Serbs and ten for other minorities. The majority party or coalition nominates the prime minister, who is appointed by the president. Both the prime minister and the government must be approved by the legislature.

HEAD OF STATE

President, Fatmir Sejdiu, *elected* 10 February 2006, *re-elected* 2008

SELECTED GOVERNMENT MEMBERS *as at June 2010*

Prime Minister, Hashim Thaci
Deputy Prime Ministers, Hajredin Kuci; Rame Manaj
Economy and Finance, Ahmet Shala
Interior, Bajram Rexhepi
Foreign Affairs, Skender Hyseni

EMBASSY OF THE REPUBLIC OF KOSOVO

100 Pall Mall, London SW1 5NQ
T 020-7659 6140 E embassy.uk@ks-gov.net
Ambassador Extraordinary and Plenipotentiary, HE Dr Muhamet Hamiti, *apptd* 2009

BRITISH EMBASSY

Ismail Qemali 6, Arberi, Dragodan, Pristina
T (+381) 3825 4700 E britishembassy.pristina@fco.gov.uk
W http://ukinkosovo.fco.gov.uk
Ambassador Extraordinary and Plenipotentiary, HE Andrew Sparkes, *apptd* 2008

BRITISH COUNCIL

Perandori Justinian 6, Qyteza Pejton, 10000 Pristina
T (+381) 3824 3292 E info@ks.britishcouncil.org
W www.britishcouncil.org/kosovo
Director, Arjeta Emra

ECONOMY AND TRADE

Under UN administration Kosovo began the transition to a market economy and over half of state-owned businesses have been privatised. However, income levels are the lowest in Europe, and the economy is dependent on international and foreign aid and the remittances of expatriates, worth about 7.5 per cent and 14 per cent of GDP respectively. Agriculture is close to subsistence level and inefficient, industrial output has declined because of insufficient investment and an unemployment level of over 40 per cent encourages emigration and the informal economy. International agencies and foreign governments are working with the Kosovan government to stimulate economic growth, attract investment and reduce unemployment.

Natural resources include lignite, lead, zinc, nickel, chrome, magnesium, kaolin and bauxite, and the mainstay of the economy is mining and the production of construction materials. Production is held back by ageing equipment and inadequacies in the power sector, although these are being addressed.

The UN administration signed Kosovo's accession to the Central Europe Free Trade Area (CEFTA) in 2006, and its members are the main markets for exports of minerals and processed metal products, scrap metals, leather goods, machinery and appliances. Imports of foodstuffs, wood, fuels, chemicals, machinery and electrical equipment come mainly from EU and neighbouring countries.

Inflation rate – 5.3 per cent (2007 est)
Population below poverty line – 37 per cent (2007 est)
Unemployment – 43 per cent (2009 est)

Trade with UK	*2008*	*2009*
Imports from UK	–	£4,568,632
Exports to UK	–	£133,999

MEDIA

Television is the primary source of news; services are provided by two private stations and the public broadcaster Kosovo Radio-Television (RTK). The European Broadcasting Union, which originally set up RTK in 1999, has accused the Kosovan government of eroding the broadcaster's editorial independence since 2008. There are over 80 licensed radio stations, and seven daily newspapers selling to a limited readership; the largest of these is *Koha Ditore.* Kosovo had 377,000 internet users in 2008.

KUWAIT

Dawlat al-Kuwayt – State of Kuwait

Area – 17,818 sq. km
Capital – Kuwait City (Al Kuwayt); population, 2,229,990 (2009 est)
Currency – Kuwaiti dinar (KD) of 1,000 fils
Population – 2,691,158 rising at 3.55 per cent a year (2009 est); 45 per cent are Kuwaiti citizens and the remainder other Arabs, Iranians, Indians, Pakistanis and westerners
Religion – Of citizens, Islam (Sunni 70 per cent, the remainder predominantly Shia) (est). Around 450,000 Christian expatriates reside in the country.
Language – Arabic (official), English
Population density – 153 per sq. km (2008)
Urban population – 98 per cent (2007 est)
Median age (years) – 26.2 (2009 est)
National anthem – 'Al-Nasheed al-Watani' ['National Anthem']
National day – 25 February
Life expectancy (years) – 77.71 (2009 est)
Mortality rate – 2.35 (2009 est)
Birth rate – 21.81 (2009 est)
Infant mortality rate – 8.96 (2009 est)
Death penalty – Retained
CPI score – 4.1 (2009)

CLIMATE AND TERRAIN

Kuwait is an almost entirely flat desert plain, with elevation extremes ranging from 306m at the highest point to 0m (Persian Gulf) at the lowest. Its territory includes the island of Bubiyan and others at the head of the Persian Gulf. The climate is arid, with little rainfall but high levels of humidity. Average temperatures range from 12°C in January to 37°C in July.

HISTORY AND POLITICS

The area was under the nominal control of the Ottoman Empire from the late 16th century, but in 1756 an autonomous sheikdom was founded that has been ruled by the al-Sabah family ever since. Kuwait entered into a treaty of friendship with Britain in 1899, in order to protect itself from Ottoman and Saudi domination, and it became a British protectorate in 1914. The borders with Saudi Arabia and Iraq were agreed between 1922 and 1933. Full independence was achieved in 1961, although Britain retained a military presence in the country until 1971.

An attempted Iraqi invasion shortly after independence in 1961 was discouraged by British troops in the Gulf. However, in August 1990 Iraq invaded and occupied Kuwait, proclaiming it a province of Iraq. In 1991, a short military campaign by a US-led coalition force expelled the Iraqi forces, although there were further Iraqi incursions in 1993 before Iraq renounced its claim and recognised the new UN-demarcated border in 1994. Extensive damage was caused to the country's infrastructure and environment during the Iraqi occupation and the liberation campaign, and reconstruction was a priority throughout the 1990s. In 2003, Kuwait was a base for forces involved in the Iraq War, and it remains an important transit route for military and civilian traffic into and out of Iraq.

In recent years, there have been clashes between security forces and militant Islamists, some of whom are alleged to have links to al-Qaida.

Although Kuwait was the first Arab country in the Gulf to have an elected legislature, this was suspended from 1977 to 1981, from 1986 to 1992 and in 1999. It has since sat regularly, with frequent democratic elections, and its assertiveness has caused clashes with the government; two elections were held in 12 months in 2008–9 owing to its efforts to subject the government to parliamentary scrutiny. The May 2008 election produced a legislature in which Islamists were again the largest bloc. In the May 2009 election, Islamists remained the largest bloc but liberals gained an additional seat, and four women were elected.

POLITICAL SYSTEM
The 1962 constitution was amended in 2005 to extend the franchise to women. The head of state is the emir, chosen from among the ruling family. He exercises executive power through the council of ministers; in 2003, the post of prime minister was separated from the role of heir to the throne for the first time. The unicameral National Assembly has 50 members directly elected for a four-year term. There are no political parties.

The country is divided into six governorates: Capital, Hawalli, Al-Ahmadi, Al-Jahrah, Al-Farwaniya and Mubarak Al-Kabeer.

HEAD OF STATE
HH The Emir of Kuwait, Shaikh Sabah al-Ahmad al-Jaber al-Sabah, *born* 1929, *acceded* 29 January 2006
Crown Prince, HH Shaikh Nawaf al-Ahmad al-Jaber al-Sabah

SELECTED GOVERNMENT MEMBERS *as at June 2010*
Prime Minister, Shaikh Nasser al-Muhammad al-Ahmad al-Sabah
First Deputy Prime Minister, Defence, Shaikh Jaber al-Mubarak al-Hamad al-Sabah
Deputy Prime Ministers, Shaikh Mohammad al-Salem al-Sabah *(Foreign Affairs);* Rashed al-Hammad
Interior, Lt.-Gen. Shaikh Jabir Khalid al-Jabir al-Sabah
Finance, Mustafa Jasim Al-Shimali

EMBASSY OF THE STATE OF KUWAIT
2 Albert Gate, London SW1X 7JU
T 020-7590 3400 E kuwait@dircon.co.uk
Ambassador Extraordinary and Plenipotentiary, HE Khaled Al-Duwaisan, GCVO, *apptd* 1993

BRITISH EMBASSY
PO Box 2, Arabian Gulf Street, Safat 13001
T (+965) 2259 4320 E britemb@qualitynet.net
W http://ukinkuwait.fco.gov.uk
Ambassador Extraordinary and Plenipotentiary, HE Frank Baker, OBE, *apptd* 2010

BRITISH COUNCIL
PO Box 345, 2 Al Arabi Street, Block 2, Mansouriya, Safat 13004
T (+965) 251 5512 W www.britishcouncil.org/me
Director, Stephen Forbes

DEFENCE
The army has 368 main battle tanks, 321 armoured personnel carriers and up to 450 armoured infantry fighting vehicles. The navy has 10 patrol and coastal vessels, based at Ras al-Qalaya. The air force has 50 combat aircraft and 25 armed helicopters.
Military budget – US$6,650m (2009)
Military personnel – 15,500: army 11,000, navy 2,000, air force 2,500; paramilitary 7,100

ECONOMY AND TRADE
Oil was discovered in 1938 and the development of the oil industry after 1945 transformed the country from one of the poorest in the world to one of the richest. Petroleum accounts for 95 per cent of export revenues and 95 per cent of government income. Income from foreign reserves and investment is also high, and helped to cushion the economy from the effects of the global economic downturn.

The climate and terrain limit agriculture and, with the exception of fish, all food is imported; the primary sector contributes only 0.3 per cent of GDP. Services account for 51.4 per cent of GDP and industry for 48.3 per cent. Apart from the oil and petrochemical industries, other activities include production of cement and construction materials, shipbuilding and repair, water desalination and food processing. Immigrant labour, mainly from Pakistan, India and Iran, makes up about 60 per cent of the two million-strong workforce.

The main export markets are Japan, South Korea, India, Taiwan, Singapore and the USA, and the main sources of imports are the USA, Japan, Germany and China. Principal exports are oil and refined products, and fertilisers. The main imports are food, construction materials, vehicles and vehicle parts, and clothing.
GNI – US$117,000m; US$43,930 per capita (2008)
Annual average growth of GDP – –0.7 per cent (2009 est)
Inflation rate – 5.7 per cent (2009 est)
Unemployment – 2.2 per cent (2004 est)
Total external debt – US$33,490m (2009 est)
Imports – US$24,900m (2008)
Exports – US$87,100m (2008)

BALANCE OF PAYMENTS
Trade – US$45,396m surplus (2009)
Current Account – US$64,470m surplus (2008)

Trade with UK	*2008*	*2009*
Imports from UK	£537,069,845	£451,182,053
Exports to UK	£1,058,519,200	£676,784,764

COMMUNICATIONS
Kuwait has 5,749km of roads, most of which are surfaced, but no railway or internal waterways. There are seven airports and airstrips; the international airport is at Kuwait City. The main seaports are Ash Shu'aybah, Ash Shuwaykh, Mina' 'Abd Allah, Mina' al Ahmadi and Mina' Sa'ud.

Modern telephone systems provided 541,000 fixed lines, 2.9 million mobile phone subscribers and 1 million internet users in 2008.

EDUCATION AND HEALTH
Education is free of charge and compulsory from six to 14 years.
Literacy rate – 94.5 per cent (2007 est)
Gross enrolment ratio (percentage of relevant age group) – primary 95 per cent; secondary 91 per cent; tertiary 18 per cent (2008 est)
Health expenditure (per capita) – US$901 (2007)
Hospital beds (per 1,000 people) – 1.8 (2003–8)

MEDIA
Newspaper publishers require a government licence and some topics are subject to government censorship. Even so, Kuwaiti newspapers are far more outspoken in their coverage of politics than newspapers in neighbouring Arab nations. State-run radio and television broadcasters compete with recently launched commercial stations; satellite television is also widely watched.

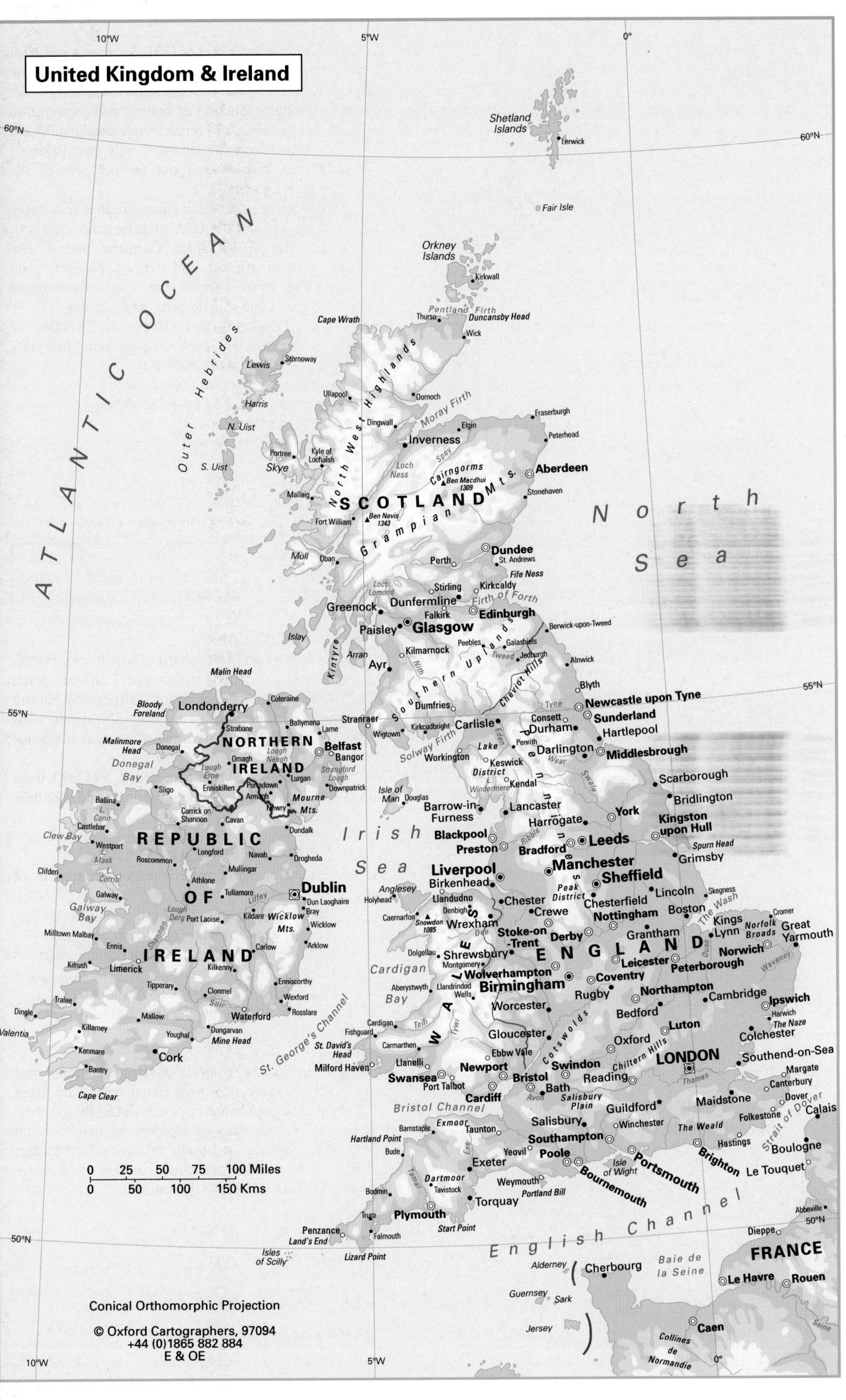

United Kingdom & Ireland
10°W
5°W
0°
60°N
55°N
50°N
ATLANTIC OCEAN
North Sea
Irish Sea
English Channel
Shetland Islands
Lerwick
Fair Isle
Orkney Islands
Kirkwall
Pentland Firth
Thurso
Duncansby Head
Cape Wrath
Wick
Outer Hebrides
Lewis
Stornoway
Harris
N. Uist
S. Uist
North West Highlands
Ullapool
Dornoch
Dingwall
Moray Firth
Elgin
Fraserburgh
Peterhead
Inverness
Portree
Kyle of Lochalsh
Skye
Loch Ness
Spey
Cairngorms
Ben Macdhui 1309
Aberdeen
Mallaig
SCOTLAND
Grampian Mts.
Stonehaven
Fort William
Ben Nevis 1343
Mull
Oban
Perth
Dundee
St. Andrews
Fife Ness
Loch Lomond
Stirling
Kirkcaldy
Dunfermline
Firth of Forth
Greenock
Falkirk
Edinburgh
Paisley
Glasgow
Berwick-upon-Tweed
Islay
Kintyre
Arran
Kilmarnock
Peebles
Galashiels
Tweed
Jedburgh
Ayr
Southern Uplands
Cheviot Hills
Alnwick
Malin Head
Nith
Blyth
Bloody Foreland
Londonderry
Coleraine
Dumfries
Tyne
Newcastle upon Tyne
Sunderland
Ballymena
Larne
Stranraer
Wigtown
Kirkcudbright
Carlisle
Eden
Consett
Durham
Hartlepool
Malinmore Head
Donegal
Strabane
NORTHERN IRELAND
Lough Neagh
Belfast
Bangor
Solway Firth
Penrith
Darlington
Middlesbrough
Donegal Bay
Omagh
Lough Erne
Strangford Lough
Workington
Lake District
Keswick
Wear
Swale
Sligo
Enniskillen
Portadown
Armagh
Lurgan
Downpatrick
Windermere
Kendal
Scarborough
Ballina
Conn
Carrick on Shannon
Newry
Mourne Mts.
Isle of Man
Douglas
Barrow-in-Furness
Lancaster
Bridlington
Castlebar
Cavan
Dundalk
Harrogate
York
Kingston upon Hull
Clew Bay
Westport
REPUBLIC
Longford
Blackpool
Ribble
Preston
Bradford
Leeds
Spurn Head
Mask
Roscommon
Navan
Drogheda
Grimsby
Clifden
Mullingar
Liverpool
Manchester
Corrib
Athlone
Dublin
Birkenhead
Sheffield
Lincoln
Skegness
Galway
OF
Tullamore
Liffey
Dun Laoghaire
Anglesey
Holyhead
Llandudno
Chester
Peak District
Chesterfield
The Wash
Galway Bay
Lough Derg
Port Laoise
Kildare
Wicklow Mts.
Bray
Wicklow
Caernarfon
Denbigh
Snowdon 1085
Wrexham
Dee
Crewe
Nottingham
Boston
Kings Lynn
Norfolk Broads
Cromer
Great Yarmouth
Milltown Malbay
Stoke-on-Trent
Derby
Grantham
Ennis
Shannon
Carlow
Arklow
Dolgellau
Shrewsbury
ENGLAND
Ouse
Norwich
IRELAND
Kilrush
Limerick
Kilkenny
Cardigan Bay
Montgomery
Wolverhampton
Leicester
Peterborough
Waveney
Enniscorthy
Aberystwyth
Llandrindod Wells
Birmingham
Coventry
Tipperary
Clonmel
Wexford
Rugby
Northampton
Cambridge
Ipswich
Tralee
Suir
WALES
Worcester
Bedford
Harwich
Dingle
Mallow
Waterford
Rosslare
St. George's Channel
Cardigan
Teifi
Luton
The Naze
Valentia
Killarney
Youghal
Dungarvan
Mine Head
Fishguard
Gloucester
Colchester
Carmarthen
Cotswolds
Oxford
St. David's Head
Ebbw Vale
Chiltern Hills
LONDON
Southend-on-Sea
Kenmare
Cork
Llanelli
Newport
Swindon
Thames
Margate
Bantry
Milford Haven
Swansea
Port Talbot
Bristol
Bath
Reading
Canterbury
Cape Clear
Cardiff
Avon
Salisbury Plain
Maidstone
Dover
Bristol Channel
Guildford
Calais
Barnstaple
Exmoor
Taunton
Salisbury
Winchester
Folkestone
Strait of Dover
Hartland Point
The Weald
Southampton
Hastings
Bude
Exe
Yeovil
Poole
Boulogne
Isle of Wight
Portsmouth
Brighton
Exeter
Bournemouth
Le Touquet
Tamar
Dartmoor
Weymouth
Tavistock
Bodmin
Torquay
Portland Bill
Abbeville
Plymouth
Truro
Start Point
Penzance
Falmouth
Dieppe
Land's End
FRANCE
Isles of Scilly
Lizard Point
Alderney
Cherbourg
Baie de la Seine
Le Havre
Rouen
Guernsey
Sark
Jersey
Caen
Seine
Collines de Normandie
0 25 50 75 100 Miles
0 50 100 150 Kms
Conical Orthomorphic Projection
© Oxford Cartographers, 97094
+44 (0)1865 882 884
E & OE

Europe
0 100 200 300 400 Miles
0 100 200 300 400 500 600 Kms
Conical Orthomorphic Projection
© Oxford Cartographers, 97094
+44 (0)1865 882 884
E & OE
ATLANTIC OCEAN
ICELAND
Reykjavik
Arctic Circle
Norwegian Sea
North Sea
Faeroe Is. (Denmark)
Shetland Is.
Orkney Is.
Hebrides
UNITED KINGDOM
REP. OF IRELAND
NORWAY
SWEDEN
DENMARK
NETHERLANDS
BELGIUM
LUX.
GERMANY
FRANCE
SWITZERLAND
LIECH.
AUSTRIA
CZECH REP.
SLOV.
CROATIA
ITALY
SAN MARINO
MONACO
ANDORRA
SPAIN
PORTUGAL
MOROCCO
ALGERIA
TUNISIA
MALTA
English Channel
Bay of Biscay
Skagerrak
Mediterranean
Adriatic
Pyrenees
Apennines
Atlas Mountains
Balearic Is. (Sp.)
Corsica (Fr.)
Sardinia (It.)
Sicily
Bornholm (Den.)
London
Paris
Madrid
Lisbon
Dublin
Amsterdam
Brussels
Luxembourg
Berlin
Copenhagen
Oslo
Stockholm
Bern
Vienna
Prague
Rome
Rabat
Algiers
Tunis
Valletta

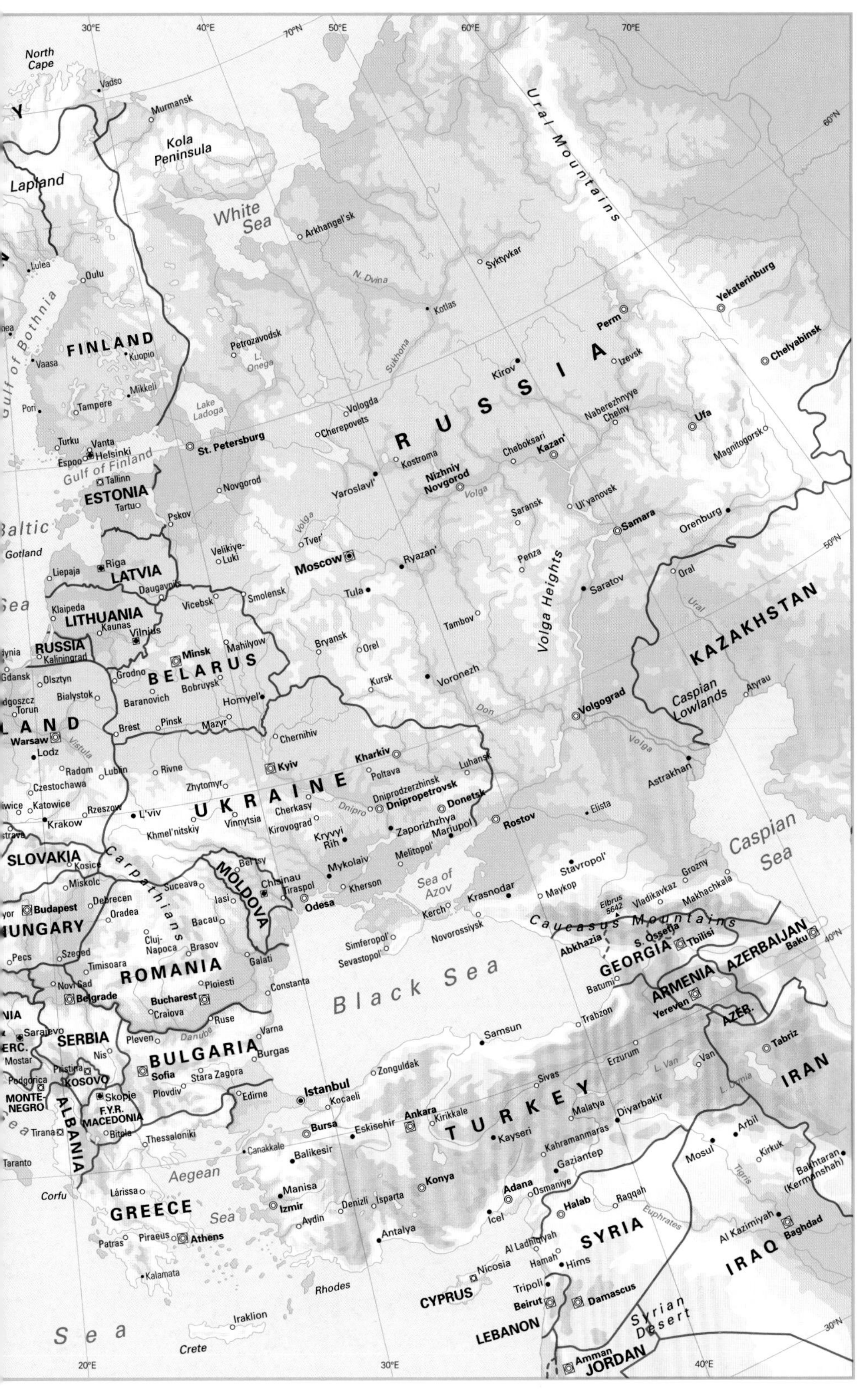

North Cape
Vadso
Murmansk
Kola Peninsula
Lapland
White Sea
Arkhangel'sk
Ural Mountains
Syktyvkar
N. Dvina
Kotlas
Yekaterinburg
Perm
Chelyabinsk
Lulea
Oulu
Gulf of Bothnia
FINLAND
Kuopio
Vaasa
Mikkeli
Tampere
Pori
Turku
Vanta
Espoo
Helsinki
Gulf of Finland
Tallinn
ESTONIA
Tartu
Petrozavodsk
L. Onega
Sukhona
Lake Ladoga
St. Petersburg
Vologda
Cherepovets
RUSSIA
Kirov
Izevsk
Naberezhnyye Chelny
Ufa
Magnitogorsk
Kostroma
Cheboksari
Kazan'
Yaroslavl'
Nizhniy Novgorod
Volga
Novgorod
Pskov
Ul'yanovsk
Saransk
Samara
Orenburg
Baltic Sea
Gotland
Tver'
Velikiye-Luki
Moscow
Ryazan'
Penza
Riga
Liepaja
LATVIA
Daugavpils
Smolensk
Tula
Oral
Saratov
Volga Heights
Vicebsk
Klaipeda
LITHUANIA
Kaunas
Vilnius
Ural
KAZAKHSTAN
Tambov
RUSSIA
Kaliningrad
Minsk
Mahilyow
Bryansk
Orel
Gdansk
Olsztyn
BELARUS
Grodno
Bobruysk
Voronezh
Kursk
Bialystok
Baranovich
Homyel'
Torun
Caspian Lowlands
Atyrau
Volgograd
Don
POLAND
Brest
Pinsk
Mazyr
Warsaw
Vistula
Chernihiv
Lodz
Radom
Lublin
Rivne
Kyiv
Kharkiv
Luhansk
Poltava
Volga
Astrakhan
Czestochawa
Zhytomyr
UKRAINE
Dniprodzerzhinsk
Dnipropetrovsk
Donetsk
Katowice
Rzeszow
L'viv
Cherkasy
Dnipro
Elista
Krakow
Khmel'nitskiy
Vinnytsia
Kirovograd
Kryvyi Rih
Zaporizhzhya
Mariupol
Rostov
Caspian Sea
SLOVAKIA
Kosice
Carpathians
Beltsy
Melitopol'
Miskolc
MOLDOVA
Mykolaiv
Stavropol'
Chisinau
Kherson
Sea of Azov
Grozny
Suceava
Iasi
Tiraspol
Krasnodar
Maykop
Vladikavkaz
Makhachkala
Budapest
Debrecen
Odesa
Elbrus 5642
HUNGARY
Oradea
Bacau
Kerch
Caucasus Mountains
Cluj-Napoca
Novorossiysk
Pecs
Brasov
Simferopol'
Abkhazia
S. Ossetia
Tbilisi
AZERBAIJAN
Baku
Szeged
Sevastopol'
GEORGIA
Timisoara
Galati
ROMANIA
Black Sea
Novi Sad
Ploiesti
Constanta
Batumi
ARMENIA
Belgrade
Bucharest
Yerevan
Craiova
Ruse
Trabzon
AZER.
Sarajevo
Danube
Varna
Samsun
BOSNIA-HERC.
SERBIA
Pleven
Tabriz
Mostar
Nis
BULGARIA
Burgas
Erzurum
Pristina
Sofia
Zonguldak
L. Van
Van
IRAN
Podgorica
KOSOVO
Stara Zagora
L. Urmia
Sivas
MONTENEGRO
Skopje
Plovdiv
Edirne
Istanbul
ALBANIA
F.Y.R. MACEDONIA
Kocaeli
TURKEY
Malatya
Diyarbakir
Tirana
Bitola
Bursa
Eskisehir
Ankara
Kirikkale
Thessaloniki
Kayseri
Arbil
Kahramanmaras
Mosul
Canakkale
Balikesir
Kirkuk
Gaziantep
Taranto
Aegean Sea
Bakhtaran (Kermanshah)
Tigris
Manisa
Konya
Adana
Osmaniye
Corfu
Larissa
Raqqah
Izmir
Denizli
Isparta
Halab
GREECE
Icel
Euphrates
Aydin
SYRIA
Al Kazimiyah
Baghdad
Patras
Piraeus
Athens
Antalya
Al Ladhiqiyah
Hamah
Hims
IRAQ
Kalamata
Nicosia
Tripoli
Rhodes
CYPRUS
Beirut
Damascus
Syrian Desert
Iraklion
LEBANON
Sea
Crete
Amman
JORDAN
30°E
40°E
50°E
60°E
70°E
70°N
60°N
50°N
40°N
30°N
20°E

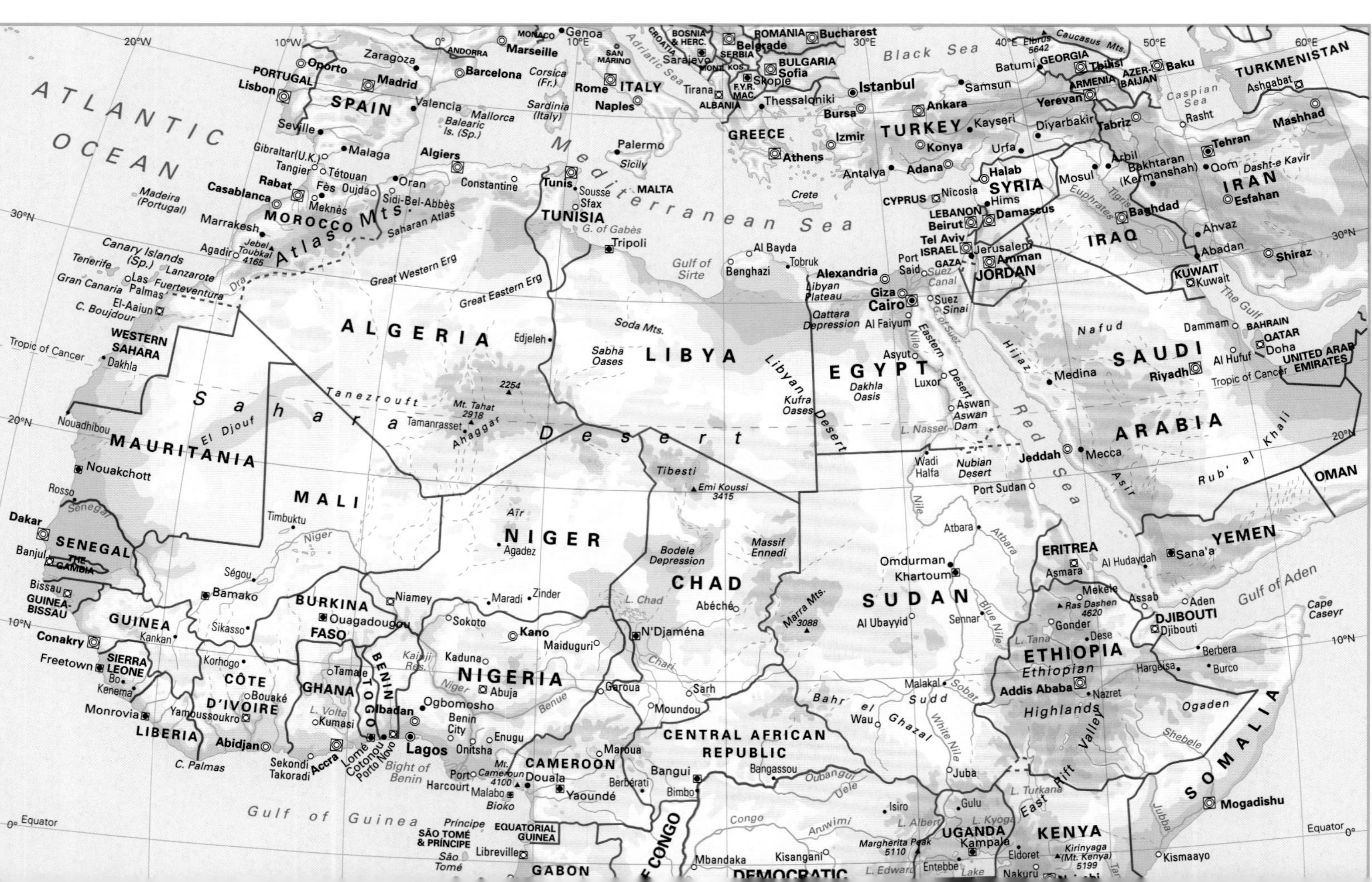

ATLANTIC OCEAN
Madeira (Portugal)
Canary Islands (Sp.)
Tenerife
Gran Canaria
Las Palmas
Lanzarote
Fuerteventura
El-Aaiun
C. Boujdour
WESTERN SAHARA
Dakhla
Tropic of Cancer
PORTUGAL
Lisbon
Oporto
SPAIN
Madrid
Zaragoza
Valencia
Seville
Malaga
Gibraltar(U.K.)
ANDORRA
Barcelona
Mallorca
Balearic Is. (Sp.)
MONACO
Marseille
Genoa
Corsica (Fr.)
Sardinia (Italy)
SAN MARINO
ITALY
Rome
Naples
Palermo
Sicily
MALTA
Adriatic Sea
CROATIA
BOSNIA & HERC.
Sarajevo
SERBIA
Belgrade
MONT.
KOS.
F.Y.R. MAC.
Skopje
Tirana
ALBANIA
GREECE
Athens
Thessaloniki
Crete
ROMANIA
Bucharest
BULGARIA
Sofia
Black Sea
Istanbul
Bursa
Izmir
TURKEY
Ankara
Samsun
Kayseri
Konya
Antalya
Adana
CYPRUS
Nicosia
Tangier
Tétouan
Rabat
Casablanca
Fès
Meknès
Oujda
Oran
Sidi-Bel-Abbès
Algiers
Constantine
MOROCCO
Marrakesh
Agadir
Jebel Toubkal 4165
Atlas Mts.
Saharan Atlas
Great Western Erg
Great Eastern Erg
Tunis
Sousse
Sfax
TUNISIA
G. of Gabès
Tripoli
Mediterranean Sea
Gulf of Sirte
Benghazi
Al Bayda
Tobruk
ALGERIA
Edjeleh
Soda Mts.
Sabha Oases
LIBYA
Libyan Desert
Kufra Oases
Tanezrouft
2254
Mt. Tahat 2918
Tamanrasset
Ahaggar
Sahara Desert
MAURITANIA
Nouadhibou
Nouakchott
El Djouf
Rosso
Senegal
Dakar
SENEGAL
Banjul
THE GAMBIA
Bissau
GUINEA-BISSAU
GUINEA
Conakry
Kankan
Freetown
SIERRA LEONE
Bo
Kenema
Monrovia
LIBERIA
C. Palmas
MALI
Timbuktu
Niger
Ségou
Bamako
Sikasso
Korhogo
CÔTE D'IVOIRE
Bouaké
Yamoussoukro
Abidjan
BURKINA FASO
Ouagadougou
GHANA
Tamale
L. Volta
Kumasi
Accra
Sekondi Takoradi
TOGO
Lomé
BENIN
Cotonou
Porto Novo
Niamey
NIGER
Aïr
Agadez
Maradi
Zinder
Sokoto
Kano
Kaduna
Maiduguri
Kainji Res.
NIGERIA
Abuja
Ibadan
Ogbomosho
Lagos
Benin City
Enugu
Onitsha
Benue
Port Harcourt
Bight of Benin
Gulf of Guinea
Mt. Cameroun 4100
Malabo
Bioko
Douala
Yaoundé
CAMEROON
Garoua
Maroua
Berbérati
Príncipe
SÃO TOMÉ & PRÍNCIPE
São Tomé
EQUATORIAL GUINEA
Libreville
GABON
CONGO
Equator
Tibesti
Emi Koussi 3415
CHAD
Bodele Depression
Massif Ennedi
L. Chad
N'Djaména
Chari
Abéché
Sarh
Moundou
Bangui
Bimbo
CENTRAL AFRICAN REPUBLIC
Bangassou
Oubangui
Uele
Congo
Aruwimi
Mbandaka
Kisangani
DEMOCRATIC
Marra Mts. 3088
Alexandria
Libyan Plateau
Qattara Depression
Giza
Cairo
Al Faiyum
Port Said
Suez Canal
Suez
Sinai
G. of Suez
EGYPT
Dakhla Oasis
Asyut
Luxor
Eastern Desert
Nile
Aswan
Aswan Dam
L. Nasser
Wadi Halfa
Nubian Desert
Port Sudan
Atbara
Omdurman
Khartoum
SUDAN
Al Ubayyid
Sennar
Blue Nile
Malakal
Sobat
Sudd
Bahr el Ghazal
Wau
White Nile
Juba
Isiro
L. Albert
Margherita Peak 5110
L. Edward
Gulu
L. Kyoga
UGANDA
Kampala
Entebbe
Lake
L. Turkana
KENYA
Eldoret
Nakuru
Kirinyaga (Mt. Kenya) 5199
ERITREA
Asmara
Mekele
Ras Dashen 4620
Gonder
Dese
L. Tana
ETHIOPIA
Ethiopian Highlands
Addis Ababa
Nazret
East Rift Valley
Assab
DJIBOUTI
Djibouti
Aden
Gulf of Aden
Cape Caseyr
Berbera
Hargeisa
Burco
Ogaden
Shebele
Jubba
SOMALIA
Mogadishu
Kismaayo
Tel Aviv
ISRAEL
GAZA
Jerusalem
Amman
JORDAN
LEBANON
Beirut
Damascus
Hims
SYRIA
Halab
Urfa
Diyarbakir
Mosul
Arbil
Euphrates
Tigris
Baghdad
IRAQ
Bakhtaran (Kermanshah)
Batumi
GEORGIA
Tbilisi
Elbrus 5642
Caucasus Mts.
ARMENIA
Yerevan
AZER-BAIJAN
Baku
Tabriz
Caspian Sea
Rasht
Tehran
Qom
Dasht-e Kavir
IRAN
Esfahan
Ahvaz
Abadan
Shiraz
TURKMENISTAN
Ashgabat
Mashhad
KUWAIT
Kuwait
The Gulf
Dammam
BAHRAIN
QATAR
Doha
Al Hufuf
UNITED ARAB EMIRATES
Tropic of Cancer
Nafud
SAUDI ARABIA
Riyadh
Hijaz
Medina
Jeddah
Mecca
Red Sea
Asir
Rub' al Khali
OMAN
YEMEN
Sana'a
Al Hudaydah
20°W
10°W
0°
10°E
20°E
30°E
40°E
50°E
60°E
30°N
20°N
10°N
0°

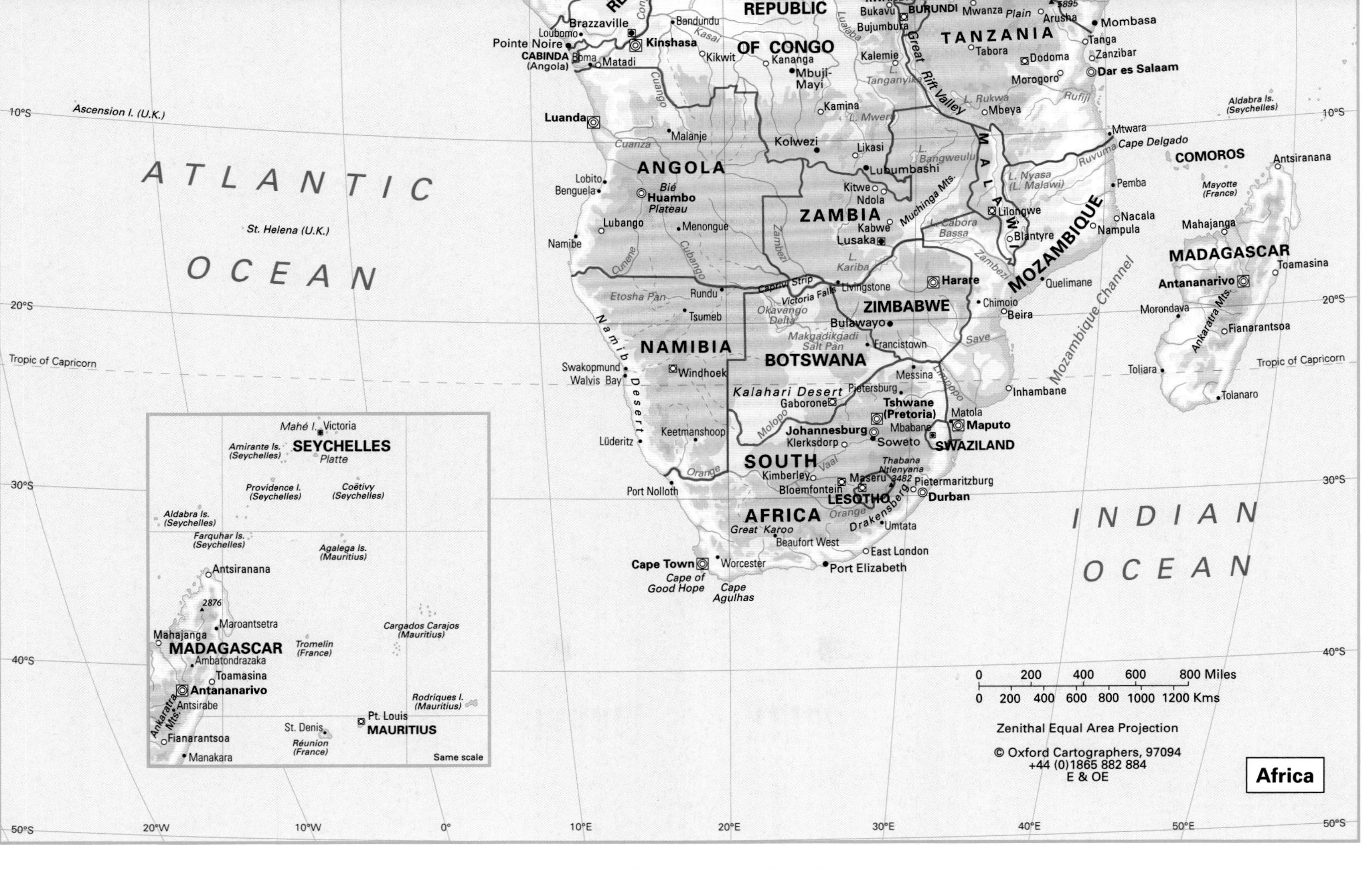
ATLANTIC OCEAN
INDIAN OCEAN
Ascension I. (U.K.)
St. Helena (U.K.)
REPUBLIC OF CONGO
TANZANIA
ANGOLA
ZAMBIA
MALAWI
MOZAMBIQUE
ZIMBABWE
NAMIBIA
BOTSWANA
SOUTH AFRICA
LESOTHO
SWAZILAND
MADAGASCAR
COMOROS
BURUNDI
CABINDA (Angola)
Brazzaville
Loubomo
Pointe Noire
Boma
Matadi
Kinshasa
Bandundu
Kikwit
Kananga
Mbuji-Mayi
Kamina
Kolwezi
Likasi
Lubumbashi
Kitwe
Ndola
Kabwe
Lusaka
Bukavu
Bujumbura
Kalemie
Mwanza
Arusha
Mombasa
Tanga
Zanzibar
Dar es Salaam
Tabora
Dodoma
Morogoro
Mbeya
Mtwara
Cape Delgado
Pemba
Nacala
Nampula
Lilongwe
Blantyre
Quelimane
Chimoio
Beira
Inhambane
Maputo
Matola
Mbabane
Harare
Bulawayo
Francistown
Livingstone
Victoria Falls
Caprivi Strip
Okavango Delta
Makgadikgadi Salt Pan
Kalahari Desert
Gaborone
Messina
Pietersburg
Tshwane (Pretoria)
Johannesburg
Soweto
Klerksdorp
Kimberley
Bloemfontein
Maseru
Thabana Ntlenyana 3482
Pietermaritzburg
Durban
Drakensberg
Umtata
East London
Port Elizabeth
Beaufort West
Great Karoo
Worcester
Cape Town
Cape of Good Hope
Cape Agulhas
Port Nolloth
Lüderitz
Keetmanshoop
Windhoek
Swakopmund
Walvis Bay
Namib Desert
Tsumeb
Rundu
Etosha Pan
Luanda
Malanje
Lobito
Benguela
Bié Plateau
Huambo
Menongue
Lubango
Namibe
Cuanza
Cuango
Kasai
Lualaba
Cubango
Cunene
Zambezi
Orange
Vaal
Molopo
Limpopo
Save
Ruvuma
Rufiji
L. Tanganyika
L. Mweru
L. Bangweulu
L. Rukwa
L. Nyasa (L. Malawi)
L. Cabora Bassa
L. Kariba
Great Rift Valley
Muchinga Mts.
Mozambique Channel
Mayotte (France)
Aldabra Is. (Seychelles)
Antsiranana
Mahajanga
Toamasina
Antananarivo
Ankaratra Mts.
Fianarantsoa
Morondava
Toliara
Tolanaro
Tropic of Capricorn
10°S
20°S
30°S
40°S
50°S
20°W
10°W
0°
10°E
20°E
30°E
40°E
50°E
Mahé I.
Victoria
SEYCHELLES
Platte
Amirante Is. (Seychelles)
Providence I. (Seychelles)
Coëtivy (Seychelles)
Aldabra Is. (Seychelles)
Farquhar Is. (Seychelles)
Agalega Is. (Mauritius)
Cargados Carajos (Mauritius)
Tromelin (France)
Rodriques I. (Mauritius)
Pt. Louis
MAURITIUS
St. Denis
Réunion (France)
Antsiranana
2876
Maroantsetra
Mahajanga
MADAGASCAR
Ambatondrazaka
Toamasina
Antananarivo
Antsirabe
Ankaratra Mts.
Fianarantsoa
Manakara
Same scale
0 200 400 600 800 Miles
0 200 400 600 800 1000 1200 Kms
Zenithal Equal Area Projection
© Oxford Cartographers, 97094
+44 (0)1865 882 884
E & OE
Africa

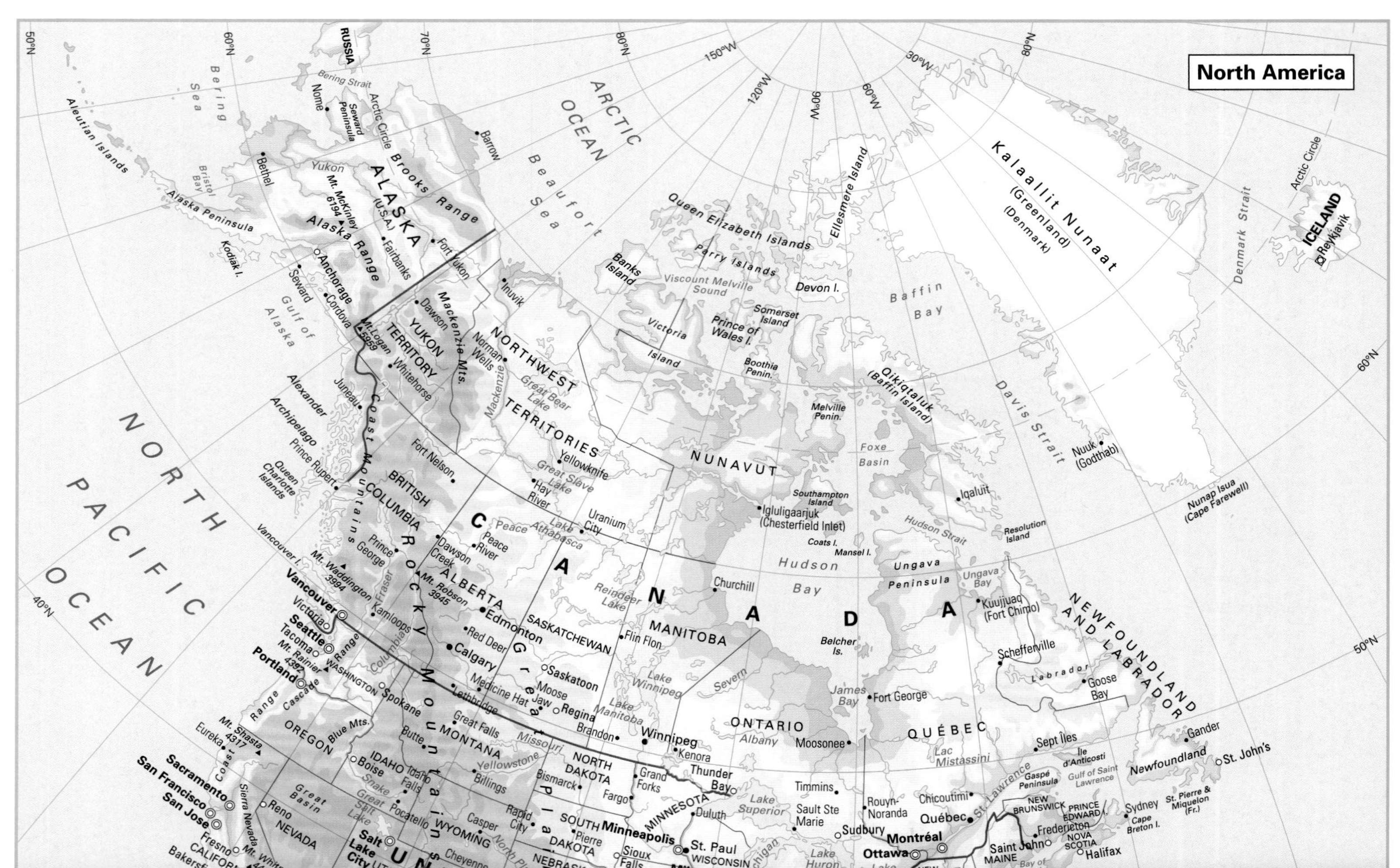
North America
ARCTIC OCEAN
Beaufort Sea
Bering Sea
Bering Strait
Arctic Circle
RUSSIA
Nome
Seward Peninsula
Barrow
Aleutian Islands
Bristol Bay
Alaska Peninsula
Kodiak I.
Bethel
Yukon
ALASKA (U.S.A.)
Brooks Range
Mt. McKinley 6194
Alaska Range
Fairbanks
Fort Yukon
Anchorage
Seward
Cordova
Gulf of Alaska
Mt. Logan 5959
Dawson
YUKON TERRITORY
Whitehorse
Mackenzie Mts.
Inuvik
Norman Wells
Mackenzie
NORTHWEST TERRITORIES
Great Bear Lake
Juneau
Alexander Archipelago
Prince Rupert
Queen Charlotte Islands
Coast Mountains
Fort Nelson
BRITISH COLUMBIA
Yellowknife
Great Slave Lake
Hay River
Uranium City
Lake Athabasca
Peace
Peace River
Dawson Creek
Prince George
Mt. Waddington 3994
Vancouver I.
Vancouver
Victoria
Mt. Robson 3945
ALBERTA
Edmonton
Red Deer
Calgary
Kamloops
Fraser
Columbia
Rocky Mountains
Seattle
Tacoma
Mt. Rainier 4392
WASHINGTON
Spokane
Portland
Cascade Range
Blue Mts.
OREGON
Mt. Shasta 4317
Eureka
Coast Range
Sacramento
San Francisco
San Jose
Fresno
Sierra Nevada
Reno
NEVADA
Great Basin
IDAHO
Boise
Idaho Falls
Snake
Pocatello
Great Salt Lake
Salt Lake City
Butte
MONTANA
Great Falls
Lethbridge
Medicine Hat
Yellowstone
Billings
Missouri
Casper
WYOMING
Cheyenne
Rapid City
Great Plains
SASKATCHEWAN
Saskatoon
Moose Jaw
Regina
Brandon
NORTH DAKOTA
Bismarck
SOUTH DAKOTA
Pierre
Sioux Falls
Fargo
Grand Forks
MINNESOTA
Minneapolis
St. Paul
WISCONSIN
Duluth
Reindeer Lake
Flin Flon
MANITOBA
Lake Winnipeg
Lake Manitoba
Winnipeg
Kenora
Thunder Bay
CANADA
Banks Island
Queen Elizabeth Islands
Parry Islands
Viscount Melville Sound
Victoria Island
Ellesmere Island
Devon I.
Somerset Island
Prince of Wales I.
Boothia Penin.
NUNAVUT
Melville Penin.
Southampton Island
Igluligaarjuk (Chesterfield Inlet)
Coats I.
Mansel I.
Hudson Bay
Churchill
Severn
Belcher Is.
James Bay
Fort George
ONTARIO
Albany
Moosonee
Timmins
Lake Superior
Sault Ste Marie
Sudbury
Lake Huron
Rouyn-Noranda
Ottawa
Montréal
Québec
Chicoutimi
QUÉBEC
Lac Mistassini
Baffin Bay
Qikiqtaluk (Baffin Island)
Foxe Basin
Iqaluit
Hudson Strait
Resolution Island
Ungava Peninsula
Ungava Bay
Kuujjuaq (Fort Chimo)
Schefferville
Labrador
Goose Bay
NEWFOUNDLAND AND LABRADOR
Sept Îles
Île d'Anticosti
Gulf of Saint Lawrence
Gaspé Peninsula
St. Lawrence
NEW BRUNSWICK
Fredericton
Saint John
MAINE
PRINCE EDWARD I.
NOVA SCOTIA
Halifax
Sydney
Cape Breton I.
St. Pierre & Miquelon (Fr.)
Newfoundland
Gander
St. John's
Davis Strait
Nuuk (Godthab)
Kalaallit Nunaat (Greenland) (Denmark)
Nunap Isua (Cape Farewell)
Denmark Strait
ICELAND
Reykjavik
NORTH PACIFIC OCEAN
30°W
60°W
90°W
120°W
150°W
80°N
70°N
60°N
50°N
40°N

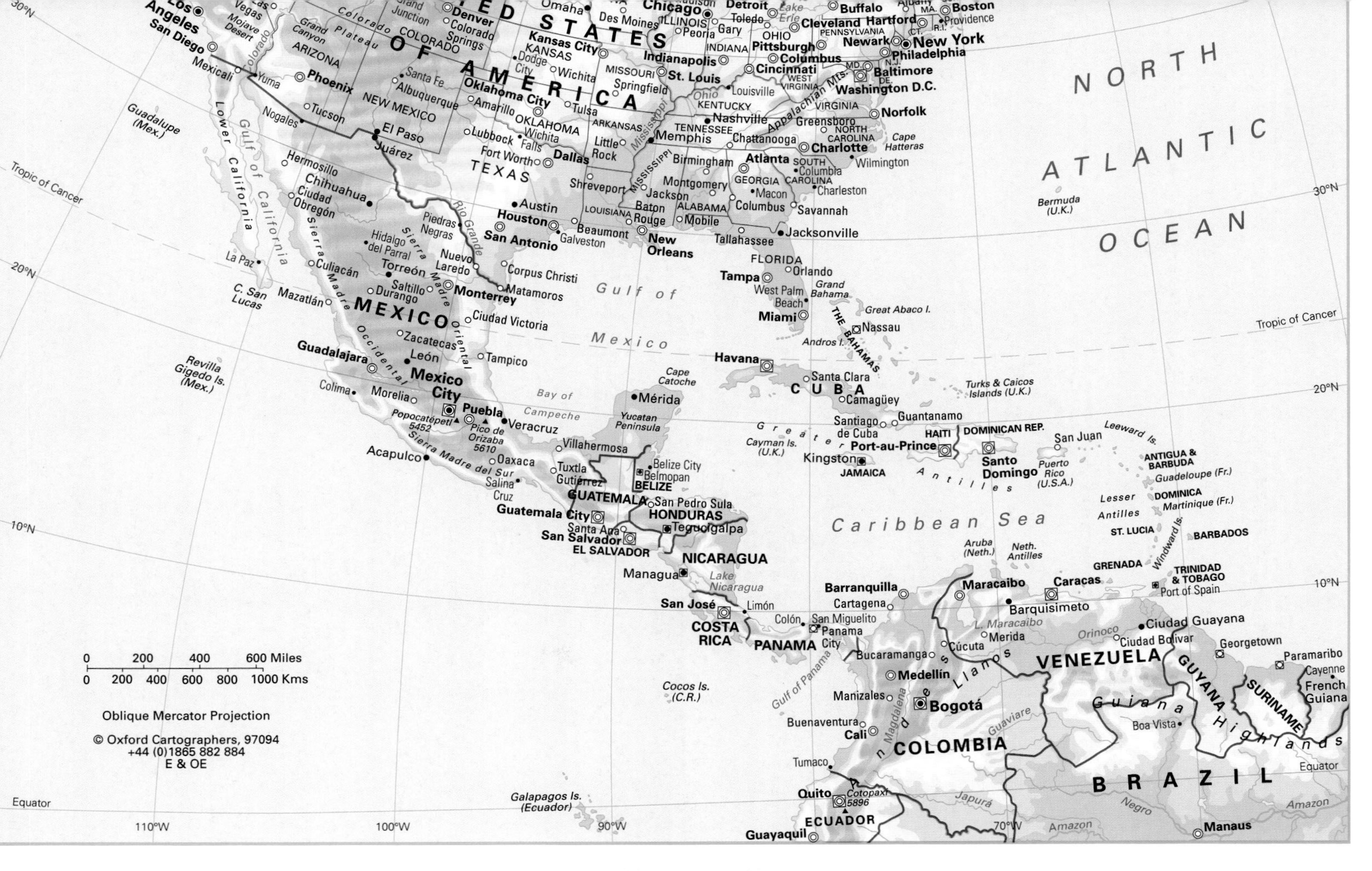
NORTH ATLANTIC OCEAN
UNITED STATES OF AMERICA
MEXICO
Gulf of Mexico
Caribbean Sea
Greater Antilles
Lesser Antilles
Tropic of Cancer
Equator
30°N
20°N
10°N
110°W
100°W
90°W
70°W
Los Angeles
San Diego
Mexicali
Yuma
Phoenix
Tucson
Nogales
El Paso
Juárez
Denver
Colorado Springs
Santa Fe
Albuquerque
Oklahoma City
Dallas
Fort Worth
Austin
Houston
San Antonio
Galveston
Beaumont
New Orleans
Baton Rouge
Mobile
Memphis
Nashville
Atlanta
Jacksonville
Tallahassee
Tampa
Orlando
Miami
Chicago
Detroit
Buffalo
Boston
New York
Philadelphia
Baltimore
Washington D.C.
Norfolk
Charlotte
Wilmington
Charleston
Savannah
Pittsburgh
Cleveland
Columbus
Cincinnati
Indianapolis
St. Louis
Kansas City
Omaha
Des Moines
Tulsa
Wichita
Amarillo
Lubbock
Little Rock
Shreveport
Birmingham
Montgomery
Chattanooga
Louisville
Greensboro
Hermosillo
Chihuahua
Ciudad Obregón
Culiacán
Mazatlán
La Paz
C. San Lucas
Torreón
Saltillo
Durango
Monterrey
Nuevo Laredo
Piedras Negras
Matamoros
Corpus Christi
Ciudad Victoria
Tampico
Zacatecas
León
Guadalajara
Colima
Morelia
Mexico City
Puebla
Veracruz
Acapulco
Oaxaca
Villahermosa
Tuxtla Gutiérrez
Mérida
Belize City
Belmopan
BELIZE
GUATEMALA
Guatemala City
San Pedro Sula
HONDURAS
Tegucigalpa
San Salvador
EL SALVADOR
NICARAGUA
Managua
COSTA RICA
San José
Limón
PANAMA
Panama City
Colón
Havana
CUBA
Santa Clara
Camagüey
Santiago de Cuba
Guantanamo
Kingston
JAMAICA
HAITI
Port-au-Prince
DOMINICAN REP.
Santo Domingo
San Juan
Puerto Rico (U.S.A.)
THE BAHAMAS
Nassau
Turks & Caicos Islands (U.K.)
Bermuda (U.K.)
ANTIGUA & BARBUDA
Guadeloupe (Fr.)
DOMINICA
Martinique (Fr.)
ST. LUCIA
BARBADOS
GRENADA
TRINIDAD & TOBAGO
Port of Spain
Aruba (Neth.)
Neth. Antilles
Barranquilla
Cartagena
Maracaibo
Caracas
Barquisimeto
VENEZUELA
Ciudad Guayana
Ciudad Bolívar
Mérida
Cúcuta
Bucaramanga
Medellín
Bogotá
COLOMBIA
Manizales
Cali
Buenaventura
Tumaco
Quito
ECUADOR
Guayaquil
Cotopaxi 5896
GUYANA
Georgetown
SURINAME
Paramaribo
Cayenne
French Guiana
BRAZIL
Manaus
Boa Vista
Guiana Highlands
Llanos
Galapagos Is. (Ecuador)
Cocos Is. (C.R.)
Revilla Gigedo Is. (Mex.)
Guadalupe (Mex.)
Gulf of California
Lower California
Sierra Madre Occidental
Sierra Madre Oriental
Sierra Madre del Sur
Yucatan Peninsula
Bay of Campeche
Popocatépetl 5452
Pico de Orizaba 5610
Rio Grande
Mississippi
0 200 400 600 Miles
0 200 400 600 800 1000 Kms
Oblique Mercator Projection
© Oxford Cartographers, 97094
+44 (0)1865 882 884
E & OE

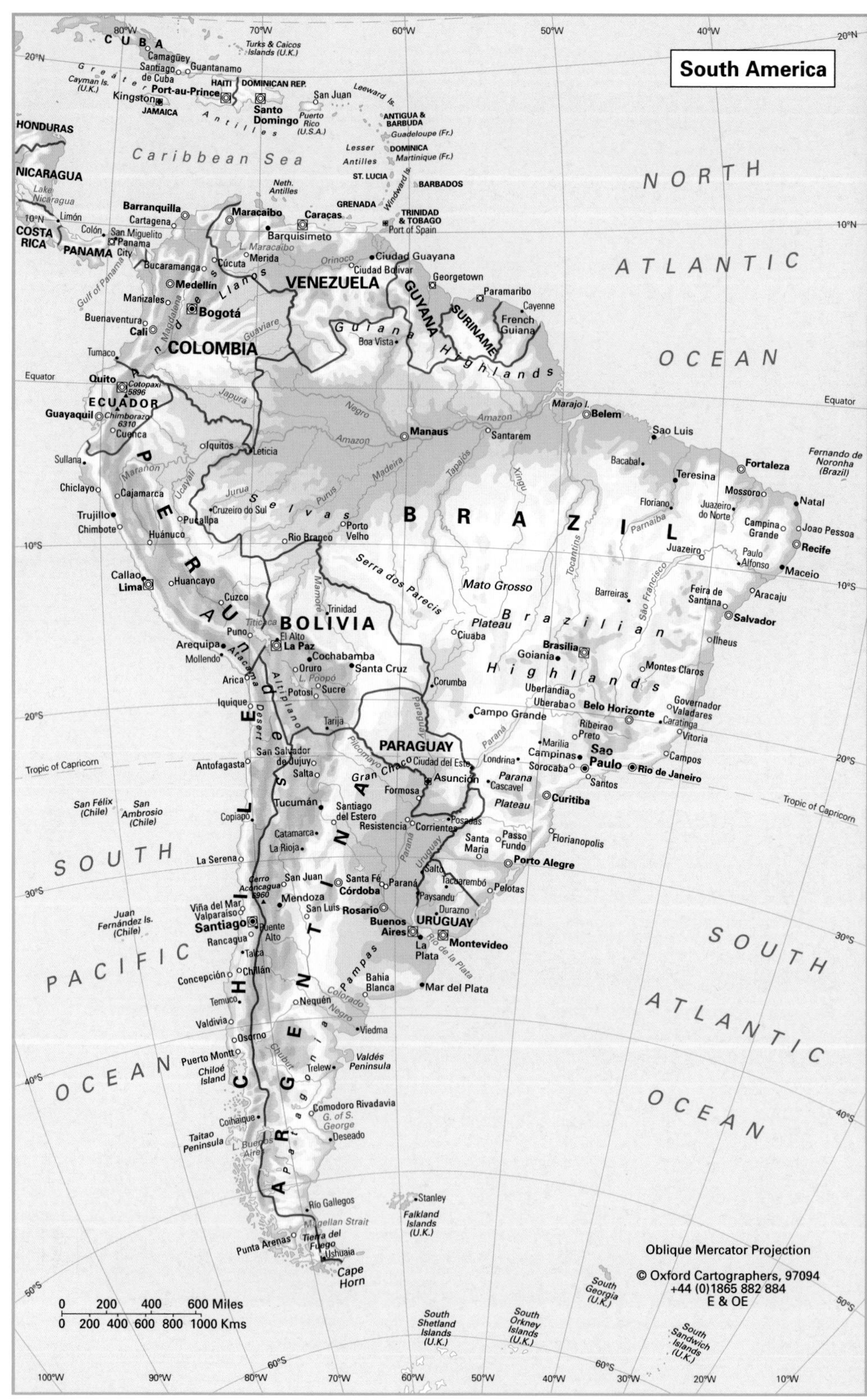

South America
CUBA
Camagüey
Santiago de Cuba
Guantanamo
Turks & Caicos Islands (U.K.)
Cayman Is. (U.K.)
Greater Antilles
HAITI
DOMINICAN REP.
Port-au-Prince
Kingston
JAMAICA
Santo Domingo
San Juan
Puerto Rico (U.S.A.)
Leeward Is.
ANTIGUA & BARBUDA
Guadeloupe (Fr.)
DOMINICA
Martinique (Fr.)
Lesser Antilles
ST. LUCIA
Windward Is.
BARBADOS
GRENADA
TRINIDAD & TOBAGO
Port of Spain
HONDURAS
NICARAGUA
Lake Nicaragua
Caribbean Sea
Neth. Antilles
COSTA RICA
Limón
Colón
PANAMA
San Miguelito
Panama City
Gulf of Panama
Barranquilla
Cartagena
Maracaibo
L. Maracaibo
Caracas
Barquisimeto
Merida
Cúcuta
Bucaramanga
Orinoco
Ciudad Guayana
Ciudad Bolivar
VENEZUELA
Georgetown
GUYANA
Paramaribo
SURINAME
Cayenne
French Guiana
Medellín
Manizales
Bogotá
Buenaventura
Cali
Llanos
Magdalena
Andes
Guaviare
COLOMBIA
Guiana Highlands
Boa Vista
Tumaco
Equator
Quito
Cotopaxi 5896
ECUADOR
Guayaquil
Chimborazo 6310
Cuenca
Japurá
Negro
Amazon
Manaus
Marajo I.
Belem
Santarem
Sao Luis
NORTH ATLANTIC OCEAN
Sullana
Iquitos
Leticia
Marañón
Ucayali
Chiclayo
Cajamarca
Trujillo
Chimbote
Cruzeiro do Sul
Jurua
Purus
Madeira
Tapajós
Xingu
Selvas
Pucallpa
Porto Velho
Rio Branco
Huánuco
PERU
BRAZIL
Bacabal
Teresina
Fortaleza
Fernando de Noronha (Brazil)
Mossoro
Natal
Floriano
Juazeiro do Norte
Parnaiba
Campina Grande
Joao Pessoa
Recife
Juazeiro
Paulo Alfonso
Maceio
Tocantins
Serra dos Parecis
Mato Grosso Plateau
Callao
Lima
Huancayo
Cuzco
Mamoré
Trinidad
BOLIVIA
Barreiras
São Francisco
Feira de Santana
Aracaju
Salvador
Titicaca
Puno
El Alto
La Paz
Arequipa
Mollendo
Cochabamba
Oruro
Santa Cruz
L. Poopó
Potosi
Sucre
Arica
Atacama Desert
Altiplano
Corumba
Ciuaba
Brazilian Highlands
Brasilia
Goiania
Ilheus
Montes Claros
Uberlandia
Uberaba
Belo Horizonte
Governador Valadares
Caratinga
Campo Grande
Paraguay
Iquique
Tarija
Ribeirao Preto
Vitoria
Marilia
Campinas
Sao Paulo
Rio de Janeiro
Campos
Sorocaba
Santos
Londrina
Parana
Tropic of Capricorn
Antofagasta
San Salvador de Jujuy
Salta
PARAGUAY
Pilcomayo
Gran Chaco
Ciudad del Este
Asunción
Formosa
Cascavel
Parana Plateau
Curitiba
San Félix (Chile)
San Ambrosio (Chile)
Copiapo
Tucumán
Santiago del Estero
Resistencia
Corrientes
Posadas
Uruguay
Catamarca
La Rioja
Santa Maria
Passo Fundo
Florianopolis
SOUTH PACIFIC OCEAN
La Serena
Salto
Porto Alegre
San Juan
Cerro Aconcagua 6960
Santa Fé
Córdoba
Paraná
Tacuarembó
Pelotas
Paysandu
Viña del Mar
Valparaiso
Mendoza
San Luis
Rosario
Durazno
URUGUAY
Juan Fernández Is. (Chile)
Santiago
Puente Alto
Buenos Aires
Montevideo
La Plata
Rio de la Plata
Rancagua
Talca
ARGENTINA
CHILE
Pampas
Concepción
Chillán
Bahia Blanca
Mar del Plata
SOUTH ATLANTIC OCEAN
Temuco
Nequén
Colorado
Valdivia
Viedma
Osorno
Chubut
Puerto Montt
Chiloé Island
Trelew
Valdés Peninsula
Patagonia
Comodoro Rivadavia
G. of S. George
Coihaique
Deseado
Taitao Peninsula
L. Buenos Aires
Stanley
Río Gallegos
Falkland Islands (U.K.)
Magellan Strait
Punta Arenas
Tierra del Fuego
Ushuaia
Cape Horn
Oblique Mercator Projection
© Oxford Cartographers, 97094
+44 (0)1865 882 884
E & OE
South Georgia (U.K.)
0 200 400 600 Miles
0 200 400 600 800 1000 Kms
South Shetland Islands (U.K.)
South Orkney Islands (U.K.)
South Sandwich Islands (U.K.)
100°W
90°W
80°W
70°W
60°W
50°W
40°W
30°W
20°W
10°W
20°N
10°N
10°S
20°S
30°S
40°S
50°S
60°S

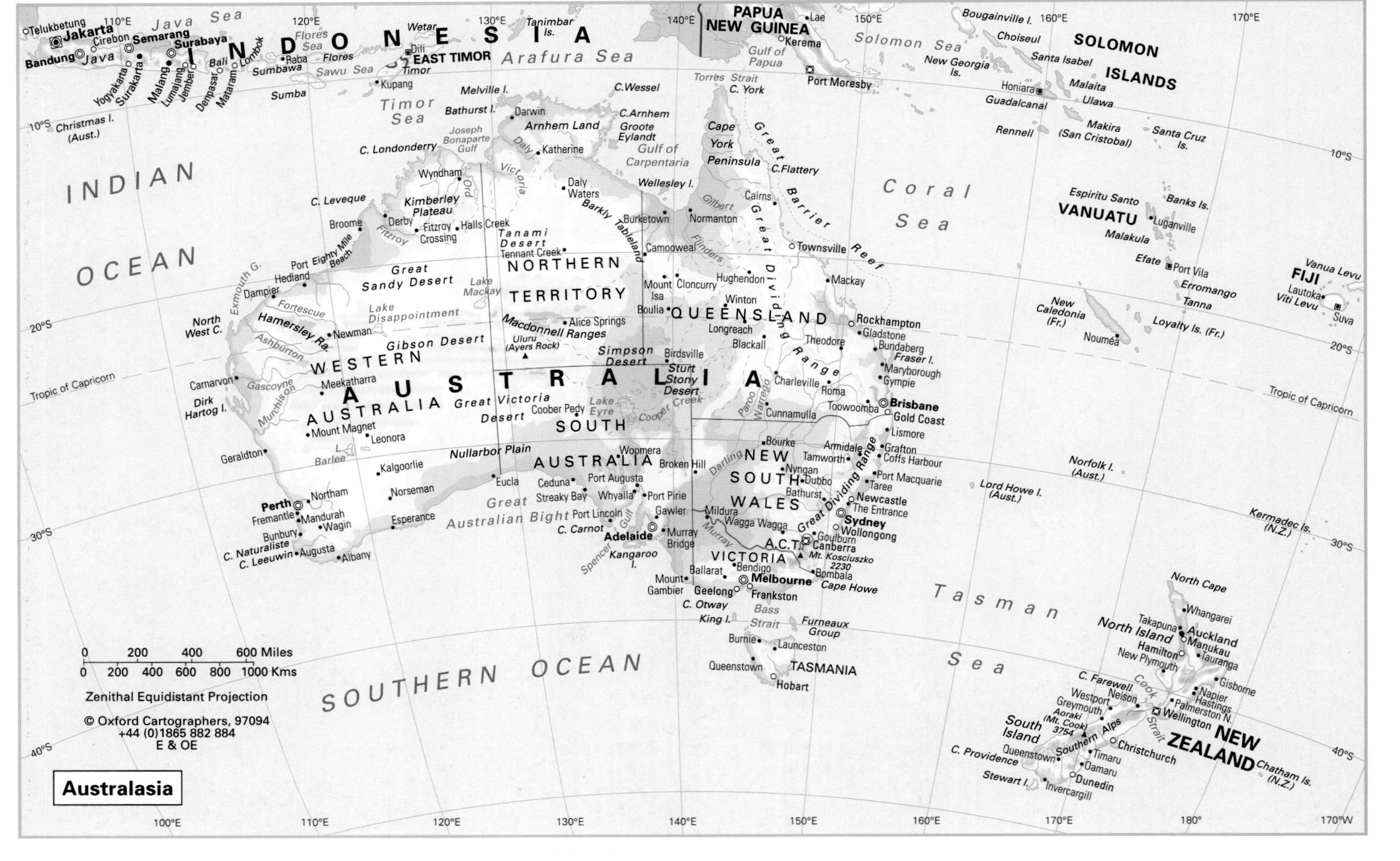
Australasia
INDONESIA
PAPUA NEW GUINEA
EAST TIMOR
SOLOMON ISLANDS
VANUATU
FIJI
AUSTRALIA
NEW ZEALAND
WESTERN AUSTRALIA
NORTHERN TERRITORY
SOUTH AUSTRALIA
QUEENSLAND
NEW SOUTH WALES
VICTORIA
A.C.T.
TASMANIA
INDIAN OCEAN
SOUTHERN OCEAN
Coral Sea
Tasman Sea
Arafura Sea
Timor Sea
Java Sea
Solomon Sea
Great Australian Bight
Gulf of Carpentaria
Great Barrier Reef
Great Dividing Range
Great Sandy Desert
Gibson Desert
Great Victoria Desert
Simpson Desert
Tanami Desert
Nullarbor Plain
Perth
Adelaide
Melbourne
Sydney
Canberra
Brisbane
Darwin
Hobart
Alice Springs
Uluru (Ayers Rock)
Wellington
Auckland
Christchurch
Port Moresby
Jakarta
Tropic of Capricorn
0 200 400 600 Miles
0 200 400 600 800 1000 Kms
Zenithal Equidistant Projection
© Oxford Cartographers, 97094
+44 (0)1865 882 884
E & OE

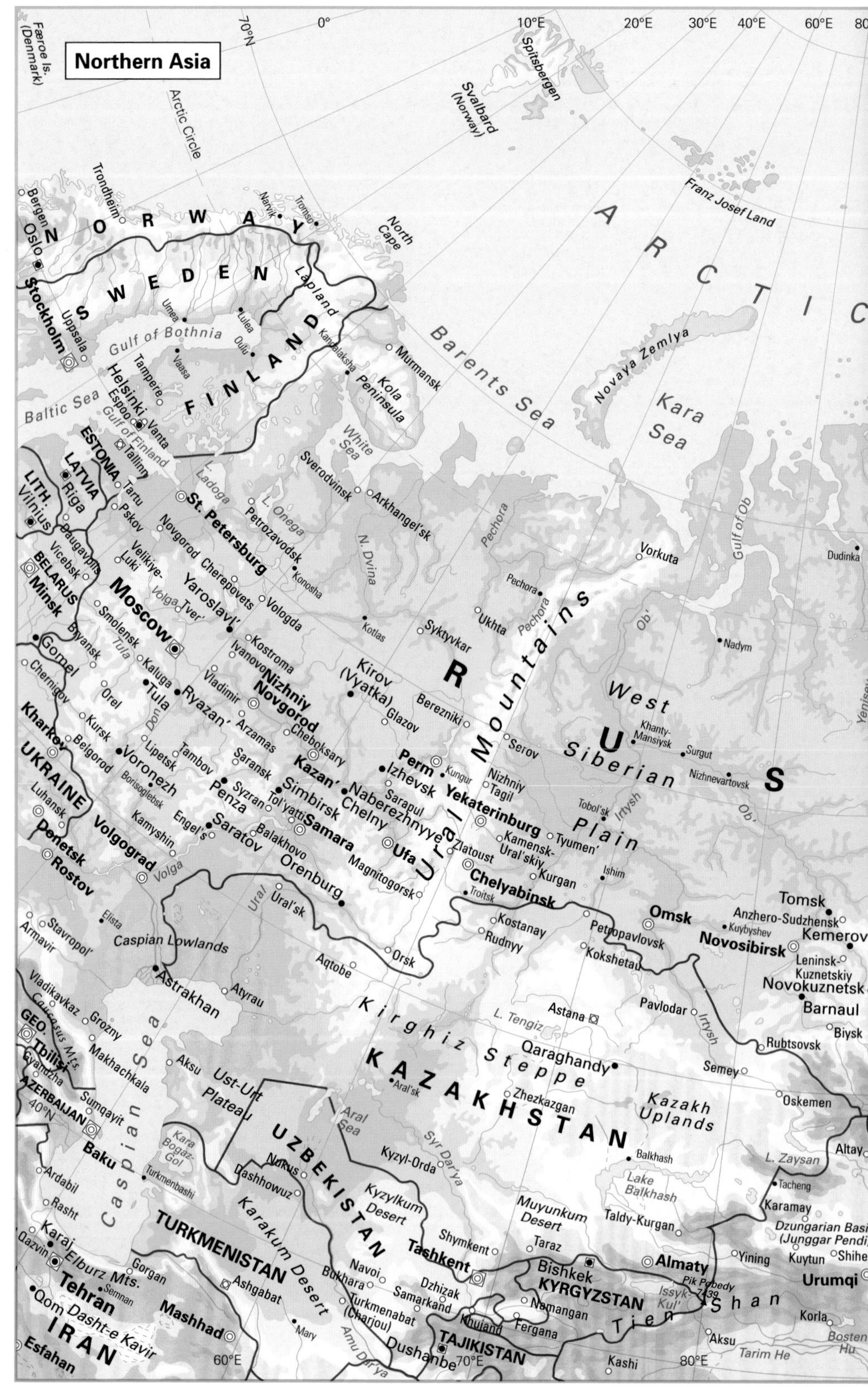

Northern Asia
ARCTIC
RUSSIA
KAZAKHSTAN
UZBEKISTAN
TURKMENISTAN
KYRGYZSTAN
TAJIKISTAN
IRAN
NORWAY
SWEDEN
FINLAND
ESTONIA
LATVIA
LITH.
BELARUS
UKRAINE
GEO.
AZERBAIJAN
Moscow
St. Petersburg
Ural Mountains
West Siberian Plain
Kirghiz Steppe
Kazakh Uplands
Caspian Sea
Aral Sea
Barents Sea
Kara Sea
Novaya Zemlya
Franz Josef Land
Svalbard (Norway)
Spitsbergen
Færoe Is. (Denmark)
Arctic Circle
Caspian Lowlands
Ust-Urt Plateau
Karakum Desert
Kyzylkum Desert
Muyunkum Desert
Tien Shan
Elburz Mts.
Dasht-e Kavir
Caucasus Mts.
Kola Peninsula
White Sea
Gulf of Bothnia
Gulf of Finland
Baltic Sea
Lapland
Gulf of Ob
Dzungarian Basin (Junggar Pendi)
Lake Balkhash
L. Tengiz
L. Zaysan
Almaty
Astana
Tashkent
Bishkek
Dushanbe
Ashgabat
Tehran
Baku
Tbilisi
Minsk
Kiev
Helsinki
Stockholm
Oslo
Riga
Vilnius
Tallinn

0 100 200 300 400 500 Miles
0 100 200 300 400 500 600 700 800 Kms
Conical Orthomorphic Projection
© Oxford Cartographers, 97094
+44 (0)1865 882 884
E & OE
Bering Sea
East Siberian
Wrangel I.
Anadyr Range
Pevek
Arctic Circle
Anadyr
Koryak Range
Severnaya Zemlya
New Siberia Is.
O C E A N
Laptev Sea
Lyakhov Is.
Taymyr Pen.
L. Taymyr
Tiksi
Indigirka
Kolyma
Kolyma Mts.
Yana
Cherskogo Range
Olenek
Verkhoyansk Range
Magadan
Okhotsk
Sea of Okhotsk
Noril'sk
Central Siberian Plateau
Lena
Yakutsk
Vilyuy
Aldan
Dzhugdzhur Range
Lower Tunguska
Olekminsk
Lensk
Sakhalin
Aleksandrovsk-Sakhalinskiy
A
I
S
Neryungri
Stanovoy Mts.
Tynda
Skovorodino
Komsomol'sk-na-Amure
Amur
Khabarovsk
Sikhote-Alin Mts.
Ust'-Ilimsk
Ust'-Kut
Angara
Lesosibirsk
Severobaikal'sk
Yablonovyy Mts.
Belogorsk
Blagoveshchensk
Birobidzhan
Achinsk
Kansk
Tayshet
Bratsk
Krasnoyarsk
Tulun
Lake Baikal
Chita
Sretensk
Da Hinggan Ling
Bei'an
Yichun
Hegang
Jiamusi
Shuangyashan
Qitaihe
Jixi
Mudanjiang
Ussuriysk
Sayan Mts.
Usol'ye-Sibirskoye
Angarsk
Irkutsk
Abakan
Ulan-Ude
Hailar
Manzhouli
Qiqihar
Daqing
Harbin
Vladivostok
Kyzyl
Hovsgol Nuur
Darhan
Ulanhot
Baicheng
Jilin
Yanji
Chongjin
Uvs Nuur
Ulaanbaatar
Ondorhaan
Changchun
Liaoyuan
Tongliao
Siping
Fushun
DEM. PEOPLE'S REP. OF KOREA
Hangayan Mts.
Altai Range
Hovd
Altay
MONGOLIA
Saynshand
INNER MONGOLIA
Chifeng
Shenyang
Fuxin
Anshan
Jinzhou
Pyongyang
Seoul
Gobi Desert
Korea Bay
Chengde
Zhangjiakou
Jining
Beijing (Peking)
Tangshan
Tianjin
Dalian
Inchon
REP. OF KOREA
Baotou
Hohhot
Datong
Bo Hai
Yantai
Weihai
Cangzhou
Turpan
Hami
Turpan Depression
Linhe
Huang He (Yellow)
Baoding
Shijiazhuang
Zibo
Weifang
Qingdao
Kwangju
C H I N A
Wuhai
Taiyuan
Yuci
Dezhou
Jinan
Yellow Sea
Shizuishan
Handan
Lop Nur
90°E
100°E
110°E
120°E
140°E
150°E
160°E
170°E
180°
70°N
60°N
50°N

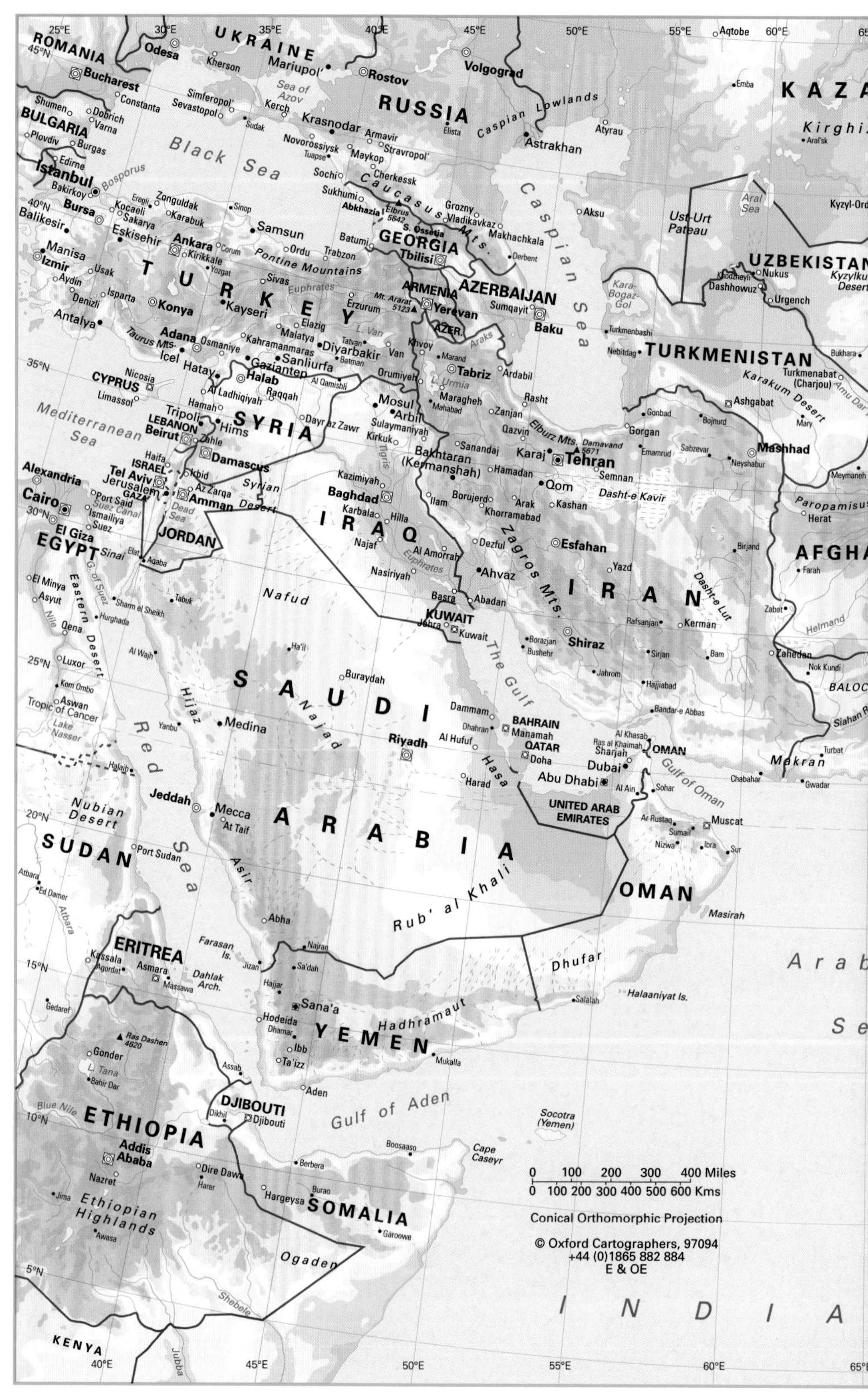
25°E
30°E
35°E
40°E
45°E
50°E
55°E
60°E
45°N
40°N
35°N
30°N
25°N
20°N
15°N
10°N
5°N
ROMANIA
Bucharest
Constanta
UKRAINE
Odesa
Kherson
Mariupol'
Rostov
Volgograd
Sea of Azov
Simferopol'
Sevastopol
Kerch
Sudak
RUSSIA
Krasnodar
Armavir
Elista
Caspian Lowlands
Astrakhan
Atyrau
Aqtobe
Emba
KAZA
Kirghiz
Aral'sk
Shumen
Dobrich
Varna
BULGARIA
Plovdiv
Burgas
Black Sea
Novorossiysk
Tuapse
Maykop
Stravropol'
Edirne
Istanbul
Bosporus
Sochi
Cherkessk
Bakirkoy
Zonguldak
Sukhumi
Caucasus Mts.
Caspian Sea
Aral Sea
Kyzyl-Orda
Ereğli
Karabuk
Sinop
Abkhazia
Elbrus 5642
Grozny
Vladikavkaz
Bursa
Kocaeli
Sakarya
S. Ossetia
Makhachkala
Aksu
Ust-Urt Pateau
Balikesir
Eskisehir
Samsun
Batumi
GEORGIA
Derbent
Manisa
Izmir
Ankara
Kirikkale
Corum
Ordu
Trabzon
Tbilisi
Yozgat
Pontine Mountains
UZBEKISTAN
Nukus
Khodzheyli
Dashhowuz
Kyzylkum Desert
Usak
Aydin
TURKEY
Sivas
Euphrates
ARMENIA
AZERBAIJAN
Kara-Bogaz-Gol
Urgench
Isparta
Denizli
Konya
Kayseri
Erzurum
Mt. Ararat 5123
Yerevan
Sumqayit
Baku
Antalya
Elazig
L. Van
AZER.
Araks
Turkmenbashi
Taurus Mts.
Adana
Osmaniye
Malatya
Tatvan
Khvoy
Nebitdag
TURKMENISTAN
Bukhara
Icel
Kahramanmaras
Diyarbakir
Van
Marand
Tabriz
Ardabil
Hatay
Gaziantep
Sanliurfa
Batman
Karakum Desert
Turkmenabat (Charjou)
Amu Darya
Nicosia
CYPRUS
Halab
Al Qamishli
Orumiyeh
L. Urmia
Limassol
Al Ladhiqiyah
Raqqah
Mosul
Maragheh
Rasht
Ashgabat
Hamah
Arbil
Mahabad
Zanjan
Gonbad
Bojnurd
Mediterranean Sea
Tripoli
LEBANON
Beirut
Zahle
SYRIA
Hims
Dayr az Zawr
Sulaymaniyah
Kirkuk
Qazvin
Elburz Mts.
Damavand 5671
Gorgan
Mary
Sanandaj
Karaj
Tehran
Emamrud
Sabzevar
Neyshabur
Mashhad
Haifa
ISRAEL
Tel Aviv
Jerusalem
GAZA
Damascus
Irbid
Tigris
Bakhtaran (Kermanshah)
Hamadan
Semnan
Meymaneh
Alexandria
Syrian Desert
Kazimiyah
Qom
Dasht-e Kavir
Cairo
Port Said
Az Zarqa
Amman
Baghdad
Borujerd
Arak
Kashan
Suez Canal
Ismailiya
Dead Sea
Karbala
Hilla
Ilam
Khorramabad
Paropamisus
Herat
El Giza
Suez
JORDAN
IRAQ
Najaf
Dezful
Esfahan
EGYPT
Sinai
Elat
Aqaba
Al Amorrah
Euphrates
Zagros Mts.
Birjand
AFGHA
G. of Suez
Ahvaz
Yazd
Farah
El Minya
Asyut
Eastern Desert
Nafud
Nasiriyah
IRAN
Dasht-e Lut
Nile
Sharm el Sheikh
Tabuk
Basra
Abadan
Zabol
Qena
Hurghada
KUWAIT
Jahra
Kuwait
Rafsanjan
Kerman
Helmand
Ha'il
Borazjan
Bushehr
Shiraz
Zahedan
Luxor
Al Wajh
The Gulf
Sirjan
Bam
Nok Kundi
Buraydah
Jahrom
Kom Ombo
SAUDI
Hijaz
Hajjiabad
BALOC
Aswan
Tropic of Cancer
Najd
Dammam
BAHRAIN
Manamah
Bandar-e Abbas
Lake Nasser
Yanbu
Medina
Dhahran
Al Hufuf
Riyadh
QATAR
Doha
Al Khasab
Ras al Khaimah
Sharjah
OMAN
Siahan Ra
Red Sea
Halaib
Hasa
Dubai
Gulf of Oman
Turbat
Makran
Harad
Abu Dhabi
Al Ain
Sohar
Chabahar
Gwadar
Nubian Desert
Jeddah
Mecca
At Taif
ARABIA
UNITED ARAB EMIRATES
Ar Rustaq
Sumail
Muscat
SUDAN
Port Sudan
Nizwa
Ibra
Sur
Asir
Rub' al Khali
OMAN
Atbara
Ed Damer
Masirah
Abha
Farasan Is.
Najran
ERITREA
Kassala
Agordat
Asmara
Massawa
Dahlak Arch.
Jizan
Sa'dah
Dhufar
Arab
Hajjar
Salalah
Halaaniyat Is.
Gedaref
Sana'a
Sea
Ras Dashen 4620
Hodeida
Dhamar
Hadhramaut
YEMEN
Gonder
L. Tana
Ibb
Ta'izz
Mukalla
Bahir Dar
Assab
Aden
Blue Nile
DJIBOUTI
Dikhil
Djibouti
Gulf of Aden
Socotra (Yemen)
ETHIOPIA
Addis Ababa
Boosaaso
Cape Caseyr
Berbera
Dire Dawa
Harer
Nazret
Burao
Hargeysa
SOMALIA
Jima
Ethiopian Highlands
Garoowe
Awasa
Ogaden
Shebele
INDIA
KENYA
Jubba
0 100 200 300 400 Miles
0 100 200 300 400 500 600 Kms
Conical Orthomorphic Projection
© Oxford Cartographers, 97094
+44 (0)1865 882 884
E & OE
40°E
45°E
50°E
55°E
60°E
65°E

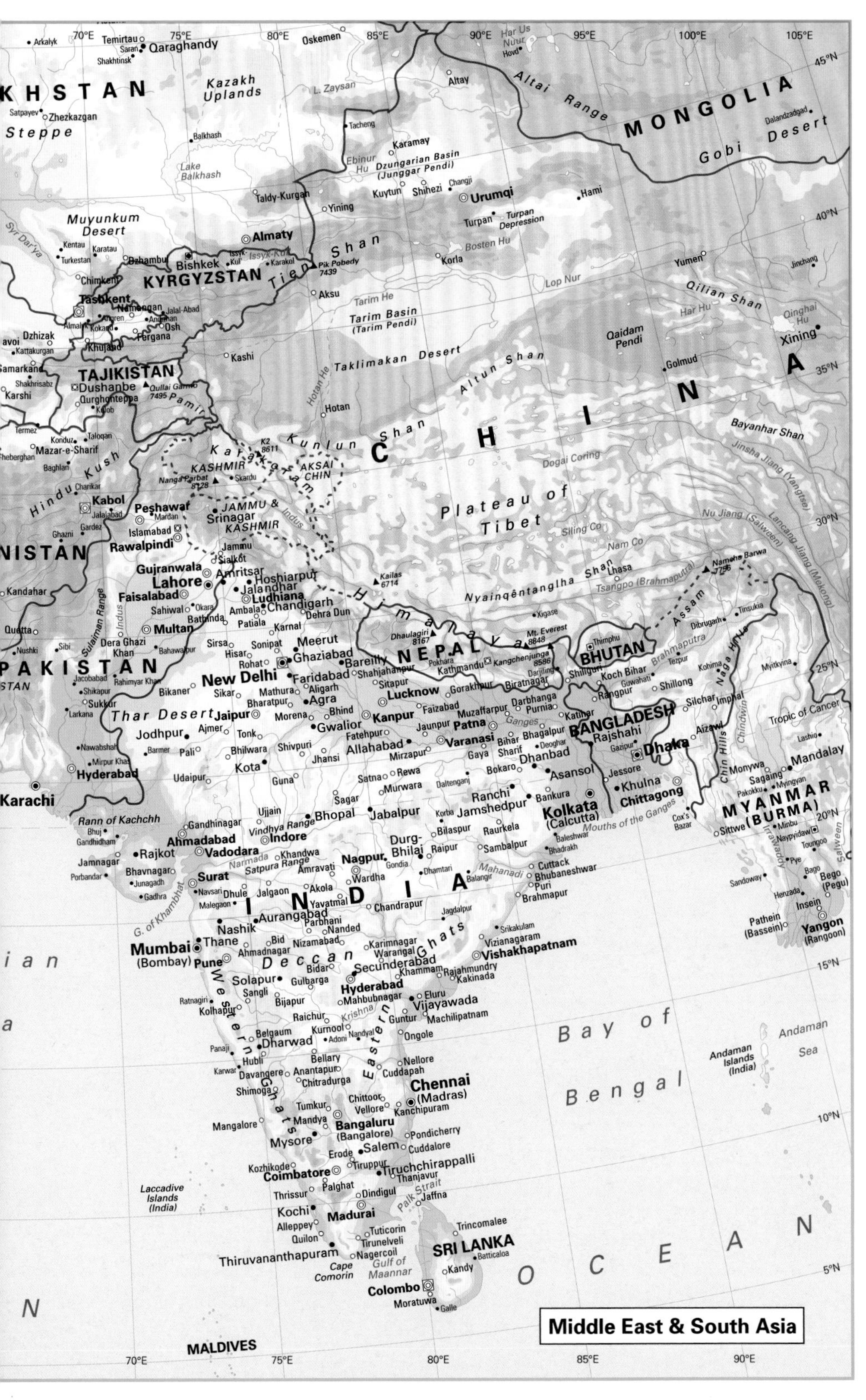

Middle East & South Asia

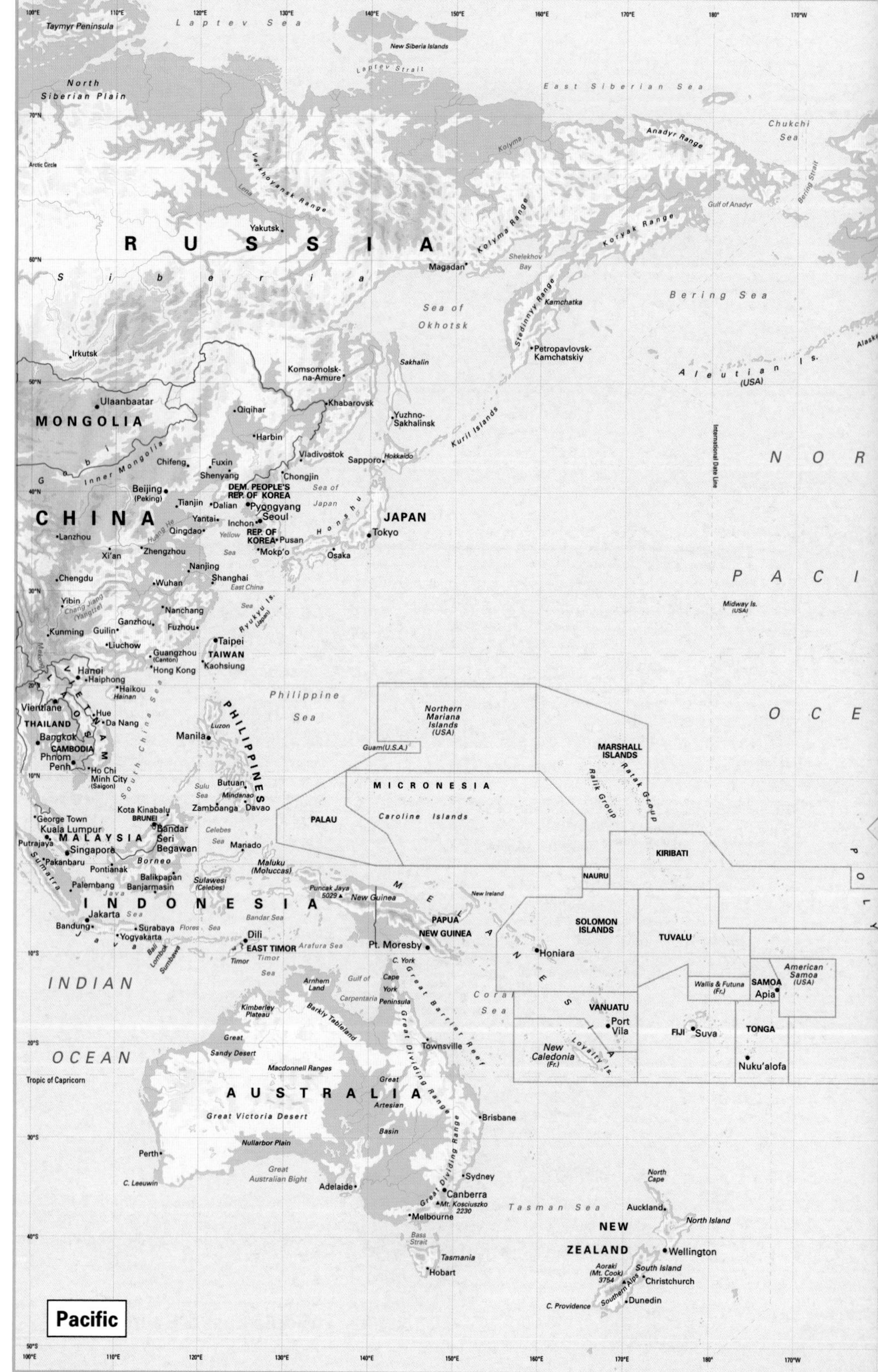

RUSSIA
MONGOLIA
CHINA
JAPAN
DEM. PEOPLE'S REP. OF KOREA
REP. OF KOREA
TAIWAN
PHILIPPINES
VIETNAM
THAILAND
CAMBODIA
MALAYSIA
BRUNEI
INDONESIA
EAST TIMOR
PAPUA NEW GUINEA
AUSTRALIA
NEW ZEALAND
PALAU
MICRONESIA
MARSHALL ISLANDS
KIRIBATI
NAURU
SOLOMON ISLANDS
TUVALU
VANUATU
FIJI
SAMOA
TONGA
INDIAN OCEAN
PACIFIC OCEAN
Laptev Sea
East Siberian Sea
Bering Sea
Sea of Okhotsk
Sea of Japan
Philippine Sea
South China Sea
Coral Sea
Tasman Sea

Pacific

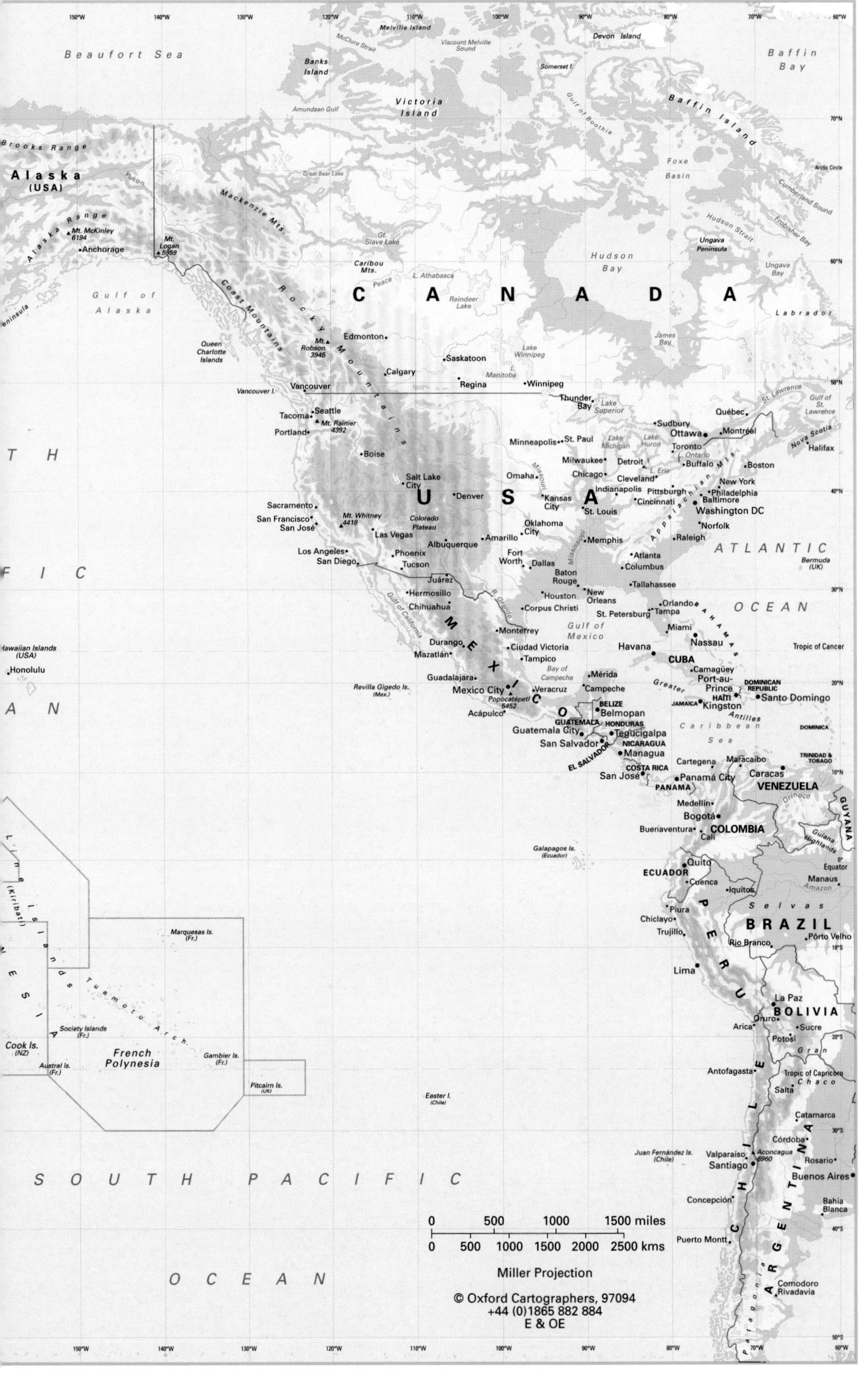

Beaufort Sea
Banks Island
Melville Island
McClure Strait
Viscount Melville Sound
Devon Island
Somerset I.
Baffin Bay
Victoria Island
Amundsen Gulf
Gulf of Boothia
Baffin Island
Brooks Range
Alaska (USA)
Yukon
Great Bear Lake
Foxe Basin
Arctic Circle
Cumberland Sound
Mackenzie Mts.
Hudson Strait
Frobisher Bay
Alaska Range
Mt. McKinley 6194
Anchorage
Mt. Logan 5959
Gt. Slave Lake
Ungava Peninsula
Hudson Bay
Ungava Bay
Caribou Mts.
Peace
L. Athabasca
Gulf of Alaska
Coast Mountains
Rocky Mountains
CANADA
Reindeer Lake
Labrador
Queen Charlotte Islands
Mt. Robson 3945
Edmonton
James Bay
Lake Winnipeg
Saskatoon
Calgary
Manitoba
Regina
Winnipeg
Vancouver I.
Vancouver
Thunder Bay
Lake Superior
St. Lawrence
Gulf of St. Lawrence
Québec
Tacoma
Seattle
Mt. Rainier 4392
Portland
Sudbury
Ottawa
Montréal
Nova Scotia
Halifax
Boise
Minneapolis
St. Paul
Lake Michigan
Lake Huron
Toronto
Lake Ontario
Milwaukee
Detroit
Buffalo
Boston
Salt Lake City
Omaha
Missouri
Chicago
Lake Erie
Cleveland
New York
Appalachian Mts.
USA
Denver
Kansas City
Indianapolis
Pittsburgh
Philadelphia
Baltimore
Cincinnati
Washington DC
St. Louis
Sacramento
San Francisco
San José
Mt. Whitney 4418
Colorado Plateau
Las Vegas
Oklahoma City
Norfolk
Amarillo
Memphis
Raleigh
Albuquerque
ATLANTIC
Los Angeles
San Diego
Phoenix
Tucson
Fort Worth
Dallas
Mississippi
Atlanta
Columbus
Bermuda (UK)
Juárez
Baton Rouge
Tallahassee
Hermosillo
New Orleans
Houston
Orlando
Tampa
St. Petersburg
OCEAN
Chihuahua
Corpus Christi
R. Grande
Gulf of California
MEXICO
BAHAMAS
Monterrey
Gulf of Mexico
Miami
Durango
Ciudad Victoria
Nassau
Havana
Tropic of Cancer
Hawaiian Islands (USA)
Honolulu
Mazatlán
Tampico
CUBA
Bay of Campeche
Camagüey
Guadalajara
Mérida
Port-au-Prince
Revilla Gigedo Is. (Mex.)
Mexico City
Veracruz
Campeche
Greater
DOMINICAN REPUBLIC
HAITI
Santo Domingo
Popocatépetl 5452
JAMAICA
Kingston
Acápulco
BELIZE
Belmopan
Antilles
GUATEMALA
HONDURAS
Guatemala City
Tegucigalpa
Caribbean Sea
DOMINICA
San Salvador
NICARAGUA
EL SALVADOR
Managua
TRINIDAD & TOBAGO
Cartegena
Maracaibo
COSTA RICA
Caracas
San José
Panamá City
PANAMA
VENEZUELA
Orinoco
Medellín
GUYANA
Bogotá
Buenaventura
Cali
COLOMBIA
Guiana Highlands
Galapagos Is. (Ecuador)
Quito
Equator
ECUADOR
Manaus
Amazon
Cuenca
Iquitos
Selvas
Piura
Chiclayo
BRAZIL
Trujillo
PERU
Rio Branco
Pôrto Velho
Line Islands (Kiribati)
Marquesas Is. (Fr.)
Lima
Tuamotu Arch.
La Paz
BOLIVIA
Oruro
Sucre
Arica
Potosi
Society Islands (Fr.)
Cook Is. (NZ)
Austral Is. (Fr.)
French Polynesia
Gambier Is. (Fr.)
Gran Chaco
Antofagasta
Tropic of Capricorn
Salta
Pitcairn Is. (UK)
Easter I. (Chile)
Catamarca
Córdoba
Juan Fernández Is. (Chile)
Valparaíso
Aconcagua 6960
Rosario
Santiago
Buenos Aires
SOUTH PACIFIC OCEAN
CHILE
ARGENTINA
Concepción
Bahia Blanca
Puerto Montt
Patagonia
Comodoro Rivadavia
0 500 1000 1500 miles
0 500 1000 1500 2000 2500 kms
Miller Projection
© Oxford Cartographers, 97094
+44 (0)1865 882 884
E & OE
150°W 140°W 130°W 120°W 110°W 100°W 90°W 80°W 70°W 60°W
70°N 60°N 50°N 40°N 30°N 20°N 10°N 0° 10°S 20°S 30°S 40°S 50°S

World Physical
ARCTIC OCEAN
PACIFIC OCEAN
NORTH ATLANTIC OCEAN
SOUTH ATLANTIC OCEAN
INDIAN OCEAN
SOUTHERN OCEAN
North America
South America
Europe
Asia
Africa
Australia
Antarctica
Greenland
Arctic Circle
Tropic of Cancer
Equator
Tropic of Capricorn
Antarctic Circle
International Date Line
Bering Strait
Brooks Range
MT. McKINLEY 6194
Alaska Peninsula
Gulf of Alaska
Victoria I.
Great Bear Lake
Great Slave Lake
Rocky Mountains
Great Plains
Hudson Bay
Baffin Island
Ungava Pen.
Labrador
Newfoundland
Davis Strait
Denmark Strait
Cape Farewell
Lake Winnipeg
L. Superior
The Great Lakes
Appalachian Mts.
Sierra Nevada
Sierra Madre
5610
Gulf of Mexico
Yucatan Pen.
Bahamas
Cuba
Hispaniola
Greater Antilles
Caribbean Sea
Hawaiian Islands
Galapagos Is.
COTOPAXI 5896
Guiana Highlands
Andes
L. Titicaca
Mato Grosso
Brazilian Highlands
MT. ACONCAGUA 6960
Falkland Islands
Tierra del Fuego
Cape Horn
Polynesia
Azores
Canary Is.
Cape Verde Is.
Iceland
Greenland Sea
Spitsbergen
Franz Josef Land
Novaya Zemlya
Barents Sea
Kara Sea
North Cape
Scandinavia
Lapland
L. Ladoga
British Isles
North Sea
Baltic Sea
Bay of Biscay
Alps
MT. BLANC 4808
Black Sea
Caucasus
5642 ELBRUS
Caspian Sea
Mediterranean Sea
JEBEL TOUBKAL 4165
Atlas Mts.
Taurus
Ural Mts.
Sahara Desert
Libyan Desert
Ahaggar
Tibesti
L. Chad
L. Nasser
Red Sea
Arabia
Rub' al Khali
Zagros
DAMAVAND 5671
RAS DASHEN 4620
Ethiopian Highlands
L. Turkana
L. Victoria
MT. KILIMANJARO 5895
L. Tanganyika
L. Nyasa (L. Malawi)
Seychelles
Comoro Is.
Madagascar
Kalahari Desert
Cape Agulhas
Aral Sea
West Siberian Plain
Central Siberian Plateau
Verkhoyansk Range
Cherskogo Range
Kolyma Ra.
Anadyr Range
Koryak Range
Kamchatka
Bering Sea
Sea of Okhotsk
Stanovoy Mts.
L. Baikal
Sayan Mts.
Altai Ra.
L. Balkhash
Gobi
Tien Shan
Hindu Kush
Kunlun Shan
K2 8611
Plateau of Tibet
Himalaya
MT. EVEREST 8848
Da Hinggan Ling
Manchurian Plain
Sikhote Alin Ra.
Sakhalin
Sea of Japan
Honshu
Yellow Sea
East China Sea
Taiwan
Philippine Sea
Luzon
Mindanao
South China Sea
Arabian Sea
W. Ghats
E. Ghats
Bay of Bengal
Sri Lanka
Maldives
MT. KINABALU 4101
Celebes Sea
Borneo
Sumatra
Java
Java Sea
Banda Sea
Timor Sea
PUNCAK JAYA 5030
New Guinea
Melanesia
Solomon Is.
Caroline Islands
Marshall Islands
Fiji
Coral Sea
New Caledonia
Great Sandy Desert
Great Victoria Desert
Great Australian Bight
Great Dividing Range
2230 MT. KOSCIUSZKO
Tasman Sea
Tasmania
North Island
New Zealand
AORAKI (MT. COOK) 3764
South Island
Modified Gall Projection
Equatorial Scale 1:166,000,000
© Oxford Cartographers, 97094
+44 (0)1865 882 884
E & OE

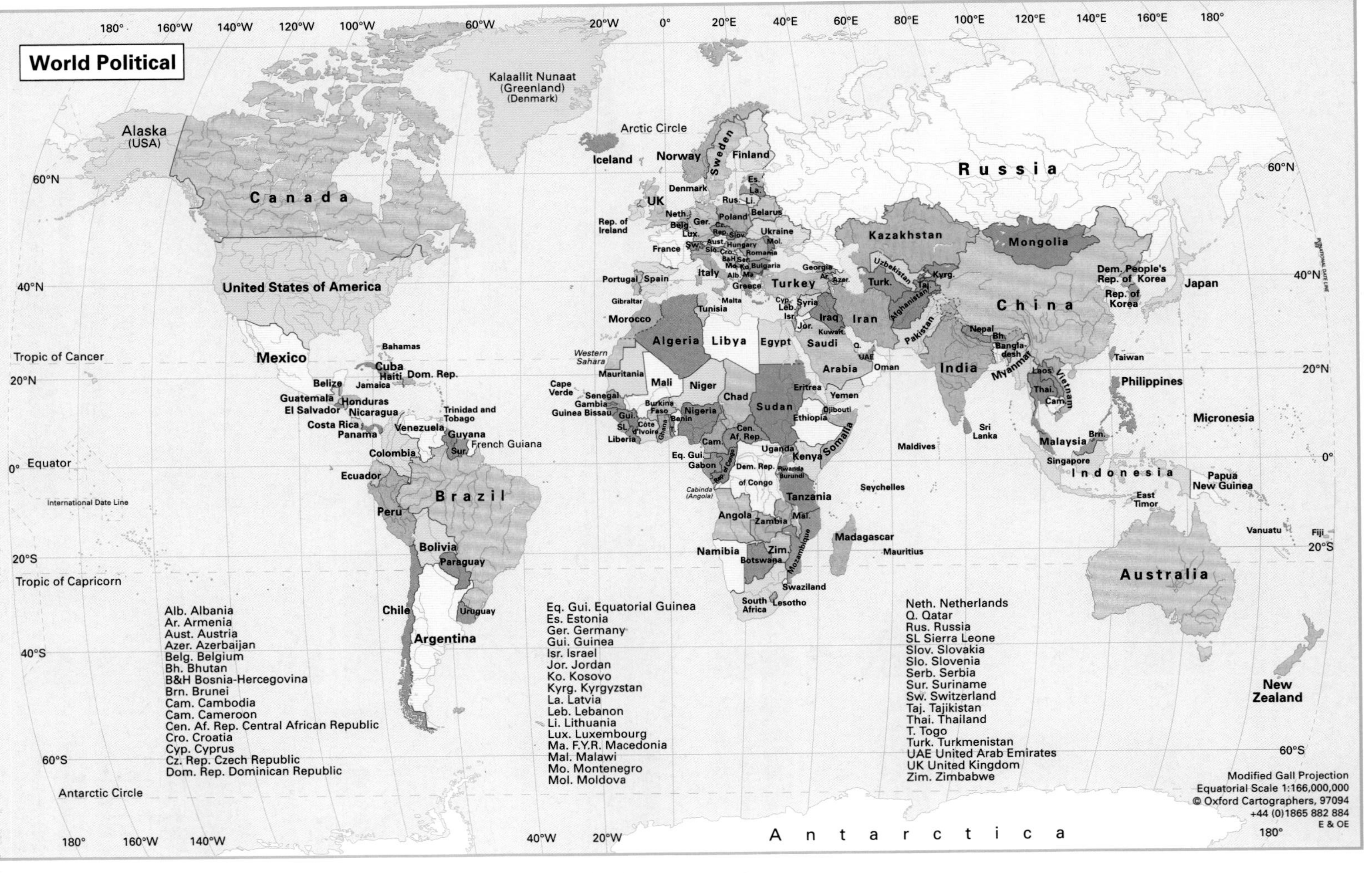
World Political
Kalaallit Nunaat
(Greenland)
(Denmark)
Alaska
(USA)
Canada
United States of America
Mexico
Bahamas
Cuba
Haiti
Dom. Rep.
Jamaica
Belize
Guatemala
El Salvador
Honduras
Nicaragua
Costa Rica
Panama
Trinidad and
Tobago
Venezuela
Guyana
Sur.
French Guiana
Colombia
Ecuador
Peru
Brazil
Bolivia
Paraguay
Chile
Argentina
Uruguay
Arctic Circle
Iceland
Norway
Sweden
Finland
Denmark
UK
Rep. of
Ireland
Neth.
Belg.
Lux.
Ger.
Poland
Belarus
Ukraine
Mol.
France
Sw.
Hungary
Romania
Bulgaria
Portugal
Spain
Italy
Greece
Gibraltar
Malta
Turkey
Georgia
Azer.
Cyp.
Leb.
Syria
Isr.
Jor.
Iraq
Iran
Kuwait
Saudi
Arabia
Q.
UAE
Oman
Yemen
Morocco
Algeria
Tunisia
Libya
Egypt
Western
Sahara
Mauritania
Mali
Niger
Chad
Sudan
Eritrea
Djibouti
Ethiopia
Somalia
Cape
Verde
Senegal
Gambia
Guinea Bissau
Gui.
SL
Liberia
Côte
d'Ivoire
Ghana
Burkina
Faso
Benin
Nigeria
Cam.
Cen.
Af. Rep.
Eq. Gui.
Gabon
Dem. Rep.
of Congo
Uganda
Kenya
Rwanda
Burundi
Tanzania
Cabinda
(Angola)
Angola
Zambia
Mal.
Mozambique
Zim.
Namibia
Botswana
Swaziland
South
Africa
Lesotho
Madagascar
Mauritius
Seychelles
Maldives
Russia
Kazakhstan
Uzbekistan
Turk.
Kyrg.
Taj.
Afghanistan
Pakistan
Mongolia
China
Nepal
Bh.
Bangla-
desh
India
Sri
Lanka
Myanmar
Laos
Thai.
Vietnam
Cam.
Malaysia
Brn.
Singapore
Indonesia
Philippines
Taiwan
Dem. People's
Rep. of Korea
Rep. of
Korea
Japan
Micronesia
Papua
New Guinea
East
Timor
Australia
Vanuatu
Fiji
New
Zealand
Antarctica
Tropic of Cancer
Equator
International Date Line
Tropic of Capricorn
Antarctic Circle
180°
160°W
140°W
120°W
100°W
60°W
20°W
0°
20°E
40°E
60°E
80°E
100°E
120°E
140°E
160°E
60°N
40°N
20°N
20°S
40°S
60°S
Alb. Albania
Ar. Armenia
Aust. Austria
Azer. Azerbaijan
Belg. Belgium
Bh. Bhutan
B&H Bosnia-Hercegovina
Brn. Brunei
Cam. Cambodia
Cam. Cameroon
Cen. Af. Rep. Central African Republic
Cro. Croatia
Cyp. Cyprus
Cz. Rep. Czech Republic
Dom. Rep. Dominican Republic
Eq. Gui. Equatorial Guinea
Es. Estonia
Ger. Germany
Gui. Guinea
Isr. Israel
Jor. Jordan
Ko. Kosovo
Kyrg. Kyrgyzstan
La. Latvia
Leb. Lebanon
Li. Lithuania
Lux. Luxembourg
Ma. F.Y.R. Macedonia
Mal. Malawi
Mo. Montenegro
Mol. Moldova
Neth. Netherlands
Q. Qatar
Rus. Russia
SL Sierra Leone
Slov. Slovakia
Slo. Slovenia
Serb. Serbia
Sur. Suriname
Sw. Switzerland
Taj. Tajikistan
Thai. Thailand
T. Togo
Turk. Turkmenistan
UAE United Arab Emirates
UK United Kingdom
Zim. Zimbabwe
Modified Gall Projection
Equatorial Scale 1:166,000,000
© Oxford Cartographers, 97094
+44 (0)1865 882 884
E & OE

FLAGS OF THE WORLD

The following four pages show the national flag of each country, as it is used for international purposes. In some cases this means that the state flag is shown. Where this is the case the country name is marked (†).

AFGHANISTAN

ALBANIA

ALGERIA

ANDORRA

ANGOLA

ANTIGUA AND BARBUDA

ARGENTINA

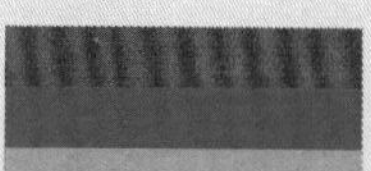

ARMENIA

AUSTRALIA

AUSTRIA

AZERBAIJAN

THE BAHAMAS

BAHRAIN

BANGLADESH

BARBADOS

BELARUS

BELGIUM

BELIZE

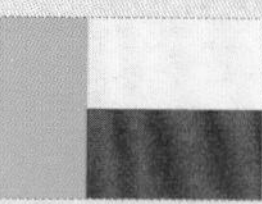
BENIN

BHUTAN

BOLIVIA†

BOSNIA AND HERCEGOVINA

BOTSWANA

BRAZIL

BRUNEI

BULGARIA

BURKINA FASO

BURUNDI

CAMBODIA

CAMEROON

CANADA

CAPE VERDE

CENTRAL AFRICAN REPUBLIC

CHAD

CHILE

CHINA

COLOMBIA

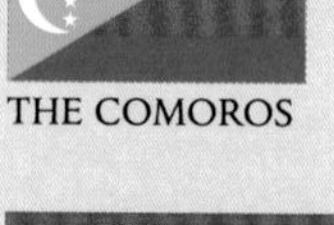
THE COMOROS

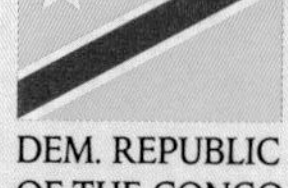
DEM. REPUBLIC OF THE CONGO

REPUBLIC OF THE CONGO

COSTA RICA

CÔTE D'IVOIRE

CROATIA

CUBA

CYPRUS

CZECH REPUBLIC

DENMARK

DJIBOUTI

DOMINICA

DOMINICAN REPUBLIC

EAST TIMOR

ECUADOR

EGYPT

EL SALVADOR

EQUATORIAL GUINEA

ERITREA

ESTONIA

ETHIOPIA

FIJI

FINLAND

FRANCE

GABON

THE GAMBIA

GEORGIA

GERMANY

GHANA

GREECE

GRENADA

GUATEMALA

GUINEA

GUINEA-BISSAU

GUYANA

HAITI†

HONDURAS

HUNGARY

ICELAND

INDIA

INDONESIA

IRAN

IRAQ

IRELAND

ISRAEL

ITALY

JAMAICA

JAPAN

JORDAN

KAZAKHSTAN

KENYA

KIRIBATI

DEM. PEOPLE'S REPUBLIC OF KOREA

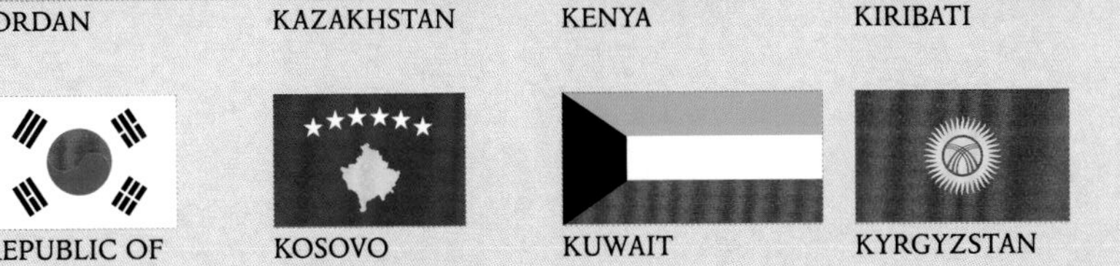

REPUBLIC OF KOREA

KOSOVO

KUWAIT

KYRGYZSTAN

LAOS

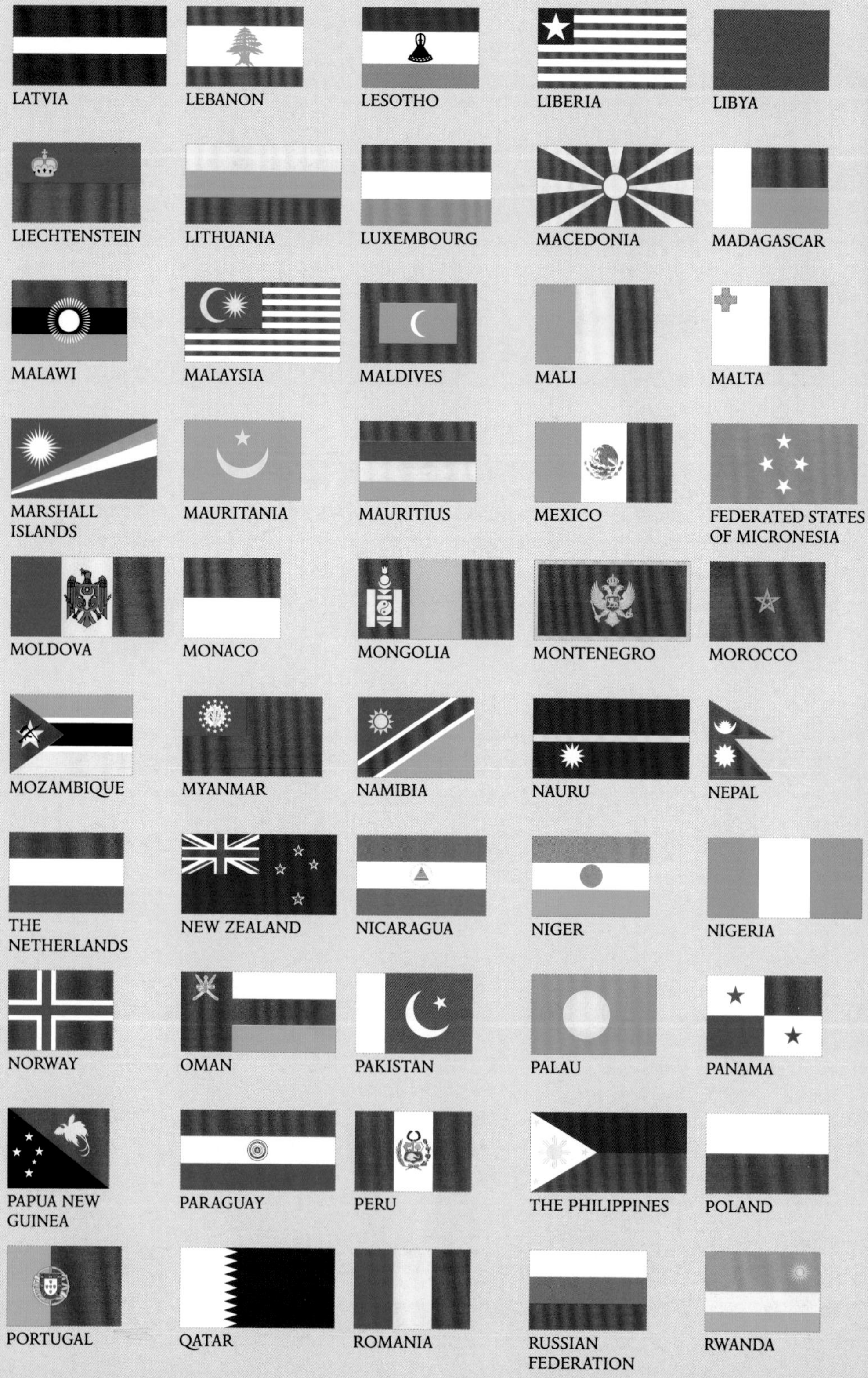

LATVIA

LEBANON

LESOTHO

LIBERIA

LIBYA

LIECHTENSTEIN

LITHUANIA

LUXEMBOURG

MACEDONIA

MADAGASCAR

MALAWI

MALAYSIA

MALDIVES

MALI

MALTA

MARSHALL ISLANDS

MAURITANIA

MAURITIUS

MEXICO

FEDERATED STATES OF MICRONESIA

MOLDOVA

MONACO

MONGOLIA

MONTENEGRO

MOROCCO

MOZAMBIQUE

MYANMAR

NAMIBIA

NAURU

NEPAL

THE NETHERLANDS

NEW ZEALAND

NICARAGUA

NIGER

NIGERIA

NORWAY

OMAN

PAKISTAN

PALAU

PANAMA

PAPUA NEW GUINEA

PARAGUAY

PERU

THE PHILIPPINES

POLAND

PORTUGAL

QATAR

ROMANIA

RUSSIAN FEDERATION

RWANDA

ST CHRISTOPHER AND NEVIS

ST LUCIA

ST VINCENT AND THE GRENADINES

SAMOA

SAN MARINO†

SAO TOME AND PRINCIPE

SAUDI ARABIA

SENEGAL

SERBIA†

SEYCHELLES

SIERRA LEONE

SINGAPORE

SLOVAKIA

SLOVENIA

SOLOMON ISLANDS

SOMALIA

SOUTH AFRICA

SPAIN

SRI LANKA

SUDAN

SURINAME

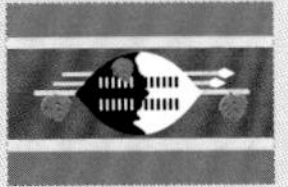
SWAZILAND

SWEDEN

SWITZERLAND

SYRIA

TAIWAN

TAJIKISTAN

TANZANIA

THAILAND

TOGO

TONGA

TRINIDAD AND TOBAGO

TUNISIA

TURKEY

TURKMENISTAN

TUVALU

UGANDA

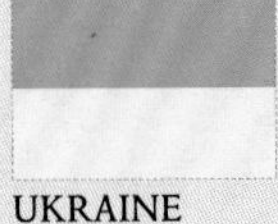
UKRAINE

UNITED ARAB EMIRATES

UNITED KINGDOM

UNITED STATES OF AMERICA

URUGUAY

UZBEKISTAN

VANUATU

VATICAN CITY STATE

VENEZUELA

VIETNAM

YEMEN

ZAMBIA

ZIMBABWE

POPULATION GROWTH RATES

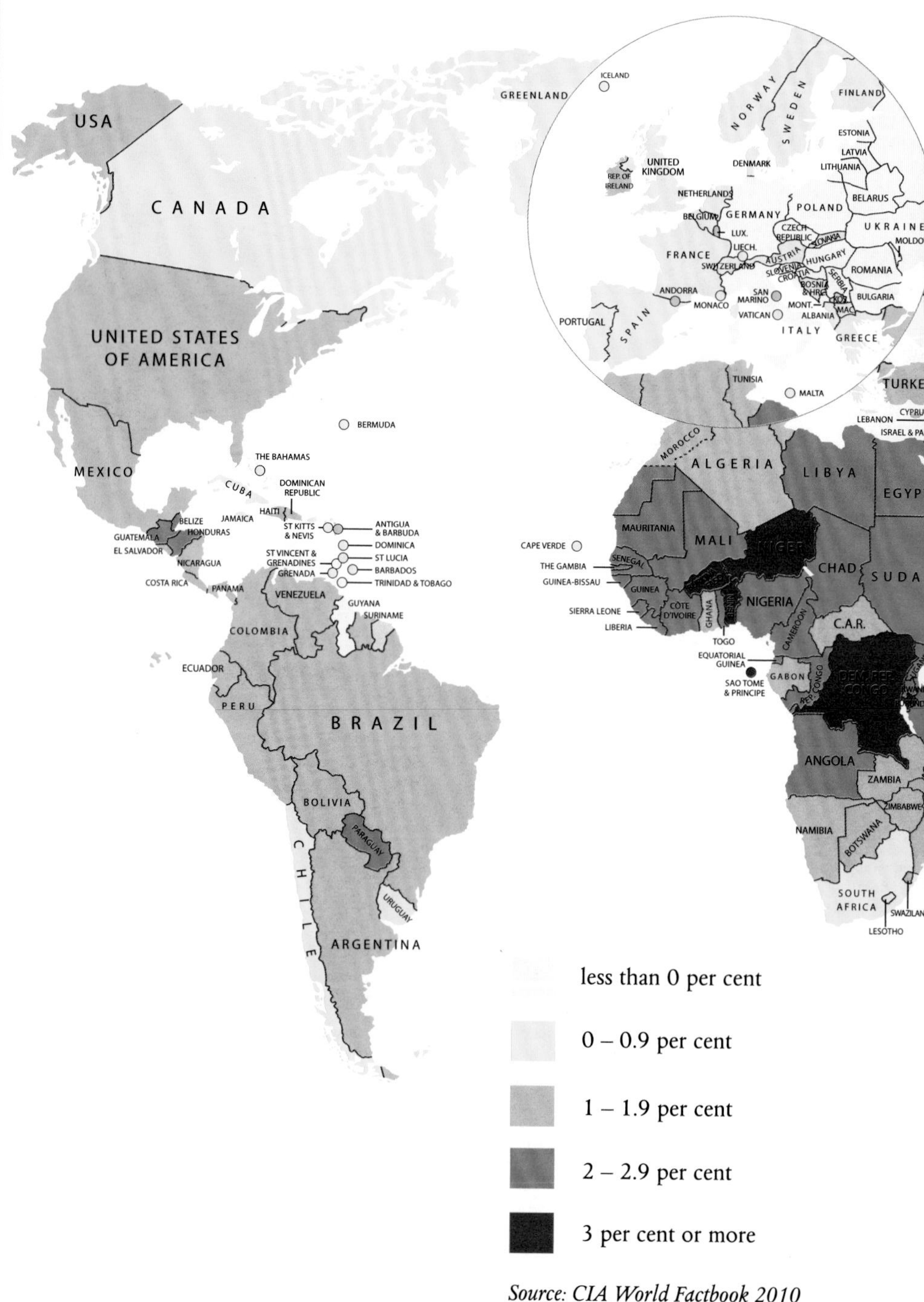

Source: CIA World Factbook 2010

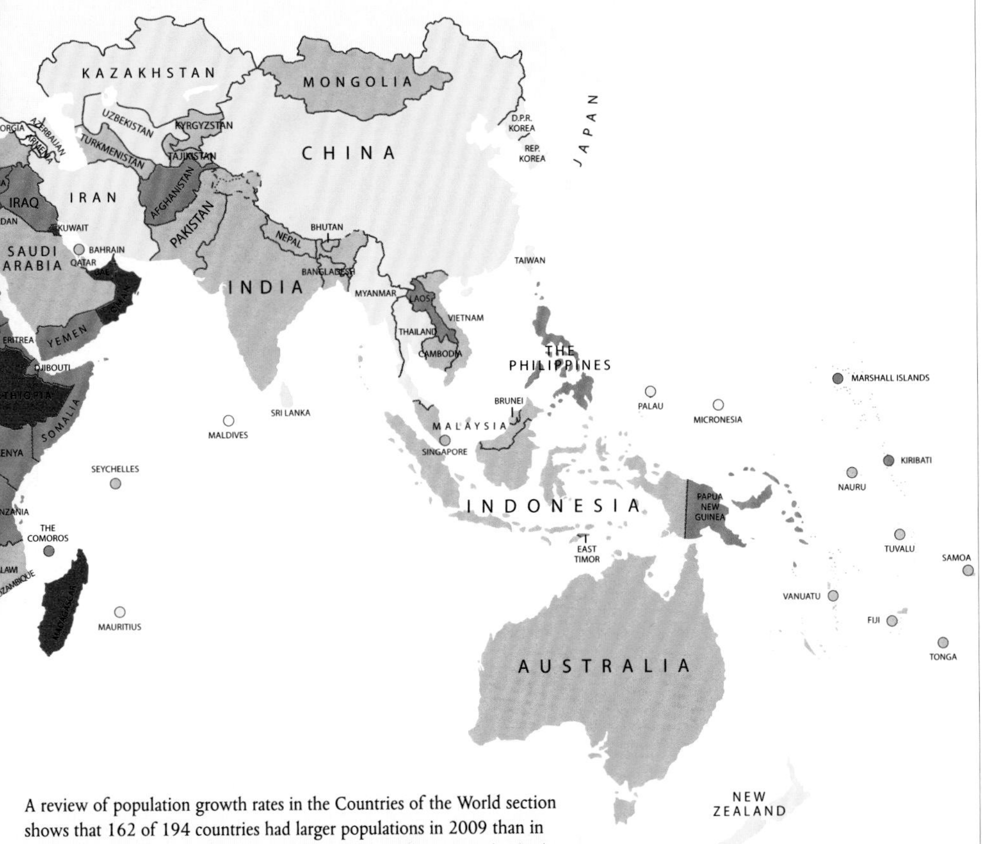

A review of population growth rates in the Countries of the World section shows that 162 of 194 countries had larger populations in 2009 than in 2008. The global population is continuing to grow, albeit more slowly than in the 1970s and 1980s. About half of the world's population now lives in countries where the number of births each year is smaller than the number of deaths, a phenomenon known as sub-replacement fertility.

In the Mediterranean and eastern Europe, declining populations are thought to be due to a combination of falling fertility rates and rising standards of living. For developed countries with industrialised economies, the effects of a fall in population growth can be far-reaching – leading to labour shortages, a decline in economic growth and a greater burden on social security systems.

INTERNET USERS
as percentage of population

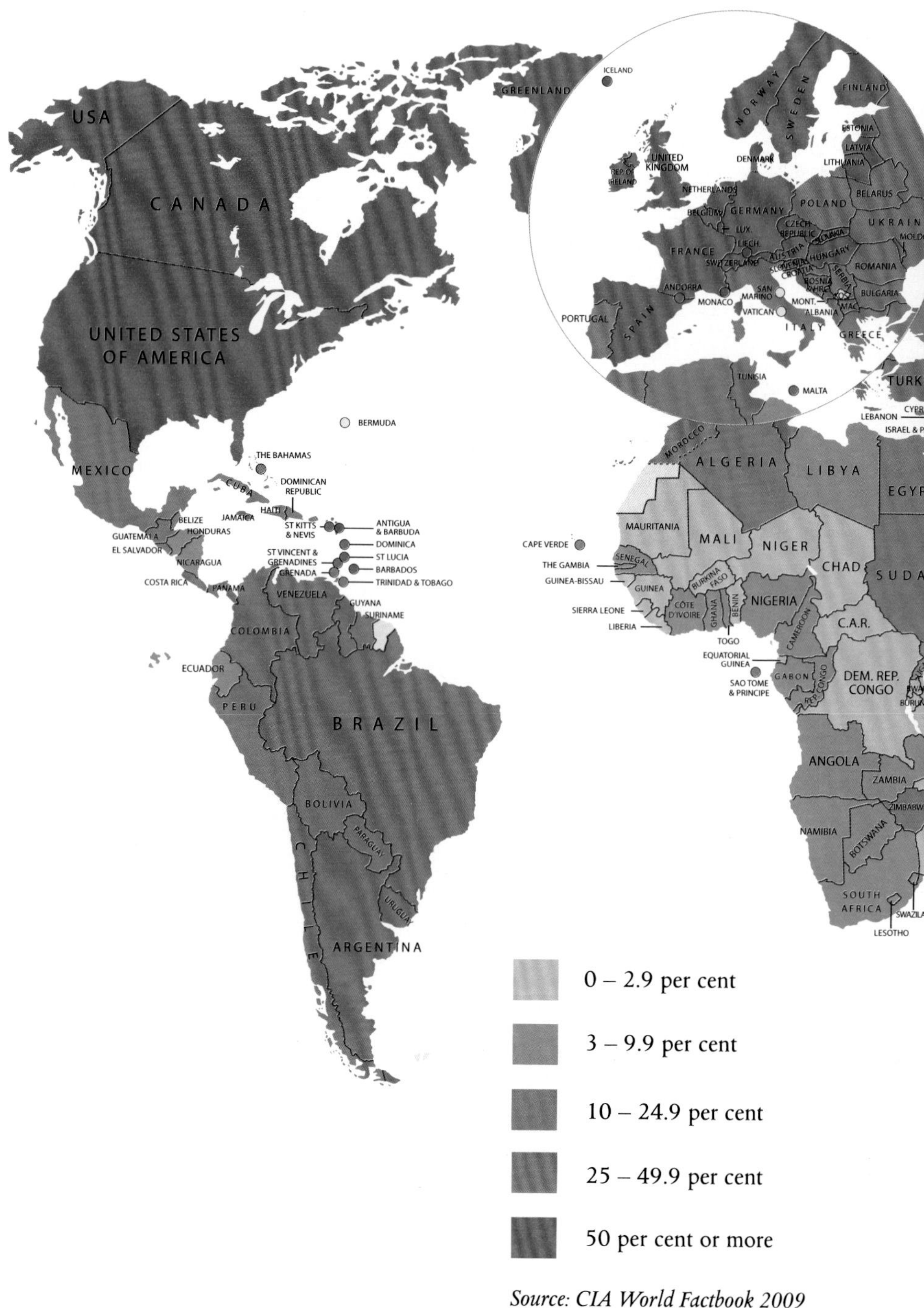

Source: CIA World Factbook 2009

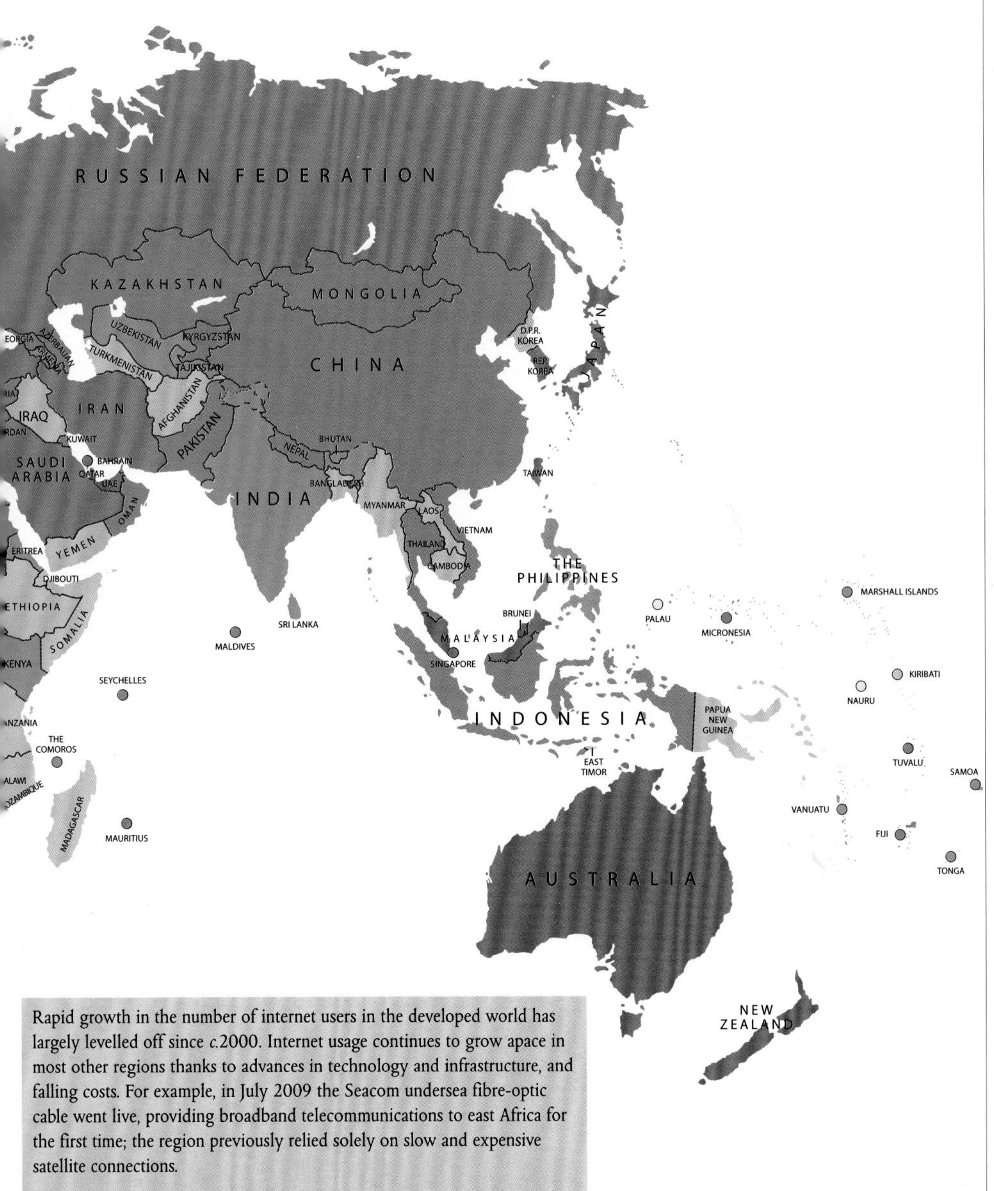

Rapid growth in the number of internet users in the developed world has largely levelled off since *c.*2000. Internet usage continues to grow apace in most other regions thanks to advances in technology and infrastructure, and falling costs. For example, in July 2009 the Seacom undersea fibre-optic cable went live, providing broadband telecommunications to east Africa for the first time; the region previously relied solely on slow and expensive satellite connections.

The definition of 'internet user' may extend from those who use the internet several times a week to those who are accessing it only once within several months. The number of people accessing the internet through their mobile phones is rising subsantially in those countries where such services are available.

UK GENERAL ELECTION 2010

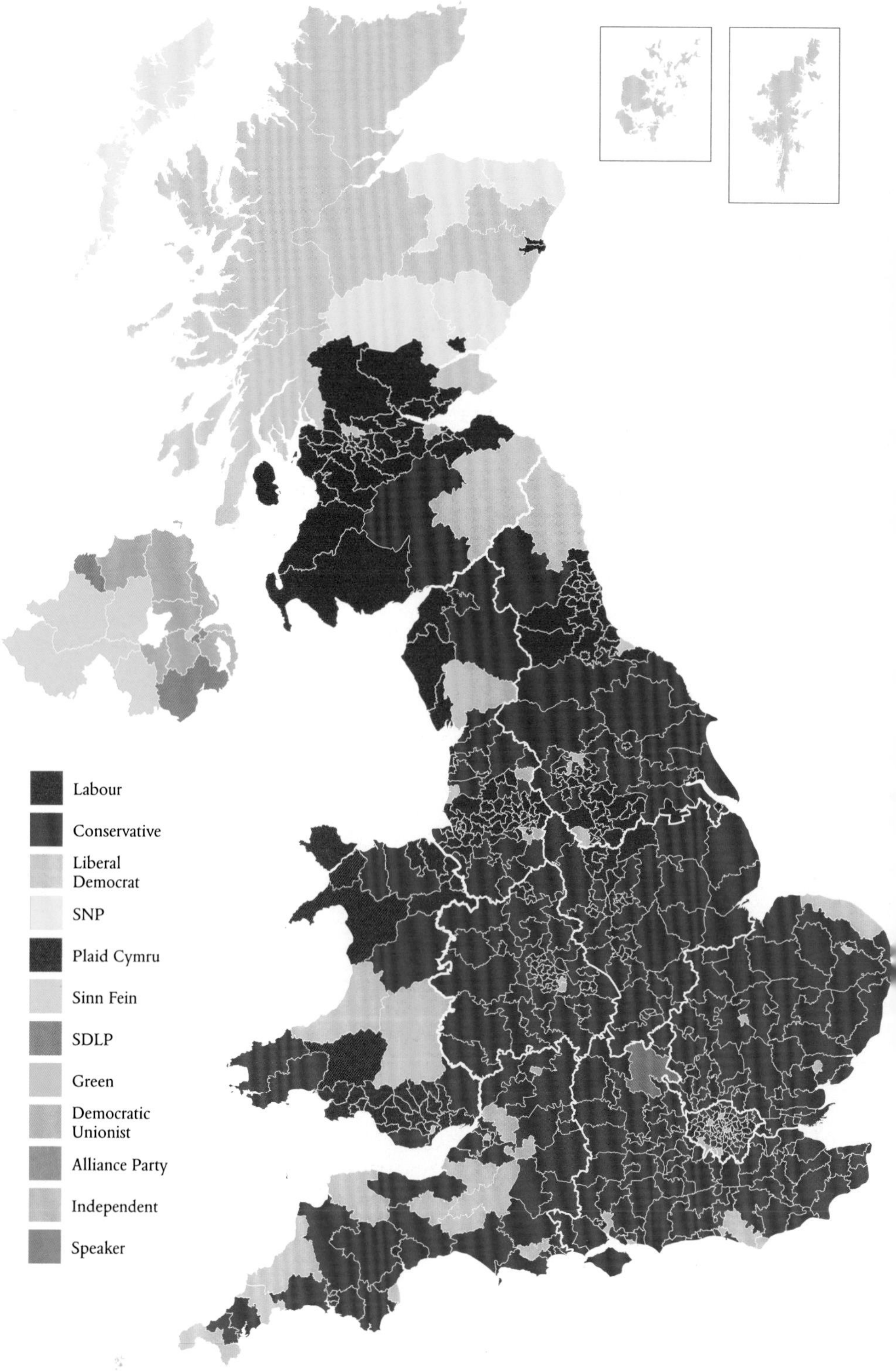

Labour

Conservative

Liberal Democrat

SNP

Plaid Cymru

Sinn Fein

SDLP

Green

Democratic Unionist

Alliance Party

Independent

Speaker

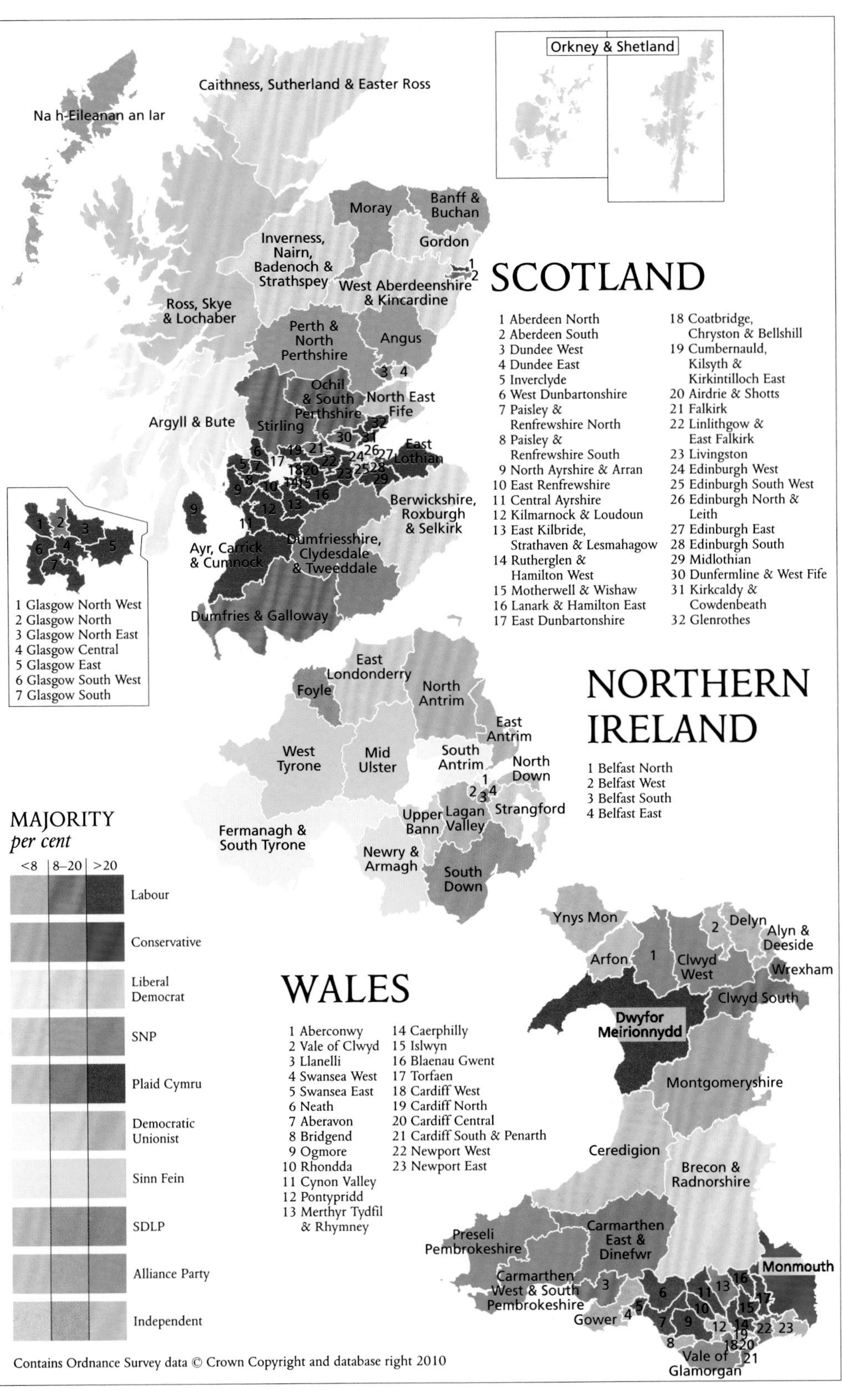

Orkney & Shetland
Caithness, Sutherland & Easter Ross
Na h-Eileanan an Iar
Moray
Banff & Buchan
Gordon
Inverness, Nairn, Badenoch & Strathspey
West Aberdeenshire & Kincardine
Ross, Skye & Lochaber
Perth & North Perthshire
Angus
Ochil & South Perthshire
North East Fife
Argyll & Bute
Stirling
East Lothian
Berwickshire, Roxburgh & Selkirk
Ayr, Carrick & Cumnock
Dumfriesshire, Clydesdale & Tweeddale
Dumfries & Galloway
SCOTLAND
1 Aberdeen North
2 Aberdeen South
3 Dundee West
4 Dundee East
5 Inverclyde
6 West Dunbartonshire
7 Paisley & Renfrewshire North
8 Paisley & Renfrewshire South
9 North Ayrshire & Arran
10 East Renfrewshire
11 Central Ayrshire
12 Kilmarnock & Loudoun
13 East Kilbride, Strathaven & Lesmahagow
14 Rutherglen & Hamilton West
15 Motherwell & Wishaw
16 Lanark & Hamilton East
17 East Dunbartonshire
18 Coatbridge, Chryston & Bellshill
19 Cumbernauld, Kilsyth & Kirkintilloch East
20 Airdrie & Shotts
21 Falkirk
22 Linlithgow & East Falkirk
23 Livingston
24 Edinburgh West
25 Edinburgh South West
26 Edinburgh North & Leith
27 Edinburgh East
28 Edinburgh South
29 Midlothian
30 Dunfermline & West Fife
31 Kirkcaldy & Cowdenbeath
32 Glenrothes
1 Glasgow North West
2 Glasgow North
3 Glasgow North East
4 Glasgow Central
5 Glasgow East
6 Glasgow South West
7 Glasgow South
East Londonderry
Foyle
North Antrim
East Antrim
West Tyrone
Mid Ulster
South Antrim
North Down
Strangford
Upper Bann
Lagan Valley
Fermanagh & South Tyrone
Newry & Armagh
South Down
NORTHERN IRELAND
1 Belfast North
2 Belfast West
3 Belfast South
4 Belfast East
MAJORITY per cent
<8
8–20
>20
Labour
Conservative
Liberal Democrat
SNP
Plaid Cymru
Democratic Unionist
Sinn Fein
SDLP
Alliance Party
Independent
Ynys Mon
Delyn
Alyn & Deeside
Arfon
Clwyd West
Wrexham
Clwyd South
Dwyfor Meirionnydd
Montgomeryshire
Ceredigion
Brecon & Radnorshire
Carmarthen East & Dinefwr
Preseli Pembrokeshire
Carmarthen West & South Pembrokeshire
Gower
Monmouth
Vale of Glamorgan
WALES
1 Aberconwy
2 Vale of Clwyd
3 Llanelli
4 Swansea West
5 Swansea East
6 Neath
7 Aberavon
8 Bridgend
9 Ogmore
10 Rhondda
11 Cynon Valley
12 Pontypridd
13 Merthyr Tydfil & Rhymney
14 Caerphilly
15 Islwyn
16 Blaenau Gwent
17 Torfaen
18 Cardiff West
19 Cardiff North
20 Cardiff Central
21 Cardiff South & Penarth
22 Newport West
23 Newport East

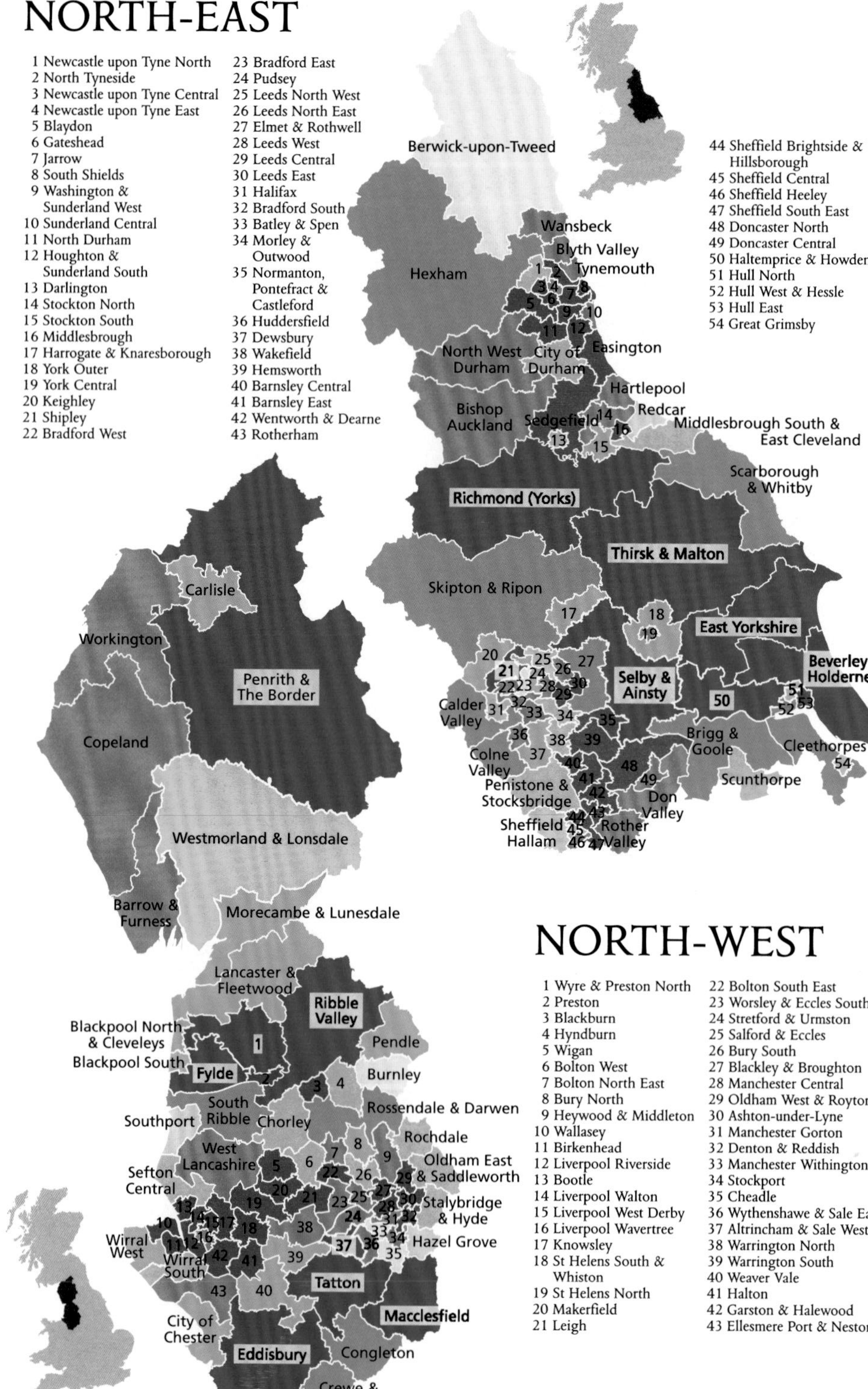
NORTH-EAST
1 Newcastle upon Tyne North
2 North Tyneside
3 Newcastle upon Tyne Central
4 Newcastle upon Tyne East
5 Blaydon
6 Gateshead
7 Jarrow
8 South Shields
9 Washington & Sunderland West
10 Sunderland Central
11 North Durham
12 Houghton & Sunderland South
13 Darlington
14 Stockton North
15 Stockton South
16 Middlesbrough
17 Harrogate & Knaresborough
18 York Outer
19 York Central
20 Keighley
21 Shipley
22 Bradford West
23 Bradford East
24 Pudsey
25 Leeds North West
26 Leeds North East
27 Elmet & Rothwell
28 Leeds West
29 Leeds Central
30 Leeds East
31 Halifax
32 Bradford South
33 Batley & Spen
34 Morley & Outwood
35 Normanton, Pontefract & Castleford
36 Huddersfield
37 Dewsbury
38 Wakefield
39 Hemsworth
40 Barnsley Central
41 Barnsley East
42 Wentworth & Dearne
43 Rotherham
44 Sheffield Brightside & Hillsborough
45 Sheffield Central
46 Sheffield Heeley
47 Sheffield South East
48 Doncaster North
49 Doncaster Central
50 Haltemprice & Howden
51 Hull North
52 Hull West & Hessle
53 Hull East
54 Great Grimsby
Berwick-upon-Tweed
Wansbeck
Blyth Valley
Tynemouth
Hexham
North West Durham
City of Durham
Easington
Hartlepool
Bishop Auckland
Sedgefield
Redcar
Middlesbrough South & East Cleveland
Scarborough & Whitby
Richmond (Yorks)
Thirsk & Malton
Skipton & Ripon
East Yorkshire
Beverley & Holderness
Selby & Ainsty
Calder Valley
Colne Valley
Brigg & Goole
Cleethorpes
Scunthorpe
Penistone & Stocksbridge
Don Valley
Sheffield Hallam
Rother Valley
Carlisle
Workington
Penrith & The Border
Copeland
Westmorland & Lonsdale
Barrow & Furness
Morecambe & Lunesdale
NORTH-WEST
1 Wyre & Preston North
2 Preston
3 Blackburn
4 Hyndburn
5 Wigan
6 Bolton West
7 Bolton North East
8 Bury North
9 Heywood & Middleton
10 Wallasey
11 Birkenhead
12 Liverpool Riverside
13 Bootle
14 Liverpool Walton
15 Liverpool West Derby
16 Liverpool Wavertree
17 Knowsley
18 St Helens South & Whiston
19 St Helens North
20 Makerfield
21 Leigh
22 Bolton South East
23 Worsley & Eccles South
24 Stretford & Urmston
25 Salford & Eccles
26 Bury South
27 Blackley & Broughton
28 Manchester Central
29 Oldham West & Royton
30 Ashton-under-Lyne
31 Manchester Gorton
32 Denton & Reddish
33 Manchester Withington
34 Stockport
35 Cheadle
36 Wythenshawe & Sale East
37 Altrincham & Sale West
38 Warrington North
39 Warrington South
40 Weaver Vale
41 Halton
42 Garston & Halewood
43 Ellesmere Port & Neston
Lancaster & Fleetwood
Ribble Valley
Blackpool North & Cleveleys
Blackpool South
Fylde
Pendle
Burnley
South Ribble
Southport
Chorley
Rossendale & Darwen
Rochdale
West Lancashire
Sefton Central
Oldham East & Saddleworth
Stalybridge & Hyde
Hazel Grove
Wirral West
Wirral South
Tatton
Macclesfield
City of Chester
Eddisbury
Congleton
Crewe & Nantwich

WEST MIDLANDS

1 Newcastle-under-Lyme
2 Stoke-on-Trent North
3 Stoke-on-Trent Central
4 Stoke-on-Trent South
5 Telford
6 Cannock Chase
7 South Staffordshire
8 Wolverhampton South West
9 Wolverhampton North East
10 Wolverhampton South East
11 Walsall North
12 Walsall South
13 Aldridge-Brownhills
14 Dudley South
15 Dudley North
16 West Bromwich West
17 West Bromwich East
18 Birmingham Perry Barr
19 Birmingham Erdington
20 Sutton Coldfield
21 Stourbridge
22 Halesowen
& Rowley Regis
23 Warley
24 Birmingham Edgbaston
25 Birmingham Ladywood
26 Birmingham Hodge Hill
27 Birmingham Northfield
28 Birmingham Selly Oak
29 Birmingham Hall Green
30 Birmingham Yardley
31 Solihull
32 Worcester
33 Mid Worcestershire
34 Redditch
35 Bromsgrove
36 Meriden
37 Coventry North West
38 Coventry North East
39 Coventry South
40 Warwick & Leamington

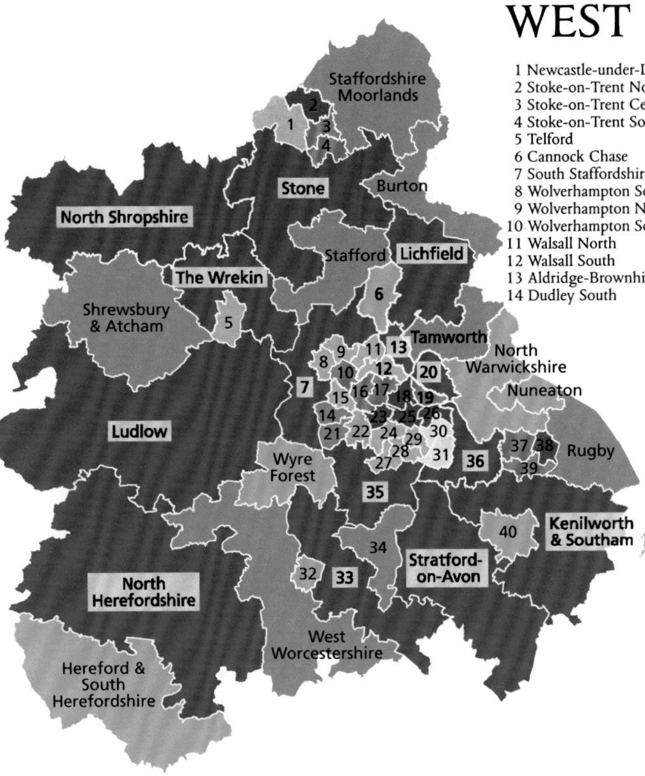

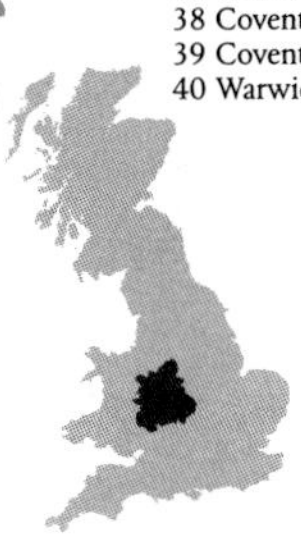

SOUTH WEST

1 Camborne & Redruth
2 St Austell & Newquay
3 Plymouth Moor View
4 Plymouth Sutton
& Devonport
5 South West Devon
6 Exeter
7 Bristol North West
8 Bristol West
9 Bristol East
10 Bristol South
11 Filton &
Bradley Stoke
12 Kingswood
13 Thornbury & Yate
14 North East Somerset
15 Bath
16 Chippenham
17 Gloucester
18 Cheltenham
19 Tewkesbury
20 North Swindon
21 South Swindon
22 South West Wiltshire
23 Mid Dorset & North Poole
24 Poole
25 Bournemouth West
26 Bournemouth East
27 Christchurch

MAJORITY
per cent

	<8	8–20	>20
Labour			
Conservative			
Liberal Democrat			

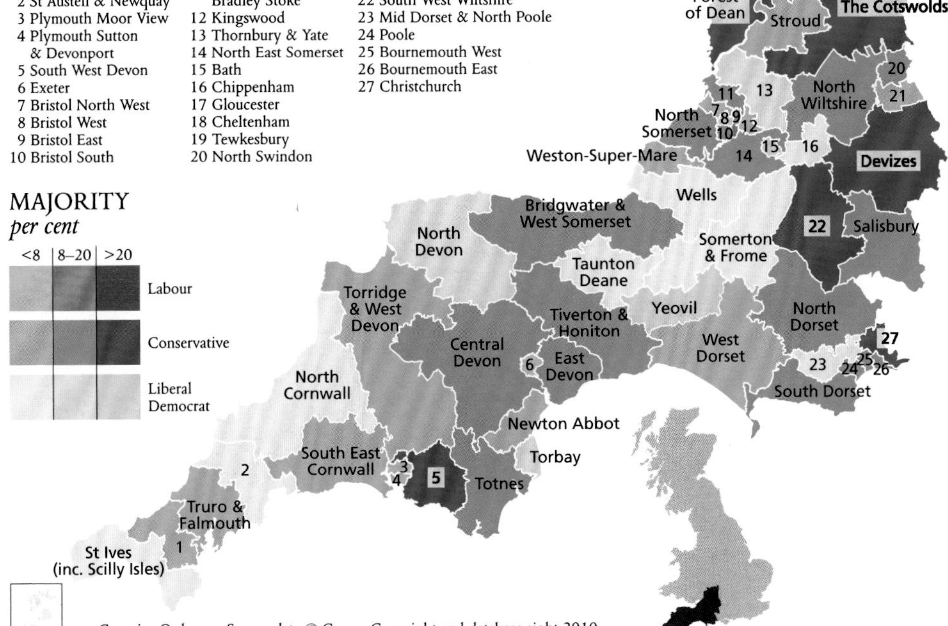

High Peak
Bassetlaw
Gainsborough
Louth & Horncastle
Derbyshire Dales
Newark
Sleaford & North Hykeham
Boston & Skegness
South Derbyshire
Rushcliffe
Grantham & Stamford
South Holland & The Deepings
Rutland & Melton
Bosworth
South Leicestershire
Corby
Kettering
Daventry
Wellingborough
South Northamptonshire

EAST MIDLANDS

1 North East Derbyshire
2 Chesterfield
3 Bolsover
4 Mansfield
5 Ashfield
6 Amber Valley
7 Mid Derbyshire
8 Erewash
9 Broxtowe
10 Nottingham North
11 Nottingham South
12 Nottingham East
13 Gedling
14 Sherwood
15 Derby North
16 Derby South
17 North West Leicestershire
18 Loughborough
19 Charnwood
20 Leicester West
21 Leicester East
22 Leicester South
23 Harborough
24 Northampton North
25 Northampton South
26 Lincoln

EAST

1 Peterborough
2 North East Cambridgeshire
3 Bedford
4 South Cambridgeshire
5 Cambridge
6 South East Cambridgeshire
7 Norwich South
8 Norwich North
9 Bury St Edmunds
10 Central Suffolk & North Ipswich
11 Ipswich
12 Colchester
13 Harwich & North Essex
14 Clacton
15 South West Bedfordshire
16 Luton North
17 Luton South
18 Hitchin & Harpenden
19 Stevenage
20 North East Hertfordshire
21 South West Hertfordshire
22 Hemel Hempstead
23 Watford
24 St Albans
25 Hertsmere
26 Welwyn Hatfield
27 Broxbourne
28 Hertford & Stortford
29 Harlow
30 Epping Forest
31 Brentwood & Ongar
32 Chelmsford
33 Basildon & Billericay
34 Thurrock
35 South Basildon & East Thurrock
36 Castle Point
37 Rayleigh & Wickford
38 Southend West
39 Rochford & Southend East

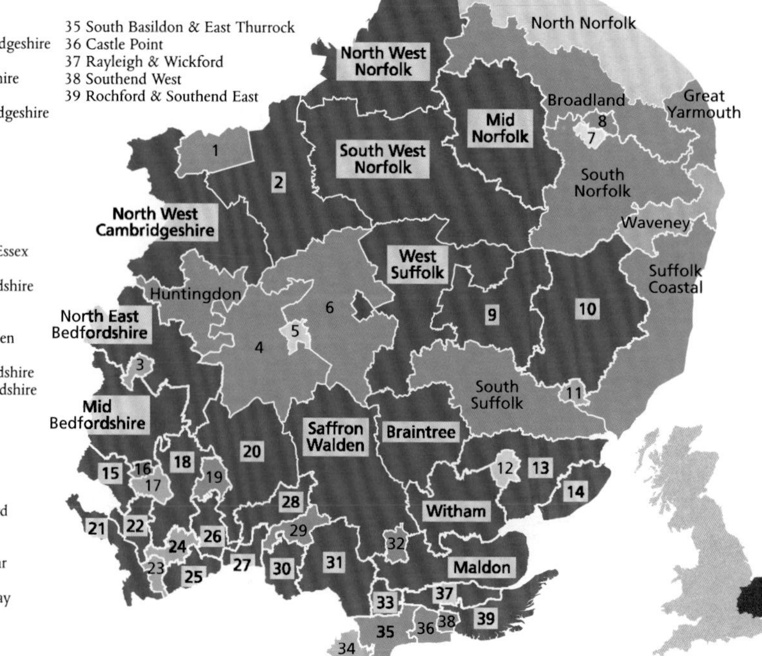

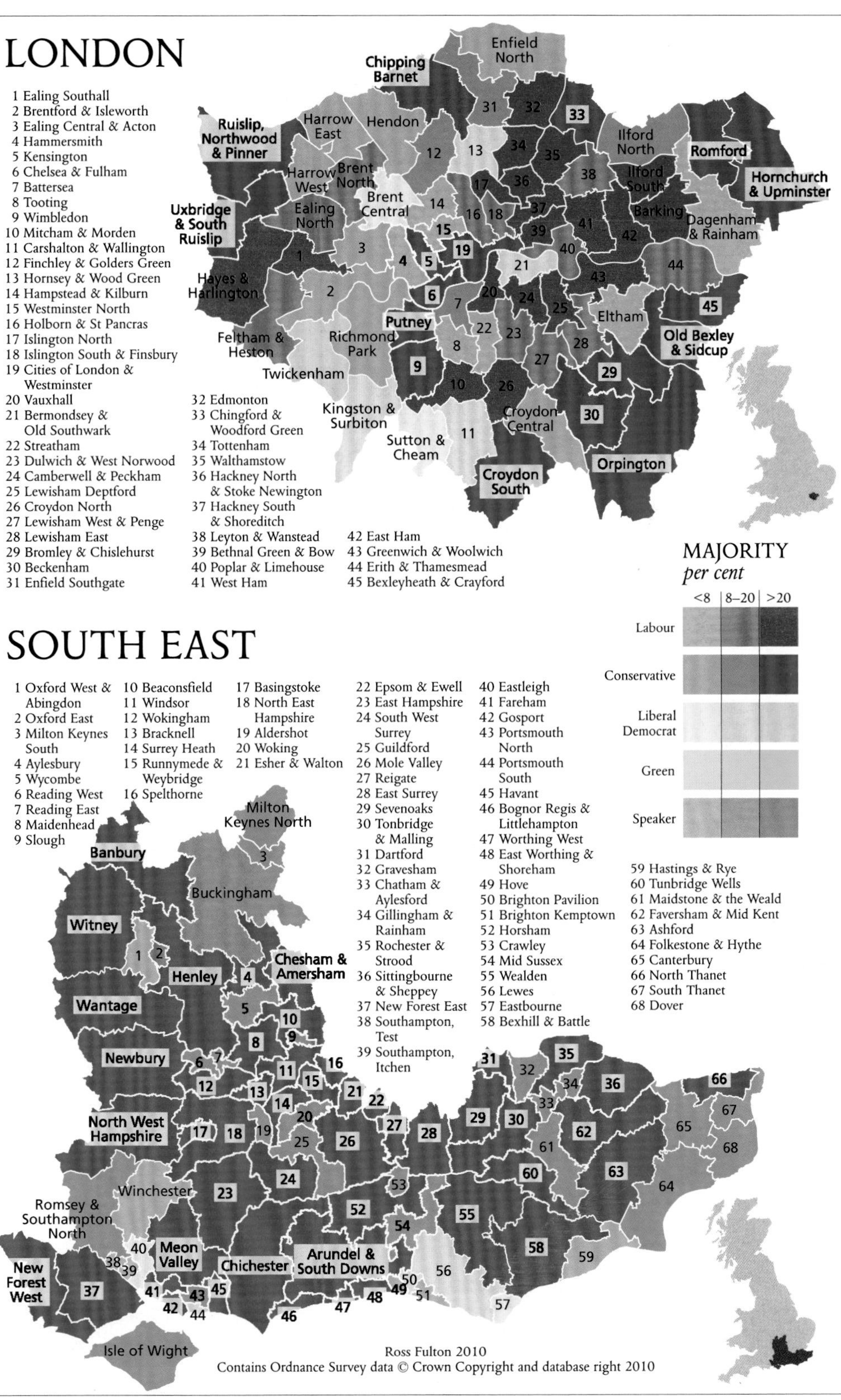
LONDON
1 Ealing Southall
2 Brentford & Isleworth
3 Ealing Central & Acton
4 Hammersmith
5 Kensington
6 Chelsea & Fulham
7 Battersea
8 Tooting
9 Wimbledon
10 Mitcham & Morden
11 Carshalton & Wallington
12 Finchley & Golders Green
13 Hornsey & Wood Green
14 Hampstead & Kilburn
15 Westminster North
16 Holborn & St Pancras
17 Islington North
18 Islington South & Finsbury
19 Cities of London & Westminster
20 Vauxhall
21 Bermondsey & Old Southwark
22 Streatham
23 Dulwich & West Norwood
24 Camberwell & Peckham
25 Lewisham Deptford
26 Croydon North
27 Lewisham West & Penge
28 Lewisham East
29 Bromley & Chislehurst
30 Beckenham
31 Enfield Southgate
32 Edmonton
33 Chingford & Woodford Green
34 Tottenham
35 Walthamstow
36 Hackney North & Stoke Newington
37 Hackney South & Shoreditch
38 Leyton & Wanstead
39 Bethnal Green & Bow
40 Poplar & Limehouse
41 West Ham
42 East Ham
43 Greenwich & Woolwich
44 Erith & Thamesmead
45 Bexleyheath & Crayford
Enfield North
Chipping Barnet
Harrow East
Hendon
Ruislip, Northwood & Pinner
Ilford North
Romford
Hornchurch & Upminster
Harrow West
Brent North
Brent Central
Ilford South
Barking
Dagenham & Rainham
Uxbridge & South Ruislip
Ealing North
Hayes & Harlington
Feltham & Heston
Richmond Park
Putney
Eltham
Old Bexley & Sidcup
Twickenham
Kingston & Surbiton
Sutton & Cheam
Croydon Central
Croydon South
Orpington
MAJORITY per cent
<8
8–20
>20
Labour
Conservative
Liberal Democrat
Green
Speaker
SOUTH EAST
1 Oxford West & Abingdon
2 Oxford East
3 Milton Keynes South
4 Aylesbury
5 Wycombe
6 Reading West
7 Reading East
8 Maidenhead
9 Slough
10 Beaconsfield
11 Windsor
12 Wokingham
13 Bracknell
14 Surrey Heath
15 Runnymede & Weybridge
16 Spelthorne
17 Basingstoke
18 North East Hampshire
19 Aldershot
20 Woking
21 Esher & Walton
22 Epsom & Ewell
23 East Hampshire
24 South West Surrey
25 Guildford
26 Mole Valley
27 Reigate
28 East Surrey
29 Sevenoaks
30 Tonbridge & Malling
31 Dartford
32 Gravesham
33 Chatham & Aylesford
34 Gillingham & Rainham
35 Rochester & Strood
36 Sittingbourne & Sheppey
37 New Forest East
38 Southampton, Test
39 Southampton, Itchen
40 Eastleigh
41 Fareham
42 Gosport
43 Portsmouth North
44 Portsmouth South
45 Havant
46 Bognor Regis & Littlehampton
47 Worthing West
48 East Worthing & Shoreham
49 Hove
50 Brighton Pavilion
51 Brighton Kemptown
52 Horsham
53 Crawley
54 Mid Sussex
55 Wealden
56 Lewes
57 Eastbourne
58 Bexhill & Battle
59 Hastings & Rye
60 Tunbridge Wells
61 Maidstone & the Weald
62 Faversham & Mid Kent
63 Ashford
64 Folkestone & Hythe
65 Canterbury
66 North Thanet
67 South Thanet
68 Dover
Milton Keynes North
Banbury
Buckingham
Witney
Henley
Chesham & Amersham
Wantage
Newbury
North West Hampshire
Winchester
Romsey & Southampton North
Meon Valley
New Forest West
Chichester
Arundel & South Downs
Isle of Wight
Ross Fulton 2010
Contains Ordnance Survey data © Crown Copyright and database right 2010

KYRGYZSTAN

Kyrgyz Respublikasy – Kyrgyz Republic

Area – 199,951 sq. km
Capital – Bishkek; population, 854,001 (2009 est)
Major city – Osh
Currency – Som of 100 tyiyn
Population – 5,431,747 rising at 1.4 per cent a year (2009 est); Kyrgyz (64.9 per cent), Uzbek (13.8 per cent), Russian (12.5 per cent), Dungan (1.1 per cent), Ukrainian (1 per cent), Uygur (1 per cent) (est)
Religion – Muslim (Sunni 80 per cent), Christian (Russian Orthodox 11 per cent) (est)
Language – Kyrgyz, Russian (both official), Uzbek, Dungun
Population density – 28 per sq. km (2008)
Urban population – 36 per cent (2007 est)
Median age (years) – 24.4 (2009 est)
National anthem – 'Kyrgyz Respublikasynyn Mamlekettik Gimni' ['National Anthem of the Kyrgyz Republic']
National day – 31 August (Independence Day)
Life expectancy (years) – 69.43 (2009 est)
Mortality rate – 6.91 (2009 est)
Birth rate – 23.44 (2009 est)
Infant mortality rate – 31.26 (2009 est)
Death penalty – Abolished for all crimes (since 2007)
CPI score – 1.9 (2009)
Gross enrolment ratio (percentage of relevant age group) – primary 95 per cent; secondary 85 per cent; tertiary 52 per cent (2008 est)
Literacy rate – 99.3 per cent (2007 est)
Health expenditure (per capita) – US$46 (2007)
Hospital beds (per 1,000 people) – 5.1 (2003–8)

CLIMATE AND TERRAIN

Kyrgyzstan is a landlocked and mountainous country lying in the Tien Shan mountain range, with the Pamirs in the extreme south. Elevation extremes range from 7,439m (Jengish Chokusu/Pik Pobedy) at the highest point to 132m (Kara-Darya) at the lowest, though most of the country lies at over 1,000m. The principal rivers are the Naryn and the Chu, and the vast Issyk-Kul lake lies in the north-east. The climate is continental but with temperatures and humidity moderated by the altitude; typical temperatures in the valleys range from as low as −14°C in January to 27°C in July. Rainfall is low for the altitude, owing to Kyrgyzstan's distance from the sea and the rain-shadow effect of the Himalayan and Pamir mountain ranges.

HISTORY AND POLITICS

After periods under Turkic, Mongol and Chinese rule, the Kyrgyz became part of the Russian Empire in the 1860s and 1870s. After the October 1917 revolution in Russia, the area became part of the Turkestan autonomous republic within the USSR until 1924, when the Kirgiz Autonomous Region was formed; it became an autonomous republic in 1926 and a constituent republic of the USSR in 1936. Soviet rule brought land reforms in the 1920s that resulted in the settlement of many of the nomadic Kyrgyz.

Reform in the USSR in the 1980s provoked an upsurge in nationalism in Kyrgyzstan and agitation for independence. Following the attempted coup in Moscow in 1991, Kyrgyzstan became an independent republic and joined the Commonwealth of Independent States.

Since independence, there has been tension between the Kyrgyz and ethnic Uzbeks, concentrated around Osh, and between the Kyrgyz and Dungans (ethnic Chinese) near Bishkek. These tensions have flared into intercommunal violence on occasions. There have also been clashes between security forces and militant Islamists, active near the border with Tajikistan.

Askar Akayev, a pro-reform Communist, was president from 1990 until he was deposed in March 2005 in a popular uprising over alleged electoral fraud; the uprising was also fuelled by years of unrest over the dire economic situation, corruption, nepotism and crime. The opposition leader Kurmanbek Bakiyev was elected president in July 2005 but his tenure was volatile, in the face of the same problems as his predecessor as well as a power struggle with the legislature over the extent of presidential powers.

In the 2007 legislative elections, President Bakiyev's Ak Zhol party won an overwhelming majority, although observers considered the polls to be marred by fraud. President Bakiyev was re-elected in July 2009, with 76 per cent of the vote, amid allegations of vote-rigging. He was forced from office in April 2010 after attempts to suppress anti-government demonstrations left over 80 protesters dead. An interim government was formed, headed by Roza Otunbayeva, as crime and civil disruption grew. Intercommunal violence between Kyrgyz and Uzbeks erupted in the Osh area in June 2010 and spread to Jalalabad. Presidential and legislative elections were scheduled for October 2010, but the violence caused the presidential election to be postponed to 2011; however, a referendum was held in June 2010 which approved a draft constitution granting greater powers to parliament at the expense of the president. (*See also* Events of the Year.)

POLITICAL SYSTEM

Under the constitution approved in June 2010 the president will be directly elected for a six-year term, which is not renewable. The unicameral Supreme Council has 90 members directly elected for a five-year term. The largest party in the legislature nominates the prime minister, and the president appoints the cabinet; the appointments are subject to the approval of the Supreme Council.

HEAD OF STATE

President and Chair of Government, Roza Otunbayeva (interim)

SELECTED GOVERNMENT MEMBERS *as at June 2010*

First Deputy Chair, Economy, Almaz Atambayev
Deputy Chairs, Azimbek Beknazarov, Temir Sariyev *(Finance)*; Omurbek Tekebayev
Foreign Affairs, Ruslan Kazakbayev
Internal Affairs, Bolot Sherniyazov
Defence, Ismail Isakov

EMBASSY OF THE KYRGYZ REPUBLIC
Ascot House, 119 Crawford Street, London W1U 6BJ
T 020-7935 1462 E mail@kyrgyz-embassy.org.uk
W www.kyrgyz-embassy.org.uk
Ambassador Extraordinary and Plenipotentiary, HE Kuban Mambetaliev, *apptd* 2006

BRITISH AMBASSADOR
HE David Moran, *apptd* 2009, resident at Almaty, Kazakhstan

BRITISH COUNCIL
Director, Lena Milosevic, resident at Almaty, Kazakhstan

DEFENCE

The army has 150 main battle tanks, 35 armoured personnel carriers and 320 armoured infantry fighting vehicles. The air force has 52 combat aircraft and 9 armed helicopters.

The USA and Russia each have an air base in the country.
Military budget – US$43m (2009 est)
Military personnel – 10,900: army 8,500, air force 2,400; paramilitary 9,500
Conscription duration – 18 months

ECONOMY AND TRADE

Economic reforms in the early 1990s caused severe hardship, and although productivity and exports have grown since the late 1990s, poverty is widespread and unemployment high, particularly in the south. The economy, which remains heavily dependent on gold, contracted in 2009 after gold production, investment and remittances dropped owing to the global downturn. The government, with international support, is pursuing poverty reduction and economic growth programmes, but the greater foreign direct investment these require may be deterred by political volatility, lack of transparency and the high level of organised crime.

The economy is predominantly agrarian, with agriculture accounting for 30.7 per cent of GDP and employing nearly 50 per cent of the workforce. There are deposits of gold, uranium, mercury and natural gas, and high hydroelectric potential. Apart from mining and energy, industry consists of light manufacturing and contributes 15.9 per cent of GDP; services contribute 53.4 per cent.

The main trading partners are Russia, Switzerland, Kazakhstan, China, Uzbekistan and the EU. Principal exports are cotton, wool, meat, tobacco, gold, mercury, uranium, natural gas, hydroelectric power, machinery and shoes. The main imports are oil, gas, machinery and equipment, chemicals and foodstuffs.
GNI – US$4,100m; US$780 per capita (2008)
Annual average growth of GDP – –1 per cent (2009 est)
Inflation rate – 7.9 per cent (2009 est)
Population below poverty line – 40 per cent (2004 est)
Unemployment – 18 per cent (2004 est)
Total external debt – US$3,467m (2008)
Imports – US$4,100m (2008)
Exports – US$1,600m (2008)

BALANCE OF PAYMENTS
Trade – US$1,621m deficit (2009)
Current Account – US$413m deficit (2008)

Trade with UK	*2008*	*2009*
Imports from UK	£3,426,582	£4,779,203
Exports to UK	£10,203,412	£98,057

COMMUNICATIONS

Kyrgyzstan has 18,500km of roads, 470km of railways and 600km of waterways. There are 29 airports and airfields; the international airport is outside Bishkek.

Both fixed-line and mobile telephone systems are expanding, though for fixed lines density is currently low and concentrated in urban areas. In 2008, there were 494,000 fixed lines in use, 3.4 million mobile phone subscribers and 850,000 internet users.

MEDIA

The media has become increasingly subject to government harassment and censorship since the 1990s, and large fines are often imposed for slander, resulting in a degree of self-censorship. The most popular medium is television, but the state-run television and radio networks have yet to achieve complete national coverage, especially in the south. There are a number of private and independent television and radio broadcasters but, like the private press, they struggle financially.

LAOS

Sathalanalat Paxathipatai Paxaxon Lao – *Lao People's Democratic Republic*

Area – 236,800 sq. km
Capital – Vientiane; population, 799,170 (2009 est)
Major towns – Luang Prabang, Pakse, Savannakhet
Currency – Kip (K) of 100 att
Population – 6,834,942 rising at 2.32 per cent a year (2009 est); there are (officially) 47 ethnic groups, including Lao (55 per cent), Khmou (11 per cent), Hmong (8 per cent) (est)
Religion – Buddhist 50 per cent (predominantly Theravada), Christian 2 per cent (est). Most of the remainder practise animist beliefs
Language – Lao (official), French, English, ethnic languages
Population density – 27 per sq. km (2008)
Urban population – 30 per cent (2007 est)
Median age (years) – 19.3 (2009 est)
National anthem – 'Pheng Xat Lao' ['Hymn of the Lao People']
National day – 2 December (Republic Day)
Life expectancy – 56.68 (2009 est)
Mortality rate – 10.78 (2009 est)
Birth rate – 33.94 (2009 est)
Infant mortality rate – 77.82 (2009 est)
Death penalty – Retained (not used since 1989)
CPI score – 2 (2009)
Literacy rate – 72.7 per cent (2007 est)

Gross enrolment ratio (percentage of age group) – primary 112 per cent; secondary 44 per cent; tertiary 13 per cent (2008 est)
Health expenditure (per capita) – US$27 (2007)
Hospital beds (per 1,000 people) – 1.2 (2003–8)

CLIMATE AND TERRAIN

Laos is landlocked and mostly mountainous, the land rising from the Mekong river basin in the west to mountains in the north and east. Elevation extremes range from 2,817m (Phou Bia) at the highest point to 70m (Mekong) at the lowest. Much of the land is covered by rainforest. The climate is tropical, with a wet season from May to November, during which humidity levels are very high. Average temperatures in Vientiane range from lows of 14°C in January to highs of 34°C in April.

HISTORY AND POLITICS

From the ninth to the 13th centuries, Laos was part of the Khmer Empire centred on Angkor in Cambodia. Small principalities developed from the 12th century and were united in the 14th century into the Lao kingdom of Lan Xang ('the land of a million elephants'), which dominated until 1713, when it split into the separate kingdoms of Luang Prabang, Vientiane and Champassac, which became tributaries of Siam (Thailand) in the late 18th century and then a protectorate of France from 1893.

Japanese occupation during the Second World War inspired a Lao nationalist movement, which proclaimed independence in 1945, but the French regained control of the country in 1946. Independence as a constitutional monarchy was granted in 1953, but much of the following 20 years was spent in civil war between the Communist Pathet Lao, backed first by China and then by North Vietnam, and royalists, who attracted US and Thai support from the early 1960s. A ceasefire in 1973 partitioned the country between the two sides, but in 1975 the Pathet Lao seized power in the rest of the country and proclaimed a republic, introducing a one-party state and initiating socialist policies. Greater economic liberalisation was introduced from the mid-1980s, and the first legislative elections since 1975 were held in 1989.

Ethnic Hmong minority groups have maintained a low-level insurgency against the communist regime since 1975. In 2000 and 2004, Laos suffered some serious civil disturbances, including bombings and armed attacks on buses. These were variously attributed to Hmong insurgents and anti-government groups based abroad.

In the 2006 legislative election, Lao People's Revolutionary Party (LPRP) candidates won all but one of the seats, the remaining seat being taken by an approved non-partisan candidate; the legislature elected Choummaly Sayasone as president and approved a reshuffled council of ministers.

POLITICAL SYSTEM

Under the 1991 constitution, the head of state is a president elected by the legislature for a five-year term. The unicameral National Assembly has 115 members, who are party-approved candidates directly elected for a five-year term. The LPRP is the only legal political party, although it has given approval to non-partisan candidates for legislative seats. Party congresses are held every five years.

HEAD OF STATE

President, Lt.-Gen. Choummaly Sayasone, *elected* 8 June 2006
Vice-President, Bounnhang Vorachit

SELECTED GOVERNMENT MEMBERS *as at June 2010*

Prime Minister, Bouasone Bouphavanh
Deputy Prime Ministers, Maj.-Gen. Asang Laoly; Somsavat Lengsavad; Maj.-Gen. Douangchay Phichit *(Defence);* Thongloun Sisoulit *(Foreign Affairs)*
Finance, Somdy Douangdy

EMBASSY OF THE LAO PEOPLE'S DEMOCRATIC REPUBLIC

74 Avenue Raymond-Poincaré, 75116 Paris, France
T (+33) (1) 4553 0298 **E** ambalaoparis@wanadoo.fr
W www.laoparis.com
Ambassador Extraordinary and Plenipotentiary, HE Khouanta Phalivong, *apptd* 2010

BRITISH AMBASSADOR

HE Quinton Quayle, *apptd* 2007, resident at Bangkok, Thailand

DEFENCE

The army has 25 main battle tanks and 50 armoured personnel carriers, and its marine section has 52 patrol and coastal combatant vessels. The air force has 22 combat-capable aircraft.
Military budget – US$17m (2008 est)
Military personnel – 29,100: army 25,600, air force 3,500; paramilitary 100,000
Conscription duration – 18 months

ECONOMY AND TRADE

Economic liberalisation and a measure of private enterprise were introduced from the mid-1980s, producing growth averaging 6 per cent a year from 1988 to 2008, except during the 1997 Asian financial crisis. Recent economic growth has been driven by dam and road construction projects and foreign investment in hydroelectric power and mining, although the global economic downturn has slowed these programmes. Poverty levels have been reduced from 46 per cent in 1992, although the country remains very poor, with only a rudimentary (though improving) infrastructure, and is dependent on international aid.

Subsistence agriculture, principally rice, accounts for 29.9 per cent of GDP and about 80 per cent of employment. Deposits of copper, tin, gold and gypsum are exploited, as is the abundance of timber in the rainforests. Other activities include food processing, manufacture of garments and cement, and tourism. A hydro-electric dam on the Mekong river exports electricity to Thailand, earning valuable additional revenue.

The main trading partners are Thailand (35 per cent of exports; 68 per cent of imports), Vietnam and China. Principal exports are timber products, coffee, electricity, tin, copper and gold. The main imports are machinery and equipment, vehicles, fuel and consumer goods.
GNI – US$4,700m; US$760 per capita (2008)
Annual average growth of GDP – 3 per cent (2009 est)
Inflation rate – 2.6 per cent (2009 est)
Population below poverty line – 30.7 per cent (2005 est)
Unemployment – 2.4 per cent (2005 est)
Total external debt – US$3,179m (2006)
Imports – US$1,400m (2008)
Exports – US$1,100m (2008)

BALANCE OF PAYMENTS
Trade – US$396m deficit (2009)
Current Account – US$921m deficit (2009)

Trade with UK	*2008*	*2009*
Imports from UK	£769,401	£1,167,766
Exports to UK	£21,974,227	£44,067,567

COMMUNICATIONS

The road network has been improved and expanded significantly since the 1990s, benefitting from substantial government investment and funding from the World Bank and other international agencies; it is currently 36,800km in extent, though most of it remains unpaved. The Friendship Bridge over the Mekong river connects Laos with Thailand, and links up the road routes from Singapore to China. A rail track across the bridge was opened in 2009, linking the Thai rail system to a railhead established on the Lao bank; there are plans to extend the line to Vientiane. There are around 4,600km of navigable waterways, principally on the Mekong and its tributaries, although some are not navigable in the dry season. There are 41 airports and airfields; the principal airports are at Vientiane and Luang Prabang.

The telephone system is poor and limited in extent but services are improving. Mobile phone distribution is growing rapidly and subscribers numbered 2 million in 2008, compared to 97,600 fixed lines. There were 130,000 internet users in 2008.

MEDIA

All media are strictly controlled by the government, which owns all three daily newspapers and the radio and television broadcasting networks. Slandering the state, distorting party policies and spreading false rumours are all criminal offences. Thai television channels are popular among many Laotian viewers.

LATVIA

Latvijas Republika – Republic of Latvia

Area – 64,589 sq. km
Capital – Riga; population, 710,637 (2009 est)
Major cities – Daugavpils, Jelgava, Liepaja
Currency – Lats of 100 santims
Population – 2,231,503 falling at 0.61 per cent a year (2009 est); Latvian (57.7 per cent), Russian (29.6 per cent), Belarusian (4.1 per cent), Ukrainian (2.7 per cent), Polish (2.5 per cent), Lithuanian (1.4 per cent) (est)
Religion – Christian (Roman Catholic 22 per cent, Lutheran 20 per cent, Orthodox 16 per cent) (est)
Language – Latvian (official), Russian, Lithuanian
Population density – 36 per sq. km (2008)
Urban population – 68 per cent (2007 est)
Median age (years) – 40.1 (2009 est)
National anthem – 'Dievs, Sveti Latviju' ['God Bless Latvia']
National day – 18 November (Independence Day)
Life expectancy (years) – 72.15 (2009 est)
Mortality rate – 13.62 (2009 est)
Birth rate – 9.78 (2009 est)
Infant mortality rate – 8.77 (2009 est)
Death penalty – Retained for certain crimes (last used 1996)
CPI score – 4.5 (2009)

CLIMATE AND TERRAIN

Latvia is a flat, low-lying country on the eastern shore of the Baltic Sea, with low hills and many lakes in the south-east. Elevation extremes range from 312m (Galzinakalns) at the highest point to 0m (Baltic Sea) at the lowest. The climate is temperate, and average temperatures in Riga range from lows of −10°C in January to highs of 22°C in July.

HISTORY AND POLITICS

Conquered and Christianised in the 13th century by the Teutonic Knights, Latvia was successively under Polish, Lithuanian and Swedish rule in the 16th and 17th centuries, until it was incorporated into the Russian Empire in 1721. Under partial German occupation during the First World War, it declared its independence in 1918 and successfully defended this against the Bolsheviks in 1918–20. A dictatorship was established in 1934 following a period of political instability and economic depression. The USSR invaded and annexed Latvia in 1940, and regained control in 1944 after ousting the German forces that had invaded in 1941. Latvia suffered huge civilian losses during the Second World War, including the destruction of its large Jewish community. Many more Latvians died after the war in purges and deportations ordered by Stalin.

Agitation by nationalist groups grew from the mid-1980s. In May 1990 the legislature declared independence, and reiterated this in August 1991 following the failed coup in Moscow, when the country's independence was internationally recognised. The last Russian troops left in 1994 but a large Russian minority remains and there are intercommunal tensions. Since the first post-Soviet elections in 1993, there has been a succession of centre-right coalition governments. Latvia joined NATO and the EU in 2004.

Ivars Godmanis' coalition government resigned in February 2009 after violent protests at government austerity measures, and Valdis Dombrovskis became prime minister at the head of a five-party coalition government. The People's Party withdrew from the coalition in March 2010, leaving the administration to continue as a minority government until the legislative election due in October 2010.

POLITICAL SYSTEM

The 1922 constitution was restored in 1993. The head of state is a president, who is elected by the legislature for a four-year term which may be renewed only once. The president appoints the prime minister, who appoints the cabinet subject to approval by the legislature. The unicameral *Saeima* has 100 deputies who are elected for a four-year term by proportional representation.

HEAD OF STATE
President, Valdis Zatlers, *elected* 31 May 2007, *sworn in* 7 July 2007

SELECTED GOVERNMENT MEMBERS *as at June 2010*
Prime Minister, Valdis Dombrovskis
Defence, Imants Liegis
Finance, Einars Repse
Foreign Affairs, Alvis Ronis
Interior, Linda Murniece

EMBASSY OF THE REPUBLIC OF LATVIA
45 Nottingham Place, London W1U 5LY
T 020-7312 0041 **E** embassy.uk@mfa.gov.lv
W www.london.mfa.gov.lv
Ambassador Extraordinary and Plenipotentiary, HE Eduards Stiprais, *apptd* 2009

BRITISH EMBASSY
5 J. Alunana Street, Riga 1010
T (+371) 6777 4700 **E** british.embassy@apollo.lv
W http://ukinlatvia.fco.gov.uk
Ambassador Extraordinary and Plenipotentiary, HE Andrew Soper, *apptd* 2010

BRITISH COUNCIL
5A-2 Blaumana Street, Riga 1011
T (+371) 6728 1730 **W** www.britishcouncil.org/latvia
Director, Dace Melbarde

DEFENCE

The army has 3 main battle tanks, the navy has 12 patrol and coastal vessels and the air force has 3 aircraft and 6 helicopters. Latvia, Lithuania and Estonia operate a joint naval unit, BALTRON, which is located at 5 naval bases: Liepaja, Riga, Ventspils, Tallinn and Klaipeda.
Military expenditure – US$542m (2008)
Military personnel – 5,745: army 1,058, navy 587, air force 319, joint staff 3,202, National Guard 579

ECONOMY AND TRADE

The country made the transition from a planned to a market economy in the decade after independence, although a few large enterprises remain in state ownership. The economy grew rapidly from 2004 to 2007, but has been severely affected by the global economic downturn since 2008 because of its large current account deficit and private-sector debt. The economy contracted by 20 per cent in 2008–9. Public spending was cut by 40 per cent in 2009 in return for aid from the IMF, the World Bank and the EU in 2008–9 to avoid devaluation of the lat.

The economy has shifted towards service industries since independence. Transit, services and banking are large sectors, with services contributing 74.3 per cent of GDP. Industry contributes 21.9 per cent of GDP and includes the manufacture of commercial and public transport vehicles, synthetic fibres, agricultural machinery, fertilisers, washing machines, radios, electronics and pharmaceuticals. The agricultural sector accounts for 3.8 per cent of GDP, employs 12 per cent of the workforce and specialises in rearing livestock, dairy farming and crops including grain, sugar beet, potatoes and other vegetables.

The main trading partners are other EU states and Russia. Principal exports are timber and wood products, machinery and equipment, metals, textiles and foodstuffs. The main imports are machinery and equipment, chemicals, fuel and vehicles.

GNI – US$26,900m; US$11,860 per capita (2008)
Annual average growth of GDP – –17.8 per cent (2009 est)
Inflation rate – 3.3 per cent (2009 est)
Unemployment – 16.6 per cent (2009 est)
Total external debt – US$38,010m (2009 est)
Imports – US$15,800m (2008)
Exports – US$9,300m (2008)

BALANCE OF PAYMENTS
Trade – US$2,015m deficit (2009)
Current Account – US$2,477m deficit (2009)

Trade with UK	*2008*	*2009*
Imports from UK	£167,565,184	£107,503,162
Exports to UK	£347,536,914	£278,150,219

COMMUNICATIONS

Latvia has 2,300km of railway track and some 73,100km of roads. There are two major ports, Riga and Ventspils, which are warm-water ports. The main airports are at Riga, Ventspils and Liepaja.

The telecommunications sector has become increasingly competitive since 2003. Fixed-line use is declining as mobile services expand. In 2008, there were 644,000 fixed lines in use, 2.2 million mobile phone subscribers and 1.3 million internet users.

EDUCATION AND HEALTH

Education is compulsory from the age of seven until 16 years, after which there is the option for a further three years of either secondary or vocational study.
Literacy rate – 99.8 per cent (2007 est)
Gross enrolment ratio (percentage of relevant age group) – primary 97 per cent; secondary 115 per cent; tertiary 69 per cent (2008 est)
Health expenditure (per capita) – US$784 (2007)
Hospital beds (per 1,000 people) – 7.6 (2003–8)

MEDIA

There are around 140 newspapers in circulation, including 24 national dailies. Television and radio output is provided by public service broadcasters and a number of commercial stations. Latvian versions of the main Russian networks are also available.

LEBANON

Al-Jumhuriyah al-Lubnaniyah – Lebanese Republic

Area – 10,452 sq. km
Capital – Beirut (Bayrut); population, 1,909,410 (2009 est)

Major cities – Sidon, Tripoli (Tarabulus)
Currency – Lebanese pound (L£) of 100 piastres
Population – 4,017,095 rising at 1.11 per cent a year (2009 est); Arab (95 per cent), Armenian (4 per cent) (est)
Religion – Muslim (Sunni 28 per cent, Shia 28 per cent, Druze 5 per cent), Christian (Maronite 22 per cent, Greek Orthodox 8 per cent, Greek Catholic 4 per cent) (est)
Language – Arabic (official), French, English, Armenian
Population density – 410 per sq. km (2008)
Urban population – 87 per cent (2007 est)
Median age (years) – 29.3 (2009 est)
National anthem – 'Koullouna Liloutaan Lil Oula Lil Alam' ['All of Us! For Our Country, For Our Flag and Glory']
National day – 22 November (Independence Day)
Life expectancy (years) – 73.66 (2009 est)
Mortality rate – 6.03 (2009 est)
Birth rate – 17.1 (2009 est)
Infant mortality rate – 21.82 (2009 est)
Death penalty – Retained
CPI score – 2.5 (2009)

CLIMATE AND TERRAIN

There is a narrow plain along the Mediterranean Sea coast, backed by the Lebanon Mountains. Running parallel to these, forming the border with Syria, is the Anti-Lebanon range. Between the two ranges lies the fertile Bekaa valley, the northern extremity of Africa's Great Rift Valley. Elevation extremes range from 3,088m (Qurnat as Sawda') at the highest point to 0m (Mediterranean Sea) at the lowest. The climate is Mediterranean, although the mountains usually receive snow in winter. Temperatures in Beirut reach average lows of 11°C in January and highs of 32°C in August.

HISTORY AND POLITICS

Lebanon was part of the Phoenician Empire from the fifth century BC until the first century AD, when it came under Roman rule and Christianity began to spread. Islam was introduced by Arabs in the seventh century AD, and the Druze faith was developed by local Muslims in the 11th century. The area was contested between Muslims and Christians during the Crusades before becoming part of the Ottoman Empire in the 16th century. Following the empire's collapse at the end of the First World War, Lebanon became a French-administered mandated territory, achieving independence in 1943 with a constitution that enshrined power-sharing by all the country's religions.

The complicated system of government established by the constitution created tensions between Christians and Muslims that in 1975 erupted into a 16-year civil war that pitted a coalition of Christian groups against Druze and Muslim militias. The conflict drew in the Palestine Liberation Organisation (PLO), then based in Beirut; Syrian forces, at the request of the Lebanese government, to restore order; and Israel, which invaded in 1978 and 1982 in response to PLO guerrilla raids on Israel, and forced the PLO to withdraw from Lebanon in 1982. By 1985, the country was close to partition as rival political and religious factions sought to gain control.

An Arab League-sponsored ceasefire came into effect in 1989 and a peace plan, the Ta'if accord, proposed revisions to the constitution that would reduce Christian Maronite dominance. This was rejected by some Christian factions and fighting continued until this opposition was crushed by Syrian forces. A fragile peace was achieved in 1991, and elections in 1992 were peaceful, although they were boycotted by some Christian parties.

Southern Lebanon was the only area in which conflict was not ended by the accord. In the buffer zones established by Israel in 1985, clashes continued throughout the 1990s between occupying Israeli troops, or the Israeli-backed South Lebanon Army (SLA), and the Hezbollah militia, supported by Syria and Iran. Although the SLA collapsed after Israel withdrew its forces in 2000, Hezbollah's control of the south continued to be accepted by the Lebanese government. In July 2006, Hezbollah's capture of Israeli soldiers in a cross-border raid sparked a month of intense fighting with Israel that killed or displaced thousands and severely damaged infrastructure. A fragile peace on the border was restored with the deployment of UN peacekeeping forces and Lebanese troops from August; it was the first deployment of government forces on the southern border in decades, although Hezbollah still controls much of the south. The government extended its control in the north of the country in 2007, taking over a militia-controlled refugee camp after a four-month siege.

Syria's influence remains pervasive, even though it was obliged to end its 29-year military presence in 2005 after huge protest rallies brought down the pro-Syria government following the assassination of former prime minister Rafik Hariri, for which Syria was blamed. Since 2005, Lebanese politics has been dominated by a power struggle between pro- and anti-Syria factions and militias. After pro-Syria ministers resigned from the predominantly anti-Syria coalition government in November 2006, pro-Syria factions pursued a greater role in the government through popular protests and a legislative boycott that left the state moribund for months. The failure to agree on a successor to President Emile Lahoud after his term of office ended in November 2007 created a political vacuum that led to a rise in factional violence. After rival political leaders concluded the Doha agreement in May 2008, a neutral candidate, General Michel Suleiman, the head of the armed forces, was elected president. In the 2009 legislative election, the governing anti-Syria '14 March' coalition won 68 seats, the opposition '8 March' bloc won 57 and independents aligned with the '14 March' coalition won three seats. After months of negotiation the '14 March' leader Saad Hariri formed a national unity government which took office in November 2009.

POLITICAL SYSTEM

The constitution dates from 1926 but has been heavily amended, most significantly in 1943, when the National Covenant set out the division of power between the religious communities, and in 1990 to incorporate the provisions of the Ta'if accord. By convention, the presidency is held by a Maronite Christian, the prime minister is a Sunni Muslim and the speaker is a Shia Muslim.

The president is elected by the legislature for a six-year term, which is not renewable. The unicameral National Assembly has 128 members, directly elected for a four-year term; seats are divided equally between Christians and Muslims, whose quotas are subdivided by confession according to the distribution formalised in the 2008 election law. This law, part of the Doha agreement, also established political consensus on 26 redrawn electoral districts. The prime minister is appointed by the president following consultation with the legislature.

HEAD OF STATE
President, Gen. Michel Suleiman, *elected* 25 May 2008, *sworn in* 26 May 2008

SELECTED GOVERNMENT MEMBERS *as at June 2010*
Prime Minister, Saad Hariri
Deputy Prime Minister, Defence, Elias Murr
Finance, Rayyah al-Haffar al-Hassan
Foreign Affairs, Ali Husayn al-Shami
Interior, Ziad Baroud

EMBASSY OF LEBANON
21 Palace Gardens Mews, London W8 4RB
T 020-7229 7265 E info@lebaneseembassy.org.uk
W www.lebaneseembassy.org.uk
Ambassador Extraordinary and Plenipotentiary, HE Inaam Osseiran, *apptd* 2007

BRITISH EMBASSY
PO Box 11-471, Armies Street, Zkak al-Blat, Serail Hill, Beirut Centre-Ville, Beirut
T (+961) (1) 960 800 E britemb@cyberia.net.lb
W http://ukinlebanon.fco.gov.uk
Ambassador Extraordinary and Plenipotentiary, HE Frances Guy, *apptd* 2006

BRITISH COUNCIL
Berytech Technology and Health, Sodeco Street, Damascus Road, 2064 1509 Beirut
T (+961) (1) 428 900 W www.britishcouncil.org/lebanon
Director, Barbara Hewitt

DEFENCE

The army has 326 main battle tanks and 1,240 armoured personnel carriers. The navy has over 25 patrol and coastal vessels at 2 bases. The air force has 10 aircraft and 8 armed helicopters.
Military budget – US$911m (2009)
Military personnel – 59,100: army 57,000, navy 1,100, air force 1,000; paramilitary 20,000; Hezbollah military force 2,000 (est)

ECONOMY AND TRADE

The civil war seriously damaged Lebanon's economy and infrastructure, and its role as an entrepôt and financial services centre for the region. Reconstruction was almost complete when the Israeli attacks in 2006 caused an estimated US$3.6bn (£1.8bn) of infrastructure damage. Recovery was hindered by internal instability, which also postponed the introduction of the economic reforms that were a condition of international funding for reconstruction. Economic growth began anew in 2008, and remained relatively robust in 2009 despite the global economic downturn.

The service sector contributes 77.9 per cent of GDP, largely through banking and tourism, which are the two main economic activities. Industry accounts for 16.7 per cent, through food processing, wine production and the manufacture of jewellery, cement, textiles, mineral and chemical products, timber and furniture, oil refining and metal fabrication. Agriculture contributes 5.4 per cent of GDP, producing fruit, vegetables, tobacco and livestock.

The main export markets are Switzerland, the UAE, Iraq, Saudi Arabia and Syria, while imports come mainly from the USA, the EU, China and Turkey. Principal exports include jewellery, base metals, chemicals, consumer goods, fruit, vegetables, tobacco and construction materials. The main imports are petroleum products, cars, medicines, clothing, meat, livestock and consumer goods.
GNI – US$28,400m; US$6,780 per capita (2008)
Annual average growth of GDP – 3 per cent (2009 est)
Inflation rate – 1.5 per cent (2009 est)
Unemployment – 9.2 per cent (2007 est)
Total external debt – US$34,470m (2009 est)
Imports – US$16,100m (2008)
Exports – US$3,500m (2008)

BALANCE OF PAYMENTS
Trade – US$14,247m deficit (2009)
Current Account – US$3,398m deficit (2008)

Trade with UK	*2008*	*2009*
Imports from UK	£304,126,539	£341,594,282
Exports to UK	£46,640,772	£28,181,513

COMMUNICATIONS

There are 7,000km of roads, though many are in poor repair. The 401km railway system, much of it unusable following the civil war, was rendered completely inoperable by the 2006 attacks. There are seven airports and airfields, including the international airport at Beirut. The principal seaports are Beirut and Tripoli.

The telephone system was repaired after the civil war but planned privatisation has been held back by political tensions. In 2008, there were 714,000 fixed lines in use, 1.4 million mobile phone subscribers and 2.2 million internet users.

EDUCATION AND HEALTH

There are nine years of compulsory education.
Literacy rate – 89.6 per cent (2007 est)
Gross enrolment ratio (percentage of relevant age group) – primary 101 per cent; secondary 82 per cent; tertiary 52 per cent (2008 est)
Health expenditure (per capita) – US$525 (2007)
Hospital beds (per 1,000 people) – 3.4 (2003–8)

MEDIA

Lebanon was the first Arab country to permit private radio and television stations. There are a number of daily newspapers in circulation, including French and English language publications. Tele-Liban is the state-run broadcaster and competes with several commercial stations, including the market-leading Lebanese Broadcasting Corporation and pro-Hezbollah al-Manar TV.

LESOTHO

Kingdom of Lesotho

Area – 30,355 sq. km
Capital – Maseru; population, 220,012 (2009 est)
Currency – Loti (M) of 100 lisente. The South African rand is also legal tender
Population – 2,130,819 rising at 0.12 per cent a year (2009 est); Sotho (99.7 per cent) (est)
Religion – Christian (Roman Catholic 45 per cent, Lesotho Evangelical 27 per cent, Anglican 9 per cent, other Protestant denominations 9 per cent), indigenous religions 10 per cent (est). Many Christians also follow indigenous beliefs
Language – English, Sesotho (both official), Zulu, Xhosa
Population density – 68 per sq. km (2008)
Urban population – 25 per cent (2007 est)
Median age (years) – 21.4 (2009 est)
National anthem – 'Lesotho Fatse la Bontata Rona' ['Lesotho, Land of Our Fathers']
National day – 4 October (Independence Day)
Life expectancy – 40.38 (2009 est)
Mortality rate – 22.2 (2009 est)
Birth rate – 24.14 (2009 est)
Infant mortality rate – 77.4 (2009 est)
HIV/AIDS adult prevalence – 21.5 per cent (2007 est)
Death penalty – Retained
CPI score – 3.3 (2009)
Military budget – US$36m (2008 est)
Military personnel – army 2,000 (est)

CLIMATE AND TERRAIN

Lesotho is a landlocked country encircled by South Africa. It consists of a highland plateau with mountains in the east. The lower land in the west contains most of the arable land and 70 per cent of the population. Elevation extremes range from 3,482m (Thabana Ntlenyana) at the highest point to 1,400m (the junction of the Orange and Makhaleng rivers) at the lowest. As 80 per cent of the country lies above 1,800m, the climate is temperate, with snow in the highlands in winter. Average temperatures at lower elevations range from highs of 30°C in January to lows of 1°C in July.

HISTORY AND POLITICS

The area was organised into a single territory by Moshoeshoe the Great from the 1820s as the Sotho people came under pressure from both the expanding Zulu nation and the Boers. In 1868, after fighting two wars with the Boers, Moshoeshoe sought protection from the British government, and Basutoland became first a British territory in 1868, and then a crown colony in 1884.

The country gained independence in 1966 as the kingdom of Lesotho, under Moshoeshoe II and with Chief Lebua Jonathan as prime minister. The post-independence period has been one of political instability, with a number of coups, mutinies and periods of civil unrest as rival political parties, army factions and the royal family competed for power. Chief Jonathan was overthrown in a military coup in 1986, and military rule ended with multiparty elections in 1993, although civil unrest followed the ousting of the military rulers, and democratic rule was restored in 1994. The 1998 elections were also followed by severe disturbances, which were quelled by an intervention force from neighbouring countries at the government's request. The situation has been more stable since an interim political authority reviewed and modified the electoral system in time for the 2002 election. King Moshoeshoe II, deposed in 1990, was reinstated in 1995 but died in 1996; he was succeeded by King Letsie III, who had been king during his father's exile.

In the 2007 legislative election, the Lesotho Congress for Democracy retained its majority, with 61 seats, and formed a new government.

POLITICAL SYSTEM

Under the 1993 constitution, subsequently amended, the head of state is a hereditary monarch, with ceremonial duties but no executive or legislative powers. The bicameral parliament comprises the National Assembly, with 120 members elected for a five-year term, one-third by proportional representation, and the senate, whose 33 members comprise 22 principal chiefs and 11 members nominated by the king. The prime minister is the leader of the majority party in the legislature and appoints the council of ministers.

HEAD OF STATE

HM The King of Lesotho, King Letsie III, *acceded* 7 February 1996, *crowned* 31 October 1997

SELECTED GOVERNMENT MEMBERS *as at July 2010*

Prime Minister, Defence, Bethuel Pakalitha Mosisili
Deputy Prime Minister, Home Affairs, Archibald Lesao Lehohla
Finance, Timothy Thahane
Foreign Affairs, Mohlabi Tsekoa

HIGH COMMISSION OF THE KINGDOM OF LESOTHO

7 Chesham Place, London SW1X 8HN
T 020-7235 5686 **E** lhc@lesotholondon.org.uk
W www.lesotholondon.org.uk
High Commissioner, HE HRH Prince Seeiso Bereng Seeiso, *apptd* 2005

BRITISH HIGH COMMISSION

High Commissioner, HE Dr Nicola Brewer, *apptd* 2009, resident at Pretoria (Tshwane), South Africa

ECONOMY AND TRADE

The country is one of the poorest in the world, with 49 per cent of the population living below the poverty line, and the situation has worsened with the severe droughts since 2001 and the global economic downturn in 2008–9. With few natural resources apart from water, the main sources of government revenue are customs dues from the South African customs union and, since 1998, the export of water and electricity to South Africa from the hydroelectric facilities created by the Lesotho Highlands Water Project. One traditional source of revenue, remittances from miners employed in South Africa (35 per cent of the male workforce), is declining as the mines become exhausted. This decline is partially compensated for by the development of a small manufacturing base processing agricultural products, producing textiles and assembling garments, and the development of tourism, especially in the highlands. Even so, nearly half of the population is unemployed.

The economy has always been dependent on subsistence agriculture, which engages 86 per cent of the population, although productivity has declined in recent years because of drought, soil erosion and loss of labour as farmers succumb to HIV/AIDS; nearly a quarter of the workforce is infected with HIV or AIDS.

The main market for exports is the USA (59 per cent) and Belgium (37 per cent); imports come mainly from

China (26 per cent), Taiwan, Hong Kong and South Korea. Principal exports are clothing, footwear, road vehicles, wool and mohair, food and livestock. The main imports are food, construction materials, vehicles, machinery, medicines and petroleum products.
GNI – US$2,200m; US$1,060 per capita (2008)
Annual average growth of GDP – –0.9 per cent (2009 est)
Inflation rate – 8.5 per cent (2009 est)
Unemployment – 45 per cent (2002)
Total external debt – US$581m (2009 est)
Imports – US$2,000m (2008)
Exports – US$900m (2008)

BALANCE OF PAYMENTS
Trade – US$1,078m deficit (2009)
Current Account – US$152m surplus (2008)

Trade with UK	*2008*	*2009*
Imports from UK	£1,164,263	£1,943,182
Exports to UK	£392,182	£1,652,169

COMMUNICATIONS

Most travel is by foot or by air, as there is little transport infrastructure other than to link the main towns to each other and to South Africa, and to access the highland hydroelectric facilities. Of the 7,100km of roads, 1,400km are surfaced. There are 26 airports and airfields; the international airport is at Maseru.

The telephone system is rudimentary but expanding. Mobile phone distribution is growing rapidly; density was over 25 per 100 people in 2008.

EDUCATION AND HEALTH

Literacy rate – 82.2 per cent (2007 est)
Gross enrolment ratio (percentage of relevant age group) – primary 108 per cent; secondary 40 per cent; tertiary 4 per cent (2008 est)
Health expenditure (per capita) – US$51 (2007)
Hospital beds (per 1,000 people) – 1.3 (2003–8)

MEDIA

Lesotho has a mixture of state-run and private media. Radio is the most important medium and reforms in 1998 allowed the establishment of a number of commercial stations. State-run Lesotho Television is the only television station, but South African broadcasts can also be received. The press publishes a range of weekly papers in both Sesotho and English. Government officials often use defamation laws against the media.

LIBERIA

Republic of Liberia

Area – 111,369 sq. km
Capital – Monrovia; population, 882,464 (2009 est)
Currency – Liberian dollar (L$) of 100 cents
Population – 3,441,790 rising at 2.67 per cent a year (2009 est); indigenous African (95 per cent), Americo-Liberians (descendants of free immigrants from the USA) (2.5 per cent), Congo People (descendants of free immigrants from the Caribbean) (2.5 per cent) (est)
Religion – Christian 86 per cent, Muslim 12 per cent (est). Many Christians and Muslims also practise elements of indigenous religious beliefs
Language – English (official), about 20 ethnic languages
Population density – 39 per sq. km (2008)
Urban population – 60 per cent (2007 est)
Median age (years) – 18 (2009 est)
National anthem – 'All Hail, Liberia, Hail!'
National day – 26 July (Independence Day)
Life expectancy (years) – 41.84 (2009 est)
Mortality rate – 20.73 (2009 est)
Birth rate – 42.25 (2009 est)
Infant mortality rate – 138.24 (2009 est)
HIV/AIDS adult prevalence – 1.6 per cent (2007 est)
Death penalty – Retained (not used since 2000)
CPI score – 3.1 (2009)
Military personnel – 2,400
Literacy rate – 55.5 per cent (2007 est)
Gross enrolment ratio (percentage of relevant age group) – primary 91 per cent; secondary 32 per cent (2008 est)
Health expenditure (per capita) – US$22 (2007 est)

CLIMATE AND TERRAIN

Liberia lies on the west African coast, just north of the equator. There are forested highlands and grassy plateaux in the interior and swampy plains on the coast, where several rivers enter the ocean. Elevation extremes range from 1,380m (Mt Wuteve) at the highest point to 0m (Atlantic Ocean) at the lowest. The climate is tropical, with very high rainfall.

HISTORY AND POLITICS

The land was purchased by the American Colonisation Society in 1821 and turned into a settlement for liberated black slaves from the USA, gaining recognition as an independent state in 1847.

In the first century of statehood, politics was dominated by the True Whig Party of the Americo-Liberian minority. Political stability ended in 1980 when a coup installed a military government under Samuel Doe. When civilian rule was restored in 1985, Doe became president, but his regime's arbitrary, corrupt rule combined with an economic collapse led to a revolt in 1989 by Charles Taylor's National Patriotic Forces of Liberia (NPFL) and the Armed Forces of Liberia (AFL). The country descended into a civil war that, apart from a respite in 1996–9, lasted until 2003. Around 250,000 people were killed and thousands were displaced. Following mediation by a number of African and European countries, all factions in the conflict signed a peace agreement in 2003 and a UN peacekeeping force was deployed. The disarming of militias was completed in 2005, and a truth and reconciliation commission was set up in 2006 and reported in 2009.

After a period of transitional government, presidential and legislative elections were held in late 2005. In the legislative election, the Congress for Democratic Change (CDC) won the most seats but without an overall majority. The Unity Party leader Ellen Johnson-Sirleaf was elected president in the second round of voting and took office in January 2006, nominating a new government that included members of two smaller parties and some independents.

POLITICAL SYSTEM

Under the 1986 constitution, the head of state is an executive president who is directly elected for a six-year term, renewable only once. There is a bicameral National Assembly, consisting of a lower chamber, the House of Representatives, with 64 members directly elected for a six-year term, and a senate, with 30 members (two from each of the 15 counties) normally elected for a nine-year term, although half of this reconvened senate will serve for only six years. The president appoints the cabinet, which must be approved by the legislature.

HEAD OF STATE

President, Ellen Johnson-Sirleaf, *elected* 8 November 2005, *sworn in* 16 January 2006
Vice-President, Joseph N. Boakai

SELECTED GOVERNMENT MEMBERS, *as at July 2010*
Defence, Brownie Samukai
Finance, Augustine Nganguan
Foreign Affairs, Olubanke King-Akerele
Internal Affairs, Harrison Kahnweah

EMBASSY OF THE REPUBLIC OF LIBERIA
23 Fitzroy Square, London W1T 6EW
T 020-7388 5489 E liberianembassy@yahoo.co.uk
W www.embassyofliberia.org.uk
Ambassador Extraordinary and Plenipotentiary, HE Wesley M. Johnson, *apptd* 2007

BRITISH AMBASSADOR
HE Ian Hughes, *apptd* 2009, resident at Freetown, Sierra Leone

ECONOMY AND TRADE

The civil war devastated an economy already weakened by government mismanagement and corruption, and drove those with expertise and capital into exile. Since the war ended, foreign aid has been received to finance reconstruction, conditional on the adoption of anti-corruption measures, and economic activity has revived. Growth since 2006 has been driven by donor aid and exports, particularly of rubber; UN sanctions on timber and diamond exports, used by civil war factions as a source of finance, were lifted in 2006 and 2007 respectively.

Natural resources include iron ore, timber, gold, diamonds and hydroelectric power potential, and Liberia benefits from reliable water resources and a climate suited to agriculture. Agriculture was the main economic activity during the civil war but its contribution to GDP and its share of the labour market has declined as the industrial and service sectors have revived. Industry centres on the processing of rubber and palm oil, forestry and mining (diamonds, iron ore).

The main export markets are India, the USA and EU countries, while imports come mainly from South Korea, Singapore, Japan and China. Principal exports are rubber, timber, iron, diamonds, cocoa and coffee. The main imports are fuels, chemicals, machinery, transport equipment, manufactured goods and foodstuffs.

GNI – US$700m; US$170 per capita (2008)
Annual average growth of GDP – 5 per cent (2009 est)
Inflation rate – 11.2 per cent (2007 est)
Population below poverty line – 80 per cent (2000 est)
Unemployment – 85 per cent (2003 est)
Total external debt – US$3,200m (2005 est)

BALANCE OF PAYMENTS
Trade - US$11,626 deficit (2009)
Current Account – US$491m deficit (2008)

Trade with UK	*2008*	*2009*
Imports from UK	£17,604,067	£15,228,146
Exports to UK	£8,618,648	£3,428,448

COMMUNICATIONS

The main seaports are Monrovia and Buchanan, and there is a merchant fleet of 2,204 ships of over 1,000 tonnes, as well as 2,109 foreign-owned ships registered in Liberia. There are 10,600km of roads, of which only 657km are surfaced, and 429km of railway track, although little of this is operational because of war damage. There are 33 airports and airfields; the international airports, Robertsfield and Spriggs Payne, are at Monrovia.

Telephone services are limited and confined mostly to Monrovia. Mobile phone coverage extends services to other towns and rural areas, and subscriptions have grown rapidly, with density now at over 20 per 100 people.

MEDIA

The state-run broadcaster runs a radio service and, following renovation of its infrastructure, provides national coverage. There is a growing number of community radio stations, often supported by international agencies or churches, plus three private television stations and a number of privately owned newspapers.

LIBYA

Al-Jumahiriyah al-Arabiyah al-Libiyah ash Shabiyah al-Ishtirakiyah al-Uzma – Great Socialist People's Libyan Arab Jamahiriya

Area – 1,759,540 sq. km
Capital – Tripoli (Tarabulus); population, 1,095,110 (2009 est)
Major cities – al-Hums, az-Zawiyah, Benghazi, Misratah, Tarhunah, Zuwarah
Currency – Libyan dinar (LD) of 1,000 dirhams
Population – 6,310,434 rising at 2.17 per cent a year (2009 est); Arab–Berber (97 per cent), with some Tuareg in the south-west
Religion – Sunni Muslim 97 per cent, Christian (Coptic Orthodox 1 per cent) (est)

Language – Arabic (official), Italian, English
Population density – 4 per sq. km (2008)
Urban population – 77 per cent (2007 est)
Median age (years) – 23.9 (2009 est)
National anthem – 'Allahu Akbar' ['God is Greatest']
National day – 1 September (Revolution Day)
Life expectancy (years) – 77.26 (2009 est)
Mortality rate – 3.45 (2009 est)
Birth rate – 25.15 (2009 est)
Infant mortality rate – 21.05 (2009 est)
Death penalty – Retained
CPI score – 2.5 (2009)

CLIMATE AND TERRAIN

Apart from hills on the north-west and north-east coasts and in the far south the country is made up of plains and plateaux, with some depressions; 90 per cent is desert or semi-desert. Elevation extremes range from 2,267m (Bikku Bitti) at the highest point to −47m (Sabkhat Ghuzayyil) at the lowest. The climate is Mediterranean on the coast, and arid desert in the interior. Average temperatures in Tripoli range from lows of 8°C in January to highs of 30°C in August.

HISTORY AND POLITICS

Libya comprises the three ancient regions of Tripolitania, Cyrenaica and Phazzania (Fezzan). Tripolitania was settled by the Phoenicians in the seventh century BC, then became the eastern part of the kingdom of Carthage. Cyrenaica was colonised by the Greeks in the fourth century BC. All three regions became provinces of the Roman Empire in the first century BC, and subsequently were under the control of the Byzantine Empire until conquered by Arabs in the seventh century AD, when Islam was introduced.

Libya was part of the Ottoman Empire from the mid-16th century until 1911, when the country was conquered and colonised by Italy. Libya suffered heavy fighting in the Second World War, then came under British and French control until 24 December 1951, when it achieved independence as the Kingdom of Libya through a UN resolution.

The discovery of oil in 1959 made the country wealthy but created social discord. In 1969 the king was deposed in a military coup led by Col. Muammar al-Gaddafi and a Revolutionary Command Council was installed that proclaimed the country a republic. Economic activity, including the oil industry, was nationalised in the 1970s.

Col. Gaddafi developed a brand of Islamic socialism and sought to promote pan-Arab unity and Islam abroad. This led Libya to support militant and revolutionary groups and to become involved in international terrorism. Relationships with Western governments became increasingly strained, bringing US military reprisals for terrorist activities in the 1980s and UN sanctions from 1992 after Libya refused to extradite two men suspected of the 1988 bombing of a Pan Am aircraft over Lockerbie, Scotland. Sanctions were suspended in 1999 after the suspects were handed over for trial, and were lifted in 2003 after Libya admitted responsibility for the bombing and paid compensation.

Since 2003 Col. Gaddafi has made further moves to end Libya's isolation and normalise relations with the West, such as abandoning its development of weapons of mass destruction and a promise in 2004 to allow UN nuclear weapons inspections.

POLITICAL SYSTEM

Under the 1977 constitution, the head of state is the 'Leader of the Revolution', Col. Muammar al-Gaddafi, who is in effect an absolute ruler. The General People's Congress, which has 760 members appointed by local 'basic people's congresses' for a three-year term, is formally responsible for policy-making and passing laws. It appoints the General People's Committee, which exercises executive power; the secretary-general of the General People's Committee is in effect the prime minister. The General People's Congress also has its own administrative secretariat. The Arab Socialist Union is the only legal political party.

HEAD OF STATE

Leader of the Revolution, Col. Muammar al-Gaddafi

SELECTED GOVERNMENT MEMBERS *as at July 2010*

Secretary-General of the General People's Congress, Muhammad Abul-Qasim al-Zwai
Secretary-General of the General People's Committee (Prime Minister), Al-Baghdadi Ali al-Mahmudi
Secretary, Economy, Muhammad al-Huwayj
Secretary, Finance, Abd-al-Hafiz Mahmud al Zulaytini
Secretary, Foreign Affairs, Mussa Kussa

THE PEOPLE'S BUREAU OF THE GREAT SOCIALIST PEOPLE'S LIBYAN ARAB JAMAHIRIYA
61–62 Ennismore Gardens, London SW7 1NH
T 020-7201 8280 E protocol_01@libyanpeoplesbureau.org.uk
B www.libyan-embassy.co.uk
Ambassador Extraordinary and Plenipotentiary, HE Omar R. Jelban, *apptd* 2010

BRITISH EMBASSY
PO Box 4206, Sharia Uahran 1, Tripoli
T (+218) (21) 340 3644 E tripoliconsular@fco.gov.uk
W http://ukinlibya.fco.gov.uk
Ambassador Extraordinary and Plenipotentiary, HE Richard Northern, MBE, *apptd* 2010

BRITISH COUNCIL
PO Box 6797, Casablanca Street, Siyahia, Tripoli
T (+218) (21) 484 3164 W www.britishcouncil.org/libya
Director, Anna Searle

DEFENCE

The army has 2,205 main battle tanks, over 1,000 armoured infantry fighting vehicles and 945 armoured personnel carriers. The navy has 2 submarines, 2 frigates, 1 corvette, 14 patrol and coastal vessels, and 7 helicopters at 4 major bases. The air force has 374 combat aircraft and 35 armed helicopters.
Military expenditure – US$800m (2008 est)
Military personnel – 76,000: army 50,000, navy 8,000, air force 18,000
Conscription duration – 12 to 24 months (selective)

ECONOMY AND TRADE

Normalisation of international relations has stimulated economic liberalisation and the start of a slow transition towards a more market-orientated economy; some subsidies have been reduced and some privatisation is planned. Libya has also attracted more foreign direct investment, mainly in the energy sector, since UN sanctions ended.

The oil industry, which is state-controlled, dominates the economy, accounting for 95 per cent of export earnings and about 25 per cent of GDP; as the population is small, this gives the country a relatively high per capita GDP, although the benefits are not felt by all the population. The considerable oil and natural gas reserves are relatively undeveloped, and Libya has licensed further exploration in recent years in auctions open to foreign companies. Attempts to diversify the economy have led to expansion of the manufacturing and construction sectors, which account for more than 20 per cent of GDP, to include the production of petrochemicals, iron, steel and aluminium in addition to food processing. Owing to the terrain and climate, agriculture is a small sector, contributing only 2.9 per cent of GDP, and Libya imports about 75 per cent of its food.

The main trading partners are Italy, Germany, other EU countries and China. Principal exports are crude oil, refined petroleum products, natural gas and chemicals. The main imports are machinery, semi-finished goods, food, transport equipment and consumer products.

GNI – US$77,900m; US$12,380 per capita (2008)
Annual average growth of GDP – 4 per cent (2009 est)
Inflation rate – 2 per cent (2009 est)
Population below poverty line – 7.4 per cent (2005 est)
Unemployment – 30 per cent (2004 est)
Total external debt – US$6,491m (2009 est)
Imports – US$11,500m (2008)
Exports – US$63,100m (2008)

BALANCE OF PAYMENTS
Trade – US$33,818m surplus (2009)
Current Account – US$36,601m surplus (2008)

Trade with UK	*2008*	*2009*
Imports from UK	£279,813,908	£427,093,243
Exports to UK	£960,474,107	£817,340,993

COMMUNICATIONS

There are about 100,000km of roads; the coastal road running from the Tunisian frontier through Tripoli, Benghazi and Tubruq to the Egyptian border, serves the main population centres. Main roads also link the provincial centres, and the oil-producing areas of the south with the coastal towns. Libya has had no railway services since 1965, but plans to build seven lines with a total of 2,757km of track with a view to resuming services. There are 137 airports and airfields; the principal airports are at Tripoli, Benghazi and Sebha. The main seaports are Benghazi, Tripoli and Tubruq.

The telephone system is being modernised and expanded. Combined fixed-line and mobile phone density was 100 per 100 people in 2008, with 1 million fixed lines, 4.8 million mobile phone subscribers and 323,000 internet users.

EDUCATION AND HEALTH

There are nine years of compulsory education, with six years each at primary and secondary level.

Literacy rate – 86.8 per cent (2007 est)
Gross enrolment ratio (percentage of relevant age group) – primary 110 per cent; secondary 93 per cent (2008 est)
Health expenditure (per capita) – US$299 (2007 est)
Hospital beds (per 1,000 people) – 3.7 (2003–8)

MEDIA

The state maintains strict control over the media. The state-run Libyan Jamahiriyah Broadcasting Corporation operates television and radio services; a private satellite television station that began operations in 2007 was nationalised in 2009. Pan-Arab satellite television is available and internet access is closely monitored but generally free from interference. The press is entirely state-run, and the international publications that are available are censored by the authorities.

LIECHTENSTEIN

Fürstentum Liechtenstein – Principality of Liechtenstein

Area – 160 sq. km
Capital – Vaduz; population, 5,151 (2009 est)
Major town – Schaan
Currency – Swiss franc of 100 rappen (or centimes)
Population – 34,761 rising at 0.7 per cent a year (2009 est)
Religion – Christian (Roman Catholic 78 per cent, Protestant denominations 8 per cent, Orthodox 1 per cent), Muslim 5 per cent (est)
Language – German (official)
Population density – 223 per sq. km (2008)
Median age (years) – 41 (2009 est)
National anthem – 'Oben am Jungen Rhein' ['High Above the Young Rhine']
National day – 15 August (Feast of the Assumption)
Life expectancy (years) – 80.06 (2009 est)
Mortality rate – 7.39 (2009 est)
Birth rate – 9.75 (2009 est)
Infant mortality rate – 4.25 (2009 est)
Death penalty – Abolished for all crimes (since 1987)

CLIMATE AND TERRAIN

Liechtenstein is a small, mountainous landlocked principality in the Alps, with the Rhine river valley running through the west of the country. Elevation extremes range from 2,599m (Grauspitz) at the highest point to 430m (Ruggeller Riet) at the lowest. The climate is continental, with heavy snowfall in winter; average temperatures range from 0°C in January to 21°C in July.

HISTORY AND POLITICS

Although there was a sovereign state within the present boundaries from the 14th century, the present state of Liechtenstein was formed from the lordships of Schellenberg and Vaduz in 1719. Part of the Holy Roman Empire, the principality became a member of the Confederation of the Rhine that succeeded the Empire in 1806, and then of the German Confederation from 1815 until 1866. It was the only German principality to remain outside the German Empire formed in 1871. The country abolished its armed forces and declared permanent neutrality in 1868. The country's neutrality was not violated in either of the world wars.

Economic decline in the years following the First World War led Liechtenstein to adopt the Swiss currency in 1921 and to enter into a Swiss customs union in 1923. The country became extremely prosperous as an international finance centre after the Second World War. Since 2000 it has tightened its laws to prevent money laundering, and since 2008 it has started to meet international financial transparency standards.

Governments in the 20th and 21st centuries have been formed by the two main parties, the northern-based Progressive Citizens' Party (FBP) and the southern-based Patriotic Union (VU). Usually they have formed a coalition government, although the FBP formed a single-party government from 2001 to 2005. However, the government's power is limited by the role and power of the monarchy, whose powers were increased when a referendum in 2003 approved constitutional changes that give the monarchy greater control over the government and judiciary. Prince Hans Adam II remains head of state but in 2004 he handed over day-to-day responsibility for running the principality to his son and heir, Prince Alois.

The VU won an overall majority in the 2009 election. The coalition government formed with the FBP continued, although the premiership passed from the FBP to the VU's Klaus Tschutscher.

POLITICAL SYSTEM

Under the 1921 constitution, Liechtenstein is a constitutional monarchy, with the hereditary prince as head of state. The unicameral legislature, the *Landtag*, has 25 members directly elected for a four-year term. The cabinet is appointed by the prince on the advice of the *Landtag* and consists of the head of government and four ministers.

HEAD OF STATE

HSH The Prince of Liechtenstein, Hans Adam II, *born* 14 February 1945; *succeeded* 13 November 1989

Heir, HSH Prince Alois, *born* 11 June 1968

SELECTED GOVERNMENT MEMBERS *as at June 2010*

Head of Government, Finance, Klaus Tschutscher

Deputy Head of Government, Economy, Martin Meyer

Foreign Affairs, Aurelia Frick

Home Affairs, Hugo Quaderer

Health, Social Affairs, Renate Mussner

BRITISH AMBASSADOR

HE Sarah Gillett, CMG, MVO, resident at Bern, Switzerland

ECONOMY AND TRADE

Liechtenstein has a prosperous, highly industrialised and diversified economy. Its mainstay is the financial services sector, which, with other service industries such as tourism, employs over half of the workforce. A light industrial base produces electronics, metal manufactures, dental products, ceramics, pharmaceuticals, food products, precision instruments and optical instruments, and employs 43.5 per cent of the workforce. Almost half the workforce commutes daily from Austria, Switzerland and Germany.

Liechtenstein became a member of the European Free Trade Association in 1991, and joined the European Economic Area in 1995. Most of its trade is with EU countries and Switzerland. The principal exports are its industrial products. The main imports are agricultural products, industrial raw materials, energy, machinery, metal goods, textiles, foodstuffs and vehicles.

Annual average growth of GDP – 3.1 per cent (2007 est)
Inflation rate – 2.4 per cent (2008)
Unemployment – 1.5 per cent (2007)

Trade with UK	*2008*	*2009*
Imports from UK	£9,091,800	£5,413,380
Exports to UK	£31,786,026	£17,569,273

COMMUNICATIONS

Liechtenstein has no airports and only 380km of roads, 28km of waterways, and 9km of rail track which is part of the Austrian system connecting Austria and Switzerland. In 2008, there were 19,600 fixed telephone lines in use, 34,000 mobile phone subscribers and 23,000 internet users.

Liechtenstein relies on foreign and satellite broadcasters for television and radio services. Circulation for its two newspapers, *Liechtenstein News* and *Liechtensteiner Vaterland,* is under 10,000.

LITHUANIA

Lietuvos Respublika – Republic of Lithuania

Area – 65,300 sq. km
Capital – Vilnius; population, 545,970 (2009 est)
Major cities – Kaunas, Klaipeda
Currency – Litas of 100 centas, pegged to the euro
Population – 3,555,179 falling at 0.28 per cent a year (2009 est); Lithuanian (83.4 per cent), Polish (6.7 per cent), Russian (6.3 per cent)
Religion – Christian (Roman Catholic 80 per cent, Orthodox 5 per cent) (est)
Language – Lithuanian (official), Russian, Polish
Population density – 54 per sq. km (2008)
Urban population – 67 per cent (2007 est)
Median age (years) – 39.3 (2009 est)
National anthem – 'Tautiska Giesme' ['National Song']
National day – 16 February (Independence Day)
Life expectancy (years) – 74.9 (2009 est)
Mortality rate – 11.18 (2009 est)
Birth rate – 9.11 (2009 est)
Infant mortality rate – 6.47 (2009 est)
Death penalty – Abolished for all crimes (since 1998)
CPI score – 4.9 (2009)

CLIMATE AND TERRAIN

Lithuania is a low-lying country with low hills in the west and south-east. It contains over 2,800 lakes, mostly in the east, although the Courland lagoon on the west coast is a major feature. Elevation extremes range from 293.8m (Aukstojas Hill) at the highest point to 0m (Baltic Sea) at the lowest. The climate is mainly continental, and average temperatures range from lows of −11°C in January to highs of 23°C in July.

HISTORY AND POLITICS

Lithuania became a nation in the 13th century. It remained pagan for far longer than the rest of Europe, only becoming fully Christian in the 15th century when the Samogitians and the Aukstaitiai, the two main ethnic groups in the region, were converted. In the 14th century, a grand duchy was formed that stretched from the Baltic to the Black Sea and eastwards almost as far as Moscow. It confederated with Poland in the 16th century, before coming under Russian rule in 1795. The country joined Poland in rebelling against Russian domination twice in the 19th century.

Occupied by Germany during the First World War, Lithuania declared its independence in 1918 and successfully defended its autonomy against the Bolsheviks in 1918–19. However, the province and city of Vilnius were occupied by the newly independent Poland from 1920 until 1939. The USSR invaded and annexed Lithuania in 1940, but the country revolted in 1941 and briefly established its own government before being invaded and occupied by the Germans in its 1941 offensive against the USSR. Around 210,000 Lithuanians, mainly Jews, were killed during the German occupation. Soviet troops ousted the Germans in 1944 and re-established Soviet control, against which Lithuanians carried on a guerrilla war until 1952.

Growing nationalist sentiment led to the formation of the pro-democracy *Sajudis* ('The Movement') in 1988 to campaign for greater autonomy. A unilateral declaration of independence in 1990 was blocked by the USSR but following the failed August coup in Moscow in 1991, Lithuania declared its independence a second time, and this was internationally recognised. The last Russian troops left the country in 1993. Lithuania joined NATO and the EU in 2004.

In the 2008 legislative elections, the Homeland Union–Lithuanian Christian Democrats became the largest party but without a majority. Its leader, Andrius Kubilius, became prime minister at the head of a four-party coalition government. The 2009 presidential election was won by Dalia Grybauskaite, who became the country's first female president.

POLITICAL SYSTEM

Under the 1992 constitution, the head of state is a president, who is directly elected for a five-year term, renewable only once. The unicameral *Seimas* has 141 members who are directly elected for a four-year term; 71 members are elected in first past the post constituencies and 70 by proportional representation. The prime minister is appointed by the president with the approval of the *Seimas,* and ministers are appointed upon the recommendation of the prime minister.

HEAD OF STATE
President, Dalia Grybauskaite, *elected* 17 May 2009, *sworn in* 12 July 2009

SELECTED GOVERNMENT MEMBERS *as at June 2010*
Prime Minister, Andrius Kubilius
Defence, Rasa Jukneviciene
Foreign Affairs, Audronius Azubalis
Interior, Raimundas Palaitis
Finance, Ingrida Simonyte

EMBASSY OF THE REPUBLIC OF LITHUANIA
84 Gloucester Place, London W1U 6AU
T 020-7486 6401 E amb.uk@urm.lt
W www.lithuanianembassy.co.uk
Ambassador Extraordinary and Plenipotentiary, HE Oskaras Jusys, *apptd* 2009

BRITISH EMBASSY
2 Antakalnio, Vilnius 10308
T (+370) (5) 246 2900 E be-vilnius@britain.lt
W http://ukinlithuania.fco.gov.uk
Ambassador Extraordinary and Plenipotentiary, HE Simon Butt, *apptd* 2008

BRITISH COUNCIL
4 Jogailos, Vilnius 01116
T (+370) (5) 264 4890 W www.britishcouncil.org/lithuania
Director, Dr Arturas Vasilauskas

DEFENCE

The army has 187 armoured personnel carriers; the navy has 1 frigate and 7 patrol and coastal vessels based at Klaipeda; the air force has 7 aircraft and 9 helicopters. Operates joint naval unit BALTRON (*see* Latvia: Defence).
Military expenditure – US$547m (2008)
Military personnel – 8,610: army 7,190, navy 470, air force 950; paramilitary 14,600
Conscription duration – 12 months

ECONOMY AND TRADE

Lithuania's transition to a market economy is nearly complete, with the private sector now accounting for about 80 per cent GDP. The transition initially caused a deep recession, but the economy recovered and grew steadily from 2004 to 2008. A cutback in imports in 2009 nearly halved the current account deficit, which had soared to 15 per cent of GDP in 2007–8, and the government is working vigorously to develop foreign investment and export markets.

The economy is diverse, and industries include metal-cutting machine tools, electric motors, domestic appliances, oil refining, shipbuilding, furniture-making, textiles and amber extraction and jewellery-making. Industry contributes 26.7 per cent to GDP, services 69.1 per cent and agriculture 4.2 per cent.

The main trading partners are other EU countries and Russia. Principal exports are mineral products, machinery and equipment, chemicals, textiles and clothing, foodstuffs and plastics. The main imports are mineral products, machinery, transport equipment, chemicals, textiles, clothing and metals.
GNI – US$39,900m; US$11,870 per capita (2008)
Annual average growth of GDP – −16.8 per cent (2009 est)
Inflation rate – 4.7 per cent (2009 est)
Population below poverty line – 4 per cent (2003)
Unemployment – 15 per cent (2009 est)
Total external debt – US$36,430m (2009)
Imports – US$31,100m (2008)
Exports – US$23,800m (2008)

BALANCE OF PAYMENTS
Trade – US$1,902m deficit (2009)
Current Account – US$1,423m surplus (2009)

Trade with UK	*2008*	*2009*
Imports from UK	£276,809,090	£165,998,761
Exports to UK	£342,511,769	£363,318,524

COMMUNICATIONS

There are 80,700km of roads, and a railway system of 1,765km linking the major towns with Vilnius and Klaipeda, the main seaport. The 87 airports and airfields include major airports at Vilnius, Kaunas and Palanga.

The telephone system is being modernised, although fixed-line use is declining as mobile phone services expand. In 2008 mobile phone density had reached 140 per 100 people, while fixed-line density had dropped to 22 per 100 people.

EDUCATION AND HEALTH

Education is free of charge and compulsory from seven to 16 years, with the system comprising primary school (four years), lower secondary school (six years), and upper secondary education (two years). The language of instruction is predominantly Lithuanian, but there are also Russian and Polish schools. Vilnius University, founded in 1579, is one of the oldest in eastern Europe.

Literacy rate – 99.7 per cent (2007 est)
Gross enrolment ratio (percentage of relevant age group) – primary 96 per cent; secondary 99 per cent; tertiary 76 per cent (2008 est)
Health expenditure (per capita) – US$717 (2007)
Hospital beds (per 1,000 people) – 8.1 (2003–8)

MEDIA

The media operate independently of the state and are free to criticise the government, although politicians have attempted to influence the editorial policies of the public-service broadcaster. It operates several radio and television networks, in competition with a number of thriving commercial stations.

LUXEMBOURG

Groussherzogtom Lëtzebuerg / Grand-Duché de Luxembourg / Großherzogtum Luxembourg – Grand Duchy of Luxembourg

Area – 2,586 sq. km
Capital – Luxembourg; population, 89,814 (2009 est)
Major towns – Esch-sur-Alzette, Dudelange
Currency – Euro (€) of 100 cents
Population – 491,775 rising at 1.17 per cent a year (2009 est); Luxembourger (63.1 per cent), Portuguese (13.3 per cent), French (4.5 per cent), Italian (4.3 per cent), German (2.3 per cent), other EU 7.3 per cent (est)
Religion – Christian (Roman Catholic 90 per cent, Orthodox denominations 1 per cent), Muslim 2 per cent (est)
Language – Luxembourgish, French, German (all official)
Population density – 189 per sq. km (2008)
Urban population – 83 per cent (2007 est)
Median age (years) – 39.2 (2009 est)
National anthem – 'Ons Heemecht' ['Our Homeland']
National day – 23 June (official birthday of Grand Duchess Charlotte)
Life expectancy (years) – 79.33 (2009 est)
Mortality rate – 8.44 (2009 est)
Birth rate – 11.73 (2009 est)
Infant mortality rate – 4.56 (2009 est)
Death penalty – Abolished for all crimes (since 1979)
CPI score – 8.2 (2009)
Military expenditure – US$232m (2008)
Military personnel – army 900; paramilitary 612

CLIMATE AND TERRAIN

A landlocked grand duchy, Luxembourg has the forested plateau of the Ardennes in the north, forming part of the Natural Germano-Luxembourg Park which extends east into Germany. The south of the country is mainly fertile farmland, and in the east is the wine-growing region of the Moselle valley. Elevation extremes range from 559m (Buurgplaatz) at the highest point to 133m (river Moselle) at the lowest. The climate is modified continental, and average temperatures in Luxembourg city range from −1°C in January to 23°C in July.

HISTORY AND POLITICS

The area was part of the Roman Empire and then became part of the Frankish Empire in the fifth century AD. It became autonomous within the Holy Roman Empire under Siegfried, Count of Ardennes, and was given the status of a duchy in 1354. Controlled by a succession of European powers after 1437, when the House of Luxembourg died out, it was made a grand duchy under Dutch rule after the Napoleonic wars. Much of Luxembourg joined the Belgians in their revolt against the Netherlands in 1830; in 1838 the western, French-speaking region was assigned to Belgium, and the remainder became an independent grand duchy in 1839. The treaty of London in 1867 confirmed its independence and neutrality. Occupation by Germany in both world wars prompted Luxembourg to give up its neutrality and it was a founding member of NATO in 1949.

Luxembourg entered into economic union with Belgium in 1921 and joined the Benelux economic union in 1948. It was a founder member of the EEC in 1958 and joined the eurozone in 1999.

The Christian Social Party (CSV) has held power almost continuously since the First World War, usually as the main partner in coalition governments. It remained the largest party in the legislature after the 2009 election, but without an overall majority. A new coalition government was formed under the leadership of Jean-Claude Juncker of the CSV, who has been prime minister since 1995.

POLITICAL SYSTEM

Under the 1868 constitution, the head of state is a hereditary grand duke. There is a unicameral legislature, the Chamber of Deputies, which has 60 members directly elected for a five-year term. There is also a Council of State, which has 21 members nominated by the grand duke; this acts as the supreme administrative tribunal and has some legislative functions. The prime minister is appointed by the grand duke on the basis of the election results and appoints the cabinet.

HEAD OF STATE
HRH The Grand Duke of Luxembourg, Grand Duke Henri, *born* 16 April 1955; *succeeded* 7 October 2000
Heir, HRH Prince Guillaume, *born* 11 November 1981

SELECTED GOVERNMENT MEMBERS *as at June 2010*
Prime Minister, Jean-Claude Juncker
Deputy Prime Minister, Foreign Affairs, Jean Asselborn
Interior, Jean-Marie Halsdorf
Finance, Luc Frieden

EMBASSY OF LUXEMBOURG
27 Wilton Crescent, London SW1X 8SD
T 020-7235 6961 E londres.amb@mae.etat.lu
W http://londres.mae.lu
Ambassador Extraordinary and Plenipotentiary, HE Hubert Wurth, *apptd* 2007

BRITISH EMBASSY
5 Boulevard Joseph II, L-1840, Luxembourg
T (+352) 229 864 W http://ukinluxembourg.fco.gov.uk
Ambassador Extraordinary and Plenipotentiary, HE Peter Bateman, *apptd* 2007

ECONOMY AND TRADE

The economy is stable, with steady growth, low unemployment and low inflation providing an exceptionally high standard of living. The government has sought to offset the contraction in the economy since 2008 with economic stimulus measures, which led to a budget deficit in 2009. Banking and financial services are the dominant sector, contributing 28 per cent of GDP. Steel production used to dominate the industrial sector, but this has diversified to include IT, telecommunications, freight transport, food processing, chemicals, metal products and engineering. Tourism is also important. The small agricultural sector consists mainly of family-owned farms. Services account for 86 per cent of GDP, industry for 13.6 per cent and agriculture for 0.4 per cent. Over 50 per cent of the workforce commutes daily from France, Belgium and Germany.

The main trading partners are other EU countries and China. Principal exports are the products of industrial activities. The main imports are minerals, metals, foodstuffs and quality consumer goods.

GNI – US$33,909m; US$69,390 per capita (2008)
Annual average growth of GDP – –4.5 per cent (2009 est)
Inflation rate – 0.5 per cent (2009 est)
Unemployment – 6.8 per cent (2009 est)
Total external debt – $1,994,000m (2009 est)
Imports – US$25,100m (2008)
Exports – US$17,900m (2008)

BALANCE OF PAYMENTS
Trade – US$12,678m surplus (2009)
Current Account – US$2,968m surplus (2009)

Trade with UK	*2008*	*2009*
Imports from UK	£198,739,738	£188,721,475
Exports to UK	£810,618,631	£608,032,838

COMMUNICATIONS

Luxembourg has one airport. There are 5,227km of roads (including 147km of motorways), and 275km of railways. The river Moselle provides 37km of navigable waterway. In 2008 there were 260,600 fixed telephone lines in use, 707,000 mobile phone users and 387,000 internet users.

MEDIA

Despite its size, Luxembourg has a significant international media presence, providing pan-European television and radio broadcasting through media groups such as RTL. Luxembourg is also the headquarters of the Société Européenne des Satellites (SES), which operates the Astra satellite fleet, Europe's largest satellite operation. The two best-selling daily newspapers are *Luxemburger Wort* and *Tageblatt.*

MACEDONIA

Republika Makedonija – Republic of Macedonia

Area – 25,713 sq. km
Capital – Skopje; population, 480,383 (2009 est)
Major city – Kumanovo
Currency – Denar of 100 deni
Population – 2,066,718 rising at 0.26 per cent a year (2009 est); Macedonian (64.2 per cent), Albanian (25.2 per cent), Turkish (3.9 per cent), Roma (2.7 per cent), Serb (1.8 per cent)
Religion – Christian (Macedonian Orthodox 65 per cent), Muslim 32 per cent (est)
Language – Macedonian (official), Albanian, Turkish, Romani, Serbian (each official in different regions)
Population density – 80 per sq. km (2008)
Urban population – 66 per cent (2007 est)
Median age (years) – 35.1 (2009 est)
National anthem – 'Denes Nad Makedonija' ['Today Over Macedonia']
National day – 2 August (start of the Ilinden or St Elijah's Day Uprising, 1903)
Life expectancy (years) – 74.68 (2009 est)
Mortality rate – 8.83 (2009 est)
Birth rate – 11.97 (2009 est)
Infant mortality rate – 9.01 (2009 est)
Death penalty – Abolished for all crimes (since 1991)
CPI score – 3.6 (2008)
Conscription duration – Six months
Literacy rate – 97.0 per cent (2007 est)
Gross enrolment ratio (percentage of relevant age group) – primary 93 per cent; secondary 84 per cent; tertiary 36 per cent (2008 est)
Health expenditure (per capita) – US$277 (2007)
Hospital beds (per 1,000 people) – 4.6 (2003–8)

CLIMATE AND TERRAIN

The landlocked country is a mountainous plateau divided by deep river valleys and basins, including the valleys of the Vardar river and its tributaries. Elevation extremes range from 2,764m (Golem Korab) at the highest point to 50m (Vardar river) at the lowest. Lakes Ohrid and Prespa straddle the border with Albania, and Lake Doiran the border with Greece. The climate is continental, with average temperatures in Skopje ranging from lows of −3°C in January to highs of 31°C in July.

HISTORY AND POLITICS

The area of the former Yugoslav republic was part of the ancient kingdom of Macedonia, which also included northern Greece and south-west Bulgaria, in the fourth century BC. Macedonia became a province of the Roman Empire in the second century BC, coming under the control of the Byzantine Empire from the fourth century AD. Slav peoples settled the area in the seventh century and mixed with the Greek, Illyrian, Thracian, Scythian and Turkish peoples.

From the ninth to the 14th centuries the area was under the rule successively of the Bulgars, Byzantium and the Serbs, and became part of the Ottoman Empire in the late 14th century. Following the Balkan wars of 1912 and 1913 the country was partitioned between Bulgaria, Serbia and Greece. After the First World War, the Serbian part was awarded to the newly created state that became Yugoslavia. During the Second World War, this area was occupied by Bulgaria from 1941 to 1944, and after liberation became a republic within the communist Federal Republic of Yugoslavia.

Nationalist sentiment grew after the death of the Yugoslav leader Josip Tito in 1980, and in 1991 Macedonia declared its independence, which Yugoslavia recognised in 1992. International recognition was initially delayed by Greece's objections to the republic's name (Greece claims that its region of Macedonia is the only one entitled to the name), but the country joined the UN in 1993 as the Former Yugoslav Republic of Macedonia; Greece recognised it under this name and lifted its trade blockade in 1995, but in 2008 the name issue stopped NATO from inviting the republic to join the alliance.

Throughout the 1990s there was tension and sporadic violence with the large ethnic Albanian minority, aggrieved at their lack of civil rights. Instability in neighbouring Kosovo spilled over into Macedonia in 2001, sparking off a two-month uprising by ethnic Albanian separatists. Peace talks facilitated by international bodies resulted in the Ohrid framework agreement, giving Albanians greater recognition within Macedonia and making Albanian an official language.

After Macedonia's admission to NATO was blocked in April 2008, an early election was called for June, as the government sought a mandate for its policies. The election was marred by violence and electoral irregularities, which caused voting to be suspended in a number of areas and then rerun a few weeks later. The VMRO-DPMNE remained the largest party and Nikola Gruevski continued as prime minister, forming a new coalition government with the largest ethnic Albanian party and three smaller parties. The 2009 presidential election was won in the second round by the VMRO-DPMNE candidate, Gjorge Ivanov.

POLITICAL SYSTEM

The 1991 constitution was amended in 2001 in accordance with the Ohrid agreement to incorporate provisions relating to ethnic Albanian rights, and several times since, most notably in 2004 to give ethnic Albanians greater local autonomy in areas where they predominate.

The head of state is a president, who is directly elected for a five-year term. The unicameral legislature, the *Sobranie,* has 120 members directly elected for a four-year term. The prime minister is appointed by the president. Government ministers are elected by the assembly but are not members of it.

HEAD OF STATE

President, Gjorge Ivanov, *elected* 5 April 2009, *sworn in* 12 May 2009

SELECTED GOVERNMENT MEMBERS *as at June 2010*

Prime Minister, Nikola Gruevski
Deputy Prime Ministers, Zoran Stavrevski *(Finance)*, Vladimir Pesevski *(Economy)*, Abdulakim Ademi, Vasko Naumovski
Foreign Affairs, Antonio Milososki
Interior, Gordana Jankulovska
Defence, Zoran Konjanovski

EMBASSY OF THE REPUBLIC OF MACEDONIA

Suites 2.1/2.2, Buckingham Court, 75–83 Buckingham Gate, London SW1E 6PE
T 020-7976 0535 E info@macedonianembassy.org.uk
W www.macedonianembassy.org.uk
Ambassador Extraordinary and Plenipotentiary, HE Marija Efremova, *apptd* 2008

BRITISH EMBASSY

Salvador Aljende 73, Skopje 1000
T (+389) (2) 329 9299 E britishembassyskopje@fco.gov.uk
W http://ukinmacedonia.fco.gov.uk
Ambassador Extraordinary and Plenipotentiary, HE Andrew Key, *apptd* 2007

BRITISH COUNCIL

PO Box 562, Bulevar Goce Delcev 6, 1000 Skopje
T (+389) (2) 313 5035 W www.britishcouncil.org/macedonia
Director, Les Dangerfield, resident at Zagreb, Croatia

DEFENCE

The army has 31 main battle tanks, 11 armoured infantry fighting vehicles and 201 armoured personnel carriers. The marine wing has 4 patrol and coastal combatant vessels. The air wing has 12 armed helicopters.
Military budget – US$167m (2009 est)
Military personnel – joint operational command 8,000

ECONOMY AND TRADE

Macedonia was the least developed republic in the former Yugoslavia before 1991, and economic growth was initially hindered by the trade embargo by Greece (1993–5) and the 2001 ethnic Albanian uprising. Economic growth was steady from 2003 to 2008, although the economy contracted sharply in 2009 as exports halved and foreign investment fell owing to the global downturn. Unemployment remains a major problem, although official figures may be overstated because of the size of the grey economy, estimated to be worth more than 20 per cent of GDP. The country remains poor, with over a quarter of the population living below the poverty line. Crime and corruption deter foreign investment.

Services produce 58.4 per cent of GDP, industry 29.5 per cent and agriculture 12.1 per cent. The main crops are grapes, tobacco, vegetables, fruit and dairy products. Food processing and wine-making are major industries, along with textiles, chemicals, iron, steel, cement, energy and pharmaceuticals. The main trading partners are Germany, Serbia, Greece, Bulgaria, Italy, and other Balkan and EU

states. Principal exports are food, wine, tobacco, textiles, manufactured goods, iron and steel. The main imports are machinery and equipment, cars, chemicals, fuels and food.
GNI – US$8,400m; US$4,130 per capita (2008)
Annual average growth of GDP – –2.4 per cent (2009 est)
Inflation rate – 0.3 per cent (2009 est)
Population below poverty line – 29.8 per cent (2006)
Unemployment – 35 per cent (2009 est)
Total external debt – US$4,656m (2009 est)
Imports – US$6,800m (2008)
Exports – US$3,900m (2008)

BALANCE OF PAYMENTS
Trade – US$2,358m deficit (2009)
Current Account – US$673m deficit (2008)

Trade with UK	*2008*	*2009*
Imports from UK	£26,755,601	£30,222,307
Exports to UK	£33,551,974	£26,607,177

COMMUNICATIONS

Macedonia has 13,182km of roads, and 699km of railways, of which 234km are electrified. A 53km railway line from Beljakovci to the Bulgarian border is under construction. The principal airports are at Skopje and Ohrid, and there are a further 12 airports and airfields around the country.

Fixed-line telephone connections are declining as mobile phones become more widespread. There were 457,000 fixed lines in use, 2.5 million mobile phone subscribers and 848,000 internet users in 2008.

MEDIA

The three channels of the state-run television service compete with a growing number of commercial stations. Broadcasters are loosely regulated and many are unlicensed. There are 12 major daily and weekly press publications, reflecting a range of views. The partially government-owned *Nova Makedonija* is the leading newspaper.

MADAGASCAR

Repoblikan'i Madagasikara/République de Madagascar – Republic of Madagascar

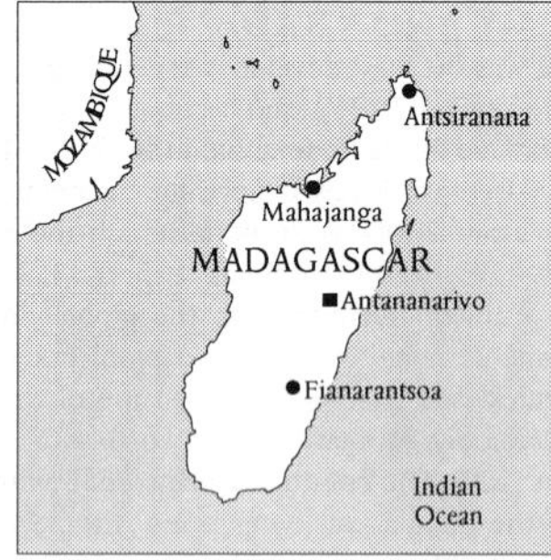

Area – 587,041 sq. km
Capital – Antananarivo; population, 1,815,690 (2009 est)
Major cities – Antsirabe, Fianarantsoa, Mahajanga, Toamasina
Currency – Ariary (MGA) of five iraimbilanja
Population – 20,653,556 rising at 3 per cent a year (2009 est); the people are of mixed Malayo-Indonesian, Arab and African origin. There are sizeable French, Chinese and Indian communities
Religion – Christian 50 per cent, Muslim 10 per cent (est). A large minority also follow traditional indigenous religions
Language – English, French, Malagasy (all official)
Population density – 33 per sq. km (2008)
Urban population – 29 per cent (2007 est)
Median age (years) – 18 (2009 est)
National anthem – 'Ry Tanindrazanay malala ô' ['Oh, Our Beloved Fatherland']
National day – 26 June (Independence Day)
Life expectancy (years) – 62.89 (2009 est)
Mortality rate – 8.14 (2009 est)
Birth rate – 38.14 (2009 est)
Infant mortality rate – 54.2 (2009 est)
Death penalty – Retained (no known use since 1958)
CPI score – 3 (2009)

CLIMATE AND TERRAIN

Madagascar, the fourth-largest island in the world, lies 386km off the south-east coast of Africa, from which it is separated by the Mozambique Channel. Coastal plains rise to a central plateau and mountains indented with river valleys. Elevation extremes range from 2,876m (Maromokotro) at the highest point to 0m (Indian Ocean) at the lowest. Because of its isolation, most mammals and plants and half of its bird species are unique to the island. However, this biological diversity is threatened by deforestation and soil erosion.

The climate is tropical on the coast, temperate in the interior and arid in the south. Average temperatures in Antananarivo range from lows of 9°C in July to highs of 27°C in December. Madagascar is subject to tropical cyclones, which cause torrential rain and flooding.

HISTORY AND POLITICS

The island was settled by peoples from south-east Asia and east Africa from around the first century AD. Although first visited by Europeans *c.*1500, local kingdoms ruled until the early 19th century, when the Merina kingdom conquered the island. France made the island a protectorate in 1895 after the last indigenous resistance was defeated. During the Second World War, the British invaded to replace the pro-Vichy government with a Free French government. At the end of the war Madagascar was returned to France, which suppressed a nationalist uprising in 1947–8. Nationalist agitation continued throughout the 1950s and resulted in independence in 1960.

The military took control in 1972 following civil disturbances, and in 1975 martial law was imposed after a coup. A Marxist one-party state was created with Lt-Cdr Didier Ratsiraka as president. Marxism was abandoned in 1980 and, following a decade of pro-democracy agitation, a new constitution introduced parliamentary democracy in 1992.

Didier Ratsiraka was defeated in the 1993 presidential elections but returned to office in 1997 after winning the 1996 election. He refused to accept his defeat in the 2001 presidential election and the six-month struggle between his supporters and those of Marc Ravalomanana, the successful candidate, brought the country close to civil war until, in July 2002, Ratsiraka went into exile and his supporters surrendered. President Ravalomanana was re-elected in 2006 and his I Love Madagascar party (TIM) retained its large majority in the 2007 legislative election.

A power struggle between President Ravalomanana

and opposition leader Andry Rajoelina began in December 2008. Following an army mutiny and Ravalomanana's resignation, Rajoelina assumed power in March 2009 with the backing of the military and the high court, but the takeover provoked continued demonstrations and widespread international condemnation. Talks between the four main political parties concluded in August 2009 with a power-sharing agreement, but Rajoelina suspended the agreement in December 2009 because of the inability of all parties to agree on appointments to the government. Legislative elections promised for May 2010 were postponed to September; a presidential election was scheduled for November 2010.

POLITICAL SYSTEM
The 1992 constitution was amended in 1998 to create an upper chamber in the legislature, increase the powers of the presidency and increase the autonomy of the six provinces; amendments approved in a 2007 referendum further increased the powers of the president. The president is directly elected and serves a five-year term. The legislature is bicameral, comprising the National Assembly, which has 127 members directly elected for a five-year term, and the senate, which has 90 members, of whom two-thirds are elected by an electoral college and one-third are nominated by the president; they serve a five-year term. The 2009 power-sharing agreement replaced the legislature with a 258-member Congress of Transition and a 65-member Higher Transition Council.

HEAD OF STATE
President, Andry Rajoelina, *took office* 21 March 2009
Co-presidents, Emmanuel Rakotovahiny; Fetison Rakoto Andrianirina; Rajemison Rakotomaharo

SELECTED GOVERNMENT MEMBERS *as at July 2010*
Prime Minister, Col. Albert Camille Vital
Deputy Prime Minister, Foreign Affairs, Adml. Hyppolite Ramaroson
Armed Forces, Gen. Andre Lucien Rakotoarimasy
Finance, Hery Rajaonarimampianina

EMBASSY OF THE REPUBLIC OF MADAGASCAR
33 Stadium Street, London SW10 0PU
T 020-7751 4410 **E** contact@embassy-madagascar-uk.com
W www.embassy-madagascar-uk.com
Ambassador Extraordinary and Plenipotentiary, vacant

BRITISH AMBASSADOR
HE Nick Leake, *apptd* 2010, resident in Port Louis, Mauritius

DEFENCE

The army has 12 light tanks and around 30 armoured personnel carriers. The navy has 6 patrol and coastal combatant vessels at 5 bases. The Gendarmerie has 5 patrol and coastal combatant vessels.
Military budget – US$103m (2008)
Military personnel – 13,500: army 12,500, navy 500, air force 500; paramilitary 8,100
Conscription duration – 18 months

ECONOMY AND TRADE

Economic liberalisation and privatisation since the mid-1990s have resulted in slow but steady growth, although the political disturbances in 2002 and 2009–10, and cyclone devastation in 2000 and 2004 have been serious setbacks. President Ravalomanana's reforms and anti-corruption measures attracted increased international aid, and in 2004 half of the country's foreign debt was written off, but aid was suspended in 2009 after President Ravalomanana was ousted. Poverty remains endemic and unemployment is high.

Agriculture, fishing and forestry are the mainstays of the economy, accounting for 26.4 per cent of GDP and employing 80 per cent of the workforce. The main cash crops include coffee, vanilla, fish, sugar cane, cocoa, cloves and pepper. The industrial sector contributes 16.6 per cent of GDP, through mining (chromite, graphite, sapphires), processing meat, fish and other agricultural products, manufacturing (textiles, garments, paper, cement, chemicals), car assembly and oil refining. Tourism is of growing importance but visitor numbers halved in 2009.

The main trading partners are France, the USA, China and Bahrain. Principal exports are agricultural products, textiles, garments, chromite and petroleum products. The main imports are capital goods, petroleum, consumer goods and food.
GNI – US$7,900m; US$420 per capita (2008)
Annual average growth of GDP – 0.4 per cent (2009 est)
Inflation rate – 8 per cent (2009 est)
Population below poverty line – 50 per cent (2004 est)
Total external debt – US$2,054m (2009)
Imports – US$4,000m (2008)
Exports – US$1,300m (2008)

BALANCE OF PAYMENTS
Trade – US$2,787m deficit (2009)
Current Account – US$1,939m deficit (2008)

Trade with UK	*2008*	*2009*
Imports from UK	£14,419,785	£13,099,073
Exports to UK	£25,755,778	£28,231,815

COMMUNICATIONS

The main seaports are Toamasina, Antsiranana, Mahajanga and Toliara. There are 89 airports and airfields, of which the major airports are at Antananarivo and Mahajanga. Surface transport is by the 65,700km of roads and 854km of railways.

In 2008 there were 164,900 fixed telephone lines in use, 4.8 million mobile phone subscribers, and 316,000 internet users.

EDUCATION AND HEALTH

Education is free of charge and compulsory for five years, but attendance is variable. Primary education is followed by a possible seven years of secondary education.
Literacy rate – 70.7 per cent (2007 est)
Gross enrolment ratio (percentage of relevant age group) – primary 152 per cent; secondary 30 per cent; tertiary 3 per cent (2008 est)
Health expenditure (per capita) – US$16 (2007)
Hospital beds (per 1,000 people) – 0.3 (2003–8)

MEDIA

State-run television and radio are the only networks with national coverage but there are a large number of private local television and radio stations; many of the radio stations are owned by politicians. Numerous news publications print a diverse range of opinions. The freedom and independence of the press has been protected by law since 1990.

MALAWI

Dziko la Malawi – Republic of Malawi

Area – 118,484 sq. km
Capital – Lilongwe; population, 820,802 (2009 est)
Major cities – Blantyre, the commercial and industrial centre; Mzuzu; Zomba, the former capital
Currency – Kwacha (K) of 100 tambala
Population – 14,268,711 rising at 2.39 per cent a year (2009 est); about nine ethnic groups, of which the largest are Chewa and Angoni (Nguni)
Religion – Christian 80 per cent, Muslim 13 per cent (predominantly Sunni) (est)
Language – Chichewa, English (both official), Chinyanja, Chiyao, Chitumbuka
Population density – 158 per sq. km (2008)
Urban population – 18 per cent (2007 est)
Median age (years) – 16.8 (2009 est)
National anthem – 'Mlungu dalitsani Malawi' ['Oh God Bless Our Land of Malawi']
National day – 6 July (Independence Day)
Life expectancy (years) – 43.82 (2009 est)
Mortality rate – 17.6 (2009 est)
Birth rate – 41.48 (2009 est)
Infant mortality rate – 89.05 (2009 est)
HIV/AIDS adult prevalence – 11.4 per cent (2007 est)
Death penalty – Retained (not used since 1992)
CPI score – 3.3 (2009)

CLIMATE AND TERRAIN

Malawi is a landlocked state lying along the western and southern shores of Lake Malawi (Nyasa). The northern and central regions are plateaux with rolling terrain, and the south is mainly hills and mountains. Elevation extremes range from 3,002m (Sapitwa) at the highest point to 37m (junction of Shire river and Mozambique border) at the lowest. The climate is subtropical, with a wet season from November to May; average temperatures in Lilongwe range from lows of 7°C in July to highs of 30°C in October.

HISTORY AND POLITICS

Until contact was made with European missionaries in the 19th century, Malawi was dominated by a succession of powerful tribes that included the Maravi, the Yao and the Nguni. The missionaries campaigned for official intervention to end the east-coast slave trade, which had begun in the early 19th century, and in 1891 Britain established the Nyasaland and District Protectorate over the area. Renamed the British Central Africa Protectorate in 1893, it became the British colony of Nyasaland in 1907. The country was joined with Northern and Southern Rhodesia (now Zambia and Zimbabwe) between 1953 and 1963. It became independent, as Malawi, in 1964, with Dr Hastings Banda as prime minister.

In 1966, the country became a one-party state ruled by the Malawi Congress Party (MCP) and Dr Banda became president, declaring himself president for life in 1971. In the early 1990s, increasing pro-democracy agitation, along with international pressure, forced Banda to introduce multiparty democracy in 1994.

In the 2004 legislative election, the MCP became the largest party with 60 seats, but without an overall majority. The simultaneous presidential election was won by the United Democratic Front (UDF) candidate Bingu wa Mutharika, who appointed a coalition government made up of the UDF and smaller parties.

In 2005, President Mutharika resigned from the UDF over the apparent hostility of the party and his predecessor, Bakili Muluzi, to his anti-corruption campaign and founded a new party, the Democratic Progressive Party (DPP). The president's uncompromising anti-corruption stance involved him in a power struggle with Muluzi and the vice-president Cassim Chilumpha that disrupted legislative business in 2006; several senior politicians, including Muluzi and Chilumpha, have been arrested since 2006 on corruption or treason charges. President Mutharika was re-elected in May 2009, and the simultaneous legislative election was won by the DPP.

POLITICAL SYSTEM

Under the 1995 constitution, the executive president is directly elected for a five-year term, renewable only once. The unicameral National Assembly consists of 193 members, who are directly elected for a five-year term.

HEAD OF STATE

President, Bingu wa Mutharika, *elected* 20 May 2004, *re-elected* 2009
Vice-president, Joyce Banda

SELECTED GOVERNMENT MEMBERS *as at July 2010*

Finance, Ken Kandodo
Foreign Affairs, Etta Banda
Home Affairs, Aaron Sangala
Defence, Sidik Mia

HIGH COMMISSION OF THE REPUBLIC OF MALAWI

70 Winnington Road, London N2 0TX
T 020-8455 5624 E malawi@malawihighcommission.co.uk
W www.malawihighcommission.co.uk
High Commissioner, HE Dr Francis Moto, *apptd* 2006

BRITISH HIGH COMMISSION

PO Box 30042, Lingadzi House, Lilongwe 3
T (+265) (1) 772 400 E bhclilongwe@fco.gov.uk
W http://ukinmalawi.fco.gov.uk
High Commissioner, HE Fergus Cochrane-Dyet, *apptd* 2009

BRITISH COUNCIL

PO Box 30222, Plot No. 13/20 City Centre, Lilongwe 3
T (+265) (1) 773 244 W www.britishcouncil.org/africa
Director, Julian Baker

DEFENCE

The maritime wing has 15 patrol and coastal combatant vessels at a base on Lake Malawi (Nyasa).
Military budget – US$43m (2008 est)
Military personnel – 5,300: army 5,300; paramilitary 1,500

ECONOMY AND TRADE

Malawi is one of the poorest countries in Africa. It has few natural resources and its agricultural land is under pressure because of population growth. It also experienced years of mismanagement under earlier governments, and corruption remains a problem despite the government's determination to eliminate it. These factors, and the vulnerability of agricultural production to both drought and severe flooding, make the country heavily dependent on food and economic aid from international agencies and donor nations. Debt relief and tighter fiscal control have reduced public debt from over 200 per cent of GDP to 49 per cent by 2008, although the proportion rose to 58 per cent in 2009 as foreign exchange earnings and investment fell.

The economy is primarily agricultural, with 85 per cent of the workforce engaged in agriculture, which accounts for 35.1 per cent of GDP and 90 per cent of export revenue. Tobacco is the most important cash crop, providing over half of export earnings, along with tea, sugar, cotton, coffee and peanuts. The main industrial activities are agricultural processing, sawmill products, cement and consumer goods, now supplemented by mining uranium, of which exports began in 2009.

The main export markets are South Africa, Egypt, Zimbabwe and the EU; imports come mainly from South Africa, India, China and Tanzania. Apart from tobacco and other agricultural products, wood products and clothing are principal exports. The main imports are food, fuels, semi-manufactures, consumer goods and transport equipment.

GNI – US$4,200m; US$280 per capita (2008)
Annual average growth of GDP – 5.9 per cent (2009 est)
Inflation rate – 8.5 per cent (2009 est)
Population below poverty line – 53 per cent (2004)
Total external debt – US$1,091m (2009 est)
Imports – US$1,700m (2008)
Exports – US$800m (2008)

BALANCE OF PAYMENTS
Trade – US$976m deficit (2009)
Current Account – US$360m deficit (2009)

Trade with UK	*2008*	*2009*
Imports from UK	£16,904,129	£24,248,446
Exports to UK	£16,639,919	£23,777,442

COMMUNICATIONS

Much internal transport is by water; there are 700km of navigable waterways on Lake Malawi (Nyasa) and the river Shire. Communication with the Indian Ocean coast is by rail through Mozambique; the route to the port of Beira was severed during Mozambique's civil war but the route to Nacala reopened in 2002. There are 797km of railways, including a single-track line linking Blantyre with the Zambian border, via Lilongwe and Salima. There are 15,451km of roads, of which 6,956km are surfaced. The main airports are at Blantyre and Lilongwe, with 30 smaller airports and airstrips around the country.

Privatisation of telecommunications was completed in 2006. Fixed-line density is about 2 per 100 people. Mobile phone services are expanding but coverage is limited to urban areas; density was about 15 per 100 people in 2008.

EDUCATION AND HEALTH

The government is responsible for primary and secondary schools, technical education and primary teacher training.
Literacy rate – 71.8 per cent (2007 est)
Gross enrolment ratio (percentage of relevant age group) – primary 120 per cent; secondary 29 per cent; tertiary 0 per cent (2008 est)
Health expenditure (per capita) – US$17 (2007)
Hospital beds (per 1,000 people) – 1.1 (2003–8)

MEDIA

There are four national newspapers, two of which are dailies; the press operates freely, although the government has used libel laws to exert pressure on journalists. Radio is the main source of information, provided by the state-run Malawi Broadcasting Corporation and a number of private stations. Television was introduced in 1999; the only provider is state-run Television Malawi.

MALAYSIA

Area – 329,847 sq. km
Capital – Kuala Lumpur; population, 1,493,500 (2009 est); Putrajaya is the administrative capital
Major cities – Ampang Jaya, Ipoh, Johor Bahru, Klang, Kota Kinabalu, Kuching, Petaling Jaya, Shah Alam, Subang Jaya
Currency – Malaysian ringgit (RM) of 100 sen; also known as Malaysian dollar
Population – 25,715,819 rising at 1.72 per cent a year (2009 est); Malay (50.4 per cent), Chinese (23.7 per cent), indigenous (11 per cent), Indian (7.1 per cent) (est)
Religion – Muslim 60 per cent (predominantly Shafi'i, a school of Sunni Islam), Buddhist 19 per cent, Christian 9 per cent, Hindu 6 per cent, Chinese traditional religions 3 per cent (est)
Language – Bahasa Malaysia (Malay) (official), English, Cantonese, Mandarin, Tamil, Telugu, Malayalam, Punjabi, Thai, Iban, Kadazan

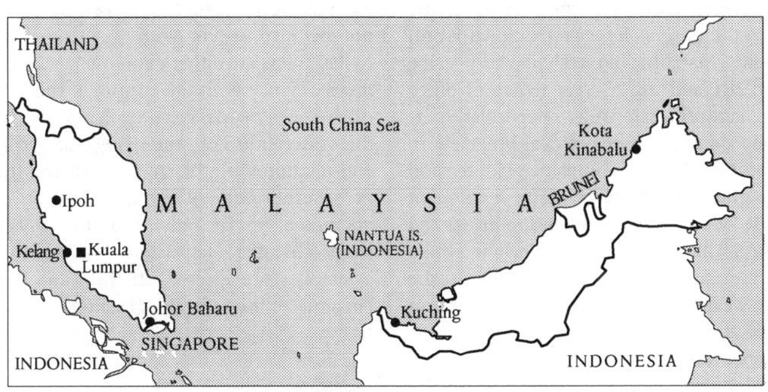

Population density – 82 per sq. km (2008)
Urban population – 70 per cent (2007 est)
Median age (years) – 24.9 (2009 est)
National anthem – 'Negaraku' ['My Country']
National day – 31 August (Malaysia Day)
Life expectancy (years) – 73.29 (2009 est)
Mortality rate – 5.02 (2009 est)
Birth rate – 22.24 (2009 est)
Infant mortality rate – 15.87 (2009 est)
Death penalty – Retained
CPI score – 4.5 (2009)

CLIMATE AND TERRAIN

Malaysia comprises the 11 states of peninsular Malaya plus the states of Sabah and Sarawak on the island of Borneo. The Malay peninsula, which extends from the isthmus of Kra to the Singapore Strait, is a plain with two highland areas in the north. The Malaysian part of Borneo is mostly high plateau, rising to mountains in western Sabah and eastern Sarawak, while Sarawak also has lower-lying land along the coast and in the Rajang valley; both states are densely forested. Elevation extremes range from 4,100m (Gunung Kinabalu, Sabah) at the highest point to 0m (Indian Ocean) at the lowest. The climate is tropical, experiencing the south-west monsoon from April to September and the north-east monsoon from November to February. Average temperatures in Kuala Lumpur range between 22°C and 33°C all year round.

HISTORY AND POLITICS

Malaysia formed part of the Srivijaya Empire from the ninth to the 14th century. From the 16th century, the Portuguese, Dutch and British vied for control in the region. The British possessions of Singapore, Penang and Malacca were formed in 1826 into the Straits Settlement, which became a crown colony in 1867. British protection was extended over four Malay states, which federated in 1896, and protection treaties were agreed with several other states between 1885 and 1930. Following occupation by the Japanese from 1941 to 1945, the United Malays National Organisation (UMNO) was founded in 1946 to oppose the postwar political settlement, which extended equal rights to the Chinese and Indian minorities; its opposition led to an insurgency (the Emergency) by the Chinese-led Malayan Communist Party from 1948 to 1955. The nine peninsular states were federated as the Federation of Malaya in 1948. The Federation of Malaya became independent in 1957, and in 1963 it combined with Singapore, Sarawak and Sabah to form the Federation of Malaysia; Singapore withdrew from the federation in 1965.

UMNO has dominated post-independence politics, initially as the governing party and since 1971 as the dominant partner in the *Barisan Nasional* (National Front) coalition governments. Mahathir bin Muhammad became prime minister in 1981 and his 22-year tenure of office saw increasingly authoritarian rule, particularly as opposition to Malay dominance of political life grew in the 1980s and 1990s. There is considerable tension between the ethnic groups in Malaysia; Malay resentment of the large Chinese minority's economic dominance led to the adoption in 1971 of policies that favour ethnic Malays in education and employment, although the Chinese remain the wealthiest section of society. In recent years there has been intercommunal violence between ethnic Indians, the poorest group, and Malays.

The Barisan Nasional coalition won the 2008 legislative election, but with a majority reduced from 198 to 140 seats after a significant swing to the opposition parties. Abdullah Ahmed Badawi, prime minister since 2003, stood down in 2009 and was replaced as leader of UMNO and prime minister by his deputy, Najib Tun Abdul Razak.

POLITICAL SYSTEM

The 1957 constitution provides for a federal government and a degree of autonomy for the state governments. The supreme head of state *(Yang di-Pertuan Agong)* is elected by the nine hereditary rulers of the peninsular states from among their number and serves a five-year term.

The federal *Parlimen* has two houses, the House of Representatives and the senate. The former is the lower house and has 222 members, directly elected for a five-year term. The senate has 70 members who serve a six-year term; the legislative assembly of each state elects two members, and 44 are nominated by the head of state.

HEAD OF STATE

Supreme Head of State, HM Sultan Mizan Zainal Abidin ibni al-Marhum Sultan Mahmud, *sworn in* 13 December 2006
Deputy Head of State, Abdul Halim Mu'adzam Shah

SELECTED GOVERNMENT MEMBERS *as at June 2010*

Prime Minister, Finance, Najib Tun Abdul Razak
Deputy Prime Minister, Muhyiddin bin Mohamed Yasin
Foreign Affairs, Anifah Aman
Home Affairs, Hishammuddin Tun Hussein
Defence, Ahmad Zahid Hamidi

MALAYSIAN HIGH COMMISSION

45 Belgrave Square, London SW1X 8QT
T 020-7235 8033 E mwlon@btconnect.com
W www.jimlondon.net
High Commissioner (acting), HE Dato Rustam Yahaya, *apptd* 2010

BRITISH HIGH COMMISSION

PO Box 11030, 185 Jalan Ampang, 50450 Kuala Lumpur
T (+60) (3) 2170 2200 E bhc.kl@fco.gov.uk
W http://ukinmalaysia.fco.gov.uk
High Commissioner, HE Boyd McCleary, CVO, *apptd* 2006

BRITISH COUNCIL

Ground Floor, West Block, Wisma Selangor Dredging, 142 C Jalan Ampang, 50450 Kuala Lumpur
T (+60) (3) 2723 7900 W www.britishcouncil.org/malaysia
Director, Mandy Johnson

FEDERAL STRUCTURE

Each of the 13 states has its own constitution, which must not be inconsistent with the federal constitution. The Malay rulers are either chosen or succeed to their position in accordance with the custom of their particular state; in other states of Malaysia, choice of the head of state is at the discretion of the *Yang di-Pertuan Agong* after consultation with the chief minister of the state. The ruler or governor acts on the advice of an executive council appointed on the advice of the chief minister and a single-chamber legislative assembly. The legislative assemblies are elected on the same basis as the lower chamber of the federal legislature.

DEFENCE

The army has 48 main battle tanks, 44 armoured infantry fighting vehicles and 835 armoured personnel carriers. The navy has 2 submarines, 2 frigates, 10 corvettes, 14 patrol and coastal vessels and 6 armed helicopters at 7 bases. The air force has 74 combat aircraft and 20 armed helicopters.
Military budget – US$4,030m (2009)
Military personnel – 109,000: army 80,000, navy 14,000, air force 15,000; paramilitary 24,600

ECONOMY AND TRADE

The economy has grown vigorously since the 1970s, transforming the country into a diversified emerging economy. The government's goal is to achieve developed nation status by 2020. To this end, it has encouraged investment in high technology industries, medical technology and pharmaceuticals. Growth has largely been driven by export-orientated manufacturing, dependence on which the government aims to reduce. A contraction following a fall in exports owing to the global downturn led the government to introduce economic stimulus packages in 2008–9.

The agricultural sector produces the raw materials for its highly developed industries. Industrial production includes rubber manufacturing, palm oil processing, electronics, tin mining and smelting, and logging and timber processing; oil and timber are produced in Sabah and Sarawak, and oil is refined in Sarawak, which also processes agricultural and forestry products. Tourism is a major industry. The services sector contributed 49.7 per cent of GDP, industry 40.9 per cent and agriculture 9.4 per cent in 2009.

The main trading partners are China, Singapore, the USA, Japan and other south-east Asian countries. Principal exports are electronic equipment, petroleum and liquefied natural gas, timber and wood products, palm oil, rubber, textiles and chemicals. The main imports are electronics, machinery, petroleum products, plastics, vehicles, iron and steel products, and chemicals.
GNI – US$196,000m; US$7,250 per capita (2008)
Annual average growth of GDP – –2.8 per cent (2009 est)
Inflation rate – 0.4 per cent (2009 est)
Unemployment – 5 per cent (2009 est)
Total external debt – US$48,260m (2009 est)
Imports – US$164,400m (2008)
Exports – US$209,700m (2008)

BALANCE OF PAYMENTS
Trade – US$36,649m surplus (2009)
Current Account – US$38,854m surplus (2008)

Trade with UK	*2008*	*2009*
Imports from UK	£1,136,753,054	£1,039,740,854
Exports to UK	£1,838,667,860	£1,564,206,200

COMMUNICATIONS

There are six main seaports in peninsular Malaysia, plus Kota Kinabalu (Sabah) and Kuching (Sarawak), and a merchant fleet of 306 ships of over 1,000 tonnes. The Strait of Malacca and the South China Sea are busy shipping lanes with high risks of piracy and armed robbery. There are 98,721km of roads, 7,200km of navigable waterways, and in peninsular Malaysia 1,849km of railways. The main international airports are at Kuala Lumpur, Kota Kinabalu and Kuching, with over 110 smaller airports and airfields around the country.

In 2008, there were 4.3 million fixed telephone lines in use, 27.1 million mobile phone subscribers and 16.9 million internet users.

EDUCATION AND HEALTH

There are six years of compulsory education.
Literacy rate – 91.9 per cent (2007 est)
Gross enrolment ratio (percentage of relevant age group) – primary 98 per cent; tertiary 30 per cent (2008 est)
Health expenditure (per capita) – US$307 (2007)
Hospital beds (per 1,000 people) – 1.8 (2003–8)

MEDIA

The government operates extremely strict censorship of all media outlets; content may be censored on security, political or moral grounds. Newspapers must annually renew their licences, which can be suspended or revoked by the home affairs minister. Controversial political websites and blogs risk government harassment and prosecution.

The four main national daily newspapers are in English: *The Star, Business Times, New Straits Times* and *The Malay Mail*. The state-run Radio Television Malaysia provides services in competition with commercial broadcasters.

MALDIVES

Dhivehi Raajjey ge Jumhooriyyaa – Republic of Maldives

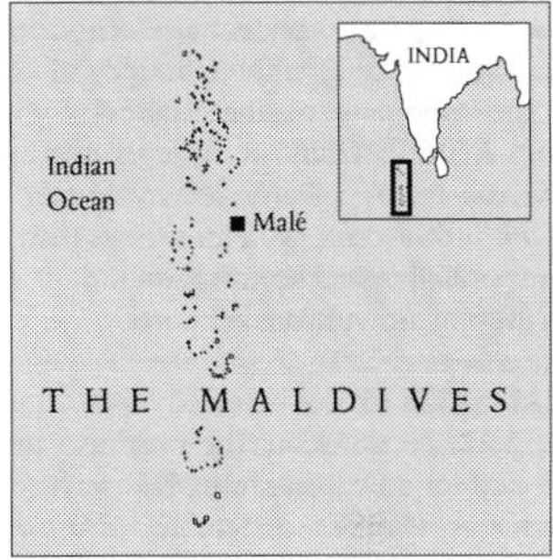

Area – 298 sq. km
Capital – Malé; population, 120,215 (2009 est)
Currency – Rufiyaa of 100 laarees
Population – 396,334 falling at 0.17 per cent a year (2009 est)
Religion – Sunni Muslim; public practice of other religions is illegal
Language – Dhivehi (official), English
Population density – 1,017 per sq. km (2008)
Urban population – 37 per cent (2007 est)
Median age (years) – 25.7 (2009 est)
National anthem – 'Gavmii mi ekuverikan matii tibegen kuriime salaam' ['In National Unity Do We Salute Our Nation']
National day – 26 July (Independence Day)
Life expectancy (years) – 73.97 (2009 est)
Mortality rate – 3.65 (2009 est)
Birth rate – 14.55 (2009 est)
Infant mortality rate – 29.53 (2009 est)
Death penalty – Retained (no known use since 1952)
CPI Score – 2.5 (2009)
Literacy rate – 97.0 per cent (2007 est)

CLIMATE AND TERRAIN

The republic is an archipelago of coral atolls in the Indian Ocean, 643km to the south-west of Sri Lanka. There are about 1,190 coral islands grouped into 26 clusters of atolls, about 200 of which are inhabited. The islands are all flat and low-lying; none is more than 2.4m above sea level, making them vulnerable to rising sea levels due to climate change. The climate is tropical, affected by the dry north-east monsoon (November–March) and the wet south-west monsoon (June–August).

HISTORY AND POLITICS

The Maldives were an independent sultanate from the mid-12th century. The sultan was overthrown by the Portuguese in 1558 but they were driven out in 1573 and the sultanate was re-established. In 1645, the islands became a dependency of Ceylon, which was under Dutch and then British rule. In 1887 they became an internally self-governing British protectorate. Independence was achieved in 1965, and in 1968 the Maldives became a republic under President Ibrahim Nasir.

The autocratic Nasir retired in 1978 and was succeeded by Maumoon Abdul Gayoom. His 30-year tenure, although equally autocratic, maintained political stability and allowed economic development. However, unprecedented violence during anti-government demonstrations in 2003 and 2004 led to the legalising of political parties in 2005 and the introduction of a new constitution in 2008. The 2004 Indian Ocean tsunami devastated the islands, destroying many homes and tourist resorts.

The first multi-party presidential election in October 2008 was won in the second round by Mohamed Nasheed, the candidate of the Maldivian Democratic Party (MDP). In the first multi-party legislative elections in May 2009, the People's Party, led by former president Maumoon Abdul Gayoom, won more seats than the MDP but not an overall majority, and the MDP formed a coalition government with smaller parties.

POLITICAL SYSTEM

Under the 2008 constitution, the executive president is directly elected for a five-year term, renewable only once. The unicameral People's Assembly *(Majlis)* has 77 members, who are directly elected for a five-year term.

HEAD OF STATE

President, Mohamed Nasheed, *elected* 29 October 2008, *sworn in* 11 November 2008
Vice-President, Mohamed Waheed Hassan Manik

SELECTED GOVERNMENT MEMBERS *as at June 2010*

Defence, Ameen Faisal
Foreign Affairs, Ahmed Shaheed
Finance, Ali Hashim
Home Affairs, Mohamed Shihab

HIGH COMMISSION OF THE REPUBLIC OF MALDIVES

22 Nottingham Place, London W1U 5NJ
T 020-7224 2135 E info@maldiveshighcommission.org
W www.maldiveshighcommission.org
High Commissioner, HE Dr Farahanaz Faizal, *apptd* 2009

BRITISH HIGH COMMISSIONER

HE Dr Peter Hayes, *apptd* 2008, resident at Colombo, Sri Lanka

ECONOMY AND TRADE

Political stability and economic liberalisation have produced steady economic growth since the 1980s, although the devastation caused by the 2004 tsunami briefly arrested this in 2005. The economy is heavily dependent on tourism, which accounts for 28 per cent of GDP and 60 per cent of foreign exchange receipts. A fall in tourist numbers as well as exports owing to the global economic downturn caused the economy to contract in 2009; the government secured a US$79.3m standby agreement with the IMF in December of that year. Import duties and tourism-related taxes provide over 90 per cent of government tax revenue. Fishing is the second largest activity, accounting for around 6 per cent of GDP. Agriculture and manufacturing are constrained by a shortage of cultivatable land and domestic labour, and so most food is imported. Industry is concentrated on clothing manufacture, boat-building and handicrafts, contributing 16.9 per cent to GDP.

The main export markets are Thailand, EU countries and Sri Lanka. The only significant export is fish. Imports include petroleum products, ships, food and clothing, and are provided mainly by Singapore, the UAE, Malaysia and India.

GNI – US$1,110m; US$3,640 per capita (2008)
Annual average growth of GDP – –4 per cent (2009 est)
Inflation rate – 7.3 per cent (2009 est)
Population below poverty line – 21 per cent (2004)
Unemployment – 14.4 per cent (2006 est)
Total external debt – US$589m (2009 est)
Imports – US$1,400m (2008)
Exports – US$100m (2008)

BALANCE OF PAYMENTS

Trade – US$842m deficit (2009)
Current Account – US$648m deficit (2008)

Trade with UK	*2008*	*2009*
Imports from UK	£8,462,631	£6,311,596
Exports to UK	£12,950,858	£10,550,276

COMMUNICATIONS

None of the islands is more than 13 sq. km in area. The larger islands have some roads. Transport between islands is by water or air; the country has five airports, two of which now handle international traffic following the upgrade of Gan airport. The main port is Malé. Telephone services are available on the inhabited islands and mobile phone distribution has expanded rapidly, reaching a density of over 100 per 100 people.

MEDIA

At present the government operates the main television and radio stations. Private stations are few because of the prohibitive cost of licences. Two of the three daily newspapers include English-language sections. Government officials retain the power to close media outlets, and journalists largely practise self-censorship. President Nasheed pledged in April 2009 to liberalise media laws to establish greater press freedom and competition.

MALI

République de Mali – Republic of Mali

Area – 1,240,192 sq. km
Capital – Bamako; population, 1,627,580 (2009 est)
Major cities – Kayes, Mopti, Ségou, Sikasso
Currency – Franc CFA of 100 centimes
Population – 12,666,987 rising at 2.77 per cent a year (2009 est); Mandé (50 per cent), Fulani (17 per cent), Voltaic (12 per cent), Songhai (6 per cent), Tuareg and Moor (10 per cent) (est); about 10 per cent are nomadic
Religion – Muslim 90 per cent (predominantly Sunni), Christian 5 per cent (predominantly Roman Catholic) (est). The remainder practise traditional indigenous beliefs
Language – French (official), Bambara
Population density – 10 per sq. km (2008)
Urban population – 32 per cent (2007 est)
Median age (years) – 15.8 (2009 est)
National anthem – 'Pour l'Afrique et Pour Toi, Mali' ['For Africa and For You, Mali']
National day – 22 September (Independence Day)
Life expectancy – 50.35 (2009 est)
Mortality rate – 15.82 (2009 est)
Birth rate – 49.15 (2009 est)
Infant mortality rate – 102.05 (2009 est)
HIV/AIDS adult prevalence – 1.4 per cent (2007 est)
Death penalty – Retained (not used since 1980)
CPI score – 2.8 (2009)

CLIMATE AND TERRAIN

A landlocked state in west Africa, Mali is mainly savannah in the south and desert plains in the north, with some hills in the north-east; over 60 per cent is desert or semi-desert. The centre is drained by the river Niger and the south-west by the river Senegal. Elevation extremes range from 1,155m (Hombori Tondo) at the highest point to 23m (river Senegal) at the lowest. The climate is subtropical in the south, with a rainy season from June to November, and arid in the north. Average temperatures in Bamako range from lows of 16°C in January to highs of 39°C in May.

HISTORY AND POLITICS

Mali was successively part of the empire of the Malinke people from the 13th to 15th centuries, and the Songhai Empire in the 15th to 16th centuries. With the fall of the Songhai Empire, it was divided between the Tuareg and the Fulani and Bambara kingdoms, and then the Tukolor and Samori kingdoms. It was conquered by the French in 1880–95 and became a French colony. In 1959, it formed the Federation of Mali with Senegal before becoming a separate independent state in 1960 under a one-party socialist regime.

In 1968, a military coup led by Lt. Moussa Traoré, who became president, resulted in 23 years of oppressive military rule. Traoré was ousted in 1991 in a military coup led by Gen. Amadou Toumani Touré. Multiparty elections were held in 1992, returning the country to civilian government.

A degree of decentralisation was introduced in 1999, partly in response to rebellions in the north by the Tuareg over land and cultural rights. Another rebellion in 2006 by Tuareg seeking greater autonomy for their region was settled within a few months, but a more militant Tuareg faction carried on an insurrection from 2007 to 2009, when the rebels disarmed and returned to negotiations.

Amadou Toumani Touré, standing as an independent candidate, won the 2002 presidential elections, and was re-elected in 2007 in the first round of voting. In the 2007 legislative elections, the Alliance for Democracy in Mali (ADEMA), which had dominated government coalitions since 1992, won the largest number of seats, and the three-party Alliance for Democracy and Progress coalition of which ADEMA is a part retained its overall majority.

POLITICAL SYSTEM

Under the 1992 constitution, the president is directly elected for a five-year term, and is eligible for a second term. The unicameral National Assembly has 160 members, 147 directly elected for a five-year term and 13 to represent Malians abroad. The president appoints the prime minister, who appoints the cabinet.

HEAD OF STATE

President, Amadou Toumani Touré, *elected* 12 May 2002, *took office* 8 June 2002, *re-elected* 2007

SELECTED GOVERNMENT MEMBERS *as at July 2010*

Prime Minister, Modibo Sidibe
Defence, Natie Pleah
Economy and Finance, Sanoussi Touré
Foreign Affairs, Moctar Ouane

EMBASSY OF THE REPUBLIC OF MALI

Avenue Molière 487, 1050 Brussels, Belgium
T (+32) (2) 345 7432 **E** info@amba-mali.be
W www.amba-mali.be
Ambassador Extraordinary and Plenipotentiary, HE Ibrahim Bocar Ba, *apptd* 2003

BRITISH AMBASSADOR

British Embassy Liaison Office, Enceinte de l'Ambassade du Canada, Route de Koulikoro, Hippodrome, BP 2069, Bamako
T (+223) 2021 3412
HE Nicholas Griffiths, *apptd* 2010

DEFENCE

The army has 33 main battle tanks and 64 armoured personnel carriers. The navy has 3 patrol and coastal combatant vessels at 4 bases. The air force has 13 combat capable aircraft and 2 armed helicopters.
Military budget – US$180m (2009 est)
Military personnel – 7,350: army 7,350; paramilitary 4,800; militia 3,000

ECONOMY AND TRADE

Mali is one of the world's poorest countries, with over 30 per cent of the population living below the poverty line.

Economic reform since the mid-1990s has produced steady growth, but Mali is heavily dependent on foreign aid and remittances from expatriates. A huge foreign debt has been reduced to a more manageable size by debt cancellation and rescheduling.

The economy is based primarily on subsistence farming and animal husbandry, which contribute 45 per cent of GDP and occupy 80 per cent of the population. Gold and phosphate mining, and cotton and food processing are the main activities in Mali's industrial sector, which accounts for 17 per cent of GDP. Export of electricity from hydroelectric plants is expected to contribute to future earnings.

The main export markets are China and Thailand; imports come mainly from Senegal, Côte d'Ivoire and France. Principal exports are cotton, gold and livestock. The main imports are fuel, machinery and equipment, construction materials, foodstuffs and textiles.

GNI – US$7,400m; US$580 per capita (2008)
Annual average growth of GDP – 3 per cent (2009 est)
Inflation rate – 2.5 per cent (2007 est)
Population below poverty line – 36.1 per cent (2005 est)
Unemployment – 30 per cent (2004 est)
Total external debt – US$2,800m (2002)
Imports – US$2,600m (2008)
Exports – US$1,700m (2008)

BALANCE OF PAYMENTS
Trade – US$921m deficit (2009)
Current Account – US$695m deficit (2008)

Trade with UK	*2008*	*2009*
Imports from UK	£6,960,978	£6,260,260
Exports to UK	£1,326,925	£426,312

COMMUNICATIONS

Mali has 18,700km of roads, 593km of railway line and 1,800km of waterways. The road network is being extended to connect Mali with all adjacent countries, and its railway is linked to Senegal. Bamako is the centre of the transport network and the main shipping point for freight, with links to ports in Côte d'Ivoire (where civil war has disrupted trade routes), Guinea and Senegal. The main port is Koulikoro on the river Niger, and the principal airport is at Bamako.

The telephone system is limited in extent and services are unreliable, though improving. In 2008, fixed-line density was less than one per 100 people, while mobile phone density was nearly 30 per 100 people.

EDUCATION AND HEALTH

Literacy rate – 26.2 per cent (2007 est)
Gross enrolment ratio (percentage of relevant age group) – primary 91 per cent; secondary 35 per cent; tertiary 5 per cent (2008 est)
Health expenditure (per capita) – US$34 (2007)
Hospital beds (per 1,000 people) – 0.6 (2003–8)

MEDIA AND CULTURE

The media is among the freest in Africa. Slander laws that might restrict comment on public officials are rarely invoked. The print media consists of 40 privately owned newspapers, and there are about 50 private television and radio stations. The state operates its own daily newspaper and a radio and television broadcast network.

The music of Mali has become increasingly popular internationally in the last decade, and has absorbed some Western influences. Important names include guitarist Ali Farka Toure (1939–2006), kora player Toumani Diabaté (*b.* 1965), duo Amadou and Mariam and Tuareg group Tinariwen.

MALTA

Repubblika ta' Malta – Republic of Malta

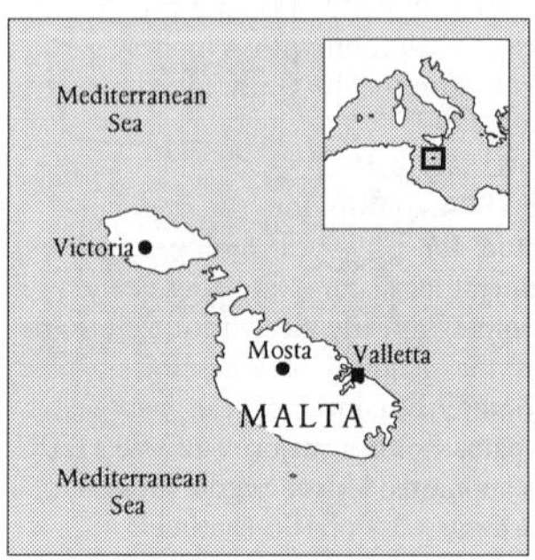

Area – 316 sq. km
Capital – Valletta; population, 199,283 (2009 est)
Major towns – Birkirkara, Mosta, Qormi, Saint Paul's Bay (San Pawl il-Bahar)
Currency – Euro (€) of 100 cents
Population – 405,165 rising at 0.4 per cent a year (2009 est)
Religion – Christian (Roman Catholic 95 per cent), Muslim 1 per cent (est)
Language – Maltese, English (both official)
Population density – 1,287 per sq. km (2008)
Urban population – 94 per cent (2007 est)
Median age (years) – 39.5 (2009 est)
National anthem – 'L-Innu Malti' ['Hymn of Malta']
National day – 21 September (Independence Day)
Life expectancy (years) – 79.44 (2009 est)
Mortality rate – 8.38 (2009 est)
Birth rate – 10.36 (2009 est)
Infant mortality rate – 3.75 (2009 est)
Death penalty – Abolished for all crimes (since 2000)
CPI score – 5.2 (2009)

CLIMATE AND TERRAIN

Malta is an archipelago of six islands in the Mediterranean Sea; Malta, Gozo and Comino are the largest. The island of Malta has a coastal plain in the north-east, rising to low hills on the south-west. Elevation extremes range from 253m (Ta'Dmejrek) at the highest point to 0m (Mediterranean Sea) at the lowest. Average temperatures in Valetta range from 12°C in January to 27°C in August.

HISTORY AND POLITICS

The islands were ruled successively by the Phoenicians, Greeks, Carthaginians, Romans, Arabs, the Spanish and the Sovereign Military Order of Malta (known as the Knights of St John), which held them from 1530 until 1798. Liberated from French rule with British naval support in 1800, the island of Malta became a British colony in 1814, and was developed into a substantial naval base and dockyard. Malta was strategically important in both world wars, but particularly the second, when it was blockaded and subjected to aerial bombardment for five months. Its resistance led to the people of Malta being awarded the George Cross, the UK's highest award for civilian bravery, in 1942.

Malta gained its independence in 1964 and became a republic in 1974. In the 1970s it developed close links with communist and Arab states, but more pro-European and pro-US policies were adopted after the election of the Nationalist Party in 1987. Malta became a member of the EU in 2004, and adopted the euro in 2008. Since joining the EU, Malta has experienced a marked increase in illegal immigration from northern Africa.

The Nationalist Party was returned to power in the 2008 legislative election with a modest overall majority. George Abela won the 2009 presidential election.

POLITICAL SYSTEM
Under the 1974 constitution, the president is elected by the legislature for a five-year term, renewable only once. The unicameral legislature, the House of Representatives, has 69 members directly elected for a five-year term; if a party wins the majority of votes in a general election without winning a majority of seats, new seats are created until that party holds a majority of one seat. The prime minister is appointed by the president and nominates the other ministers.

HEAD OF STATE
President, George Abela, *took office* 4 April 2009

SELECTED GOVERNMENT MEMBERS *as at June 2010*
Prime Minister, Defence, Lawrence Gonzi
Deputy Prime Minister, Foreign Affairs, Tonio Borg
Home Affairs, Carmelo Mifsud Bonnici
Finance and Economy, Tonio Fenech

MALTA HIGH COMMISSION
Malta House, 36–38 Piccadilly, London W1J 0LE
T 020-7292 4800 **E** maltahighcommission.london@gov.mt
W www.foreign.gov.mt
High Commissioner, HE Joseph Zammit Tabona, *apptd* 2009

BRITISH HIGH COMMISSION
Whitehall Mansions, Ta'Xbiex Seafront, Ta'Xbiex, XBX 1026
T (+356) 2323 0000 **E** bhcvalletta@fco.gov.uk
W http://ukinmalta.fco.gov.uk
High Commissioner, HE Louise Stanton, *apptd* 2009

BRITISH COUNCIL
Exchange Buildings, Republic Street, Valletta VLT 05
T (+356) 2122 6377 **W** www.britishcouncil.org/malta
Director, Petra Bianchi

DEFENCE
The Maritime Squadron has 9 patrol and coastal combatant vessels.
Military budget – US$37.8m (2010)
Military personnel – 1,954

ECONOMY AND TRADE
The mainstay of the economy for over a century was the dockyard, and ship-building and ship repairs remain significant industries, but since the 1980s Malta has developed into a tourist destination, financial services centre and freight trans-shipment point. Tourism is now the main source of income, followed by foreign trade and manufacturing, especially of electronics and pharmaceuticals. All have been adversely affected by the global downturn, causing the economy to contract sharply.

The service sector accounts for 80.9 per cent of GDP, industry for 17.4 per cent and agriculture for 1.7 per cent; Malta produces only about 20 per cent of its food requirements. The main trading partners are other EU states, the USA and Singapore. Principal exports are electrical machinery, mechanical appliances, fish and shellfish, pharmaceuticals and printed material. The main imports are mineral fuels and oil, machinery, aircraft and other transport equipment, semi-manufactured goods, food, beverages and tobacco.
GNI – US$6,216m; US$15,310 per capita (2007)
Annual average growth of GDP – –4 per cent (2009 est)
Inflation rate – 2.7 per cent (2009 est)
Unemployment – 6 per cent (2009)
Total external debt – US$188.8m (2005)
Imports – US$4,600m (2008)
Exports – US$2,800m (2008)

BALANCE OF PAYMENTS
Trade – US$1,593m deficit (2009)
Current Account – US$453m deficit (2008)

Trade with UK	*2008*	*2009*
Imports from UK	£464,620,934	£377,432,592
Exports to UK	£135,580,642	£104,440,464

COMMUNICATIONS
The main ports are Marsaxlokk and Valletta, and there is a large merchant fleet of 1,438 ships of over 1,000 tonnes. Ferry services run to the islands. There are 2,227km of roads, but no railways. The only airport is outside Valletta.

The telephone system extends to all the islands. In 2008, there were 241,100 fixed lines in use, 385,600 mobile phone subscribers and 198,800 internet users.

EDUCATION
Education is free at all levels and compulsory between the ages of five and 16.
Literacy rate – 92.4 per cent (2007 est)

MEDIA
Radio broadcasting began in the 1930s, partly to counter Fascist broadcasts from Italy. There are public-service radio and television broadcasters, as well as a thriving private sector; Italian television channels are popular, as are cable and satellite television services. The main private broadcasters, like the major newspapers, tend to be owned by or have strong affiliations with political parties or the Roman Catholic Church. Most newspapers are published in Maltese or English.

MARSHALL ISLANDS

Republic of the Marshall Islands

Area – 181 sq. km (plus 11,673 sq. km of lagoon waters)
Capital – Majuro; population, 29,601 (2009 est)
Major towns – Ebeye, Rita
Currency – US dollar (US$) of 100 cents
Population – 64,522 rising at 2.08 per cent a year (2009 est); mainly Micronesian. About 60 per cent of the population lives on Majuro and Kwajalein
Religion – Christian (United Church of Christ 52 per cent, Assemblies of God 24 per cent, Roman Catholic 8 per cent, Mormon 8 per cent, Bukot nan Jesus 2 per cent, Seventh-day Adventist 1 per cent, Baptist 1 per cent, Full Gospel 1 per cent), Baha'i 1 per cent
Language – Marshallese, English (both official)

Population density – 331 per sq. km (2008)
Urban population – 71 per cent (2007 est)
Median age (years) – 21.2 (2009 est)
National anthem – 'Forever Marshall Islands'
National day – 1 May (Constitution Day)
Life expectancy (years) – 71.19 (2009 est)
Mortality rate – 4.49 (2009 est)
Birth rate – 30.7 (2009 est)
Infant mortality rate – 25.45 (2009 est)
Death penalty – Abolished for all crimes (since 1986)

CLIMATE AND TERRAIN

The republic consists of two chains of 29 coral atolls, five islands and over 1,000 islets in the western Pacific Ocean. All of the islands are low-lying (the highest point is 10m) and vulnerable to rising sea levels, which could submerge them by the mid-21st century. The climate is tropical, with a wet season from May to November.

HISTORY AND POLITICS

The Marshall Islands were first claimed by Spain in 1592 but were left largely undisturbed. Subsequently they were seized by Germany and formally became a protectorate in 1886. Japan took control of the islands in 1914 on behalf of the Allied powers and administered them from 1920 until 1944, when they were captured by US forces. In 1947 the islands became part of the UN Trust Territory of the Pacific Islands, administered by the USA. Between 1946 and 1962, US nuclear weapons were tested on Bikini and Enewetak atolls. Enewetak has been partially decontaminated but Bikini is uninhabitable; the USA paid compensation to the test victims in the 1980s but the government is seeking US$2.7bn (£1.4bn) in further compensation to cover the medical care of radiation victims and rectify environmental damage.

The islands became internally self-governing in 1979, and US administration ended in 1986, when a compact of free association between the Republic of the Marshall Islands and the USA came into effect. Under this agreement, the USA recognised the republic as a sovereign and independent state but retained responsibility for external security and defence as well as giving financial help. UN trust territory status was terminated in 1990 and full independence was granted in December 1990. A renegotiated compact with the USA was signed in 2003. The USA retains control of the Kwajalein atoll, where it has a military base and missile tracking station.

In the 2007 legislative election, the Our Islands (AKA) grouping won the largest number of seats. Litokwa Tomeing was elected president in January 2008 but lost a vote of confidence in October 2009. Jurelang Zedkaia was elected to succeed him.

POLITICAL SYSTEM

Under the 1979 constitution, the executive president is elected by the legislature from among its members to serve a four-year term. The unicameral legislature, the *Nitijela*, has 33 members, directly elected for a four-year term. There are no formal political parties, although groupings of like-minded independents have emerged in recent years. There is also a 12-member Council of Chiefs *(Iroij)* which has a consultative and advisory role.

HEAD OF STATE

President, Jurelang Zedkaia, *elected* 26 October 2009, *sworn in* 1 November 2009

SELECTED GOVERNMENT MEMBERS *as at June 2010*

Finance, Jack Ading
Foreign Affairs, John Silk
Internal Affairs, Norman Matthew

BRITISH AMBASSADOR

HE Stephen Lillie, *apptd* 2009, resident at Manila, the Philippines

ECONOMY AND TRADE

The islands have few natural resources, apart from possible seabed mineral deposits, and the economy is dependent on aid from the USA, supplemented by ship registration fees and the sale of fishing licences. Most islanders live by subsistence farming and fishing, with coconuts, breadfruit and fish the main commercial crops. A small-scale industrial sector produces copra and handicrafts and processes tuna. Tourism is being encouraged but has declined recently which, with a similar decline in fishing licence sales, has caused the economy to contract. The government is the largest employer. The main trading partners are the USA, Japan, Australia and China. Principal exports are copra and coconut products, handicrafts and fish. Main imports include food and fuel.

GNI – US$195m; US$3,270 per capita (2008)
Annual average growth of GDP – –0.3 per cent (2008 est)
Inflation rate – 12.9 per cent (2008 est)
Unemployment – 36 per cent (2006 est)
Total external debt – $87m (2008 est)

Trade with UK	*2008*	*2009*
Imports from UK	£45,540,034	£25,899,697
Exports to UK	£1,945,714	£288,594

COMMUNICATIONS

Air transport provides the main means of internal travel, and there are 15 airports and airfields throughout the islands, with internal and international flights operated by Air Marshall Islands and Continental Air Micronesia. Majuro is the main airport as well as the main port, with a merchant fleet of 1,049 ships of over 1,000 tonnes; a further 956 foreign-owned ships are registered in the republic. There are 2,000km of surfaced roads. There is a modern telephone network on the major islands and atolls. Mobile phone distribution is less than a quarter of fixed-line density.

MEDIA

The media occasionally practises self-censorship over controversial issues. There are state-owned and private broadcasters, with some areas also able to receive US forces' radio and television broadcasts. A government-owned monthly gazette publishes official information, but leaves political coverage to the privately owned weekly newspaper *Marshall Islands Journal*, published in English and Marshallese.

MAURITANIA

Al-Jumhuriyah al-Islamiyah al-Muritaniyah – Islamic Republic of Mauritania

Area – 1,030,700 sq. km
Capital – Nouakchott; population, 708,789 (2009 est)
Major towns – Atar, Kaedi, Kiffa, Nouadhibou, Rosso
Currency – Ouguiya (UM) of 5 khoums
Population – 3,129,486 rising at 2.40 per cent a year (2009 est)
Religion – Muslim 99 per cent (almost entirely Sunni) (est)
Language – Arabic (official), Pulaar, Soninke, Wolof, French
Population density – 3 per sq. km (2008)
Urban population – 41 per cent (2007 est)
Median age (years) – 19.2 (2009 est)
National anthem – 'National Anthem of Mauritania'
National day – 28 November (Independence Day)
Life expectancy (years) – 60.37 (2009 est)
Mortality rate – 9.16 (2009 est)
Birth rate – 34.11 (2009 est)
Infant mortality rate – 63.42 (2009 est)
Death penalty – Retained (not used since 1987)
CPI score – 2.5 (2009)
Literacy rate – 55.8 per cent (2007 est)
Gross enrolment ratio (percentage of relevant age group) – primary 98 per cent; secondary 23 per cent; tertiary 4 per cent (2007 est)
Health expenditure (per capita) – US$22 (2007)
Hospital beds (per 1,000 people) – 0.4 (2003–8)

CLIMATE AND TERRAIN

About 60 per cent of the country is covered by the plains of the Sahara Desert, with some hills in the centre. The terrain is arid, apart from in the Senegal river valley; most of the population lives there or on the coast at Nouakchott and Nouadhibou. Elevation extremes range from Kediet Ijill (915m) at the highest point to −5m (Sebkhet Te-n-Dghamcha) at the lowest. There is a desert climate; the north of the country is virtually rainless, while the south receives some unreliable rainfall between June and October. Humidity can be high in the wet season, especially on the coast. Average temperatures in Nouakchott range from lows of 13°C in December to highs of 34°C in both May and September.

HISTORY AND POLITICS

Eastern Mauritania was part of the Ghana Empire and then the Muslim Almoravid and Almohad empires from the 11th to the 13th century. The area became part of the French West Africa protectorate in 1903 and then a colony in 1920. The country became independent as the Islamic Republic of Mauritania on 28 November 1960.

The country has experienced several military coups and periods of military rule since independence. The 1984 coup brought to power Col. Maaouya ould Sid Ahmed Taya, who restored civilian rule in 1992 with multi-party elections in which he was elected president. President Taya was deposed in a military coup in 2005 and after a period of transitional government, elections were held in late 2006 and early 2007.

The 2007 presidential election was won by Sidi ould Cheikh Abdallahi, who became the country's first democratically elected president since independence. In 2008 President Abdallahi was overthrown in a military coup after attempting to sack four military leaders. Democracy was restored with the presidential election in July 2009; this was won by General Mohamed ould Abdelaziz, who had led the 2008 coup, with 52 per cent of the vote.

POLITICAL SYSTEM

The 1991 constitution was amended in 2006 to reduce the term of the president, who is is directly elected, to five years, renewable only once. The bicameral legislature comprises the National Assembly, the lower house, and the senate. The National Assembly has 95 members who are directly elected for a five-year term. The senate has 56 members (including three representing Mauritanians abroad), who are indirectly elected for a six-year term; one-third is elected every two years.

HEAD OF STATE

President, Gen. Mohamed ould Abdelaziz, *elected* 18 July 2009, *sworn in* 5 August 2009

SELECTED GOVERNMENT MEMBERS *as at July 2010*

Prime Minister, Moulaye ould Mohamed Laghdhaf
Finance, Ahmed ould Moulaye Ahmed
Foreign Affairs, Naha mint Hamdi ould Mouknass
Interior, Mohamed ould Boilil
Defence, Hamadi ould Hamadi

EMBASSY OF THE ISLAMIC REPUBLIC OF MAURITANIA

5 rue de Montevideo, Paris 75116, France
T (+33) 4504 8354
Ambassador Extraordinary and Plenipotentiary, vacant

BRITISH AMBASSADOR

HE Timothy Morris, *apptd* 2008, resident at Rabat, Morocco

DEFENCE

The army has 35 main battle tanks and 25 armoured personnel carriers. The navy has 12 patrol and coastal combatant vessels at 2 bases.
Military budget – US$20m (2007 est)
Military personnel – 15,870: army 15,000, navy 620, air force 250; paramilitary 5,000
Conscription duration – 24 months

ECONOMY AND TRADE

Mauritania is one of the poorer countries in the region, with 40 per cent of the population living below the poverty line and unemployment at 30 per cent. Past economic mismanagement and droughts created a huge foreign debt, although the country has benefited from debt relief under the IMF's heavily indebted poor country initiative.

Natural resources include iron ore, copper, gold, gypsum, oil (off-shore production began in 2006) and rich fishing waters, although the latter are threatened by over-exploitation. Agriculture and animal husbandry, mainly at subsistence level, are the mainstay of the economy, accounting for 12.5 per cent of GDP and engaging 50 per cent of the population. The main industries are fish processing, oil production and mining.

The main trading partners are China and EU countries. Principal exports are iron ore (nearly 40 per cent), fish and fish products, gold, copper and oil. The main imports are machinery, petroleum products, capital goods, food and consumer goods.

GNI – US$2,600m; US$840 per capita (2008)
Annual average growth of GDP – 1.5 per cent (2009 est)
Inflation rate – 7.3 per cent (2007 est)
Population below poverty line – 40 per cent (2004 est)
Unemployment – 30 per cent (2008 est)

BALANCE OF PAYMENTS
Trade – US$442m surplus (2009)
Current Account – US$557m deficit (2008)

Trade with UK	*2008*	*2009*
Imports from UK	£25,532,073	£10,149,138
Exports to UK	£5,705,837	£273,829

COMMUNICATIONS

The main seaports are Nouakchott and Nouadhibou. There are 728km of railways and 11,100km of roads, and ferry services operate on the Senegal river. There are 27 airports and airfields. The telephone system is limited but improvements are being made. Mobile phone distribution is growing rapidly, with a density of 60 per 100 people, compared to 2 per 100 people for fixed lines.

MEDIA

The media is forbidden by law to publish opinions or information that undermine Islam or threaten national security. Television and radio services are state-owned, but a liberalisation law passed by parliament in July 2010 opened the broadcasting sector to private operators. Most newspapers are privately owned and, since 2006, are no longer required to obtain pre-publication approval from the government.

MAURITIUS

Republic of Mauritius

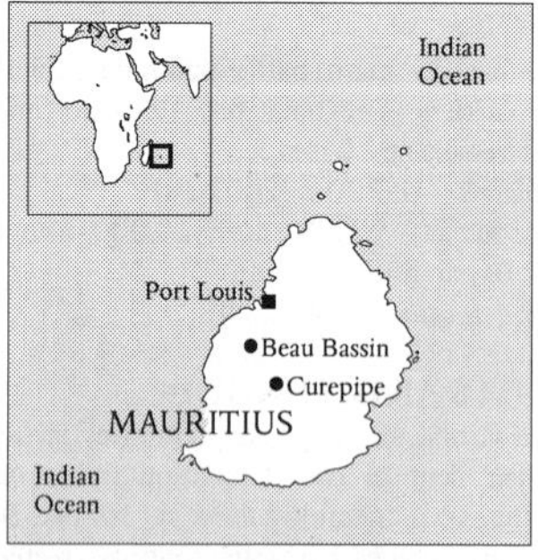

Area – 2,040 sq. km (includes Rodrigues and other islands)
Capital – Port Louis; population, 149,286 (2009 est)
Major towns – Beau Bassin-Rose Hill, Curepipe, Quatre Bornes, Vacoas-Phoenix
Currency – Mauritius rupee of 100 cents
Population – 1,284,264 rising at 0.78 per cent a year (2009 est); Indo-Mauritian (68 per cent), Creole (27 per cent), Sino-Mauritian (3 per cent), Franco-Mauritian (2 per cent) (est)
Religion – Hindu 50 per cent, Christian 32 per cent (of which Roman Catholic 73 per cent), Muslim 17 per cent (of which Sunni 90 per cent) (est)
Language – English (official), French, Creole, Bhojpuri
Population density – 625 per sq. km (2008)
Urban population – 42 per cent (2007 est)
Median age (years) – 31.9 (2009 est)
National anthem – 'Motherland'
National day – 12 March (Independence Day)
Life expectancy (years) – 74 (2009 est)
Mortality rate – 6.59 (2009 est)
Birth rate – 14.41 (2009 est)
Infant mortality rate – 12.2 (2009 est)
HIV/AIDS adult prevalence – 1.3 per cent (2007 est)
Death penalty – Abolished for all crimes (since 1995)
CPI score – 5.4 (2009)

CLIMATE AND TERRAIN

The republic is an island group in the Indian Ocean, approximately 885km east of Madagascar. The volcanic island of Mauritius rises from narrow coastal plains to a central plateau ringed by mountains. Elevation extremes range from 828m (Mt Piton) at the highest point to 0m (Indian Ocean) at the lowest. The island of Rodrigues, formerly a dependency but now part of Mauritius, is about 563km east of Mauritius, with an area of 108km; the population is 37,700 (2008 est). The islands of Agalega and St Brandon are dependencies of Mauritius; the total population is 289 (2008).

There is a tropical climate, modified by south-east trade winds, and little variation in temperature throughout the year. The cyclone season (November–April) brings rain but cyclones usually miss the islands.

HISTORY AND POLITICS

The islands were visited before the 16th century, but were only settled after 1638 by the Dutch, who introduced sugar cane to the islands; the colonists withdrew in 1710. A decade later they were replaced by the French, who established plantations that were worked by African slaves. In 1814 Mauritius was ceded to the British, who had occupied it in 1810. The British abolished slavery in 1834 and imported indentured Indian and Chinese labourers to work on the plantations. Independence was achieved on 12 March 1968 and the state became a republic in 1992.

The Militant Socialist Movement (MSM) under Sir Anerood Jugnauth held power from 1983 until 1995, and then returned to power in the 2000 election in coalition with the Mauritian Militant Movement (MMM). Jugnauth stood down as party leader and prime minister in 2003 and was elected president later that year; he was re-elected in 2008. The MSM-MMM coalition lost the 2005 election to the opposition Socialist Alliance, including the Mauritius Labour Party (MPT) led by Navinchandra Ramgoolam, who became prime minister. The MPT-led Alliance of the Future, now including also the MSM, won the legislative election in May 2010.

POLITICAL SYSTEM

The 1968 constitution was amended in 1992 to introduce a republican form of government, and in 2001 to give the island of Rodrigues a degree of autonomy. The president is elected by the legislature for a five-year term, renewable once. The unicameral National Assembly has 62 elected members (Mauritius has 20 three-member constituencies and Rodrigues returns two members) and eight appointed members, who serve a five-year term; the electoral commission allocates the appointed seats on a 'best loser' basis to give more equitable representation to ethnic minorities. The prime minister is the leader of the majority party in the legislature.

Rodrigues has an 18-member regional assembly, inaugurated in 2002, when a chief commissioner and chief executive were appointed.

HEAD OF STATE
President, Sir Anerood Jugnauth, *took office* 7 October 2003, re-elected 2008
Vice-President, Angidi Chettiar

SELECTED GOVERNMENT MEMBERS *as at July 2010*
Prime Minister, Defence, Interior, Navinchandra Ramgoolam
Deputy Prime Minister, Ahmed Rashid Beebeejaun
Vice Prime Ministers,, Rama Pravind Kumar Jugnauth *(Finance and Economic Development)*; Charles Duval
Foreign Affairs, Arvin Boolell

MAURITIUS HIGH COMMISSION
32–33 Elvaston Place, London SW7 5NW
T 020-7581 0294 E londonmhc@btinternet.com
High Commissioner, HE Abhimanu Kundasamy, *apptd* 2005

BRITISH HIGH COMMISSION
PO Box 1063, Les Cascades Building, Edith Cavell Street, Port Louis
T (+230) 202 9400 E bhc@bow.intnet.mu
W http://ukinmauritius.fco.gov.uk
High Commissioner, HE Nick Leake, *apptd* 2010

BRITISH COUNCIL
PO Box 111, Royal Road, Rose Hill
T (+230) 403 0200 W www.britishcouncil.org/africa
Director, Dawn Long

DEFENCE

The army has 2 armoured infantry fighting vehicles and 16 armoured personnel carriers. The coast guard has 27 patrol and coastal combatant vessels.
Military budget – US$41m (2009)
Military personnel – none active; paramilitary 2,000

ECONOMY AND TRADE

Since independence Mauritius has developed from an economy dependent on agriculture to one with prospering manufacturing (primarily of textiles and garments), tourism and financial sectors. Although sugar remains an important commodity (sugar cane is grown on 90 per cent of cultivated land and produces 15 per cent of export earnings), both the sugar and textile industries are beginning to decline. Diversification is being encouraged into fish processing, information and communications technology, hospitality and property development. The services sector accounts for 70.5 per cent of GDP, industry for 24.6 per cent and agriculture for 4.9 per cent.

The main trading partners are the UK, France and India. Principal exports are clothing, textiles, sugar, cut flowers, molasses and fish. The main imports are manufactured goods, capital equipment, food, fuels and chemicals.

GNI – US$8,500m; US$6,700 per capita (2008)
Annual average growth of GDP – 2.1 per cent (2009 est)
Inflation rate – 3.4 per cent (2009 est)
Population below poverty line – 8 per cent (2006 est)
Unemployment – 7.8 per cent (2009 est)
Total external debt – US$4,567m (2009 est)
Imports – US$4,700m (2008)
Exports – US$2,400m (2008)

BALANCE OF PAYMENTS
Trade – US$2,472m deficit (2009)
Current Account – US$971m deficit (2008)

Trade with UK	*2008*	*2009*
Imports from UK	£52,073,601	£53,141,951
Exports to UK	£375,868,065	£320,955,141

COMMUNICATIONS

Port Louis handles the bulk of the island's external trade. The international airport is located at Plaisance. The 2,066km of roads are all surfaced. There are no railways. The telephone system offers a good service; mobile phone distribution has risen rapidly, reaching a density of 80 per 100 people in 2008, compared to a steady 30 per 100 people for fixed telephone lines.

EDUCATION AND HEALTH

Twelve years of primary education are free of charge and compulsory. The Institute of Education is responsible for training primary and secondary school teachers and for curriculum development.
Literacy rate – 87.4 per cent (2007 est)
Gross enrolment ratio (percentage of relevant age group) – primary 99 per cent; secondary 88 per cent (2008 est); tertiary 16 per cent (2009 est)
Health expenditure (per capita) – US$247 (2007)
Hospital beds (per 1,000 people) – 3.3 (2003–8)

MEDIA

Freedom of expression is guaranteed by the constitution and a number of daily newspapers and weekly publications offer a range of political viewpoints. The state-owned Mauritius Broadcasting Corporation runs television and radio services funded through advertising and a licence fee. Private radio stations were introduced in 2002 and the government intends to open up television broadcasting to private operators; satellite television is already available.

MEXICO

Estados Unidos Mexicanos – United Mexican States

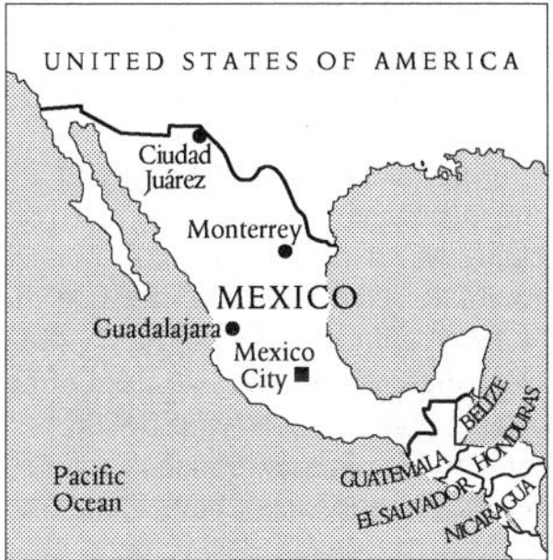

Area – 1,964,375 sq. km
Capital – Mexico City; population, 19,318,500 (2009 est)
Major cities – Ciudad Juárez, Guadalajara, León, Monterrey, Puebla, Tijuana
Currency – Peso of 100 centavos
Population – 111,211,789 rising at 1.13 per cent a year (2009 est)
Religion – Christian (Roman Catholic 88 per cent) (est)
Language – Spanish (official), 66 Mayan, Nahuatl and other regional languages
Population density – 55 per sq. km (2008)
Urban population – 77 per cent (2007 est)
Median age (years) – 26.3 (2009 est)
National anthem – 'Himno Nacional Mexicano' ['Mexican National Anthem']
National day – 16 September (Independence Day)
Life expectancy (years) – 76.06 (2009 est)
Mortality rate – 4.8 (2009 est)
Birth rate – 19.71 (2009 est)
Infant mortality rate – 18.42 (2009 est)
Death penalty – Abolished for all crimes (since 2005)
CPI score – 3.3 (2009)

CLIMATE AND TERRAIN

The Rio Grande forms the eastern part of the border with the USA. South of this, coastal plains rise to a central plateau which lies between two spines of high mountains, the Western and the Eastern Sierra Madre, running from the north-west to south-east. The mountains include volcanoes such as Popocatepetl, and in the south are covered with dense jungle. The Yucatán peninsula in the south-east is low-lying, and marshy on the coast. The narrow Baha California peninsula, separated from the rest of the country by the Gulf of California, has a range of hills running along it. Elevation extremes range from 5,700m (Volcan Pico de Orizaba) at the highest point to −10m (Laguna Salada) at the lowest. The north has a desert climate, while the south is tropical. Average temperatures in Mexico City range from lows of 6°C in January to highs of 26°C in May.

HISTORY AND POLITICS

Mexico was the centre of Mesoamerican civilisations for over 2,500 years: the Olmecs (*c.*1200–600 BC), based on the Mexican Gulf Coast; the Zapotecs (*c.*300 BC to 300 AD) in the Oaxaca valley; the Mayas (*c.*300–900 AD) in southern Mexico and the Yucatán peninsula; the Mixtecs (*c.*800–1300) in the Oaxaca valley; and the Toltecs (*c.*900–1170) in central Mexico and the Yucatán peninsula. The Aztecs, who came to the region in the 13th century, ruled until their civilisation fell to the Spanish under Hernán Cortés in 1519–21. As the viceroyalty of New Spain, Mexico remained under Spanish rule until the 19th century. In the first century of Spanish occupation, the indigenous population fell from around 21 million to one million, largely through lack of resistance to European diseases.

After an unsuccessful revolt in 1810 and a protracted struggle, independence was declared in 1821 and a federal republic was instituted in 1824. Mexico suffered extreme instability, civil war and invasion throughout much of the 19th century. War with the USA in 1836 and 1846–8 led to the loss of about one-third of its territory. There was civil war in 1858–61 and in 1862–7 war with Britain, France and Spain after Mexico suspended interest payments on its foreign debt. Porfirio Díaz ruled as a dictator between 1876 and 1911, until his repressive regime was overthrown in a revolution that introduced radical land and labour reforms, but instability continued.

The National Revolutionary Party, founded in 1929, came to dominate political life. Renamed the Institutional Revolutionary Party (PRI) in 1946, it formed a succession of authoritarian governments. Although unrest was not eliminated under its regime, the 1960s saw rapid industrialisation and the 1970s an oil-fuelled economic boom. Falling oil prices led to a serious financial crisis in 1982 and Mexico defaulted on its debt. Economic difficulties were eased in the 1990s with the introduction of reforms and free trade agreements.

These reforms led to a degree of social upheaval. Fearing for the status of the already marginalised indigenous peoples, the Zapatista National Liberation Front (EZLN) led revolts in the south of the country in 1994 and 1995. Although violence tailed off in the late 1990s, civil campaigning continued, culminating in a mass march on Mexico City in 2001 in support of a bill of indigenous rights. The bill was enacted later that year but the Zapatistas claimed its provisions had been watered down and vowed to continue their campaign.

The government also faces problems with corruption and violent crime, much of which is drug-related. Mexico is a major producer of illegal drugs as well as the main staging post for South American drugs trafficked into the USA; rivalry between drugs cartels, their resistance to the government's drug-eradication and anti-trafficking programmes, and the army's tactics in pursuit of these programmes have led to a marked rise in violence since 2006, with intimidation and corruption used to suborn law enforcement.

The PRI's political dominance ended at the 1997 election, when it lost its absolute majority in the lower house of the legislature, although it continued in government until 2000 and was again in power from 2003 until 2006. The 2006 presidential election was won by Felipe Calderón of the Partido Accion Nacional (PAN); his closest rival, Lopez Obrador, challenged the result, his supporters staging mass protests for several months. Calderón's victory was confirmed in September after recounts, although Obrador and his supporters refused to accept the result, alleging voting irregularities. In the 2006 legislative election, PAN became the largest party in both houses of Congress, but lost its majority in the lower chamber to the PRI in the 2009 legislative elections.

POLITICAL SYSTEM

Under the 1917 constitution, the federal republic consists of 31 states and the federal capital. The head of state is an executive president, directly elected for a single six-year term. The bicameral legislature is the Congress of the Union: the lower house, the Chamber of Deputies, has 500 members, directly elected for a three-year term, and the senate has 128 members, directly elected for a six-year term. The president appoints the cabinet.

Each of the states has its own constitution and is administered by a governor, elected for a six-year term, and a state chamber of deputies, elected for a three-year term.

HEAD OF STATE

President, Felipe Calderón, *elected* 2 July 2006, *sworn in* 1 December 2006

SELECTED GOVERNMENT MEMBERS *as at July 2010*

Defence, Gen. Guillermo Galván
Economy, Bruno Ferrari Garcia de Alba

Foreign Affairs, Patricia Espinosa Cantellano
Interior, Francisco Blake Mora

EMBASSY OF MEXICO
16 St George Street, London W1S 1FD
T 020-7499 8586 E embgbretana@sre.gob.mx
W http://portal.sre.gob.mx/reinounidoeng
Ambassador Extraordinary and Plenipotentiary,
HE Eduardo Medina-Mora Icaza, *apptd* 2010

BRITISH EMBASSY
Río Lerma 71, Col. Cuauhtémoc, 06500 Mexico City
T (+52) (55) 5242 8500 E ukinmexico@att.net.mx
W http://ukinmexico.fco.gov.uk
Ambassador Extraordinary and Plenipotentiary,
HE Judith Macgregor, LVO, *apptd* 2009

BRITISH COUNCIL
Lope de Vega 316, Col. Chapultepec Morales,
11570 Mexico City
T (+52) (55) 5263 1900 W www.britishcouncil.org/mexico
Director, Chris Rawlings

DEFENCE

The army has 709 armoured personnel carriers. The navy has 6 frigates, 189 patrol and coastal vessels, and 7 combat aircraft. There are 18 naval bases. The air force has 78 combat aircraft and 162 helicopters.
Military budget – US$4,410m (2009)
Military personnel – 267,506: army 200,000, navy 55,961, air force 11,545, marines 19,328; paramilitary 36,500

ECONOMY AND TRADE

Mexico had a relatively closed economy until the mid-1980s but increased trade and domestic liberalisation in the 1990s stimulated economic growth and development, particularly in the industrial sector. However, although it has free trade agreements with over 50 countries, covering 90 per cent of its trade, its economy is still closely tied to that of the USA and went into a deep recession in 2009 as the global downturn affected its main export market. Despite recent growth and its oil, natural gas and mineral resources, Mexico remains a poor country; over 12 million Mexicans work overseas, predominantly in the USA, and much of the remaining population, especially in poor and rural areas, is dependent on their remittances, which are a major source of foreign exchange revenue. President Calderón has prioritised job creation and poverty reduction measures, which have had opposition support.

Agriculture is diverse and productive; major crops include maize, wheat, soya beans, rice, beans, cotton, coffee, fruit, tomatoes, beef, poultry and dairy products. Agriculture accounts for 4.3 per cent of GDP and 13.7 per cent of employment. The main industries include production of food, beverages, tobacco, chemicals, iron and steel, textiles, clothing, motor vehicles, consumer durables, oil production, mining and tourism. Tourism is now the fourth largest revenue earner, but was hard hit in 2009 by the 'swine flu' outbreak. The services sector accounts for 62.8 per cent of GDP and industry for 32.9 per cent.

The main trading partner is the USA (80.5 per cent of exports; 48 per cent of imports). Canada is the other main export market, and China the other main source of imports. Principal exports include manufactured goods, oil and oil products, silver, fruit, vegetables, coffee and cotton. The main imports include metal-working machines, steel mill products, agricultural machinery, electrical equipment, car parts for assembly, vehicle repair parts, aircraft and aircraft parts.
GNI – US$1,062,400m; US$9,900 per capita (2008)
Annual average growth of GDP – –7.1 per cent (2009 est)
Inflation rate – 5.3 per cent (2009 est)
Population below poverty line – 13.8 per cent (2006)
Unemployment – 6.2 per cent (2009 est)
Total external debt – US$177,000m (2009)
Imports – US$352,200m (2008)
Exports – US$291,800m (2008)

BALANCE OF PAYMENTS
Trade – US$4,680m deficit (2009)
Current Account – US$5,238m deficit (2009)

Trade with UK	*2008*	*2009*
Imports from UK	£849,873,807	£720,656,134
Exports to UK	£735,743,350	£1,096,027,463

COMMUNICATIONS

Veracruz, Tampico and Coatzacoalcos are the chief seaports on the east coast, and Guaymas, Mazatlán, Lázaro Cárdenas and Salina Cruz on the Pacific. There are 17,500km of railways; the rail network is currently undergoing reorganisation. There are 366,100km of roads, of which 132,300km are surfaced, and 2,900km of navigable rivers and coastal canals. The main international airport is at Mexico City, with 20 others around the country.

The fixed-line telephone network is limited in scope, with a density of less than 20 per 100 people, and mobile phone distribution has grown rapidly, reaching 70 per 100 people in 2008. In 2008 there were 23 million internet users.

EDUCATION AND HEALTH

Although Mexico allows for at least nine years of free education (longer and compulsory, to various degrees, in some states), on average adults have only completed 7.2 years. The country's largest university is the National Autonomous University of Mexico, situated in Mexico City.
Literacy rate – 92.8 per cent (2007 est)
Gross enrolment ratio (percentage of relevant age group) – primary 113 per cent; secondary 87 per cent; tertiary 26 per cent (2008 est)
Health expenditure (per capita) – US$564 (2007)
Hospital beds (per 1,000 people) – 1.7 (2003–8)

MEDIA

The Televisa group used to dominate Mexican broadcasting but now competes with other television channels and a huge number of independent radio stations operating in a competitive sector. Some northern radio stations broadcast to Mexicans working in the USA. There are six national daily newspapers, representing a variety of political opinions. The murder, kidnap and intimidation of journalists has risen markedly since the government's offensive against drug cartels began in 2006; at least 11 journalists were murdered in 2009.

CULTURE

The dominant figures in Mexican art are husband and wife Diego Rivera (1886–1957) and Frida Kahlo (1907–1954). In literature, essayist and poet Octavio Paz (1914–98) won the Nobel prize in 1990, while Carlos Fuentes (*b.* 1928) is a respected political commentator and novelist.

As in other Latin American countries, football has a huge following, and the country has hosted the World Cup twice, in 1970 and 1986. Bullfighting is also very popular and Mexico City is home to the largest ring in the world, seating 55,000.

FEDERATED STATES OF MICRONESIA

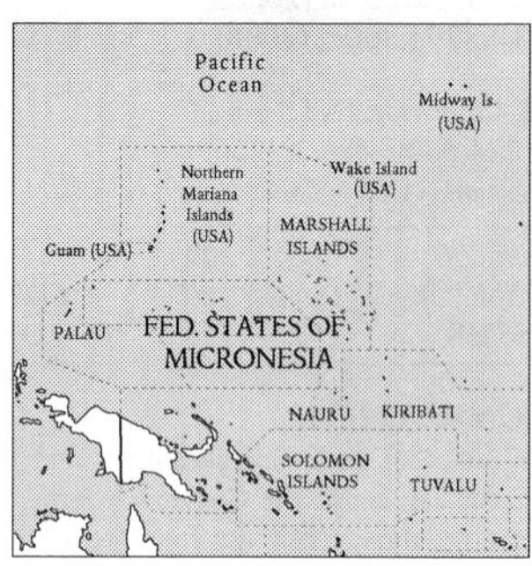

Area – 702 sq. km
Capital – Palikir, on Pohnpei; population, 6,941 (2009 est)
Major town – Weno
Currency – US dollar (US$) of 100 cents
Population – 107,434 falling at 0.24 per cent a year (2009 est); Chuukese (48.8 per cent), Pohnpeian (24.2 per cent), Kosraean (6.2 per cent), Yapese (5.2 per cent), Yap outer islands (4.5 per cent), Polynesian (1.5 per cent)
Religion – predominantly Christian, divided about equally between Roman Catholics and Protestant denominations, of which the United Church of Christ is the largest; proportions vary greatly between the states
Language – English (official), Chuukese, Kosrean, Pohnpeian, Yapese, Ulithian, Woleaian, Nukuoro, Kapingamarangi
Population density – 159 per sq. km (2007)
Urban population – 22 per cent (2007 est)
Median age (years) – 22 (2009 est)
National anthem – 'Patriots of Micronesia'
National day – 10 May (Constitution Day)
Life expectancy (years) – 70.94 (2009 est)
Mortality rate – 4.46 (2009 est)
Birth rate – 23.1 (2009 est)
Infant mortality rate – 26.1 (2009 est)
Death penalty – Abolished for all crimes (since 1986)

CLIMATE AND TERRAIN

The republic consists of four major island groups totalling over 600 mountainous volcanic islands and low-lying coral atolls, extending over 2,900 sq. km of the western Pacific Ocean. Elevation extremes range from 791m (Totolom) at the highest point to 0m (Pacific Ocean) at the lowest. The climate is tropical, with only slight seasonal variations in temperatures. The islands are vulnerable to the effects of global warming, particularly an increase in the frequency and intensity of storms in the region.

HISTORY AND POLITICS

Inhabited since around 4,000 BC by migrants from the Philippines and Indonesia, Micronesia experienced contact with Europeans from the 1520s, and the islands were colonised by Spain from the 16th century. German encroachment in the 1870s and 1880s was resisted until 1899, when Germany purchased the islands from Spain. The islands were occupied by Japan on behalf of the Allies during the First World War, and administered as a League of Nations mandated territory by Japan from 1920 until the Japanese defeat in the Second World War. In 1947 the islands became part of the UN Trust Territory of the Pacific, administered by the USA.

A constitution was adopted in 1979 and the islands became independent in 1986 under a compact of free association with the USA, by which the USA retains responsibility for defence and provides substantial financial aid; a renegotiated agreement was signed in 2003. The UN trusteeship was formally terminated in 1990.

Emmanuel ('Manny') Mori was elected president in 2007. The most recent legislative election took place in March 2009.

POLITICAL SYSTEM

The 1979 constitution established a federal republic of four states: Chuuk, Kosrae, Pohnpei and Yap. The federal head of state is an executive president, who is elected by the federal legislature for a four-year term. The unicameral congress has 14 members, ten senators directly elected for a two-year term and four senators 'at large' (one from each state) elected for a four-year term; the president and vice-president must be selected from among the 'at large' senators. The federal cabinet is appointed by the president and approved by the congress. There are no formal political parties.

Each state has its own constitution, legislature and government.

HEAD OF STATE

President, Emmanuel Mori, *elected* 11 May 2007
Vice-President, Alik L. Alik

SELECTED GOVERNMENT MEMBERS *as at June 2009*

Finance, Finley S. Perman
Foreign Affairs, Lorin S. Robert
Health, Vita Akapito Skilling

BRITISH AMBASSADOR

HE Peter Beckingham, *apptd* 2005, resident at Manila, the Philippines

ECONOMY AND TRADE

Micronesia has few natural resources apart from phosphate, which is not exploited, and is highly dependent on aid from the USA, which constitutes over a quarter of GDP. The main economic activities are subsistence farming and fishing, which account for nearly 30 per cent of GDP, but both are threatened by climate change and over-fishing. The islands' remoteness and lack of facilities has constrained the development of tourism, the main industry; other industries include construction, fish processing, specialised aquaculture and handicrafts. Two-thirds of the workforce is employed by the government. The main trading partners are the USA and Japan. Principal exports are fish, garments, bananas and black pepper. The main imports are food, manufactured goods and machinery.

GNI – US$274m; US$2,470 per capita (2007)
Annual average growth of GDP – 0.3 per cent (2005 est)
Inflation rate – 2.2 per cent (2005)

Unemployment – 22 per cent (2000 est)
Total external debt – US$60.8m (2005 est)

Trade with UK	*2008*	*2009*
Imports from UK	£21,638	£38,903
Exports to UK	£19,262	£509,065

COMMUNICATIONS

Most transport is by air or sea. There are six airports and airfields, with major airports on the four main islands, and the main seaports are Colonia (Yap), Kolonia (Pohnpei), Lele and Moen. There are 240km of roads. The islands are all connected to the telephone system. Fixed-line use has declined as mobile phone subscriptions have increased.

MEDIA

There are no daily newspapers; the federal government produces a fortnightly information bulletin and state governments produce weekly news publications. State governments and one of the churches operate radio and television stations, except in Kosrae, which does not have a television station.

MOLDOVA

Republica Moldova – Republic of Moldova

Area – 33,851 sq. km
Capital – Chisinau; population, 650,043 (2009 est)
Major towns – Balti, Tighina, Tiraspol
Currency – Moldovan leu (plural lei) of 100 bani
Population – 4,320,748 falling at 0.08 per cent a year (2009 est): Moldovan/Romanian (78.2 per cent), Ukrainian (8.4 per cent), Russian (5.8 per cent), Gagauz (4.4 per cent); Bulgarian (1.9 per cent)
Religion – Christian (Orthodox denominations 90 per cent: predominantly Moldovan Orthodox; minority Bessarabian Church) (est)
Language – Moldovan (official; linguistically identical to Romanian), Russian, Gagauz
Population density – 110 per sq. km (2008)
Urban population – 42 per cent (2007 est)
Median age (years) – 34.6 (2009 est)
National anthem – 'Limba Noastra' ['Our Language']
National day – 27 August (Independence Day)
Life expectancy (years) – 70.8 (2009 est)
Mortality rate – 10.78 (2009 est)
Birth rate – 11.12 (2009 est)
Infant mortality rate – 13.13 (2009 est)
Death penalty – Abolished for all crimes (since 1995)
CPI score – 3.3 (2009)

CLIMATE AND TERRAIN

A landlocked country to the north-west of the Black Sea, Moldova consists of rolling steppe lying mostly between the Prut and Dniester rivers. Elevation extremes range from 430m (Dealul Bulanesti) at the highest point to 2m (river Dniester) at the lowest. The climate is continental, and average temperatures in Chisinau range from lows of −8°C in January to highs of 27°C in July.

HISTORY AND POLITICS

Part of the Roman province of Dacia from AD 106, the area, subsequently known as Bessarabia, experienced centuries of invasion and occupation after the fall of the Roman Empire. Part of a larger independent Moldovan kingdom from the mid-14th century, between the 16th and early 19th century possession of the territory was disputed between various countries, but mainly the Ottoman and Russian empires. Bessarabia was granted to Russia in 1812.

After the Russian revolution in 1917, Bessarabia declared independence and then became a province of Romania in 1918. Romania was forced to return Bessarabia to the USSR in 1940 and it was incorporated with a small strip of land on the east bank of the river Dniester as the Moldavian Soviet Socialist Republic. This was retaken by Romania in 1941 but recaptured by Soviet forces in 1944.

Moldovan nationalism grew in the late 1980s and the parliament asserted its political and economic sovereignty in 1990, declaring independence and joining the Commonwealth of Independent States in 1991 after the collapse of the USSR. A referendum in 1994 endorsed independence rather than unification with Romania or Russia.

The governments in the first decade after independence were made up of moderate reformists, but their ineffectiveness led to a resurgence in support for the Communist Party of Moldova (PCM), which won the majority of seats in the 1998, 2001, 2005 and 2009 legislative elections. Its victory in April 2009 was greeted with violent opposition protests at alleged vote-rigging, but a recount confirmed the result. However, two attempts to elect a president failed because of an opposition boycott, forcing a second legislative election in July 2009. In the second poll the PCM's seats fell from 60 to 48, and four pro-Western parties formed a coalition government, but with only 53 seats it lacked a large enough majority to elect its presidential candidate in the face of PCM opposition. Failure to elect a president led the constitutional court in March 2010 to call another election for July 2010. However in July 2010 the legislature approved a government proposal for a referendum, to be held in September 2010, on whether future presidents should be popularly elected; presidential and legislative elections were tentatively scheduled to follow in November 2010.

SECESSION

Moldovan nationalism in the late 1980s and possible reunification with Romania alarmed the republic's Russian and Ukrainian ethnic minorities in the Transdniestria region (east of the Dniester) and the Gagauz (Turkish-speaking Christians) in the south-west. Both areas declared independence unilaterally in 1990, though this was not recognised. Both regions were granted a special status by the 1994 constitution, and the Gagauz have since exercised a degree of autonomy over their political, economic and cultural affairs.

A stalemate has developed over the status of Transdniestria. Fighting between separatists and government forces in 1991 was followed by a ceasefire in 1992, maintained by Russian peacekeeping troops. Despite talks sponsored by the OSCE, EU, Russia and Ukraine since the late 1990s, no political settlement has been reached, and Russia and the Transdniestrian authorities have failed to comply with agreements to withdraw Russian troops, arms and ammunition. The area has adopted symbols of nationhood but isolation because of its unresolved status has weakened its economy and internal security.

POLITICAL SYSTEM
The 1997 constitution was amended in 2000 to increase the powers of the legislature and the executive. The head of state is a president who (since 2000) is elected by the legislature by a three-fifths majority (61 votes) for a four-year term, renewable only once. The unicameral legislature, the *Parlamentul*, has 101 members, who are directly elected for a four-year term. The prime minister and government are nominated by the president.

HEAD OF STATE
Interim President, Mihai Ghimpu

SELECTED GOVERNMENT MEMBERS *as at July 2010*
Prime Minister, Vlad Filat
Deputy Prime Ministers, Iurie Leanca *(External Affairs)*; Valeriu Lazar *(Economy)*; Victor Osipov; Ion Negrei
Defence, Vitalie Marinuta
Finance, Veaceslav Negruta
Internal Affairs, Police Maj.-Gen. (retd) Victor Catan

EMBASSY OF THE REPUBLIC OF MOLDOVA
5 Dolphin Square, Edensor Road, London W4 2ST
T 020-8995 6818 **E** embassy.london@mfa.md
W www.britania.mfa.gov.md
Ambassador Extraordinary and Plenipotentiary, HE Natalia Solcan, *apptd* 2008

BRITISH EMBASSY
18 Nicolae Iorga Str., Chisinau MD-2012
T (+373) 222 225902 **E** enquiries.chisinau@fco.gov.uk
W http://ukinmoldova.fco.gov.uk
Ambassador Extraordinary and Plenipotentiary, HE Keith Shannon, *apptd* 2009

DEFENCE
The army has 44 armoured infantry fighting vehicles and 164 armoured personnel carriers.
Military budget – US$22m (2009)
Military personnel – 5,998: army 5,148, air force 850; paramilitary 2,379
Conscription duration – 12 months

ECONOMY AND TRADE
Moldova is one of the poorest countries in Europe, despite moves towards a market economy since independence. With few natural resources and most industry lying in the breakaway Transdniestria region, the economy is dependent on agriculture and remittances from expatriate workers. An estimated 25 per cent of the workforce was employed abroad but many have returned due to the global downturn; the reduction in remittances and rise in unemployment have increased Moldova's economic difficulties, and it required IMF support in 2009 and 2010.

The agricultural sector accounts for 16 per cent of GDP. Principal crops include vegetables, fruit, wine, grain, sugar beet, sunflower seed, tobacco, beef and milk. Major industrial activities include food processing and production of sugar, vegetable oil, agricultural machinery, foundry equipment, domestic appliances and textiles. Industry accounts for 19.9 per cent of GDP and services for 64.1 per cent.

The main trading partners are Morocco, Russia, Romania, Ukraine, Italy and Germany. Principal exports are foodstuffs, textiles and machinery. The main imports are fuel and energy, machinery and equipment, chemicals and textiles.
GNI – US$5,300m; US$1,500 per capita (2008)
Annual average growth of GDP – –6.6 per cent (2009 est)
Inflation rate – 0 per cent (2009 est)
Population below poverty line – 29.5 per cent (2005)
Unemployment – 2.6 per cent (2009 est)
Total external debt – US$3,970m (2009)
Imports – US$4,100m (2008)
Exports – US$1,300m (2008)

BALANCE OF PAYMENTS
Trade – US$2,146m deficit (2009)
Current Account – US$987m deficit (2008)

Trade with UK	*2008*	*2009*
Imports from UK	£21,093,124	£29,738,710
Exports to UK	£18,458,028	£28,232,116

COMMUNICATIONS
Moldova has 12,700km of roads and 1,140km of railways. There are 11 airports and airstrips; the principal airport is at Chisinau. There are 424km of navigable waterways on the Prut and Dniester rivers, and access to the Black Sea via the river Danube has been agreed with Ukraine.

The telephone system is antiquated and service is poor outside the capital, although some modernisation is under way. In 2008 there were 1.1 million fixed telephone lines in use, 2.4 million mobile phone subscribers and 850,000 internet users.

EDUCATION AND HEALTH
Literacy rate – 99.2 per cent (2007 est)
Gross enrolment ratio (percentage of relevant age group) – primary 89 per cent; secondary 83 per cent; tertiary 40 per cent (2008 est)
Health expenditure (per capita) – US$127 (2007)
Hospital beds (per 1,000 people) – 6.1 (2003–8)

MEDIA
Freedom of media expression is guaranteed by the constitution, but laws exist prohibiting defamation or insulting the state. There are four main newspapers, and Moldovan editions of Russian papers are also popular. State-run television and radio stations compete with a small number of commercial channels. The breakaway Transdniestria region operates its own television and radio stations.

MONACO

Principaute de Monaco – Principality of Monaco

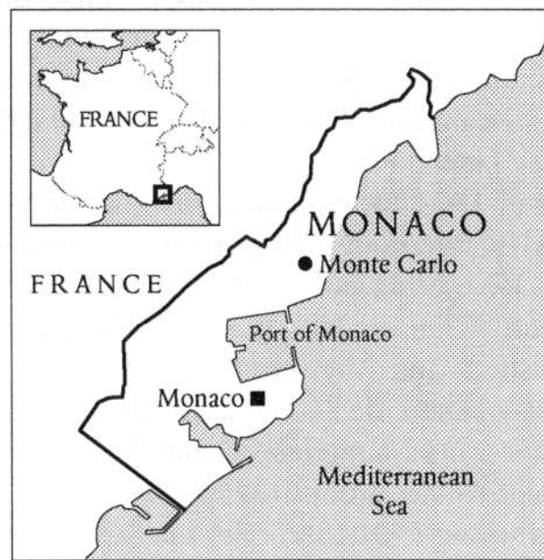

Area – 2 sq. km
Capital – Monaco
Major town – Monte Carlo
Currency – Euro (€) of 100 cents
Population – 32,965 rising at 0.39 per cent a year (2009 est); French (47 per cent), Monegasque (16 per cent), Italian (16 per cent) (est)
Religion – Christian (predominantly Roman Catholic)
Language – French (official), English, Italian, Monegasque
Population density – 16,358 per sq. km (2008)
Urban population – 100 per cent (2007 est)
Median age (years) – 45.7 (2009 est)
National anthem – 'Hymne Monégasque' ['Hymn of Monaco']
National day – 19 November (St Rainier's Day)
Life expectancy (years) – 80.09 (2009 est)
Mortality rate – 12.74 (2009 est)
Birth rate – 9.1 (2009 est)
Infant mortality rate – 5 (2009 est)
Death penalty – Abolished for all crimes (since 1962)

CLIMATE AND TERRAIN

Monaco lies on 2.5 miles of steep, rugged Mediterranean coastline. It has been expanded by 0.3 sq. km with land reclaimed from the sea by infilling. Elevation extremes range from 140m (Mt Agel) at the highest point to 0m (Mediterranean Sea) at the lowest. The climate is Mediterranean, with average temperatures ranging from lows of 8°C in January to highs of 26°C in July.

HISTORY AND POLITICS

Monaco has been ruled by the Grimaldi family since the 13th century. Monarchical France recognised Monaco's independence in the 15th century, but Revolutionary France annexed it in 1793. Although the prince was restored to power in 1814, Monaco did not regain its independence until 1861. It was occupied by the Italians and subsequently by the Germans in the Second World War. The principality's foreign relations and security have been aligned to those of France since 1861 by various treaties; the terms were changed in 2005 to allow Monaco greater control over its foreign relations and internal administration.

The 1962 constitution was amended in 2002 to allow the throne to pass in the female line in the absence of male heirs. Legislative power is held jointly by the prince and a 24-member national council, which is directly elected for a five-year term. Executive power is exercised by the prince and a six-member Council of Government, headed by a minister of state who is nominated by the prince from a list of three French diplomats submitted by the French government. The judicial code is based on that of France.

In the 2008 legislative election, the Union for Monaco (UPM) retained its 21 seats, an overwhelming majority, in the legislature. Jean-Paul Proust resigned as Minister of State in March 2010 and was replaced by Michel Roger.

HEAD OF STATE
HSH The Prince of Monaco, Prince Albert II (Alexandre Louis Pierre), *born* 14 March 1958, *succeeded* 6 April 2005
Heir, HSH Princess Caroline von Hannover, *born* 23 January 1957

SELECTED GOVERNMENT MEMBERS *as at July 2010*
Minister of State, Michel Roger
Finance and Economy, Sophie Thevenoux
Interior, Paul Masseron
Foreign Affairs, Franck Biancheri

EMBASSY OF THE PRINCIPALITY OF MONACO
7 Upper Grosvenor Street, London W1K 2LX
T 020-7318 1083 E embassy.uk@gouv.mc
W www.monaco-embassy-uk.gouv.mc
Ambassador Extraordinary and Plenipotentiary, Evelyne Genta, *apptd* 2010

BRITISH CONSULATE-GENERAL
PO Box 265, 33 Boulevard Princesse Charlotte, 98005 Monaco
T (+377) 9350 9954
Hon. Consul-General, Sir Peter Westmacott, resident in Marseille, France

ECONOMY AND TRADE

The economy has diversified away from its historic dependence on tourism and gambling, and over half its revenue now comes from financial services, real estate and light industry. A large floating jetty, installed in 2002, has extended the harbour facilities, doubling the port's capacity to handle cruise ships. As the state collects no taxes from individuals and little from businesses, it has become a tax haven for the wealthy, and non-Monegasques make up about 84 per cent of the population. The state retains monopolies in a number of sectors, including tobacco, the telephone network and the postal service. It is in a customs union with France, through which it participates in the EU market. Over half its trade is with EU countries, particularly Italy.
Unemployment – 0 per cent (2005 est)

MEDIA

Radio Monte-Carlo started broadcasting to France in the 1960s and Italy in the 1970s. Monaco has one television station, and hosts the international Monte Carlo Television Festival each year. Monaco has no daily newspapers, but the principality's news is covered by the French press.

MONGOLIA

Mongol Uls – Mongolia

Area – 1,564,116 sq. km
Capital – Ulaanbaatar; population, 948,719 (2009 est)
Major towns – Darhan, Erdenet
Currency – Tugrik of 100 mongo
Population – 3,041,142 rising at 1.49 per cent a year (2009 est); Mongol (94.9 per cent), Turkic (5 per cent) (est)
Religion – Buddhist 90 per cent (predominantly Tibetan school of Mahayana), Muslim 5 per cent, Christian 4 per cent (mostly Protestant) (est)
Language – Khalkha Mongol (official), Turkic, Russian
Population density – 2 per sq. km (2008)
Urban population – 57 per cent (2007 est)
Median age (years) – 25.3 (2009 est)
National anthem – 'Mongol ulsiin toriin duulal' ['National Anthem of Mongolia']
National day – 11 July (Revolution Day)
Life expectancy (years) – 67.65 (2009 est)
Mortality rate – 6.12 (2009 est)
Birth rate – 21.05 (2009 est)
Infant mortality rate – 39.88 (2009 est)
Death penalty – Retained
CPI score – 2.7 (2009)
Literacy rate – 97.3 per cent (2007 est)
Gross enrolment ratio (percentage of relevant age group) – primary 102 per cent; secondary 95 per cent; tertiary 50 per cent (2008 est)
Health expenditure (per capita) – US$64 (2007)
Hospital beds (per 1,000 people) – 6.1 (2003–8)

CLIMATE AND TERRAIN

The eastern part of landlocked Mongolia lies on a semi-desert plateau, with steppes rising to the Mongolian Altai and Hangai mountain ranges in the west. The Gobi desert covers the southern third of the country. Elevation extremes range from 4,374m (Nayramadlin Orgil) at the highest point to 518m (Hoh Nuur) at the lowest. The country has long, cold Siberian winters, which quickly turn into short and warm summers. The wet season runs from June to September. Average temperatures in Ulaanbaatar range from lows of −32°C in January to highs of 22°C in July.

HISTORY AND POLITICS

The nomadic tribes of Mongolia, mostly Turks and Uygurs, were united in the early 13th century by Genghis Khan, forming the nucleus of a Mongol Empire that reached its zenith under Kublai Khan, Genghis' grandson, when it stretched from Hungary to China and as far south as Vietnam. After Kublai's death in 1294, the empire declined. Many of the khanates formed under Genghis survived as increasingly independent petty kingdoms, but Mongolia itself was conquered by China in the late 17th century and became the provinces of Inner and Outer Mongolia.

When imperial rule in China collapsed in 1911, Outer Mongolia declared itself an independent monarchy under a Buddhist lama king. Chinese rule was reasserted in 1915, but in 1921 Mongolian revolutionaries, supported by the Soviets, overthrew Chinese rule and the Mongolian People's Revolutionary Party (MPRP) formed a government. When the king died in 1924, the monarchy was abolished and the ensuing republic introduced communist-inspired defeudalisation and collectivisation programmes and suppressed Buddhism. With the assistance of Soviet troops, Mongolia resisted Japanese attacks in the late 1930s and after the Second World War, Mongolia seemed likely to remain under Soviet control, but in a 1946 UN plebiscite the people voted for independence.

Mongolia became more open to external contacts from the mid-1980s and, influenced by events in eastern Europe, a popular campaign for political and economic reform led to the first multi-party elections in 1990 and a massive privatisation programme, which began in 1991. The MPRP, which had eschewed communism, continued to dominate political life until 1996, when an alliance of nationalists and social democrats was elected to power. The alliance became the subject of corruption scandals and its transition to a market economy caused widespread social disruption and poverty. The MPRP returned to power in the 2001 election, having already regained the presidency in 1997, but lost nearly half of its seats in the legislature in the 2004 election.

In the 2008 legislative election the MPRP won 44 seats and the Democratic Party (DP) 27 seats; the showing of smaller parties was poorer than expected, leading to allegations of electoral fraud that provoked protests so violent that a four-day state of emergency was declared. The MPRP formed a coalition government with the DP, and Sanjaa Bayar continued as prime minister. The 2009 presidential election was won by the DP candidate, Tsakhiagiin Elbegdorj, prime minister in 1998 and 2006–8. Sanjaa Bayar resigned as prime minister in October 2009 and was replaced by Sukhgaatar Batbold.

POLITICAL SYSTEM

The 1992 constitution was amended in 2000 to give the president the right to dissolve the legislature if it is unable to reach agreement on appointing a prime minister. The president is directly elected for a four-year term, which is renewable. The unicameral State Great Hural has 76 members who are directly elected for a four-year term. The prime minister is elected by the legislature and appoints the cabinet.

HEAD OF STATE

President, Tsakhiagiin Elbegdorj, *elected* 24 May 2009, *sworn in* 18 June 2009

SELECTED GOVERNMENT MEMBERS *as at June 2010*

Prime Minister, Sukhbaatar Batbold
First Deputy Prime Minister, Norovyn Altanhuyag
Defence, Luvsanvandan Bold
Finance, Sangajabyn Bayartsogt
Foreign Affairs, Gombojav Zandanshatar
Justice and Internal Affairs, Tsendiyn Nyamdorj

EMBASSY OF MONGOLIA
7–8 Kensington Court, London W8 5DL
T 020-7937 0150 E office@embassyofmongolia.co.uk
W www.embassyofmongolia.co.uk
Ambassador Extraordinary and Plenipotentiary, HE Bulgaa Altangerel, *apptd* 2008

BRITISH EMBASSY
PO Box 703, 30 Enkh Taivny Urgun Chuluu, Bayanzurkh District, Ulaanbaatar 13381
T (+976) (11) 458 133 E britemb@mongol.net
W http://ukinmongolia.fco.gov.uk
Ambassador Extraordinary and Plenipotentiary, HE William Dickson, *apptd* 2009

DEFENCE

The army has 370 main battle tanks, 150 armoured personnel carriers and 310 armoured infantry fighting vehicles. The air force has 9 aircraft and 11 armed helicopters.
Military budget – US$51m (2008 est)
Military personnel – 10,000: army 8,900, air force 800, construction troops 300; paramilitaries 7,200
Conscription duration – 12 months

ECONOMY AND TRADE

The economy suffered during the transition to a market economy but recovered to show strong growth in recent years. This had faltered before the global downturn began; in 2008 declining commodity prices and export demand and soaring inflation caused difficulties that forced the government to seek an IMF loan in spring 2009. Mongolia has attracted foreign investment, particularly in mining, agricultural processing and infrastructure, but administrative corruption, dependency on imported energy supplies (mostly from Russia) and the vulnerability of the agrarian sector to climate extremes continue to hinder growth. Over a third of the population lives below the poverty line.

Deposits of copper, coal, molybdenum, fluorspar, tin, tungsten, gold and oil are being exploited; copper and gold sales are major drivers of recent economic growth. The agrarian sector, which makes up 21.2 per cent of GDP, engages 34 per cent of the workforce in agriculture and herding. The main products are grains, vegetables, forage crops, sheep, goats and other livestock. The main industries are construction, mining, processing animal products and the production of oil, food and beverages, cashmere and natural yarns.

The main export market is China (64 per cent); the main import providers are Russia (38 per cent) and China (28 per cent). Principal exports are copper, clothing, livestock, animal products, cashmere, wool, hides, metals and coal. The main imports are machinery and equipment, fuels, cars, foodstuffs, industrial consumer goods, chemicals and construction materials.
GNI – US$4,400m; US$1,670 per capita (2008)
Annual average growth of GDP – 9 per cent (2009)
Inflation rate – 28 per cent (2008 est)
Population below poverty line – 36.1 per cent (2004)
Unemployment – 2.8 per cent (2008)
Total external debt – US$1,600m (2008)
Imports – US$3,600m (2008)
Exports – US$2,500m (2008)

BALANCE OF PAYMENTS
Trade – US$273m deficit (2009)
Current Account – US$722m deficit (2008)

Trade with UK	*2008*	*2009*
Imports from UK	£5,685,617	£4,166,984
Exports to UK	£3,262,095	£16,834,135

COMMUNICATIONS

Mongolia has 1,810km of railways and 49,250km of roads, though only about 4 per cent of the roads are surfaced. The main airport is at Ulaanbaatar, although there are over 40 other airports and airfields around the country. The lakes and main rivers are navigable in the summer months but ice-bound in winter. International trade is via Russia and China.

The telephone system is improving but fixed-line density is very low. In 2008 there were 165,000 fixed telephone lines in use, 1.8 million mobile phone subscribers and 330,000 internet users.

MEDIA

There are five daily newspapers, including *Onoodor,* which has the biggest circulation, and *Unen,* the organ of the Mongolian People's Revolutionary Party and the country's oldest newspaper. In 2005 the state-run radio and television service was transformed into a public-service broadcaster, and now competes with a number of private operators. Radio is a key medium because of the nomadic life of some of the population.

MONTENEGRO

Crna Gora – Montenegro

Area – 13,812 sq. km
Capital – Podgorica; population, 143,853 (2009 est)
Major cities – Cetinje (historic and cultural capital), Niksic
Currency – Euro (€) of 100 cents
Population – 672,180 falling at 0.85 per cent a year (2009 est); Montenegrin (43 per cent), Serbian (32 per cent), Bosniak (8 per cent), Albanian (5 per cent)
Religion – Christian (Orthodox denominations 74 per cent, Roman Catholic 4 per cent), Muslim 18 per cent (est)
Language – Montenegrin (based on a Serbo-Croatian dialect) (official), Serbian, Bosnian, Albanian, Croatian
Population density – 46 per sq. km (2008)
Urban population – 61 per cent (2007 est)
Median age (years) – 36.7 (2009 est)
National anthem – 'Oj, Svijetla Majska Zoro' ['O, Bright Dawn of May']
National day – 13 July
Life expectancy (years) – 74.73 (2005 est)
Mortality rate – 8.63 (2009 est)
Birth rate – 11.14 (2009 est)
Infant mortality rate – 12.89 (2005 est)

Death penalty – Abolished for all crimes (since 2002)
CPI score – 3.9 (2009)
Literacy rate – 96.4 per cent (2007 est)
Gross enrolment ratio (percentage of relevant age group) – primary 99 per cent; secondary 89 per cent; tertiary 36 per cent (2002)

CLIMATE AND TERRAIN

The terrain is mountainous in the north and centre of the country, intersected by deep canyons and river valleys, and falls to a narrow plain on the highly indented Adriatic coast. About half of the country is densely forested. Elevation extremes range from 2,522m (Bobotov Kuk) at the highest point to 0m (Adriatic Sea) at the lowest. The main rivers are the Piva (Drina), the Tara and the Lim. Lake Skadarsko straddles the border with Albania. The climate is Mediterranean on the coast, but more continental inland. Average temperatures in Podgorica range from lows of 2°C in January to highs of 33°C in July.

HISTORY AND POLITICS

The area was part of the Roman province of Illyria, and then was settled by Slavs in the seventh century. In the late 12th century it was incorporated into the medieval kingdom of Serbia and so became part of the Ottoman Empire after Serbia's defeat by the Turks in 1389. When Serbia became independent in 1878, Montenegro followed and remained an independent monarchy until the end of the First World War. In 1918, Montenegro joined with Serbia and the former Austro-Hungarian provinces of Slovenia, Croatia and Bosnia-Hercegovina to form the Kingdom of Serbs, Croats and Slovenes, which was renamed Yugoslavia in 1929. Yugoslavia was occupied by Axis forces in 1941 and after liberation it reformed as a communist federal republic under the presidency of partisan leader Josip Tito in 1945. When the federation disintegrated in 1991, Serbia and Montenegro formed the Federal Republic of Yugoslavia, declared on 27 April 1992.

Montenegro's desire for independence led in 2002 to an EU-brokered agreement between the leaders of Serbia, Montenegro and the Federal Republic of Yugoslavia that restructured the republic into a union of two semi-independent states, named Serbia and Montenegro, with effect from March 2003. The agreement provided for the two republics to hold referendums on whether to retain or end the union after a minimum of three years. In a referendum held in Montenegro on 21 May 2006, 55.5 per cent voted in favour of independence, which was declared on 3 June and acknowledged by the Serbian legislature on 5 June. Montenegro joined the UN on 26 June 2006, and formally applied for EU membership in 2008.

In the 2008 presidential election, President Vujanovic was returned for a second term. In the 2009 legislative election, the Coalition for a European Montenegro again won the most seats, and Milo Djukanovic's three-party coalition government continued in office.

POLITICAL SYSTEM

Under the 2007 constitution, the president is directly elected for a five-year term, which is renewable. The unicameral Assembly of the Republic of Montenegro has 81 members directly elected for a four-year term; five members are elected from the ethnic Albanian community. The prime minister appoints the cabinet, subject to the approval of the assembly.

HEAD OF STATE

President, Filip Vujanovic, *elected* 11 May 2003, *re-elected* 6 April 2008

SELECTED GOVERNMENT MEMBERS *as at July 2010*

Prime Minister, Milo Djukanovic
Deputy Prime Ministers, Svetozar Marovic; Vujica Lazovic; Igor Luksic *(Finance)*
Foreign Affairs, Milan Rocen
Defence, Boro Vucinic

EMBASSY OF MONTENEGRO

18 Callcott Street, London W8 7SU
T 020-7727 6007 E dragisa_burzan@yahoo.co.uk
Ambassador Extraordinary and Plenipotentiary, HE Dragisa Burzan, *apptd* 2007

BRITISH EMBASSY

Ulcinjska 8, Gorica C, 81000 Podgorica
T (+382) (20) 618 010 E podgorica@britishembassy.co.me
W http://ukinmontenegro.fco.gov.uk
Ambassador Extraordinary and Plenipotentiary, HE Catherine Knight-Sands, *apptd* 2009

DEFENCE

The army has 8 armoured personnel carriers. The navy has 2 submarines, 1 frigate and 4 patrol and coastal combatant vessels at 4 bases.
Military budget – US$61m (2009)
Military personnel – 3,127: army 2,500, navy 401, air force 226; paramilitary 10,100

ECONOMY AND TRADE

Montenegro achieved fiscal autonomy from the Yugoslav federation in the 1990s, managing its own budget, collecting customs tariffs on its own account, maintaining its own central bank and adopting the euro. However, it faced the same problems as Serbia – slow growth, foreign debt, lack of foreign investment, high unemployment, corruption and organised crime – as well as having more limited health and educational facilities and a poor administrative capacity. Since independence, it has pursued international integration, prioritising in particular its bid for EU membership. It has privatised its aluminium industry and financial sector, and is attracting direct foreign investment in its growing tourism industry. All three sectors have been badly hit by the global downturn, causing the economy to contract sharply.

The main agricultural products are tobacco, fruit and vegetables. Major industrial activities include production of steel, aluminium and consumer goods, processing of agricultural products and tourism. The main trading partners are EU and other Balkan countries.
GNI – US$4,146m; US$6,660 per capita (2008)
Annual average growth of GDP – –4 per cent (2009 est)
Inflation rate – 3.4 per cent (2007)
Population below poverty line – 7 per cent (2007 est)
Unemployment – 14.7 per cent (2007 est)
Total external debt – US$650m (2006 est)

BALANCE OF PAYMENTS

Trade – US$171m deficit (2004)
Current Account – US$2,382m deficit (2008)

Trade with UK	*2008*	*2009*
Imports from UK	£17,742,106	£4,821,909
Exports to UK	£4,224,502	£1,971,387

COMMUNICATIONS

Montenegro's independence leaves Serbia landlocked, although access to the Adriatic ports of Bar and Kotor is expected to be negotiated. There is 250km of rail track, part of the European system linking Bar with Belgrade, via Podgorica. The 7,400km of roads include major routes linking Podgorica and the coastal ports with the hinterland and neighbouring countries. There are five airports, including international airports at Podgorica and Tivat. Modernised telecommunications systems provided services to 362,000 fixed-line subscribers, 735,000 mobile phone subscribers and 294,000 internet users in 2008.

MEDIA

Freedom of the press is guaranteed, though observers have reported continuing political influence over editorial policies. Overseas donors and organisations have contributed funds to stimulate private media growth, but this has been limited by low advertising revenue. There are also state-funded television and radio broadcasters.

MOROCCO

Al-Mamlakah al-Maghribiyah – Kingdom of Morocco

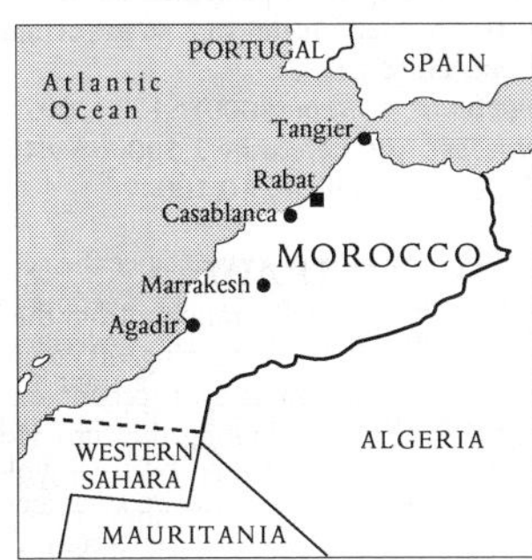

Area – 446,550 sq. km
Capital – Rabat; population, 1,769,590 (2009 est)
Major cities – Agadir, Casablanca, Fez, Marrakesh, Meknès, Tangier
Currency – Dirham (DH) of 100 centimes
Population – 34,359,364 rising at 1.48 per cent a year (2009 est); Arab–Berber (99.1 per cent)
Religion – Muslim 99 per cent (predominantly Sunni), Christian 1 per cent (est)
Language – Arabic (official), French, Berber dialects
Population density – 71 per sq. km (2008)
Urban population – 56 per cent (2007 est)
Median age (years) – 25 (2009 est)
National anthem – 'Hymne Chérifien' ['Hymn of the Sharif']
National day – 30 July (Coronation Day)
Life expectancy (years) – 71.8 (2009 est)
Mortality rate – 5.45 (2009 est)
Birth rate – 20.96 (2009 est)
Infant mortality rate – 36.88 (2009 est)
Death penalty – Retained (not used since 1993)
CPI score – 3.3 (2009)

CLIMATE AND TERRAIN

Fertile coastal plains in the west rise to a mountainous centre, with ranges, including the Atlas range, running north-east to south-west. The Rif mountains lie along the northern, Mediterranean coast. Elevation extremes range from 4,165m (Jebel Toubkal) at the highest point to −55m (Sebkha Tah) at the lowest. The climate is Mediterranean, becoming more extreme in the interior. Average temperatures in Rabat range from lows of 8°C in January to 28°C in August, although summer temperatures in the desert can reach 41°C.

HISTORY AND POLITICS

From the tenth century BC, the northern coast was settled by the Phoenicians. Morocco was part of the Roman Empire from the first century AD until it was invaded by first the Vandals and then the Visigoths in the fifth and sixth centuries. Arab conquest of the area began in the seventh century but Morocco was independent from about the ninth century, successfully resisting inclusion in the Ottoman Empire in the 16th century. The current Alawite dynasty was founded in the mid-17th century. Morocco remained isolated until the mid-19th century, when the country opened up to European trade. The subsequent growth in Spanish and French influence resulted in its partition into two protectorates from 1912. In the Second World War, Morocco was a base for the Allied offensives that drove German forces out of North Africa.

Nationalist campaigning for independence began in the 1940s. French and Spanish forces withdrew in 1956, leaving Morocco independent under Sultan Mohammed V, who adopted the title of king in 1957; the coastal towns of Ceuta and Melilla remain under Spanish control. King Hassan II, who ruled from 1961 to 1999, annexed the mineral-rich Western Sahara region in 1975.

Since the accession of King Mohammed VI in 1999, Morocco has been moving away from absolute monarchy, increasing civil liberties and addressing human rights issues. In the 2007 legislative election the Independence Party (Istiqlal), one of the parties in the coalition government, became the largest party but without an outright majority. Its leader, Abbas el Fassi, was appointed prime minister and formed a coalition government that includes five parties and a number of independents.

POLITICAL SYSTEM

The 1992 constitution was amended in 1996 to introduce a bicameral legislature. The head of state is a hereditary constitutional monarch. The king appoints the prime minister and, on the latter's recommendation, appoints the members of the council of ministers. There is a bicameral legislature; the lower house, the House of Representatives *(Majlis al-Nuwab)* has 325 members who are directly elected for a five-year term. The House of Councillors *(Majlis al-Mustasharin)* has 270 members, elected by local councils, professional organisations and the 'salaried classes'; one-third of its members is elected every three years, to serve a nine-year term.

HEAD OF STATE

HM The King of Morocco, King Mohammed VI (Sidi Mohammed Ben Hassan), *born* 21 August 1963, *acceded* 23 July 1999, crowned 30 July 1999
Heir, HRH Crown Prince Moulay Hassan, *born* 2003

SELECTED GOVERNMENT MEMBERS *as at July 2010*

Prime Minister, Abbas el-Fassi
Economy and Finance, Salaheddine Mezouar
Foreign Affairs, Taieb Fassi Fihri
Interior, Taib Cherkaoui

EMBASSY OF THE KINGDOM OF MOROCCO
49 Queen's Gate Gardens, London SW7 5NE
T 020-7581 5001 E ambalondres@maec.gov.ma
W www.moroccanembassylondon.org.uk
Ambassador Extraordinary and Plenipotentiary,
HH Princess Lalla Joumala Aaoui, *apptd* 2009

BRITISH EMBASSY
28 Avenue SAR Sidi, Mohammed, Souissi, Rabat
T (+212) (37) 633 333 E generalenquiries.rabat@fco.gov.uk
W http://ukinmorocco.fco.gov.uk
Ambassador Extraordinary and Plenipotentiary,
HE Timothy Morris, *apptd* 2008

BRITISH COUNCIL
36 rue de Tanger, BP 427, Rabat
T (+212) (37) 760 836 W www.britishcouncil.org/morocco
Director, Adam Ladbury

DEFENCE

The army has 580 main battle tanks, 70 armoured infantry fighting vehicles and 765 armoured personnel carriers. The navy has 3 frigates and 27 patrol and coastal combatant vessels at five bases. The air force has 89 combat aircraft and 19 armed helicopters.

Military budget – US$3,190m (2009)
Military personnel – 195,800: army 175,000, navy 7,800, air force 13,000; paramilitary 50,000
Conscription duration – 18 months

ECONOMY AND TRADE

Economic liberalisation since 1999 has attracted foreign direct investment, but growth is inhibited by a scarcity of private-sector enterprises and by the country's dependency on foreign energy imports. Morocco remains a poor country, with unemployment averaging 10 per cent, though it is often nearer 20 per cent in urban areas. The remittances of expatriate workers are crucial to the domestic economy but these, along with tourism and export demand, declined in 2008–9 owing to the global downturn, causing the economy to contract.

The large agrarian sector generates 19.2 per cent of GDP and engages 44.6 per cent of the workforce, producing cereals, citrus fruits, vegetables, wine, olives and livestock. It faces environmental problems such as desertification and soil erosion. Another major sector is the exploitation of mineral reserves, especially phosphate. Other industries include food processing, textiles, leather goods, construction and tourism, which the government is working to expand. Industry accounts for 31.3 per cent of GDP and services for 49.4 per cent.

The main trading partners are EU countries, especially France and Spain. Principal exports are clothing, textiles, electrical components, inorganic chemicals, transistors, crude minerals, fertilisers, petroleum products, fruit and vegetables. The main imports are crude petroleum, fabrics, telecommunications equipment, wheat, gas and electricity.

GNI – US$80,800m; US$2,520 per capita (2008; includes Western Sahara)
Annual average growth of GDP – 4 per cent (2009 est)
Inflation rate – 2 per cent (2009 est)
Population below poverty line – 15 per cent (2007 est)
Unemployment – 9.1 per cent (2009 est)
Total external debt – US$20,060m (2009 est)
Imports – US$40,600m (2008)
Exports – US$18,500m (2008)

BALANCE OF PAYMENTS
Trade – US$18,736m deficit (2009)
Current Account – US$4,568m deficit (2009)

Trade with UK	*2008*	*2009*
Imports from UK	£485,205,081	£298,857,855
Exports to UK	£439,824,640	£311,811,054

COMMUNICATIONS

There are 1,907km of railways linking the major towns and 57,600km of roads; a 35,700km network of surfaced roads connects the main towns. The main ports are Tangier, Casablanca and Agadir, on the Atlantic coast. The principal airports are at Rabat, Agadir, Casablanca and Marrakesh; Royal Air Maroc is the national airline.

There is a modern telephone system, but fixed-line density is less than 10 per 100 people, compared to mobile phone density of 65 per 100 people.

EDUCATION AND HEALTH

Education is compulsory between the ages of six and 15. There are government primary, secondary and technical schools. At Fez there is a theological university. Schools for minority faiths are permitted and may receive government grants.

Literacy rate – 55.6 per cent (2007 est)
Gross enrolment ratio (percentage of relevant age group) – primary 107 per cent; secondary 56 per cent; tertiary 12 per cent (2008 est)
Health expenditure (per capita) – US$120 (2007)
Hospital beds (per 1,000 people) – 1.1 (2003–8)

MEDIA

State control of the media has eased since the accession of King Mohammad VI, although its freedom to cover sensitive topics remains limited. The government owns Radio-Television Marocaine and has a stake in 2M, the other main television network. Private radio and television services are expanding, however, and satellite television is widely accessed. There are a number of daily newspapers, including one which is state-owned, but circulations are limited by low literacy levels.

WESTERN SAHARA

Al-Jumhuriyya al-'Arabiyya as-Sahrawiyya ad-Dimuqratiyya – Sahrawi Arab Democratic Republic
Area – 266,000 sq. km. Neighbours: Morocco (north), Algeria (north-east), Mauritania (east and south)
Population – 405,210 (2009 est)
Administrative centre – El-Aaiun (Laayoune); population, 200,000 (2007 est)
Religion – Muslim (99 per cent) (est)
Language – Arabic, Hassaniyya Arabic, Spanish
Flag – Three horizontal stripes of black, white and green with a red crescent and a five-pointed star in the centre and a red triangle based on the hoist

Western Sahara came under Spanish rule in 1884, and became a province in 1934. Following Spain's withdrawal in 1976, Morocco and Mauritania annexed the territory and divided it between them. The Polisario Front declared the Western Sahara's independence as the Sahrawi Arab Democratic Republic in 1976, and began a guerrilla war to win the territory, setting up a government in exile. In 1979, Mauritania withdrew from its part of the territory, which was annexed by Morocco. Fighting between Polisario and Moroccan forces continued at varying levels of intensity until 1991, when a UN-brokered ceasefire came into effect.

The 1991 ceasefire was established following both sides' agreement in 1988 to UN proposals for a peace settlement, which included holding a referendum on the future status of Western Sahara. But the precise terms of the referendum have proved a sticking point and an impasse was reached that has still not been overcome despite further negotiations in 2001–4; Polisario agreed to a referendum offering the options of independence, semi-autonomy or integration for Western Sahara, but Morocco is only prepared to accept semi-autonomy or integration. The UN suspended the process of preparing for the referendum in 1996 because of disagreements over voter registration; the ceasefire remains in place. Negotiations again took place from 2007 to 2009 but made no progress.

MOZAMBIQUE

República de Moçambique – Republic of Mozambique

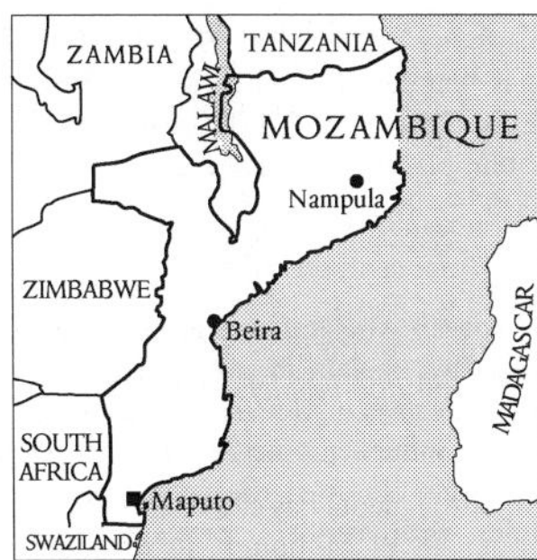

Area – 799,380 sq. km
Capital – Maputo; population, 1,589,060 (2009 est)
Major cities – Beira, Chimoio, Nacala, Nampula
Currency – New metical (MT) of 100 centavos
Population – 21,669,278 rising at 1.79 per cent a year (2009 est)
Religion – Christian (Roman Catholic 24 per cent, Protestant denominations 22 per cent), Muslim 20 per cent (est); many Christians and Muslims incorporate indigenous practices into their worship
Language – Portuguese (official), Emakhuwa, Xichangana, Elomwe, Cisena, Echuwabo
Population density – 28 per sq. km (2008)
Urban population – 36 per cent (2007 est)
Median age (years) – 17.4 (2009 est)
National anthem – 'Patria Amada' ['Beloved Fatherland']
National day – 25 June (Independence Day)
Life expectancy (years) – 41.18 (2009 est)
Mortality rate – 20.07 (2009 est)
Birth rate – 37.98 (2009 est)
Infant mortality rate – 105.8 (2009 est)
HIV/AIDS adult prevalence – 11.8 per cent (2007 est)
Death penalty – Abolished for all crimes (since 1990)
CPI score – 2.5 (2009)
Literacy rate – 44.4 per cent (2007 est)
Gross enrolment ratio (percentage of relevant age group) – primary 114 per cent; secondary 21 per cent (2008 est)
Health expenditure (per capita) – US$18 (2007)
Hospital beds (per 1,000 people) – 0.8 (2003–8)

CLIMATE AND TERRAIN

Coastal plains rise to plateaux in the centre and west, with mountains on the western borders. Elevation extremes range from 2,436m (Mt Binga) at the highest point to 0m (Indian Ocean) at the lowest. A number of rivers run from the western highlands to the Indian Ocean coast, including the Zambezi, Limpopo, Save and Ruvuma. The climate is tropical, with average temperatures in Maputo ranging from lows of 13°C in July to highs of 31°C in February.

HISTORY AND POLITICS

Between the first and fourth centuries Mozambique was settled by Bantu peoples. Trade with India and the Arabian peninsula grew and migrants from both these regions settled in the coastal areas. From the 16th century the Portuguese established settlements along the coast and the Zambezi, trading in gold, ivory, spices and slaves, and in the late 19th century they succeeded in conquering the interior. The area was administered as part of Portuguese India from 1751, becoming a separate colony in the late 19th century and an overseas province of Portugal in 1951. Concessions to private companies that had operated as *de facto* rulers over much of the country were ended in 1930.

The *Frente de Libertacao de Mocambique* (Frelimo) was founded in 1962 to fight for independence and a ten-year guerrilla war against Portuguese forces began in 1964. Independence was achieved in 1975, when a one-party socialist republic was set up. Opposition to this was led from 1977 by the *Resistencia Nacional de Mocambique* (Renamo) and a brutal civil war broke out that lasted until 1992. Mozambique joined the Commonwealth in 1995; although it had never been under British rule, it has close relationships and a shared experience with its neighbours, all former British colonies. Reconstruction of the economy and infrastructure progressed quickly after the civil war, although a series of natural catastrophes since 2000 have been major setbacks. An additional problem is the large number of remaining landmines, and the consequent amputees. The level of HIV/AIDS infection is also high.

In 1990 Frelimo abandoned Marxist-Leninism and ended one-party rule, introducing a multiparty system. The first elections under the new constitution were held in 1994 and won by Frelimo. Frelimo retained power in the 1999, 2004 and 2009 elections, prompting allegations of vote-rigging by Renamo, though monitors believe that any irregularities were minor. In the 2009 elections President Guebuza, of Frelimo, was re-elected, and Frelimo retained its overall majority in the legislature.

POLITICAL SYSTEM

Under the 2004 constitution, the executive president is directly elected for a five-year term, renewable only once. The unicameral Assembly of the Republic has 250 members, who are directly elected for a five-year term. The president appoints the prime minister and the council of ministers.

HEAD OF STATE

President, Armando Guebuza, *elected* 22 December 2004, *sworn in* 2 February 2005, *re-elected* 2009

SELECTED GOVERNMENT MEMBERS *as at July 2010*

Prime Minister, Aires Bonifacio Ali
Foreign Affairs, Oldemiro Baloi
Interior, Jose Pacheco
Finance, Manuel Chang
Defence, Filipe Nhussi

HIGH COMMISSION FOR THE REPUBLIC OF MOZAMBIQUE
21 Fitzroy Square, London W1T 6EL
T 020-7383 3800 E helga@mozambiquehc.co.uk
W www.mozambiquehighcommission.org.uk
High Commissioner, HE Antonio Gumende, *apptd* 2002

BRITISH HIGH COMMISSION
PO Box 55, Av. Vladimir I Lenine 310, Maputo
T (+258) (21) 356 000 E bhcgeneral@gmail.com
W http://ukinmozambique.fco.gov.uk
High Commissioner, HE Anthony Shaun Cleary, *apptd* 2010

BRITISH COUNCIL
2nd Floor, Hollard Building, 269 Av. Sociedade e Goegrafia, Maputo
T (+258) (1) 355 000 W www.britishcouncil.org/africa
Director, Lisa McManus

DEFENCE

The army has 60 main battle tanks, 40 armoured infantry fighting vehicles and 271 armoured personnel carriers. The navy has 5 patrol and coastal combatant vessels. The air force has 2 armed helicopters.
Military budget – US$70m (2009)
Military personnel – 11,200: army 10,000, navy 200, air force 1,000
Conscription duration – 24 months

ECONOMY AND TRADE

Political stability and economic liberalisation have attracted foreign direct investment and donor support, and achieved economic growth despite setbacks from devastating flooding (2000, 2001, 2007, 2008, 2010), droughts (2002, 2003, 2009, 2010) and an earthquake (2006). But the country remains poor, with 70 per cent of the population living below the poverty line, and is dependent on foreign aid. The huge foreign debt has been reduced to a more manageable size by debt cancellation and rescheduling, but there is a substantial ongoing trade imbalance.

Agriculture and forestry are the mainstay of the economy, accounting for 28.7 per cent of GDP and engaging about 80 per cent of the workforce; shellfish, cashew nuts, cotton, sugar, citrus fruits and timber are important exports. There are considerable oil, gas, mineral and hydroelectric power resources, which are increasingly being exploited. Industries include aluminium extraction and smelting, food processing, production of beverages, chemicals, petroleum products and textiles. There are plans to expand titanium extraction and processing, and garment-manufacturing. Industry generates 25.4 per cent of GDP and services 45.9 per cent. The country also benefits from trade with its landlocked neighbours.

The main trading partners are South Africa and the Netherlands. Principal exports are aluminium, agricultural products, timber and electricity. The main imports are machinery, vehicles, fuel, chemicals, metal products, foodstuffs and textiles.
GNI – US$8,400m; US$380 per capita (2008)
Annual average growth of GDP – 4.3 per cent (2009 est)
Inflation rate – 3.5 per cent (2009 est)
Population below poverty line – 70 per cent (2001 est)
Total external debt – US$4,159m (2009 est)
Imports – US$4,100m (2008)

BALANCE OF PAYMENTS
Trade – US$1,164m deficit (2009)
Current Account – US$1,179m deficit (2008)

Trade with UK	*2008*	*2009*
Imports from UK	£11,136,164	£15,452,864
Exports to UK	£59,632,023	£45,235,005

COMMUNICATIONS

The main seaports are Maputo, Beira and Nacala; these also handle trade for landlocked neighbouring countries, to which they are linked by rail. A new rail link to South Africa has been commissioned, and there are plans to develop new rail and road links to Malawi, Zambia and Botswana. There is currently a total of 4,800km of railways. Of the 30,400km of roads, only 5,700km is surfaced. The 460km of navigable waterways are on Cahora Bassa Lake and the lower reaches of the Zambezi. The principal airports are at Maputo and Beira, with over 100 smaller airports and airstrips around the country.

The telephone system is efficient but fixed-line availability is limited and mobile phone distribution has grown rapidly. There were 78,000 fixed lines in use, 4.4 million mobile phone subscribers and 350,000 internet users in 2008.

MEDIA

Freedom of speech is guaranteed in the constitution, but criminal libel laws remain in place. There are two daily newspapers and several weekly publications, although these have little influence outside urban areas because of low literacy levels. Radio is the main news medium for most people, with services provided by the state broadcaster, several private stations, and dozens of community and local radio stations funded by UNESCO and the government. State and privately owned television services, including Portuguese and Brazilian channels, compete for a mainly urban audience.

MYANMAR

Pyidaungzu Myanma Naingngandaw – Union of Myanmar

Area – 678,500 sq. km
Capital – Naypyitaw; population, 992,379 (2009 est)
Major cities – Bago, Mandalay, Mawlamyine (Moulmein), Pathein (Bassein), Yangon (Rangoon)
Currency – Kyat (K) of 100 pyas
Population – 48,137,741 rising at 0.78 per cent a year (2009 est); Burman (68 per cent), Shan (9 per cent), Karen (7 per cent), Rakhine (4 per cent), Chinese (3 per cent), Indian (2 per cent), Mon (2 per cent) (est)

Religion – Buddhist 90 per cent (predominantly Theravada), Christian 4 per cent, Muslim 4 per cent (est). Other estimates put the proportion of Muslims as high as 10 per cent
Language – Burmese (official), numerous ethnic languages
Population density – 76 per sq. km (2008)
Urban population – 32 per cent (2007 est)
Median age (years) – 28.2 (2009 est)
National anthem – 'Kaba Ma Kyei' ['Till the End of the World, Myanmar']
National day – 4 January (Independence Day)
Life expectancy (years) – 63.39 (2009 est)
Mortality rate – 9.14 (2009 est)
Birth rate – 16.97 (2009 est)
Infant mortality rate – 47.61 (2009 est)
Death penalty – Retained (not used since the 1980s)
CPI score – 1.4 (2009)

CLIMATE AND TERRAIN

Central lowlands are ringed by mountains in the west, north (part of the foothills of the Himalayas) and east, and running down the Kra isthmus that Myanmar shares with Thailand. Elevation extremes range from 5,881m (Hkakabo Razi) at the highest point to 0m (Andaman Sea) at the lowest. The lowlands are drained by the Irrawaddy river and its chief tributary, the Chindwin, and the eastern mountains by the Salween. The Irrawaddy has a large delta on the Andaman coast. The climate is tropical, with a wet season from June to September. Average temperatures in Mandalay, representative of the interior lowlands, range from lows of 13°C in January to highs of 38°C in April, although temperatures in the interior can reach 43°C between March and May.

HISTORY AND POLITICS

Myanmar (also known as Burma) was first unified in the 11th century by King Anawrahta, who adopted Theravada Buddhism; his successors ruled the area until an invasion by the Mongols under Kublai Khan in 1287. The country was reunified in the 15th century but was weakened by internal dissension and wars with Siam (Thailand). King Alaunghpaya reunited the nation in the 18th century. In the first half of the 19th century, border disputes with British India spiralled into a series of wars. Following the third Anglo-Burmese war, Burma was annexed as part of British India in 1885. It became a self-governing protectorate in 1937, and was occupied by the Japanese during the Second World War. Following liberation by British troops and Burmese nationalists, the country gained its independence as the quasi-federal Union of Burma in 1948.

Following a left-wing military coup in 1962, the federal system was abolished and the economy nationalised. In 1974, a one-party socialist republic was formally established. Following another coup in 1988, all existing state institutions were replaced by the State Law and Order Council (SLORC), martial law was imposed and the country's name was changed to Myanmar; the SLORC was replaced by the State Peace and Development Council in 1997.

Pro-democracy forces, notably the National League for Democracy (NLD) under Aung San Suu Kyi, oppose military rule. In 1990 the NLD won a landslide victory in the first multiparty elections for 30 years. The military ignored the election results, prevented the constituent assembly from convening, and have continued to rule by diktat, suppressing and persecuting pro-democracy campaigners. Aung San Suu Kyi was under house arrest from 1989 to 1995 and almost continuously from 2000 to date.

A constitutional convention set up in 1993 was reconvened in 2004 (after an eight-year recess), but without the participation of the NLD and other opposition and ethnic groups. Shortly after it closed in 2007 there were widespread anti-government demonstrations, which were brutally suppressed, attracting international condemnation. A new constitution was put to a referendum in May 2008; the government claimed that 92 per cent of the 99 per cent turnout voted in favour.

Cyclone Nargis devastated the Irrawaddy delta on 3 May 2008, leaving an estimated 140,000 dead or missing. The government appealed for international aid but initially restricted aid workers' access to the country to distribute supplies.

The results of the 1990 election were officially annulled in March 2010 as preparations began for presidential and legislative elections expected later in the year. Electoral laws have been framed to exclude many political activists, such as Aung San Suu Kyi, and the NLD announced a boycott of the elections. Several members of the government have resigned their military commissions to contest the elections as civilians, registering a new political party, the Union Solidarity and Development Party.

INSURGENCIES

Since independence in 1948 there have been various insurgencies, mostly by ethnic groups. These have included the Kachin, Kayin (Karen), Karenni, Wa, Shan, Mon, Arakan Chin and Kokang ethnic minorities. Since 1992, 18 ethnic groups have signed ceasefire agreements with the government. Some groups have achieved a degree of autonomy in their region; others have splintered, creating intra-ethnic tension. The country's ethnic minorities are believed to bear the brunt of the government's human rights abuses; military offensives against insurgents have displaced over half a million people.

POLITICAL SYSTEM

The constitution was effectively abrogated in 1988 when the executive and legislature were abolished and replaced by SLORC, itself replaced in 1997 by the State Peace and Development Council (SPDC), whose chairman is *de facto* head of state. A unicameral 485-member constituent assembly was elected in 1990 but has not been allowed to convene. There are no permitted political parties. The constitution approved in 2008 will come into effect with the next elections; it bars as candidates anyone with a criminal conviction or who belongs to a religious order, reserves 25 per cent of seats for the military and requires a 75 per cent approval for constitutional change.

HEAD OF STATE

Chair of State Peace and Development Council, Defence, Senior Gen. Than Shwe

SELECTED GOVERNMENT MEMBERS *as at June 2010*

Prime Minister, Lt.-Gen. (retd) Thein Sein
Finance and Revenue, Maj.-Gen. Hla Tun
Foreign Affairs, Maj.-Gen. U Nyan Win
Home Affairs, Maj.-Gen. Maung Oo

EMBASSY OF THE UNION OF MYANMAR
19A Charles Street, London W1X 8ER
T 020-7499 8841 E melondon@btconnect.com
Ambassador Extraordinary and Plenipotentiary, HE U Nay Win, *apptd* 2005

BRITISH EMBASSY
PO Box 638, 80 Strand Road, Yangon
T (+95) (1) 380 322 E be.rangoon@fco.gov.uk
W http://ukinburma.fco.gov.uk
Ambassador Extraordinary and Plenipotentiary, HE Andrew Heyn, *apptd* 2009

BRITISH COUNCIL
PO Box 638, 78 Kanna Road, Yangon
T (+95) (1) 254 658/256 290 W www.britishcouncil.org/burma
Director, Alan Smart

DEFENCE

The army has 150 main battle tanks and 325 armoured personnel carriers. The navy has 3 corvettes and 50 patrol and coastal vessels at 6 bases. The air force has 125 combat aircraft.
Military budget – US$7,000m (2007 est)
Military personnel – 406,000: army 375,000, navy 16,000, air force 15,000; paramilitary 107,250

ECONOMY AND TRADE

Myanmar has fertile soil and an abundance of natural resources such as timber (it is the world's largest exporter of teak), precious gems (jade, pearls, rubies and sapphires), and oil and natural gas, but the economy is characterised by corruption and mismanagement. The country has become increasingly poverty-stricken under military rule and around a third of the population lives below the poverty line. The economy suffers from unpredictable policies, market distortions and inadequate commercial, transport and energy infrastructure. The regime's repressiveness has lost it development aid and attracted economic and trade sanctions since the 1990s. There is a large grey economy and considerable unofficial cross-border trade.

Agriculture is the dominant economic activity, accounting for 43.1 per cent of GDP and engaging 70 per cent of the workforce; the most important export crops are rice, pulses, beans and fish. The 2008 cyclone flooded large tracts of arable land in the Irrawaddy delta, killed livestock and destroyed fishing boats; official obstructiveness towards or diversion of international relief has slowed the pace of recovery. The main industries are forestry, mining and oil and gas extraction, and these have attracted some foreign investment; manufacturing and services are struggling, and the then growing tourist industry declined dramatically after suppression of the 2007 demonstrations. Industry contributes 19.8 per cent of GDP and services 37.1 per cent.

The main trading partners are Thailand (52 per cent of exports; 21 per cent of imports), China (31 per cent of imports), Singapore and India. Principal exports are natural gas, wood products, agricultural produce, clothing and gems. The main imports are fabric, petroleum products, fertiliser, plastics, machinery, transport equipment, construction materials, crude oil and food.
Annual average growth of GDP – 1 per cent (2009 est)
Inflation rate – 7.7 per cent (2009 est)
Population below poverty line – 32.7 per cent (2007 est)
Unemployment – 4.7 per cent (2009 est)
Total external debt – US$7,373m (2009 est)
Imports – US$4,300m (2008)
Exports – US$7,000m (2008)

BALANCE OF PAYMENTS
Trade – US$4,317m surplus (2009)
Current Account – US$697m deficit (2008)

Trade with UK	*2008*	*2009*
Imports from UK	£3,512,328	£3,635,937
Exports to UK	£36,333,951	£33,402,607

COMMUNICATIONS

The 12,800km of navigable waterways include the Irrawaddy and Chindwin rivers; the main stream of the Irrawaddy is navigable for 1,440km and carries most of the country's traffic. The chief seaports are Yangon (Rangoon), Mawlamyine (Moulmein) and Akyab (Sittwe). The railway network of 3,955km covers most of the country. There are 27,000km of roads. The main airports are at Yangon, Mandalay and Tavoy.

The telephone system is rudimentary and domestic services are poor. Mobile phone services are more efficient than fixed-line and growing more quickly, with 375,800 mobile phones in 2008, compared to 829,000 fixed lines.

EDUCATION AND HEALTH

Literacy rate – 89.9 per cent (2007 est)
Gross enrolment ratio (percentage of relevant age group) – primary 115 per cent; secondary 49 per cent; tertiary 11 per cent (2008 est)
Health expenditure (per capita) – US$7 (2007)
Hospital beds (per 1,000 people) – 0.6 (2003–8)

MEDIA

The government controls and censors all media outlets, including the four national newspapers and four television stations. Editors and journalists are answerable to the military authorities, ensuring that self-censorship is widespread. Democratic Voice of Burma, an opposition radio station broadcasting via short-wave from Norway, and foreign services such as the BBC and Voice of America, are key sources of information for the population.

NAMIBIA

Republic of Namibia

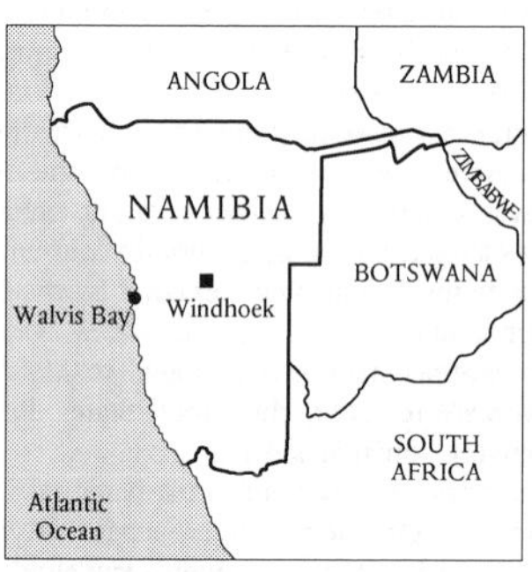

Area – 824,292 sq. km
Capital – Windhoek; population, 341,722 (2009 est)
Major towns – Rundu, Walvis Bay
Currency – Namibian dollar of 100 cents, at parity with South African rand

Population – 2,108,665 rising at 0.95 per cent a year (2009 est); Ovambo (50 per cent), Kavangos (9 per cent), Herero (7 per cent), Damara (7 per cent), Nama (5 per cent), Caprivian (4 per cent), San (Bushmen) (3 per cent), Baster (2 per cent) (est)
Religion – Christian 90 per cent (predominantly Lutheran, Roman Catholic and Anglican), Muslim 1 per cent (predominantly Sunni) (est). Many of the remainder practise indigenous religions
Language – English (official), Afrikaans (lingua franca), German, Oshiwambo, Herero, Nama, other indigenous languages
Population density – 3 per sq. km (2008)
Urban population – 36 per cent (2007 est)
Median age (years) – 21 (2009 est)
National anthem – 'Namibia, Land of the Brave'
National day – 21 March (Independence Day)
Life expectancy (years) – 51.24 (2009 est)
Mortality rate – 13.3 (2009 est)
Birth rate – 23.51 (2009 est)
Infant mortality rate – 45.51 (2009 est)
HIV/AIDS adult prevalence – 13.9 per cent (2007 est)
Death penalty – Abolished for all crimes (since 1990)
CPI score – 4.5 (2009)
Literacy rate – 88.0 per cent (2007 est)
Gross enrolment ratio (percentage of relevant age group) – primary 112 per cent; secondary 66 per cent; tertiary 9 per cent (2008 est)
Health expenditure (per capita) – US$319 (2007)
Hospital beds (per 1,000 people) – 2.7 (2009)

CLIMATE AND TERRAIN

The Namib desert runs along the Atlantic coast and is separated by a line of hills and high veldt from the Kalahari desert in the interior. Elevation extremes range from 2,606m (Konigstein) at the highest point to 0m (Atlantic Ocean) at the lowest. The only rivers not dependent on rains are the Orange, which forms the southern border with South Africa, and the Zambezi, which runs through the Caprivi Strip in the extreme north-east of the country. The climate is arid in the west and semi-arid in the centre and north-east; rainfall is sparse and droughts are frequent. The coast is cooler and frequently foggy. Average temperatures range from 13°C in July to 24°C in December.

HISTORY AND POLITICS

Pre-colonial Namibia was inhabited by San (Bushmen) and then by Bantu tribes. It was annexed by Germany in 1884 and named South West Africa. Indigenous uprisings against colonial settlement in the early 20th century were brutally suppressed, with some tribes suffering severe losses; the Herero and Nama were nearly wiped out. The territory was occupied by South Africa on behalf of the Allies in 1915 and after the First World War it became a League of Nations mandated territory, administered by South Africa.

The arrangement continued under the UN after the Second World War, but South Africa exceeded its mandate by effectively annexing the country, extending representation in the South Africa parliament to the white population in 1949, and applying apartheid in 1966. These actions were taken despite the UN's refusal to permit the country's incorporation into South Africa in 1946 and its termination of the mandate in 1966. In 1968, the UN changed the country's name to Namibia, and the South West Africa People's Organisation (SWAPO), which had campaigned for racial equality and independence since 1960, began a guerrilla war against South Africa.

South Africa's peace talks with Angola in 1988 led to agreement on independence for Namibia, and this was achieved on 21 March 1990; South Africa's Walvis Bay enclave was returned to Namibia in 1994.

The country has enjoyed stability since independence, apart from a brief period of secessionist violence in the Caprivi Strip in the late 1990s. In recent years there has been agitation for an acceleration of land reform, and the government programme moved from voluntary sales to expropriation of white-owned farms in 2005. The country's main problems arise from the demographic, economic and social impact of the high level of HIV/AIDS infection among the population.

SWAPO has been the dominant party since independence, holding the presidency and commanding a parliamentary majority without interruption. The 2004 presidential election was won by Hifikepunye Pohamba, who was re-elected in November 2009. In the 2009 legislative elections, SWAPO retained its majority in both legislative chambers.

POLITICAL SYSTEM

Under the 1990 constitution, the executive president is directly elected for a five-year term, renewable only once. There is a bicameral parliament consisting of a National Assembly, with 72 members directly elected for a five-year term and up to six additional non-voting members appointed by the president, and a National Council, whose 26 members are elected by the regional councils from among their own members for a six-year term; the latter's main function is to review and consider legislation from the lower chamber. The president appoints the prime minister and the other ministers.

HEAD OF STATE

President, Hifikepunye Pohamba, *elected* 16 November 2004, *sworn in* 21 March 2005, *re-elected* 2009

SELECTED GOVERNMENT MEMBERS *as at July 2010*

Prime Minister, Nahas Angula
Deputy Prime Minister, Marco Hausiku
Defence, Maj-Gen. Charles Namoloh
Finance, Saarah Kuugongelwa-Amathila
Foreign Affairs, Utoni Nujoma
Home Affairs, Rosalia Nghidinwa

HIGH COMMISSION FOR THE REPUBLIC OF NAMIBIA

6 Chandos Street, London W1G 9LU
T 020-7636 6244 E info@namibiahc.org.uk
W www.namibiahc.org.uk
High Commissioner, HE George Mbanga Liswaniso, *apptd* 2006

BRITISH HIGH COMMISSION

PO Box 22202, 116 Robert Mugabe Avenue, Windhoek
T (+264) (61) 274 800 E general.windhoek@fco.gov.uk
W http://ukinnamibia.fco.gov.uk
High Commissioner, HE Mark Bensberg, *apptd* 2007

BRITISH COUNCIL

1–5 Fidel Castro Street, Windhoek
T (+264) (61) 226 776 W www.britishcouncil.org/africa
Director, Ronnie Micallef

DEFENCE

The army has 60 armoured personnel carriers. The navy has 9 patrol and coastal combatant vessels at a base at Walvis Bay. The air force has 24 combat aircraft and 2 armed helicopters.

Military budget – US$305m (2009)
Military personnel – 9,200: army 9,000, navy 200; paramilitary 6,000

ECONOMY AND TRADE

Namibia is a poor country, with about half of the population living below the poverty line. Its arid terrain limits agriculture, but the emphasis on environmental protection (enshrined in the constitution) is helping the development of tourism. The country has rich mineral deposits; extraction of these is the main industrial activity and minerals account for over 50 per cent of foreign exchange earnings, so falling prices in the global downturn have caused the economy to contract. Other industries process the products of the farming and fisheries sectors. Agriculture operates mostly at subsistence level, accounting for 9.6 per cent of GDP but engaging 35–40 per cent of the workforce.

The main trading partners are South Africa, the EU, Japan, China and the USA. Principal exports are diamonds, copper, gold, zinc, lead, uranium, cattle, processed fish and skins. The main imports are foodstuffs (particularly grain), petroleum products and fuel, machinery and equipment, and chemicals.

GNI – US$9,000m; US$4,210 per capita (2008)
Annual average growth of GDP – 0.7 per cent (2009 est)
Inflation rate – 8.8 per cent (2009 est)
Population below poverty line – 55.8 per cent (2005 est)
Unemployment – 5 per cent (2008 est)
Total external debt – US$1,184m (2009 est)
Imports – US$4,500m (2008)
Exports – US$3,000m (2008)

BALANCE OF PAYMENTS
Trade – US$1,810m deficit (2009)
Current Account – US$241m surplus (2008)

Trade with UK	*2008*	*2009*
Imports from UK	£16,803,954	£22,710,996
Exports to UK	£116,131,872	£113,679,751

COMMUNICATIONS

Namibia has 2,600km of railways and 42,200km of roads. In 2004, a road bridge across the Zambezi opened, linking Namibia with Zambia and raising hopes of an increase in regional trade. The main airports are at Windhoek and Odangwa, with over 120 smaller airports and airfields around the country. The two main seaports are Walvis Bay and Luderitz.

Telephone services are good in both urban and rural areas. Fixed-line subscriptions have declined slightly, while mobile subscriptions have grown rapidly; combined density is about 55 per 100 people.

MEDIA

Freedom of the press is guaranteed by the constitution and government interference in reportage is rare. There are six national newspapers, published in English, German, Afrikaans and Oshiwambo. The state-administered Namibian Broadcasting Corporation operates alongside a private television network and around 20 private and community radio stations.

NAURU

Republic of Nauru

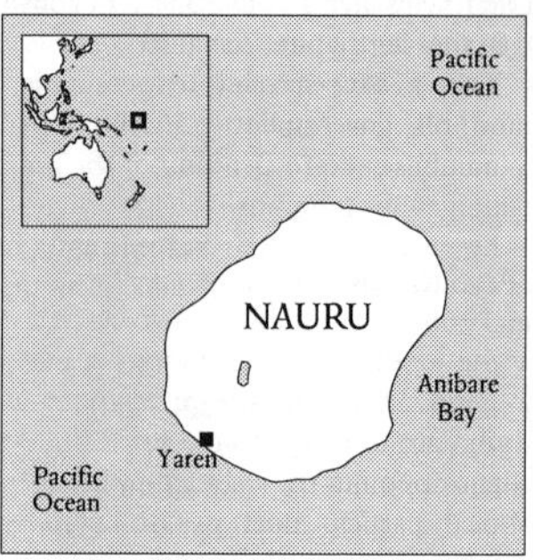

Area – 21 sq. km
Capital – Yaren District (unofficial)
Currency – Australian dollar ($A) of 100 cents
Population – 14,019 rising at 1.75 per cent a year (2009 est); Nauruan (58 per cent), other Pacific Islander (26 per cent), Chinese (8 per cent), European (8 per cent) (est)
Religion – Predominantly Christian, of whom around two-thirds are Protestant and one-third Roman Catholic
Language – Nauruan (official), English
Population density – 609.9 per sq. km (2004 est)
Urban population – 100 per cent (2007 est)
Median age (years) – 21.6 (2009 est)
National anthem – 'Nauru Bwiema' ('Song of Nauru')
National day – 31 January (Independence Day)
Life expectancy (years) – 64.2 (2009 est)
Mortality rate – 6.42 (2009 est)
Birth rate – 23.9 (2009 est)
Infant mortality rate – 9.25 (2009 est)
Death penalty – Retained (not used since 1968)

CLIMATE AND TERRAIN

Nauru is a low-lying island in the southern Pacific Ocean, 42km south of the Equator and 4,000km north-east of Sydney, Australia. There is a fertile coastal plain but about 60 per cent of the land area consists of the central plateau, formed of phosphate, which has been extensively mined. The plateau rim is the highest point, at 61m; the lowest is 0m at sea level. The climate is tropical, with a rainy season from November to February.

HISTORY AND POLITICS

Nauru was first settled by Polynesian and Melanesian groups. The first Europeans to visit the island were British whalers in 1798 and by 1888 Nauru was annexed by Germany. At the outbreak of the First World War, Nauru was occupied by Australia, which continued to administer the island under a League of Nations mandate from 1920. The island was occupied by the Japanese in 1942–3, but in 1947 UN trusteeship status superseded the mandate and Nauru continued to be administered by Australia until it became independent on 31 January 1968.

A financial crisis since 2003 has caused some political instability, with five changes of president between January and August 2003 and two different presidents in 2004. A more stable period during Ludwig Scotty's second presidency (2004–7) saw the introduction of austerity measures and public sector reform, but Scotty lost a vote of confidence in December 2007 and was replaced by

Marcus Stephen. The 2008 legislative election succeeded in breaking a parliamentary deadlock over the budget, but by early 2010 a realignment of political allegiances had produced another stalemate. Despite an early election in April 2010 the legislature remained evenly split and unable to elect a new speaker or president. President Stephen and his government continue in office as a caretaker administration pending the outcome of negotiations.

POLITICAL SYSTEM

Under the 1968 constitution, the executive president is elected by the legislature from among its members for a three-year term. The unicameral parliament has 18 members, who are directly elected for a three-year term. The president appoints the cabinet. Although there are active political parties, most parliamentary candidates stand as independents.

HEAD OF STATE

President, Internal Affairs Marcus Stephen, *elected* 19 December 2007, *re-elected* 29 April 2008

SELECTED GOVERNMENT MEMBERS *as at June 2010*

Foreign Affairs, Kieren Keke
Justice, Roland Kun
Finance, Frederic Pitcher

HONORARY CONSULATE

Romshed Courtyard, Underriver, Sevenoaks, Kent TN15 0SD
T 01732-746061 E nauru@weald.co.uk
Honorary Consul, Martin Weston

BRITISH HIGH COMMISSIONER

HE Malcolm McLachlan, MBE, *apptd* 2009, resident at Suva, Fiji

ECONOMY AND TRADE

Phosphate is the only resource and its extraction is the sole industry, but reserves will be exhausted imminently. Profits derived from the mining industry were invested in trust funds to provide for the post-mining future, but heavy spending from the funds has left the country virtually bankrupt, causing it to default on loans and have assets seized in 2004. Nauru accommodated asylum seekers for Australia between 2001 and 2008, but the loss of this revenue has left the economy dependent on international aid (principally from Australia) and revenue from the sale of fishing licences. Diversification efforts include offshore banking and small-scale tourism.

The main trading partners are Australia and New Zealand. The only export is phosphate. All food, fuel, manufactured goods, machinery and construction materials have to be imported.

Unemployment – 90 per cent (2004 est)
Total external debt – US$33.3m (2002)

Trade with UK	*2008*	*2009*
Imports from UK	£2,649,264	£36,844
Exports to UK	£38,496	£31,636

EDUCATION AND MEDIA

Education is free of charge and compulsory between the ages of six and 17.

Nauru has no daily press but there are three weekly or fortnightly publications. A government-owned radio service broadcasts material from the BBC and Radio Australia, and the government-owned Nauru Television broadcasts programmes from New Zealand.

NEPAL

Sanghiya Loktantrik Ganatantra Nepal – Federal Democratic Republic of Nepal

Area – 147,181 sq. km
Capital – Kathmandu; population, 989,730 (2009 est)
Major cities – Biratnagar, Lalitpur, Pokhara
Currency – Nepalese rupee of 100 paisa
Population – 29,563,377 rising at 1.28 per cent a year (2009 est); Chhettri (15.5 per cent), Brahman-Hill (12.5 per cent), Magar (7 per cent), Tharu (6.6 per cent), Tamang (5.5 per cent), Newar (5.4 per cent), Kami (3.9 per cent), Yadav (3.9 per cent)
Religion – Hindu 86 per cent, Buddhist 8 per cent, Muslim 4 per cent (predominantly Sunni), Christian 2 per cent (est)
Language – Nepali (official), English, Maithali, Bhojpuri, Tharu, Tamang, Newar, Magar, Awadhi
Population density – 201 per sq. km (2008)
Urban population – 17 per cent (2007 est)
Median age (years) – 20.8 (2009 est)
National anthem – 'Sayaun Thunga Phool Ka' ['Hundreds of Flowers']
Life expectancy (years) – 65.46 (2009 est)
Mortality rate – 6.97 (2009 est)
Birth rate – 23.18 (2009 est)
Infant mortality rate – 47.46 (2009 est)
Death penalty – Abolished for all crimes (since 1997)
CPI score – 2.3 (2009)

CLIMATE AND TERRAIN

The north of landlocked Nepal lies in the Himalayas, with the snowline at about 4,880m. The terrain descends from the mountains through a hilly central region with fertile valleys to the southern plains, the Terai, that lie in the valley of the Ganges. Elevation extremes range from 8,848m (Mt Everest) at the highest point, to 70m (Kanchan Kalan) at the lowest. The climate varies from subtropical in the south to much cooler with severe winters in the north. Average temperatures in Kathmandu range from lows of 2°C in January to highs of 29°C in July. The rainy season lasts from June to September.

HISTORY AND POLITICS

Modern Nepal was formed from a number of small states that were conquered and unified in the 18th century by the Gurkha ruler Prithvi Naryan Shah. After war with the British in 1815–16, Nepal became a British-dependent buffer state; its independence was formally recognised in 1923.

Power was seized by Jung Bahdur in 1846. He assumed the title Rana and his family became hereditary chief ministers, reducing the monarchy to a purely ceremonial role and keeping the country isolated.

In 1950–1, the Ranas were overthrown in the so-called 'palace revolution' and the monarchy was restored to power. Apart from 1959–60, when a parliamentary system of government was in place, the kings ruled as absolute monarchs until 1990, when a new constitution was introduced that made the country a constitutional monarchy and multiparty parliamentary democracy.

However, factionalism led to frequent changes of government, causing political and social instability, which was exacerbated from 1996 by a Maoist insurgency led by the Nepal Communist Party. The insurgency began in the west and quickly spread, despite the government's often brutal attempts at suppression. King Gyanendra assumed direct control of the government in 2005 in an attempt to defeat the insurgents, who by 2006 controlled 80 per cent of the country.

Politicians allied themselves with the Maoists to achieve the restoration of democracy, and in April 2006 the king reinstated the legislature after three months of violent pro-democracy protests. In Novemer 2006 a peace accord was signed with the Maoists, who then participated in the interim legislature set up in January 2007 and the multiparty government that took office in April.

Elections to the constituent assembly took place in April 2008, and candidates of the Communist Party of Nepal–Maoists (CPN-M) won the most seats. At its first meeting on 28 May 2008, the assembly declared the country a republic and abolished the monarchy. The assembly elected Ram Baran Yadav of the Nepali Congress party as the country's first president in July, and in August the CPN-M leader, Pushpa Kamal Dahal ('Prachanda'), was elected prime minister and formed a six-party coalition government. The prime minister and deputy prime minister resigned in May 2009 after a disagreement with the president, and Madhav Kumar Nepal, leader of the Marxist-Leninist Communists (CPN-UML), was appointed prime minister and appointed a new coalition government. This excluded the CPN-M, and the political stalemate that ensued crippled government and threatened to undermine the peace process; Mr Nepal resigned in June 2010 in the hope that a new government could be formed to end the impasse.

POLITICAL SYSTEM

The 2007 interim constitution is in force until a new constitution is drafted by the constituent assembly and is approved. The monarchy was abolished in May 2008 and the country declared a republic. The head of state is the president, who was elected by the constituent assembly. The interim legislature was replaced in May 2008 by a constituent assembly with 601 members, 240 directly elected, 335 elected by proportional representation and 26 appointed by the council of ministers. In May 2010 the assembly voted to extend its original term, which had expired, by an additional year, as it had failed to draft a new constitution. The prime minister is appointed by consensus among the political parties or elected by a two-thirds majority of the assembly. The council of ministers is responsible to the legislature.

HEAD OF STATE

President, Ram Baran Yadav, *elected* 21 July 2008, *sworn in* 23 July 2008
Vice-President, Paramananda Jha

SELECTED GOVERNMENT MEMBERS *as at July 2010*
Chair of the Council of Ministers, vacant
Vice Chairs, Bijaya Kumar Gachhedar; Sujata Koirala *(Foreign Affairs)*
Finance, Surendra Pandey
Defence, Bidya Devi Bhandari
Home Affairs, Bhim Rawal

EMBASSY OF NEPAL
12A Kensington Palace Gardens, London W8 4QU
T 020-7229 1594 E eon@nepembassy.org.uk
W www.nepembassy.org.uk
Ambassador Extraordinary and Plenipotentiary, HE Dr Suresh Chandra Chalise, *apptd* 2010

BRITISH EMBASSY
PO Box 106, Lainchaur, Kathmandu
T (+977) (1) 441 0583 E bekathmandu@fco.gov.uk
W http://ukinnepal.fco.gov.uk
Ambassador Extraordinary and Plenipotentiary, HE John Tucknott, MBE, *apptd* 2010

BRITISH COUNCIL
PO Box 640, Lainchaur, Kathmandu
T (+977) (1) 4410 798 W www.britishcouncil.org/nepal
Country Manager, Paula Middleton

DEFENCE

The army has 40 armoured personnel carriers.
Military budget – US$209m (2009)
Military personnel – 95,753: army 95,753; paramilitary 62,000

ECONOMY AND TRADE

The country is one of the poorest in Asia, and the economy is dependent on foreign aid and trade with India. The major foreign exchange earners are tourism, the main industry, and expatriates' remittances; both were relatively unaffected by the global economic downturn. Tourism and hydroelectric power have potential for development, although this might compound growing environmental problems.

Agriculture is the main economic sector, generating 35 per cent of GDP and engaging about 76 per cent of the workforce; principal crops are pulses, rice, maize, wheat, sugar cane, jute, root crops and milk. Industries other than tourism include carpets, textiles, cigarettes, cement and bricks, and the processing of rice, jute, sugar and oilseed. Industry accounts for 16 per cent of GDP and services for 49 per cent.

The main export markets are India (55 per cent), the USA, Bangladesh and Germany; the main import providers are India (55 per cent) and China. Principal exports are clothing, pulses, carpets, textiles, juice, and pashmina and jute goods. The main imports are petroleum products, machinery and equipment, gold, electrical goods and medicine.
GNI – US$11,500m; US$400 per capita (2008)
Annual average growth of GDP – 4.7 per cent (2009 est)
Inflation rate – 13.2 per cent (2009 est)
Population below poverty line – 30.9 per cent (2004)
Unemployment – 46 per cent (2008 est)
Total external debt – US$4,500m (2009 est)
Imports – US$3,600m (2008)
Exports – US$1,100m (2008)

BALANCE OF PAYMENTS
Trade – US$2,709m deficit (2009)
Current Account – US$536m surplus (2009)

Trade with UK	*2008*	*2009*
Imports from UK	£6,624,256	£6,328,011
Exports to UK	£11,704,571	£12,373,916

COMMUNICATIONS

There is a total of 17,300km of roads, of which over half are surfaced. A major highway runs the length of the country through the Terai, linking the main lowland centres and extending into the hills to Kathmandu and Pokhara. Other highways connect Kathmandu with India and Tibet. There are 59km of railways. The principal airport is at Kathmandu, and there are over 40 smaller airports and airfields around the country.

The telephone system is extensive but fixed-line services are poor and mobile phone distribution is expanding rapidly. In 2008 there were 805,000 fixed telephone lines in use, 4.2 million mobile phone subscribers and 499,000 internet users.

EDUCATION AND HEALTH

Literacy rate – 56.5 per cent (2007 est)
Gross enrolment ratio (percentage of relevant age group) – primary 124 per cent; secondary 43 per cent (2008 est)
Health expenditure (per capita) – US$20 (2007)
Hospital beds (per 1,000 people) – 0.2 (2002–7)

MEDIA

The draconian media laws introduced during the insurgency have been eased since 2006 but remain strict; journalists operating in the Terai region can face death threats and physical attacks from armed groups. Private television and radio stations operate alongside government-run networks. The two semi-official newspapers have the widest circulations of the dailies.

THE NETHERLANDS

Koninkrijk der Nederlanden – Kingdom of the Netherlands

Area – 41,543 sq. km
Capital – Amsterdam; population, 1,043,700 (2009 est)
Seat of government – The Hague (Den Haag or, in full, 's-Gravenhage), population 629,185 (2009 est)
Major cities – Almere, Eindhoven, Rotterdam, Tilburg, Utrecht
Currency – Euro (€) of 100 cents
Population – 16,715,999 rising at 0.41 per cent a year (2009 est); Dutch (80.7 per cent), Indonesian (2.4 per cent), Turkish (2.2 per cent), Surinamese (2 per cent), Moroccan (2 per cent) (est)
Religion – Christian 43 per cent (majority Roman Catholic), Muslim 6 per cent
Language – Dutch, Frisian (both official); English is widely spoken
Population density – 487 per sq. km (2008)
Urban population – 81 per cent (2007 est)
Median age (years) – 40.4 (2009 est)
National anthem – 'Het Wilhelmus' ['The William']
National day – 30 April (Queen's Day)
Life expectancy (years) – 79.4 (2009 est)
Mortality rate – 8.74 (2009 est)
Birth rate – 10.4 (2009 est)
Infant mortality rate – 4.73 (2009 est)
Death penalty – Abolished for all crimes (since 1982)
CPI score – 8.9 (2009)

CLIMATE AND TERRAIN

The Netherlands is a low-lying country; about a quarter is below sea level, making it susceptible to flooding despite the coastal defences and a network of dykes and canals. Its land area has been extended over the centuries by land reclamation (polders), found especially in the west around the huge freshwater lake of Yssel, created in the 1930s by damming the Zuider Zee. The country is crossed by three major European rivers, the Rhine, Maas (Meuse) and Scheldt, whose estuaries are in the south-west. Elevation extremes range from 322m (Vaalserberg) at the highest point to −7m (Zuidplaspolder) at the lowest point. The climate is temperate, with average temperatures in De Bilt ranging from lows of −1°C in January to highs of 22°C in July.

HISTORY AND POLITICS

The area was part of the Frankish Empire by the eighth century and subsequently of Middle Francia. From the 10th century, the various counties, dioceses and mercantile towns became virtually independent states owing fealty to various overlords, including the Holy Roman Emperor. In the 15th century these came under the rule of the dukes of Burgundy and then of the Habsburgs from 1477, passing to the Spanish branch of the Habsburgs in 1555. The northern provinces, led by William, Prince of Orange, rebelled against Spanish rule in 1568. The war of independence ended with the seven northern provinces forming the Union of Utrecht in 1579, and in 1581 independence was declared; the United Provinces were formally recognised as an independent republic in 1648.

The 17th century was a golden age in which the Dutch led the world in trade, art and science, founding colonies in the East and West Indies. Commercial and colonial rivalries led to three wars with Britain in the late 17th century, and resisting French attempts at domination exhausted the country in the 18th century. In 1795, French revolutionary armies overran the country and it remained under French rule until 1813. In 1815, the northern and southern provinces were reunited into one kingdom, with the hereditary *stadtholder* of the northern provinces becoming King William I of the Netherlands and grand duke of Luxembourg. The southern provinces seceded to form Belgium in 1830 and the Duchy of Luxembourg was made an independent state in 1867. The Netherlands was neutral during the First World War, but during the Second World War the country was invaded and occupied by Germany from 1940 until 1945.

The post-war period was marked by economic expansion, the construction of a liberal welfare state and decolonisation. The Netherlands formed the Benelux economic union with Belgium and Luxembourg in 1948, was a founder member of the EEC in 1958 and joined the eurozone in 1999.

Although it is a stable democracy, one party has rarely commanded a sufficient parliamentary majority to govern alone and post-war governments have usually been coalitions of two or more parties. The coalition of the CDA, the Labour Party (PvdA) and the Christian Union (CU), sworn into office in February 2007, collapsed in February 2010 after the PvdA withdrew. Jan Peter Balkenende, prime minister since 2002, headed a caretaker government until an early election was held in June. The election gave a narrow lead to the People's Party for Freedom and Democracy (VVD), which won 31 seats to the PvdA's 30; by mid-July the VVD remained in negotiations with the PvdA, D66 and Green Left parties to form a coalition government.

POLITICAL SYSTEM

Under the 1983 constitution, the kingdom consists of three autonomous elements: the Netherlands, the Netherlands Antilles and Aruba. The head of state is a hereditary constitutional monarch. The States-General *(Staten-Generaal)* consists of the First Chamber *(Eerste Kamer)* of 75 members, elected for a four-year term by the Provincial States; and the Second Chamber *(Tweede Kamer)* of 150 members, directly elected for a four-year term. The head of government is the prime minister, who is responsible to the legislature.

HEAD OF STATE

HM The Queen of the Netherlands, Queen Beatrix Wilhelmina Armgard, KG, GCVO, *born* 31 January 1938; *succeeded* 30 April 1980
Heir, HRH Prince Willem Alexander, *born* 27 April 1967

SELECTED GOVERNMENT MEMBERS *as at June 2010*

Prime Minister, Jan Peter Balkenende
Deputy Prime Minister, André Rouvoet
Defence, Eimert van Middelkoop
Economic Affairs, Maria van der Hoeven
Foreign Affairs, Maxime Verhagen
Interior, Guusje ter Horst
Finance, Jan Kees de Jager

ROYAL NETHERLANDS EMBASSY

38 Hyde Park Gate, London SW7 5DP
T 020-7590 3200 E london@netherlands-embassy.org.uk
W www.netherlands-embassy.org.uk
Ambassador Extraordinary and Plenipotentiary, HE Pieter Waldeck, *apptd* 2007

BRITISH EMBASSY

Lange Voorhout 10, The Hague, 2514 ED
T (+31) (70) 427 0427 E ukinnl@fco.gov.uk
W http://ukinnl.fco.gov.uk
Ambassador Extraordinary and Plenipotentiary, HE Paul Arkwright, *apptd* 2009

BRITISH COUNCIL

Weteringschans 85A, Amsterdam, 1017 RZ
T (+31) (20) 550 6060 W www.britishcouncil.org/netherlands
Director, Martin Hope

DEFENCE

The army has 60 main battle tanks, 224 armoured infantry fighting vehicles and 70 armoured personnel carriers. The navy has 4 submarines, 4 destroyers, 2 frigates and 21 helicopters. The air force has 87 combat aircraft and 29 armed helicopters.

Military expenditure – US$12,200m (2008)
Military personnel – 46,882: army 21,825, navy 9,420, air force 9,559, paramilitary 6,078

ECONOMY AND TRADE

The Netherlands has a highly industrialised and diversified market economy, and is a European transportation hub. The economy depends heavily on foreign trade and contracted sharply in 2009 as exports fell by almost 25 per cent in the global economic downturn. The government nationalised two banks to stabilise the financial sector and introduced stimulus measures, creating a budget deficit.

The highly mechanised agricultural sector employs only 2 per cent of the workforce but output supplies the food processing industries and the export as well as the domestic market. Flower bulbs and cut flowers are a major contributor to this sector, as is the fishing industry. The industrial sector contributes 23.6 per cent of GDP; major industries include food processing, and the manufacture of metal and engineering products, electrical machinery and equipment, chemicals, oil refining, construction and micro-electronics. The service industries represent 74.9 per cent of the economy. Other EU countries and China account for most overseas trade. Principal exports are machinery and equipment, chemicals, fuels and foodstuffs. The main imports are machinery and transport equipment, chemicals, fuels, foodstuffs and clothing.

GNI – US$811,400m; US$49,340 per capita (2008)
Annual average growth of GDP – –4.3 per cent (2009 est)
Inflation rate – 0.7 per cent (2009 est)
Population below poverty line – 10.5 per cent (2005)
Unemployment – 5 per cent (2009 est)
Total external debt – US$2,452,000m (2009 est)
Imports – US$489,000m (2008)
Exports – US$541,500m (2008)

BALANCE OF PAYMENTS

Trade – US$48,626m surplus (2009)
Current Account – US$41,652m surplus (2009)

Trade with UK	*2008*	*2009*
Imports from UK	£19,358,569,029	£17,380,275,200
Exports to UK	£25,354,522,956	£21,226,934,388

COMMUNICATIONS

The main seaport is Rotterdam, although there are a number of other ports on river estuaries or linked to the coast by the canals; 6,215km of inland waterways, including canals, are navigable by ships of up to 50 tonnes. The large merchant fleet includes 622 ships of over 1,000 tonnes. There are 137,000km of roads and 2,900km of railways, of which 2,064km are electrified. The principal airports are at Amsterdam, Rotterdam, Eindhoven and Maastricht, with a further 23 smaller airports and airfields around the country.

There is a modern telephone system and a very high density of mobile phone ownership. In 2008 there were 7.3 million fixed telephone lines in use, 19.9 mobile phone subscribers and 14.3 million internet users.

EDUCATION AND HEALTH

Thirteen years of compulsory primary and secondary education are provided by denominational and state schools. The principal universities are at Leiden, Utrecht, Groningen, Amsterdam, Nijmegen, Maastricht and Rotterdam.

Gross enrolment ratio (percentage of relevant age group) – primary 107 per cent; secondary 120 per cent; tertiary 60 per cent (2008 est)
Health expenditure (per capita) – US$4,243 (2007)
Hospital beds (per 1,000 people) – 4.8 (2003–8)

MEDIA

Ownership of the five national newspapers is highly concentrated. A competitive broadcasting sector includes Nederlandse Omroep Stichting (NOS), which oversees the country's public television networks and radio stations, and a large number of commercial stations. Public broadcasters are statutorily obliged to allocate airtime to different political, religious or other interest groups according to the number of members each has. Freedom of the press is guaranteed by the constitution.

CULTURE

The Netherlands has produced many major artists, particularly during the golden age between 1580 and 1700; these include Rembrandt (1606–69) and Vermeer (1632–75), and later figures such as Vincent van Gogh (1853–90), Piet Mondrian (1872–1944) and M. C. Escher (1898–1972). Other notables are mathematician and physicist Christiaan Huygens (1629–95), who made the first pendulum clock, and philosopher Baruch Spinoza (1632–77).

OVERSEAS TERRITORIES

The Kingdom of the Netherlands currently consists of three autonomous elements: the Netherlands in Europe, the Netherlands Antilles and Aruba. The five islands making up the Netherlands Antilles agreed with the Netherlands government in 2005 to end the federation; Curacao and St Maarten will become autonomous, and Bonaire, St Eustatius and Saba will become part of the Netherlands with 'special municipality' status. Dissolution of the federation was scheduled for 10 October 2010.

ARUBA

Area – 193 sq. km
Capital – Oranjestad; population, 33,112 (2009 est)
Major town – Sint Nicolaas
Currency – Aruban guilder/florin of 100 cents
Population – 103,065 rising at 1.48 per cent a year (2009 est)
Language – Dutch (official), Papiamento, Spanish, English
National Day – 18 March (Flag Day)

The Caribbean island was colonised by the Dutch in the 17th century. It was part of the Netherlands Antilles until 1986, when it became a separate, autonomous territory. The Dutch government is responsible for external affairs; internal government is in the hands of the prime minister and council of ministers, who are responsible to the 21-member unicameral legislature. The principal economic activities are tourism, offshore financial services and oil refining.
Governor, Fredis Refunjol, *apptd* 2004
Prime Minister, Mike Eman, *elected* 2009

NETHERLANDS ANTILLES

Nederlandse Antillen
Area – 960 sq. km
Capital – Willemstad, on Curacao; population, 123,355 (2009 est)
Currency – Netherlands Antilles guilder of 100 cents
Population – 227,049 rising at 0.73 per cent a year (2009 est)
Language – Dutch (official), Papiamento, English, Spanish, Creole

The Netherlands Antilles comprises the Caribbean islands of Curacao, Bonaire, part of St Maarten, St Eustatius and Saba. The islands were colonised by the Dutch in the 17th century and became a self-governing federation in 1954; the federation was scheduled to be dissolved on 10 October 2010. The Dutch government is responsible for external affairs; internal affairs are in the hands of a prime minister and council of ministers, who are elected by the 22-member unicameral legislature. The principal economic activities are tourism, oil refining and offshore financial services.
Governor, Gen. Frits Goedgedrag, *appt* 2002
Prime Minister, Emily de Jongh-Elhage, *elected* 2006

NEW ZEALAND

Aotearoa – New Zealand

Area – 270,534 sq. km (includes outlying islands)
Capital – Wellington; population, 391,201 (2009 est)
Major cities – Auckland, Christchurch, Dunedin, Hamilton, Manakau, North Shore, Tauranga, Waitakere
Currency – New Zealand dollar (NZ$) of 100 cents
Population – 4,213,418 rising at 0.94 per cent a year (2009 est); European (69.8 per cent), Maori (7.9 per cent), Asian (5.7 per cent), Pacific Islander (4.4 per cent)
Religion – Christian (Anglican 15 per cent, Roman Catholic 14 per cent, Presbyterian 11 per cent, Methodist 3 per cent, other 8 per cent), Buddhist 2 per cent, Hindu 2 per cent, Muslim 1 per cent (est)
Language – English, Maori, New Zealand Sign Language (all official)
Population density – 16 per sq. km (2008)
Urban population – 86 per cent (2007 est)
Median age (years) – 36.6 (2009 est)
National anthem – 'God Defend New Zealand'/'God Save the Queen'
National day – 6 February (Waitangi Day)
Life expectancy (years) – 80.36 (2009 est)
Mortality rate – 7.05 (2009 est)
Birth rate – 13.94 (2009 est)
Infant mortality rate – 4.92 (2009 est)
Death penalty – Abolished for all crimes (since 1989)
CPI score – 9.4 (2009)

CLIMATE AND TERRAIN

New Zealand consists of North Island, South Island and neighbouring coastal islands such as Stewart Island, and outlying islands that include the Chatham, Kermadec, Three Kings, Bounty, Antipodes, Snares, Auckland and Campbell groups in the South Pacific Ocean. The two larger islands, North Island and South Island, are separated by the relatively narrow Cook Strait. The island groups are much smaller and more widely dispersed.

Much of the North and South Islands is mountainous. The North Island mountains include several volcanoes, three of which are active. The principal range is the Southern Alps, extending the entire length of the South Island to the west of the Canterbury Plains. There are geysers and hot springs in the Rotorua district and glaciers in the Southern Alps. Elevation extremes range from 3,754m (Aoraki/Mt Cook) at the highest point to 0m (Pacific Ocean) at the lowest. The climate is temperate, though with marked regional variations; average temperatures in Christchurch (South Island) range from lows of 2°C in July to highs of 21°C in January.

HISTORY AND POLITICS

Settled by Polynesian tribes, the ancestors of the Maori, from about the tenth century, New Zealand was sighted by the Dutch navigator Abel Tasman in 1642 but he did not land. The British explorer James Cook surveyed the coastline in 1769, the year in which the islands were claimed by the British. The Maori accepted British sovereignty in 1840, under the treaty of Waitangi, in return for land rights and the rights of British subjects. Large-scale European immigration and the 1860s gold rush led to encroachment by settlers and 'land wars' with the Maori in 1860 and 1872; Maori resistance was defeated but concessions such as parliamentary representation were won. A tribunal was set up in 1975 to consider grievances caused by breaches of the Waitangi treaty, and in the 1990s the Maori were compensated for land lost to European settlers.

New Zealand was administered as part of Britain's New South Wales colony until 1841, when it became a separate colony. In 1907 it was granted dominion status; in 1931 the Statute of Westminster tacitly acknowledged its independence, which was formally confirmed in 1947.

New Zealand forces took part in the Boer War, both world wars, the Korean War and the Vietnam War. Since the UK's entry into the EEC in 1973, the focus of New Zealand's foreign and trade policies has shifted to Asia and the Pacific region.

Post-war politics has been dominated by the National Party and the Labour Party, either forming governments on their own or in coalition with smaller parties; coalitions have been the norm since a proportional representation voting system was introduced in 1993. In the 2008 legislative election, the National Party won the most seats but without an overall majority, and formed a coalition government with the support of three smaller parties.

POLITICAL SYSTEM

There is no written constitution. The head of state is Queen Elizabeth II, represented by the governor-general, who is appointed on the advice of the New Zealand government. The unicameral House of Representatives currently has 122 members (usually 120), elected for a three-year term; there are 70 members from single-member constituencies, which include seven Maori constituencies, and 52 (usually 50) allocated from party lists; if a party wins a significantly larger proportion of constituency seats relative to their party list vote, this can result in an 'overhang' of extra seats. The prime minister and the cabinet are appointed by the governor-general on the advice of the legislature.

GOVERNOR-GENERAL

Governor-General, HE Anand Satyanand, *sworn in* August 2006

SELECTED GOVERNMENT MEMBERS *as at June 2010*

Prime Minister, John Key
Deputy Prime Minister, Finance, Bill English
Defence, Wayne Mapp
Internal Affairs, Nathan Guy
Foreign Affairs, Murray McCully

NEW ZEALAND HIGH COMMISSION

New Zealand House, 80 Haymarket, London SW1Y 4TQ
T 020-7930 8422 E aboutnz@newzealandhc.org.uk
W www.nzembassy.com/united-kingdom
High Commissioner, HE Derek Leask, *apptd* 2008

BRITISH HIGH COMMISSION

PO Box 1812, 44 Hill Street, Wellington 6011
T (+64) (4) 924 2888 E consularmail.wellington@fco.gov.uk
W http://ukinnewzealand.fco.gov.uk
High Commissioner, HE Victoria Treadell, MVO *apptd* 2010

BRITISH COUNCIL

PO Box 91488, Victoria Street West, Auckland 1142
T (+64) (4) 363 3707 W www.britishcouncil.org/nz
Director, Ingrid Leary

DEFENCE

With Australia and the USA, New Zealand formed the ANZUS Pacific security treaty in 1951, but its non-nuclear military policy led to disagreements with the USA and France in 1985, and in 1986 the USA suspended its ANZUS obligations towards New Zealand.

The army has 102 armoured infantry fighting vehicles. The navy has 2 frigates and 6 patrol and coastal vessels based at Auckland. The air force has 6 combat aircraft.
Military expenditure – US$1,750m (2008)
Military personnel – 9,702: army 5,003, navy 2,104, air force 2,595

ECONOMY AND TRADE

Since the 1980s industrial and service sectors have developed to complement the large, efficient agricultural sector. Growth has been driven by trade, particularly in agricultural products, but various factors had pushed the economy into recession in 2008 before the global downturn. Government stimulus measures were introduced to cushion the effects of the recession in 2009, after which a fragile recovery began.

The agricultural sector contributes 4.6 per cent of GDP, employs 7 per cent of the workforce and provides 70–80 per cent of exports. The main products are dairy products, meat, cereals, pulses, fruits, vegetables, wool and fish. The major industries are food processing, wood and paper products, textiles, machinery, transport equipment, financial services and tourism, which is overtaking agriculture as the main source of foreign exchange revenue. Non-metallic minerals such as coal, limestone and dolomite are heavily exploited, and gold and iron production is economically important. Natural gas deposits in offshore and onshore fields are used for electricity generation, though a significant amount of the country's energy is derived from sustainable sources such as hydroelectric power. Industry contributes 23.7 per cent of GDP and services 71.7 per cent.

The main trading partners are Australia, the USA, China and Japan. Principal exports are dairy products, meat, wood, wood products, fish and machinery. The main imports are machinery and equipment, vehicles and aircraft, petroleum, electronics, textiles and plastics.

GNI – US$118,800m; US$27,830 per capita (2008)
Annual average growth of GDP – –1.3 per cent (2009 est)
Inflation rate – 1.8 per cent (2009 est)
Unemployment – 7.3 per cent (2009 est)
Total external debt – US$58,920m (2009 est)
Imports – US$34,400m (2008)
Exports – US$30,600m (2008)

BALANCE OF PAYMENTS
Trade – US$713m deficit (2009)
Current Account – US$3,565m deficit (2009)

*Trade with UK**	*2008*	*2009*
Imports from UK	£360,047,915	£327,480,741
Exports to UK	£707,509,011	£744,805,957

* Includes Tokelau, Cook Islands and Niue

COMMUNICATIONS

The national railway system was renationalised in 2008, and is now operated by the New Zealand Railways Corporation; there are 4,128km of railway track. There are 93,800km of roads, of which about 65 per cent are surfaced. The principal airports are at Auckland, Wellington (North Island), Christchurch and Dunedin (South Island) and there are over 110 smaller airports and airfields around the country; the government holds a 75.5 per cent stake in Air New Zealand. Tauranga, Christchurch, New Plymouth, Auckland and Napier are the main seaports.

In 2008 the telephone system provided 1.8 million fixed lines, and there were 4.6 million mobile phone subscribers and 3 million internet users.

EDUCATION AND HEALTH

Education is free of charge and compulsory between the ages of 5 and 16.

Gross enrolment ratio (percentage of relevant age group) – primary 101 per cent; secondary 120 per cent; tertiary 79 per cent (2008 est)
Health expenditure (per capita) – US$2,790 (2007)
Hospital beds (per 1,000 people) – 6.2 (2002–7)

MEDIA AND CULTURE

The broadcasting sector was deregulated in 1988. Two public television networks compete with three major private networks. The public radio broadcaster operates one international and three domestic and stations, and there are a large number of private radio stations, including a Maori-language broadcaster. There are three main national daily papers.

The first Maori settlers brought the art form *Whakapapa,* a type of oral genealogy, to the islands. Notable cultural figures include the writer Katherine Mansfield (1888–1923), poet Sam Hunt (*b.* 1946), filmmakers Jane Campion (*b.* 1954) and Peter Jackson (*b.* 1961), opera singer Kiri Te Kanawa (*b.* 1944), and musical comedy duo Flight of the Conchords.

TERRITORIES

TOKELAU

Area – 12 sq. km
Population – 1,433 (2008 est)

Tokelau consists of three atolls, Fakaofo, Nukunonu and Atafu, in the southern Pacific Ocean. Formerly part of Britain's Gilbert and Ellice Islands colony, Tokelau was transferred to New Zealand administration in 1926 and proclaimed part of New Zealand in 1949.

The territory is self-administering, but has rejected greater autonomy in two referendums (2006 and 2007). The Council for the Ongoing Government (cabinet) comprises three *Faipule* (village leaders) and three *Pulenuku* (village mayors), one from each atoll; the position of *Ulu-o-Tokelau* (leader) is rotated among the three *Faipule* members annually. The *General Fono,* which has 20 members elected for a three-year term, has legislative powers. Each atoll has a *Taupulega* (council of elders). The economy is dependent on New Zealand budgetary aid, with some revenue derived from remittances and the sale of fishing rights, postage stamps, coins and the use of its internet suffix. The principal activities are subsistence farming, copra production and handicrafts.

Administrator (acting), John Allen, *apptd* 2009

THE ROSS DEPENDENCY

New Zealand has administrative responsibility for the Ross Dependency. This is defined as all the Antarctic islands and territories between 160° E. and 150° W. longitude which are situated south of the 60° S. parallel, including Edward VII Land and portions of Victoria Land (*see also* The North and South Poles).

ASSOCIATED STATES

COOK ISLANDS

Area – 237 sq. km
Population – 12,271 (2008 est)
Capital – Avarua, on Rarotonga

The Cook Islands consist of 15 volcanic islands and coral atolls in the southern Pacific Ocean. A former British protectorate, since 1965 the islands have been self-governing in free association with New Zealand. Queen Elizabeth II has a representative on the islands, and the New Zealand government is represented by a high commissioner. There is a 24-member legislative assembly, and the House of Ariki, made up of 15 traditional leaders who advise on traditional matters. Executive power is exercised by a prime minister and a cabinet responsible to the legislature. The main economic activities are tourism, agriculture (especially tropical fruits), fruit processing, fishing, garment manufacturing, handicrafts, and pearl-farming; black pearls are the main export.

HM Representative, Sir Frederick Goodwin, KBE
Prime Minister, Jim Marurai

NIUE

Area – 260 sq. km
Population – 1,444 (2008 est)
Capital – Alofi; population, 547 (2009 est)

Although part of the Cook Islands group, Niue was administered separately after 1903. Since 1974 the island has been self-governing in free association with New Zealand. A New Zealand high commissioner represents both the Queen and the New Zealand government. There is a 20-member legislative assembly, and executive power is exercised by a prime minister and a three-member cabinet drawn from the assembly's members. The principal economic activities are agriculture, fishing, tourism, handicrafts, food processing and the sale of postage stamps and the use of its internet suffix.

New Zealand High Commissioner (acting), Michael Pointer, *apptd* 2010

NICARAGUA

República de Nicaragua – Republic of Nicaragua

Area – 130,370 sq. km
Capital – Managua; population, 934,156 (2009 est)
Major cities – Chinandega, Esteli, León, Masaya, Tipitapa
Currency – Córdoba (C$) of 100 centavos
Population – 5,891,199 rising at 1.78 per cent a year (2009 est)
Religion – Christian (Roman Catholic 54 per cent, Protestant denominations 28 per cent) (est)
Language – Spanish (official), English, Miskito
Population density – 47 per sq. km (2008)
Urban population – 56 per cent (2007 est)
Median age (years) – 22.1 (2009 est)
National anthem – 'Salve a ti, Nicaragua' ['Hail to You, Nicaragua']
National day – 15 September (Independence Day)
Life expectancy (years) – 71.5 (2009 est)
Mortality rate – 4.3 (2009 est)
Birth rate – 23.25 (2009 est)
Infant mortality rate – 25.02 (2009 est)
Death penalty – Abolished for all crimes (since 1979)
CPI score – 2.5 (2009)

CLIMATE AND TERRAIN

The narrow Pacific coastal plain is broken by active volcanoes and lakes Managua and Nicaragua. A mountainous central region separates it from the broad Atlantic coastal plain, which constitutes 60 per cent of the country and is covered by tropical rainforest. Elevation extremes range from 2,438m (Mogoton) at the highest point to 0m (Pacific Ocean) at the lowest. The climate is generally tropical on the plains but cooler at altitude; average temperatures in Managua range from highs of 34°C in April to lows of 20°C in December. The country is subject to frequent earthquakes.

HISTORY AND POLITICS

The area was settled by tribes from Mexico and Mesoamerica from the ninth century AD. Spanish colonisation began in 1523 but in the 17th and 18th centuries the British were the dominant presence on the Caribbean coast, with the Spanish controlling the Pacific plain. Independence from Spain was achieved in 1821 and the area was initially incorporated into Mexico. In 1823 it became part of a Central American federation of former Spanish provinces but seceded and became fully independent in 1838. British control of the Caribbean coast was ceded to Nicaragua in 1860.

In 1893, General José Santos Zelaya established a dictatorship that lasted until 1909, when he was overthrown by US troops. General Anastasio Somoza established a dictatorship in 1938 and ruled until his assassination in 1956, when he was succeeded as president by his sons Luis (1956–67) and Anastasio (1967–79). The family amassed a huge fortune in its 44 years in power, until it was overthrown in 1979 in a popular revolt led by the *Frente Sandinista de Liberacíon Nacional* (FSLN), popularly known as the Sandinistas.

The Sandinistas' socialist government redistributed land and promoted education and health services, but was opposed by US-backed right-wing guerrillas (the Contras). The civil war lasted from 1982 until 1990 (although there was a ceasefire from 1988), when the Sandinistas were unexpectedly defeated in elections by a coalition of opposition parties.

After the civil war, governments were liberal or liberal-dominated coalitions, keeping the FSLN from power even though it was often the largest party in the legislature. However, in the 2006 presidential and legislative elections, the FSLN candidate, Daniel Ortega (president 1984–90), was elected president and the FSLN became the largest party in the assembly, with 38 seats.

POLITICAL SYSTEM

The 1987 constitution was amended in 1995 to reduce the presidential term; further changes reducing the power of the presidency came into effect in 2007. The executive president is directly elected for a five-year term; the ban on consecutive second terms was removed in 2009. The unicameral National Assembly has 90 members directly elected for a five-year term; unsuccessful presidential and vice-presidential candidates may be awarded a seat if they receive more than the average percentage of the vote in each electoral district. The cabinet is appointed by the president.

HEAD OF STATE

President, Daniel Ortega, *elected* 5 November 2006, *sworn in* 10 January 2007
Vice-President, Jaime Morales

SELECTED GOVERNMENT MEMBERS *as at July 2010*

Defence, Ruth Tapia Roa
Finance, Alberto Guevara
Foreign Affairs, Samuel Santos
Interior, Ana Isabel Morales Mazún

EMBASSY OF NICARAGUA

Suite 31, Vicarage House, 58–60 Kensington Church Street, London W8 4DP
T 020-7938 2373 E embaniclondon@btconnect.com
Ambassador Extraordinary and Plenipotentiary, HE Carlos Arguello-Gomez, *apptd* 2010

BRITISH AMBASSADOR

Ambassador Extraordinary and Plenipotentiary, HE Tom Kennedy, LVO, resident at San José, Costa Rica

DEFENCE

The army has 127 main battle tanks and 166 armoured personnel carriers. The navy has 24 patrol and coastal vessels at 3 bases. The air force has 7 aircraft and 16 helicopters.

Military budget – US$40m (2009)
Military personnel – 12,000: army 10,000, navy 800, air force 1,200
Conscription duration – 18–36 months (voluntary)

ECONOMY AND TRADE

Progress towards economic recovery and reconstruction after the civil war was reversed in 1998 by Hurricane Mitch, which left 20 per cent of the population homeless. Economic growth since has been slow, and the economy contracted in 2009 as the global downturn reduced export demand and remittances (worth almost 15 per cent of GDP), and key commodity prices fell. Although almost 80 per cent of debt was cancelled in 2004 and 2006, the government is dependent on foreign aid and nearly half the population lives below the poverty line.

Agriculture is the mainstay of the economy, accounting for 17.5 per cent of GDP and 29 per cent of employment. The main commercial crops are coffee, beef, shellfish, tobacco, sugar and peanuts. Industry includes food and timber processing, mining, the manufacture of chemicals, machinery, metal products, textiles and clothing, oil refining and tourism. Industry contributes 26.5 per cent of GDP and services 56.1 per cent.

The main trading partners are the USA and other Central and South American countries. Principal exports are the main commercial crops and gold. The main imports are consumer goods, machinery and equipment, raw materials and petroleum products.

GNI – US$6,100m; US$1,080 per capita (2008)
Annual average growth of GDP – −2.9 per cent (2009 est)
Inflation rate – 4 per cent (2009 est)
Population below poverty line – 48 per cent (2005)
Unemployment – 5.9 per cent (2009 est)
Total external debt – US$4,700m (2009 est)
Imports – US$4,300m (2008)
Exports – US$1,500m (2008)

BALANCE OF PAYMENTS
Trade – US$1,867m deficit (2009)
Current Account – US$925m deficit (2009)

Trade with UK	*2008*	*2009*
Imports from UK	£3,760,294	£2,352,093
Exports to UK	£10,494,093	£11,176,819

COMMUNICATIONS

The Inter-American Highway runs between Nicaragua's Honduran and Costa Rican borders while the Inter-Oceanic Highway runs from Corinto on the Pacific coast via Managua to Rama, where there is a natural waterway to Bluefields on the Caribbean. There are 19,100km of roads but no operable railway. The main airport is at Managua, and there are a further 142 airports and airfields around the country. The chief ports are Corinto (Pacific) and Bluefields and El Bluff (Caribbean). There are 2,220km of inland waterways, mostly on lakes Managua and Nicaragua, and Lake Nicaragua is the chief element in a 2006 proposal to construct a canal linking the Pacific and Caribbean coasts.

The telephone system is being expanded and upgraded with the help of foreign investment. Fixed-line density was about 5 per 100 people in 2008 and mobile density was 55 per 100 people.

EDUCATION AND HEALTH

Literacy rate – 78.0 per cent (2007 est)
Gross enrolment ratio (percentage of relevant age group) – primary 117 per cent; secondary 68 per cent (2008 est)
Health expenditure (per capita) – US$92 (2007)
Hospital beds (per 1,000 people) – 0.9 (2003–8)

MEDIA

There are three daily newspapers. Several commercial networks provide television services, and there are a large number of radio stations.

NIGER

République du Niger – Republic of Niger

Area – 1,267,000 sq. km
Capital – Niamey; population, 1,004,200 (2009 est)
Major cities – Maradi, Zinder
Currency – Franc CFA of 100 centimes
Population – 15,306,252 rising at 3.68 per cent per year (2009 est); Hausa (55.4 per cent), Djerma (21 per cent), Tuareg (9.3 per cent), Fulani (8.5 per cent), Kanouri Manga (4.7 per cent)
Religion – Muslim 98 per cent (of which Sunni 95 per cent, Shia 5 per cent), Christian 2 per cent (est)
Language – French (official), Hausa, Djerma
Population density – 12 per sq. km (2008)
Urban population – 16 per cent (2007 est)
Median age (years) – 15.2 (2009 est)
National anthem – 'La Nigérienne' ['Song of Niger']
National day – 18 December (Republic Day)
Life expectancy (years) – 52.6 (2009 est)
Mortality rate – 14.83 (2009 est)
Birth rate – 51.6 (2009 est)
Infant mortality rate – 116.66 (2009 est)
Death penalty – Retained (no known use since 1976)
CPI score – 2.9 (2009)
Literacy rate – 28.7 per cent (2007 est)
Gross enrolment ratio (percentage of relevant age group) – primary 62 per cent; tertiary 1 per cent (2009 est); secondary 11 per cent (2008 est)
Health expenditure (per capita) – US$16 (2007)
Hospital beds (per 1,000 people) – 0.3

CLIMATE AND TERRAIN

A landlocked state, the country is mostly desert, with low hills in the north and savannah in the south. Elevation extremes range from 2,022m (Mt Bagzane) at the highest point to 200m (river Niger) at the lowest. The Niger valley in the south-west is the only well-watered area. There is a desert climate, except in the extreme south which is sub-tropical. Average temperatures in Niamey range from lows of 14°C in January to highs of 41°C in May.

HISTORY AND POLITICS

The area was divided between several kingdoms formed by different tribes (Tuareg, Songhai, Hausa, Fulani) from the tenth to 19th centuries. French colonial expansion from the 1880s brought the whole area under its control in 1898 and in 1904 it became part of French West Africa. The country became autonomous in 1958 and achieved full independence in 1960.

The first president introduced a one-party regime, which continued under the military government installed after a coup in 1974. Following popular agitation, civilian government was reintroduced in 1989, other parties were legalised in 1990, and multi-party elections held in 1993. This political liberalisation was reversed following a military coup in 1996 led by Brig. Ibrahim Barre Mainassara. He was assassinated in 1999 by the military, who restored political pluralism.

From 1990 there was a rebellion in the north by Tuareg seeking greater social equality and political representation. Peace agreements with rebel groups in 1995 and 1997 brought calm until 2007, when a new rebel group emerged, seeking greater autonomy and access to mining revenue; this group signed a ceasefire with the government in April 2009.

In May 2009 President Mamadou Tandja (first elected in 1999) assumed emergency powers in order to proceed with a controversial referendum on constitutional changes that would increase presidential power. The referendum approved the new constitution and the president's National Movement for Society in Development won an overwhelming victory in the October 2009 legislative election, which was boycotted by the opposition. President Tandja was deposed in February 2010 by the military, which in March 2010 appointed a transitional government. A referendum on a new constitution was promised for October 2010, followed by presidential and legislative elections.

Drought in 2009 caused crop failures which left about half the population in need of food aid in 2010.

POLITICAL SYSTEM

Under the 2009 constitution, which was suspended in February 2010, the president is directly elected for a five-year term, which is renewable without limit. The unicameral National Assembly has 113 members directly elected for a five-year term. The prime minister is appointed by the president.

HEAD OF STATE

President, Col. Salou Djibo, *took power* 18 February 2010

SELECTED GOVERNMENT MEMBERS *as at July 2010*

Prime Minister, Mahamadou Danda
Finance and Economy, Badamassi Annou
Foreign Affairs, Toure Aminatou Maiga
Interior, Cisse Ousmane
Defence, Brig.-Gen. Mamadou Ousseini

EMBASSY OF THE REPUBLIC OF NIGER

154 rue de Longchamp, 75116 Paris, France
T (+33) (1) 4504 8060
Ambassador Extraordinary and Plenipotentiary, HE Adamou Seydou, *apptd* 2003

BRITISH AMBASSADOR

HE Dr Nicholas Westcott, CMG, *apptd* 2008, resident at Accra, Ghana

DEFENCE

The army has 22 armoured personnel carriers.
Military budget – US$67m (2009 est)
Military personnel – 5,300: army 5,200, air force 100; paramilitary 5,400
Conscription duration – 24 months (selective)

ECONOMY AND TRADE

Niger is one of the poorest countries in the world, with the majority of the population living below the poverty line. Economic progress has been constrained by political instability, recurrent droughts, desertification, over-grazing and rapid population growth, leaving the country dependent on foreign aid. Its huge foreign debt burden was much reduced by debt relief and cancellation in 2000 and 2005.

The mainstay of the economy is subsistence agriculture and herding, which account for 39 per cent of GDP and engage 90 per cent of the population; the main cash crops are cowpeas, cotton, vegetables, cereals and livestock. Dependence on uranium mining makes the economy vulnerable to fluctuations in global uranium prices; efforts are being made to diversify into exploitation of other mineral resources, including gold and oil. The other industries are processing agricultural products and manufacturing cement, bricks, soap, textiles and chemicals. Industry contributes 17 per cent of GDP and services 44 per cent.

The main trading partners are Japan (80.8 per cent of exports), France and Nigeria. Principal exports are uranium ore, livestock, cowpeas and onions. The main imports are foodstuffs, machinery, vehicles and parts, petroleum and cereals.
GNI – US$4,800m; US$330 per capita (2008)
Annual average growth of GDP – 3.2 per cent (2009 est)
Inflation rate – 0.1 per cent (2007 est)
Total external debt – US$2,100m (2003 est)
Imports – US$1,500m (2008)
Exports – US$800m (2008)

BALANCE OF PAYMENTS

Trade – US$637m deficit (2009)
Current Account – US$713m deficit (2008)

Trade with UK	*2008*	*2009*
Imports from UK	£2,513,332	£3,837,710
Exports to UK	£9,268,693	£300,916

COMMUNICATIONS

Niger has no railways. Of the 18,600km of roads, less than 4,000km are surfaced. The river Niger is navigable between September and March for 300km from Niamey to the Benin frontier. The principal airport is at Niamey and there are a further 27 airports and airfields.

The telephone system is limited in extent and concentrated mainly in the more densely populated south-west. Although mobile phone distribution has grown rapidly, the combined density of fixed-line and mobile phones is only 13 per 100 people.

MEDIA

Media freedom has improved since 1999. Although the state-run television and radio services still dominate broadcasting, private stations, particularly radio stations, are proliferating. Radio is the most important form of communication, owing to low levels of literacy.

NIGERIA

Federal Republic of Nigeria

Area – 923,768 sq. km
Capital – Abuja (since 1991); population, 1,857,230 (2009 est)
Major cities – Aba, Benin City, Ibadan, Ilorin, Kaduna, Kano, Lagos (the former capital), Maiduguri, Port Harcourt, Zaria
Currency – Naira (N) of 100 kobo
Population – 149,229,090 rising at 2 per cent a year (2009 est); Hausa and Fulani (29 per cent), Yoruba (21 per cent), Igbo (18 per cent), Ijaw (10 per cent), Kanuri (4 per cent), Ibibio (3.5 per cent), Tiv (2.5 per cent) (est)
Religion – Muslim 50 per cent (predominantly Sunni), Christian 50 per cent, traditional indigenous religions 10 per cent (est); many Christians and Muslims also follow indigenous beliefs
Language – English (official), Hausa, Yoruba, Igbo, Fula
Population density – 166 per sq. km (2008)
Urban population – 48 per cent (2007 est)
Median age (years) – 19 (2009 est)
National anthem – 'Arise O Compatriots, Nigeria's Call Obey'
National day – 1 October (Independence Day)
Life expectancy (years) – 46.94 (2009 est)
Mortality rate – 16.56 (2009 est)
Birth rate – 36.65 (2009 est)
Infant mortality rate – 94.35 (2009 est)
HIV/AIDS adult prevalence – 2.9 per cent (2007 est)
Death penalty – Retained
CPI score – 2.5 (2009)
Literacy rate – 72.0 per cent (2007 est)
Gross enrolment ratio (percentage of relevant age group) – primary 93 per cent; secondary 30 per cent (2008 est)
Health expenditure (per capita) – US$74 (2007)
Hospital beds (per 1,000 people) – 0.5 (2003–8)

CLIMATE AND TERRAIN

The north is arid savannah and semi-desert plains, which rise to central hills and plateaux. There are mountains along the south-eastern border, but the south is generally low-lying and covered in tropical rainforest, with mangrove swamps along the coast and hills in the south-east. Elevation extremes range from 2,419m (Chappal Waddi) at the highest point to 0m (Atlantic Ocean) at the lowest. The river Niger flows across the country from the north-west to the south coast, where it forms a broad delta on the Gulf of Guinea. The climate is equatorial in the south, tropical in the centre and arid in the north. The north has one rainy season (June to September), while the south has two (March–July, September–October); average temperatures in Lagos range between 23°C and 32°C all year round.

HISTORY AND POLITICS

Nigeria was at the centre of the Nok culture from 500 BC to AD 200. Various kingdoms flourished in the area in medieval times, and Islam was introduced to the north in the 13th century. The Oyo Empire was dominant in the south in the 17th century and the Muslim Sokoto Empire in the north in the 19th century. European traders had arrived on the coast in the 15th century and participated in the gold and slave trades. After Britain abolished slavery, several other powers attempted to exploit the slave trade in Nigeria, which led Britain to annex Lagos in 1861. Britain established protectorates over adjacent territories in stages during the late 19th century, amalgamating the whole area of modern Nigeria into a single political and administrative unit in 1914. The country became a federation in 1954, and increasing degrees of internal self-government were introduced until the country became independent in 1960.

Independence unleashed ethnic and regional tensions, and there were two military coups in 1966; the first coup was Igbo-led and provoked an anti-Igbo counter-coup from the north. The following year, three eastern states seceded and set up the Igbo state of Biafra, sparking a civil war. The conflict lasted until 1970, when Biafra surrendered and was reunited with Nigeria; despite an international relief effort, bombing and famine killed around one million people.

In the 30 years after 1967 there were several military coups and the governments during most of the period were military or military-dominated. Some of the regimes made efforts to reintroduce civilian government, legalise political parties and restore democracy, but invariably suspended these when the results were unfavourable to them. The most recent restoration of civilian rule was in 1999, following presidential and legislative elections.

Ethnic and regional tensions have been more openly and violently expressed since 1999, including calls for secession by various groups. The main source of tension is the religious divide between the predominantly Muslim north, where Shariah law has been introduced in 12 states, and the predominantly Christian south. There have been sporadic violent clashes in which thousands have died, leading to internal migration of Christians from the north. The latest trouble spot is the Niger delta, where activists have been demanding greater local control over oil revenues since the 1990s, but these campaigns have been overshadowed since 2003 by the activities of armed militants, who have attacked oil installations and kidnapped foreign oil workers, while trade in stolen oil has fuelled violence and corruption in the region. In August 2009 a government amnesty for militants began and many surrendered their weapons.

The 2007 presidential and legislative elections were condemned as undemocratic by international observers amid reports of violence, intimidation and ballot-rigging. The presidential election was won by Umaru Musa Yar'Adua of the People's Democratic Party (PDP), which also retained its majority in both legislative chambers. President Yar'Adua died in May 2010 and was succeeded by the vice-president, Goodluck Jonathan. Presidential and legislative elections are due in April 2011.

POLITICAL SYSTEM
The country is a federal democratic republic. Under the 1999 constitution, the executive president is directly elected for a four-year term, renewable only once. The president appoints the federal executive council, which must be approved by the senate. The National Assembly is bicameral; the House of Representatives has 360 members and the senate has 109 members, both elected for a four-year term.

HEAD OF STATE
President, Goodluck Jonathan, *sworn in* 6 May 2010
Vice-President, Namadi Sambo

SELECTED GOVERNMENT MEMBERS *as at July 2010*
Defence, Chief Adetokunbo Kayode
Finance, Olusegun Olutoyin Aganga
Foreign Affairs, Henry Odein Ajumogobia
Internal Affairs, Capt. Emmanuel Iheanacho

HIGH COMMISSION FOR THE FEDERAL REPUBLIC OF NIGERIA
Nigeria House, 9 Northumberland Avenue, London WC2N 5BX
T 020-7839 1244 E hc@nigeriahc.org.uk W www.nhcuk.org
High Commissioner, HE Dr Dalhatu S. Tafida, *apptd* 2008

BRITISH HIGH COMMISSION
Dangote House, Aguiyi Ironsi Street, Wuse, Abuja
T (+234) (9) 462 3200 E information.abuja@fco.gov.uk
W http://ukinnigeria.fco.gov.uk
High Commissioner, HE Robert Dewar, CMG, *apptd* 2007

BRITISH COUNCIL
Plot 3645, IBB Way, Maitama, PMB 550, Garki, Abuja
T (+234) (9) 4137 8707 W www.britishcouncil.org/africa
Director, Peter Upton

FEDERAL STRUCTURE
The federal republic is divided into 36 states and the Federal Capital Territory: Abia, Adamawa, Akwa Ibom, Anambra, Bauchi, Bayelsa, Benue, Borno, Cross River, Delta, Ebonyi, Edo, Ekiti, Enugu, Gombe, Imo, Jigawa, Kaduna, Kano, Katsina, Kebbi, Kogi, Kwara, Lagos, Nassarawa, Niger, Ogun, Ondo, Osun, Oyo, Plateau, Rivers, Sokoto, Taraba, Yobe and Zamfara. Each state has an elected governor and legislature.

DEFENCE
The army has 276 main battle tanks, 157 light tanks and over 484 armoured personnel carriers. The navy has 1 frigate, 1 corvette and 27 patrol and coastal vessels at 3 bases. The air force has 87 combat aircraft and 9 armed helicopters.
Military budget – US$1,490m (2009)
Military personnel – 80,000: army 62,000, navy 8,000, air force 10,000; paramilitaries 82,000

ECONOMY AND TRADE
Nigeria is the leading sub-Saharan oil producer, enjoying an oil boom in the 1970s and recently benefiting again from high oil prices. However, the mismanagement and corruption that dissipated the profits of the 1970s boom have not been overcome, so the majority of the population still receives little benefit, and nearly three-quarters live below the poverty line. Past governments also failed to diversify the economy away from its dependence on the oil industry, which accounts for 20 per cent of GDP, 80 per cent of government revenue and 95 per cent of foreign exchange earnings. However, the current government is showing the political will to introduce reforms that will improve fiscal and monetary management, curb inflation and address regional agitation for wider distribution of oil revenues. Factors such as security and inadequate infrastructure remain obstacles to growth, but infrastructure improvements are a priority, especially in electricity supply and roads. Recent high oil revenues and debt relief or cancellation have, however, freed Nigeria from much of its large foreign debt.

The mainstay of the economy is agriculture, mostly at subsistence level, which generates 33.1 per cent of GDP and engages 70 per cent of the labour force. The main crops include cocoa, peanuts, cotton, palm oil, maize, rice, sorghum and millet. However, agricultural output has failed to keep pace with rapid population growth, changing Nigeria from a net food exporter to a food importer. Industrial activities include oil and natural gas production, mining (coal, tin, columbite), processing agricultural products, textiles, cement and other construction materials and footwear. Industry contributes 33.8 per cent of GDP and services 33.1 per cent.

The main trading partners are the USA (42 per cent of exports), China, EU countries and Brazil. Principal exports are oil and oil products, cocoa and rubber. The main imports are machinery, chemicals, transport equipment, manufactured goods, food and live animals.
GNI – US$177,400m; US$1,170 per capita (2008)
Annual average growth of GDP – 3.8 per cent (2009 est)
Inflation rate – 11.5 per cent (2009 est)
Population below poverty line – 70 per cent (2007 est)
Unemployment – 4.9 per cent (2007 est)
Total external debt – US$9,689m (2009 est)
Imports – US$42,400m (2008)
Exports – US$31,000m (2004)

BALANCE OF PAYMENTS
Trade – US$33,006m surplus (2009)
Current Account – US$42,261m surplus (2008)

Trade with UK	*2008*	*2009*
Imports from UK	£1,433,422,326	£1,235,385,393
Exports to UK	£872,890,713	£621,229,035

COMMUNICATIONS
Internal long-distance travel is mostly by air; there are 56 airports and airfields, including the principal airports at Lagos, Abuja, Kano and Port Harcourt. The Nigerian railway network, which is controlled by the Nigerian Railway Corporation, has 3,505km of track. There are 193,200km of roads, and 8,600km of waterways, mostly on the Niger and Benue rivers; some parts of the Niger delta are only accessible by water. The main seaports are Lagos, Port Harcourt, Warri and Calabar. There is a high risk of piracy or armed robbery of shipping in the Niger delta and the Gulf of Guinea.

Both the fixed-line and mobile phone telephone networks are expanding quickly, although fixed-line density was still only 1 per 100 people in 2008, while mobile phone density had reached 45 per 100 people. There were also 11 million internet users.

MEDIA
State-run television and radio broadcasters provide national and regional services. All 36 states run their own radio stations and most also provide television. State services operate alongside a large number of private and commercial networks. Radio provides Nigerians with

their main access to the media, as television viewing is concentrated in urban areas. There are over 100 national and local newspapers and periodicals.

CULTURE

Significant writers include Chinua Achebe (*b.* 1930), whose novel *Things Fall Apart* (1958) has been translated into 50 languages, the Nobel prize winner Wole Soyinka (*b.* 1934) and Ken Saro-Wiwa (1941–1995), whose political activism resulted in his death at the hands of the military government.

'Nollywood' is the colloquial name for the Nigerian film industry, which produces an estimated 2,000 films a year. Most go straight to low-priced DVD or VCD, and often outsell Hollywood blockbusters in many parts of Africa.

Fela Kuti (1938–97) is Nigeria's most famous musician. He pioneered Afrobeat, a style combining traditional Yoruba rhythms with jazz and funk. The movement became inextricably linked with Kuti's personal politics, which saw him embrace black power, campaign against suppression of human rights in Africa, and mount two unsuccessful runs for the Nigerian presidency.

NORWAY

Kongeriket Norge – Kingdom of Norway

Area – 384,802 sq. km, of which Svalbard and Jan Mayen have a combined area of 61,397 sq. km
Capital – Oslo; population, 874,695 (2009 est)
Major cities – Bergen, Stavanger, Trondheim
Currency – Krone of 100 ore
Population – 4,660,539 rising at 0.34 per cent per year (2009 est)
Religion – Christian (Evangelical Lutheran 82 per cent, other Protestant denominations 4 per cent, Roman Catholic 1 per cent), Muslim 2 per cent (est)
Language – Bokmal and Nynorsk Norwegian (both official), Finnish, Sami (official in six municipalities)
Population density – 16 per sq. km (2008)
Urban population – 77 per cent (2007 est)
Median age (years) – 39.4 (2009 est)
National anthem – 'Ja, Vi Elsker Dette Landet' ['Yes, We Love This Country']
National day – 17 May (Constitution Day)
Life expectancy (years) – 79.95 (2009 est)
Mortality rate – 9.29 (2009 est)
Birth rate – 10.99 (2009 est)
Infant mortality rate – 3.58 (2009 est)
Death penalty – Abolished for all crimes (since 1979)
CPI score – 8.6 (2009)

CLIMATE AND TERRAIN

The terrain is mostly mountainous, with elevated, barren plateaux separated by deep, narrow valleys; the north is arctic tundra. The coastline is deeply indented with numerous fjords and fringed with thousands of rocky islands and islets; Geirangerfjord and Naeroyfjord are UNESCO World Heritage Sites. Elevation extremes range from 2,469m (Galdhopiggen) at the highest point to 0m (Norwegian Sea) at the lowest.

Nearly half of the country lies north of the Arctic Circle, and at North Cape the sun does not appear to set between about 14 May and 29 July, causing the phenomenon known as the midnight sun; conversely, there is no apparent sunrise from about 18 November to 24 January. The climate is temperate on the coast but colder and wetter inland; average temperatures in Oslo range from lows of −7°C in January to highs of 22°C in July, but winter temperatures in parts of the north can drop to −40°C.

HISTORY AND POLITICS

Norway became a unified country under rule of King Harald Fairhair in *c.*900 but dissolved after his death and was reunified by Olav II in *c.*1016–28. Canute brought Norway under Danish rule in 1028 but the throne reverted on his death to Magnus I. When the royal house died out in the 14th century, the Danish monarch was the nearest heir and in 1397 Norway, Denmark and Sweden were united under a single monarch in the Kalmar Union. Sweden seceded from the union in 1523, but Norway continued to be ruled by the Danish crown until 1814, when it was ceded to Sweden.

Although internal self-government was established in 1814, growing tension over constraints on the Norwegian government led to the union being dissolved, and Norway became independent in 1905. The first king of the newly independent country was a Danish prince, who took the throne as King Haakon VII.

The country was neutral in the First World War, but in the Second World War Norway was invaded and occupied by Germany from 1940 until 1945. Norway joined NATO in 1949 and was a founder member of the European Free Trade Association in 1960. Membership of the EU was rejected in referendums in 1972 and 1994.

After 1945, governments pursued policies of economic planning and an extensive welfare state. The Labour Party dominated politics from the 1930s to the early 1980s, governing either on its own or in coalition with smaller parties. It was returned to power in 2005 after winning a majority of seats in the legislative election, forming a coalition government with the Socialist Left and Centre parties. In the 2009 legislative election the governing coalition was returned with a one-seat majority.

POLITICAL SYSTEM

Norway is a constitutional monarchy with a hereditary monarch as head of state. Under the 1814 constitution, the unicameral *Storting* has 169 members who are directly elected for a four-year term; a 2007 constitutional amendment, which abolished a bicameral division within the *Storting*, took effect from the 2009 election. The prime minister, who is responsible to parliament, appoints the cabinet.

HEAD OF STATE

HM The King of Norway, King Harald V, KG, GCVO, *born* 21 February 1937; *succeeded* 17 January 1991

Heir, HRH Crown Prince Haakon Magnus, *born* 20 July 1973

SELECTED GOVERNMENT MEMBERS *as at July 2010*
Prime Minister, Jens Stoltenberg
Defence, Grete Faremo
Finance, Sigbjorn Johnsen
Foreign Affairs, Jonas Gahr Store

ROYAL NORWEGIAN EMBASSY
25 Belgrave Square, London SW1X 8QD
T 020-7591 5500 E emb.london@mfa.no
W www.norway.org.uk
Ambassador Extraordinary and Plenipotentiary, HE Kim Traavik, *apptd* 2010

BRITISH EMBASSY
Thomas Heftyesgate 8, 0264 Oslo
T (+47) 2313 2700 E britemb@online.no
W http://ukinnorway.fco.gov.uk
Ambassador Extraordinary and Plenipotentiary, HE Jane Owen, *apptd* 2010

BRITISH COUNCIL
Storgaten 10 B, 0155 Oslo
T (+47) (22) 396 190 W www.britishcouncil.org/norway
Director, Karoline Tellum

DEFENCE

The army has 72 main battle tanks, 104 armoured infantry fighting vehicles and 390 armoured personnel carriers. The navy has 6 submarines, 3 frigates and 6 patrol and coastal vessels at two bases. The air force has 52 combat aircraft.

Military expenditure – US$5,860m (2008)
Military personnel – 24,025: army 7,900, navy 3,550, air force 2,500, home guard 475, central support 9,600
Conscription duration – 12 months plus refresher training

ECONOMY AND TRADE

Norway's prosperity depends primarily upon oil and gas extraction and its fisheries. Oil and gas account for nearly half of exports. Oil production is declining, but exploration for oil and gas in the Barents Sea, and other areas that are becoming more accessible as the Arctic ice cap retreats, is ongoing. Norway has planned for the time when reserves are exhausted by investing the revenue from this sector in a government fund. The state retains a majority share in key enterprises, including the oil industry.

The nature of the terrain restricts agriculture, which generates 2.1 per cent of GDP. The main industries apart from oil and gas are fishing, forestry, food processing, shipbuilding, pulp and paper products, metals, chemicals, mining and textiles. Shipping freight services are also significant, with Norwegian companies controlling almost 5 per cent of the world's shipping fleet by tonnage. Industry contributes 39.5 per cent of GDP and services 58.3 per cent.

The main trading partners are EU countries, the USA and China. Principal exports are oil and petroleum products, machinery and equipment, metals, chemicals, ships and fish. The main imports are machinery and equipment, chemicals, metals and foodstuffs.

GNI – US$416,400m; US$87,340 per capita (2008)
Annual average growth of GDP – 1.1 per cent (2009 est)
Inflation rate – 2.3 per cent (2009 est)
Unemployment – 3.2 per cent (2009 est)
Total external debt – US$548,100m (2009 est)
Imports – US$88,000m (2008)
Exports – US$165,300m (2008)

BALANCE OF PAYMENTS
Trade – US$52,190m surplus (2009)
Current Account – US$83,825m surplus (2008)

Trade with UK	*2008*	*2009*
Imports from UK	£2,755,061,561	£2,692,075,673
Exports to UK	£20,645,733,957	£14,777,830,846

COMMUNICATIONS

There are 4,100km of railways and 92,900km of roads. The rail network stops at Bodo, a little way north of the Arctic Circle, and there are few roads in the far north, to which the main means of transport is by sea; the state ferry service operates between Bergen and Kirkenes carrying freight, vehicles and passengers. There are 98 airports and airfields, including the principal airports at Oslo, Bergen, Stavanger and Trondheim. The main ports are Oslo, Bergen, Kristiansand, Tonsberg, Stavanger and Narvik, and there is a large merchant fleet, with 688 ships of over 1,000 tonnes registered in Norway and 923 registered abroad.

The fixed-line telephone system serves all parts of the country and mobile phone distribution has grown rapidly. In 2008 there were 1.9 millon fixed lines in use, 5.3 million mobile phone subscribers and 3.9 million internet users.

EDUCATION AND HEALTH

Education from six to 16 is free of charge and compulsory in the basic schools, and free from 16 to 19 years. The majority of pupils receive post-compulsory schooling at upper secondary schools, universities, and regional and specialist colleges.

Gross enrolment ratio (percentage of relevant age group) – primary 98 per cent; secondary 113 per cent; tertiary 76 per cent (2008 est)
Health expenditure (per capita) – US$7,354 (2007)
Hospital beds (per 1,000 people) – 3.9 (2003–8)

MEDIA AND CULTURE

The public broadcaster NRK operates radio and television channels, in competition with a number of commercial rivals. Newspaper readership is high given the size of the population, with one weekly and five daily national newspapers.

Celebrated cultural figures include the artist Edvard Munch (1863–1944), responsible for one of the world's most recognisable paintings, *The Scream* (1893); writer Knut Hamsun (1859–1952), winner of the Nobel prize in 1920; dramatist Henrik Ibsen (1828–1906); the composer Edvard Grieg (1843–1907) and the 1980s pop group A-ha, which has sold over 30 million albums worldwide.

TERRITORIES

SVALBARD

Area – 61,020 sq. km
Population – 2,116 (2009 est); Norwegian 70 per cent, Russian 24 per cent

The Svalbard archipelago consists of Spitsbergen, North East Land, the Wiche Islands, Barents Island, Edge Island, Prince Charles Foreland, Hope Island and Bear Island.

It lies north of the Arctic Circle, and glaciers and snow cover around 60 per cent of the area, although the west coast is ice-free for about half the year. Some 65 per cent of the Svalbard archipelago is protected to ensure biodiversity; there are seven national parks, six large nature reserves, 15 bird sanctuaries and one geotopic protected area. A global seed repository has been established on Spitsbergen. Norway's sovereignty was recognised by treaty in 1920 but the other signatories were granted equal rights to exploit mineral deposits, although this right is now only exercised by Russia. The territory is administered by a governor, who is responsible to the Ministry of Justice and Police. The main economic activities are coal mining, tourism, and research and education.

JAN MAYEN ISLAND

Area – 377 sq. km
Population – the only residents are the staff of the radio and meteorological stations

The island is barren, volcanic and partially covered by glaciers, with no exploitable natural resources. It lies in the North Atlantic Ocean about 950 km west of Norway. The island was annexed by Norway in 1922 and integrated into the kingdom in 1930; since 1995 it has been administered by the governor of Nordland county.

NORWEGIAN ANTARCTIC TERRITORY

The Norwegian Antarctic Territory consists of Queen Maud Land, Bouvet Island and Peter the First Island. Claimed in 1938, Queen Maud Land is a sector of the Antarctic continent which extends from 45° E. to 20° E. Peter the First Island was formally claimed in 1931 and is the only claimed area covered under the Antarctic treaty that is not part of the main land mass. Bouvet Island was claimed in 1930 (*see also* The North and South Poles).

OMAN

Saltanat Uman – Sultanate of Oman

Area – 309,500 sq. km
Capital – Muscat (Masqat); population, 634,074 (2009 est)
Major cities – Ibri, Salalah, Suhar, as-Suwayq
Currency – Rial Omani (OR) of 1,000 baisas
Population – 3,418,085 rising at 3.14 per cent a year (2009 est)
Religion – Muslim (predominantly Ibadhi; Shia 5 per cent) (est), with Hindu and Christian minorities. Islam is the official religion
Language – Arabic (official), English, Baluchi, Urdu
Population density – 9 per sq. km (2008)
Urban population – 72 per cent (2007 est)
Median age (years) – 18.8 (2009 est)
National anthem – 'Nashid as-Salaam as-Sultani' ['The Sultan's Anthem']
National day – 18 November (Birthday of Sultan Qaboos)
Life expectancy (years) – 74.16 (2009 est)
Mortality rate – 3.65 (2009 est)
Birth rate – 34.79 (2009 est)
Infant mortality rate – 16.88 (2009 est)
Death penalty – Retained
CPI score – 5.5 (2009)

CLIMATE AND TERRAIN

Oman lies at the south-eastern corner of the Arabian peninsula and includes territory at the tip of the Musandam peninsula, which is separated from the rest of the country by the UAE. There are mountains in the north and the south-west of the country, divided by high desert plateau; over 80 per cent of the country is desert. The plateau descends to a fertile plain on the Arabian Sea coast. Elevation extremes range from 2,980m (Jabal Shams) at the highest point to 0m (Arabian Sea) at the lowest. The climate is arid, with high temperatures and humidity throughout the year; temperatures are lower on the coast, but the high humidity there often makes coastal areas the most inhospitable. Average temperatures in Muscat range from lows of 19°C in January to highs of 38°C in June.

HISTORY AND POLITICS

Oman began to build an empire in the Middle East from the eighth century AD and remained largely unchallenged until the arrival in 1506 of the Portuguese, who were ousted in 1650. An independent sultanate was established in 1749 by the founder of the dynasty that still rules the country. By the early 19th century, Omani rule extended to the east African coast and parts of Persia and Balochistan (in modern Pakistan). The kingdom came under British influence from the late 19th century until 1951.

The country was divided from 1913, with religious leaders in control of the interior and the sultan of the coastal regions. The interior's attempts to assert its independence led to clashes in the 1950s, but by 1959 the sultan had established control over the whole country. An insurrection in the south by left-wing rebels supported by South Yemen began in 1965 and was defeated with British military assistance in 1975. The discovery and subsequent exploitation of oil in the mid-1960s led to the steady economic transformation of Oman, and in 1970 the sultan was overthrown in a bloodless coup by his son, Sultan Qaboos bin Said al-Said, who initiated a modernisation programme.

The country is still essentially an absolute monarchy, although a degree of political liberalisation has occurred in the past 20 years and the 1996 Basic Statute sets out the development of the political and legal systems; the first direct election to the consultative council was held in 2000 and the first by universal adult suffrage in 2003. In the 2007 election, 38 members were returned and 46 new members were elected.

POLITICAL SYSTEM

In 1996 the sultan issued a Basic Statute that is in effect a constitution; it established a succession mechanism, codified the system of government and set up a bicameral legislature. At present, legislation is proposed by the sultan and passed by decree. The sultan is advised by the bicameral Council of Oman, comprising the Consultative

Council *(Majlis al-Shura)*, which has 84 members directly elected for a four-year term, and the Council of State *(Majlis al-Dawlah)*, which has 59 members appointed by the sultan. The *Shura* council has the right to review legislation, question ministers and make policy proposals. The *Majlis al-Dawlah* is intended to facilitate 'constructive cooperation between the government and the citizens'. There are no political parties.

HEAD OF STATE
HM The Sultan of Oman, Prime Minister, Sultan Qaboos bin Said al-Said, *succeeded following a coup,* 23 July 1970

SELECTED GOVERNMENT MEMBERS *as at June 2010*
Deputy Prime Minister, Fahd bin Mamud al-Said
Defence, Badr bin Saud bin Hareb al-Busaidi
Foreign Affairs, Yusuf bin Alawi bin Abdullah
Interior, Saud bin Ibrahim al-Busaidi
Economy, Ahmed bin Abdul Nabi Makki

EMBASSY OF THE SULTANATE OF OMAN
167 Queen's Gate, London SW7 5HE
T 020-7225 0001
Ambassador Extraordinary and Plenipotentiary, HE Abdul Aziz al-Hinai, *apptd* 2009

BRITISH EMBASSY
PO Box 185, Mina al Fahal, 113 Muscat
T (+968) (24) 609 000 E enquiries.muscat@fco.gov.uk
W http://ukinoman.fco.gov.uk
Ambassador Extraordinary and Plenipotentiary, HE Noel Guckian, *apptd* 2005

BRITISH COUNCIL
PO Box 73, Road One, Madinat al Sultan, Qaboos West, 115 Muscat
T (+968) (24) 681 000 W www.britishcouncil.org/me
Director, John Gildea

DEFENCE

The army has 117 main battle tanks and 206 armoured personnel carriers. The navy has 2 corvettes and 11 patrol and coastal vessels at 6 bases. The air force has 64 combat aircraft.
Military budget – US$4,060m (2009)
Military personnel – 42,600: army 25,000, navy 4,200, air force 5,000, Royal Household 6,400, foreign forces 2,000; paramilitary 4,400

ECONOMY AND TRADE

Although its production is more modest than other Gulf states, oil and gas are the mainstay of Oman's economy and account for nearly 80 per cent of government revenue. Oil reserves are dwindling and development plans centre on diversification, industrialisation and privatisation, with the aim of reducing the oil sector's contribution to GDP to 9 per cent by 2020. Industrial development is focused on natural gas production, metal manufacturing, petrochemicals and trans-shipment ports, with plans also to develop tourism and communication technology industries. Improved training, especially in IT and business skills, is intended to enable the local population to replace expatriate workers. The global economic crisis has slowed development.

Agriculture and fishing account for 1.4 per cent of GDP, producing dates, limes, bananas, alfalfa and vegetables as well as fish. The main industries apart from oil and natural gas extraction are oil refining, liquefied natural gas production, construction and production of cement, copper, steel, chemicals and optic fibre. Industry accounts for 48.6 per cent of GDP and services for 49.9 per cent.

The main trading partners are the UAE, China, Japan and South Korea. Principal exports are petroleum, re-exports, fish, metals and textiles. The main imports are machinery and transport equipment, manufactured goods, food and livestock.
GNI – US$39,100; US$14,330 per capita (2008)
Annual average growth of GDP – 2.6 per cent (2009 est)
Inflation rate – 5.3 per cent (2009 est)
Unemployment – 15 per cent (2004 est)
Total external debt – US$7,474m (2009 est)
Imports – US$23,100m (2008)
Exports – US$37,700m (2008)

BALANCE OF PAYMENTS
Trade – US$8,419m surplus (2009)
Current Account – US$5,469m surplus (2008)

Trade with UK	*2008*	*2009*
Imports from UK	£432,926,775	£349,956,037
Exports to UK	£139,329,700	£86,355,954

COMMUNICATIONS

There are some 42,300km of roads, of which 16,500km are surfaced, but there are no railways. The main airports are at Muscat and Salalah, with over 120 other airports and airfields around the country. The main ports are Salalah and Port Qaboos at Mutrah, which has eight deep-water berths.

The modern telephone system served 274,200 fixed-line subscribers, 3.2 million mobile phone subscribers and 465,000 internet users in 2008.

EDUCATION AND HEALTH

Literacy rate – 84.4 per cent (2007 est)
Gross enrolment ratio (percentage of relevant age group) – primary 75 per cent; secondary 88 per cent; tertiary 26 per cent (2008 est)
Health expenditure (per capita) – US$375 (2007)
Hospital beds (per 1,000 people) – 2 (2003–8)

MEDIA

The first private radio station launched in 2007, ending a government monopoly on television and radio broadcasting. Satellite dishes are permitted, so stations from neighbouring Saudi Arabia, the UAE and Yemen can be received. There are a large number of newspapers, including four national dailies. The press can be subject to political and cultural censorship by the government.

PAKISTAN

Jamhuryat Islami Pakistan – Islamic Republic of Pakistan

Area – 796,095 sq. km
Capital – Islamabad; population, 832,002 (2009 est)
Major cities – Faisalabad, Gujranwala, Hyderabad, Karachi, Lahore, Multan, Peshawar, Quetta, Rawalpindi
Currency – Pakistan rupee of 100 paisa
Population – 176,242,949 rising at 1.95 per cent a year (2009 est); Punjabi (44.7 per cent), Pashtun (15.4 per cent), Sindhi (14.1 per cent), Sariaki (8.4 per cent), Muhagirs (7.6 per cent), Balochi (3.6 per cent) (est)
Religion – Muslim 97 per cent (predominantly Sunni) (est); small Christian and Hindu minorities; Islam is the state religion
Language – Urdu, English (both official), Punjabi, Sindhi, Siraiki, Pashto, Balochi, Hindko, Brahui, Burushaski
Population density – 215 per sq. km (2008)
Urban population – 36 per cent (2007 est)
Median age (years) – 20.8 (2009 est)
National anthem – 'Qaumi Tarana' ['National Anthem']
National day – 23 March (Republic Day)
Life expectancy (years) – 64.49 (2009 est)
Mortality rate – 7.68 (2009 est)
Birth rate – 27.62 (2009 est)
Infant mortality rate – 65.14 (2009 est)
Death penalty – Retained
CPI score – 2.4 (2009)

CLIMATE AND TERRAIN

The arid Thar desert in the east gives way to the fertile Indus valley in the centre of the country. The terrain then rises to the Makran, Kirthar and Sulaiman mountain ranges in the west and the Karakoram and Himalayan ranges in the north. Elevation extremes range from 8,611m (K2) at the highest point to 0m (Indian Ocean) at the lowest. The climate varies greatly across the country. For most areas, the rainy season runs from July to September and is accompanied by very high humidity. Average temperatures in Islamabad range from lows of 2°C in January to highs of 40°C in June.

HISTORY AND POLITICS

Islam was introduced to the area from the eighth century onwards. From the 12th century, the territory formed part of successive empires covering northern India, including the Delhi sultanate and the Mughal Empire, and came under British control by the mid-19th century, forming part of the territory of British India.

Unable to agree with the Hindu-dominated Indian National Concress on the terms under which Muslim religious and political rights would be protected in an independent Indian state, in 1940 Mohammad Ali Jinnah, leader of the All-India Muslim League, and other Muslim leaders endorsed the Lahore resolution, which called for a separate state for Muslims. The predominantly Muslim areas of British India were partitioned at independence in 1947, forming the state of Pakistan. This state comprised West Pakistan (now Pakistan) and East Pakistan, the Muslim areas of Bengal, which became the independent state of Bangladesh in 1971 following a short civil war. It became a republic in 1956.

Since 1958 Pakistan has alternated between military and civilian rule. The first military regime was replaced by civilian government under Zulfiqar Ali Bhutto (1971–7), who was overthrown by General Zia ul-Haq (1977–88). Civilian governments under Benazir Bhutto and Nawaz Sharif (1988–99) proved unstable, with several rapid changes of government amid allegations of corruption. In 1999 a military coup brought General Pervez Musharraf to power. He restored civilian government in 2002, but controversially refused to resign his army post and become a civilian president until after his re-election as president in 2007; he resigned as president in August 2008 to avoid impeachment proceedings.

In September 2001 President Musharraf aligned Pakistan with the West in its 'war on terror', providing support to the Allies in the Afghan war. This policy angered Islamic militants, who are believed to be responsible for terrorist attacks in the major cities.

The legislative elections originally scheduled for January 2008 were postponed to February after the assassination of Benazir Bhutto in December 2007. The two main opposition parties, Bhutto's Pakistan People's Party (PPP) and Nawaz Sharif's Pakistan Muslim League–Nawaz Sharif (PML-N), won the most seats and formed a coalition government that also included two smaller parties; the PML-N withdrew from the coalition government in August 2008. The presidential election in September 2008 was won by Asif Ali Zadari, the widower of Benazir Bhutto.

INSURGENCIES

Balochistan, Punjab and Sindh provinces have all been affected since the 1980s by conflict between Shia and Sunni fundamentalists. Balochistan and, since the early 1990s, Sindh (especially Karachi) have experienced violence by armed militants seeking greater autonomy for each province.

Civil order has always been harder to maintain in the North-West Frontier Province and the federally administered tribal areas than in the rest of the country. These areas became havens for the Taliban fleeing Afghanistan after 2001 and for like-minded militants, who became entrenched along the Afghan border, radicalising and destabilising increasingly wide areas. Government military and security forces are struggling to maintain control in over half of these areas. The government conceded the imposition of Shariah law in the Swat valley as part of a cease-fire agreement with the Taliban in early 2009, but when the Taliban attempted to extend their influence further into the country, the army began a counter-insurgency offensive to retake the area in April 2009, subsequently moving against the Taliban in other strongholds such as South Waziristan. These offensives led to an increase in militants' attacks in the major cities, resulting in over 3,000 deaths in terrorist attacks in 2009. In 2010 the Taliban began to reassert its influence in some of the areas cleared by the army offensives in 2009.

FOREIGN RELATIONS

Since partition, sovereignty over the predominantly Muslim state of Jammu and Kashmir has been disputed between Pakistan and India. A short war in 1947–8 resulted in the state being partitioned between the two countries; its status remains unresolved, despite further outbreaks of war in 1965 and 1971, low-level conflict for control of the Siachen glacier since 1985 and occasional increases in military exchanges, most recently in 1999–2002 and 2003. Tension was exacerbated by Pakistan's support of the Muslim insurgency in the Indian part of the state, which began in the 1980s, and by both countries' acquisition of nuclear weapons. Moves towards a peaceful settlement began in 2003, when diplomatic missions were reopened and the resumption of transport links was initiated. Formal diplomatic talks began in 2004 and have achieved several accords intended to reduce tension between the two countries (although the status of Kashmir has yet to be addressed). Talks were temporarily suspended by the Indian government after the Mumbai terrorist attacks in 2008, but resumed in early 2010.

International concern was raised in 2004 by disclosures that Pakistan has sold its nuclear technology to other countries.

POLITICAL SYSTEM

Pakistan is a federal republic. The 1973 constitution has been suspended and restored several times, and amended in 1985, 2002, 2003 and most recently in April 2010, when some of the president's powers were returned to the prime minister. Under the present constitution, the president is elected by the legislature for a five-year term.

The parliament *(Majlis as-Shura)* comprises a lower house, the National Assembly and the senate. The National Assembly has 342 members, of whom 60 are women and ten are elected by non-Muslim minorities; members serve for a five-year term. The senate has 100 members, 88 elected by provincial assemblies, eight chosen by tribal agencies and four elected by the National Assembly; they serve a six-year term, with half elected every three years. The prime minister is nominated by and is responsible to the legislature.

There are four provinces: Balochistan, Khyber Pukhtoonkhwa (formerly North-West Frontier Province), Punjab and Sindh. Each has a provincial assembly and government. In addition, there are the Federally Administered Tribal Areas and the Islamabad Capital Territory.

HEAD OF STATE

President, Asif Ali Zardari, *elected* 6 September 2008, *sworn in* 9 September 2008

SELECTED GOVERNMENT MEMBERS *as at June 2010*

Prime Minister, Yusuf Raza Gilani
Defence, Chaudhry Ahmed Mukhtar
Foreign Affairs, Shah Mehmood Qureshi
Finance, Abdul Hafiz Skeikh
Interior, Rehman Malik

HIGH COMMISSION FOR THE ISLAMIC REPUBLIC OF PAKISTAN

34–36 Lowndes Square, London SW1X 9JN
T 020-7664 9204 W www.pakmission-uk.gov.pk
High Commissioner, HE Wajid Shamsul Hasan, *apptd* 2008

BRITISH HIGH COMMISSION

PO Box 1122, Diplomatic Enclave, Ramna 5, Islamabad
T (+92) (51) 282 2000 E bhcmedia@dsl.net.pk
W http://ukinpakistan.fco.gov.uk
High Commissioner, HE Adam Thomson, CMG, *apptd* 2010

BRITISH COUNCIL

PO Box 1135, Islamabad
T (+92) (51) 283 3133 W www.britishcouncil.org/pakistan
Director, David Martin

DEFENCE

The army has over 2,461 main battle tanks, 1,266 armoured personnel carriers and 26 armed helicopters. The navy has 8 submarines, 7 frigates, 8 patrol and coastal vessels, 12 combat aircraft and 6 armed helicopters at three bases. The air force has 383 combat aircraft and 19 helicopters.

Military expenditure – US$4,110m (2009)
Military personnel – 617,000: army 550,000, navy 22,000, air force 45,000; paramilitary 304,000

ECONOMY AND TRADE

Decades of political instability, inefficiency, corruption and high military expenditure have left Pakistan a poor and underdeveloped country. In the 2000s economic reforms, international aid and greater foreign investment produced steady growth of 6–8 per cent a year until 2008, notably in the industrial and service sectors, and reduced poverty levels by 10 per cent between 2001 and 2007. However, slower growth in 2008 caused budget and fiscal deficits that forced Pakistan to seek IMF assistance; inflation, already a persistant problem, rose to 20.3 per cent in 2008, and it remains high. A large proportion of the country's labour force works abroad, especially in the Middle East, providing valuable remittances but also causing use of child labour within Pakistan.

Agriculture employs 43 per cent of the workforce, producing cotton, wheat, rice, sugar cane, fruit, vegetables, milk, meat and eggs, and contributing 20.8 per cent of GDP. Significant manufacturing industries include textiles and clothing, food processing, pharmaceuticals, construction materials, paper products, fertiliser and seafood. Industry accounts for 24.3 per cent of GDP and services for 54.9 per cent.

The main trading partners are the UAE, the USA, China, Saudi Arabia and Afghanistan. Principal exports are textiles (clothing, bed linen, cotton cloth and yarn), rice, leather goods, sports goods, chemicals, manufactures and carpets and rugs. The main imports are petroleum, petroleum products, machinery, plastics, transport equipment, edible oils, paper, iron, steel and tea.

GNI – US$157,300m; US$980 per capita (2008)
Annual average growth of GDP – 2.7 per cent (2009 est)
Inflation rate – 14.2 per cent (2009 est)
Population below poverty line – 24 per cent (2005–6 est)
Unemployment – 15.2 per cent (2009 est)
Total external debt – US$52,120m (2009 est)
Imports – US$42,300m (2008)
Exports – US$20,400m (2008)

BALANCE OF PAYMENTS

Trade – US$16,025m deficit (2009)
Current Account – US$13,874m deficit (2008)

Trade with UK	*2008*	*2009*
Imports from UK	£464,997,302	£461,208,391
Exports to UK	£596,328,460	£643,510,372

COMMUNICATIONS

There are some 259,000km of roads and 7,800km of railways. The principal airports are at Karachi, Islamabad, Lahore, Peshawar and Sialkot. Pakistan International Airlines operates domestic air services between the principal cities as well as international services. The main seaports are Karachi and Port Muhammad bin Qasim. A deepwater port at Gwadar in Balochistan, funded and constructed by China, became fully functional in 2008, and there are numerous plans to further develop the city as a regional energy and transport hub.

Recent investment has resulted in dramatic improvements in the fixed-line and mobile telephone infrastructure. Since 2000, fixed-line availability has risen gradually but mobile phone distribution has rocketed; in 2008 there were 4.5 million fixed lines in use, while mobile phone subscribers numbered 91.4 million in 2009. In 2008 there were 18.5 million internet users.

EDUCATION AND HEALTH

Education is free of charge to upper secondary level.
Literacy rate – 54.2 per cent (2007 est)
Gross enrolment ratio (percentage of relevant age group) – primary 85 per cent; secondary 33 per cent; tertiary 5 per cent (2008 est)
Health expenditure (per capita) – US$23 (2007)
Hospital beds (per 1,000 people) – 0.6 (2003–8)

MEDIA

There are eight national daily newspapers, and the state-owned broadcaster, Pakistan Television Corporation Ltd, competes with around 50 private channels. The government has granted licences for a number of satellite television and radio stations since 2004. A number of unlicensed broadcasters are believed to exist in the north of the country.

PALAU

Beluu er a Belau – Republic of Palau

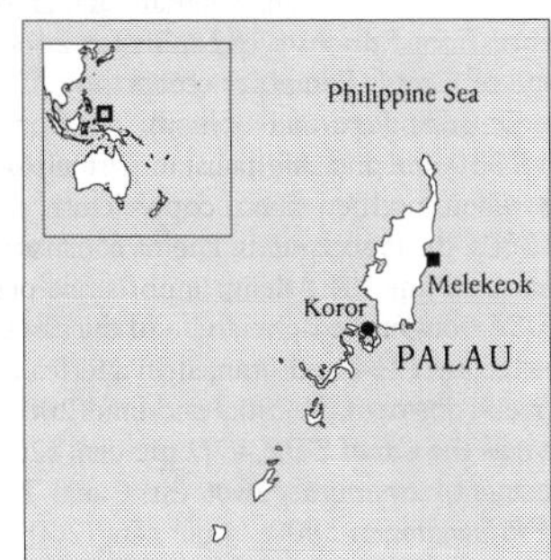

Area – 459 sq. km
Capital – Melekeok, on Babeldaob; population, 566 (2009 est)
Major town – Koror
Currency – US dollar (US$) of 100 cents
Population – 20,796 rising at 0.43 per cent a year (2009 est); Palauan (69.9 per cent), Filipino (15.3 per cent), Chinese (4.9 per cent)
Religion – Christian (Roman Catholic 65 per cent, Evangelical Church 10 per cent, Seventh-day Adventist 5 per cent, Mormons 2 per cent), Modekngei 9 per cent (est). Modekngei is unique to Palau and combines elements of animism and Christian beliefs
Language – Palauan (official in most islands), English (official in all islands), Tobi, Sonsoralese, Angaur (official in respective island), Japanese (official in Angaur), Filipino, Chinese
Population density – 44 per sq. km (2008)
Urban population – 79 per cent (2007 est)
Median age (years) – 32.2 (2009 est)
National anthem – 'Belau rekid' ['Our Palau']
National day – 9 July (Constitution Day)
Life expectancy (years) – 71.22 (2009 est)
Mortality rate – 7.89 (2009 est)
Birth rate – 11.2 (2009 est)
Infant mortality rate – 13.14 (2009 est)
Death penalty – Abolished for all crimes (since 1994)
Literacy rate – 91.9 per cent (2007 est)

CLIMATE AND TERRAIN

The republic consists of six island groups in the western Pacific Ocean; these comprise eight large islands and over 300 smaller islands or islets that are either volcanic and mountainous or coral and low-lying. Elevation extremes range from 242m (Mt Ngerchelchuus) at the highest point to 0m (Pacific Ocean) at the lowest. The climate is tropical, with a wet season from May to November. Average daily temperatures are an almost constant 27°C.

HISTORY AND POLITICS

Palau has been inhabited since the first millennium BC. In the 19th century, Spain and Germany vied for possession until 1889, when Spain sold the islands to Germany, which exploited the phosphate deposits and developed coconut plantations. Japan occupied the islands on behalf of the Allies in 1914 and administered them after the First World War under a League of Nations mandate. Japanese forces were ousted by the USA during the Second World War.

In 1947 the islands became part of the UN Trust Territory of the Pacific, administered by the USA. In 1982 a compact of free association was signed with the USA under which the USA retained responsibility for defence and foreign policy in return for providing economic aid; the compact was ratified in 1993 and entered into force when Palau became independent on 1 October 1994.

In the latest presidential and legislative elections, held in November 2008, Johnson Toribiong was elected president.

POLITICAL SYSTEM

Under the 1981 constitution, the executive president is directly elected for a four-year term, renewable only once. The president appoints the cabinet. The bicameral National Congress comprises the House of Delegates, which has 16 members (one from each state), and the nine-member senate; members of both chambers stand for election as independents, and serve a four-year term. A council of indigenous chiefs, composed of the paramount chief from each of the 16 states, acts as an advisory body to the president on matters concerning traditional law and customs.

Each of the 16 constituent states has its own governor and legislature.

HEAD OF STATE

President, Johnson Toribiong, *elected* 4 November 2008, *inaugurated* 15 January 2009
Vice-President, Finance, Kerai Mariur

SELECTED GOVERNMENT MEMBERS *as at June 2010*
Industry and Commerce, Jackson Ngiraingas
Minister of State, Victor Yano

BRITISH AMBASSADOR
HE Stephen Lillie, *apptd* 2009, resident at Manila, the Philippines

ECONOMY AND TRADE

The economy is reliant on economic aid from the USA and the government is keen to diversify. Tourism is growing and now caters for over 80,000 people a year, but the government is limiting development to protect the environment. The other main industries are handicrafts, construction and garment manufacturing. Subsistence agriculture and fishing remain important, engaging 20 per cent of the workforce and producing crops such as coconuts, copra, cassava and sweet potatoes as well as fish. Revenue is also derived from the sale of licences to foreign fishing fleets.

The main trading partners are the USA, Japan, Taiwan, Singapore and South Korea. Principal exports are shellfish, tuna, copra and clothing. The main imports are machinery and equipment, fuels, metals and foodstuffs.

GNI – US$175m; US$8,630 per capita (2008)
Annual average growth of GDP – 5.5 per cent (2005 est)
Inflation rate – 2.7 per cent (2005 est)
Unemployment – 4.2 per cent (2005 est)

Trade with UK	*2008*	*2009*
Imports from UK	£11,318	£5,500
Exports to UK	–	–

COMMUNICATIONS

There are 61km of roads, but no railways. There are three airports, on Koror, Peleliu and Angaur, which receive international flights from Guam, Japan, the Philippines and Taiwan. Koror is also the main seaport. Telecommunications systems are widely available, with over 90 per 100 people subscribing to either fixed-line or mobile phone services.

MEDIA

There is no television station in Palau, but most households can receive US and satellite television via cable. Radio broadcasting is provided by one government and two private stations, and there are three weekly news publications.

PANAMA

República de Panamá – Republic of Panama

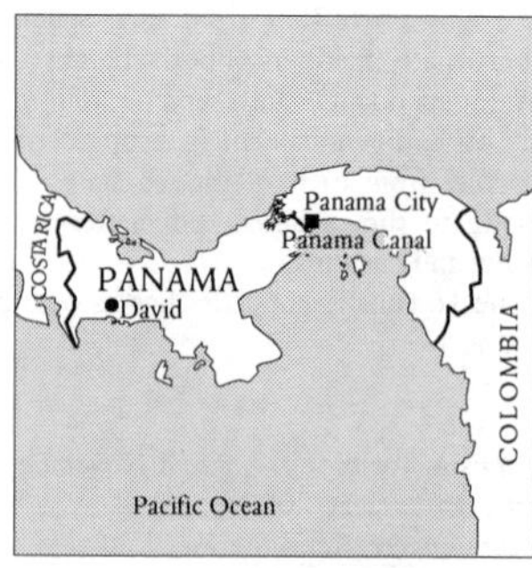

Area – 75,420 sq. km
Capital – Panama City; population, 1,346,260 (2009 est)
Major cities – Colón, Davíd
Currency – Balboa of 100 centésimos; at parity with the US dollar, which is used as paper currency. Both Panamanian and US coins are used
Population – 3,360,474 rising at 1.50 per cent a year (2009 est)
Religion – Christian (Roman Catholic 75 per cent, Protestant denominations 15 per cent, Mormon 1 per cent) (est)
Language – Spanish (official), English
Population density – 46 per sq. km (2008 est)
Urban population – 73 per cent (2007 est)
Median age (years) – 27 (2009 est)
National anthem – 'Himno Istmeño' ['Hymn of the Isthmus']
National day – 3 November (Independence Day)
Life expectancy (years) – 77.25 (2009 est)
Mortality rate – 4.66 (2009 est)
Birth rate – 20.18 (2009 est)
Infant mortality rate – 12.67 (2009 est)
Death penalty – Abolished for all crimes (since 1922)
CPI score – 3.4 (2009)

CLIMATE AND TERRAIN

Panama lies on the isthmus connecting North and South America. A mountain range runs along the centre, falling to coastal plains on both coasts. There is dense tropical rainforest in the east. Elevation extremes range from 3,475m (Volcan Baru) at the highest point to 0m (Pacific Ocean) at the lowest. The climate is tropical, with a prolonged wet season from May to January. Average temperatures are relatively constant throughout the year, and range between 22°C and 32°C.

HISTORY AND POLITICS

Panama was visited by Spanish explorers from 1502, and in 1519 became part of the Viceroyalty of New Andalucia, later New Grenada. It became a strategically important centre of trade. When it gained its independence from Spain in 1821, Panama joined the confederacy of Gran Colombia (comprising Colombia, Venezuela, Ecuador, Peru and Bolivia). The confederacy split up in 1830 and Panama became part of Colombia until 1903, when it achieved its independence.

In the 1880s, the French attempted to construct a canal across Panama to link the Atlantic and Pacific oceans. In 1903 the USA bought the rights to build the canal, which was completed in 1914 and opened in 1919. The USA was also given control of the canal and land to either side of it, known as the Canal Zone, in perpetuity but, under a 1977 agreement, sovereignty over the Canal Zone was transferred to Panama in 2000.

Panama was under the military rule of General Omar Torrijos from 1968 until his death in 1981. In 1983, General Manuel Noriega seized power and instigated a period of military rule, supported by the USA until 1987. An internal coup to unseat Noriega was unsuccessful in 1988, but in 1989 US forces invaded and deposed him. Noriega surrendered in 1990 and was tried and sentenced in the USA on drug-trafficking and money-laundering charges in 1992. In 1991, Panama abolished its armed forces.

The 2009 presidential election was won by Ricardo Martinelli of the Democratic Change party. In the simultaneous legislative election, the governing *Partido Revolucionario Democrática* (PRD) was again the individual party with the most seats, but the combined seats of the four-party Alliance for Change coalition led by Martinelli constituted a majority.

POLITICAL SYSTEM
Under the 1972 constitution, as amended, the executive president is directly elected for a five-year term, which is not renewable. The unicameral National Assembly has 71 members, who are directly elected for a five-year term. The president, who is responsible to the legislature, appoints the cabinet.

HEAD OF STATE
President, Ricardo Martinelli, *elected* 3 May 2009, *sworn in* 1 July 2009
First Vice-President, Foreign Affairs, Juan Carlos Varela

SELECTED GOVERNMENT MEMBERS *as at July 2010*
Interior, Roxana Mendez
Economy and Finance, Alberto Vallarino Clement

EMBASSY OF PANAMA
40 Hertford Street, London W1J 7SH
T 020-7493 4646 E panama1@btconnect.com
Ambassador Extraordinary and Plenipotentiary, HE Gilberto Arias, *apptd* 2009

BRITISH EMBASSY
PO Box 0816-07946, Torre MMG, Calle 53, Marbella, Panama City 1
T (+507) 269 0866 E britemb@cwpanama.net
W http://ukinpanama.fco.gov.uk
Ambassador Extraordinary and Plenipotentiary, HE Richard Austen, MBE, *apptd* 2006

DEFENCE
The National Maritime Service has 45 patrol and coastal combatant vessels at 3 bases.
Military budget – US$269m (2009)
Military personnel – none active; paramilitary 12,000

ECONOMY AND TRADE
The economy is based on a large service sector and has experienced steady growth in recent years, although this has slowed since 2008 because of the global economic downturn. However, the distribution of wealth is uneven, and nearly one-third of the population lives below the poverty line.

The service sector accounts for 76.8 per cent of GDP, derived from the operation of the Panama Canal and the Colón free trade zone, financial services, container ports, ship registry and tourism. Enlargement of the canal to take more and larger vessels began in 2007 and is scheduled for completion in 2014. Industry, which contributes 17.2 per cent of GDP, includes construction, brewing, sugar refining and the manufacture of cement and other construction materials. Agriculture, which accounts for 5.9 per cent of GDP, is centred on bananas, rice, maize, coffee, sugar cane, vegetables, livestock and shrimp.

The main trading partners are the USA, Costa Rica, China and EU countries. Principal exports are bananas, shrimp, sugar, coffee and clothing. The main imports are capital goods, foodstuffs, consumer goods and chemicals.
GNI – US$22,700m; US$6,690 per capita (2008)
Annual average growth of GDP – 2.4 per cent (2009 est)
Inflation rate – 2.6 per cent (2009 est)
Population below poverty line – 28.6 per cent (2006 est)
Unemployment – 7.1 per cent (2009 est)
Total external debt – US$12,040m (2009 est)
Imports – US$9,100m (2008)
Exports – US$1,200m (2008)

BALANCE OF PAYMENTS
Trade – US$6,553m deficit (2009)
Current Account – US$12m deficit (2009)

Trade with UK	*2008*	*2009*
Imports from UK	£148,913,294	£117,258,733
Exports to UK	£12,126,271	£13,937,526

COMMUNICATIONS
The Panama Canal connects the Pacific and Atlantic oceans, significantly shortening sea journeys between the two. Each year the canal handles over 14,000 transits, containing around 300 million tonnes (net) of cargo; this represents about 5 per cent of world trade and over 40 per cent of trade between Asia and the east coast of the USA. The chief ports are Colón, Cristóbal and Balboa, at either end of the canal. Because of its role as a ship registry, there were 6,323 Panamanian- and 5,394 foreign-owned ships of over 1,000 tonnes registered under its flag in 2008.

Apart from the 82km of the canal, there are over 700km of navigable waterways. These are supplemented by 76km of railways and 12,000km of roads. There are 117 airports and airfields; the principal airport is at Panama City.

Modern telephone systems served 524,000 fixed-line subscribers, 3.9 million mobile phone subscribers and 935,000 internet users in 2008.

EDUCATION AND HEALTH
There are nine years of compulsory education.
Literacy rate – 93.4 per cent (2007 est)
Gross enrolment ratio (percentage of relevant age group) – primary 111 per cent; secondary 71 per cent; tertiary 45 per cent (2008 est)
Health expenditure (per capita) – US$396 (2007)
Hospital beds (per 1,000 people) – 2.2 (2003–8)

MEDIA
The freedom of the media has improved markedly in recent years owing to the repeal of restrictive legislation in 2005. Broadcasting is dominated by the private sector, and there are several television networks and about 100 radio stations. *La Prensa, Panama News* and *El Siglo* are among the leading newspapers.

PAPUA NEW GUINEA

Gau Hedinarai ai Papua-Matamata Guinea – Independent State of Papua New Guinea

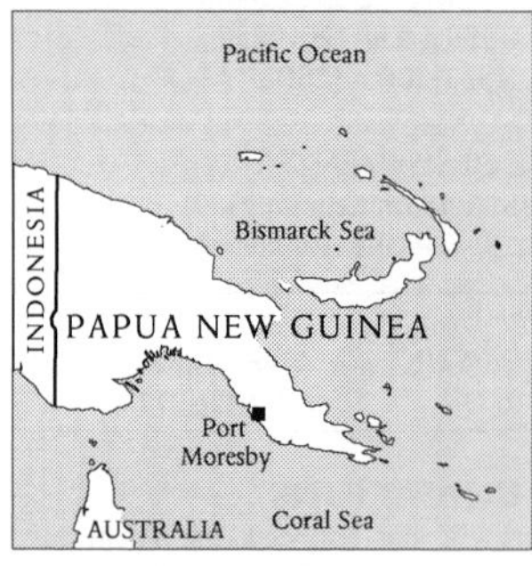

Area – 462,840 sq. km
Capital – Port Moresby; population, 313,593 (2009 est)
Major town – Lae
Currency – Kina (K) of 100 toea
Population – 6,057,263 rising at 2.07 per cent a year (2009 est)
Religion – Christian (Roman Catholic 30 per cent, Evangelical Lutheran 20 per cent, United Church 12 per cent, Seventh-day Adventist 10 per cent, Pentecostal 9 per cent, Evangelical Alliance 5 per cent, Anglican 3 per cent, Baptist 3 per cent, other 8 per cent) (est); Christian beliefs are often combined with elements of traditional indigenous religions
Language – English, Tok Pisin, Hiri Motu (all official), Motu; 860 indigenous languages are spoken, representing over 10 per cent of the world total
Population density – 15 per sq. km (2008)
Urban population – 12 per cent (2007 est)
Median age (years) – 21.7 (2009 est)
National anthem – 'O Arise, All You Sons'
National day – 16 September (Independence Day)
Life expectancy (years) – 66.34 (2009 est)
Mortality rate – 6.86 (2009 est)
Birth rate – 27.55 (2009 est)
Infant mortality rate – 45.23 (2009 est)
HIV/AIDS adult prevalence rate – 1.4 per cent (2007 est)
Death penalty – Retained (not used since 1950)
CPI score – 2.1 (2009)
Literacy rate – 57.8 per cent (2007 est)
Gross enrolment ratio (percentage of relevant age group) – primary 55 per cent (2008 est)
Health expenditure (per capita) – US$31 (2007)

CLIMATE AND TERRAIN

Papua New Guinea lies in the south-western Pacific Ocean and consists of the eastern half of the island of New Guinea, the islands of Bougainville, New Britain and New Ireland, the Admiralty Islands, the D'Entrecasteaux Islands and the Louisiade archipelago. A range of densely forested mountains runs across the centre of the Papuan part of New Guinea, descending to coastal plains and swamps, and coral reefs. Elevation extremes range from 4,509m (Mt Wilhelm) at the highest point to 0m (Pacific Ocean) at the lowest. There are a number of active volcanoes and the country is subject to frequent eruptions and earthquakes. Over 50 per cent of the country is forested, and 20 per cent is permanently or seasonally flooded. The climate is tropical and subject to the north-west monsoon (December–March) and south-east monsoon (May–October).

HISTORY AND POLITICS

New Guinea was visited by Europeans from the 16th century, before being colonised in the 19th century. The Dutch incorporated the western part of the island (now Papua province, Indonesia) into the Dutch East Indies in 1828. In 1884–6, Britain and Germany divided the east of the island. A British protectorate was proclaimed over south-eastern New Guinea and the adjacent islands, which were annexed outright in 1888 and placed under Australian administration in 1906. The north-east was claimed by Germany in 1884 and became a colony in 1899. This was occupied by Australia in the First World War, and both the British territory and the German-mandated territory were administered by Australia from 1920 until 1942. The territories were occupied by Japan between 1942 and 1945. After the Second World War the territories were combined as a UN trust territory and administered by Australia before becoming self-governing in 1973 and independent on 16 September 1975.

Separatism on Bougainville island led to nine years of conflict (1989–98) in which an estimated 20,000 people died. A peace agreement in 2001 provided for autonomy for the island and guaranteed a referendum on independence 10 to 15 years after the election of an autonomous government. The first autonomous government was elected in 2005.

Border areas are sometimes affected by the overspill from fighting between separatists and Indonesian forces in the Indonesian province of Papua. Thousands of refugees from this conflict live in camps along the border.

Fractionalism and shifting alliances have caused political instability since independence, and a proportional representation element was introduced into the voting system in 2007 to try to increase the stability of governments. Following the 2007 legislative election, the coalition led by National Alliance Party (NAP) remained the largest party in parliament, and the NAP leader Sir Michael Somare was elected prime minister for the fourth time, forming a new coalition government.

POLITICAL SYSTEM

The 1975 constitution was amended in 1998 to grant greater autonomy to Bougainville, and in March 2010 to expand the maximum number of cabinet ministers from 28 to 31. The head of state is Queen Elizabeth II, represented by a governor-general who is elected by the legislature for a six-year term. The unicameral National Parliament has 109 members, 20 from provincial electorates and the remainder from open electorates, who are directly elected for a five-year term. The prime minister is nominated by the legislature and appointed by the governor-general.

Governor-General, Sir Paulias Matane, *sworn in* 29 June 2004

SELECTED GOVERNMENT MEMBERS *as at June 2010*
Prime Minister, Sir Michael Somare
Deputy Prime Minister, Finance and Treasury (acting), Puka Temu
Foreign Affairs, Sam Abal

PAPUA NEW GUINEA HIGH COMMISSION
14 Waterloo Place, London SW1Y 4AR
T 020-7930 0922 E info@png.org.uk

W www.pnghighcomm.org.uk
High Commissioner, HE Jean Kekedo, OBE, *apptd* 2002

BRITISH HIGH COMMISSION
Sec 411 Lot 1 & 2, Kiroki Street, Waigani, Port Moresby
T (+675) 325 1677 E ukinpng@datec.net.pg
W http://ukinpng.fco.gov.uk
High Commissioner, HE David Dunn, *apptd* 2007

DEFENCE

The Maritime Element has 4 patrol and coastal combatant vessels at four bases.
Military budget – US$50m (2009)
Military personnel – 3,100: army 2,500, air force 200, Maritime Element 400

ECONOMY AND TRADE

Political instability, corruption, a weak economy and high unemployment and crime levels had brought the country to a parlous state by 2004, when an Australian report warned that it was in imminent danger of economic and social collapse. The economy has grown slightly since, owing to higher commodity prices and tight control of the national budget, but the country remains poor and underdeveloped, with about one-third of the population living below the poverty line and unemployment in some urban areas as high as 80 per cent. It continues to struggle to attract foreign investment and is dependent on foreign aid, mostly from Australia, which accounts for nearly 20 per cent of the budget.

Only about 1 per cent of the land area is suitable for commercial crops. About 85 per cent of the population practises subsistence farming, including some tribes in the interior so isolated that their economy is unmonetised. Mineral deposits, including copper, gold, silver, nickel, oil and natural gas, are abundant and constitute the main sources of revenue, although exploitation is hampered by the terrain and poor infrastructure. The main industries are mining, oil extraction and refining, forestry, processing of agricultural and forestry products, construction and tourism. Industry contributes 37 per cent of GDP and services 31 per cent.

The main trading partners are Australia, Singapore, China and Japan. Principal exports are oil, gold, copper ore, logs, palm oil, coffee, cocoa and shellfish. The main imports are machinery and transport equipment, manufactured goods, food, fuels and chemicals.
GNI – US$6,800m; US$1,040 per capita (2008)
Annual average growth of GDP – 0.7 per cent (2009 est)
Inflation rate – 6.5 per cent (2009 est)
Population below poverty line – 37 per cent (2002 est)
Unemployment – 1.8 per cent (2004 est)
Total external debt – US$2,320m (2009 est)
Imports – US$3,600m (2008)
Exports – US$5,700m (2008)

BALANCE OF PAYMENTS
Trade – US$2,243m surplus (2009)
Current Account – US$805m surplus (2008)

Trade with UK	*2008*	*2009*
Imports from UK	£6,945,335	£14,088,206
Exports to UK	£64,386,311	£54,000,192

COMMUNICATIONS

Dense forest in the interior means that most internal travel is by air or water. There are 11,000km of inland waterways and 9,600km of roads, of which less than 700km are surfaced; the most important road links Lae with the populous highlands. There are 560 airports and airstrips, the principal airports being at Port Moresby, Lae and Rabaul. Air Niugini operates regular flights internally and to other countries in the region. The main seaports are Port Moresby, Lae and Madang on New Guinea and Kimbe and Rabaul on New Britain. Several shipping companies operate cargo services around the world, but cargo and passenger services between the main ports and outports are very limited.

The telephone system provides a minimal service; combined density of fixed lines and mobile phones has nearly quadrupled since 2005, to 11 per 100 people, as mobile phone ownership in particular has grown rapidly.

MEDIA

Radio is the most important medium owing to the widely scattered population and low literacy levels. There are state-run and private radio and television broadcasters, although television coverage is limited to Port Moresby and regional capitals. There are two foreign-owned daily newspapers and a number of weekly publications.

PARAGUAY

República del Paraguay – Republic of Paraguay

Area – 406,752 sq. km
Capital – Asunción; population, 1,977,340 (2009 est)
Major cities – Ciudad del Este, Lambaré, Limpio, Ñemby
Currency – Guaraní (Gs) of 100 céntimos
Population – 6,995,655 rising at 2.36 per cent a year (2009 est)
Religion – Christian (Roman Catholic 90 per cent, Protestant denominations 6 per cent) (est)
Language – Spanish, Guaraní (both official)
Population density – 16 per sq. km (2008)
Urban population – 60 per cent (2007 est)
Median age (years) – 21.9 (2009 est)
National anthem – 'Paraguayos, República o Muerte' ['Paraguayans, the Republic or Death']
National day – 15 May (Independence Day)
Life expectancy (years) – 75.77 (2009 est)
Mortality rate – 4.46 (2009 est)
Birth rate – 28.17 (2009 est)
Infant mortality rate – 24.68 (2009 est)
Death penalty – Abolished for all crimes (since 1992)
CPI score – 2.1 (2009)

CLIMATE AND TERRAIN

The landlocked country is divided by the river Paraguay into two distinct regions. The area east of the Paraguay is a fertile, grassy plateau where most of the population lives. The area to the west, the Gran Chaco, consists of a grassy and occasionally marshy plain that extends into neighbouring countries. Elevation extremes range from 842m (Cerro Pero) at the highest point to 46m (the junction of the Paraguay and Paraná rivers) at the lowest. The climate varies from subtropical to temperate, with higher rainfall in the east and semi-arid conditions in the west. Average temperatures in Asunción range from lows of 12°C in June to highs of 35°C in January.

HISTORY AND POLITICS

Spanish colonisation of Paraguay began in the early 16th century and Asunción was founded in 1537. Paraguay became independent from Spain in 1811 under the dictator José Gaspar Rodriguez de Francia, who ruled until his death in 1840. His successors instigated a period of reform and modernisation which ended in 1865–70 with the catastrophic War of the Triple Alliance against Brazil, Uruguay and Argentina over access to the sea. The war resulted in the loss of over half the population as well as 150,000 sq. km of territory, and initiated a period of political instability that lasted until 1912. In the Chaco War of 1932–5, Paraguay gained territory in the west from Bolivia.

Political instability and conflict in the late 1940s ended with a coup in 1954 in which General Alfredo Stroessner seized power. His rule was autocratic and increasingly repressive, marked by corruption and human rights abuses. He was ousted in a coup in 1989 that paved the way for free multiparty elections to the presidency and legislature in 1993. These were won by the National Republican Association-Colorado Party (ANR-PC) and its presidential candidate, and the ANR-PC won all subsequent elections until 2008. Instability has prevailed since the 1990s, however, with the assassination of a vice-president, an attempted coup, widespread corruption and the growth of drug-trafficking, money-laundering and organised crime.

The 2008 presidential election was won by Fernando Lugo of the Patriotic Alliance for Change coalition (APC), the first president from outside the ANR-PC in 61 years. In the simultaneous legislative election, the ANR-PC remained the largest single party in both legislative chambers but the APC coalition held a greater number of the seats.

POLITICAL SYSTEM

Under the 1992 constitution, the executive president is directly elected for a five-year term, which is not renewable. The bicameral Congress consists of a 45-member senate and an 80-member Chamber of Deputies, both directly elected for a five-year term. The president, who is responsible to congress, appoints the council of ministers.

HEAD OF STATE

President, Fernando Lugo, *elected* 20 April 2008, *sworn in* 15 August 2008
Vice-President, Frederico Franco

SELECTED GOVERNMENT MEMBERS *as at July 2010*

Defence, Gen. (retd) Luis Bereiro Spaini
Foreign Affairs, Hector Lacognata
Interior, Rafael Filizzola

EMBASSY OF THE REPUBLIC OF PARAGUAY

3rd Floor, 344 Kensington High Street, London W14 8NS
T 020-7610 4180 E embapar@btconnect.com
W www.paraguayembassy.co.uk

Ambassador Extraordinary and Plenipotentiary, HE Miguel Solano López, *apptd* 2009

BRITISH AMBASSADOR

HE Shan Morgan, *apptd* 2008, resident in Buenos Aires, Argentina

DEFENCE

The army has 5 main battle tanks and 30 armoured personnel carriers. The navy has 28 patrol and coastal combatant vessels at 3 bases. The air force has 3 combat aircraft.
Military budget – US$127m (2009)
Military personnel – 10,650: army 7,600, navy 1,950, air force 1,100; paramilitary 14,800
Conscription duration – 12–24 months

ECONOMY AND TRADE

The economy showed modest growth from 2003 to 2008, partly owing to economic reforms, a condition of IMF loans in 2002. Drought reduced production of key exports in 2008, and the global downturn affected export demand and commodity prices in 2009, pushing the economy into recession. Economic performance is also hampered in the longer term by political instability, corruption, national and foreign debt, inadequate infrastructure and high crime levels, and a large unofficial economy exists. About one-fifth of the population lives below the poverty line, although this rate is higher in the cities because of migration from the countryside of families made landless by the commercialisation of agriculture and forest clearances.

The country has few mineral resources although exploration for oil and gas is under way. The economy is largely agricultural, much of it at subsistence level. Agricultural production, which accounts for 20.2 per cent of GDP and engages 26.5 per cent of the workforce, is centred on cotton, sugar cane, soya beans, maize, wheat, tobacco, cassava, fruit, vegetables and livestock products. The main industries are sugar refining, forestry, manufacturing (cement, textiles, beverages, wood products, steel) and hydro-electric power generation. Industry accounts for 18.7 per cent of GDP and services for 61.2 per cent.

The main trading partners are Brazil, China and Argentina. Principal exports are soya beans, feed, cotton, meat, edible oils, electricity, timber and leather. The main imports are road vehicles, consumer goods, tobacco and petroleum products.
GNI – US$13,100m; US$2,110 per capita (2008)
Annual average growth of GDP – –3.5 per cent (2009 est)
Inflation rate – 2.5 per cent (2009 est)
Population below poverty line – 32 per cent (2005 est)
Unemployment – 7.9 per cent (2009 est)
Total external debt – US$3,310m (2009 est)
Imports – US$10,200m (2008)
Exports – US$4,300m (2008)

BALANCE OF PAYMENTS

Trade – US$3,679m deficit (2009)
Current Account – US$412m deficit (2008)

Trade with UK	*2008*	*2009*
Imports from UK	£16,269,476	£17,778,619
Exports to UK	£4,696,982	£3,092,625

COMMUNICATIONS

Although landlocked, Paraguay has 3,100km of navigable waterways on its rivers. Direct shipping services operate between Asunción and Europe and the USA, and river steamer services provide internal transport. There are 29,500km of roads, including connections with Sao Paulo and Buenos Aires, but many are impassable in severe weather. Paraguay has 36km of railways. There are about 14 airports, including the principal airport at Asunción, and around 780 airfields and airstrips around the country.

The fixed-line telephone system is not extensive so mobile phone distribution has risen rapidly. In 2008 there were 491,000 fixed lines in use, 6 million mobile phone subscribers and 894,000 internet users.

EDUCATION AND HEALTH

Basic education is free of charge and compulsory for nine years.

Literacy rate – 94.6 per cent (2007 est)
Gross enrolment ratio (percentage of relevant age group) – primary 108 per cent; secondary 66 per cent (2008 est)
Health expenditure (per capita) – US$114 (2007)
Hospital beds (per 1,000 people) – 1.3 (2003–8)

MEDIA

The media operates freely, although journalists investigating politically sensitive issues can experience harassment. Most of the media is privately owned, but there is a state-run national radio station. There has been a proliferation of unlicensed radio stations close to the Argentinian and Brazilian borders.

PERU

República del Peru – Republic of Peru

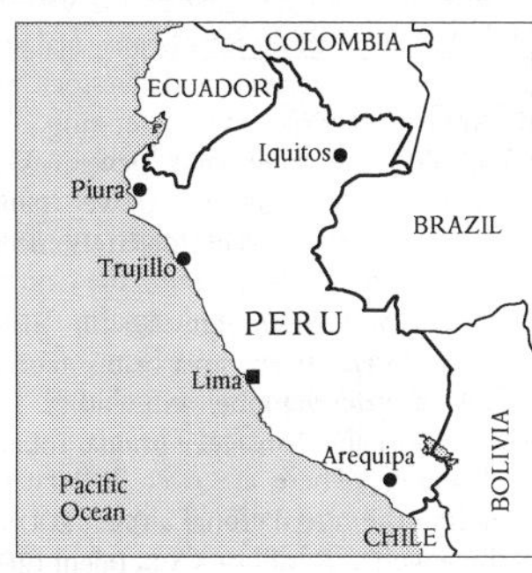

Area – 1,285,216 sq. km
Capital – Lima; population (including Callao), 8,769,350 (2009 est)
Major cities – Arequipa, Chiclayo, Iquitos, Piura, Trujillo
Currency – New sol of 100 centimos
Population – 29,546,963 rising at 1.23 per cent a year (2009 est)
Religion – Christian (Roman Catholic 81 per cent, Protestant denominations 13 per cent, other 3 per cent) (est)
Language – Spanish, Quechua (both official), Aymara, other Amerindian languages
Population density – 23 per sq. km (2008)
Urban population – 71 per cent (2007 est)
Median age (years) – 26.1 (2009 est)
National anthem – 'Somos libres, seámoslo siempre' ['We Are Free, Let Us Remain So Forever']
National day – 28 July (Independence Day)
Life expectancy (years) – 70.74 (2009 est)
Mortality rate – 6.14 (2009 est)
Birth rate – 19.38 (2009 est)
Infant mortality rate – 28.62 (2009 est)
Death penalty – Retained for certain crimes (last used 1979)
CPI score – 3.7 (2009)

CLIMATE AND TERRAIN

Peru has three main regions: the Costa, the coastal desert plain west of the Andes; the Sierra (mountain range) of the Andes, which runs parallel to the Pacific coast; and the Montaña (or Selva), a vast area of jungle stretching from the eastern foothills of the Andes to the country's eastern and north-eastern borders. Elevation extremes range from 6,768m (Nevado Huascaran) at the highest point to 0m (Pacific Ocean) at the lowest. The climate is arid in the west, temperate in the mountains and tropical in the east. Occasionally, due to the El Niño weather system, the northern districts receive several days of higher temperatures accompanied by torrential rain. Average temperatures in Lima range from lows of 13°C in August to highs of 28°C in January.

HISTORY AND POLITICS

The Inca Empire centred on Cuzco superseded earlier civilisations in Peru and flourished from the 13th to the 15th century, when the empire reached its zenith before falling to Spanish conquistadores led by Francisco Pizarro in 1532–3. The territory formed the Viceroyalty of Peru and its gold and silver mines made Peru the principal source of wealth in Spain's American empire. After 1810, Peru became the centre of Spanish colonial government as its other colonies rebelled. Although Peru declared its independence in 1821, this was achieved only with the final defeat of Spanish forces in 1824.

Peru entered into several border disputes with its neighbours in the 19th and 20th centuries, including the Pacific War (1879–83) in which it lost three southern coastal provinces to Chile. A border dispute with Ecuador was renewed in 1981, leading to a short, inconclusive war in 1995, but was resolved in 1998 following adjudication. A border dispute with Chile ended in 1999 with the implementation of accords first agreed in 1929.

Following independence, Peru alternated between periods of military dictatorship and democratic rule. The most recent return to democracy, in 1980, has not brought greater political stability or improved economic and social equality. Two left-wing insurgencies, by the Maoist *Sendero Luminoso* (Shining Path) and the *Movimento Revolucionario Tupac Amaru* (MRTA), began in the 1980s. The activities of the *Sendero Luminoso* in particular destabilised the government and the economy; the conflict caused about 69,000 deaths and saw human rights abuses by both the security forces and the guerrillas. By the late 1990s both insurgencies had been overcome, although a few Maoists remain active. The conflict has left a legacy of criminal violence, much of it related to drug production and trafficking.

The economy deteriorated badly in the late 1980s, and by 1990 inflation had reached 400 per cent. Alberto Fujimori was elected president in 1990 on a platform of economic reform. Within two years he had dismantled the existing order in Peru by dismissing the legislature, sacking senior judges, imposing order through an 'emergency national reconstruction government' and changing the constitution. He fled to Japan in 2000 to escape corruption charges and was succeeded by Alejandro Toledo, becoming the country's first president of Quechan descent.

In the 2006 legislative election, the Union for Peru (UPP) party won the most seats; the presidential election was won by the Peruvian Aprista Party (APRA) candidate Alan Garcia (president 1985–90). In October 2008 the APRA-led government resigned because APRA party members were implicated in a corruption scandal, and a new government was appointed under Yehude Simon. Simon's government resigned in June 2009 after the security forces' handling of demonstrations caused the death of over 50 indigenous protesters; Javier Velásquez was appointed to head a reshuffled government. Fresh presidential and legislative elections are due in April 2011.

POLITICAL SYSTEM

Under the 1993 constitution, the executive president is directly elected for a five-year term, renewable only once. The unicameral legislature, the Congress of the Republic, has 120 members, directly elected for a five-year term. The president, who is responsible to the congress, appoints the council of ministers.

HEAD OF STATE

President, Alan Garcia, *elected* 4 June 2006, *sworn in* 28 July 2006

Vice-Presidents, Luis Giampietri Rojas; Lourdes Mendoza del Solar

SELECTED GOVERNMENT MEMBERS *as at July 2010*

President of Council of Ministers, Javier Velasquez

Defence, Rafael Rey

Economy and Finance, Mercedes Aráoz

Foreign Affairs, José Antonio García Belaunde

Interior, Gen. Octavio Salazar

EMBASSY OF PERU

52 Sloane Street, London SW1X 9SP

T 020-7235 1917 E postmaster@peruembassy-uk.com

W www.peruembassy-uk.com

Ambassador Extraordinary and Plenipotentiary, HE Ricardo Luna, *apptd* 2006

BRITISH EMBASSY

PO Box 854, Torre Parque Mar (Piso 22), Avenida José Larco 1301, Lima

T (+51) (1) 617 3000 E belima@fco.gov.uk

W http://ukinperu.fco.gov.uk

Ambassador Extraordinary and Plenipotentiary, HE James Dauris, *apptd* 2010

DEFENCE

The army has 240 main battle tanks and 299 armoured personnel carriers. The navy has 6 submarines, 1 cruiser, 8 frigates, 14 patrol and coastal combatant vessels and 3 armed helicopters at 7 bases. The air force has 70 combat aircraft and 16 armed helicopters.

Military budget – US$1,570m (2009)

Military personnel – 114,000: army 74,000, navy 23,000, air force 17,000; paramilitary 77,000

ECONOMY AND TRADE

The economy has grown steadily since 2002, driven by increased agricultural, fisheries and mining exports, many major infrastructure developments and tourism. Poverty remains widespread, but the benefits of the economic growth are starting to be felt in the poorer regions and the poverty rate has declined by 15 per cent since 2002. Economic growth has slowed in the global downturn, owing to reduced demand for exports and lower commodity prices.

Mineral resources, including copper, gold, silver, zinc, oil and natural gas, are abundant, and extracting and refining these is the mainstay of the economy, although this makes it vulnerable to global price fluctuations. Other industries include steel and metal fabrication, fishing and fish processing, textiles and clothes manufacture and food processing. Agriculture is centred on asparagus, coffee, cocoa, cotton, sugar cane, rice, cereals, vegetables, fruit, coca, medicinal plants, meat and dairy products. Services contribute 59.7 per cent to GDP, industry 32.1 per cent and agriculture 8.2 per cent.

The main trading partners are the USA, China, other South American countries and Canada. Principal exports are copper, gold, zinc, crude oil and petroleum products, coffee, vegetables, textiles and fishmeal. The main imports are oil and petroleum products, plastics, machinery, vehicles, iron and steel, wheat and paper.

GNI – US$115,100m; US$3,990 per capita (2008)

Annual average growth of GDP – 1 per cent (2009 est)

Inflation rate – 1.2 per cent (2009 est)

Population below poverty line – 44.5 per cent (2006 est)

Unemployment – 9 per cent (2009 est)

Total external debt – US$30,040m (2009 est)

Imports – US$29,900m (2008)

Exports – US$31,500m (2008)

BALANCE OF PAYMENTS

Trade – US$5,236m surplus (2009)

Current Account – US$248m surplus (2009)

Trade with UK	*2008*	*2009*
Imports from UK	£87,810,535	£77,558,604
Exports to UK	£163,505,876	£171,220,047

COMMUNICATIONS

There are 78,829km of roads, of which 11,351km are surfaced. These include sections of two transnational highways: the east-west Andean Highway, linking the Pacific and Atlantic coasts, and the north–south Pan-American Highway running along the Pacific coast. The state-run railways have 1,989km of track, and 8,800km of inland waterways are navigable, on tributaries of the Amazon and Lake Titicaca. The main seaports are Callao and Matarani. There are over 200 airports and airstrips, including the international airport at Lima.

In 2008 there were 2.9 million fixed telephone lines in use, 21 million mobile phone subscribers and 7.1 million internet users.

EDUCATION AND HEALTH

Education is free of charge and compulsory for 11 years.

Literacy rate – 89.6 per cent (2007 est)

Gross enrolment ratio (percentage of relevant age group) – primary 113 per cent; secondary 98 per cent; tertiary 34 per cent (2008 est)

Health expenditure (per capita) – US$160 (2007)

Hospital beds (per 1,000 people) – 1.5 (2003–8)

MEDIA

Media freedom has greatly improved since 2000, but coverage of corruption, drug-trafficking or guerrilla activities has attracted violence against the media. The major broadcasters and newspapers are privately run, with the state-run radio and television stations having relatively small audiences. There are several television networks, six national daily newspapers and a host of commercial radio broadcasters.

THE PHILIPPINES

Republika ng Pilipinas – Republic of the Philippines

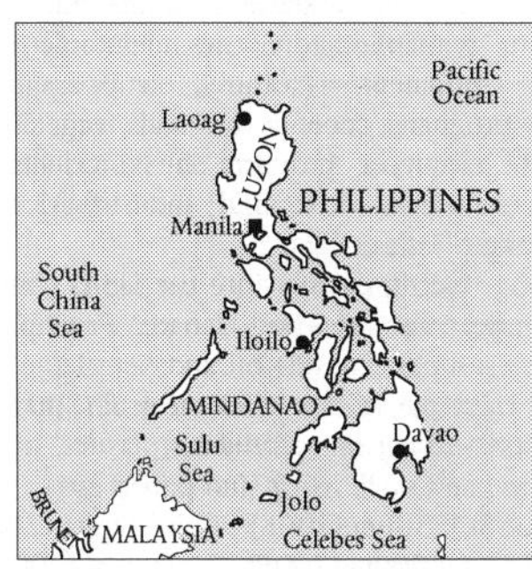

Area – 300,000 sq. km
Capital – Manila; population (Metro Manila, including Quezon City), 11,449,200 (2009 est)
Major cities – Bacolod, Cagayan de Oro, Cebu, Davao, General Santos (Dadiangas), Iloilo, Zamboanga
Currency – Philippine peso (P) of 100 centavos
Population – 97,976,603 rising at 1.96 per cent a year (2009 est); Tagalog (28.1 per cent), Cebuano (13.1 per cent), Ilocano (9 per cent), Bisaya (7.6 per cent), Hiligaynon Ilonggo (7.5 per cent), Bikol (6 per cent), Waray (3.4 per cent) (est)
Religion – Christian (Roman Catholic 80 per cent, other denominations 5 per cent), Muslim 5 per cent (predominantly Sunni) (est)
Language – Filipino (based on Tagalog), English (both official), Tagalog, Cebuano, Ilocano, Hiligaynon, Bicol, Waray, Pampango, Pangasinan
Population density – 303 per sq. km (2008)
Urban population – 64 per cent (2007 est)
Median age (years) – 22.5 (2009 est)
National anthem – 'Lupang Hinirang' ['Chosen Land']
National day – 12 June (Independence Day)
Life expectancy (years) – 71.09 (2009 est)
Mortality rate – 5.1 (2009 est)
Birth rate – 26.01 (2009 est)
Infant mortality rate – 20.56 (2009 est)
Death penalty – Abolished for all crimes (since 2006)
CPI score – 2.4 (2009)

CLIMATE AND TERRAIN

The Philippines comprises over 7,100 islands in the western Pacific Ocean. The principal islands are Luzon, Mindanao, Mindoro, Samar, Negros, Palawan, Panay and Leyte; other groups include the Sulu islands, Babuyanes and Batanes, Calamian and Kalayaan islands. The islands mostly have mountainous interiors and narrow coastal plains. The mountain ranges are volcanic, and some volcanoes are still active. Elevation extremes range from 2,954m (Mt Apo) at the highest point to 0m (Philippine Sea) at the lowest. The climate is tropical, with relatively constant temperatures throughout the year which in Manila reach average lows of 21°C in January and 34°C in May and June, when the humidity is particularly oppressive. The country is affected by the monsoons, which cause the rainy season between July and October. During this period the country is also susceptible to typhoons, which frequently cause widespread damage and loss of life.

HISTORY AND POLITICS

The Philippine islands were settled first by Malays, then by Chinese, Indonesian and Arab traders. Islam was introduced in the 14th century and became the dominant religion in the south. The islands were discovered by Spain and then settled from 1565 by the Spanish, who introduced Roman Catholicism. Colonial rule lasted until 1898, when Spain ceded the colony to the USA following the Spanish-American War. The country became internally self-governing in 1935, was occupied by Japan from 1942 to 1944, and achieved independence from the USA in 1946.

Ferdinand Marcos was elected president in 1965, imposing martial law in 1972. His regime became increasingly repressive, corrupt and violent, and when he falsified election results in 1986 to prevent Corazon Aquino from taking office as president a popular uprising forced him to flee the country. Aquino survived political unrest and ten attempted military coups to introduce a new constitution and entrench democratic politics.

Fidel Ramos, Aquino's successor in 1992, built on her work, raised the country's international profile and instigated peace talks with insurgents (*see* below). Joseph Estrada, elected president in 1998, was overthrown in 2001 in a popular uprising; his term was completed by Vice-President Gloria Arroyo. President Arroyo retained the presidency in the 2004 presidential election, but her popularity plummeted and her anti-corruption measures and economic reforms were undermined by corruption scandals and impeachment attempts.

The presidential election in May 2010 was won by Benigno ('Noynoy') Aquino III, son of former president Corazon Aquino.

INSURGENCY

A communist insurgency by the New People's Army (NPA) began in the late 1960s. The NPA is based in Mindanao but has groups in rural areas throughout the country. Peace talks between the government and the NPA's political front, the National Democratic Front, stalled in 2004 and clashes continue.

There has been a Muslim (Moro) insurgency in the southern islands, particularly Mindanao, since the 1970s. The Moro National Liberation Front (MNLF) concluded a peace agreement with the government in 1996 that ended its insurgency and established the Autonomous Region of Muslim Mindanao (ARMM). The Moro Islamic Liberation Front (MILF) agreed a ceasefire with the government in 2003, but negotiations over a Muslim 'homeland' broke down in 2008, and a resumption of violence displaced over 300,000 people until another ceasefire was agreed in July 2009; peace talks were resumed in December 2009.

The radical Muslim separatist group Abu Sayyaf, based on Jolo and Basilan, is viewed as a terrorist organisation and the government refuses to negotiate with it. It has links with Jamaah Islamiyah, the group responsible for the Bali bombings, and possibly with al-Qaeda. Since 2001 it has carried out a series of violent kidnappings and bombings, but military operations since 2006 have depleted its numbers and its leadership.

POLITICAL SYSTEM
Under the 1987 constitution, the executive president is directly elected for a six-year term, which is not renewable. There is a bicameral Congress. The lower house, the House of Representatives, has 272 members, of whom 219 are directly elected and the rest appointed from party and minority group lists; all serve a three-year term. The senate has 24 members directly elected for a six-year term, with half re-elected every three years.

The Autonomous Region of Muslim Mindanao comprises the provinces of Lanao del Sur and Maguindanao on Mindanao and the island provinces of Sulu, Tawi-Tawi and Basilan. It has a 24-member regional assembly and a governor.

HEAD OF STATE
President, Benigno ('Noynoy') Aquino III, *elected* 10 May 2010, *sworn in* 30 June 2010
Vice-President, Jejomar Binay

SELECTED GOVERNMENT MEMBERS *as at June 2010*
Finance, Cesar Purisima
Trade and Industry, Gregory Domingo
Foreign Affairs, Alberto Romulo
Defence, Voltaire Gazmin

EMBASSY OF THE REPUBLIC OF THE PHILIPPINES
6–8 Suffolk Street, London SW1Y 4HG
T 020-7451 1800 E embassy@philemb.co.uk
W http://philembassy-uk.org
Ambassador Extraordinary and Plenipotentiary, HE Antonio Lagdameo, *apptd* 2009

BRITISH EMBASSY
120 Upper McKinley Road, McKinley Hill, Taguig City 1634, Manila
T (+63) (2) 858 2200 E uk@info.com.ph
W http://ukinthephilippines.fco.gov.uk
Ambassador Extraordinary and Plenipotentiary, HE Stephen Lillie, *apptd* 2009

BRITISH COUNCIL
10th Floor, Taipan Place, F Ortigas Jr Road, Ortigas Centre, Pasig City 1605
T (+63) (2) 914 1011 W www.britishcouncil.org/philippines
Director, Andrew Picken

DEFENCE
The army has 85 armoured infantry fighting vehicles and 520 armoured personnel carriers. The navy has 1 frigate and 62 patrol and coastal vessels at 3 bases. The air force has 30 combat aircraft and 25 armed helicopters.
Military budget – US$1,160m (2009)
Military personnel – 120,000: army 80,000, navy 24,000, air force 16,000; paramilitary 40,500

ECONOMY AND TRADE
The economy has been one of the best-performing in the region since 2002, owing to growth in exports, agricultural output and the service industries. Despite this, poverty has increased as economic expansion struggles to offset the high rate of population growth, and nearly a third of the population lives below the poverty line. Remittances from the millions of Filipinos working abroad are vital, accounting for about 10 per cent of GNP, and helped to cushion the economy in 2009 from the effects of the global downturn, which slowed the rate of growth.

Major industries include electronics assembly, manufacture of clothing, footwear, pharmaceuticals, chemicals and wood products, food processing, oil refining and fishing. The large agricultural sector employs 34 per cent of the workforce, producing sugar cane, coconuts, rice, maize, tropical fruits and livestock products. Agriculture accounts for 14.9 per cent of GDP, industry for 29.9 per cent and services for 55.2 per cent.

The main trading partners are the USA, Japan, China, Singapore, other Asian states and the EU. Principal exports are semiconductors and electronic products, transport equipment, clothing, copper products, petroleum products, coconut oil and fruit. The main imports are electronic products, fuels, machinery and transport equipment, iron and steel, fabrics, grains, chemicals and plastics.
GNI – US$170,400m; US$1,890 per capita (2008)
Annual average growth of GDP – 1.6 per cent (2009 est)
Inflation rate – 3 per cent (2009 est)
Population below poverty line – 30 per cent (2003 est)
Unemployment – 8 per cent (2009 est)
Total external debt – US$62,730m (2009 est)
Imports – US$60,300m (2008)
Exports – US$49,000m (2008)

BALANCE OF PAYMENTS
Trade – US$12,076m deficit (2009)
Current Account – US$8,552m surplus (2009)

Trade with UK	*2008*	*2009*
Imports from UK	£232,786,012	£257,939,907
Exports to UK	£598,045,31	£690,258,821

COMMUNICATIONS
There are about 202,000km of roads, and Philippine National Railway operates 897km of railways. The main ports are Manila (Luzon), Cebu, Davao, and Cagayan de Oro and Nasipit (Mindanao), and there are over 400 smaller ports. The South China Sea is an area with a high risk of piracy and armed robbery against shipping. There are 254 airports and airfields, including international airports at Manila, Cebu and Davao City.

There is a good telephone system, and mobile phone distribution has grown rapidly. There were 3.9 million fixed lines in use, 68.1 million mobile phone subscribers and 5.6 million internet users in 2008.

EDUCATION AND HEALTH
There are seven years of free and compulsory primary education, followed by three years of free but non-compulsory secondary education.
Literacy rate – 93.4 per cent (2007 est)
Gross enrolment ratio (percentage of relevant age group) – primary 108 per cent; secondary 81 per cent; tertiary 28 per cent (2008 est)
Health expenditure (per capita) – US$63 (2007)
Hospital beds (per 1,000 people) – 1.1 (2003–8)

MEDIA
The media is independent and lively, but journalists are frequently subjected to intimidation and violence, especially in the southern islands. The government-owned IBC television network competes with two commercial broadcasters. There are over 700 radio stations and four main national newspapers, including *The Daily Tribune* and *Malaya.*

POLAND

Rzeczpospolita Polska – Republic of Poland

Area – 312,685 sq. km
Capital – Warsaw; population, 1,709,560 (2009 est)
Major cities – Bydgoszcz, Gdansk, Katowice, Krakow, Lodz, Lublin, Poznan, Szczecin, Wroclaw
Currency – Zloty of 100 groszy
Population – 38,482,919 falling at 0.05 per cent a year (2009 est)
Religion – Christian (Roman Catholic 94 per cent, Orthodox denominations 1 per cent) (est)
Language – Polish (official)
Population density – 125 per sq. km (2008)
Urban population – 61 per cent (2007 est)
Median age (years) – 37.9 (2009 est)
National anthem – 'Mazurek Dabrowskiego' ['Dabrowski's Mazurka']
National day – 3 May (Constitution Day)
Life expectancy (years) – 75.63 (2009 est)
Mortality rate – 10.05 (2009 est)
Birth rate – 10.04 (2009 est)
Infant mortality rate – 6.8 (2009 est)
Death penalty – Abolished for all crimes (since 1997)
CPI score – 5 (2009)

CLIMATE AND TERRAIN

Poland lies mostly in a great plain crossed by the Oder, Neisse and Vistula rivers. The land rises to the Carpathian, Tatra and Sudeten mountains along the southern border. Elevation extremes range from 2,499m (Rysy) at the highest point to −2m (Raczki Elblaskie) at the lowest. The climate is continental, and average temperatures in Warsaw range from lows of −6°C in January to highs of 24°C in July.

HISTORY AND POLITICS

Poland emerged as an independent kingdom in the ninth century and reached the height of its power under the Jagiellon dynasty, founded in 1386 by a dynastic marriage that united Poland and Lithuania. This commonwealth, which at its zenith stretched from the Baltic to the Black Sea, was weakened by attacks by its neighbours, and in 1772, 1793 and 1795 its territory was partitioned between Russia, Prussia and Austria. The congress of Vienna (1814–5) created the semi-independent Congress Kingdom of Poland, but this was subsequently incorporated into the Russian Empire.

Poland regained its independence after the First World War under the terms of the treaty of Versailles. The Second World War began with the German invasion of western Poland on 1 September 1939; on 17 September, Soviet forces invaded eastern Poland, and on 21 September Germany and the USSR declared that Poland had ceased to exist. Germany occupied the rest of Poland in 1941 when it began its offensive against the USSR. The USSR aligned with the Allies, and the country was liberated by Soviet forces in 1944–5. After the war, its boundaries were redrawn. Eastern Poland was ceded to the USSR but the country gained German territory in Silesia along the Oder and Neisse rivers, effectively shifting the state 240km westwards.

The post-war coalition government was Soviet-influenced and in 1947 a communist republic was proclaimed. Nationalisation and agricultural collectivisation programmes were introduced and the Roman Catholic Church was persecuted. In 1980, following a strike at the Gdansk shipyard prompted by economic crisis and popular discontent, a mass movement for civil and national rights coalesced around the newly formed independent trade union Solidarity, led by Lech Walesa. The following year, the Communist government declared martial law, driving Solidarity underground. Economic decline and continuing unrest in the 1980s eventually resulted in talks in 1989 that led to multiparty elections later that year; the Communists lost power and Solidarity helped to form a coalition government.

The post-communist governments introduced economic reforms from 1990 but the transition to a market economy caused unemployment and a sharp drop in living standards. Popular discontent and a fragmented parliament led to a succession of short-lived governments. Poland joined NATO in 1999 and the EU in 2004.

The Law and Justice Party (PiS) candidate, Lech Kaczynski, won the 2005 presidential election. The PiS-led coalition in power since 2005 collapsed in 2007, leading to an early election in which the liberal Civic Platform (PO) won most of the seats in both chambers, although without an outright majority in the lower house. The PO formed a coalition government with the Polish Popular Party and independents, under the PO leader Donald Tusk. President Kaczynski was killed in a plane crash in Russia in April 2010; his successor, acting president Bronislaw Komorowski of the PO, was elected in July.

POLITICAL SYSTEM

Under the 1997 constitution, the head of state is the president, who is directly elected for a five-year term, renewable only once. The president nominates the prime minister and has the right to be consulted over the appointment of the foreign, defence and interior ministers. The National Assembly is bicameral; the lower house, the Diet *(Sejm)*, has 460 members elected by proportional representation for a four-year term. The senate has 100 members elected on a provincial basis for a four-year term.

HEAD OF STATE

President, Bronislaw Komorowski, *elected* 4 July 2010, *sworn in* 6 August 2010

SELECTED GOVERNMENT MEMBERS *as at July 2010*

Prime Minister, Donald Tusk
Deputy Prime Minister, Economy, Waldemar Pawlak
Defence, Bogdan Klich
Foreign Affairs, Radoslaw Sikorski
Finance, Jan Vincent-Rostowski
Interior, Jerzy Miller

EMBASSY OF THE REPUBLIC OF POLAND
47 Portland Place, London W1B 1JH
T 020-7291 3520 E london@msz.gov.pl
W http://london.polemb.net
Ambassador Extraordinary and Plenipotentiary, HE Barbara Tuge-Erecinska, *apptd* 2006

BRITISH EMBASSY
ul. Kawalerii 12, 00-468 Warsaw
T (+48) (22) 311 0000 E info@britishembassy.pl
W http://ukinpoland.fco.gov.uk
Ambassador Extraordinary and Plenipotentiary, HE Ric Todd, *apptd* 2007

BRITISH COUNCIL
Al. Jerozolimskie 59, 00-697 Warsaw
T (+48) (22) 695 5900 W www.britishcouncil.org/poland
Director, Tony O'Brien

DEFENCE

The army has 946 main battle tanks, 1,508 armoured infantry fighting vehicles, 239 armoured personnel carriers and 53 armed helicopters. The navy has 5 submarines, 3 frigates, 5 corvettes, and 10 armed helicopters at 5 bases. The air force has 128 combat aircraft.
Military expenditure – US$10,100m (2008)
Military personnel – 100,000: army 46,400, navy 8,000, air force 17,500, joint staff 28,100

ECONOMY AND TRADE

Poland's successful transition to a market economy in the 1990s came at the cost of high levels of public debt, unemployment and inflation, which have been reduced by subsequent governments. The economy has grown steadily since 1992 and particularly since accession to the EU in 2004. Further economic development is hindered by inefficiency, rigidity and low-level corruption, although the Tusk government is committed to further privatisation and structural reform.

Poland has vast mineral resources, especially coal, and nearly half its area is fertile arable land. The large agricultural sector has been modernised but remains inefficient; it employs 17 per cent of the workforce but contributes only 4.6 per cent of GDP. The main crops are vegetables, fruit, wheat, meat, eggs and dairy products. The main industries are machine-building, iron and steel production, coal-mining, chemicals, shipbuilding, food processing, glass, beverages and textiles. Industry accounts for 28.1 per cent of GDP.

The main trading partners are other EU countries (especially Germany) and Russia. Principal exports include machinery and vehicles, manufactured goods, food and livestock. The main imports are machinery and vehicles, semi-manufactured goods, chemicals, minerals, fuels and lubricants.
GNI – US$447,100m; US$11,730 per capita (2008)
Annual average growth of GDP – 1.1 per cent (2009 est)
Inflation rate – 3.4 per cent (2009 est)
Population below poverty line – 17 per cent (2003 est)
Unemployment – 11 per cent (2009 est)
Total external debt – US$201,200m (2009 est)
Imports – US$206,100m (2008)
Exports – US$169,500m (2008)

BALANCE OF PAYMENTS
Trade – US$4,392m deficit (2009)
Current Account – US$26,909m deficit (2008)

Trade with UK	*2008*	*2009*
Imports from UK	£2,922,692,776	£2,691,400,545
Exports to UK	£4,238,469,258	£4,611,074,117

COMMUNICATIONS

The country has a total of 22,300km of railways, 424,000km of roads, and 3,997km of navigable rivers and canals. Over 120 airports and airfields are in use; the principal airports are at Warsaw, Krakow, Katowice and Wroclaw. The principal seaports are Gdansk, Gdynia, Szczecin and Swinoujscie.

The fixed-line telephone system is being modernised but progress has been slow, especially in rural areas, whereas mobile phone distribution has grown very rapidly. In 2008 there were 10.3 million fixed lines in use, 44 million mobile phone subscribers and 18.7 million internet users.

EDUCATION AND HEALTH

Elementary education (ages seven to 15) is free of charge and compulsory. Secondary education is also free, but optional.
Literacy rate – 99.3 per cent (2007 est)
Gross enrolment ratio (percentage of relevant age group) – primary 98 per cent; secondary 100 per cent; tertiary 67 per cent (2008 est)
Health expenditure (per capita) – US$716 (2007)
Hospital beds (per 1,000 people) – 5.2 (2003–8)

MEDIA

Freedom of speech is generally respected, although laws against criticism of the political system are still in force. The broadcasting market is the largest in eastern and central Europe. State-owned television (TVP) still has the largest national audience share for its output, although there are competitive commercial and subscription services. State-owned radio reaches just over half the population and there are more than 200 other commercial local and regional stations on air. Poland has over 300 newspapers, most of them local or regional, but less than a third of Poles read any newspaper.

CULTURE

Major writers include Nobel Prize winners Henryk Sienkiewicz (1846–1916), Wladyslaw Stanislaw Reymont (1867–1925), Czeslaw Milosz (1911–2004), Wislawa Szymborska (*b.* 1923), and journalist Ryszard Kapuscinski (1932–2007). The great English-language novelist Joseph Conrad (or Jozef Korzeniowski, 1857–1924) was born in Poland.

Other notable cultural figures include the pianist and composer Frédéric Chopin (1810–49); film directors Krzysztof Kieslowski (1941–1996) and Academy Award winner Roman Polanski (*b.* 1933); astronomer Nicolaus Copernicus (1473–1543), who formulated the first heliocentric theory of the solar system, and scientist Marie Curie (1867–1934), who became the first woman to win a Nobel Prize, in recognition for her work in physics (1903) and chemistry (1911).

PORTUGAL

Republica Portuguesa – Portuguese Republic

Area – 92,090 sq. km
Capital – Lisbon; population, 2,808,190 (2009 est)
Major cities – Oporto
Currency – Euro (€) of 100 cents
Population – 10,707,924 rising at 0.28 per cent a year (2009 est)
Religion – Christian (Roman Catholic 80 per cent, Protestant denominations 2 per cent) (est)
Language – Portuguese, Mirandese (both official)
Population density – 116 per sq. km (2008)
Urban population – 59 per cent (2007 est)
Median age (years) – 39.4 (2009 est)
National anthem – 'A Portuguesa' ['The Portuguese Song']
National day – 10 June (Portugal Day)
Life expectancy (years) – 78.21 (2009 est)
Mortality rate – 10.68 (2009 est)
Birth rate – 10.29 (2009 est)
Infant mortality rate – 4.78 (2009 est)
Death penalty – Abolished for all crimes (since 1976)
CPI score – 5.8 (2009)

CLIMATE AND TERRAIN

The terrain is mountainous north of the river Tagus, with rolling hills and plains in the south. Elevation extremes range from 2,351m (Ponta do Pico, Azores) at the highest point to 0m (Atlantic Ocean) at the lowest. Forests of pine, cork oak and eucalyptus cover about 38 per cent of the country. The climate is temperate, with average temperatures in Lisbon ranging from lows of 8°C in January to highs of 28°C in August.

HISTORY AND POLITICS

Part of the Roman Empire from the second century BC, the country was overrun by Vandals and Visigoths in the fifth century AD. The Visigoths were ousted by Muslims from north Africa in the eighth century, but Christian reconquest began in the tenth century and an independent Christian kingdom was established in the 12th century.

Portuguese navigators led the 15th-century European age of exploration and the country soon became a major commercial and colonial power, its empire expanding to include Brazil, parts of China and vast areas of Africa. In 1807 Portugal was invaded by Napoleonic France and then became the base from which Allied forces liberated Portugal and Spain in the Peninsular War. The 19th century was politically turbulent, with power struggles between conservative and liberal politicians and between different factions of the royal family. In 1910 an armed uprising in Lisbon drove King Manuel II into exile and a republic was declared.

A period of political instability ensued until the military intervened in 1926. The constitution of 1933 gave formal expression to the authoritarian *Estado Novo* (New State) introduced by Dr Antonio Salazar, prime minister from 1932 until 1968. Marcello Caetano succeeded Salazar in 1968 but the regime's failure to liberalise at home or to conclude wars in the African colonies resulted in the government's overthrow by a military coup in 1974. Great political turmoil followed in 1974–5, a period in which most of the country's colonies gained their independence. Elections in 1976 stabilised the situation and full civilian government was restored in 1982. Portugal joined the EEC in 1986 and adopted the euro in 2002.

The Socialist Party won the 2005 legislative election with 120 seats, its first absolute majority in the assembly since 1974. However, it lost its overall majority in the 2009 election, and, unable to put together a coalition, formed a minority government. The 2006 presidential election was won by the Social Democrat candidate Anibal Cavaco Silva (prime minister 1985–95); the next presidential poll is due in January 2011.

POLITICAL SYSTEM

Under the 1976 constitution, amended in 1982 and 1989, the head of state is a president who is directly elected for a five-year term, renewable only once. The unicameral Assembly of the Republic has 230 members, directly elected by proportional representation for a four-year term. The prime minister, appointed by the president, is usually the leader of the largest party in the assembly.

HEAD OF STATE

President of the Republic, Anibal Cavaco Silva, *elected* 22 January 2006, *sworn in* 9 March 2006

SELECTED GOVERNMENT MEMBERS *as at July 2010*

Prime Minister, Jose Socrates
Foreign Affairs, Luis Amado
Interior, Rui Pereira
Finance, Fernando Teixeira dos Santos
Defence, Augusto Santos Silva

EMBASSY OF PORTUGAL

11 Belgrave Square, London SW1X 8PP
T 020-7235 5331 E london@portembassy.co.uk
Ambassador Extraordinary and Plenipotentiary, HE Antonio Santana Carlos, *apptd* 2006

BRITISH EMBASSY

Rua de Sao Bernardo 33, 1249-082 Lisbon
T (+351) (21) 392 4000 E ppa.lisbon@fco.gov.uk
W http://ukinportugal.fco.gov.uk
Ambassador Extraordinary and Plenipotentiary, HE Alexander Ellis, *apptd* 2007

BRITISH COUNCIL

Rua Luís Fernandes 1–3, 1249-062 Lisbon
T (+351) (21) 321 4500 W www.britishcouncil.org/portugal
Director, Gill Caldicott

DEFENCE

The army has 225 main battle tanks and 353 armoured personnel carriers. The navy has 1 submarine, 12 frigates, 7 corvettes and 18 patrol and coastal vessels at 6 bases. The air force has 25 combat aircraft.

Military expenditure – US$3,720m (2008)
Military personnel – 43,330: army 26,700, navy 10,540, air force 7,100; paramilitary 47,700

ECONOMY AND TRADE

Portugal's economy has been transformed since it joined the EU in 1986 into a diversified and increasingly service-based economy: much of it has been liberalised, and many state enterprises privatised. The global downturn caused the economy to contract in 2009 and the budget deficit rose to 6.7 per cent of GDP; the government introduced austerity measures in spring 2010.

Around 10 per cent of the workforce is engaged in agriculture, contributing 2.7 per cent of GDP. The chief products are grain, fruit and vegetables, livestock, fish, dairy products and timber and cork from the forests. The main industries are tourism, manufacturing (textiles, motor vehicle components, footwear, cork, paper, chemicals), metalworking, oil refining, shipbuilding and repair and wine-making. Natural resources are being exploited to generate electricity from hydroelectric and solar sources to reduce Portugal's dependence on imported fuel and energy. Industry accounts for 23 per cent of GDP and services for 74.3 per cent.

The main trading partners are other EU countries, particularly Spain, and Angola. Principal exports are textiles, clothing, wood products, agricultural products and electrical equipment. The main imports include machinery, vehicles, chemicals, oil, textiles and agricultural products.

GNI – US$219,600m; US$28,680 per capita (2008)
Annual average growth of GDP – –3.3 per cent (2009 est)
Inflation rate – –0.9 per cent (2009 est)
Population below poverty line – 18 per cent (2006 est)
Unemployment – 9.2 per cent (2009 est)
Total external debt – US$507,000m (2009 est)
Imports – US$89,900m (2008)
Exports – US$57,200m (2008)

BALANCE OF PAYMENTS
Trade – US$26,182m deficit (2009)
Current Account – US$22,915m deficit (2009)

Trade with UK	*2008*	*2009*
Imports from UK	£1,597,842,031	£1,488,712,934
Exports to UK	£1,676,606,404	£1,392,390,660

COMMUNICATIONS

There are 2,786km of railways, of which 1,351km are electrified, and 82,900km of roads. There are 65 airports and airfields, including international airports at Lisbon, Oporto, Faro, Santa Maria (Azores) and Funchal (Madeira). The main ports are Lisbon, Oporto and Setubal.

Modern telephone systems served 4.1 million fixed-line subscribers, 14.9 million mobile phone subscribers and 4.5 million internet users in 2008.

EDUCATION AND HEALTH

Education is free of charge and compulsory for nine years from the age of six. Secondary education is mainly conducted in state general unified schools, lyceums, technical and professional schools and private schools. There are also military, naval, polytechnic and other specialist schools. The university at Coimbra was founded in 1290.

Literacy rate – 94.9 per cent (2007 est)
Gross enrolment ratio (percentage of relevant age group) – primary 115 per cent; secondary 101 per cent; tertiary 57 per cent (2008 est)
Health expenditure (per capita) – US$2,108 (2007)
Hospital beds (per 1,000 people) – 3.5 (2003–8)

MEDIA

The monopoly of the public broadcaster RTP ended in 1992, and commercial stations now dominate the market. Public radio networks are operated by RTP, while the Roman Catholic Church owns Radio Renascenca. There are about 300 other local and regional commercial radio stations. Principal national newspapers include the daily titles *Diario de Noticias, Publico, Correio da Manha* and *Jornal de Noticias*.

AUTONOMOUS REGIONS

Madeira and the Azores are both autonomous regions, each with its own locally elected assembly and government.

MADEIRA is a group of islands in the Atlantic Ocean about 990km south-west of Lisbon, and consists of Madeira, Porto Santo and three uninhabited islands. Total area is 801 sq. km; population, 247,399 (2009 est). Funchal on Madeira, the largest island, is the capital.

THE AZORES is an archipelago of nine islands in the Atlantic Ocean 1,400–1,800km west of Lisbon, and consists of Flores, Corvo, Terceira, Sao Jorge, Pico, Faial, Graciosa, Sao Miguel and Santa Maria. Total area is 2,322 sq. km; population, 245,374 (2009 est). Ponta Delgada, on Sao Miguel, is the capital.

QATAR

Dawlat Qatar – State of Qatar

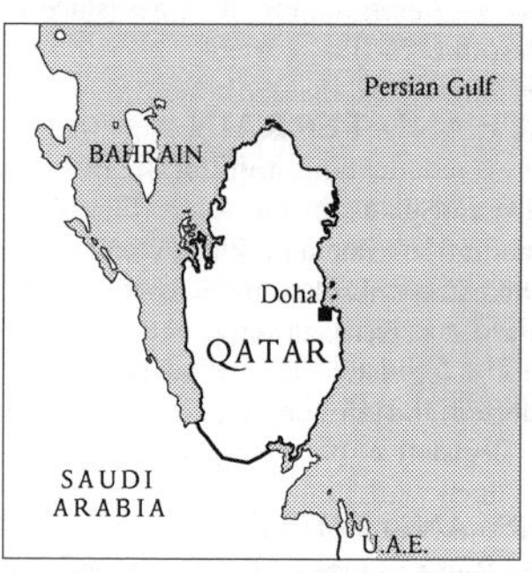

Area – 11,586 sq. km
Capital – Doha; population, 426,617 (2009 est)
Major city – Ar Rayyan
Currency – Qatar riyal of 100 dirhams
Population – 833,285 rising at 0.96 per cent a year (2009 est); Arab (40 per cent), Indian (18 per cent), Pakistani (18 per cent), Iranian (10 per cent) (est)
Religion – Muslim (predominantly Sunni; Shia 5 per cent) (est)
Language – Arabic (official), English
Population density – 111 per sq. km (2008)
Urban population – 96 per cent (2007 est)
Median age (years) – 30.8 (2009 est)
National anthem – 'As-Salam al-Amiri' ['The Peace of the Amir']
National day – 3 September (Independence Day)

Life expectancy (years) – 75.35 (2009 est)
Mortality rate – 2.46 (2009 est)
Birth rate – 15.61 (2009 est)
Infant mortality rate – 12.66 (2009 est)
Death penalty – Retained
CPI score – 7 (2009)
Literacy rate – 93.1 per cent (2007 est)

CLIMATE AND TERRAIN

Qatar occupies a peninsula in the Persian Gulf and is mostly a low-lying desert plain, with sand dunes in the south. Elevation extremes range from 103m (Qurayn Abu al-Bawl) at the highest point to 0m (Persian Gulf) at the lowest. The country has a desert climate, with low rainfall and average temperatures ranging from lows of 13°C in January to highs of 42°C in July. Humidity along the coast often reaches 90 per cent in summer.

HISTORY AND POLITICS

Towns on the Qatari coast developed into important trading centres from the 18th century. Persian rule of the area ended in the mid-18th century and after a period of conflict, the peninsula became a dependency of Bahrain in the 1850s. A revolt against Bahraini rule in the 1860s was suppressed, but Britain intervened in 1867, recognising the dependency as a separate entity. Nominally under the rule of the Ottoman Empire from 1871 until the outbreak of the First World War, Qatar became a British protectorate in 1916, when the al-Thani family was recognised as the ruling house. It became independent in 1971.

In 1972 Shaikh Ahmad was overthrown by the crown prince and prime minister, Shaikh Khalifa. Shaikh Khalifa was overthrown in 1995 by his son and heir, Shaikh Hamad, who has since introduced liberal reforms. Municipal elections, the first democratic polls since independence, were held in 1999. A referendum in 2003 approved a new constitution, which came into force in 2005. Elections to the partially elected consultative council established by the constitution have yet to take place.

POLITICAL SYSTEM

A new constitution came into force in 2005. The head of state is a hereditary absolute monarch, the amir. There is no legislature at present, although the 2005 constitution provides for a legislative council with 45 members, 30 directly elected and 15 appointed by the amir, and this will have legislative powers. At present there is an advisory council with 35 members appointed by the amir. There are no political parties. Women have been permitted to vote and stand for election since 1999; the first female cabinet member was appointed in 2003.

HEAD OF STATE

HH Amir of Qatar, Defence, Shaikh Hamad bin Khalifa al-Thani, KCMG, *assumed power* 27 June 1995
Crown Prince, HH Shaikh Tamim bin Hamad al-Thani

SELECTED GOVERNMENT MEMBERS *as at June 2010*

Prime Minister, Foreign Affairs, HH Shaikh Hamad bin Jassem bin Jabr al-Thani
Deputy Prime Minister, Abdullah bin Hamad al-Attiyah
Internal Affairs, Shaikh Abdulla bin Khalid al-Thani
Economy and Finance, Yousef bin Hussain Kamal

EMBASSY OF THE STATE OF QATAR

1 South Audley Street, London W1K 1NB
T 020-7493 2200 E london@mofa.gov.qa
W www.qatarembassy.info
Ambassador Extraordinary and Plenipotentiary, HE Khalid Rashid al-Hamoudi al-Mansouri, *apptd* 2005

BRITISH EMBASSY

PO Box 3, Doha
T (+974) 496 2000 E embassy.qatar@fco.gov.uk
W http://ukinqatar.fco.gov.uk
Ambassador Extraordinary and Plenipotentiary, John Hawkins, *apptd* 2008

BRITISH COUNCIL

PO Box 2992, 93 Al Sadd Street, Doha
T (+974) 425 1888 W www.britishcouncil.org/me-qatar
Director, John Gildea

DEFENCE

The army has 30 main battle tanks, 226 armoured personnel carriers and 40 armoured infantry fighting vehicles. The navy has 21 patrol and coastal combatant vessels at 2 bases. The air force has 18 combat aircraft and 19 armed helicopters.
Military budget – US$1,750m (2008)
Military personnel – 11,800: army 8,500, navy 1,800, air force 1,500

ECONOMY AND TRADE

The economy is based largely on the production of oil and gas, which account for more than 50 per cent of GDP, about 85 per cent of export earnings and 70 per cent of government revenues. The state-owned Qatar General Petroleum Corporation controls the industry, and is responsible for oil production onshore and offshore. There has been substantial foreign investment in exploitation of Qatar's large gasfields, and the country is now the world's leading exporter of liquefied natural gas.

Other industries include oil refining, production of ammonia, fertilisers, petrochemicals, steel and cement, and ship repairing. Industry contributes 68.4 per cent of GDP, services 31.5 per cent and agriculture, which is constrained by the terrain and climate, just 0.1 per cent. The economy depends on foreign workers, who outnumber the indigenous population.

The main export markets are Japan, South Korea and Singapore. Principal exports are liquefied natural gas, petroleum products, fertilisers and steel. The chief sources of imports are the USA, EU states and Japan. The main imports are machinery and transport equipment, food and chemicals.
Annual average growth of GDP – 9.2 per cent (2009 est)
Inflation rate – −3.9 per cent (2009 est)
Unemployment – 0.5 per cent (2009 est)
Total external debt – US$63,160m (2009 est)
Imports – US$26,900m (2008)
Exports – US$63,800m (2008)

BALANCE OF PAYMENTS

Trade – US$30,887m surplus (2009)
Current Account – US$13,797m surplus (2009)

Trade with UK	*2008*	*2009*
Imports from UK	£691,040,119	£777,811,991
Exports to UK	£110,722,925	£704,661,834

COMMUNICATIONS

Major infrastructure projects include expansion of the road network and construction of a new international airport. There are 8,000km of roads, but no railways. Doha is the principal of the five airports, and also the main seaport. Gulf Air and Qatar Airways provide regular international air services. Halul is the terminal for offshore oilfields.

Qatar's modern telecommunications systems served 263,000 fixed lines, 1.7 million mobile phone subscribers and 436,000 internet users in 2008.

MEDIA

Qatar officially ended media censorship in 1995 and since then the press has essentially been free from government interference, although some self-censorship is practised. Al Jazeera, a government-owned news and current affairs satellite television channel launched in 1996, has become one of the most important broadcasters in the Middle East; it launched an English-language channel in 2006. Domestic television and radio are exclusively state-run. The leading newspapers are privately owned, though many have links to the royal family or other leading figures.

ROMANIA

Area – 238,391 sq. km
Capital – Bucharest; population, 1,933,200 (2009 est)
Major cities – Brasov, Cluj-Napoca, Constanta, Craiova, Galati, Iasi, Timisoara
Currency – New leu (plural lei) of 100 bani
Population – 22,215,421 falling at 0.15 per cent a year (2009 est); Romanian (89.5 per cent), Hungarian (6.6 per cent), Roma (2.5 per cent); small minority of Sasi (Transylvanian Saxons)
Religion – Christian (Orthodox 87 per cent, Roman Catholic 5 per cent, Greek Catholic 1 per cent; numerous Protestant denominations) (est); small Muslim and Jewish minorities
Language – Romanian (official), Hungarian, Romani, German
Population density – 94 per sq. km (2008)
Urban population – 54 per cent (2007 est)
Median age (years) – 37.7 (2009 est)
National anthem – 'Desteapta-te, Romane' ['Awake Thee, Romanian']
National day – 1 December (Unification Day)
Life expectancy (years) – 72.45 (2009 est)
Mortality rate – 11.88 (2009 est)
Birth rate – 10.53 (2009 est)
Infant mortality rate – 22.9 (2009 est)
Death penalty – Abolished for all crimes (since 1989)
CPI score – 3.8 (2009)

CLIMATE AND TERRAIN

The Carpathian mountain range runs south from the Ukrainian border into the centre of the country and then turns west (the Transylvanian Alps) and north. The mountains enclose the central Transylvanian plateau and divide it from the southern Wallachian plain, part of the basin of the river Danube, which runs along most of the southern border, and the eastern Moldavian plateau, through which the river Siret runs, and the Black Sea coast. The mountains are thickly forested. Elevation extremes range from 2,544m (Moldoveanu) at the highest point to 0m (Black Sea) at the lowest. The climate is continental, with average temperatures in Bucharest ranging from lows of −7°C in January to highs of 30°C in July and August.

HISTORY AND POLITICS

Romania was incorporated into the Roman Empire as Dacia in the early part of the second century AD but was abandoned 150 years later when the Romans were driven out by the Goths. After centuries of rule by invading and often disparate tribal forces, the principalities of Moldavia and Wallachia came under the suzerainty of the Ottoman Empire from the 16th century to the late 19th century, when they united in 1862 and became the independent kingdom of Romania in 1881. Transylvania was successively under Hungarian, Ottoman and Austrian rule until after the First World War, in which Romania joined with the Allies; the post-war peace settlement awarded Transylvania, Bukovina and Bessarabia to Romania.

In 1940 Romania was forced to cede territory to the USSR and Hungary, and power was seized by the Romanian fascists, who took the country into the Second World War on the Axis side. When its leaders were overthrown in 1944, Romania changed sides. It was occupied in 1945 by Soviet forces and a communist-dominated government was installed. In 1947 King Michael abdicated, the monarchy was abolished and Romania became a communist republic. In 1965 Nicolae Ceausescu became leader of the Romanian Communist Party and pursued a foreign policy increasingly independent of the USSR, forming relationships with China and several Western countries. Ceausescu's regime was brutal and corrupt, and when the rest of eastern Europe threw off communist rule in 1989, violent suppression of reformers provoked an uprising in December 1989 that deposed and executed the dictator and his wife.

Although Romania became a multiparty democracy in 1991, governments continued to be dominated by former Communists until 1996. Popular unrest and demonstrations have persisted throughout the post-communist period, as much of the population has yet to benefit greatly from the transition to a market economy. Romania joined NATO in 2004 and the EU in 2007.

Traian Basescu, the candidate of a coalition of the Democratic and National Liberal parties, won the 2004 presidential election and was re-elected in December 2009. In the 2008 legislative election, an alliance of the Social Democratic Party (PSD) and the Conservative Party (PC) remained the largest bloc, although the Democratic Liberal Party (PD-L) was the largest party. The PD-L formed a coalition government with the PSD under Emil Boc. The PSD withdrew from the coalition in October, leaving a minority government which resigned after losing a vote of confidence. After failed attempts to form a government by other candidates, Emil Boc was reappointed prime minister in December 2009 at the head of coalition of the PD-L, the Democratic Union of Hungarians in Romania and several independents.

POLITICAL SYSTEM

The 1991 constitution was amended in 2003 to bring it into line with EU requirements. The president is directly elected for a five-year term, renewable only once. The bicameral parliament comprises the Chamber of Deputies with 334 seats, of which 18 are reserved for ethnic minorities, and the senate with 137 seats. Both houses are directly elected for a four-year term by proportional representation. The prime minister is appointed by the president.

HEAD OF STATE

President of the Republic, Traian Basescu,
elected 12 December 2004, *re-elected* 2009

SELECTED GOVERNMENT MEMBERS *as at July 2010*

Prime Minister, Emil Boc
Deputy Prime Minister, Bela Marko
Interior, Vasile Blaga
Defence, Gabriel Oprea
Economy, Adriean Vedeanu
Finance, Sebastian Vladescu
Foreign Affairs, Teodor Baconschi

EMBASSY OF ROMANIA

Arundel House, 4 Palace Green, London W8 4QD
T 020-7937 9666 **E** roemb@roemb.co.uk
W www.londra.mae.ro
Ambassador Extraordinary and Plenipotentiary,
HE Dr Ion Jinga, *apptd 2008*

BRITISH EMBASSY

24 Strada Jules Michelet, 010463 Bucharest
T (+40) (21) 201 7200 **E** Press.Bucharest@fco.gov.uk
W http://ukinromania.fco.gov.uk
Ambassador Extraordinary and Plenipotentiary,
HE Robin Barnett, *apptd* 2006

BRITISH COUNCIL

Calea Dorobantilor 14, 010572 Bucharest
T (+40) (21) 307 9600 **W** www.britishcouncil.org/romania
Director, Dr Nigel Townson

DEFENCE

The army has 299 main battle tanks, 1,069 armoured personnel carriers and 26 armoured infantry fighting vehicles. The navy has 3 frigates, 4 corvettes and 17 patrol and coastal vessels at 4 bases. The air force has 49 combat aircraft.

Under an agreement signed in 2005, the USA is allowed to use military bases in Romania.

Military expenditure – US$3,000m (2008)
Military personnel – 73,350: army 43,000, navy 7,150, air force 9,700, joint staff 13,500; paramilitary 79,900

ECONOMY AND TRADE

Transition to a market economy made sluggish progress until 2000, accelerating after 2004 in order to meet the requirements for EU accession. Although the economy grew steadily from 2000 to 2008, it was from a low base and the effects only recently started to have an impact on the country's widespread poverty. The economy contracted sharply in 2009 owing to the global downturn, and the government sought IMF funding in spring 2009, but political volatility in late 2009 delayed the implementation of measures to address the economic problems.

Agriculture remains inefficient, employing about 30 per cent of the workforce but contributing only 12.4 per cent of GDP. The principal crops are grains, sugar beet, sunflower seeds, vegetables and livestock products. Vines and fruit are grown, and extensive forests support an important timber industry. There are reserves of natural gas and oil, but Romania is a net importer of fossil fuels, although it exports electricity. Mineral deposits including coal, iron ore, bauxite, chromium and uranium support a mining industry. Other industries include manufacturing, electrical and light machinery and car assembly, metallurgy, food processing and oil refining.

The main trading partners are EU states (especially Italy and Germany), Turkey and Russia. Principal exports include machinery and equipment, textiles, footwear, metals and metal products, minerals and fuels, chemicals and agricultural products. The main imports are machines and equipment, fuels, minerals, chemicals, textiles, base metals and agricultural products.

GNI – US$178,100m; US$8,280 per capita (2008)
Annual average growth of GDP – –6.9 per cent (2009 est)
Inflation rate – 5 per cent (2009 est)
Population below poverty line – 25 per cent (2005 est)
Unemployment – 7.6 per cent (2009 est)
Total external debt – US$95,480m (2009 est)
Imports – US$83,000m (2008)
Exports – US$49,500m (2008)

BALANCE OF PAYMENTS

Trade – US$13,113m deficit (2009)
Current Account – US$7,104m deficit (2009)

Trade with UK	*2008*	*2009*
Imports from UK	£735,065,600	£661,622,700
Exports to UK	£739,085,725	£758,103,995

COMMUNICATIONS

There are 10,800km of railways, over one-third of which are electrified. There are 198,800km of roads, of which 60,000km are surfaced and 228km are motorway. Navigable waterways include 1,599km on the river Danube and its tributaries and 132km of canals, principally the canal linking the Danube to the Black Sea. The principal ports are Braila, Constanta, Galati and Tulcea. The main airports are at Bucharest and Timisoara.

Liberalisation of telecommunications in 2003 has led to rapid growth, and fixed-line density is now over 20 per 100 people. In 2008 there were 5 million fixed lines in use, 24.5 million mobile phone subscribers and 6.1 million internet users.

EDUCATION AND HEALTH

Primary and secondary education is free of charge and compulsory for ten years.

Literacy rate – 97.6 per cent (2007 est)
Gross enrolment ratio (percentage of relevant age group) – primary 105 per cent; secondary 87 per cent; tertiary 58 per cent (2008 est)
Health expenditure (per capita) – US$369 (2007)
Hospital beds (per 1,000 people) – 6.5 (2003–8)

MEDIA

State-owned broadcasters operate two television and four national radio networks. There is a thriving private television sector and over 100 private radio stations. Cable, satellite and subscription television is becoming more widespread. There are five main daily newspapers.

RUSSIA

Rossiyskaya Federatsiya – Russian Federation

Area – 17,098,242 sq. km. Includes the Kalingrad exclave, between Lithuania and Poland. Neighbours: Norway, Finland, Estonia, Latvia, Belarus, Ukraine (west), Georgia, Azerbaijan, Kazakhstan, China, Mongolia, North Korea (south)
Capital – Moscow; population, 10,522,900 (2009 est). Founded in around 1147, it became the centre of the rising Moscow principality and in the 15th century the capital of the whole of Russia (Muscovy). In 1703 Peter the Great transferred the capital to St Petersburg, but Moscow was again designated as the capital in 1918
Major cities – Chelyabinsk, Kazan, Nizhniy Novgorod (Gorky 1932–90), Novosibirsk (Novonikolayevsk until 1926), Omsk, Perm, Rostov, St Petersburg (Petrograd 1914–24; Leningrad 1924–91), Samara (Kuibyshev 1935–90), Ufa, Volgograd (Stalingrad 1925–61), Yekaterinburg (Sverdlovsk 1924–91)
Currency – Rouble of 100 kopeks
Population – 140,041,247 falling at 0.47 per cent a year (2009 est); Russian (79.8 per cent), Tatar (3.8 per cent), Ukrainian (2 per cent), Bashkir (1.2 per cent), Chuvash (1.1 per cent), and a further 150 nationalities
Religion – Christian (Russian Orthodox 70 per cent, other 2 per cent), Muslim 10 per cent, Buddhist 1 per cent (est); small Jewish minority
Language – Russian (official); many minority languages
Population density – 9 per sq. km (2008)
Urban population – 73 per cent (2007 est)
Median age (years) – 38.4 (2009 est)
National anthem – 'Gosudarstvenny Gimn Rossiyskoy Federatsii' ['State Anthem of the Russian Federation']
National day – 12 June (Russia Day)
Life expectancy (years) – 66.03 (2009 est)
Mortality rate – 16.06 (2009 est)
Birth rate – 10.53 (2009 est)
Infant mortality rate – 10.56 (2009 est)
Death penalty – Retained (not used since 1999)
CPI score – 2.2 (2009)

CLIMATE AND TERRAIN

Russia includes the easternmost areas of Europe and the whole of northern Asia. Russia lies mostly on plains which extend eastwards to the Ural mountains and then from the Urals to the Yenesei river. To the east of the Yenesei are plateaux, with lowlands in northern Siberia. Mountainous areas lie along the southern borders, in eastern Siberia and the Kamchatka peninsula. The terrain varies from the tundra of the Arctic region, through the taiga (the largest zone) of the north and centre, to the grassy plains (steppe) between the forests and the mountains. Elevation extremes range from 5,633m (Mt El'brus, Caucasus) at the highest point to −28m (Caspian Sea) at the lowest. Russia has the longest Arctic coastline in the world (over 27,000km); it also has Baltic, Black Sea and Pacific coastlines.

The most important rivers are the Volga, the Northern Dvina, the Neva, the Don and the Kuban in the European part, and in the Asiatic part the Ob, the Irtysh, the Yenisei, the Lena, the Amur and, further north, the Khatanga, Olenek, Yana, Indigirka and Kolyma. Lake Baikal in eastern Siberia is the deepest lake in the world. Part of the Caspian Sea lies within Russia.

The climate is mostly continental, but varies with latitude and terrain from arctic conditions in the north to subtropical in the far east and on the Black Sea coast. Average temperatures in Moscow range from lows of −16°C in January to highs of 23°C in July. Rainfall is low to moderate in most of the country.

HISTORY AND POLITICS

Russia was settled by many ethnic groups, including Slavs, Turks and Bulgars in the third to seventh centuries AD, and in the 13th century came under the overlordship of the Mongols. In the 15th century the grand duke of Muscovy threw off Mongol overlordship and began a process of unification and territorial expansion continued by his successors. Internal disorder and war with neighbouring countries held back Russian development until the reign of Peter I (The Great) (1682–1725), who introduced Western ideas of government, modernised the army and founded the navy. Under Catherine II (The Great) (1762–96) Russia extended its territory further. Russian expansion in Asia led to a war with Japan in 1904–5 that ended in an unexpected defeat. Protests about the conduct of the war developed into a revolution in 1905 which, though suppressed, forced the emperor to establish Russia's first parliament *(Duma)*.

The *Duma's* powers were limited and it was unable to ameliorate the Tsarist regime's endemic misgovernment or the conditions of the increasingly militant urban working class. During the First World War discontent caused by autocratic rule, the poor military conduct of the war and wartime privation led to a revolution which broke out in March 1917. The Tsar abdicated and a power struggle ensued between the provisional government and the Bolshevik Party. This led to a second revolution in November 1917 in which the Bolsheviks, led by Vladimir Lenin (1870–1924), seized power.

Civil war between 'red' Bolshevik forces and 'white' monarchist and anti-communist forces, the latter supported by foreign powers, lasted until the end of

1922. During the civil war, Russia was declared a Soviet republic and other Soviet republics were formed in Ukraine, Belorussia and Transcaucasia. These four republics merged to form the Union of Soviet Socialist Republics (USSR) on 30 December 1922.

During the 1930s Joseph Stalin (1879–1953) introduced a policy of rapid industrialisation under a series of five-year plans, brought all sectors of industry under government control, abolished private ownership and enforced the collectivisation of agriculture, causing severe famine. Many ethnic minority groups suffered under Stalin's regime and it is estimated that up to 1.5 million people were deported to the Gulags of Siberia and the central Asian republics. After being attacked by Nazi Germany in 1941, the USSR joined the Second World War on the side of the Allies. In 1944–5 Soviet forces liberated much of eastern Europe and the post-war communist regimes in these countries were closely tied to the Soviet government.

The post-war period was dominated for 40 years by the Cold War with the West, especially the USA, prompting massive expenditure on the military-industrial sector and the provision of aid to developing countries as a means of extending Soviet influence. Tight political and economic control was maintained over the countries in the Soviet bloc, including military intervention in support of communist regimes in Europe and Afghanistan.

Mikhail Gorbachev became Soviet leader in 1985 and introduced the policies of *perestroika* (restructuring) and *glasnost* (openness) in order to revamp the economy, which had stagnated since the 1970s, to root out corruption and inefficiency, and to end the Cold War. The retreat from total control by the Communist Party unleashed ethnic and nationalist tensions.

Following the defeat of an attempted coup by hardline Communists in August 1991, effective political power was in the hands of the leaders of the constituent republics, especially President Yeltsin of Russia, and the USSR began to break up as the constituent republics declared their independence. The USSR formally ceased to exist on 31 December 1991. The Russian Federation took over the USSR's seat at the UN in December 1991, was recognised as an independent state by the EC and USA in January 1992, and joined the G7 group of industrialised countries in 1996.

The presidency of Vladimir Putin (2000–8) saw an increasing degree of centralisation, the partial renationalisation of industry (especially oil and gas), the re-assertion of state control over the media, an increasingly authoritarian stance on democracy and an aggressive approach to relations with former Soviet states.

In the 2007 legislative elections, the pro-Putin United Russia party retained its majority in the Duma, and President Putin won a parliamentary seat. This enabled him to be appointed chair of the council of ministers in 2008 after his successor as president, Dmitry Medvedev, took office. President Medvedev is widely regarded as a figurehead, with Putin continuing to wield the most political power and to determine government policy.

INSURGENCIES

Chechnya occupies an area that is strategically important to Russia because routes from central Russia to the Black Sea and Caspian Sea, and oil and gas pipelines from neighbouring countries, pass through it. The republic declared itself independent in 1991 but its attempts to assert its independence led to two wars with the federal government. The first of these, in 1994–6, resulted in the signing of the Khasavyurt accords. After the peace broke down and Russia invaded Chechnya again in 1999, President Putin refused negotiations and imposed direct rule from Moscow in 2000. Rebels continued with terrorist attacks but these have declined since 2007. Russia announced the end of counter-terrorism operations in Chechnya in 2009, but has had to reinstate these in some areas where rebels remain active.

The conflict in Chechnya has destabilised the whole of the northern Caucasus, especially Ingushetia and Dagestan, where violence has increased in recent years. The violence has also affected other parts of Russia, where extremists linked to Chechen separatists have carried out suicide bombings and attacks such as the Moscow theatre siege in 2002, the Beslan school siege in 2004, and the bombing of Moscow's metro system in March 2010.

POLITICAL SYSTEM

The 1993 constitution introduced multiparty democracy and enshrines various human rights and civil liberties; amendments in 2008 extended the terms of office for the presidency to six years and for the State Duma to five years from the next elections. The head of state is a president, who is directly elected for a four-year term (at present), renewable only once consecutively. The bicameral Federal Assembly comprises the State Duma (lower house) of 450 members, all elected by proportional representation for a four-year term (at present), and the Council of the Federation, which has 166 members (two from each member of the federation), appointed for terms of varying lengths. The president appoints the chairman of the council of ministers (prime minister), subject to the approval of the legislature, but is also entitled to chair sessions of the council.

HEAD OF STATE

President, Dmitry Medvedev, *elected* 2 March 2008, *took office* 7 May 2008

SELECTED GOVERNMENT MEMBERS *as at July 2010*

Prime Minister, Vladimir Putin
First Deputy Chairs, Igor Shuvalov; Viktor Zubkov
Deputy Chairs, Alexei Kudrin *(Finance)*; Sergei Ivanov; Aleksandr Khloponin; Dmitri Kozak; Igor Sechin; Igor Shuvalov; Sergei Sobyanin; Aleksandr Zhukov
Foreign Affairs, Sergei Lavrov
Interior, Rashid Nurgaliyev
Defence, Anatoly Serdyukov

EMBASSY OF THE RUSSIAN FEDERATION

6–7 Kensington Palace Gardens, London W8 4QX
T 020-7229 6412 E info@rusemb.org.uk
W www.rusemb.org.uk
Ambassador Extraordinary and Plenipotentiary, HE Yury Fedotov, *apptd* 2005

BRITISH EMBASSY

Smolenskaya Naberezhnaya 10, 121099 Moscow
T (+7) (495) 956 7200 E moscow@britishembassy.ru
W http://ukinrussia.fco.gov.uk
Ambassador Extraordinary and Plenipotentiary, HE Dame Anne Pringle, DCMG, *apptd* 2008

BRITISH COUNCIL

Ulitsa Nikoloyamskaya 1, 109189 Moscow
T (+7) (495) 287 1800 W www.britishcouncil.org.ru
Director, Rosemary Hilhorst

FEDERAL STRUCTURE
Following the break-up of the USSR in 1991, a new federal treaty was signed in 1992 between the central government and the autonomous republics of the Russian Federation. Tatarstan and Bashkortostan signed the treaty in 1994 after securing considerable legislative and economic autonomy.

The Russian Federation comprises 46 *oblasti* (regions), 9 *krai* (autonomous territories), 21 *respubliki* (autonomous republics), 4 *okrugi* (autonomous areas), two cities of federal status (Moscow and St Petersburg) and one autonomous Jewish *oblast*, Yevrey. The *oblasti* are Amur, Arkhangelsk, Astrakhan, Belgorod, Bryansk, Chelyabinsk, Irkutsk, Ivanovo, Kaliningrad, Kaluga, Kemerovo, Kirov, Kostroma, Kurgan, Kursk, Leningrad, Lipetsk, Magadan, Moscow, Murmansk, Nizhny-Novgorod, Novgorod, Novosibirsk, Omsk, Orenburg, Orel, Penza, Pskov, Rostov, Ryazan, Sakhalin, Samara, Saratov, Smolensk, Sverdlovsk, Tambov, Tomsk, Tula, Tver, Tyumen, Ulyanovsk, Vladimir, Volgograd, Vologda, Voronezh and Yaroslavl. The *krai* are Altai, Kamchatka, Khabarovsk, Krasnodar, Krasnoyarsk, Perm, Primorski, Stavropol and Zabaykalsk. The *respubliki* are Adygeia, Altai, Bashkortostan, Buryatia, Chechnya, Chuvashia, Dagestan, Ingushetia, Kabardino-Balkaria, Kalmykiya, Karachayevo-Cherkessia, Karelia, Khakassia, Komi, Mari-El, Mordovia, North Ossetia, Sakha, Tatarstan, Tuva and Udmurtia. The *okrugi* are Chukotka, Khanty-Mansi, Nenets and Yamalo-Nenets.

DEFENCE

Since the demise of the USSR, Russia's armed forces have been considerably reduced. Major army reform is ongoing, including a large-scale structural reorganisation, shorter conscription periods, the civilianisation of military posts and staff cuts in the defence ministry.

A CIS collective security treaty enables Russia to station troops in Armenia, Belarus, Kazakhstan, Kyrgyzstan and Tajikistan. The Black Sea fleet was divided between Russian and Ukraine under an agreement signed in 1997.

The Strategic Deterrent Forces have 14 nuclear-powered ballistic missile submarines and 430 intercontinental ballistic missiles equipped with some 1,605 nuclear warheads. Russia also has 79 long-range strike aircraft capable of carrying strategic missiles.

The army has 23,000 main battle tanks, over 9,900 armoured personnel carriers and over 15,180 armoured infantry fighting vehicles. The navy has 66 submarines, 1 aircraft carrier, 5 cruisers, 14 destroyers, 14 frigates, 23 corvettes, 75 patrol and coastal vessels, 259 combat aircraft and 116 armed helicopters. The air force has 1,743 combat aircraft.

Russia deploys forces in Armenia (3,214), Georgia (3,400 est), Moldova (1,500 est) and Tajikistan (5,500).

Military expenditure – US$86,000m (2008 est)
Military personnel – 1,027,000: Strategic Deterrent Forces 80,000, army 360,000, airborne 35,000, navy 142,000, air force 160,000, command and support 250,000; paramilitary 449,000
Conscription duration – 12 months

ECONOMY AND TRADE

Under the Soviet regime, an essentially agrarian economy in 1917 was transformed by the early 1960s into the second-greatest industrial power in the world. However, by the early 1970s the concentration of resources on the military-industrial complex had caused stagnation in the civilian economy. Economic reforms were introduced by President Gorbachev, including the legalisation of small private businesses, the reduction of state control over the economy, and denationalisation and privatisation. In 1992 the first stage of mass privatisation of state industries began; 80 per cent of the economy had been privatised by 1996. The largest and most economically significant industries, oil and gas, were partially renationalised from 2004.

The transition to a market economy caused a severe economic crisis in 1993 and again in 1998, when the rouble collapsed. But from 1999, the economy sustained growth averaging 7 per cent a year, and unemployment and poverty declined. Average incomes grew by more than 10 per cent a year from 2002, and the middle class has expanded. Banking and fiscal reforms stimulated foreign investment, although political and economic uncertainties, corruption, excessive red tape and a lack of trust in institutions inhibit growth. Other problems include the economy's vulnerability to fluctuations in global prices of key commodities and a dilapidated infrastructure. Some of these factors exacerbated the impact on Russia of the global financial crisis in autumn 2008, when a sharp fall in oil prices coincided with turmoil in the banking system and a 70 per cent drop in the stock market. Despite US$200bn in government aid to the financial sector, credit and confidence problems, a severe drop in production and rising unemployment caused a sharp contraction in the economy that greatly increased the numbers living below the poverty line. The economy started to recover in late 2009.

Russia has some of the world's richest natural resources, especially mineral deposits and timber. The recent growth in the economy is founded on the exploitation and export of its oil and natural gas reserves. Russia is now the world's leading exporter of hydrocarbons and the leading supplier to European countries and China, a position that has led the country into disputes with some of its neighbours; Ukraine, Georgia and Belarus have all had gas supplies cut for short periods during price negotiations. Oil and natural gas account for 60 per cent of exports, 50 per cent of federal budget revenue and 20 per cent of GDP. Economic diversification is a government priority.

Mining (coal, iron ore, aluminium and other non-ferrous metals) and oil and natural gas extraction are concentrated in the region south of Moscow, the Volga valley, the northern Caucasus, the Urals, Siberia and the far east and north. Russia is also keen to exploit the shrinking of the Arctic ice-cap to prospect for previously inaccessible deposits under the Arctic Sea. Moscow and St Petersburg are still the two largest industrial centres, but new industrial areas have been developed in the Urals, the Kuznetsk basin, Siberia and the far east. The main industries are processing oil, gas and minerals, forestry, all forms of machine building (including transport, communications, agricultural, construction, and power generating and transmitting equipment), defence industries, shipbuilding, medical and scientific instruments, consumer durables, textiles, food processing and handicrafts.

The vast area and the great variety in climatic conditions are reflected in the structure of agriculture. In the far north, only reindeer breeding, hunting and fishing are possible; further south, forestry is combined with grain growing. In the southern half of the forest zone and in the adjacent forest–steppe zone, the acreage under grain crops is larger and agriculture more complex. The southern part of the Western Siberian plain is an important grain-growing and stock-breeding area. In the extreme south, cotton is cultivated. Vine, tobacco and other southern crops are grown on the Black Sea shore of the Caucasus.

The service sector is the largest, accounting for 60.5 per cent of GDP and employing 58.1 per cent of the workforce; industry contributes 34.8 per cent of GDP and employs 31.9 per cent; and agriculture accounts for 4.7 per cent of GDP and 10 per cent of employment.

Russia's main trading partners are EU countries (especially Germany), China, Ukraine, Japan, Turkey and the USA. Principal exports are oil and petroleum products, natural gas, timber and wood products, metals, chemicals, manufactured goods, military vehicles and defence equipment. The main imports are vehicles, machinery and equipment, plastics, medicines, iron and steel, consumer goods, meat, fruit and nuts, and semi-finished metal products.

GNI – US$1,371,200m; US$9,660 per capita (2008)
Annual average growth of GDP – –8.5 per cent (2009 est)
Inflation rate – 11.9 per cent (2009 est)
Population below poverty line – 15.8 per cent (2007)
Unemployment – 8.9 per cent (2009 est)
Total external debt – US$369,200m (2009 est)
Imports – US$321,200m (2008)
Exports – US$471,800m (2008)

BALANCE OF PAYMENTS
Trade – US$111,365m surplus (2009)
Current Account – US$102,400m surplus (2008)

Trade with UK	*2008*	*2009*
Imports from UK	£4,131,665,283	£2,286,399,343
Exports to UK	£6,694,221,368	£4,515,161,446

COMMUNICATIONS

Because of the vast distances, the terrain and the harsh winter climate, the main means of internal long-distance travel are by air or the Trans-Siberian railway. Neither the rail nor the road systems are well-developed countrywide; both are concentrated in the more densely populated European areas and the Urals. There are over 1,210 airports and airfields, although only about 600 have surfaced runways. The principal international airports are at Moscow, St Petersburg and Novosibirsk, and the main national carriers are Aeroflot and S7 Airlines. The railways are state-run, with 87,000km of the network used for passenger transport and 30,000km by industry. There are 933,000km of roads, 755,000km of which are surfaced.

The most important ports include Taganrog, Rostov and Novorossiysk around the Black Sea and the Sea of Azov. Two of the three northern ports, St Petersburg and Arkhangelsk, are icebound during winter; only Murmansk is accessible. Several ports have been built along the Arctic Sea route between Murmansk and Vladivostok and are in regular use in summer. The far eastern port of Vladivostok, Russia's Pacific naval base, is kept open by icebreakers all the year round. There is a large merchant fleet of 1,074 ships of 1,000 tonnes and over, with a further 486 ships registered in other countries.

There are 102,000km of waterways. The great rivers of European Russia flow outwards from the centre, linking all parts of the plains with the chief ports. They are supplemented by a 72,000km system of canals which provides a through route between the White Sea and Baltic Sea in the north and the Black Sea, Caspian Sea and the Sea of Azov in the south; the most notable are the White Sea–Baltic Canal, the Moscow–Volga Canal and the Volga–Don Canal.

The telecommunications infrastructure is expanding and modernising, although less quickly for fixed lines than for mobile phones, and rural services are still inadequate. There were 44 million fixed lines in use, 188 million mobile phone subscribers and 45 million internet users in 2008.

EDUCATION AND HEALTH

There are 11 years of compulsory education: nine at basic school level and a further two at senior secondary level. Higher education is provided by public and private accredited higher education institutions.

Literacy rate – 99.5 per cent (2007 est)
Gross enrolment ratio (percentage of relevant age group) – primary 97 per cent; secondary 84 per cent; tertiary 75 per cent (2008 est)
Health expenditure (per capita) – US$493 (2007)
Hospital beds (per 1,000 people) – 9.7 (2003–8)

MEDIA

Broadcasting is dominated by the Russian State Television and Radio Broadcasting Company (VGTRK) and stations part-owned by the government or whose owners have close ties to it. Most of the country's 400 newspapers are privately owned but some of the most influential titles are owned by companies closely linked to the government. This has reduced editorial independence, and journalists are subject to harassment, intimidation and assault for coverage of sensitive subjects such as human rights or corruption.

CULTURE

Russian is a branch of the Slavonic family of languages and is written in the Cyrillic script.

Russian literature consisted mainly of *byliny* (folk songs), epic songs, chronicles and works of moral theology before the 19th century, when poetry reached its zenith with Alexander Pushkin (1799–1837) and Mikhail Lermontov (1814–41), while the dramatist and short-story writer Anton Chekhov (1860–1904) achieved acclaim throughout Europe for plays such as *The Three Sisters* and *The Cherry Orchard*. Novelists Nikolai Gogol (1809–52), Ivan Turgenev (1818–83), Fyodor Dostoyevsky (1821–81) and Leo Tolstoy (1828–1910) created masterpieces such as *Dead Souls, Fathers and Sons, Crime and Punishment* and *War and Peace* respectively. In the 20th century, Anna Akhmatova (1888–1966), Boris Pasternak (1890–1960), Mikhail Bulgakov (1891–1940), Vladimir Nabokov (1899–1977) and Nobel laureate Alexander Solzhenitsyn (1918–2008) have been especially acclaimed.

In classical music, Mikhail Glinka (1804–57) was an innovator to match Pushkin, while those following him include Mussorgsky (1839–81), Tchaikovsky (1840–93) – arguably the most internationally successful Russian composer, whose ballets include *Swan Lake* and *The Nutcracker* – Rimsky-Korsakov (1844–1908), Rachmaninov (1873–1943), Stravinsky (1882–1971), Prokofiev (1891–1953) and Shostakovich (1906–75).

Directors Sergei Eisenstein (1898–1948), Andrei Tarkovsky (1932–86) and Nikita Mikhalkov (*b.* 1945) are celebrated figures in Russian cinema.

RWANDA

Republika y'u Rwanda/République rwandaise – Republic of Rwanda

Area – 26,338 sq. km
Capital – Kigali; population, 908,705 (2009 est)
Major towns – Butare; Gisenyi; Gitarama; Ruhengeri
Currency – Rwanda franc of 100 centimes
Population – 10,473,282 rising at 2.78 per cent a year (2009 est); Hutu (84 per cent), Tutsi (15 per cent), Twa (1 per cent) (est)
Religion – Christian (Roman Catholic 57 per cent, Seventh-day Adventist 11 per cent, other Protestant denominations 26 per cent), Muslim 5 per cent (est); a very small minority practises indigenous religions
Language – Kinyarwanda, French, English (all official), Swahili
Population density – 394 per sq. km (2008)
Urban population – 18 per cent (2007 est)
Median age (years) – 18.7 (2009 est)
National anthem – 'Rwanda nziza' ['Beautiful Rwanda']
National day – 1 July (Independence Day)
Life expectancy (years) – 50.52 (2009 est)
Mortality rate – 14.02 (2009 est)
Birth rate – 39.37 (2009 est)
Infant mortality rate – 81.61 (2009 est)
HIV/AIDS adult prevalence – 2.3 per cent (2007 est)
Death penalty – Abolished for all crimes (since 2007)
CPI score – 3.3 (2009)
Literacy rate – 64.9 per cent (2007 est)
Gross enrolment ratio (percentage of relevant age group) – primary 151 per cent; secondary 22 per cent; tertiary 4 per cent (2008 est)
Health expenditure (per capita) – US$37 (2007)
Hospital beds (per 1,000 people) – 1.6 (2003–8)

CLIMATE AND TERRAIN

Landlocked Rwanda's terrain is mostly savannah uplands and mountains, including the volcanic Virunga range in the north-west. Elevation extremes range from 4,519m (Volcan Karisimbi) at the highest point to 950m (river Rusizi) at the lowest. Rwanda's western border runs through Lake Kivu. The climate is temperate, with a wet season from October to May. Average daily temperatures in Rubona range between 12°C and 27°C throughout the year.

HISTORY AND POLITICS

Rwanda was settled by Hutu peoples from the tenth century. From the 14th century, they came under the dominance of Tutsi migrants, who became the rulers of a centralised kingdom established in the 15th century. This historic dominance of the majority Hutus by the minority Tutsis underlies the modern conflict between the two ethnic groups.

Rwanda became part of German East Africa in 1899 and was occupied by Belgium when the First World War broke out. After the war, it became a mandated territory administered by Belgium. In 1959 the Hutu population rebelled against Tutsi domination, overthrowing the king and causing thousands of Tutsis to flee the country. Rwanda became a republic in 1961, and independence was achieved in July 1962 under a Hutu president. He was overthrown in 1973 in a military coup led by Maj.-Gen. Juvenal Habyarimana, whose National Revolutionary Development Movement (MRND) was the only legal party until 1991.

Armed Tutsi exiles in Uganda made repeated attempts to invade Rwanda in the 1960s and 1970s, but were defeated by the predominantly Hutu army. Continued conflict left thousands dead over a period of 30 years. These exiles and opponents of the MRND regime formed the Tutsi-led Rwandan Patriotic Front (FPR) in 1985. The FPR invaded the country in 1990, and a cycle of rebel incursions and military reprisals, mostly against Tutsis, continued until the Arusha peace accords were concluded in 1993.

In April 1994, the assassination of President Habyarimana triggered a massacre of the Tutsi minority and moderate Hutus by the army and youth militia *(interahamwe)*; about 1 million people were killed in three months and millions more fled to neighbouring countries. The FPR's forces mobilised to end the bloodshed and took control of the country, causing defeated forces *(exFAR/I)* and over two million Hutus to flee, mostly to Zaire (now the Democratic Republic of the Congo). In July 1994 the FPR established a broad-based government of national unity in which moderate Hutus held the presidency and premiership and the FPR took eight of the 22 seats. An International Criminal Tribunal for Rwanda was established in 1995 to bring to trial those directly responsible for the 1994 genocide.

Incursions by *exFAR/I* continued in the west, drawing Rwanda into the civil war in the Democratic Republic of the Congo from 1996 until 2002, and the Congolese border areas remain volatile. Internally, reconciliation efforts and political reforms since 1994 have been more successful in achieving social stability, although the FPR is regarded as authoritarian, suppressing political opposition. Rwanda joined the Commonwealth in 2009.

The FPR won the 2003 legislative elections and retained an overall majority in the 2008 election, continuing in government in coalition with six other parties and a number of independent members. The FPR leader Paul Kagame was elected president in 2003, and re-elected with a 93 per cent share of votes on 9 August 2010.

POLITICAL SYSTEM

Under the 2003 constitution, the president is directly elected for a seven-year term, renewable only once. The bicameral pariament consists of the Chamber of Deputies (the lower house) and the senate. The Chamber of Deputies has 80 members, of whom 53 are directly elected, 24 are women members elected by the provinces, two represent youth organisations and one represents organisations of disabled people; all serve a five-year term. The senate has 26 members indirectly elected for an eight-year term. Political parties are barred from organising on an ethnic, regional or religious basis.

In 2006 the 12 provinces were replaced by five provinces: North, East, South, West and Kigali, with the aim of creating more ethnically diverse administrative areas.

HEAD OF STATE
President, Maj-Gen. Paul Kagame, *appointed* 17 April 2000, *sworn in* 22 April 2000, *elected* 25 August 2003, *re-elected* August 2010

SELECTED GOVERNMENT MEMBERS *as at July 2010*
Prime Minister, Bernard Makuza
Defence, Gen. James Kabarebe
Finance and Economic Planning, John Rwangombwa
Foreign Affairs, Louise Mushikiwabo

HIGH COMMISSION OF THE REPUBLIC OF RWANDA
120–122 Seymour Place, London W1H 1NR
T 020-7224 9832 E uk@ambarwanda.org.uk
W www.ambarwanda.org.uk
High Commissioner, Ernest Rwamucyo, *apptd* 2010

BRITISH HIGH COMMISSION
Parcelle No. 1131, Blvd de l'Umuganda, Kacyira-Sud, BP 576 Kigali
T (+250) 0252 585 771 E embassy.kigali@fco.gov.uk
W http://ukinrwanda.fco.gov.uk
High Commissioner, HE Nicholas Cannon, OBE, *apptd* 2008

DEFENCE

The army has 24 main battle tanks, over 35 armoured infantry fighting vehicles and over 56 armoured personnel carriers. The air force has at least 5 armed helicopters.
Military budget – US$76m (2009)
Military personnel – 33,000: army 32,000, air force 1,000; paramilitary 2,000

ECONOMY AND TRADE

Rwanda is the most densely populated country in Africa, with few natural resources and minimal industry. Over half the population lives below the poverty line and economic growth, especially in food production, struggles to keep up with population growth. It is dependent on international aid but the demands of its high foreign debt have been reduced by debt relief. Regional instability, inadequate transport links with other countries and energy shortages hamper development, although electricity supply is expected to become more reliable when methane from Lake Kivu starts to be tapped.

Around 90 per cent of the population is engaged in agriculture, which is mainly at subsistence level and contributes 41.7 per cent of GDP. The main industries are mining, processing agricultural products and small-scale manufacturing, and there is an incipient tourist industry.

The main trading partners are Kenya, Uganda, Democratic Republic of Congo, China and Belgium. The main exports are coffee, tea, hides and tin ore. The principal imports are foodstuffs, machinery and equipment, steel, petroleum products and construction materials.
GNI – US$4,300m; US$440 per capita (2008)
Annual average growth of GDP – 5.5 per cent (2009 est)
Inflation rate – 14.2 per cent (2009 est)
Total external debt – US$1,400m (2004 est)
Imports – US$1,100m (2008)
Exports – US$300m (2008)

BALANCE OF PAYMENTS
Trade – US$978m deficit (2009)
Current Account – US$230m deficit (2008)

Trade with UK	*2008*	*2009*
Imports from UK	£8,128,673	£9,292,599
Exports to UK	£460,241	£4,370,667

COMMUNICATIONS

Rwanda has received considerable foreign aid to upgrade its transport infrastructure since 1994. The main internal transport system is the 14,000km road network, which links with those of neighbouring countries to provide access to Kenyan and Tanzanian ports for international trade. There are no railways, but in 2006 a feasibility study was planned to consider the possibility of including Rwanda in a proposed expansion of the rail network in central Africa. Lake Kivu is navigable by shallow boats, and provides access, but no regular services, to the Democratic Republic of the Congo. The principal airport is at Kigali.

The limited fixed-line telephone system mostly serves government and business, and mobile phone distribution has grown rapidly. There were 17,000 fixed lines in use, 1.3 million mobile phone subscribers and 300,000 internet users in 2008.

MEDIA

The broadcast media is mainly state-owned, and the state-run Radio Rwanda has the largest audience. Private radio stations have opened since 2004, and the BBC World Service, Voice of America and Deutsche Welle all broadcast in Kigali. Television is mostly confined to urban areas. There are a growing number of newspapers, but they are subject to government restrictions and harassment, and generally exercise self-censorship.

ST KITTS AND NEVIS

Federation of St Christopher and Nevis (Federation of St Kitts and Nevis)

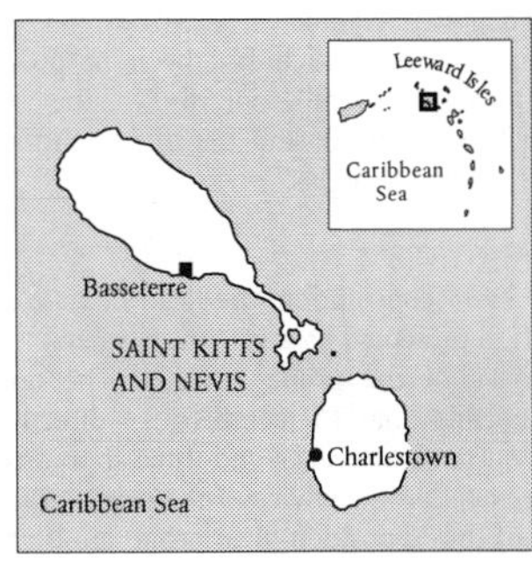

Area – 261 sq. km
Capital – Basseterre; population, 12,847 (2009 est)
Major town – Charlestown, the chief town of Nevis
Currency – East Caribbean dollar (EC$) of 100 cents
Population – 40,131 rising at 0.85 per cent a year (2009 est)
Religion – Christian (Anglican 50 per cent, Roman Catholic 25 per cent) (est)
Language – English (official)
Population density – 189 per sq. km (2008)

Urban population – 32 per cent (2007 est)
Median age (years) – 28.6 (2009 est)
National anthem – 'Oh Land of Beauty!'
National day – 19 September (Independence Day)
Life expectancy (years) – 73.2 (2009 est)
Mortality rate – 8.05 (2009 est)
Birth rate – 17.67 (2009 est)
Infant mortality rate – 13.94 (2009 est)
Death penalty – Retained (last used 2008)
Literacy rate – 97.8 per cent (2007 est)

CLIMATE AND TERRAIN

The volcanic islands of St Kitts (St Christopher) (168 sq. km) and Nevis (93 sq. km) are part of the Leeward group in the eastern Caribbean Sea. The centre of St Kitts is forest-clad and mountainous, with the Great Salt Pond occupying the tip of its southern peninsula; elevation extremes range from 1,156m (Mt Liamuiga) at the highest point to 0m (Caribbean Sea) at the lowest. Nevis, separated from the southern tip of St Kitts by a strait 3km wide, is dominated by Nevis Peak (985m). The climate is tropical, moderated by north-east trade winds, and a wet season occurs from May to September. The islands are in the hurricane belt.

HISTORY AND POLITICS

The islands were inhabited by Carib, or Kalinago, people when discovered in 1493 by Christopher Columbus, who gave St Christopher its name. Colonisation by the British began in 1623–4, when St Kitts became the first British colony in the West Indies, and French settlement began shortly after. The island was held jointly from 1628 to 1713, although there were skirmishes between the British and French settlers in the 17th century; France dropped its claims after 1783. Nevis was settled by the British from 1628. The two islands were part of the Leeward Islands colony from 1871 to 1956, and then of the West Indies Federation from 1958 to 1962. They achieved internal self-government in 1967 and became independent in September 1983.

A separatist movement was formed on Nevis in 1970. A referendum on the issue in 1998 resulted in a 61.8 per cent vote in favour of secession, which fell short of the two-thirds majority required.

The Labour Party, which has been in power since 1995, retained its overall majority in the legislative election in January 2010, and began its fourth term of office under Denzil Douglas.

POLITICAL SYSTEM

Under the 1983 constitution, the head of state is Queen Elizabeth II, represented by a governor-general appointed on the advice of the prime minister. The unicameral National Assembly has 15 members: 11 directly elected for a five-year term, a speaker, and three appointed by the governor-general on the advice of the prime minister and the leader of the opposition. The prime minister, who is responsible to the legislature, and the cabinet are appointed by the governor-general.

Nevis is responsible for its own internal affairs. It has an eight-member Nevis Island assembly and is governed by the Nevis Island administration, headed by the premier.

Governor-General, HE Sir Cuthbert Sebastian, GCMG, OBE, *apptd* 1996

SELECTED GOVERNMENT MEMBERS *as at July 2010*
Prime Minister, Finance, Denzil Douglas
Deputy Prime Minister, Foreign Affairs, National Security, Sam Condor

HIGH COMMISSION FOR ST KITTS AND NEVIS
10 Kensington Court, London W8 5DL
T 020-7937 9718 E sknhighcomm@btconnect.com
High Commissioner, HE James Williams, *apptd* 2001

BRITISH HIGH COMMISSIONER
HE Paul Brummell, *apptd* 2009, resident at Bridgetown, Barbados

ECONOMY AND TRADE

The sugar industry was the mainstay of the economy for over 300 years but was closed down in 2005 after decades of operating at a loss. Tourism (the chief source of foreign exchange revenue), offshore financial services and manufacturing, especially distilling, food processing, clothing and electronics, are being developed, although all, especially tourism, have suffered in the global downturn. Services now account for 71 per cent of GDP, industry for 26 per cent and agriculture for 3 per cent. The economy of Nevis relies on farming, but a sea-island cotton industry is being developed for export.

The main trading partners are the USA and Trinidad and Tobago. Principal exports are machinery, food, electronic equipment, beverages and tobacco. The main imports are machinery, manufactured goods, food and fuels.

GNI – US$535m; US$10,870 per capita (2008)
Annual average growth of GDP – –2 per cent (2009 est)
Inflation rate – 4.5 per cent (2007 est)
Total external debt – US$314m (2004 est)

BALANCE OF PAYMENTS
Trade – US$254m deficit (2009)
Current Account – US$195m deficit (2008)

Trade with UK	*2008*	*2009*
Imports from UK	£8,727,998	£7,693,108
Exports to UK	£764,170	£223,704

COMMUNICATIONS

The islands have a total of 383km of roads, of which 163km are surfaced, and 50km of narrow-gauge railways on St Kitts. Basseterre is a port of registry and has deep-water harbour facilities. There are regular ferries between Basseterre and Charlestown. There are two airports; that on St Kitts can take most large jet aircraft, and Nevis' airport can take small aircraft and has night-time landing facilities. There are modern telecommunications systems.

MEDIA

The government-owned broadcaster ZIZ operates national television and radio networks. Cable television services are also available, and there are several private radio stations. *The Sun* is the sole daily newspaper and is privately owned.

ST LUCIA

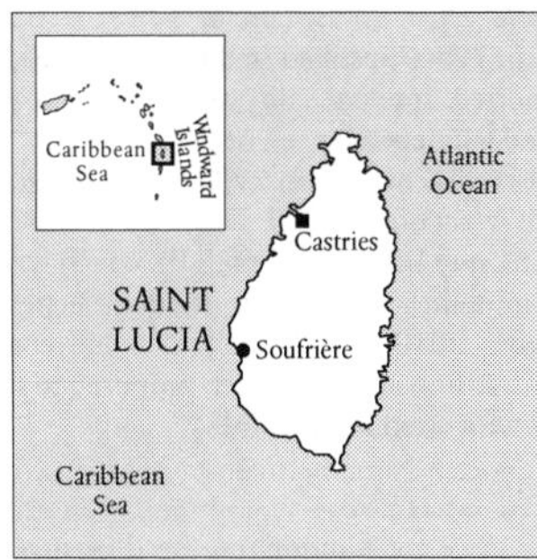

Area – 616 sq. km
Capital – Castries; population, 15,395 (2009 est)
Currency – East Caribbean dollar (EC$) of 100 cents
Population – 160,267 rising at 0.42 per cent a year (2009 est)
Religion – Christian (Roman Catholic 67 per cent, Seventh-day Adventist 9 per cent, Pentecostal 6 per cent, Evangelical 2 per cent, Anglican 2 per cent), Rastafarian 2 per cent (est); small Muslim minority
Language – English (official), French patois
Population density – 279 per sq. km (2008)
Urban population – 28 per cent (2007 est)
Median age (years) – 29.8 (2009 est)
National anthem – 'Sons and Daughters of Saint Lucia'
National day – 22 February (Independence Day)
Life expectancy (years) – 76.45 (2009 est)
Mortality rate – 6.8 (2009 est)
Birth rate – 15.1 (2009 est)
Infant mortality rate – 13.43 (2009 est)
Death penalty – Retained
CPI score – 7 (2009)
Literacy rate – 94.8 per cent (2007 est)

CLIMATE AND TERRAIN

St Lucia is the second-largest island in the Windward group. The interior is mountainous and densely forested, with elevation extremes ranging from 950m (Mt Gimie) at the highest point to 0m (Caribbean Sea) at the lowest. The area around the volcanic peaks of Gros Piton and Petit Piton is a UNESCO World Heritage Site. The climate is tropical, moderated by trade winds and with a wet season from July to November. The island is in the hurricane belt.

HISTORY AND POLITICS

The original Arawak settlers were superseded by Caribs by AD 800. The island was sighted by Columbus in 1502 and European settlement began in the 1550s. Control was disputed between France and Britain from the mid-17th century until 1814, when the island was ceded to Britain. It achieved internal self-government in 1967 and became independent on 22 February 1979. Violent crime and a gang culture have grown in recent years, largely as a result of drug-trafficking.

The St Lucia Labour Party, in power since 1997, lost the 2006 general election to the United Workers Party, which formed a government under Sir John Compton; he died in September 2007 and Stephenson King became prime minister.

POLITICAL SYSTEM

Under the 1979 constitution, the head of state is Queen Elizabeth II, represented by a governor-general appointed on the advice of the prime minister. The bicameral parliament consists of the house of assembly and the senate. The senate has 11 members, six nominated by the government, three by the opposition and two by the governor-general. The House of Assembly has 17 elected members and an appointed speaker who serve a five-year term. The prime minister, who is responsible to the legislature, and the cabinet are appointed by the governor-general.

Governor-General, HE Dame Pearlette Louisy, *apptd* 1997

SELECTED GOVERNMENT MEMBERS *as at July 2010*
Prime Minister, Finance, Economy, Stephenson King
Home Affairs, George Guy Mayers
External Affairs, Rufus Bousquet
Attorney-General, Nicholas Frederick

HIGH COMMISSION FOR ST LUCIA
1 Collingham Gardens, London SW5 0HW
T 020-7370 7123 E enquiries@stluciahcuk.org
W www.stluciahcuk.org
High Commissioner, HE Eldridge Stephens, OBE, *apptd* 2008

BRITISH HIGH COMMISSIONER
HE Paul Brummell, *apptd* 2009, resident at Bridgetown, Barbados

ECONOMY AND TRADE

The economy was dependent on bananas (which still account for about 41 per cent of export earnings), but has diversified since preferential access to EU markets ended in 1999. Tourism and offshore financial services have been developed, and the manufacturing sector is the most diverse in the Caribbean, processing agricultural products, assembling electronic components and producing clothing, beverages and corrugated cardboard boxes. Services now account for 80 per cent of GDP, industry for 15 per cent and agriculture for 5 per cent. The economy contracted in the global downturn as tourist numbers fell.

The main trading partners are Brazil, the USA and the UK. Principal exports are bananas, clothing, cocoa, vegetables, fruit and coconut oil. The main imports are food, manufactured goods, machinery and transport equipment, chemicals and fuels.

GNI – US$921m; US$5,410 per capita (2008)
Annual average growth of GDP – –2.5 per cent (2009 est)
Inflation rate – 1.9 per cent (2007 est)
Unemployment – 20 per cent (2003 est)
Total external debt – US$257m (2004 est)
Imports – US$700m (2008)
Exports – US$100m (2008)

BALANCE OF PAYMENTS
Trade – US$585m deficit (2009)
Current Account – US$306m deficit (2008)

Trade with UK	*2008*	*2009*
Imports from UK	£15,066,323	£14,978,913
Exports to UK	£16,663,048	£19,077,675

COMMUNICATIONS

St Lucia has around 1,200km of roads and two airports, at Castries and Vieux Fort. Castries also has a deep-water harbour. There are modern telecommunications systems.

MEDIA

The television and radio broadcasters are privately owned, other than one government-owned radio network which broadcasts in English and Creole. The island has two main newspapers, *The Star* and *The Voice*, both published three times a week.

ST VINCENT AND THE GRENADINES

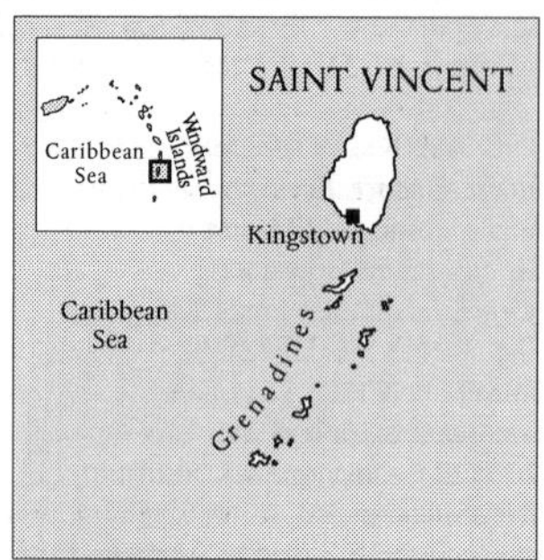

Area – 389 sq. km
Capital – Kingstown; population, 28,199 (2009 est)
Currency – East Caribbean dollar (EC $) of 100 cents
Population – 104,574 falling at 0.34 per cent a year (2009 est)
Religion – Christian (Anglican 16 per cent, Pentecostal 16 per cent, Baptist 9 per cent, Methodist 9 per cent, Seventh-day Adventist 9 per cent, Roman Catholic 7 per cent); Rastafarian 1 per cent (est)
Language – English (official), French patois
Population density – 280 per sq. km (2008)
Urban population – 47 per cent (2007 est)
Median age (years) – 28.9 (2009 est)
National anthem – 'St Vincent, Land So Beautiful'
National day – 27 October (Independence Day)
Life expectancy (years) – 73.65 (2009 est)
Mortality rate – 6.91 (2009 est)
Birth rate – 15.27 (2009 est)
Infant mortality rate – 15.14 (2009 est)
Death penalty – Retained
CPI score – 6.4 (2009)
Literacy rate – 88.1 per cent (2007 est)

CLIMATE AND TERRAIN

The state, which lies in the Windward group, consists of St Vincent and the 32 small islands and cays of the northern Grenadines, a chain stretching 64km across the eastern Caribbean Sea between St Vincent and Grenada. St Vincent itself is a mountainous and densely forested volcanic island. The Grenadines, of which the largest are Bequia, Canouan, Mayreau, Mustique and Union Island, are low-lying coral islands. Elevation extremes range from 1,234m (La Soufriére volcano, St Vincent) at the highest point to 0m (Caribbean Sea) at the lowest. The climate is tropical, with a rainy season from May to November. The islands lie in the hurricane belt.

HISTORY AND POLITICS

Settled successively by the Ciboney people, the Arawaks and the Caribs, St Vincent was sighted by Christopher Columbus in 1498 but resisted European settlement longer than other Caribbean islands. Although granted by Charles I to the Earl of Carlisle in 1627, control was disputed between the British and the French until the islands were ceded to Britain in 1783. A Black Carib uprising in 1795–7 resulted in thousands of Black Caribs being deported. Internal self-government was granted in 1969, and independence as St Vincent and the Grenadines was achieved on 27 October 1979.

An early election in 2001 was won decisively by the opposition Unity Labour Party (ULP), which was returned for a second term in 2005; a legislative election was due in December 2010. A referendum in November 2009 rejected a draft constitution which proposed to replace the monarchy with a republic.

POLITICAL SYSTEM

Under the 1979 constitution, the head of state is Queen Elizabeth II, represented by a governor-general appointed on the advice of the prime minister. The unicameral House of Assembly has 21 members: 15 directly elected for a five-year term and six senators appointed by the governor-general (four on the advice of the government and two on the advice of the opposition). The prime minister, who is responsible to the legislature, and the cabinet are appointed by the governor-general.
Governor-General, Sir Frederick Ballantyne, GCMG, *apptd* 2002

SELECTED GOVERNMENT MEMBERS *as at July 2010*
Prime Minister, Finance, Economy, National Security, Ralph Gonsalves
Deputy Prime Minister, Foreign Affairs, Louis Straker

HIGH COMMISSION FOR ST VINCENT AND THE GRENADINES
10 Kensington Court, London W8 5DL
T 020-7565 2874 E info@svghighcom.co.uk
W www.svghighcom.co.uk
High Commissioner, HE Cenio E. Lewis, *apptd* 2001

BRITISH HIGH COMMISSIONER
HE Paul Brummell, *apptd* 2009, resident at Bridgetown, Barbados

ECONOMY AND TRADE

The economy was based on bananas (which still account for over a third of exports) but since 1999, when preferential access to EU markets ended, efforts have been made to diversify. Tourism (the development of which has been hampered by drug-related crime), manufacturing and offshore banking services have all expanded, although the economy contracted in 2009 owing to the global downturn. Services now account for 64 per cent of GDP, industry for 26 per cent and agriculture for 10 per cent.

The main export markets are Greece and France. Imports come mostly from Singapore, Trinidad and Tobago, and the USA. Principal exports are bananas, vegetables, starch and tennis racquets. The main imports are foodstuffs, machinery and equipment, chemicals, fertilisers, minerals and fuel.
GNI – US$551m; US$5,050 per capita (2008)
Annual average growth of GDP – –6.5 per cent (2009 est)
Inflation rate – 6.1 per cent (2007 est)
Unemployment – 15 per cent (2001 est)
Total external debt – US$223m (2004 est)
Imports – US$400m (2008)
Exports – US$50m (2007)

BALANCE OF PAYMENTS
Trade – US$325m deficit (2009)
Current Account – US$217m deficit (2008)

Trade with UK	*2008*	*2009*
Imports from UK	£7,775,665	£9,933,460
Exports to UK	£4,489,151	£4,666,003

COMMUNICATIONS

The islands have around 829km of roads, of which 580km are surfaced. The main harbour is at Kingstown, which is a port of registry for shipping. There is a large merchant marine of 525 ships of over 1,000 tonnes; 476 ships are foreign-owned. There are six airports; although none can accommodate international flights at present, an international airport is under construction and scheduled for completion in 2011. There are modern telecommunications systems.

MEDIA

The press is privately owned, and its freedom is guaranteed by the constitution. There is one daily newpaper, *The Herald,* and several other weekly titles. There are several private radio stations and a national radio service which is partly government-funded. Television broadcasting is operated by the St Vincent and the Grenadines Broadcasting Corporation.

SAMOA

Malo Sa'oloto Tuto'atasi o Samoa – Independent State of Samoa

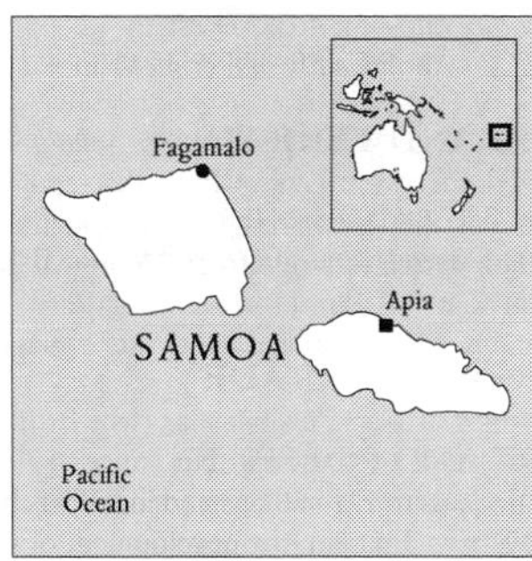

Area – 2,831 sq. km
Capital – Apia, on Upolu; population, 36,433 (2009 est)
Currency – Tala (S$) of 100 sene
Population – 219,998 rising at 1.35 per cent a year (2009 est). Samoans are a Polynesian people, though the population also includes Euronesians, Chinese and Europeans
Religion – Christian (Congregational 34 per cent, Roman Catholic 19 per cent, Methodist 14 per cent, Mormon 13 per cent, Assemblies of God 7 per cent, Seventh-day Adventist 4 per cent); small Baha'i minority (est)
Language – English, Samoan
Population density – 63 per sq. km (2008)
Urban population – 23 per cent (2007 est)
Median age (years) – 20.8 (2009 est)
National anthem – 'The Banner of Freedom'
National day – 1 June (Independence Day)
Life expectancy (years) – 71.86 (2009 est)
Mortality rate – 5.79 (2009 est)
Birth rate – 28.06 (2009 est)
Infant mortality rate – 24.22 (2009 est)
Death penalty – Abolished for all crimes (since 2004)
CPI score – 4.5 (2009)
Literacy rate – 98.7 per cent (2007 est)

CLIMATE AND TERRAIN

Samoa consists of the islands of Savai'i, Upolu, Apolima, Manono, Fanuatapu, Namua, Nu'utele, Nu'ulua and Nu'usafe'e in the south Pacific Ocean. All the islands are volcanic in origin, with narrow coastal plains and mountainous, densely forested interiors. Elevation extremes range from 1,857m (Mauga Silisili, Savai'i) at the highest point to 0m (Pacific Ocean) at the lowest. The climate is tropical, with a wet season from November to April. Average temperatures range between 23°C and 30°C all year round. The islands are vulnerable to cyclones and tsunamis.

HISTORY AND POLITICS

Inhabited since *c.*1000 BC, Samoa was visited by European traders, explorers and missionaries from the 18th century. Germany, the UK and the USA disputed control of the islands until 1899, when the nine western islands (Western Samoa) became a German colony and the eastern islands American Samoa. Western Samoa was occupied by New Zealand on the outbreak of the First World War and became a mandated territory administered by New Zealand from 1920. Internal self-government was granted in 1959, and Western Samoa became independent on 1 June 1962. The state was treated as a member country of the Commonwealth until its formal admission in 1970. In 1997 the state dropped 'Western' from its name.

The Human Rights Protection Party, which has been in power since 1981, remained the largest party in the legislature after the 2006 election; it won 35 seats, the Samoa Democratic United Party won 10 seats and independents won four. Former prime minister Tuiatua Tupua Tamasese Efi was elected head of state in June 2007, following his predecessor's death the previous month. Parliamentary elections are next scheduled for March 2011.

POLITICAL SYSTEM

Under the 1962 constitution, the head of state is elected and has functions analogous to those of a constitutional monarch. Initially an office held for life, the monarch is now elected by the legislature for a five-year term. The unicameral legislative assembly *(Fono)* has 49 members elected for a five-year term; only members of the *Matai* (elected clan leaders) may stand for election. The prime minister is appointed by the monarch on the recommendation of the legislature and appoints the cabinet.

HEAD OF STATE
Head of State, Tuiatua Tupua Tamasese Efi, *elected* 16 June 2007, *sworn in* 20 June 2007

SELECTED GOVERNMENT MEMBERS *as at July 2010*
Prime Minister, Foreign Affairs, Tuilaepa Sailele Malielegaoi
Deputy Prime Minister, Misa Telefoni Retzlaff
Finance, Niko Lee Hang

EMBASSY OF SAMOA
20 avenue de l'Oree, 1000 Brussels, Belgium
T (+32) (2) 660 8454 E samoanembassy@skynet.be
High Commissioner, HE Tuala Falani Chan Tung, *apptd* 2006

BRITISH HIGH COMMISSIONER
HE Victoria Treadell, MVO *apptd* 2010, resident at Wellington, New Zealand

ECONOMY AND TRADE

The economy is underdeveloped but has grown steadily in the past decade, diversifying away from its traditional dependence on fishing, agriculture (which is vulnerable to cyclones), remittances from migrant workers (worth about 25 per cent of GDP) and international aid. Although agriculture generates 11.6 per cent of GDP, employing about two-thirds of the labour force and supplying about 90 per cent of exports, manufacturing is branching out from small-scale processing of agricultural products into light manufacturing (particularly of motor vehicle components), and offshore financial services are being developed. Tourism has grown rapidly and now accounts for about 25 per cent of GDP. However, the global downturn caused the economy to contract from 2008, and a tsunami in 2009 caused severe damage.

The main trading partners are Australia, American Samoa, New Zealand, Fiji and Singapore. Principal exports are fish, coconut oil and cream, copra, taro, vehicle parts, garments and beer. The main imports are machinery and equipment, industrial supplies and foodstuffs.

GNI – US$504m; US$2,820 per capita (2008)
Annual average growth of GDP – –0.8 per cent (2009 est)
Inflation rate – 6 per cent (2007 est)
Total external debt – US$177m (2004 est)
Imports – US$200m (2008)
Exports – US$15m (2007)

BALANCE OF PAYMENTS
Trade – US$144m deficit (2009)
Current Account – US$11m deficit (2009)

Trade with UK	*2008*	*2009*
Imports from UK	£1,105,729	£394,389
Exports to UK	£315,199	£547,564

COMMUNICATIONS

There are 2,337km of roads, of which 332km are surfaced. Upolu contains the harbours of Apia and Mulifanua, and Savai'i the harbour of Salelologa. There are four airports, including an international airport 35km west of Apia on Upolu. Transport systems were severely damaged by a tsunami in 2009.

Telecommunications systems are adequate; in 2008 there were 28,800 fixed lines in use, 124,000 mobile phone subscribers and 9,000 internet users.

MEDIA

There are two daily papers, one weekly title and one fortnightly. The press is generally free to report as it chooses, although the *Samoa Observer* has been sued by the government for reporting on alleged corruption. The state-run Samoa Broadcasting Corporation operates television and radio networks, competing with a small number of privately owned television and radio stations.

SAN MARINO

Repubblica di San Marino – Republic of San Marino

Area – 61 sq. km
Capital – San Marino; population, 4,389 (2009 est)
Currency – Euro (€) of 100 cents
Population – 30,324 rising at 1.15 per cent a year (2009 est)
Religion – Christian (Roman Catholic 90 per cent) (est)
Language – Italian (official)
Population density – 517 per sq. km (2008)
Urban population – 94 per cent (2007 est)
Median age (years) – 41.5 (2009 est)
National anthem – 'Inno Nazionale della Repubblica' ['National Anthem of the Republic']
National day – 3 September (Republic Day)
Life expectancy (years) – 81.97 (2009 est)
Mortality rate – 8.48 (2009 est)
Birth rate – 9.63 (2009 est)
Infant mortality rate – 5.34 (2009 est)
Death penalty – Abolished for all crimes (since 1865)

CLIMATE AND TERRAIN

A landlocked enclave in central Italy, the republic lies in the foothills of the Apennines, 20km from the Adriatic Sea. Elevation extremes range from 755m (Mt Titano) at the highest point to 55m (Torrente Ausa) at the lowest. The climate is Mediterranean, with an average annual rainfall of 762mm.

HISTORY AND POLITICS

The republic is said to have been founded in the fourth century by a Christian stonecutter seeking refuge from religious persecution. By the 12th century a self-governing commune was established, and a parliamentary constitution was adopted in 1600. The republic resisted papal claims and those of neighbouring dukedoms from the 15th to 18th centuries, and the papacy recognised its independence in 1631. In 1862 it signed a treaty with the newly united kingdom of Italy which recognised its integrity and sovereignty and accorded it the protection of Italy. San Marino became a member of the UN in 1992.

Following the 2006 legislative election, the Christian Democratic Party (PDCS) remained the largest party in the legislature, but a coalition government was formed by the Party of Socialists and Democrats (PSD), United Left and Popular Alliance (AP) parties. A split in the government in August 2008 led to an early election in November that resulted in the Pact for San Marino (PSM) coalition (of the PDCS, AP, Freedom List and Union of Moderates) winning the most seats and forming a new coalition government.

POLITICAL SYSTEM
The 1600 constitution has been amended several times. The joint heads of state are two captains-regent who are elected at six-monthly intervals (March and September) by the legislature, taking office the month after the election. Executive power is vested in the captains-regent and the Congress of State (cabinet), which is also elected by the legislature. The unicameral legislature, the Great and General Council, has 60 members, who are directly elected for a five-year term.

HEADS OF STATE *as at July 2010*
Captains-Regent, Marco Conti; Glauco Sansovini

SELECTED GOVERNMENT MEMBERS *as at July 2010*
Finance, Gabriele Gatti
Foreign Affairs, Antonella Mularoni
Internal Affairs, Valeria Ciavatta

EMBASSY OF THE REPUBLIC OF SAN MARINO
c/o Consulate of the Republic of San Marino, Flat 51, 162 Sloane Street, London SW1X 9BS
T 020-7823 4762 E dipartimentoaffariesteri@pa.sm
Ambassador Extraordinary and Plenipotentiary, HE Countess Marina Meneghetti de Camillo, *apptd* 2002, resident at Rome, Italy

BRITISH AMBASSADOR
HE Edward Chaplin, *apptd* 2006, resident at Rome, Italy

ECONOMY AND TRADE

Tourism and banking are the basis of the economy, and the service sector contributes over 50 per cent of GDP. In 2009, investment outflows following Italy's tax amnesty, a money-laundering scandal at its largest bank and the global downturn pushed San Marino's economy into recession and caused a budget deficit.

The principal agricultural products are wine, cheeses, grains and fruits, and the other main industries are the manufacture of clothing, electronics and ceramics. Sales of postage stamps and coins also generate significant revenue. San Marino is in a customs union with the EU.

GNI – US$1,291m; US$45,130 per capita (2007)
Annual average growth of GDP – 4.3 per cent (2007 est)
Inflation rate – -3.5 per cent (2008 est)
Unemployment – 3.1 per cent (2008 est)

Trade with UK	*2008*	*2009*
Imports from UK	£11,956,199	£10,009,227
Exports to UK	£6,713,818	£4,014,480

MEDIA

San Marino has a state-run broadcaster, which provides radio and television services. The two daily newspapers are *La Tribuna Sammarinese* and *San Marino Oggi.*

SAO TOME AND PRINCIPE

Republica Democratica de Sao Tome e Principe – Democratic Republic of Sao Tome and Principe

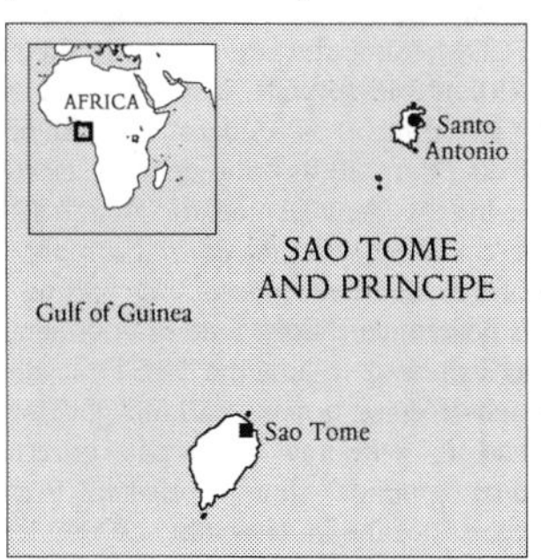

Area – 964 sq. km
Capital – Sao Tome; population, 59,851 (2009 est)
Currency – Dobra of 100 centimos
Population – 212,679 rising at 3.09 per cent a year (2009 est)
Religion – Christian (Roman Catholic 85 per cent, Protestant denominations 12 per cent), Muslim 2 per cent (est)
Language – Portuguese (official), Creole dialects
Population density – 167 per sq. km (2008)
Urban population – 60 per cent (2007 est)
Median age (years) – 16.4 (2009 est)
National anthem – 'Independencia total' ['Total Independence']
National day – 12 July (Independence Day)
Life expectancy (years) – 68.32 (2009 est)
Mortality rate – 5.8 (2009 est)
Birth rate – 38.54 (2009 est)
Infant mortality rate – 37.12 (2009 est)
Death penalty – Abolished for all crimes (since 1990)
CPI score – 2.8 (2009)
Literacy rate – 87.9 per cent (2007 est)

CLIMATE AND TERRAIN

The republic consists of the islands of Sao Tome, Principe and several uninhabited islets off the west coast of Africa. The islands, which are volcanic in origin, are mountainous and thickly forested. Elevation extremes range from 2,024m (Pico de Sao Tome) at the highest point to 0m (Atlantic Ocean) at the lowest. The climate is tropical, with a wet season from October to May. Average daily temperatures are between 25°C and 27°C all year round.

HISTORY AND POLITICS

The uninhabited islands were discovered by the Portuguese between 1469 and 1472, and settlement began in 1493. Plantations were established that became important producers of sugar cane, cocoa and coffee. Agitation against Portuguese rule began in the late 1950s. The islands gained independence from Portugal in July 1975 and became a one-party state under the rule of the Movement for the Liberation of Sao Tome and Principe (MLSTP). The government nationalised the plantations and formed close links with the communist bloc. These were scaled down in the 1980s as the economy deteriorated and in 1990 the MLSTP abandoned Marxism and introduced political pluralism and economic liberalisation. The first multiparty elections were held in 1991. Democracy has brought a degree of political instability, and tensions have been heightened recently by disagreements over the exploitation of offshore oil reserves.

In the 2006 legislative election, the Force for Change Democratic Movement-Democratic Convergence Party (MDFM-PCD) became the largest bloc in the legislature, though without an overall majority, and formed a coalition government. President de Menezes was re-elected at the 2006 presidential election. The opposition Independent Democratic Action (ADI) party joined the coalition government in February 2008, its leader Patrice Trovoada becoming prime minister. Trovoada's government lost a vote of confidence in May and he was dismissed. In June the MLSTP leader Joaquim Rafael Branco formed a new coalition government. The MDFM had to withdraw from the government on constitutional grounds after it elected President de Menezes as its leader in December 2009, leaving the MLSTP in coalition with the PCD. In the August 2010 legislative election the ADI became the largest party in the legislature but lacked a majority, and formed a government with a number of independent members of the National Assembly.

POLITICAL SYSTEM
Under the 1990 constitution, the president is directly elected for a five-year term, renewable only once. The unicameral National Assembly has 55 members, directly elected for a four-year term. The prime minister is appointed by the president and nominates the cabinet.

Since 1995 Princípe has been internally self-governing, with an eight-member regional council.

HEAD OF STATE
President, Fradique de Menezes, *elected* 29 July 2001, *sworn in* 3 September 2001, *re-elected* 2006

SELECTED GOVERNMENT MEMBERS *as at July 2010*
Prime Minister, Joaquim Rafael Branco
Defence, Elsa Teixeira Pinto
Finance, Angela Viegas Santiago
Foreign Affairs, Carlos Alberto Pires Tiny

EMBASSY OF SAO TOME AND PRINCIPE
175 avenue de Tervuren, 1150 Brussels, Belgium
T (+32) (2) 734 8966 E ambassade@saotomeprincipe.be
Ambassador Extraordinary and Plenipotentiary, vacant

BRITISH AMBASSADOR
HE Richard Wildash, *apptd* 2010, resident at Luanda, Angola

ECONOMY AND TRADE

The economy is largely dependent on cocoa, which accounts for 80 per cent of exports; tourism is being encouraged in an attempt to diversify. A major economic shift will begin with the start of oil production from offshore reserves in the Gulf of Guinea, probably from 2010–11. The fields are being developed jointly with Nigeria, and Sao Tome and Principe will receive 40 per cent of the revenue. Most of the population is engaged in subsistence farming and fishing, and over half live below the poverty line.

The principal trading partners are Portugal (59 per cent of imports), the UK (33 per cent of exports) and the Netherlands (27 per cent of exports). Principal exports are cocoa, copra, coffee and palm oil. The main imports are machinery and electrical equipment, foodstuffs and petroleum products.

GNI – US$164m; US$1,030 per capita (2008)
Annual average growth of GDP – 4.3 per cent (2009 est)
Inflation rate – 19 per cent (2009 est)
Population below poverty line – 54 per cent (2004 est)
Total external debt – US$318m (2002 est)

BALANCE OF PAYMENTS
Trade – US$106m deficit (2009)
Current Account – US$88m deficit (2008)

Trade with UK	*2008*	*2009*
Imports from UK	£68,288	£147,050
Exports to UK	£1,754	£10,964

COMMUNICATIONS

There are 320km of roads, 218km of which are surfaced but in poor condition. There are two airports, and the ports are Santo Antonio, on Principe, and Sao Tome. The telephone system supported 7,700 fixed lines, 49,000 mobile phone users and 24,800 internet users in 2008.

MEDIA

Freedom of expression is generally respected. The islands' only radio and television stations are state-run, but opposition parties are given free airtime. There are three privately owned newspapers and one published by the government.

SAUDI ARABIA

Al-Mamlakah al-Arabiyah as Suudiyah – Kingdom of Saudi Arabia

Area – 2,149,690 sq. km
Capital – Riyadh (Ar-Riyad); population, 4,725,270 (2009 est)
Major cities – Ad Dammam, Jeddah, Mecca, Medina, Tabuk, At Ta'if
Currency – Saudi riyal (SR) of 100 halalas
Population – 28,686,633 rising at 1.85 per cent a year (2009 est); includes some 5,576,076 non-nationals (2008 est)
Religion – Muslim (Sunni 90 per cent, predominantly Wahhabi; Shia 10 per cent) (est). Public practice of other religions is forbidden
Language – Arabic (official)
Population density – 12 per sq. km (2008)
Urban population – 81 per cent (2007 est)
Median age (years) – 21.6 (2009 est)
National anthem – 'As-Salaam al Malaki' ['The Royal Salute']

National day – 23 September (Unification Day)
Life expectancy (years) – 76.3 (2009 est)
Mortality rate – 2.47 (2009 est)
Birth rate – 28.55 (2009 est)
Infant mortality rate – 11.57 (2009 est)
Death penalty – Retained
CPI score – 4.3 (2009)

CLIMATE AND TERRAIN

Saudi Arabia comprises about 80 per cent of the Arabian peninsula. The Hejaz region (north-west) runs along the northern Red Sea coast to the Asir and contains the holy cities of Mecca and Medina. The mountainous Asir (south-west) and the coastal plain of the Tihama lie along the southern Red Sea coast from the Hejaz to the border with Yemen. The Nejd plateau extends over the centre, including the Nafud and Dahna deserts. The Hasa (east) is low-lying and largely desert. The Empty Quarter (south) is the world's largest sand desert. Elevation extremes range from 3,133m (Jabal Sawda) at the highest point to 0m (Persian Gulf) at the lowest. There is a desert climate, with extremes of temperature in the interior; coastal areas are more temperate but extremely humid. Average temperatures in Riyadh range from lows of 8°C in January to highs of 42°C in July.

HISTORY AND POLITICS

The Arabian peninsula was the birthplace of the Muslim faith in the seventh century and the base from which the religion and a Muslim empire expanded, eventually stretching from India to Spain. When this empire declined in the 12th century, Arabia became isolated and internally divided. The rise of the al-Saud family began in the 18th century, when it united the Nejd in support of the Wahhabi religious movement. The modern state was the culmination of a 30-year campaign by Abd-al Aziz al-Saud (often known as Ibn Saud) to unite the four tribal regions of the Hejaz, Asir, Najd and Hasa; the Kingdom of Saudi Arabia was proclaimed on 23 September 1932.

The ruling family preserved stability for many years by suppressing dissent and resisting calls for greater democracy, with some of its actions raising international concerns over human rights abuses. Internal tension grew in the 1990s because of the continuing presence of foreign, particularly US, troops in the country after the 1991 Gulf War; troops and foreign nationals became terrorist targets. Despite the troops' redeployment to Qatar in early 2003, the frequency of attacks increased following the start of the Iraq War in 2003 and included Saudi as well as foreign victims. Some dissident groups are believed to have links with al-Qaida. Since 2003 demand for political reform has grown and become more militant. In 2005, the country's first nationwide elections were held for half the seats on municipal councils, with voting by universal male suffrage.

King Abdullah acceded to the throne after the death of his half-brother King Fahd in 2005.

POLITICAL SYSTEM

There is no written constitution; constitutional practice is provided for by articles of government based on the Qur'an and the teachings and sayings of the Prophet Muhammad *(Sunnah)* and issued by royal decree.

Saudi Arabia is a hereditary monarchy. The king is head of government and appoints the council of ministers (established in 1953), whose term of office was fixed in 1993 at four years.

There is no legislature; the Consultative Council *(Majlis-al-Shura)* debates policy, proposes legislation in certain areas and makes recommendations to the king. The council's 150 members are appointed by the king and serve a four-year term. Its decisions are taken by majority vote. There are no political parties.

Each of the 13 provinces has a governor appointed by the king and a council of prominent local citizens to advise the governor on local government, budgetary and planning issues.

HEAD OF STATE

The King of Saudi Arabia, Custodian of the Two Holy Mosques, Prime Minister, Commander of the National Guard, King Abdullah bin Abdul Aziz al-Saud, *born* 1923, *succeeded* 2 August 2005
HRH Crown Prince, Deputy Prime Minister, Defence, Prince Sultan bin Abdul Aziz al-Saud

SELECTED GOVERNMENT MEMBERS *as at July 2010*

Interior, HRH Prince Nayef bin Abdul Aziz al-Saud
Finance, Ibrahim bin Abdel Aziz al-Assaf
Foreign Affairs, HRH Prince Saud al-Faisal bin Abdul Aziz al-Saud
Economy, Khaled bin Mohammad al-Qussaibi

ROYAL EMBASSY OF SAUDI ARABIA

30 Charles Street, London W1J 5DZ
T 020-7917 3000 E ukemb@mofa.gov.sa
W www.saudiembassy.org.uk
Ambassador Extraordinary and Plenipotentiary, HE HRH Prince Mohamed bin Nawaf bin Abdul Aziz al-Saud, *apptd* 2005

BRITISH EMBASSY

PO Box 94351, Diplomatic Quarter, Riyadh 11693
T (+966) (1) 488 0077 E PressOffice.Riyadh@fco.gov.uk
W http://ukinsaudiarabia.fco.gov.uk
Ambassador Extraordinary and Plenipotentiary, HE Sir Tom Phillips, KCMG, *apptd* 2010

BRITISH COUNCIL

PO Box 58012, C-14, 3rd Floor, Al-Fazari Square, Diplomatic Quarter, Riyadh 11594
T (+966) (1) 483 1818
W www.britishcouncil.org/me-saudiarabia
Director, Adrian Chardwick

DEFENCE

The army has 910 main battle tanks, 2,240 armoured personnel carriers, 780 armoured infantry fighting vehicles and 12 armed helicopters. The navy has 7 frigates, 4 corvettes, 65 patrol and coastal vessels and 15 armed helicopters at 7 bases. The air force has 280 combat aircraft.
Military budget – US$41,200m (2009)
Military personnel – 233,500: army 75,000, navy 13,500, air force 20,000, Air Defence Force 16,000, Industrial Security Force 9,000, National Guard 100,000; paramilitary 15,500

ECONOMY AND TRADE

The economy is based on oil extraction and processing, but since 1970 the government has used a series of five-year development plans to encourage diversification, and the non-oil sector now accounts for over half of GDP. The 2000–5 development plan encouraged the growth of the private sector (now responsible for about 40 per cent of GDP) and an increase in the proportion of Saudi Arabian citizens in the workforce (about a third of workers are foreign nationals). The 2005–9 plan extends privatisation further, covering a wide range of infrastructure and services, including the development of mineral industries, housing and transport schemes, petrochemical plants, electricity generation, water supplies and desalination, telecommunications and ports. The 2010–14 plan adopted in April 2010 aims to increase natural gas production and to promote the growth of small- and medium-sized businesses partly through further privatisation; it also partially opened the Saudi stock market to foreign investors. To promote diversification and foreign investment, Saudi Arabia joined the World Trade Organisation in 2005.

Oil extraction since the 1940s has brought great wealth. Saudi Arabia has the largest proven reserves of oil in the world (over 20 per cent of the world total) and the fifth-largest reserves of recoverable gas. Depending on world prices, the oil and gas industry contributes around 45 per cent of GDP and about 80 per cent of government revenue. Falling prices and lower demand owing to the global downturn caused the economy to contract in 2009.

The main industries apart from oil extraction and refining include production of petrochemicals, ammonia, industrial gases, caustic soda, cement, fertiliser, plastics and metals, commercial ship and aircraft repair and construction. Industry accounts for 59.1 per cent of GDP and the service sector for 37.9 per cent. Agriculture contributes 3 per cent but is limited by the terrain, although productivity has been increased by extensive irrigation, desalination and the use of aquifers. The main products are cereals, fruit, meat and dairy products.

The main trading partners are the USA, Japan, China and South Korea. Oil and petroleum products constitute 90 per cent of exports. The principal imports are machinery and equipment, foodstuffs, chemicals, motor vehicles and textiles.

GNI – US$440,500m; US$17,870 per capita (2008)
Annual average growth of GDP – –0.6 per cent (2009 est)
Inflation rate – 5 per cent (2009 est)
Unemployment rate – 11.6 per cent (among males only) (2009 est)
Total external debt – US$72,450m (2009 est)
Imports – US$115,100m (2008)
Exports – US$328,900m (2008)

BALANCE OF PAYMENTS
Trade – US$177,098m surplus (2009)
Current Account – US$20,478m surplus (2009)

Trade with UK	*2008*	*2009*
Imports from UK	£2,278,326,748	£2,648,095,106
Exports to UK	£732,856,240	£555,991,836

COMMUNICATIONS

The main cargo ports are Jeddah on the Red Sea coast and Dammam on the Gulf coast. The main oil port (the world's largest) is Ras Tanura. There are 1,392km of railways, operated by the state-run Saudi Railway Organisation, which link Riyadh with the Gulf ports; there are plans to build a railway from Jeddah to Dammam. The road network totals 221,372km (of which 47,529km are surfaced), including a motorway system connecting all the cities and main towns. The 25km-long King Fahd Causeway connects the Eastern Province to Bahrain. There are over 200 airports and airfields; the three international airports are at Riyadh, Jeddah (serving Mecca) and Dammam.

Modern telecommunications systems provided services to 4.1 million fixed telephone lines, 36 million mobile phone subscribers and 7.7 million internet users in 2008.

EDUCATION AND HEALTH

With the exception of a few schools for expatriate children, all schools are supervised by the government and are segregated. There is great emphasis on vocational training, provided at literacy and artisan skill training centres and more advanced industrial, commercial and agricultural education institutes. The King Abdullah University of Science and Technology, a graduate-level research university and the first mixed-sex campus in Saudi Arabia, opened in September 2009.

Literacy rate – 85 per cent (2007 est)
Gross enrolment ratio (percentage of relevant age group) – primary 98 per cent; secondary 95 per cent; tertiary 30 per cent (2008 est)
Health expenditure (per capita) – US$531 (2007)
Hospital beds (per 1,000 people) – 2.2 (2003–8)

MEDIA AND CULTURE

Saudi Arabia's media is one of the most tightly controlled in the Middle East. Criticism of the government and royal family and the questioning of religious doctrine are not tolerated.

The only television and radio networks are operated by the state-run Broadcasting Service of the Kingdom of Saudi Arabia (BSKSA). Private radio and TV stations are not permitted, but there is a big market for pan-Arab services from satellite and subscription-based broadcasters. Although not necessarily state-run, Saudi newspapers normally follow the lead of the state-run press agency. Pan-Arab newspapers are also available but are censored. The government uses security systems to block websites with content it deems unsuitable.

Saudi culture revolves around Islam – it was the birthplace of the religion and two of Islam's holiest sites are situated in the country. Mecca was the Prophet Muhammad's birthplace and contains the Great Mosque, within which is the *Ka'abah* or sacred shrine of the Muslim religion. This is the focus of the annual *Hajj* ('pilgrimage'). Medina ('city of light'), some 300km north of Mecca, is celebrated as the first city to embrace Islam and as the burial place of the Prophet.

SENEGAL

République du Sénégal – Republic of Senegal

Area – 196,722 sq. km
Capital – Dakar; population, 2,776,700 (2009 est)
Major cities – Kaolack, Mbour, Saint-Louis, Thiès, Ziguinchor
Currency – Franc CFA of 100 centimes
Population – 13,711,597 rising at 2.71 per cent a year (2009 est); Wolof (43.3 per cent), Fulani (23.8 per cent), Serer (14.7 per cent), Jola (3.7 per cent), Mandinka (3 per cent), Soninke (1.1 per cent), European and Lebanese (1 per cent) (est)
Religion – Muslim 94 per cent, Christian 4 per cent (est). Most incorporate traditional indigenous beliefs into their worship
Language – French (official), Wolof, Pulaar, Jola, Mandinka
Population density – 63 per sq. km (2008)
Urban population – 42 per cent (2007 est)
Median age (years) – 18.6 (2009 est)
National anthem – 'Pincez Tous vos Koras, Frappez les Balafons' ['All Pluck Your Koras, Strike the Balafons']
National day – 4 April (Independence Day)
Life expectancy (years) – 59 (2009 est)
Mortality rate – 9.75 (2009 est)
Birth rate – 36.84 (2009 est)
Infant mortality rate – 58.94 (2009 est)
Death penalty – Abolished for all crimes (since 2004)
CPI score – 3 (2009)

CLIMATE AND TERRAIN

The terrain is generally low and rolling, with plains rising to hills in the south-east. There is desert in the north, savannah in the centre and tropical forest in the south. Elevation extremes range from 581m (near Nepen Diakha) at the highest point to 0m (Atlantic Ocean) at the lowest. There are three rivers: the Senegal on the northern border; and the Gambia and the Casamance in the south. The climate is tropical, with a wet season from June to September. Average temperatures in Dakar range from lows of 17°C in February to highs of 32°C in October.

HISTORY AND POLITICS

Senegal was part of the Mali Empire in the 14th to 15th centuries. The first European visitors were the Portuguese in 1445. The French established a fort at Saint-Louis in 1659 and European traders exported slaves, ivory, gold and other commodities from there in the 17th and 18th centuries. The interior was colonised by the French in the mid-19th century and the territory became part of French West Africa in 1902. It became an autonomous state in 1958 and achieved independence as part of the Federation of Mali in June 1960, seceding to form the Republic of Senegal in August 1960. From 1966 to 1978, the country was a one-party state under the rule of the Senegalese Progressive Union (UPS), which changed its name to the Socialist Party (PS) in 1976.

In the early 1980s a separatist insurgency led by the Movement of Democratic Forces of Casamance (MFDC) began in the impoverished Casamance region south of the river Gambia. A 2001 peace agreement was not implemented because of splits and leadership changes among the separatists. Further splits have prevented the full implementation of a fresh peace agreement with the government made in 2004, as some separatist factions remain active, and clashes continue between troops and rebels.

The Socialist Party's 40 years of political domination ended in 2000 with the election of Abdoulaye Wade, leader of the Senegalese Democratic Party (PDS), as president. The 2001 legislative election was won by an alliance of 40 parties, the *Sopi* (Change) coalition, led by the PDS; the PS retained only ten seats. President Wade was re-elected in the first round of the 2007 presidential election. The *Sopi* coalition retained its majority in the 2007 legislative elections, which were boycotted by opposition parties.

POLITICAL SYSTEM

The 2001 constitution was amended in 2007 to re-establish the senate as the upper chamber of a bicameral legislature. The executive president is directly elected for a seven-year term, renewable only once. The bicameral *Parlement* comprises the National Assembly, the lower chamber, which has 150 members directly elected for a five-year term; and the senate, which has 100 members, 35 indirectly elected and 65 appointed by the president, for a five-year term. The president appoints the prime minister, who nominates the other ministers.

HEAD OF STATE

President, Abdoulaye Wade, *elected* 19 March 2000, *sworn in* 1 April 2000, *re-elected* 2007

SELECTED GOVERNMENT MEMBERS *as at July 2010*

Prime Minister, Souleymane Ndene Ndiaye
Finance and Economy, Abdoulaye Diop
Interior, Becaye Diop
Foreign Affairs, Madicke Niang

EMBASSY OF THE REPUBLIC OF SENEGAL

39 Marloes Road, London W8 6LA
T 020-7938 4048 E senegalembassy@hotmail.co.uk
W www.senegalembassy.com
Ambassador Extraordinary and Plenipotentiary, HE Abdou Sourang, *apptd* 2007

BRITISH EMBASSY

PO Box 6025, 20 rue du Docteur Guillet, Dakar
T (+221) 823 7392 E britemb@orange.sn
W http://ukinsenegal.fco.gov.uk
Ambassador Extraordinary and Plenipotentiary, HE Christopher Trott, *apptd* 2005

BRITISH COUNCIL

Rue AAB-68, Amitie Zone A&B, BP 6232, Dakar
T (+221) 869 2700 W www.britishcouncil.org/africa
Director, Eric Lawrie

DEFENCE

The army has over 36 armoured personnel carriers. The navy has 9 patrol and coastal combatant vessels at 2 bases. The air force has 1 combat capable aircraft and 2 armed helicopters.
Military budget – US$217m (2008)
Military personnel – 13,620: army 11,900, navy 950, air force 770; paramilitary 5,000
Conscription duration – 24 months (selective)

ECONOMY AND TRADE

Despite steady growth since the mid-1990s and the cancellation of two-thirds of its high foreign debt in recent years, Senegal's population is poor; over half live below the poverty line, and unemployment is over 40 per cent. The country is heavily dependent on foreign aid and remittances from expatriate workers, but the development of the textiles, information technology, telecommunications services and tourist industries and infrastructure projects are government priorities.

Agriculture and fishing are the mainstays of the economy, engaging 77.5 per cent of the workforce and contributing 13.8 per cent of GDP. The main industries are food and fish processing, mining (phosphate, iron, zircon, gold), oil refining, the production of fertiliser and construction materials, ship construction and repair, and tourism. Industry accounts for 23.3 per cent of GDP and services for 62.9 per cent. The main trading partners are France, Mali, EU countries, India and China. The principal exports are fish, groundnuts (raw and processed), petroleum products, phosphates and cotton. Principal imports are food, beverages, capital goods and fuels.

GNI – US$11,900m; US$980 per capita (2008)
Annual average growth of GDP – 5.1 per cent (2009 est)
Inflation rate – 0.8 per cent (2009 est)
Unemployment – 48 per cent (2007 est)
Total external debt – US$2,763m (2009 est)
Imports – US$5,700m (2008)
Exports – US$2,400m (2008)

BALANCE OF PAYMENTS
Trade – US$3,171m deficit (2009)
Current Account – US$1,908m deficit (2008)

Trade with UK	*2008*	*2009*
Imports from UK	£475,017,586	£272,538,289
Exports to UK	£10,013,768	£9,574,339

COMMUNICATIONS

Senegal has a road network of some 13,576km, of which 3,972km are surfaced. Overseas donors are providing funds for road-building programmes in the north and the south. There are also 906km of railways and 1,000km of navigable waterways, mainly on the Senegal, Saloum and Casamance rivers. Dakar is the main port and the location of the principal airport; the seaport facilities are being modernised and a second international airport near Dakar is planned. The national carrier, Air Senegal, collapsed in April 2009; a new carrier, Senegal Airlines, planned to begin operations in partnership with the Dubai-based airline Emirates by the end of 2010.

The telephone system is good although not extensive. In 2008 there were 238,000 fixed lines in use, 5.4 million mobile phone subscribers and 1 million internet users.

EDUCATION AND HEALTH

Literacy rate – 41.9 per cent (2007 est)
Gross enrolment ratio (percentage of relevant age group) – primary 84 per cent; secondary 31 per cent; tertiary 8 per cent (2008 est)
Health expenditure (per capita) – US$54 (2007)
Hospital beds (per 1,000 people) – 0.3 (2003–8)

MEDIA

The longstanding tradition of press freedom has been undermined since 2008 by state intimidation.The state-run broadcaster operates the only free television channels and the main national and regional radio networks. There are many private radio stations, and subscription-based television is available. There are five major daily newspapers, one of which is state-owned.

SERBIA

Republika Srbija – Republic of Serbia

Area – 77,474 sq. km
Capital – Belgrade; population, 1,115,380 (2009 est)
Major cities – Kragujevac, Nis, Novi Sad
Currency – Serbian dinar of 100 paras
Population – 7,379,339 falling at 0.47 per year (2009 est); Serb (82.9 per cent), Hungarian (3.9 per cent), Bosniak (1.8 per cent), Roma (1.4 per cent), Yugoslav (1.1 per cent), Montenegrin (0.9 per cent) (est)
Religion – Christian (Serbian Orthodox 84 per cent, Roman Catholic 5 per cent, Protestant denominations 2 per cent), Muslim 5 per cent (est)
Language – Serbian (official), Hungarian, Romanian, Slovak, Ukrainian, Croatian (all official in different regions), Bosnian, Romani
Population density – 83 per sq. km (2008)
Urban population – 52 per cent (2007 est)
Median age (years) – 41 (2009 est)
National anthem – 'Boze Pravde' ['God of Justice']
National day – 15 February
Life expectancy (years) – 73.9 (2009 est)
Mortality rate – 13.86 (2009 est)
Birth rate – 9.19 (2009 est)
Infant mortality rate – 6.75 (2009 est)
Death penalty – Abolished for all crimes (since 2002)
CPI score – 3.5 (2009)
Literacy rate – 96.4 per cent (2007 est)
Gross enrolment ratio (percentage of relevant age group) – primary 101 per cent; secondary 90 per cent; tertiary 49 per cent (2008 est)
Health expenditure (per capita) – US$408 (2007)
Hospital beds (per 1,000 people) – 5.4 (2003–8)

CLIMATE AND TERRAIN

The landlocked country is mountainous in the south, while the north is dominated by the low-lying plains of the Danube and its major tributaries, the Sava, the Tisa and the Morava. Its highest point is 2,169m (Midzor). The climate is continental; average temperatures in Belgrade range from lows of −3°C in January to highs of 28°C in July.

HISTORY AND POLITICS

The medieval kingdom of Serbia emerged in the 12th century to form a large and prosperous state in the Balkans. Defeat by the Turks in 1389 led to almost 500 years of Turkish rule. After gaining increasing autonomy within the Ottoman Empire from 1815, Serbia became fully independent in 1878 and a kingdom in 1881. At the end of the First World War Serbia joined with the former

Austro-Hungarian provinces of Slovenia, Croatia and Bosnia and Hercegovina and the kingdom of Montenegro to form the Kingdom of Serbs, Croats and Slovenes, which was renamed Yugoslavia in 1929. Yugoslavia was occupied and partitioned by the Axis powers in 1941 and reformed after liberation in 1945 as a communist federal republic under the presidency of partisan leader Josip Tito. When the federation disintegrated in 1991–2, Serbia and Montenegro were left to form the rump Federal Republic of Yugoslavia (FRY), which was declared on 27 April 1992.

Serbia under Slobodan Milosevic (president 1989–96) opposed the break-up of the federation and supported various military efforts, ultimately unsuccessful, to unite ethnic Serbs in neighbouring republics into a 'Greater Serbia'. Milosevic dominated Serbian and federal politics in the 1990s, becoming president of the FRY in 1997. His corrupt and repressive regime ended when he lost the 2000 federal presidential election; he was arrested in 2001 and extradited to the UN International Criminal Tribunal for the Former Yugoslavia, where he died in 2006 during his trial.

In 2003 the Federal Republic of Yugoslavia was restructured into a union of Serbia and Montenegro, each with semi-independent status. Montenegro voted to become independent in May 2006 and the union was dissolved in June, with Serbia succeeding to the union's membership of international bodies. The Serbian province of Kosovo unilaterally declared its independence in February 2008 after nine years under UN administration.

Boris Tadic, leader of the Democratic Party (DS), was elected president in 2004; he was re-elected in early 2008. After the 2007 legislative election, a coalition government was formed by the DS, the Democratic Party of Serbia (DSS) and two smaller parties. This government resigned in March 2008, after only ten months in office, because of disagreements between the coalition partners over policy towards the EU following Kosovo's declaration of independence. In elections held in May, the For a European Serbia coalition, led by the DS, won the most seats but without an overall majority. It formed a coalition government with the Socialist Party.

POLITICAL SYSTEM

Under the 2006 constitution, the president is directly elected for a five-year term, renewable only once. The unicameral National Assembly has 250 members, directly elected for a four-year term. The prime minister is appointed by the president.

HEAD OF STATE

President, Boris Tadic, *elected* 27 June 2004, *took office* 11 July 2004, *re-elected* 3 February 2008

SELECTED GOVERNMENT MEMBERS *as at July 2010*

Prime Minister, Mirko Cvetkovic
Deputy Prime Ministers, Mladjan Dinkic *(Economy)*; Ivica Dacic *(Interior)*; Bozidar Djelic
Finance, Diana Dragutinovic
Foreign Affairs, Vuk Jeremic
Defence, Dragan Sutanovac

EMBASSY OF THE REPUBLIC OF SERBIA
28 Belgrave Square, London SW1X 8QB
T 020-7235 9049 E london@serbianembassy.org.uk
W http://serbianembassy.org.uk
Ambassador Extraordinary and Plenipotentiary, Dejan Popovic, *apptd* 2008

BRITISH EMBASSY
Resavska 46, 11000 Belgrade
T (+381) (11) 264 5055 E belgrade.man@fco.gov.uk
W http://ukinserbia.fco.gov.uk
Ambassador Extraordinary and Plenipotentiary, HE Stephen Wordsworth, LVO, *apptd* 2006

BRITISH COUNCIL
Terazije 8/1, 11000 Belgrade
T (+381) (11) 302 3800 W www.britishcouncil.org/serbia
Director, Andrew Glass

DEFENCE

The army has 212 main battle tanks, 39 armoured personnel carriers and 323 armoured infantry fighting vehicles. The air force has 83 combat aircraft.
Military budget – US$1,060m (2009)
Military personnel – 29,125: army 12,260, air force and air defence 4,262, training command 6,212, MoD 6,391
Conscription duration – 6 months

ECONOMY AND TRADE

Economic mismanagement, UN sanctions in the 1990s and damage to infrastructure and industry from NATO bombing in 1999 had reduced the economy to about 40 per cent of its 1990 size by 2000. Since 2000, governments have pursued economic reforms and international reintegration, obtained international support for economic restructuring, and rescheduled payments or received debt relief on much of its foreign debt. Progress has been intermittent, but most of the economy is now privatised. Economic growth averaged 6 per cent until 2008, but the economy has been severely affected by the global downturn, which brought credit constraints, a fall in foreign investment and manufacturing output, a sharp drop in export demand and reduced remittances from expatriate workers. The government sought IMF support in 2008 as the budget and trade deficits grew. Serbia submitted a formal application for EU membership in 2009.

Agriculture accounts for 12.7 per cent of GDP and employs 23.9 per cent of the workforce. The main agricultural products are wheat, maize, sugar beet, sunflowers, fruit, meat and milk. Industry includes production of base metals, furniture, machinery, chemicals, sugar, tyres, clothing and pharmaceuticals. Industry contributes 23.5 per cent of GDP and services 63.8 per cent. The main trading partners are Russia, EU states and former Yugoslav republics. Principal exports are iron and steel, clothing, wheat, fruit, vegetables and non-ferrous metals.
GNI – US$41,100m; US$5,590 per capita (2008)
Annual average growth of GDP – –4.6 per cent (2009 est)
Inflation rate – 6.8 per cent (2007 est)
* *Population below poverty line* – 6.5 per cent (2007 est)
Unemployment – 18.8 per cent (2007 est)
† *Total external debt* – US$26,240m (2007 est)
* Figure includes Kosovo
† Figure includes Montenegro and Kosovo

BALANCE OF PAYMENTS
Trade – US$171m deficit (2004)
Current Account – US$8,646m deficit (2008)

Trade with UK	*2008*	*2009*
Imports from UK	£113,965,726	£94,010,676
Exports to UK	£80,506,921	£65,505,305

COMMUNICATIONS

Serbia has some 37,000km of roads, around 31,000km of which are surfaced. There are also 3,400km of railways, linking Belgrade directly to Athens, Bucharest, Budapest, Istanbul, Ljubljana, Munich, Skopje, Sofia, Thessaloniki, Vienna and Zagreb. There are 587km of navigable waterways on the Danube and Sava rivers; the principal ports include Belgrade and Novi Sad on the Danube. The main international airport is at Belgrade.

Modernisation of the telephone system is progressing, although rural services are not as good as those in urban areas. There were 3.1 million fixed lines in use, 9.6 million mobile phone subscribers and 2.9 million internet users in 2008.

MEDIA

The ousting of Milosevic allowed the media much greater freedom and outlets subsequently proliferated. A media regulatory system is in operation and issues licences to the hundreds of private-sector radio and television broadcasters. The state-funded national broadcaster RTS aims to develop into a public service, and state-funded local and regional media outlets are to be privatised. Newspapers include the dailies *Danas, Blik,* and *Politika,* and the weeklies *Vreme* and *NIN.*

SEYCHELLES

République des Seychelles/Repiblik Sesel – Republic of Seychelles

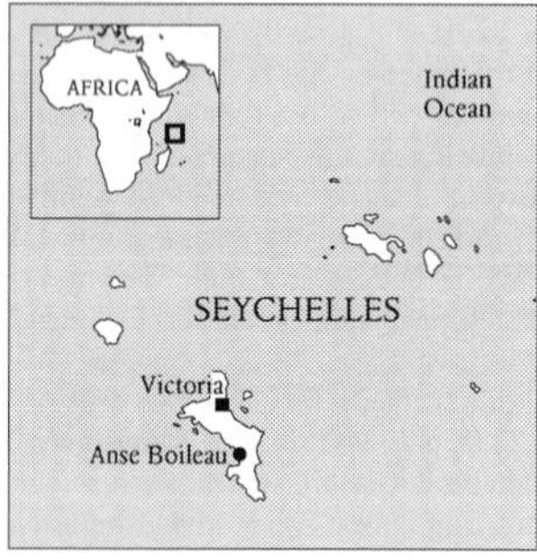

Area – 455 sq. km
Capital – Victoria, on Mahé; population, 26,001 (2009 est)
Currency – Seychelles rupee of 100 cents
Population – 87,476 rising at 1 per cent a year (2009 est)
Religion – Christian (Roman Catholic 82 per cent, Anglican 6 per cent) (est)
Language – English, French, Creole (all official)
Population density – 189 per sq. km (2008)
Urban population – 54 per cent (2007 est)
Median age (years) – 31.4 (2009 est)
National anthem – 'Koste Seselwa' ['Seychellois Unite']
National day – 18 June (Constitution Day)
Life expectancy (years) – 73.02 (2009 est)
Mortality rate – 6.93 (2009 est)
Birth rate – 15.87 (2009 est)
Infant mortality rate – 12.3 (2009 est)
Death penalty – Abolished for all crimes (since 1993)
CPI score – 4.8 (2009)
Literacy rate – 91.8 per cent (2007 est)

CLIMATE AND TERRAIN

Seychelles consists of 115 islands spread over 643,737 sq. km of the south-west Indian Ocean, north of Madagascar. There is a relatively compact granitic group of 32 islands, with high hills and mountains, of which Mahé is the largest and most populated (about 90 per cent of the population lives on Mahé), and an outlying coralline group, for the most part only slightly above sea-level. Elevation extremes range from 905m (Morne Seychellois) at the highest point to 0m (Indian Ocean) at the lowest. The climate is tropical, with average temperatures between 24°C and 30°C throughout the year, and a wet season from November to March.

HISTORY AND POLITICS

The uninhabited islands were proclaimed French territory in 1756, but settlement of the Mahé group began only in 1770. The group was a dependency of Mauritius, and was ceded to Britain with Mauritius in 1814. In 1903 these islands, together with the coralline group, were formed into a colony separate from Mauritius. On 29 June 1976, the islands became an independent republic.

Following a coup d'état in 1977, when France-Albert René became president, Seychelles became a one-party state ruled by the Seychelles People's Progressive Front (SPPF) in 1979. Opposition parties were permitted from 1991 and in 1993 President René reintroduced a multiparty constitution. Power has remained with the SPPF under the pluralist system, although opposition parties are beginning to achieve a greater share of the vote.

President René stepped down in mid-term in 2004 and the rest of his term was served by the vice-president, James Michel, who was elected president in 2006. In the 2007 legislative election, the SPPF retained its overall majority.

POLITICAL SYSTEM

Under the 1993 constitution, the executive president is directly elected for a five-year term, with a maximum of three consecutive terms. The unicameral National Assembly has up to 34 members: 23 directly elected by constituencies and up to 11 allocated by proportional representation; members serve a five-year term. The council of ministers is appointed by the president.

HEAD OF STATE

President, Defence, James Michel, *assumed office* 14 April 2004
Vice-President, Finance, Danny Faure

SELECTED GOVERNMENT MEMBERS *as at July 2010*

Foreign Affairs, Jean-Paul Adam
Home Affairs, Joel Morgan

SEYCHELLES HIGH COMMISSION

4th Floor, 111 Baker Street, London W1U 6RR
T 020-7935 7770 E consulate@seychelles.gov.net
High Commissioner, HE Patrick Pillay, *apptd* 2010

BRITISH HIGH COMMISSION

PO Box 161, Oliaji Trade Centre, Victoria, Mahé
T (+248) 283 666 E bhcvictoria@fco.gov.uk
W http://ukinseychelles.fco.gov.uk
High Commissioner, HE Matthew Forbes, OBE, *apptd* 2009

DEFENCE

The coast guard has 9 patrol and coastal combatant vessels at a base at Port Victoria.
Military budget – US$8.5m (2008 est)
Military personnel – 200: army 200; paramilitary 450

ECONOMY AND TRADE

Seychelles prospered after independence owing to the development of tuna fishing and tourism, which employs about 30 per cent of the workforce. However, the economy became unstable in 2008 owing to the large external debt, high deficits, rises in food and oil prices and a reduction in foreign exchange earnings after tourism declined in 2008 due to the global economic downturn. The government introduced an IMF reform programme in late 2008 and has sought debt cancellation.

Agriculture, small-scale manufacturing and offshore financial services are being developed to diversify the economy. Apart from fishing and tourism, the main industries involve processing fish, coconuts and vanilla, producing coir rope, furniture and beverages, boat-building and printing. The main trading partners are EU countries, Saudi Arabia, Mauritius and Singapore. The principal exports are canned tuna, frozen fish, cinnamon bark, copra and re-exports of petroleum products. The principal imports are machinery and equipment, foodstuffs, petroleum products and chemicals.
GNI – US$889m; US$10,220 per capita (2008)
Annual average growth of GDP – –8.7 per cent (2009 est)
Inflation rate – 34 per cent (2009 est)
Unemployment rate – 2 per cent (2006 est)
Total external debt – US$1,250m (2009 est)
Imports – US$1,000m (2008)
Exports – US$400m (2008)

BALANCE OF PAYMENTS
Trade – US$516m deficit (2009)
Current Account – US$412m deficit (2008)

Trade with UK	*2008*	*2009*
Imports from UK	£16,405,012	£18,854,915
Exports to UK	£44,517,596	£64,511,611

COMMUNICATIONS

There are around 458km of roads, most of which are surfaced. The main port is Victoria, and ferries run regularly between Mahé, Praslin and La Digue. Some 14 airports, eight with surfaced runways, serve the islands; the principal airport is at Mahé.

The telephone system serves all the islands. In 2008 there were 23,200 fixed lines in use, 85,300 mobile phone subscribers and 32,000 internet users.

MEDIA

Although the media has operated more freely since one-party rule was abolished in 1993, the only terrestrial radio and television stations and the sole daily newspaper are controlled by the government. There is no privately owned broadcasting sector because of prohibitive broadcasting licence fees, and libel laws have been used against private and pro-opposition newspapers. Cable and satellite television and international radio stations are available.

SIERRA LEONE

Republic of Sierra Leone

Area – 71,740 sq. km
Capital – Freetown; population, 875,432 (2009 est)
Major towns – Bo, Kenema
Currency – Leone (Le) of 100 cents
Population – 6,440,053 rising at 2.28 per cent a year (2009 est); 20 ethnic groups, of which the largest are the Temne (30 per cent), Mende (30 per cent), Krio (Creole) (10 per cent) (est)
Religion – Muslim 60 per cent, Christian 20 per cent, indigenous and other beliefs 5 per cent (predominantly animist) (est)
Language – English (official), Krio (Creole), Mende, Temne
Population density – 78 per sq. km (2008)
Urban population – 37 per cent (2007 est)
Median age (years) – 17.5 (2009 est)
National anthem – 'High We Exalt Thee, Realm of the Free'
National day – 27 April (Independence Day)
Life expectancy (years) – 41.24 (2009 est)
Mortality rate – 21.91 (2009 est)
Birth rate – 44.73 (2009 est)
Infant mortality rate – 154.43 (2009 est)
HIV/AIDS adult prevalence – 1.5 per cent (2007 est)
Death penalty – Retained
CPI score – 2.2 (2009)

CLIMATE AND TERRAIN

The land rises from mangrove swamps along the coast, to low-lying wooded country, and then to a mountainous plateau in the east. Elevation extremes range from 1,948m (Loma Mansa) at the highest point to 0m (Atlantic Ocean) at the lowest. The climate is tropical, with a rainy season from May to November; rainfall peaks in July and August, and is particularly heavy on the coast.

HISTORY AND POLITICS

Coastal trading posts were established by the Portuguese in the 15th century and the British in the 17th century. In 1787 British philanthropists and abolitionists established a settlement for repatriated former slaves from Britain and its colonies on the Freetown peninsula. In 1808 the settlement was declared a crown colony and became the main base in west Africa for enforcing the 1807 Act outlawing the slave trade. In 1896 a protectorate was declared over the hinterland. The Freetown colony and the protectorate were united in 1951, and on 27 April 1961 Sierra Leone became independent.

The country became a republic in 1971 and a

one-party state in 1978. Transition to a multiparty democracy began in 1991 but was aborted by a military coup in 1992. Civilian rule was restored with the 1996 elections. Another coup in May 1997 was short-lived, and the government was reinstated in March 1998 with the assistance of ECOWAS troops.

The transition to multiparty and civilian rule was complicated by the civil war with the Revolutionary United Front (RUF), which began in 1991. Fighting continued until 2001, when a lasting ceasefire was agreed, and the war was declared over in 2002. An estimated 50,000 people were killed, 30,000 mutilated and a third of the population displaced between 1991 and 2002. A truth and reconciliation commission and a UN-supported war crimes tribunal were set up in 2002.

The 2007 presidential election was won by Ernest Bai Koroma, the All People's Congress (APC) candidate, in the second round. The APC won a majority of seats in the simultaneous legislative election, defeating the Sierra Leone People's Party, which had been in power since 2002.

POLITICAL SYSTEM

Under the 1991 constitution, the executive president is directly elected for a five-year term, renewable only once. The unicameral parliament has 124 members: 112 directly elected for a five-year term and 12 indirectly elected to represent the 12 provincial districts. The president appoints and chairs the cabinet.

HEAD OF STATE

President, Ernest Bai Koroma, *elected* 18 September 2007
Vice-President, Samuel Sam-Sumana

SELECTED GOVERNMENT MEMBERS *as at July 2010*

Finance, Samura Kamara
Foreign Affairs, Zainab Bangura
Internal Affairs, Dauda Kamara
Defence, Maj. (retd) Paolo Conteh

SIERRA LEONE HIGH COMMISSION

41 Eagle Street, London WC1R 4TL
T 020-7404 0140 E info@slhc-uk.org.uk
W www.slhc-uk.org.uk
High Commissioner, HE Edward Turay, *apptd* 2010

BRITISH HIGH COMMISSION

6 Spur Road, Freetown
T (+232) (22) 232 961
E freetown.general.enquiries@fco.gov.uk
W http://ukinsierraleone.fco.gov.uk
High Commissioner, HE Ian Hughes, *apptd* 2009

BRITISH COUNCIL

PO Box 124, Tower Hill, Freetown
T (+232) (22) 222 223 W www.britishcouncil.org/africa
Director, June Rollinson, OBE

DEFENCE

The process of disarming the country's various factions after the civil war was completed in 2004. The army took over full responsibility for internal security in December 2005 when the UN peacekeeping forces left. The navy has 4 patrol and coastal combatant vessels at a base in Freetown.
Military budget – US$11m (2009)
Military personnel – 10,500: Joint Staff 10,500

ECONOMY AND TRADE

The country has been devastated by a decade of civil war, and unemployment has increased with the demobilisation of former combatants. Economic activity has grown since the end of the war but the country remains extremely poor, dependent on foreign aid and expatriates' remittances. It benefited from having around 90 per cent of its foreign debt written off in 2006.

There are significant mineral deposits – mainly diamonds, bauxite, rutile, iron and gold – and agricultural and fishery resources, although the lack of infrastructure hampers development. Diamonds account for about half of export earnings, but nearly 50 per cent of GDP is generated by agriculture, much of which is at subsistence level. Industry consists mainly of mining (diamonds, rutile, bauxite), processing agricultural products, light manufacturing for the domestic market, oil refining and ship repair.

The main export market is Belgium (27 per cent) and the USA; the chief import suppliers are South Africa, China, the USA, EU countries and Côte d'Ivoire. Principal exports are diamonds, rutile, cocoa, coffee and fish. The main imports are foodstuffs, machinery and equipment, fuels and lubricants, and chemicals.
GNI – US$1,800m; US$320 per capita (2008)
Annual average growth of GDP – 2 per cent (2009 est)
Inflation rate – 11.7 per cent (2007 est)
Population below poverty line – 70.2 per cent (2004)
Total external debt – US$1,610m (2003 est)
Imports – US$600m (2008)
Exports – US$200m (2008)

BALANCE OF PAYMENTS

Trade – US$370m deficit (2009)
Current Account – US$228m deficit (2008)

Trade with UK	*2008*	*2009*
Imports from UK	£26,921,350	£20,731,223
Exports to UK	£4,047,663	£11,216,500

COMMUNICATIONS

The railway system was phased out in 1974, but an extensive road network has been developed since; there are now 11,300km of roads in the country, although only 904km are surfaced. A bridge over the Mano river links Sierra Leone with Liberia. There is an international airport at Freetown and eight airfields around the country. Freetown, which has one of the world's largest natural harbours, is the main port and there are smaller ports at Pepel, Bonthe and Niti.

The fixed-line telephone system is poor and mobile phone distribution is growing rapidly. There were about 31,500 fixed lines in use, 1 million mobile phone subscriptions and 13,900 internet users in 2008.

EDUCATION AND HEALTH

School attendance has improved considerably since the civil war ended. The public University of Sierra Leone incorporates several campuses in Freetown, and Njala University was constituted in Bo in 2005; there are a number of other technical and teacher-training institutes throughout the country.
Literacy rate – 38.1 per cent (2007 est)
Gross enrolment ratio (percentage of relevant age group) – primary 158 per cent; secondary 35 per cent (2008 est)
Health expenditure (per capita) – US$14 (2007 est)
Hospital beds (per 1,000 people) – 0.4 (2003–8)

MEDIA

Media freedom is limited by the government's use of libel laws to restrict coverage of politically sensitive issues. Broadcasters also have to contend with unreliable electricity supplies and a lack of advertising revenue. The national broadcaster operates televison and radio networks, alongside one privately owned television station and dozens of radio stations, including a UN network. Dozens of privately run newspapers are published in Freetown, despite low literacy levels.

SINGAPORE

Xinjiapo Gongheguo/Republik Singapura/Cinkappur Kutiyaracu – Republic of Singapore

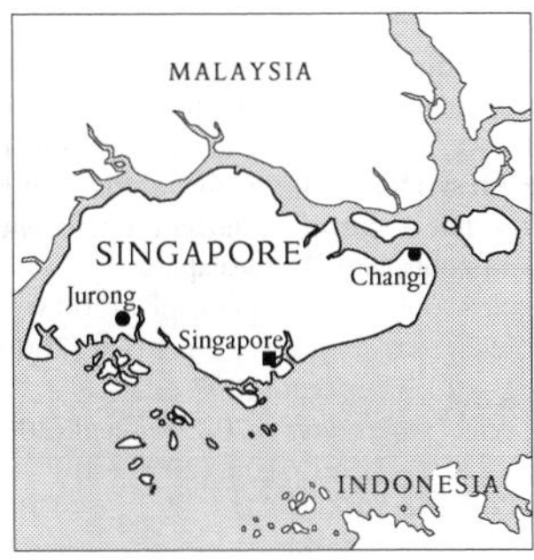

Area – 705 sq. km
Capital – Singapore
Currency – Singapore dollar (S$) of 100 cents
Population – 4,657,542 rising at 1 per cent a year (2009 est); Chinese (76.8 per cent), Malay (13.9 per cent), Indian (7.9 per cent)
Religion – Buddhist 43 per cent, Muslim 15 per cent (predominantly Sunni), Christian 15 per cent, Hindu 4 per cent (est)
Language – Mandarin, English, Malay, Tamil (all official), Hokkien, Cantonese, Teochew
Population density – 6,943 per sq. km (2008)
Urban population – 100 per cent (2007 est)
Median age (years) – 39 (2009 est)
National anthem – 'Majulah Singapura' ['Onward, Singapore']
National day – 9 August
Life expectancy (years) – 81.98 (2009 est)
Mortality rate – 4.66 (2009 est)
Birth rate – 8.82 (2009 est)
Infant mortality rate – 2.31 (2009 est)
Death penalty – Retained
CPI score – 9.2 (2009)
Literacy rate – 94.4 per cent (2007 est)
Gross enrolment ratio (percentage of relevant age group) – primary 78 per cent; secondary 63 per cent (2006 est)
Health expenditure (per capita) – US$1,148 (2007)
Hospital beds (per 1,000 people) – 3.2 (2003–8)

CLIMATE AND TERRAIN

Singapore consists of the island of Singapore and 63 islets situated off the southern extremity of the Malay peninsula, from which it is separated by the Straits of Johor. The land rises from the shores to a low, undulating central plateau. Elevation extremes range from 166m (Bukit Timah) at the highest point to 0m (Singapore Strait) at the lowest. The state is just north of the Equator and the climate is tropical, subject to monsoons in June to September and December to March. There is frequent rain and high humidity.

HISTORY AND POLITICS

Singapore, a trading site since the 13th century, was established as a British trading post by Sir Stamford Raffles in 1819 and was ceded to Britain in perpetuity in 1824. In 1826 it was incorporated with Penang and Malacca to form the Straits Settlements and they became a crown colony in 1867. Singapore became the commercial and financial hub of south-east Asia in the 19th century, and the principal British military base in the Far East in the 1920s. In 1942, during the Second World War, it fell to Japanese forces. Liberated in 1945, it became a separate colony in 1946, and internal self-government was introduced in 1959. It became part of the Federation of Malaysia in 1963, before withdrawing to become an independent sovereign state on 9 August 1965.

Although Singapore is a multiparty state, the People's Action Party (PAP) has dominated politics since 1959; opposition candidates were elected to parliament for the first time in 1981. The PAP leader Lee Kuan Yew was prime minister from 1959 until he retired in 1990; he remains a cabinet minister.

Sellapan Rama Nathan was elected president in 1999 and was declared re-elected in August 2005, although no election was held on either occasion as he was the sole eligible candidate. In the 2006 general election, the PAP won 82 seats (37 of them unopposed) and opposition parties two. Lee Hsien Loong, the son of Lee Kuan Yew, continued in office as prime minister, a post he has held since 2004. The next general election is due in May 2011.

POLITICAL SYSTEM

The 1959 constitution was amended in 1965 to end the affiliation with Malaysia and make Singapore a republic, and in 1991 to make the presidency directly elected. The president is directly elected for a six-year term, which is renewable. The president appoints the prime minister and, on his advice, the members of the cabinet. There is a unicameral parliament with 84 directly elected members and up to three extra members from opposition parties (NCMPs), depending on their share of the vote; they serve a five-year term. Up to nine members can also be nominated by the government for a two-year term (NMPs).

HEAD OF STATE

President, Sellapan Rama Nathan, *took office* 1 September 1999, *re-elected* 17 August 2005

SELECTED GOVERNMENT MEMBERS *as at July 2010*

Prime Minister, Lee Hsien Loong
Deputy Prime Ministers, Rear-Adm. Teo Chee Hean *(Defence)*; Wong Kan Seng *(Home Affairs)*
Foreign Affairs, George Yong Boon Yeo
Finance, Tharman Shanmugaratnam

HIGH COMMISSION FOR THE REPUBLIC OF SINGAPORE

9 Wilton Crescent, London SW1X 8SP
T 020-7235 8315 **E** singhc_lon@sgmfa.gov.sg
W www.mfa.gov.sg/london
High Commissioner, HE Michael Eng Cheng Teo, *apptd* 2002

BRITISH HIGH COMMISSION
100 Tanglin Road, Singapore 247919
T (+65) 6424 4200 E commercial.singapore@fco.gov.uk
W http://ukinsingapore.fco.gov.uk
High Commissioner, HE Paul Madden, *apptd* 2007

BRITISH COUNCIL
30 Napier Road, Singapore 258509
T (+65) 6473 1111 W www.britishcouncil.org/sg
Director, Mark Howard

DEFENCE

The army has 196 main battle tanks, over 1,280 armoured personnel carriers and over 272 armoured infantry fighting vehicles. The navy has 4 submarines, 6 frigates, 6 corvettes and 23 patrol and coastal combatant vessels at 2 bases. The air force has 104 combat aircraft and 12 armed helicopters.

Military budget – US$8,230m (2008)
Military personnel – 72,500: army 50,000, navy 9,000, air force 13,500; paramilitary 93,800
Conscription duration – 24 months

ECONOMY AND TRADE

Historically based on trade in raw materials from surrounding countries and on entrepot trade in finished products, the economy industrialised rapidly after independence and diversified, becoming a regional financial and technology centre and a tourist destination. Economic growth has rarely flagged since 1965, although the global economic downturn pushed the economy into recession in 2008; recovery began in 2010.

Agriculture is limited and contributes little to GDP. Industries include manufacturing (especially consumer electronics, information technology products, biomedical sciences, pharmaceuticals and chemicals), engineering, oil refining, rubber processing, food processing and ship repair; industry contributes 27.6 per cent of GDP. The service sector (financial and business services, entrepot trade, tourism) accounts for 72.4 per cent of GDP and employs 76 per cent of the workforce.

The main trading partners are Malaysia, China, the USA, Indonesia, Japan and Hong Kong. Principal exports are machinery and equipment (especially electronic), consumer goods, pharmaceuticals and other chemicals and mineral fuels. The main imports are machinery and equipment, mineral fuels, chemicals, food and consumer goods.

GNI – US$168,200m; US$34,760 per capita (2008)
Annual average growth of GDP – −2.6 per cent (2009 est)
Inflation rate – 0.5 per cent (2009 est)
Unemployment – 3.4 per cent (2009 est)
Total external debt – US$19,200m (2009 est)
Imports – US$319,800m (2008)
Exports – US$338,200m (2008)

BALANCE OF PAYMENTS
Trade – US$24,047m surplus (2009)
Current Account – US$33,838m surplus (2008)

Trade with UK	*2008*	*2009*
Imports from UK	£2,727,466,434	£2,846,943,615
Exports to UK	£3,847,362,065	£2,422,103,565

COMMUNICATIONS

There are 3,325km of roads, all surfaced, and 30km of railway and an extensive light rail system on the island. The road system is connected to the Malaysian network via a 1.1km causeway and a road bridge across the Straits of Johor; the causeway also carries a rail link to Malaysia. Singapore is one of the largest and busiest seaports in the world, although there is a high risk of piracy and armed robbery in the South China Sea. It has a large merchant fleet of 1,292 ships of over 1,000 tonnes, of which 331 are registered in other countries, while 774 foreign-owned ships are registered in Singapore. There is one international airport, at Changi; Singapore Airlines is the national carrier.

The modern telecommunications system provided services to 1.9 million fixed-line users, 6.4 million mobile phone subscribers and 3.4 million internet users in 2008.

MEDIA

Singapore's media is tightly regulated by the government. Private satellite dishes are illegal and internet access is controlled, although the government sees the country as a digital media pioneer and plans to create thousands of new jobs in this sector. Broadcasting is dominated by MediaCorp, owned by a state investment agency. Singapore Press Holdings, which has close links to the ruling party, has a virtual monopoly on the newspaper industry, and publishes 17 newspapers.

SLOVAKIA

Slovenska Republika – Slovak Republic

Area – 49,035 sq. km
Capital – Bratislava; population, 428,003 (2009 est)
Major city – Kosice
Currency – Euro (€) of 100 cents
Population – 5,463,046 rising at 0.14 per cent a year (2009 est); Slovak (85.8 per cent), Hungarian (9.7 per cent), Roma (1.7 per cent), Ruthenian/Ukrainian (1 per cent)
Religion – Christian (Roman Catholic 69 per cent, Lutheran 7 per cent) (est)
Language – Slovak (official), Hungarian, Romani, Ukrainian
Population density – 112 per sq. km (2008)
Urban population – 56 per cent (2007 est)
Median age (years) – 36.9 (2009 est)
National anthem – 'Nad Tatrou sa blyska' ['Lightning Over the Tatras']
National day – 1 September (Constitution Day)
Life expectancy (years) – 75.4 (2009 est)
Mortality rate – 9.53 (2009 est)
Birth rate – 10.6 (2009 est)
Infant mortality rate – 6.84 (2009 est)
Death penalty – Abolished for all crimes (since 1990)

CPI score – 4.5 (2009)
Gross enrolment ratio (percentage of relevant age group) – primary 102 per cent; secondary 93 per cent; tertiary 50 per cent (2008 est)
Health expenditure (per capita) – US$1,077 (2007)
Hospital beds (per 1,000 people) – 6.8 (2003–8)

CLIMATE AND TERRAIN

Slovakia is landlocked and mountainous, lying in the western Carpathian range which includes the Tatra and Beskid mountains to the north. The mountains fall to plains in the south-east and south-west; the latter is the plain of the river Danube and its tributary the Vah, which rises in the Tatras. Elevation extremes range from 2,655m (Gerlachovsky stit) at the highest point to 94m (Bodrog river) at the lowest. The climate is temperate, with warm humid summers and cold dry winters. Average temperatures in Bratislava range from −3°C in January to 26°C in July and August.

HISTORY AND POLITICS

The area was part of the kingdom of Greater Moravia in the ninth century, became part of the Magyar kingdom of Hungary in the tenth century and, with Hungary, came under Austrian Habsburg rule from the 16th century. After the dissolution of the Austro-Hungarian Empire in 1918, Slovakia became part of Czechoslovakia.

Following the German annexation of Czechoslovakia in 1938–9, Slovakia became a nominally independent fascist state but was exploited as part of the German war effort. After an abortive uprising in 1944, Slovakia was liberated by Soviet forces in 1945 and returned to Czechoslovakia, where a communist regime assumed power in 1948. Following the collapse of communist rule in 1989, Slovak separatism gained ground and the Czech and Slovak republics negotiated the dissolution of the federation into two sovereign states in 1992. Dissolution took effect on 1 January 1993.

The Movement for a Democratic Slovakia (HZDS), led by the authoritarian Vladimir Meciar, dominated the coalition governments that held office in the 1990s, pursuing populist nationalist policies. It was ousted at the 1998 election by an alliance of liberals, centrists, left-wingers and ethnic Hungarians, which formed a coalition government under Mikulas Dzurinda of the Slovak Democratic and Christian Union (SDKU). This government, which was re-elected in 2002, introduced the constitutional and economic reforms necessary to meet the requirements for EU membership. Slovakia joined NATO and the EU in 2004, and the eurozone in 2009.

The 2004 presidential election was won by Ivan Gasparovic; he was re-elected in 2009. After the 2006 legislative election, the centre-left Direction–Social Democracy party (Smer-SD) became the largest party in the legislature, but without a majority, and formed a three-party coalition government. Smer-SD remained the largest party after the legislative election in June 2010, but four centre-right parties won a majority of seats and formed a coalition government headed by Iveta Radicova of the SDKU. (*See also* Events of the Year.)

POLITICAL SYSTEM

The 1993 constitution has been amended several times, most recently in 1999 to allow direct elections to the presidency. The president is directly elected for a five-year term, renewable only once. The unicameral National Council of the Slovak Republic has 150 members, who are directly elected for a four-year term by proportional representation. The prime minister, who is appointed by the president, nominates the cabinet.

HEAD OF STATE

President, Ivan Gasparovic, *elected* 17 April 2004, *sworn in* 15 June 2004, *re-elected* 2009

SELECTED GOVERNMENT MEMBERS *as at July 2010*

Prime Minister, Iveta Radicova
Deputy Prime Ministers, Ivan Miklos *(Finance);* Rudolf Chmel; Jan Figel
Defence, Lubomir Galko
Foreign Affairs, Mikulas Dzurinda
Interior, Daniel Lipsic

EMBASSY OF THE SLOVAK REPUBLIC

25 Kensington Palace Gardens, London W8 4QY
T 020-7313 6470 E emb.london@mzv.sk
W www.slovakembassy.co.uk
Ambassador Extraordinary and Plenipotentiary, Juraj Zervan, *apptd* 2007

BRITISH EMBASSY

Panska 16, Bratislava 811 01
T (+421) (2) 5998 2000 E bebra@internet.sk
W http://ukinslovakia.fco.gov.uk
Ambassador Extraordinary and Plenipotentiary, HE Michael Roberts, *apptd* 2007

BRITISH COUNCIL

PO Box 68, Panska 17, 814 99 Bratislava
T (+421) (2) 5443 1074 W www.britishcouncil.org/slovakia
Director, Andrew Spells

DEFENCE

The army has 245 main battle tanks, 132 armoured personnel carriers and 383 armoured infantry fighting vehicles. The air force has 22 combat aircraft and 16 armed helicopters.

Military expenditure – US$1,470m (2008)
Military personnel – 16,531: army 7,322, air force 4,190, central staff 1,462, support and training 3,557
Conscription duration – 6 months

ECONOMY AND TRADE

Slovakia has nearly completed the transition from a centrally planned to a free-market economy, following structural reforms and privatisation begun after 1998. As a result, foreign investment has risen, especially in the vehicle and electronics industries, and GDP grew steadily in 2000–8. The economy contracted sharply in 2009 because of the global economic downturn.

Natural resources include brown coal and lignite, natural gas, oil, iron ore, copper and manganese. Major industries include production of metal and metal products, food and beverages, fuel and energy (electricity, gas, coke, oil and nuclear), chemicals and synthetic fibres, machinery, paper and printing, ceramics, transport vehicles, textiles and electrical and optical equipment. Industry accounts for 34.4 per cent of GDP, services 63 per cent and agriculture 2.6 per cent.

The main trading partners are other EU countries (especially Germany and the Czech Republic) and Russia. Principal exports are machinery and electrical equipment (36 per cent), vehicles (21 per cent), base metals, chemicals, minerals and plastics. The main imports are machinery and transport equipment, intermediate manufactured goods and fuels.

GNI – US$89,700m; US$16,590 per capita (2008)
Annual average growth of GDP – –4.9 per cent (2009 est)
Inflation rate – 1.6 per cent (2009 est)
Unemployment – 11.8 per cent (2009 est)
Total external debt – US$52,530m (2008 est)
Imports – US$74,000m (2007)
Exports – US$71,100m (2008)

BALANCE OF PAYMENTS
Trade – US$2,399m surplus (2009)
Current Account – US$6,220m deficit (2008)

Trade with UK	*2008*	*2009*
Imports from UK	£445,875,465	£365,615,310
Exports to UK	£1,602,150,202	£1,537,626,411

COMMUNICATIONS

Slovakia has a total of 43,800km of roads, including 316km of motorways. There are 3,600km of railways, and 172km of navigable waterways on the river Danube. The main Danube ports are Bratislava and Komarno, and the principal airport is at Bratislava.

The modern telecommunications system has expanded rapidly in recent years, especially for mobile phones. In 2008 there were 1.1 million fixed telephone lines in use, 5.5 million mobile phone subscribers and 3.6 million internet users.

MEDIA

The public broadcasters, Slovak TV and Slovak Radio, operate national networks in competition with private companies; Slovak TV has lost much of its audience share to privately owned TV Markiza since 1990, and there are now over 20 private radio stations. Cable and satellite television channels are also popular. The major daily newspapers are all privately owned. The press operates freely, although there is concern about the use of defamation laws against journalists.

SLOVENIA

Republika Slovenija – Republic of Slovenia

Area – 20,273 sq. km
Capital – Ljubljana; population, 260,092 (2009 est)
Major city – Maribor
Currency – Euro (€) of 100 cents
Population – 2,005,692 falling at 0.11 per cent a year (2009 est); Slovene (83.1 per cent), Serb (2 per cent), Croat (1.8 per cent), Bosniak (1.1 per cent)
Religion – Christian (Roman Catholic 58 per cent, Orthodox 2 per cent), Muslim 2 per cent (est)
Language – Slovene (official), Serbo-Croat; Hungarian and Italian are also official in designated municipalities
Population density – 100 per sq. km (2008)
Urban population – 49 per cent (2007 est)
Median age (years) – 41.7 (2009 est)
National anthem – 'Zdravljica' ['A Toast']
National day – 25 June (Statehood Day)
Life expectancy (years) – 76.92 (2009 est)
Mortality rate – 10.62 (2009 est)
Birth rate – 8.97 (2009 est)
Infant mortality rate – 4.25 (2009 est)
Death penalty – Abolished for all crimes (since 1989)
CPI score – 6.6 (2009)

CLIMATE AND TERRAIN

The Alps cover 42 per cent of the country, towards the north, and the south lies on the high Karst plateau. The only low-lying areas are the Pannonian plain in the east and north-east, and the short (47km) narrow coastal belt on the Adriatic Sea. Elevation extremes range from 2,864m (Triglav) at the highest point to 0m (Adriatic Sea) at the lowest. The climate is continental in most of the country but Mediterranean on the coast. Average temperatures in Ljubljana range from lows of −7°C in January to highs of 27°C in July.

HISTORY AND POLITICS

Settled by Slovenes in the sixth century, the area was later ruled by Slavs, Franks and Hungarians before coming under the control of the Austrian Habsburg dynasty in the 14th century. Following the collapse of the Austro-Hungarian Empire in 1918, Slovenia became part of the Kingdom of the Serbs, Croats and Slovenes (later Yugoslavia). German forces invaded Yugoslavia in 1941 and Slovenia was divided between Germany, Italy and Hungary. In 1945 it was reformed as a constituent part of the communist federal republic of Yugoslavia. After a dispute with Italy and nine years of international administration, the Adriatic coast and hinterland were returned to Slovenia in 1954, while Italy retained Trieste.

The first multiparty elections, held in April 1990, were won by the pro-independence 'Demos' coalition. In a referendum in December 1990, 88 per cent of the electorate voted for independence, which was declared on 25 June 1991. A ten-day war with the Yugoslav National Army followed before the army withdrew under the terms of an EU-brokered ceasefire. Slovenia became a member of NATO and the EU in 2004, and joined the eurozone in 2007.

The Liberal Democracy of Slovenia party (LDS) was the major party in every government from 1991 to 2004. The 2007 presidential election was won by an independent candidate, Danilo Turk. Following the 2008 legislative election, the Social Democrats (SD) formed a coalition government with three other parties (including the LDS) and several independents.

POLITICAL SYSTEM
Under the 1991 constitution, the president is directly elected for a five-year term. The unicameral National Assembly has 90 members directly elected for a four-year term. The National Council, which has 40 members indirectly elected for a five-year term, has an advisory role. The prime minister, who is nominated by the president and elected by the legislature, appoints the cabinet.

HEAD OF STATE
President, Danilo Turk, *elected* 11 November 2007; *sworn in* 22 December 2007

SELECTED GOVERNMENT MEMBERS *as at July 2010*
Prime Minister, Borut Pahor
Defence, Ljubica Jelusic
Finance, Franc Krizanic
Foreign Affairs, Samuel Zbogar
Internal Affairs, Katarina Kresal

EMBASSY OF THE REPUBLIC OF SLOVENIA
10 Little College Street, London SW1P 3SH
T 020-7222 5700 E vlo@gov.si W http://london.embassy.si
Ambassador Extraordinary and Plenipotentiary, HE Iztok Jarc, *apptd* 2009

BRITISH EMBASSY
4th Floor, Trg Republike 3, 1000 Ljubljana
T (+386) (1) 200 3910 E info@british-embassy.si
W http://ukinslovenia.fco.gov.uk
Ambassador Extraordinary and Plenipotentiary, HE Andrew Page, *apptd* 2009

BRITISH COUNCIL
Tivoli Center, Tivolska 30, 1000 Ljubljana
T (+386) (1) 300 2030 W www.britishcouncil.org/slovenia
Director, Robert Monro

DEFENCE

The army has 70 main battle tanks and 124 armoured personnel carriers. The army's Maritime Element has 1 patrol and coastal combatant vessel.
Military expenditure – US$834m (2008)
Military personnel – army 7,200; paramilitary 4,500

ECONOMY AND TRADE

Always the most prosperous republic of the former Yugoslavia, Slovenia's transition to a market economy was smoothed by good infrastructure and a well-educated workforce, and it has successfully re-orientated its exports towards Western markets. Much of the economy remains in state ownership and taxes are high, deterring foreign investment and inhibiting its international competitiveness. The economy contracted sharply in 2009 as exports and industrial production fell owing to the global downturn.

Agriculture contributes 2.5 per cent of GDP, industry 30.9 per cent and the service sector 66.6 per cent. The main agricultural products are potatoes, hops, wheat, sugar beet, maize, grapes and livestock. Industries include mining and mineral processing (iron ore, aluminium, lead, zinc), electronics (including for military purposes), vehicles, electric power equipment, wood products, textiles, chemicals and machine tools.

The main trading partners are other EU countries (particularly Germany and Italy), Croatia and Russia. Principal exports are manufactured goods, machinery and transport equipment, chemicals and food. These items, along with fuels and lubricants, are also the main imports.
GNI – US$49,000m; US$24,230 per capita (2008)
Annual average growth of GDP – –6.2 per cent (2009 est)
Inflation rate – 0.8 per cent (2009 est)
Population below the poverty line – 12.9 per cent (2004 est)
Unemployment – 9.4 per cent (2009 est)
Total external debt – US$53,200m (2009 est)
Imports – US$33,900m (2008)
Exports – US$29,200m (2008)

BALANCE OF PAYMENTS
Trade – US$1,156m deficit (2009)
Current Account – US$3,365m deficit (2008)

Trade with UK	*2008*	*2009*
Imports from UK	£217,754,528	£171,575,270
Exports to UK	£309,133,877	£246,102,212

COMMUNICATIONS

There are 38,700km of roads and 1,228km of railways, of which 503km are electrified. Major international road and rail routes cross the country. There are 16 airports and airfields, with international airports at Ljubljana, Maribor and Portoroz. Koper is the main port, receiving shipments from landlocked central European countries.

In 2008 there were 1 million fixed telephone lines in use, 2.1 million mobile phone subscribers and 1.1 million internet users.

EDUCATION AND HEALTH

Education is free of charge and compulsory between the ages of six and 15.
Literacy rate – 99.7 per cent (2007 est)
Gross enrolment ratio (percentage of relevant age group) – primary 103 per cent; secondary 94 per cent; tertiary 85 per cent (2008 est)
Health expenditure (per capita) – US$1,836 (2007)
Hospital beds (per 1,000 people) – 4.7 (2003–8)

MEDIA

Slovenia saw a rapid development of its media market after the fall of communism. The main newspapers are privately owned, and the broadcasting sector is a mix of public and private ownership. The television market is mainly shared between the public service, RTV Slovenia, and the private stations Pop TV and Kanal A. About two-thirds of households are connected to cable or satellite.

SOLOMON ISLANDS

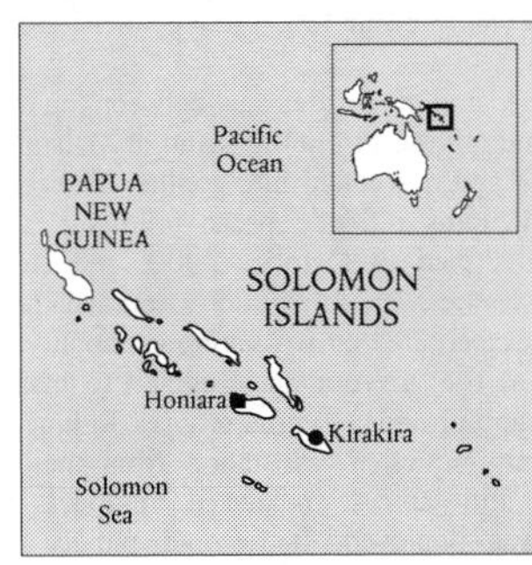

Area – 28,896 sq. km
Capital – Honiara, on Guadalcanal; population, 71,921 (2009 est)
Currency – Solomon Islands dollar (SI$) of 100 cents
Population – 595,613 rising at 2.39 per cent a year (2009 est); Melanesian (94.5 per cent), Polynesian (3 per cent), Micronesian (1.2 per cent)
Religion – Christian (Anglican 35 per cent, Roman Catholic 19 per cent, Pentecostal 17 per cent, Methodist 11 per cent, Seventh-day Adventist 10 per cent), indigenous animist religions 5 per cent (est)

Language – English (official), Melanesian Pidgin (lingua franca); around 120 indigenous languages exist
Population density – 18 per sq. km (2008)
Urban population – 18 per cent (2007 est)
Median age (years) – 19.7 (2009 est)
National anthem – 'God Save Our Solomon Islands'
National day – 7 July (Independence Day)
Life expectancy (years) – 73.69 (2009 est)
Mortality rate – 3.77 (2009 est)
Birth rate – 27.69 (2009 est)
Infant mortality rate – 19.03 (2009 est)
Death penalty – Abolished for all crimes (since 1966)
CPI score – 2.8 (2009)
Literacy rate – 76.6 per cent (2007 est)

CLIMATE AND TERRAIN

Forming a scattered archipelago of mountainous islands and low-lying coral atolls in the south-west Pacific Ocean, the Solomon Islands stretch about 1,448km in a south-easterly direction from the Shortland Islands to the Santa Cruz islands. The six biggest islands are Choiseul, New Georgia, Santa Isabel, Guadalcanal, Malaita and Makira (San Cristobal). They are characterised by thickly forested mountain ranges intersected by deep, narrow valleys. Elevation extremes range from 2,447m (Mt Makarakomburu) at the highest point to 0m (Pacific Ocean) at the lowest. The climate is tropical, with little variation in temperature, and a wet season between November and April. The islands are prone to seismic activity and tsunamis.

HISTORY AND POLITICS

The islands were discovered by the Spanish in 1568 and visited by Europeans intermittently for about 300 years. Following the inauguration of sugar plantations in Queensland and Fiji (which created a need for labour) and the arrival of missionaries and traders, Britain declared a protectorate in 1893 over the southern islands; the northern islands were ceded to Britain by Germany in 1899. Some of the islands were occupied by the Japanese in 1942, and recaptured by Allied forces in 1943–5 after fierce fighting, especially on Guadalcanal. After the Second World War, campaigns began for self-government, which was achieved in 1976; independence followed in July 1978.

Ethnic tension on Guadalcanal between the indigenous Isatabus and migrants from the island of Malaita escalated from 1998 and descended into conflict between militant factions. Despite a fragile peace following a ceasefire agreement signed in October 2000, and elections in 2001, lawlessness and corruption pervaded the country. This was exacerbated by worsening economic and social problems as the government struggled to maintain law and order and provide essential services. In June 2003 the government requested assistance from neighbouring countries and an Australian-led regional assistance mission was deployed. It restored public order and disarmed the militias by late 2003, and has since worked to restore stable government and revive the economy.

In the April 2006 legislative election, the governing People's Alliance Party (PAP) and the opposition won an equal number of seats. Snyder Ridi of the PAP was elected prime minister on 20 April but resigned six days later after rioting in protest at his appointment. Manasseh Sogavare (prime minister 2000–1) of the Social Credit Party was elected to replace him and formed a coalition government. Sogavare was defeated in a vote of no confidence in December 2007 and Derek Sikua was elected prime minister. A legislative election in August 2010 made the Solomon Islands Democratic Party the largest party in the legislature with only 11 seats; independents won 28 seats. The legislature elected Danny Philip the new prime minister on 25 August.

POLITICAL SYSTEM

Under the 1978 constitution, the Solomon Islands is a constitutional monarchy. The head of state is Queen Elizabeth II, represented by a governor-general, who is chosen by the legislature. The unicameral National Parliament has 50 members who are directly elected for a four-year term. The prime minister is elected by the legislature from among its members, and nominates the cabinet, which is formally appointed by the governor-general.
Governor-General, Frank Kabui, *apptd* 2009

SELECTED GOVERNMENT MEMBERS *as at September 2010*

Prime Minister, Danny Philip
Deputy Prime Minister, Home Affairs, Manasseh Maelanga
Finance, Gordon Darcy Lilo
Foreign Affairs, Peter Shanel

HIGH COMMISSION FOR THE SOLOMON ISLANDS

17 Avenue Edouard Lacombe, 1040 Brussels, Belgium
T (+32) (2) 732 7085 E siembassy@compuserve.com
High Commissioner, HE Joseph Ma'ahanua, *apptd* 2006

BRITISH HIGH COMMISSION

PO Box 676, Telekom House, Mendana Avenue, Honiara
T (+677) 21705 E bhc@solomon.com.sb
W http://ukinsolomonislands.fco.gov.uk
High Commissioner, HE Timothy Smart, *apptd* 2008

ECONOMY AND TRADE

The civil unrest of 1998–2003 left the country virtually bankrupt but the restoration of law and order enabled the economy to recover until its modest but steady growth was curtailed by the global downturn and natural disasters in 2009 and 2010. The country's greater dependency since 2003 on foreign aid, principally from Australia, has increased as the downturn has reduced government revenues.

Agriculture, much at subsistence level, is the largest economic sector, accounting for over 40 per cent of GDP and engaging 75 per cent of the population. Abundant mineral resources are largely undeveloped, although there are plans to reopen a major gold mine. The main industries are fishing, mining, forestry and processing agricultural products; industry contributes 11 per cent of GDP.

The main export market is China (51.4 per cent); most imports come from Singapore and Australia. Principal exports are timber, fish, copra, palm oil and cocoa. The main imports are food, machinery and equipment, manufactured goods, fuels and chemicals.
GNI – US$518m; US$1,010 per capita (2008)
Annual average growth of GDP – 0 per cent (2009 est)
Inflation rate – 6.3 per cent (2007 est)
Total external debt – US$166m (2004 est)
Imports – US$300m (2008)
Exports – US$200m (2008)

BALANCE OF PAYMENTS

Trade – US$128m deficit (2009)
Current Account – US$106m deficit (2008)

Trade with UK	*2008*	*2009*
Imports from UK	£2,281,085	£3,329,959
Exports to UK	£424,191	£561,185

COMMUNICATIONS

There are 1,360km of roads, of which only 33km are surfaced. The main ports are Honiara and Yandina. There are 36 airports and airfields, the main one being at Honiara. Solomon Airlines operates international services to other Pacific states and Australia. Air Niugini flies from Papua New Guinea to Honiara.

Telephone services are limited; in 2008 there were 8,000 fixed telephone lines in use, 30,000 mobile phone subscribers and 10,000 internet users.

MEDIA

The Solomon Islands Broadcasting Corporation (SIBC) operates a public radio service, and there are two commercial stations. One Television provides television programmes, and external satellite services can be received. Low literacy levels mean that SIBC has greater influence than the press, which consists of one daily, two weekly and two monthly newspapers. Australia and Taiwan have donated funds and equipment to develop the domestic media, and press freedom and security have improved since 2003.

SOMALIA

Jamhuuriyada Demuqraadiga Soomaaliyeed – Somalia

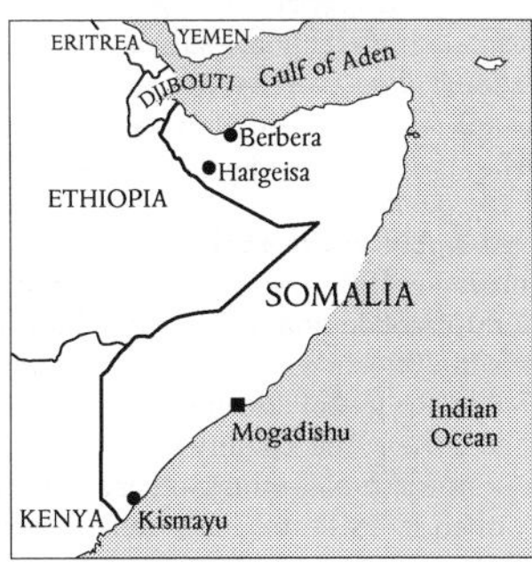

Area – 637,657 sq. km
Capital – Mogadishu; population, 1,352,800 (2009 est)
Major cities – Baidoa, Berbera, Burao, Hargeisa, Kismayu
Currency – Somali shilling of 100 cents; other currencies are also in circulation
Population – 9,832,017 rising at 2.82 per cent a year (2009 est)
Religion – Muslim (predominantly Sunni, including Sunni forms of Sufism); small Christian minority
Language – Somali, Arabic (both official), Italian, English
Population density – 14 per sq. km (2008)
Urban population – 36 per cent (2007 est)
Median age (years) – 17.5 (2009 est)
National anthem – 'Somaliyaay toosoo' ['Somalia, Wake Up']
National day – 1 July (Foundation Day)
Life expectancy (years) – 49.63 (2009 est)
Mortality rate – 15.55 (2009 est)
Birth rate – 43.7 (2009 est)
Infant mortality rate – 109.19 (2009 est)
Death penalty – Retained
CPI score – 1.1 (2009)
Gross enrolment ratio (percentage of relevant age group) – primary 17 per cent (2005 est)

CLIMATE AND TERRAIN

The country is mostly an arid and flat or undulating plateau, rising to hills in the north. Elevation extremes range from 2,416m (Shimbiris) at the highest point to 0m (Indian Ocean) at the lowest. The climate is tropical, influenced by the north-east and south-west monsoons. Rainfall is greater in the south than the north, but is low and irregular throughout the country, leading to frequent droughts. Average temperatures in Mogadishu are between 23°C and 32°C throughout the year.

HISTORY AND POLITICS

From the eighth century onwards Arab settlers introduced Islam and established coastal trading towns that developed into sultanates. European contact began in the early 16th century, with Italian, French and British interest intensifying after the Suez Canal opened in 1869. Protectorates were established in the north by the British (1887) and in the centre and the south by the Italians (1889–1905). Italian Somalia was returned to Italian administration as a UN Trust Territory in 1950. The two protectorates became independent and merged to form the United Republic of Somalia in July 1960.

In 1969 the armed forces seized power in a coup led by Maj.-Gen. Muhammad Siad Barre, and established a socialist Islamic regime which became a one-party state in 1979. Insurrection in the north began in 1978 and by 1988 opposition to the government had developed into a civil war, the rebels toppling the Said Barre regime in 1991. Attempts to establish a new central government failed as political and clan rivalries split the former rebels. The situation degenerated into civil war between rival 'warlords' and the state effectively disintegrated. Local administrations based on clans or Islamic courts have since developed in most areas.

Subsequent attempts to re-establish a central government were unsuccessful until 2004, when two years of peace talks concluded with the establishment of a transitional federal legislature and president in 2004 and a transitional federal government in 2005. The federal government's attempts to assert its authority, supported between 2007 and January 2009 by Ethiopian armed forces, led to an upsurge in violence as its forces were resisted by Islamist militias loyal to the Union of Islamic Courts (UIC) and opponents of Ethiopian 'occupation'.

Most of the Alliance for the Re-liberation of Somalia (ARS), formed in 2007 to resist the Ethiopian presence in Somalia, agreed a ceasefire with the government in June 2008 in return for Ethiopian withdrawal, and subsequently joined the legislature and government. More hard-line Islamist insurgents, in particular the al-Shabaab militia, continue to oppose the government and have regained control of much of the south of the country. Although the transitional government has been located in Mogadishu since early 2009, its control of the capital is partial, tenuous and constantly challenged. Piracy in the Gulf of Aden and the Indian Ocean became a major problem in early 2008; international naval patrols to prevent attacks on shipping began in late 2008.

Abdullahi Yusuf Ahmed, elected president in 2004, resigned in December 2008, and the legislature elected the ARS leader Sheikh Sharif Ahmed as president in January 2009; a new coalition government was appointed in February and March.

SECESSION

The northern-based Somali National Movement (SNM) took control of the north-west (the former British

Somaliland protectorate) after Siad Barre's deposition, and in May 1991 declared unilateral independence as the 'Republic of Somaliland'. It has its own political system, government institutions and currency, supported by revenue from expatriates' remittances, customs duties from the port at Berbera and livestock exports. The leaders of the regime have refused to take part in the peace process since 1999 and have not signed the 2004 peace agreement; they are seeking international recognition of Somaliland's independence.

The north-east of the country proclaimed its autonomy as the region of Puntland in 1998. Puntland seeks participation in a federal Somalia rather than independence. Its leaders have taken part in the peace process, signing the 2004 peace agreement; its former leader, Col. Abdullahi Yusuf Ahmed, was federal president from 2004 to 2008. Since 2005 the area has been the hub of piracy in the region, especially the Gulf of Aden.

There has been sporadic fighting between Somaliland and Puntland over Somaliland's Sool and Sanaag regions, which Puntland claims on ethnic grounds.

POLITICAL SYSTEM

Somalia has been without an effective central government since 1991. The 2004 peace agreement established transitional federal institutions (TFIs) in 2005 with a five-year mandate to draw up a constitution and hold elections; their mandate was extended for two years in January 2009. The TFIs include the Transitional Federal Parliament, which had 275 seats but was expanded to 450 seats in January 2009 to include 200 ARS members and a further 75 representatives of civil society. The parliament elects the president and approves the appointment of ministers to the transitional federal government.

HEAD OF STATE

President, Sheikh Sharif Ahmed, *sworn in* 31 January 2009

SELECTED GOVERNMENT MEMBERS *as at July 2010*

Prime Minister, Omar Sharmarke
Deputy Prime Ministers, Abdiwahid Ilmi Gonjeh; Abdurahman Adan Ibrahim; Adan Muhammad Nur Madobe
Defence, Abukar Abdi Osman
Foreign Affairs, Yusuf Ibrahim Hasan
Internal Affairs, Abdulkadir Ali Omar

DEFENCE

There have been no national armed forces since 1991, despite attempts at re-establishment by the transitional government. Somaliland and Puntland have their own militias with limited amounts of equipment.

ECONOMY AND TRADE

The lack of central government has prevented broad-based economic development or assistance from international donors. About 60 per cent of the population lives below the poverty line, and many are dependent on remittances from relatives abroad. Natural resources are not exploited and industry is virtually non-existent but the lack of regulation has led to a thriving and relatively sophisticated entrepreneurial economy, especially in livestock, remittance/money transfer services (in the absence of a banking sector) and telecommunications. Infrastructure has been developed by commercial concerns, with businesses building small airfields and using natural harbours for overseas trade, and the three main telecommunications companies jointly funding internet infrastructure. The main factor inhibiting trade is the lack of a functional central bank.

Agriculture, primarily livestock-raising by nomads or semi-nomads, is the most important economic sector. It accounts for about 65 per cent of GDP and over half of export earnings, but is vulnerable to drought.

The main export markets are the UAE and Yemen; imports come mainly from Djibouti. Principal exports are livestock, bananas, hides, fish, charcoal and scrap metal. The main imports are manufactures, petroleum products, foodstuffs, construction materials and qat.

Annual average growth of GDP – 2.6 per cent (2009 est)
Total external debt – US$3,000m (2001 est)

Trade with UK	*2008*	*2009*
Imports from UK	£1,375,056	£1,147,049
Exports to UK	£40,419	£14,720

COMMUNICATIONS

The main ports are Mogadishu, Kismayu and Merca in the south, and Berbera (in Somaliland) in the north, although these have all been damaged by war. There is a high risk of piracy and armed robbery of shipping in the Gulf of Aden and the Indian Ocean; since early 2008 there have been coordinated international efforts to prevent Somali pirates threatening international shipping in the region. The international airports are at Mogadishu and Hargeisa (in Somaliland). There are international flights to Kenya and the UAE.

Little of the public telephone system has survived the civil wars, but mobile phone services are available in most major population centres. There were 100,000 fixed lines in use, 627,000 mobile phone subscribers and 102,000 internet users in 2008.

MEDIA

Many new print and broadcast outlets emerged after Siad Barre was ousted in 1991, but most were tied to one of the country's warring factions. Recent years have seen the emergence of stronger regional media, particularly in radio, but broadcasters and journalists operate in a dangerous environment which limits their ability to report freely and objectively. Many Somalis rely on foreign broadcasts for news and information.

SOUTH AFRICA

Republic of South Africa

Area – 1,219,090 sq. km
Capital – The seat of government is Pretoria (Tshwane): population, 1,403,880 (2009 est); the seat of the legislature is Cape Town: population, 3,352,890 (2009 est); and the seat of the judiciary is Bloemfontein: population, 436,356 (2009 est)
Major cities – Durban, Johannesburg, Port Elizabeth, Soweto
Currency – Rand (R) of 100 cents
Population – 49,052,489 rising at 0.28 per cent a year (2009 est)
Religion – Christian (African Independent Churches 20 per cent, other 60 per cent); small minorities of Muslims, Hindus, Jews and followers of indigenous religions (est). Many combine Christian and indigenous religious practices
Language – Afrikaans, English, IsiNdebele, IsiXhosa, IsiZulu, Sepedi, Sesotho, Setswana, SiSwati, Tshivenda, Xitsonga (all official); the most widely spoken are IsiZulu, IsiXhosa and Afrikaans, but English is the lingua franca
Population density – 40 per sq. km (2008)
Urban population – 60 per cent (2007 est)
Median age (years) – 24.4 (2009 est)
National anthems – 'Nkosi Sikelel' iAfrika' ['God Bless Africa'], incorporating 'Die Stem van Suid Afrika' ['The Call of South Africa']
National day – 27 April (Freedom Day)
Life expectancy (years) – 48.98 (2009 est)
Mortality rate – 16.99 (2009 est)
Birth rate – 19.93 (2009 est)
Infant mortality rate – 44.42 (2009 est)
HIV/AIDS adult prevalence – 16.3 per cent (2007 est)
Death penalty – Abolished for all crimes (since 1997)
CPI score – 4.7 (2009)

CLIMATE AND TERRAIN

South Africa occupies the southernmost part of the African continent, with the exception of Lesotho, Swaziland and the extreme south of Mozambique. Its territory includes Prince Edward and Marion Islands, 1,920km to the south-east of Cape Town. The narrow coastal plain is separated by a mountainous escarpment, including the Drakensberg range, from a high inland plateau (the Great Karoo and the Highveld), an area of semi-arid scrubland in the west merging into grasslands or savannah in the centre and east. Elevation extremes range from 3,408m (Njesuthi) at the highest point to 0m (Atlantic Ocean) at the lowest. The main rivers are the Orange and the Limpopo and their tributaries. The country lies at the convergence of the Atlantic and Indian oceans, and the climate is influenced by the cold Benguela current along the west coast and the warm Agulhas current along the east, as well as by the altitude of the interior. These influences cause cooler, drier conditions in the west and almost subtropical warmth and rainfall in the east. Average temperatures in Pretoria (Tshwane) range from lows of 3°C in July to highs of 28°C in December.

HISTORY AND POLITICS

Hunter-gatherers, the San (Bushmen) and Khoikhoi, inhabited southern Africa from *c.*8000 BC. By the eighth century AD, Bantu-speaking peoples had arrived from the north and settled. The Portuguese navigator Bartolomeu Días charted the coast in 1488 and the Dutch founded the colony of the Cape of Good Hope in 1652. The British occupied the Cape in 1795 after Revolutionary France had conquered the Netherlands, and the colony was ceded to Britain in 1806. From 1836 the Boers (descendants of Dutch settlers) migrated north-east in the Great Trek to escape British rule, and founded the republic of Natal in 1839; the British annexed Natal in 1844, made it a colony in 1856 and added Zululand to it in 1897 after victory in the Zulu wars. The Boer republics of Transvaal (founded 1852) and Orange Free State (founded 1854) became British colonies in 1902 after the Boer Wars of 1880–1 and 1899–1902. The four self-governing colonies were united in 1910 to form the Union of South Africa, with dominion status. It became a sovereign state within the Commonwealth in 1931. South Africa left the Commonwealth and became a republic on 31 May 1961, largely as a result of international condemnation of the Sharpeville massacre (1960), in which 67 protesters were killed by police.

The National Party came to power in 1948 and intensified racial segregation through its policy of apartheid ('separateness'), which it pursued until 1991. As a result, South Africa's social and political structure came to be based on racial segregation, with separate institutions and facilities for different racial groups. The African National Congress (ANC) and other opposition groups mounted a civil disobedience campaign, following which most opposition groups were banned. Internal opposition continued, with strikes and violence in the 1980s leading to the declaration of a state of emergency in 1985. Internationally, the country became isolated as economic and cultural sanctions were imposed.

In 1984, a new constitution extended the franchise to mixed race and Asian people, but the progressive dismantling of apartheid began with the desegregation of public facilities in 1989. This was followed by the lifting of the bans on the ANC and other anti-apartheid groups, the release from prison of ANC leader Nelson Mandela (1990) and the effective abolition of the laws implementing apartheid in 1991. Negotiations between the government of F. W. de Klerk, the ANC and other political and civic groups reached agreement in 1991 on the establishment of an interracial administration and the formation of a five-year coalition government following multiracial elections. In 1993 the franchise was extended to all adults, and elections took place in April 1994. The ANC won a majority in both legislative chambers, and Nelson Mandela was elected president. South Africa rejoined the Commonwealth and took its UN seat again in 1994.

High levels of HIV/AIDS infection, a very high crime rate, social disruption and lack of education resulting from apartheid are serious problems. There has also been growing discontent in recent years at the lack of progress in reducing poverty since the end of apatheid. Despite these problems, South Africa is widely regarded as the dominant political, economic and diplomatic force in the region.

The ANC has won all the legislative elections since 1994, but is increasingly racked by internal tensions and tainted by corruption allegations. In April 2009 its majority in the National Assembly was reduced by 13 seats and it lost one of the provincial assemblies as two of the opposition parties began to challenge its dominance. In May 2009, Jacob Zuma of the ANC was elected president.

POLITICAL SYSTEM

Under the 1997 constitution, the executive president is elected by the National Assembly for a five-year term, renewable only once. The president, who is responsible to the legislature, appoints the cabinet. The bicameral parliament consists of the National Assembly, the lower house, and the National Council of Provinces. The National Assembly has 400 members directly elected by proportional representation for a five-year term. The National Council of Provinces has 90 members, ten for each province, elected by the provincial legislatures for a five-year term.

South Africa is divided into nine provinces: Eastern Cape, Free State, Gauteng, KwaZulu-Natal, Limpopo, Mpumalanga, Northern Cape, North-West, and Western Cape. Each province has its own premier, legislature and constitution.

HEAD OF STATE
President, Jacob Zuma, *elected* 6 May 2009, *sworn in* 9 May 2009
Deputy President, Kgalema Motlanthe

SELECTED GOVERNMENT MEMBERS *as at July 2010*
Defence, Lindiwe Nonceba Sisulu
Finance, Pravin Gordhan
Foreign Affairs, Maite Nkoana-Mashabane
Home Affairs, Nkosazana Dlamini-Zuma

SOUTH AFRICAN HIGH COMMISSION
South Africa House, Trafalgar Square, London WC2N 5DP
T 020-7451 7299 E london.general@foreign.gov.za
W www.southafricahouse.com
High Commissioner, HE Dr Zola Skweyiya, *apptd* 2009

BRITISH HIGH COMMISSION
255 Hill Street, Arcadia 0002, Pretoria (Tshwane)
T (+27) (12) 421 7500 E media.pretoria@fco.gov.uk
W http://ukinsouthafrica.fco.gov.uk
High Commissioner, HE Dr Nicola Brewer, CMG, *apptd* 2009

BRITISH COUNCIL
Ground Floor, Forum 1, Braampark, 33 Hoofd Street, Braamfontein, Johannesburg 2001
T (+27) (11) 718 4300 W www.britishcouncil.org/africa
Director, David Cordingley

DEFENCE

The South African National Defence Force (SANDF) was created in 1994 from the merger of the South African Defence Forces (SADF), the Umkhonto we Sizwe (MK) armed wing of the ANC, the Azanian People's Liberation Army (APLA) of the Pan Africanist Congress of Azania, and the defence forces of the four former 'independent' homelands.

The army has 167 main battle tanks, 810 armoured personnel carriers and 1,200 armoured infantry fighting vehicles. The navy has 3 submarines, 4 corvettes and 26 patrol and coastal vessels at 4 bases. The air force has 33 combat aircraft and 11 armed helicopters.
Military expenditure – US$4,350m (2009)
Military personnel – 62,082: army 37,141, navy 6,244, air force 10,653, military health service 8,044

ECONOMY AND TRADE

The economy varies between the sophisticated and well-developed, based on manufacturing, mining and financial services; the living eked out by the very poor, mostly through subsistence agriculture; and a large informal sector. Growth was strong until 2008, since when the global economic downturn has caused a contraction in the economy owing to falling commodity prices and export demand. State-owned enterprises are being used to create jobs and raise incomes. However, unemployment remains high and poverty widespread (about half the population lives below the poverty line), and productivity and trade are constrained by outdated infrastructure in some sectors; power cuts have been frequent since 2007 because of the unreliability of the electricity supply.

Agriculture, forestry and fishing account for 3 per cent of GDP and employ 9 per cent of the workforce. Principal crops are maize, wheat, sugar cane, fruit and vegetables. Livestock farming and cotton and viticulture are also widespread.

The largest industry is mining; South Africa is the world's largest producer of gold, platinum and chromium, as well as producing diamonds, manganese, coal, copper, iron ore, tin, uranium and titanium. Other industries include car assembly, metalworking, food processing, ship repair and production of machinery, textiles, iron and steel, chemicals and fertiliser; manufacturing is concentrated most heavily around Johannesburg, Pretoria (Tshwane) and the major ports. Tourism is a significant industry, with over nine million visitors in 2007, and South Africa is a major transit point for its landlocked neighbours. Industry contributes 31.1 per cent of GDP and services 65.8 per cent.

Fossil-fuel based electricity generation is being supplemented by nuclear power; one nuclear power station is in operation and others are planned. South Africa exports electricity through its electricity grid connections to all states in southern Africa. Water resources are inadequate to meet demand, so water is imported from the highlands of Lesotho.

The main trading partners are China, Germany, the USA and Japan. Principal exports are gold, diamonds, platinum, other metals and minerals, and machinery and equipment. Principal imports are machinery and equipment, chemicals, petroleum products, scientific instruments and foodstuffs.
GNI – US$283,200m; US$5,820 per capita (2008)
Annual average growth of GDP – –1.9 per cent (2009 est)
Inflation rate – 7.2 per cent (2009 est)
Unemployment – 24 per cent (2009 est)
Total external debt – US$73,840m (2009 est)
Imports – US$99,500m (2008)
Exports – US$84,600m (2008)

BALANCE OF PAYMENTS
Trade – US$1,796m deficit (2009)
Current Account – US$19,593m deficit (2008)

Trade with UK	*2008*	*2009*
Imports from UK	£2,540,803,638	£2,153,771,710
Exports to UK	£4,536,375,472	£7,333,406,607

COMMUNICATIONS

The country has 20,872km of railways, including the high-speed Gautrain launched in June 2010, which links Johannesburg's main international airport with its commercial district and will eventually connect with Pretoria. There are 362,100km of roads, of which 73,500km are surfaced, and over 600 airports and airfields, with international airports at Johannesburg, Durban and Cape Town. South African Airways operates international services worldwide and it is the principal operator of domestic flights. Durban is the largest seaport. Other major ports are Cape Town, Port Elizabeth, East London, Saldanha, Mossel Bay and Richards Bay.

The telephone system is the most developed in Africa, and there is a very high level of mobile phone ownership. There were 4.4 million fixed lines in use, 45 million mobile phone subscribers and 4.2 million internet users in 2008.

EDUCATION AND HEALTH

Education is compulsory between the ages of seven and 15. It is provided by the state and organised into three levels: general education and training, further education and training, and higher education. The nine provincial legislatures manage education facilities, subject to a national policy framework.

Literacy rate – 88 per cent (2007 est)
Gross enrolment ratio (percentage of relevant age group) – primary 105 per cent; secondary 95 per cent (2008 est)
Health expenditure (per capita) – US$497 (2007)
Hospital beds (per 1,000 people) – 2.8 (2003–8)

MEDIA AND CULTURE

South Africa's media industry is the largest and most influential in Africa. The South African Broadcasting Corporation (SABC) is a major, state-owned television and radio broadcaster, and there is a thriving private sector, with widespread take-up of cable and satellite television and a large number of radio stations since deregulation in 1996. *The Star* is Johannesburg's oldest daily newspaper, while the *Sunday Times* is the longest running weekly title; *Beeld* is a popular Afrikaans daily title. Press freedom is generally respected, with little evidence of repressive measures against journalists.

South Africa is home to a diversity of cultures, and black cultures such as Zulu, Xhosa and Ndebele are experiencing a revival after their suppression during the apartheid years. Celebrated figures include the writers Nadine Gordimer (*b.* 1923) and J. M. Coetzee (*b.* 1940), winners of the Nobel prize for literature in 1991 and 2003 respectively. The Nobel peace prize was won by Archbishop Desmond Tutu (*b.* 1931) in 1984, and shared by Nelson Mandela (*b.* 1918) and F. W. de Klerk (*b.* 1936) in 1993.

SPAIN

Reino de España – Kingdom of Spain

Area – 505,370 sq. km
Capital – Madrid; population, 5,762,050 (2009 est)
Major cities – Barcelona, Bilbao, Las Palmas (Gran Canaria), Málaga, Murcia, Palma (Majorca), Seville, Valencia, Zaragoza
Currency – Euro (€) of 100 cents
Population – 40,525,002 rising at 0.07 per cent a year (2009 est)
Religion – Christian (Roman Catholic 77 per cent) (est)
Language – Castilian (Spanish) (official), Catalan, Galician, Basque (all are official in certain regions)
Population density – 91 per sq. km (2008)
Urban population – 77 per cent (2007 est)
Median age (years) – 41.1 (2009 est)
National anthem – 'La Marcha Real' ['The Royal March']
National day – 12 October
Life expectancy (years) – 80.05 (2009 est)
Mortality rate – 9.99 (2009 est)
Birth rate – 9.72 (2009 est)
Infant mortality rate – 4.21 (2009 est)
Death penalty – Abolished for all crimes (since 1995)
CPI score – 6.1 (2009)

CLIMATE AND TERRAIN

Spain occupies over 80 per cent of the Iberian peninsula, and includes two archipelagos and territories on or just off the Moroccan coast. The interior consists of an elevated plateau surrounded and traversed by mountain ranges: the Pyrenees on the border with France, the Cantabrian Mountains (north-west), the Sierra de Guadarrama, Sierra Morena, Montes de Toledo (centre) and the Sierra Nevada (south). Elevation extremes range from 3,718m (Pico de Teide, Tenerife, Canary Islands) at the highest point to 0m (Mediterranean Sea) at the lowest. The principal rivers are the Duero, the Tajo (Tagus), the Guadiana, the Guadalquivir, the Ebro and the Miño. The climate is Mediterranean in the southern and eastern coastal areas, and temperate further inland and at altitude. Average temperatures in Madrid range from lows of 2°C in January to highs of 31°C in July.

HISTORY AND POLITICS

The Romans conquered the Iberian peninsula in the second century BC. It was overrun by Vandals and Visigoths in the fifth century AD, and invaded and occupied by Muslims from Africa in the eighth century. Christians in the north formed small kingdoms which had reconquered the peninsula by 1492. Spain's modern form derives from the dynastic union of the kingdoms of Castile and Aragón in 1479. In the 16th century, Spain's exploration and colonisation of the New World made it one of the richest and most powerful nations in Europe, with an empire that covered most of central and southern America. However, a succession of costly wars and revolts in the 17th and 18th centuries saw this empire go into steady decline. Its central and southern American possessions declared independence in the early 19th century, and most other overseas possessions had been lost by 1900.

The restoration of the Bourbon monarchy after the Napoleonic occupation of 1808–14 initiated over a century of political instability, with power struggles between conservative and liberal factions in royal, political and military circles. The dictatorship of Gen. Primo de Rivera (1923–30) ended with the exiling of King Alfonso XIII and the declaration of the Second Republic in 1931. Left-wing victory in the 1936 election led to an army revolt in Spanish Morocco that spread throughout Spain, developing into a civil war that lasted until March 1939. Gen. Francisco Franco, who had led the right-wing Nationalist forces in the civil war, became president and ruled the country until his death in 1975. His death was followed, according to his wishes, by the restoration of the monarchy, and Prince Juan Carlos of

Bourbon (grandson of Alfonso XIII) became head of state as King Juan Carlos I. The first free election was held in 1977, and a referendum in 1978 endorsed a democratic constitution.

Spain joined NATO in 1982 and the EEC in 1986, becoming a member of the euro zone in 1999.

The Spanish Socialist Workers' Party (PSOE) won an unexpected victory in the 2004 election, held three days after the bombing of commuter trains in Madrid by a group linked to al-Qaida. In the 2008 legislative elections the PSOE increased its seats, remaining the largest party in the Congress of Deputies but without a majority; the main opposition party, the Popular Party, won the most seats in the senate. José Luis Rodríguez Zapatero continued as prime minister at the head of a minority PSOE government, which has the support of five small parties.

INSURGENCIES

The Basque separatist organisation ETA (*Euzkadi ta Azkatasuna* – Basque Nation and Liberty), formed in 1959, has carried out a terrorist campaign of bombings, shootings and kidnappings since 1961 in an attempt to gain independence for the Basque country. ETA rejected regional autonomy for the Basque country in 1979 as insufficient and continued its campaign, but has been greatly weakened since the early 1990s by increased cooperation between Spanish security forces and their European counterparts. *Herri Batasuna,* regarded as ETA's political wing, was banned in 2003. ETA has announced a number of ceasefires since 1998, during some of which it has held talks with the government or political parties, but no progress has been made towards a political settlement that it considers acceptable; its latest ceasefire was called off in 2007.

POLITICAL SYSTEM

The 1978 constitution has been amended at various times to devolve powers to the 19 autonomous regions. The head of state is a hereditary constitutional monarch. There is a bicameral legislature, the *Cortes Generales,* comprising a 350-member Congress of Deputies directly elected for a four-year term, and a senate with 264 members, 208 directly elected and 56 appointed by the assemblies of the autonomous regions, for a four-year term.

There are 19 autonomous regions: Andalucía, Aragón, Asturias, Balearic Islands, the Basque Country, Canary Islands, Cantabria, Castilla-La Mancha, Castilla y León, Catalonia, Ceuta, Extremadura, Galicia, La Rioja, Madrid, Melilla, Murcia, Navarra and Valencia. Each has its own elected legislature and government. In 2006 a referendum endorsed the *Cortes'* approval of greater autonomy for Catalonia.

HEAD OF STATE

HM The King of Spain, King Juan Carlos I de Borbón, KG, GCVO, *born* 5 January 1938, *acceded to the throne* 22 November 1975

Heir, HRH The Prince of the Asturias (Prince Felipe Juan Pablo Alfonso y Todos los Santos), *born* 30 January 1968

SELECTED GOVERNMENT MEMBERS *as at July 2010*

Prime Minister, José Luis Rodríguez Zapatero

First Deputy Prime Minister, Maria Teresa Fernandez de la Vega

Second Deputy Prime Minister, Economy and Finance, Elena Salgado Mendez

Foreign Affairs, Miguel Ángel Moratinos

Interior, Alfredo Pérez Rubalcaba

Defence, Carmen Chacon Piqueras

EMBASSY OF SPAIN

39 Chesham Place, London SW1X 8SB
T 020-7235 5555 E emb.londres@maec.es
W www.mae.es/embajadas/londres/es/home
Ambassador Extraordinary and Plenipotentiary, Carles Casajuana Palet, *apptd* 2008

BRITISH EMBASSY

Torre Espacio, Paseo de la Castellana 259D, 28046 Madrid
T (+34) (91) 714 6300 E enquiries.madrid@ukinspain.com
W http://ukinspain.fco.gov.uk
Ambassador Extraordinary and Plenipotentiary, HE Giles Paxman, LVO, *apptd* 2009

BRITISH COUNCIL

Paseo del General Martínez, Campos 31, E-28010 Madrid
T (+34) (91) 337 3500 W www.britishcouncil.org/spain
Director, Rod Pryde

DEFENCE

The army has 498 main battle tanks, 144 armoured infantry fighting vehicles and 1,465 armoured personnel carriers. The navy has 4 submarines, 1 aircraft carrier, 11 frigates, 32 patrol and coastal vessels, 16 combat aircraft and 24 armed helicopters at 6 bases. The air force has 179 combat aircraft.

Military expenditure – US$19,200m (2008)

Military personnel – 128,013: army 79,736, navy 17,943, air force 21,606, joint staff 8,728; paramilitary 80,210

ECONOMY AND TRADE

Conservatism and isolation held back economic development in the mid-20th century, but the economy improved from the 1950s with industrialisation and the development of tourism. The mixed capitalist economy showed above-average growth, stimulated by liberalisation, privatisation and deregulation, from the mid-1990s until 2007. In late 2008 it entered a severe recession because of the global economic downturn. This pushed unemployment to 20 per cent by spring 2010 (from 8 per cent in 2007). The downturn in construction and the property market left many banks struggling in spring 2010, and concerns over rising public-sector debt led to Spain's international credit rating being downgraded; the government introduced austerity measures in response.

The generally fertile country produces grains, vegetables, olives, sugar beets, citrus and other fruits, meat and dairy products. Viticulture is widespread. Spain also has one of Europe's largest fishing industries. The agricultural sector contributes 3.3 per cent of GDP and employs 4.2 per cent of the workforce. Abundant mineral resources include coal, iron ore, copper, zinc, lead, uranium and tungsten. Metal extraction and the manufacture of metal products, including steel, are major industries. A diverse industrial sector includes manufacturing (principally textiles, clothing, footwear, beverages, chemicals, cars, machine tools, clay products, pharmaceuticals and medical equipment), food processing, shipbuilding and tourism. The tourist industry usually caters for over 52 million visitors a year, but it has been hit by the recession. Industry accounts for 26.8 per cent of GDP and the service sector for 70 per cent.

The main trading partners are other EU countries,

especially Germany and France. Principal exports include machinery, vehicles, foodstuffs, pharmaceuticals, medicines and other consumer goods. The main imports are machinery and equipment, fuels, chemicals, semi-finished goods, foodstuffs, consumer goods, and measuring and medical control instruments.
GNI – US$1,454,800m; US$31,930 per capita (2008)
Annual average growth of GDP – −3.7 per cent (2009 est)
Inflation rate – −0.6 per cent (2009 est)
Population below the poverty line – 19.8 per cent (2005)
Unemployment – 18.5 per cent (2009 est)
Total external debt – US$2,410,000m (2009 est)
Imports – US$417,000m (2008)
Exports – US$277,700m (2008)

BALANCE OF PAYMENTS
Trade – US$60,037m deficit (2009)
Current Account – US$74,136m deficit (2009)

Trade with UK	*2008*	*2009*
Imports from UK	£10,020,705,906	£8,952,783,708
Exports to UK	£10,249,254,052	£9,134,372,285

COMMUNICATIONS
Spain has a total of 681,000km of roads, nearly all of which are surfaced (including 13,900km of motorways). Railways total 15,300km, and there are 1,000km of navigable inland waterways. The main ports are Algeciras, Alicante, Barcelona, Bilbao, Cádiz, Santander and Valencia, and Las Palmas in the Canary Islands. The principal airports are at Madrid, Barcelona, Alicante, Málaga, Valencia and Bilbao, and there are over 100 other airports and airfields around the country.

The modern telecommunications systems provided services to 20.2 million fixed-line subscribers, 49.7 million mobile phone subscribers and 25.2 million internet users in 2008.

EDUCATION AND HEALTH
Education is free from age six to 18, and compulsory to the age of 16. Private schools (about 30 per cent of primary and 60 per cent of secondary schools) have to fulfil certain criteria to receive government maintenance grants. There are 73 universities, the oldest of which, Salamanca, was founded in 1218. Other historic foundations are Valladolid (1346), Barcelona (1430), Zaragoza (1474), Santiago (1495), Valencia (1500), Seville (1505) and Madrid (1508).
Literacy rate – 97.9 per cent (2007 est)
Gross enrolment ratio (percentage of relevant age group) – primary 105 per cent; secondary 119 per cent; tertiary 68 per cent (2008 est)
Health expenditure (per capita) – US$2,712 (2007)
Hospital beds (per 1,000 people) – 3.4 (2003–8)

MEDIA
Broadcasting has expanded in recent years, with cable, satellite and digital services growing steadily. Public radio and television services are run by RadioTelevision Espanola (RTVE), which is funded by advertising and state subsidies. Many private radio and TV stations operate at both national and regional levels. The analogue signal was switched off in April 2010. There are four Madrid-based daily newspapers and another two based in Barcelona. Popular titles include *El Mundo, ABC, El País* and *El Periodico de Catalunya.*

CULTURE
Spain's literature is one of the oldest in the world. The *Poem of the Cid,* the earliest of Spain's heroic works, was written *c.*1140. The outstanding writers of Spain's Golden Age are Miguel de Cervantes (1547–1616), Lope de Vega (1562–1635) and Pedro Calderón de la Barca (1600–81). The Nobel prize for literature has been awarded to five Spanish authors: J. Echegaray (1832–1916), J. Benavente (1866–1954), Juan Ramón Jiménez (1881–1958), Vicente Aleixandre (1898–1984) and Camilo José Cela (1916–2002). Federico Garciá Lorca (1898–1936) is the most esteemed modern dramatist.

Spain's long tradition in fine art includes the work of El Greco (1541–1614), Velázquez (1599–1660), Goya (1746–1828), Picasso (1881–1973), Miró (1893–1983) and Dali (1904–89).

ISLANDS AND ENCLAVES

THE BALEARIC ISLES form an archipelago off the east coast of Spain. There are four large islands (Majorca/Mallorca, Minorca, Ibiza and Formentera) and seven smaller ones (Aire, Aucanada, Botafoch, Cabrera, Dragonera, Pinto and El Rey). Area 4,992 sq. km; population 1,095,426 (2009 est). The archipelago forms a province of Spain. The capital is Palma on Majorca.

THE CANARY ISLANDS are an archipelago in the Atlantic off the African coast, consisting of seven islands and six islets. Area 7,447 sq. km; population 2,103,992 (2009 est). The Canary Islands form two provinces of Spain: Las Palmas, comprising Gran Canaria, Lanzarote, Fuerteventura and six islets, with the seat of administration at Las Palmas in Gran Canaria; and Santa Cruz de Tenerife, comprising Tenerife, La Palma, La Gomera and El Hierro, with the seat of administration at Santa Cruz in Tenerife.

ISLA DE FAISANES is an uninhabited Franco-Spanish condominium, at the mouth of the Bidassoa in La Higuera bay.

CEUTA is a fortified post on the Moroccan coast, opposite Gibraltar. Area 19 sq. km; population 78,674 (2009 est). Ceuta is an autonomous city of Spain.

MELILLA is a town on a rocky promontory of the Moroccan coast, connected with the mainland by a narrow isthmus. Area 13 sq. km; population 73,460 (2009 est). Melilla is an autonomous city of Spain.

OVERSEAS TERRITORIES

The following territories, which are Spanish settlements on the Moroccan seaboard, come under direct Spanish administration. They are uninhabited other than by military personnel.

PENON DE ALHUCEMAS is a bay including six islands.

PENON DE LA GOMERA (or Peñón de Velez) is a fortified rocky islet.

THE CHAFFARINAS (or Zaffarines) is a group of three islands near the Algerian frontier.

SRI LANKA

Shri Lamka Prajatantrika Samajaya di Janarajaya/Ilankai Jananayaka Choshalichak Kutiyarachu – Democratic Socialist Republic of Sri Lanka

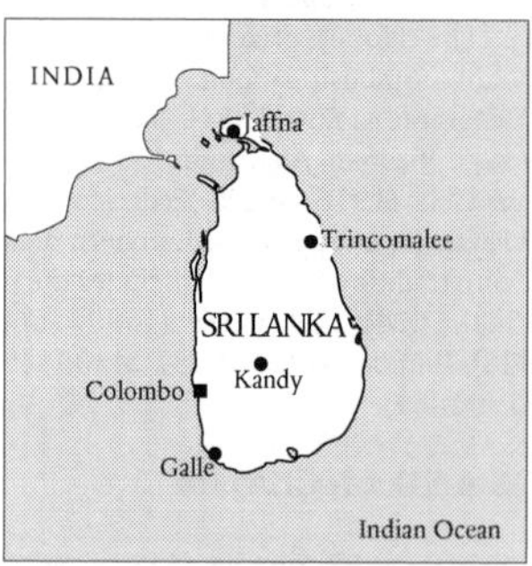

Area – 65,610 sq. km
Capital – Colombo; population, 681,484 (2009 est), Sri Jayewardenepura Kotte; population, 123,090 (2009 est) is the administrative capital
Major cities – Dehiwala-Mount Lavinia, Jaffna, Kalmunai, Kandy, Moratuwa, Negombo, Trincomalee, Vavuniya
Currency – Sri Lankan rupee of 100 cents
Population – 21,324,791 rising at 0.90 per cent a year (2009 est); Sinhalese (73.8 per cent), Sri Lankan Moor (7.2 per cent), Indian Tamil (4.6 per cent), Sri Lankan Tamil (3.9 per cent) (2001 est; excludes predominantly Tamil areas then held by rebels)
Religion – Buddhist 70 per cent (predominantly Theravada), Hindu 15 per cent, Christian 8 per cent (predominantly Roman Catholic), Muslim 7 per cent (predominantly Sunni) (est)
Language – Sinhala (official), Tamil, English
Population density – 312 per sq. km (2008)
Urban population – 15 per cent (2007 est)
Median age (years) – 30.9 (2009 est)
National anthem – 'Sri Lanka Matha' ['Mother Sri Lanka']
National day – 4 February (Independence Day)
Life expectancy (years) – 75.14 (2009 est)
Mortality rate – 6.13 (2009 est)
Birth rate – 16.26 (2009 est)
Infant mortality rate – 18.57 (2009 est)
Death penalty – Retained (not used since 1976)
CPI score – 3.1 (2009)
Literacy rate – 90.8 per cent (2007 est)
Gross enrolment ratio (percentage of relevant age group) – primary 105 per cent (2007 est)
Health expenditure (per capita) – US$68 (2007)
Hospital beds (per 1,000 people) – 3.1 (2003–8)

CLIMATE AND TERRAIN

Sri Lanka (formerly Ceylon) is an island in the Indian Ocean, separated from India by the narrow Palk Strait. The land is low-lying in the north and along the coasts, rising to a central massif with hills and mountains in the south and centre. Forests, jungle and scrub cover the greater part of the island. In areas over 600m above sea level, grasslands *(patanas* or *talawas)* are found. Elevation extremes range from 2,524m (Pidurutalagala) at the highest point to 0m (Indian Ocean) at the lowest. The climate is tropical with little seasonal variation in conditions and humidity, which often reaches around 90 per cent. The island experiences the south-west monsoon from May to September and the north-east monsoon from October to January.

HISTORY AND POLITICS

Modern Sri Lanka is a product of its history of settlement, which began with the arrival of the Sinhalese in the sixth century BC. They settled in the north, but gradually moved southwards under pressure from Tamil invasions from southern India, which began in the third century BC. These Tamils settled in the northern and eastern coastal areas. The Portuguese landed in the early 16th century and established control over most of the island by 1618. These territories were conquered by the Dutch in 1658 and held until 1798, when they were ceded to the British, becoming a British crown colony in 1802. With the annexation of the kingdom of Kandy in 1815, all Ceylon came under British rule. Plantation agriculture flourished, and in the mid-19th century large numbers of predominantly Tamil indentured labourers were brought over from southern India. Ceylon achieved independence on 4 February 1948. In 1972 it became a republic and the country was renamed Sri Lanka ('Resplendent Island'). Politics has been dominated since 1948 by the United National Party (UNP) and the Sri Lanka Freedom Party (SLFP); the latter formed the United People's Freedom Alliance (UPFA) with the People's Liberation Front (JVP) in 2004.

Tension between the Buddhist Sinhalese majority and the Hindu Tamil minority dates from the early 20th century, and intensified after policies discriminating against Tamils were introduced following independence. Separatist movements developed in the 1970s to campaign for an independent Tamil state in the north and east of the island, and in 1983 the Liberation Tigers of Tamil Eelam (LTTE) began a guerrilla war against government forces for control of these areas. Although fighting tended to be confined to the north, especially the Jaffna peninsula, terrorist attacks occurred throughout the island. The LTTE captured territory in the north and along the east coast between the early 1990s and the mid 2000s, holding almost a third of the island by 2005. After the 2002 ceasefire broke down in 2006 amid escalating violence, government forces mounted major offensives, recapturing the eastern province in 2007 and the north between January 2008 and May 2009, when the LTTE forces were finally defeated. The conflict is estimated to have left 70,000 dead and displaced over 1 million people. International concern was expressed over allegations of war crimes by Sri Lankan forces against civilians trapped in the conflict zone in the final stages of the civil war, and the detention of over 250,000 Tamils in government-run camps.

The 2005 presidential election was won by the SLFP leader Mahinda Rajapakse, and he was re-elected in an early election in January 2010. The legislative election in April 2010 was won by the UPFA, with an increased majority.

POLITICAL SYSTEM

The 1978 constitution was amended in 1983 to ban parties advocating separatism and in 1987 to create provincial councils. The executive president is directly elected for a six-year term, which may be renewed. The unicameral parliament has 225 members directly elected by proportional representation for a six-year term. The president appoints the prime minister and cabinet.

Elected councils were set up in the nine provinces in 1987 in an attempt to defuse ethnic tensions.

The Northern and Eastern provinces were merged into one from 1988 to 2006.

HEAD OF STATE
President; Defence; Finance, Mahinda Rajapakse, *elected* 17 November 2005, *re-elected* 26 January 2010

SELECTED GOVERNMENT MEMBERS *as at July 2010*
Prime Minister, Dissanayake Jayaratne
Home Affairs, John Seneviratne
Foreign Affairs, G. L. Peiris

HIGH COMMISSION OF THE DEMOCRATIC SOCIALIST REPUBLIC OF SRI LANKA
13 Hyde Park Gardens, London W2 2LU
T 020-7262 1841 E mail@slhc-london.co.uk
W www.slhclondon.org
High Commissioner, HE Chandra Nihal Jayasinghe, *apptd* 2008

BRITISH HIGH COMMISSION
389 Bauddhaloka Mawatha, Colombo 7
T (+94) (11) 539 0639 E bhctrade@slt.lk
W http://ukinsrilanka.fco.gov.uk
High Commissioner, HE Peter Hayes, *apptd* 2008

BRITISH COUNCIL
PO Box 753, 49 Alfred House Gardens, Colombo 3
T (+94) (1) 1258 1171 W www.britishcouncil.org/srilanka
Director, Gill Westaway

DEFENCE

The army has 62 main battle tanks, 217 armoured personnel carriers and 62 armoured infantry fighting vehicles. The navy has 130 patrol and coastal vessels at 5 bases. The air force has 22 combat aircraft and 13 armed helicopters.
Military expenditure – US$1,570m (2009)
Military personnel – 160,900: army 117,900, navy 15,000, air force 28,000; paramilitary 62,200

ECONOMY AND TRADE

Despite the civil war and the 2004 Indian Ocean tsunami, which destroyed tourist resorts and the fishing industry, the economy saw sustained growth throughout the 2000s. The global downturn affected productivity only slightly, but high government debt and budget deficits obliged the government to seek an IMF loan. Reconstruction in the east and north is expected to stimulate economic growth. The once predominantly agricultural economy has become increasingly industrialised and diversified, with service industries such as tourism now making the greatest contribution to GDP. Remittances from expatriate workers are also economically significant.

Agriculture still accounts for 12.6 per cent of GDP and 33 per cent of employment. The main crops are rice, sugar cane, grains, pulses, oilseed, spices, vegetables, fruit, tea, rubber, coconuts, livestock products and fish. Manufacturing is based on processing the main cash crops of rubber, tea, coconuts, tobacco and other commodities, and production of textiles, clothing, beverages and cement; other industries include oil refining and mining gemstones. Service industries such as telecommunications, banking and insurance, information technology services and tourism are also important; the tourist industry usually caters for over 400,000 visitors a year. The service sector accounts for 57.7 per cent of GDP and industry for 29.7 per cent.

The main trading partners are India, the USA, China, the UK and Singapore. Principal exports are textiles and clothing, tea, spices, diamonds, emeralds, rubies, coconut products, rubber manufactures and fish. The main imports are textile fabrics, mineral products, oil, foodstuffs, machinery and transport equipment.
GNI – US$35,800m; US$1,780 per capita (2008)
Annual average growth of GDP – 3.9 per cent (2009 est)
Inflation rate – 3.3 per cent (2009 est)
Unemployment – 7 per cent (2009 est)
Total external debt – US$19,450m (2009 est)
Imports – US$14,000m (2008)
Exports – US$8,400m (2008)

BALANCE OF PAYMENTS
Trade – US$2,874m deficit (2009)
Current Account – US$3,719m deficit (2008)

Trade with UK	*2008*	*2009*
Imports from UK	£122,210,410	£119,788,834
Exports to UK	£651,886,775	£688,221,062

COMMUNICATIONS

There are 97,300km of roads, of which 78,800km are surfaced. The rail network is government-run and there are 1,449km of track. Colombo is the main port, although China is building a new deep-water container port at Hambantota. The principal airport is Bandaranaike International, to the north of the capital.

Fixed-line telephone services now extend to most of the country, and mobile phone distribution is expanding rapidly. There were 3.4 million fixed lines in use, 11.1 million mobile phone users and 1.2 million internet users in 2008.

MEDIA

Many of the main media outlets are state-owned, including two major television stations, the radio networks operated by the Sri Lanka Broadcasting Corporation and several newspapers. There are also privately owned broadcast media and newspapers. Outlets tend to be divided on ethnic lines, and services are provided in Sinhala, Tamil and English. The private media debate political issues and criticise the government, but often face harassment, intimidation and violence for doing so.

SUDAN

Jumhuriyat as-Sudan – Republic of the Sudan

Area – 2,505,813 sq. km
Capital – Khartoum; population, 5,021,390 (2009 est)
Major cities – Juba, Kassala, Kusti, Nyala, El Obeid, Port Sudan
Currency – Sudanese pound (SDP) of 100 piastres
Population – 41,087,825 rising at 2.14 per cent a year (2009 est); Arab and Nubian peoples populate the north and centre, with Nilotic and black African peoples in the south
Religion – Muslim 70 per cent (predominantly Sunni; in north), traditional indigenous beliefs 25 per cent (est); sizeable Christian minority mostly in south and Khartoum; many animists also follow Christian practices
Language – Arabic, English (both official), Nubian, Ta Bedawie
Population density – 17 per sq. km (2008)
Urban population – 43 per cent (2007 est)
Median age (years) – 19.1 (2009 est)
National anthem – 'Nahnu Jund Allah Jund Al-Watan' ['We Are the Army of God and of Our Land']
National day – 1 January (Independence Day)
Life expectancy (years) – 51.42 (2009 est)
Mortality rate – 12.94 (2009 est)
Birth rate – 33.74 (2009 est)
Infant mortality rate – 82.43 (2009 est)
HIV/AIDS adult prevalence – 1.3 per cent (2007 est)
Death penalty – Retained
CPI score – 1.5 (2009)

CLIMATE AND TERRAIN

Sudan is the largest country in Africa and is predominately desert. The Libyan Desert in the west is separated from the rocky Nubian Desert in the east by the fertile valley of the Nile and its tributaries. There are mountains in the west and the south, and along the Red Sea coast. Elevation extremes range from 3,187m (Kinyeti) at the highest point to 0m (Red Sea) at the lowest. The climate is arid on the desert plains, tropical in the south, and cooler at altitude. There is a rainy season from April to October. Average temperatures in Khartoum range from lows of 15°C in January to highs of 42°C in May.

HISTORY AND POLITICS

Parts of northern Sudan were included in the Egyptian Empire from 1900 BC and the Nubian Empire from the sixth century BC. The country was converted to Coptic Christianity in the sixth century AD, and Islam was introduced in the seventh century by Arab invaders, but did not become widespread until the 15th century. From the eighth century onwards, northern Sudan was conquered and occupied by several Arab and Arab-African powers. The south remained independent. Egypt established its control over the north in the early 19th century. The Mahdi revolt in the 1880s led to a joint Anglo-Egyptian campaign to subdue the country, and it was administered as an Anglo-Egyptian condominium from 1899. On 19 December 1955 the Sudanese legislature declared Sudan an independent sovereign state, and on 1 January 1956 a republic was proclaimed.

Tensions between the dominant Arab Muslim north and the black African Christian and animist south have dominated the post-independence period. The first civil war in the south began in 1955 and lasted until 1972, when the south was given greater autonomy. A second civil war broke out in 1983, largely because of attempts to impose Shari'ah law on the whole country. A peace process began in 2000 and the parties to it – the government, the Sudan People's Liberation Army/Movement (SPLA/M) and the southern National Democratic Alliance – finalised a peace agreement in 2004. Under this, a largely autonomous administration (installed in October 2005) governs in the south, and a referendum on independence for the south was to be held after six years.

The civil wars caused years of political instability in the country as a whole, resulting in several coups, and Sudan spent much of the period between 1958 and 1996 under military or one-party rule. Elections were held in 1996 and 2000 but the 2004 legislative election was postponed because of the peace process. Following the 2004 peace agreement, a new constitution was approved in July 2005, under which the president and vice-president were sworn in, and a power-sharing government took office in September.

The first multiparty presidential and legislative elections for 24 years were held in April 2010. President al-Bashir was re-elected as national president; most opposition candidates withdrew before the poll, alleging electoral malpractice and intimidation. In the legislative election, the president's National Congress Party won an overwhelming majority in the north and an overall majority nationally; some northern opposition parties boycotted the elections, citing vote-rigging and government intimidation. A new government of national unity was appointed in June. A referendum on independence is to be held in the south in early 2011.

INSURGENCIES

In the western region of Darfur, tension between nomadic Arab livestock herders and black African farmers over land and grazing rights led to a rise in intercommunal violence in the 1990s. Between 2002 and 2009 black African rebels protesting at marginalisation were ruthlessly suppressed by government forces, often operating through Arab militia *(Janjaweed)* which carried out mass executions and forcible depopulation. The government resisted international pressure to disarm the militias, and obstructed the deployment of peacekeeping troops and the work of aid agencies inside Darfur. Incursions into neighbouring countries to attack refugees from the conflict there destabilised the region. Two of the main rebel groups signed peace agreements with the government, one in 2006 and the other in 2009. Violence by smaller rebel groups and banditry continue. An estimated 300,000 have died from violence, starvation or disease since 2003, and over four million people have been internally displaced or become refugees in Chad and the Central African Republic. In 2009, the International Criminal Court issued a warrant for the arrest of President al-Bashir for war crimes and crimes against humanity in Darfur.

POLITICAL SYSTEM

Under the 2005 constitution, the executive president is directly elected for a five-year term, renewable only once. The bicameral National Legislature comprises a National Assembly with 450 members, including 112 seats reserved for women, directly elected for a five-year term, and a Council of States with two members from each of the 25 states. The president appoints the cabinet.

The south has a largely autonomous government. The president of the south is also the national first vice-president.

HEAD OF STATE
President, Prime Minister, Field Marshal Omar al-Bashir, *seized power* 1989, *elected* 1996, *re-elected* 2000, *sworn in under new constitution* 9 July 2005, *re-elected* 2010
First Vice-President, Salva Kiir Mayardit
Second Vice-President, Ali Osman Mohammed Taha

SELECTED GOVERNMENT MEMBERS *as at July 2010*
Defence, Lt.-Gen. Abdel-Rahim Hussein
Finance, Ali Mahmoud Abdul-Rasoul
Foreign Affairs, Ali Ahmed Karti
Interior, Ibrahim Mohamed Hamid

EMBASSY OF THE REPUBLIC OF THE SUDAN
3 Cleveland Row, London SW1A 1DD
T 020-7839 8080 E admin@sudanembassy.co.uk
W www.sudan-embassy.co.uk
Ambassador Extraordinary and Plenipotentiary, Omer Mohammed Ahmed Siddig, *apptd* 2006

BRITISH EMBASSY
PO Box 801, Off Sharia Al Baladiya, Khartoum East
T (+249) (1) 8377 7105 E information.khartoum@fco.gov.uk
W http://ukinsudan.fco.gov.uk
Ambassador Extraordinary and Plenipotentiary, HE Nicholas Kay, CMG, *apptd* 2010

BRITISH COUNCIL
PO Box 1253, 14 Abu Sinn Street, Khartoum Central
T (+249) 183 780817 W www.britishcouncil.org/africa
Director, Richard Weyers

DEFENCE

The army has 360 main battle tanks, 419 armoured personnel carriers and 75 armoured infantry fighting vehicles. The navy has 15 patrol and coastal combatant vessels at 3 bases. The air force has 79 combat aircraft and 23 armed helicopters.
Military budget – US$579m (2007 est)
Military personnel – 109,300: army 105,000, navy 1,300, air force 3,000; paramilitary 17,500
Conscription duration – 24 months

ECONOMY AND TRADE

Since 1997 Sudan has worked with the IMF to implement economic reforms which, despite the country's political instability and vulnerability to drought, have stabilised the economy. In 1999 Sudan began exporting oil, and increases in oil and agricultural production, light industry and exports have resulted in steady growth in GDP in recent years. However, development started from a low base and about 40 per cent of the population lives below the poverty line.

Agriculture, much at subsistence level, provides employment for around 80 per cent of the workforce and contributes 32.1 per cent of GDP. Mechanised and traditional agriculture is practised in areas with sufficient rainfall and irrigation. The principal crops include cotton, groundnuts, sorghum, millet, wheat, gum arabic, sugar cane, tropical fruits and livestock. Industry consists of oil extraction and refining, cotton ginning, manufacture of textiles, cement, edible oils, sugar, soap, shoes, pharmaceuticals, armaments and vehicle assembly. Industry contributes 29.4 per cent of GDP and services 38.5 per cent.

The main trading partners are China, Japan and India. Principal exports are oil and petroleum products, cotton, sesame, livestock, groundnuts, gum arabic and sugar. The main imports are foodstuffs, manufactured goods, refinery and transport equipment, medicines, chemicals, textiles and wheat.
GNI – US$45,700m; US$1,100 per capita (2008)
Annual average growth of GDP – 3.8 per cent (2009 est)
Inflation rate – 12.3 per cent (2009 est)
Population below poverty line – 40 per cent (2004 est)
Unemployment – 18.7 per cent (2002 est)
Total external debt – US$36,270m (2009 est)
Imports – US$9,200m (2008)
Exports – US$12,500m (2008)

BALANCE OF PAYMENTS
Trade – US$4,216m surplus (2009)
Current Account – US$5,229m deficit (2008)

Trade with UK	*2008*	*2009*
Imports from UK	£142,372,592	£122,925,450
Exports to UK	£5,336,558	£17,821,590

COMMUNICATIONS

Large areas of the country lack basic infrastructure, which has been a focus of development since the late 1990s. The railway network is about 5,980km in length. There are 11,900km of roads, of which 4,320km are surfaced, and there are over 4,000km of navigable waterways, including 1,700km on the White and Blue Nile rivers. Port Sudan, on the Red Sea, is the main seaport. The principal airports are at Khartoum and Juba, and there are over 100 other airports and airfields. Sudan Airways provides domestic and international flights.

The fixed-line telephone system is being upgraded; mobile phone services are growing rapidly. In 2008 there were 356,000 fixed lines in use, 11.2 million mobile phone subscribers and 4.2 million internet users.

EDUCATION AND HEALTH

Education is free of charge for most children, and compulsory for eight years; six years of primary education is followed by at least two years of secondary education. There are three types of secondary school: general, academic and vocational. The primary language of instruction is Arabic.
Literacy rate – 60.9 per cent (2007 est)
Gross enrolment ratio (percentage of relevant age group) – primary 74 per cent; secondary 38 per cent (2009 est)
Health expenditure (per capita) – US$40 (2007 est)
Hospital beds (per 1,000 people) – 0.7 (2003–8)

MEDIA

Radio and television are controlled by the government, and news reports are scrutinised by a military censor. There are no wholly privately owned television stations. It is possible to access foreign broadcasts via satellite television and international radio stations. There are several privately owned newspapers but their freedom of expression is limited. A number of broadcasters and newspapers operate in the country's south, some with foreign funding.

SURINAME

Republiek Suriname – Republic of Suriname

Area – 163,820 sq. km
Capital – Paramaribo; population, 259,343 (2009 est)
Major towns – Lelydorp, Nieuw Nickerie
Currency – Suriname dollar of 100 cents
Population – 481,267 rising at 1.1 per cent a year (2009 est); Hindustani (37 per cent), Creole (31 per cent), Javanese (15 per cent), Maroons (10 per cent), Amerindian (2 per cent), Chinese (2 per cent), white (1 per cent) (est)
Religion – Christian 41 per cent, Hindu 20 per cent, Muslim 14 per cent (predominantly Sunni), indigenous religions 3 per cent (est)
Language – Dutch (official), English, Surinamese (Sranang Tongo), Caribbean Hindustani (a dialect of Hindi), Javanese
Population density – 3 per sq. km (2008)
Urban population – 75 per cent (2007 est)
Median age (years) – 27.9 (2009 est)
National anthem – 'God zij met ons Suriname' ['God Be With Our Suriname']
National day – 25 November (Independence Day)
Life expectancy (years) – 73.73 (2009 est)
Mortality rate – 5.51 (2009 est)
Birth rate – 16.8 (2009 est)
Infant mortality rate – 18.81 (2009 est)
HIV/AIDS adult prevalence – 2.1 per cent (2007 est)
Death penalty – Retained (not used since 1982)
CPI score – 3.7 (2009)
Literacy rate – 90.4 per cent (2007 est)

CLIMATE AND TERRAIN

The narrow, swampy coastal plain is home to about 90 per cent of the population. From the coastal belt, the land rises to a hilly interior covered by tropical rainforest and savannah; the rainforest contains a great diversity of flora and fauna. Elevation extremes range from 1,230m (Juliana Top) at the highest point to −2m (coastal plain) at the lowest. The land is drained by several rivers, some of which have been dammed to create large artificial lakes used to generate hydro-electric power. The climate is tropical, moderated by the north-east trade winds. There are two wet seasons, from April to August and November to February.

HISTORY AND POLITICS

Although visited and claimed by Spanish explorers in 1593, early European settlements all failed. A British colony was founded in 1651 but this was ceded to the Dutch in 1667. Dutch rule was interrupted by British occupation during the French Revolutionary and Napoleonic wars, but was restored in 1816. The colony, known as Dutch Guiana, became autonomous in 1954, and achieved independence on 25 November 1975 as Suriname. At independence, about 40 per cent of the population emigrated to the Netherlands.

The early years of independence were politically unstable, with a period of military rule under Desi Bouterse following a coup in 1980. Democratic, civilian rule was restored with elections in 1987, but the military overthrew the government in 1990 in a coup engineered by Bouterse. Democratic elections in 1991 were won by the New Front for Democracy and Development alliance, led by Ronald Venetiaan, who became president. President Venetiaan introduced an unpopular austerity programme, which improved the economy but lost him the 1996 election.

Ronald Venetiaan was elected president again in 2000, and again introduced an austerity programme to tackle dire economic conditions; he was re-elected in 2005. After the legislative election in May 2010, the Mega Combination bloc, dominated by Desi Bouterse's National Democratic Party, held the most seats in the legislature, and agreed with the A Combination bloc to form a coalition government. In July 2010 Desi Bouterse was elected president by parliament.

POLITICAL SYSTEM

Under the 1987 constitution, the executive president is elected for a five-year term by a two-thirds majority in the legislature or, if the required majority cannot be achieved, by a specially convened United Peoples' Assembly including district and local council representatives. The vice-president is elected in the same way. The unicameral National Assembly has 51 members directly elected for a five-year term. The council of ministers is appointed by the president and chaired by the vice-president.

HEAD OF STATE

President, Desi Bouterse, *elected* 19 July 2010, *sworn in* 12 August 2010
Vice-President, Ram Sardjoe

SELECTED GOVERNMENT MEMBERS *as at July 2010*

Defence, Ivan Fernald
Finance, Humphrey Hildenberg
Foreign Affairs, Lygia Kraag-Keteldijk
Internal Affairs, Maurits Hassankhan

EMBASSY OF THE REPUBLIC OF SURINAME

Alexander Gogelweg 2, 2517 JH The Hague, The Netherlands
T (+31) (70) 365 0844 E ambassade.suriname@wxs.nl
Ambassador Extraordinary and Plenipotentiary, HE Urmila Joella-Sewnundun, *apptd* 2008

BRITISH AMBASSADOR

HE Fraser Wheeler, *apptd* 2006, resident at Georgetown, Guyana

DEFENCE

The army has 15 armoured personnel carriers. The navy has 8 patrol and coastal combatant vessels at a base in Paramaribo. The air force has 4 combat capable aircraft.
Military budget – US$39m (2009)
Military personnel – 1,840: army 1,400, navy 240, air force 200

ECONOMY AND TRADE

Former president Venetiaan introduced policies that contained rampant inflation and other economic problems, and produced steady growth for a few years before the global downturn, which caused the economy to contract owing to reduced global prices for key commodities. The mainstays of the economy are mining, especially bauxite and gold, and oil and alumina production; these account for 85 per cent of exports and 25 per cent of government revenue, making the economy vulnerable to global price fluctuations. Bauxite reserves are declining, but oil production is increasing from existing offshore fields and onshore exploration has begun. Agriculture employs only 8 per cent of the population but produces 10.8 per cent of GDP. Industries other than mining and oil production are forestry, food processing and fishing. Industry accounts for 24.4 per cent of GDP and services for 64.8 per cent.

The main trading partners are the USA, Canada, the Netherlands, Trinidad and Tobago, Belgium and Norway. Principal exports are alumina, gold, crude oil, timber, fish and shrimp, rice and bananas. The main imports are capital equipment, petroleum, foodstuffs, cotton and consumer goods.

GNI – US$2,454m; US$4,760 per capita (2008)
Annual average growth of GDP – –2.2 per cent (2009 est)
Inflation rate – 6.4 per cent (2007 est)
Unemployment – 9.5 per cent (2004 est)
Total external debt – US$504.3m (2005 est)
Imports – US$1,400m (2008)
Exports – US$1,700m (2008)

BALANCE OF PAYMENTS
Trade – US$497m surplus (2009)
Current Account – US$121m surplus (2008)

Trade with UK	*2008*	*2009*
Imports from UK	£7,969,352	£11,224,629
Exports to UK	£462,356	£2,979,890

COMMUNICATIONS

There are 4,300km of roads in total, of which approximately one-quarter is surfaced. There are no railways. The 1,200km of waterways provide the most effective means of travel in the interior. The main seaport is Paramaribo. There are 50 airports and airfields; the principal airport is at Paramaribo.

The telephone system is good and mobile phone services have expanded rapidly. Combined fixed-line and mobile density is now over 100 per 100 people.

MEDIA

State-owned broadcast media offer a range of views, and operate alongside commercial radio and television stations. The two daily newspapers, *De West* and *De Ware Tijd*, are privately owned. The government upholds freedom of expression.

SWAZILAND

Umbuso weSwatini – Kingdom of Swaziland

Area – 17,364 sq. km
Capital – Mbabane; population, 73,815 (2009 est). Lobamba is the legislative capital
Major town – Manzini
Currency – Lilangeni (E; plural *Emalangeni*) of 100 cents; South African currency is also in circulation. Swaziland is a member of the Common Monetary Area and the Lilangeni has a par value with the South African rand
Population – 1,123,913 falling at 0.02 per cent a year (2009 est)
Religion – Christian (Protestant denominations 45 per cent, Zionist 37 per cent, Roman Catholic 5 per cent)
Language – English, siSwati (both official)
Population density – 68 per sq. km (2008)
Urban population – 25 per cent (2007 est)
Median age (years) – 18.8 (2009 est)
National anthem – 'Nkulunkulu Mnikati wetibuiso temaSwati' ['Oh God, Bestower of Blessings on the Swazi']
National day – 6 September (Independence Day)
Life expectancy (years) – 31.99 (2009 est)
Mortality rate – 30.83 (2009 est)
Birth rate – 26.25 (2009 est)
Infant mortality rate – 68.63 (2009 est)
HIV/AIDS adult prevalence – 24.3 per cent (2007 est)
Death penalty – Retained (not used since 1983)
CPI score – 3.6 (2009)
Literacy rate – 79.6 per cent (2007 est)
Gross enrolment ratio (percentage of relevant age group) – primary 108 per cent; secondary 53 per cent; tertiary 4 per cent (2008 est)
Health expenditure (per capita) – US$151 (2007)
Hospital beds (per 1,000 people) – 2.1 (2003–8)

CLIMATE AND TERRAIN

The main regions of the landlocked country are: the densely forested and mountainous Highveld along the western border, with an average altitude of 1,219m; the Middleveld, a mixed farming area which averages about 609m in altitude, and the Lowveld, which was mainly scrubland until the introduction of sugar cane plantations, in the centre; and the Lubombo ridge, along the eastern edge of the Lowveld. Elevation extremes range from 1,862m (Emlembe) at the highest point to 21m (Great Usutu river) at the lowest. Four rivers, the Komati, Usutu, Mbuluzi and Ngwavuma, flow from west to east.

The climate varies; the Highveld is humid and temperate, the Middleveld and Lubombo are subtropical, and the Lowveld is tropical and semi-arid. Average temperatures in Mbabane, in the Highveld, range from lows of 6°C in June to highs of 25°C in January and December.

HISTORY AND POLITICS

The Swazi people are believed to have arrived in the area in the 16th century, and by the mid-17th century had developed a strong kingdom thrice the size of the present country. This became a protectorate of the Boer republic of the Transvaal in 1884, and subsequently of Britain. The Kingdom of Swaziland became independent on 6 September 1968.

In 1973 King Sobhuza II suspended the constitution, banned political parties and assumed absolute power. The parliamentary system was replaced by traditional tribal communities *(tinkhundla)*. Sobhuza II died in 1982, and was succeeded by a son who was a minor. The regency between 1982 and 1986 led to power struggles within the royal family, but the real power passed to the Dlamini clan, which continues to dominate the government.

Demands for democratisation of the constitution have grown over the past 20 years, with the campaigning of political movements and trade unions supported by popular demonstrations, general strikes and blockades of the border with South Africa.

Swaziland has the highest levels of HIV/AIDS infection in the world, and as a consequence faces severe demographic, economic and social problems.

POLITICAL SYSTEM

The 2005 constitution retains the executive powers of the king; it appears to permit political parties while maintaining the ban on their members standing for election. The head of state is a hereditary king who is effectively an absolute monarch. There is a bicameral parliament comprising a 30-member senate and a 65-member House of Assembly; members of both serve a five-year term. Each of the country's 55 administrative districts *(tinkhundla)* directly elects one member to the House of Assembly and the king appoints ten members; the new constitution increases these to 60 elected and 15 appointed members. The members of the House of Assembly elect ten of their own number to the senate and a further 20 senators are appointed by the king.

HEAD OF STATE

HM The King of Swaziland, King Mswati III, *crowned* 25 April 1986

SELECTED GOVERNMENT MEMBERS *as at July 2010*

Prime Minister, Barnabas Sibusiso Dlamini
Deputy Prime Minister, Themba Masuku
Finance, Majozi Sithole
Foreign Affairs, Lutfo Dlamini
Home Affairs, Chief Mgwagwa Gamedze

KINGDOM OF SWAZILAND HIGH COMMISSION

20 Buckingham Gate, London SW1E 6LB
T 020-7630 6611 E enquiries@swaziland.org.uk
High Commissioner (acting), Henry Zeeman

BRITISH HIGH COMMISSIONER

HE Dr Nicola Brewer, *apptd 2009,* resident at Pretoria (Tshwane), South Africa

ECONOMY AND TRADE

The country is very poor, with about 69 per cent of the population living below the poverty line. Customs dues from the South African Customs Union and remittances from expatriates working in South Africa are a vital supplement to the domestic economy; customs revenue dropped sharply in the global downturn and the government applied for international financial assistance.

Subsistence agriculture occupies about 70 per cent of the population and contributes 8.4 per cent of GDP. Sugar cane, cotton, citrus fruits and pineapples are the main cash crops and the basis of industries producing sugar, canned fruit and soft drink concentrates. Coal mining has become less important since the 1980s with diversification into manufacturing such products as textiles, clothing, wood pulp and refrigerators. However, a shift in global trading concessions devastated the clothing industry in 2005, leaving thousands unemployed, and has affected the sugar industry, although this has adapted. Industry contributes 42.4 per cent of GDP and services 49.2 per cent.

South Africa accounts for about 60 per cent of exports and over 90 per cent of imports. Principal exports are the products of agriculture and manufacturing. The main imports are vehicles, machinery, transport equipment, foodstuffs, petroleum products and chemicals.

GNI – US$3,000m; US$2,600 per capita (2008)
Annual average growth of GDP – –0.4 per cent (2009 est)
Inflation rate – 8.5 per cent (2009 est)
Population below poverty line – 69 per cent (2006)
Unemployment – 40 per cent (2006 est)
Total external debt – US$534m (2009 est)
Imports – US$2,200m (2008)
Exports – US$1,800m (2008)

BALANCE OF PAYMENTS

Trade – US$475m deficit (2009)
Current Account – US$187m deficit (2009)

Trade with UK	*2008*	*2009*
Imports from UK	£4,755,538	£6,082,510
Exports to UK	£40,993,739	£15,049,505

COMMUNICATIONS

The railway network is 301km long and connects with the Mozambique port of Maputo and the South African railway to Richards Bay and Durban. There are 3,594km of roads, of which 1,078km are surfaced. There is an international airport at Manzini, which is expected to be replaced by the new Sikhuphe International Airport by early 2011. Swaziland Airlink, in association with South African Airlink, provides scheduled air services to southern and eastern Africa.

Although modern, the fixed-line telephone system is not extensive and mobile phone services have grown rapidly. There were 44,000 fixed lines in use, 457,000 mobile phone subscribers and 48,200 internet users in 2008.

MEDIA

The media is under tight government control. State-run broadcasters provide the only television and radio channels, apart from an American evangelical Christian radio station which uses local transmitters to transmit regionally. One daily newspaper supports the government, the other carries little political content.

SWEDEN

Konungariket Sverige – Kingdom of Sweden

Area – 450,295 sq. km
Capital – Stockholm; population, 1,278,820 (2009 est)
Major cities – Gothenburg, Malmo, Uppsala
Currency – Swedish krona of 100 ore
Population – 9,059,651 rising at 0.16 per cent a year (2009 est)
Religion – Christian (Lutheran 73 per cent, other Protestant denominations 4 per cent), Muslim 5 per cent (est)
Language – Swedish (official), Finnish, Sami dialects, Meankieli, Romani, Yiddish (all official national minority languages)
Population density – 22 per sq. km (2008)
Urban population – 84 per cent (2007 est)
Median age (years) – 41.5 (2009 est)
National anthem – 'Du Gamla, Du Fria' ['Thou Ancient, Thou Freeborn']
National day – 6 June (Flag Day)
Life expectancy (years) – 80.86 (2009 est)
Mortality rate – 10.21 (2009 est)
Birth rate – 10.13 (2009 est)
Infant mortality rate – 2.75 (2009 est)
Death penalty – Abolished for all crimes (since 1972)
CPI score – 9.2 (2009)

CLIMATE AND TERRAIN

The terrain is mostly flat or rolling lowlands in the south and along the east coast, with mountains in the west. Elevation extremes range from 2,111m (Kebnekaise) at the highest point to −2.4m (reclaimed bay of Lake Hammarsjon) at the lowest. There are many lakes, including Vanern, Vattern, Malaren and Hjalmaren in the south, and over 20,000 islands off the coast near Stockholm. The climate is temperate in the south and subarctic in the north; average temperatures in Stockholm range from lows of −5°C in January to highs of 22°C in July.

HISTORY AND POLITICS

Sweden takes its name from the Svear people who were the dominant population in the east from *c.*500 AD, while the Goths inhabited the west. A kingdom had emerged from a gradual union of the two peoples by *c.*1000, although the south and west remained under Danish rule until the 17th century. During the Viking expansion (*c.*700–1000), the Swedes colonised the eastern Baltic, Finland and Russia; Finland was incorporated into the kingdom in the 12th century. The Union of Kalmar (1397) brought Sweden and Norway under Danish rule. Sweden regained its independence following a rebellion by noblemen in 1523 which resulted in the election of Gustav I to the Swedish throne.

Sweden's power reached its zenith in the 17th century under Gustav II. The Danes were driven out of southern Sweden, the Baltic coast of Russia was seized and the Swedish army pushed into Germany after vanquishing the Catholic League. Swedish power waned with its defeat in the Great Northern War (1700–21). Finland was lost to Russia in 1809; Norway was ceded to Sweden by the congress of Vienna (1814–15) but gained its independence in 1905.

Sweden remained neutral during both world wars. Post-war politics has been dominated by Social Democrat-led coalitions which established a mixed economy and a generous welfare state between 1946 and 1969. Right-wing and centrist parties have held power in 1976–82, 1991–4 and since 2006. Sweden joined the EU in 1995, but the government decided against membership of the eurozone in 1997, a decision confirmed in a 2003 national referendum.

After the 2006 general election, the Social Democrats remained the largest party in the legislature but a larger number of seats was won by a coalition led by the Moderate Party. A four-party Alliance for Sweden coalition government comprising the Moderate Party, Centre Party, Liberal Party and Christian Democrat Party took office in October 2006. A legislative election was scheduled for 18 September 2010.

POLITICAL SYSTEM

Sweden is a hereditary constitutional monarchy. The 1975 constitution was amended in 1979 to vest the succession in the monarch's eldest child irrespective of sex. The unicameral legislature, the *Riksdag*, has 349 members directly elected by proportional representation for a four-year term. The prime minister appoints the council of ministers.

Sweden is divided into 21 counties *(lan)* and 290 municipalities *(kommun)*.

HEAD OF STATE

HM The King of Sweden, King Carl XVI Gustaf, KG, *born* 30 April 1946, *succeeded* 15 September 1973
Heir, HRH Crown Princess Victoria Ingrid Alice Desiree, Duchess of Vastergotland, *born* 14 July 1977

SELECTED GOVERNMENT MEMBERS *as at July 2010*

Prime Minister, Fredrik Reinfeldt
Deputy Prime Minister, Maud Olofsson
Defence, Sten Tolgfors
Finance, Anders Borg
Foreign Affairs, Carl Bildt

EMBASSY OF SWEDEN

11 Montagu Place, London W1H 2AL
T 020-7917 6400 E ambassaden.london@foreign.ministry.se
W www.swedenabroad.com/london
Ambassador Extraordinary and Plenipotentiary, HE Nicola Clase, *apptd* 2010

BRITISH EMBASSY

PO Box 27819, Skarpogatan 6–8, 115 93 Stockholm
T (+46) (8) 671 3000 E info@britishembassy.se
W http://ukinsweden.fco.gov.uk
Ambassador Extraordinary and Plenipotentiary, HE Andrew Mitchell, *apptd* 2006

BRITISH COUNCIL
c/o British Embassy
T (+46) (8) 671 3110 W www.britishcouncil.org/sweden
Country Manager, Roger Budd

DEFENCE

The army has 280 main battle tanks, 687 armoured personnel carriers and 336 armoured infantry fighting vehicles. The navy has 4 submarines, 5 corvettes and 14 patrol and coastal vessels at 3 bases. The air force has 165 combat aircraft.

Sweden has a policy of non-alignment in peace and neutrality in war, and has declined to become a member of NATO.

Military budget – US$5,610m (2009)
Military personnel – 13,050: army 5,900, navy 2,850, air force 4,300; paramilitary 800; voluntary auxiliary organisations 42,000
Conscription duration – 10–11 months

ECONOMY AND TRADE

Sweden developed from an agricultural to an industrial economy in the early 20th century. The prosperity that had funded the generous welfare state after 1946 ended in the early 1990s, when Sweden experienced a deep recession. It recovered to experience strong growth until 2008 before again entering recession as a result of the global downturn. Government intervention was needed to stabilise the banking sector in early 2009.

The main, export-orientated industries are engineering and high-tech manufacturing, mining and forestry. Forests cover over half the total land area and sustain the timber, finished wood products, pulp and paper milling industries. Mineral resources include iron ore, lead, zinc, sulphur, granite, marble, precious and heavy metals (the latter not exploited) and extensive deposits of low-grade uranium ore. The engineering sector provides 50 per cent of output and exports, particularly specialised machinery and systems, motor vehicles, aircraft, electrical and electronic equipment, armaments, pharmaceuticals, plastics and chemical industries.

Sweden has no significant resources of hydrocarbon fuels and relies upon imported gas and coal for 50 per cent of its energy needs and hydroelectricity for about 15 per cent. In 2009 the government reversed its previous policy of phasing out nuclear power. Less than 10 per cent of the land area is farmland and only 1.1 per cent of the labour force is employed in farming. Agriculture contributes 1.6 per cent of GDP, industry 26.7 per cent and services 71.6 per cent.

The main trading partners are other EU states, Norway and the USA. Principal exports include machinery, vehicles, paper products, pulp and wood, iron and steel products, and chemicals. The main imports are machinery, oil and petroleum products, chemicals, vehicles, iron and steel, foodstuffs and clothing.

GNI – US$469,400m; US$50,910 per capita (2008)
Annual average growth of GDP – –4.6 per cent (2009 est)
Inflation rate – –0.5 per cent (2009 est)
Unemployment – 9.3 per cent (2009 est)
Total external debt – US$669,100m (2009 est)
Imports – US$165,100m (2008)
Exports – US$183,100m (2008)

BALANCE OF PAYMENTS
Trade – US$11,889m surplus (2009)
Current Account – US$37,279m surplus (2008)

Trade with UK	*2008*	*2009*
Imports from UK	£5,080,059,997	£4,106,945,098
Exports to UK	£6,698,405,028	£5,359,370,008

COMMUNICATIONS

The railway network is 11,600km in length. There are 425,300km of roads, of which 139,300km are surfaced (including 1,700km of motorways). There are also 2,052km of waterways, navigable for small steamers and barges. The main ports are Gothenburg, Helsingborg, Malmo and Stockholm. The principal airports are at Stockholm, Gothenburg, Lulea, Malmo and Umea. Scandinavian Airlines provides international and domestic flights, and domestic flights are also provided by Malmo Aviation. The Oresund Bridge connects Sweden to Denmark.

The modern telecommunications systems provided services to 5.3 million fixed-line subscribers, 11 million mobile phone subscribers and 8.1 million internet users in 2008.

EDUCATION AND HEALTH

The state education system provides nine years of free and compulsory schooling from the age of seven to 16 in the comprehensive elementary schools. A majority of pupils continue into further education of three years' duration in the upper secondary schools, and a unified higher education system administered in six regional areas containing one of the universities: Uppsala (founded 1477); Lund (1668); Stockholm (1878); Gothenburg (1887); Umea (1963) and Linkoping (1967).

Gross enrolment ratio (percentage of relevant age group) – primary 94 per cent; secondary 103 per cent; tertiary 75 per cent (2008 est)
Health expenditure (per capita) – US$4,495 (2007)
Hospital beds (per 1,000 people) – 3.6 (2000–6)

MEDIA

Public television is run by Sveriges Television (SVT). There are a number of commercial stations and around two-thirds of households have cable or satellite television. The switch from analogue to digital services was completed in 2007. Commercial radio began in 1993, and some of the main stations now have near-national networks, in competition with public broadcaster Sveriges Radio. The country is among the world's top consumers of newspapers and the government provides subsidies to newspapers regardless of their political affiliation. There are four Stockholm-based daily newspapers, one based in Gothenburg and one in Malmo.

CULTURE

Several Swedish writers have become globally successful, among them crime-fiction writers Henning Mankel (*b.* 1948) and Stieg Larsson (1954–2004), and Astrid Lindgren (1907–2002), the creator of *Pippi Longstocking*. A number of Swedes have received Academy awards, including directors Ingmar Bergman (1918–2007), and Lasse Hallstrom (*b.* 1946) and actors Greta Garbo (1905–90) and Ingrid Bergman (1915–82). ABBA is the country's best-known musical export and has sold over 370 million albums; founders Bjorn Ulvaeus and Benny Andersson also had international hits with the stage musicals *Mamma Mia!* and *Chess*. In science, astronomer Anders Celsius (1701–44) devised the eponymous temperature scale, and the chemist and industrialist Alfred Nobel (1833–96) invented dynamite and founded the Nobel prizes.

SWITZERLAND

Schweizerische Eidgenossenschaft/Confédération suisse/ Confederazione Svizzera/Confederaziun svizra – Swiss Confederation

Area – 41,277 sq. km
Capital – Bern; population, 345,720 (2009 est)
Major cities – Basel, Geneva, Lausanne, Zurich
Currency – Swiss franc of 100 rappen (or centimes)
Population – 7,604,467 rising at 0.28 per cent a year (2009 est); German (65 per cent), French (18 per cent), Italian (10 per cent), Romansch (1 per cent) (est)
Religion – Christian (Roman Catholic 42 per cent, Protestant denominations 35 per cent, Orthodox 2 per cent), Muslim 4 per cent (majority Sunni) (est)
Language – German, French, Italian, Romansch (all official), Serbo-Croatian, Albanian, Portuguese, Spanish, English
Population density – 191 per sq. km (2008)
Urban population – 73 per cent (2007 est)
Median age (years) – 41 (2009 est)
National anthem – 'Schweizerpsalm'/'Cantique suisse'/'Salmo svizzero'/Psalm svizzer' ['Swiss Psalm']
National day – 1 August (Confederation Day)
Life expectancy (years) – 80.85 (2009 est)
Mortality rate – 8.59 (2009 est)
Birth rate – 9.59 (2009 est)
Infant mortality rate – 4.18 (2009 est)
Death penalty – Abolished for all crimes (since 1992)
CPI score – 9 (2009)

CLIMATE AND TERRAIN

Landlocked Switzerland is the most mountainous country in Europe. The central plateau of rolling hills, plains and over 1,500 lakes is enclosed by mountains. The Jura mountains lie in the north-west and the Alps, which cover two-thirds of the country, occupy the south and east. Elevation extremes range from 4,634m (Dufourspitze, Alps) at the highest point to 195m (Lake Maggiore) at the lowest. Lakes Neuchâtel, Lucerne and Zurich lie wholly within the country, but Lake Maggiore is shared with Italy, Lake Geneva with France and Lake Constance with Germany and Austria. The Rhine, Rhône and Inn rivers all rise in the Alps. The climate is temperate, with conditions that vary with altitude. Average temperatures in Zurich range from lows of −3°C in January to highs of 25°C in July.

HISTORY AND POLITICS

The area was conquered by the Romans in 58 BC and then overrun by Germanic tribes in the fourth century AD. It was a province of the medieval Holy Roman Empire from 1033. The Swiss confederation began in 1291 as a defensive alliance of three cantons to protect their autonomy, and expanded during the following centuries, becoming independent of the Habsburgs in the 14th century. Its independence was recognised by the Treaty of Westphalia in 1648. French revolutionary forces captured Switzerland in 1789 and named it the Helvetic Republic. Independence was restored in 1814, and the congress of Vienna (1815) joined Geneva, Neuchatel and Valais to the confederation and recognised the country's perpetual neutrality in international affairs. A new constitution was adopted in 1848 which replaced the loose confederation of cantons with a federal state and enhanced the powers of the central government.

Many policy decisions are submitted to national referendums. Although the federal government has pursued a policy of gradual integration with the EU and applied for membership in 1992, referendums have rejected membership of the European Economic Area (1992), approved bilateral trade agreements with the EU (2000), and rejected EU membership (2001).

Proportional representation, introduced in 1919, resulted in coalition governments throughout the 20th and into the 21st century. Apart from a 12-month period in 2007–8, since 1959 the federal government has been a coalition of four parties: the Swiss People's Party (SVP), the Social Democratic Party, the Christian Democratic People's Party and the Radical Democratic Party. Following the October 2007 legislative election, the SVP remained the largest party in the legislature, increasing its number of seats to 62, although it withdrew from the coalition government for a year from December 2007 after one of its ministers was voted out of office.

POLITICAL SYSTEM

Under the 1998 constitution, the head of state is a president elected annually (along with the vice-president) for a one-year term, which cannot be consecutive, by the federal legislature from the members of the Federal Council. The bicameral legislature, the Federal Assembly, has two chambers: the National Council has 200 members, directly elected for a four-year term; the Council of States has 46 members (two from each canton and one from each half-canton) directly elected within each canton for a four-year term.

Executive power is in the hands of a Federal Council of seven members, elected for a four-year term by the Federal Assembly after every legislative election. The Federal Council is chaired by the president. Not more than one person from the same canton may be elected a member of the Council; however, there is a tradition that Italian- and French-speaking areas should between them be represented on the council by at least two members.

Any citizen able to obtain 100,000 voters' signatures in support of holding a referendum on a given issue can initiate a national referendum.

SELECTED GOVERNMENT MEMBERS *as at July 2010*
President of the Swiss Confederation, Doris Leuthard
Vice-President, Moritz Leuenberger
Defence, Ueli Maurer
Finance, Hans-Rudolf Merz
Foreign Affairs, Micheline Calmy-Rey
Interior, Didier Burkhalter

EMBASSY OF SWITZERLAND
16–18 Montagu Place, London W1H 2BQ
T 020-7616 6000 **E** lon.vertretung@eda.admin.ch
W www.eda.admin.ch/london

Ambassador Extraordinary and Plenipotentiary, HE Alexis Lautenberg, *apptd* 2004

BRITISH EMBASSY
Thunstrasse 50, 3005 Bern
T (+41) (31) 359 7700 E info@britishembassy.ch
W http://ukinswitzerland.fco.gov.uk
Ambassador Extraordinary and Plenipotentiary, HE Sarah Gillett, CMG, MVO, *apptd* 2009

BRITISH COUNCIL
PO Box 532, Sennweg 2, 3000 Bern 9
T (+41) (31) 301 1473 W www.britishcouncil.org/switzerland
Director, Caroline Morrissey, MBE

CONFEDERAL STRUCTURE
There are 23 cantons, three of which are subdivided, making 20 cantons and six half-cantons, or 26 in all. Each canton and half-canton has its own government and a substantial degree of autonomy. The main language in 19 of the cantons is German; in the others it is French (*) or Italian (†).

The confederation consists of: Aargau, Appenzell-Ausserrhoden, Appenzell-Innerrhoden, Basel-Country, Basel-Town, Bern, *Fribourg, *Geneva, Glarus, Graubünden/Grischun, *Jura, Lucerne, *Neuchatel, Nidwalden, Obwalden, St Gallen, Schaffhausen, Schwyz, Solothurn, Thurgau, †Ticino, Uri, *Valais, *Vaud, Zug and Zurich.

DEFENCE
The army has 353 main battle tanks, 407 armoured personnel carriers and 154 armoured infantry fighting vehicles. The air force has 87 combat aircraft.
Military budget – US$4,420m (2009)
Military personnel – 22,059: joint 4,059; 18,000 conscript
Conscription duration – 18 weeks, then 3-week refresher courses

ECONOMY AND TRADE
Switzerland has a prosperous and stable market economy with low unemployment and a highly skilled labour force. Although it has rejected EU membership, it has brought many of its practices into line with EU members to maintain its competitiveness. Its prosperity is based on banking, financial services and export-orientated industrial manufacturing. However, the banks were badly affected by the 2008 global financial crisis, requiring government support for part of the sector, and export demand slowed, causing a recession in 2009.

Agriculture is practised in the mountain valleys and the central plateau, where grains, fruits and vegetables are grown. Dairy farming and stock-raising are also important. Expertise in precision, electrical and mechanical engineering underpins many of the chief manufacturing industries, which produce machinery, chemicals and pharmaceuticals, watches, textiles, precision instruments, wood products and foodstuffs. Banking, insurance and tourism are the major service industries. Agriculture contributes 1.3 per cent of GDP, industry 27.6 per cent and services 71 per cent.

The main trading partners are EU countries (especially Germany) and the USA. Principal exports are machinery, chemicals, metals, watches and agricultural products. The main imports are machinery, chemicals, vehicles, metals, agricultural products and textiles.

GNI – US$424,500m; US$55,510 per capita (2008)
Annual average growth of GDP – –1.8 per cent (2009 est)
Inflation rate – –0.6 per cent (2009 est)
Unemployment – 3.7 per cent (2009 est)
Total external debt – US$1,339,000m (2009 est)
Imports – US$173,300m (2008)
Exports – US$191,400m (2008)

BALANCE OF PAYMENTS
Trade – US$20,029m surplus (2009)
Current Account – US$11,947m surplus (2008)

Trade with UK	*2008*	*2009*
Imports from UK	£4,607,170,218	£5,057,072,305
Exports to UK	£5,954,948,667	£10,268,943,761

COMMUNICATIONS
There are 71,400km of roads, including 1,793km of motorways. Railway track totals 4,900km, almost all of which is electrified. Transnational Alpine routes are served by all-weather road and rail tunnels. The Rhine carries heavy shipping traffic on the 65km stretch from Basel-Rheinfelden and Schaffhausen-Bodensee, and there are 12 navigable lakes. The principal airports are at Zurich, Basel, Bern and Geneva.

Modern telecommunications systems provided services to 4.8 million fixed-line subscribers, 8.8 million mobile phone subscribers and 5.7 million internet users in 2008.

EDUCATION AND HEALTH
Education is controlled by cantonal and communal authorities and is free and compulsory from ages seven to 16. Special schools make a feature of commercial and technical instruction. Major universities include Basel (founded 1460), Bern (1834), Fribourg (1889), Geneva (1873), Lausanne (1890), Zurich (1832) and Neuchatel (1909), the technical universities of Lausanne and Zurich and the economics university of St Gall.
Gross enrolment ratio (percentage of relevant age group) – primary 102 per cent; secondary 96 per cent; tertiary 47 per cent (2008 est)
Health expenditure (per capita) – US$6,108 (2007)
Hospital beds (per 1,000 people) – 5.5 (2003–8)

MEDIA AND CULTURE
The public-service Swiss Broadcasting Corporation (SRG/SSR), which is funded mainly through licence fees, dominates broadcasting; it operates seven television networks and 18 radio stations, broadcasting in all of the country's official languages. Private radio and television stations operate at regional level, and television stations from France, Germany and Italy are widely available through multi-channel cable and satellite television. The press has full editorial freedom. Newspapers tend to be regional, reflecting linguistic divisions: there are two German-language dailies based in Zurich, two French-language dailies in Geneva and an Italian-language daily in Lugano.

Important cultural figures include the writer and philosopher Jean-Jacques Rousseau (1712–78), the psychoanalyst Carl Jung (1875–1961), the poet Carl Spitteler (1845–1924), who won the Nobel prize for literature in 1919, and the writer and founder of modern structural linguistics Ferdinand de Saussure (1857–1913).

SYRIA

Al-Jumhuriyah al-Arabiyah as-Suriyah – Syrian Arab Republic

Area – 185,180 sq. km
Capital – Damascus; population, 2,527,260 (2009 est)
Major cities – Aleppo (Halab), Hama (Hamah), Homs (Hims), Latakia (Al Ladhiqiyah)
Currency – Syrian pound (S£) of 100 piastres
Population – 20,178,485 rising at 2.13 per cent a year (2009 est)
Religion – Muslim (Sunni 74 per cent, Druze 3 per cent; other 13 per cent, including Alawite sect), Christian 10 per cent (of which Greek Orthodox is the largest denomination) (est)
Language – Arabic (official), Kurdish, Armenian, Aramaic, Circassian, French
Population density – 112 per sq. km (2008)
Urban population – 54 per cent (2007 est)
Median age (years) – 21.7 (2009 est)
National anthem – 'Homat el Diyar' ['Guardians of the Homeland']
National day – 17 April (Independence Day)
Life expectancy (years) – 71.19 (2009 est)
Mortality rate – 4.61 (2009 est)
Birth rate – 25.9 (2009 est)
Infant mortality rate – 25.87 (2009 est)
Death penalty – Retained
CPI score – 2.6 (2009)

CLIMATE AND TERRAIN

There is a narrow coastal plain and ranges of mountains in the west, and the fertile basin of the river Euphrates in the north-east. The centre and south of the interior consist of semi-arid and desert plateaux. Elevation extremes range from 2,814m (Mt Hermon) at the highest point to −200m (unnamed location near Lake Tiberias) at the lowest. There is a desert climate in much of the country, moderated by altitude in the mountains, and a Mediterranean climate on the coast. Average temperatures in Damascus range from lows of 2°C in January to highs of 37°C in August.

HISTORY AND POLITICS

The area was successively part of the Phoenician, Persian, Roman and Byzantine empires. It was conquered by Muslim Arabs in the seventh century, and by the Turks in the 11th century. The location of many battles during the medieval Crusades, Syria became part of the Ottoman Empire in 1516. Following the empire's collapse after the First World War, Syria became a mandated territory in 1920, administered by France with the mandated territory of Lebanon as 'Greater Lebanon'. It became independent in 1946 when French forces withdrew. Syria formed part of the United Arab Republic with Egypt from 1958 to 1961, when it seceded. It was involved in the Arab-Israeli wars in 1948, 1967 and 1973, losing the Golan Heights to Israel in 1967.

Syrian intervention in Lebanon began in 1976, its military presence influencing politics there after the civil war ended. Forces remained until 2005, when they were withdrawn in response to massive popular protests in Lebanon and intense international pressure following the assassination of former Lebanese prime minister Rafik Hariri. Following the withdrawal, many Western states continued to accuse Syria of supporting and arming Lebanese militants. Syrian relations with the West have also been strained in recent years by its support for Iraqi insurgents and Palestinian militants, and suspicions that it was attempting to develop weapons of mass destruction. However, the country has been moving to end its isolation and re-engage with peace processes in the Middle East, and relations with the USA and EU states have improved since 2007.

The Arab Socialist Renaissance (Ba'ath) Party has been the ruling party since 1963. Hafez al-Assad seized power in a coup in 1970 and was elected president in 1971. He remained president until his death in 2000, when he was succeeded by his son, Bashar al-Assad, who was re-elected unopposed in 2007. Following the 2007 legislative election, the Ba'ath Party and its allies retained a large majority in the legislature.

POLITICAL SYSTEM

The 1973 constitution declares that the Arab Socialist Renaissance (Ba'ath) Party is the leading party in the state and society. The executive president is elected for a seven-year term by the legislature and confirmed in office by a national referendum. The president appoints the council of ministers. The unicameral People's Council *(Majlis al-Sha'ab)* has 250 members directly elected for a four-year term. The only candidates permitted to stand in elections are those from the Ba'ath Party, parties allied with it or independents.

HEAD OF STATE

President, Lt-Gen. Bashar al-Assad, *elected* 27 June 2000, *confirmed by referendum* 10 July 2000, *re-elected* 2007
Vice-Presidents, Farouk al-Shara; Najah al-Attar

SELECTED GOVERNMENT MEMBERS *as at July 2010*

Prime Minister, Mohammed Naji al-Otari
Deputy Prime Minister, Economy, Abdallah al-Dardari
Defence, Lt.-Gen. Ali Habib Mahmud
Finance, Mohammad al-Hussein
Foreign Affairs, Walid al-Muallem
Interior, Maj.-Gen. Said Sammur

EMBASSY OF THE SYRIAN ARAB REPUBLIC

8 Belgrave Square, London SW1X 8PH
T 020-7245 9012 W www.syremb.com
Ambassador Extraordinary and Plenipotentiary, Sami Khiyami, *apptd* 2004

BRITISH EMBASSY

PO Box 37, Kotob Building, Mohammad Kurd Ali Street, Malki, Damascus
T (+963) (11) 339 1513
E british.embassy.damascus@fco.gov.uk
W http://ukinsyria.fco.gov.uk
Ambassador Extraordinary and Plenipotentiary, HE Simon Collis *apptd* 2007

BRITISH COUNCIL
PO Box 33105, Maysaloun Street, Shalaan, Damascus
T (+963) (11) 331 0631 W www.britishcouncil.org/syria
Director, Elizabeth White

DEFENCE

The army has 4,950 main battle tanks, 1,500 armoured personnel carriers and up to 2,450 armoured infantry fighting vehicles. The navy has 2 frigates, 21 patrol and coastal vessels and 13 armed helicopters at 3 bases. The air force has 555 combat aircraft and 71 armed helicopters.

Military budget – US$1,460m (2007)
Military personnel – 325,000: army 220,000, navy 5,000, air force 40,000, air defence 60,000; paramilitary 108,000
Conscription duration – 30 months

ECONOMY AND TRADE

The economy is state-controlled and predominantly state-owned, although recent modest economic reforms have included some privatisation and the reduction of state subsidies; a stock exchange opened in 2009. Oil and agriculture account for nearly half of GDP, but other activities, such as financial services, non-oil industry and trade, are becoming increasingly important. Gas is produced for domestic use, and phosphate is mined and processed; other non-oil industry includes the manufacture of textiles, processed food, beverages, tobacco and cement, and car assembly. Agriculture contributes 17.7 per cent of GDP, industry 26.5 per cent and services 55.9 per cent.

The main export markets are Iraq, Germany, Lebanon and Italy; imports come chiefly from Saudi Arabia, China, Russia and Italy. Principal exports are crude oil, minerals, petroleum products, fruit and vegetables, cotton fibre, textiles, clothing, meat, livestock and wheat. The main imports are machinery and transport equipment, electric power machinery, food and livestock, metals and metal products, chemicals, plastics, yarn and paper.

GNI – US$44,400m; US$2,160 per capita (2008)
Annual average growth of GDP – 2.2 per cent (2009 est)
Inflation rate – 3.8 per cent (2009 est)
Population below poverty line – 11.9 per cent (2006 est)
Unemployment – 9.2 per cent (2009 est)
Total external debt – US$7,621m (2009 est)
Imports – US$18,300m (2008)
Exports – US$14,300m (2008)

BALANCE OF PAYMENTS
Trade – US$3,821m deficit (2009)
Current Account – US$1,942m deficit (2008)

Trade with UK	*2008*	*2009*
Imports from UK	£92,505,708	£147,147,184
Exports to UK	£117,428,059	£69,937,869

COMMUNICATIONS

There are 2,052km of railways, which link with the networks of neighbouring countries. The country has 97,400km of roads, 19,500km of which are surfaced. The principal airports are at Aleppo and Damascus; internal air services operate between all major cities. The main port is Latakia.

Telecommunications systems are being improved and networks are growing rapidly. In 2008 there were 3.6 million fixed telephone lines in use, 7.1 million mobile phone subscribers and 3.6 million internet users.

EDUCATION AND HEALTH

Education is under state control. Elementary education is free at state schools and is compulsory from the age of seven. Upper secondary education is not compulsory and is free only at state schools. There are universities at Damascus, Halab, Tishrin and Hims.

Literacy rate – 83.1 per cent (2007 est)
Gross enrolment ratio (percentage of relevant age group) – primary 124 per cent; secondary 74 per cent (2008 est)
Health expenditure (per capita) – US$68 (2007)
Hospital beds (per 1,000 people) – 1.5 (2003–8)

MEDIA

The only domestic television network and the main radio channels and newspapers are owned and controlled by the government or the Ba'ath party. There has been a cautious easing of controls since 2000; private publications were licensed, as were private radio stations in 2005, and satellite receivers are now permitted so many viewers have access to foreign television broadcasts. However, news broadcasting remains the monopoly of the state-controlled media, and foreign and domestic media output and the internet are censored.

TAIWAN

T'ai-wan – Taiwan (Republic of China)

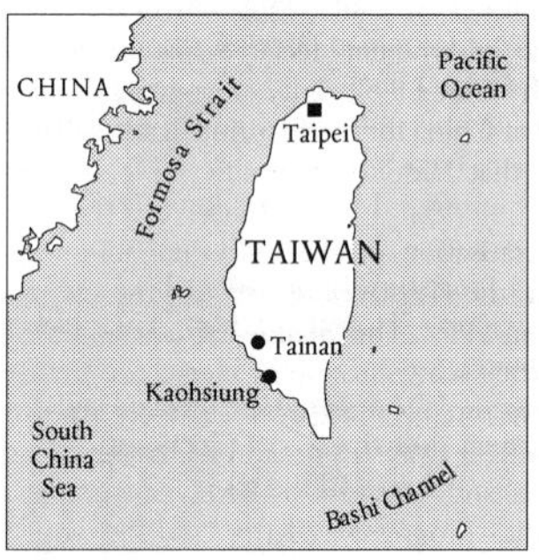

Area – 35,980 sq. km
Capital – Taipei; population, 2,646,474 (2001 est)
Major cities – Kaohsiung, Taichung, Tainan
Currency – New Taiwan dollar (NT$) of 100 cents
Population – 22,974,347 rising at 0.23 per cent a year (2009 est); Han Chinese 98 per cent (Holo 70 per cent, Hakka 14 per cent), indigenous (2 per cent) (est)
Religion – Buddhist 35 per cent, Taoist 33 per cent, Christian 2 per cent (est). Many combine Buddhism and Taoism, and may also practise Chinese folk beliefs. About 3 per cent belong to the Falun Gong spiritual movement
Language – Mandarin (official), Taiwanese (Min-Nan), Hakka dialects
Population density – 618 per sq. km (2001)
Median age – 36.5 (2009 est)
National anthem – 'National Anthem of the Republic of China'
National day – 10 October (Republic Day)
Life expectancy (years) – 77.96 (2009 est)
Mortality rate – 6.76 (2009 est)
Birth rate – 8.99 (2009 est)
Infant mortality rate – 5.35 (2009 est)
Death penalty – Retained (last used 2010)
CPI score – 5.6 (2009)

CLIMATE AND TERRAIN

The island of Taiwan (formerly Formosa) lies 145km east of the Chinese mainland. Mountains run the length of the island, covering over half the terrain, with lowlands in the west. Elevation extremes range from 3,952m (Yu Shan) at the highest point to 0m (South China Sea) at the lowest. Taiwan shares the tropical monsoon climate of southern China, with large seasonal variations in temperature, dry winters and wet summers. The typhoon season lasts from May to November, with particularly high humidity between July and September.

Territories include the Penghu (Pescadores) islands (80.47 sq. km), some 56km west of Taiwan, as well as Kinmen (Quemoy) (109 sq. km) and Matsu (7 sq. km), which are only a few kilometres from mainland China.

HISTORY AND POLITICS

Settled by Chinese from about the 12th century, the island was annexed by China in the 17th century, and ceded to Japan in 1895 at the end of the Sino-Japanese War. It was returned to China after Japan's defeat in the Second World War. The Kuomintang (KMT) government, led by Gen. Chiang Kai-shek, withdrew to Taiwan in 1949 after being defeated by the Communists in mainland China. The territory remained under Chiang Kai-shek's presidency until his death in 1975. He was succeeded as president by his son, Gen. Chiang Ching-kuo, who ruled until his death in 1988. Martial law was lifted in 1987 after 38 years. In 1991 the Taiwanese government declared an end to the state of war with China, officially recognising the People's Republic of China for the first time, and ended emergency measures that had frozen political life in Taiwan since 1949.

Democratisation of the authoritarian one-party state began in the 1980s and led to the first multiparty elections in 1992. The 'Senior Parliamentarians' who had retained their seats since being elected on the mainland in 1948 were forcibly retired in 1991–2. From this point, power shifted away from the mainlanders to the native Taiwanese, and 50 years of KMT rule ended when the Democratic Progressive Party (DPP), which favours self-determination, won the presidency in 2000 and the 2001 legislative election.

The DPP retained the presidency and continued in government after the 2004 elections. However, in the 2008 elections the KMT returned to power, winning a majority of seats in the legislature, and the KMT candidate, Ma Ying-jeou, was elected president. Premier Liu Chao-shiuan and his cabinet resigned in September 2009 over the poor response to Typhoon Morakot in the preceding month; a new government was formed under Wu Den-yih.

FOREIGN RELATIONS

Legally, most nations acknowledge the position of the Chinese government that Taiwan is a province of the People's Republic of China, and as a result Taiwan has formal diplomatic relations with only 23 countries and no seat at the UN. China has sanctioned the use of force to prevent Taiwan declaring itself independent.

Contacts between Taiwan and China began in the 1980s and have led to a gradual relaxation of restrictions on direct economic, trade and transport links, and on travel and tourism. Since 2008, Taiwan has sought greater economic cooperation and integration with China.

POLITICAL SYSTEM

The 1947 constitution (which originally applied to the whole of China) has been amended a number of times since 1991. In 2004 an amendment provided for future proposed constitutional changes to be put to a referendum instead of the National Assembly (formerly the upper house of the legislature), which was disbanded under 2005 provisions that also reduced the number of legislative seats with effect from the 2008 election.

The president is directly elected for a four-year term, renewable only once. The unicameral Legislative Yuan has 113 members: 73 directly elected, 34 elected proportionately by party and six elected by aboriginal voters in two constituencies; all serve a four-year term. The president appoints the premier and, on the premier's advice, the cabinet.

HEAD OF STATE

President, Ma Ying-jeou, *elected* 22 March 2008
Vice-President, Vincent Siew

SELECTED GOVERNMENT MEMBERS *as at July 2010*

Premier, Wu Den-yih
Defence, Kao Hua-chu
Economy, Shih Yen-shiang
Foreign Affairs, Timothy Yang Chin-tien
Interior, Jiang Yi-huah

BRITISH COUNCIL

2F-1, 106 XinYi Rd, Sec. 5, Taipei 110
T (+886) (2) 8722 1000 W www.britishcouncil.org/taiwan
Director, Christine Skinner

DEFENCE

The army has over 926 main battle tanks, 950 armoured personnel carriers, 225 armoured infantry fighting vehicles and 101 armed helicopters. The navy has 4 submarines, 4 destroyers, 22 frigates, 73 patrol and coastal vessels, 32 combat aircraft and 20 armed helicopters at 5 bases. The air force has 477 combat aircraft.

Military budget – US$9,780m (2009)
Military personnel – 290,000: army 200,000, navy 45,000, air force 45,000; paramilitary 17,000
Conscription duration – 12 months

ECONOMY AND TRADE

Since the 1950s Taiwan has transformed itself from a mainly agricultural country into a highly developed industrial economy. This transition was driven by exports. There has been a gradual shift away from state domination of the economy, with a reduction in government influence on investment and foreign trade, and privatisation in the financial and industrial sectors. Taiwan's export markets suffered severely in the global economic downturn and the economy contracted sharply in 2008–9, but it escaped turmoil in its financial sector.

Only a quarter of the land area is suitable for agriculture but the soil is very fertile, producing rice, corn, vegetables, fruit, tea, meat and dairy products. The industrial base includes electronics, oil refining, armaments, chemicals, textiles, iron and steel, machinery, cement, food processing, vehicles, consumer goods, pharmaceuticals and fishing. Agriculture contributes 1.6 per cent of GDP, industry 29.2 per cent and services 69.2 per cent.

The main trading partners are China (27 per cent of exports), Japan, the USA and Hong Kong. Principal exports are computer products and electronic equipment, machinery, metals, textiles, plastics, chemicals and precision instruments. The main imports are electronic and electrical equipment, machinery, oil and precision instruments.

Average annual growth of GDP – –4 per cent (2009 est)
Inflation rate – –0.7 per cent (2009 est)
Population below poverty line – 0.95 per cent (2007 est)
Unemployment – 6.4 per cent (2009 est)
Total external debt – US$82,680m (2009 est)
Imports – US$240,700m (2008)
Exports – US$255,100m (2008)

BALANCE OF PAYMENTS
Trade – US$29,014m surplus (2009)
Current Account – US$42,572m surplus (2009)

Trade with UK	*2008*	*2009*
Imports from UK	£836,298,133	£754,577,469
Exports to UK	£2,482,862,1228	£2,400,413,264

COMMUNICATIONS

Taiwan has 1,582km of railways and a total road network of 41,300km, most of which is surfaced (including 976km of motorways). The main ports are Keelung, Kaohsiung and Taichung, and there are international airports at Taoyuan (near Taipei), Kaohsiung and Taichung. There are internal flights between the major cities.

Modern, digital telecommunications systems provided services to 14.3 million fixed-line telephone subscribers, 25.4 million mobile phone subscribers and 15.1 million internet users in 2008.

MEDIA

The media is among the most liberal and competitive in Asia. There are some 350 newspapers, all of which are privately owned and reflect a wide range of views. The broadcast media, especially television, has a high level of ownership by the government, the military and political parties. Both terrestrial and cable television services operate, and cable subscription is the highest in the region. There are over 170 radio stations.

TAJIKISTAN

Jumhurii Tojikiston – Republic of Tajikistan

Area – 143,100 sq. km
Capital – Dushanbe; population, 703,939 (2009 est)
Major town – Khujand
Currency – Somoni of 100 dirams
Population – 7,349,145 rising at 1.88 per cent a year (2009 est); Tajik (79.9 per cent), Uzbek (15.3 per cent), Russian (1.1 per cent), Kyrgyz (1.1 per cent)
Religion – Muslim 97 per cent (of which Sunni 96 per cent, Shia 4 per cent), Christian 2 per cent (predominantly Russian Orthodox) (est)
Language – Tajik (official), Russian
Population density – 49 per sq. km (2008)
Urban population – 26 per cent (2007 est)
Median age (years) – 21.9 (2009 est)
National anthem – 'Surudi Milli' ['National Anthem']
National day – 9 September (Independence Day)
Life expectancy (years) – 65.33 (2009 est)
Mortality rate – 6.83 (2009 est)
Birth rate – 26.9 (2009 est)
Infant mortality rate – 41.03 (2009 est)
Death penalty – Retained (not used since 2004)
CPI score – 2 (2009)
Literacy rate – 99.6 per cent (2007 est)
Gross enrolment ratio (percentage of relevant age group) – primary 102 per cent; secondary 84 per cent; tertiary 20 per cent (2008 est)
Health expenditure (per capita) – US$29 (2007)
Hospital beds (per 1,000 people) – 5.4 (2003–8 est)

CLIMATE AND TERRAIN

The landlocked country is mountainous, with the Pamir highlands in the east and the high ridges of the Pamir-Altai ranges in the centre. More than half of the country lies above 3,000m. Elevation extremes range from 7,495m (Qullai Ismoili Somoni) at the highest point to 300m (Syr Darya river) at the lowest. The main rivers are the Syr Darya, flowing through the Fergana valley in the north, and the Amu Darya and its tributaries in the west and south. Most of the population lives on the fertile plains formed by these rivers. The climate is continental, with average temperatures in central areas of −2°C in January and 25°C in July.

HISTORY AND POLITICS

The area that is now Tajikistan was conquered by Alexander the Great in the fourth century BC and remained under Greek and Greco-Persian rule for 200 years, until the kingdom of Kushan was established throughout the Bactria region.

Tajikistan was invaded by Muslim Arabs in the eighth century AD, and Islam was the prevalent religion by the time of the Samanid Persian conquest in the ninth century. From the ninth to the 16th century, the region was ruled by a succession of Turkic, Mongol and Uzbek states, and remained under the control of various feudal principalities until the 19th century. In 1868, the northern part was subsumed within the Russian Empire, while the south was annexed by the Bukhara khanate. At the time of the Russian revolution in 1917 the Central Asian territories attempted to establish their independence, but Bolshevik power was consolidated in the north by April 1918, and in the rest of Tajikistan by 1920. In 1924 the Tajikistan Autonomous Soviet Socialist Republic was formed as part of the Uzbek Republic, before Tajikistan was given full republican status within the USSR in 1929.

Tajikistan declared its independence on 9 September 1991. In 1992, anti-government demonstrations escalated into a five-year civil war between government forces and Islamic and pro-democracy groups. A peace accord signed in 1997 was implemented by 2000. Political assassinations and bombings occurred after the end of the civil war, but the level of violence has dropped since 2002.

Former Communists have dominated politics since 1991 and power is concentrated in the president's hands. Opposition parties are weak and face harassment; a number of opposition leaders have been arrested on criminal charges, moves that their supporters claim are politically motivated.

President Rakhmonov has served as head of state since 1992, and was re-elected for a third term in 2006. The 2010 legislative elections were won by the incumbent (former communist) People's Democratic Party of Tajikistan (HDKT) with an overwhelming majority, although international observers considered the polls flawed.

POLITICAL SYSTEM

The 1994 constitution was amended in 1999 and 2003, following referendums, to introduce changes to the presidential term of office and the legislative structure. The executive president is directly elected for a single seven-year term, although the 2003 amendment permits the current incumbent to stand for two further terms. The bicameral legislature consists of the Assembly of Representatives *(Majlisi Namoyandogan)*, which has 63 members directly elected for a five-year term, and the National Assembly *(Majlisi Milli)*, which has 33 members, 25 elected by five regional assemblies and eight appointed by the president, to serve a five-year term. Administratively, Tajikistan is divided into two provinces and the Gorno-Badakhstan autonomous region.

HEAD OF STATE

President, Emomali Rakhmon, *elected by Supreme Soviet* 19 November 1992, *elected* 6 November 1994, *re-elected* 1999, 2006

SELECTED GOVERNMENT MEMBERS *as at July 2010*

Prime Minister, Akil Akilov
First Deputy Prime Minister, Asadullo Ghulomov
Deputy Prime Ministers, Murodali Alimardonov *(Economy)*; Ruqiya Qurbonova
Defence, Col.-Gen. Sherali Khayrulloyev
Finance, Safarali Najmiddinov
Foreign Affairs, Hamrokhon Zaripov
Internal Affairs, Abdurahim Qahhorov

EMBASSY OF THE REPUBLIC OF TAJIKISTAN

Grove House, 27 Hammersmith Grove, London W6 0NE
T 020-8600 2520 E info@tajembassy.ork.uk
W www.tajembassy.org.uk
Ambassador Extraordinary and Plenipotentiary, HE Erkin Kasymov, *apptd* 2008

BRITISH EMBASSY

65 Mirzo Tursunzade Street, Dushanbe 734002
T (+992) 372 42221 E dushanbe.reception@fco.gov.uk
W http://ukintajikistan.fco.gov.uk
Ambassador Extraordinary and Plenipotentiary, HE Trevor Moore, *apptd* 2009

DEFENCE

The army has 37 main battle tanks, 23 armoured infantry fighting vehicles and 23 armoured personnel carriers. The air force has 4 armed helicopters.
Military budget – US$80m (2009)
Military personnel – 8,800: army 7,300, air force 1,500; paramilitary 7,500
Conscription duration – 24 months

ECONOMY AND TRADE

Since the civil war, there has been steady economic growth but the economy remains fragile owing to the inconsistent implementation of structural reforms, corruption, poor industrial and transport infrastructure, energy shortages and high foreign debt. The country has benefited from debt cancellation, and is receiving substantial aid, primarily to develop industrial and transport infrastructure. However, nearly 60 per cent of the population lives below the poverty line and many are dependent on remittances. The global downturn reduced the value of remittances and export commodity prices in 2009.

Agriculture is the major sector of the economy, accounting for 20.1 per cent of GDP but 50 per cent of employment. Cattle-raising and cotton-growing predominate; other crops are grain, fruit, grapes and vegetables. Abundant mineral deposits are not fully exploited. Industry consists of aluminium and hydro-electric power production, mining (zinc and lead), food processing and light industries making chemicals and fertilisers, cement, metal-cutting machine tools, refrigerators and freezers. The sector contributes 22.2 per cent of GDP and employs 12.8 per cent of the workforce.

The main export markets are Russia, China, Turkey and Iran; imports come chiefly from Russia, China and Kazakhstan. Principal exports are aluminium, electricity, cotton, fruit, vegetable oil and textiles. The main imports are electricity, petroleum products, aluminium oxide, machinery and equipment, and foodstuffs.
GNI – US$4,100m; US$600 per capita (2008)
Annual average growth of GDP – 3 per cent (2009 est)
Inflation rate – 6.6 per cent (2009 est)
Population below poverty line – 60 per cent (2007 est)
Unemployment – 2.3 per cent (2008 est)
Total external debt – US$1,805m (2009 est)

BALANCE OF PAYMENTS

Trade – US$1,663m deficit (2009)
Current Account – US$453m deficit (2008)

Trade with UK	*2008*	*2009*
Imports from UK	£6,815,422	£5,045,511
Exports to UK	£74,095	£29,740

COMMUNICATIONS

Infrastructure development is a government priority, with China supporting a road-building programme and the USA funding a bridge linking Tajikistan with Afghanistan. There are 680km of railway and 27,767km of roads; many roads, including the main highways, are only open in the summer months. About 200km of the river Vakhsh is navigable. The main airport is at Dushanbe, and there are over 20 other airports and airfields around the country.

Telecommunications systems are expanding and being modernised. There were 360,000 fixed telephone lines in use, 3.5 million mobile phone subscribers and 600,000 internet users in 2008.

MEDIA

The government retains tight control over the media: state-run radio and television stations dominate broadcasting, newspapers must be registered and the authorities control the printing presses. Independent journalists frequently come under government pressure. The private broadcasting sector has about 15 active television stations and 10 radio stations. There are more than 200 newspapers, some government-owned and others linked to political parties.

TANZANIA

Jamhuri ya Muungano wa Tanzania – United Republic of Tanzania

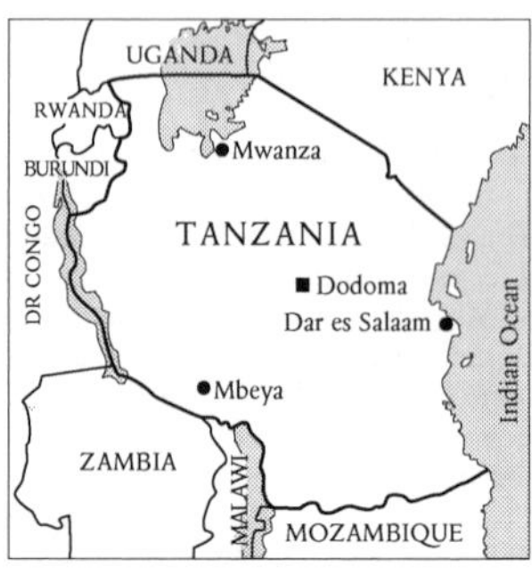

Area – 947,300 sq. km
Capital – Dodoma; population, 200,447 (2009 est)
Major cities – Arusha, Dar es Salaam, Mbeya, Mwanza, Zanzibar
Currency – Tanzanian shilling of 100 cents
Population – 41,048,532 rising at 2.04 per cent a year (2009 est); over 130 African ethnic groups on the mainland; Arab, African and mixed race on Zanzibar
Religion – Christian 62 per cent, Muslim 35 per cent (of which Sunni 80 per cent, Shia 20 per cent), indigenous beliefs 3 per cent on mainland; Muslim 98 per cent on Zanzibar (est)
Language – Swahili, English (both official), Arabic (especially on Zanzibar)
Population density – 48 per sq. km (2008)
Urban population – 25 per cent (2007 est)
Median age (years) – 18 (2009 est)
National anthem – 'Mungu Ibariki Afrika' ['God Bless Africa']
National day – 26 April (Union Day)
Life expectancy (years) – 52.01 (2009 est)
Mortality rate – 12.59 (2009 est)
Birth rate – 34.29 (2009 est)
Infant mortality rate – 69.28 (2009 est)
HIV/AIDS adult prevalence – 5.8 per cent (2007 est)
Death penalty – Retained (not used since 1995)
CPI score – 2.6 (2009)

CLIMATE AND TERRAIN

Tanzania comprises the former Tanganyika, on the mainland of east Africa, and the islands of Zanzibar, Pemba and Mafia. Most of the country lies on the central African plateau, from which rise mountains that run across the centre of the country from north-east to south-west. Peaks include Mt Kilimanjaro (5,895m), the highest point on the continent of Africa, and Mt Meru (4,564m). The lowest point is 0m (Indian Ocean). The land falls to plains in the south-east and along the coast, and to swamps in the west. Large areas of lakes Victoria, Tanganyika and Malawi (Nyasa) lie on the northern and western borders, and there are smaller lakes in the north-east and south-west. The Serengeti National Park covers an area of 9,656 sq. km in the north of the country. The climate is tropical, modified by altitude, with a rainy season from November to April except in coastal regions, which get most rain between March and May; rainfall is sporadic in the interior but more reliable and heavier on the coast.

HISTORY AND POLITICS

The area was settled by Bantu people from the fifth century AD, and city states developed along the coast from the eighth century, trading with Arab, Indian and Persian merchants. Portuguese explorers arrived in the 15th century, and in the 16th century the Portuguese conquered Zanzibar, periodically controlling the coastal states on the mainland. They were ousted from Zanzibar in 1699 by Arabs from Oman, and Oman exercised overlordship over the east African coast from Zanzibar until 1861, when the sultanates of Oman and Zanzibar were separated. The sultanate of Zanzibar became a British protectorate in 1890 and Germany established the colony of German East Africa on the mainland in the 1890s. After the First World War, Tanganyika became a mandated territory under British administration, and achieved independence on 9 December 1961. It became a republic in 1962. Zanzibar became independent as a constitutional monarchy on 10 December 1963. The sultan was overthrown in a revolution in 1964 and Zanzibar united with Tanganyika on 26 April 1964; the new country was formally named the United Republic of Tanzania in October 1964.

The country was a one-party state from 1965 to 1992 under the Revolutionary Party of Tanzania (CCM). The constitution was amended in 1992 to allow multiparty politics, with the stipulation that all parties must be active in both the mainland and Zanzibar and that parties must not be formed on regional, religious, tribal or racial grounds. The first multiparty elections were held in 1995 and were won by the CCM, which has continued to dominate politics.

In the 2005 national elections, the CCM candidate Jakaya Kikwete was elected president, and the party retained its overwhelming majority in the legislature. In Zanzibar's simultaneous 2005 presidential and legislative elections, President Amani Karume was re-elected, and the CCM retained its majority in the legislature; the elections were characterised by violence and accusations of electoral fraud. A constitutional amendment to allow the formation of a coalition government in Zanzibar was approved by referendum in July 2010.

Presidential and legislative elections were due to be held in October 2010.

POLITICAL SYSTEM

The 1977 constitution was amended in 1992 to introduce multiparty elections and in 2000 to allow the president to nominate some members of parliament. The executive president is directly elected for a five-year term, renewable only once. The president is always from Tanganyika and the vice-president is always from Zanzibar. The unicameral National Assembly *(Bunge)* has 323 members: 232 directly elected, 75 seats reserved for women, five chosen by Zanzibar's legislature, and the speaker; up to ten further members may be appointed by the president. All serve a five-year term. The *Bunge* enacts laws that apply to the whole of Tanzania and laws that apply only to the mainland; laws that apply specifically to Zanzibar are enacted by the island's own legislature, the 50-member House of Representatives. Zanzibar also has its own directly elected president (who is a member of the Union government) and legislature.

HEAD OF STATE
President of the United Republic, Jakaya Kikwete, *elected* 14 December 2005, *took office* 21 December 2005
Vice-President, Ali Mohamed Shein
President of Zanzibar, Amani Karume

SELECTED GOVERNMENT MEMBERS *as at July 2010*
Prime Minister, Mizengo Pinda
Defence, Hussein Mwinyi
Finance, Mustapha Mkullo
Foreign Affairs, Bernard Membe
Home Affairs, Lawrence Masha

HIGH COMMISSION FOR THE UNITED REPUBLIC OF TANZANIA
3 Stratford Place, London W1C 1AS
T 020-7569 1470 E tanzarep@tanzania-online.gov.uk
W www.tanzania-online.gov.uk
High Commissioner (acting), HE Chabaka Kilumanga, *apptd* 2010

BRITISH HIGH COMMISSION
PO Box 9200, Umoja House, Garden Avenue, Dar es Salaam
T (+255) (22) 211 0101 E bhc.dar@dar.mail.fco.gov.uk
W http://ukintanzania.fco.gov.uk
High Commissioner, HE Diane Corner, *apptd* 2009

BRITISH COUNCIL
PO Box 9100, Samora Avenue/Ohio Street, Dar es Salaam
T (+255) (22) 211 6574 W www.britishcouncil.org/africa
Director, Kate Ewart-Biggs

DEFENCE

The army has 45 main battle tanks and 14 armoured personnel carriers. The navy has 8 patrol and coastal combatant vessels at 3 bases. The air force has 25 combat capable aircraft.
Military budget – US$183m (2008 est)
Military personnel – 27,000: army 23,000, navy 1,000, air force 3,000; paramilitary 1,400
Conscription duration – 24 months

ECONOMY AND TRADE

State control has been dismantled gradually since the mid-1980s. Liberalisation and modernisation policies, supported by the World Bank, IMF and aid donors, have increased private-sector growth and investment, and produced steady GDP growth in recent years. However, around one-third of the population still lives below the poverty line.

Agriculture is the mainstay of the economy, accounting for 26.4 per cent of GDP, about 80 per cent of employment and 85 per cent of exports. It provides coffee, tea, cotton, pyrethrum, cashew nuts, grains, fruit and vegetables as well as the raw materials for industries producing sugar, beer, cigarettes and sisal twine. Zanzibar and Pemba produce cloves and clove oil, and coconuts and their derivatives. Increased output of minerals (chiefly diamonds, gold and iron) has driven recent economic growth, and soda ash, cement, petroleum products, footwear, clothing, wood products and fertiliser are also produced. Tourism is a major source of revenue. Industry accounts for 22.6 per cent of GDP and services for 50.9 per cent.

The main trading partners are India, China, Japan, UAE, South Africa and EU countries. Principal exports are gold, coffee, cashew nuts, manufactures (especially clothing) and cotton. The main imports are consumer goods, machinery and transport equipment, industrial raw materials and crude oil.
GNI – US$18,400m; US$440 per capita (2008; mainland Tanzania only)
Annual average growth of GDP – 4.5 per cent (2009 est)
Inflation rate – 11.6 per cent (2009 est)
Total external debt – US$7,070m (2009 est)
Imports – US$7,100m (2008)
Exports – US$2,700m (2008)

BALANCE OF PAYMENTS
Trade – US$3,608m deficit (2009)
Current Account – US$2,012m deficit (2008)

Trade with UK	*2008*	*2009*
Imports from UK	£95,709,332	£96,851,813
Exports to UK	£25,853,963	£18,580,295

COMMUNICATIONS

There are 78,890km of roads, only 6,808km of which are surfaced. The 3,690km of railways connect Dar es Salaam with Zambia, northern Tanzania and Kenya, and lakes Tanganyika and Victoria. The three great lakes in the north and east are the main trade routes with neighbouring countries, via ports at Mwanza, Musoma, Bukoba (Lake Victoria) and Kigoma (Lake Tanganyika). The main seaports are Dar es Salaam, Tanga, Mtwara, Zanzibar, Mkoani and Wete (Pemba); international shipping faces a high risk of piracy and armed robbery in the Indian Ocean. Coastal shipping services connect the mainland to Zanzibar, and lake services operate on Lake Tanganyika and Lake Malawi (Nyasa). The principal international airports are at Dar es Salaam, Kilimanjaro and Zanzibar.

The fixed-line telephone system is being modernised; mobile phone distribution has grown rapidly. There were 179,900 fixed lines and 14.7 million mobile phone subscribers in 2009, and 520,000 internet users in 2008.

EDUCATION AND HEALTH

Education is compulsory for seven years. The teaching medium is Swahili but the government is making efforts to improve English standards in secondary and higher education.
Literacy rate – 72.3 per cent (2007 est)
Gross enrolment ratio (percentage of relevant age group) – primary 110 per cent; tertiary 1 per cent (2008 est)
Health expenditure (per capita) – US$22 (2007)
Hospital beds (per 1,000 people) – 1.1 (2003–8)

MEDIA

The mainland has a liberal media environment, with privately owned broadcasters and newspapers operating alongside the state-run media. Radio has long been the dominant medium and private stations are prevalent in urban areas, but audiences have turned increasingly to television, which was launched only in 1994.

Zanzibar has a less liberal media policy and there are no private broadcasters or newspapers on the island, although locals can access mainland media.

THAILAND

Ratcha Anachak Thai – Kingdom of Thailand

Area – 513,120 sq. km
Capital – Bangkok (Krung Thep); population, 6,901,690 (2009 est)
Major cities – Chon Buri, Nonthaburi, Samut Prakan, Udon Thani
Currency – Baht of 100 satang
Population – 65,905,410 rising at 0.62 per cent a year (2009 est); Thai, including Lao (75 per cent), Chinese (14 per cent) (est)
Religion – Buddhist 94 per cent (predominantly Theravada), Muslim 5 per cent (predominantly Sunni) (est)
Language – Thai (official), English
Population density – 132 per sq. km (2008)
Urban population – 33 per cent (2007 est)
Median age (years) – 33.3 (2009 est)
National anthem – 'Phleng Chat' ['National Song']
National day – 5 December (Birthday of the King)
Life expectancy (years) – 73.1 (2009 est)
Mortality rate – 7.25 (2009 est)
Birth rate – 13.4 (2009 est)
Infant mortality rate – 17.63 (2009 est)
HIV/AIDS adult prevalence – 1.2 per cent (2007 est)
Death penalty – Retained (last used 2009)
CPI score – 3.4 (2009)

CLIMATE AND TERRAIN

Thailand is divided geographically into four regions: the north is mountainous and forested; to the north-east is the semi-arid Korat plateau; the centre is a fertile plain lying in the Chao Phraya basin; and the south is the narrow, mountainous isthmus of Kra. Extremes of elevation range from 2,576m (Doi Inthanon) at the highest point to 0m (Gulf of Thailand) at the lowest. The principal rivers are the Chao Phraya and its tributaries in the central plains and the Mekong on the north and eastern borders. The climate is tropical, with a monsoon season from June to October and high humidity.

HISTORY AND POLITICS

The Thai nation was founded in the 13th century and expanded in the following centuries at the expense of the declining Khmer Empire. Although trade with China, Japan and Europe developed in the 17th century, in 1699 an isolationist policy was adopted. Burma invaded in the 18th century, leaving the country in a state of anarchy until reunification in 1782 under the first king of the present Chakri dynasty. From the late 19th century, Thailand (then known as Siam) opened up to European contact and trade under a series of modernising kings who reformed the country's administration and commerce. It was the only country in the region to avoid colonisation by a European power.

Following a revolution in 1932, Thailand became a constitutional monarchy with parliamentary government. It was occupied by Japan from 1941 until 1945, after which it was under military or military-controlled governments for most of the following 50 years. In 1992, mass demonstrations in Bangkok forced from power the military-aligned government that had won the 1992 election. Civilian rule was restored until 2006, when the military staged a coup against the government led by Thaksin Shinawatra.

The military handed over to a civilian government after the 2007 legislative election, but political volatility has continued, with mass demonstrations and sit-ins in Bangkok by the anti-Thaksin People's Alliance for Democracy (PAD) or 'yellow shirts', or the pro-Thaksin United Front for Democracy against Dictatorship (UDD) or 'red shirts', and clashes between the two. The PAD demonstrated against the six-party coalition government headed by the pro-Thaksin People Power Party (PPP), which was formed after the 2007 election. The PPP and its two main coalition partners were ordered to dissolve in December 2008 after being found guilty of electoral fraud, and the government was replaced by a seven-party coalition led by the Democratic Party. This government faced 18 months of protests by the UDD, culminating in the violent dispersal of its supporters in May 2010 after a two-month occupation of central Bangkok. (*See also* Events of the Year.)

INSURGENCY

The Muslim minority is concentrated in the isthmus of Kra. A separatist campaign in the region began in the 1970s but died down in the 1980s. Violence was renewed in early 2004 and has since claimed over 3,000 lives.

POLITICAL SYSTEM

Thailand is a constitutional monarchy with a hereditary monarch as head of state. The 2007 constitution provides for a bicameral National Assembly comprising a 480-member House of Representatives, elected for a four-year term, and a senate with 150 members: 76 elected members (one from each province) and 74 members appointed by a selection committee; senators serve a six-year term. The prime minister is appointed by the king and approved by and responsible to the House of Representatives.

HEAD OF STATE

HM The King of Thailand, King Bhumibol Adulyadej (Rama IX), *born* 5 December 1927, *succeeded* 9 June 1946
Heir, HRH Crown Prince Maha Vajiralongkorn, *born* 28 July 1952

SELECTED GOVERNMENT MEMBERS *as at July 2010*

Prime Minister, Defence, Abhisit Vejjajiva
Deputy Prime Ministers, Trairong Suwankiri *(Economic Affairs)*; Suthep Thaugsuban; Maj.-Gen. Sanan Kachornprasart
Defence, Gen. Prawit Wongsuwan
Finance, Korn Chatikavanij
Foreign Affairs, Kasit Piromya
Interior, Chavarat Charnvirakul

ROYAL THAI EMBASSY
29–30 Queen's Gate, London SW7 5JB
T 020-7589 2944 E csinfo@thaiembassy.org.uk
W www.thaiembassyuk.org.uk
Ambassador Extraordinary and Plenipotentiary,
HE Kitti Wasinondh, *apptd* 2007

BRITISH EMBASSY
14 Wireless Road, Bangkok 10330
T (+662) 305 8333 E info.bangkok@fco.gov.uk
W http://ukinthailand.fco.gov.uk
Ambassador Extraordinary and Plenipotentiary,
HE Quinton Quayle, *apptd* 2007

BRITISH COUNCIL
254 Chulalongkorn Soi 64, Siam Square, Phayathai Road, Pathumwan, Bangkok 10330
T (+662) 652 5678 W www.britishcouncil.org/thailand
Director, John Whitehead

DEFENCE

The army has 333 main battle tanks, 950 armoured personnel carriers and 5 armed helicopters. The navy has 1 aircraft carrier, 10 frigates, 9 corvettes, 90 patrol and coastal vessels, 21 combat aircraft and 8 armed helicopters at 5 bases. The air force has 165 combat aircraft.

Military budget – US$5,130m (2009)
Military personnel – 305,860: army 190,000, navy 69,860, air force 46,000; paramilitary 113,700
Conscription duration – 24 months

ECONOMY AND TRADE

Thailand was transformed from an agricultural to an export-orientated industrial economy in the last quarter of the 20th century, sustaining steady growth after its quick recovery from the 1997 economic crisis. The global economic downturn caused the export-dependent economy to contract owing to a sharp drop in demand, and persistent political turmoil is hampering its recovery.

The agricultural sector generates 11.6 per cent of GDP and employs 42 per cent of the workforce. The main crops are rice, cassava, rubber, maize, sugar cane, coconuts and soya beans. In recent years fishing and livestock production have grown in importance. There are reserves of natural gas, lignite, tin, tungsten and lead.

The main industry is tourism, which has been the chief foreign exchange earner since the 1980s. Other industries include textiles and clothing, agricultural processing, beverages, tobacco, cement, mining (Thailand is a leading producer of tin and tungsten) and light manufacturing (jewellery, electrical appliances, computers and parts), furniture, plastics and cars and vehicle parts. Industry contributes 43.3 per cent of GDP and services 45.1 per cent.

The main trading partners are Japan, China, the USA and Malaysia. Principal exports are textiles and footwear, fish products, rice, rubber, jewellery, cars, computers and electrical appliances. The main imports are capital goods, intermediate goods and raw materials, consumer goods and fuels.

GNI – US$247,200m; US$3,670 per capita (2008)
Annual average growth of GDP – –3.5 per cent (2009 est)
Inflation rate – –0.9 per cent (2009 est)
Population below poverty line – 10 per cent (2004 est)
Unemployment – 2.7 per cent (2009 est)
Total external debt – US$60,650m (2009 est)
Imports – US$178,800m (2008)
Exports – US$172,900m (2008)

BALANCE OF PAYMENTS
Trade – US$18,143m surplus (2009)
Current Account – US$20,291m surplus (2009)

Trade with UK	*2008*	*2009*
Imports from UK	£712,732,966	£884,910,336
Exports to UK	£2,297,669,299	£2,119,317,894

COMMUNICATIONS

There are 180,100km of roads, almost all of which are surfaced, and 4,071km of railways. Bangkok is the main international airport, though airports at Chiang Mai, Phuket and Hat Yai also receive international flights. The main ports are Bangkok and Sattahip, and there are 3,701km of inland waterways navigable by small boats.

A competitive telecommunications sector has seen a rapid growth in mobile phone take-up. In 2008 there were 7 million fixed lines in use, 62 million mobile phone subscribers and 16.1 million internet users.

EDUCATION AND HEALTH

Primary and lower secondary education is compulsory and free, and upper secondary education is free in government schools. Private universities and colleges are playing an increasing role in higher education.

Literacy rate – 94.1 per cent (2007 est)
Gross enrolment ratio (percentage of relevant age group) – primary 106 per cent; secondary 83 per cent; tertiary 50 per cent (2007 est)
Health expenditure (per capita) – US$136 (2007)
Hospital beds (per 1,000 people) – 2.2 (2002–7)

MEDIA

Nearly all the national terrestrial television networks and many of the radio networks are controlled by the government and the military, although media reforms are being introduced to reduce military interest and allow the private sector more involvement. Although free to criticise policy and expose abuses of power, the media tends towards self-censorship regarding the monarchy, military and judiciary. Newspapers are largely privately run, with popular titles including *Bangkok Post* and *Thairath.*

TIMOR-LESTE

Republika Demokratika Timor Lorosa'e/Republica Democratica de Timor-Leste – Democratic Republic of Timor-Leste

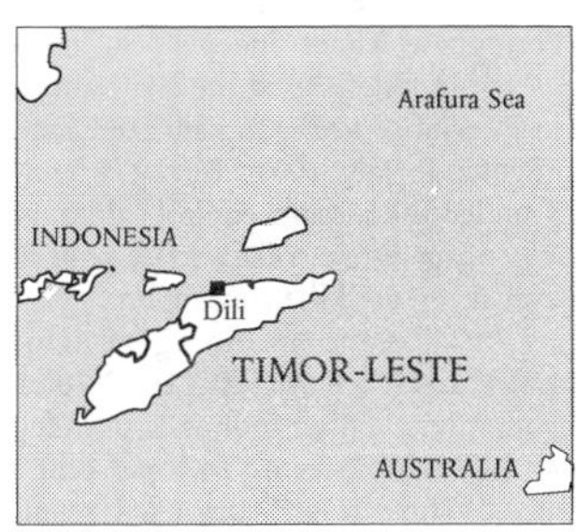

Area – 14,874 sq. km. Includes the enclave of Oecussi
Capital – Dili; population, 166,441 (2009 est)
Major towns – Baucau, Dare, Los Palos, Maliana, Pantemakassar (Oecussi)
Currency – US dollar (US$) of 100 cents

Population – 1,131,612 rising at 2.03 per cent a year (2009 est)
Religion – Christian (Roman Catholic 98 per cent, Protestant denominations 1 per cent), Muslim 1 per cent (est)
Language – Tetum, Portuguese (both official), Indonesian, English, around 14 indigenous languages
Population density – 74 per sq. km (2008)
Urban population – 27 per cent (2007 est)
Median age (years) – 21.8 (2009 est)
National anthem – 'Patria' ['Fatherland']
National day – 28 November (Independence Day)
Life expectancy – 67.27 (2009 est)
Mortality rate – 5.98 (2009 est)
Birth rate – 26.25 (2009 est)
Infant mortality rate – 40.65 (2009 est)
Death penalty – Abolished for all crimes (since 1999)
CPI score – 2.2 (2009)
Military personnel – 1,332: army 1,250, naval element 82
Literacy rate – 50.1 per cent (2007 est)
Gross enrolment ratio (percentage of relevant age group) – primary 107 per cent (2008 est); tertiary 15 per cent (2009 est)
Health expenditure (per capita) – US$58 (2007)

CLIMATE AND TERRAIN

The republic comprises the eastern half of the island of Timor, plus the enclave of Oecussi, which lies on the northern coast, separated from the rest of the country by the Indonesian province of West Timor. The island, about 296km long and 72km wide, lies at the eastern end of the Malay archipelago and is the largest of the Lesser Sunda Islands. The interior is covered in forests and mountains. Elevation extremes range from 2,963m (Mt Tatamailau) at the highest point to 0m (Timor Sea) at the lowest. The climate is tropical.

HISTORY AND POLITICS

The island was settled in prehistoric times by peoples from other parts of the region. It was discovered by the Portuguese *c.*1515 and, after disputes over possession between the Portuguese and the Dutch, was partitioned between the two. The eastern part of the island was a Portuguese colony from 1702 until 1975, apart from three years of Japanese occupation during the Second World War. Portuguese rule collapsed following the 1974 coup in Portugal, and a power struggle between pro-independence parties led to a brief civil war. The Revolutionary Front for an Independent East Timor (Fretilin) emerged as the strongest party, and unilaterally declared Portuguese Timor independent in November 1975. However, Indonesia used the civil war as a pretext to invade in December 1975, and annexed East Timor as its 27th province in July 1976. By 1979, most of East Timor was under Indonesia's control, although Fretilin continued to engage in guerrilla warfare until the 1990s. The UN never recognised the annexation.

Following the fall of the Suharto regime in Indonesia, a plebiscite was held in August 1999 offering the population autonomy within Indonesia or independence; in a turnout of 98.5 per cent, 78.5 per cent voted for independence. This result provoked violence by supporters of integration into Indonesia and Indonesian troops, who murdered hundreds of people and devastated towns. UN peacekeeping troops were deployed in September 1999, and the UN set up a transitional administration. East Timor became independent as the Democratic Republic of Timor-Leste on 20 May 2002.

The UN mission left in 2005 when its peacekeeping duties ended. International troops returned in May 2006 to re-establish law and order after clashes between protesting ex-soldiers and the authorities had escalated into wider factional violence. A non-military UN peacekeeping mission was set up in August 2006. Instability continued, with violent protests in August 2007 over the appointment of Xanana Gusmao as prime minister, and attacks on the president and prime minister by renegade soldiers in February 2008.

The 2007 presidential election was won in the second round by Jose Ramos-Horta (prime minister 2006–7). In the 2007 legislative election, Fretilin won the largest number of seats, but without an overall majority. Negotiations with the National Congress for Timorese Reconstruction (CNRT) over forming a coalition failed, and instead the CNRT formed a coalition government with smaller parties under its leader, Xanana Gusmao (president 2002–7).

POLITICAL SYSTEM

The 2002 constitution established a parliamentary democracy. The president is directly elected for a five-year term, renewable only once. The unicameral National Parliament has 65 members, directly elected for a five-year term. The council of ministers is nominated by the prime minister, who is appointed by the president.

HEAD OF STATE

President, Jose Ramos-Horta, *elected* 9 May 2007, *took office* 20 May 2007

SELECTED GOVERNMENT MEMBERS *as at August 2010*

Prime Minister, Defence, Xanana Gusmao
Deputy Prime Minister, Jose Luis Guterres
Finance, Emilia Pires
Foreign Affairs, Zacarias da Costa

BRITISH EMBASSY

Ambassador Extraordinary and Plenipotentiary, HE Martin Hatfull, *apptd* 2008, resident at Jakarta, Indonesia

ECONOMY AND TRADE

An internationally funded programme in 2002–5 achieved substantial reconstruction of the infrastructure destroyed in the 1999 post-referendum violence, but the 2006 outbreak of civil unrest and looting caused further damage and disrupted economic activity. Economic growth since independence is largely owing to the exploitation of offshore oil and gas deposits, which has boosted government revenue but has had little impact on unemployment levels; there are no domestic production facilities so oil and gas are piped to Australia for processing. High levels of poverty and unemployment, weak civil administration, inadequate infrastructure and a low skills base all hinder development.

Services contribute 55 per cent of GDP, industry 12.8 per cent, and agriculture 32.2 per cent, although it engages 90 per cent of the population. The main commercial crops are coffee, timber, rice, maize, vegetables, tropical fruits and vanilla. There are some light manufacturing industries and quarrying. The main trading partners are Australia, Indonesia and EU countries. Principal exports are coffee, oil, natural gas, sandalwood and marble. The main imports are food, fuels and machinery.

GNI – US$2,706m; US$2,460 per capita (2008)
Annual average growth of GDP – 7.4 per cent (2009 est)

Inflation rate – 7.8 per cent (2007 est)
Population below poverty line – 42 per cent (2003 est)
Unemployment – 20 per cent (2006 est)

BALANCE OF PAYMENTS
Current Account – US$1,177m surplus (2007)

Trade with UK	*2008*	*2009*
Imports from UK	£121,384	£171,338
Exports to UK	£135,183	£23,196

COMMUNICATIONS

There are no railways or waterways, and Dili is the only port. There is one major road, which links the main townships along the northern coast. There are 6,000km of roads in total, 2,600km of which are surfaced. There are six airports and airfields; the only international airport is at Dili. The telephone system is rudimentary and largely limited to urban areas.

MEDIA

There are national public radio and television services and a number of community radio stations, many of which receive funding and support from international organisations. Public radio covers around 90 per cent of the country, but access to television broadcasts is largely limited to the capital. Three newspapers are published daily.

TOGO

République Togolaise – Togolese Republic

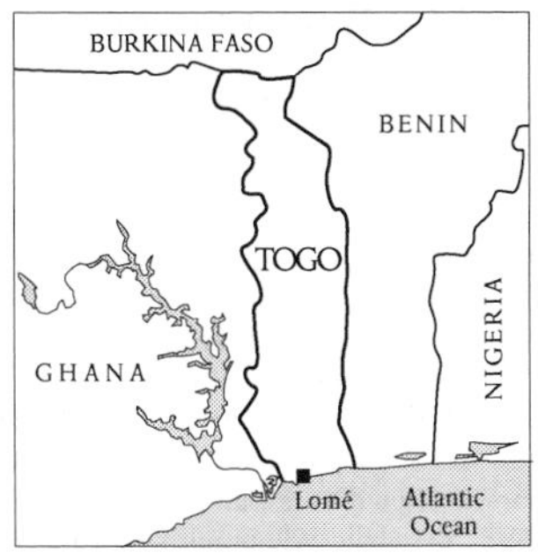

Area – 56,785 sq. km
Capital – Lomé; population, 1,592,630 (2009 est)
Major cities – Atakpamé, Kara, Sokodé
Currency – Franc CFA of 100 centimes
Population – 6,019,877 rising at 2.71 per cent a year (2009 est)
Religion – Christian 48 per cent (Roman Catholic 28 per cent, Protestant 10 per cent, other 10 per cent), Animist 33 per cent, Muslim (Sunni 14 per cent) (est)
Language – French (official), Ewe, Mina (in south), Kabye, Dagomba (in north)
Population density – 119 per sq. km (2008)
Urban population – 41 per cent (2007 est)
Median age (years) – 18.7 (2009 est)
National anthem – 'Salut à toi, pays de nos aïeux' ['Hail to Thee, Land of Our Forefathers']
National day – 27 April (Independence Day)
Life expectancy (years) – 58.69 (2009 est)
Mortality rate – 9.33 (2009 est)
Birth rate – 36.44 (2009 est)
Infant mortality rate – 56.24 (2009 est)
HIV/AIDS adult prevalence – 3.2 per cent (2007 est)
Death penalty – Abolished for all crimes (since 2009)
CPI score – 2.8 (2009)
Literacy rate – 53.2 per cent (2007 est)
Gross enrolment ratio (percentage of relevant age group) – primary 105 per cent; secondary 41 per cent; tertiary 5 per cent (2008 est)
Health expenditure (per capita) – US$33 (2007)
Hospital beds (per 1,000 people) – 0.9 (2003–8)

CLIMATE AND TERRAIN

From hills in the centre of the country, the terrain declines to savannah in the north and in the south to a plateau that leads to a coastal plain with marshes and lagoons. Elevation extremes range from 986m (Mt Agou) at the highest point to 0m (Atlantic Ocean) at the lowest. The climate in the south is tropical with two wet seasons (March to July and September to November). In the north it is semi-arid with one wet season (May to September). The average temperature in Lomé is 27°C all year round.

HISTORY AND POLITICS

Germany established a protectorate, Togoland, over the area in 1884, and this was occupied on the outbreak of the First World War by Britain and France. The country was divided between Britain and France as a League of Nations mandate after the war and the mandate was renewed by the UN in 1946. In 1957, following a plebiscite, British Togoland integrated with Ghana when it became independent. French Togoland achieved independence as the Republic of Togo in 1960.

There was a military coup in 1963 led by Gnassingbé Eyadéma, who installed a civilian president. In 1967 Eyadéma overthrew the government and became president himself, introducing a one-party state under his *Rassemblement du peuple togolais* (RPT). Violent demonstrations in 1990 forced the government to introduce a multiparty constitution in 1992. Eyadéma and the RPT were returned to power in the first multiparty elections in 1993 and in two subsequent elections. The regime continued its brutal suppression of opposition, particularly before and after elections.

After President Eyadéma's death in February 2005, the military attempted to install his son, Faure Gnassingbé, as president but this attracted domestic and international condemnation. Gnassingbé resigned as acting president, only to be elected to the presidency in April 2005. Following reconciliation talks in 2006, the government and opposition leaders signed an accord providing for the participation of opposition parties in a transitional government, and a national unity government was appointed until a legislative election was held in 2007. The election, the first without an opposition boycott for two decades, was nevertheless won by the RPT, which retained its majority; the polls were declared free and fair by observers. President Gnassingbé was re-elected in March 2010.

POLITICAL SYSTEM
Under the 1992 constitution, the president is directly elected for a five-year term. The unicameral National Assembly has 81 members, who are directly elected for a five-year term. The prime minister is appointed by the president and appoints the cabinet in consultation with the president.

HEAD OF STATE
President, Defence, Faure Gnassingbé, *elected* 24 April 2005, *sworn in* 4 May 2005, *re-elected* 2010

SELECTED GOVERNMENT MEMBERS *as at July 2010*
Prime Minister, Gilbert Houngbo
Economy and Finance, Adji Otheth Ayassor
Foreign Affairs, Eliot Ohin

EMBASSY OF THE REPUBLIC OF TOGO
8 rue Alfred Roll, 75017 Paris, France
T (+33) (1) 4380 1213
Ambassador Extraordinary and Plenipotentiary, HE Tchao Sotou Bere, *apptd* 2003

BRITISH AMBASSADOR
HE Dr Nicholas Westcott, CMG, *apptd* 2008, resident at Accra, Ghana

DEFENCE

The army has 2 main battle tanks, 20 armoured infantry fighting vehicles and 30 armoured personnel carriers. The navy has 2 patrol and coastal combatant vessels at a base at Lomé. The air force has 10 combat capable aircraft.
Military budget – US$67m (2009 est)
Military personnel – 8,550: army 8,100, navy 200, air force 250; paramilitary 750
Conscription duration – 24 months (selective)

ECONOMY AND TRADE

Progress on economic reform, intended to attract foreign investment and balance the budget, is slow, lacking impetus on privatisation and financial transparency. Resumption of aid to Togo, mostly suspended in the 1990s because of its human rights record, has increased since the 2007 election, and the country is working with donors on a debt reduction scheme. Growth is hampered by declining productivity and underinvestment.

The economy is predominantly based on agriculture, accounting for 47.4 per cent of GDP, engaging 65 per cent of the workforce and providing most of the country's exports as well as the raw materials for industry. Industrial activity centres on phosphate mining, agricultural processing and manufacture of cement, handicrafts, textiles and beverages. Industry accounts for 25.4 per cent of GDP and 5 per cent of employment.

The main export markets are Germany, Ghana, Burkina Faso and India; imports come mainly from China (37 per cent) and EU states. Principal exports are re-exports, cotton, phosphates, coffee and cocoa. The main imports are machinery and equipment, foodstuffs and petroleum products.
GNI – US$2,600m; US$410 per capita (2008)
Annual average growth of GDP – 1.8 per cent (2009 est)
Inflation rate – 3.3 per cent (2009 est)
Total external debt – US$2,000m (2005)
Imports – US$1,500m (2008)
Exports – US$800m (2008)

BALANCE OF PAYMENTS
Trade – US$713m deficit (2009)
Current Account – US$214m deficit (2008)

Trade with UK	*2008*	*2009*
Imports from UK	£44,464,111	£19,288,453
Exports to UK	£709,786	£801,143

COMMUNICATIONS

Togo has about 7,500km of roads, of which approximately one-third is surfaced. There are 532km of railways. The chief waterway is the Mono river, depending on rainfall, and the main ports are Lomé and Kpeme. The principal airport is at Lomé.

The telephone system served 141,000 fixed telephone lines, 1.5 million mobile phone subscribers and 350,000 internet users in 2008.

MEDIA

The government owns the main national television and radio stations, one of the three daily newspapers and, in association with the ruling RPT party, some of the private radio stations. Privately owned media outlets have increased since the 1990s but often have limited finances. Freedom of expression is not respected; journalists can be subject to harassment, and broadcasting stations and presses to arbitrary closure.

TONGA

Pule'anga Tonga – Kingdom of Tonga

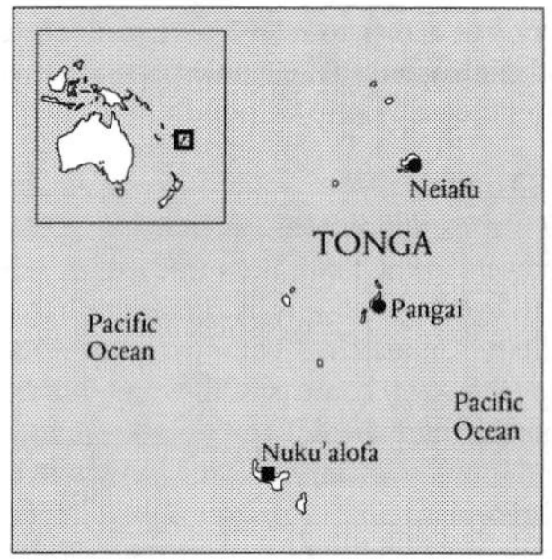

Area – 747 sq. km
Capital – Nuku'alofa, on Tongatapu; population, 24,260 (2009 est)
Currency – Pa'anga (T$) of 100 seniti
Population – 120,898 rising at 1.48 per cent a year (2009 est)
Religion – Christian (Wesleyan Methodist 53 per cent, Mormon 17 per cent, Roman Catholic 11 per cent, other 14 per cent) (est); small Baha'i minority
Language – English, Tongan (both official)
Population density – 144 per sq. km (2008)
Urban population – 24 per cent (2007 est)
Median age (years) – 22.3 (2009 est)
National anthem – 'Koe Fasi Oe Tu'i Oe Otu Tonga' ['Song of the King of the Tonga Islands']
National day – 4 June (Emancipation Day)
Life expectancy (years) – 70.73 (2009 est)
Mortality rate – 5.02 (2009 est)
Birth rate – 19.84 (2009 est)
Infant mortality rate – 11.58 (2009 est)
Death penalty – Retained (not used since 1982)
CPI score – 3 (2009)
Literacy rate – 99.2 per cent (2007 est)

CLIMATE AND TERRAIN

Tonga comprises over 170 islands in three groups, situated in the south Pacific Ocean some 724km east-south-east of Fiji. Most of the islands are of coral formation, but some are volcanic (Tofua, Kao and Niuafo'ou or 'Tin Can' Island). Elevation extremes range from 1,033m (unnamed location on Kao Island) at the highest point to 0m (Pacific Ocean) at the lowest. The climate is tropical, moderated by trade winds, with an average temperature of 26°C all year round.

HISTORY AND POLITICS

The islands were settled by Polynesians from *c.*1000 AD. They were visited by European explorers from the 17th century. The country was reunited in 1845 after a civil war, and a modern constitution adopted in 1875. Tonga became a British protectorate in 1900, and regained full independence on 4 June 1970.

A pro-democracy movement began in 1992 and gathered momentum throughout the 1990s, with the first political party being established in 1994. Following consultation on political and constitutional reform in 2005 and negotiations in 2007, a political reform commission was appointed after the 2008 election; in 2009 it recommended reducing the monarchy to a ceremonial role and introducing a popularly elected legislature.

In the 2008 legislative election, the Human Rights and Democracy Movement won four of the popularly elected seats, other pro-democracy candidates the remaining five. A legislative election was scheduled for November 2010; a majority of seats were to be popularly elected.

POLITICAL SYSTEM

The 1875 constitution was amended in 2003 to give greater powers to the king; the present king relinquished some of his executive powers in 2008. The head of state is a hereditary monarch. The unicameral Legislative Assembly *(Fale Alea)* consists of the king, the 16-member privy council, nine hereditary nobles elected by their peers, and nine popularly elected representatives who serve a three-year term. Legislation passed in April 2010 will increase the number of elected representatives in the assembly to 17, alongside nine hereditary nobles and up to four members appointed by the king, effective from the next election. The privy council acts as a cabinet. The prime minister is head of government.

HEAD OF STATE

HM The King of Tonga, King (Siaosi) George Tupou V, *born* 4 May 1948, *acceded* 11 September 2006, *crowned* 1 August 2008
Heir, HRH Crown Prince Tupouto'a Lavaka, *born* 12 July 1959

SELECTED GOVERNMENT MEMBERS *as at July 2010*

Prime Minister, Foreign Affairs, Defence, Feleti (Fred) Sevele
Deputy Prime Minister, Villiami Tau Tangi
Finance, Afu'alo Matoto

TONGA HIGH COMMISSION

36 Molyneux Street, London W1H 6AB
T 020-7724 5828 E snkioa@tongahighcom.co.uk
High Commissioner, HE Dr Sione Ngongo Kioa, *apptd* 2006

BRITISH HIGH COMMISSIONER

HE Malcolm McLachlan, MBE, resident at Suva, Fiji, *apptd* 2009

ECONOMY AND TRADE

There are few natural resources and the country is dependent on foreign aid and remittances from Tongans working abroad. Tourism is the second-largest source of foreign exchange revenue after remittances. The government is encouraging the development of a private sector. Unemployment is high.

Agriculture, fishing and tourism are the main economic activities. The main crops are squashes, coconuts, bananas, vanilla beans, cocoa, coffee, ginger and black pepper. Fish is an important staple food. A small light industry sector processes agricultural produce.

The main export markets are the USA, Japan and New Zealand; imports come chiefly from Fiji and New Zealand. Principal exports are squashes, fish, vanilla beans and root crops. The main imports are foodstuffs, machinery and transport equipment, fuels and chemicals.
GNI – US$279m; US$2,690 per capita (2008)
Annual average growth of GDP – –0.5 per cent (2009 est)
Inflation rate – 5.9 per cent (2007 est)
Population below poverty line – 24 per cent (2004 est)
Unemployment – 13 per cent (2004 est)
Total external debt – US$80.7m (2004 est)
Imports – US$200m (2008)
Exports – US$80m (2007)

BALANCE OF PAYMENTS

Trade – US$135m deficit (2009)
Current Account – US$39m deficit (2008)

Trade with UK	*2008*	*2009*
Imports from UK	£722,719	£664,587
Exports to UK	£74,411	£88,838

COMMUNICATIONS

There are 680km of roads in Tonga, 184km of which are surfaced. Its principal port is Nuku'alofa. There are six airfields on the islands; one has a surfaced runway.

Competition between providers has stimulated rapid expansion of telecommunications services. In 2008 there were 25,500 fixed telephone lines in use, 50,500 mobile phone subscribers and 8,400 internet users.

MEDIA

A 2003 constitutional amendment increased state control of the media. The weekly newspaper, *Tonga Chronicle,* and the Tonga Broadcasting Commission, which operates television and radio stations, are both state-run. There are a number of private television and radio stations.

TRINIDAD AND TOBAGO

Republic of Trinidad and Tobago

Area – 5,128 sq. km
Capital – Port of Spain, on Trinidad; population, 57,351 (2009 est)

Major towns – Chaguanas, San Fernando, Scarborough (Tobago)
Currency – Trinidad and Tobago dollar (T$) of 100 cents
Population – 1,229,953 falling at 0.1 per cent a year (2008 est)
Religion – Christian (Roman Catholic 26 per cent, Anglican 8 per cent, Pentecostal 7 per cent, Baptist 7 per cent, Seventh-day Adventist 4 per cent, Presbyterian and Congregational 3 per cent, Jehovah's Witness 2 per cent, Methodist 1 per cent), Hindu 23 per cent, Muslim 6 per cent, indigenous religions 6 per cent (est)
Language – English (official), Caribbean Hindustani (a dialect of Hindi), French, Spanish, Chinese
Population density – 260 per sq. km (2008)
Urban population – 13 per cent (2007 est)
Median age (years) – 32.1 (2009 est)
National anthem – 'Forged From the Love of Liberty'
National day – 31 August (Independence Day)
Life expectancy (years) – 70.86 (2009 est)
Mortality rate – 8.11 (2009 est)
Birth rate – 14.36 (2009 est)
Infant mortality rate – 29.93 (2009 est)
HIV/AIDS adult prevalence – 1.2 per cent (2007 est)
Death penalty – Retained (last used 1999)
CPI score – 3.6 (2009)

CLIMATE AND TERRAIN

Trinidad, the most southerly of the West Indian islands, lies 11km off the north coast of Venezuela. The island is mostly flat, with low mountains, the Northern Range, across almost its entire northern width and some low hills in the centre. Elevation extremes range from 940m (Mt Aripo) at the highest point to 0m (Caribbean Sea) at the lowest. Pitch Lake, on the south-west coast, is the world's largest natural source of asphalt.

Tobago lies 30km north-east of Trinidad. The island has a range of hills, Main Ridge, running along its length; the highest point is 565m. Several islands, of which Chacachacare, Huevos, Monos and Gaspar Grande are the most important, lie west of Corozal Point, the north-west extremity of Trinidad.

The climate is tropical, with a wet season from June to December. Temperatures are constant all year round.

HISTORY AND POLITICS

Trinidad is believed to be the oldest site of human habitation in the Caribbean archipelago, with excavated human remains dating back 7,200 years. The islands were home to a number of indigenous peoples, including the Nepuyo, Yaio and Caribs.

Trinidad and Tobago were discovered by Columbus in 1498. Trinidad was colonised in 1532 by Spain, capitulated to the British in 1797, and was ceded to Britain in 1802. Tobago was colonised by the Dutch from the 1630s but subsequently changed hands numerous times until it was ceded to Britain by France in 1814. The two islands were amalgamated into a single British colony in 1889. Internal self-government was granted in 1959 and independence was attained on 31 August 1962; the country became a republic in 1976. Although politically stable, the republic has experienced growing levels of drug- and gang-related violence since the 1990s.

The People's National Movement (PNM) has dominated post-independence politics, only out of office in 1986–91 and 1995–2001, and from May 2010. The PNM won the 2009 election for the Tobago legislature, but lost an early general election in May 2010 to the People's Partnership coalition, which took office under Kamla Persad-Bissessar, the country's first female prime minister. President Richards, first elected in 2003, was declared re-elected in February 2008, when he was the only candidate for the presidency.

POLITICAL SYSTEM

Under the 1976 constitution, the president is elected for a five-year term by an electoral college consisting of both houses of the legislature. The bicameral parliament comprises the House of Representatives and the senate. The former has 41 members directly elected for a five-year term. The senate has 31 members, of whom 16 are appointed on the advice of the prime minister, six on the advice of the leader of the opposition and nine at the discretion of the president, to serve a five-year term.

Since 1980 Tobago has had internal self-government through its House of Assembly, which has 16 members, 12 directly elected and four chosen by the house for a four-year term.

HEAD OF STATE

President, George Maxwell Richards, *elected* 14 February 2003, *took office* 17 March 2003, *re-elected* 2008

SELECTED GOVERNMENT MEMBERS *as at July 2010*

Prime Minister, Kamla Persad-Bissessar
Attorney-General, Anand Ramlogan
Finance, Winston Dookeran
Foreign Affairs, Surujrattan Rambuchan
National Security, Brig. John Sandy

HIGH COMMISSIONER OF THE REPUBLIC OF TRINIDAD AND TOBAGO

42 Belgrave Square, London SW1X 8NT
T 020-7245 9351 E tthc@btconnect.com
W www.tthighcommission.co.uk
High Commissioner, Serena Joseph-Harris, *apptd* 2009

BRITISH HIGH COMMISSION

PO Box 778, 19 St Clair Avenue, St Clair, Port of Spain
T (+868) 350 0444 E generalenquiries.ptofs@fco.gov.uk
W http://ukintt.fco.gov.uk
High Commissioner, HE Eric Jenkinson OBE, *apptd* 2007

BRITISH COUNCIL

c/o British High Commission
T (+868) 628 0565 W www.britishcouncil.org/tt.
Manager, Jasbinder Birk

DEFENCE

The coastguard has 25 patrol and coastal combatant vessels at 5 bases.
Military budget – US$158m (2009 est)
Military personnel – 4,063: army 3,000, coastguard 1,063

ECONOMY AND TRADE

The country is the most prosperous in the Caribbean, owing largely to its oil and natural gas reserves, but the government has encouraged diversification into petrochemicals, aluminium, plastics, financial services and tourism to reduce its dependence on the energy sector. After years of steady growth, the economy contracted in 2009 as demand for exports and oil prices dropped.

The agricultural sector is small, accounting for 0.5 per cent of GDP and 4 per cent of employment; the main products are cocoa, rice, citrus fruits, coffee, vegetables and poultry. Sugar production has declined since 2003 when the state-owned sugar company was closed. Apart from oil and gas extraction and processing, the main industries are tourism, food processing, production of chemicals, steel products, cement, beverages and cotton textiles.

The main trading partners are the USA (45 per cent of exports; 26 per cent of imports), Brazil, Spain, Venezuela and Jamaica. Principal exports are oil and petroleum products, liquified natural gas, chemicals, steel products, beverages, cereals and cereal products, sugar, cocoa, coffee, citrus fruits, vegetables and flowers. The main imports are fuels, lubricants, machinery, transport equipment, manufactured goods, food, chemicals and livestock.

GNI – US$22,100m; US$16,590 per capita (2008)
Annual average growth of GDP – −2.7 per cent (2009 est)
Inflation rate – 7.6 per cent (2009 est)
Population below poverty line – 17 per cent (2007 est)
Unemployment – 7.5 per cent (2009 est)
Total external debt – US$2,079m (2009 est)
Imports – US$9,900m (2008)
Exports – US$17,800m (2008)

BALANCE OF PAYMENTS
Trade – US$551m surplus (2009)
Current Account – US$8,775m surplus (2008)

Trade with UK	*2008*	*2009*
Imports from UK	£115,638,236	£105,938,549
Exports to UK	£190,423,859	£334,214,157

COMMUNICATIONS

The two islands have about 8,300km of roads, of which about half are surfaced. The three main ports are Scarborough (Tobago), Port of Spain and Point Lisas, where new industries powered by local natural gas are located. The international airport is at Port of Spain on Trinidad, and Tobago is served by Crown Point airport.

Modern telecommunications systems provided services to 307,000 fixed-line subscribers, 1.5 million mobile phone subscribers and 227,000 internet users in 2008.

EDUCATION AND HEALTH

Education is free at all state-owned and government-assisted denominational schools, and at certain faculties at the University of the West Indies. Attendance is compulsory for children aged six to 12 years, after which attendance at free secondary schools is determined by success in the secondary school entrance examination at 11 years.

Literacy rate – 98.7 per cent (2007 est)
Gross enrolment ratio (percentage of relevant age group) – primary 103 per cent; secondary 89 per cent (2008 est)
Health expenditure (per capita) – US$785 (2007)
Hospital beds (per 1,000 people) – 2.7 (2003–8)

MEDIA

There are both private and state-owned media organisations. Private television and radio stations predominate and the freedom of the press is constitutionally protected. *Newsday* and *Trinidad Guardian* are popular newspapers.

TUNISIA

Al-Jumhuriyah at-Tunisiyah – Tunisian Republic

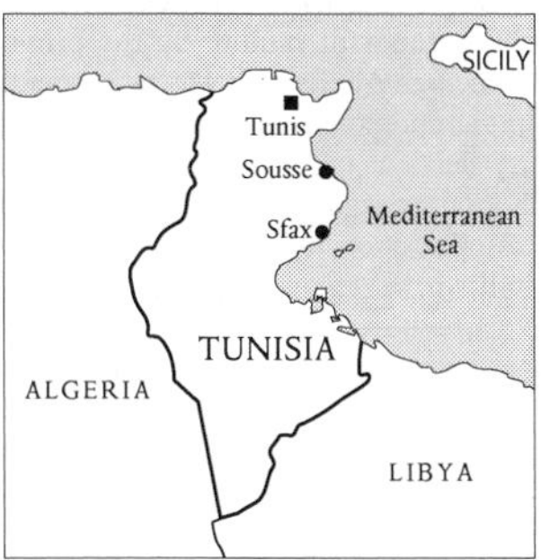

Area – 163,610 sq. km
Capital – Tunis; population, 758,729 (2009 est)
Major cities – Aryanah, Sfax
Currency – Tunisian dinar of 1,000 millimes
Population – 10,486,339 rising at 0.98 per cent a year (2009 est)
Religion – Muslim 99 per cent (predominantly Sunni; Shia less than 1 per cent) (est); small minorities of Christians and Jews. Sunni Islam is the official religion
Language – Arabic (official), French
Population density – 66 per sq. km (2008)
Urban population – 66 per cent (2007 est)
Median age (years) – 29.2 (2009 est)
National anthem – 'Himat al-Hima' ['Defenders of the Homeland']
National day – 20 March (Independence Day)
Life expectancy (years) – 75.78 (2009 est)
Mortality rate – 5.2 (2009 est)
Birth rate – 15.42 (2009 est)
Infant mortality rate – 22.57 (2009 est)
Death penalty – Retained (not used since 1991)
CPI score – 4.2 (2009)

CLIMATE AND TERRAIN

A central plain rises to mountains in the north, and in the semi-arid south merges into the Sahara desert. There are salt lakes in the west. Elevation extremes range from 1,544m (Jebel ech Chambi) at the highest point to −17m (Shatt al Gharsah) at the lowest. The northern and coastal regions have a Mediterranean climate, while there is a desert climate in the south. Average temperatures in Tunis range from lows of 6°C in January to highs of 33°C in August.

HISTORY AND POLITICS

The area was ruled successively by the Phoenicians, Carthaginians, Romans, Byzantines and Arabs before becoming a largely autonomous part of the Ottoman Empire in the 16th century. In the 19th century French influence grew and it was formally declared a French protectorate in 1883. It was briefly occupied by Germany during the Second World War (1942–3), and became independent as a monarchy under the bey in 1956. In 1957 the bey was deposed and the country became a republic under one-party rule with Habib Bourguiba as president.

There was a growing demand throughout the 1970s for the legalisation of other political parties and the government's resistance to these led to serious unrest. Multiparty legislative elections were held in 1981, but the ruling party, now known as the Constitutional Democratic Rally (RCD), has retained its grip on power over the past two decades. Although proclaimed president for life in 1975, President Bourguiba was deposed in 1987 on the grounds of senility by the prime minister Zine el-Abidine Ben Ali. Ben Ali was subsequently elected president in unopposed elections in 1989 and 1994, and in multiparty elections in 1999, 2004 and 2009.

The authoritarian regime maintains tight constraints on the political opposition, with electoral laws and media access weighted in favour of the RCD. The main opposition party boycotted the presidential election in 2004, and a change in the electoral laws prevented its preferred candidate from standing in 2009. In the legislative election in October 2009, the RCD retained its overwhelming majority in the lower legislative chamber.

POLITICAL SYSTEM

The 1959 constitution has been amended a number of times, most recently in 2002 to remove the restriction on the number of presidential terms and to establish a second legislative chamber. The executive president is directly elected for a five-year term. The parliament *(Barlaman)* comprises the Chamber of Deputies *(Majlis al-Nuwaab)*, with 214 members directly elected for a five-year term, and the Chamber of Councillors *(Majlis al-Mustasharin)*, which has 126 members (85 elected by municipal councils, professional organisations and trade unions, and 41 appointed by the president), who serve a six-year term, with half elected every three years.

HEAD OF STATE

President, Zine el-Abidine Ben Ali, *took office* 7 November 1987, *elected* 2 April 1989, *re-elected* 1994, 1999, 2004, 2009

SELECTED GOVERNMENT MEMBERS *as at July 2010*

Prime Minister, Mohammed Ghannouchi
Defence, Ridha Grira
Finance, Mohamed Ridha Chalghoum
Foreign Affairs, Kamel Morjane
Interior, Rafik Belhaj Kacem

EMBASSY OF TUNISIA

29 Prince's Gate, London SW7 1QG
T 020-7584 8117 E london@tunisianembassy.co.uk
Ambassador Extraordinary and Plenipotentiary, HE Hamida M'rabet Labidi, *apptd* 2007

BRITISH EMBASSY

Rue du Lac Windemere, Les Berges du Lac, 1053 Tunis
T (+216) (71) 108 700 E british.embassy@planet.tn
W http://ukintunisia.fco.gov.uk
Ambassador Extraordinary and Plenipotentiary, HE Chris O'Connor, *apptd* 2008

BRITISH COUNCIL

87 Avenue Mohamed V, 1002 Tunis Belvédère
T (+216) 7184 8588 W www.britishcouncil.org/tunisia
Director, Eunice Crook

DEFENCE

The army has 84 main battle tanks and 268 armoured personnel carriers. The navy has 25 patrol and coastal combatant vessels at 3 bases. The air force has 27 combat aircraft.

Military budget – US$534m (2008)
Military personnel – 35,800: army 27,000, navy 4,800, air force 4,000; paramilitary 12,000
Conscription duration – 12 months (selective)

ECONOMY AND TRADE

The economy is diverse and an increasing proportion is in private ownership. Further liberalisation is planned to attract foreign investment and remove barriers to trade with the EU. Growth was steady from the late 1990s until 2008, although the economy contracted in 2009 as export demand dropped, and poverty levels have been reduced.

Agriculture and fisheries account for 11 per cent of GDP; the main products are olives, grain, tomatoes, citrus fruits, sugar beets, dates, almonds, meat and dairy products. The main industries are oil production, mining (principally phosphates and iron ore), tourism, processing agricultural products and manufacture of textiles, footwear and beverages. Tourism is the chief foreign exchange earner.

The main trading partners are EU countries, especially France and Italy. Principal exports are clothing, semi-finished goods and textiles, agricultural products, mechanical goods, phosphates and chemicals, hydrocarbons and electrical equipment. The main imports are textiles, machinery and equipment, hydrocarbons, chemicals and foodstuffs.

GNI – US$36,000m; US$3,480 per capita (2008)
Annual average growth of GDP – 0.7 per cent (2009 est)
Inflation rate – 3.4 per cent (2009 est)
Population below poverty line – 7.4 per cent (2005 est)
Unemployment – 15.7 per cent (2009 est)
Total external debt – US$18,110m (2009 est)
Imports – US$24,600m (2008)
Exports – US$19,300m (2008)

BALANCE OF PAYMENTS

Trade – US$5,106m deficit (2009)
Current Account – US$620m deficit (2006)

Trade with UK	*2008*	*2009*
Imports from UK	£217,671,199	£152,643,422
Exports to UK	£395,317,180	£351,221,362

COMMUNICATIONS

Tunisia has 19,200km of roads, over 12,600km of which are surfaced. There are 2,200km of railways. The main ports include Bizerte, Sfax, Sousse and Tunis-La Goulette. The principal airports are at Tunis, Monastir and Djerba.

The telephone system is being upgraded and expanded, and mobile and internet subscriptions are growing rapidly. In 2008 there were 1.2 million fixed lines in use, 8.6 million mobile phone subscribers and 2.8 million internet users.

EDUCATION AND HEALTH

There are 11 years of free and compulsory education.

Literacy rate – 77.7 per cent (2007 est)
Gross enrolment ratio (percentage of relevant age group) – primary 108 per cent; secondary 90 per cent; tertiary 32 per cent (2008 est)
Health expenditure (per capita) – US$211 (2007)
Hospital beds (per 1,000 people) – 2.0 (2003–8)

MEDIA

The media is tightly controlled by the government; the state monopoly of broadcasting ended only in recent years and the private sector is still small. Most alternatives to the state-run television networks are satellite channels broadcasting pan-Arab programmes. An independent press exists but is closely monitored, and self-censorship is common because of the harsh penalties for breaching the press code. Foreign publications are frequently seized and internet access is monitored.

TURKEY

Turkiye Cumhuriyeti – Republic of Turkey

Area – 783,562 sq. km
Capital – Ankara (Angora), in Asia; population, 3,845,610 (2009 est)
Major cities – Adana, Antalya, Bursa, Gaziantep, Istanbul, Izmir, Konya
Currency – New Turkish lira (TL) of 100 kurus
Population – 76,805,524 rising at 1.31 per cent a year (2009 est); Turkish (70–75 per cent), Kurdish (18 per cent) (est)
Religion – Muslim 99 per cent (predominantly Hanafi, a school of Sunni Islam; a large minority are Alevi, a Shia sect); small Christian and Jewish minorities (est)
Language – Turkish (official), Kurdish, Dimli, Azeri, Kabardian
Population density – 96 per sq. km (2008)
Urban population – 68 per cent (2007 est)
Median age (years) – 27.7 (2009 est)
National anthem – 'Istiklal Marsi' ['The Independence March']
National day – 29 October (Republic Day)
Life expectancy (years) – 71.96 (2009 est)
Mortality rate – 6.1 (2009 est)
Birth rate – 18.66 (2009 est)
Infant mortality rate – 25.78 (2009 est)
Death penalty – Abolished for all crimes (since 2004)
CPI score – 4.4 (2009)

CLIMATE AND TERRAIN

Turkey in Europe consists of the relatively low-lying area of Eastern Thrace, including the cities of Istanbul and Edirne, and is separated from Asia by the Bosporus at Istanbul and by the Sea of Marmara and the Dardanelles (a strait about 64km in length, with a width varying from 1.6km to 6.4km).

Turkey in Asia comprises the whole of Asia Minor or Anatolia. Western Anatolia consists of a high central plateau with narrow coastal plains fringed by mountains in the north and south. Eastern Anatolia is mountainous, the land falling to a plateau between the mountains and the Syrian border. Elevation extremes range from 5,166m (Mt Ararat) at the highest point to 0m (Mediterranean Sea) at the lowest. The Euphrates and Tigris rivers rise in the eastern mountains, which also contain many lakes, including Lake Van. Anatolia is prone to earthquakes.

The climate is temperate, but more extreme in the interior. Average temperatures in Ankara range from lows of −4°C in January to highs of 31°C in August.

HISTORY AND POLITICS

Asia Minor was part of the empire of Alexander the Great and then of the Roman and Byzantine empires, coming under Turkish rule in the 11th century. The Ottoman Empire was founded in the 13th century and reached its zenith in the 16th century, its rule encompassing much of western Asia, northern Africa and south-eastern Europe. In the 17th century it began a steady decline, and after defeat in the First World War the empire's remaining territory was partitioned. Following a nationalist revolt and the expulsion of foreign forces, the sultanate was abolished and Turkey was proclaimed a republic on 29 October 1923, under Gazi Mustafa Kemal (later known as Kemal Ataturk), who was elected president. Policies of secularism, rapid modernisation, economic development and neutrality were introduced. Turkey was neutral for much of the Second World War, but joined the Allies in 1945.

Since 1945 there has been a multiparty system but political deadlock, economic problems and civil unrest or terrorism have led to military intervention to restore stability in 1960, 1971, 1980 and 1997.

Turkey joined NATO in 1952. It became a candidate for EU membership in 1999 and subsequently introduced constitutional, economic and human and civil rights reforms to meet the preconditions for membership negotiations. The EU accession process began in 2005 but impetus has flagged since 2007 because of internal political crises.

Tension between secularists and Islamists has grown in recent years, particularly since the Islamic-based Justice and Development Party (AKP), led by Recep Tayyip Erdogan, came to power in 2002. Seculists' concerns about the AKP's agenda caused a four-month political crisis in 2007, preventing the election of a new president and leading outgoing President Sezer to refuse approval of constitutional amendments. The impasse was ended by early legislative elections in July 2007, in which the AKP won a greatly increased majority. In August the AKP candidate, Abdullah Gul, was elected president in the third round of voting. Another legislative election is due by July 2011.

INSURGENCIES

Turkey's 12 million Kurds are the majority population in the south-east of the country, and have sought greater political and cultural rights for many years. The Kurdistan Workers' Party (PKK) has fought a guerrilla war for an ethnic homeland in the south-east since 1984 and has been blamed for bombings in other parts of Turkey. Conflict on the Turkey–Iraq border has caused tension in relations with Iraq, especially in 2008 after Turkish military incursions into the autonomous Kurdish area in northern Iraq, where PKK fighters have taken refuge. The government started to seek a political solution to the violence in 2009, introducing measures to increase Kurdish language rights and reduce the military presence in the south-east.

Pro-Islamic parties have become increasingly popular since the 1990s, and a number have been banned since 1998 for acting as a focus for anti-secular activities.

A number of bombings, attributed to Muslim extremists, occurred in Istanbul in 2003 and 2004.

POLITICAL SYSTEM
The 1982 constitution has been amended several times, mostly recently in 2007; further constitutional amendments, including reforms which would reinforce civil liberties and increase civilian control of the military, were to be put to a referendum in September 2010. The current president was elected by the legislature for a single seven-year term; in future, the president will be directly elected for a four-year term, renewable only once. The unicameral Turkish Grand National Assembly has 550 members who were directly elected for a five-year term; from the next election the term will be four years. The prime minister is appointed by the president and appoints the cabinet.

HEAD OF STATE
President, Abdullah Gul, *elected* 27 August 2007

SELECTED GOVERNMENT MEMBERS *as at July 2010*
Prime Minister, Recep Tayyip Erdogan
Deputy Prime Ministers, Ali Babacan *(Economic Affairs)*; Bulent Arinc; Cemil Cicek
Finance, Mehmet Simsek
Foreign Affairs, Ahmet Davutoglu
Interior, Besir Atalay

EMBASSY OF THE REPUBLIC OF TURKEY
43 Belgrave Square, London SW1X 8PA
T 020-7393 0202 E turkemb.london@mfa.gov.tr
W www.londra.be.mfa.gov.tr
Ambassador Extraordinary and Plenipotentiary, HE Unal Cevikoz, *apptd* 2010

BRITISH EMBASSY
Sehit Ersan Caddesi 46/A, Cankaya, Ankara
T (+90) (312) 455 3344 E britembinf@turk.net
W http://ukinturkey.fco.gov.uk
Ambassador Extraordinary and Plenipotentiary, HE David Reddaway, CMG, MBE, *apptd* 2009

BRITISH COUNCIL
Karum Is Merkezi, D Blok 430 Kat 5, Kavalklidere, Ankara
T (+90) (312) 455 3600 W www.britishcouncil.org.tr
Director, Jeff Streeter

DEFENCE
The army has 4,503 main battle tanks, 3,643 armoured personnel carriers, 650 armoured infantry fighting vehicles and 37 armed helicopters. The navy has 14 submarines, 23 frigates, 43 patrol and coastal vessels, 7 combat aircraft and 10 armed helicopters at 12 bases. The air force has 426 combat aircraft. Since its invasion of Cyprus in 1974, Turkey has maintained forces in the north of the island and at present has about 36,000 personnel stationed there.

As a member of NATO, Turkey is host to the Sixth Allied Tactical Air Force Headquarters. US air force detachments (1,514 personnel) are based at Incirlik in southern Turkey.
Military expenditure – US$13,500m (2008)
Military personnel – 510,600: army 402,000, navy 48,600, air force 60,000; paramilitary 102,200
Conscription duration – 15 months

ECONOMY AND TRADE
The economy combines modern industry and commerce with a traditional agriculture sector. The private sector is growing steadily, although basic industry, banking, transport and communications remain largely under state control. Since 2002, the government has implemented a stringent IMF programme, which achieved growth averaging over 5 per cent a year from 2005 to 2007, although the economy contracted sharply in 2009 because of the global downturn despite government stimulus measures. Large current account and public debt deficits remain.

The agricultural sector accounts for 9.3 per cent of GDP and employs 29.5 per cent of the workforce. The principal crops are tobacco, cotton, grain, olives, sugar beets, pulses, nuts, citrus and other fruits, and livestock products. A diverse industrial sector is dominated by textiles and clothing (which employ one-third of the industrial workforce), food processing, vehicle assembly, electronics, mining, iron and steel, oil, construction, timber and paper. Turkey is also a destination and a transit route for oil and gas from central Asian countries. Tourism is a major industry and source of foreign revenue. Industry contributes 25.6 per cent of GDP and services 65.1 per cent.

The main trading partners are EU countries (especially Germany), Russia, China and the USA. Principal exports are clothing, foodstuffs, textiles, metal manufactures and transport equipment. The main imports are machinery, chemicals, semi-finished manufactures, fuels and transport equipment.
GNI – US$666,600m; US$9,020 per capita (2008)
Annual average growth of GDP – –5.8 per cent (2009 est)
Inflation rate – 5.9 per cent (2009 est)
Unemployment – 14.6 per cent (2009 est)
Total external debt – US$253,200m (2009)
Imports – US$201,800m (2008)
Exports – US$132,000m (2008)

BALANCE OF PAYMENTS
Trade – US$38,611m deficit (2009)
Current Account – US$13,853m deficit (2009)

Trade with UK	*2008*	*2009*
Imports from UK	£2,450,632,387	£2,252,092,566
Exports to UK	£4,676,274,116	£3,935,699,827

COMMUNICATIONS
Turkey has nearly 427,000km of roads, of which about a third are surfaced. There are almost 8,700km of railways, and 1,200km of navigable waterways. The principal ports are Istanbul (Europe) and Izmir (Asia). There is a large merchant fleet of 612 ships of 1,000 tonnes or over. The principal airports are at Istanbul and Ankara.

Telecommunications systems are being modernised and expanded, especially the mobile phone network. There were 17.5 million fixed lines in use, 65.8 million mobile phone subscribers and 24.5 million internet users in 2008.

EDUCATION AND HEALTH
Education is free, secular and compulsory from the ages of six to 14. There are elementary, secondary and vocational schools.
Literacy rate – 88.7 per cent (2007 est)
Gross enrolment ratio (percentage of relevant age group) – primary 98 per cent; secondary 82 per cent; tertiary 37 per cent (2008 est)

Health expenditure (per capita) – US$465 (2007)
Hospital beds (per 1,000 people) – 2.8 (2003–8)

MEDIA

Media freedom has increased since 1999 as many restrictions have been lifted to comply with EU accession requirements. However, journalists remain subject to harassment and prosecution, and broadcasters to suspension of services for airing sensitive issues. Turkey has one state television and radio broadcaster, TRT, over 300 private television channels and more than 1,000 private radio stations. TRT has begun to broadcast Kurdish-language programmes, to conform with EU criteria on minority rights. There are around 40 national daily newspapers, including *Hurriyet, Milliyet* and *Cumhuriyet,* and the English-language *Hurriyet Daily News.*

CULTURE

Turkey is rich in archaeological remains, including Ephesus, a religious and cultural centre in Greek and Roman times, and an important centre of early Christianity; Troy, the Homeric city of Ilium; and a wealth of sites from the Roman, Byzantine, early Christian and Ottoman periods. Ankara (then called Ancyra) was the capital of the Roman province of *Galatia Prima,* and a marble temple (now in ruins), dedicated to Augustus, contains the *Monumentum (Marmor) Ancyranum,* inscribed with a record of the reign of Augustus Caesar.

The Roman city of Byzantium was selected by Constantine the Great as the capital of the eastern Roman Empire in AD 328 and was renamed Constantinople after the emperor's death. Now Istanbul, it contains the celebrated church of St Sophia, which, after becoming a mosque, was made a museum in 1934, and Topkapi, the former palace of the Ottoman sultans. In 2006 author Orhan Pamuk (*b.* 1952) became the first Turkish Nobel laureate.

TURKMENISTAN

Area – 488,100 sq. km
Capital – Ashgabat; population, 637,238 (2009 est)
Major cities – Dashhowuz, Turkmenabat
Currency – Manat of 100 tennesi
Population – 4,884,887 rising at 1.14 per cent a year (2009 est); Turkmen (85 per cent), Uzbek (5 per cent), Russian (4 per cent) (est)
Religion – Muslim 89 per cent (majority Sunni), Christian 9 per cent (mainly Eastern Orthodox) (est)
Language – Turkmen (official), Russian, Uzbek
Population density – 11 per sq. km (2008)
Urban population – 48 per cent (2007 est)
Median age (years) – 24.46 (2008 est)
National anthem – 'Garassyz baky Bitarap Turkmenistanyn Dowlet Gimni' ['National Anthem of Independent Neutral Turkmenistan']
National day – 27 October (Independence Day)
Life expectancy (years) – 67.87 (2009 est)
Mortality rate – 6.31 (2009 est)
Birth rate – 19.69 (2009 est)
Infant mortality rate – 45.36 (2009 est)
Death penalty – Abolished for all crimes (since 1999)
CPI score – 1.8 (2009)
Literacy rate – 99.5 per cent (2007 est)
Health expenditure (per capita) – US$139 (2007 est)
Hospital beds (per 1,000 people) – 4.1 (2003–8)

CLIMATE AND TERRAIN

Over 80 per cent of the country is taken up by the Kara Kum (Black Sands) desert. There are mountains in the south and along the Iranian border, and areas below sea level along the edges of the Caspian Sea. Elevation extremes range from 3,139m (Gora Ayribaba) at the highest point to −81m (Lake Akchanaya) at the lowest (although, because of fluctuations in its water level, Lake Sarygamysh sometimes has a lower elevation). There is a subtropical desert climate. Average temperatures in Ashgabat range from lows of −4°C in January to highs of 36°C in July.

HISTORY AND POLITICS

Turkmenistan was conquered successively by the Persians, Greeks (under Alexander the Great), Parthians, Arabs and Mongols from the sixth century BC. From the early 19th century until 1886 Turkmenistan was gradually incorporated into the Russian Empire. A Turkmen revolt against Russian rule in 1916 brought a period of autonomy until 1921, when Soviet control over Turkmenistan was established and it became an Autonomous Soviet Socialist Republic. Turkmenistan became a full republic of the USSR in 1925. It declared its independence from the USSR on 27 October 1991.

Saparmurat Niyazov became leader of the Turkmen Communist Party in 1985, and was elected president in 1990, becoming president for life in 2004. His autocratic regime, through harassment and authoritarianism, prevented the development of any effective political opposition or press freedom, rejecting political pluralism in favour of a cult of personality. After President Niyazov's death in 2006, Gurbanguly Berdimuhammedov was elected president. He is introducing reforms, but the country remains in effect a one-party state under an authoritarian regime.

The Democratic Party of Turkmenistan (DP), the renamed Communist Party, is currently the only legal political party, although the president has said that other political parties might be registered. The DP held all the seats in the legislature after the 2008 elections.

POLITICAL SYSTEM

A new constitution was adopted in 2008 which encouraged multiparty politics and economic liberalisation and abolished the People's Council. The executive president is directly elected for a five-year term. The unicameral parliament *(Majlis)* has 125 members directly elected for a five-year term.

The country is divided into five provinces (Ahal, Balkan, Dashhowuz, Lebap and Mary) and the city of Ashgabat.

HEAD OF STATE
President, Chair of the Council of Ministers, Gurbanguly Berdimuhammedov, *elected* 14 February 2007

SELECTED GOVERNMENT MEMBERS *as at July 2010*
First Deputy Chair, Foreign Affairs, Rashid Meredov
Defence, Yaylim Berdiyew
Finance, Annamuhammet Gocyyew
Interior, Iskander Mulikov

EMBASSY OF TURKMENISTAN
2nd Floor, St George's House, 14–17 Wells Street, London W1T 3PD
T 020-7255 1071 E tkm-embassy-uk@btconnect.com
W www.turkmenembassy.org.uk
Ambassador Extraordinary and Plenipotentiary, HE Yazmurad N. Seryayev, *apptd* 2003

BRITISH EMBASSY
301–308 Office Building, Four Points Ak Altin Hotel, Ashgabat
T (+993) (12) 363 462 E beasb@online.tm
W http://ukinturkmenistan.fco.gov.uk
Ambassador Extraordinary and Plenipotentiary, HE Keith Allan, *apptd* 2010

DEFENCE

The army has 680 main battle tanks, 829 armoured personnel carriers and 942 armoured infantry fighting vehicles. The navy has 10 patrol and coastal combatant vessels. The air force has 94 combat aircraft and 10 armed helicopters.
Military expenditure – US$84m (2008)
Military personnel – 22,000: army 18,500, navy 500, air force 3,000
Conscription duration – 24 months

ECONOMY AND TRADE

The Niyazov regime was reluctant to adopt market reforms; his successor has introduced reforms, but most economic activity remains in state control and is inefficient. Turkmenistan has large reserves of natural gas and some oil, but exports were restricted by a lack of export routes until 2009–10, when existing pipelines to Russia and Iran were supplemented by a new gas pipeline to China and a second pipeline to Iran; a trans-Caucasian route to European markets is also under exploration. However, government misuse of the revenues from these commodities means little has been done to alleviate the widespread poverty or high level of unemployment.

Agriculture is intensive around the irrigated oases, with half the irrigated land used to grow cotton, although exports of this commodity have halved in recent years owing to poor harvests. Agriculture accounts for 10.1 per cent of GDP and 48 per cent of employment; grain and livestock are the other main products. The principal industries are gas and oil production, petroleum products, textiles (including silk) and food processing. Industry contributes 30.5 per cent of GDP.

The main export markets are Ukraine, Turkey, Hungary and the UAE; imports come chiefly from China, Turkey and Russia. Principal exports are gas, crude oil, petrochemicals, textiles and cotton fibre. The main imports are machinery and equipment, chemicals and foodstuffs.
GNI – US$14,400m; US$2,840 per capita (2008)
Annual average growth of GDP – 2.9 per cent (2009 est)
Inflation rate – 15 per cent (2009 est)
Population below poverty line – 30 per cent (2004 est)
Unemployment – 60 per cent (2004 est)
Total external debt – US$1,400m (2004 est)

BALANCE OF PAYMENTS
Trade – US$4,214m surplus (2009)
Current Account – US$1,678m deficit (2009)

Trade with UK	*2008*	*2009*
Imports from UK	£19,008,387	£28,513,671
Exports to UK	£28,875,569	£59,426,834

COMMUNICATIONS

Turkmenistan has 58,600km of roads, nearly 47,600km of which are surfaced, and 3,000km of railways. There are two important waterways, the Amu Darya river in the north-east and the Niyazov (formerly Kara Kum) canal running across the Kara Kum desert from the Amu Darya to the Caspian Sea, providing 1,300km of transport routes. The main port is Turkmenbashi, on the Caspian Sea, and the main airport is at Ashgabat.

Telecommunications networks are underdeveloped but are being expanded. There were 478,000 fixed lines in use, 1.1 million mobile phone subscribers and 75,000 internet users in 2008.

MEDIA

The government has total control of the media, monitoring output, operating printing presses, censoring foreign media output before broadcast and controlling access to the internet. There are no private broadcast media, and most newspapers are mouthpieces of state or party organisations.

TUVALU

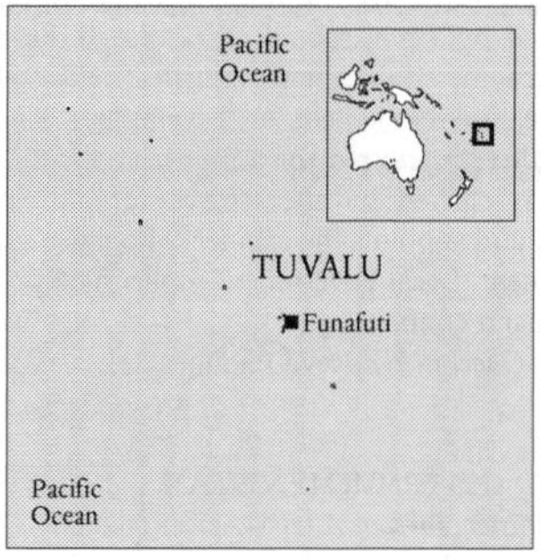

Area – 26 sq. km
Capital – Funafuti; population, 4,956 (2009 est)
Currency – The Australian dollar (A$) of 100 cents is legal tender. In addition there are Tuvalu dollar and cent coins in circulation
Population – 12,373 rising at 1.62 per cent a year (2009 est); Polynesian (96 per cent), Micronesian (4 per cent) (est)
Religion – Christian (Congregationalist 91 per cent, Seventh-day Adventist 3 per cent, Jehovah's Witness 2 per cent, Roman Catholic 1 per cent), Baha'i 3 per cent (est)
Language – English, Tuvaluan (both official), Samoan, Kiribati (on Nui)
Population density – 423 per sq. km (1999)
Urban population – 49 per cent (2007 est)
Median age (years) – 25.4 (2009 est)

National anthem – 'Tuvalu mo te Atua' ['Tuvalu for the Almighty']
National day – 1 October (Independence Day)
Life expectancy (years) – 69.29 (2009 est)
Mortality rate – 6.95 (2009 est)
Birth rate – 23.11 (2009 est)
Infant mortality rate – 18.43 (2009 est)
Death penalty – Abolished for all crimes (since 1978)

CLIMATE AND TERRAIN

Tuvalu comprises nine low-lying coral islands and atolls, in the south-west Pacific Ocean. The highest elevation is 5m and the lowest 0m (Pacific Ocean). The climate is tropical, with an average temperature of 26°C all year round.

HISTORY AND POLITICS

The islands were discovered by Europeans in the 18th century and, as the Ellice Islands, came under the control of the British in 1877. They formed part of the Gilbert and Ellice Islands protectorate (later a colony) from 1892, but were granted separate status from the Gilbert Islands in 1975. The islands became independent as Tuvalu on 1 October 1978. The country is seriously affected by rising sea levels, which are threatening its economic viability.

There are no political parties; allegiances are influenced by personal and island loyalties. Although politically stable as a democracy, there are frequent changes in government as support in parliament shifts. Most of the government lost their seats in the 2006 legislative election and a new cabinet was appointed following the election of Apisai Ielemia as prime minister. A legislative election was expected in September 2010.

POLITICAL SYSTEM

Under the 1978 constitution, Tuvalu is a constitutional monarchy with Queen Elizabeth II as head of state, represented by a governor-general who is appointed on the advice of the prime minister. The unicameral legislature, the Parliament of Tuvalu, has 15 members who are directly elected for a four-year term. The prime minister is elected by the legislature from among its members, and appoints the cabinet, who must be members of parliament. Local government services are provided by elected island councils.

Governor-General, HE Revd Filoimea Telito, GCMG, MBE

SELECTED GOVERNMENT MEMBERS *as at July 2010*
Prime Minister; Foreign Affairs, Apisai Ielemia
Deputy Prime Minister, Taavau Teii
Finance, Lotoala Metia
Home Affairs, Willy Telavi

HONORARY CONSULATE OF TUVALU
Tuvalu House, 230 Worple Road, London SW20 8RH
T 020-8879 0985 E tuvaluconsulate@netscape.net
Honorary Consul, Dr Iftikhar A. Ayaz

BRITISH HIGH COMMISSIONER
HE Malcolm McLachlan, MBE, *apptd* 2009, resident at Suva, Fiji

ECONOMY AND TRADE

The main economic activities are subsistence agriculture and fishing, although agricultural productivity is threatened by the increasing salinity of the soil as the sea level rises; the only cash crop is coconuts. Tourism is limited by the state's remoteness. Most employment is in the public sector or abroad, often as merchant seamen; many families rely on remittances from expatriate workers. The government receives substantial annual income from a trust fund set up in 1987, and raises revenue through the sale of fishing licences, postage stamps and coins, and the leasing of its 900 telephone code and .tv internet suffix.

The main trading partners are Japan, the USA, New Zealand and Australia. The only exports are copra and fish. The main imports are food, livestock, fuels, machinery and manufactured goods.

Annual average growth of GDP – 3 per cent (2006 est)
Inflation rate – 3.8 per cent (2006 est)

Trade with UK	*2008*	*2009*
Imports from UK	£23,804	£932
Exports to UK	—	—

COMMUNICATIONS

Funafuti has an airfield, from which a service operates regularly to Fiji and Kiribati, and it is also the main port. There are 8km of roads on the islands. The telephone system provides an adequate service, with 1,500 fixed lines in use, 2,000 mobile phone subscribers and 4,200 internet users in 2008.

MEDIA

The state-owned Tuvalu Media Corporation publishes a fortnightly newspaper and runs Radio Tuvalu, the main information source for islanders. There is no domestic television, although many islanders watch foreign programming via satellite.

UGANDA

Republic of Uganda

Area – 241,038 sq. km
Capital – Kampala; population, 1,535,060 (2009 est)
Major towns – Entebbe, Gulu, Lira
Currency – Uganda shilling of 100 cents
Population – 32,369,558 rising at 2.69 per cent a year (2008 est); Baganda (16.9 per cent), Banyakole (9.5 per cent), Basoga (8.4 per cent), Bakiga (6.9 per cent), Iteso (6.4 per cent), Langi (6.1 per cent), Acholi (4.7 per cent), Bagisu (4.6 per cent), Lugbara (4.2 per cent), Bunyoro (2.7 per cent); over 10 other ethnic groups
Religion – Christian 85 per cent (Roman Catholic 42 per cent, Anglican 36 per cent, Evangelical and Pentecostal 7 per cent), Muslim 12 per cent (predominantly Sunni), traditional indigenous beliefs 3 per cent (est); indigenous beliefs are often blended into or observed alongside Christianity or Islam

Language – English (official), Luganda, Swahili, Arabic
Population density – 161 per sq. km (2008)
Urban population – 13 per cent (2007 est)
Median age (years) – 15 (2009 est)
National anthem – 'O Uganda, Land of Beauty'
National day – 9 October (Independence Day)
Life expectancy (years) – 52.72 (2009 est)
Mortality rate – 12.09 (2009 est)
Birth rate – 47.84 (2009 est)
Infant mortality rate – 64.82 (2009 est)
HIV/AIDS adult prevalence – 5.2 per cent (2007 est)
Death penalty – Retained
CPI score – 2.5 (2009)

CLIMATE AND TERRAIN

The landlocked country lies on a high plateau with mountain ranges in the west, south-west and north-east. Elevation extremes range from 5,110m (Mt Stanley) at the highest point to 621m (Lake Albert) at the lowest. Nearly 20 per cent of the country is covered by lakes, rivers and wetlands, and it contains about half of lakes Victoria, Edward and Albert (Mobuto), as well as lakes Kyoga, Kwania, George and Bisina (formerly Salisbury) and the course of the Nile from its outlet from Lake Victoria to the Sudan border at Nimule. The climate is tropical, moderated by the altitude. There are two rainy seasons (March–May, October–December) in the south; the north is drier, semi-arid in places, with a single, longer rainy season.

HISTORY AND POLITICS

Indigenous people had formed several kingdoms in the area by the 14th century. External contact began in the early 19th century with Arab traders and then European explorers. A British protectorate was established over the kingdom of Buganda in 1894 and gradually extended to other territory by 1914. Uganda became independent on 9 October 1962 as a federation of the kingdoms of Ankole, Buganda, Bunyoro, Busoga and Toro.

In 1963 Uganda was proclaimed a federal republic but in 1966 prime minister Milton Obote overthrew the president, ended the federal status and became executive president. In 1971 President Obote was deposed in an army coup led by Maj.-Gen. Idi Amin, who proclaimed himself head of state. His brutal dictatorship was overthrown in 1979 with military assistance from Tanzania.

Milton Obote was re-elected president in 1980 but political instability and human rights abuses continued. He was ousted by a military coup in 1985 amid a civil war with the rebel National Resistance Army (NRA) led by Yoweri Museveni. A military council was installed but the NRA captured Kampala in January 1986, securing control of the rest of the country in the following few months. Museveni began a process of reconstruction which has resulted in Uganda becoming relatively peaceful and stable, and restored a degree of prosperity.

Museveni's 'Movement' system of government, under which political parties were allowed to exist but not to contest elections, was in place from 1986 until a 2005 referendum resulted in a return to multiparty politics. In multiparty elections held in 2006, President Museveni was re-elected for a third term in the second round of the presidential election, and the National Resistance Movement retained its majority in parliament.

INSURGENCIES

The Lord's Resistance Army (LRA), whose aims have never been specified, began a low-level insurgency in northern Uganda in the late 1980s; thousands have been massacred or mutilated, an estimated 20,000 children abducted to serve in its forces, and 1.7 million people displaced into camps. The government and the LRA reached a negotiated settlement in 2008 after two years of talks, but the LRA leader has refused to sign the agreement. Despite offensives against LRA bases in their territories by Ugandan, Sudanese and Congolese forces in 2008–9, the LRA continues to attack civilians in north-eastern Congo (where most of the LRA is now located), southern Sudan, the Central African Republic and Kenya.

POLITICAL SYSTEM

The 1995 constitution was amended in 2005 to allow multiparty elections. The president is directly elected for a five-year term; the two-term limit was abolished in 2005. The unicameral parliament has 215 directly elected members and 94 (including 69 women) elected indirectly to represent particular groups; all serve a five-year term. The prime minister is appointed by the president, subject to the approval of parliament.

HEAD OF STATE

President, Yoweri Museveni, *sworn in* 29 January 1986, *elected* 9 May 1996, *re-elected* 2001, 2006
Vice-President, Gilbert Balibaseka Bukenya

SELECTED GOVERNMENT MEMBERS *as at July 2010*

Prime Minister, Apolo Nsibambi
Deputy Prime Ministers, Henry Muganwa Kajura; Eriya Kategaya; Ali Kirunda Kivejinja *(Internal Affairs)*
Defence, Crispus W. C. B. Kiyonga
Finance, Syda Namirembe Bbumba
Foreign Affairs, Sam Kutesa

UGANDA HIGH COMMISSION

Uganda House, 58–59 Trafalgar Square, London WC2N 5DX
T 020-7839 5783 **E** info@ugandahighcommission.co.uk
W www.ugandahighcommission.co.uk
High Commissioner, HE Joan Rwabyomere, *apptd* 2006

BRITISH HIGH COMMISSION

PO Box 7070, 4 Windsor Loop, Kampala
T (+256) (31) 231 2000 **E** bhcinfo@starcom.co.ug
W http://ukinuganda.fco.gov.uk
High Commissioner, HE Martin Shearman, CVO, *apptd* 2008

BRITISH COUNCIL

PO Box 7070, Rwenzori Courts, Plot 2 and 4A, Nakasero Road, Kampala
T (+256) (41) 456 0800 **W** www.britishcouncil.org/africa
Director, Sital Dhillon

DEFENCE

The army has 162 main battle tanks, 31 armoured infantry fighting vehicles and 79 armoured personnel carriers. The air force has 16 combat-capable aircraft and 6 armed helicopters.
Military expenditure – US$243m (2009)
Military personnel – 45,000: Ugandan People's Defence Force 45,000; paramilitary 1,800

ECONOMY AND TRADE

Economic reforms adopted since 1986 have produced steady economic growth, which has been only slightly affected by the global downturn. However, there has been little industrialisation, so the economy is vulnerable to fluctuations in global commodity prices, especially that of coffee, its main export. Uganda's debt burden has been reduced by debt relief since 2000 but it is still dependent on foreign aid.

Agriculture is the most important economic sector, contributing 22.5 per cent of GDP and engaging about 80 per cent of the workforce. The principal crops are coffee, tea, cotton, tobacco, cassava, potatoes, maize, millet, pulses, cut flowers and livestock products. Industrial activity centres on production of sugar, tobacco, cotton textiles, cement and steel, brewing and fishing. Tourism is growing, and oil has been discovered but is not yet being exploited.

The main export markets are neighbouring countries, the EU and Switzerland; imports come chiefly from Kenya, India, the UAE and China. Principal exports are coffee, fish and fish products, tea, cotton, cut flowers, horticultural products and gold. Electricity is exported to Kenya, Tanzania and Rwanda. The main imports are capital equipment, vehicles, petroleum, medical supplies and cereals.

GNI – US$13,300m; US$420 per capita (2008)
Annual average growth of GDP – 4 per cent (2009 est)
Inflation rate – 12.6 per cent (2009 est)
Total external debt – US$2,050m (2009 est)
Imports – US$4,800m (2008)
Exports – US$2,200m (2008)

BALANCE OF PAYMENTS
Trade – US$3,121m deficit (2009)
Current Account – US$469m deficit (2008)

Trade with UK	*2008*	*2009*
Imports from UK	£49,779,250	£49,659,175
Exports to UK	£18,875,845	£9,227,960

COMMUNICATIONS

There are over 1,200km of rail track, and 70,700km of roads, of which 16,300km are surfaced. Having no coast, Uganda is dependent upon rail and road links to Mombasa in Kenya and Dar es Salaam in Tanzania for much of its trade, although the lakes and the river Nile provide navigable routes internally and to neighbouring countries. There is an international airport at Entebbe, and over 30 other airports and airfields around the country.

The fixed-line telephone system is inadequate and mobile phone distribution is growing rapidly. In 2008 there were 169,000 fixed lines in use, 8.6 million mobile phone subscribers and 2.5 million internet users.

EDUCATION AND HEALTH

Education is a joint undertaking by the government, local authorities and voluntary agencies. In 1996 the Universal Primary Education programme was launched, under which four children per family are entitled to receive free primary education.

Literacy rate – 73.6 per cent (2007 est)
Gross enrolment ratio (percentage of relevant age group) – primary 120 per cent; secondary 25 per cent; tertiary 4 per cent (2008 est)
Health expenditure (per capita) – US$28 (2007)
Hospital beds (per 1,000 people) – 0.4 (2009)

MEDIA

Private broadcasters have proliferated since media laws were liberalised in 1993, although they can be subject to constraints if the government perceives reporting as a threat to national security or likely to raise racial tension. They operate alongside the television and radio networks run by the public broadcaster. Radio is the most popular medium. The main newspapers include *New Vision*, which is state-owned but editorially independent.

UKRAINE

Ukrayina – Ukraine

Area – 603,550 sq. km
Capital – Kyiv (Kiev); population, 2,778,850 (2009 est)
Major cities – Dnipropetrovsk, Donetsk, Kharkiv, L'viv, Odesa, Zaporizhzhya
Currency – Hryvnia of 100 kopiykas
Population – 45,700,395 falling at 0.63 per cent a year (2009 est); Ukrainian (77.8 per cent), Russian (17.3 per cent); small Belarusian, Moldovan, Crimean Tatar, Bulgarian, Romanian, Polish, Hungarian and Greek minorities
Religion – Christian (predominantly Ukrainian Orthodox; Greek Catholic 9 per cent, Roman Catholic 2 per cent), Muslim 1 per cent (predominantly Sunni) (est)
Language – Ukrainian (official), Russian
Population density – 80 per sq. km (2008)
Urban population – 68 per cent (2007 est)
Median age (years) – 39.5 (2009 est)
National anthem – 'Shche ne vmerla, Ukrainy' ['Ukraine's Glory Has Not Perished']
National day – 24 August (Independence Day)
Life expectancy (years) – 68.25 (2009 est)
Mortality rate – 15.81 (2009 est)
Birth rate – 9.6 (2009 est)
Infant mortality rate – 8.98 (2009 est)
HIV/AIDS adult prevalence – 1.1 per cent (2007 est)
Death penalty – Abolished for all crimes (since 1999)
CPI score – 2.2 (2009)

CLIMATE AND TERRAIN

Much of the country lies in a plain (steppe), with the Carpathian mountains in the west and mountains in the south of the Crimean peninsula. Elevation extremes range from 2,061m (Hora Hoverla) at the highest point to 0m (Black Sea) at the lowest. The main rivers are the Dnieper, which runs through the centre of the country, the Dniester in the west, the Southern Buh and the Northern Donets (a tributary of the Don). The climate is continental, and Mediterranean in the southern Crimea. Average temperatures in Kyiv range from lows of −10°C in January to highs of 25°C in July.

HISTORY AND POLITICS

The earliest Slavic state was formed on the river Dnieper with its capital at Kyiv in the ninth century AD. The area was invaded successively by the Goths, Huns and Khazars, and then by the Tatar-Mongols in the 13th century. It came under Lithuanian rule in the 14th century, and was part of the Polish–Lithuanian Commonwealth in the 16th century. The east rebelled in 1685 and became part of Russia in the 17th century. The west became part of the Habsburg empire after 1795.

A reunified Ukraine declared its independence in 1918, but a civil war ensued which ended in 1921 with the partitioning of Ukraine between the USSR and Poland. In 1922 Ukraine became a constituent republic of the USSR. Germany invaded and occupied Ukraine from 1941 until forced to withdraw by the Red Army in 1944. Ukraine regained its western territory in the aftermath of the Second World War, and in 1954 the Crimea was transferred from Russia to Ukraine. Ukraine declared itself independent of the USSR on 24 August 1991.

In 1986 Ukraine suffered the world's worst nuclear disaster, when a reactor at the Chernobyl nuclear plant exploded. At least 10,000 people have died from radiation poisoning, the long-term health of millions more has been affected and a large area of the country is permanently contaminated.

Tensions between pro-Russian and pro-western political blocs, and divisions within the pro-western parties, have caused political instability since 2004, with two legislative elections and several changes of government. The latest legislative election, in September 2007, was called after a power struggle between President Yushchenko and Viktor Yanukovych, prime minister from July 2006, produced a political impasse. Yanukovych's Party of Regions remained the largest party in the legislature but without an outright majority, and President Yushchenko's Our Ukraine–People's Self Defence Bloc (OUPSD) and the Yulia Tymoshenko Bloc (YTB) formed a coalition government headed by Yulia Tymoshenko (prime minister February–September 2005). This government collapsed in September 2008 after disagreements over its response to Russia's use of force in Georgia; an early legislative election was called for December, but was cancelled when the OUPSD and YTB joined with the Lytvyn Bloc to reconstitute the coalition government. The government resigned after losing a vote of confidence in March 2010 and was replaced by a four-party coalition led by the Party of the Regions, whose leader, Viktor Yanukovych, had been elected president in January 2010.

FOREIGN RELATIONS

In the aftermath of the USSR's disintegration in 1991, relations between Ukraine and Russia were strained by disputes over the Black Sea fleet and the status of Crimea. An agreement was reached in 1997 over the division of the fleet and Russia's lease of a naval base in Sevastapol. Disputes over Crimea have flared up intermittently, most recently in 2003 over a border in the region. The main causes of tension are the pro-Western policies pursued by some recent governments, particularly the possibility of Ukraine joining NATO, and the economic interdependence of the two countries; Ukraine is heavily dependent on Russia for gas supplies, and pipelines carrying much of Russia's gas exports to Europe pass through Ukraine. Price disputes have led to Russia suspending gas supplies on four occasions, but relations have improved since the election of President Yanukovych.

Ukraine signed a partnership and cooperation agreement with the EU in 1994 and an association agreement is under negotiation; President Yanukovych is less committed to EU membership than his predecessor. Ukraine was involved in NATO's Partnership for Peace programme in the 1990s. It applied for NATO membership during Viktor Yushchenko's presidency, but President Yanukovych's preference is for a strengthened relationship short of membership.

POLITICAL SYSTEM

The 1996 constitution was amended in 2006 to transfer some powers from the president to the legislature. The president is directly elected for a five-year term. The unicameral Supreme Council has 450 members, who are directly elected for a five-year term. The Supreme Council nominates the prime minister.

The country is divided into 24 provinces, the autonomous republic of Crimea and two municipalities (Kyiv and Sevastapol) with provincial status.

HEAD OF STATE

President, Viktor Yanukovych, *elected* 7 February 2010, *sworn in* 25 February 2010

SELECTED GOVERNMENT MEMBERS *as at August 2010*

Prime Minister, Mykola Azarov
First Deputy Prime Minister, Andriy Klyuyev
Deputy Prime Ministers, Borys Kolesnikov; Volodymyr Sivkovych; Serhiy Tyhypko; Viktor Tykhonov; Viktor Slauta
Finance, Fedir Yaroshenko
Interior, Anatoliy Mohylyov
Defence, Mykhaylo Yezhel
Foreign Affairs, Kostyantyn Hryshchenko
Economy, Vasyl Tsushko

EMBASSY OF UKRAINE

60 Holland Park, London W11 3SJ
T 020-7727 6312 **E** emb_gb@mfa.gov.ua
W www.ukremb.org.uk
Ambassador Extraordinary and Plenipotentiary, Dr Ihor Kharchenko, *apptd* 2005

BRITISH EMBASSY

Desyatinna 9, Kyiv 01025
T (+380) (44) 490 3660 **E** ukembinf@gmail.com
W ukinukraine.fco.gov.uk
Ambassador Extraordinary and Plenipotentiary, HE Leigh Turner, *apptd* 2008

BRITISH COUNCIL

4/12 Vul. Hryhoriya Skovorody, Kyiv 04070
T (+380) (44) 490 5600 **W** www.britishcouncil.org/ukraine
Director, Margaret Jack

DEFENCE

The army has 2,988 main battle tanks, 1,432 armoured personnel carriers, 3,028 armoured infantry fighting vehicles and 139 armed helicopters. The navy has 1 submarine, 1 frigate, 3 corvettes, 5 patrol and coastal vessels, 10 combat aircraft and 72 armed helicopters at 6 bases. The air force has 211 combat aircraft.

Russia has around 13,000 navy personnel at Sevastopol; Russia's lease of the naval base, agreed in 1997, was extended in 2010 to run until at least 2042.
Military budget – US$1,410m (2009)
Military personnel – 129,925: army 70,753, navy 13,932, air force 45,240; paramilitaries 84,900
Conscription duration – 18–24 months

ECONOMY AND TRADE

The first decade of independence was characterised by economic mismanagement and opposition to economic restructuring. Reform began in the late 1990s and brought economic growth, with rises in output and exports and a reduction in inflation. However, the slow progress of reform has been a drag on the economy, leaving it vulnerable to external factors such as the global economic downturn; the economy contracted severely in 2009 after key commodity prices and export demand fell. The government sought IMF support in autumn 2008, but some funding has been delayed owing to political volatility.

The agricultural sector is large and productive, with over half the land under cultivation. The main crops are grain, sugar beet, sunflower seeds and vegetables; stock-raising and dairy-farming are also important. Agriculture accounts for 9.8 per cent of GDP and 16 per cent of employment. There are large deposits of coal, iron ore and other minerals. The main industrial activities are mining and metal processing, manufacture of machinery and transport equipment, chemicals, petrochemicals, electricity generation and food processing, especially sugar. Ukraine imports three-quarters of its oil and gas, principally from Russia; supplies have been suspended on occasions by price disputes with Russia, but in 2009 the two countries signed 10-year gas supply and transit agreements.

The main trading partners are Russia (21 per cent of exports; 29 per cent of imports), China, Germany and Turkey. Principal exports are ferrous and non-ferrous metals (especially steel), fuel and petroleum products, chemicals, machinery and transport equipment, and foodstuffs. The main imports are energy (primarily gas), machinery and equipment, and chemicals.

GNI – US$148,600m; US$3,210 per capita (2008)
Annual average growth of GDP – –14.1 per cent (2009 est)
Inflation rate – 16.5 per cent (2009 est)
Population below poverty line – 37.7 per cent (2003)
Unemployment – 4.8 per cent (2009 est)
Total external debt – US$88,920m (2009 est)
Imports – US$85,500m (2008)
Exports – US$67,000m (2008)

BALANCE OF PAYMENTS
Trade – US$5,449m deficit (2009)
Current Account – US$12,763m deficit (2008)

Trade with UK	*2008*	*2009*
Imports from UK	£573,916,527	£583,689,767
Exports to UK	£178,655,211	£138,742,068

COMMUNICATIONS

Ukraine has a total of 169,400km of roads, 165,600km of which are surfaced. It has 21,700km of railways, and 2,200km of waterways, mostly on the river Dnieper. Its main seaports are Mariupol on the Sea of Azov, and Kherson, Mykolayiv, Odesa and Sevastopol on the Black Sea. There is a large merchant fleet of 189 ships of 1,000 tonnes and over, with a further 204 Ukrainian-owned ships registered in other countries. The principal airports are at Kyiv and Odesa.

The fixed-line telephone system is being improved. In 2008 there were 13.2 million fixed lines in use, 55.7 million mobile phone subscribers and 10.4 million internet users.

EDUCATION AND HEALTH

Literacy rate – 99.7 per cent (2007 est)
Gross enrolment ratio (percentage of relevant age group) – primary 98 per cent; secondary 94 per cent; tertiary 79 per cent (2008 est)
Health expenditure (per capita) – US$210 (2007)
Hospital beds (per 1,000 people) – 8.7 (2003–8)

MEDIA

There are several private and state-owned television and radio networks. Ukraine has seven daily newspapers, many of which are mass-circulation publications; some publish both Ukrainian and Russian editions. Major titles include *Fakty i Kommentarii, Silski Visti* and *Segodnya.* The press has asserted its independence to a much greater extent since the disputed presidential election of 2004.

UNITED ARAB EMIRATES

Al-Imarat al-Arabiyah al-Muttahidah – United Arab Emirates

Area – 83,600 sq. km
Capital – Abu Dhabi; population, 666,360 (2009 est)
Major cities – Ajman, Al-Ain, Ash Shariqah, Dubai
Currency – UAE dirham (Dh) of 100 fils
Population – 4,798,491 rising at 3.69 per cent a year (2009 est); Emirati nationals 20.1 per cent, non-nationals 79.9 per cent (2005 est); of the non-nationals, about half are from South Asia and a quarter are Arab or Iranian
Religion – Muslim 76 per cent, Christian 9 per cent (est), large Hindu and Buddhist minorities; Islam is the state religion, and 90 per cent of nationals are Muslim (Sunni 85 per cent, Shia 15 per cent)
Language – Arabic (official), Persian, English, Hindi, Urdu
Population density – 54 per sq. km (2008)
Urban population – 78 per cent (2007 est)
Median age (years) – 30.1 (2009 est)
National anthem – 'Ishy Bilady' ['Long Live My Homeland']
National day – 2 December (Independence Day)
Life expectancy (years) – 76.11 (2009 est)
Mortality rate – 2.11 (2009 est)
Birth rate – 16.02 (2009 est)
Infant mortality rate – 12.7 (2009 est)
Death penalty – Retained
CPI score – 6.5 (2009)

CLIMATE AND TERRAIN

The United Arab Emirates (UAE) is situated in the south-east of the Arabian peninsula. Six of the emirates lie on the shore of the Gulf, between the Musandam peninsula in the east and the Qatar peninsula in the west, while the seventh, Fujairah, lies on the Gulf of Oman. A flat coastal plain merges into the desert of the interior, and there are mountains in the east. Elevation extremes range from 1,527m (Jabal Yibir) at the highest point to 0m (Persian Gulf) at the lowest. There is a desert climate, although it is cooler in the mountains, with high humidity on the coast. Average temperatures in Sharjah range between lows of 12°C in January to highs of 39°C in August.

HISTORY AND POLITICS

The United Arab Emirates (formerly the Trucial States) is composed of seven emirates. Six of these came together as an independent state on 2 December 1971 when they ended their individual special treaty relationships with the British government, and they were joined by Ras al-Khaimah on 10 February 1972. On independence, the union government assumed full responsibility for all internal and external affairs apart from those internal matters that remain the prerogative of the individual emirates.

Sheikh Zayed of Abu Dhabi was president from independence until his death in 2004. He was succeeded as Sultan of Abu Dhabi by his son, Sheikh Khalifa, who was also elected president of the UAE. The first national elections were held in 2006, when half the members of the Federal National Council were elected by a small electoral college.

POLITICAL SYSTEM

The 1971 provisional constitution, approved in 1996, was amended in 2008 to extend the Federal National Council's term and convert it from a consultative into a legislative body. Overall authority lies with the Supreme Council, comprising the hereditary rulers of the seven emirates, each of whom also governs in his own territory. The president and vice-president are elected every five years by the Supreme Council from among its members. The president appoints the prime minister and the council of ministers. The unicameral Federal National Council has 40 members, eight members each from Abu Dhabi and Dubai, six each from Sharjah and Ras al-Khaimah and four each for Fujairah, Umm al-Qaiwain and Ajman; half are elected by an electoral college and half are appointed by the rulers of each emirate. In 2008 the council's original two-year term (2006–8) was extended to February 2011.

HEAD OF STATE

President, HH Sheikh Khalifa bin Zayed al-Nahyan *(Abu Dhabi), elected* 3 November 2004

Vice-President, Prime Minister, Defence, HH Sheikh Mohammed bin Rashid al-Maktoum *(Dubai)*

SELECTED GOVERNMENT MEMBERS *as at August 2010*

Deputy Prime Ministers, Lt.-Gen. Sheikh Saif bin Zayed al-Nahyan *(Interior);* Sheikh Mansour bin Zayed al-Nahyan

Finance, HH Sheikh Hamdan bin Rashid al-Maktoum

Foreign Affairs, Sheikh Abdullah bin Zayed al-Nahyan

Economy, Sultan bin Saeed al-Mansouri

EMBASSY OF THE UNITED ARAB EMIRATES

30 Prince's Gate, London SW7 1PT

T 020-7581 1281 E information@uaeembassyuk.net

W www.uaeembassyuk.net

Ambassador Extraordinary and Plenipotentiary, HE Abdul Rahman Ghanim al-Mutaiwee, *apptd* 2009

BRITISH EMBASSY

PO Box 248, Khalid bin al-Waleed Street (Street 22), Abu Dhabi

T (+971) (2) 610 1100 E chancery.abudhabi@fco.gov.uk

W ukinuae.fco.gov.uk

Ambassador Extraordinary and Plenipotentiary, HE Dominic Jermey, OBE, *apptd* 2010

BRITISH COUNCIL

PO Box 46523, Villa No. 7, Al-Nasr Street, Khalidiya, Abu Dhabi

T (+971) (2) 691 0600 W www.britishcouncil.org/me-uae

Director, Paul Sellers

FEDERAL STRUCTURE

The emirates are: Abu Dhabi, Ajman, Dubai, Fujairah, Ras al-Khaimah, Sharjah and Umm al-Qaiwain. Each emirate has its own government, judicial system and penal code. Abu Dhabi has an executive council chaired by the crown prince.

DEFENCE

The army has 471 main battle tanks, 892 armoured personnel carriers and 430 armoured infantry fighting vehicles. The navy has 2 frigates, 2 corvettes and 14 patrol and coastal vessels at 8 bases. The air force has 184 combat aircraft and over 40 armed helicopters.

Military budget – US$15,470m (2009 est)

Military personnel – 51,000: army 44,000, navy 2,500, air force 4,500

ECONOMY AND TRADE

Exploitation of the territories' oil reserves began in the 1960s and transformed the UAE from poor rural principalities into modern states with a high standard of living. Oil and gas production dominate the economy, although diversification means that the hydrocarbon sector now accounts for less than 25 per cent of GDP. The economy is also dependent on foreign workers, who make up about 85 per cent of the workforce, but the government aims to increase opportunities for its citizens through improved education and expansion of the private sector. The economy was badly hit by the global downturn, particularly in Dubai, which was heavily exposed when property prices crashed; its debt crisis has been alleviated by loans from federal and Abu Dhabi institutions.

Agriculture is limited by the terrain but the area under cultivation has been extended by irrigation and water desalination projects. The main products are dates, vegetables, watermelons, poultry, eggs and dairy products. Non-hydrocarbon industries include fishing, aluminium, cement, petrochemicals, fertilisers, commercial ship repair, construction materials, handicrafts, textiles, boat-building, financial services and tourism. Several free-trade zones, where overseas companies can trade tax-free, are attracting foreign investment.

The main export markets are Japan, South Korea and India; imports come chiefly from China, India, the USA, Germany and Japan. Principal exports are crude oil (45 per cent), natural gas, re-exports, dried fish and dates. The main imports are machinery and transport equipment, chemicals and food.

GNI – US$103,500m; US$26,210 per capita (2006)

Annual average growth of GDP – –4 per cent (2009 est)

Inflation rate – 1.5 per cent (2009 est)

Population below poverty line – 19.5 per cent (2003)

Unemployment – 2.4 per cent (2001 est)

Total external debt – US$128,600m (2009 est)

Imports – US$158,900m (2008)

Exports – US$231,600m (2008)

BALANCE OF PAYMENTS
Trade – US$65,824m surplus (2009)
Current Account – US$22,155m surplus (2008)

Trade with UK	*2008*	*2009*
Imports from UK	£3,686,072,459	£4,017,082,386
Exports to UK	£1,033,730,988	£567,337,254

COMMUNICATIONS

There are 4,080km of roads, all of which are surfaced, but no railway system. Jebel Ali, Mina Zayed and Mina Saqr are the most significant ports, and there is an international airport in every emirate except Ajman, where one is under construction.

Modern telecommunications systems provided services to 1.5 million fixed-line subscribers, 9.4 million mobile phone subscribers and 2.9 million internet users in 2008.

EDUCATION AND HEALTH

Education is free in state schools and compulsory from ages six to 14
Literacy rate – 90 per cent (2007 est)
Gross enrolment ratio (percentage of relevant age group) – primary 108 per cent; secondary 94 per cent; tertiary 25 per cent (2008 est)
Health expenditure (per capita) – US$1,253 (2007)
Hospital beds (per 1,000 people) – 1.9 (2003–8)

MEDIA

Dubai is a regional media hub, home to pan-Arab satellite television channels and international media organisations such as Reuters and Sony; Abu Dhabi is establishing a similar media zone. UAE residents can receive broadcasts from a variety of domestic and pan-Arab television and radio stations, and there are a number of national daily newspapers. There are restrictions on media content, however, with censorship of foreign publications and frequent internal self-censorship. A 1988 law requires the licensing of publications and outlines acceptable subjects for coverage.

UNITED KINGDOM

United Kingdom of Great Britain and Northern Ireland

Area – 243,122 sq. km
Capital – London; population, 7,620,000 (2008)
Major cities – Birmingham, Bristol, Edinburgh, Glasgow, Leeds, Liverpool, Manchester, Sheffield
Currency – Pound sterling (£) of 100 pence
Population – 61,383,000 rising at 0.28 per cent a year (2009 est)
Religion – Christian (Anglican 29 per cent, Roman Catholic 10 per cent, other Protestant denominations 14 per cent), Muslim 3 per cent, Hindu 1 per cent (est); small Jewish, Sikh and Buddhist minorities
Language – English, Welsh, Scottish Gaelic (none official)
Population density – 254 per sq. km (2008)
Urban population – 90 per cent (2007 est)
Median age (years) – 40.2 (2009 est)
National anthem – 'God Save the Queen'
Life expectancy (years) – 79.01 (2009 est)
Mortality rate – 10.02 (2009 est)
Birth rate – 10.65 (2009 est)
Infant mortality rate – 4.85 (2009 est)
Death penalty – Abolished for all crimes (since 1998)
CPI score – 7.7 (2009)

CLIMATE AND TERRAIN

The terrain of Great Britain is higher in the north and west, with low mountains and rugged hills in Scotland, northern England and Wales; the land declines towards the south and east, with its lowest points in the south-east. Northern Ireland is more low-lying, with low mountains in the north and east. The heavily indented coastline varies in height between high cliffs and sea level. Elevation extremes range from 1,343m (Ben Nevis, Scotland) at the highest point to –4m (the Fens, eastern England) at the lowest. Although Scotland contains numerous large lochs and northern England includes a region known as the Lake District, the largest freshwater lake is Lough Neagh in Northern Ireland. The main rivers are the Thames, the Severn and the Trent in England and Wales, and the Tay in Scotland. The climate is temperate and extremes are rare, but the convergence of Atlantic, Arctic and European weather systems produces unusually changeable weather conditions. Average temperatures in London range from lows of 2°C in January to highs of 22°C in July.

HISTORY AND POLITICS

England, the largest of the United Kingdom's four constituent countries, was unified by the early tenth century. It experienced a period of Danish rule in the early 11th century, and then in 1066 was conquered by Duke William of Normandy. The Norman kings and their successors sought to expand their rule over the whole of Britain. Wales was conquered in the 13th century and politically united with England in 1535. English involvement in Ireland began in the 12th century and control of the whole island was finally established in Elizabeth I's reign. The succession of Elizabeth I by James VI of Scotland in 1603 united the two countries under one crown, followed by the transfer of Scottish government to Westminister by the Act of Union in 1707, creating Great Britain. Government of Ireland was transferred to Westminster in 1801, when the state became known as the United Kingdom. When the rest of Ireland became independent in 1921, the six counties of Northern Ireland chose to remain under British rule. Sectarian violence broke out in 1968 between the Protestant majority and the Roman Catholic minority over civil rights, and was continued by paramilitary forces seeking union with the Republic of Ireland until a peace process began in the 1990s. Self-government was granted to Scotland, Wales and Northern Ireland in 1999.

In 1215, facing a revolt by the barons, King John signed Magna Carta, which attempted to define good kingship and began the country's constitutional development. The attempts of the Stuart kings to extend royal powers at the expense of Parliament in the mid 17th century led to the English Civil Wars, which established the relationship of the executive to the legislature. From the late 17th century Britain embarked on a period of massive trade expansion, emerging as a major colonial power in the 18th century with control over large territories, particularly in North America and the Indian subcontinent; 13 of the North American colonies seceded in 1776 and formed the United States of America.

Industrialisation began in Britain in the second half of the 18th century, and entered a second phase after 1830 that stimulated great economic growth and further colonial expansion throughout the 19th century. But Britain's economic and political dominance declined in the 20th century, undermined by the two world wars, the second war leaving the country close to economic collapse. Most of its colonies were granted independence between 1947 and the mid 1980s, many joining the Commonwealth. After the UK joined the European Community in 1973, its economic and diplomatic focus shifted from the Commonwealth to Europe.

The Labour government elected in 1945 pursued socialist economic and welfare policies, nationalising key industries, setting up the National Health Service and expanding the social security system. Economic decline continued until the 1980s, when it was reversed by the Conservative government led by Margaret Thatcher, the country's first woman prime minister. Her administration privatised nationalised industries, opened up welfare services to market forces and reduced the role of local government, polarising politics and public opinion. She also established a close relationship with the USA that was supportive of its foreign policy. This has been continued by her successors, most recently in the support for the US 'war on terror' and the deployment of British forces in Afghanistan since 2001 and Iraq from 2003 to 2009.

At the 2010 legislative election, the Conservative party won the most seats but without an outright majority. After negotiations with the Liberal Democrat party, a coalition government was formed under the Conservative leader, David Cameron, with the Liberal Democrat leader, Nick Clegg, as deputy prime minister.

POLITICAL SYSTEM

There is no written constitution. The head of state is a hereditary constitutional monarch. The bicameral parliament consists of the House of Commons, the lower house, and the House of Lords. The House of Commons has 650 members, directly elected for a five-year term. The House of Lords is appointed and numbers vary; in July 2010 it had 755 members, comprising 26 archbishops and bishops of the Church of England, 23 appeal judges, 614 life peers and 92 hereditary peers. The prime minister is the leader of the majority party or coalition in the House of Commons.

Powers over certain internal matters were devolved in 1999 to Scotland, Wales and Northern Ireland, each of which has its own legislature and government; devolution was suspended in Northern Ireland several times between 2000 and 2007 owing to the breakdown of power-sharing arrangements.

HEAD OF STATE

HM The Queen of the United Kingdom of Great Britain and Northern Ireland, Queen Elizabeth II, *born* 21 April 1926; *succeeded* 6 February 1952; *crowned* 2 June 1953

Heir, HRH The Prince of Wales (Prince Charles Philip Arthur George), *born* 14 November 1948

SELECTED GOVERNMENT MEMBERS *as at July 2010*

Prime Minister, First Lord of the Treasury, Civil Service, David Cameron

Deputy Prime Minister, Nick Clegg

Chancellor of the Exchequer, George Osborne

Foreign and Commonwealth Affairs, William Hague

Justice, Lord Chancellor, Kenneth Clarke

Home Affairs, Theresa May

Defence, Liam Fox

DEFENCE

The army has 386 main battle tanks, 2,718 armoured personnel carriers, 575 armoured infantry fighting vehicles and 66 armed helicopters. The navy has 12 submarines, 2 aircraft carriers, 6 destroyers, 17 frigates, 23 patrol and coastal combatant vessels, 13 combat aircraft and 119 armed helicopters at 7 bases. The air force has 287 combat aircraft.

Military expenditure – US$60,700m (2008)

Military personnel – 175,690: army 100,290, navy 35,650, air force 39,750

ECONOMY AND TRADE

The UK has a highly developed and technologically advanced economy that is now dominated by services and trade. It was the first industrialised nation, developing an economy in the 19th century based on heavy industry, mass manufacturing and global trade. It became less predominant as industrialisation spread to other countries, and the demands of the Second World War caused a postwar industrial decline that left the economy less efficient than many of its competitors and increasingly undercut by cheaper production in the developing world. In the 1980s, privatisation of state industries and constraints on public spending improved government finances, and primary industrial activities were increasingly replaced by service industries. After emerging from recession in the early 1990s, the economy experienced its longest-recorded period of expansion, outperforming the rest of the EU states, until 2008. The global economic downturn, tight credit and the end of the property boom caused the economy to go into recession from early 2008 until late 2009. The banking sector in particular was badly affected by the global financial crisis in 2008 and government intervention was necessary to stabilise the financial system, including nationalising or part-nationalising major banks. These measures left the government with a massive public-sector debt to service, and the new coalition government announced tight constraints on public spending from 2010.

The service sector, especially banking, insurance and business services, electronics, telecommunications and tourism, now contributes 75 per cent of GDP and employs about 80 per cent of the workforce. Agriculture is intensive, highly mechanised and efficient, meeting about 60 per cent of the UK's food needs with 1.4 per cent of the workforce, although contributing only 1.2 per cent of GDP. The UK has large but declining reserves of oil, gas and coal, and the country became a net importer of energy in 2005. Other industrial output is mostly of manufactured goods, including machine tools, electrical power equipment, automation and transport equipment, aircraft, ships, motor vehicles and parts, electronics and communications equipment, metals, chemicals, paper and paper products, food processing, textiles, clothing and other consumer goods.

The main trading partners are other EU countries, the USA and China. The principal exports are manufactured

goods, fuels, chemicals, food, beverages and tobacco. The main imports are manufactured goods, machinery, fuels and foodstuffs.
GNI – US$2,827,300m; US$46,040 per capita (2008)
Annual average growth of GDP – –4.3 per cent (2009 est)
Inflation rate – 2.1 per cent (2009 est)
Population below poverty line – 14 per cent (2006 est)
Unemployment – 8 per cent (2009 est)
Total external debt – US$9,088,000m (2009)
Imports – US$632,900m (2008)
Exports – US$459,900m (2008)

BALANCE OF PAYMENTS
Trade – US$127,606m deficit (2009)
Current Account – US$28,838m deficit (2009)

COMMUNICATIONS

Traditionally a seafaring nation, the UK has a large merchant navy, with 518 ships of over 1,000 tonnes registered in the UK and 391 ships registered overseas. The main ports are at Grimsby and Immingham, Tees and Hartlepool, London, Southampton, Milford Haven, Liverpool, Forth, Felixstowe, Dover, Sullom Voe and Belfast. There is an extensive road network of 398,366km, including 3,520km of motorways. Railway passenger services are operated by 29 private companies. The network is being upgraded, and nearly a third of the 16,454km of track is now electrified. The Channel tunnel links the UK railway network to those of mainland Europe. About 3,200km of waterways are navigable, although most are used for leisure and only about 600km for commerce. There are about 144 licensed civil airports, of which Heathrow (the world's busiest international airport), Gatwick, Stansted and Manchester handle the highest volume of passengers.

Technologically advanced telecommunications systems provided services to 33.2 million fixed telephone lines, 75.6 million mobile phone subscribers and 48.8 million internet users in 2008.

EDUCATION AND HEALTH

Full-time education is compulsory between the ages of five and 16 in Great Britain and four and 16 in Northern Ireland. Education between the ages of 16 and 18 is voluntary, but under recent government legislation, will become compulsory from 2013. There are 116 universities, including the Open University, which offers distance-learning access to further and higher education.
Gross enrolment ratio (percentage of relevant age group) – primary 104 per cent; secondary 97 per cent; tertiary 59 per cent (2008 est)
Health expenditure (per capita) – US$3,867 (2007)
Hospital beds (per 1,000 people) – 3.9 (2003–8)

MEDIA

The media is free, rarely censored and exerts considerable influence, particularly in political life. The press is mostly owned by large communications companies and therefore financially independent of any political party, although most newspapers adopt a political stance. The British Broadcasting Corporation is a public service broadcaster with a worldwide reputation. It provides radio and television programmes, in competition with several commercial radio and television stations, including cable and satellite services. There are plans for the analogue television signal to be switched off by 2012. British libel laws, under which the burden of proof lies with the defendant, have led to an increasing number of foreign claimants filing libel suits in the UK over articles or books which would not warrant an action in their own country; the laws are currently under review.

OVERSEAS TERRITORIES

See pp 1077–1084

UNITED STATES OF AMERICA

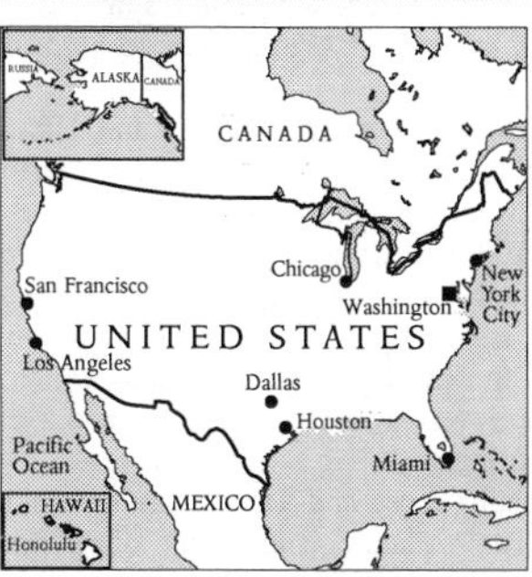

Area – 9,826,675 sq. km
Capital – Washington, District of Columbia; population, 4,420,650 (2009 est)
Major cities – Chicago, Dallas, Houston, Los Angeles, New York, Philadelphia, Phoenix, San Antonio, San Diego, San José
Currency – US dollar (US$) of 100 cents
Population – 307,212,123 rising at 0.98 per cent a year (2009 est); white 80 per cent, black 12.9 per cent, Asian 4.4 per cent, Amerindian and Alaska native 1 per cent, native Hawaiian and other Pacific islander 0.2 per cent, two or more races 1.6 per cent; Hispanic 15.1 per cent (persons of Hispanic origin may be of any race or ethnic group) (2007 est)
Religion – Christian (Protestant denominations 51 per cent, Roman Catholic 24 per cent, Mormon 2 per cent), Jewish 2 per cent, Buddhist 1 per cent, Muslim 1 per cent (est)
Language – English, Spanish, Hawaiian (official in Hawaii)
Population density – 33 per sq. km (2008)
Urban population – 81 per cent (2007 est)
Median age (years) – 36.7 (2009 est)
National anthem – 'The Star-Spangled Banner'
National day – 4 July (Independence Day)
Life expectancy (years) – 78.11 (2009 est)
Mortality rate – 8.38 (2009 est)
Birth rate – 13.82 (2009 est)
Infant mortality rate – 6.26 (2009 est)
Death penalty – Abolished in 15 states, District of Columbia and US insular territories
CPI score – 7.5 (2009)

CLIMATE AND TERRAIN

The coastline has a length of about 3,329km on the Atlantic Ocean, 12,268km on the Pacific, 1,705km on the Arctic, and 2,624km on the Gulf of Mexico. The principal river is the Mississippi-Missouri-Red (5,970km long), traversing the whole country from Montana to its mouth in the Gulf of Mexico. The Rocky Mountains range runs the length of the western portion of the country. West of this, bordering the Pacific coast, the Cascade Mountains and Sierra Nevada form the outer edge of a high tableland, consisting partly of stony and sandy desert and partly of grazing land and forested mountains, and including the Great Salt Lake, which extends to the Rocky Mountains. A vast central plain lies between the Rockies and the hills and low mountains of the eastern states, where large forests still exist, remnants of the forests which formerly extended over the entire Atlantic slope. Elevation extremes range from 6,198m (Mt McKinley, Alaska) to −86m (Death Valley, California). The climate varies with latitude but is mostly temperate, with semi-arid conditions on the great plains and arid in the south-west. Average temperatures in Washington DC range from lows of −3°C in January to highs of 31°C in July.

Two states are detached: Alaska and Hawaii. Alaska occupies the north-western extremity of North America, separated from the rest of the USA by the Canadian province of British Columbia. The terrain is arctic tundra with mountain ranges, and the climate is arctic. The state of Hawaii is a chain of about 20 mountainous volcanic islands in the north Pacific Ocean, of which the chief islands are Hawaii, Maui, Oahu, Kauai and Molokai. The climate is tropical.

The Pacific coast and Hawaii are prone to seismic activity. The Atlantic and Gulf of Mexico coasts frequently experience hurricanes.

HISTORY AND POLITICS

The area that is now the USA was first inhabited by nomadic hunters who probably arrived from Asia *c.*30,000 BC. The continent was reached by the Norse in the tenth century and explored by the Spanish after their first landfall in North America in 1513. European colonisation began in the 16th century, with Spanish settlements in the south, and British, Dutch, French, German and Swedish settlements along the eastern seaboard. In the first century of European settlement, much of the native population was killed by diseases brought by the colonists. Many black Africans were introduced as slaves to work on the plantations in the Caribbean and southern US states.

By 1733 there were 13 British colonies, composed mostly of religious non-conformists who had left Britain to escape persecution. A rebellion broke out in these colonies in 1775, largely because of the colonists' objection to being taxed by, but having no representation in, the British parliament. The British government's forces were defeated with French, Spanish and Dutch assistance. The Declaration of Independence which inaugurated the United States of America was signed on 4 July 1776; Britain recognised American sovereignty in 1783. The first federal constitution was drawn up in 1787; ten amendments, termed the Bill of Rights, were added in 1791. The 13 original states of the Union ratified the constitution between 1787 and 1790. Vermont, Kentucky and Tennessee were admitted in the 1790s, but most of the states acceded in the 19th century, as the opening up of the centre and west led to the creation of new states, and European or neighbouring countries ceded or sold their territories to the USA.

The Civil War (1861–5) was fought over the issue of slavery, which was integral to the economy of the southern states but was opposed by the northern states. The Confederacy of 11 southern states (Virginia, North Carolina, South Carolina, Georgia, Alabama, Florida, Tennessee, Mississippi, Louisiana, Texas, Arkansas) seceded in 1860–1, but was defeated by the northern states.

The USA industrialised rapidly in the late 19th century. It emerged as a world economic and military superpower in the 20th century and played a decisive role in the two world wars. Its economic and military (including nuclear) supremacy has given the USA a key role in shaping the post-war world. The Cold War with the USSR, which began after the Second World War, ended in 1990. Following terrorist attacks in New York and Washington DC on 11 September 2001, President George W. Bush declared a 'war on terror'. As part of this, the USA led multi-national forces into conflicts in Afghanistan in 2001 (*see* Afghanistan) and Iraq in 2003 (*see* Iraq); US troops remain in both countries to help stabilise internal security. Problems in the US financial sector triggered a global economic downturn in 2007 and pushed the US economy into recession; the US government is promoting international attempts to safeguard against similar events.

The 2008 presidential election was won by the Democrat candidate Barack Obama, the first African-American to hold the office. In the 2008 legislative elections, the Democrat Party retained its majorities in both houses of congress. The Democrat majority in the senate was lost in early 2010 but President Obama's controversial health insurance reform law was still passed by both houses in March 2010. The next election of the whole House of Representatives and one-third of the senate was scheduled for 2 November 2010.

POLITICAL SYSTEM

By the constitution of 17 September 1787 (which has been amended 15 times, most recently in 1992), the government of the USA is entrusted to three separate authorities: the federal executive (the president and cabinet), the legislature (congress, which consists of a senate and a House of Representatives) and the judicature. The president is indirectly elected by an electoral college to serve a four-year term, and may serve a maximum of two consecutive terms. If a president dies in office, the vice-president serves the remainder of his term. The president appoints the cabinet officers and all the chief officials, subject to confirmation by the senate. He makes recommendations of a general nature to congress, and when laws are passed, he may return them to congress with a veto. But, if a measure so vetoed is again passed by both houses of congress by a two-thirds majority in each house, it becomes law, notwithstanding the objection of the president.

Each of the 50 states has its own executive, legislature and judiciary. In theory, they are sovereign, but in practice their autonomy is increasingly circumscribed.

PRESIDENTIAL ELECTIONS

Candidates for the presidency must be at least 35 years of age and a native citizen of the USA. The electoral college for each state is directly elected by universal adult suffrage in the November preceding the January in which the presidential term expires. The number of members of the electoral college is equal to the whole number of senators and representatives to which the state is entitled in the national congress. The electoral college for each state meets in its state in December and each member votes for a presidential candidate by ballot. The ballots are sent to Washington, and opened on 6 January by the president of the senate in the presence of congress. The candidate who has received a majority of the whole number of electoral votes cast is declared president for the ensuing term. If no one has a majority, then from the highest on the list (not exceeding three) the House of Representatives elects a president, the votes being taken by states, the representation from each state having one vote. A presidential term begins at noon on 20 January.

HEAD OF STATE
President, Barack Obama, *elected* 2008, *sworn in* 20 January 2009
Vice-President, Joseph Biden

SELECTED GOVERNMENT MEMBERS *as at August 2010*
Secretary of State, Hillary Clinton
Defence, Robert Gates
Interior, Ken Salazar
Treasury, Timothy Geithner
Secretary for Homeland Security, Janet Napolitano

THE CONGRESS
Legislative power is vested in the bicameral congress, comprising the senate and the House of Representatives. The senate has 100 members, two from each state, elected for a six-year term, with one-third elected every two years. The House of Representatives has 435 members directly elected in each state for a two-year term; a resident commissioner from Puerto Rico and a delegate each from American Samoa, the District of Columbia, Guam, the Northern Mariana Islands and the Virgin Islands serve as non-voting members of the house.

Members of the 111th congress were elected on 4 November 2008 and sworn into office on 6 January 2009. As at July 2010, the 111th congress is constituted as follows:
Senate: Democrats 57; Republicans 41; Independent 1; Independent Democrat 1
House of Representatives: Democrats 257; Republicans 178
President of the Senate, The Vice-President
Senate majority leader, Harry Reid *(D), Nevada*
Speaker of the House of Representatives, Nancy Pelosi *(D), California*
House majority leader, Steny Hoyer *(D), Maryland*

THE JUDICATURE
The federal judiciary consists of three sets of federal courts: the Supreme Court at Washington, DC, consisting of a Chief Justice and eight Associate Justices; the US court of appeals, consisting of 179 circuit judges within 12 regional circuits and one federal circuit; and the 94 US district courts served by 678 district court judges.

THE SUPREME COURT
US Supreme Court Building, Washington DC 20543
Chief Justice, John Roberts, *apptd* 2005

UNITED STATES EMBASSY
24 Grosvenor Square, London W1A 1AE
T 020-7499 9000 W www.usembassy.org.uk
Ambassador Extraordinary and Plenipotentiary, HE Louis B. Susman, *apptd* 2009

BRITISH EMBASSY
3100 Massachusetts Avenue NW, Washington DC 20008
T (+1) (202) 588 6500 E washi@fco.gov.uk
W http://ukinusa.fco.gov.uk
Ambassador Extraordinary and Plenipotentiary, Sir Nigel Sheinwald, KCMG, *apptd* 2006

BRITISH COUNCIL
c/o The British Embassy
T (+1) (202) 588 6500 W www.britishcouncil.org/usa
Director, Sharon Memis

THE STATES OF THE UNION

The USA is a federal republic consisting of 50 states and the federal District of Columbia, and also of organised territories. Of the present 50 states, 13 are original states, seven were admitted without previous organisation as territories, and 30 were admitted after such organisation.

§ The 13 original states
(D) Democratic Party; (I) Independent; (R) Republican Party; (C) Covenant

State (with date and order of admission)	*Area sq. km*	*Population (2009 est)*	*Capital*	*Governor (end of term in office)*
Alabama (AL) (1819, 22)	133,915	4,708,708	Montgomery	Bob Riley (R), Jan. 2011
Alaska (AK) (1959, 49)	1,530,694	698,473	Juneau	Sean Parnell (R), Dec. 2010
Arizona (AZ) (1912, 48)	295,259	6,595,778	Phoenix	Jan Brewer (R), Jan. 2011
Arkansas (AR) (1836, 25)	137,754	2,889,450	Little Rock	Mike Beebe (D), Jan. 2011
California (CA) (1850, 31)	411,047	36,961,664	Sacramento	Arnold Schwarzenegger (R), Jan. 2011
Colorado (CO) (1876, 38)	269,595	5,024,748	Denver	Bill Ritter (D), Jan. 2011
Connecticut (CT) § (1788, 5)	12,997	3,518,288	Hartford	M. Jodi Rell (R), Jan. 2011
Delaware (DE) § (1787, 1)	5,297	885,122	Dover	Jack Markell (D), Jan. 2013
Florida (FL) (1845, 27)	151,939	18,537,969	Tallahassee	Charlie Crist (R), Jan. 2011
Georgia (GA) § (1788, 4)	152,576	9,829,211	Atlanta	Sonny Perdue (R), Jan. 2011
Hawaii (HI) (1959, 50)	16,760	1,295,178	Honolulu	Linda Lingle (R), Dec. 2010
Idaho (ID) (1890, 43)	216,430	1,545,801	Boise	C. L. Otter (R), Jan. 2011
Illinois (IL) (1818, 21)	145,933	12,910,409	Springfield	Patrick Quinn III (D), Jan. 2011
Indiana (IN) (1816, 19)	93,719	6,423,113	Indianapolis	Mitchell E. Daniels (R), Jan. 2013
Iowa (IA) (1846, 29)	145,752	3,007,856	Des Moines	Chet Culver (D), Jan. 2011
Kansas (KS) (1861, 34)	213,097	2,818,747	Topeka	Mark Parkinson (D), Jan. 2011
Kentucky (KY) (1792, 15)	104,661	4,314,113	Frankfort	Steve Beshear (D), Dec. 2011
Louisiana (LA) (1812, 18)	123,677	4,492,076	Baton Rouge	Bobby Jindal (R), Jan. 2012
Maine (ME) (1820, 23)	86,156	1,318,301	Augusta	John Baldacci (D), Jan. 2011
Maryland (MD) § (1788, 7)	27,091	5,699,478	Annapolis	Martin O'Malley (D), Jan. 2011
Massachusetts (MA) § (1788, 6)	21,455	6,593,587	Boston	Deval Patrick (D), Jan. 2011
Michigan (MI) (1837, 26)	151,584	9,969,727	Lansing	Jennifer Granholm (D), Jan. 2011

Minnesota (MN) (1858, 32)	218,600	5,266,214	St Paul	Tim Pawlenty (R), Jan. 2011
Mississippi (MS) (1817, 20)	123,514	2,951,996	Jackson	Haley Barbour (R), Jan. 2012
Missouri (MO) (1821, 24)	180,514	5,987,580	Jefferson City	Jeremiah (Jay) Nixon (D), Jan. 2013
Montana (MT) (1889, 41)	380,848	974,989	Helena	Brian Schweitzer (D), Jan. 2013
Nebraska (NE) (1867, 37)	200,349	1,796,619	Lincoln	Dave Heineman (R), Jan. 2011
Nevada (NV) (1864, 36)	286,352	2,643,085	Carson City	Jim Gibbons (R), Jan. 2011
New Hampshire (NH) § (1788, 9)	24,033	1,324,575	Concord	John Lynch (D), Jan. 2011
New Jersey (NJ) § (1787, 3)	20,168	8,707,739	Trenton	Chris Christie (R), Jan. 2014
New Mexico (NM) (1912, 47)	314,925	2,009,671	Santa Fé	Bill Richardson (D), Jan. 2011
New York (NY) § (1788, 11)	127,189	19,541,453	Albany	David Paterson (D), Jan. 2011
North Carolina (NC) § (1789, 12)	136,412	9,380,884	Raleigh	Beverly Perdue (D), Jan. 2013
North Dakota (ND) (1889, 39)	183,117	646,844	Bismarck	John Hoeven (R), Dec. 2012
Ohio (OH) (1803, 17)	107,044	11,542,645	Columbus	Ted Strickland (D), Jan. 2011
Oklahoma (OK) (1907, 46)	181,185	3,687,050	Oklahoma City	Brad Henry (D), Jan. 2011
Oregon (OR) (1859, 33)	251,418	3,825,657	Salem	Ted R. Kulongoski (D), Jan. 2011
Pennsylvania (PA) § (1787, 2)	117,347	12,604,767	Harrisburg	Edward G. Rendell (D), Jan. 2011
Rhode Island (RI) § (1790, 13)	3,139	1,053,209	Providence	Don Carcieri (R), Jan. 2011
South Carolina (SC) § (1788, 8)	80,582	4,561,242	Columbia	Mark Sanford (R), Jan. 2011
South Dakota (SD) (1889, 40)	199,730	812,383	Pierre	Mike Rounds (R), Jan. 2011
Tennessee (TN) (1796, 16)	109,153	6,296,254	Nashville	Phil Bredesen (D), Jan. 2011
Texas (TX) (1845, 28)	691,027	24,782,302	Austin	Rick Perry (R), Jan. 2011
Utah (UT) (1896, 45)	219,888	2,784,572	Salt Lake City	Gary Herbert (R), Nov. 2010
Vermont (VT) (1791, 14)	24,900	621,760	Montpelier	James H. Douglas (R), Jan. 2011
Virginia (VA) § (1788, 10)	105,586	7,882,590	Richmond	Bob McDonnell (R), Jan. 2014
Washington (WA) (1889, 42)	176,479	6,664,195	Olympia	Christine Gregoire (D), Jan. 2013
West Virginia (WV) (1863, 35)	62,761	1,819,777	Charleston	Joe Manchin III (D), Jan. 2013
Wisconsin (WI) (1848, 30)	145,436	5,654,774	Madison	Jim Doyle (D), Jan. 2011
Wyoming (WY) (1890, 44)	253,324	544,270	Cheyenne	Dave Freudenthal (D), Jan. 2011
Dist. of Columbia (DC) (1791)	179	599,657	–	Adrian M. Fenty (D), *(Mayor)*

OUTLYING TERRITORIES AND POSSESSIONS

	Area sq. km	*Population (2009 est)*	*Capital*	*Governor (end of term in office)*
American Samoa	199	65,628	Pago Pago	Togiola Tulafono (D), Jan. 2013
Guam	541	178,430	Hagatna	Felix P. Camacho (R), Jan. 2011
Northern Mariana Islands	477	88,662	Saipan	Benigno Fitial (C), Jan. 2014
Puerto Rico	13,790	3,967,288	San Juan	Luis G. Fortuño (R), Jan. 2013
US Virgin Islands	363	109,825	Charlotte Amalie	John DeJongh Jr (D), Jan. 2011

DEFENCE

Each military department is separately organised and functions under the direction, authority and control of the Secretary of Defence (except the Coast Guard, which is part of the Department of Homeland Security created in 2002). The air force has primary responsibility for the Department of Defence space development programmes and projects. Under US strategic command the USA has 730 submarine-launched ballistic missiles, 500 laser-guided nuclear missiles *(Minuteman III)* and 95 heavy nuclear-capable bombers. There are currently 4 space-based early warning satellites in orbit and the USA operates land-based early warning systems throughout the world. The army has 5,850 main battle tanks, 6,452 armoured infantry fighting vehicles, 19,637 armoured personnel carriers and 1,035 armed helicopters.

The navy has 14 strategic submarines, 57 tactical submarines, 11 aircraft carriers, 22 cruisers, 56 destroyers, 21 frigates, 16 patrol and coastal vessels, 31 amphibious and support ships, 900 combat aircraft and 220 armed helicopters. The Marine Corps has 403 main battle tanks, 371 combat aircraft and over 145 armed helicopters. The air force has 2,708 combat aircraft.

In May 2010 the Department of Defence, for the first time, disclosed the size of its nuclear arsenal, which then stood at 5,113 warheads.

Military expenditure – US$690,300m (2009)

Military personnel – 1,580,255: army 662,232, navy 335,822, Marine Corps 204,261, air force 334,342, coastguard 43,598

ECONOMY AND TRADE

The USA is one of the world's leading industrial nations, with a sophisticated market economy that saw huge growth during the 20th century. This economic development was due in part to the mechanisation of the agrarian economy, the expansion of the transport infrastructure and large amounts of relatively cheap migrant labour; more recently it has been driven by rapid advances in technology. In the late 20th century, the economy shifted emphasis from industry to services, and government involvement in the economy was steadily reduced. Until 2008, the economy experienced steady growth, with low unemployment and inflation, although there were large budget and trade deficits, high levels of personal debt and an increasingly uneven distribution of wealth.

The US sub-prime mortgage crisis in 2007 triggered a global economic downturn, and falling property prices and tight credit pushed the domestic economy into recession by mid 2008. Following the failure of several investment banks, the congress passed a US$700bn relief programme to stabilise the financial markets in October 2008, and in spring 2009 a US$787bn fiscal stimulus package and a record US$3.6 trillion budget for 2010 were approved. Despite these measures, the economy still experienced the collapse of key industries (such as vehicle manufacturing), and rising unemployment and inflation before growth restarted in late 2009 after the USA's longest and deepest recession since the 1930s; the budget and trade deficits remain very high.

Agriculture is a major industry in the USA, with about 18 per cent of land under cultivation. Principal crops are wheat, maize, other grains, fruit, vegetables, cotton, meat and dairy products. Agriculture, fishing and forestry contribute 1.2 per cent of GDP and employ 0.7 per cent of the workforce.

Mining and extraction are important to the economy. Large quantities of coal, iron ore, phosphate rock, copper, zinc and lead are mined. About one-third of the country's oil requirements are supplied by domestic production, principally from fields in the Gulf of Mexico; production dropped after a six-month moratorium on offshore oil exploration and drilling was introduced in spring 2010 following an offshore rig explosion that led to severe environmental damage in the gulf. Natural gas is also produced. Despite its domestic oil and natural gas resources and its electricity generating capacity, the USA is a net importer of energy.

The industrial sector is highly diversified and technologically advanced. The main manufacturing industries produce steel, vehicles, aircraft and aerospace equipment, telecommunications equipment, chemicals, electronic equipment and consumer goods, and process food. Industry contributes 21.9 per cent of GDP and services account for 76.9 per cent of GDP.

The main trading partners are Canada, China, Mexico, Japan, Germany and the UK. Principal exports are capital goods (chiefly transistors, aircraft, vehicle parts, computers, telecommunications equipment), industrial supplies, consumer goods (cars, medicines) and agricultural produce (soya beans, fruit, maize). The main imports are industrial goods (especially crude oil), consumer goods (cars, clothing, medicines, furniture, toys), capital goods (computers, telecommunications equipment, vehicle parts, office machines, electric power machinery) and agricultural products.

GNI – US$14,572,900m; US$47,930 per capita (2008)
Annual average growth of GDP – –2.5 per cent (2009 est)
Inflation rate – –0.7 per cent (2009 est)
Population below poverty line – 12 per cent (2004 est)
Unemployment – 9.4 per cent (2009 est)
Total external debt – US$13,450,000m (2009 est)
Imports – US$2,165,200m (2008)
Exports – US$1,301,100m (2008)

BALANCE OF PAYMENTS
Trade – US$502,456m deficit (2009)
Current Account – US$417,999m deficit (2009)

Trade with UK	*2008*	*2009*
Imports from UK	£34,690,527,979	£33,598,991,523
Exports to UK	£28,652,734,180	£32,100,909,704

GDP BY INDUSTRY (2009)

	US$bn
Private industries (total)	12,323.8
Agriculture, forestry, fisheries	136.4
Mining	231.3
Construction	578.3
Manufacturing	1,568.6
Transportation and warehousing	393.9
Wholesale trade	793.3
Retail trade	842.2
Finance, insurance and real estate	3,057.8
Information	633.8

Source: Bureau of Economic Analysis, 'Value Added by Industry'

COMMUNICATIONS

There are approximately 6.47 million km of roads, with surfaced roads accounting for 65.1 per cent of the total. There are 226,400km of railways, and more than 41,000km of navigable internal waterways, of which 19,300km are used for commerce. The main seaports are at Anchorage (Alaska), Baltimore, Boston, Charleston, Chicago, Corpus Christi, Duluth, Hampton Roads, Honolulu (Hawaii), Houston, Jacksonville, Long Beach, Los Angeles, New Orleans, New York, Philadelphia, Port Canaveral, Portland (Oregon), Prudhoe Bay (Alaska), San Francisco, Savannah, Seattle, Tampa and Toledo. There are over 15,000 airports and airfields; nearly 200 are capable of handling international flights, but the rest cater for the high domestic demand as air travel is the main form of transport for long-distance internal journeys.

Technologically advanced systems provide multi-purpose telecommunications facilities, though fixed-line subscriptions are declining as mobile phone use grows. There were 150 million fixed-line subscribers, 270 million mobile phone subscribers and 231 million internet users in 2008.

EDUCATION AND HEALTH

All the states have compulsory school attendance laws. In general, children are obliged to attend school from seven to 16 years of age. Of the total revenue for public elementary and secondary schools in 2008, 43.5 per cent came from local governments, 48.3 per cent from state governments and 8.2 per cent from the federal government. Among the better-known universities are Harvard (founded in 1636), Yale (1701) and Princeton (1746).

Gross enrolment ratio (percentage of relevant age group) – primary 98 per cent; secondary 94 per cent; tertiary 82 per cent (2008 est)
Health expenditure (per capita) – US$7,285 (2007)
Hospital beds (per 1,000 people) – 3.1 (2003–8)

MEDIA

The media industry is the largest and most influential in the world, and television programming is exported around the world. Internally, television and radio are regulated by the Federal Communications Commission. The major television networks are ABC, CBS, NBC, CNN, Fox, MTV, HBO and the Public Broadcasting System, which serves around 350 local member stations and is partially funded by the government and by private grants. There are around 10,000 commercial radio stations and the National Public Radio network which has over 600 non-commercial member stations, and more than 1,500 daily newspapers, including *The Wall Street Journal, USA Today, The Washington Post* and *The New York Times*. However, a decline in advertising revenues caused the parent companies of a number of major daily newspapers to file for bankruptcy protection in 2008–9, and several others are experiencing financial difficulties. *Time, Newsweek* and *US News and World Report* are influential current affairs magazines, while *Rolling Stone* and *Vanity Fair* are popular entertainment titles.

CULTURE

The culture of the USA is indebted to the diverse origins of its immigrants; European, African and Latin American influences are particularly strong. Often at the forefront of modern philosophical, literary and artistic movements (such as feminism, postmodernism and postcolonialism), the USA boasts many important writers, film-makers and artists.

The best-known writers include Edgar Allan Poe (1809–49), Mark Twain (1835–1910), Henry James (1843–1916), and poets Walt Whitman (1819–92) and Emily Dickinson (1830–86) in the 19th century; William Faulkner (1897–1962), Ernest Hemingway (1899–1961), John Steinbeck (1902–68), poet Robert Frost (1874–1963) and dramatist Eugene O'Neill (1888–1953) in the early 20th century; and Saul Bellow (1915–2005), J. D. Salinger (1919–2010), John Updike (1932–2009), Philip Roth (*b.* 1933) and playwrights Arthur Miller (1915–2005) and Tennessee Williams (1911–83) among the postwar generation. African-American literature has been assimiliated into the literary canon through the works of Ralph Ellison (1913–94), Maya Angelou (*b.* 1928), Toni Morrison (*b.* 1931) and Alice Walker (*b.* 1944). David Foster Wallace (1962–2008) was one of the most acclaimed writers of recent times.

The Hollywood film industry is the most wide-reaching in the world; celebrated film-makers include Walt Disney (1901–66), Orson Welles (1915–85), Frank Capra (1897–1991), Stanley Kubrick (1928–99), Francis Ford Coppola (*b.* 1939), Martin Scorsese (*b.* 1942) and Steven Spielberg (b. 1946).

Modern art found a spiritual home on the east coast and the Guggenheim and Metropolitan museums in New York house vast collections. Renowned artists include Edward Hopper (1882–1967), Jackson Pollock (1912–56), Roy Lichtenstein (1923–97) and Andy Warhol (1928–87).

The music of the USA reflects the country's ethnic diversity, with superior recording and distribution methods ensuring that rock and roll, country, blues, jazz and hip-hop became known worldwide. Musical icons include Elvis Presley (1935–77) and Bob Dylan (*b.* 1941) in rock, Hank Williams (1923–53) and Johnny Cash (1932–2003) in country music, Leadbelly (1888–1949) and Muddy Waters (1915–83) in blues, and Louis Armstrong (1901–71), Miles Davis (1926–91) and John Coltrane (1926–67) in jazz.

US TERRITORIES ETC

US insular areas are territories that are not part of one of the 50 US states or a federal district. The US Department of the Interior's Office of Insular Affairs has jurisdiction over American Samoa, Guam, the Northern Mariana Islands, the US Virgin Islands, part of Palmyra Atoll (4 sq. km) and Wake Atoll (6.4 sq. km), the latter shared with the US army's Space and Strategic Defence Command. The US Fish and Wildlife Service has jurisdiction over Baker Island (1.5 sq. km), Howland Island (2.5 sq. km), Jarvis Island (4.2 sq. km), Johnston Atoll (2.5 sq. km, shared with the Defence Threat Reduction Agency), Midway Atoll (5.2 sq. km), Navassa Island (7.8 sq. km), Kingman Reef and part of Palmyra Atoll. The Aleutian Islands (17,666 sq. km) form part of the Alaskan archipelago.

Four of the eight populated insular areas are represented in the House of Representatives: Puerto Rico by a resident commissioner, and American Samoa, Guam and the US Virgin Islands by one non-voting delegate each.

PUERTO RICO

Commonwealth of Puerto Rico
Area – 13,790 sq. km
Capital – San Juan; population, 2,729,980 (2009 est). Other major towns are: Bayamón, Carolina, Poncel
Population – 3,971,020 rising at 0.34 per cent per year (2009 est); most people are of Spanish descent. The official languages are Spanish and English
National day – 25 July (Constitution Day)

Puerto Rico (Rich Port) is an island of the Greater Antilles group in the Caribbean Sea and was discovered in 1493 by Columbus. It was a Spanish possession until 1898, when it was ceded to the USA after the Spanish–American War. Residents have been US citizens since 1917, and Puerto Rico is represented in congress by a non-voting resident commissioner, who is directly elected for a four-year term. Under its 1952 constitution, Puerto Rico is a self-governing commonwealth. The governor is directly elected for a four-year term. The bicameral legislative assembly consists of a 27-member senate and a 51-member House of Representatives, whose members serve a four-year term. Tourism, pharmaceuticals, electronics, clothing and food processing are the main economic activities.

Governor, Luis G. Fortuño (New Progressive Party)

Trade with UK	*2008*	*2009*
Imports from UK	£255,645,557	–
Exports to UK	£224,565,005	–

GUAM

Guahan – Territory of Guam
Area – 541.3 sq. km
Capital – Hagatna (also known as Agana); population, 149,000 (2007 est)
Population – 178,430; rising at 1.37 per cent per year (2009 est); Chamorro (37 per cent), Filipino (26 per cent), other Pacific islander (11 per cent). The official languages are Chamorro (a language of the Malayo-Polynesian family with admixtures of Spanish) and English; most Chamorro residents are bilingual
National day – first Monday in March (Discovery Day)

Guam is the largest of the Mariana Islands, in the north Pacific Ocean. A Spanish colony for centuries, it was ceded to the USA in 1898 after the Spanish–American War. Guam was occupied by the Japanese in 1941 but was recaptured by US forces in 1944. Any person born in Guam is a US citizen. Guam is represented in congress by a non-voting delegate, who is directly elected for a two-year term. Under the Organic Act of Guam 1950, Guam has statutory powers of self-government. The governor and lieutenant-governor are directly elected for a four-year term. The 15-member unicameral legislature is directly elected every two years. The main sources of revenue are tourism (particularly from Japan) and US military spending; the military installation is one of the most strategically important US bases in the Pacific.

Governor, Felix P. Camacho (R)

Trade with UK	*2008*	*2009*
Imports from UK	£3,176,266	£1,687,254
Exports to UK	£143,495	£94,782

AMERICAN SAMOA

Territory of American Samoa
Area – 199 sq. km
Capital – Pago Pago
Population – 65,628 rising at 1.22 per cent per year (2009 est)
National day – 17 April (Flag Day)

American Samoa consists of the islands of Tutuila, Aunu'u, Ofu, Olosega, Ta'u, Rose Island and Swains Island. The islands were discovered by Europeans in the 18th century and the USA took possession in 1900. Those born in American Samoa are US non-citizen nationals, although some have acquired citizenship through service in the US armed forces or other naturalisation procedures. American Samoa is represented in congress by a non-voting delegate, who is directly elected for a two-year term. Under the 1966 constitution, American Samoa has a measure of self-government, with certain powers reserved to the US Secretary of the Interior. The governor and deputy governor are directly elected for a four-year term. The bicameral legislative assembly comprises a 21-member House of Representatives (one appointed member and 20 members directly elected for a two-year term) and an 18-seat senate with members elected from among the traditional chiefs for a four-year term. Tuna fishing and canning are the principal economic activities. The economy and transport systems were severely damaged by a tsunami in 2009.
Governor, Togiola Tulafono (D)

THE UNITED STATES VIRGIN ISLANDS

Area – 1,910 sq. km
Capital – Charlotte Amalie, on St Thomas; population, 53,526 (2009 est)
Population – 109,825 falling at 0.03 per cent per year (2009 est)
National day – 31 March (Transfer Day)

There are three main islands, St Thomas, St Croix and St John, and about 50 small islets or cays. These constituted the Danish part of the Virgin Islands from the 17th century until purchased by the USA in 1917. Those born in the US Virgin Islands are US nationals. The Virgin Islands are represented in congress by a non-voting representative, who is directly elected for a two-year term. Under the provisions of the Revised Organic Act of 1954, the islands have powers of self-government. The governor and lieutenant-governor are directly elected for a four-year term. The unicameral senate has 15 members directly elected for a two-year term. Tourism, oil refining and manufacturing are the main industries.
Governor, John DeJongh Jr (D)

NORTHERN MARIANA ISLANDS

Commonwealth of the Northern Mariana Islands
Area – 477 sq. km
Seat of government – Saipan
Population – 48,317 falling at 5.57 per cent per year (2010 est)
National day – 8 January (Commonwealth Day)

The USA administered the Northern Mariana Islands, a group of 14 islands in the north-west Pacific Ocean, as part of a UN trusteeship until the trusteeship agreement was terminated in 1986, when the islands became a commonwealth under US sovereignty. Those resident in 1976 or subsequently born in the islands are US citizens. The islands are represented in congress by a non-voting representative, who is directly elected for a two-year term. Under the 1978 constitution, the islands are self-governing. The governor and lieutenant-governor are directly elected for a four-year term. The bicameral legislature comprises a 20-member House of Representatives and a nine-member senate; members are directly elected, representatives for two years and senators for four years. Tourism and manufacturing, especially of clothing, are the main industries.
Governor, Benigno Fitial (C)

URUGUAY

República Oriental del Uruguay – Oriental Republic of Uruguay

Area – 176,215 sq. km
Capital – Montevideo; population, 1,632,620 (2009 est)
Major towns – Ciudad de la Costa, Salto
Currency – Uruguayan peso of 100 centésimos
Population – 3,494,382 rising at 0.47 per cent a year (2009 est)
Religion – Christian (Roman Catholic 45 per cent, Protestant 6 per cent, Afro-umbandista 3 per cent, Mormon 3 per cent) (est)
Language – Spanish (official), Portunol or Brazilero (Portuguese-Spanish mix)
Population density – 19 per sq. km (2008)
Urban population – 92 per cent (2007 est)
Median age (years) – 33.4 (2009 est)
National anthem – 'Himno Nacional' ['National Anthem']
National day – 25 August (Independence Day)
Life expectancy (years) – 76.35 (2009 est)
Mortality rate – 9.09 (2009 est)
Birth rate – 13.91 (2009 est)
Infant mortality rate – 11.32 (2009 est)
Death penalty – Abolished for all crimes (since 1907)
CPI score – 6.7 (2009)

CLIMATE AND TERRAIN

The country consists mainly of undulating grassy plains, with low hills. Elevation extremes range from 514m (Cerro Catedral) at the highest point to 0m (Atlantic Ocean) at the lowest. The principal river is the Rio Negro (with its tributary, the Yi), flowing from north-east to south-west into the Rio Uruguay; damming of the Negro has created a reservoir that is the largest artificial lake in South America. The climate is warm temperate, with occasional cold and strong winds. Average temperatures in Montevideo range from lows of 6°C in July to highs of 28°C in January.

HISTORY AND POLITICS

The hostility of the indigenous Charrúa Amerindians when the Rio de la Plata was first explored by the Spanish in 1516 discouraged colonisation until the 17th century. Although initially settled by the Portuguese, the *Banda Oriental*, as the territory lying on the eastern bank of the river Uruguay was then called, was disputed between the Portuguese and the Spanish until the late 18th century and then between Brazil and Argentina after Spanish rule was overthrown. Uruguay's independence was recognised in 1828 and a republic was inaugurated in 1830. In the mid-19th century there was a power struggle between the conservatives *(Blancos)* and liberals *(Colorados)* which descended into civil war. From 1904 until the 1960s the country experienced political stability and prosperity.

The period from 1962 until 1973 saw economic decline and turmoil caused by the Marxist Tupamaros guerrillas. They were crushed by a military dictatorship that held power from 1973 until 1985, when a return to civilian rule was agreed after violent anti-government protests at the regime's repressive rule and the deteriorating economy.

The Colorado and National *(Blanco)* parties now both occupy the centre ground, but their dominance of politics has been eroded by left-wing parties such as New Space and coalitions such as the Progressive Encounter-Broad Front (EP-FA). The EP-FA won outright majorities in both legislative chambers in the 2004 and the 2009 elections. The 2009 presidential election was won by the EP-FA candidate José Mujica, and he appointed an EP-FA-led coalition government.

POLITICAL SYSTEM

Under the 1997 constitution, the executive president is directly elected for a five-year term, which is not renewable. The president, who appoints the council of ministers, is responsible to the legislature. The bicameral general assembly consists of a Chamber of Representatives, with 99 members directly elected for a five-year term, and the Chamber of Senators, which has 31 members, 30 directly elected for a five-year term and the vice-president as an *ex officio* member.

The republic is divided into 19 departments, each with an elected governor and legislature.

HEAD OF STATE

President, José Mujica, *elected* 29 November 2009, *took office* 1 March 2010
Vice-President, Danilo Astori

SELECTED GOVERNMENT MEMBERS *as at August 2010*

Economy and Finance, Fernando Lorenzo
Foreign Relations, Luis Almagro
Interior, Eduardo Bonomi
Defence, Luis Rosadilla

EMBASSY OF URUGUAY

125 Kensington High Street, London W8 5SF
T 020-7937 4170 E emburuguay@emburuguay.org.uk
Ambassador Extraordinary and Plenipotentiary, HE Julio Moreira Moran, *apptd* 2009

BRITISH EMBASSY

PO Box 16024, Calle Marco Bruto 1073, 11300 Montevideo
T (+598) (2) 622 3630 E ukinuruguay@gmail.com
W http://ukinuruguay.fco.gov.uk
Ambassador Extraordinary and Plenipotentiary, HE Patrick Mullee, *apptd* 2008

DEFENCE

The army has 15 main battle tanks, 133 armoured personnel carriers and 18 armoured infantry fighting vehicles. The navy has 2 frigates, 25 patrol and coastal combatant vessels and 5 combat aircraft at 5 bases. The air force has 15 combat aircraft.

Military budget – US$373m (2009)
Military personnel – 24,621: army 16,234, navy 5,403, air force 2,984; paramilitary 920

ECONOMY AND TRADE

After years of steady growth, Uruguay suffered a severe recession from 1998, largely owing to the economic problems of Brazil and Argentina, its main export markets and sources of tourists. It reduced many to poverty in what had previously been a moderately prosperous society, and over a quarter of households still lived below the poverty line in 2008. The recession culminated in a banking crisis in 2002; IMF loans, the rescheduling of foreign debt repayments and the government's emergency measures achieved a recovery and the economy grew strongly from 2004 to 2008. The 2008 global downturn slowed economic growth in 2009 as commodity prices and tourist numbers fell, but Uruguay has avoided recession, mainly through increased public expenditure.

Ranching and livestock products (beef, mutton, wool) have been the mainstay of the economy since the mid-19th century, generating the prosperity that enabled Uruguay to develop an extensive welfare system in the early 20th century, although dependence on these products leaves the economy vulnerable to price fluctuations. Other crops include rice, grains, soya beans, citrus fruits, wine grapes, linseed and sunflower seed. Agricultural produce is the basis of the food processing and beverages industries. Other industries include fishing, forestry and the manufacture of electrical machinery, transport equipment, petroleum products, textiles and chemicals. Exploited minerals include clinker, dolomite, marble and granite. Tourism and offshore financial services also contribute substantially to revenue. Agriculture contributes 9.3 per cent of GDP, industry 22.7 per cent and services 68 per cent.

The main trading partners are Brazil, Argentina, China and the USA. Principal exports are meat, rice, leather products, wool, fish and dairy products. The main imports are crude oil and petroleum products, machinery, chemicals, vehicles and paper.

GNI – US$27,500m; US$8,260 per capita (2008)
Annual average growth of GDP – 0.6 per cent (2009 est)
Inflation rate – 7.3 per cent (2009 est)
Unemployment – 7.9 per cent (2009 est)
Total external debt – US$12,610m (2009 est)
Imports – US$8,900m (2008)
Exports – US$6,400m (2008)

BALANCE OF PAYMENTS

Trade – US$1,646m deficit (2009)
Current Account – US$253m deficit (2009)

Trade with UK	*2008*	*2009*
Imports from UK	£62,820,007	£55,034,646
Exports to UK	£111,539,987	£106,535,851

COMMUNICATIONS

There are nearly 77,800km of roads, 7,700km of which are surfaced, and 1,600km of railway, of which 1,200km are operational. There are 1,600km of navigable waterways, mainly on the Uruguay and Negro rivers. A bridge across the Rio de la Plata links Uruguay and Argentina. The main ports are Montevideo and Colonia on the coast, and Fray Bentos and Paysandú on the river Uruguay. There is an international airport near Montevideo, and 56 smaller airports and airfields around the country.

Modernised telephone systems provided services to 959,000 fixed-line subscribers, 3.5 million mobile phone subscribers, and 1.3 million internet users in 2008.

EDUCATION AND HEALTH

Primary and secondary education is compulsory and free, and technical and trade schools and evening courses for adult education are state-run. The university at Montevideo was founded in 1849.

Literacy rate – 97.9 per cent (2007 est)
Gross enrolment ratio (percentage of relevant age group) – primary 114 per cent; secondary 92 per cent; tertiary 64 per cent (2008 est)
Health expenditure (per capita) – US$582 (2007)
Hospital beds (per 1,000 people) – 2.9 (2003–8)

MEDIA

The constitution enshrines freedom of expression. There are more than 100 daily and weekly newspapers, all privately owned, and more than 100 radio stations, as well as 20 television channels. The government owns one television and one radio station.

UZBEKISTAN

O'zbekiston Respublikasi – Republic of Uzbekistan

Area – 447,400 sq. km
Capital – Tashkent; population, 2,200,910 (2009 est)
Major cities – Andijan, Bukhara, Karsi, Namangan, Nukus, Samarkand
Currency – Som of 100 tiyins
Population – 27,606,007 rising at 0.94 per cent a year (2009 est); Uzbek (80 per cent), Russian (5.5 per cent), Tajik (5 per cent), Kazakh (3 per cent), Karakalpak (2.5 per cent), Tatar (1.5 per cent) (est)
Religion – Muslim (Sunni 90 per cent, Shia 1 per cent), Christian (Russian Orthodox 5 per cent) (est)
Language – Uzbek (official), Russian, Tajik
Population density – 64 per sq. km (2008)
Urban population – 37 per cent (2007 est)
Median age (years) – 24.7 (2009 est)
National anthem – 'O'zbekiston Respublikasining Davlat Madhiyasi' ['National Anthem of the Republic of Uzbekistan']
National day – 1 September (Independence Day)
Life expectancy (years) – 71.96 (2009 est)
Mortality rate – 5.29 (2009 est)
Birth rate – 17.58 (2009 est)
Infant mortality rate – 23.43 (2009 est)
Death penalty – Abolished for all crimes (since 2008)
CPI score – 1.7 (2009)

CLIMATE AND TERRAIN

Landlocked Uzbekistan has four regions: the Ustyurt plateau and Amu Darya delta in the west; the Kyzyl Kum desert east of the Aral Sea; the Tien Shan and Pamir mountains in the east and south-east; and the fertile Fergana valley in the east, crossed by the Syr Darya river. Elevation extremes range from 4,301m (Adelunga Toghi) at the highest point to −12m (Sariqarnish Kuli) at the lowest. The country includes the southern part of the Aral Sea. There is a semi-arid desert climate, although it is colder in the mountains. Average temperatures in Tashkent range from lows of −6°C in January to highs of 33°C in July.

HISTORY AND POLITICS

Settlements in the south developed as important transit points on the ancient 'Silk Road' in the first century BC. Bukhara and Samarkand became two of the most important cultural and academic centres in the Islamic world after the religion was introduced in the eighth century. In the 13th century the area became part of the Mongol Empire, with Samarkand as its capital during the reign of Amir Timur (Tamerlane). As the empire declined, independent principalities emerged. The three khanates in what is now Uzbekistan, Khiva, Kokand and Bukhara, were annexed by the Russian Empire in the second half of the 19th century. In 1917 a Bolshevik revolution broke out in Tashkent and by 1921 all of Uzbekistan had been absorbed into the USSR. Under Soviet rule a massive land irrigation programme was implemented to allow the cultivation of cotton, but this also led to the drying up of the Aral Sea.

Uzbekistan declared its independence from the USSR on 1 September 1991 but post-independence political life has been dominated by the former Communists. The main opposition parties, *Erk* (Freedom) and *Birlik* (Unity), were banned in 1992 and have since become inactive; other forms of opposition are suppressed and the government has been accused of human rights abuses, including the systematic use of torture. The former communist leader Islam Karimov, who came to power in 1990, was elected president in 1991 and has retained the presidency since, in unopposed elections or through the extension of his term of office in referendums. He was re-elected in 2007 for a third term, despite the constitutional restriction to two terms.

All legislative elections since independence have been won by the People's Democratic Party (the former Communist Party) or its allies. After the latest legislative election in December 2009 and January 2010, the largest party in the legislative chamber was the pro-Karimov Liberal Democratic Party; opposition parties were barred from contesting the election. Most elections have been reported by observers to be neither free nor fair and have attracted international criticism.

INSURGENCIES

The Islamic Movement of Uzbekistan (IMU), founded in 1996, has carried out armed attacks and bombings sporadically since 1999, but has little support. However, its activities have provided the government with an excuse to curtail human rights and suppress political opposition and protests, such as those in Andijan in 2005, when over 180 protesters were killed by troops.

POLITICAL SYSTEM

The 1992 constitution was amended in 2002 to create a bicameral legislature and extend the president's term of office. The president is directly elected; his term of office was five years, renewable only once, but was extended to seven years. The legislature, the Supreme Assembly, became bicameral after the 2004–5 elections. The Legislative Chamber has 150 members, 135 directly elected and 15 members of the Ecological Movement of Uzbekistan. The senate has 100 members, 16 appointed by the president and 84 elected by regional deputies to represent the regions and the capital. Members of both houses serve a five-year term. The president appoints the cabinet, which is chaired by the prime minister.

The country is divided into 12 provinces, the autonomous republic of Karakalpakstan, and the city of Tashkent.

HEAD OF STATE

President, Islam Karimov, *elected* 29 December 1991, *elected by referendum for a five-year term* 1995, *re-elected* 2000, 2007

SELECTED GOVERNMENT MEMBERS *as at August 2010*

Prime Minister, Shavkat Mirziyaev
First Deputy Prime Minister, Finance, Rustam Azimov
Deputy Prime Ministers, Farida Akbarova; Abdulla Aripov; Ergash Shoismatov; Ulugbek Roziqulov; Botir Khodayev; Elyor Ganiev
Defence, Gen. Qobil Berdiyev
Foreign Affairs, Vladimir Norov
Interior, Bahodir Matlubov

EMBASSY OF THE REPUBLIC OF UZBEKISTAN

41 Holland Park, London W11 3RP
T 020-7229 7679 E info@uzbekembassy.org
W www.uzbekembassy.org
Ambassador Extraordinary and Plenipotentiary, HE Otabek Akbarov, *apptd* 2007

BRITISH EMBASSY

Ul. Gulyamova 67, Tashkent 100000
T (+998) (71) 120 1500 E brit@emb.uz
W ukinuzbekistan.fco.gov.uk
Ambassador Extraordinary and Plenipotentiary, HE Rupert Joy, *apptd* 2009

BRITISH COUNCIL

University of World Languages Building, 11 Mirobod St, Tashkent 700031
T (+998) (71) 140 0660/61/62/63
W www.britishcouncil.org.uk/uzbekistan
Director, Steve McNulty

DEFENCE

The army has 340 main battle tanks, 399 armoured infantry fighting vehicles and 309 armoured personnel carriers. The air force has 135 combat capable aircraft and 29 armed helicopters.
Military budget – US$94m (2007 est)
Military personnel – 67,000: army 50,000, air force 17,000; paramilitary 20,000
Conscription duration – 12 months

ECONOMY AND TRADE

The economy remains centrally planned and control has increased in some areas, stifling economic activity. Economic growth and living standards are among the worst in the former Soviet republics, with a third of the population living below the poverty line. The global downturn has had little impact owing to the country's relative economic isolation.

The economy is based on intensive agricultural production, particularly of cotton, made possible by extensive irrigation schemes. Vegetables, fruit, grain and livestock are also produced. The main industries are textile manufacture, food processing, machine building, metallurgy, mining (especially for gold), oil and natural gas production and chemicals. Oil and gas exports offer greater potential for economic growth and have attracted foreign interest, notably from Russia and China, but exploitation is hampered by a lack of modern oil pipelines and basic infrastructure. Agriculture contributes 26.7 per cent of GDP, industry 39.7 per cent and services 33.5 per cent.

The main trading partners are Russia, Ukraine, China, South Korea and Kazakhstan. Principal exports are oil and natural gas, cotton, gold, mineral fertilisers, metals, textiles, food products, machinery and motor vehicles. The main imports are machinery and equipment, foodstuffs, chemicals and metals.
GNI – US$24,700m; US$910 per capita (2008)
Annual average growth of GDP – 6.2 per cent (2009 est)
Inflation rate – 8.6 per cent (2009 est)
Population below poverty line – 33 per cent (2004 est)
Unemployment – 1.1 per cent (2009 est)
Total external debt – US$3,630m (2009 est)

BALANCE OF PAYMENTS

Trade – US$2,323m surplus (2009)
Current Account – US$3,562m surplus (2008)

Trade with UK	*2008*	*2009*
Imports from UK	£26,985,637	£43,800,986
Exports to UK	£28,951,754	£29,360,708

COMMUNICATIONS

Uzbekistan has 86,500km of roads, 75,500km of which are paved. It has nearly 4,000km of railway, and 1,100km of waterways. The principal airport is at Tashkent.

The fixed-line telephone system is antiquated and mobile phone distribution is growing rapidly. There were 1.9 million fixed lines in use, 12.7 million mobile phone subscribers and 2.5 million internet users in 2008.

EDUCATION AND HEALTH

Literacy rate – 96.9 per cent (2007 est)
Gross enrolment ratio (percentage of relevant age group) – primary 94 per cent; secondary 102 per cent; tertiary 10 per cent (2008 est)
Health expenditure (per capita) – US$41 (2007)
Hospital beds (per 1,000 people) – 4.8 (2003–8)

MEDIA

The government strictly controls the media and much of the population relies on foreign broadcasts. Self-censorship by journalists is common because of state harassment, and internet access to independent websites is blocked. There is a mixture of government-run and private television and radio stations. Almost all newspapers are produced by the state or by pro-government organisations.

VANUATU

Ripablik blong Vanuatu/République de Vanuatu – Republic of Vanuatu

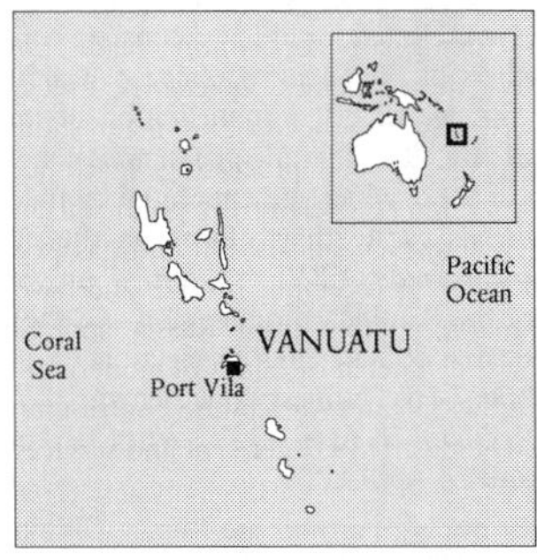

Area – 12,189 sq. km
Capital – Port Vila, on Efaté; population, 43,629 (2009 est)
Major town – Luganville, on Espiritu Santo
Currency – Vatu
Population – 218,519 rising at 1.4 per cent a year (2009 est). About 95 per cent are Melanesian, the rest being mostly Micronesian, Polynesian and European
Religion – Christian (Presbyterian 32 per cent, Anglican 13 per cent, Roman Catholic 13 per cent, Seventh-day Adventist 11 per cent, other Protestant denominations 14 per cent), John Frum Movement (an indigenous cargo cult) 5 per cent (est)
Language – English, French, Bislama (all official); over 100 local languages exist
Population density – 19 per sq. km (2008)
Urban population – 24 per cent (2007 est)
Median age (years) – 24.2 (2009 est)
National anthem – 'Yumi, Yumi, Yumi' ['We, We, We']
National day – 30 July (Independence Day)
Life expectancy (years) – 63.98 (2009 est)
Mortality rate – 7.55 (2009 est)
Birth rate – 21.53 (2009 est)
Infant mortality rate – 49.45 (2009 est)
Death penalty – Abolished for all crimes (since 1980)
CPI score – 3.2 (2009)
Literacy rate – 78.1 per cent (2007 est)

CLIMATE AND TERRAIN

Situated in the south Pacific Ocean, Vanuatu comprises 13 large and some 70 small islands, of either coral or volcanic origin, including the Banks Islands and Torres Islands in the north. The principal islands are Vanua Lava, Espiritu Santo, Maewo, Pentecost, Ambae, Malekula, Ambrym, Epi, Efaté, Erromango, Tanna and Aneityum. Most islands are mountainous and covered with dense rainforest. Elevation extremes range from 1,877m (Tabwemasana) at the highest point to 0m (Pacific Ocean) at the lowest. The climate varies from tropical in the north of the archipelago to subtropical in the south, and all the islands experience cyclones. Several islands have active volcanoes and seismic events are frequent.

HISTORY AND POLITICS

Some of the islands of Vanuatu have been inhabited for over 4,000 years. Europeans first visited in the early 17th century, and Captain Cook named the islands the New Hebrides in 1774. In the 19th century, the British and the French established plantations, and from 1906 jointly administered the islands as the Condominium of the New Hebrides. This became independent as the Republic of Vanuatu in 1980.

In the 2008 legislative election, the Vanuaaku Pati won the most seats; its leader, Edward Natapei, was elected prime minister and formed a coalition government. The 2009 presidential election was won by Iolu Abil in the third round of voting. Edward Natapei's tenure as prime minister and party leader was challenged on a technicality in November 2009, but he continued to hold office pending the election of a new prime minister. This was delayed by legal challenges over his dismissal and a split in his party over the leadership, and he remains in office at the head of a new coalition including former opposition parties, still with the support of the majority of members of parliament.

POLITICAL SYSTEM

Under the 1980 constitution, the head of state is a president who is elected for a five-year term by an electoral college consisting of the members of the legislature and the presidents of the six provincial governments. The unicameral parliament has 52 members, directly elected for a four-year term. The prime minister is elected by parliament from among its members, and appoints the council of ministers. The National Council of Chiefs advises on matters of custom.

HEAD OF STATE

President, Iolu Abil, *elected* 2 September 2009

SELECTED GOVERNMENT MEMBERS *at August 2010*

Prime Minister, Edward Natapei
Finance and Economic Management, Sela Molisa
Foreign Affairs, Joe Natuman
Internal Affairs, Moana Carcasses

BRITISH HIGH COMMISSIONER

HE Malcolm McLachlan, MBE, *apptd* 2009, resident at Suva, Fiji

ECONOMY AND TRADE

The economy is based on small-scale agriculture and fishing; 65 per cent of the population is employed on plantations or in subsistence agriculture. Subsistence crops include yams, taro, fruit and vegetables; the principal cash crops are coconuts, cocoa and coffee. Cattle are kept on the plantations. There is a small light industrial sector producing frozen food and fish and canned meat, and processing wood. Eco-tourism and offshore financial services are of growing importance.

The main export markets are Thailand (53.2 per cent) Japan and Poland; imports come chiefly from Japan, Australia, China and Singapore. Principal exports are copra, beef, cocoa, timber, kava and coffee. The main imports are machinery and equipment, foodstuffs and fuels.

GNI – US$417m; US$1,840 per capita (2007)
Annual average growth of GDP – 3.8 per cent (2009 est)
Inflation rate – 3.9 per cent (2007 est)
Total external debt – US$81.2m (2004 est)
Imports – US$300m (2008)
Exports – US$30m (2007)

BALANCE OF PAYMENTS

Trade – US$219m deficit (2009)
Current Account – US$14m deficit (2009)

Trade with UK	*2008*	*2009*
Imports from UK	£783,240	£5,016,125
Exports to UK	£860,564	£496,597

COMMUNICATIONS

Vanuatu has 1,070km of roads, of which 256km are surfaced. There are no railways. The main ports are Forari, Port Vila and Santo. There are about 30 airports and airfields on the islands; the main international airport is at Port Vila. Air connections and cruise ship facilities are being improved to boost tourism.

There were 10,400 fixed telephone lines, 36,000 mobile phone subscribers and 17,000 internet users in 2008.

VATICAN CITY STATE

Status Civitatis Vaticanae or Sancta Sedes/Stato Della Città del Vaticano or Santa Sede – State of the Vatican City or the Holy See

Area – 0.44 sq. km (enclave only)
Capital – Vatican City
Currency – Euro (€) of 100 cents
Population – 826 (2009 est)
Religion – Christian (Roman Catholic)
Language – Latin (official), Italian, French
Population density – 2,273 per sq. km (1997)
National anthem – 'Inno e Marcia Pontificale' ['Pontifical Anthem and March']
National day – 24 April (Inauguration of Pope Benedict XVI)
Death penalty – Abolished for all crimes (since 1969)

HISTORY

The Vatican City State is an independent sovereign state that consists of an enclave within the city of Rome and extraterritorial areas including offices and basilicas in Rome, the pope's summer residence and the location of Vatican Radio's transmitter. The Holy See, which comprises the pope and the departments that carry out the government of the Roman Catholic Church worldwide, has sovereign authority over the Vatican City State's territory, providing its government and diplomatic representation overseas.

The head of the Roman Catholic Church became a temporal ruler in the eighth century, holding territory in central Italy. The Papal States were annexed in 1860 by the newly unified kingdom of Italy, and Rome was captured by Italian troops in 1870–1, when the pope withdrew into the Vatican Palace. In the Lateran treaties (1929), Italy recognised the pope's sovereignty over the city of the Vatican, and declared the state to be neutral and inviolable territory. The Vatican City State has special observer status at the United Nations.

The pope, the Sovereign Pontiff, is the head of state of the Vatican City, which is governed as an absolute monarchy. He is elected for life by a conclave consisting of those members of the Sacred College of Cardinals who are under the age of 80. Administration of the state is carried out by the Pontifical Commission and the Secretariat of State, which are appointed by the pope. All Vatican officials vacate their offices on the death of a pope. Pope Benedict XVI confirmed in office the president of the Pontifical Commission and the members of the Secretariat of State after his election.

Sovereign Pontiff, His Holiness Pope Benedict XVI (Joseph Ratzinger), *born* 16 April 1927, *elected* 19 April 2005, *inaugurated* 24 April 2005

SECRETARIAT OF STATE *as at July 2010*
Secretary of State, Cardinal Tarcisio Bertone
Substitute for General Affairs, Archbishop Fernando Filoni
Secretary for Relations with States, Archbishop Dominique Mamberti

PONTIFICAL COMMISSION
President, Archbishop Giovanni Lajolo

APOSTOLIC NUNCIATURE
54 Parkside, London SW19 5NE
T 020-8944 7189
Apostolic Nuncio, HE Archbishop Faustino Sainz Munoz, *apptd* 2005

BRITISH EMBASSY TO THE HOLY SEE
Via XX Settembre 80/A, 00187 Rome
T (+39) (6) 4220 4000 E holysee@fco.gov.uk
W http://ukinholysee.fco.gov.uk
Ambassador Extraordinary and Plenipotentiary, HE Francis Campbell, *apptd* 2005

ECONOMY

The Vatican City is unique in having a non-commercial economy. It is supported by financial contributions from Roman Catholic dioceses worldwide. Revenue is also generated by the sale of postage stamps, coins, medals and tourist mementoes. Income from investments and property and global banking and financial services also provide considerable revenue.

MEDIA AND CULTURE

Vatican Radio broadcasts worldwide in many languages, and the Vatican Information Service is the official news service.

The city is a World Heritage Site. Its architectural masterpiece, St Peter's Basilica, is famed for its domed roof and the Sistine Chapel ceiling, respectively designed and painted by Michelangelo. The Vatican museum contains a vast art collection.

VENEZUELA

República Bolivariana de Venezuela – Bolivarian Republic of Venezuela

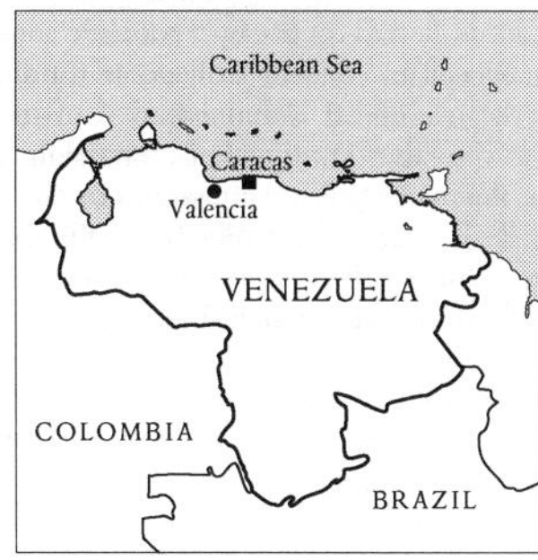

Area – 912,050 sq. km
Capital – Caracas; population, 3,050,770 (2009 est)
Major cities – Barquisimeto, Ciudad Guayana, Maracaibo, Valencia
Currency – Bolívar fuerte (Bs. F) of 100 céntimos
Population – 26,814,843 rising at 1.51 per cent a year (2009 est)
Religion – Christian (Roman Catholic 92 per cent) (est)
Language – Spanish (official), several indigenous languages
Population density – 32 per sq. km (2008)
Urban population – 93 per cent (2007 est)
Median age (years) – 25.5 (2009 est)
National anthem – 'Gloria al Bravo Pueblo' ['Glory to the Brave People']
National day – 5 July (Independence Day)
Life expectancy (years) – 73.61 (2009 est)
Mortality rate – 5.12 (2009 est)
Birth rate – 20.61 (2009 est)
Infant mortality rate – 21.54 (2009 est)
Death penalty – Abolished for all crimes (since 1863)
CPI score – 1.9 (2009)

CLIMATE AND TERRAIN

The Andean mountains, of which the main range is the Sierra Nevada de Mérida, run across the north-west of the country, separating the northern coast from the central plains *(llanos)*. The Guiana Highlands occupy the south-east of the country. Elevation extremes range from 5,007m (Pico Bolivar) at the highest point to 0m (Caribbean Sea) at the lowest. The Orinoco flows across the centre of the country to its delta on the Atlantic coast. Its upper waters are united with those of the Rio Negro (a Brazilian tributary of the Amazon) by a natural river or canal, known as the Brazo Casiquiare. The coastal lowlands contain many lagoons and lakes, including Lake Maracaibo (area 13,351 sq. km), the largest lake in South America. The climate varies from tropical to alpine, depending on altitude, and most areas experience a wet season from May to November. Average temperatures in Caracas range from lows of 13°C in January to highs of 27°C in April and May.

HISTORY AND POLITICS

Columbus landed on the coast in 1498, and the first Spanish settlement was established at Cumaná in 1520. Venezuela became part of the Viceroyalty of New Granada in the early 18th century. There were several revolts against Spanish colonial rule, and a declaration of independence in 1811 was followed by several years of struggle until troops led by Simón Bolivar defeated the Spanish at the battle of Carabobo in 1821. Venezuela became part of Gran Colombia (with Colombia, Ecuador and Panama), and then an independent republic in 1830 under the first of a series of *caudillos* (military leaders). The first truly democratic elections were held in 1947 but the government was overthrown by the military within months. An enduring civilian democracy was established in 1958 and introduced a period of relative political stability.

Oil revenues supported a buoyant economy in the 1970s but a price collapse in the mid-1980s led to economic difficulties and widespread poverty, causing social unrest and a number of attempted coups. Since he came to power in 1998, President Hugo Chávez's economic and social reforms and his authoritarian style have polarised domestic opinion, provoking strikes and demonstrations, an attempted military coup in 2002 and a recall referendum in 2004, which he won.

President Chávez was re-elected again in 2006. In the 2005 legislative election, the president's Fifth Republic Movement won an overall majority in the legislature and parties allied to it took the remaining seats because of an opposition boycott of the election. The parties supporting the president subsequently amalgamated to form the United Socialist Party of Venezuela, launched in 2008. A legislative election was scheduled for 26 September 2010.

POLITICAL SYSTEM

Under the 1999 constitution, the executive president is directly elected for a six-year term; the limit on the number of successive terms was abolished in 2009. The unicameral National Assembly has 165 members, directly elected for a five-year term. The president appoints the vice-president and the council of ministers.

The country is divided into 23 states, one capital district and one federal dependency composed of 11 island groups (72 individual islands). The states have considerable autonomy and each has its own legislature and elected governor.

HEAD OF STATE

President, Col. (retd) Hugo Chávez Frías, *elected* 6 December 1998, *sworn in* 2 February 1999, *re-elected* 2000, 2006
Vice-President, Elías Jaua Milano

SELECTED GOVERNMENT MEMBERS *as at August 2010*

Interior and Justice, Tarek El Aissami
Defence, Carlos Mata Figueroa
Economy, Jorge Giordani
Foreign Relations, Nicolas Maduro

EMBASSY OF THE BOLIVARIAN REPUBLIC OF VENEZUELA

1 Cromwell Road, London SW7 2HW
T 020-7584 4206 E info@venezlon.co.uk
W www.venezlon.co.uk
Ambassador Extraordinary and Plenipotentiary, HE Samuel Moncada, *apptd* 2007

BRITISH EMBASSY

Edificio Torre la Castellana, Piso 11, Avenida la Principal de la Castellana, Caracas 1601
T (+58) (212) 263 8411 E britishembassy@internet.ve
W http://ukinvenezuela.fco.gov.uk
Ambassador Extraordinary and Plenipotentiary, HE Catherine Nettleton, *apptd* 2010

BRITISH COUNCIL
Torre Credicard, Piso 3, Avenida Principal El Bosque, Chacaito, Caracas
T (+58) (212) 952 9965 W www.britishcouncil.org/venezuela
Director, Cherry Gough

DEFENCE

The army has 81 main battle tanks, 91 armoured personnel carriers and 10 armed helicopters. The navy has 2 submarines, 6 frigates, 8 patrol and coastal vessels and 10 combat aircraft at 10 bases. The air force has 81 combat aircraft.

Military expenditure – US$3,200m (2009)
Military personnel – 115,000: army 63,000, navy 17,500, air force 11,500, National Guard 23,000
Conscription duration – 30 months (selective)

ECONOMY AND TRADE

Much of industry is state-owned, and since President Chávez came to power an increasing proportion of the private sector, some foreign-owned, has been nationalised, including oil, electricity and banking companies. Oil and gas are the mainstays of the economy, providing 90 per cent of exports and over 50 per cent of government revenue, but heavy dependence on them makes the economy vulnerable to global price fluctuations. The economy contracted in 2009 owing to lower prices and the global downturn, with the impact of the recession being exacerbated by electricity rationing after a severe drought in 2009–10 left hydroelectric plants inoperable. A dual exchange rate was introduced in January 2010.

Other major industries are mining (coal, iron ore, bauxite, gold), production of construction materials, textiles, steel and aluminium, food processing and vehicle assembly. Industry contributes 36.8 per cent of GDP and services 59.2 per cent.

Agriculture comprises large-scale commercial farms and subsistence farming. Land distribution is uneven, but redistribution of land to the rural poor, breaking up larger estates, has begun. Agricultural products include maize, sorghum, sugar cane, rice, bananas, vegetables and coffee. There is an extensive beef and dairy farming industry. Agriculture provides 4 per cent of GDP and engages over 10 per cent of the workforce.

The main trading partners are the USA (35 per cent of exports; 24 per cent of imports), other Latin American countries and China. Principal exports are oil, bauxite and aluminium, steel, chemicals, agricultural products and basic manufactures. The main imports are raw materials, machinery, transport equipment and construction materials.

GNI – US$257,900m; US$9,230 per capita (2008)
Annual average growth of GDP – –1.5 per cent (2009 est)
Inflation rate – 27.3 per cent (2009 est)
Population below poverty line – 37.9 per cent (2005 est)
Unemployment – 10.9 per cent (2009 est)
Total external debt – US$43,410m (2009 est)
Imports – US$49,600m (2008)
Exports – US$93,200m (2008)

BALANCE OF PAYMENTS
Trade – US$56,740m surplus (2009)
Current Account – US$8,561m surplus (2009)

Trade with UK	*2008*	*2009*
Imports from UK	£262,267,021	£277,360,066
Exports to UK	£570,326,894	£396,227,834

COMMUNICATIONS

There are 96,155km of roads, some 32,308km of them surfaced. The 7,100km of inland waterways include 400km on the river Orinoco which, with Lake Maracaibo, is navigable for ocean-going ships. Road and river communications have made railways practically redundant, except for carrying iron ore in the south-east, although the government is expanding the network and there are now some 800km of lines. The main ports are Maracaibo, Puerto Cabello and Caracas-La Guaira; there is a high risk of piracy or armed robbery for shipping in Venezuelan waters. There are over 400 airports and airfields, the principal airports being at Caracas and Maracaibo.

Telecommunications are being modernised and expanded. In 2008 there were 6.3 million fixed lines in use, 27.1 million mobile phone subscribers and 7.2 million internet users.

EDUCATION AND HEALTH

There are nine years of compulsory education. Under President Chávez, healthcare and education programmes have been greatly expanded.

Literacy rate – 95.2 per cent (2007 est)
Gross enrolment ratio (percentage of relevant age group) – primary 103 per cent; secondary 81 per cent; tertiary 78 per cent (2008 est)
Health expenditure (per capita) – US$477 (2007)
Hospital beds (per 1,000 people) – 1.3 (2003–8)

MEDIA

Media watchdogs have accused President Chávez of creating a climate of fear among journalists. In 2007 the terrestrial transmission licence of RCT, the country's oldest private television station and an outspoken critic of the president, was revoked by the government, and in 2009 opposition television network Globovision was heavily fined for alleged tax evasion and several dozen radio stations were closed. There are many private radio and television broadcasters in addition to the state-run networks (on which President Chávez has his own television and radio shows). There are six daily newspapers, including *El Mundo* and *El Nacional.*

VIETNAM

Cong Hoa Xa Hoi Chu Nghia Viet Nam – Socialist Republic of Vietnam

Area – 331,210 sq. km
Capital – Hanoi; population, 2,667,800 (2009 est)
Major cities – Bien Hoa, Da Nang, Haiphong, Ho Chi Minh City

Currency – Dong of 10 ho or 100 xu
Population – 86,967,524 rising at 0.98 per cent a year (2009 est); Kinh (86.2 per cent), Tay (1.9 per cent), Thai (1.7 per cent), Muong (1.5 per cent), Khome (1.4 per cent), Hoa (1.1 per cent), Nun (1.1 per cent), Hmong (1 per cent)
Religion – Buddhist 50 per cent (predominantly Mahayana), Christian (Roman Catholic 8 per cent, Protestant denominations 1 per cent), Cao Dai 2 per cent, Hoa Hao 2 per cent (est). Cao Dai is a syncretistic religion that combines elements of several faiths. Hoa Hao is a branch of Buddhism
Language – Vietnamese (official), English, French, Chinese, Khmer; Mon-Khmer and Malayo-Polynesian are spoken in mountain areas
Population density – 278 per sq. km (2008)
Urban population – 27 per cent (2007 est)
Median age (years) – 27.4 (2009 est)
National anthem – 'Tien Quan Ca' ['Army March']
National day – 2 September (Independence Day)
Life expectancy (years) – 71.61 (2009 est)
Mortality rate – 6.17 (2009 est)
Birth rate – 16.31 (2009 est)
Infant mortality rate – 22.88 (2009 est)
Death penalty – Retained
CPI score – 2.7 (2009)

CLIMATE AND TERRAIN

The country is mostly mountainous, apart from the densely populated fertile plains around the deltas of the Hong (Red River) in the north and the Mekong in the south. Elevation extremes range from 3,144m (Fan Si Pan) at the highest point to 0m (South China Sea) at the lowest. The climate is tropical and affected by the monsoon cycle. The wet season lasts from May to September, although the coast, being affected by typhoons and tropical storms, receives most rain between September and January.

HISTORY AND POLITICS

Independent kingdoms in Vietnam were unified in the 15th century but power became decentralised until the early 19th century, when central authority was reasserted with the assistance of France. From 1858 to 1884 France conquered Vietnam, establishing three protectorates which in 1887 became part of France's Indo-Chinese Union with Cambodia and Laos. Vietnam was under Japanese occupation from 1940 to 1945; Vietnamese Communists fought a guerrilla war of resistance against the occupiers and, controlling most of the country when the Second World War ended, declared independence.

France's attempts to reassert its control led to the Indo-China War (1946–54) which ended with France's withdrawal and an armistice dividing the country into communist North Vietnam and non-communist South Vietnam. A communist insurgency began in South Vietnam in 1957 and escalated into war between the communist north and the US-backed south. Direct military intervention by the USA began in the early 1960s but ended after talks resulted in a peace agreement in 1973. The civil war continued until the south was defeated in 1975, and North and South Vietnam were reunified in 1976 as the Socialist Republic of Vietnam.

A degree of economic liberalisation was introduced from 1986 and a new constitution in 1992 approved many economic and political reforms, but power remains with the ruling Communist Party. After a major government corruption scandal in 2006, the party leadership requested comments on its political platform; this prompted a public debate about the party's role, criticism of government and some calls for political pluralism. Subsequently, the government has continued its anti-corruption campaign but cracked down on media coverage of corruption and pro-democracy campaigners.

At its five-yearly meeting in 2006, the Communist Party Congress elected a new politburo and secretariat. A few months later the president and prime minister resigned to allow a younger leadership to be appointed; Nguyen Minh Triet was elected president to complete his predecessor's term of office, and he appointed Nguyen Tan Dung as prime minister. In the 2007 legislative election, the Communist Party won 450 of the 500 seats; subsequently Nguyen Minh Triet was re-elected president and Nguyen Tan Dung was reappointed prime minister.

POLITICAL SYSTEM

The 1992 constitution was amended in 2001 to allow small-scale capitalism greater freedom. The president is elected by the legislature to serve a five-year term. The unicameral National Assembly *(Quoc-Hoi)* has 500 members, who are directly elected for a five-year term. The head of government is the prime minister, who is responsible to the National Assembly, which appoints the council of ministers. However, effective power lies with the Communist Party of Vietnam. Its highest executive body is the Central Committee, elected by the national party congress held every five years. The politburo and the secretariat of the central committee, which exercise the real power, are elected at the party congress.

HEAD OF STATE

President, Nguyen Minh Triet, *elected* 27 June 2006 *re-elected* 24 June 2007
Vice-President, Nguyen Thi Doan

SELECTED GOVERNMENT MEMBERS *as at August 2010*

Prime Minister, Nguyen Tan Dung
Deputy Prime Ministers, Pham Gia Khiem *(Foreign Affairs);* Troung Vinh Trong; Nguyen Sinh Hung; Nguyen Thien Nhan; Hoang Trung Hai
Finance, Vu Van Ninh
Internal Affairs, Tran Van Tuan
National Defence, Gen. Phung Quang Thanh

EMBASSY OF THE SOCIALIST REPUBLIC OF VIETNAM

12–14 Victoria Road, London W8 5RD
T 020-7937 1912 E consular@vietnamembassy.org.uk
W www.vietnamembassy.org.uk
Ambassador Extraordinary and Plenipotentiary, HE Tran Quang Hoan, *apptd* 2007

BRITISH EMBASSY

Central Building, 31 Hai Ba Trung, Hanoi
T (+84) (4) 936 0500 E behanoi02@vnn.vn
W http://ukinvietnam.fco.gov.uk
Ambassador Extraordinary and Plenipotentiary, HE Mark Kent, *apptd* 2008

BRITISH COUNCIL

40 Cat Linh Street, Dong Da, Hanoi
T (+84) (4) 843 6780 W www.britishcouncil.org/vietnam
Director, Robin Rickard

DEFENCE

The army has 1,315 main battle tanks, 1,380 armoured personnel carriers and 300 armoured infantry fighting

vehicles. The navy has 2 submarines, 5 frigates, 6 corvettes and 38 patrol and coastal vessels at 7 principal bases. The air force has 219 combat aircraft and 26 armed helicopters.
Military budget – US$2,800m (2009)
Military personnel – 455,000: army 412,000, navy 13,000, air force 30,000; paramilitary 40,000
Conscription duration – 24–36 months

ECONOMY AND TRADE

The economy struggled for a decade after 1975 owing to the devastation of war and the imposition of a centrally planned economy. Since economic liberalisation and international integration were adopted in 1986, the economy has grown substantially, albeit from a low base, and export-driven industries are being developed. Poverty was reduced by over 40 per cent between 1993 and 2007, although more remote rural areas have yet to benefit. The global downturn reduced economic growth in 2008–9, but domestic demand and fiscal stimulus packages averted a recession.

Agriculture's contribution is gradually shrinking, but still accounts for 21.3 per cent of GDP and employs 52 per cent of the workforce. The main industries are food processing, clothing and footwear, machine building, coal mining, steel, cement, chemical fertiliser, glass, tyres and paper, and oil and gas production from large offshore reserves. Industry now contributes 40 per cent of GDP and services 38.7 per cent.

The main trading partners are the USA, China, Japan, Singapore and Taiwan. Principal exports are crude oil, fish and seafood, rice, coffee, rubber, tea, clothing and footwear. The main imports are machinery and equipment, petroleum products, fertiliser, steel products, raw cotton, grain, cement and motorcycles.
GNI – US$76,800m; US$890 per capita (2008)
Annual average growth of GDP – 4.4 per cent (2009 est)
Inflation rate – 7.3 per cent (2009 est)
Population below poverty line – 14.8 per cent (2007 est)
Unemployment – 6.5 per cent (2009 est)
Total external debt – US$26,060m (2009 est)
Imports – US$79,300m (2008)
Exports – US$60,900m (2008)

BALANCE OF PAYMENTS
Trade – US$12,379m deficit (2009)
Current Account – US$10,706m deficit (2009)

Trade with UK	*2008*	*2009*
Imports from UK	£167,647,862	£209,679,762
Exports to UK	£1,026,164,284	£1,050,664,663

COMMUNICATIONS

Vietnam has 222,000km of roads, 180,000km of which are unsurfaced. It has 2,300km of railways and 5,000km of navigable waterways. The main ports are Haiphong and Ho Chi Minh City; there is a high risk of piracy or armed robbery in the South China Sea. The principal airports are at Ho Chi Minh City, Hanoi and Da Nang.

Telecommunications systems are being modernised and expanded, and mobile phone distribution is growing rapidly. There were 29.6 million fixed lines in use, 70 million mobile phone subscribers and 20.8 million internet users in 2008.

EDUCATION AND HEALTH

Literacy rate – 90.3 per cent (2007 est)
Gross enrolment ratio (percentage of relevant age group) – primary 90 per cent; secondary 76 per cent; tertiary 16 per cent (2006 est)
Health expenditure (per capita) – US$58 (2007)
Hospital beds (per 1,000 people) – 2.7 (2003–8)

MEDIA

The government controls the media and it has closed broadcasters and jailed journalists who have reported on matters outside the narrowly defined official limits. There is one national television station and many local stations; some satellite channels are also available. The state-run radio network operates several national stations. The Communist Party and the People's Army both publish a daily newspaper and there are also newspapers published in English and French.

YEMEN

Al-Jumhuriyah al-Yamaniyah – Republic of Yemen

Area – 527,968 sq. km
Capital – Sana'a; population, 2,228,530 (2009 est)
Major cities – Aden (the former capital of South Yemen), Al Hudaydah, Ibb, Al Mukulla, Ta'izz
Currency – Riyal of 100 fils
Population – 23,822,783 rising at 3.45 per cent a year (2009 est)
Religion – Muslim (Sunni 55 per cent, Shia 45 per cent) (est); small Jewish, Christian and Hindu minorities
Language – Arabic (official)
Population density – 43 per sq. km (2008)
Urban population – 30 per cent (2007 est)
Median age (years) – 16.8 (2009 est)
National anthem – 'United Republic'
National day – 22 May (Unification Day)
Life expectancy (years) – 63.27 (2009 est)
Mortality rate – 7.61 (2009 est)
Birth rate – 42.14 (2009 est)
Infant mortality rate – 54.7 (2009 est)
Death penalty – Retained
CPI score – 2.1 (2009)

CLIMATE AND TERRAIN

A mountainous region in the west and south divides the desert plains of the interior from the narrow coastal plains. Elevation extremes range from 3,667m (Jabal an Nabi Shu'ayb) at the highest point to 0m (Arabian Sea) at the lowest. There is a desert climate, which is particularly harsh in the east, but moderated in the western mountains by the monsoon. The coast experiences high humidity.

Average temperatures in Aden range from lows of 22°C in January to highs of 37°C in June.

The islands of Perim and Kamaran in the Red Sea, and Suqutra in the Gulf of Aden, are Yemeni territory. The border with Saudi Arabia, except for the north-west corner, is unclear and is being delineated following an agreement between the two countries in 2006.

HISTORY AND POLITICS

Northern Yemen became part of the Ottoman Empire in the early 16th century and although it achieved some independence in the 17th century, Ottoman control was re-established in the 1870s and the area remained part of the empire until it collapsed at the end of the First World War. In 1918 north Yemen became an independent kingdom under the rule of the Hamid al-Din dynasty. A revolution in 1962 overthrew the monarchy and the Yemen Arab Republic was declared. Fighting between royalists and republicans continued until 1967, when the republican regime was recognised internationally.

Aden, on the south coast, came under British rule in 1839, and a protectorate was gradually established over the sultanates of the southern hinterland in the second half of the 19th century. An armed rebellion against British rule began in 1963. After British troops withdrew in 1967, power was seized by the National Liberation Front, which established a repressive communist regime in the People's Republic of South Yemen (later renamed the People's Democratic Republic of Yemen).

The two countries united to form the Republic of Yemen on 22 May 1990. A power struggle between the former northern and southern elites led to a three-month civil war in 1994 in which a southern attempt to secede was crushed by northern government forces. Tensions remain between the north and south, where secessionist sentiment is re-emerging; southerners perceive the south to be marginalised and their resentment has led to public protests and occasional violence. Tourists have been kidnapped on several occasions by groups seeking concessions from the government.

There was fighting in the north-west from 2004 as government forces attempted to suppress an insurgency by the al-Houthis, a Shia sect in the predominantly Sunni country; the government and rebels signed a ceasefire in February 2010. Yemen has also experienced a number of terrorist attacks since 2002, blamed on Islamic extremists, and since 2009 fears have arisen that al-Qaeda-linked militants have been regrouping there after being forced out of Afghanistan and Pakistan.

Lt.-Gen. Ali Abdullah Saleh, president of North Yemen from 1978, became president of the united country in 1990. He was elected president for a five-year term in 1994 and, following constitutional changes, re-elected for a seven-year term in the first direct presidential election in 1999; he was re-elected again in 2006. In the 2003 legislative election, the ruling General People's Congress (GPC) won 228 seats and formed a coalition government with the Yemeni Alliance for Reform (YAR or al-Islah). A legislative election was scheduled for April 2009, but in February 2009 was postponed for two years pending constitutional reform.

POLITICAL SYSTEM

The 1991 constitution was amended following a referendum in 2001. The president is directly elected for a seven-year term, renewable only once. The unicameral House of Representatives *(Majlis al-Nowab)* has 301 members directly elected for a six-year term. In addition, there is an advisory Shura council, whose 111 members are appointed by the president. The prime minister is appointed by the president.

HEAD OF STATE

President, Field Marshal Ali Abdullah Saleh, *took office* 22 May 1990, *elected* 1 October 1994, *re-elected* 1999, 2006

Vice-President, Gen. Abdrabo Mansour Hadi

SELECTED GOVERNMENT MEMBERS *as at August 2010*

Prime Minister, Ali Mohammad Mujawar

Deputy Prime Ministers, Gen. Rashad Mohammad al-Alimi *(Defence)*; Abdul-Karim Ismail al-Arhabi *(Economic Affairs)*; Sadiq Abu Ras *(Interior)*

Foreign Affairs, Abu-Bakr Abdallah al-Qirbi

Finance, Numan Saleh al-Suhaibi

EMBASSY OF THE REPUBLIC OF YEMEN

57 Cromwell Road, London SW7 2ED

T 020-7584 6607 **E** yemen.embassy@btconnect.com

Ambassador Extraordinary and Plenipotentiary, HE Mohamed Taha Mustafa, *apptd* 2005

BRITISH EMBASSY

PO Box 1287, 938 Thaher Himiyar Street, East Ring Road (opposite Mövenpick Hotel), Sana'a

T (+967) (1) 308 100 **E** britishembassysanaa@fco.gov.uk

W http://ukinyemen.fco.gov.uk

Ambassador Extraordinary and Plenipotentiary, HE Tim Torlot, *apptd* 2007

BRITISH COUNCIL

PO Box 2157, 3rd Floor, Administrative Tower, Sana'a Trade Centre, Algiers Street, Sana'a

T (+967) (1) 448 356 **W** www.britishcouncil.org/me-yemen

Director, Michael White

DEFENCE

The army has 790 main battle tanks, 728 armoured personnel carriers and 200 armoured infantry fighting vehicles. The navy has 20 patrol and coastal vessels at 2 bases. The air force has 79 combat aircraft and 8 armed helicopters.

Military budget – US$1,550m (2009)

Military personnel – 66,700: army 60,000, navy 1,700, air force 3,000, air defence 2,000; paramilitary 71,200

Conscription duration – 24 months

ECONOMY AND TRADE

Despite its oil industry, the mainstay of the economy, Yemen is one of the poorest countries in the Arab world. The government began an IMF restructuring programme in 2006 that aims to diversify the economy and attract foreign investment. Implementation has been hampered by popular protests, security problems both internally and from piracy in nearby waters, corruption and rapid population growth. Falling oil prices nearly halved the government's revenue in 2009, although Yemen also benefited from its first exports of liquified natural gas.

Agriculture is largely of a subsistence nature, and, with herding and fishing, engages about 75 per cent of the population, contributing 9.7 per cent of GDP. Apart from oil extraction and refining, industry consists of small-scale manufacturing of cotton textiles, leather goods, handicrafts, aluminium products and cement, food processing and ship repair.

The main trading partners are China, Thailand, India and the UAE. Principal exports are crude oil, coffee, dried and salted fish, and liquified natural gas. The main imports are food and livestock, machinery and equipment, and chemicals.

GNI – US$21,900m; US$960 per capita (2008)
Annual average growth of GDP – 3.8 per cent (2009 est)
Inflation rate – 3.6 per cent (2009 est)
Population below poverty line – 45.2 per cent (2003)
Unemployment – 35 per cent (2003 est)
Total external debt – US$6,245m (2009 est)
Imports – US$9,300m (2008)
Exports – US$9,300m (2008)

BALANCE OF PAYMENTS
Trade – US$663m deficit (2009)
Current Account – US$1,251m deficit (2009)

Trade with UK	*2008*	*2009*
Imports from UK	£69,201,560	£74,609,413
Exports to UK	£3,577,084	£1,794,907

COMMUNICATIONS

Yemen has 71,000km of roads, of which 6,000km are surfaced. Its main ports are at Aden, Al Hudaydah and Al-Mukalla. There is a high risk of piracy and armed robbery in offshore waters in the Gulf of Aden. The principal airports are at Sana'a and Aden.

Since unification a national telephone network has been created, but although mobile phone distribution is expanding rapidly, fixed-line telephone density remains low. There were 1.1 million fixed lines in use, 3.7 million mobile phone users and 370,000 internet users in 2008.

EDUCATION AND HEALTH

Literacy rate – 58.9 per cent (2007 est)
Gross enrolment ratio (percentage of relevant age group) – primary 85 per cent; tertiary 10 per cent (2008 est)
Health expenditure (per capita) – US$43 (2007)
Hospital beds (per 1,000 people) – 0.7 (2003–8)

MEDIA

All broadcasting is state-run and administered by the Ministry of Information. Television and radio are the main means of communication owing to low levels of literacy. The government also funds some newspapers and controls most of the printing. There are four main newspapers: *Al-Thawrah, Yemen Times, Yemen Observer* and *Al-Ayyam*. Journalists are increasingly subject to intimidation or arrest for criticism of government officials or policy.

ZAMBIA

Republic of Zambia

Area – 752,618 sq. km
Capital – Lusaka; population, 1,412,590 (2009 est)
Major cities – Kitwe, Ndola
Currency – Kwacha (K) of 100 ngwee
Population – 11,862,740 rising at 1.63 per cent a year (2009 est); over 70 ethnic groups, of which the Lozi, Bemba, Ngoni, Tonga, Luvale and Kaonde are the largest
Religion – Christian 87 per cent, indigenous religions 7 per cent, Hindu and Muslim 1 per cent (est)
Language – English (official), Bemba, Kaonde, Lozi, Lunda, Luvale, Nyanja, Tonga (national), over 70 other local languages
Population density – 17 per sq. km (2008)
Urban population – 35 per cent (2007 est)
Median age (years) – 17 (2009 est)
National anthem – 'Stand and Sing of Zambia, Proud and Free'
National day – 24 October (Independence Day)
Life expectancy (years) – 38.63 (2009 est)
Mortality rate – 21.34 (2009 est)
Birth rate – 40.24 (2009 est)
Infant mortality rate – 101.2 (2009 est)
HIV/AIDS adult prevalence – 15.1 per cent (2007 est)
Death penalty – Retained (not used since 1997)
CPI score – 3 (2009)
Literacy rate – 70.6 per cent (2007 est)
Gross enrolment ratio (percentage of relevant age group) – primary 119 per cent; secondary 52 per cent (2008 est)
Health expenditure (per capita) – US$57 (2007)
Hospital beds (per 1,000 people) – 1.9 (2003–8)

CLIMATE AND TERRAIN

Landlocked Zambia lies on a forested plateau cut through by river valleys and with higher land in the north and north-east. Elevation extremes range from 2,301m (unidentified location, Mafinga Hills) at the highest point to 329m (Zambezi river) at the lowest. The Zambezi and its tributaries are the main rivers. Lake Bangweulu and parts of Lakes Tanganyika, Mweru and Kariba lie within its boundaries. The climate is tropical, moderated by altitude, with a rainy season from October to April.

HISTORY AND POLITICS

Most of the ethnic groups in Zambia migrated there between the 16th and the 18th centuries. Portuguese explorers arrived in the late 18th century and, with Arab traders, began slave-trading in the 19th century. The area came under British administration in 1889, was named

Northern Rhodesia in 1911 and became a British protectorate in 1924. It was part of the Central African Federation with South Rhodesia (Zimbabwe) and Nyasaland (Malawi) from 1953 to 1963, when the federation was dissolved and Northern Rhodesia achieved internal self-government. It became an independent republic on 24 October 1964 under the name of Zambia. Kenneth Kaunda of the United National Independence Party (UNIP) became president at independence and remained in power until 1991.

Zambia was a one-party state ruled by the UNIP from 1972 until 1990, when pressure from opposition groups led to a new constitution, under which multiparty legislative and presidential elections were held in 1991. The UNIP and President Kaunda were defeated by the Movement for Multiparty Democracy (MMD) and its presidential candidate Frederick Chiluba.

Serious food shortages have occurred in recent years owing to floods and drought, leading to appeals for international food aid in 2001 and 2005. The country also faces serious demographic, economic and social problems because of high levels of HIV/AIDS infection.

The MMD remained the largest party in the legislature after the 2006 elections, although it commands a majority only because of the support of the appointed members of the legislature. Rupiah Banda was elected president in 2008.

POLITICAL SYSTEM

Under the 1991 constitution, the executive president is directly elected for a five-year term, renewable only once. The unicameral National Assembly has 158 members: 150 directly elected, up to eight nominated by the president and a speaker; all serve a five-year term. The president appoints the cabinet.

A new constitution is under debate, with the aim of adopting it prior to the 2011 elections.

HEAD OF STATE

President, Rupiah Banda, *elected* 30 October 2008, *sworn in* 2 November 2008
Vice-President, George Kunda

SELECTED GOVERNMENT MEMBERS *as at August 2010*

Home Affairs, Mkhondo Lungu
Foreign Affairs, Kabinga Pande
Finance, Situmbeko Musokotwane

HIGH COMMISSION FOR THE REPUBLIC OF ZAMBIA

Zambia House, 2 Palace Gate, London W8 5NG
T 020-7589 6655 E zhcl@btconnect.com
W www.zambiahc.org.uk
High Commissioner, HE Royson Mukwena, *apptd* 2009

BRITISH HIGH COMMISSION

PO Box 50050, 5210 Independence Avenue, 15101 Ridgeway, Lusaka
T (+260) (21) 1423 200 E lusakageneralenquiries@fco.gov.uk
W http://ukinzambia.fco.gov.uk
High Commissioners, HE Thomas Carter and HE Carolyn Davidson, *apptd* 2008

BRITISH COUNCIL

PO Box 34571, Heroes Place, Cairo Road, Lusaka
T (+260) (21) 122 8332 W www.britishcouncil.org/africa
Director, Paul Clementson

DEFENCE

The army has 30 main battle tanks and 13 armoured personnel carriers. The air force has 28 combat-capable aircraft.
Military budget – US$229m (2009)
Military personnel – 15,100: army 13,500, air 1,600; paramilitary 1,400

ECONOMY AND TRADE

The transition since the 1990s from a state-controlled to a free-market economy has improved productivity, especially in the now-privatised copper industry. Strong growth from 1996 to 2008 was driven in particular by mining, hydro-electric power generation, construction and tourism. The economy contracted in 2009 as copper prices and demand fell in the global economic downturn, but has started to recover owing to rising copper prices and a good maize harvest.

Copper is the main source of foreign earnings and increased demand in recent years for electronics has spurred investment and greater output. However, 85 per cent of the workforce remains engaged in agriculture, mostly at subsistence level, which accounts for 19.7 per cent of GDP. The main industries are copper and cobalt mining and processing, construction, food processing, beverages, chemicals, textiles, fertiliser and horticulture. The main trading partners are South Africa and China. Principal exports are copper, cobalt, electricity, tobacco, cut flowers and cotton. The main imports are machinery, transport equipment, petroleum products, electricity, fertiliser, foodstuffs and clothing.
GNI – US$12,000m; US$950 per capita (2008)
Annual average growth of GDP – 4.5 per cent (2009 est)
Inflation rate – 13.5 per cent (2009 est)
Total external debt – US$3,313m (2009 est)
Imports – US$5,100m (2008)
Exports – US$5,100m (2008)

BALANCE OF PAYMENTS

Trade – US$22m surplus (2009)
Current Account – US$1,049m deficit (2008)

Trade with UK	*2008*	*2009*
Imports from UK	£44,265,287	£41,644,455
Exports to UK	£17,681,784	£22,488,425

MEDIA

The state-run Zambia National Broadcasting Association provides the only television service and dominates radio broadcasting; private radio stations provide little political content. Three of the four main newspapers are state-owned. Libel and security laws are used against journalists, and defaming the president is a criminal offence.

ZIMBABWE

Republic of Zimbabwe

Area – 390,757 sq. km
Capital – Harare; population, 1,606,260 (2009 est)
Major cities – Bulawayo, Chitungwiza, Gweru, Mutare
Currency – Zimbabwe dollar (Z$) of 100 cents; circulation suspended April 2009; US dollar and South African rand in use
Population – 11,392,629 rising at 1.53 per cent a year (2009 est); Shona (82 per cent), Ndebele (14 per cent) (est)
Religion – Christian 70 per cent, Muslim 1 per cent (est). Indigenous beliefs are widely followed, often combined with Christian faiths
Language – English (official), Shona, Ndebele
Population density – 32 per sq. km (2008)
Urban population – 37 per cent (2007 est)
Median age (years) – 17.6 (2009 est)
National anthem – 'Simudzai Mureza wedu WeZimbabwe' ['Blessed be the Land of Zimbabwe']
National day – 18 April (Independence Day)
Life expectancy (years) – 45.77 (2009 est)
Mortality rate – 16.19 (2009 est)
Birth rate – 31.49 (2009 est)
Infant mortality rate – 32.31 (2009 est)
HIV/AIDS adult prevalence – 14.6 per cent (2007 est)
Death penalty – Retained
CPI score – 2.2 (2009)

CLIMATE AND TERRAIN

A landlocked country, Zimbabwe lies mainly on a high plateau with a central high veld and mountains in the east. Elevation extremes range from 2,592m (Inyangani) at the highest point to 162m (confluence of the Runde and Save rivers) at the lowest. The climate is tropical, moderated by altitude, with a wet season from November to March. Average temperatures in Harare range from lows of 7°C in June to highs of 27°C in November.

HISTORY AND POLITICS

Organised settlement of the region began at least 20,000 years ago and a succession of Shona kingdoms ruled the area until the early 19th century; they included the builders of the Great Zimbabwe complex that gives the country its name. In the 19th century the Ndebele people occupied an area of the south (Matabeleland), and were often in dispute with the people of the north (Mashonaland). The area came under British influence from the 1880s, when the British started to exploit the mineral resources, and by 1893 the whole country was under British control. It became the British protectorate of Southern Rhodesia in 1898, and a self-governing colony in 1923. It was part of the Central African Federation with Northern Rhodesia (Zambia) and Nyasaland (Malawi) from 1953 until 1963.

Opposition to independence under black majority rule in Southern Rhodesia prompted a unilateral declaration of independence (UDI) in 1965 by the white-dominated colonial government. International sanctions and guerrilla warfare by African nationalist groups forced the government to negotiate, and the UDI was terminated in 1979. Power was transferred to the majority population and the country became independent as the Republic of Zimbabwe on 18 April 1980.

Robert Mugabe became prime minister at independence and executive president in 1987. The political dominance of his party, the Zimbabwe African National Union-Patriotic Front (ZANU-PF), after 1987 made the country in effect a one-party state. Mugabe's regime became increasingly autocratic, brutally suppressing opposition and dissent, and rejecting international criticism of human rights and other abuses. The appropriation of white-owned farms, which began in 2000, caused an agricultural collapse that has resulted in chronic food shortages and malnutrition; distribution of international food aid is often inequitable, used by ZANU-PF to garner support.

In the 2008 legislative elections, ZANU-PF lost its majority in the lower chamber, winning 97 seats to the 99 seats of the Movement for Democratic Change (MDC); it retained its majority in the senate, with 30 seats to the MDC's 24. The MDC leader Morgan Tsvangirai won the first round of the 2008 presidential election with 47.9 per cent of the vote (President Mugabe polled 43.2 per cent), which was insufficient for outright victory. In advance of the second-round polls, ZANU-PF conducted a campaign of violence and intimidation against MDC supporters so severe that Morgan Tsvangirai withdrew from the election; although the victor by default, President Mugabe persisted with polling and won 85 per cent of the vote.

An internationally brokered power-sharing arrangement was agreed between ZANU-PF and the MDC in September 2008 and January 2009, although negotiations over the composition of the cabinet were not completed until February 2009, when Morgan Tsvangirai was sworn in as prime minister at the head of a national unity government. The new government has moved to end Zimbabwe's international isolation and to seek support for its political and economic reforms, although some initiatives have been obstructed by ZANU-PF, and MDC members are still subject to intimidation.

POLITICAL SYSTEM

The 1980 constitution was amended in 1987, 1990, 2005 and 2007. The national unity government is an interim one until a draft constitution has been prepared and approved, after which elections will take place.

The executive president is directly elected for a six-year term. The bicameral parliament comprises the House of Assembly and the senate. The former has 210 members, directly elected for a five-year term; the appointment of the vice-presidents, prime minister and deputy prime minister as *ex officio* members brought the total to 214. The senate (re-introduced in 2005) has 93 members, 60 elected (six from each province), five appointed by the president, ten provincial governors and 18 traditional chiefs, who serve a five-year term; a further 11 senators were appointed, five by the president and six by the MDC, bringing the total to 100.

The country is divided into eight provinces and two cities (Bulawayo and Harare) with provincial status. The provinces are: Manicaland, Mashonaland Central, Mashonaland East, Mashonaland West, Masvingo, Matabeleland North, Matabeleland South and Midlands.

HEAD OF STATE
President, Robert Mugabe, *elected* 30 December 1987, *re-elected* 1990, 1996, 2002, 2008
Vice-Presidents, John Nkomo; Joyce Mujuru

SELECTED GOVERNMENT MEMBERS *as at August 2010*
Prime Minister, Morgan Tsvangirai
Defence, Emmerson Mnangagwa
Finance, Tendai Biti
Foreign Affairs, Simbarashe Mumbengegwi
Home Affairs, Theresa Makone

EMBASSY OF THE REPUBLIC OF ZIMBABWE
Zimbabwe House, 429 Strand, London WC2R 0JR
T 020-7836 7755 E zimlondon@yahoo.co.uk
Ambassador Extraordinary and Plenipotentiary, HE Gabriel Mharadze Machinga, *apptd* 2005

BRITISH EMBASSY
PO Box 4490, 3 Norfolk Road, Mount Pleasant, Harare
T (+263) (4) 8585 5200 E bhcinfo@zol.co.zw
W http://ukinzimbabwe.fco.gov.uk
Ambassador Extraordinary and Plenipotentiary, HE Mark Canning, CMG, *apptd* 2009

BRITISH COUNCIL
PO Box 664, Corner House, Samora Machel Avenue, Harare
T (+263) (4) 775 313-4 W www.britishcouncil.org/africa
Director, Rajiv Bendre

DEFENCE

The army has 40 main battle tanks, many of which are non-operational, and 85 armoured personnel carriers. The air force has 46 combat-capable aircraft and 6 armed helicopters.
Military budget – US$155m (2006 est)
Military personnel – 29,000: army 25,000, air force 4,000; paramilitary 21,800

ECONOMY AND TRADE

Poor governance, and in particular the seizure of almost all the white-owned commercial farms, caused a rapid decline in the agriculture-based economy from 2000. Both agricultural output and GDP have halved since the late 1990s, unemployment is now estimated to be over 90 per cent, and three-quarters of the population is living below the poverty line, with half dependent on food aid. Other forms of international aid were suspended because of the government's arrears on past loans. The economy and social services have been badly hit by the migration of professional and skilled labour, and the high level of HIV/AIDS infection. The national unity government has started to stabilise the economy and has opened discussions with the IMF. Hyperinflation was stemmed by the adoption of the US dollar in April 2009.

Agriculture accounted for 28 per cent of GDP in 1998 and engaged two-thirds of the workforce, but in 2009 accounted for only 19.1 per cent of GDP. The most important crops are cotton and tobacco for export and maize for domestic consumption. Other crops include wheat, coffee, sugar cane, peanuts and livestock.

The mining sector is important to the economy as a foreign exchange earner. Almost all mineral production is exported. Gold is the most important product; others are coal, platinum, copper, nickel, tin, iron ore and other metal and non-metal ores. Mining is now the largest industrial activity and supports a ferro-alloy industry and a steel works. Manufacturing, traditionally highly dependent on the agricultural sector for raw materials, produces wood products, cement, chemicals, fertiliser, clothing, footwear, foodstuffs and beverages; output has dropped in some industries because of transport difficulties and power rationing. Industry generates 23.9 per cent of GDP and services 56.9 per cent.

The main trading partners are South Africa, the Democratic Republic of Congo, Botswana and China. Principal exports are platinum, cotton, tobacco, gold, ferro-alloys, textiles and clothing. The main imports are machinery and transport equipment, other manufactures, chemicals, fuels and food.
GNI – US$4,500m; US$340 per capita (2007)
Annual average growth of GDP – –3.7 per cent (2009 est)
Inflation rate – 5.1 per cent (2009 est)
Population below poverty line – 68 per cent (2004)
Unemployment – 95 per cent (2009 est)
Total external debt – US$5,821m (2009 est)
Imports – US$2,900m (2008)
Exports – US$2,200m (2008)

BALANCE OF PAYMENTS
Trade – US$529m deficit (2009)
Current Account – US$945m deficit (2009)

Trade with UK	*2008*	*2009*
Imports from UK	£20,530,175	£19,484,600
Exports to UK	£37,019,717	£50,681,621

COMMUNICATIONS

Zimbabwe has 97,300km of roads, of which 18,500km are surfaced. There are 3,100km of railways but services have become increasingly restricted by lack of diesel and spare parts, leading to the reintroduction into service of steam locomotives. The country relies on rail connections through Mozambique and South Africa for access to seaports. The main airports are at Harare and Bulawayo.

The telephone system is badly maintained. Mobile phone distribution is growing quickly, but internet access is largely limited to Harare. In 2008 there were 354,000 fixed lines in use, 1.7 million mobile phone subscribers and 1.4 million internet users.

EDUCATION AND HEALTH

Education is compulsory at primary level, and the language of instruction is English.
Literacy rate – 91.2 per cent (2007 est)
Gross enrolment ratio (percentage of relevant age group) – primary 104 per cent; secondary 41 per cent (2008 est)
Health expenditure (per capita) – US$79 (2007 est)
Hospital beds (per 1,000 people) – 3.0 (2003–8)

MEDIA

The only television and radio stations and the two main daily newspapers are state-run. The national unity government set up a commission in late 2009 to initiate media liberalisation and license new outlets. Six new newspapers began publishing in 2010, but readership is limited by high cover prices. Journalists face draconian measures, including imprisonment, for failing to register with a government body, and for publishing 'false news' critical of the government.

THE NORTH AND SOUTH POLES

THE ARCTIC

The Arctic is the region around the Earth's north pole; it includes the ice-covered Arctic Ocean, parts of Canada, the USA, Greenland, Iceland, Finland, Norway, Sweden and Russia. The area is commonly defined as lying north of the line of latitude known as Arctic Circle (running at 66° 33′ N) or inside the 10°C July isotherm, which roughly corresponds to the edge of the habitat in which trees can grow. North of the tree line is Arctic tundra where a layer of subsoil remains permanently frozen.

The climate is harsh, particularly during winter (October–March) when the Arctic receives little sunlight; the average monthly temperature in December, January and February is around −10 to −15°C, but on individual nights may fall as low as −60°C over the larger land masses. In summer, conditions are often damp and foggy although there is daylight for 24 hours a day. The average monthly temperature in high summer ranges from just above zero over permanent ice to 15°C in continental areas. The Arctic is rarely as cold as the Antarctic as there is water, not land, underneath the Arctic ice. The water is warmer than the air above it, causing heat to rise and moderating the cold. The polar icepack was, on average, less than 2.5m thick in 2008, down from 3m in 2004.

The polar bear is the region's apex predator. Other native species include varieties of caribou, lemming, wolf, hare and fox; many bird species also migrate to tundra areas in summer. Vegetation is limited to the tundra and consists of around 1,700 species of low-lying shrubs, grasses, herbs, flowers, lichens and mosses.

ARCTIC SEA ROUTES

In 1906 Norwegian explorer Roald Amundsen first successfully navigated the Northwest passage, but the shallow waterways he encountered ensured that the route held little commercial potential until recently. Similarly, the Northern Sea route (formerly the Northeast passage) linking the Atlantic and Pacific oceans around Russia's Arctic coast, was first navigated by Swedish explorer Adolf Erik Nordenskjold in 1878–9, but thereafter only icebreakers and Russian submarines regularly traversed it.

In summer 2007, the Northwest Passage was declared open and ice-free for the first time since records began in 1978; the first commercial ship travelled through it in September 2008. In August 2008 the Northwest passage and the Northern Sea route were open simultaneously for the first time, making the Arctic circumnavigable. Two German ships became the first cargo vessels to navigate the Northern Sea route in September 2009.

CLIMATE CHANGE

The extent of ice in the Arctic has become a key measure of global climate change. The rate at which the ice melts grows exponentially: whereas the white ice reflects sunlight back into space, the darker seas absorb its heat, and the rising sea temperature melts the surrounding ice. The extent of the sea-ice roughly doubles between summer and winter, typically reaching its greatest extent in March and retreating to its lowest point in September. The record low was recorded on 16 September 2007, when ice cover was 41 per cent below the 1978–2000 average September low. Rising temperatures have caused some areas of permafrost to thaw, releasing methane – a potent greenhouse gas – into the atmosphere.

NATURAL RESOURCES

The Arctic's receding ice presents opportunities for national governments to lay claim to a wealth of hydrocarbon and mineral deposits. In 2008 the US Geological Survey estimated that 20 per cent of the world's undiscovered oil and gas reserves – as much as 90 billion barrels of oil, 44 billion barrels of natural gas liquids and 1,670 trillion cubic feet of natural gas – are located within the Arctic Circle. The majority of them lie offshore and are not yet recoverable with current extraction technology. Under the 1982 UN Convention on the Law of the Sea, no state owns the pole or the ocean surrounding it: the five countries which border the Arctic Ocean – Russia, Denmark, Norway, Canada and the USA (a non-signatory) – are limited to an economic zone of 200 nautical miles from their coastline, unless able to prove that their continental shelf extends beyond that limit. In August 2007, Russia planted a flag in the seabed below the pole, on the Lomonosov Ridge which spans much of the Arctic, and which Russia claims is an extension of the Eurasian continent and therefore part of its territory. However, Canadian and Danish geologists assert that Lomonosov is an extension of the North American continent, and therefore falls under their jurisdiction. A UN panel is scheduled to make a final ruling on Arctic sovereignty by 2020.

THE ANTARCTIC

The Antarctic is generally defined as the area lying within the Antarctic Convergence, the zone where cold northward-flowing Antarctic sea water sinks below warmer southward-flowing water. This zone fluctuates unevenly between the latitudes of 48° S and 61° S, typically extending further south in the Pacific Ocean than in the Atlantic. The continent itself lies almost entirely within the Antarctic Circle, an area of around 13,209,000 sq. km, 98 per cent of which is permanently ice-covered. The average thickness of the grounded ice is 2,034m, but in places it exceeds 4,500m; it amounts to some 24.7 million cubic km, and represents around 68 per cent of the world's fresh water and 90 per cent of the world's ice. Much of the sea freezes in winter, forming 'fast ice' which breaks free of the coast in summer and drifts north as pack ice.

CLIMATE AND TERRAIN

Antarctica is the highest, coldest and driest continent on Earth, with average coastal temperatures ranging from just above freezing in the summer (December–February) to −17°C in winter. Conditions on the interior plateau are more severe, with katabatic (gravity-driven) winds and frequent cyclonic storms pushing average winter temperatures down to −65°C. The Vostok research station holds the record for the lowest surface temperature recorded on earth at −89.2°C. Elevation extremes range from 4,897m (Vinson Massif) at the highest point to −2,540m (Bentley Subglacial Trench) at the lowest. The Transantarctic mountains bisect the continent north–south, dividing the west Antarctic ice sheet – an ice-filled marine basin – from the significantly larger and more elevated east sheet. With average precipitation of just 166mm a year, Antarctica is considered a desert.

CLIMATE CHANGE

While the recent decline in levels of ice in the Arctic has been clear and visible, concurrent changes in the Antarctic have been more complex. Despite reports of a recent thickening of the interior of the east ice sheet due to increased snowfall, a study of satellite data published by scientists of the University of Colorado in 2006 indicated that the Antarctic ice sheet as a whole had declined by as much as 152 cubic km (36 cubic miles) a year since 2002, the majority of that loss having taken place in the west Antarctic.

The British Antarctic Survey have found that the west coast of the Antarctic Peninsula has become one of the fastest-warming areas on the planet, with annual mean temperatures rising by around 3°C over the past 50 years. Curiously, the temperatures recorded by the Amundsen-Scott station at the South Pole actually show a recent cooling, as do some studies of east Antarctica as a whole. The precise cause of this is unknown, but scientists have proposed that the warming of the seas in the surrounding ocean has produced more precipitation, which cools the area when it falls as snow. Greater snowfall has also been associated with an expansion of Antarctica's sea-ice, which some recent studies indicate has grown in surface area by around 0.5 per cent a year since 1978. The snow's additional weight appears to push existing sea-ice deeper into the water, causing more of it to freeze. However, this expansion is neither uniform nor universally accepted, and a number of other studies cite a long-term and continuing decline in Antarctic sea-ice since at least the 1950s.

HISTORY AND DISCOVERY

The idea of Antarctica is much older than proof of the continent's existence. The notion of *Terra Australis*, a vast southern continent which counterbalanced the northern lands of Europe, Asia and North Africa, originated by Aristotle, and was commonly found on world maps until the end of the 18th century. The supposed size of this land was corrected after the explorer James Cook's circumnavigation of the globe in 1774. His journey from New Zealand to the Cape of Good Hope (via Tierra del Fuego), travelling at a high southern latitude (between 53° and 60°), confirmed that any landmass must be confined to the polar region.

The date of the first sighting of Antarctica is unclear. In 1820 three separate expeditions, from the UK, the USA and Russia, each claimed to have seen the continent within days of each other, and the argument has never been settled. The golden age of Antarctic exploration was prompted by the discovery of the magnetic North Pole in 1831, but it was not until the beginning of the 20th century that real progress was made. James Clark Ross was the first to identify the approximate location of the South Pole, but was unable to reach it. British explorers Robert Scott in 1901–4 and Ernest Shackleton in 1907–9 got closer, but it was not until Norwegian adventurer Roald Amundsen pioneered a new route, through the Axel Heiberg Glacier, that the pole was reached in December 1911. Scott's second attempt was also successful, but he arrived a month later and perished with his team on the return journey.

FLORA AND FAUNA

The only land animals to survive on the Antarctic continent are tiny invertebrates, including microscopic mites, lice, ticks, nematodes, rotifers and tardigrades. The largest land animal is the *Belgica antarctica*, a flightless midge just 12mm in size. The snow petrel, one of only three birds that breed exclusively in Antarctica, has been spotted at the South Pole. Large numbers of seals, penguins and other seabirds go ashore to breed in the summer; the emperor penguin is the only species that breeds ashore throughout the winter. Four species of albatross breed in South Georgia during the summer, but their numbers are in serious decline due to the effects of longline fishing in the Southern Ocean region. Recent climate change has also affected the continent's wildlife with the number of Adelie penguins falling significantly, as open-water species such as the chinstrap and gentoo penguins invade its Antarctic Peninsula habitat to take advantage of the warming temperatures.

By contrast, the Antarctic seas abound with life; recent expeditions identified over 700 previously unknown species. Krill, which congregates in large schools, is crucial to the ecosystem and provides a diet for migratory whales (including killer, humpback and blue whales), a number of species of seal, penguin, albatross and other, smaller birds. Each of these species is threatened by a substantial fall in recorded levels of krill since the 1970s, thought to be caused by a reduction in the sea-ice which shields its larvae from predators during winter. In 2008 an unexpected wealth of animal life was recorded in the seas around the South Orkney islands at the tip of the Antarctic Peninsula – among the 1,224 species documented were five new species and one new genus.

With almost all of the Antarctic continent permanently covered in ice, only a small number of flowering plants, ferns and club mosses survive. Most of these are found on the sub-Antarctic islands, while only two species (a grass and a pearlwort) extend south of 60° S. Antarctic vegetation is dominated by lichens and mosses, with a few liverworts, algae and fungi surviving in the cracks and pore spaces of sandstone and granite rocks.

ANTARCTIC LAW

The Antarctic treaty was signed on 1 December 1959 when 12 states (Argentina, Australia, Belgium, Chile, France, Japan, New Zealand, Norway, South Africa, the Soviet Union, the UK and the USA) pledged to promote scientific and technical cooperation unhampered by politics. The signatories agreed to establish free use of the Antarctic continent for peaceful scientific purposes; freeze all territorial claims and disputes in the Antarctic; ban all military activities in the area; and prohibit nuclear explosions and the disposal of radioactive waste. The Antarctic treaty was defined as covering areas south of latitude 60° S., excluding the high seas but including the ice shelves, and came into force in 1961. The treaty provides that any member of the UN can accede to it, and has since been signed by a further 35 states. In 1998 an extension to the treaty came into effect, placing a 50-year ban on mining, oil exploration and mineral extraction in Antarctica, and stipulating that all tourists, explorers and expeditions now require permission to enter the Antarctic from a relevant national authority. However, in recent years the region's coastal states have asserted often

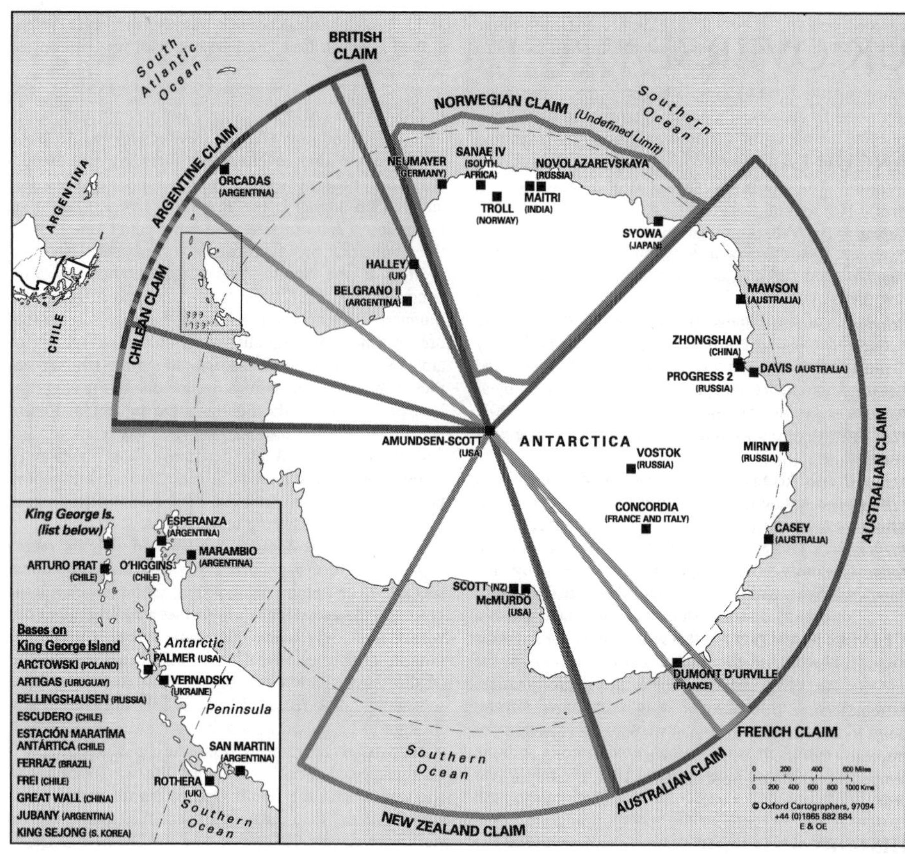

conflicting claims to oil- and gas-rich territory on the Antarctic sea bed. Under the terms of the UN Convention on the Law of the Sea, each nation's sovereignty over its continental shelf extends up to 350 nautical miles beyond its territorial coasts; the UN Commission on the Limits of the Continental Shelf is examining evidence submitted in support of these claims.

SCIENTIFIC RESEARCH

There are 20 nations with permanently manned research stations in Antarctica:

Country	*Number of research stations*
Argentina	6
Chile	5
Russian Federation	5
Australia	3
USA	3
China	2
France	2
UK	2

Brazil, Germany, India, Italy (shared with France), Japan, New Zealand, Norway, Poland, Republic of Korea, South Africa, Ukraine and Uruguay each have a single station.

POPULATION AND TOURISM

Antarctica has no indigenous inhabitants, although the continent maintains a population of tourists, scientists and research workers which peaks in the summer months at over 4,400.

Antarctic tourism is a growth industry. The first *Lonely Planet* guide to Antarctica was published in 1996, and ship-borne cruises depart from Argentina, Chile, Australia and New Zealand. The continent has also become a popular venue for extreme sports enthusiasts: it is now possible to sky-dive, ski, ride a motorbike and fly a helicopter across the continent, and the Vinson Massif and other peaks have become desirable destinations for mountaineers. The huts built by Scott and Shackleton are also popular attractions. The International Association of Antarctic Tour Operators recorded 6,704 tourists in the 1992–3 summer season, rising to more than 46,000 in 2007–8 and dipping to just under 38,000 in 2008–9.

In 1991 the International Association of Antarctica Tour Operators was founded with the objective of providing a self-regulating code of conduct for all operators to follow, but membership is voluntary, and fears remain regarding tourism-related environmental damage.

THE BRITISH ANTARCTIC SURVEY

The British Antarctic Survey (BAS) is part of the Natural Environment Research Council and carries out the majority of Britain's scientific research in Antarctica. Around 450 staff are employed by BAS and the organisation supports five research stations, two of which are staffed throughout the winter months. *See* the BAS website (W www.antarctica.ac.uk) for further information.

UK OVERSEAS TERRITORIES

ANGUILLA

Area – 102 sq. km
Capital – The Valley; population, 1,635 (2009 est)
Currency – East Caribbean dollar (EC$) of 100 cents
Population – 14,436 rising at 2.27 per cent a year (2009 est)
Religion – Christian (Protestant 83 per cent, Roman Catholic 5 per cent, other denominations 1 per cent) (est)
Language – English (official)
Population density – 150 per sq. km (2005 est)
Flag – British blue ensign with the coat of arms and three dolphins in the fly
National day – 30 May (Anguilla Day)
Life expectancy (years) – 80.65 (2009 est)
Mortality rate – 4.36 (2009 est)
Birth rate – 13.02 (2009 est)
Infant mortality rate – 3.52 (2009 est)
Population below poverty line – 23 per cent (2002)

CLIMATE AND TERRAIN

Anguilla is a flat coralline island in the eastern Caribbean and the most northerly of the Leeward Islands. Elevation extremes range from 65m (Crocus Hill) at the highest point to 0m (Caribbean Sea) at the lowest. The climate is tropical, modified by north-east trade winds, with temperatures ranging from 25°C to 31°C throughout the year.

HISTORY AND POLITICS

Anguilla has been a British colony since 1650. For much of its history it was linked administratively with St Kitts, but three months after the Associated State of Saint Christopher (St Kitts)-Nevis-Anguilla came into being in 1967, the Anguillans repudiated government from St Kitts. After a period of direct rule, in 1976 Anguilla was given a new status and separate constitution. Final separation from St Kitts and Nevis was effected in December 1980 and Anguilla reverted to a British dependency.

The 1982 constitution (amended in 1990) provides for a governor, an executive council comprising four of the elected assembly members and two *ex-officio* members (the attorney-general and deputy governor), and a 12-member House of Assembly, consisting of a speaker, seven elected members, two nominated members and two *ex-officio* members (the attorney-general and deputy governor). The 2010 general election was won by the Anguilla United Movement with four seats.

Governor, HE Alistair Harrison, CVO, *apptd* 2009
Chief Minister, Hon. Hubert Hughes

ECONOMY

The main economic activity is tourism, which has stimulated construction. Offshore financial services, lobster fishing and expatriates' remittances are also important. Export earnings are mainly from sales of fish, lobsters, livestock, salt, concrete blocks and rum.

Imports – US$143m (2006)
Exports – US$13m (2006)

BALANCE OF PAYMENTS
Trade – US$162m deficit (2009)
Current Account – US$35m deficit (2002)

Trade with UK	*2008*	*2009*
Imports from UK	£953,970	£573,321
Exports to UK	£282,169	£50,527

COMMUNICATIONS

The road network is gradually expanding but less than half is paved. The main ports are Blowing Point ferry terminal and Wallblake airport, near The Valley.

BERMUDA

Area – 53.3 sq. km
Capital – Hamilton, on Main Island; population, 11,535 (2009 est)
Currency – Bermuda dollar of 100 cents
Population – 67,837 rising at 0.65 per cent a year (2009 est)
Religion – Protestant 52 per cent, Roman Catholic 15 per cent (est)
Language – English (official), Portuguese
Population density – 1,211 per sq. km (2005 est)
Flag – British red ensign with the coat of the arms in the fly
National day – 24 May (Bermuda Day)
Life expectancy (years) – 80.43 (2009 est)
Mortality rate – 7.3 (2009 est)
Birth rate – 11.57 (2009 est)
Infant mortality rate – 2.46 (2009 est)

CLIMATE AND TERRAIN

Bermuda is a group of over 130 small islands, of which about 20 are inhabited, in the North Atlantic Ocean. All the islands are volcanic in origin, with hilly interiors, surrounded by coral reefs. Elevation extremes range from 76m (Town Hill) at the highest point to 0m (Atlantic Ocean) at the lowest. The climate is subtropical, regulated by the Gulf Stream, with an average temperature of 24°C.

HISTORY AND POLITICS

Bermuda was discovered by the Spanish *c.*1503 but colonised by the British from the early 17th century, becoming a colony in 1684. Independence from the UK was rejected in a 1995 referendum.

Internal self-government was introduced in 1968. The governor is responsible for external affairs, defence, internal security and the police, although administrative matters for the police service have been delegated to the minister of labour, home affairs and public safety. The cabinet comprises the premier and six elected assembly members. The legislature consists of the senate of 11 appointed members and the House of Assembly with 36 members elected for a five-year term. At the 2007 election, the ruling Progressive Labour Party retained its 22 seats and continued in office.

Governor, HE Sir Richard Gozney, KCMG, *apptd* 2007
Premier, Hon. Ewart Brown

ECONOMY

The economy is based on offshore financial services for international business, especially re-insurance, and tourism. Other activities include light manufacturing (re-exports of pharmaceuticals are the main export) and construction.

Trade – US$1,589m deficit (2009)

Trade with UK	*2008*	*2009*
Imports from UK	£191,142,795	£20,922,122
Exports to UK	£74,555,014	£863,642

COMMUNICATIONS

The main islands are connected by a series of bridges and causeways. There are 447km of roads, all of which are paved, and one airport, near Ferry Reach on St David's Island. The main ports are at Hamilton and St George. The telephone system is extensive, and mobile telephone distribution is widespread.

BRITISH ANTARCTIC TERRITORY

Area – 1,709,400 sq. km
Population – There is no indigenous population; the British Antarctic Survey maintains two permanently staffed research stations, at Halley and Rothera, and two part-time (summer only) stations, at Fossil Bluff (Alexander Island) and Signy (South Orkney Islands). Several other countries maintain research stations in the territory.
Flag – British white ensign, without the cross of St George, with the territory's coat of arms in the fly

CLIMATE AND TERRAIN

The British Antarctic Territory (BAT) consists of the areas south of 60°S. latitude, between longitudes 20°W. and 80°W. The territory includes the South Orkney Islands, the South Shetland Islands, the mountainous Antarctic Peninsula and all adjacent islands, and the land mass extending to the South Pole. The highest point of the territory is 3,184m (Mt Jackson).

Only around 0.7 per cent of the territory remains ice-free, and the permanent ice sheet that covers the remainder is, in places, 5km thick. The climate is polar desert with very little precipitation, and the annual average temperature at the South Pole is –49°C.

HISTORY AND POLITICS

Britain made its first territorial claim to part of the Antarctic in 1908. Since 1943, a permanent presence has been maintained which became the British Antarctic Survey (BAS) in 1962. In the same year, the territory, originally administered as a dependency of the Falkland Islands, became a UK overseas territory in its own right.

The BAT is administered by the Foreign and Commonwealth Office, and has a full suite of laws, and legal and postal administrations. All activities are governed by the Antarctic Treaty of 1961, which has the objectives of keeping Antarctica demilitarised and promoting international scientific cooperation. The territory is self-financing from income tax revenue and the sale of postage stamps and coins.

GOVERNMENT OF THE BRITISH ANTARCTIC TERRITORY
Polar Regions Unit, Overseas Territories Directorate, Foreign and Commonwealth Office, London SW1A 2AH
T 020-7008 1921 **E** Lesley.Peto@fco.gov.uk

Commissioner (non-resident), Colin Roberts, *apptd* 2008
Administrator, Rob Bowman

BRITISH INDIAN OCEAN TERRITORY

Area – 54,400 sq. km, of which 60 sq. km is land
Population – No indigenous population now lives in the archipelago; around 4,000 military personnel and civilian contract employees (2004 est) are based at the joint UK–US naval support facility on Diego Garcia
Currency – US dollar (US$) of 100 cents
Flag – Divided horizontally into blue and white wavy stripes, with the Union Flag in the canton and a crowned palm-tree over all in the fly

CLIMATE AND TERRAIN

The British Indian Ocean Territory (BIOT) comprises the Chagos Archipelago of 55 islands in six main groups, situated on the Great Chagos Bank in the Indian Ocean, about 1,900km north-east of Mauritius. The largest and most southerly of the islands is Diego Garcia, a sand cay with an area of about 44 sq. km. The main island groups are Peros Banhos (29 islands with a total land area of 6.5 sq. km) and Salamon (11 islands with a total land area of 3.2 sq. km).

The flat and low terrain rarely rises more than 2m above sea level. The climate is hot and humid, although moderated by trade winds.

HISTORY AND POLITICS

The Chagos Archipelago, originally colonised by the French, was one of the dependencies of Mauritius ceded to Britain in 1814 and was administered from Mauritius until 1965, when the British Indian Ocean Territory was established. The islands of Farquhar, Desroches and Aldabra became part of the Seychelles when it became independent in 1976; since then the territory has consisted of the Chagos Archipelago only. Since the 1980s, successive Mauritian governments have claimed sovereignty over the islands, arguing that they were annexed illegally.

Diego Garcia is used as a joint naval support facility by Britain and the USA. The islands' former inhabitants were forcibly relocated between 1967 and 1973 to allow for the construction of the naval base, most being resettled in Mauritius and the Seychelles. Since the 1990s they have taken legal action to obtain the right to return to and settle in the islands; the first visit by former residents, a day trip, took place in 2006. In 2006, the Chagossians won a High Court case allowing them to return to the archipelago, but not to Diego Garcia. The House of Lords overturned this ruling on appeal in 2008; the European Court of Human Rights is scheduled to hear a Chagossian petition in summer 2010. The British government unilaterally, and controversially, declared the Chagos archipelago a marine protected area in April 2010.
Commissioner (non-resident), Colin Roberts, *apptd* 2008
Administrator, Joanne Yeadon, *apptd* 2007

BRITISH VIRGIN ISLANDS

Area – 153 sq. km
Capital – Road Town, on Tortola; population, 9,384 (2009 est)
Currency – US dollar (US$) of 100 cents
Population – 24,491 rising at 1.84 per cent a year (2009 est)

Religion – Protestant 86 per cent, Roman Catholic 10 per cent (est)
Language – English (official)
Population density – 146 per sq. km (2005)
Flag – British blue ensign with the coat of arms in the fly
National day – 1 July (Territory Day)
Life expectancy (years) – 77.26 (2009 est)
Mortality rate – 4.37 (2009 est)
Birth rate – 14.62 (2009 est)
Infant mortality rate – 14.65 (2009 est)

CLIMATE AND TERRAIN

The easternmost part of the Virgin Islands archipelago in the Caribbean Sea, the British Virgin Islands comprise Tortola, Virgin Gorda, Anegada, Jost Van Dyke and about 40 islets and cays; 16 of the islands are inhabited. Apart from Anegada, which is flat, the British Virgin Islands are hilly with coral reefs offshore. The highest point of elevation is 521m (Mt Sage, on Tortola). The climate is sub-tropical, with little variation in temperature, which typically ranges between 25°C in January and 29°C in July. The hurricane season is from August to October.

HISTORY AND POLITICS

Initially settled by Arawak Indians, the islands were named by Christopher Columbus in 1493 and colonised by the Dutch in the early 17th century. Annexed by the British in 1672, the islands were part of the Leeward Islands colony from 1872 to 1960. After a period of direct rule, a measure of self-government was introduced by the 1977 constitution and extended in 2000.

Under the 2007 constitution, the governor, appointed by the crown, retains responsibility for defence, security, external affairs and the civil service. The executive council comprises the premier, four other elected Assembly members and the attorney-general. The House of Assembly consists of a speaker, one *ex-officio* member (the attorney-general) and 13 members elected for a four-year term.

The 2007 election was won by the opposition Virgin Islands Party with ten seats.

Governor, HE David Pearey, *apptd* 2006
Premier, Hon. Ralph O'Neal, OBE

ECONOMY

The main industries are tourism, which generates about 45 per cent of GDP, and offshore financial services. Other industries include construction and light manufacturing. The major exports are rum, fresh fish, fruit, livestock, gravel and sand. Chief imports are building materials, machinery, cars and foodstuffs.

Trade with UK	*2008*	*2009*
Imports from UK	£9,475,301	£31,380
Exports to UK	£72,695,112	£10,630,295

COMMUNICATIONS

The principal airport is on Beef Island, linked by bridge to Tortola, and there are also airfields on Anegada and Virgin Gorda. Road Harbour, at Road Town, is the main port, and ferry services connect the main islands. Many of the 200km of roads are steep and narrow.

CAYMAN ISLANDS

Area – 262 sq. km
Capital – George Town, on Grand Cayman; population, 31,723 (2009 est)
Currency – Cayman Islands dollar (CI$) of 100 cents
Population – 49,035 rising at 2.39 per cent a year (2009 est)
Religion – Christian (Protestant 66 per cent, Roman Catholic 11 per cent) (est)
Language – English (official), Spanish
Population density – 199 per sq. km (2005 est)
Flag – British blue ensign with the coat of arms in the fly
National day – first Monday in July (Constitution Day)
Life expectancy (years) – 80.44 (2009 est)
Mortality rate – 4.89 (2009 est)
Birth rate – 12.36 (2009 est)
Infant mortality rate – 6.94 (2009 est)
GNI – US$43,703 per capita (2002)
Annual average growth of GDP – 1.1 per cent (2008)

CLIMATE AND TERRAIN

The Cayman Islands comprise Grand Cayman, Cayman Brac and Little Cayman. Situated about 241km south of Cuba, the low-lying islands are divided from Jamaica, 268km to the south-east, by the Cayman Trench, the deepest part of the Caribbean Sea. Typical temperatures are 20°C in January and 30°C in July. Peak hurricane season is from August to October.

HISTORY AND POLITICS

The territory derives its name from the Carib word *caymanas* (crocodile). The islands were ceded to Britain by Spain in 1670, and permanent settlement began in the 1730s. A dependency of Jamaica from 1863, the islands came under direct rule after 1962, and a measure of self-government was granted in 1972.

The 1972 constitution provides for a governor, a legislative assembly and a cabinet. The governor is responsible for the police, civil service, defence and external affairs, and chairs the cabinet. The cabinet comprises three appointed official members and five of the assembly's elected members. The legislative assembly has 18 members, 15 elected for a four-year term and the three appointed official members of the cabinet, and a speaker. Following a constitutional review, a new constitution came into effect in November 2009.

The election in May 2009 was won by the opposition United Democratic Party.

Governor, HE Duncan Taylor, CBE, *apptd* 2010
Leader of Government Business, Hon. McKeeva Bush, OBE

CAYMAN ISLANDS GOVERNMENT OFFICE
6 Arlington Street, London SW1A 1RE **T** 020-7491 7772
W www.gov.ky

ECONOMY

The mainstays of the economy are offshore financial services (largely owing to the absence of direct taxation) and tourism. Government revenue is derived from fees and duties.

Trade with UK	*2008*	*2009*
Imports from UK	£9,804,953	£10,163,692
Exports to UK	£60,312,167	£2,003,173

COMMUNICATIONS

The islands are served by airports at George Town and on Cayman Brac and by an airfield on Little Cayman. George Town is the main port. There are 785km of surfaced roads.

FALKLAND ISLANDS

Area – 12,173 sq. km
Capital – Stanley, on East Falkland; population, 2,212 (2009 est)
Currency – Falkland Island pound of 100 pence
Population – 3,140 rising at 0.01 per cent a year (2008 est)
Religion – Christian 67 per cent, other 1 per cent (est)
Flag – British blue ensign with the coat of arms centred in the fly
National day – 14 June (Liberation Day)

CLIMATE AND TERRAIN

The Falkland Islands consist of East Falkland (6,759 sq. km), West Falkland (5,413 sq. km) and around 700 small islands in the South Atlantic Ocean, about 480km from the South American mainland. Elevation extremes range from 705m (Mt Usbourne) at the highest point to 0m (Atlantic Ocean) at the lowest. Temperatures in Stanley range from 2°C in June to 10°C in January, and annual rainfall is low (around 600mm per year).

HISTORY AND POLITICS

The Falkland Islands have a long history of occupation by European countries, including France, Spain and the UK, which claimed sovereignty in 1765 and established its first settlement in 1766.

In 1820, the Falklands were claimed for the newly independent Argentina and a settlement was founded in 1826 but this was destroyed by the USA in 1831. In 1833 occupation was resumed by the British, and the islands were permanently colonised. Argentina continued to claim sovereignty over the islands (known to them as *las Islas Malvinas),* and invaded the islands on 2 April 1982. A British naval and military task force recaptured the islands on 14 June 1982. A small naval and military garrison remains in the islands. Argentina has reasserted its claims of sovereignty since 2007, and particularly since oil exploration began in offshore waters.

Under the 2009 constitution, the governor chairs an executive council consisting of three of the elected members of the legislative assembly and two *ex-officio* members, the chief executive and the financial secretary. The legislative assembly consists of eight members elected for a four-year term, the same two *ex-officio* members and a speaker. The last election was held in 2009; the next is to be held by November 2013. There are no political parties and all members sit as independents.
Governor, HE Alan Huckle, *apptd* 2006
Chief Executive, Dr Tim Thorogood, *apptd* 2008

FALKLAND ISLANDS GOVERNMENT OFFICE
Falkland House, 14 Broadway, London SW1H 0BH
T 020-7222 2542 W www.falklands.gov.fk

ECONOMY

Since the establishment of a conservation and managed fishing zone around the islands in 1987, the economy has been transformed, with revenue from fishing and related activities overtaking sheep-farming as the main industry. Fishing licence fees now provide about half of government revenue, making the islands self-supporting in all but defence costs, but overfishing since 2005 has led to a dramatic decline in fish stocks. Tourism, especially wildlife tourism, is growing. Fish, meat, wool and hides are the principal exports. Chief imports are fuel, food and drink, construction materials and clothing.

There are believed to be substantial reserves of oil and gas offshore and the Falkland Islands government has licensed exploration for exploitable sites; drilling began in 2010.

Trade with UK	*2008*	*2009*
Imports from UK	£25,307,483	£21,474,576
Exports to UK	£3,807,050	£2,635,030

COMMUNICATIONS

There is an international airport at Mt Pleasant, served by military flights to the UK that also carry civilian passengers and by commercial flights to Chile. The main port is Stanley Harbour and a regular shipping service operates to the UK. The road network is gradually expanding but only roads in and around Stanley are paved, and most longer internal journeys are by light aircraft. International telecommunications are possible through a satellite link, and nearly three-quarters of all households have internet access.

GIBRALTAR

Area – 6.5 sq. km
Capital – Gibraltar
Currency – Gibraltar pound of 100 pence
Population – 28,034 rising at 0.11 per cent a year (2009 est)
Religion – Christian (Roman Catholic 78 per cent, other denominations 10 per cent), Muslim 4 per cent, Jewish 2 per cent, Hindu 2 per cent (est)
Language – English (official), Spanish, Italian, Portuguese
Population density – 5,119 per sq. km (2005 est)
Flag – White with a red stripe along the lower edge; over all a red castle with a key hanging from its gateway
National day – 10 September
Life expectancy (years) – 80.19 (2009 est)
Mortality rate – 9.56 (2009 est)
Birth rate – 10.67 (2009 est)
Infant mortality rate – 4.83 (2009 est)

CLIMATE AND TERRAIN

Gibraltar is a rocky promontory, 426m at its highest point, that juts southwards from the south-east coast of Spain, with which it is connected by a low isthmus. It is about 32km from the coast of Africa, across the Strait of Gibraltar.

HISTORY AND POLITICS

Gibraltar was captured in 1704, during the War of the Spanish Succession, by a combined Dutch and English force, and was ceded to Great Britain by the treaty of Utrecht (1713). This treaty stipulates that if Britain ever relinquishes colonial rights over Gibraltar, the colony would return to Spain.

Spanish claims to the territory were a source of tension for many years, but after the overwhelming rejection of a joint sovereignty arrangement in a referendum in 2002, Spain moderated its attitude and the previously bilateral Anglo-Spanish talks about the territory became tripartite with the inclusion of Gibraltar from 2006.

Gibraltar is part of the EU (with the UK government responsible for enforcing EU directives affecting Gibraltar), but is not a full member and is exempt from the common policies on customs, commerce, agriculture, fisheries and VAT. Gibraltarians have voted in EU elections since 2004.

The 1969 constitution made provision for self-government in respect of certain domestic matters, but full internal autonomy came into effect with the 2007 constitution. This limited the governor's responsibilities to external affairs, defence, internal security and public service. The House of Assembly was restyled the Gibraltar Parliament, and may determine its own size; at present, it consists of an appointed speaker and 17 members elected for a four-year term. The government is formed by the chief minister (who is the leader of the majority party) and ministers from among the elected members of parliament.

The 2007 elections were won by the Gibraltar Social Democrats with ten seats, and it continued in office under Peter Caruana.

Governor, HE Vice-Admiral Sir Adrian Johns KBE, CBE, *apptd* 2009
Chief Minister, Hon. Peter Caruana

GOVERNMENT OF GIBRALTAR
150 Strand, London WC2R 1JA T 020-7836 0777
W www.gibraltar.gov.uk

ECONOMY

The economy is dominated by tourism (especially retail for day visitors), offshore financial services and shipping, and these three sectors account for about two-thirds of GDP. Diversification efforts have encouraged telecommunications in particular and Gibraltar has become a centre for internet businesses, especially internet gaming. A shift from a predominantly public-sector to a private-sector economy has occurred in recent years, although government spending still has a significant impact on the local economy. The chief sources of government revenue are port dues, the rent of the crown estate in the town, and duties on consumer items (although value added tax is not applied in the territory).

GNI – US$5,000 per capita (2001)

Trade with UK	*2008*	*2009*
Imports from UK	£420,319,853	£359,370,965
Exports to UK	£17,021,036	£13,532,504

COMMUNICATIONS

Gibraltar has one international airport; air links to Spain and through Spanish air space reopened in 2006. The 29km road network is all surfaced; road links to Spain reopened in the 1980s. The port services the large shipping industry, cruise liners and a regular ferry service to Tangiers (Morocco).

MONTSERRAT

Area – 102 sq. km
Capital – Plymouth (abandoned 1997); the seat of government is now at Brades, in the north, population, 823 (2009 est); a new capital is under construction at nearby Little Bay
Currency – East Caribbean dollar (EC$) of 100 cents
Population – 5,079 rising at 0.39 per cent a year (2009 est)
Language – English (official)
Population density – 55 per sq. km (2005 est)
Flag – British blue ensign with the coat of arms in the fly
Life expectancy (years) – 72.76 (2009 est)
Mortality rate – 8.44 (2009 est)
Birth rate – 12.36 (2009 est)
Infant mortality rate – 16.08 (2009 est)

CLIMATE AND TERRAIN

Montserrat is a mountainous volcanic island in the Leeward group in the Caribbean Sea. Its lowest point of elevation is 0m (Caribbean Sea); its highest point was 914m (Chances Peak), although a lava dome in a crater in the Soufrière Hills volcano is estimated to be over 930m. Volcanic activity since 1995 has left over half of the island devastated by lava flows and ash. The climate is tropical and the average temperature is 26°C.

HISTORY AND POLITICS

Discovered by Columbus in 1493, Montserrat became a British colony in 1632. The first settlers were predominantly Irish indentured servants from St Kitts. France and Britain fought over the island during the 17th and 18th centuries but Montserrat was finally restored to Britain in 1783.

Volcanic activity by the Soufrière Hills volcano since 1995, particularly in 1996, 1997 and 2003, has left over half of the island uninhabitable, and prompted the migration of two-thirds of the population in the late 1990s. A 'special vulnerable area', to which access is restricted, covers two-thirds of the island and two maritime exclusion zones extend between 2km and 4km offshore.

The present constitution came into force in 1990; some modifications were made in 1999 after more than half of the constituencies were made uninhabitable by volcanic activity, and talks are in progress about modernisation measures proposed by the Montserrat government in 2005. The executive council is chaired by the governor and comprises four elected members and two *ex-officio* members (the attorney-general and the financial secretary). The legislative council consists of the speaker, two *ex-officio* members (the attorney-general and the financial secretary) and nine members elected for a five-year term. In the 2009 general election, the Movement for Change and Prosperity won the most seats.

Governor, HE Peter A. Waterworth, *apptd* 2007
Chief Minister, Hon. Reuben Meade

GOVERNMENT OF MONTSERRAT
180–186 Kings Cross Road, London WC1X 9DE
T 020-7520 2622

ECONOMY

Continuing volcanic activity has restricted economic activity to the northern third of the island. Activity includes mining and quarrying, construction (mostly public sector), financial and professional services, and tourism. Communications improved with the opening of Gerald's airport in the north in 2005, allowing regular commercial air services to resume. There are port facilities at Little Bay, and a ferry service to and from Antigua was reintroduced in December 2009.

Trade with UK	*2008*	*2009*
Imports from UK	£913,425	£637,817
Exports to UK	£300,844	£268,965

PITCAIRN ISLANDS

Pitcairn, Henderson, Ducie and Oeno Islands
Area – 47 sq. km
Capital – Adamstown, on Pitcairn Island

Currency – New Zealand dollar (NZ$) of 100 cents
Population – 48 (2009 est)
Religion – Seventh Day Adventist 100 per cent
Language – English, Pitkern (both official)
Flag – British blue ensign with the coat of arms in the fly
National day – 23 January (Bounty Day)

CLIMATE AND TERRAIN

Pitcairn is the chief of a group of rugged islands situated in the South Pacific Ocean, about midway between New Zealand and Panama. The other main islands of the group are Henderson, lying 168km east-north-east of Pitcairn; Oeno, lying 120km north-west; and Ducie, lying 470km east; all are uninhabited. Henderson Island is a UNESCO World Heritage Site. The climate is tropical, with average temperatures ranging from 19°C in August to 24°C in February.

HISTORY AND POLITICS

Pitcairn was settled in 1790 by mutineers from the *Bounty* and their Tahitian companions. The population was resettled on Norfolk Island in 1856 but two groups of people returned, in 1859 and 1864. It became a British settlement under the British Settlements Act 1887. Under the 2010 constitutional arrangements, the islands are administered by the government of Pitcairn Islands, which consists of the governor (usually the British High Commissioner to New Zealand), the Pitcairn Islands Office, headed by the commissioner, and the island council, which manages internal affairs. The island council has ten members, of whom six are elected; elections are held every two years in December. The council is chaired by an island mayor, elected every three years.

Governor (non-resident), HE Victoria Treadell, MVO, *apptd* 2010 *(British High Commissioner to New Zealand)*
Commissioner (non-resident), Leslie Jaques, *apptd* 2003
Mayor, Mike Warren

ECONOMY

The islanders live by subsistence fishing and horticulture, and the sale of honey and handicrafts, although tourism is being promoted. Apart from small fees charged for licences there are no taxes and government revenue is derived almost solely from the sale of postage stamps and .pn internet domain names, and income from investments. Since financial reserves became exhausted a few years ago the islands have received budgetary aid from the UK.

Trade with UK	*2008*	*2009*
Imports from UK	£414,052	£56,051
Exports to UK	–	£104,684

COMMUNICATIONS

There is no airfield and the only means of access is by sea; cruise and container ships stop irregularly but a regular shipping supply route to French Polynesia was established in 2006. There are 6.4km of dirt roads on the islands. A telephone system, a limited television service and internet access have been introduced in recent years.

ST HELENA, ASCENSION AND TRISTAN DA CUNHA

Religion – Christian (predominantly Protestant); Baha'i minority
Language – English (official)
Life expectancy (years) – 78.44 (2009 est)
Mortality rate – 6.68 (2009 est)
Birth rate – 11.13 (2009 est)
Infant mortality rate – 17.63 (2009 est)

ST HELENA
Area – 122 sq. km
Capital – Jamestown; population, 699 (2009 est)
Currency – St Helena pound (£) of 100 pence
Population – 4,000 (2009 est)
Flag – British blue ensign with the coat of arms in the fly

CLIMATE AND TERRAIN

St Helena is situated in the South Atlantic Ocean, 1,500km south of the Equator and about 1,900km west of Africa. The island is rugged and volcanic, with sheer cliffs rising to a central plateau. The climate is tropical but mild, tempered by trade winds, and the average temperature is about 24°C.

HISTORY AND POLITICS

St Helena is believed to have been discovered by the Portuguese navigator Joao da Nova in 1502. It was used as a port of call for vessels of all nations trading to the East until the late 19th century. It was annexed by the Dutch in 1633 but never occupied by them, and the British East India Company seized it in 1659. From 1815 to 1821 the island was lent to the British government as a place of exile for the Emperor Napoléon Bonaparte, who died there on 5 May 1821, and in 1834 it was annexed to the British crown. The Zulu chief Dinizulu was exiled to the island in 1890, and up to 6,000 Boer prisoners were held there between 1900 and 1903.

Under the 2009 constitution, government is administered by a governor, advised by an executive council comprising three *ex-officio* members (the chief secretary, financial secretary and attorney-general) and five elected members of the legislative council. The legislative council consists of 12 members elected for a four-year term, the three *ex-officio* members of the executive council and a speaker.

Governor, HE Andrew Gurr, *apptd* 2007

GOVERNMENT OF ST HELENA
7 Portland Place, London W1B 1PP **T** 020-7031 0314

ECONOMY AND TRADE

St Helena's importance as a port of call on the sea routes between Europe and Africa and Asia declined after the opening of the Suez Canal. The island has few natural resources and its economy is dependent on an annual grant from the UK. The main economic activities are agriculture, the sale of fishing licences, fish processing and tourism. The only significant exports are coffee and frozen, canned and dried fish.

Trade with UK	*2008*	*2009*
Imports from UK	£10,223,739	£10,206,841
Exports to UK	£345,375	£4,430,891

COMMUNICATIONS

Access is solely by sea, provided by a regular supply ship. Jamestown is the only port. Plans for a long-promised airport were cancelled by the UK government in 2009. St Helena has 138km of roads, most of which are single track. Telecommunication services are provided via satellite links, which also enable television programmes to be received for distribution by cable. There are two local radio stations and two weekly newspapers.

ASCENSION ISLAND
Area – 90 sq. km
Capital – Georgetown; population, 560 (2003 est)
Currency – St Helena/Ascension pound (£) of 100 pence
Population – 880 (2009 est)

CLIMATE AND TERRAIN

The island is a rocky volcanic peak that lies in the South Atlantic Ocean some 1,200km north-west of St Helena. The highest point (Green Mountain), some 859m, is covered with lush vegetation. It is an important breeding place for the green turtle and a number of seabird species.

HISTORY AND POLITICS

Ascension is said to have been discovered by Joao da Nova in 1501 and two years later was visited on Ascension Day by Alphonse d'Albuquerque, who gave the island its present name. It was uninhabited until the arrival of Napoleon in St Helena in 1815, when a small British naval garrison was stationed on the island. As HMS *Ascension* it remained under the supervision of the Board of Admiralty until 1922, when it was made a dependency of St Helena. The island was an important logistical centre in both world wars and during the Falklands conflict, and it has a continuing role as a military air base and in broadcasting, telecommunications and satellite tracking.

In 2002 new constitutional arrangements introduced a measure of self-government, and in 2009 Ascension ceased to be a dependency of St Helena. The governor, who is resident in St Helena, retains responsibility for defence, external affairs, internal security and public service. The governor, represented locally by the island administrator, chairs the island council, which consists of seven elected members and two *ex-officio* members (the director of financial services and the attorney-general).
Administrator, Ross Denny, *apptd* 2008

ECONOMY

Before 2002 the island was governed and financed by the main commercial users (the BBC and Cable and Wireless) and the military. With the change in governance in 2002, a fiscal regime was introduced to finance public services through taxation. This funds public services, a school, a hospital, police and judicial services. A private sector is developing following the sale of previously government-owned concerns to commercial operators and the establishment of a sports fishing industry.

COMMUNICATIONS

Communications with the outside world are by sea and air. Georgetown is the only port and there are regular scheduled shipping services, as well as regular air links to the UK and the USA by military aircraft and occasional charter flights. Ascension has 40km of roads. Telecommunication services are provided via satellite links. There is a local radio station and a weekly newspaper.

TRISTAN DA CUNHA
Area – 201 sq. km
Capital – Edinburgh of the Seven Seas
Currency – Currency is that of the UK
Population – 265 (2009 est)
Flag – British blue ensign with the coat of arms in the fly

CLIMATE AND TERRAIN

Tristan da Cunha is the chief of a group of islands in the South Atlantic Ocean which lie some 2,333km south-west of St Helena. All of the islands are volcanic and steep-sided with cliffs or narrow beaches. The highest point of elevation is 2,062m (Queen Mary's Peak) while the lowest is 0m (Atlantic Ocean). Gough and Inaccessible islands are UNESCO World Heritage Sites.

HISTORY AND POLITICS

Tristan da Cunha was discovered in 1506 by the Portuguese navigator Tristao da Cunha. In 1760 a British naval officer visited the islands and gave his name to Nightingale Island. In 1816 the group was annexed to the British crown and a garrison was placed on Tristan da Cunha. When this force was withdrawn in 1817, four adults and two children remained at their own request and formed a settlement, which was joined in 1827 by five women from St Helena and afterwards by others from Cape Colony. Owing to its position on a major sea route the colony thrived, with an economy based on trade with passing ships, until the late 19th century, when the opening of the Suez Canal led to decline.

In 1961 a volcano, believed to have been extinct for thousands of years, erupted and the danger of further volcanic activity led to the evacuation of inhabitants to the UK until 1963.

Tristan da Cunha and Inaccessible, Nightingale and Gough islands were dependencies of St Helena from 1938 to 2009. They are administered by the governor of St Helena through a resident administrator, who is advised by an island council. This consists of eight members elected for a three-year term, of whom one must be a woman, and three appointed members.
Administrator, David Morley, *apptd* 2007

ECONOMY

The island is almost financially self-sufficient; UK government aid finances training scholarships and a resident medical officer at the hospital. The main activities are crayfish fishing, fish processing, agriculture and the sale of postage stamps and coins.

COMMUNICATIONS

Communications with the outside world are by sea as there is no airport. Scheduled visits to the island are limited to about nine calls a year by fishing vessels from Cape Town and annual calls by a South African research vessel. Tristan da Cunha has 20km of roads. There is a local radio station and a newspaper.

SOUTH GEORGIA AND THE SOUTH SANDWICH ISLANDS

Area – 3,903 sq. km
Capital – King Edward Point (administrative centre), on South Georgia
Currency – Pound sterling
Population – There is no indigenous population. The British Antarctic Survey maintains two permanently staffed research stations, at King Edward Point and on Bird Island, to the north-west of South Georgia; in addition, there is the Government Officer at King Edward Point, and the curators of the museum at Grytviken, South Georgia
Flag – British blue ensign, with the coat of arms in the fly

CLIMATE AND TERRAIN

South Georgia lies 1,390km south-east of the Falkland Islands. Over half of the mountainous island is permanantly ice-covered, with many large glaciers. The main mountain range is the Allardyce, and elevation extremes range from 2,934m (Mt Paget) at the highest point to 0m (Atlantic Ocean) at the lowest. The South Sandwich Islands, lying about 750km miles south-east of South Georgia, are a chain of 11 uninhabited volcanic islands some 350km long. Some of the volcanoes are still active.

HISTORY AND POLITICS

South Georgia was used by whalers and sealers of many nationalities following its discovery by Captain Cook in 1775. Britain annexed South Georgia and the South Sandwich Islands in 1908 and since then they have been under continuous British occupation, apart from a brief period during the Falklands conflict in 1982; Argentina claims sovereignty over the territory. A small British army garrison was maintained on South Georgia between 1982 and 2001.

Under the present constitution, which came into effect in 1985, the commissioner is concurrently the governor of the Falkland Islands. A chief executive officer, also based in the Falklands Islands, is responsible for administration. A government officer is based in South Georgia.

Commissioner (non-resident), HE Alan Huckle *apptd* 2006
Chief Executive Officer (non-resident), Harriet Hall
Senior Executive Officer, Martin Collins

ECONOMY

A conservation and management fishing zone was established around the islands in 1993 and a licensing regime introduced for fishing vessels. Sale of fishing licences, passenger landing fees, harbour dues, and the sale of postage stamps and commemorative coins are the main sources of revenue. Tourism, especially wildlife tourism, is growing, but prior permission to land on the islands must be sought and is subject to environmental impact assessments and landing fees.

Access is possible only by sea; there are no scheduled services but cruise ships and other vessels call at South Georgia.

TURKS AND CAICOS ISLANDS

Area – 430 sq. km
Capital – Cockburn Town, on Grand Turk; population, 6,195 (2009 est)
Currency – US dollar (US$) of 100 cents
Population – 22,942 rising at 2.56 per cent a year (2009 est)
Religion – Protestant (86 per cent) (est)
Language – English (official)
Population density – 71 per sq. km (2005 est)
Flag – British blue ensign with the coat of arms in the fly
National day – 30 August (Constitution Day)
Life expectancy (years) – 75.42 (2009 est)
Mortality rate – 4.18 (2009 est)
Birth rate – 20.79 (2009 est)
Infant mortality rate – 13.89 (2009 est)

CLIMATE AND TERRAIN

The Turks and Caicos Islands are about 80km south-east of the Bahamas, of which they are geographically an extension. There are around 40 islands and cays, of which six are permanently inhabited. The climate is marine tropical, moderated by trade winds; the average annual temperature is 27°C.

HISTORY AND POLITICS

The islands changed hands several times between the French, Spanish and British between their discovery in 1512 and the arrival of the first settlers, a group of Bermudans, in the 1670s. They were administered as part of the Bahamas from 1799 until 1848, when they achieved separate colonial status, but they were administered from Jamaica between 1872 and 1962, and from the Bahamas between 1965 and 1973. Since 1973 the territory has had its own governor, and internal self-government was introduced in the 1970s.

The 2006 constitution provided for ministerial government and a partially elected legislature, with the governor retaining responsibility for defence, external affairs, internal security and the regulation of financial services. Following an inquiry into alleged political corruption in 2008–9, on 14 August 2009 the UK government suspended parts of the constitution, dismissed the House of Assembly and imposed direct rule by the governor for a period of two years, during which time legislative, administrative and financial reforms are to be implemented. The cabinet and legislature were replaced by an Advisory Council and an Consultative Forum, which the governor may consult.

Governor, HE Gordon Wetherell, *apptd* 2008

GOVERNMENT OF TURKS AND CAICOS ISLANDS
42 Westminster Palace Gardens, 1–7 Artillery Row, London SW1P 1RR T 020-7222 9024

ECONOMY

The main industries are tourism, offshore financial services and fishing. The USA is the main source of tourists.

Trade with UK	*2008*	*2009*
Imports from UK	£2,317,567	£3,257,817
Exports to UK	£143,036	£2,915

COMMUNICATIONS

The principal airports are on the islands of Grand Turk and Providenciales and provide international air links. There are smaller airports on the other main islands, and regular internal air services between them. The main seaports are on Grand Turk and Providenciales. The islands also have a total of 121km of roads, 24km of which are surfaced.

THE YEAR 2009–10

The year under review covers the period from 1 August 2009 to 31 July 2010

EVENTS OF THE YEAR 2009–10

UK AFFAIRS

AUGUST 2009

7. Ronnie Biggs, jailed in 2001 for his part in the 1963 'great train robbery', was released on compassionate grounds. **14.** The chief medical officer for England, Sir Liam Donaldson, announced that 13 million people would be vaccinated against swine flu from October 2009, as part of a rolling campaign starting with pregnant women and those with chronic illnesses. **18.** The first national audit of NHS staff health found high rates of obesity, smoking, absenteeism and poor mental health and concluded that this had a direct impact on the quality of patient care. Karen Upton, the widow of Warrant Officer Sean Upton, who was killed on duty in Afghanistan in July 2009, became the first person to receive the Elizabeth Cross. **20.** The Scottish justice minister, Kenny MacAskill, announced the release on compassionate grounds of Abdelbaset al-Megrahi, the Libyan convicted of the 1988 bombing of Pan Am flight 103 over Lockerbie, who was said to be terminally ill with prostate cancer. **23.** A confidential MoD report highly critical of the MoD's system of procuring equipment for the armed forces was leaked to the *Sunday Times;* the MoD insisted that the report, compiled by an internal adviser, was intended to be published as part of a wider review of defence equipment procurement. **27.** Official figures showed that the UK population had exceeded 61 million for the first time, and recorded the greatest annual increase in births since 1962.

SEPTEMBER 2009

1. The UK government came under increasing pressure to explain its role in the release of Abdelbaset al-Megrahi on 20 August; it insisted that the decision had been made solely by the Scottish government after al-Megrahi was diagnosed with terminal cancer, and that his release was not related to a 2007 prisoner transfer agreement between the UK and Libya. **5.** In Birmingham, supporters of the right-wing English Defence League, which had organised an anti-Islamic rally, clashed with mainly Muslim counter-protesters; around 80 arrests were made. **6.** The UNISON union, which has campaigned against cuts in public sector pay and pensions, announced that it could no longer afford to fund its own final-salary pension scheme. **9.** Stephen Farrell, a British journalist who had been kidnapped in northern Afghanistan on 5 September 2009, was rescued during a special forces raid; his Afghan translator, Sultan Munadi, and a British soldier were killed during the operation. **12.** The Health Protection Agency temporarily shut Godstone Farm, a children's petting farm in Surrey, after confirming that it was the source of a strain of *E. Coli* infection in 36 children. **24.** The Labour peer Baroness Vadera announced that she was stepping down from her government position as business secretary to take up a new role coordinating the handover of the G20 presidency from Britain to South Korea. **28.** Around 200,000 doses of Cevarix were recalled by health authorities following the death of a 14-year-old girl shortly after being administered the vaccine as part of the national immunisation programme against the human papilloma virus; an inquest concluded on 1 October that the girl's death had been caused by a previously undetected tumour, not the vaccine. **29.** In his opening address to the Labour Party conference, the prime minister, Gordon Brown, pledged to remodel the economy, clean up politics and create a more responsible society.

OCTOBER 2009

8. The Communication Workers Union (CWU) announced that its members had voted in favour of strike action over the Royal Mail's modernisation plans; a series of 24-hour national strikes began on 22 October after several months of local strikes. **9.** The MoD announced that, with the exception of operational troops, all training for members of the Territorial Army (TA) would be suspended for six months in order to save around £20m of the Army's budget. **12.** Many MPs were issued with requests for repayment or further information following the completion of Sir Thomas Legg's independent audit of MPs' expense claims between April 2004 and March 2009. **14.** The annual report published by the Care Quality Commission, the healthcare regulator for England, stated that nearly half of NHS hospitals failed to meet core standards. **15.** The high court ruled that the foreign secretary, David Miliband, had acted in a way that was harmful to the rule of law by suppressing evidence about the treatment of terrorist suspect Binyam Mohamed, who was held in a secret prison in Pakistan and interrogated by MI5; the court ordered the release of a written summary of what the CIA told British intelligence officials about Mr Mohamed. **20.** The Archbishop of Westminster, Vincent Nichols, leader of the Roman Catholic Church in England and Wales, announced a papal decree by Pope Benedict XVI allowing Anglicans who wished to enter into full communion with the Roman Catholic Church to retain some elements of their Anglican identity. **22.** Nick Griffin, the leader of the far-right British National Party and MEP for North West England, appeared on the BBC's *Question Time;* around 600 anti-fascism protesters staged a demonstration outside the BBC's west London headquarters during the live broadcast of the programme. **23.** A British couple, Paul and Rachel Chandler, disappeared while sailing from the Seychelles towards Tanzania; Somali pirates later made a $7m (£4.2m) ransom demand for their release. **28.** A 20-month inquiry into the deaths of 14 servicemen killed when an RAF Nimrod surveillance aircraft burst into flames over Afghanistan in 2006 found the MoD, its safety advisory agency and BAE Systems, the UK's largest defence company, were to blame for the safety failures which led to the disaster. **30.** The home secretary, Alan Johnson, dismissed the chair of the government's Advisory Council on the Misuse of Drugs (ACMD), David Nutt, after Professor Nutt criticised the government's decision to reclassify cannabis as a class B drug, against the ACMD's advice.

NOVEMBER 2009

1. Two members of the ACMD resigned in protest at the dismissal of Professor Nutt; a further three members resigned on 10 November. **3.** A British mercenary, Simon Mann, was pardoned and released by the president of Equatorial Guinea after serving 15 months of a 34-year sentence for his part in an attempted coup of the west African state in 2004. **11.** The health minister, Ann Keen, announced that from 2013 all new NHS nurses will be required to hold a degree in nursing or an equivalent international qualification. **14.** Severe storms with winds reaching 100mph battered the UK, causing flash flooding in many areas; a tornado damaged 60 homes in Essex, and in Devon and Cornwall power lines were brought down, leaving 10,000 homes without electricity. **19.** David Curry, the Conservative MP for Skipton and Ripon, resigned as the chair of the parliamentary standards and privileges committee ahead of a formal inquiry into allegations that he had claimed almost £30,000 in expenses for a second home in which he rarely stayed. **19–20.** Torrential rain swept across the UK; Cumbria received more than a month's worth of rain in 24 hours, causing floods throughout the region. **26.** The Care Quality Commission (CQC) reported a number of failings at Basildon and Thurrock University Hospitals Foundation Trust in Essex, including a lack of basic nursing care and high rates of infection resulting from poor hygiene; the CQC also identified 11 other underperforming NHS trusts. **30.** Gordon Brown announced that 500 extra army personnel would be deployed to Afghanistan in December 2009, bringing the total number of British troops in the country to over 10,000.

DECEMBER 2009

7. Military losses in Afghanistan in 2009 reached 100 with the death of 23-year-old Lance Cpl Adam Drane of the Royal Anglian Regiment. **10.** MPs' expense claims for 2008–9, which totalled over £10m, were published on the parliamentary website. **13.** The schools secretary, Ed Balls, announced the introduction in July 2010 of a new vetting and barring scheme for those working with children; certain groups, such as authors, people under 18, and those who work with children less than once a week, would no longer require criminal record checks. **14.** British Airways cabin crew voted in favour of a 12-day strike beginning on 22 December; the high court blocked the strike on 17 December, ruling it illegal because Unite (the union organising the ballot) had included votes cast by people no longer employed by BA. **15.** The defence secretary, Bob Ainsworth, announced the purchase of 22 US Chinook helicopters, to be deployed in 2013, and other frontline equipment worth over £1bn; the cost will be defrayed by cutting the total number of aircraft, closing an RAF bomber base and cutting thousands of jobs in the MoD and armed forces. **19.** Eurostar services were suspended after cold weather resulted in electrical failures, which caused five trains to break down in the Channel Tunnel, stranding 2,000 passengers underground, some for up to 15 hours; services resumed on 23 December. **23.** The government announced £20m of funding for people who were born with disabilities as a result of their mothers taking thalidomide during pregnancy, and agreed to make a formal apology in parliament in January 2010. **24.** The chief of the general staff, General Sir David Richards, admitted that 56 army training exercises, involving both the TA and the regular army, had been cancelled in 2009 in order to cut costs. **29.** A British man, Akmal Shaikh, was executed in Urumqi, China, for drug-trafficking after smuggling 4kg of heroin into the country in 2007, despite appeals for clemency by relatives and the British government. **30.** A British IT consultant, Peter Moore, was released 31 months after being kidnapped in Iraq; three of the four British security guards abducted with him in May 2007 are known to have been killed by an extremist Shia group, Asaib al-Haq.

JANUARY 2010

4. The home secretary announced the tightening of airport security, including the introduction of full-body scanners at Heathrow airport, in the light of an attempted terrorist attack on a US plane on 25 December (*see* The Americas). **6.** Heavy snowfall affected many areas of the UK, resulting in school closures, grounded flights and disruption to public transport; the freezing weather conditions, which began in mid-December, continued into March in some areas of the UK. **11.** Peter Robinson, the first minister of Northern Ireland, temporarily stepped down from his post to order to clear his name after a BBC investigation revealed that his wife had had an affair with 19-year-old Kirk McCambley, and had obtained a £50,000 loan to help Mr McCambley to set up his own business; Mr Robinson was accused of failing to report his wife's financial affairs to the parliamentary authorities when they became known to him. **14.** The business secretary, Lord Mandelson, announced funding cuts of £398m for universities in England in 2010–11, and encouraged universities to devise two-year fast-track degrees. **26.** *An Anatomy of Economic Inequality in the UK*, a paper commissioned by the minister for women and equality, Harriet Harman, found that the richest 10 per cent of people in Britain were more than 100 times wealthier than the poorest 10 per cent. **29.** The former prime minister Tony Blair appeared before the Chilcot inquiry into the war in Iraq, answering questions about the UK's invasion of Iraq in 2003 and its aftermath.

FEBRUARY 2010

1. Pope Benedict XVI strongly criticised Britain's proposed equality law, arguing that it restricted the freedom of religious communities to act in accordance with their beliefs; the following day Harriet Harman announced that she would no longer introduce a planned amendment to the bill requiring religious organisations to comply with equal opportunity legislation when employing people in non-religious posts. **3.** Peter Robinson resumed his post as first minister of Northern Ireland (*see* 11 January). **4.** Sir Thomas Legg published his report into MPs' expenses, which recommended that £1.3m should be repaid by 390 MPs. Sir Paul Kennedy, a high court judge hearing MPs' appeals against Sir Thomas Legg's requests for expenses repayments, concluded that it was wrong to create retrospective rules; as a result the judge reduced some repayment amounts and cleared others completely. **5.** The director of public prosecutions, Keir Starmer, charged three MPs (Elliot Morley, David Chaytor, Jim Devine) and one peer (Lord Hanningfield) with offences relating to their expense claims; the four attempted to avoid standing trial by claiming parliamentary privilege, but a judge rejected their claim on 11 June and their appeal against this ruling was defeated on 30 July. BAE Systems agreed to pay £285m in fines, including a £255m ($400m) payment to the US Department of Justice, after pleading guilty to accounting offences; the agreement ended a six-year investigation into allegations of bribery and corruption in a series of arms deals. Following ten days of negotiations, Sinn Fein and the Democratic Unionist Party agreed to a power-sharing deal under which key policing and justice powers would be devolved from Westminster to the government of Northern Ireland. **6.** The Irish National Liberation Army, a republican paramilitary group responsible for more than 120 deaths during the Troubles, announced that it had decommissioned its weapons. **10.** The foreign secretary, David Miliband, lost an appeal to prevent the publication of a seven-paragraph summary of a court document showing that MI5 officers were involved in the ill treatment of Binyam Mohamed, although the government succeeded in having the most damning passage removed from the court of appeal judgment, previously leaked to the media in draft form, in which Lord Neuberger claimed that MI5 did not respect human rights (*see* 15 October 2009). **14.** The British National Party (BNP) voted in favour of changes to its constitution that would open membership of the party to black and Asian people. **25.** The Ministry of Justice announced that the delay in the release of government papers would be reduced from 30 to 20 years.

MARCH 2010

1. Lord Ashcroft, a high-profile donor to the Conservative Party, admitted that for tax purposes he was not domiciled in the UK, and therefore did not pay tax on his overseas income. **9.** The coroner at the inquest into the deaths of Corporal Sarah Bryant (the first British servicewoman to be killed in Afghanistan) and three SAS reservists, returned a verdict of unlawful killing; the coroner found that the use of lightly armoured Snatch Land Rovers on the front line was unsuitable, and that the victims had received inadequate training in detecting improvised explosive devices. **12.** A judge ordered the BNP to remove two clauses from its constitution as they were indirectly racist towards non-white members, and ordered the party to pay £60,000 in legal costs. **17.** A Roman Catholic child adoption society, Catholic Care, won a case in the high court allowing it to appeal against the Charity Commission's decision that the society should not be exempted from the 2007 Sexual Orientation Regulations; Catholic Care sought an exemption so that it could exclude gay couples as potential adoptive parents. **18.** The George Cross was awarded to two bomb disposal experts, Staff Sergeant Kim Hughes and Staff Sergeant Otto Shmid, for their service in Afghanistan; Staff Sergeant Shmid's award was posthumous, as he was killed while trying to disarm an improvised explosive device (*see* Decorations and Medals). **20.** BA cabin crew began a three-day strike in protest at the management's decision to reduce cabin crew numbers on all flights; a further four-day strike took place from 27 March. **22.** Three former cabinet ministers, Geoff Hoon, Patricia Hewitt and Stephen Byers, were suspended from the Labour party following claims that they had traded on their political influence for profit by signing up for lucrative lobbying consultancies.

APRIL 2010

1. The high court granted an injunction preventing a planned national rail strike because of allegations of irregularities in the ballot. **6.** The prime minister, Gordon Brown, formally asked the Queen to dissolve Parliament, and set 6 May as the official date for a general election. **12.** A car bomb exploded outside MI5's regional headquarters in Northern Ireland. David Ford was appointed justice minister of Northern Ireland, the first appointment to the post for nearly 40 years. **14.** The eruption of the Eyjafjallajökull volcano in Iceland created an ash cloud destructive to jet engines; when this spread to European air space the following day, all flights to and from the UK and much of Europe were cancelled, stranding thousands of travellers. **16.** The first of three televised debates took place between the leaders of the Labour Party, Conservative Party and the Liberal Democrat Party; the debates, taking place on the Thursday evening in three consecutive weeks, enabled the leaders to present and debate their parties' policies in the lead-up to the general election. **20.** UK airports reopened following a re-evaluation of the risk to commercial jets of flying through the volcanic ash cloud, but delays to flights continued for some days. **22.** The Roman Catholic Church in England and Wales issued an apology and condemned incidents of child abuse and the subsequent failure to deal with complaints; the church set aside four days for prayer and atonement (*see* Europe). **28.** While campaigning in Rochdale, Prime Minister Gordon Brown was overheard on a broadcast microphone referring to 65-year-old Gillian Duffy, a voter he had just spoken to, as a 'bigoted woman'; he later apologised to her in person and in a BBC Radio 2 interview.

MAY 2010

4. Further activity by the Eyjafjallajökull volcano grounded flights to and from Scottish and Northern Ireland airports (*see* 14 April); flights resumed on 6 May. **6.** A general election took place in the UK; in some constituencies, polling stations were unable to cope with the numbers of voters in the last hours of polling and thousands had been unable to vote when the stations closed at 10pm. **7.** The election resulted in a hung parliament; the Conservative Party had won the most seats but had not achieved an outright majority, and discussions began between the three main parties to decide what form the new government would take. **10.** Gordon Brown announced that he would step down as leader of the Labour Party by September 2010. **11.** Gordon Brown resigned as prime minister and Labour party leader with immediate effect after the failure of talks between Labour and the Liberal Democrats. The Conservatives and the Liberal Democrats agreed to form a coalition government, and David Cameron was appointed prime minister. **12.** Appointments to the new coalition cabinet were confirmed, including the Liberal Democrat leader Nick Clegg as deputy prime minister, George Osborne as chancellor, Theresa May as home secretary and William Hague as foreign secretary; five Liberal Democrats were appointed to cabinet positions. **16.** Volcanic ash grounded flights to and from large areas of the UK; flights resumed on 18 May (*see* 14 April *and* 4 May). **17.** The high court blocked the first of four planned five-day strikes by British Airways cabin crew; the court of appeal overturned the ban on 20 May and the first strike began on 24 May (*see* 14 December 2009 *and* 20 March 2010). **18.** A high court judge ruled that an al-Qaeda member, Abid Nasser, could not be deported to Pakistan despite posing a serious threat to national security, as there was a risk that he would be tortured by security services in Pakistan. **25.** At the state opening of parliament, the Queen outlined the new government's legislative programme, including a number of bills relating to economic reform and financial regulation, and a bill allowing schools to apply for academy status and 'free schools' to be set up by parents or other groups. **29.** David Laws resigned as chief secretary to the treasury after less than three weeks in the post, when it emerged that he had claimed more than £40,000 in expenses to rent rooms from his partner.

JUNE 2010

10. Nominations for the leadership of the Labour party closed with five candidates standing for election in September 2010: Diane Abbott, Ed Balls, Andy Burnham, David Miliband and Ed Miliband. **15.** The Saville report into the Bloody Sunday killings in Londonderry in 1972 was published; it concluded that the deaths of 14 unarmed protesters, shot by troops sent to police the march, were unjustified. The new prime minister, David Cameron, made a formal apology for the Bloody Sunday killings in the House of Commons. **17.** The government announced an initial round of spending cuts amounting to £10.5bn. **27.** The Unite union postponed a ballot on further strike action after BA made its cabin crew members a final offer on pay and working conditions.

JULY 2010

3. The new chancellor of the exchequer, George Osborne, asked ministers to create two models for cuts in their departmental budgets, one for 25 per cent and one for 40 per cent, although some spending, such as on the NHS, is protected. **5.** The education secretary, Michael Gove, cancelled the previous government's school-building programme. **6.** As a new rule requiring peers to pay tax on their global earnings came into force, five members of the House of Lords gave up their seats in order to retain their non-domiciled tax status. **7.** The defence secretary, Liam Fox, announced that British forces would be replaced by US troops in the Sangin district of Afghanistan by the end of 2010. **12.** The general synod of the Church of England passed a measure that will enable women to become bishops from 2014, despite high-profile protests from opponents. **13.** Three British soldiers serving in Afghanistan were killed by an Afghan colleague in an apparently premeditated attack. **15.** The Vatican published a list of serious offences in the Roman Catholic Church, which included the ordination of women as priests among grave crimes that would result in excommunication. **19.** The prime minister, David Cameron, gave a speech describing his vision of a 'big society' where power is devolved from the state to the people. **21.** The deputy prime minister, Nick Clegg, announced that the family unit of Yarl's Wood immigration centre would close as part of plans to end the detention of children awaiting deportation. The prime minister launched a national citizen service scheme to send 16-year-olds on summer camps to encourage them to become engaged with their community. **28.** In a question and answer session during a visit to India, David Cameron asserted that some elements in Pakistan were aiding terrorist groups; Pakistan's intelligence agency responded by calling off an intelligence-sharing visit to the UK by its counter-intelligence officers. **29.** The government announced proposals to end compulsory retirement at the age of 65 in 2011.

ARTS AND MEDIA

AUGUST 2009

3. Two newly discovered pieces of piano music that were composed by Mozart when he was eight years old were performed for the first time in Salzburg, on Mozart's original piano. **13.** *Men's Health* overtook *FHM* to become the bestselling men's magazine in the UK, according to circulation figures released by ABC. **26.** Dominic Mohan was appointed editor of *The Sun,* replacing Rebekah Brooks (née Wade), who had become chief executive of News International in June 2009. Channel 4 confirmed that it would not broadcast the reality television show *Big Brother* after its 11th series in 2010. **29.** The Public, a £63m arts centre in West Bromwich, opened fully for the first time since the building was completed in June 2008, following problems with funding. **31.** Disney announced that it had bought Marvel Entertainment, owner of the rights to comic book characters such as Spider-Man and the X-Men, in a $4bn (£2.5bn) deal.

SEPTEMBER 2009

7. Terry Wogan confirmed that he would be leaving his Radio 2 breakfast show, the most popular radio programme in the UK, which he had presented for 27 years; his final show was broadcast on 18 December. **8.** Speech Debelle won the Mercury Music Prize for her debut album *Speech Therapy.* **12.** The culture secretary, Ben Bradshaw, approved the use of product placement by commercial television channels in the UK to raise additional revenue. **25.** The chairman of ITV, Michael Grade, announced that he would be leaving the channel; this left the chairmanship and chief executive post vacant after a dispute between the ITV board and the company's prospective new chief executive, Tony Ball, stopped him taking up his appointment. **30.** Tate Modern withdrew a display about to open to the public that featured a naked image of actor Brooke Shields at ten years old, after the Metropolitan Police warned that it could break obscenity laws. At the MOBO Awards, British artists won eight out of 13 categories, including Best UK Act, won by N-Dubz, and Best UK Newcomer, won by JLS.

OCTOBER 2009

4. It was reported that legislation passed by parliament in 2003 allowing legal deposit libraries to archive digital literature and online scientific research had not yet come into force, resulting in the loss of years of archivable material. **6.** The Booker prize was won by Hilary Mantel for *Wolf Hall,* a historical novel based on the life of Thomas Cromwell. **8.** The Nobel prize for literature was awarded to the Romanian-born German writer Herta Müller. **11.** The Royal Bank of Scotland announced that it would put its art collection on public display; the bank owns over 2,200 items of British art, which is believed to be the largest corporate collection in Britain. **12.** The *London Evening Standard,* bought by Alexander Lebedev in January 2009, became a free newspaper. Art experts announced that a painting sold at auction in 1998 for $19,000 was almost certainly by Leonardo da Vinci and worth a possible £100m; a fingerprint on the painting was found to match one on da Vinci's *St Jerome.* **14.** The prime minister, Gordon Brown, announced in the Commons that the justice secretary would examine the use of 'super-injunctions' after one prevented the UK media from reporting part of parliamentary proceedings on 12 October (*see* Crimes and Legal Affairs 12 October). **23.** The BPI, the trade organisation for the UK recorded music industry, announced that 117m singles had been sold in the UK in 2009 to date, breaking the previous record of 115.1m, set in 2008. **27.** Associated Newspapers announced the closure of the free London newspaper *London Lite;* the announcement came shortly after the closure of rival title *The London Paper,* leaving the *London Evening Standard* as the only evening London freesheet (*see* 12 October). **29.** Quarterly figures released by RAJAR showed that Radio 4 had 10.22m listeners tuning in for at least five minutes a week in the third quarter of the year, its highest listener numbers for a decade.

NOVEMBER 2009

3. The Ambassador Theatre Group acquired the theatres belonging to the company Live Nation in a £90m deal that gave the company five times as many seats as any other theatre operator in the UK. **5.** The Museums, Libraries and Archives Council reported that works by living artists were accepted for the first time in the 2008–9 tax year under the Acceptance in Lieu Scheme, whereby works can be given to the nation in place of paying death duties. **12.** The BBC published the salaries of its senior staff for the first time; its top 107 'decision makers' earned £22m between them, and at least 37 executives earned more than the prime minister. **16.** It was reported that Google had signed a revised settlement deal with authors' associations in the USA that limited the international scope of its original plans; out-of-print books from only the USA, the UK, Canada and Australia will be made available online, initially to US users. **18.** Archie Norman, a former Conservative MP, was appointed chairman of ITV (*see* 25 September). **24.** The National Gallery announced that curators had rediscovered *Charles I Insulted by Cromwell's Soldiers*, a masterpiece by Paul Delaroche, in the home of the Duke of Sutherland. **26.** Tony Gallagher, a former *Daily Mail* executive, was appointed editor of *The Daily Telegraph*, replacing Will Lewis who became managing director of the newspaper's new digital division. **27.** Export sales for television programmes produced in the UK rose by 25 per cent in 2008 to £980m, according to the annual UK TV Exports Survey. **30.** *The Art Newspaper* reported that the Benevento missal, a medieval book sold to the British Library after being looted from an Italian cathedral during the Second World War, was to become the first item from a British national museum to be returned to its previous owners under the Holocaust (Return of Cultural Objects) Act 2009. Johnston Press, which owns more than 300 newspapers, began charging for access to some online content for three of its titles.

DECEMBER 2009

2. Petina Gappah won the Guardian first book award for *An Elegy for Easterly*. Google announced that it would allow publishers of paid content to restrict the number of web pages a user could access for free via Google News. **7.** The Turner prize was awarded to 49-year-old Richard Wright in the last year he was eligible to enter the competition; Wright created a fresco in gold leaf for the exhibition of shortlisted artists at Tate Britain. **8.** Raphael's *Head of a Muse* sold for £29.16m at Christie's in London, making it the most expensive drawing sold at auction. **16.** Cambridge University library received Siegfried Sassoon's papers, including diaries from the Western Front and notebooks documenting his personal life and literary career, following a fundraising campaign to buy them for £1.25m. **20.** Rage Against the Machine's 'Killing in the Name', released in 1992, reached number one in the singles chart following an internet campaign in protest at *X Factor*'s monopoly of the chart at Christmas. **31.** The Queen's Gold Medal for Poetry was awarded to Don Paterson for his collection *Rain*.

JANUARY 2010

4. The Costa book awards were won by Colm Toibin (novel) for *Brooklyn*, Raphael Selbourne (first novel) for *Beauty*, Graham Farmelo (biography) for *The Strangest Man*, Christopher Reid (poetry) for *A Scattering*, and Patrick Ness (children's book) for *The Ask and The Answer*. **18.** Philip Gross, professor of creative writing at the University of Glamorgan, won the TS Eliot prize for poetry for his collection *The Water Table*. **20.** *The New York Times*, owner of the most popular newspaper website in the USA, announced that it would start to charge readers for online content if they accessed more than a set number of online articles each month. **25.** A woman who lost her balance at the Metropolitan museum in New York accidentally made a six-inch tear in *The Actor*, a Picasso work valued at $130m (£80m). **26.** Christopher Reid won the Costa book of the year award for *A Scattering* (*see* 4 January). **27.** The Society of London Theatre announced that 2009 was a record year for theatre box office revenue and theatre attendance; revenues increased by 7.6 per cent, and attendance by 5.5 per cent on 2008. **28.** ITV appointed Adam Crozier, previously head of Royal Mail, as its new chief executive (*see* 25 September 2009).

FEBRUARY 2010

3. *L'Homme qui Marche I*, a sculpture by Alberto Giacometti, sold for just over £65m at Sotheby's in London, becoming the most expensive work of art ever sold at auction; the same auction featured three works that had been missing since the Nazi annexation of Austria in 1938, including Klimt's painting *Kirche in Cassone* which sold for £27m. **8.** The Booksellers Association announced that 102 independent bookshops had closed in 2009, an average of nearly two per week. **9.** The Guardian Media Group sold 22 regional titles, including the *Manchester Evening News*, to a rival publisher, Trinity Mirror. **11.** According to the annual public lending right survey, James Patterson was the most borrowed author from UK lending libraries in 2008–9, for the third consecutive year. **16.** At the Brit Awards, Lady Gaga won three awards, including best international female solo artist, Dizzee Rascal won best male solo artist, Lily Allen won best female solo artist, and Florence and the Machine won best British album for *Lungs*. **17.** A new video-on-demand website was launched; SeeSaw provides more than 3,000 hours of free programming from the BBC, Channel 4 and Five. The British edition of *Reader's Digest* magazine went into administration after 72 years. **21.** At the BAFTA film awards, *The Hurt Locker* won six awards, including best film; *Avatar* only won two awards despite receiving eight nominations. **23.** Abbey Road studios were given Grade II listed status by National Heritage, following reports that the owners, the record company EMI, planned to sell the building. **24.** An Italian court found three Google executives guilty of violating the privacy of a minor for allowing a film showing the bullying of an autistic boy to appear on the website; the ruling implied that internet service providers such as Facebook and YouTube could be held responsible for content created by their users. **26.** It was reported that the previous week a copy of the first comic to feature Superman had sold for $1m (£657,000), and a copy of the first comic to feature Batman for $1,075,500 (£703,000).

MARCH 2010

1. The director-general of the BBC, Mark Thompson, announced the possible closure of two radio stations

(6 Music and Asian Network), a cap on spending on broadcasting rights, and a 25 per cent cut in staff working on the BBC website. **7.** At the Academy Awards, *The Hurt Locker* won six Oscars, including best picture, best director and best original screenplay; Kathryn Bigelow, director of *The Hurt Locker*, was the first woman ever to win the best director award. **9.** *The News of the World* agreed to pay PR agent Max Clifford a £1m settlement in exchange for Mr Clifford agreeing to drop legal action against journalists who allegedy intercepted his voicemail messages. **11.** In a case brought by the surviving members of Pink Floyd, a high court judge ruled that EMI could no longer sell songs from any of the band's albums as single downloads or mobile phone ringtones. **15.** The Arden Shakespeare imprint published an edition of *Double Falsehood*, an 18th-century play by Lewis Theobald, with new research supporting claims that it was based on a lost Shakespeare play called *Cardenio*. **21.** The Olivier award for best new play was won by *The Mountaintop*, written by Katori Hall; the best actor award was won by Mark Rylance for *Jerusalem*, and best actress by Rachel Weisz for *A Streetcar Named Desire*. **25.** *The Independent* and *The Independent on Sunday* were sold for a token sum of £1 to Alexander Lebedev, owner of the *Evening Standard* newspaper since January 2009 and his son Evgeny. **26.** ITV announced that *The Bill*, Britain's longest-running television drama, would end in autumn 2010 after more than 25 years.

APRIL 2010

13. Mark Damazer announced his resignation as the controller of BBC Radio 4 in order to become the master of St Peter's College at Oxford University. **17.** Arts Council England announced that it would create an online gallery so that its collection could be viewed in its entirety; normally only a fifth of the collection can be displayed to the public. **19.** The presenter Adrian Chiles left the BBC for ITV after being replaced as the Friday evening host of *The One Show*. **23.** The historian and author Orlando Figes admitted to writing anonymous reviews on Amazon's UK website in praise of his own work and attacking the work of other historians.

MAY 2010

12. Official figures published by RAJAR showed a 50 per cent increase in listeners to the 6 Music radio station after its possible closure was announced (*see* 1 March). The Archbishop of Canterbury announced that previously unseen items collected by his predecessors would go on display at Lambeth Palace; the collection includes Elizabeth I's prayer book and a copy of the execution warrant for Mary, Queen of Scots. **19.** The Lost Man Booker prize, set up to acknowledge novels published in 1970 that went unrecognised because of a change in the award's rules, was awarded to J. G. Farrell, for *Troubles*. **20.** Five masterpieces insured for €100m (£85.4m) were stolen from the Musée d'Art Moderne in Paris, including works by Picasso and Matisse. **23.** The Cannes Palme d'Or was awarded to *Uncle Boonmee Who Can Recall His Past Lives*, a film by Thai director Apichatpong Weerasethakul. **24.** It was announced that all arts organisations funded by the Department for Culture, Media and Sport, including the national museums and Arts Council England, would be required to cut their budget by at least 3 per cent by the end of 2011. **28.** A £20m extension to the Museum of London was opened.

JUNE 2010

1. *The Times* and *The Sunday Times* began to charge for access to online content. **5.** At the BAFTA television awards, *The Thick of It* won best sitcom, best male comedy performance and best female comedy performance (for Peter Capaldi and Rebecca Front); Kenneth Branagh won the best actor award and Julie Walters won best actress. **7.** *The New Yorker* published its list of the top 20 American writers under 40; these included Chimamanda Ngozi Adichie, Jonathan Safran Foer, Yiyun Li and Téa Obreht. **9.** The Orange prize for fiction was won by Barbara Kingsolver for her novel *The Lacuna*. **14.** In a poll of BBC Radio 3 listeners, *When I am Laid in Earth* by Henry Purcell was voted the nation's favourite aria. **18.** The British poet Geoffrey Hill was elected as the new Oxford professor of poetry, a five-year post at Oxford University. **22.** Daphne Todd won the BP Portrait award for *Last Portrait of Mother*, a painting of her mother after her death at the age of 100. In London, Sotheby's auctioned for £16.2m André Derain's *Arbres à Collioure*, from the collection of art dealer Ambroise Vollard, part of whose collection was deposited in a Paris bank safety deposit box after his death in 1939 and only discovered in 1979; another 139 pieces, including works by Cezanne, Degas, Gaugin, Picasso and Renoir, were auctioned in Paris on 29 June for a total of €3.5m (£2.9m). **24.** An auction at Christie's in London set a record for total sales at a single art auction, realising a total of £152.5m for works by artists including Picasso and Monet; an auction at Sotheby's the day before took £112m.

JULY 2010

1. Charles Saatchi announced that he would give his gallery and 200 works of art to the nation upon his retirement; he suggested that the Saatchi gallery in Chelsea should be renamed the Museum of Contemporary Art, London (MOCA). **2.** The BBC Samuel Johnson prize for non-fiction was won by Barbara Demick for her book *Nothing to Envy: Real Lives in North Korea*. **5.** The BBC Trust decided that 6 Music would continue to broadcast pending a review of all of the BBC's digital radio services; the trust sanctioned the closure of Asian Network, provided that more local programming was provided for Asian communities (*see* 1 March). **15.** Londonderry was designated as the first UK City of Culture for 2013. Gwyneth Williams was appointed as the new controller for BBC Radio 4 (*see* 13 April). **16.** Jonathan Ross presented the last edition of his ten-year-old television chat show on BBC One. **19.** Lord Bragg announced that the *South Bank Show* would move to the Sky Arts channel after ITV cancelled the 33-year-old show. **20.** The culture minister, Jeremy Hunt, proposed cuts of up to 50 per cent in the staff of the Department for Culture, Media and Sport as part of his overall budget reduction programme. William Jacques was jailed for three-and-a-half years for stealing rare books worth £40,000 from the Royal Horticultural Society's library. **22.** Figures published by the UK Film Council showed that cinema box office takings in 2009 were a record £944m; admissions were at their second-highest level since 1971. **23.** Richard Desmond, the owner of Express Newspapers, bought Channel Five for £103.5m. **28.** BSkyB bought the rights to the entire HBO television catalogue. The Churchill Archive Trust and Bloomsbury publishers announced plans to digitise Winston Churchill's entire archive and make it available online.

BUSINESS AND ECONOMIC AFFAIRS

AUGUST 2009

3. Barclays and HSBC banks reported pre-tax profits of £2.99bn and £2.95bn respectively for the first half of 2009. **4.** The nationalised bank Northern Rock reported a pre-tax loss for the first half of 2009 of £724m and that 40 per cent of its mortgage borrowers were in negative equity. **5.** Lloyds Banking Group, which is 43 per cent publicly owned, reported a pre-tax loss of £4bn in the first half of 2009. **12.** Official figures showed unemployment at a 14-year high of 2.44 million people and that the rate for those aged 18 to 24 had risen to 17 per cent. **20.** Treasury figures showed that public debt increased by £8bn in July 2009 to £800bn (56.8 per cent of GDP). **25.** Figures from the British Bankers' Association showed that net mortgage lending increased by £1.6bn in July 2009.

SEPTEMBER 2009

2. The US pharmaceutical company Pfizer agreed to pay a record $2.3bn (£1.4bn) fine for misbranding several of its medicines and bribing medical professionals to promote four of its drugs. The share value of BP reached £100bn after the energy group announced that it had struck oil in the Gulf of Mexico. **4.** The World Trade Organisation (WTO) ruled that subsidies received by the aircraft manufacturer Airbus from EU governments were illegal; the case, brought against the EU by the USA in 2004, was the longest-running investigation to date by the WTO. The Financial Services Authority (FSA) ruled that Royal Bank of Scotland (RBS) could not make a payment to bondholders in October 2009 as the bank was reliant on public money to remain solvent. **8.** The mobile phone companies Orange and T-Mobile announced the merger of their UK businesses, creating the UK's largest mobile phone company (*see* 2 March). **11.** An independent investigation into the collapse of MG Rover in 2005 revealed that the four directors (Peter Beale, John Edwards, Nick Stephenson and John Towers) took £42m out of the company in the five-year period directly before it went into administration with debts of £1.3bn. **18.** Figures from the Office for National Statistics (ONS) showed that government tax receipts in August had decreased by 9 per cent compared with August 2008, while public spending increased by 3 per cent, with the result that national debt increased by £16.2bn in August 2009, making it 57.5 per cent of GDP. **25.** The Society of Motor Manufacturers and Traders reported that, despite improved sales resulting from the government's car scrappage scheme, car production decreased by 31.5 per cent in August 2009 compared with August 2008.

OCTOBER 2009

1. National Grid reported that gas production in the UK sector of the North Sea would be 6 per cent lower in 2009–10 compared with 2008–9, obliging the UK to import around 50 per cent of its gas supplies. **4.** The National Farmers' Union warned that a biofuel refinery scheduled to open in December at Wilton, Teesside, would consume a tenth of the country's wheat harvest, more than the national surplus, and could turn the UK into a net importer of wheat for the first time. **7.** The energy company E.ON announced that it had postponed controversial plans to build a coal-fired power station at Kingsnorth, Kent, after a recent fall in the demand for electricity. **22.** The Land Registry announced plans to cut around 1,500 jobs and close a quarter of its offices. **23.** ONS figures showed that GDP decreased by 0.4 per cent in the third quarter of 2009, the sixth consecutive quarter of decline for the UK economy. **30.** The American health and safety regulator OSHA fined BP $87m (£53m) for over 700 safety violations at a Texas refinery where an explosion killed 15 people and injured 170 in 2005.

NOVEMBER 2009

2. RBS announced that 3,700 job cuts would be implemented over the next two years in addition to the 12,000 jobs already cut since the start of the financial crisis. **3.** The chancellor of the exchequer, Alistair Darling, announced an additional £33.5bn support package for RBS, increasing public ownership from 70 to 84 per cent. **5.** The Bank of England voted to increase its programme of quantitative easing by £25bn to £200bn in order to continue to stimulate economic growth in the UK. **6.** British Airways announced that revenues had fallen by 13.7 per cent over the previous six months and that it would cut 4,900 jobs, around 12 per cent of its workforce, by March 2010 (*see* UK Affairs, 14 December *and* 20 March). **8.** A major credit rating agency downgraded Greece's credit rating because of its large sovereign debt, causing a marked drop in share prices and a weakening of the euro on world markets amid growing concern about other indebted eurozone countries. **12.** British Airways announced plans to merge with the Spanish airline Iberia, creating Europe's largest airline. **13.** The East Coast main-line rail franchise was nationalised. **20.** National Savings and Investments withdrew two products launched on 26 October 2009 (a one-year bond offering 3.95 per cent interest and a two-year savings product offering 4.25 per cent interest) following complaints from banks and building societies that they constituted unfair competition. **24.** Lloyds Banking Group launched a rights issue, the biggest in British corporate history, in an attempt to raise £13.5bn. **25.** The supreme court ruled in favour of high street banks in a test case brought by the Office of Fair Trading (OFT), which challenged the legality of high overdraft charges and fees for bounced cheques. Dubai World, a large investment conglomerate owned by the Dubai government which was responsible for ambitious construction projects in the Gulf state, asked creditors for a six-month moratorium on debt repayments on liabilities amounting to $60bn (£37bn); the announcement caused global shares to plunge, including a £14bn drop in value for British banks with loan exposures to Dubai (*see* 14 December). **26.** The Borders UK book retail chain went into administration with a loss of 1,150 jobs.

DECEMBER 2009

1. J D Wetherspoon announced plans to open 250 new pubs over a five-year period, creating 10,000 new jobs. **2.** The Yorkshire and Chelsea building societies confirmed that they were to merge. **4.** The steelmaking company Corus confirmed that it was to end production at its Teesside factory with a loss of 1,700 jobs. **9.** The chancellor of the exchequer presented his pre-Budget report; proposed measures included a 50 per cent tax on bankers' bonuses over £25,000, a 0.5 per cent increase from April 2011 in national insurance contributions for workers earning more than £20,000, a 1 per cent cap on public sector pay, and a cap on state contributions to public service pensions. **14.** The government of Abu Dhabi announced a $10bn (£6.1bn) support package for Dubai World, which prevented the conglomerate defaulting on a loan repayment and boosted global financial markets. **17.** ONS figures showed that public sector net borrowing reached £20.3bn in November; the figure was the highest for any month since records began in 1993 but was lower than economists had expected. **22.** Figures from the British Bankers' Association showed that total consumer credit contracted by 2.2 per cent in 2009.

JANUARY 2010

8. Virgin Money purchased the private bank Church House Trust, acquiring a banking licence through the purchase. **11.** The British Retail Consortium announced that retailers had experienced their highest December sales for eight years, with an overall rise of 4.2 per cent in like-for-like sales. **14.** The US president, Barack Obama, announced a proposal to levy a 'financial crisis responsibility fee' of 0.15 per cent on the liabilities of financial institutions with over $50bn (£32bn) in assets; the levy is intended to recoup the $117bn (£72bn) loss to the US treasury of the $700bn (£429bn) troubled assets relief programme introduced to rescue failing banks in 2009. Bosch announced plans to close its car parts factory in Wales in 2011 with a loss of 900 jobs. **19.** Cadbury accepted a £11.5bn ($18.7bn) takeover bid from the US food company Kraft; the trade union Unite expressed concern over the effect of the takeover on Cadbury's British employees. **20.** ONS figures showed that, by the ILO measure, unemployment in the UK fell by 7,000 to 2.458 million, or 7.8 per cent, the first quarterly decline since the period from March–May 2008. **21.** President Obama proposed significant curbs on the activities of banks, including limits on the size of banks and a ban on proprietary trading, as safeguards against a future financial crisis; US stocks fell sharply, as did shares in European and Asian banks (*see* 15 July). **25.** The Church of England lost £40m of investments in two Manhattan housing complexes after a consortium of buyers, led by the New York investment firm Tishman Speyer, passed the estate to creditors. **26.** ONS figures showed that the UK economy had come out of recession; GDP grew by 0.3 per cent in the last quarter of 2009. **28.** The pharmaceutical company AstraZeneca announced that it would cut 8,000 jobs worldwide, including an estimated 1,500 jobs in the UK. Toyota announced that it would cut 750 jobs at two UK factories; it also recalled millions of its vehicles in the USA, Europe and China owing to faulty accelerator pedals (*see* 9 February). **29.** The euro dropped to a six-month low against the dollar, largely because of mounting concerns over Greece's ability to finance its €300bn (£259bn) national debt (*see* 12 April).

FEBRUARY 2010

4. The Bank of England announced the end of its quantitative easing scheme, but warned that the UK's economic recovery would be slow. **9.** Toyota announced a further recall of 437,000 Prius cars, owing to braking problems; the recall took the total number of cars recalled to 8.5 million, with an estimated loss to the company of $4bn (£2.5bn). Kraft, the new owners of Cadbury, announced that the phased closure of the Somerdale factory near Bristol by 2011, originally announced by Cadbury in 2007, would go ahead; the announcement reversed Kraft's statements about keeping the factory open during the takeover negotiations. **11.** The Council of Mortgage Lenders reported that 46,000 homes were repossessed in 2009, the highest number since 1995. **16.** The FSA fined Mehmet Sepil, chief executive of the Turkish oil firm Genel Energi, £967,005 for using insider information to deal in Heritage Oil shares. The UK inflation rate rose to 3.5 per cent in January 2010. **17.** ONS figures showed that the number of unemployed people claiming benefits reached 1.64 million in January 2010, the highest figure since 1997. **25.** Royal Bank of Scotland announced losses of £3.6bn for 2009 after struggling with billions of pounds of bad loans. **26.** Lloyds Banking Group announced losses of £6.3bn for 2009.

MARCH 2010

2. The merger of Orange and T-Mobile was confirmed after the OFT's concerns were satisfied. **6.** The Bank of England maintained the bank base rate at 0.5 per cent for the 12th consecutive month. In a referendum in Iceland, 93 per cent rejected a proposal to reimburse the British and Dutch governments for the compensation of over €3.8bn (£3.4bn) they paid to account-holders in their countries after the collapse of the Icesave bank in 2008. **11.** John Lewis announced annual pre-tax profits of £306.6m, a 9.7 per cent increase on 2009. **12.** An investigation into events prior to the bankruptcy of Lehman Brothers in September 2008 linked the British law firm Linklaters to the approval of controversial deals known as 'repos' that concealed billion-dollar debts held by the company; the accountancy firm Ernst & Young were also implicated by the report. **15.** The FSA asked Ernst & Young to provide information about controversial accounting techniques that allegedly enabled Lehman Brothers to cover up billion-dollar liabilities in the two years before its collapse. **17.** ONS figures showed that the number of people claiming unemployment benefit fell in February 2010 to 1.59 million. **24.** In the final Budget before the general election, the chancellor announced £11bn of cuts in public sector spending; he also cancelled stamp duty for first-time buyers on homes costing less than £250,000 and increased the duty by 5 per cent on homes costing over £1m. **29.** A court in China sentenced four executives of the mining company Rio Tinto to jail sentences ranging from seven to 14 years for commercial espionage and accepting bribes. **30.** The statutory consumer watchdog Consumer Focus made a formal complaint to the OFT, alleging that cash ISAs pay poor rates of interest and that banks use unfair obstacles to prevent customers from switching to better deals. **31.** The FSA charged seven men with being part of an alleged insider trading ring; two of the defendants worked at the investment banks J P Morgan Casenove and UBS. Deloitte, administrators for the rail maintenance company Jarvis, announced around 1,100 redundancies.

APRIL 2010

7. The German carmaker Daimler announced that Daimler, Renault and Nissan were taking a 3.1 per cent stake in each other's companies; although the companies remain separate, the deal allows them to share technology and development costs. **12.** The leaders of eurozone countries worked out a rescue package combining bilateral European and IMF loans worth €40bn (£35bn) in the event of Greece being unable to refinance its €15bn (£13bn) public debt (*see* 23 April). **13.** The FSA fined David Baker, the former deputy chief executive at Northern Rock, £504,000 and his colleague Richard Barclay £140,000 for deliberately misreporting mortgage arrears figures prior to Northern Rock's collapse. **16.** The OFT fined tobacco manufacturers and retailers, including Imperial Tobacco, Asda, Morrison and Sainsburys, for unlawfully inflating the cost of cigarettes. **20.** Goldman

Sachs reported net earnings of $3.46bn (£2.25bn) for the first quarter of 2010, a 90 per cent increase on 2009. The FSA launched a formal investigation into the London operations of Goldman Sachs after it emerged that Fabrice Tourre, a London-based employee of the company, was thought to be the main instigator of a $1bn (£650m) fraud under investigation in the USA. **21.** ONS figures showed that the number of unemployed people had risen to over 2.5 million people for the first time since 1994. **22.** The Faith shoe retail chain went into administration. **23.** Greece requested that an EU-IMF financial rescue package be activated to help its debt-ridden economy out of crisis. **27.** Stock markets worldwide dipped after international credit rating agencies downgraded Greek government bonds to junk status, prompting fears over the expanding cost of the EU-IMF bailout for Greece; the agencies subsequently downgraded the credit ratings of Portugal and Spain, other economically weak countries in the eurozone.

MAY 2010

2. The Greek government announced a new package of austerity measures to save up to €30m (£25m); the package was approved by eurozone finance ministers, who also approved a €110bn (£96bn) loan to Greece by the European Central Bank and the IMF on 7 May. **3.** United Airlines and Continental Airlines announced their merger, creating the world's largest airline. **10.** EU finance ministers agreed a €750bn (£653bn) emergency funding facility to stabilise the euro and prevent an increase in sovereign debt in eurozone countries; the fund consists of a fund administered by the European Commission, a system of loans from the 16 eurozone governments and additional funding by the IMF. **18.** The consumer prices index (CPI) measure of inflation rose to 3.7 per cent, while the retail prices index (RPI) measure reached 5.3 per cent, its highest rate for 19 years. **19.** Germany banned the short-selling of eurozone government bonds, causing the euro to fall to a market low of $1.2146. **20.** The FSA imposed a record fine of £2.8m on former stockbroker Simon Eagle for using methods in breach of stock market rules to artificially ramp up a company's share price. **21.** European finance ministers agreed a strategy for handling any future euro crisis, and to overhaul the EU single currency rules and introduce more effective economic governance. British Airways announced its worst-ever annual loss of £531m. **24.** The new chancellor of the exchequer, George Osborne, announced £6.25bn of immediate cuts in public spending, including reductions in government department budgets, and the scrapping of child trust funds. **25.** The FTSE 100 index fell to 4,940.68, its lowest level in nine months, as a result of escalating tension between North and South Korea and fears that Europe's sovereign debt crisis would spread to Spain. **26.** The Takeover Panel reprimanded Kraft for its misleading statements about reversing the Somerdale factory closure during its takeover of Cadbury (*see* 9 February). **27.** Asda paid £778m to take over the discount grocery chain Netto; the deal was subject to approval by the OFT.

JUNE 2010

1. The US government launched a criminal investigation into the Gulf of Mexico oil disaster; BP's market value dropped by £12bn in one day, contributing to ~ overall fall in value of over £40bn since the disast~ (*see* Environment and Science, 20 April). **3.** T~ J. P. Morgan £33.33m for failing to ke~ a separate account. **16.** BP issued an apology and agreed to pay $20bn (£13.5bn) into a compensation fund for victims of the Gulf of Mexico oil spill, while its chairman announced that the company would not pay share dividends for the rest of the year; the White House insisted that the compensation fund payment was not capped. In the chancellor's speech at the annual Mansion House dinner, George Osborne announced plans to abolish the tripartite system of financial regulation introduced by Gordon Brown in 1997, and replace the FSA with a financial policy committee overseen by the Bank of England and a separate consumer protection and markets authority. **22.** George Osborne delivered his emergency 'austerity' Budget, intended to save £40bn in public spending; measures included raising VAT to 20 per cent from January 2011, welfare cuts, an annual £2bn levy on banks and a public-sector pay freeze.

JULY 2010

1. Tate & Lyle sold its sugar business to American Sugar Refining in a deal thought to be worth £200m. **2.** Forty-seven per cent of Tesco shareholders refused to support the group's renumeration proposals, which awarded its directors multi-million-pound pay packages. **8.** The IMF warned western countries that cutting deficits this year risked undermining economic recovery and said that most advanced economies did not need to tighten budgets until 2011. **14.** ONS figures showed that the number of employed had increased by 160,000 to 28,980,000 in the three months to May 2010; the rise was mainly attributed to an increase in part-time workers, which reached a record 7.8 million. **15.** The US senate passed the Financial Reform Bill, which includes measures to prevent banks from proprietary trading, increase the regulation of mortgage and credit providers and reduce the size of 'too big to fail' banks. The US Securities and Exchange Commission fined Goldman Sachs $550m (£358m) over the bank's handling of investments made in mortgage-related securities. **17.** The Civil Aviation Authority confirmed that Goldtrail Travel had gone into administration; up to 50,000 customers were thought to be affected. **21.** Reckitt Benckiser agreed a £2.5bn takeover of SSL, whose businesses include Durex condoms and Scholl shoes. **23.** ONS figures showed that GDP rose by 1.1 per cent in the second quarter of 2010. A court in the Netherlands fined the oil trading company Trafigura €1m (£830,000) for illegally transporting a cargo of toxic waste from a Dutch port to Côte d'Ivoire in 2006. **27.** BP reported a record loss in the second quarter of 2010 of $17bn (£11bn), which included $32bn (£20bn) set aside to cover the cost of the oil clean-up operation in the Gulf of Mexico and compensation. BP also announced that its chief executive Tony Hayward would leave the company after concerns over his handling of the Gulf rig explosion and oil spill; he will be rep~ by Bob Dudley, currently in charge of BP'~ operation in the Gulf. **29.** Metro Bank, t~ high street bank in more than 1~ London.

CRIMES AN~

AUG~

jewellery worth £40m from Graff Diamonds in Mayfair. **13.** Riam Dean, a 22-year-old law student, won a claim for wrongful dismissal against Abercrombie & Fitch; the company considered that Ms Dean, who has a prosthetic arm, had breached its 'look policy' by wearing a cardigan on the shop floor and moved her to stockroom work.

SEPTEMBER 2009

4. Samantha Joseph, aged 17, was jailed for life for leading 16-year-old Shakilus Townsend into an ambush where he was stabbed to death; seven gang members involved in the attack received prison sentences ranging from ten to 15 years. The high court ruled that a transsexual serving life for manslaughter and attempted rape should be moved to a women's prison, as holding her in a men's prison violated her human rights. **6.** The home secretary, Alan Johnson, announced that he had released a suspected terrorist from a control order; the release came as a result of a ruling by law lords in July 2009 that the control orders placed on the suspect and two other men were illegal. **9.** Michael Shields, a Liverpool football fan jailed for the attempted murder of a barman in Bulgaria in 2005, was pardoned by the justice secretary, Jack Straw, after new evidence came to light. **14.** Four men received life sentences, with minimum terms of between 22 and 40 years, for planning to use liquid explosives to launch terrorist attacks on transatlantic planes; three men were convicted of planning the attack, the fourth of conspiracy to murder. **17.** Police confirmed that David Lace, whose body was exhumed in August 2009, was almost certainly the man who murdered 22-year-old Teresa de Simone in 1979; Sean Hodgson, who served 27 years of a life sentence for the crime, had been released in March 2009. **23.** The director of public prosecutions (DPP), Keir Starmer, issued draft guidance, effective immediately, to clarify under what circumstances people would be prosecuted for assisting a suicide; the law lords had ruled in favour of an appeal, brought by Debbie Purdy, for the clarification of the law in July 2009. **25.** A report by the National Association of Probation Officers revealed that the proportion of veterans in the prison population had more than doubled in the last six years; military veterans represented 6 per cent of the total on probation, and 8.5 per cent of the prison population. **28.** An inquest into the deaths of Fiona Pilkington and her daughter, Francecca Hardwick, ruled that the police and council officials were partly responsible for their deaths as they had failed to respond effectively to Ms Pilkington's complaints; Ms Pilkington killed herself and her 18-year-old daughter, who had severe learning difficulties, following years of abuse from local teenagers.

OCTOBER 2009

5. Paul Allen was jailed for 18 years for his role in the theft of £53m, Britain's biggest cash robbery, from a Securitas depot in Kent in 2006. Human remains were found in a bin bag by the M5 motorway near Bristol, and were identified two days later as the body of Melanie Hall, who disappeared in 1996, aged 25. **6.** The lord chief justice, Lord Judge, issued new sentencing guidelines recommending indeterminate prison terms with no fixed release date for gun traffickers. **7.** A [illegible]-old man from Essex was jailed for 12 years for [illegible] over a 33-year period and fathering [illegible] [co]urt of appeal dismissed an [illegible] ruling in July [illegible]

apply not only to the initial injury of service personnel but also to subsequent disabilities resulting from appropriate medical treatment; the MoD had argued for a narrower interpretation that would allow it to cut the compensation to two injured soldiers. Trafigura, a multinational oil trading firm, obtained a secret injunction preventing *The Guardian* from reporting the proceedings of parliament, in particular a parliamentary question tabled by the MP Paul Farrelly about Trafigura's injunction (obtained in September 2009) preventing publication of the Minton report on its alleged dumping of hazardous waste in Côte d'Ivoire in 2006; the injunction was communicated to other UK media and also became binding on them, but was dropped after the parliamentary proceedings and the existence of the injunctions were reported on Twitter and the internet, and by foreign media and the magazine *Private Eye* (*see also* Arts and Media 14 October; International Events, Africa 20 September). **28.** James Yates, who was serving seven years in prison for supplying the gun used to kill 11-year-old Rhys Jones in 2007, had his sentence increased to 12 years after his original sentence was referred to the court of appeal for being unduly lenient. **29.** Neil Strachan and James Rennie were jailed for life for sexually assaulting children and running a paedophile network; six other defendants were imprisoned for various shorter terms. Marlon King, a Premier League footballer, was sentenced to 18 months in prison for sexually assaulting a woman in a nightclub in 2008.

NOVEMBER 2009

10. The justice secretary announced an increase in the minimum prison sentence for murders involving knives from 15 to 25 years, to make the sentence comparable to the 30-year minimum for murders involving guns. **11.** Anne Darwin, jailed in 2008 for collaborating with her husband to fake his death and claim insurance money, was ordered by Leeds crown court to repay £591,000 within 12 months; John Darwin had to repay a nominal sum of £1 as all their assets were in his wife's name. **18.** The high court ruled that agencies such as MI5 and MI6 could use secret evidence to defend themselves in civil cases if disclosure would affect national security, and that the 'closed' court procedure used in such instances in criminal cases could be extended to civil cases; the ruling was in relation to a case brought by seven British former detainees at Guantanamo Bay, who are claiming damages from the intelligence services and government for aiding and abetting their unlawful imprisonment, extraordinary rendition and ill-treatment in detention (*see* 4 May). **21.** A 400lb car bomb partially detonated outside the Northern Ireland policing board's headquarters but no one was injured. **22.** Jane Andrews, a former dresser to the Duchess of York, escaped from East Sutton Park open prison where she was serving a life sentence for the murder of her boyfriend in 2000; she was found by police on 25 November. **26.** The home secretary refused to block the extradition of Gary McKinnon to the USA on medical grounds; the 43-year-old Asperger's sufferer admitted to hacking into 97 US military and NASA computers during 2001 and 2002, but argued in his defence that he was only looking for information on alien technology.

DECEMBER 2009

3. The Metropolitan Police shut down 1,219 websites falsely claiming to sell discounted designer goods, some of which passed on the credit card details of customers.

4. An Italian court sentenced Amanda Knox and Raffaele Sollecito to 26 and 25 years' imprisonment respectively for the murder of British student Meredith Kercher in Perugia, Italy, in 2007; Rudy Guede had been sentenced to 30 years in prison for the murder in October 2008. **15.** Vanessa George received an indeterminate prison sentence for abusing children in her care at a nursery in Plymouth, and for creating and distributing images of the abuse to Angela Allen and Colin Blanchard; Ms Allen also received an indeterminate sentence, but Mr Blanchard's sentencing was adjourned as he was expected to face further charges. **16.** Peter Tobin, already serving life sentences for the murders of Vicky Hamilton and Angelika Kluk, was found guilty of the murder of 18-year-old Dinah McNicol in 1991, and was sentenced to a full life term. **17.** Mehmet Goren was sentenced to life in prison for killing his 15-year-old daughter, Tulay Goren, in an 'honour killing' in 1999 because the family disapproved of her boyfriend. The BBC paid £25,000 in libel damages to Trafigura for alleging on *Newsnight* that the company caused deaths, miscarriages and long-term injuries by dumping hazardous waste in Côte d'Ivoire in 2006 (*see also* International Events, Africa 20 September).

JANUARY 2010

11. The first criminal trial without a jury to take place in England and Wales for over 400 years began at the high court in London, after a judge ruled that there was a significant danger of jury-tampering; four defendants were accused of the robbery of a warehouse near Heathrow airport in 2004, and were found guilty and sentenced on 31 March. **12.** The European court of human rights ruled that the use of police stop and search powers was illegal as they were too widely drawn and lacked safeguards against abuse; the home secretary, Alan Johnson, decided that the UK police would continue to use stop and search powers pending the outcome of an appeal against the ruling. **14.** Lord Justice Jackson, a court of appeal judge, published a report outlining proposals for changes to civil litigation. **18.** A high court judge ruled that control orders against two terrorist suspects were unlawful, and that the men were entitled to claim damages from the government for the three-and-a-half years that their movements were restricted. **20.** Frances Inglis was given a life sentence for the murder of her brain-damaged son Thomas, who she killed with an injection of a lethal dose of heroin. **22.** Two brothers, aged 10 and 11, were given indeterminate sentences for a prolonged attack on two boys, aged 9 and 11, in Edlington, where they threw heavy stones at them, tried to strangle them and sexually assaulted them, leaving both seriously injured. **25.** Kay Gilderdale was cleared of attempted murder at the high court for providing her daughter, who had ME, with a lethal dose of morphine to inject herself. Paul Hutchinson was given a life sentence for the murder of Colette Aram in 1983; the case was the first reconstruction to appear on *Crimewatch* but Mr Hutchinson was only arrested in 2009 owing to advances in DNA technology. **27.** The supreme court ruled that ministers acted unlawfully in freezing the financial assets of five al-Qaeda suspects without a vote in parliament.

FEBRUARY 2010

4. A coroner ruled that Dr Daniel Ubani, an out-of-hours doctor who was on his first shift in Britain, had unlawfully killed 70-year-old David Gray when he mistakenly gave Mr Gray ten times the normal dose of the painkiller diamorphine. **8.** Commander Ali Dizaei, a senior officer in the Metropolitan Police, was sentenced to four years in prison for misconduct in a public office and perverting the course of justice. **9.** Mohammed Atif Siddique, the first person to be found guilty of terrorism charges in Scotland, had his most serious conviction overturned by the appeal court after serving almost half of an eight-year sentence; he was released from prison immediately as he had served his full sentence for two lesser terrorism offences. **10.** The court of appeal ruled that 71-year-old Davender Ghai had the right to be cremated on a traditional open-air pyre after his death, according to his religious beliefs as a Hindu. **15.** At the inquiry into the death of the Iraqi civilian Baha Mousa, the commander of the regiment that detained him admitted condoning inhumane practices and admitted responsibility for his death. **16.** The Ministry of Justice published a comprehensive review into the workings of juries; it found that two thirds of jurors did not fully understand judges' legal directions before retiring to consider their verdict, and 26 per cent of jurors on high-profile cases had seen information about the trial on the internet. **25.** The director of public prosecutions published final guidelines to clarify the law on assisted suicide; the guidelines included 16 factors that would favour prosecution and six factors that would mitigate against prosecution, including whether the victim reached a clear decision to commit suicide, and whether the suspect reported the suicide to the police (*see* 23 September).

MARCH 2010

5. Lance Corporal Joe Glenton was sentenced to nine months in a military prison for going absent without leave; he left Britain to avoid being redeployed to Afghanistan in 2007. **8.** Peter Chapman was sentenced to life in prison for the kidnap, rape and murder of 17-year-old Ashleigh Hall; Mr Chapman created a false profile on Facebook to befriend Miss Hall and persuade her to meet him. **12.** Angela Gordon and Junaid Abuhamza were given indefinite prison sentences for the manslaughter of Ms Gordon's seven-year-old daughter, Khyra Ishaq; she died from an infection in 2008 following months of starvation imposed on her as a punishment by her mother and stepfather. **15.** The government pledged to scrap family court fees, which can be up to £4,800 a case, as the high costs were deterring some social service departments from applying for a court order for vulnerable children. **16.** Five-year-old Sahil Saheed was released 12 days after being kidnapped at gunpoint during a family holiday in Pakistan; five people were arrested the following day. **18.** Chrisdian Johnson was jailed for life for the murder of Christopher Ogunyemi; he was placed at the crime scene by analysing DNA from his dog, which had been stabbed during the attack, the first time animal DNA has been used as evidence. **19.** The son of Sir Edward and Joan Downes was told that he would not be prosecuted for assisting his parents' suicide, as the DPP ruled that it would not be in the public interest. **31.** A policeman was cleared of assaulting a protester during a vigil for Ian Tomlinson, who died during the G20 protests in April 2009; the judge ruled that the footage of Sgt Smellie hitting the protester did not show the full story. The court of appeal ruled that the media would be permitted to report on certain hearings in the court of protection, which deals with the affairs of those who lack capacity to make their own decisions.

APRIL 2010
9. Loloahi Tapui was found guilty of fraud for showing her employer, the attorney general Baroness Scotland, documents which she falsely claimed gave her the right to work in the UK; Ms Tapui had been an 'overstayer' in the UK for four years. **14.** The trial began of three companies accused of health and safety breaches in connection with an explosion and fire at the Buncefield oil depot near Hemel Hempstead in 2005, the two other companies involved having already pleaded guilty; the three companies were found guilty of all charges in June (*see* 16 July). **16.** A ban on the laboratory-produced drug mephedrone came into force after being rushed through parliament; it was classified as a Class B substance. Corby borough council agreed to an out-of-court settlement with 19 people born with deformities caused by toxic dust from a former steelworks in the town, ending an 11-year legal case. **21.** The supreme court ruled in favour of two men who challenged the indefinite inclusion of their names on the sex offenders register without any chance of a review; the ruling paves the way for a review mechanism to be implemented. **23.** Sharon Shoesmith lost her case in the high court to prove that she was unlawfully dismissed as director of children's services at Haringey council following the death of Baby P. Six members of the same family were convicted of torturing, killing and decapitating 26-year-old Michael Gilbert, who they kept as a slave at their house in Bedfordshire; three were given life sentences, and three were given sentences ranging from six to ten years. **26.** Companies including Argos and Homebase admitted liability for the sale of leather sofas with the chemical DMF in them; they agreed to pay compensation of up to £20m to be shared between nearly 2,000 claimants who suffered medical problems after exposure to the chemical. **27.** A report into the death of Blair Peach, killed during a protest against the National Front in 1979, concluded that he was probably killed by a member of the Metropolitan Police riot squad; 3,000 documents were released that had previously been kept secret by the police.

MAY 2010
4. The court of appeal overturned a ruling that agencies such as MI5 and MI6 should be allowed to use secret information to defend themselves in civil cases (*see* 18 November) and ruled that such cases should be tried in public. **5.** Jewellery and diamonds worth over £1m were stolen from De Beers and Tiffany & Co in a raid at the Westfield shopping centre, London. **14.** A Labour MP, Stephen Timms, was stabbed during his constituency surgery in East Ham, London; his injuries were not thought to be life-threatening, and a 21-year-old woman was arrested. Ian Davison, a white supremacist, was sentenced to ten years in prison for making ricin; he was the first Briton to be convicted for producing a chemical weapon. **17.** Bristol Crown court fined Great Western Hospitals NHS trust £75,000 and ordered it to pay £25,000 costs for a fatal accident in which a new mother, Mayra Cabrera, was given an anaesthetic instead of a saline solution in May 2004. **21.** Rachel Baker, a former care home manager, was sentenced to ten years in prison for killing a 97-year-old woman by injecting her with a lethal dose of painkiller; Ms Baker had been stealing prescription drugs from the residents to feed her addiction. **24.** Two boys, aged 10 and 11, were convicted of the attempted rape of an eight-year-old girl in Hayes, London, in October 2009. **27.** Stephen Griffiths, a PhD student from Bradford, was charged with the murders of Suzanne Blamires, Shelley Armitage and Susan Rushworth. **29.** Toxicology tests carried out on the bodies of two teenagers who were thought to have died as a result of taking mephedrone found that they had not taken the drug; the deaths of the two boys had led to a successful campaign to ban the drug (*see* 16 April).

JUNE 2010
2. Derrick Bird, a 52-year-old taxi driver, shot dead 12 people and injured a further 11 in west Cumbria before killing himself. **16.** The supreme court ruled that a suspected terrorist's human rights had been breached by a control order that forced him to move 150 miles away from his family and friends. **22.** Sean Ganterton and Martin Durnell were given prison sentences of two years and 21 months respectively after systematically bullying and threatening two undercover reporters posing as a Muslim couple living on a Bristol housing estate for a *Panorama* documentary on racism. A 16-year-old boy was sentenced to a minimum of 14 years in prison for fatally stabbing 18-year-old Salum Kombo, after trading insults and threats on Facebook, in Bromley-by-Bow in September 2009. **29.** The Mayor of London, Boris Johnson, won a high court order to evict peace protesters from Parliament Square Gardens; the protesters' appeal against the ruling was turned down on 16 July. **30.** Rangzieb Ahmed won the right to appeal against his conviction for being involved with terrorist organisations, on the grounds that Britain was complicit in his torture after he was detained in Pakistan. The supreme court ruled that British soldiers in war zones are not protected by human rights laws when they are away from their base; the decision reversed a ruling by the high court in 2008 that had awarded protection to soldiers in any circumstances, including in combat.

JULY 2010
3. Raoul Moat shot dead his former partner's new boyfriend, and injured his former partner and a police officer two days after being released from prison; the police conducted a week-long search of the village of Rothbury, leading to his discovery on 9 July when, after hours of negotiations, Mr Moat shot himself. **7.** The supreme court ruled that homosexual asylum seekers could not be deported from the UK on the grounds that they could conceal their sexual orientation in their home country. **8.** The home secretary, Theresa May, banned the police from using random stop and search powers pending a review of counter-terrorism legislation. **11.** The high court blocked the sale of a house by a father who owed more than £78,000 in child maintenance; the case was the first to make use of new powers to halt or reverse the sale of assets by parents who refuse to pay child support. **12.** Ibrahim Savant, Arafat Waheed Khan and Waheed Zaman were each sentenced to life in prison for planning a terrorist attack that involved detonating liquid bombs on transatlantic jets. Three police officers were shot and a further 24 injured in Belfast after protesters against the annual Orange Order parades became violent when riot police attempted to remove them. **16.** Peter Sutcliffe, the 'Yorkshire Ripper', who was given 20 life sentences for murdering 13 women, lost his appeal to be considered for parole, although the judge revealed that a mental health tribunal had concluded that it was safe to move him to a less secure unit. The five companies responsible for the Buncefield oil depot explosion in 2005 were fined a total of £9.5m for health and safety breaches (*see* 14 April). **21.** The former owner of *The*

Daily Telegraph, Lord Black of Crossharbour, was released on $2 million bail by a Chicago court after serving less than half of a six-and-a-half year sentence for fraud and obstruction of justice, but the judge refused him leave to return to his native Canada and demanded that he provide a full statement of financial assets by 16 August. **22.** The Crown Prosecution Service decided not to prosecute an officer who struck Ian Tomlinson at the G20 protests in 2009 shortly before Mr Tomlinson died. Declan Duffy, a republican paramilitary, was sentenced to life in prison for killing an army recruitment sergeant in 1992, athough under the terms of the Good Friday Agreement he was expected to serve around two years. **23.** Jon Venables, one of the killers of two-year-old James Bulger in 1993, was sentenced to two years in prison for downloading and distributing child pornography. **28.** The home secretary, Theresa May, announced plans to end the use of antisocial behaviour orders. **29.** The court of appeal ruled that separated couples will no longer be able to use covertly found documents to demonstrate that their partner has been concealing money as evidence in divorce proceedings. **30.** An inquest jury determined that a points failure had caused the deaths of seven people in the Potters Bar rail crash in 2002; the Crown Prosecution Service announced that it would investigate whether criminal proceedings could be brought.

ENVIRONMENT AND SCIENCE

AUGUST 2009

2. The journal *Nature Genetics* published findings from a study comparing the DNA of women with ovarian cancer to those without the disease; the scientists had isolated a gene variant that increases the chance of developing the disease by up to 40 per cent. **3.** Leading shoe manufacturers demanded an immediate moratorium on destruction of the Amazon rainforest by leather suppliers in Brazil. **16.** A UN report warned that without modernisation of irrigation systems in Asia, countries with rapidly growing populations such as India and China are likely to experience unprecedented food shortages; the population of the continent is expected to grow by 1.5 billion by 2050. **21.** A rupture on the Montara offshore drilling rig, owned by the Thai oil company PTTEP, caused oil to leak into the Timor Sea at the rate of 300–400 barrels a day (*see* 23 October) **26.** The journal *Nature* reported that an experiment on rhesus macaques had transferred healthy mitochondrial DNA (mDNA) from a donor egg to a maternal egg in which the mDNA was faulty, resulting in the successful birth of four monkeys; the breakthrough could eventually help to eradicate disorders carried within mitochondrial DNA.

SEPTEMBER 2009

6. *Nature Genetics* reported the discovery that two genes, known as CLU and PICALM, when impaired are linked to the development of Alzheimer's disease. **17.** The journal *Science* published a description of the newly discovered dinosaur *Raptorex kriegstini,* a small ancestor of *Tyrannosaurus rex.* **18.** An Oxford University study that followed its subjects for 38 years found that a combination of smoking, high blood pressure and high cholesterol in middle-age reduced men's life expectancy by ten years. **21.** An ecological assessment of rivers in England and Wales revealed that only 26 per cent were in 'good' condition as defined by the EU water framework. A number of EU countries, including France, Italy and Spain, voted against a proposal to ban EU trade in the endangered bluefin tuna, provoking criticism from environmentalists. **24.** Data from India's first lunar mission, *Chandrayaan I,* provided evidence for the presence of water on the surface of the moon. Archaeologists announced that a metal detectorist in south Staffordshire had discovered the largest Anglo-Saxon hoard yet found in the UK; the hoard of over 1,500 gold and silver pieces dating to the seventh century was later valued at nearly £3.3m (*see also* Archaeology).

OCTOBER 2009

1. *Science* reported that some 4.4 million-year-old *Ardipithecus ramidus* fossils, discovered in Ethiopia in 1992, show characteristics of both hominid and ape species, ie the ability to walk upright and an aptitude for climbing trees; the finding could bring scientists closer to establishing a common ancestor shared by chimpanzees and humans. **5.** The river Trent was found to be contaminated with cyanide and untreated sewage, which affected about 30 miles of the river; on 8 October the Environment Agency issued a notice suspending discharges into the river by Red Industries of Stoke-on-Trent after tests showed it to be the source of the contamination. **6.** The French National Centre of Scientific Research announced an 'exceptional' discovery of 150 million-year-old dinosaur imprints of up to two metres in diameter near Plagne in eastern France. **7.** A study in *Nature* described a previously undetected ring of dust surrounding the planet Saturn at a distance of 8 million miles; the halo is around 1.55 million miles thick, while Saturn's regular rings are only metres thick. **12.** The government's climate change committee warned that the recession was threatening the investment in green housing, power and transport needed to meet government targets for tackling global warming. Scientists from the Institute of Cancer Research described how, in rare cases, cancer can be transmitted in the womb; they studied cancer cells from a mother and baby (who both had cancer) and found they shared an identical cancer gene which had mutated in a way that made it undetectable to the immune system of the child. **21.** A study published in *Nature* refuted the theory that the fossil of *Darwinius masillae,* popularly known as Ida, is related to humans; based on comparisons with a similar fossil found in Egypt, the report suggested the remains belong to a small lemur or loris which evolved in parallel to primates. **23.** An oil slick measuring 9,650 sq. miles (25,000 sq. km), caused by a leak from an oil rig in the Timor Sea (*see* 21 August), threatened marine reserves and many species; over 400,000 litres of oil had leaked before the rupture was plugged.

NOVEMBER 2009

2. According to the annual survey of threatened species by the International Union for the Conservation of Nature (IUCN), nearly 17,300 of the world's 47,677 assessed species are under threat of extinction. **13.** NASA scientists announced that a probe which was crashed into the southern polar region of the moon had recovered about 25 gallons of water. **18.** The Kenyan government began to evict thousands of illegal settlers from the Mau forest in an attempt to restore the area's damaged ecosystem. **19.** The Prince of Wales launched an emergency scheme whereby developed nations will pay countries such as Brazil and Indonesia to reduce the destruction of tropical rainforest; the USA pledged $275m (£165m) to the fund. **20.** The journal *Zookeys* described four new species of crocodile derived from 100 million-year-old fossil remains found in Niger and Morocco; the discoveries, which offer clues about why the ancestors of modern crocodiles survived when dinosaurs became extinct, included *Kaprosuchus saharicus,* a 6m (20ft) long crocodile with an armoured snout.

DECEMBER 2009

8. The World Meterological Organisation, in conjunction with the UN climate change conference in Copenhagen, released a preliminary assessment of global temperature averages which predicted that the first decade of the 21st century would be the warmest on record. **10.** Marine scientists at the UN Climate Change Conference presented a report on ocean acidification which stated that carbon dioxide emissions would have severe consequences for marine life (including the extinction of fish species as a result of plankton depletion) unless immediate cuts in emissions are made. **11.** Findings published in the journal *Cell* identified a gene, FOXL2, that determines whether a person will develop male or female sex traits. **15.** The journal *Current Biology* published the first evidence of invertebrates using tools; a species of octopus, *amphioctopus marginatus,* was observed assembling halved coconut shells as shelter on the sea floor off the coast of Bali. **16.** Scientists at the Wellcome Trust Sanger Institute announced that they had reconstructed the biological history of small cell lung cancer and malignant melonoma; they sequenced the full genomes of cancerous cells and healthy cells in sufferers of each disease and were able to catalogue mutations. **18.** The UN climate change conference failed to agree binding targets for greenhouse gas reductions, with China reportedly resistant to proposed global targets. **22.** The journal *Stem Cell* published results of trial therapy that used stem cell grafts from a healthy eye to restore sight to a man with limbal stem cell deficiency (LSCD).

JANUARY 2010

4. In *Science,* NASA scientists reported the discovery by the Kepler probe of five planets orbiting distant stars in the Milky Way; all of the planets have temperatures too high to harbour life. **6.** A study by scientists at Imperial College and King's College published in the journal *PLoS One* discredited the theory that chronic fatigue syndrome, or ME, is caused by the retrovirus XMRV; analysis of blood samples from patients with the condition found that none had the virus. **7.** Scientists announced the discovery of 395 million-year-old fossil footprints in southeastern Poland; these show that four-legged animals walked on land 18 million years earlier than previously understood. **12.** The journal *Proceedings of the National Academy of Scientists* reported the discovery that the Arctic tern migrates more than 50,000 miles a year, the longest recorded migration of any living creature. The *British Medical Journal* reported that angiotensin receptor blockers (ARBs), which are usually prescribed to treat high blood pressure, reduce the likelihood of developing Alzheimer's disease and dementia by up to 50 per cent. **21.** The Intergovernmental Panel on Climate Change made an unprecedented apology over a 'poorly substantiated' prediction that the Himalayan glaciers were likely to melt by 2035. **27.** The Information Commissioner's Office said that the climatic research centre at the University of East Anglia had breached rules by withholding data requested under the Freedom of Information Act; the centre was accused of covering up data after emails were leaked on the internet. *Nature* published research by scientists at Bristol University and the China Academy of Science which used fossilised pigments to establish that the plumage of the *Sinosauropteryx,* a flesh-eating dinosaur species that lived 125 million years ago, was russet-coloured. **29.** The General Medical Council found Dr Andrew Wakefield guilty on a number of misconduct charges relating to research which he claimed established a link between the MMR vaccination and the development of bowel disease and autism; the *Lancet* retracted a paper by Dr Wakefield that it had published in 1998, which was based on the discredited research (*see* 24 May).

FEBRUARY 2010

3. The *New England Journal of Medicine* published a case in which neuroscientists were able to communicate with a patient thought to be in a vegetative state; scans monitoring his brain activity showed the patient correctly answered a series of 'yes' and 'no' questions after being told to think of playing tennis (a motor activity) to indicate a 'yes' and to think of walking around his home (a spatial activity) to indicate 'no'. **18.** The IUCN reported that 48 per cent of the 634 primate species are threatened with imminent extinction owing to hunting, smuggling and destruction of habitat; the species include the golden-headed langur, found only on the island of Cat Ba in Vietnam, and the Sumatran orang-utan. The journal *Science Translational Medicine* published details of a new DNA test that can monitor the effects of treatment on tumours.

MARCH 2010

4. An international review by 41 scientists in *Science* concluded that the mass extinction of dinosaurs was caused by an asteroid that collided with the earth 65 million years ago in what is today Mexico, and not by volcanic activity. **9.** DEFRA announced the release of lice from Japan to control Japanese knotweed in the UK. **11.** Natural England released a report, *Lost Life: England's Lost and Threatened Species,* which identified 943 native species that are now classed as a conservation priority owing to habitat loss, inappropriate management, pollution and pressure from non-native species. **14.** *Nature Chemical Biology* reported that scientists from the University of Calgary had identified the two genes in opium poppies with painkilling qualities, raising the possibility of finding more efficient ways of producing common painkillers such as codeine and morphine. **19.** A team of British and Italian scientists announced that they had successfully transplanted a windpipe – stripped of the donor's cells then coated with stem cells – into a boy at Great Ormond Street hospital; his own body incubated and regenerated the organ, a cheaper and faster process than regenerating a donor organ externally. **25.** *Nature* reported the identification of a previously unknown type of ancient human through the analysis of DNA from a finger-bone unearthed in a Siberian cave; the hominin, nicknamed X-woman by researchers, lived between 48,000 and 30,000 years ago, and may have existed alongside *Homo sapiens* and Neanderthals. **30.** Greenpeace accused the US oil company Koch Industries of 'spreading inaccurate and misleading information' about climate science; the report said the company had donated nearly $48m (£32m) to climate opposition groups between 1997 and 2008.

APRIL 2010

1. The foreign secretary, David Miliband, announced the creation of the world's largest marine conservation reserve in waters surrounding the Chagos Islands in the Indian Ocean; the decision was countered by an appeal to the European Court of Human Rights by Chagossians who were evicted by the British government to make way for a US military base on the largest of the islands in the 1960s. **8.** *Science* announced the discovery in a South African cave of two 1.9 million-year-old skeletons, thought to represent a new species of human ancestor with ape-like traits; other scientists questioned the significance of the find, which was named *Australopithecus sediba.* **20.** An explosion on Deepwater Horizon, a BP-leased oil rig in the Gulf of Mexico, killed 11 workers and ruptured the Macondo well, causing an oil spillage considered the USA's worst environmental disaster; oil leaked from the ruptured well at an estimated rate of 210,000 gallons a day until BP succeeded in capping the leak in July; fisheries and other marine life, and, from early May, coastal wetlands and species were severely affected by the contamination by the leaked oil and the chemicals used to disperse it. **28.** *The Lancet* reported on an 11-year research programme monitoring over 170,000 people for bowel cancer; the results suggested that a five-minute screening test for bowel cancer could cut deaths from the disease by 43 per cent and the incidence of bowel cancer by a third if the test was extended to those aged over 50. **29.** The US president, Barack Obama, ordered the US military to help with attempts to contain oil leaking from the Macondo well, and said BP would be held responsible for the consequences of the disaster (*see also* Business and Economic Affairs).

MAY 2010

6. *Science* published research by scientists from the Max Planck Institute for Evolutionary Anthropology which compared the Neanderthal genome with modern human genomes from a range of locations; they found that most people living outside Africa can trace up to 4 per cent of their DNA to Neanderthal origin, which is attributed to instances of interbreeding between the species. **11.** A study based on 10,000 civil servants published in the *European Heart Journal* found evidence that working overtime (three extra hours or more each day) increased the risk of developing coronary heart disease by 60 per cent. **13.** Research published in *Science* showed that genetically modified crops may be more prone to infestation; the ten-year study was conducted in six major cotton-growing regions of China. **15.** Thousands of litres of chemical dispersant were released at depths close to the seabed as part of attempts to tackle the growing oil spill in the Gulf of Mexico; scientists expressed concern over the environmental implications of the release of toxic dispersant at such depths. **16.** Ocean scientists reported giant plumes of oil coagulating at depths of up to 1,300m in the Gulf of Mexico. **18.** Environmental lobby groups agreed to end a boycott of 21 forestry companies in return for a commitment to suspend logging and road-building on 29 million hectares (71 million acres) of forest in northern Canada. **20.** A US scientist, Craig Venter, announced that he had created the world's first synthetic life form, a microbe that thrives and replicates itself with only a man-made genome to guide it. **24.** Andrew Wakefield was struck off the medical register after being found guilty of serious professional misconduct over his unethical conduct of research (*see* 29 January). **27.** President Obama declared a six-month moratorium on oil exploration in the Arctic and on the drilling of 33 new wells in the Gulf of Mexico. **29.** An attempt to plug the Macondo oil well leak with heavy mud failed.

JUNE 2010

3. The European Commission gave the UK government a final warning to reduce the pollution of London's air by particles known as PM10s, emitted by traffic and factories, or face a fine of up to £300m. **6.** BP claimed partial success in its efforts to stem the Gulf oil leak after a 'cut and cap' approach succeeded in filtering off 42,000 gallons of oil a day; however, the environmental situation had worsened, with 32 per cent of the Gulf's fisheries closed, oil contamination of the Louisiana and Florida coasts, and colonies of brown pelicans badly affected. **9.** Scientists on three continents reported 'alarming' rates of decline in snake populations after monitoring 17 populations in a variety of habitats; species in decline include the smooth snake (UK), asp viper (France, Italy) and the royal python (Nigeria). **10.** *Nature* published new research that suggested that a type of genetic diversity known as copy number variations (CNVs), in which large segments of DNA are missing or duplicated, might play a significant role in causing autism. **22.** An Imperial College London study published in the *British Medical Journal* found no link between mobile phone masts and early childhood cancer. **23.** The leak of oil in the Gulf of Mexico returned to full force after an underwater robot accidentally bumped into the containment device; the cap was refitted a day later. An International Whaling Commission meeting failed to agree new rules on whaling; the existing moratorium, which dates from 1986, continues to be circumvented by Iceland, Norway and Japan. **24.** A review by the Royal College of Obstetricians and Gynaecologists concluded that the human foetus is unable to feel pain for the first 24 weeks after conception. **29.** Wildlife officials announced plans to dig up 70,000 turtle eggs from beaches on the Gulf of Mexico and move them to the Atlantic coast in an attempt to save that generation of hatchlings from death as a result of the Gulf oil spill; the plan emerged amid accusations that BP's attempt to reduce the spillage by burning off oil had burnt turtles alive.

JULY 2010

8. The journal *Nature* reported the discovery of a number of flint tools preserved in sediment near Happisburgh, Norfolk; they are believed to be between 840,000 and 950,000 years old, pushing back the date of the first known human occupation of Britain by nearly 250,000 years. **15.** BP succeeded in stopping the oil leak in the Gulf of Mexico for the first time since 20 April, though the company warned that the new cap was only a temporary solution until a relief well was drilled. **21.** British scientists announced the discovery of a huge star, named R136a1, in the Tarantula nebula which has the mass of 265 suns and the luminosity of nearly 10 million suns; it was discovered using the Very Large Telescope in the Atacama desert in northern Chile. **29.** The UN withdrew the Galapagos Islands from its world heritage danger list, citing improved efforts by Ecuador to protect the archipelago's unique biodiversity.

SPORT

AUGUST 2009

2. At the world swimming championships in Rome, the British swimmer Liam Tancock won the 50m backstroke event in 24.04sec, setting a new world record. **13.** The International Olympic Committee (IOC) announced that women's boxing would be included in the Olympic Games for the first time in 2012; it also recommended the addition of rugby sevens and golf in 2016. **15.** Andy Murray was ranked number two in the ATP world rankings after his victory in the semi-final of the Rogers Cup in Montreal, the highest ranking achieved by a British player. **16.** At the IAAF World Championships in Berlin, Usain Bolt won the 100m in a world record time of 9.58sec; it was the biggest reduction in the men's 100m record since electronic timing was introduced in 1968. Jessica Ennis produced a personal best to win the heptathlon at the world championships. **17.** The European Rugby Cup banned Dean Richards, formerly Harlequins' director of rugby, from coaching in European competitions for three years for his role in the 'Bloodgate' incident; a fake-blood capsule bought by Richards from a joke shop was used by player Tom Williams to fabricate an injury in order to be substituted during a match against Leinster in the Heineken Cup. **18.** Phillips Odowu produced a personal best to win the triple jump at the world championships. **20.** Usain Bolt ran the 200m in 19.19secs, winning a second gold medal and breaking his second world record at the world championships. **23.** The England cricket team beat Australia in the final test match at the Oval, winning the Ashes series 2–1, their second consecutive victory in an Ashes series on home soil since the 1980s. **25.** Violent clashes between fans at a League Cup fixture between West Ham and Milwall resulted in 13 people being arrested and five charged; the violence had been organised in advance of the game via online forums.

SEPTEMBER 2009

3. FIFA banned Chelsea from signing any new players until 2011 for illegally inducing the French youth international Gaël Kakuta to sign for the club in 2007 (*see* 4 February). **4.** The FIA accused Renault of interfering with the 2008 Singapore grand prix, alleging that Nelson Piquet Jr was ordered to crash in order to benefit his Renault teammate Fernando Alonso (*see* 21 September). **9.** England beat Croatia 5–1 at Wembley to qualify for the 2010 World Cup finals in South Africa. **10.** In football, Germany defeated England 6–2 in the final of the women's European championship. **13.** In tennis, Heather Watson, a 17-year-old from Guernsey, won the girls' singles at the US Open, the first Briton to do so. **14.** Kim Clijsters won the US Open women's singles title after a two-year break from tennis. **15.** The actor and comedian Eddie Izzard completed his 43rd marathon in 52 days in aid of Sport Relief. **21.** The FIA banned Renault's managing director, Flavio Briatore, from Formula One for his role in the 'Crashgate' scandal (*see* 4 September). The memorial service of former Newcastle Utd and England manager Sir Bobby Robson took place at Durham cathedral, and was broadcast live to the Newcastle's stadium, St James' Park, where it was watched by thousands of fans. **25.** IFK Gothenburg goalkeeper Kim Christensen faced suspension after he admitted pushing the goalposts closer together than regulation width prior to a game against Orebo. **28.** The FA charged West Ham and Millwall for failing to halt racist behaviour among their fans during their match on 25 August.

OCTOBER 2009

2. The IOC awarded the Brazilian city of Rio de Janeiro the 2016 Olympic Games, which will be the first to be held in South America. An independent arbitration panel upheld Kevin Keegan's claim of constructive dismissal against Newcastle Utd FC; he was awarded £2m. **4.** The Derby-winning racehorse Sea The Stars won the Prix de L'Arc de Triomphe in Paris, its sixth consecutive victory in a group one race; it was the horse's last race, and its jockey, Mick Kinane, later announced his retirement after a career of 34 years. **5.** Sulaiman al-Fahim sold 90 per cent of Portsmouth FC to the Saudi Arabian businessman Ali al-Faraj after only six weeks as owner; a week earlier it had emerged that the club was facing severe financial difficulties when players' wages went unpaid. **11.** In rugby league, Leeds Rhinos beat St Helens 18–10 at Old Trafford to win a third successive Super League Grand Final. **15.** The British gymnast Daniel Keatings won a silver medal in the all-around men's section of the world championships, held at the O2 Arena, London. **18.** Jenson Button came fifth in the Brazilian grand prix after starting 14th on the grid; the result gave him an unassailable lead in the Formula One drivers' World Championship, making him the tenth Briton to win the drivers' title; it also won the constructors' title for Brawn-Mercedes in their first season. Beth Tweddle won a gold medal in the floor event at the Artistic Gymnastic world championships, Britain's second-ever world championship gold. **25.** In motor sport, Citröen driver Sébastian Loeb won his sixth consecutive world rally title. Valentino Rossi clinched his second successive MotoGP world championship, his seventh in total.

NOVEMBER 2009

7. The British boxer David Haye defeated 2.18m (7ft 2in) Nikolai Valuev on points to win the WBA world heavyweight championship. **13.** An independent review by the Department of Culture, Media and Sport recommended that the list of 'crown jewel' sports events (those protected for live broadcast on free-to-air television) should be extended to include events such as the Ashes test cricket series and all home nations' football qualifiers; sports bodies expressed concern over the impact this would have on funding for sports at grassroots level (*see* 21 July). **16.** FIFA learned that the Iraqi Olympic Committee had disbanded the Iraqi Football Association and taken control of the game in Iraq; FIFA condemned political intervention in the game (*see* 20 November). **18.** Thierry Henry admitted that he had deliberately handled the ball before setting up the decisive goal in France's World Cup qualification play-off against the Republic of Ireland; the Irish FA led calls for a rematch. Algeria beat Egypt in another of the World Cup play-offs, sparking violent demonstrations by fans from both countries (*see* Africa, 18 November). **20.** FIFA banned Iraqi teams from competing in all international football competitions after the Iraqi Olympic Committee stood by its decision to disband the Iraqi Football Association. In the premiership, Tottenham Hotspur beat Wigan Athletic 9–1; Jermain Defoe scored five goals in Spurs' best scoreline in 33 years. **27.** Tiger Woods was involved in a car accident at his home in Florida; on 11 December he admitted to trangessions in his personal life and announced that he was taking an indefinite break from professional golf.

DECEMBER 2009

2. Lionel Messi won the 2009 European Footballer of the Year award. **7.** The British Racing Drivers' Club secured a 17-year deal to host the British grand prix at Silverstone. **13.** The footballer Ryan Giggs won the BBC Sports

Personality of the Year award, unexpectedly beating the bookmakers' favourite, Jenson Button; Giggs was honoured for a year in which he won an 11th league title with Manchester Utd. **22.** Michael Schumacher signed a one-year deal to return to Formula One, driving for the Mercedes team. **26.** The racehorse Kauto Star won the King George VI Chase for the fourth successive year, equalling the record held by Desert Orchid. **29.** The England cricket team produced a strong performance against South Africa on the penultimate day of the second Test, at one stage reducing their opponents to 50 for six; they won the match in Durban by an innings. **30.** Portsmouth FC failed to pay players' wages for the third time in the 2009–10 season; the club was served with a winding-up petition by HM Revenue & Customs.

JANUARY 2010

3. Phil Taylor won his 15th Professional Darts Corporation world title. **5.** Manchester City FC announced losses of £92.6m for the 2008–9 season, its first season under its new owner Sheikh Mansour. **7.** Graham Onions, the number 11 batsman in the England cricket team, faced 17 deliveries to draw the match for England in the third Test against South Africa; he had also faced 19 last-stand deliveries to draw the first Test. **8.** Separatists in Cabinda attacked a bus taking the Togo national football team to the Africa Cup of Nations tournament in Angola, killing three people; the Togo team withdrew from the competition and flew home on 10 January. **17.** Mark Selby recovered from three frames behind with four to play to beat Ronnie O'Sullivan in the UK Masters snooker final at Wembley. **31.** Roger Federer defeated Andy Murray in the final of the Australian Open tennis tournament, preventing the British player from winning his first grand slam tournament. Egypt beat Ghana 1–0 in the Africa Cup of Nations final in Angola, winning the competition for the seventh time.

FEBRUARY 2010

3. Portsmouth FC changed ownership for the fourth time in the 2009–10 season; the Hong Kong businessman Balram Chainrai exercised an option to take a controlling interest to stabilise the financial situation of the club and protect his loans of over £17m to it. **4.** The Court of Arbitration for Sport overturned a ruling that banned Chelsea FC from signing new players until 2011 after the club agreed to pay £2.6m compensation to the French team Lens (*see* 3 September). **5.** The England football manager Fabio Capello stripped John Terry of the England captaincy following allegations about the player's private life; Terry was replaced as captain by Rio Ferdinand, and Steven Gerrard became vice-captain. **7.** The New Orleans Saints beat the Indianapolis Colts 31–17 to win the Super Bowl XLIV; the victory was viewed as a symbol of recovery for the city devastated by Hurricane Katrina in 2005. **12.** The XXI Winter Olympic Games opened in Vancouver, Canada. The Georgian luge athlete Nodar Kumaritashvili was killed in a training accident prior to the opening of the Winter Olympics; the elevation of the men's start-line was reduced by 20m after complaints that the track was too fast and dangerous. **19.** Amy Williams won a gold medal in the women's skeleton, Britain's first gold medal at a Winter Olympics since 1980. **24.** The Indian cricketer Sachin Tendulkar became the first batsman to score a double century in a one-day International during a match with South Africa in Gwalior, India. **26.** Portsmouth FC went into administration, the first club to do so in the history of the Premier League; they were later docked nine points (*see* 21 April).

MARCH 2010

4. The Football League approved the offshore owners of Leeds United FC as 'fit and proper' while keeping their identity private; politicians and football supporters' groups called for the information to be made public. **14.** David Beckham suffered a ruptured achilles tendon during a football match for AC Milan; the injury prevented him from playing for the rest of the season and in the 2010 World Cup. **22.** The London organising committee for the 2012 Olympic Games invited the public to register interest in buying tickets for the Games; 150,000 people registered in nine hours. **25.** Sir Chris Hoy won the men's keirin sprint, his tenth cycling world title, in Copenhagen. **27.** The British cyclist Victoria Pendleton won a fourth consecutive world title in the women's sprint; a day later she was controversially beaten into second place in the keirin final.

APRIL 2010

3. In the university boat race, Cambridge came from behind to beat Oxford, who were the favourites, by one-and-a-half lengths. **10.** The Grand National was won by Don't Push It, ridden by Tony McCoy, who achieved his first Grand National victory in 14 attempts. **21.** Administrators for Portsmouth FC revealed the full scale of the club's financial problems, with debts of £119m, and fans and local traders among the creditors. **24.** Steve Davis, aged 52, became the oldest snooker world championship quarter-finalist in 27 years when he beat the defending champion John Higgins 13–11. **26.** India's cricket board suspended the chairman of the Indian Premier League, Lalit Modi, over corruption allegations. **29.** Fulham beat Hamburg to reach the final of football's Europa League; they subsequently lost the final to Atlético Madrid.

MAY 2010

2. The British gymnast Beth Tweddle won gold in two events, the uneven bars and the floor exercise, at the European championships in Birmingham; the British team won the silver team medal. The World Professional Billiards and Snooker Association suspended the world number one John Higgins after newspaper allegations that he had agreed to take a £261,000 bribe to deliberately lose frames in four tournaments. **9.** Chelsea beat Wigan Athletic 8–0, the victory securing the club the Premier League championship by one point. **15.** Chelsea beat the recently relegated Portsmouth 1–0 in the FA Cup final, achieving the club's first-ever double. **16.** Lord Triesman resigned as chairman of the FA and of England's bid to host the 2018 World Cup after the *Mail on Sunday* published a transcript of a private conversation, recorded without his knowledge, in which he alleged that Russia and Spain were plotting to bribe referees during the 2010 World Cup. England beat Australia by seven wickets to win the World Twenty20 tournament in the West Indies; the man of the match was Craig Kieswetter, who scored 63 runs off 49 balls for England. **18.** The former England striker Gary Lineker resigned from his *Daily Mail* newspaper column over Lord Triesman's resignation from the FA; Lineker said that the newspaper group's action had undermined England's bid to host the 2018 World Cup. **22.** Inter Milan, coached by José Mourinho, beat Bayern Munich 2–0 to win the Champions League; it was Mourinho's second success in the competition as a coach.

29. The defending champions Leicester beat Saracens 33–27 to win the rugby premiership final, the club's third premiership title in four years.

JUNE 2010

4. The England football captain Rio Ferdinand was ruled out of the World Cup after sustaining a knee ligament injury; Steven Gerrard replaced him as captain. **5.** The Derby was won by Workforce, ridden by Ryan Moore, in a record time of 2min 31.33sec. **6.** Rafael Nadal won the men's singles title at the French Open, his fifth victory in six years, and moved up to number one in the men's tennis world rankings. Fifteen people were injured in a stampede at a World Cup warm-up match between Nigeria and North Korea in Johannesburg, South Africa. **11.** The football World Cup opened in South Africa, the first time the tournament has been held in the continent, with a 1–1 draw between the host nation and Mexico; like all subsequent games, it was accompanied by the distinctive sound of vuvuzela horns. **12.** England drew their first World Cup game against the USA 1–1 after a mistake by England's goalkeeper Robert Green led to the US equaliser; over 1.5 million viewers watching on ITV's HD channel missed England's goal after an advert was aired during the match by mistake. **19.** The England rugby team beat Australia 21–20 in Sydney, securing a 1–1 draw in the test series. **23.** England qualified for the last 16 in the World Cup in a tense 1–0 victory over Slovenia; the only goal of the game was scored by Jermain Defoe. **24.** At Wimbledon, John Isner beat Nicolas Mahut 6–4, 3–6, 6–7, 7–6, 70–68, the final set making the match the longest in tennis history. **27.** England were knocked out of the football World Cup after being beaten 4–1 by Germany, the heaviest World Cup defeat ever suffered by England. The England cricket team won the third one-day International against Australia at Old Trafford, securing an unassailable lead in the five-match series.

JULY 2010

2. Andy Murray was beaten in straight sets in the semi-finals at Wimbledon by Rafael Nadal, the eventual winner of the men's singles title. **11.** Spain beat the Netherlands 1–0 in the World Cup final, its first-ever victory in the tournament; Spain scored in extra time in a tense final during which the English referee, Howard Webb, booked 13 players and sent off one. **15.** Rory McIlroy, a 21-year-old from Northern Ireland, scored a nine-under-par 63, equalling the course record in the first round of the 2010 golf Open Championship at St Andrews. **18.** Louis Oosthuizen, a 300-1 outsider, won the Open Championship by seven shots. **21.** The new sports minister, Hugh Robertson, halted a planned overhaul of sports broadcasting rights (*see* 13 November). **22.** The Sri Lankan cricket player Muttiah Muralitharan took his 800th test wicket during the last test match of his career, against India. **25.** The Ferrari Formula One team was fined $100,000 (£65,000) for race-fixing after Felipe Massa was ordered to move aside to allow his teammate Fernando Alonso, a title contender, to win the German grand prix. **27.** Mo Farah won the gold medal and Chris Thompson won the silver medal in the men's 10,000m at the European athletic championships in Barcelona. **31.** At the European championships Jessica Ennis won gold in the heptathlon, Dai Greene won gold in the 400m hurdles and Mo Farah won a second gold medal, in the 5,000m.

INTERNATIONAL

AFRICA

AUGUST 2009

6. In Nigeria, an amnesty between the government and militant groups in the oil-rich Niger delta came into effect; unconditional pardons and cash payments were offered to rebels who surrendered their arms. **9.** The factions in the six-month political crisis in Madagascar signed an agreement providing for a power-sharing coalition to govern during a 15-month transitional period leading to elections; a transitional government was appointed on 8 September. **18.** Niger adopted a new constitution, approved in a referendum earlier in August, which expanded presidential powers and extended the presidential term. A Zambian court cleared former president Frederick Chiluba of all corruption charges relating to $500,000 (£306,000) of treasury bills which he was alleged to have embezzled between 1991 and 2001. **30.** A presidential election in Gabon was won by Ali Bongo, the candidate of the ruling party and the son of President Omar Bongo, who died in June 2009; the announcement of the results on 3 September triggered violent protests amid opposition allegations of electoral fraud.

SEPTEMBER 2009

4. The IMF sanctioned a $510m (£311m) loan to Zimbabwe to replenish its foreign currency reserves; it was the IMF's first substantial engagement with Zimbabwe since 1999. **7.** A female journalist, Lubna Hussein, who had led a high-profile campaign against Sudan's indecency laws, was fined 500 Sudanese pounds (£127) for wearing trousers in public; she was released from prison the following day after her union paid the fine, against her wishes. **10.** The Ugandan government's decision to refuse the king of the Buganda people permission to visit Kayunga district triggered several days of rioting in central Uganda; at least 15 people were killed in four days. **14.** In a helicopter attack in Somalia, US special forces reportedly killed Saleh Ali Nabhan, a leader of the insurgent group al-Shabaab, which has close ties to al-Qaeda; a revenge suicide bomb attack by al-Shabaab in Mogadishu on 17 September killed 16 people, including five African Union peacekeepers. **20.** The multinational oil trading company Trafigura announced that it had reached a settlement with 31,000 personal injury claimants in Côte d'Ivoire, in advance of an imminent hearing at the high court in London; the company continued to deny liability for the dumping of hazardous waste from a cargo ship near Abidjan in 2006. **23.** A Tanzanian court sentenced three men to death for murdering a 13-year-old albino boy in order to sell his body parts for use in witchcraft rituals; he was one of more than 50 albino people murdered in the country in similar circumstances since 2007. **28.** In Guinea, opposition supporters protesting at the proposed candidacy of the junta leader, Captain Moussa Dadis Camara, in the forthcoming presidential election were attacked by government forces, who reportedly shot dead 157 people and raped hundreds.

OCTOBER 2009

1. Fighting broke out in the Somali port of Kismayo when the al-Shabaab group reneged on an agreement with the Hezb al-Islam group over shared control of the city; at least ten people were killed and thousands forced to flee. **4.** The last three militia leaders in the Niger Delta, all linked with the Movement for the Emancipation of the Niger Delta (MEND), surrendered their arms under the government amnesty; on 16 October the remaining members of MEND announced the end of a 90-day ceasefire. **12–13.** Strikes were held in Guinea in protest at the killings on 28 September (*see* above). **14.** In Zimbabwe, a white MDC government minister, Roy Bennett, was indicted for allegedly plotting a coup in 2006; Mr Bennett, whose detention caused the MDC to boycott the unity government until 5 November, was acquitted on 10 May 2010. **16.** The ruling Botswana Democratic party won the general election in Botswana; President Khama was re-elected by the legislature on 20 October. **20.** In Niger, the legislative election was won by President Tandja's National Movement for Society in Development with an overwhelming majority of seats after an opposition boycott of the poll. **22.** The Ethiopian government appealed for emergency food aid after particularly poor rains increased the number dependent on food aid from 4.9 million to 6.2 million. **25.** In Tunisia, President Ben Ali was re-elected for a fifth consecutive term, and his Constitutional Democratic Rally party retained its overwhelming majority in the legislature. **27.** The EU imposed an arms embargo on Guinea and a travel ban on 42 of its military leaders because of the killings on 28 September; two days later the African Union peace and security council approved economic and travel sanctions against the country. **28.** In Mozambique, President Guebuza was re-elected and Frelimo retained its overall majority in the legislature, although the results were contested by the opposition.

NOVEMBER 2009

8. A cargo ship from the UAE carrying weapons bound for Somalia, in contravention of a UN arms embargo, was seized by Somali pirates. **13.** A new prime minister took office in Madagascar but the appointment of other members of the transitional government was suspended on 23 November (*see* 9 August). **18.** After the Algerian football team's victory over Egypt in Sudan, Algerians allegedly attacked Egyptian fans; the following day rioting continued in Algiers, the Algerian embassy in Cairo was attacked and Egypt recalled its ambassador from Algeria. **23.** President Yar'Adua of Nigeria entered a Saudi Arabian hospital for medical treatment. **28.** The legislative election in Namibia was won by the incumbent South West African People's Organisation, and its candidate, Hifikepunye Pohamba, was re-elected president. **29.** Rwanda joined the Commonwealth, becoming the second member never to have been part of the British Empire. Somali pirates seized the Greek-registered oil tanker *Maran Centaurus* off the coast of the Seychelles. The presidential election in Equatorial Guinea was won by the incumbent president, Brig.-Gen. Obiang Nguema, with 95.8 per cent of the vote.

DECEMBER 2009

3. The president of Guinea, Capt. Moussa Dadis Camara, was badly injured in an assassination attempt and left the country for medical treatment; General Sékouba Konaté became acting president. In Mogadishu, a suicide bomber thought to belong to the al-Shabaab group killed at least 22 people, including three Somali government ministers. **14.** Four days of raids by the Lord's Resistance Army began in north-eastern DR Congo; over 320 civilians were murdered and a further 250 abducted. **20.** In legislative elections in the Comoros, a majority of the seats were won by the president's supporters. **21.** President Rajoelina of Madagascar formally abandoned the August power-sharing agreement and replaced the civilian prime minister with a senior military figure. **29.** Infighting between members of the radical Islamist Kata Kalo sect in northern Nigeria spilled over into an attack on a military unit; at least 70 people were killed, including the sect's leader.

JANUARY 2010

5. The World Food Programme announced that it was suspending its operations in six areas of southern Somalia, where it was providing food rations to about one million people, because of intimidation and attempted extortion by the al-Shabaab group. In a remote region of southern Sudan, 139 people were killed in inter-tribal violence. **7.** Thousands of Coptic Christians clashed with security forces as they protested at the murder of six Copts in southern Egypt, reportedly in revenge for the alleged rape of a Muslim girl. **13.** A Nigerian high court judge granted executive powers to vice-president Goodluck Jonathan, ending the constitutional crisis caused by President Yar'Adua's absence since November 2009 (*see* 5 May); the parliament recognised Goodluck Jonathan as acting president on 9 February. **19.** State security forces were sent to the central Nigerian town of Jos after three days of intercommunal violence between Muslims and Christians in which over 300 people were killed (*see* 7 March). **20.** Guinea's military government and opposition parties agreed a power-sharing coalition to govern until elections in June; the legislative election was subsequently postponed to late 2010.

FEBRUARY 2010

15. The Libyan government imposed a ban on Europeans from signatory states of the Schengen agreement entering the country; the travel ban was an escalation of a diplomatic dispute with Switzerland (*see* 22 February). **18.** President Mamadou Tandja of Niger was deposed in a military coup and the Supreme Council for the Restoration of Democracy was established as the new ruling body, headed by the coup leader, Maj. Salou Djibo; it immediately suspended the constitution and dissolved the organs of the state. **22.** The Swiss embassy in Tripoli surrendered Max Göldi, a Swiss citizen convicted of immigration offences, to the Libyan authorities; the embassy had sheltered him since November 2009. **23.** Mahamadou Danda was appointed interim prime minister of Niger, though Maj. Djibo headed the 20-member cabinet named on 1 March.

MARCH 2010

1. In Zimbabwe, a law came into effect requiring 51 per cent of the controlling interest in white-owned businesses to be surrendered to black citizens. **4.** President Gnassingbé was re-elected in Togo's presidential election. **7.** Continuing violence between Muslims and Christians in Jos, Nigeria, left nearly 500 dead; 49 people were charged with murder (*see* 19 January). **10.** The interim government of Niger appealed for emergency food aid, claiming that 58 per cent of the population faced food shortages. **17.** The acting president of Nigeria, Goodluck Jonathan, dissolved the government; on 31 March the senate confirmed his nominations for a new government, which was took office on 6 April. **23.** Somali pirates captured the Malta-registered cargo ship MV *Friga,* which was sailing from Egypt to Thailand, 1,000 nautical miles off the Somali coast, their longest-range attack to date.

APRIL 2010

1. Mutinous soldiers briefly detained the prime minister of Guinea-Bissau, Carlos Gomes Jr, and his military chief of staff. **3.** The white supremacist leader Eugene Terre'Blanche was bludgeoned to death on his farm in South Africa; two black farm workers were charged with his murder. **11–15.** Presidential and legislative elections were held in Sudan; President Omar Hassan al-Bashir was re-elected and vice-president Salva Kiir was re-elected president of semi-autonomous southern Sudan, with the president's National Congress Party winning an overall majority of seats, particularly in the north of the country. **23.** The interim government in Niger announced that a referendum on a new constitution would be held in October 2010.

MAY 2010

1. A double bombing at a mosque in Mogadishu, Somalia, killed 46 people. **2.** A Somali militant group, Hizbul Islam, seized the coastal town of Harardhere, a major pirate haven, vowing to impose Sharia law and eliminate the piracy trade there. **5.** President Yar'Adua of Nigeria died in Saudia Arabia, where he was receiving medical treatment; acting president Goodluck Jonathan was sworn in as president the following day. The legislative election in Mauritius was won by the incumbent coalition government. **7.** In South Africa, police arrested five suspected white extremists who were allegedly planning bomb attacks on black townships prior to the World Cup tournament. **12.** An Afriqiyah Airways flight from Johannesburg crashed on landing in Tripoli, Libya, killing all but one of its 104 passengers; 61 of the casualties were Dutch. **20.** A Malawi court convicted a homosexual couple, Steven Monjeza and Tiwonge Chimbalanga, of 'unnatural acts and gross indecency' for participating in a symbolic engagement ceremony in December 2009, and sentenced them to 14 years' imprisonment with hard labour; both men received a presidential pardon on 29 May after the intervention of the UN secretary-general, Ban Ki-Moon. **23.** Ethiopia's legislative election was won by the incumbant Ethiopian People's Revolutionary Democratic Front with an overwhelming majority of seats; observers considered the polls flawed and opposition leaders called for a rerun, alleging government intimidation.

JUNE 2010

15. In Sudan, a new government of national unity was sworn in. **24.** Jean Leonard Rgambage, the acting editor of a Rwandan newspaper, was murdered in Kigali; he had been investigating the government's alleged role in the assassination of an exiled Rwandan army general in South Africa on 19 June; Andre Kagwa Rwisereka, the vice president of an opposition party, was also found murdered near Butare on 14 July. **27.** The first round of the presidential election in Guinea was inconclusive; the supreme court subsequently ruled that candidates Cellou Dalein Diallo and Alpha Conde should face a run-off on 1 August. **28.** President Nkurunziza of Burundi was re-elected unopposed in the country's first direct presidential election after opposition parties boycotted the election.

JULY 2010

2. At least 223 people were killed in eastern DR Congo when a fuel tanker overturned and caught fire. **11.** Suicide bombings at a restaurant and a rugby club in Kampala, Uganda, killed 79 people; the authorities subsequently detained 20 suspects with connections to the Somali al-Shabaab group, which had claimed responsibility for the bombings. **18.** It was reported that during the previous week clashes between the Justice and Equality Movement (JEM) and Sudanese forces had left over 300 dead; the JEM had suspended its participation in peace talks with the Sudanese government in May 2010, claiming that the government had broken the terms of a ceasefire agreed in February 2010. **28.** At least 140 people were killed when a boat capzised on the Kasai river in western DR Congo.

THE AMERICAS

AUGUST 2009

8. Sonia Sotomayor was sworn in as a judge of the US supreme court, the first Hispanic appointee to the court. **14.** The UK government suspended the constitution, government and legislature of the Turks and Caicos Islands, and imposed direct rule through the territory's governor for up to two years, after an inquiry found evidence of widespread government corruption. **25.** Albert Gonzalez, a former US secret service employee, was sentenced to 20 years' imprisonment for conspiring in the theft of the details of 130 million credit card holders, believed to be the largest such fraud in history, by hacking into the computers of major corporations. **26.** Jaycee Lee Dugard was discovered by police 18 years after she went missing from outside her home in California at the age of 11; Phillip and Nancy Garrido were arrested on charges of abduction, rape and imprisonment.

SEPTEMBER 2009

17. President Obama of the USA announced the scrapping of the previous administration's plans to deploy a missile interception system in Poland and the Czech Republic. **21.** The deposed and exiled Honduran president Manuel Zelaya secretly re-entered the country and took refuge at the Brazilian embassy in Tegucigalpa, seeking dialogue with the interim government (*see* 30 October). **24.** The UN security council voted unanimously in favour of a non-binding resolution that called for states with nuclear weapons to continue to disarm, a ban on nuclear tests and stronger safeguards against the spread of nuclear weapons. **25.** At a G20 summit in Pittsburg, USA, heads of government agreed to set broad annual economic objectives jointly and to subject member states' economies to regular scrutiny by the IMF; the summit also announced that the G20 would replace the G8 as the international council for economic cooperation.

OCTOBER 2009

21. The Nicaraguan supreme court ended the constitutional limit on a president serving consecutive terms or more than two terms, opening the way for President Ortega to stand for a third term in 2011. The US authorities began a two-day operation during which more than 300 suspected members or associates of a Mexican drug cartel, La Familia Michoacana, were arrested and large quantities of crystal methamphetamine were seized. **23.** President Obama declared a national emergency after the number of deaths in the USA from the swine influenza A (H1N1) virus reached 1,000. **25.** The Uruguayan legislative election was won by the incumbent Progressive Encounter-Broad Front. **26.** Following three days of raids in 36 US cities, the FBI announced the arrest of almost 700 people involved in child sex trafficking, and the rescue of 52 minors. **30.** The de facto government of Honduras and deposed president Manuel Zelaya agreed on a power-sharing government to hold office until the start of the next presidential term in January 2010 (*see* 29 November); the deal collapsed the following week after Zelaya withdrew.

NOVEMBER 2009

5. Major Nidal Malik Hasan, a US army psychiatrist, killed 13 people and wounded 31 in a shooting rampage at a military base in Texas. **7.** The US House of Representatives voted by 220 to 215 in favour of a Democrat-sponsored healthcare reform bill which would extend healthcare coverage to 36 million uninsured Americans by 2019 (*see* 24 December). Hurricane Ida caused floods and mudslides in five provinces of El Salvador, killing over 140 people. **13.** The US government announced that Khalid Sheikh Mohammad, the self-confessed mastermind of the 11 September 2001 terrorist attacks, and four alleged co-conspirators held in Guantánamo Bay would stand trial in the USA. **18.** A federal judge found the US army's corps of engineers directly responsible, through neglecting the maintainance of a shipping canal, for some of the most extreme flooding to result from Hurricane Katrina in 2005; the ruling awarded $720,000 (£432,000) in damages to seven plaintiffs, and entitled over 100,000 homes and businesses to compensation from the federal government. **29.** The presidential election in Honduras was won by Porfirio Lobo, the candidate of the opposition National party; most other Latin American countries did not recognise the election as they considered the de facto regime, established by a coup in June 2009, illegitimate. José Mujica was elected president of Uruguay in the second round of voting.

DECEMBER 2009

1. The US government announced that a further 30,000 US troops would be deployed to Afghanistan within six months, bringing the total number to 98,000. **2.** The Honduran supreme court voted against the reinstatement of deposed president Manuel Zelaya. **6.** President Evo Morales of Bolivia was re-elected for a second term; the president's Movement Towards Socialism party won the simultaneous legislative election. **16.** The leader of a Mexican drug gang, Arturo Beltrán Leyva, was among eight men killed during a raid in central Mexico by Mexican marines. **21.** In Colombia, FARC guerrillas kidnapped and killed the governor of Caquetá province. The Mexico City assembly passed legislation granting equal marriage rights to same-sex couples, the first jurisdiction in Latin America to do so; the law came into effect on 4 March 2010. **24.** The US senate voted by 60 to 39 in favour of a Democrat-sponsored healthcare reform bill; this differed from the bill passed by the House of Representatives on 7 November, with which it had to be merged before passing into law, on points such as the omission of a government-funded public health insurance scheme and alternative tax proposals to fund the reforms (*see* 21 March 2010). **25.** A Nigerian Muslim, Umar Farouk Abdulmuttalab, attempted to bring down a transatlantic flight shortly before it landed in the USA by detonating a chemical bomb concealed in his underwear; the device, which only partially ignited, was supplied by the Yemen-based al-Qaida in the Arabian Peninsula. **30.** The minority Canadian government prorogued parliament until 3 March 2010; opposition parties accused the government of trying to avoid questions over its alleged complicity in the torture of Afghan detainees. **31.** A US federal judge dismissed on procedural grounds all charges against five of the six private security guards employed by the security contractor Blackwater (now known as Xe Ltd) who shot dead 17 Iraqi civilians in Baghdad in September 2007. Heavy rains in south-eastern Brazil triggered flooding and mudslides in which 76 people were killed.

JANUARY 2010

8. President Hugo Chavez of Venezuela announced the introduction of a two-tier exchange rate against the US dollar, devaluing the bolivar by 17 per cent for 'priority' imports and by 50 per cent for 'non-essential' goods. **12.** A 7.0-magnitude earthquake struck southern Haiti, causing extreme damage in the Port-au-Prince area, where an estimated 230,000 people were killed and one million displaced; early responses by international rescue and aid missions were hampered by the damage to infrastructure, which closed the country's major port and its only airport, and the loss of many Haitian government and NGO staff and facilities. **17.** Sebastian Piñera won the presidential election in Chile in the second round of voting. **19.** The UN security council unanimously approved the dispatch of 3,500 peacekeeping troops to Haiti, to supplement the 9,000 already present, to help restore security after outbreaks of looting and violence in the aftermath of the earthquake. **20.** In a controversial decision passed by a 5–4 majority, the US supreme court ended restrictions on spending in political campaigns, in particular on advertising, by corporations and unions. The evacuation began of an estimated 400,000 refugees from Port-au-Prince to tented settlements in the surrounding countryside. **28.** Ben Bernanke's appointment for a second four-year term as chairman of the US federal reserve was approved.

FEBRUARY 2010

2. President Obama submitted his proposed budget for the fiscal year 2011 to congress; it amounted to $3.8 trillion (£2.4 trillion), and included $100bn of further spending on infrastructure and tax breaks for small businesses. **4.** A Haitian court charged ten American Baptist missionaries with child kidnapping and criminal association after they attempted to take 33 Haitian children out of the country without documentation or authorisation; nine were released without charge, but the most senior was convicted of arranging illegal travel and detained until 17 May. **7.** Laura Chinchilla, the former vice-president and candidate of the National Liberation Party (PLN), won the presidential election in Costa Rica; in the simultaneous legislative election the PLN remained the largest party, though without a majority. **16.** President Kirchner of Argentina decreed that ships using Argentinian ports would require a permit to enter or leave the disputed waters around the Falkland Islands in response to British plans for oil exploration to begin near the islands. **27.** A massive 8.8-magnitude earthquake off the coast of Chile caused a tsunami which hit the south of the country; the two events left over 520 people dead and caused widespread damage.

MARCH 2010

21. The US congress voted 219 to 212 in favour of a revised version of the healthcare reform bill passed by the senate on 24 December; the bill, signed into law by President Obama on 23 March, introduces greater regulation of health insurance providers, establishes government-run insurance exchanges and expands federal subsidies and tax breaks for health insurance, which will become mandatory for all American citizens by 2016. **31.** President Obama announced that his administration would consider leasing 67,000,000ha (167,000,000 acres) of US coastal waters off the central and southern Atlantic seaboard and the north coast of Alaska for oil and gas drilling, a policy intended to reduce the country's dependency on imported energy.

APRIL 2010

1. In two cities in north-eastern Mexico, members of the New Federation – an alliance between the Gulf, Sinaloa and La Familia Michoacana drug cartels – blockaded troops inside their barracks to prevent them responding to earlier clashes between the army and gunmen in a nearby town; 18 cartel members were killed in the ensuing fighting. **4.** The US House of Representatives' foreign affairs committee recognised the killings of Armenians by Turkish troops during the First World War as genocide; Turkey recalled its ambassador to Washington. **5.** Heavy rainstorms caused floods and landslides in Rio de Janeiro, Brazil, which killed over 200 people, most of them residents of hillside slums. **6.** The US government published a revised nuclear weapons strategy, undertaking not to develop any new nuclear weapons and curtailing the conditions under which the country would use them. **8.** In Prague, President Obama and President Medvedev of Russia signed a new nuclear arms reduction treaty, replacing the Strategic Arms Reduction Treaty signed in 1991. **12.** President Obama hosted a two-day summit on the global threat of nuclear weapons, at which he solicited support for further sanctions against Iran **23.** The governor of the US state of Arizona enacted a punitive immigration reform bill (*see* 28 July); protests against the law were held in 70 US cities on 1 May. **26.** Manuel Noriega, the former military dicator of Panama, was extradited from the USA to France to face money-laundering charges (*see* 7 July).

MAY 2010

1. An unsuccessful car bombing attempt was made in Times Square, New York, by Faisal Shahzad, a Pakistan-born US citizen allegedly operating on behalf of Tehrik-e-Taliban Pakistan. **11.** The US government's official investigation into the explosion and loss of life on the Deepwater Horizon oil rig (*see* Environment and Science, 20 April) began its opening session in New Orleans. **15.** Canon Mary Glasspool was consecrated as a bishop of the Episcopal Church in the USA, becoming the first openly lesbian bishop in the Anglican communion. **23.** A state of emergency was declared in parts of Kingston, Jamaica, as four police stations were attacked by supporters of the gang leader Christopher 'Dudus' Coke, whom police had attempted to arrest on a US extradition warrant; on 25 and 26 May, 76 people were shot dead and 500 arrested as the armed forces raided Mr Coke's stronghold; Mr Coke was arrested on 22 June, and he was extradited to the USA to face charges of drug and weapons trafficking on 24 June. **24.** Early parliamentary elections in Trinidad and Tobago were won by the People's Partnership coalition formed by five opposition parties; Kamla Persad-Bissessar became the country's first female prime minister on 26 May. **25.** The Suriname legislative election was won by the Mega Combination coalition of opposition parties. **28.** Two Central American volcanoes, Pacaya in Guatemala and Tungaurahua in central Ecuador, erupted, prompting the evacuation of nearby residents and producing ash clouds which disrupted air traffic. **30.** Tropical storm Agatha brought torrential rain to Central America, causing floods and mudslides which killed 165 people in Guatemala, 20 in Honduras and 12 in El Salvador.

JUNE 2010

10. In a legal settlement with the city of New York's insurance company, about 10,000 rescue and clean-up workers at the site of the World Trade Centre in New York, who had allegedly received inadequate equipment and supervision, won entitlement to compensation for health problems developed as a consequence. **20.** Juan Manuel Santos, Colombia's defence minister in 2006–9, won the country's presidential election in the second round. **22.** A Louisiana court overturned the six-month moratorium on deepwater drilling in the Gulf of Mexico imposed by the US federal government in response to the continuing oil leak from the damaged Deepwater Horizon rig (*see* Environment and Science, 27 May). **23.** President Obama dismissed with immediate effect General Stanley McChrystal, the US and NATO commander in Afghanistan, after a *Rolling Stone* magazine article attributed to the general and several aides criticised senior US government officials and policies in relation to the war in Afghanistan. **27.** Countries attending the G20 summit in Toronto made a non-binding commitment to halve their budget deficits by 2013. **28.** The FBI announced the arrest of ten Russians who had lived as American citizens for years while carrying out undercover intelligence-gathering for Russia's Federal Security Service; on 8 July all ten confessed and were convicted of minor conspiracy offences, and on 9 July they were exchanged for four people imprisoned in Russia for espionage, at least three of whom had worked for the CIA or MI6. In Mexico, a candidate in the governorship election in Tamaulipas state was assassinated; responsibility was attributed to the Los Zetas drug cartel, as the state's government was widely believed to collude with the rival Gulf cartel. The US supreme court ruled by 5–4 that the constitutional right to gun ownership within the home applied in all areas of all states, potentially rendering untenable many local and state gun control laws. **30.** General David Petraeus replaced General Stanley McChrystal as US and NATO commander in Afghanistan.

JULY 2010

7. A Paris court convicted Manuel Noriega of laundering drug money in France during the 1980s, sentencing him to seven years' imprisonment and ordering the seizure of €2.3m (£1.9m) of his assets (*see* 26 April). **8.** Four US senators wrote to the British ambassador to the USA requesting an investigation into the circumstances surrounding the release of Abdelbaset al-Magrahi (*see* UK Affairs, 20 August 2009). **15.** The US senate foreign relations committee announced an inquiry into whether BP lobbied for the release of al-Magrahi to secure oil deals in Libya; after British ministers refused to travel to Washington to attend, on 27 July the senate postponed the hearing to September and the chair said that he might send investigators to the UK to interview British witnesses. **19.** The Suriname legislature elected Dési Bouterse as president. **21.** A bill legalising same-sex marriage in Argentina was signed into law by President Fernández. **22.** At a meeting of the Organisation of American States, Colombia presented evidence to substantiate its claim that Venezuela was harbouring

1,500 FARC rebels; Venezuela rejected the claims and severed diplomatic ties with Colombia. **24.** The Peruvian government declared a state of emergency in 16 of its 25 regions in response to extreme winter temperatures, which had fallen as low as −24°C in parts of the south, causing over 400 deaths. **25.** The whistleblowing website WikiLeaks published 92,201 of the US military's internal records of its actions in Afghanistan between January 2004 and December 2009; the files detailed 144 unpublicised incidents in which civilians were killed or injured by coalition forces, described the technology used in and the nature and number of attacks by and against the Taliban, and revealed the existence of both a 'kill or capture' list of wanted Taliban and al-Qaida figures and a NATO special forces unit tasked with seizing or killing its members. **28.** A US federal judge granted a preliminary injunction against several provisions of an immigration law due to take effect in Arizona on 29 July, including one which required state police to determine the citizenship status of anyone they arrest or reasonably suspect to be an illegal immigrant, and another which made it illegal for a foreign-born individual not to carry immigration papers; the federal government had filed a lawsuit challenging the constitutionality of the measures. **29.** Ignacio 'Nacho' Coronel, one of the leaders of the Sinaloa drug cartel, was killed in a shoot-out with the Mexican army in Guadalajara.

ASIA

AUGUST 2009

3. Trial by jury was reintroduced in Japan; it had been abolished in 1943. **4.** The former US president Bill Clinton visited North Korea and met the leader Kim Jong-il, securing the release of two American journalists who had been sentenced in June 2009 to 12 years' hard labour for entering the country illegally. **8.** Typhoon Morakot struck Taiwan, causing mudslides that killed over 460 people; the south-eastern coast of China, the Philippines and Japan were also affected. **11.** The Burmese pro-democracy leader Aung San Suu Kyi was convicted of breaching the terms of her house arrest by receiving an uninvited American visitor, John Yettaw, and was sentenced to three years' imprisonment, commuted to a further 18 months' house arrest. **12.** Fighting between Taliban militants and the forces of a pro-government tribal chief in Pakistan's South Waziristan border region left over 70 people dead. **15.** It was reported that on 27 July President Karzai of Afghanistan had enacted by decree the Shia Personal Status Law, granting numerous powers over family and sexual matters to Shia men, often at the expense of women's rights enshrined in the constitution. **17.** The parents of more than 600 children suffering from lead poisoning in China's north-western Shaanxi province stormed the lead and zinc smelter responsible for the pollution that caused the children's illness. **20.** The presidential and provincial elections in Afghanistan were marred by insurgency attacks, a low turnout and allegations of widespread fraud; preliminary results released on 16 September showed that President Karzai had won the first round of the presidential election with 54.6 per cent of the votes (*see* 19 October). Chinese media reported that pollution from a manganese factory had caused lead poisoning in 1,354 schoolchildren in China's central Hunan province. **23.** Baitullah Mehsud, the head of the Islamist militant group Tehrik-i-Taliban, died from injuries sustained in a US air strike; his brother Hakimullah Mehsud was named as his successor. **29.** After weeks of tension in the Kokang (Han Chinese) special region in north-eastern Myanmar and nine days of fighting with Kokang forces, the Burmese army established its control of the region; over 30,000 people sought refuge in China. **30.** The Democratic Party of Japan (DPJ) won an overwhelming majority in elections to Japan's lower legislative house, ousting the Liberal Democratic Party, which lost power for only the second time since 1955; the DPJ leader Yukio Hatoyama became prime minister on 16 September.

SEPTEMBER 2009

2. A suicide bomb attack near Kabul killed 23 people, including Afghanistan's deputy head of intelligence. **2–4.** Thousands of Han Chinese staged protests in Urumqi, in China's Xinjiang province, accusing the authorities of failing to protect them from a spate of syringe attacks allegedly carried out by ethnic Uygurs; the Urumqi Communist party secretary and the Xinjiang chief of police were dismissed on 5 September, and the provincial party chief was removed in April 2010. **4.** A NATO air strike on two hijacked fuel tankers, thought to be intended for use in suicide attacks, killed about 120 people, believed to include 69 Taliban members, near Kunduz, Afghanistan. **11.** Chen Shui-bian, the president of Taiwan from 2000 to 2008, and his wife were sentenced to life imprisonment for corruption in Taipei. **26.** Typhoon Ketsana hit the northern Philippines, killing over 460 people; the storm and the floods and landslides that it caused also killed 163 people in Vietnam, 43 in Cambodia and 14 in Laos. **30.** Peter Galbraith, the UN deputy special representative for Afghanistan, was removed from his post after disagreeing with his superior, Kai Eide, about how to deal with the allegations of electoral irregularities in the Afghan presidential election.

OCTOBER 2009

5. Following five days of torrential rain, floods in the south Indian states of Karnataka and Andhra Pradesh killed about 250 people and displaced 750,000. **8.** A suicide car bomb at the Indian embassy in Kabul killed 17 people; the Taliban claimed responsibility. Typhoon Parma caused mudslides which killed about 290 people in northern Luzon, the Philippines' largest island. **9.** In Pakistan, a Taliban bomb killed 49 people in a Peshawar bazaar. **10.** Ten Taliban gunmen disguised as soldiers attacked the Pakistani army's headquarters in Rawalpindi, killing six soldiers and holding 45 hostages overnight; six personnel were killed the following day as army commandos retook the building. **15.** President Obama signed into law the Kerry-Lugar bill providing a $7.5bn (£4.9bn) aid package for Pakistan over five years, despite protests by Pakistani politicians, military chiefs and the public over non-binding conditions thought to encroach on Pakistani sovereignty. Raids on three police stations in Lahore, Pakistan, and the bombing of another in Kohat by Islamist militants killed 41 people. **17.** The Pakistani military mobilised over 30,000 troops in a major offensive against al-Qaida and Taliban strongholds in South Waziristan; controversially, the army entered into temporary alliances with four Islamist militant groups opposed to the Taliban. **19.** In its report on the Afghan presidential election, the UN-backed electoral complaints commission found that fraudulent votes accounted for 25 per cent of the overall total and 36 per cent of the votes cast for President Karzai; his share was reduced accordingly to 49.6 per cent, below the 50 per cent threshold for outright victory in the first round of voting, forcing a run-off election (*see* 1 November). **28.** A Taliban suicide bombing in Kabul killed five UN employees, prompting the UN to withdraw 600 of its 1,100 foreign staff from Afghanistan until March 2010. In Pakistan, a suspected Taliban car bomb killed over 120 people in a busy Peshawar market. **31.** Typhoon Mirinae, the third tropical storm to hit the Philippines in a month, killed at least 11 people.

NOVEMBER 2009

1. The second-placed candidate in the Afghan presidential election, Dr Abdullah Abdullah, withdrew his candidacy in the run-off ballot after his preconditions were refused; the following day the run-off ballot on 7 November was cancelled and President Karzai was declared the winner of the August election. **2.** The UN suspended long-term development work in Pakistan's tribal areas and the North-West Frontier province because of security concerns. **10.** The Cambodian government appointed the exiled former Thai prime minister Thaksin Shinawatra as an economic adviser; the Thai government responded by recalling its ambassador to Cambodia and cancelling a joint energy exploration agreement. **13.** A suicide truck bomb killed 13 people and partially destroyed the Peshawar headquarters of Pakistan's Inter-Services Intelligence agency. **21.** A gas explosion in a state-owned coal mine in north-eastern China killed 108 miners. **23.** On the Philippine island of Mindanao, an attack on a group travelling to submit election nomination papers left 57 people dead, including the family of an opposition candidate in the gubernatorial election and 32 journalists; a state of emergency was imposed until 5 December, and by February 2010 over 210 men connected with the Ampatuan clan had been charged with murder, including the local mayor and gubernatorial candidate Andal Ampatuan Jr and his father, Andal Ampatuan Sr. **27.** A river ferry capsized in south-west Bangladesh, killing over 70 people; on 4 December, 46 people died when a ferry capsized in north-east Bangladesh. **30.** North Korea launched a drastic revaluation of its currency at a rate of 100 old won to 1 new won, with the exchange of cash holdings limited to 100,000 won (£475 at the official rate) and a seven-day period; this wiped out the value of personal savings and entrepreneurial working capital, causing economic chaos and, reportedly, unprecedented public protests and civil disobedience.

DECEMBER 2009

1. The last 130,000 Tamil civilans held in Sri Lankan government internment camps since May 2009 were officially granted freedom of movement; over 11,000 'combatant category' prisoners reportedly remained incarcerated without charge. **4.** Six armed gunmen attacked a mosque in the Pakistani city of Rawalpindi, killing over 40 people during Friday prayers. **7.** Abdul Ahad Sahebi, the mayor of Kabul, was sentenced to four years' imprisonment for corruption. **16.** Pakistan's supreme court ruled that an amnesty decree passed in 2007, which pardoned thousands of politicians and bureaucrats facing corruption and other criminal charges, was unconstitutional, and ordered the reinstatement of several charges against President Zardari. **20.** The Communist Party of Nepal–Maoists (CPN–M) initiated a three-day general strike, in support of its demand that a new national unity government should be formed under its leadership. **27.** In a night raid in the Kunar province of Afghanistan, US special forces mistakenly shot dead eight schoolboys; the killings sparked protests throughout the country. **28.** Tehrik-e-Taliban bombed a Shia Muslim procession observing the Ashura day of mourning in Karachi, Pakistan, killing 43 people. Thai authorities began to deport 4,506 ethnic Hmong asylum seekers to Laos, where they claimed they would face oppression. **30.** An al-Qaida triple agent killed seven CIA agents and a Jordanian intelligence officer in a suicide bombing at a CIA base in Khost, Afghanistan.

JANUARY 2010

1. A suicide car bomber killed 97 people in Lakki Marwat, a town in Pakistan's North West Frontier province which had recently formed an anti-Taliban militia. **2.** A 5.3-magnitude earthquake in eastern Tajikistan left 10,000 people homeless. **26.** Mahinda Rajapaksa was re-elected for a second term in an early presidential election in Sri Lanka; the main rival candidate, General Sarath Fonseka, said he would contest the result in the courts, but he was arrested on 8 February, and in March court martial proceedings were initiated against him on charges of corruption and engaging in politics while in uniform. **28.** Five former army officers, found guilty of killing the first president of Bangladesh, Sheikh Mujibur Rahman, and around 25 other people during a coup in 1975, were executed in Dhaka. **29.** The US administration formally approved a proposed $6.3bn (£4bn) arms sales package to Taiwan; the Chinese government reacted by cancelling bilateral military and security contacts with the USA and threatening sanctions against US defence firms.

FEBRUARY 2010

5. Two bombings in Karachi, Pakistan – of a bus carrying Shia Muslims and of the hospital to which the injured were taken – left 25 people dead. **8.** Mullah Barader, believed to be the Afghan Taliban's top military commander, was captured in Karachi in a joint operation by the Pakistani and US intelligence agencies; the arrests of three other senior Afghan Taliban leaders in Pakistan were announced on 18 and 23 February. Heavy snowfall caused the first of a series of avalanches in the Salang pass, a stretch of Afghanistan's north–south highway vital as a supply route, killing 172 motorists. **12.** *The Guardian* reported that a law passed in 2007 granting immunity from prosecution to former Taliban fighters had been implemented unannounced by the Afghan government in late 2009. **13.** A major offensive by NATO and Afghan forces, Operation Moshtarak, was launched to secure government control of southern Helmand, Afghanistan. The bombing of a restaurant in Pune, India, killed 17 people; Laskhar-e-Taiba al-Alami, a previously unknown splinter group of the Pakistani Islamist militants Lakshar-e-Taiba, claimed that the attack was in response to the Indian government's refusal to discuss the disputed Kashmir region at a summit meeting with Pakistan on 25 February. **18.** A suicide bomber from the Ansar ul-Islam militant group killed 30 people at the local base of the rival Lashkar-e-Islam militant group in Pakistan's Khyber tribal region. **21.** A NATO air strike mistakenly hit a minibus convoy in southern Afghanistan, killing 27 civilians. Albader Parad, leader of a wing of the Islamic extremist group Abu Sayyaf, was among six members killed by marines in a raid on their camp on Jolo island, Philippines. **23.** President Karzai issued a decree giving him total control of the UN-backed electoral complaints commission. **25.** India and Pakistan resumed formal talks, which had been suspended following the Mumbai terrorist attacks in 2008. **26.** Thailand's supreme court found the exiled former prime minister Thakshin Shinawatra guilty on five charges of corruption, asserting that he had concealed and inappropriately pursued business interests while in office; 46bn (£923m) of his 76bn baht (£1.52bn) of frozen assets were seized.

MARCH 2010

1. An unprecedented joint editorial in 13 Chinese newspapers appealed for the reform of the *hukou* (household registration) system; under the present system, people who migrate to cities from rural areas and their children can gain only limited access to government services. **8.** In Myanmar, five electoral laws were passed in preparation for the elections expected in late 2010; the provisions maintained the military regime's control over the electoral process, barred prisoners, political prisoners, members of religious orders and insurgent groups from participating in the elections, and annulled the results of the 1990 election as they did not comply with the new laws. A Taliban car bomber in Lahore, Pakistan, killed 13 people and destroyed the Federal Investigation Agency building, where suspected militants were interrogated. **12.** Two suicide bombers attacked Pakistani military vehicles in a crowded Lahore market, killing 45 people. **13.** A series of bombings in Kandahar, Afghanistan, killed 35 people. **14.** Thousands of supporters of the United Front for Democracy against Dictatorship (UFDD), or 'red shirts', converged on Bangkok, Thailand beginning a two-month occupation of parts of the city centre in support of their demand for immediate legislative elections. **22.** The US-based internet service provider Google closed its Chinese website and began automatically redirecting Chinese users to its uncensored Hong Kong website after hacking attacks, allegedly state-sponsored, on its technology and email services in which the accounts of several Chinese dissidents were compromised; Google ended the automatic redirection on 29 June, a day before the expiry of the company's licence to operate in China, which the Chinese government confirmed on 11 July had been renewed until 2012. **26.** The South Korean navy corvette *Cheonan*, which was patrolling the country's disputed maritime boundary with North Korea, sank in the Yellow Sea with the loss of 46 crew members (*see* 20 May). **29.** Myanmar's main opposition party, the National League for Democracy, announced that it would boycott the forthcoming election because of the restrictive new electoral laws (*see* 8 March), which would require it to expel several of its leaders, including Aung San Suu Kyi, in order to contest the election; the party was dissolved on 6 May. **31.** The Afghan legislature rejected an attempt by the president to have an all-Afghan body monitor the 2010 legislative election.

APRIL 2010

1. President Karzai blamed foreign observers for the electoral fraud in the 2009 elections and accused the UN and EU of wanting a puppet government in Afghanistan. **3.** The UFDD supporters occupying central Bangkok moved their main camp to the tourist and retail district; the Thai prime minister Abhisit Vejjajiva declared a state of emergency on 7 April following a siege of the parliament building. **5.** A suicide bomber at a Pashtun nationalist rally in north-west Pakistan killed 45 people. **6.** Maoist rebels ambushed Indian paramilitary police in the central state of Chhattisgarh, killing 75 officers. **7.** Thousands attended anti-government demonstrations in the Kyrgyz capital of Bishkek and several other parts of the country; clashes between riot police and protesters in Bishkek resulted in 85 deaths, leading protesters to storm government offices, the parliament and other key buildings. President Kurmanbek Bakiyev fled Bishkek for southern Kyrgyzstan, where he attempted to muster support before going into exile on 15 April. **8.** An interim Kyrgyz government led by opposition leader Roza Otunbayeva was formed and promised to draft a revised constitution in advance of legislative elections in October 2010. Sri Lanka's early legislative election was won by the incumbent United People's Freedom Alliance, which increased its majority. The Pakistani legislature approved the reinstatement of the 1973 constitution in its original form, which returned many powers from the president to the prime minister. **10.** Thai forces attempting to clear central Bangkok of UFDD supporters clashed violently with the protesters, leaving 25 people dead. Two misdirected Pakistani air strikes in the Khyber region killed 71 people, most of them civilians. **13.** A cyclone struck Bangladesh's Rangpur region and the neighbouring Indian states of West Bengal, Assam and Bihar, killing over 150 people and destroying crops and over 100,000 homes. **14.** A 6.9-magnitude earthquake struck the Chinese province of Qinghai on the Tibetan plateau, followed by 17 forceful aftershocks; the earthquake killed 2,700 people and destroyed the majority of buildings in the worst affected areas. **15.** A UN enquiry into the assassination of Benazir Bhutto, the former prime minister of Pakistan, in 2007 condemned inadequate security measures taken by the authorities and found that Pakistani military intelligence had wilfully destroyed evidence from the scene.

MAY 2010

3. The only surviving perpetrator of the Mumbai terrorist attack in 2008, Mohammad Ajmal Amir Kasab, was convicted of murder, waging war on India and related charges; on 6 May he was sentenced to death by hanging. **10.** Benigno 'Noynoy' Aquino III, the Liberal party candidate, won the presidential election in the Philippines; in the simultaneous legislative election, the Lakas Kampi–Christian Muslim Democrats won the most seats in the lower legislative chamber but without an overall majority. **13.** The Thai government ordered troops to clear UFDD protesters occupying central Bangkok after they ignored a deadline to disperse, beginning six days of violence that resulted in over 40 deaths; as troops surrounded the camps, a renegade general who had sided with the protesters was shot and fatally wounded. **17.** A landmine planted by Maoist rebels killed 36 people in the central Indian state of Chattisgarh. **19.** The Thai army stormed the UFDD camp in central Bangkok, prompting the protest leaders to surrender and tell their supporters to disperse; rioting broke out in the northern cities of Udon Thani, Khon Kaen and Chiang Mai. **20.** An international investigation into the sinking of the South Korean corvette *Cheonan* found that a North Korean submarine had torpedoed the vessel; on 24 May South Korea announced the cessation of all trade with North Korea, and banned the country's ships from using its sea lanes. **22.** An Air India flight crashed on landing near Mangalore, southern India, killing 158 of the 166 people on board. **28.** Nepal's constituent assembly reached the end of its term without agreeing a new constitution, and its term was extended by one year. A passenger train was derailed in West Bengal, India, killing over 60 people; Maoist rebels were believed to be responsible. Armed militants describing themselves as the Punjabi Taliban killed 80 people in attacks on two mosques belonging to the Ahmaddiya movement, a heterodox sect of Islam, in Lahore, Pakistan. **31.** Al-Qaida announced the death of Mustafa Abu al-Yazid (also known as Sheikh Said al-Masri), its operations commander in Afghanistan, who had apparently been killed by a US air strike in north-west Pakistan during the previous fortnight.

JUNE 2010

2. The Japanese prime minister Yukio Hatoyama resigned after eight months in office; his support had plummeted after he reneged in May 2010 on an election pledge to relocate the US air base on Okinawa island, a decision which caused the Social Democrat party to resign from the coalition government. **3.** At least 117 people were killed in a tenement block fire in Dhaka, Bangladesh. **4.** Naoto Kan was appointed prime minister of Japan in succession to Yukio Hatoyama. A three-day Consultative Peace Jirga in Afghanistan ended with delegates making 16 recommendations, including the establishment of a peace commission to oversee negotiations with insurgents. **6.** Registration of parties for the Burmese election closed with 33 parties registered, including six allied to the government and one established by former members of the National League for Democracy. **7.** A court in Bhopal, India, sentenced seven former managers at the Indian subsidiary of Union Carbide, a US-based chemical and polymer company, to two years in prison on criminal negligence charges relating to their responsibility for a gas leak in the city in 1984 which caused 25,000 deaths and serious medical problems for thousands; the men, who also received fines of £1,400 each, were released on bail pending an appeal. **10.** Violent clashes between ethnic Kyrgyz and Uzbeks in Kyrgyzstan's southern city of Osh and the surrounding area resulted in an estimated 2,000 deaths in five days. **11.** The transitional Kyrgyz government declared a state of emergency in the Osh area and deployed troops to secure Osh, where Uzbek districts suffered most from arson and looting; by 14 June about 100,000 of the 500,000 displaced Uzbeks had fled across the border to Uzbekistan. **14.** The Afghan Taliban reportedly kidnapped 40 Pakistani soldiers from a checkpoint in Pakistan's Mohmand tribal area. **17.** Floods and landslides killed 57 people in western Myanmar and 55 people in neighbouring areas of Bangladesh. **20.** Severe floods in southern China affected about 10 million people and caused 132 deaths. **27.** In a referendum, Kyrgyz voters approved a proposed new constitution, which would establish a parliamentary system of government with diminished presidential power. **30.** The Nepali prime minister Madhav Kumar Nepal resigned, having failed to end a deadlock with the CPN–M, which, as the largest party in parliament, continued to protest its entitlement to lead the coalition government; he remained in post until a new government could be formed.

JULY 2010

1. China's state news agency Xinhua launched an international English-language news channel, China Xinhua News Network Corporation World, initially broadcast in Hong Kong but with global satellite coverage planned by the end of 2010. **2.** Suicide bombers killed 42 people in an attack on a shrine complex in Lahore, Pakistan; no group claimed responsibility. **7.** The Indian army was deployed and a curfew imposed in Srinagar, Kashmir, following weeks of protests in which 15 people were killed. **9.** Two suicide bombers killed 62 people in Pakistan's Mohmand tribal region. **11.** Japan's coalition government lost control of the upper legislative house in national elections. **23.** A NATO rocket attack was alleged to have killed 52 civilians in Helmand province, Afghanistan; NATO said it was investigating the incident. The government of Pakistan extended the tenure of the army chief, General Ashraq Kayani, by an unprecedented three years. **26.** The war crimes tribunal in Cambodia sentenced Kaing Guek Eav, or 'Comrade Duch', to 35 years in prison (reduced by the 16 years he had already served) for war crimes and crimes against humanity; he had been the chief jailer at a detention centre where over 16,000 people were killed under the Khmer Rouge regime in the late 1970s. **27.** Abnormally heavy monsoon rain caused devastating floods across much of Pakistan, causing severe flooding throughout the Indus river valley; up to 20 million people were affected and at least 1,600 killed. **28.** A Pakistani Airbus on an internal flight crashed outside Islamabad, killing all 152 passengers and crew. **30.** A major offensive by NATO and Afghan forces, Operation Tor Shezada (Black Prince), was launched to secure government control of central Helmand, Afghanistan.

AUSTRALASIA AND THE PACIFIC

AUGUST 2009

5. A ferry capsized off the coast of Tonga, killing over 90 passengers. **13.** The Australian senate voted out a government bill that would have introduced a carbon emissions trading scheme and imposed a carbon emission tax on industry from 2011. **27.** The UN's special rapporteur on the human rights of indigenous peoples denounced restrictions imposed on Aboriginal communities in Australia's Northern Territory, which included bans on alcohol and pornography and the imposition of conditions on the spending of welfare payments, as overtly discriminatory, and illegal under international treaties.

SEPTEMBER 2009

1. Fiji was suspended from the Commonwealth after the military government refused to commit to holding elections in 2010. **2.** A 7.0-magnitude earthquake off the coast of Java, Indonesia, left about 80 dead. Iolu Abil was elected president of Vanuatu in the third round of voting. **29.** Samoa, American Samoa and northern Tonga were hit by tsunamis caused by an 8.1-magnitude subterranean earthquake; over 220 people died and many buildings were destroyed. **30.** A 7.6-magnitude earthquake struck the Indonesian island of Sumatra, killing over 1,110 people and causing serious damage to thousands of buildings.

OCTOBER 2009

21. President Litokwa Tomeing of the Marshall Islands was ousted in a no-confidence vote in the legislature; on 26 October the speaker, Jurelang Zedkaia, was elected as his successor.

NOVEMBER 2009

5. Ratu Epeli Nailatikau was sworn in as president of Fiji, after serving as interim president since July.

DECEMBER 2009

1. Tony Abbott was elected leader of Australia's Liberal party by a narrow margin. **2.** The Australian government bill introducing a carbon emissions trading scheme was defeated in the senate for a second time (*see* 13 August). **15.** Nauru formally recognised the independence of the breakaway Georgian regions of Abkhazia and, the following day, South Ossetia; Russia, which supports the new republics, had reportedly agreed to provide funding of $50m (£30.7m) in funding in Nauru.

JANUARY 2010
4. A 7.2-magnitude earthquake caused landslides and a tsunami which destroyed around 200 houses in the Solomon Islands; no casualties were reported but about 1,000 were left homeless.

MARCH 2010
3. The Fijian high court convicted eight men of conspiracy to assassinate Frank Bainimarama, then interim prime minister, in 2007; the men were sentenced to between three and seven years in prison. A court in Timor Leste convicted 23 people of attempting to assassinate the president and prime minister in 2008 and sentenced them to between nine and 16 years in prison; five defendants were acquitted.

APRIL 2010
21. The prime minister of the Solomon Islands, Derek Sikua, dismissed five cabinet ministers for their failure to support his attempts to reform the political system; their absence from a parliamentary vote on the reform bill contributed to its defeat. **24.** A legislative election in Nauru failed to resolve the deadlock over the budget, as the parliament remained evenly split and was unable to elect a speaker or a new president.

JUNE 2010
19. Another legislative election was held in Nauru in an attempt to resolve the political impasse, which resulted in another hung parliament. **23.** The Australian prime minister Kevin Rudd resigned as Labour party leader rather than contest the party leadership, which he was expected to lose; his deputy, Julia Gillard, was elected party leader unopposed on 24 June, becoming Australia's first female prime minister.

JULY 2010
5. The indigenous tribes of the Torres Strait, a group of over 250 islands off the north coast of Australia, won native title rights over 40,000 sq. km of the surrounding sea. **17.** The new Australian prime minister, Julia Gillard, called a general election for 21 August.

EUROPE

AUGUST 2009
6. Russia and Turkey signed an agreement to construct a natural gas pipeline from Russia's Black Sea coast to western Europe via Turkish waters. **8.** The Italian government legalised and set out operational guidelines for vigilante patrols. Four opposition parties in Moldova agreed to form a coalition, giving the bloc a narrow majority over the Communists, the largest party after the July 2009 election; the coalition government took office on 25 September. **12.** The Russian prime minister, Vladimir Putin, announced spending plans that allocated 15bn roubles (£314m) to strengthening Russia's military presence in the breakaway Georgian republic of Abkhazia. **16.** The MV *Arctic Sea*, a Maltese cargo ship officially carrying a £1.1m cargo of timber from Finland to Algeria, which disappeared shortly after passing through the English Channel on 28 July, was detected by the Russian navy off the Cape Verde islands; eight hijackers were arrested and later charged by Russian prosecutors. **17.** A truck bomb attack by Chechen rebels in the southern Russian republic of Ingushetia killed 25 people. **22.** The Greek government declared a state of emergency as forest fires spread across 120,000ha (297 acres) around the northern suburbs of Athens; over 20,000 people fled their homes before the fires were brought under control on 25 August.

SEPTEMBER 2009
12. A German merchant ship became the first western commercial vessel to successfully navigate the Russian north-east passage through the Arctic Sea. **14.** In Norway's legislative election, the incumbent three-party coalition narrowly won a second term in office. **16.** Jose Manuel Barroso was re-elected for a second five-year term as president of the European Commission. A new three-party coalition government was approved by the Albanian legislature. **22.** French police cleared 'the Jungle', a large shanty town in Calais housing predominantly Afghan asylum seekers attempting to enter Britain, and detained 278 people. **27.** In Germany's federal elections the Christian Democrats–Christian Social Union won the most seats and combined with the Free Democrat party to form a coalition government under Angela Merkel, who was re-elected chancellor on 28 October. Portugal's legislative election was won by the Socialist party, which remained the largest party but lost its overall majority; the incumbent prime minister, José Socrates, was unable to form a coalition so took office at the head of a minority government.

OCTOBER 2009
1. Social Democratic Party ministers in Romania's coalition government resigned in solidarity with interior minister Dan Nica, dismissed by Prime Minister Emil Boc over electoral fraud allegations; the government, now a minority, lost a vote of confidence on 13 October and resigned. **3.** In a second referendum, 67.1 per cent of Irish voters approved the Lisbon EU reform treaty. **4.** A snap general election in Greece was won by the opposition Pan-Hellenic Socialist Movement (PASOK), whose leader, George Papandreou, was sworn in as prime minister on 6 October. **7.** Italy's constitutional court overturned a 2008 law which granted immunity from prosecution to the prime minister, president and the speakers of both chambers of parliament. **10.** The Armenian and Turkish governments signed an accord to normalise their relations and establish diplomatic ties between the two countries; its protocols remained subject to parliamentary ratification. Poland ratified the Lisbon treaty. **19.** Aitor Elizarán Aguilar, believed to be the political chief of the Basque separatist organisation Eta, was arrested by French anti-terrorism police in Brittany. **26.** The trial of the former Serbian warlord Radovan Karadzic, indicted on two counts of genocide against Bosnian Muslims in 1992 and 1995 and nine other war crimes charges, opened at the International Criminal Tribunal for the former Yugoslavia in the Hague; Mr Karadzic boycotted the proceedings, and on 6 November the trial was adjourned until 1 March 2010. **27.** A Paris court convicted 42 defendants, including prominent politicians, businessmen and artists, of various charges relating to the illegal sale of £450m worth of weapons to the Angolan government between 1993 and 1998; the same court found the

Church of Scientology guilty of defrauding believers of money with false scientific claims, fining it €600,000 (£545,000). **31.** Italian police arrested Salvatore Russo, head of a Mafia clan which controlled organised crime in the Naples area.

NOVEMBER 2009

3. The Czech Republic ratified the Lisbon treaty (*see* 1 December), having secured an opt-out from the EU's charter of fundamental rights. **4.** An Italian court convicted *in absentia* 23 former CIA agents of kidnapping, for their involvement in the 'extraordinary rendition' of an Egyptian suspected terrorist abducted from Milan in 2003. **13.** The Turkish interior minister outlined government plans to end the 25-year conflict with the Kurds in south-eastern Turkey. **16.** The Russian television journalist Olga Kotovskaya died in mysterious circumstances in Kaliningrad a day after winning a court battle to regain control of her independent news channel, Kaskad, from local bureaucrats who had seized it in 2004; a criminal investigation was launched. **19.** A summit of EU heads of government appointed Herman Van Rompuy, the prime minister of Belgium, president of the European Council and Lady Ashton of Upholland, the European commissioner for trade, as the EU's high representative for foreign and security policy. **24.** Yves Leterme was appointed prime minister of Belgium in place of Herman Van Rompuy. **25.** The Christian Brothers, a Roman Catholic order found by the Ryan report of May 2009 to be responsible for most known cases of child abuse committed in Ireland between 1914 and 2000, offered €161m (£145m) in cash and land as reparation to the government and to its victims; on 3 December, another order found responsible for abuse, the Sisters of Mercy order, offered €128 (£117) in compensation. **26.** The German army's chief of staff, Wolfgang Schneiderhan, resigned following the disclosure that the defence ministry had withheld information about civilian casualties of a German-led NATO air strike in Afghanistan on 4 September 2009; the defence minister, Franz Josef Jung, resigned the following day. The Irish government published a damning report criticising the Roman Catholic Church in Ireland for its handling of child abuse allegations against members of the clergy; the Murphy report found that police officials, four archbishops and other senior clergy had colluded in covering up the sexual and physical abuse of children by clerics within the Dublin diocese (*see* 17 December). **27.** An express train from Moscow to St Petersburg was bombed and derailed, killing 39 people, including several senior government officials; the 'Caucasian Mujahideen' claimed responsibility. **29.** In Switzerland, a ban on the construction of minarets on mosques was approved by 57.5 per cent of voters in a national referendum.

DECEMBER 2009

1. The Lisbon treaty entered into force. Italian police announced that they had broken up the Parisi Mafia clan, arresting 74 people and seizing about €220m (£199m) in assets. **4.** An explosion caused by indoor fireworks killed 149 people in Perm, Russia. **6.** President Traian Basescu of Romania was narrowly elected to a second term in office. **7.** For the second time in 2009, the Moldovan legislature was too divided to elect a president; the constitution required a legislative election to be held, but prevented this being called within 12 months of the previous election, so it had to be postponed until July 2010. **9.** The Irish government announced an austerity budget, making substantial cuts in public sector pay, social welfare and capital spending. **11.** Turkey's constitutional court banned the Democratic Society party, the only pro-Kurdish party in parliament. **13.** The Italian prime minister, Silvio Berlusconi, was assaulted during a rally in Milan. **17.** After two nominees as prime minister had failed to form a government, the outgoing Romanian prime minister Emil Boc was renominated; his new coalition government was approved by parliament on 23 December. The Bishop of Limerick resigned, as did the Bishop of Kildare and Leighlin on 23 December, both admitting their failure to challenge the Roman Catholic Church's handling of child abuse cases earlier in their careers. **22.** Serbia formally applied for membership of the European Union. The European court of human rights ruled that Bosnia and Hercegovina's constitution violated fundamental human rights by preventing citizens of ethnicities other than Muslim, Serb or Croat from standing for elected office; reform was called for as a prerequisite of the country's accession to the EU. **24.** Greece's parliament approved the government's austerity budget, although the budget was criticised by the EU and credit rating agencies as not sufficiently radical.

JANUARY 2010

7. After youths assaulted a group of African immigrant farmworkers in the southern Italian town of Rosarno, around 100 fellow immigrants rioted; the following day a protest march by immigrants met with violence from residents; by 10 January over 1,100 immigrants, most of whom were Ghanaian, had been by evacuated from the area or detained by the authorities. **8.** Portugal's parliament passed a bill permitting gay marriage. **10.** Ivo Josipovic, the Social Democrat party candidate, won the Croatian presidential election. **15.** The Greek government submitted an economic recovery plan to the EU and the European Central Bank; its austerity measures faced strong domestic opposition, prompting weeks of strikes and demonstrations. **28.** In Paris, the former French prime minister Dominique de Villepin was acquitted on all charges of complicity in slanderous corruption allegations made against Nicolas Sarkozy, then finance minister, and around 40 other prominent politicians in 2004, though two other men were convicted.

FEBRUARY 2010

7. Viktor Yanukovych, the Party of the Regions candidate and a former president and prime minister, was elected president of Ukraine. **15.** A head-on train crash in Belgium killed 18 passengers. **18.** The Irish defence minister Willie O'Dea resigned after an audio recording proved that he had falsely accused a Sinn Fein rival of running a brothel. **20.** The Labour party withdrew from the Dutch coalition government over differences with the prime minister about Dutch military involvement in Afghanistan; the prime minister, Jan Peter Balkenende, resigned on 23 February and was reappointed as head of a caretaker government until elections in June. Torrential rain caused flooding and landslides on the Portuguese island of Madeira, killing at least 43 people. **22.** In a nationwide operation, Turkish police arrested 49 senior and former military officers over an alleged plot, 'Sledgehammer', to overthrow the government in 2002–3; further arrests followed, and by 26 February 31 people had been charged. **24.** An estimated two million Greek workers observed a general strike against recently announced government spending cuts, which included the reduction of public sector pay, pensions and recruitment freezes and tax rises. **28.** Ibon Gogeaskoetxea, the suspected leader of the Basque separatist group Eta, and two other senior Eta members were arrested in Normandy in a joint French-Spanish police operation.

MARCH 2010

1. At the International Criminal Tribunal for the former Yugoslavia, Radovan Karadzic denied all charges in a belligerent opening statement in his own defence. The sole border crossing between Russia and Georgia was reopened, having been closed since 2006. **3.** The Ukranian government lost a vote of confidence and the prime minister, Yuliya Tymoshenko, resigned immediately; on 11 March a new three-party coalition government, headed by the Party of Regions leader Mykola Azarov, was approved by parliament. The Greek government announced additional spending cuts and tax increases. **6.** In a referendum in Iceland, 93 per cent of voters rejected a government proposal to reimburse the British and Dutch governments for the €3.8bn (£3.2bn) they dispersed in compensation to depositors with Icesave, an Icelandic bank which failed in 2008. **17.** The People's Party withdrew from Latvia's coalition government after differences over financial policy, leaving the government without a majority. **20.** Pope Benedict XVI issued a letter apologising to the people of Ireland and the victims of child sex abuse by the Roman Catholic clergy there. **23.** The UK government expelled a senior Israeli diplomat believed to be the Mossad chief in London, after a criminal investigation concluded that Israel's intelligence services had forged British passports used by the assassins of Mahmoud al-Mabhouh (*see* Middle East, 19 January). **26.** The Portuguese parliament approved the government's austerity measures. **29.** Two female suicide bombers, members of the Black Widow group associated with Chechen separatists, killed 40 people in two attacks on Moscow's metro system.

APRIL 2010

8. President Medvedev of Russia and President Obama of the USA signed a new nuclear arms reduction treaty, replacing the Strategic Arms Reduction Treaty signed in 1991. **10.** President Lech Kaczynski and dozens of Polish political and military leaders were among 96 people killed when their plane crashed while landing in fog at Smolensk airport, Russia, as they travelled to a memorial ceremony. **11.** The opposition party Fidesz won the first round of Hungary's legislative election, and increased its majority in the second round of voting on 25 April; a government with Fidesz party leader Viktor Orban as prime minister was sworn in on 29 May. **14.** The ash cloud created by the eruption of Iceland's Eyjafjallajokull volcano began to drift towards Europe and caused the closure of airports and airspace throughout north-western Europe by the evening of 15 April, and in much of central and eastern Europe by 16 April; most states relaxed restrictions on 20 and 21 April. **18.** Dervis Eroglu, an opponent of the reunification of Cyprus, won a leadership election in Turkish-backed northern Cyprus, unseating the pro-reunification incumbent Mehmet Ali Talat. **21.** Russia's lease on naval facilities in the Ukranian port of Sevastopol was extended beyond its original 2017 expiry date until at least 2042, in return for Ukraine receiving a 30 per cent discount on gas imported from Russia; Ukraine's parliament ratified the extension on 27 April, despite a brawl erupting during the debate. **22.** The Armenian parliament suspended ratification of the agreement normalising relations with Turkey, after the Turkish prime minister said that Armenia should resolve its dispute with Azerbaijan. The Flemish Liberal Party withdrew from the Belgian coalition government. **25.** In Austria's presidential election, the incumbent president, Heinz Fischer, was re-elected for a second term. **26.** The Belgian prime minister, Yves Leterme, resigned; the lower house was dissolved on 6 May and a legislative election called for June (*see* 13 June).

MAY 2010

5. Three bank employees were killed in central Athens when their building was firebombed during a general strike and nationwide protests against budget cuts under debate in the parliament. **6.** The Greek legislature approved a stringent new round of budget cuts representing savings of €30bn (£25.7bn), which were required by the EU and IMF in return for financial aid. **11.** In an interview given en route to Portugal, Pope Benedict XVI said that the clerical child sex abuse scandal showed that the greatest threat to the Roman Catholic Church was from 'sin within' the church. **27.** The Spanish legislature approved the government's spending cuts by one vote. **29.** In the Czech legislative election, the Social Democratic party and the Civic Democrats won 56 and 53 seats respectively, while smaller parties gained ground (*see* 28 June). **31.** Horst Köhler resigned as president of Germany following hostile public reaction to his comments in a radio interview on 22 May, in which he argued for economic self-interest as a motivation for recent German military interventions overseas.

JUNE 2010

9. Elections to the lower house in the Netherlands produced an inconclusive result, with the People's Party for Freedom and Democracy (VVD) winning 31 seats, the Labour party 30, the far-right Freedom party 24 and the Christian Democratic Appeal party 21; negotiation of a coalition government was still continuing in August 2010. **10.** The International Criminal Tribunal for the former Yugoslavia sentenced two Bosnian Serbs, Ljubisa Beara and Vujadin Popovic, to life imprisonment for their roles in the massacre of over 5,330 Muslim men and boys at Srebrenica in 1995; five other defendents were convicted of lesser, related crimes. **12.** Russia's security service announced the capture of Ali Taziyev, believed to be the military commander of the Caucasian Mujahideen separatists. In the Slovakian legislative election, the Smer-SD party remained the largest party but without an overall majority, and it was unable to negotiate a coalition; four centre-right parties formed a coalition on 6 July and a coalition government took office under Iveta Radicova on 8 July. **13.** In elections to Belgium's lower house, the New Flemish Alliance, a Flemish separatist party, became the largest party with 27 seats, narrowly ahead of the francophone Socialist party, with 26 seats; negotiation of a coalition government was still continuing in August 2010. **16.** Turkish troops mounted an incursion across the border into Iraq's Kurdish region, killing four Kurdish rebels who had attacked a Turkish unit. The interim president of Moldova announced that new elections would not be held until after a referendum in September 2010 on whether the country should revert to direct presidential elections. **17.** A Dutch court sentenced five Somali men to five years in prison for robbery at sea; the men had attempt to hijack a Netherlands Antilles-registered ship in the Gulf of Aden in January 2009. **18.** Matti Vanhanen stood down as prime minister of Finland and KESK party leader; he was succeeded in both positions on 22 June by Mari Kiviniemi. **19.** Eleven Turkish soldiers and 12 PKK guerillas were killed in fighting in southern Turkey. **21.** Russia began incremental daily reductions in natural gas supplies to Belarus until 24 June, when the supply was restored after Belarus repaid an outstanding debt of £133m for earlier gas supplies. **24.** Belgian police raided the Roman Catholic Church's national headquarters in Mechelen in search of evidence of sexual abuse by members of the clergy. **28.** Petr Necas, leader of the Civic Democrats, was appointed prime minister of the Czech Republic; his government, a coalition of the Civic Democrats, TOP09 and Public Affairs parties, was sworn in on 13 July. Italian police arrested 24 people, seized over €100m (£81.4m) in cash and property and sequestered over 100 companies in an operation against two money-laundering networks, which had allegedly smuggled an estimated €2.7bn (£2.3bn) to China since 2006; most of the money was generated by a Tuscany-based fashion-counterfeiting operation. **29.** Pal Schmitt was elected president of Hungary by the legislature. **30.** The German presidential election was won by Christian Wulff, the candidate of the ruling coalition.

JULY 2010

4. The presidential election in Poland was won by the Civic Platform candidate Bronislaw Komorowski, who had been acting president since the death of President Lech Kaczynski. **6.** A new customs union between Russia, Belarus and Kazakhstan came into effect. **13.** In a nationwide operation, Italian police arrested over 300 suspected members of the powerful Calabria-based Ndrangheta crime syndicate, including its presumed leader, Domenico Oppedisano. **19.** A Greek investigative journalist, Sokratis Giolas, was murdered by gunmen in Athens; a left-wing terrorist group, the Sect of Revolutionaries, claimed responsibility. **23.** The International Court of Justice ruled that Kosovo's unilateral declaration of independence from Serbia in February 2008 was legal under international law; Serbia, which had sought the court's non-binding opinion, maintained its opposition to Kosovo's statehood. **27.** Iceland began accession negotiations with the EU. **29.** President Medvedev of Russia signed a law granting the Federal Security Service the right to caution people it believes are preparing to commit a crime, and providing for prison sentences for obstruction of the agency's work. **30.** In Italy, Gianfranco Fini, co-founder of Silvio Berlusconi's Freedom People party, and 33 of its MPs defected to set up a new parliamentary group, Future and Freedom for Italy; the split left the coalition government five seats short of a parliamentary majority.

MIDDLE EAST

AUGUST 2009

1. In Tehran, Iran, the trials began of over 100 protesters against the controversial outcome of the presidential election in June 2009, charged with involvement in a foreign-backed conspiracy to overthrow the state. **3.** The supreme leader of Iran, Ayatollah Khamenei, formally endorsed the re-election of President Mahmoud Ahmadinejad; two former presidents, Hojatoleslam Rafsanjani and Mohammad Khatami, boycotted Ahmadinejad's swearing-in ceremony on 5 August. **7.** Bomb attacks on Shia pilgrims and worshippers throughout Iraq left 37 dead; a further 48 were killed on 10 August. **11.** Yemeni forces launched a major offensive against Houthi rebels, from the minority Shia Zaidi sect, in north-west Yemen. **25.** Syria and Iraq recalled their envoys in a diplomatic crisis sparked by Iraqi accusations that Syria was harbouring two insurgents responsible for recent devastating bombings in Baghdad. **30.** Ehud Olmert, who stood down as prime minister of Israel in 2008, was indicted on fraud and corruption charges relating to his time as mayor of Jerusalem; his trial began on 25 September.

SEPTEMBER 2009

8. With the parties in the new Lebanese coalition government unable to agree on the distribution of portfolios, the prime minister-designate, Saad al-Hariri, unilaterally nominated a cross-party government, but this was rejected in the legislature; al-Hariri resigned his mandate on 10 September, but was reappointed on 16 September (*see* 9 November). **15.** The report of a UN inquiry into the Israeli offensive against Gaza between December 2008 and January 2009 (the Goldstone report) concluded that both Israel and Hamas had committed war crimes, and recommended that the situation in Gaza should be referred to the International Criminal Court if the Israeli government and the Palestinian authorities failed to meet the UN security council's requirements. **17.** An air raid on a refugee camp in northern Yemen left over 80 civilians dead; the Yemeni government claimed that the dead were Houthi rebels. **18.** Thousands of Iranians took part in renewed anti-government demonstrations in Tehran and other cities, taking over anti-Israel rallies held as part of the state-organised al-Quds (Jerusalem) day. **25.** The International Atomic Energy Agency (IAEA) disclosed that President Ahmadinejad of Iran had revealed in a recent letter to it the existence of a second uranium enrichment plant in Iran, under construction near the city of Qom since mid 2006 (*see* 1 October). **27.** Iran began two days of missile-testing, including of two types of long-range missiles capable of reaching Israel and US bases in the Gulf.

OCTOBER 2009

1. At a meeting in Geneva with the 'E3+3' (Britain, France, Germany, the USA, Russia and China), Iran agreed in principle to send about 75 per cent of its low-enriched uranium abroad for further processing into fuel for its medical research reactor. **4.** The Iranian government agreed that the IAEA could inspect its Qom uranium enrichment plant. **8.** A Tehran court passed the first death sentences in the mass trials that began in August. **18.** Jundallah, an ethnic Baloch insurgent group in Iran, claimed responsibility for the suicide bombing of a convoy of Revolutionary Guards in Sistan-Baluchistan province. **23.** Iran failed to meet the deadline for sealing the agreement reached on 1 October, instead presenting its own proposals, which included buying higher enriched uranium from abroad and other measures that would involve waiving UN sanctions against Iran. The Palestinian president Mahmoud Abbas called presidential and legislative elections for January 2010, after Hamas, which controls Gaza, refused to sign an Egyptian-brokered agreement ending its two-year rift with Fatah, which controls the West Bank and had already signed the agreement; in November 2009 the elections were postponed indefinitely after Hamas refused to allow voting in Gaza. **25.** Two truck bombs killed 155 people in Baghdad, one gutting the justice ministry and the second badly damaging the Baghdad governate building; the Islamic State of Iraq, an al-Qaeda affiliate, claimed responsibility. Israeli police stormed Jerusalem's al-Aqsa mosque, Islam's third-holiest site, following a violent protest by Palestinian youths over access and rights to the compound.

NOVEMBER 2009

4. Israeli special forces intercepted and seized a ship off the coast of Cyprus which was allegedly carrying over 500 tonnes of Iranian munitions destined for the Lebanon-based militant group Hezbollah. Yemen's Houthi rebels killed a Saudi border patrol; Saudi air and artillery reprisal attacks on 5 November killed 40 Yemeni men. **9.** In Lebanon, a 30-member national unity cabinet was appointed under Saad al-Hariri; it included 15 ministers from al-Hariri's '14 March' alliance, ten from the '8 March' alliance and five independents selected by President Suleiman. **10.** Saudi Arabia imposed a naval blockade on Yemen's Red Sea coast. **22.** Mohammad Ali Abtahi, a former vice-president of Iran and a leading reformist, received a six-year prison sentence for his part in the post-election unrest. **27.** The IAEA board passed by 25–3 a resolution calling on Iran to halt immediately the construction of its uranium enrichment plant near Qom, clarify its original purpose, and confirm it has no other hidden atomic facilities or clandestine plans for any; Iran rejected the resolution, announcing on 29 November plans to create a further 10 uranium enrichment facilities. **30.** The king of Jordan dissolved the legislature halfway through its term and called for early elections, although no date has been set.

DECEMBER 2009

8. Five coordinated car bombings in Baghdad killed 127 people; the Islamic State of Iraq insurgents claimed responsibility. **16.** The terms of office of the Palestinian president and legislature were extended indefinitely until new elections are held. **18.** Iranian soldiers seized an oil well 300m inside Iraq's south-east border, escalating an ownership dispute; the troops pulled back to a distance of 50m on 20 December. **27.** In Iran, the Ashura festival, which coincided with the seventh day of mourning for the Grand Ayatollah Montazeri, provided the opposition Green Movement with an opportunity to stage anti-government protests in a number of cities; violent confrontations between protesters and the security forces left eight dead. **30.** Two suicide bombings in Ramadi, Iraq, killed 23 people; the provincial governor, thought to be the main target, was severely injured.

JANUARY 2010

15. Iraq's independent electoral commission banned 500 candidates, over 400 of them Sunni, from contesting the elections in March because of their alleged past connections with the banned Ba'ath party; the ban was overturned on 3 February. Yemeni forces reportedly killed Qasim al-Raimi, the military leader of al-Qaida in the Arabian Peninsula, and four of his lieutenants in a missile strike. **17.** Ali Hassan al-Majid, a cousin of the former Iraqi president Saddam Hussein known as 'Chemical Ali', received his fourth death sentence after being found guilty of ordering the 1988 poison gas attack on the Kurdish town of Halabja which killed more than 5,000 people; he was hanged on 25 January. **19.** A senior Hamas leader, Mahmoud al-Mabhouh, was assassinated in a Dubai hotel by members of a 26-strong team who travelled to Dubai using fake British, Irish, French and German passports; Hamas accused the Mossad, Israel's intelligence agency, of carrying out the killing. **25.** A series of coordinated suicide bomb and gun attacks on three Baghdad hotels by the Islamic State of Iraq left over 40 people dead. An Ethiopian Airlines plane flying to Addis Ababa caught fire shortly after taking off from Beirut during a thunderstorm, crashing into the sea and killing all 90 people on board.

FEBRUARY 2010

1. About 54 Shia pilgrims travelling to a festival in the Iraqi holy city of Karbala were killed in Baghdad by a suspected al-Qaida affiliate; 63 more people were killed in Karbala in the following three days. **11.** The Yemeni government signed a ceasefire with the Houthi rebels. **16.** The US government restored full diplomatic relations with Syria; it had withdrawn its ambassador in 2005 in protest at the suspected involvement of Syria in the assassination of former Lebanese prime minister Rafik Hariri. **18.** An IAEA report setting out the questions the agency wanted Iran to answer about its nuclear programme caused international alarm at how much closer Iran was to developing weaponry than had previously been thought.

MARCH 2010

3. Three coordinated suicide bombings in Baquba, northern Iraq, killed 32 people. **7.** A legislative election was held in Iraq, amid violence that left 39 dead; the party coalitions with the greatest numbers of seats were Ayad Allawi's Iraqiya bloc (91 seats) and the incumbent prime minister al-Maliki's State of Law bloc (89 seats) but no bloc was large enough to form a government and negotiations between the parliamentary coalitions continued for some months, with the political uncertainty leading to an upsurge in violence. **9.** The Israeli interior ministry announced that it had approved the construction of 1,600 new apartments in an ultra-orthodox Jewish settlement in occupied East Jerusalem; this caused Palestinian leaders to pull out of indirect peace talks with their Israeli counterparts scheduled to begin the following day. **26.** A double bombing killed at least 40 people in a Shia area in eastern Iraq.

APRIL 2010

2. Gunmen in uniform raided a Sunni village near Baghdad, killing 25 people, many of them former members of the now disbanded Sons of Iraq, a US-funded militia; 13 suspected al-Qaida affiliates were later arrested in connection with the attack. **4.** Bombings outside the Iranian, Egyptian and Syrian embassies and the German ambassador's residence in Baghdad killed 42 people; the Islamic State of Iraq claimed responsibility. **6.** About 35 people were killed in seven coordinated bombings in Baghdad on 6 April. **18.** Abu Ayyoub al-Masri, head of al-Qaida in Iraq, and Abu Omar al-Baghdadi, leader of the affiliated Islamic State of Iraq, were killed near Tikrit in northern Iraq by US and Iraqi forces. **23.** Bombings of Shia targets by insurgents in Baghdad and elsewhere in Iraq killed 72 people. **26.** A suicide bomber attacked a convoy in Sana'a in an unsuccessful attempt to assassinate the British ambassador to Yemen; al-Qaida in the Arabian Peninsula later claimed responsibility.

MAY 2010

3. The USA renewed its sanctions against Syria, saying that it supported terrorist groups, sought weapons of mass destruction and had armed Hezbollah in Lebanon in contravention of UN resolutions. **6.** It was announced in Iraq that the State of Law bloc and the Iraqi National Alliance bloc had agreed to form a governing coalition, although this would be a few seats short of a majority in the legislature. **9.** The Israeli government and the Palestinian Authority began indirect peace talks, the first negotiations between the two for 18 months. **10.** A number of explosions and shootings in Iraq killed over 102 people, including at least 45 in three bombings in the central town of al-Hilla; al-Qaida was believed to be responsible. **17.** Iran signed an agreement with Brazil and Turkey under which it would send low-enriched uranium abroad for reprocessing into fuel rods, but would also continue to enrich uranium itself. **31.** Israeli naval commandos raided a flotilla of six ships in international waters 64km off the coast of Gaza which were carrying aid and supplies to Gaza in defiance of an Israeli blockade; during the storming of the largest vessel, MV *Mavi Marmara*, the commandos shot dead nine Turks and wounded dozens of other activists of various nationalities, some of whom the Israeli government alleged were armed.

JUNE 2010

9. The UN security council passed resolution 1929, which imposed further sanctions on Iran (the fourth set since 2006), including an expanded arms embargo and an extension of the freeze on assets to an additional 41 Iranian companies. Over 100,000 Ashkenazi *Haredi* men marched through Jerusalem in support of 43 *Haredi* parents who were to be jailed for defying a court order to return their daughters to one of their community's schools in a West Bank settlement; the government had forcibly reintegrated Sephardi and Ashkenazi girls in the school's classes. **14.** The new Iraqi legislature met for the first time since the March elections, although it was still unclear which parties would form the government. **17.** The EU announced further sanctions against Iran, including measures which prohibit investment in and technical assistance to some sectors of Iran's oil and gas industries by member states. **20.** Iran executed Abdolmalek Rigi, the leader of the Jundallah group, for orchestrating raids and bombings in the Sistan-Baluchistan province; on 16 July a retaliatory suicide bomb attack by Jundallah on a Shia mosque in Zahedan, the provincial capital, killed 28 people. The Israeli cabinet agreed on a policy which, if implemented, would significantly ease its blockade of Gaza to allow imports of products deemed to have a solely civilian use.

JULY 2010

8. The Iranian authorities postponed temporarily the execution by stoning of Sakineh Mohammadi Ashtiani, a woman convicted of adultery in 2006, after an international outcry at the sentence following a global campaign by her children to highlight her plight; it was unclear whether her execution would go ahead by other means. **15.** Dr Shahram Amiri, an Iranian nuclear scientist who had either defected to or been abducted by the USA and had passed information to the CIA, was feted upon his return to Iran; Dr Amiri had disappeared in Saudi Arabia in June 2009. **18.** A suicide bomber killed at least 45 former members of the Sons of Iraq militia as they queued outside a military base to collect government disbursements; it was the latest in a series of attacks against the group in the previous three months. The Syrian government introduced a bill that would ban the wearing of the *niqab* veil in universities. **29.** Israeli planes bombed Gaza City, the first air raid for 18 months, in retaliation for a rocket attack on the city of Ashqelon.

OBITUARIES

Abramsky, Chimen, historian, aged 93 – *d.* 14 March 2010, *b.* September 1916
Acheson, Sir Donald, KBE, Chief Medical Officer (1983–91), aged 83 – *d.* 10 January 2010, *b.* 17 September 1926
Aharonovitch, Yitzhak, captain of the Holocaust survivor ship *Exodus*, aged 86 – *d.* 23 December 2009, *b.* 27 August 1923
Aird, Sir Alastair, GCVO, Private Secretary to Queen Elizabeth the Queen Mother (1993–2002), aged 78 – *d.* 30 September 2009, *b.* 14 January 1931
Alan, Ray, ventriloquist and writer, aged 79 – *d.* 24 May 2010, *b.* 18 September 1930
Annabi, Hédi, head of the UN mission in Haiti, aged 65 – *d.* c.12 January 2010, *b.* 4 September 1944
Ash, Russell, writer and publisher, aged 64 – *d.* 21 June 2010, *b.* 18 June 1946
Ashtown (7th), Lord (Nigel Trench), diplomat, aged 93 – *d.* 6 March 2010, *b.* 27 October 1916
Bainbridge, Dame Beryl, DBE, novelist, aged 75 – *d.* 2 July 2010, *b.* 21 November 1934
Bateson, Bill, sports journalist, aged 73 – *d.* 24 September 2009, *b.* 19 March 1936
Bedser, Sir Alec, CBE, cricketer, aged 91 – *d.* 4 April 2010, *b.* 4 July 1918
Black, Sir James, OM, pharmacologist, joint winner of the Nobel Prize in Physiology or Medicine (1988), aged 85 – *d.* 21 March 2010, *b.* 14 June 1924
Bohr, Prof. Aage, Danish physicist, joint winner of the Nobel Prize in Physics (1975), aged 87 – *d.* 8 September 2009, *b.* 19 June 1922
Booth, Albert, Labour MP (1966–83), Secretary of State for Employment (1976–9), aged 81 – *d.* 6 February 2010, *b.* 28 May 1928
Borlaug, Norman, US agronomist and winner of the Nobel Peace Prize for his services to food production (1970), aged 95 – *d.* 12 September 2009, *b.* 25 March 1914
Bourgeois, Louise, French sculptor and painter, aged 98 – *d.* 31 May 2010, *b.* 25 December 1911
Bray, Barbara, translator, editor, radio producer and theatre director, aged 85 – *d.* 25 February 2010, *b.* 24 November 1924
Brown, David, US Hollywood film producer, aged 93 – *d.* 1 February 2010, *b.* 28 July 1916
Brown, Jim, director of Radio Free Europe (1978–84), aged 81 – *d.* 16 November 2009, *b.* 8 March 1928
Buxton of Alsa, Lord (Aubrey Buxton), KCVO, MC, naturalist, television executive and politician, aged 91 – *d.* 1 September 2009, *b.* 15 July 1918
Byrd, Robert, longest-serving US Senator (1958–2010), aged 92 – *d.* 28 June 2010, *b.* 20 November 1917
Caldera, Rafael, president of Venezuela (1969–74, 1994–9), aged 93 – *d.* 24 December 2009, *b.* 14 January 1916
Calvocoressi, Peter, writer, lawyer and wartime intelligence officer, aged 97 – *d.* 5 February 2010, *b.* 17 November 1912
Carmichael, Ian, actor, aged 89 – *d.* 5 February 2010, *b.* 18 June 1920
Carpenter, Harry, OBE, television sports commentator, aged 84 – *d.* 20 March 2010, *b.* 17 October 1925
Chapman, Baroness (Nicola Jane), campaigner for the rights of disabled people, aged 48 – *d.* 3 September 2009, *b.* 3 August 1961
Churchill, Winston Spencer, Conservative MP (1970–97), aged 69 – *d.* 2 March 2010, *b.* 10 October 1940
Clanwilliam (7th), Earl (John Meade), aged 90 – *d.* 24 December 2009, *b.* 27 September 1919
Clothier, Sir Cecil, KCB, QC, first Chair of the Police Complaints Authority (1985–9), aged 90 – *d.* 8 May 2010, *b.* 28 August 1919
Colville of Culross (4th), Viscount (John Colville), QC, lawyer and politician, aged 76 – *d.* 8 April 2010, *b.* 19 July 1933
Cowling, George, meterologist, first weatherman on British television, aged 89 – *d.* 24 December 2009, *b.* 2 March 1920
Cradock, Rt. Hon. Sir Percy, diplomat, architect of the 1997 transfer of Hong Kong from the UK to China, aged 86 – *d.* 22 January 2010, *b.* 26 October 1923
Crofton, Prof. Sir John, lung physician, played a key role in the control of tuberculosis, aged 97 – *d.* 3 November 2009, *b.* 27 March 1912
Currey, Charles, yachtsman and boat builder, Olympic silver medallist (1952), aged 94 – *d.* 10 May 2010, *b.* 26 February 1916
Cushnie, John, panellist on Radio 4's *Gardeners' Question Time* (1996–2009), aged 66 – *d.* 31 December 2009, *b.* 14 May 1943
Dae-jung, Kim, President of South Korea (1998–2003) and winner of the Nobel Peace Prize (2000), aged 85 – *d.* 18 August 2009, *b.* 3 December 1923
Dale, Margaret, ballet dancer and television producer, aged 87 – *d.* 28 January 2010, *b.* 10 December 1922
Daly, Cardinal Cahal, Roman Catholic Archbishop of Armagh (1990–6), aged 92 – *d.* 31 December 2009, *b.* 1 October 1917
Dankworth, Sir John, jazz composer and saxophonist, aged 82 – *d.* 6 February 2010, *b.* 20 September 1927
David, Baroness (Nora), Labour life peer, aged 96 – *d.* 29 November 2009, *b.* 23 September 1913
Day, Lucienne, textile designer, aged 93 – *d.* 30 January 2010, *b.* 5 January 1917
Dee, Simon, 1960s television chat show host and radio DJ, aged 74 – *d.* 29 August 2009, *b.* 28 July 1935
Delacourt-Smith of Alteryn, Baroness (Margaret Delacourt-Smith), life peer in the House of Lords, aged 93 – *d.* 8 June 2010, *b.* 5 April 1916
Denyer, Prof. Peter, pioneer of mobile phone camera technology, aged 56 – *d.* 22 April 2010, *b.* 27 April 1953
Diggory, Peter, gynaecologist and champion of abortion law reform, aged 85 – *d.* 22 November 2009, *b.* 6 January 1924
Dio, Ronnie James, heavy metal rock singer, aged 67 – *d.* 16 May 2010, *b.* 10 July 1942
Disney, Roy, US film studio executive, aged 79 – *d.* 16 December 2009, *b.* 10 January 1930

Dover, Sir Kenneth, classicist, president of the British Academy (1978–81), chancellor of the university of St Andrews (1981–2005), aged 89 – *d.* 7 March 2010, *b.* 11 March 1920

Duckworth, Ruth, potter and sculptor, aged 90 – *d.* 18 October 2009, *b.* 10 April 1919

Duffy, Brian, photographer, aged 76 – *d.* 31 May 2010, *b.* 15 June 1933

Eccleston, Harry, OBE, artist and banknote designer, aged 87 – *d.* 30 April 2010, *b.* 21 January 1923

Elles, Baroness (Diana), human rights campaigner and Conservative MEP (1979–89), aged 88 – *d.* 17 October 2009, *b.* 19 July 1921

Ettedgui, Joseph, designer, retailer and entrepreneur, aged 74 – *d.* 18 March 2010, *b.* 22 February 1936

Feoktistov, Konstantin, Russian cosmonaut, aged 83 – *d.* 21 November 2009, *b.* 7 February 1926

Flanagan, Barry, sculptor and printmaker, aged 68 – *d.* 1 September 2009, *b.* 11 January 1941

Fleming, Tom, OBE, actor and broadcaster, aged 82 – *d.* 18 April 2010, *b.* 29 June 1927

Flowers, Lord (Sir Brian), FRS, nuclear physicist, aged 85 – *d.* 25 June 2010, *b.* 13 September 1924

Floyd, Keith, television chef, aged 65 – *d.* 14 September 2009, *b.* 28 December 1943

Foot, Michael, PC, politician, journalist, leader of the Labour party in opposition (1980–3), aged 96 – *d.* 3 March 2010, *b.* 23 July 1913

Foster, Peter, architect, surveyor of Westminster Abbey (1973–88), aged 90 – *d.* 6 March 2010, *b.* 2 May 1919

Francis, Dick, jockey and bestselling thriller writer, aged 89 – *d.* 14 February 2010, *b.* 31 October 1920

Gainsborough (5th), Earl (Anthony Gerard Noel), aged 86 – *d.* 29 December 2009, *b.* 24 October 1923

Gately, Stephen, pop singer and member of 1990s pop band Boyzone, aged 33 – *d.* 10 October 2009, *b.* 17 March 1976

Gies, Miep, Dutch wartime helper to Anne Frank and her family and protector of her diary, aged 100, *d.* 11 January 2010, *b.* 15 February 1909

Ginzburg, Vitaly, Russian physicist and astrophysicist; winner of the Nobel Prize in Physics (2003), aged 93 – *d.* 8 November 2009, *b.* 4 October 1916

Glendevon (2nd), Lord (Julian Hope), opera producer, aged 59 – *d.* 29 September 2009, *b.* 6 March 1950

Goulding, Sir Marrack, KCMG, Under-Secretary General of the United Nations (1986–97), aged 73 – *d.* 9 July 2010, *b.* 2 September 1936

Graham, Bruce, architect of the Sears Tower in Chicago and key figure in the development of Canary Wharf in London, aged 84 – *d.* 6 March 2010, *b.* 1 December 1925

Grant, Cy, actor, writer and singer, aged 90 – *d.* 13 February 2010, *b.* 8 November 1919

Gray, Rose, chef, cookery writer and co-founder of the River Café restaurant, aged 71 – *d.* 28 February 2010, *b.* 28 January 1939

Gregory, Alfred, photographer who recorded the first ascent of Everest in 1953, aged 96 – *d.* 9 February 2010, *b.* 12 February 1913

Grey, Antony, gay rights campaigner, aged 82 – *d.* 30 April 2010, *b.* 6 October 1927

Haig, Gen. Alexander, NATO Supreme Allied Cdr Europe (1974–9), US Secretary of State (1981–2), aged 85 – *d.* 20 February 2010, *b.* 2 December 1924

Hamer, Rupert, journalist, defence correspondent for the *Sunday Mirror,* aged 39 – *d.* 9 January 2010, *b.* 28 February 1970

Hamilton (15th), Duke and **Brandon (12th)**, Duke (Angus Douglas-Hamilton), premier peer of Scotland and Hereditary Keeper of the palace of Holyrood House, aged 71 – *d.* 5 June 2010, *b.* 13 September 1938

Harman, General Sir Jack, GCB, OBE, MC, Deputy Supreme Allied Cdr, Europe (1978–81), aged 89 – *d.* 28 December 2009, *b.* 20 July 1920

Harper, Fr Michael, Archpriest of the Antiochian Orthodox Deanery of the UK and Ireland, aged 78 – *d.* 6 January 2010, *b.* 12 March 1931

Harris, Whitney, lawyer, prosecutor at the Nuremberg trials, aged 97 – *d.* 21 April 2010, *b.* 12 August 1912

Healey, Lady (Edna), writer, broadcaster, wife of Labour politician Lord Healey, aged 92 – *d.* 21 July 2010, *b.* 14 June 1918

Heathfield, Peter, general secretary of the National Union of Mineworkers (1984–92), aged 81 – *d.* 4 May 2010, *b.* 2 March 1929

Henry, Sir Denis, QC, Court of Appeal judge (1993–2002), aged 78 – *d.* 6 March 2010, *b.* 19 April 1931

Higgins, Alex, snooker player, twice world champion (1972, 1982), aged 61 – *d.* 24 July 2010, *b.* 18 March 1949

Hopper, Dennis, US actor and director, aged 74 – *d.* 29 May 2010, *b.* 17 May 1936

Horne, Lena, US singer and actor, aged 92 – *d.* 9 May 2010, *b.* 30 June 1917

Howard-Dobson, Gen. Sir Patrick, GCB, Quartermaster General of the Army (1977–9) and national president of the British Legion (1981–7), aged 88 – *d.* 8 November 2009, *b.* 12 August 1921

Ingrams, Michael, television presenter and documentary film-maker, aged 83 – *d.* 21 September 2009, *b.* 13 December 1925

Jeanne-Claude, international artist known for her 'wrapping' collaborations with her husband Christo, particularly *Wrapped Reichstag* (1995), aged 74 – *d.* 18 November 2009, *b.* 13 June 1935

Jeffries, Lionel, actor and director, aged 83 – *d.* 19 February 2010, *b.* 10 June 1926

Jones, Maggie, actor, played the character Blanche Hunt in *Coronation Street* (1972–4, 1999–2009), aged 75 – *d.* 2 December 2009, *b.* 21 June 1934

Jones, Rt. Revd Noël, CB, Chaplain of the Fleet (1984–9), Bishop of Sodor and Man (1989–2003), aged 76 – *d.* 28 August 2009, *b.* 25 December 1932

Kaczynski, Lech, president of Poland (2005–10), aged 60 – *d.* 10 April 2010, *b.* 18 June 1949

Keeley, Robin, forensic scientist, pioneer of analytical chemistry, aged 65 – *d.* 17 May 2010, *b.* 15 August 1944

Kemp, Rt. Revd Eric, Bishop of Chichester (1974–2001), *d.* 28 November 2009, *b.* 27 April 1915

Kennedy, Edward, Democratic Senator for Massachusetts (1962–2009), aged 77 – *d.* 25 August 2009, *b.* 22 February 1932

Kennedy, Sir Ludovic, writer and broadcaster, aged 89 – *d.* 18 October 2009, *b.* 3 November 1919

Koirala, Girija Prasad, four-times prime minister of Nepal, aged 85 – *d.* 20 March 2010, *b.* 20 February 1925

Krebs, Prof. Edwin, US biochemist, joint winner of the Nobel Prize in Physiology or Medicine (1992), aged 91 – *d.* 21 December 2009, *b.* 6 June 1918

Kumar, Ashok, Labour MP (1991–2, 1997–2010), aged 53 – *found dead* 15 March 2010, *b.* 28 May 1956

Laing of Dunphail, Lord (Hector Laing), chairman of United Biscuits (1972–90), treasurer of the Conservative Party (1988–93), aged 87 – *d.* 21 June 2010, *b.* 12 May 1923

Langridge, Philip, CBE, tenor, aged 70 – *d.* 5 March 2010, *b.* 16 December 1939

Law, Phillip, CBE, Australian educational pioneer and Antarctic explorer, aged 97 – *d.* 28 February 2010, *b.* 21 April 1912

Lawless, Terry, boxing trainer, aged 76 – *d.* 24 December 2009, *b.* 29 March 1933

Lévi-Strauss, Claude, anthropologist, aged 100 – *d.* 1 November 2009, *b.* 28 November 1908

Levine, David, US political caricaturist, aged 83 – *d.* 29 December 2009, *b.* 20 December 1926

Mackerras, Sir Charles, CH, CBE, conductor, aged 84 – *d.* 14 July 2010, *b.* 17 November 1925

McLaren, Bill, CBE, rugby union commentator, aged 86 – *d.* 19 January 2010, *b.* 16 October 1923

McLaren, Malcolm, entrepreneur, manager of the Sex Pistols, aged 64 – *d.* 8 April 2010, *b.* 22 January 1946

Macneil of Barra (26th), (Ian Macneil), contract lawyer, aged 80 – *d.* 16 February 2010, *b.* 20 June 1929

McQueen, Alexander, CBE, fashion designer, aged 40 – *found dead* 11 February 2010, *b.* 17 March 1969

Mabey, Bevil, designed bridges for rapid construction in war zones and remote areas, aged 94 – *d.* 27 April 2010, *b.* 16 April 1916

Macphail, Hon. Lord (Iain Macphail), Lord of Session (2005–9), aged 71 – *d.* 21 October 2009, *b.* 24 January 1938

Magan, Brig. William, CBE, senior executive officer of MI5, oldest surviving member, aged 101 – *d.* 21 January 2010, *b.* 13 June 1908

Marshall, Sir Denis, president of the Law Society (1981–2) who introduced compulsory insurance for solicitors, aged 93 – *d.* 17 November 2009, *b.* 1 June 1916

Mercante, Arthur, boxing referee, aged 90 – *d.* 10 April 2010, *b.* 27 January 1920

Merrick, Gil, footballer, goalkeeper for England (1951–4), aged 88, *d.* 3 February 2010, *b.* 26 January 1922

Moore, Charles, US civil rights photographer, aged 79 – *d.* 11 March 2010, *b.* 9 March 1931

Moran, Air Chief Marshal Sir Christopher, KCB, OBE, MVO, Commander-in-Chief HQ Air Command (2009–10), aged 54 – *d.* 26 May 2010, *b.* 28 April 1956

Neame, Ronald, CBE, film cameraman, producer, writer and director, aged 99 – *d.* 16 June 2010, *b.* 23 April 1911

Nirenberg, Marshall, US biologist and geneticist, joint winner of the Nobel Prize in Physiology or Medicine (1968), aged 82 – *d.* 15 January 2010, *b.* 10 April 1927

Noel-Baker, Francis, Labour MP for Brentford and Chiswick (1945–50) and Swindon (1955–69), aged 89 – *d.* 25 September 2009, *b.* 7 January 1920

Northesk (14th), Earl (David Carnegie), one of the 90 hereditary peers in the House of Lords, aged 55 – *d.* 28 March 2010, *b.* 3 November 1954

O'Donnell, Peter, writer, creator of the comic-strip character Modesty Blaise, aged 90 – *d.* 3 May 2010, *b.* 11 April 1920

Ohno, Kazuo, Japanese dancer, co-established *Butoh,* a form of dance drama, aged 103 – *d.* 1 June 2010, *b.* 27 October 1903

Painting, Norman, actor who played Phil Archer in the BBC Radio 4 soap opera *The Archers* (1950–2009), aged 85 – *d.* 29 October 2009, *b.* 24 April 1924

Palevsky, Max, US computer pioneer, co-founder of the Intel Corporation, aged 85 – *d.* 5 May 2010, b. 24 July 1924

Park of Monmouth, Baroness (Daphne Park), CMG, OBE, MI6 officer, principal of Somerville college, Oxford and governor of the BBC, aged 88 – *d.* 24 March 2010, *b.* 1 September 1921

Paul, Les, jazz guitarist and creator of the solid-bodied electric guitar, aged 94 – *d.* 13 August 2009, *b.* 9 June 1915

Pavle, Patriarch, head of the Serbian Orthodox Church, aged 95 – *d.* 15 November 2009, *b.* 11 September 1914

Payne, Sir Norman, airport designer and engineer, chief executive of BAA, aged 88 – *d.* 7 February 2010, *b.* 9 October 1921

Penn, Irving, US fashion photographer, aged 92 – *d.* 7 October 2009, *b.* 16 June 1917

Pitman, Sir Brian, chief executive of Lloyds bank (1984–2001), aged 78 – *d.* 10 March 2010, *b.* 13 December 1931

Plater, Alan, CBE, TV playwright and novelist, aged 75 – *d.* 24 June 2010, *b.* 15 April 1935

Plowright, Walter, CMG, FRS, veterinary scientist, developed a vaccine that eradicated the cattle virus rinderpest, aged 86 – *d.* 19 February 2010, *b.* 20 July 1923

Plummer of St Marylebone, Lord (Desmond Plummer), Conservative politician and leader of the General London Council (1967–73), aged 95 – *d.* 2 October 2009, *b.* 25 May 1914

Quaife, Pete, musician, bass player and co-founder of the Kinks, aged 66 – *d.* 24 June 2010, *b.* 31 December 1943

Quinto, Felice, Italian celebrity photographer, aged 80 – *d.* 16 January 2010, *b.* 11 April 1929

Quinton, Lord (Anthony), philosopher, aged 85 – *d.* 19 June 2010, *b.* 25 March 1925

Redgrave, Corin, actor, aged 70 – *d.* 6 April 2010, *b.* 16 July 1939

Redgrave, Lynn, OBE, actor, aged 67 – *d.* 2 May 2010, *b.* 8 March 1943

Richardson of Duntisbourne, Rt. Hon. Lord, KG, MBE, governor of the Bank of England (1973–83), aged 94, *d.* 22 January 2010, *b.* 25 November 1915

Riddell, Sir John, Bt., private secretary to the Prince and Princess of Wales (1985–90), aged 76 – *d.* 24 July 2010, *b.* 3 January 1934

Roberts, Ed, electronics engineer, developed one of the first personal computers, aged 68 – *d.* 1 April 2010, *b.* 13 September 1941

Robertson, Max, television reporter, presenter and commentator, aged 94 – *d.* 20 November 2009, *b.* 28 August 1915

Ronay, Egon, Hungarian-born food critic and publisher, aged 94 – *d.* 12 June 2010, *b.* 24 July 1915

Rooke, Brig. Vera, CB, CBE, Matron-in-Chief (Army) and Director Army Nursing Services (1981–4), aged 84 – *d.* 13 September 2009, *b.* 24 December 1924

Rumbold, Dame Angela, DBE, MP (1982–97), education minister and vice-chair of the Conservative party, aged 77 – *d.* 19 June 2010, *b.* 11 August 1932

Salinger, J. D., US writer, author of *The Catcher in the Rye,* aged 91 – *d.* 27 January 2010, *b.* 1 January 1919

Samaranch, Juan Antonio, Spanish president of the International Olympic Committee (1980–2001), aged 89 – *d.* 21 April 2010, *b.* 17 July 1920

Saramago, Jose, Portuguese writer, winner of the Nobel Prize for Literature (1998), aged 87 – *d.* 18 June 2010, *b.* 16 November 1922

Scanlon, Albert, footballer for Manchester United and survivor of the 1958 Munich air crash, aged 74 – *d.* 22 December 2009, *b.* 10 October 1935

Semyonova, Marina, Russian ballerina and teacher with the Bolshoi, aged 101 – *d.* 9 June 2010, *b.* 12 June 1908

Shepherd, David, MBE, cricketer and umpire, aged 68 – *d.* 27 October 2009, *b.* 27 December 1940

Shepherd-Barron, John, invented the first automatic cash machine, aged 84 – *d.* 15 May 2010, *b.* 23 June 1925

Shriver, Eunice Kennedy, founder of the Special Olympics, aged 88 – *d.* 11 August 2009, *b.* 10 July 1921

Sillitoe, Alan, novelist and playwright, aged 82 – *d.* 25 April 2010, *b.* 4 March 1928

Simionato, Giulietta, Italian mezzo-soprano, aged 99 – *d.* 5 May 2010, *b.* 12 May 1910

Simmons, Jean, OBE, actor, aged 80 – *d.* 22 January 2009, *b.* 31 January 1929

Smyslov, Vasily, Russian Grandmaster and world chess champion (1957–8), aged 89 – *d.* 27 March 2010, *b.* 24 March 1971

Soulbury (3rd), Viscount (Sir Peter Ramsbotham), GCMG, GCVO, British ambassador to the USA (1974–7), governor-general of Bermuda (1977–80), aged 90 – *d.* 9 April 2010, *b.* 8 October 1919

Speirs, Bill, General Secretary of the Scottish Trades Union Congress (1998–2006), aged 57 – *d.* 23 September 2009, *b.* 8 March 1952

Spero, Nancy, US artist, aged 83 – *d.* 18 October 2009, *b.* 24 August 1926

Starkey, Greville, jockey, aged 70 – *d.* 14 April 2010, *b.* 21 December 1939

Steinberg, Lord (Leonard Steinberg), bookmaking entrepreneur and Conservative life peer, aged 73 – *d.* 2 November 2009, *b.* 1 August 1936

Stever, Horton, US aeronautical engineer, aged 93 – *d.* 8 April 2010, *b.* 24 October 1916

Swayze, Patrick, actor, aged 57 – *b.* 18 August 1952, *d.* 14 September 2009

Taylor, David, Labour MP (1997–2009), aged 63 –*d.* 26 December 2009, *b.* 22 August 1946

Todd, Richard, actor, aged 90 – *d.* 3 December 2009, *b.* 11 June 1919

Townshend (7th), Marquess (George Townshend), businessman and farmer, aged 93 – *d.* 23 April 2010, *b.* 13 May 1916

Vann, Stanley, master of the music at Peterborough Cathedral (1953–77), aged 100 – *d.* 27 March 2010, *b.* 15 February 1910

Verney, Rt. Revd Stephen, MBE, Bishop Suffragan of Repton (1977–85), aged 90 – *d.* 9 November 2009, *b.* 17 April 1919

Wagner, Wolfgang, German director of the Bayreuth Festival Opera (1966–2008), aged 90 – *d.* 21 March 2010, *b.* 30 August 1919

Walker of Worcester, Lord (Peter Walker), MBE, PC, cabinet minister, Conservative MP (1961–92), aged 78 – *d.* 22 June 2010, *b.* 25 March 1932

Waterhouse, Keith, CBE, journalist and playwright, aged 80 – *d.* 4 September 2009, *b.* 6 February 1929

Watkins, Alan, political columnist and author, aged 77 – *d.* 8 May 2010, *b.* 3 April 1933

Webb, George, jazz pianist and band leader, aged 92 – *d.* 11 March 2010, *b.* 8 October 1917

Wild, Earl, concert pianist and composer, aged 94 – *d.* 23 January 2010, *b.* 26 November 1915

Wilson, Charlie, US Democrat Congressman (1973–96), aged 76 – *d.* 10 February 2010, *b.* 1 June 1933

Wolff, Dr Sula, German-born child psychiatrist, aged 85 – *d.* 21 September 2009, *b.* 1 March 1924

Woodward, Edward, OBE, actor, aged 79 – *d.* 16 November 2009, *b.* 1 June 1930

Wright, Sir Oliver, GCMG, GCVO, DSC, Ambassador to Denmark (1966–9), Germany (1975–81) and the USA (1982–6), aged 88 – *d.* 1 September 2009, *b.* 6 March 1921

Yamaguchi, Tsutomu, only official survivor of both atomic bomb attacks on Japan at the end of the second world war, aged 93 – *d.* 4 January 2010, *b.* 16 March 1916

Yates, William, Conservative MP (1955–66), aged 88 – *d.* 18 April 2010, *b.* 15 September 1921

Yar'Adua, Umaru Musa, president of Nigeria (2007–10), aged 58 – *d.* 5 May 2010, *b.* 16 August 1951

ARCHAEOLOGY

Dr Nadia Durrani and Dr Neil Faulkner

THE STAFFORDSHIRE HOARD

The star discovery of the past year was unquestionably the Staffordshire Hoard. Located in July 2009 by amateur treasure hunter Terry Herbert, it represents the biggest cache of Anglo-Saxon gold unearthed in Britain. The only other find that comes close in significance is the famed Sutton Hoo treasure uncovered some 70 years ago.

The hoard comprises around 1,500 items, more than two-thirds of which are either gold or silver. Such is its richness that it roughly doubles the total quantity of metalwork known from this period of Anglo-Saxon history. The workmanship and materials are consistently of the highest quality, and their aesthetic beauty has inspired awe among the most hardened archaeological veterans. Though still in the preliminary stages of study by archaeologists, the hoard is poised to redefine the understanding of Anglo-Saxon society, politics and thought.

The assemblage consists almost entirely of beautifully crafted military artefacts including sword hilts, pommels and helmet fragments. So far, 84 pommel caps have been identified, 135 plate fragments from sword grips, and 71 collars or guards. Helmets are well represented in the assemblage and can be compared with the most complete and famous of Anglo-Saxon helmets: those found in the royal ship burial at Sutton Hoo. Fragments of sword scabbards form another distinct category of material, often comprising mounts of gold inlaid with delicate garnet cloisonné. However, among the assemblage are many objects without known parallels.

Most items had been damaged prior to deposition. The gold had been bent, twisted and sometimes broken. The silver, less malleable, had usually been broken, and generally survived more fragmented than the gold. Much of this damage appears to have occurred when the more precious parts of multi-part artefacts were detached – indicating that only the best elements of each object were selected for burial.

How to interpret the presence of this sumptuous yet twisted military hoard? The 'damage' may have had ritual significance. Current thinking is that the hoard represents an offering to the deity of the finest material, and that its broken condition may have rendered it symbolically fit to pass to 'the other side'.

The literary sources are also helping to inform ideas. Swords were highly worked and highly prized objects in the Middle Anglo-Saxon world and feature prominently in the famous Anglo-Saxon poem *Beowulf*, which is probably broadly contemporary with the Staffordshire Hoard. For example, *Beowulf* mentions a sword hilt being taken as a trophy in battle. The poem also refers to the burial of a king and the deposition of gold in his grave, to quote: 'They let the ground keep that ancestral treasure, gold under gravel, gone to earth, as useless to men now as it ever was.' Thus, initial thinking is that the hoard might represent a haul of booty taken from defeated enemies on the battlefield; and that these trophies were then ritually buried as thank-offerings to pagan deities by the victorious Kingdom of Mercia, in whose former territory the hoard was discovered.

Certainly, the discovery of the hoard in Staffordshire occasions no surprise, since this was formerly the heartland of the Kingdom of Mercia, the most aggressive and expansionist of the Middle Anglo-Saxon states, led during the eighth and ninth centuries AD by Kings Penda, Wulfhere, Aethelred, Coenred, Coelred, and Aethelbald.

In terms of dating, the early eighth century AD has been suggested for the hoard's deposition. This date is based on the forms of objects and on decorative techniques and styles, and through comparison with those of other known Anglo-Saxon artefacts. Though the hoard includes material dating back to perhaps the late sixth century, such items would have been high-value objects – heirlooms of sorts – that had been looked after and passed on to future generations. So the date at which the hoard was deposited must, of course, be based on the likely date of the latest (eighth century) material.

This was a period of transition. The Christian conversion of the Anglo-Saxon kingdoms had begun. Yet the buried booty suggests pagan rituals were still at work, and that it was an offering to the gods. The Staffordshire Hoard therefore represents the twilight period of the pagan past.

THE HOARD, METAL-DETECTING, AND THE PAS

That the Staffordshire Hoard became known to archaeological scholarship is testimony to the integrity of Terry Herbert and the success of the Portable Antiquities Scheme (PAS). Herbert had been hunting treasure for 20 years, ever since buying a metal detector in a car-boot sale. He was astonished when he literally struck gold, and worked feverishly for four days after recovering the first object. As the significance of his discovery dawned on him, he contacted the PAS finds liaison officer for Staffordshire, Duncan Slarke, who promptly arrived on site to receive no fewer than 231 bags of gold objects.

Staffordshire County Council called in Birmingham Archaeology to carry out a controlled excavation of the hoard find-spot. They were assisted by veteran Anglo-Saxon specialist Kevin Leahy, who catalogued all the finds on to a database in just 12 days. This allowed a formal inquest to be held, as the law required, within 11 weeks of Herbert's original discovery. The inquest confirmed that the hoard was technically 'treasure', allowing interested museums to bid to acquire the material, and imposing an obligation on the finder to sell at the minimum price determined by a British Museum-based valuation committee. In this case, Birmingham Museum and Art Gallery, the Potteries Museum and Art Gallery, and Staffordshire County Council have joined together, and will be assisted by the British Museum, in order to acquire the hoard and keep it local. The hoard is expected to be judged to be worth a seven-figure sum. The amount will be split between the finder and the landowner.

Metal detectors have long been controversial in archaeology. They developed from the mine-detecting technology of the Second World War, and the hobby of metal-detecting took off in the 1970s. The archaeological establishment was almost uniformly hostile and there were public campaigns, supported by national bodies such as the Council for British Archaeology, to have metal detectors banned. This reflected the misuse of metal detectors to vandalise archaeological sites by stripping them of valuable objects. In some cases, this was done for personal gain, and the objects were sold and all knowledge of them lost. In other cases, there was no ill intent, but the effect was to remove objects from their archaeological context, greatly reducing their information value even if they were subsequently brought to the attention of appropriate specialists. These concerns reflect an ongoing problem: 'night-hawking' is a major concern of archaeologists, involving, as it does, nocturnal raids by metal-detectorists on important archaeological sites in order to recover valuable objects for sale on the black market.

Some archaeologists, on the other hand, have always recognised that the great majority of metal-detectorists are neither criminals nor people motivated by personal gain. Their hobby is a way into the past. In the 1970s, such archaeologists as Tony Gregory in Norfolk and Kevin Leahy in Lincoln (the same Kevin Leahy as mentioned above) pioneered the building of working relationships with metal-detectorists in their counties. The idea was to create channels of communication so that finds could be identified, find-spots recorded, and the public store of archaeological knowledge enhanced by the work of the metal-detectorists.

WHAT IS TREASURE?

Under the 1996 Treasure Act, treasure is defined as:

- Any metallic object, other than a coin, provided that at least 10 per cent by weight of metal is precious metal (that is, gold or silver) and that it is at least 300 years old when found. If the object is of prehistoric date it will be treasure provided any part of it is precious metal.
- Any group of two or more metallic objects of any composition of prehistoric date that come from the same find (*see* below).
- All coins from the same find provided they are at least 300 years old when found (but if the coins contain less than 10 per cent of gold or silver there must be at least ten of them). Only the following groups of coins will normally be regarded as coming from the same find:
  1) hoards that have been deliberately hidden
  2) smaller groups of coins, such as the contents of purses, that may been dropped or lost
  3) votive or ritual deposits.
- Any object, whatever it is made of, that is found in the same place as, or had previously been together with, another object that is treasure.

The success of these informal arrangements underpinned the drive to create a national scheme two decades later. British Museum archaeologist Roger Bland both advised the government on a new Treasure Act and pushed forwards the establishment of a national Portable Antiquities Scheme. The act and the scheme complemented one another, the former providing a new legal framework that safeguarded the interests of finders and gave them an incentive to come forward, the latter creating the local mechanisms for contacting metal-detectorists, winning their confidence, and setting up regular systems for the identification and recording of new finds. The Treasure Act was passed in 1996, and the PAS was piloted in a number of regions at the same time, before going national a couple of years later, with finds liaison officers now in place across England and Wales (W www.finds.org.uk). The usual pattern is for liaison officers to build links with, and make regular visits to, metal-detecting clubs, and in this way create and maintain relationships with local hobbyists. Finds identification and recording is often done on the spot, but if they need to be taken away, this is done only with permission and all finds are returned. Trust is crucial to the effectiveness of the scheme. The exception is with treasure finds, which are subject to state control, but here the finder's interest in the commercial value of any objects is protected.

NEOLITHIC ORKNEY

The discovery of a vast artificial prehistoric mound at the Ness of Brodgar on Orkney is set to be as important for Neolithic studies as the Staffordshire Hoard is proving for Anglo-Saxon studies. Archaeologists, led by Nick Card of the Orkney Research Centre for Archaeology, located the 5,000-year-old site between two famous stone circles (the Ring of Brodgar and the Stones of Stenness) and close to the equally renowned Maes Howe passage grave. The new site is set to transform ideas about prehistoric religion on Orkney.

The site is the size of five football pitches and formed of massive stone structures and dumps of domestic waste (or 'middens'). The so-called Structure 1 comprises a drystone-wall structure over 15m long and 10m wide. It had entrances at either end with large amounts of midden material dumped around it, making it appear somewhat subterranean. It had also been remodelled several times. A second structure of comparable size was excavated nearby (Structure 8). A third structure, however, was almost twice the size, over 25m long and almost 20m wide (Structure 10). The external walls of this third structure were almost 5m thick, consisting of two stone-built walls, each 2m wide, separated by a midden wall-core. The external corners were curving. The stonework was of exceptional quality. The monumentality of this building, coupled with its central location on a mound, and its intervisibility with the two stone rings, the passage-grave, and other contemporary ritual structures, make Structure 10 a veritable Neolithic cathedral. Its central significance is confirmed by other strands of evidence.

Once Structure 10 had been built, other structures on the mound were levelled, enhancing the new edifice's domination of the landscape (at least seven more large structures have been located in geophysical survey and await more detailed investigation). More than 80 stone panels decorated with finely incised geometric art/graffiti have been found in the excavations, and the more substantial of these, such as those decorated with numerous cup and cup-and-ring marks, have been found around Structure 10.

Bounding the site to the north is a massive double-faced stone wall running the 100m width of the narrow peninsula on which the site is located. Another wall, 2m wide, runs on a parallel course to the south. These walls seem to delineate a huge sacred space, at the heart of which lay Structure 10. The rich assemblage of artefacts recovered includes polished stone axes and maceheads and a wide range of beautifully decorated grooved ware pottery.

When all the evidence is pieced together – the location; the scale, symmetry and complexity of the architecture; the monumental enclosure wall; and the artefact assemblage – the term 'ritual' or 'temple' seems inescapable. It is possible that the famous stone circles were, in fact, secondary features, peripheral to the Neolithic temple complex at the Ness. Certainly, the sacred landscape must be interpreted in its entirety to be understood, just as we attempt to do in relation to the yet more famous, and in some ways comparable, complex around Stonehenge. Current thinking assumes ritual progression from one monumentalised space to another, symbolically representing a transition or rite of passage, most probably from life to death, or from the 'land of the living' to the 'land of the ancestors'.

AD 410: END OF ROMAN BRITAIN

The major focus this year for Roman Britain specialists has been the 1,600th anniversary of the date normally taken to represent the end of Roman Britain. In fact, the date itself is controversial. It depends on a literary reference which may well have been distorted by a medieval copyist's mistake. In any case, no-one believes that Roman Britain ended with a clear-cut decision by the imperial authorities to abandon the province. Troop levels were run down over a generation because of military demands elsewhere in the embattled Western Empire, such that the British frontiers became increasingly insecure, and law and order gradually broke down in the countryside. Even so, because AD 410 is the conventional date for the end of Roman Britain, the anniversary has been adopted as an opportunity to review the state of knowledge about the critical transition from Roman Britain to a time that some still call the Dark Ages.

A series of conferences across the country, starting with a major one at the British Museum in February 2010, brought together ancient historians, academic archaeologists, finds specialists and excavators to debate the issues. Traditionally, debate has been polarised between 'long' and 'short chronologists'. The former see Romano-British civilisation as well-rooted and long-lived, continuing in some form well beyond the end of Roman rule, perhaps even into the sixth century AD in some form. The short chronologists see Romanisation as a thin aristocratic veneer that is eroded by the economic, political and military crises of the third and fourth centuries AD, such that towns, villas and the luxury trades are all in an advanced state of decay by the late fourth century.

Now, it seems, a new consensus is beginning to emerge. Increasingly, with refined excavation techniques and greater sensitivity in relation to the ephemeral evidence left by final-phase Roman occupation, excavators are finding evidence for structures, occupation and continuing human activity on Roman sites in the late fourth and early fifth centuries. Of particular importance are current excavation projects at the Roman legionary fortress at Caerleon in Wales, and at the Roman forts at Binchester in County Durham and Vindolanda just south of Hadrian's Wall. In each case, excavators are recovering strong evidence for activity immediately post-dating the latest substantial Roman military structures. Interpretation is hard. Specialists are uncertain what is represented. It may be the Late Roman army, or a local militia, or an independent warlord, or perhaps just local people reusing an abandoned military site.

What does seem to be agreed is that, sooner or later, Britain broke up into separate warlord states, and that some Roman sites, both forts and towns, were reused by Early Dark Age rulers seeking security behind Roman walls and legitimacy through adopting the trappings of Roman power. Wroxeter (near modern Shrewsbury) and Birdoswald (on Hadrian's Wall) have long been recognised as probable Early Dark Age politico-military centres. The growing impression is that these sites may be typical ('type-sites' in the archaeological jargon) rather than rare exceptions to a general rule of abandonment and ruination. Caerleon, Vindolanda and Binchester have now become candidates. These reused Roman sites join another long-established category of sites, where Early Dark Age politico-military centres were established either on old Iron Age hillforts or on new defensible sites in the countryside. Examples include Tintagel in Cornwall, Dinas Emrys in Gwynedd, and South Cadbury in Somerset. It may be that all of these sites had a broadly similar character, sharing a range of political, military and ideological functions, in the divided post-Roman world of fifth and sixth century AD Britain. Further support for such conceptions comes from detailed artefact studies, particularly those of Stuart Laycock, looking at Late Roman and post-Roman paramilitary buckles and belt-fittings, which seem to form distinct regional groups, as if shadowing the existence of rival tribal militias. Laycock has, in fact, drawn parallels with contemporary conflicts in the Balkans, Iraq and Afghanistan.

DEAD BLOODY VIKINGS

On the usually uneventful line of the Weymouth relief road in Dorset a rescue dig by Oxford Archaeology has revealed the remains of 51 men in a mass grave. Headless and hacked, the doomed were probably the executed members of a Viking raiding party. If so, this grave is confirmation of the ferocity of the conflict between Anglo-Saxons and the Vikings between the ninth and 11th centuries AD – and that the Viking raiders, despite their awesome reputation, did not always have things their own way.

When first discovered, the remains – consisting of neatly stacked skulls on one side and a tangle of twisted torsos in the centre – led the excavators to assume they were dealing with some sort of prehistoric ritual site. However, subsequent dating revealed the remains belonged to the period AD 890 to 1034. Moreover, isotope tests on their teeth revealed origins for the individuals represented in various parts of Scandinavia. One of them had lived much of his life inside the Arctic Circle. All were well-built young men in their late teens or early 20s.

The date, the osteological evidence and the circumstances of burial all point to capture and execution by the defending Anglo-Saxon forces. The heads of the men were hacked off with swords or axes. Cut marks on the bones of upper torsos, arms and hands imply that the victims tried to resist their brutal fate.

SCOTLAND GETS OLDER

The discovery of flints at Howburn Farm in South Lanarkshire by the Biggar Archaeology Group has pushed back the date of the earliest human activity in Scotland to a warm 'snap' in the Late Palaeolithic – around 12,000 BC.

Although the Earth was warming rapidly from around 13,000 BC, temperatures dropped again at around 11,000 BC. It was only after this dip that the current sustained warm period (the Holocene) began; and it was only in the Holocene – or so we thought – that people ventured past the Midlands. However, these tools indicate that Late Palaeolithic (or Old Stone Age) people were living in southern Scotland in 12,000 BC during the brief warm period between the two cold spells.

The revisionary stone finds were made during a long

programme of field-based research that involved both fieldwalking and selective excavation, with up to 150 volunteers actively involved in the project. The flint tools almost certainly represent a temporary campsite that was periodically reused. They include projectile points for hunting, long-bladed scrapers and knives for processing carcasses, and burins and piercers for working animal skins.

The Howburn Farm tools belong to the 'Hamburgian Culture', which is also known in northern Germany and southern Denmark (the North Sea did not exist at the time, and Britain was joined to the Continent by the 'Doggerland' land-bridge). The toolkits of Hamburgian people, dating to the period 13,000 to 11,000 BC, have characteristic technological features, such as spur-faceted striking platforms (the careful preparation of the core from which flakes are struck being a critical aspect of flint-tool manufacture).

It is likely that Late Palaeolithic hunters moved long distances across an extended North European Plain that would, in 12,000 BC, have stretched from Yorkshire to the Urals, pursuing herds of reindeer and wild horses on seasonal migration routes. The hunters would undoubtedly have made tools of bone, antler and wood, in addition to flint, but the acidic soils of Scotland rarely permit the survival of such artefacts.

RELOCATING BOSWORTH

One of the most important battles in English history has been relocated, thanks to field research by Glenn Foard, Project Officer of the Battlefields Trust.

A careful desktop scrutiny of Late Medieval documentary evidence for the Battle of Bosworth – where Henry Tudor defeated and killed King Richard III and founded the Tudor dynasty – seemed to indicate that the traditional site for the battle was wrong. A new search of local place-names and topography was guided by a key passage in the *Anglica Historia* of Polydore Vergil (1470–1555): 'Between the armies was a marsh, which Henry purposely kept on his right, so it would serve as a fortress to protect his men. At the same time also, by doing this, he left the sun behind.'

This clue took archaeologists to a new potential location for the fighting on 22 August 1485 – and it was systematic survey on this site, using metal detectors, that finally identified the battlefield beyond any doubt. A survey of some 7 sq. km of landscape yielded 5,000 finds. Only a small proportion of these related to the battle, but it was enough to prove the battle site. Bosworth was one of the first battles to be fought in Europe using artillery and handguns in quantity, and key finds from the archaeological survey included 22 pieces of lead round-shot and bullets. The number of round-shot recovered is extraordinary since it represents more than that known from all the other battlefields of the 15th and 16th centuries in Europe combined. The scatter of round-shot extends over a distance of more than a kilometre, and the combined evidence suggests that the battle was fought in the area between the villages of Dadlington, Shenton, Upton and Stoke Golding.

The discoveries have international significance. Gunpowder was transforming the nature of warfare. It was clearly being used on a potentially decisive scale at Bosworth. And this, of course, was a battle that changed the course of English history.

BLUESTONEHENGE

Britain's most famous archaeological site – Stonehenge – is rarely out of the news, and the past year was no exception. A second stone circle – dubbed 'Bluestonehenge' – has been found at West Amesbury, at the point where the Avenue leading from Stonehenge proper reaches the River Avon.

Archaeologists have for long speculated that this river was part of a sacred routeway, which then continued along the Avenue to Stonehenge. And the new discovery of the major stone circle of Bluestonehenge, on the river's edge, appears to be spectacular confirmation of that. It is now apparent that the river links Stonehenge with the Avenue, and then Bluestonehenge with the massive circular earthwork known as Durrington Walls located just a short distance to the north.

Built of bluestones from the Preseli Hills of Carmarthenshire – like the bluestone circle at Stonehenge itself – the new circle represents a huge investment of resources in cutting, transporting and erecting the monoliths. The circle comprises a 25m-wide henge monument (a ditched enclosure with an external bank), at the centre of which lay a 10m-wide ring of stones, represented today by a ring of pits filled with clay and flint nodules used as packing stones. The archaeological team has excavated a quarter of the stone circle, identifying nine stone holes, whose curvature and spacing imply that the monoliths were placed 1.12m apart, and that originally there were up to 25 of them forming the complete monument. Two antler picks were discovered, and when radiocarbon dates have been secured for these, a relatively precise date for the construction of the monument will be available. Meantime, the discovery of distinctive 'chisel arrowheads' places Bluestonehenge in the period 3400 to 2500 BC.

The investigations are led by a team of academic archaeologists from several universities that includes Mike Parker Pearson. He has advanced the argument (also relevant to new discoveries at the Ness of Brodgar in Orkney, *see* above) that the Stonehenge landscape as a whole represents a sequence of monuments associated with elaborate rites of passage in which the dead passed from the 'land of the living' (perhaps symbolised by wooden structures) to the 'land of the ancestors' (stone structures). Bluestonehenge would seem to add another large piece to this interpretive picture of the distant past.

ARCHITECTURE

John Hitchman

NOTTINGHAM CONTEMPORARY, HIGH PAVEMENT, NOTTINGHAM

Architect: Caruso St John Architects

The Nottingham Contemporary offers a major new gallery – which opened in late 2009 with an exhibition of works by David Hockney – and performance facility, providing 3,000 sq. m of gallery space, a multi-purpose auditorium, educational facilities and a cafeteria. Located on a steeply sloping site on the southern edge of the city centre, the building's four main levels are cut into the contours; the main entrance being approached from an open terrace opening out off High Pavement at the uppermost level, in effect making the notional ground floor the top floor, with basement and mezzanine levels below.

The new building has aroused some negative comments as well as praise for its bold, simple and, from a distance at least, overtly industrial aesthetic. The building comprises a roughly triangular-shaped, largely solid base, set tight into the acute corner formed by the junction of Middle Hill and High Pavement. The external perimeter walls of the main building are faced with pre-cast concrete panels. From a low-level base of black, polished pre-cast concrete, the panels rise the full height of the elevations; each panel featuring a concave recess set between projecting ribs to create a rippling effect along the façade.

These panels convey a visual likeness to the ribbed casings of industrial containers, in sharp contrast to both the adjacent 19th-century red brick buildings of the Lace Market quarter's huddle of warehouses and offices, and the nearby Victorian gothic church. On closer viewing, the olive-green, pre-cast panels take on an altogether more intricate character, as the hard-edged appearance gives way to hints of subtlety in the texture and reveals a surface of incredible delicacy. This is achieved by casting the panels with an impressively precise rendering of a sample of lace-work, thus cleverly referencing the lace-making heritage of Nottingham and of this locality in particular.

The gallery's main entrance is tucked beneath a cavernous overhanging section of external cladding, covering nearly half of the newly created paved plaza on High Pavement. A small lobby set into the outside corner leads into the reception foyer, which gives direct access to the suite of ground-floor gallery spaces.

The ground-floor galleries are in the main provided with natural daylight from a regular coffered grid of overhead roof-lights, although the taller gallery three is provided with a single large sky-light and a wide window on to the street. This has the benefit of allowing glimpses into the gallery from outside, helping to break down the boundary between inside and out and involving any exhibition in a dialogue with the street scene. A journey into the lower reaches of the building reveals a forthright approach to finishes, starting with the handling of the shuttered concrete of the main staircase and finding its full expression in the bare unfinished concrete walls of the performance space at basement level.

An intermediate mezzanine level provides rooms for education, archive storage, meetings and offices, while on the basement level, opposite the performance space, is located a bar and café, with windows along the south side providing daylight and doors on to the outdoor terrace that forms a staging post on the new public route up the hill.

CIRCLEBATH HOSPITAL, PEASEDOWN ST JOHN, BATH

Architect: Foster + Partners

This 6,000 sq. m hospital has recently been completed for Circle, a private healthcare partnership of some 2,000 clinical practitioners and one of the largest such partnerships in Europe. It is the first of a planned programme of small-scale private hospitals that will also provide treatment for NHS patients benefiting from primary care trust funding, and it is intended to instigate a radical new approach to healthcare provision and hospital design.

By comparison with the majority of general hospitals, CircleBath is small and compact, with just 28 bedrooms, including two double rooms. In keeping with the clinicians' aim of 'putting the hospitality back into hospital', the design is modelled on the hotel concept, with distinct functional zones efficiently organised. The hospital functions are spread over three storeys, with the building cut into the gentle incline of the site, which is set in rolling countryside on the edge of the green belt south-east of Bath.

The long, slim form is orientated east-west, providing the rooms on the long south-facing elevation with wonderful pastoral views. The main approach is from the north by road, where car parking is provided at grade and on one lower level. From the vehicle drop-off point access is made through a lobby directly into a central linear double-height, top-lit atrium space, around which all the ground and first-floor accommodation is arranged. The ground floor functions as the administrative and social heart of the hospital. Two elliptical counter arrangements stand in the middle of the space – that nearest the entrance serves as the main reception desk, the second as a bar and refreshment counter with seating beyond. Opposite the entrance an additional lounge with wall-to-wall glass windows brings views of the surrounding countryside right into the heart of the building.

Along the south side of the ground floor are arranged nine consulting rooms, with fully glazed external walls overlooking a wide terrace created by the projecting basement structure, their doors recessed in pairs behind four internal treatment rooms. On the north side are located ancillary back-up rooms, lavatories and, along the perimeter, a continuous bank of mechanical plant spaces. The layout of the accommodation is designed to maximise the daylight benefits of the orientation, by placing the majority of the habitable rooms on the south side and using substantial portions of the north-facing elevation for plant and equipment.

On the first floor the atrium is enclosed to form an internal corridor, with occasional slot windows providing

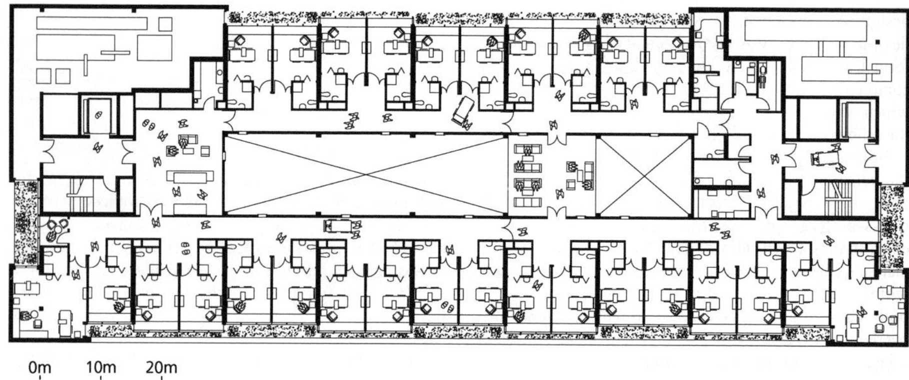

Fig. 1 CircleBath Hospital (first-floor plan), Foster + Partners

glimpses down into the atrium below and at one point doors providing access on to a balcony bridge. Eighteen bedrooms are arranged along the south side, ten on the north, and here timber and laminate finishes and decor are of high quality and convey a bespoke, if not luxurious, ambience. Vertical access is organised with a lift and stair core at each end of the plan: up to the first floor and its banks of recovery bedrooms; down to the basement and the clinical operations centre.

The first floor cantilevers out beyond the ground-floor perimeter on all four sides, expressed as a thin rectangular box clad in silver anodised panels arranged as overlapping squares or shingles and set on the diagonal to create a diamond pattern. Long shallow slits have been cut into the façades where windows are required to light the banks of bedrooms, with a shorter one placed in each end elevation.

In contrast to the shiny floating volume of the first floor, the ground floor is recessive and faced with full-height solid black or glazed panels. The palette is restrained, clinical even, the modelling simple and crisp. The building's small overall size allows it to retain an architectural clarity not available to the sprawling agglomerations characteristic of so many general hospitals.

MEDIACITY: UK, SALFORD QUAYS, MANCHESTER

Architects: Wilkinson Eyre Architects Ltd (Concept Design BBC Buildings); Fairhurst Design Group (Studio Block); Chapman Taylor (Residential and Stages E–L); Benoy (Master planners)

The 90-hectare site, previously largely derelict, occupies a prominent position on the north bank of the Manchester Ship Canal at the junction with the first of the Salford Quays, an area of former commercial docks just 15 minutes to the west by tram from Manchester's city centre. Since the docks closed in the 1980s the area has seen some significant regeneration, most notably in the form of the Lowry Centre and the Imperial War Museum North.

Outline planning permission for MediaCity: UK was granted in October 2006, based on initial concept designs for three office buildings, a studio block and two residential towers, organised within an overall master plan developed by Benoy.

The three key aspects of the master plan were:

- to provide a good mix of uses – including residential, commercial, hotels, studios and retail – together with essential back-up services such as doctors' surgeries, nurseries and health clubs, so that the area could develop into a sustainable community
- to create a dense urban grain consistent with providing a range of spatial experiences appropriate for what is intended to be a new part of the city
- to organise all these activities around a strong underlying geometry in order to create an urban framework closely related to its local context

The core geometry is generated from a series of radial axes and concentric circles focused on the centre of the prominent circular corner drum of the Lowry Centre. This has created a radial pattern of streets, boulevards and open spaces defining the principal building plots of the new development. Bordering the Ship Canal, the first radial segment includes two office buildings for the BBC (buildings A and C) and a residential tower. The two office buildings are separated by an open street following the line of one of the concentric circles, and it is proposed at some stage to continue this route via an arching pedestrian bridge to the west bank to link up with the museum and other developments on the opposite side.

The second radial segment features a large, open piazza reaching from the water's edge back into the heart of the site, where the hub of the BBC's activities is located, the main studio block and, beyond it, at the rear of the site, a multi-storey car park positioned over the development's energy centre. Two tower buildings emerge from the rear sides of the studio block: one an office building, the other a hotel. The open piazza extends eastwards – its curving northern edge defining the line of the building frontages – while along the dockside the extension to the metro system, linking the site to the centre of Manchester, reaches its terminus, with a station concourse and platform canopies forming part of the intricately designed public realm. This includes both green landscaped areas of parkland and the hard-paved piazza in front of the studio block designed to accommodate a range of outdoor entertainment activities and public events.

Running northwards from the piazza and park, the third radial segment includes a further office building for the BBC (building B), out of which emerges a residential tower extending to 22 floors, and behind which is proposed a further open square; while the fourth segment includes the media education facility for Salford University.

With the layout of the individual buildings organised within the master plan, the concept for their architectural design was developed, the keynotes being simplicity and flexibility. There was a decision not to compete, in formalistic terms at least, with the development's visually complex neighbours, the war museum and the Lowry – which is not to say that there is a lack of visual variety in the scheme as realised.

Building C, fronting directly on to the water's edge at the junction of canal and dock, occupies the pivotal position on the site and its top storey is surmounted by an over-sailing canopy, a motif that reappears elsewhere in an effort to provide visual continuity between buildings. The main façades are glazed with a curtain walling system, within which is a dynamic pattern of horizontal bands of both clear and various shades of blue-tinted glazing, overlaid on the southwest and southeast-facing façades by a layer of brise-soleil (solar shading) blades in a related pattern.

Building A, adjacent and bordering the Ship Canal, has two major components. Firstly the office component, with a low-level, podium-type ground floor and six floors of offices above set out on a simple L-shaped plan. Secondly, a residential tower rises through 25 floors, topped by a two-storey penthouse. It has been modelled with an offset elliptical plan shape to accentuate its slenderness as a landmark, maximise opportunities for views across the canal, and respond to the orientation of the sun to increase sunlight within the flats.

Building B, on the other side of the main studio block, offers further variants on the established themes but here the residential tower is more integrated with the office accommodation from which it grows. Wrapping over the top of the office element in a dramatic cantilever, it gives this composition the form of two interlocking L-blocks – one in plan, one in section – but it is unfortunate that the elevational treatment lacks the finesse of the waterside buildings.

The studio block will be the centre of the BBC's television production activities and will feature one of the largest television studios in Europe at 1,200 sq. m in plan area. A studio for the use of the BBC Philharmonic Orchestra is mounted on hydraulic jacks to ensure total acoustic separation.

With the various BBC buildings having been handed over on time, a comprehensive and technically sophisticated fit-out programme followed on to enable the studios to go live in 2011, with broadcasting due to start on 31 December 2010. The site has been awarded the world's first BREEAM (Building Research Establishment Environmental Assessment Method) approved sustainable community classification.

BROADCASTING PLACE, LEEDS

Architect: Feilden Clegg Bradley Studios

Broadcasting Place is a mixed-use development for a commercial client, Downing Developments, in conjunction with Leeds Metropolitan University. It combines office and teaching spaces for the university's new Faculty of Arts and Society with residential accommodation for the students, while also providing for a new Baptist church to be incorporated within one of its three component buildings.

The site is located on the northern edge of the city centre next to the busy inner ring road, the A58(M), which passes to the south, and a major city centre feeder road, the A660, which rises along the eastern edge in an open cutting. It was previously home to the BBC Radio and Television Studios, which occupied the retained Broadcasting House, a listed stone building in the classical style. The gothic former Baptist Church, also listed and now converted into offices, cuts into the north-west corner of the site, leaving an awkward site profile in which to organise the footprint of the new buildings.

Citing a number of influences on the conceptual thinking, including the characteristic geology and landscape of the nearby moors and the heritage of famous local sculptors Moore and Hepworth, the architect has modelled Broadcasting Place in three complementary but distinct building forms. In combination they have something of the character of a rocky landscape outcrop with their sloping roof profiles and angular forms, reaching a crescendo in the 23-storey block of student accommodation at the south-east corner.

The planning brief, which was developed with the council during the design of an earlier scheme, included the requirement for a significant pedestrian route through the previously private site and a new courtyard space, and respect for the site's location within a conservation area in terms of scale, massing and materials. There also needed to be recognition of its potential contribution to the general build-up of the urban grain and its value as a 'gateway' landmark at an important road junction on the edge of the city centre.

The new pedestrian route and central courtyard divide the buildings into two major components. Block A, the Humanities Building, frames the two internal sides of the site occupied by the former Baptist church, and dog-legs back on itself to terminate with a wing running parallel to the north side of Broadcasting House. Block B, the arts building, and Block C, the student tower, are physically linked and higher, the footprint kinked in two places to create a long wing running along the eastern road frontage, screening the internal courtyard from the noise and fumes of the ring road.

Both buildings are characterised by strong raking roof profiles, reflecting to some extent the natural topography and also enabling the scale of the elevations to be adjusted to respond to the low-rise buildings along Woodhouse Lane on one side and in contrast to the commanding scale of the landmark tower on the other. Although the patterns of fenestration vary from one elevation to the next, the buildings have a strongly unified visual appearance through the consistent use of Cor-ten rusting steel panels for the cladding throughout. Such a simple palette of materials and the tough weathered appearance of the steel endows the buildings with a pervasive feeling of strength and purpose, aided by the angular and uncompromising geometry of the three-dimensional forms.

Block A is the lowest of the three blocks, being scaled down where it emerges on to Woodhouse Lane between the two listed buildings. It houses lecture rooms, exhibition areas and administrative offices and features a recessed two-storey glazed frontage set beneath a two-storey panelled upper part under a gently raking roof line. This rises from a low point to the south next to old Broadcasting House and takes the eye-line higher to the north as it approaches the former Baptist church, with its corner tower.

Block B, housing art, architecture, graphics, photography and print studios, workshops and offices, rakes down over its length from eight storeys at its north-east prow to seven storeys where it abuts the student tower. At a point approaching half-way along its length the block changes direction by means of a fault line

Fig. 2 Southgate (south elevation), Chapman Taylor

that creates sharp-angled projections and opposing recesses in the elevations. The roof-line descends in a continuous line and provides the opportunity for double-height split-level studio space immediately below the inclined roof plane.

Block C rises 22 floors above the ground-level foyer, each floor split into two groups of five single study bedrooms, each with their own access corridor either side of a spine wall, with one studio flat in addition. Each group of study bedrooms has a communal area and kitchen, whose blank end walls face the city centre to the south. The adjoining kitchen and communal rooms are set out with the south wall splayed at an angle to the main elevations and, by reversing the splay at intervals up the height of the building, the tower has been articulated with a series of dynamic cantilevered projections as though each succeeding stage had been twisted on its axis. The intervals between each twist of the end wall increase towards the top, adding to the sense of upward thrust.

The project has won the Europe award from the Council on Tall Buildings and Urban Habitat.

SOUTHGATE, BATH
Architect: Chapman Taylor

The new Southgate complex comprises a mixed-use development of shops, leisure facilities, residential accommodation and restaurants on a site occupying the lower slopes of the city centre near the meandering River Avon. This was formerly occupied by a previous incarnation of the Southgate Centre, a single-storey enclosed shopping centre constructed in the 1970s, together with a multi-storey car park and bus station. The total redevelopment area, including the relocated bus station and transport interchange, extends to about five hectares, and is bounded to the north by New Orchard Street and Henry Street (the line of the old city wall), by Manvers Street to the east, Southgate Street to the west and the river to the south.

The site lies outside the Roman and medieval city of Bath. Southgate is an ancient route of Roman origin, linking the city to the old river bridge, but the location of the site outside the old wall and the pre-existing 20th-century construction on the site made the potential for serious archaeological discoveries less likely.

Although it provided much-needed larger retail units, the somewhat brutal and interventionist design of the earlier centre had been a point of contention among Bath's citizens and a possible reason for its subsequent commercial decline. For the new development there was a desire to return an open street-based urban grain to this important area of Bath. The new design creates a sequence of open streets linking the surrounding parts of the city to a new public square at the heart of the site and providing a new major route connecting the upper part of the city to the new transport interchange alongside Bath Spa railway station and the river frontage.

The main point of entry is at the north-west corner, at the junction of New Orchard Street, Southgate, Stall Street and Lower Borough Walls. From this busy corner a new street carves its way diagonally through the site, expanding into an elongated triangular central piazza, from the corners of which two further streets strike off due south towards the river and the railway. Additional connecting streets cut through at mid-points on the west, north and east sides, to create a fully permeable pattern of pedestrian thoroughfares defined by six mainly three- to four-storey urban blocks, largely standalone in nature but with some upper-level interconnecting bridges. The internal plans of the blocks have been manipulated to provide the large retail footprints demanded by high street stores, for which Bath has a need. The scale of the building increases towards the centre and again to the south-east corner, block G, to accommodate the anchor department store, Debenhams. A large three-storey underground car park sits underneath the south-east part of the site, with access ramps placed in the south-west corner, off St James' Parade.

Given the context of Bath being a World Heritage Site, the fine detail of internal planning for the Southgate complex inevitably took a back seat to matters of external treatment and materials. During the early concept-design stage, a decision was taken to adopt a Georgian architectural language and to develop the elevations using a restrained classical vocabulary and, wherever possible, locally sourced natural Bath stone – or at least other finishes that replicated those found in the surrounding streets, including materials such as painted stucco and render. Bath planners were adamant that the cream-coloured limestone with which much of the city is built should be the primary facing material.

Cost constraints have had an impact on the extent of natural-stone usage, while modern construction techniques and procurement constraints have had a similarly significant impact on detailing, particularly where panellised construction methods were employed. While the use of classical ornamentation has mostly been kept deliberately restrained to avoid competing with the more glamorous examples elsewhere in the city, every building has its own individual design, to create variety, vitality and interest within a generally coherent and co-ordinated composition.

Block A, at the north-west corner, three storeys high

and triangular in plan, has residential flats occupying the top storey facing St Lawrence Street, the new diagonal street leading into the scheme, and is faced in natural stone, with a slate roof behind a parapet. The main elevations are plain, as if replicating a simple terrace of houses, with continuous shop-fronts set in at ground level; the corners of the block are treated as pavilions, with raised parapets and blind arches at first-floor accommodating triple windows.

Block B responds to block A across the diagonal street with an identical façade; its similar pavilion end on the Southgate corner framing this important entry point. This and the Southgate elevation are faced in stone, whereas on the internal elevations towards the piazza the facing material changes to painted stucco and the scale increases, the façade design on to the square being loosely derived from that of the Guildhall.

Block C occupies the south-west corner – the south and west facades being stone-faced, the north and east mostly rendered. The two towers at the south-west corner frame the vehicular entry and exit ramps to the underground car park, while the other two act as a visual stop to the top level of flats set into a mansard roof wrapping around the north and east sides.

The ground-floor colonnade extends across both blocks E/F and G, which completes the southern frontage on to Dorchester Street. Block E/F occupies a pivotal position on the site and features a grand north elevation on to the central square. This incorporates a giant order of two storeys over the ground-floor shop-fronts, enclosing balconies at each level and flanked by pavilion elements with blind arches similar to those elsewhere. Block G, housing the anchor department store, is the most florid of the group, taking its cue from the Greek revival detailing of the retained Argyll Hotel building to which it abuts on the south and west sides. It features stronger cornices, more elaborate architraves, a pronounced mansard roof on north and west elevations and two-storey pilasters, all designed to create the illusion of a grand classical composition with diminishing floor heights, whereas in reality it conceals three retail floors of identical height.

One of the difficulties besetting this kind of historicist approach concerns the incongruities between the demands of modern retailers on one hand and the normal proportions of domestic residential building on the other. The designers of the new Southgate have given a commendable amount of care and attention to the development of an appropriate response to the classic Georgian architecture of Bath and then to the detailing, the articulation and selection of materials necessary to achieve as strong a feeling of authenticity as possible.

It can be no surprise, given the sensitivity of the location, that this £140m project (building cost) had a long and not entirely smooth gestation period. Initial work on the scheme began in 1996, but it was not until 2003 that planning consent was granted. Construction began in 2006, with phase one completing in 2009 and the remainder scheduled for completion during 2010. The scheme is not without its critics, both from the purist point of view in the classical versus modern debate, and also in relation to the execution of the design intent and the sheer volume of building. These quibbles aside, Southgate represents a massive visual improvement to a strategically important part of the city, which desperately needs to retain its competitive edge as a retail destination for the local population as well as a world-class attraction for visitors from afar.

AWARDS

RIBA AWARDS 2009

The Stirling Prize – Maggie's Centre, Hammersmith, London; Rogers Stirk Harbour and Partners

The Stirling shortlist

Kentish Town Health Centre, London; Allford Hall Monaghan Morris

5 Aldermanbury Square, London; Eric Parry Architects

Liverpool One Masterplan, Liverpool; BDP

Bodegas Protos Winery, Valladolid, Spain; Rogers Stirk Harbour and Partners

Fuglsang Kunstmuseum, Lolland, Denmark; Tony Fretton Architects

RIBA SPECIAL AWARDS 2009

The Manser Medal – Gap House, London; Pitman Tozer Architects

The Stephen Lawrence Prize – El Ray, Kent; Simon Conder Associates

The RIBA CABE Public Space Award – Castleford Bridge, West Yorkshire; McDowell and Benedetti

Crown Estate Conservation Award – The Midland Hotel, Morecambe; Union North

RIBA Sorrell Schools Award – Minster School, Nottinghamshire; Penoyre and Prasad Architects

BRITISH CONSTRUCTION INDUSTRY AWARDS 2009

Prime Minister's Better Public Building Award – Joseph Chamberlain Sixth Form College, Birmingham; Nicholas Hare Architects

Major Project Award – Kings Place, London; Dixon Jones

Building Award – The Yellow Building, London; Allford Hall Monaghan Morris

Small Building Award – Dunraven School New Sports Hall, London; SCABAL

Conservation Award – St Martin-in-the-Fields, London; Eric Parry Architects

RIAS AWARDS 2009

RIAS Andrew Doolan Best Building in Scotland Award – Small Animal Hospital, Glasgow, Scotland; Archial Architects

RIBA AWARDS 2010

The Lubetkin Prize – UK Pavilion, World Expo 2010, Shanghai, China; Heatherwick Studio

Royal Gold Medal – IM Pei

CIVIC TRUST AWARDS 2010

Special Award for Sustainability – Liverpool One Masterplan, Liverpool; BDP

Special Award for Restoration – Midland Hotel, Morecambe; Union North

Special Award for Inclusive Design – Hull Truck Theatre; Wright & Wright Architects

Michael Middleton Award (Conservation) – St Martin-in-the-Fields, London; Eric Parry Architects

ART AND CULTURE

Ossian Ward

MARKET WOES, AUCTION HIGHS AND LOWS

The UK retained second spot in the international art market with 29 per cent of total global sales, which were estimated at €31bn (£26.3bn) worldwide. This strong showing, despite the continuing recession, was just a shade behind the USA, whose share had fallen from 46 per cent in 2006 to just 30 per cent in 2009, at the expense of a bullish Chinese art trade. Auction houses were hit hardest, even though the auction season had begun with hopes of a resurgence in the flagging market that had seen sale volumes down by around 70 to 80 per cent year-on-year. The renewed confidence in the lower-priced end of the contemporary art spectrum didn't translate into strong bids and increased buying, however, and some sellers were even put off after auction houses abandoned minimum price guarantees.

On a surprising night in February 2010, all the market doom and gloom was temporarily forgotten as a 1961 bronze *Walking Man* sculpture by Alberto Giacometti bcame the most expensive work of art to be sold at auction, reaching an astonishing £65m at Sotheby's in London. Only a few months later in a May auction at Christie's New York, a Pablo Picasso from 1932 called *Nude, Green Leaves and a Bust* beat the Giacometti and achieved a new record of $106.5m (£69.7m). However, these remarkable prices turned out to be blips in the market and more realistic, brutal results would be reserved for the summer sales.

Expectations were high for the June 2010 'Impressionist and Modern' auction at Christie's, but while a 1903 Blue Period portrait by Pablo Picasso sold for nearly £35m to an anonymous bidder, a much-admired rare Claude Monet from his 'Nympheas' series of 1906 failed to attract any interest near to its presale estimate of £30–£40m and was withdrawn. If that showed that the deep pockets of years gone by were not in evidence, a solid but unspectacular 'Postwar and Contemporary' sale at Sotheby's, also in June, backed this up. The £41m total sold was initially impressive but hid major disappointments for blue-chip works by Gerhard Richter and Peter Doig that, unusually, failed to sell. Christie's fared a little better, securing the highest score of the two houses with a classic 1963 silver silkscreen of Elizabeth Taylor by Andy Warhol selling for £6.7m. The worst was to come at Phillips de Pury, the third biggest auction house, where almost half of the lots at a June sale failed to attract buyers, resulting in one of the worst results for an evening contemporary sale, at under £4m total.

With this kind of instability creeping into the market, two smaller auction houses – Dreweatts and Bloomsbury Auctions – decided to join forces and pool their combined pulling power of £40m per annum. However, according to a survey of dealers, it was the antiques trade, rather than contemporary art, which was the more secure and had recently become a safe haven for British art investors. Millionaires, it turned out, were also more likely to put their money into art than ever before, with this 'passion investment' outstripping other luxury goods as long-term assets.

Following the massive bailouts paid to failing institutions, the public and media rightly turned their attentions to the cultural affairs of our state-owned coffers. The Royal Bank of Scotland, which came under scrutiny after it was saved by a £20bn government loan, offered to put its sizeable corporate art collection on permanent display as a sign of goodwill, but the regulators stepped in and suggested that the bank should in fact consider selling some of its 2,200-strong cache of works by Joshua Reynolds, Johann Zoffany, David Hockney and L. S. Lowry.

ARTS POLICY AND OLYMPIC PLANS

British museums also began flirting seriously with the much frowned-upon practice of deaccessioning, or selling from their permanent collections. In January 2010 a strict law forbidding this practice was softened, mainly to allow institutions to return objects that had been looted by Nazis to their rightful owners. The Holocaust (Return of Cultural Objects) Act 2009 specified that items stolen between 1933 and 1945 could be repatriated if found by the Spoliation Advisory Panel to have been illegally acquired by any museum.

A controversial wrangle that predated the change in law involved the proposal to sell a Rodin sculpture and a picture by Alfred Munnings from the city of Southampton's art collection. It may have divided opinion – some believed the £15m raised would be well spent on a new Sea City Museum and Titanic exhibition, others believed it set a dangerous precedent – but the Southampton debate was nevertheless soon followed by the Tate's decision to deaccession works from its collection for the first time in its history. A large steel staircase work by the Spanish sculptor Juan Muñoz was mooted as the first to be sold and would begin a programme of 'trading up' works by particular artists, to better represent them.

The newly incumbent coalition government announced cuts almost immediately in May 2010. Jeremy Hunt, the Minister for Culture, Olympics, Media and Sport, said he was facing a loss of £66m from his combined budgets, despite pre-election assurances from the Conservatives that they would pump an extra £40m into heritage projects – especially castles, ancient structures and religious buildings. In fact, the cultural sector was asked to contemplate 25 to 40 per cent cuts on top of the forecasted 3.5 per cent cuts. Fears were raised by the directors of many national institutions that cuts of around 10 per cent would mean redundancies, and anything more would have an impact on visitors in terms of shorter opening hours. The threat of closure even hung over a number of leading museums, galleries and theatres. The Institute of Contemporary Arts (ICA) in London came the closest of the major Arts Council-funded bodies to the breadline, having to slash its budgets and staff to reduce deficits of around £1m.

Arguably, many major museums were guilty of mismanaging their finances in the tax year 2008–9, as accounts released showed investments losing value hand over fist. The Victoria & Albert Museum (V&A) saw the value of its investments lose £4.8m, or around 20 per cent. The British Museum's fell by £11m and the Tate saw its hedge funds lose £1.1m.

Respite arrived late in the news that increased sales of lottery tickets would boost the Heritage Lottery Fund – depleted by its support of the Olympics – by £25m each year until 2018. Indeed, the Olympic and Paralympic Games had been blamed for siphoning as much as £322m away from the other arts, but after much uncertainty and a revolving staff door – that ended with the Southbank Centre's artistic director Jude Kelly chairing the cultural portion of the 2012 Games and former director of the Manchester festival, Ruth Mackenzie, becoming director of the Cultural Olympiad – some of the artistic projects that would accompany the festival of sport began to take shape. Among the announcements was a raft of winning commissions for 12 new regional works of public art that included Anthony McCall's idea for a giant spinning column of clouds over Liverpool. Towering over them all, though, would be Anish Kapoor's Olympic landmark, the *ArcelorMittal Orbit*. The 115-metre steel sculpture at Stratford is set to be Britain's tallest and most expensive at £19.1m. The inevitable press jibes ensued, likening it to a helter-skelter or twisted spaghetti, although matters were not helped when London mayor Boris Johnson nicknamed it the 'hubble-bubble', claiming it resembled a giant shisha pipe.

The follow-up to Antony Gormley's *One & Other*, whereby the fourth plinth at Trafalgar Square became an impromptu stage for 2,400 performing members of the public, was Nigerian-born Yinka Shonibare's *Nelson's Ship in a Bottle* (although, in between, the mayor had his wish to temporarily put up a statue commemorating Battle of Britain RAF Commander Sir Keith Park). Shonibare's scale replica of HMS *Victory* featured 37 sails made from the artist's trademark Dutch wax fabric, using colourful and naval-themed African prints. Gormley himself remained much in demand for public art, unveiling a New York version of his 31-man *Event Horizon* piece first seen on the South Bank of London in 2007, as well as similar works at Bexhill-on-Sea's De La Warr Pavilion and on the Water of Leith in Edinburgh. After installing 100 more such bodies for *Horizon Field* in the Austrian Alps, the artist said that he would stop producing the epic scatterings of his life-size iron casts: 'We've covered the urban condition, the endlessness of the sea, and now the chaos of the mountains. That'll do.'

One notable public art failure, Thomas Heatherwick's giant, thorny *B of the Bang* that rose as a monument of Manchester's 2002 Commonwealth Games, was shelved and placed into storage indefinitely after years of safety concerns about its dangerously dropping steel spikes. Also briefly seen in Manchester was a controversial street parade organised by Turner Prize-winner Jeremy Deller, in which discrete groups of locals including scouts, mill workers and goths were asked to celebrate their identity. It was the band of 'unrepentant' smokers that city officials objected to, with the most unrepentant of them all, artist David Hockney, contributing a flag of an ashtray which was carried as part of the event.

ART FAIRS AND COLLECTING

There was a cull in the previously prospering number of art fairs in the autumn season. The young pretender that had limited itself to hosting galleries under six years old, the Zoo Art Fair, continued in a reduced capacity in 2009 but cancelled its 2010 edition, citing straitened times. Other weaker fairs such as Scope, Bridge and Red Dot also disappeared, while the main event, the Frieze Art Fair, staged every October in Regent's Park, continued to grow with 24 new exhibitors and a section dedicated to less established galleries, which lessened the blow of some high-profile drop-outs. Another October fair, Design Art London, changed its name and its focus in 2009, to the Pavilion of Art & Design, widening its remit to include decorative arts, antiques and fine art in addition to 20th-century and contemporary design.

The major fair rebranding of the year was for the venerable old Grosvenor House Art & Antiques Fair, which was scrapped to make way for Masterpiece London (held at the Chelsea Barracks from 24–29 June 2010), an all-encompassing jamboree of cars, art, antiques and other luxury goods. A new art fair aimed at the Latin American market called Pinta, previously held only in New York, came to London's Earls Court from 3–6 June, boasting many galleries from Sao Paulo, Buenos Aires and Bogota alongside more familiar dealers such as White Cube and Sprüth Magers showing work from the Spanish-speaking continent.

The sheer wealth of work at any one art fair began to cause concern for insurance companies charged with finding adequate coverage for their clients. With so many expensive pieces under one roof, any major disaster would result in huge losses for the underwriters. A tightening of the regulations around works of art brought to the UK 'in bond' also threatened the ability of fairs, galleries and museums to put on shows without paying the full import tax. The rule is that art works can be taken out of customs warehouses for three months without incurring this cost, but in practice many of these permissions have been regularly extended or reissued without too many questions. The change in attitude by customs officials might mean less international business for British galleries, less fluid lines of credit or even less ambition in terms of exhibition-making.

Although the Frieze Art Fair declined an invitation to feature in a task on the BBC's hit TV show, *The Apprentice*, the collector Charles Saatchi launched his own talent search programme on BBC2 called *School of Saatchi*, in which a bunch of hopefuls negotiated artistic assignments in order to get an exhibition with the hallowed Saatchi Gallery. If few observers were heartened by the incursion of reality television into the art world, then no one expected Saatchi's next move, which was to announce that he would donate his building and part of his collection to the nation. The shock statement in July 2010 stated that 200 works worth £25m – including Tracey Emin's famous installation, *My Bed*, and works by the Chapman Brothers – would be bequeathed to the nation under the title of the Museum of Contemporary Art London or MoCA London. A trio of shows in 2012 would reveal the full extent of the gift, although a firm date was not set for the reclusive collector's official retirement. It seems that he will leave the institution in fine form, having only just failed to garner the top spot for most visited exhibition of the year in Britain, missing out to an exhibition of work by the equally elusive street artist Banksy, at the Bristol's City Museum and Art Gallery.

Artist and photographer Martin Parr announced another generous donation, of some 700 photographs from his private collection, to be left either to the Tate or the V&A. Parr said he wanted to raise the status of the medium in Britain beyond its current marginalisation and that his bequest would help fill gaps in the national collection. Other potential museum donors and benefactors were busy putting their prized possessions up for sale, with numerous historic collections owned by aristocratic families being split up by the auction houses. Earl Spencer held a sale at Christie's of works from his Althorp estate, while the Earl of Rosebery and the Duke of Rutland were putting works on to the open market by Turner and Poussin, respectively. The Duke of Devonshire also looked to dispense with some of the family silver from Chatsworth House at a Sotheby's sale in October 2010, hoping to raise at least £2.5m towards running costs.

MUSEUM NEWS AND ACQUISITIONS

Museums were kept under serious pressure, having seen a 37 per cent drop in donations in the year ending 31 March 2009, while a report by the charity Arts & Business claimed that UK companies, as well as individual philanthropists, and nonprofit institutions, were holding back from investing in the arts in general and might continue to stay away for another two years. Especially in jeopardy were the many museum building projects looking to raise large amounts of capital. The British Museum was still some £43m short of its £135m needed for the 2013 opening of a new World Conservation and Exhibitions Centre, while Tate Modern was only halfway towards its £215m Herzog & de Meuron-designed extension.

One way of easing the burden on museums was suggested in a speech by London mayor Boris Johnson, who cited the example of voluntary admission fees at the Metropolitan Museum in New York as a possible way forward for some cash-strapped institutions.

Many other revenue streams were being squeezed and special attention was drawn to the arts sponsorship of BP after its disastrous Deep Water Horizon leak in the Gulf of Mexico brought worldwide condemnation for the oil firm. Both Tate and the National Portrait Gallery, who were celebrating continued BP sponsorship for two decades, remained defiant in the face of repeated calls to drop such damaging partnerships. They were besieged by protesters and performances from groups such as Liberate Tate and Art Not Oil, and there were also guerrilla-style attacks on the British Museum and Tate Britain's Summer Party – although nothing more toxic than gallons of treacle were spilt all over the steps and galleries.

There were notable success stories for the museum sector too. Nottingham Contemporary, a regional centre for modern art opened in a new corrugated concrete structure by Caruso St John architects. Its 3,000 sq. m of exhibition space makes it one of the biggest dedicated galleries outside of London and it inaugurated its galleries with a display of America-era pools and portraits by David Hockney from the 1960s.

Another newcomer was the quirky, pleasingly unfinished and itinerant Museum of Everything, which opened for half the year in a disused dairy in north London. Showcasing 200 extraordinary works from the collection of James Brett by now famous 'outsiders' such as Henry Darger, as well as naive artists and schizophrenics, hobos and savants, the display then toured to Turin but promised to return to London with a new exhibition in the near future.

The Museum of London reopened its modern galleries after a £20m refit, allowing it to show 7,000 objects tracing the city's history, from the Great Fire of 1666 to the present day. Another refurbishment opened in April at Leighton House, the former residence and studio of Victorian painter Lord Frederic Leighton. Over a 17-month closure and after years of restoration, the dramatic interiors were gilded and repainted to recapture its former glory, all to the tune of £1.7m. The V&A's new £30m Medieval and Renaissance galleries, designed by architectural practice MUMA, opened to great fanfare in late 2009 as did its renovated Ceramics Galleries on the top floor.

Without doubt the most anticipated overhaul was for Oxford University's Ashmolean Museum, nicknamed the 'temple of arts' when it opened in its current site in 1845 and rightly famed for its outstanding collections of art and archaeology. American architect Rick Mather's £61m masterplan not only doubled the display, with 39 new galleries, but added new education and conservation centres. Adding to its treasured paintings by Raphael and Uccello was the welcome reattribution of a picture called *The Triumph of Love* to Titian. The Ashmolean acquired the painting before it was cleaned and later reckoned to be by the Italian Renaissance master.

Among other notable acquisitions was the National Portrait Gallery's purchase of a new version of Marc Quinn's famous self-portrait bust made of nine frozen pints of his own blood. *Self*, now an icon of Brit Art, has to be kept refrigerated and the artist only makes a new one every five years.

DISCOVERIES AND ART CRIMES

A lawsuit over another misattributed Titian finally ended when Christie's was forced to settle out of court for an undisclosed sum. The auction house had failed to notice that a work it sold for £8,000 in 1993 was not only a real bargain but also a painting entitled *Salome with the Head of John the Baptist* by Titian.

A painting by the British artist Sir Alfred Munnings was found hidden behind a painting by another artist with whom he is believed to have had a love affair. Such fortuitous recovery of lost works formed part of a fascinating exhibition at the National Gallery, called 'Close Examination: Fakes, Mistakes and Discoveries' (30 June–12 September 2010). The museum not only delved beneath the surface of paintings to reveal how forgeries are routinely revealed through forensic testing, X-rays and microscopic examination by the scientific department, but it also came clean about the rogues in its collection including a fake Botticelli, Dürer and Poussin.

Despite the new advances in revealing forgeries through technology, it has long been known that Chinese factories are producing fakes by everyone from Andy Warhol to Leonardo da Vinci. Bizarrely, however, the UK's most infringed artist turned out to be Mandy Wilkinson, a relatively unknown Welsh painter whose work sells for £2,000. More worryingly, the UK was named as the world's most dangerous place to own art by the Art Loss Register, who keep track of lost and stolen works of art. Although a startling 53,709 works have gone missing here since 1976, it was the French authorities that were left red-faced after an audacious heist in May, in which five paintings were removed from the Museum of Modern Art in Paris. The value of the missing works by Picasso, Matisse, Leger, Modigliani and Braque was estimated to be close to €500m (£422.6m).

One of the UK's biggest thefts in recent years went unsolved after five men were cleared of plotting to extort money for the return of Leonardo da Vinci's *Madonna of the Yarnwinder*, stolen from the Duke of Buccleuch's Drumlanrig Estate in 2003. They were not accused of carrying out that raid.

EXHIBITIONS AND PRIZES

Damien Hirst's much vaunted return to the solitary act of painting met with critical disdain in two shows at the Wallace Collection (14 October 2009–24 January 2010) and his gallery White Cube (25 November 2009–30 January 2010). The dark-blue pictures of skulls, lemons and interiors were inspired by Francis Bacon and Old Master paintings, but were described as 'amateurish', 'dreadful' and 'doomy' by the newspapers.

At around the same time, Tate Modern opened its autumn show, 'Pop Life: Art in a Material World', to a storm of controversy over the American artist Richard Prince's photograph of a 10-year-old Brooke Shields posing naked in a bathtub. The 1983 work, *Spiritual America,* was deemed offensive and removed by the Metropolitan Police's Obscene Publications Unit, forcing Tate Modern to pulp all its exhibition catalogues as well. Regarded as the first ever Pop artist, legendary British artist Richard Hamilton was given an exhibition at the Serpentine Gallery (3 March–25 April 2010) that focused instead on his political work and other 'Modern Moral Matters'.

One of the most provocative acts of the year was Michael Landy's *Art Bin* at the South London Gallery (29 January–14 March 2010) which not only symbolically trashed the gallery before its extension was built, but also turned it into a giant dustbin. Landy invited artists to bring their 'failures' and throw their unwanted pieces into the giant skip. Pieces by Cornelia Parker, Julian Opie and Peter Blake joined works by Damien Hirst and Landy's wife, Gillian Wearing.

Painter of temporary and ephemeral wall works, Richard Wright, won the 2009 Turner Prize and £25,000 award, while the second Jarman Award for filmmaking went to Lindsay Seers, who received £10,000. The fourth Artes Mundi prize, presented by the National Museum of Cardiff to an outstanding international artist and worth £40,000, went to Yael Bartana from Israel. New awards for Russian art (the Kandinsky Prize), Italian art (Renaissance Arts Prize) and Islamic art (the Jameel Prize) were all inaugurated in London, while the annual Art Fund Prize for museums and galleries went to the Ulster Museum in Belfast.

PEOPLE

After seven years at the helm of Tate Modern, Spanish director Vicente Todolí resigned and was replaced by a surprise candidate, Chris Dercon, who had been director of Munich's Haus der Kunst. Tate Britain also unveiled a new director to replace the outgoing Stephen Deuchar, who was appointed as director of the Art Fund, and in April 2010 Penelope Curtis, who had been at the Henry Moore Institute since 1999, took up her post. Tate also named Simon Baker as its first curator of photography and international art. The artistic director of the Barbican Centre, Graham Sheffield, left for a similar role at a multi-arts complex in Hong Kong, while Catherine Ince joined as a new curator at the Barbican Art Gallery. The Baltic Centre in Gateshead continued to shuffle its staff with a new chief curator, Laurence Sillars, joining from Tate Liverpool and Peter Buchan as its new chairman of the board.

Notable obituaries included Scottish painter Craigie Aitchison at the age of 83, who was honoured with a small display of his work as part of the Royal Academy's Summer Exhibition (14 June–22 August 2010), and Welsh sculptor Barry Flanagan whose work was displayed by his Cork Street gallery Waddington (16 March–17 April 2010). The American fashion and celebrity photographer Irving Penn died only months before his retrospective opened at the National Portrait Gallery (18 February–6 June 2010) and the life of modern dance pioneer Merce Cunningham was distilled in a sensitive film by British artist Tacita Dean, shown at Frith Street Gallery (13 May–26 June 2010). German painter Sigmar Polke and nonagenarian French sculptor Louise Bourgeois died within weeks of each other in June 2010.

BUSINESS AND FINANCE

Timothy Hindle

It was a year for the Grand Old Duke of York. No sooner had things gone right up to the top of the hill than they came right back down again. Stock markets, commodity prices, economic growth and so on. It was a year of uncertainty, a time when pessimists bought gold, while optimists waited for consumers, bankers and governments to transport them back to 2007, the last year when growth was steady, homes were as safe as houses, and bankers' bonuses were unquestioned.

The FTSE 100 index marched right up to 5,800 in April 2010 (a rise of over 40 per cent in nine months) before falling right back down again to almost 4,800 by July. And while the price of oil climbed to almost $90 (£60) a barrel by April, it fell by 20 per cent in the month of May alone. Coffee, tea and beef prices likewise rose to new highs before tumbling back. The key word was volatility – all bright and perky on a Monday morning, markets could be forecasting a fate worse than Greece by the close on Tuesday.

EUROPE'S ECONOMIC WOES

Beware, you could say, of Greeks bearing statistics. The land of Socrates and Melina Mercouri persistently misreported the state of its finances to the EU and, when the truth was out, collapsed in a heap. Its credit rating fell below A grade for the first time in a decade. Membership of the eurozone, which for some time had been making cannier British holidaymakers wary of high-price Greece as a summer destination, put the small Mediterranean country under unbearable pressure.

Greece was rescued in April by a German-led bail-out worth €30bn (£25bn). But the package was slow to arrive and it gave investors time to panic about where might be next. Thoughts turned first to the PIGS, those Mediterranean countries in the euro straitjacket: Portugal, Italy, Greece and Spain. Some soon wondered whether the malaise might spread beyond the eurozone, to others with similarly overstretched public finances, so that then the group might be known as PIGS UK.

However, Britain's coalition government, elected in May 2010, wasted little time in tackling the sorry state of the nation's kitty. Since March 2009, £200bn had been pumped into the economy under the strategy of quantitative easing, designed to stop recession turning into depression. In his first budget, on 22 June 2010, the new chancellor of the exchequer, George Osborne, set out to balance the books with tax rises and expenditure cuts. He announced that VAT would rise to 20 per cent from January 2011 and that cuts in welfare payments and the public-sector payroll would help to reduce the budget deficit by about a quarter in the next fiscal year. Despite its claim that these measures constituted a fair and progressive budget, the UK government was later criticised by the Institute for Fiscal Studies (IFS) for being regressive. It would be the poorest 10 per cent of the population that were most affected by the changes, claimed the IFS.

Unemployment, at its highest for 16 years in April 2010, was expected to rise still further as the public sector shed jobs, and as those businesses dependent on public-sector contracts (the construction industry in particular) were also forced to lay off workers. Economic growth, which had stuttered back up to 0.2 per cent in the first quarter of 2010, remained fragile, and the long-feared second half of a double-dip recession seemed to be one possible consequence of the Osborne measures.

Another possible outcome was a series of strikes, with public-sector unions and private-sector workers threatening a return to industrial action the likes of which had not been seen since the Thatcher years. British Airways (BA) put its doors to manual in March 2010 when a three-day walk-out by cabin crew disgruntled about cuts in pay and perks grounded many of its flights. Undeterred by record annual losses of £531m and evidence of a £3.7bn hole in their company's pension scheme, BA workers continued to strike spasmodically into June.

In the event, the BA strike was less effective at grounding Britain than a cloud of ash that floated over from the Eyjafjallajokull volcano in Iceland. Much of Europe's airspace was closed for six days in April 2010 as caution prevailed about the possible effects of high-level ash on jet engines. Stranded British travellers and logistics firms were forced to call upon hitherto unused wells of ingenuity when most of Britain's airports fell briefly silent.

It was an eventful year for the flight industry. The new coalition government clamped down on airport expansion in London, removing support for a third runway at the decaying Heathrow, and saying it would not support plans for new runways at Stansted or Gatwick. In December 2009, Ferrovial, the Spanish owner of London's three largest airports, had sold Gatwick to Global Infrastructure Partners – a company that already owned London City airport – for £1.5bn.

Anglo-Spanish air-transport links were further intertwined in April 2010 when, after 15 months of talks, BA agreed to merge with Iberia in a deal that will leave both airlines' brands up in the air, and both their hubs on the ground (in London and Madrid). With a marked lack of originality, the new holding company was christened International Airlines. When it was announced that Heathrow was no longer to get a third runway, BA played its new Anglo-Spanish card. In future, it said, it might be compelled to favour Madrid airport over Heathrow.

NEW LINE-UPS FOR BRITISH BRANDS

Greece, Iceland, Spain – the year emphasised again the global (and often unexpected) sources of influence on British business. In January an American food giant, Kraft, best known for cheese slices and instant coffee, successfully bid £11.9bn for Cadbury and brought yet another iconic British brand into foreign hands.

The American food group had to raise its original offer by some 17 per cent to persuade shareholders to yield. After the event, Warren Buffett, the legendary American investor, said that Kraft had done 'a bad deal'. It was a bad deal for some of those at Cadbury too. The American company soon reversed an earlier pledge not to close a Cadbury factory near Bristol.

Another iconic brand changed hands during the year.

Harrods, owned since 1985 by Mohamed al Fayed, was bought in April 2010 by Qatar's sovereign-wealth fund for £1.5bn. The Qatari fund is no stranger to the UK, being the biggest single shareholder in both Barclays bank and J. Sainsbury. In the same month, Deutsche Bahn, Germany's state-owned railway company, paid £1.6bn for Arriva, one of Britain's biggest bus and train operators. And T-Mobile, owned by Deutsche Telekom, merged its UK operations with those of Orange, owned by France Telecom. The new operation became the largest mobile phone network in Britain with 28.4 million customers, overtaking both O2 and Vodafone.

GULF OIL DISASTER

On 20 April 2010 the Deepwater Horizon oil rig exploded, killing 11 men and springing a leak in its pipeline. By the summer, it had gushed more than 3 million barrels of oil into the Gulf of Mexico.

The majority of Deepwater Horizon (65 per cent) was owned by BP, a company that until a decade ago was called British Petroleum. Today BP has more shareholders and employees in America than it does in Britain, and its chair is Swedish. It is still, however, registered in the UK and thought of as British, especially by US President Barack Obama who vowed to make the company pay for damages and lost earnings. By July, BP said it had spent well over $3bn trying to contain the gushing oil, and there were forecasts that its total clean-up costs could mount to $15bn. In addition, BP agreed with the American government that it would set up a $20bn compensation fund and waive its dividend for at least the next three quarters.

By mid-June, BP's share price had fallen by 50 per cent, knocking £60bn off the value of the company. That threatened to knock a big hole in the many pension funds that considered BP's stock to be a *sine qua non* of any blue-chip portfolio. It also suggested that investors thought there were more costs yet to come.

The oil leak was a double blow for the company: for BP had at last looked like it would make money from its considerable investment in the Gulf of Mexico, a place where the technical challenges are formidable. As recently as September 2009, the press had trumpeted the oil discovery of the year, maybe even the decade. BP had struck lucky with its Tiber well, a find that had required the company to drill more than 10km below the Gulf's sea bed. 'Now,' said *Business Week,* the company 'is getting a shot in the arm from its Gulf finds, which are just coming on stream with profitable oil'. Famous last words.

The Deepwater Horizon oil spill raised serious questions about whether BP's culture had put too much emphasis on cost-cutting and too little on safety. Had it got the balance wrong in past attempts to push forward the barriers of oil exploration in what is a risky and competitive industry? In July 2010, BP's chief executive, Tony Hayward, paid the inevitable price. He announced that he would stand down in October in favour of Bob Dudley, who would become BP's first non-British CEO.

Other iconic companies changed those at their helm during the year. Among high street grocers there was an almost complete turnaround, with changes taking place at firms that accounted for over 60 per cent of the UK grocery market. The best known of them all, Sir Terry Leahy, boss of Tesco, announced his retirement after 14 years in the job. His successor, Philip Clarke, looked unlikely to bring radical change. Like Sir Terry he was born in Liverpool, started his working life stacking shelves and had virtually no experience other than at Tesco.

In November 2009 it was announced that a Dutchman, Marc Bolland, would become CEO of Marks & Spencer. Mr Bolland joined from Wm Morrison supermarkets and was replaced in that post by Dalton Philips. Then in April 2010, Andy Bond announced that he was standing down as Asda CEO after five years in the job. Andy Clarke, Asda's chief operating officer, stepped up to become the new boss of the Walmart-owned chain.

Meanwhile the online grocery business offered more promise than profit. Ocado, a familiar name in grocery deliveries, went public in July 2010 with an offering of shares that valued the business at over £800m, despite the fact that during its ten-year history it had yet to make a profit.

GREEN PIECES

Other firms were eager to show their green credentials. The UK's target of generating 15 per cent of its energy from renewable sources by 2020 looked less fanciful following announcements by Siemens, General Electric and Mitsubishi that they were all to invest in wind turbine production in the UK.

At the same time, British Gas said that it would step up production of smart meters and create 2,500 new jobs in the process. Smart meters aim to help consumers save gas and electricity. They are the energy industry's equivalent of the ladderless stocking – produced by suppliers to help them sell less. Can such a thing last?

The new coalition government, eager to show its own green credentials, confirmed that it would go ahead with a £21m grant to Nissan, the Japanese car company, to build its Leaf electric car in the north-east. However, Japanese car companies, the biggest auto manufacturers in the UK, had a difficult year. Toyota in particular had an *annus horribilis.* Once renowned for its exemplary production system, Toyota was forced to recall millions of cars in the USA, Europe and China after evidence that their accelerator pedals could become stuck. Then the company recalled almost half a million of its new hybrid cars (which run on petrol and electricity) because of possible problems with their brakes. Finally, in July, an engine fault prompted the recall of its top-of-the-range model, the Lexus.

Japan's loss was largely Germany's gain. Between them, Audi, BMW and Volkswagen gained 20 per cent of the British market, a big increase and almost twice the share of the top three Japanese brands. In general, the UK car industry, hard hit by the economic recession in 2008 and 2009, bounced back. Demand was boosted first by the government's 'scrappage' scheme, which gave buyers of new cars a £2,000 discount if they simultaneously scrapped a car that was more than ten years old. The scheme ended in March 2010, but even after that the industry prospered. Car production in the UK increased by over 50 per cent in May on the same period a year earlier. Demand was later boosted by buyers wanting to avoid the increase in VAT from January 2011.

BANKERS' BONUSES AND STATE REGULATION

There were continuing efforts to prevent banks from repeating their past follies. In his first budget, George Osborne introduced a bank levy, to apply from January 2011. It will be calculated on the balance sheets of UK banks and building societies, and of the UK operations of foreign banks. Osborne said he expected the tax, a sort of insurance premium, to raise £2bn a year once fully in place.

In November 2009 the then Labour government tried to prevent the majority state-owned Royal Bank of Scotland from paying £1.5bn in bonuses to its investment banking unit. Directors at the bank threatened to resign if the bonuses were banned. But a government minister, Lord Myners, told them 'to come back into the real world'. For a short time, the chancellor imposed a 50 per cent tax on bonuses over £25,000 (the tax to be paid by the banks themselves).

The Labour government also set out to recoup some of the £2.3bn it lost when the Icelandic bank Icesave collapsed in 2008. Icelandic voters rejected the idea in a referendum in March 2009, but the government pressed on, threatening to veto Iceland's entry into the EU until the issue is settled. The population of Iceland is about 307,000 – will they deem membership of the EU to be worth around £7,500 for every single inhabitant?

George Osborne, once in office, soon set about redecorating the bank regulatory system. It was sorely in need of it. In a 2009 league table produced by the World Economic Forum, organisers of the annual Davos conference, Britain came 126th in a ranking of the soundness of banking systems around the world. It was just below Burundi. Osborne announced plans to abolish the Financial Services Authority (FSA), the body that had been created in 1997 by a previous fresh-faced chancellor – New Labour's Gordon Brown. The FSA, Osborne said, had been almost entirely focused on 'rules-based regulation'; it had failed to see the wood-of-risks for the trees. He handed back supervisory responsibility for banks to the Bank of England, where it had been until 1997. And he announced that there would be a review into whether Britain's bigger banks should be broken up – in particular, whether their high-risk investment banking businesses should be separated from their bread-and-butter savings and current-account services.

The move concentrated power in the hands of the governor of the Bank of England, Mervyn King, a man who had argued that without supervisory powers the Bank could be likened to 'a church whose congregation attends weddings and funerals but ignores the sermons in between'.

Bank regulators these days tend to move in parallel. In the USA the Dodd-Frank bill moved closer to the statute book. *The Economist* said it would 'bring the most sweeping changes to America's financial regulatory system since the 1930s'. At the same time, the European Commission suggested an EU-wide insurance scheme against bank crises (funded by a levy on financial institutions), but the idea was opposed by both Britain and France. Meanwhile, a directive imposing limits on bankers' bonuses was approved by the European parliament.

FROM WEST TO EAST

HSBC (formerly the Hong Kong and Shanghai Banking Corporation) moved the office of its CEO from London back to Hong Kong, where the bank first began in 1865. It said the move was made to prepare the bank 'for the shift in the world's centre of economic gravity from west to east'. Evidence of that shift came when China's share of voting rights in the World Bank was raised to 4.42 per cent, putting it behind only the USA and Japan.

The eyes of British business were seldom off China. Not surprisingly, for the country's growth rate climbed back up to 11.9 per cent in the first quarter of 2010, and it reported a monthly trade deficit for the first time in six years – that is, its imports were greater than its exports.

However there were some cracks in the Far Eastern economic miracle. Workers started to demonstrate that they could go on strike, just like everybody else. And in March 2010, a court in Shanghai sentenced four employees of the Anglo-Australian mining group Rio Tinto to jail terms and fines. The four – one Australian citizen and three Chinese nationals – admitted taking bribes during negotiations over iron ore sales with China's steel mills.

CONSERVATION

THE NATURAL ENVIRONMENT

Peter Marren

CUTBACKS TO NATURE CONSERVATION

England faces significant cutbacks in funding for nature conservation. At the time of writing, Natural England, the government's wildlife watchdog, was expecting a budget cut of 30 per cent, a figure that would entail redundancies, the closure of nearly half its body's regional offices, and much less to spend on conservation projects. Despite plans to phase in the job losses over four years, 400 posts are likely to be lost over the next financial year, according to Natural England's chief executive, Dr Helen Phillips.

Wildlife and Countryside Link, the umbrella body representing Britain's voluntary conservation societies, fears that another target for cuts will be the millions spent on entry-level and higher-level stewardship programmes which pay farmers to manage the land in a relatively wildlife-friendly way. Sites of Special Scientific Interest (SSSIs) will, says Wildlife and Countryside Link, become 'sadly degraded' for want of funds to manage them. It predicts the early extinction of the corncrake, and possibly the twite, cirl bunting and turtle dove, if farm payments are cut drastically. If Natural England's species recovery programme is cut, endangered invertebrates such as the freshwater pearl mussel, and the Duke of Burgundy butterfly and the large blue butterfly might also be lost.

Landscapes that depend on subsidies, such as wildflower meadows and chalk downs, and coastal habitats such as saltmarsh, would be hard hit. Staff cuts at DEFRA could derail plans to record historic footpaths and bridleways. The challenge will be to find less expensive ways of preserving species and their habitats.

THE GREAT CRANE PROJECT

The RSPB, along with the Wildfowl and Wetlands Trust and the Pensthorpe Conservation Trust, are sponsoring an attempt to reintroduce the crane to the Somerset Levels. The common crane is a magnificent bird, taller than a heron, with plumed wing feathers and a loud trumpeting call that carries far over the marshes where it breeds. They were once widespread in the lowland landscape judging by fossils, place names and their place in folklore: 204 cranes appeared on the menu of the Bishop of York's inauguration feast in 1465. The birds were driven to extinction in around 1600, probably through a combination of drainage works and hunting. The crane is still found in parts of Europe where it has adapted to breeding in an agricultural landscape.

Since 1979, a small number of cranes have colonised the Norfolk Broads naturally, but the colony has not spread much further. A pair nested at an RSPB reserve at Lakenheath in the Fens in 2009, while four birds lingered for a while at the Loch of Kinnordy in Angus in May 2010.

The feeling among experts is that the crane will need human intervention to build up its numbers in Britain. The Great Crane Project draws on the experience of the successful reintroduction of the endangered whooping crane in eastern USA. It will attempt to establish the bird at the Somerset Levels and Moors, which has a suitably mild climate with relatively few hazards to flying birds. Funding from the Viridor Credits company will enable up to 100 young cranes to be reared at the wildfowl centre at Slimbridge from eggs taken from a large nature reserve in Brandenburg, Germany. The chicks will be hand-reared by costumed humans and then released in a two-hectare enclosure on the levels. Starting in autumn 2010, the sponsors hope to establish a resident breeding population of about 20 pairs over the next 20 years. If successful, the first British-born cranes will leave their nests around 2015.

PROGRESS ON OTHER BIRD INTRODUCTIONS

The red kite continues to be among the most talked-about British birds, its floating crooked-winged form and distinctive forked tail being a familiar sight over much of Britain during the past 20 years. There are currently around 2,100 pairs of kites in Britain, half of them in Wales. The first kites were released in 1989, and the reintroduction has now reached its final phase with 90 birds released in Grizedale Forest in north-west England, the only remaining kite gap. The kite has also begun to breed in County Wicklow in Ireland, following releases there since 2007, although two were found poisoned in 2010.

The least successful part of the reintroduction has been Scotland, where there are just 135 breeding pairs, only a seventh of potential capacity. Of 103 kites found dead between 1989 and 2006, 41 were killed illegally. Investigators have attributed the deaths to persecution by gamekeepers. Most of the illegally killed kites were found near the core breeding area, which itself is near to large areas of grouse moor management.

The white-tailed eagle, also known as the sea eagle, was first released in western Scotland in 1975 and has reached a self-sustaining, and slowly growing, population of about 40 pairs. In 2008, eagle chicks taken from nests in Norway were released at a secret location on the coast of Fife in the hope that they will eventually colonise the east coast of Scotland.

A controversial plan to release sea eagles in East Anglia was shelved in 2010 because its sponsor, Natural England, faced budget cuts. The body decided to pull out rather than commit taxpayers' money to an extensive public consultation on a scheme it would be unable to fund.

The great bustard bred for the second year running on Salisbury Plain, Wiltshire. The small colony of 18 birds produced at least four chicks this year. Last year two chicks managed to fledge, although one was killed shortly afterwards by a fox, and the other has not been seen since. The great bustard is making steady progress although the five-year delay between hatching and maturity means this introduction is definitely a long haul.

PLANTLIFE'S GHOST ORCHID DECLARATION

The charity Plantlife produced a report drawing attention to the gross neglect of the plant kingdom by the nature conservation establishment. The *Ghost Orchid Declaration*

– named after a plant thought to be extinct – pointed out that one wild flower species in five is at risk of following the orchid to national extinction. It called for a greater investment in these 'poor relations of the wildlife world', claiming that there is a fundamental imbalance between resources for animals compared with plants. For example, the Joint Nature Conservation Committee spent nearly £3m on research contracts for the marine environment and birds between 2007 and 2009, but nothing on plants and fungi. Botany and mycology (the science of fungi) are now unpopular subjects for university degrees: of some 18,405 new biology students in 2007–8, only 195 opted for botany.

Habitat management, even on supposedly protected sites, does not necessarily favour wild flowers, says Plantlife. For example, although there has been a 5 per cent increase in broadleaved woodland since 1990, woodland flowers have decreased by up to 20 per cent (while species confined to old woodland have declined even more). Agri-environment schemes do not seem much help to plants: in England, less than 3 per cent of Environmental Stewardship agreements had suitable options for farmland wild flowers. The *Ghost Orchid* report concluded that despite being a nation of keen gardeners, we seem to be losing our connection with wild plants.

There was, however, one happy note. The ghost orchid, last seen in 1986, turned up alive and well at a secret location on the Welsh borders within a day or two of the press launch of Plantlife's report. It is perhaps unwise to write off a wild plant so quickly.

BEAVERS RETURN

In May 2009 three families of beavers were released into the wild in western Scotland. This was the first time beavers have lived wild in Britain since the animal became extinct more than 200 years ago. Conservationists have long wanted to re-establish it, not only for its own sake but because the beaver is a keystone species, creating its own diverse habitat of coppiced woodland, riversides and lakes. Although the European Beaver has been successfully introduced to many parts of Europe, there has been considerable resistance to the scheme in Britain because of fears that the animal might harm farming, forestry and fishing interests.

The Scottish Beaver Trial is run by the Royal Zoological Society of Scotland and the Scottish Wildlife Trust with support from Scottish Natural Heritage and the Scottish government. The first two beaver families, imported from Norway where they are still common, were shepherded into manmade lodges on small lochs within Knapdale Forest in Argyll, followed soon afterwards by a third pair, ceremoniously released by Roseanna Cunningham, the Scottish environment minister.

The project has suffered teething problems. Five of the 17 beavers imported from Norway died while in quarantine. Plans for a second pilot, in a more populated area at the Insh Marshes by the River Spey, were dropped after complaints from the salmon industry. And several of the beavers have died or gone missing and will have to be replaced. The colony has survived the freezing winter of 2009–10 and the animals are busy increasing the size of their lodges while feeding on young rowan and willow trees and, during winter, on tree bark. A fourth pair was released into the trial site in May 2010. The progress of the beavers is being closely monitored, with regular updates available on the Scottish beavers website
W www.scottishbeavers.org.uk

SSSI CONTROVERSY

SSSI (Sites of Special Scientific Interest) is the somewhat clumsy name for those outstanding wild places where a measure of protection is applied to their use. They range from a hectare or so to broad expanses of intertidal flats or mountain country covering thousands of hectares. England alone has 4,118 SSSIs covering more than a million hectares.

A government target, set in 2003, was to bring 95 per cent of the area designated in England as SSSI to a 'favourable or recovering condition' by 2010. Scotland and Wales have broadly similar objectives. Natural England reported steady progress towards this aim, claiming that 88 per cent of the SSSI area met the government's target by March 2009, and that it is now well on course to achieve the full 95 per cent. This should mean that SSSIs are in better condition today than they have been for many years.

Unfortunately, the government figures can seem hard to square with ongoing losses in wildlife among well-monitored groups such as farmland birds, butterflies and moths, and wild flowers. Some naturalists on the ground report serious deterioration on certain SSSIs, such as natural meadows, marshes and sheep-grazed uplands.

Meanwhile, existing guidelines used to select SSSIs are under review. Voluntary bodies argue that many places of SSSI quality do not enjoy the official protection that is their due.

NATURE AND CHILDREN

Much has been made of the apparent distancing of young people from the world of nature. Despite the continued popularity of programmes such as *Springwatch* on television, most specialist societies have an ageing population and young adults seem to have little knowledge or interest in nature on their doorsteps. The result, according to the American author, Richard Louv, is 'nature deficit disorder'. Children, robbed of fresh air and the freedom to wander, become bored, fractious and self-absorbed.

One possible reason for the dislocation is that children are discouraged from picking flowers or collecting objects from the wild because these activities are regarded as environmentally damaging. Even timeless pursuits such as conkers, climbing trees and outdoor swimming seem to be in decline.

There are modest glimmerings of a reaction. Teachers Fiona Danks and Jo Schofield published *Make it Wild!* in May 2010, full of things to make and do outdoors before you grow up, such as creating living willow sculptures and playing hay bale games. A similar approach was used by naturalist Stephen Moss in his *Bumper Book of Nature*. But can the simple pleasures of nature compete with iPads, Tweets and other 21st-century delights? Time will tell.

SEABIRDS AND RATS

Most species of seabird are in trouble because changes in the sea have reduced the stocks of small fish on which they depend, notably sand-eels. But they also face a threat from rats which are voracious predators both of eggs and chicks. Island seabird colonies around the world have suffered catastrophic declines owing to the presence of rats, which seem to follow humankind wherever it settles.

The only practical solution is to remove the rats. Such operations are costly and difficult, but several British islands have been made rat-free in recent years including Lundy (which involved the controversial eradication of the black rat, itself endangered) and Puffin Island off

Anglesey. A recent study published in the journal *Ibis* has prioritised islands in the UK where eradication would be most cost-effective. These include islets in the Western Isles such as the Shiants and Taransay, as well as the Calf of Man, all of which have significant colonies of vulnerable burrowing birds such as Manx shearwater and European storm-petrel.

BUTTERFLY SUMMER

In March 2010, Britain hosted a three-day symposium at Reading University organised by the charity Butterfly Conservation. Sessions covered butterfly topics from the UK and across the world, highlighting many ingenious conservation projects and also the major threats faced by butterflies and moths. In the keynote address, Sir David Attenborough compared the task facing conservationists as akin to landing a man on the moon.

After suffering two dismal summers in 2008 and 2009, Britain's butterflies recovered somewhat in 2010, although the numbers of some species, including Duke of Burgundy and Lulworth skipper, remain lower than usual. The small tortoiseshell has recovered well from two bad years when its fall in numbers was attributed to a recently arrived parasitic fly. There was also excitement late in 2009 when numbers of the Queen of Spain fritillary were seen near the Sussex coast, and later its larvae were found on field pansies. This rare migrant bred in Suffolk in the mid-90s and may be on the verge of becoming a new British resident. Another more common migrant, the painted lady, arrived in large numbers in spring 2009, although hopes for an even larger summer generation were dashed by the cool weather.

A further advance in knowledge is the surprising dependency of many native butterflies on ants. The large blue has long been known to complete its early stages inside the nest of a particular kind of ant, but the silver-studded blue has an equally intimate association with ants that tend and 'milk' its caterpillars. In perhaps even more remarkable behaviour, the marbled white and some of the browns sequester obnoxious chemicals by deliberately feeding on grasses infected by mildews, thus rendering the adult butterfly poisonous to predators. Insect lives continue to surprise with their subtle ingenuities.

INVASIONS AND TAKE-OVERS

The impact of non-native species on our wildlife is a growing concern. Invasive species are not subject to the usual checks and balances of a mature ecosystem. A prominent recent example is the horse chestnut leaf-mining moth whose tunnels blotch and speckle the leaves and often turn the whole foliage brown by July. Another is the harlequin ladybird, which not only clusters in corners and window frames but is reducing the number of our native ladybirds by feeding on them. Another unwanted intruder is the American signal crayfish, an escapee from ill-advised crayfish farms in the 1970s that has all but wiped out the native crayfish. By 2010 it had reached Loch Ken in Galloway where it threatened the fish stocks. More than a million were trapped, to little effect. Generally there is little that can be done in such cases except to monitor the consequences and try and learn from past mistakes.

Less well known is the effect of invasive plants. Buddleia is associated in the public eye with butterflies, and therefore a welcome addition, but it is Britain's fastest spreading plant, and quickly smothers places such as quarries, which are already refuges for insects and wild flowers. Ditches and shallow ponds face an onslaught of invasive plants originating from aquaria and garden centres, such as parrot's feather and floating pennywort. An article in *British Wildlife* magazine gave a host of other examples of plants out of control: African carpobrotus and Asian cotoneasters on dunes and headlands, Indian balsams on riverbanks and rhododendrons on peaty hillsides in the west. Controlling one of the worst of them, Japanese knotweed, by introducing a knotweed-eating bug from Japan, could merely compound the problem if the bug decides to eat something else.

A NEW BAT

Britain has a new species of mammal. This is the alcathoe bat, *Myotis alcathoe,* which was detected in woods and caves in Sussex and Yorkshire by John Altringham and his team at Leeds University. The species was first discovered in Greece in 2001 and has since been found over much of Europe. It resembles the whiskered bat so closely that even experts have difficulty telling them apart. Fortunately the alcathoe bat has a distinctive call which can be picked up on a bat detector. Altringham believes that the new bat is an overlooked native species and not a recent arrival, which may turn out to be widespread, at least in England. The discovery of the alcathoe bat brings the number of British bats to 17, accounting for a third of all our native mammal species.

FOR PEAT'S SAKE

Natural England has begun a comprehensive review of the condition of Britain's peatlands, that is, areas of land covered with a substantial layer of peat. Twenty years ago, such places were valued mainly for wildlife. Today they are important to everyone as carbon stores. Every time a peat bog is disturbed, carbon escapes into the atmosphere as carbon dioxide, the greenhouse gas responsible for climate change. With the government's commitment to meeting tough carbon targets, the conservation of peatlands has acquired a new urgency.

Natural England's report, *England's Peatlands – Carbon Storage and Greenhouse Gases,* provides detailed mapping of their full extent and condition, but concludes, alarmingly, that almost three-quarters has been seriously damaged. Much peat has been removed for garden fertiliser. Peatlands have also been drained, burned and eroded; around 40 per cent of deep lowland peat is now under cultivation. The report estimates that England's damaged peatlands are leaking about 3 million tonnes of carbon dioxide a year, equivalent to the emissions of over 350,000 households.

FORESTRY SELL-OFF

Under pressure to reduce costs, the Forestry Commission is planning to sell off parts of its estate. This could have implications for anyone who uses national forests, since privatisation might in practice restrict public access. Although a private owner would be obliged to honour the commission's open access policy, they might choose to, say, close car parks or remove picnic tables. Conservationists are also concerned that privatisation would result in a more hardline approach to timber management. The Forestry Commission was once criticised for sacrificing wildlife and amenity to timber targets, but recently it has managed its estate in a more balanced way.

In 2009, the Scottish government abandoned its initial plans to lease a quarter of Scotland's national forest to the private sector. Instead it proposes to sell forest land to finance more tree-planting, in part to help tackle climate change. In England woods are being sold incrementally without any public statement of changed policy.

REPRIEVE FOR BADGERS

Tuberculosis in cattle is a major issue for farmers in western Britain. The ways in which the disease is contracted and spread between herds have been investigated and debated intensively, and many believe that contact with infected badgers is the problem. Many farmers want a cull on badgers, a protected species. In July 2010 a cull planned for part of south-west Wales was halted by appeal court judges after a campaign launched by the Badger Trust.

The case against culling is that it probably would not work. The micro-organisms that cause bovine TB can 'sleep' for years, and there is thought to be a large reservoir of infection in cattle herds because of decades of lax biosecurity. In some areas at least, the disease is also spread by deer as well as badgers. The answer could be vaccination, not culling, but it may take a number of years to develop such a solution.

BUILT HERITAGE

Matthew Saunders

POLICY DEVELOPMENTS

The most significant disappointment reported in the last year's *Built Heritage* article was the Labour government's decision to shelve the long-heralded Heritage Protection Bill. This Bill had promised the most sweeping changes to the legislative framework for the protection of England's historic environment since the Second World War. The incoming coalition government made some comforting noises about introducing the necessary legislation, but there were no firm promises. However, it was announced under the outgoing Labour government on 2 November 2009 that responsibility for compiling the registers of listed buildings had passed, by statutory instrument, from the Secretary of State to English Heritage (although the former retained responsibility for approving the lists). At the same time, in the pursuit of greater transparency, there was a new commitment by English Heritage to consult with local authorities and owners in all listing cases. English Heritage has made a commitment to introducing a unified designation system by the end of 2010, which aims to provide a definitive one-stop shop through which members of the public can access details of listed buildings, ancient monuments, world heritage sites, and the register of parks, gardens, battlefields and wrecks.

In the absence of the Heritage Protection Bill, the principal change was the publication of *Planning Policy Statement 5: Planning for the Historic Environment* (PPS5) in March 2010. The deadening bureaucracy of the title should not hide the significance of the document. In company with the associated practice guide compiled by English Heritage it brings together in one location the present thinking by central government on policy and practice relating to historic buildings and archaeology, and still stands under the new coalition government. The preceding *Planning Policy Guidance 15,* in force for well over a decade, has been withdrawn. The new document lays greater stress than its predecessor on the 'significance' of historic sites and re-establishes the presumption in favour of conservation that designation, or listing, will always bring. Like many government documents it stresses the need to meet the challenge of climate change, but it also makes it quite clear that decision makers should balance the needs of the environment with those of protecting the beauty, character and interest of historic buildings.

Also published just before the hiatus occasioned by the spring 2010 election was a government statement on the historic environment in England, which begins with a suitable clarion call: 'The government believes that the historic environment is an asset of enormous cultural, social, economic and environmental value. It makes a very real contribution to our quality of life and the quality of our places. We recognise that while some of today's achievements may become tomorrow's heritage, our existing heritage assets are simply irreplaceable.' There was an associated statement in Wales, this time a more personal celebration by the Minister for Heritage, Alun Ffred Jones. It did, nevertheless, contain specific promises: that Cadw would complete the scheduling of all known prehistoric and Roman monuments of national importance within Wales by the end of 2012; that work would start in 2010 on a programme of thematic surveys of 20th-century heritage assets; and that there would be a consultation on the establishment of a register of battlefields in Wales. There were further pledges from Cadw to commission a detailed survey of listed buildings throughout Wales and a list of scheduled monuments at risk in 2010.

ENGLISH HERITAGE – CAMPAIGNS AND RESEARCH

English Heritage continued its annual Heritage at Risk campaign, concentrating in 2010 on places of worship. (In 2009 the spotlight was on conservation areas.) This gave renewed impetus to the English Heritage 'Inspired' campaign, the principal element of which was the employment of a number of support officers mostly based at diocesan level, but with one given a national overview under the National Churches Trust, whose mission is to help churches stave off closure and broaden the constituency of users and supporters. The associated report concluded that 90 per cent of English churches are in good condition, a tribute to the congregations and to funders.

English Heritage also worked on the Strategic Stone Study, which aims to provide a single source of information on stones used in the construction of historic buildings with an examination of the extent of unworked sources, including disused quarries.

Its excellent publication programme continued with English Heritage publishing several important books on historic seaside resorts and an assessment of the history and conversion of historic schools. Where such schools have had to close, enterprising developers have adapted them, in one case in Folkestone as a Baptist chapel and in another, in Oxford, as a public house. Significant English Heritage research also emerged on the thermal performance of timber sash windows. This showed how simple measures can allow these windows to meet current building regulations, and how shutters and good quality secondary glazing are useful in meeting green objectives. Further guides were produced including *London's Historic Fire Stations* and *An Archaeology of Town Commons in England.*

THE NATIONAL TRUST

It was reported in last year's *Almanack* that the National Trust was on the verge of acquiring the Baroque masterpiece Seaton Delaval Hall in Northumberland. The deal was sealed just before Christmas 2009 when the hall was acquired by the government under the Acceptance in Lieu (AIL) scheme and passed thereafter to the Trust. One of the greatest works of Sir John Vanbrugh, Seaton Delaval Hall, was the first country house to be saved for the nation through AIL procedures in 25 years, the last one being Calke Abbey in Derbyshire. In satisfaction of a tax bill of £4.9m (£1.7m for the Hall and land and £3.2m for the contents of the east wing and statues in the garden) the agreement ensures that the mansion, most of its contents and more than 32ha (80 acres) of land will now be preserved in perpetuity. The National Trust pledged £6.9m to create an endowment fund and opened the estate to the public in spring 2010.

The story north of the border was dispiriting by comparison. During 2009 the National Trust for Scotland announced a programme involving the loss of 91 full-time equivalent posts as well as the closure in whole or part of a number of its properties, in order to cope with an acute financial crisis. Part of the retrenchment involved the sale of the Trust's headquarters, a magnificent Georgian building in Edinburgh's New Town. It was the National Trust (for England and Wales) which provided the initial funding for the attempt to resuscitate something from the ruins of the Civic Trust which went bankrupt in the spring of 2009. The National Trust financed the Civic Society Initiative, which was succeeded in spring 2010 by the newly announced Civic Voice – this organisation set itself the task of coordinating, with a light hand, the activities of the country's civic societies and civic trusts.

THE HERITAGE LOTTERY FUND

As taxpayer-funded agencies like English Heritage faced the prospect of savage cuts under the new coalition government as it struggles to reduce the national deficit, the Heritage Lottery Fund seemed to buck the trend with the promise of higher than anticipated income (albeit from an annual spend of £180m, down from the £330m of its best years). An increase of some £25m a year came from improved ticket sales and there was a promise of a further boost given the coalition government's commitment to reinstate the original proportions of funding to be enjoyed by traditional 'good causes' as envisaged by John Major when he founded the National Lottery in 1994. This would mean that of the 28 per cent of National Lottery revenue channelled to good causes, 20 per cent (up from 16.7 per cent under Labour) would go to heritage.

The following major grants reached the first or second round of the Heritage Lottery funding process (a 'first round pass' permits a project to proceed to the second round, but does not necessarily mean it will secure funding) in the course of the year under review:

- Bletchley Park, Buckinghamshire (£4,586,000), to conserve the centre for code-breaking established in 1937
- Charles Dickens' Museum at 48 Doughty Street in Bloomsbury, London (£1,773,000)
- Chedworth Roman Villa in Gloucestershire (£700,000)
- Colchester Castle, Essex (£1,873,000)
- Ditchling Museum in West Sussex (£993,000), an important centre for the Arts and Crafts Movement with works by Eric Gill and Frank Brangwyn
- Dreamland in Margate in Kent (£3,334,500), built in 1920, which includes a Grade II listed scenic railway, one of the oldest rides in the world, and a Grade II* listed cinema
- The Institute and Memorial Hall at Newbridge, Glamorgan (£2,897,000)
- Kettle's Yard in Cambridge (£2,306,000)
- Lews Castle in the Outer Hebrides (£2,640,000), to repair the Castle and rehouse a museum in part of it
- Lytham Hall, Lytham St Annes, Lancashire (£1,817,000)
- The Old Magnus Building at Newark in Nottinghamshire (£2,843,000), to rehouse the town's Museum within the largely derelict listed buildings previously occupied by the Thomas Magnus School founded in 1529
- Penllergare Valley Woods, Glamorgan (£2,170,000)
- Piece Hall in Halifax in West Yorkshire (£7,000,000), the great courtyard of 1779 built for the sale of cloth pieces
- Red House at Aldeburgh in Suffolk (£1,205,000), the home of Benjamin Britten
- Roman Maryport in Cumbria (£3,749,000), to develop Camp Farm, which is home to a Roman fort and the largest and most intact civic settlement, or vicus, on Hadrian's Wall
- St Fagan's National Museum in Wales (£8,700,000)
- Salisbury and South Wiltshire Museum in Salisbury (£1,642,000)
- †Stonehenge, Wiltshire (£4,950,000)
- The Transporter bridge in Middlesbrough (£2,031,000)
- University Church of St Mary the Virgin in Oxford (£3,290,000)
- The Walronds, Cullompton, Devon (£1,668,000), to repair and open up to the public one of the most significant houses in the town built between 1570 and 1605
- The William Morris Gallery at Walthamstow, London (£1,320,000)

† A planned £20m visitor centre at Stonehenge was one of the first projects to be scrapped by the coalition government in its attempts to reduce the national deficit. The £4.95m Heritage Lottery Fund grant is still in place and there is hope that a scheme of some sorts will go ahead.

The Heritage Lottery Fund also introduced the Skills for the Future Programme, which disbursed some £16m in May 2010 to a great variety of schemes to train people, mostly the young, in hard and soft heritage skills such as roof-thatching, creating websites, studying and conserving wildlife, and maintaining historic parks and gardens.

NEW BEGINNINGS

As some antidote to the unfortunate news of the closure of the Textile Conservation Centre at the University of Southampton early in 2010 came the opening of a number of significant attractions. Of particular note were the revamped displays at the Jewish Museum, the restored Leighton House in Kensington, revamped modern galleries at the Museum of London, the expanded People's History Museum in Manchester, the Hull History Centre, the spectacular Medieval and Renaissance Galleries at London's Victoria & Albert Museum and 20 new galleries at the Ashmolean Museum in Oxford. The Herbert Art Gallery and Museum in Coventry opened in its new premises near the Cathedral and plans were announced for a new City museum at Chichester in Sussex.

A brave scheme to re-erect the Euston Arch (demolished in 1962) in its original location as part of a broader redevelopment of the station was also announced, but as yet there is no certainty this will go ahead. The Landmark Trust (the building preservation society) added three new sites to its portfolio in 2010: the French country retreat of the Duke and Duchess of Windsor, near Paris; Cavendish Hall near Newmarket in Suffolk; and the Oxenford Gatehouse in Surrey designed by A. W. Pugin.

CHANGE FOR CHURCHES

The Churches Conservation Trust took into care two important redundant medieval churches – at Knotting in Bedfordshire and Thornton-le-Moors in Cheshire. The Historic Chapels Trust increased its holdings by taking into care Westgate Methodist Chapel at Upper Weardale in Northumberland and Lord Petrie's private Catholic Chapel at Thorndon Park, near Brentwood in Essex. It also agreed to take the Strict Baptist Chapel at Grittleton, near Chippenham in Wiltshire. The Friends of Friendless Churches agreed to take Long Crichel church in Dorset.

The Grade I listed church of St Mary, Devizes in Wiltshire, was reprieved following a formal threat of closure, while new uses were announced for the long redundant churches of St John's, High Wycombe in Buckinghamshire, which is to become a Centre of Creativity in the hands of the local authority; Holy Trinity, East Hyde in Hertfordshire, which is to become a place of worship for the Greek Orthodox Community; and St Mary's, Harrogate in North Yorkshire, which is to be transformed into a health spa. St Michael-on-the-Mount, Bristol, is to go to the City Church, a member of the Evangelical Alliance; while St Peter's, Thetford in Norfolk, is to be reinvented as an art gallery, centre for local artists and home for the Staniforth book collection.

Taylors of Loughborough (Leicestershire), one of only two bell foundries in England, went into and out of bankruptcy within a matter of weeks during September 2009, narrowly avoiding the closure that would have been a cultural disaster.

PUBLICATIONS AND NEWS

In terms of publications, there were new additions to the Pevsner series of architectural guides in the *Buildings of England* series on Berkshire, Cumbria and West Yorkshire. The *Biographical Dictionary of Sculptors in Britain 1660–1851*, running to 1,620 pages and published in September 2009, was a literary landmark in the study of the public statue and the church monument. There were also significant biographies of the architect R. D. Chantrell and the artist and conservationist John Piper (the latter by Frances Spalding).

The year witnessed the passing of the distinguished conservation architect Peter Foster, Surveyor to Westminster Abbey 1973–88, and the former Conservation Minister, Lord Kennet, who as the journalist Wayland Young had written the influential book entitled *Preservation* in the early 1970s, which played an important part in changing the public mood. And that distinguished figure, Sir Roy Strong, former Director of the Victoria & Albert Museum, put his affairs in order by leaving his papers to the Bodleian in Oxford and his famous garden in Herefordshire to the Vivat Trust. Heritage Link, the umbrella body for 82 voluntary heritage organisations, was rebranded as the Heritage Alliance and in December 2009 installed television personality Loyd Grossman as its new chairman.

DANCE

Bridie Macmahon

Classical ballet has never lacked for great dancers; but in recent years, the dearth of great new works for them to dance has been a source of major concern. So while the emergence during the year of exciting new dancing talents is to be welcomed, the real hope for the future of the art form lay in the possible signs of genuine new choreographic talent.

Many leading companies marked anniversaries during the year. One of some significance was Birmingham Royal Ballet's celebration of the 20th anniversary of its move to Birmingham from London in 1990. By the late 1980s the then Sadler's Wells Royal Ballet had outgrown the facilities at the old Sadler's Wells theatre in Islington, and arts policy at the time increasingly advocated spreading arts provision more equitably throughout the country rather than concentrating resources in London. An invitation was issued to the company in 1987 by the Birmingham Hippodrome and Birmingham City Council, offering considerable financial incentives and vastly improved facilities at the Hippodrome theatre. The then director of the company, Peter Wright, overcame initial misgivings to give the move enthusiastic support, seeing an opportunity for the company to flourish in its new setting. In 1990 the company moved to Birmingham, changing its name to Birmingham Royal Ballet.

One of the objectives of the move was to create a more robust and separate identity for the Royal Ballet's 'second' company; and over the following two decades this objective has been met through a combination of physical independence, separate governance from the Royal Opera House (achieved in 1997), and the artistic vision and leadership of both Peter Wright and David Bintley, who took over as director of the company in 1995. Ballet directors generally survive a little longer than football managers, but Bintley's 15 years at the helm of a large touring company is nevertheless a testament to both his stamina and his continuing creativity. Great companies on the whole are fed by great schools, and so the move of Elmhurst School for Dance from London to Birmingham in 2005 to form the Associate School of Birmingham Royal Ballet was also a significant development. The company held 20th anniversary gala celebrations at the Birmingham Hippodrome in March 2010 with highlights from its repertoire and multimedia presentations marking the company's achievements on local, national and international levels.

BALLETIC EQUATION

Bintley's own choreography has been a rich source of material for the company over the years. His latest work, *E=mc²*, was inspired by the book *E=mc²: a Biography of the World's Most Famous Equation* by David Bodanis, and is set to a commissioned score by the Australian composer Matthew Hindson. It sets out to reflect Einstein's theory of relativity in three main sections of fast and furious dance depicting energy, mass and speed of light. Between the second and third sections a single dancer clad in a white kimono dances to the backdrop of a rumbling explosion that evokes the terrible consequences of the atomic bombs that shattered Hiroshima and Nagasaki. The work is a complex, intelligent and powerful piece that won the dance prize at the South Bank Show Awards in January 2010. In November 2009 the Belgian conductor Koen Kessels was appointed music director of the company in succession to Barry Wordsworth.

One of the works performed by Birmingham Royal Ballet during the year was Kenneth MacMillan's masterful *Romeo and Juliet.* MacMillan (1929–92) would have turned 80 during this season. The anniversary was also marked by the Royal Ballet in its repertoire, with performances of not only *Romeo and Juliet* but also *Mayerling* and a triple bill comprising *Concerto, The Judas Tree* and *Elite Syncopations,* a programme reflecting different phases of MacMillan's career and the range of his work. A substantial biography of the choreographer, *Different Drummer* by Jann Parry, was also published during the year, and provided insights into the complex, difficult man who produced so many works reflective of his character. The later years of his life were more tranquil on a personal level, but he continued to make many ballets fuelled by his identification with the outsider and by themes of violence, betrayal and death. Perhaps his most moving works – *Song of the Earth,* set to Mahler's great song cycle and created in 1965; and his 1977 *Requiem,* to Fauré, and *Gloria,* set to Poulenc and created in 1980 – revealed a different side: still passionate but also poetic; raging against the dying of the light, but accepting it with grace; a man on the side of the angels. A symposium entitled *Kenneth MacMillan's Choreographic Imagination and Psychological Insight* was held at Imperial College London in November 2009, and brought together leading figures from the worlds of dance and psychology in an effort to explore how MacMillan's personal life influenced his creative life.

What matters, however, is the body of work he has left behind; and the Royal Ballet in practice remains the primary and most effective vehicle for presenting and promoting his work. It is therefore to be hoped that a wider range of MacMillan's ballets can be mounted by the company in years to come, so that he is remembered not only for great, dramatic full-length works, nor for the works with the most lurid scenarios and violent choreography (as in *The Judas Tree,* his final work), but also for some of the subtle, beautiful and thought-provoking one-act works that he made throughout his career.

ROYAL DANCERS

Since Kenneth MacMillan's death the Royal Ballet has struggled to find a resident classical choreographer to make works of a consistent quality for its outstanding dancers. The current resident choreographer, Wayne McGregor, creates ambitious and physically extreme works of contemporary dance, making use of the dancers' strength and classical technique but often in the process literally pulling them out of shape. In the longer term, this runs the risk of undermining their classical (and essentially harmonious) training. Nevertheless, many dancers were impressive in the year under review, including the relative newcomers Steven McRae and (perhaps most notably, given his youth) Sergei Polunin. Polunin was born in the Ukraine and joined the Royal

Ballet School at the age of 13 in 2003. In 2006 he won the Prix de Lausanne and in 2007 he was named Young British Dancer of the Year. Now 20, he danced several principal roles for the first time during the year – including in *The Sleeping Beauty* and *Cinderella* – and displayed a confidence, pride and stage presence reminiscent of the young Nureyev. His technique is also strong, clean and beautiful, and it was no surprise that he was promoted to principal for the beginning of the 2010–11 season.

In choreographic terms, the most encouraging event of the season was the premiere of a work by 24-year-old Liam Scarlett, a dancer with the Royal Ballet, in May 2010. His first piece for the main Opera House stage, *Asphodel Meadows,* was set to Poulenc's Double Piano Concerto and displayed classical confidence combined with a contemporary sensitivity, originality and flair. Here is a dance-maker who knows what he wants to do with the art form, and in this case he uses the music and his dancers to reflect seriously and beautifully on love and mortality. Jonathan Watkins, another young dancer in the company, also created his first work for the main stage in February 2010. *As One* was set to a commissioned score by Graham Fitkin and sought to explore the disparate and fragmented lives being led by a group of city dwellers. Both the music and dance evoke a frenetic and slightly demented world that fails to cohere into a substantial vision, and the flickering video screens of the design have the effect of overshadowing the dancers in the foreground; but Watkins does produce moments and movements of interest and his confident handling of his material is to be welcomed. The other new work of the season was *Limen* by Wayne McGregor, set to Kaija Saariaho's cello concerto and premièred in November 2009. Bathed in colour from the lighting installations by Tatsuo Miyajima, the dancers are only one element in a wider visual experience. With a more classical influence to some of the movements than is usual with McGregor, the work is nevertheless a continuation of his harsh modernism which, although often striking, and conveyed here as usual with exemplary skill and dedication by his cast, makes little use of their individual qualities as people.

One of the company's most popular principals, Miyako Yoshida, retired at the end of the season after more than 25 years with the Royal Ballet companies. She will be returning to her home country of Japan, leaving behind lasting memories of the purity of her technique, the joy of her musicality and the sweetness of her temperament. A former Royal Ballet principal, Georgina Parkinson, died on 18 December 2009 at the age of 71. She was a tall, elegant and gracious dancer who was a muse to both Frederick Ashton and Kenneth MacMillan, perhaps most memorably creating roles in Ashton's *Enigma Variations* and *Monotones I* and the role of Empress Elisabeth in MacMillan's *Mayerling.* David Ashmole, a talented, versatile and dedicated former Royal Ballet dancer and teacher, died in the summer of 2009 at the age of 59.

FOUNDERS HONOURED

Monica Mason, director of the Royal Ballet, retires in 2012, and speculation has started as to who will succeed her. In the meantime, a memorial tablet to the 'Founders of the Royal Ballet' was dedicated in Poets' Corner at Westminster Abbey on 17 November 2009 in a special service marking the contribution of Dame Ninette de Valois (founder director), Sir Frederick Ashton (founder choreographer), Constant Lambert (founder music director) and Dame Margot Fonteyn (Prima Ballerina Assoluta) in the establishment of the company. It could be argued that Dame Alicia Markova (first ballerina) and Sir Robert Helpmann (leading male dancer) should have been honoured too, but it is long overdue for such recognition to be extended to the country's leading ballet company. Mason's successor will inherit the company's history as well as its present and will be responsible for directing its future; he or she must therefore be someone who can understand, nurture and safeguard all three.

Michael Corder, a former Royal Ballet dancer and a classical choreographer of distinction, was appointed director of dance at English National Ballet School in September 2009. He will therefore be working in collaboration with Wayne Eagling, also a Royal Ballet alumnus and currently director of English National Ballet, to ensure a good supply of dancers for the company. ENB celebrates its 60th anniversary in 2010 since it dates its existence from a performance in Southsea given on 14 August 1950. The company is performing well under Eagling but struggles to broaden its repertoire in view of its financial constraints. Eagling did create a new work, *Men Y Men,* in September 2009 – this was set to Rachmaninov piano preludes and gave nine of the company's men a chance to shine as they danced with bare-chested athleticism and on a bill paired with *Giselle* with its many roles for the women. Nineteen-year-old Vadim Muntagirov emerged during the year as an exciting new star, and the company held its first Emerging Dancer Award ceremony to encourage the talent within its ranks; it was awarded to Anaïs Chalendard, with Crystal Costa receiving the People's Choice Award. The season ended with the 60th-anniversary celebrations culminating in the company's first season at the London Coliseum for ten years in August 2010.

More anniversary celebrations were seen at Scottish Ballet during the year as the company marked 40 years of its existence. The Prince of Wales became its patron in the autumn of 2009, and the company joined forces with the Scottish Academy of Music And Drama to launch an undergraduate course in modern ballet, the first of its kind in Scotland and effectively providing a school for the company as had always been envisaged by its founders, Peter Darrell and Elizabeth West. A new version of *Petrushka* was created by Ian Spink in September 2009 to mark the centenary of Diaghilev's Ballets Russes; it was set to Stravinsky's score, but with the action updated to post-Communist Russia and featuring a pole dancer, a strong man and a clown in place of the puppets of the original work. Paul Liburd, a dancer of great power and sensitivity, won the 2009 Critics' Circle National Dance Award for Best Male Dancer; there was therefore much sadness at his decision to retire from the company at the end of the season.

Northern Ballet Theatre is the same age as Scottish Ballet, and marked the milestone with an ambitious programme of full-length and one-act works. Two celebratory shows were held at the Grand Theatre, Leeds, at the end of 2009, including a performance of Christopher Gable's *A Christmas Carol* involving many of the company's former dancers. The company moves to its new permanent home in the centre of Leeds in autumn 2010.

THE PLACE

Contemporary dance is for perhaps obvious reasons less given to celebrating anniversaries than its classical counterpart; but this year The Place theatre did trumpet its own 40th anniversary with deserved pride. Founded by Robin Howard, who had been inspired by the first visit of the Martha Graham company to London in 1954, this Victorian drill hall near Euston station in London became the creative centre of contemporary dance in the UK. Robert Cohan, the first artistic director, established both what became London Contemporary Dance School and its performing arm, London Contemporary Dance Theatre. Dancers not only performed but were also encouraged to choreograph, and almost all the leading British modern dance choreographers have been nurtured at The Place at some stage. London Contemporary Dance Theatre closed in 1994, but Richard Alston then took over as artistic director of The Place and launched his own company to fill the gap. The school now has 180 full-time students and plays a significant role in UK dance education.

Richard Alston's company is still a vibrant presence on the UK dance scene. Alston mounted a new production of his 1994 work *Movements from Petrushka* during the year, and in June 2010 new works by Alston and Martin Lawrance were given in a season at The Place that also included *Something to Do,* created by Alston within a month of The Place's opening in 1969 and his earliest existing work.

Rambert Dance Company, founded in 1926 by Marie Rambert and so the oldest surviving dance company in Britain, won the 2010 Laurence Olivier Award for Outstanding Achievement in Dance for what was described as 'an outstanding year of new work'. Mark Baldwin's *The Comedy of Change,* premiered in September 2009, was presented as part of the Darwin year celebrations and sought to combine the worlds of evolution and dance; it did so imaginatively and effectively, using courtship dances and animal display rituals as part of its vocabulary. Henri Oguike's *Tread Softly,* premiered in October 2009, was set to an orchestrated version of Schubert's *Death and the Maiden,* and was a fast and edgy work making full use of Rambert's excellent dancers.

Dance Umbrella 2009 included an ambitious season of African dance, perhaps looking forward to the focus on Africa that reached fever pitch during the 2010 football world cup. It also used London itself as the backdrop for a number of performances, with a human sculpture trail created by Willi Dorner around the South Bank and Paul-André Fortier's *Cabane* presented at four contrasting venues in Canary Wharf, Smithfield, Marylebone and Greenwich. A new work by Michael Clark, *Come, Been and Gone,* commissioned by Dance Umbrella, was performed at the Barbican, and Mark Morris Dance Group performed both at Sadler's Wells and across the UK.

A two-week season of Indian dance was staged at Sadler's Wells in November 2009. Akram Khan, its co-curator (with Nitin Sawhney), was to have danced his new work *Gnosis* during the season, but was forced to truncate it due to a shoulder injury. The piece, inspired by a character in the Mahabharata, was given in its entirety in April 2010 and was a powerful vehicle both for Khan's magnificent dancing and that of his co-performer, Yoshie Sunahata.

SON ET LUMIÈRE

The increasingly lauded Israeli choreographer Hofesh Shechter created a stunning new work, *Political Mother,* which premiered at the Brighton Dome in May 2010. Performed by ten dancers, the work is accompanied by Shechter's own score featuring a band of live drummers and electric guitarists. It uses sound, movement and light to rip into the deception and manipulation at the heart of repressive societies, and does so with a fervent power and intensity that carries all before it. *Goldberg: the Brandstrup-Rojo Project,* which won the 2010 Laurence Oliver Award for Best New Dance Production for its creators, the choreographer Kim Brandstrup and the Royal Ballet dancer Tamara Rojo, was mounted in the Linbury Studio Theatre at the Royal Opera House in September 2009. Set to J. S. Bach's *Goldberg Variations,* the work portrayed the shifting relationships between seven people and was superbly performed by Rojo herself and an excellent cast including her Royal Ballet colleagues Steven McRae and Thomas Whitehead. Ballet Black, Cassa Pancho's company of black and Asian classically trained dancers, presented new works by a range of choreographers at the same venue in March 2010. The company won Outstanding Company award at the Critics' Circle National Dance Awards for 2009.

Visitors to the UK during the year included the Royal Ballet of Flanders, Christopher Wheeldon's Morphoses (before Wheeldon's subsequent departure as director of the company he founded), the National Ballet of Cuba, the Danza Contemporánea de Cuba and the National Ballet of Spain. The season was framed by visits from the Mariinsky Ballet in the summer of 2009 and the Bolshoi Ballet in the summer of 2010; but at its heart were the rare and precious performances of Mark Morris's 1988 work *L'Allegro, il Penseroso, ed il Moderato* at the London Coliseum in April 2010. A setting of Handel's score based on Milton's poems, Morris explores the human condition in a series of profoundly beautiful dances that culminate in a scene of joyous peace and unity as Morris, unlike Handel, allows *L'Allegro* to triumph. 'Mirth with thee I mean to live' stands as a proud and confident expression of the faith, hope and love without which all dance would be meaningless.

NEW PRODUCTIONS

ROYAL BALLET

Founded 1931 as the Vic-Wells Ballet

Royal Opera House, Covent Garden, London WC2E 9DD

Limen (Wayne McGregor), 4 November 2009. A one-act work. *Music,* Kaija Saariaho; *set designs,* Tatsuo Miyajima; *costume designs,* Moritz Junge. Cast led by Sarah Lamb and Eric Underwood

As One (Jonathan Watkins), 19 February 2010. A one-act work. *Music,* Graham Fitkin; *design,* Simon Daw. Cast led by Steven McRae

Asphodel Meadows (Liam Scarlett), 5 May 2010. A one-act work. *Music,* Poulenc; *design,* John Macfarlane. Cast led by Marianela Nuñez, Rupert Pennefather, Tamara Rojo, Bennet Gartside, Laura Morera and Ricardo Cervera

BIRMINGHAM ROYAL BALLET

Founded 1946 as the Sadler's Wells Opera Ballet

Birmingham Hippodrome, Thorp Street, Birmingham B5 4AU

$E=mc^2$ (David Bintley), 23 September 2009. A one-act work. *Score,* Matthew Hindson; *costume designs,* Kate Ford

ENGLISH NATIONAL BALLET

Founded 1950 as London Festival Ballet

Markova House, 39 Jay Mews, London SW7 2ES

Men Y Men (Wayne Eagling), 23 September 2009. A one-act work. *Music,* Rachmaninov

RAMBERT DANCE COMPANY
Founded 1926 as the Marie Rambert Dancers
94 Chiswick High Road, London W4 1SH

The Comedy of Change (Mark Baldwin), 16 September 2009. *Score,* Julian Anderson; *set designs,* Kader Attia; *costume designs,* Georg Meyer-Wiel

Tread Softly (Henri Oguike), 7 October 2009. *Music,* Schubert; *costume designs,* Asalia Khadjé

RICHARD ALSTON DANCE COMPANY
Founded 1994
The Place, 17 Duke's Road, London WC1H 9AB

Even More (Richard Alston), 16 June 2010. *Music,* Prokofiev

Lie of the Land (Martin Lawrance), 16 June 2010. *Music,* Ryoji Ikeda

SCOTTISH BALLET
Founded 1956 as the Western Theatre Ballet; moved to Glasgow as Scottish Theatre Ballet 1969
Tramway, 25 Albert Drive, Glasgow G41 2PE

Petrushka (Ian Spink), 4 September 2009. *Music,* Stravinksy; *design,* Yannis Thavoris. Cast led by Daniel Davidson, Victoria Willard, Tama Barry and Erik Cavallari

AWARDS

CRITICS' CIRCLE NATIONAL DANCE AWARDS 2009

De Valois Award for Outstanding Achievement in Dance – Alexander Grant (The Royal Ballet and National Ballet of Canada)
Dancing Times Award for Best Male Dancer – Paul Liburd (Scottish Ballet)
Richard Sherrington Award for Best Female Dancer – Leanne Benjamin (The Royal Ballet)
Dance Europe Award for Outstanding Company – Ballet Black
Best Classical Choreography – Wayne McGregor for *Infra* (The Royal Ballet)
Best Modern Choreography – Christopher Bruce for *Hush* (Rambert Dance Company)
Patron's Award – Richard Bonynge (international conductor)
PMB Presentations Award for Best Foreign Dance Company – Merce Cunningham Dance Company
Outstanding Female Performance (Classical) – Melissa Hamilton (The Royal Ballet)
Outstanding Male Performance (Classical) – Sergei Polunin (The Royal Ballet)
Outstanding Female Performance (Modern) – Amy Hollingsworth (freelance)
Outstanding Male Performance (Modern) – Thomas Gülgeç (Rambert Dance Company)
Angelina Ballerina Children's Award – Lucy Wood (Susan Robinson School of Dance)
CDET Student of the Year Award – Sam Chung (Tring Park School for the Performing Arts)
Dance UK Industry Award – Marie McCluskey (Artistic Director, Swindon Dance)

LAURENCE OLIVIER AWARDS 2010 (DANCE)

Best New Dance Production – *Goldberg: the Brandstrup-Rojo project* at the Royal Opera House (Kim Brandstrup and Tamara Rojo)
Outstanding Achievement in Dance – Rambert Dance Company for an outstanding year of new work
Best Theatre Choreographer – Stephen Mear for *Hello Dolly!* at the Open Air Theatre

ROYAL ACADEMY OF DANCE QUEEN ELIZABETH II CORONATION AWARD 2009
Victor and Lilian Hochhauser

YOUNG BRITISH DANCER OF THE YEAR

2001	Lauren Cuthbertson	2006	James Hay
2002	Anniek Soobroy	2007	Sergiy Polunin
2003	Joseph Caley	2008	William Bracewell
2004	Aaron Robison	2009	Yasmine Naghdi
2005	Ruth Bailey	2010	Francesca Hayward

FILM

Jonathan Theodore

A HOLY GRAIL?

The year 2009 saw the revival of one of Hollywood's commercial ambitions: 3D cinema. Box-office giants *Avatar* and *Alice in Wonderland* spearheaded a new wave of films that collectively make up the biggest – and most expensive – initiative in the history of the movie business since the adoption of widescreen.

For the normally conservative Tinseltown, returning to the iconic red-and-green goggles is a U-turn to the less glorious pages of its past. Since the 1950s, 3D cinema has a chequered history of false starts and passing fads. In particular it has been plagued by the chicken-and-egg commercial conundrum: producers would not make the investment in 3D films because too few cinemas possessed the ability to screen them, and the theatres would not equip themselves with 3D-capable displays because there were too few movies to make it worth the expense. But for the first time, the whole industry appears fully committed to backing the technology and is pouring in the billions needed for its success.

Opinions on this huge gamble vary widely. Noted critic Roger Ebert has dismissed 3D as being as doomed as its previous incarnations. And some viewers – who have reportedly suffered dizziness and nausea watching 3D films – expressed concerns at the high-tech digital trickery. However, pressing economic realities have compelled the industry to roll the dice on its future. Higher ticket prices have masked the fact that cinema attendances have suffered decades of decline: a trend now accelerated by the toxic triumvirate of piracy, recession and the growing popularity of ever-cheaper 'home movie theatres'. Consequently there is an urgent need for Hollywood to generate new sources of revenue. Furthermore, it is widely believed that the digital revolution of the past two decades has enabled the generation of an illusion of three dimensions that is now genuinely convincing and immersive – a contrast to the cheap gimmick that made past duds such as *Jaws 3D* such a source of mockery and derision.

The technology is also seen as one of the best ways to combat the challenge of illegal downloading – an industry equivalent to $10bn (£6.4bn) of lost revenue in the USA alone – and to recover a 'wow' factor that can lure audiences away from their high-definition television sets back to the big screen. Whether it proves to be the saviour of the movie business or not, with another 30 such movies in line for the coming two years – including the entire DreamWorks Animation line-up – 3D is with us for the foreseeable future.

ECOLOGICAL WISDOM – NOW IN 3D

The poster child for this bold new direction was *Avatar,* James Cameron's first film since 1997's *Titanic.* The legendary writer-director of *Terminator* and *Aliens* fame returned to his sci-fi roots with a futuristic story about a human corporation mining a precious resource – imaginatively named Unobtanium – on a remote tropical planet. The Corporation comes into conflict with the indigenous Na'vi, giant aliens whose bodies the colonials can inhabit and impersonate. The plot is borderline bizarre, but beneath its quirky trappings lies a familiar anti-imperialist ideology, and *Avatar* hammers away with an anti-corporate message of the ecological wisdom and spiritual values of primitive tribes. The film is oddly reminiscent of *Dances with Wolves,* where a frontiersman falls for an indigenous culture he then helps defend against greedy colonialists, only this time catapulted into space and the third dimension. Shot with a proprietary new 3D technology, the stunning effects – *Avatar*'s budget is rumoured at $300m (£192m) – will impress even the most hardened cynics of CGI (computer-generated imagery), presenting an apparently seamless mesh of ordinary reality with digitally crafted fantasia. Fully rendered facial features have often been lambasted as fake but here the effects are startlingly lifelike, even when evidently at their most unreal.

With its quirky plot and lack of stars – little-known Sam Worthington and Zoe Saldana lead the cast – *Avatar* perplexed many pundits with a phenomenal box-office gross that topped nearly $3bn (£1.9bn) worldwide, trouncing *Titanic*'s previously thought unbeatable record of $1.8bn (£1.2bn). But the combination of groundbreaking visuals and Cameron sci-fi earned the film a vast audience of repeat viewers, and higher ticket prices for 3D screenings contributed much of that gross: over 60 per cent of the film's ticket sales were for 3D viewings, an impressive statistic that has been touted by its proponents as evidence for the future success of the medium.

CRITICAL ACCLAIM

While *Avatar* topped the box office by a mile, Cameron's ex-wife Kathryn Bigelow's tiny limited-release project *The Hurt Locker* was lavished with awards and acclaim. The film stars little-known Jeremy Renner as William James, the head of a small ordnance disposal team on tour in Iraq in 2004. The Iraq war has spawned many cinematic critiques and Bigelow's picture has generated some left-liberal criticism for its seemingly patriotic depiction of soldiers as heroic peacekeepers, but *The Hurt Locker* pointedly skirts away from any political message, and its boldest conclusion – that Sgt. James's heroic exploits stem from an addiction to a life-and-death rush of adrenaline – is hardly a positive psychological observation. Rather the film tries to convey the nightmare of Iraq from the soldier's point of view, eschewing the conventions of narrative to present a collage of set-pieces from James's 12-month tour of duty, each a master class of escalating, intolerable tension.

To similar plaudits, the Coen Brothers – lionised since 2007's *No Country for Old Men* – came out with another classic in *A Serious Man,* a very loose contemporary reworking of the Book of Job in which theatre actor Michael Stuhlbarg stars as a physics professor, Larry Gopnik, living in a Jewish enclave of Minnesota in 1967. Larry is a mild-mannered man baffled and confounded by a series of frustrations and misfortunes that threaten his job and livelihood, and lead him into an existential crisis about his belief system and moral code. *A Serious Man* blends the desolation of *No Country* with the quirky comedy of the following year's Coen hit *Burn After Reading* – no easy feat, but the directors again display their singular talents by crafting a story so pitilessly bleak without forfeiting any of their hallmark eccentric humour.

Numerous plaudits also went to *Precious: Based on the Novel Push by Sapphire,* an uncompromisingly grim depiction of desperate urban plight. *Precious* is about an obese and abused black teenager living in the slums of Harlem in 1987: her father has raped her and left her with two children, an obscenity for which her mother – a bully consumed with loathing for her daughter and herself – attacks her physically and verbally in fits of jealous rage. Admittedly some of the film's wild acclaim may have been seeded by political correctness, and the upbeat third act feels contrived and veers into easy sentimentality. But no one can doubt the quality of the lead performances: Gabourey Sidibe as the stoic and taciturn protagonist, or her brutal tyrant of a mother as conveyed by Oscar-winning Mo'Nique. Even Mariah Carey, notorious for her past attempts at acting, delivers a spot-on turn as a weathered and sceptical social worker.

Less impressive was Lars von Trier's continuing quest for avant-garde acclaim, which reached new heights of self-indulgence in *Antichrist.* Willem Dafoe and Charlotte Gainsbourg play a married couple, devastated by the loss of their infant child, who move to a cottage in the woods where they are beset by strange visions while indulging in violent sexual behaviour. Featuring scenes of self-harm and the torture of others for pleasure, *Antichrist* proved as controversial and divisive as was intended, but fails in its more aesthetic goals. The film piles on horror after horror in an acutely self-conscious attempt to generate great art, but for all its aspirations to greatness – it is dedicated to Andrei Tarkovsky – *Antichrist* is no more profound than your average slasher flick. Von Trier wants to evoke an authentic experience of pain, but the shock tactics on display simply deaden and desensitise the audience.

RECESSION AND REUNION

Aside from the agitprop polemics of Michael Moore's *Capitalism: A Love Story,* Hollywood's response to the global economic downturn was somewhat muffled. This is for understandable reasons: Tinseltown has long been a symbol of an American-led brand of consumption and excess, thereby hardly making a good source for its critique. Furthermore, the industry has long known that the salve that mass audiences seek in bleak times is sheer escapism – after 9/11, cinemagoers flooded to fantasy and superhero films, not serious and probing studies of global geo-politics.

One exception to this trend came from *Up in the Air,* in which George Clooney plays Ryan Bingham, a man employed by a human resources consultancy to travel round the globe firing people on behalf of their cowardly employers. It is the middle of the recession, and consequently business is booming.

An engaging blend of light existential musings and dark social satire, *Up in the Air* aims to capture the zeitgeist of the nation's mood – it gives us every emotion, from anxiety bordering on despair to stoical resolution. Director Jason Reitman uses real people who have been recently fired to capture a realistic range of responses, but their performances are more than equalled by Clooney's own turn. A vapid charmer, Ryan revels in the rootlessness of his lifestyle, but finishes the film alienated and unhappy, deprived by his jet-set lifestyle of real human connection – an emotional poverty that mirrors and surpasses the material kind he inflicts on hapless corporate employees.

Elsewhere this year Hollywood appeared to be afflicted by a nasty case of sequel-itis. *Shrek Forever After,* which was generally well received, missed analyst forecasts for its opening by $30m (£19m), while *Sex in the City 2* flopped, lagging dramatically behind its predecessor in revenues. The latter outcome was no great surprise once word of mouth turned sour, as the movie plundered whatever goodwill was left in the ageing franchise: it is *Carry on Carrie Bradshaw,* an absurdist trek through a Middle East conjured straight from the pages of *Arabian Nights,* and a devout neo-liberal hymn to global wanton consumerism. The film aspires to feminism, but seems to think that liberation for women involves buying expensive shoes, and its caricature of the Middle East as an exotic land of decadence and repression has disturbing echoes of colonialist propaganda.

Finally arriving at our screens was Gothic maestro Tim Burton's long-delayed *Alice in Wonderland,* which transposes the story to the threshold of her adulthood, when at 19 years old she again tumbles down the rabbit hole after hastily fleeing an unwelcome arranged marriage. This new context would have allowed for an engaging psychological subtext on adolescence and adulthood but the real-world background is quickly discarded for a surreal mélange. *Alice* showcases some familiar Burton strengths – in particular, the sets are suffused with a spooky baroque splendour, and Johnny Depp delivers another demented performance as the Mad Hatter. Laurels go to Helena Bonham Carter's wonderful turn as the petulant and childishly tyrannical Queen of Hearts – though the performance is seemingly indebted to Miranda Richardson's 'Queenie' in *Blackadder II.* Unfortunately, *Alice* is all surface splendour, stripping the tales of the rich metaphors that made them so iconic in the first place. Eschewing the mathematical puzzles and metaphysical satire of the original, it is a wacky, psychedelic retread through otherwise familiar thematic conventions of the fantasy genre, even climaxing in a customary CGI battle that looks like *The Lord of the Rings* with giant chess pieces. *Alice* was not shot with 3D cameras – instead the effects were added post-production, and their incongruity shows: they come across as a superfluous and heavy-handed distraction, more likely to induce nausea than admiration.

A yet more disappointing return to the screen came from writer-director Richard Kelly of *Donnie Darko* fame, who came back after a long period in the wilderness with *The Box,* a thriller that falls foul of its sweeping eschatological pretensions. The film is adapted from a short story in which a struggling couple are offered a box with a button by a mystery stranger, and a choice: if they press the button, someone, somewhere, unconnected to them, will die, but they will receive a large sum of money in exchange. It is an intriguing premise that in this version is quickly buried under mountains of meaningless mumbo-jumbo. At heart *The Box* is a simple morality tale, but its running time is fattened by irrelevant sojourns into conspiracy theory as we lazily drift towards a fairly obvious conclusion. Kelly is at least original in his styling, and avoids obvious scare techniques, reaching for the bizarre, the surreal and the apocalyptic. But his cod-existential ponderings prove little more than dubious wrapping for some silly special effects.

Alongside the Burton-Depp reunion, Ridley Scott and Russell Crowe got together for the first time in a decade with *Robin Hood.* In this inventive reworking of medieval lore, Ridley portrays Robin as a daring socialist revolutionary whose father pioneered the Magna Carta. Crowe plays the role with his customary brooding intensity (and a much-derided English/Celtic accent). It is mildly entertaining fare, but compares poorly to Scott and Crowe's previous collaboration on *Gladiator*.

EUROPEAN CINEMA

Away from Hollywood, the past year saw a gold standard in European cinema. Acclaimed auteur Michael Haneke surpassed himself with *The White Ribbon*, an artful and ambiguous horror which premiered at the 2009 Cannes festival and easily scooped the Palme d'Or. Filmed in a lustrous black and white, the languidly paced picture unravels the threads of social life in a northern German village when it is being plagued by anonymous acts of violence, just before the outbreak of the First World War. Over its three-hour running time Haneke subtly and gradually posits the thesis that out of the poisonous climate of repression and persecution in this rural village a future generation of fascists was hatched: the idea is never overtly stated, but it lies latent and implicit in every frame and, whatever the historical veracity of such a view, Haneke's technical delivery of it is pitch perfect.

Another instant classic was Jacques Audiard's *A Prophet*, a French crime film based on a partially true story about Malik, an illiterate young man sentenced to six years in prison, who is faced with the dilemma thrust on him by a gang leader of being killed or becoming a murderer. *A Prophet* is a powerful drama marked with the same precision of intent as *The White Ribbon*. It takes a cliché – the brutal prison with its corrupt guards and powerful gang leaders – and reanimates it with a wealth of meaning and feeling.

VIOLENCE AND VENGEANCE

A less than subtle use of violence came out of Quentin Tarantino's fevered imagination with *Inglourious Basterds*, a luridly violent fantasy in which an anarchic bunch of macho Jewish soldiers, aided by a French cinema proprietor, bring down the Third Reich. Vengeance has long been an obsession of the director – whose last big hit was *Kill Bill* – and here he gets lost in a delirious revenge fantasy. The film was advertised as a *Dirty Dozen*-style war movie, but it is more an exploration of the *mise-en-scène* of classic war films. *Inglourious* boasts flourishes of genius – there are some marvellous set pieces of coiled, drawn-out tension, plenty of clever little touches of irony, and a breakout performance from Austrian TV actor Christoph Waltz, who plays Nazi colonel Hans Landa, aka 'The Jew Hunter'. Highly cerebral and oddly cheerful, Hans is the only character who resists stereotyping amid an array of cartoonish caricatures. How much the film appeals depends entirely on one's appreciation of Tarantino's style, for the writer-director long ago surrendered to artistic self-indulgence; *Inglourious* resembles the fevered fantasy of a bright and precocious kid for whom everything is just a clever game. Brad Pitt as Lt. Aldo Raine turns in a confused performance bereft of charisma, and memorable only for a preposterous Southern accent.

Another violent genre piece came with Martin Scorsese's *Shutter Island*, a throwaway B-movie foray that consciously blends Hitchcockian thriller and psychological horror. Leonardo DiCaprio stars as US Marshal Teddy Daniels, who is investigating the disappearance of a psychiatric patient at an isolated island facility for the insane – or is he? With a thudding, melodramatic soundtrack, dark and stormy skyline and heavy-handed scare scenes, the film frequently (and possibly intentionally) veers into parody. Events unfold in a confused and convoluted manner but this fails to disguise a remarkably simple wireframe plot, and DiCaprio's character grapples with comprehending the truth long after the viewer has fitted the pieces of the puzzle together. *Shutter Island* is a predictable film with an obvious outcome, and one which a more inventive director like David Lynch would have either avoided or buried in ambiguity.

A more inventive retelling came in *Bad Lieutenant*, famed German auteur Werner Herzog's eccentric remake of Abel Ferrara's classic 1992 tale, in which a corrupt cop pursues the murderer of a nun while being plagued by Catholic guilt. Herzog replaces the tortured angst of the original with irony bordering on farce. The film is a bizarre concoction of European art-house sensibilities with the Hollywood cop genre, but the marriage works surprisingly well, and Nicolas Cage continues his transition from movie star to character actor in a superbly dysfunctional performance. Equally laudable was the performance of Colin Firth in *A Single Man*, where he proves himself a subtle actor more than capable of handling the existential dilemmas of loneliness, buried sexuality and middle age.

The age-old story of elite schools as cesspits of repression and jealousy saw its latest spin in *Cracks*. Directed by Ridley Scott's daughter, Jordan, the independently produced drama is a Sapphic intrigue between an alluring swimming teacher, Miss G (Eva Green) and several of her boarding-school students. Miss G's seemingly worldly-wise and vivacious ways are idolised by the girls, with the exception of the newest arrival, Fiamma (María Valverde), a Spanish aristocrat who inflames her desires while seeing straight through her hypocrisies and deceptions. *Cracks* is nicely choreographed and features some fine performances from Green and several of the cast, but the overly cold and clinical direction costs it any emotional resonance. While the film is a tragedy of heated jealousy and desire, its lukewarm and lethargic tone underplays the carefully cultivated mood. Much the same problem affected *I Am Love*, starring Tilda Swinton and directed by Luca Guadagnino, a gorgeous and elegantly wrought tragedy about the patrician classes of Milan. The film effectively portrays their lethargy and withdrawal, but is so bloodless that it inspires little empathy with its events.

AWARD CEREMONIES

In recent years the Academy has distanced itself from rewarding commercial success – 2009's controversial snubbing of *The Dark Knight* being a case in point – and it cemented this tradition by handing the biggest prize of 2010 to *The Hurt Locker*, a limited-release project which took an insignificant $15m (£9.6m) at the US box office (a fraction of the mammoth revenues generated by *Avatar*, its biggest rival for the award), possibly making it the most commercially unsuccessful winner of all time. Kathryn Bigelow also became the first woman to win the Best Director award. Jeff Bridges won Best Actor for a sugary performance as an alcoholic country singer in *Crazy Heart* – a forgettable outing save for a wonderful acoustic soundtrack, performed by Bridges himself.

More inspired choices came in the supporting Oscars, deservedly won by Mo'Nique (the mother in *Precious*) and Christoph Waltz for *Inglourious Basterds*. The Foreign

Language category has long been a sideshow to the main event and is notorious for snubbing seminal movies: this year was no exception, with *The White Ribbon* and *A Prophet* – ranked by critical consensus as modern masterpieces – losing out to worthy but unmemorable Argentine crime drama *The Secret in Their Eyes.*

At what was generally considered one of the most uninspiring years at Cannes to date, Thai auteur Apichatpong Weerasethakul scored the top award with *Uncle Boonmee Who Can Recall His Past Lives,* an eclectic film steeped in spiritualism and eastern theology.

OBITUARIES

British actor Edward Woodward passed away at the age of 79. The Bafta-winning stalwart of stage and screen was most famous for his role in cult classic *The Wicker Man* (1973) as Sergeant Howie, a puritanically upright policeman who investigates the disappearance of a young girl on a remote Scottish island, and quickly comes into conflict with its inhabitants and their unbridled pagan practices.

Iconic 1950s actor Richard Todd died of cancer at the age of 90. Todd was best remembered for his portrayals of clean-cut and upright British heroes, most famously RAF Commander Guy Gibson in *The Dam Busters* (1955), a dramatisation of the daring and risky bomber raid on the Ruhr valley dams in 1943. Todd was himself a war veteran and one of the first British officers to set foot in Normandy on D-Day. His grizzled military past and box-office clout made the actor Ian Fleming's first choice for James Bond, which went to Connery after Todd passed it down owing to a scheduling conflict.

The French actress Cecile Aubry died of lung cancer aged 81. Highly regarded for starring in literary adaptations such as Henri-Georges Clouzot's *Manon* (1949), she shot to fame in her only American film, *The Black Rose* (1950), a bizarre Oriental romance in which she co-starred with Orson Welles.

AWARDS

ACADEMY AWARDS 2010

Best Picture – *The Hurt Locker* (Kathryn Bigelow)
Directing – Kathryn Bigelow *(The Hurt Locker)*
Actor in a Leading Role – Jeff Bridges *(Crazy Heart)*
Actress in a Leading Role – Sandra Bullock *(The Blind Side)*
Actor in a Supporting Role – Christoph Waltz *(Inglourious Basterds)*
Actress in a Supporting Role – Mo'Nique *(Precious: Based on the Novel Push by Sapphire)*
Animated Feature Film – *Up* (Pete Docter)
Writing (Original Screenplay) – *The Hurt Locker,* by Mark Boal
Writing (Adapted Screenplay) – *Precious: Based on the Novel Push by Sapphire,* by Geoffrey Fletcher
Foreign Language Film – *The Secret in Their Eyes (El Secreto de Sus Ojos),* Argentina
Documentary (Feature) – *The Cove* (Louie Psihoyos)

CANNES FILM FESTIVAL 2010

Palme d'Or – *Uncle Boonmee Who Can Recall His Past Lives* (Apichatpong Weerasethakul)
Grand Prix – *Of Gods and Men* (Xavier Beauvois)
Jury Prize – *A Screaming Man* (Mahamat-Saleh Haroun)
Best Director – Mathieu Amalric *(On Tour)*
Best Actor – Javier Bardem *(Biutiful)* and Elio Germano *(La Nostra Vita)*
Best Actress – Juliette Binoche *(Certified Copy)*
Best Screenplay – Lee Chang-Dong *(Poetry)*
Camera d'Or – *Ano Bisiesto,* by Michael Rowe

BERLIN FILM FESTIVAL 2010

Golden Bear – *Honey* (Semih Kaplanoglu)
Grand Jury Prize – *If I Want to Whistle, I Whistle* (Florin Serban)
Silver Bear for Best Director – Roman Polanski *(The Ghost Writer)*

VENICE FILM FESTIVAL 2009

Golden Lion – *Lebanon* (Samuel Maoz)
Special Jury Prize – *Soul Kitchen* (Fatih Atkin)

LITERATURE

Nick Rennison

FICTION

The taste for historical fiction which many commentators have noticed in recent years – usually in order to condemn it and call for a greater commitment to the contemporary world – showed no signs of dwindling in the year under review. The 2009 Man Booker Prize, still the most prestigious of British book awards, was won by Hilary Mantel's *Wolf Hall*, an ambitious narrative set in the court of Henry VIII and focusing on the rise to power of Thomas Cromwell. Four of the other novels on the Man Booker shortlist were also set in the past. There was even the announcement of a new award – the Walter Scott Prize – worth £25,000 and open only to writers of historical fiction.

Many of the most admired contemporary novelists continued to find inspiration in yesterday's stories rather than today's. Andrea Levy followed her Orange Prize-winning success *Small Island* with *The Long Song* (Headline Review), a cleverly constructed story set in 19th-century Jamaica about an old woman looking back at her life as a slave on a sugar plantation. Helen Dunmore's *The Betrayal* (Fig Tree) was set in Leningrad in the early 1950s and chronicled the attempts by its central characters, a young doctor and a nursery school teacher, to create a life together amid the fear and suspicion of Soviet society. In *Parrot and Olivier in America* (Faber & Faber) Peter Carey created a picaresque tale of a French aristocrat and his servant discovering the New World of American democracy in the early years of the 19th century. Maggie O'Farrell chose to weave together two stories, one from the present day and one from Soho in its years as a bohemian enclave in the heart of 1950s London, in *The Hand that First Held Mine* (Headline Review). Martin Amis looked at even more recent history as he struggled to dissect and understand the sexual revolution of the 1960s and 1970s in *The Pregnant Widow* (Jonathan Cape). Booker Prize-winning Irish novelist Roddy Doyle concluded his trilogy re-examining the history of Ireland in the 20th century through the eyes of his central character, Henry Smart, with *The Dead Republic* (Jonathan Cape).

Even David Mitchell, one of the most innovative of British writers, whose earlier narratives have whisked readers around the global village of today and forward into the near future, seemed to feel the lure of the past in his latest novel. *The Thousand Autumns of Jacob de Zoet* (Sceptre) is set in the 18th century and follows the fortunes of its central character, a Dutch clerk working on the tiny Japanese island of Dejima, an isolated trading *entrepôt* between East and West.

MODERN SOCIETY

Not all novelists, of course, were flicking through the history books in search of stories. The urge to anatomise the present was still there. Sebastian Faulks made a bold if not entirely successful attempt to write a 'state of the nation' novel in *A Week in December* (Hutchinson) which traces the lives of seven characters in modern London, from a greedy hedge fund manager to an underground train driver, as they gradually converge. Jonathan Coe's *The Terrible Privacy of Maxwell Sim* (Viking) was a comic novel about a salesman, trapped in a dull and disintegrating life, who goes on an improbable journey through the country to deliver goods to a remote retail outlet in the Shetlands. It had much to say about the loneliness and alienation of modern society.

Solar (Jonathan Cape), the latest novel by Ian McEwan, took an oblique look at one of the great debates of our time. The book told the story of Michael Beard, a philandering middle-aged physicist who won a Nobel Prize when he was younger but now, embarking on a trip with fellow scientists to the Arctic in order to study global warming at first hand, is only too aware of his failing faculties. The book was advertised in advance as its author's take on climate change, which suggested a novel of high-minded seriousness, but Beard's misadventures often prove funny. McEwan once said that he hates comic novels, likening them to 'being wrestled to the ground and being tickled', but *Solar* went on to win a prize (the Bollinger Everyman Wodehouse Prize) that is awarded specifically for comic fiction.

Jon McGregor's first two novels were rightly praised for their ability to invest ordinary life with a sense of the extraordinary. His third, *Even the Dogs* (Bloomsbury), began with the lonely death of a heavy drinker and then opened out into a bleak but compelling narrative that threw sympathetic light on the desperate lives of a group of drug-addicted and marginalised young people in an unnamed Midlands city.

A FEW FAMILIAR NAMES

Other writers, perhaps more familiar than Jon McGregor, produced new novels in the period under review. Nick Hornby's *Juliet, Naked* (Viking) was the story of Tucker Crowe, a reclusive American singer-songwriter and the unexpected relationship he develops with the girlfriend of his greatest fan in England. Rose Tremain created a dark tale of familial transgression and cultural misunderstanding, set in the Cévennes mountains of France, in *Trespass* (Chatto & Windus). Barbara Trapido's *Sex and Stravinsky* (Bloomsbury) was a cleverly choreographed comedy about two couples discovering, after years of marriage, that they have made the wrong choice in partners. *Love and Summer* (Penguin) was the octogenarian William Trevor's first novel since *The Story of Lucy Gault* was published in 2002. One of Britain's most inventive novelists, Jim Crace, produced an offbeat thriller, set in the near future and featuring an ageing jazz musician jolted out of his routine life, in *All That Follows* (Picador). *The Good Man Jesus and the Scoundrel Christ* (Canongate), Philip Pullman's retelling of the Gospels, threatened to be the most controversial novel of the year, generating claims by some Christians that it was blasphemous. In fact, the book provided a brilliant new interpretation of the life of Christ and was also a thought-provoking reflection on the process of how stories come into existence and accrue their meanings.

DEATH NO OBJECT TO PUBLICATION

This was another year which proved that death is not necessarily an obstacle to a literary career. Publishers are always eager to riffle through the posthumous papers of great writers, and so two authors reappeared in lists of new titles many years after they had departed for the great lending library in the sky. Penguin was eager to persuade us that John Wyndham's *Plan for Chaos* and Vladimir Nabokov's *The Original of Laura* each represented a substantial addition to the *oeuvre* of its author. In the event, *Plan for Chaos* proved to be a pulp potboiler and *The Original of Laura* little more than notes for an unfinished novel which the author asked to be destroyed after his death. Luckily the authors' reputations already stood too high to be damaged by the appearance of such unsatisfactory works.

THRILL SEEKERS

In the thriller genre, *The Lost Symbol* (Transworld), Dan Brown's follow-up to *The Da Vinci Code*, saw his central character, Harvard University symbologist Robert Langdon, plunged into further funny business involving ancient wisdom and long-hidden secrets. Once again critics fell over themselves to point out Brown's historical inaccuracies and stylistic infelicities; once again his millions of readers took little, if any, notice of the critics.

Robert Harris, a better writer than Brown, published *Lustrum* (Hutchinson), the second of a proposed trilogy of novels set in the dying days of the Roman Republic and featuring the orator and politician, Marcus Tullius Cicero. As Cicero steered his way through the dangerous whirlpool of the era's politics, Harris brought the grandeur and corruption of Republican Rome vividly to life.

It was impossible to escape the work of the late Stieg Larsson. If the person opposite you on the tube or train was reading a crime novel, then chances were it was by Larsson. The final volume in his trilogy, *The Girl Who Kicked the Hornets' Nest* (Maclehose Press), was published in autumn 2009 and became as big a bestseller as the earlier volumes. Sadly, Larsson himself is not around to enjoy the success but it has been so enormous that perhaps squabbles over his legacy were inevitable. Acrimonious disputes between his long-term partner, Eva Gabrielsson, and his brother and father continue six years after the Swedish writer's death at the age of only 50.

Meanwhile, one of Britain's bestselling crime writers, Ian Rankin, had bid farewell to his popular character, Inspector Rebus, but continued to produce crime fiction of the highest quality. *The Complaints* (Orion), like the Rebus novels, is set in Edinburgh and focuses on Malcolm Fox, a cop in the police department investigating corruption and wrongdoing within the force itself.

Swedish author Henning Mankell, whose books featuring Inspector Kurt Wallander have gained fresh attention after TV adaptations won much praise, published *The Man from Beijing* (Harvill Secker), a political thriller that ranged confidently through time and space.

SCI-FI AND SPECULATIVE FICTION

The most influential writer today in British sci-fi (SF) and fantasy (or speculative fiction, as its admirers sometimes prefer to call it) is probably China Miéville. His earlier novel *The City and the City* won both the major prizes for SF on this side of the Atlantic – the Arthur C. Clarke Award and the British Science Fiction Association Award – and his new book, *Kraken* (Macmillan), a characteristically weird adventure that begins with the kidnapping of a giant squid from London's Natural History Museum, is likely to garner more awards.

Other British writers with big reputations produced new work in recent months. With *Stone Spring* (Gollancz) Stephen Baxter began a new trilogy set in an alternative Europe where the land mass now covered by the North Sea still existed; Alastair Reynolds published *Terminal World* (Gollancz), set in his Revelation Space Universe; and Adam Roberts' *New Model Army* (Gollancz) offered a vision of a near-future Britain in which civil war had broken out.

NON-FICTION

Altogether better writers than those ghosts who record the lives of celebrities turned their attention to the memoir. Novelist Rupert Thomson produced a compelling account of familial love and resentment in *This Party's Got to Stop* (Granta). Poet John Burnside wrote with unflinching and unsettling honesty about battling against addiction and mental instability in *Waking Up in Toytown* (Jonathan Cape). In *Blood Knots* (Atlantic Books) Luke Jennings created a book that was both a paean in praise of the delights of angling and the story, told through the prism of his experiences with rod and line, of growing up in the late 1950s and 1960s, of his relationship with his father and of his friendship with a remarkable man named Robert Nairac.

The publication of *Hitch 22* (Atlantic Books), the unsurprisingly controversial memoirs of Christopher Hitchens, was sadly followed by the announcement that the journalist and polemicist was suffering from oesophageal cancer and would be unable to undertake the book tour planned for him. Antonia Fraser's *Must You Go* (Weidenfeld & Nicolson), a record of her marriage to Harold Pinter, attracted contrasting reviews. Some thought it an honest and touching portrait of their love; others were less impressed.

WRITERS' LIVES

The more traditional literary biography continued to flourish. Although much was made in the publicity accompanying the book of its subject's drinking and sexual misdemeanours, there were few sensational revelations in John Carey's *William Golding* (Faber & Faber). It was simply a sensitive and well-crafted biography of the man who wrote *Lord of the Flies*. *The Secret Lives of Somerset Maugham* (John Murray) by Selina Hastings and Wendy Moffat's *E. M. Forster: A New Life* (Bloomsbury) were similarly skilful reconstructions of writers' lives.

Pearl S. Buck's novel of Chinese peasant life, *The Good Earth*, was a bestseller in the 1930s and its author became the first American woman to win the Nobel Prize for Literature. Today her name is probably known to few general readers but Hilary Spurling's biography, *Burying the Bones: Pearl Buck in China* (Profile), hoped to change that. Perhaps a Buck revival will eventually match the recent resurgence of interest in the French-Jewish novelist Irène Némirovsky, killed at Auschwitz in 1942. Not only are many of the 16 novels she wrote in her short life back in print but a biography, simply titled *The Life of Irène Némirovsky* (Chatto & Windus), by Olivier Philipponnat and Patrick Lienhardt, has now been translated into English. Biography and literary detective work met in James Shapiro's *Contested Will* (Faber & Faber), a brilliant investigation into the controversies surrounding the plays of Shakespeare and who actually wrote them. Was it the man from Stratford or any one of a long list of alternative candidates – from Christopher Marlowe to Sir Francis Bacon – who have been suggested over the years?

BRITISH PERSPECTIVES

Novelist, biographer and popular historian Peter Ackroyd turned his attention from his native London to the Pearl of the Adriatic and published *Venice* (Chatto & Windus), a characteristically erudite and occasionally eccentric portrait of the lagoon city. Other writers produced equally memorable books offering a British perspective on European history. Graham Robb's *Parisians* (Picador), curiously subtitled 'An Adventure History of Paris', looked at the last two and a half centuries in the life of the French capital through the lives of some of its most famous inhabitants. *Germania* (Picador) by Simon Winder, a product of its author's obsession with all things German, was half history and half travelogue but wholly delightful and amusing. There were books which looked back on Britain in the recent past and discovered that it seemed almost as much a foreign country as the lands explored by Winder. Francis Wheen turned his eye on the 1970s in *Strange Days Indeed* (Fourth Estate) and produced a very funny chronicle of its oddities and excesses. Barry Miles, witness to many of the great counter-cultural events of the 1960s, published *London Calling* (Atlantic Books), an eye-opening survey of underground creativity in the capital from the end of the Second World War to the present day. And Bill Bryson looked for history in his own house in *At Home* (Doubleday). His revelations of the larger stories behind everyday life and ordinary domesticity proved as entertaining as anything in his travel books.

POETRY

After the mud-slinging and backbiting that attracted public attention to the election for the Oxford poetry professorship in 2009, it was a relief that poetry was able to garner more positive publicity in the first month of 2010. Christopher Reid's *A Scattering* (Arete), his moving collection of verses in tribute to his late wife, was chosen by the judges of the Costa Prizes as their Book of the Year, the first time in a decade that a poetry book had been the choice. And, when the election for the Oxford professorship was re-run in June, there was little doubt that the most suitable candidate won. A landslide victory for Geoffrey Hill was hailed by nearly everyone as the best result possible.

Another cause for celebration was the recognition given to poets in the Queen's Birthday Honours list. Wendy Cope was awarded an OBE and Simon Armitage and Michael Longley were each given a CBE. Meanwhile, the two most prestigious prizes for poetry in the UK went to poets who have both built up substantial and much-admired bodies of work over the last 20 years. Philip Gross's collection, *The Water Table* (Bloodaxe Books) won the 2009 T. S. Eliot Prize; Don Paterson's *Rain* (Faber & Faber) took the Forward Poetry Prize for Best Collection.

NEW COLLECTIONS

One of the original participants in that ill-fated race for the Oxford professorship, the Nobel laureate Derek Walcott published *White Egrets* (Faber & Faber), a new collection of his poetry. Other veteran poets showed that the advancing years had done little to blunt their poetic powers. Dannie Abse's *Two for Joy* (Hutchinson), subtitled 'Scenes from Married Life', was like a companion volume to *The Presence*, his 2007 memoir of loss and mourning, and celebrated his 50-year-long love affair with his late wife, Joan. *Standard Midland* (Bloodaxe Books) was a collection by Roy Fisher, many of the poems evoking the Midlands landscapes and cityscapes he knows so well and *Pebble and I* (Chatto) was another gathering of poems by the reliably intelligent and accomplished John Fuller. Elaine Feinstein, whose distinctive verse has been appearing since the 1960s, published *Cities* (Carcanet Press).

Other poets had significant volumes appearing in the year. *Dragon Talk* (Bloodaxe Books) was Fleur Adcock's first collection in a decade, *The Book of Mirrors* (Bloodaxe Books) was the fourth collection by Frieda Hughes, the daughter of Ted Hughes and Sylvia Plath, and Robin Robertson, a poet much admired by fellow poets, published *The Wrecking Light* (Picador).

Seeing Stars (Faber & Faber) was a new collection by Simon Armitage; Fiona Sampson, editor of the Poetry Society's magazine *Poetry Review* published *Rough Music* (Carcanet Press); poet and translator from his native Hungarian George Szirtes gathered together some substantial work in *The Burning of the Books and other Poems* (Bloodaxe Books); and Lachlan Mackinnon's *Small Hours* (Faber & Faber) was his first collection in seven years.

CHILDREN'S

Although not everyone will know her name, Kaye Webb arguably did more to influence children's literature in Britain during the 20th century than anyone else. Editor of Puffin Books for 20 years and founder of the Puffin Club, Webb died in 1996 but she found a sympathetic biographer this year in Valerie Grove. *So Much to Tell* (Viking) revealed the private woman behind the public face. Puffin itself was celebrating its 70th anniversary in 2010 and promoted a list of 70 titles in a variety of categories from The Best Mischief and Mayhem to The Best Alternatives to Twilight. A poll to pick the nation's favourite Puffin of all time from a shortlist of seven was won by Eoin Colfer's *Artemis Fowl*.

Colfer's runaway triumph in the poll – he took more than 60 per cent of the vote – was an indication of the ascendancy of fantasy fiction in the children's market. The same is even more true of teen fiction where, as the ranks of 'twihards' continue to grow and a new work by Stephenie Meyer appears, the novella *The Short Second Life of Bree Tanner* (ATOM), casual observers might be forgiven for thinking that all books must necessarily involve vampires and virgins. Certainly Meyer's imitators continue to be legion but there are plenty of highly original and gifted writers of fantasy fiction as well.

Patrick Ness completed his prize-winning 'Chaos Walking' trilogy with *Monsters of Men* (Walker); Philip Reeve published *A Web of Air* (Scholastic), set in the world of his 'Mortal Engines' quartet; and Garth Nix, the prolific Australian author of young adult fantasy fiction, concluded his 'Keys to the Kingdom' series with *Lord Sunday* (HarperCollins). One of the few authors to match Nix for productivity is the horror novelist Darren Shan and, as well as completing his 'City Trilogy' with *The City of the Snakes* (HarperCollins), he published the standalone novel *The Thin Executioner* (HarperCollins). *The Prince of Mist* (Weidenfeld & Nicolson) by Carlos Ruiz Zafon, the author of *The Shadow of the Wind*, was first published in Spanish in the 1990s but made its first appearance in English in 2010. This atmospheric ghost story was originally aimed at young readers but it has the page-turning power to appeal to those of any age. The American writer Rick Riordan struck gold with his books based on Greek mythology featuring Percy Jackson, a modern child who discovers that he is a demigod. His latest series, making use of the mythology of ancient Egypt, began with *The Red Pyramid* (Puffin). Diana Wynne Jones, the author of *Howl's Moving Castle*, has been described as the godmother of British fantasy writing for children and her latest book, *Enchanted Glass* (HarperCollins), is another classic in the making.

BEWITCHING STORIES

If writers for children were not conjuring up fantastic worlds, they were often, like their adult counterparts, looking to the past for their stories. Some of the most imaginative writers managed to combine fantasy and history in the same book. Celia Rees, author of the powerful *Witch Child*, set in the 17th century, published *The Fool's Girl* (Bloomsbury), a tale in which Shakespeare joins forces with some of the characters in his play *Twelfth Night*. Jeanette Winterson has proved herself a superb writer for younger readers in recent years and *The Battle of the Sun* (Bloomsbury) is set in the same period as Celia Rees' novel but includes even more elements of the rich, the strange and the fantastic.

Were any writers setting their fiction in the here and now? Well, the final part of Morris Gleitzman's much-admired trilogy was actually called *Now* (Puffin) and brought a story which began in Nazi-occupied Poland to a satisfying conclusion in present-day Australia. And, of course, there was always Jacqueline Wilson, the undisputed queen of fiction who examines the real problems and challenges faced by young people today. Her latest book was *Little Darlings* (Doubleday).

OBITUARIES

As always, the year saw the departure of some literary giants. J. D. Salinger died on 27 January 2010, 26 days after his 91st birthday. He had allowed none of his work to appear in print since *The New Yorker* published a short story called 'Hapworth 16, 1924' in 1965. For the next 45 years he retained his fame as the invisible man of American letters, a recluse who was rarely seen in public and protected his privacy with a ferocious willingness to make use of the law as a weapon against those who threatened it. After his death, there were reports that he had left behind as many as 15 novels which he had written during his years of self-imposed silence but chosen not to publish.

Three very different English writers made their appearances in the obituary columns during the first half of 2010. Dick Francis, originally famous as the jockey who was riding the Queen Mother's horse Devon Loch when it fell inexplicably during the 1956 Grand National, went on to greater renown as the much-loved author of dozens of crime novels, nearly all of them set in the world of racing he knew so well. Alan Sillitoe wrote two of the best-known works of 1950s English fiction, *Saturday Night and Sunday Morning* and *The Loneliness of the Long Distance Runner*, and was often categorised as one of the 'Angry Young Men' of that era. It was a label he disliked intensely and it may well have stood in the way of a proper appreciation of Sillitoe's varied work over the 50 years since it was first applied to him. Beryl Bainbridge was a novelist whose public persona, often revealed in TV interviews and newspaper profiles, was that of a lovable eccentric, pardonably fond of liquor and cigarettes. She was also one of the most skilled of contemporary British novelists, equally at home creating laconic, blackly comic narratives which drew on her own earlier life in Liverpool and, in her later novels, providing her own offbeat perspective on iconic events and individuals in English history from the sinking of the *Titanic* and Scott of the Antarctic to the Crimean War and Dr Johnson.

Others who died in the period under review included Budd Schulberg, the American novelist and screenwriter who wrote the script for the Brando film *On the Waterfront*; Keith Waterhouse, the 'legend-in-his-own-lunchtime' journalist and author of the novel *Billy Liar*; the fantasy novelist Louise Cooper; the thriller writer Lionel Davidson; the American crime novelist Stuart M. Kaminsky; the British sci-fi writer Robert Holdstock; the travel writer and historian Geoffrey Moorhouse; the American novelist Louis Auchincloss; Robert B. Parker, creator of the hard-boiled American private eye Spenser; Erich Segal, the Harvard classics professor who wrote the novel *Love Story*; the English children's author William Mayne; the Australian-born poet, long resident in Britain, Peter Porter; the American beat poet Peter Orlovsky; the Australian novelist Randolph Stow; Peter O'Donnell, the creator of Modesty Blaise; the playwright and TV screenwriter Alan Plater; and the Nobel Prize-winning Portuguese writer José Saramago.

AWARDS

MAN BOOKER PRIZE 2009

Hilary Mantel – *Wolf Hall* (winner)

SHORTLIST

A. S. Byatt – *The Children's Book*
J. M. Coetzee – *Summertime*
Adam Foulds – *The Quickening Maze*
Simon Mawer – *The Glass Room*
Sarah Waters – *The Little Stranger*

COSTA BOOK AWARDS 2009

Costa Book of the Year Award: Christopher Reid – *A Scattering*

CATEGORY WINNERS

Costa Novel Award: Colm Toibin – *Brooklyn*
Costa First Novel Award: Raphael Selbourne – *Beauty*
Costa Biography Award: Graham Farmelo – *The Strangest Man: The Hidden Life of Paul Dirac, Quantum Genius*
Costa Poetry Award: Christopher Reid – *A Scattering*
Costa Children's Book Award: Patrick Ness – *The Ask and the Answer*

ORANGE PRIZE 2010

Barbara Kingsolver – *The Lacuna* (winner)

BBC SAMUEL JOHNSON PRIZE FOR NON-FICTION 2010

Barbara Demick – *Nothing to Envy: Real Lives in North Korea* (winner)

CARNEGIE MEDAL IN CHILDREN'S LITERATURE 2010

Neil Gaiman – *The Graveyard Book* (winner)

WALTER SCOTT PRIZE 2010

Hilary Mantel – *Wolf Hall* (winner)

THE MEDIA

TELEVISION

Steve Clarke

In a media world obsessed by social networking sites such as Facebook and Twitter, the ubiquitous micro-blogging service, it was tempting to underplay the enduring appeal and power of television. However, come the general election and, a month later, the World Cup, the medium's sustained hold on the British public was clear. In fact, according to newly published research, as a nation we were watching more television than ever. The May 2010 general election was galvanised by Britain's first televised debates between the main political leaders. The three programmes, broadcast by ITV, Sky News and the BBC, proved that on this unique occasion television's power to influence the political agenda was unmatched; without his success in the first of these talk-ins, Liberal Democrat leader Nick Clegg may arguably never have achieved high office.

SIGNS OF ECONOMIC RECOVERY BY TV NETWORKS

Elsewhere in television, there were signs of financial recovery by both ITV and Channel 4, while their struggling terrestrial rival, Five, was put up for sale by owners RTL Group. Pay giant BSkyB continued its upward trajectory, although there were attempts by the regulator OFCOM to curb its market dominance. As for what most viewers enjoyed watching, 2009–10 was notable, once more, for the perennial popularity of the soaps and Saturday-night family fare such as *The X Factor* and *Doctor Who*. Meanwhile *Strictly Come Dancing* experienced a difficult season. As audiences used their mobiles and laptops to comment on shows while they were broadcast, the growing emergence of social media as a way of engaging with TV was evident. At the same time media owners encouraged viewers to seek out their shows via Facebook. The success of tween show *Glee*, first shown by digital station E4, was as much a success for social media as it was for television.

CLEGGMANIA BREAKS OUT AFTER TV TRIUMPH

For decades Britain's political leaders had resisted the overtures of the TV networks to follow the US example and partake in live leaders' debates during a general election campaign. In the year under review agreement was finally reached, not least because incumbent prime minister Gordon Brown, behind in the opinion polls, reasoned he had nothing to lose. As the veteran media commentator Raymond Snoddy said: 'Brown is widely seen as charmless and very bad at TV. David Cameron, on the other hand, a former TV spin doctor, is very much at ease on television and is rather good at it. Brown must hope that he will come over as the resolute, reliable leader compared with the fluffy, young pretender.'

On the day it was Nick Clegg who 'won' the first TV debate, due to his perceived freshness, obvious confidence and apparent ability to talk straight. His small-screen performance led to an immediate surge in popularity for the Liberal Democrats. By the third week of the leaders' debates his performance was less assured. The first debate was watched by 9.38 million, enough to make the programme number two in the ratings. From then on, the shows became the centrepiece of the national election campaign. They were scrutinised by news desks and commentators across all media.

QUESTION TIME CONTROVERSY

Earlier, in October 2009, another political programme, BBC1's *Question Time*, aroused controversy when the corporation decided to invite BNP leader Nick Griffin to appear as a panellist on the show. The move provoked a lot of public anger. Protesters gathered outside Television Centre in west London, but many opinion formers thought that Griffin did himself no favours when he attacked homosexuals and Muslims on air. Some members of the studio audience booed the BNP leader, calling him 'a disgrace'. The real winner from the episode was *Question Time*, which achieved its highest audience in 30 years of broadcasting as eight million viewers watched.

UPLIFT FOR ITV AS ARCHIE NORMAN JOINS

The recession had undermined advertising revenues across television, but towards the end of 2009 there were indications that money was returning to the commercial networks, especially ITV. The success of the autumn season of *The X Factor* encouraged advertisers to return to ITV, as did the World Cup, whose coverage was shared between ITV and the BBC. However, England's failure to progress beyond the last 16 competitors ended hopes of a bigger-still surge in advertising money.

Under the new leadership of chair Archie Norman, the businessman and former Conservative MP credited with turning round the once-ailing supermarket chain Asda, and CEO Adam Crozier, former head of Royal Mail, ITV looked more determined than it had for some time. Seasoned shows like *The Bill*, a fixture of the schedule for 27 years, and *Heartbeat* were axed, while other long-runners, including *A Touch of Frost*, bowed out gracefully. Whether ITV, facing more competition than ever before, could create new shows that would match these old stagers was a moot point.

There was praise for new three-part ITV drama *Unforgiven*, written and created by Sally Wainwright, and described by *The Times'* Andrew Billen as 'risky and original'. Suranne Jones starred as Ruth Slater, a woman released from prison on licence after serving 15 years for the murder of two policemen. Another show enjoyed by critics was *Collision*, a series that recycled the Hollywood idea of an accident that brings hitherto unconnected lives together. Reviewers admired the performances, direction and the script. And in common with two successful BBC1 dramas, *Criminal Justice* and *Five Days*, *Collision* was shown in five consecutive weekday episodes.

Tried-and-trusted dramas including *Wild at Heart* and *Lewis* performed strongly, but the keenly anticipated revival of *The Prisoner* failed to make waves. *Foyle's War*, starring Michael Kitchen, returned for three new episodes despite having been axed by ITV in 2007.

SOUTH BANK SHOW MAKES FINAL BOW

After more than 30 years on air, ITV arts showcase *The South Bank Show* came to a close. The decision to jettison the programme was attacked by the crime writer P. D. James and no lesser figure than Prince Charles. The heir to the throne complained that 'oblivion is not the place for the arts'. He added: 'I cannot say I am encouraged as mainstream television abandons such a unique and special commitment. Civilisation needs all the help it can get – more so today than ever before, but now it loses one of its greatest champions. It is a sad loss.' During the year under review there were no new comedy hits from ITV. For millions of viewers *Harry Hill's TV Burp* was a must-see show which impressed critics and awards juries alike.

ITV's biggest show, excluding *Coronation Street*, was *The X Factor*, whose performers, especially 'Jedward' (twins John and Edward), generated a lot of interest. With the network devoting more time to the talent extravaganza on Sunday nights, ratings and advertising boomed as more than 15 million people watched, some ironically. There were indications that another of ITV's biggest money-spinners, *Britain's Got Talent*, was losing popularity. The audience of 11.8 million for the final was no match for last year's figure of 17.3 million, when Susan Boyle was making headlines.

However, the growing sense of renewed purpose at ITV manifested itself by the decision to sign three big BBC stars – Adrian Chiles, presenter of *The One Show*, his co-presenter Christine Bleakley, and, even more significantly, Jonathan Ross, whose last BBC1 chat show was broadcast in July 2010. Chiles and Bleakley were to front a new-look ITV breakfast show, *Daybreak*, due to replace GMTV in September.

LIVE EASTENDERS GETS FANS GUESSING

Despite this mini-exodus of talent from the corporation, BBC1 remained the nation's most popular channel. One of the year's biggest successes was the first live edition of *EastEnders*, shown in February 2010 to celebrate the soap's 25th anniversary. The 'Who Killed Archie?' storyline was described as 'one of the best kept secrets in TV history', by *The Sun*. Not even the cast knew the identity of the murderer. Bets were taken on the guilty party while the embattled prime minister, Gordon Brown, alluded to the *EastEnders* plot. 'The only thing I haven't been accused of is murdering that guy Archie Mitchell in *EastEnders*,' he told a hostile press. The 30-minute live episode of *EastEnders* was watched by more than 16 million viewers, a massive audience.

The triumph was especially sweet as it followed a disappointing performance by BBC1 flagship entertainment show, *Strictly Come Dancing*, in the autumn. *Strictly's* ratings were the lowest for four years. The programme had suffered from accusations of ageism when judge Arlene Phillips, 66, was dropped to be replaced by one of the show's former winners, 30-year-old singer Alesha Dixon. Gossip writers wondered if Bruce Forsyth might leave the programme.

FRY ROASTS DOCTOR WHO AS 'CHILDISH'

Doctor Who's popularity was sustained as Matt Smith made his debut as the 11th Time Lord in March 2010. Critics responded favourably. In the *Daily Telegraph* Benji Wilson gave David Tennant's successor an A+. However, Stephen Fry, speaking at BAFTA in June, cast a caustic eye at the *Doctor Who* phenomenon when he said: 'The only dramas the BBC will boast about are *Merlin* and *Doctor Who*, which are fine; but they're children's programmes. They're not for adults.' Fry's criticism went further. He suggested that it was not only these two shows that were guilty of 'infantilism'.

BBC1's adaptation of Angela Levy's *Small Island* divided opinion, as did new, high-profile BBC1 cop show *Luther* starring Idris Elba from *The Wire*. A series based on the 2006 murder of five Ipswich prostitutes, *Five Daughters*, was described by *The Guardian* as 'BBC drama at its best, free of cop show cliché'. The third and apparently final run of Jimmy McGovern's *The Street* won acclaim and there were good reviews for BBC2's *Five Minutes of Heaven*, which explored the legacy of violence in Northern Ireland.

A two-part serialisation of Martin Amis's novel *Money* failed to live up to the hype. On BBC4, *Enid*, starring Helena Bonham Carter as a ruthless Enid Blyton, was highly regarded by critics, but another BBC2 biopic, *Lennon Naked*, featuring Christopher Eccleston as the ex-Beatle, garnered a mixed reception. In the spring the final season of high-concept show *Ashes to Ashes* bowed out with almost six million viewers.

MIRANDA GIVES BBC2 SOMETHING TO LAUGH ABOUT

In comedy Miranda Hart moved from radio to BBC2 with a quirky series, *Miranda*, that provided some welcome originality. Another promising new comedy from the channel was *Rev* starring Tom Hollander as a beleaguered, streetwise inner city vicar, a far cry from clerical stereotypes. But no new sitcom could match the critical praise heaped on the third series of *The Thick of It*. Stand-up comic Michael McIntyre scored on BBC1 with his *Comedy Roadshow*.

Science documentaries were much in evidence across BBC channels during the year 2009–10. *Wonders of the Solar System*, presented by Professor Brian Cox, was one of the best. Writing in *The Independent*, critic Tom Sutcliffe said that 'as a primer in cosmic dazzlement it works very well indeed'. Also outstanding was a two-part exploration of the USA's recent history, *Obama's America*, presented and written by Simon Schama.

A POLITICAL COUP BY JULIE WALTERS

Channel 4, whose new CEO David Abraham joined in the spring, underwent a period of readjustment as it became clear that there was no chance, given the state of the public finances, of any public subsidy or a partnership with BBC Worldwide. One of its outstanding programmes was *Mo*, a drama starring Julie Walters as the late Labour minister Mo Mowlam. Even by her own exacting standards, Walters' performance was regarded as one of her best. *Misfits*, a comedy drama about a group of young offenders who gain supernatural powers, was another stand-out. It aired on Channel 4's sister station, E4, and allowed cast members to interact with audiences via Twitter. *Come Dine With Me*, which had graduated from Channel 4's daytime schedule, also struck the right note with audiences. Such was the series' popularity that on election night a special edition was aired in which politicians, including Edwina Currie, competed to host the best dinner party.

During the year under review Channel 4 broadcast its final series of *Big Brother*. There was speculation that rival station, Five, might buy the once all-conquering reality show, but as Five was put up for sale following losses of £37m it had other, more pressing concerns. In July 2010, Five was bought by *Daily Express* owner Richard Desmond for £104m. He had originally made his money from publishing pornographic magazines and still owned a portfolio of 'adult' TV channels.

RADIO

For many loyal listeners the defining radio event of 2009–10 was Terry Wogan, arguably Britain's most popular radio presenter, hosting his final Radio 2 breakfast programme. Gillian Reynolds, *Daily Telegraph* radio critic, described the end of *Wake Up with Wogan* in December 2009 as 'a historic week in radio'. She added: 'With such high ratings for so long, his programme has long since beaten all rivals into the ground.'

The 71-year-old Wogan, whose breakfast farewell was broadcast on 18 December 2009, resurfaced with a new show in February 2010, but for millions of Wogan fans their morning routines would never be quite the same again. 'Thank you for being my friend,' he told listeners as he signed off with Anthony Newley's *The Party's Over*. 'I know you are going to welcome Chris Evans with the same generosity of spirit that you have shown me,' he said.

Later in the year, as criticism of high salaries and fees for senior BBC executives and talent intensified with the election of a new government, Wogan stepped into the controversy. He said the most highly paid BBC stars should take a 'responsible' 10 to 15 per cent pay cut because high-profile presenters should not be exempt from public sector cuts.

EVANS GETS ON THE RIGHT TRACK

The decision to replace Wogan with Chris Evans was a contentious one. *The Daily Mail's* radio reviewer David Thomas derided the broadcaster as 'the absolute epitome of the jabbering idiot deejay', but even he was forced to recant once Evans' Radio 2 breakfast show was under way. 'Sorry we were wrong,' noted Thomas. Critics welcomed the erstwhile TV star's more direct style. To the surprise of sceptics Evans added 1.5 million listeners to the Radio 2 breakfast audience as 9.3 million tuned in, according to RAJAR statistics released in May 2010.

Away from the mainstream arena of Radio 2, the corporation's digital station BBC 6 Music became the centre of attention. In March 2010, BBC director-general Mark Thompson announced his intention to close the service as part of proposals outlined in a new strategy review. The thinking behind the decision, the BBC explained, was part of the corporation's aim to 'do fewer things better'. The BBC's radio chief Tim Davie emphasised: 'We didn't arrive lightly at the decision to recommend the closure of 6 Music. . . currently only one in five adults have heard of it and less than one in 50 listens to it.'

But the BBC executives had, arguably, failed to take into account the commitment of those who did listen regularly to 6 Music. Helped by social networking sites, a campaign to save the station quickly mobilised. Said Georgina Rodgers, co-founder of Save BBC 6 Music: 'BBC 6 Music is the only place that caters for our diverse tastes, giving us access to the BBC's rich musical archive and offering valuable exposure to new music that may not otherwise be heard on a national radio station. The presenters play music they are passionate about to an audience who are passionate about music.'

In March and later in May protesters gathered outside Broadcasting House in London. The unprecedented publicity for the station led to a surge in listening as the number of people tuning in increased by 50 per cent; 6 Music further added to its credibility when jurors at the Sony Awards gave it two awards. In July the BBC Trust, who had to approve Thompson's decision, announced the station would be saved and that executives should consider the future of 6 Music 'as part of a wider examination of how best to improve the performance of the corporation's digital stations'.

DIGITAL SWITCHOVER

In terms of media policy one of the more pressing problems for the coalition government was when to turn off the analogue radio transmitters and switch to all-digital broadcasts. The new culture minister, Ed Vaizey, said that although there was an aim to move to digital by the end of 2015, FM transmissions would continue to operate beyond that date. The politician said that so far 11 million digital radio sets had been sold and that digital listening accounted for 24 per cent of radio listening in the UK.

In the commercial sector the biggest gains were at Absolute Radio Classic Rock, an increase of 37.1 per cent to 255,000 weekly listeners; NME Radio, up 16.5 per cent to 226,000; and Jazz FM, up 15.4 per cent to 471,000. However, during the year under review overall, commercial radio's audience share fell to a record low: 41.3 per cent compared to a peak of 51.1 per cent in 1997. There was much soul-searching over this apparently unstoppable slide. Writing in *The Guardian* Tony Stoller, the former chief executive of the Radio Authority, suggested that one factor driving the decline was commercial radio's lack of localness. 'Independent radio in the UK has morphed into commercial radio,' observed Stoller. He pointed out that, ironically, a less regulated radio business had resulted in smaller revenues – down from £594m in 2000 to £506m in 2009.

Nevertheless, consolidation continued to occur. In June 2010, GMC Radio, part of the cash-strapped Guardian Media Group, announced plans to turn its five Smooth Radio regional stations in England into a single national broadcaster based in Manchester. Up to 60 jobs would be lost. The same month Global Radio, owners of Capital, Heart and LBC, revealed that it would be cutting in half the number of local Heart stations. The reorganisation involved the loss of up to 200 full-time and freelance posts.

Meanwhile, the commercial radio industry's trade body, the Radio Centre, called for Radio 1 and Radio 2 to be forced to reduce their appeal to listeners aged between 25 and 44. Radio 1 should focus on teenagers and the under-25s, who are less desirable to advertisers, while Radio 2 should shift its lower age limit up from 40-plus to 45-plus over a period of three years. The report also called for the BBC to boost its commitment to digital radio.

THE PRESS

As newspapers grappled with the challenges of an online world and fragile economy, it was perhaps remarkable that the national press suffered no closures during the year under review. *The Independent* appeared to be saved from extinction when, in March 2010, Alexander Lebedev bought the title for the nominal sum of £1, such was the stricken state of the publication's finances. Later during the summer, in what may well turn out to be a seminal development, *The Times* and *The Sunday Times* finally introduced a 'paywall' as readers were charged £2 a week to read the titles online.

Across what used to be known as Fleet Street, cutbacks

were once again the order of the day. In the spring the Guardian Media Group reported a pre-tax loss of £171m; at the *Guardian* and *Observer* 203 posts were lost. At Trinity Mirror 200 editorial jobs were cut from the company's three national titles, the *Daily* and *Sunday Mirror,* and *The People. The Times* too announced job losses; editor James Harding revealed that *The Times* and sister title *The Sunday Times* were losing in the region of £240,000 a day.

LONDON'S PAPER WARS END

Newspaper owners were desperate to find new business models. In October 2009, the *London Evening Standard* became a free paper for the first time in its 182-year history. It was estimated to be losing £10m a year. Said owner Alexander Lebedev: 'The *London Evening Standard* is the first leading quality newspaper to go free and I'm sure others will follow.' In fact, none did – although rival free newspaper *London Lite,* owned by Associated Newspapers, ceased publication a month later. *The London Paper,* part of Rupert Murdoch's News International stable, had closed in September 2009. As Mediaguardian observed: 'The real driving force behind the decision to close *The London Paper* is Rupert Murdoch's newfound evangelism for paid-for content. This month he declared that News Corp's mission is "to increase our revenue from all our content". A loss-making free paper does not fit into this vision.'

Of course, there is no such thing as a free newspaper (advertising and cover price both generate revenue). It remains to be seen which of the newspaper owners discovers the route to riches in the digital age. There were indications that the *Daily Mail's* hugely popular website was leading the pack. It was attracting high levels of advertising by offering a very different, and even more celebrity-fixated selection of stories than were available to readers of the newspaper.

A relatively recent press phenomenon was the rise of local newspapers funded by local councils. Eric Pickles, the new local government secretary, said he wanted to axe 'the weekly town hall Pravdas' to ensure that a healthy independent local press can scrutinise the work of councils. There was concern that these papers, which also cover non-council topics such as TV listings and sport, were forcing even more local papers out of business.

The *Evening Standard* later claimed the decision to go free had boosted circulation to 600,000 a day and that the paper was on course to make a profit by 2012. Nevertheless, should the paywall succeed for *The Times* and *The Sunday Times,* other newspaper owners may follow suit and start charging for the online versions of their titles. In any case, it was a long-term strategy and no one expected the proverbial quick fix. 'The success or failure of this paywall, in short, will not be settled over a couple of months of subscription crunching: more like over a couple of years of revenue assessments,' suggested Peter Preston in *The Observer.*

The launch of the Apple iPad – a tablet computer designed to make reading text on the move much easier than on other, smaller mobile devices – was regarded by some commentators as a lifeline to struggling newspaper owners. It seemed that significant numbers of readers were eager to access the news via a touch screen. BBC journalist Andrew Marr was one convert to Apple's device. He wondered whether technology was ending the traditional demarcation lines between different news media. 'I think it isn't long before in news terms, there is hardly any distinction between broadcasting and newspapers,' he wrote in a BBC blog. 'This singularity is almost here. On my iPad, I will follow a political crisis in real time, merging commentators and video clips, a little bit of Nick Robinson here and some Simon Jenkins there.'

SUN SUPPORTS CAMERON

Political leaders still, of course, craved the support of national newspapers, especially during a general election. Famously, Britain's biggest selling tabloid, *The Sun,* had supported New Labour, apparently helping Tony Blair to defeat John Major in 1997. In autumn 2009 the paper switched allegiances by declaring its newfound support for David Cameron's Conservatives – just as the Labour Party conference started. By the time of May's general election, *The Sun's* support for the Conservatives was rabid. On election day, it advised readers to vote Conservative in terms seeking to echo the success of Barack Obama's Presidential campaign. 'Our Only Hope,' *The Sun* declared on a front page adorned by a huge poster-style portrait of a steadfast-looking Cameron.

Alone among the big-selling tabloids, only the *Daily Mirror* opted for Gordon Brown; the left-leaning *Guardian* and *Independent* favoured the Liberal Democrats. The remainder of the national press, including the previously Labour-supporting *Financial Times,* all backed the Conservatives.

Some commentators wondered whether in the internet age the perceived influence of newspapers to decide the outcome of general elections was on the wane. This is a complex issue. However, despite enjoying the support of the majority of national newspapers, the Conservatives were unable to win an outright majority.

Ultimately newspapers depend on the stories they publish to keep their readers coming back for more. Within weeks of the coalition taking office, *The Daily Telegraph* helped to force the resignation of new Treasury chief secretary, David Laws, over revelations of an abuse in his parliamentary expenses. Laws, who was revealed to have been claiming rental expenses to live at his male partner's flat, had spent a mere 17 days in high office.

Away from the Westminster village, the war in Afghanistan remained high on the news agenda. Tragically the *Sunday Mirror's* highly regarded reporter, Rupert Hamer, was killed by a roadside bomb in Afghanistan in January 2010. The next day's issue of the *Daily Mirror* was dedicated to the 39-year-old foreign correspondent. Another death mourned in newspaper circles was that of the veteran political columnist Alan Watkins, who died, aged 77, in May. He was credited with inventing such phrases as 'the men in suits' and 'young fogeys'.

Earlier, in September 2009, the death was announced of one of Fleet Street's greatest stars, Keith Waterhouse. He had first found fame on the *Daily Mirror,* latterly writing for the *Daily Mail.* Unusually, Waterhouse successfully combined a career in newspapers alongside his work as both a novelist and playwright.

THE INTERNET

For the majority of British households life without regular access to the internet would be difficult to imagine. A report published in July 2010 by the Joseph Rowntree Foundation found that a computer and an internet connection at home were no longer viewed as luxuries, but as essentials for all working-age households to enable people 'to participate in society', both to access job opportunities and to gain discounts on services.

However, as Martha Lane Fox, the UK's digital champion, pointed out, there were still around 10 million people in Britain who had never used the internet. The lack of access to the web was particularly acute among 'the disadvantaged, unemployed and retired,' noted Lane Fox. Her role to get all Britons online by 2012 was expanded by the new coalition government to include advising ministers on how to use the web more effectively. 'Promoting digital inclusion is essential for a dynamic modern economy and can help to make government more efficient and effective,' announced the new prime minister, David Cameron.

TWITTER GOES MAINSTREAM

As for those whose daily routine would be impossible without a reliable broadband link or a mobile device providing instant web access, the period 2009–10 was when micro-blogging site, Twitter, came of age and entered the mainstream. 'It has also become a powerful political and journalistic tool – a platform for protesters in Iran or readers angry at *The Daily Mail's* treatment of the death of former Boyzone star Stephen Gately,' opined *The Guardian*. Stephen Fry, whose number of followers on Twitter increased from 630,000 to 1.5 million in the period under review, agreed. He claimed that the 'Twitternet' was responsible for a fundamental 'shift in the very focus of democracy' with the potential to 'become the new fifth estate'.

Ironically, the San Francisco-based company was still to post a profit, despite an estimated 100 million Twitter users worldwide. Its role – and that of social media per se – in the general election was widely debated. In fact, many commentators thought the general election would be Britain's first internet campaign. While there was no Obama-style web-driven funding campaign, a report by the Reuters Institute for the Study of Journalism showed how much impact social media had on the election, especially regarding younger voters.

The 18 to 24 age group covered by the survey said they used Facebook extensively during the election, and consumed most of their election news via the web: 89 per cent, compared with 81 per cent for TV and 59 per cent for newspapers. Following decades attempting to encourage young people to vote, the Electoral Commission achieved some success with aboutmyvote.co.uk, which recorded 1.8 million visits during the campaign, 40 per cent from 18- to 24-year-olds. Grassroots commentary on the election was provided by websites such as mydavidcameron.com, which invited people to customise Conservative Party billboards, while Twitter became a must-have for the vast majority of politicians. John Prescott, the former deputy prime minister, was an enthusiastic user of the micro-blogging site.

THE RISE AND RISE OF FACEBOOK

Facebook's popularity soared (there were 500 million active users, according to figures released in July 2010), although there was controversy over what some critics of the site regarded as its cavalier attitude to privacy. In May 2010, Facebook CEO Mark Zuckerberg admitted that Facebook had 'missed the mark' over privacy. Regulators were concerned about the complexity of Facebook's privacy settings. As a result, a simpler set of controls was introduced. In July Facebook generated more headlines when thousands of users posted their support for convicted criminal Raoul Moat, who had killed his ex-girlfriend's new partner and wounded a policeman before apparently shooting himself. The 'RIP Raoul Moat You Legend!' page, which attracted more than 30,000 contributions and the condemnation of David Cameron in the Commons, was removed from Facebook by its creator, 21-year-old Siobhan O'Dowd, following public revulsion.

While Facebook's future looked golden, other social networking sites struggled. MySpace and especially Bebo, aimed at teenage girls, experienced big challenges. At one point it looked as if Bebo might close, but the site was eventually sold by AOL to Criterion Capital Partners for an undisclosed sum, rumoured to be $10m or less. Such were the gold rush economics of the web and the fickleness of its younger users that just two years earlier AOL had bought Bebo for $850m. According to some reports, traffic to MySpace UK had halved in the first six months of 2010. There were rumours that owners News Corporation were considering selling the site, but this was denied.

RIVALS AND REGULATORS ATTACK GOOGLE

During the period under review Google was rarely out of the headlines. Rupert Murdoch accused the search engine of 'kleptomania' and acting as a 'parasite' for including News Corp content in its Google News pages. Regulators, too, articulated concern over the company's power. The European Commission announced that it would investigate Google over claims that it had acted anti-competitively. Meanwhile Google's reputation suffered after it agreed to censor its search results in China; however, the decision was subsequently reversed.

The BBC's presence as a provider of web-based news, information and entertainment was attacked by News Corporation's James Murdoch. He warned of the BBC's 'chilling' ambitions. The subtext was that the popularity of the news pages on bbc.co.uk might undermine News Corp's paywall ambitions for its own newspapers. During 2009–10, the BBC did announce plans to scale back its activities on the web, with a proposal to halve the number of websites. In July 2010, bbc.co.uk was given a new look aimed at improving navigation; while the iPlayer was also upgraded.

The site revamp involved providing built-in access to Twitter and Facebook so that users could recommend shows via these networks. Another BBC-backed initiative, Project Canvas, was finally approved by the BBC Trust. Commentators hailed the project, due to launch in 2011, as a landmark in media convergence because it would enable audiences to access the internet from their TV sets once they had bought a new set-top box. But BSkyB and Virgin Media opposed Canvas, fearing that it would undermine their own video-on-demand services.

MUSIC

MUSIC (CLASSICAL)

Jonathan Lennie

ANNIVERSARIES

Celebrations to mark the 350th anniversary of Purcell's birth, the 250th anniversary of Handel's death, 200 years since Haydn's death and 200 years from Mendelssohn's birth, continued to the end of 2009. Notable events included countertenor David Daniels singing a programme entitled *Handel Remixed* at London's Barbican Hall in September, as part of the venue's *Great Performers* series. The American singer joined the Academy of St Martin-in-the-Fields to grapple with reinterpretations of the German master by Nico Muhly, Michael Nyman, Jocelyn Pook, John Tavener and Craig Armstrong to mixed reviews. BBC Radio 3, the Sony Station of the Year 2009, held an end-of-year listeners' ballot on the quartet's relative popularity – with the result, in descending order: Handel, Haydn, Mendelssohn and Purcell.

Around the UK, 2010 was 'Polska! Year', a plethora of Polish-related events curated in conjunction with the Polish Cultural Institute. In the first half of the year, almost-ubiquitous celebrations of the 200th anniversary of the birth of Frédéric Chopin, the country's most famous classical export, included his entire piano works performed more than once. Portuguese pianist Artur Pizarro presented all of the solo piano works over nine concerts at St John's, Smith Square, in London's Westminster, dividing his programmes into chronological blocks. Across town, at Kings Place, Martino Tirimo curated the sporadic *Chopin Unwrapped* series, presenting the composer's entire *oeuvre* across 12 recitals, albeit with piano reductions of the two concertos. Meanwhile, with ambiguity surrounding Chopin's exact birth date, the Southbank Centre in London hedged its bets with celebratory recitals from Polish pianist Krystian Zimerman on 22 February, followed by the Italian Maurizio Pollini on 1 March, the other contending date. In the suburbs, St Barnabas Church in Ealing produced a Chopin marathon, with pianists taking turns playing all the piano work over two days in February.

The bicentenary of the birth of Robert Schumann also fell in 2010, although celebrations were slower in getting started, with larger-scale series planned for later in the year – for instance, at Kings Place and Wigmore Hall. Meanwhile, St Barnabas presented another of its weekend marathons in June, featuring ten musical hours of Schumann from 47 various soloists and ensembles over four sessions.

While London concentrated its early 2010 anniversary celebrations on Chopin, further north the 150th anniversary of Gustav Mahler's birth was taken up by the Bridgewater Hall in a six-month series, *Mahler in Manchester*. The venue's three resident orchestras – the Hallé, BBC Philharmonic and Manchester Camerata – began a full cycle of the composer's symphonies, alongside a series of newly commissioned pieces to show the continuing relevance of Mahler's music today. It began with the BBC Philharmonic, under its principal conductor Gianandrea Noseda, setting the composer in an avant-garde perspective by juxtaposing each of his symphonies with a newly commissioned work. The opening concert in January, for example, paired the First Symphony with Kurt Schwertsik's *Nachtmusiken.* Other commissions were completed by Luke Bedford, Anthony Payne, Colin and David Matthews, Olivier Latry, Detlev Glanert, Uri Caine, Friedrich Cerha, Bushra El-Turk and Edward Gregson. Augmenting the cycle, Manchester Camerata presented the symphony-in-all-but-name *Das Lied von der Erde* in its Schoenberg reduction. The highlight came in May when the monumental Eighth, 'Symphony of a Thousand', was unleashed by Sir Mark Elder conducting more than 120 instrumentalists and 300 singers.

The Viennese composer's anniversary year was also acknowledged by the Royal Liverpool Philharmonic, which adopted a more traditional contextual stance. A numerical symphony cycle kicked off in January 2010, under the baton of its Russian chief Vasily Petrenko, but was less concentrated than Manchester's, running over three seasons along with other Mahler works.

Of the significant contemporary composers enjoying anniversaries, British composer George Benjamin celebrated his 50th birthday with a concert, on 7 February, of his music at the Queen Elizabeth Hall in London. Benjamin, who was accepted into the Paris Conservatoire at the age of just 16 to study with Olivier Messiaen, consistently reinvents his musical language, working slowly while lavishing meticulous detail on his gleaming works.

FESTIVALS

Over eight weeks in 2009 (17 July–12 September), the world's biggest classical jamboree, the BBC Proms, enjoyed its 115th season. This year it exploited the year 1934 to mark the end and the beginning of an era. It was the year we lost Elgar, Holst and Delius, but also witnessed the birth of Peter Maxwell Davies and Harrison Birtwistle (both now knighted; the former Master of the Queen's Music, the latter still exploring Greek myth in music of unnerving power and complexity). All were honoured at the Royal Albert Hall in various concerts.

A second theme was cycles: all 11 of Stravinsky's ballet scores and all five of Mendelssohn's symphonies were performed by a variety of orchestras, while the three piano concertos and *Concert Fantasia* by Tchaikovsky were played by soloist Stephen Hough. As the UK's largest commissioning body of classical music, the BBC Proms revealed 12 world premieres, including Paris-based Brit Ben Foskett's *From Trumpet,* Ryan Wigglesworth's *The Genesis of Secrecy* and even drum'n'bass DJ Goldie entertained the Children's Prom with his orchestral debut, *Sine Tempore.* The five BBC orchestras descended on London along with other top-flight outfits from around Europe and beyond, including the West-Eastern Divan under founder Daniel Barenboim, again generating harmony both musically and culturally, made up as it is of young Arab and Israeli musicians (here playing Mendelssohn, Wagner, Berlioz and Berg).

British minimalist Michael Nyman, long ignored by

the festival, made his Proms debut on 25 August performing with his band in a late-night recital that featured selections from his film scores and the premiere of 'The Musicologist Scores', a piece based on one chord, interrupted by Purcell and Handel citations. There were straight performances of the anniversary foursome, too, including Handel's oratorios *Samson* and *Messiah,* Purcell's opera *The Fairy Queen,* fresh from Glyndebourne, Haydn's oratorio *The Creation* and *The Seven Last Words,* and Mendelssohn's Violin Concerto and Symphony No. 2. One of the most talked about evenings was conductor Bernard Haitink's profound account of Mahler's Ninth Symphony, with the London Symphony Orchestra. Conductor David Robertson oversaw the Last Night, which featured the usual flag-waving fun, with trumpeter Alison Balsom as soloist in the Haydn Concerto and *Fireworks Fanfares,* while mezzo-soprano Sarah Connolly sang Purcell arias, charming Prommers by dressing as Horatio Nelson.

The Edinburgh International Festival 2009 ran from 14 August–6 September, entertaining the Scottish capital with a variety of top-flight events, including a series exploring J. S. Bach's cantatas at the Greyfriars Kirk by a host of classy ensembles such as The Sixteen, Cantus Cölln, the Dunedin Consort and Bach Collegium Japan. In the Usher Hall, there were song recitals by bass-baritones Bryn Terfel and Willard White. An impressive succession of orchestras took their turn under their respective maestros, including the Hallé under Sir Mark Elder and the English Baroque Soloists under Sir John Eliot Gardiner. Poignantly, Garry Walker had to step in for Sir Charles Mackerras, who had hardly missed an Edinburgh Festival appearance in nearly 60 years, to conduct the Scottish Chamber Orchestra in Haydn's *Seven Last Words of our Saviour on the Cross.*

The Huddersfield Contemporary Music Festival in November 2009 once again confirmed the appetite for new music. Highlights included the London Sinfonietta playing against an electronically produced reflection in *Bhakti* – a set of musical meditations from the 1980s on ancient Hindu texts by the festival's composer-in-residence Jonathan Harvey – which was contrasted with *Mesopotamia,* Richard Barrett's sequence of ten musical movements overlapped in 'archaeological' layers. The American pianist and composer Frederic Rzewski impressed with a performance of his own *Nanosonatas.*

Nigel Kennedy's Polish Weekend was notable for its breadth and unconventionality: the maverick British violinist took over London's Southbank Centre for three days of music, food and drink in May 2010. Kennedy's Polish credentials began ten years earlier with his marriage to Polish wife Agnieszka and subsequent life in Kraków, where he became involved in the capital city's music scene, leading to setting up a jazz quintet and the Orchestra of Life (for young classical musicians who, like Kennedy, have a jazz bent). Both of these outfits performed over the weekend along with distinguished jazz musicians, engaging in eclectic events, such as accompanying a screening of football's 1973 World Cup qualifying match between England and Poland.

In May 2010 the Norfolk and Norwich Festival staged the UK premiere of Jordi Savall's project *Jerusalem: The City of the Two Peaces.* His ensembles, Hesperion XXI and La Capella Reial de Catalunya, were joined by musicians from the diverse occidental and oriental traditions that have played their part in the city's history.

The Aldeburgh Festival 2010 opened on 11 June with George Benjamin's *Into the Little Hill.* Set to a libretto by Martin Crimp, the chamber opera is loosely based on the tale of the Pied Piper of Hamelin and tells of a morally bankrupt politician who, desperate to shore up a flagging public vote, promises to exterminate the town's rats. It was presented by Claire Booth (soprano), Susan Bickley (mezzo-soprano) and the London Sinfonietta under Franck Ollu. The piece was paired with Luciano Berio's darkly comic *Recital I.*

Surely the UK's most extensive local summer series, the City of London Festival (June 2010) programmed events around the themes of music of the Portuguese-speaking world, Chopin and bees. The first encompassed composers and musicians from Portugal, Brazil, Angola, Mozambique, Cape Verde and Goa. Highlights included *The Rhythm of Tides,* charting the history of the Portuguese empire, composed by Tony Haynes, who conducted his Grand Union Orchestra. Chopin was also acknowledged, notably with Portuguese pianist Cristina Ortiz as soloist in the Second Piano Concerto at the Guildhall, where the composer gave his final concert in 1848. Then, as night fell, 21 pianists on 21 upright pianos gave the premiere of a piece by Richard Causton, inspired by Chopin's *Nocturnes.* Festivities ended with a concert at LSO St Luke's in which the Aurora Orchestra under Nicholas Collon played works by Stravinsky, Bach, Rameau and Julian Anderson, while a troupe of capoeira dancers, Cordao de Ouro, choreographed by Mestre Poncianinho Almeida, performed with breath-taking energy and precision.

Also in London, the Spitalfields Summer Festival 2010's curtain-raiser was David Sawer's ballet *Rumplestiltskin,* performed by Birmingham Contemporary Music Group under Martyn Brabbins. Ubiquitous choral ensemble The Sixteen, (Gramophone Artist of the Year 2009), directed by Harry Christophers, explored the choral music of Allegri and Monteverdi's *Selva morale e spirituale* of 1641, even returning to investigate the Italian master further with jazz pianist Julian Joseph. The associate curator, composer James Weeks, presented the world premiere of his *Tide Trilogy.* An aural depiction of the landscapes of the English coast, the piece weaves together three virtuoso solo works with live electronics.

The St Magnus Festival in Orkney, established by composer Sir Peter Maxwell Davies, continued the year's Chopin theme in June 2010: pianist Ewa Kupiec's programmes featured some of Chopin's most inspired piano works, plus the Second Sonata by Grazyna Bacewicz, Poland's most prominent female composer. (The sonata was first performed by its dedicatee, Wladyslaw Szpilman, whose story is told in the film *The Pianist.*) Górecki's Third Quartet was also presented by the Royal String Quartet.

OTHER HIGHLIGHTS 2009

The Barbican Centre in London began its *Great Performers* series in October 2009 with French baroque choir and orchestra Les Arts Florissants, celebrating 30 years under its American maestro William Christie, and included the English Concert directed by the recently appointed Harry Bicket in a December rendition of Handel's *Messiah.*

Alfred Schnittke: Between Two Worlds ran in London, November 2009. The series was the brainchild of conductor Vladimir Jurowski who, as principal conductor of London Philharmonic Orchestra, curated and oversaw performances of works by the eclectic polystylist who Jurowski believes might be 'the last link in the chain of what we call the European tradition'.

In an impressive collaboration between music and technology, *Re-Rite* was an award-winning project for which the Philharmonia Orchestra under principal conductor Esa-Pekka Salonen took over a warehouse on the South Bank in London in November 2009 to present Stravinsky's revolutionary ballet score *The Rite of Spring*. The orchestra had been filmed by nearly 30 high-definition cameras: each room was dedicated to a different section of the orchestra, with the playback adjusted to reflect what would be heard from that position on the stage. The project later visited Leicester in April 2010.

The BBC Symphony Orchestra continued its 'Total Immersion' events in 2009, honouring two elder statesmen: in December 2009 the American George Crumb (born 1929), in a day of music, discussion and film, ending with his massive, transcendent, orchestral work *Star-Child,* requiring four conductors, two choirs and off-stage brass; then, the following month, German composer and 1960s radical Hans Werner Henze (born 1926) was also present for *Elogium Musicum,* an orchestral song of praise in memory of his late partner, and his latest opera, *Phaedra.* The series continued in January 2010 with leading German modernist Wolfgang Rihm.

OTHER HIGHLIGHTS 2010

The BBC Philharmonic, celebrating its 75th birthday, launched its 2009–10 season with Bohuslav Martinu's *The Frescoes of Piero della Francesca,* part of its ongoing *Neglected Heroes* series, with Luigi Dallapiccola enjoying a second hearing of his ballet score *Marsia.* E. J. Moeran, who died 60 years before, made up the trio through a performance of his Symphony in G minor.

The City of Birmingham Symphony Orchestra, founded in 1920, kicked off 2010 with works by Vaughan Williams and Elgar as part of its series of British music from the decade leading up to its inauguration. Sir Simon Rattle, who made his name with the band in the 1980s, returned to conduct a starry cast in Bach's *St Matthew Passion,* while in June the orchestra's much talked-about young principal conductor, Andris Nelsons, took to the podium to deliver a performance of Wagner's opera *Lohengrin,* which he later conducted as the curtain-raiser to the Bayreuth Festival 2010.

Young composer Luke Bedford assumed the new position of composer-in-residence at Wigmore Hall. To mark the inauguration, in January the Birmingham Contemporary Music Group under Oliver Knussen played works by Bedford and Helen Grime, contrasting them with 1960s pieces by the young Alexander Goehr, Harrison Birtwistle and Peter Maxwell Davies. The hall also hosted the Royal Philharmonic Society Lecture 2010, which was given by Alex Ross, chief music critic of *The New Yorker* and phenomenally successful author of *The Rest is Noise: Listening to the Twentieth Century,* who delivered a light-hearted history of the practice of applauding at classical concerts.

Osmo Vänskä conducted the London Philharmonic Orchestra in fellow-Finn Jean Sibelius's symphony cycle January–February 2010. A three-week Czech Festival in London, in February 2010, was led by the Czech National Symphony Orchestra at Cadogan Hall presenting a complete performance of Smetana's *Má Vlast,* alongside Martinu and Dvorák, and the London Philharmonic Orchestra playing Suk's *Asrael Symphony* at the Royal Festival Hall.

In March 2010 the John Armitage Memorial Trust (JAM) celebrated ten years of commissioning works for choir, brass and organ with a concert at St Bride's, Fleet Street, in London. Boasting more than 50 premieres over the past decade, the trust presented Tarik O'Regan's *The Night's Untruth,* an accomplished work setting reflections on sleep by Shakespeare among others.

Beethoven (born in 1770) was honoured early in 2010 at the Southbank Centre with several cycles: the Takács Quartet played the string quartets (in January and May); the Orchestra of the Age of Enlightenment, under various conductors, the symphonies (January–May), and Daniel Barenboim was the soloist with Berlin Staatskapelle for the five piano concertos (January–February). As it was 260 years since J. S. Bach's death, the venue also hosted a Bach Weekend in March. On a weekend in April, *Varèse 360°* presented all of the French composer's modest *oeuvre;* the closing performance of *Amériques* was assertively delivered by the National Youth Orchestra of Great Britain under Paul Daniel, its numbers swollen to 170. Moving to New York in 1917, Edgard Varèse sought to incorporate the noise of everyday life into music, pioneering unaccompanied percussion, adding fire sirens and notably searching for a way to produce electronic music, decades before the technology was available.

Meanwhile, the Orchestra of the Age of Enlightenment continued its sporadic *Night Shift* event aimed at a younger, first-time audience, reprising concert highlights late in the evening for an informal concert sandwiched between foyer DJ sets. Other initiatives to relax the concert-going experience continued on a monthly basis, notably *Limelight* at the 100 Club on London's Oxford Street and composer Gabriel Prokofiev's contemporary classical club night, *Nonclassical,* at an East End pub.

OBITUARIES

In November 2009, Elizabeth Söderström, the Swedish soprano best known for her Janácek roles died, at 82; Geneviève Joy, the French pianist, teacher and wife of 92-year-old composer Henri Dutilleux, died in the same month, aged 90. American pianist Earl Wild died at 94 in January 2010, following an acclaimed career spanning some 80 years. Wolfgang Wagner, the grandson of Richard and director of the Bayreuth Festival for 57 years, died in April 2010 at 90.

MOVES AND NEW APPOINTMENTS

The BBC Philharmonic has announced that 2010–11 will be Gianandrea Noseda's last as chief conductor, having held the post since 2002, although his close association with the orchestra continues as he becomes conductor laureate. He is succeeded by the Spanish maestro Juanjo Mena in September 2011.

The Royal Liverpool Philharmonic announced that Vasily Petrenko had renewed his contract to 2015, and that he had been given the title of chief conductor. It is a post he holds in conjunction with that of principal conductor of the National Youth Orchestra. (In May 2010 Petrenko was named male artist of the year in the Classical Brit awards.)

Scottish-born Donald Runnicles became the BBC Scottish Symphony Orchestra's chief conductor in September 2009, a post which runs concurrently with his position as general music director of Deutsche Oper Berlin. He succeeded Ilan Volkov, who held the post from January 2003 and who is now the principal guest conductor. The BBC SSO also introduces composer/conductor Matthias Pintscher, who becomes its new artist-in-association in the 2010–11 season.

Elsewhere, the composer John Woolrich will take over from Gavin Henderson as artistic director of Devon's Dartington Festival in 2011. Pinchas Zukerman took up the appointment as principal conductor of the Royal Philharmonic Orchestra, and young British star and Simon Rattle protégé, Robin Ticciati, began his tenure as principal conductor of the Scottish Chamber Orchestra in September 2009. At 82 years old, the conductor Sir Colin Davis received a Queen's Medal for Music in 2009. Plus, Sarah Connolly (mezzo), pianist Peter Donohoe and conductor James Loughran all received CBEs in the New Year's Honours List 2010.

COMPETITIONS

In November 2009, 68 competitors took part in the triennial Leeds Piano Competition, which was won by 29-year-old Russian pianist Sofya Gulyak. She clinched the Gold Medal and £15,000 through her playing of Brahms's Concerto No 1 in D minor; three of the five other finalists played Beethoven's *Emperor Concerto*.

The title of BBC Young Musician of the Year 2010 was claimed in May 2010 by 16-year-old flautist Lara Ömeroglu from Watford, beating strong competition from 25 finalists; the runners-up were flautist Emma Halnan and violinist Callum Smart. In April 2010 at Wigmore Hall, South African baritone Njabulo Madlala won the Kathleen Ferrier Award, singing Schumann and songs from his homeland.

The soprano Sophie Junker emerged as winner of the 9th Handel Singing Competition 2010, in a contest at St George's, Hanover Square (Handel's local church), accompanied by the London Handel Orchestra directed from the harpsichord by Laurence Cummings.

AWARDS

CLASSIC FM/GRAMOPHONE AWARDS 2009

DISC AWARDS

Historic Reissue – *Composers in Person,* Various artists, EMI
Baroque Instrumental – Fretwork's *Purcell: The Complete Fantazias*
Baroque Vocal: Handel's *Coronation Anthems,* The Sixteen directed by Harry Christophers
Choral: Elgar's *The Dream of Gerontius,* Hallé, Hallé Choir, Hallé Youth Choir under Sir Mark Elder
Concerto: Britten's Piano Concerto, Steven Osborne, BBC Scottish Symphony Orchestra under Ilan Volkov
Contemporary: *NMC Songbook*
DVD: Wagner's *The Copenhagen Ring,* Royal Danish Opera
Early Music: *Song of Songs,* Stile Antico Best
Historic Archive: Berlioz's *Les Troyens,* Royal Opera House 1957
Instrumental: Debussy's Complete Works for Solo Piano, Volume 4, Jean-Efflam Bavouzet
Opera: Puccini's *Madame Butterfly,* Angela Gheorghiu, Jonas Kaufmann, Orchestra e Coro dell'Accadmia Nazionale di Santa Cecilia under Antonio Pappano
Orchestral: Tchaikovsky's *Manfred Symphony,* Royal Liverpool Philharmonic Orchestra under Vasily Petrenko
Solo Vocal: Schumann's *Dichterliebe and other Heine Settings,* Gerald Finley
Recital: Martinu's *Juliette,* Czech Philharmonic under Sir Charles Mackerras
Chamber Award/Recording of the Year – Quatuor Ebène's *Ravel, Debussy, Fauré: String Quartets*

SPECIAL AWARDS

Artist of the Year – The Sixteen
Label of the Year – ECM
Lifetime Achievement – Nikolaus Harnoncourt
Specialist Classical Chart – Howard Goodall for *Enchanted Voices*
Special Achievement – Bernard Coutaz of Harmonia Mundi
Editor's Choice – Stephen Kovacevich plays Beethoven's *Diabelli Variations*
Concerto – Britten's Complete works for piano & orchestra, Steven Osborne, BBC Scottish Symphony Orchestra under Ilan Volkov
Young Artist of the Year – Yuja Wang
Music in the Community – Streetwise Opera

ROYAL PHILHARMONIC SOCIETY AWARDS 2010

Audience Development Award – Philharmonia Orchestra, *Re-Rite*
Chamber Music and Song Award – Wigmore Hall: Haydn Bicentenary Season Celebrations
Chamber-Scale Composition Award – Kevin Volans, *viola:piano*
Concert Series and Festivals Award – Huddersfield Contemporary Music Festival
Conductor – Oliver Knussen
Creative Communication – Philharmonia Orchestra, *Re-Rite*
Education – English Touring Opera with Hall for Cornwall, *One Day, Two Dawns*
Ensemble – London Sinfonietta
Instrumentalist – Stephen Hough
Large-Scale Composition – Kaija Saariaho, *Notes on Light*
Opera and Music Theatre – BBC Symphony Orchestra, *Juliette*
Singer – Philip Langridge
Young Artist – Iestyn Davies

MUSIC (POPULAR)

Piers Martin

BRITAIN'S GOT TALENT

This year two quite different female singers dominated the world of pop. Susan Boyle, the Scottish church volunteer who was catapulted to fame in 2009 after her performance on the ITV1 show *Britain's Got Talent* captivated millions of viewers around the world, released the fastest-selling debut album to date. In the UK, *I Dreamed a Dream,* mostly a collection of cover versions – including the Rolling Stones' 'Wild Horses' and the Monkees' 'Daydream Believer' – sold more than 410,000 copies in its first week of release in November 2009, according to the Official Charts Company (OCC), beating previous first-week record-holders Leona Lewis, whose 2007 debut *Shine* sold 376,000 copies, and *Whatever People Say I Am, That's What I'm Not* by Arctic Monkeys, which sold 363,000 in 2006.

I Dreamed a Dream went on to become the UK's bestseller of 2009, selling 1.6 million copies. The album also went straight to number one in Australia, Canada, Ireland and New Zealand, while in the USA it sold more than 700,000 in its first week, making it not only the biggest debut of 2009 in the States but also the biggest-selling debut for a female solo artist on the Billboard chart. The album sold some 3 million copies worldwide in its first week alone, with total sales rising to 9 million by the summer of 2010.

The TV clip that launched Boyle on the path to success, her moving rendition of 'I Dreamed a Dream' from the musical *Les Misérables,* has received around 150 million views on YouTube. But there were concerns about Boyle's ability to cope with the stresses of her newfound celebrity, and Simon Cowell, the influential producer and creator of *Britain's Got Talent* and *The X Factor,* faced criticism that his programmes exploit vulnerable people for entertainment. Like many acts discovered by Cowell on talent shows, Boyle is signed to his record label Syco Music, part of Sony.

GOING GAGA FOR GAGA

US phenomenon Lady Gaga may have come second to Boyle in terms of album sales – her 2008 debut *The Fame,* reissued as a double-CD with a disc of eight new tracks and renamed *The Fame Monster,* sold 1.4 million in the UK in 2009, according to figures from the British Phonographic Industry (BPI) – but the 24-year-old New Yorker, whose real name is Stefani Germanotta, has taken to her role as international pop star with extraordinary relish. With over 16 million Facebook fans and over 5 million followers on Twitter, Gaga has become one of the world's most prominent personalities, known as much for her outlandish fashion sense, eccentric behaviour and candid interviews as her music, a generic electronic pop confection.

Her track 'Poker Face' was the UK's bestselling single of 2009; another, 'Just Dance', came in third. Add to these the sales for 'Bad Romance' and Gaga accounted for almost 3 million singles sold in the UK in 2009, the BPI noted. Meanwhile the singles 'Telephone' and 'Alejandro', each promoted with an ostentatious video, occupied the top ten for much of 2010. Gaga was duly honoured at the Brits in February with three awards: international female, international breakthrough act and international album. She was also the bestselling digital artist of the year, with downloads of her singles and album tracks totalling 2.88 million.

POP TOPS ROCK

Gaga's fortunes heralded a resurgence for pop, which became the bestselling music genre of the year: 33.5 per cent of singles sold in the UK were classed as pop by the OCC, up from 28 per cent in 2008. Overall, the singles market experienced its best year to date with over 152 million sales (up from 110 million in 2008), 98 per cent of which were digital downloads.

Singles by *X Factor* winners Joe McElderry ('The Climb') and Alexandra Burke ('Bad Boys') were among the top ten bestsellers of 2009, while 'Fight for this Love', the debut solo single by Girls Aloud star and *X Factor* judge Cheryl Cole, also fared well. Cole's second single, '3 Words', featured an appearance by Will.i.am from American pop-rappers The Black Eyed Peas, who were responsible for three of 2009's bestselling singles. Between 'I Gotta Feeling', 'Boom Boom Pow', 'Meet Me Halfway' and their album *The E.N.D (The Energy Never Dies),* The Black Eyed Peas sold more than 2 million copies in the UK. Figures from the US in May 2010, meanwhile, certified 'I Gotta Feeling' as the bestselling digital song to date. The track spent 14 weeks at the top of the US chart and sold 5.56 million downloads, according to Nielsen SoundScan; in February 'I Gotta Feeling' was officially named the most downloaded track by the iTunes online store.

Rock's share of the singles spoils slipped from 31 per cent to 24.5 per cent, and the biggest-selling rock single of 2009 turned out to be a record that was first released in 1992. In what some experts considered the greatest chart upset of recent times, US political rockers Rage Against the Machine's expletive-strewn 'Killing in the Name' clinched the coveted Christmas number one spot after a close-fought battle with *X Factor* victor Joe McElderry.

The Los Angeles rock band, who had faded from view after success in the 1990s, sold 500,000 downloads – 50,000 more than McElderry's 'The Climb' – following a Facebook campaign to prevent another *X Factor* festive number one; the four from 2005–8 had all been *X Factor* winners. Speaking to the BBC, Rage Against the Machine guitarist Tom Morello said the campaign had 'tapped into the silent majority of the people in the UK who are tired of being spoon-fed one schmaltzy ballad after another'. Frontman Zack de la Rocha announced the band would play a free concert in London to celebrate their win, which took place six months later, in June, in Finsbury Park. However, the ultimate winner was Sony Music, to which both Rage Against the Machine and McElderry, via subsidiary labels, are signed. McElderry's single triumphed overall, though, ending the year as the fifth biggest seller.

NEGATIVE FEEDBACK

On the whole this proved to be a difficult year for British rock. One of the UK's biggest bands, Oasis, split up in August 2009 when lead guitarist and chief songwriter Noel Gallagher walked out on the group at a festival in Paris following a series of rows with his younger brother Liam. This was not the first time he had left the band – the brothers have a famously fractious relationship – but on this occasion Noel stated that he could no longer work with his sibling, adding, 'It's with some sadness and great relief to tell you that I quit Oasis tonight.' The Manchester five-piece shot to fame in the mid-1990s when their spirited take on '60s rock 'n' roll, dubbed Britpop, captured the mood of the nation. Many observers were keen to point out that Oasis has been trading on past glories for over a decade, but they still attracted a devoted following. Noel is expected to embark on a solo career, while Liam launched a clothing label, Pretty Green, and started work on a new band called Beady Eye.

A number of guitar bands also struggled to reconnect with a British public whose appetite for indie-rock appeared to have diminished, particularly when offered arguably more exciting acts such as Florence and the Machine, N-Dubz and a rejuvenated Dizzee Rascal. Although Snow Patrol's 'Chasing Cars' was declared the most widely played song of the decade by licensing group PPL, audiences showed signs of indie fatigue. Underwhelming album sales led to time off for The Enemy and to a split for The Rakes. Arctic Monkeys, those bankable poster boys of modern British indie, could only muster sales of 270,000 for their third album *Humbug* (released in August 2009), a fifth of the tally for their previous albums. *Humbug* saw the Sheffield youngsters come of age following recording sessions in the Californian desert, but it was a difficult record with no obvious singles and it alienated the fairweather element of their fanbase.

Across the Atlantic, New York indie darlings MGMT ditched the addictive pop hooks that made their 2008 debut so appealing in favour of indulgent psychedelic sprawls on their second album *Congratulations.* The result was a second-rate prog-rock opus – and no hit singles.

In happier news, Leicester rockers Kasabian, looking to

inherit Oasis' mantle as the band of the people, sold over half a million copies of their third album, *West Ryder Pauper Lunatic Asylum,* and were crowned best British group at the Brits.

LOVE SAVES THE DAY

The cosmic pop of Florence and the Machine (aka Londoner Florence Welch and her band) was the runaway success of the year. A flame-haired performer with an arresting voice and an endless wardrobe of designer frocks, Welch's chart-topping debut album *Lungs* sold 1.1 million copies in the UK and fared well all over the world. Her heartfelt cover of The Source featuring Candi Staton's 1986 hit 'You Got the Love' (released here as the grammatically correct 'You've Got the Love') became one of those rare songs that captures the public's imagination and develops a life of its own, making it inescapable for much of the year. At the Brits, where *Lungs* was named best album, Welch duetted with rapper Dizzee Rascal, himself the winner of best British male, on a 'mash-up' of their two hits entitled 'You've Got the Dirtee Love', while no British summer festival in 2010 was seemingly complete without Welch performing the tune with great gusto; she did so on three occasions at the Glastonbury festival, for example.

SUCCESS FOR UK URBAN SCENE

Dizzee Rascal capped a successful year in which he completed his transformation from credible rapper to cartoonish pop star with the bell-bottomed summer number one 'Dirtee Disco', one of the less understated moments from his fourth album *Tongue n' Cheek.* At just 24, Dizzee Rascal is something of a veteran in British urban music and is viewed as a role model who has paved the way for a new generation of streetwise rappers and producers who are blending the edgier sound of grime and hip-hop with a commercial sheen.

East London rappers Tinie Tempah and Tinchy Stryder made their mark with 'Pass Out' and the album *Catch 22* respectively, while N-Dubz, a lively R&B trio from Camden, north London, released second LP *Against All Odds* before landing their own Channel 4 show, the fly-on-the-wall documentary series *Being . . . N-Dubz.* In the realm of ultra-slick R&B, however, few could compete with boy band JLS; the 2008 *X Factor* runners-up scooped Brits for breakthrough act and best single for their ballad 'Beat Again' and released the seventh highest-selling album of 2009.

In a surprising move, the 2009 Mercury Prize was awarded to the relatively unknown London rapper Speech Debelle, for her debut album *Speech Therapy,* beating the bookies' favourites Florence and the Machine, Friendly Fires, and the Horrors. The Mercury judges praised her street-smart lyrical flow and rags-to-riches tales, but her jazzy hip-hop didn't connect with any significant audience and, despite the win, which traditionally boosts sales, the album failed to make the top 40. Two months later Debelle sacked her label, Big Dada, claiming that their distribution network was inadequate.

XX MARKS THE SPOT

The xx, four south London school friends who wear black and seldom speak, made what swiftly became the year's word-of-mouth, must-have album. Released without fanfare in the summer of 2009 but immediately praised on influential blogs and magazines, their eponymous debut enchanted listeners with sparse, doleful tunes on which singers Romy Madley Croft and Oliver Sim softly revealed their intimate secrets, their tenderness resonating with fans all over the world. With the instant, universal acclaim came constant attention and international touring, leading founder member Baria Qureshi – unprepared for this level of exposure – to leave the group before Christmas. So ubiquitous had the xx's music become that in a matter of months their album topped many end-of-year polls, and their song 'Intro' was later used by the BBC for the station's general election coverage. By July 2010 *xx* had sold 150,000 copies in the UK and 180,000 in the USA and this media-shy band had become a major festival draw.

A NU-FOLK REVOLUTION

Folk music in all its forms enjoyed a resurgence this year. This revival of sorts – christened 'nu-folk' by some – was led chiefly by London's Mumford & Sons, a well-heeled quartet who dress like Victorian farmhands, swap instruments on stage and sing in close harmony. Their debut *Sigh No More* topped the charts in Ireland and Australia and, on the back of their rousing live shows, sold 550,000 copies in the UK. A wise head on young shoulders, 20-year-old Laura Marling, emerged from the same folk-rock scene as Mumford & Sons, and indeed was romantically linked to Marcus Mumford of that band. However, her delicate singer-songwriting placed her more in the mould of Joni Mitchell. *I Speak Because I Can,* Marling's acclaimed second album, took confessional folk into the top five for the first time in a long while.

From Kendal in the Lake District, foppish four-piece Wild Beasts wowed critics and curious listeners with the fleshy folk of *Two Dancers,* their second album for the Domino label. The year's indie crossover smash, *Merriweather Post Pavilion,* the eighth album by New York experimental outfit Animal Collective was widely hailed as an electronic psych-pop masterpiece during the year under review and come Christmas it topped many album-of-the-year lists. The album, an intoxicating blend of Beach Boys-esque harmony and ethnic tones, sold 60,000 in the UK and 280,000 worldwide.

A likely contender for critics' album-of-the-year lists 2010 is US singer-songwriter Joanna Newsom, who released her third album, the triple-disc *Have One on Me* in February. As with her previous albums, the harpist received glowing reviews for her poetic, if cryptic lyrics and innovative compositions. Particular note was made of her more mature vocals and her musical palette, which drew on a broader range of instruments and influences from jazz and blues.

On the back of their critically acclaimed third album *Veckatimest,* Grizzly Bear – an erudite New York band prone to hazy pastoralism – took their lucid baroque pop on a tour of UK gigs and festivals, proving to be a major draw for festival-goers. Not to be outdone, fellow Brooklynites Vampire Weekend raised eyebrows when the preppy calypso of their second LP *Contra* reached the top spot in the USA, peaking at three in the UK, marking an encouraging year for independent music.

A WEALTHY ESTATE

One of the highest-earning pop stars of the year turned out to be Michael Jackson, who died from heart failure in June 2009 aged 50. The king of pop's estate estimated that $1bn (£675m) had been generated since his death, including £250m in album sales (24 million were sold). Additional income came from 39.4 million song downloads, 4.5 million ringtones, internet licensing worth £4m, and £175m from the concert film *This Is It.*

Jackson's finances, which were in a rather parlous state before his demise – a situation that led to his planned mammoth comeback residency at London's O2 venue – are looking remarkably healthy.

AWARDS

BRIT AWARDS 2010
British Male Solo Artist – Dizzee Rascal
British Female Solo Artist – Lily Allen
British Album – Florence And The Machine, *Lungs*
British Group – Kasabian
British Breakthrough Act – JLS
British Single – JLS, 'Beat Again'
International Male Solo Artist – Jay-Z
International Female Solo Artist – Lady Gaga
International Breakthrough Act – Lady Gaga
International Album – Lady Gaga, *The Fame*
British Producer – Paul Epworth
Critics' Choice – Ellie Goulding
Outstanding Contribution to Music – Robbie Williams
BRITs Album of 30 Years – Oasis, *(What's The Story) Morning Glory?* (1996)
BRITs Hits 30 – Spice Girls for 'Wannabe' / 'Who Do You Think You Are?' (1997)

MERCURY MUSIC PRIZE 2009
Speech Debelle – *Speech Therapy*

NME AWARDS 2010
British Band – Muse
Album – Kasabian, *West Ryder Pauper Lunatic Asylum*
Track – The Big Pink, 'Dominos'
Solo Artist – Jamie T
Live Band – Arctic Monkeys
New Band – Bombay Bicycle Club
International Band – Paramore
Best festival – Glastonbury
Live Event – Blur at Hyde Park
Godlike Genius – Paul Weller

MUSIC OF BLACK ORIGIN (MOBO) AWARDS 2009
UK Act – N-Dubz
Newcomer – JLS
Song – JLS, 'Beat Again'
Album – N-Dubz, *Uncle B*
DJ – Trevor Nelson
Hip-Hop – Chipmunk
R&B – Keri Hilson
International – Beyoncé
Reggae – Sean Paul
Jazz – YolanDa Brown
Gospel – Victizzle
African Act – Nneka

OPERA

Elizabeth Forbes

THE ROYAL OPERA

Tony Hall, chief executive of the Royal Opera House since April 2001, was appointed a non-political peer in February 2010 as a reward, no doubt, for the quite amazing rise in standards at Covent Garden in those years. The first half of its most recent season was dominated by a magnificent new production of *Tristan und Isolde*, directed by Francesca Zambello, with an excellent cast headed by Ben Heppner and Nina Stemme as the tragic lovers. However, it was the Orchestra of the Royal Opera House, with music director Antonio Pappano conducting, that gave the most pleasure, illuminating Wagner's score with great beauty and deep emotion. Later in the season Pappano also conducted the Covent Garden premiere of Prokofiev's *The Gambler*. Richard Jones' production stressed the dramatic content of the work, while John Tomlinson as the General and Susan Bickley as his elderly aunt, Babulenka, stood out from a fine cast.

At the end of the season, Pappano conducted two operas running one after the other: a new production by Laurent Pelly of Massenet's *Manon* and a revival of Verdi's *Simon Boccanegra*. The unusually full performance of *Manon*, set in the 1880s, with Anna Netrebko affecting in the title role and Vittorio Grigolo making a truly sensational Covent Garden debut as the Chevalier des Grieux, was extremely entertaining, both for the singing and the orchestral playing of Massenet's gorgeous score. *Simon Boccanegra*, with Elijah Moshinsky's nearly 20-year-old staging in good order, starred tenor Placido Domingo as Simon, the first baritone role he had sung in London. Both musically and dramatically the role suited him perfectly at this stage in his career; with Ferruccio Furlanetto as a noble Fiesco, the great duets between the two characters made their fullest impact. When Furlanetto was indisposed, Paata Burchuladze took over as Fiesco, and was equally imposing

Domingo had meant to sing the tenor role of Bajazet in a new production of Handel's *Tamerlano* three months previously, but was ill and had to cancel. Though his replacement, Kurt Streit, was more than adequate and the Orchestra of the Enlightenment played well, the performance was not a success. The Royal Opera's Christmas offering, Tchaikovsky's *The Tsarina's Slippers*, fared better in its first appearance at Covent Garden, directed by Zambello and with an all-Russian cast. More popular still, Robert Lepage's production of Stravinsky's *The Rake's Progress* (already seen in Brussels), set the Auden/Kallman, Hogarth-inspired text in 1950s Hollywood. This worked surprisingly well and Toby Spence made a splendid Tom Rakewell. David McVicar's new staging of Verdi's *Aida*, well conducted by Nicola Luisotti, offered little spectacle in the Triumph Scene, but magnificent choral singing, while the principals were all appropriately cast.

Interesting revivals at Covent Garden included Nicholas Hytner's production of Verdi's *Don Carlo*, with the duet between two basses, Furlanetto's King Philip and Tomlinson's Grand Inquisitor, the highlight of the evening; a vivid performance of Janácek's *Cunning Little Vixen*, conducted by Charles Mackerras; a delightful staging, as light as air, of Rossini's *Turco in Italia*, with Alexandro Corbelli in the title role; Corbelli also sang Sulpice in the revival of Donizetti's *La Fille du régiment*, in which Juan Diego Flórez threw off his top Cs with great élan. The revival of David McVicar's staging of Strauss' *Salome* was notable for the astounding performance of the title role by Angela Denoke. In the Linbury Studio Theatre, there was the world premiere of Eleanor Alberga's *Letters of a Love Betrayed*, with new productions of Thomas Arne's *Artaxerxes* (premiered at Covent Garden in 1762) and Jonathan Dove's *The Enchanted Pig*, a 'witty, gritty, anti-fairy tale' according to the composer and his librettist, Alasdair Middleton.

ENGLISH NATIONAL OPERA

English National Opera at the London Coliseum opened the season with a new production of Ligeti's *Le Grand Macabre*, given its UK premiere by the company in 1982. Staged by Alex Ollé and Valentina Carrasco (the directors of Catalan total theatre company, La Fura dels Baus), the production was played out on the enormous figure of a recumbent nude woman. A strong cast was assembled, including Susan Bickley as Mescalina, Pavlo Hunka as Nekrotzar and Frode Olsen as Astradamors, with perhaps Wolfgang Ablinger-Sperrhacke's Piet the Pot the most compelling. Baldur Brönnimann conducted. Rupert Goold's new production of Puccini's *Turandot*, apparently set in a Chinese restaurant, was over-fussy; no one was allowed to stand still for a second. Musically though, Edward Gardner, ENO's music director, ensured a fine performance, both chorus and orchestra contributing greatly to its success. Kirsten Blanck made an icy Turandot, with Amanda Echalaz as a most sympathetic Liù.

Echalaz returned to ENO later in the season to sing the title role in a new staging of *Tosca*. Conducted by Gardner, Puccini's opera was directed by Catherine Malfitano, herself once a famous Tosca, who handled the action well, apart from allowing noisy goings-on by the guards that spoilt the beautiful sound-picture of Rome by night that opens the third act. Julian Gavin's Cavaradossi and Anthony Michaels-Moore's Scarpia were also excellent. Jonathan Miller's production of Donizetti's *Elixir of Love*, originally designed for New York City Opera, moved the action to Adina's Diner, a roadside eatery in 1950s America, which worked quite well. Although Andrew Shore's Dulcamara dominated the stage, Sarah Tynan's Adina and John Tessier's Nemorino were also well in the picture.

David Alden's new production of Janácek's *Katya Kabanova*, appropriately bleak, was overshadowed by Susan Bickley's unyielding Kabanicha. With Patricia Racette a most moving Katya and Stuart Skelton a strong-voiced if weak-willed Boris, it was the younger couple, Anna Grevelius as Varvara and Alfie Boe as Vanya, who provided light relief. Boe also sang Nadir in Penny Woolcock's splendid new staging of Bizet's *The Pearl Fishers*. Dick Bird's impressive, multi-level set was perfect for the choral scenes, delivered with tremendous enthusiasm by the ENO Chorus. Hannan Alattar as Leila and Quinn Kelsey as Zurga were excellent, as was Boe. However, the tenor was off ill at some performances and at one, when his cover was also unwell, Nadir was sung from the side of the stage, in French, by William Burden, who was at Glyndebourne rehearsing for *Don Giovanni.* Conductor Rory Macdonald kept the dramatic as well as musical tension high.

Katie Mitchell's controversial new production of Mozart's *Idomeneo* pleased some people but annoyed many others. Set in the 1990s, a corporate power struggle seemed to be taking place. Intrusive and highly distracting black-clad waiters were continually bringing champagne and other refreshments, even during arias; however, as conducted by Gardner the performance was musically superb, with Paul Nilon in the title role outstanding among a strong cast and the chorus in tremendous voice. Revivals included David McVicar's award-winning production (originally staged at the Mariinsky Theatre, St Petersburg) of Britten's *The Turn of the Screw,* conducted in exemplary fashion by Charles Mackerras. Rebecca Evans made a particularly good Governess, while Timothy Robinson produced exactly the right unearthly tones for Peter Quint. David Alden's clever, 19th-century staging of Donizetti's *Lucia di Lammermoor* was also revived, with most of the original cast.

Fiona Shaw's production of Hans Werner Henze's *Elegy for Young Lovers* for ENO at the Young Vic was of particular interest. Unjustly ignored since its British premiere at Glyndebourne in 1961, Henze's brilliant score was deftly conducted by Stefan Blunier, with the equally brilliant text by Auden and Kallman vividly sung by Steven Page as poet Gregor Mittenhofer, Lucy Schauffer as Carolina, his secretary, and Jennifer Rhys-Davies as Hilda Mack, his inspiration. After the end of the season at the Coliseum, intrepid opera-lovers travelled to a disused factory on Great Eastern Quay in London's Docklands to experience *The Duchess of Malfi,* Torsten Rasch's new work based on John Webster's extremely bloody tragedy. Presented by ENO in conjunction with Punchdrunk, this example of immersive theatre took place all over the building, stunningly directed and designed by Felix Barrett, and conducted by Stephen Higgins, with Claudia Huckle as the tragic Duchess.

OPERA NORTH, SCOTTISH OPERA AND WELSH NATIONAL OPERA

Opera North offered four interesting new productions, as well as the world premiere of Jonathan Dove's *Swanhunter,* with libretto, based on a Finnish legend from *The Kalevala,* by Alasdair Middleton. Given in the newly restored Howard Assembly Rooms adjoining the Grand Theatre, Dove's chamber opera uses only six singers and six instrumentalists; it was conducted with spirit by Stuart Stratford. Massenet's *Werther,* conducted by music director Richard Farnes and staged by Tom Cairns, was consistently well sung, especially by Paul Nilon in the title role and Alice Coote as Charlotte. *Ruddigore,* directed by Jo Davies, pleased all the Gilbert and Sullivan fans, who specially enjoyed Anne Marie Owens' Dame Hannah and Steven Page's Sir Roderic.

The Adventures of Mr Broucek, Janácek's rarely performed operatic mixture of history and science fiction, was cleverly staged by John Fulljames, idiomatically conducted by Martin André and tirelessly sung by a fine cast. Apart from the excellent John Graham Hall in the title role, most of the singers had three roles each. Late in the season Donizetti's *Maria Stuarda,* directed by Tom Cairns, scored a veritable triumph; the unhistoric but dramatically powerful central scene where Queen Elizabeth I and Mary, Queen of Scots, come face to face at Fotheringay, made a shattering impact. The finest singing came from Sarah Connolly as Mary, whose death scene brought tears to all eyes.

Scottish Opera, in collaboration with the Royal Scottish Academy of Music and Drama and the Rachmaninov Conservatoire in Rostov-on-Don, achieved notable success with a production, directed by Irina Brown, of Prokofiev's vast epic *War and Peace,* involving 230 individuals. RSAMD students enlarged the SO Orchestra and provided the chorus and 22 of the soloists. The remaining six were Russians – among them Maria Kozlova as a sweet Natasha and Aleksey Gusev a strong Napoleon. Tim Dean, RSAMD's head of opera, conducted his large forces with a sure hand. Scottish Opera's other new production, Rossini's *Italiana in Algeri,* directed by Colin McColl, was hugely entertaining. Presented as a television soap opera, with exotic filmed backgrounds, the plot was as clear as, if not clearer than, the original. Wyn Davies conducted a fine cast with Karen Cargill as Isabella and Tizziano Bracci as Mustafa.

Welsh National Opera's first ever production of Wagner's *Die Meistersinger von Nürnberg,* staged by Richard Jones, was conducted by Lothar Koenigs, WNO's new music director, and featured Bryn Terfel's first Hans Sachs. As the magnificent chorus thundered out its greeting to Sachs in Act III, the singers were also expressing their affection for the Welsh bass-baritone who continues to sing in Wales long after he has become an international star. With Terfel in commanding voice, Amanda Roocroft as a delightful Eva and Raymond Very a handsome Walter, the performance was immensely rewarding. Earlier in the season WNO presented new productions of Verdi's *La traviata,* directed by David McVicar, and Mozart's *Die Entführung aus dem Serail,* directed by James Robinson, as well as a revival of *Madama Butterfly,* originally staged by Joachim Herz in 1978, but still in good condition.

FESTIVALS

Glyndebourne's new production of *Billy Budd* followed the Sussex festival's tradition of scoring great successes with Britten operas. Staged by Michael Grandage with utter respect for the Forster/Crozier text derived from Herman Melville's novella, and conducted by Mark Elder with total fidelity to Britten's score, the opera was a shattering experience. The large cast and chorus, headed by Jacques Imbrailo's Billy, John Mark Ainsley's Captain Vere and Phillip Ens' Claggart, all sang superbly. The second new production, Mozart's *Don Giovanni,* directed by Jonathan Kent and with a magnificent set designed by Paul Brown, was moved to the 1950s as if in a black-and-white Italian film. Music director Vladimir Jurowski conducted the Orchestra of the Age of Enlightenment with great affection, while Gerald Finley made an elegant if not very devilish Giovanni, William Burden was a lyrical Ottavio and Luca Pisaroni's splendid Leporello took photos of his master's conquests.

Revivals at Glyndebourne included Nicholas Hytner's much admired staging of Mozart's *Così fan tutte,* conducted by Charles Mackerras for seven performances, and then by James Gaffigan, as well as *Macbeth,* directed by Richard Jones with Erika Sunnegårdh as Lady Macbeth and Andrzej Dobber in the title role. John Cox's famous 1975 production of Stravinsky's *The Rake's Progress,* wonderfully designed by David Hockney, was conducted by Jurowski with Topi Lehtipuu, a Finnish tenor born in Australia, as Tom Rakewell. Glyndebourne Touring Opera (GTO) performed the new staging of *Don Giovanni* with revivals of Peter Hall's 2005 production of Rossini's *La Cenerentola* and Robert Carsen's 2008 staging of Monteverdi's *L'incoronazione di Poppea.*

At Edinburgh, Australian Opera offered a European premiere in *Bliss,* with music by Brett Dean and text by Amanda Holden. Directed by Neil Armfeld and conducted by Elgar Howarth, *Bliss* tells the story of Harry Joy, an advertising executive, who dies of a heart attack but manages to reclaim his soul from hell. Peter Coleman-Wright as Harry, Merlyn Quaife as his wife Betty and Lorina Gore as Honey B, the girl with whom Harry intends to spend his blissful future, were all excellent. Gershwin's *Porgy and Bess,* originally from Lyons, directed by José Montalvo and Dominique Hervier, and C.H. Braun's *Montezuma,* dating from 1755, with libretto by Frederick the Great, directed by Claudio Valdés Kuri, were the only other staged productions in Edinburgh. Among operatic concerts Puccini's *La fanciulla del West,* conducted by Scottish Opera's music director, Francesco Corti, with Susan Bullock in the title role, and Purcell's *The Indian Queen,* conducted by Harry Christofers, were the most interesting.

Buxton opened with Verdi's *Luisa Miller,* directed by Stephen Medcalf and conducted by Andrew Greenwood, followed by Peter Cornelius' rarely performed *Barber of Baghdad,* staged by Alessandro Talevi and conducted by Stephen Barlow. A new version of Mozart's unfinished opera *Zaide,* completed by the conductor Ian Page with arias and ensembles from Mozart's earlier works and with a new English text by Michael Symons Roberts and Ben Power, was staged by Melly Still in a contemporary Middle Eastern jail with, in some people's opinion, gratuitous violence. Greenwood also conducted another unusual Mozart item, Richard Strauss' version of *Idomeneo,* given in concert with Paul Nilon in the title role. As the annual children's opera, Richard Rodney Bennett's *All the King's Men,* originally produced in 1968, was revived; it involved a number of local children and a youth orchestra under the baton of Ewa Strusinska.

Garsington, for its last season at the Oxfordshire manor – it moves to a new home at Wormsley in 2011 – presented the long overdue British premiere of Rossini's 1817 opera seria *Armida,* directed by Martin Duncan and conducted by David Parry. As the wicked sorceress Armida, Jessica Pratt sang her coloratura-studded vocal line with amazing dexterity. The final new production, Britten's *A Midsummer Night's Dream,* conducted by Steuart Bedford, was musically magical, with James Laing as Oberon, Rebecca Bottone as Titania and Neal Davies as Bottom leading a fine cast. Grange Park, growing more ambitious each year, chose to mount *Capriccio,* Richard Strauss' conversation-piece, conducted by Stephen Barlow and directed by Stephen Medcalf, who set the action in war-time Germany, with Susan Gritton as a superb Countess. This was followed by Prokofiev's *The Love for Three Oranges,* wittily staged and designed by David Fielding, with Jeffrey Lloyd-Roberts as the lugubrious Prince and Rebecca Cooper as Fata Morgana.

Longborough celebrated its 20th season with a production of Wagner's *Die Walküre,* the second instalment of its projected *Ring* cycle, due to be completed in 2013, the Wagner bicentenary. Conducted by Anthony Negus and staged by Alan Privett, with Alwyn Mellor as Brünnhilde, Jason Howard as Wotan, Andrew Rees as Siegmund and Lee Bisset as Sieglinde, this was country-house opera at its finest. There were also new productions of Mozart's *Don Giovanni,* conducted by Gianluca Marciano and directed by Jenny Miller, as well as Puccini's *Madama Butterfly,* conducted by Jonathan Lyness and staged by Richard Studer, who also designed the production. Operas performed at the BBC Promenade Concerts at the Royal Albert Hall included Welsh National Opera's *Die Meistersinger von Nürnberg* with Bryn Terfel; Covent Garden's *Simon Boccanegra* with Placido Domingo and Glyndebourne's *Hänsel und Gretel* conducted by Robin Ticciati.

OBITUARIES

Australian conductor Sir Charles Mackerras died in July 2010, aged 84. He came to London in 1947 and after studying in Prague became a staff conductor at Sadler's Wells Opera (now English National Opera), making his debut in 1948 conducting Johann Strauss' *Die Fledermaus.* During his time in Prague he became passionately interested in the operas of Leos Janácek and in 1951 conducted the first UK stage performance of *Katya Kabanova;* later he also conducted *Jenufa, The Makropulos Case* and *The House of the Dead.* His other great passion was Mozart and in 1965 he amazed audiences with a version of *The Marriage of Figaro* in which all the vocal decorations current in the 18th century were in place. The same year he gave a particularly vivid performance of Britten's *Peter Grimes.*

Mackerras made his debut at Covent Garden in 1964, conducting *Katerina Ismailova,* a watered down version of *Lady Macbeth of Mtsensk* that Shostakovich had been obliged to make by Stalin. He continued conducting at Covent Garden over the next 40 years. In 1970 Mackerras became music director of ENO and for the next seven years conducted a great many different operas, illustrating his wide interests.

Mackerras was music director of Welsh National Opera from 1987 to 1992, conducting a series of works by Richard Strauss – *Salome, Die Frau ohne Schatten, Ariadne auf Naxos* and *Der Rosenkavalier* – that were greatly admired. At Covent Garden he conducted Verdi's *Un ballo in maschera* in 1995 and in 2002 the original version of Martinu's *Greek Passion,* written for that theatre but never performed there. In 1990 Mackerras conducted Verdi's *Falstaff* at Glyndebourne and went with ENO on a tour of the USSR, conducting Handel's *Xerxes.* At Glyndebourne in 2010 he conducted seven performances of *Così fan tutte,* the last on 12 June, a few weeks before he died.

The British tenor Philip Langridge died in March 2010 at the age of 70. A concert singer early in his career, he started to appear in opera from the early 1970s. In 1973 he sang the title role of Henze's *King Stag* at its British premiere on Radio 3. In 1974 he sang the Male Chorus in Britten's *The Rape of Lucretia* for English Opera Group. He created the title role of Thomas Wilson's *Confessions of a Justified Sinner* for Scottish Opera in 1976 and the following year sang Don Ottavio in *Don Giovanni* at Glyndebourne, returning in 1979 as Florestan in Beethoven's *Fidelio* with the Touring Opera. Bénédict in Berlioz' *Béatrice et Bénédict* at Buxton in 1980 and Zhivny in Janácek's *Fate* at the Queen Elizabeth Hall in 1983 were both extremely well received and Langridge repeated them later for English National Opera.

Langridge made his Covent Garden debut in 1983, singing the Fisherman and the Teapot in, respectively, Stravinsky's *Le Rossignol* and Ravel's *L'Enfant et les*

Sortilèges. Between 1986 and 1992 he sang Shuisky in Musorgsky's *Boris Godunov,* Laca in Janácek's *Jenufa,* the title roles of Britten's *Peter Grimes* and Mozart's *Idomeneo* and Gustav von Aschenbach in Britten's *Death in Venice.* In 1994 he returned to Glyndebourne to create Kong in Birtwistle's *The Second Mrs Kong* for GTO and repeated the role at the festival the following year. Continuing to appear at Covent Garden from 1996, he sang Jupiter in Handel's *Semele,* Loge in Wagner's *Rheingold,* the title role of Pfitzner's *Palestrina,* the King of Naples in the premiere of Thomas Adès' *The Tempest,* Don Basilio in Mozart's *Le nozze di Figaro,* the Priest Hiereus in the premiere of Birtwistle's *The Minotaur* and finally three roles in a new production of Berg's *Lulu,* the Prince, a Manservant and the Marquis in 2009.

English tenor David Hillman died in August 2009, aged 74. After making his debut in 1962 with Welsh National Opera as Arvino in Verdi's *I Lombardi,* he joined Sadler's Wells Opera and sang with them for a dozen years. He created Fenney in Richard Rodney Bennett's *Mines of Sulphur* in 1965 and Sostène in Malcolm Williamson's *Violins of St Jacques* in 1966. His other roles at Sadler's Wells were Tamino in *The Magic Flute,* Belmonte in *The Abduction from the Seraglio,* Alfredo in *La traviata,* Rodolfo in *La Bohème,* Eisenstein in *Die Fledermaus,* Essex in Britten's *Gloriana,* Janek in Janácek's *The Makropulos Case,* Herman in Tchaikovsky's *The Queen of Spades* and the title role of Offenbach's *Tales of Hoffmann.* In 1975 he sang the Shepherd in the UK premiere of Karol Szymanowski's *King Roger* for the New Opera Company and the Duke in Verdi's *Rigoletto* for Kent Opera. For Scottish Opera he created Quintus in Iain Hamilton's *The Catiline Conspiracy* in 1974 and Darnley in Thea Musgrave's *Mary, Queen of Scots* in 1977. At Glyndebourne in 1985 he sang Elemer in Strauss' *Arabella.*

Scottish bass Ian Wallace died in October 2009, aged 90. Having made his debut in 1946 as Schaunard in *La Bohème* with the New London Opera Company at the Cambridge Theatre, he sang at Glyndebourne from 1948 to 1961. His roles were Musetto in *Don Giovanni,* Samuele in Verdi's *Ballo in maschera,* Dr Bartolo in both Mozart's *Nozze di Figaro* and Rossini's *Barbiere di Siviglia,* Don Magnifico in Rossini's *Cenerentola,* Ser Matteo in Busoni's *Arlecchino* and the Tutor in Rossini's *Comte Ory.* For Scottish Opera he sang, as well as Don Magnifico, Leporello in *Don Giovanni,* Pistol in Verdi's *Falstaff,* and the Duke of Plaza Toro in *The Gondoliers.*

Russian mezzo-soprano Irina Archipova, who died in February 2010 aged 84, sang two Verdi roles at Covent Garden: Azucena in *Il trovatore* in 1975 and Ulrica in *Un ballo in maschera* in 1988. Italian mezzo soprano Giulietta Simionato died in May 2010 a week short of her 100th birthday. She sang Adalgisa in Bellini's *Norma* (with Maria Callas in the title role) and Amneris in Verdi's *Aida* in the 1952–3 season at Covent Garden, returning to sing Amneris again in the 1960s.

Italian bass Cesare Siepi died in July 2010, aged 87. He first sang at Covent Garden as Pistol in Verdi's *Falstaff* during a visit from La Scala, Milan. In 1962 he appeared with the Covent Garden company, singing Mozart's Don Giovanni, of which he was a noted exponent and also sang King Philip II in Verdi's *Don Carlos.*

Greek designer Stephanos Lazaridis, who died in May 2010 aged 67, worked extensively in Britain. For English National Opera in the 1970s he designed sets and costumes for Bizet's *Carmen,* Mozart's *Marriage of Figaro, Don Giovanni* and *The Abduction from the Seraglio,* Verdi's *Il trovatore* and Massenet's *Werther,* all for productions directed by John Copley. In the 1980s he designed *The Mikado* and *Tosca* working with Jonathan Miller, *Madam Butterfly* with Graham Vick, Weber's *Euryanthe* and Smetana's *Dalibor* with John Blatchley. Between 1983 and 1990 he designed a series of productions directed by David Pountney that contained his finest work: Dvorák's *Rusalka,* Janácek's *Osud (Fate),* Shostakovich's *Lady Macbeth of Mtsensk,* Humperdinck's *Hansel and Gretel,* Verdi's *Macbeth* and Berg's *Wozzeck.* At Covent Garden in 1990 he designed Martinu's *Greek Passion* with Pountney, in 2002 *Wozzeck* and in 2006–7 a *Ring* cycle with Keith Warner. Lazaridis both directed and designed Stravinsky's *Oedipus Rex* for Opera North in 1987 and Bartok's *Bluebeard's Castle* for Scottish Opera in 1990.

British tenor Anthony Rolfe Johnson died in July 2010 at the age of 69. He made his debut in 1973 with the English Opera Group as Vaudémont in Tchaikovsky's *Iolantha* and in 1974 sang the title role of Britten's *Albert Herring.* At Glyndebourne from 1974–6 he sang Stroh in Strauss' *Intermezzo,* Lensky in Tchaikovsky's *Eugene Onegin* and Fenton in Verdi's *Falstaff.* For English Music Theatre he sang Peter Quint in Britten's *Turn of the Screw* in 1976 and Tamino in Mozart's *Magic Flute* in 1977. He first appeared with English National Opera in 1978 as Don Ottavio in Mozart's *Don Giovanni,* followed by Belmonte in his *Seraglio* and Ferrando in his *Così fan tutte.*

He made his Covent Garden debut in 1987 in Britten's *War Requiem,* then sang Jupiter in Handel's *Semele* and Oronte in his *Alcina.* He sang the title role of Britten's *Peter Grimes* for Scottish Opera in 1994, repeating it the same year at Glyndebourne, where he also sang the title role of Mozart's *Clemenza di Tito* in 1995. After Mozart's *Idomeneo* for Welsh National Opera and Florestan in Beethoven's *Fidelio* for ENO, he sang Captain Vere in a concert performance of Britten's *Billy Budd* at Manchester in 1997 and Aschenbach in Britten's *Death in Venice* at the Royal Festival Hall in 1999.

PRODUCTIONS

In the summaries of company activities below, the dates in brackets indicate the year that the current production entered their repertory.

ROYAL OPERA
Founded 1946
Royal Opera House, Covent Garden, London WC2E 9DD
W www.roh.org.uk

REPERTORY: *Don Carlo* (2008), *Carmen* (2006), *l'Heure espagnole/Gianni Schicchi* (2007), *Der Rosenkavalier* (1984), *La Bohème* (1974), *Così fan tutte* (1995), *Cunning Little Vixen* (1990), *Turco in Italia* (2003), *La traviata* (1994), *La Fille du régiment* (2007), *Le nozze di Figaro* (2006), *Simon Boccanegra* (1991), *Salome* (2008)

NEW PRODUCTIONS: *Tristan und Isolde* (Wagner), 29 September 2009. Conductor, Antonio Pappano; director, Christof Loy; designer, Johannes Leiacker. Nina Stemme (Isolde), Sophie Koch (Brangäne), Ben Heppner (Tristan), Michael Volle (Kurwenal), John Tomlinson (King Mark)

The Tsarina's Slippers (Tchaikovsky), 20 November 2009. Conductor, Alexander Polianichko; director, Francesca Zambello; set designer, Mikhail Mokrov; costume designer, Tatiana Noginova. Larissa Diadkova (Solokha), Olga Guryakova (Oxana), Vsevolod Grivnov (Vakula), Maxim Mikhailov (The Devil)

The Rake's Progress (Stravinsky), 22 January 2010. Conductor Ongo Metzmacher; director, Robert Lepage; set designer, Carl Fillion; costume designer, François Barbeau. Rosemary Joshua (Anne), Toby Spence (Tom Rakewell), Patricia Bardon (Baba the Turk), Kyle Ketelsen (Nick Shadow)

The Gambler (Prokofiev), 11 February 2010. Conductor, Antonio Pappano; director, Richard Jones; set designer, Antony McDonald; costume designer, Nicky Gillibrand. Roberto Saccà (Alexey), Angela Denoke (Paulina), John Tomlinson (The General), Susan Bickley (Babulenka)

Tamerlano (Handel), 5 March 2010. Conductor, Ivor Bolton; director, Graham Vick; designer, Richard Hudson. Sara Mingardo (Andronico), Kurt Streit (Bajazet), Christianne Stotijn (Tamerlano), Renata Pokupic (Irene)

Aida (Verdi), 27 April 2010. Conductor, Nicola Luisotti; director, David McVicar; set designer, Jean-Marie Puissant; costume designer, Moritz Junge. Micaela Carosi (Aida), Marianne Cornetti (Amneris), Marcelo Alvarez (Radames), Marco Vratogna (Amonasro)

Manon (Massenet), 22 July 2010. Conductor, Antonio Pappano; director, Laurent Pelly; designer, Chantal Thomas. Anna Netrebko (Manon), Vittorio Grigolo (Chevalier des Grieux), Russell Braun (Lescaut)

ENGLISH NATIONAL OPERA
Founded 1931
London Coliseum, St Martin's Lane, London WC2N 4BS
W www.eno.org

REPERTORY: *Rigoletto* (1982), *The Turn of the Screw* (2008), *Lucia di Lammermoor* (2008), *Satyagraha* (2007)

NEW PRODUCTIONS: *Le grand Macabre* (Ligeti), 17 September 2009. Conductor, Edward Gardner; directors, Alex Ollé/Valentina Carrasco; set designer, Alfons Flores; costume designer, Lluc Castells. Wolfgang Ablinger-Sperrhacke (Piet the Pot), Susan Bickley (Mescalina), Andrew Watts (Prince Go-Go), Pavlo Hunka (Nekrotzar)

Turandot (Puccini), 8 October 2009. Conductor Edward Gardner; director, Rupert Goold; set designer, Miriam Buether; costume designer, Katrina Lindsay. Kirsten Blanck (Turandot), Amanda Echalaz (Liù), Gwyn Hughes Jones (Calaf)

Duke Bluebeard's Castle (Bartok), 6 November 2009. Conductor, Edward Gardner; director, Daniel Kramer; designer, Giles Cadle. Clive Bayley (Duke Bluebeard), Michaela Martens (Judith). Given with the ballet *Rite of Spring*.

Messiah (Handel), 27 November 2009. Conductor, Laurence Cummings; director, Deborah Warner; set designer, Tom Pye; costume designer, Moritz Junge. Sophie Bevan, Catherine Wyn-Roberts, John Mark Ainslie, Brindley Sherratt

The Elixir of Love (Donizetti), 12 February 2010. Conductor, Pablo Hera-Casado; director, Jonathan Miller; designer, Isabella Bywater. Sarah Tynan (Adina), John Tessier (Nemorino), Andrew Shore (Dulcamara), David Kempster (Belcore)

Katya Kabanova (Janácek), 15 March 2010. Conductor, Mark Wigglesworth; director, David Alden; set designer, Charles Edwards; costume designer, Jon Morrell. Patricia Racette (Katya), Susan Bickley (Kabanicha), Anna Grevelius (Varvara), Stuart Skelton (Boris), Alfie Boe (Vanya), John Graham-Hall (Tichon)

Elegy for Young Lovers (Henze), 24 April 2010 at the Young Vic. Conductor, Stefan Blunier; director, Fiona Shaw; designer, Tom Pye. Steven Page (Mittenhofer), Lucy Schaufer (Carolina), Jennifer Rhys-Davies (Hilda Mack), Kate Valentine (Elisabeth), Robert Murray (Toni)

Tosca (Puccini), 18 May 2010. Conductor, Edward Gardner; director, Catherine Malfitano; set designer, Frank Philip Schlössmann; costume designer, Gideon Davey. Amanda Echalaz (Tosca), Julian Gavin (Cavaradossi), Anthony Michaels-Moore (Scarpia)

The Pearl Fishers (Bizet), 1 June 2010. Conductor, Rory Macdonald; director, Penny Woolcock; set designer, Dick Bird; costume designer, Kevin Pollard. Hanan Alattar (Leila), Alfie Boe (Nadir), Quinn Kelsey (Zurga), Freddie Tong (Nourabad)

Idomeneo (Mozart), 18 June 2010. Conductor, Edward Gardner; director, Katie Mitchell; set designer, Vicki Mortimer; costume designer, Alex Eales. Paul Nilon (Idomeneo), Sarah Tynan (Ilya), Robert Murray (Idamante), Emma Bell (Electra)

The Duchess of Malfi (Torsten Rasch), 13 July 2010 at Great Eastern Quay, in collaboration with Punchdrunk. Conductor, Stephen Higgins; director/designer, Felix Barrett. Claudia Huckle (The Duchess), Richard Burkhard (Bosola), Raquel Mesoguer (Malateste)

OPERA NORTH
Founded 1978
Grand Theatre, New Briggate, Leeds LS1 6N
W www.operanorth.co.uk

REPERTORY: *Così fan tutte* (2004), *La Bohème* (1993), *Rusalka* (2003), *Rigoletto* (2006)

NEW PRODUCTIONS: *Werther* (Massenet), 29 September 2009. Conductor, Richard Farnes; director, Tom Cairns; designer, Hildegard Bechler. Paul Nilon (Werther), Alice Coote (Charlotte), Fflur Wyn (Sophie), Peter Savidge (Albert)

The Adventures of Mr Broucek (Janácek), 10 October 2009. Conductor, Martin André; director, John Fulljames; designer, Alex Lowde. John Graham Hall (Mr Broucek); Anne Sophie Duprels, Jeffery Lloyd Roberts, Donald Maxwell (three roles each)

Swanhunter (Jonathan Dove), world premiere at Howard Assembly Rooms, 13 November 2009. Conductor, Stuart Stratford; director, Clare Whistler; designer, Dody Nash. Andrew Rees (Lemminkäinen), Yvonne Howard (Mother), Elizabeth Cragg (Swan)

Ruddigore (Sullivan), 30 January 2010. Conductor, John Wilson; director, Jo Davies; designer Richard Hudson. Amy Freston (Rose), Stephen Page (Sir Roderic), Anne Marie Owens (Dame Hannah), Grant Doyle (Robin)

Maria Stuarda (Donizetti), 4 June 2010. Conductor, Guido Johannes Rundstadt; director/designer, Antony McDonald. Antonia Cifrone (Elizabeth), Sarah Connoly (Mary), Bülent Bezür (Leicester), David Kempster (Cecil)

Performances were given in Leeds and on tour in Belfast, Nottingham, Salford Quay and Newcastle.

SCOTTISH OPERA
Founded 1962
39 Elmbank Crescent, Glasgow G2 4PT
W www.scottishopera.org.uk

REPERTORY: *Elixir of Love* (1994), *La Bohème* (2004)

NEW PRODUCTIONS: *Italian Girl in Algiers* (Rossini),

29 October 2009. Conductor, Wyn Davies; director, Colin McColl; set designer, Tony Rabbitt; costume designer, Nic Smillie. Karen Cargill (Isabella), Thomas Walker (Lindoro), Tiziano Bracci (Mustaphà), Adrian Powers (Taddei)

War and Peace (Prokofiev), 29 October 2009, with Royal Scottish Academy of Music and Dance. Conductor, Timothy Dean; director, Irina Brown; designer, Chloe Lamford. Maria Kozlova (Natasha), Michel de Souza (Andrey), Alecksey Gusev (Napoleon), Aram Ohanian (Kutusov)

Performances were given in Glasgow and on tour in Inverness, Aberdeen and Edinburgh.

WELSH NATIONAL OPERA
Founded 1946
Wales Millennium Centre, Bute Place, Cardiff Bay CF10 5AL
W www.wno.org.uk

REPERTORY: *Madama Butterfly* (1978), *Wozzeck* (2005), *Tosca* (1992), *Carmen* (1997), *Rigoletto* (2002)

NEW PRODUCTIONS: *La traviata* (Verdi), 12 September 2009. Conductor, Andrea Licata; director, David McVicar; designer, Tania McCallin. Myrtò Papatanasiu (Violetta), Alfie Boe, (Alfredo), Dario Solari (Germont)

Die Entführung aus dem Serail (Mozart), Conductor, Rinaldo Alessandrini; director, James Robinson; designer, Allen Moyer. Lisette Oropesa (Constanze), Claire Ormshaw (Blonde), Robin Tritschler (Belmonte), Petros Magoulos (Osmin)

Die Meistersinger von Nürnberg (Wagner), 19 June 2010. Conductor, Lothar Koenigs; director, Richard Jones; set designer, Paul Steinberg; costume designer, Buki Shiff. Bryn Terfel (Hans Sachs), Amanda Roocroft (Eva), Raymond Very (Walter), Christopher Purves (Beckmesser), Brindley Sherratt (Pogner)

Performances were given in Cardiff and on tour in Swansea, Llandudno, Liverpool, Oxford, Bristol, Birmingham, Southampton, Milton Keynes and Plymouth.

GLYNDEBOURNE
Founded 1934
Glyndebourne, Lewes, East Sussex BN8 5UU
W www.glyndebourne.com

The Festival ran from 20 May to 29 August 2010.

REPERTORY: *Così fan tutte* (2006), *Macbeth* (2007), *The Rake's Progress* (1975), *Hänsel und Gretel* (2008)

NEW PRODUCTIONS: *Billy Budd* (Britten), 25 May 2010. Conductor, Mark Elder; director, Michael Grandage; designer, Christopher Oram. John Mark Ainslie (Captain Vere), Jacques Imbrailo (Billy), Phillip Ens (Claggart), Jeremy White (Dansker)

Don Giovanni (Mozart), 4 June 2010. Conductor, Vladimir Jurowski; director, Jonathan Kent; designer, Paul Brown. Gerald Finley (Giovanni), Anna Samuil (Anna), Kate Royal (Elvira), William Burden (Ottavio), Luca Pisaroni (Leporello)

GLYNDEBOURNE TOURING OPERA: *Don Giovanni* (2010), *La Cenerentola* (2005), *L'incoronazione di Poppea* (2008)

Performances were given at Glyndebourne, Woking, Milton Keynes, Norwich, Plymouth and Stoke-on-Trent.

PARLIAMENT

Patrick Robathan

The last session of the 2005 Labour government, led by Gordon Brown since 2007, proved to be the most rebellious parliament of the post-war period. The 2009–10 session saw a total of 48 Labour rebellions out of 135 divisions (a rate of 36 per cent), with some surprising names defying their whips for the first time. The most rebellious MP was Jeremy Corbyn (with 23 votes against party lines in the session). The year ended with a Conservative-Liberal Democrat coalition government led by David Cameron, the youngest prime minister since 1812. Even he did not have it all his own way as in the 11 weeks before the summer recess a handful of Liberal Democrat MPs opposed the coalition on votes on at least two issues.

NEW SESSION: QUEEN'S SPEECH

The session opened with the Queen's Speech on 18 November 2009. It contained proposals for ten new bills covering a crackdown on excesses in the City, a legal obligation to halve the budget deficit within four years, new measures to combat youth unemployment, plans to tighten the laws on bribery, and measures to set up a fund to bring in universal broadband by 2012. The theme of the programme was that government could make a positive difference.

Gordon Brown said, 'we are speaking up not in the party interest but in the national interest. . . One party has the policies enabling it to make the right decisions to deal with the recession.' While welcoming certain aspects of the programme, Conservative leader David Cameron said that overall, 'the prime minister is desperately trying a few tricks to save his own skin. When the country is crying out for change, are we really going to be subjected to six more months of endless relaunches, bogus legislation and fake dividing lines?' Liberal Democrat leader Nick Clegg said, 'this is a fantasy Queen's Speech from a government who are running out of road and a parliament that has lost the trust of the British people.'

On 23 November environment secretary Hilary Benn made a statement on the flooding in Cumbria. On 25 November there were two statements: firstly, chancellor Alistair Darling on the emergency liquidity assistance that the Bank of England had provided to the banking system since October 2008 – 'inevitably [it had] to be provided on a confidential basis' but 'as a result no savers in UK banks or building societies have lost money'. Secondly, Scottish secretary Jim Murphy on government plans for devolution in Scotland following the Calman Commission recommendations. 'A stronger Scotland in a stronger United Kingdom,' he said.

A week later Gordon Brown came to the Commons to update MPs on the situation in Afghanistan and Pakistan. This was followed by health secretary Andy Burnham on patient safety in the NHS, following incidents at Basildon and Thurrock University Hospitals NHS Foundation Trust and Colchester Hospital University NHS Foundation Trust, with details of the further steps taken to improve regulation and safety standards in the NHS. Alistair Darling then introduced the second reading of the Financial Services Bill, which set up a Council for Financial Stability, giving the Financial Services Authority greater powers to regulate banks, essential to 'enhance and strengthen the supervisory regime'. The bill received an unopposed second reading and went on to have an unopposed third reading in the Commons on 25 January 2010, before passing through the Lords and receiving Royal Assent on 8 April. On 1 December 2009 home secretary Alan Johnson replied to an urgent question (also known as a private notice question, *see* Houses of Parliament) from Conservative backbench MP David Burrowes on his decision not to intervene to stop Gary McKinnon's extradition to the USA.

PRE-BUDGET REPORT

On 9 December 2009 chancellor Alistair Darling presented his pre-Budget report: national insurance would go up by 0.5 per cent more than previously planned from 2011, public sector workers would face a 1 per cent pay cap, and there were plans for a bank bonus tax and a home boiler scrappage scheme. Mr Darling said he wanted to promote growth without 'wrecking' recovery, but the Conservatives accused him of putting off tough decisions on spending because of the coming general election. As usual, on the day following the pre-Budget report the minister for pensions, Maria Eagle, made a statement on the annual benefits up-rating, with increases of 1.8 per cent from April 2010.

On 14 December Gordon Brown made a statement on his visit to Afghanistan and also on the conclusions of the European Council, which had concentrated on global warming. On 15 December defence secretary Bob Ainsworth announced changes to the defence programme to enhance the support to the troops in Afghanistan, worth some £900m over the ensuing three years, with reductions elsewhere to 'match our expenditure against available resources'. On 16 December Mr Ainsworth returned to the Commons to announce that the government was implementing many of the 84 recommendations of the Haddon-Cave review into the loss of Nimrod XV230 in September 2006.

RETURN FROM CHRISTMAS RECESS

The Commons returned from the Christmas recess on 5 January 2010. Foreign secretary David Miliband answered an urgent question from Labour chair of the Home Affairs Select Committee Keith Vaz on the situation in Yemen given the closure of the British embassy and the position of British citizens there; the UK would host a high-level meeting in London later in the month, he said. Alan Johnson then made a statement on aviation and border security following the failed attempt to destroy a passenger plane at Detroit on Christmas day. Energy and climate change secretary Ed Miliband reported back on the climate change conference held in Copenhagen in December 2009, admitting that the outcome 'was disappointing in a number of respects'. Finally, junior business, innovation and skills minister Ian Lucas outlined the government's plans to mark the

Queen's diamond jubilee in 2012 with the addition of an extra bank holiday. The Fiscal Responsibility Bill, designed to put the government's deficit-reduction plan on a statutory footing in order to halve the UK deficit over four years, was given a second reading by 265 votes to 196, a majority of 69. The third reading was passed by 265 votes to 197 (majority 68) on 20 January 2010 and after clearing the Lords it gained royal assent on 10 February. On 7 January transport minister Sadiq Khan answered an urgent question from Conservative communities spokesperson Caroline Spelman on the country's salt reserves and local government's ability to maintain the road network in the most severe weather conditions for 29 years.

On 13 January international development secretary Douglas Alexander replied to an urgent question from Labour MP Diane Abbott updating the house on the recent earthquake in Haiti and the government's immediate response. On 14 January health minister Mike O'Brien made a statement about assistance for thalidomide survivors, confirming a £20m three-year pilot scheme to help meet their longterm health needs.

On 29 January Labour MP Harry Cohen made a personal statement to the house apologising for not declaring substantial income that he received from renting a property which he declared as his main residence. He accepted the Parliamentary Commissioner for Standards sanction that the House of Commons should withhold the £65,000 payment he would be due to receive when he stepped down as an MP at the next election.

On 1 February David Miliband made a statement on the previous weekend's London Afghanistan conference and the earlier meeting about Yemen, which he said meant 'there is a new confidence and clarity. The test is to turn these words into deeds.' On 4 February, exchequer secretary to the Treasury Sarah McCarthy-Fry replied to an urgent question from Labour backbencher Michael Connarty: she was 'deeply regretting' the government's breaching of its undertaking to parliament about the time scale and process for opt-in decisions in relation to the European Union (Amendment) Act 2008.

On 8 February Gordon Brown welcomed the agreement on policing and justice between the Democratic Unionist Party and Sinn Fein that would lead to the completion of the devolution of power in Northern Ireland. On 9 February Mike O'Brien made a statement on out-of-hours primary care following the conclusion of the coroner's inquest into the care of David Gray, implementing many of the recommendations made in the report by Dr Colin-Thome and Professor Field. On 10 February David Miliband responded to the ruling by the court of appeal on the case of Binyam Mohamed, which had found that seven paragraphs containing summaries of American intelligence relating to Mr Mohamed's case held in UK files had been redacted and should be published. Mr Miliband felt that while the government had lost the case, 'the court is fulfilling its vital constitutional role, protecting this country and upholding the law'. Bob Ainsworth then published his review of the Armed Forces Compensation Scheme, accepting the recommendations of the report by Lord Boyce in their entirety.

Returning from the half-term recess on 22 February, Chris Bryant responded to an urgent question from shadow foreign secretary William Hague about the use of forged British passports by persons implicated in the murder of Mahmoud al-Mabhouh in Dubai on 19 January (David Miliband subsequently updated the house on the misuse of these passports on 22 March). On 24 February, Gordon Brown apologised on behalf of the UK government for the child migration schemes of the 1960s. 'We cannot change history, but I believe that by confronting the failings of the past we show that we are determined to do all we can to heal the wounds,' he said. Andy Burnham then made a statement on the publication of the Francis report into the failings of the Mid-Staffordshire NHS Foundation Trust – 'totally unacceptable and a breach of the values of the NHS'.

On 8 March Jack Straw replied to an urgent question from shadow attorney-general Dominic Grieve on the circumstances of the breach of licence conditions by and recall to prison of Jon Venables. On 11 March Sadiq Khan made a statement on plans for a high-speed rail link between London and Scotland which he called 'a credible plan, for a national cause'. On 16 March Mr Khan responded to an urgent question from Conservative transport spokesperson Theresa Villiers on the situation relating to the British Airways strike, saying that while the government had urged both sides to reach an agreement, they themselves had no powers to impose a settlement. She questioned whether the government could stand up to the unions 'when one quarter of the Labour party's funding is provided by the very same union'.

On 22 March leader of the house Harriet Harman made a statement about paid advocacy and lobbying following various allegations about recent ministerial decisions. The cabinet secretary had been satisfied that there had been no improper influence on government policy or ministerial decisions.

MARCH BUDGET 2010

On 24 March 2010 Alistair Darling presented his third Budget with a warning to voters not to put the recovery at risk by deserting Labour. He said Labour had been 'right about the recovery' and cut this year's forecast £178bn deficit by £11bn.

The key points included:

- £2.5bn one-off growth package for jobs
- stamp duty allowance for first-time buyers doubled to £250,000 for a period of two years
- RBS and Lloyds Bank to provide £94bn in small business loans
- 20,000 university places to be created in subjects such as science, maths and engineering
- six-month work or training guarantee for under-24s extended to 2012
- winter fuel allowance rates extended for a further year
- planned fuel duty increase to be staged
- 15,000 civil servants to be relocated outside London

David Cameron accused Mr Darling of stealing Conservative policies, claiming that Labour had made a 'complete mess' of the economy and had 'done nothing to clear it up'; he suggested that 'the biggest risk to the recovery is five more years of this prime minister'. Liberal Democrat leader Nick Clegg thought the chancellor was 'in denial' about the scale of cuts needed to address the deficit. After four days of debate the Budget was approved but the opposition forced no less than seven votes on the various Budget resolutions. The Finance Bill was only published on 1 April and with insufficient time left before the dissolution of parliament prior to the general election; a deal was done for all its stages to be considered in the Commons on 7 April, when many clauses were dropped including a proposed tax rise on cider, 50p-a-month broadband tax and changes to furnished holiday lettings. The bill was then nodded through the Lords and received royal assent on 8 April.

RUN-UP TO THE GENERAL ELECTION
During the easter recess Gordon Brown announced the date of the general election as 6 May 2010. When parliament returned on 6 April, there was a great deal of horse trading between the parties to salvage parts of the government's legislative programme, with more than ten bills being considered by parliamentarians in the 'wash-up period' – the remaining time before parliament was dissolved on 8 April. These included the Digital Economy Bill aimed at supporting artists' copyright and tackling illegal file-sharing. Despite former Labour minister Tom Watson arguing it would be a 'catastrophic disaster' if the bill was passed as constituted, it was approved by MPs by a majority of 142 votes and gained royal assent on 8 April.

NEW COALITION GOVERNMENT
The general election on 6 May 2010 gave no party an overall majority. After five days of intense negotiation, a new Conservative-Liberal Democrat coalition government under David Cameron was formed and took power. This would also be a new-look parliament with deputy speakers and select committee chairmen being voted on by the whole House of Commons, and members of those committees being elected by their parties in a ballot rather than just imposed by the whips – changes agreed in the previous parliament on 4 March and designed to give backbenchers more power to call the government to account. A threatened coup against speaker John Bercow never materialised and he was duly unanimously re-elected to his post on 18 May. The Independent Parliamentary Standards Authority, set up to scrutinise MPs' expenses in the light of the scandals of the previous parliament, also began its work, but came in for criticism over the way it was handling claims and the time taken to settle them.

NEW SESSION: QUEEN'S SPEECH
The 2010–11 session of parliament opened with the Queen's Speech on 25 May 2010. Proposals for the coalition government's legislative programme for the next 18 months included at least 22 new bills, among them plans for the major reform of schools, police, welfare and Britain's political system. The theme of the programme was 'freedom, fairness and responsibility' with the priority to 'reduce the deficit and restore economic growth'.

David Cameron said it 'marks an end to the years of recklessness and big government and the beginning of the years of responsibility and good government. It shows the world that Britain is re-opening for business; it tackles the causes of our social problems; it means better schools for our children, real hope for those out of work, a stronger NHS for everyone, and it means a parliament that belongs to the people not the politicians.'

Acting opposition leader Harriet Harman said Labour would 'not oppose for the sake of it' but neither would it 'pull its punches . . . We will be determined to prevent unfairness. We will speak up for the public services that matter. We will be vigilant in protecting jobs and businesses.' She warned, 'these coalition partners, lacking confidence in each other, are already preparing for the day when they shrink back from their loveless embrace. It's like a political pre-nup.' After six days of debate the programme was approved by 335 votes to 257.

DAVID LAWS' DEBUT IS SHORTLIVED
On 26 May the chief secretary to the Treasury, Liberal Democrat MP David Laws, made his debut at the dispatch box when he answered an urgent question from Alistair Darling concerning more than £6bn of immediate spending cuts, which were to be used to reduce Britain's £156bn deficit. Mr Laws went on the offensive, accusing the former Labour government of a 'scorched earth strategy' on spending and telling MPs that ministers were looking 'very closely at decisions that had been made' at the end of Labour's term. For his part Mr Darling said the cuts went 'far beyond' what had been pledged by the Conservatives. However a few days later, on 29 May, Mr Laws resigned from his position after admitting he claimed expenses to pay rent to his partner. He could not, he said, 'escape the conclusion that what I have done was in some way wrong'.

After the first prime minister's questions of the coalition on 2 June, foreign secretary William Hague gave the government's response to the interception of boats in the 'Free Gaza' flotilla by the Israeli navy, which had involved 37 British nationals. On 3 June home secretary Theresa May made a statement to the house on the shooting dead of 12 people in Cumbria the previous day, suggesting that any debate about the UK's gun laws while right and proper should wait 'until we know the full facts'.

IDENTITY CARDS
The first piece of legislation to be introduced by the coalition government was the measure to abolish identity cards, which was given an unopposed second reading in the House of Commons on 9 June 2010. Home secretary Theresa May called the cards, 'the worst of government; intrusive and bullying, ineffective and expensive'. The bill was unamended in committee and due to go before the Lords in the autumn.

ACADEMIES BILL
One of the flagship policies of the coalition government was the Academies Bill – designed to allow schools to opt out of local council control and to pave the way for free schools as early as September 2010 – which was fast-tracked through the parliamentary system. During debate in the Lords, where the bill was introduced on 7 June, the government agreed to table amendments with changes on the consultation process to include a clause to enshrine the equal rights of pupils with special educational needs and to ensure that academies have to submit to requests under the Freedom of Information Act. It had its third reading on 13 July and was given a second reading in the Commons on 19 July. At this stage various MPs questioned the speed with which the bill was progressing – even the Conservative Chairman of the Education Select Committee, Graham Stuart, said only a 'pretty overwhelming argument' could justify the risk of cutting short the debate – but it was passed by 326 votes to 236, a government majority of 90. All committee consideration in the Commons was taken on the floor of the house on 21 and 22 July, with the third reading on 26 July. At this final stage six Liberal Democrat MPs voted for an opposition amendment calling for more time for consultation among parents. The amendment was defeated by 77 votes and the third reading was passed by 317 votes to 225, a government majority 92, and received royal assent on 27 July.

LOCAL GOVERNMENT BILL DELAYED

On 9 June 2010 health secretary Andrew Lansley announced a full public inquiry into events at Mid Staffordshire NHS Foundation Trust, to report by March 2011. The coalition government also met an early setback when the Local Government Bill had its second reading in the Lords, likewise on 9 June. The bill intended to revoke structural change orders that established Exeter and Norwich as unitary councils from 1 April 2010 and prevent the implementation of the Suffolk unitary proposals. A motion moved by Labour peer Lord Howarth to refer the bill to the examiners of petitions for private bills because it appeared to single out Exeter and Norwich (and so should follow the procedure that governs any legislation that appears to apply to one group of individuals differently from other similar individuals) was passed by 154 to 150 against the wishes of the government. The examiners found that the bill was not hybrid (Conservative minister Baroness Hanham said the opposition had used a 'dubious' delaying tactic), and it began its progress in the Lords a second time on 30 June.

AFGHANISTAN, BP AND BLOODY SUNDAY

On 14 June 2010 David Cameron reported back on his first visit to Afghanistan as prime minister, promising that under the coalition government there would be quarterly updates to the house. He confirmed that the UK was in Afghanistan for 'national security' and that its forces would not remain 'one day longer than is necessary'. Also on that day, George Osborne made a statement on the creation of the Office of Budget Responsibility and the publication of its first report, providing 'an independent and comprehensive assessment of the public finances'. And finally energy and climate change secretary Chris Huhne outlined the circumstances surrounding the BP oil spill in the Gulf of Mexico, reassuring MPs that US President Barack Obama had told the prime minister 'he has no interest in undermining BP's value, and that frustrations in America have nothing to do with national identity'.

On 15 June Mr Cameron announced the long-awaited publication of the Saville Inquiry report into the Bloody Sunday killings, concluding, 'what happened on Bloody Sunday was both unjustified and unjustifiable. It was wrong.' On 16 June George Osborne answered an urgent question from Alistair Darling on the future of financial services regulation and the role of the Bank of England in micro-prudential supervision.

CUTBACKS AND REFORM

On 17 June justice secretary Ken Clarke responded to an urgent question from Liberal Democrat party president Simon Hughes on the consequence of the timing of legal aid payments to the charity Refugee and Migrant Justice that could force it to close. The new chief secretary to the Treasury Danny Alexander announced that the coalition government would cancel 12 projects totalling £2bn, which the previous Labour government had agreed since the start of 2010, including an £80m loan to Sheffield Forgemasters. Mr Alexander said, 'As a result of the poor decisions made by the previous government... We have also found another spending black-hole in the previous government's plans – projects had been approved with no money in place to pay for them.' Finally, financial secretary to the Treasury Mark Hoban made a statement about plans to reform the institutional framework for financial regulation: the Bank of England would be in charge of macro-prudential regulation through the establishment of a Financial Policy Committee and a Prudential Regulation Authority, a subsidiary of the Bank of England, would also be created, together with the Consumer Protection and Markets Authority.

On 21 June David Cameron updated MPs on his first European Council meeting as prime minister, where members had concentrated on securing the economic recovery, agreeing 'unanimously' that early action on budget deficits was required.

EMERGENCY BUDGET 2010

On 22 June 2010 chancellor George Osborne presented the first Budget of the coalition government, setting out a five-year plan to rebuild the British economy. It showed how the government intended to tackle Britain's record deficit, outlining a plan to get the public finances under control and to provide a springboard for a private sector-led recovery. Key points included:

- 25 per cent cut in departmental spending over four years
- two-year public sector pay freeze for staff earning more than £21,000
- VAT increase from 17.5 per cent to 20 per cent from 4 January 2011
- standard rate of insurance premium tax to rise from 5 per cent to 6 per cent and the higher rate to increase from 17.5 per cent to 20 per cent
- personal income tax allowance increased to £7,475 from April 2011
- one-year council tax freeze from April 2011
- capital gains tax increased from 18 per cent to 28 per cent for higher-rate taxpayers
- child benefit frozen for three years
- new maximum limits on housing benefit payments

Mr Osborne described it as a 'progressive Budget', with 'decisive' action needed to prevent a 'catastrophic collapse' in economic confidence, but stressed it would be done in a 'fair' way with the better-off shouldering most of the burden. 'Everyone will pay something but the people at the bottom of the income scale will pay proportionately less than those at the top.'

Harriet Harman said Mr Osborne's Budget would stifle growth, was 'reckless' and would 'throw people out of work', as well as hit hardest 'those who can least afford it'. She also criticised the Liberal Democrats for providing a 'fig leaf' for their Conservative coalition partners, arguing 'this reckless Tory budget would not be possible without the Lib Dems... their leaders have sacrificed everything they ever stood for to ride in ministerial cars and to ride on the coat tails of the Tory government.'

This sentiment was echoed by Plaid Cymru Treasury spokesperson Jonathan Edwards, who accused deputy prime minister Nick Clegg of sitting next to David Cameron 'like a nodding dog, agreeing with every word as VAT was raised'.

After four days of debate the Budget was approved on 28 June with separate votes forced by Labour on the increases in VAT and insurance premium tax in an attempt to embarrass Liberal Democrat backbenchers – in the event while some abstained, none voted against the government. A small 11-clause Finance Bill to enact the key tax measures at the heart of the emergency Budget package was published on 1 July (with another promised for autumn with the rest of the measures). At its second reading on 6 July the bill was passed by 332 votes to 230 (none of the Liberal Democrat backbenchers voted against). However, a row in the Commons regarding tactics meant that the debate lasted nearly nine and a half hours. Some observers suggested this was to ensure that MPs could claim their extra allowance for late-night sitting; others accused MPs of being too drunk to vote. (New Conservative MP for Rochester and Stroud Mark Reckless did later apologise for being drunk and missing the vote.)

Unusually, all the committee stages were taken on the floor of the house, again in an attempt by Labour to expose what it saw as Liberal Democrat hypocrisy on issues such as the VAT rise. The VAT clauses were discussed on 13 July and four Liberal Democrat MPs tabled an amendment calling for an investigation into the impact of the VAT increase; in the end that amendment was not put to a vote. The proposal to increase VAT was passed by 346 votes to 270, a majority of 76, with two Liberal Democrats voting against. The Finance Bill had its third reading in the Commons on 20 July, when it was passed by 322 votes to 242, a majority of 80. It was nodded though the Lords on 26 July and received royal assent on 27 July.

PARLIAMENTARY REFORM AND 'UNFUNDED PROMISES'

On 5 July 2010 Nick Clegg unveiled plans for parliamentary reform because, he said, 'we have a unique duty to restore the trust in our political system that has been tested to its limits in recent times.' He confirmed government plans to introduce legislation for five-year fixed-term parliaments – the next general election to be held on 7 May 2015 – with a concession that any vote of no confidence in the government would require only a simple majority. The government would also introduce a bill for a referendum on the alternative vote system and a review of constituency boundaries to create fewer, more equal-sized constituencies. The referendum would be held on 5 May 2011, the same day as elections were due for the Scottish parliament and Welsh Assembly.

Education secretary Michael Gove then made a statement on major reductions to the Building Schools for the Future programme, which, he said, 'were based on unsustainable assumptions and led to unfunded promises'. Ed Balls called it a 'black day' for UK schools. On 7 July Mr Gove was forced to return to the Commons to apologise for mistakes in the list of schools affected by the plans, which he had published alongside his statement.

UK INTELLIGENCE SERVICES

On 6 July 2010 David Cameron made a statement on allegations about the UK intelligence services treatment of detainees, announcing an official inquiry to report within a year. 'It is time to clear up this matter once and for all,' he said. The next day, defence secretary Liam Fox made the first of regular statements updating MPs on UK operations in Afghanistan. On 8 July Theresa May made a statement on the ending of stop and search powers under section 44 of the Terrorism Act 2000, following a ruling from the European Court of Human Rights that they amounted to the violation of the right to a private life.

FUTURE OF THE NHS

On 12 July 2010 health secretary Andrew Lansley published a white paper on the future of the NHS, setting out 'a long-term vision for an NHS that is led by patients and professionals, not by politicians'. His Labour shadow Andy Burnham said it 'represents a roll of the dice that puts the NHS at risk – a giant political experiment with no consultation, no piloting and no evidence'.

SIMPLIFICATION OF TAXES

On 20 July 2010 exchequer secretary to the Treasury David Gauke answered an urgent question from shadow chief secretary Liam Byrne on the structure and approach of the new Office of Tax Simplification, which had been announced in the emergency Budget.

A piece of history was made on 21 July when Nick Clegg became the first Liberal Democrat MP to take Prime Minister's Questions. William Hague then reported back to MPs on the outcome of the conference he had attended in Kabul on the future of Afghanistan.

On 22 July Mark Hoban announced how the coalition government would implement the recommendations of the parliamentary ombudsman concerning Equitable Life policy holders with the introduction of a bill to allow for payments to be made.

POLICING

On 26 July 2010 attorney-general Damian Green replied to an urgent question from Labour backbench MP Emily Thornberry on the decision of the director of public prosecutions not to prosecute any police officer in connection with the assault and subsequent death of Ian Tomlinson at the protest at the G20 meeting in London in 2009, stressing that it was a decision made 'independently of government'. Theresa May then gave the details of a consultation paper on policing in the 21st century, introducing directly elected police and crime commissioners by 2012 and proposals to introduce a cost-effective way to establish 101 as a single police non-emergency number so that it was easier to report crime.

FINAL WORK BEFORE SUMMER RECESS

On 27 July 2010, the last day before the summer recess, energy and climate change secretary Chris Huhne fulfilled the coalition commitment to present an annual energy statement to parliament. He said it set out, 'a clear strategy for creating the 21st-century energy system that this country urgently needs if we are to have affordable, secure and low-carbon energy in future'.

Theresa May then made a statement on the government's decision to opt into the draft directive for a European Investigation Order. '[It] does not amount to a loss of sovereignty,' she said. While welcomed by the official opposition, there was much concern on the Conservative backbenches. Conservative chairman of the backbench European Scrutiny Committee and leading Euro-sceptic William Cash expressed concern that the investigation order gave 'undue rights to police officers from other European countries to order our police to gather sensitive personal information'.

When the House of Commons then rose for the summer recess (one day earlier than the Lords), it was already looking forward to returning in September when it would start to discuss the two major bills on parliamentary reform: the Parliamentary Voting and Constituencies Bill and the Fixed Term Parliaments Bill. The opposition had said it would oppose both bills and some 45 Conservative backbench MPs had signed an early day motion calling for the proposed referendum on changes to the voting system to be held on a different date to that suggested.

PUBLIC ACTS OF PARLIAMENT

Public acts included in this list are those which received the royal assent after 31 July 2009. The date stated after each act is the date on which it came into operation.

Law Commission Act 2009 ch. 14 (12 January 2010) makes provision in relation to the Law Commission.

Autism Act 2009 ch. 15 (12 January 2010) makes provision about meeting the needs of adults with autistic spectrum conditions; and for connected purposes.

Holocaust (Return of Cultural Objects) Act 2009 ch. 16 (day or days to be appointed) confers power to return certain cultural objects on grounds relating to events occurring during the Nazi era.

Driving Instruction (Suspension and Exemption Powers) Act 2009 ch. 17 (various dates, some to be appointed) provides for the suspension in certain circumstances of registration and licences relating to the provision of driving instruction; makes provision about exemptions from prohibitions concerning registration (including provision about suspension); about compensation in connection with suspension; and for connected purposes.

Perpetuities and Accumulations Act 2009 ch. 18 (various dates, some to be appointed) amends the law relating to the avoidance of future interests on grounds of remoteness and the law relating to accumulations of income.

Green Energy (Definition and Promotion) Act 2009 ch. 19 (12 January 2010) defines the term 'green energy'; promotes its development, installation and usage; and for connected purposes.

Local Democracy, Economic Development and Construction Act 2009 ch. 20 (various dates, some to be appointed) makes provision for the purposes of promoting public involvement in relation to local authorities and other public authorities; about bodies representing the interests of tenants; about local freedoms and honorary titles; about the procedures of local authorities, their powers relating to insurance and the audit of entities connected with them; establishes the Local Government Boundary Commission for England and makes provision relating to local government boundary and electoral change; makes provision about local and regional development; amends the law relating to construction contracts; and for connected purposes.

Health Act 2009 ch. 21 (day or days to be appointed) makes provision about the NHS Constitution; about health care (including provision about the National Health service and health bodies); about the control of the promotion and sale of tobacco products; about the investigation of complaints about privately arranged or funded adult social care; and for connected purposes.

Apprenticeships, Skills, Children and Learning Act 2009 ch. 22 (various dates, some to be appointed) makes provision about apprenticeships, education, training and children's services; amends the Employment Rights Act 1996; establishes the Young People's Learning Agency for England, the office of the Chief Executive of Skills Funding, the Office of Qualifications and Examinations Regulation and the School Support Staff Negotiating Body and makes provision about those bodies and that office; makes provision about the Qualifications and Curriculum Authority; about schools and institutions within the further education sector; about student loans; and for connected purposes.

Marine and Coastal Access Act 2009 ch. 23 (various dates, some to be appointed) makes provision in relation to marine functions and activities; about migratory and freshwater fish; makes provision for and in connection with the establishment of an English coastal walking route and of rights of access to land near the English coast; enables the making of Assembly Measures in relation to Welsh coastal routes for recreational journeys and rights of access to land near the Welsh coast; makes further provision in relation to Natural England and the Countryside Council for Wales; makes provision in relation to works which are detrimental to navigation; to amend the Harbours Act 1964; and for connected purposes.

Welfare Reform Act 2009 ch. 24 (various dates, some to be appointed) amends the law relating to social security; makes provision enabling disabled people to be given greater control over the way in which certain public services are provided for them; amends the law relating to child support; makes provision about the registration of births; and for connected purposes.

Coroners and Justice Act 2009 ch. 25 (various dates) amends the law relating to coroners, to investigation of deaths and to certification and registration of deaths; amends the criminal law; makes provision about criminal justice and about dealing with offenders; about the Commissioner for Victims and Witnesses; relating to the security of court and other buildings; about legal aid and about payments for legal services provided in connection with employment matters; for payments to be made by offenders in respect of benefits derived from the exploitation of material pertaining to offences; amends the Data Protection Act 1998; and for connected purposes.

Policing and Crime Act 2009 ch. 26 (various dates, some to be appointed) makes provision about the police; about prostitution, sex offenders, sex establishments and certain other premises; for reducing and dealing with the abuse of alcohol; about the proceeds of crime; about extradition; amends the Aviation Security Act 1982; makes provision about criminal records and amends the Safeguarding Vulnerable Groups Act 2006 and the Safeguarding Vulnerable Groups (Northern Ireland) Order 2007; confers, extends or facilitates search, forfeiture and other powers relating to the United Kingdom's borders or elsewhere; makes further provision for combating crime and disorder; repeals redundant provisions; and for connected purposes.

Consolidated Fund Act 2009 ch. 27 (16 December 2009) authorises the use of resources for the service of the years ending with 31 March 2010 and 31 March 2011 and to apply certain sums out of the Consolidated Fund to the service of the years ending 31 March 2010 and 31 March 2011.

Video Recordings Act 2010 ch. 1 (21 January 2010) repeals and revives provisions of the Video Recordings Act 1984.

Terrorist Asset-Freezing (Temporary Provisions) Act 2010 ch. 2 (10 February 2010) makes provision for the temporary validity of certain Orders in Council imposing financial restrictions on, and in relation to, persons suspected of involvement in terrorist activity; and for connected purposes.

Fiscal Responsibility Act 2010 ch. 3 (10 February 2010) makes provision for and in connection with the imposition of duties for securing sound public finances.

Corporation Tax Act 2010 ch. 4 (1 April 2010) restates, with minor changes, certain enactments relating to corporation tax and certain enactments relating to company distributions; and for connected purposes.

Appropriation Act 2010 ch. 5 (18 March 2010) authorises the use of resources for the service of the years ending with 31 March 2009 and 31 March 2010 and to apply certain sums out of the Consolidated Fund to the service of the year ending with 31 March 2010; appropriates the supply authorised in this Session of Parliament for the service of the years ending with 31 March 2009 and 31 March 2010.

Marriage (Wales) Act 2010 ch. 6 (18 March 2010) enables persons to be married in a place of worship in a parish in the Church in Wales with which they have a qualifying connection; and for connected purposes.

Co-operative and Community Benefit Societies and Credit Unions Act 2010 ch. 7 (day or days to be appointed) makes provision for societies to be registered as co-operative or community benefit societies and renames the Industrial and Provident Societies Acts; applies to registered societies the provisions relating to directors' disqualification and makes provision for the application of certain other enactments relating to companies; confers power to make provision for credit unions corresponding to any provision applying to building societies; and for connected purposes.

Taxation (International and Other Provisions) Act 2010 ch. 8 (1 April 2010) restates, with minor changes, certain enactments relating to tax; makes provision for purposes connected with the restatement of enactments by other tax law rewrite Acts; and for connected purposes.

Child Poverty Act 2010 ch. 9 (25 March 2010 & 25 May 2010) sets targets relating to the eradication of child poverty, and makes other provision about child poverty.

Third Parties (Rights against Insurers) Act 2010 ch. 10 (day or days to be appointed) makes provision about the rights of third parties against insurers of liabilities to third parties in the case where the insured is insolvent, and in certain other cases.

Cluster Munitions (Prohibitions) Act 2010 ch. 11 (25 March 2010) makes provision for giving effect to the Convention on Cluster Munitions.

Appropriation (No. 2) Act 2010 ch. 12 (8 April 2010) appropriates the supply authorised in this Session of Parliament for the service of the year ending with 31 March 2011.

Finance Act 2010 ch. 13 (various dates, some to be appointed) grants certain duties, alters other duties, and amends the law relating to the National Debt and the Public Revenue, and makes further provision in connection with finance.

Anti-Slavery Day Act 2010 ch. 14 (8 April 2010) introduces a national day to raise awareness of the need to eradicate all forms of slavery, human trafficking and exploitation; and for connected purposes.

Equality Act 2010 ch. 15 (various dates, some to be appointed) makes provision to require Ministers of the Crown and others when making strategic decisions about the exercise of their functions to have regard to the desirability of reducing socio-economic inequalities; reforms and harmonises equality law and restates the greater part of the enactments relating to discrimination and harassment related to certain personal characteristics; enables certain employers to be required to publish information about the differences in pay between male and female employees; prohibits victimisation in certain circumstances; requires the exercise of certain functions to be with regard to the need to eliminate discrimination and other prohibited conduct; enables duties to be imposed in relation to the exercise of public procurement functions; increases equality of opportunity; amends the law relating to rights and responsibilities in family relationships; and for connected purposes.

Northern Ireland Assembly Members Act 2010 ch. 16 (various dates, some to be appointed) makes provision relating to salaries, allowances and pensions for members of the Northern Ireland Assembly.

Crime and Security Act 2010 ch. 17 (various dates, some to be appointed) makes provision about police powers of stop and search; about the taking, retention, destruction and use of evidential material; for the protection of victims of domestic violence; about injunctions in respect of gang-related violence; about anti-social behaviour orders; about the private security industry; about possession and use of electronic communications devices in prison; about air weapons; for the compensation of victims of overseas terrorism; about licensing the sale and supply of alcohol; about searches in relation to persons subject to control orders; and for connected purposes.

Personal Care at Home Act 2010 ch. 18 (day or days to be appointed) amends section 15 of the Community Care (Delayed Discharges etc) Act 2003 so as to remove the restriction on the period for which personal care may be provided free of charge to persons living at home; and to make consequential provision.

Mortgage Repossessions (Protection of Tenants etc) Act 2010 ch. 19 (day or days to be appointed) protects persons whose tenancies are not binding on mortgagees and to require mortgagees to give notice of the proposed execution of possession orders.

Sunbeds (Regulation) Act 2010 ch. 20 (8 April 2011) makes provision about the use or supply of tanning devices that use artificial ultra-violet radiation; and for connected purposes.

Sustainable Communities Act 2007 (Amendment) Act 2010 ch. 21 (8 June 2010) amends the Sustainable Communities Act 2007.

Debt Relief (Developing Countries) Act 2010 ch. 22 (8 June 2010) makes provision for or in connection with the relief of debts of certain developing countries.

Bribery Act 2010 ch. 23 (various dates, some to be appointed) makes provision about offences relating to bribery; and for connected purposes.

Digital Economy Act 2010 ch. 24 (various dates, some to be appointed) makes provision about the functions of the Office of Communications; about the online infringement of copyright and about penalties for infringement of copyright and performers' rights; about internet domain registries; about the functions of the Channel Four Television Corporation; about the regulation of television and radio services; about the regulation of the use of the electromagnetic spectrum; to amend the Video Recordings Act 1984; makes provision about public lending right in relation to electronic publications; and for connected purposes.

Constitutional Reform and Governance Act 2010 ch. 25 (various dates, some to be appointed) makes provision relating to the civil service of the State; in relation to section 3 of the Act of Settlement; relating to the ratification of treaties; relating to the counting of votes in parliamentary elections; amends the Parliamentary Standards Act 2009 and the European Parliament (Pay and Pensions) Act 1979 and makes provision relating to pensions for members of the House of Commons, Ministers and other office holders; makes provision for treating members of the House of Commons and members of the House of Lords as resident, ordinarily resident and domiciled in the United Kingdom for taxation purposes; amends the Government Resources and Accounts Act 2000 and makes corresponding provision in relation to Wales; amends the Public Records Act 1958 and the Freedom of Information Act 2000.

Children, Schools and Families Act 2010 ch. 26 (various dates, some to be appointed) makes provision about children with disabilities or special educational needs, school and other education, and governing bodies' powers; makes provision amending the Education Acts; about Local Safeguarding Children Boards; and about publication of information relating to family proceedings.

Energy Act 2010 ch. 27 (various dates, some to be appointed) makes provision relating to the demonstration, assessment and use of carbon capture and storage technology; about reports on decarbonisation of electricity generation and development and use of carbon capture and storage technology; for requiring benefits to be provided by holders of gas or electricity supply licences; about the functions of the Gas and Electricity Markets Authority; about general duties of the Secretary of State in relation to gas and electricity markets; about electricity generation licences; about persons authorised to supply gas or electricity; and for connected purposes.

Financial Services Act 2010 ch. 28 (various dates, some to be appointed) makes provision amending the Financial Services and Markets Act 2000, including provision about financial education, and other provision about financial services and markets; and for the administration of court funds by the Director of Savings.

Flood and Water Management Act 2010 ch. 29 (day or days to be appointed) makes provision about water, including about the management of risks in connection with flooding and coastal erosion.

WHITE PAPERS

This section provides an outline of a selection of white papers that have been published in the last year. For further information see W www.official-documents.co.uk or www.parliament.uk. Alternatively, visit the websites of individual government departments – *see* Government Departments section.

Archives for the 21st Century was presented to parliament by the Lord Chancellor and Secretary of State for Justice in November 2009. The paper asserts the importance of publicly funded archive services and highlights the fragility of digital information, taking on the challenge of preserving it as part of the national heritage. Initiatives include strengthening leadership and developing a responsive, skilled workforce; a coordinated response to managing digital information so that it is accessible now and remains discoverable in the future; and comprehensive online access to archives and digitised archive content for citizens at a time and place that suits them.

Protecting the Public: Supporting the Police to Succeed was presented to parliament by the Home Secretary in December 2009. Building on reforms set out in the 2008 green paper *From the Neighbourhood to the National: Policing our Communities Together,* this paper sets out plans to tackle anti-social behaviour by providing the public with more of an understanding of their entitlements and the police with more freedom. Initiatives include cutting unnecessary costs in order to focus on frontline delivery; raising awareness of the policing pledge which informs the public of the standards they can expect; and empowering police professionals in return for greater accountability.

Working Our Way to Better Mental Health: a Framework for Action was presented to parliament by the Secretaries of State of the Department for Work and Pensions and the Department of Health in December 2009. The paper states the government's plans to improve well-being at work for everyone and to deliver better employment results for people with mental health conditions. The paper proposes to challenge the stigma surrounding mental health; encourage employers to offer more employment opportunities to people who have mental health conditions; and to co-ordinate help tailored to individuals' needs both in and out of work.

Building Bridges to Work: New Approaches to Tackling Long-term Worklessness was presented to parliament by the Secretary of State for Work and Pensions in March 2010. Building on earlier phases of reform to welfare and employment, the paper outlines how to assist the long-term unemployed back into work. Initiatives include increasing the accuracy of the Work Capability Assessment in order to allow appropriate consideration of people's ability to adapt to their disability; providing extra support for those who have been deemed fit for work but have spent a number of years on incapacity benefit; and guaranteeing employment or work placements for those who do not find work after two years.

Building the National Care Service was presented to parliament by the Secretary of State for Health in March 2010. The paper details the government's goal to create a National Care Service, available to all and free when needed. Initiatives include introducing a universal deferred payment system for those who struggle to meet costs; abolishing the postcode lottery by establishing in law the point at which someone becomes eligible for state support; and allowing free care for those who need to stay in residential care for more than two years.

The Modernisation Review of Public Libraries: a Policy Statement was presented to parliament by the Secretary of State for Culture, Media and Sport in March 2010. The paper sets out the government's goal of reversing the decline in library use and utilising the opportunities presented by digitisation. Proposals include all library services to provide free internet access by 2011; offering library membership as an entitlement from birth; assessing opening hours to accommodate local need; and allowing the public the opportunity to order any book, even if the title is out of print.

Social Fund Reform: Debt, Credit and Low-income Households was presented to parliament by the Secretary of State for Work and Pensions in March 2010. The paper sets out to review the role and design of the social fund and to provide help for the more vulnerable members of society. Initiatives include creating a more straightforward and simple method for the customer to receive one-off or occasional loans; providing goods and services instead of cash for grants; supporting the frequent users of the social fund to help them address more deep-seated financial problems; and improving the recovery of outstanding debts to the social fund in order to increase the amount of money that is available for lending to customers.

Equity and Excellence: Liberating the NHS was presented to parliament by the Secretary of State for Health in July 2010. The paper outlines plans to reform the NHS by giving patients more choice and control and by freeing healthcare professionals to focus on improving health outcomes. Proposals include enabling patients to choose which GP practice they register with, regardless of where they live; allowing groups of GPs to take responsibility for commissioning care for their local communities; providing patients with the opportunity to rate hospitals and clinics; and reducing management costs so that more resources are directed to support frontline services.

SCIENCE AND DISCOVERY

Storm Dunlop

LIFE

ALL LIFE FROM SINGLE ANCESTOR

In a study published in *Nature* in June 2010, Douglas Theobald of Brandeis University, Waltham, Massachusetts, established that all life on Earth derives from a common ancestor. Because gene-swapping appears to be so simple, and is used to argue in favour of a multi-ancestor model for the origin of life forms, he investigated 23 common proteins that have variant forms in 12 species, four from each of the three branches of life: archaea, bacteria and eukaryotes (organisms whose cells have discrete nuclei). He found that a model with a single ancestor and single gene swapping was at least 103,489 times more probable than the best multi-ancestor model.

FIRST LIFEFORM WITH SYNTHETIC DNA

In a report published in *Science* in May 2010, scientists at the Craig Venter Institute in Maryland and San Diego described how they constructed a synthetic bacterial genome, and substituted it for the genome within an existing bacterium. They have called this a 'synthetic cell', although only the genome is artificial.

They sequenced the nucleotides in the genome of the bacterium *Mycoplasma mycoides* and from this they constructed a synthetic copy of the chromosome from fragments of DNA. This chromosome was inserted into a recipient *Mycoplasma capricolum* cell from which the natural chromosome had been removed. The resulting hybrid reproduced, giving rise to a colony essentially identical to the natural form.

THE FIRST MULTICELLULAR LIFEFORMS

Possibly the earliest multicellular lifeforms are described in *Nature* for 1 July 2010 by a team from the University of Poitiers in France. The fossils, from Gabon in West Africa, are large (1–12cm across) and seem to have flat, irregularly shaped but generally rounded bodies, with slits around the edges and complex internal folds. They appear more complicated than simple colonies of bacteria. They are dated to 2.1×10^9 BP, an amazing 1.5×10^9 years older than the earliest previously accepted multicellular fossils, which slightly predate the Cambrian explosion of 545 million BP.

These are trace fossils, with none of the actual cellular material remaining, but an inorganic nature was ruled out by the detection of carbon and sulphur isotopes of organic origin. Studies of the rock chemistry indicate that the organisms lived in the sea at depths of 30–40m, and almost certainly metabolised oxygen, which was rapidly increasing in the atmosphere following the Great Oxidation Event of about $2.5–2.4 \times 10^9$ BP.

ANIMALS THAT EXIST WITHOUT OXYGEN

Until recently, it was believed that all multicellular life forms on Earth metabolised oxygen, and that only archaea and bacteria could survive anoxic conditions. In an announcement in April 2010, a team from Marche Polytechnic University in Ancona, Italy, described the discovery of three animals that live and reproduce under anoxic conditions in the L'Atalante basin (about 3.5km deep) in the Mediterranean, west of Crete. Dead specimens of the new life forms, named loriciferans from the lorica, the thick layer that protects them, were recovered, but they contained viable eggs, which hatched under completely oxygen-free conditions. Only one species, *Spinoloricus Cinzia*, has been formally described. Details of the other two, *Rugiloricus* and *Pliciloricus*, have yet to be published.

POSSIBLE EARLY DATE FOR ORIGIN OF TETRAPODS

The remarkable *Tiktaalik roseae* fossils discovered in the Canadian Arctic in 2004 suggested that tetrapods (four-legged vertebrates) first emerged from the sea on to freshwater deltas or lake shores around 380 million BP. The discovery of fossil trackways and individual footprints from a quarry in south-eastern Poland, described in *Nature* in January 2010, may indicate that tetrapods emerged from a shallow, possibly tropical, marine environment about 395 million BP. The trackways appear to have been made by one life form and the individual footprints by a larger creature, estimated to be 2.5m long. Trace fossils of this sort are notoriously difficult to interpret in the absence of body fossils, and some experts point to the fact that the apparent style of locomotion is not found elsewhere in the fossil record until some 50 million years later. The trackways could have been caused by lobe-finned fish, and the individual footprints by some creature that became extinct and was not an ancestor of modern tetrapods.

DINOSAUR EXTINCTION NOT CAUSED BY THE CHICXULUB IMPACT

Recent results contradict the widely held view that the meteorite impact that created the Chicxulub crater in northern Yucatan was responsible for the K-T (Cretaceous-Tertiary) mass extinction, 65 million years ago, when dinosaurs and some 60 per cent of all animal species became extinct. Details published in *Palaeogeography, Palaeoclimatology, Palaeoecology* in September 2009 and March 2010 by a collaborative German/US project point to prolonged climatic stress as the most probable cause. In particular, they confirm earlier findings (published in April 2009) that the Chicxulub event occurred some 300,000 years before the mass extinction.

Examination of various microfossils such as algal cysts, spores, and pollen indicates that there were widespread, prolonged fluctuations in environmental conditions and ecosystems lasting for several million years, beginning long before the K-T boundary and its extinctions. The climatic variations may be linked to the extended period of intermittent volcanism associated with the eruption of the Deccan volcanic province in India. In this scenario, the Chicxulub impact was not the primary cause of the extinctions, but could have been a contributory factor.

THE HOMINID AND HOMININ FAMILY TREE

There have been major developments in understanding the family tree of primates, hominids (the existing and extinct ape and human forms) and hominins (the sub-group consisting of chimpanzees and humans). In

July 2010, researchers from the University of Michigan described in *Nature* the discovery in Saudi Arabia of a skull from an extremely primitive primate, *Saadanius hijazensis*. About 29 million years old, the fossil exhibits features in common with Old-World monkeys and apes, and humans. It, or some unknown related form, could be the ancestor of all later species.

Amid controversy over the long delay in publication of results on fossils discovered in Ethiopia in 1992, an international team described *Ardipithecus ramidus* in *Science* in October 2009. The most complete fossil was of a female, nicknamed 'Ardi', but fragments of at least 36 other individuals were found. Some features resemble those of apes, and others those of humans. *Ardipithecus*, dated to around 4.4 million BP, may not be a direct ancestor of the *Homo* genus, but offers light on how humans evolved from the ancestor we have in common with chimpanzees (which probably dates back to around 7–6 million BP). The team suggested that Ardi had an arboreal lifestyle in fairly dense woodland, but a later study, based on geological evidence, published in *Science* in May 2010 by a group from the University of Utah, argues that the species inhabited an open savanna-like landscape.

Similar controversy still surrounds *Australopithecus afarensis*, which lived slightly later (4–3 million BP). In June 2010, in the online version of *Proceedings of the National Academy of Sciences*, a team, led from the Cleveland Museum of Natural History, described Kadanuumuu ('Big Man' in the Afar language), a male fossil, much taller (1.5–1.7m) than the famous female 'Lucy' (1.1m), generally considered to display a chimpanzee-like skeletal structure, with a primitive two-legged gait and probably an arboreal habit. The discovery team claim that the new fossils demonstrate an efficient, upright gait, perhaps readily suited to running, and therefore a savanna-like habitat. On this basis, it was suggested that *A. afarensis* might be the source of the footprints (3.6 million BP) found at Laetoli in Tanzania 30 years ago. Other experts, however, dispute the human-like gait and ground-dwelling interpretation of these fragmentary fossils.

In *Science*, in April 2010, the discovery in a cave at Malapa, near Johannesburg, of two specimens of a new hominid, *Australopithecus sebida*, was announced by a team from the University of Witwatersrand. They claimed that the fossils, dated to 1.95–1.78 million BP, represent a link between *Australopithecus* and *Homo*, but this is disputed by other experts, who regard the finds as a variant of *Australopithecus*, especially as genuine *Homo* forms are known from an earlier date (2.3 million BP). Further specimens are required for the status of *A. sebida* to be clarified.

The existence and earliest dates of various *Homo* species outside Africa appeared well-established, with *Homo erectus* (1.8 million BP at Dmanisi, Georgia and, in the case of the important 'Peking Man' fossils from Zhoukoudian, 750,000 BP); *Homo heidelbergensis* (500,000 BP); *Homo neanderthalensis* (130,000 BP), and *Homo floresiensis* (90,000 BP). The announcement in *Nature* in March 2010, by a team from the Max Planck Institute for Evolutionary Anthropology in Leipzig, of genetic evidence for a new species of *Homo* came as a complete surprise. The team extracted mitochondrial DNA (passed through the maternal line) from a finger bone discovered in the Denisova Cave in the Altai Mountains. When compared with modern DNA, the recovered sequence shows approximately twice as many variations as Neandertal DNA, more than enough to establish it as a new species, nicknamed 'X-woman'. Dated to about 48,000–30,000 BP, this suggests an earlier wave of colonisation from Africa by some unknown species. The mitochondrial ancestor common to X-woman, Neandertals, and modern humans is estimated to have lived 1.3–0.8 million BP, and the mitochondrial ancestor common to Neandertals and *Homo sapiens* 620,000–320,000 BP.

Results published in *HOMO – Journal of Comparative Human Biology* in July 2010 finally appear to confirm that the remains of tiny humans (nicknamed 'hobbits') found on the Indonesian island of Flores were a genuine species or sub-species *(Homo floresiensis)* not individuals affected by cretinism. This form of *Homo* lived as recently as 38,000–13,000 BP and thus at the same time as modern humans. There is some doubt about whether it could have evolved from the earlier *Homo erectus*. In March 2010, it was reported in *Nature* that tools discovered at the Wolo Sege site revealed the presence of an unknown human-like form on Flores at least 1 million BP. Again, this raises the possibility that a more primitive hominin migrated from Africa to colonise Asia before *Homo erectus*.

NEANDERTAL AND OTHER GENES IN HOMO SAPIENS

Work published in February 2009 suggested that the human genome did not contain elements derived from Neandertals *(Homo neanderthalensis)*. This was dramatically (but only partially) contradicted by findings published on 7 May 2010 in *Science* as a preliminary result of a major, four-year, international effort, led by the Max Planck Institute for Evolutionary Anthropology in Leipzig. The Neandertal genome is the origin of genes found in some 1 to 4 per cent of modern humans living in Eurasia (western Europeans, Han Chinese, and Papua-New-Guinea populations were examined), suggesting a limited amount of interbreeding between 100,000 and 45,000 BP. The link is not found in modern populations from western and southern Africa, so does not contradict the overall 'Out of Africa' theory which holds that *Homo sapiens* originated in Africa and that all modern populations derive from a small group that left the continent around 60,000–50,000 BP. Given that one criterion of a species is the ability to produce viable offspring, it has been suggested that Neandertals should be reclassified as *Homo sapiens neanderthalensis*.

Results presented in April 2010 by the University of Albuquerque confirm the genetic link and also find a sudden increase in genetic diversity in Indo-Pacific populations occurring around 40,000 BP. Rather than originating with Neandertals, this diversity suggests interbreeding with other *Homo* species, possibly *Homo erectus*, a species related to *Homo floresiensis*, or an unknown earlier precursor.

EARLIEST EVIDENCE OF HUMANS IN NORTHERN EUROPE

In July 2010, it was announced in *Nature* that stone tools discovered at Happisburgh, Norfolk were dated to 950,000 BP, or even earlier. The site was probably occupied by the species known as *Homo antecessor*, and thus becomes the earliest known northern European site for a member of the *Homo* genus. Indications of a very cool climate suggest that the inhabitants almost certainly wore clothing and may perhaps have had the use of fire. The earliest southern European sites (again for *Homo antecessor*) are Atapuerca and Sima del Elefante in Spain, dated to 1.1–1.2 million BP and 780,000 BP, respectively.

SOPHISTICATED BEHAVIOUR PREDATES HOMO SAPIENS

Sophisticated behaviour, with evidence of communication, social organisation, and segregated living and working areas has, until now, been associated with *Homo sapiens*, and dated to the Middle Palaeolithic around 250,000 BP. Results published in *Science* in December 2009 by a team from the Hebrew University Institute of Archaeology have not only overturned this view, but give dates of 750,000 BP, half a million years earlier.

The excavation at Gesher Benot Ya'aqov, in the Dead Sea rift in the southern Hula Valley of northern Israel, revealed an Acheulian culture with a wide range of tools, animal bones and plant remains. This represents a typical hunter-gatherer settlement, and is probably associated with *Homo erectus* or some other ancestral *Homo* species. (*Homo sapiens* apparently emerged only about 300,000–200,000 BP.) Different tasks, ranging from nut processing to fish preparation, were carried out in different areas, and certain tasks, such as the working of basalt and limestone tools, were carried out near hearths, whereas flint-working occurred elsewhere.

A POTENTIAL METHOD OF PREVENTING MITOCHONDRIAL DISEASES

The energy required by eucaryotic cells is provided by structures known as mitochondria. Unlike the approximately 23,000 genes present in human cellular nuclei, which originate from both parents, just 13 genes control the production of mitochondria, and these are passed solely from mother to child. As with all DNA, however, mitochondrial DNA is subject to mutations, which may lead to diseases of varying severity, some of which are fatal in early infancy.

In April 2010, scientists at Newcastle University announced in *Nature* that they had developed a technique for transferring DNA between human eggs. A fertilised egg contains two pronuclei, one each from egg and sperm. The researchers removed the pronuclei from a fertilised egg, leaving behind the faulty mitochondria, and transferred them to a donor egg from which the pronuclei had been removed. The resulting egg therefore contained DNA from the mother and father, and correctly functioning mitochondria from the donor. Any child would be free from mitochondrial disease, but have its genetic inheritance solely determined by its parents' DNA.

An effectively similar procedure with monkey eggs was announced in *Nature* in August 2009 by a team from Oregon Health and Science University, resulting in the birth of two, apparently healthy young. The technique, although accompanied by ethical issues, offers great potential for eliminating human mitochondrial diseases, none of which are currently treatable.

A 'CURE' FOR COLOUR BLINDNESS

In September 2009, researchers at the University of Washington described in *Nature* how they had used genetic techniques to give full colour vision to male squirrel monkeys, normally unable to distinguish between red and green (similar to red/green colour blindness in humans). They introduced therapeutic genes into the colour-sensing cells in the retinas of adult male monkeys, who then developed the appropriate photosensitive pigments and were able to differentiate between the colours. The surprising aspect of this work is that it showed that even adult brains were able to adapt to new sensory information. The results suggest that the technique might be appropriate for treating genetic colour deficiencies in humans.

THE UNIVERSE

SUPERNOVAE MAY NOT FORGE HEAVIEST NUCLEI

It has been generally believed that all elements heavier than iron (with 26 protons in its nucleus) are produced in supernovae by what is known as the r-process, whereby captured neutrons turn into protons within a nucleus, creating an element with a greater atomic number. A study published in *Physical Review Letters* in June 2010 finds that for a small supernova of 8.8 solar masses, the r-process fails beyond nickel (28 protons). The team from the Max Planck Institute for Astrophysics in Garching suggest that heavier elements are created in neutron-rich explosions when collapsed stars merge. Other scientists point out that the mass of the star modelled is very small and further studies are required with much greater (and thus more realistic) initial masses.

SUPERMASSIVE STARS

Theory and observations of stars in our galaxy set the absolute upper limit for the mass of modern stars as about 150 solar masses. Intense radiation pressure prevents the accretion of greater amounts of material. Theoretical studies had suggested that, if larger stars ever existed, they would finally explode as Type II (core-collapse) supernovae in what was termed a 'pair-instability' process. In April 2007, a supernova, SN 2007bi, was observed to take exceptionally long times to rise to maximum and to fade. The decline was powered by the decay of radioactive nickel in exceptionally high abundance. Only a pair-instability process could account for the observations, and calculations, published in *Nature* in February 2010 by a team from the Weizmann Institute of Science in Rehovot, Israel, suggested an incredible 300 solar masses for the progenitor star.

In a paper published in *Monthly Notices of the Royal Astronomical Society* in July 2010, a team from Sheffield University described the discovery of several massive stars in the clusters NGC 3603 and RMC 136a (the latter in the Large Magellanic Cloud). One star in particular, RNC 136a1, was found to have a current mass of about 265 solar masses, and a probable mass at the time of its formation of some 320 solar masses. It has a diameter about 30 times that of the Sun.

Such massive stars are exceptional nowadays, but almost certainly existed in large numbers in the early Universe shortly after the Big Bang. They therefore offer a chance to study conditions that existed at that distant period.

RAINING PEBBLES

The discovery of exoplanets (planets around other stars) has proceeded apace, with hundreds now known. None are perhaps so strange as the planet known as CoRoT-7b, discovered in February 2009 by the CoRoT spaceprobe, launched by the French and European space agencies. The rocky planet, about twice the size of Earth and five times its mass, orbits at a distance of just 2.6 million kilometres (less than one-twenty-fifth of Mercury's distance from the Sun). It is gravitationally locked, so that one hemisphere is permanently turned towards the star and has a temperature of about 2600 Kelvin (2327°C), which would turn the surface into a lava ocean. In a paper published in *Astrophysical Journal* in October 2009, scientists from Washington University in St Louis describe the exotic atmospheric chemistry, which consists of elements from vaporised rock. Just as water condenses and freezes with lower temperatures with increasing altitude on Earth, a similar process occurs on CoRoT-7b. At various altitudes different combinations of vapours condense into solid particles, which then fall towards the lava ocean. It is 'raining pebbles' of different types of rock.

LIFE ON MARS?

Controversy erupted in 1996 when it was claimed that the Allan Hills Martian meteorite, ALH 84001, found in Antarctica in 1984, contained carbon-based molecules and biomorphs (objects shaped like bacteria). Since then the general opinion has been that the features could not be interpreted as signs of life. Now various results have revitalised the arguments.

A study, published in *Earth and Planetary Science Letters,* in June 2009, by a team from NASA's Johnson Space Center has established that certain ALH 84001 minerals were not, as previously thought, deposited from water at temperatures of 150°C or more, but below 100°C, at which temperature organisms are certainly able to survive.

Even more significant is a report from the same team that appeared in *Geochimica et Cosmochimica Acta* in November 2009, which claimed that there is no plausible geological (ie non-biological) explanation for nanocrystal magnetites found in the rock. Taken with suggestions that other Martian meteorites exhibit biomorphs, these results ensure that the controversy over Martian life continues.

In an unrelated study of the same meteorite, appearing in *Science* in April 2010, a team from the University of Houston, used a new method (lutetium-hafnium isotope analysis) to obtain the age and source of minerals present. A revised age of 4.091×10^9 BP was obtained (some 400 million years younger than previous estimates), suggesting that the meteorite was formed when Mars was wet and had a magnetic field. Again, such conditions would be favourable for primitive life. The data indicate that volcanic activity has been present on Mars for a significant fraction of the planet's history.

WIDESPREAD WATER ONCE EXISTED ON MARS

The surface of Mars consists of two distinct regions: the southern highlands, and much lower, extensive northern plains, created, it is believed, by a gigantic impact early in the planet's history, and subsequently covered by layers of volcanic and sedimentary material. Several missions such as ESA's Mars Express and NASA's Mars Reconnaissance Orbiter have discovered clays or clay-like minerals, indicative of formerly wet conditions, at thousands of sites in the southern highlands. In a paper published in *Science* in June 2010, a team from the University of Paris reported similar findings at a number of sites in the north, where later impacts have exposed the underlying rocks. The implications are that liquid water existed across the whole of Mars during part of the Noachian period, 4.6×10^9 BP to 3.5×10^9 BP.

These findings are confirmed by a separate report in *Nature Geoscience* online, also in June 2010, by scientists from the University of Colorado at Boulder, that 29 of the 52 dry river deltas and many thousands of river valleys in the northern lowlands all lie at the same altitude, as would be expected if they were discharging into a widespread ocean. They estimate that this would have been about 550m deep if spread around the whole planet.

A re-examination and recalibration of measurements made at Gusev Crater by NASA's Mars Exploration Rover, Spirit, in 2005, was published in *Science* (again in June 2010) by a team led from the Johnson Space Center in Houston. The rocks contain some 25 per cent of carbonates, far more than previously thought. The minerals present probably arose from carbonate-rich water that reacted with existing rocks. This, in turn, suggests warm, wet conditions and a dense carbon-dioxide-rich atmosphere at an early epoch.

LUNAR WATER

It has suddenly been realised that there are substantial amounts of water ice on the Moon. Three different forms of deposit have been discovered and these were discussed at a conference at the Lunar and Planetary Institute (LPI) in Houston in March 2010. One type of deposit was found by NASA's Mini-SAR (radar) experiment on the Indian Chandrayaan-1 probe. This found 40 craters (2–5km in diameter) near the north pole with lenses of ice at least 2m deep. The craters are in permanent shadow and have temperatures as low as 25K (–248°C). An LPI team is currently studying results for the south pole and findings will be published in *Geophysical Research Letters.*

A second experiment on Chandrayaan-1, the Moon Mineralogy Mapper, discovered, in 2009, a thin layer of ice that has a widespread, patchy distribution across the whole Moon. This is very thin, being bound to rocks and dust in the very outermost millimetres of the surface. It probably arises when oxygen atoms present in the soil capture protons (ie hydrogen nuclei) from the solar wind, giving rise to hydroxyl (OH) radicals and water.

This thin layer was detected in the debris ejected when the LCROSS (Lunar Crater Observation and Sensing Satellite) probe and last-stage rocket were deliberately crashed into the permanently shadowed crater Cabeus on 9 October 2009. The impacts also revealed a deeper, thicker layer of ice that contained unexpected compounds, including sulphur dioxide (SO_2), methanol (CH_3OH), and diacetylene (H_2C_4). This layer is probably significantly older than the superficial deposit and may originate in ancient cometary impacts.

A (SLIGHTLY) YOUNGER EARTH

A study reported in *Nature Geosciences* in July 2010 suggests that the Earth took longer to accrete from smaller bodies (planetesimals) than previously supposed (100 million years as against 30 million years). The final state was reached around 4.467×10^9 BP, rather than 4.537×10^9 BP. The study examined the rate at which the early Earth differentiated into a molten, metallic core, and an overlying mantle.

Hafnium-182 decays into tungsten-182 at a known rate over several million years. Any tungsten produced as the Earth was differentiating would be incorporated into the metallic core. By comparing the content of tungsten-182 in the mantle with that found in meteorites, a time-scale for the differentiation could be established. The process appears to have seen a rapid, initial accretion, followed by a break – possibly coincident with the impact believed to have formed the Moon – and a subsequent slower accretion.

PLATE TECTONICS NOT DRIVEN BY MANTLE CONVECTION

It has generally been assumed that convection currents within the Earth's mantle primarily control the motion and speed of plate-tectonic movements. A study published in *Science* in July 2010 by a team from Monash University in Melbourne, Australia, contradicts this view. Using observations and advanced computer modelling, the team found that both the velocities of the plates and the location of the plate boundaries are controlled by conditions at subduction zones, where one plate dives under another.

The models show that the subducting (lower) plate is not 'pushed' by convection in the underlying mantle but, by sinking, exerts a drag on the portion of the plate that remains at the surface, causing either motion of the plate or a change in the position of the subduction boundary. Although mantle convection certainly occurs, it is not the principal factor in plate motion.

CATASTROPHIC FLOOD FILLED MEDITERRANEAN BASIN

Although the Mediterranean basin was once dry land, details of the flooding have been difficult to determine. New research, published in *Nature* in December 2009 by a team from the Research Council of Spain, suggests that the flooding, known as the Zanclean flood, occurred about 5 million BP and could have filled the basin in just two years.

The inflow from the Atlantic to the Mediterranean initially occurred over a sill, and caused the erosion of a small channel. When a critical point was reached, the flow abruptly eroded a far deeper, broad channel, 200km long, through the Straits of Gibraltar. The flow rate may have been so extreme as to raise the level of the Mediterranean by as much as 10m per day.

. . . AND EVERYTHING

MASERS, LASERS, AND NOW SPASERS (AND PLASMONS)

In August 2009, nearly 50 years after the development of the laser (by Maiman, in May 1960) a research group from the University of Norfolk, Virginia – followed in October 2009 by another at the University of California, Berkeley – announced that they had succeeded in creating 'spasers', devices for 'surface plasmon amplification by the stimulated emission of radiation'.

Metals conduct electricity because their electrons have great freedom of movement. Plasmons are collective, wavelike oscillations of these electrons. They may be excited by light at the appropriate frequency (within the visible to infrared range), and are essentially trapped at the surface. The exciting wavelength is highly specific and depends on the metal involved. Without amplification, plasmons typically decay in attoseconds (10^{-18} seconds). The spasers described were excited by lasers emitting radiation of the appropriate wavelength. Interaction between the plasmon particle and dye particles immediately surrounding it produced mutual feedback, resulting in amplified emission of light at the desired wavelength.

A significant potential application of spasers is in the field of optical computing which, despite its great promise of extremely fast computation, has lacked a means of rapidly switching light between 'on' and 'off' states. If a compact method of exciting spasers can be devised that does not require energy-intensive lasers, the devices offer hope that optical computing may finally become feasible.

Plasmons themselves are finding practical applications. One that appears to hold considerable promise is a treatment for cancer. Initial tests in mice suggest that nanoparticle plasmons attached to suitable antibodies can latch on to cancerous cells. When actuated by focused, tuned, infrared radiation, the plasmons heat up and destroy just the target cell.

INCONSTANT PHYSICAL CONSTANTS?

The physical constants are generally assumed to be invariant across space and time. A report published in *Astrophysical Journal Letters* in June 2010, by a group from the National Centre for Radio Astrophysics in Pune, India, hints that the fine-structure constant, alpha, once had a different value. The team measured the properties of hydroxyl radicals in a gas cloud some 2.9×10^9 light-years distant, illuminated by an even more distant radio source, the supermassive black hole PKS 1413 + 135. Discrepancies in the radio spectrum are tentative evidence that alpha once differed from the current value. A similar, unconfirmed hint of variation in alpha has been suspected in light from distant quasars. Verification of any alteration in the 'constants' would require a complete revision of the current Standard Model of particle physics.

A NEW GENERATION OF SUB-ATOMIC PARTICLES?

The Standard Model of particle physics currently recognises three generations of sub-atomic particles, and suggests that a Higgs boson, yet to be observed, accounts for the mass of every particle. Two separate experiments at the Tevatron synchrotron at the Fermi National Accelerator Laboratory (Fermilab) in Batavia, Illinois, hint that a fourth generation of particles may exist, and one suggests that there may even be multiple Higgs particles. In March 2010, researchers examining CDF (Collider Detector at Fermilab) data from the Tevatron's proton/antiproton collisions found a small surplus of events hinting at the existence of a fourth quark, heavier than the three known pairs of quarks. (There would actually be a pair of fourth-generation quarks: the top prime and bottom prime quarks.)

An even stronger hint of a fourth generation of particles comes from the DZero experiment. Results submitted to *Physics Review D* found that particles known as B-mesons decayed asymmetrically, producing more muons than antimuons. If confirmed, this is an exceptionally significant finding. It could explain a problem that has concerned physicists and cosmologists for years: why the Universe consists of matter, when theory suggests that equal quantities of matter and antimatter should have been created in the Big Bang, and would annihilate one another, leaving just a sea of radiation.

The concept known as supersymmetry, where all known particles, including those that carry forces, have a heavier partner, could also explain the matter/antimatter asymmetry. (Results of B-meson decay presented by CERN's BELLE collaboration at the Lepton-Photon International Symposium in Hamburg in August 2009 hint that a supersymmetric solution would fit the data better than the current Standard Model.) Some researchers at Fermilab, in results described in *Symmetry* in June 2010 suggest that the DZero results support the existence of multiple Higgs bosons, in agreement with supersymmetry.

THE TROUBLE WITH NEUTRINOS

There is evidence that the three varieties of neutrinos (electron, muon and tau neutrinos) are able to oscillate between the forms. Oscillation is possible only if neutrinos have mass, so this is yet another problem for the current Standard Model of particle physics, which predicts that neutrinos are massless. Although earlier experiments had determined that a number of electron and muon neutrinos, produced in the Sun, the atmosphere, or accelerators, had 'disappeared' (ie oscillated) before reaching the detectors, detection of a change in a beam of neutrinos of a given type was lacking. In the OPERA experiment, a beam of muon neutrinos is produced by the Super Proton Synchrotron at the European Centre for Nuclear Research (CERN), and directed at the Gran Sasso laboratory in Italy, 730 kilometres away. In an incredible feat of detection, a report submitted to *Physics Letters B* reveals that (with a high degree of confidence) a single tau neutrino has actually been detected in the blizzard of muon neutrinos created by 1.89×10^{19} protons at CERN. Confirmation of other events will probably come with analysis of an even larger quantity of data that has already been obtained.

In a further development, it now seems possible that a fourth variety of neutrino may exist. This variety, known as the 'sterile' neutrino because it has even less tendency to interact with ordinary matter than the known neutrinos, was suggested to account for results obtained in the 1990s from the Liquid Scintillator Neutrino Detector (LSND) operated at the Los Alamos National Laboratory in New Mexico. Detection would be through the neutrinos' gravitational effects, and they would be good candidates for the dark matter that is believed to dominate the Universe.

In 2007, results of the Mini Booster Neutrino Experiment (MiniBooNE) at the Fermi National Accelerator Laboratory in Batavia, Illinois, found no evidence for sterile neutrinos. MiniBooNE initially used neutrinos to search for the effect and, once again, if the Standard Model is correct, there should be no difference between the behaviour of neutrinos and antineutrinos. To check, however, the researchers repeated the experiment with antineutrinos and, in a result reported at a neutrino conference in Greece in June 2010, found a higher rate of oscillation of muon antineutrinos into electron antineutrinos than predicted. This excess may occur through muon antineutrinos turning into sterile neutrinos before finally becoming electron antineutrinos.

The results agree with other research at Batavia, found by the Main Injector Neutrino Oscillation Search (MINOS), also announced in Greece, of subtle differences in the behaviour of neutrinos and antineutrinos. Once again, there is an apparent asymmetry in the way matter and antimatter behave.

REPAIRED LARGE HADRON COLLIDER BACK ON TRACK

Following its breakdown in September 2008, shortly after commissioning, the world's most powerful particle accelerator, the Large Hadron Collider (LHC) at CERN was repaired and improved systems were installed before it was cooled to its operating temperature of just 1.9K (colder than deep space) and restarted on 20 November 2009. Two separate beams were circulated by 23 November, and achieved record-breaking energies of 2.36 TeV (2.36×10^{12} electron volts) on 8 December, and 3.5 TeV on 19 March 2010. The first collisions between the beams occurred on 30 March, and scientific results started to arrive on 5 April, with the detection of an extremely short-lived 'beauty' particle (otherwise known as a bottom quark), essential confirmation that the experiment was functioning correctly.

By late June 2010, 10,000 particle collisions per second were being generated. In July it was announced at the International Conference on High Energy Physics in Paris that the ATLAS and CMS experiments had observed several candidates for the top quark (the heaviest particle yet known), so the LHC appears well on track to achieve all its targets for 2010, before the winter shutdown and restart in 2011 when the eventual goal of 7 TeV per beam should be reached. Even before then, it may detect the W prime and Z prime bosons (heavy versions of the W and Z bosons that are responsible for the weak interaction) and which have been proposed to account for certain anomalies in the current Standard Model of particle physics.

SUPER-HEAVY ELEMENT 117 CREATED

In April 2010, a joint Russian/US team, led by the Joint Institute for Nuclear Research at Dubna, Russia, announced the creation of element 117 (provisional name ununseptium) in a paper submitted to *Physical Review Letters*. In two runs of 70 days each, the team smashed a calcium-48 isotope, with 20 protons and 28 neutrons, into artificially created berkelium (97 protons and 152 neutrons), producing just six atoms of element 117, in two isotopic forms (176 and 177 neutrons), with half-lives of 14 and 78 milliseconds.

The discovery of element 117 fills a gap in the periodic table, where all transuranic elements up to, and including, element 118 have now been created, although in some cases just a few atoms have been observed. Analysis of the radioactive decay of ununseptium suggests that the predicted 'island of stability', where super-heavy elements may have half-lives of days, months, or even years, may actually exist. Such elements could have 184 neutrons and either 120 or 126 protons.

THEATRE

Matt Trueman

ALL THAT GLITTERS

Talk of a new theatrical golden age is probably premature. Only time will tell whether the past 12 months come to sit comfortably alongside the game-changing years of post-war theatre. Certainly the bar was raised, but whether any goalposts were shifted remains to be seen. As was the case in those vintage years, the charge was led from the east side of Sloane Square. Under the continuing artistic direction of Dominic Cooke, the Royal Court barely put a foot wrong, repeatedly offering political enquiry without sacrificing the entertainment values that make it palatable.

At its helm was Jez Butterworth's *Jerusalem*, a guttural lament for a lost England whose green pleasantries and idiosyncrasies have been deposed by urban ubiquity and the mollycoddling politics of council officials and health and safety legislation. Set on St George's Day in a Wiltshire wood, a wellington boot's throw away from the annual Flintlock fair, *Jerusalem* gave us the most transfixing character of recent years: Johnny 'Rooster' Byron – simultaneously freeloading vagrant and freewheeling vanguard; former daredevil; neglectful father; teller of the tallest tales; pill-peddling Pied Piper, perennial Peter Pan and possible paedophile. It produced a monumental performance from a muscular Mark Rylance, which began chugging a cocktail of raw egg, vodka, milk and speed before culminating – three and a half hours later – bloodied and bloodcurdling, beating a drum that seemed to shake the foundations of both the theatre and the nation beyond. Surrounded by a band of merry miscreants, including Mackenzie Crook's dozy Ginger, Gerard Horan's drooping publican and Jessica Barden's teenage gremlin, 'Rooster' won the support of critics and audiences alike, with a sell-out West End transfer to be followed by a Broadway stint in 2011.

Equally quick to transfer across town was *Enron*, an epic vaudeville – not quite the musical some claimed – about the American company's financial unravelling, which originally opened at the Chichester Festival Theatre. Written over five years by Lucy Prebble, *Enron* was fast-tracked by Rupert Goold and Henny Finch of Headlong Theatre in response to the global economic crisis. The result was electric topicality and – thanks to Goold's witty, almost brash direction that brought velociraptors, light sabers and three blind mice to the stage – thrilling visuals. Like *Jerusalem*, *Enron* revolved around a towering lead role: as the corporation's president Jeffrey Skilling, Samuel West sculpted himself from bespectacled nerd to Brylcreemed butterfly in a designer suit. UK Critics heralded *Enron* as *the* financial play. However, a subsequent Broadway transfer, recast with American actors, closed after 15 performances in the wake of notices disappointed by its insubstantial evaluation of a very American failure.

If *Enron*'s success was a product of its currency, the Royal Court repeated the trick with *Posh*, a portrait of an Oxbridge dining society based on the Bullingdon Club (of which David Cameron, George Osborne and Boris Johnson were once members), programmed to coincide with the general election. Laura Wade's script was heavy on left-wing righteousness, attacking an out-of-sorts and out-of-touch aristocracy, but Lyndsey Turner's direction and a terrific young cast turned it into a satirical cartoon, interspersing scenes with ridiculous *a cappella* renditions of R&B hits in the plum vowels of heightened RP.

Elsewhere the election brought a small glut of plays responding to the newfound prevalence of the British National Party. At the Wellcome Collection, Mick Gordon and Billy Bragg joined forces on *Pressure Drop*, the Finborough Theatre offered Anders Lustgarten's *A Day at the Racists* and Philip Ridley's *Moonfleece* toured the country, being controversially vetoed by Dudley council.

In fact, politics was at the heart of many new plays. Jack Thorne took us back to the *2nd May 1997* to explore Labour's landslide as seen by three politically diverse couples; Kieron Barry dramatised the inquest into Jean Charles de Menezes' death in *Stockwell;* and James Graham – a young writer growing in promise with every offering – critiqued the generational imbalance in *The Whisky Taster*. Kilburn's Tricycle Theatre, once brilliantly described as a 'court of public morality', brought two grand cycles of plays: the first, *Not Black and White*, explored contemporary issues of race, while the second, *Women, Power and Politics*, trained its eye on the past and present with nine short plays about the imbalance between the sexes in Westminister and beyond.

But it was biography that fuelled two of the most celebrated new plays in London. When everyone was backing Butterworth for a grand slam of Best New Play awards, with Prebble deemed his only threat, it was Katori Hall who took the Olivier Award for *The Mountaintop* – an imaginative account of the night before Martin Luther King (David Harewood) was assassinated. Meanwhile, John Logan's *Red* at the Donmar Warehouse gave a portrait of the artist Mark Rothko (Alfred Molina), focusing on his relationship with both his work and his assistant, played by Eddie Redmayne.

Elsewhere Simon Stephens gave a compulsive account of a Columbine-style shooting in a Stockport school in *Punk Rock*. Stephens later returned to the Lyric Hammersmith in collaboration with David Eldridge and Robert Holman for a beautifully everyday vision of apocalypse, *A Thousand Stars Explode in the Sky*. At the Hampstead, the RSC gave Shakespeare a makeover with David Greig's sequel to Macbeth, *Dunsinane*, and Dennis Kelly's epic, but not entirely successful, re-imagining of King Lear, *The Gods Weep*, which nurtured the financial crisis into a full-blown civil war. Back at the Royal Court, in the cosy, claustrophobic upstairs space, the strike-rate was maintained by Mike Bartlett's *Cock*, Tim Crouch's *The Author* (almost an invective against the Royal Court itself) and D. C. Moore's *The Empire*. All three writers had impressively productive years.

NATIONAL PRIDE

Sadly the same could not always be said of new writing at the National. Mark Ravenhill's adaptation of Terry Pratchett's *Nation*, Drew Pautz's confused critique of the church, *Love the Sinner*, Hanif Kureishi's *The Black Album* and Tamsin Oglesby's *Really Old, Like Forty Five* all misfired. Alan Bennett produced his first play since *The History Boys* and, although *The Habit of Art* won critical plaudits, it lacked the spark of its predecessor. On one level it's a cerebral biographical study of W. H. Auden (Richard Griffiths) through his friendship with Benjamin Britten (Alex Jennings), musing on the unpredictable and ungainly nature of genius. On another, it is a meta-theatrical farce with Auden's situation framed as a shoddy play peopled by insecure actors.

More socially acute were Moira Buffini's *Welcome to Thebes,* which transposed Grecian myth into contemporary African politics with wry knowingness and narrative drive, and Tadeusz Slobodzianek's *Our Class* (translated by Ryan Craig). Directed with beautiful efficacy by Bijan Sheibani, *Our Class* followed a set of Polish Catholics and Jews from classroom to coffin, via the atrocities of the Second World War. The piece's skill lies in weaving individual narratives horrifically towards the slaughter and its delicate, sympathetic unravelling of the consequences. It was a spectacularly difficult watch.

However, if lively new works were rare on the South Bank, rejuvenated old ones seemed par for the course. Under artistic director Nicholas Hytner's incisive programming, the National doesn't deal so much in revivals as resuscitations.

In a year that began with J. B. Priestley's famously tricky *Time and the Conways* receiving the Rupert Goold treatment (think time-twisting moments that fused *Alice in Wonderland* with *Donnie Darko*), we were privy to some startling rediscoveries. Who knew, for example, Terence Rattigan's self-discarded *After the Dance* – first seen in 1939 – to be so intricate and devastating a masterpiece? Yet, in Thea Sharrock's Lyttelton production spun from microscopic details and delicate emotional threads, it offered a soaring – and surprisingly contemporary – picture of the inter-war years.

The same keen eye for the miniscule coursed through Katie Mitchell's production of Bruckner's *Pains of Youth.* For all the failings of Bruckner's narrative – particularly its abrupt ending – Mitchell proved boredom a fascinating beast by painting the symptomatic loucheness, lethargy and gluttony with the finest of brushes. Mitchell's other National production, also housed in the Cottesloe, was a bold adaptation of Dr Seuss's *The Cat in the Hat,* which perfectly recreated the aesthetic of the original illustrations right down to the shading.

In fact no UK theatre created work with such constant vivid flair as the National. Marianne Elliott's fairytale-inspired *All's Well That Ends Well* and her production of Thomas Middleton's *Women Beware Women,* the fifth act of which was stripped of text and played as a masquerade of brutalities as the Olivier stage revolved, were sumptuously designed by Rae Smith and Lez Brotherston respectively. Equally dazzling to look at was Bunny Christie's glacial palatial set for *The White Guard* in the Lyttelton, a stunning production capturing the chaos of civil war note-perfectly.

No less imposing in scale, but altogether stilted and pompous, was *Mother Courage and Her Children* directed by Deborah Warner and starring Fiona Shaw as the profiteering born-survivor. Warner pulled in the parallels with Iraq, which sat awkwardly and seemed (unsurprisingly) banal, but the production's flaw was in feeling like faux-Brecht. Stage hands posed onstage and danced in the wings as if no one was watching, displaying all the discomfort of marked men.

More promising was Nicholas Hytner's announcement of a £70m makeover for the National, which will bring a new education centre as an extension to the Cottesloe, a new riverfront café and a glass-fronted production centre. At the same time, NT Live! – the National's initiative to broadcast its live performances to cinema screens worldwide – flourished, after its launch in June 2009 with *Phèdre* starring Helen Mirren. This was followed by *All's Well That Ends Well, Nation, The Habit of Art* and Dion Boucicault's *London Assurance* – another of the theatre's stunning re-inventions, led by a hilariously camp Simon Russell-Beale as Sir Harcourt Courtly and a horsey, gung-ho Fiona Shaw (in a role she was born to play). Its continued success led to a second season being announced for 2010–11.

TINSELTOWN IN THEATRELAND

In the West End no story was bigger than that of *Love Never Dies,* Andrew Lloyd Webber's hotly anticipated and much-dreaded sequel to *Phantom of the Opera* and his first new musical since *The Woman in White.* Or rather, the only stories bigger than *Love Never Dies* were those surrounding the show itself, from the pre-emptive viral disparaging that targeted audiences and critics directly, to its acquisition of a tagline that might as well be its epitaph. Rechristened 'Paint Never Dries' by guerrilla theatre bloggers the West End Whingers, *Love Never Dies* is unlikely ever to shake free of the slogan. In actual fact, the critical response ran the whole gamut of ratings, from one star in *Time Out* to five in *The Independent* and *What's On Stage.* Although the narrative was accused of a certain flaccidity to match the banality of Glenn Slater's lyrics, Lloyd Webber's score was generally heralded for its intricacy and attention to detail.

While Lloyd Webber may not take comfort, *Love Never Dies* was far from the year's biggest flop. That accolade went to the ill-advised and implausible musical biopic of Ernest Hemingway, *Too Close to the Sun,* which closed after a fortnight and quickly joined *Behind the Iron Mask* (also composed by John Robinson) in the pantheon of West End atrocities.

Beyond that the West End turned to Hollywood to populate its stages and fill its auditoria. There were stage adaptations of *Breakfast at Tiffany's* starring Anna Friel as a blonde Holly Golightly in keeping with Capote's novella; *The Shawshank Redemption* (faithful to the last); and, most winningly of all, *Legally Blonde: The Musical* with Sheridan Smith as the manicured law student Elle Woods.

At the Garrick, Douglas Carter Beane's *The Little Dog Laughed* delved into Hollywood's closet with a cynical look at the film industry's covering up of homosexuality to preserve box-office returns. While the narrative is perhaps overly straightforward, its caustic wit drew a superb performance from Tamsin Greig as a lesbian talent agent as dry as the Nevada desert. 'Are you British?' she hollered at Rupert Friend's manicured movie-star, 'Do you have a Knighthood? Then shut up!' Jamie Lloyd's production also provided a chance to catch a few young British hopes for Hollywood, with Harry Lloyd and Gemma Arterton doing themselves no harm, although, by comparison, Friend himself seemed bland.

Keira Knightley, however, won over her sceptics with a brave performance in Martin Crimp's contemporary adaptation of *The Misanthrope.* She proved an admirable foil for Damian Lewis's scornfully honest Alceste and was rewarded with a nomination for the Ian Charleson award.

THE RUINS OF A DREAM

In fact, a wider picture of America came under the scrutiny of British theatre time and again, arguably on account of the economic crisis, which became somewhat of an excuse to examine the catastrophic cracks at the heart of the capitalist ideology. In comparison to recent years, 2009–10 saw an unusually high number of American classics revived.

In the early summer months, a Broadway transfer of *Hair* sat side by side on Shaftesbury Avenue with Howard Davies' recreation of his devastating National Theatre production of *All My Sons* with a cast helmed by David Suchet (buzzing round the stage like an angry pinball) and Zoë Wanamaker. The Donmar Warehouse had a roaring success with *A Streetcar Named Desire*, in which Elliot Cowan played Stanley Kowalski as if channeling a young Marlon Brando. Even so, the show belonged to Rachel Weisz as Blanche DuBois, a turn that would see her match Mark Rylance with Olivier, Evening Standard and Critics' Circle Awards for Best Actress.

Around town, the Cut hosted two of the most dogged American plays centring on race when the Old Vic displayed a fine, if uninspiring, *Six Degrees of Separation* and the Young Vic gave August Wilson's *Joe Turner's Come and Gone* an estimable outing. Debbie Allen, meanwhile, directed an all-African-American version of *Cat on a Hot Tin Roof* starring James Earl Jones as Big Daddy at the Novello. The Almeida Theatre presented another Pulitzer-prize winning play, Lynn Nottage's *Ruined* to widespread critical acclaim.

The other dramatic beneficiary of the recession was Henrik Ibsen, whose plays returned to fashion on account of their crisp atmosphere of austerity. Alongside a spook of *Ghosts* (Bolton Octagon, Arcola and Duchess Theatres), there were two very different versions of *Hedda Gabbler* (Bath Theatre Royal and the Riverside Studios) and *A Doll's House* at the Colchester Mercury. The Sheffield Crucible chose to re-open with *An Enemy of the People*, casting Antony Sher as Dr Stockmann. Before the end of 2010, Manchester's Royal Exchange will show *The Lady from the Sea* and, at the Almeida, *The Master Builder* will get a run starring Gemma Arterton and Stephen Dillane.

UNDER NEW MANAGEMENT

Outside of London, it took major refurbishments and regime changes to really pull focus. The Sheffield Crucible relaunched in February 2010 under the artistic direction of Daniel Evans, whose first season in charge was characterised by a diverse combination of local concerns and audience-drawing names, both in terms of people and plays. Stephanie Street's *Sisters*, a testimonial to British Muslim women, presented a balanced perspective and threw up a range of fascinating prejudices from both within and without. Richard Wilson directed the first UK revival of Polly Stenham's smash-hit debut *That Face* with Frances Barber playing mother-cum-monster Martha; Nigel Harman and John Light alternated roles in Sam Shepard's *True West;* and Laura Wade's *Alice* carved Lewis Carroll's Wonderland out of contemporary Sheffield.

Further South, Tom Morris – a former director of the Battersea Arts Centre and National Theatre Studio – took over the newly refurbished Bristol Old Vic, beginning his tenure with an alternative take on *Romeo and Juliet*. In a smart comment on an aging society, *Juliet and her Romeo* made pensioners of the star-crossed lovers. Despite a low-key start, Morris's appointment seems particularly well judged for a local theatre scene deemed one of the most forward-thinking in the country.

Back in London, Sean Holmes took over from David Farr at the Lyric Hammersmith, bringing a level of conservatism to the venue's programming without sacrificing its openness to embrace new forms, as demonstrated by his first two productions in charge – a revival of Trevor Griffiths' *Comedians* (with a standout performance from David Dawson) and a radical re-imagining of *Three Sisters* by Filter Theatre Company, both directed by Holmes himself. Following this, the Lyric had a commercial success with *Ghost Stories* – a co-production with the Liverpool Everyman – which transferred to the Duke of York's Theatre in the summer, taking aim at *The Woman in Black's* claim to be the scariest show in the West End.

Anthony Clark relinquished the reins of the Hampstead Theatre at the end of a damp retrospective season in celebration of its 50th anniversary; he was replaced by Ed Hall, artistic director of all-male Shakespeare theatre company Propeller. Meanwhile, Steve Marmion took over the Soho Theatre from Lisa Goldman. Roxanna Silbert left her post as artistic director at Paines Plough with James Grieve and George Perrin stepping into her shoes. Joe Murphy succeeds them at nabokov. Harun Morrison and Laura McDermott, former producers at the Battersea Arts Centre, were appointed co-artistic directors of Birmingham's Fierce Festival and Mark Ball – himself a former Fierce artistic director – presented the first full-blown London International Festival of Theatre (LIFT) since 2001.

EXPERIMENTALLY SPEAKING

One of the major strands of Mark Ball's inaugural season was our relationship to technology, which continued to take a massive role in more experimental practice. LIFT brought over The Builder's Association from New York with *Continuous City*, a sprawling thesis of a play on the erosion of human communication through the increased ease of connectivity. The piece, which was constructed around a series of webcam conversations, suggested a slide towards ubiquity as the world became a smaller, more conquerable place. By contrast, Dries Verhoeven used the same web technology in *Life Streaming* to forge a genuine connection of sorts between audiences in a temporary internet café and 16 native performers in Sri Lanka, all of whom were directly affected by the 2004 tsunami.

Further afield, theatre looked towards audio-tours for inspiration, though efforts ranged from the interesting (*Would Like to Meet* at the Barbican) to the halfhearted (*Hall* at Hornsey Town Hall) to the downright misguided (*They Only Come at Night*, a first-person vampire thriller, at the Barbican). More successful was David Rosenberg's *Electric Hotel*, an off-site dance piece presented by Sadler's Wells, in which the audience tuned into different spaces of a glass-fronted Copacabana-style hotel specially constructed from shipping containers.

At the other end of the spectrum, the possibility for genuine intimacy came under scrutiny. In July 2010, the Battersea Arts Centre hosted the *One on One Festival*, a collection of bespoke encounters and experiences for individuals. At its centre was the year's most controversial piece, *Internal* by Belgian collective Ontroerend Goed (literally, *Feel Estate*). Originally experienced in a hotel conference room as part of the Edinburgh Fringe Festival, *Internal* moved its audience from a seemingly private, intimate moment resembling a speed date or confessional session into a more public space akin to group therapy. Although it relied on its theatricality, the effects were all too real, with audience members emerging half-giddy with love or intensely angry at the betrayal suffered.

Internal relied on being a conveyor belt, mass-producing personalised experiences. So too did *You Me Bum Bum Train*, winner of this year's Oxford Samuel Beckett Trust Award, which made a fairground ride of theatre, plonking audience members in a rickety wheelchair to speed them through a dizzying maze of social situations and casting them as all manner of heroes: clergymen giving sermons, ministers facing the press, rock stars, burglars and celebrated authors. It was an exuberant carousel of fantasies treating you to the experiences of someone else's lifetime.

The year may well, however, mark the end of an exciting period of risk and enquiry. June 2010 saw the Arts Council England's subsidy of all Regularly Funded Organisations (RFOs) cut by 0.5 per cent. It was further compounded by a letter sent from the Arts Council England's chief executive, Alan Davey, to all RFOs in July requesting that they brace themselves for a 10 per cent reduction in funding for the next financial year. Estimates for the cuts to the Department for Culture, Media and Sport have been as high as 40 per cent, with the most likely scenario a 25 to 30 per cent cut over a four-year period. The effects of that would be catastrophic – this past year might emerge as a precious vintage after all.

AWARDS

2010 LAURENCE OLIVIER AWARDS

Best Actor – Mark Rylance for *Jerusalem* at the Royal Court and the Apollo
Best Actress – Rachel Weisz for *A Streetcar Named Desire* at the Donmar Warehouse
Best Actor in a Supporting Role – Eddie Redmayne for *Red* at the Donmar Warehouse
Best Actress in a Supporting Role – Ruth Wilson for *A Streetcar Named Desire* at the Donmar Warehouse
Best New Play – *The Mountaintop* by Katori Hall at Theatre 503 and the Trafalgar Studios
Best New Comedy – *The Priory* at the Royal Court
Best Revival – *Cat on a Hot Tin Roof* at the Novello
Best Actor in a Musical – Aneurin Barnard for *Spring Awakening* at the Novello
Best Actress in a Musical – Samantha Spiro for *Hello, Dolly!* at the Open Air Theatre
Best Performance in a Supporting Role in a Musical – Iwan Rheon for *Spring Awakening* at the Novello
Best New Musical – *Spring Awakening* at the Novello
Best Musical Revival – *Hello, Dolly!* at the Open Air Theatre
Best New Dance Production – The Brandstrup-Rojo Project's *Goldberg* at the Royal Opera House
Outstanding Achievement in Dance – Rambert Dance Company for an outstanding year of new work
Best New Opera Production – The Royal Opera, *Tristan und Isolde* at the Royal Opera House
Outstanding Achievement in Opera – Nina Stemme for her performance in *Tristan und Isolde* at the Royal Opera House
Outstanding Achievement in an Affiliate Theatre – *Cock* at the Royal Court
Best Entertainment – *Morecambe* at the Duchess
Best Director – Rupert Goold for *Enron* at the Royal Court and the Noel Coward
Best Theatre Choreographer – Stephen Mear for *Hello Dolly!* at the Open Air Theatre
Best Set Design – *Jerusalem* at the Royal Court and the Apollo, designed by Ultz
Best Lighting Design – *Burnt by the Sun* at the National Theatre, designed by Mark Henderson
Best Sound Design – *Spring Awakening* at the Novello, designed by Brian Ronan
Best Costume Design – *Priscilla: Queen of the Desert* at the Palace, designed by Tim Chappel and Lizzy Gardiner
Audience Award for Most Popular Show (as voted by users of officiallondontheatre.co.uk) – *Wicked* at the Apollo Victoria
Outstanding Acheivement – Michael Codron
Special Award – Dame Maggie Smith

CRITICS' CIRCLE AWARDS FOR 2009

Best Actor – Mark Rylance for *Jerusalem* at the Royal Court
Best Actress – Rachel Weisz for *A Streetcar Named Desire* at the Donmar Warehouse
The John and Wendy Trewin Award for Best Shakespearean Performance – Jude Law for *Hamlet* at the Donmar West End at Wyndham's Theatre
The Jack Tinker Award for Most Promising Newcomer – Tom Sturridge for *Punk Rock* at the Lyric Hammersmith
Best New Play – *Jerusalem* by Jez Butterworth at the Royal Court
The Peter Hepple Award for Best Musical – *Spring Awakening* at the Lyric Hammersmith and the Novello
Best Director – Rupert Goold for *Enron* at the Minerva Theatre, Chichester, and the Royal Court
Best Designer – Christopher Oram for *Red* at the Donmar Warehouse
Most Promising Playwright – Alia Bano for *Shades* at the Royal Court

EVENING STANDARD THEATRE AWARDS FOR 2009

Best Actor – Mark Rylance for *Jerusalem* at the Royal Court
The Natasha Richardson Award for Best Actress – Rachel Weisz for *A Streetcar Named Desire* at the Donmar Warehouse
The Milton Shulman Award for Outstanding Newcomer – Lenny Henry for *Othello* at the Trafalgar Studios
Best Play – *Jerusalem* by Jez Butterworth at the Royal Court
The Ned Sherrin Award for Best Musical – *Hello, Dolly!* at the Open Air Theatre
The Sydney Edwards Award for Best Director – Rupert Goold for *Enron* at the Royal Court
Best Design – Mamoru Iriguchi for *Mincemeat* at Cordy House, Shoreditch
The Charles Wintour Award for Most Promising Playwright – Alia Bano for *Shades* at the Royal Court
Special Award – Sir Ian McKellen

WEATHER

There were many exceptional weather events between mid-2009 and mid-2010. Statistically, the 2009–10 winter was the coldest and snowiest for 31 years, but was cold and snowy only in comparison with the relatively mild and snow-free winters of the last quarter-century. Were we able to pick it up and transplant it into, say, the 1940s, 1950s or 1960s, it would have scarcely looked out of place.

In middle latitudes of the northern hemisphere the winter weather is controlled by the jet stream. This is a conveyor-belt of winds in the upper atmosphere which drives the weather systems that deliver day-to-day weather. In some years the jet stream is powerful and blows hard and true from west to east. In Britain such a winter will be characterised by an endless succession of Atlantic storms, delivering frequent rain and wind, while temperatures remain resolutely above average. In other years the jet stream is relatively weak, and like a sluggish river it will meander widely on its travels. It still flows essentially from west to east, but it will stray deep into the sub-tropics, then into polar latitudes, and then back to the sub-tropics. In winter 2009–10, the UK found itself on the cold side of one of those meanders, and that resulted in Atlantic depressions heading across Spain and into the Mediterranean. This left the backdoor open for north-easterly winds to blow straight out of the Arctic, bringing severe frosts and heavy snow with them.

NEWSWORTHY EVENTS

There were several flooding episodes during the late-summer and autumn of 2009, but they all paled into relative insignificance in the wake of the Cumbrian floods in November. The Cumbrian floods triggered by the downpour on 19–20 November 2009 resulted in the death of a police officer in Workington; large parts of Cockermouth were inundated, three road bridges were washed away and a further 16 rendered unsafe.

Severe cold and snow were the main features of the winter, and night-time readings of −18°C or below were recorded in the Scottish highlands in each month from December 2009 to March 2010 – an unprecedented circumstance. Heavy snow fell widely in England and Wales on 18 and 21 December, and 6 and 13 January. The heaviest falls in Scotland were during the last ten days of December, the last week of February and the last few days of March. Water shortages developed during the first six months of 2010 in those areas normally blessed with excessive rainfall, including west and south-west Scotland, north-west England, north Wales, and parts of Northern Ireland, and reservoir levels in these districts were worryingly low by the end of June. The six-month rainfall total in north-west England was the lowest since April–September 1995.

THE YEAR 2009

The central England temperature for the entire year was 10.1°C, which is 0.3°C above the average for the standard reference period 1971–2000, and this was within one decimal point of the value for 2008. Every year since 1996 has posted an above-average mean temperature. Rainfall, averaged over England and Wales, totalled 968mm over the year, some 4 per cent above the long-term normal, the lowest annual figure for three years. The sunshine aggregate of 1,661 hours, again averaged over England and Wales, was 9 per cent above normal – more than in each of the preceding two years, but marginally less than in 2006.

TEMPERATURE

Both July and August 2009 had mean temperatures close to the long-term average, but this masked the fact that days were often rather cool whereas nights were consistently warm. September, October and November were all warm months, and the autumn quarter ranked just below the warmest on record. Mild weather continued into early-December, but there was a dramatic change during the second week and from then until the middle of March temperatures were consistently below the average. December 2009 averaged 2.0°C below the 1971–2000 mean and was the coldest since 1996, January was 3.0°C below average and the coldest since 1987, while February was 1.4°C below average and the coldest since 1996. The winter quarter ended up 2.1°C below average, and it was thus the coldest winter since 1978–9.

Each of the spring months of 2010 was within half a degree of the long-term mean, but June was a notably warm month. The highest individual temperature of 2009 was 32.0°C at Hampton (Greater London) on 1 July, while the lowest was −18.4°C at Altnaharra (Sutherland) on 9 February and again at Braemar (Aberdeenshire) on 29 December; the lowest daytime maximum was −12.2°C at Braemar on December 29. In January 2010 the temperature fell to −22.3°C early on 8 January at Altnaharra, and the daytime maximum that day was −13.5°C.

Weather statistics, 2009

	Mean Temp. °C	*Diff. from normal* °C	*Rainfall (mm)*	*Proportion of ave. %*	*Sunshine hours*	*Proportion of ave. %*
England	9.7	+0.3	948	104	1,672	109
Wales	9.3	+0.3	1,148	104	1,545	102
Scotland	9.1	+0.6	1,137	119	1,440	112
Northern Ireland	10.1	+0.4	1,025	115	1,484	110
United Kingdom	9.5	+0.4	980	109	1,573	109

MEAN MONTHLY TEMPERATURE (°C)

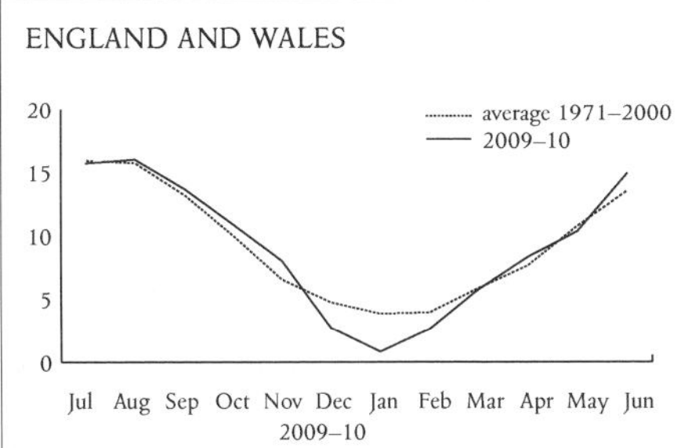

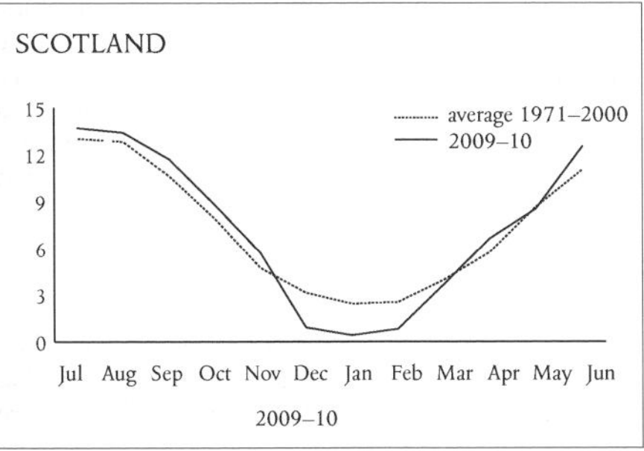

RAINFALL

July and August 2009 were both exceptionally wet in northern and western parts of the UK, and there were many instances of short-lived flooding following heavy downpours. At Alston (Cumbria) 116mm of rain fell in 48 hours on 16–17 July, and near Fochabers (Moray) 126mm was logged on 3 September. However, after the first few days September was generally dry, and October was also dry over most of England and Wales. November was, averaged nationally, the wettest since 1970, but many long-standing records were broken in the western half of the country, and destructive floods followed a long-lasting downpour over the Lake District, with Cockermouth in west Cumbria being particularly badly hit. At Seathwaite in Borrowdale 378mm of rain fell in just 34 hours, and new national records were established for rainfall in 24 hours, 48 hours, 72 hours, one week, and one calendar month. The winter months were rather wet in eastern and southern districts, but generally dry in the west and north, and there was a general shortage of rainfall over most parts of the UK during April, May and June 2010.

MEAN MONTHLY RAINFALL (MM)

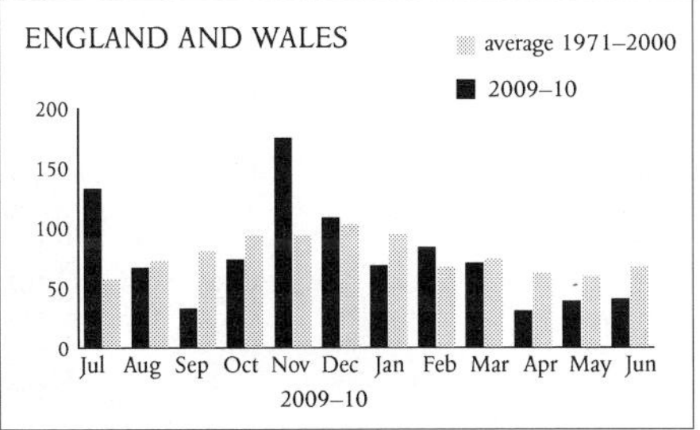

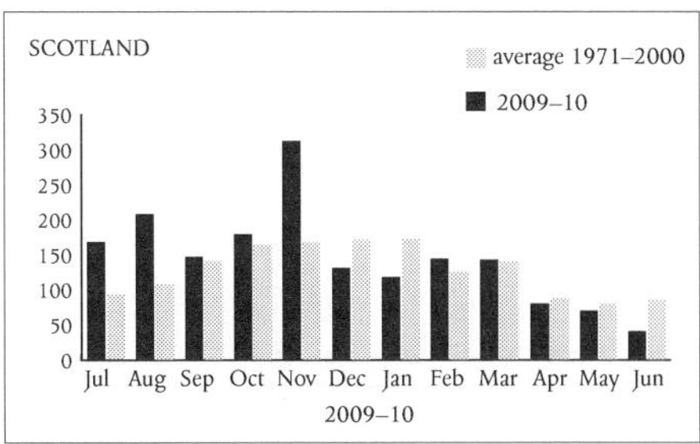

SUNSHINE

For the third year running there was a marked sunshine deficit in most parts of the country during July and August 2009, although the latter month was appreciably less gloomy than August 2008. September was generally brighter, except in north-west Scotland where Stornoway registered its dullest such month in 130 years of records. October was rather cloudy, while November was bright in the east but dull in the west. By contrast, the three winter months were rather cloudy in eastern districts, but exceptionally sunny in western parts of the UK, and new high monthly records were established in Cornwall in both December and January. Averaged nationally, April was the fifth sunniest in the last 100 years (though not quite as sunny as the record-breaking month of April 2007), while June was the sunniest since 1975 and the fourth sunniest in the last 100 years.

MONTHLY SUNSHINE (HOURS)

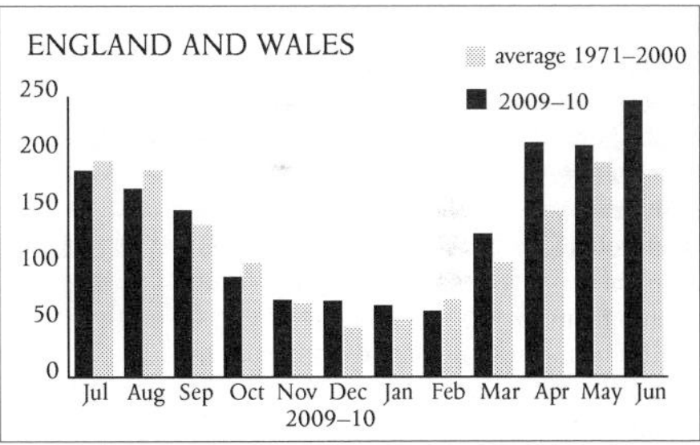

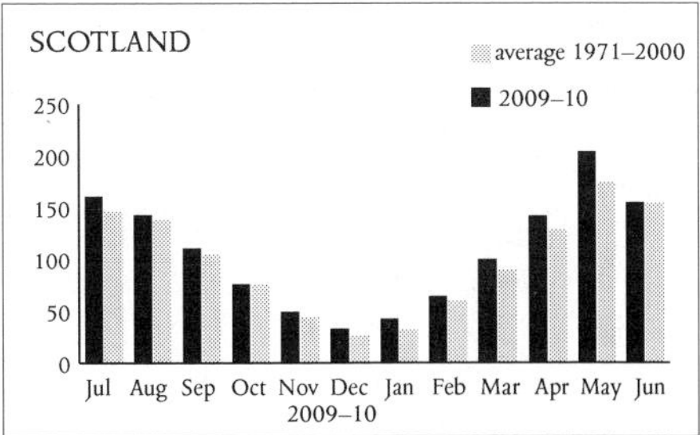

UK WEATHER STATIONS

Given below are temperature, rainfall and sunshine at selected climatological stations for July 2009 to June 2010.

Ht height of station above mean sea-level
Temp mean monthly air temperature
Rain total monthly rainfall
Sun total monthly sunshine duration

		July 2009			*August 2009*			*September 2009*			*October 2009*		
	Ht m	*Temp °C*	*Rain mm*	*Sun hrs*	*Temp °C*	*Rain mm*	*Sun hrs*	*Temp °C*	*Rain mm*	*Sun hrs*	*Temp °C*	*Rain mm*	*Sun hrs*
Stornoway	15	14.4	134	146	14.0	120	96	12.7	86	65	10.1	138	74
Aberdeen	65	15.1	105	145	15.1	54	129	13.1	103	120	10.1	181	88
Glasgow	59	15.7	135	153	15.1	211	116	13.3	95	104	10.5	131	96
Belfast	68	15.5	101	132	15.5	176	102	13.3	32	119	11.5	76	69
Durham	102	15.6	111	132	16.1	26	131	13.7	22	107	10.7	29	74
York	8	16.0	129	183	16.9	53	158	14.1	27	142	11.3	44	93
Manchester	69	15.9	153	124	16.1	53	121	13.5	55	96	10.9	48	73
Holyhead	10	15.8	113	176	15.8	103	136	14.1	29	127	12.5	73	88
Nottingham	117	16.3	122	155	16.9	56	151	14.3	23	125	11.5	58	83
Norwich	32	17.2	48	207	18.5	11	196	15.2	14	130	11.7	47	77
Birmingham	140	16.3	118	157	16.8	47	156	14.3	20	127	11.7	42	83
Cardiff	46	16.3	188	142	16.5	69	144	14.5	20	158	12.5	71	91
Bristol	42	16.9	135	167	17.0	39	166	14.9	19	156	12.3	59	96
London	137	17.1	77	156	18.0	55	155	15.2	66	121	12.1	37	74
Bournemouth	10	16.7	75	184	16.7	26	179	14.5	41	169	12.3	79	91
Camborne	86	15.7	222	156	15.9	68	124	14.3	38	163	12.9	93	96

		November 2009			*December 2009*			*January 2010*			*February 2010*		
	Ht	*Temp*	*Rain*	*Sun*	*Temp*	*Rain*	*Sun*	*Temp*	*Rain*	*Sun*	*Temp*	*Rain*	*Sun*
Stornoway	15	7.5	173	46	4.5	116	32	3.8	89	49	3.3	57	50
Aberdeen	65	6.7	149	71	2.0	82	37	2.1	76	42	1.9	88	78
Glasgow	59	6.9	251	53	1.5	73	33	1.3	59	67	1.7	78	75
Belfast	68	7.5	130	62	3.3	53	61	2.1	62	55	2.6	56	57
Durham	102	7.7	104	74	2.5	43	70	1.4	39	64	2.1	45	55
York	8	8.0	92	78	2.7	52	79	1.2	45	53	2.4	54	50
Manchester	69	7.9	131	50	2.9	71	66	0.9	46	62	2.2	59	56
Holyhead	10	9.6	199	49	5.3	87	43	3.5	55	67	3.9	39	92
Nottingham	117	8.3	117	81	3.3	74	78	1.6	51	67	2.5	49	41
Norwich	32	8.9	102	84	3.6	72	73	1.3	47	58	2.3	73	59
Birmingham	140	8.7	110	75	3.1	55	82	1.3	58	74	2.9	42	59
Cardiff	46	9.9	150	50	4.7	80	61	2.3	65	69	4.3	46	75
Bristol	42	9.3	213	58	3.9	77	61	1.9	51	70	3.9	59	56
London	137	9.2	159	68	3.7	89	76	1.5	65	67	3.2	108	53
Bournemouth	10	9.9	138	68	4.3	140	74	1.7	57	69	4.3	77	59
Camborne	86	10.3	194	57	6.5	96	81	4.3	109	104	5.5	63	95

		March 2010			*April 2010*			*May 2010*			*June 2010*		
	Ht	*Temp*	*Rain*	*Sun*	*Temp*	*Rain*	*Sun*	*Temp*	*Rain*	*Sun*	*Temp*	*Rain*	*Sun*
Stornoway	15	6.1	61	91	7.1	72	113	8.9	68	158	12.9	28	131
Aberdeen	65	5.5	47	112	8.1	36	139	9.3	59	184	13.3	23	109
Glasgow	59	5.5	76	112	8.7	83	166	10.6	22	199	15.3	39	203
Belfast	68	5.7	70	125	8.7	34	149	10.7	34	201	15.0	47	179
Durham	102	5.9	30	121	8.8	8	139	10.1	25	147	14.4	21	157
York	8	6.2	45	143	8.7	20	164	10.5	10	185	15.3	30	213
Manchester	69	6.2	50	117	8.5	28	162	10.4	14	154	15.1	36	214
Holyhead	10	6.3	77	147	8.8	17	223	10.8	38	272	14.7	30	252
Nottingham	117	6.5	50	124	9.3	38	159	11.1	23	173	15.7	50	195
Norwich	32	6.4	31	120	9.2	19	208	10.3	22	213	14.9	15	217
Birmingham	140	6.3	43	140	9.1	23	193	11.0	28	192	15.5	68	243
Cardiff	46	6.3	46	135	9.2	23	222	11.5	47	216	15.5	18	261
Bristol	42	6.7	42	133	9.9	27	226	12.3	31	196	16.5	26	265
London	137	6.7	41	124	10.0	25	190	11.5	86	163	16.5	29	201
Bournemouth	10	6.3	72	121	8.7	34	246	11.2	16	189	15.5	29	279
Camborne	86	6.7	77	139	9.1	36	231	11.1	52	210	14.7	34	286

METEOROLOGICAL OBSERVATIONS IN LONDON *(Hampstead Observatory)*

Maximum temperature is for the period 9am to 9pm; minimum temperature is for the period 9pm to 9am; the 'rainfall day' is the 24 hours starting at 9am on the day of entry; the 'wet hours' column counts all clock-hours during the rainfall day during which 0.2mm or more has fallen; sunshine is for the calendar day. All times are GMT.

July 2009

Day	*Temperature* Min °C	Max °C	*Rain* mm	*Wet* hours	*Sun* hours
1	15.1	27.1	0.0	0	8.6
2	14.1	27.9	0.4	2	11.6
3	18.0	24.4	0.0	2	3.8
4	13.8	24.0	0.0	0	8.1
5	15.2	23.3	0.2	1	6.2
6	13.6	21.0	4.4	6	5.0
7	13.3	18.7	9.0	9	3.4
8	11.6	18.9	0.7	2	2.1
9	10.0	18.1	0.2	1	4.7
10	9.4	20.8	0.0	0	7.5
11	13.8	20.6	8.6	12	0.5
12	13.8	22.1	0.0	0	5.3
13	13.1	21.1	0.0	0	5.4
14	13.3	22.1	1.8	4	5.7
15	13.6	21.0	1.5	4	2.0
16	12.5	22.8	11.9	4	6.6
17	13.8	18.9	2.9	4	2.5
18	12.5	20.2	0.0	0	5.9
19	11.9	19.5	1.1	1	2.8
20	11.4	20.6	2.9	5	5.3
21	13.4	21.5	0.7	2	1.0
22	13.8	20.8	0.2	1	5.1
23	13.4	20.6	7.3	6	4.4
24	12.5	18.3	12.5	5	4.4
25	11.8	22.8	0.0	0	8.1
26	12.7	20.1	6.2	12	2.5
27	11.7	19.9	0.4	2	2.9
28	11.3	20.3	1.1	3	6.5
29	14.2	20.3	3.1	4	2.8
30	11.1	18.6	0.2	1	7.5
31	11.1	21.3	0.0	1	8.2

August 2009

Day	*Temperature* Min °C	Max °C	*Rain* mm	*Wet* hours	*Sun* hours
1	16.2	19.4	0.7	3	0.6
2	10.5	20.0	0.0	0	6.9
3	11.3	21.4	0.4	2	5.8
4	15.8	20.7	0.0	0	0.1
5	16.9	26.3	0.0	0	5.1
6	16.4	26.2	45.3	10	4.0
7	14.6	21.5	0.0	2	6.1
8	11.6	23.2	0.0	0	7.0
9	15.9	24.7	0.0	0	6.0
10	15.1	21.1	0.0	0	3.0
11	14.7	23.9	0.0	0	5.7
12	14.9	20.7	2.6	5	0.5
13	15.1	22.7	0.0	0	5.1
14	14.3	21.6	0.0	0	2.4
15	14.6	21.7	0.0	0	2.9
16	14.4	23.8	0.0	0	6.1
17	12.5	21.9	0.0	0	6.2
18	13.1	23.7	0.0	0	6.9
19	14.0	27.5	0.0	0	10.1
20	15.8	21.5	0.0	0	3.9
21	12.0	19.6	0.9	2	5.8
22	10.7	21.0	0.0	0	6.7
23	16.1	26.0	0.0	0	10.0
24	14.7	22.9	0.0	0	4.6
25	11.6	20.2	0.9	2	5.0
26	13.7	21.7	1.8	5	2.0
27	15.3	21.7	0.0	0	3.9
28	11.4	18.3	2.6	6	5.4
29	8.5	19.6	0.0	0	7.4
30	9.4	18.2	0.0	0	2.5
31	15.4	24.4	0.2	1	5.2

September 2009

Day	*Temperature* Min °C	Max °C	*Rain* mm	*Wet* hours	*Sun* hours
1	13.8	20.2	1.1	2	4.4
2	12.6	17.2	11.2	11	1.2
3	12.4	17.9	0.2	2	3.5
4	9.7	17.5	0.0	0	6.1
5	9.5	18.9	0.0	0	5.6
6	12.3	19.3	0.0	0	3.6
7	13.7	20.3	0.0	0	1.0
8	16.2	26.6	0.0	0	7.2
9	12.8	18.3	0.0	0	4.2
10	8.6	19.4	0.0	0	5.6
11	9.5	19.2	0.0	0	3.4
12	11.0	21.3	0.0	0	8.2
13	10.1	16.1	0.0	0	0.3
14	11.5	19.2	0.0	0	3.5
15	12.7	15.0	53.2	13	0.0
16	12.4	18.6	0.0	0	4.2
17	10.5	15.7	0.0	0	1.2
18	10.4	19.0	0.0	0	7.0
19	12.1	23.0	0.0	0	4.3
20	12.4	19.8	0.2	1	3.4
21	10.5	20.4	0.0	0	5.6
22	10.6	19.2	0.0	0	3.1
23	13.6	17.5	0.0	0	1.5
24	9.7	19.2	0.0	0	7.1
25	8.2	19.9	0.0	0	8.2
26	8.2	19.5	0.0	0	5.2
27	8.2	20.7	0.0	0	7.4
28	11.0	18.5	0.0	0	1.5
29	10.1	21.0	0.0	0	3.8
30	12.2	16.8	0.0	0	0.0

October 2009

Day	*Temperature* Min °C	Max °C	*Rain* mm	*Wet* hours	*Sun* hours
1	12.2	16.6	0.0	0	3.2
2	6.4	16.7	0.0	0	5.2
3	11.0	15.5	0.0	0	0.2
4	8.6	15.8	0.2	1	3.2
5	10.9	13.4	5.7	7	0.0
6	12.3	18.0	6.6	6	0.1
7	10.6	12.5	8.6	7	0.4
8	5.8	15.3	0.0	0	7.2
9	6.6	13.3	3.3	5	1.5
10	11.1	17.5	0.2	1	3.0
11	10.8	16.6	0.2	1	1.4
12	6.6	15.0	0.0	0	4.6
13	5.8	16.0	0.2	1	6.4
14	9.8	13.1	0.0	0	0.2
15	8.2	16.6	0.2	1	4.8
16	9.6	13.6	0.0	0	2.1
17	6.2	12.0	0.0	0	0.9
18	3.5	12.3	0.0	0	3.2
19	4.9	11.4	0.0	0	0.0
20	5.7	13.0	1.8	2	0.0
21	10.9	13.2	0.4	2	0.0
22	9.8	16.2	0.0	0	2.0
23	9.0	16.9	1.8	4	5.0
24	12.7	17.1	0.2	1	0.4
25	10.2	16.7	0.0	0	5.5
26	10.4	16.9	4.2	7	5.0
27	11.6	17.7	0.0	0	2.6
28	10.7	17.6	0.0	0	0.7
29	10.6	17.1	0.0	0	3.1
30	10.2	15.1	2.4	3	1.6
31	11.2	17.2	2.0	3	1.8

November 2009

Day	Temperature Min °C	Max °C	Rain mm	Wet hours	Sun hours
1	10.8	15.7	12.3	0	0.3
2	4.9	12.7	4.0	3	5.7
3	8.0	12.7	4.4	7	0.7
4	4.0	11.5	0.7	10	4.9
5	6.6	11.7	0.0	3	1.7
6	7.4	10.4	7.7	0	0.0
7	3.4	10.4	2.0	5	6.5
8	6.1	8.9	0.2	4	1.2
9	3.0	7.9	0.0	1	2.9
10	2.2	7.8	0.5	0	0.0
11	6.3	9.3	2.0	3	1.0
12	7.1	13.4	11.5	5	2.9
13	9.7	14.6	9.3	9	0.0
14	8.4	11.8	13.5	11	1.1
15	7.2	13.6	5.7	8	4.8
16	8.9	13.1	1.3	7	2.6
17	8.2	13.0	0.0	0	4.1
18	9.6	13.3	0.0	0	0.0
19	11.9	13.9	1.3	0	3.8
20	11.9	13.7	1.5	3	0.3
21	9.2	15.1	11.2	3	0.8
22	7.8	10.7	8.8	13	1.8
23	7.5	12.8	2.2	5	0.9
24	7.6	13.4	7.3	3	0.0
25	8.0	11.1	0.7	6	5.4
26	6.1	10.0	0.0	2	3.8
27	4.1	8.0	4.4	0	3.1
28	3.7	8.4	15.9	5	4.7
29	4.5	7.0	29.5	11	0.7
30	3.9	5.7	0.4	2	1.9

December 2009

Day	Temperature Min °C	Max °C	Rain mm	Wet hours	Sun hours
1	–0.3	6.2	1.7	1	5.4
2	4.9	10.8	12.2	10	1.5
3	6.5	6.8	0.9	3	0.0
4	0.4	8.4	4.4	5	4.8
5	5.8	10.3	8.7	8	3.3
6	9.5	10.6	1.1	6	3.8
7	6.6	10.4	3.5	5	0.0
8	3.6	8.9	2.4	6	3.8
9	8.9	11.2	0.7	1	1.1
10	5.5	10.2	0.2	2	6.3
11	2.5	6.3	0.0	1	1.7
12	3.6	7.5	0.2	1	3.6
13	2.9	6.2	1.5	2	2.3
14	0.9	5.1	0.4	3	2.9
15	0.0	2.5	0.0	0	2.4
16	–3.7	1.3	5.2	8	0.4
17	–0.1	3.4	0.2	3	2.2
18	–1.9	0.3	2.2	4	3.6
19	–4.4	1.7	0.2	1	6.3
20	–4.1	1.3	1.7	3	6.3
21	–2.2	1.8	3.1	6	0.0
22	–1.2	1.6	3.3	6	1.6
23	–2.5	4.0	11.8	13	2.4
24	1.1	4.9	0.4	4	0.1
25	0.7	3.4	1.5	0	2.0
26	2.9	8.2	0.2	3	1.1
27	3.5	6.6	0.0	0	1.4
28	–1.0	4.7	0.2	0	5.2
29	1.2	3.3	13.1	13	0.0
30	2.6	3.7	7.9	16	0.0
31	1.9	2.9	0.0	4	0.2

January 2010

Day	Temperature Min °C	Max °C	Rain mm	Wet hours	Sun hours
1	–2.2	2.6	0.0	0	6.1
2	–2.7	4.8	0.0	0	5.8
3	–1.7	2.3	0.0	0	5.3
4	–5.2	1.9	0.0	0	6.4
5	–5.0	0.6	0.0	0	1.1
6	–0.7	–0.5	0.2	1	0.0
7	–6.4	–0.1	2.5	3	1.3
8	–4.3	–0.6	2.3	4	2.9
9	–4.8	–1.0	0.5	2	2.9
10	–1.0	0.8	2.1	6	0.0
11	–0.8	0.0	0.7	3	0.0
12	–0.4	0.8	0.5	2	0.0
13	–1.3	0.5	8.1	8	0.0
14	–0.9	2.3	8.8	10	0.0
15	–0.3	5.5	0.5	2	0.0
16	3.0	7.1	12.9	10	0.0
17	2.2	9.4	0.2	1	6.2
18	2.2	6.1	0.0	0	0.5
19	5.8	6.2	0.0	0	0.0
20	2.6	2.6	0.5	2	0.0
21	1.6	5.8	2.5	5	2.9
22	3.5	7.3	9.2	17	0.0
23	5.0	5.2	0.0	0	0.0
24	2.3	4.9	3.0	9	0.8
25	2.1	3.2	1.4	2	0.3
26	–0.5	1.3	0.0	0	6.1
27	–2.9	4.6	1.4	1	0.5
28	3.0	6.7	9.5	10	2.5
29	2.8	4.3	0.7	3	2.3
30	–3.0	4.1	0.0	0	7.2
31	–3.6	2.5	0.2	1	5.8

February 2010

Day	Temperature Min °C	Max °C	Rain mm	Wet hours	Sun hours
1	–2.1	4.9	0.7	3	6.9
2	–0.3	7.0	3.7	7	0.0
3	0.9	6.4	1.5	6	0.2
4	6.4	7.8	4.6	5	0.1
5	5.5	11.4	0.4	1	4.1
6	2.8	6.0	0.2	1	3.0
7	1.7	4.3	0.9	2	0.2
8	0.5	1.0	0.4	2	0.0
9	–1.4	4.5	0.2	1	4.2
10	–0.1	2.4	0.0	0	4.0
11	–2.3	2.2	1.3	4	5.3
12	–0.4	2.8	0.4	1	0.3
13	–0.5	2.5	1.1	3	1.4
14	–0.5	3.8	0.4	1	0.0
15	–1.9	2.8	9.0	7	0.3
16	1.9	3.8	22.4	19	0.0
17	1.1	8.3	0.0	0	5.9
18	–0.6	4.8	2.0	6	0.1
19	0.2	6.3	0.0	0	4.0
20	–2.5	6.4	0.4	2	5.1
21	–0.2	6.2	12.8	11	0.4
22	0.7	1.5	2.0	5	0.0
23	0.6	3.0	4.2	6	0.0
24	2.5	9.4	4.8	11	0.6
25	5.9	8.6	9.5	9	0.4
26	4.2	7.5	1.1	4	3.3
27	3.1	9.8	20.9	14	2.4
28	3.8	4.9	3.1	4	0.2

March 2010

Day	*Temperature* Min °C	Max °C	*Rain* mm	*Wet* hours	*Sun* hours
1	–0.9	9.9	0.0	0	6.5
2	0.8	10.1	0.0	0	7.9
3	0.6	5.4	0.0	0	4.8
4	0.6	6.5	0.0	0	5.4
5	–2.9	9.3	0.0	0	7.6
6	1.9	5.9	0.0	0	6.5
7	–4.0	4.1	0.0	0	8.1
8	–3.2	5.6	0.0	0	7.1
9	0.5	6.3	0.0	0	1.3
10	1.4	4.7	0.0	0	1.9
11	0.5	12.1	0.2	2	1.6
12	–0.1	8.9	0.7	3	1.7
13	2.3	8.2	0.0	0	1.8
14	2.6	11.8	0.0	0	5.6
15	2.1	13.1	0.0	0	7.0
16	2.6	12.5	0.0	0	7.8
17	5.0	14.2	0.0	0	6.9
18	6.0	16.3	1.2	3	6.0
19	7.7	11.3	3.0	7	2.2
20	10.4	12.2	6.7	13	0.0
21	4.8	13.1	0.0	0	6.6
22	5.4	11.3	0.9	3	3.1
23	2.6	12.2	7.6	9	4.3
24	8.2	15.6	0.0	0	2.3
25	10.3	14.1	6.9	8	0.3
26	6.2	12.3	2.1	2	3.7
27	6.3	12.5	1.2	3	1.6
28	4.3	13.4	5.1	9	3.2
29	7.0	11.3	3.7	6	0.0
30	7.2	11.2	5.3	8	0.9
31	2.4	5.7	1.2	3	0.0

April 2010

Day	*Temperature* Min °C	Max °C	*Rain* mm	*Wet* hours	*Sun* hours
1	0.7	8.5	3.5	6	5.3
2	4.6	10.2	6.2	8	1.6
3	2.8	11.5	1.5	8	3.1
4	4.1	11.9	0.2	1	3.7
5	2.9	12.5	0.0	0	0.8
6	6.7	15.3	0.0	0	10.2
7	8.2	10.5	1.1	3	0.1
8	3.1	16.7	0.0	0	10.0
9	6.4	18.4	0.0	0	9.3
10	7.0	15.9	0.0	0	8.5
11	4.4	13.4	0.0	0	7.1
12	4.9	13.4	0.0	0	3.7
13	3.1	14.3	0.0	0	10.0
14	5.2	11.3	0.0	0	1.5
15	3.3	13.4	0.0	0	6.8
16	4.0	12.9	0.0	0	5.6
17	2.5	16.7	0.0	0	10.3
18	4.8	18.8	0.0	0	10.9
19	6.5	14.3	0.0	0	4.5
20	3.6	14.7	0.0	0	9.3
21	1.4	12.9	0.0	0	10.6
22	2.3	13.3	0.0	0	10.6
23	4.0	16.4	0.0	0	10.5
24	5.0	20.0	1.1	2	10.3
25	9.9	18.2	0.2	1	2.9
26	7.5	17.0	0.0	0	2.2
27	7.4	20.2	0.0	0	8.3
28	10.2	20.6	0.0	0	7.2
29	10.5	18.1	2.9	6	2.9
30	6.8	14.4	7.9	5	2.3

May 2010

Day	Min °C	Max °C	Rain mm	Wet hours	Sun hours
1	8.9	16.5	62.5	15	2.6
2	6.8	8.0	4.6	7	0.1
3	3.4	10.6	0.2	2	5.7
4	1.5	10.9	0.9	3	4.2
5	3.5	14.6	0.2	1	4.0
6	7.4	15.6	0.0	0	5.5
7	4.4	12.5	0.0	0	1.8
8	5.6	9.1	0.4	2	0.0
9	5.2	11.0	0.0	0	0.9
10	3.9	11.9	0.0	0	5.9
11	1.9	9.4	0.2	1	3.3
12	1.2	10.8	0.0	0	5.4
13	2.7	13.5	0.0	0	5.5
14	4.3	15.1	0.0	0	4.4
15	7.0	16.4	0.0	0	5.7
16	5.1	15.0	10.6	4	3.2
17	5.1	17.0	0.0	0	7.2
18	7.2	17.8	0.0	0	6.4
19	7.8	19.7	0.0	0	7.0
20	10.3	22.4	0.0	0	3.4
21	13.6	23.8	0.0	0	8.4
22	10.0	22.9	0.0	0	11.8
23	10.5	27.8	0.0	0	12.3
24	14.0	28.0	0.0	0	12.0
25	11.0	18.3	0.0	0	9.9
26	7.8	16.0	1.8	4	5.5
27	8.5	17.7	0.0	0	3.1
28	6.8	18.6	0.0	0	8.4
29	10.0	14.4	4.0	9	0.5
30	11.5	18.7	0.0	0	8.1
31	9.2	15.7	0.0	0	0.7

June 2010

Day	Min °C	Max °C	Rain mm	Wet hours	Sun hours
1	10.3	13.0	8.1	11	0.0
2	8.6	21.3	0.0	0	11.8
3	8.9	21.0	0.0	0	12.3
4	9.3	25.7	0.0	0	12.1
5	12.2	26.0	0.2	1	7.2
6	15.2	22.4	0.0	0	3.5
7	11.6	20.0	8.8	10	4.9
8	10.9	17.8	2.9	3	2.6
9	11.1	19.0	1.1	2	4.7
10	13.0	18.3	0.2	1	0.2
11	11.5	19.3	0.0	0	3.0
12	9.0	19.4	0.0	0	5.2
13	10.4	19.9	0.0	0	4.1
14	10.5	19.3	5.3	3	3.5
15	7.5	17.1	0.0	0	6.2
16	7.6	18.8	0.0	0	10.1
17	7.2	22.4	0.0	0	11.3
18	9.3	18.7	1.3	4	2.3
19	6.8	14.9	0.0	0	4.8
20	6.1	18.2	0.0	0	3.9
21	11.5	23.2	0.0	0	6.5
22	12.7	26.8	0.0	0	8.3
23	12.7	26.6	0.0	0	12.1
24	13.1	25.3	0.0	0	6.3
25	13.9	25.6	0.0	0	7.4
26	14.9	25.6	0.0	0	11.6
27	13.4	29.6	0.0	0	12.0
28	14.6	28.2	1.1	2	12.3
29	14.9	27.2	0.0	0	5.7
30	16.2	25.7	0.0	0	4.5

SPORTS RESULTS

ALPINE SKIING

WORLD CUP 2009–10

MEN
Downhill: Didier Cuche (Switzerland), 528pts
Slalom: Reinfried Herbst (Austria), 534pts
Giant Slalom: Ted Ligety (USA), 412pts
Super Giant Slalom: Erik Guay (Canada), 331pts
Overall: Carlo Janka (Switzerland), 1,179pts

WOMEN
Downhill: Lindsey Vonn (USA), 725pts
Slalom: Maria Riesch (Germany), 493pts
Giant Slalom: Kathrin Hoelzl (Germany), 471pts
Super Giant Slalom: Lindsey Vonn (USA), 620pts
Overall: Lindsey Vonn (USA), 1,671pts

AMERICAN FOOTBALL

AFC Championship 2009–10: Indianapolis Colts beat New York Jets 30–17
NFC Championship 2009–10: New Orleans Saints beat Minnesota Vikings 31–28
XLIV Superbowl 2010: New Orleans Saints beat Indianapolis Colts 31–17

ANGLING

BRITISH CHAMPIONSHIPS 2009
Individual: Adrian Goulding

TEAMS
First Division: Shakespeare Redditch
Second Division: Browning Hotrods
Third Division: Scunthorpe Blue
Ladies: Reading Angling Team Hydro

ASSOCIATION FOOTBALL

LEAGUE COMPETITIONS 2009–10

ENGLAND AND WALES
Premier League
1. Chelsea, 86pts
2. Manchester United, 85pts
3. Arsenal, 75pts
Relegated: Burnley, Hull City, Portsmouth

Championship
1. Newcastle United, 102pts
2. West Bromwich Albion, 91pts
Play-off winner and third promotion place: Blackpool
Relegated: Sheffield Wednesday, Plymouth Argyle, Peterborough United

League 1
1. Norwich City, 95pts
2. Leeds United, 86pts
Play-off winner and third promotion place: Millwall
Relegated: Gillingham, Wycombe Wanderers, Southend United, Stockport County

League 2
1. Notts County, 93pts
2. Bournemouth, 83pts
3. Rochdale, 82pts
Play-off winner and fourth promotion place: Dagenham & Redbridge
Relegated: Grimsby Town, Darlington

Football Conference
1. Stevenage Borough, 99pts
Play-off winner and second promotion place: Oxford United

Welsh Premier League
1. The New Saints, 82pts
2. Llanelli AFC, 80pts
3. Port Talbot Town, 65pts

Women's Premier League National Division
1. Arsenal, 61pts
2. Everton, 50pts
3. Chelsea, 49pts

SCOTLAND
Premier Division
1. Rangers, 87pts
2. Celtic, 81pts
Relegated: Falkirk

Division 1
1. Inverness Caledonian Thistle, 73pts
Relegated: Airdrie United, Ayr United

Division 2
1. Stirling Albion, 65pts
Also promoted: Cowdenbeath
Relegated: Arbroath, Clyde

Division 3
1. Livingston, 78pts
Play-off winner and second promotion place: Forfar Athletic
Bottom: Montrose

NORTHERN IRELAND
Premier League
1. Linfield, 74pts
2. Cliftonville, 69pts
3. Glentoran, 65pts

REPUBLIC OF IRELAND
Premier Division 2009: 1. Bohemians, 77pts; 2. Shamrock Rovers, 73pts; 3. Cork City, 60pts*; 4. Derry City, 59pts*; 5. Dundalk, 44pts*

*Cork City dissolved; Derry City relegated for FAI rule breaches; Dundalk therefore qualified for UEFA Europa League

FRANCE
Ligue 1: 1. Marseille, 78pts; 2. Lyon, 72pts; 3. Auxerre, 71pts

GERMANY
Bundesliga: 1. Bayern Munich, 70; 2. Schalke 04, 65pts; 3. Werder Bremen, 61pts

ITALY

Serie A: 1. Internazionale, 82pts; 2. Roma, 80pts; 3. AC Milan, 70pts

NETHERLANDS

Eredivisie: 1. FC Twente, 86pts; 2. Ajax, 85; 3. PSV Eindhoven, 78pts

SPAIN

La Liga: 1. Barcelona, 99pts; 2. Real Madrid, 96pts; 3. Valencia, 71pts

CUP COMPETITIONS 2009–10

ENGLAND

FA Cup final 2010: Chelsea beat Portsmouth 1–0
League Cup final 2010: Manchester United beat Aston Villa 2–1
Football League Trophy final 2010: Southampton beat Carlisle United 4–1
FA Vase final 2010: Whitley Bay beat Wroxham 6–1
FA Trophy final 2010: Barrow beat Stevenage Borough 2–1
Community Shield 2010: Manchester United beat Chelsea 3–1

WOMEN

FA Cup final 2010: Everton beat Arsenal 3–2
Premier League Cup final 2010: Leeds Carnegie beat Everton 3–1

WALES

FAW Welsh Cup final 2010: Bangor City beat Port Talbot Town 3–2
Welsh League Cup final 2010: The New Saints beat Rhyl 3–1

SCOTLAND

Scottish Cup final 2010: Dundee United beat Ross County 3–0
League Cup final 2010: Rangers beat St Mirren 1–0

NORTHERN IRELAND

Irish Cup final 2010: Linfield beat Portadown 2–1

EUROPE

Champions League final 2010: Internazionale beat Bayern Munich 2–0
UEFA Cup final 2010: Atletico Madrid beat Fulham 2–1 (aet)

WORLD PLAYER OF THE YEAR

2009 – Lionel Messi (Argentina)
2008 – Cristiano Ronaldo (Portugal)
2007 – Kaká (Brazil)
2006 – Fabio Cannavaro (Italy)
2005 – Ronaldinho (Brazil)
2004 – Ronaldinho (Brazil)
2003 – Zinedine Zidane (France)
2002 – Ronaldo (Brazil)
2001 – Luís Figo (Portugal)
2000 – Zinedine Zidane (France)
1999 – Rivaldo (Brazil)
1998 – Zinedine Zidane (France)
1997 – Ronaldo (Brazil)
1996 – Ronaldo (Brazil)
1995 – George Weah (Liberia)

WORLD CUP FINALS

South Africa, 11 June–11 July 2010

GROUP A

	P	*W*	*D*	*L*	*F*	*A*	*GD*	*PTS*
Uruguay	3	2	1	0	4	0	4	7
Mexico	3	1	1	1	3	2	1	4
South Africa	3	1	1	1	3	5	–2	4
France	3	0	1	2	1	4	–3	1

South Africa and Mexico drew 1–1
Uruguay and France drew 0–0
Uruguay beat South Africa 3–0
Mexico beat France 2–0
Uruguay beat Mexico 1–0
South Africa beat France 2–1

GROUP B

	P	*W*	*D*	*L*	*F*	*A*	*GD*	*PTS*
Argentina	3	3	0	0	7	1	6	9
South Korea	3	1	1	1	5	6	–1	4
Greece	3	1	0	2	2	5	–3	3
Nigeria	3	0	1	2	3	5	–2	1

Argentina beat Nigeria 1–0
South Korea beat Greece 2–0
Greece beat Nigeria 2–1
Argentina beat South Korea 4–1
Nigeria and South Korea drew 2–2
Argentina beat Greece 2–0

GROUP C

	P	*W*	*D*	*L*	*F*	*A*	*GD*	*PTS*
USA	3	1	2	0	4	3	1	5
England	3	1	2	0	2	1	1	5
Slovenia	3	1	1	1	3	3	0	4
Algeria	3	0	1	2	0	2	–2	1

England and USA drew 1–1
Slovenia beat Algeria 1–0
USA and Slovenia drew 2–2
England and Algeria drew 0–0
England beat Slovenia 1–0
USA beat Algeria 1–0

GROUP D

	P	*W*	*D*	*L*	*F*	*A*	*GD*	*PTS*
Germany	3	2	0	1	5	1	4	6
Ghana	3	1	1	1	2	2	0	4
Australia	3	1	1	1	3	6	–3	4
Serbia	3	1	0	2	2	3	–1	3

Germany beat Australia 4–0
Ghana beat Serbia 1–0
Serbia beat Germany 1–0
Ghana and Australia drew 1–1
Germany beat Ghana 1–0
Australia beat Serbia 2–1

GROUP E

	P	*W*	*D*	*L*	*F*	*A*	*GD*	*PTS*
Netherlands	3	3	0	0	5	1	4	9
Japan	3	2	0	1	4	2	2	6
Denmark	3	1	0	2	3	6	–3	3
Cameroon	3	0	0	3	2	5	–3	0

Netherlands beat Denmark 2–0
Japan beat Cameroon 1–0
Netherlands beat Japan 1–0
Denmark beat Cameroon 2–1
Japan beat Denmark 3–1
Netherlands beat Cameroon 2–1

GROUP F

	P	W	D	L	F	A	GD	PTS
Paraguay	3	1	2	0	3	1	2	5
Slovakia	3	1	1	1	4	5	−1	4
New Zealand	3	0	3	0	2	2	0	3
Italy	3	0	2	1	4	5	−1	2

Italy and Paraguay drew 1–1
New Zealand and Slovakia drew 1–1
Paraguay beat Slovakia 2–0
Italy and New Zealand drew 1–1
Slovakia beat Italy 3–2
Paraguay and New Zealand drew 0–0

GROUP G

	P	W	D	L	F	A	GD	PTS
Brazil	3	2	1	0	5	2	3	7
Portugal	3	1	2	0	7	0	7	5
Ivory Coast	3	1	1	1	4	3	1	4
North Korea	3	0	0	3	1	12	−11	0

Ivory Coast and Portugal drew 0–0
Brazil beat North Korea 2–1
Brazil beat Ivory Coast 3–1
Portugal beat North Korea 7–0
Portugal and Brazil drew 0–0
Ivory Coast beat North Korea 3–0

GROUP H

	P	W	D	L	F	A	GD	PTS
Spain	3	2	0	1	4	2	2	6
Chile	3	2	0	1	3	2	1	6
Switzerland	3	1	1	1	1	1	0	4
Honduras	3	0	1	2	0	3	−3	1

Chile beat Honduras 1–0
Switzerland beat Spain 1–0
Chile beat Switzerland 1–0
Spain beat Honduras 2–0
Spain beat Chile 2–1
Switzerland beat Honduras drew 0–0

ROUND OF 16
Uruguay beat South Korea 2–1
Ghana beat USA 2–1 (aet)
Netherlands beat Slovakia 2–1
Brazil beat Chile 3–0
Argentina beat Mexico 3–1
Germany beat England 4–1
Paraguay beat Japan 5–3 on penalties (0–0 aet)
Spain beat Portugal 1–0

QUARTER-FINALS
Uruguay beat Ghana 4–2 on penalties (1–1 aet)
Netherlands beat Brazil 2–1
Germany beat Argentina 4–0
Spain beat Paraguay 1–0

SEMI-FINALS
Netherlands beat Uruguay 3–2
Spain beat Germany 1–0

THIRD PLACE PLAY-OFF
Germany beat Uruguay 3–2

FINAL
Spain beat Netherlands 1–0 (aet)

ATHLETICS

EUROPEAN CROSS COUNTRY CHAMPIONSHIPS
Dublin, Ireland, 13 December 2009

SENIOR MEN (10km)
Individual: Alemayehu Bezabeh (Spain), 30min 45sec
Team: Spain, 34pts

U23 MEN (8km)
Individual: Noureddine Smail (France), 25min 11sec
Team: France 31pts

JUNIOR MEN (6km)
Individual: Jeroen D'Hoedt (Belgium), 18min 46sec
Team: Great Britain, 24pts

SENIOR WOMEN (8km)
Individual: Hayley Yelling (Great Britain), 27min 49sec
Team: Portugal, 25pts

U23 (6km)
Individual: Sultan Haydar (Turkey), 21min 14sec
Team: Great Britain, 22pts

JUNIOR WOMEN (4km)
Individual: Karoline Grovdal (Norway), 14min 10sec
Team: Russia, 47pts

UK INDOOR CHAMPIONSHIPS
Sheffield, 13–14 February 2010

MEN
60m: Dwain Chambers (Belgrave), 6.50sec
200m: Leon Baptiste (Enfield & Haringey), 20.90sec
400m: Richard Buck (City of York), 47.54sec
800m: Andrew Osagie (Harlow), 1min 50.21sec
1,500m: Colin McCourt (Dundee), 4min 04.83sec
3,000m: Andrew Vernon (Aldershot), 8min 00.70sec
60mH: Callum Priestley (Woodford Green), 7.69sec
High jump: Samson Oni (Belgrave), 2.25m
Pole vault: Steve Lewis (Newham), 5.56m
Long jump: Greg Rutherford (Milton Keynes), 7.94m
Triple jump: Tosin Oke (Nigeria), 16.76m
Shot: Mark Edwards (Birchfield), 17.40m

WOMEN
60m: Joice Maduaka (Woodford Grn), 7.29sec
200m: Joice Maduaka (Woodford Grn), 23.48sec
400m: Kim Wall (Basildon), 53.07sec
800m: Jenny Meadows (Wigan), 2min 00.91sec
1,500m: Helen Clitheroe (Preston), 4min 13.90sec
3,000m: Hazel Murphy (Ireland), 9min 02.09sec
60mH: Derval O'Rourke (Ireland), 8.11sec
High jump: Vikki Hubbard (Birchfield), 1.87m
Pole vault: Kate Dennison (Sale), 4.40m
Long jump: Kelly Proper (Ireland), 6.48m
Triple jump: Trecia Smith (Jamaica), 13.69m
Shot: Alison Rodger (Sale), 16.02m

ENGLISH NATIONAL CROSS COUNTRY CHAMPIONSHIPS
Parliament Hill Fields, London, 19 February 2010

SENIOR MEN (12km)
Individual: Andrew Vernon (Aldershot), 38min 01sec
Team: Aldershot, Farnham & Dist, 182pts

JUNIOR MEN (10km)
Individual: Nick Goolab (Belgrave), 33min 07sec
Team: Warrington, 62pts

SENIOR WOMEN (8km)
Individual: Stephanie Twell (Aldershot), 27min 52sec
Team: Charnwood, 73pts

JUNIOR WOMEN (6km)
Individual: Joanne Harvey (Exeter), 22min 06sec
Team: Aldershot, Farnham & Dist, 154pts

WORLD INDOOR CHAMPIONSHIPS
Doha, Qatar, 12–14 March 2010

MEN
60m: Dwain Chambers (Great Britain), 6.48sec
400m: Chris Brown (Bahamas), 46.64sec
800m: Abubaker Kaki (Sudan), 1min 46.23sec
1,500m: Deresse Mekonnen (Ethiopia), 3min 41.86sec
3,000m: Bernard Lagat (USA), 7min 37.97sec
60mH: Dayron Robles (Cuba), 7.34sec
4 × 400m: USA, 3min 03.40sec
High jump: Ivan Ukhov (Russia), 2.36m
Pole vault: Steve Hooker (Australia), 6.01m
Long jump: Fabrice Lapierre (Australia), 8.17m
Triple jump: Teddy Tamgho (France), 17.90m
Shot: Christian Cantwell (USA), 21.83m
Pentathlon: Brian Clay (USA), 6,204pts

WOMEN
60m: Veronica Campbell-Brown (Jamaica), 7.00sec
400m: Debbie Dunn (USA), 51.04sec
800m: Mariya Savinova (Russia), 1min 58.26sec
1,500m: Kalkidan Gezahegn (Ethiopia), 4min 08.14sec
3,000m: Meseret Defar (Ethiopia), 8min 51.17sec
60mH: Lolo Jones (USA), 7.72sec
4 × 400m: USA, 3min 27.34sec
High jump: Blanka Vlasic (Croatia), 2.00m
Pole vault: Fabiana Murer (Brazil), 4.80m
Long jump: Brittney Reese (USA), 6.70m
Triple jump: Olga Rypakova (Kazakhstan), 15.14m
Shot: Nadezhda Ostapchuk (Belarus), 20.85m
Heptathlon: Jessica Ennis (Great Britain), 4,937pts

IAAF WORLD CROSS COUNTRY CHAMPIONSHIPS
Bydgoszcz, Poland, 28 March 2010

SENIOR MEN (11.75km)
Individual: Joseph Ebuya (Kenya), 33min 00sec
Team: Kenya, 20pts

JUNIOR MEN (7.9km)
Individual: Caleb Ndiku (Kenya), 22min 07sec
Team: Kenya, 10pts

SENIOR WOMEN (7.9km)
Individual: Emily Chebet (Kenya), 24min 19sec
Team: Kenya, 14pts

JUNIOR WOMEN (5.98km)
Individual: Mercy Cherono (Kenya), 18min 47sec
Team: Kenya, 10pts

LONDON MARATHON
London, 25 April 2010

Men: Tsegaye Kebede (Ethiopia), 2hr 05min 19sec
Women: Liliya Shobukhova (Russia), 2hr 22min 00sec

EUROPEAN TEAM CHAMPIONSHIPS
Bergen, Norway, 19–20 June 2010

MEN
100m: Dwain Chambers (Great Britain), 9.99sec
200m: Martial Mbandjock (France), 20.55sec
400m: Martyn Rooney (Great Britain), 45.67sec
800m: Yuri Borzakovski (Russia), 1min 45.41sec
1,500m: Colin McCourt (Great Britain), 3min 46.70sec
3,000m: Jesús España (Spain), 8min 19.39sec
5,000m: Mo Farah (Great Britain), 13min 46.93sec
3,000mSt: Tomasz Szymkowiak (Poland), 8min 31.53sec
110mH: Andy Turner (Great Britain), 13.48sec
400mH: Dai Greene (Great Britain), 49.53sec
4 × 100m: Italy, 38.83sec
4 × 400m: Russia, 3min 01.72sec
High jump: Aleksandr Shustov (Russia), 2.28m
Pole vault: Renaud Lavillenie (France), 5.70m
Long jump: Pavel Shalin (Russia), 8.26m
Triple jump: Viktor Kuznetsov (Ukraine),17.26m
Shot: Tomasz Majewski (Poland), 20.63m
Discus: Robert Harting (Germany), 66.80m
Hammer: Pavel Krivitski (Belarus), 77.79m
Javelin: Matthias de Zordo (Germany), 83.30m

WOMEN
100m: Véronique Mang (France), 11.23 sec
200m: Yelizaveta Bryshina (Russia), 22.71sec
400m: Kseniya Ustalova (Russia), 51.79sec
800m: Nataliya Lupu (Ukraine), 2min 02.74sec
1,500m: Anna Mischenko (Ukraine), 4min 05.32sec
3,000m: Yelena Zadorozhnaya (Russia), 9min 08.42sec
5,000m: Sabrina Mockenhaupt (Germany), 15min 17.38sec
3,000mSt: Yuliya Zarudneva (Russia), 9min 23.00sec
100mH: Tatyana Dektyareva (Russia), 12.68sec
400mH: Natalya Antyukh (Russia), 55.27sec
4 × 100m: Russia, 42.98sec
4 × 400m: Russia, 3min 23.76sec
High jump: Antonietta Di Martino (Italy), 2.00m
Pole vault: Svetlana Feofanova (Russia), 4.65m
Long jump: Eloyse Lesueur (France), 6.78m
Triple jump: Olha Saladukha (Ukraine), 14.39m
Shot: Anna Avdeyeva (Russia), 19.14m
Discus: Nadine Müller (Germany), 63.53m
Hammer: Betty Heidler (Germany), 73.24m
Javelin: Christina Obergföll (Germany), 59.88m

Points: Russia, 379.5; Great Britain, 317; Germany, 304.5; France, 290; Ukraine, 287; Poland, 284; Italy, 283.5; Belarus 235; Greece, 187.5; Norway 175; Finland 150

UK TRIALS AND CHAMPIONSHIPS
Birmingham, 25–27 June 2010

MEN
100m: Dwain Chambers (Belgrave), 10.14sec
200m: Christian Malcolm (Cardiff), 20.77sec
400m: Martyn Rooney (Croydon), 44.99sec
800m: Michael Rimmer (Liverpool Pembroke), 1min 47.22sec
1,500m: Andy Baddeley (Harrow), 3min 41.49sec
5,000m: Chris Thompson (Aldershot, Farnham & District), 13min 48.15sec
10,000m: Steven Kiprotich (Uganda), 27min 58.03sec
3,000mSt: Luke Gunn (Derby), 8min 37.35sec
110mH: William Sharman (Belgrave), 13.45sec
400mH: Dai Greene (Swansea), 48.77sec
5,000m Walk: Alex Wright (Belgrave), 20min 11.09sec

High jump: Martyn Bernard (Wakefield), 2.28m
Pole vault: Joe Ive (Sutton), 5.35m
Long jump: Chris Tomlinson (Newham & Essex), 8.17m
Triple jump: Phillips Idowu (Belgrave), 17.12m
Shot: Carl Myerscough (Blackpool &Fylde), 19.77m
Discus: Brett Morse (Birchfield), 61.45m
Hammer: Alex Smith (Sale), 70.68m
Javelin: James Campbell (Cheltenham), 74.00m
**Decathlon:* David Guest (Bridgend), 7,727pts

WOMEN
100m: Laura Turner (Harrow), 11.41sec
200m: Laura Turner (Harrow), 23.66sec
400m: Lee McConnell (Shaftesbury Barnet), 51.55sec
800m: Jemma Simpson (Newquay & Par), 2min 01.50sec
1,500m: Hannah England (Oxford), 4min 33.23sec
5,000m: Freya Murray (Chester-Le-Street), 15min 48.75sec
10,000m: Jo Pavey (Exeter), 31min 51.91sec
3,000mSt: Barbara Parker (Norwich), 9min 37.77sec
100mH: Louise Hazel (Birchfield), 13.32sec
400mH: Perri Shakes Drayton (Victoria Park), 56.93sec
5,000m Walk: Jo Jackson (Redcar), 21min 52.95sec
High jump: Stephanie Pywell (Sale), 1.84m
Pole vault: Kate Dennison (Sale), 4.45m
Long jump: Jade Johnson (Herne Hill), 6.48m
Triple jump: Laura Samuel (Leicester), 13.52m
Shot: Eden Francis (Birchfield), 16.02m
Discus: Jade Nicholls (Shaftesbury Barnet), 57.81m
Hammer: Zoe Derham (Birchfield), 66.11m
Javelin: Goldie Sayers (Belgrave), 58.60m
**Heptathlon:* Dominique Blaize (Kingston & Poly), 5,671pts

* Held at Stoke-on-Trent, 5–6 June 2010

EUROPEAN CHAMPIONSHIPS
Barcelona, Spain, 27 July–1 August 2010

MEN
100m: Christophe Lemaêtre (France), 10.11sec
200m: Christophe Lemaêtre (France), 20.37sec
400m: Kevin Borlée (Belgium), 45.08sec
800m: Marcin Levandowski (Poland), 1min 47.07sec
1,500m: Arturo Casado (Spain), 3min 42.74sec
5,000m: Mo Farah (Great Britain), 13min 31.18sec
10,000m: Mo Farah (Great Britain), 28min 24.99sec
Marathon: Viktor Röthlin (Switzerland), 2hr 15min 31sec
3,000m St: Mahiedine Mekhissi-Benabbad (France), 8min 07.87sec
110mH: Andy Turner (Great Britain), 13.28sec
400mH: Dai Greene (Great Britain), 48.12sec
4 × 100m: France, 38.11sec
4 × 400m: Russia, 3min 02.14sec
20km Walk: Stanislav Yemelyanov (Russia), 1hr 20min 10sec
50km Walk: Yohann Diniz (France), 3hr 40min 37sec
High jump: Aleksandr Shustov (Russia), 2.33m
Pole vault: Renaud Lavillenie (France), 5.85m
Long jump: Christian Reif (Germany), 8.47m
Triple jump: Phillips Idowu (Great Britain), 17.81m
Shot: Andrei Mikhnevich (Belarus), 21.01m
Discus: Piotr Malachowski (Poland), 68.87m
Hammer: Libor Charfreitag (Slovakia) 80.02m
Javelin: Andreas Thorkildsen (Norway), 88.37m
Decathlon: Romain Barras (France), 8,453pts

WOMEN
100m: Verena Sailer (Germany), 11.10sec
200m: Myriam Soumaré (France), 22.32sec
400m: Tatyana Firova (Russia), 49.89sec
800m: Mariya Savinova (Russia), 1min 58.22sec
1,500m: Nuria Fernandez (Spain), 4min 00.20sec
5,000m: Alemitu Bekele (Turkey), 14min 52.20sec
10,000m: Elvan Abeylegesse (Turkey), 31min 10.23sec
Marathon: Zivile Balciunaite (Lithuania), 2hr 31min 14sec
3,000m St: Yuliya Zarudneva (Russia), 9min 17.57sec
110mH: Nevin Yanit (Turkey), 12.63sec
400mH: Nataya Antyukh (Russia), 52.92sec
4 × 100m: Ukraine, 42.29sec
4 × 400m: Russia, 3min 21.26sec
20km Walk: Olga Kaniskina (Russia), 1hr 27min 44sec
High jump: Blanka Vlasic (Croatia), 2.03m
Pole vault: Svetlana Feofanova (Russia), 4.75m
Long jump: Ineta Radevica (Latvia), 6.92m
Triple jump: Olha Saladukha (Ukraine), 14.81m
Shot: Nadyezda Ostapchuk (Belarus), 20.48m
Discus: Sandra Perkovic (Croatia), 64.67m
Hammer: Betty Heidler (Germany), 76.38m
Javelin: Linda Stahl (Germany), 66.81m
Heptathlon: Jessica Ennis (Great Britain), 6,823pts

BADMINTON

WORLD CHAMPIONSHIPS 2010
Paris, France, August 23–29

Men's Singles: Chen Jin (China) beat Taufik Hidayat (Indonesia) 2–0
Women's Singles: Wang Lin (China) beat Xin Wang (China) 2–1
Men's Doubles: Yun Cai and Haifeng Fu (China) beat Kien Keat Koo and Boon Heong Tan (Malaysia) 2–1
Women's Doubles: Jing Du and Yang (F) Yu (China) beat Shu Jin Ma and Xiaoli Wang (China) 2–0
Mixed Doubles: Bo Zheng and Jin Ma (China) beat Sung Hyun Ko and Jung Eun Ha (Korea) 2–1

ALL-ENGLAND CHAMPIONSHIPS 2010
Birmingham, March

Men's Singles: Chong Wei Lee (Malaysia) beat Kenichi Tago (Japan) 2–0
Women's Singles: Tine Rasmussen (Denmark) beat Yihan Wang (China) 2–1
Men's Doubles: Lars Paaske and Jonas Rasmussen (Denmark) beat Markis Kido and Hendra Setiawan (Indonesia) 2–1
Women's Doubles: Jing Du and Yang (F) Yu (China) beat Shu Cheng and Yunlei Zhao (China) 2–1
Mixed Doubles: Nan Jhang and Yunlei Zhao (China) beat Nova Widianto and Liliyana Natsir (Indonesia) 2–1

ENGLISH NATIONAL CHAMPIONSHIPS 2010
Manchester, February

Men's Singles: Rajiv Ouseph beat Carl Baxter 2–1
Women's Singles: Elizabeth Cann beat Helen Davies 2–0
Men's Doubles: Anthony Clark and Nathan Robertson beat Chris Adcock and Robert Blair 2–0
Women's Doubles: Jenny Wallwork and Gabby White beat Mariana Anathangelou and Heather Olver 2–1
Mixed Doubles: Nathan Clark and Jenny Wallwork beat Anthony Clark and Heather Olver 2–0

SCOTTISH NATIONAL CHAMPIONSHIPS 2010
Perth, January–February

Men's Singles: Calum Menzies beat Kieran Merrilees 2–0
Women's Singles: Susan Egelstaff beat Linda Sloan 2–0
Men's Doubles: Jamie Neill and Keith Turnbull beat Watson Briggs and Paul Van Rietvelde 2–0
Women's Doubles: Imogen Bankier and Emma Mason beat Susan Egelstaff and Linda Sloan 2–0
Mixed Doubles: Watson Briggs and Imogen Bankier beat Paul Van Rietvelde and Jillie Cooper 2–0

WELSH NATIONAL CHAMPIONSHIPS 2010
Cwmbran, February

Men's Singles: Irwansyah beat Jamie Van Hooijdonk 2–1
Women's Singles: Sarah Thomas beat Carissa Turner 2–1
Men's Doubles: J. Phillips and J. Morgan beat M. Lewis and M. Hughes 2–1
Women's Doubles: C. Harvey and C. Turner beat K. Blake and B. Higginson 2–0
Mixed Doubles: R. Vaughan and S. Thompson beat J. Morgan and K. A. Sheppard 2–1

BASEBALL

American League Championship Series 2009: New York Yankees beat Los Angeles Angels of Anaheim 4–2
National League Championship Series 2009: Philadelphia Phillies beat Los Angeles Dodgers 4–1
World Series 2009: New York Yankees beat Philadelphia Phillies 4–2

BASKETBALL

BRITISH

MEN
BBL Play-off final 2010: Everton Tigers beat Glasgow Rocks 80–72
BBL Trophy final 2010: Newcastle Eagles beat Cheshire Jets 119–95
BBL Cup final 2010: Sheffield Sharks beat Cheshire Jets 89–86
BBL Champions 2009–10: Newcastle Eagles

WOMEN
EBL Division 1 2009–10: Sheffield Hatters
EBL Division 1 Play-off final 2009–10: UWIC Archers beat Sheffield Hatters 56–52
National Cup final 2010: Sheffield Hatters beat Nottingham Wildcats 67–54

USA – NATIONAL BASKETBALL LEAGUE (NBA)
Eastern Conference final 2010: Boston Celtics beat Orlando Magic 4–2
Western Conference final 2010: LA Lakers beat Phoenix Suns 4–2
NBA final 2010: LA Lakers beat Boston Celtics 4–3

BOWLS — INDOOR

WORLD CHAMPIONSHIPS 2010
Norfolk, January

Men's Singles: Greg Harlow (England) beat Stewart Anderson (Scotland) 2–0
Women's Singles: Debbie Stavrou (England) beat Alison Merrien (Channel Islands) 2–1
Men's Pairs: Andy Thomson and Ian Bond (England) beat David Gourlay (Australia) and Billy Jackson (England) 2–1
Mixed Pairs: Alex Marshall and Carol Ashby (Scotland) beat Ceri Ann Davies and David Gourlay (Scotland) 2–1

BRITISH ISLES INDOOR BOWLS CHAMPIONSHIPS 2010
Perth, March

Singles: Mike Stepney (Scotland) beat Ian McClure (Ireland) 21–9
Pairs: Ireland beat Wales 26–21 (after extra end)
Triples: England beat Channel Islands 19–9
Fours: Channel Islands beat England 24–23

ENGLISH NATIONAL CHAMPIONSHIPS 2010
Nottingham, April

Singles: Robert Newman beat Les Gillett 21–15
Pairs: Cumbria beat City of Ely 18–17
Triples: City of Ely beat Hartlepool 18–11
Fours: Darlington beat Wey Valley 20–16
Liberty Trophy (Inter-County Championship) final: Durham beat Berkshire 148–90
Champion of Champions (Warner Lakeside, February): Nick Brett beat Tom Bishop 21–7

SCOTTISH NATIONAL CHAMPIONSHIPS 2010
Prestwick, March

Pairs: Elgin beat Dumbarton 24–7
Triples: Bainfield beat Fraserburgh 21–12
Fours: Lanarkshire beat Paisley 23–21

BOWLS — OUTDOOR

BRITISH ISLES CHAMPIONSHIPS 2010
Worthing, July

Singles: Scotland beat Guernsey 21–14
Pairs: Ireland beat Guernsey 16–15
Triples: Wales beat England 18–7
Fours: Scotland beat Jersey 25–9

ENGLISH NATIONAL CHAMPIONSHIPS 2010
Worthing, August

Singles: Romford beat Hove & Kingsway 21–8
Pairs: White Hart beat Manchester Commonwealth 22–19
Triples: Halesworth Angel beat Bitton Park 19–9
Fours: Cambridge & County beat Herne Bay 18–17
Inter-County Championship: Cornwall beat Huntingdonshire 126–109

SCOTTISH NATIONAL CHAMPIONSHIPS 2010
Ayr, August

MEN
Singles: Priorscroft beat Slateford 21–20
Pairs: Anchor beat Blantyre 17–13
Triples: Tanfield beat Raploch 16–11
Fours: Houldsworth beat Rock 25–6

WELSH NATIONAL CHAMPIONSHIPS 2010
Llandrindod Wells, August

Singles: Glyncorrwg beat Llantrisant 21–18
Pairs: Brigend beat Llandrindod Wells 24–12
Triples: Ystradfechan beat Parc-y-Dre 19–17
Fours: Presteigne beat Barry Athletic 26–16

BOXING

WORLD CHAMPIONS
as at 1 September 2010

WORLD BOXING COUNCIL (WBC)
Heavy: Vitaly Klitschko (Ukraine)
Cruiser: Krzysztof Wlodarczyk (Poland)
Light-heavy: Jean Pascal (Haiti/Canada)
Supermiddle: Mikkel Kessler (Denmark)
Middle: Sergio Martinez (Argentina)
Superwelter: vacant
Welter: Andre Berto (USA)
Superlight: Devon Alexander (USA)
Light: Humberto Soto (Mexico)
Superfeather: Vitaly Tajbert (Kazakhstan)
Feather: Elio Rojas (Dominica)
Superbantam: Toshiaki Nishioka (Japan)
Bantam: Fernando Montiel (Mexico)
Superfly: vacant
Fly: Pongsaklek Wonjongkam (Thailand)
Lightfly: Omar Nino (Mexico)
Straw: Oleydong Sithsamerchai (Thailand)

WORLD BOXING ASSOCIATION (WBA)
Heavy: David Haye (Great Britain)
Cruiser: Guillermo Jones (Panama)
Light-heavy: Beibut Shumenov (Kazakhstan)
Supermiddle: Andre Ward (USA)
Middle: Felix Sturm (Germany)
Superwelter: Miguel Cotto (Puerto Rico)
Welter: Vyacheslav Senchenko (Ukraine)
Superlight: Amir Khan (Great Britain)
Light: Juan Manuel Marquez (Mexico)
Superfeather: Takashi Uchiyama (Japan)
Feather: Chris John (Indonesia)
Superbantam: Celestino Caballero (Panama)
Bantam: Anselmo Moreno (Panama)
Superfly: Vic Darchinyan (Armenia)
Fly: Daiki Kameda (Japan)
Lightfly: Giovanni Segura (Mexico)
Minimum: Román González (Nicaragua)

WORLD BOXING ORGANISATION (WBO)
Heavy: Wladimir Klitschko (Ukraine)
Cruiser: Marco Huck (Germany)
Light-heavy: Juergen Braehmer (Germany)
Supermiddle: Robert Stieglich (Germany)
Middle: vacant
Superwelter: Sergei Dzinziruk (Ukraine)
Welter: Manny Pacquiao (Puerto Rico)
Superlight: Timothy Bradley (USA)
Light: Juan Manuel Marquez (Mexico)
Superfeather: Roman Martinez (Puerto Rico)
Feather: Juan Manuel Lopez (Puerto Rico)
Superbantam: Wilfredo Vasquez Jr. (Puerto Rico)
Bantam: Fernando Montiel (Mexico)
Superfly: Omar Narvaez (Argentina)
Fly: Julio Cesar Miranda (Mexico)
Lightfly: Ivan Calderon (Puerto Rico)
Straw: Donnie Nietes (Philippines)

INTERNATIONAL BOXING FEDERATION (IBF)
Heavy: Wladimir Klitschko (Ukraine)
Cruiser: Steve Cunningham (USA)
Light-heavy: Tavoris Cloud (USA)
Supermiddle: Lucian Bute (Romania)
Middle: Sebastian Sylvester (Germany)
Superwelter: Cory Spinks (USA)
Welter: Jan Zaveck (Slovenia)
Superlight: Devon Alexander (USA)
Light: vacant
Superfeather: vacant
Feather: Orlando Salido (Mexico)
Super-bantam: Steve Molitor (Canada)
Bantam: Yonnhy Perez (Mexico)
Super-fly: Simphiwe Nongqayi (South Africa)
Fly: Moruti Mthalane (South Africa)
Light-fly: Luis Lazarte (Argentina)
Straw: Nkosinathi Joyi (South Africa)

BRITISH CHAMPIONS
Heavy: Derek Chisora
Cruiser: Robert Norton
Light-heavy: vacant
Super-middle: Paul Smith
Middle: Darren Barker
Light-middle: Sam Webb
Welter: Kell Brook
Light-welter: Lenny Daws
Light: John Murray
Super-feather: Gary Sykes
Feather: Martin Lindsay
Super-bantam: vacant
Bantam: Stuart Hall
Super-fly: Lee Haskins
Fly: Shinny Bayarr

CHESS

FIDE World Champion 2010: Viswanathan Anand (Sri Lanka)
British Champion 2010: Mickey Adams

CRICKET

TEST SERIES

SOUTH AFRICA V ENGLAND
Centurion (16–20 December 2009): South Africa drew with England. South Africa 418 and 301–7; England 356 and 228–9
Durban (26–30 December 2009): England beat South Africa by an innings and 98 runs. South Africa 343 and 133; England 574–9
Cape Town (3–7 January 2010): South Africa drew with England. South Africa 291 and 447–7; England 273 and 296–9
Johannesburg (14–17 January 2010): South Africa won by an innings and 74 runs. England 180 and 169; South Africa 423–7

BANGLADESH V ENGLAND
Chittagong (12–16 March 2010): England beat Bangladesh by 181 runs. England 599–6 and 209–7; Bangladesh 296 and 331
Dhaka (20–24 March 2010): England won by 9 wickets. Bangladesh 419 and 285; England 496 and 209–1

ENGLAND V BANGLADESH
Lord's (27–31 May 2010): England beat Bangladesh by 8 wickets. England 505 and 163–2; Bangladesh 282 and 382
Old Trafford (4–6 June 2010): England beat Bangladesh by an innings and 80 runs. England 419; Bangladesh 216 and 123

ENGLAND V PAKISTAN

Trent Bridge (29 July–1 August 2010): England beat Pakistan by 354 runs. England 354 and 262–9; Pakistan 182 and 80

Edgbaston (6–9 August 2010): England beat Pakistan by 9 wickets. Pakistan 72 and 296; England 251 and 118–1

The Oval (18–22 August 2010): Pakistan beat England by 4 wickets. England 233 and 222; Pakistan 308 and 148–6

Lord's (26–29 August 2010): England beat Pakistan by an innings and 225 runs. England 446; Pakistan 74 and 147

ONE-DAY INTERNATIONALS

IRELAND V ENGLAND

Belfast (27 August 2009): England beat Ireland by 3 runs (Duckworth-Lewis method). England 203–9; Ireland 112–9

ENGLAND V AUSTRALIA

The Oval (4 September 2009): Australia beat England by 4 runs. Australia 260–5; England 256–9

Lord's (6 September 2009): Australia beat England by 39 runs. Australia 249–8; England 210

Southampton (9 September 2009): Australia beat England by 6 wickets. England 228–9; Australia 230–4

Lord's (12 September 2009): Australia beat England by 7 wickets. England 220; Australia 221–3

Trent Bridge (15 September 2009): Australia beat England by 4 wickets. England 299; Australia 302–6

Trent Bridge (17 September 2009): Australia beat England by 111 runs. Australia 296–8; England 185

Chester-le-Street (19 September 2009): England beat Australia by 4 wickets. Australia 176; England 177–6

SOUTH AFRICA V ENGLAND

Johannesburg (20 November 2009): No result

Centurion (22 November 2009): England beat South Africa by 4 wickets. South Africa 250–9; England 252–3

Cape Town (27 November 2009): South Africa beat England by 112 runs. South Africa 354–6; England 242

Port Elizabeth (29 November 2009): England beat South Africa by 7 wickets. South Africa 119; England 121–3

Durban (4 December 2009): No result

BANGLADESH V ENGLAND

Dhaka (28 February 2010): England won by 6 wickets. Bangladesh 228; England 229–4

Dhaka (2 March 2010): England beat Bangladesh by 2 wickets. Bangladesh 260–6; England 261–8

Chittagong (5 March 2010): England beat Bangladesh by 45 runs. England 284–5; Bangladesh 239–9

TWENTY20 INTERNATIONALS

ENGLAND V AUSTRALIA

Old Trafford (30 August 2009): No result

Old Trafford (1 September 2009): No result

SOUTH AFRICA V ENGLAND

Johannesburg (13 November 2009): England won by 1 run (Duckworth-Lewis method). England 202–6; South Africa 127–3

Centurion (15 November 2009): South Africa won by 84 runs. South Africa 241–6; England 157–8

ENGLAND V PAKISTAN

Dubai (19 February 2010): England won by 7 wickets. Pakistan 129–8; England 130–3

Dubai (20 February 2010): Pakistan won by 4 wickets. England 148–6; Pakistan 149–6

WORLD TWENTY20

West Indies, April–May 2010

First round

Group A

	Matches	*Won*	*Lost*	*Tied*	*N/R*	*Pts*	*Net RR*
Australia	2	2	0	0	0	4	+1.525
Pakistan	2	1	1	0	0	2	−0.325
Bangladesh	2	0	2	0	0	0	−1.200

Group B

	Matches	*Won*	*Lost*	*Tied*	*N/R*	*Pts*	*Net RR*
New Zealand	2	2	0	0	0	4	+0.428
Sri Lanka	2	1	1	0	0	2	+0.355
Zimbabwe	2	0	2	0	0	0	−1.595

Group C

	Matches	*Won*	*Lost*	*Tied*	*N/R*	*Pts*	*Net RR*
India	2	2	0	0	0	4	+1.495
South Africa	2	1	1	0	0	2	+1.125
Afghanistan	2	0	2	0	0	0	−2.446

Group D

	Matches	*Won*	*Lost*	*Tied*	*N/R*	*Pts*	*Net RR*
West Indies	2	2	0	0	0	4	+2.780
England	2	0	1	0	1	1	−0.452
Ireland	2	0	1	0	1	1	−3.500

Super eights

Group E

	Matches	*Won*	*Lost*	*Tied*	*N/R*	*Pts*	*Net RR*
England	3	3	0	0	0	6	+0.962
Pakistan	3	1	2	0	0	2	+0.041
New Zealand	3	1	2	0	0	2	−0.373
South Africa	3	1	2	0	0	2	−0.617

Group F

	Matches	*Won*	*Lost*	*Tied*	*N/R*	*Pts*	*Net RR*
Australia	3	3	0	0	0	6	+2.733
Sri Lanka	3	2	1	0	0	4	−0.333
West Indies	3	1	2	0	0	2	−1.281
India	3	0	3	0	0	0	−1.117

Semi-finals

Gros Islet (13 May 2010): England beat Sri Lanka by 7 wickets. Sri Lanka 128–6; England 132–3

Gros Islet (14 May 2010): Australia beat Pakistan by 57 runs. Pakistan 191–6; Australia 197–7

Final

Bridgetown (16 May 2010): England beat Australia by 7 wickets. Australia 147–6; England 148–3

ENGLAND AND WALES DOMESTIC COMPETITIONS

County Championship 2009, Division 1: Durham, 240pts; *Relegated* Sussex, 143pts; Worcestershire, 94pts – *Division 2:* Kent, 219pts; *Promoted* Essex, 194pts

Pro40 2009, Division 1: Sussex, 12pts; *Relegated* Gloucestershire, 5pts; Nottinghamshire, 2pts – *Division 2:* Warwickshire, 13pts; *Promoted* Middlesex, 12pts

Friends Provident Twenty20 Cup final 2010: Hampshire beat Somerset (lost fewer wickets). Somerset 173–6; Hampshire 173–5

OTHER INTERNATIONAL DOMESTIC CHAMPIONSHIPS

Australia: Sheffield Shield final 2009–10: Victoria beat Queensland by 457 runs. Victoria 305 and 591–8; Queensland 257 and 182. *Ford Ranger Cup final 2009–10:* Tasmania beat Victoria by 110 runs. 304–6; Victoria 194. *Twenty20 Big Bash final 2009–10:* Victoria beat South Australia by 48 runs. Victoria 166–7; South Australia 118–9

Bangladesh: National League 2009–10 final: Rajshahi Division drew with Chittagong Division. Rajshahi Division 372 and 413–5; Chittagong Division 301 – Rajshahi Division won on first-innings score. *National Twenty20 final 2009–10:* Rajshahi Division beat Khulna Division by 6 wickets. Khulna Division 161–6; Rajshahi Division 163–4

India: Irani Trophy final 2009–10: Mumbai drew with Rest of India. Rest of India 260 and 352–4; Mumbai 230 – Rest of India won on first-innings score. *BCCI Corporate Trophy 2009–10:* Air India Red beat Air India Blue by 93 runs. Air India Red 284–8; Air India Blue 191. *KPL Cup 2009–10:* Bangalore Provident (Rural) beat Belagavi Panthers by 5 wickets. Belagavi Panthers 122–7; Bangalore Provident (Rural) 125–5. *NKP Salve Challenger Trophy 2009–10:* India Red beat India Blue by 7 wickets. India Blue 84; India Red 85–3. *Deodhar Trophy 2009–10:* North Zone beat West Zone by 49 runs. North Zone 267–9; West Zone 218. *Duleep Trophy final 2009–10:* West Zone beat South Zone by 3 wickets. South Zone 400 and 386–9; West Zone 251 and 541–7. *Ranji Trophy Super League 2009–10:* Mumbai beat Karnataka by 6 runs. Mumbai 233 and 234; Karnataka 130 and 331. *Syed Mushtaq Ali Trophy 2009–10:* Maharashtra beat Hyderabad by 19 runs. Maharashtra 119; Hyderabad (India) 100. *Vijay Hazare Trophy final 2009–10:* Tamil Nadu beat Bengal by 29 runs. Tamil Nadu 379–6; Bengal 350–8. *Indian Premier League Twenty20 final 2010:* Chennai Super Kings beat Mumbai Indians by 22 runs. Chennai Super Kings 168–5; Mumbai Indians 146–9

New Zealand: Plunket Shield 2009–10: Northern Districts 52pts. *One Day Competition final 2009–10:* Northern Districts beat Auckland by 21 runs. Northern Districts 304–3; Auckland 283–9. *HRV Cup final 2009-10:* Central Districts beat Auckland by 78 runs. Central Districts 206–6; Auckland 128

Pakistan: Quaid-e-Azam Trophy final 2009–10: Karachi Blues beat Habib Bank Limited by 141 runs. Karachi Blues 215 and 187; Habib Bank Limited 195 and 66. *RBS Pentangular Cup final 2009–10:* Sui Northern Gas Pipelines Limited beat Habib Bank Limited by 7 wickets. Habib Bank Limited 484 and 105; Sui Northern Gas Pipelines Limited 368 and 223–3. *RBS Pentangular One-Day Cup final 2009–10:* Sind Dolphins beat Baluchistan Bears by 78 runs. Sind Dolphins 270–6; Baluchistan Bears 192. *RBS Cup final 2009–10:* Sui Northern Gas Pipelines Limited beat Sialkot Stallions by 132 runs. Sui Northern Gas Pipelines Limited 284–7; Sialkot Stallions 152. *RBS Twenty20 Cup final 2009–10:* Sialkot Stallions beat Faisalabad Wolves by 5 wickets. Faisalabad Wolves 109–9; Sialkot Stallions 110–5

South Africa: SuperSport Series 2009–10: Cape Cobras, 130.72pts. *MTN40 final 2009–10:* Warriors beat Dolphins by 71 runs. Warriors 299–4; Dolphins 228. *Pro20 Series final 2009–10:* Warriors beat Lions by 82 runs. Warriors 186–2; Lions 104. *Provincial Three Day Challenge 2009–10:* Eastern Province 190.7pts. *Provincial One Day Challenge 2009–10:* Northerns 44pts

Sri Lanka: Premier League Tournament 2009–10: Chilaw Marians Cricket Club, 107.675pts. *Premier Limited Overs Tournament final 2009–10:* Tamil Union Cricket and Athletic Club beat Chilaw Marians Cricket Club by 63 runs (Duckworth-Lewis method). Tamil Union Cricket and Athletic Club 234; Chilaw Marians Cricket Club 143–8. *Inter-Provincial tournament final 2010:* No result. Basnahira North and Basnahira South share title. *Inter-Provincial Twenty20 Cup final 2010:* Wayamba beat Ruhuna by 95 runs. Wayamba 208–8; Ruhuna 113

West Indies: President's Cup 2009–10: Trinidad & Tobago beat Guyana by 81 runs. Trinidad & Tobago 286–6; Guyana 205. *Regional Four Day Tournament 2009-10:* Jamaica, 60pts. *Caribbean T20 final 2009-10:* Guyana beat Barbados by 1 wicket. Barbados 134–5; Guyana 135–9

Zimbabwe: Logan Cup 2009–10: Mashonaland Eagles 169pts. *Faithwear Cup 2009–10:* Mountaineers 28pts. *Stanbic Bank 20 Series final 2009–10:* Mountaineers beat Mashonaland Eagles by 9 wickets. Mashonaland Eagles 105; Mountaineers 106–1

CURLING

MEN'S WORLD CHAMPIONSHIP 2010
Cortina d'Ampezzo, Italy, April

Final: Canada beat Norway 9–3

WOMEN'S WORLD CHAMPIONSHIP 2010
Saskatchewan, Canada, March

Final: Germany beat Scotland 8–6

CYCLING

Vuelta a Espana 2009: Alexandro Valverde (Spain)
Giro d'Italia 2010: Ivan Basso (Italy)
Tour de France 2010: Alberto Contador (Spain)

WORLD ROAD RACE CHAMPIONSHIPS 2009
Mendrisio, Switzerland, September

MEN
Elite Time Trial: Fabian Cancellara (Switzerland)
Road Race: Cadel Evans (Australia)

WOMEN
Elite Time Trial: Kristin Armstrong (USA)
Road Race: Tatiana Guderzo (Italy)

BRITISH NATIONAL ROAD RACE CHAMPIONSHIPS 2010
Nelson, June

MEN
Road Race: Geraint Thomas

WOMEN
Road Race: Emma Pooley

WORLD TRACK CHAMPIONSHIPS 2010
Copenhagen, Denmark, March

MEN
Points Race: Cameron Meyer (Australia)
Olympic Sprint: Gregory Bauge (France)
1km Time Trial: Teun Mulder (Netherlands)
Individual Pursuit: Taylor Phinney (USA)
Scratch Race: Alex Rasmussen (Denmark)
Keirin: Chris Hoy (Great Britain)
Team Pursuit: Australia
Madison: Leigh Howard and Cameron Meyer (Australia)
Team Sprint: Germany
Omnium: Edward Clancy (Great Britain)

WOMEN
Points Race: Tara Whitten (Canada)
500m Time Trial: Anna Meares (Australia)
Individual Pursuit: Sarah Hammer (USA)
Scratch Race: Pascale Jeuland (France)
Keirin: Simona Krupeckaite (Latvia)
Sprint: Victoria Pendleton (Great Britain)
Team Sprint: Australia
Team Pursuit: Australia
Omnium: Tara Whitten (Canada)

DARTS

BDO World Championship 2010: Martin Adams (England) beat Dave Chisnall (England) 7–5
PDC World Championship 2009–10: Phil Taylor (England) beat Simon Whitlock (Australia) 7–3

EQUESTRIANISM

Burghley Horse Trials 2009: Oliver Townend (Great Britain) on Carousel Quest
Badminton Horse Trials 2010: Paul Tapner (Australia) on Inonothing
British Open Horse Trials 2010 (Gatcombe Park): Daisy Berkeley (Great Britain) on Spring Along

ETON FIVES

Amateur Championship (Kinnaird Cup) final 2010: Matthew Wiseman and James Toop beat Tom Dunbar and Peter Dunbar 3–1
Alan Barber Cup final 2010: Old Olavians beat Old Salopians 3–0
County Championship final 2010: Hertfordshire beat Kent 2–1
Schools' Championship 2010: Highgate 2 beat Highgate 1 3–1
Preparatory Schools' Tournament 2010: Highgate 1 beat Highgate 2 2–0

FENCING

WORLD CHAMPIONSHIPS 2009
Antalya, Turkey, September–October

MEN
Individual Foil: Andrea Baldini (Italy)
Individual Epée: Anton Avdeev (Russia)
Individual Sabre: Nicolas Limbach (Germany)
Team Foil: Italy
Team Epée: France
Team Sabre: Romania

WOMEN
Individual Foil: Aida Shanaeva (Russia)
Individual Epée: Lubov Shutova (Russia)
Individual Sabre: Mariel Zagunis (USA)
Team Foil: Italy
Team Epée: Italy
Team Sabre: Ukraine

EUROPEAN CHAMPIONSHIPS 2010
Leipzig, Germany, July

MEN
Individual Foil: Andrea Baldini (Italy)
Individual Epée: Jean-Michel Lucenay (France)
Individual Sabre: Alexey Yakimenko (Russia)
Team Foil: Italy
Team Epée: Hungary
Team Sabre: Italy

WOMEN
Individual Foil: Valentina Vezzali (Italy)
Individual Epée: Imke Duplitzer (Germany)
Individual Sabre: Svetlana Kormilitsyna (Russia)
Team Foil: Italy
Team Epée: Poland
Team Sabre: Ukraine

BRITISH CHAMPIONSHIPS 2010
Sheffield, July

MEN
Individual Foil: Keith Cook
Individual Epée: Jon Willis
Individual Sabre: Alexander O'Connell
Team Foil: Salle Paul A
Team Epée: Haverstock LP A
Team Sabre: Scimitar

WOMEN
Individual Foil: Natalia Sheppard
Individual Epée: Elisa Albini
Individual Sabre: Chrystal Nicoll
Team Foil: Lansdowne
Team Epée: LTFC A
Team Sabre: Truro A

GOLF (MEN)

THE MAJOR CHAMPIONSHIPS 2010
US Masters (Augusta, 8–11 April): Phil Mickelson (USA), 272
US Open (Pebble Beach, 17–20 June): Graeme McDowell (Northern Ireland), 284
The Open (St Andrews, 15–18 July): Louis Oosthuizen (South Africa), 272
US PGA Championship (Whistling Straits, 12–15 August): Martin Kaymer (Germany), 277

WORLD RANKINGS
as at 15 August 2010

1. Tiger Woods (USA); 2. Phil Mickelson (USA); 3. Lee Westwood (England); 4. Steve Stricker (USA); 5. Martin Kaymer (Germany)

PGA EUROPEAN TOUR 2009
Omega European Masters (Crans-sur-Sierre, Switzerland): Alexander Noren (Sweden), 264
Mercedes Benz Championship (Gut Lärchenhof, Germany): James Kingston (South Africa), 275

Austrian Open (Fontana): Rafael Cabrera-Bello (Spain), 264
Alfred Dunhill Links Championship (St Andrews, Carnoustie and Kingsbarns, Scotland): Simon Dyson (England), 264
Madrid Masters (Centro Nacional de Golf, Spain): Ross McGowan (England), 263
Portugal Masters (Vilamoura): Lee Westwood (England), 265
Castelló Masters Costa Azahar (Club de Campo del Mediterráneo): Michael Jonzon (Sweden), 264
Barclays Singapore Open (Sentosa): Ian Poulter (England), 274
Volvo World Matchplay Championship (Casares, Spain): Ross Fisher (England)
WGC – HSBC Champions (Sheshan International, China): Phil Mickelson (USA), 271
JBWere Masters (Melbourne, Australia): Tiger Woods (USA), 274
UBS Hong Kong Open (Fanling): Grégory Bourdy (France), 261
Dubai World Championship (Earth Course): Lee Westwood (England), 265

TEAM CHAMPIONSHIPS
Ryder Cup 2008 (Valhalla, USA): USA beat Europe, 16½–11½
Omega Mission Hills World Cup (Mission Hills, China): Italy

EUROPEAN TOUR ORDER OF MERIT 2009
1. Lee Westwood (England); 2. Rory McIlroy (Northern Ireland); 3. Martin Kaymer (Germany); 4. Ross Fisher (England); 5. Paul Casey (England)

PGA EUROPEAN TOUR 2010
Alfred Dunhill Championship (Leopard Creek, South Africa): Pablo Martin (Spain), 271
South African Open (Pearl Valley): Richie Ramsay (Scotland), 275
Africa Open (East Africa): Charl Schwartzel (South Africa), 272
Joburg Open (Royal Johannesburg and Kensington): Charl Schwartzel (South Africa), 261
Abu Dhabi Golf Championship (Abu Dhabi): Martin Kaymer (Germany), 267
Qatar Masters (Doha): Robert Karlsson (Sweden), 273
Dubai Desert Classic (Emirates): Miguel Angel Jiménez (Spain), 277
Avantha Masters (New Delhi): Andrew Dodt (Australia), 274
WGC – Accenture Match Play (The Gallery, Tucson): Ian Poulter (England)
Maybank Malaysian Open (Kuala Lumpur): Noh Seung-yul (Korea), 274
WGC – CA Championship (Doral Resort, Florida): Ernie Els (South Africa), 270
Trophee Hassan II (Rabat, Morocco): Rhys Davies (Wales), 266
Open de Andalucia (Málaga, Spain): Louis Oosthuizen (South Africa), 263
Estoril Open de Portugal (Penha Longa): Thomas Bjorn (Denmark), 265
Madeira Island Open (Porto Santo Golfe): James Morrison (England), 268
Volvo China Open (Suzhou): Yang Y E (Korea), 273
Ballantine's Championship (Pinx, South Korea): Marcus Fraser (Australia), 204 (54 holes)
Open de España (Seville): Alvaro Quiros (Spain), 277
BMW Italian Open (Royal Park i Roveri): Fredrik Andersson Hed (Sweden), 272
Iberdrola Open Cala Millor Mallorca (Son Servera): Peter Hanson (Sweden), 274
BMW PGA Championship (Wentworth, England): Simon Khan (England), 278
Open de France (Le Golf National): Miguel Angel Jimenez (Spain), 273
Scottish Open (Loch Lomond): Edoardo Molinari (Italy), 272
Nordea Scandinavian Masters (Stockholm, Sweden): Richard S Johnson (Sweden), 277
3 Irish Open (Killarney): Ross Fisher (England), 266
WGC – Bridgestone Invitational (Firestone, USA): Hunter Mahan (USA), 268
Czech Open (Celadna): Peter Hanson (Sweden), 278
Johnnie Walker Championship (Gleneagles, Scotland): Edoardo Molinari (italy), 278

AMATEUR CHAMPIONSHIPS 2010
British Amateur Championship (Muirfield): Jin Jeong (South Korea)
English Amateur Championship (Little Aston/Sutton Coldfield): Tommy Fleetwood (England)
Brabazon Trophy (English Open Strokeplay), (Royal Liverpool): Darren Wright (England), 285
Scottish Amateur Championship (Gullane): Michael Stewart (Scotland)
Scottish Open Strokeplay (Glasgow Gailes): Romaine Wattel (France), 275
Welsh Amateur Championship (Tenby): Alastair Jones (Wales)
Welsh Open Strokeplay (Royal St David's): Eddie Pepperell (England), 267
Irish Amateur Open Championship (Royal Dublin): Alan Dunbar (Northern Ireland), 292
Irish Amateur Close Championship (Royal Dublin): Dara Lernihan (Ireland)
Lytham Trophy (Royal Lytham Golf Club): Paul Cutler (Northern Ireland), 284
Berkshire Trophy (The Berkshire): Eddie Pepperell (England), 275

GOLF (WOMEN)

THE MAJOR CHAMPIONSHIPS 2010
Kraft Nabisco Championship (Mission Hills Country Club, USA, 1–4 April): Yani Tseng (Taiwan), 275
US Women's Open (Oakmont, 8–11 July): Paula Creamer (USA), 281
LPGA Championship (Locust Hill, USA, 24–27 June): Cristie Kerr (USA), 269
Women's British Open (Royal Birkdale, 29 July–1 August): Yani Tseng (Taiwan), 277

EUROPEAN LPGA TOUR 2009
UNIQA Open (Fohrenwald-Wiener Neustadt, Austria): Linda Wessberg (Sweden), 279
Randstad Open de France Dames (Le Golf d'Arras): Nicole Gergely (Austria), 275
Tenerife Ladies Open (Golf Costa Adeje): Felicity Johnson (England), 274
Madrid Masters (Casino Club, Spain): Azahara Munoz Guijarro (Spain), 203
Carta Si Italian Open (Le Rovedine Milano): Marianne Skarpnord (Norway), 204
Suzhou Taihu Ladies Open (Suzhou Taihu International, China): Bo Mi Suh (Korea), 210

Daishin Securities Tomato Tour Ladies Masters (Cypress Country Club): Hyun-Ji Kim (Korea), 215
Dubai Masters (Emirates): In Kyung Kim (Korea), 270

EUROPEAN LPGA TOUR ORDER OF MERIT 2009
1. Sophie Gustafson (Sweden); 2. Catriona Matthew (Scotland); 3. Becky Brewerton (Wales); 4. Marianne Skarpnord (Norway); 5. Tania Elosegui (Spain)

TEAM CHAMPIONSHIP 2009
Solheim Cup: USA beat Europe 16–12

EUROPEAN LPGA TOUR 2010
Pegasus New Zealand Women's Open (Pegasus): Laura Davies (England), 279
ANZ Ladies Masters (Royal Pines, Australia): Karrie Webb (Australia), 262
Australian Open (Commonwealth): Yani Tseng (Taiwan), 283
Lalla Meryem Cup (Royal Golf Anfa Mohammedia): Anja Monke (Germany), 208
Comunitat Valenciana European Nations Cup (La Sella): Sophie Gustafson (Sweden) and Anna Nordqvist (Sweden), 267
Turkish Airlines Ladies Open (National Golf Club, Antalya): Melissa Reid (England), 216
German Open (Gut Hausern): Laura Davies (England), 277
Ladies Slovak Open (Gray Bear Slovakia): Maria Hernandez (Spain), 280
ABN AMRO Open (Golfclub Broekpolder, Netherlands): Florentyna Parker (England), 207
Swiss Open (Gerre Losone): Lee-Anne Pace (South Africa), 204
Open de Portugal (Campo Real): Karen Lunn (Australia), 204
Tenerife Ladies Open (Buenavista): Trish Johnson (England), 274
Evian Masters (Evian Les Bains, France): Jiyai Shin (Korea), 274
British Open (Royal Birkdale): Yani Tseng (Taiwan), 277
Irish Open (Killeen Castle): Sophie Gustafson (Sweden), 204
Wales Championship of Europe (Conwy): Lee-Anne Pace (South Africa), 282
Ladies Scottish Open (Archerfield Links): Virginie Lagoutte-Clement (France), 217
Finnair Masters (Helsinki, Finland): Lee-Anne Pace (South Africa), 199

TEAM CHAMPIONSHIPS 2010
European Cup (La Manga, Spain): Sweden

AMATEUR CHAMPIONSHIPS 2010
British Open Championship (Ganton): Kelly Tidy (England)
Ladies' British Open Amateur Strokeplay Championship (Tenby): Pamela Pretswell (Scotland), 218
English Close Amateur Championship (Broadstone): Hayley Davis (England)
English Strokeplay Championship (Whittington Heath): Julie Yang (Korea), 284
Helen Holm (Scottish Open Strokeplay Championship) (Troon): Danielle McVeigh (Ireland), 205
Scottish Ladies Close Amateur Championship (Craigielaw): Kelsey MacDonald (Scotland)
Welsh Open Strokeplay (Southerndown): Julie Yang (Korea), 223
Welsh Close Championship (Glamorganshire): Tara Davies (Wales)
Irish Open Strokeplay Championship (Newlands): Hannah Burke (England), 214
Irish Close Championship (Portstewart): Mary Dowling (Ireland)

GREYHOUND RACING

2009
St Leger (Wimbledon): Kinda Easy

2010
The Regency (Hove): He Went Whoosh
Pall Mall (Oxford): Ballymac Ace
Golden Jacket (Crayford): Group Skater
Grand National (Wimbledon): Plane Daddy
The Derby (Wimbledon): Bandicoot Tipoki

GYMNASTICS

WORLD CHAMPIONSHIPS 2009
London, 13–18 October

MEN
Individual All-around: Kohei Uchimura (Japan)

Floor: Marian Dragulescu (Romania)
Pommel Horse: Zhang Hongtao (China)
Still Rings: Yang Mingyong (China)
Vault: Marian Dragulescu (Romania)
Parallel Bars: Wang Guanyin (China)
High Bar: Zou Kai (China)

WOMEN
Individual All-around: Bridget Sloan (USA)

Floor: Beth Tweddle (Great Britain)
Beam: Deng Linlin (China)
Vault: Kayla Williams (USA)
Uneven Bars: He Kexin (China)

EUROPEAN CHAMPIONSHIPS 2010
Birmingham, April–May

MEN
Individual All-around: Cyril Tommasone (France)

Floor: Matthias Fahrig (Germany)
Pommel Horse: Daniel Keatings (Great Britain)
Still Rings: Matteo Morandi (Italy)
Vault: Tomi Tuuha (Finland)
Parallel Bars: Yann Cucherat (France)
High Bar: Vlasios Maras (Greece)

WOMEN
Individual All-around: Elena Amelia Racea (Romania)

Floor: Beth Tweddle (Great Britain)
Beam: Elena Amelia Racea (Romania)
Vault: Ekaterina Kurbatova (Russia)
Uneven Bars: Beth Tweddle (Great Britain)

BRITISH CHAMPIONSHIPS 2009
Goresbrook, October–November

Overall Champion: Daniel Keatings

Floor: Daniel Keatings
Pommel Horse: Daniel Keatings

Still Rings: Danny Lawrence
Vault: Kristian Thomas
Parallel Bars: Daniel Keatings
High Bar: Daniel Keatings

BRITISH WOMEN'S CHAMPIONSHIPS 2010
Guildford, July

Overall Champion: Hannah Whelan

Floor: Niamh Rippin
Beam: Hannah Whelan
Vault: Imogen Cairns
Asymmetric Bars: Beth Tweddle

HOCKEY

MEN
English Hockey League 2009–10: Premier Division: Reading, 41pts; *Conference East:* Canterbury, 46pts; *Conference North:* Deeside Ramblers, 41pts; *Conference West:* Team Bath Buccaneers, 46pts
English Hockey League Indoor Championship final 2010: East Grinstead beat Surbiton 9–5
English Hockey League Cup final 2009–10: Beeston drew with East Grinstead 4–4. East Grinstead won 9–7 on penalty strokes
County Championship 2009–10: A Division: Berkshire beat Sussex 3–2; B Division: Lancashire beat Staffordshire 5–4; C Division: Lincolnshire beat Worcestershire 5–3

WOMEN
English Hockey League 2009–10: Premier Division: Leicester, 52pts; *Conference East:* Ipswich, 41pts; *Conference North:* University of Durham, 47pts; *Conference West:* Cannock, 47pts
English Hockey League Indoor Championship final 2009–10: Leicester drew 2–2 with Slough. Leicester won 2–1 on penalty strokes
English Hockey League Cup final 2009–10: Slough beat Leicester 1–0

HORSE RACING

NATIONAL HUNT

HENNESSY GOLD CUP
(1957) Newbury, 3 miles and about 2½ f

2006 State of Play (6y), P. Moloney
2007 Denman (7y), S. Thomas
2008 Madison du Berlais (7y), T. Scudamore
2009 Denman (9y), R. Walsh

TINGLE CREEK CHASE
(1957) Sandown, 2 miles

2006 Kauto Star (6y), R. Walsh
2007 Twist Magic (5y), S. Thoma
2008 Master Minded (5y), A. P. McCoy
2009 Twist Magic (7y), R. Walsh

KING GEORGE VI CHASE
(1937) Kempton, about 3 miles

2006 Kauto Star (6y), R. Walsh
2007 Kauto Star (7y), R. Walsh
2008 Kauto Star (8y), R. Walsh
2009 Kauto Star (9y), R. Walsh

CHAMPION HURDLE
(1927) Cheltenham, 2 miles and about ½ f

2007 Sublimity (7y), P. Carberry
2008 Katchit (5y), R. Thornton
2009 Punjabi (6y), B. Geraghty
2010 Binocular (6y), A. P. McCoy

QUEEN MOTHER CHAMPION CHASE
(1959) Cheltenham, about 2 miles

2007 Voy Por Ustedes (6y), R. Thornton
2008 Master Minded (5y), R. Walsh
2009 Master Minded (6y), R. Walsh
2010 Big Zeb (9y), B. Geraghty

CHELTENHAM GOLD CUP
(1924) 3 miles and about 2½ f

2007 Kauto Star (7y), R. Walsh
2008 Denman (8y), S. Thomas
2009 Kauto Star (9y), R. Walsh
2010 Imperial Commander (9y), P. Brennan

GRAND NATIONAL
(1837) Liverpool, 4 miles and about 4 f

2007 Silver Birch (10y), R. Power
2008 Comply or Die (9y), T. Murphy
2009 Mon Mome (9y), L. Treadwell
2010 Don't Push It (10y), A. P. McCoy

BET 365 GOLD CUP
(1957) Sandown, 3 miles and about 5 f

2007 Hot Weld (8y), G. Lee
2008 Monkerhostin (11y), R. Johnson
2009 Hennessy (8y), A. P. McCoy
2010 Church Island (11y), A. Heskin

STATISTICS
WINNING NATIONAL HUNT TRAINERS 2009–10

P. F. Nicholls	£2,717,399
N. J. Henderson	1,958,462
J. O'Neill	1,737,436
N. A. Twiston-Davies	1,542,492
D. E. Pipe	1,216,066
P. J. Hobbs	1,041,264
A. King	761,870
D. McCain Jr	735,295
E. Williams	686,751
J. Howard Johnson	541,487

WINNING NATIONAL HUNT JOCKEYS 2009–10

	1st	*2nd*	*3rd*	*Unpl.*	*Total mts*
A. P. McCoy	195	140	96	443	874
R. Johnson	160	124	126	404	814
J. Maguire	108	78	61	310	557
T. Scudamore	72	47	58	376	553
B. Geraghty	70	21	23	93	207
A. Coleman	69	61	66	345	541
R. Walsh	69	42	28	95	234
R. Thornton	68	83	78	328	557
P. J. Brennan	67	104	74	406	651
D. O'Regan	66	58	41	235	400

The above statistics have been provided by *Timeform,* publishers of the *Racehorses* and *Chasers and Hurdlers* annuals

THE FLAT

THE CLASSICS

ONE THOUSAND GUINEAS

(1814) Rowley Mile, Newmarket, for three-year-old fillies

Year	*Winner*	*Betting*	*Owner*	*Jockey*	*Trainer*	*Runners*
2006	Speciosa	10–1	M. H. Sly	M. Fenton	Mrs P. Sly	13
2007	Finsceal Beo	5–4	M. A. Ryan	K. Manning	J. Bolger	21
2008	Natagora	11–4	Stefan Friborg	C-P Lemaire	P. Bary	15
2009	Ghanaati	20–1	H. Al Maktoum	R. Hills	B. Hills	19
2010	Special Duty	9–2	K. Abdulla	S. Pasquier	Mrs C. Head-Maarek	17

TWO THOUSAND GUINEAS

(1809) Rowley Mile, Newmarket, for three-year-olds

Year	*Winner*	*Betting*	*Owner*	*Jockey*	*Trainer*	*Runners*
2006	George Washington	6–4	Mrs J. Magnier and M. Tabor	K. Fallon	A. O'Brien	14
2007	Cockney Rebel	25–1	P. Cunningham	O. Peslier	G. Huffer	24
2008	Henrythenavigator	11–1	Mrs J. Magnier	J. Murtagh	A. O'Brien	15
2009	Sea the Stars	8–1	C. Tsui	M. Kinane	M. Oxx	16
2010	Makfi	33–1	M. Offenstadt	C-P. Lemaire	M. Delzangles	19

THE DERBY

(1780) Epsom, 1 mile and about 4 f, for three-year-olds

The first winner was Sir Charles Bunbury's Diomed in 1780. The owners with the record number of winners are Lord Egremont, who won in 1782, 1804, 1805, 1807, 1826 (also won five Oaks); and the late Aga Khan, who won in 1930, 1935, 1936, 1948, 1952. Other winning owners are: Duke of Grafton (1802, 1809, 1810, 1815); Mr J. Bowes (1835, 1843, 1852, 1853); Sir J. Hawley (1851, 1858, 1859, 1868); the 1st Duke of Westminster (1880, 1882, 1886, 1899); and Sir Victor Sassoon (1953, 1957, 1958, 1960).

The Derby was run at Newmarket in 1915–18 and 1940–5.

Year	*Winner*	*Betting*	*Owner*	*Jockey*	*Trainer*	*Runners*
2006	Sir Percy	6–1	A. E. Pakenham	M. Dwyer	M. Tregoning	18
2007	Authorized	5–4	Saleh Al Homeizi and Imad Al Sagar	L. Dettori	P. Chapple-Hyam	17
2008	New Approach	5–1	H. R. H. Princess Haya of Jordan	K. Manning	J. Bolger	16
2009	Sea the Stars	11–4	C. Tsui	M. Kinane	M. Oxx	12
2010	Workforce	6–1	K. Abdulla	R. Moore	M. Stoute	12

THE OAKS

(1779) Epsom, 1 mile and about 4 f, for three-year-old fillies

Year	*Winner*	*Betting*	*Owner*	*Jockey*	*Trainer*	*Runners*
2006	Alexandrova	9–4	Mrs J. Magnier and M. Tabor	K. Fallon	A. O'Brien	10
2007	Light Shift	13–2	Niarchos family	T. Durcan	H. Cecil	14
2008	Look Here	33–1	J. H. Richmond-Watson	S. Sanders	R. M. Beckett	16
2009	Sariska	9–4	Michael Bell	Jamie Spencer	Lady Bamford	12
2010	Snow Fairy	9–1	Anamoine Ltd.	R. Moore	E. A. L. Dunlop	15

ST LEGER

(1776) Doncaster, 1 mile and about 6 f, for three-year-olds (2006 run at York)

Year	*Winner*	*Betting*	*Owner*	*Jockey*	*Trainer*	*Runners*
2005	Scorpion	10–11	Mrs J. Magnier and M. Tabor	L. Dettori	A. O'Brien	6
2006	Sixties Icon	11–8	Mrs S. Roy	L. Dettori	J. Noseda	11
2007	Lucarno	7–2	Mr G. Strawbridge	J. Fortune	J. H. M. Gosden	10
2008	Conduit	8–1	Sir Michael Stoute	L. Dettori	Ballymacoll Stud	14
2009	Mastery	14–1	Godolphin	T. Durcan	S. Bin Suroor	8

RESULTS

CAMBRIDGESHIRE HANDICAP

(1839) Newmarket, 1 mile and 1 f

2006 Formal Decree (3y), J. Spencer
2007 Pipedreamer (3y), J. Fortune
2008 Tazeez (4y), R. Hills
2009 Supaseus (6y), T. Block

PRIX DE L'ARC DE TRIOMPHE

(1920) Longchamp, 1½ miles

2006 Rail Link (3y), S. Pasquier
2007 Dylan Thomas (4y), K. Fallon
2008 Zarkava (3y), C. Soumillon
2009 Sea the Stars (3y), M. J. Kinane

CESAREWITCH
(1839) Newmarket, 2 miles and about 2 f

2006 Detroit City (4y), J. Spencer
2007 Leg Spinner (6y), J. Murtagh
2008 Caracciola (11yr), E. Ahern
2009 Darley Sun (3y), A. Atzeni

CHAMPION STAKES
(1877) Newmarket, 1 mile and 2 f

2006 Pride (6y), C-P. Lemaire
2007 Literato (3y), C-P. Lemaire
2008 New Approach (3y), K. J. Manning
2009 Twice Over (4y), T. Queally

DUBAI WORLD CUP
(1996) Dubai, 1 mile and 2 f

2007 Invasor (5y), F. Jara
2008 Curlin (4y), R. Albarado
2009 Well Armed (6y), A. Gryder
2010 Gloria de Campeao (7y), T. Pereira

LINCOLN HANDICAP
(1965) Doncaster, 1 mile

2007 Very Wise (5y), J. Fanning
2008 Smokey Oakey (4y), J. Quinn
2009 Expresso Star (4y), J. Fortune
2010 Penitent (4y), J. Murtagh

JOCKEY CLUB STAKES
(1894) Newmarket, 1½ miles

2007 Sixties Icon (4y), L. Dettori
2008 Getaway (5y), S. Pasquier
2009 Bronze Cannon (4y), J. Fortune
2010 Jukebox Jury (4y), R. Ffrench

PRIX DU JOCKEY CLUB
(1836) Chantilly, 1 mile and about 2½ f, for three-year-olds

2007 Lawman, L. Dettori
2008 Vision D'Etat, I. Mendizabal
2009 Le Havre, C-P. Lemaire
2010 Lope de Vega, M. Guyon

ASCOT GOLD CUP
(1807) Ascot, 2 miles and about 4 f

2007 Yeats (6y), M. J. Kinane
2008 Yeats (7y), J. Murtagh
2009 Yeats (8y), J. Murtagh
2010 Rite of Passage (6y), P. J. Smullen

IRISH DERBY
(1866) Curragh, 1½ miles, for three-year-olds

2007 Soldier of Fortune, J. A. Heffernan
2008 Frozen Fire, J. A. Heffernan
2009 Fame and Glory, J. Murtagh
2010 Cape Blanco, J. Murtagh

ECLIPSE STAKES
(1886) Sandown, 1 mile and about 2 f

2007 Notnowcato, (5y), R. Moore
2008 Mount Nelson (4y), J. Murtagh
2009 Sea the Stars (3y), M. J. Kinane
2010 Twice Over (5y), T. Queally

KING GEORGE VI AND QUEEN ELIZABETH DIAMOND STAKES
(1952) Ascot, 1 mile and about 4 f

2007 Dylan Thomas (4y), J. P. Murtagh
2008 Duke of Marmalade (4y), J. Murtagh
2009 Conduit (4y), R. Moore
2010 Harbinger (4y), O. Peslier

GOODWOOD CUP
(1812) Goodwood, about 2 miles

2007 Alegretto (4y), R. Moore
2008 Yeats (7y), J. Murtagh
2009 Schiaparelli (6 y), L. Dettori
2010 Illustrious Blue (7y), J. Crowley

STATISTICS

WINNING FLAT OWNERS 2009

Hamdan Al Maktoum	£2,959,686
Godolphin	2,559,242
K. Abdulla	1,973,568
Christopher Tsui	1,575,935
Sheikh Hamdan bin Mohammed Al Maktoum	1,245,851
Ballymacoll Stud	1,187,651
D. Smith, Mrs J. Magnier & M. Tabor	937,254
M. Tabor, D. Smith & Mrs J. Magnier	836,850
Cheveley Park Stud	830,803
Saeed Manana	606,772

WINNING FLAT TRAINERS 2009

M. Stoute	£3,296,912
A. P. O'Brien	2,677,212
M. Johnston	2,607,701
S. bin Suroor	2,559,242
R. Hannon	2,504,367
J. H. M. Gosden	2,067,124
B. W. Hills	1,795,016
J. Oxx	1,614,717
R. A Fahey	1,553,016
H. R. Cecil	1,311,631

WINNING FLAT SIRES 2009

	Races won	*Stakes*
Cape Cross by Green Desert	135	£2,897,835
Oasis Dream by Green Desert	100	2,564,661
Pivotal by Polar Falcon	110	1,826,198
Danehill Dancer by Danehill	77	1,451,866
Galileo by Sadler's Wells	39	1,401,061
Sadler's Wells by Northern Dancer	35	1,238,106
Montjeu by Sadler's Wells	49	1,209,584
Dansili by Danehill	83	1,159,078
Invincible Spirit by Green Desert	80	1,059,372
Exceed and Excel by Danehill	75	1,036,356

WINNING FLAT JOCKEYS 2009

	1st	*2nd*	*3rd*	*Unpl.*	*Total mts*
R. L. Moore	178	140	112	444	874
R. Hughes	144	98	92	434	768
J. Spencer	130	110	82	373	695
C. Catlin	126	137	110	916	1,289
N. Callan	120	125	85	558	888
J. Crowley	120	112	124	710	1,066
R. Winston	120	110	116	592	938
P. Hanagan	119	115	128	637	999
J. Fanning	113	93	74	432	712
P. Makin	111	75	80	495	761

The above statistics have been provided by *Timeform,* publishers of the *Racehorses* and *Chasers and Hurdlers* annuals

ICE HOCKEY

MEN'S WORLD CHAMPIONSHIP 2010
Cologne, Germany, May
Final: Czech Republic beat Russia 2–1

WOMEN'S WORLD CHAMPIONSHIP 2009
Hameenlinna, Finland, April
Final: USA beat Canada 4–1

DOMESTIC COMPETITIONS
Elite League Champions 2009–10: Coventry Blaze
Play-off Champions 2010: Belfast Giants
Challenge Cup final 2010: Nottingham Panthers beat Cardiff Devils 8–7

NATIONAL HOCKEY LEAGUE
Stanley Cup final 2009–10: Chicago Blackhawks beat Philadelphia Flyers 4–2

ICE SKATING

WORLD CHAMPIONSHIPS 2010
Turin, Italy, March

Men: Takahashi Daisuke (Japan)
Women: Asada Mao (Japan)
Pairs: Pang Qing and Tong Jian (China)
Ice Dance: Tessa Virtue and Scott Moir (Canada)

EUROPEAN CHAMPIONSHIPS 2010
Tallinn, Estonia, January

Men: Evgeni Plushenko (Russia)
Women: Carolina Koster (Italy)
Pairs: Yuko Kavaguti and Alexander Smirnov (Russia)
Ice Dance: Joksana Domnina and Maxim Shabalin (Russia)

BRITISH CHAMPIONSHIPS 2010
Sheffield, November 2009

Men: Mathew Parr
Women: Jenna McCorkell
Pairs: Stacey Kemp and David King
Ice Dance: Sinead Kerr and John Kerr

JUDO

EUROPEAN CHAMPIONSHIPS 2010
Vienna, Austria, April

MEN
Heavyweight (over 100kg): Igor Makarov (Belarus)
Light-heavyweight (100kg): Elco van der Geest (Belgium)
Middleweight (90kg): Marcus Nyman (Sweden)
Welterweight (81kg): Sirazhudin Magomedov (Russia)
Lightweight (73kg): Joao Pino (Portugal)
Junior Lightweight (66kg): Sugoi Uriarte (Spain)
Bantamweight (60kg): Sofiane Milous (France)

WOMEN
Heavyweight (over 78kg): Lucija Polavder (Slovenia)
Light-heavyweight (78kg): Abigel Joo (Hungary)
Middleweight (70kg): Anett Meszeros (Hungary)
Welterweight (63kg): Elisabeth Willeboordse (Netherlands)
Lightweight (57kg): Corina Caprioriu (Romania)
Junior Lightweight (52kg): Natalia Kuzyutina (Russia)
Bantamweight (48kg): Alina Dumitrou (Romania)

BRITISH OPEN CHAMPIONSHIPS 2010
London, May

MEN
Heavyweight (over 100kg): Angel Parra (Spain)
Light-heavyweight (100kg): Danny Mieeuwsen (Netherlands)
Middleweight (90kg): Derek Nathan Gielis (Belgium)
Welter (81kg): Francisco Javier Madera (Spain)
Lightweight (73kg): Christophe Besnard (France)
Junior Lightweight (66kg): Jasper Lefevere (Belgium)
Bantamweight (60kg): Ashley McKenzie (Great Britain)

WOMEN
Heavyweight (over 78kg): Sarah Adlington (Great Britain)
Light-heavyweight (78kg): Audrey Thorel (France)
Middleweight (70kg): Karine Berger (France)
Welter (63kg): Gemma Howell (Great Britain)
Lightweight (57kg): Shareen Richardson (Belgium)
Junior Lightweight (52kg): Miriam Polak (Netherlands)
Bantamweight (48kg): Amelie Rosseneu (Belgium)

MOTORCYCLING

MOTOGP 2009
Sanmarinese (Misano): Valentino Rossi (Italy), Yamaha
Portuguese (Estoril): Jorge Lorenzo (Spain), Yamaha
Australian (Phillip Island): Casey Stoner (Australia), Ducati
Malaysian (Sepang): Casey Stoner (Australia), Ducati
Spanish (Valencia): Dani Pedrosa (Spain), Honda
Riders' Championship 2009: 1. Valentino Rossi (Italy), Yamaha, 306pts; 2. Jorge Lorenzo (Spain), Yamaha, 261pts; 3. Dani Pedrosa (Spain), Honda, 234pts

MOTOGP 2010
Qatari (Losail): Valentino Rossi (Italy), Yamaha
Spanish (Jerez): Jorge Lorenzo (Spain), Yamaha
French (Le Mans): Jorge Lorenzo (Spain), Yamaha
Italian (Mugello): Dani Pedrosa (Spain), Honda
British (Silverstone): Jorge Lorenzo (Spain), Yamaha
Dutch (Assen): Jorge Lorenzo (Spain), Yamaha
Cataluñyan (Montmelo): Jorge Lorenzo (Spain), Yamaha
German (Sachsenring): Dani Pedrosa (Spain), Honda
USA (Laguna Seca): Jorge Lorenzo (Spain), Yamaha
Czech Republic (Brno): Jorge Lorenzo (Spain), Yamaha
USA (Indianapolis): Dani Pedrosa (Spain), Honda

250CC GRAND PRIX 2009
Sanmarinese (Misano): Hector Barbera (Spain), Aprilia
Portuguese (Estoril): Marco Simoncelli (Italy), Gilera
Australian (Phillip Island): Marco Simoncelli (Italy), Gilera
Malaysian (Sepang): Hiroshi Aoyama (Japan), Honda
Spanish (Valencia): Hector Barbera (Spain), Aprilia
Riders' Championship 2009: 1. Hiroshi Aoyama (Japan), Honda, 261pts; Hector Barber (Spain), Aprilia, 239pts; Marco Simoncelli (Italy), Gilera, 231pts

MOTO2 2010
Qatari (Losail): Shoya Tomizawa (Japan), Suter
Spanish (Jerez): Toni Elias (Spain), Moriwaki
French (Le Mans): Toni Elias (Spain), Moriwaki
Italian (Mugello): Andrea Iannone (Italy), Speed Up
British (Silverstone): Jules Cluzen (France), Suter

Dutch (Assen): Andrea Iannone (Italy), Speed Up
Cataluñyan (Montmelo): Yuki Takahashi (Japan), Tech 3
German (Sachsenring): Toni Elias (Spain), Moriwaki
Czech Republic (Brno): Toni Elias (Spain), Moriwaki
USA (Indianapolis): Toni Elias (Spain), Moriwaki

125CC GRAND PRIX 2009
Sanmarinese (Misano): Julian Simon (Spain), Aprilia
Portuguese (Estoril): Pol Esparagaro (Spain), Derbi
Australian (Phillip Island): Julian Simon (Spain), Aprilia
Malaysian (Sepang): Julian Simon (Spain), Aprilia
Spanish (Valencia): Julian Simon (Spain), Aprilia
Riders' Championship 2009: 1. Julian Simon (Spain), Aprilia, 289pts; 2. Bradley Smith (Great Britain), Aprilia, 223.5pts; 3. Nicolas Terol (Spain), Aprilia, 179.5pts

125CC GRAND PRIX 2010
Qatari (Losail): Nicolas Terol (Spain), Aprilia
Spanish (Jerez): Pol Esparagaro (Spain), Derbi
French (Le Mans): Pol Esparagaro (Spain), Derbi
Italian (Mugello): Marc Marquez (Spain), Derbi
British (Silverstone): Marc Marquez (Spain), Derbi
Dutch (Assen): Marc Marquez (Spain), Derbi
Cataluñyan (Montmelo): Marc Marquez (Spain), Derbi
German (Sachsenring): Marc Marquez (Spain), Derbi
Czech Republic (Brno): Nicolas Terol (Spain), Aprilia
USA (Indianapolis): Nicolas Terol (Spain), Aprilia

ISLE OF MAN TOURIST TROPHY 2010
Senior: Ian Hutchinson (England), Honda
Supersport: Race 1 – Ian Hutchinson (England), Honda: Race 2 – Ian Hutchinson (England), Honda

WORLD SUPERBIKES 2009
Germany (Nurburgring): Race 1 – Ben Spies (USA), Yamaha; Race 2 – Jonathan Rea (Great Britain), Honda
Italy (Imola): Race 1 – Noriyuki Haga (Japan), Yamaha; Race 2 – Michel Fabrizio (Italy), Ducati
France (Magny Cours): Race 1 – Ben Spies (USA), Yamaha; Race 2 – Noriyuki Haga (Japan), Yamaha
Portugal (Algarve): Race 1 – Ben Spies (USA), Yamaha; Race 2 – Michel Fabrizio (Italy), Ducati
Riders' World Championship 2009: 1. Ben Spies (USA), Yamaha, 462pts; 2. Noriyuki Haga (Japan), Yamaha, 456pts; 3. Michel Fabrizio (Italy), Ducati, 382pts

WORLD SUPERBIKES 2010
Australia (Phillip Island): Race 1 – Leon Haslam (Great Britain), Suzuki; Race 2 – Carlos Checa (Spain), Ducati
Portugal (Algarve): Race 1 – Max Biaggi (Italy), Aprilia; Race 2 – Max Biaggi (Italy), Aprilia
Spain (Valencia): Race 1 – Leon Haslam (Great Britain), Suzuki; Race 2 – Noriyuki Haga (Japan), Ducati
Netherlands (Assen): Race 1 – Jonathan Rea (Great Britain), Honda; Race 2 – Jonathan Rea (Great Britain), Honda
Italy (Monza): Race 1 – Max Biaggi (Italy), Aprilia; Race 2 – Max Biaggi (Italy), Aprilia
South Africa (Kyalami): Race 1 – Michel Fabrizio (Italy), Ducati; Race 2 – Leon Haslam (Great Britain), Suzuki
USA (Salt Lake City): Race 1 – Max Biaggi (Italy), Aprilia; Race 2 – Max Biaggi (Italy), Aprilia
San Marino (Misano): Race 1 – Max Biaggi (Italy), Aprilia; Race 2 – Max Biaggi (Italy), Aprilia
Czech (Brno): Race 1 – Jonathan Rea (Great Britain), Honda; Race 2 – Max Biaggi (Italy), Aprilia
British (Silverstone): Race 1 – Cal Crutchlow (Great Britain), Yamaha; Race 2 – Cal Crutchlow (Great Britain), Yamaha

MOTOR RACING

FORMULA ONE GRAND PRIX 2009
Italian (Monza): Rubens Barrichello (Brazil), Brawn
Singapore: Lewis Hamilton (Great Britain), McLaren
Japanese (Suzuka): Sebastian Vettel (Germany), Red Bull
Brazilian (Interlagos): Mark Webber (Australia), Red Bull
Abu Dhabi (Yas Marina): Sebastian Vettel (Germany), Red Bull
Drivers' World Championship 2009: 1. Jenson Button (Great Britain), Brawn, 95pts; 2. Sebastian Vettel (Germany), Red Bull, 84pts; 3. Rubens Barrichello (Brazil), Brawn, 77pts
Constructors' World Championship 2009: 1. Brawn, 172pts; 2. Red Bull, 153.5; 3. McLaren, 71pts

FORMULA ONE GRAND PRIX 2010
Bahraini (Sakhir): Fernando Alonso (Spain), Ferrari
Australian (Melbourne): Jenson Button (Great Britain), McLaren
Malaysian (Sepang): Sebastian Vettel (Germany), Red Bull
Chinese (Shanghai): Jenson Button (Great Britain), McLaren
Spanish (Barcelona): Mark Webber (Australia), Red Bull
Monaco (Monte Carlo): Mark Webber (Australia), Red Bull
Turkish (Istanbul): Lewis Hamilton (Great Britain), McLaren
Canadian (Montreal): Lewis Hamilton (Great Britain), McLaren
European (Valencia): Sebastian Vettel (Germany), Red Bull
British (Silverstone): Mark Webber (Australia), Red Bull
German (Nürburgring): Fernando Alonso (Spain), Ferrari
Hungarian (Budapest): Mark Webber (Australia), Red Bull
Belgium (Spa): Lewis Hamilton (Great Britain), McLaren

INDIANAPOLIS 500 2010
Indianapolis, USA, May
Dario Franchitti (Great Britain), Chip Ganassi

LE MANS 24-HOUR RACE 2010
Le Mans, France, June
Mike Rockenfeller (Germany), Timo Bernhard (Germany) and Romain Dumas (France), Audi

MOTOR RALLYING

WORLD RALLY CHAMPIONSHIP 2009
Australia: Mikko Hirvonen (Finland), Ford
Spain: Sébastien Loeb (France), Citroën
Great Britain: Mikko Hirvonen (Finland), Ford
Drivers' World Championship 2009: 1. Sébastien Loeb, (France), Citroën, 93pts; 2. Mikko Hirvonen (Finland), Ford, 92pts; 3. Daniel Sordo (Spain), Citroën, 64pts
Manufacturers' World Championship 2009: 1. Citroën, 167pts; 2. BP Ford, 140pts; 3. Stobart Ford, 80pts

WORLD RALLY CHAMPIONSHIP 2010
Sweden: Mikko Hirvonen (Finland), Ford
Mexico: Sébastien Loeb (France), Citroën
Jordan: Sébastien Loeb (France), Citroën
Turkey: Sébastien Loeb (France), Citroën
New Zealand: Jari-Matti Latvala (Finland), Ford
Portugal: Sébastien Ogier (France), Citroën

Bulgaria: Sébastien Loeb (France), Citroën
Finand: Jari-Matti Latvala (Finland), Ford
Germany: Sébastien Loeb (France), Citroën

BRITISH RALLY CHAMPIONSHIP 2009
Ulster: Eugene Donnelly (Ireland), Skoda
Yorkshire: Keith Cronin (Ireland), Mitsubishi

BRITISH RALLY CHAMPIONSHIP 2010
North Wales: Keith Cronin (Ireland), Subaru
Pirelli International: Gwyndaf Evans (Great Britain), Mitsubishi
Jim Clark International: Gwyndaf Evans (Great Britain), Mitsubishi
Isle of Man: Keith Cronin (Ireland), Subaru
Rally NI: Craig Breen (Ireland), Ford

DAKAR RALLY 2010
Argentina and Chile, January

Bike: Cyril Despres (France), KTM
Quad: Marcos Patronelli (Argentina), Yamaha
Car: Carlos Sainz (Spain), Volkswagen
Truck: Vladimir Chagin (Russia), Kamaz

NETBALL

Superleague 2009–10: Surrey Storm
Superleague play-off 2010: TeamBath

NORDIC EVENTS

BIATHLON WORLD CUP 2009–10

MEN
Overall: Emil Hegle Svendsen (Norway), 828pts

WOMEN
Overall: Magdalena Neuner (Germany), 933pts

BIATHLON WORLD CHAMPIONSHIPS 2010
Khanty-Mansiysk, Russia, March

MIXED
Relay: Germany

NORDIC WORLD CUP 2009–10

CROSS COUNTRY
Men: Petter Northug Jr. (Norway), 1,621pts
Women: Justyna Kowalczyk (Poland), 2,064pts

SKI-JUMPING
Simon Ammann (Switzerland), 1,649pts

NORDIC COMBINED
Jason Lamy Chappuis (France), 1,155pts

POLO

Prince of Wales Trophy 2010: Broncos beat Zacara 8–7
Queen's Cup final 2010: Dubai beat Les Lions ll 12–10
Warwickshire Cup 2010: Emlor beat Salkeld 9–7
Gold Cup (British Open) final 2010: Dubai beat Lechuza Caracas 14–12
Coronation Cup 2010: England beat New Zealand 9–7

RACKETS

Noel Bruce Cup 2009: C. Danby and A. Titchener-Barrett (Harrow) beat J. Coyne and T. Cockroft (Wellington) 4–0
Amateur Singles Championship final 2009: A. Titchener-Barrett beat J. Coyne 3–0
The Foster Cup final 2009 (public schools' singles championship): C. Portz (Winchester) beat N. Hopcroft (Wellington) 3–0
British Professional Singles Championship final 2010: M. Hubbard beat D. Makey 3–0
British Open Singles Championship final 2010: A. Titchener-Barrett beat J. Stout 4–3
British Open Doubles Championship final 2010: A. Titchener-Barrett and T. Cockcroft beat J. Stout and M. Gooding 4–2
Amateur Doubles Championship 2010: G. Barker and A. Robinson beat T. Cockroft and A. Titchener-Barrett 4–0
Public Schools Doubles 2009: C. Portz and B. Stevens (Winchester) beat R. Owen and C. Stout (Cheltenham) 4–3

REAL TENNIS

MEN
British Open Singles final 2009: Robert Fahey (Australia) beat Steve Virgona (Australia) 3–1
British Open Doubles final 2009: Steve Virgona (Australia) and Nick Wood (Great Britain) beat Robert Fahey (Australia) and Ruaraidh Gunn (Great Britain) 3–0
Inter-Club Tournament 2009: Singles – Tom Lewis (Bristol and Bath); Doubles – Leamington 1; Club team trophy – Moreton Morrell
World Singles Championship 2010: Robert Fahey (Australia) beat Steve Virgona (Australia) 7–2
Henry Leaf Cup final 2010 (public schools' old boys' doubles championship): Charterhouse 1 beat Charterhouse 2 2–0
National League final 2010: Middlesex University beat RTC 2–1

WOMEN
British Open Singles Championship final 2010: Claire Vigrass (Great Britain) beat Karen Hird (Great Britain) 2–0
British Open Doubles Championship final 2010: Claire Vigrass (Great Britain) and Freddy Adam (USA) beat Alex Garside (Great Britain) and Aldona Greenwood (Great Britain) 2–0

ROWING

BRITISH CHAMPIONSHIPS 2010
Strathclyde, July

MEN
Single sculls: Ben Hicks (Isle of Ely), 8min 18.78sec
Double sculls: Hertfordshire University/Inverness, 6min 53.95sec
Quadruple sculls: Monmouth/Hereford, 6min 20.53sec
Coxless pairs: Durham University, 7min 00.70sec
Coxless fours: London, 6min 28.04sec
Coxed fours: London, 7min 12.05sec
Eights: London, 6min 05.25sec

WOMEN

Single sculls: Emily Taylor (Durham University), 8min 09.55sec
Double sculls: Mortlake, Anglian & Alpha, 7min 19.02sec
Quadruple sculls: Nottingham/Latymer Upper/Dame A Harpur, 7min 02.35sec
Coxless pairs: City Of Oxford, 7min 42.90sec
Coxless fours: Rhwyfo Cymru, 7min 18.89sec
Coxed fours: Reading, 7min 29.62sec
Eights: LEH/DUS/TSS/PAN/DAH/CAN/NRC, 6min 48.86sec

HENLEY ROYAL REGATTA 2010

Grand Challenge Cup: Ruder Club Hansa von 1898 e.V. Dortmund (Germany) beat Waiariki R. C. (New Zealand) and The Tideway Scullers School by 1¾ lengths
Stewards' Challenge Cup: Princeton Training Center (USA) beat Club France (France) by ¾ length
Queen Mother Challenge Cup: Reading University and Leander Club beat Princeton Training Center (USA) by 2 lengths
Silver Goblets and Nickalls' Challenge Cup: Murray and Bond (New Zealand) beat Reed and Triggs Hodge easily
Double Sculls Challenge Cup: Berest and Bahain (France) beat Wells and Bateman (not rowed out)
Diamond Challenge Sculls: M. Drysdale (New Zealand) beat L. Caronen (Sweden) by 3 lengths
Remenham Challenge Cup: Western R. C. (Canada) beat Leander Club and Oxford Brookes University by 2 lengths
Princess Grace Challenge Cup: Gloucester R.C. and Leander Club beat Waiariki R.C. (New Zealand) by 5 lengths
Princess Royal Challenge Cup: M. Knapkova (Czech Republic) beat G. L. Stone (USA) by 3½ lengths
Ladies' Challenge Plate: Harvard University (USA) beat Oxford Brookes University and Oxford University by ⅓ length
Visitors' Challenge Cup: Leander Club and Durham University beat Leander Club 'A' by 2 lengths
Prince of Wales Challenge Cup: Leander Club beat The Tideway Scullers School 'A' by ¾ length
Thames Challenge Cup: 1829 B.C. beat West End R.C. (New Zealand) by 2¾ lengths
Wyfold Challenge Cup: Nottingham and Union R.C. beat London R.C. 'A' by 1¼ lengths
Britannia Challenge Cup: The Tideway Scullers School beat London R.C. 'A' by ½ length
Temple Challenge Cup: University of Washington (USA) beat Amsterdamsche Studenten Roeivereeniging Nereus (Netherlands) by 4¼ lengths
Prince Albert Challenge Cup: University College Dublin (Ireland) beat Bristol University by 2 lengths
Princess Elizabeth Challenge Cup: Princess Elizabeth Challenge Cup: Eton College beat Kent School (USA) by 4 lengths
Fawley Challenge Cup: Banks R.C. and Melbourne University (Australia) beat Westminster School and Walton R.C. by 2½ lengths

THE 155TH UNIVERSITY BOAT RACE

Putney–Mortlake, 4 miles, 1 f, 180 yd, 3 April 2010

Cambridge beat Oxford easily; 17min 35sec
Cambridge have won 80 times, Oxford 75 and there has been one dead heat. The record time is 16min 19sec, rowed by Cambridge in 1998.

OTHER ROWING EVENTS

Wingfield Sculls 2009: Men, Alan Campbell (Tideway Scullers); *Women,* Sophie Hosking (London R. C.)
Oxford Torpids 2010: Men, Christ Church; *Women,* Magdalen
Oxford Summer Eights 2010: Men, Christ Church; *Women,* Balliol
Head of the River 2010: Men, Molesey I; *Women,* Gloucester/Imperial College/Marlow/Reading University/Thames/UL

RUGBY FIVES

National Open Singles Championship final 2009: J. Toop beat J. Minta 2–0
National Ladies' Singles Championship final 2009: C. Knowles beat E. Howie 2–0
National Ladies' Doubles Championship final 2009: C. Knowles and M. Whitehead beat A. Ganguly and C. Cooley 2–0
National Open Doubles Championship final 2010: H. Buchanan and R. Perry beat M. Bate and W. Ellison 2–0
National Club Championship final 2010: Manchester YMCA beat Old Paulines 121–83
National Schools' Singles Championship final 2010: E. Kay (St. Paul's) beat L. Thomson (Christ's Hospital) 2–0
National Schools' Doubles Championship final 2010: St. Paul's I beat St. Paul's II
Varsity Match 2010: Oxford beat Cambridge 300–38

RUGBY LEAGUE

Challenge Cup final 2010: Warrington beat Leeds 30–6
Super League Grand Final 2009: Leeds beat St. Helens 18–10
World Club Challenge 2010: Melbourne beat Leeds 18–10

AMATEUR COMPETITIONS 2009–10

National Conference League Premier Division Grand Final: Leigh East beat Siddal 37–10
Division One: Thatto Heath Crusaders
Division Two: Eccles
BARLA National Cup final: Queens beat Leigh East 17–7
Varsity Match 2010: Oxford beat Cambridge 32–22

RUGBY UNION

SIX NATIONS' CHAMPIONSHIP 2010

6 February	London	England beat Wales 30–17
	Dublin	Ireland beat Italy 29–11
7 February	Edinburgh	France beat Scotland 19–18
13 February	Paris	France beat Ireland 33–10
	Cardiff	Wales beat Scotland 31–24
14 February	Rome	England beat Italy 17–12
26 February	Cardiff	France beat Wales 26–20
27 February	London	Ireland beat England 20–16
	Rome	Italy beat Scotland 16–12
13 March	Dublin	Ireland beat Wales 27–12
	Edinburgh	Scotland drew with England 15–15
14 March	Paris	France beat Italy 46–20
20 March	Paris	France beat England 12–10
	Dublin	Scotland beat Ireland 23–20
	Cardiff	Wales beat Italy 33–10

Final standings: 1. France, 10pts; 2. Ireland, 6pts; 3. England, 5pts; 4. Wales, 4pts; 5. Scotland, 3pts; 6. Italy, 2pts

EUROPEAN COMPETITIONS 2009–10
Heineken European Cup final: Toulouse beat Biarritz 21–19
European Challenge Cup: Cardiff Blues beat Toulon 28–21

DOMESTIC COMPETITIONS 2009–10

ENGLAND
Premiership: Leicester, 73pts
Premiership final: Leicester beat Saracens 33–27
RFU Championship: Bristol, 92pts
RFU Championship final: Exeter beat Bristol 9–6 (at Exeter); Exeter beat Bristol 29–10 (at Bristol). Exeter promoted to Premiership.
National League: Division 1, Esher, 135pts; *Division 2* (North), Macclesfield, 130pts; (South) Barking, 124pts
British and irish Cup final: Cornish Pirates beat Munster 23–14
County Championship final (Bill Beaumont Cup): Lancashire beat Gloucestershire 36–6
County Shield: Dorset & Wilts beat Leicestershire 36–26
County Plate: Kent beat Warwickshire 33–27 (aet)
126th Varsity Match: Cambridge beat Oxford 31–27

ANGLO-WELSH
LV Cup final: Northampton beat Gloucester 30–24

CELTIC
Magners League: Leinster, 55pts
Magners League final: Ospreys beat Leinster 17–12

SCOTLAND
Premier League: Division 1, Currie, 101pts; *Division 2,* Stirling County, 90pts; *Division 3,* Hillhead/Jordanhill, 95pts
Cup final: Ayr beat Melrose 36–23

WALES
Premiership: Neath, 104pts; *National League:* Division 1 (East), UWIC, 88pts; (West), Tonmawr, 95pts; (North) Nant Conwy, 80pts
WRU Challenge Cup final: Llanelli beat Carmarthen Quins 20–8

IRELAND
All Ireland League: Division 1A, Cork Constitution*, 46pts; Division 1B, Old Belvedere*, 56pts; Division 2, Lansdowne*, 66pts; Division 3, Queen's University*, 69pts

* All table-topping teams also won play-offs

SHOOTING

140TH NATIONAL RIFLE ASSOCIATION IMPERIAL MEETING
Bisley, July 2010

Queen's Prize: Barnard, 129.7 v-bulls
Grand Aggregate: D. N. Kent, 938 v-bulls; Maj. Ret'd P. Eggemann, 864 v-bulls
Prince of Wales Prize: H.J. Mitera, 86 v-bulls
St George's Vase: Hinchliffe, 68.6 v-bulls
All Comers' Aggregate: G. E. Morris, 373.51 v-bulls
Kolapore Cup: Great Britain, 1196.195 v-bulls
Chancellor's Trophy: Cambridge University, 1,153.125 v-bulls
National Trophy: Scotland, 2,070.277 v-bulls
Musketeers Cup: Exeter University, 591.78 v-bulls
County Championship Long Range: Surrey, 597.91 v-bulls
Mackinnon Challenge Cup: England, 1,173.140 v-bulls
The Albert: G. L. James, 222.23 v-bulls
Hopton Challenge Cup: Maj. A. R. McLeod, 987.106 v-bulls

SNOOKER

2009–10
Shanghai Masters: Ronnie O'Sullivan (England) beat Liang Wenbo (China) 10–5
Grand Prix (Glasgow): Neil Robertson (Australia) beat Ding Junhui (China) 9–4
UK Championship (Telford): Ding Junhui (China) beat John Higgins (Scotland) 10–8
Masters (Wembley): Mark Selby (England) beat Ronnie O'Sullivan (England) 10–9
Welsh Open (Newport): John Higgins (Scotland) beat Ali Carter (England) 9–4
China Open (Beijing): Mark Williams (Wales) beat Ding Junhui (China) 10–6
World Championship (Sheffield): Neil Robertson (Australia) beat Graeme Dott (Scotland) 18–13

SPEED SKATING

WORLD ALL-ROUND CHAMPIONSHIPS 2010
Heerenveen, Netherlands, March

MEN
500m: Konrad Niedzwiedzki (Poland), 35.68sec
1,500m: Jonathan Kuck (USA), 1min 45.36sec
5,000m: Sven Kramer (Netherlands), 6min 19.63sec
10,000m: Sven Kramer (Netherlands), 12min 57.97sec

WOMEN
500m: Yekaterina Shikhova (Russia), 38.83sec
1,500m: Kristina Groves (Canada), 1min 56.64sec
3,000m: Martina Sablikova (Czech Rep.), 4min 03.59sec
5,000m: Martina Sablikova (Czech Republic), 6min 50.98sec

EUROPEAN ALL-ROUND CHAMPIONSHIPS 2010
Hamar, Norway, January

MEN
500m: Konrad Niedzwiedzki (Poland), 36.07sec
1,500m: Enrico Fabris (Italy), 1min 46.37sec
5,000m: Sven Kramer (Netherlands), 6min 19.78sec
10,000m: Sven Kramer (Netherlands), 13min 19.32sec

WOMEN
500m: Karolina Erbanova (Czech Rep.), 39.54sec
1,500m: Ireen Wuest (Netherlands), 1min 59.08sec
3,000m: Martina Sablikova (Czech Rep.), 4min 03.09sec
5,000m: Martina Sablikova (Czech Rep.), 6min 59.44sec

WORLD SHORT TRACK CHAMPIONSHIPS 2010
Sofia, Bulgaria, March

MEN
500m: Liang Wenhao (China), 41.383sec
1,000m: Lee Ho-Suk (Rep. of Korea), 1min 26.675sec

1,500m: Kwak Yoon-Gy (Rep. of Korea), 2min 21.387sec
3,000m: Lee Ho-Suk (Rep. of Korea)
5,000m relay: Korea, 6min 44.821sec
Overall: Lee Ho-Suk (Rep. of Korea), 86pts

WOMEN
500m: Wang Meng (China), 43.353sec
1,000m: Wang Meng (China), 1min 30.572sec
1,500m: Park Seung-Hi (Rep. of Korea), 2min 21.570sec
3,000m: Park Seung-Hi (Rep. of Korea), 5min 04.070sec
3,000m relay: Korea, 4min 08.356sec
Overall: Park Seung-Hi (Rep. of Korea), 73pts

EUROPEAN SHORT TRACK CHAMPIONSHIPS 2010
Dresden, Germany, January

MEN
500m: Maxime Chataignier (France), 42.420sec
1,000m: Nicola Rodigari (Italy), 1min 26.818sec
1,500m: Nicola Rodigari (Italy), 2min 15.177sec
3,000m: Thibaut Fauconnet (France), 4min 49.585sec
5,000m relay: Italy, 6min 45.195sec
Overall: Nicola Rodigari (Italy), 102pts

WOMEN
500m: Arianna Fontana (Italy), 43.877sec
1,000m: Katerina Novotna (Czech Rep.), 1min 31.843sec
1,500m: Arianna Fontana (Italy), 2min 23.946sec
3,000m: Katerina Novotna (Czech Rep.), 5min 13.484sec
3,000m relay: Germany, 4min 15.979sec
Overall: Katerina Novotna (Czech Rep.), 89pts

SQUASH

MEN
British Open 2009: Nick Matthew (England) beat James Willstrop (England) 3–2
World Open 2009: Amr Shabana (Egypt) beat Ramy Ashour (Egypt) 3–0
World Team Championship 2009: Egypt beat France 2–1
European Championship 2010: Thierry Lincou (France) beat Gregory Gaultier (France) (Gaultier retired with score 2–0)
European Team Championship 2010: England beat France 4–0
British National Championship 2010: Nick Matthew (England) beat James Willstrop (England) 3–0

WOMEN
British Open 2009: Rachel Grinham (Australia) beat Madeline Perry (Ireland) 3–0
World Team Championship 2009: Egypt beat England 2–1
World Open 2009: Nicol David (Malaysia) beat Natalie Grinham (Netherlands) 3–1
European Championship 2010: Jenny Duncalf (England) beat Vanessa Atkinson (Netherlands) 3–2
European Team Championship 2010: Netherlands beat France 2–1
British National Championship 2009: Alison Waters beat Jenny Duncalf 3–2

SWIMMING

EUROPEAN CHAMPIONSHIPS 2010
Budapest, Hungary, August

MEN
50m freestyle: Frederick Bousquet (France), 21.49sec
100m freestyle: Alain Bernard (France), 48.49sec
200m freestyle: Paul Biedermann (Germany), 1min 46.06sec
400m freestyle: Yannick Agnel (France), 3min 46.17sec
800m freestyle: Sebastien Rouault (France), 7min 48.28sec
1,500m freestyle: Sebastien Rouault (France), 14min 55.17sec
4 × 100m freestyle relay: Russia, 3min 12.46sec
4 × 200m freestyle relay: Russia, 7min 06.71sec
50m backstroke: Camille Lacourt (France), 24.07sec
100m backstroke: Camille Lacourt (France), 52.11sec
200m backstroke: Stanislav Donets (Russia), 1min 57.18sec
50m breaststroke: Fabio Scozzoli (Italy), 27.38sec
100m breaststroke: Alexander Dale Oen (Norway), 59.20sec
200m breaststroke: Daniel Gyurta (Hungary), 2min 08.95sec
50m butterfly: Rafael Munoz Perez (Spain), 23.17sec
100m butterfly: Evgeny Korotyshkin (Russia), 51.73sec
200m butterfly: Pawel Korzeniowsky (Poland), 1min 55.00sec
200m individual medley: Laszlo Cseh (Hungary), 1min 57.73sec
400m individual medley: Laszlo Cseh (Hungary), 4min 10.95sec
4 × 100m medley relay: France, 3min 31.32sec

WOMEN
50m freestyle: Therese Alshammar (Sweden), 24.45sec
100m freestyle: Francesca Halsall (Great Britain), 53.58sec
200m freestyle: Federica Pellegrini (Italy), 1min 55.45sec
400m freestyle: Rebecca Adlington (Great Britain), 4min 04.55sec
800m freestyle: Lotte Friis (Denmark), 8min 23.27sec
1,500m freestyle: Lotte Friis (Denmark), 15min 59.13sec
4 × 100m freestyle relay: Germany, 3min 37.72sec
4 × 200m freestyle relay: Hungary, 7min 52.49sec
50m backstroke: Aliaksandra Herasimenia (Bulgaria), 27.64sec
100m backstroke: Gemma Spofforth (Great Britain), 59.80sec
200m backstroke: Elizabeth Simmonds (Great Britain), 2min 07.04sec
50m breaststroke: Yuliya Efimova (Russia), 30.29sec
100m breaststroke: Yuliya Efimova (Russia), 1min 06.32sec
200m breaststroke: Anastasia Chaun (Russia), 2min 23.50sec
50m butterfly: Therese Alshammar (Sweden), 25.63sec
100m butterfly: Sarah Sjostrom (Sweden), 57.32 sec
200m butterfly: Katinka Hosszu (Hungary), 2min 06.71sec
200m individual medley: Katinka Hosszu (Hungary), 2min 10.09sec
400m individual medley: Hannah Miley (Great Britain), 4min 33.09sec
4 × 100m medley relay: Great Britain, 3min 59.72sec

BRITISH CHAMPIONSHIPS 2010
Sheffield, March

MEN
50m freestyle: Simon Burnett (Windsor), 22.53sec
100m freestyle: Adam Brown (Hatfield), 49.64sec
200m freestyle: Robert Bale (Loughborough University), 1min 47.82sec
400m freestyle: Robert Renwick (Glasgow), 3min 50.32sec
1,500m freestyle: Daniel Fogg (Loughborough University), 15min 18.73sec
50m backstroke: Luke Wood (Salford), 26.17sec
100m backstroke: Liam Tancock (Loughborough University), 52.85sec
200m backstroke: James Goddard (Stockport), 1min 57.06sec
50m breaststroke: Robert Holderness (Millfield), 28.73sec
100m breaststroke: Kristopher Gilchrist (Edinburgh), 1min 01.22sec
200m breaststroke: Michael Jamieson (Edinburgh), 2min 11.14sec
50m butterfly: Ian Hulme (Peterlee), 24.22sec
100m butterfly: Michael Rock (Stockport), 52.66sec
200m butterfly: Michael Rock (Stockport), 1min 56.86sec
200m medley: James Goddard (Stockport), 1min 57.76sec
400m medley: Roberto Pavoni (Brentwood), 4min 14.55sec

WOMEN
50m freestyle: Francesca Halsall (Loughborough University), 24.77sec
100m freestyle: Francesca Halsall (Loughborough University), 54.71sec
200m freestyle: Rebecca Adlington (Nova), 1min 57.87sec
400m freestyle: Rebecca Adlington (Nova), 4min 05.50sec
800m freestyle: Rebecca Adlington (Nova), 8min 21.95sec
50m backstroke: Georgia Davies (Swansea), 28.54sec
100m backstroke: Elizabeth Simmonds (Loughborough University), 59.43sec
200m backstroke: Elizabeth Simmonds (Loughborough University), 2min 06.79sec
50m breaststroke: Achieng Ajulu-Bushell (Plymouth Lea), 31.18sec
100m breaststroke: Achieng Ajulu-Bushell (Plymouth Lea), 1min 08.51sec
200m breaststroke: Stacey Tadd (Bath University), 2min 29.66sec
50m butterfly: Amy Smith (Loughborough University), 26.88sec
100m butterfly: Francesca Halsall (Loughborough University), 57.83sec
200m butterfly: Ellen Gandy (Beckenham), 2min 07.70sec
200m medley: Hannah Miley (Garioch), 2min 12.32sec
400m medley: Hannah Miley (Garioch), 4min 37.05sec

TABLE TENNIS

WORLD TEAM CHAMPIONSHIPS 2010
Moscow, Russia, May

Men's final: China beat Germany 3–1
Women's final: Singapore beat China 3–1

ENGLISH NATIONAL CHAMPIONSHIPS 2010
Sheffield, March
Men's Singles: Andrew Baggaley beat Liam Pitchford 4–3
Women's Singles: Joanna Parker beat Kelly Sibley 4–1
Men's Doubles: Liam Pitchford and Gareth Evans beat Paul Drinkhall and Darius Knight 3–1
Women's Doubles: Joanna Parker and Kelly Sibley beat Karina Le Fevre and Emma Vickers 3–0
Mixed Doubles: Joanna Parker and Paul Drinkhall beat Kelly Sibley and Darius Knight 3–2

TENNIS

US OPEN CHAMPIONSHIPS 2009
New York, August–September

Men's Singles: Juan Martin del Potro (Argentina) beat Roger Federer (Switzerland) 3–6, 7–6, 4–6, 7–6, 6–2
Women's Singles: Kim Clijsters (Belgium) beat Caroline Wozniacki (Denmark) 7–5, 6–3
Men's Doubles: Lukas Dlouhy (Czech Republic) and Leander Paes (India) beat Mahesh Bhupathi (India) and Mark Knowles (Bahamas) 3–6, 6–3, 6–2
Women's Doubles: Serena Williams (USA) and Venus Williams (USA) beat Cara Black (Zimbabwe) and Liezel Huber (USA) 6–2, 6–2
Mixed Doubles: Carly Gullickson (USA) and Travis Parrott (USA) beat Cara Black (Zimbabwe) and Leander Paes (India) 6–2, 6–4

AUSTRALIAN OPEN CHAMPIONSHIPS 2010
Melbourne, January

Men's Singles: Roger Federer (Switzerland) beat Andy Murray (Great Britain) 6–3, 6–4, 7–6
Women's Singles: Serena Williams (USA) beat Justine Henin (Belgium) 6–4, 3–6, 6–2
Men's Doubles: Bob Bryan (USA) and Mike Bryan (USA) beat Daniel Nestor (Canada) and Nenad Zimonjic (Serbia) 6–3, 6–7, 6–3
Women's Doubles: Serena Williams (USA) and Venus Williams (USA) beat Cara Black (Zimbabwe) and Liezel Huber (USA) 6–4, 6–3
Mixed Doubles: Cara Black (Zimbabwe) and Leander Paes (India) beat Ekaterina Makarova (Russia) and Jaroslav Levinsky (Czech Republic) 7–5, 6–3

FRENCH OPEN CHAMPIONSHIPS 2010
Paris, May–June

Men's Singles: Rafael Nadal (Spain) beat Robin Soderling (Sweden) 6–4, 6–2, 6–4
Women's Singles: Francesca Schiavone (Italy) beat Samantha Stosur (Australia) 6–4, 7–6
Men's Doubles: Daniel Nestor (Canada) and Nenad Zimonjic (Serbia) beat Lukas Dlouhy (Czech Republic) and Leander Paes (India) 7–5, 6–2
Women's Doubles: Serena Williams (USA) and Venus Williams (USA) beat Kveta Peschke (Czech Republic) and Katarina Srebotnik (Slovenia) 6–2, 6–3
Mixed Doubles: Katarina Srebotnik (Slovenia) and Nenad Zimonjic (Serbia) beat Yaroslava Shvedova (Kazakhstan) and Julian Knowle (Austria) 4–6, 7–6, 11–9

ALL-ENGLAND CHAMPIONSHIPS 2010
Wimbledon, June–July

Men's Singles: Rafael Nadal (Spain) beat Tomas Berdych (Czech Republic) 6–3, 7–5, 6–4
Ladies' Singles: Serena Williams (USA) beat Vera Zvonareva (Russia) 6–3, 6–2

Men's Doubles: Juergen Melzer (Austria) and Philipp Petzschner (Germany) beat Robert Lindstedt (Sweden) and Horia Tecau (Romania) 6–1, 7–5, 7–5
Ladies' Doubles: Vania King (USA) and Yaroslava Shvedova (Kazakhstan) beat Elena Vesnina (Russia) and Vera Zvonareva (Russia) 7–6, 6–2
Mixed Doubles: Cara Black (Zimbabwe) and Leander Paes (India) beat Wesley Moodie (South Africa) and Lisa Raymond (USA) 6–4, 7–6

TEAM CHAMPIONSHIPS
Davis Cup final 2009: Spain beat Czech Republic 5–0
Federation Cup final 2009: Italy beat USA 4–0

2010 (XXI) WINTER OLYMPICS

Vancouver, Canada, 12–28 February 2010

ALPINE SKIING

MEN
Downhill: Didier Defago (Switzerland), 1min 54.31sec
Slalom: Giuliano Razzoli (Italy), 1min 39.32sec
Giant Slalom: Carlo Janka (Switzerland), 2min 37.83sec
Super G Slalom: Aksel Lund Svindal (Norway), 1min 30.34sec
Combination: Bode Miller (USA), 2min 44.92sec

WOMEN
Downhill: Lindsey Vonn (USA), 1min 44.19sec
Slalom: Maria Riesch (Germany), 1min 42.89sec
Giant Slalom: Viktoria Rebensburg (Germany), 2min 27.11sec
Super G Slalom: Andrea Fischbacher (Austria), 1min 20.14sec
Combination: Maria Riesch (Germany), 2min 09.14sec

BIATHLON

MEN
10km Sprint: Vincent Jay (France), 24min 07.8sec
12.5km Pursuit: Bjorn Ferry (Sweden), 33min 38.4sec
15km Mass Start: Yevgeni Ustyugov (Russia), 35min 35.7sec
20km Individual: Emil Hegle Svendsen (Norway), 48min 22.5sec
4 × 7.5km Relay: Norway, 1hr 21min 38.1sec

WOMEN
7.5km Sprint: Anastazia Kuzmina (Slovakia), 19min 55.6sec
10km Pursuit: Magdalena Neuner (Germany), 30min 16.0sec
12.5km Mass Start: Magdalena Neuner (Germany), 35min 19.6sec
15km Individual: Tora Berger (Norway), 40min 52.8sec
4 × 6km Relay: Russia, 1hr 09min36.3sec

BOBSLEIGH

MEN
Two-man: Germany I, 3min 26.65sec
Four-man: USA I, 3min 24.46sec

WOMEN
Two-woman: Canada, 13min 32.28sec

CURLING
Men: Canada
Women: Sweden

FIGURE SKATING
Men: Evan Lysacek (USA), 257.67pts
Women: Kim Yu-Na (Rep. of Korea), 228.56pts
Pairs: Xue Shen and Hongbo Zhao (China), 216.57pts
Ice Dance: Tessa Virtue and Scott Moir (Canada), 221.57pts

FREESTYLE SKIING

MEN
Moguls: Alexandre Bilodeau (Canada), 26.75pts
Aerials: Alexei Grishin (Belarus), 248.41pts
Ski Cross: Michael Schmid (Switzerland)

WOMEN
Moguls: Hannah Kearney (USA), 26.63pts
Aerials: Lydia Lassila (Australia), 214.74pts
Ski Cross: Ashleigh McIvor (Canada)

ICE HOCKEY
Men: Canada
Women: Canada

LUGE

MEN
Singles: Felix Loch (Germany), 3min 13.085sec
Two-Man: Austria, 1min 22.705sec

WOMEN
Singles: Tatjana Hüfner (Germany), 2min 46.524sec

NORDIC COMBINED
Sprint: Jason Lamy-Chappus (France), 25min 47.1sec
Individual: Bill Demong (USA), 24min 46.9sec
Relay: Austria, 49min 31.6sec

NORDIC SKIING

MEN
Sprint: Nikita Kriukov (Russia), 3min 36.3sec
Sprint Team: Norway, 19min 01.0sec
15km Freestyle: Dario Cologna (Switzerland), 33min 36.3sec
30km Pursuit: Marcus Hellner (Sweden), 1hr 15min 11.4sec
50km Classical: Petter Northug (Norway), 2hr 35min 35.5sec
4 × 10km Relay: Sweden, 1hr 45min 05.4sec

WOMEN
Sprint: Marit Bjorgen (Norway), 3min 39.2sec
Sprint Team: Germany, 18min 03.7sec
10km Freestyle: Charlotte Kalla (Sweden), 24min 58.4sec
15km Pursuit: Marit Bjorgen (Norway), 39min 58.1sec
30km Classical: Justyna Kowalczyk (Poland), 1hr 30min 32.7sec
4 × 5km Relay: Norway, 55min 19.5sec

SKELETON SLED
Men: Jon Montgomery (USA), 3min 29.73sec
Women: Amy Williams (Great Britain), 3min 35.64sec

SKI-JUMPING

Normal Hill: Simon Ammann (Switzerland), 276.5pts
Large Hill: Simon Ammann (Switzerland), 283.6pts
Large Hill-Team: Austria, 1107.9pts

SNOWBOARDING

MEN

Half-Pipe: Shaun White (USA), 48.4pts
Slalom: Jasey Jay Anderson (Canada)
Cross: Seth Westcott (USA)

WOMEN

Half-Pipe: Torah Bright (Australia), 45.0pts
Slalom: Nicolien Sauerbreij (Netherlands)
Cross: Maelle Ricker (Canada)

SHORT-TRACK SPEED SKATING

MEN

500m: Charles Hamelin (Canada), 40.981sec
1000m: Lee Jung-Su (Rep. of Korea), 1min 23.747sec
1500m: Lee Jung-Su (Rep. of Korea), 2min 17.619sec
5km Relay: Canada, 6min 44.224sec

WOMEN

500m: Wang Meng (China), 43min 048sec
1000m: Wang Meng (China), 1min 29.213sec
1500m: Yang Zhou (China), 2min 16.993sec
3km Relay: China, 4min 06.610sec

SPEED SKATING

MEN

500m: Mo Tae-Bum (Rep. of Korea), 1min 09.82sec
1000m: Shani Davis (USA), 1min 08.94sec
1500m: Mark Tuitert (Netherlands), 1min 45.57sec
5000m: Sven Kramer (Netherlands), 6min 14.46sec
10km: Lee Seung-Hoon (Rep. of Korea), 12min 58.55sec
Team Pursuit: Canada, 3min 41.37sec

WOMEN

500m: Lee Sang-Hwa (Rep. of Korea), 1min 16.09sec
1000m: Christine Nesbitt (Canada), 1min 16.56sec
1500m: Ireen Wust (Netherlands), 1min 56.89sec
3000m: Martina Sablikova (Czech Rep.), 4min 02.53sec
5000m: Martina Sablikova (Czech Rep.), 6min 50.91sec
Team Pursuit: Germany, 3min 02.82sec

MEDAL TABLE

Country	*G*	*S*	*B*	*Total*
Canada	14	7	5	26
Germany	10	13	7	30
United States	9	15	13	37
Norway	9	8	6	23
Rep. of Korea	6	6	2	14
Switzerland	6	0	3	9
China	5	2	4	11
Sweden	5	2	4	11
Austria	4	6	6	16
Netherlands	4	1	3	8
Russia	3	5	7	15
France	2	3	6	11
Australia	2	1	0	3
Czech Rep.	2	0	4	6
Poland	1	3	2	6
Italy	1	1	3	5
Belarus	1	1	1	3
Slovakia	1	1	1	3
Great Britain	1	0	0	1
Japan	0	3	2	5
Croatia	0	2	1	3
Slovenia	0	2	1	3
Latvia	0	2	0	2
Finland	0	1	4	5
Estonia	0	1	0	1
Kazakhstan	0	1	0	1

SPORTS RECORDS

ATHLETICS WORLD RECORDS

As at 30 August 2010

All the world records given below have been accepted by the International Amateur Athletic Federation except those marked with an asterisk* which are awaiting homologation or ratification. Fully automatic timing to 1/100th second is mandatory up to and including 400 metres. For distances up to and including 10,000 metres, records will be accepted to 1/100th second if timed automatically, and to 1/10th if hand timing is used.

MEN

TRACK EVENTS	*hr*	*min*	*sec*
100m			9.58
Usain Bolt (Jamaica) 2009			
200m			19.19
Usain Bolt (Jamaica) 2009			
400m			43.18
Michael Johnson (USA) 1999			
800m		1	41.09
David Rudisha (Kenya) 2010			
1,000m		2	11.96
Noah Ngeny (Kenya) 1999			
1,500m		3	26.00
Hicham El Guerrouj (Morocco) 1998			
1 mile		3	43.13
Hicham El Guerrouj (Morocco) 1999			
2,000m		4	44.79
Hicham El Guerrouj (Morocco) 1999			
3,000m		7	20.67
Daniel Komen (Kenya) 1996			
5,000m		12	37.35
Kenenisa Bekele (Ethiopia) 2004			
10,000m		26	17.53
Kenenisa Bekele (Ethiopia) 2005			
20,000m		56	26.0
Haile Gebrselassie (Ethiopia) 2007			
21,285m	1	00	00.0
Haile Gebrselassie (Ethiopia) 2007			
25,000m	1	13	55.8
Toshihiko Seko (Japan) 1981			
30,000m	1	29	18.8
Toshihiko Seko (Japan) 1981			
Marathon	2	03	59
Haile Gebrselassie (Ethiopia) 2009			
110m hurdles (1.07m)			12.87
Dayron Robles (Cuba) 2008			
400m hurdles (0.97m)			46.78
Kevin Young (USA) 1992			
3,000mSt		7	53.63
Saif Saaeed Shaheen (Qatar) 2004			

RELAYS	*min*	*sec*
4 × 100m		37.10
Jamaica, 2008		
4 × 200m	1	18.68
USA, 1994		
4 × 400m	2	54.29
USA, 1993		
4 × 800m	7	02.43
Kenya, 2006		
4 × 1,500m	14	36.23
Kenya, 2009		

FIELD EVENTS	*m*	*ft*	*in*
High jump	2.45	8	0½
Javier Sotomayor (Cuba) 1993			
Pole vault	6.14	20	1¾
Sergei Bubka (Ukraine) 1994			
Long jump	8.95	29	4½
Mike Powell (USA) 1991			
Triple jump	18.29	60	0¼
Jonathan Edwards (GB) 1995			
Shot	23.12	75	10¼
Randy Barnes (USA) 1990			
Discus	74.08	243	0
Jürgen Schult (GDR) 1986			
Hammer	86.74	284	7
Yuriy Sedykh (USSR) 1986			
Javelin	98.48	323	1
Jan Zelezny (Czech Rep.) 1996			
Decathlon†	9,026pts		
Roman Sebrle (Czech Rep.) 2001			

† Ten events comprising 100m, long jump, shot, high jump, 400m, 110m hurdles, discus, pole vault, javelin, 1,500m

WALKING (TRACK)	*hr*	*min*	*sec*
20,000m	1	17	25.6
Bernard Segura (Mexico) 1994			
29,572m	2	00	00.0
Maurizio Damilano (Italy) 1992			
30,000m	2	01	44.1
Maurizio Damilano (Italy) 1992			
50,000m	3	40	57.9
Thierry Toutain (France) 1996			

WOMEN

TRACK EVENTS	*hr*	*min*	*sec*
100m			10.49
Florence Griffith-Joyner (USA) 1988			
200m			21.34
Florence Griffith-Joyner (USA) 1988			
400m			47.60
Marita Koch (GDR) 1985			
800m		1	53.28
Jarmila Kratochvilova (Czechoslovakia) 1983			
1,500m		3	50.46
Qu Yunxia (China) 1993			
1 mile		4	12.56
Svetlana Masterkova (Russia) 1996			
3,000m		8	06.11
Wang Junxia (China) 1993			
5,000m		14	11.15
Tirunesh Dibaba (Ethiopia) 2008			
10,000m		29	31.78
Wang Junxia (China) 1993			
Marathon	2	15	25
Paula Radcliffe (GB) 2003			
100m hurdles (0.84m)			12.21
Yordanka Donkova (Bulgaria) 1988			
400m hurdles (0.76m)			52.34
Yuliya Pechonkina (Russia) 2003			

3,000mSt	8	58.81
Gulnara Galkina (Russia) 2008		

RELAYS	min	sec
4 × 100m		41.37
GDR, 1985		
4 × 200m	1	27.46
USA, 2000		
4 × 400m	3	15.17
USSR, 1988		
4 × 800m	7	50.17
USSR, 1984		

FIELD EVENTS	m	ft	in
High jump	2.09	6	10¼
Stefka Kostadinova (Bulgaria) 1987			
Pole vault	5.06	16	7¼
Yelena Isinbayeva (Russia) 2009			
Long jump	7.52	24	8¼
Galina Chistyakova (USSR) 1988			
Triple jump	15.50	50	10¼
Inessa Kravets (Ukraine) 1995			
Shot	22.63	74	3
Natalya Lisovskaya (USSR) 1987			
Discus	76.80	252	0
Gabriele Reinsch (GDR) 1988			
Hammer	78.30*	256	11
Anita Wlodarczyk (Poland) 2010			
Javelin (new implement in 1999)	72.28	237	2
Barbora Spotakova (Czech Rep.) 2008			
Heptathlon†		7,291pts	
Jackie Joyner-Kersee (USA) 1986			

† Seven events comprising 100m hurdles, shot, high jump, 200m, long jump, javelin, 800m

ATHLETICS NATIONAL (UK) RECORDS

As at 30 August 2010

Records set anywhere by athletes eligible to represent Great Britain and Northern Ireland

MEN

TRACK EVENTS	hr	min	sec
100m			9.87
Linford Christie, 1993			
Dwain Chambers, 2002			
200m			19.87
John Regis, 1994			
400m			44.36
Iwan Thomas, 1997			
800m		1	41.73
Sebastian Coe, 1981			
1,000m		2	12.18
Sebastian Coe, 1981			
1,500m		3	29.67
Sebastian Coe, 1985			
1 mile		3	46.32
Steve Cram, 1985			
2,000m		4	51.39
Steve Cram, 1985			
3,000m		7	32.79
David Moorcroft, 1982			
5,000m		12	57.94
Mo Farah, 2010			
10,000m		27	18.14
Jon Brown, 1998			
20,000m		57	28.7
Carl Thackery, 1990			
20,855m	1	00	00.0
Carl Thackery, 1990			
25,000m	1	15	22.6
Ron Hill, 1965			
30,000m	1	31	30.4
Jim Alder, 1970			
Marathon	2	07	13
Steve Jones, 1985			
3,000mSt		8	07.96
Mark Rowland, 1988			
110m hurdles			12.91
Colin Jackson, 1993			
400m hurdles			47.82
Kriss Akabusi, 1992			

RELAYS	min	sec
4 × 100m		37.73
GB team, 1999		
4 × 200m	1	21.29
GB team, 1989		
4 × 400m	2	56.60
GB team, 1996		
4 × 800m	7	03.89
GB team, 1982		

FIELD EVENTS	m	ft	in
High jump	2.37	7	9¼
Steve Smith, 1993			
Pole vault	5.80	19	0¼
Nick Buckfield, 1998			
Long jump	8.30	27	2¾
Greg Rutherford, 2008			
Triple jump	18.29	60	0¼
Jonathan Edwards, 1995			
Shot	21.92	71	11
Carl Myerscough, 2003			
Discus	66.64	218	8
Perris Wilkins, 1998			
Hammer	77.54	254	5
Martin Girvan, 1984			
Javelin	91.46	300	1
Steve Backley, 1992			
Decathlon		8,847pts	
Daley Thompson, 1984			

WALKING (TRACK)	hr	min	sec
20,000m	1	23	26.5
Ian McCombie, 1990			
30,000m	2	19	18
Christopher Maddocks, 1984			
50,000m	4	05	44.6
Paul Blagg, 1990			
26,037m	2	00	00.0
Ron Wallwork, 1971			

WOMEN

TRACK EVENTS	hr	min	sec
100m			11.05
Montell Douglas, 2008			
200m			22.10
Kathy Cook, 1984			
400m			49.43
Kathy Cook, 1984			
800m		1	56.21
Kelly Holmes, 1995			
1,500m		3	57.90
Kelly Holmes, 2004			
1 mile		4	17.57
Zola Budd, 1985			

		min	sec
3,000m		8	22.20
Paula Radcliffe, 2002			
5,000m		14	29.11
Paula Radcliffe, 2004			
10,000m		30	01.09
Paula Radcliffe, 2002			
Marathon	2	15	25
Paula Radcliffe, 2003			
100m hurdles			12.80
Angela Thorp, 1996			
400m hurdles			52.74
Sally Gunnell, 1993			
3,000mSt		9	29.14
Helen Clitheroe, 2008			

RELAYS	*min*	*sec*
4 × 100m		42.43
GB team, 1980		
4 × 200m	1	31.57
GB team, 1977		
4 × 400m	3	22.01
GB team, 1991		
4 × 800m	8	23.8
GB team, 1971		

FIELD EVENTS	*m*	*ft*	*in*
High jump	1.95	6	4¾
Diana Elliott, 1982			
Susan Jones, 2001			
Jessica Ennis, 2007			
Pole vault	4.60	15	1
Kate Dennison, 2009			
Long jump	6.90	22	7¾
Beverley Kinch, 1983			
Triple jump	15.15	49	8½
Ashia Hansen, 1997			
Shot	19.36	63	6¼
Judy Oakes, 1988			
Discus	67.48	221	5
Margaret Ritchie, 1981			
Hammer	68.93	226	1
Lorraine Shaw, 2001			
Javelin	65.75	215	8
Goldie Sayers, 2008			
Heptathlon		6,831pts	
Denise Lewis, 2000			

SWIMMING WORLD RECORDS

As at 30 August 2010

MEN	*min*	*sec*
50m freestyle		20.91
Cesar Cielo Filho, Brazil		
100m freestyle		46.91
Cesar Cielo Filho, Brazil		
200m freestyle	1	42.00
Paul Biedermann, Germany		
400m freestyle	3	40.07
Paul Biedermann, Germany		
800m freestyle	7	32.12
Zhang Lin, China		
1,500m freestyle	14	34.56
Grant Hackett, Australia		
50m breaststroke		26.67
Cameron Van Der Burgh, South Africa		
100m breaststroke		58.58
Brenton Rickard, Australia		
200m breaststroke	2	07.31
Christian Sprenger, Australia		
50m butterfly		22.43
Rafael Munoz, Spain		
100m butterfly		49.82
Michael Phelps, USA		
200m butterfly	1	51.51
Michael Phelps, USA		
50m backstroke		24.04
Liam Tancock, Great Britain		
100m backstroke		51.94
Aaron Peirsol, USA		
200m backstroke	1	51.92
Aaron Peirsol, USA		
200m medley	1	54.10
Ryan Lochte, USA		
400m medley	4	03.84
Michael Phelps, USA		
4 × 100m freestyle relay	3	08.24
USA		
4 × 200m freestyle relay	6	58.55
USA		
4 × 100m medley relay	3	27.28
USA		

WOMEN	*min*	*sec*
50m freestyle		23.73
Britta Steffen, Germany		
100m freestyle		52.07
Britta Steffen, Germany		
200m freestyle	1	52.98
Federica Pellegrini, Italy		
400m freestyle	3	59.15
Federica Pellegrini, Italy		
800m freestyle	8	14.10
Rebecca Adlington, Great Britain		
1,500m freestyle	15	42.54
Kate Ziegler, USA		
50m breaststroke		29.80
Jessica Hardy, USA		
100m breaststroke	1	04.45
Jessica Hardy, USA		
200m breaststroke	2	20.12
Annamay Pierse, Canada		
50m butterfly		25.07
Therese Alshammar, Sweden		
100m butterfly		56.06
Sarah Sjostrom, Sweden		
200m butterfly	2	01.81
Liu Zigi, China		
50m backstroke		27.06
Zhao Jing, China		
100m backstroke		58.12
Gemma Spofforth, Great Britain		
200m backstroke	2	04.81
Kirsty Coventry, Zimbabwe		
200m medley	2	06.15
Ariana Kukors, USA		
400m medley	4	29.45
Stephanie Rice, Australia		
4 × 100m freestyle relay	3	31.72
The Netherlands		
4 × 200m freestyle relay	7	42.08
China		
4 × 100m medley relay	3	52.19
China		

TIME AND SPACE

ASTRONOMY

TIME MEASUREMENT AND CALENDARS

TIDES AND TIDAL PREDICTIONS

ASTRONOMY

The following pages give astronomical data for each month of the year 2011. There are four pages of data for each month. All data are given for 0h Greenwich Mean Time (GMT), ie at the midnight at the beginning of the day named. This applies also to data for the months when British Summer Time is in operation (for dates, *see* below).

The astronomical data are given in a form suitable for observation with the naked eye or with a small telescope. These data do not attempt to replace the *Astronomical Almanac* for professional astronomers.

A fuller explanation of how to use the astronomical data is given on pages 1279–88.

CALENDAR FOR EACH MONTH

The calendar for each month comprises dates of general interest plus the dates of birth or death of well-known people. For key religious, civil and legal dates *see* page 9. For details of flag-flying days *see* page 23. For royal birthdays *see* pages 23 and 24–5. Public holidays are given in italics. *See* also pages 10 and 11.

Fuller explanations of the various calendars can be found under Time Measurement and Calendars.

The zodiacal signs through which the Sun is passing during each month are illustrated. The date of transition from one sign to the next, to the nearest hour, is given under Astronomical Phenomena.

JULIAN DATE

The Julian date on 2011 January 0.0 is 2455561.5. To find the Julian date for any other date in 2011 (at 0h GMT), add the day-of-the-year number on the extreme right of the calendar for each month to the Julian date for January 0.0.

SEASONS

The seasons are defined astronomically as follows:

Spring from the vernal equinox to the summer solstice
Summer from the summer solstice to the autumnal equinox
Autumn from the autumnal equinox to the winter solstice
Winter from the winter solstice to the vernal equinox

The time when seasons start in 2011 (to the nearest hour) are:

Northern Hemisphere

Vernal equinox	March 20d 23h GMT
Summer solstice	June 21d 17h GMT
Autumnal equinox	September 23d 09h GMT
Winter solstice	December 22d 05h GMT

Southern Hemisphere

Autumnal equinox	March 20d 23h GMT
Winter solstice	June 21d 17h GMT
Vernal equinox	September 23d 09h GMT
Summer solstice	December 22d 05h GMT

The longest day of the year, measured from sunrise to sunset, is at the summer solstice. The longest day in the United Kingdom will fall on 21 June in 2011.

The shortest day of the year is at the winter solstice. The shortest day in the United Kingdom will fall on 22 December in 2011.

The equinox is the point at which day and night are of equal length all over the world.

In popular parlance, the seasons in the northern hemisphere comprise the following months:

Spring	March, April, May
Summer	June, July, August
Autumn	September, October, November
Winter	December, January, February

BRITISH SUMMER TIME

British Summer Time is the legal time for general purposes during the period in which it is in operation (*see also* pages 1285–6). During this period, clocks are kept one hour ahead of Greenwich Mean Time. The hour of changeover is 01h Greenwich Mean Time. The duration of Summer Time in 2011 is from March 27 01h GMT to October 30 01h GMT.

JANUARY 2011

FIRST MONTH, 31 DAYS. *Janus*, god of the portal, facing two ways, past and future

1	*Saturday*	The *Daily Universal Register* changed its name to *The Times* 1788	day 1
2	*Sunday*	In Paris, Louis Daguerre took the first photograph of the moon 1839	2
3	*Monday*	J. R. R. Tolkien, philologist and author *b.* 1892; Josiah Wedgwood, potter *d.* 1795	week 1 day 3
4	*Tuesday*	Albert Camus was killed in a car accident 1960	4
5	*Wednesday*	Alexander Dumas, author of *The Count of Monte Cristo*, fought his first duel 1825	5
6	*Thursday*	Porky the Pig made his debut in the Warner Brothers cartoon 'Gold Diggers of 49' 1936	6
7	*Friday*	George Gershwin, aged 26, completed his jazz symphony *Rhapsody in Blue* 1924	7
8	*Saturday*	US mogul William Randolph Hearst forbade his newspapers from advertising *Citizen Kane* 1941	8
9	*Sunday*	Wilbur Smith, Zambian-British novelist *b.* 1933; Katherine Mansfield, New Zealand author *d.* 1923	9
10	*Monday*	Thomas Paine published his influential anti-monarchist tract, *Common Sense* 1776	week 2 day 10
11	*Tuesday*	Dashiell Hammett and Raymond Chandler met at a *Black Mask* magazine get-together 1936	11
12	*Wednesday*	John Singer Sargent, US painter *b.* 1856; Nevil Shute, novelist *d.* 1960	12
13	*Thursday*	Pietro Mascagni's *Cavalleria rusticana* became the first opera to be heard on the radio 1910	13
14	*Friday*	An as yet unpublished Joseph Conrad returned to London after a long career at sea 1894	14
15	*Saturday*	Ivor Novello, Welsh composer and actor *b.* 1893; Jack Teagarden, jazz trombonist *d.* 1964	15
16	*Sunday*	The first volume of *Don Quixote* by Miguel de Cervantes was published in Madrid 1605	16
17	*Monday*	Benny Goodman and his orchestra performed the first jazz concert at Carnegie Hall 1938	week 3 day 17
18	*Tuesday*	A. A. Milne, author *b.* 1882; Sir Cecil Beaton, fashion designer and photographer *d.* 1980	18
19	*Wednesday*	Henrik Ibsen's play *The Master Builder* premiered in Berlin 1893	19
20	*Thursday*	Robert Frost recited his poem 'The Gift Outright' at the inauguration of John F. Kennedy 1961	20
21	*Friday*	US author Don DeLillo won the American Book Award for his novel *White Noise* 1985	21
22	*Saturday*	Lord Byron, poet *b.* 1788; Else Lasker-Schüler, German poet *d.* 1945	22
23	*Sunday*	Édouard Manet, French impressionist painter *b.* 1832; Salvador Dalí, Spanish surrealist painter *d.* 1989	23
24	*Monday*	Franz Kafka stopped writing his unfinished first novel *Amerika* 1913	week 4 day 24
25	*Tuesday*	Karel Capek's play *R.U.R.*, which introduced the word 'robot', premiered in Prague 1921	25
26	*Wednesday*	US producer Samuel Goldwyn bought the film rights to *The Wonderful Wizard of Oz* 1934	26
27	*Thursday*	Poet and politician Dante Alighieri was exiled from Florence 1302	27
28	*Friday*	Sidonie-Gabrielle Colette, French author *b.* 1873; Jerry Siegel, creator of Superman *d.* 1996	28
29	*Saturday*	Edgar Allan Poe's poem 'The Raven' was published in the *New York Evening Mirror* 1845	29
30	*Sunday*	The Beatles gave their last public performance on top of their London recording studio 1969	30
31	*Monday*	Norman Mailer, US novelist *b.* 1923; John Galsworthy, novelist *d.* 1933	week 5 day 31

ASTRONOMICAL PHENOMENA

d	*h*	
2	14	Mercury in conjunction with Moon. Mercury 4°N.
3	19	Earth at perihelion (147 million km.)
4	09	Partial eclipse of Sun
5	00	Mars in conjunction with Moon. Mars 3°S.
8	15	Venus at greatest elongation W. 47°
9	14	Mercury at greatest elongation W. 23°
10	11	Jupiter in conjunction with Moon. Jupiter 6°S.
20	10	Sun's longitude 300° ♒
25	05	Saturn in conjunction with Moon. Saturn 8°N.
26	06	Saturn at stationary point
30	03	Venus in conjunction with Moon. Venus 3°N.

MINIMA OF ALGOL

d	*h*	*d*	*h*	*d*	*h*
3	20.6	15	07.8	26	19.1
6	17.4	18	04.7	29	15.9
9	14.2	21	01.5		
12	11.0	23	22.3		

CONSTELLATIONS

The following constellations are near the meridian at

	d	*h*		*d*	*h*
December	1	24	January	16	21
December	16	23	February	1	20
January	1	22	February	15	19

Draco (below the Pole), Ursa Minor (below the Pole), Camelopardalis, Perseus, Auriga, Taurus, Orion, Eridanus and Lepus

THE MOON

Phases, Apsides and Node	*d*	*h*	*m*
● New Moon	4	09	03
☽ First Quarter	12	11	31
○ Full Moon	19	21	21
☾ Last Quarter	26	12	57
Apogee (405,014km)	10	05	41
Perigee (362,774km)	22	00	17

Mean longitude of ascending node on January 1, 272°

THE SUN

s.d. 16′.3

Day	Right Ascension			Dec. –		Equation of time		Rise 52°		Rise 56°		Transit		Set 52°		Set 56°		Sidereal time			Transit of first point of Aries		
	h	*m*	*s*	°	′	*m*	*s*	*h*	*m*	*h*	*m*	*h*	*m*	*h*	*m*	*h*	*m*	*h*	*m*	*s*	*h*	*m*	*s*
1	18	44	24	23	03	–3	11	8	08	8	31	12	03	15	59	15	36	6	41	13	17	15	57
2	18	48	49	22	58	–3	39	8	08	8	31	12	04	16	00	15	37	6	45	09	17	12	01
3	18	53	13	22	52	–4	07	8	08	8	31	12	04	16	01	15	38	6	49	06	17	08	05
4	18	57	38	22	47	–4	35	8	08	8	30	12	05	16	02	15	40	6	53	02	17	04	09
5	19	02	02	22	40	–5	03	8	07	8	30	12	05	16	03	15	41	6	56	59	17	00	13
6	19	06	25	22	34	–5	29	8	07	8	29	12	06	16	05	15	42	7	00	56	16	56	17
7	19	10	48	22	26	–5	56	8	07	8	29	12	06	16	06	15	44	7	04	52	16	52	22
8	19	15	11	22	19	–6	22	8	06	8	28	12	07	16	07	15	45	7	08	49	16	48	26
9	19	19	33	22	11	–6	47	8	06	8	27	12	07	16	09	15	47	7	12	45	16	44	30
10	19	23	54	22	02	–7	12	8	05	8	26	12	07	16	10	15	49	7	16	42	16	40	34
11	19	28	15	21	53	–7	37	8	04	8	26	12	08	16	12	15	50	7	20	38	16	36	38
12	19	32	35	21	44	–8	00	8	04	8	25	12	08	16	13	15	52	7	24	35	16	32	42
13	19	36	55	21	34	–8	24	8	03	8	24	12	09	16	15	15	54	7	28	31	16	28	46
14	19	41	14	21	24	–8	46	8	02	8	23	12	09	16	16	15	56	7	32	28	16	24	50
15	19	45	33	21	13	–9	08	8	01	8	22	12	09	16	18	15	57	7	36	25	16	20	54
16	19	49	50	21	02	–9	29	8	01	8	20	12	10	16	19	15	59	7	40	21	16	16	58
17	19	54	07	20	51	–9	50	8	00	8	19	12	10	16	21	16	01	7	44	18	16	13	02
18	19	58	24	20	39	–10	09	7	59	8	18	12	10	16	22	16	03	7	48	14	16	09	07
19	20	02	39	20	27	–10	28	7	58	8	17	12	11	16	24	16	05	7	52	11	16	05	11
20	20	06	54	20	14	–10	47	7	57	8	15	12	11	16	26	16	07	7	56	07	16	01	15
21	20	11	08	20	02	–11	04	7	55	8	14	12	11	16	27	16	09	8	00	04	15	57	19
22	20	15	22	19	48	–11	21	7	54	8	12	12	11	16	29	16	11	8	04	01	15	53	23
23	20	19	34	19	34	–11	37	7	53	8	11	12	12	16	31	16	13	8	07	57	15	49	27
24	20	23	46	19	20	–11	53	7	52	8	09	12	12	16	33	16	15	8	11	54	15	45	31
25	20	27	57	19	06	–12	07	7	51	8	08	12	12	16	34	16	17	8	15	50	15	41	35
26	20	32	08	18	51	–12	21	7	49	8	06	12	12	16	36	16	19	8	19	47	15	37	39
27	20	36	17	18	36	–12	34	7	48	8	05	12	13	16	38	16	21	8	23	43	15	33	43
28	20	40	26	18	21	–12	46	7	46	8	03	12	13	16	40	16	24	8	27	40	15	29	47
29	20	44	34	18	05	–12	58	7	45	8	01	12	13	16	42	16	26	8	31	36	15	25	52
30	20	48	41	17	49	–13	08	7	44	7	59	12	13	16	43	16	28	8	35	33	15	21	56
31	20	52	48	17	32	–13	18	7	42	7	57	12	13	16	45	16	30	8	39	30	15	18	00

DURATION OF TWILIGHT (in minutes)

Latitude	*52°*	*56°*	*52°*	*56°*	*52°*	*56°*	*52°*	*56°*
	1 January		*11 January*		*21 January*		*31 January*	
Civil	41	47	40	45	38	43	37	41
Nautical	84	96	82	93	80	90	78	87
Astronomical	125	141	123	138	120	134	117	130

THE NIGHT SKY

Mercury is visible as a morning object for the first two weeks of the month and reaches its greatest western elongation (23 degrees) on the 9th. It becomes visible very low above the south-eastern horizon at about the beginning of morning civil twilight. During this time its magnitude brightens slowly from +0.1 to –0.2.

Venus reaches its greatest western elongation (47 degrees) on the 8th with a magnitude of about –4.5. Thus it is visible as a brilliant morning object, low in the south-eastern sky, for several hours before sunrise. Venus passes 8 degrees north of Antares, in Scorpius, on the 15/16th. On the morning of the 1st the waning crescent Moon could be used as a guide to seeing Venus in daylight, shortly after sunrise: Venus can then be found about 9 degrees above and 9 degrees to the right of the Moon. A similar opportunity occurs on the morning of the 30th when Venus will appear only about 4 degrees above and 3 degrees to the right of the Moon.

Mars is unsuitably placed for observation throughout January.

Jupiter, magnitude –2.3, is an evening object, visible in the south-western quadrant of the sky, but by the end of the month is lost to view well before midnight. Jupiter is in the constellation of Pisces, and on the 4th passes only 0.5 degrees south of Uranus, thus providing a useful guide to observers with binoculars to locate the fainter planet. Note that there is a difference of 8 magnitudes between the two planets. The waxing crescent Moon passes 6 degrees north of Jupiter on the 10th.

Saturn, magnitude +0.8, is a morning object, reaching its first stationary point on the 26th, in the constellation of Virgo, only about 5 degrees northwest of Spica. On the 26th the planet reaches its first stationary point and begins its slow retrograde motion. At the very end of January it becomes visible low in the eastern sky shortly before midnight.

THE MOON

Day	R.A.		Dec.	Hor. Par.	Semi-diam.	Sun's Co-Long.	PA of Br. Limb	Ph.	Age	Rise				Transit		Set			
										52°		56°				52°		56°	
	h	*m*	°	′	′	°	°	%	*d*	*h*	*m*	*h*	*m*	*h*	*m*	*h*	*m*	*h*	*m*
1	15	45	–22.8	57.8	15.8	224	99	12	26.3	5	32	5	59	9	27	13	17	12	51
2	16	44	–24.1	57.4	15.6	236	94	6	27.3	6	36	7	05	10	23	14	10	13	42
3	17	42	–24.0	56.9	15.5	249	90	2	28.3	7	28	7	55	11	19	15	13	14	47
4	18	38	–22.6	56.3	15.4	261	93	0	29.3	8	08	8	31	12	12	16	22	16	00
5	19	32	–20.0	55.8	15.2	273	248	0	0.7	8	38	8	56	13	02	17	34	17	17
6	20	23	–16.6	55.3	15.1	285	249	3	1.7	9	01	9	15	13	49	18	46	18	34
7	21	11	–12.4	54.9	15.0	297	247	7	2.7	9	20	9	30	14	33	19	56	19	48
8	21	57	–7.9	54.5	14.9	310	245	13	3.7	9	37	9	42	15	14	21	05	21	01
9	22	41	–3.1	54.3	14.8	322	244	20	4.7	9	51	9	52	15	55	22	12	22	13
10	23	24	+1.7	54.1	14.8	334	244	28	5.7	10	06	10	03	16	35	23	19	23	24
11	0	07	+6.5	54.2	14.8	346	245	36	6.7	10	21	10	14	17	17	—		—	
12	0	52	+11.1	54.4	14.8	358	247	46	7.7	10	38	10	27	17	59	0	27	0	36
13	1	38	+15.2	54.8	14.9	10	249	55	8.7	10	59	10	43	18	45	1	36	1	50
14	2	26	+18.9	55.4	15.1	23	253	65	9.7	11	25	11	05	19	34	2	46	3	05
15	3	18	+21.7	56.1	15.3	35	257	74	10.7	11	59	11	34	20	26	3	56	4	19
16	4	13	+23.6	56.9	15.5	47	262	82	11.7	12	44	12	17	21	22	5	02	5	29
17	5	12	+24.2	57.7	15.7	59	267	90	12.7	13	43	13	16	22	20	6	01	6	29
18	6	11	+23.4	58.6	16.0	71	271	95	13.7	14	55	14	31	23	19	6	50	7	15
19	7	12	+21.1	59.3	16.2	83	271	99	14.7	16	16	15	57	—		7	29	7	49
20	8	11	+17.5	59.9	16.3	95	162	100	15.7	17	42	17	29	0	16	7	59	8	13
21	9	08	+12.7	60.3	16.4	107	120	98	16.7	19	09	19	01	1	12	8	23	8	32
22	10	04	+7.1	60.4	16.5	120	118	94	17.7	20	35	20	33	2	06	8	44	8	48
23	10	58	+1.2	60.3	16.4	132	118	87	18.7	22	00	22	04	2	58	9	04	9	03
24	11	52	–4.8	60.0	16.4	144	117	78	19.7	23	24	23	33	3	49	9	23	9	17
25	12	45	–10.4	59.5	16.2	156	115	67	20.7	—		—		4	40	9	44	9	33
26	13	40	–15.4	59.0	16.1	168	112	56	21.7	0	47	1	02	5	33	10	08	9	52
27	14	35	–19.4	58.4	15.9	180	108	45	22.7	2	08	2	28	6	27	10	38	10	17
28	15	32	–22.3	57.8	15.7	192	103	34	23.7	3	23	3	48	7	22	11	17	10	51
29	16	30	–23.9	57.2	15.6	205	98	25	24.7	4	29	4	57	8	18	12	05	11	37
30	17	27	–24.1	56.6	15.4	217	92	16	25.7	5	24	5	52	9	13	13	03	12	36
31	18	23	–23.1	56.1	15.3	229	88	9	26.7	6	07	6	32	10	06	14	10	13	46

MERCURY

Day	R.A.		Dec.	Diam.	Phase	Transit		5° high			
								52°		56°	
	h	*m*	°	′	%	*h*	*m*	*h*	*m*	*h*	*m*
1	17	17	–20.2	8	38	10	35	7	10	7	38
3	17	20	–20.5	8	45	10	31	7	08	7	36
5	17	25	–20.8	7	52	10	29	7	08	7	37
7	17	31	–21.2	7	57	10	27	7	10	7	40
9	17	39	–21.6	7	62	10	28	7	13	7	44
11	17	48	–21.9	6	67	10	29	7	17	7	49
13	17	58	–22.3	6	70	10	31	7	21	7	55
15	18	08	–22.6	6	74	10	33	7	26	8	00
17	18	19	–22.8	6	77	10	36	7	31	8	06
19	18	30	–23.0	6	79	10	40	7	36	8	12
21	18	42	–23.1	6	81	10	44	7	41	8	17
23	18	54	–23.1	5	83	10	48	7	46	8	21
25	19	06	–23.1	5	85	10	53	7	50	8	25
27	19	19	–23.0	5	87	10	57	7	53	8	28
29	19	31	–22.8	5	88	11	02	7	56	8	30
31	19	44	–22.5	5	90	11	07	7	58	8	32

VENUS

Day	R.A.		Dec.	Diam.	Phase	Transit		5° high			
								52°		56°	
	h	*m*	°	′	%	*h*	*m*	*h*	*m*	*h*	*m*
1	15	28	–15.3	27	46	8	48	4	48	5	07
6	15	48	–16.4	26	49	8	48	4	55	5	16
11	16	09	–17.5	24	51	8	49	5	04	5	26
16	16	30	–18.5	23	54	8	51	5	13	5	37
21	16	53	–19.3	22	56	8	54	5	22	5	48
26	17	16	–20.1	21	58	8	57	5	30	5	58
31	17	40	–20.6	20	61	9	01	5	39	6	07

MARS

Day	R.A.		Dec.	Diam.	Phase	Transit		5° high			
								52°		56°	
	h	*m*	°	′	%	*h*	*m*	*h*	*m*	*h*	*m*
1	19	20	–23.2	4	100	12	40	15	42	15	07
6	19	37	–22.6	4	100	12	37	15	44	15	10
11	19	53	–21.9	4	100	12	34	15	47	15	15
16	20	10	–21.2	4	100	12	30	15	50	15	20
21	20	26	–20.3	4	100	12	27	15	53	15	26
26	20	42	–19.3	4	100	12	23	15	57	15	31
31	20	58	–18.3	4	100	12	20	16	01	15	37

SUNRISE AND SUNSET

d	London				Bristol				Birmingham				Manchester				Newcastle				Glasgow				Belfast			
	0° 05′		51° 30′		2° 35′		51° 28′		1° 55′		52° 28′		2° 15′		53° 28′		1° 37′		54° 59′		4° 14′		55° 52′		5° 56′		54° 35′	
d	*h*	*m*	*h*	*m*	*h*	*m*	*h*	*m*	*h*	*m*	*h*	*m*	*h*	*m*	*h*	*m*	*h*	*m*	*h*	*m*	*h*	*m*	*h*	*m*	*h*	*m*	*h*	*m*
1	8	06	16	02	8	16	16	12	8	18	16	04	8	25	16	00	8	31	15	49	8	47	15	54	8	46	16	08
2	8	06	16	03	8	16	16	13	8	18	16	05	8	25	16	01	8	31	15	50	8	47	15	55	8	46	16	10
3	8	06	16	04	8	16	16	14	8	18	16	06	8	25	16	02	8	31	15	51	8	47	15	56	8	46	16	11
4	8	06	16	05	8	15	16	15	8	18	16	08	8	24	16	04	8	30	15	52	8	46	15	57	8	45	16	12
5	8	05	16	06	8	15	16	16	8	17	16	09	8	24	16	05	8	30	15	54	8	46	15	59	8	45	16	13
6	8	05	16	07	8	15	16	18	8	17	16	10	8	24	16	06	8	30	15	55	8	45	16	00	8	44	16	15
7	8	05	16	09	8	14	16	19	8	17	16	11	8	23	16	08	8	29	15	57	8	45	16	02	8	44	16	16
8	8	04	16	10	8	14	16	20	8	16	16	13	8	23	16	09	8	28	15	58	8	44	16	03	8	43	16	18
9	8	04	16	11	8	13	16	22	8	16	16	14	8	22	16	10	8	28	16	00	8	43	16	05	8	43	16	19
10	8	03	16	13	8	13	16	23	8	15	16	16	8	21	16	12	8	27	16	01	8	43	16	06	8	42	16	21
11	8	02	16	14	8	12	16	24	8	14	16	17	8	21	16	13	8	26	16	03	8	42	16	08	8	41	16	22
12	8	02	16	16	8	12	16	26	8	14	16	18	8	20	16	15	8	25	16	04	8	41	16	10	8	40	16	24
13	8	01	16	17	8	11	16	27	8	13	16	20	8	19	16	17	8	24	16	06	8	40	16	12	8	40	16	26
14	8	00	16	19	8	10	16	29	8	12	16	22	8	18	16	18	8	23	16	08	8	39	16	13	8	39	16	27
15	8	00	16	20	8	09	16	30	8	11	16	23	8	17	16	20	8	22	16	10	8	38	16	15	8	38	16	29
16	7	59	16	22	8	09	16	32	8	10	16	25	8	16	16	21	8	21	16	11	8	37	16	17	8	37	16	31
17	7	58	16	23	8	08	16	33	8	09	16	26	8	15	16	23	8	20	16	13	8	35	16	19	8	35	16	32
18	7	57	16	25	8	07	16	35	8	08	16	28	8	14	16	25	8	19	16	15	8	34	16	21	8	34	16	34
19	7	56	16	27	8	06	16	37	8	07	16	30	8	13	16	27	8	18	16	17	8	33	16	23	8	33	16	36
20	7	55	16	28	8	05	16	38	8	06	16	31	8	12	16	28	8	17	16	19	8	32	16	25	8	32	16	38
21	7	54	16	30	8	04	16	40	8	05	16	33	8	11	16	30	8	15	16	21	8	30	16	27	8	31	16	40
22	7	53	16	32	8	02	16	42	8	04	16	35	8	09	16	32	8	14	16	23	8	29	16	29	8	29	16	42
23	7	51	16	33	8	01	16	43	8	03	16	37	8	08	16	34	8	12	16	25	8	27	16	31	8	28	16	44
24	7	50	16	35	8	00	16	45	8	01	16	39	8	07	16	36	8	11	16	26	8	26	16	33	8	26	16	46
25	7	49	16	37	7	59	16	47	8	00	16	40	8	05	16	38	8	10	16	28	8	24	16	35	8	25	16	48
26	7	48	16	38	7	58	16	49	7	59	16	42	8	04	16	39	8	08	16	30	8	22	16	37	8	23	16	50
27	7	46	16	40	7	56	16	50	7	57	16	44	8	03	16	41	8	06	16	33	8	21	16	39	8	22	16	52
28	7	45	16	42	7	55	16	52	7	56	16	46	8	01	16	43	8	05	16	35	8	19	16	41	8	20	16	54
29	7	44	16	44	7	53	16	54	7	54	16	48	8	00	16	45	8	03	16	37	8	17	16	43	8	19	16	56
30	7	42	16	46	7	52	16	56	7	53	16	50	7	58	16	47	8	01	16	39	8	16	16	45	8	17	16	58
31	7	41	16	47	7	51	16	57	7	51	16	51	7	56	16	49	8	00	16	41	8	14	16	48	8	15	17	00

JUPITER

Day	*R.A.*		*Dec.*		*Transit*		*5° high*			
							52°		56°	
	h	*m*	°	′	*h*	*m*	*h*	*m*	*h*	*m*
1	23	49.4	–2	32	17	07	22	21	22	15
11	23	54.7	–1	55	16	33	21	50	21	45
21	0	00.8	–1	13	16	00	21	20	21	16
31	0	07.6	–0	27	15	27	20	52	20	48

Diameters – equatorial 37″ polar 35″

SATURN

Day	*R.A.*		*Dec.*		*Transit*		*5° high*			
							52°		56°	
	h	*m*	°	′	*h*	*m*	*h*	*m*	*h*	*m*
1	13	05.1	–4	19	6	24	1	20	1	27
11	13	06.5	–4	25	5	46	0	43	0	50
21	13	07.3	–4	27	5	07	0	04	0	11
31	13	07.4	–4	24	4	28	23	21	23	28

Diameters – equatorial 18″ polar 16″
Rings – major axis 40″ minor axis 7″

URANUS

Day	*R.A.*		*Dec.*		*Transit*		*10° high*			
							52°		56°	
	h	*m*	°	′	*h*	*m*	*h*	*m*	*h*	*m*
1	23	50.0	–1	53	17	07	21	51	21	42
11	23	50.9	–1	47	16	29	21	13	21	05
21	23	52.2	–1	38	15	51	20	36	20	27
31	23	53.6	–1	29	15	13	19	59	19	51

Diameter 4″

NEPTUNE

Day	*R.A.*		*Dec.*		*Transit*		*10° high*			
							52°		56°	
	h	*m*	°	′	*h*	*m*	*h*	*m*	*h*	*m*
1	21	56.5	–13	03	15	14	18	50	18	28
11	21	57.7	–12	57	14	36	18	12	17	50
21	21	59.0	–12	50	13	58	17	35	17	13
31	22	00.3	–12	43	13	20	16	58	16	36

Diameter 2″

FEBRUARY 2011

SECOND MONTH, 28 or 29 DAYS. *Februa*, Roman festival of Purification

1	*Tuesday*	The first volume of the *Oxford English Dictionary*, from *A* to *Ant*, was published 1884	day 32
2	*Wednesday*	James Joyce's *Ulysses* was published in one volume 1922	33
3	*Thursday*	Rock stars Buddy Holly, Ritchie Valens, and J. P. Richardson were killed in a plane crash 1959	34
4	*Friday*	James Fenimore Cooper's *The Last of the Mohicans* was published 1826	35
5	*Saturday*	Joris-Karl Huysmans, French novelist *b.* 1848; Marianne Moore, US poet *d.* 1972	36
6	*Sunday*	Russian author Fyodor Dostoevsky married the widow Maria Dmitrievna Isaeva 1857	37
7	*Monday*	Andreas Gursky's photograph *99 Cent II Diptychon* sold for $3.3m (£1.7m) at auction 2007	week 6 day 38
8	*Tuesday*	Jules Verne, French novelist *b.* 1828; Dame Iris Murdoch, novelist *d.* 1999	39
9	*Wednesday*	Actor Joanne Woodward received the first star on the Hollywood Walk of Fame 1960	40
10	*Thursday*	Dante Gabriel Rossetti discovered his wife, Elizabeth, had taken a fatal laudanum overdose 1862	41
11	*Friday*	Voltaire received 300 visitors in Paris the day after returning from 28 years in exile 1778	42
12	*Saturday*	Franco Zeffirelli, Italian director *b.* 1923; Immanuel Kant, German philosopher *d.* 1804	43
13	*Sunday*	The last 'Peanuts' comic strip appeared in newspapers, the day after Charles M. Schulz died 2000	44
14	*Monday*	New York hosted the 'Boz' Ball, a lavish party in honour of Charles Dickens 1842	week 7 day 45
15	*Tuesday*	Harold Arlen, US composer *b.* 1905; Nat King Cole, US jazz musician *d.* 1965	46
16	*Wednesday*	Richard Ford, Pulitzer prize-winning US novelist *b.* 1944; Angela Carter, writer *d.* 1992	47
17	*Thursday*	Giacomo Puccini's *Madame Butterfly* premiered at La Scala in Milan 1904	48
18	*Friday*	Mark Twain's *The Adventures of Huckleberry Finn* was first published 1885	49
19	*Saturday*	Ezra Pound won the first Bollingen Prize for his poetry collection *The Pisan Cantos* 1948	50
20	*Sunday*	The New York Metropolitan Museum of Art opened 1872	51
21	*Monday*	The Communist League published Marx and Engels' *The Communist Manifesto* 1848	week 8 day 52
22	*Tuesday*	Arthur Schopenhauer, philosopher *b.* 1788; Adam Ferguson, philosopher *d.* 1816	53
23	*Wednesday*	Canadian journalist Robert Ross published the first English edition of Oscar Wilde's *De Profundis* 1905	54
24	*Thursday*	The Theatre Royal, Drury Lane, burnt down for the second time 1809	55
25	*Friday*	Sylvia Plath and Ted Hughes first met at a party in Cambridge 1956	56
26	*Saturday*	Christopher Marlowe was baptised in Canterbury 1564	57
27	*Sunday*	Lord Byron gave his maiden speech in the House of Lords 1812	58
28	*Monday*	The erroneous entry 'dord' was discovered in *Webster's New International Dictionary* 1939	week 9 day 59

ASTRONOMICAL PHENOMENA

d	*h*	
1	17	Mercury in conjunction with Moon. Mercury 3°S.
3	03	Mars in conjunction with Moon. Mars 5°S.
4	17	Mars in conjunction
7	05	Jupiter in conjunction with Moon. Jupiter 6°S.
17	10	Neptune in conjunction
19	00	Sun's longitude 330° ♓
20	23	Mars in conjunction with Mercury. Mars 1°N.
21	12	Saturn in conjunction with Moon. Saturn 8°N.
25	09	Mercury in superior conjunction

MINIMA OF ALGOL

d	*h*	*d*	*h*	*d*	*h*
1	12.8	13	00.1	24	11.4
4	09.6	15	20.9	27	08.2
7	06.4	18	17.7		
10	03.2	21	14.5		

CONSTELLATIONS

The following constellations are near the meridian at

	d	*h*		*d*	*h*
January	1	24	February	15	21
January	16	23	March	1	20
February	1	22	March	16	19

Draco (below the Pole), Camelopardalis, Auriga, Taurus, Gemini, Orion, Canis Minor, Monoceros, Lepus, Canis Major and Puppis

THE MOON

Phases, Apsides and Node	*d*	*h*	*m*
● New Moon	3	02	31
☽ First Quarter	11	07	18
○ Full Moon	18	08	36
☾ Last Quarter	24	23	26
Apogee (405,951km)	6	23	20
Perigee (358,237km)	19	07	31

Mean longitude of ascending node on February 1, 271°

THE SUN

s.d. 16′.2

Day	Right Ascension h	m	s	Dec. – °	′	Equation of time m	s	Rise 52° h	m	Rise 56° h	m	Transit h	m	Set 52° h	m	Set 56° h	m	Sidereal time h	m	s	Transit of first point of Aries h	m	s
1	20	56	53	17	16	−13	27	7	41	7	56	12	14	16	47	16	32	8	43	26	15	14	04
2	21	00	58	16	58	−13	36	7	39	7	54	12	14	16	49	16	34	8	47	23	15	10	08
3	21	05	02	16	41	−13	43	7	37	7	52	12	14	16	51	16	37	8	51	19	15	06	12
4	21	09	05	16	23	−13	50	7	36	7	50	12	14	16	53	16	39	8	55	16	15	02	16
5	21	13	08	16	06	−13	55	7	34	7	48	12	14	16	55	16	41	8	59	12	14	58	20
6	21	17	09	15	47	−14	00	7	32	7	46	12	14	16	56	16	43	9	03	09	14	54	24
7	21	21	10	15	29	−14	05	7	31	7	44	12	14	16	58	16	45	9	07	05	14	50	28
8	21	25	10	15	10	−14	08	7	29	7	42	12	14	17	00	16	48	9	11	02	14	46	32
9	21	29	09	14	51	−14	10	7	27	7	39	12	14	17	02	16	50	9	14	59	14	42	36
10	21	33	07	14	32	−14	12	7	25	7	37	12	14	17	04	16	52	9	18	55	14	38	41
11	21	37	05	14	12	−14	13	7	23	7	35	12	14	17	06	16	54	9	22	52	14	34	45
12	21	41	01	13	53	−14	13	7	22	7	33	12	14	17	08	16	56	9	26	48	14	30	49
13	21	44	57	13	33	−14	13	7	20	7	31	12	14	17	10	16	59	9	30	45	14	26	53
14	21	48	53	13	13	−14	11	7	18	7	28	12	14	17	11	17	01	9	34	41	14	22	57
15	21	52	47	12	52	−14	09	7	16	7	26	12	14	17	13	17	03	9	38	38	14	19	01
16	21	56	41	12	32	−14	06	7	14	7	24	12	14	17	15	17	05	9	42	34	14	15	05
17	22	00	34	12	11	−14	03	7	12	7	22	12	14	17	17	17	07	9	46	31	14	11	09
18	22	04	26	11	50	−13	58	7	10	7	19	12	14	17	19	17	10	9	50	28	14	07	13
19	22	08	17	11	29	−13	53	7	08	7	17	12	14	17	21	17	12	9	54	24	14	03	17
20	22	12	08	11	07	−13	48	7	06	7	15	12	14	17	23	17	14	9	58	21	13	59	22
21	22	15	58	10	46	−13	41	7	04	7	12	12	14	17	24	17	16	10	02	17	13	55	26
22	22	19	48	10	24	−13	34	7	02	7	10	12	14	17	26	17	18	10	06	14	13	51	30
23	22	23	37	10	02	−13	27	7	00	7	07	12	13	17	28	17	20	10	10	10	13	47	34
24	22	27	25	9	40	−13	18	6	57	7	05	12	13	17	30	17	23	10	14	07	13	43	38
25	22	31	13	9	18	−13	10	6	55	7	02	12	13	17	32	17	25	10	18	03	13	39	42
26	22	35	00	8	56	−13	00	6	53	7	00	12	13	17	34	17	27	10	22	00	13	35	46
27	22	38	47	8	33	−12	50	6	51	6	57	12	13	17	35	17	29	10	25	56	13	31	50
28	22	42	33	8	11	−12	40	6	49	6	55	12	13	17	37	17	31	10	29	53	13	27	54

DURATION OF TWILIGHT (in minutes)

Latitude	*52°*	*56°*	*52°*	*56°*	*52°*	*56°*	*52°*	*56°*
	1 February		*11 February*		*21 February*		*31 February*	
Civil	37	41	35	39	34	38	34	37
Nautical	77	86	75	83	74	81	73	80
Astronomical	117	130	114	126	113	124	112	124

THE NIGHT SKY

Mercury is unsuitably placed for observation throughout the month, as it passes through superior conjunction on the 25th.

Venus continues to be visible as a brilliant object in the early mornings before dawn. Its magnitude is −4.2.

Mars passes through conjunction on the 4th and thus is unsuitably placed for observation throughout the month.

Jupiter, magnitude −2.1, continues to be visible in the south-western sky in the early part of the evening. On the 7th the 4-day old waxing crescent Moon passes 6 degrees north of the planet.

Saturn, in the constellation of Virgo, is rising in the eastern sky before midnight and remains visible until the morning twilight inhibits observation. Its magnitude is +0.6. On the 21st the waning gibbous Moon passes 8 degrees south of the planet.

Zodiacal Light. The evening cone may be observed stretching up from the western horizon, along the ecliptic, after the end of twilight, from the 19th onwards. This faint phenomenon is only visible under good conditions and in the absence of both moonlight and artificial lighting.

THE MOON

Day	R.A.		Dec.	Hor. par.	Semi-diam.	Sun's Co-Long.	PA of Br. Limb	Ph.	Age	Rise 52°		Rise 56°		Transit		Set 52°		Set 56°	
	h	m	°	′	′	°	°	%	d	h	m	h	m	h	m	h	m	h	m
1	19	17	−20.9	55.6	15.2	241	86	4	27.7	6	40	7	00	10	56	15	20	15	01
2	20	08	−17.7	55.2	15.0	253	89	1	28.7	7	06	7	21	11	44	16	31	16	17
3	20	56	−13.8	54.8	14.9	266	145	0	29.7	7	26	7	37	12	28	17	42	17	32
4	21	43	−9.4	54.5	14.8	278	229	1	0.9	7	43	7	50	13	11	18	50	18	45
5	22	27	−4.7	54.2	14.8	290	237	3	1.9	7	59	8	01	13	52	19	58	19	57
6	23	11	+0.1	54.1	14.7	302	239	8	2.9	8	14	8	12	14	33	21	05	21	09
7	23	54	+4.9	54.0	14.7	314	241	14	3.9	8	29	8	23	15	13	22	12	22	20
8	0	38	+9.6	54.1	14.7	326	243	21	4.9	8	45	8	35	15	55	23	20	23	33
9	1	23	+13.8	54.3	14.8	339	246	29	5.9	9	04	8	50	16	39	—		—	
10	2	10	+17.6	54.7	14.9	351	249	38	6.9	9	27	9	09	17	25	0	29	0	46
11	3	00	+20.7	55.2	15.0	3	253	47	7.9	9	56	9	34	18	15	1	37	1	59
12	3	53	+22.9	55.9	15.2	15	258	57	8.9	10	35	10	09	19	08	2	44	3	09
13	4	48	+24.0	56.8	15.5	27	264	67	9.9	11	25	10	58	20	03	3	45	4	12
14	5	46	+23.8	57.7	15.7	39	269	76	10.9	12	29	12	03	21	00	4	38	5	04
15	6	45	+22.2	58.7	16.0	52	274	85	11.9	13	45	13	23	21	58	5	21	5	43
16	7	44	+19.3	59.6	16.2	64	277	92	12.9	15	08	14	52	22	54	5	55	6	12
17	8	42	+15.0	60.4	16.5	76	276	97	13.9	16	35	16	25	23	50	6	23	6	35
18	9	40	+9.7	60.9	16.6	88	250	100	14.9	18	03	17	59	—		6	46	6	52
19	10	36	+3.8	61.2	16.7	100	139	99	15.9	19	32	19	33	0	44	7	07	7	08
20	11	31	−2.4	61.1	16.7	112	125	96	16.9	20	59	21	06	1	37	7	27	7	23
21	12	27	−8.3	60.8	16.6	124	120	90	17.9	22	26	22	39	2	31	7	48	7	39
22	13	23	−13.7	60.2	16.4	137	116	81	18.9	23	51	—		3	25	8	12	7	58
23	14	20	−18.2	59.4	16.2	149	111	71	19.9	—		0	09	4	21	8	41	8	22
24	15	18	−21.5	58.6	16.0	161	106	61	20.9	1	10	1	34	5	17	9	18	8	54
25	16	16	−23.4	57.8	15.7	173	100	50	21.9	2	21	2	48	6	13	10	03	9	36
26	17	14	−24.0	57.0	15.5	185	94	39	22.9	3	20	3	48	7	09	10	59	10	32
27	18	10	−23.2	56.3	15.3	197	89	30	23.9	4	07	4	32	8	03	12	03	11	38
28	19	04	−21.3	55.7	15.2	210	85	21	24.9	4	42	5	04	8	53	13	11	12	50

MERCURY

Day	R.A.		Dec.	Diam.	Phase	Transit		5° high 52°		5° high 56°	
	h	m	°	′	%	h	m	h	m	h	m
1	19	51	−22.3	5	90	11	10	7	59	8	32
3	20	04	−21.9	5	92	11	15	8	01	8	33
5	20	17	−21.4	5	93	11	20	8	02	8	32
7	20	30	−20.8	5	94	11	26	8	03	8	31
9	20	44	−20.1	5	95	11	31	8	03	8	30
11	20	57	−19.3	5	96	11	37	8	02	8	28
13	21	11	−18.4	5	97	11	43	8	01	8	25
15	21	24	−17.4	5	97	11	48	8	00	8	22
17	21	38	−16.4	5	98	11	54	7	58	8	19
19	21	52	−15.2	5	99	12	00	16	04	15	46
21	22	05	−13.9	5	99	12	06	16	18	16	02
23	22	19	−12.6	5	100	12	12	16	33	16	18
25	22	33	−11.2	5	100	12	17	16	47	16	34
27	22	47	−9.7	5	100	12	23	17	02	16	51
29	23	01	−8.1	5	99	12	29	17	18	17	08
31	23	14	−6.4	5	98	12	35	17	33	17	25

VENUS

Day	R.A.		Dec.	Diam.	Phase	Transit		5° high 52°		5° high 56°	
	h	m	°	′	%	h	m	h	m	h	m
1	17	44	−20.7	20	61	9	02	5	40	6	09
6	18	09	−21.0	19	63	9	07	5	47	6	17
11	18	33	−21.1	18	65	9	12	5	53	6	23
16	18	58	−21.0	17	67	9	17	5	57	6	26
21	19	23	−20.6	17	69	9	22	5	59	6	27
26	19	48	−20.0	16	70	9	27	5	59	6	26
31	20	12	−19.2	16	72	9	32	5	58	6	23

MARS

Day	R.A.		Dec.	Diam.	Phase	Transit		5° high 52°		5° high 56°	
	h	m	°	′	%	h	m	h	m	h	m
1	21	02	−18.1	4	100	12	19	16	02	15	39
6	21	17	−16.9	4	100	12	15	16	06	15	45
11	21	33	−15.7	4	100	12	11	16	10	15	51
16	21	48	−14.4	4	100	12	07	16	14	15	57
21	22	04	−13.0	4	100	12	02	16	18	16	02
26	22	19	−11.6	4	100	11	57	16	22	16	08
31	22	34	−10.2	4	100	11	53	16	26	16	13

SUNRISE AND SUNSET

	London		*Bristol*		*Birmingham*		*Manchester*		*Newcastle*		*Glasgow*		*Belfast*	
	0° 05′	*51° 30′*	*2° 35′*	*51° 28′*	*1° 55′*	*52° 28′*	*2° 15′*	*53° 28′*	*1° 37′*	*54° 59′*	*4° 14′*	*55° 52′*	*5° 56′*	*54° 35′*
d	*h m*	*h m*	*h m*	*h m*	*h m*	*h m*	*h m*	*h m*	*h m*	*h m*	*h m*	*h m*	*h m*	*h m*
1	7 39	16 49	7 49	16 59	7 50	16 53	7 55	16 51	7 58	16 43	8 12	16 50	8 14	17 02
2	7 38	16 51	7 48	17 01	7 48	16 55	7 53	16 53	7 56	16 45	8 10	16 52	8 12	17 04
3	7 36	16 53	7 46	17 03	7 47	16 57	7 51	16 55	7 54	16 47	8 08	16 54	8 10	17 06
4	7 34	16 55	7 44	17 05	7 45	16 59	7 49	16 57	7 52	16 49	8 06	16 56	8 08	17 08
5	7 33	16 56	7 43	17 07	7 43	17 01	7 48	16 59	7 50	16 51	8 04	16 58	8 06	17 10
6	7 31	16 58	7 41	17 08	7 41	17 03	7 46	17 01	7 48	16 53	8 02	17 01	8 04	17 12
7	7 29	17 00	7 39	17 10	7 40	17 05	7 44	17 03	7 47	16 55	8 00	17 03	8 02	17 14
8	7 28	17 02	7 38	17 12	7 38	17 07	7 42	17 05	7 45	16 58	7 58	17 05	8 00	17 16
9	7 26	17 04	7 36	17 14	7 36	17 08	7 40	17 07	7 42	17 00	7 56	17 07	7 58	17 18
10	7 24	17 06	7 34	17 16	7 34	17 10	7 38	17 09	7 40	17 02	7 54	17 09	7 56	17 20
11	7 22	17 07	7 32	17 18	7 32	17 12	7 36	17 11	7 38	17 04	7 52	17 12	7 54	17 22
12	7 21	17 09	7 30	17 19	7 30	17 14	7 34	17 13	7 36	17 06	7 49	17 14	7 52	17 24
13	7 19	17 11	7 29	17 21	7 28	17 16	7 32	17 15	7 34	17 08	7 47	17 16	7 50	17 26
14	7 17	17 13	7 27	17 23	7 27	17 18	7 30	17 17	7 32	17 10	7 45	17 18	7 48	17 29
15	7 15	17 15	7 25	17 25	7 25	17 20	7 28	17 19	7 30	17 12	7 43	17 20	7 46	17 31
16	7 13	17 17	7 23	17 27	7 23	17 22	7 26	17 21	7 28	17 14	7 40	17 22	7 44	17 33
17	7 11	17 18	7 21	17 28	7 21	17 24	7 24	17 23	7 25	17 16	7 38	17 25	7 42	17 35
18	7 09	17 20	7 19	17 30	7 19	17 26	7 22	17 25	7 23	17 19	7 36	17 27	7 39	17 37
19	7 07	17 22	7 17	17 32	7 16	17 27	7 20	17 27	7 21	17 21	7 33	17 29	7 37	17 39
20	7 05	17 24	7 15	17 34	7 14	17 29	7 18	17 29	7 19	17 23	7 31	17 31	7 35	17 41
21	7 03	17 26	7 13	17 36	7 12	17 31	7 16	17 31	7 16	17 25	7 29	17 33	7 33	17 43
22	7 01	17 27	7 11	17 37	7 10	17 33	7 13	17 32	7 14	17 27	7 26	17 35	7 30	17 45
23	6 59	17 29	7 09	17 39	7 08	17 35	7 11	17 34	7 12	17 29	7 24	17 38	7 28	17 47
24	6 57	17 31	7 07	17 41	7 06	17 37	7 09	17 36	7 09	17 31	7 22	17 40	7 26	17 49
25	6 55	17 33	7 05	17 43	7 04	17 39	7 07	17 38	7 07	17 33	7 19	17 42	7 23	17 51
26	6 53	17 35	7 03	17 45	7 02	17 40	7 05	17 40	7 05	17 35	7 17	17 44	7 21	17 53
27	6 51	17 36	7 01	17 46	6 59	17 42	7 02	17 42	7 02	17 37	7 14	17 46	7 19	17 55
28	6 49	17 38	6 58	17 48	6 57	17 44	7 00	17 44	7 00	17 39	7 12	17 48	7 16	17 57

JUPITER

Day	*R.A.*		*Dec.*		*Transit*		*5° high*			
							52°		*56°*	
	h	*m*	°	′	*h*	*m*	*h*	*m*	*h*	*m*
1	0	08.3	−0	22	15	24	20	49	20	45
11	0	15.7	+0	27	14	52	20	21	20	19
21	0	23.6	+1	20	14	21	19	55	19	52
31	0	31.9	+2	14	13	50	19	28	19	27

Diameters – equatorial 35″ polar 32″

SATURN

Day	*R.A.*		*Dec.*		*Transit*		*5° high*			
							52°		*56°*	
	h	*m*	°	′	*h*	*m*	*h*	*m*	*h*	*m*
1	13	07.3	−4	24	4	24	23	17	23	24
11	13	06.7	−4	17	3	44	22	36	22	43
21	13	05.4	−4	06	3	04	21	54	22	01
31	13	03.6	−3	53	2	23	21	12	21	19

Diameters – equatorial 18″ polar 17″
Rings – major axis 42″ minor axis 7″

URANUS

Day	*R.A.*		*Dec.*		*Transit*		*10° high*			
							52°		*56°*	
	h	*m*	°	′	*h*	*m*	*h*	*m*	*h*	*m*
1	23	53.8	−1	28	15	09	19	55	19	47
11	23	55.5	−1	16	14	31	19	18	19	10
21	23	57.3	−1	04	13	54	18	42	18	34
31	23	59.3	−0	51	13	17	18	06	17	58

Diameter 4″

NEPTUNE

Day	*R.A.*		*Dec.*		*Transit*		*10° high*			
							52°		*56°*	
	h	*m*	°	′	*h*	*m*	*h*	*m*	*h*	*m*
1	22	00.5	−12	42	13	16	16	54	16	33
11	22	01.9	−12	34	12	38	16	17	15	56
21	22	03.4	−12	27	12	00	15	40	15	19
31	22	04.8	−12	19	11	22	15	03	14	42

Diameter 2″

MARCH 2011

THIRD MONTH, 31 DAYS. *Mars*, Roman god of battle

1	*Tuesday*	Robert Lowell, US poet *b.* 1917; George Herbert, poet *d.* 1633	day 60
2	*Wednesday*	*Casablanca* won three Oscars, including Best Picture, at the 16th Academy Awards 1944	61
3	*Thursday*	The first edition of *TIME* magazine was published, with Joseph G. Cannon on its cover 1923	62
4	*Friday*	Peter Tchaikovsky's ballet *Swan Lake* premiered at the Bolshoi Theatre in Moscow 1877	63
5	*Saturday*	Charlotte Brontë wrote to the Reverend Henry Nussey declining his offer of marriage 1839	64
6	*Sunday*	Michelangelo, Italian artist *b.* 1475; Georgia O'Keeffe, US artist *d.* 1986	65
7	*Monday*	Robert Frost's poem 'Stopping by Woods on a Snowy Evening' was published 1923	week 10 day 66
8	*Tuesday*	Douglas Adams' *The Hitchhiker's Guide to the Galaxy* began on BBC Radio 4 1978	67
9	*Wednesday*	Samuel Barber, US composer *b.* 1910; Harry Somers, English-Canadian composer *d.* 1999	68
10	*Thursday*	US novelist Zelda Fitzgerald (wife of F. Scott Fitzgerald) died in a fire at Highland Hospital 1948	69
11	*Friday*	The *Daily Courant*, the first regular English daily newspaper, was launched 1702	70
12	*Saturday*	Jack Kerouac, US author *b.* 1922; Robert Ludlum, US author *d.* 2001	71
13	*Sunday*	Henrik Ibsen's play *Ghosts* opened at the Royalty Theatre, London 1891	72
14	*Monday*	Sylvia Beach, US publisher *b.* 1887; Sir Thomas Malory, author *d.* 1471	week 11 day 73
15	*Tuesday*	Francis Ford Coppola's *The Godfather* premiered in New York 1972	74
16	*Wednesday*	The Lyttelton Theatre in London officially opened with Albert Finney as Hamlet 1976	75
17	*Thursday*	A Van Gogh exhibition in Paris caused a sensation, 11 years after the artist's death 1901	76
18	*Friday*	John Updike, US Pulitzer Prize-winning novelist *b.* 1932; Laurence Sterne, novelist *d.* 1768	77
19	*Saturday*	Honoré de Balzac's play *Les Ressources de Quinola* opened to an empty house 1842	78
20	*Sunday*	Harriet Beecher Stowe's anti-slavery novel, *Uncle Tom's Cabin*, was published 1852	79
21	*Monday*	Johann Sebastian Bach, German composer *b.* 1685; Robert Southey, poet *d.* 1843	week 12 day 80
22	*Tuesday*	The Lumière brothers held their first private screening of projected motion pictures 1895	81
23	*Wednesday*	Thomas Harris delivered the 600-page manuscript for his new novel, *Hannibal* 1999	82
24	*Thursday*	Tennessee Williams' play *Cat on a Hot Tin Roof* opened in New York 1955	83
25	*Friday*	US Customs confiscated 520 copies of Allen Ginsberg's poetry collection *Howl* 1955	84
26	*Saturday*	F. Scott Fitzgerald's debut novel, *This Side of Paradise*, was published 1920	85
27	*Sunday*	Alfred Hitchcock's first US film, *Rebecca*, starring Laurence Olivier and Joan Fontaine, opened 1940	86
28	*Monday*	Mario Vargas Llosa, Peruvian novelist *b.* 1936; Virginia Woolf, writer *d.* 1941	week 13 day 87
29	*Tuesday*	Ludwig van Beethoven gave his first public performance as a virtuoso and composer 1795	88
30	*Wednesday*	Sean O'Casey, Irish dramatist *b.* 1880; John McGahern, Irish novelist *d.* 2006	89
31	*Thursday*	The first instalment of Dickens' *The Pickwick Papers* was published under the pseudonym 'Boz' 1836	90

ASTRONOMICAL PHENOMENA

d	*h*	
1	03	Venus in conjunction with Moon. Venus 2°S.
4	07	Mars in conjunction with Moon. Mars 6°S.
5	13	Mercury in conjunction with Moon. Mercury 6°S.
7	00	Jupiter in conjunction with Moon. Jupiter 6°S.
16	01	Jupiter in conjunction with Mercury. Jupiter 2°S.
20	19	Saturn in conjunction with Moon. Saturn 8°N.
20	23	Sun's longitude 0° ♈
21	12	Uranus in conjunction
23	01	Mercury at greatest elongation E. 19°
30	21	Mercury at stationary point
31	08	Venus in conjunction with Moon. Venus 5°S.

MINIMA OF ALGOL

d	*h*	*d*	*h*	*d*	*h*
2	05.0	13	16.3	25	03.6
5	01.8	16	13.1	28	00.4
7	22.6	19	09.9	30	21.2
10	19.5	22	06.8		

CONSTELLATIONS

The following constellations are near the meridian at

	d	*h*		*d*	*h*
February	1	24	March	16	21
February	15	23	April	1	20
March	1	22	April	15	19

Cepheus (below the Pole), Camelopardalis, Lynx, Gemini, Cancer, Leo, Canis Minor, Hydra, Monoceros, Canis Major and Puppis

THE MOON

Phases, Apsides and Node	*d*	*h*	*m*
● New Moon	4	20	46
☽ First Quarter	12	23	45
○ Full Moon	19	18	10
☾ Last Quarter	26	12	07
Apogee (406,594km)	6	08	04
Perigee (356,574km)	19	19	15

Mean longitude of ascending node on March 1, 269°

THE SUN

s.d. 16′.1

Day	Right Ascension			Dec.		Equation of time		Rise				Transit		Set				Sidereal time			Transit of first point of Aries		
								52°		56°				52°		56°							
	h	*m*	*s*	°	′	*m*	*s*	*h*	*m*	*h*	*m*	*h*	*m*	*h*	*m*	*h*	*m*	*h*	*m*	*s*	*h*	*m*	*s*
1	22	46	19	−7	48	−12	29	6	47	6	53	12	12	17	39	17	33	10	33	50	13	23	58
2	22	50	04	−7	25	−12	17	6	45	6	50	12	12	17	41	17	35	10	37	46	13	20	02
3	22	53	48	−7	02	−12	05	6	42	6	47	12	12	17	43	17	38	10	41	43	13	16	07
4	22	57	32	−6	39	−11	53	6	40	6	45	12	12	17	44	17	40	10	45	39	13	12	11
5	23	01	16	−6	16	−11	40	6	38	6	42	12	12	17	46	17	42	10	49	36	13	08	15
6	23	04	59	−5	53	−11	27	6	36	6	40	12	11	17	48	17	44	10	53	32	13	04	19
7	23	08	42	−5	30	−11	13	6	33	6	37	12	11	17	50	17	46	10	57	29	13	00	23
8	23	12	24	−5	06	−10	59	6	31	6	35	12	11	17	51	17	48	11	01	25	12	56	27
9	23	16	06	−4	43	−10	44	6	29	6	32	12	11	17	53	17	50	11	05	22	12	52	31
10	23	19	48	−4	20	−10	29	6	27	6	30	12	10	17	55	17	52	11	09	19	12	48	35
11	23	23	29	−3	56	−10	14	6	24	6	27	12	10	17	57	17	54	11	13	15	12	44	39
12	23	27	10	−3	33	−9	58	6	22	6	24	12	10	17	59	17	56	11	17	12	12	40	43
13	23	30	51	−3	09	−9	42	6	20	6	22	12	10	18	00	17	59	11	21	08	12	36	47
14	23	34	31	−2	45	−9	26	6	18	6	19	12	09	18	02	18	01	11	25	05	12	32	52
15	23	38	11	−2	22	−9	09	6	15	6	17	12	09	18	04	18	03	11	29	01	12	28	56
16	23	41	51	−1	58	−8	53	6	13	6	14	12	09	18	06	18	05	11	32	58	12	25	00
17	23	45	30	−1	34	−8	36	6	11	6	11	12	08	18	07	18	07	11	36	54	12	21	04
18	23	49	09	−1	11	−8	18	6	08	6	09	12	08	18	09	18	09	11	40	51	12	17	08
19	23	52	48	−0	47	−8	01	6	06	6	06	12	08	18	11	18	11	11	44	48	12	13	12
20	23	56	27	−0	23	−7	43	6	04	6	03	12	08	18	12	18	13	11	48	44	12	09	16
21	0	00	06	+0	01	−7	25	6	01	6	01	12	07	18	14	18	15	11	52	41	12	05	20
22	0	03	45	+0	24	−7	07	5	59	5	58	12	07	18	16	18	17	11	56	37	12	01	24
23	0	07	23	+0	48	−6	49	5	57	5	55	12	07	18	18	18	19	12	00	34	11	57	28
24	0	11	02	+1	12	−6	31	5	54	5	53	12	06	18	19	18	21	12	04	30	11	53	32
25	0	14	40	+1	35	−6	13	5	52	5	50	12	06	18	21	18	23	12	08	27	11	49	37
26	0	18	19	+1	59	−5	55	5	50	5	48	12	06	18	23	18	25	12	12	23	11	45	41
27	0	21	57	+2	22	−5	37	5	47	5	45	12	05	18	25	18	27	12	16	20	11	41	45
28	0	25	35	+2	46	−5	19	5	45	5	42	12	05	18	26	18	29	12	20	17	11	37	49
29	0	29	14	+3	09	−5	01	5	43	5	40	12	05	18	28	18	31	12	24	13	11	33	53
30	0	32	52	+3	33	−4	43	5	41	5	37	12	05	18	30	18	33	12	28	10	11	29	57
31	0	36	31	+3	56	−4	25	5	38	5	34	12	04	18	31	18	35	12	32	06	11	26	01

DURATION OF TWILIGHT (in minutes)

Latitude	*52°*	*56°*	*52°*	*56°*	*52°*	*56°*	*52°*	*56°*
	1 March		*11 March*		*21 March*		*31 March*	
Civil	34	37	34	37	34	37	34	38
Nautical	73	80	73	80	74	81	75	84
Astronomical	112	124	113	125	115	128	120	135

THE NIGHT SKY

Mercury reaches its greatest eastern elongation (19 degrees) on the 23rd and therefore becomes visible in the evenings after the first 10 days of the month until only a few days short of the end of the month. It may be detected low above the west-south-western horizon around the beginning of evening civil twilight. At first its magnitude is −1.2 but this has diminished to about +1.1 by the end of its period of visibility. This is the only evening apparition during the year for observers in the British Isles.

Venus, magnitude −4.0, is visible as a morning object, low above the southeastern horizon before dawn. It is getting noticeably closer to the Sun and by the end of the month observers will be unlikely to see it for more than a quarter of an hour before sunrise. On the morning of the 1st the waning crescent Moon passes 1 degree north of the planet: again on the 31st the Moon passes 5 degrees north of Venus.

Mars continues to remain too close to the Sun for observation throughout the month.

Jupiter, magnitude −2.1, is now only visible low above the south-western horizon for a short while after sunset, but only for the first half of the month. Thereafter it is lost in the gathering twilight. The waxing crescent Moon, only 2 days old, passes 5 degrees north of the planet on the evening of the 6th. Do not confuse Mercury with the much brighter Jupiter around the middle of the month, Mercury passing 2 degrees north of Jupiter.

Saturn continues to be visible as an evening object, magnitude +0.5, in the constellation of Virgo. By the end of the month it should be visible low above the eastern horizon by about 19h. By this time it will be transiting the meridian around midnight as it moves towards opposition early next month. On the evening of the 20th the Full Moon passes 8 degrees south of Saturn.

Zodiacal Light. The evening cone may be observed stretching up from the western horizon, along the ecliptic, after the end of twilight, until the 5th and again after the 19th. This faint phenomenon is only visible under good conditions and in the absence of both moonlight and artificial lighting.

THE MOON

Day	R.A.		Dec.	Hor. par.	Semi-diam.	Sun's Co-Long.	PA of Br. Limb	Ph.	Age	Rise 52°		Rise 56°		Transit		Set 52°		Set 56°	
	h	m	°	′	′	°	°	%	d	h	m	h	m	h	m	h	m	h	m
1	19	56	−18.4	55.1	15.0	222	81	13	25.9	5	10	5	27	9	41	14	21	14	05
2	20	44	−14.8	54.7	14.9	234	80	7	26.9	5	32	5	44	10	26	15	31	15	20
3	21	31	−10.6	54.4	14.8	246	82	3	27.9	5	50	5	58	11	09	16	40	16	33
4	22	16	−6.0	54.2	14.8	258	94	1	28.9	6	06	6	10	11	51	17	47	17	45
5	22	59	−1.2	54.0	14.7	271	174	0	0.2	6	21	6	21	12	31	18	54	18	56
6	23	43	+3.6	53.9	14.7	283	225	1	1.2	6	37	6	33	13	12	20	01	20	08
7	0	26	+8.2	53.9	14.7	295	235	4	2.2	6	53	6	45	13	53	21	09	21	19
8	1	11	+12.5	54.1	14.7	307	241	9	3.2	7	11	6	59	14	36	22	16	22	32
9	1	57	+16.4	54.3	14.8	319	246	15	4.2	7	32	7	16	15	21	23	24	23	44
10	2	46	+19.7	54.7	14.9	332	250	22	5.2	7	59	7	38	16	09	–		–	
11	3	37	+22.1	55.2	15.0	344	255	31	6.2	8	33	8	09	17	00	0	31	0	54
12	4	30	+23.5	55.8	15.2	356	261	40	7.2	9	18	8	51	17	52	1	32	1	59
13	5	26	+23.8	56.6	15.4	8	267	50	8.2	10	14	9	48	18	47	2	27	2	53
14	6	23	+22.8	57.5	15.7	20	272	61	9.2	11	22	10	58	19	42	3	13	3	37
15	7	20	+20.4	58.4	15.9	32	277	71	10.2	12	39	12	20	20	38	3	50	4	10
16	8	17	+16.8	59.4	16.2	45	281	81	11.2	14	01	13	48	21	32	4	20	4	35
17	9	13	+12.1	60.2	16.4	57	283	89	12.2	15	27	15	20	22	26	4	45	4	54
18	10	09	+6.6	60.9	16.6	69	281	95	13.2	16	55	16	53	23	20	5	07	5	11
19	11	05	+0.5	61.4	16.7	81	269	99	14.2	18	24	18	28	–		5	28	5	27
20	12	01	−5.6	61.5	16.8	93	168	100	15.2	19	53	20	03	0	14	5	49	5	43
21	12	59	−11.3	61.2	16.7	105	127	97	16.2	21	22	21	37	1	10	6	13	6	01
22	13	57	−16.3	60.7	16.5	118	117	92	17.2	22	47	23	08	2	06	6	40	6	24
23	14	57	−20.2	59.9	16.3	130	110	85	18.2	–		–		3	05	7	15	6	53
24	15	57	−22.7	59.0	16.1	142	103	76	19.2	0	05	0	30	4	03	7	59	7	33
25	16	57	−23.7	58.0	15.8	154	97	66	20.2	1	10	1	37	5	01	8	52	8	25
26	17	55	−23.3	57.1	15.6	166	90	55	21.2	2	03	2	28	5	57	9	55	9	30
27	18	51	−21.7	56.3	15.3	178	85	45	22.2	2	43	3	05	6	50	11	03	10	41
28	19	43	−19.0	55.6	15.1	191	81	35	23.2	3	13	3	31	7	39	12	13	11	56
29	20	33	−15.5	55.0	15.0	203	77	26	24.2	3	37	3	50	8	25	13	23	13	10
30	21	20	−11.5	54.5	14.9	215	76	18	25.2	3	56	4	06	9	08	14	31	14	23
31	22	05	−7.0	54.2	14.8	227	75	11	26.2	4	13	4	18	9	50	15	38	15	35

MERCURY

Day	R.A.		Dec.	Diam.	Phase	Transit		5° high 52°		5° high 56°	
	h	m	°	′	%	h	m	h	m	h	m
1	23	01	−8.1	5	99	12	29	17	18	17	08
3	23	14	−6.4	5	98	12	35	17	33	17	25
5	23	28	−4.6	5	97	12	41	17	49	17	42
7	23	42	−2.8	5	95	12	47	18	04	17	59
9	23	56	−1.0	5	91	12	53	18	19	18	16
11	0	09	+0.8	6	87	12	58	18	34	18	32
13	0	22	+2.6	6	82	13	03	18	48	18	47
15	0	34	+4.4	6	75	13	07	19	01	19	02
17	0	45	+6.1	6	68	13	10	19	12	19	14
19	0	56	+7.6	7	60	13	12	19	22	19	25
21	1	05	+9.0	7	52	13	13	19	29	19	34
23	1	12	+10.2	7	43	13	12	19	34	19	39
25	1	18	+11.1	8	35	13	10	19	36	19	42
27	1	22	+11.9	8	28	13	06	19	35	19	41
29	1	25	+12.3	9	21	13	00	19	30	19	37
31	1	25	+12.5	9	15	12	52	19	23	19	30

VENUS

Day	R.A.		Dec.	Diam.	Phase	Transit		5° high 52°		5° high 56°	
	h	m	°	′	%	h	m	h	m	h	m
1	20	02	−19.5	16	71	9	30	5	58	6	25
6	20	27	−18.5	15	73	9	35	5	56	6	20
11	20	52	−17.3	15	75	9	40	5	52	6	14
16	21	16	−15.9	14	76	9	44	5	47	6	07
21	21	40	−14.3	14	78	9	48	5	41	5	58
26	22	03	−12.6	14	79	9	52	5	34	5	49
31	22	27	−10.6	13	80	9	56	5	26	5	39

MARS

Day	R.A.		Dec.	Diam.	Phase	Transit		5° high 52°		5° high 56°	
	h	m	°	′	%	h	m	h	m	h	m
1	22	28	−10.8	4	100	11	55	7	25	7	39
6	22	43	−9.3	4	100	11	50	7	12	7	24
11	22	57	−7.8	4	100	11	45	6	59	7	09
16	23	12	−6.3	4	100	11	40	6	45	6	54
21	23	26	−4.7	4	100	11	34	6	31	6	39
26	23	41	−3.1	4	100	11	29	6	18	6	24
31	23	55	−1.5	4	100	11	24	6	04	6	09

SUNRISE AND SUNSET

	London				*Bristol*				*Birmingham*				*Manchester*				*Newcastle*				*Glasgow*				*Belfast*			
	0° 05′		*51° 30′*		*2° 35′*		*51° 28′*		*1° 55′*		*52° 28′*		*2° 15′*		*53° 28′*		*1° 37′*		*54° 59′*		*4° 14′*		*55° 52′*		*5° 56′*		*54° 35′*	
d	*h*	*m*	*h*	*m*	*h*	*m*	*h*	*m*	*h*	*m*	*h*	*m*	*h*	*m*	*h*	*m*	*h*	*m*	*h*	*m*	*h*	*m*	*h*	*m*	*h*	*m*	*h*	*m*
1	6	46	17	40	6	56	17	50	6	55	17	46	6	58	17	46	6	57	17	41	7	09	17	50	7	14	17	59
2	6	44	17	42	6	54	17	52	6	53	17	48	6	55	17	48	6	55	17	43	7	07	17	53	7	12	18	01
3	6	42	17	43	6	52	17	54	6	51	17	50	6	53	17	50	6	53	17	45	7	04	17	55	7	09	18	03
4	6	40	17	45	6	50	17	55	6	48	17	52	6	51	17	52	6	50	17	47	7	02	17	57	7	07	18	05
5	6	38	17	47	6	48	17	57	6	46	17	53	6	48	17	54	6	48	17	49	6	59	17	59	7	04	18	07
6	6	36	17	49	6	45	17	59	6	44	17	55	6	46	17	56	6	45	17	51	6	57	18	01	7	02	18	09
7	6	33	17	50	6	43	18	00	6	41	17	57	6	44	17	57	6	43	17	53	6	54	18	03	7	00	18	11
8	6	31	17	52	6	41	18	02	6	39	17	59	6	41	17	59	6	40	17	55	6	51	18	05	6	57	18	13
9	6	29	17	54	6	39	18	04	6	37	18	01	6	39	18	01	6	38	17	58	6	49	18	07	6	55	18	15
10	6	27	17	56	6	37	18	06	6	35	18	02	6	37	18	03	6	35	18	00	6	46	18	09	6	52	18	17
11	6	24	17	57	6	34	18	07	6	32	18	04	6	34	18	05	6	33	18	01	6	44	18	11	6	50	18	19
12	6	22	17	59	6	32	18	09	6	30	18	06	6	32	18	07	6	30	18	03	6	41	18	13	6	47	18	21
13	6	20	18	01	6	30	18	11	6	28	18	08	6	29	18	09	6	28	18	05	6	39	18	16	6	45	18	23
14	6	18	18	03	6	28	18	13	6	25	18	10	6	27	18	11	6	25	18	07	6	36	18	18	6	42	18	25
15	6	15	18	04	6	25	18	14	6	23	18	11	6	25	18	12	6	23	18	09	6	33	18	20	6	40	18	27
16	6	13	18	06	6	23	18	16	6	21	18	13	6	22	18	14	6	20	18	11	6	31	18	22	6	37	18	29
17	6	11	18	08	6	21	18	18	6	18	18	15	6	20	18	16	6	18	18	13	6	28	18	24	6	35	18	31
18	6	09	18	09	6	19	18	19	6	16	18	17	6	17	18	18	6	15	18	15	6	26	18	26	6	32	18	33
19	6	06	18	11	6	16	18	21	6	14	18	18	6	15	18	20	6	12	18	17	6	23	18	28	6	30	18	35
20	6	04	18	13	6	14	18	23	6	11	18	20	6	13	18	22	6	10	18	19	6	20	18	30	6	27	18	37
21	6	02	18	14	6	12	18	24	6	09	18	22	6	10	18	23	6	07	18	21	6	18	18	32	6	25	18	38
22	5	59	18	16	6	09	18	26	6	07	18	24	6	08	18	25	6	05	18	23	6	15	18	34	6	22	18	40
23	5	57	18	18	6	07	18	28	6	04	18	25	6	05	18	27	6	02	18	25	6	12	18	36	6	20	18	42
24	5	55	18	20	6	05	18	30	6	02	18	27	6	03	18	29	6	00	18	27	6	10	18	38	6	17	18	44
25	5	53	18	21	6	03	18	31	6	00	18	29	6	00	18	31	5	57	18	29	6	07	18	40	6	15	18	46
26	5	50	18	23	6	00	18	33	5	57	18	31	5	58	18	33	5	55	18	31	6	05	18	42	6	12	18	48
27	5	48	18	25	5	58	18	35	5	55	18	32	5	56	18	34	5	52	18	33	6	02	18	44	6	10	18	50
28	5	46	18	26	5	56	18	36	5	52	18	34	5	53	18	36	5	50	18	35	5	59	18	46	6	07	18	52
29	5	44	18	28	5	54	18	38	5	50	18	36	5	51	18	38	5	47	18	37	5	57	18	48	6	05	18	54
30	5	41	18	30	5	51	18	40	5	48	18	38	5	48	18	40	5	44	18	39	5	54	18	50	6	02	18	56
31	5	39	18	31	5	49	18	41	5	45	18	39	5	46	18	42	5	42	18	41	5	51	18	52	6	00	18	58

JUPITER

Day	*R.A.*		*Dec.*		*Transit*		*5° high*			
							52°		*56°*	
	h	*m*	°	′	*h*	*m*	*h*	*m*	*h*	*m*
1	0	30.2	+2	03	13	56	19	33	19	32
11	0	38.8	+2	59	13	25	19	07	19	06
21	0	47.5	+3	55	12	54	18	41	18	41
31	0	56.4	+4	51	12	24	18	16	18	17

Diameters – equatorial 33″ polar 31″

SATURN

Day	*R.A.*		*Dec.*		*Transit*		*5° high*			
							52°		*56°*	
	h	*m*	°	′	*h*	*m*	*h*	*m*	*h*	*m*
1	13	04.0	–3	56	2	31	21	21	21	27
11	13	01.8	–3	40	1	49	20	38	20	44
21	12	59.3	–3	23	1	08	19	54	20	00
31	12	56.5	–3	05	0	25	19	11	19	16

Diameters – equatorial 19″ polar 17″
Rings – major axis 43″ minor axis 7″

URANUS

Day	*R.A.*		*Dec.*		*Transit*		*10° high*			
							52°		*56°*	
	h	*m*	°	′	*h*	*m*	*h*	*m*	*h*	*m*
1	23	58.9	–0	54	13	24	18	13	18	05
11	0	00.9	–0	40	12	47	17	37	17	30
21	0	03.0	–0	27	12	10	17	01	16	54
31	0	05.1	–0	13	11	32	16	25	16	18

Diameter 4″

NEPTUNE

Day	*R.A.*		*Dec.*		*Transit*		*10° high*			
							52°		*56°*	
	h	*m*	°	′	*h*	*m*	*h*	*m*	*h*	*m*
1	22	04.5	–12	20	11	30	7	49	8	10
11	22	06.0	–12	13	10	52	7	10	7	31
21	22	07.3	–12	06	10	14	6	32	6	52
31	22	08.5	–11	59	9	36	5	53	6	13

Diameter 2″

APRIL 2011

FOURTH MONTH, 30 DAYS. *Aperire*, to open; Earth opens to receive seed.

1	*Friday*	Sergei Rachmaninov, Russian composer *b.* 1873; Scott Joplin, US ragtime composer *d.* 1917	day 91
2	*Saturday*	Charlie Chaplin returned to the USA for the first time in 20 years to collect an Oscar 1972	92
3	*Sunday*	Oscar Wilde began an unsuccessful libel suit against the Marquess of Queensberry 1895	93
4	*Monday*	Maya Angelou, US poet *b.* 1928; Martin Luther King Jr, US clergyman and activist *d.* 1968	week 14 day 94
5	*Tuesday*	Julie Andrews won Best Actress at the Oscars for her role in *Mary Poppins* 1965	95
6	*Wednesday*	Italian poet Petrarch first saw 'Laura', the feminine ideal immortalised in his *Song Book* 1327	96
7	*Thursday*	William Wordsworth, poet *b.* 1770; William Godwin, novelist and political writer *d.* 1836	97
8	*Friday*	The *Venus de Milo* was discovered on the Aegean island of Melos 1820	98
9	*Saturday*	Samuel Clemens, aka Mark Twain, received his steamboat pilot's licence 1859	99
10	*Sunday*	The Statute of Anne, the first British copyright law on printed materials, came into effect 1710	100
11	*Monday*	Dorothy Parker resigned as drama critic at *The New Yorker* magazine 1931	week 15 day 101
12	*Tuesday*	French author Gustave Flaubert's *Madame Bovary* was published 1857	102
13	*Wednesday*	Oscar-winning film *Wuthering Heights*, starring Laurence Olivier, was released 1939	103
14	*Thursday*	Lexicographer Noah Webster published his *American Dictionary of the English Language* 1828	104
15	*Friday*	Jeffrey Archer, author and politician *b.* 1940; Jean-Paul Sartre, French philosopher *d.* 1980	105
16	*Saturday*	The Rolling Stones released their eponymous debut album 1964	106
17	*Sunday*	Geoffrey Chaucer first recited his *Canterbury Tales* 1397	107
18	*Monday*	Ezra Pound was cleared of treason after spending 13 years in a psychiatric hospital 1958	week 16 day 108
19	*Tuesday*	*The Simpsons* premiered as a short vignette on the *Tracey Ullman Show* 1987	109
20	*Wednesday*	Edgar Allan Poe's 'The Murders in the Rue Morgue' was published 1841	110
21	*Thursday*	Iggy Pop, US singer *b.* 1947; Nina Simone, US jazz singer *d.* 2003	111
22	*Friday*	Soviet newspaper *Pravda* was first published in St Petersburg 1912	112
23	*Saturday*	Vladimir Nabokov, Russian-American writer *b.* 1899; Rupert Brooke, poet *d.* 1915	113
24	*Sunday*	French officer Claude-Joseph Rouget de Lisle began composing the French national anthem 1792	114
25	*Monday*	Daniel Defoe's novel *Robinson Crusoe* was published 1719	week 17 day 115
26	*Tuesday*	William Shakespeare was baptised at Holy Trinity Church, Stratford 1564	116
27	*Wednesday*	Ludwig van Beethoven finished composing his piece for piano, 'Für Elise' 1810	117
28	*Thursday*	T. S. Eliot accepted a job as editor at Faber & Faber in London 1925	118
29	*Friday*	The musical *Hair* opened on Broadway at the Biltmore Theatre 1968	119
30	*Saturday*	New York opened its first World's Fair, attracting 44 million people over two seasons 1939	120

ASTRONOMICAL PHENOMENA

d	*h*	
2	12	Mars in conjunction with Moon. Mars 6°S.
3	19	Jupiter in conjunction with Moon. Jupiter 6°S.
4	00	Saturn at opposition
4	10	Mercury in conjunction with Moon. Mercury 1°S.
6	15	Jupiter in conjunction
9	09	Pluto at stationary point
9	20	Mercury in inferior conjunction
12	04	Jupiter in conjunction with Mercury. Jupiter 3°S.
17	03	Saturn in conjuction with Moon. Saturn 8°N.
19	15	Mars in conjunction with Mercury. Mars 0°.6 S.
20	10	Sun's longitude 30° ♉
23	10	Mercury at stationary point
30	17	Venus in conjunction with Moon. Venus 7°S.

MINIMA OF ALGOL

d	*h*	*d*	*h*	*d*	*h*
2	18.0	14	05.3	25	16.6
5	14.9	17	02.1	28	13.4
8	11.7	19	23.0		
11	08.5	22	19.8		

CONSTELLATIONS

The following constellations are near the meridian at

	d	*h*		*d*	*h*
March	1	24	April	15	21
March	16	23	May	1	20
April	1	22	May	16	19

Cepheus (below the Pole), Cassiopeia (below the Pole), Ursa Major, Leo Minor, Leo., Sextans, Hydra and Crater

THE MOON

Phases, Apsides and Node	*d*	*h*	*m*
● New Moon	3	14	32
☽ First Quarter	11	12	05
○ Full Moon	18	02	44
☾ Last Quarter	25	02	47
Apogee (406, 648 km)	2	09	16
Perigee (358, 097 km)	17	06	06
Apogee (406, 017 km)	29	18	10

Mean longitude of ascending node on April 1, 268°

THE SUN

s.d. 16′.0

Day	Right Ascension			Dec. +		Equation of time		Rise 52°		Rise 56°		Transit		Set 52°		Set 56°		Sidereal time			Transit of first point of Aries		
	h	*m*	*s*	°	′	*m*	*s*	*h*	*m*	*h*	*m*	*h*	*m*	*h*	*m*	*h*	*m*	*h*	*m*	*s*	*h*	*m*	*s*
1	0	40	10	4	19	–4	07	5	36	5	32	12	04	18	33	18	37	12	36	03	11	22	05
2	0	43	48	4	43	–3	49	5	34	5	29	12	04	18	35	18	39	12	39	59	11	18	09
3	0	47	27	5	06	–3	32	5	31	5	27	12	03	18	37	18	42	12	43	56	11	14	13
4	0	51	06	5	29	–3	14	5	29	5	24	12	03	18	38	18	44	12	47	52	11	10	17
5	0	54	46	5	51	–2	57	5	27	5	21	12	03	18	40	18	46	12	51	49	11	06	22
6	0	58	25	6	14	–2	39	5	24	5	19	12	03	18	42	18	48	12	55	46	11	02	26
7	1	02	05	6	37	–2	22	5	22	5	16	12	02	18	43	18	50	12	59	42	10	58	30
8	1	05	44	7	00	–2	06	5	20	5	13	12	02	18	45	18	52	13	03	39	10	54	34
9	1	09	24	7	22	–1	49	5	18	5	11	12	02	18	47	18	54	13	07	35	10	50	38
10	1	13	04	7	44	–1	33	5	15	5	08	12	01	18	49	18	56	13	11	32	10	46	42
11	1	16	45	8	07	–1	17	5	13	5	06	12	01	18	50	18	58	13	15	28	10	42	46
12	1	20	26	8	29	–1	01	5	11	5	03	12	01	18	52	19	00	13	19	25	10	38	50
13	1	24	07	8	50	–0	45	5	09	5	01	12	01	18	54	19	02	13	23	21	10	34	54
14	1	27	48	9	12	–0	30	5	07	4	58	12	00	18	55	19	04	13	27	18	10	30	58
15	1	31	29	9	34	–0	15	5	04	4	56	12	00	18	57	19	06	13	31	14	10	27	03
16	1	35	11	9	55	0	00	5	02	4	53	12	00	18	59	19	08	13	35	11	10	23	07
17	1	38	54	10	17	+0	14	5	00	4	51	12	00	19	00	19	10	13	39	08	10	19	11
18	1	42	36	10	38	+0	28	4	58	4	48	11	59	19	02	19	12	13	43	04	10	15	15
19	1	46	19	10	59	+0	41	4	56	4	46	11	59	19	04	19	14	13	47	01	10	11	19
20	1	50	03	11	19	+0	55	4	54	4	43	11	59	19	06	19	16	13	50	57	10	07	23
21	1	53	47	11	40	+1	07	4	51	4	41	11	59	19	07	19	18	13	54	54	10	03	27
22	1	57	31	12	00	+1	20	4	49	4	38	11	59	19	09	19	20	13	58	50	9	59	31
23	2	01	16	12	21	+1	31	4	47	4	36	11	58	19	11	19	22	14	02	47	9	55	35
24	2	05	01	12	41	+1	43	4	45	4	33	11	58	19	12	19	24	14	06	43	9	51	39
25	2	08	47	13	00	+1	53	4	43	4	31	11	58	19	14	19	26	14	10	40	9	47	43
26	2	12	33	13	20	+2	04	4	41	4	29	11	58	19	16	19	28	14	14	37	9	43	48
27	2	16	19	13	39	+2	14	4	39	4	26	11	58	19	17	19	30	14	18	33	9	39	52
28	2	20	07	13	58	+2	23	4	37	4	24	11	58	19	19	19	32	14	22	30	9	35	56
29	2	23	54	14	17	+2	32	4	35	4	22	11	57	19	21	19	35	14	26	26	9	32	00
30	2	27	43	14	36	+2	40	4	33	4	19	11	57	19	23	19	37	14	30	23	9	28	04

DURATION OF TWILIGHT (in minutes)

Latitude	52°	56°	52°	56°	52°	56°	52°	56°
	1 April		*11 April*		*21 April*		*31 April*	
Civil	34	38	35	39	37	42	39	44
Nautical	76	84	79	89	83	96	89	106
Astronomical	120	136	127	147	137	165	152	204

THE NIGHT SKY

Mercury passes through inferior conjunction on the 9th and therefore is unsuitably placed for observation throughout the month.

Venus continues to be visible for a very short while in the eastern sky, in the early mornings before sunrise. Its magnitude is –3.9. On the last day of the month the old waning crescent Moon passes 6 degrees north of Venus.

Mars is unsuitably placed for observation throughout the month.

Jupiter passes through conjunction on the 6th and thus remains too close to the Sun for observation.

Saturn, magnitude +0.4, reaches opposition on the 3rd, and therefore is visible throughout the hours of darkness. Saturn remains in the constellation of Virgo throughout the year. The Full Moon is in the vicinity of the planet on April 16–18th, passing 8 degrees south of it in the early hours of the 17th. The rings of Saturn are more easily visible in smaller telescopes as the minor axis reaches 7 arcseconds in width this month.

THE MOON

Day	R.A.		Dec.	Hor. Par.	Semi-diam.	Sun's Co-Long.	PA of Br. Limb	Ph.	Age	Rise				Transit		Set			
										52°		56°				52°		56°	
	h	m	°	′	′	°	°	%	d	h	m	h	m	h	m	h	m	h	m
1	22	48	−2.4	54.0	14.7	239	77	6	27.2	4	29	4	30	10	31	16	45	16	46
2	23	32	+2.4	53.9	14.7	252	82	3	28.2	4	44	4	41	11	11	17	52	17	57
3	0	15	+7.0	53.9	14.7	264	103	1	29.2	5	00	4	53	11	52	18	59	19	08
4	1	00	+11.4	54.0	14.7	276	200	0	0.4	5	18	5	07	12	35	20	07	20	20
5	1	46	+15.4	54.2	14.8	288	234	2	1.4	5	38	5	24	13	20	21	15	21	33
6	2	34	+18.8	54.5	14.8	300	245	5	2.4	6	04	5	45	14	07	22	21	22	44
7	3	25	+21.4	54.9	14.9	313	252	10	3.4	6	36	6	13	14	56	23	24	23	49
8	4	17	+23.0	55.3	15.1	325	259	17	4.4	7	17	6	51	15	48	—		—	
9	5	12	+23.6	55.9	15.2	337	265	25	5.4	8	08	7	42	16	41	0	21	0	47
10	6	07	+22.9	56.5	15.4	349	271	34	6.4	9	10	8	46	17	34	1	08	1	33
11	7	03	+21.0	57.3	15.6	2	276	45	7.4	10	22	10	01	18	28	1	47	2	08
12	7	58	+17.9	58.1	15.8	14	281	56	8.4	11	39	11	24	19	21	2	19	2	35
13	8	53	+13.7	59.0	16.1	26	285	66	9.4	13	00	12	51	20	13	2	45	2	56
14	9	47	+8.7	59.8	16.3	38	287	77	10.4	14	24	14	20	21	05	3	07	3	14
15	10	41	+3.0	60.5	16.5	50	287	86	11.4	15	50	15	51	21	57	3	28	3	30
16	11	36	−2.9	61.0	16.6	62	285	93	12.4	17	17	17	24	22	51	3	49	3	46
17	12	32	−8.8	61.2	16.7	75	277	98	13.4	18	46	18	58	23	47	4	11	4	03
18	13	30	−14.1	61.1	16.7	87	222	100	14.4	20	14	20	32	—		4	37	4	23
19	14	30	−18.5	60.7	16.6	99	124	99	15.4	21	38	22	01	0	46	5	09	4	50
20	15	32	−21.6	60.1	16.4	111	109	95	16.4	22	52	23	18	1	46	5	49	5	25
21	16	34	−23.3	59.2	16.1	123	100	89	17.4	23	52	—		2	46	6	40	6	13
22	17	34	−23.4	58.3	15.9	135	93	80	18.4	—		0	18	3	45	7	41	7	15
23	18	33	−22.1	57.3	15.6	148	86	71	19.4	0	38	1	02	4	41	8	49	8	26
24	19	27	−19.7	56.4	15.4	160	81	61	20.4	1	13	1	32	5	33	10	00	9	42
25	20	19	−16.4	55.7	15.2	172	77	51	21.4	1	40	1	55	6	21	11	11	10	58
26	21	07	−12.4	55.0	15.0	184	74	41	22.4	2	01	2	12	7	06	12	21	12	12
27	21	53	−8.0	54.5	14.9	196	72	32	23.4	2	19	2	25	7	48	13	29	13	24
28	22	37	−3.4	54.2	14.8	209	71	24	24.4	2	35	2	38	8	29	14	36	14	35
29	23	20	+1.3	54.0	14.7	221	72	16	25.4	2	51	2	49	9	10	15	42	15	46
30	0	04	+5.9	54.0	14.7	233	73	10	26.4	3	06	3	01	9	51	16	49	16	57

MERCURY

Day	R.A.		Dec.	Diam.	Phase	Transit		5° high			
								52°		56°	
	h	m	°	′	%	h	m	h	m	h	m
1	1	25	+12.5	10	12	12	48	19	18	19	25
3	1	23	+12.3	10	7	12	37	19	06	19	13
5	1	20	+11.8	11	4	12	26	18	52	18	58
7	1	16	+11.1	11	2	12	14	18	35	18	41
9	1	11	+10.3	11	0	12	01	18	18	18	23
11	1	06	+9.3	12	0	11	48	5	35	5	31
13	1	01	+8.3	12	1	11	36	5	28	5	25
15	0	56	+7.2	12	3	11	24	5	21	5	19
17	0	53	+6.3	11	6	11	12	5	15	5	13
19	0	50	+5.4	11	9	11	02	5	09	5	08
21	0	49	+4.7	11	12	10	53	5	03	5	03
23	0	49	+4.2	11	16	10	46	4	58	4	58
25	0	50	+3.8	10	20	10	39	4	53	4	53
27	0	52	+3.6	10	23	10	34	4	49	4	49
29	0	55	+3.6	10	27	10	29	4	44	4	44
31	1	00	+3.7	9	31	10	26	4	40	4	40

VENUS

Day	R.A.		Dec.	Diam.	Phase	Transit		5° high			
								52°		56°	
	h	m	°	′	%	h	m	h	m	h	m
1	22	31	−10.2	13	81	9	56	5	24	5	37
6	22	54	−8.2	13	82	10	00	5	15	5	26
11	23	17	−6.0	13	83	10	03	5	06	5	15
16	23	39	−3.8	12	84	10	05	4	57	5	04
21	0	02	−1.5	12	85	10	08	4	48	4	52
26	0	24	+0.8	12	87	10	11	4	38	4	41
31	0	46	+3.2	12	88	10	13	4	29	4	30

MARS

Day	R.A.		Dec.	Diam.	Phase	Transit		5° high			
								52°		56°	
	h	m	°	′	%	h	m	h	m	h	m
1	23	58	−1.2	4	99	11	23	6	01	6	06
6	0	12	+0.3	4	99	11	17	5	48	5	51
11	0	27	+1.9	4	99	11	12	5	34	5	36
16	0	41	+3.5	4	99	11	06	5	21	5	21
21	0	55	+5.0	4	99	11	01	5	07	5	07
26	1	09	+6.5	4	99	10	55	4	54	4	52
31	1	23	+8.0	4	99	10	49	4	41	4	38

SUNRISE AND SUNSET

	London				Bristol				Birmingham				Manchester				Newcastle				Glasgow				Belfast			
	0° 05′		51° 30′		2° 35′		51° 28′		1° 55′		52° 28′		2° 15′		53° 28′		1° 37′		54° 59′		4° 14′		55° 52′		5° 56′		54° 35′	
d	*h*	*m*	*h*	*m*	*h*	*m*	*h*	*m*	*h*	*m*	*h*	*m*	*h*	*m*	*h*	*m*	*h*	*m*	*h*	*m*	*h*	*m*	*h*	*m*	*h*	*m*	*h*	*m*
1	5	37	18	33	5	47	18	43	5	43	18	41	5	43	18	44	5	39	18	43	5	49	18	54	5	57	19	00
2	5	34	18	35	5	44	18	45	5	41	18	43	5	41	18	45	5	37	18	45	5	46	18	56	5	55	19	01
3	5	32	18	36	5	42	18	46	5	38	18	45	5	39	18	47	5	34	18	47	5	44	18	58	5	52	19	03
4	5	30	18	38	5	40	18	48	5	36	18	46	5	36	18	49	5	32	18	49	5	41	19	00	5	50	19	05
5	5	28	18	40	5	38	18	50	5	34	18	48	5	34	18	51	5	29	18	51	5	38	19	02	5	47	19	07
6	5	25	18	41	5	35	18	51	5	32	18	50	5	31	18	53	5	27	18	52	5	36	19	04	5	45	19	09
7	5	23	18	43	5	33	18	53	5	29	18	52	5	29	18	55	5	24	18	54	5	33	19	06	5	42	19	11
8	5	21	18	45	5	31	18	55	5	27	18	53	5	27	18	56	5	22	18	56	5	31	19	08	5	40	19	13
9	5	19	18	46	5	29	18	56	5	25	18	55	5	24	18	58	5	19	18	58	5	28	19	10	5	37	19	15
10	5	17	18	48	5	27	18	58	5	22	18	57	5	22	19	00	5	17	19	00	5	26	19	12	5	35	19	17
11	5	14	18	50	5	24	19	00	5	20	18	59	5	20	19	02	5	14	19	02	5	23	19	15	5	32	19	19
12	5	12	18	51	5	22	19	01	5	18	19	00	5	17	19	04	5	12	19	04	5	20	19	17	5	30	19	21
13	5	10	18	53	5	20	19	03	5	16	19	02	5	15	19	05	5	09	19	06	5	18	19	19	5	27	19	23
14	5	08	18	55	5	18	19	05	5	13	19	04	5	13	19	07	5	07	19	08	5	15	19	21	5	25	19	24
15	5	06	18	56	5	16	19	06	5	11	19	06	5	10	19	09	5	04	19	10	5	13	19	23	5	23	19	26
16	5	03	18	58	5	14	19	08	5	09	19	07	5	08	19	11	5	02	19	12	5	10	19	25	5	20	19	28
17	5	01	19	00	5	11	19	10	5	07	19	09	5	06	19	13	5	00	19	14	5	08	19	27	5	18	19	30
18	4	59	19	01	5	09	19	11	5	04	19	11	5	03	19	15	4	57	19	16	5	05	19	29	5	15	19	32
19	4	57	19	03	5	07	19	13	5	02	19	13	5	01	19	16	4	55	19	18	5	03	19	31	5	13	19	34
20	4	55	19	05	5	05	19	15	5	00	19	14	4	59	19	18	4	52	19	20	5	00	19	33	5	11	19	36
21	4	53	19	06	5	03	19	16	4	58	19	16	4	57	19	20	4	50	19	22	4	58	19	35	5	08	19	38
22	4	51	19	08	5	01	19	18	4	56	19	18	4	54	19	22	4	48	19	24	4	56	19	37	5	06	19	40
23	4	49	19	10	4	59	19	20	4	54	19	20	4	52	19	24	4	45	19	26	4	53	19	39	5	04	19	42
24	4	47	19	11	4	57	19	21	4	52	19	21	4	50	19	25	4	43	19	28	4	51	19	41	5	02	19	44
25	4	45	19	13	4	55	19	23	4	49	19	23	4	48	19	27	4	41	19	29	4	48	19	43	4	59	19	45
26	4	43	19	15	4	53	19	25	4	47	19	25	4	46	19	29	4	39	19	31	4	46	19	45	4	57	19	47
27	4	41	19	16	4	51	19	26	4	45	19	27	4	44	19	31	4	36	19	33	4	44	19	47	4	55	19	49
28	4	39	19	18	4	49	19	28	4	43	19	28	4	42	19	33	4	34	19	35	4	41	19	49	4	53	19	51
29	4	37	19	20	4	47	19	30	4	41	19	30	4	39	19	35	4	32	19	37	4	39	19	51	4	50	19	53
30	4	35	19	21	4	45	19	31	4	39	19	32	4	37	19	36	4	30	19	39	4	37	19	53	4	48	19	55

JUPITER

Day	*R.A.*		*Dec.*		*Transit*		*5° high*			
							52°		*56°*	
	h	*m*	°	′	*h*	*m*	*h*	*m*	*h*	*m*
1	0	57.3	+4	57	12	21	6	29	6	28
11	1	06.3	+5	53	11	50	5	53	5	52
21	1	15.2	+6	47	11	20	5	18	5	16
31	1	24.1	+7	41	10	50	4	43	4	40

Diameters – equatorial 33″ polar 31″

SATURN

Day	*R.A.*		*Dec.*		*Transit*		*5° high*			
							52°		*56°*	
	h	*m*	°	′	*h*	*m*	*h*	*m*	*h*	*m*
1	12	56.2	–3	03	0	21	5	32	5	26
11	12	53.3	–2	45	23	35	4	51	4	46
21	12	50.6	–2	28	22	53	4	11	4	05
31	12	48.1	–2	13	22	11	3	30	3	25

Diameters – equatorial 19″ polar 17″

Rings – major axis 43″ minor axis 6″

URANUS

Day	*R.A.*		*Dec.*		*Transit*		*10° high*			
							52°		*56°*	
	h	*m*	°	′	*h*	*m*	*h*	*m*	*h*	*m*
1	0	05.3	–0	12	11	29	6	36	6	43
11	0	07.3	+0	02	10	51	5	57	6	04
21	0	09.3	+0	14	10	14	5	19	5	26
31	0	11.1	+0	26	9	36	4	40	4	47

Diameter 4″

NEPTUNE

Day	*R.A.*		*Dec.*		*Transit*		*10° high*			
							52°		*56°*	
	h	*m*	°	′	*h*	*m*	*h*	*m*	*h*	*m*
1	22	08.7	–11	58	9	32	5	49	6	09
11	22	09.8	–11	53	8	54	5	10	5	30
21	22	10.7	–11	48	8	16	4	31	4	51
31	22	11.5	–11	44	7	37	3	52	4	12

Diameter 2″

MAY 2011

FIFTH MONTH, 31 DAYS. *Maia*, goddess of growth and increase

1	*Sunday*	Joseph Heller, US novelist *b.* 1923; John Dryden, Poet Laureate *d.* 1700	day 121
2	*Monday*	US director Steven Spielberg began filming *Jaws* 1972	week 18 day 122
3	*Tuesday*	Lord Byron swam across the Hellespont strait (the Dardanelles) in Turkey 1810	123
4	*Wednesday*	Ernest Hemingway won the Pulitzer Prize for Fiction for *The Old Man and the Sea* 1953	124
5	*Thursday*	Carnegie Hall officially opened with a concert conducted by Peter Tchaikovsky 1891	125
6	*Friday*	Orson Welles, US actor and director *b.* 1915; Marlene Dietrich, German-born US actor *d.* 1992	126
7	*Saturday*	US big band Glenn Miller and His Orchestra recorded the 'Chattanooga Choo-Choo' 1941	127
8	*Sunday*	The Irish Literary Theatre opened with a performance of Yeats' play *The Countess Cathleen* 1899	128
9	*Monday*	*Sam and Friends*, Jim Henson's first puppet TV show, aired in Washington DC 1955	week 19 day 129
10	*Tuesday*	The National Gallery in London opened to the public 1824	130
11	*Wednesday*	The Academy of Motion Picture Arts and Sciences held its inaugural banquet 1927	131
12	*Thursday*	Pink Floyd hosted the first ever 'quadraphonic' concert 1967	132
13	*Friday*	Stevie Wonder, US musician *b.* 1950; Chet Baker, US jazz trumpeter *d.* 1988	133
14	*Saturday*	Virginia Woolf's fourth novel *Mrs Dalloway* was published 1925	134
15	*Sunday*	Vincent van Gogh's *Portrait of Dr Gachet* sold for a record \$82.5m (£49m) at auction 1990	135
16	*Monday*	Samuel Johnson first met his companion and biographer James Boswell 1763	week 20 day 136
17	*Tuesday*	Erik Satie, French composer *b.* 1866; Sandro Botticelli, Italian painter *d.* 1510	137
18	*Wednesday*	Under torture, Thomas Kyd accused fellow playwright Christopher Marlowe of heresy 1593	138
19	*Thursday*	T. E. Lawrence ('Lawrence of Arabia') died after a motorcycle crash 1935	139
20	*Friday*	Flemish cartographer Abraham Ortelius produced the first modern atlas 1570	140
21	*Saturday*	French author Colette began to publish her novel *The Vagabond* in serial form 1910	141
22	*Sunday*	Japanese company Namco released its landmark arcade game *Pac-Man* 1980	142
23	*Monday*	The New York Public Library was dedicated by President Howard Taft 1911	week 21 day 143
24	*Tuesday*	John Henry Brodribb became the first actor to receive a knighthood 1895	144
25	*Wednesday*	Gilbert and Sullivan's comic opera *HMS Pinafore* opened in London 1878	145
26	*Thursday*	Bram Stoker's *Dracula* first went on sale in London 1897	146
27	*Friday*	US musician Bob Dylan released his album *The Freewheelin' Bob Dylan* 1963	147
28	*Saturday*	Ian Fleming, writer *b.* 1908; Eric Morecambe, comedian *d.* 1984	148
29	*Sunday*	Igor Stravinsky's ballet *The Rite of Spring* premiered in Paris, causing a riot 1913	149
30	*Monday*	Mikhail Bakunin, Russian philosopher *b.* 1814; Peter Paul Rubens, Flemish painter *d.* 1640	week 22 day 150
31	*Tuesday*	Samuel Pepys recorded the last entry in his 1.3 million-word diary 1669	151

ASTRONOMICAL PHENOMENA

d	*h*	
1	00	Mercury in conjunction with Moon. Mercury 7°S.
1	04	Jupiter in conjunction with Mars. Jupiter 0°.4S.
1	15	Jupiter in conjunction with Moon. Jupiter 6°S.
1	15	Mars in conjunction with Moon. Mars 5°S.
7	19	Mercury at greatest elongation W.27°.
9	16	Venus in conjunction with Mercury. Venus 1°N.
11	15	Jupiter in conjunction with Venus. Jupiter 0°.6N.
11	20	Jupiter in conjunction with Mercury. Jupiter 2°N.
14	10	Saturn in conjunction with Moon. Saturn 8°N.
16	09	Venus in conjunction with Mercury. Venus 1°N.
21	01	Mars in conjunction with Mercury. Mars 2°N.
21	09	Sun's longitude 60° ♊
23	08	Mars in conjunction with Venus. Mars 1°N.
29	10	Jupiter in conjunction with Moon. Jupiter 5°S.
30	18	Mars in conjunction with Moon. Mars 4°S.
31	01	Venus in conjunction with Moon. Venus 4°S.
31	16	Mercury in conjunction with Moon. Mercury 4°S.

MINIMA OF ALGOL

Algol is inconveniently situated for observation during May

CONSTELLATIONS

The following constellations are near the meridian at

	d	*h*		*d*	*h*
April	1	24	May	16	21
April	15	23	June	1	20
May	1	22	June	15	19

Cepheus (below the Pole), Cassiopeia (below the Pole), Ursa Minor, Ursa Major, Canes Venatici, Coma Berenices, Bootes, Leo, Virgo, Crater, Corvus and Hydra

THE MOON

Phases, Apsides and Node	*d*	*h*	*m*
● New Moon	3	06	51
☽ First Quarter	10	20	33
○ Full Moon	17	11	09
☾ Last Quarter	24	18	52
Perigee (362,151 km)	15	11	32
Apogee (404,969 km)	27	10	02

Mean longitude of ascending node on May 1, 266°

THE SUN

s.d. 15′.8

Day	Right Ascension			Dec. +		Equation of time		Rise 52°		Rise 56°		Transit		Set 52°		Set 56°		Sidereal time			Transit of first point of Aries		
	h	m	s	°	′	m	s	h	m	h	m	h	m	h	m	h	m	h	m	s	h	m	s
1	2	31	31	14	54	+2	48	4	31	4	17	11	57	19	24	19	39	14	34	19	9	24	08
2	2	35	21	15	13	+2	55	4	29	4	15	11	57	19	26	19	41	14	38	16	9	20	12
3	2	39	11	15	30	+3	02	4	27	4	13	11	57	19	28	19	43	14	42	12	9	16	16
4	2	43	01	15	48	+3	08	4	26	4	10	11	57	19	29	19	45	14	46	09	9	12	20
5	2	46	52	16	06	+3	14	4	24	4	08	11	57	19	31	19	47	14	50	06	9	08	24
6	2	50	44	16	23	+3	19	4	22	4	06	11	57	19	33	19	49	14	54	02	9	04	28
7	2	54	36	16	40	+3	23	4	20	4	04	11	57	19	34	19	51	14	57	59	9	00	33
8	2	58	28	16	56	+3	27	4	18	4	02	11	57	19	36	19	53	15	01	55	8	56	37
9	3	02	22	17	12	+3	30	4	17	4	00	11	56	19	37	19	55	15	05	52	8	52	41
10	3	06	15	17	28	+3	33	4	15	3	58	11	56	19	39	19	56	15	09	48	8	48	45
11	3	10	10	17	44	+3	35	4	13	3	56	11	56	19	41	19	58	15	13	45	8	44	49
12	3	14	04	18	00	+3	37	4	12	3	54	11	56	19	42	20	00	15	17	41	8	40	53
13	3	18	00	18	15	+3	38	4	10	3	52	11	56	19	44	20	02	15	21	38	8	36	57
14	3	21	56	18	29	+3	39	4	08	3	50	11	56	19	45	20	04	15	25	35	8	33	01
15	3	25	52	18	44	+3	39	4	07	3	48	11	56	19	47	20	06	15	29	31	8	29	05
16	3	29	49	18	58	+3	38	4	05	3	46	11	56	19	48	20	08	15	33	28	8	25	09
17	3	33	47	19	12	+3	37	4	04	3	44	11	56	19	50	20	10	15	37	24	8	21	13
18	3	37	45	19	26	+3	36	4	02	3	43	11	56	19	51	20	12	15	41	21	8	17	18
19	3	41	44	19	39	+3	34	4	01	3	41	11	56	19	53	20	13	15	45	17	8	13	22
20	3	45	43	19	52	+3	31	4	00	3	39	11	57	19	54	20	15	15	49	14	8	09	26
21	3	49	43	20	04	+3	27	3	58	3	37	11	57	19	56	20	17	15	53	10	8	05	30
22	3	53	43	20	16	+3	24	3	57	3	36	11	57	19	57	20	19	15	57	07	8	01	34
23	3	57	44	20	28	+3	19	3	56	3	34	11	57	19	59	20	20	16	01	04	7	57	38
24	4	01	46	20	40	+3	14	3	54	3	33	11	57	20	00	20	22	16	05	00	7	53	42
25	4	05	48	20	51	+3	09	3	53	3	31	11	57	20	01	20	24	16	08	57	7	49	46
26	4	09	50	21	02	+3	03	3	52	3	30	11	57	20	03	20	25	16	12	53	7	45	50
27	4	13	53	21	12	+2	56	3	51	3	29	11	57	20	04	20	27	16	16	50	7	41	54
28	4	17	57	21	22	+2	49	3	50	3	27	11	57	20	05	20	28	16	20	46	7	37	58
29	4	22	01	21	32	+2	42	3	49	3	26	11	57	20	06	20	30	16	24	43	7	34	03
30	4	26	05	21	41	+2	34	3	48	3	25	11	57	20	08	20	31	16	28	39	7	30	07
31	4	30	10	21	50	+2	26	3	47	3	24	11	58	20	09	20	33	16	32	36	7	26	11

DURATION OF TWILIGHT (in minutes)

Latitude	52°	56°	52°	56°	52°	56°	52°	56°
	1 May		*11 May*		*21 May*		*31 May*	
Civil	39	44	41	48	44	53	46	57
Nautical	89	106	97	120	106	141	115	187
Astronomical	152	204	176	TAN	TAN	TAN	TAN	TAN

THE NIGHT SKY

Mercury, although reaching greatest western elongation on the 7th, remains unsuitably placed for observation throughout the month.

Venus, magnitude −3.9, continues to be visible in the eastern sky, low above the horizon for a very short while before sunrise.

Mars continues to be unsuitably placed for observation throughout the month.

Jupiter remains too close to the Sun for observation until the very end of the month when it becomes visible as a morning object, though only visible low above the south-eastern horizon for a short while before dawn. Jupiter, magnitude −2.1, is moving slowly eastwards on the borders of the constellations of Pisces and Aries.

Saturn, magnitude +0.6, is still visible as an evening object in the south-western sky, though by the end of the month it will only be visible for about an hour after midnight. On the 14th the waxing gibbous Moon passes 8 degrees south of the planet.

THE MOON

Day	R.A.		Dec.	Hor. Par.	Semi-diam.	Sun's Co-Long.	PA of Bright Limb	Ph.	Age	Rise				Transit		Set			
										52°		56°				52°		56°	
	h	*m*	°	′	′	°	°	%	*d*	*h*	*m*	*h*	*m*	*h*	*m*	*h*	*m*	*h*	*m*
1	0	48	+10.4	54.1	14.7	245	77	5	27.4	3	24	3	14	10	33	17	57	18	09
2	1	34	+14.4	54.3	14.8	258	85	2	28.4	3	44	3	30	11	17	19	05	19	21
3	2	22	+18.0	54.6	14.9	270	120	0	29.4	4	08	3	50	12	04	20	12	20	33
4	3	12	+20.8	54.9	15.0	282	235	1	0.8	4	38	4	16	12	53	21	17	21	41
5	4	05	+22.6	55.3	15.1	294	254	3	1.8	5	17	4	52	13	44	22	16	22	42
6	4	59	+23.4	55.8	15.2	307	263	7	2.8	6	05	5	39	14	37	23	06	23	31
7	5	54	+23.0	56.3	15.3	319	270	13	3.8	7	04	6	40	15	31	23	48	—	
8	6	50	+21.4	56.8	15.5	331	276	21	4.8	8	13	7	51	16	24	—		0	10
9	7	44	+18.6	57.4	15.6	343	281	30	5.8	9	27	9	11	17	16	0	21	0	39
10	8	38	+14.7	58.1	15.8	355	285	41	6.8	10	45	10	34	18	06	0	48	1	01
11	9	31	+10.0	58.7	16.0	8	288	52	7.8	12	05	11	59	18	57	1	11	1	19
12	10	23	+4.7	59.3	16.2	20	290	63	8.8	13	27	13	26	19	47	1	31	1	35
13	11	16	−0.9	59.9	16.3	32	290	74	9.8	14	50	14	54	20	38	1	51	1	50
14	12	10	−6.6	60.3	16.4	44	289	83	10.8	16	16	16	25	21	32	2	12	2	06
15	13	06	−12.1	60.5	16.5	56	286	91	11.8	17	42	17	57	22	28	2	35	2	24
16	14	04	−16.8	60.5	16.5	69	279	97	12.8	19	07	19	28	23	27	3	03	2	47
17	15	04	−20.4	60.3	16.4	81	261	100	13.8	20	27	20	51	—		3	39	3	18
18	16	07	−22.7	59.7	16.3	93	114	100	14.8	21	35	22	01	0	27	4	25	4	00
19	17	09	−23.4	59.1	16.1	105	96	97	15.8	22	28	22	53	1	28	5	22	4	56
20	18	09	−22.6	58.2	15.9	117	88	92	16.8	23	09	23	30	2	27	6	29	6	05
21	19	07	−20.6	57.4	15.6	129	82	85	17.8	23	40	23	57	3	22	7	41	7	21
22	20	01	−17.5	56.5	15.4	142	77	77	18.8	—		—		4	13	8	54	8	39
23	20	51	−13.6	55.7	15.2	154	73	67	19.8	0	04	0	16	5	00	10	06	9	55
24	21	38	−9.3	55.1	15.0	166	70	58	20.8	0	24	0	31	5	44	11	16	11	10
25	22	23	−4.7	54.6	14.9	178	69	48	21.8	0	41	0	44	6	26	12	24	12	22
26	23	07	0.0	54.3	14.8	191	68	39	22.8	0	56	0	56	7	07	13	30	13	33
27	23	51	+4.7	54.2	14.8	203	69	30	23.8	1	12	1	08	7	48	14	37	14	43
28	0	35	+9.2	54.2	14.8	215	70	21	24.8	1	29	1	21	8	29	15	44	15	55
29	1	20	+13.3	54.3	14.8	227	73	14	25.8	1	48	1	36	9	13	16	52	17	07
30	2	07	+17.0	54.6	14.9	239	76	8	26.8	2	10	1	54	9	59	18	00	18	20
31	2	57	+20.1	55.0	15.0	252	81	4	27.8	2	38	2	18	10	47	19	07	19	30

MERCURY

Day	R.A.		Dec.	Diam.	Phase	Transit		5° high			
								52°		56°	
	h	*m*	°	′	%	*h*	*m*	*h*	*m*	*h*	*m*
1	1	00	+3.7	9	31	10	26	4	40	4	40
3	1	05	+4.0	9	34	10	23	4	36	4	36
5	1	11	+4.4	9	38	10	21	4	31	4	31
7	1	17	+4.9	8	41	10	20	4	28	4	27
9	1	25	+5.6	8	44	10	20	4	24	4	22
11	1	33	+6.3	8	47	10	21	4	20	4	18
13	1	42	+7.2	7	51	10	22	4	17	4	14
15	1	51	+8.1	7	54	10	23	4	13	4	10
17	2	01	+9.2	7	57	10	25	4	10	4	06
19	2	12	+10.2	7	61	10	28	4	07	4	02
21	2	23	+11.4	6	64	10	32	4	05	3	59
23	2	35	+12.6	6	68	10	36	4	03	3	55
25	2	48	+13.8	6	72	10	41	4	01	3	53
27	3	01	+15.1	6	75	10	46	4	00	3	50
29	3	15	+16.3	6	79	10	53	3	59	3	48
31	3	30	+17.6	6	83	11	00	3	59	3	47

VENUS

Day	R.A.		Dec.	Diam.	Phase	Transit		5° high			
								52°		56°	
	h	*m*	°	′	%	*h*	*m*	*h*	*m*	*h*	*m*
1	0	46	+3.2	12	88	10	13	4	29	4	30
6	1	09	+5.5	11	89	10	16	4	20	4	19
11	1	31	+7.8	11	90	10	19	4	11	4	08
16	1	54	+10.0	11	91	10	22	4	03	3	58
21	2	17	+12.1	11	92	10	26	3	55	3	49
26	2	41	+14.1	11	93	10	30	3	48	3	40
31	3	05	+16.0	11	93	10	34	3	43	3	32

MARS

Day	R.A.		Dec.	Diam.	Phase	Transit		5° high			
								52°		56°	
	h	*m*	°	′	%	*h*	*m*	*h*	*m*	*h*	*m*
1	1	23	+8.0	4	99	10	49	4	41	4	38
6	1	37	+9.4	4	99	10	44	4	28	4	24
11	1	52	+10.8	4	98	10	39	4	16	4	10
16	2	06	+12.1	4	98	10	33	4	03	3	56
21	2	20	+13.4	4	98	10	28	3	51	3	43
26	2	35	+14.7	4	98	10	23	3	39	3	30
31	2	49	+15.8	4	98	10	17	3	28	3	18

SUNRISE AND SUNSET

	London				Bristol				Birmingham				Manchester				Newcastle				Glasgow				Belfast			
	0° 05′		51° 30′		2° 35′		51° 28′		1° 55′		52° 28′		2° 15′		53° 28′		1° 37′		54° 59′		4° 14′		55° 52′		5° 56′		54° 35′	
d	*h*	*m*	*h*	*m*	*h*	*m*	*h*	*m*	*h*	*m*	*h*	*m*	*h*	*m*	*h*	*m*	*h*	*m*	*h*	*m*	*h*	*m*	*h*	*m*	*h*	*m*	*h*	*m*
1	4	33	19	23	4	43	19	33	4	37	19	33	4	35	19	38	4	27	19	41	4	34	19	55	4	46	19	57
2	4	31	19	25	4	41	19	35	4	35	19	35	4	33	19	40	4	25	19	43	4	32	19	57	4	44	19	59
3	4	29	19	26	4	39	19	36	4	33	19	37	4	31	19	42	4	23	19	45	4	30	19	59	4	42	20	01
4	4	28	19	28	4	38	19	38	4	32	19	39	4	29	19	43	4	21	19	47	4	28	20	01	4	40	20	03
5	4	26	19	29	4	36	19	39	4	30	19	40	4	27	19	45	4	19	19	49	4	26	20	03	4	38	20	04
6	4	24	19	31	4	34	19	41	4	28	19	42	4	25	19	47	4	17	19	51	4	24	20	05	4	36	20	06
7	4	22	19	33	4	32	19	43	4	26	19	44	4	24	19	49	4	15	19	53	4	21	20	07	4	34	20	08
8	4	20	19	34	4	31	19	44	4	24	19	45	4	22	19	51	4	13	19	54	4	19	20	09	4	32	20	10
9	4	19	19	36	4	29	19	46	4	22	19	47	4	20	19	52	4	11	19	56	4	17	20	11	4	30	20	12
10	4	17	19	37	4	27	19	47	4	21	19	49	4	18	19	54	4	09	19	58	4	15	20	13	4	28	20	14
11	4	15	19	39	4	26	19	49	4	19	19	50	4	16	19	56	4	07	20	00	4	13	20	15	4	26	20	15
12	4	14	19	41	4	24	19	50	4	17	19	52	4	14	19	57	4	05	20	02	4	11	20	17	4	24	20	17
13	4	12	19	42	4	22	19	52	4	16	19	53	4	13	19	59	4	03	20	04	4	09	20	18	4	22	20	19
14	4	11	19	44	4	21	19	54	4	14	19	55	4	11	20	01	4	01	20	05	4	07	20	20	4	21	20	21
15	4	09	19	45	4	19	19	55	4	12	19	57	4	09	20	02	4	00	20	07	4	06	20	22	4	19	20	22
16	4	08	19	47	4	18	19	57	4	11	19	58	4	08	20	04	3	58	20	09	4	04	20	24	4	17	20	24
17	4	06	19	48	4	16	19	58	4	09	20	00	4	06	20	06	3	56	20	11	4	02	20	26	4	15	20	26
18	4	05	19	50	4	15	19	59	4	08	20	01	4	05	20	07	3	55	20	12	4	00	20	28	4	14	20	28
19	4	03	19	51	4	14	20	01	4	06	20	03	4	03	20	09	3	53	20	14	3	58	20	29	4	12	20	29
20	4	02	19	52	4	12	20	02	4	05	20	04	4	02	20	10	3	51	20	16	3	57	20	31	4	11	20	31
21	4	01	19	54	4	11	20	04	4	04	20	06	4	00	20	12	3	50	20	17	3	55	20	33	4	09	20	33
22	4	00	19	55	4	10	20	05	4	02	20	07	3	59	20	13	3	48	20	19	3	54	20	35	4	08	20	34
23	3	58	19	57	4	08	20	06	4	01	20	09	3	57	20	15	3	47	20	21	3	52	20	36	4	06	20	36
24	3	57	19	58	4	07	20	08	4	00	20	10	3	56	20	16	3	45	20	22	3	51	20	38	4	05	20	37
25	3	56	19	59	4	06	20	09	3	59	20	11	3	55	20	18	3	44	20	24	3	49	20	40	4	03	20	39
26	3	55	20	01	4	05	20	10	3	58	20	13	3	54	20	19	3	43	20	25	3	48	20	41	4	02	20	40
27	3	54	20	02	4	04	20	12	3	56	20	14	3	52	20	21	3	41	20	27	3	46	20	43	4	01	20	42
28	3	53	20	03	4	03	20	13	3	55	20	15	3	51	20	22	3	40	20	28	3	45	20	44	4	00	20	43
29	3	52	20	04	4	02	20	14	3	54	20	17	3	50	20	23	3	39	20	30	3	44	20	46	3	59	20	45
30	3	51	20	05	4	01	20	15	3	53	20	18	3	49	20	25	3	38	20	31	3	43	20	47	3	57	20	46
31	3	50	20	07	4	00	20	16	3	52	20	19	3	48	20	26	3	37	20	32	3	41	20	49	3	56	20	47

JUPITER

Day	*R.A.*		*Dec.*		*Transit*		*5° high*			
							52°		*56°*	
	h	*m*	°	′	*h*	*m*	*h*	*m*	*h*	*m*
1	1	24.1	+7	41	10	50	4	43	4	40
11	1	32.9	+8	32	10	19	4	08	4	05
21	1	41.4	+9	20	9	48	3	33	3	29
31	1	49.6	+10	05	9	17	2	58	2	53

Diameters – equatorial 34″ polar 32″

SATURN

Day	*R.A.*		*Dec.*		*Transit*		*5° high*			
							52°		*56°*	
	h	*m*	°	′	*h*	*m*	*h*	*m*	*h*	*m*
1	12	48.1	−2	13	22	11	3	30	3	25
11	12	45.9	−2	01	21	30	2	50	2	45
21	12	44.2	−1	52	20	49	2	10	2	05
31	12	43.0	−1	47	20	08	1	29	1	25

Diameters – equatorial 19″ polar 17″

Rings – major axis 42″ minor axis 6″

URANUS

Day	*R.A.*		*Dec.*		*Transit*		*10° high*			
							52°		*56°*	
	h	*m*	°	′	*h*	*m*	*h*	*m*	*h*	*m*
1	0	11.1	+0	26	9	36	4	40	4	47
11	0	12.8	+0	37	8	59	4	02	4	08
21	0	14.3	+0	46	8	21	3	23	3	29
31	0	15.6	+0	54	7	43	2	44	2	50

Diameter 4″

NEPTUNE

Day	*R.A.*		*Dec.*		*Transit*		*10° high*			
							52°		*56°*	
	h	*m*	°	′	*h*	*m*	*h*	*m*	*h*	*m*
1	22	11.5	−11	44	7	37	3	52	4	12
11	22	12.1	−11	41	6	58	3	13	3	33
21	22	12.5	−11	39	6	19	2	34	2	54
31	22	12.6	−11	38	5	40	1	55	2	15

Diameter 2″

♊ JUNE 2011 ♋

SIXTH MONTH, 30 DAYS. *Juno*, goddess of marriage

1	*Wednesday*	Samuel Taylor Coleridge began publishing his periodical, *The Friend* 1809	day 152
2	*Thursday*	Marquis de Sade, French author *b.* 1740; Vita Sackville-West, author *d.* 1962	153
3	*Friday*	Pen pals T. S. Eliot and Groucho Marx met for the first time in London 1964	154
4	*Saturday*	The first Pulitzer prizes were awarded 1917	155
5	*Sunday*	Elvis Presley debuted his song 'Hound Dog' on *The Milton Berle Show* 1956	156
6	*Monday*	The French surrealist film *Un Chien Andalou* was released 1929	week 23 day 157
7	*Tuesday*	Dean Martin, US actor and singer *b.* 1917; E. M. Forster, British writer *d.* 1970	158
8	*Wednesday*	George Orwell's novel *Nineteen Eighty-Four* was published 1949	159
9	*Thursday*	Cartoon character Donald Duck made his debut in *The Wise Little Hen* 1934	160
10	*Friday*	Leo Tolstoy set out on a pilgrimage to the Optina Eastern Orthodox monastery 1881	161
11	*Saturday*	Gene Wilder, US actor *b.* 1935; John Wayne, US actor *d.* 1979	162
12	*Sunday*	Anne Frank was given a diary for her thirteenth birthday 1942	163
13	*Monday*	The Beatles achieved their final US number one, 'The Long and Winding Road' 1970	week 24 day 164
14	*Tuesday*	*Action Comics* published its first issue, introducing the character Superman 1938	165
15	*Wednesday*	Rembrandt's *Danae* was damaged by a vandal in the State Hermitage Museum, St Petersburg 1985	166
16	*Thursday*	James Joyce met his future wife, Nora; he later used the day as the setting for *Ulysses* 1904	167
17	*Friday*	The French frigate *Isère* arrived in New York Harbor carrying the Statue of Liberty 1885	168
18	*Saturday*	Jürgen Habermas, German philosopher *b.* 1929; Maxim Gorky, Russian writer *d.* 1936	169
19	*Sunday*	The first five-cent cinema, or 'nickelodeon', opened in Pittsburgh, USA 1905	170
20	*Monday*	US TV variety show *The Ed Sullivan Show* debuted under the title *Toast of the Town* 1948	week 25 day 171
21	*Tuesday*	Columbia Records unveiled its new long-playing (LP) record in New York 1948	172
22	*Wednesday*	US film *Who's Afraid of Virginia Woolf?* debuted with the Production Code seal of approval 1966	173
23	*Thursday*	Treatises attributed to John Frith were found in the belly of a cod at Cambridge market 1626	174
24	*Friday*	The first major exhibition of Pablo Picasso's works opened in Paris 1901	175
25	*Saturday*	Charles Baudelaire's poetry collection *Les Fleurs du Mal* was published in Paris 1857	176
26	*Sunday*	Shirley Jackson's classic short story 'The Lottery' was published in *The New Yorker* 1948	177
27	*Monday*	Edward Gibbon completed his *History of the Decline and Fall of the Roman Empire* 1787	week 26 day 178
28	*Tuesday*	Luigi Pirandello, Italian dramatist *b.* 1867; Edward Carpenter, poet *d.* 1929	179
29	*Wednesday*	The Globe Theatre burned down after fire broke out during a performance of *Henry VIII* 1613	180
30	*Thursday*	US author Margaret Mitchell's novel *Gone with the Wind* was published 1936	181

ASTRONOMICAL PHENOMENA

d	*h*	
1	21	Partial eclipse of Sun
3	08	Neptune at stationary point
10	16	Saturn in conjunction with Moon. Saturn 8°N.
13	00	Mercury in superior conjunction
13	04	Saturn at stationary point
15	20	Total eclipse of Moon
21	17	Sun's longitude 90° ♋
26	05	Jupiter in conjunction with Moon. Jupiter 5°S.
28	05	Pluto at opposition
28	18	Mars in conjunction with Moon. Mars 2°S.
30	08	Venus in conjunction with Moon. Venus 0.°05 S.

MINIMA OF ALGOL

Algol is inconveniently situated for observation during June

CONSTELLATIONS

The following constellations are near the meridian at

	d	*h*		*d*	*h*
May	1	24	June	15	21
May	16	23	July	1	20
June	1	22	July	16	19

Cassiopeia (below the Pole), Ursa Minor, Draco, Ursa Major, Canes Venatici, Bootes, Corona, Serpens, Virgo and Libra

THE MOON

Phases, Apsides and Node	*d*	*h*	*m*
● New Moon	1	21	03
☽ First Quarter	9	02	11
○ Full Moon	15	20	14
☾ Last Quarter	23	11	48
Perigee (367,217 km)	12	01	49
Apogee (404,232 km)	24	04	13

Mean longitude of ascending node on June 1, 264°

THE SUN

s.d. 15′.8

Day	Right Ascension			Dec. +		Equation of time		Rise				Transit		Set				Sidereal time			Transit of first point of Aries		
								52°		56°				52°		56°							
	h	m	s	°	′	m	s	h	m	h	m	h	m	h	m	h	m	h	m	s	h	m	s
1	4	34	16	21	59	+2	17	3	46	3	22	11	58	20	10	20	34	16	36	33	7	22	15
2	4	38	21	22	07	+2	08	3	46	3	21	11	58	20	11	20	35	16	40	29	7	18	19
3	4	42	28	22	14	+1	58	3	45	3	20	11	58	20	12	20	37	16	44	26	7	14	23
4	4	46	34	22	22	+1	48	3	44	3	19	11	58	20	13	20	38	16	48	22	7	10	27
5	4	50	41	22	29	+1	38	3	43	3	19	11	58	20	14	20	39	16	52	19	7	06	31
6	4	54	48	22	35	+1	27	3	43	3	18	11	59	20	15	20	40	16	56	15	7	02	35
7	4	58	56	22	42	+1	16	3	42	3	17	11	59	20	16	20	41	17	00	12	6	58	39
8	5	03	03	22	48	+1	05	3	42	3	16	11	59	20	17	20	42	17	04	08	6	54	43
9	5	07	11	22	53	+0	54	3	41	3	16	11	59	20	18	20	43	17	08	05	6	50	47
10	5	11	20	22	58	+0	42	3	41	3	15	11	59	20	18	20	44	17	12	02	6	46	52
11	5	15	28	23	03	+0	30	3	40	3	15	12	00	20	19	20	45	17	15	58	6	42	56
12	5	19	37	23	07	+0	18	3	40	3	14	12	00	20	20	20	46	17	19	55	6	39	00
13	5	23	46	23	11	+0	06	3	40	3	14	12	00	20	20	20	47	17	23	51	6	35	04
14	5	27	55	23	14	−0	07	3	40	3	13	12	00	20	21	20	47	17	27	48	6	31	08
15	5	32	04	23	17	−0	19	3	39	3	13	12	00	20	22	20	48	17	31	44	6	27	12
16	5	36	13	23	19	−0	32	3	39	3	13	12	01	20	22	20	49	17	35	41	6	23	16
17	5	40	22	23	22	−0	45	3	39	3	13	12	01	20	23	20	49	17	39	37	6	19	20
18	5	44	32	23	23	−0	58	3	39	3	13	12	01	20	23	20	49	17	43	34	6	15	24
19	5	48	41	23	25	−1	11	3	39	3	13	12	01	20	23	20	50	17	47	31	6	11	28
20	5	52	51	23	26	−1	24	3	40	3	13	12	01	20	24	20	50	17	51	27	6	07	32
21	5	57	00	23	26	−1	37	3	40	3	13	12	02	20	24	20	50	17	55	24	6	03	37
22	6	01	10	23	26	−1	50	3	40	3	13	12	02	20	24	20	51	17	59	20	5	59	41
23	6	05	19	23	26	−2	03	3	40	3	14	12	02	20	24	20	51	18	03	17	5	55	45
24	6	09	29	23	25	−2	16	3	40	3	14	12	02	20	24	20	51	18	07	13	5	51	49
25	6	13	38	23	24	−2	28	3	41	3	14	12	03	20	24	20	51	18	11	10	5	47	53
26	6	17	48	23	22	−2	41	3	41	3	15	12	03	20	24	20	51	18	15	07	5	43	57
27	6	21	57	23	20	−2	54	3	42	3	15	12	03	20	24	20	50	18	19	03	5	40	01
28	6	26	06	23	18	−3	06	3	42	3	16	12	03	20	24	20	50	18	23	00	5	36	05
29	6	30	15	23	15	−3	19	3	43	3	17	12	03	20	24	20	50	18	26	56	5	32	09
30	6	34	24	23	12	−3	31	3	43	3	17	12	04	20	24	20	50	18	30	53	5	28	13

DURATION OF TWILIGHT (in minutes)

Latitude	*52°*	*56°*	*52°*	*56°*	*52°*	*56°*	*52°*	*56°*
	1 June		*11 June*		*21 June*		*31 June*	
Civil	46	58	48	61	49	63	48	61
Nautical	116	TAN	124	TAN	127	TAN	124	TAN
Astronomical	TAN	TAN	TAN	TAN	TAN	TAN	TAN	TAN

THE NIGHT SKY

Mercury passes through superior conjunction on the 12th and remains unsuitably placed for observation throughout the month.

Venus, magnitude −3.9, is still a brilliant object in the early morning sky in the east but only for observers with a very good clear horizon in the east-north-east since it is only about 5 or 6 degrees high at sunrise.

Mars remains too close to the sun for observation throughout June but will become visible in the early mornings next month.

Jupiter, magnitude −2.2, continues to be visible as a bright object low in the south-eastern sky in the early hours. The planet is moving slowly eastwards in the constellation of Aries. The waning crescent Moon passes 5 degrees north of Jupiter on the 26th.

Saturn, magnitude +0.7, continues to be visible in the western sky in the evenings. On the 13th it reaches its second stationary point and resumes its direct motion. Saturn is still in the constellation of Virgo. The Moon passes 8 degrees south of the planet on the 10th.

Twilight. Reference to the section above shows that astronomical twilight lasts all night for a period around the summer solstice (ie in June and July), even in southern England. Under these conditions the sky never gets completely dark as the Sun is always less than 18 degrees below the horizon.

THE MOON

Day	R.A.		Dec.	Hor. Par.	Semi-diam.	Sun's Co-Long.	PA. of Br. Limb	Ph.	Age	Rise				Transit		Set			
										52°		56°				52°		56°	
	h	*m*	°	′	′	°	°	%	*d*	*h*	*m*	*h*	*m*	*h*	*m*	*h*	*m*	*h*	*m*
1	3	50	+22.2	55.4	15.1	264	89	1	28.8	3	14	2	50	11	38	20	08	20	34
2	4	44	+23.3	55.9	15.2	276	228	0	0.2	4	00	3	34	12	32	21	03	21	28
3	5	40	+23.2	56.4	15.4	288	269	1	1.2	4	57	4	31	13	26	21	47	22	10
4	6	36	+21.8	56.9	15.5	301	276	5	2.2	6	03	5	41	14	20	22	23	22	42
5	7	32	+19.2	57.4	15.7	313	282	10	3.2	7	17	6	59	15	13	22	52	23	07
6	8	26	+15.6	57.9	15.8	325	287	18	4.2	8	35	8	22	16	04	23	16	23	26
7	9	19	+11.1	58.4	15.9	337	290	27	5.2	9	54	9	46	16	54	23	37	23	42
8	10	11	+5.9	58.8	16.0	350	292	38	6.2	11	14	11	11	17	43	23	57	23	57
9	11	03	+0.4	59.1	16.1	2	293	49	7.2	12	35	12	37	18	33	—		—	
10	11	55	−5.2	59.4	16.2	14	292	61	8.2	13	57	14	04	19	24	0	17	0	12
11	12	48	−10.5	59.6	16.2	26	291	72	9.2	15	20	15	33	20	17	0	38	0	29
12	13	44	−15.3	59.7	16.3	38	288	81	10.2	16	44	17	02	21	13	1	03	0	49
13	14	42	−19.3	59.6	16.3	51	283	90	11.2	18	04	18	27	22	12	1	34	1	15
14	15	43	−22.0	59.4	16.2	63	278	96	12.2	19	16	19	42	23	11	2	14	1	50
15	16	44	−23.3	59.0	16.1	75	272	99	13.2	20	16	20	42	—		3	05	2	39
16	17	45	−23.1	58.5	15.9	87	83	100	14.2	21	03	21	26	0	11	4	08	3	42
17	18	44	−21.5	57.8	15.7	99	80	98	15.2	21	38	21	57	1	08	5	18	4	56
18	19	40	−18.8	57.1	15.5	112	75	94	16.2	22	06	22	20	2	02	6	33	6	15
19	20	32	−15.1	56.3	15.4	124	71	89	17.2	22	27	22	37	2	51	7	46	7	34
20	21	21	−10.9	55.7	15.2	136	69	82	18.2	22	46	22	51	3	37	8	58	8	50
21	22	08	−6.3	55.1	15.0	148	67	73	19.2	23	02	23	04	4	21	10	08	10	04
22	22	52	−1.6	54.6	14.9	160	66	64	20.2	23	18	23	15	5	03	11	16	11	16
23	23	36	+3.2	54.4	14.8	173	66	55	21.2	23	34	23	28	5	44	12	23	12	27
24	0	20	+7.8	54.2	14.8	185	67	45	22.2	23	52	23	42	6	25	13	30	13	39
25	1	05	+12.1	54.3	14.8	197	69	36	23.2	—		23	58	7	07	14	37	14	51
26	1	52	+15.9	54.5	14.9	209	72	27	24.2	0	13	—		7	52	15	45	16	03
27	2	40	+19.2	54.9	15.0	222	75	19	25.2	0	38	0	20	8	39	16	52	17	14
28	3	32	+21.6	55.4	15.1	234	79	12	26.2	1	11	0	48	9	29	17	56	18	21
29	4	36	+23.1	55.9	15.2	246	83	6	27.2	1	52	1	27	10	22	18	54	19	20
30	5	22	+23.4	56.6	15.4	258	87	2	28.2	2	45	2	19	11	17	19	43	20	08

MERCURY

Day	R.A.		Dec.	Diam.	Phase	Transit		5° high			
								52°		56°	
	h	*m*	°	′	%	*h*	*m*	*h*	*m*	*h*	*m*
1	3	37	+18.2	5	85	11	04	3	59	3	47
3	3	53	+19.4	5	89	11	12	4	00	3	47
5	4	10	+20.6	5	93	11	21	4	02	3	47
7	4	28	+21.6	5	96	11	31	4	06	3	49
9	4	46	+22.6	5	98	11	41	4	10	3	53
11	5	05	+23.4	5	100	11	52	4	16	3	57
13	5	24	+24.1	5	100	12	04	19	45	20	05
15	5	43	+24.6	5	99	12	15	19	59	20	20
17	6	02	+24.9	5	98	12	26	20	12	20	33
19	6	21	+25.0	5	96	12	37	20	23	20	44
21	6	39	+24.9	5	93	12	48	20	33	20	53
23	6	57	+24.7	5	89	12	58	20	41	21	00
25	7	14	+24.3	5	86	13	07	20	47	21	06
27	7	31	+23.8	6	82	13	15	20	51	21	10
29	7	47	+23.1	6	79	13	23	20	54	21	12
31	8	02	+22.3	6	75	13	30	20	56	21	13

VENUS

Day	R.A.		Dec.	Diam.	Phase	Transit		5° high			
								52°		56°	
	h	*m*	°	′	%	*h*	*m*	*h*	*m*	*h*	*m*
1	3	10	+16.4	11	94	10	35	3	41	3	31
6	3	34	+18.0	10	94	10	40	3	37	3	25
11	3	59	+19.5	10	95	10	45	3	34	3	20
16	4	25	+20.8	10	96	10	51	3	32	3	17
21	4	50	+21.8	10	96	10	57	3	32	3	15
26	5	17	+22.6	10	97	11	03	3	33	3	16
31	5	43	+23.2	10	98	11	10	3	37	3	19

MARS

Day	R.A.		Dec.	Diam.	Phase	Transit		5° high			
								52°		56°	
	h	*m*	°	′	%	*h*	*m*	*h*	*m*	*h*	*m*
1	2	52	+16.0	4	98	10	16	3	25	3	15
6	3	07	+17.1	4	98	10	11	3	14	3	03
11	3	22	+18.1	4	97	10	06	3	04	2	51
16	3	36	+19.1	4	97	10	01	2	53	2	40
21	3	51	+19.9	4	97	9	56	2	44	2	29
26	4	06	+20.7	4	97	9	52	2	34	2	19
31	4	21	+21.4	4	97	9	47	2	25	2	09

SUNRISE AND SUNSET

	London		*Bristol*		*Birmingham*		*Manchester*		*Newcastle*		*Glasgow*		*Belfast*	
	0° 05′	*51° 30′*	*2° 35′*	*51° 28′*	*1° 55′*	*52° 28′*	*2° 15′*	*53° 28′*	*1° 37′*	*54° 59′*	*4° 14′*	*55° 52′*	*5° 56′*	*54° 35′*
d	*h m*	*h m*	*h m*	*h m*	*h m*	*h m*	*h m*	*h m*	*h m*	*h m*	*h m*	*h m*	*h m*	*h m*
1	3 49	20 08	3 59	20 18	3 52	20 20	3 47	20 27	3 36	20 34	3 40	20 50	3 55	20 48
2	3 48	20 09	3 59	20 19	3 51	20 21	3 46	20 28	3 35	20 35	3 39	20 51	3 54	20 50
3	3 48	20 10	3 58	20 20	3 50	20 22	3 46	20 29	3 34	20 36	3 38	20 53	3 54	20 51
4	3 47	20 11	3 57	20 21	3 49	20 23	3 45	20 30	3 33	20 37	3 37	20 54	3 53	20 52
5	3 46	20 12	3 57	20 22	3 48	20 24	3 44	20 31	3 32	20 39	3 36	20 55	3 52	20 53
6	3 46	20 13	3 56	20 23	3 48	20 25	3 43	20 32	3 31	20 40	3 36	20 56	3 51	20 54
7	3 45	20 14	3 55	20 23	3 47	20 26	3 43	20 33	3 31	20 41	3 35	20 57	3 50	20 55
8	3 45	20 14	3 55	20 24	3 47	20 27	3 42	20 34	3 30	20 42	3 34	20 58	3 50	20 56
9	3 44	20 15	3 54	20 25	3 46	20 28	3 42	20 35	3 29	20 43	3 34	20 59	3 49	20 57
10	3 44	20 16	3 54	20 26	3 46	20 29	3 41	20 36	3 29	20 43	3 33	21 00	3 49	20 58
11	3 44	20 17	3 54	20 27	3 45	20 29	3 41	20 37	3 28	20 44	3 33	21 01	3 48	20 59
12	3 43	20 17	3 53	20 27	3 45	20 30	3 40	20 38	3 28	20 45	3 32	21 02	3 48	21 00
13	3 43	20 18	3 53	20 28	3 45	20 31	3 40	20 38	3 28	20 46	3 32	21 03	3 48	21 00
14	3 43	20 19	3 53	20 28	3 45	20 31	3 40	20 39	3 27	20 46	3 31	21 03	3 47	21 01
15	3 43	20 19	3 53	20 29	3 44	20 32	3 40	20 39	3 27	20 47	3 31	21 04	3 47	21 01
16	3 43	20 20	3 53	20 29	3 44	20 32	3 40	20 40	3 27	20 48	3 31	21 04	3 47	21 02
17	3 43	20 20	3 53	20 30	3 44	20 33	3 39	20 40	3 27	20 48	3 31	21 05	3 47	21 02
18	3 43	20 20	3 53	20 30	3 44	20 33	3 39	20 41	3 27	20 48	3 31	21 05	3 47	21 03
19	3 43	20 21	3 53	20 31	3 44	20 34	3 40	20 41	3 27	20 49	3 31	21 06	3 47	21 03
20	3 43	20 21	3 53	20 31	3 44	20 34	3 40	20 41	3 27	20 49	3 31	21 06	3 47	21 04
21	3 43	20 21	3 53	20 31	3 45	20 34	3 40	20 42	3 27	20 49	3 31	21 06	3 47	21 04
22	3 43	20 21	3 53	20 31	3 45	20 34	3 40	20 42	3 27	20 50	3 31	21 06	3 47	21 04
23	3 43	20 22	3 54	20 31	3 45	20 34	3 40	20 42	3 28	20 50	3 32	21 07	3 48	21 04
24	3 44	20 22	3 54	20 31	3 45	20 35	3 41	20 42	3 28	20 50	3 32	21 07	3 48	21 04
25	3 44	20 22	3 54	20 31	3 46	20 35	3 41	20 42	3 28	20 50	3 32	21 07	3 48	21 04
26	3 44	20 22	3 55	20 31	3 46	20 35	3 41	20 42	3 29	20 50	3 33	21 07	3 49	21 04
27	3 45	20 22	3 55	20 31	3 47	20 34	3 42	20 42	3 29	20 49	3 33	21 06	3 49	21 04
28	3 45	20 21	3 56	20 31	3 47	20 34	3 42	20 42	3 30	20 49	3 34	21 06	3 50	21 04
29	3 46	20 21	3 56	20 31	3 48	20 34	3 43	20 42	3 30	20 49	3 34	21 06	3 50	21 03
30	3 47	20 21	3 57	20 31	3 48	20 34	3 44	20 41	3 31	20 49	3 35	21 05	3 51	21 03

JUPITER

Day	*R.A.*		*Dec.*		*Transit*		*5° high*			
							52°		*56°*	
	h	*m*	°	′	*h*	*m*	*h*	*m*	*h*	*m*
1	1	50.4	+10	10	9	14	2	55	2	50
11	1	58.2	+10	52	8	42	2	20	2	14
21	2	05.5	+11	29	8	10	1	44	1	38
31	2	12.2	+12	03	7	37	1	09	1	02

Diameters – equatorial 36″ polar 33″

SATURN

Day	*R.A.*		*Dec.*		*Transit*		*5° high*			
							52°		*56°*	
	h	*m*	°	′	*h*	*m*	*h*	*m*	*h*	*m*
1	12	43.0	−1	47	20	04	1	25	1	21
11	12	42.4	−1	46	19	24	0	46	0	41
21	12	42.6	−1	49	18	45	0	06	0	01
31	12	43.3	−1	57	18	07	23	23	23	18

Diameters – equatorial 18″ polar 16″

Rings – major axis 40″ minor axis 5″

URANUS

Day	*R.A.*		*Dec.*		*Transit*		*10° high*			
							52°		*56°*	
	h	*m*	°	′	*h*	*m*	*h*	*m*	*h*	*m*
1	0	15.7	+0	55	7	39	2	41	2	47
11	0	16.7	+1	01	7	01	2	02	2	08
21	0	17.4	+1	05	6	22	1	23	1	29
31	0	17.8	+1	07	5	43	0	44	0	49

Diameter 4″

NEPTUNE

Day	*R.A.*		*Dec.*		*Transit*		*10° high*			
							52°		*56°*	
	h	*m*	°	′	*h*	*m*	*h*	*m*	*h*	*m*
1	22	12.6	−11	38	5	36	1	51	2	11
11	22	12.6	−11	39	4	57	1	11	1	31
21	22	12.3	−11	40	4	17	0	32	0	52
31	22	11.9	−11	43	3	38	23	49	0	13

Diameter 2″

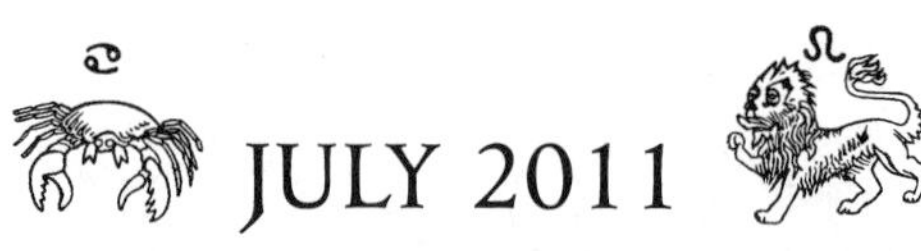

JULY 2011

SEVENTH MONTH, 31 DAYS. *Julius* Caesar, formerly *Quintilis*, fifth month of Roman pre-Julian calendar

1	*Friday*	Salvador Dali wore a diving suit to give a lecture at the International Surrealist Exhibition 1934	day 182
2	*Saturday*	The Live 8 benefit concerts took place in the G8 nations and in South Africa 2005	183
3	*Sunday*	*Adresseavisen*, the oldest Norwegian newspaper still in print, was founded 1767	184
4	*Monday*	The Marquis de Sade was taken to Charenton insane asylum 1789	week 27 day 185
5	*Tuesday*	The pilot of US sitcom *Seinfeld* aired under the title *The Seinfeld Chronicles* 1989	186
6	*Wednesday*	Geoffrey Rush, Australian actor *b.* 1951; Louis Armstrong, US jazz musician *d.* 1971	187
7	*Thursday*	The Yardbirds broke up, leading to the creation of Led Zeppelin 1968	188
8	*Friday*	Ernest Hemingway was wounded on the Austro-Italian frontline in the First World War 1918	189
9	*Saturday*	William Faulkner reported for active service with the Canadian Royal Air Force 1918	190
10	*Sunday*	Rubens' painting *The Massacre of the Innocents* sold for £49.5m ($76.7m) at Sotheby's 2002	191
11	*Monday*	Welsh poet Dylan Thomas married Caitlin Macnamara in Mousehole, Cornwall 1937	week 28 day 192
12	*Tuesday*	Richard II appointed Geoffrey Chaucer as chief clerk of the king's works 1389	193
13	*Wednesday*	The Hollywood sign (originally 'Hollywoodland') was dedicated 1923	194
14	*Thursday*	German author Hugo Ball first recited his Dada manifesto at the Cabaret Voltaire in Zurich 1916	195
15	*Friday*	Inigo Jones, architect *b.* 1573; Anton Chekhov, Russian writer *d.* 1904	196
16	*Saturday*	J. D. Salinger's *The Catcher in the Rye* was published 1951	197
17	*Sunday*	US silent movie *A Noise from the Deep* featured the first pie-in-the-face routine on film 1913	198
18	*Monday*	Hunter S. Thompson, US writer *b.* 1937; Jane Austen, novelist *d.* 1817	week 29 day 199
19	*Tuesday*	Emile Zola fled France after being convicted of libel against the French army 1898	200
20	*Wednesday*	US magazine *Billboard* published its first 'Music Popularity Chart' 1940	201
21	*Thursday*	A US ban on the distribution of D. H. Lawrence's novel *Lady Chatterley's Lover* was lifted 1959	202
22	*Friday*	Shakespeare's *The Merchant of Venice* was entered on the Stationers' Register 1598	203
23	*Saturday*	Caravaggio received his first public commission, for the Contarelli Chapel in Rome 1599	204
24	*Sunday*	Billy Taylor, US jazz musician *b.* 1921; Peter Sellers, comedian and actor *d.* 1980	205
25	*Monday*	Bob Dylan switched to an electric guitar at the Newport Folk Festival 1965	week 30 day 206
26	*Tuesday*	Aldous Huxley, author *b.* 1894; Diane Arbus, US photographer *d.* 1971	207
27	*Wednesday*	Bugs Bunny debuted in the cartoon *A Wild Hare* 1940	208
28	*Thursday*	Percy Bysshe Shelley and Mary Wollstonecraft eloped to France 1814	209
29	*Friday*	The BBC Light Programme radio station began broadcasting 1945	210
30	*Saturday*	Margaret Mitchell sold the film rights to *Gone With the Wind* for $50,000 1936	211
31	*Sunday*	Daniel Defoe was put in the pillory for seditious libel against the Church 1703	212

ASTRONOMICAL PHENOMENA

d	*h*	
1	09	Partial eclipse of Sun
3	00	Mercury in conjunction with Moon. Mercury 5°N.
4	15	Earth at aphelion (152 million km.)
7	22	Saturn in conjunction with Moon. Saturn 7°N.
10	01	Uranus at stationary point
20	05	Mercury at greatest elongation E. 27°
23	04	Sun's longitude 120° ♌
23	21	Jupiter in conjunction with Moon. Jupiter 5°S.
27	17	Mars in conjunction with Moon. Mars 0.5°N.
30	10	Venus in conjunction with Moon. Venus 4°N.

MINIMA OF ALGOL

d	*h*	*d*	*h*	*d*	*h*
3	12.2	14	23.4	26	10.7
6	09.0	17	20.2	29	07.5
9	05.8	20	17.0		
12	02.6	23	13.9		

CONSTELLATIONS

The following constellations are near their meridian at

	d	*h*		*d*	*h*
June	1	24	July	16	21
June	15	23	August	1	20
July	1	22	August	16	19

Ursa Minor, Draco, Corona, Hercules, Lyra, Serpens, Ophiuchus, Libra, Scorpius and Sagittarius

THE MOON

Phases, Apsides and Node	*d*	*h*	*m*
● New Moon	1	08	54
☽ First Quarter	8	06	29
○ Full Moon	15	06	40
☾ Last Quarter	23	05	02
● New Moon	30	18	40
Perigee (369,605 km)	7	13	50
Apogee (404,317 km)	21	22	44

Mean longitude of ascending node on July 1, 263°

THE SUN

s.d. 15′.8

Day	Right Ascension			Dec. +		Equation of time		Rise 52°		Rise 56°		Transit		Set 52°		Set 56°		Sidereal time			Transit of first point of Aries		
	h	*m*	*s*	°	′	*m*	*s*	*h*	*m*	*h*	*m*	*h*	*m*	*h*	*m*	*h*	*m*	*h*	*m*	*s*	*h*	*m*	*s*
1	6	38	32	23	08	−3	43	3	44	3	18	12	04	20	23	20	49	18	34	49	5	24	17
2	6	42	41	23	04	−3	55	3	45	3	19	12	04	20	23	20	49	18	38	46	5	20	22
3	6	46	49	23	00	−4	06	3	46	3	20	12	04	20	22	20	48	18	42	42	5	16	26
4	6	50	56	22	55	−4	17	3	46	3	21	12	04	20	22	20	47	18	46	39	5	12	30
5	6	55	04	22	50	−4	28	3	47	3	22	12	05	20	22	20	47	18	50	36	5	08	34
6	6	59	11	22	44	−4	39	3	48	3	23	12	05	20	21	20	46	18	54	32	5	04	38
7	7	03	17	22	38	−4	49	3	49	3	24	12	05	20	20	20	45	18	58	29	5	00	42
8	7	07	24	22	32	−4	58	3	50	3	25	12	05	20	20	20	44	19	02	25	4	56	46
9	7	11	30	22	25	−5	08	3	51	3	26	12	05	20	19	20	43	19	06	22	4	52	50
10	7	15	35	22	18	−5	17	3	52	3	27	12	05	20	18	20	42	19	10	18	4	48	54
11	7	19	40	22	10	−5	25	3	53	3	29	12	05	20	17	20	41	19	14	15	4	44	58
12	7	23	45	22	03	−5	33	3	54	3	30	12	06	20	17	20	40	19	18	11	4	41	02
13	7	27	49	21	54	−5	41	3	55	3	31	12	06	20	16	20	39	19	22	08	4	37	06
14	7	31	52	21	46	−5	48	3	56	3	33	12	06	20	15	20	38	19	26	05	4	33	11
15	7	35	55	21	36	−5	54	3	57	3	34	12	06	20	14	20	37	19	30	01	4	29	15
16	7	39	58	21	27	−6	00	3	59	3	36	12	06	20	13	20	35	19	33	58	4	25	19
17	7	44	00	21	17	−6	06	4	00	3	37	12	06	20	12	20	34	19	37	54	4	21	23
18	7	48	02	21	07	−6	11	4	01	3	39	12	06	20	10	20	33	19	41	51	4	17	27
19	7	52	03	20	57	−6	15	4	02	3	40	12	06	20	09	20	31	19	45	47	4	13	31
20	7	56	03	20	46	−6	19	4	04	3	42	12	06	20	08	20	30	19	49	44	4	09	35
21	8	00	03	20	35	−6	23	4	05	3	44	12	06	20	07	20	28	19	53	40	4	05	39
22	8	04	03	20	23	−6	26	4	06	3	45	12	06	20	06	20	26	19	57	37	4	01	43
23	8	08	02	20	11	−6	28	4	08	3	47	12	06	20	04	20	25	20	01	34	3	57	47
24	8	12	00	19	59	−6	30	4	09	3	49	12	07	20	03	20	23	20	05	30	3	53	51
25	8	15	58	19	46	−6	31	4	11	3	50	12	07	20	01	20	21	20	09	27	3	49	56
26	8	19	55	19	33	−6	32	4	12	3	52	12	07	20	00	20	20	20	13	23	3	46	00
27	8	23	52	19	20	−6	32	4	14	3	54	12	07	19	58	20	18	20	17	20	3	42	04
28	8	27	48	19	07	−6	31	4	15	3	56	12	07	19	57	20	16	20	21	16	3	38	08
29	8	31	43	18	53	−6	30	4	17	3	58	12	06	19	55	20	14	20	25	13	3	34	12
30	8	35	38	18	38	−6	29	4	18	3	59	12	06	19	54	20	12	20	29	09	3	30	16
31	8	39	32	18	24	−6	26	4	20	4	01	12	06	19	52	20	10	20	33	06	3	26	20

DURATION OF TWILIGHT (in minutes)

Latitude	*52°*	*56°*	*52°*	*56°*	*52°*	*56°*	*52°*	*56°*
	1 July		*11 July*		*21 July*		*31 July*	
Civil	48	61	47	58	44	53	42	49
Nautical	124	TAN	117	TAN	107	146	98	123
Astronomical	TAN	TAN	TAN	TAN	TAN	TAN	182	TAN

THE NIGHT SKY

Mercury reaches greatest eastern elongation (27 degrees) on the 20th but the long duration of twilight means that it remains unsuitably placed for observation throughout the month.

Venus, magnitude −3.9, continues to be visible in the early morning sky but only to those with a good clear horizon and the ability to detect Venus only a few degrees high at sunrise. After the middle of the month it is unlikely to be seen at all because of its increasing proximity to the Sun.

Mars, magnitude +1.4, slowly becomes visible as a difficult morning object early in the month, low above the eastern horizon for a short while before the increasing brightness of the pre-dawn sky inhibits observation. Mars is moving steadily eastwards in the constellation of Taurus. The thin waning crescent Moon passes 1 degree south of the planet on the 27th.

Jupiter, magnitude −2.3, continues to be visible as a bright morning object in the south-eastern sky. Later in the month it is becoming visible low above the eastern horizon before midnight. The Moon, at Last Quarter, passes 4 degrees north of Jupiter on the 24th.

Saturn, magnitude +0.8, continues to be visible in the evenings, low above the western horizon although the long evening twilight severely restricts the time available for observation before the planet sets. On the 7th, the Moon, just before First Quarter, passes 8 degrees south of the planet.

THE MOON

Day	R.A.		Dec.	Hor. Par.	Semi-diam.	Sun's Co-Long.	PA. of Br. Limb	Ph.	Age	Rise				Transit		Set			
										52°		56°				52°		56°	
	h	m	°	′	′	°	°	%	d	h	m	h	m	h	m	h	m	h	m
1	6	19	+22.4	57.2	15.6	271	80	0	29.2	3	49	3	25	12	12	20	23	20	44
2	7	15	+20.1	57.8	15.7	283	293	1	0.7	5	02	4	42	13	06	20	55	21	11
3	8	11	+16.7	58.3	15.9	295	291	3	1.7	6	20	6	05	13	59	21	21	21	33
4	9	06	+12.3	58.7	16.0	307	293	8	2.7	7	41	7	31	14	51	21	44	21	50
5	9	59	+7.2	59.0	16.1	320	295	16	3.7	9	02	8	57	15	41	22	04	22	06
6	10	51	+1.7	59.2	16.1	332	295	25	4.7	10	23	10	24	16	31	22	24	22	21
7	11	43	−3.9	59.3	16.2	344	295	36	5.7	11	44	11	50	17	21	22	44	22	36
8	12	36	−9.3	59.3	16.2	356	294	47	6.7	13	06	13	18	18	13	23	08	22	55
9	13	30	−14.2	59.2	16.1	9	291	58	7.7	14	28	14	45	19	07	23	36	23	18
10	14	27	−18.3	59.1	16.1	21	287	69	8.7	15	48	16	10	20	03	—		23	49
11	15	25	−21.3	58.8	16.0	33	283	79	9.7	17	02	17	27	21	01	0	11	—	
12	16	25	−23.0	58.5	15.9	45	278	88	10.7	18	06	18	32	21	59	0	57	0	31
13	17	25	−23.3	58.1	15.8	57	273	94	11.7	18	57	19	21	22	56	1	53	1	27
14	18	24	−22.2	57.6	15.7	70	272	98	12.7	19	37	19	57	23	51	3	00	2	36
15	19	20	−19.9	57.1	15.6	82	296	100	13.7	20	07	20	23	—		4	12	3	52
16	20	14	−16.6	56.5	15.4	94	57	99	14.7	20	31	20	42	0	42	5	26	5	11
17	21	04	−12.5	55.9	15.2	106	63	97	15.7	20	51	20	58	1	30	6	39	6	29
18	21	52	−8.0	55.4	15.1	118	63	92	16.7	21	08	21	11	2	15	7	50	7	45
19	22	37	−3.3	54.9	15.0	130	63	86	17.7	21	24	21	23	2	58	9	00	8	58
20	23	22	+1.5	54.5	14.9	143	63	79	18.7	21	40	21	36	3	39	10	07	10	10
21	0	06	+6.2	54.3	14.8	155	64	70	19.7	21	57	21	49	4	20	11	14	11	21
22	0	50	+10.6	54.2	14.8	167	66	62	20.7	22	17	22	04	5	02	12	21	12	33
23	1	36	+14.6	54.3	14.8	179	68	52	21.7	22	40	22	23	5	46	13	29	13	45
24	2	24	+18.0	54.6	14.9	192	72	43	22.7	23	09	22	48	6	31	14	36	14	56
25	3	13	+20.8	55.0	15.0	204	76	33	23.7	23	46	23	21	7	20	15	41	16	04
26	4	06	+22.6	55.6	15.1	216	80	24	24.7	—		—		8	11	16	41	17	07
27	5	01	+23.3	56.3	15.3	228	85	16	25.7	0	33	0	07	9	04	17	34	17	59
28	5	57	+22.9	57.0	15.5	241	89	9	26.7	1	31	1	07	9	59	18	19	18	41
29	6	54	+21.1	57.8	15.8	253	91	4	27.7	2	41	2	19	10	54	18	54	19	12
30	7	51	+18.1	58.5	15.9	265	85	1	28.7	3	58	3	41	11	49	19	23	19	37
31	8	47	+14.0	59.2	16.1	277	338	0	0.3	5	19	5	08	12	42	19	48	19	56

MERCURY

Day	R.A.		Dec.	Diam.	Phase	Transit		5° high			
								52°		56°	
	h	m	°	′	%	h	m	h	m	h	m
1	8	02	+22.3	6	75	13	30	20	56	21	13
3	8	16	+21.5	6	72	13	36	20	57	21	12
5	8	29	+20.6	6	68	13	41	20	56	21	11
7	8	41	+19.6	6	65	13	45	20	55	21	08
9	8	53	+18.6	7	62	13	49	20	52	21	05
11	9	04	+17.6	7	58	13	52	20	49	21	00
13	9	14	+16.5	7	55	13	54	20	45	20	55
15	9	24	+15.5	7	52	13	55	20	40	20	50
17	9	32	+14.4	7	49	13	55	20	35	20	43
19	9	40	+13.4	8	46	13	55	20	29	20	36
21	9	47	+12.4	8	43	13	54	20	23	20	29
23	9	53	+11.4	8	40	13	52	20	15	20	21
25	9	58	+10.5	9	36	13	48	20	08	20	13
27	10	02	+9.7	9	33	13	44	19	59	20	04
29	10	05	+8.9	9	29	13	39	19	50	19	54
31	10	07	+8.3	10	26	13	33	19	41	19	44

VENUS

Day	R.A.		Dec.	Diam.	Phase	Transit		5° high			
								52°		56°	
	h	m	°	′	%	h	m	h	m	h	m
1	5	43	+23.2	10	98	11	10	3	37	3	19
6	6	10	+23.4	10	98	11	17	3	42	3	24
11	6	36	+23.4	10	99	11	24	3	50	3	31
16	7	03	+23.0	10	99	11	31	3	59	3	41
21	7	30	+22.4	10	99	11	38	4	09	3	52
26	7	56	+21.5	10	100	11	44	4	21	4	05
31	8	22	+20.4	10	100	11	50	4	35	4	20

MARS

Day	R.A.		Dec.	Diam.	Phase	Transit		5° high			
								52°		56°	
	h	m	°	′	%	h	m	h	m	h	m
1	4	21	+21.4	4	97	9	47	2	25	2	09
6	4	36	+22.0	4	96	9	42	2	17	2	00
11	4	51	+22.5	4	96	9	37	2	09	1	52
16	5	06	+22.9	4	96	9	32	2	01	1	44
21	5	20	+23.3	4	96	9	28	1	54	1	36
26	5	35	+23.5	4	95	9	23	1	48	1	29
31	5	50	+23.7	4	95	9	18	1	42	1	23

SUNRISE AND SUNSET

	London				*Bristol*				*Birmingham*				*Manchester*				*Newcastle*				*Glasgow*				*Belfast*			
	0° 05′		*51° 30′*		*2° 35′*		*51° 28′*		*1° 55′*		*52° 28′*		*2° 15′*		*53° 28′*		*1° 37′*		*54° 59′*		*4° 14′*		*55° 52′*		*5° 56′*		*54° 35′*	
d	*h*	*m*	*h*	*m*	*h*	*m*	*h*	*m*	*h*	*m*	*h*	*m*	*h*	*m*	*h*	*m*	*h*	*m*	*h*	*m*	*h*	*m*	*h*	*m*	*h*	*m*	*h*	*m*
1	3	47	20	21	3	57	20	31	3	49	20	34	3	44	20	41	3	32	20	48	3	36	21	05	3	52	21	03
2	3	48	20	20	3	58	20	30	3	50	20	33	3	45	20	40	3	33	20	48	3	37	21	05	3	53	21	02
3	3	49	20	20	3	59	20	30	3	51	20	33	3	46	20	40	3	33	20	47	3	38	21	04	3	53	21	02
4	3	49	20	20	4	00	20	29	3	51	20	32	3	47	20	40	3	34	20	47	3	39	21	03	3	54	21	01
5	3	50	20	19	4	00	20	29	3	52	20	32	3	48	20	39	3	35	20	46	3	40	21	03	3	55	21	01
6	3	51	20	19	4	01	20	28	3	53	20	31	3	49	20	38	3	36	20	45	3	41	21	02	3	56	21	00
7	3	52	20	18	4	02	20	28	3	54	20	31	3	50	20	38	3	37	20	45	3	42	21	01	3	57	20	59
8	3	53	20	17	4	03	20	27	3	55	20	30	3	51	20	37	3	38	20	44	3	43	21	00	3	58	20	59
9	3	54	20	17	4	04	20	27	3	56	20	29	3	52	20	36	3	40	20	43	3	44	20	59	3	59	20	58
10	3	55	20	16	4	05	20	26	3	57	20	28	3	53	20	35	3	41	20	42	3	45	20	58	4	01	20	57
11	3	56	20	15	4	06	20	25	3	58	20	28	3	54	20	34	3	42	20	41	3	47	20	57	4	02	20	56
12	3	57	20	14	4	07	20	24	3	59	20	27	3	55	20	34	3	43	20	40	3	48	20	56	4	03	20	55
13	3	58	20	13	4	08	20	23	4	00	20	26	3	56	20	33	3	45	20	39	3	49	20	55	4	04	20	54
14	3	59	20	13	4	09	20	22	4	01	20	25	3	57	20	32	3	46	20	38	3	51	20	54	4	06	20	53
15	4	00	20	12	4	10	20	21	4	03	20	24	3	59	20	30	3	47	20	37	3	52	20	53	4	07	20	52
16	4	01	20	11	4	12	20	20	4	04	20	23	4	00	20	29	3	49	20	35	3	54	20	51	4	08	20	50
17	4	03	20	10	4	13	20	19	4	05	20	22	4	01	20	28	3	50	20	34	3	55	20	50	4	10	20	49
18	4	04	20	08	4	14	20	18	4	06	20	20	4	03	20	27	3	52	20	33	3	57	20	49	4	11	20	48
19	4	05	20	07	4	15	20	17	4	08	20	19	4	04	20	26	3	53	20	31	3	58	20	47	4	13	20	46
20	4	06	20	06	4	17	20	16	4	09	20	18	4	05	20	24	3	55	20	30	4	00	20	46	4	14	20	45
21	4	08	20	05	4	18	20	15	4	11	20	17	4	07	20	23	3	56	20	29	4	01	20	44	4	16	20	44
22	4	09	20	04	4	19	20	13	4	12	20	15	4	08	20	22	3	58	20	27	4	03	20	43	4	17	20	42
23	4	10	20	02	4	21	20	12	4	13	20	14	4	10	20	20	3	59	20	26	4	05	20	41	4	19	20	41
24	4	12	20	01	4	22	20	11	4	15	20	13	4	11	20	19	4	01	20	24	4	06	20	39	4	20	20	39
25	4	13	20	00	4	23	20	09	4	16	20	11	4	13	20	17	4	03	20	22	4	08	20	38	4	22	20	37
26	4	15	19	58	4	25	20	08	4	18	20	10	4	14	20	16	4	04	20	21	4	10	20	36	4	24	20	36
27	4	16	19	57	4	26	20	07	4	19	20	08	4	16	20	14	4	06	20	19	4	12	20	34	4	25	20	34
28	4	18	19	55	4	28	20	05	4	21	20	07	4	18	20	12	4	08	20	17	4	13	20	32	4	27	20	32
29	4	19	19	54	4	29	20	04	4	22	20	05	4	19	20	11	4	09	20	15	4	15	20	30	4	29	20	31
30	4	20	19	52	4	31	20	02	4	24	20	03	4	21	20	09	4	11	20	14	4	17	20	28	4	30	20	29
31	4	22	19	51	4	32	20	00	4	25	20	02	4	22	20	07	4	13	20	12	4	19	20	27	4	32	20	27

JUPITER

Day	*R.A.*		*Dec.*		*Transit*		*5° high*			
							52°		*56°*	
	h	*m*	°	′	*h*	*m*	*h*	*m*	*h*	*m*
1	2	12.2	+12	03	7	37	1	09	1	02
11	2	18.2	+12	32	7	04	0	33	0	26
21	2	23.4	+12	56	6	30	23	53	23	46
31	2	27.6	+13	15	5	55	23	16	23	08

Diameters – equatorial 39″ polar 36″

SATURN

Day	*R.A.*		*Dec.*		*Transit*		*5° high*			
							52°		*56°*	
	h	*m*	°	′	*h*	*m*	*h*	*m*	*h*	*m*
1	12	43.3	–1	57	18	07	23	23	23	18
11	12	44.6	–2	08	17	29	22	44	22	39
21	12	46.5	–2	22	16	51	22	05	22	00
31	12	48.9	–2	40	16	14	21	27	21	21

Diameters – equatorial 17″ polar 15″

Rings – major axis 38″ minor axis 5″

URANUS

Day	*R.A.*		*Dec.*		*Transit*		*10° high*			
							52°		*56°*	
	h	*m*	°	′	*h*	*m*	*h*	*m*	*h*	*m*
1	0	17.8	+1	07	5	43	0	44	0	49
11	0	17.9	+1	08	5	04	0	04	0	10
21	0	17.8	+1	06	4	24	23	21	23	27
31	0	17.3	+1	03	3	45	22	42	22	47

Diameter 4″

NEPTUNE

Day	*R.A.*		*Dec.*		*Transit*		*10° high*			
							52°		*56°*	
	h	*m*	°	′	*h*	*m*	*h*	*m*	*h*	*m*
1	22	11.9	–11	43	3	38	23	49	0	13
11	22	11.3	–11	47	2	58	23	09	23	29
21	22	10.5	–11	51	2	18	22	30	22	50
31	22	09.6	–11	56	1	37	21	50	22	10

Diameter 2″

AUGUST 2011

EIGHTH MONTH, 31 DAYS. *Augustus*, formerly *Sextilis*, sixth month of Roman pre-Julian calendar

1	*Monday*	MTV ('Music Television') began broadcasting with *Video Killed the Radio Star* 1981	week 31 day 213
2	*Tuesday*	George Eliot began writing her masterpiece *Middlemarch* 1869	214
3	*Wednesday*	The Italian opera house La Scala opened 1778	215
4	*Thursday*	William Blake began an apprenticeship at James Basire's engravers in London 1772	216
5	*Friday*	US writers Nathaniel Hawthorne and Herman Melville met at a picnic in Massachusetts 1850	217
6	*Saturday*	Andy Warhol, US artist *b.* 1928; Diego Velázquez, Spanish painter *d.* 1660	218
7	*Sunday*	Novelist Henry Fielding arrived in Lisbon, hoping the climate would help his ill-health 1754	219
8	*Monday*	The iconic cover photo of the Beatles album *Abbey Road* was taken 1969	week 32 day 220
9	*Tuesday*	US writer Henry David Thoreau's book *Walden* was published 1854	221
10	*Wednesday*	Virginia Woolf (née Stephen) married Leonard Woolf at St Pancras registry office 1912	222
11	*Thursday*	Jackson Pollock died in a drink-driving related car crash in New York 1956	223
12	*Friday*	Cecil B. DeMille, US film director *b.* 1881; Thomas Mann, German novelist and Nobel Laureate *d.* 1955	224
13	*Saturday*	US band Jefferson Airplane played their debut gig at the Matrix Club in San Francisco 1965	225
14	*Sunday*	Arthur Sullivan's *The Lost Chord* was used to demonstrate the newly perfected phonograph 1888	226
15	*Monday*	The original Woodstock Music & Art Fair began in Bethel, New York 1969	week 33 day 227
16	*Tuesday*	US magazine *Sports Illustrated* was launched 1954	228
17	*Wednesday*	Wagner's opera *Götterdämmerung* premiered in Bayreuth 1876	229
18	*Thursday*	Samuel Johnson and James Boswell embarked on a tour of the Hebrides 1773	230
19	*Friday*	US composer Leonard Bernstein conducted his last concert 1990	231
20	*Saturday*	H. P. Lovecraft, US writer *b.* 1890; Jules Laforgue, French poet *d.* 1887	232
21	*Sunday*	The *Mona Lisa* was stolen by Vincenzo Peruggia, a Louvre employee, who kept it for two years 1911	233
22	*Monday*	The BBC performed its first experimental TV broadcast from Broadcasting House 1932	week 34 day 234
23	*Tuesday*	Film premiere of *The Big Sleep*, adapted from Raymond Chandler's novel 1946	235
24	*Wednesday*	Tom Stoppard's *Rosencrantz and Guildenstern are Dead* debuted 1966	236
25	*Thursday*	Martin Amis, novelist *b.* 1949; David Hume, Scottish philosopher *d.* 1776	237
26	*Friday*	US writer Ralph Waldo Emerson first met the influential writer Thomas Carlyle 1838	238
27	*Saturday*	Italian artist Michelangelo was commissioned to carve the *Pietà* 1498	239
28	*Sunday*	US ventriloquist Edgar Bergen's dummy, Charlie McCarthy, received an honorary degree 1938	240
29	*Monday*	French surrealist writer André Breton was questioned by the FBI 1943	week 35 day 241
30	*Tuesday*	Henry James returned to the USA after two decades in Europe 1904	242
31	*Wednesday*	Edvard Munch's *The Scream* was recovered by police, two years after its theft 2006	243

ASTRONOMICAL PHENOMENA

d	*h*	
1	10	Mercury in conjunction with Moon. Mercury 1°N.
3	04	Mercury at stationary point
4	07	Saturn in conjunction with Moon. Saturn 7°N.
16	12	Venus in superior conjunction
16	23	Venus in conjunction with Mercury. Venus 6°N.
17	01	Mercury in inferior conjunction
20	09	Jupiter in conjunction with Moon. Jupiter 5°S.
22	23	Neptune at opposition
23	11	Sun's longitude 150° ♍
25	13	Mars in conjunction with Moon. Mars 3°N.
26	22	Mercury at stationary point
28	00	Mercury in conjunction with Moon. Mercury 2°N.
29	09	Venus in conjunction with Moon. Venus 6°N.
30	09	Jupiter at stationary point
31	19	Saturn in conjunction with Moon. Saturn 7°N.

MINIMA OF ALGOL

d	*h*	*d*	*h*	*d*	*h*
1	04.3	12	15.5	24	02.8
4	01.1	15	12.3	26	23.6
6	21.9	18	09.2	29	20.4
9	18.9	21	06.0		

CONSTELLATIONS

The following constellations are near their meridian at

	d	*h*		*d*	*h*
July	1	24	August	16	21
July	16	23	September	1	20
August	1	22	September	15	19

Draco, Hercules, Lyra, Cygnus, Sagitta, Ophiuchus, Serpens, Aquila and Sagittarius

THE MOON

Phases, Apsides and Node	*d*	*h*	*m*
☽ First Quarter	6	11	08
○ Full Moon	13	18	57
☾ Last Quarter	21	21	54
● New Moon	29	03	04
Perigee (365,784km)	2	20	56
Apogee (405,129km)	18	16	15
Perigee (360,871km)	30	17	29

Mean longitude of ascending node on August 1, 261°

THE SUN

s.d. 15′.8

Day	Right Ascension			Dec. +		Equation of time		Rise 52°		Rise 56°		Transit		Set 52°		Set 56°		Sidereal time			Transit of first point of Aries		
	h	*m*	*s*	°	′	*m*	*s*	*h*	*m*	*h*	*m*	*h*	*m*	*h*	*m*	*h*	*m*	*h*	*m*	*s*	*h*	*m*	*s*
1	8	43	26	18	09	−6	23	4	21	4	03	12	06	19	51	20	08	20	37	03	3	22	24
2	8	47	19	17	54	−6	20	4	23	4	05	12	06	19	49	20	06	20	40	59	3	18	28
3	8	51	11	17	39	−6	16	4	24	4	07	12	06	19	47	20	04	20	44	56	3	14	32
4	8	55	03	17	23	−6	11	4	26	4	09	12	06	19	45	20	02	20	48	52	3	10	36
5	8	58	54	17	07	−6	06	4	27	4	11	12	06	19	44	20	00	20	52	49	3	06	41
6	9	02	45	16	51	−6	00	4	29	4	13	12	06	19	42	19	58	20	56	45	3	02	45
7	9	06	35	16	34	−5	53	4	30	4	15	12	06	19	40	19	56	21	00	42	2	58	49
8	9	10	24	16	18	−5	46	4	32	4	16	12	06	19	38	19	54	21	04	38	2	54	53
9	9	14	13	16	01	−5	38	4	34	4	18	12	06	19	36	19	51	21	08	35	2	50	57
10	9	18	01	15	43	−5	29	4	35	4	20	12	05	19	34	19	49	21	12	32	2	47	01
11	9	21	49	15	26	−5	20	4	37	4	22	12	05	19	33	19	47	21	16	28	2	43	05
12	9	25	35	15	08	−5	11	4	38	4	24	12	05	19	31	19	45	21	20	25	2	39	09
13	9	29	22	14	50	−5	01	4	40	4	26	12	05	19	29	19	42	21	24	21	2	35	13
14	9	33	08	14	32	−4	50	4	42	4	28	12	05	19	27	19	40	21	28	18	2	31	17
15	9	36	53	14	13	−4	39	4	43	4	30	12	05	19	25	19	38	21	32	14	2	27	21
16	9	40	38	13	55	−4	27	4	45	4	32	12	04	19	23	19	35	21	36	11	2	23	26
17	9	44	22	13	36	−4	14	4	47	4	34	12	04	19	21	19	33	21	40	07	2	19	30
18	9	48	06	13	17	−4	02	4	48	4	36	12	04	19	19	19	31	21	44	04	2	15	34
19	9	51	49	12	57	−3	48	4	50	4	38	12	04	19	16	19	28	21	48	01	2	11	38
20	9	55	31	12	38	−3	34	4	51	4	40	12	03	19	14	19	26	21	51	57	2	07	42
21	9	59	14	12	18	−3	20	4	53	4	42	12	03	19	12	19	23	21	55	54	2	03	46
22	10	02	56	11	58	−3	05	4	55	4	44	12	03	19	10	19	21	21	59	50	1	59	50
23	10	06	37	11	38	−2	50	4	56	4	46	12	03	19	08	19	18	22	03	47	1	55	54
24	10	10	18	11	18	−2	35	4	58	4	48	12	02	19	06	19	16	22	07	43	1	51	58
25	10	13	58	10	57	−2	18	5	00	4	50	12	02	19	04	19	13	22	11	40	1	48	02
26	10	17	39	10	36	−2	02	5	01	4	52	12	02	19	01	19	11	22	15	36	1	44	06
27	10	21	18	10	15	−1	45	5	03	4	54	12	02	18	59	19	08	22	19	33	1	40	11
28	10	24	58	9	54	−1	28	5	04	4	56	12	01	18	57	19	06	22	23	30	1	36	15
29	10	28	37	9	33	−1	10	5	06	4	58	12	01	18	55	19	03	22	27	26	1	32	19
30	10	32	15	9	12	−0	53	5	08	4	59	12	01	18	53	19	01	22	31	23	1	28	23
31	10	35	53	8	50	−0	34	5	09	5	01	12	00	18	50	18	58	22	35	19	1	24	27

DURATION OF TWILIGHT (in minutes)

Latitude	52°	56°	52°	56°	52°	56°	52°	56°
	1 August		*11 August*		*21 August*		*31 August*	
Civil	41	49	39	45	37	42	35	40
Nautical	97	121	90	107	84	97	79	90
Astronomical	179	TAN	154	210	139	168	128	148

THE NIGHT SKY

Mercury passes through inferior conjunction on the 17th and remains too close to the Sun for observation until the last few days of August when it may be seen emerging for the morning twilight about 35 to 40 minutes before sunrise, low above the eastern horizon. During this short period Mercury's magnitude brightens from +1.1 to +0.4.

Venus passes through superior conjunction on the 16th and is not suitably placed for observation at all this month.

Mars continues to be visible in the early mornings, passing from Taurus into Gemini at the beginning of the month. Its magnitude is still +1.4. On the 25th, the waning crescent Moon passes 3 degrees south of the planet.

Jupiter is a brilliant object, magnitude −2.5, now visible in the eastern sky before midnight. The waning Moon, near Last Quarter, passes 4 degrees north of Jupiter on the 20th. At the end of the month Jupiter, still in the constellation of Aries, reaches its first stationary point and commences its retrograde motion.

Saturn, magnitude +0.9, is visible low above the west-south-western horizon for a short while in the evenings, but by the middle of the month is lost in the gathering twilight. On the 4th the waxing crescent Moon passes 8 degrees south of the planet.

Neptune is at opposition on the 22nd, in the constellation of Aquarius. It is not visible to the naked eye since its magnitude is +7.9.

Meteors. The maximum of the famous Perseid meteor shower occurs in the the early hours of the 13th, free from interference by moonlight.

THE MOON

Day	*R.A.*		*Dec.*	*Hor. Par.*	*Semi-diam.*	*Sun's Co-Long.*	*PA. of Br. Limb*	*Ph.*	*Age*	*Rise*				*Transit*		*Set*			
										52°		*56°*				*52°*		*56°*	
	h	*m*	°	′	′	°	°	%	*d*	*h*	*m*	*h*	*m*	*h*	*m*	*h*	*m*	*h*	*m*
1	9	42	+9.0	59.6	16.2	290	304	2	1.3	6	42	6	36	13	34	20	09	20	13
2	10	36	+3.5	59.9	16.3	302	300	7	2.3	8	06	8	05	14	26	20	30	20	29
3	11	29	−2.3	59.9	16.3	314	299	14	3.3	9	29	9	33	15	17	20	51	20	45
4	12	23	−7.9	59.8	16.3	326	297	23	4.3	10	53	11	02	16	09	21	14	21	03
5	13	18	−13.0	59.6	16.2	338	294	34	5.3	12	16	12	31	17	03	21	40	21	24
6	14	14	−17.3	59.2	16.1	351	290	45	6.3	13	37	13	57	17	59	22	13	21	53
7	15	12	−20.6	58.8	16.0	3	285	56	7.3	14	52	15	16	18	56	22	55	22	31
8	16	11	−22.6	58.3	15.9	15	280	67	8.3	15	58	16	24	19	53	23	47	23	21
9	17	10	−23.3	57.8	15.8	27	275	77	9.3	16	53	17	18	20	50	—		—	
10	18	08	−22.6	57.3	15.6	40	270	85	10.3	17	36	17	58	21	44	0	49	0	24
11	19	04	−20.6	56.8	15.5	52	267	92	11.3	18	09	18	26	22	36	1	58	1	37
12	19	58	−17.6	56.3	15.3	64	266	97	12.3	18	35	18	48	23	24	3	11	2	54
13	20	48	−13.9	55.8	15.2	76	277	99	13.3	18	56	19	05	—		4	23	4	11
14	21	37	−9.5	55.4	15.1	88	10	100	14.3	19	14	19	19	0	10	5	35	5	27
15	22	23	−4.9	54.9	15.0	100	50	98	15.3	19	31	19	32	0	53	6	44	6	41
16	23	08	−0.1	54.6	14.9	113	56	95	16.3	19	47	19	44	1	35	7	53	7	54
17	23	52	+4.6	54.3	14.8	125	60	90	17.3	20	04	19	57	2	17	9	00	9	05
18	0	36	+9.1	54.2	14.8	137	62	84	18.3	20	22	20	12	2	58	10	07	10	16
19	1	22	+13.2	54.1	14.7	149	65	76	19.3	20	44	20	29	3	41	11	14	11	28
20	2	08	+16.8	54.3	14.8	161	69	68	20.3	21	10	20	51	4	25	12	20	12	38
21	2	57	+19.7	54.5	14.9	174	73	59	21.3	21	43	21	20	5	12	13	25	13	47
22	3	48	+21.9	55.0	15.0	186	77	49	22.3	22	24	21	59	6	01	14	27	14	51
23	4	41	+23.0	55.6	15.2	198	82	40	23.3	23	17	22	51	6	52	15	22	15	47
24	5	36	+23.0	56.4	15.4	210	87	30	24.3	—		23	57	7	46	16	10	16	33
25	6	32	+21.8	57.2	15.6	223	92	21	25.3	0	20	—		8	40	16	49	17	09
26	7	28	+19.3	58.1	15.8	235	96	13	26.3	1	32	1	13	9	34	17	21	17	37
27	8	24	+15.7	59.0	16.1	247	97	6	27.3	2	52	2	37	10	28	17	48	17	59
28	9	20	+11.1	59.8	16.3	259	93	2	28.3	4	14	4	05	11	22	18	12	18	17
29	10	15	+5.7	60.3	16.4	271	41	0	29.3	5	39	5	35	12	15	18	33	18	34
30	11	10	−0.1	60.7	16.5	284	315	1	0.9	7	05	7	06	13	07	18	55	18	51
31	12	05	−5.9	60.8	16.6	296	303	5	1.9	8	31	8	38	14	01	19	18	19	09

MERCURY

Day	*R.A.*		*Dec.*	*Diam.*	*Phase*	*Transit*		*5° high*			
								52°		*56°*	
	h	*m*	°	′	%	*h*	*m*	*h*	*m*	*h*	*m*
1	10	07	+8.0	10	24	13	29	19	36	19	39
3	10	08	+7.6	10	20	13	21	19	26	19	29
5	10	07	+7.3	10	16	13	12	19	15	19	18
7	10	04	+7.2	11	12	13	02	19	05	19	07
9	10	01	+7.2	11	9	12	50	18	53	18	56
11	9	56	+7.5	11	6	12	37	18	42	18	45
13	9	51	+7.9	11	3	12	24	18	31	18	35
15	9	45	+8.5	11	2	12	10	18	21	18	24
17	9	39	+9.2	11	1	11	56	5	43	5	38
19	9	33	+10.0	11	2	11	43	5	25	5	20
21	9	28	+10.9	10	3	11	30	5	08	5	02
23	9	24	+11.7	10	7	11	19	4	52	4	46
25	9	22	+12.5	10	11	11	09	4	38	4	31
27	9	22	+13.1	9	17	11	02	4	27	4	20
29	9	24	+13.6	9	23	10	56	4	19	4	11
31	9	28	+13.9	8	31	10	53	4	14	4	05

VENUS

Day	*R.A.*		*Dec.*	*Diam.*	*Phase*	*Transit*		*5° high*			
								52°		*56°*	
	h	*m*	°	′	%	*h*	*m*	*h*	*m*	*h*	*m*
1	8	27	+20.1	10	100	11	52	19	05	19	19
6	8	52	+18.7	10	100	11	57	19	02	19	15
11	9	17	+17.0	10	100	12	02	18	58	19	09
16	9	42	+15.2	10	100	12	07	18	52	19	01
21	10	06	+13.1	10	100	12	12	18	45	18	53
26	10	30	+11.0	10	100	12	16	18	38	18	43
31	10	53	+8.7	10	100	12	19	18	29	18	33

MARS

Day	*R.A.*		*Dec.*	*Diam.*	*Phase*	*Transit*		*5° high*			
								52°		*56°*	
	h	*m*	°	′	%	*h*	*m*	*h*	*m*	*h*	*m*
1	5	53	+23.7	4	95	9	17	1	41	1	22
6	6	08	+23.8	4	95	9	12	1	35	1	16
11	6	22	+23.8	4	95	9	06	1	30	1	11
16	6	37	+23.7	5	94	9	01	1	26	1	07
21	6	51	+23.5	5	94	8	56	1	21	1	03
26	7	05	+23.2	5	94	8	50	1	17	0	59
31	7	19	+22.9	5	93	8	44	1	13	0	56

SUNRISE AND SUNSET

d	*London*				*Bristol*				*Birmingham*				*Manchester*				*Newcastle*				*Glasgow*				*Belfast*			
	0° 05′		*51° 30′*		*2° 35′*		*51° 28′*		*1° 55′*		*52° 28′*		*2° 15′*		*53° 28′*		*1° 37′*		*54° 59′*		*4° 14′*		*55° 52′*		*5° 56′*		*54° 35′*	
d	*h*	*m*	*h*	*m*	*h*	*m*	*h*	*m*	*h*	*m*	*h*	*m*	*h*	*m*	*h*	*m*	*h*	*m*	*h*	*m*	*h*	*m*	*h*	*m*	*h*	*m*	*h*	*m*
1	4	23	19	49	4	34	19	59	4	27	20	00	4	24	20	06	4	15	20	10	4	21	20	25	4	34	20	25
2	4	25	19	47	4	35	19	57	4	28	19	58	4	26	20	04	4	16	20	08	4	23	20	23	4	36	20	23
3	4	26	19	46	4	37	19	56	4	30	19	57	4	27	20	02	4	18	20	06	4	24	20	21	4	37	20	21
4	4	28	19	44	4	38	19	54	4	32	19	55	4	29	20	00	4	20	20	04	4	26	20	18	4	39	20	20
5	4	29	19	42	4	40	19	52	4	33	19	53	4	31	19	58	4	22	20	02	4	28	20	16	4	41	20	18
6	4	31	19	40	4	41	19	50	4	35	19	51	4	32	19	56	4	24	20	00	4	30	20	14	4	43	20	16
7	4	33	19	39	4	43	19	49	4	36	19	49	4	34	19	54	4	25	19	58	4	32	20	12	4	44	20	14
8	4	34	19	37	4	44	19	47	4	38	19	48	4	36	19	52	4	27	19	56	4	34	20	10	4	46	20	11
9	4	36	19	35	4	46	19	45	4	40	19	46	4	37	19	50	4	29	19	54	4	36	20	08	4	48	20	09
10	4	37	19	33	4	47	19	43	4	41	19	44	4	39	19	48	4	31	19	52	4	38	20	06	4	50	20	07
11	4	39	19	31	4	49	19	41	4	43	19	42	4	41	19	46	4	33	19	49	4	40	20	03	4	52	20	05
12	4	40	19	29	4	50	19	39	4	45	19	40	4	43	19	44	4	35	19	47	4	42	20	01	4	53	20	03
13	4	42	19	27	4	52	19	37	4	46	19	38	4	44	19	42	4	36	19	45	4	44	19	59	4	55	20	01
14	4	44	19	26	4	54	19	35	4	48	19	36	4	46	19	40	4	38	19	43	4	46	19	56	4	57	19	59
15	4	45	19	24	4	55	19	33	4	50	19	34	4	48	19	38	4	40	19	41	4	47	19	54	4	59	19	56
16	4	47	19	22	4	57	19	31	4	51	19	32	4	50	19	36	4	42	19	38	4	49	19	52	5	01	19	54
17	4	48	19	20	4	58	19	29	4	53	19	30	4	51	19	34	4	44	19	36	4	51	19	49	5	03	19	52
18	4	50	19	18	5	00	19	27	4	55	19	27	4	53	19	32	4	46	19	34	4	53	19	47	5	04	19	50
19	4	51	19	15	5	02	19	25	4	56	19	25	4	55	19	29	4	48	19	31	4	55	19	45	5	06	19	47
20	4	53	19	13	5	03	19	23	4	58	19	23	4	56	19	27	4	50	19	29	4	57	19	42	5	08	19	45
21	4	55	19	11	5	05	19	21	5	00	19	21	4	58	19	25	4	51	19	27	4	59	19	40	5	10	19	43
22	4	56	19	09	5	06	19	19	5	01	19	19	5	00	19	23	4	53	19	24	5	01	19	37	5	12	19	40
23	4	58	19	07	5	08	19	17	5	03	19	17	5	02	19	21	4	55	19	22	5	03	19	35	5	14	19	38
24	5	59	19	05	5	10	19	15	5	05	19	15	5	03	19	18	4	57	19	20	5	05	19	32	5	15	19	36
25	5	01	19	03	5	11	19	13	5	06	19	12	5	05	19	16	4	59	19	17	5	07	19	30	5	17	19	33
26	5	03	19	01	5	13	19	11	5	08	19	10	5	07	19	14	5	01	19	15	5	09	19	27	5	19	19	31
27	5	04	18	59	5	14	19	08	5	10	19	08	5	09	19	11	5	03	19	12	5	11	19	25	5	21	19	29
28	5	06	18	56	5	16	19	06	5	11	19	06	5	10	19	09	5	04	19	10	5	13	19	22	5	23	19	26
29	5	07	18	54	5	17	19	04	5	13	19	03	5	12	19	07	5	06	19	07	5	15	19	20	5	25	19	24
30	5	09	18	52	5	19	19	02	5	15	19	01	5	14	19	04	5	08	19	05	5	17	19	17	5	26	19	21
31	5	11	18	50	5	21	19	00	5	16	18	59	5	16	19	02	5	10	19	02	5	19	19	15	5	28	19	19

JUPITER

Day	*R.A.*		*Dec.*		*Transit*		*5° high*			
							52°		*56°*	
	h	*m*	°	′	*h*	*m*	*h*	*m*	*h*	*m*
1	2	28.0	+13	17	5	51	23	12	23	05
11	2	31.0	+13	29	5	15	22	35	22	27
21	2	32.9	+13	36	4	37	21	57	21	49
31	2	33.5	+13	37	3	59	21	18	21	10

Diameters – equatorial 43″ polar 40″

SATURN

Day	*R.A.*		*Dec.*		*Transit*		*5° high*			
							52°		*56°*	
	h	*m*	°	′	*h*	*m*	*h*	*m*	*h*	*m*
1	12	49.1	–2	42	16	11	21	23	21	18
11	12	52.1	–3	02	15	34	20	45	20	39
21	12	55.4	–3	25	14	58	20	07	20	01
31	12	59.1	–3	49	14	23	19	29	19	23

Diameters – equatorial 16″ polar 14″

Rings – major axis 37″ minor axis 6″

URANUS

Day	*R.A.*		*Dec.*		*Transit*		*10° high*			
							52°		*56°*	
	h	*m*	°	′	*h*	*m*	*h*	*m*	*h*	*m*
1	0	17.3	+1	03	3	41	22	38	22	43
11	0	16.5	+0	57	3	01	21	58	22	04
21	0	15.5	+0	51	2	20	21	18	21	24
31	0	14.3	+0	43	1	40	20	38	20	45

Diameter 4″

NEPTUNE

Day	*R.A.*		*Dec.*		*Transit*		*10° high*			
							52°		*56°*	
	h	*m*	°	′	*h*	*m*	*h*	*m*	*h*	*m*
1	22	09.5	–11	57	1	33	21	46	22	06
11	22	08.6	–12	02	0	53	21	06	21	27
21	22	07.5	–12	08	0	13	20	27	20	47
31	22	06.5	–12	14	23	28	19	47	20	08

Diameter 2″

SEPTEMBER 2011

NINTH MONTH, 30 DAYS. *Septem* (seven), seventh month of Roman pre-Julian calendar

1	*Thursday*	Johann Pachelbel, German composer *b.* 1653; Siegfried Sassoon, war poet *d.* 1967	day 244
2	*Friday*	The original *Star Trek* was cancelled after its third season 1969	245
3	*Saturday*	William Wordsworth wrote his poem *Composed upon Westminster Bridge* 1802	246
4	*Sunday*	Beatrix Potter wrote a letter containing the first incarnation of Peter Rabbit 1893	247
5	*Monday*	Victor Hugo returned to France from exile in Guernsey 1870	week 36 day 248
6	*Tuesday*	Manchester Free Library opened, becoming Britain's first free public lending library 1852	249
7	*Wednesday*	Guillaume Apollinaire was arrested on suspicion of stealing the *Mona Lisa* 1911	250
8	*Thursday*	Frank Sinatra, 19, appeared on the radio talent show *Major Bowes' Amateur Hour* 1935	251
9	*Friday*	James Joyce moved into the Martello Tower with Oliver St John Gogarty 1904	252
10	*Saturday*	Pablo Picasso's monumental anti-war mural *Guernica* was returned to Spain 1981	253
11	*Sunday*	US actor-director Roscoe 'Fatty' Arbuckle was arrested on suspicion of manslaughter 1921	254
12	*Monday*	The cave paintings at Lascaux were discovered by four boys and a dog named Robot 1940	week 37 day 255
13	*Tuesday*	Francis Scott Key began the poem that in 1931 became the US national anthem 1814	256
14	*Wednesday*	Handel finished his choral masterwork *Messiah* after just 24 days 1741	257
15	*Thursday*	Marilyn Monroe's iconic 'billowing white dress' scene in *The Seven Year Itch* was filmed 1954	258
16	*Friday*	The United Shakespeare Company bought the poet's childhood home in Stratford-upon-Avon 1847	259
17	*Saturday*	Poet John Keats and portrait painter Joseph Severn set off for Italy 1820	260
18	*Sunday*	Aldous Huxley was hired as a schoolmaster at Eton 1917	261
19	*Monday*	'Mama' Cass Elliot, US musician *b.* 1941; Italo Calvino, Italian writer *d.* 1985	week 38 day 262
20	*Tuesday*	The first Cannes Film Festival opened, seven years later than originally planned 1946	263
21	*Wednesday*	J. R. R. Tolkien's *The Hobbit* was first published 1937	264
22	*Thursday*	Actor and playwright Ben Jonson was indicted for manslaughter after a duel 1598	265
23	*Friday*	Leo Tolstoy married Sophia Andreyevna Behrs, 16 years his junior 1862	266
24	*Saturday*	F. Scott Fitzgerald, US writer *b.* 1896; Theodor Seuss Geisel (Dr Seuss), US cartoonist *d.* 1991	267
25	*Sunday*	Diarist Samuel Pepys drank a cup of 'tee' for the first time 1660	268
26	*Monday*	*West Side Story* premiered on Broadway 1957	week 39 day 269
27	*Tuesday*	Fearing Nazi capture, Jewish critic Walter Benjamin took a fatal overdose of morphine 1940	270
28	*Wednesday*	According to the Chinese calendar, Confucius was born 551BC	271
29	*Thursday*	George Bernard Shaw turned down a peerage 1930	272
30	*Friday*	Wolfgang Amadeus Mozart's final opera *The Magic Flute* premiered 1791	273

ASTRONOMICAL PHENOMENA

d	*h*	
3	06	Mercury at greatest elongation W. 18°
16	15	Jupiter in conjunction with Moon. Jupiter 5°S.
16	18	Pluto at stationary point
23	06	Mars in conjunction with Moon. Mars 5°N.
23	09	Sun's longitude 180° ♎
26	00	Uranus at opposition
27	09	Mercury in conjunction with Moon. Mercury 6°N.
28	07	Venus in conjunction with Moon. Venus 5°N.
28	10	Saturn in conjunction with Moon. Saturn 7°N.
28	20	Mercury in superior conjunction
30	00	Saturn in conjunction with Venus. Saturn 1°N.

MINIMA OF ALGOL

d	*h*	*d*	*h*	*d*	*h*
1	17.2	13	04.4	24	15.7
4	14.0	16	01.3	27	12.5
7	10.8	18	22.1	30	09.3
10	07.6	21	18.9		

CONSTELLATIONS

The following constellations are near their meridian at

	d	*h*		*d*	*h*
August	1	24	September	15	21
August	16	23	October	1	20
September	1	22	October	16	19

Draco, Cepheus, Lyra, Cygnus, Vulpecula, Sagitta, Delphinus, Equuleus, Aquila, Aquarius and Capricornus

THE MOON

Phases, Apsides and Node	*d*	*h*	*m*
☽ First Quarter	4	17	39
○ Full Moon	12	09	27
☾ Last Quarter	20	13	39
● New Moon	27	11	09
Apogee (406,043 km)	15	06	12
Perigee (357,561 km)	28	00	57

Mean longitude of ascending node on September 1, 259°

THE SUN

s.d. 15.9

Day	Right Ascension			Dec.		Equation of time		Rise 52°		Rise 56°		Transit		Set 52°		Set 56°		Sidereal time			Transit of first point of Aries		
	h	m	s	°	′	m	s	h	m	h	m	h	m	h	m	h	m	h	m	s	h	m	s
1	10	39	31	+8	29	−0	16	5	11	5	03	12	00	18	48	18	56	22	39	16	1	20	31
2	10	43	09	+8	07	+0	03	5	13	5	05	12	00	18	46	18	53	22	43	12	1	16	35
3	10	46	46	+7	45	+0	22	5	14	5	07	11	59	18	44	18	50	22	47	09	1	12	39
4	10	50	23	+7	23	+0	42	5	16	5	09	11	59	18	41	18	48	22	51	05	1	08	43
5	10	54	00	+7	01	+1	02	5	18	5	11	11	59	18	39	18	45	22	55	02	1	04	47
6	10	57	37	+6	39	+1	22	5	19	5	13	11	58	18	37	18	42	22	58	59	1	00	51
7	11	01	13	+6	17	+1	42	5	21	5	15	11	58	18	34	18	40	23	02	55	0	56	56
8	11	04	49	+5	54	+2	03	5	22	5	17	11	58	18	32	18	37	23	06	52	0	53	00
9	11	08	25	+5	32	+2	23	5	24	5	19	11	57	18	30	18	35	23	10	48	0	49	04
10	11	12	01	+5	09	+2	44	5	26	5	21	11	57	18	27	18	32	23	14	45	0	45	08
11	11	15	36	+4	46	+3	05	5	27	5	23	11	57	18	25	18	29	23	18	41	0	41	12
12	11	19	11	+4	23	+3	26	5	29	5	25	11	56	18	23	18	27	23	22	38	0	37	16
13	11	22	47	+4	01	+3	48	5	31	5	27	11	56	18	20	18	24	23	26	34	0	33	20
14	11	26	22	+3	38	+4	09	5	32	5	29	11	56	18	18	18	21	23	30	31	0	29	24
15	11	29	57	+3	15	+4	30	5	34	5	31	11	55	18	16	18	19	23	34	28	0	25	28
16	11	33	32	+2	52	+4	52	5	35	5	33	11	55	18	13	18	16	23	38	24	0	21	32
17	11	37	07	+2	28	+5	13	5	37	5	35	11	55	18	11	18	13	23	42	21	0	17	37
18	11	40	42	+2	05	+5	35	5	39	5	37	11	54	18	09	18	11	23	46	17	0	13	41
19	11	44	17	+1	42	+5	56	5	40	5	38	11	54	18	06	18	08	23	50	14	0	09	45
20	11	47	53	+1	19	+6	18	5	42	5	40	11	54	18	04	18	05	23	54	10	0	05	49
21	11	51	28	+0	55	+6	39	5	44	5	42	11	53	18	02	18	03	23	58	07	0	01	53
																					23	57	57
22	11	55	03	+0	32	+7	00	5	45	5	44	11	53	17	59	18	00	0	02	03	23	54	01
23	11	58	38	+0	09	+7	21	5	47	5	46	11	52	17	57	17	57	0	06	00	23	50	05
24	12	02	14	−0	15	+7	42	5	49	5	48	11	52	17	55	17	55	0	09	56	23	46	09
25	12	05	50	−0	38	+8	03	5	50	5	50	11	52	17	52	17	52	0	13	53	23	42	13
26	12	09	26	−1	01	+8	24	5	52	5	52	11	51	17	50	17	50	0	17	50	23	38	17
27	12	13	02	−1	25	+8	45	5	53	5	54	11	51	17	48	17	47	0	21	46	23	34	22
28	12	16	38	−1	48	+9	05	5	55	5	56	11	51	17	45	17	44	0	25	43	23	30	26
29	12	20	14	−2	11	+9	25	5	57	5	58	11	50	17	43	17	42	0	29	39	23	26	30
30	12	23	51	−2	35	+9	45	5	58	6	00	11	50	17	41	17	39	0	33	36	23	22	34

DURATION OF TWILIGHT (in minutes)

Latitude	52°	56°	52°	56°	52°	56°	52°	56°
	1 September		*11 September*		*21 September*		*31 September*	
Civil	35	39	34	38	34	37	34	37
Nautical	79	89	76	85	74	82	73	80
Astronomical	127	147	120	136	116	129	113	125

THE NIGHT SKY

Mercury continues to be visible as a morning object for the first two weeks of the month, low above the eastern horizon about the time of beginning of morning civil twilight. During this period its magnitude brightens from +0.2 to −1.2. This is the most favourable morning apparition of the year for observers in the northern hemisphere. Mercury passes 0.7 degrees north of Regulus on the morning of the 9th, Mercury being the brighter object.

Venus remains too close to the Sun for observation throughout September.

Mars, magnitude +1.4, continues to be visible in the eastern skies in the early mornings. It moves from Gemini into Cancer during September, passing south of Castor and Pollux early in the month, and passing less than 1 degree south of Praesepe (the 'Beehive' open cluster) at the very end of the month. On the 23rd the waning crescent Moon passes 5 degrees south of Mars.

Jupiter, magnitude −2.7, is moving slowly retrograde in Aries, becoming visible low above the eastern horizon soon after 21h at the beginning of the month and after about 19h at the end of the month. On the 16th the waning gibbous Moon passes 4 degrees north of the planet.

Saturn continues to be too close to the Sun for observation.

Uranus is at opposition on the 26th, in the constellation of Pisces. The planet is barely visible to the naked eye as its magnitude is +5.7, but it is readily located with only small optical aid.

Zodiacal Light. The morning cone may be observed stretching up from the eastern horizon, along the ecliptic, before the beginning of morning twilight, from the 1st to the 10th and again after the 25th. This faint phenomenon is only visible under good conditions and in the absence of both moonlight and artificial lighting.

THE MOON

Day	R.A.		Dec.	Hor. Par.	Semi-diam.	Sun's Co-Long.	PA. of Br. Limb	Ph.	Age	Rise				Transit		Set			
										52°		56°				52°		56°	
	h	m	°	′	′	°	°	%	d	h	m	h	m	h	m	h	m	h	m
1	13	01	−11.3	60.5	16.5	308	298	12	2.9	9	57	10	10	14	56	19	44	19	30
2	13	59	−16.0	60.1	16.4	320	293	21	3.9	11	21	11	39	15	53	20	16	19	57
3	14	57	−19.7	59.5	16.2	333	288	31	4.9	12	40	13	03	16	50	20	56	20	32
4	15	57	−22.0	58.9	16.0	345	282	42	5.9	13	50	14	16	17	48	21	45	21	19
5	16	57	−23.0	58.2	15.8	357	276	53	6.9	14	49	15	14	18	45	22	44	22	19
6	17	55	−22.6	57.5	15.7	9	271	64	7.9	15	35	15	58	19	40	23	50	23	28
7	18	51	−21.0	56.8	15.5	21	266	74	8.9	16	11	16	30	20	32	—		—	
8	19	45	−18.3	56.2	15.3	34	262	82	9.9	16	38	16	53	21	21	1	01	0	43
9	20	36	−14.8	55.7	15.2	46	260	89	10.9	17	01	17	12	22	07	2	13	1	59
10	21	24	−10.7	55.2	15.0	58	260	94	11.9	17	20	17	27	22	51	3	23	3	14
11	22	10	−6.2	54.8	14.9	70	266	98	12.9	17	38	17	40	23	33	4	33	4	28
12	22	55	−1.5	54.5	14.9	82	296	100	13.9	17	54	17	53	—		5	41	5	40
13	23	40	+3.2	54.3	14.8	95	30	99	14.9	18	11	18	06	0	15	6	48	6	52
14	0	24	+7.7	54.1	14.7	107	52	97	15.9	18	29	18	20	0	56	7	55	8	03
15	1	09	+11.9	54.0	14.7	119	60	94	16.9	18	50	18	36	1	38	9	01	9	14
16	1	55	+15.6	54.0	14.7	131	65	89	17.9	19	14	18	57	2	22	10	08	10	24
17	2	43	+18.7	54.2	14.8	143	70	82	18.9	19	44	19	23	3	08	11	13	11	33
18	3	33	+21.1	54.5	14.8	155	75	74	19.9	20	22	19	58	3	55	12	15	12	38
19	4	24	+22.5	54.9	15.0	168	80	65	20.9	21	08	20	44	4	45	13	12	13	36
20	5	17	+22.9	55.5	15.1	180	86	56	21.9	22	05	21	42	5	36	14	01	14	25
21	6	12	+22.1	56.3	15.3	192	91	46	22.9	23	12	22	51	6	28	14	43	15	05
22	7	06	+20.2	57.1	15.6	204	96	36	23.9	—		—		7	21	15	18	15	35
23	8	01	+17.1	58.1	15.8	216	100	26	24.9	0	26	0	09	8	14	15	46	15	59
24	8	56	+13.0	59.0	16.1	229	102	17	25.9	1	45	1	33	9	06	16	11	16	19
25	9	51	+8.1	59.9	16.3	241	103	9	26.9	3	07	3	01	9	59	16	34	16	37
26	10	45	+2.5	60.7	16.5	253	99	3	27.9	4	32	4	31	10	52	16	55	16	54
27	11	41	−3.3	61.1	16.7	265	77	1	28.9	5	59	6	03	11	46	17	18	17	12
28	12	38	−9.0	61.3	16.7	278	324	1	0.6	7	27	7	37	12	42	17	44	17	32
29	13	36	−14.1	61.2	16.7	290	301	4	1.6	8	55	9	10	13	39	18	14	17	58
30	14	36	−18.3	60.7	16.5	302	292	10	2.6	10	19	10	39	14	39	18	52	18	31

MERCURY

Day	R.A.		Dec.	Diam.	Phase	Transit		5° high			
								52°		56°	
	h	m	°	′	%	h	m	h	m	h	m
1	9	30	+14.0	8	35	10	52	4	12	4	04
3	9	38	+14.0	7	44	10	52	4	12	4	03
5	9	46	+13.8	7	52	10	53	4	14	4	06
7	9	57	+13.3	7	61	10	56	4	19	4	12
9	10	08	+12.6	6	69	11	00	4	27	4	20
11	10	21	+11.8	6	76	11	05	4	37	4	30
13	10	34	+10.7	6	83	11	10	4	48	4	42
15	10	48	+9.5	5	88	11	16	5	00	4	56
17	11	02	+8.2	5	92	11	22	5	13	5	10
19	11	16	+6.7	5	95	11	28	5	26	5	24
21	11	30	+5.2	5	97	11	34	5	40	5	39
23	11	43	+3.7	5	98	11	40	5	54	5	54
25	11	57	+2.1	5	99	11	45	6	07	6	09
27	12	10	+0.6	5	100	11	50	6	21	6	24
29	12	23	−1.0	5	100	11	56	6	34	6	38
31	12	36	−2.6	5	100	12	00	17	12	17	06

VENUS

Day	R.A.		Dec.	Diam.	Phase	Transit		5° high			
								52°		56°	
	h	m	°	′	%	h	m	h	m	h	m
1	10	58	+8.2	10	100	12	20	18	27	18	31
6	11	21	+5.8	10	100	12	23	18	18	18	19
11	11	43	+3.3	10	99	12	26	18	09	18	08
16	12	06	+0.7	10	99	12	29	17	59	17	56
21	12	29	−1.8	10	99	12	32	17	48	17	43
26	12	51	−4.3	10	98	12	35	17	38	17	31
31	13	14	−6.9	10	98	12	38	17	27	17	18

MARS

Day	R.A.		Dec.	Diam.	Phase	Transit		5° high			
								52°		56°	
	h	m	°	′	%	h	m	h	m	h	m
1	7	21	+22.8	5	93	8	43	1	13	0	55
6	7	35	+22.4	5	93	8	37	1	09	0	52
11	7	48	+21.9	5	93	8	30	1	06	0	49
16	8	02	+21.4	5	93	8	24	1	02	0	46
21	8	15	+20.8	5	92	8	17	0	59	0	44
26	8	27	+20.2	5	92	8	10	0	56	0	41
31	8	40	+19.6	5	92	8	03	0	52	0	38

SUNRISE AND SUNSET

	London				*Bristol*				*Birmingham*				*Manchester*				*Newcastle*				*Glasgow*				*Belfast*			
	0° 05′		*51° 30′*		*2° 35′*		*51° 28′*		*1° 55′*		*52° 28′*		*2° 15′*		*53° 28′*		*1° 37′*		*54° 59′*		*4° 14′*		*55° 52′*		*5° 56′*		*54° 35′*	
d	*h*	*m*	*h*	*m*	*h*	*m*	*h*	*m*	*h*	*m*	*h*	*m*	*h*	*m*	*h*	*m*	*h*	*m*	*h*	*m*	*h*	*m*	*h*	*m*	*h*	*m*	*h*	*m*
1	5	12	18	48	5	22	18	58	5	18	18	57	5	17	19	00	5	12	19	00	5	21	19	12	5	30	19	16
2	5	14	18	45	5	24	18	55	5	20	18	54	5	19	18	57	5	14	18	57	5	23	19	10	5	32	19	14
3	5	15	18	43	5	25	18	53	5	21	18	52	5	21	18	55	5	16	18	55	5	25	19	07	5	34	19	11
4	5	17	18	41	5	27	18	51	5	23	18	50	5	23	18	52	5	18	18	52	5	26	19	04	5	36	19	09
5	5	19	18	39	5	29	18	49	5	25	18	47	5	24	18	50	5	19	18	50	5	28	19	02	5	37	19	07
6	5	20	18	36	5	30	18	46	5	26	18	45	5	26	18	48	5	21	18	47	5	30	18	59	5	39	19	04
7	5	22	18	34	5	32	18	44	5	28	18	43	5	28	18	45	5	23	18	45	5	32	18	57	5	41	19	02
8	5	23	18	32	5	33	18	42	5	30	18	40	5	30	18	43	5	25	18	42	5	34	18	54	5	43	18	59
9	5	25	18	30	5	35	18	40	5	31	18	38	5	31	18	40	5	27	18	40	5	36	18	51	5	45	18	56
10	5	27	18	27	5	37	18	37	5	33	18	36	5	33	18	38	5	29	18	37	5	38	18	49	5	46	18	54
11	5	28	18	25	5	38	18	35	5	35	18	33	5	35	18	36	5	31	18	35	5	40	18	46	5	48	18	51
12	5	30	18	23	5	40	18	33	5	36	18	31	5	36	18	33	5	32	18	32	5	42	18	43	5	50	18	49
13	5	31	18	20	5	41	18	30	5	38	18	29	5	38	18	31	5	34	18	30	5	44	18	41	5	52	18	46
14	5	33	18	18	5	43	18	28	5	39	18	26	5	40	18	28	5	36	18	27	5	46	18	38	5	54	18	44
15	5	34	18	16	5	44	18	26	5	41	18	24	5	42	18	26	5	38	18	24	5	48	18	36	5	56	18	41
16	5	36	18	13	5	46	18	23	5	43	18	21	5	43	18	23	5	40	18	22	5	50	18	33	5	57	18	39
17	5	38	18	11	5	48	18	21	5	44	18	19	5	45	18	21	5	42	18	19	5	52	18	30	5	59	18	36
18	5	39	18	09	5	49	18	19	5	46	18	17	5	47	18	18	5	44	18	17	5	54	18	28	6	01	18	34
19	5	41	18	07	5	51	18	17	5	48	18	14	5	49	18	16	5	45	18	14	5	55	18	25	6	03	18	31
20	5	42	18	04	5	52	18	14	5	49	18	12	5	50	18	14	5	47	18	12	5	57	18	22	6	05	18	29
21	5	44	18	02	5	54	18	12	5	51	18	10	5	52	18	11	5	49	18	09	5	59	18	20	6	07	18	26
22	5	46	18	00	5	56	18	10	5	53	18	07	5	54	18	09	5	51	18	06	6	01	18	17	6	08	18	24
23	5	47	17	57	5	57	18	07	5	54	18	05	5	56	18	06	5	53	18	04	6	03	18	14	6	10	18	21
24	5	49	17	55	5	59	18	05	5	56	18	02	5	57	18	04	5	55	18	01	6	05	18	12	6	12	18	18
25	5	51	17	53	6	01	18	03	5	58	18	00	5	59	18	01	5	57	17	59	6	07	18	09	6	14	18	16
26	5	52	17	50	6	02	18	00	6	00	17	58	6	01	17	59	5	59	17	56	6	09	18	06	6	16	18	13
27	5	54	17	48	6	04	17	58	6	01	17	55	6	03	17	56	6	00	17	54	6	11	18	04	6	18	18	11
28	5	55	17	46	6	05	17	56	6	03	17	53	6	05	17	54	6	02	17	51	6	13	18	01	6	20	18	08
29	5	57	17	44	6	07	17	54	6	05	17	51	6	06	17	52	6	04	17	48	6	15	17	59	6	21	18	06
30	5	59	17	41	6	09	17	51	6	06	17	48	6	08	17	49	6	06	17	46	6	17	17	56	6	23	18	03

JUPITER

Day	*R.A.*		*Dec.*		*Transit*		*5° high*			
							52°		*56°*	
	h	*m*	°	′	*h*	*m*	*h*	*m*	*h*	*m*
1	2	33.5	+13	37	3	55	21	14	21	06
11	2	32.7	+13	31	3	15	20	34	20	27
21	2	30.6	+13	19	2	33	19	54	19	46
31	2	27.4	+13	01	1	51	19	13	19	06

Diameters – equatorial 47″ polar 44″

SATURN

Day	*R.A.*		*Dec.*		*Transit*		*5° high*			
							52°		*56°*	
	h	*m*	°	′	*h*	*m*	*h*	*m*	*h*	*m*
1	12	59.5	–3	52	14	19	19	25	19	19
11	13	03.5	–4	18	13	44	18	48	18	41
21	13	07.7	–4	45	13	09	18	10	18	03
31	13	12.1	–5	13	12	34	17	33	17	25

Diameters – equatorial 16″ polar 14″
Rings – major axis 36″ minor axis 6″

URANUS

Day	*R.A.*		*Dec.*		*Transit*		*10° high*			
							52°		*56°*	
	h	*m*	°	′	*h*	*m*	*h*	*m*	*h*	*m*
1	0	14.2	+0	42	1	36	20	34	20	41
11	0	12.9	+0	33	0	55	19	55	20	01
21	0	11.4	+0	24	0	14	19	15	19	21
31	0	10.0	+0	14	23	30	18	35	18	41

Diameter 4″

NEPTUNE

Day	*R.A.*		*Dec.*		*Transit*		*10° high*			
							52°		*56°*	
	h	*m*	°	′	*h*	*m*	*h*	*m*	*h*	*m*
1	22	06.4	–12	15	23	24	3	10	2	49
11	22	05.4	–12	20	22	44	2	29	2	08
21	22	04.4	–12	25	22	04	1	48	1	27
31	22	03.6	–12	30	21	24	1	07	0	46

Diameter 2″

OCTOBER 2011

TENTH MONTH, 31 DAYS. *Octo* (eighth), eighth month of Roman pre-Julian calendar

1	*Saturday*	The first section of Gustave Flaubert's novel *Madame Bovary* was published in *Revue de Paris* 1856	day 274
2	*Sunday*	Wallace Stevens, US poet *b.* 1879; Marcel Duchamp, French-US artist *d.* 1968	275
3	*Monday*	Edgar Allan Poe was found in a delirious state on the streets of Baltimore 1849	week 40 day 276
4	*Tuesday*	Jack London bought nine plot outlines from 25-year-old Sinclair Lewis for $52.50 1910	277
5	*Wednesday*	*Monty Python's Flying Circus* first aired on BBC1 1969	278
6	*Thursday*	The first feature-length 'talkie', *The Jazz Singer*, premiered in New York 1927	279
7	*Friday*	Allen Ginsberg gave the first reading of his poem 'Howl' at Six Gallery in San Francisco 1955	280
8	*Saturday*	Talking Heads released their widely acclaimed album *Remain in Light* 1980	281
9	*Sunday*	Spanish writer Miguel de Cervantes was baptised 1547	282
10	*Monday*	Harold Pinter, playwright *b.* 1930; Orson Welles, US film director and writer *d.* 1985	week 41 day 283
11	*Tuesday*	Aaron Copland wrote to his parents to tell them he had sold his first composition 1921	284
12	*Wednesday*	Oktoberfest took place in its original form: a celebration of a Bavarian royal wedding 1810	285
13	*Thursday*	US poet Robert Lowell was sentenced to a year and a day in prison for resisting the draft 1943	286
14	*Friday*	The first of A. A. Milne's *Winnie-the-Pooh* books was published 1926	287
15	*Saturday*	*The Great Dictator* (written, directed by and starring Charlie Chaplin) premiered 1940	288
16	*Sunday*	Oscar Wilde, writer *b.* 1864; Arthur 'Art' Blakey, jazz musician *d.* 1990	289
17	*Monday*	Anton Chekhov's play *The Sea Gull* had a disastrous debut 1896	week 42 day 290
18	*Tuesday*	Matisse's paper cut-out *Le Bateau* was hung upside down at New York MoMA 1961	291
19	*Wednesday*	Writer Leigh Hunt was born, on whom Dickens based the character Skimpole in *Bleak House* 1859	292
20	*Thursday*	Sydney Opera House was formally opened by Queen Elizabeth II 1973	293
21	*Friday*	The Guggenheim museum opened in New York 1959	294
22	*Saturday*	Franz Liszt, Hungarian composer *b.* 1811; Sir Kingsley Amis, writer *d.* 1995	295
23	*Sunday*	The Smurfs first appeared in Belgian magazine *Spirou* 1958	296
24	*Monday*	Harry Houdini gave his last performance 1926	week 43 day 297
25	*Tuesday*	The Charge of the Light Brigade, commemorated in Tennyson's famous poem, took place 1854	298
26	*Wednesday*	US film *Rebel Without a Cause*, starring the late James Dean, opened 1955	299
27	*Thursday*	Sergei Rachmaninov performed the debut of his Piano Concerto No. 2 1901	300
28	*Friday*	Jonathan Swift's classic novel *Gulliver's Travels* was published 1726	301
29	*Saturday*	US musical *Runnin' Wild*, which popularised the Charleston, opened on Broadway 1923	302
30	*Sunday*	Orson Welles' radio production of *War of the Worlds* first aired, inciting panic and complaints 1938	303
31	*Monday*	The Mount Rushmore National Memorial sculpture was declared complete 1941	week 44 day 304

ASTRONOMICAL PHENOMENA

d	*h*	
6	22	Saturn in conjunction with Mercury. Saturn 2°N.
13	16	Jupiter in conjunction with Moon. Jupiter 5°S.
13	21	Saturn in conjunction
21	20	Mars in conjunction with Moon. Mars 6°N.
23	19	Sun's longitude 210° ♏
26	02	Saturn in conjunction with Moon. Saturn 6°N.
28	02	Mercury in conjunction with Moon. Mercury 0°.2 N.
28	04	Venus in conjunction with Moon. Venus 2°N.

MINIMA OF ALGOL

d	*h*	*d*	*h*	*d*	*h*
3	06.1	14	17.4	26	04.6
6	02.9	17	14.2	29	01.4
8	23.8	20	11.0	31	22.3
11	20.6	23	07.8		

CONSTELLATIONS

The following constellations are near their meridian at

	d	*h*		*d*	*h*
September	1	24	October	16	21
September	15	23	November	1	20
October	1	22	November	15	19

Ursa Major (below the Pole), Cepheus, Cassiopeia, Cygnus, Lacerta, Andromeda, Pegasus, Capricornus, Aquarius and Piscis Austrinus

THE MOON

Phases, Apsides and Node	*d*	*h*	*m*
☽ First Quarter	4	03	15
○ Full Moon	12	02	06
☾ Last Quarter	20	03	30
● New Moon	26	19	56
Apogee (406,431 km)	12	11	26
Perigee (357,048 km)	26	12	19

Mean longitude of ascending node on October 1, 258°

THE SUN

s.d. 16′.1

Day	Right Ascension			Dec. –		Equation of time		Rise 52°		Rise 56°		Transit		Set 52°		Set 56°		Sidereal time			Transit of first point of Aries		
	h	*m*	*s*	°	′	*m*	*s*	*h*	*m*	*h*	*m*	*h*	*m*	*h*	*m*	*h*	*m*	*h*	*m*	*s*	*h*	*m*	*s*
1	12	27	28	2	58	+10	04	6	00	6	02	11	50	17	38	17	36	0	37	32	23	18	38
2	12	31	05	3	21	+10	24	6	02	6	04	11	49	17	36	17	34	0	41	29	23	14	42
3	12	34	43	3	45	+10	43	6	03	6	06	11	49	17	34	17	31	0	45	25	23	10	46
4	12	38	20	4	08	+11	02	6	05	6	08	11	49	17	32	17	29	0	49	22	23	06	50
5	12	41	58	4	31	+11	20	6	07	6	10	11	49	17	29	17	26	0	53	19	23	02	54
6	12	45	37	4	54	+11	38	6	09	6	12	11	48	17	27	17	23	0	57	15	22	58	58
7	12	49	16	5	17	+11	56	6	10	6	14	11	48	17	25	17	21	1	01	12	22	55	02
8	12	52	55	5	40	+12	13	6	12	6	16	11	48	17	22	17	18	1	05	08	22	51	07
9	12	56	34	6	03	+12	30	6	14	6	18	11	47	17	20	17	16	1	09	05	22	47	11
10	13	00	14	6	26	+12	47	6	15	6	20	11	47	17	18	17	13	1	13	01	22	43	15
11	13	03	55	6	48	+13	03	6	17	6	22	11	47	17	16	17	10	1	16	58	22	39	19
12	13	07	36	7	11	+13	19	6	19	6	24	11	47	17	13	17	08	1	20	54	22	35	23
13	13	11	17	7	33	+13	34	6	20	6	26	11	46	17	11	17	05	1	24	51	22	31	27
14	13	14	59	7	56	+13	49	6	22	6	28	11	46	17	09	17	03	1	28	48	22	27	31
15	13	18	41	8	18	+14	03	6	24	6	30	11	46	17	07	17	00	1	32	44	22	23	35
16	13	22	24	8	40	+14	16	6	26	6	32	11	46	17	05	16	58	1	36	41	22	19	39
17	13	26	08	9	02	+14	29	6	27	6	34	11	45	17	03	16	55	1	40	37	22	15	43
18	13	29	52	9	24	+14	42	6	29	6	37	11	45	17	00	16	53	1	44	34	22	11	47
19	13	33	37	9	46	+14	53	6	31	6	39	11	45	16	58	16	50	1	48	30	22	07	52
20	13	37	22	10	08	+15	04	6	33	6	41	11	45	16	56	16	48	1	52	27	22	03	56
21	13	41	09	10	29	+15	15	6	34	6	43	11	45	16	54	16	46	1	56	23	22	00	00
22	13	44	55	10	51	+15	25	6	36	6	45	11	45	16	52	16	43	2	00	20	21	56	04
23	13	48	43	11	12	+15	34	6	38	6	47	11	44	16	50	16	41	2	04	17	21	52	08
24	13	52	31	11	33	+15	42	6	40	6	49	11	44	16	48	16	38	2	08	13	21	48	12
25	13	56	20	11	54	+15	50	6	41	6	51	11	44	16	46	16	36	2	12	10	21	44	16
26	14	00	09	12	15	+15	57	6	43	6	53	11	44	16	44	16	34	2	16	06	21	40	20
27	14	04	00	12	35	+16	03	6	45	6	55	11	44	16	42	16	31	2	20	03	21	36	24
28	14	07	51	12	55	+16	09	6	47	6	58	11	44	16	40	16	29	2	23	59	21	32	28
29	14	11	42	13	16	+16	13	6	49	7	00	11	44	16	38	16	27	2	27	56	21	28	32
30	14	15	35	13	35	+16	17	6	50	7	02	11	44	16	36	16	25	2	31	52	21	24	37
31	14	19	28	13	55	+16	21	6	52	7	04	11	44	16	34	16	22	2	35	49	21	20	41

DURATION OF TWILIGHT (in minutes)

Latitude	52°	56°	52°	56°	52°	56°	52°	56°
	1 October		*11 October*		*21 October*		*31 October*	
Civil	34	37	34	37	34	38	35	39
Nautical	73	80	73	80	74	81	75	83
Astronomical	113	125	112	124	113	124	114	126

THE NIGHT SKY

Mercury remains unsuitably placed for observation throughout October.

Venus is unsuitably placed for observation throughout October.

Mars, magnitude +1.3, is visible in the eastern skies not long after midnight, moving from Cancer into Leo during the month and approaching Regulus. During the night of October 21–22 the Moon, just past Last Quarter, passes about 7 degrees south of Mars.

Jupiter, magnitude −2.9, reaches opposition on the 29th and thus remains available for observation throughout the hours of darkness. On the 13th the Moon, just past Full, passes 4 degrees north of the planet. The four Galilean satellites are readily observable with a small telescope or even a good pair of binoculars provided that they are held rigidly.

Saturn remains too close to the Sun for observation throughout October as it passes through conjunction on the 13th.

THE MOON

Day	R.A.		Dec.	Hor. Par.	Semi-diam.	Sun's Co-Long.	PA. of Br. Limb	Ph.	Age	Rise				Transit		Set			
										52°		56°				52°		56°	
	h	m	°	′	′	°	°	%	d	h	m	h	m	h	m	h	m	h	m
1	15	38	−21.2	60.0	16.4	314	285	18	3.6	11	36	12	00	15	39	19	40	19	15
2	16	39	−22.6	59.2	16.1	326	278	27	4.6	12	40	13	06	16	38	20	37	20	12
3	17	40	−22.6	58.3	15.9	339	272	38	5.6	13	32	13	55	17	35	21	43	21	20
4	18	38	−21.2	57.4	15.7	351	266	49	6.6	14	11	14	31	18	29	22	53	22	34
5	19	32	−18.8	56.6	15.4	3	262	59	7.6	14	42	14	57	19	19	—		23	50
6	20	24	−15.5	55.9	15.2	15	258	69	8.6	15	06	15	17	20	05	0	04	—	
7	21	13	−11.5	55.3	15.1	27	256	78	9.6	15	26	15	34	20	50	1	15	1	05
8	21	59	−7.2	54.9	14.9	40	255	85	10.6	15	44	15	48	21	32	2	24	2	18
9	22	44	−2.6	54.5	14.8	52	255	91	11.6	16	01	16	01	22	13	3	32	3	30
10	23	28	+2.0	54.2	14.8	64	258	96	12.6	16	18	16	14	22	55	4	39	4	41
11	0	13	+6.6	54.0	14.7	76	268	99	13.6	16	36	16	28	23	37	5	45	5	52
12	0	57	+10.8	54.0	14.7	88	325	100	14.6	16	56	16	44	—		6	52	7	02
13	1	43	+14.6	54.0	14.7	100	49	99	15.6	17	19	17	03	0	20	7	58	8	13
14	2	31	+17.9	54.1	14.7	113	64	97	16.6	17	47	17	28	1	05	9	03	9	22
15	3	20	+20.4	54.2	14.8	125	72	93	17.6	18	22	18	00	1	52	10	06	10	28
16	4	11	+22.0	54.5	14.9	137	78	87	18.6	19	06	18	41	2	41	11	04	11	29
17	5	03	+22.7	54.9	15.0	149	85	80	19.6	19	58	19	34	3	31	11	56	12	20
18	5	56	+22.2	55.5	15.1	161	90	71	20.6	21	00	20	38	4	22	12	39	13	02
19	6	50	+20.7	56.1	15.3	173	95	62	21.6	22	09	21	51	5	13	13	15	13	34
20	7	43	+18.0	56.9	15.5	186	100	52	22.6	23	23	23	10	6	04	13	45	14	00
21	8	36	+14.4	57.8	15.7	198	104	41	23.6	—		—		6	55	14	11	14	21
22	9	29	+9.9	58.7	16.0	210	106	31	24.6	0	41	0	33	7	46	14	34	14	39
23	10	22	+4.8	59.6	16.2	222	108	21	25.6	2	02	1	58	8	37	14	55	14	56
24	11	16	−0.8	60.4	16.5	234	107	12	26.6	3	25	3	27	9	29	15	17	15	13
25	12	11	−6.5	61.0	16.6	247	104	5	27.6	4	51	4	58	10	23	15	41	15	32
26	13	09	−11.8	61.4	16.7	259	93	1	28.6	6	19	6	31	11	20	16	09	15	55
27	14	09	−16.5	61.4	16.7	271	343	0	0.2	7	47	8	05	12	20	16	44	16	25
28	15	11	−20.0	61.0	16.6	283	293	2	1.2	9	10	9	32	13	21	17	28	17	05
29	16	15	−22.1	60.4	16.5	295	282	7	2.2	10	23	10	47	14	23	18	23	18	58
30	17	18	−22.6	59.6	16.2	308	274	14	3.2	11	22	11	46	15	24	19	28	19	04
31	18	18	−21.6	58.6	16.0	320	267	23	4.2	12	08	12	29	16	20	20	39	20	18

MERCURY

Day	R.A.		Dec.	Diam.	Phase	Transit		5° high			
								52°		56°	
	h	m	°	′	%	h	m	h	m	h	m
1	12	36	−2.6	5	100	12	00	17	12	17	06
3	12	48	−4.1	5	100	12	05	17	08	17	01
5	13	01	−5.6	5	99	12	09	17	05	16	56
7	13	13	−7.1	5	99	12	14	17	01	16	51
9	13	25	−8.6	5	98	12	18	16	57	16	46
11	13	37	−10.0	5	97	12	22	16	53	16	40
13	13	49	−11.3	5	96	12	26	16	49	16	35
15	14	01	−12.7	5	95	12	30	16	45	16	29
17	14	12	−13.9	5	94	12	34	16	41	16	23
19	14	24	−15.2	5	93	12	38	16	37	16	18
21	14	36	−16.3	5	92	12	41	16	33	16	12
23	14	47	−17.4	5	91	12	45	16	29	16	06
25	14	59	−18.5	5	90	12	49	16	26	16	01
27	15	11	−19.5	5	88	12	53	16	22	15	55
29	15	22	−20.4	5	87	12	56	16	19	15	50
31	15	34	−21.3	5	85	13	00	16	16	15	45

VENUS

Day	R.A.		Dec.	Diam.	Phase	Transit		5° high			
								52°		56°	
	h	m	°	′	%	h	m	h	m	h	m
1	13	14	− 6.9	10	98	12	38	17	27	17	18
6	13	37	− 9.3	10	97	12	42	17	17	17	05
11	14	01	−11.7	10	97	12	45	17	07	16	52
16	14	25	−13.9	10	96	12	50	16	57	16	40
21	14	49	−16.0	10	96	12	54	16	48	16	28
26	15	14	−18.0	10	95	12	59	16	40	16	17
31	15	39	−19.7	11	94	13	05	16	33	16	06

MARS

Day	R.A.		Dec.	Diam.	Phase	Transit		5° high			
								52°		56°	
	h	m	°	′	%	h	m	h	m	h	m
1	8	40	+19.6	5	92	8	03	0	52	0	38
6	8	52	+18.9	5	92	7	55	0	49	0	36
11	9	04	+18.1	5	91	7	47	0	45	0	33
16	9	15	+17.4	5	91	7	39	0	41	0	30
21	9	26	+16.6	6	91	7	31	0	37	0	27
26	9	37	+15.8	6	91	7	22	0	33	0	23
31	9	48	+15.0	6	90	7	13	0	28	0	19

SUNRISE AND SUNSET

	London				*Bristol*				*Birmingham*				*Manchester*				*Newcastle*				*Glasgow*				*Belfast*			
	0° 05′		*51° 30′*		*2° 35′*		*51° 28′*		*1° 55′*		*52° 28′*		*2° 15′*		*53° 28′*		*1° 37′*		*54° 59′*		*4° 14′*		*55° 52′*		*5° 56′*		*54° 35′*	
d	*h*	*m*	*h*	*m*	*h*	*m*	*h*	*m*	*h*	*m*	*h*	*m*	*h*	*m*	*h*	*m*	*h*	*m*	*h*	*m*	*h*	*m*	*h*	*m*	*h*	*m*	*h*	*m*
1	6	00	17	39	6	10	17	49	6	08	17	46	6	10	17	47	6	08	17	43	6	19	17	53	6	25	18	01
2	6	02	17	37	6	12	17	47	6	10	17	44	6	12	17	44	6	10	17	41	6	21	17	51	6	27	17	58
3	6	04	17	34	6	14	17	44	6	11	17	41	6	13	17	42	6	12	17	38	6	23	17	48	6	29	17	56
4	6	05	17	32	6	15	17	42	6	13	17	39	6	15	17	39	6	14	17	36	6	25	17	46	6	31	17	53
5	6	07	17	30	6	17	17	40	6	15	17	37	6	17	17	37	6	16	17	33	6	27	17	43	6	33	17	51
6	6	08	17	28	6	18	17	38	6	17	17	34	6	19	17	35	6	18	17	31	6	29	17	40	6	35	17	48
7	6	10	17	25	6	20	17	35	6	18	17	32	6	21	17	32	6	19	17	28	6	31	17	38	6	36	17	46
8	6	12	17	23	6	22	17	33	6	20	17	30	6	22	17	30	6	21	17	26	6	33	17	35	6	38	17	43
9	6	13	17	21	6	23	17	31	6	22	17	27	6	24	17	28	6	23	17	23	6	35	17	33	6	40	17	41
10	6	15	17	19	6	25	17	29	6	24	17	25	6	26	17	25	6	25	17	21	6	37	17	30	6	42	17	39
11	6	17	17	17	6	27	17	27	6	25	17	23	6	28	17	23	6	27	17	18	6	39	17	28	6	44	17	36
12	6	18	17	14	6	28	17	24	6	27	17	21	6	30	17	21	6	29	17	16	6	41	17	25	6	46	17	34
13	6	20	17	12	6	30	17	22	6	29	17	18	6	31	17	18	6	31	17	13	6	43	17	23	6	48	17	31
14	6	22	17	10	6	32	17	20	6	31	17	16	6	33	17	16	6	33	17	11	6	45	17	20	6	50	17	29
15	6	24	17	08	6	34	17	18	6	32	17	14	6	35	17	14	6	35	17	09	6	47	17	17	6	52	17	27
16	6	25	17	06	6	35	17	16	6	34	17	12	6	37	17	11	6	37	17	06	6	49	17	15	6	54	17	24
17	6	27	17	04	6	37	17	14	6	36	17	09	6	39	17	09	6	39	17	04	6	51	17	13	6	56	17	22
18	6	29	17	02	6	39	17	12	6	38	17	07	6	41	17	07	6	41	17	01	6	53	17	10	6	57	17	19
19	6	30	16	59	6	40	17	10	6	39	17	05	6	43	17	05	6	43	16	59	6	55	17	08	6	59	17	17
20	6	32	16	57	6	42	17	07	6	41	17	03	6	44	17	02	6	45	16	57	6	57	17	05	7	01	17	15
21	6	34	16	55	6	44	17	05	6	43	17	01	6	46	17	00	6	47	16	54	6	59	17	03	7	03	17	13
22	6	36	16	53	6	46	17	03	6	45	16	59	6	48	16	58	6	49	16	52	7	02	17	00	7	05	17	10
23	6	37	16	51	6	47	17	01	6	47	16	57	6	50	16	56	6	51	16	50	7	04	16	58	7	07	17	08
24	6	39	16	49	6	49	16	59	6	48	16	55	6	52	16	54	6	53	16	47	7	06	16	56	7	09	17	06
25	6	41	16	47	6	51	16	57	6	50	16	52	6	54	16	52	6	55	16	45	7	08	16	53	7	11	17	03
26	6	43	16	45	6	52	16	55	6	52	16	50	6	56	16	49	6	57	16	43	7	10	16	51	7	13	17	01
27	6	44	16	43	6	54	16	53	6	54	16	48	6	58	16	47	6	59	16	41	7	12	16	49	7	15	16	59
28	6	46	16	42	6	56	16	52	6	56	16	46	7	00	16	45	7	01	16	39	7	14	16	47	7	17	16	57
29	6	48	16	40	6	58	16	50	6	58	16	45	7	01	16	43	7	03	16	36	7	16	16	44	7	19	16	55
30	6	50	16	38	6	59	16	48	6	59	16	43	7	03	16	41	7	05	16	34	7	18	16	42	7	21	16	53
31	6	51	16	36	7	01	16	46	7	01	16	41	7	05	16	39	7	07	16	32	7	20	16	40	7	23	16	51

JUPITER

Day	*R.A.*		*Dec.*		*Transit*		*5° high*			
							52°		*56°*	
	h	*m*	°	′	*h*	*m*	*h*	*m*	*h*	*m*
1	2	27.4	+13	01	1	51	19	13	19	06
11	2	23.1	+12	39	1	07	18	31	18	24
21	2	18.2	+12	14	0	23	17	49	17	43
31	2	13.0	+11	48	23	34	17	07	17	01

Diameters – equatorial 49″ polar 46″

SATURN

Day	*R.A.*		*Dec.*		*Transit*		*5° high*			
							52°		*56°*	
	h	*m*	°	′	*h*	*m*	*h*	*m*	*h*	*m*
1	13	12.1	–5	13	12	34	7	35	7	43
11	13	16.7	–5	40	11	59	7	02	7	11
21	13	21.2	–6	08	11	24	6	30	6	39
31	13	25.7	–6	34	10	49	5	58	6	07

Diameters – equatorial 16″ polar 14″
Rings – major axis 35″ minor axis 7″

URANUS

Day	*R.A.*		*Dec.*		*Transit*		*10° high*			
							52°		*56°*	
	h	*m*	°	′	*h*	*m*	*h*	*m*	*h*	*m*
1	0	10.0	+0	14	23	30	4	28	4	22
11	0	08.5	+0	05	22	49	3	47	3	40
21	0	07.2	–0	04	22	08	3	06	2	59
31	0	05.9	–0	11	21	28	2	24	2	17

Diameter 4″

NEPTUNE

Day	*R.A.*		*Dec.*		*Transit*		*10° high*			
							52°		*56°*	
	h	*m*	°	′	*h*	*m*	*h*	*m*	*h*	*m*
1	22	03.6	–12	30	21	24	1	07	0	46
11	22	02.9	–12	34	20	44	0	27	0	05
21	22	02.4	–12	36	20	04	23	43	23	21
31	22	02.1	–12	38	19	24	23	03	22	41

Diameter 2″

NOVEMBER 2011

ELEVENTH MONTH, 30 DAYS. *Novem* (nine), ninth month of Roman pre-Julian calendar

1	*Tuesday*	L. S. Lowry, painter *b.* 1887; Ezra Pound, US poet *d.* 1972	day 305
2	*Wednesday*	George Bernard Shaw died, leaving money in trust for the research of a 42-letter alphabet 1950	306
3	*Thursday*	Charles Earl Boles ('Black Bart') committed his last stagecoach robbery 1883	307
4	*Friday*	T. S. Eliot was awarded the Nobel prize in literature 1948	308
5	*Saturday*	Samuel Pepys went to see *Macbeth*, which he judged 'a pretty good play' 1664	309
6	*Sunday*	George Eliot's first story, one of the *Scenes of Clerical Life*, was submitted for publication 1856	310
7	*Monday*	Frank Sinatra and Ava Gardner got married 1951	week 45 day 311
8	*Tuesday*	The Bodleian library opened to scholars at Oxford University 1602	312
9	*Wednesday*	Ivan Turgenev, Russian writer *b.* 1818; Dylan Thomas, Welsh poet *d.* 1953	313
10	*Thursday*	Thirty-six copies of Kurt Vonnegut's book *Slaughterhouse-Five* were burnt in North Dakota 1973	314
11	*Friday*	Bill Gates bought Leonardo da Vinci's notebook *The Codex Leicester* for $30.8m (£19.9m) 1994	315
12	*Saturday*	Auguste Rodin, French sculptor *b.* 1840; Elizabeth Gaskell, novelist *d.* 1865	316
13	*Sunday*	Wordsworth and Coleridge conceived 'The Rime of the Ancient Mariner' while on holiday 1797	317
14	*Monday*	Herman Melville's novel *Moby Dick* was first published 1851	week 46 day 318
15	*Tuesday*	William Shakespeare was named on a list of tax defaulters in St Helen's parish, London 1597	319
16	*Wednesday*	Diana Krall, Canadian jazz pianist *b.* 1964; Clark Gable, US actor *d.* 1960	320
17	*Thursday*	English-language bookshop and lending library Shakespeare and Company opened in Paris 1919	321
18	*Friday*	Mickey Mouse first appeared in the cartoon short *Steamboat Willie* 1928	322
19	*Saturday*	Alfred, Lord Tennyson succeeded William Wordsworth as Poet Laureate 1850	323
20	*Sunday*	Don DeLillo, US author *b.* 1936; Robert Altman, US director *d.* 2006	324
21	*Monday*	Voltaire spent his 23rd birthday incarcerated in the Bastille 1717	week 47 day 325
22	*Tuesday*	Maurice Ravel's orchestral piece *Boléro* premiered at the Paris Opéra 1928	326
23	*Wednesday*	John Milton's anti-censorship tract *Areopagitica* was published 1644	327
24	*Thursday*	Laurence Sterne, novelist *b.* 1713; Dodie Smith, novelist and playwright *d.* 1990	328
25	*Friday*	Japanese novelist Yukio Mishima staged an unsuccessful *coup d'état* in Tokyo 1970	329
26	*Saturday*	Lewis Carroll sent a handwritten *Alice's Adventures Under Ground* to ten-year-old Alice Liddell 1864	330
27	*Sunday*	US author Ken Kesey held his first all night 'acid test' party in California 1965	331
28	*Monday*	A £40 bond was bought for the marriage of William Shakespeare and Anne Hathaway 1582	week 48 day 332
29	*Tuesday*	Rossini's *The Barber of Seville* became the first opera to be sung in Italian in the USA 1825	333
30	*Wednesday*	Production began on Alfred Hitchcock's film *Psycho* 1959	334

ASTRONOMICAL PHENOMENA

d	*h*	
9	15	Jupiter in conjunction with Moon. Jupiter 5°S.
9	19	Neptune at stationary point
14	08	Mercury at greatest elongation E. 23°
19	05	Mars in conjunction with Moon. Mars 7°N.
22	16	Sun's longitude 240° ♐
22	18	Saturn in conjunction with Moon. Saturn 6°N.
24	07	Mercury at stationary point
25	06	Partial eclipse of Sun
26	10	Mercury in conjunction with Moon. Mercury 2°S.
27	04	Venus in conjunction with Moon. Venus 3°S.

MINIMA OF ALGOL

d	*h*	*d*	*h*	*d*	*h*
3	19.1	15	06.3	26	17.6
6	15.9	18	03.2	29	14.4
9	12.7	21	00.0		
12	09.5	23	20.8		

CONSTELLATIONS

The following constellations are near their meridian at

	d	*h*		*d*	*h*
October	1	24	November	15	21
October	16	23	December	1	20
November	1	22	December	16	19

Ursa Major (below the Pole), Cepheus, Cassiopeia, Andromeda, Pegasus, Pisces, Aquarius and Cetus

THE MOON

Phases, Apsides and Node	*d*	*h*	*m*
☽ First Quarter	2	16	38
○ Full Moon	10	20	16
☾ Last Quarter	18	15	09
● New Moon	25	06	10
Apogee (406,195 km)	8	13	07
Perigee (359,680 km)	23	23	14

Mean longitude of ascending node on November 1, 256°

THE SUN

s.d. 16′.2

Day	Right Ascension			Dec. –		Equation of time		Rise 52°		Rise 56°		Transit		Set 52°		Set 56°		Sidereal time			Transit of first point of Aries		
	h	m	s	°	′	m	s	h	m	h	m	h	m	h	m	h	m	h	m	s	h	m	s
1	14	23	22	14	15	+16	23	6	54	7	06	11	44	16	32	16	20	2	39	46	21	16	45
2	14	27	17	14	34	+16	25	6	56	7	08	11	44	16	31	16	18	2	43	42	21	12	49
3	14	31	13	14	53	+16	26	6	58	7	10	11	44	16	29	16	16	2	47	39	21	08	53
4	14	35	09	15	12	+16	26	6	59	7	12	11	44	16	27	16	14	2	51	35	21	04	57
5	14	39	06	15	30	+16	25	7	01	7	15	11	44	16	25	16	12	2	55	32	21	01	01
6	14	43	04	15	48	+16	24	7	03	7	17	11	44	16	23	16	10	2	59	28	20	57	05
7	14	47	03	16	06	+16	22	7	05	7	19	11	44	16	22	16	08	3	03	25	20	53	09
8	14	51	03	16	24	+16	18	7	07	7	21	11	44	16	20	16	06	3	07	21	20	49	13
9	14	55	03	16	41	+16	15	7	08	7	23	11	44	16	18	16	04	3	11	18	20	45	17
10	14	59	05	16	59	+16	10	7	10	7	25	11	44	16	17	16	02	3	15	14	20	41	22
11	15	03	07	17	16	+16	04	7	12	7	27	11	44	16	15	16	00	3	19	11	20	37	26
12	15	07	10	17	32	+15	58	7	14	7	29	11	44	16	14	15	58	3	23	08	20	33	30
13	15	11	14	17	48	+15	50	7	16	7	31	11	44	16	12	15	56	3	27	04	20	29	34
14	15	15	19	18	04	+15	42	7	17	7	34	11	44	16	11	15	54	3	31	01	20	25	38
15	15	19	24	18	20	+15	33	7	19	7	36	11	45	16	09	15	53	3	34	57	20	21	42
16	15	23	31	18	35	+15	23	7	21	7	38	11	45	16	08	15	51	3	38	54	20	17	46
17	15	27	38	18	50	+15	13	7	23	7	40	11	45	16	07	15	49	3	42	50	20	13	50
18	15	31	46	19	05	+15	01	7	24	7	42	11	45	16	05	15	48	3	46	47	20	09	54
19	15	35	55	19	19	+14	48	7	26	7	44	11	45	16	04	15	46	3	50	43	20	05	58
20	15	40	05	19	33	+14	35	7	28	7	46	11	46	16	03	15	45	3	54	40	20	02	02
21	15	44	16	19	47	+14	21	7	29	7	48	11	46	16	02	15	43	3	58	37	19	58	07
22	15	48	27	20	00	+14	06	7	31	7	50	11	46	16	01	15	42	4	02	33	19	54	11
23	15	52	39	20	13	+13	50	7	33	7	52	11	46	15	59	15	40	4	06	30	19	50	15
24	15	56	53	20	26	+13	34	7	34	7	54	11	47	15	58	15	39	4	10	26	19	46	19
25	16	01	07	20	38	+13	16	7	36	7	55	11	47	15	57	15	38	4	14	23	19	42	23
26	16	05	21	20	50	+12	58	7	37	7	57	11	47	15	56	15	37	4	18	19	19	38	27
27	16	09	37	21	01	+12	39	7	39	7	59	11	48	15	56	15	35	4	22	16	19	34	31
28	16	13	53	21	12	+12	20	7	41	8	01	11	48	15	55	15	34	4	26	13	19	30	35
29	16	18	10	21	23	+11	59	7	42	8	03	11	48	15	54	15	33	4	30	09	19	26	39
30	16	22	27	21	33	+11	38	7	44	8	04	11	49	15	53	15	32	4	34	06	19	22	43

DURATION OF TWILIGHT (in minutes)

Latitude	*52°*	*56°*	*52°*	*56°*	*52°*	*56°*	*52°*	*56°*
	1 November		*11 November*		*21 November*		*31 November*	
Civil	36	40	37	41	38	43	40	45
Nautical	75	84	78	87	80	90	82	93
Astronomical	115	127	117	130	120	134	123	138

THE NIGHT SKY

Mercury remains unsuitably placed for observation throughout November.

Venus becomes visible as a evening object as it emerges from the evening twilight after the first week of the month. Observers in Scotland will have to wait at least another week before it becomes visible to them. It will be visible very low above the south-western horizon shortly after sunset, but only for a very short while. Its magnitude is −3.9. The thin waxing crescent Moon passes 2 degrees north of Venus on the 27th.

Mars, its magnitude brightening from +1.1 to +0.8, continues its eastern motion in Leo, becoming visible in the eastern sky around midnight. Mars passes 1 degree north of Regulus on the 10th, while on the 19th the Last Quarter Moon passes 8 degrees south of the planet.

Jupiter, just past opposition, continues to be visible for the greater part of the night, magnitude −2.7. It is visible as a brilliant evening object in the southern and south-western skies. On the 9th, the Moon, almost Full, passes 5 degrees north of Jupiter.

Saturn, magnitude +0.8, is becoming visible for a short while as a morning object, low above the east-south-eastern horizon before the increasing twilight glow inhibits observation. Saturn is in the constellation of Virgo. On the evening of the 22nd the waning crescent Moon passes 7 degrees south of the planet.

THE MOON

Day	*R.A.*		*Dec.*	*Hor. Par.*	*Semi-diam.*	*Sun's Co-Long.*	*PA. of Br. Limb*	*Ph.*	*Age*	*Rise*				*Transit*		*Set*			
										52°		*56°*				*52°*		*56°*	
	h	*m*	°	′	′	°	°	%	*d*	*h*	*m*	*h*	*m*	*h*	*m*	*h*	*m*	*h*	*m*
1	19	16	−19.4	57.7	15.7	332	262	33	5.2	12	42	12	59	17	13	21	52	21	36
2	20	10	−16.3	56.8	15.5	344	257	43	6.2	13	09	13	22	18	02	23	04	22	53
3	21	00	−12.4	55.9	15.2	356	254	53	7.2	13	31	13	40	18	47	—		—	
4	21	47	−8.1	55.3	15.1	9	252	63	8.2	13	50	13	55	19	31	0	15	0	07
5	22	33	−3.6	54.7	14.9	21	251	72	9.2	14	07	14	08	20	12	1	23	1	20
6	23	17	+1.0	54.4	14.8	33	251	80	10.2	14	24	14	21	20	54	2	30	2	31
7	0	01	+5.5	54.1	14.7	45	252	87	11.2	14	42	14	35	21	35	3	36	3	41
8	0	46	+9.8	54.0	14.7	57	254	93	12.2	15	01	14	50	22	18	4	42	4	52
9	1	31	+13.7	54.0	14.7	69	259	97	13.2	15	23	15	09	23	03	5	49	6	02
10	2	18	+17.1	54.1	14.7	81	269	99	14.2	15	50	15	32	23	49	6	55	7	12
11	3	07	+19.8	54.3	14.8	94	22	100	15.2	16	23	16	01	—		7	59	8	20
12	3	58	+21.6	54.5	14.9	106	73	99	16.2	17	04	16	40	0	37	8	59	9	22
13	4	51	+22.5	54.8	14.9	118	83	96	17.2	17	54	17	30	1	28	9	52	10	17
14	5	44	+22.3	55.2	15.0	130	90	91	18.2	18	53	18	31	2	19	10	38	11	01
15	6	37	+21.0	55.7	15.2	142	96	85	19.2	20	00	19	41	3	10	11	16	11	36
16	7	30	+18.6	56.3	15.3	154	101	77	20.2	21	11	20	56	4	00	11	48	12	04
17	8	22	+15.3	56.9	15.5	167	105	67	21.2	22	26	22	15	4	50	12	14	12	26
18	9	14	+11.1	57.6	15.7	179	108	57	22.2	23	42	23	37	5	39	12	37	12	44
19	10	05	+6.3	58.4	15.9	191	110	46	23.2	—		—		6	28	12	58	13	01
20	10	56	+1.1	59.1	16.1	203	111	35	24.2	1	01	1	01	7	17	13	19	13	17
21	11	49	−4.4	59.8	16.3	215	110	24	25.2	2	23	2	27	8	08	13	41	13	34
22	12	44	−9.7	60.4	16.5	227	109	15	26.2	3	47	3	56	9	02	14	06	13	54
23	13	41	−14.6	60.8	16.6	240	105	8	27.2	5	12	5	27	9	59	14	36	14	20
24	14	42	−18.5	61.0	16.6	252	99	2	28.2	6	37	6	57	10	59	15	15	14	54
25	15	45	−21.3	60.8	16.6	264	81	0	29.2	7	56	8	20	12	02	16	04	15	40
26	16	49	−22.5	60.4	16.4	276	277	1	0.8	9	04	9	29	13	04	17	05	16	41
27	17	52	−22.1	59.7	16.3	288	268	4	1.8	9	58	10	20	14	04	18	16	17	54
28	18	53	−20.4	58.8	16.0	301	261	10	2.8	10	38	10	57	15	01	19	31	19	13
29	19	49	−17.5	57.9	15.8	313	256	18	3.8	11	10	11	24	15	53	20	46	20	33
30	20	42	−13.7	56.9	15.5	325	253	27	4.8	11	34	11	44	16	41	21	59	21	51

MERCURY

Day	*R.A.*		*Dec.*	*Diam.*	*Phase*	*Transit*		*5° high*			
								52°		*56°*	
	h	*m*	°	′	%	*h*	*m*	*h*	*m*	*h*	*m*
1	15	40	−21.7	5	84	13	02	16	14	15	42
3	15	51	−22.5	6	82	13	05	16	11	15	37
5	16	02	−23.1	6	80	13	09	16	09	15	33
7	16	13	−23.7	6	77	13	12	16	07	15	28
9	16	24	−24.2	6	74	13	14	16	05	15	24
11	16	34	−24.7	6	71	13	17	16	03	15	21
13	16	44	−25.0	6	67	13	18	16	02	15	18
15	16	53	−25.2	7	62	13	19	16	01	15	16
17	17	01	−25.3	7	57	13	19	16	00	15	15
19	17	08	−25.4	7	51	13	17	15	59	15	13
21	17	13	−25.3	8	44	13	14	15	57	15	12
23	17	16	−25.0	8	36	13	09	15	54	15	11
25	17	16	−24.6	9	28	13	01	15	50	15	09
27	17	14	−24.1	9	19	12	50	15	44	15	05
29	17	09	−23.4	9	11	12	36	15	36	15	01
31	17	00	−22.6	10	5	12	19	15	27	14	54

VENUS

Day	*R.A.*		*Dec.*	*Diam.*	*Phase*	*Transit*		*5° high*			
								52°		*56°*	
	h	*m*	°	′	%	*h*	*m*	*h*	*m*	*h*	*m*
1	15	44	−20.0	11	94	13	06	16	32	16	04
6	16	10	−21.5	11	93	13	12	16	27	15	55
11	16	36	−22.7	11	93	13	19	16	23	15	49
16	17	03	−23.7	11	92	13	26	16	22	15	44
21	17	30	−24.3	11	91	13	33	16	24	15	43
26	17	57	−24.7	11	90	13	41	16	28	15	46
31	18	24	−24.7	12	89	13	48	16	36	15	54

MARS

Day	*R.A.*		*Dec.*	*Diam.*	*Phase*	*Transit*		*5° high*			
								52°		*56°*	
	h	*m*	°	′	%	*h*	*m*	*h*	*m*	*h*	*m*
1	9	50	+14.8	6	90	7	11	0	27	0	18
6	10	01	+14.0	6	90	7	02	0	22	0	14
11	10	11	+13.2	6	90	6	52	0	17	0	09
16	10	20	+12.4	6	90	6	42	0	11	0	04
21	10	30	+11.6	7	90	6	32	0	05	23	58
26	10	38	+10.8	7	90	6	21	23	57	23	51
31	10	47	+10.1	7	90	6	09	23	49	23	44

SUNRISE AND SUNSET

	London 0° 05′		51° 30′		*Bristol* 2° 35′		51° 28′		*Birmingham* 1° 55′		52° 28′		*Manchester* 2° 15′		53° 28′		*Newcastle* 1° 37′		54° 59′		*Glasgow* 4° 14′		55° 52′		*Belfast* 5° 56′		54° 35′	
d	*h*	*m*	*h*	*m*	*h*	*m*	*h*	*m*	*h*	*m*	*h*	*m*	*h*	*m*	*h*	*m*	*h*	*m*	*h*	*m*	*h*	*m*	*h*	*m*	*h*	*m*	*h*	*m*
1	6	53	16	34	7	03	16	44	7	03	16	39	7	07	16	37	7	09	16	30	7	23	16	38	7	25	16	49
2	6	55	16	32	7	05	16	42	7	05	16	37	7	09	16	35	7	11	16	28	7	25	16	35	7	27	16	47
3	6	57	16	30	7	07	16	41	7	07	16	35	7	11	16	33	7	13	16	26	7	27	16	33	7	29	16	45
4	6	58	16	29	7	08	16	39	7	09	16	33	7	13	16	31	7	15	16	24	7	29	16	31	7	31	16	43
5	7	00	16	27	7	10	16	37	7	10	16	31	7	15	16	30	7	17	16	22	7	31	16	29	7	33	16	41
6	7	02	16	25	7	12	16	35	7	12	16	30	7	17	16	28	7	19	16	20	7	33	16	27	7	35	16	39
7	7	04	16	24	7	14	16	34	7	14	16	28	7	19	16	26	7	21	16	18	7	35	16	25	7	37	16	37
8	7	05	16	22	7	15	16	32	7	16	16	26	7	21	16	24	7	24	16	16	7	37	16	23	7	39	16	35
9	7	07	16	20	7	17	16	31	7	18	16	25	7	22	16	22	7	26	16	14	7	39	16	21	7	41	16	33
10	7	09	16	19	7	19	16	29	7	20	16	23	7	24	16	21	7	28	16	12	7	42	16	19	7	43	16	31
11	7	11	16	17	7	21	16	27	7	21	16	21	7	26	16	19	7	30	16	11	7	44	16	17	7	45	16	29
12	7	12	16	16	7	22	16	26	7	23	16	20	7	28	16	17	7	32	16	09	7	46	16	16	7	47	16	28
13	7	14	16	14	7	24	16	24	7	25	16	18	7	30	16	16	7	34	16	07	7	48	16	14	7	49	16	26
14	7	16	16	13	7	26	16	23	7	27	16	17	7	32	16	14	7	36	16	05	7	50	16	12	7	51	16	24
15	7	18	16	12	7	27	16	22	7	29	16	15	7	34	16	13	7	38	16	04	7	52	16	10	7	53	16	23
16	7	19	16	10	7	29	16	20	7	30	16	14	7	36	16	11	7	40	16	02	7	54	16	09	7	55	16	21
17	7	21	16	09	7	31	16	19	7	32	16	12	7	37	16	10	7	41	16	01	7	56	16	07	7	57	16	20
18	7	23	16	08	7	33	16	18	7	34	16	11	7	39	16	08	7	43	15	59	7	58	16	05	7	59	16	18
19	7	24	16	06	7	34	16	16	7	36	16	10	7	41	16	07	7	45	15	58	8	00	16	04	8	01	16	17
20	7	26	16	05	7	36	16	15	7	37	16	09	7	43	16	06	7	47	15	56	8	02	16	02	8	03	16	15
21	7	28	16	04	7	38	16	14	7	39	16	07	7	45	16	04	7	49	15	55	8	04	16	01	8	04	16	14
22	7	29	16	03	7	39	16	13	7	41	16	06	7	46	16	03	7	51	15	53	8	06	15	59	8	06	16	13
23	7	31	16	02	7	41	16	12	7	42	16	05	7	48	16	02	7	53	15	52	8	08	15	58	8	08	16	11
24	7	33	16	01	7	42	16	11	7	44	16	04	7	50	16	01	7	55	15	51	8	10	15	57	8	10	16	10
25	7	34	16	00	7	44	16	10	7	46	16	03	7	52	16	00	7	56	15	50	8	12	15	55	8	12	16	09
26	7	36	15	59	7	45	16	09	7	47	16	02	7	53	15	59	7	58	15	49	8	13	15	54	8	13	16	08
27	7	37	15	58	7	47	16	08	7	49	16	01	7	55	15	58	8	00	15	47	8	15	15	53	8	15	16	07
28	7	39	15	57	7	49	16	07	7	50	16	00	7	56	15	57	8	02	15	46	8	17	15	52	8	17	16	06
29	7	40	15	56	7	50	16	07	7	52	15	59	7	58	15	56	8	03	15	45	8	19	15	51	8	19	16	05
30	7	42	15	56	7	51	16	06	7	53	15	59	8	00	15	55	8	05	15	45	8	21	15	50	8	20	16	04

JUPITER

Day	*R.A.*		*Dec.*		*Transit*		*5° high*			
							52°		*56°*	
	h	*m*	°	′	*h*	*m*	*h*	*m*	*h*	*m*
1	2	12.5	+11	45	23	29	6	01	6	07
11	2	07.4	+11	20	22	45	5	14	5	20
21	2	02.8	+10	58	22	01	4	28	4	34
31	1	59.0	+10	40	21	18	3	44	3	49

Diameters – equatorial 49″ polar 46″

SATURN

Day	*R.A.*		*Dec.*		*Transit*		*5° high*			
							52°		*56°*	
	h	*m*	°	′	*h*	*m*	*h*	*m*	*h*	*m*
1	13	26.2	–6	37	10	46	5	54	6	03
11	13	30.6	–7	02	10	11	5	22	5	31
21	13	34.8	–7	25	9	36	4	49	4	59
31	13	38.8	–7	47	9	01	4	15	4	26

Diameters – equatorial 16″ polar 14″

Rings– major axis 36″ minor axis 8″

URANUS

Day	*R.A.*		*Dec.*		*Transit*		*10° high*			
							52°		*56°*	
	h	*m*	°	′	*h*	*m*	*h*	*m*	*h*	*m*
1	0	05.8	–0	12	21	24	2	20	2	13
11	0	04.9	–0	18	20	43	1	39	1	32
21	0	04.1	–0	22	20	03	0	59	0	52
31	0	03.7	–0	25	19	24	0	19	0	12

Diameter 4″

NEPTUNE

Day	*R.A.*		*Dec.*		*Transit*		*10° high*			
							52°		*56°*	
	h	*m*	°	′	*h*	*m*	*h*	*m*	*h*	*m*
1	22	02.1	–12	38	19	20	22	59	22	37
11	22	02.0	–12	38	18	41	22	20	21	58
21	22	02.1	–12	37	18	02	21	41	21	19
31	22	02.5	–12	35	17	23	21	02	20	40

Diameter 2″

DECEMBER 2011

TWELFTH MONTH, 31 DAYS. *Decem* (ten), tenth month of Roman pre-Julian calendar

1	*Thursday*	Edmund Spenser's poem *The Faerie Queene* was entered on the Stationers' Register 1589	day 335
2	*Friday*	Samuel Taylor Coleridge enlisted in the Light Dragoons cavalry unit 1793	336
3	*Saturday*	*A Streetcar Named Desire*, starring Marlon Brando, opened on Broadway 1947	337
4	*Sunday*	Rainer Maria Rilke, German poet *b.* 1875; Omar Khayyam, Persian astronomer and poet *d.* 1122	338
5	*Monday*	The Guennol Lioness, a Mesopotamian statue, sold for $57m (£28m) 2007	week 49 day 339
6	*Tuesday*	The capstone of the Washington Monument was set in place 1884	340
7	*Wednesday*	Roman orator Marcus Tullius Cicero was executed as an enemy of the state of Rome 43BC	341
8	*Thursday*	The first female actor appeared in a Shakespeare production, as Desdemona in *Othello* 1660	342
9	*Friday*	The *American Minerva*, New York City's first daily newspaper, was founded 1793	343
10	*Saturday*	The first Nobel prizes were awarded, in physics, chemistry, medicine, literature and peace 1901	344
11	*Sunday*	Salman Rushdie appeared outside the UK for the first time since the 1989 *fatwa* against him 1991	345
12	*Monday*	Beethoven recorded in his diary his first music lesson with Joseph Haydn 1792	week 50 day 346
13	*Tuesday*	Gustav Mahler conducted the premiere of his Symphony No. 2 in Berlin 1895	347
14	*Wednesday*	Aphra Behn, one of the first English women to earn her living as a writer, was baptised 1640	348
15	*Thursday*	George Orwell delivered his manuscript of *The Road to Wigan Pier* 1936	349
16	*Friday*	Czech composer Antonin Dvorak's Symphony No. 9 premiered in New York 1893	350
17	*Saturday*	Poet and MP Andrew Marvell petitioned for John Milton's release from prison 1660	351
18	*Sunday*	Thomas Paine was found guilty *in absentia* of seditious libel for his *Rights of Man* 1792	352
19	*Monday*	Édith Piaf, French singer and actor *b.* 1915; Emily Brontë, novelist *d.* 1848	week 51 day 353
20	*Tuesday*	Elvis Presley received a draft notice for the US army 1957	354
21	*Wednesday*	William Wordsworth and his sister Dorothy moved into Dove Cottage in Cumbria 1799	355
22	*Thursday*	Fyodor Dostoevsky faced a firing squad, but was reprieved at the last moment 1849	356
23	*Friday*	André Gide's magazine *NRF* rejected Marcel Proust's *Remembrance of Things Past* 1912	357
24	*Saturday*	Aldous Huxley took LSD for the first time 1955	358
25	*Sunday*	Humphrey Bogart, US actor *b.* 1899; Tristan Tzara, Romanian writer *d.* 1963	359
26	*Monday*	US writer Ambrose Bierce sent his last letter from Mexico before disappearing 1913	week 52 day 360
27	*Tuesday*	J. M. Barrie's play *Peter Pan* premiered in London 1904	361
28	*Wednesday*	French writer Stendhal had the 'day of genius' when he conceived his book *De l'Amour* 1819	362
29	*Thursday*	James Joyce's *A Portrait of the Artist as a Young Man* was first published 1916	363
30	*Friday*	Percy Bysshe Shelley married writer Mary Wollstonecraft Godwin in London 1816	364
31	*Saturday*	Henri Matisse, French painter *b.* 1869; John Wycliffe, British theologian and translator *d.* 1384	365

ASTRONOMICAL PHENOMENA

d	*h*	
4	09	Mercury in inferior conjunction
6	17	Jupiter in conjunction with Moon. Jupiter 5°S.
10	07	Uranus at stationary point
10	15	Total eclipse of Moon
14	02	Mercury at stationary point
17	08	Mars in conjunction with Moon. Mars 8°N.
20	06	Saturn in conjunction with Moon. Saturn 6°N.
22	05	Sun's longitude 270° ♑
23	03	Mercury in conjunction with Moon. Mercury 3°N.
23	06	Mercury at greatest elongation W.22°
25	22	Jupiter at stationary point
27	08	Venus in conjunction with Moon. Venus 6°S.
29	08	Pluto in conjunction

MINIMA OF ALGOL

d	*h*	*d*	*h*	*d*	*h*
2	11.2	13	22.5	25	09.8
5	08.1	16	19.3	28	06.6
8	04.9	19	16.2	31	03.4
11	01.7	22	13.0		

CONSTELLATIONS

The following constellations are near their meridian at

	d	*h*		*d*	*h*
November	1	24	December	16	21
November	15	23	January	1	20
December	1	22	January	16	19

Ursa Major (below the Pole), Ursa Minor (below the Pole), Cassiopeia, Andromeda, Perseus, Triangulum, Aries, Taurus, Cetus and Eridanus

THE MOON

Phases, Apsides and Node	*d*	*h*	*m*
☽ First Quarter	2	09	52
○ Full Moon	10	14	36
☾ Last Quarter	18	00	48
● New Moon	24	18	06
Apogee (405,445 km)	6	01	06
Perigee (364,779 km)	22	02	51

Mean longitude of ascending node on December 1, 255°

THE SUN

s.d. 16′.3

Day	Right Ascension (h m s)	Dec. − (° ′)	Equation of time (m s)	Rise 52° (h m)	Rise 56° (h m)	Transit (h m)	Set 52° (h m)	Set 56° (h m)	Sidereal time (h m s)	Transit of first point of Aries (h m s)
1	16 26 46	21 42	+11 17	7 45	8 06	11 49	15 52	15 31	4 38 02	19 18 47
2	16 31 04	21 52	+10 54	7 46	8 08	11 49	15 52	15 30	4 41 59	19 14 52
3	16 35 24	22 01	+10 31	7 48	8 09	11 50	15 51	15 30	4 45 55	19 10 56
4	16 39 44	22 09	+10 08	7 49	8 11	11 50	15 51	15 29	4 49 52	19 07 00
5	16 44 04	22 17	+9 44	7 50	8 12	11 50	15 50	15 28	4 53 48	19 03 04
6	16 48 26	22 25	+9 19	7 52	8 14	11 51	15 50	15 28	4 57 45	18 59 08
7	16 52 47	22 32	+8 54	7 53	8 15	11 51	15 49	15 27	5 01 42	18 55 12
8	16 57 10	22 39	+8 28	7 54	8 17	11 52	15 49	15 26	5 05 38	18 51 16
9	17 01 32	22 45	+8 02	7 55	8 18	11 52	15 49	15 26	5 09 35	18 47 20
10	17 05 55	22 51	+7 36	7 56	8 19	11 53	15 49	15 26	5 13 31	18 43 24
11	17 10 19	22 57	+7 09	7 58	8 21	11 53	15 48	15 25	5 17 28	18 39 28
12	17 14 43	23 02	+6 41	7 59	8 22	11 54	15 48	15 25	5 21 24	18 35 32
13	17 19 07	23 06	+6 13	8 00	8 23	11 54	15 48	15 25	5 25 21	18 31 37
14	17 23 32	23 10	+5 45	8 00	8 24	11 54	15 48	15 25	5 29 17	18 27 41
15	17 27 57	23 14	+5 17	8 01	8 25	11 55	15 48	15 25	5 33 14	18 23 45
16	17 32 23	23 17	+4 48	8 02	8 26	11 55	15 49	15 25	5 37 11	18 19 49
17	17 36 48	23 20	+4 19	8 03	8 27	11 56	15 49	15 25	5 41 07	18 15 53
18	17 41 14	23 22	+3 50	8 04	8 27	11 56	15 49	15 25	5 45 04	18 11 57
19	17 45 40	23 24	+3 20	8 04	8 28	11 57	15 49	15 26	5 49 00	18 08 01
20	17 50 06	23 25	+2 51	8 05	8 29	11 57	15 50	15 26	5 52 57	18 04 05
21	17 54 32	23 26	+2 21	8 06	8 29	11 58	15 50	15 26	5 56 53	18 00 09
22	17 58 59	23 26	+1 51	8 06	8 30	11 58	15 51	15 27	6 00 50	17 56 13
23	18 03 25	23 26	+1 21	8 07	8 30	11 59	15 51	15 27	6 04 46	17 52 17
24	18 07 52	23 25	+0 51	8 07	8 31	11 59	15 52	15 28	6 08 43	17 48 21
25	18 12 18	23 24	+0 21	8 07	8 31	12 00	15 53	15 29	6 12 40	17 44 26
26	18 16 45	23 23	−0 09	8 08	8 31	12 00	15 53	15 30	6 16 36	17 40 30
27	18 21 11	23 21	−0 39	8 08	8 32	12 01	15 54	15 30	6 20 33	17 36 34
28	18 25 37	23 18	−1 08	8 08	8 32	12 01	15 55	15 31	6 24 29	17 32 38
29	18 30 03	23 15	−1 38	8 08	8 32	12 02	15 56	15 32	6 28 26	17 28 42
30	18 34 29	23 12	−2 07	8 08	8 32	12 02	15 57	15 33	6 32 22	17 24 46
31	18 38 55	23 08	−2 36	8 08	8 32	12 03	15 58	15 34	6 36 19	17 20 50

DURATION OF TWILIGHT (in minutes)

Latitude	52°	56°	52°	56°	52°	56°	52°	56°
	1 December		*11 December*		*21 December*		*31 December*	
Civil	40	45	41	47	41	47	41	47
Nautical	82	93	84	96	85	97	84	96
Astronomical	123	138	125	141	126	142	125	141

THE NIGHT SKY

Mercury is unsuitably placed for observation at first, as it passes through inferior conjunction on the 4th. After the first ten days of the month Mercury becomes visible as a morning object low above the south-eastern horizon around the beginning of morning civil twilight. During this period its magnitude brightens from +1.1 to −0.4.

Venus, magnitude −4.0, is now moving out away from the Sun and is visible for some time after sunset in the early evenings, though only at a relatively low altitude. The waxing crescent Moon passes 6 degrees north of Venus on the 27th.

Mars, its magnitude brightening from +0.7 to +0.2, is visible in the eastern sky before midnight, still in the constellation of Leo.

Moon. On the 17th the Moon, at Last Quarter, passes 8 degrees south of the planet.

Jupiter, magnitude −2.7, continues to be visible as a brilliant object in the night sky, though by the end of the year it has sunk too low in the western sky after about 01h. The waxing gibbous Moon passes about 4 degrees north of Jupiter on the 6th.

Saturn, magnitude +0.8, can now be seen in the south-eastern quadrant of the sky after about 04h at the beginning of the month and shortly after 02h by the end of the month. The old crescent Moon passes 7 degrees south of Mars on the 20th.

Meteors. The maximum of the well-known Geminid meteor shower occurs on the 14th. The waning crescent Moon will provide some interference after about 20h.

THE MOON

Day	R.A.		Dec.	Hor. Par.	Semi-diam.	Sun's Co-Long.	PA. of Br. Limb	Ph.	Age	Rise				Transit		Set			
										52°		56°				52°		56°	
	h	m	°	′	′	°	°	%	d	h	m	h	m	h	m	h	m	h	m
1	21	32	−9.4	56.1	15.3	337	250	36	5.8	11	55	12	01	17	26	23	10	23	05
2	22	19	−4.9	55.4	15.1	349	248	46	6.8	12	13	12	15	18	09	—		—	
3	23	04	−0.2	54.8	14.9	1	248	56	7.8	12	30	12	28	18	51	0	18	0	18
4	23	48	+4.3	54.4	14.8	14	248	65	8.8	12	47	12	42	19	33	1	25	1	29
5	0	33	+8.7	54.2	14.8	26	249	74	9.8	13	06	12	56	20	15	2	31	2	39
6	1	18	+12.7	54.1	14.7	38	251	82	10.8	13	27	13	14	20	59	3	37	3	50
7	2	05	+16.3	54.1	14.8	50	254	88	11.8	13	52	13	35	21	44	4	44	5	00
8	2	53	+19.1	54.3	14.8	62	258	94	12.8	14	23	14	02	22	33	5	49	6	08
9	3	44	+21.2	54.6	14.9	74	262	98	13.8	15	01	14	38	23	22	6	51	7	13
10	4	36	+22.4	55.0	15.0	86	265	100	14.8	15	49	15	25	—		7	47	8	11
11	5	30	+22.4	55.4	15.1	99	97	100	15.8	16	46	16	23	0	14	8	36	9	00
12	6	24	+21.4	55.8	15.2	111	99	98	16.8	17	51	17	31	1	06	9	18	9	38
13	7	17	+19.3	56.3	15.3	123	103	94	17.8	19	02	18	45	1	57	9	51	10	08
14	8	10	+16.1	56.8	15.5	135	107	89	18.8	20	16	20	04	2	48	10	19	10	32
15	9	02	+12.1	57.3	15.6	147	110	81	19.8	21	31	21	24	3	37	10	43	10	51
16	9	53	+7.5	57.8	15.7	159	112	72	20.8	22	48	22	46	4	25	11	04	11	08
17	10	43	+2.4	58.3	15.9	171	113	62	21.8	—		—		5	13	11	24	11	24
18	11	34	−2.9	58.8	16.0	184	113	50	22.8	0	06	0	09	6	02	11	45	11	40
19	12	27	−8.1	59.3	16.2	196	112	39	23.8	1	26	1	34	6	53	12	07	11	58
20	13	21	−13.0	59.7	16.3	208	110	28	24.8	2	48	3	01	7	47	12	34	12	20
21	14	19	−17.2	60.0	16.3	220	107	18	25.8	4	11	4	29	8	43	13	07	12	49
22	15	19	−20.3	60.1	16.4	232	102	10	26.8	5	31	5	53	9	43	13	50	13	27
23	16	21	−22.2	60.0	16.4	244	98	4	27.8	6	43	7	08	10	44	14	44	14	19
24	17	24	−22.5	59.7	16.3	257	97	1	28.8	7	43	8	07	11	45	15	50	15	26
25	18	26	−21.3	59.2	16.1	269	236	0	0.3	8	31	8	52	12	44	17	04	16	43
26	19	25	−18.9	58.5	16.0	281	251	2	1.3	9	07	9	24	13	39	18	20	18	05
27	20	21	−15.4	57.8	15.7	293	250	6	2.3	9	35	9	47	14	31	19	37	19	25
28	21	13	−11.2	56.9	15.5	305	247	13	3.3	9	58	10	06	15	18	20	50	20	44
29	22	02	−6.7	56.2	15.3	318	246	20	4.3	10	17	10	21	16	03	22	01	21	59
30	22	48	−1.9	55.5	15.1	330	245	29	5.3	10	35	10	35	16	46	23	10	23	12
31	23	34	+2.8	54.9	15.0	342	245	38	6.3	10	53	10	49	17	28	—		—	

MERCURY

Day	R.A.		Dec.	Diam.	Phase	Transit		5° high			
								52°		56°	
	h	m	°	″	%	h	m	h	m	h	m
1	17	00	−22.6	10	5	12	19	15	27	14	54
3	16	50	−21.6	10	1	12	00	15	16	14	46
5	16	38	−20.6	10	0	11	41	8	18	8	46
7	16	28	−19.7	10	3	11	23	7	53	8	19
9	16	19	−18.9	9	9	11	07	7	32	7	57
11	16	13	−18.4	9	17	10	54	7	15	7	39
13	16	10	−18.2	9	26	10	44	7	03	7	27
15	16	10	−18.2	8	35	10	36	6	56	7	19
17	16	12	−18.4	8	43	10	31	6	52	7	16
19	16	17	−18.7	7	51	10	29	6	52	7	17
21	16	23	−19.2	7	57	10	27	6	54	7	19
23	16	31	−19.7	7	63	10	27	6	58	7	25
25	16	40	−20.3	6	68	10	28	7	03	7	31
27	16	49	−20.8	6	72	10	30	7	09	7	39
29	16	59	−21.4	6	76	10	33	7	16	7	47
31	17	10	−21.9	6	79	10	36	7	24	7	56

VENUS

Day	R.A.		Dec.	Diam.	Phase	Transit		5° high			
								52°		56°	
	h	m	°	″	%	h	m	h	m	h	m
1	18	24	−24.7	12	89	13	48	16	36	15	54
6	18	52	−24.5	12	88	13	56	16	46	16	06
11	19	19	−23.9	12	87	14	03	16	59	16	21
16	19	45	−23.0	12	86	14	10	17	15	16	40
21	20	12	−21.9	12	85	14	17	17	31	17	00
26	20	37	−20.4	13	84	14	23	17	49	17	21
31	21	02	−18.8	13	83	14	28	18	07	17	42

MARS

Day	R.A.		Dec.	Diam.	Phase	Transit		5° high			
								52°		56°	
	h	m	°	″	%	h	m	h	m	h	m
1	10	47	+10.1	7	90	6	09	23	49	23	44
6	10	55	+ 9.4	7	90	5	58	23	41	23	37
11	11	03	+ 8.7	8	90	5	46	23	32	23	29
16	11	10	+ 8.1	8	90	5	33	23	23	23	19
21	11	16	+ 7.6	8	91	5	20	23	12	23	09
26	11	22	+ 7.1	9	91	5	06	23	01	22	58
31	11	27	+ 6.7	9	91	4	52	22	48	22	46

SUNRISE AND SUNSET

	London		*Bristol*		*Birmingham*		*Manchester*		*Newcastle*		*Glasgow*		*Belfast*	
	0° 05′	*51° 30′*	*2° 35′*	*51° 28′*	*1° 55′*	*52° 28′*	*2° 15′*	*53° 28′*	*1° 37′*	*54° 59′*	*4° 14′*	*55° 52′*	*5° 56′*	*54° 35′*
d	*h m*	*h m*	*h m*	*h m*	*h m*	*h m*	*h m*	*h m*	*h m*	*h m*	*h m*	*h m*	*h m*	*h m*
1	7 43	15 55	7 53	16 05	7 55	15 58	8 01	15 54	8 07	15 44	8 22	15 49	8 22	16 03
2	7 44	15 54	7 54	16 05	7 56	15 57	8 03	15 54	8 08	15 43	8 24	15 48	8 23	16 02
3	7 46	15 54	7 56	16 04	7 58	15 57	8 04	15 53	8 10	15 42	8 26	15 47	8 25	16 02
4	7 47	15 53	7 57	16 04	7 59	15 56	8 06	15 52	8 11	15 41	8 27	15 47	8 26	16 01
5	7 48	15 53	7 58	16 03	8 00	15 56	8 07	15 52	8 13	15 41	8 29	15 46	8 28	16 00
6	7 50	15 53	8 00	16 03	8 02	15 55	8 08	15 51	8 14	15 40	8 30	15 45	8 29	16 00
7	7 51	15 52	8 01	16 02	8 03	15 55	8 10	15 51	8 16	15 40	8 31	15 45	8 31	15 59
8	7 52	15 52	8 02	16 02	8 04	15 54	8 11	15 50	8 17	15 39	8 33	15 44	8 32	15 59
9	7 53	15 52	8 03	16 02	8 05	15 54	8 12	15 50	8 18	15 39	8 34	15 44	8 33	15 58
10	7 54	15 51	8 04	16 02	8 06	15 54	8 13	15 50	8 19	15 39	8 35	15 43	8 34	15 58
11	7 55	15 51	8 05	16 01	8 08	15 54	8 14	15 50	8 21	15 38	8 37	15 43	8 35	15 58
12	7 56	15 51	8 06	16 01	8 09	15 54	8 15	15 50	8 22	15 38	8 38	15 43	8 37	15 58
13	7 57	15 51	8 07	16 01	8 10	15 54	8 16	15 49	8 23	15 38	8 39	15 43	8 38	15 58
14	7 58	15 51	8 08	16 01	8 11	15 54	8 17	15 49	8 24	15 38	8 40	15 43	8 39	15 58
15	7 59	15 51	8 09	16 01	8 11	15 54	8 18	15 50	8 25	15 38	8 41	15 43	8 40	15 58
16	8 00	15 51	8 10	16 02	8 12	15 54	8 19	15 50	8 26	15 38	8 42	15 43	8 40	15 58
17	8 01	15 52	8 11	16 02	8 13	15 54	8 20	15 50	8 26	15 38	8 43	15 43	8 41	15 58
18	8 01	15 52	8 11	16 02	8 14	15 54	8 21	15 50	8 27	15 38	8 43	15 43	8 42	15 58
19	8 02	15 52	8 12	16 02	8 15	15 55	8 21	15 50	8 28	15 39	8 44	15 43	8 43	15 59
20	8 03	15 53	8 13	16 03	8 15	15 55	8 22	15 51	8 29	15 39	8 45	15 44	8 43	15 59
21	8 03	15 53	8 13	16 03	8 16	15 55	8 23	15 51	8 29	15 40	8 45	15 44	8 44	15 59
22	8 04	15 54	8 14	16 04	8 16	15 56	8 23	15 52	8 30	15 40	8 46	15 45	8 45	16 00
23	8 04	15 54	8 14	16 04	8 17	15 56	8 24	15 52	8 30	15 41	8 46	15 45	8 45	16 00
24	8 05	15 55	8 15	16 05	8 17	15 57	8 24	15 53	8 31	15 41	8 47	15 46	8 45	16 01
25	8 05	15 55	8 15	16 06	8 17	15 58	8 24	15 54	8 31	15 42	8 47	15 47	8 46	16 02
26	8 05	15 56	8 15	16 06	8 18	15 58	8 25	15 54	8 31	15 43	8 47	15 47	8 46	16 02
27	8 06	15 57	8 15	16 07	8 18	15 59	8 25	15 55	8 31	15 43	8 48	15 48	8 46	16 03
28	8 06	15 58	8 16	16 08	8 18	16 00	8 25	15 56	8 31	15 44	8 48	15 49	8 46	16 04
29	8 06	15 59	8 16	16 09	8 18	16 01	8 25	15 57	8 32	15 45	8 48	15 50	8 46	16 05
30	8 06	16 00	8 16	16 10	8 18	16 02	8 25	15 58	8 32	15 46	8 48	15 51	8 46	16 06
31	8 06	16 00	8 16	16 11	8 18	16 03	8 25	15 59	8 31	15 47	8 48	15 52	8 46	16 07

JUPITER

Day	*R.A.*	*Dec.*	*Transit*	*5° high*	
				52°	*56°*
	h m	*° ′*	*h m*	*h m*	*h m*
1	1 59.0	+10 40	21 18	3 44	3 49
11	1 56.4	+10 29	20 37	3 01	3 06
21	1 55.0	+10 24	19 56	2 20	2 25
31	1 55.0	+10 27	19 17	1 41	1 46

Diameters – equatorial 46″ polar 43″

SATURN

Day	*R.A.*	*Dec.*	*Transit*	*5° high*	
				52°	*56°*
	h m	*° ′*	*h m*	*h m*	*h m*
1	13 38.8	−7 47	9 01	4 15	4 26
11	13 42.4	−8 06	8 25	3 41	3 52
21	13 45.6	−8 22	7 49	3 07	3 18
31	13 48.4	−8 35	7 12	2 31	2 42

Diameters – equatorial 16″ polar 15″
Rings – major axis 37″ minor axis 9″

URANUS

Day	*R.A.*	*Dec.*	*Transit*	*10° high*	
				52°	*56°*
	h m	*° ′*	*h m*	*h m*	*h m*
1	0 03.7	−0 25	19 24	0 19	0 12
11	0 03.5	−0 25	18 44	23 36	23 28
21	0 03.7	−0 24	18 05	22 57	22 49
31	0 04.2	−0 20	17 26	22 18	22 11

Diameter 4″

NEPTUNE

Day	*R.A.*	*Dec.*	*Transit*	*10° high*	
				52°	*56°*
	h m	*° ′*	*h m*	*h m*	*h m*
1	22 02.5	−12 35	17 23	21 02	20 40
11	22 03.1	−12 32	16 44	20 23	20 02
21	22 03.8	−12 28	16 05	19 45	19 24
31	22 04.8	−12 23	15 27	19 08	18 46

Diameter 2″

RISING AND SETTING TIMES

TABLE 1. SEMI-DIURNAL ARCS (HOUR ANGLES AT RISING/SETTING)

Dec.	*Latitude* 0°	10°	20°	30°	40°	45°	50°	52°	54°	56°	58°	60°	*Dec.*
	h m	*h m*	*h m*	*h m*	*h m*	*h m*	*h m*	*h m*	*h m*	*h m*	*h m*	*h m*	
0°	6 00	6 00	6 00	6 00	6 00	6 00	6 00	6 00	6 00	6 00	6 00	6 00	0°
1°	6 00	6 01	6 01	6 02	6 03	6 04	6 05	6 05	6 06	6 06	6 06	6 07	1°
2°	6 00	6 01	6 03	6 05	6 07	6 08	6 10	6 10	6 11	6 12	6 13	6 14	2°
3°	6 00	6 02	6 04	6 07	6 10	6 12	6 14	6 15	6 17	6 18	6 19	6 21	3°
4°	6 00	6 03	6 06	6 09	6 13	6 16	6 19	6 21	6 22	6 24	6 26	6 28	4°
5°	6 00	6 04	6 07	6 12	6 17	6 20	6 24	6 26	6 28	6 30	6 32	6 35	5°
6°	6 00	6 04	6 09	6 14	6 20	6 24	6 29	6 31	6 33	6 36	6 39	6 42	6°
7°	6 00	6 05	6 10	6 16	6 24	6 28	6 34	6 36	6 39	6 42	6 45	6 49	7°
8°	6 00	6 06	6 12	6 19	6 27	6 32	6 39	6 41	6 45	6 48	6 52	6 56	8°
9°	6 00	6 06	6 13	6 21	6 31	6 36	6 44	6 47	6 50	6 54	6 59	7 04	9°
10°	6 00	6 07	6 15	6 23	6 34	6 41	6 49	6 52	6 56	7 01	7 06	7 11	10°
11°	6 00	6 08	6 16	6 26	6 38	6 45	6 54	6 58	7 02	7 07	7 12	7 19	11°
12°	6 00	6 09	6 18	6 28	6 41	6 49	6 59	7 03	7 08	7 13	7 20	7 26	12°
13°	6 00	6 09	6 19	6 31	6 45	6 53	7 04	7 09	7 14	7 20	7 27	7 34	13°
14°	6 00	6 10	6 21	6 33	6 48	6 58	7 09	7 14	7 20	7 27	7 34	7 42	14°
15°	6 00	6 11	6 22	6 36	6 52	7 02	7 14	7 20	7 27	7 34	7 42	7 51	15°
16°	6 00	6 12	6 24	6 38	6 56	7 07	7 20	7 26	7 33	7 41	7 49	7 59	16°
17°	6 00	6 12	6 26	6 41	6 59	7 11	7 25	7 32	7 40	7 48	7 57	8 08	17°
18°	6 00	6 13	6 27	6 43	7 03	7 16	7 31	7 38	7 46	7 55	8 05	8 17	18°
19°	6 00	6 14	6 29	6 46	7 07	7 21	7 37	7 45	7 53	8 03	8 14	8 26	19°
20°	6 00	6 15	6 30	6 49	7 11	7 25	7 43	7 51	8 00	8 11	8 22	8 36	20°
21°	6 00	6 16	6 32	6 51	7 15	7 30	7 49	7 58	8 08	8 19	8 32	8 47	21°
22°	6 00	6 16	6 34	6 54	7 19	7 35	7 55	8 05	8 15	8 27	8 41	8 58	22°
23°	6 00	6 17	6 36	6 57	7 23	7 40	8 02	8 12	8 23	8 36	8 51	9 09	23°
24°	6 00	6 18	6 37	7 00	7 28	7 46	8 08	8 19	8 31	8 45	9 02	9 22	24°
25°	6 00	6 19	6 39	7 02	7 32	7 51	8 15	8 27	8 40	8 55	9 13	9 35	25°
26°	6 00	6 20	6 41	7 05	7 37	7 57	8 22	8 35	8 49	9 05	9 25	9 51	26°
27°	6 00	6 21	6 43	7 08	7 41	8 03	8 30	8 43	8 58	9 16	9 39	10 08	27°
28°	6 00	6 22	6 45	7 12	7 46	8 08	8 37	8 52	9 08	9 28	9 53	10 28	28°
29°	6 00	6 22	6 47	7 15	7 51	8 15	8 45	9 01	9 19	9 41	10 10	10 55	29°
30°	6 00	6 23	6 49	7 18	7 56	8 21	8 54	9 11	9 30	9 55	10 30	12 00	30°
35°	6 00	6 28	6 59	7 35	8 24	8 58	9 46	10 15	10 58	12 00	12 00	12 00	35°
40°	6 00	6 34	7 11	7 56	8 59	9 48	12 00	12 00	12 00	12 00	12 00	12 00	40°
45°	6 00	6 41	7 25	8 21	9 48	12 00	12 00	12 00	12 00	12 00	12 00	12 00	45°
50°	6 00	6 49	7 43	8 54	12 00	12 00	12 00	12 00	12 00	12 00	12 00	12 00	50°
55°	6 00	6 58	8 05	9 42	12 00	12 00	12 00	12 00	12 00	12 00	12 00	12 00	55°
60°	6 00	7 11	8 36	12 00	12 00	12 00	12 00	12 00	12 00	12 00	12 00	12 00	60°
65°	6 00	7 29	9 25	12 00	12 00	12 00	12 00	12 00	12 00	12 00	12 00	12 00	65°
70°	6 00	7 56	12 00	12 00	12 00	12 00	12 00	12 00	12 00	12 00	12 00	12 00	70°
75°	6 00	8 45	12 00	12 00	12 00	12 00	12 00	12 00	12 00	12 00	12 00	12 00	75°
80°	6 00	12 00	12 00	12 00	12 00	12 00	12 00	12 00	12 00	12 00	12 00	12 00	80°

Note: If latitude and declination are of the same sign, take out the respondent directly. If they are of opposite signs, subtract the respondent from 12h.

Table 1 gives the complete range of declinations in case any user wishes to calculate semi-diurnal arcs for bodies other than the Sun and Moon.

Example:

Lat.	Dec.	Semi-diurnal arc
+52°	+20°	7h 51m
+52°	−20°	4h 09m

TABLE 2. CORRECTION FOR REFRACTION AND SEMI-DIAMETER

	m	*m*	*m*	*m*	*m*	*m*	*m*	*m*	*m*	*m*	*m*	*m*	*m*
0°	3	3	4	4	4	5	5	5	6	6	6	7	0°
10°	3	3	4	4	4	5	5	6	6	6	7	7	10°
20°	4	4	4	4	5	5	6	7	7	8	8	9	20°
25°	4	4	4	4	5	6	7	8	8	9	11	13	25°
30°	4	4	4	5	6	7	8	9	11	14	21	—	30°

SUNRISE AND SUNSET

The local mean time of sunrise or sunset may be found by obtaining the hour angle from Table 1 and applying it to the time of transit. The hour angle is negative for sunrise and positive for sunset. A small correction to the hour angle, which always has the effect of increasing it numerically, is necessary to allow for the Sun's semi-diameter (16′) and for refraction (34′); it is obtained from Table 2. The resulting local mean time may be converted into the standard time of the country by taking the difference between the longitude of the standard meridian of the country and that of the place, adding it to the local mean time if the place is west of the standard meridian, and subtracting it if the place is east.

Example– Required the New Zealand Mean Time (12h fast on GMT) of sunset on May 23 at Auckland, latitude 36° 50′ S. (or minus), longitude 11h 39m E. Taking the declination as +20°.6 (page 1247), we find

		h	*m*
New Zealand Standard Time	+	12	00
Longitude	–	11	39
Longitudinal Correction	+	0	21
Tabular entry for Lat. 30° and Dec. 20°, opposite signs	+	5	11
Proportional part for 6° 50′ of Lat.	–		15
Proportional part for 0°.6 of Dec.	–		2
Correction (Table 2)	+		4
Hour angle		4	58
Sun transits (page 1247)		11	57
Longitudinal correction	+		21
New Zealand Mean Time		17	16

MOONRISE AND MOONSET

It is possible to calculate the times of moonrise and moonset using Table 1, though the method is more complicated because the apparent motion of the Moon is much more rapid and also more variable than that of the Sun.

TABLE 3. LONGITUDE CORRECTION

X / *A*	40*m*	45*m*	50*m*	55*m*	60*m*	65*m*	70*m*
h	*m*	*m*	*m*	*m*	*m*	*m*	*m*
1	2	2	2	2	3	3	3
2	3	4	4	5	5	5	6
3	5	6	6	7	8	8	9
4	7	8	8	9	10	11	12
5	8	9	10	11	13	14	15
6	10	11	13	14	15	16	18
7	12	13	15	16	18	19	20
8	13	15	17	18	20	22	23
9	15	17	19	21	23	24	26
10	17	19	21	23	25	27	29
11	18	21	23	25	28	30	32
12	20	23	25	28	30	33	35
13	22	24	27	30	33	35	38
14	23	26	29	32	35	38	41
15	25	28	31	34	38	41	44
16	27	30	33	37	40	43	47
17	28	32	35	39	43	46	50
18	30	34	38	41	45	49	53
19	32	36	40	44	48	51	55
20	33	38	42	46	50	54	58
21	35	39	44	48	53	57	61
22	37	41	46	50	55	60	64
23	38	43	48	53	58	62	67
24	40	45	50	55	60	65	70

The parallax of the Moon, about 57′, is near to the sum of the semi-diameter and refraction but has the opposite effect on these times. It is thus convenient to neglect all three quantities in the method outlined below.

Notation

ϕ = latitude of observer
λ = longitude of observer (measured positively towards the west)
T_{-1} = time of transit of Moon on previous day
T_0 = time of transit of Moon on day in question
T_1 = time of transit of Moon on following day
δ_0 = approximate declination of Moon
δ_R = declination of Moon at moonrise
δ_S = declination of Moon at moonset
h_0 = approximate hour angle of Moon
h_R = hour angle of Moon at moonrise
h_S = hour angle of Moon at moonset
t_R = time of moonrise
t_S = time of moonset

Method

1. With arguments ϕ, δ_0 enter Table 1 on page 1278 to determine h_0 where h_0 is negative for moonrise and positive for moonset.

2. Form approximate times from
   $t_R = T_0 + \lambda + h_0$
   $t_S = T_0 + \lambda + h_0$

3. Determine δ_R, δ_S for times t_R, t_S respectively.

4. Re-enter Table 1 (as above) with
   (*a*) arguments ϕ, δ_R to determine h_R
   (*b*) arguments ϕ, δ_S to determine h_S

5. Form $t_R = T_0 + \lambda + h_R + AX$
   $t_S = T_0 + \lambda + h_S + AX$

where $A = (\lambda + h)$

and $X = (T_0 - T_{-1})$ if $(\lambda + h)$ is negative
$X = (T_1 - T_0)$ if $(\lambda + h)$ is positive

AX is the respondent in Table 3.

Example – To find the times (GMT) of moonrise and moonset at Vancouver (ϕ =+49°, λ = +8h 12m) on 2011 January 29. The starting data (page 1232) are

T_{-1} = 7h 22m
T_0 = 8h 18m
T_1 = 9h 13m
δ_0 = –24°

1. h_0 = 3h 56m
2. Approximate values
   t_R = 29d 08h 18m + 8h 12m + (–3h 56m)
   = 29d 12h 34m
   t_S = 29d 08h 18m + 8h 12m + (+3h 56m)
   = 29d 20h 26m
3. δ_R = –24°.0
   δ_S = –24°.1
4. h_R = – 3h 56m
   h_S = +3h 55m
5. t_R = 29d 08h 18m + 8h 12m + (–3h 56m) + 9m
   = 29d 12h 43m
   t_S = 29d 08h 18m + 8h 12m + (+3h 55m) + 29m
   = 29d 20h 54m

To get the LMT of the phenomenon the longitude is subtracted from the GMT thus:

Moonrise = 29d 12h 43m – 8h 12m = 29d 04h 31m
Moonset = 29d 20h 54m – 8h 12m = 29d 12h 42m

ECLIPSES 2011

ECLIPSES

During 2011 there will be six eclipses, four of the Sun and two of the Moon. (Penumbral eclipses of the Moon are not mentioned in this section as they are so difficult to observe.)

1. A partial eclipse of the Sun on January 4 is visible from most of Asia, Europe, and most of northern and central Africa. The partial phase begins at 06h 40m and ends at 11h 01m. From the British Isles the eclipse begins before sunrise. At Greenwich the eclipse ends at 09h 31m and at Edinburgh at 09h 34m.
2. A partial eclipse of the Sun on June 1 is visible from eastern and northern Asia, northern Canada and Greenland. The eclipse begins at 19h 25m and ends at 23h 07m.
3. A total eclipse of the Moon on June 15 is visible from most of South America except the extreme north-west, Europe, Africa, most of Asia except the northern and eastern part, and Australasia. The partial phase begins at 18h 22m and ends at 22h 03m. Totality begins at 19h 22m and ends at 21h 03m.
4. A partial eclipse of the Sun on July 1 is only visible from a small area of ocean lying well south of South Africa and adjacent to Antarctica. The eclipse begins at 07h 54m and ends at 09h 23m.
5. A partial eclipse of the Sun on November 25 is visible from the extreme south of south Africa, Tasmania, most of New Zealand, and Antarctica. The eclipse begins at 04h 23m and ends at 08h 17m.
6. A total eclipse of the Moon on December 10 is visible from Australasia, Asia, Europe, most of Africa except some extreme parts of the northwest and southwest of the continent, North America, and most of central America. The partial phase begins at 12h 45m and ends at 16h 18m. Totality begins at 14h 06m and ends at 14h 58m.

POSITIONS OF STARS

The positions of heavenly bodies on the celestial sphere are defined by two co-ordinates, right ascension and declination, which are analogous to longitude and latitude on the surface of the Earth. If we imagine the plane of the terrestrial equator extended indefinitely, it will cut the celestial sphere in a great circle known as the celestial equator. Similarly the plane of the Earth's orbit, when extended, cuts in the great circle called the ecliptic. The two intersections of these circles are known as the First Point of Aries and the First Point of Libra. If from any star a perpendicular is drawn to the celestial equator, the length of this perpendicular is the star's declination. The arc, measured eastwards along the equator from the First Point of Aries to the foot of this perpendicular, is the right ascension. An alternative definition of right ascension is that it is the angle at the celestial pole (where the Earth's axis, if prolonged, would meet the sphere) between the great circles to the First Point of Aries and to the star.

The plane of the Earth's equator has a slow movement, so that our reference system for right ascension and declination is not fixed. The consequent alteration in these quantities from year to year is called precession. In right ascension it is an increase of about 3 seconds a year for equatorial stars, and larger or smaller changes in either direction for stars near the poles, depending on the right ascension of the star. In declination it varies between +20″ and −20″ according to the right ascension of the star.

A star or other body crosses the meridian when the sidereal time is equal to its right ascension. The altitude is then a maximum, and may be deduced by remembering that the altitude of the elevated pole is numerically equal to the latitude, while that of the equator at its intersection with the meridian is equal to the co-latitude, or complement of the latitude.

Thus in London (lat. 51° 30′) the meridian altitude of Sirius is found as follows:

	°	′
Altitude of equator	38	30
Declination south	16	43
Difference	21	47

The altitude of Capella (Dec. +46° 00′) at lower transit is:

Altitude of pole	51	30
Polar distance of star	44	00
Difference	7	30

The brightness of a heavenly body is denoted by its magnitude. Omitting the exceptionally bright stars Sirius and Canopus, the twenty brightest stars are of the first magnitude, while the faintest stars visible to the naked eye are of the sixth magnitude. The magnitude scale is a precise one, as a difference of five magnitudes represents a ratio of 100 to 1 in brightness. Typical second magnitude stars are Polaris and the stars in the belt of Orion. The scale is most easily fixed in memory by comparing the stars with Norton's *Star Atlas*. The stars Sirius and Canopus and the planets Venus and Jupiter are so bright that their magnitudes are expressed by negative numbers. A small telescope will show stars down to the ninth or tenth magnitude, while stars fainter than the twentieth magnitude may be photographed by long exposures with the largest telescopes.

MEAN AND SIDEREAL TIME

The length of a sidereal day in mean time is 23h 56m 04s.09. Hence 1h MT = 1h+9^s.86 ST and 1h ST = 1h − 9^s.83 MT.

Acceleration

h	*m*	*s*	*m*	*s*	*s*
1	0	10	0	00	0
2	0	20	3	02	1
3	0	30	9	07	2
4	0	39	15	13	3
5	0	49	21	18	4
6	0	59	27	23	5
7	1	09	33	28	6
8	1	19	39	34	7
9	1	29	45	39	8
10	1	39	51	44	9
11	1	48	57	49	10
12	1	58	60	00	
13	2	08			
14	2	18			
15	2	28			
16	2	38			
17	2	48			
18	2	57			
19	3	07			
20	3	17			
21	3	27			
22	3	37			
23	3	47			
24	3	57			

Retardation

h	*m*	*s*	*m*	*s*	*s*
1	0	10	0	00	0
2	0	20	3	03	1
3	0	29	9	09	2
4	0	39	15	15	3
5	0	49	21	21	4
6	0	59	27	28	5
7	1	09	33	34	6
8	1	19	39	40	7
9	1	28	45	46	8
10	1	38	51	53	9
11	1	48	57	59	10
12	1	58	60	00	
13	2	08			
14	2	18			
15	2	27			
16	2	37			
17	2	47			
18	2	57			
19	3	07			
20	3	17			
21	3	26			
22	3	36			
23	3	46			
24	3	56			

To convert an interval of mean time to the corresponding interval of sidereal time, enter the acceleration table with the given mean time (taking the hours and the minutes and seconds separately) and add the acceleration obtained to the given mean time. To convert an interval of sidereal time to the corresponding interval of mean time, take out the retardation for the given sidereal time and subtract.

The columns for the minutes and seconds of the argument are in the form known as critical tables. To use these tables, find in the appropriate left-hand column the two entries between which the given number of minutes and seconds lies; the quantity in the right-hand column between these two entries is the required acceleration or retardation. Thus the acceleration for 11m 26s (which lies between the entries 9m 07s and 15m 13s) is 2s. If the given number of minutes and seconds is a tabular entry, the required acceleration or retardation is the entry in the right-hand column above the given tabular entry, eg the retardation for 45m 46s is 7s.

Example – Convert 14h 27m 35s from ST to MT

	h	*m*	*s*
Given ST	14	27	35
Retardation for 14h		2	18
Retardation for 27m 35s			5
Corresponding MT	14	25	12

EXPLANATION OF ASTRONOMICAL DATA

Positions of the heavenly bodies are given only to the degree of accuracy required by amateur astronomers for setting telescopes, or for plotting on celestial globes or star atlases. Where intermediate positions are required, linear interpolation may be employed.

Definitions of the terms used cannot be given here. They must be sought in astronomical literature and textbooks.

A special feature has been made of the times when the various heavenly bodies are visible in the British Isles. Since two columns, calculated for latitudes 52° and 56°, are devoted to risings and settings, the range 50° to 58° can be covered by interpolation and extrapolation. The times given in these columns are Greenwich Mean Times for the meridian of Greenwich. An observer west of this meridian must add his/her longitude (in time) and vice versa.

In accordance with the usual convention in astronomy, + and – indicate respectively north and south latitudes or declinations.

All data are, unless otherwise stated, for 0h Greenwich Mean Time (GMT), ie at the midnight at the beginning of the day named. Allowance must be made for British Summer Time during the period that this is in operation.

PAGE ONE OF EACH MONTH

The calendar for each month is explained on page 1229.

Under the heading Astronomical Phenomena will be found particulars of the more important conjunctions of the Sun, Moon and planets with each other, and also the dates of other astronomical phenomena of special interest.

Times of Minima of Algol are approximate times of the middle of the period of diminished light.

The Constellations listed each month are those that are near the meridian at the beginning of the month at 22h local mean time. Allowance must be made for British Summer Time if necessary. The fact that any star crosses the meridian 4m earlier each night or 2h earlier each month may be used, in conjunction with the lists given each month, to find what constellations are favourably placed at any moment. The table preceding the list of constellations may be extended indefinitely at the rate just quoted.

The principal phases of the Moon are the GMTs when the difference between the longitude of the Moon and that of the Sun is 0°, 90°, 180° or 270°. The times of perigee and apogee are those when the Moon is nearest to, and farthest from, the Earth, respectively. The nodes or points of intersection of the Moon's orbit and the ecliptic make a complete retrograde circuit of the ecliptic in about 19 years. From a knowledge of the longitude of the ascending node and the inclination, whose value does not vary much from 5°, the path of the Moon among the stars may be plotted on a celestial globe or star atlas.

PAGE TWO OF EACH MONTH

The Sun's semi-diameter, in arc, is given once a month.

The right ascension and declination (Dec.) is that of the true Sun. The right ascension of the mean Sun is obtained by applying the equation of time, with the sign given, to the right ascension of the true Sun, or, more easily, by applying 12h to the Sidereal Time. The direction in which the equation of time has to be applied in different problems is a frequent source of confusion and error. Apparent Solar Time is equal to the Mean Solar Time plus the Equation of Time. For example, at 12h GMT on August 8 the Equation of Time is –5m 42s and thus at 12h Mean Time on that day the Apparent Time is 12h – 5m 42s = 11h 54m 18s.

The Greenwich Sidereal Time at 0h and the Transit of the First Point of Aries (which is really the mean time when the sidereal time is 0h) are used for converting mean time to sidereal time and vice versa.

The GMT of transit of the Sun at Greenwich may also be taken as the local mean time (LMT) of transit in any longitude. It is independent of latitude. The GMT of transit in any longitude is obtained by adding the longitude to the time given if west, and vice versa.

LIGHTING-UP TIME

The legal importance of sunrise and sunset is that the Road Vehicles Lighting Regulations 1989 (SI 1989 No. 1796) as amended, make the use of front and rear position lamps on vehicles compulsory during the period between sunset and sunrise. Headlamps on vehicles are required to be used during the hours of darkness on unlit roads, on lit roads with a speed limit exceeding 30mph, or whenever visibility is seriously reduced. The hours of darkness are defined in these regulations as the period between half an hour after sunset and half an hour before sunrise.

In all laws and regulations 'sunset' refers to the local sunset, ie the time at which the Sun sets at the place in question. This common-sense interpretation has been upheld by legal tribunals.

SUNRISE AND SUNSET

The times of sunrise and sunset are those when the Sun's upper limb, as affected by refraction, is on the true horizon of an observer at sea-level. Assuming the mean refraction to be 34′, and the Sun's semi-diameter to be 16′, the time given is that when the true zenith distance of the Sun's centre is 90°+34′+16′ or 90° 50′, or, in other words, when the depression of the Sun's centre below the true horizon is 50′. The upper limb is then 34′ below the true horizon, but is brought there by refraction. An observer on a ship might see the Sun for a minute or so longer, because of the dip of the horizon, while another viewing the sunset over hills or mountains would record an earlier time. Nevertheless, the moment when the true zenith distance of the Sun's centre is 90° 50′ is a precise time dependent only on the latitude and longitude of the place, and independent of its altitude above sea-level, the contour of its horizon, the vagaries of refraction or the small seasonal change in the Sun's semi-diameter; this moment is suitable in every way as a definition of sunset (or sunrise) for all statutory purposes.

TWILIGHT

Light reaches us before sunrise and continues to reach us for some time after sunset. The interval between darkness and sunrise or sunset and darkness is called twilight. Astronomically speaking, twilight is considered to begin or end when the Sun's centre is 18° below the horizon, as no light from the Sun can then reach the observer. As thus defined twilight may last several hours; in high latitudes at the summer solstice the depression of 18° is not reached, and twilight lasts from sunset to sunrise.

The need for some sub-division of twilight is met by dividing the gathering darkness into four stages.

(1) *Sunrise or Sunset,* defined as above
(2) *Civil twilight,* which begins or ends when the Sun's centre is 6° below the horizon. This marks the time when operations requiring daylight may commence or must cease. In England it varies from about 30 to 60 minutes after sunset and the same interval before sunrise
(3) *Nautical twilight,* which begins or ends when the Sun's centre is 12° below the horizon. This marks the time when it is, to all intents and purposes, completely dark
(4) *Astronomical twilight,* which begins or ends when the Sun's centre is 18° below the horizon. This marks theoretical perfect darkness. It is of little practical importance, especially if nautical twilight is tabulated

To assist observers the durations of civil, nautical and astronomical twilights are given at intervals of ten days. The beginning of a particular twilight is found by subtracting the duration from the time of sunrise, while the end is found by adding the duration to the time of sunset. Thus the beginning of astronomical twilight in latitude 52°, on the Greenwich meridian, on March 11 is found as 06h 24m – 113m = 04h 31m and similarly the end of civil twilight as 17h 57m +34m = 18h 31m. The letters TAN (twilight all night) are printed when twilight lasts all night.

Under the heading The Night Sky will be found notes describing the position and visibility of the planets and other phenomena.

PAGE THREE OF EACH MONTH

The Moon moves so rapidly among the stars that its position is given only to the degree of accuracy that permits linear interpolation. The right ascension (RA) and declination (Dec.) are geocentric, ie for an imaginary observer at the centre of the Earth. To an observer on the surface of the Earth the position is always different, as the altitude is always less on account of parallax, which may reach 1°.

The lunar terminator is the line separating the bright from the dark part of the Moon's disk. Apart from irregularities of the lunar surface, the terminator is elliptical, because it is a circle seen in projection. It becomes the full circle forming the limb, or edge, of the Moon at New and Full Moon. The selenographic longitude of the terminator is measured from the mean centre of the visible disk, which may differ from the visible centre by as much as 8°, because of libration.

Instead of the longitude of the terminator the Sun's selenographic co-longitude (Sun's co-long.) is tabulated. It is numerically equal to the selenographic longitude of the morning terminator, measured eastwards from the mean centre of the disk. Thus its value is approximately 270° at New Moon, 360° at First Quarter, 90° at Full Moon and 180° at Last Quarter.

The Position Angle (PA) of the Bright Limb is the position angle of the midpoint of the illuminated limb, measured eastwards from the north point on the disk. The Phase column shows the percentage of the area of the Moon's disk illuminated; this is also the illuminated percentage of the diameter at right angles to the line of cusps. The terminator is a semi-ellipse whose major axis is the line of cusps, and whose semi-minor axis is determined by the tabulated percentage; from New Moon to Full Moon the east limb is dark, and vice versa.

The times given as moonrise and moonset are those when the upper limb of the Moon is on the horizon of an observer at sea-level. The Sun's horizontal parallax (Hor. par.) is about 9″, and is negligible when considering sunrise and sunset, but that of the Moon averages about 57′. Hence the computed time represents the moment when the true zenith distance of the Moon is 90° 50′ (as for the Sun) minus the horizontal parallax. The time required for the Sun or Moon to rise or set is about four minutes (except in high latitudes).

See also page 1279 and footnote on page 1283.

The GMT of transit of the Moon over the meridian of Greenwich is given; these times are independent of latitude but must be corrected for longitude. For places in the British Isles it suffices to add the longitude if west, and vice versa. For other places a further correction is necessary because of the rapid movement of the Moon relative to the stars. The entire correction is conveniently determined by first finding the west longitude λ of the place. If the place is in west longitude, λ is the ordinary west longitude; if the place is in east longitude λ is the complement to 24h (or 360°) of the longitude and will be greater than 12h (or 180°). The correction then consists of two positive portions, namely λ and the fraction λ/24 (or λ°/360) multiplied by the difference between consecutive transits. Thus for Christchurch, New Zealand, the longitude is 11h 31m east, so λ = 12h 29m and the fraction λ/24 is 0.52. The transit on the local date 26 April 2011 is found as follows:

		d	*h*	*m*
GMT of transit at Greenwich	April	25	06	21
λ			12	29
0.52 × (6h 21m – 5h 33m)				25
GMT of transit at Christchurch		25	19	15
Corr. to NZ Standard Time			12	00
Local standard time of transit	April	26	07	15

As is evident, for any given place the quantities λ and the correction to local standard time may be combined permanently, being here 24h 29m.

Positions of Mercury are given for every second day, and those of Venus and Mars for every fifth day; they may be interpolated linearly. The diameter (Diam.) is given in seconds of arc. The phase is the illuminated percentage of the disk. In the case of the inner planets this approaches 100 at superior conjunction and 0 at inferior conjunction. When the phase is less than 50 the planet is crescent-shaped or horned; for greater phases it is gibbous. In the case of the exterior planet Mars, the phase approaches 100 at conjunction and opposition, and is a minimum at the quadratures.

Since the planets cannot be seen when on the horizon, the actual times of rising and setting are not given; instead, the time when the planet has an apparent altitude of 5° has been tabulated. If the time of transit is between 00h and 12h the time refers to an altitude of 5° above the eastern horizon; if between 12h and 24h, to the western horizon. The phenomenon tabulated is the one that occurs between sunset and sunrise. The times given may be interpolated for latitude and corrected for longitude, as in the case of the Sun and Moon.

PAGE FOUR OF EACH MONTH

The GMTs of sunrise and sunset for seven cities, whose adopted positions in longitude (W.) and latitude (N.) are given immediately below the name, may be used not only for these phenomena, but also for lighting-up times (*see* page 1281 for a fuller explanation).

The particulars for the four outer planets resemble those for the planets on Page Three of each month, except that, under Uranus and Neptune, times when the planet is 10° high instead of 5° high are given; this is because of the inferior brightness of these planets. The diameters given for the rings of Saturn are those of the major axis (in the plane of the planet's equator) and the minor axis respectively. The former has a small seasonal change due to the slightly varying distance of the Earth from Saturn, but the latter varies from zero when the Earth passes through the ring plane every 15 years to its maximum opening half-way between these periods. The rings were last open at their widest extent (and Saturn at its brightest) in 2002; this will occur again in 2017. The Earth passed through the ring plane in 2009.

TIME

From the earliest ages, the natural division of time into recurring periods of day and night has provided the practical time-scale for the everyday activities of the human race. Indeed, if any alternative means of time measurement is adopted, it must be capable of adjustment so as to remain in general agreement with the natural time-scale defined by the diurnal rotation of the Earth on its axis. Ideally the rotation should be measured against a fixed frame of reference; in practice it must be measured against the background provided by the celestial bodies. If the Sun is chosen as the reference point, we obtain Apparent Solar Time, which is the time indicated by a sundial. It is not a uniform time but is subject to variations which amount to as much as a quarter of an hour in each direction. Such wide variations cannot be tolerated in a practical time-scale, and this has led to the concept of Mean Solar Time in which all the days are exactly the same length and equal to the average length of the Apparent Solar Day.

The positions of the stars in the sky are specified in relation to a fictitious reference point in the sky known as the First Point of Aries (or the Vernal Equinox). It is therefore convenient to adopt this same reference point when considering the rotation of the Earth against the background of the stars. The time-scale so obtained is known as Apparent Sidereal Time.

GREENWICH MEAN TIME

The daily rotation of the Earth on its axis causes the Sun and the other heavenly bodies to appear to cross the sky from east to west. It is convenient to represent this relative motion as if the Sun really performed a daily circuit around a fixed Earth. Noon in Apparent Solar Time may then be defined as the time at which the Sun transits across the observer's meridian. In Mean Solar Time, noon is similarly defined by the meridian transit of a fictitious Mean Sun moving uniformly in the sky with the same average speed as the true Sun. Mean Solar Time observed on the meridian of the transit circle telescope of the Royal Observatory at Greenwich is called Greenwich Mean Time (GMT). The mean solar day is divided into 24 hours and, for astronomical and other scientific purposes, these are numbered 0 to 23, commencing at midnight. Civil time is usually reckoned in two periods of 12 hours, designated am (*ante meridiem,* ie before noon) and pm (*post meridiem,* ie after noon), although the 24 hour clock is increasingly being used.

UNIVERSAL TIME

Before 1925 January 1, GMT was reckoned in 24 hours commencing at noon; since that date it has been reckoned from midnight. To avoid confusion in the use of the designation GMT before and after 1925, since 1928 astronomers have tended to use the term Universal Time (UT) or Weltzeit (WZ) to denote GMT measured from Greenwich Mean Midnight.

In precision work it is necessary to take account of small variations in Universal Time. These arise from small irregularities in the rotation of the Earth. Observed astronomical time is designated UT0. Observed time corrected for the effects of the motion of the poles (giving rise to a 'wandering' in longitude) is designated UT1. There is also a seasonal fluctuation in the rate of rotation of the Earth arising from meteorological causes, often called the annual fluctuation. UT1 corrected for this effect is designated UT2 and provides a time-scale free from short-period fluctuations. It is still subject to small secular and irregular changes.

APPARENT SOLAR TIME

As mentioned above, the time shown by a sundial is called Apparent Solar Time. It differs from Mean Solar Time by an amount known as the Equation of Time, which is the

---

SUNRISE, SUNSET, MOONRISE AND MOONSET

The tables have been constructed for the meridian of Greenwich and for latitudes 52° and 56°. They give Greenwich Mean Time (GMT) throughout the year. To obtain the GMT of the phenomenon as seen from any other latitude and longitude in the British Isles, first interpolate or extrapolate for latitude by the usual rules of proportion. To the time thus found, the longitude (expressed in time) is to be added if west (as it usually is in Great Britain) or subtracted if east. If the longitude is expressed in degrees and minutes of arc, it must be converted to time at the rate of 1° = 4m and 15′ = 1m. A method of calculating rise and set time for other places in the world is given on page 1279.

The GMT at which the planet transits the Greenwich meridian is also given. The times of transit are to be corrected to local meridians in the usual way, as already described.

total effect of two causes which make the length of the apparent solar day non-uniform. One cause of variation is that the orbit of the Earth is not a circle but an ellipse, having the Sun at one focus. As a consequence, the angular speed of the Earth in its orbit is not constant; it is greatest at the beginning of January when the Earth is nearest the Sun.

The other cause is due to the obliquity of the ecliptic; the plane of the equator (which is at right angles to the axis of rotation of the Earth) does not coincide with the ecliptic (the plane defined by the apparent annual motion of the Sun around the celestial sphere) but is inclined to it at an angle of 23° 26′. As a result, the apparent solar day is shorter than average at the equinoxes and longer at the solstices. From the combined effects of the components due to obliquity and eccentricity, the equation of time reaches its maximum values in February (−14 minutes) and early November (+16 minutes). It has a zero value on four dates during the year, and it is only on these dates (approximately April 15, June 14, September 1 and December 25) that a sundial shows Mean Solar Time.

SIDEREAL TIME

A sidereal day is the duration of a complete rotation of the Earth with reference to the First Point of Aries. The term sidereal (or 'star') time is a little misleading since the time-scale so defined is not exactly the same as that which would be defined by successive transits of a selected star, as there is a small progressive motion between the stars and the First Point of Aries due to the precession of the Earth's axis. This makes the length of the sidereal day shorter than the true period of rotation by 0.008 seconds. Superimposed on this steady precessional motion are small oscillations (nutation), giving rise to fluctuations in apparent sidereal time amounting to as much as 1.2 seconds. It is therefore customary to employ Mean Sidereal Time, from which these fluctuations have been removed. The conversion of GMT to Greenwich sidereal time (GST) may be performed by adding the value of the GST at 0h on the day in question (page two of each month) to the GMT converted to sidereal time using the table on page 1280.

Example – To find the GST at August 8d 02h 41m 11s GMT

	h	*m*	*s*
GST at 0h	21	04	38
GMT	2	41	11
Acceleration for 2h			20
Acceleration for 41m 11s			7
Sum = GST =	23	46	16

If the observer is not on the Greenwich meridian then his/her longitude, measured positively westwards from Greenwich, must be subtracted from the GST to obtain Local Sidereal Time (LST). Thus, in the above example, an observer 5h east of Greenwich, or 19h west, would find the LST as 4h 46m 16s.

EPHEMERIS TIME

An analysis of observations of the positions of the Sun, Moon and planets taken over an extended period is used in preparing ephemerides. (An ephemeris is a table giving the apparent position of a heavenly body at regular intervals of time, eg one day or ten days, and may be used to compare current observations with tabulated positions.) Discrepancies between the positions of heavenly bodies observed over a 300-year period and their predicted positions arose because the time-scale to which the observations were related was based on the assumption that the rate of rotation of the Earth is uniform. It is now known that this rate of rotation is variable. A revised time-scale, Ephemeris Time (ET), was devised to bring the ephemerides into agreement with the observations.

The second of ET is defined in terms of the annual motion of the Earth in its orbit around the Sun (1/31556925.9747 of the tropical year for 1900 January 0d 12h ET). The precise determination of ET from astronomical observations is a lengthy process as the requisite standard of accuracy can only be achieved by averaging over a number of years.

In 1976 the International Astronomical Union adopted Terrestrial Dynamical Time (TDT), a new dynamical time-scale for general use whose scale unit is the SI second (*see* Atomic Time, below). TDT was renamed Terrestrial Time (TT) in 1991. ET is now of little more than historical interest.

TERRESTRIAL TIME

The uniform time system used in computing the ephemerides of the solar system is Terrestrial Time (TT), which has replaced ET for this purpose. Except for the most rigorous astronomical calculations, it may be assumed to be the same as ET. During 2011 the estimated difference TT − UT is about 66 seconds.

ATOMIC TIME

The fundamental standards of time and frequency must be defined in terms of a periodic motion adequately uniform, enduring and measurable. Progress has made it possible to use natural standards, such as atomic or molecular oscillations. Continuous oscillations are generated in an electrical circuit, the frequency of which is then compared or brought into coincidence with the frequency characteristic of the absorption or emission by the atoms or molecules when they change between two selected energy levels. Since the 13th General Conference on Weights and Measures in October 1967, the unit of time, the second, has been defined in the International System of units (SI) as 'the duration of 9 192 631 770 periods of the radiation corresponding to the transition between the two hyperfine levels of the ground state of the caesium-133 atom'.

In the UK, the national time scale is maintained by the National Physical Laboratory (NPL), using an ensemble of atomic clocks based on either caesium or hydrogen atoms. In addition the NPL (along with several other national laboratories) has constructed and operates a caesium fountain primary frequency standard, which utilises the cooling of caesium atoms by laser light to determine the duration of the SI second at the highest attainable level of accuracy. Caesium fountain primary standards typically achieve an accuracy of around 1 part in 1,000 000 000 000 000, which is equivalent to one second in 30 million years.

Timekeeping worldwide is based on two closely related atomic time scales that are established through international collaboration. International Atomic Time (TAI) is formed by combining the readings of more than 250 atomic clocks located in about 55 institutes and was set close to the astronomically based Universal Time (UT) near the beginning of 1958. It was formally recognised in 1971 and since 1988 January 1 has been maintained by the International Bureau of Weights and Measures

(BIPM). Civil time in almost all countries is now based on Coordinated Universal Time (UTC), which differs from TAI by an integer number of seconds and was designed to make both atomic time and UT available with accuracy appropriate for most users. On 1 January 1972 UTC was set to be exactly 10 seconds behind TAI, and since then the UTC time-scale has been adjusted by the insertion (or, in principle, omission) of leap seconds in order to keep it within ±0.9 s of UT. These leap seconds are introduced, when necessary, at the same instant throughout the world, either at the end of December or at the end of June. The last leap second occurred immediately prior to 0h UTC on 2009 January 1 and was the 24th leap second. All leap seconds so far have been positive, with 61 seconds in the final minute of the UTC month. The time 23h 59m 60s UTC is followed one second later by 0h 0m 00s of the first day of the following month. Notices concerning the insertion of leap seconds are issued by the International Earth Rotation and Reference Systems Service (IERS).

The computation of UTC is carried out monthly by the BIPM and takes place in three stages. First, a weighted average known as Echelle Atomique Libre (EAL) is calculated from all of the contributing atomic clocks. In the second stage, TAI is generated by applying small corrections, derived from the results contributed by primary frequency standards, to the scale interval of EAL to maintain its value close to that of the SI second. Finally, UTC is formed from TAI by the addition of an integer number of seconds. The results are published monthly in the BIPM Circular T in the form of offsets at 5-day intervals between UTC and the time scales of contributing organisations.

RADIO TIME-SIGNALS

UTC is made generally available through time-signals and standard frequency broadcasts such as MSF in the UK, CHU in Canada and WWV and WWVH in the USA. These are based on national time-scales that are maintained in close agreement with UTC and provide traceability to the national time-scale and to UTC. The markers of seconds in the UTC scale coincide with those of TAI.

To disseminate the national time-scale in the UK, special signals (call-sign MSF) are broadcast by the National Physical Laboratory. From 2007 April 1 the MSF service, previously broadcast from British Telecom's radio station at Rugby, has been transmitted from Anthorn radio station in Cumbria. The signals are controlled from a caesium beam atomic frequency standard and consist of a precise frequency carrier of 60 kHz which is switched off, after being on for at least half a second, to mark every second. The first second of the minute begins with a period of 500 ms with the carrier switched off, to serve as a minute marker. In the other seconds the carrier is always off for at least one tenth of a second at the start and then it carries an on-off code giving the British clock time and date, together with information identifying the start of the next minute. Changes to and from summer time are made following government announcements. Leap seconds are inserted as announced by the IERS and information provided by them on the difference between UTC and UT is also signalled. Other broadcast signals in the UK include the BBC six pips signal, the BT Timeline ('speaking clock'), the NPL telephone and internet time services for computers, and a coded time-signal on the BBC 198 kHz transmitters which is used for timing in the electricity supply industry. From 1972 January 1 the six pips on the BBC have consisted of five short pips from second 55 to second 59 (six pips in the case of a leap second) followed by one lengthened pip, the start of which indicates the exact minute. From 1990 February 5 these signals have been controlled by the BBC with seconds markers referenced to the satellite-based US navigation system GPS (Global Positioning System) and time and day referenced to the MSF transmitter. Formerly they were generated by the Royal Greenwich Observatory. The NPL telephone and internet services are directly connected to the national time scale.

Accurate timing may also be obtained from the signals of international navigation systems such as the ground-based eLORAN, or the satellite-based American GPS or Russian GLONASS systems.

STANDARD TIME

Since 1880 the standard time in Britain has been Greenwich Mean Time (GMT); a statute that year enacted that the word 'time' when used in any legal document relating to Britain meant, unless otherwise specifically stated, the mean time of the Greenwich meridian. Greenwich was adopted as the universal meridian on 13 October 1884. A system of standard time by zones is used worldwide, standard time in each zone differing from that of the Greenwich meridian by an integral number of hours or, exceptionally, half-hours or quarter-hours, either fast or slow. The large territories of the USA and Canada are divided into zones approximately 7.5° on either side of central meridians.

Variations from the standard time of some countries occur during part of the year; they are decided annually and are usually referred to as Summer Time or Daylight Saving Time.

At the 180th meridian the time can be either 12 hours fast on Greenwich Mean Time or 12 hours slow, and a change of date occurs. The internationally recognised date or calendar line is a modification of the 180th meridian, drawn so as to include islands of any one group on the same side of the line, or for political reasons. The line is indicated by joining up the following coordinates:

Lat.	*Long.*	*Lat.*	*Long.*
90° S.	180°	48° N.	180°
51° S.	180°	53° N.	170° E.
45° S.	172.5° W.	65.5° N.	169° W.
15° S.	172.5° W.	68° N.	169° W.
5° S.	180°	90° N.	180°

Changes to the date line would require an international conference.

BRITISH SUMMER TIME

In 1916 an Act ordained that during a defined period of that year the legal time for general purposes in Great Britain should be one hour in advance of Greenwich Mean Time. The Summer Time Acts 1922 and 1925 defined the period during which Summer Time was to be in force, stabilising practice until the Second World War.

During the Second World War (1941–5) and in 1947 Double Summer Time (two hours in advance of Greenwich Mean Time) was used for the period in which ordinary Summer Time would have been in force. During these years clocks were also kept one hour in advance of Greenwich Mean Time in the winter. After the war, ordinary Summer Time was invoked each year from 1948–68.

Between 1968 October 27 and 1971 October 31

clocks were kept one hour ahead of Greenwich Mean Time throughout the year. This was known as British Standard Time.

The most recent legislation is the Summer Time Act 1972, which enacted that 'the period of summer time for the purposes of this Act is the period beginning at two o'clock, Greenwich Mean Time, in the morning of the day after the third Saturday in March or, if that day is Easter Day, the day after the second Saturday in March, and ending at two o'clock, Greenwich Mean Time, in the morning of the day after the fourth Saturday in October.'

The duration of Summer Time can be varied by Order in Council and in recent years alterations have been made to synchronise the period of Summer Time in Britain with that used in Europe. The rule for 1981–94 defined the period of Summer Time in the UK as from the last Sunday in March to the day following the fourth Saturday in October and the hour of changeover was altered to 01h Greenwich Mean Time.

There was no rule for the dates of Summer Time between 1995–7. Since 1998 the 9th European Parliament and Council Directive on Summer Time has harmonised the dates on which Summer Time begins and ends across member states as the last Sundays in March and October respectively. Under the directive Summer Time begins and ends at 01hr Greenwich Mean Time in each member state. Amendments to the Summer Time Act to implement the directive came into force in 2002.

The duration of Summer Time in 2011 is:
March 27 01h GMT to October 30 01h GMT

MEAN REFRACTION

Alt.	Ref.	Alt.	Ref.	Alt.	Ref.
° ′	′	° ′	′	° ′	′
1 20		3 12		7 54	
	21		13		6
1 30		3 34		9 27	
	20		12		5
1 41		4 00		11 39	
	19		11		4
1 52		4 30		15 00	
	18		10		3
2 05		5 06		20 42	
	17		9		2
2 19		5 50		32 20	
	16		8		1
2 35		6 44		62 17	
	15		7		0
2 52		7 54		90 00	
	14				
3 12					

The refraction table is in the form of a critical table (*see* page 1280).

ASTRONOMICAL CONSTANTS

Solar parallax	8″.794
Astronomical unit	149597870 km
Precession for the year 2011	50″.291
Precession in right ascension	$3^{s}.075$
Precession in declination	20″.043
Constant of nutation	9″.202
Constant of aberration	20″.496
Mean obliquity of ecliptic (2011)	23° 26′ 17″
Moon's equatorial hor. parallax	57′ 02″.70
Velocity of light in vacuo per second	299792.5 km
Solar motion per second	20.0 km
Equatorial radius of the Earth	6378.140 km
Polar radius of the Earth	6356.755 km
North galactic pole (IAU standard)	RA 12h 49m (1950.0). Dec.+27°.4 N.
Solar apex	RA 18h 06m Dec. +30°
Length of year (in mean solar days)	
Tropical	365.24219
Sidereal	365.25636
Anomalistic (perihelion to perihelion)	365.25964
Eclipse	346.62003

Length of month (mean values)	*d*	*h*	*m*	*s*
New Moon to New	29	12	44	02.9
Sidereal	27	07	43	11.5
Anomalistic (perigee to perigee)	27	13	18	33.2

THE EARTH

The shape of the Earth is that of an oblate spheroid or solid of revolution whose meridian sections are ellipses not differing much from circles, while the sections at right angles are circles. The length of the equatorial axis is about 12,756 km, and that of the polar axis is 12,714 km. The mean density of the Earth is 5.5 times that of water, although that of the surface layer is less. The Earth and Moon revolve about their common centre of gravity in a lunar month; this centre in turn revolves round the Sun in a plane known as the ecliptic, that passes through the Sun's centre. The Earth's equator is inclined to this plane at an angle of 23.4°. This tilt is the cause of the seasons. In mid-latitudes, and when the Sun is high above the Equator, not only does the high noon altitude make the days longer, but the Sun's rays fall more directly on the Earth's surface; these effects combine to produce summer. In equatorial regions the noon altitude is large throughout the year, and there is little variation in the length of the day. In higher latitudes the noon altitude is lower, and the days in summer are appreciably longer than those in winter.

The average velocity of the Earth in its orbit is 30km a second. It makes a complete rotation on its axis in about 23h 56m of mean time, which is the sidereal day. Because of its annual revolution round the Sun, the rotation with respect to the Sun, or the solar day, is more than this by about four minutes. The extremity of the axis of rotation, or the North Pole of the Earth, is not rigidly fixed, but wanders over an area roughly 20 metres in diameter.

ELEMENTS OF THE SOLAR SYSTEM

Orb	Mean distance from Sun (Earth = 1)	km 10^6	Sidereal period days	Synodic period days	Incl. of orbit to ecliptic °	′	Diameter km	Mass (Earth = 1)	Period of rotation on axis days
Sun	—	—	—	—	—		1,392,000	332,981	25–35*
Mercury	0.39	58	88.0	116	7	00	4,879	0.0553	58.646
Venus	0.72	108	224.7	584	3	24	12,104	0.8150	243.019*r*
Earth	1.00	150	365.3	—	—		12,756*e*	1.0000	0.997
Mars	1.52	228	687.0	780	1	51	6,794*e*	0.1074	1.026
Jupiter	5.20	778	4,332.6	399	1	18	142,984*e* 133,708*p*	317.83	0.410*e*
Saturn	9.55	1429	10,759.2	378	2	29	120,536*e* 108,728*p*	95.16	0.426*e*
Uranus	19.22	2875	30,684.6	370	0	46	51,118*e*	14.54	0.718*r*
Neptune	30.11	4504	60,191.2	367	1	46	49,528*e*	17.15	0.671
Pluto †	39.80	5954	91,708.2	367	17	09	2,390	0.002	6.387

e equatorial, *p* polar, *r* retrograde, * depending on latitude, † reclassified as a dwarf planet since August 2006

THE SATELLITES

	Name	Star mag.	Mean distance from primary km	Sidereal period of revolution d
EARTH				
I	Moon	—	384,400	27.322
MARS				
I	Phobos	11	9,378	0.319
II	Deimos	12	23,459	1.262
JUPITER				
XVI	Metis	17	127,960	0.295
XV	Adrastea	19	128,980	0.298
V	Amalthea	14	181,300	0.498
XIV	Thebe	16	221,900	0.675
I	Io	5	421,600	1.769
II	Europa	5	670,900	3.551
III	Ganymede	5	1,070,000	7.155
IV	Callisto	6	1,883,000	16.689
XIII	Leda	20	11,165,000	240.92
VI	Himalia	15	11,460,000	250.57
X	Lysithea	18	11,717,000	259.22
VII	Elara	17	11,741,000	259.65
XII	Ananke	19	21,276,000	629.77*r*
XI	Carme	18	23,404,000	734.17*r*
VIII	Pasiphae	17	23,624,000	743.68*r*
IX	Sinope	18	23,939,000	758.90*r*
SATURN				
XVIII	Pan	20	133,583	0.575
XV	Atlas	18	137,640	0.602
XVI	Prometheus	16	139,353	0.613
XVII	Pandora	16	141,700	0.629
XI	Epimetheus	15	151,422	0.694
X	Janus	14	151,472	0.695
I	Mimas	13	185,520	0.942
II	Enceladus	12	238,020	1.370
III	Tethys	10	294,660	1.888
XIII	Telesto	19	294,660	1.888
XIV	Calypso	19	294,660	1.888
IV	Dione	10	377,400	2.737
XII	Helene	18	377,400	2.737
V	Rhea	10	527,040	4.518
VI	Titan	8	1,221,850	15.945
SATURN				
VII	Hyperion	14	1,481,000	21.277
VIII	Iapetus	11	3,561,300	79.330
IX	Phoebe	16	12,952,000	550.48*r*
URANUS				
VI	Cordelia	24	49,770	0.335
VII	Ophelia	24	53,790	0.376
VIII	Bianca	23	59,170	0.435
IX	Cressida	22	61,780	0.464
X	Desdemona	22	62,680	0.474
XI	Juliet	21	64,350	0.493
XII	Portia	21	66,090	0.513
XIII	Rosalind	22	66,940	0.558
XIV	Belinda	22	75,260	0.624
XV	Puck	20	86,010	0.762
V	Miranda	16	129,390	1.413
I	Ariel	14	191,020	2.520
II	Umbriel	15	266,300	4.144
III	Titania	14	435,910	8.706
IV	Oberon	14	583,520	13.463
XVI	Caliban	22	7,230,000	579.5*r*
XX	Stephano	24	8,002,000	676.5*r*
XVII	Sycorax	21	12,179,000	1,283.4*r*
XVIII	Prospero	23	16,418,000	1,992.8*r*
XIX	Setebos	23	17,459,000	2,202.2*r*
NEPTUNE				
III	Naiad	25	48,230	0.294
IV	Thalassa	24	50,080	0.311
V	Despina	23	52,530	0.335
VI	Galatea	22	61,950	0.429
VII	Larissa	22	73,550	0.555
VIII	Proteus	20	117,650	1.122
I	Triton	13	354,760	5.877
II	Nereid	19	5,513,400	360.136
PLUTO				
I	Charon	17	19,600	6.387

Currently the total number of satellites of the outer planets are: Jupiter 62, Saturn 60, Uranus 27, Neptune 13, Pluto 3.

TERRESTRIAL MAGNETISM

The Earth's main magnetic field corresponds approximately to that of a very strong small bar magnet near the centre of the Earth, but with appreciable smooth spatial departures. The origin of the main field is generally ascribed to electric currents associated with fluid motions in the Earth's core. As a result not only does the main field vary in strength and direction from place to place, but also with time. Superimposed on the main field are local and regional anomalies whose magnitudes may in places approach that of the main field; these are due to the influence of mineral deposits in the Earth's crust. A small proportion of the field is of external origin, mostly associated with electric currents in the ionosphere. The configuration of the external field and the ionisation of the atmosphere depend on the incident particle and radiation flux from the Sun. There are, therefore, short-term and non-periodic as well as diurnal, 27-day, seasonal and 11-year periodic changes in the magnetic field, dependent upon the position of the Sun and the degree of solar activity.

A magnetic compass points along the horizontal component of a magnetic line of force. These lines of force converge on the 'magnetic dip-poles', the places where the Earth's magnetic field is vertical. These poles move with time, and their present approximate adopted mean positions are 85.3° N., 136.4° W. and 64.4° S., 137.2° E.

There is also a 'magnetic equator', at all points of which the vertical component of the Earth's magnetic field is zero and a magnetised needle remains horizontal. This line runs between 2° and 12° north of the geographical equator in Asia and Africa, turns sharply south off the west African coast, and crosses South America through Brazil, Bolivia and Peru; it re-crosses the geographical equator in mid-Pacific.

Reference has already been made to secular changes in the Earth's field. The following table indicates the changes in magnetic declination (or variation of the compass). Declination is the angle in the horizontal plane between the direction of true north and that in which a magnetic compass points. Similar, though much smaller, changes have occurred in 'dip' or magnetic inclination. Secular changes differ throughout the world. Although the London observations suggest a cycle with a period of several hundred years, an exact repetition is unlikely.

London		*Greenwich*	
1580	11° 15′ E.	1900	16° 29′ W.
1622	5° 56′ E.	1925	13° 10′ W.
1665	1° 22′ W.	1950	9° 07′ W.
1730	13° 00′ W.	1975	6° 39′ W.
1773	21° 09′ W.	1998	3° 32′ W.
1850	22° 24′ W.		

In order that up-to-date information on declination may be available, many governments publish magnetic charts on which there are lines (isogonic lines) passing through all places at which specified values of declination will be found at the date of the chart.

In the British Isles, isogonic lines now run approximately north-east to south-west. Though there are considerable local deviations due to geological causes, a rough value of magnetic declination may be obtained by assuming that at 50° N. on the meridian of Greenwich, the value in 2011 is 1° 00′ west and allowing an increase of 11′ for each degree of latitude northwards and one of 26′ for each degree of longitude westwards. For example, at 53° N., 5° W., declination will be about 1° 00′ + 33′ + 130′, ie 3° 43′ west. The average annual change at the present time is about 11′ decrease.

The number of magnetic observatories is about 180, irregularly distributed over the globe. There are three in Great Britain, run by the British Geological Survey: at Hartland, north Devon; at Eskdalemuir, Dumfries and Galloway; and at Lerwick, Shetland Islands. The following are some recent annual mean values of the magnetic elements for Hartland.

Year	*Declination West* ° ′	*Dip or inclination* ° ′	*Horizontal intensity nanoTesla (nT)*	*Vertical intensity nT*
1960	9 58.8	66 43.9	18707	43504
1965	9 30.1	66 34.0	18872	43540
1970	9 06.5	66 26.1	19033	43636
1975	8 32.3	66 17.0	19212	43733
1980	7 43.8	66 10.3	19330	43768
1985	6 56.1	66 07.9	19379	43796
1990	6 15.0	66 09.7	19539	43896
1995	5 33.2	66 07.3	19457	43951
2000	4 43.6	66 06.9	19508	44051
2005	3 56.4	66 06.0	19576	44177
2009	3 20.1	66 02.4	19658	44235

As well as navigation at sea, in the air and on land by compass the oil industry depends on the Earth's magnetic field as a directional reference. They use magnetic survey tools when drilling well-bores and require accurate estimates of the local magnetic field, taking into account the crustal and external fields.

MAGNETIC STORMS

Occasionally, sometimes with great suddenness, the Earth's magnetic field is subject for several hours to marked disturbance. During a severe storm in October 2003 the declination at Eskdalemuir changed by over 5° in six minutes. In many instances such disturbances are accompanied by widespread displays of aurorae, marked changes in the incidence of cosmic rays, an increase in the reception of 'noise' from the Sun at radio frequencies, and rapid changes in the ionosphere and induced electric currents within the Earth which adversely affect satellite operations, telecommunications and electric power transmission systems. The disturbances are caused by changes in the stream of ionised particles which emanates from the Sun and through which the Earth is continuously passing. Some of these changes are associated with visible eruptions on the Sun, usually in the region of sun-spots. There is a marked tendency for disturbances to recur after intervals of about 27 days, the apparent period of rotation of the Sun on its axis, which is consistent with the sources being located on particular areas of the Sun.

TIME MEASUREMENT AND CALENDARS

MEASUREMENTS OF TIME

Measurements of time are based on the time taken by the earth to rotate on its axis (day); by the moon to revolve around the earth (month); and by the earth to revolve around the sun (year). From these, which are not commensurable, certain average or mean intervals have been adopted for ordinary use.

THE DAY

The day begins at midnight and is divided into 24 hours of 60 minutes, each of 60 seconds. The hours are counted from midnight up to 12 noon (when the sun crosses the meridian), and these hours are designated am *(ante meridiem);* and again from noon up to 12 midnight, which hours are designated pm *(post meridiem),* except when the 24-hour reckoning is employed. The 24-hour reckoning ignores am and pm, numbering the hours 0 to 23 from midnight.

Colloquially the 24 hours are divided into day and night, day being the time while the sun is above the horizon (including the four stages of twilight defined in the Astronomy section). Day is subdivided into morning, the early part of daytime, ending at noon; afternoon, from noon to about 6pm; and evening, which may be said to extend from 6pm until midnight. Night begins at the close of astronomical twilight (*see* the Astronomy section) and extends beyond midnight to sunrise the next day.

The names of the days are derived from Old English translations or adaptations of the Roman titles.

Sunday	Sol	Sun
Monday	Luna	Moon
Tuesday	Tiw/Tyr (god of war)	Mars
Wednesday	Woden/Odin	Mercury
Thursday	Thor	Jupiter
Friday	Frigga/Freyja (goddess of love)	Venus
Saturday	Saeterne	Saturn

THE MONTH

The month in the ordinary calendar is approximately the twelfth part of a year, but the lengths of the different months vary from 28 (or 29) days to 31.

THE YEAR

The equinoctial or tropical year is the time that the earth takes to revolve around the sun from equinox to equinox, ie 365.24219 mean solar days, or 365 days 5 hours 48 minutes and 45 seconds.

The calendar year usually consists of 365 days but a year containing 366 days is called a bissextile (*see* Roman calendar) or leap year, one day being added to the month of February so that a date 'leaps over' a day of the week. In the Roman calendar the day that was repeated was the sixth day before the beginning of March, the equivalent of 24 February.

A year is a leap year if the date of the year is divisible by four without remainder, unless it is the last year of the century. The last year of a century is a leap year only if its number is divisible by 400 without remainder, eg the years 1800 and 1900 had only 365 days but the year 2000 had 366 days.

THE SOLSTICE

A solstice is the point in the tropical year at which the sun attains its greatest distance, north or south, from the Equator. In the northern hemisphere the furthest point north of the Equator marks the summer solstice and the furthest point south marks the winter solstice.

The date of the solstice varies according to locality. For example, if the summer solstice falls on 21 June late in the day by Greenwich time, that day will be the longest of the year at Greenwich though it may be by only a second, but it will fall on 22 June, local date, in Japan, and so 22 June will be the longest day there. The date of the solstice is also affected by the length of the tropical year, which is 365 days 6 hours less about 11 minutes 15 seconds. If a solstice happens late on 21 June in one year, it will be nearly 6 hours later in the next (unless the next year is a leap year), ie early on 22 June, and that will be the longest day.

This delay of the solstice does not continue because the extra day in a leap year brings it back a day in the calendar. However, because of the 11 minutes 15 seconds mentioned above, the additional day in a leap year brings the solstice back too far by 45 minutes, and the time of the solstice in the calendar is earlier, in a four-year pattern, as the century progresses. The last year of a century is in most cases not a leap year, and the omission of the extra day puts the date of the solstice later by about 6 hours. Compensation for this is made by the fourth centennial year being a leap year. The solstice has become earlier in date throughout the last century and, because the year 2000 was a leap year, the solstice will get earlier still throughout the 21st century. The date of the winter solstice, the shortest day of the year, is affected by the same factors as the longest day.

At Greenwich the sun sets at its earliest by the clock about ten days before the shortest day. The daily change in the time of sunset is due in the first place to the sun's movement southwards at this time of the year, which diminishes the interval between the sun's transit and its setting. However, the daily decrease of the Equation of Time causes the time of apparent noon to be continuously later day by day, which to some extent counteracts the first effect. The rates of the change of these two quantities are not equal or uniform; their combination causes the date of earliest sunset to be 12 or 13 December at Greenwich. In more southerly latitudes the effect of the movement of the sun is less, and the change in the time of sunset depends on that of the Equation of Time to a greater degree, and the date of earliest sunset is earlier than it is at Greenwich, eg on the Equator it is about 1 November.

THE EQUINOX

The equinox is the point at which the sun crosses the Equator and day and night are of equal length all over the world. This occurs in March and September.

DOG DAYS

The days about the heliacal rising of the Dog Star, noted from ancient times as the hottest period of the year in the northern hemisphere, are called the Dog Days. Their incidence has been variously calculated as depending on the Greater or Lesser Dog Star (Sirius or Procyon) and their duration has been reckoned as from 30 to 54 days. A generally accepted period is from 3 July to 15 August.

CHRISTIAN CALENDAR

In the Christian chronological system the years are distinguished by cardinal numbers before or after the birth of Christ, the period being denoted by the letters BC (Before Christ) or, more rarely, AC *(Ante Christum),* and AD (*Anno Domini* – In the Year of Our Lord). The correlative dates of the epoch are the fourth year of the 194th Olympiad, the 753rd year from the foundation of Rome, AM 3761 in Jewish chronology, and the 4,714th year of the Julian period. The actual date of the birth of Christ is somewhat uncertain.

The system was introduced into Italy in the sixth century. Though first used in France in the seventh century, it was not universally established there until about the eighth century. It has been said that the system was introduced into England by St Augustine (AD 596), but it was probably not generally used until some centuries later. It was ordered to be used by the bishops at the Council of Chelsea (AD 816).

THE JULIAN CALENDAR

In the Julian calendar (adopted by the Roman Empire in 45 BC) all the centennial years were leap years, and for this reason towards the close of the 16th century there was a difference of ten days between the tropical and calendar years; the equinox fell on 11 March of the calendar, whereas at the time of the Council of Nicaea (AD 325), it had fallen on 21 March. In 1582 Pope Gregory ordained that 5 October should be called 15 October and that of the end-century years only the fourth should be a leap year.

THE GREGORIAN CALENDAR

The Gregorian calendar was adopted by Italy, France, Spain and Portugal in 1582, by Prussia, the Roman Catholic German states, Switzerland, Holland and Flanders on 1 January 1583, by Poland in 1586, Hungary in 1587, the Protestant German and Netherland states and Denmark in 1700, and by Great Britain and its Dominions (including the North American colonies) in 1752, by the omission of 11 days (3 September being reckoned as 14 September). Sweden omitted the leap day in 1700 but observed leap days in 1704 and 1708, and reverted to the Julian calendar by having two leap days in 1712; the Gregorian calendar was adopted in 1753 by the omission of 11 days (18 February being reckoned as 1 March). Japan adopted the calendar in 1872, China in 1912, Bulgaria in 1916, Turkey and Soviet Russia in 1918, Yugoslavia and Romania in 1919, and Greece in 1923.

In the same year that the change was made in England from the Julian to the Gregorian calendar, the start of the new year was also changed from 25 March to 1 January.

THE ORTHODOX CHURCHES

Some Orthodox churches still use the Julian reckoning but the majority of Greek Orthodox churches and the Romanian Orthodox Church have adopted a modified 'New Calendar', observing the Gregorian calendar for fixed feasts and the Julian for movable feasts.

The Orthodox Church year begins on 1 September. There are four fast periods and, in addition to Pascha (Easter), twelve great feasts, as well as numerous commemorations of the saints of the Old and New Testaments throughout the year.

THE DOMINICAL LETTER

The dominical letter is one of the letters A–G which are used to denote the Sundays in successive years. If the first day of the year is a Sunday the letter is A; if the second, B; the third, C; and so on. A leap year requires two letters, the first for 1 January to 29 February, the second for 1 March to 31 December.

EPIPHANY

The feast of the Epiphany, commemorating the manifestation of Christ, later became associated with the offering of gifts by the Magi. The day was of great importance from the time of the Council of Nicaea (AD 325), as the primate of Alexandria was charged at every Epiphany feast with the announcement in a letter to the churches of the date of the forthcoming Easter. The day was also of importance in Britain as it influenced dates, ecclesiastical and lay, eg Plough Monday, when work was resumed in the fields, fell on the Monday in the first full week after Epiphany.

LENT

The Teutonic word *Lent,* which denotes the fast preceding Easter, originally meant no more than the spring season; but from Anglo-Saxon times, at least, it has been used as the equivalent of the more significant Latin term *Quadragesima,* meaning the 'forty days' or, more literally, the fortieth day. Ash Wednesday is the first day of Lent, which ends at midnight before Easter Day.

PALM SUNDAY

Palm Sunday, the Sunday before Easter and the beginning of Holy Week, commemorates the triumphal entry of Christ into Jerusalem and is celebrated in Britain (when palm is not available) by branches of willow gathered for use in the decoration of churches on that day.

MAUNDY THURSDAY

Maundy Thursday is the day before Good Friday, the name itself being a corruption of *dies mandati* (day of the mandate) when Christ washed the feet of the disciples and gave them the mandate to love one another.

EASTER DAY

Easter Day is the first Sunday after the full moon which happens on, or next after, the 21st day of March; if the full moon happens on a Sunday, Easter Day is the Sunday after.

This definition is contained in an Act of Parliament (24 Geo. II c. 23) and explanation is given in the preamble to the Act that the day of full moon depends on certain tables that have been prepared. These tables are summarised in the early pages of the Book of Common Prayer. The moon referred to is not the real moon of the heavens, but a hypothetical moon on whose 'full' the date of Easter depends, and the lunations of this 'calendar' moon consist of 29 and 30 days alternately, with certain necessary modifications to make the date of its full agree as nearly as possible with that of the real moon, which is known as the Paschal Full Moon.

A FIXED EASTER

In 1928 the House of Commons agreed to a motion for the third reading of a bill proposing that Easter Day shall, in the calendar year next but one after the commencement of the Act and in all subsequent years, be the first Sunday after the second Saturday in April. Easter would thus fall on the second or third Sunday in April, ie between 9 and 15 April (inclusive). A clause in the bill provided that before it shall come into operation, regard shall be had to any opinion expressed officially by the various Christian churches. Efforts by the World Council of Churches to secure a unanimous choice of date for Easter by its member churches have so far been unsuccessful.

ROGATION DAYS

Rogation Days are the Monday, Tuesday and Wednesday preceding Ascension Day and from the fifth century were observed as public fasts with solemn processions and supplications. The processions were discontinued as religious observances at the Reformation, but survive in the ceremony known as 'beating the parish bounds'. Rogation Sunday is the Sunday before Ascension Day.

EMBER DAYS

The Ember days occur on the Wednesday, Friday and Saturday of the same week, four times a year. Used for the ordination of clergy, these days are set aside for fasting and prayer. The weeks in which they fall are: (a) after the third Sunday in Advent, (b) before the second Sunday in Lent, (c) before Trinity Sunday and (d) after Holy Cross day.

TRINITY SUNDAY

Trinity Sunday is eight weeks after Easter Day, on the Sunday following Pentecost (Whit Sunday). Subsequent Sundays are reckoned in the Book of Common Prayer calendar of the Church of England as 'after Trinity'.

Thomas Becket (1118–70) was consecrated Archbishop of Canterbury on the Sunday after Whit Sunday and his first act was to ordain that the day of his consecration should be held as a new festival in honour of the Holy Trinity. This observance spread from Canterbury throughout the whole of Christendom.

MOVEABLE FEASTS TO THE YEAR 2035

Year	*Ash Wednesday*	*Easter*	*Ascension*	*Pentecost (Whit Sunday)*	*Advent Sunday*
2011	9 March	24 April	2 June	12 June	27 November
2012	22 February	8 April	17 May	27 May	2 December
2013	13 February	31 March	9 May	19 May	1 December
2014	5 March	20 April	29 May	8 June	30 November
2015	18 February	5 April	14 May	24 May	29 November
2016	10 February	27 March	5 May	15 May	27 November
2017	1 March	16 April	25 May	4 June	3 December
2018	14 February	1 April	10 May	20 May	2 December
2019	6 March	21 April	30 May	9 June	1 December
2020	26 February	12 April	21 May	31 May	29 November
2021	17 February	4 April	13 May	23 May	28 November
2022	2 March	17 April	26 May	5 June	27 November
2023	22 February	9 April	18 May	28 May	3 December
2024	14 February	31 March	9 May	19 May	1 December
2025	5 March	20 April	29 May	8 June	30 November
2026	18 February	5 April	14 May	24 May	29 November
2027	10 February	28 March	6 May	16 May	28 November
2028	1 March	16 April	25 May	4 June	3 December
2029	14 February	1 April	10 May	20 May	2 December
2030	6 March	21 April	30 May	9 June	1 December
2031	26 February	13 April	22 May	1 June	30 November
2032	11 February	28 March	6 May	16 May	28 November
2033	2 March	17 April	26 May	5 June	27 November
2034	22 February	9 April	18 May	28 May	3 December
2035	7 February	25 March	3 May	13 May	2 December

NOTES

Ash Wednesday (first day in Lent) can fall at earliest on 4 February and at latest on 10 March

Mothering Sunday (fourth Sunday in Lent) can fall at earliest on 1 March and at latest on 4 April

Easter Day can fall at earliest on 22 March and at latest on 25 April

Ascension Day is forty days after Easter Day and can fall at earliest on 30 April and at latest on 3 June

Pentecost (Whit Sunday) is seven weeks after Easter and can fall at earliest on 10 May and at latest on 13 June

Trinity Sunday is the Sunday after Whit Sunday

Corpus Christi falls on the Thursday after Trinity Sunday

Sundays after Pentecost – there are not less than 18 and not more than 23

Advent Sunday is the Sunday nearest to 30 November

EASTER DAYS AND DOMINICAL LETTERS 1500 TO 2035

Dates up to and including 1752 are according to the Julian calendar. For dominical letters in leap years, *see* note below

		1500–1599	1600–1699	1700–1799	1800–1899	1900–1999	2000–2035
March							
d	22	1573	1668	1761	1818		
e	23	1505/16	1600	1788	1845/56	1913	2008
f	24	1611/95	1706/99	1940			
g	25	1543/54	1627/38/49	1722/33/44	1883/94	1951	2035
A	26	1559/70/81/92	1654/65/76	1749/58/69/80	1815/26/37	1967/78/89	
b	27	1502/13/24/97	1608/87/92	1785/96	1842/53/64	1910/21/32	2005/16
c	28	1529/35/40	1619/24/30	1703/14/25	1869/75/80	1937/48	2027/32
d	29	1551/62	1635/46/57	1719/30/41/52	1807/12/91	1959/64/70	
e	30	1567/78/89	1651/62/73/84	1746/55/66/77	1823/34	1902/75/86/97	
f	31	1510/21/32/83/94	1605/16/78/89	1700/71/82/93	1839/50/61/72	1907/18/29/91	2002/13/24
April							
g	1	1526/37/48	1621/32	1711/16	1804/66/77/88	1923/34/45/56	2018/29
A	2	1553/64	1643/48	1727/38	1809/20/93/99	1961/72	
b	3	1575/80/86	1659/70/81	1743/63/68/74	1825/31/36	1904/83/88/94	
c	4	1507/18/91	1602/13/75/86/97	1708/79/90	1847/58	1915/20/26/99	2010/21
d	5	1523/34/45/56	1607/18/29/40	1702/13/24/95	1801/63/74/85/96	1931/42/53	2015/26
e	6	1539/50/61/72	1634/45/56	1729/35/40/60	1806/17/28/90	1947/58/69/80	
f	7	1504/77/88	1667/72	1751/65/76	1822/33/44	1901/12/85/96	
g	8	1509/15/20/99	1604/10/83/94	1705/87/92/98	1849/55/60	1917/28	2007/12
A	9	1531/42	1615/26/37/99	1710/21/32	1871/82	1939/44/50	2023/34
b	10	1547/58/69	1631/42/53/64	1726/37/48/57	1803/14/87/98	1955/66/77	
c	11	1501/12/63/74/85/96	1658/69/80	1762/73/84	1819/30/41/52	1909/71/82/93	2004
d	12	1506/17/28	1601/12/91/96	1789	1846/57/68	1903/14/25/36/98	2009/20
e	13	1533/44	1623/28	1707/18	1800/73/79/84	1941/52	2031
f	14	1555/60/66	1639/50/61	1723/34/45/54	1805/11/16/95	1963/68/74	
g	15	1571/82/93	1655/66/77/88	1750/59/70/81	1827/38	1900/06/79/90	2001
A	16	1503/14/25/36/87/98	1609/20/82/93	1704/75/86/97	1843/54/65/76	1911/22/33/95	2006/17/28
b	17	1530/41/52	1625/36	1715/20	1808/70/81/92	1927/38/49/60	2022/33
c	18	1557/68	1647/52	1731/42/56	1802/13/24/97	1954/65/76	
d	19	1500/79/84/90	1663/74/85	1747/67/72/78	1829/35/40	1908/81/87/92	
e	20	1511/22/95	1606/17/79/90	1701/12/83/94	1851/62	1919/24/30	2003/14/25
f	21	1527/38/49	1622/33/44	1717/28	1867/78/89	1935/46/57	2019/30
g	22	1565/76	1660	1739/53/64	1810/21/32	1962/73/84	
A	23	1508	1671		1848	1905/16	2000
b	24	1519	1603/14/98	1709/91	1859		2011
c	25	1546	1641	1736	1886	1943	

No dominical letter is placed against the intercalary day 29 February, but since it is still counted as a weekday and given a name, the series of letters moves back one day every leap year after intercalation. Thus, a leap year beginning with the dominical letter C will change to a year with the dominical letter B on 1 March

HINDU CALENDAR

The Hindu calendar is a luni-solar calendar of 12 months, each containing 29 days, 12 hours. Each month is divided into a light fortnight (Shukla or Shuddha) and a dark fortnight (Krishna or Vadya) based on the waxing and waning of the moon. In most parts of India the month starts with the light fortnight, ie the day after the new moon, although in some regions it begins with the dark fortnight, ie the day after the full moon.

The new year according to the civil calendar begins in the month of Chaitra (March/April) and ends in the month of Phalgun (March). The 12 months – Chaitra, Vaishakh, Jyeshtha, Ashadh, Shravan, Bhadrapad, Ashvin, Kartik, Margashirsh, Paush, Magh and Phalgun – have Sanskrit names derived from 12 asterisms (constellations). There are regional variations to the names of the months but the Sanskrit names are understood throughout India.

Every lunar month that has a solar transit is termed pure *(shuddha)*. The lunar month without a solar transit is impure *(mala)* and called an intercalary month. An intercalary month occurs approximately every 32 lunar months, whenever the difference between the Hindu year of 360 lunar days (354 days 8 hours solar time) and the 365 days 6 hours of the solar year reaches the length of one Hindu lunar month (29 days 12 hours).

The leap month may be added at any point in the Hindu year. The name given to the month varies according to when it occurs but is taken from the month immediately following it. There is no leap month in 2011.

The days of the week are called Raviwar (Sunday), Somawar (Monday), Mangalwar (Tuesday), Budhawar (Wednesday), Guruwar (Thursday), Shukrawar (Friday) and Shaniwar (Saturday). The names are derived from the Sanskrit names of the sun, the moon and five planets, Mars, Mercury, Jupiter, Venus and Saturn.

Most fasts and festivals are based on the lunar calendar but a few are determined by the apparent movement of the sun, eg Sankranti and Pongal (in southern India), which are celebrated on 14/15 January to mark the start of the Sun's apparent journey northwards and a change of season.

Festivals celebrated throughout India are Chaitra (the New Year), Raksha-bandhan (the renewal of the kinship bond between brothers and sisters), Navaratri (a nine-night festival dedicated to the goddess Parvati), Dasara (the victory of Rama over the demon army), Diwali (a festival of lights), Makara Sankranti, Shivaratri (dedicated to Shiva), and Holi (a spring festival). British Hindus commonly celebrate the festival of Diwali as the start of the new year instead of observing it at the beginning of Chaitra.

Regional festivals are Durga-puja (dedicated to the goddess Durga (Parvati)), Sarasvati-puja (dedicated to the goddess Sarasvati), Ganesh Chaturthi (worship of Ganesh on the fourth day (Chaturthi) of the light half of Bhadrapad), Ramanavami (the birth festival of the god Rama) and Janmashtami (the birth festival of the god Krishna).

The main festivals celebrated in Britain are Navaratri, Dasara, Durga-puja, Diwali, Holi, Sarasvati-puja, Ganesh Chaturthi, Raksha-bandhan, Ramanavami and Janmashtami.

For dates of the main festivals in 2011, *see* page 9.

JEWISH CALENDAR

The story of the Flood in the Book of Genesis indicates the use of a calendar of some kind and that the writers recognised 30 days as the length of a lunation. However, after the diaspora, Jewish communities were left in considerable doubt as to the times of fasts and festivals. This led to the formation of the Jewish calendar as used today. It is said that this was done in AD 358 by Rabbi Hillel II, though some assert that it did not happen until much later.

The calendar is luni-solar, and is based on the lengths of the lunation and of the tropical year as found by Hipparchus (*c.*120 BC), which differ little from those adopted at the present day. The year AM 5771 (2010–11) is the 14th year of the 304th Metonic (Minor or Lunar) cycle of 19 years and the 3rd year of the 207th Solar (or Major) cycle of 28 years since the Era of the Creation. Jews hold that the Creation occurred at the time of the autumnal equinox in the year known in the Christian calendar as 3760 BC (954 of the Julian period). The epoch or starting point of Jewish chronology corresponds to 7 October 3761 BC. At the beginning of each solar cycle, the Tekufah of Nisan (the vernal equinox) returns to the same day and to the same hour.

The hour is divided into 1,080 minims, and the month between one new moon and the next is reckoned as 29 days 12 hours 793 minims. The normal calendar year, called a regular common year, consists of 12 months of 30 days and 29 days alternately. Since 12 months such as these comprise only 354 days, in order that each of them shall not diverge greatly from an average place in the solar year, a 13th month is occasionally added after the fifth month of the civil year (which commences on the first day of the month Tishri), or as the penultimate month of the ecclesiastical year (which commences on the first day of the month Nisan). The years when this happens are called Embolismic or leap years.

Of the 19 years that form a Metonic cycle, seven are leap years; they occur at places in the cycle indicated by the numbers 3, 6, 8, 11, 14, 17 and 19, these places being chosen so that the accumulated excesses of the solar years should be as small as possible.

A Jewish year is of one of the following six types:

Minimal common	353 days
Regular common	354 days
Full common	355 days
Minimal leap	383 days
Regular leap	384 days
Full leap	385 days

The regular year has alternate months of 30 and 29 days. In a Full year Marcheshvan, the second month of the civil year, has 30 days instead of 29; in minimal years Kislev, the third month, has 29 instead of 30. The additional month in leap years is called Adar Sheni and follows the month called Adar Rishon; the usual Adar festivals are observed in Adar Sheni. In a leap year Adar I has 30 days, in all other years it has 29. None of the variations mentioned are allowed to change the number of days in the other months, which still follow the alternation of the normal 12.

These are the main features of the Jewish calendar, which must be considered permanent because as a Jewish law it cannot be altered except by a Great Sanhedrin.

The Jewish day begins between sunset and nightfall. The time used is that of the meridian of Jerusalem, which is 2h 21m in advance of Greenwich Mean Time. Rules for the beginning of sabbaths and festivals were laid down for the latitude of London in the 18th century and hours for nightfall are fixed annually by the Chief Rabbi.

JEWISH CALENDAR 5771–72

AM 5771 is a full leap year of 13 months, 55 sabbaths and 385 days. AM 5772 is a regular common year of 12 months, 51 sabbaths and 354 days.

Month (length)	AM 5771	AM 5772
Tishri 1 (30)	9 September 2010	29 September
Marcheshvan 1 (30)	9 October	29 October
Kislev 1 (30)	8 November	27 November
Tebet 1 (29)	8 December	27 December
Shebat 1 (30)	6 January 2011	25 January 2012
**Adar 1* (29/30)	5 February	
†*Adar II* (30)	7 March	
Nisan 1 (30)	5 April	
Iyar 1 (29)	5 May	
Sivan 1 (30)	3 June	
Tammuz 1 (29)	3 July	
Ab 1 (30)	1 August	
Elul 1 (29)	31 August	

* Known as Adar Rishon in leap years

† Additional month in leap years, known as Adar Sheni

JEWISH FASTS AND FESTIVALS

For dates of principal festivals in 2011, *see* page 9.

Tishri 1–2	Rosh Hashanah (New Year)
Tishri 3	*Fast of Gedaliah
Tishri 10	Yom Kippur (Day of Atonement)
Tishri 15–21	Succoth (Feast of Tabernacles)
Tishri 21	Hoshana Rabba
Tishri 22	Shemini Atseret (Solemn Assembly)
Tishri 23	Simchat Torah (Rejoicing of the Law)
Kislev 25	Hanukkah (Dedication of the Temple) begins
Tebet 10	Fast of Tebet
†*Adar* 13	§Fast of Esther
†*Adar* 14	Purim
†*Adar* 15	Shushan Purim
Nisan 15–22	Pesach (Passover)
Sivan 6–7	Shavuoth (Feast of Weeks)
Tammuz 17	*Fast of Tammuz
Ab 9	*Fast of Ab

* If these dates fall on the sabbath the fast is kept on the following day

† Adar Sheni in leap years

§ This fast is observed on Adar 11 (or Adar Sheni 11 in leap years) if Adar 13 falls on a sabbath

MUSLIM CALENDAR

The Muslim era is dated from the *Hijrah,* or flight of the Prophet Muhammad from Mecca to Medina, the corresponding date of which in the Julian calendar is 16 July AD 622. The lunar *hijri* calendar is used principally in Iran, Egypt, Malaysia, Pakistan, Mauritania, various Arab states and certain parts of India. Iran uses the solar hijri calendar as well as the lunar hijri calendar. The dating system was adopted about AD 639, commencing with the first day of the month Muharram.

The lunar calendar consists of 12 months containing an alternate sequence of 30 and 29 days, with the intercalation of one day at the end of the 12th month at stated intervals in each cycle of 30 years. The object of the intercalation is to reconcile the date of the first day of the month with the date of the actual new moon.

Some adherents still take the date of the evening of the first physical sighting of the crescent of the new moon as that of the first of the month. If cloud obscures the moon the present month may be extended to 30 days, after which the new month will begin automatically regardless of whether the moon has been seen. (Under religious law a month must have less than 31 days.) This means that the beginning of a new month and the date of religious festivals can vary from the published calendars.

In each cycle of 30 years, 19 years are common and contain 354 days, and 11 years are intercalary (leap years) of 355 days, the latter being called *kabisah.* The mean length of the Hijrah years is 354 days 8 hours 48 minutes and the period of mean lunation is 29 days 12 hours 44 minutes.

To ascertain if a year is common or kabisah, divide it by 30: the quotient gives the number of completed cycles and the remainder shows the place of the year in the current cycle. If the remainder is 2, 5, 7, 10, 13, 16, 18, 21, 24, 26 or 29, the year is kabisah and consists of 355 days.

MUSLIM CALENDAR 1432–33

Hijrah 1432 AH (remainder 22) is a common year and Hijrah 1433 (remainder 23) is also a common year. Calendar dates below are estimates based on calculations of moon phases.

Month (length)	1432 AH	1433 AH
Muharram 1 (30)	7 December 2010	26 November
Safar 1 (29)	5 January 2011	26 December
Rabi' I 1 (30)	4 February	
Rabi' II 1 (29)	6 March	
Jumada I 1 (30)	15 April	
Jumada II 1 (29)	4 May	
Rajab 1 (30)	3 June	
Sha'ban 1 (29)	2 July	
Ramadan 1 (30)	1 August	
Shawwal 1 (29)	30 August	
Dhu'l-Qa'da 1 (30)	29 September	
Dhu'l-Hijjah 1 (30)	28 October	

MUSLIM FESTIVALS

Ramadan is a month of fasting for all Muslims because it is the month in which the revelation of the *Qur'an* (Koran) began. During Ramadan, Muslims abstain from food, drink and sexual pleasure from dawn until after sunset throughout the month.

The two major festivals are *Eid ul-Fitr* and *Eid ul-Adha.* Eid ul-Fitr marks the end of the Ramadan fast and is celebrated on the day after the sighting of the new moon of the following month. Eid ul-Adha, the festival of sacrifice (also known as the great festival), celebrates the submission of the Prophet Ibrahim (Abraham) to God. Eid ul-Adha falls on the tenth day of Dhu'l-Hijjah, coinciding with the day when those on *hajj* (pilgrimage to Mecca) sacrifice animals.

Other days accorded special recognition are:

Muharram 1	New Year's Day
Muharram 10	Ashura (the day Prophet Noah left the Ark and Prophet Moses was saved from Pharaoh (Sunni), the death of the Prophet's grandson Husain (Shi'ite))
Rabi'u-l-Awwal (Rabi' I) 12	Mawlid ul-Nabi (birthday of the Prophet Muhammad)
Rajab 27	Laylat ul-Isra' wa'l-Mi'raj (The Night of Journey and Ascension)
*Ramadan**	Laylat ul-Qadr (Night of Power)
Dhu'l-Hijjah 10	Eid ul-Adha (Festival of Sacrifice)

* Moveable feast

For dates of the major celebrations in 2011, *see* page 9.

SIKH CALENDAR

The Sikh calendar is a lunar calendar of 365 days divided into 12 months. The length of the months varies between 29 and 32 days.

There are no prescribed feast days and no fasting periods. The main celebrations are Baisakhi Mela (the new year and the anniversary of the founding of the Khalsa), Diwali Mela (festival of light), Hola Mohalla Mela (a spring festival held in the Punjab), and the Gurpurbs (anniversaries associated with the ten Gurus).

For dates of the major celebrations in 2011, *see* page 9.

THAI CALENDAR

Thailand adopted the Suriyakati calendar, a modified version of the Gregorian calendar during the reign of King Rama V in 1888, using 1 April as the first day of the year. In 1940 the date of the new year was changed to 1 January. The years are counted from the beginning of the Buddhist era (BE), which is calculated to have commenced upon the death of the Lord Buddha, taken to have occurred in 543 BC, so AD 2011 is BE 2554. The Chinese system of associating years with one of twelve animals is also in use in Thailand. The Chantarakati lunar calendar is used to determine religious holidays; the new year begins on the first day of the waxing moon in November or, if there is a leap month, in December.

CIVIL AND LEGAL CALENDAR

THE HISTORICAL YEAR

Before 1752, two calendar systems were used in England. The civil or legal year began on 25 March and the historical year on 1 January. Thus the civil or legal date 24 March 1658 was the same day as the historical date 24 March 1659; a date in that portion of the year is written as 24 March 1658/9, the earlier date showing the civil or legal year.

THE NEW YEAR

In England in the seventh century, and as late as the 13th, the year was reckoned from Christmas Day, but in the 12th century the Church in England began the year with the feast of the Annunciation of the Blessed Virgin ('Lady Day') on 25 March, and this practice was adopted generally in the 14th century. The civil or legal year in the British dominions (exclusive of Scotland) began with

Lady Day until 1751. But in and since 1752 the civil year has begun with 1 January. New Year's Day in Scotland was changed from 25 March to 1 January in 1600.

Elsewhere in Europe, 1 January was adopted as the first day of the year by Venice in 1522, German states in 1544, Spain, Portugal and the Roman Catholic Netherlands in 1556, Prussia, Denmark and Sweden in 1559, France in 1564, Lorraine in 1579, the Protestant Netherlands in 1583, Russia in 1725, and Tuscany in 1751.

REGNAL YEARS

Regnal years are the years of a sovereign's reign and each begins on the anniversary of his or her accession, eg regnal year 60 of the present queen begins on 6 February 2011.

The system was used for dating Acts of Parliament until 1962. The Summer Time Act 1925, for example, is quoted as 15 and 16 Geo. V c. 64, because it became law in the parliamentary session which extended over part of both of these regnal years. Acts of a parliamentary session during which a sovereign died were usually given two year numbers, the regnal year of the deceased sovereign and the regnal year of his or her successor, eg those passed in 1952 were dated 16 Geo. VI and 1 Elizabeth II. Since 1962 Acts of Parliament have been dated by the calendar year.

QUARTER AND TERM DAYS

Holy days and saints days were the usual means in early times for setting the dates of future and recurrent appointments. The quarter days in England and Wales are the feast of the Nativity (25 December), the feast of the Annunciation (25 March), the feast of St John the Baptist (24 June) and the feast of St Michael and All Angels (29 September).

The term days in Scotland are Candlemas (the feast of the Purification), Whitsunday, Lammas (Loaf Mass) and Martinmas (St Martin's Day). These fell on 2 February, 15 May, 1 August and 11 November respectively. However, by the Term and Quarter Days (Scotland) Act 1990, the dates of the term days were changed to 28 February (Candlemas), 28 May (Whitsunday), 28 August (Lammas) and 28 November (Martinmas).

RED-LETTER DAYS

Red-letter days were originally the holy days and saints days indicated in early ecclesiastical calendars by letters printed in red ink. The days to be distinguished in this way were approved at the Council of Nicaea in AD 325.

These days still have a legal significance, as judges of the Queen's Bench Division wear scarlet robes on red-letter days falling during the law sittings. The days designated as red-letter days for this purpose are:

Holy and saints days

The Conversion of St Paul, the Purification, Ash Wednesday, the Annunciation, the Ascension, the feasts of St Mark, SS Philip and James, St Matthias, St Barnabas, St John the Baptist, St Peter, St Thomas, St James, St Luke, SS Simon and Jude, All Saints, St Andrew.

Civil calendar (for dates, *see* page 9)

The anniversaries of the Queen's accession, the Queen's birthday and the Queen's coronation, the Queen's official birthday, the birthday of the Duke of Edinburgh, the birthday of the Prince of Wales, St David's Day and Lord Mayor's Day.

PUBLIC HOLIDAYS

Public holidays are divided into two categories, common law and statutory. Common law holidays are holidays 'by habit and custom'; in England, Wales and Northern Ireland these are Good Friday and Christmas Day.

Statutory public holidays, known as bank holidays, were first established by the Bank Holidays Act 1871. They were, literally, days on which the banks (and other public institutions) were closed and financial obligations due on that day were payable the following day. The legislation currently governing public holidays in the UK, which is the Banking and Financial Dealings Act 1971, stipulates the days that are to be public holidays in England, Wales, Scotland and Northern Ireland.

If a public holiday falls on a Saturday or a Sunday then another day will be given in lieu, usually the following Monday. For example, Christmas Day in 2011 falls on a Sunday, so Monday 26 December will be a 'substitute' holiday. For dates of public holidays in 2011 and 2012, *see* pages 10–11. The public holidays are:

England and Wales
*New Year's Day
Good Friday
Easter Monday
*The first Monday in May
The last Monday in May
The last Monday in August
Christmas Day
Boxing Day

Scotland
New Year's Day
*2 January
Good Friday
The first Monday in May
*The last Monday in May
The first Monday in August
†St Andrew's Day
Christmas Day
Boxing Day

Northern Ireland
*New Year's Day
Good Friday
17 March
Easter Monday
*The first Monday in May
The last Monday in May
‡12 July
The last Monday in August
Christmas Day
Boxing Day

* Granted annually by royal proclamation
† Voluntary public holiday in exchange for an existing local holiday
‡ Subject to proclamation by the secretary of state for Northern Ireland

CHRONOLOGICAL CYCLES AND ERAS

SOLAR (OR MAJOR) CYCLE

The solar cycle is a period of 28 years; in any corresponding year of each cycle the days of the week recur on the same day of the month.

METONIC (LUNAR, OR MINOR) CYCLE

In 432 BC, Meton, an Athenian astronomer, found that 235 lunations are very nearly, though not exactly, equal in duration to 19 solar years and so after 19 years the phases of the Moon recur on the same days of the month (nearly). The dates of full moon in a cycle of 19 years were inscribed in figures of gold on public monuments in Athens, and the number showing the position of a year in the cycle is called the golden number of that year.

JULIAN PERIOD

The Julian period was proposed by Joseph Scaliger in 1582. The period is 7,980 Julian years, and its first year coincides with the year 4713 BC. The figure of 7,980 is the product of the number of years in the solar cycle, the Metonic cycle and the cycle of the Roman indiction (28 × 19 × 15).

ROMAN INDICTION

The Roman indiction is a period of 15 years, instituted for fiscal purposes about AD 300.

EPACT

The epact is the age of the calendar Moon, diminished by one day, on 1 January, in the ecclesiastical lunar calendar.

CHINESE CALENDAR

A lunar calendar was the sole calendar in use in China until 1911, when the government adopted the new (Gregorian) calendar for official and most business activities. The Chinese tend to follow both calendars, the lunar calendar playing an important part in personal life, eg birth celebrations, festivals, marriages; and in rural villages the lunar calendar dictates the cycle of activities, denoting the change of weather and farming activities.

The lunar calendar is used in Hong Kong, Singapore, Malaysia, Tibet and elsewhere in south-east Asia. The calendar has a cycle of 60 years. The new year begins at the first new moon after the sun enters the sign of Aquarius, ie the new year falls between 21 January and 19 February in the Gregorian calendar.

Each year in the Chinese calendar is associated with one of 12 animals: the rat, the ox, the tiger, the rabbit, the dragon, the snake, the horse, the goat or sheep, the monkey, the chicken or rooster, the dog, and the pig.

The date of the Chinese new year and the astrological sign for the years 2011–14 are:

2011	3 February	Rabbit
2012	23 January	Dragon
2013	10 February	Snake
2014	31 January	Horse

COPTIC CALENDAR

In the Coptic calendar, which is used in parts of Egypt and Ethiopia, the year is made up of 12 months of 30 days each, followed, in general, by five complementary days. Every fourth year is an intercalary or leap year and in these years there are six complementary days. The intercalary year of the Coptic calendar immediately precedes the leap year of the Julian calendar. The era is that of Diocletian or the Martyrs, the origin of which is fixed at 29 August AD 284 (Julian date).

INDIAN ERAS

In addition to the Muslim reckoning, other eras are used in India. The Saka era of southern India, dating from 3 March AD 78, was declared the national calendar of the Republic of India with effect from 22 March 1957, to be used concurrently with the Gregorian calendar. As revised, the year of the new Saka era begins at the spring equinox, with five successive months of 31 days and seven of 30 days in ordinary years, and six months of each length in leap years. The year AD 2011 is 1933 of the revised Saka era.

The year AD 2011 corresponds to the following years in other eras:

Year 2068 of the Vikram Samvat era
Year 1418 of the Bengali San era
Year 1187 of the Kollam era
Year 5112 of the Kaliyuga era
Year 2554 of the Buddha Nirvana era

JAPANESE CALENDAR

The Japanese calendar is essentially the same as the Gregorian calendar, the years, months and weeks being of the same length and beginning on the same days as those of the Gregorian calendar. The numeration of the years is different, based on a system of epochs or periods, each of which begins at the accession of an emperor or other important occurrence. The method is not unlike the British system of regnal years, except that each year of a period closes on 31 December. The Japanese chronology begins about AD 650 and the three latest epochs are defined by the reigns of emperors, whose actual names are not necessarily used:

Epoch
Taisho – 1 August 1912 to 25 December 1926
Showa – 26 December 1926 to 7 January 1989
Heisei – 8 January 1989

The year Heisei 23 begins on 1 January 2011.

The months are known as First Month, Second Month, etc, First Month being equivalent to January. The days of the week are Nichiyobi (Sun-day), Getsuyobi (Moon-day), Kayobi (Fire-day), Suiyobi (Water-day), Mokuyobi (Wood-day), Kinyobi (Metal-day) and Doyobi (Earth-day).

THE MASONIC YEAR

Two dates are quoted in warrants, dispensations, etc, issued by the United Grand Lodge of England, those for the current year being expressed as *Anno Domini* 2011 – *Anno Lucis* 6011. This *Anno Lucis* (year of light) is based on the Book of Genesis 1:3, the 4,000-year difference being derived, in modified form, from *Ussher's Notation,* published in 1654, which places the Creation of the World in 4004 BC.

OLYMPIADS

Ancient Greek chronology was reckoned in Olympiads, cycles of four years corresponding with the periodic Olympic Games held on the plain of Olympia, in Elis, once every four years. The intervening years were the first, second, etc, of the Olympiad, which received the name of the victor at the Games. The first recorded Olympiad is that of Choroebus, 776 BC.

ZOROASTRIAN CALENDAR

Zoroastrians, followers of the Iranian prophet Zarathushtra (known to the Greeks as Zoroaster) are mostly to be found in Iran and in India, where they are known as Parsees.

The Zoroastrian era dates from the coronation of the last Zoroastrian Sasanian king in AD 631. The Zoroastrian calendar is divided into 12 months, each comprising 30 days, followed by five holy days of the Gathas at the end of each year to make the year consist of 365 days.

In order to synchronise the calendar with the solar year of 365 days, an extra month was intercalated once every

120 years. However, this intercalation ceased in the 12th century and the new year, which had fallen in the spring, slipped back to August. Because intercalation ceased at different times in Iran and India, there was one month's difference between the calendar followed in Iran (Kadmi calendar) and that followed by the Parsees (Shenshai calendar). In 1906 a group of Zoroastrians decided to bring the calendar back in line with the seasons again and restore the new year to 21 March each year (Fasli calendar).

The Shenshai calendar (new year in August) is mainly used by Parsees. The Fasli calendar (new year, 21 March) is mainly used by Zoroastrians living in Iran, in the Indian subcontinent, or away from Iran.

ROMAN CALENDAR

Roman historians adopted as an epoch the foundation of Rome, which is believed to have happened in the year 753 BC. The ordinal number of the years in Roman reckoning is followed by the letters AUC *(ab urbe condita)*, so that the year 2011 is 2764 AUC (MMDCCLXIV). The calendar that we know has developed from one said to have been established by Romulus using a year of 304 days divided into ten months, beginning with March. To this Numa added January and February, making the year consist of 12 months of 30 and 29 days alternately, with an additional day so that the total was 355. It is also said that Numa ordered an intercalary month of 22 or 23 days in alternate years, making 90 days in eight years, to be inserted after 23 February.

However, there is some doubt as to the origination and the details of the intercalation in the Roman calendar. It is certain that some scheme of this kind was inaugurated and not fully carried out, for in the year 46 BC Julius Caesar found that the calendar had been allowed to fall into some confusion. He sought the help of the Egyptian astronomer Sosigenes, which led to the construction and adoption (45 BC) of the Julian calendar, and, by a slight alteration, to the Gregorian calendar now in use. The year 46 BC was made to consist of 445 days and is called the Year of Confusion.

In the Roman (Julian) calendar the days of the month were counted backwards from three fixed points, or days, and an intervening day was said to be so many days before the next coming point, the first and last being counted. These three points were the Kalends, the Nones, and the Ides. Their positions in the months and the method of counting from them will be seen in the table below. The year containing 366 days was called *bissextilis annus*, as it had a doubled sixth day *(bissextus dies)* before the March Kalends on 24 February – *ante diem sextum Kalendas Martias*, or a.d. VI Kal. Mart.

Present days of the month	*March, May, July, October have thirty-one days*	*January, August, December have thirty-one days*	*April, June, September, November have thirty days*	*February has twenty-eight days, and in leap year twenty-nine*
1	Kalendis	Kalendis	Kalendis	Kalendis
2	VI	IV ante	IV ante	IV ante
3	V ante	III Nonas	III Nonas	III Nonas
4	IV Nonas	pridie Nonas	pridie Nonas	pridie Nonas
5	III	Nonis	Nonis	Nonis
6	pridie Nonas	VIII	VIII	VIII
7	Nonis	VII	VII	VII
8	VIII	VI ante	VI ante	VI ante
9	VII	V Idus	V Idus	V Idus
10	VI ante	IV	IV	IV
11	V Idus	III	III	III
12	IV	pridie Idus	pridie Idus	pridie Idus
13	III	Idibus	Idibus	Idibus
14	pridie Idus	XIX	XVIII	XVI
15	Idibus	XVIII	XVII	XV
16	XVII	XVII	XVI	XIV
17	XVI	XVI	XV	XIII
18	XV	XV	XIV	XII
19	XIV	XIV	XIII	XI
20	XIII	XIII	XII ante Kalendas	X ante Kalendas
21	XII	XII ante Kalendas	XI (of the month	IX Martias
22	XI ante Kalendas	XI (of the month	X following)	VIII
23	X (of the month	X following)	IX	VII
24	IX following)	IX	VIII	*VI
25	VIII	VIII	VII	V
26	VII	VII	VI	IV
27	VI	VI	V	III
28	V	V	IV	pridie Kalendas
29	IV	IV	III	Martias
30	III	III	pridie Kalendas	
31	pridie Kalendas (Aprilis, Iunias, Sextilis, Novembris)	pridie Kalendas (Februarias, Septembris, Ianuarias)	(Maias, Quinctilis, Octobris, Decembris)	

* Repeated in leap year

CALENDAR FOR ANY YEAR 1780–2040

To select the correct calendar for any year between 1780 and 2040, consult the index below

*leap year

1780 N*	1813 K	1846 I	1879 G	1912 D*	1945 C	1978 A	2011 M
1781 C	1814 M	1847 K	1880 J*	1913 G	1946 E	1979 C	2012 B*
1782 E	1815 A	1848 N*	1881 M	1914 I	1947 G	1980 F*	2013 E
1783 G	1816 D*	1849 C	1882 A	1915 K	1948 J*	1981 I	2014 G
1784 J*	1817 G	1850 E	1883 C	1916 N*	1949 M	1982 K	2015 I
1785 M	1818 I	1851 G	1884 F*	1917 C	1950 A	1983 M	2016 L*
1786 A	1819 K	1852 J*	1885 I	1918 E	1951 C	1984 B*	2017 A
1787 C	1820 N*	1853 M	1886 K	1919 G	1952 F*	1985 E	2018 C
1788 F*	1821 C	1854 A	1887 M	1920 J*	1953 I	1986 G	2019 E
1789 I	1822 E	1855 C	1888 B*	1921 M	1954 K	1987 I	2020 H*
1790 K	1823 G	1856 F*	1889 E	1922 A	1955 M	1988 L*	2021 K
1791 M	1824 J*	1857 I	1890 G	1923 C	1956 B*	1989 A	2022 M
1792 B*	1825 M	1858 K	1891 I	1924 F*	1957 E	1990 C	2023 A
1793 E	1826 A	1859 M	1892 L*	1925 I	1958 G	1991 E	2024 D*
1794 G	1827 C	1860 B*	1893 A	1926 K	1959 I	1992 H*	2025 G
1795 I	1828 F*	1861 E	1894 C	1927 M	1960 L*	1993 K	2026 I
1796 L*	1829 I	1862 G	1895 E	1928 B*	1961 A	1994 M	2027 K
1797 A	1830 K	1863 I	1896 H*	1929 E	1962 C	1995 A	2028 N*
1798 C	1831 M	1864 L*	1897 K	1930 G	1963 E	1996 D*	2029 C
1799 E	1832 B*	1865 A	1898 M	1931 I	1964 H*	1997 G	2030 E
1800 G	1833 E	1866 C	1899 A	1932 L*	1965 K	1998 I	2031 G
1801 I	1834 G	1867 E	1900 C	1933 A	1966 M	1999 K	2032 J*
1802 K	1835 I	1868 H*	1901 E	1934 C	1967 A	2000 N*	2033 M
1803 M	1836 L*	1869 K	1902 G	1935 E	1968 D*	2001 C	2034 A
1804 B*	1837 A	1870 M	1903 I	1936 H*	1969 G	2002 E	2035 C
1805 E	1838 C	1871 A	1904 L*	1937 K	1970 I	2003 G	2036 F*
1806 G	1839 E	1872 D*	1905 A	1938 M	1971 K	2004 J*	2037 I
1807 I	1840 H*	1873 G	1906 C	1939 A	1972 N*	2005 M	2038 K
1808 L*	1841 K	1874 I	1907 E	1940 D*	1973 C	2006 A	2039 M
1809 A	1842 M	1875 K	1908 H*	1941 G	1974 E	2007 C	2040 B*
1810 C	1843 A	1876 N*	1909 K	1942 I	1975 G	2008 F*	
1811 E	1844 D*	1877 C	1910 M	1943 K	1976 J*	2009 I	
1812 H*	1845 G	1878 E	1911 A	1944 N*	1977 M	2010 K	

A

	January	*February*	*March*
Sun.	1 8 15 22 29	5 12 19 26	5 12 19 26
Mon.	2 9 16 23 30	6 13 20 27	6 13 20 27
Tue.	3 10 17 24 31	7 14 21 28	7 14 21 28
Wed.	4 11 18 25	1 8 15 22	1 8 15 22 29
Thur.	5 12 19 26	2 9 16 23	2 9 16 23 30
Fri.	6 13 20 27	3 10 17 24	3 10 17 24 31
Sat.	7 14 21 28	4 11 18 25	4 11 18 25

	April	*May*	*June*
Sun.	2 9 16 23 30	7 14 21 28	4 11 18 25
Mon.	3 10 17 24	1 8 15 22 29	5 12 19 26
Tue.	4 11 18 25	2 9 16 23 30	6 13 20 27
Wed.	5 12 19 26	3 10 17 24 31	7 14 21 28
Thur.	6 13 20 27	4 11 18 25	1 8 15 22 29
Fri.	7 14 21 28	5 12 19 26	2 9 16 23 30
Sat.	1 8 15 22 29	6 13 20 27	3 10 17 24

	July	*August*	*September*
Sun.	2 9 16 23 30	6 13 20 27	3 10 17 24
Mon.	3 10 17 24 31	7 14 21 28	4 11 18 25
Tue.	4 11 18 25	1 8 15 22 29	5 12 19 26
Wed.	5 12 19 26	2 9 16 23 30	6 13 20 27
Thur.	6 13 20 27	3 10 17 24 31	7 14 21 28
Fri.	7 14 21 28	4 11 18 25	1 8 15 22 29
Sat.	1 8 15 22 29	5 12 19 26	2 9 16 23 30

	October	*November*	*December*
Sun.	1 8 15 22 29	5 12 19 26	3 10 17 24 31
Mon.	2 9 16 23 30	6 13 20 27	4 11 18 25
Tue.	3 10 17 24 31	7 14 21 28	5 12 19 26
Wed.	4 11 18 25	1 8 15 22 29	6 13 20 27
Thur.	5 12 19 26	2 9 16 23 30	7 14 21 28
Fri.	6 13 20 27	3 10 17 24	1 8 15 22 29
Sat.	7 14 21 28	4 11 18 25	2 9 16 23 30

EASTER DAYS

March 26	1815, 1826, 1837, 1967, 1978, 1989
April 2	1809, 1893, 1899, 1961
April 9	1871, 1882, 1939, 1950, 2023, 2034
April 16	1786, 1797, 1843, 1854, 1865, 1911 1922, 1933, 1995, 2006, 2017
April 23	1905

B (LEAP YEAR)

	January	*February*	*March*
Sun.	1 8 15 22 29	5 12 19 26	4 11 18 25
Mon.	2 9 16 23 30	6 13 20 27	5 12 19 26
Tue.	3 10 17 24 31	7 14 21 28	6 13 20 27
Wed.	4 11 18 25	1 8 15 22 29	7 14 21 28
Thur.	5 12 19 26	2 9 16 23	1 8 15 22 29
Fri.	6 13 20 27	3 10 17 24	2 9 16 23 30
Sat.	7 14 21 28	4 11 18 25	3 10 17 24 31

	April	*May*	*June*
Sun.	1 8 15 22 29	6 13 20 27	3 10 17 24
Mon.	2 9 16 23 30	7 14 21 28	4 11 18 25
Tue.	3 10 17 24	1 8 15 22 29	5 12 19 26
Wed.	4 11 18 25	2 9 16 23 30	6 13 20 27
Thur.	5 12 19 26	3 10 17 24 31	7 14 21 28
Fri.	6 13 20 27	4 11 18 25	1 8 15 22 29
Sat.	7 14 21 28	5 12 19 26	2 9 16 23 30

	July	*August*	*September*
Sun.	1 8 15 22 29	5 12 19 26	2 9 16 23 30
Mon.	2 9 16 23 30	6 13 20 27	3 10 17 24
Tue.	3 10 17 24 31	7 14 21 28	4 11 18 25
Wed.	4 11 18 25	1 8 15 22 29	5 12 19 26
Thur.	5 12 19 26	2 9 16 23 30	6 13 20 27
Fri.	6 13 20 27	3 10 17 24 31	7 14 21 28
Sat.	7 14 21 28	4 11 18 25	1 8 15 22 29

	October	*November*	*December*
Sun.	7 14 21 28	4 11 18 25	2 9 16 23 30
Mon.	1 8 15 22 29	5 12 19 26	3 10 17 24 31
Tue.	2 9 16 23 30	6 13 20 27	4 11 18 25
Wed.	3 10 17 24 31	7 14 21 28	5 12 19 26
Thur.	4 11 18 25	1 8 15 22 29	6 13 20 27
Fri.	5 12 19 26	2 9 16 23 30	7 14 21 28
Sat.	6 13 20 27	3 10 17 24	1 8 15 22 29

EASTER DAYS

April 1	1804, 1888, 1956, 2040
April 8	1792, 1860, 1928, 2012
April 22	1832, 1984

C

	January	*February*	*March*
Sun.	7 14 21 28	4 11 18 25	4 11 18 25
Mon.	1 8 15 22 29	5 12 19 26	5 12 19 26
Tue.	2 9 16 23 30	6 13 20 27	6 13 20 27
Wed.	3 10 17 24 31	7 14 21 28	7 14 21 28
Thur.	4 11 18 25	1 8 15 22	1 8 15 22 29
Fri.	5 12 19 26	2 9 16 23	2 9 16 23 30
Sat.	6 13 20 27	3 10 17 24	3 10 17 24 31

	April	*May*	*June*
Sun.	1 8 15 22 29	6 13 20 27	3 10 17 24
Mon.	2 9 16 23 30	7 14 21 28	4 11 18 25
Tue.	3 10 17 24	1 8 15 22 29	5 12 19 26
Wed.	4 11 18 25	2 9 16 23 30	6 13 20 27
Thur.	5 12 19 26	3 10 17 24 31	7 14 21 28
Fri.	6 13 20 27	4 11 18 25	1 8 15 22 29
Sat.	7 14 21 28	5 12 19 26	2 9 16 23 30

	July	*August*	*September*
Sun.	1 8 15 22 29	5 12 19 26	2 9 16 23 30
Mon.	2 9 16 23 30	6 13 20 27	3 10 17 24
Tue.	3 10 17 24 31	7 14 21 28	4 11 18 25
Wed.	4 11 18 25	1 8 15 22 29	5 12 19 26
Thur.	5 12 19 26	2 9 16 23 30	6 13 20 27
Fri.	6 13 20 27	3 10 17 24 31	7 14 21 28
Sat.	7 14 21 28	4 11 18 25	1 8 15 22 29

	October	*November*	*December*
Sun.	7 14 21 28	4 11 18 25	2 9 16 23 30
Mon.	1 8 15 22 29	5 12 19 26	3 10 17 24 31
Tue.	2 9 16 23 30	6 13 20 27	4 11 18 25
Wed.	3 10 17 24 31	7 14 21 28	5 12 19 26
Thur.	4 11 18 25	1 8 15 22 29	6 13 20 27
Fri.	5 12 19 26	2 9 16 23 30	7 14 21 28
Sat.	6 13 20 27	3 10 17 24	1 8 15 22 29

EASTER DAYS

March 25	1883, 1894, 1951, 2035
April 1	1866, 1877, 1923, 1934, 1945, 2018, 2029
April 8	1787, 1798, 1849, 1855, 1917, 2007
April 15	1781, 1827, 1838, 1900, 1906, 1979, 1990, 2001
April 22	1810, 1821, 1962, 1973

D (LEAP YEAR)

	January	*February*	*March*
Sun.	7 14 21 28	4 11 18 25	3 10 17 24 31
Mon.	1 8 15 22 29	5 12 19 26	4 11 18 25
Tue.	2 9 16 23 30	6 13 20 27	5 12 19 26
Wed.	3 10 17 24 31	7 14 21 28	6 13 20 27
Thur.	4 11 18 25	1 8 15 22 29	7 14 21 28
Fri.	5 12 19 26	2 9 16 23	1 8 15 22 29
Sat.	6 13 20 27	3 10 17 24	2 9 16 23 30

	April	*May*	*June*
Sun.	7 14 21 28	5 12 19 26	2 9 16 23 30
Mon.	1 8 15 22 29	6 13 20 27	3 10 17 24
Tue.	2 9 16 23 30	7 14 21 28	4 11 18 25
Wed.	3 10 17 24	1 8 15 22 29	5 12 19 26
Thur.	4 11 18 25	2 9 16 23 30	6 13 20 27
Fri.	5 12 19 26	3 10 17 24 31	7 14 21 28
Sat.	6 13 20 27	4 11 18 25	1 8 15 22 29

	July	*August*	*September*
Sun.	7 14 21 28	4 11 18 25	1 8 15 22 29
Mon.	1 8 15 22 29	5 12 19 26	2 9 16 23 30
Tue.	2 9 16 23 30	6 13 20 27	3 10 17 24
Wed.	3 10 17 24 31	7 14 21 28	4 11 18 25
Thur.	4 11 18 25	1 8 15 22 29	5 12 19 26
Fri.	5 12 19 26	2 9 16 23 30	6 13 20 27
Sat.	6 13 20 27	3 10 17 24 31	7 14 21 28

	October	*November*	*December*
Sun.	6 13 20 27	3 10 17 24	1 8 15 22 29
Mon.	7 14 21 28	4 11 18 25	2 9 16 23 30
Tue.	1 8 15 22 29	5 12 19 26	3 10 17 24 31
Wed.	2 9 16 23 30	6 13 20 27	4 11 18 25
Thur.	3 10 17 24 31	7 14 21 28	5 12 19 26
Fri.	4 11 18 25	1 8 15 22 29	6 13 20 27
Sat.	5 12 19 26	2 9 16 23 30	7 14 21 28

EASTER DAYS

March 24	1940
March 31	1872, 2024
April 7	1844, 1912, 1996
April 14	1816, 1968

E

	January	*February*	*March*
Sun.	6 13 20 27	3 10 17 24	3 10 17 24 31
Mon.	7 14 21 28	4 11 18 25	4 11 18 25
Tue.	1 8 15 22 29	5 12 19 26	5 12 19 26
Wed.	2 9 16 23 30	6 13 20 27	6 13 20 27
Thur.	3 10 17 24 31	7 14 21 28	7 14 21 28
Fri.	4 11 18 25	1 8 15 22	1 8 15 22 29
Sat.	5 12 19 26	2 9 16 23	2 9 16 23 30

	April	*May*	*June*
Sun.	7 14 21 28	5 12 19 26	2 9 16 23 30
Mon.	1 8 15 22 29	6 13 20 27	3 10 17 24
Tue.	2 9 16 23 30	7 14 21 28	4 11 18 25
Wed.	3 10 17 24	1 8 15 22 29	5 12 19 26
Thur.	4 11 18 25	2 9 16 23 30	6 13 20 27
Fri.	5 12 19 26	3 10 17 24 31	7 14 21 28
Sat.	6 13 20 27	4 11 18 25	1 8 15 22 29

	July	*August*	*September*
Sun.	7 14 21 28	4 11 18 25	1 8 15 22 29
Mon.	1 8 15 22 29	5 12 19 26	2 9 16 23 30
Tue.	2 9 16 23 30	6 13 20 27	3 10 17 24
Wed.	3 10 17 24 31	7 14 21 28	4 11 18 25
Thur.	4 11 18 25	1 8 15 22 29	5 12 19 26
Fri.	5 12 19 26	2 9 16 23 30	6 13 20 27
Sat.	6 13 20 27	3 10 17 24 31	7 14 21 28

	October	*November*	*December*
Sun.	6 13 20 27	3 10 17 24	1 8 15 22 29
Mon.	7 14 21 28	4 11 18 25	2 9 16 23 30
Tue.	1 8 15 22 29	5 12 19 26	3 10 17 24 31
Wed.	2 9 16 23 30	6 13 20 27	4 11 18 25
Thur.	3 10 17 24 31	7 14 21 28	5 12 19 26
Fri.	4 11 18 25	1 8 15 22 29	6 13 20 27
Sat.	5 12 19 26	2 9 16 23 30	7 14 21 28

EASTER DAYS

March 24	1799
March 31	1782, 1793, 1839, 1850, 1861, 1907 1918, 1929, 1991, 2002, 2013
April 7	1822, 1833, 1901, 1985
April 14	1805, 1811, 1895, 1963, 1974
April 21	1867, 1878, 1889, 1935, 1946, 1957, 2019, 2030

F (LEAP YEAR)

	January	*February*	*March*
Sun.	6 13 20 27	3 10 17 24	2 9 16 23 30
Mon.	7 14 21 28	4 11 18 25	3 10 17 24 31
Tue.	1 8 15 22 29	5 12 19 26	4 11 18 25
Wed.	2 9 16 23 30	6 13 20 27	5 12 19 26
Thur.	3 10 17 24 31	7 14 21 28	6 13 20 27
Fri.	4 11 18 25	1 8 15 22 29	7 14 21 28
Sat.	5 12 19 26	2 9 16 23	1 8 15 22 29

	April	*May*	*June*
Sun.	6 13 20 27	4 11 18 25	1 8 15 22 29
Mon.	7 14 21 28	5 12 19 26	2 9 16 23 30
Tue.	1 8 15 22 29	6 13 20 27	3 10 17 24
Wed.	2 9 16 23 30	7 14 21 28	4 11 18 25
Thur.	3 10 17 24	1 8 15 22 29	5 12 19 26
Fri.	4 11 18 25	2 9 16 23 30	6 13 20 27
Sat.	5 12 19 26	3 10 17 24 31	7 14 21 28

	July	*August*	*September*
Sun.	6 13 20 27	3 10 17 24 31	7 14 21 28
Mon.	7 14 21 28	4 11 18 25	1 8 15 22 29
Tue.	1 8 15 22 29	5 12 19 26	2 9 16 23 30
Wed.	2 9 16 23 30	6 13 20 27	3 10 17 24
Thur.	3 10 17 24 31	7 14 21 28	4 11 18 25
Fri.	4 11 18 25	1 8 15 22 29	5 12 19 26
Sat.	5 12 19 26	2 9 16 23 30	6 13 20 27

	October	*November*	*December*
Sun.	5 12 19 26	2 9 16 23 30	7 14 21 28
Mon.	6 13 20 27	3 10 17 24	1 8 15 22 29
Tue.	7 14 21 28	4 11 18 25	2 9 16 23 30
Wed.	1 8 15 22 29	5 12 19 26	3 10 17 24 31
Thur.	2 9 16 23 30	6 13 20 27	4 11 18 25
Fri.	3 10 17 24 31	7 14 21 28	5 12 19 26
Sat.	4 11 18 25	1 8 15 22 29	6 13 20 27

EASTER DAYS

March 23	1788, 1856, 2008
April 6	1828, 1980
April 13	1884, 1952, 2036
April 20	1924

G

	January	*February*	*March*
Sun.	5 12 19 26	2 9 16 23	2 9 16 23 30
Mon.	6 13 20 27	3 10 17 24	3 10 17 24 31
Tue.	7 14 21 28	4 11 18 25	4 11 18 25
Wed.	1 8 15 22 29	5 12 19 26	5 12 19 26
Thur.	2 9 16 23 30	6 13 20 27	6 13 20 27
Fri.	3 10 17 24 31	7 14 21 28	7 14 21 28
Sat.	4 11 18 25	1 8 15 22	1 8 15 22 29

	April	*May*	*June*
Sun.	6 13 20 27	4 11 18 25	1 8 15 22 29
Mon.	7 14 21 28	5 12 19 26	2 9 16 23 30
Tue.	1 8 15 22 29	6 13 20 27	3 10 17 24
Wed.	2 9 16 23 30	7 14 21 28	4 11 18 25
Thur.	3 10 17 24	1 8 15 22 29	5 12 19 26
Fri.	4 11 18 25	2 9 16 23 30	6 13 20 27
Sat.	5 12 19 26	3 10 17 24 31	7 14 21 28

	July	*August*	*September*
Sun.	6 13 20 27	3 10 17 24 31	7 14 21 28
Mon.	7 14 21 28	4 11 18 25	1 8 15 22 29
Tue.	1 8 15 22 29	5 12 19 26	2 9 16 23 30
Wed.	2 9 16 23 30	6 13 20 27	3 10 17 24
Thur.	3 10 17 24 31	7 14 21 28	4 11 18 25
Fri.	4 11 18 25	1 8 15 22 29	5 12 19 26
Sat.	5 12 19 26	2 9 16 23 30	6 13 20 27

	October	*November*	*December*
Sun.	5 12 19 26	2 9 16 23 30	7 14 21 28
Mon.	6 13 20 27	3 10 17 24	1 8 15 22 29
Tue.	7 14 21 28	4 11 18 25	2 9 16 23 30
Wed.	1 8 15 22 29	5 12 19 26	3 10 17 24 31
Thur.	2 9 16 23 30	6 13 20 27	4 11 18 25
Fri.	3 10 17 24 31	7 14 21 28	5 12 19 26
Sat.	4 11 18 25	1 8 15 22 29	6 13 20 27

EASTER DAYS

March 23	1845, 1913
March 30	1823, 1834, 1902, 1975, 1986, 1997
April 6	1806, 1817, 1890, 1947, 1958, 1969
April 13	1800, 1873, 1879, 1941, 2031
April 20	1783, 1794, 1851, 1862, 1919, 1930, 2003, 2014, 2025

H (LEAP YEAR)

	January	*February*	*March*
Sun.	5 12 19 26	2 9 16 23	1 8 15 22 29
Mon.	6 13 20 27	3 10 17 24	2 9 16 23 30
Tue.	7 14 21 28	4 11 18 25	3 10 17 24 31
Wed.	1 8 15 22 29	5 12 19 26	4 11 18 25
Thur.	2 9 16 23 30	6 13 20 27	5 12 19 26
Fri.	3 10 17 24 31	7 14 21 28	6 13 20 27
Sat.	4 11 18 25	1 8 15 22 29	7 14 21 28

	April	*May*	*June*
Sun.	5 12 19 26	3 10 17 24 31	7 14 21 28
Mon.	6 13 20 27	4 11 18 25	1 8 15 22 29
Tue.	7 14 21 28	5 12 19 26	2 9 16 23 30
Wed.	1 8 15 22 29	6 13 20 27	3 10 17 24
Thur.	2 9 16 23 30	7 14 21 28	4 11 18 25
Fri.	3 10 17 24	1 8 15 22 29	5 12 19 26
Sat.	4 11 18 25	2 9 16 23 30	6 13 20 27

	July	*August*	*September*
Sun.	5 12 19 26	2 9 16 23 30	6 13 20 27
Mon.	6 13 20 27	3 10 17 24 31	7 14 21 28
Tue.	7 14 21 28	4 11 18 25	1 8 15 22 29
Wed.	1 8 15 22 29	5 12 19 26	2 9 16 23 30
Thur.	2 9 16 23 30	6 13 20 27	3 10 17 24
Fri.	3 10 17 24 31	7 14 21 28	4 11 18 25
Sat.	4 11 18 25	1 8 15 22 29	5 12 19 26

	October	*November*	*December*
Sun.	4 11 18 25	1 8 15 22 29	6 13 20 27
Mon.	5 12 19 26	2 9 16 23 30	7 14 21 28
Tue.	6 13 20 27	3 10 17 24	1 8 15 22 29
Wed.	7 14 21 28	4 11 18 25	2 9 16 23 30
Thur.	1 8 15 22 29	5 12 19 26	3 10 17 24 31
Fri.	2 9 16 23 30	6 13 20 27	4 11 18 25
Sat.	3 10 17 24 31	7 14 21 28	5 12 19 26

EASTER DAYS

March 29	1812, 1964
April 5	1896
April 12	1868, 1936, 2020
April 19	1840, 1908, 1992

I

	January	*February*	*March*
Sun.	4 11 18 25	1 8 15 22	1 8 15 22 29
Mon.	5 12 19 26	2 9 16 23	2 9 16 23 30
Tue.	6 13 20 27	3 10 17 24	3 10 17 24 31
Wed.	7 14 21 28	4 11 18 25	4 11 18 25
Thur.	1 8 15 22 29	5 12 19 26	5 12 19 26
Fri.	2 9 16 23 30	6 13 20 27	6 13 20 27
Sat.	3 10 17 24 31	7 14 21 28	7 14 21 28

	April	*May*	*June*
Sun.	5 12 19 26	3 10 17 24 31	7 14 21 28
Mon.	6 13 20 27	4 11 18 25	1 8 15 22 29
Tue.	7 14 21 28	5 12 19 26	2 9 16 23 30
Wed.	1 8 15 22 29	6 13 20 27	3 10 17 24
Thur.	2 9 16 23 30	7 14 21 28	4 11 18 25
Fri.	3 10 17 24	1 8 15 22 29	5 12 19 26
Sat.	4 11 18 25	2 9 16 23 30	6 13 20 27

	July	*August*	*September*
Sun.	5 12 19 26	2 9 16 23 30	6 13 20 27
Mon.	6 13 20 27	3 10 17 24 31	7 14 21 28
Tue.	7 14 21 28	4 11 18 25	1 8 15 22 29
Wed.	1 8 15 22 29	5 12 19 26	2 9 16 23 30
Thur.	2 9 16 23 30	6 13 20 27	3 10 17 24
Fri.	3 10 17 24 31	7 14 21 28	4 11 18 25
Sat.	4 11 18 25	1 8 15 22 29	5 12 19 26

	October	*November*	*December*
Sun.	4 11 18 25	1 8 15 22 29	6 13 20 27
Mon.	5 12 19 26	2 9 16 23 30	7 14 21 28
Tue.	6 13 20 27	3 10 17 24	1 8 15 22 29
Wed.	7 14 21 28	4 11 18 25	2 9 16 23 30
Thur.	1 8 15 22 29	5 12 19 26	3 10 17 24 31
Fri.	2 9 16 23 30	6 13 20 27	4 11 18 25
Sat.	3 10 17 24 31	7 14 21 28	5 12 19 26

EASTER DAYS

March 22	1818
March 29	1807, 1891, 1959, 1970
April 5	1795, 1801, 1863, 1874, 1885, 1931, 1942, 1953, 2015, 2026, 2037
April 12	1789, 1846, 1857, 1903, 1914, 1925, 1998, 2009
April 19	1829, 1835, 1981, 1987

J (LEAP YEAR)

	January	*February*	*March*
Sun.	4 11 18 25	1 8 15 22 29	7 14 21 28
Mon.	5 12 19 26	2 9 16 23	1 8 15 22 29
Tue.	6 13 20 27	3 10 17 24	2 9 16 23 30
Wed.	7 14 21 28	4 11 18 25	3 10 17 24 31
Thur.	1 8 15 22 29	5 12 19 26	4 11 18 25
Fri.	2 9 16 23 30	6 13 20 27	5 12 19 26
Sat.	3 10 17 24 31	7 14 21 28	6 13 20 27

	April	*May*	*June*
Sun.	4 11 18 25	2 9 16 23 30	6 13 20 27
Mon.	5 12 19 26	3 10 17 24 31	7 14 21 28
Tue.	6 13 20 27	4 11 18 25	1 8 15 22 29
Wed.	7 14 21 28	5 12 19 26	2 9 16 23 30
Thur.	1 8 15 22 29	6 13 20 27	3 10 17 24
Fri.	2 9 16 23 30	7 14 21 28	4 11 18 25
Sat.	3 10 17 24	1 8 15 22 29	5 12 19 26

	July	*August*	*September*
Sun.	4 11 18 25	1 8 15 22 29	5 12 19 26
Mon.	5 12 19 26	2 9 16 23 30	6 13 20 27
Tue.	6 13 20 27	3 10 17 24 31	7 14 21 28
Wed.	7 14 21 28	4 11 18 25	1 8 15 22 29
Thur.	1 8 15 22 29	5 12 19 26	2 9 16 23 30
Fri.	2 9 16 23 30	6 13 20 27	3 10 17 24
Sat.	3 10 17 24 31	7 14 21 28	4 11 18 25

	October	*November*	*December*
Sun.	3 10 17 24 31	7 14 21 28	5 12 19 26
Mon.	4 11 18 25	1 8 15 22 29	6 13 20 27
Tue.	5 12 19 26	2 9 16 23 30	7 14 21 28
Wed.	6 13 20 27	3 10 17 24	1 8 15 22 29
Thur.	7 14 21 28	4 11 18 25	2 9 16 23 30
Fri.	1 8 15 22 29	5 12 19 26	3 10 17 24 31
Sat.	2 9 16 23 30	6 13 20 27	4 11 18 25

EASTER DAYS

March 28	1880, 1948, 2032
April 4	1920
April 11	1784, 1852, 2004
April 18	1824, 1976

K

	January	*February*	*March*
Sun.	3 10 17 24 31	7 14 21 28	7 14 21 28
Mon.	4 11 18 25	1 8 15 22	1 8 15 22 29
Tue.	5 12 19 26	2 9 16 23	2 9 16 23 30
Wed.	6 13 20 27	3 10 17 24	3 10 17 24 31
Thur.	7 14 21 28	4 11 18 25	4 11 18 25
Fri.	1 8 15 22 29	5 12 19 26	5 12 19 26
Sat.	2 9 16 23 30	6 13 20 27	6 13 20 27

	April	*May*	*June*
Sun.	4 11 18 25	2 9 16 23 30	6 13 20 27
Mon.	5 12 19 26	3 10 17 24 31	7 14 21 28
Tue.	6 13 20 27	4 11 18 25	1 8 15 22 29
Wed.	7 14 21 28	5 12 19 26	2 9 16 23 30
Thur.	1 8 15 22 29	6 13 20 27	3 10 17 24
Fri.	2 9 16 23 30	7 14 21 28	4 11 18 25
Sat.	3 10 17 24	1 8 15 22 29	5 12 19 26

	July	*August*	*September*
Sun.	4 11 18 25	1 8 15 22 29	5 12 19 26
Mon.	5 12 19 26	2 9 16 23 30	6 13 20 27
Tue.	6 13 20 27	3 10 17 24 31	7 14 21 28
Wed.	7 14 21 28	4 11 18 25	1 8 15 22 29
Thur.	1 8 15 22 29	5 12 19 26	2 9 16 23 30
Fri.	2 9 16 23 30	6 13 20 27	3 10 17 24
Sat.	3 10 17 24 31	7 14 21 28	4 11 18 25

	October	*November*	*December*
Sun.	3 10 17 24 31	7 14 21 28	5 12 19 26
Mon.	4 11 18 25	1 8 15 22 29	6 13 20 27
Tue.	5 12 19 26	2 9 16 23 30	7 14 21 28
Wed.	6 13 20 27	3 10 17 24	1 8 15 22 29
Thur.	7 14 21 28	4 11 18 25	2 9 16 23 30
Fri.	1 8 15 22 29	5 12 19 26	3 10 17 24 31
Sat.	2 9 16 23 30	6 13 20 27	4 11 18 25

EASTER DAYS

March 28	1869, 1875, 1937, 2027
April 4	1790, 1847, 1858, 1915, 1926, 1999, 2010, 2021
April 11	1819, 1830, 1841, 1909, 1971, 1982, 1993
April 18	1802, 1813, 1897, 1954, 1965
April 25	1886, 1943, 2038

L (LEAP YEAR)

	January	*February*	*March*
Sun.	3 10 17 24 31	7 14 21 28	6 13 20 27
Mon.	4 11 18 25	1 8 15 22 29	7 14 21 28
Tue.	5 12 19 26	2 9 16 23	1 8 15 22 29
Wed.	6 13 20 27	3 10 17 24	2 9 16 23 30
Thur.	7 14 21 28	4 11 18 25	3 10 17 24 31
Fri.	1 8 15 22 29	5 12 19 26	4 11 18 25
Sat.	2 9 16 23 30	6 13 20 27	5 12 19 26

	April	*May*	*June*
Sun.	3 10 17 24	1 8 15 22 29	5 12 19 26
Mon.	4 11 18 25	2 9 16 23 30	6 13 20 27
Tue.	5 12 19 26	3 10 17 24 31	7 14 21 28
Wed.	6 13 20 27	4 11 18 25	1 8 15 22 29
Thur.	7 14 21 28	5 12 19 26	2 9 16 23 30
Fri.	1 8 15 22 29	6 13 20 27	3 10 17 24
Sat.	2 9 16 23 30	7 14 21 28	4 11 18 25

	July	*August*	*September*
Sun.	3 10 17 24 31	7 14 21 28	4 11 18 25
Mon.	4 11 18 25	1 8 15 22 29	5 12 19 26
Tue.	5 12 19 26	2 9 16 23 30	6 13 20 27
Wed.	6 13 20 27	3 10 17 24 31	7 14 21 28
Thur.	7 14 21 28	4 11 18 25	1 8 15 22 29
Fri.	1 8 15 22 29	5 12 19 26	2 9 16 23 30
Sat.	2 9 16 23 30	6 13 20 27	3 10 17 24

	October	*November*	*December*
Sun.	2 9 16 23 30	6 13 20 27	4 11 18 25
Mon.	3 10 17 24 31	7 14 21 28	5 12 19 26
Tue.	4 11 18 25	1 8 15 22 29	6 13 20 27
Wed.	5 12 19 26	2 9 16 23 30	7 14 21 28
Thur.	6 13 20 27	3 10 17 24	1 8 15 22 29
Fri.	7 14 21 28	4 11 18 25	2 9 16 23 30
Sat.	1 8 15 22 29	5 12 19 26	3 10 17 24 31

EASTER DAYS

March 27	1796, 1864, 1932, 2016
April 3	1836, 1904, 1988
April 17	1808, 1892, 1960

M

	January	*February*	*March*
Sun.	2 9 16 23 30	6 13 20 27	6 13 20 27
Mon.	3 10 17 24 31	7 14 21 28	7 14 21 28
Tue.	4 11 18 25	1 8 15 22	1 8 15 22 29
Wed.	5 12 19 26	2 9 16 23	2 9 16 23 30
Thur.	6 13 20 27	3 10 17 24	3 10 17 24 31
Fri.	7 14 21 28	4 11 18 25	4 11 18 25
Sat.	1 8 15 22 29	5 12 19 26	5 12 19 26

	April	*May*	*June*
Sun.	3 10 17 24	1 8 15 22 29	5 12 19 26
Mon.	4 11 18 25	2 9 16 23 30	6 13 20 27
Tue.	5 12 19 26	3 10 17 24 31	7 14 21 28
Wed.	6 13 20 27	4 11 18 25	1 8 15 22 29
Thur.	7 14 21 28	5 12 19 26	2 9 16 23 30
Fri.	1 8 15 22 29	6 13 20 27	3 10 17 24
Sat.	2 9 16 23 30	7 14 21 28	4 11 18 25

	July	*August*	*September*
Sun.	3 10 17 24 31	7 14 21 28	4 11 18 25
Mon.	4 11 18 25	1 8 15 22 29	5 12 19 26
Tue.	5 12 19 26	2 9 16 23 30	6 13 20 27
Wed.	6 13 20 27	3 10 17 24 31	7 14 21 28
Thur.	7 14 21 28	4 11 18 25	1 8 15 22 29
Fri.	1 8 15 22 29	5 12 19 26	2 9 16 23 30
Sat.	2 9 16 23 30	6 13 20 27	3 10 17 24

	October	*November*	*December*
Sun.	2 9 16 23 30	6 13 20 27	4 11 18 25
Mon.	3 10 17 24 31	7 14 21 28	5 12 19 26
Tue.	4 11 18 25	1 8 15 22 29	6 13 20 27
Wed.	5 12 19 26	2 9 16 23 30	7 14 21 28
Thur.	6 13 20 27	3 10 17 24	1 8 15 22 29
Fri.	7 14 21 28	4 11 18 25	2 9 16 23 30
Sat.	1 8 15 22 29	5 12 19 26	3 10 17 24 31

EASTER DAYS

March 27	1785, 1842, 1853, 1910, 1921, 2005
April 3	1825, 1831, 1983, 1994
April 10	1803, 1814, 1887, 1898, 1955, 1966, 1977, 2039
April 17	1870, 1881, 1927, 1938, 1949, 2022, 2033
April 24	1791, 1859, 2011

N (LEAP YEAR)

	January	*February*	*March*
Sun.	2 9 16 23 30	6 13 20 27	5 12 19 26
Mon.	3 10 17 24 31	7 14 21 28	6 13 20 27
Tue.	4 11 18 25	1 8 15 22 29	7 14 21 28
Wed.	5 12 19 26	2 9 16 23	1 8 15 22 29
Thur.	6 13 20 27	3 10 17 24	2 9 16 23 30
Fri.	7 14 21 28	4 11 18 25	3 10 17 24 31
Sat.	1 8 15 22 29	5 12 19 26	4 11 18 25

	April	*May*	*June*
Sun.	2 9 16 23 30	7 14 21 28	4 11 18 25
Mon.	3 10 17 24	1 8 15 22 29	5 12 19 26
Tue.	4 11 18 25	2 9 16 23 30	6 13 20 27
Wed.	5 12 19 26	3 10 17 24 31	7 14 21 28
Thur.	6 13 20 27	4 11 18 25	1 8 15 22 29
Fri.	7 14 21 28	5 12 19 26	2 9 16 23 30
Sat.	1 8 15 22 29	6 13 20 27	3 10 17 24

	July	*August*	*September*
Sun.	2 9 16 23 30	6 13 20 27	3 10 17 24
Mon.	3 10 17 24 31	7 14 21 28	4 11 18 25
Tue.	4 11 18 25	1 8 15 22 29	5 12 19 26
Wed.	5 12 19 26	2 9 16 23 30	6 13 20 27
Thur.	6 13 20 27	3 10 17 24 31	7 14 21 28
Fri.	7 14 21 28	4 11 18 25	1 8 15 22 29
Sat.	1 8 15 22 29	5 12 19 26	2 9 16 23 30

	October	*November*	*December*
Sun.	1 8 15 22 29	5 12 19 26	3 10 17 24 31
Mon.	2 9 16 23 30	6 13 20 27	4 11 18 25
Tue.	3 10 17 24 31	7 14 21 28	5 12 19 26
Wed.	4 11 18 25	1 8 15 22 29	6 13 20 27
Thur.	5 12 19 26	2 9 16 23 30	7 14 21 28
Fri.	6 13 20 27	3 10 17 24	1 8 15 22 29
Sat.	7 14 21 28	4 11 18 25	2 9 16 23 30

EASTER DAYS

March 26	1780
April 2	1820, 1972
April 9	1944
April 16	1876, 2028
April 23	1848, 1916, 2000

GEOLOGICAL TIME

The earth is thought to have come into existence approximately 4,600 million years ago, but for nearly half this time, the Archean era, it was uninhabited. Life is generally believed to have emerged in the succeeding Proterozoic era. The Archean and the Proterozoic eras are often together referred to as the Precambrian.

Although primitive forms of life, eg algae and bacteria, existed during the Proterozoic era, it is not until the strata of Palaeozoic rocks are reached that abundant fossilised remains appear. Since the Precambrian, there have been three great geological eras:

PALAEOZOIC ('ANCIENT LIFE')

*c.*542–*c.*251 million years ago

Cambrian – Mainly sandstones, slate and shales; limestones in Scotland. Shelled fossils and invertebrates, eg trilobites and brachiopods appear, as do the earliest known vertebrates (jawless fish)

Ordovician – Mainly shales and mudstones, eg in north Wales; limestones in Scotland. First fish

Silurian – Shales, mudstones and some limestones, found mostly in Wales and southern Scotland

Devonian – Old red sandstone, shale, limestone and slate, eg in south Wales and the West Country

Carboniferous – Coal-bearing rocks, millstone grit, limestone and shale. First traces of land-living creatures

Permian – Marls, sandstones and clays. First reptile fossils

There were two great phases of mountain building in the Palaeozoic era: the Caledonian, characterised in Britain by NE–SW lines of hills and valleys; and the later Hercynian, widespread in west Germany and adjacent areas, and in Britain exemplified in E–W lines of hills and valleys.

The end of the Palaeozoic era was marked by the extensive glaciations of the Permian period in the southern continents and the decline of amphibians. It was succeeded by an era of warm conditions.

MESOZOIC ('MIDDLE FORMS OF LIFE')

*c.*251–*c.*65.5 million years ago

Triassic – Mostly sandstone, eg in the West Midlands; primitive mammals appear

Jurassic – Mainly limestones and clays, typically displayed in the Jura mountains, and in England in a NE–SW belt from Lincolnshire and the Wash to the Severn and the Dorset coast

Cretaceous – Mainly chalk, clay and sands, eg in Kent and Sussex

Giant reptiles were dominant during the Mesozoic era, but it was at this time that marsupial mammals first appeared, as well as *Archaeopteryx lithographica,* the earliest known species of bird. Coniferous trees and flowering plants also developed during the era and, with the birds and the mammals, were the main species to survive into the Cenozoic era. The giant reptiles became extinct.

CENOZOIC ('RECENT LIFE')

from *c.*65.5 million years ago

Palaeocene, *Eocene* } The emergence of new forms of life, including existing species; primates appear

Oligocene – Fossils of a few still existing species

Miocene – Fossil remains show a balance of existing and extinct species

Pliocene – Fossil remains show a majority of still existing species

Pleistocene – The majority of remains are those of still existing species

Holocene – The present, post-glacial period. Existing species only, except for a few exterminated by humans

In the last 25 million years, from the Miocene through the Pliocene periods, the Alpine-Himalayan and the circum-Pacific phases of mountain building reached their climax. During the Pleistocene period ice-sheets repeatedly locked up masses of water as land ice; its weight depressed the land, but the locking-up of the water lowered the sea level by 100–200 metres. The glaciations and interglacials of the Ice Age are difficult to date and classify, but recent scientific opinion considers the Pleistocene period to have begun approximately 1.64 million years ago. The last glacial retreat, merging into the Holocene period, was *c.* 10,000 years ago.

HUMAN DEVELOPMENT

Any consideration of the history of humans must start with the fact that all members of the human race belong to one species of animal, ie *Homo sapiens,* the definition of a species being in biological terms that all its members can interbreed. As a species of mammal it is possible to group humans with other similar types, known as the primates. Amongst these is found a sub-group, the apes, which includes, in addition to humans, the chimpanzees, gorillas, orang-utans and gibbons. All lack a tail, have shoulder blades at the back, and a Y-shaped chewing pattern on the surface of their molars, as well as showing the more general primate characteristics of four incisors, a thumb which is able to touch the fingers of the same hand, and finger and toe nails instead of claws. The factors available to scientific study suggest that human beings have chimpanzees and gorillas as their nearest relatives in the animal world. However, there once lived creatures, now extinct, which were closer to modern man than the chimpanzees and gorillas, and which shared with modern man the characteristics of having flat faces (ie the absence of a pronounced muzzle), being bipedal, and possessing large brains.

The debate surrounding evidence for the oldest human ancestors is ongoing. The fossil record becomes more patchy as time stretches backward, which makes new hominid discoveries harder to confirm. The earliest putative hominin for which there is significant fossil evidence is *Ardipithecus ramidus,* for which an almost complete skeleton, dating to at least 4.4 million years ago, was discovered in the Afar Rift, Ethiopia in 1992. Analysis of the skeleton suggests the creature had characteristics of both humans and apes; able to climb trees and walk on two feet. Australopithecines have left more numerous remains in south and east Africa, among which sub-groups may be detected. Living between 4.2 and 1.5 million years ago, they were relatives of modern humans in respect of the fact that they walked upright, did not have an extensive muzzle and had similar types of pre-molars. The first australopithecine remains were recognised at Taung in South Africa in 1924 and named *Australopithecus africanus,* dating between 3.3 and 2.3 million years ago. The most impressive discovery was made at Hadar, Ethiopia, in 1974 when about half a skeleton of *Australopithecus afarensis,* known as 'Lucy', was found. Some 3.2 million years ago, 'Lucy' certainly walked upright.

Also in east Africa, especially at Olduvai Gorge in Tanzania, between *c.* 2.5 and 1.8 million years ago, lived a hominid group which not only walked upright, had a flat face, and a large brain case, but also made simple pebble and flake stone tools. These early pebble tool users, because of their distinctive characteristics, have been grouped as a separate sub-species, now extinct, of the genus *Homo* and are known as *Homo habilis* or 'handy man'.

The use of fire, again a human characteristic, is associated with another group of extinct hominids whose remains, about a million years old, are found in south and east Africa, China, Indonesia, north Africa and Europe. Mastery of the techniques of making fire probably helped the colonisation of the colder northern areas and in this respect the site of Vertesszollos in Hungary is of particular importance. *Homo ergaster* in Africa and *Homo erectus* in Asia are the names given to this group of fossils and they relate to a number of famous individual discoveries, eg Solo Man, Heidelberg Man, and especially Peking Man who lived at the cave site at Choukoutien which has yielded evidence of fire and burnt bone.

The well-known group Neandertal Man, or *Homo neanderthalensis,* is an extinct form of man that lived between about 350,000 and 24,000 years ago, thus spanning the last Ice Age. Indeed, its ability to adapt to the cold climate on the edge of the ice-sheets is one of its characteristic features, the remains being found only in Europe, Asia and the Middle East. Complete neandertal skeletons were found during excavations at Tabun in Israel, together with evidence of tool-making and the use of fire. Distinguished by very large brains, it seems that neandertal man was the first to develop recognisable social customs, especially deliberate burial rites. Why the neandertals became extinct is not clear but it may be connected with the climatic changes at the end of the Ice Ages, which would have seriously affected their food supplies; possibly they became too specialised for their own good.

The shin bone of Boxgrove Man found in 1993 – *Homo heidelbergensis* – and the Swanscombe skull are the best known early human fossil remains found in England. Some specialists prefer to group Swanscombe Man (or, more probably, woman) together with the Steinheim skull from Germany, seeing both as a separate sub-species. There is too little evidence as yet on which to form a final judgement.

Modern humans – *Homo sapiens* – had evolved to our present physical condition and had colonised much of the world by about 40,000 years ago. There are many previously distinguished individual specimens, eg Cromagnon Man, which may now be grouped together as *Homo sapiens.* It was modern humans that spread to the American continent by crossing the landbridge between Siberia and Alaska and thence moved south through North America and into South America. Equally it is modern humans who over the last 40,000 years have been responsible for the major developments in technology, art and civilisation generally.

One of the problems for those studying human fossils is the lack in many cases of sufficient quantities of fossil bone for analysis. It is important that theories should be tested against evidence, rather than the evidence being made to fit the theory. The Piltdown hoax of 1912 (and not fully exposed until the 1970s) is a well-known example of 'fossils' being forged to fit what was seen in some quarters as the correct theory of human evolution.

The discovery of the structure of DNA in 1953 has come to have a profound effect upon the study of human evolution. For example, it was claimed in 1987 that a common ancestor of all human beings was a person who lived in Africa some 200,000 years ago, thus encouraging the 'out of Africa' theory of hominid migration from east Africa to the Middle East and then throughout the world. There is no doubt that the studies based on DNA have vast potential to elucidate further the course of human evolution.

CULTURAL DEVELOPMENT

The Eurocentric bias of early archaeologists meant that the search for a starting point for the development and transmission of cultural ideas, especially by migration, trade and warfare, concentrated unduly on Europe and the Near East. The Three Age system, whereby prehistory was divided into a Stone Age, a Bronze Age and an Iron Age, was devised by Christian Thomsen, curator of the National Museum of Denmark in the early 19th century, to facilitate the classification of the museum's collections. The descriptive adjectives referred to the materials from which the implements and weapons were made and came to be regarded as the dominant features of the societies to which they related. The refinement of the Three Age system once dominated archaeological thought and remains a generally accepted concept in the popular mind. However, it is now seen by archaeologists as an inadequate model for human development.

Common sense suggests that there were no complete breaks between one so-called Age and another, any more than contemporaries would have regarded 1485 as a complete break between medieval and modern English history. Nor can the Three Age system be applied universally. In some areas it is necessary to insert a Copper Age, while in Africa south of the Sahara there would seem to be no Bronze Age at all; in Australia, Old Stone Age societies survived, while in South America, New Stone Age communities existed into modern times. The civilisations in other parts of the world clearly invalidate a Eurocentric theory of human development.

The concept of the 'Neolithic revolution', associated with the domestication of plants and animals, was a development of particular importance in the human cultural pattern. It reflected change from the hunter-gatherer economies to a more settled agricultural way of life and therefore, so the argument goes, made possible the development of urban civilisation. However, it can no longer be argued that this 'revolution' took place only in one area from which all development stemmed. Though it appears that the cultivation of wheat and barley was first undertaken, together with the domestication of cattle and goats/sheep, around 10,000 years ago in the Fertile Crescent (the area bounded by the rivers Tigris and Euphrates), there is evidence that rice was first deliberately planted and pigs domesticated in south-east Asia, maize first cultivated in Central America and llamas first domesticated in South America. Cultural change took place independently in different parts of the world at different rates and different times.

The Neolithic period of cultural development has been difficult to date reliably because the transition to agriculture took place long before writing was invented. The development and refinement of radio-carbon dating and other scientific methods of producing absolute chronologies is enabling the cross-referencing of societies to be undertaken. It may eventually be possible to obtain a reliable chronological framework, in absolute terms of years, against which the cultural development of any particular area may be set.

GEOLOGICAL TIME

Era	*Period*	*Epoch*	*Dates*	*Evolutionary stages*
Cenozoic	Quaternary	Holocene	9,600 BC–present	Humans
		Pleistocene	1,808,000–9,600 BC	
	Neogene	Pliocene	5,332,000–1,806,000	
		Miocene	23,030,000–5,332,000	
	Paleogene	Oligocene	34–23 Ma*	
		Eocene	55.8–33.9 Ma	
		Palaeocene	65.5–55.8 Ma	
Mesozoic	Cretaceous		145.5–65.5 Ma	
	Jurassic		199.6–145.5 Ma	First birds
	Triassic		251–199.6 Ma	First mammals
Palaeozoic	Permian		299–251 Ma	First reptiles
	Carboniferous		359.2–299 Ma	First amphibians and insects
	Devonian		416–359.2 Ma	
	Silurian		443.7–416 Ma	
	Ordovician		488.3–443.7 Ma	First fish
	Cambrian		542–488.3 Ma	First invertebrates
Precambrian	Proterozoic		2,500–542 Ma	First primitive life forms, eg algae and bacteria
	Archaean		3,800–2,500 Ma	
	Hadean		4,500–3,800 Ma	

* Ma = millions of years ago

TIDES AND TIDAL PREDICTIONS

TIDES

Tides are the periodic rise and fall of the sea level caused mainly by the gravitational pull, or tide raising force (TRF), of the Moon and the Sun. The Moon's TRF accounts for 70 per cent of the total; the Sun's for 30 per cent. When the Moon and the Sun are in line with the Earth they are said to be 'in conjunction' (or syzygy) and their combined TRFs are greatest. This produces the largest rise and fall of the tide, otherwise known as spring tides; they occur just after a full or new moon. The opposite effect, just after the Moon's first and last quarters, when the Sun and Moon form a right angle with the Earth, produces neap tides, with a relatively small tidal range between high water and low water.

A lunar day is about 24 hours and 50 minutes, giving two complete tidal cycles, with about 12 hours and 25 minutes between successive high waters. These are known as semi-diurnal tides and are applicable in the Atlantic Ocean and around the coasts of north-west Europe. Other parts of the world have diurnal tides, with only one high water and one low water each (lunar) day, or mixed tides which are partly diurnal and partly semi-diurnal.

Land and seabed conditions influence the tides locally. On the south coast of England, for example, double high waters occur between Swanage and Selsey Bill, and low water is much more sharply defined than high water. Tides can also be greatly affected by the Coriolis force, which is induced by the Earth's rotation and, in the northern hemisphere, tends to deflect any moving object to the right. Thus the easterly flood tidal stream in the English Channel is deflected towards the French coast causing higher high waters; on the ebb the opposite happens causing lower low waters. This, coupled with local geography, means that the mean spring range of the tide at St Malo is nearly 11m while the range on the English coast at Portland, 120 miles to the north, is a mere 2m.

Meteorological conditions also affect the tides. Prolonged strong winds and unusually high (or low) atmospheric pressure can significantly lower (or raise) the height of the tide; the wind alone can affect the predicted times of high and low water by as much as an hour. Variation of pressure by 34 millibars from the norm can cause a height difference of 0.3m. Intense minor depressions, line squalls, or other abrupt changes in the weather can cause wave oscillations known as seiches. The wave period of a seiche can vary from a few minutes to about 2 hours, with heights of up to a metre. Wick on the north-east coast of Scotland and Fishguard in south-west Wales are particularly prone to seiches.

TIDAL STREAMS

Tidal streams are the movements of water caused by the vertical rise and fall of the tide. They normally change direction about every 6 hours. Tidal streams should not be confused with ocean currents, such as the Gulf Stream, which run indefinitely in the same direction. The rate, or set, of the stream in any particular place is proportional to the range of the tide. Thus, the rate during spring tides is greater than that at neaps. In the central English Channel the maximum spring rate is nearly 5 knots while the neap rate at the same position is just 3 knots. As with tidal heights, local geography plays a significant role in the rate of the tidal stream. For example, in the narrow waters of the Pentland Firth between mainland Scotland and the Orkney Islands, rates of 16 knots have been recorded.

The tidal stream does not necessarily turn at the same time as high or low water. In the English Channel the stream turns at approximately high and low water at Dover. However, high water at Dover is at about the same time as low water at Plymouth, and vice versa.

Around the UK, the main flood tidal stream sets eastward up the English Channel, north-east into the Bristol Channel, and north up the west coasts of Ireland and Scotland. However, the flood sets south-east through the North Channel and south into the Irish Sea, where it meets the northerly flood through St George's Channel at the Isle of Man. Off the east coasts of Scotland and England the stream sets south as far as the Thames Estuary before meeting the north-going stream from the eastern part of the Dover Strait.

DEFINITIONS

Chart Datum (CD) is the reference level from which tidal levels are predicted. **Ordnance Datum** at Newlyn is the datum of the land levelling system on mainland England, Scotland and Wales. This is the datum from which heights on UK land maps are measured. CD varies from about 5m above Ordnance Datum to about 6.5m below. **Highest Astronomical Tide (HAT)** and **Lowest Astronomical Tide (LAT)** are the highest and lowest levels of the tide, respectively, which can be predicted to occur under average meteorological, and any combination of astronomical, conditions. **Duration** of the tide is the interval between low water and the next high water. It can be used to calculate the approximate time of low water when only the time of high water is known. **Mean Sea Level (MSL or ML)** is the average level of the sea's surface over a long period, normally observed over 18.6 years. The **Range** of the tide is the difference between the heights of successive high waters and low waters. It is greatest at spring tides, least at neaps. The range is often indicated by **Tidal Coefficients** which are proportional to, but not the same as, the range on a particular day. A coefficient, for example, of 95 indicates an average spring tide, while 45 is an average neap tide.

PREDICTIONS

The following data are daily predictions of the time and height of high water at London Bridge, Liverpool, Greenock and Leith. The time of the data is Greenwich Mean Time; this applies also to data for the months when British Summer Time is in operation and the hour's time difference should be added. The datum of predictions for each port shows the difference of height, in metres from Ordnance datum (Newlyn).

 The section was compiled with the assistance of Andy Du Port and Chris Stevens.

JANUARY 2011 *High Water* GMT

	LONDON BRIDGE Datum of Predictions 3.20m below				LIVERPOOL (Gladstone Dock) Datum of Predictions 4.93m below				GREENOCK Datum of Predictions 1.62m below				LEITH Datum of Predictions 2.90m below			
	hr	*ht m*	*hr*	*ht m*	*hr*	*ht m*	*hr*	*ht m*	*hr*	*ht m*	*hr*	*ht m*	*hr*	*ht m*	*hr*	*ht m*
SA 1	10 56	6.3	23 35	6.2	08 24	8.2	20 55	8.3	09 53	3.2	22 05	3.2	11 59	5.0	—	—
SU 2	12 02	6.5	—	—	09 23	8.6	21 52	8.6	10 50	3.3	23 08	3.3	00 35	5.1	12 57	5.1
M 3	00 36	6.4	12 59	6.6	10 13	8.9	22 41	8.8	11 38	3.5	—	—	01 31	5.2	13 47	5.3
TU 4	01 28	6.5	13 49	6.8	10 57	9.1	23 24	8.9	00 01	3.3	12 22	3.6	02 20	5.3	14 32	5.4
W 5	02 12	6.6	14 33	6.9	11 37	9.3	—	—	00 48	3.3	13 02	3.7	03 03	5.4	15 13	5.5
TH 6	02 52	6.7	15 13	6.9	00 02	8.9	12 14	9.3	01 28	3.3	13 39	3.7	03 43	5.4	15 51	5.4
F 7	03 27	6.7	15 50	6.8	00 38	8.8	12 49	9.2	02 05	3.2	14 15	3.7	04 21	5.3	16 28	5.4
SA 8	04 00	6.7	16 23	6.7	01 11	8.7	13 23	9.0	02 40	3.2	14 49	3.6	04 57	5.2	17 03	5.3
SU 9	04 31	6.6	16 54	6.6	01 43	8.5	13 57	8.8	03 15	3.2	15 25	3.6	05 33	5.0	17 39	5.1
M 10	05 01	6.5	17 25	6.4	02 17	8.3	14 33	8.5	03 52	3.2	16 01	3.5	06 11	4.9	18 17	5.0
TU 11	05 33	6.4	17 59	6.2	02 54	8.0	15 13	8.1	04 31	3.2	16 40	3.3	06 51	4.7	18 58	4.8
W 12	06 08	6.2	18 37	6.0	03 35	7.6	15 59	7.8	05 11	3.1	17 23	3.2	07 36	4.5	19 46	4.6
TH 13	06 52	5.9	19 25	5.8	04 26	7.3	16 57	7.4	05 55	3.0	18 14	3.0	08 28	4.4	20 45	4.4
F 14	07 47	5.7	20 34	5.6	05 34	7.1	18 10	7.3	06 47	2.9	19 16	2.9	09 29	4.3	21 53	4.4
SA 15	09 11	5.7	21 55	5.7	06 52	7.2	19 25	7.4	07 53	2.9	20 31	2.9	10 35	4.4	23 03	4.4
SU 16	10 30	5.9	23 05	6.0	08 03	7.6	20 30	7.8	09 10	3.0	21 49	2.9	11 41	4.6	—	—
M 17	11 35	6.2	—	—	09 00	8.1	21 25	8.2	10 16	3.1	22 52	3.1	00 10	4.7	12 42	4.9
TU 18	00 09	6.3	12 32	6.6	09 49	8.6	22 13	8.7	11 06	3.3	23 44	3.2	01 08	5.0	13 32	5.1
W 19	01 04	6.6	13 24	6.9	10 33	9.1	22 58	9.1	11 49	3.5	—	—	01 55	5.3	14 15	5.4
TH 20	01 53	6.8	14 13	7.1	11 16	9.5	23 42	9.5	00 31	3.3	12 32	3.7	02 38	5.5	14 54	5.6
F 21	02 39	6.9	14 59	7.3	11 59	9.8	—	—	01 17	3.4	13 14	3.8	03 20	5.7	15 34	5.8
SA 22	03 22	7.1	15 43	7.4	00 25	9.6	12 43	9.9	02 01	3.4	13 57	3.9	04 02	5.8	16 15	5.9
SU 23	04 03	7.2	16 26	7.4	01 09	9.6	13 26	9.9	02 44	3.4	14 41	3.9	04 45	5.8	16 59	5.9
M 24	04 43	7.1	17 10	7.2	01 53	9.4	14 10	9.6	03 26	3.4	15 24	3.9	05 30	5.6	17 45	5.7
TU 25	05 24	7.0	17 55	6.9	02 38	9.1	14 57	9.2	04 07	3.4	16 08	3.8	06 17	5.4	18 34	5.5
W 26	06 07	6.8	18 43	6.6	03 26	8.6	15 48	8.7	04 49	3.3	16 54	3.6	07 09	5.1	19 33	5.2
TH 27	06 58	6.6	19 39	6.3	04 21	8.1	16 51	8.1	05 35	3.2	17 43	3.4	08 09	4.8	20 44	4.9
F 28	08 01	6.3	20 43	6.0	05 30	7.7	18 09	7.7	06 29	3.0	18 42	3.1	09 18	4.6	22 01	4.7
SA 29	09 16	6.1	21 57	5.8	06 51	7.6	19 35	7.6	07 57	2.9	20 19	2.9	10 31	4.6	23 19	4.7
SU 30	10 36	6.0	23 19	5.9	08 10	7.8	20 51	7.9	09 35	3.0	22 07	2.9	11 46	4.7	—	—
M 31	11 52	6.2	—	—	09 14	8.2	21 48	8.2	10 38	3.2	23 08	3.0	00 32	4.8	12 52	4.9

FEBRUARY 2011 *High Water* GMT

	LONDON BRIDGE				LIVERPOOL (Gladstone Dock)				GREENOCK				LEITH			
TU 1	00 26	6.2	12 52	6.5	10 04	8.7	22 34	8.5	11 27	3.4	23 57	3.1	01 29	5.0	13 42	5.1
W 2	01 18	6.5	13 40	6.7	10 46	9.0	23 12	8.8	12 10	3.5	—	—	02 14	5.2	14 23	5.3
TH 3	02 01	6.6	14 21	6.8	11 22	9.2	23 45	8.9	00 39	3.2	12 50	3.6	02 51	5.3	15 00	5.4
F 4	02 37	6.7	14 58	6.8	11 55	9.3	—	—	01 15	3.2	13 25	3.6	03 25	5.3	15 33	5.4
SA 5	03 10	6.8	15 29	6.8	00 16	8.9	12 27	9.3	01 46	3.2	13 57	3.6	03 57	5.3	16 05	5.4
SU 6	03 39	6.8	15 57	6.8	00 45	8.9	12 57	9.2	02 16	3.2	14 28	3.6	04 29	5.2	16 36	5.4
M 7	04 07	6.8	16 24	6.7	01 14	8.8	13 28	9.0	02 48	3.3	14 59	3.5	05 01	5.1	17 08	5.3
TU 8	04 35	6.7	16 52	6.6	01 44	8.6	13 58	8.7	03 21	3.3	15 32	3.5	05 35	5.0	17 42	5.1
W 9	05 05	6.6	17 23	6.4	02 13	8.3	14 30	8.4	03 54	3.3	16 08	3.3	06 11	4.8	18 19	4.9
TH 10	05 37	6.4	17 58	6.1	02 46	8.0	15 06	8.0	04 29	3.2	16 47	3.2	06 50	4.6	19 01	4.7
F 11	06 15	6.2	18 39	5.9	03 27	7.6	15 54	7.5	05 07	3.1	17 33	3.0	07 36	4.4	19 53	4.4
SA 12	07 03	5.9	19 33	5.6	04 25	7.2	17 06	7.1	05 52	2.9	18 31	2.8	08 35	4.3	21 01	4.3
SU 13	08 07	5.7	20 57	5.5	05 52	7.0	18 38	7.1	06 51	2.8	19 47	2.7	09 48	4.3	22 22	4.3
M 14	09 43	5.7	22 28	5.7	07 22	7.3	20 01	7.5	08 14	2.8	21 24	2.8	11 04	4.4	23 40	4.5
TU 15	11 04	6.1	23 43	6.1	08 32	7.9	21 04	8.1	09 42	3.0	22 38	3.0	12 14	4.7	—	—
W 16	12 09	6.6	—	—	09 27	8.5	21 55	8.7	10 42	3.2	23 30	3.1	00 44	4.9	13 09	5.1
TH 17	00 43	6.6	13 05	7.0	10 14	9.2	22 40	9.3	11 29	3.4	—	—	01 35	5.3	13 53	5.5
F 18	01 34	6.9	13 55	7.2	10 57	9.7	23 24	9.7	00 17	3.3	12 14	3.6	02 18	5.6	14 33	5.8
SA 19	02 19	7.1	14 41	7.4	11 40	10.0	—	—	01 01	3.3	12 59	3.7	02 59	5.8	15 13	6.0
SU 20	03 02	7.3	15 24	7.5	00 06	9.9	12 23	10.2	01 44	3.4	13 43	3.8	03 40	5.9	15 55	6.1
M 21	03 42	7.4	16 06	7.4	00 48	9.9	13 06	10.1	02 25	3.4	14 26	3.9	04 23	5.9	16 39	6.1
TU 22	04 22	7.4	16 48	7.2	01 30	9.6	13 48	9.8	03 04	3.5	15 09	3.9	05 07	5.7	17 25	5.8
W 23	05 02	7.2	17 29	6.8	02 12	9.3	14 33	9.3	03 42	3.4	15 51	3.7	05 53	5.4	18 15	5.5
TH 24	05 44	7.0	18 13	6.5	02 58	8.7	15 22	8.6	04 20	3.3	16 33	3.5	06 42	5.1	19 13	5.1
F 25	06 32	6.6	19 02	6.1	03 51	8.1	16 24	7.9	05 02	3.2	17 19	3.2	07 40	4.7	20 24	4.7
SA 26	07 31	6.2	20 05	5.8	05 01	7.6	17 48	7.3	05 50	3.0	18 12	2.9	08 51	4.5	21 42	4.5
SU 27	08 48	5.9	21 26	5.6	06 27	7.4	19 23	7.3	07 05	2.8	20 05	2.6	10 08	4.4	23 06	4.5
M 28	10 15	5.8	22 59	5.7	07 53	7.6	20 41	7.6	09 15	2.8	22 04	2.7	11 31	4.5	—	—

MARCH 2011 *High Water* GMT

	LONDON BRIDGE Datum of Predictions 3.20m below				LIVERPOOL (Gladstone Dock) Datum of Predictions 4.93m below				GREENOCK Datum of Predictions 1.62m below				LEITH Datum of Predictions 2.90m below			
	hr	*ht m*	*hr*	*ht m*	*hr*	*ht m*	*hr*	*ht m*	*hr*	*ht m*	*hr*	*ht m*	*hr*	*ht m*	*hr*	*ht m*
TU 1	11 36	6.1	—	—	08 59	8.1	21 35	8.1	10 19	3.1	22 57	2.9	00 23	4.7	12 39	4.8
W 2	00 07	6.1	12 36	6.5	09 47	8.5	22 16	8.4	11 07	3.3	23 40	3.0	01 18	4.9	13 27	5.0
TH 3	00 58	6.5	13 21	6.7	10 26	8.8	22 50	8.7	11 50	3.4	—	—	01 58	5.1	14 06	5.2
F 4	01 39	6.6	14 00	6.8	10 59	9.1	23 21	8.9	00 17	3.1	12 29	3.5	02 32	5.2	14 39	5.3
SA 5	02 14	6.7	14 33	6.8	11 30	9.2	23 49	9.0	00 50	3.2	13 04	3.5	03 02	5.2	15 10	5.4
SU 6	02 44	6.8	15 02	6.8	12 00	9.2	—	—	01 19	3.2	13 34	3.4	03 30	5.3	15 39	5.4
M 7	03 12	6.9	15 27	6.8	00 17	9.0	12 30	9.2	01 48	3.3	14 03	3.4	04 00	5.2	16 09	5.4
TU 8	03 39	6.9	15 53	6.8	00 45	8.9	12 59	9.0	02 18	3.3	14 33	3.4	04 30	5.2	16 41	5.3
W 9	04 08	6.9	16 22	6.7	01 12	8.7	13 28	8.8	02 48	3.4	15 05	3.4	05 02	5.1	17 14	5.1
TH 10	04 38	6.7	16 53	6.5	01 40	8.5	13 58	8.5	03 19	3.4	15 40	3.3	05 36	4.9	17 50	4.9
F 11	05 11	6.5	17 27	6.2	02 11	8.2	14 33	8.1	03 52	3.3	16 18	3.1	06 13	4.7	18 31	4.7
SA 12	05 48	6.3	18 06	6.0	02 49	7.8	15 20	7.7	04 27	3.2	17 01	2.9	06 56	4.5	19 21	4.5
SU 13	06 34	6.1	18 58	5.7	03 44	7.4	16 27	7.2	05 09	3.0	17 56	2.7	07 50	4.3	20 25	4.3
M 14	07 34	5.9	20 12	5.5	05 09	7.1	18 01	7.1	06 04	2.8	19 14	2.6	09 04	4.2	21 47	4.3
TU 15	09 05	5.8	21 51	5.7	06 45	7.3	19 30	7.5	07 24	2.8	21 02	2.7	10 29	4.4	23 09	4.5
W 16	10 33	6.1	23 12	6.1	08 01	7.9	20 38	8.1	09 04	2.9	22 18	2.9	11 42	4.7	—	—
TH 17	11 43	6.6	—	—	08 59	8.6	21 31	8.8	10 13	3.2	23 09	3.1	00 16	4.9	12 40	5.1
F 18	00 15	6.6	12 41	7.0	09 48	9.2	22 17	9.4	11 05	3.4	23 54	3.3	01 09	5.3	13 26	5.5
SA 19	01 07	7.0	13 31	7.2	10 33	9.7	23 00	9.7	11 52	3.6	—	—	01 53	5.6	14 08	5.8
SU 20	01 53	7.2	14 17	7.4	11 17	10.1	23 42	9.9	00 38	3.4	12 39	3.7	02 34	5.8	14 50	6.1
M 21	02 36	7.4	15 01	7.4	12 00	10.2	—	—	01 20	3.4	13 24	3.8	03 16	5.9	15 34	6.1
TU 22	03 18	7.5	15 42	7.3	00 24	9.9	12 44	10.0	02 00	3.5	14 09	3.8	03 59	5.9	16 20	6.0
W 23	03 59	7.5	16 23	7.1	01 06	9.7	13 27	9.7	02 39	3.5	14 52	3.7	04 43	5.7	17 08	5.8
TH 24	04 40	7.3	17 04	6.7	01 49	9.3	14 12	9.1	03 16	3.5	15 34	3.6	05 30	5.4	18 00	5.4
F 25	05 23	7.0	17 46	6.4	02 34	8.8	15 02	8.4	03 55	3.4	16 16	3.3	06 19	5.1	18 59	5.0
SA 26	06 11	6.6	18 32	6.0	03 27	8.2	16 04	7.7	04 36	3.2	17 02	3.0	07 17	4.7	20 06	4.6
SU 27	07 08	6.1	19 31	5.7	04 35	7.6	17 25	7.2	05 24	3.0	17 56	2.7	08 27	4.5	21 19	4.4
M 28	08 22	5.8	20 51	5.5	05 58	7.4	18 57	7.1	06 33	2.8	19 54	2.5	09 42	4.4	22 40	4.4
TU 29	09 46	5.8	22 22	5.7	07 22	7.5	20 15	7.5	08 40	2.8	21 39	2.6	11 01	4.4	23 57	4.5
W 30	11 06	6.0	23 34	6.0	08 28	7.9	21 08	7.9	09 49	3.0	22 29	2.8	12 10	4.7	—	—
TH 31	12 07	6.4	—	—	09 17	8.3	21 48	8.3	10 38	3.2	23 09	3.0	00 51	4.8	12 59	4.9

APRIL 2011 *High Water* GMT

	LONDON BRIDGE				LIVERPOOL (Gladstone Dock)				GREENOCK				LEITH			
F 1	00 25	6.4	12 52	6.6	09 55	8.6	22 21	8.6	11 21	3.3	23 45	3.1	01 31	5.0	13 38	5.1
SA 2	01 07	6.6	13 30	6.7	10 29	8.9	22 51	8.8	11 59	3.3	—	—	02 04	5.1	14 12	5.2
SU 3	01 42	6.7	14 02	6.7	11 01	9.0	23 19	8.9	00 17	3.2	12 35	3.3	02 33	5.2	14 42	5.3
M 4	02 13	6.8	14 30	6.7	11 32	9.1	23 48	9.0	00 48	3.2	13 06	3.3	03 01	5.2	15 13	5.3
TU 5	02 42	6.9	14 56	6.8	12 02	9.0	—	—	01 17	3.3	13 36	3.3	03 31	5.2	15 44	5.3
W 6	03 11	7.0	15 24	6.8	00 16	8.9	12 33	8.9	01 47	3.4	14 07	3.3	04 02	5.2	16 17	5.2
TH 7	03 42	6.9	15 56	6.7	00 45	8.8	13 03	8.7	02 17	3.4	14 40	3.3	04 34	5.1	16 51	5.1
F 8	04 15	6.8	16 29	6.5	01 15	8.6	13 36	8.5	02 48	3.5	15 17	3.2	05 08	5.0	17 28	5.0
SA 9	04 50	6.7	17 04	6.3	01 49	8.4	14 15	8.2	03 21	3.4	15 56	3.1	05 45	4.8	18 11	4.8
SU 10	05 29	6.5	17 44	6.1	02 30	8.1	15 04	7.8	03 58	3.3	16 40	2.9	06 29	4.6	19 02	4.6
M 11	06 17	6.3	18 37	5.9	03 26	7.7	16 10	7.4	04 39	3.1	17 35	2.8	07 22	4.5	20 04	4.5
TU 12	07 17	6.1	19 47	5.7	04 45	7.4	17 35	7.4	05 33	3.0	18 51	2.7	08 31	4.4	21 20	4.5
W 13	08 41	6.0	21 18	5.8	06 12	7.6	18 58	7.7	06 48	2.9	20 31	2.7	09 55	4.5	22 38	4.6
TH 14	10 04	6.3	22 38	6.2	07 26	8.0	20 06	8.2	08 26	2.9	21 48	2.9	11 07	4.8	23 44	5.0
F 15	11 13	6.7	23 42	6.6	08 27	8.6	21 01	8.8	09 41	3.2	22 40	3.1	12 06	5.1	—	—
SA 16	12 13	7.0	—	—	09 19	9.2	21 50	9.3	10 37	3.4	23 27	3.3	00 38	5.3	12 57	5.5
SU 17	00 37	7.0	13 05	7.1	10 07	9.6	22 35	9.6	11 27	3.5	—	—	01 25	5.6	13 43	5.8
M 18	01 25	7.2	13 52	7.2	10 53	9.9	23 18	9.8	00 11	3.4	12 17	3.6	02 09	5.8	14 28	6.0
TU 19	02 10	7.4	14 36	7.2	11 39	9.9	—	—	00 54	3.4	13 04	3.6	02 52	5.8	15 15	6.0
W 20	02 54	7.5	15 19	7.1	00 02	9.8	12 25	9.7	01 35	3.5	13 51	3.6	03 37	5.8	16 04	5.9
TH 21	03 38	7.5	16 01	7.0	00 45	9.6	13 10	9.4	02 14	3.5	14 35	3.5	04 23	5.6	16 54	5.6
F 22	04 21	7.3	16 42	6.7	01 29	9.2	13 56	8.8	02 53	3.5	15 18	3.4	05 10	5.4	17 47	5.3
SA 23	05 06	6.9	17 24	6.3	02 14	8.8	14 45	8.2	03 33	3.4	16 02	3.2	06 01	5.1	18 43	5.0
SU 24	05 53	6.5	18 09	6.0	03 06	8.3	15 44	7.6	04 16	3.2	16 50	2.9	06 57	4.8	19 44	4.6
M 25	06 47	6.1	19 03	5.8	04 09	7.8	16 54	7.2	05 05	3.0	17 46	2.7	08 01	4.6	20 48	4.4
TU 26	07 53	5.9	20 14	5.6	05 21	7.5	18 13	7.1	06 09	2.8	19 04	2.6	09 08	4.4	21 57	4.3
W 27	09 05	5.8	21 32	5.7	06 34	7.5	19 27	7.3	07 44	2.8	20 41	2.6	10 17	4.4	23 09	4.4
TH 28	10 17	5.9	22 43	5.9	07 41	7.7	20 25	7.7	09 04	2.9	21 40	2.8	11 24	4.5	—	—
F 29	11 22	6.2	23 41	6.2	08 34	8.0	21 08	8.0	09 59	3.0	22 25	2.9	00 08	4.6	12 18	4.7
SA 30	12 12	6.4	—	—	09 17	8.3	21 45	8.3	10 44	3.2	23 04	3.1	00 52	4.8	13 02	4.9

MAY 2011 *High Water* GMT

	LONDON BRIDGE Datum of Predictions 3.20m below				LIVERPOOL (Gladstone Dock) Datum of Predictions 4.93m below				GREENOCK Datum of Predictions 1.62m below				LEITH Datum of Predictions 2.90m below			
	hr	*ht m*	*hr*	*ht m*	*hr*	*ht m*	*hr*	*ht m*	*hr*	*ht m*	*hr*	*ht m*	*hr*	*ht m*	*hr*	*ht m*
SU 1	00 27	6.5	12 53	6.5	09 55	8.6	22 17	8.6	11 24	3.2	23 40	3.2	01 28	4.9	13 39	5.0
M 2	01 07	6.7	13 27	6.6	10 30	8.7	22 49	8.8	12 01	3.2	—	—	02 00	5.1	14 13	5.1
TU 3	01 41	6.8	13 59	6.7	11 04	8.8	23 20	8.9	00 14	3.3	12 35	3.2	02 32	5.2	14 47	5.2
W 4	02 14	6.9	14 30	6.7	11 37	8.9	23 51	8.9	00 47	3.3	13 08	3.2	03 04	5.2	15 21	5.2
TH 5	02 46	6.9	15 02	6.7	12 10	8.8	—	—	01 17	3.4	13 42	3.2	03 37	5.2	15 56	5.2
F 6	03 21	6.9	15 37	6.6	00 24	8.9	12 46	8.7	01 49	3.5	14 19	3.2	04 11	5.2	16 33	5.2
SA 7	03 57	6.9	16 13	6.5	00 59	8.8	13 23	8.5	02 23	3.5	14 59	3.2	04 47	5.1	17 13	5.1
SU 8	04 36	6.8	16 51	6.3	01 37	8.6	14 06	8.3	02 59	3.5	15 41	3.1	05 26	5.0	17 57	5.0
M 9	05 18	6.6	17 34	6.2	02 22	8.3	14 57	8.0	03 38	3.4	16 28	3.0	06 10	4.8	18 48	4.8
TU 10	06 08	6.5	18 27	6.1	03 18	8.1	15 59	7.8	04 22	3.3	17 23	2.9	07 02	4.7	19 46	4.7
W 11	07 07	6.3	19 31	6.0	04 27	7.9	17 11	7.7	05 15	3.1	18 31	2.8	08 07	4.6	20 55	4.7
TH 12	08 22	6.3	20 51	6.1	05 42	8.0	18 25	7.9	06 24	3.0	19 53	2.8	09 23	4.7	22 07	4.8
F 13	09 37	6.4	22 06	6.3	06 51	8.2	19 32	8.3	07 51	3.1	21 08	2.9	10 34	4.9	23 11	5.0
SA 14	10 44	6.6	23 11	6.6	07 55	8.6	20 31	8.7	09 07	3.2	22 07	3.1	11 35	5.1	—	—
SU 15	11 45	6.8	—	—	08 52	9.0	21 23	9.1	10 09	3.3	22 58	3.2	00 08	5.2	12 31	5.4
M 16	00 09	6.9	12 40	6.9	09 44	9.3	22 11	9.4	11 04	3.4	23 46	3.3	00 59	5.4	13 22	5.6
TU 17	01 01	7.1	13 30	6.9	10 34	9.5	22 58	9.5	11 55	3.5	—	—	01 46	5.6	14 12	5.7
W 18	01 49	7.3	14 16	7.0	11 23	9.5	23 43	9.6	00 30	3.4	12 46	3.5	02 32	5.6	15 01	5.8
TH 19	02 36	7.3	15 01	7.0	12 10	9.3	—	—	01 14	3.5	13 34	3.4	03 19	5.6	15 51	5.7
F 20	03 21	7.3	15 44	6.9	00 28	9.4	12 56	9.1	01 55	3.5	14 21	3.3	04 06	5.5	16 41	5.5
SA 21	04 07	7.1	16 26	6.7	01 12	9.2	13 42	8.7	02 35	3.5	15 05	3.2	04 54	5.4	17 32	5.3
SU 22	04 52	6.9	17 07	6.4	01 57	8.9	14 28	8.2	03 15	3.5	15 50	3.1	05 43	5.1	18 22	5.0
M 23	05 37	6.5	17 49	6.2	02 44	8.5	15 17	7.8	03 57	3.3	16 36	2.9	06 34	4.9	19 15	4.7
TU 24	06 25	6.2	18 35	6.0	03 37	8.1	16 13	7.5	04 44	3.2	17 26	2.8	07 28	4.7	20 09	4.5
W 25	07 19	6.0	19 33	5.8	04 36	7.8	17 16	7.2	05 37	3.0	18 22	2.7	08 26	4.6	21 05	4.4
TH 26	08 20	5.9	20 42	5.8	05 40	7.6	18 23	7.2	06 42	2.9	19 22	2.7	09 25	4.5	22 04	4.4
F 27	09 22	5.9	21 48	5.9	06 43	7.6	19 26	7.4	07 57	2.8	20 27	2.8	10 24	4.4	23 04	4.4
SA 28	10 23	6.0	22 49	6.1	07 42	7.7	20 20	7.7	09 04	2.9	21 26	2.9	11 23	4.5	23 58	4.6
SU 29	11 20	6.1	23 43	6.3	08 34	8.0	21 04	8.0	09 58	3.0	22 17	3.0	12 16	4.7	—	—
M 30	12 10	6.3	—	—	09 19	8.2	21 43	8.3	10 45	3.0	23 02	3.2	00 45	4.8	13 02	4.8
TU 31	00 29	6.6	12 53	6.5	10 00	8.4	22 20	8.6	11 26	3.1	23 42	3.3	01 26	5.0	13 44	5.0

JUNE 2011 *High Water* GMT

	LONDON BRIDGE				LIVERPOOL (Gladstone Dock)				GREENOCK				LEITH			
W 1	01 11	6.7	13 33	6.6	10 38	8.6	22 55	8.8	12 05	3.1	—	—	02 04	5.1	14 23	5.1
TH 2	01 50	6.8	14 11	6.7	11 15	8.7	23 31	8.9	00 17	3.4	12 43	3.1	02 40	5.2	15 01	5.2
F 3	02 28	6.9	14 49	6.7	11 53	8.8	—	—	00 51	3.5	13 22	3.1	03 17	5.3	15 38	5.3
SA 4	03 07	7.0	15 27	6.7	00 08	9.0	12 32	8.8	01 27	3.5	14 03	3.2	03 53	5.3	16 18	5.3
SU 5	03 47	7.0	16 06	6.6	00 48	9.0	13 14	8.8	02 04	3.6	14 45	3.2	04 31	5.3	16 59	5.3
M 6	04 28	7.0	16 46	6.6	01 30	8.9	13 59	8.6	02 43	3.6	15 30	3.1	05 11	5.2	17 44	5.2
TU 7	05 13	6.9	17 29	6.5	02 16	8.7	14 48	8.4	03 24	3.6	16 17	3.1	05 56	5.1	18 33	5.1
W 8	06 01	6.7	18 17	6.4	03 08	8.6	15 43	8.2	04 09	3.5	17 09	3.0	06 46	5.0	19 27	4.9
TH 9	06 57	6.5	19 15	6.3	04 06	8.4	16 45	8.1	05 00	3.4	18 06	3.0	07 44	4.9	20 29	4.8
F 10	08 02	6.4	20 25	6.3	05 11	8.3	17 52	8.1	06 00	3.2	19 13	2.9	08 52	4.9	21 36	4.8
SA 11	09 10	6.4	21 37	6.4	06 19	8.3	18 59	8.2	07 14	3.1	20 26	2.9	10 04	4.9	22 41	4.9
SU 12	10 16	6.4	22 43	6.5	07 26	8.4	20 04	8.4	08 34	3.1	21 35	3.0	11 10	5.0	23 42	5.1
M 13	11 20	6.5	23 46	6.7	08 30	8.6	21 02	8.7	09 45	3.2	22 34	3.2	12 11	5.2	—	—
TU 14	12 21	6.6	—	—	09 29	8.8	21 55	9.0	10 46	3.3	23 26	3.3	00 38	5.2	13 09	5.4
W 15	00 43	6.9	13 15	6.7	10 22	9.0	22 44	9.2	11 42	3.3	—	—	01 30	5.4	14 02	5.5
TH 16	01 36	7.0	14 04	6.8	11 13	9.1	23 30	9.3	00 13	3.4	12 35	3.3	02 19	5.5	14 52	5.5
F 17	02 24	7.1	14 49	6.8	11 59	9.0	—	—	00 58	3.5	13 24	3.2	03 06	5.5	15 40	5.5
SA 18	03 11	7.2	15 32	6.8	00 14	9.3	12 43	8.9	01 40	3.5	14 09	3.2	03 52	5.5	16 26	5.4
SU 19	03 55	7.1	16 12	6.7	00 56	9.2	13 24	8.7	02 19	3.5	14 52	3.1	04 37	5.4	17 11	5.3
M 20	04 37	6.9	16 50	6.6	01 37	9.0	14 03	8.4	02 58	3.5	15 32	3.0	05 21	5.3	17 55	5.1
TU 21	05 17	6.6	17 27	6.4	02 17	8.7	14 43	8.1	03 37	3.4	16 13	3.0	06 04	5.1	18 39	4.8
W 22	05 57	6.4	18 05	6.3	03 00	8.4	15 27	7.8	04 17	3.3	16 55	3.0	06 49	4.9	19 24	4.6
TH 23	06 38	6.2	18 48	6.1	03 48	8.0	16 17	7.5	05 01	3.1	17 39	2.9	07 37	4.7	20 12	4.5
F 24	07 26	6.0	19 44	5.9	04 42	7.7	17 16	7.3	05 49	3.0	18 27	2.9	08 29	4.5	21 04	4.4
SA 25	08 24	5.8	20 52	5.8	05 43	7.5	18 21	7.2	06 44	2.9	19 20	2.8	09 25	4.4	22 00	4.4
SU 26	09 26	5.8	21 57	5.9	06 47	7.4	19 25	7.4	07 49	2.8	20 21	2.9	10 24	4.4	22 59	4.5
M 27	10 27	5.9	22 58	6.1	07 49	7.6	20 23	7.7	09 00	2.8	21 25	3.0	11 25	4.5	23 58	4.6
TU 28	11 28	6.1	23 54	6.4	08 45	7.8	21 11	8.1	10 03	2.9	22 23	3.1	12 24	4.6	—	—
W 29	12 22	6.4	—	—	09 33	8.2	21 54	8.4	10 55	3.0	23 11	3.2	00 52	4.8	13 16	4.8
TH 30	00 44	6.6	13 11	6.6	10 16	8.5	22 34	8.8	11 41	3.0	23 51	3.3	01 38	5.0	14 01	5.1

JULY 2011 *High Water* GMT

	LONDON BRIDGE Datum of Predictions 3.20m below				LIVERPOOL (Gladstone Dock) Datum of Predictions 4.93m below				GREENOCK Datum of Predictions 1.62m below				LEITH Datum of Predictions 2.90m below			
	hr	*ht m*	*hr*	*ht m*	*hr*	*ht m*	*hr*	*ht m*	*hr*	*ht m*	*hr*	*ht m*	*hr*	*ht m*	*hr*	*ht m*
F 1	01 30	6.8	13 56	6.7	10 57	8.7	23 14	9.0	12 24	3.1	—	—	02 20	5.2	14 42	5.2
SA 2	02 13	7.0	14 38	6.8	11 37	9.0	23 54	9.2	00 29	3.5	13 07	3.1	02 58	5.4	15 22	5.4
SU 3	02 56	7.1	15 19	6.9	12 19	9.1	—	—	01 08	3.6	13 50	3.1	03 36	5.5	16 02	5.5
M 4	03 38	7.2	15 59	6.9	00 35	9.3	13 02	9.1	01 48	3.7	14 34	3.2	04 15	5.5	16 43	5.5
TU 5	04 20	7.2	16 38	6.9	01 19	9.3	13 46	9.1	02 29	3.7	15 17	3.2	04 56	5.5	17 27	5.4
W 6	05 03	7.1	17 19	6.8	02 03	9.2	14 32	8.9	03 11	3.7	16 02	3.2	05 40	5.5	18 14	5.3
TH 7	05 49	6.9	18 03	6.7	02 50	9.0	15 22	8.6	03 55	3.7	16 48	3.2	06 27	5.4	19 04	5.1
F 8	06 39	6.6	18 54	6.6	03 42	8.8	16 17	8.3	04 42	3.5	17 37	3.1	07 21	5.2	20 02	4.9
SA 9	07 37	6.4	19 56	6.4	04 42	8.4	17 21	8.1	05 35	3.3	18 33	3.0	08 26	5.0	21 07	4.8
SU 10	08 42	6.3	21 08	6.4	05 51	8.2	18 32	8.0	06 37	3.1	19 44	2.9	09 40	4.9	22 15	4.8
M 11	09 49	6.2	22 20	6.4	07 06	8.1	19 44	8.1	08 00	3.0	21 08	2.9	10 52	4.9	23 22	4.9
TU 12	11 00	6.2	23 30	6.5	08 19	8.2	20 49	8.4	09 30	3.0	22 18	3.1	12 01	5.0	—	—
W 13	12 09	6.3	—	—	09 23	8.4	21 46	8.8	10 41	3.1	23 14	3.3	00 25	5.0	13 04	5.1
TH 14	00 35	6.7	13 07	6.5	10 18	8.7	22 35	9.1	11 39	3.1	—	—	01 22	5.2	13 57	5.3
F 15	01 30	6.9	13 56	6.7	11 05	8.8	23 19	9.2	00 02	3.4	12 30	3.1	02 10	5.4	14 44	5.4
SA 16	02 18	7.0	14 39	6.8	11 47	8.9	23 59	9.3	00 47	3.5	13 15	3.1	02 54	5.5	15 26	5.4
SU 17	03 01	7.1	15 19	6.9	12 25	8.9	—	—	01 26	3.5	13 55	3.1	03 36	5.5	16 07	5.4
M 18	03 41	7.0	15 54	6.9	00 36	9.3	13 00	8.8	02 03	3.5	14 31	3.1	04 16	5.5	16 45	5.3
TU 19	04 17	6.9	16 27	6.8	01 11	9.1	13 33	8.6	02 38	3.5	15 05	3.1	04 54	5.4	17 23	5.1
W 20	04 50	6.7	16 59	6.7	01 46	8.9	14 07	8.4	03 12	3.5	15 40	3.1	05 31	5.2	18 00	5.0
TH 21	05 22	6.5	17 31	6.5	02 22	8.6	14 43	8.1	03 47	3.4	16 18	3.1	06 08	5.0	18 39	4.8
F 22	05 54	6.3	18 05	6.3	03 01	8.3	15 23	7.8	04 24	3.3	16 57	3.1	06 49	4.8	19 22	4.6
SA 23	06 29	6.0	18 45	6.0	03 45	7.8	16 11	7.4	05 04	3.1	17 39	3.0	07 35	4.6	20 11	4.5
SU 24	07 14	5.8	19 37	5.8	04 39	7.5	17 13	7.2	05 52	2.9	18 26	2.9	08 30	4.4	21 08	4.4
M 25	08 18	5.6	20 57	5.7	05 48	7.2	18 29	7.1	06 51	2.8	19 22	2.9	09 33	4.3	22 10	4.4
TU 26	09 37	5.6	22 14	5.8	07 04	7.2	19 42	7.4	08 03	2.7	20 31	2.9	10 40	4.3	23 16	4.5
W 27	10 49	5.9	23 20	6.2	08 12	7.5	20 42	7.9	09 25	2.8	21 44	3.0	11 48	4.5	—	—
TH 28	11 54	6.2	—	—	09 09	8.0	21 31	8.4	10 33	2.9	22 41	3.2	00 20	4.7	12 50	4.8
F 29	00 18	6.5	12 49	6.5	09 56	8.5	22 14	8.9	11 24	3.0	23 27	3.3	01 14	5.0	13 39	5.1
SA 30	01 09	6.8	13 37	6.8	10 39	8.9	22 55	9.3	12 09	3.1	—	—	01 58	5.3	14 22	5.4
SU 31	01 56	7.1	14 22	6.9	11 20	9.2	23 36	9.6	00 08	3.5	12 53	3.2	02 38	5.5	15 02	5.6

AUGUST 2011 *High Water* GMT

	LONDON BRIDGE				LIVERPOOL (Gladstone Dock)				GREENOCK				LEITH			
M 1	02 40	7.3	15 03	7.1	12 02	9.5	—	—	00 50	3.6	13 35	3.2	03 16	5.7	15 42	5.7
TU 2	03 23	7.4	15 43	7.2	00 18	9.8	12 44	9.5	01 32	3.7	14 17	3.2	03 55	5.8	16 23	5.7
W 3	04 05	7.3	16 22	7.2	01 01	9.8	13 27	9.5	02 14	3.8	14 59	3.3	04 36	5.9	17 06	5.7
TH 4	04 46	7.2	17 01	7.1	01 43	9.7	14 11	9.2	02 57	3.8	15 40	3.3	05 20	5.8	17 51	5.5
F 5	05 29	6.9	17 43	6.9	02 28	9.4	14 57	8.8	03 40	3.8	16 21	3.3	06 07	5.6	18 40	5.2
SA 6	06 14	6.6	18 29	6.7	03 17	8.9	15 49	8.4	04 23	3.6	17 05	3.2	07 00	5.3	19 35	5.0
SU 7	07 07	6.3	19 28	6.4	04 16	8.4	16 53	8.0	05 11	3.4	17 55	3.0	08 05	5.0	20 41	4.7
M 8	08 10	6.0	20 41	6.2	05 29	7.9	18 11	7.7	06 05	3.1	19 02	2.9	09 23	4.8	21 54	4.7
TU 9	09 23	5.9	22 01	6.1	06 54	7.7	19 32	7.9	07 26	2.8	20 50	2.9	10 42	4.7	23 09	4.7
W 10	10 45	6.0	23 20	6.3	08 16	7.8	20 43	8.2	09 36	2.8	22 08	3.1	11 58	4.8	—	—
TH 11	11 59	6.2	—	—	09 21	8.2	21 38	8.7	10 44	3.0	23 03	3.3	00 19	4.9	13 02	5.0
F 12	00 27	6.6	12 57	6.6	10 11	8.6	22 24	9.0	11 35	3.1	23 49	3.4	01 15	5.2	13 51	5.2
SA 13	01 21	6.9	13 43	6.8	10 52	8.8	23 03	9.2	12 19	3.1	—	—	02 00	5.4	14 32	5.3
SU 14	02 05	7.0	14 23	6.9	11 28	8.9	23 38	9.3	00 31	3.5	12 58	3.1	02 39	5.5	15 08	5.4
M 15	02 44	7.0	14 58	6.9	12 01	9.0	—	—	01 09	3.5	13 32	3.1	03 16	5.5	15 42	5.4
TU 16	03 19	7.0	15 29	7.0	00 11	9.3	12 32	8.9	01 43	3.5	14 01	3.1	03 50	5.5	16 15	5.3
W 17	03 49	6.9	15 59	6.9	00 43	9.2	13 01	8.8	02 14	3.5	14 32	3.2	04 23	5.4	16 48	5.2
TH 18	04 17	6.8	16 27	6.9	01 14	9.1	13 31	8.6	02 45	3.5	15 04	3.2	04 57	5.3	17 22	5.1
F 19	04 44	6.6	16 57	6.7	01 46	8.8	14 02	8.4	03 16	3.4	15 39	3.3	05 32	5.1	17 58	4.9
SA 20	05 13	6.4	17 28	6.4	02 18	8.4	14 35	8.0	03 50	3.3	16 15	3.2	06 09	4.9	18 38	4.7
SU 21	05 45	6.1	18 04	6.2	02 55	8.0	15 15	7.7	04 28	3.2	16 54	3.1	06 52	4.7	19 24	4.5
M 22	06 23	5.9	18 47	5.9	03 41	7.5	16 09	7.3	05 12	3.0	17 39	3.0	07 42	4.5	20 19	4.4
TU 23	07 13	5.6	19 47	5.7	04 48	7.1	17 32	7.1	06 09	2.7	18 35	2.9	08 46	4.3	21 27	4.3
W 24	08 31	5.4	21 22	5.6	06 17	7.0	19 01	7.3	07 22	2.6	19 44	2.9	10 00	4.3	22 39	4.4
TH 25	10 08	5.6	22 44	6.0	07 40	7.4	20 12	7.8	08 56	2.7	21 05	3.0	11 14	4.5	23 49	4.7
F 26	11 22	6.1	23 49	6.5	08 44	8.0	21 05	8.4	10 16	2.9	22 12	3.2	12 21	4.8	—	—
SA 27	12 22	6.5	—	—	09 33	8.6	21 50	9.0	11 07	3.1	23 02	3.4	00 46	5.0	13 14	5.2
SU 28	00 44	6.9	13 12	6.9	10 17	9.1	22 32	9.5	11 50	3.2	23 46	3.6	01 32	5.4	13 57	5.5
M 29	01 33	7.2	13 57	7.1	10 58	9.5	23 14	9.9	12 32	3.3	—	—	02 12	5.7	14 38	5.8
TU 30	02 18	7.4	14 39	7.3	11 40	9.8	23 56	10.1	00 30	3.7	13 14	3.3	02 51	6.0	15 18	5.9
W 31	03 01	7.4	15 19	7.4	12 21	9.9	—	—	01 14	3.8	13 55	3.4	03 32	6.1	15 59	5.9

SEPTEMBER 2011 *High Water* GMT

	LONDON BRIDGE Datum of Predictions 3.20m below				LIVERPOOL (Gladstone Dock) Datum of Predictions 4.93m below				GREENOCK Datum of Predictions 1.62m below				LEITH Datum of Predictions 2.90m below			
	hr	*ht m*	*hr*	*ht m*	*hr*	*ht m*	*hr*	*ht m*	*hr*	*ht m*	*hr*	*ht m*	*hr*	*ht m*	*hr*	*ht m*
TH 1	03 43	7.4	15 59	7.4	00 38	10.1	13 04	9.7	01 58	3.9	14 35	3.4	04 14	6.1	16 42	5.8
F 2	04 24	7.2	16 38	7.3	01 21	9.9	13 47	9.4	02 41	3.9	15 14	3.4	05 00	5.9	17 27	5.6
SA 3	05 04	6.9	17 20	7.0	02 06	9.4	14 32	9.0	03 23	3.8	15 54	3.4	05 48	5.7	18 15	5.3
SU 4	05 47	6.5	18 07	6.7	02 55	8.8	15 24	8.4	04 05	3.6	16 37	3.3	06 43	5.3	19 11	5.0
M 5	06 36	6.2	19 03	6.4	03 55	8.1	16 31	7.9	04 50	3.3	17 26	3.1	07 51	4.9	20 20	4.7
TU 6	07 38	5.9	20 18	6.1	05 15	7.6	17 54	7.6	05 43	2.9	18 32	2.9	09 10	4.6	21 38	4.6
W 7	08 58	5.7	21 43	6.0	06 47	7.4	19 20	7.8	07 10	2.7	20 34	2.9	10 32	4.6	22 56	4.7
TH 8	10 26	5.8	23 06	6.3	08 10	7.7	20 30	8.2	09 37	2.8	21 51	3.1	11 51	4.8	—	—
F 9	11 41	6.2	—	—	09 10	8.2	21 23	8.7	10 33	3.0	22 43	3.3	00 07	4.9	12 51	5.0
SA 10	00 11	6.7	12 37	6.6	09 55	8.5	22 04	9.0	11 18	3.1	23 28	3.5	01 01	5.2	13 36	5.2
SU 11	01 02	6.9	13 21	6.8	10 31	8.8	22 40	9.2	11 57	3.2	—	—	01 42	5.3	14 12	5.3
M 12	01 43	7.0	13 58	6.9	11 03	9.0	23 12	9.3	00 08	3.6	12 31	3.2	02 18	5.5	14 44	5.4
TU 13	02 19	6.9	14 30	6.9	11 33	9.0	23 43	9.3	00 45	3.5	13 00	3.2	02 51	5.5	15 14	5.4
W 14	02 50	6.9	14 59	7.0	12 01	9.1	—	—	01 17	3.5	13 28	3.3	03 23	5.5	15 44	5.3
TH 15	03 16	6.9	15 27	7.0	00 13	9.3	12 30	9.0	01 46	3.5	13 57	3.3	03 54	5.4	16 15	5.3
F 16	03 42	6.8	15 56	7.0	00 43	9.1	12 58	8.8	02 16	3.5	14 29	3.4	04 26	5.3	16 48	5.2
SA 17	04 09	6.7	16 26	6.8	01 13	8.8	13 27	8.6	02 48	3.4	15 02	3.4	05 00	5.2	17 22	5.0
SU 18	04 39	6.5	16 57	6.6	01 44	8.5	13 58	8.3	03 22	3.4	15 37	3.4	05 37	5.0	18 00	4.8
M 19	05 10	6.3	17 32	6.3	02 19	8.1	14 35	7.9	03 59	3.2	16 14	3.3	06 19	4.8	18 43	4.6
TU 20	05 46	6.0	18 15	6.1	03 03	7.7	15 26	7.5	04 42	3.0	16 58	3.1	07 08	4.6	19 36	4.5
W 21	06 32	5.7	19 09	5.8	04 06	7.2	16 45	7.2	05 36	2.8	17 53	3.0	08 09	4.4	20 44	4.4
TH 22	07 37	5.5	20 31	5.7	05 36	7.1	18 20	7.3	06 50	2.7	19 03	2.9	09 24	4.4	22 03	4.5
F 23	09 18	5.6	22 05	6.0	07 05	7.4	19 36	7.9	08 30	2.7	20 26	3.0	10 41	4.5	23 15	4.7
SA 24	10 43	6.0	23 15	6.5	08 13	8.0	20 34	8.5	09 52	2.9	21 39	3.2	11 50	4.9	—	—
SU 25	11 47	6.5	—	—	09 05	8.7	21 22	9.2	10 43	3.2	22 33	3.5	00 14	5.1	12 44	5.3
M 26	00 13	7.0	12 40	6.9	09 51	9.3	22 06	9.7	11 26	3.3	23 21	3.6	01 02	5.5	13 29	5.6
TU 27	01 04	7.2	13 27	7.2	10 33	9.7	22 49	10.1	12 07	3.4	—	—	01 44	5.8	14 10	5.9
W 28	01 51	7.4	14 11	7.4	11 15	10.0	23 32	10.2	00 08	3.8	12 48	3.5	02 25	6.1	14 52	6.0
TH 29	02 35	7.4	14 53	7.5	11 58	10.0	—	—	00 54	3.8	13 29	3.5	03 08	6.2	15 34	6.0
F 30	03 18	7.3	15 35	7.5	00 16	10.2	12 41	9.9	01 40	3.9	14 10	3.6	03 54	6.2	16 18	5.9

OCTOBER 2011 *High Water* GMT

	LONDON BRIDGE				LIVERPOOL (Gladstone Dock)				GREENOCK				LEITH			
SA 1	03 59	7.2	16 17	7.4	01 01	9.8	13 24	9.5	02 24	3.8	14 50	3.6	04 42	6.0	17 04	5.6
SU 2	04 41	6.8	17 00	7.1	01 48	9.3	14 11	9.0	03 07	3.7	15 31	3.5	05 33	5.6	17 54	5.3
M 3	05 23	6.5	17 48	6.7	02 38	8.7	15 04	8.5	03 50	3.5	16 14	3.4	06 31	5.2	18 52	5.0
TU 4	06 10	6.1	18 44	6.3	03 40	8.0	16 12	7.9	04 37	3.2	17 04	3.2	07 39	4.9	20 02	4.7
W 5	07 09	5.8	19 57	6.0	04 58	7.4	17 32	7.7	05 32	2.9	18 12	3.0	08 54	4.6	21 17	4.6
TH 6	08 28	5.7	21 17	6.0	06 27	7.3	18 54	7.8	07 18	2.7	20 02	3.0	10 11	4.6	22 32	4.7
F 7	09 54	5.8	22 37	6.2	07 48	7.6	20 03	8.1	09 14	2.8	21 20	3.1	11 27	4.7	23 41	4.9
SA 8	11 08	6.1	23 43	6.5	08 46	8.1	20 55	8.5	10 07	3.0	22 14	3.3	12 26	4.9	—	—
SU 9	12 05	6.5	—	—	09 29	8.4	21 37	8.8	10 48	3.1	22 58	3.5	00 34	5.1	13 10	5.1
M 10	00 33	6.8	12 50	6.7	10 04	8.7	22 12	9.0	11 24	3.3	23 39	3.5	01 16	5.2	13 45	5.2
TU 11	01 14	6.8	13 26	6.8	10 35	8.9	22 44	9.2	11 56	3.3	—	—	01 52	5.3	14 16	5.3
W 12	01 48	6.8	13 59	6.9	11 04	9.0	23 15	9.2	00 15	3.5	12 26	3.4	02 24	5.4	14 45	5.4
TH 13	02 17	6.8	14 28	7.0	11 32	9.1	23 46	9.2	00 48	3.5	12 56	3.5	02 56	5.4	15 15	5.4
F 14	02 43	6.9	14 57	7.0	12 01	9.1	—	—	01 18	3.5	13 26	3.5	03 27	5.4	15 46	5.3
SA 15	03 10	6.8	15 27	7.0	00 17	9.0	12 31	8.9	01 49	3.5	13 58	3.6	04 01	5.3	16 18	5.2
SU 16	03 40	6.8	15 59	6.9	00 48	8.8	13 00	8.8	02 23	3.4	14 31	3.6	04 36	5.2	16 52	5.1
M 17	04 11	6.6	16 33	6.7	01 21	8.6	13 33	8.5	02 58	3.4	15 06	3.6	05 13	5.0	17 29	5.0
TU 18	04 44	6.4	17 10	6.5	01 57	8.2	14 11	8.2	03 37	3.3	15 44	3.5	05 55	4.9	18 11	4.8
W 19	05 20	6.1	17 53	6.3	02 43	7.9	15 02	7.8	04 20	3.1	16 26	3.3	06 44	4.7	19 02	4.6
TH 20	06 07	5.9	18 47	6.1	03 43	7.5	16 14	7.5	05 12	2.9	17 18	3.2	07 41	4.6	20 06	4.5
F 21	07 08	5.7	19 59	6.0	05 03	7.4	17 41	7.6	06 22	2.8	18 26	3.1	08 52	4.5	21 24	4.6
SA 22	08 33	5.7	21 28	6.2	06 26	7.6	18 56	8.0	07 55	2.8	19 47	3.1	10 07	4.7	22 37	4.8
SU 23	10 02	6.1	22 39	6.6	07 37	8.1	19 58	8.6	09 18	3.0	21 03	3.3	11 15	5.0	23 38	5.2
M 24	11 09	6.5	23 40	6.9	08 33	8.8	20 51	9.2	10 12	3.2	22 03	3.5	12 11	5.3	—	—
TU 25	12 06	6.9	—	—	09 22	9.3	21 39	9.7	10 58	3.4	22 56	3.7	00 30	5.5	13 00	5.6
W 26	00 34	7.1	12 57	7.2	10 08	9.7	22 28	10.0	11 41	3.5	23 46	3.8	01 17	5.8	13 44	5.8
TH 27	01 24	7.2	13 44	7.4	10 52	9.9	23 12	10.1	12 23	3.6	—	—	02 03	6.0	14 27	6.0
F 28	02 10	7.3	14 29	7.5	11 36	10.0	23 59	10.0	00 35	3.8	13 06	3.7	02 49	6.1	15 12	6.0
SA 29	02 55	7.2	15 14	7.5	12 21	9.9	—	—	01 23	3.8	13 48	3.7	03 37	6.1	15 57	5.8
SU 30	03 38	7.1	15 59	7.4	00 46	9.6	13 07	9.6	02 09	3.7	14 30	3.7	04 28	5.9	16 45	5.6
M 31	04 21	6.8	16 45	7.1	01 34	9.1	13 54	9.1	02 54	3.6	15 12	3.6	05 21	5.6	17 36	5.4

NOVEMBER 2011 *High Water* GMT

	LONDON BRIDGE Datum of Predictions 3.20m below				LIVERPOOL (Gladstone Dock) Datum of Predictions 4.93m below				GREENOCK Datum of Predictions 1.62m below				LEITH Datum of Predictions 2.90m below			
	hr	*ht m*	*hr*	*ht m*	*hr*	*ht m*	*hr*	*ht m*	*hr*	*ht m*	*hr*	*ht m*	*hr*	*ht m*	*hr*	*ht m*
TU 1	05 05	6.5	17 33	6.7	02 25	8.6	14 46	8.6	03 40	3.4	15 57	3.5	06 18	5.2	18 33	5.1
W 2	05 51	6.2	18 27	6.3	03 23	8.0	15 48	8.2	04 28	3.2	16 47	3.3	07 20	4.9	19 39	4.8
TH 3	06 43	5.9	19 31	6.1	04 31	7.5	16 58	7.8	05 25	2.9	17 49	3.2	08 27	4.7	20 47	4.7
F 4	07 52	5.8	20 41	6.0	05 47	7.3	18 11	7.8	06 42	2.8	19 12	3.1	09 35	4.6	21 55	4.7
SA 5	09 09	5.8	21 52	6.0	07 04	7.5	19 19	7.9	08 18	2.8	20 34	3.1	10 44	4.6	23 00	4.7
SU 6	10 20	6.0	23 00	6.2	08 06	7.8	20 16	8.2	09 21	3.0	21 34	3.3	11 45	4.7	23 56	4.9
M 7	11 21	6.2	23 54	6.4	08 53	8.2	21 02	8.5	10 06	3.1	22 23	3.4	12 33	4.9	—	—
TU 8	12 10	6.5	—	—	09 31	8.5	21 41	8.7	10 46	3.3	23 06	3.4	00 43	5.0	13 13	5.1
W 9	00 37	6.6	12 51	6.7	10 04	8.7	22 16	8.9	11 21	3.4	23 44	3.4	01 23	5.1	13 46	5.2
TH 10	01 14	6.7	13 27	6.8	10 36	8.9	22 50	9.0	11 55	3.5	—	—	01 58	5.2	14 18	5.3
F 11	01 46	6.7	14 00	6.9	11 07	9.0	23 23	9.0	00 19	3.4	12 28	3.6	02 32	5.3	14 49	5.4
SA 12	02 16	6.8	14 31	6.9	11 38	9.1	23 56	9.0	00 53	3.4	13 00	3.7	03 05	5.3	15 21	5.4
SU 13	02 46	6.8	15 04	7.0	12 10	9.0	—	—	01 27	3.4	13 33	3.7	03 40	5.3	15 55	5.3
M 14	03 19	6.7	15 39	6.9	00 30	8.8	12 43	8.9	02 03	3.4	14 07	3.7	04 16	5.2	16 29	5.2
TU 15	03 53	6.6	16 16	6.8	01 06	8.7	13 18	8.7	02 40	3.4	14 43	3.7	04 55	5.1	17 07	5.1
W 16	04 28	6.5	16 55	6.7	01 45	8.4	13 59	8.5	03 21	3.3	15 22	3.6	05 37	5.0	17 48	5.0
TH 17	05 07	6.3	17 40	6.6	02 31	8.2	14 48	8.2	04 04	3.2	16 05	3.5	06 24	4.9	18 37	4.9
F 18	05 53	6.2	18 33	6.4	03 26	7.9	15 50	8.0	04 54	3.1	16 54	3.4	07 18	4.8	19 34	4.8
SA 19	06 49	6.0	19 36	6.3	04 33	7.8	17 03	8.0	05 55	3.0	17 54	3.3	08 21	4.7	20 45	4.8
SU 20	07 59	6.0	20 54	6.3	05 47	7.8	18 16	8.2	07 11	2.9	19 08	3.3	09 32	4.8	21 59	4.9
M 21	09 23	6.2	22 05	6.5	06 58	8.2	19 22	8.5	08 33	3.0	20 26	3.3	10 39	5.0	23 04	5.1
TU 22	10 34	6.5	23 09	6.7	08 00	8.6	20 22	9.0	09 37	3.2	21 34	3.5	11 39	5.2	—	—
W 23	11 35	6.8	—	—	08 56	9.1	21 17	9.3	10 30	3.4	22 33	3.6	00 02	5.4	12 33	5.5
TH 24	00 08	6.9	12 31	7.1	09 46	9.4	22 08	9.6	11 18	3.5	23 27	3.7	00 55	5.7	13 21	5.7
F 25	01 01	7.0	13 22	7.2	10 34	9.7	22 58	9.7	12 04	3.6	—	—	01 46	5.8	14 08	5.8
SA 26	01 50	7.1	14 11	7.4	11 21	9.8	23 47	9.6	00 19	3.7	12 49	3.7	02 36	5.9	14 54	5.8
SU 27	02 38	7.1	14 59	7.4	12 07	9.8	—	—	01 10	3.7	13 32	3.8	03 26	5.9	15 41	5.8
M 28	03 23	7.0	15 46	7.3	00 35	9.4	12 53	9.6	01 58	3.6	14 15	3.8	04 16	5.7	16 30	5.6
TU 29	04 07	6.8	16 33	7.1	01 23	9.1	13 39	9.3	02 45	3.5	14 57	3.7	05 07	5.5	17 19	5.4
W 30	04 50	6.6	17 19	6.8	02 09	8.6	14 26	8.9	03 30	3.3	15 41	3.6	05 59	5.2	18 12	5.2

DECEMBER 2011 *High Water* GMT

	LONDON BRIDGE				LIVERPOOL (Gladstone Dock)				GREENOCK				LEITH			
TH 1	05 33	6.4	18 07	6.4	02 58	8.2	15 17	8.5	04 16	3.2	16 28	3.5	06 53	5.0	19 07	5.0
F 2	06 17	6.1	18 58	6.2	03 52	7.8	16 14	8.1	05 05	3.1	17 20	3.3	07 49	4.7	20 07	4.8
SA 3	07 11	5.9	19 56	6.0	04 52	7.5	17 17	7.8	05 59	3.0	18 19	3.2	08 47	4.6	21 07	4.6
SU 4	08 17	5.8	20 58	5.9	05 59	7.3	18 22	7.7	06 59	2.9	19 27	3.1	09 46	4.5	22 07	4.6
M 5	09 24	5.8	21 59	5.9	07 07	7.5	19 25	7.8	08 05	2.9	20 37	3.1	10 46	4.5	23 06	4.6
TU 6	10 27	6.0	23 00	6.1	08 07	7.7	20 21	8.0	09 09	3.1	21 39	3.2	11 44	4.7	—	—
W 7	11 24	6.2	23 53	6.3	08 54	8.1	21 09	8.3	10 02	3.2	22 30	3.2	00 02	4.7	12 34	4.9
TH 8	12 14	6.4	—	—	09 35	8.4	21 50	8.5	10 48	3.4	23 15	3.3	00 50	4.9	13 15	5.0
F 9	00 39	6.5	12 57	6.6	10 12	8.7	22 28	8.7	11 28	3.5	23 55	3.3	01 32	5.0	13 52	5.2
SA 10	01 19	6.6	13 36	6.8	10 46	8.9	23 04	8.8	12 05	3.6	—	—	02 10	5.1	14 28	5.3
SU 11	01 56	6.7	14 13	6.8	11 20	9.0	23 40	8.9	00 33	3.3	12 39	3.7	02 47	5.2	15 03	5.4
M 12	02 32	6.7	14 49	6.9	11 55	9.1	—	—	01 10	3.3	13 12	3.7	03 23	5.3	15 37	5.4
TU 13	03 08	6.7	15 26	7.0	00 16	8.9	12 31	9.1	01 48	3.4	13 48	3.8	04 00	5.3	16 13	5.4
W 14	03 44	6.7	16 05	7.0	00 54	8.9	13 09	9.1	02 27	3.3	14 26	3.8	04 39	5.3	16 50	5.3
TH 15	04 21	6.7	16 46	6.9	01 35	8.8	13 50	8.9	03 08	3.3	15 06	3.8	05 20	5.2	17 30	5.2
F 16	05 00	6.6	17 29	6.8	02 19	8.6	14 35	8.7	03 50	3.3	15 49	3.7	06 05	5.1	18 16	5.2
SA 17	05 42	6.5	18 18	6.6	03 08	8.4	15 27	8.5	04 35	3.2	16 35	3.6	06 55	5.0	19 07	5.0
SU 18	06 31	6.4	19 14	6.4	04 04	8.2	16 28	8.4	05 26	3.1	17 27	3.5	07 51	4.9	20 08	4.9
M 19	07 30	6.3	20 22	6.3	05 10	8.0	17 37	8.3	06 26	3.0	18 30	3.4	08 56	4.8	21 21	4.9
TU 20	08 46	6.2	21 33	6.3	06 20	8.1	18 49	8.3	07 42	3.0	19 46	3.3	10 05	4.9	22 34	5.0
W 21	10 02	6.4	22 41	6.4	07 30	8.3	19 59	8.5	09 01	3.1	21 06	3.3	11 10	5.0	23 41	5.2
TH 22	11 10	6.6	23 46	6.5	08 34	8.7	21 02	8.8	10 07	3.3	22 16	3.4	12 10	5.2	—	—
F 23	12 13	6.8	—	—	09 31	9.0	21 59	9.1	11 01	3.5	23 16	3.5	00 41	5.4	13 05	5.4
SA 24	00 45	6.7	13 10	7.0	10 23	9.4	22 52	9.3	11 50	3.6	—	—	01 37	5.6	13 55	5.6
SU 25	01 39	6.8	14 01	7.1	11 11	9.6	23 40	9.4	00 11	3.5	12 37	3.7	02 28	5.7	14 43	5.7
M 26	02 27	6.9	14 50	7.2	11 57	9.7	—	—	01 03	3.5	13 21	3.8	03 16	5.7	15 29	5.7
TU 27	03 13	7.0	15 36	7.2	00 25	9.3	12 40	9.6	01 50	3.4	14 03	3.8	04 03	5.6	16 15	5.7
W 28	03 55	6.9	16 20	7.1	01 08	9.1	13 21	9.4	02 34	3.4	14 44	3.8	04 49	5.5	17 00	5.5
TH 29	04 34	6.8	17 01	6.8	01 47	8.8	14 01	9.1	03 14	3.3	15 24	3.7	05 34	5.3	17 45	5.3
F 30	05 11	6.6	17 40	6.6	02 26	8.4	14 42	8.7	03 54	3.3	16 05	3.6	06 19	5.0	18 30	5.1
SA 31	05 48	6.4	—	—	03 08	8.1	15 27	8.3	04 34	3.2	16 47	3.4	07 04	4.8	—	—

GENERAL REFERENCE

WEIGHTS AND MEASURES

CONVERSION TABLES

THE PERIODIC TABLE

NOBEL PRIZE WINNERS

ABBREVIATIONS

WEIGHTS AND MEASURES

SI UNITS

The Système International d'Unités (SI) is an international and coherent system of units devised to meet all known needs for measurement in science and technology. The system was adopted by the eleventh Conférence Générale des Poids et Mesures (CGPM) in 1960. A comprehensive description of the system is given in *SI The International System of Units* (HMSO). The British Standards that describe the essential features of the International System of Units are *Specifications for SI units and recommendations for the use of their multiples and certain other units* (BS ISO 1000:1992) and *Conversion factors for units* (BS 350: 2004).

The system consists of seven base units and the derived units formed as products or quotients of various powers of the base units. Together the base units and the derived units make up the coherent system of units. In the UK the SI base units, and almost all important derived units, are realised at the National Physical Laboratory and disseminated through the National Measurement Office.

BASE UNITS

Ampere (A) = unit of electric current
Candela (cd) = unit of luminous intensity
Kelvin (K) = unit of thermodynamic temperature
Kilogram (kg) = unit of mass
Metre (m) = unit of length
Mole (mol) = unit of amount of substance
Second (s) = unit of time

DERIVED UNITS

For some of the derived SI units, special names and symbols exist; those approved by the CGPM are as follows:

Becquerel (Bq) = unit of activity (of a radionuclide)
Coulomb (C) = unit of electric charge, quantity of electricity
Degree Celsius (°C) = unit of Celsius temperature
Farad (F) = unit of electric capacitance
Gray (Gy) = unit of absorbed dose, specific energy imparted, kerma, absorbed dose index
Henry (H) = unit of inductance
Hertz (Hz) = unit of frequency
Joule (J) = unit of energy, work, quantity of heat
Katal (kat) = unit of catalytic activity
Lumen (lm) = unit of luminous flux
Lux (lx) = unit of illuminance
Newton (N) = unit of force
Ohm (Ω) = unit of electric resistance
Pascal (Pa) = unit of pressure, stress
Radian (rad) = unit of plane angle
Siemens (S) = unit of electric conductance
Sievert (Sv) = unit of dose equivalent, dose equivalent index
Steradian (sr) = unit of solid angle
Tesla (T) = unit of magnetic flux density
Volt (V) = unit of electric potential, potential difference, electromotive force
Watt (W) = unit of power, radiant flux
Weber (Wb) = unit of magnetic flux

Other derived units are expressed in terms of base units. Below are some of the more commonly used derived units:

Ampere per metre ($A\ m^{-1}$) = unit of magnetic field strength
Candela per square metre ($cd\ m^{-2}$) = unit of luminance
Cubic metre (m^3) = unit of volume
Joule per kelvin ($J\ K^{-1}$) = unit of heat capacity
Joule per kilogram kelvin ($J\ kg^{-1}\ K^{-1}$) = unit of specific heat capacity
Kilogram per cubic metre ($kg\ m^{-3}$) = unit of density
Kilogram metre per second ($kg\ m\ s^{-1}$) = unit of momentum
Metre per second ($m\ s^{-1}$) = unit of velocity
Metre per second squared ($m\ s^{-2}$) = unit of acceleration
Newton per metre ($N\ m^{-1}$) = unit of surface tension
Pascal second (Pa s) = unit of dynamic viscosity
Square metre (m^2) = unit of area
Volt per metre ($V\ m^{-1}$) = unit of electric field strength
Watt per square metre ($W\ m^{-2}$) = unit of heat flux density, irradiance
Watt per metre kelvin ($W\ m^{-1}\ K^{-1}$) = unit of thermal conductivity

Non SI units accepted for use with the SI by the CGPM:

Minute Hour Day	measurement of time
Degree Minute Second	plane angle measurement
Hectare	measurement of area
Litre	measurement of volume
Tonne	measurement of mass

SI PREFIXES

Decimal multiples and submultiples of the SI units are indicated by SI prefixes. These are as follows:

Multiples	*Submultiples*
yotta (Y) × 10^{24}	deci (d) × 10^{-1}
zetta (Z) × 10^{21}	centi (c) × 10^{-2}
exa (E) × 10^{18}	milli (m) × 10^{-3}
peta (P) × 10^{15}	micro (μ) × 10^{-6}
tera (T) × 10^{12}	nano (n) × 10^{-9}
giga (G) × 10^{9}	pico (p) × 10^{-12}
mega (M) × 10^{6}	femto (f) × 10^{-15}
kilo (k) × 10^{3}	atto (a) × 10^{-18}
hecto (h) × 10^{2}	zepto (z) × 10^{-21}
deca (da) × 10	yocto (y) × 10^{-24}

METRIC UNITS

The metric primary standards are the metre as the unit of measurement of length, and the kilogram as the unit of measurement of mass. Other units of measurement are defined by reference to the primary standards.

MEASUREMENT OF LENGTH

Kilometre (km) = 1,000 metres
Metre (m) = the length of the path travelled by light in a vacuum during a time interval of 1/299,792,458 of a second

Decimetre (dm) = 1/10 metre
Centimetre (cm) = 1/100 metre
Millimetre (mm) = 1/1,000 metre

MEASUREMENT OF AREA

Hectare (ha) = 100 ares
Decare = 10 ares
Are (a) = 100 square metres
Square metre = a superficial area equal to that of a square each side of which measures one metre
Square decimetre = 1/100 square metre
Square centimetre = 1/100 square decimetre
Square millimetre = 1/100 square centimetre

MEASUREMENT OF VOLUME

Cubic metre (m^3) = a volume equal to that of a cube each edge of which measures one metre
Cubic decimetre = 1/1,000 cubic metre
Cubic centimetre (cc) = 1/1,000 cubic decimetre
Hectolitre = 100 litres
Litre = a cubic decimetre
Decilitre = 1/10 litre
Centilitre = 1/100 litre
Millilitre = 1/1,000 litre

MEASUREMENT OF CAPACITY

Hectolitre (hl) = 100 litres
Litre (l or L) = a cubic decimetre
Decilitre (dl) = 1/10 litre
Centilitre (cl) = 1/100 litre
Millilitre (ml) = 1/1,000 litre

MEASUREMENT OF MASS OR WEIGHT

Tonne (t) = 1,000 kilograms
Kilogram (kg) = equal to the mass of the international prototype of the kilogram
Hectogram (hg) = 1/10 kilogram
Gram (g) = 1/1,000 kilogram
*Carat (metric) = 1/5 gram
Milligram (mg) = 1/1,000 gram

* Used only for transactions in precious stones, metals or pearls

IMPERIAL UNITS

The imperial primary standards are the yard as the unit of measurement of length and the pound as the unit of measurement of mass. Other units of measurement are defined by reference to the primary standards.

MEASUREMENT OF LENGTH

Mile = 1,760 yards
Furlong = 220 yards
Chain = 22 yards
Yard (yd) = 0.9144 metre
Foot (ft or ′) = 1/3 yard
Inch (in or ″) = 1/36 yard

MEASUREMENT OF AREA

Square mile = 640 acres
Acre = 4,840 square yards
Rood = 1,210 square yards
Square yard (sq. yd) = a superficial area equal to that of a square each side of which measures one yard
Square foot (sq. ft) = 1/9 square yard
Square inch (sq. in) = 1/144 square foot

MEASUREMENT OF VOLUME

Cubic yard = a volume equal to that of a cube each edge of which measures one yard
Cubic foot = 1/27 cubic yard
Cubic inch = 1/1,728 cubic foot

MEASUREMENT OF CAPACITY

Bushel = 8 gallons
Peck = 2 gallons
Gallon (gal) = 4.54609 cubic decimetres
Quart (qt) = 1/4 gallon
Pint (pt) = 1/2 quart
Gill = 1/4 pint
Fluid ounce (fl oz) = 1/20 pint
Fluid drachm = 1/8 fluid ounce
Minim (min) = 1/60 fluid drachm

MEASUREMENT OF MASS OR WEIGHT

Ton = 2,240 pounds
Hundredweight (cwt) = 112 pounds
Cental = 100 pounds
Quarter = 28 pounds
Stone = 14 pounds
Pound (lb) = 0.45359 kilogram
Ounce (oz) = 1/16 pound
*Ounce troy (oz tr) = 12/175 pound
Dram (dr) = 1/16 ounce
Grain (gr) = 1/7,000 pound
Pennyweight (dwt) = 24 grains
Ounce apothecaries' = 480 grains
Drachm (ℨ1) = 1/8 ounce apothecaries'
Scruple (∋1) = 1/3 drachm

* Used only for transactions in gold, silver or other precious metals, and articles made therefrom

MEASUREMENT OF ELECTRICITY

Units of measurement of electricity are defined by the Weights and Measures Act 1985 as follows:
Ampere (A) = that constant current which, if maintained in two straight parallel conductors of infinite length, of negligible circular cross-section and placed 1 metre apart in a vacuum, would produce between these conductors a force equal to 2×10^{-7} newton per metre of length
Ohm (Ω) = the electric resistance between two points of a conductor when a constant potential difference of 1 volt, applied between the two points, produces in the conductor a current of 1 ampere, the conductor not being the seat of any electromotive force
Volt (V) = the difference of electric potential between two points of a conducting wire carrying a constant current of 1 ampere when the power dissipated between these points is equal to 1 watt
Watt (W) = the power which in one second gives rise to energy of 1 joule
Kilowatt (kW) = 1,000 watts
Megawatt (MW) = one million watts

MEASUREMENT OF SOUND

INTENSITY

Decibels (db) are used to measure the power or intensity of sound. Decibel level is calculated on a logarithmic scale as a ratio against a standard power; each increase of 10db on the scale corresponds to ten times the intensity and twice the loudness. Some examples of decibel levels are:

Silence	0db
Noise level of ordinary conversation	60db
Damage threshold for noise	90db
Noise level of typical streetworks	110db
Pain threshold for noise	130db

FREQUENCY AND PITCH

Frequency is a measure of how many waves or sound waves pass through a medium over a certain period of time. It is measured in Hertz (Hz) (*see* Derived SI Units) and a frequency of one Hz equals one wave, or one vibration every second. The typical range for human hearing is between 20Hz and 20,000Hz.

Frequency is closely linked to pitch, which indicates how high or low a sound is; a high frequency will have a high pitch, and a frequency doubled sounds an octave higher.

WATER AND LIQUOR MEASURES

1 cubic foot = 62.32 pounds
1 gallon = 10 pounds
1 cubic cm = 1 gram
1,000 cubic cm = 1 litre; 1 kilogram
1 cubic metre = 1,000 litres; 1,000 kilograms; 1 tonne
An inch of rain on the surface of an acre (43,560 sq. feet) = 3,630 cubic feet = 100.992 tons
Cisterns: A cistern 4 × 2.5 feet and 3 feet deep will hold brimful 186.963 gallons, weighing 1,869.63 pounds in addition to its own weight

WATER FOR SHIPS

Kilderkin = 18 gallons
Barrel = 36 gallons
Puncheon = 72 gallons
Butt = 110 gallons
Tun = 210 gallons

BOTTLES OF WINE

Traditional equivalents in standard champagne bottles:
Magnum = 2 bottles
Jeroboam = 4 bottles
Rehoboam = 6 bottles
Methuselah = 8 bottles
Salmanazar = 12 bottles
Balthazar = 16 bottles
Nebuchadnezzar = 20 bottles
A quarter of a bottle is known as a *nip*
An eighth of a bottle is known as a *baby*

ANGULAR AND CIRCULAR MEASURES

60 seconds (") = 1 minute (′)
60 minutes = 1 degree (°)
90 degrees = 1 right angle or quadrant
Diameter of circle × 3.1416 = circumference
Diameter squared × 0.7854 = area of circle
Diameter squared × 3.1416 = surface of sphere
Diameter cubed × 0.523 = solidity of sphere
One degree of circumference × 57.3 = radius*
Diameter of cylinder × 3.1416; product by length or height, gives the surface
Diameter squared × 0.7854; product by length or height, gives solid content

* Or, one radian (the angle subtended at the centre of a circle by an arc of the circumference equal in length to the radius) = 57.3 degrees

MILLION, BILLION ETC

The long- and short-scale systems result in different numerical values for sums greater than a million. Many European countries use the long-scale system while the short-scale system is used by the USA and most English-speaking countries. In 1974 the UK government officially adopted the short-scale system, but the use of the terms billion and trillion in the UK can still be ambiguous.

Long-scale		
Million	thousand × thousand	10^6
Billion	million × million	10^{12}
Trillion	million × billion	10^{18}
Quadrillion	million × trillion	10^{24}

Short-scale		
Million	thousand × thousand	10^6
Billion	thousand × million	10^9
Trillion	million × million	10^{12}
Quadrillion	million × billion	10^{15}

NAUTICAL MEASURES

DISTANCE

Distance at sea is measured in nautical miles. The British Standard nautical mile was 6,080 feet but this measure has been obsolete since 1970 when the international nautical mile of 1,852 metres was adopted by the Hydrographic Department of the Ministry of Defence. The cable (600 feet or 100 fathoms) was a measure approximately one-tenth of a nautical mile. Such distances are now expressed in decimal parts of a sea mile or in metres.

Soundings at sea were recorded in fathoms (6 feet). Depths are now expressed in metres on Admiralty charts.

SPEED

Speed is measured in nautical miles per hour, called knots. A ship moving at the rate of 30 nautical miles per hour is said to be doing 30 knots.

Knots	*Mph*	*Knots*	*Mph*
1	1.1515	9	10.3636
2	2.3030	10	11.5151
3	3.4545	15	17.2727
4	4.6060	20	23.0303
5	5.7575	25	28.7878
6	6.9090	30	34.5454
7	8.0606	35	40.3030
8	9.2121	40	46.0606

TONNAGE

Under the Merchant Shipping Act 1854, the tonnage of UK-registered vessels was measured in tons of 100 cubic feet. The need for a universal method of measurement led to the adoption of the International Convention on Tonnage Measurements of Ships 1969, which measures, in cubic metres, all the internal spaces of a vessel for the gross tonnage and those of the cargo compartments for the net tonnage. The convention has applied since July 1982 to new ships, ships which needed to be remeasured because of substantial alterations, and ships whose owners requested remeasurement. On 18 July 1994 the convention became mandatory.

TEMPERATURE SCALES

The SI (International System) unit of temperature is the Kelvin (K), which is defined as the fraction 1/273.16 of the temperature of the triple point of water (ie where ice, water and water vapour are in equilibrium). The zero of the Kelvin scale is the absolute zero of temperature. The freezing point of water is 273.15K and the boiling point (as adopted in the International Temperature Scale of 1990) is 373.124K.

The Celsius scale (°C; formerly centigrade) is defined by subtracting 273.15 from the Kelvin temperature. The Fahrenheit (°F) scale is related to the Celsius scale by the relationships:

Temperature °F = (temperature °C × 1.8) + 32
Temperature °C = (temperature °F – 32) ÷ 1.8

It follows from these definitions that the freezing point of water is 0°C and 32°F. The boiling point is 99.974°C and 211.953°F.

The temperature of the human body varies from person to person and in the same person can be affected by a variety of factors. In most people body temperature varies between 36.5°C and 37.2°C (97.7–98.9°F).

Conversion between scales

°C	°F	°C	°F	°C	°F
100	212	60	140	20	68
99	210.2	59	138.2	19	66.2
98	208.4	58	136.4	18	64.4
97	206.6	57	134.6	17	62.6
96	204.8	56	132.8	16	60.8
95	203	55	131	15	59
94	201.2	54	129.2	14	57.2
93	199.4	53	127.4	13	55.4
92	197.6	52	125.6	12	53.6
91	195.8	51	123.8	11	51.8
90	194	50	122	10	50
89	192.2	49	120.2	9	48.2
88	190.4	48	118.4	8	46.4
87	188.6	47	116.6	7	44.6
86	186.8	46	114.8	6	42.8
85	185	45	113	5	41
84	183.2	44	111.2	4	39.2
83	181.4	43	109.4	3	37.4
82	179.6	42	107.6	2	35.6
81	177.8	41	105.8	1	33.8
80	176	40	104	Zero	32
79	174.2	39	102.2	−1	30.2
78	172.4	38	100.4	−2	28.4
77	170.6	37	98.6	−3	26.6
76	168.8	36	96.8	−4	24.8
75	167	35	95	−5	23
74	165.2	34	93.2	−6	21.2
73	163.4	33	91.4	−7	19.4
72	161.6	32	89.6	−8	17.6
71	159.8	31	87.8	−9	15.8
70	158	30	86	−10	14
69	156.2	29	84.2	−11	12.2
68	154.4	28	82.4	−12	10.4
67	152.6	27	80.6	−13	8.6
66	150.8	26	78.8	−14	6.8
65	149	25	77	−15	5
64	147.2	24	75.2	−16	3.2
63	145.4	23	73.4	−17	1.4
62	143.6	22	71.6	−18	0.4
61	141.8	21	69.8	−19	−2.2

DISTANCE OF THE HORIZON

The distance to the horizon can be calculated, in metric units, using the equation D = 3.8373√H where D is the distance in kilometres and H is the height of the observer in metres, and in imperial units using the equation D = 1.3157√H where D is the distance in miles and H is the height of the observer in feet. The resulting distances are those following a straight line from the observer to the horizon; it is not the distance along the curvature of the Earth. The difference between these two figures, however, is minimal for heights below 100km (62 miles).

Height in metres (feet)	*Range in km (miles)*
1.7 (5.6)*	5.0 (3.1)
5 (16)	8.6 (5.3)
10 (32.8)	12.1 (7.5)
50 (164)	27.1 (16.8)
100 (328)	38.4 (23.8)
509 (1,670)†	86.6 (53.8)
1,000 (3,281)	121.34 (75.4)
5,000 (16,404)	271.3 (168.5)
8,848 (29,028)‡	361.0 (224.2)
9,144 (30,000)§	366.9 (228.0)

* Average human height in the UK
† Height of the tallest inhabited building (Taipei 101)
‡ Height of Mt Everest
§ Height of cruising aeroplane

PAPER MEASURES

Printing paper	*Writing paper*
5 bundles = 1 bale	480 sheets = 1 ream
2 reams = 1 bundle	20 quires = 1 ream
516 sheets = 1 ream	24 sheets = 1 quire

INTERNATIONAL PAPER SIZES

The basis of the international series of paper sizes is a rectangle having an area of one square metre, the sides of which are in the proportion of 1:√2. The proportions 1:√2 have a geometrical relationship, the side and diagonal of any square being in this proportion. The effect of this arrangement is that if the area of the sheet of paper is doubled or halved, the shorter side and the longer side of the new sheet are still in the same proportion 1:√2. This feature is useful where photographic enlargement or reduction is used, as the proportions remain the same.

Description of the A series is by capital A followed by a figure. The basic size has the description A0 and the higher the figure following the letter, the greater is the number of sub-divisions and therefore the smaller the sheet. Half A0 is A1 and half A1 is A2. Where larger dimensions are required the A is preceded by a figure. Thus 2A0 means twice the size A0; 4A0 is four times the size of A0.

B sizes are intermediate between any two adjacent sizes of the A series. The A series is for magazines and books, B for posters, wall charts and other large items, and C for envelopes. The paper size recommended for business correspondence is A4.

ENVELOPE SIZES

Standard C series envelope sizes are designed for use with the A series of paper sizes. The DL (dimension lengthwise) format is not part of the C series, but is widely used for business letters.

A SERIES

	mm		*mm*
A0	841 × 1189	A6	105 × 148
A1	594 × 841	A7	74 × 105
A2	420 × 594	A8	52 × 74
A3	297 × 420	A9	37 × 52
A4	210 × 297	A10	26 × 37
A5	148 × 210		

B SERIES

B0	1000 × 1414	B6	125 × 176
B1	707 × 1000	B7	88 × 125
B2	500 × 707	B8	62 × 88
B3	353 × 500	B9	44 × 62
B4	250 × 353	B10	31 × 44
B5	176 × 250		

ENVELOPE SIZES

	mm	*Usage*
C0	917 × 1297	A0 sheet
C1	648 × 917	A1 sheet
C2	458 × 648	A2 sheet, A1 sheet folded in half
C3	324 × 458	A3 sheet, A2 folded in half
C4	229 × 324	A4 sheet, A3 folded in half
C5	162 × 229	A5 sheet, A4 folded in half
C6	114 × 162	A5 sheet folded in half
DL	110 × 220	A4 sheet folded in thirds, A5 in half

BOOK SIZES

Traditional		*Modern*	
	mm		*mm*
Royal Quarto	250 × 320	Crown Royal	210 × 280
Demy Quarto	220 × 290	Royal	191 × 235
Crown Quarto	190 × 250	Demy	152 × 229
Royal Octavo	150 × 250	*Paperbacks*	
Demy Octavo	143 × 222	C Format	143 × 222
Large Crown		B format	129 × 198
Octavo	129 × 198	A format	111 × 175

OBSOLETE MEASURES

Length
Cubit, Digit, Ell, Finger, Hand (still in use for measurement of horses), League, Palm, Span
Capacity
Barrel, Bushel, Cask, Hogshead, Sester, Tun
Weight
Clove, Fother, Last, Mark, Nail, Sack, Tod
Area
Bovate, Carucate, Perch, Virgate, Yoke

CLOTHING SIZES

MEN'S

Item	*UK*	*USA*	*Europe*
Suits	36	36	46
	38	38	48
	40	40	50
	42	42	52
	44	44	54
	46	46	56
Shirts	12	12	30–31
	12½	12½	32
	13	13	33
	13½	13½	34–35
	14	14	36
	14½	14½	37
	15	15	38
	15½	15½	39–40
	16	16	41
	16½	16½	42
	17	17	43
	17½	17½	44–45
Shoes	6½	7	39
	7	7½	40
	7½	8	41
	8	8½	42
	8½	9	43
	9	9½	43
	9½	10	44
	10	10½	44
	10½	11	45

WOMEN'S

Item	*UK*	*USA*	*Europe*
Clothing	8	6	36
	10	8	38
	12	10	40
	14	12	42
	16	14	44
	18	16	46
	20	18	48
	22	20	50
	24	22	52
Shoes	4	5½	37
	4½	6	37
	5	6½	38
	5½	7	38
	6	7½	39
	6½	8	39
	7	8½	40
	7½	9	40
	8	9½	41

CONVERSION TABLES FOR WEIGHTS AND MEASURES

Bold figures equal units of either of the columns beside them; thus: 1 cm = 0.394 inches and 1 inch = 2.540 cm

LENGTH			AREA			VOLUME			WEIGHT (MASS)		
Centimetres		*Inches*	*Square cm*		*Square in*	*Cubic cm*		*Cubic in*	*Kilograms*		*Pounds*
2.540	**1**	0.394	6.452	**1**	0.155	16.387	**1**	0.061	0.454	**1**	2.205
5.080	**2**	0.787	12.903	**2**	0.310	32.774	**2**	0.122	0.907	**2**	4.409
7.620	**3**	1.181	19.355	**3**	0.465	49.161	**3**	0.183	1.361	**3**	6.614
10.160	**4**	1.575	25.806	**4**	0.620	65.548	**4**	0.244	1.814	**4**	8.819
12.700	**5**	1.969	32.258	**5**	0.775	81.936	**5**	0.305	2.268	**5**	11.023
15.240	**6**	2.362	38.710	**6**	0.930	98.323	**6**	0.366	2.722	**6**	13.228
17.780	**7**	2.756	45.161	**7**	1.085	114.710	**7**	0.427	3.175	**7**	15.432
20.320	**8**	3.150	51.613	**8**	1.240	131.097	**8**	0.488	3.629	**8**	17.637
22.860	**9**	3.543	58.064	**9**	1.395	147.484	**9**	0.549	4.082	**9**	19.842
25.400	**10**	3.937	64.516	**10**	1.550	163.871	**10**	0.610	4.536	**10**	22.046
50.800	**20**	7.874	129.032	**20**	3.100	327.742	**20**	1.220	9.072	**20**	44.092
76.200	**30**	11.811	193.548	**30**	4.650	491.613	**30**	1.831	13.608	**30**	66.139
101.600	**40**	15.748	258.064	**40**	6.200	655.484	**40**	2.441	18.144	**40**	88.185
127.000	**50**	19.685	322.580	**50**	7.750	819.355	**50**	3.051	22.680	**50**	110.231
152.400	**60**	23.622	387.096	**60**	9.300	983.226	**60**	3.661	27.216	**60**	132.277
177.800	**70**	27.559	451.612	**70**	10.850	1147.097	**70**	4.272	31.752	**70**	154.324
203.200	**80**	31.496	516.128	**80**	12.400	1310.968	**80**	4.882	36.287	**80**	176.370
228.600	**90**	35.433	580.644	**90**	13.950	1474.839	**90**	5.492	40.823	**90**	198.416
254.000	**100**	39.370	645.160	**100**	15.500	1638.710	**100**	6.102	45.359	**100**	220.464
Metres		*Yards*	*Square m*		*Square yd*	*Cubic m*		*Cubic yd*	*Metric tonnes*		*Tons (UK)*
0.914	**1**	1.094	0.836	**1**	1.196	0.765	**1**	1.308	1.016	**1**	0.984
1.829	**2**	2.187	1.672	**2**	2.392	1.529	**2**	2.616	2.032	**2**	1.968
2.743	**3**	3.281	2.508	**3**	3.588	2.294	**3**	3.924	3.048	**3**	2.953
3.658	**4**	4.374	3.345	**4**	4.784	3.058	**4**	5.232	4.064	**4**	3.937
4.572	**5**	5.468	4.181	**5**	5.980	3.823	**5**	6.540	5.080	**5**	4.921
5.486	**6**	6.562	5.017	**6**	7.176	4.587	**6**	7.848	6.096	**6**	5.905
6.401	**7**	7.655	5.853	**7**	8.372	5.352	**7**	9.156	7.112	**7**	6.889
7.315	**8**	8.749	6.689	**8**	9.568	6.116	**8**	10.464	8.128	**8**	7.874
8.230	**9**	9.843	7.525	**9**	10.764	6.881	**9**	11.772	9.144	**9**	8.858
9.144	**10**	10.936	8.361	**10**	11.960	7.646	**10**	13.080	10.161	**10**	9.842
18.288	**20**	21.872	16.723	**20**	23.920	15.291	**20**	26.159	20.321	**20**	19.684
27.432	**30**	32.808	25.084	**30**	35.880	22.937	**30**	39.239	30.481	**30**	29.526
36.576	**40**	43.745	33.445	**40**	47.840	30.582	**40**	52.318	40.642	**40**	39.368
45.720	**50**	54.681	41.806	**50**	59.799	38.228	**50**	65.398	50.802	**50**	49.210
54.864	**60**	65.617	50.168	**60**	71.759	45.873	**60**	78.477	60.963	**60**	59.052
64.008	**70**	76.553	58.529	**70**	83.719	53.519	**70**	91.557	71.123	**70**	68.894
73.152	**80**	87.489	66.890	**80**	95.679	61.164	**80**	104.636	81.284	**80**	78.737
82.296	**90**	98.425	75.251	**90**	107.639	68.810	**90**	117.716	91.444	**90**	88.579
91.440	**100**	109.361	83.613	**100**	119.599	76.455	**100**	130.795	101.605	**100**	98.421
Kilometres		*Miles*	*Hectares*		*Acres*	*Litres*		*Gallons*	*Metric tonnes*		*Tons (US)*
1.609	**1**	0.621	0.405	**1**	2.471	4.546	**1**	0.220	0.907	**1**	1.102
3.219	**2**	1.243	0.809	**2**	4.942	9.092	**2**	0.440	1.814	**2**	2.205
4.828	**3**	1.864	1.214	**3**	7.413	13.638	**3**	0.660	2.722	**3**	3.305
6.437	**4**	2.485	1.619	**4**	9.844	18.184	**4**	0.880	3.629	**4**	4.409
8.047	**5**	3.107	2.023	**5**	12.355	22.730	**5**	1.100	4.536	**5**	5.521
9.656	**6**	3.728	2.428	**6**	14.826	27.276	**6**	1.320	5.443	**6**	6.614
11.265	**7**	4.350	2.833	**7**	17.297	31.822	**7**	1.540	6.350	**7**	7.716
12.875	**8**	4.971	3.327	**8**	19.769	36.368	**8**	1.760	7.257	**8**	8.818
14.484	**9**	5.592	3.642	**9**	22.240	40.914	**9**	1.980	8.165	**9**	9.921
16.093	**10**	6.214	4.047	**10**	24.711	45.460	**10**	2.200	9.072	**10**	11.023
32.187	**20**	12.427	8.094	**20**	49.421	90.919	**20**	4.400	18.144	**20**	22.046
48.280	**30**	18.641	12.140	**30**	74.132	136.379	**30**	6.599	27.216	**30**	33.069
64.374	**40**	24.855	16.187	**40**	98.842	181.839	**40**	8.799	36.287	**40**	44.092
80.467	**50**	31.069	20.234	**50**	123.555	227.298	**50**	10.999	45.359	**50**	55.116
96.561	**60**	37.282	24.281	**60**	148.263	272.758	**60**	13.199	54.431	**60**	66.139
112.654	**70**	43.496	28.328	**70**	172.974	318.217	**70**	15.398	63.503	**70**	77.162
128.748	**80**	49.710	32.375	**80**	197.684	363.677	**80**	17.598	72.575	**80**	88.185
144.841	**90**	55.923	36.422	**90**	222.395	409.137	**90**	19.798	81.647	**90**	99.208
160.934	**100**	62.137	40.469	**100**	247.105	454.596	**100**	21.998	90.719	**100**	110.231

THE PERIODIC TABLE OF ELEMENTS

Key	
6	atomic number
Carbon	name of element
C	chemical number
12.01	atomic mass

	Alkali metals I A	Alkaline earth metals II A	III B	IV B	V B	VI B	V II		VIII		I B	II B	III A	IV A	V A	VI A	VII A	Noble gases
			Transition metals										Non-metals					
1	1 Hydrogen **H** 1.01																	2 Helium **He** 4.00
2	3 Lithium **Li** 6.94	4 Beryllium **Be** 9.01											5 Boron **B** 10.81	6 Carbon **C** 12.01	7 Nitrogen **N** 14.01	8 Oxygen **O** 16.00	9 Fluorine **F** 19.00	10 Neon **Ne** 20.18
3	11 Sodium **Na** 22.99	12 Magnesium **Mg** 24.31											13 Aluminium **Al** 26.98	14 Silicon **Si** 28.09	15 Phosphorus **P** 30.97	16 Sulphur **S** 32.07	17 Chlorine **Cl** 35.45	18 Argon **Ar** 39.95
4	19 Potassium **K** 39.10	20 Calcium **Ca** 40.08	21 Scandium **Sc** 44.96	22 Titanium **Ti** 47.88	23 Vanadium **V** 50.94	24 Chromium **Cr** 52.00	25 Manganese **Mn** 54.94	26 Iron **Fe** 55.85	27 Cobalt **Co** 58.93	28 Nickel **Ni** 58.69	29 Copper **Cu** 63.55	30 Zinc **Zn** 65.38	31 Gallium **Ga** 69.72	32 Germanium **Ge** 72.64	33 Arsenic **As** 74.92	34 Selenium **Se** 78.96	35 Bromine **Br** 79.904	36 Krypton **Kr** 83.80
5	37 Rubidium **Rb** 85.47	38 Strontium **Sr** 87.62	39 Yttrium **Y** 88.91	40 Zirconium **Zr** 91.22	41 Niobium **Nb** 92.91	42 Molybdenum **Mo** 95.96	43 Technetium **Tc** 97.91	44 Ruthenium **Ru** 101.07	45 Rhodium **Rh** 102.91	46 Palladium **Pd** 106.42	47 Silver **Ag** 107.87	48 Cadmium **Cd** 112.41	49 Indium **In** 114.82	50 Tin **Sn** 118.71	51 Antimony **Sb** 121.76	52 Tellurium **Te** 127.60	53 Iodine **I** 126.9045	54 Xenon **Xe** 131.29
6	55 Caesium **Cs** 132.91	56 Barium **Ba** 137.33	Lanthanide series (*see* below)	72 Hafnium **Hf** 178.49	73 Tantalum **Ta** 180.94	74 Tungsten **W** 183.85	75 Rhenium **Ru** 186.21	76 Osmium **Os** 190.23	77 Iridium **Ir** 192.22	78 Platinum **Pt** 195.08	79 Gold **Au** 196.97	80 Mercury **Hg** 200.59	81 Thallium **Tl** 204.38	82 Lead **Pb** 207.2	83 Bismuth **Bi** 208.98	84 Polonium **Po** 209	85 Astatine **At** 210	86 Radon **Rn** 222
7	87 Francium **Fr** 223	88 Radium **Ra** 226	Actinide series (*see* below)	104 Rutherfordium **Rf** 261	105 Dubnium **Db** 262	106 Seaborgium **Sg** 266	107 Bohrium **Bh** 264	108 Hassium **Hs** 277	109 Meitnerium **Mt** 268	110 Darmstadtium **Ds** 271	111 Roentgenium **Rg** 272	112 Copernicium **Cn** 285						

Rare earth elements—Lanthanide series	57 Lanthanum **La** 138.91	58 Cerium **Ce** 140.12	59 Praeseodymium **Pr** 140.91	60 Neodymium **Nd** 144.24	61 Promethium **Pm** 145	62 Samarium **Sm** 150.36	63 Europium **Eu** 151.96	64 Gadolinium **Gd** 157.25	65 Terbium **Tb** 158.93	66 Dysprosium **Dy** 162.50	67 Holmium **Ho** 164.93	68 Erbium **Er** 167.26	69 Thulium **Tm** 168.93	70 Ytterbium **Yb** 173.05	71 Lutetium **Lu** 174.97
Actinide series	89 Actinium **Ac** 227	90 Thorium **Th** 232.04	91 Protactinium **Pa** 231.04	92 Uranium **U** 238.03	93 Neptunium **Np** 237	94 Plutonium **Pu** 244	95 Americium **Am** 243	96 Curium **Cm** 247	97 Berkelium **Bk** 247	98 Californium **Cf** 251	99 Eisteinium **Es** 252	100 Fermium **Fm** 257	101 Mendelevium **Md** 258	102 Nobelium **No** 259	103 Lawrencium **Lr** 262

The periodic table arranges the elements into horizontal rows (periods) and vertical columns (groups) according to their atomic number. The elements in a group all have similar properties; across each period, atoms are electropositive (form positive ions) to the left and electronegative to the right. The earliest version of the periodic table was devised in 1869 by Dmitriy Mendeleyev, who predicted the existence of several elements from gaps in the table.

NOBEL PRIZE WINNERS

For prize winners for the years 1901–2006, *see* earlier editions of *Whitaker's Almanack.*

The Nobel Prizes are awarded each year from the income of a trust fund established by the Swedish scientist Alfred Nobel, the inventor of dynamite, who died on 10 December 1896 leaving a fortune of £1,750,000. The prizes are awarded to those who have contributed most to the common good in the domain of:

Physics – awarded by the Royal Swedish Academy of Sciences
Chemistry – awarded by the Royal Swedish Academy of Sciences
Physiology or Medicine – awarded by the Karolinska Institute
Literature – awarded by the Swedish Academy of Arts
Peace – awarded by a five-person committee elected by the Norwegian Storting
Economic Sciences (instituted 1969) – awarded by the Royal Swedish Academy of Sciences

The prizes are awarded every year on 10 December, the anniversary of Nobel's death. The first awards were made on 10 December 1901. The Trust is administered by the board of directors of the Nobel Foundation, Stockholm, consisting of five members and three deputy members. The Swedish government appoints a chair and a deputy chair, the remaining members being appointed by the awarding authorities.

The awards in the last three years have been distributed as follows:

	2007	*2008*	*2009*
Physics	Albert Fert *(France)*, Peter Grünberg *(Germany)*	Yoichiro Nambu *(USA)*, Makoto Kobayashi *(Japan)*, Toshihide Maskawa *(Japan)*	Willard S. Boyle *(Canada)*, Charles K. Kao *(China)*, George E. Smith *(USA)*
Chemistry	Gerhard Ertl *(Germany)*	Osamu Shimomura *(USA)*, Martin Chalfie *(USA)*, Roger Y. Tsien *(USA)*	Venkatraman Ramakrishnan *(India)*, Thomas A. Steitz *(USA)*, Ada E. Yonath *(Israel)*
Physiology or Medicine	Mario R. Capecchi *(USA)*, Sir Martin J. Evans *(UK)*, Oliver Smithies *(USA)*	Harald zur Hausen *(Germany)*, François Barré-Sinoussi *(France)*, Luc Montagnier *(France)*	Elizabeth H. Blackburn *(Australia)*, Carol W. Greider *(USA)*, Jack W. Szostak *(UK)*
Literature	Doris Lessing *(UK)*	Jean-Marie Gustave Le Clézio *(France and Mauritius)*	Herta Müller *(Romania)*
Peace	IPCC *(international)*, Albert Arnold Gore Jr *(USA)*	Martti Ahtisaari *(Finland)*	Barack H. Obama *(USA)*
Economics	Leonid Hurwicz *(USA)*, Eric S. Maskin *(USA)*, Roger B. Myerson *(USA)*	Paul Krugman *(USA)*	Elinor Ostrom *(USA)*, Oliver E. Williamson *(USA)*

ABBREVIATIONS AND ACRONYMS

Ψ seaport

A

A ampere
AA Alcoholics Anonymous
AAA Amateur Athletic Association
AAS *Annual Abstract of Statistics*
ABA Amateur Boxing Association
ABE Association of Building Engineers
ABM anti-ballistic missile
abr abridged
ac alternating current
a/c account
AC *(ante Christum)* before Christ
Companion, Order of Australia
ACAS Advisory, Conciliation and Arbitration Service
ACT Australian Capital Territory
AD *(anno Domini)* in the year of our Lord
ADB Asian Development Bank
ADC Aide-de-Camp
ADC (P) Personal ADC to the Queen
Adj. Adjutant
Adj. Gen. Adjutant General
ad lib *(ad libitum)* at pleasure
Adm. Admiral
AE Air Efficiency award
AEM Air Efficiency Medal
aet after extra time
AFC Air Force Cross
AFM Air Force Medal
AG Attorney-General
AGM air-to-ground missile
annual general meeting
AH *(anno Hegirae)* in the year of the Hegira
AI artificial intelligence
AIDS acquired immune deficiency syndrome
AIM Alternative Investment Market
ALG Adult Learning Grant
alt altitude
am *(ante meridiem)* before noon
AM amplitude modulation
(anno mundi) in the year of the world
Assembly Member *(Wales)*
amp amplifier
AMU Arab Maghreb Union
ANC African National Congress
anon anonymous
ANZAC Australian and New Zealand Army Corps
AO Air Officer
Officer, Order of Australia
AOC Air Officer Commanding
AONB area of outstanding natural beauty
APEC Asia-Pacific Economic Cooperation
apptd appointed
APR annual percentage rate
ASA Advertising Standards Authority
Amateur Swimming Association
ASAP as soon as possible
ASBO antisocial behaviour order
ASEAN Association of South-East Asian Nations
ASLEF Associated Society of Locomotive Engineers and Firemen
ASLIB Association for Information Management
ATC Air Training Corps
AUC *(ab urbe condita)* in the year from the foundation of Rome
(anno urbis conditae) in the year of the founding of the city
AV Authorised Version *(of Bible)*
AVR Army Volunteer Reserve
AWOL absent without (official) leave

B

b. born
bowled *(cricket)*
BA Bachelor of Arts
BAA British Airports Authority
British Astronomical Association
BAF British Athletics Federation
BAFTA British Academy of Film and Television Arts
BAS Bachelor in Agricultural Science
British Antarctic Survey
BBA British Bankers' Association
BBC British Broadcasting Corporation
BBFC British Board of Film Classification
BBSRC Biotechnology and Biological Sciences Research Council
BC before Christ
borough council
British Columbia *(Canada)*
BCH (D) Bachelor of (Dental) Surgery
BCL Bachelor of Civil Law
BCOM Bachelor of Commerce
BD Bachelor of Divinity
BDA British Dental Association
BDS Bachelor of Dental Surgery
BED Bachelor of Education
BEM British Empire Medal
BENG Bachelor of Engineering
BFI British Film Institute
BFPO British Forces Post Office
BIS Business, Innovation and Skills (Department for)
BLIT Bachelor of Literature
BLITT Bachelor of Letters
BM Bachelor of Medicine
British Museum
BMA British Medical Association
BMI body mass index
BMUS Bachelor of Music
BNFL British Nuclear Fuels
Bp Bishop
BPHARM Bachelor of Pharmacy
BPHIL Bachelor of Philosophy
bpm beats per minute
BPS British Psychological Society
Brig. Brigadier
BSC Bachelor of Science
BSE bovine spongiform encephalopathy
BSI British Standards Institution
BST British Summer Time
Bt. Baronet
BTEC Business and Technology Education Council
BTU British thermal unit
BVMS Bachelor of Veterinary Medicine and Surgery

C

c. *(circa)* about
chapter *(Public Acts)*
C Celsius
centigrade
C. Conservative
CA chartered accountant *(Scotland)*
CAA Civil Aviation Authority
CAB Citizens Advice Bureau
CAD computer-aided design
Cadw Ancient Monuments Board for Wales
Cantuar: of Canterbury *(Archbishop)*
CAP Common Agricultural Policy
Capt. Captain
CARICOM Caribbean Community and Common Market
Carliol: of Carlisle *(Bishop)*
CB Companion, Order of the Bath
CBE Commander, Order of the British Empire
CBI Confederation of British Industry
CBSS Council of the Baltic Sea States

CC	Chamber of Commerce
	city council
	Companion, Order of Canada
	county council
	county court
CCC	county cricket club
CCF	Combined Cadet Force
CCHEM	chartered chemist
CCTA	City Colleges for Technology and the Arts
CD	Civil Defence
	Corps Diplomatique
Cdr	Commander
Cdre	Commodore
CDS	Chief of the Defence Staff
CE	civil engineer
	Common (or Christian) Era
CEFAS	Centre for Environment, Fisheries and Aquaculture Science
CENG	chartered engineer
CEO	chief executive officer
CERN	European Organisation for Nuclear Research
Cestr:	of Chester *(Bishop)*
CET	Central European Time
	Common External Tariff
cf	*(confer)* compare
CF	Chaplain to the Forces
CFC	chlorofluorocarbon
CGC	Conspicuous Gallantry Cross
CGEOL	chartered geologist
CGI	computer-generated imagery
CGM	Conspicuous Gallantry Medal
cgs	centimetre-gramme-second *(system)*
CGS	Chief of General Staff
CH	Companion of Honour
CHB/M	Bachelor/Master of Surgery
CI	Channel Islands
	Imperial Order of the Crown of India
CIA	Central Intelligence Agency
CICA	Conference on Interaction and Confidence Building Measures in Asia
	Criminal Injuries Compensation Authority
CICAP	Criminal Injuries Compensation Appeals Panel
Cicestr:	of Chichester *(Bishop)*
CID	Criminal Investigation Department
CIE	Companion, Order of the Indian Empire
CIF	cost, insurance and freight
C-in-C	Commander-in-Chief
CILIP	Chartered Institute of Library and Information Professionals
CIPFA	Chartered Institute of Public Finance and Accountancy
CIS	Commonwealth of Independent States
CJD	Creutzfeld-Jakob disease
CLJ	Commander, Order of St Lazarus of Jerusalem
CM	*(Chirurgiae Magister)* Master of Surgery
CMG	Companion, Order of St Michael and St George
CMEC	Child Maintenance and Enforcement Commission
CND	Campaign for Nuclear Disarmament
c/o	care of
CO	Commanding Officer
C of E	Church of England
COI	Central Office of Information
Col.	Colonel
cons.	consecrated
Cpl.	Corporal
CPM	Colonial Police Medal
CPRE	Council for the Protection of Rural England
CPS	Crown Prosecution Service
CSI	Companion, Order of the Star of India
CTC	City Technology Colleges
CVO	Commander, Royal Victorian Order

D

d	*(denarius)* penny
d.	died
DAB	Digital Audio Broadcasting
DBE	Dame Commander, Order of the British Empire
dc	direct current
DC	District of Columbia *(USA)*
	district council
DCB	Dame Commander, Order of the Bath
D CH	*(Doctor Chirurgiae)* Doctor of Surgery
DCL	Doctor of Civil Law
DCM	Distinguished Conduct Medal
DCMG	Dame Commander, Order of St Michael and St George
DCMS	Department for Culture, Media and Sport
DCVO	Dame Commander, Royal Victorian Order
DD	Doctor of Divinity
DDS	Doctor of Dental Surgery
DDT	dichlorodiphenyl trichloroethane
DECC	Department of Energy and Climate Change
del	*(delineavit)* he/she drew it
DEFRA	Department of the Environment, Food and Rural Affairs
DFC	Distinguished Flying Cross
DfE	Department for Education
DFID	Department for International Development
DFM	Distinguished Flying Medal
DfT	Department for Transport
DG	*(Dei gratia)* by the grace of God
	director-general
DIP ED	Diploma in Education
DIP HE	Diploma in Higher Education
DIPHS	Diploma of the Heraldry Society
DL	Deputy Lieutenant
DLIT	Doctor of Literature
DLITT	Doctor of Letters
DLR	Docklands Light Railway
DMUS	Doctor of Music
DNA	deoxyribonucleic acid
DNB	*Dictionary of National Biography*
do	*(ditto)* the same
DoH	Department of Health
DPH *or* DPHIL	Doctor of Philosophy
DPP	Director of Public Prosecutions
Dr	Doctor
DSC	Distinguished Service Cross
	Doctor of Science
DSM	Distinguished Service Medal
DSO	Companion, Distinguished Service Order
DTP	desktop publishing
Dunelm:	of Durham *(Bishop)*
DV	*(Deo volente)* God willing
DVD	digital versatile disc
DVLA	Driver and Vehicle Licensing Agency
DVT	deep vein thrombosis
DWI	Drinking Water Inspectorate
DWP	Department for Work and Pensions

E

E	east
	email
Ebor:	of York *(Archbishop)*
EBRD	European Bank for Reconstruction and Development
EC	Elizabeth Cross
ECB	England and Wales Cricket Board
	European Central Bank
ECG	electrocardiogram
ECGD	Export Credits Guarantee Department
ECOWAS	Economic Community of West African States

ED Efficiency Decoration
EEC European Economic Community
EEG electroencephalogram
EFA European Fighter Aircraft
EFTA European Free Trade Association
eg *(exempli gratia)* for the sake of example
EHRC Equality and Human Rights Commission
EIB European Investment Bank
EMA Education Maintenance Allowance
EMS European Monetary System
EMU European Monetary Union
EPSRC Engineering and Physical Sciences Research Council
ER *(Elizabetha Regina)* Queen Elizabeth
ERM exchange rate mechanism
ERNIE electronic random number indicator equipment
ESA European Space Agency
ESRC Economic and Social Research Council
est established
estimate
ETA *(Euzkadi ta Askatasuna)* Basque separatist organisation
et al *(et alibi)* and elsewhere
(et alii) and others
etc *(et cetera)* and the other things/and so forth
et seq *(et sequentia)* and the following
EU European Union
EURATOM European Atomic Energy Community
Exon: of Exeter *(Bishop)*

F

f *(forte)* loud
F Fahrenheit
Fellow of
FA Football Association
FANY First Aid Nursing Yeomanry
FAO for the attention of
FAQ frequently asked questions
FARC *(Fuerzas Armadas Revolucionarias de Colombia)* Colombian rebel organisation
FBA Fellow, British Academy
FBAA Fellow, British Association of Accountants and Auditors
FBI Federal Bureau of Investigation
FBS Fellow, Botanical Society
FBU Fire Brigades Union
FC football club
FCA Fellow, Institute of Chartered Accountants in England and Wales
FCCA Fellow, Chartered Association of Certified Accountants
FCGI Fellow, City and Guilds of London Institute
FCIA Fellow, Corporation of Insurance Agents
FCIARB Fellow, Chartered Institute of Arbitrators
FCIB Fellow, Chartered Institute of Bankers
Fellow, Corporation of Insurance Brokers
FCIBSE Fellow, Chartered Institution of Building Services Engineers
FCII Fellow, Chartered Insurance Institute
FCIPS Fellow, Chartered Institute of Purchasing and Supply
FCIS Fellow, Institute of Chartered Secretaries and Administrators
FCIT Fellow, Chartered Institute of Transport
FCMA Fellow, Chartered Institute of Management Accountants
FCO Foreign and Commonwealth Office
FCP Fellow, College of Preceptors
FD *(Fidei Defensor)* Defender of the Faith
FE further education
fec *(fecit)* made this
ff *(fecerunt)* made this (pl)
folios following
ff *(fortissimo)* very loud
FFA Fellow, Faculty of Actuaries *(Scotland)*
Fellow, Institute of Financial Accountants
FFAS Fellow, Faculty of Architects and Surveyors
FFCM Fellow, Faculty of Community Medicine
FFPHM Fellow, Faculty of Public Health Medicine
FGS Fellow, Geological Society
FHS Fellow, Heraldry Society
FHSM Fellow, Institute of Health Service Management
FIA Fellow, Institute of Actuaries
FIBIOL Fellow, Institute of Biology
FICE Fellow, Institution of Civil Engineers
FICS Fellow, Institution of Chartered Shipbrokers
FIEE Fellow, Institution of Electrical Engineers
FIERE Fellow, Institution of Electronic and Radio Engineers
FIFA *(Fédération Internationale de Football Association)* International Federation of Football Association
FIM Fellow, Institute of Metals
FIMGT Fellow, Institute of Management
FIMM Fellow, Institution of Mining and Metallurgy
FINSTF Fellow, Institute of Fuel
FINSTP Fellow, Institute of Physics
FIQS Fellow, Institute of Quantity Surveyors
FIS Fellow, Institute of Statisticians
FJI Fellow, Institute of Journalists
FLS Fellow, Linnean Society
FM Field Marshal
frequency modulation
FMEDSCI Fellow, Academy of Medical Sciences
fo folio
FO Flying Officer
FOB free on board
FPHS Fellow, Philosophical Society
FRAD Fellow, Royal Academy of Dancing
FRAES Fellow, Royal Aeronautical Society
FRAI Fellow, Royal Anthropological Institute
FRAM Fellow, Royal Academy of Music
FRAS Fellow, Royal Asiatic Society
Fellow, Royal Astronomical Society
FRBS Fellow, Royal Botanic Society
Fellow, Royal Society of British Sculptors
FRCA Fellow, Royal College of Anaesthetists
FRCGP Fellow, Royal College of General Practitioners
FRCM Fellow, Royal College of Music
FRCO Fellow, Royal College of Organists
FRCOG Fellow, Royal College of Obstetricians and Gynaecologists
FRCP Fellow, Royal College of Physicians, London
FRCPATH Fellow, Royal College of Pathologists
FRCPE *or* FRCPED Fellow, Royal College of Physicians, Edinburgh
FRCPI Fellow, Royal College of Physicians, Ireland
FRCPSYCH Fellow, Royal College of Psychiatrists
FRCR Fellow, Royal College of Radiologists
FRCS Fellow, Royal College of Surgeons of England

FRCSE *or* FRCSED Fellow, Royal College of Surgeons of Edinburgh
FRCSGLAS Fellow, Royal College of Physicians and Surgeons of Glasgow
FRCSI Fellow, Royal College of Surgeons in Ireland
FRCVS Fellow, Royal College of Veterinary Surgeons
FRECONS Fellow, Royal Economic Society
FRENG Fellow, Royal Academy of Engineering
FRGS Fellow, Royal Geographical Society
FRHISTS Fellow, Royal Historical Society
FRHS Fellow, Royal Horticultural Society
FRIBA Fellow, Royal Institute of British Architects
FRICS Fellow, Royal Institution of Chartered Surveyors
FRMETS Fellow, Royal Meteorological Society
FRMS Fellow, Royal Microscopical Society
FRNS Fellow, Royal Numismatic Society
FRPHARMS Fellow, Royal Pharmaceutical Society
FRPS Fellow, Royal Photographic Society
FRS Fellow, Royal Society
FRSA Fellow, Royal Society of Arts
FRSC Fellow, Royal Society of Chemistry
FRSE Fellow, Royal Society of Edinburgh
FRSH Fellow, Royal Society of Health
FRSL Fellow, Royal Society of Literature
FRTPI Fellow, Royal Town Planning Institute
FSA Fellow, Society of Antiquaries
Financial Services Authority
Food Standards Agency
FSS Fellow, Royal Statistical Society
FSVA Fellow, Incorporated Society of Valuers and Auctioneers
FT *Financial Times*
FTI Fellow, Textile Institute
FTII Fellow, Chartered Institute of Taxation
FZS Fellow, Zoological Society

G

GATT General Agreement on Tariffs and Trade
GBE Dame/Knight Grand Cross, Order of the British Empire
GC George Cross
GCB Dame/Knight Grand Cross, Order of the Bath
GCC Gulf Cooperation Council
GCE General Certificate of Education
GCHQ Government Communications Headquarters
GCIE Knight Grand Commander, Order of the Indian Empire
GCLJ Knight Grand Cross, Order of St Lazarus of Jerusalem
GCMG Dame/Knight Grand Cross, Order of St Michael and St George
GCSE General Certificate of Secondary Education
GCSI Knight Grand Commander, Order of the Star of India
GCVO Dame/Knight Grand Cross, Royal Victorian Order
GDP gross domestic product
Gen. General
GHQ general headquarters
GLA Greater London Authority
GM genetically modified
George Medal
GMB Britain's General Union
GMT Greenwich Mean Time
GNI gross national income
GNVQ General National Vocational Qualification
GOC General Officer Commanding
GP General Practitioner
GPS Global Positioning System
Gp Capt. Group Captain
GSA Girls' Schools Association
GST Greenwich Sidereal Time

H

HA Health Authority
HAC Honourable Artillery Company
HB His Beatitude
HBM Her/His Britannic Majesty('s)
Honorary Chaplain to the Forces
HD High Definition *(television)*
HE Her/His Excellency
higher education
His Eminence
HGV heavy goods vehicle
HH Her/His Highness
Her/His Honour
His Holiness
HIM Her/His Imperial Majesty
HIV human immunodeficiency virus
HJS *(hic jacet sepultus)* here lies buried
HM Her/His Majesty('s)
HMAS Her/His Majesty's Australian Ship
HMC Headmasters' and Headmistresses' Conference
HMI Her/His Majesty's Inspector
HML Her/His Majesty's Lieutenant
HMS Her/His Majesty's Ship
HMSO Her/His Majesty's Stationery Office
HNC Higher National Certificate
HND Higher National Diploma
Hon. Honorary
Honourable
HP hire purchase
HPA Health Protection Agency
HQ headquarters
HR human resources
HRH Her/His Royal Highness
HRT hormone replacement therapy
HSE Health and Safety Executive
(hic sepultus est) here is buried
HSH Her/His Serene Highness
HTA Human Tissue Authority
HTML hypertext mark-up language
HTTP hypertext transfer protocol
HWM high water mark

I

I Island
IAEA International Atomic Energy Agency
IATA International Air Transport Association
IB International Baccalaureate
IBF International Boxing Federation
ibid *(ibidem)* in the same place
IBRD International Bank for Reconstruction and Development
ICAO International Civil Aviation Organisation
ICC International Cricket Council
International Criminal Court
ICJ International Court of Justice
ICOMOS International Council on Monuments and Sites
ICRC International Committee of the Red Cross
ICT Information and Communication Technology
id *(idem)* the same
IDA International Development Association
IDD international direct dialling

ie *(id est)* that is
IEA International Energy Agency
IFA independent financial adviser
IFAD International Fund for Agricultural Development
IFC International Finance Corporation
ILO International Labour Organisation/Office
IMF International Monetary Fund
IMO International Maritime Organisation
inc. incorporated
INLA Irish National Liberation Army
in loc *(in loco)* in its place
INRI *(Iesus Nazarenus Rex Iudaeorum)* Jesus of Nazareth, King of the Jews
inst *(instant)* current month
Interpol International Criminal Police Organisation
IOC International Olympic Committee
IoM Isle of Man
IOU I owe you
IoW Isle of Wight
IPS Identity and Passport Service
iPSC induced pluripotent stem cell
IQ intelligence quotient
IRA Irish Republican Army
IRB International Rugby Board
IRC International Rescue Committee
Is Islands
ISA individual savings account
ISBN International Standard Book Number
ISO Imperial Service Order
International Organisation for Standardisation
ISP internet service provider
ISSN International Standard Serial Number
ITN Independent Television News
ITU International Telecommunication Union
ITUC International Trade Union Confederation
ITV Independent Television
IUCN International Union for Conservation of Nature
IVF in vitro fertilisation
IWC International Whaling Commission

J

J Judge
Justice
JP Justice of the Peace
Jr Junior

K

KBE Knight Commander, Order of the British Empire
KCB Knight Commander, Order of the Bath
KCIE Knight Commander, Order of the Indian Empire
KCLJ Knight Commander, Order of St Lazarus of Jerusalem
KCMG Knight Commander, Order of St Michael and St George
KCSI Knight Commander, Order of the Star of India
KCVO Knight Commander, Royal Victorian Order
KG Knight of the Garter
KGB *(Komitet Gosudarstvennoi Bezopasnosti)* Committee of State Security *(USSR)*
kHz kilohertz
KLJ Knight, Order of St Lazarus of Jerusalem
ko knock out *(boxing)*
KP Knight, Order of St Patrick
KStJ Knight, Order of St John of Jerusalem
Kt. Knight
KT Knight of the Thistle
kV kilovolt
kW kilowatt
kWh kilowatt hour

L

Lab. Labour
Lat. Latitude
lbw leg before wicket *(cricket)*
lc lower case *(printing)*
LCD Liquid Crystal Display
LCJ Lord Chief Justice
LCM least/lowest common multiple
LD Liberal Democrat
LDS Licentiate in Dental Surgery
LEA Local Education Authority
LHB Local Health Board *(Wales)*
LHD *(Literarum Humaniorum Doctor)* Doctor of Humane Letters/Literature
Lib. Liberal
lit literary
Lit Hum *(Literae Humaniores)* classics course, Oxford University
LITT D Doctor of Letters
LJ Lord Justice
LLB Bachelor of Laws
LLD Doctor of Laws
LLM Master of Laws
loc cit *(loco citato)* in the place cited
Londin: of London *(Bishop)*
Long. longitude
LS *(loco sigilli)* place of the seal
LSC Learning and Skills Council
Legal Services Commission
lsd *(librae, solidi, denarii)* pounds, shillings and pence
LSE London School of Economics and Political Science
LST Local Sidereal Time
Lt Lieutenant
LTA Lawn Tennis Association
LTTE Liberation Tigers of Tamil Eelam
ltd limited *(liability)*
LVO Lieutenant, Royal Victorian Order
LW long wave
LWM low water mark

M

M Member
Monsieur
MA Master of Arts
Maj. Major
maj. majority
max maximum
MB *(Medicinae Baccalaureus)* Bachelor of Medicine
MBA Master of Business Administration
MBC Metropolitan Borough Council
MBE Member, Order of the British Empire
MBO management buy-out
MC Master of Ceremonies
Military Cross
MCB Muslim Council of Britain
MCC Marylebone Cricket Club
MCH(D) Master of (Dental) Surgery
MD managing director
Doctor of Medicine
MDC Movement for Democratic Change *(Zimbabwe)*
MDS Master of Dental Surgery
ME Middle English
myalgic encephalomyelitis
MEC Member of Executive Council
MED Master of Education
mega one million times
MEP Member of the European Parliament
Mgr Monsignor
MI Military Intelligence
micro one-millionth part
milli one-thousandth part
min minimum
minutes
MIT Massachusetts Institute of Technology

MLA — Member of Legislative Assembly *(Northern Ireland)*
Museums, Libraries and Archives Council
MLC — Member of Legislative Council
MLITT — Master of Letters
Mlle — Mademoiselle
MLR — minimum lending rate
MM — Military Medal
Mme — Madame
MMR — measles, mumps and rubella *(vaccine)*
MN — Merchant Navy
MO — Medical Officer/Orderly
MoD — Ministry of Defence
MoJ — Ministry of Justice
MP — Member of Parliament
Military Police
mph — miles per hour
MPHIL — Master of Philosophy
MR — Master of the Rolls
MRC — Medical Research Council
MRI — magnetic resonance imaging
MRSA — methicillin-resistant staphylococcus aureus
MS — manuscript (*pl* MSS)
Master of Surgery
multiple sclerosis
MSC — Master of Science
MSP — Member of Scottish Parliament
MUSB/D — Bachelor/Doctor of Music
MV — merchant vessel
motor vessel
MVO — Member, Royal Victorian Order
MW — medium wave
megawatt

N

N — north
n/a — not applicable
not available
NAAFI — Navy, Army and Air Force Institutes
NAFTA — North American Free Trade Agreement
NAO — National Audit Office
NASA — National Aeronautics and Space Administration
NASUWT — National Association of Schoolmasters/Union of Women Teachers
NATO — North Atlantic Treaty Organisation
nb — *(nota bene)* note well
NCO — non-commissioned officer
NDPB — non-departmental public body
NEB — New English Bible
nem con — *(nemine contradicente)* no one contradicting
NERC — Natural Environment Research Council
nes — not elsewhere specified
NESTA — National Endowment for Science, Technology and the Arts
NFU — National Farmers' Union
NHS — National Health Service
NI — National Insurance
Northern Ireland
no — *(numero)* number
non seq — *(non sequitur)* it does not follow
Norvic: — of Norwich *(Bishop)*
NP — Notary Public
NRA — National Rifle Association
NS — New Style *(calendar)*
NSPCC — National Society for the Prevention of Cruelty to Children
NSW — New South Wales *(Australia)*
NT — National Theatre
National Trust
New Testament
Northern Territory *(Australia)*
NUJ — National Union of Journalists
NUM — National Union of Mineworkers
NUS — National Union of Students
NUT — National Union of Teachers
NVQ — National Vocational Qualification
NZ — New Zealand

O

OAP — old age pension(er)
OAPEC — Organisation of Arab Petroleum Exporting Countries
OAS — Organisation of American States
Ob *or* obit — died
OBE — Officer, Order of the British Empire
OBR — Office for Budget Responsibility
OC — Officer Commanding
OE — Old English
omissions excepted
OECD — Organisation for Economic Cooperation and Development
OED — *Oxford English Dictionary*
OFCOM — Office of Communications
OFGEM — Office of Gas and Electricity Markets
OFM — Order of Friars Minor *(Franciscans)*
Ofsted — Office for Standards in Education, Children's Services and Skills
OFT — Office of Fair Trading
OFWAT — Office of Water Services
OHMS — On Her/His Majesty's Service
OHP — overhead projector
OIC — Organisation of the Islamic Conference
OM — Order of Merit
ono — or near(est) offer
ONS — Office for National Statistics
op — *(opus)* work
OP — opposite prompt side *(of theatre)*
Order of Preachers *(Dominicans)*
out of print *(books)*
op cit — *(opere citato)* in the work cited
OPEC — Organisation of Petroleum Exporting Countries
OPSI — Office of Public Sector Information
ORR — Office of Rail Regulation
OS — Old Style *(calendar)*
Ordnance Survey
OSA — Order of St Augustine
OSB — Order of St Benedict
OSCE — Organisation for Security and Cooperation in Europe
OStJ — Officer, Order of St John of Jerusalem
OT — Old Testament
OTC — Officers' Training Corps
Oxon — (of) Oxford
Oxfordshire

P

p — page
PA — personal assistant
Press Association
public address (system)
PAYE — pay as you earn
PAYG — pay as you go
pc — *(per centum)* in the hundred
PC — personal computer
Police Constable
politically correct
Privy Counsellor
PCB — polychlorinated biphenyl
PCT — Primary Care Trust
PDSA — People's Dispensary for Sick Animals
PE — physical education
Petriburg: — of Peterborough *(Bishop)*
PFI — Private Finance Initiative
PG — parental guidance
PGA — Professional Golfers Association
PGCE — Postgraduate Certificate of Education
PHD — Doctor of Philosophy
PIF — Pacific Islands Forum
pl — plural
PLA — Port of London Authority
plc — public limited company
PLO — Palestine Liberation Organisation
pm — *(post meridiem)* after noon
PM — post mortem
Prime Minister
PMRAFNS — Princess Mary's Royal Air Force Nursing Service
PO — Petty Officer
Pilot Officer
post office
postal order
POW — prisoner of war

pp pages
(per procurationem) by proxy
PPS Parliamentary Private Secretary
PR proportional representation
public relations
PRA President of the Royal Academy
pro tem *(pro tempore)* for the time being
prox *(proximo)* next month
PRS President of the Royal Society
PRSE President of the Royal Society of Edinburgh
PS *(postscriptum)* postscript
psc passed staff college
PSNCR public sector net cash requirement
PSV public service vehicle
PTA Parent Teacher Association
Pte. Private
PTO please turn over

Q

QARANC Queen Alexandra's Royal Army Nursing Corps
QARNNS Queen Alexandra's Royal Naval Nursing Service
QBD Queen's Bench Division
QC Queen's Counsel
QE quantitative easing
QED *(quod erat demonstrandum)* which was to be proved
QGM Queen's Gallantry Medal
QHC Queen's Honorary Chaplain
QHDS Queen's Honorary Dental Surgeon
QHNS Queen's Honorary Nursing Sister
QHP Queen's Honorary Physician
QHS Queen's Honorary Surgeon
Qld Queensland *(Australia)*
QMG Quartermaster-General
QPM Queen's Police Medal
QS quarter sessions
Queen's Scholar
QSO quasi-stellar object *(quasar)*
Queen's Service Order
quango quasi-autonomous non-governmental organisation
qv *(quod vide)* which see

R

r. *(recto)* on the right-hand page
R *(Regina)* Queen
(Rex) King
RA Royal Academy/Academician
Royal Artillery
RAC Royal Armoured Corps
Royal Automobile Club
RADA Royal Academy of Dramatic Art
RADC Royal Army Dental Corps
RAEC Royal Army Educational Corps
RAES Royal Aeronautical Society
RAF Royal Air Force
RAM random-access memory
Royal Academy of Music
RAMC Royal Army Medical Corps
RAN Royal Australian Navy
RAOC Royal Army Ordnance Corps
RAPC Royal Army Pay Corps
RAVC Royal Army Veterinary Corps
R&B rhythm and blues
RBS Royal Bank of Scotland
Royal Society of British Sculptors
RC Red Cross
Roman Catholic
RCM Royal College of Music
RCN Royal College of Nursing
RCT Royal Corps of Transport
R&D research and development
RD refer to drawer *(banking)*
Royal Naval and Royal Marine Forces Reserve Decoration
Rural Dean
RE Religious Education
Royal Engineers
REM rapid eye movement
REME Royal Electrical and Mechanical Engineers
Rep representative
Republican
Rep. Republic
Revd Reverend
RFL Rugby Football League
RFU Rugby Football Union
RGS Royal Geographical Society
RHS Royal Horticultural Society
Royal Institute of Painters in Watercolours
Royal Institution
RIBA Royal Institute of British Architects
RIP *(requiescat in pace)* may he/she rest in peace
RIR Royal Irish Regiment
RM Royal Marines
RMA Royal Military Academy
RMT National Union of Rail, Maritime and Transport Workers
RN Royal Navy
RNIB Royal National Institute of Blind People
RNID Royal National Institute for Deaf People
RNLI Royal National Lifeboat Institution
RNR Royal Naval Reserve
RNVR Royal Naval Volunteer Reserve
RNXS Royal Naval Auxiliary Service
RNZN Royal New Zealand Navy
ROC Royal Observer Corps
Roffen: of Rochester *(Bishop)*
ROI Republic of Ireland
Royal Institute of Oil Painters
RoSPA Royal Society for the Prevention of Accidents
RP Received Pronunciation
Royal Society of Portrait Painters
RPA Rural Payments Agency
rpm revolutions per minute
RRC Lady of Royal Red Cross
RSA Royal Scottish Academician
Royal Society of Arts
RSC Royal Shakespeare Company
RSE Royal Society of Edinburgh
RSM Regimental Sergeant Major
RSPB Royal Society for the Protection of Birds
RSPCA Royal Society for the Prevention of Cruelty to Animals
RSV Revised Standard Version *(of Bible)*
RSVP *(répondez, s'il vous plaît)* please reply
RSW Royal Scottish Society of Painters in Watercolours
Rt. Hon. Right Honourable
RTPI Royal Town Planning Institute
RUC Royal Ulster Constabulary
RV Revised Version *(of Bible)*
RWS Royal Water Colour Society
RYS Royal Yacht Squadron

S

s second *(also* sec)
section (Public Acts)
(solidus) shilling
S south
SA Salvation Army
South Africa
South America
South Australia
SAARC South Asian Association for Regional Cooperation
SAE stamped addressed envelope
Salop Shropshire
SARS severe acute respiratory syndrome
Sarum: of Salisbury *(Bishop)*
SAS Special Air Service
SBS Special Boat Service
SCD Doctor of Science
SCM State Certified Midwife
SCO Shanghai Cooperation Organisation
SDLP Social Democratic and Labour Party

SEAQ	Stock Exchange Automated Quotations system
sec	second (*also* s)
SEN	special educational needs
	State Enrolled Nurse
SERPS	State Earnings Related Pension Scheme
SFO	Serious Fraud Office
SHA	Strategic Health Authority
SI	statutory instrument
	(Système International d'Unités) International System of Units
sic	*(sic)* so written
SIDS	sudden infant death syndrome
sig	signature
	Signor
SJ	Society of Jesus *(Jesuits)*
SLD	Social and Liberal Democrats
SMP	Statutory Maternity Pay
SNP	Scottish National Party
SOCA	Serious Organised Crime Agency
SOE	Special Operations Executive
sp	*(sine prole)* without issue
spgr	specific gravity
Sr	Senior
	Sister *(title)*
SRO	self-regulating organisation
SS	Saints
	steamship
SSC	Solicitor before Supreme Court *(Scotland)*
SSN	standard serial number
SSP	statutory sick pay
SSSI	Site of Special Scientific Interest
ST	*Social Trends*
STD	*(Sacrae Theologiae Doctor)* Doctor of Sacred Theology
	subscriber trunk dialling
stet	*(stet)* let it stand *(printing)*
STFC	Science and Technology Facilities Council
STI	sexually transmitted infection
stp	standard temperature and pressure
STP	*(Sacrae Theologiae Professor)* Professor of Sacred Theology
Sub Lt.	sub-lieutenant
SVQ	Scottish Vocational Qualification

T

TA	Territorial Army
TB	tuberculosis
TD	Territorial Decoration
TEFL	teaching English as a foreign language
temp	temperature
	temporary employee
TES	*Times Educational Supplement*
THES	*Times Higher Education Supplement*
TLS	*Times Literary Supplement*
TNT	trinitrotoluene *(explosive)*
trans.	translated
TRH	Their Royal Highnesses
trs	transpose *(printing)*
TT	Tourist Trophy *(motorcycle races)*
	tuberculin tested
TTP	*Tehrik-i-Taliban Pakistani* (Pakistani Taliban)
TUC	Trades Union Congress

U

U	Unionist
UAB	unitary awarding body
UAE	United Arab Emirates
uc	upper case *(printing)*
UC	Unitary Council
UCAS	Universities and Colleges Admissions Service
UCATT	Union of Construction, Allied Trades and Technicians
UCL	University College London
UCU	University and College Union
UDA	Ulster Defence Association
UDI	Unilateral Declaration of Independence
UDR	Ulster Defence Regiment
UEFA	Union of European Football Associations
UFF	Ulster Freedom Fighters
UFO	unidentified flying object
UHF	ultra-high frequency
UKAEA	UK Atomic Energy Authority
UN	United Nations
UNESCO	United Nations Educational, Scientific and Cultural Organisation
UNHCR	United Nations High Commissioner for Refugees
UNICEF	United Nations Children's Fund
UNIDO	United Nations Industrial Development Organisation
UNPO	Unrepresented Nations and Peoples Organisation
UPU	Universal Postal Union
USB	universal serial bus
USDAW	Union of Shop, Distributive and Allied Workers
USSR	Union of Soviet Socialist Republics
UTC	coordinated universal time system *(Temps Universel Coordonné)*
UVF	Ulster Volunteer Force

V

v	*(versus)* against
v.	*(verso)* on the left-hand page
V&A	Victoria and Albert Museum
VA	Vicar Apostolic
	Victoria and Albert Order
VAD	Voluntary Aid Detachment *(nursing)*
VAT	value added tax
VC	Victoria Cross
VD	Volunteer Officers' Decoration
VDU	visual display unit
Ven.	Venerable
VHF	very high frequency
VRD	Royal Naval Volunteer Reserve Officers' Decoration
VSO	Voluntary Service Overseas

W

W	website
	west
WBC	World Boxing Council
WBO	World Boxing Organisation
WCC	World Council of Churches
WEA	Workers' Educational Association
WEU	Western European Union
WFTU	World Federation of Trade Unions
WHO	World Health Organisation
WI	West Indies
	Women's Institute
Winton:	of Winchester *(Bishop)*
WIPO	World Intellectual Property Organisation
WMD	weapons of mass destruction
WMO	World Meteorological Organisation
WO	Warrant Officer
WRAC	Women's Royal Army Corps
WRAF	Women's Royal Air Force
WRNS	Women's Royal Naval Service
WRVS	Women's Royal Voluntary Service
WS	Writer to the Signet
WTO	World Trade Organisation
WWW	World Wide Web

Y

YHA	Youth Hostels Association
YMCA	Young Men's Christian Association
YWCA	Young Women's Christian Association

Z

ZANU-PF	Zimbabwean African National Union – Patriotic Front

INDEX

C

J

P

STOP PRESS

CHANGES SINCE PAGES WENT TO PRESS

EVENTS OF THE YEAR

BUSINESS AND ECONOMIC AFFAIRS

25 August. An Institute for Fiscal Studies report described the coalition government's first Budget as 'clearly regressive'; the report claimed that changes to housing benefits, disability living allowance and tax benefits will result in the poorest tenth of the population losing a greater proportion of their income than the richest. BP confirmed that it no longer intended to compete for an oil exploration licence in Greenland, owing to the damage caused to its reputation by the Deepwater Horizon oil spill. **4 September.** HMRC announced that nearly six million people in the UK had paid the wrong amount of tax through the pay as you earn (PAYE) system; 4.3 million people were due a rebate but 1.4 million people had underpaid by an average of £1,500.

CRIME

23 August. The body of Gareth Williams, an MI6 officer, was found in a padlocked holdall in his flat; the cause of death remained unknown.

ENVIRONMENT AND SCIENCE

3 September. BP announced that it would take two weeks to permanently seal the Deepwater Horizon oil well leak.

SPORT

3 September. The International Cricket Council charged Pakistan test captain Salman Butt and opening bowlers Mohammad Amir and Mohammad Asif under its anti-corruption code in relation to allegedly fixed incidents during the final Test match against England at Lord's.

AFRICA

1 August. The Independent Democratic Action (ADI) party won 26 of 55 seats in Sao Tome and Principe's legislative elections; ADI leader Patrice Trovoada was appointed prime minister on 13 August, and included four independent MPs in his minority cabinet. **4.** In a referendum in Kenya, 67 per cent of voters approved a new constitution which would introduce a bill of rights and land reform, and curb the powers of the president. **9.** Paul Kagame won a second term in Rwanda's presidential election, securing 93 per cent of votes in a poll in which only candidates allied to his ruling Rwandan Patriotic Front party were permitted to stand. **1 September.** Thirteen people were killed and around 140 were arrested during riots in Maputo, Mozambique, after droughts in Russia led to increased wheat and bread prices.

THE AMERICAS

5 August. The collapse of a tunnel in a copper mine near Copiapó, Chile, trapped 33 miners 700m underground; rescuers made contact with the men on 22 August, though it was estimated that the drilling of a borehole large enough to allow their escape would take between two and four months. **7.** Elena Kagan was sworn in as a judge of the US supreme court. **10.** Venezuela and Colombia agreed to restore diplomatic relations, which had been severed in July over an allegation by the Colombian government that Venezuela was harbouring 1,500 FARC rebels. **31.** American troops formally ended combat operations in Iraq; the remaining US military personnel assumed non-combat roles, though they remained able to participate in operations led by Iraqi forces when requested.

ASIA

7 August. Heavy rainfall and flooding in China's north-western Gansu province caused mudslides in which over 1,400 people were killed. **13.** Myanmar's ruling junta announced that parliamentary elections, the first since 1990, would be held on 7 November 2010. **17.** President Karzai issued a decree ordering all private security firms working in Afghanistan to cease operations within four months. **23.** In Manila, the Philippines, a former policeman hijacked a bus while armed with an automatic rifle; a 12-hour stand-off with police ended in the death of the gunman and eight of his hostages.

AUSTRALASIA AND THE PACIFIC

21 August. A snap legislative election in Australia resulted in a hung parliament, with both the incumbent Labour party and the Liberal–National coalition winning 72 seats each; Julia Gillard remained as prime minister after securing the support of two key independent MPs.

EUROPE

29 August. Islamist rebels mounted an attack on the residence of Chechen president Ramzan Kadyrov in the village of Tsentoroi; at least 19 people were killed. **5 September.** The Basque separatist organisation Eta announced that it had ceased violent attacks, though it stopped short of surrendering its weapons or describing the ceasefire as permanent.

MIDDLE EAST

17 August. The Lebanese parliament voted to lift restrictions on the employment of the country's 400,000 Palestinian refugees, who gained the same employment rights as other foreigners. **25.** Bombings in seven Iraqi cities killed over 50 people. **2 September.** A two-day summit was held in Washington DC between Israeli prime minister Benjamin Netanyahu and Palestinian National Authority president Mahmoud Abbas, the first direct peace negotiations between Israeli and Palestinian leaders since 2008; both agreed to hold fortnightly talks thereafter.